The Great Metal Discography

By the same author

The Great Rock Discography

The Great Psychedelic Discography

The Great Alternative & Indie Discography

The Great Metal Discography

From Hard Rock To Hardcore

Second Edition

M. C. Strong

Second edition first published in the UK in 2001 by MOJO Books,
an imprint of Canongate Books Ltd,
14 High Street, Edinburgh EH1 1TE

Published in the United States of America and Canada in 2002 by MOJO Books

10 9 8 7 6 5 4 3 2 1

British Library Cataloguing-in-Publication Data
A catalogue record for this book is available upon request from the British Library

ISBN 1 84195 185 4

Typeset by TexturAL, Dundee

Printed and bound in Finland by WS Bookwell

www.canongate.net

This book is dedicated to . . .

my mother JEAN FOTHERINGHAM
(born: 6th of January 1929,
died of cancer: 31st of August 1985)

Still missing you
and thanks for still
guiding me through all
the hard times.

my dad GERRY/GEOFF STRONG
(born: 28th of July 1930,
died of a heart attack: 20th October 1998)

Will miss you always.
You were also a great friend, inspiration
and someone who could make me laugh.

Hope you're both getting on up there.
If only . . .

Acknowledgements

I'd like to thank the following "GREAT" people who've helped me with this book (i.e. contributors):– BRENDON GRIFFIN, BARNEY MIERS, ADAM STAFFORD, ALAN LAWSON, proof-reader DAVE WHITE, and not forgetting PAUL McCARTHY (and his wife NAN) for his contribution to the first edition.

I'd also like to thank my "Great" friends ALLAN and ELAINE BREWSTER, VIC ZDZIEBLO, SANDY and CAROLINE McCRAE, PETER McGUCKIN, DOUGIE NIVEN, MIKEY KINNAIRD, IAN 'HARRY' HARRISON, EILEEN SCOTT-MONCRIEFF (+ family), TONY HUGHES, PAUL HUGHES, TAM MORRISON, MICHAEL FLETCHER, STEFAN LEWANDOWSKI (and MARIE), the artist (always) known as HAMISH + everyone at Alex SMITH's bar in Falkirk (now up for sale) including ALLAN MANN, LAURA, KELLY, PAUL KLEMM, BILL FISHER, JOCK HILL, BRIAN McLAUGHLIN, JOHN McARDLE, LAURIE DOOLAN, BILLY and ANN ROSS, RAB 'GIZMO' WATSON, GRANT BAILEY, PETER WAUGH, JOE SIMPSON, TONY WEIR, ANDY RISK, MARTIN McDERMOTT, STEVEN HUGHES, IAIN McLEAN, DAVIE WALKER, ALEC GRAY, WATTY MORRISON, ELLA CRAWFORD and BARRY MOORE.

Also not forgetting American KIP HANNAN, HAMISH McLEOD PRENTICE, BRIAN VAUSE, RUSSELL MAYES, ROY JACK, SHUG MACKIE, STEVIE CANAVAN, TOM COCHRANE, IAIN SUTHERLAND, GEORGE MAIN, RAY NOTLEY, DEREK IRVINE, DAVIE BLAIR, LES O'CONNOR (deceased), CHRIS REID (deceased), GEORDIE YOUNG (deceased), BUFF + SUSAN, TED MOCHAR, DAVIE SEATH, my accountant GRAHAM MINTO, DAVID FLETCHER, DAVID BLUE, ALAN LIDDELL, GOGZ, BARRY LIDDELL, HUNTER WATT, MICK and WENDY (from Malta holiday), GYLLA-FIONA SIMPSON, MALCOLM STEWART (of Jimpress fanzine), the Hebrides pub guys DAVIE BISSETT, MALCOLM YORK, ANDY SUTHERLAND and JOHN BISSETT, EWAN (of Europa Records, Friar Street, Stirling; a brilliant shop for every type of music buff), everyone at CANONGATE Books (they know who they are), everyone at 'Screenbase' (especially ROB), DEREK KILLAH and all the staff who helped me at the Falkirk Library, plus *RECORD COLLECTOR* (and PETER DOGGETT) for finally reviewing this book (as if!). Other music publications I read and thank are the *NME, LASERLOG/R.E.D., MUSIC WEEK, BILLBOARD, KERRANG!, MOJO, SELECT* and *Q*.

A very special mention to my daughters SUZANNE and SHIRLEY, my grandson IVOR, my granny ZENA MACKAY (who sadly passed away on the 15th of April, 2000), my auntie JOYCE (+ MICHAEL), my cousins PAUL, STEPHEN (+ NINA), BRIAN (+ JEANETTE), KEVIN (+ KAREN) and MAUREEN McELROY, AVRIL and JACKIE, uncle FRANK in Australia, RONNIE and MAISIE, ISOBEL and DANNY BUCHANAN, JENNIFER and KEITH plus DANIEL. Oh, and thanks for a great year and a half to someone who would (and I would now) like to remain nameless. I wish you all the best for the future.

Although there have been a plethora of letters in the past year, I will get around to printing only the good names in the 6th edition – if there is one. Nah! except one JAN KUEHNEMUND, formerly of hard-rock US girl band VIXEN; wow! makes you wanna visit the States!

* * * * *

M. C. Strong

Introduction

METAL?

'An alloy or an opaque elementary substance, possessing a peculiar lustre, fusibility, conductivity for heat and electricity, readiness to form positive ions' – you might say, or have I just taken the definition from Chambers' English Dictionary?!

This book will be my 10th published by Canongate since the first edition of THE GREAT ROCK DISCOGRAPHY hit the shops way back in December 1994. I've had my most prolific period yet since the inception of the new millennium (around a year and a half ago), compiling three tomes:- THE GREAT ROCK DISCOGRAPHY (5th Edition), THE GREAT SCOTS DISCOGRAPHY (rejected by Canongate and Mainstream, the top two Scottish publishers? – I think not!) and this one, THE GREAT METAL DISCOGRAPHY – Hard Rock to Hardcore (2nd Edition). You can't write three books of this nature in such a short space of time by sitting in your local pub day and night. It is of course nice to be allowed to escape from the house/cage the odd day or two a week – you'd crack otherwise. I packed in quite a lot of things during the 10 hours a day I allowed myself to complete these projects (I used to work up to 16 a day). With the taxman on my back once again, it became a lot harder for me to concentrate on everything I had to do. There were also other problems, but too numerous to mention here – my close friends know the story. I tried to pack in as much as I could and quite literally packed in everything – a certain person knows that story and if I could turn back the clock, well?

So despite everything (all the crack-ups, break-ups and hold-ups), here is the revised and (I hope) fully updated METAL DISCOGRAPHY 2nd edition – wow! I can safely say it's twice the book the first edition was, due to the updated biogs/discogs (right up to cut-off period, 30th June 2001), complete track listings (or very nearly), etc, etc. Due to my deadline, I didn't manage to get in everything I wanted, although I probably wouldn't have been allowed more pages than you see here (640, to be exact). The major difference to this tome is the inclusion of everything hardcore/punk; *Kerrang!* readers at least will enjoy this concept, as – since the advent of grunge/NIRVANA in the early '90s (and quite possibly before) – there has been an ever-thinning line between metal and punk. GUNS N' ROSES covering classic punk numbers on their 'Spaghetti Incident' set in '93, and numerous acts combining hardcore, metal and even hard rock – EXPLOITED and NAPALM DEATH are prime examples. Of course, some of you older, stick-in-the-mud headbangers will disagree totally – if you do just don't read the groups with the white headings (see further on). I have plenty taped examples of groups like ALTERNATIVE TV and CHELSEA getting to grips with what we now come to expect as heavy metal/rock. The more punk experimental or New Wave/pop outfits such as WIRE, The STRANGLERS and TELEVISION are not included here; look up THE GREAT ALTERNATIVE & INDIE DISCOGRAPHY for this info. I was a punk in '77/'78, having spent several years playing (h)air-guitar to many a hard rock tune; the two genres rarely matched and both sets of fans definitely didn't. I hope I can cross these thin barriers with this Metal book – read, listen and enjoy.

Book Layout: Like the last edition, I've used different heading-styles for the three categories of entries:–

The usual white-on-black heading is allocated to Metal acts (e.g., BLACK SABBATH, MARILYN MANSON);

The white-on-grey heading is for Hard Rock (e.g., LED ZEPPELIN, BON JOVI);

The black-heading-in-white-box, which was used for grunge in the first edition, is allocated to hardcore/punk this time around (e.g., IGGY POP, DEAD KENNEDYS); goth and some industrial acts are also under this heading.

Black Metal: A dangerous subject indeed and not to be taken (or written about) lightly. **Why?** Possibly because there were a lot of satanic messages in the track listings and I had to read them out several times before I put them into my computer; a dangerous thing if you don't want to call up Satan or the dead. I intentionally give no examples here. Unwittingly, I probably cursed a witch or two (and myself) along the way and I hope the evil spirits are now long gone. I know I'll be asked to visit Norway or Scandinavia quite soon, and although I'd love to visit all my Viking buddies up there, I'll have to decline for (future) health reasons; even although COUNT GRISHNAKH (of BURZUM) is still incarcerated for stabbing to death fellow Black-metaller, EURONYMOUS. "The pen is mightier than the sword" is a saying I'd like to leave out for a few years until the proverbial dust settles. Putting these little vacation foibles to one side and shaking like a leaf in the process, I welcome some nice letters from anybody interested enough to put pen to paper.

"What's next then?" two or three of you might be asking. The 6th Edition, the GRD on the internet; a publisher for the Great Scots book; finish off a novel or two; or get a real job that pays weekly/monthly? – who knows and who really cares, I don't anymore.

From Me To You, M. C. STRONG

Falkirk, August 2001

. . . "From out of the earth came Heavy Metal, Hard Rock, Hardcore and The Great Metal Discography" would probably be how Rock DJ, Tommy Vance, would describe it. Rock on . . .

A Brief History Of Heavy Metal, Hard Rock & Hardcore

Since time immemorial (well, since the dawning of '67, anyway) hairy men have taken up their trusty axe (er, electric guitar, that is) and let ear-mincing battle commence. In the beginning (i.e. the mid-'60s) there were riffs, basically amplified blues licks lashed out by white boys in suits attempting to interpret the sounds they were hearing on import "race" singles (i.e. black legends such as ALBERT KING, HOWLIN' WOLF, ELMORE JAMES, JOHN LEE HOOKER, SONNY BOY WILLIAMSON, and a host of others too numerous to mention). When this worked, it redefined the possibilities of the electric guitar as a tool of hormone-fuelled rebellion – see 'Louie Louie' (The Kingsmen), 'You Really Got Me' (The Kinks), '(I Can't Get No) Satisfaction' (The Rolling Stones), 'My Generation' (The Who), 'Wild Thing' (The Troggs), etc. The latter track would subsequently become a catalyst for JIMI HENDRIX's manic six-string innovation, the afro'd hipster transforming this garage-pop classic into a snarling heavy rock monster. But the song that really set this hepcat amongst the folk-pop pigeons was the thundering 'Purple Haze', a bruising head-on collision between psychedelia and proto-metal. Another guitar god waiting on the sidelines was ERIC CLAPTON (fresh from stints with The YARDBIRDS and JOHN MAYALL'S BLUESBREAKERS), the blues wizard acquiring both an (ill-advised) afro and a heavy sound for his power-trio CREAM after witnessing a particularly incendiary HENDRIX gig. As the long, strange trip of psychedelia started going bad, the music got louder, darker and heavier, American covers specialists VANILLA FUDGE being overtaken by fellow sludge merchants IRON BUTTERFLY (both bands introducing claustrophic organ into the heavy rock scene; the 17-minute title track from 'In-A-Gadda-Da-Vida' virtually brushed aside any lingering remnants of flower-pop in the summer of '68). Another US outfit doing the rounds at this time were STEPPENWOLF, a band that went down in the history of rock, not so much for their musical innovation as for their infamous coining of the term "Heavy Metal" in the song 'Born To Be Wild'. This metallic anthem became more famous when it was subsequently used on the soundtrack for the cult hippy/biker movie, 'Easy Rider'. While America had road fever, Britain had the blues again (well before the advent of Thatcherism!), this time around a decidedly heavier dose, courtesy of bands such as TEN YEARS AFTER, FREE, JETHRO TULL, TASTE (RORY GALLAGHER's band) and the inimitably 'Dazed And Confused' LED ZEPPELIN. To most commentators' minds, the first real "heavy metal" band, PLANT, PAGE, JONES and BONHAM laid the foundation slabs of the genre with their explosive but soulful sonic assault. The funky depth charge riff and orgasmic wailing of 'Whole Lotta Love' drew new battle lines, and for a number of years there were few worthy challengers. While punk-rock was stillborn with the primal howl of The STOOGES and MC5 (garage bands evolving into three-chord heavyweights), Britain had spawned a more sinister strain of blues-fuelled doom-metal in the shape of Brummie occult-fiends, BLACK SABBATH. Fronted by shrieking banshee, OZZY OSBOURNE, and powered by the leaden riffs of TONY IOMMI, the group came out of nowhere in the early '70s to deliver unto the Earth the apocalyptic atmospherics of their thunderous opening track, 'Black Sabbath' (from the album, 'Black Sabbath'). Their blackest moment, however, arrived in the form of 'Paranoid', a juddering riffathon of a 45 that penetrated the proverbial heart of darkness. Heavy rock began to proliferate faster with each passing month: already the scene had witnessed the 'Black Night' of DEEP PURPLE, while lesser acts such as URIAH HEEP, ATOMIC ROOSTER and America's loudest exports BLUE CHEER and GRAND FUNK RAILROAD were making the metal grade (Southern rock was also evolving, meshing together blues, country and hard rock into a blistering all-American vanguard headed by The ALLMAN BROTHERS, ZZ TOP and later LYNYRD SKYNYRD). A vague UK equivalent could be found in populist hard rock boogie-meisters, STATUS QUO, a jeans 'n' T-shirt alternative to the glam-stomp of SLADE and SWEET, who followed MOTT THE HOOPLE and QUEEN's hard-rock example as mid-'70s stagnation beckoned (the US glam equivalent being schlockmeister, ALICE COOPER). As usual the Americans did it bigger and flashier, the twin-headed decadent beast of AEROSMITH and KISS dominating the massive US territory with their sleazy sex/drugs anthems (these two bands alone were arguably responsible for the biggest cloning operation the rock scene had ever witnessed; see below). Over the northern border, Canadian bands such as Mormon rockers BACHMAN-TURNER OVERDRIVE and prog-rock heavies RUSH were part of the wider, more disparate international hard-rock scene that saw bands as diverse as NAZARETH (Scotland), BUDGIE (Wales), GOLDEN EARRING (Netherlands) and SCORPIONS (Germany) carving out their own niche prior to the dawn of punk. Instigated primarily as a vicious backlash against the bloated corpse of 'dinosaur rock', the older generation of heavy rockers suddenly found themselves in the critical doghouse. America was reprieved for the time being, rock fans embracing the very antithesis of punk in the shape of glossy AOR; beginning with BOSTON's 'More Than A Feeling', and running through KANSAS, JOURNEY, REO SPEEDWAGON and FOREIGNER, the genre gathered strength on into the '80s. Indirectly allied to this was the defiantly unique MEAT LOAF, the beefy powerhouse sweating his way through the landmark 'Bat Out Of Hell'. Leaner, meaner acts like legendary Australian nutters, AC/DC, and London's MOTORHEAD (fronted by LEMMY, formerly a bassist with early '70s psychedelic heavies, HAWKWIND) co-existed quite happily alongside punk's blitzkrieg onslaught, the latter act's scuzzy metal'n'roll pivotal in the emergence of '80s thrash. Another byproduct of the revolution came in the form of the New Wave Of British Heavy Metal (NWOBHM), a D.I.Y. grassroots movement inspired by the success of proto-thrash Brit-metallers JUDAS PRIEST. Taking the rawness and aggression of punk and applying it to metal, IRON MAIDEN became the movement's flagbearer and subsequently one of the biggest heavy-metal bands in the world. Cut from a similar, if more lighweight cloth, DEF LEPPARD also went on to take the world by storm, although SAXON and their ilk faded along with the scene several years later. Meanwhile, America had finally cottoned on to punk rock and was in the throes of its own mini-revolution with a burgeoning hardcore movement; inspired by the nihilism of the SEX PISTOLS, bands such as The DEAD KENNEDYS, BLACK FLAG and SOCIAL DISTORTION attempted to articulate the rage and frustration of Uncle Sam's broken dream (arty noisesters including HUSKER DU, SONIC YOUTH and The BUTTHOLE SURFERS were to take the form into more experimental territory and partly lay the groundwork for 'grunge'). The 'never-say-die' punk attitude was re-activated in Britain with the "oi" movement, spearheaded by the mohican-topped likes of EXPLOITED, GBH and DISCHARGE, outfits that later solidified into heavy metal (the latter outfit especially was a major influence on the late '80s grindcore scene, a sonically extreme music form originated by NAPALM DEATH and instigating lemmingmania stagediving). Across the Atlantic, American musicians, influenced by a combination of NWOBHM and hardcore, had been creating a lightning-fast strain of metal later christened "thrash". METALLICA started the ball rolling with their debut album, 'Kill 'Em All', while MEGADETH, ANTHRAX and SLAYER waited in the wings, each trading in their own particularly intense take on the genre. The latter outfit's controversial 'Reign In Blood' album especially inspiring a generation of budding extremists who took the idea a step further and created the gore-spattered "death-metal" craze. Chief purveyors like DEATH, OBITUARY and MORBID ANGEL revelled in explicit lyrics, unintelligable vocals and unrelenting onslaughts of thrash-based noise. Another sub-division of metal's more unsavoury side was the black-metal movement, actually started in Newcastle(!) by VENOM, and taken to ludicrous new depths by Scandinavian satanists BATHORY (later 'developed' by obsessive Norwegian outfits like MAYHEM and BURZUM; the latter's COUNT GRISHNAKH murdered the former's EURONYMOUS in '93, enough said). Running parallel to all this extremity was the US hair-metal brigade led by BON JOVI, a band taking at least some of their cue from L.A. party-rock legends, VAN HALEN. The fabled city of angels was also the breeding ground for the glam/sleaze rock revival, GUNS N' ROSES condensing the scene's lowlife fascination into the blistering 'Appetite For Destruction' album in 1987, AXL ROSE, SLASH and Co. combining the best of AC/DC, AEROSMITH and the SEX PISTOLS into one compellingly seedy whole. Other minor players included POISON, FASTER PUSSYCAT, L.A. GUNS, etc, while already-established acts such as MOTLEY CRUE, W.A.S.P. and RATT benefitted from renewed interest. Something of an anomaly, hip-hop punks The BEASTIE BOYS shook up the rock scene earlier in the year with the brilliantly dumb teenage anthem, '(You Gotta) Fight For Your Right (To Party)'; though it would take a few years for the metal scene to fully endorse the new style, the seismic effect of the BEASTIEs' sound is still being felt today (RAGE AGAINST THE MACHINE being a prime example). Soul and funk were now on the rock/metal agenda big style, black artists such as LIVING COLOUR and LENNY KRAVITZ breaking through worldwide, while white funk-metal veterans RED HOT CHILI PEPPERS and FAITH NO MORE were hailed as heroes by the media. Heavy metal as people knew and loved/hated it was already undergoing a sea change (JANE'S ADDICTION and subsequently The SMASHING PUMPKINS re-writing the rules), when NIRVANA changed it forever in the Autumn of 1991 with groundbreaking grunge anthem, 'Smells Like Teen Spirit'; rising from the insular Seattle scene alongside MUDHONEY, TAD, etc, NIRVANA succeeded in fusing punk, pop and metal in a fashion which rendered the old guard obselete. Out went spandex, solos and socks down underpants, in came checked-shirts, ripped jeans and distortion pedals. In the wake of NIRVANA's colossal success, metal emerged anew in the shape of SOUNDGARDEN, PEARL JAM, ALICE IN CHAINS, et al, while the PC politics of grunge opened the floodgates for a barrage of feisty female rage courtesy of HOLE, BABES IN TOYLAND, L7, etc (who made '70s/'80s 'hard' rock chicks such as HEART, RUNAWAYS, PAT BENATAR and VIXEN seem like librarians). The first half of the '90s also saw the rebirth of industrial metal, once the preserve of '80s alternative punks, KILLING JOKE. This time around the genre was twisted into hideous new shapes via MINISTRY (with various off-shoots REVOLTING COCKS, LARD, etc), NINE INCH NAILS and MARILYN MANSON, the latter taking gothic imagery, sex and perversion to new limits of bad taste and once again upsetting the moral majority in the process. JONATHAN DAVIES of KORN seems to be another to translate his unsavoury childhood in lyrical form, the track 'Daddy' from 1994's eponymous classic reaching soul baring, tear-jerking lengths rarely witnessed in the macho world of metal. An obvious example of how things have changed beyond recognition lies in the fact that the best rock'n'roll experience of the last few years was techno-industrial outfit, The PRODIGY. As they metamorphosed from a rave act into a decidedly darker proposition, these Essex lads created some of the most exhilarating blasts of danceable noise of the decade in 'Voodoo People', 'Poison', 'Firestarter' and 'Breathe'. By 1998, the scene was more diverse than it had ever been, with continual cross-fertilisation being the driving force; MAX CAVALERA (formerly of legendary Brazilian tribal-thrashers, SEPULTURA) and his SOULFLY outfit are currently on the cutting edge, while the same year saw metal coming full circle with both BLACK SABBATH (reunited with OZZY) and LED ZEPPELIN (reunited as PAGE & PLANT) making a significant comeback. Meanwhile, the re-emergence in the mid '90s of Punk rock (especially from the States) has only gone to prove that Punk and Hardcore never really died – they were only resting in other genres waiting to have another go at the pop world via GREEN DAY, OFFSPRING, BLINK 182, ASH, etc. The new millennium has also given us a crop of fresh-faced alt-rock-meets-metal acts such as AND THEY WILL KNOW US BY THE TRAIL OF DEAD and AT THE DRIVE-IN (where do they get these names, man?), but surely the biggest prospect comes in the shape of metal rappers, LIMP BIZKIT . . . read on brothers and sisters.

M. C. STRONG
and
BRENDON GRIFFIN

Rap meets Metal

The Story So Far: The walls between Hip-Hop and Hard Rock/Metal first came tumbling down (quite literally) back in 1986 as faded '70s superstar STEVEN TYLER and his AEROSMITH crew smashed a mic stand through the flimsy partition which separated them from black spiritual brethren RUN DMC. The video in question was witnessed by millions, the Queens hip-hop posse revitalising AEROSMITH's mid-'70s gem, 'Walk This Way' and sowing the seeds of a musical revolution which is still ripping up the rule book to this day. While this legendary head-to-head is often cited as Rap-Metal's birth, a bearded entrepreneur by the name of RICK RUBIN was beavering away behind the scenes at 'Def Jam' records. A fan of anything extreme, he'd picked up a bunch of white middle-class, rock-loving hip-hop wannabes named The BEASTIE BOYS. While hip-hop records sampling classic rock was nothing new, the BEASTIE's were the first to do it with a Rock attitude. Not content with merely sampling (LED ZEPPELIN, AC/DC, etc), they got in SLAYER axeman KERRY KING to reel off a solo on their massive breakthrough hit, '(You've Got To) Fight For Your Right (To Party)'. The date was early '87 and suddenly white suburban kids began to appropriate the image and outlook of black hip-hop. The wholesale appropriation of the music (EMINEM for example) would come later but for the time being at least, Rock began meeting Rap head on with various artists cross-fertilising their sound. 'Def Jam' was basically the centre of the new Rap-Metal universe; not only did they count both The BEASTIE BOYS and SLAYER on their roster but they were also home to legendary Rap militants PUBLIC ENEMY. Led by the outspoken CHUCK D, these Long Island rebels sampled SLAYER's 'Angel Of Death' on their own 'She Watch Channel Zero' (from their seminal 1988 album, 'It Takes A Nation Of Millions . . .') and went on to collaborate with thrashers ANTHRAX on a groundbreaking version of their hit single 'Bring The Noise'. Incidentally, ANTHRAX had already become one of the first metal acts to show their appreciation of hip-hop with 1987's 'I'm The Man' single. The RED HOT CHILI PEPPERS of course had been crafting their funk-punk beast since the early '80s and remain a pivotal element in the whole scene although they never recorded a big name hip-hop collaboration. FAITH NO MORE certainly took their cue from the CHILI's, helping carry the hybrid forward and cutting the single, 'Another Body Murdered' with Samoan heavyweights BOO-YAA T.R.I.B.E. The track was part of a crucial 1993 soundtrack collection ('Judgement Night') masterminded by 'Immortal' records mainman, Happy Walters. The record herded together the main players from the Hip-Hop and Alt-Rock scene, letting them fight it out in the studio and unwittingly planting the seeds of America's current Nu-metal overload. Amongst others were thrilling pairings between ICE-T and SLAYER (a cover of DISCHARGE's 'Disorder'), HOUSE OF PAIN and HELMET, and CYPRESS HILL with both SONIC YOUTH and PEARL JAM. Yet perhaps more than any other band, L.A.'s RAGE AGAINST THE MACHINE personified and articulated the anger prevalent in both genres, setting the blueprint for the rest of the decade and beyond on their groundbreaking eponymous debut set in '92. The late '90s saw a spate of Rap'n'Metal collaborations as the so-called Nu-metal brigade noised up their opponents. Thus we had ICE CUBE and KORN on the track 'Fuck Dying', PUFF DADDY, MA$E & LIL' KIM with SYSTEM OF A DOWN on 'Will They Die 4 You', PUFF DADDY (again!) with LED ZEP legend JIMMY PAGE on near chart-topping 'Come With Me' (from the movie re-make of 'Godzilla'), BUSTA RHYMES and OZZY OSBOURNE (although the veteran bat-chomper claims to despise Rap-Metal) on 'This Means War!!', EMINEM and KID ROCK on the subtle-as-a-sledgehammer 'Fuck Off', and last but not least METHOD MAN (of WU-TANG CLAN) and LIMP BIZKIT on the massive hit 'N2gether Now'. Talking of the WU-TANG crew (but not behind their backs, honest), 'Loud' records took the 'Judgement Night' concept into the new millennium with the 'Loud Rocks' album, pairing up their roster – WU-TANG CLAN, THA ALKAHOLIKS, MOBB DEEP, XZIBIT, BIG PUNISHER and DEAD PREZ – with the likes of SYSTEM OF A DOWN, SUGAR RAY, STATIC-X, SEVENDUST, SICK OF IT ALL and INCUBUS. Although the revolution continues, much of the cross-cultural traffic (with a few noteable exceptions, i.e. ICE-T/BODY COUNT) is one-way; how many major Hip-Hop artists employ a full-on metal guitarist? Which is possibly why Rap-Metal is becoming increasingly cliched and one-dimensional. If LIMP BIZKIT and PAPA ROACH are the future then that fight for the right to party way back in the mid-'80s was surely in vain.

M.C.S. and B.G.

How To Read The Book

If you're struggling in any way how to comprehend some of the more complex parts of each discography, here are some examples to make it easier. Read below for around 10 minutes, taking a step at a time. The final lines/examples you see will give you a good guide before you proceed with the actual chronological discographies. However, I think that once you've read your own favourites you'll have a good idea.

GROUP / ARTIST (Metal)

Formed/Born: Where/When ... biography including style/analysis, songwriters, cover versions, trivia, etc.

Album rating: i.e. rating between 1-10 amalgamated between music press reviews, your letters and my own personal opinion.

SINGER (born; b. day/month/year, town/city, country) – vocals, whatever (ex-GROUP; if any) / **MUSICIAN** (b. BIRTH NAME, 8 Sep'60, Musselburgh, Scotland) – instruments / **OTHER MUSICIANS** – other instruments, vocals, etc.

UK Label US Label

UKdate. (single, ep or album) *(UK cat.no.)* <*US cat.no.*> **THE TITLE** [ ] [ ] US date
note:- UK label – might be another country's label if not released in UK.
also:- Labels only appear when the group signs to a new one.
note:- UK date – might be foreign, <even American at times>, if not initially issued in Britain.
note:- (UK catalogue number; in curved brackets) <US cat.no.; in angle brackets>
note:- chart positions, UK + US, are in the boxes below labels.
also:- the boxes in the above example have been left blank, thus they did not hit either UK or US charts.
note:- US date after the boxes indicates a variation from its UK counterpart.
also:- Any other info on the right of the boxes (e.g. German) indicates it was not issued in the US.

UKdate. (7") *(UK cat.no.)* **A-SIDE. / B-SIDE** [ ] [-]
US date. (7") <*US cat.no.*> **A-SIDE. / DIFFERENT B-SIDE** [-] [ ]
note:- The two examples above show that the UK + US release did not have an identical A-side & B-side, thus the chart boxes are marked with a – to indicate it was not released in either the UK or the US.

UKdate. (7"/c-s) *(CATNO 1/+C)* **A-SIDE. / B-SIDE** [ ] [-]
note:- above had two formats with the same tracks (i.e. 7"/c-s). However, catalogue numbers will always vary among different formats – often only slightly (e.g. CATNO 1/+C). Each cat.no. would read thus:- (7")=*(CATNO 1)* and (c-s)=*(CATNO 1C)*. To save space the (/) slash comes into effect. The (/) means "or" and in this case it is prefixed with a + sign for the equivalent cassette (c-s).

UKdate. (7"/c-s) *(example same as above)* **SEE ABOVE** [ ] [-]
(12"+=/cd-s+=) *(CATNO 1-12/1-CD)* – Extra tracks.
note:- If there are more formats with extra or different tracks, a new line would be used. Obviously there would also be alternative catalogue numbers utilising the "(/)" as before. Extra tracks would therefore mean the addition of the sign "(+=)" to each format.

UKdate. (lp/c/cd) *(CATNO 200/+MC/CD)* <*US catno 4509*> **ALBUM TITLE** [ ] [ ]
– Track listing / Track 2 / And so on. *(re-issued = re-iss. A later date, and other 'Label' mentioned, if different from original; new cat.no.) (could be re-iss. many times and if "(+=)" sign occurs there will be extra tracks from the original)* <*could also apply to the US release if in pointed brackets*>
note:- Album above released in 3 formats, thus 3 catalogue numbers are neccessary. The "long-player" lp *(CATNO 200)* is obvious. The "cassette" c = +MC *(CATNO 200MC)* or "compact disc" CD *(CATNO 200CD)*. The US <*cat.no.*> will normally be just one set of numbers (or see further below for other details).

UKdate. (cd/c/lp) *(CD/TC+/CATNO+200)* <*UScatno 4509*> **ALBUM TITLE** [ ] [ ] US date
note:- This time a prefix is used instead of a suffix, hence the difference before the standard lp catalogue number. For instance, the cd would read as *(CDCATNO 200)*.

Jun 97. (cd/c/lp) <*(5557 49860-2/-4/-1)*> **ALBUM TITLE** [1] [1] May97
note:- Some catalogue numbers don't include any letters, but instead consist of a number sequence followed by one digit which universally corresponds with the format (i.e. 2 = cd / 4 = c / 1 = lp).
also:- If the US numbers are identical, there would be no need to list them separately, i.e. <*(the numbers)*>
note:- I've also marked down an actual date of release and its variant in the US (you'll find this fictitious album also hit No.1 in both charts "and ah've no even heard it yet, man!")

— **NEW MUSICIAN/SINGER** (b.whenever, etc.) – instruments (ex-GROUP(s) replaced = repl. DEPARTING MUSICIAN/SINGER, who joined whatever
note:- Above denotes a line-up change.

GROUP or ARTIST with major change of name

note:- above would always be in grey.

UK Label US Label

Jun 97. (cd/c/lp; GROUP or ARTIST with minor change of name) <*(5557 49860)*> **ALBUM TITLE** [1] [1] May97

– compilations, etc. –

UKdate. (cd) *compilation Label only; (cat.no.)* **ALBUM TITLE** [100] [-]
– Track listing would be selective, only included if the release was deemed essential.

* * *

The other music types are shown with headings as follows:–

GROUP / ARTIST (Hard Rock)

and

GROUP/ARTIST (Hardcore/Punk)

RECORD-LABEL ABBREVIATIONS

Nearly all the record labels have been shown in full, but the following abbreviations have been used:

Amphetam. Reptile – Amphetamine Reptile
Better Youth Org'n. – Better Youth Organization
EMI Internat. – EMI International
Fundam. – Fundamental
Transatla. – Transatlantic
Sympathy F – Sympathy For The Record Industry
U.A. – United Artists
Warners – Warner Brothers
not iss. – not issued

Formats & Abbreviations

VINYL (black coloured unless stated)

(lp) = The (LONG PLAYER) record ... circular 12" plays at $33^{1/3}$ r.p.m., and has photo or artwork sleeve. Approximate playing time ... 30–50 minutes with average 10 tracks. Introduced in the mid-'50s on mono until stereo took over in the mid-'60s. Quadrophonic had a spell in the '70s, but only on mainly best-selling lp's, that had been previously released. Because of higher costs to the manufacturer and buyer, the quad sunk around 1978. Also note that around the mid-'50s, some albums were released on 10 inch. Note:– average cost to the customer as of now = £9.00 (new). Collectors can pay anything from £1 to over £500, depending on the quality of the recording. Very scratched records can be worthless, but unplayed-mint deletions are worth a small fortune to the right person. Auctions and record fairs can be the place to find that long lost recording that's eluded you. This applies to all other vinyl below.

(d-1p) = The (DOUBLE-LONG PLAYER) record ... as before. Playing time 50–90 minutes on 4 sides, with average 17 tracks. Introduced to rock/pop world in the late '60s, to complement compilations, concept & concert (aka live) albums.
Compilations:– are a selection of greatest hits or rare tracks, demos, etc.
Concepts:– are near-uninterrupted pieces of music, based around a theme.
Note that normal lp's could also be compilations, live or concept. Some record companies through the wishes of their artists, released double lp's at the price of one lp. If not, price new would be around £15.

(t-1p) = The (TRIPLE-LONG PLAYER) record ... as before. Playing time over 100 minutes with normally over 20 tracks. Because of the cost to the consumer, most artists steered clear of this format. Depending on the artwork on the sleeve, these cost over £17.50. (See its replacement, the CD.)

(4-1p-box) = The (BOXED-LONG PLAYER) record (could be between 4 and 10 in each boxed-set). As the triple album would deal with live, concept or compilation side, the boxed-set would be mostly re-issues of all the artist's album material, with probably a bonus lp thrown in, to make it collectable. Could be very pricey, due to lavish outlay in packaging. They cost over £25 new.

(m-lp) = The (MINI-LONG PLAYER) record ... playing time between 20 and 30 minutes and containing on average 7 tracks. Introduced for early '80s independent market, and cost around £5.
= Note:– This could be confused at times with the extended-play 12" single.

(pic-1p) = The (PICTURE DISC-LONG PLAYER) record ... as before but with album artwork/ design on the vinyl grooves. Mainly for the collector because of the slightly inferior sound quality. If unplayed, these can fetch between £10 and £250.

(coloured lp) = The (COLOURED-LONG PLAYER) record; can be in a variety of colours including ... white / blue / red / clear / purple / green / pink / gold / silver.

(red-1p) = The (RED VINYL-LONG PLAYER) record would be an example of this.

(7") = The (7 INCH SINGLE). Arrived in the late '50s, and plays at 45 r.p.m. Before this its equivalent was the 10" on 78 r.p.m. Playing time now averages 4 minutes per side, but during the late '50s up to mid-'60s, each side averaged $2^{1/2}$ minutes. Punk rock/new wave in 1977/78 resurrected this idea. In the '80s, some disco releases increased playing time. Another idea that was resurrected in 1977 was the picture sleeve. This had been introduced in the '60s, but mostly only in the States.
Note:– cost in mid-98 was just under £2.50; second-hand rarities can cost between 25p and £200, depending again on their condition. These might also contain limited freebies/gifts (i.e. posters, patches, stickers, badges, etc). Due to the confusion this would cause, I have omitted this information, and kept to the vinyl aspect in this book. Another omission has been DJ promos, demos, acetates, magazine freebies, various artists' compilations, etc. Only official shop releases get a mention.

(7" m) = The (7 INCH MAXI-SINGLE). Named so because of the extra track, mostly on the B-side. Introduced widely during the early '70s; one being ROCKET MAN by ELTON JOHN.

(7" ep) = The (7 INCH EXTENDED PLAY SINGLE). Plays mostly at $33^{1/3}$ r.p.m., with average playing time 10–15 minutes and 4 tracks. Introduced in the late '50s as compilations for people to sample their albums. These had a *title* and were also re-introduced from 1977 onwards, but this time for punk groups' new songs.

(d7") = The (DOUBLE 7 INCH SINGLE). Basically just two singles combined ... 4 tracks. Introduced in the late '70s for the "new wave/romantics", and would cost slightly more than normal equivalent.

(7" pic-d) = The (7 INCH PICTURE-DISC SINGLE). This was vinyl that had a picture on the grooves, which could be viewed through a see-through plastic cover.

(7" sha-pic-d) = The (7 INCH SHAPED-PICTURE-DISC SINGLE). Vinyl as above but with shape (i.e. gun, mask, group) around the edge of the groove. Awkward because it would not fit into the collector's singles box. Initially limited, and this can still be obtained at record fairs for over £3. Note:– However, in the book the type of shape has not been mentioned, to save space.

(7" coloured) = The (7 INCH COLOURED SINGLE). Vinyl that is not black (i.e. any other colour; red, yellow, etc). Note:– (7" multi) would be a combination of two or more colours (i.e. pink/purple).

(7" flexi) = The (7 INCH FLEXIBLE SINGLE). One-sided freebies, mostly given away by magazines, at concerts or as mentioned here; free with single or lp. Worth keeping in mint condition and well protected.

(12") = The (12 INCH SINGLE). Plays at 45 r.p.m., and can have extended or extra tracks to its 7" counterpart (+=) or (++=). B-side's playing speed could be at 33 r.p.m. Playing time could be between 8 and 15 minutes. Introduced in 1977 with the advent of new wave and punk. They were again a must for collectors, for the new wave of British heavy metal scene.

(12"ep) = The (12 INCH EXTENDED PLAY SINGLE). Virtually same as above but *titled* like the 7" ep. Playing time over 12 minutes, and could have between 3 and 5 tracks.

(d12") = The (DOUBLE 12 INCH SINGLE). See double 7". Can become very collectable and would cost new as normal 12", £4.50.

(12" pic-d) = The (12 INCH PICTURE-DISC SINGLE). As with 7" equivalent ... see above.

(12" sha-pic-d) = The (12 INCH SHAPED-PICTURE-DISC SINGLE). See above 7" equivalent.

(12" colrd) = The (12 INCH COLOURED SINGLE). Not black vinyl ... see above 7" equivalent.

(10") = The (10 INCH SINGLE). Plays at 45 r.p.m. and, like the 12", can have extra tracks (+=). Very collectable, it surfaced in its newer form around the early '80s, and can be obtained in shops at £4.50. Note:– also (10" ep) / (d10") / (10" coloured) / (10" pic-d) / (10" sha-pic-d).

CASSETTES

(c) = The (CASSETTE) album ... size in case 4 1/2 inches high. Playing-time same as lp album, although after the mid-'80s cd revolution, some were released with extra tracks. Introduced in the late '60s, to compete with the much bulkier lp. Until the '80s, most cassettes were lacking in group info, lyric sheets, and freebies. Note:– cost to the consumer as of now = £8 new. But for a few exceptions, most do not increase in price, and can be bought second-hand or budget-priced for around £5.

(d-c) = The (DOUBLE-CASSETTE) album ... as above, and would hold same tracks as d-lp or even t-lp. Price between £12 and £16.

(c-s) = The (CASSETTE-SINGLE). Now released mostly with same two tracks as 7" equivalent. The other side played the same 2 or 3 tracks. Introduced unsuccessfully in the US around the late '60s. Re-introduced there and in Britain in the mid-'80s. In the States, it and its cd counterpart have replaced the charting 7" single for the '90s. Cost new is around £1.50–£2.50, and might well become quite collectable.

(c-ep) = The (CASSETTE-EXTENDED PLAY SINGLE). Same as above but *titled* as 12".

COMPACT DISCS

(cd) = The (COMPACT DISC) album. All 5" circular and mostly silver on its playing side. Perspex casing also includes lyrics & info, etc. Introduced late in 1982, and widely the following year (even earlier for classical music). Initially for top recording artists, but now in 2000 nearly every release is in cd format. Playing time normally over 50 minutes with some containing extra tracks or mixes. Possible playing time is just over 75 minutes. Marketed as unscratchable, although if they go uncleaned, they will stick just as vinyl. Average price now is £15, and will become collectable if, like most gloomy predictions, they do not deteriorate with time.

(d-cd) = The (DOUBLE-COMPACT DISC) album ... same as above although very pricey, between £20 and £25.

(cd-s) = The (COMPACT DISC-SINGLE). Mainly all 5" (but some 3" cd-s could only be played with a compatible gadget inside the normal cd player). Playing time over 15 minutes to average 25 minutes, containing 4 or 5 tracks. Introduced in 1986 to compete with the 12" ep or cassette. 99% contained extra tracks to normal formats. Cost new: over £4.50.

(pic-cd-s) = The (PICTURE-COMPACT DISC-SINGLE). Has picture on disc, which gives it its collectability. Also on (pic-cd-ep).

(vid-pic-s) = The (VIDEO-COMPACT DISC-SINGLE). A video cd, which can be played through stereo onto normal compatible TV screen. Very costly procedure, but still might be the format of the future. Promo videos can be seen on pub jukeboxes, which has made redundant the returning Wurlitzer style.

DIGITAL AUDIO TAPE

(dat) = The (DIGITAL AUDIO TAPE) album. Introduced in the mid-'80s and, except for Japan and the rich yuppie, are not widely issued. It is a smaller version of the cassette, with the quality of the cd.

Another format (which I have not included) is the CARTRIDGE, which was available at the same time as the cassette. When the cassette finally won the battle in the early '80s, the cartridge became redundant. All car-owners of the world were happy when thieves made them replace the stolen cartridge player with the resurrected cassette. You can still buy these second-hand, but remember you'll have to obtain a second-hand 20-year-old player, with parts possibly not available.

Other abbreviations: repl. = replaced / comp. = compilation / re-iss. = re-issued / re-dist. = re-distributed

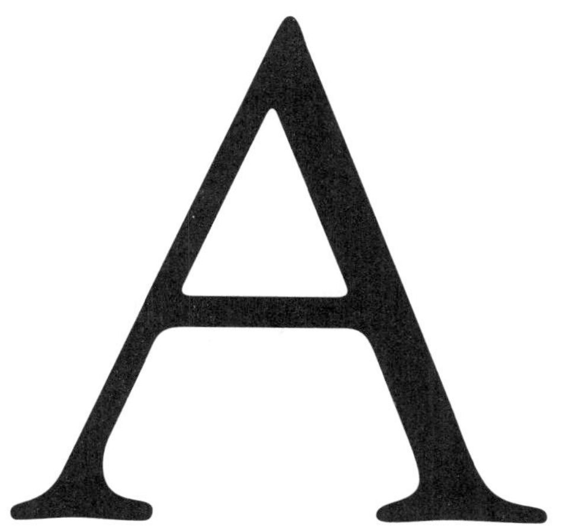

'A'

Formed: Suffolk, England . . . 1994 by the Leeds-born PERRY brothers, JASON, GILES and ADAM, who duly recruited MARK CHAPMAN and STEVIE SWINDON. Initially VAN HALEN obsessives, they progressed into an alternative heavy/punk fun-rock outfit influenced by JANE'S ADDICTION, GREEN DAY and The MANIC STREET PREACHERS. 'A' – they probably picked this short moniker because they'd be first in every Rock book – proceeded to tour with everyone from the re-formed SEX PISTOLS, ASH and SYMPOSIUM before being shipped off to California on a new recording mission courtesy of 'London' (via their own 'Tycoon' label). A's debut single in the summer of '96, '5 IN THE MORNING', was received favourably by critics into prozac-punk pop. During the next year, they released three more (including 'No.1', which used lyrics from Billy Joel's 'My Life') and an album 'HOW ACE ARE BUILDINGS', which was given rave reviews in Kerrang! In 1999, 'A' were back with a sophomore effort, 'vs MONKEY KONG'. However, despite three further minor hits, 'SUMMER ON THE UNDERGROUND', 'OLD FOLKS' and 'I LOVE LAKE TAHOE', it fell just short of giving the band a Top 60 place. • **Covered:** OWNER OF A LONELY HEART (Yes).

Album rating: HOW ACE ARE BUILDINGS (*6) / vs MONKEY KONG (*5)

JASON PERRY – vocals / **MARK CHAPMAN** – guitar / **GILES PERRY** – keyboards, vocals / **STEVIE SWINDON** – bass, vocals / **ADAM PERRY** – drums

Tycoon | not iss.

Jul 96. (7") *(TY 1)* **FIVE IN THE MORNING. / ALMOST EVERYTHING IS GREAT** [ ] [-]
(cd-s+=) *(TYCD 1)* – 8 fingers.

Nov 96. (7") *(TY 2)* **HOUSE UNDER THE GROUND. / "40"** [ ] [-]
(cd-s+=) *(TYCD 2)* – Demolished house.

May 97. (7") *(TY 3)* **BAD IDEA. / "40"** [ ] [-]
(cd-s+=) *(TYCD 3)* – Look what you made me do.

Aug 97. (7") *(TY 4)* **No.1. / ALRIGHT** [ ] [-]
(cd-s+=) *(TYCD 4)* – Ouch! / ('A'version).

Sep 97. (cd/c) *(828 916-2/-4)* **HOW ACE ARE BUILDINGS** [ ] [-]
– Turn it up / Foghorn / Cheeky monkey / No.1 / Bad idea / Sing-a-long / Winter of '96 / Out of tune / Fistral / House under the ground / 5 in the morning / Ender. *(re-iss. Jun98; same)*

— (summer '97) **DANIEL P. CARTER** – bass; repl. SWINDON

Oct 97. (cd-s) *(COUP 06)* **HOUSE UNDER THE GROUND / (track by Glitterbox)** [ ] [-]
(above issued on 'Revolution')

Jan 98. (7") *(TY 5)* **FOGHORN. / LAST GIRL** [63] [-]
(cd-s+=) *(TYCD 5)* – A demolished house.

Mar 98. (7") *(TY 6)* **NUMBER ONE. / GOOD IDEA** [47] [-]
(cd-s+=) *(TYCD 6)* – Alright / Sasqatch.
(cd-s) *(TYCDP 6)* – ('A'side) / ('A'-Happy Valley ranch mix) / Foghorn / Foghorn (video).

Jun 98. (7"pic-d) *(TY 7)* **SING-A-LONG. / I'M OVER IT** [57] [-]
(cd-s+=) *(TYCD 7)* – Callhimyin / Photo finger.
(cd-s) *(TYCDP 7)* – ('A'side) / ('A'-post-term audio mix) / Singing out of tune (literally, in a castle) / Number One (video).

London | Mammoth

Oct 98. (7"/c-s) *(TY/+CS 8)* **SUMMER ON THE UNDERGROUND. / OWNER OF A LONELY HEART** [72] [-]
(cd-s+=) *(TYCD 8)* – I can't wait until morning.
(cd-s) *(TYCDP 8)* – ('A'side) / For starters / Charlie Jordan.

May 99. (7"pic-d) *(TY 9)* **OLD FOLKS. / ONE DAY** [54] [-]
(cd-s+=) *(TYCD 9)* – Don't be punks (acapella version).
(cd-s) *(TYCDP 9)* – ('A'side) / She said / We're equal.

Aug 99. (7"pic-d) *(TY 10)* **I LOVE LAKE TAHOE. / MONKEY KING JR.** [59] [-]
(cd-s) *(TYCD 10)* – ('A'-version).
(cd-s) *(TYCDP 10)* – ('A'side) / Turn it down / Old folks / Old folks (video).

Aug 99. (cd) *(3984 27695-2)* <65501> **vs MONKEY KONG** [62] [ ] Sep00
– For starters / Monkey Kong / A / Old folks / Hopper Jonnus fang / Summer on the underground / Warning / If it ain't broke, fix it anyway / I love Lake Tahoe / Don't be punks / Down on the floor / Jason's addiction / Miles away / Getting around. *<US+=>* – She said / One day / If it ain't broke (live).

London | not iss.

May 00. (m-cd) *(8573 83098-2)* **EXIT STAGE RIGHT (live)** [ ] [-]
– Intro / If it ain't broke, fix it anyway / Monkey Kong / A / Old folks / I love Lake Tahoe / Over it / Foghorn.

Lee AARON

Born: KAREN LYNN GREENING, 21 Jul'62, Belleville, Ontario, Canada. Initially something of a sex symbol, AARON's career got off to an infamous start after she posed nude for the top shelf mag, 'Oui'. Her vocal gymnastics were given exposure on a debut album, 'THE LEE AARON PROJECT' (1982), which featured a variety of notable Canadian hard rock musicians from MOXY, SANTERS, WRABIT, RECKLESS, FRANK SODA, etc. After a visit to Britain in 1983 with co-songwriter JOHN ALBANI, she subsequently signed to 'Attic' ('Roadrunner' in Europe), releasing the 'METAL QUEEN' opus the following year. Despite a support slot in Europe to rising stars BON JOVI and a more consistent third album, 'CALL OF THE WILD' (1985), recognition outside her native Canada continued to elude the golden tonsiled songstress. Respectable domestic plaudits finally came with her eponymous fourth effort, an album of radio friendly ballads and soft-rockers. Although she went from strength to strength at home with double platinum selling album, 'BODYROCK', her work wasn't widely available outside Canada, thus depriving her of US or European fame. A comeback album in 1995, 'EMOTIONAL RAIN', added little to her recording ouvre. • **Covered:** I JUST WANNA MAKE LOVE TO YOU (Willie Dixon).

Album rating: THE LEE AARON PROJECT (*4) / METAL QUEEN (*6) / CALL OF THE WILD (*6) / LEE AARON (*6) / BODYROCK (*5) / SOME GIRLS DO (*4) / POWERLINE: THE BEST OF LEE AARON compilation (*6) / EMOTIONAL RAIN (*4)

LEE AARON PROJECT

LEE AARON – vocals; with **RICK SANTERS** – bass, co-writer / **EARL JOHNSON** – lead guitar / **MARK SANTERS** – drums / etc.

Polydor | Freedom

1982. (lp) *(815 211-1)* **THE LEE AARON PROJECT** [-] [ ] German
– Under your spell / Lonely for your love / Night riders / Texas outlaw / I like my rock hard / I just wanna make love to you / Runnin' from your love / Should have known / Took your heart away. *(UK-iss.Jul84 on 'Roadrunner'+=; RR 9842)* – Under the stars.

— now solo with more permanent band from defunct WRABIT. **JOHN ALBANI** – guitar, vocals / **GEORGE BERNHARDT** – guitar, vocals / **JACK MELI** – bass, vocals / **ATTILA DEMJEN** – drums

Roadrunner | Attic CAN

Jul 84. (lp) *(RR 9861)* **METAL QUEEN** [ ] [ ]
– Metal queen / Lady of the darkest night / Head above water / Got to be the one / Shake it up / Deceiver / Steal away your love / Hold out / Breakdown / We will be rockin'. *(re-iss. Aug86 on '10-Virgin' lp/c; DIX/CDIX 47) (cd-iss. 1989; XID 25) (cd re-iss. Aug98 on 'Attic'; ACDM 1188)*

Sep 84. (12") *(RR12 5507)* **METAL QUEEN. /** [ ] [-]

— **SIMON BRIERLEY** – guitar; repl. ALBANI

— **SPYDER SINNAEVE** – bass; repl. MELI

— **JERRY MERCER** – drums; repl. DEMJEN

Jun 85. (12"m) *(RR12 5495)* **ROCK ME ALL OVER. / LINE OF FIRE / EVIL GAME** [ ] [ ]

Sep 85. (7") *(RR 5488)* **BARELY HOLDIN' ON. / DANGEROUS ZONE** [ ] [ ]
(12"+=/12"pic-d+=) *(RR12/RRP6 5488)* – Call of the wild.

Oct 85. (lp/c) *(RR/+4 9780)* **CALL OF THE WILD** [ ] [ ]
– Rock me all over / Runnin' from the fire / Champion / Barely holdin' on / Burnin' love / Line of fire / Beat 'em up / Paradise / Evil game / Danger zone / Hot to be rocked. *(re-iss. Aug86 on '10-Virgin' lp/c; DIX/CDIX 46) (cd-iss. 1989; XID 24) (cd-iss. Nov97 & Aug98; ACD 1212)*

— she again only retained, enlisting **JIM GELCER** – keyboards / **CHRIS BROCKAWAY** – bass, vocals / **RANDY COOKE** – percussion

10-Virgin | Attic

Mar 87. (7") *(TEN 155)* **ONLY HUMAN. / EMPTY HEART** [ ] [ ]
(12"+=) *(TENT 155)* – Call of the wild.

Apr 87. (lp/c/cd) *(208/408/258 206)* **LEE AARON** [ ] [ ]
– Powerline / Hands are tied / Only human / Empty heart / Number one / Don't rain on my parade / Going off the deep end / If this is love / Eye for an eye / Heartbeat of the world / Dream with me. *(cd-iss. Aug98 on 'Attic'; ACDM 1231)*

— She recruited new live band **GREG DOYLE** – guitar / **JOHN ALBANI** – guitar / **CHAS ROTUNDA** – bass / **KIMIO OKI** – drums

— for below; **AARON + ALBANI** (now producer) recruited **SCOTT HUMPHREY** – electronic drums + **MATTHEW GERRARD** – bass / **PHIL NARO** – vocals

Attic | not iss.

1989. (lp/cd) *(841387-1/-2)* **BODYROCK** [-] [-] German
– Nasty boyz / Yesterday / Gotta thing for you / Rock candy / Tough girls don't cry / Sweet talk / Rock the hard way / Shame / Whatcha do to my body / Hands on / Rebel angel / How deep. *(UK cd-iss. May99 on 'Attic'; ACDM 1257)*

— **AARON, ALBANI + COOKE** were joined by **ROB LAIDLAW** – bass

1991. (cd) *(511487-2)* **SOME GIRLS DO** [-] [-] German
– Some girls do / Crazy in love / Hands off the merchandise / Wild at heart / Sex with love / (You make me) Wanna be bad / Tuff love / Motor city boy / Love crimes / Can't stand the heat / Dangerous / Tell me somethin' good / Peace on earth. *(UK cd-iss. Aug98 on 'Attic'; ACDM 1322)*

No Bull — not iss.

Nov 95. (cd) *(34195-2)* **EMOTIONAL RAIN** [ ] [-]
– Odds of love / Concrete & ice / Baby go round / Fire in your flame / Waterfall / Inside / Raggedy Jane / Soul in motion / Strange Alice / Emotional rain / Judgement day / Heaven / Cry / Had enough.

– compilations, etc. –

Jul 00. (cd) *Attic; (ACDM 1369)* **POWERLINE: THE BEST OF LEE AARON** [ ] [ ] Nov94
– Texas outlaw / Metal queen / I like my rock hard / Lady of the darkest night / Barely holding on / Rock me all over / Powerline / Only human / Hands on / Nasty boyz / Whatcha do to my body / Sweet talk / Some girls do / Sex with love / Peace on Earth.

AARONSROD

Formed: Hawaii, USA . . . 1984 by Italian-born ANGELO JENSEN, who enlisted the help of NEIL DELAFORCE, BRIAN SPALDING, EDWARD DYSARZ and GERARD GONSALVES. It took the band nearly three years to come up with their debut album, 'ILLUSIONS KILL'. Released on 'Roadrunner', it was a fusion of Brit/American influences such as early NWOBHM and RATT, whom they subsequently supported before their eventual demise.

Album rating: ILLUSIONS KILL (*5)

ANGELO JENSEN – vocals / **NEIL DALAFORCE** – vocals, guitar / **BRIAN SPALDING** – guitar / **EDWARD DYSARZ** – bass, vocals / **GERARD GONSALVES** – drums

Roadrunner — not iss.

Feb 87. (lp) *(RR 9690)* **ILLUSIONS KILL** [ ] [-]
– Do me in / I wanna take you higher / She say . . . no way! / Never cry wolf / Russian roulette / Hard as stone / Deceiving eyes / Mirage / Roll the dice / Khoram's blade.

—— split soon after above

ABATTOIR

Formed: Los Angeles, California, USA . . . 1983 by MEL SANCHEZ, MARK CARO and guitarist JUAN GARCIA. They soon added RAWL PRESTON on lead vox, plus 'DANGER' WAYNE on drums. After debuting at the local Troubadour Theater, they made their first studio recordings, although these were without PRESTON who had been deposed by JOHN CYRIIS (ex-SCEPTRE). One track, 'SCREAMS FROM THE GRAVE', made it onto a various compilation 'Metal Massacre IV'. Their new wave thrash (lying somewhere between BLACK SABBATH and the RAMONES) subsequently secured them support slots with W.A.S.P. and METALLICA, although another change had taken place; DANNY AMAYA for WAYNE. More personnel changes were to occur when GARCIA and CYRIIS took off to eventually form AGENT STEEL. In came singer STEVE GAINES and guitarist DANNY OLIVERIO, just in time to record their 1985 'Combat' ('Roadrunner' UK) debut, 'VICIOUS ATTACK', an album that included a cover of Motorhead's 'ACE OF SPADES'. The following year, GAINES was also to leave, replaced by MIKE TOWERS, resulting in a less abrasive feel. Another album 'THE ONLY SAFE PLACE' was delivered, although after co-founder SANCHEZ departed in 1988 to form EVILDEAD, all was lost.

Album rating: VICIOUS ATTACK (*5) / THE ONLY SAFE PLACE (*6)

STEVE GAINES – vocals / **DANNY OLIVERIO** – guitars / **MARK CARO** – lead guitar / **MEL SANCHEZ** – bass / **DANNY AMAYA** – drums

Roadrunner — Combat

Jul 85. (lp/c) *(RR 9788) <MX/+T 8014>* **VICIOUS ATTACK** [ ] [ ]
– Screams from the grave / Vicious attack (maniac) / The enemy / Ace of spades / The living and the dead / Stronger than evil / Don't walk alone / Game of death. *(cd-iss. Mar99 on 'Century Media'; CM 66011-2)*

MIKE TOWERS – vocals; repl. GAINES who joined BLOODLUST

Noise — not iss.

1986. (lp) *(N 0045)* **THE ONLY SAFE PLACE** [ ] [-]
– Intro: Beyond the alter / Bring on the damned / The only safe place / Nothing sacred / Hammer of the gods / Back to Hell / Temptations of the flesh / Under my skin / S.B.D. (feel the fire) / Night of the knife / Piano outro. *(cd-iss. Oct99 on 'Century Media'; CM 66020-2)*

—— they soon disbanded 1988 after SANCHEZ departed to form EVILDEAD

ABHINANDA

Formed: Sweden . . . summer '93 by the sextet of JOSE SAXLUND, NIKLAS RUDOLFSSON, PAR HANSSON, JAN LORD, MATTIAS ABRAHAMSSON and DANIEL BERGLUND. Gaining some reputation on the Euro hardcore/metal scene, ABHINANDA built up a loyal following during spells which saw them support the likes of EARTH CRISIS. Mid 90's sets, 'SENSELESS' (1996) and 'ABHINANDA' (1997) also sold well in Scandinavia and instigated enough ammunition to tour the UK and release a third long-player, 'RUMBLE', late in '98.

Album rating: SENSELESS (*6) / ABHINANDA (*6) / RUMBLE (*6)

JOSE SAXLUND – vocals / **PAR HANSSON** – guitar / **NIKLAS RUDOLFSSON** – guitar / **JAN LORD** – keyboards / **MATTIAS ABRAHAMSSON** – bass / **DANIEL BERGLUND** – drums

Desperate Fight — not iss.

Jun 96. (cd) *(DFR 4)* **SENSELESS** [ ] [-]
– Senseless / Inner qualities / Needle / Fallen / Competition in hatred / Love story? / Drift apart / Dragon / My source / Serenade.

May 97. (cd/lp) *(DFR 16/+LP)* **ABHINANDA** [ ] [-]
– Illumination / Fascistproof / Still the 17th Century / Despertar / All of us / (untitled) / Emptiness / Monster / Le sacre de sang / Let's march.

Dec 98. (cd) *(DFR 23)* **RUMBLE** [ ] [-]

ABRASIVE WHEELS

Formed: Leeds, England . . . 1980 by SHONNA (a male!), DAVE, HARRY and RYAN. Late the following year, the lads booted out their anti-military anthem, 'THE ARMY SONG', a pretty much standard blast of 3-chord "oi" with a SHAM 69/COCKNEY REJECTS sing-a-long factor. Initially released on their own eponymous imprint, it was subsequently given a re-issue by 'Riot City' after that label had issued a follow-up EP, 'VICIOUS CIRCLE'. Later in '82, the anarchy-by-numbers continued with the 'BURN THE SCHOOLS' single and their debut album, 'WHEN THE PUNKS GO MARCHING IN'. Smoothing out their rough edges as "oi" rapidly went down the pan, the ABRASIVE WHEELS signed to 'Clay' and speeded up their inevitable decline with an ill-advised cover of Elvis Presley's 'JAILHOUSE ROCK'.

Album rating: WHEN THE PUNKS GO MARCHING IN! (*4) / BLACK LEATHER GIRL (*3) / THE PUNK SINGLES COLLECTION compilation (*5)

SHONNA – vocals / **DAVE** – guitar / **HARRY** – bass, vocals / **RYAN** – drums

Abrasive Wheels — not iss.

Nov 81. (7"m) *(ABW 1)* **THE ARMY SONG. / JUVENILE / SO SLOW** [ ] [-]
(re-iss. Mar82 on 'Riot City' 7"red; RIOT 9)

Riot City — not iss.

Jan 82. (7"ep) *(RIOT 4)* **VICIOUS CIRCLE EP** [ ] [-]
– Vicious circle / Attack / Voice of youth.

Oct 82. (7") *(RIOT 16)* **BURN 'EM DOWN. / BURN 'EM DOWN** [ ] [-]

Nov 82. (lp) *(CITY 001)* **WHEN THE PUNKS GO MARCHING IN** [ ] [-]
– Vicious circle / 1982 / Danger, danger / BBC / Mayday / Voice of youth / Just another punk band / Gottarun / Burn 'em down / Shout it out / Slaughterhouse / First rule (no rule) / Attack / When the punks go marching in. *(re-iss. Jul97 on 'Get Back'; GET 17) (cd-iss. Jun98 on 'Captain Oi'+=; AHOY 025)* – Army song / Juvenile / So slow / Vicious circle (single version) / Attack (single version) / Voice of youth (single version) / Urban rebel / Criminal youth.

Clay — not iss.

Jun 83. (7") *(CLAY 24)* **JAILHOUSE ROCK. / SONIC OMEN** [ ] [-]

Nov 83. (7") *(CLAY 28)* **LAW OF THE JUNGLE. / BANNER OF HOPE** [ ] [-]

—— **NEV** – drums; repl. RYAN

Mar 84. (lp) *(CLAYLP 9)* **BLACK LEATHER GIRL** [ ] [-]
– Maybe tomorrow / Christianne / Sea of madness / Law of the jungle / The prisoner / Drummer boy / Jailhouse rock / Strain of love / Searching for the truth / Black leather girl / Nineteen / Devil on my shoulder. *(cd-iss. Nov00 on 'Captain Oi'+=; AHOYCD 037)* – Banner of hope / Sonic omen / Jailhouse rock (single version) / The prisoner (12" version) / Black leather girl (12" version).

Jun 84. (7") *(CLAY 33)* **THE PRISONER. / CHRISTIANNE** [ ] [-]
(12"+=) *(12CLAY 33)* – Black leather girl.

—— disbanded soon after above release

– compilations, etc. –

Nov 00. (cd) *Captain Oi; (AHOYCD 051)* **THE PUNK SINGLES COLLECTION** [ ] [-]

ABSCESS (see under ⇒ AUTOPSY)

ABSU

Formed: Texas, USA . . . 1989 out of DOLMEN by SHAFTIEL and EQUITANT – both also known as GARY and DANNY; they also moonlighted with KARNAGE and KARRION. A series of rehearsal demos circulated to their ever growing devotees, the last of which was the quaintly titled 'TEMPLES OF OFFAL' EP late in '91. More singles were unearthed around this time, all very rare.. erm, perhaps mythical even. The group subsequently came under the leadership of Norwegians, EMPEROR PROSCRIPTOR MAGIKUS, who joined the following year along with fellow ex-MEGAS member, DAVIEL ATHRON MYSTICA. Mixing up a devilish potion of death metal and 70's concept Prog-rock, they delivered unto the human race in 1993, 'BARATHRUM: V.I.T.R.I.O.L.', an acronym for VISITA INTERIORA TERRAE RECTIFICANDO INVENIES OCCULTUL LAPIDEM (apparently Latin for 'Visiting the interior of the Earth!). And so it came to pass, DAVIEL went on to pastures new. In the year of our Lord, 1995, ABSU returned to wreak aural havoc, releasing the second chapter of their demonic metal crusade, 'THE SUN OF TIPHARETH', 'THE THIRD STORM OF CYTHRAUL' following a year and a half later. MAGIKUS and Co had obviously never paid attention at Sunday school.

Album rating: BARATHRUM: V.I.T.R.I.O.L. (*5) / THE SUN OF TIPHARETH mini (*5) / THE THIRD STORM OF CYTHRAUL (*6) / IN THE EYES OF IODANACH mini (*6) / TARA (*5)

SHAFTIEL + EQUITANT plus others unknown

not iss. — own demos

1991. (12") *<none>* **IMMORTAL SORCERY** [-] [-]

1991. (12"ep) *<none>* **RETURN OF THE ANCIENTS** - -
– Immortal sorcery / Eternal rest / Sea of Glasya / Dawn of invocation.

1991. (c-ep) *<none>* **THE TEMPLES OF OFFAL** - -
– Immortal sorcery / Sumerian sands (the silence) / Disembodied.

EMPEROR PROSCRIPTOR MAGIKUS (b. McGOVERN) – percussion, voices (ex-MEGAS) / **DAVIEL ATHRON MYSTICIA** – guitars

Osmose own

Apr 94. (cd/lp) *(OPCD/OPLP 020) <THIKCD 01>* **BARATHRUM: V.I.T.R.I.O.L.** 1993
– An involution of thorns / Descent to Acheron (evolving into the progression of woe) / An equinox of fathomless disheartenment / The thrice is greatest to Ninnigal / Infinite and profane thrones / Fantasizing to the third of the Pagan vision (Quoth the sky, nevermore) Act II / An evolution of horns. *<US-iss.Aug98 +=; same>* – The coming of war (live) / The thrice is greatest to Ninnigal (live) / Never blow out the eastern candle (live).

— without DAVIEL; now trio of **SHAFTIEL, PROSCRIPTOR + EQUITANT ALASTOR** – bass

Osmose Osmose

May 95. (m-cd/m-lp) *(OPCD/OPLP 029)* **THE SUN OF TIPHARETH** -
– Apzu / Feis mor tir na n'og (Across the North Sea to Visnech) / Cyntefyn's fountain / A quest into the 77th novel / Our lust for lunar plains (nox luna inlustris) / The coming of war / The sun of Tiphareth. *<US-iss.Apr99; same>*

Jun 95. (cd-s) *<OPEP 005>* **. . .AND SHINETH UNTO THE COLD COMETH . . . / AKHERA GOITI – AKHERA BEITI (ONE BLACK OPALITH FOR TOMORROW)** -

Feb 97. (cd/lp) *(OPCD/OPLP 045)* **THE THIRD STORM OF CYTHRAUL** -
– Prelusion to Cythraul incl. . . .And shineth unto the cold cometh . . . / Highland tyrant attack / A magician's Lapis-Lazuli / Swords and leather / The winter zephyr (. . .within kingdoms of mist) / Morbid scream / Customs of Tasseomancy (Quoth the sky, nevermore) Act I / Intelligence towards the crown / . . .Of Celtic fire, we are born incl. Terminus (. . .In the eyes of Ioldanach). *(cd bonus+=)* – Akhera goiti – Akhera beiti (one black opalith for tomorrow).

Sep 98. (m-cd/m-lp) *<(OPCD/OPLP 070)>* **IN THE EYES OF IOLDANACH** Dec99
– V.I.T.R.I.O.L. / Hallstatt / Mannannan / Never blow out the eastern candle.

Osmose unknown

May 01. (cd/lp) *(OPCD/OPLP 098) <8202>* **TARA**
– Phase one: Ioldanach's pedagogy:- I. Tara, II. Pillars of mercy, III. A shield with an iron face, IV. Mannannan, V. The Cognate house of courtly witches lies west of County Meath, VI. She cries the quiet lake / Phase two: The Cythraul clan's scrutiny:- VII. From ancient times (starless skies burn to ash), VIII. Bron (of the waves), IX. Four crossed wands (spell 181), X. Vorago (spell 182), XI. Yrp Lluyddawe (of the armies), XII. Stone of destiny (. . .foe Magh Slecht and ard Righ), XIII. Tara (recapitulation).

A.C.

Formed: Boston, Massachusetts, USA . . . 1988 by SETH PUTNAM and an initially anonymous bunch of noise merchants (A.C. stood for ANAL CUNT). Their distinctive, at times unlistenable "music", was initially unleashed via a split 7" single in 1988. A handful of obscure 45's followed, including an EP, 'MORBID FLORIST' and another which reputedly featured over 5,000 tracks/blasts of guitar abuse. After a brief split and the recruitment of a more talented axegrinder, an album 'EVERYONE SHOULD BE KILLED' (containing only 50 odd "songs" this time!) was finally released by 'Earache' (also home of their spiritual forebears, NAPALM DEATH) around Xmas '93. Three more instalments of anti-social mayhem followed over the next few years, the optimistically titled, '40 TOP HITS', '40 MORE REASONS TO HATE US' (do we really need one?) and 'I LIKE IT WHEN YOU DIE' (enough said!). The second of these, saw PHIL ANSELMO (of PANTERA) make a guest spot on their rendition of Manowar's 'GLOVES OF METAL'; try and steer clear of their cover of 'THEME FROM THREE'S COMPANY'. 1998's 'PICNIC OF LOVE' set, was just way OTT, while the following year's 'IT JUST GETS WORSE' described it perfectly.

Album rating: MORBID FLORIST mini (*3) / EVERYONE SHOULD BE KILLED (*5) / TOP 40 HITS (*4) / 40 MORE REASONS TO HATE US (*4) / I LIKE IT WHEN YOU DIE (*4) / PICNIC OF LOVE (*2) / IT JUST GETS WORSE (*4) / THE EARLY STUFF 1988-1991 compilation (*5)

SETH PUTNAM – vocals, guitar, keyboards / **FRED ORDONEZ** – guitar / **TIM MORSE** – drums

not iss. unknown

1988. (7") **split singles w/ MEATSHITS and PSYCHO** -

1991. (cd-ep) *<6070>* **MORBID FLORIST** -
– Some songs / Song #5 / Chump change / Slow song from split 7" / Unbelievable / Siege / Grateful Dead / I don't wanna dance / Even more songs / Radio hit / Some more songs / Morrissey / Song #6 / Guy Lombardo. *<cd re-iss. Oct98 on 'Relapse'+=; RR 6994-2>* – Untitled.

— added **JOHN KOZIK** – guitar

Earache Earache

Dec 93. (lp/c/cd) *(<MOSH 101/+MC/CD>)* **EVERYONE SHOULD BE KILLED** Jun94
– Some songs / Some more songs / Blur including new A.C. song / Even more songs / Tim / Judge / Spin cycle / Song / Pavarotti / Unbelievable / Music sucks / Newest A.C. song / Chiffon & chips / Hey Smiley / Seth / I'm not allowed to like A.C. anymore / EX.A blur / G.M.O.T.R. / I'm wicked underground / Blur including G / Shut up Mike / Abomination of unneccessarily augmented / Radio hit / Loser / When I think of the true punk rock bands / Eddy Grant / MTV is my source for new music / Song titles are fucking stupid / Having to make up song titles sucks / Well you know, mean Gene / Song / Iron funeral / Chapel of gristle / Hellbent for leatherman / Alcoholic / Chump change / Slow song for split 7" / Des Bink's hairstyle / Newest A.C. song / Greatful dead / Aging disgracefully / Brutally morbid axe of Satan / Surfer / You must be wicked underground if you own this / Choke edge / Otis Sistrunk / Rusty knife / Fred Bash / Guess which 10 of these are actual song titles / Our band is wicked sick (we have flu) / Guy le fleur / Song / Empire sandwich shop / Morrissey / Selling out by having song titles / Grindcore is very terrifying / Song / Guy Lombardo. *(cd re-iss. Sep97; same)*

— **PAUL KRAYNAK** – guitar; repl. ORDONEZ

Apr 95. (cd) *(<MOSH 129CD>)* **TOP 40 HITS** Mar95
– Some hits / Some more hits / Pepe, the gay waiter / Even more hits / M.J.C. / Flower shop Guy / Living Colour is my favourite black metal band / Lenny's in my neighbourhood / Stayin' alive (oil version) / Benchpressing the effects on Kevin Sharp's vocals / Josue / Delicious face style / No.19 to go / Stealing Seth's idea – the new book by Jon Chang / Morbid dead guy / Believe in the king / Don't call Japanese hardcore Jap core / Shut up Mike, pt.2 / Hey, aren't you Gary Spivey? / Breastfeeding JMJ. Bullocks toenail collection / Fore play with a tree shredder / 2 down 5 to go / I liked Earche better when Dig answered the phone / Brain dead / Newest A.C. song No.3 / The sultry ways of Steve Berger / Escape (the Pina Colada song) / Lives ruined by music / Still a freshman after all these years / I'm still standing / Art fag / John / Newest A.C. song / Song No.9 (instrumental) / Cleft palate / Theme from the A Team / Old lady across the hall with no life / Shut up Paul / Lazy eye (once a Hank, always a Hank) / American woman. *(cd re-iss. Sep97; same)*

— **SCOTT HULL** – guitar; repl. PAUL (on most)

Mar 96. (cd) *(<MOSH 149CD>)* **40 MORE REASONS TO HATE US**
– Face it, you're a metal band / Punching Joe Bonni's face in / Kill women / Steroids guy / Everyone in Allston should be killed / I noticed that you're gay / Dead, gay and dropped / You looked divorced / I hope you get deported / Mike Mahan has Gingivitis / Trapped / You're a fucking cunt / Phyllis is an old annoying cunt / All Stankus is always on the phone with his / Bill Scott's dumb / Harvey Korman is gay / You fucking freak / Theme from Three's Company / Jeanine jizm is a freak / Everyone in Anal Cunt is dumb / I just saw the gayest guy on earth / Johnny Violent getting his ass kicked by . . . / Metamorphosis / I'm sick of you / Howard Wulkan's bald / You're a trendy fucking pussy / Tom Arnold / I got athletes foot showering at Mike's / Big pants, bigger loser / Marc Payson is a drunk / Your family is dumb / Furnace / You're dumb / Van full of retards / Deche Chare are a bunch of fucking losers / Everyone in the underground scene is stupid / Dumb, fat and gross / I'm not stubborn / Mike Mahan's sty / 02657 / Gloves of metal / bonus track. *(re-iss. Sep97; same)*

— **JOSH MARTIN** – guitar, vocals; repl. SCOTT

— **NATE LINEHAN** – drums; repl. MORSE

— added **HILARY LOGEE + BRIAN SEKULA + RIVER** – backing vocals

Mar 97. (cd) *(<MOSH 169CD>)* **I LIKE IT WHEN YOU DIE**
– Jack Kerorkian is cool / Valu jet / You've got no friends / You keep a diary / You own a store / You got date raped / Recycling is gay / You're a cop / You can't shut up / You've got cancer / We just disagree / Hungry hungry hippos / You are an interior decorator / Pottery's gay / Rich Goyette is gay / Branscombe Richmond / You live in Allston / You are a food critic / Just the two of us / You're band's in the cut out bin / You're gay / You look adopted / Your cousin is George Lynch / You have goals / You drive an IROC / You play on a softball team / Because you're old / You sell Cologne / Being a cobbler is dumb / You live in a houseboat / Richard Butler / 311 sucks / Your kid is deformed / You are an orphan / You're old (fuck you) / You go to art school / Your best friend is you / You're in a coma / Windchimes are gay / No we don't want to do a split 7 inch with your stupid fucking band / Rene Auberjonois / The internet is gay / Ha ha your wife left you / Hootie And the Blowfish / You went to see Dishwalla and Everclear (you're gay) / Looking drop dead in McDonald's / Technology's gay / Your favourite band is Supertramp / I'm Anal Cunt / You (fill in the bank) / Kyle from Incantation has a moustache / Bonus track #3.

Jul 98. (cd) *<22>* **PICNIC OF LOVE** -
– Picnic of love / Greed is something we don't need / I wanna grow old with you / I'd love to have your daughter's hand in marriage / I couldn't afford a present so I wrote you this song instead / Waterfall wishes / I'm not that kind of boy / Saving ourselves for marriage / I respect your feelings as a woman and a human being / In my heart there's a star named after you / My woman, my lover, my friend.

— <above issued on 'Conquest'>

Jul 99. (cd) *(<MOSH 195CD>)* **IT JUST GETS WORSE** Sep99
– I became a counselor so I could tell rape victims they asked for it / Easy E got A.I.D.S. from F.Mercury / I like drugs and child abuse / Laughing while Lennard Peltier gets raped in prison / I convinced you to beat your wife on a daily basis / I sent concentration camp footage to America's funniest home videos / Rancid sucks (and the Clash sucked too) / I paid J. Howell to rape you / I pushed your wife in front of the subway / Extreme Noise Terror are afraid of us / You rollerblading faggot / I sent a thank you card to guy who raped you / I lit your baby on fire / Body by Auschwitz / I intentionally ran over your dog / Sweatshops are cool / Women: nature's punching bag / I snuck a retard into a sperm bank / Your kid committed suicide because you suck / I ate your horse / Hitler was a sensitive man / You robbed a sperm bank because you're a cum guzzling fag / I made your kid get A.I.D.S. so you could watch it die / I fucked your wife / Into the oven / I gave NAMBLA pictures of your kid / The only reason men talk to you is they want to get laid, you stupid / I made fun of you because your kid just died / Domestic violence is really really really funny / Dictators are cool / Dead beat dads are cool / I'm really excited about the upcoming David Buskin concert / Being ignorant is awesome / You're pregnant, so I kicked you in the stomach / Chris Barnes is a pussy / Tim is gay / BT/AC / I sold your dog to a Chinese restaurant / I got an office job for the solo purpose of sexually harassing women.

– compilations, etc. –

Oct 00. (cd) *Artemis; <751047>* **THE EARLY YEARS 1988-1991** -

ACCEPT

Formed: Germany . . . 1977 by UDO DIRKSCHNEIDER, WOLF HOFFMANN, JAN KOMMET, PETER BALES and FRANK FRIEDRICH. Akin to a German JUDAS PRIEST, they were instantly recognisable for UDO's screeching, howling vocal delivery and the band's spitfire thrash backing. They initially recorded for a number of domestic labels, releasing a couple of well-received albums, punctuated by a UK set for the 'Logo' label, 'I'M A REBEL' (1980). Following a support slot with the aforementioned JP, they signed to the 'Heavy Metal' label (an off-shoot of 'Atlantic'), unleashing the 'RESTLESS AND WILD' album, the record breaching the UK Top 100. Now on CBS subsidiary, 'Portrait', they continued the aggression with the charmingly titled,

'BALLS TO THE WALL', an album which saw the band break Stateside. Personnel changes had dogged the band since their inception, this state of affairs climaxing with the departure of UDO for a solo project following the release of 'METAL HEART' (1985). Although it became ACCEPT's best selling record to date, DIRKSCHNEIDER was none too pleased with the band's metamorphosis from heavy metal into lightweight aluminium. A series of frontmen were enlisted in a round of musical chairs that saw ROB ARMITAGE fill in for one studio album, 'RUSSIAN ROULETTE' and a live effort, while DAVID REESE and JIM STACEY shared vocal duties on the 1989 album, 'EAT THE HEAT' (REESE having come to blows with BALTES on a US tour). UDO returned from his solo sojourn, augmented by old cohorts, BALTES, HOFFMANN and KAUFMANN, 'R.C.A.' releasing three final efforts, 'OBJECTION OVERRULED' (1993), 'DEATH ROW' (1994) and 'PREDATOR' (1996); American metal-graveyard stable, 'C.M.C.' concluded ACCEPT's long career with the appropriately-titled 'THE FINAL CHAPTER' in '98.

Album rating: ACCEPT (*5) / BREAKER (*5) / I'M A REBEL (*6) / RESTLESS AND WILD (*7) / BALLS TO THE WALL (*6) / METAL HEART (*6) / KAIZOKU-BAN (*4) / RUSSIAN ROULETTE (*5) / EAT THE HEAT (*4) / STAYING A LIFE: LIVE IN JAPAN (*5) / OBJECTION OVERRULED (*6) / DEATH ROW (*6) / STEEL GLOVE: THE COLLECTION (*4) / PREDATOR (*4) / THE FINAL CHAPTER (*4)

UDO DIRKSCHNEIDER – vocals / **WOLF HOFFMANN** – lead guitar, vocals / **JAN KOMMET** – guitar / **PETER BALTES** – bass / **FRANK FRIEDRICH** – drums

Metrognome not iss.

Jan 79. (lp) *(0060 188)* **ACCEPT** [-] [-] German
– Lady Lou / Tired of me / Seawinds / Take him in my heart / Sounds of war / Free me now / Glad to be alone / That's rock'n'roll / Helldriver / Street fighter. *(UK-iss.Jul83 on 'Brain'; METAL 103) (re-iss. pic-lp Mar85 on 'Razor'; METALP 101) (cd-iss. Nov95 on 'Castle'; CLACD 404)*

— **STEFAN KAUFMANN** – drums, vocals; repl. FRIEDRICH

— added **JORG FISCHER** – guitar

Polydor not iss.

1979. (lp) *(1060 390)* **BREAKER** [-] [-] German
– Starlight / Breaker / Run if you can / Can't stand the night / Son of a bitch / Burning / Feelings / Midnight highway / Breaking up again / Down and out. *(UK-iss.Dec81 on 'Brain'; same) (cd-iss. Apr92 on 'Castle'; CLACD 245)*

— **FRANK HERRMANN** – guitar, vocals; repl. FISCHER

Logo Passport

Jun 80. (lp) *(1025)* **I'M A REBEL** [ ] [-]
– I'm a rebel / Save us / No time to lose / Thunder & lightning / China lady / I wanna be no hero / The king / Do it. *(cd-iss. Apr92 on 'Castle'; CLACD 244)*

Heavy Metal not iss.

Mar 83. (lp/c/pic-lp) *(HMI LP/MC/PD 1)* **RESTLESS AND WILD** [98] [-]
– Fast as a shark / Restless and wild / Ahead of the pack / Shake your heads/ Neon nights / Get ready / Demon's night / Flash rockin' man / Don't go stealing my soul away / Princess of the dawn. *(released in Germany 1982 on CNR'; 656.042) (re-iss. Apr86 on 'Portrait' lp/cd; HMI LP/XD 6) (cd-iss. Jun93 on 'FM Revolver'; 810987-2)*

Dec 83. (12") *(12HIGH 3)* **RESTLESS AND WILD. / FAST AS A SHARK** [ ] [-]

Portrait Portrait

Jan 84. (lp/c) *(PRT/40 25791)* *<39241>* **BALLS TO THE WALL** [ ] [74]
– Balls to the wall / London leatherboys / Fight it back / Head over heels / Losing more than you've ever had / Love child / Turn me on / Losers and winners / Guardian of the night / Winter dreams.

Apr 84. (7"/ext.12") *(A/TA 4311)* **BALLS TO THE WALL. / LOSING MORE THAN YOU'VE EVER HAD** [ ] [-]

Mar 85. (lp/c) *(PRT/40 26538)* *<39974>* **METAL HEART** [50] [94]
– Metal heart / Midnight mover / Up to the limit / Wrong is right / Screaming for a love-bite / Too high to get it right / Dogs on leads / Teach us to survive / Living for tonite / Bound to fail.

Mar 85. (7") *(A 6130)* **MIDNIGHT MOVER. / WRONG IS RIGHT** [ ] [ ]
(12"+=) *(TA 6130)* – Balls to the wall / London leather boys.

— **ROB ARMITAGE** (b. England) – vocals (ex-BABY TUCKOO) repl. DIRKSCHNEIDER who formed UDO.

Feb 86. (lp/c) *(PRT/40 54916)* **KALSOKU-BAN (live)** [ ] [ ]
– Metal heart / Screaming for a love bite / Up to the limit / Head over heels / Love child / Living for tonite.

Apr 86. (lp/c) *(PRT/40 26893)* *<40354>* **RUSSIAN ROULETTE** [ ] [ ]
– TV war / Monsterman / Russian roulette / It's hard to find a way / Aiming high / Heaven is Hell / Another second to be / Walking in the shadow / Man enough to cry / Stand tight.

— **DAVID REESE** (b. USA) – vocals; repl. ARMITAGE

— **FISCHER** returned, but soon departed after a space of months.

— **JIM STACEY** (b. USA) – vocals; repl. REESE to complete below album (REESE formed BANGALORE CHOIR, while BALTES joined DON DOKKEN after below)

Epic Epic

Aug 89. (lp/c/cd) *(465229-1/-4/-2)* *<44368>* **EAT THE HEAT** [ ] [ ] Jun89
– X-T-C / Generation clash / Chain reaction / Love sensation / Turn the wheel / Hellhammer / Prisoner / I can't believe in you / Mistreated / Stand 4 what U R / Break the ice / D-train.

— KAUFMANN became ill, and was replaced during 1990 by **KEN MARY** (ex-HOUSE OF LORDS)

— **DIRKSCHNEIDER, HOFFMAN + BALTES** reformed ACCEPT once again

R.C.A. C.M.C.

Feb 93. (cd/c/lp) *(74321 12466-2/-4/-1)* *<6203>* **OBJECTION OVERRULED** [ ] [ ] Jul93
– Bulletproof / Donation / I don't wanna be like you / Slaves to metal / Objection overruled / This one's for you / Sick, dirty and mean / Projectors of terror / All or nothing / Rich and famous / Amamos la vida / Instrumental. *<US cd re-iss. 2000 on 'Nuclear Blast'; NB 6761>*

R.C.A. Volcano

1994. (cd) *(74321 23016-2)* *<35006>* **DEATH ROW** [-] [ ] German
– Death row / Sodom & Gomorra / The beast inside / Dead on! / Guns 'R' us / Like a loaded gun / What else / Stone evil / Bad habits die hard / Prejudice / Bad religion / Generation clash II / Writing on the wall / Drifting apart / Pomp and circumstance. *<US re-iss. 2000 on 'Nuclear Blast'; NB 6762>*

— added on session **MICHAEL CARTELIONE** – drums

1996. (cd) *(74321 33570-2)* *<11101>* **PREDATOR** [-] [ ] Feb97
– Hard attack / Crossroads / Making me scream / Diggin' in the dirt / Lay it down / It ain't over yet / Predator / Crucified / Take out the crime / Don't give a damn / Run through the night / Primitive.

not iss. C.M.C.

1998. (cd) **THE FINAL CHAPTER** [-] [ ]

– compilations, etc. –

Jun 84. (d-lp/d-c) *Razor; (RAZD/+K 11)* **METAL MASTERS** [ ] [-]
(cd-iss. 1987; RAZCD 11)

Oct 87. (lp/cd) *Razor; (META LP/CD 119)* **THE HUNGRY YEARS** [ ] [-]
(re-iss. May91; same) (re-iss. cd Oct92 & Mar95 on 'Castle'; CLACD 405)

Aug 87. (d-lp) *Portrait; (PRTA 241)* **BALLS TO THE WALL / METAL HEART** [ ] [-]

Oct 89. (d-lp/c/d-cd) *That's Original; (TFO LP/MC/CD 23)* **BREAKER / I'M A REBEL** [ ] [-]

Dec 90. (d-cd) *R.C.A.; <EK 46944>* **STAYING A LIFE (live 1985)** [-] [ ]

Oct 91. (cd/c) *Castle; (CCS CD/MC 311)* **THE COLLECTION** [ ] [-]
– Lady Lou / I'm a rebel / Thunder & lightning / Breaker / Burning / Son of a bitch / Fast as a shark / Restless & wild / Princess of the dawn / Balls to the wall / London leather boys / Love child / Metal heart / Up to the light / Screaming for a love bite / Monster man / T.V. war / The king.

Nov 92. (cd) *Ariola Express; (290876)* **LIVE IN JAPAN (live)** [ ] [-]

Oct 95. (cd) *Castle; (CCSCD 422)* **STEEL GLOVE** [ ] [-]

Nov 97. (d-cd) *Gun; (GUN 150CD)* **ALL AREAS WORLDWIDE** [ ] [-]

Jan 99. (3xcd-box) *Spalax; (CDST 14708)* **THE ACCEPT BOX** [ ] [-]

ACCUSER

Formed: Germany ... 1986 by EBERHARD WEYEL and VOLKER BORCHERT after their departure from BREAKER, FRANK THOMAS and THOMAS KIRCHER eventually completing the line-up. Their first few albums (KIRCHER being replaced by SHUTZ on the second) were released on the independent, 'Atom H', their sound a stale take-off of Bay Area thrash-metal (i.e. EXODUS, METALLICA, etc.). A European tour with MUCKY PUP emphasised their shortcoming s, they soldiered on into the 90's with a trio of albums commencing with 'REPENT'.

Album rating: THE CONVICTION (*5) / EXPERIMENTAL ERRORS mini (*4) / WHO DOMINATES WHO? (*4) / REPENT (*4) / TAKEN BY THE THROAT (*5)

EBERHARD WEYEL – vocals, bass (ex-BREAKER) / **FRANK THOMAS** – guitar (ex-EXPECT NO MERCY) / **VOLKER BORCHERT** – drums (ex-BREAKER) / early guitarist THOMAS KIRCHER (not on album)

Atom H not iss.

Jan 87. (lp) *(ATOMH 003)* **THE CONVICTION** [ ] [-]
– Evil liar / Sadistic terror / Down by law / Law of war / Accuser / The conviction / Screaming for guilt.

— added **RENE 'MUTZE' SCHUTZ** – guitar

Nov 88. (m-lp) *(ATOMH 006)* **EXPERIMENTAL ERRORS** [ ] [-]
– The persuasion / Black suicide / Terroristic violence / Technical excess / F-H-W-C / 'Ratouli'.

1989. (lp/cd) *(ATOMH 008/+CD)* **WHO DOMINATES WHO?** [ ] [-]
– Master of disaster / Who pulls the wire? / Elected to suffer / Symbol of hate / Who dominates who? / Bastard / Called to the bench.

Rough Trade not iss.

Aug 92. (cd/c/lp) *(RTD 158.1393-2/-4/-1)* **REPENT** [-] [-] German
– Rotting from within / Repent / Get saved / Sacrifice machine / The living dead / The drones / Judgement gone blind / Nosferatu / Metal machine music.

Shark not iss.

May 95. (cd) *(CC 025052CD)* **CONFUSION ROMANCE** [ ] [-]

No Bull not iss.

Oct 95. (cd) *(34168-2)* **TAKEN BY THE THROAT** [ ] [-]

— ACCUSER have since parted company

AC/DC

Formed: Sydney, Australia . . . 1973, by ex-pat Scots brothers MALCOLM and ANGUS YOUNG. After an initial single, 'CAN I SIT NEXT TO YOU', the siblings headed for Melbourne where they recruited another Caledonian exile, wildman BON SCOTT. Stabilizing the line-up with MARK EVANS and PHIL RUDD, the band signed up with 'Albert' records, a company run by the eldest YOUNG brother, GEORGE, and HARRY VANDA (both ex-EASYBEATS). AC/DC's first two releases, 'HIGH VOLTAGE' (1975) and 'TNT' (1976) were Australia-only affairs, competent boogie-rock that established their name on the domestic scene and generated enough interest for 'Atlantic' UK to come sniffing with chequebook in hand. With major label muscle behind them, the band relocated to London just as punk was rearing its snotty, vomit-encrusted head. With their particular brand of no-frills rock and ANGUS' school uniform stage gear, the band were initially loosely affiliated to the scene. But with ANGUS' bowel-quaking riffs and SCOTT's high-pitched bellow, their eventual status as one of the archetypal heavy metal acts was almost inevitable from the off. 'Atlantic' introduced the band to Britain with a compilation drawn from the group's first two Australian releases (confusingly also titled 'HIGH VOLTAGE') and AC/DC's first album proper was 1976's 'DIRTY DEEDS DONE DIRT CHEAP'. While its follow-up, 'LET THERE BE ROCK' gave the band their first taste of chart action, AC/DC were first and foremost a live band. The bare-legged cheek of ANGUS was eminently entertaining, his body contorting and jerking like a clockwork toy on speed (NEIL YOUNG's more frenetic noodlings bear a striking similarity, long lost brothers perhaps?!). After a corking live album, 'IF YOU WANT BLOOD, YOU'VE GOT IT' (featuring that classic paeon to the larger woman, 'WHOLE LOTTA ROSIE', no anorexic waifs for this lot!), the band hit the big time with 'HIGHWAY TO HELL' (1979). Despite a more commercial sheen courtesy of producer Mutt Lange, the likes of 'TOUCH TOO MUCH' and the title track were unforgettable AC/DC moments, utilising the band's trademark steamrolling rhythm section and their inimitable way with a testosterone-saturated chorus. As ever, the group's lyrics were, for the most part, positively neolithic although their reliably unreconstructed, femininst-baiting songs were never without humour, something of a novelty in the metal scene of that era. Being Scottish/Australian, and a rock star to boot, BON SCOTT wasn't exactly a lager shandy man, the 'Uisge Beath' ('Water of life', or whisky to sassenach readers) rather taking away his life after he drank himself into an early grave the following February (1980). Yet incredibly, by July, the band were back with a No. 1 album, 'BACK IN BLACK', a record that saw the band finally break big in America. Ex-GEORDIE singer, BRIAN JOHNSON, had been recruited on vocal duties and his gravelly yelp carried on where SCOTT left off. The likes of 'HELL'S BELLS' and the irrepressible 'YOU SHOOK ME ALL NIGHT LONG' were staples of rock discos (remember them?) up and down the land and the band became a top drawer draw in the age of stadium rock, headlining the legendary Castle Donington Festival in its heyday. Yet from here on in, AC/DC lost their spark somewhat. 'FLICK OF THE SWITCH' and 'FLY ON THE WALL' were metal by numbers although 'WHO MADE WHO' (1986) was an interesting hotch-potch of new and old. 'BLOW UP YOUR VIDEO' (1988) and 'THE RAZOR'S EDGE' (1990) saw a resurgence of sorts the respective sets making Top 5. The band continued to tour for the metal faithful, 1992's 'LIVE' documenting the visceral thrill of the AC/DC concert experience. But while their formula is wearing a bit thin, nobody seems to have informed the band, 1995's hilariously titled 'BALLBREAKER' crudely retreading over-familiar ground. Still, in the (supposedly) sophisticated PC world of the 90's, you've got to hand it to a band who can still get away with titles like 'COVER YOU IN OIL', 'HARD AS A ROCK' and 'LOVE BOMB'. Now signed to 'Liberty' at the turn of the millennium, AC/DC delivered an even tastier set of numbers via 'STIFF UPPER LIP' (2000). Vive le rock! • **Songwriters:** Most by YOUNG brothers, some with SCOTT or JOHNSON. Covered; BABY PLEASE DON'T GO / BONNY (trad).

Album rating: HIGH VOLTAGE (UK *8) / DIRTY DEEDS DONE DIRT CHEAP (*6) / LET THERE BE ROCK (*8) / POWERAGE (*6) / IF YOU WANT BLOOD – YOU'VE GOT IT (*8) / HIGHWAY TO HELL (*8) / BACK IN BLACK (*8) / FOR THOSE ABOUT TO ROCK (WE SALUTE YOU) (*4) / FLICK OF THE SWITCH (*5) / FLY ON THE WALL (*5) / WHO MADE WHO (*5) / BLOW UP YOUR VIDEO (*7) / THE RAZOR'S EDGE (*5) / LIVE (*7) / BALLBREAKER (*6) / STIFF UPPER LIP (*7)

ANGUS YOUNG (b.31 Mar'59, Glasgow, Scotland) – guitar / **MALCOLM YOUNG** (b. 6 Jan'53 Glasgow) – guitar / **DAVE EVANS** – vocals / **ROB BAILEY** – bass / **PETER CLACK** – drums

not iss. Albert

Jul 74. (7") **CAN I SIT NEXT TO YOU. / ROCKIN' IN THE PARLOUR** [-] [-] Aust.

— When all but the brothers departed, they recruited (i.e.DAVE joined RABBIT) **BON SCOTT** (b.RONALD SCOTT, 9 Jul'46, Kirriemuir, Scotland) – vocals (ex-VALENTINES, ex-FRATERNITY, ex-SPECTORS, ex-MOUNT LOFTY RANGERS) / **MARK EVANS** – (b. 2 Mar'56, Melbourne) – bass (ex-BUSTER BROWN) / **PHIL RUDD** (b.19 May'54, Melbourne) – drums

Jan 75. (lp) <APLP 009> **HIGH VOLTAGE** [-] [-] Austra
– Baby please don't go / She's got balls / Little lover / Stick around / Soul stripper / You ain't got a hold of me / Love song / Show business.

1975. (7") **DOG EAT DOG. / CARRY ME HOME** [-] [-] Austra

Dec 75. (lp) <APLP 016> **T.N.T.** [-] [-] Austra
– It's a long way to the top (if you wanna rock'n'roll) / The Rock'n'roll singer / The jack / Live wire / T.N.T. / Rocker / Can I sit next to you girl / High voltage / School days.

Atlantic Atco

Apr 76. (7") *(K 10745)* **IT'S A LONG WAY TO THE TOP (IF YOU WANNA ROCK'N'ROLL). / CAN I SIT NEXT TO YOU GIRL** [ ] [-]
(re-iss. Jun80 on 'Heavy Metal-Atlantic'; HM 3) (hit UK 55)

May 76. (lp/c) *(K/K4 50257)* **HIGH VOLTAGE** (compilation from two above) [ ] [-]
– It's a long way to the top (if you wanna rock'n'roll) / The rock'n'roll singer / The jack / Live wire / T.N.T. / Can I sit next to you girl / Little lover / She's got balls / High voltage. *<US-iss.Apr81; 142> (cd-iss. Oct87; K2 50257) (re-iss. Jul94 cd/c; 7567 92413-2/-4) (cd re-iss. May98 on 'E.M.I.'; 494671-2)*

Aug 76. (7") *(K 10805)* **JAILBREAK. / FLING THING** [ ] [-]
(re-iss. Mar80)

Oct 76. (7") *(K 10860)* **HIGH VOLTAGE. / LIVE WIRE** [ ] [-]
(re-iss. Jun80 on 'Heavy Metal-Atlantic'; HM 1) (hit UK 48)

Dec 76. (7") *<7068>* **HIGH VOLTAGE. / IT'S A LONG WAY TO THE TOP (IF YOU WANNA ROCK'N'ROLL)** [-] [ ]

Dec 76. (lp/c) *(K/K4 50323)* **DIRTY DEEDS DONE DIRT CHEAP** [ ] [-]
– Dirty deeds done dirt cheap / Love at first feel / Big balls / Rocker / Problem child / There's gonna be some rockin' / Ain't no fun (waiting round to be a millionaire) / Ride on / Squealer. *<US-iss.Apr81; 16033>* – <hit No.3> *(cd-iss. Aug87; K2 50323) (re-iss. Jul94 cd/c; 7567 92448-2/-4) (cd re-iss. May98 on 'E.M.I.'; 494670-2)*

Jan 77. (7"m) *(K 10899)* **DIRTY DEEDS DONE DIRT CHEAP. / BIG BALLS / THE JACK** [ ] [-]
(re-iss. Jun80 on 'Heavy Metal-Atlantic'; HM 2) (hit UK 47)

— **CLIFF WILLIAMS** (b.14 Dec'49, Romford, England) – bass (ex-HOME, ex-BANDIT) repl. MARK

Sep 77. (7") *(K 11018) <7086>* **LET THERE BE ROCK. / PROBLEM CHILD** [ ] [ ]
(re-iss. Mar80)

Oct 77. (lp/c) *(K/K4 50366) <151>* **LET THERE BE ROCK** [17] [ ]
– Go down / Dog eat dog / Let there be rock / Bad boy boogie / Overdose / Crapsody in blue / Hell ain't a bad place to be / Whole lotta Rosie. *(cd-iss. Jun89; K2 50366) (re-iss. Oct94 cd/c; 7567 92445-2/-4) (cd re-iss. Sep98 on 'E.M.I.'; 497316-2)*

Atlantic Atlantic

May 78. (lp/c) *(K/K4 50483) <19180>* **POWERAGE** [26] [ ]
– Gimme a bullet / Down payment blues / Gone shootin' / Riff raff / Sin city / Up to my neck in you / What's next to the moon / Cold hearted man / Kicked in the teeth. *(cd-iss. Jun89; K 781 548-2) (re-iss. Oct94 cd/c; 7567 92446-2/-4) (cd re-iss. May98 on 'E.M.I.'; 494672-2)*

May 78. (7"/12") *(K 11142/+T)* **ROCK'N'ROLL DAMNATION. / SIN CITY** [24] [-]
(re-iss. Mar80; same)

Jun 78. (7") *<3499>* **ROCK'N'ROLL DAMNATION. / KICKED IN THE TEETH** [-] [ ]

Oct 78. (lp/c) *(K/K4 50532) <19212>* **IF YOU WANT BLOOD, YOU'VE GOT IT (live)** [13] [ ]
– Riff raff / Hell ain't a bad place to be / Bad boy boogie / The jack / Problem child / Whole lotta Rosie / Rock'n'roll damnation / High voltage / Let there be rock / Rocker. *(re-iss. Mar80; same) (cd-iss. Jun89; K 781 553-2) (re-iss. Oct94; 7567 92447-2/-4) (cd re-iss. May98 on 'E.M.I.'; 494669-2)*

Oct 78. (7"/12") *(K 11207/+T) <3553>* **WHOLE LOTTA ROSIE (live). / HELL AIN'T A BAD PLACE TO BE (live)** [ ] [ ]
(re-iss. Mar80; same) (re-iss. Jun80 on 'Heavy Metal-Atlantic'; HM 4) (hit UK 36)

Aug 79. (lp/c) *(K/K4 50628) <19244>* **HIGHWAY TO HELL** [8] [17]
– Highway to Hell / Girls got rhythm / Walk all over you / Touch too much / Beating around the bush / Shot down in flames / Get it hot / If you want blood (you've got it) / Love hungry man / Night prowler. *(cd-iss. Jul87; 250 628-2) (cd re-iss. 1989; K2 50628) (cd re-iss. Jan98 on 'E.M.I.'; 477088-2)*

Aug 79. (7") *(K 11321)* **HIGHWAY TO HELL. / IF YOU WANT BLOOD (YOU'VE GOT IT)** [56] [-]
(re-iss. Mar80; same)

Aug 79. (7") *<3617>* **HIGHWAY TO HELL. / NIGHT PROWLER** [-] [47]

Oct 79. (7") *(K 11406)* **GIRLS GOT RHYTHM. / GET IT HOT** [ ] [-]
(7"ep) *(K 11406E)* – ('A'side) / If you want blood (you've got it) / Hell ain't a bad place to be (live) / Rock'n'roll damnation.

Jan 80. (7"m) *(K 11435)* **TOUCH TOO MUCH (live). / LIVE WIRE (live) / SHOT DOWN IN FLAMES (live)** [29] [-]

Feb 80. (7") *<3644>* **TOUCH TOO MUCH (live). / WALK ALL OVER YOU (live)** [-] [ ]

— **BRIAN JOHNSON** (b.5 Oct'47, Newcastle, England) – vocals (ex-GEORDIE) repl. BON SCOTT who died 20 Feb'80 after drunken binge.

Jul 80. (lp/c) *(K/K4 50735) <16018>* **BACK IN BLACK** [1] [4]
– Hells bells / Shoot to thrill / What do you do for money honey / Give the dog a bone / Let me put my love into you / Back in black / You shook me all night long / Have a drink on me / Shake a leg / Rock and roll ain't noise pollution. *(cd-iss. Feb87; K2 50735) (re-iss. Aug94 cd/c; 7567 92418-2/-4) (cd re-iss. Jun98 on 'E.M.I.'; 495153-2)*

Sep 80. (7") *(K 11600) <3761>* **YOU SHOOK ME ALL NIGHT LONG. / HAVE A DRINK ON ME** [38] [35]

Nov 80. (7"/12") *(K 11630/+T)* **ROCK'N'ROLL AIN'T NOISE POLLUTION. / HELL'S BELLS** [15] [ ]

Feb 81. (7") *<3787>* **BACK IN BLACK. / WHAT DO YOU DO FOR MONEY HONEY** [-] [37]

Nov 81. (lp/c) *(K/K4 50851) <11111>* **FOR THOSE ABOUT TO ROCK (WE SALUTE YOU)** [3] [1]
– For those about to rock (we salute you) / Put the finger on you / Let's get it up / Inject the venom / Snowballed / Evil walk / C.O.D. / Breaking the laws / Night of the long knives / Spellbound. *(cd-iss. Jul87; K2 50851) (re-iss. Jul94 cd/c; 7567 92412-2/-4) (cd re-iss. Jan98 on 'E.M.I.'; 477090-2)*

Jan 82. (7") *(K 11706)* **LET'S GET IT UP. / BACK IN BLACK (live)** [13] [-]
(12"+=) *(K 11706T)* – T.N.T. (live).

Jan 82 (7")(12") *<3894><3898>* **LET'S GET IT UP. / SNOWBALLED** [-] [44]

Jun 82 (7") *<4029>* **FOR THOSE ABOUT TO ROCK (WE SALUTE YOU). / T.N.T.** [-] [ ]

Jun 82. (7"/ext.12") *(K 11721/+T)* **FOR THOSE ABOUT TO ROCK (WE SALUTE YOU). / LET THERE BE ROCK (live)** [15] [ ]

Aug 83. (lp/c) *(780 100-1/-4) <80100>* **FLICK OF THE SWITCH** [4] [15]
– Rising power / This house is on fire / Flick of the switch / Nervous shakedown / Landslide / Guns for fire / Deep in the hole / Bedlam in Belgium / Badlands / Brain shake. *(re-iss. Jul87 lp/c/cd; K781 455-1/-4/-2) (re-iss. Oct94 cd/c; 7567 92448-2/-4) (cd re-iss. Jan98 on 'E.M.I.'; 477091-2)*

Sep 83. (7"/7"sha-pic-d) *(A 9774/+P) <89774>* **GUNS FOR HIRE. / LANDSLIDE** [37] [84]

Mar 84. (7") *<89722>* **FLICK OF THE SWITCH. / BADLANDS** [-] [ ]

— **SIMON WRIGHT** (b.19 Jun'63) – drums (ex-A II Z, ex-TYTAN) repl. RUDD

Jul 84. (7"/7"sha-pic-d) *(A 9651/+P)* **NERVOUS SHAKEDOWN. / ROCK'N'ROLL AIN'T NOISE POLLUTION (live)** [35] [ ]
(12"+=/c-s+=) *(A 9651 T/C)* – Sin city (live) / This house is on fire (live).

Jun 85. (7"/7"w-poster/7"sha-pic-d/12") *(A 9532/+W/P/T) <89532>* **DANGER. / BACK IN BUSINESS** [48] [ ]

Jul 85. (lp/c/cd) *(781 263-1/-4/-2) <81263>* **FLY ON THE WALL** [7] [32]
– Fly on the wall / Shake your foundations / First blood / Danger / Sink the pink / Playing with the girls / Stand up / Hell or high water / Back in business / Send for the man. *(cd re-iss. Jan98 on 'E.M.I.'; 477092-2)*

Nov 85. (7") **SHAKE YOUR FOUNDATIONS. / SEND FOR THE MAN** [-] [ ]

Jan 86. (7"/7"w-poster/7"sha-pic-d) *(A 9474/+C/P)* **SHAKE YOUR FOUNDATIONS. / STAND UP** [24] [ ]
(12"+=) *(A 9474T)* – Jailbreak.

May 86. (7"/7"sha-pic-d) *(A 9425/+P)* <89425> **WHO MADE WHO. / GUNS FOR HIRE (live)** [16] [ ]
(12"+=/12"w-poster) *(A 9425T/+W)* – ('A'-Collectors mix).

May 86. (lp/c) *(WX 57/+C)* <81650> **WHO MADE WHO (Soundtrack; Maximum Overdrive)** (part compilation) [11] [33]
– Who made who / You shook me all night long / DT / Sink the pink / Ride on / Hells bells / Shake your foundations / Chase the ace / For those about to rock (we salute you). *(cd-iss. 1988; 781 650-2) (cd re-iss. Sep98 on 'E.M.I.'; 746299-2)*

Aug 86. (7"/7"sha-pic-d) *(A 9377/+P)* <89377> **YOU SHOOK ME ALL NIGHT LONG (live). / SHE'S GOT BALLS (live)** [46] [ ]
(12"/12"sha-pic-d) *(A 9377 T/TP)* – ('B'extended) / ('A'live).

Jan 88. (7") *(A 9136)* <89136> **HEATSEEKER. / GO ZONE** [12] [ ]
(12"+=/12"g-f+=/12"pic-d+=/3"cd-s+=) *(A 9136 T/TW/TP/CD)* – Snake high.

Feb 88. (lp/c)(cd) *(WX 144/+C)(781 828-2)* <81828> **BLOW UP YOUR VIDEO** [2] [12]
– Heatseeker / That's the way I wanna rock'n'roll / Meanstreak / Go zone / Kissin' dynamite / Nick of time / Some sin for nuthin' / Ruff stuff / Two's up / Some sin for nuthin' / This means war. *(cd re-iss. Sep98 on 'E.M.I.'; 748977-2)*

Mar 88. (7") *(A 9098)* <89098> **THAT'S THE WAY I WANNA ROCK'N'ROLL. / KISSIN' DYNAMITE** [22] [ ]
(12"+=/12"g-f+=/12"pic-d+=) *(A 9098T/+W/P)* – Borrowed time.
(3"cd-s+=) *(A 9098CD)* – Shoot to thrill (live) / Whole lotta Rosie (live).

— (Apr88) cousin **STEVE YOUNG** – guitar briefly replaced MALCOLM on tour

— (1989) (ANGUS, MALCOLM, BRIAN & CLIFF) bring in **CHRIS SLADE** (b.30 Oct'46) – drums (ex-GARY MOORE, ex-MANFRED MANN EARTHBAND, ex-FIRM) repl. WRIGHT who had joined DIO.

Atco Atco

Sep 90. (7"/c-s/10"pic-d) *(B 8907/+C/P)* **THUNDERSTRUCK. / FIRE YOUR GUNS** [13] [ ]
(12"+=/cd-s+=) *(B 8907 T/CD)* – DT / Chase the ace.

Oct 90. (cd)(lp/pic-lp/c) *(<91413>)(WX 364/+P/+C)* **THE RAZOR'S EDGE** [4] [2]
– Thunderstruck / Fire your guns / Moneytalks / The razor's edge / Mistress for Christmas / Rock your heart out / Are you ready / Got you by the balls / Shot of love / Let's make it / Goodbye & good riddance to bad luck / If you dare. *(cd re-iss. Jun98 on 'E.M.I.'; 495144-2)*

Nov 90. (7"/c-s) *(B 8886/+C)* **MONEYTALKS. / MISTRESS FOR CHRISTMAS** [36] [-]
(12"+=/12"sha-pic-d+=/cd-s+=) *(B 8886 T/P/CD)* – Borrowed time.

Nov 90. (c-s) <98881> **MONEYTALKS. / BORROWED TIME** [-] [23]

Apr 91. (7"/7"w-patch/7"s/c-s) *(88830/+X/W/C)* **ARE YOU READY. / GOT YOU BY THE BALLS** [34] [ ]
(12"+=/12"g-f+=/cd-s+=) *(88830 T/TW/CD)* – The razor's edge.

Oct 92. (7") *(B 8479)* **HIGHWAY TO HELL (live) / HELL'S BELLS (live)** [14] [ ]
(12"pic-d) *(B 8479TP)* – ('A'side) / High voltage (live).
(cd-s) *(B 8479CD)* – ('A'side) / High voltage (live) / Hell ain't a bad place to be (live).
(cd-s) *(B 8479CDX)* – ('A'side) / High voltage (live) / The jack (live).

Oct 92. (cd/c/d-lp) *(<7567 92212-2/-4/-1>)* **LIVE (live)** [5] [15]
– Thunderstruck / Shoot to thrill / Back in black / Sin city / Who made who / Fire your guns / Jailbreak / The jack / The razor's edge / Dirty deeds done dirt cheap / Hells bells / Heatseeker / That's the way I wanna rock'n'roll / High voltage / You shook me all night long / Whole lotta Rosie / Let there be rock / Medley:- Bonny – Highway to Hell / T.N.T. / For those about to rock (we salute you). *<in the US, a SPECIAL COLLECTOR'S EDITION hit No.26; 92215-2> (cd/d-cd re-iss. Jun98 on 'E.M.I.'; 49514 5/6-2)*

Feb 93. (12"/cd-s) *(B 6073 T/CD)* **DIRTY DEEDS DONE DIRT CHEAP (live). / SHOOT TO THRILL (live) / DIRTY DEEDS DONE DIRT CHEAP** [68] [ ]

Jun 93. (7"/c-s) *(88396/+C)* <98406> **BIG GUN. / BACK IN BLACK (live)** [23] [65]
(12"+=) *(88396T)* – For those about to rock (live).
(cd-s) *(88396CD)* – ('A'side) / For those about to rock (live).

Sep 95. (7"yellow/cd-s/s-cd-s) *(A 4368 X/CD/CDX)* **HARD AS A ROCK. / CAUGHT WITH YOUR PANTS DOWN** [33] [ ]

Sep 95. (cd/c/lp) *(<7559 61780-2/-4/-2>)* **BALLBREAKER** [6] [4]
– Whisky on the rocks / The honey roll / The furor / Love bomb / Hard as a rock / Hail Caesar / Cover you in oil / Caught with your pants down / Burnin' alive / Boogie man / Ballbreaker. *(cd re-iss. Jun98 on 'E.M.I.'; 495149-2)*

Apr 96. (c-s) *(A 6051C)* **HAIL CAESAR / WHISKEY ON THE ROCKS** [56] [ ]
(cd-s+=) *(A 6051CD)* – Whole lotta Rosie (live).

Jul 96. (cd-s) *(7559-64286-2)* **COVER YOU IN OIL / LOVE BOMB / BALLBREAKER** [ ] [ ]

Liberty Liberty

Feb 00. (cd/c) *(525667-2/-4)* <62494> **STIFF UPPER LIP** [12] [7]
– Stiff upper lip / Meltdown / House of jazz / Hold me back / Safe in New York City / Can't stand still / Can't stop rock'n'roll / Satellite blues / Damned / Come and get it / All screwed up / Give it up.

Apr 00. (cd-s) *(CDSTIFF 100)* **STIFF UPPER LIP / HARD AS A ROCK (live) / BALLBREAKER (live)** [65] [-]

– compilations, others, etc. –

Aug 84. (m-lp) *Atco;* <80178> **JAILBREAK '74** (early demos..) [-] [76]
(UK re-iss. cd Oct94; 7567 92449-2)

Sep 84. (7") *Atlantic;* <89616> **JAILBREAK. / SHOW BUSINESS** [-] [ ]

1991. (3xcd-box) *Atco;* **BOX SET** [ ] [-]
– HIGHWAY TO HELL / BACK IN BLACK / FOR THOSE ABOUT TO ROCK

Nov 97. (d-cd; BON SCOTT & THE FRATERNITY) *Raven; (RVCD 56)* **COMPLETE SESSIONS 1971-1972** [ ] [ ]

Dec 97. (5xcd-box) *(493273-2)* **BONFIRE** [ ] [90]

Jan 98. (cd-s; BON SCOTT) *Head Office; (HOR 002)* **ROUND AND ROUND AND ROUND. /** [ ] [-]

Sep 98. (cd; by BON SCOTT & THE FRATERNITY) *Connoisseur; VSOPCD 261)* **LIVESTOCK – BON SCOTT WITH FRATERNITY** [ ] [-]

– Australian compilations (selective)

on 'E.M.I.' unless stated otherwise

Sep 87. (6xbox-lp) **BOX SET** [-] [-]
– (lp's) – TNT / HIGH VOLTAGE / DIRTY DEEDS DONE DIRT CHEAP / LET THERE BE ROCK / POWERAGE / HIGHWAY. (12"free w/above) **COLD HEARTED MAN**

Dec 87. (5xbox-lp) **BOX SET 2** [-] [-]
– (lp's) – BACK IN BLACK / FOR THOSE ABOUT TO ROCK / FLICK OF THE SWITCH / FLY ON THE WALL / WHO MADE WHO

ACHERON

Formed: Florida, USA . . . early 90's by VINCENT CROWLEY (no relation to ALISTEIR . . . probably). This man is also apparently the "brains" behind a Satanic youth cult, The Order Of The Evil Eye, most of ACHERON's compositions guided by fellow Devil worshipper, "REVEREND" PETER GILMORE. Though their lyrics may have been genuinely demonic, their music was standard issue death-metal, as evidenced on their debut ('RITES OF THE BLACK MASS') album for the 'Turbo' label in 1992. A follow-up, the optimistically titled, 'SATANIC VICTORY' was released around two years later, their third, 'LEX TALIONIS', appearing in '95. Of late – 1997 and 1998 to be exact – ACHERON delivered two more 'ANTI-GOD, ANTI-CHRIST' and 'THOSE WHO HAVE RISEN'.

Album rating: RITES OF THE BLACK MASS (*6) / SATANIC VICTORY (*6) / LEX TALIONIS (*6) / THOSE WHO HAVE RISEN (*5)

VINCENT CROWLEY – guitar, vocals / with **REVEREND PETER GILMORE** – keyboards / **TONY BLAKK** – rhythm guitar / **TROY GEFFERN** – bass / **MIKE BROWNING** – drums

Turbo Turbo

Oct 92. (cd/c/lp) *<(TURBO 007 CD/MC/LP)>* **RITES OF THE BLACK MASS** [ ] [ ]
– intro . . . / To thee we confess / intro . . . / Thou art Lord / intro . . . / Ave Satanas / intro . . . / Summoning the master / intro . . . / One with darkness / intro . . . / Prayer of Hell / intro . . . / Unholy praises / intro . . . / Cursed Nazarene / intro . . . / The Enchian key / intro . . . / Let us depart.

1994. (cd) **SATANIC VICTORY** [-] [ ]
– Unholy praises / Seven deadly sins / Satanic erotica / Prayer of Hell / 666 / God is dead.

1995. (cd) **LEX TALIONIS** [-] [ ]
– intro . . . / Legions of hatred / intro . . . / Enter thy coven / intro . . . / Slaughterisation for Satan / intro . . . / Voices within / intro . . . / Purification day / intro . . . / Inner beasts / intro . . . / The entity / intro . . . / I.N.R.I. (flase prophet) / Lex Talionis march (outro).

Merciless Merciless

Nov 97. (m-lp) *<(MRLPSR 001)>* **ANTI-GOD, ANTI-CHRIST** [ ] [ ]
– Fuck the ways of Christ / Shemhamforash (the ultimate blasphemy) / Blessed by damnation / Baptism for Devlyn Alexandra / Total war.

Full Moon Full Moon

Aug 98. (cd) *<(FMP 019CD)>* **THOSE WHO HAVE RISEN** [ ] [ ] Jul98
– Intro: Nosferatu prelude / Lifeforce (the blood) / Hekal Tiamat / Necromanteion communion / Out of body / Undead celebration / Final harvest / Shurpu kishpu / The calling / Immortal sigil.

– compilations, etc. –

Feb 99. (cd) *Full Moon; (FMP 024CD) / Blackend;* <6> **COMPENDIUM DIABLERL** [ ] [ ] May99
– (LEX TALIONIS / SATANIC VICTORY)

ACID

Formed: Belgium . . . 1980, the line-up comprising DEMON, DIZZY LIZZY, T-BONE, ANVIL and fronted by leather-clad dominatrix, KATE. The latter's provocative magnetism certainly did the band no harm in securing a deal with 'Roadrunner', albeit only for a one-off 45, 'HELL ON WHEELS' in 1982. The band's piledriving metal onslaught was given free rein on the following year's eponymous debut album, released on their self-financed 'Giant' label. Despite a further couple of similar albums in the mid 80's ('MANIAC' and 'ENGINE BEAST') as well as a comeback set ('DON'T LOSE YOUR TEMPER') in '89, they gained little recognition outside the Benelux region.

Album rating: ACID (*4) / MANIAC (*4) / ENGINE BEAST (*3) / DON'T LOSE YOUR TEMPER (*4)

KATE – vocals / **DEMON** – guitar / **DIZZY LIZZY** – guitar / **T-BONE** – bass / **ANVIL** – drums

Roadrunner not iss.

Jul 82. (7") *(84169-1)* **HELL ON WHEELS. / HOOKED ON METAL** [ ] [-]

Giant not iss.

Jan 83. (lp) *(G 711)* **ACID** [-] [-] Belg
– Acid / Ghostriders / Hell on wheels / Anvill / Demon / Hooked on metal / Woman at last / Five day's hell / Heaven's devils / Satan.

Jan 84. (lp) *(G 712)* **MANIAC** [ ] [-]
– Max overload / Maniac / Black car / America / Lucifera / No time / Prince of hell and fire / Bottoms up.
(above issued UK on 'Megathon'; *007)*

1985. (lp) *(G 713)* **ENGINE BEAST** [-] [-] Belg
– S.T.C. / Lost in Hell / Halloween queen / Big Ben / Lady death / Warriors of the dark / Let me die / She loves you / Engine beast / Satan's delivery.

S.P.V. not iss.

Aug 89. (lp) *(080604)* **DON'T LOSE YOUR TEMPER** [ ] [-]
– Drivin' / All through the night / Draw the line / Memories / Die by order / Up to the neck / Fine / Don't lose your temper / To the edge of the world / Dark voices.

— split after above

ACID REIGN

Formed: Harrogate, Yorkshire, England . . . 1986 by lyricist H and co. (KEV, GAZ, IAN and RAMSEY). They recorded demo 'MOSHKINSTEIN', and this was to be the name of their debut release in 1988 for 'Music For Nations' subsidiary label 'Under One Flag'. The record met with encouraging reviews, the metal press latching on to its inimitable style, which mixed US thrash with a distinctly British humour. The following year, their first full-length long-player, 'THE FEAR', was released to general critical acclaim. A line-up change was installed for their next album, 'OBNOXIOUS' (their first for 'Music For Nations'), although this was overshadowed by the final vinyl outing, 'HANGIN' ON THE TELEPHONE', a novelty thrash cover of The NERVES track, initially made famous by new wave faves, BLONDIE.

Album rating: MOSHKINSTEIN mini (*5) / THE FEAR (*5) / OBNOXIOUS (*6) / THE WORST OF ACID REIGN compilation (*6)

H – vocals / **KEV** – guitar / **GAZ JENNINGS** – guitar / **IAN GANGWER** – bass / **RAMSEY WHARTON** – drums, keyboards

Under One Flag | not iss.

Mar 88. (m-lp) *(MFLAG 20)* **MOSHKINSTEIN** □ [-]
– Goddess / Suspended sentence / Freedom of speech / Motherly love / Respect the dead / Chaos (lambs to the slaughter). *(re-iss. Aug89; same)*

Feb 89. (cd/c/lp) *(CD/T+/FLAG 31)* **THE FEAR** □ [-]
– You never know (with RINGO STARR) / Insane ecstasy / Blind aggression / Lost in solitude / Reflection of truths / Humanoia / Life in forms. *(cd+=)* – MOSHKINSTEIN (lp tracks).

— **ADAM** – guitar (ex-LORD CRUCIFER) + **MAC** – bass (ex-HOLOSLADE); repl. GAZ + IAN

Jun 89. (10"ep) *(10FLAG 106)* **HUMANOIA EP** (re-recordings) □ [-]
– Humanoia / All I see (live) / Goddess (live) / Bully boy (live) / Chaos (live).

Jan 90. (c-s/7") *(T+/FLAG 109)* **HANGIN' ON THE TELEPHONE. / MOTHERLY LOVE (live)** □ [-]
(12"+=) *(12FLAG 109)* – Genghis Khan (warriors of) (live).

Apr 90. (cd/c/lp) *(CD/T+/FLAG 39)* **OBNOXIOUS** □ [-]
– Creative restraint / Joke chain / Thoughtful sleep / You are your enemy / Phantasm / My open mind / Codes of conformity / This is serious. *(re-iss. Jul92; same)*

— Disbanded early '91, after the departure of ADAM (to CATHEDRAL' RAMSEY subsequently joined him). KEV joined LAWNMOWER DETH.

– compilations, etc. –

Nov 91. (cd/c/lp) *Under One Flag; (CDFLAG 60)* **THE WORST OF ACID REIGN** (live + demos) □ [-]
– Bully boy – Lucifer's hammer / Motherly love / Two minded takeover / R.F.Y.S. / Amnesiac / Magic roundabout / The argument / Sabbath medley / Reflection of truths / Hangin' on the telephone / Warriors of Genghis Khan / Three year war / The joke's on us / Big white teeth.

ACRIMONY

Formed: Wales . . . 1992 by DORIAN WALTERS, STU O'HARA, LEE DAVIES, MEAD and DARREN IVEY, who almost immediately introduced themselves to the metal world via two demos, 'A SOMBRE THOUGHT' and 'SOLSTICE SADNESS'. In 1995, their debut album, 'HYMNS TO THE STONE' showcased their homegrown brand of psychedelic stoner rock in the mould of BLUE CHEER or HAWKWIND. Later in the year, a mini-cd, 'THE ACID ELEPHANT' was herded out, followed in '97 by their debut for 'Peaceville', the widely acclaimed 'TUMULI SHROOMAROOM' (aka 'My Meditation Chamber'). The latter concluded with the 13-minute+ 'FIREDANCE', while other epic numbers included the classic 'MILLION YEAR SUMMER' – the record turned out to be their swansong although they covered Status Quo's 'O BABY' and Doom's 'EXPLOITATION' on a 'Peaceville' label compilation late in '98.

Album rating: HYMNS TO THE STONE (*5) / THE ACID ELEPHANT mini (*6) / TUMULI SHROOMAROOM (*8)

DORIAN WALTERS – vocals / **STU O'HARA** – guitar / **LEE DAVIES** – guitar / **MEAD** – bass / **DARREN IVEY** – drums

own label | not iss.

1992. (c-ep) *(none)* **A SOMBRE THOUGHT** □ [-]

1993. (c-ep) *(none)* **SOLSTICE SADDNESS** □ [-]

Godhead | not iss.

Apr 95. (cd) *(GOD 010CD)* **HYMNS TO THE STONE** □ [-]
– Leaves of mellow grace / The inn / Second wind / Spaced cat #6 / Urabalaboom / Herb / Magical mystery man / Whatever / Cosmic A.W.O.L.

Oct 95. (m-cd) *(GOD 019MCD)* **THE ACID ELEPHANT** □ [-]
– Tyranny / The davastation / Distant sunrise / Chasing a rainbow / Burning lives / Forbidden memories.

Peaceville | not iss.

May 97. (cd) *(CDVILE 68)* **TUMULI SHROOMAROOM** □ [-]
– Hymns to the stone / Million year summer / Turn the page / Vy / Find the path / The bud song / Motherslug (the mother of all slugs) / Heavy feather / Firedance.

— split late 1997

ACROPHET

Formed: Brookfield, Wisconsin, USA . . . 1986 by songwriter DAVE PELLINO. Inspired by the more successful thrash-metal bands of the day, ACROPHET's attempt at the genre was largely derivative, indistinguishable from the legions of similar second division outfits. Nevertheless the band were signed by 'Roadrunner', who churned out two albums, 'CORRUPT MINDS' (1988) and 'FADED GLORY' (1990).

Album rating: CORRUPT MINDS (*5) / FADED GLORY (*6)

DAVE PELLINO – lead guitar / **DAVE BAUMANN** – vocals, bass / **TODD SAIKE** – guitar / **JASON MOONEY** – drums

Roadrunner | not iss.

Oct 88. (lp/cd) *(RR 923-1/-2)* **CORRUPT MINDS** □ [-]
– Intro to corruption / Corrupt minds / Slaves of sin / From the depths / Living in today / Warped illusions / Lifeless image / Crime for loving / Holy spirit / Ceremonial slaughter / Forgotten faith / Victims of the holocaust. *(cd-iss. Jul95 on 'Triple X'; TX 51032CD)*

Roadracer | not iss.

Apr 90. (cd/lp) *(RO 9404-2/-1)* **FADED GLORY** □ [-]
– Coimbra (April in Portugal) / Disse-te adeus e morri / Alfama / Return to me life / When time stands still / Independence at its finest / Dependency / Fado Portugues / Silent insanity / Legend has it / Dead all day.

— split in 1991

ACTIFED

Formed: Hounslow, London, England . . . 1981 by WEAZEL, CLINTON GRACE, JOHN BRISTOW and STUART HEMPHILL. A victim of their own hype, ACTIFED graced the front cover of "oi" sympathisers, Sounds (the now defunct weekly NME rival!), before getting any vinyl in the shops! Legal problems over the use of their name (from the pharmaceutical company), etc., etc., plus the installation of a fresh singer, DAVID ROGERS, held up the recording of their debut EP, 'DAWN OF A LEGION'. Finally surfacing on 'Jungle' in 1983, the EP's indie chart sales benefitted from the production kudos of former GENERATION X man, TONY JAMES. A further latter day punk effort, 'CRUCIFIXION', appeared the following year, although by this point the initial buzz had dimmed down as underground indie fashion diversified into two distinct tribes, "Gothic" and "Anarcho-Punk".

Album rating: the singles, I suppose!

DAVID ROGERS – vocals, lead guitar; repl. WEAZEL / **CLINTON GRACE** – guitar / **JOHN BRISTOW** – bass / **STUART HEMPHILL** – drums

Jungle | not iss.

Aug 83. (12"ep) *(JUNG 7)* **DAWN OF A LEGION EP** □ [-]
– Creation / Prophecy / Innocent / Exit.

Jun 84. (12") *(JUNG 11)* **CRUCIFIXION. / BLACK SKINNED BLUE EYED BOYS** □ [-]

— split late in 1984, an album of recordings shelved

ACTION PACT

Formed: Essex, England . . . early 80's out of the BAD SAMARITANS by KIM IGOE, DES 'WILD PLANET', JOE FUNGUS and KIM's brother JOHN on vocals. The latter was replaced by female, GEORGE CHEEX, before they actually hit the studio, their debut 7", 'HEATHROW TOUCHDOWN', being a split affair with DEAD MAN SHADOW (a band which JOHN subsequently joined as a guitarist). Following heavy radio support from Radio One DJ, JOHN PEEL, they signed to "oi/punk" specialist, 'Fall Out', issuing the anti glue-sniffing anthem, 'SUICIDE BAG', in the heady summer of '82. With drummer FUNGUS moving out for the gruesomely monikered GRIMLY FIENDISH, the quartet released a third single, 'PEOPLE', prior to a reissue of their most sought after track, 'LONDON BOUNCERS' (originally included on the split debut) and a long awaited debut album, 'MERCURY THEATRE ON THE AIR AGAIN' (1983). A new bass player, THISTLES (the permanent replacement for KIM IGOE, who had been substituted in the meantime by PHIL LANGHAM), featured on a handful of further singles and their vinyl parting shot, 'SURVIVAL OF THE FATTEST' (1984).

Album rating: MERCURY THEATRE – ON THE AIR (*5) / SURVIVAL OF THE FATTEST (*5) / THE PUNK SINGLES COLLECTION compilation (*6)

GEORGE CHEEX (b.1966) – vocals; repl. JOHN who joined DEAD MAN'S SHADOW / **DES 'WILD PLANET'** – guitar / **KIM IGOE** – bass / **JOE FUNGUS** – drums

Subversive | not iss.

Nov 81. (7"ep) *(ANARCHO 1)* **HEATHROW TOUCHDOWN EP** □ [-]
– London bouncers / All purpose action footwear / DEAD MAN'S SHADOW: Police force / Danger UXB.

Fall Out | not iss.

Aug 82. (7") *(FALL 003)* **SUICIDE BAG. / STANWELL / BLUE BLOOD** □ [-]

— **GRIMLY FIENDISH** – drums; repl. FUNGUS

Mar 83. (7") *(FALL 010)* **PEOPLE. / TIMES MUST CHANGE / SIXTIES FLIX** □ [-]

Jul 83. (7"/12") *(FALL/+12 016)* **LONDON BOUNCERS. / ALL PURPOSE ACTION FOOTWEAR** □ [-]

Sep 83. (lp/c) *(FALL LP/CLP 013)* **MERCURY THEATRE – ON THE AIR** □ [-]

– (Drowning out the) Big jets / Fools factions / Things that need . . . / Cowslick blues / Double standards / Losers / London bouncers (bully boy version) / People / Currant bun / Mindless aggression / Blue blood / Protest is alive / Mercury Theatre (on the air again).

— **THISTLES** – bass; repl. PHIL LANGHAM (ex-DARK) who repl. IGOE

Nov 83. (7") *(FALL 019)* **QUESTION OF CHOICE. / HOOK LINE AND SINKER / SUSS OF THE SWISS** [ ] [-]

Aug 84. (7") *(FALL 026)* **YET ANOTHER DOLE QUEUE SONG. / ROCKAWAY BEACH** [ ] [-]
(12"+=) *(FALL12 026)* – 1974 / Rock'n'roll part 2.

Oct 84. (7") *(FALL 029)* **COCKTAIL CREDIBILITY. / CONSUMER MADNESS** [ ] [-]

Nov 84. (lp) *(FALLLP 030)* **SURVIVAL OF THE FATTEST** [ ] [-]
– Open your eyes / Optimism / Keep it tickin' over / Have fun / Up on the heath / Johnny Fontaine / Yet another dole queue song / Cocktail credibility / Who's to blame? / Human beings / Voice in the wilderness.

— split early in 1985

– compilations, etc. –

Nov 98. (cd) *Captain Oi; (<AHOYCD 032>)* **THE PUNK SINGLES COLLECTION** [ ] [ ]

ACTION SWINGERS

Formed: New York City, New York, USA . . . early 90's by mainman, NED HAYDEN, along with former PUSSY GALORE member JULIA CAFRITZ and SONIC YOUTH drummer BOB BERT; the fourth devotee was bassman HOWIE PYRO. Not the greatest rock band in the world by any means, the ACTION SWINGERS were nevertheless rifftastically melodious although poorly produced. Grungy and Lo-Fi – like WEEN meeting SONIC YOUTH on a bad day out – the 'SWINGERS produced three full sets, the last of which was the appropriately titled 'QUIT WHILE YOU'RE AHEAD' (1994).

Album rating: ACTION SWINGERS (*4) / MORE FAST NUMBERS mini (*4) / DECIMATION BLVD. (*4) / QUIT WHILE YOU'RE AHEAD (*5)

NED HAYDEN – vocals, guitar / **JULIA CAFRITZ** – guitar, vocals (ex-PUSSY GALORE) / **HOWIE PYRO** – bass / **BOB BERT** – drums (ex-SONIC YOUTH)

not iss. | Primo Scree

Sep 91. (cd,c) *<SCREE 6>* **ACTION SWINGERS** [-] [ ]
– Song / Cuban bush / Nacho / Watch out / Funky Manc / Fire / Hot rock action / I'm dead / UFO / Fully loaded / Instrumental / Skicap! *(hidden track+=)* – Untitled instrumental.

— CAFRITZ left

Wiiija | not iss.

Jul 92. (m-cd) *(WIJ 14CD)* **MORE FAST NUMBERS** [ ] [-]
– Knocked out cold / You want my action / Incinerated / I'm sick / Courtney Love.

Newt | Caroline

Jun 94. (lp/cd) *(TOAD 6/+CD) <CARL 1738>* **DECIMATION BLVD.** [ ] [ ] May93
– I don't wanna be this way / Anyway that you want / Glad to be gone / Searching for kicks / No heart and soul / Whow do you work this thing / I can't get no action / You only know my name / Nothing to me now / Fooled again / Too far gone / Waiting for my chance / You better keep your big mouth shut / Defective.

Oct 94. (cd) *(TOAD 7CD) <CAROL 1750>* **QUIT WHILE YOU'RE AHEAD** [ ] [ ] Sep94
– Kicked in the head / Bum my trip / Miserable life / Dear of a fucked up planet / Blow job / Bent / I got the blues / Nembutal sunset / In the hole / Losing my cool.

— disbanded later in '94, BERT joined The CHROME CRANKS

– compilations, etc. –

Aug 99. (cd) *Reptilian; (REP 034CD)* **THE COMPLETE LONDON TOE RAG** [ ] [ ]

ADAM BOMB

Formed: USA . . . 1984 as supergroup by ADAM BRENNER (ex-TKO), with JIMMY CREPSO (ex-AEROSMITH), SANDY SLAVIN (ex-RIOT) and PHIL FEIT. Signed to 'Geffen', they released a typical pop-metal effort, 'FATAL ATTRACTION' in 1985. CREPSO departed during a long hiatus, the band returning early in 1990 with the underwhelming 'PURE S.E.X.', basically a re-hash of their debut with further out-takes.

Album rating: FATAL ATTRACTION (*5) / PURE S.E.X. (*4)

ADAM BRENNER – vocals, guitar (ex-TKO) / **JIMMY CREPSO** – guitar (ex-AEROSMITH) / **PHIL FEIT** – bass / **SANDY SLAVIN** – drums

not iss. | Geffen

1985. (lp) *<GHS 24066>* **FATAL ATTRACTION** [-] [ ]
– S.S.T. / All the young dudes / I want my heavy metal / You'll never know / Fatal attraction / Shape of the world / Take me in / Russian roulette / It's a bust / Prime evil.

— now without CREPSO, replaced by **NEIL O'CONNOR** – synth-bass / **ALAN WETTON** – sax

FM-Revolver | not iss.

Mar 90. (12") *(12VHF 54)* **PURE S.E.X. /** [ ] [-]

Mar 90. (cd/c/lp) *(WKFM CD/MC/LP 140)* **PURE S.E.X.** [ ] [-]
– Pure S.E.X. / Youth will lead the way / You take me away / High or low / Dangerous when lit / Lost in time / You'll never know / Fallen angel / Know your rights / What in the world. *(cd+=)* – Pure S.E.X. (hard mix).

— split after above

Bryan ADAMS

Born: 5 Nov'59, Vancouver, Canada. In 1977 he set up a writing partnership with JIM VALLANCE, drummer with techno-rock band, PRISM. Numerous groups, including LOVERBOY, KISS, BACHMAN-TURNER OVERDRIVE, etc. used their songs before ADAMS signed a contract with 'A&M' early in 1979. While VALLANCE recorded with ADAMS on the low-key debut single and eponymous album, he soon bowed out (the writing partnership continued) and ADAMS assembled a new band for the follow-up, 'YOU WANT IT YOU GOT IT' (1982). However, it wasn't until Spring 1983, with the release of 'STRAIGHT FROM THE HEART', that ADAMS made a significant impact on the US charts. His gravel-voiced, sub-SPRINGSTEEN rock was soon to enter into an ongoing love affair with coffee tables the world over, the follow-up album, 'CUTS LIKE A KNIFE' making the Top 10 album chart in America. ADAMS really hit his stride with 'RECKLESS' (1984), a sturdy, professional set of soft-rockers and ballads. While 'SUMMER OF '69' was an entertaining piece of anthemic pop/rock and the album possessed just enough rough-edged charm to offset the cheese factor, the likes of 'THE KIDS WANNA ROCK' was downright cringeworthy. ADAMS also beat ELTON to a Princess Di tribute with the B-side of the 'HEAVEN' single, entitled, funnily enough, 'DIANA'. The album made the man a household name while the follow-up effort, 'INTO THE FIRE' (1987) marked the end of his songwriting partnerhip with VALLANCE and saw ADAMS lyrics take on a more political bent (the following year saw ADAMS playing the Nelson Mandela benefit concert at Wembley Stadium). Still, any hopes of a radical new direction were dashed several years later upon the release of the unashamed slush-pop ballad, '(EVERYTHING I DO) I DO IT FOR YOU'. The record (featured on the soundtrack to the Kevin Costner film, 'Robin Hood, Prince Of Thieves') went to No. 1 on both sides of the Atlantic for what seemed like an eternity. After 16 weeks of radio overkill, one might have suspected that the populace had satiated their Adams appetite, so to speak, but no, the follow-up, 'CAN'T STOP THIS THING WE STARTED' (more uptempo but equally bland) almost breached the UK Top 10. The album, 'WAKING UP THE NEIGHBOURS' (1992) went to the top of the album charts, although it's safe to say that by now, ADAMS was probably appealing to a slightly different market and had lost any credibility (if, that is, he actually had any in the first place!) with a younger, more discerning audience. More nauseatingly saccharine ballads followed ('ALL FOR LOVE', 'HAVE YOU EVER REALLY LOVED A WOMAN' etc., you get the picture) into the singles charts while his most recent attempts at rock (in the loosest sense of the term, naturally) make HANSON sound dangerous. • **Covered:** WALKING AFTER MIDNIGHT (D. Hecht / A. Block) / I FOUGHT THE LAW (Sonny Curtis) / LITTLE RED ROOSTER (Willie Dixon).

Album rating: BRYAN ADAMS (*3) / YOU WANT IT YOU GOT IT (*5) / CUTS LIKE A KNIFE (*7) / RECKLESS (*7) / INTO THE FIRE (*5) / WAKING UP THE NEIGHBOURS (*5) / SO FAR SO GOOD compilation (*6) / LIVE! LIVE! LIVE! (*4) / 18 TIL I DIE (*4) / UNPLUGGED (*4) / ON A DAY LIKE TODAY (*4) / THE BEST OF ME compilation (*8)

BRYAN ADAMS – vocals, guitar / with **JIM VALLANCE** – drums, keyboards, guitar, bass

A&M | A&M

Jul 79. (7"/ext.12") *(AMS/+P 7460) <2163>* **LET ME TAKE YOU DANCIN'. / DON'T TURN ME AWAY** [ ] [ ]

Apr 80. (7") *(AMS 7520) <2220>* **HIDIN' FROM LOVE. / WAIT AND SEE** [ ] [ ]

Mar 81. (lp) *(AMLH 64800) <4800>* **BRYAN ADAMS** [ ] [ ] Nov80
– Hidin' from love / Win some, lose some / Wait and see / Give me your love / Wastin' time / Don't ya say it / Remember / State of mind / Try to see it my way. *(cd-iss. Jan87; CDA 3100) (re-iss. cd 1988; CDMID 100)*

Apr 81. (7") *<2249>* **GIVE ME YOUR LOVE. / WAIT AND SEE** [-] [ ]

— now with **TOMMY HANDEL** – keyboards / **BRIAN STANLEY** – bass + **MICKEY CURRY** – drums repl. VALLANCE (he continued to co-write + play piano + percussion for ADAMS until '88).

Mar 82. (7") *(AMS 8183) <2359>* **LONELY NIGHTS. / DON'T LOOK NOW** [ ] [84]

Apr 82. (lp) *(AMLH 64864) <4864>* **YOU WANT IT, YOU GOT IT** [78] [ ] Jan82
– Lonely nights / One good reason / Don't look now / Jealousy / Coming home / Fits ya good / Tonight / You want it, you got it / Last chance / No one makes it right. *(cd-iss. Aug85; CDA 3154) (re-iss. cd 1988; CDMID 100)*

Jul 82. (7") *<2409>* **COMING HOME. / FITS YA GOOD** [-] [ ]

— **DAVE TAYLOR** – bass repl. STANLEY

— added **KEITH SCOTT** – guitar, vocals

Mar 83. (lp) *(SMLH 64919) <4919>* **CUTS LIKE A KNIFE** [ ] [8] Feb83
– The only one / Take me back / This time / Straight from the heart / Cuts like a knife / I'm ready / What's it gonna be / Don't leave me lonely / The best has yet to come. *(re-iss. Mar86; same); hit UK 21) (cd-iss. Mar86; CDA 4919)* (cd re-iss. 1988; *CDMID 102)*

Mar 83. (7") *<2536>* **STRAIGHT FROM THE HEART. / ONE GOOD REASON** [-] [10]

Apr 83. (7"/12") *(AM/+X 103)* **STRAIGHT FROM THE HEART. / LONELY NIGHTS** [ ] [-]

Jun 83. (7") *(2553>* **CUTS LIKE A KNIFE. / LONELY NIGHTS** [-] [15]

Jul 83. (7") *(AM 129)* **CUTS LIKE A KNIFE. / FITS YA GOOD** [ ] [-]
(12"+=) *(AMP 129)* – Hidin' from love.

Aug 83. (7") *<2574>* **THIS TIME. / FITS YA GOOD** [-] [24]

Nov 83. (7") *<26??>* **THE BEST HAS YET TO COME. / I'M READY** [-] [ ]

Dec 84. (7") *(AM 224) <2686>* **RUN TO YOU. / I'M READY** [11] [6] Oct84
(12"+=) *(AMD 224)* – Cuts like a knife.
(d7"++=) *(AMY 224)* – Lonely nights.

Feb 85. (lp/c/cd) *<(AMA/AMC/CDA 5013)>* **RECKLESS** [7] [1] Nov84
– One night love affair / She's only happy when she's dancin' / Run to you / Heaven /

Somebody / Summer of '69 / It's only love / Kids wanna rock / Long gone / Ain't gonna cry. *(re-iss. Jul92 & Sep97; 395013-2)*

Feb 85. (7"/7"pic-d/12") *(AM/+P/Y 236)* *<2701>* **SOMEBODY. / LONG GONE** [35] [11] Jan85

Mar 85. (7") *<2722>* **DIANA. / ('A'live)** [-] [ ]

Apr 85. (7") *<2729>* **HEAVEN. / ('A'live)** [-] [1]

May 85. (7") *(AM 256)* **HEAVEN. / DIANA** [38] [-]
(12"+=) *(AMY 256)* – Fits ya good / ('A'version).
(d7"+=) *(AMD 256)* – Straight from the heart / You want it, you got it.

Jun 85. (7") *<2739>* **SUMMER OF '69. / THE BEST HAS YET TO COME** [-] [5]

Jul 85. (7") *(AM 267)* **SUMMER OF '69. / KIDS WANNA ROCK (live)** [42] [-]
(12"+=) *(AMY 267)* – The Bryan Adamix.

Sep 85. (7") *<2770>* **ONE NIGHT LOVE AFFAIR. / LONELY NIGHTS** [-] [13]

Oct 85. (7"/12"; by BRYAN ADAMS & TINA TURNER) *(AM/+Y 285)* **IT'S ONLY LOVE. / THE BEST WAS YET TO COME** [29] [-]
(d7"+=) *(AMD 285)* – Somebody. / Long gone.

Nov 85. (7"; by BRYAN ADAMS & TINA TURNER) *<2791>* **IT'S ONLY LOVE. / THE ONLY ONE** [-] [15]

Dec 85. (7"/12") *(AM/+Y 297)* **CHRISTMAS TIME. / REGGAE CHRISTMAS** [55] [-]

Feb 86. (7") *(AM 295)* **THIS TIME. / I'M READY** [41] [-]
(12"+=) *(AMY 295)* – Lonely nights.

Jul 86. (7") *(AM 322)* **STRAIGHT FROM THE HEART. / FITS YA GOOD** [51] [-]
(12"+=) *(AMY 322)* – ('A'live).

Mar 87. (7") *(ADAM 2)* *<2921>* **HEAT OF THE NIGHT. / ANOTHER DAY** [50] [6]
(12"+=) *(ADAM 2-12)* – ('A'extended remix).

Apr 87. (lp/c/cd) *<(AMA/AMC/CDA 3907)>* **INTO THE FIRE** [10] [7]
– Heat of the night / Into the fire / Victim of love / Another day / Native son / Only the strong survive / Remembrance day / Rebel rebel / Hearts on fire / Home again. *(re-iss. Mar93 cd/c;)*

May 87. (7") *<2948>* **HEARTS ON FIRE. / THE BEST HAS YET TO COME** [-] [26]

May 87. (7"/c-s) *(ADAM/+C 3)* **HEARTS ON FIRE. / RUN TO YOU** [57] [-]
(12"+=) *(ADAM 3-12)* – Native sun.

Aug 87. (7") *<2964>* **VICTIM OF LOVE. / INTO THE FIRE** [-] [32]

Oct 87. (7"/7"box/c-s) *(AM/+F/C 407)* **VICTIM OF LOVE. / HEAT OF THE NIGHT (live)** [68] [-]
(12"+=) *(AMY 407)* – ('A'live).

—— BRYAN now used session people?

Jun 91. (7"/c-s) *(AM/+MC 789)* *<1567>* **(EVERYTHING I DO) I DO IT FOR YOU. / SHE'S ONLY HAPPY WHEN SHE'S DANCING (live)** [1] [1]
(12"+=/cd-s+=) *(AM Y/CD 789)* – ('A'extended) / Cuts like a knife.

Aug 91. (7"/c-s) *(AM/+MC 812)* *<1576>* **CAN'T STOP THIS THING WE STARTED. / IT'S ONLY LOVE (live)** [12] [2]
(etched-12"+=/cd-s+=) *(AM Y/CD 812)* – Hearts on fire.

Sep 91. (cd/c/lp) *(397164-2/-4/-1)* *<5367>* **WAKING UP THE NEIGHBOURS** [1] [6]
– Is your mama gonna miss ya? / Hey honey – I'm rockin' you in! / Can't stop this thing we started / Thought I'd died and gone to Heaven / Not guilty / House arrest / Vanishing / Do I have to say the words? / There will never be another tonight / All I want is you / Depend on me / (Everything I do) I do it for you / If you wanna leave me (can I come too?) / Touch the hand / Don't drop that bomb on me.

Nov 91. (7"/c-s) *(AM/+C 838)* *<1588>* **THERE WILL NEVER BE ANOTHER TONIGHT. / INTO THE FIRE (live)** [32] [31]
(etched-12"+=/pic-cd-s+=) *(AM Y/CD 838)* – One night love affair (live).

Feb 92. (7"/c-s) *(AM/+C 848)* *<1592>* **I THOUGHT I'D DIED AND GONE TO HEAVEN. / SOMEBODY (live)** [8] [13]
(12"+=) *(AMY 848)* – (Everything I do) I do it for you.
(cd-s+=) *(AMCD 848)* – Heart of the night (live).

Jul 92. (7"/c-s) *(AM/+C 879)* **ALL I WANT IS YOU. / RUN TO YOU** [22] [-]
(12"+=/cd-s+=) *(AM Y/CD 879)* – Long gone.

Sep 92. (7"/c-s) *(AM/+C 0068)* *<1611>* **DO I HAVE TO SAY THE WORDS?. / SUMMER OF '69** [30] [11] Jul92
(12"+=/cd-s+=) – Kids wanna rock / Can't stop this thing we started.

Oct 93. (7"/c-s) *(580423-7/-4)* *<0422>* **PLEASE FORGIVE ME. / C'MON EVERYBODY** [2] [7]
(cd-s+=) *(580423-2)* – Can't stop this thing we started / There will never be another tonight.

Nov 93. (cd/c/lp) *(540157-2/-4/-1)* *<0157>* **SO FAR SO GOOD** (compilation) [2] [7]
– Summer of '69 / Straight from the heart / It's only love / Can't stop this thing we started / Do I have to say the words? / This time / Run to you / Heaven / Cuts like a knife / (Everything I do) I do it for you / Somebody / Kids wanna rock / Heat of the night / Please forgive me.

Jan 94. (7"/c-s; BRYAN ADAMS, ROD STEWART & STING) *(580477-7/-4)* *<0476>* **ALL FOR LOVE. / ('A'instrumental)** [2] [1] Nov93
(cd-s) *(580477-2)* – ('A'side) / Straight from the heart (live) (BRYAN ADAMS) / If only (ROD STEWART) / Love is stronger than justice (live) (STING). (above hit from the film 'The Three Musketeers')

Jul 94. (cd/c) *(397094-2/-4)* **LIVE! LIVE! LIVE!** (rec.live Belgium 1988) [17] [-]
– She's only happy when she's dancin' / It's only love / Cuts like a knife / Kids wanna rock / Hearts on fire / Take me back / The best was yet to come / Heaven / Heat of the night / Run to you / One night love affair / Long gone / Summer of '69 / Somebody / Walking after midnight / I fought the law / Into the fire.

Apr 95. (7"/c-s/cd-s) *(581028-7/-4/-2)* *<1028>* **HAVE YOU EVER REALLY LOVED A WOMAN? / LOW LIFE** [4] [1]

May 96. (c-s/cd-s) *(581579-4/-2)* *<1578>* **THE ONLY THING THAT LOOKS GOOD ON ME IS YOU / HEY ELVIS / I WANT IT ALL** [6] [52]
(cd-s) *(581639-2)* – ('A'side) / Summer of '69 / Cuts like a knife / Thought I'd died and gone to Heaven.

Jun 96. (cd/c) *(540675-2/-4)* *<0551>* **18 TIL I DIE** [1] [31]
– The only thing that looks good on me is you / Do to you / Let's make a night to remember / 18 til I die / Star / (I wanna be) Your underwear / We're gonna win / I think about you / I'll always be right there / It ain't a party . . . if you can't come 'round / Black pearl / You're still beautiful to me / Have you ever really loved a woman?

Aug 96. (c-ep) *(581865-4)* **LET'S MAKE A NIGHT TO REMEMBER / ROCK STEADY / HEY LITTLE GIRL / IF YA WANNA BE BAD YA GOTTA BE GOOD** [10] [-]
(cd-ep) *(581865-2)* – (first 3 tracks) / ('A'version).
(cd-ep) *(581867-2)* – ('A'side) / ('A'version) / If ya wanna be bad ya gotta be good / Little red rooster.

Aug 96. (c-s,cd-s) *<1862>* **LET'S MAKE A NIGHT TO REMEMBER / STAR** [-] [24]

Nov 96. (cd-ep) *(582027-2)* **STAR / THE ONLY THING THAT LOOKS GOOD ON ME IS YOU / IT'S ONLY LOVE (with MELISSA ETHERIDGE) / RUN TO YOU** [13] [-]
(c-ep/cd-ep) *(582025-4/-2)* – ('A'side) / Let's make it a night to remember / All for love / (Everything I do) I do it for you.

Jan 97. (c-s; by BARBRA STREISAND & BRYAN ADAMS) *(582083-4)* *<78480>* **I FINALLY FOUND SOMEONE / 18 TIL I DIE** [10] [8] Nov96
(cd-s) *(582083-2)* – ('A'side) / Star / I think about you / Do to you. *(above issued on 'Columbia' US)*

Apr 97. (c-s/cd-s) *(582183-4/-2)* **18 TIL I DIE / DO TO YOU** [22] [ ]
(cd-s+=) *(582183-5)* – Can't stop this thing we started / Touch the hand.

Dec 97. (cd/c) *<(540831-2/-4)>* **UNPLUGGED (live)** [19] [88]
– Summer of '69 / Back to you / Cuts like a knife / I'm ready / Fits ya good / When you love someone / 18 til I die / I think about you / If ya wanna be bad ya gotta be good / Let's make a night to remember / The only thing that looks good on me is you / A little love / Heaven / I'll always be right there.

Dec 97. (c-s/cd-s) *(582475-4/-2)* **BACK TO YOU / HEY ELVIS / CAN'T STOP THIS THING WE STARTED – IT AIN'T A PARTY . . . IF YOU CAN'T COME 'ROUND (medley)** [18] [ ]

Mar 98. (c-s/cd-s) *(582535-4/-2)* **I'M READY /** [20] [ ]
(cd-s) *(582537-2)* –

Mercury Mercury

Sep 98. (c-s) *(MERMC 516)* **ON A DAY LIKE TODAY / SHE BELIEVES IN ME** [13] [ ]
(cd-s+=) *(MERCD 516)* – ('A'-Pants down mix).
(cd-s) *(MERDD 516)* – ('A'side) / The only thing that looks good on me (is you) / Bin there, done that.

Oct 98. (cd/c) *<(541016-2/-4)>* **ON A DAY LIKE TODAY** [11] [ ]
– How do ya feel tonight / C'mon c'mon c'mon / Getaway / On a day like today / Fearless / I'm a liar / Cloud number nine / When you're gone (with MELANIE C) / Inside out / If I had you / Before the night is over / I don't wanna live forever / Where angels fear to tread / Lie to me.

Nov 98. (c-s; by BRYAN ADAMS & MEL C) *(582818-4)* **WHEN YOU'RE GONE / HEY BABY** [3] [ ]
(cd-s+=) *(582819-2)* – When you're gone (without Melanie C).
(cd-s) *(582821-2)* – ('A'side) / I love ya too much / What does it do to your heart.

Apr 99. (c-s) *(582646-4)* **CLOUD NUMBER 9 / Bryan Adams & Mel C: WHEN YOU'RE GONE (acoustic)** [6] [ ]
(cd-s+=) *(582849-2)* – Let's talk about love.
(cd-s) *(582847-2)* – ('A'mixes; Chicane / Bascombe / medley).

Nov 99. (cd/c) *(490522-2/-4)* **THE BEST OF ME** (compilation) [12] [ ]
– The best of me / Can't stop this thing we started / I'm ready (MTV unplugged) / Summer of '69 / Let's make it a night to remember / All for love (w/ ROD STEWART & STING) / Have you ever really loved a woman / Run to you / Cloud number nine (Chicane mix) / Everything I do (I do it for you) / Back to you (MTV unplugged) / When you're gone (w/ MEL C) / Please forgive me / The only thing that looks good on me is you / Inside out. *(special cd+=; 490559-2)* – South Africa live:- Summer of '69 / Back to you / Can't stop this thing we started / Have you ever really loved a woman / Rock steady.

Nov 99. (c-s) *(497023-4)* **THE BEST OF ME / CLOUD NUMBER NINE** [47] [ ]
(cd-s+=) *(497196-2)* – Fearless.
(cd-s) *(497195-2)* – ('A'side) / Inside out / How do ya feel tonight.

—— In Mar'00, ADAMS was credited with CHICANE on their UK No.1 single, 'Don't Give Up'.

– compilations, others, etc. –

Jun 89. (c) *A&M; (AMC 24101)* **CUTS LIKE A KNIFE / RECKLESS** [ ] [-]

—— on the 2nd lp below he had replaced NICK GILDER

Jan 92. (cd/lp; SWEENEY TODD featuring BRYAN ADAMS) *Receiver; (RR CD/LP 154)* **IF WISHES WERE HORSES** [ ] [-]
– Tantalize / If wishes were horses / Until I find you / Pushin' and shovin' / No.5243605 Smith / Song for a star / Shut up / All of a sudden / Wastin' time / Say hello wave goodbye.

ADDICT

Formed: Oxfordshire, England . . . 1997 (now based in London) by MARK ASTON, JAMES DENHAM, Dane NIKOLAJ JUEL and LUKE BULLEN, the latter replacing an unknown original drummer. The band, who released three singles ('SAVE ME', 'DUST' and 'RED BIRD') for UK indie 'Big Cat' late '97 and '98, were obviously influenced by BUSH and LED ZEPPELIN with RADIOHEAD thrown in for good measure. This helped ADDICT and their label obtain backing from Richard Branson's 'V2', while rave reviews for their DAVE BIANCO-produced debut set, 'STONES' (1998), were no doubt due to the excellent 'ABUSED' finale track.

Album rating: STONES (*7)

MARK ASTON – vocals / **NIKOLAJ JUEL** (b. Denmark) – guitar / **JAMES DENHAM** – bass / **LUKE BULLEN** – drums

Big Cat / V2

Jun 97. (12"/cd-s) *(ABB 140 T/CD)* **SAVE ME. / LOVER / PROSTITUTE**
Oct 97. (7") *(ABB 144S)* **DUST. / THINK AGAIN**
(cd-s+=) *(ABB 144CD)* – The one that got away.
Feb 98. (7") *(ABB 158S)* **RED BIRD. / 95 BELOW**
(cd-s+=) *(ABB 158CD)* – Easy meet / ('A'-album version).
Apr 98. (7") *(ABB 160S)* **MONSTER SIDE. / NO PLACE LIKE HOME**
(cd-s+=) *(ABB 160CD)* – So far gone.
May 98. (cd/c/lp) *(ABB 145 CD/MC/LP)* *<81845>* **STONES**
– Dust / Monsterside / All change / Red bird / Heavy / Teenage angel / Caned / Underneath / Nobody knows / Stones / Black hole / Abused.

ADICTS

Formed: Ipswich, England . . . 1978 by MONKEY (aka KEITH WARREN), MELVIN ELLIS, KID DEE (aka (MICHAEL DAVISON) and PETE DAVIDSON, who intentionally incorrectly spelled their group moniker (or did they?). Kitted out in "Clockwork Orange"-style garb, these second wave punks veered on the ridiculous, releasing an EP, 'LUNCH WITH THE ADICTS' and an album, 'SONGS OF PRAISE', in late '81. The following year, The ADICTS supplied their fans with another fix in the shape of the 'VIVA LA REVOLUTION' single. During the course of the following year, they scraped into both the album and singles charts with 'SOUND OF MUSIC' (1982) and 'BAD BOY' respectively. After a very brief spell with 'Warners/Sire' (under the revamped moniker of ADX), the stalwart punks returned with a series of workmanlike efforts which did nothing to create any musical dependence among the record buying public. • **Trivia:** The cover of their demo compilation, 'THIS IS YOUR LIFE', was packaged in a similar "red book" fashion to the famous TV programme.

Album rating: SONGS OF PRAISE (*5) / SOUND OF MUSIC (*5) / FIFTH OVERTURE (*3) / ROCKERS IN RAGS (*4) / THIS IS YOUR LIFE compilation (*5) / THE VERY BEST OF THE ADICTS compilation (*6)

MONKEY (b. KEITH WARREN) – vocals / **PETE DAVIDSON** – guitar / **MELVIN ELLIS** – bass / **KID DEE** (b. MICHAEL DAVISON) – drums

Dining Out / not iss.

Jun 81. (7"ep) *(TUX 1)* **LUNCH WITH THE ADICTS**
– This week / Straight jacket / Organised confused / Easy way out.

D.W.E.D. / not iss.

Oct 81. (lp) *(SMT 008)* **SONGS OF PRAISE**
– England / Just like me / Viva la revolution / Hurt / Tango / Telepathic people / Mary Whitehouse / Distortion / Songs of praise / Sensitive / Dynasty / Get addicted / Calling calling / In the background / Peculiar music / Numbers. *(re-iss. Apr86 yellow-lp/pic-lp on 'Fall Out'; FALLLP 006/+P) (cd-iss. Jan94 on 'Cleopatra'; CLEO 2481CD)*

Fall Out / not iss.

Jul 82. (7") *(FALL 002)* **VIVA LA REVOLUTION. / STEAMROLLER**

Razor / not iss.

Nov 82. (7") *(RZS 101)* **CHINESE TAKEAWAY. / YOU'LL NEVER WALK ALONE**
Nov 82. (lp) *(RAZ 2)* **SOUND OF MUSIC** 99
– How sad / 4321 / Chines takeaway / Johnny was a soldier / Disco / Eyes in the back of your head / Joker in the pack / Lullaby / My baby got run over by a steamroller / A man's gotta do / Let's go / The easy way out / Shake, rattle, bang your head. *(cd-iss. Aug93 on 'Great Expectations'; PIPCD 040) (cd re-iss. Jan94 on 'Cleopatra'; CLEO 3315CD)*
May 83. (7"/7"pic-d) *(RZS/+P 104)* **BAD BOY. / SHAKE, RATTLE, BANG YOUR HEAD** 75

Zig Zag / not iss.

1984. (7"; as ADDIX) **TOO BLIND TO SEE. / (NO SUCH THING AS A) BAD BOY**

ADX

Warners / not iss.

Apr 84. (7") *(W 9298)* **TOKYO. / THE ODD COUPLE**
(12"+=) *(W 9298T)* – Medley.

Sire / not iss.

May 85. (7") *(U 9070)* **FALLING IN LOVE AGAIN. / COME ALONG**
(12"+=) *(U 9070T)* – It's a laugh/ Saturday night.

ADICTS

Fall Out / not iss.

Nov 85. (12"ep) *(FALL12 038)* **BAR ROOM BOP EP**
– Champs Elysees / Sound of music / Who spilt my beer / Cowboys.
Sep 87. (lp) *(FALLLP 042)* **FIFTH OVERTURE**
Jun 90. (lp/cd) *(FALL LP/CD 046)* **ROCKERS IN ORBIT – LIVE IN ALABAMA (live '88)**
– Viva la revolution / Let's go / Tango / England / Hurt / Put yourself in my hands / Change / Joker in the pack / Just like me / Rockers in rags / Chinese takeaway / Odd couple / Steam roller / Numbers / Bad boy / Ode to joy. *(cd+=)* – Crazy / Sensitive / Na na na / She's a rocker / Easy way out / Shake rattle bang your head / Get adicted / Straight jacket / Organized confusion / Calling calling / How sad / Viva / Rocking wrecker.

— Disbanded around late 80's after completing below

— re-formed in the 90's

Anagram / Cleopatra

Sep 93. (cd) *(GRAMM 68)* *<CLEO 5951>* **TWENTY-SEVEN**
– Angel / Love sucks / Do it / That's happiness / Shangri-la / Football fairy story / Rossini / Breakdown / Give me more / F*** it up / G.I.R.L. / What am I to do / Rockers in rags / Let's dance / 7:27 / Bog / Come out to play (learn to play guitar with monkey & kid / Give me more (reprise) / Just wanna dance with you. *(re-iss. Feb97; CDPUNK 87)*

– compilations, etc. –

Jan 85. (lp) *Fall Out; (FALLLP 021)* **THIS IS YOUR LIFE (1978-80)** (demos)
(re-iss. Sep92 lp/cd; FALL LP/CD 021)
Jul 87. (lp) *Link; (LINKLP 010)* **LIVE AND LOUD!! – THE OFFICIAL BOOTLEG (live)**
Nov 92. (cd) *Dojo; (DOJOCD 69)* **TOTALLY ADICTED**
– Viva la revolution / Songs of praise / Get adicted / Sensitive / Just like me / Too young / Chinese takeaway / Joker in the pack / Steamroller / How sad / Let's go / Easy way out / Smart Alex / Troubadour / Tokyo / Crazy / Bad boy / Runaway / Come along / I wanna be sedated / Falling in love again / It's a laugh / Saturday night / Zimbabwe brothers are go.
Aug 93. (cd) *Great Expectations; (PIPCD 041)* **SMART ALEX**
– Ode to joy / Smart Alex / Troubadour / Tokyo / California / Crazy / Bad boy / Jelly babies / Maybe maybe not / Rocking wrecker / Runaway / You're all fools.
Jun 94. (cd) *Anagram; (<CDPUNK 33>)* **THE COMPLETE ADICTS SINGLES COLLECTION** 1995
May 96. (cd) *Dojo; (DOJOCD 263)* **THE BEST OF THE ADICTS**
Jul 97. (cd) *Cleopatra; (<CLP 9963>)* **ULTIMATE ADICTION** May97
May 98. (cd) *Captain Oi; (<AHOYCD 088>)* **SOUND OF MUSIC / SMART ALEX** Jan00
Jun 98. (cd) *Anagram; (<CDPUNK 105>)* **THE VERY BEST OF THE ADICTS** Sep99
– Easy way out / Straight jacket / Viva la revolution / Steamroller / Songs of praise / England / Get adicted / Chinese takeaway / Joker in the pack / How sad / Let's go / Bad boy / Tokyo / Odd couple / Smart Alex / Troubadour / Runaway / Champ Elysees / Angel / Love sucks.
Jun 99. (cd) *Harry May; (MAYOCD 117)* **JOKER IN THE PACK**

ADOLESCENTS

Formed: Fullarton, Orange County, California, USA . . . 1980 by TONY 'MONTANA' BRANDENBURG and STEVE 'SOTO' RODGERS (ex-AGENT ORANGE), who poached the other three members, FRANK AGNEW, his brother RIKK and CASEY ROYER (latter two also ex-DETOURS) from an embryonic version of SOCIAL DISTORTION. Emerging from the fertile US hardcore scene of the day, The ADOLESCENTS appeared very briefly on the 'Posh Boy' label via the ultra limited gold 7", 'AMOEBA'. Their follow-up single for 'Frontier', 'WELCOME TO REALITY', enjoyed a more conventional pressing as did the accompanying eponymous album in '81. However, this was to be their last set for some time as RIKK pursued a brief solo career, releasing the appropriately titled, 'ALL BY MYSELF' (1982) while simultaneously enjoying stints with CHRISTIAN DEATH and T.S.O.L. During a mid 80's hiatus, The ADOLESCENTS carried on with live work, ALFIE AGNEW filling the shoes of his absent brother. A self-financed comeback album, 'BRATS IN BATTALIONS' (1987), appeared as the hardcore scene was increasingly being influenced by the noisier end of the metal spectrum. It came as little surprise then, when RIKK, STEVE and Co. were snapped up by 'Triple X', who issued two further albums, 'BALBOA FUN*ZONE' (1988) and 'LIVE 1981 AND 1986', the former on European imprint, 'Roadrunner'. Although they subsequently disbanded at the turn of the decade, RIKK's second solo set – released as RIKK AGNEW'S YARD SALE – 'EMOTIONAL VOMIT' (1990) was an ADOLESCENTS album in all but name featuring as it did all three AGNEW siblings. • **Covered:** INSTANT JARMA (John Lennon) / SURF YOGI (Balk-Hardwick) / I GOT A RIGHT (Iggy Pop) / ALL DAY AND ALL OF THE NIGHT (Kinks).

Album rating: ADOLESCENTS (*5) / BRATS IN BATTALIONS (*5) / BALBOA FUN*ZONE (*6) / LIVE 1981 AND 1986 collection (*5)

TONY 'MONTANA' BRANDENBURG – vocals / **RIKK AGNEW** – lead guitar (ex-SOCIAL DISTORTION, ex-DETOURS) / **FRANK AGNEW** – rhythm guitar (ex-SOCIAL DISTORTION) / **STEVE 'SOTO' RODGERS** – bass, vocals (ex-AGENT ORANGE) / **CASEY ROYER** – drums, vocals (ex-SOCIAL DISTORTION, ex-DETOURS)

not iss. / Posh Boy

1980. (ltd-7"gold) *<PBS 6>* **AMOEBA. /**

not iss. / Frontier

1981. (7"ep) *<FRT 101>* **WELCOME TO REALITY / LOSING BATTLE. / NO WAY / THINGS START MOVING**
1981. (lp) *<FLP 1003>* **ADOLESCENTS**
– I hate children / Who is who / Wrecking crew / L.A. girl / Self destruct / Kids of the black hole / No way / Amoeba / Word attack / Rip it up / Democracy / No friends / Creatures. *(UK-iss.Apr88 on 'Weird Systems'; WS 32) (re-iss. Apr92 on 'Frontier' cd/c/lp; 4601-2L/4L/1L)* <*(re-iss. May97 on 'Epitaph' cd/c/lp; E 0102-2/-4/-1)*>

— split soon after above, RIKK AGNEW released a solo album, 'ALL BY MYSELF' for 'Frontier' in 1982. The ADOLESCENTS reunited for live work, FRANK's place was taken by his other brother, **ALFIE AGNEW**

not iss. / S.O.S.

Sep 87. (lp) *<SOS 1001>* **BRATS IN BATTALIONS**
– Brats in battalions / I love you / The liar / Things start moving / Do the Freddie / Losing battle / House of the rising sun / Peasant song / Skate Babylon / Welcome to reality / Marching with the Reich / I got a right / She wolf. *(UK-iss.1989 on 'Armageddon'; 083604) (cd-iss. Nov98 on 'Triple X'; TX 51061CD)*

— **RIKK, FRANK + STEVE** with new member **SANDY HANSEN** – drums

Roadrunner / Triple X

Nov 88. (lp/cd) *(RR 9494-1/-2)* *<51010-1/-2>* **BALBOA FUN*ZONE**
– Balboa funzone / Just like before / Instant karma! / Alone against the world / Allen hotel / Frustrated / Genius in pain / It's tattoo time / Til' she comes down / Modern day Napoleon / I'm a victim / Balboa funzone (it's in your touch) / Runaway / She walks alone / Surf Yogi. *(cd-iss. Jul95 on 'Triple X'; TX 51010CD)*

— disbanded in 1989, although RIKK AGNEW'S YARD SALE (with his brothers) released one album, 'EMOTIONAL VOMIT' for 'Triple X' in 1990

– others, etc. –

1989. (cd) *Triple X; <51015>* **LIVE 1981 AND 1986 (live)** [-] [ ]
– Amoeba / Who is who / No friends / Welcome to reality / Self destruct / Things start moving / Word attack / Losing battle / I got a right / No way / Liar / Rip it up / L.A. girl / Wrecking crew / Creatures / Kids of the black hole / Peasant song / Do the Eddy / Liar / Who is who / Wrecking crew.

Jan 98. (cd) *Amsterdamned; (51225-2) / Triple X; <51225>* **RETURN TO THE BLACK HOLE (live)** [ ] [ ] Sep97
– No way / Who is who / Word attack / Self destruct / L.A. girl / Brats in battalions / Welcome to reality / Wrecking crew / Do the Eddy / I love you / Losing battle / Creatures / All day and all of the night / Rip it up / Amoeba / Kids of the black hole / I got a right.

ADRENALIN O.D.

Formed: New Jersey, USA . . . Autumn 1981 by PAUL RICHARD, JIM FOSTER, JACK STEEPLES and DAVE SCOTT. Their first effort, the 1983 self-financed mini-set, 'LET'S BARBEQUE WITH . . .', instigated a series of fun hardcore releases with a distinctly adolescent sense of humour. Unlike many bands of their ilk, ADRENALIN O.D. maintained a fairly stable line-up throughout their career, FOSTER's replacement by guitarist BRUCE WINGATE prior to their debut album proper, 'THE WACKY HI-JINKS OF . . .' (1985) the only minor hiccup. Early '87 saw the release of the album, 'HUMUNGOUSFUNGUSAMONGUS', the title a shining example of ADRENALIN O.D.'s boisterous penchant for a play on words. Two further sets were sighted in the shops at the turn of the decade, 'CRUISING WITH ELVIS IN BIGFOOT'S UFO' and 'ISHTAR', although these failed to benefit from a more commercial approach. • **Covered:** WE WILL ROCK YOU + SHEER HEART ATTACK (Queen) / DETROIT ROCK CITY (Kiss).

Album rating: THE WACKY HI-JINKS OF . . . (*5) / HUMUNGOUSFUNGUS AMONGUS (*7) / CRUISING WITH ELVIS IN BIGFOOT'S UFO (*6) / ISHTAR (*3) / THEME FROM AN I (*3) / SITTIN' PRETTY (*4)

PAUL RICHARD – vocals, guitar / **JIM FOSTER** – guitar / **JACK STEEPLES** – bass / **DAVE SCOTT** – drums

Rough Justice | Buy Our Records

1983. (12"ep) **LET'S BARBEQUE WITH ADRENALIN O.D. EP** [-] [ ]

— **BRUCE WINGATE** – guitar; repl. FOSTER

— **KEITH HARTEL** – bass; repl. STEEPLES who formed KOWALSKIS

1984. (lp) *<BOR12 002>* **THE WACKY HI-JINKS OF . . .** [-] [ ]
– A.O.D. vs Godzilla / Middle aged whore / etc.

1985. (7"ep) **split EP** [-] [ ]
– We will rock you / etc.

Jan 87. (lp) *(JUST 5) <BOR12 008>* **HUMUNGOUSFUNGUSAMONGUS** [ ] [ ] Nov86
– A.O.D. vs son of Godzilla / Office building / Tuppe answer / Pope – on a rope / Fishin' musician / Pizza 'n' beer / Bugs / Youth blimp / Commercial cuts / Survive / Masterpiece / Crowd control / Velvet Elvis / F**k the neighbours / Surfin' Jew / Bruce's lament / The nice song.

1988. (10"ep) *(10KORE 105)* **THEME FROM AN IMAGINARY MIDGET WESTERN. / DETROIT ROCK CITY / COFFIN CRUISER** [ ] [ ]

Oct 88. (lp) *(JUST 12M) <BOR 018>* **CRUISING WITH ELVIS IN BIGFOOT'S UFO** [ ] [ ]
– If this is Tuesday . . . it must be Walla-Walla / Bulimic food fight / Swindel / Stew / Second to none / My mother can't drive / Theme from an imaginary midget western / Something about . . . Amy Carter / Flip side unclassified / Baby elephant walk.

Restless | Restless

1990. (cd/c) *<(72380-2/-4)>* **ISHTAR** [ ] [ ]
– My achin' back / Twenty dollar bill / Sheer heart attack / Obvious toupee / Tiny fingers / What a way to go / Big time major love thang / Paul A Roid / All right Tokyo / Joe from Lodi / Dave A Roid / Bad karma merchant.

not iss. | Buy Our Records

1992. (lp) *<BOR 016>* **THEME FROM AN I** [-] [ ]

not iss. | Grand Theft Auto

Jan 96. (cd) *<GFA 9>* **SITTIN' PRETTY** [-] [ ]
– Status symbol / Hijack / Suburbia / Old people talk loud / Trans am / House husband / Scare tactics / Mischief night / Status symbol / Workd War 4 / Hijack / White hassle / Brady bunch / A.O.D. vs Godzilla / White hassle / Small talk / Going to a funeral / Corporate Disneyland / Trans am (the saga continues) / Sightseeing / Middle-aged whore / World War 4 / Clean and jerk / Sleep / Rah-jah / Rock'n'roll gas station / Paul's not home / Suburbia / Trans am / Going to a funeral / New Years Eve / World War 4 / Midle-aged whore / Clean and jerk / Infiltrate the state / Masterpiece / Status symbol / Velvet Elvis / Crowd control / Rah-jah / Rather be asleep / Sightseeing / We will rock you.

— after their demise, RICHARDS teamed up with ordained minister STEEPLES to form SUX (alongside TOMMY KOPROWSKI, GREG FARAH + LARRY GIORDINO)

AEROSMITH

Formed: Sunapee, New Hampshire, USA . . . summer 1970, by JOE PERRY and STEVEN TYLER, who, with others (BRAD WHITFORD, TOM HAMILTON and JOEY KRAMER) moved to Boston, Massachusetts. By 1972, through a Max's Kansas City gig, they were signed to 'Columbia' by Clive Davis for a six figure sum. The band released their eponymous debut album the following year and the ROLLING STONES comparisons were inevitable from the off. While The 'Stones had taken American music, translated it and shipped it back across the water, AEROSMITH took the 'Stones interpretation of the Blues and customized it for a younger generation. Comparisons with LED ZEPPELIN were somewhat off the mark, the PERRY/TYLER partnership closely mimicking that of JAGGER and RICHARDS and while the latter two proclaimed themselves the 'Glimmer Twins', so it came to pass that Perry and Tyler were duly christened the 'Toxic Twins' in recognition of their legendary mid-70's decadence. 'MAMA KIN' and the Rufus Thomas cover, 'WALKIN' THE DOG' were fine examples of AEROSMITH's early revved-up R&B strut while the ballad, 'DREAM ON', scraped the lower regions of the US singles chart. The follow-up album, 'GET YOUR WINGS' (1974), consolidated the band's rock'n'raunch but it wasn't until the release of 'TOYS IN THE ATTIC' the following year that the band staked their claim as one of America's biggest and sexiest rock acts. Featuring the swaggering 'SWEET EMOTION' and the supple funk-rock of 'WALK THIS WAY', the record made AEROSMITH a household name, Stateside at least, going on to sell millions. Quintessentially American, the band cut little ice in Britain where punk was the order of the day. While Britain was pogoing to the strains of 'Anarchy in the UK', American heavy metal kids were skinning up to Aerosmith's 'ROCKS' (1976), a seminal record that saw the band at the peak of their powers. Dirty, sinewy riffs gyrated provocatively against diamond melodies, TYLER's pout almost audible as he casually reeled off his lurid tales of life on the road. While the band continued to pack out stadiums across America, their fabled penchant for nose candy was beginning to take its toll on their creative output. 'DRAW THE LINE' (1978) and 'NIGHT IN THE RUTS' (1980) fell woefully short of the band's capabilities, tension between TYLER and PERRY eventually leading to the latter leaving and forming The JOE PERRY PROJECT. Despite a near-fatal road accident, TYLER soldiered on with a revamped line-up for the equally uninspired 'ROCK IN A HARD PLACE' (1982). The all-important chemistry was gone while the chemicals seemingly continued to take their toll. Just as it looked like the end for the band, PERRY and TYLER settled their differences and the original AEROSMITH line-up signed to 'Geffen', getting it together for the 'DONE WITH MIRRORS' (1985) album, their best effort since the 70's heyday. AEROSMITH always had the funk and it seemed fitting that their miraculous commercial and creative rebirth was kickstarted by black hip hop crew RUN DMC. Their reworking of 'WALK THIS WAY' was released at the height of the rock/rap crossover in 1986 when 'Def Jam' was a force to be reckoned with and VW badges were in short supply, duly exposing AEROSMITH to a generation of kids who had never even heard of the band. Bang on cue, the band released 'PERMANENT VACATION' (1987), a masterful return to form which spawned a classic slice of AEROSMITH sleaze in 'DUDE (LOOKS LIKE A LADY)'. Moreover, the band had almost singlehandedly inspired a whole scene; almost every band in the late 80's glam-metal movement modelled themselves on prime 70's AEROSMITH (i.e. GUNS N' ROSES, FASTER PUSSYCAT, JUNKYARD, L.A. GUNS etc.). While the majority of these bands quickly faded into obscurity, AEROSMITH left the young pretenders for dust, releasing the adventurous and critically acclaimed 'PUMP' (1989). The single 'LOVE IN AN ELEVATOR', TYLER's tongue planted, as ever, firmly in cheek (probably not his own though), gave the band their first Top 20 hit in the UK. With the album reaching No.3, it finally seemed Britain had cottoned on, albeit fifteen years later. If 1993's 'GET A GRIP' sounded somewhat formulaic, it was another massive hit nevertheless. After just more than three years away, they returned to 'Columbia', releasing the wittily titled Top 50 hit, 'FALLING IN LOVE (IS HARD ON THE KNEES)', previewing yet another massive selling opus, 'NINE LIVES' (1997). Having scored a modest hit with 'PINK' (an ever bigger UK hit in '99), AEROSMITH unplugged their amps to power-ballad to the top of the Hot 100 with 'I DON'T WANT TO MISS A THING'. Almost as sentimental as the film it was lifted from ('Armageddon'), TYLER and his cohorts crooned through every filled up wrinkle whilst leaving a few mascara stains on their female fans. While The ROLLING STONES continue to roll (bankroll, that is), there's no reason to suggest that AEROSMITH won't continue in a creakily similar fashion. Come the new millennium, the veteran campaigners were back to the hard stuff (music, that is) with 'JUST PUSH PLAY' (2001), the BONEYARD BOYS (aka producers Mark Hudson and Marti Frederiksen) helping tease out a set which many believed AEROSMITH's best since 'PUMP' more than a decade earlier. • **Songwriters:** PERRY / TYLER (aka TOXIC TWINS) except; COME TOGETHER (Beatles) / REMEMBER WALKIN' IN THE SAND (Shangri-la's) / TRAIN KEPT A-ROLLIN' (Johnny Burnette Trio) / MILK COW BLUES (Kokomo Arnold) / CRY ME A RIVER (Julie London) / MY ADIDAS (Run DMC). THE JOE PERRY PROJECT:- GET IT ON (BANG A GONG) (T. Rex) / BIG TEN-INCH RECORD (F.Weismantel; blues artist?) / ALL YOUR LOVE (Otis Rush) / HELTER SKELTER (Beatles) / CHIP AWAY THE STONE (Richie Supa). • **Miscellaneous:** In 1978 the group appeared in the 'SGT. PEPPER' Beatles film.

Album rating: AEROSMITH (*8) / GET YOUR WINGS (*7) / TOYS IN THE ATTIC (*9) / ROCKS (*8) / DRAW THE LINE (*7) / LIVE BOOTLEG (*7) / AEROSMITH'S GREATEST HITS compilation (*9) / NIGHT IN THE RUTS (*6) / ROCK IN A HARD PLACE (*6) / DONE WITH MIRRORS (*6) / CLASSICS LIVE collection (*4) / CLASSICS LIVE 2 collection (*5) / PERMANENT VACATION (*8) / GEMS collection (*6) / PUMP (*8) / PANDORA'S BOX compilation boxed-set (*9) / GET A GRIP (*6) / BIG ONES compilation (*8) / NINE LIVES (*6) / JUST PUSH PLAY (*5) / Joe Perry Project: LET THE MUSIC DO THE TALKING (*6)

STEVEN TYLER (b. STEVEN TALLARICO, 26 Mar'48, New York City) – vocals / **JOE PERRY** (b.10 Sep'50, Lawrence, Mass.) – guitar (ex-JAM BAND) / **BRAD WHITFORD** (b.23 Feb'52, Winchester, Mass.) – guitar repl. RAY TABANO / **TOM HAMILTON** (b.31 Dec'51, Colorado Springs) – bass (ex-JAM BAND) / **JOEY KRAMER** (b.21 Jun'50, New York City) – drums

C.B.S. Columbia

Jun 73. (lp) *<32005>* **AEROSMITH** [-] [ ]
– Make it / Somebody / Dream on / One way street / Mama kin / Write me a letter / Movin' out / Walkin' the dog. *(UK-iss.Sep74; CBS 65486) <US re-dist.Mar76 hit No.21> <US re-iss. Sep87/ cd-May88; PC/CK 32005>(cd-iss. Mar92 & Dec93 on 'Columbia'; 469011-2) (cd re-iss. Nov94; CK 64401) (cd re-iss. May97 on 'Columbia'; 474962-2)*

Nov 73. (7") *(CBS 1898) <45894>* **DREAM ON. / SOMEBODY** [ ] [59] Oct73
<US ext.re-iss. Jan76; 10278> ; hit No.6 *(re-iss. Apr76; CBS 4000)*

Feb 74. (7") *<46029>* **SAME OLD SONG AND DANCE. / PANDORA'S BOX** [-] [ ]

Apr 74. (7") *<10034>* **SPACED. / TRAIN KEPT A-ROLLIN'** [-] [ ]

Jun 74. (7") *<10105>* **S.O.S. (TOO BAD). / LORD OF THE THIGHS** [-] [ ]

Nov 74. (lp/c) *(CBS/40 80015) <32847>* **GET YOUR WINGS** [ ] [74] Mar74
– Same old song and dance / Lord of the thighs / Spaced / Woman of the world / S.O.S. (too bad) / Train kept a-rollin' / Seasons of wither / Pandora's box. *<US re-iss. Sep87/ cd-May88; PC/CK 32847> (UK-cd Mar92 & Dec93 & May97 on 'Columbia'; 474963-2)*

May 75. (7") *<10155>* **SWEET EMOTION. / UNCLE SALTY** [-] [36]

Jul 75. (lp/c) *(CBS/40 80773) <33479>* **TOYS IN THE ATTIC** [ ] [11] Apr75
– Toys in the attic / Uncle Salty / Adam's apple / Walk this way / Big ten inch record / Sweet emotion / No more no more / Round and round / You see me crying. *(re-iss. Feb88 on 'Castle' lp/c/cd; CLA LPX/MCX/CDX 135) <US re-iss. Sep87/ cd-iss. May88; PC/CK 33479> (UK re-iss. Apr91 & Nov93 & Jul95 & May97 on 'Columbia'; 480414-2) (re-iss. Oct97 on 'Simply Vinyl'; SVLP 0001)*

Sep 75. (7") *<10206>* **WALK THIS WAY. / ROUND AND ROUND** [-] [ ]

Nov 75. (7") *<10253>* **TOYS IN THE ATTIC. / YOU SEE ME CRYING** [-] [ ]

Jun 76. (lp/c) *(CBS/40 81379) <34165>* **ROCKS** [ ] [3] May76
– Back in the saddle / Last child / Rats in the cellar / Combination / Sick as a dog / Nobody's fault / Get the lead out / Lick and a promise / Home tonight. *<US re-iss. Sep87/May88; PC/CK 34165> (cd-iss. Jul89; CD 32517) (re-iss. cd Dec93 & May97 on 'Columbia'; 474965-2) (lp re-iss. Feb99 on 'Simply Vinyl'; SVLP 65)*

Aug 76. (7") *(CBS 4452) <10359>* **LAST CHILD. / COMBINATION** [ ] [21] Jun76

Sep 76. (7") *<10407>* **HOME TONIGHT. / PANDORA'S BOX** [-] [71]

Feb 77. (7") *(CBS 4878) <10449>* **WALK THIS WAY. / UNCLE SALTY** [ ] [10] Nov76

Apr 77. (7") *<10516>* **BACK IN THE SADDLE. / NOBODY'S FAULT** [-] [38]

Oct 77. (7") *<10637>* **DRAW THE LINE. / BRIGHT LIGHT FRIGHT** [-] [42]

Jan 78. (lp/c) *(CBS/40 82147) <34856>* **DRAW THE LINE** [ ] [11] Dec77
– Draw the line / I wanna know why / Critical mass / Get it up / Bright light fright / Kings and queens / The hand that feeds / Sight for sore eyes / Milk cow blues. *<US re-iss. Sep87; PC 34856> (re-iss. cd Dec93 & May97 on 'Columbia'; 474966-2)*

Mar 78. (7") *<10699>* **KINGS AND QUEENS. / CRITICAL MASS** [-] [70]

Jun 78. (7") *<10727>* **GET IT UP. / MILK COW BLUES** [-] [ ]

Aug 78. (7") *<10802>* **COME TOGETHER. / KINGS AND QUEENS** [ ] [23]

Jan 79. (d-lp) *(CBS 88325) <35564>* **LIVE! BOOTLEG (live)** [ ] [13] Nov78
– Back in the saddle / Sweet emotion / Lord of the thighs / Toys in the attic / Last child / Come together / Walk this way / Sick as a dog / Dream on / Chip away the stone / Sight for sore eyes / Mama kin / S.O.S. / I ain't got you / Mother popcorn / Train kept a rollin'. *<US re-iss. Dec87; PC 35564> (re-iss. cd Aug93/Dec93/May97 on 'Columbia'; 469004-2/474967-2)*

Jan 79. (7") *<10880>* **CHIP AWAY THE STONE (live). / CHIP AWAY THE STONE (studio)** [-] [77]

Jan 80. (lp/c) *(CBS/40 83680) <36050>* **NIGHT IN THE RUTS** [ ] [14] Nov79
– No surprize / Chiquita / Remember (walkin' in the sand) / Cheesecake / Three mile smile / Reefer head woman / Bone to bone (Coney Island white fish boy) / Think about it / Mia. *<US re-iss. Sep87; PC 36050> (cd-iss. Mar92 & Dec93 & May97 & Feb01 on 'Columbia'; 474968-2)*

Feb 80. (7") *(CBS 8220) <11181>* **REMEMBER (WALKIN' IN THE SAND). / BONE TO BONE (CONEY ISLAND WHITE FISH BOY)** [ ] [67] Jan80

—— (Dec79) **JIMMY CREPSO** – guitar (ex-FLAME) repl. JOE PERRY who went solo

—— (Feb80) **RICK DUFAY** – guitar repl. WHITFORD who teamed up with ST. HOLMES

Oct 82. (lp/c) *(CBS/40 85931) <38061>* **ROCK IN A HARD PLACE** [ ] [32] Sep82
– Jailbait / Lightning strikes / Bitch's brew / Bolivian ragamuffin / Cry me a river / Prelude to Joanie / Joanie's butterfly / Rock in a hard place (Cheshire cat) / Jig it up / Push comes to shove. *<US re-iss. Sep87; PC 38061> (cd-iss. Aug93/Dec93/May97 on 'Columbia'; 469006-2/474970-2)*

—— (Mar84) original 1970's line-up reform (see above)

Geffen Geffen

Nov 85. (7") *<28814>* **SHEILA. / GYPSY BOOTS** [-] [ ]

Dec 85. (lp/c) *(GEF/40 26695) <24091>* **DONE WITH MIRRORS** [ ] [36] Nov85
– Let the music do the talking / My fist your face / Shame on you / The reason a dog / Shela / Gypsy boots / She's on fire / The hop / Darkness. *<US cd-iss. Oct87; 20491-2> (UK re-iss. Jun89 on 'W.E.A.'; 924 091-1/-4/-2) (re-iss. Apr92 & Jun94 & Feb98 cd/c; GFLD/GFLC 19052)*

—— In Aug'86, AEROSMITH were credited on RUN DMC's hit version of 'WALK THIS WAY'.

Aug 87. (lp/c)(cd) *(WX 126/+C)(924 162-2) <24162>* **PERMANENT VACATION** [37] [11]
– Heart's done time / Magic touch / Rag doll / Simoriah / Dude (looks like a lady) / St. John / Hangman jury / Girl keep coming apart / Angel / Permanent vacation / I'm down / The movie. *(re-iss. Jun94 cd/c; ; GFLD/GFLC 19254) (lp re-iss. Jul98 on 'Simply Vinyl'; SVLP 35)*

Oct 87. (7") *(GEF 29) <28240>* **DUDE (LOOKS LIKE A LADY). / SIMORIAH** [45] [14] Sep87
(12"+=/12"pic-d+=) *(GEF 29T/+P)* – Once is enough.

Apr 88. (7"/12"/12"pic-d) *(GEF 34/+T/TP) <28249>* **ANGEL. / GIRL KEEPS COMING APART** [69] [3] Jan88
(3"cd-s+=) *(GEF 34CD)* – Angel (A.O.R. remix) / Dude (looks like a lady).

Jun 88. (12") *<27915>* **RAG DOLL. / ST.JOHN** [-] [17]

Aug 89. (7"/7"s/c-s) *(GEF 63/+X/C) <22845>* **LOVE IN AN ELEVATOR. / YOUNG LUST** [13] [5]
(10"pic-d+=/12"+=/3"cd-s+=) *(GEF 63 TP/T/CD)* – Ain't enough.

Sep 89. (lp/c)(cd) *(WX 304/+C)(924 254-2) <24254>* **PUMP** [3] [5]
– Young lust / F.I.N.E. / Love in an elevator / Monkey on my back / Janie's got a gun / The other side / My girl / Don't get mad, get even / Voodoo medicine man / What it takes. *(re-iss. Jun94 cd/c; GFLD/GFLC 19255) (lp re-iss. Nov98 on 'Simply Vinyl'; SVLP 45)*

Nov 89. (7"/7"sha-pic-d/c-s) *(GEF 68/+P/C) <22727>* **JANIE'S GOT A GUN. / VOODOO MEDICINE MAN** [ ] [4]
(12"+=/3"cd-s+=) *(GEF 68 T/CD)* – Rag doll (live).

Feb 90. (7"/7"sha-pic-d) *(GEF 72/+P)* **DUDE (LOOKS LIKE A LADY) (remix). / MONKEY ON MY BACK** [20] [-]
(12"/cd-s) *(GEF 72 T/CD)* – ('A'extended) / Love in an elevator (live) / Walk this way (live).

Mar 90. (7"/c-s) *<19944>* **WHAT IT TAKES. / MONKEY ON MY BACK** [-] [9]

Apr 90. (7") *(GEF 76)* **RAG DOLL. / SIMORIAH** [42] [-]
(12"/12"s) *(GEF 76 T/TW)* – ('A'side) / Mama kin (live) / Let it rain (live).
(cd-s) *(GEF 76CD)* – ('A'side) / Mama kin (live) / Dream on (live).

Aug 90. (7"/c-s) *(GEF 79/+C) <19927>* **THE OTHER SIDE. / MY GIRL** [46] [22] Jun90
(12"+=) *(GEFT 79)* – Theme from 'Wayne's World' / ('A'-honky tonk).
(12") *(GEFTW 79)* – ('A'side) / Love in an elevator / Dude (looks like a lady) / Walk this way.

Apr 93. (12"pic-d/cd-s) *(GFST/+D 35) <19149>* **LIVIN' ON THE EDGE. / DON'T STOP / FLESH** [19] [18]
(cd-s) *(GFSTX 35)* – ('A'side) / ('A'acoustic) / Can't stop messin'.

Apr 93. (cd/c/lp) *(GED/GEC/GEF 24444) <24455>* **GET A GRIP** [2] [1]
– Intro / Eat the rich / Get a grip / Fever / Livin' on the edge / Flesh / Walk on down / Shut up and dance / Cryin' / Gotta love it / Crazy / Line up / Can't stop messin' / Amazing / Boogie man.

Jun 93. (10"colrd) *(GFST 46)* **EAT THE RICH. / FEVER / HEAD FIRST** [34] [-]
(cd-s+=) *(GFSTD 46)* – Livin' on the edge (demo).

Oct 93. (c-s) *(GFSC 56) <19256>* **CRYIN' / WALK ON DOWN** [17] [12] Jul93
(12"white+=) *(GFST 56)* – I'm down.
(cd-s++=) *(GFSTD 56)* – My fist your face.
(cd-s+=) *(GFSXD 56)* – Love in an elevator / Janie's got a gun.

Nov 93. (c-s,cd-s) *<19264>* **AMAZING / FEVER** [-] [24]

Dec 93. (c-s) *(GFSC 63) <19264>* **AMAZING / GOTTA LOVE IT** [57] [-]
(12"colrd+=) *(GFST 63)* – ('A'acoustic).
(cd-s+=) *(GFSTD 63)* – ('A'orchestral).

May 94. (c-s,cd-s) *<19267>* **CRAZY / GOTTA LOVE IT** [-] [17]

Jun 94. (c-s) *(GFSC 75)* **SHUT UP AND DANCE. / DEUCES ARE WILD** [24] [-]
(7"+=) *(GFS 75)* – Crazy (orchestral).
(cd-s++=) *(GFSTD 75)* – Line up.

Oct 94. (c-s) *(GFSC 80)* **CRAZY / BLIND MAN** [23] [-]
(cd-s+=) *(GFSTD 80)* – Shut up and dance (live) / Blind man (mix).

Nov 94. (cd/c/d-lp) *(GED/GEC/GEF 24546) <24716>* **BIG ONES** (compilation) [7] [6]
– Walk on water / Love in an elevator / Rag doll / What it takes / Dude (looks like a lady) / Janie's got a gun / Cryin' / Amazing / Blind man / Deuces are wild / The other side / Crazy / Eat the rich / Angel / Livin' on the edge / Dude (looks like a lady) (live).

Dec 94. (c-s,cd-s) *<19377>* **BLIND MAN / HEAD FIRST** [-] [49]

Columbia Columbia

Mar 97. (7"/c-s) *(664075-7/-4)* **FALLING IN LOVE (IS HARD ON THE KNEES). / FALL TOGETHER** [22] [35] Feb97
(cd-s+=) *(664075-2)* – Sweet emotion / Seasons of wither.

Mar 97. (cd/c) *(485020-2/-4) <67547>* **NINE LIVES** [4] [1]
– Nine lives / Falling in love (is hard on the knees) / Hole in my soul / Taste of India / Full circle / Something's gotta give / Ain't that a bitch / Farm / Crash / Kiss your past good-bye / Pink / Falling off / Attitude adjustment / Fallen angels.

Jun 97. (7"pic-d) *(664501-7)* **HOLE IN MY SOUL. / NINE LIVES (live)** [29] [51] Aug97
(cd-s+=) *(664501-2)* – Falling in love (is hard on the knees) (Butcher mix) / Falling in love (is hard on the knees) (Moby flawed mix).
(cd-s) *(664501-5)* – ('A'side) / Falling in love (is hard on the knees) (Moby f**kee mix) / Falling in love (is hard on the knees) (live) / Walk this way (live).

Dec 97. (7"pink) *(664872-7) <78830>* **PINK. / PINK (Chulo mix)** [38] [27] Feb98
(cd-s) *(664872-2)* – ('A'side) / ('A'-South Beach mix) / ('A'live).

Sep 98. (7"/cd-s) *(666408-7/-2) <78952>* **I DON'T WANT TO MISS A THING. / TASTE OF INDIA (rock remix)** [4] [1] Aug98
(cd-s+=) *(6664087-5)* – Pink (live) / Crash.

Jun 99. (c-s) *(667534-4)* **PINK / I DON'T WANT TO MISS A THING (live)** [13] [-]
(cd-s+=) *(667534-2)* – Hole in my soul.
(cd-s) *(667534-5)* – ('A'side) / ('A'mix) / ('A'mix).

Mar 01. (7") *(670931-7) <79555>* **JADED. / ANGEL'S EYE** [13] [7]
(cd-s+=) *(670931-2)* – ('A'-stripped down acoustic mix) / ('A'-guitars mix) / Under my skin.
(cd-s+=) *(670931-5)* – ('A'-acoustic mix) / Under my skin (reprise).

Mar 01. (cd/c/lp) *(501535-2/-4/-1) <62088>* **JUST PUSH PLAY** [7] [2]
– Beyond beautiful / Just push play / Jaded / Fly away from here / Tip hoppin' / Sunshine / Under my skin / Luv lies / Outta your head / Drop dead gorgeous / The light inside / Avant garden / The face.

– compilations, others, etc. –

on 'CBS' UK / 'Columbia' US + UK (90's) unless otherwise mentioned

Jan 81. (lp/c) *(CBS/40 84704) <36865>* **AEROSMITH'S GREATEST HITS** [ ] [53] Nov80
– Dream on / Same old song and dance / Sweet emotion / Walk this way / Remember (walking in the sand) / Back in the saddle / Draw the line / Kings and queens / Come together / Last child. *<US re-iss. Sep87/ cd-Feb88; CK/CS 36865> (re-iss. Nov89 pic-lp/cd; 460703-8/-2) (re-iss. cd Dec93 & Jan01 on 'Columbia'; 474969-2)*

Sep 86. (lp/c) *(CBS/40 26901) <40329>* **CLASSICS LIVE!** (live 1977-1983) [ ] [84] Apr86
– Train kept a-rollin' / Kings and queens / Sweet emotion / Dream on / Mama kin / Three mile smile / Reefer head woman / Lord of the thighs / Major Barbra. *<US re-iss. Nov87 lp/c/cd; FC/FCT/CK 40329> (re-iss. cd Dec93 on 'Columbia'; 474971-2)*

Aug 87. (lp/c) <FC/+T 40855> **CLASSICS LIVE II (live)** [-] [ ]
– Back in the saddle / Walk this way / Movin' out / Draw the line / Same old song and dance / Last child / Let the music do the talking / Toys in the attic. *(UK cd-iss. Nov89; 460037-2) (cd re-iss. Dec92 on 'Columbia'; 474972-2)*
Jun 88. (d-lp/c/cd) *Raw Power; (RAW LP/TC/CD 037)* **ANTHOLOGY** [ ] [-]
1988. (7") <08536> **CHIP AWAY THE STONE. / S.O.S. (TOO BAD)** [-] [ ]
Aug 88. (3"cd-s) <38K 0795-2> **WALK THIS WAY / DREAM ON** [-] [ ]
Nov 89. (lp/c/cd) *(463224-1/-4/-2) <44487>* **GEMS** [ ] [ ] Dec88
– Rats in the cellar / Lick and a promise / Chip away the stone / No surprize / Mama kin / Adam's apple / Nobody's fault / Round and round / Critical mass / Lord of the thighs / Jailbait / Train kept a rollin'.
(re-iss. Apr91 & Dec93 on 'Columbia'; 474973-2) (cd re-iss. May98; 491236-2)
Dec 91. (t-cd/t-c) *(469293-2/-4) <46209>* **PANDORA'S BOX** [ ] [45]
– When I needed you / Make it / Movin' out / One way street / On the road again / Mama kin / Same old song and dance / Train kept a-rollin' / Seasons of wither / Write me a letter / Dream on / Pandora's Box / Rattlesnake shake / Walkin' the dog / Lord of the thighs // Toys in the attic / Round and round / Krawhitham / You see me crying / Sweet emotion / No More no more / Walk this way / I wanna know why / Big ten inch record / Rats in the cellar / Last child / All your love / Soul saver / Nobody's fault / Lick and a promise / Adam's apple / Draw the line / Critical mass // Kings and queens / Milk cow blues / I live in Connecticut / Three mile smile / Let it slide / Cheese cake / Bone to bone (Coney Island white fish boy) / No surprize / Come together / Downtown Charlie / Sharpshooter / Shit house shuffle / South station blues / Riff & roll / Jailbait / Major Barbara / Chip away the stone / Helter skelter / Back in the saddle / Circle jerk. *(3xcd-iss. Nov98; 487480-2)*
Jun 93. (cd) *(474038-2)* **TOYS IN THE ATTIC / CLASSICS LIVE** [ ] [-]
Jul 93. (cd) *(463224-2)* **ROCKS / GEMS** [ ] [ ]
Jun 94. (cd/c) *(476956-2/-4)* **PANDORA'S TOYS (BEST)** (compilation of 'PANDORA'S BOX') [ ] [ ]
– Sweet emotion / Draw the line / Walk this way / Dream on / Train kept a rollin' / Mama kin / Nobody's fault / Seasons of wither / Big ten-inch record / All your love / Helter skelter / Chip away the stone.
Aug 94. (c-s) *(660449-4) <74101>* **SWEET EMOTION / SUBWAY** [74] [ ] Dec91
(cd-s+=) *(660449-2)* – Circle jerk.
Dec 94. (12xcd-box) *(477803-2)* **BOX OF FIRE** [ ] [ ]
– (AEROSMITH / GET YOUR WINGS / TOYS IN THE ATTICS / ROCKS / DRAW THE LINE / LIVE BOOTLEG / NIGHT IN THE RUTS / GREATEST HITS / ROCK IN A HARD PLACE / CLASSICS LIVE / CLASSICS LIVE II / GEMS / bonus cd)
May 97. (13xcd-box) *(477803-2)* **BOX OF FIRE** [ ] [ ]
Nov 97. (3xcd-box) *(485312-2)* **TOYS IN THE ATTIC / DRAW THE LINE / ROCKS** [ ] [ ]
Aug 98. (cd) *(487351-2)* **CLASSICS LIVE VOL.1 & 2** [ ] [ ]
Oct 98. (d-cd/d-c) *Geffen; <(GED/GEC 25221)>* **A LITTLE SOUTH OF SANITY (live)** [36] [12]
– Eat the rich / Love in an elevator / Falling in love (is hard on the knees) / Same old song and dance / Hole in my soul / Monkey on my back / Livin' on the edge / Cryin' / Rag doll / Angel / Janie's got a gun / Amazing // Back in the saddle / Last child / The other side / Walk on down / Dream on / Crazy / Mama kin / Walk this way / Dude (looks like a lady) / What it takes / Sweet emotion.
Sep 00. (cd) *(499855-2)* **AEROSMITH / TOYS IN THE ATTIC** [ ] [-]
Oct 00. (d-cd) *Universal; <(E 490433-2)>* **PERMANENT VACATION / DONE WITH MIRRORS** [ ] [ ]
Oct 00. (t-cd) *Universal; <(E 424935-2)>* **PERMANENT VACATION / DONE WITH MIRRORS / PUMP** [ ] [ ]
Nov 00. (t-cd) *Universal; <(E 485312-2)>* **TOYS IN THE ATTIC / DRAW THE LINE / ROCKS** [ ] [ ]
Jan 01. (cd) *Universal; <(E 497441-2)>* **THE UNIVERSAL MASTERS COLLECTION** [ ] [ ]

JOE PERRY PROJECT

(while not an AEROSMITH member) with **RALPH NORMAN** – vocals / **DAVID HULL** – bass / **RONNIE STEWART** – drums

C.B.S. Columbia

Mar 80. (lp) *(CBS 84213)* <36388> **LET THE MUSIC DO THE TALKING** [ ] [47]
– Let the music do the talking / Conflict of interest / Discount dogs / Shooting star / Break song / Rockin' train / The mist is rising / Ready on the firing line / Life at a glance. *(cd-iss. Aug95 on 'Columbia'; 480967-2)*
Aug 80. (7") *(CBS 8889)* <11250> **LET THE MUSIC DO THE TALKING. / BONE TO BONE** [ ] [ ]

— **CHARLIE FARREN** – vocals repl. NORMAN

Jun 81. (lp) <37364> **I'VE GOT THE ROCK'N'ROLLS AGAIN** [-] [ ]
– East Coast, West Coast / No substitute for arrogance / I've got the rock'n'rolls again / Buzz buzz / Soldier of fortune / T.V. police / Listen to the rock / Dirty little things / Play the game / South station blues.
Jul 81. (7") <02497> **BUZZ BUZZ. / EAST COAST, WEST COAST** [-] [ ]

— **PERRY** new line-up **MARK BELL** – vocals / **DANNY HARGROVE** – bass / **JOE PET** – drums

M.C.A. M.C.A.

Jan 84. (lp/c) *(MCF/+C 3205)* **ONCE A ROCKER, ALWAYS A ROCKER** [ ] [ ]
– Once a rocker, always a rocker / Black velvet pants / Woman in chains / Guns west / Crossfire / King of the kings / Never wanna stop / Adrianna / Get it on (bang-a-gong) / Walk with me Sally.

WHITFORD / ST.HOLMES

BRAD WHITFORD – guitar, vocals / **ST.HOLMES** – guitar (ex-TED NUGENT) also **DAVID HEWITT** – bass / **STEVE PACE** – drums

not iss. Columbia

Jul 81. (7") <02555> **SHY AWAY. / MYSTERY GIRL** [-] [ ]
Aug 81. (lp) **WHITFORD / ST. HOLMES** [-] [ ]
– I need love / Whiskey woman / Hold on / Sharp shooter / Every morning / Action / Shy away / Does it really matter / Spanish box / Mystery girl.

AFGHAN WHIGS

Formed: Denver, Colorado, USA . . . Autumn '86, by GREG DULLI and RICK McCOLLUM who met in a prison. The pair moved to Cincinatti, Ohio, after signing for Seattle based indie label 'Sub Pop' in 1989, their independently released debut set, 'BIG TOP HALLOWEEN' (1988), having caused something of a stir with its proto-grunge exhortations. Produced by Seattle maestro, Jack Endino, the album, 'UP IN IT', worked around the same formula, hinting at their wider country and soul influences. After a further set for 'Sub Pop', 'CONGREGATION' (1992), and an EP of soul covers, 'UPTOWN AVONDALE', the group were plucked from the mire of grunge cultdom by 'Elektra' in the major label stampede following NIRVANA's success. A former film student, DULLI cannily negotiated the right to creative control over the band's videos, his acting ambitions duly realised in 1994 when he scored the part of JOHN LENNON in Stuart Sutcliffe's story, 'Backbeat'. The 'WHIGS major label debut, 'GENTLEMEN', pushed all the right critical buttons, fleshing out their grungy noir-soul sound against a typically hard-bitten lyrical background. Although the record surprisingly failed to make the US charts, it scored a Top 60 placing in the UK. DULLI's rendition of Barry White's 'CAN'T GET ENOUGH OF YOUR LOVE', was an indication of where AFGHAN WHIGS were headed with 'BLACK LOVE'. An even more soul-centric offering, the album almost scraped into the British Top 40, the band now signed to 'Mute' (still on 'Elektra' US). 'Columbia' took up the reins for er . . . 1998's '1965', a celebration of rock music's debt to the power of sex. Recorded in New Orleans, the record was hailed as their long promised masterpiece, a writhing, sweaty slab of post-grunge voodoo soul. DULLI matched this aggression later in the year, after a brawl with a steward earned him a few days in intensive care and a fractured skull . . . er to boot. Subsequently the singer threatened action on the Texas nightclub even though it was alleged that he was the main instigator. • **Songwriters:** DULLI, some McCOLLUM except; covers by MY WORLD IS EMPTY WITHOUT YOU (Diana Ross & The Supremes) / (Al Green) / BAND OF GOLD (Freda Payne) / I KEEP COMING BACK (Austell-Graham) / IF I ONLY HAD A HEART (from 'Wizard Of Oz') / CREEP (Radiohead) / LITTLE GIRL BLUE (Hart-Rodgers) / MR. SUPERLOVE (Ass Ponys) / LOST IN THE SUPERMARKET (Clash).

Album rating: BIG TOP HALLOWEEN (*4) / UP IN IT (*6) / CONGREGATION (*7) / GENTLEMEN (*7) / BLACK LOVE (*6) / 1965 (*8)

GREG DULLI – vocals, guitar / **RICK McCOLLUM** – guitar / **JOHN CURLEY** – bass / **STEVE EARLE** – drums

not iss. Ultrasuede

Oct 88. (lp) <001> **BIG TOP HALLOWEEN** [-] [ ]
– Here comes Jesus / In my town / Priscilla's wedding day / Push / Scream / But listen / Big top Halloween / Life in a day / Sammy / Doughball / Back o' the line / Greek is extra.

Sub Pop Sub Pop

Aug 89. (7") <SP 32> **I AM THE STICKS. / WHITE TRASH PARTY** [-] [ ]
Apr 90. (cd/c/lp/orange-lp) <SP 60> **UP IN IT** [-] [ ]
– Retarded / White trash party / Hated / Southpaw / Amphetamines and coffee / Now can we begin / You my flower / Son of the south / I know your secret. *(cd/c+=)* – I am the sticks. *(UK-iss.Aug90 on 'Glitterhouse'; GR 0092) (cd re-iss. Sep98; SPCD 60)*
Oct 90. (7",7"red) <SP 84> **SISTER BROTHER. / HEY CUZ** [-] [ ]
Dec 90. (12"ep) <SP 4-115> **THE RETARD EP** [ ] [ ]
– Retarded / Sister brother / Hey cuz / Turning in two. *(cd-ep May93; SPCD 4-115)*
Jan 92. (lp/cd) <(SP 183/+CD)> **CONGREGATION** [ ] [ ]
– Her against me / I'm her slave / Turn on the water / Conjure me / Kiss the floor / Congregation / This is my confession / Dedicate it / The temple / Let me lie to you / Tonight. *(cd re-iss. Sep98; same)*
Jan 92. (12"ep) <(SP 187)> **TURN ON THE WATER. / MILES IZ DEAD / DELTA KONG** [ ] [ ]
(cd-ep+=) *(SPCD 187)* – Chalk outline.
May 92. (7"white,7"lavender) <(SP 142)> **CONJURE ME. / MY WORLD IS EMPTY WITHOUT YOU** [ ] [ ]
(12"+=)(cd-s+=) <(SP 42)><(SP 203CD)> – My flower.
Oct 92. (7"ep) <(SP 216)> **UPTOWN AVONDALE EP: BAND OF GOLD. / COME SEE ABOUT ME** [ ] [ ]
(12"+=) <(SP 215)> – True love travels on a gravel road / Beware.
(cd-s++=) <(SP 215CD)> – Rebirth of the cool.
(above release could have been issued earlier in US, early 1990)

Blast First Elektra

Sep 93. (7") *(BFFP 89)* **GENTLEMEN. / MR. SUPERLOVE** [ ] [ ]
(12"+=/cd-s+=) *(BFFP 89 T/CD)* – The dark end of the street.
Oct 93. (lp/cd) *(BFFP 90/+CD)* <7559 61501-2> **GENTLEMEN** [58] [ ]
– If I were going / Gentlemen / Be sweet / Debonair / When we two parted / Fountain and fairfax / What jail is like / My curse / Now you know / I keep coming back / Brother Woodrow – Closing prayer. *(lp w /free 7"ep)* – ROT. / TONIGHT

— guests on the album: **HAROLD CHICHESTER** – keyboards / **BARB HUNTER** – cello / **JODY STEPHENS** – vocals / **MARCY MAYS** – vocals

Feb 94. (7"ep/12"ep/cd-ep) *(BFFP 95/+T/CD)* **BROKEN PROMISES EP** [ ] [ ]
– Debonair / My curse / Little girl blue / Ready.
(cd-ep) *(BFFP 95CDL)* – ('A'side) / Rot / I keep coming back / Tonight.

— In Mar'94, 'MR.SUPERLOVE' was issued on B-side of ASS PONY's single on 'Monocat'.

Aug 94. (7"ep/10"ep/cd-ep) *(BFFP 96/+T/CD)* <61708> **WHAT JAIL IS LIKE EP** (some live) [ ] [ ]
– What jail is like / Mr. Superlove / Dark end of the street / Little girl blue / Gentlemen / Now you know / My world is empty without you.

Mute Elektra

Feb 96. (10"ep/cd-ep) *(10/CD MUTE 128)* **HONKY'S LADDER E.P.**
– Honky's ladder / Blame, etc. / If I only had a heart / Creep.

Mar 96. (cd/c/lp) *(CD/C+/STUMM 143) <61896>* **BLACK LOVE** 41 79
– Crime scene part one / My enemy / Double day / Blame, etc. / Step into the light / Going to town / Honky's ladder / Night by candlelight / Bulletproof / Summer's kiss / Faded.

Aug 96. (cd-ep) *(CDMUTE 199)* **GOING TO TOWN / GOING TO TOWN – MODERN ROCK LIVE / YOU'VE CHANGED / I WANT TO GO TO SLEEP / MOON RIVER**

Columbia Columbia

Oct 98. (7") *(666576-7)* **SOMETHIN' HOT / MISS WORLD**
(cd-s+=) *(666576-2)* – Papa was a rascal.

Oct 98. (cd/c) *(491486-2/-4) <69450>* **1965**
– Somethin' hot / Crazy / Uptown again / Sweet son of a bitch / 66 / City soleil / John the baptist / The slide song / Neglekted / Omerta / The vampire Lanois.

—— added **JOSH PAXTON** – keyboards / **SUSAN MARSHALL + DOUG FALSETTI** – backing vocals

AFI

Formed: Ukiah, Northern California, USA . . . 1991 by high school friends DAVEY HAVOK, MARKUS STOPHOLESE, VICK and ADAM CARSON. One split 7" single (wih LOOSE CHANGE) and a debut EP, 'BEHIND THE TIMES', later, college commitments led to an inevitable break up. A chance reunion show subsequently down went so well that the AFI crew (now featuring GEOFF KRESGE in place of VICK) got back together permanently, relocating to Berkeley where the likes of RANCID and GREEN DAY had cut their teeth at fabled punk venue, Gillman Street. After spotting the band at a show in Hollywood, DEXTER HOLLAND (of OFFSPRING fame) snapped them up for his 'Nitro' label and proceeded to release a debut album, 'VERY PROUD OF YA' (1996). Another two sets of bullseye-aim hardcore followed in 1997: 'ANSWER THAT & STAY FASHIONABLE' and 'SHUT YOUR MOUTH & OPEN YOUR EYES'. While the band's acronym has been been subject to many and varied interpretations over the years, the official line is that it stands for A FIRE INSIDE, the title of a 1998 EP and also the name of AFI's website. Judging by the musical contents of 'BLACK SAILS IN THE SUNSET' (1999), that fire was at least partly fuelled by Old Nick himself. Well, not really, but influences form the darker side of punk – MISFITS, JOY DIVISION etc – were definitely infiltrating the band's previously straight up sound. Hardcore fans' suspicions were also raised by the fact that HAVOK (now backed by a slightly altered line-up of CARSON, HUNTER and JADE PUGET) had taken to wearing make-up and black PVC. The transformation was even more pronounced on 'THE ART OF DROWNING' (2000), HAVOK's angst-ridden lyrics mirroring the tortured music.

Album rating: VERY PROUD OF YA (*6) / ANSWER THAT AND STAY FASHIONABLE (*6) / SHUT YOUR MOUTH AND OPEN YOUR EYES (*6) / BLACK SAILS IN THE SUNSET (*7) / THE ART OF DROWNING (*6)

DAVEY HAVOC – vocals / **JADE PUGET** – guitar / **HUNTER** – bass / **ADAM CARSON** – drums

Nitro Nitro

Oct 96. (cd/c/lp) *<(15805-2/-4/-1)>* **VERY PROUD OF YA** Jun96
– He who laughs last / File 13 / Wake-up call / Cult status / Perfect fit / Advances in modern technolgy / Theory of revolution / This secret Ninja / Soap box derby / Fishbowl / Charles Atlas / Crop tub / Consult my lover / Take the test / Two of a kind / Shatty Fatmas / Yurf Rendenmein / Cruise control / Modern epic.

May 97. (cd/c/lp) *<(15811-2/-4/-1)>* **ANSWER THAT AND STAY FASHIONABLE** Apr97
– Two of a kind / Half empty bottle / Yurf rendenmein / I wanna get a Mohawk (but mom won't let me) / Brownie bottom sundae / The chequered demon / Cereal wars / The mother in me / Rizzo in the box / Kung-fu devil / Your name here / Ny-quil / Don't make me ill / Open your eyes / Highschool football hero.

Nov 97. (cd/c/lp) *<(15815-2/-4/-1)>* **SHUT YOUR MOUTH AND OPEN YOUR EYES**
– Keeping out of direct sunlight / Three reasons / A single second / ph Low / Let it be broke / Third season / Lower your head and take it in the body / Coin return / The new patron saints and angels / Three seconds notice / Salt for your wounds / Today's lesson / The Devil loves you / Triple zero.

May 99. (7"ep/cd-ep) *<(ADELINE 002/+CD)>* **A FIRE INSIDE EP** Sep98
– 3 1/2 / Over exposure / The hanging garden / Demonomania.
(above issued on 'Adeline')

Jun 99. (cd/lp) *<(15824-2/-1)>* **BLACK SAILS IN THE SUNSET**
– Strength through wounding / Porphyria cutanea tarda / Esanguination / Malleus maleficarum / Narrative of soul against soul / Clove smoke catharsis / The prayer position / No poetic device / Weathered tome / The last kiss / At a glance / God called in sick today.

Dec 99. (cd-ep) *<(15829-2)>* **ALL HALLOWS**
– Porphryia / Malleus maleficarum / Prayer position / Who knew.

Sep 00. (cd/lp) *<(15835-2/-1)>* **THE ART OF DROWNING**
– Initiation / The lost souls / The nephilim / Ever and a day / Sacrifice theory / Of greetings and goodbyes / Smile / A story at three / The days of the phoenix / Catch a hot one / Wester / 6 to 8 / The despair factor / Morningstar / Battled *[cd-only]* / Dream of waking *[lp-only]*.

Apr 01. (cd-ep) *<(15843-2)>* **THE DAYS OF THE PHOENIX E.P.**
– The days of the phoenix / A winter's tale / Wester.

A FOOT IN COLDWATER

Formed: Pickering, Canada . . . 1971 by former NUCLEUS (NOT the jazz-rock act from England) members HUGH LEGGAT, BOB HORNE and DANNY TAYLOR alongside ALEX MACHIN and PAUL NAUMANN (both former members of TORONTO act LEATHER). Named by 'Daffodil' boss Frank Davies, the melodic hard rockers released their eponymous debut album in 1972, scoring a domestic Top 30 hit with '(MAKE ME DO) ANYTHING YOU WANT'. That year also saw the release of singles 'ISN'T LOVE UNKIND (IN MY LIFE)' and 'LOVE IS COMING', both featured on the imaginatively titled follow-up album, 'THE SECOND FOOT IN COLDWATER' (1973). In an attempt to kickstart their fading sales, 1974's 'ALL AROUND US' was bolstered with a brace of previous hits although their label's subsequent bankruptcy hardly helped matters. While the record was released in the USA by 'Elektra' in 1975, AFIC finally found another Canadian home in the shape of RUSH's 'Anthem' imprint. A comeback album, 'BREAKING THROUGH' (1977) failed to do just that and the band finally turned the tap off for good. LEGGAT went on to form THUNDEROAD with his brother GORD, subsequently changing the name to PRIVATE EYE (also featuring HOWARD WARDEN and PAUL STAMP). This in turn metamorphosed into LEGGAT featuring the siblings alongside erstwhile AFIC buddy DANNY TAYLOR, the outfit releasing an album for 'Capitol' in 1982 entitled 'ILLUMINATIONS'. MACHIN worked as a songwriter and jingle singer, releasing a one-off eponymous album as CHAMPION for 'C.B.S.'. AFIC have reformed for sporadic reunion tours since 1988 while MACHIN played at a classic rock revue in Ottawa as part of the Canada Day 2000 celebrations.

Album rating: A FOOT IN COLDWATER (*5) / SECOND FOOT IN COLDWATER (*5) / ALL AROUND US (*5 / BREAKING THROUGH (*5)

ALEX MACHIN – vocals / **PAUL NAUMANN** – guitar / **BOB HORNE** – keyboards / **HUGH LEGGAT** – bass / **DANNY TAYLOR** – drums

Daffodil not iss.

1972. (lp) *<SBA 16012>* **A FOOT IN COLDWATER** – – Canada
– On the wind / Yalla yae / Deep freeze / (Make me do) Anything you want / Who can stop us now / Alone together / Fallen man / In heat. *(UK-iss.1974 on 'Elektra'; 52011) <cd-iss. 1998 on 'Unidisc'+=; AGEK 2158>* – Lady true.

1972. (7") *<DFS 1017>* **(MAKE ME DO) ANYTHING YOU WANT. / (part 2)** – – Canada

1972. (7") *<DFS 1028>* **(ISN'T LOVE UNKIND) IN MY LIFE. / DEEP FREEZE** – – Canada

1972. (7") *<DFS 1033>* **LADY TRUE. / IN HEAT** – – Canada

1973. (lp) *<SBA 16028>* **THE SECOND FOOT IN COLDWATER** – – Canada
– Coming is love: a) Mose into E – b) Coming is love / So long / Suzy / How much can you take / (Isn't love unkind) In my life / Sailing ships / Love is coming. *<cd-iss. 1998 on 'Unidisc'; AGEK 2159>*

Elektra Elektra

Jan 75. (7") *(K 12164) <45250>* **I KNOW WHAT YOU NEED. / PARA-DICE** Mar75

Mar 75. (lp) *<K 71025>* **ALL AROUND US** –
– I know what you need / All around us / (Make me do) Anything you want / It's only love / Love is coming / How much can you take / He's always there (watching you) / Yalla yae / (Isn't love unkind) In my life / Para-dice. *<Canadian-iss.1974; DAF 10048> <cd-iss. 1998 on 'Unidisc'; AGEK 2160>*

Mar 75. (7") *(K 12170) <45224>* **MAKE ME DO ANYTHING YOU WANT. / ALL AROUND US** Jan75

not iss. Anthem

1975. (7") *<1216-1068>* **MIDNIGHT LADY. / ALL AROUND US** – – Canada

1977. (7") **BREAKING THROUGH. /** – – Canada

1977. (lp) *<ANR 1-1008>* **BREAKING THROUGH** – – Canada
– Save it all for me / The night's still young / Play my guitar / Goodnight my love / Why / I knew she would / Driftaway / Yes I'm smiling / Breaking through.

—— Disbanded after above and LEGGAT formed PRIVATE EYE with brother GORDY plus HOWARD WARDEN and PAUL STAMP. They made one eponymous lp for 'Captitol'; (EST 11980). He later went solo and of others; MACHIN guested for CHAMPION.

– compilations, etc. –

1977. (lp) *Daffodil;* **FOOTPRINTS VOL.1** – – Canada
<re-iss. '84 on 'Capitol'> <cd-iss. '91 on 'BEI'; BEICD 25>

1984. (lp) *Daffodil;* **FOOTPRINTS VOL.2** – – Canada
<re-iss. '84 on 'Capitol'> <cd-iss. '91 on 'BEI'; BEICD 26>

1998. (d-cd) *Unidisc; <AGEK2-2161>* **THE VERY BEST OF A FOOT IN COLDWATER** – – Canada

AFTER HOURS

Formed: Southampton, England . . . mid-80's out of XS and LOVE ATTACK by JOHN FRANCIS, TIM PAYNE, ANDY NYE, MARTIN WALLS and MARK ADDISON. In 1988, they released what was to be their only effort, 'TAKE OFF', which employed the services of producer ROBIN BLACK, shifting music styles between hard rock (WHITESNAKE / DEEP PURPLE) and limp-wristed AOR.

Album rating: TAKE OFF (*4)

JOHN FRANCIS – vocals / **TIM PAYNE** – guitar / **ANDY NYE** – keyboards (ex-MICHAEL SCHENKER GROUP) / **MARTIN WALLS** – bass / **MARK ADDISON** – drums

FM-Revolver not iss.

Aug 88. (lp/c/cd/pic-lp) *(WKFMLP 89)* **TAKE OFF** –

– Love attack / Better late than never / Stay by my side / Take off / The game / Another lonely night / Paint it black / Without you.

— **ALAN JACKMAN** – drums (ex-OUTFIELD); repl. ADDISON

— They were to split not long after

AFTERMATH

Formed: Tucson, Arizona, USA . . . 1984 by RICHARD SHAYKA and CLIFF FINNEY. With the line-up completed by JOHN E. JANUARY, JOE NUTT and RICK VON GLAHN, they eventually found a taker for their easy-going metal in the Dutch 'Mushroom' label. A debut album, 'DON'T CHEER ME UP', appeared the following year (1989) to general indifference. • **Note:** It would be a different AFTERMATH alt-pop outfit that released 'Eyes Of Tomorrow' in 1995.

Album rating: DON'T CHEER ME UP (*4)

RICHARD SHAYKA – vocals / **CLIFF FINNEY** – guitar / **JOHN E. JANUARY** – guitar / **JOE NUTT** – bass / **RICK VON GLAHN** – drums

Mushroom / not iss.

Feb 89. (lp) *(20001)* **DON'T CHEER ME UP** [-] [-] Dutch
– Lines of horror / Black and yellow / Daemynspeke / Straight from the hell / Beast of wrath / Luci's dance / Aftermath.

— split after failure of above

AGATHODAIMON

Formed: Mainz, Germany . . . 1995 by HYPERION, SATHONYS, VAMPALLANS, MARKO T and MATTHIAS R. Yep, you guessed it, yet another crew of gothic black metal types dying to take your musical soul. But these guys are something of an anomaly on the scene given that they hail from Germany rather than Norway. They've nevertheless taken a lot of their musical cues from those nasty Norsemen, earning themselves a deal with 'Nuclear Blast' on the strength of two demo tapes. While one VLAD DRACUL (don't ask . . .) apparently served as lyricist for the debut album, 'BLACKEN THE ANGEL' (1998), the Rumanian singer was subsequently refused entry to Germany after a trip to his homeland. A friend, AKAIAS, was duly drafted in to handle vocals and went on to tour Europe with the band alongside the likes of GORGOTH and CHILDREN OF BODOM. With DRACUL still absent towards the end of the decade, AKAIAS also appeared on 1999's 'A HIGHER ART OF REBELLION' (1999).

Album rating: BLACKEN THE ANGEL (*6) / A HIGHER ART OF REBELLION (*4)

VLAD DRACUL (b. Rumania) – vocals / **HYPERION** – guitar / **SATHONYS** – guitar / **VAMPALLANS** – keyboards / **MARKO T** – bass / **MATTHIAS R** – drums

own label / not iss.

1996. (cd-ep) **CARPE NOCTUM** [-] [-] German

1997. (cd-ep) **NEAR DARK** [-] [-] German

— **AKAIAS** – vocals; repl. VLAD who couldn't return to Germany (he continued to write the lyrics for AKAIAS to sing)

Nuclear Blast / Nuclear Blast

Jul 98. (cd) *(NB 298-2)* <6298> **BLACKEN THE ANGEL** [ ] [ ]
– Tristeta vehementa / Banner of blasphemy / Near dark / Ill of an imaginary guilt / Die nacht des unwesens / Contemplation song / Sfintit cu roua suferintii / Stingher – Alone / After dark / Ribbons – Requiem.

Nov 99. (cd) *(NB 422-2)* <6422> **A HIGHER ART OF REBELLION** [ ] [ ]
– Ne cheama pamintul / Tongue of thorns / Glasul artei viitoare / When she was mute / A death in its olenitude / Body of clay / Novus ordo seclorum / Back into the shadows / Los posedes / Neovampirism / Heaven's coffin / Ribbons – Requiem '99 / Body of clay (remix).

AGENT ORANGE

Formed: Fullerton, Orange County, California, USA . . . late 70's by main songwriter, MIKE PALM, alongside STEVE 'SOTO' RODGERS and SCOTT MILLER. Naming themselves after a chemical weapon used in the Vietnam War, the hardcore trio took a similarly vicious approach in their sound. Having featured on disc jockey, Rodney Bingenheimer's (presenter on the KROQ radio station) 'Posh Boy' various artists compilation, 'Rodney On The Roq's' with the track, 'BLOODSTAINS', the band were signed to the Robbie Fields-run label in their own right. A single, 'EVERYTHING TURNS GRAY', was unleashed in '81, the last to feature ADOLESCENTS-bound RODGERS, who was replaced by JAMES LEVESQUE. Later that year, AGENT ORANGE issued their debut album, 'LIVING IN DARKNESS', a more melodic affair that fused punk with early 60's DICK DALE-esque surf. Three more "skate-punk" instrumentals were showcased on 1983's 'BITCHIN' SUMMER', an EP that brought them to the attention of 'Enigma'. Their first release for the label was the 'WHEN YOU LEAST EXPECT IT' EP, a record that contained an unlikely cover of Jefferson Airplane's psychedelic classic, 'SOMEBODY TO LOVE'. A much anticipated second album, 'THIS IS THE VOICE', eventually surfaced in 1986, although another five year hiatus was just around the corner. During this period, they found ex-SOCIAL DISTORTION guy, BRENT LILES, who replaced LEVESQUE on what proved to be their music biz swansong, 'REAL LIVE SOUND', in 1991. • **Covered:** POLICE TRUCK (Dead Kennedys) / PIPELINE (Chantays) / SHAKIN' ALL OVER (Johnny Kidd & The Pirates).

Album rating: LIVING IN DARKNESS (*5) / THIS IS THE VOICE (*6) / REAL LIVE SOUND (*4)

MIKE PALM – vocals, guitar / **STEVE 'SOTO' RODGERS** – bass / **SCOTT MILLER** – drums

not iss. / Posh Boy

1981. (7"ep) <PBS 12> **EVERYTHING TURNS GRAY. / PIPELINE** [-] [ ]

— **JAMES LEVESQUE** – bass; repl. RODGERS who joined the ADOLESCENTS

Oct 81. (lp) <PBS 122> **LIVING IN DARKNESS** [-] [ ]
– Too young to die / Everything turns gray / Miserlou / The last goodbye / No such thing / A cry for help in a world gone mad / Bloodstains / Living in darkness / Pipeline / Breakdown / Mr. Moto.

1983. (7"ep) <PBS 103-7> **BITCHIN' SUMMER EP** [-] [ ]

not iss. / Enigma

1984. (12"ep) <E 1047> **WHEN YOU LEAST EXPECT IT EP** [-] [ ]
– It's up to me and you / Bite the hand that feeds / Somebody to love / Out of limits. *(UK cd-iss. Feb95 on 'Restless'; 722182)*

1986. (lp) <971209> **THIS IS THE VOICE** [-] [ ]
– Voices / It's in your head / Say it isn't true / Fire in the rain / In your dreams tonight / Tearing me apart . . . so strange / Bite the hand that feeds / I kill spies / This is not the end. *(UK cd-iss. Feb95 on 'Restless'; 725402)*

— **BRENT LILES** – bass (ex-SOCIAL DISTORTION) repl. LEVESQUE

Restless / Restless

Dec 90. (cd/c) <72529-2/-4> **REAL LIVE SOUND (live)** [-] [ ]
– Fire in the rain / Everything turns grey / Tearing me apart / Too young to die / It's in your head / I kill spies / Bite the hand that feeds (part 1) / Somebody to love / No such thing / Say it isn't true / Bloodstains / Pipeline / Last goodbye / Police truck / This is not the end / Shakin' all over. *(UK cd-iss. Feb95; same as US)*

— disbanded around the early 90's; the AGENT ORANGE of the mid 90's who released the 'VIRTUALLY INDESTRUCTABLE ALBUM', were not the same act

AGENT STEEL

Formed: Los Angeles, California, USA . . . 1984, by former ABATTOIR frontman and songwriter, JOHN CYRIIS, the self-acclaimed Steven Spielberg of Heavy Metal. The group signed to the US metal label, 'Combat', who issued their debut album, 'OPERATION REDEYE' in 1985. The same year, they finally established themselves within the metal scene via the 'Roadrunner' licensed 'SKEPTIC'S APOCALYPSE'. Label problems subsequently resulted in a move to 'Music For Nations', where a new line-up issued an EP entitled 'MAD LOCUST RISING' and the acclaimed 'UNSTOPPABLE FORCE' (1989). CYRIIS then relocated to Florida, minus the rest of the band, effectively ending AGENT STEEL's brief musical journey.

Album rating: OPERATION REDEYE (*4) / SKEPTICS APOCALYPSE (*5) / UNSTOPPABLE FORCE (*6) / OMEGA CONSPIRACY (*4)

JOHN CYRIIS – vocals (ex-ABATTOIR) / **MARK MARSHALL** – guitar / **BILL SIMMONS** – guitar / **GEORGE ROBB** – bass / **CHUCK PROFUS** – drums

not iss. / Combat

1985. (lp) **OPERATION REDEYE** [-] [ ]

Roadrunner / Combat

Sep 85. (lp) *(RR 9759)* **SKEPTICS APOCALYPSE** [ ] [ ]
– The calling / Agents of steel / Taken by force / Evil eye, evil minds / Bleed for the godz / Children of the sun / 144,000 gone / Guilty as charged / Back to reign. *(cd-iss. Apr89 + Feb93 on 'Roadracer'; RO 97592) (cd re-iss. Jun99 on 'Century Media'; CM 66009-2)*

— **JOHN + CHUCK** recruited new members **JUAN GARCIA + BERNIE VERSAILLES** – guitar / **MICHAEL ZAPUTIL** – bass

Music For Nations / Combat

Aug 86. (12"ep) *(12KUT 124)* **MAD LOCUST RISING** [ ] [ ]
– (The swarm is upon us) / Mad locust rising / The ripper / Let it be done – The day at Guyana. *(cd-iss. Mar00 on 'Century Media'; CM 66052-2)*

Aug 89. (cd/c/lp) *(CD/T+/MFN 66)* <88561 8096-2> **UNSTOPPABLE FORCE** [ ] [ ]
– Unstoppable force / Never surrender / Indestructive / Chosen to stay / Still searchin' / Rager / The day at Guyana / Nothin' left / Traveler. *(cd re-iss. Nov99 on 'Century Media'; CM 66039-2)*

— they had already disbanded Spring 1989; re-formed later with **GARCIA, VERSAILLES** with **BRUCE HALL** – vocals

Candlelight / Metal Blade

Oct 99. (cd) *(CANDLE 038CD)* <14333> **OMEGA CONSPIRACY** [ ] [ ] 2000
– Destroy the hush / Illuminati is machine / Fighting backwards / New godz / Know your master / Infinity / Awaken the swarm / Into the nowhere / Bleed forever / It's not what you think / *(hidden track+=)* – Beyond the realms of death.

AGNOSTIC FRONT

Formed: New York, USA . . . 1983 by frontman ROGER MIRET (a tattooed and pit-bull breeding veggie!) and guitarist VINNIE STIGMA, who completed the line-up with ALEX KINNON, ROB KABULA and LOUIE BEATTO. Initially playing hardcore (the 45, 'UNITED BLOOD' proves the point), the band gradually assumed more of a metallic sheen, releasing 'VICTIM OF PAIN' for the 'Rat Cage' label in '84 before signing with 'Relativity' for the release of 1986's 'CAUSE FOR ALARM'. Their right wing political leanings distanced them even further from NY's punk scene, the uncompromising lyrics complementing the aggressive musical backing. A third set, 'LIBERTY & JUSTICE FOR . . .' was issued the following year, their last vinyl outing for some time. This was due to MIRET's subsequent year and a half incarceration on drugs charges. In 1992 with temporary frontman, ALAN PETERS, they returned from their sabbatical, unleashing the fine 'ONE VOICE' (which also featured new guitarist MATT HENDERSON). However, although MIRET was out of jail, they played their last gig at CBGB's just prior to Xmas that year (an album of the show was issued the following year as 'LAST WARNING'). STIGMA and HENDERSON duly joined MADBALL, a band in the same vein fronted by MIRET's younger brother, FREDDY CRICIEN. Returning half a decade later on 'Epitaph' records (who else!), AGNOSTIC FRONT released two further long-players, 'SOMETHING'S GOTTA GIVE' (1998) and 'RIOT, RIOT UPSTART' (1999).

Album rating: VICTIM IN PAIN (*4) / CAUSE FOR ALARM (*6) / LIBERTY AND JUSTICE FOR (*6) / LIVE AT CBGB'S (*4) / ONE VOICE (*5) / TO BE CONTINUED . . . THE VERY BEST OF . . . compilation (*6) / LAST WARNING (*5) / SOMETHING'S GOTTA GIVE (*5) / RIOT, RIOT UPSTART (*4)

ROGER MIRET – vocals / **VINNIE STIGMA** – guitar / **ALEX KINNON** – guitar / **ROB KABULA** – bass / **LOUIE BEATTO** (RAYBEEZ) – drums

not iss. — unknown

1983. (7") **UNITED BLOOD. /** [-]

not iss. — Rat Cage

1984. (lp) **VICTIM IN PAIN** [-]
– Victim in pain / Remind them / Blind justice / Last warning / United and strong / Hiding inside / Power / Fascist attitude / Society sucker / Your mistake / With time. *<re-iss. Aug87 on 'Combat'; 88561-8181-1>*

— **ADAM MOOCHIE** – bass; repl. ROB + ALEX

Rough Justice — Combat

May 86. (lp)<cd> *(JUST 3) <88561-3022-2>* **CAUSE FOR ALARM**
– The eliminator / Existance of hate / Time will come / Growing concern / Your mistake / Out for blood / Toxic shock / Bomber Zee / Public assistance / Shoot his load. *(cd-iss. Aug87; CDJUST 3) (re-iss. Nov99 on 'Century Media' cd/lp; CM 66001-2/-1)*

— **JIMMY MERRICK** – drums; repl. BEATTO

Oct 87. (cd/lp) *(CD+/JUST 8) <970.958>* **LIBERTY & JUSTICE FOR . . .**
– Liberty and justice / Crucial moment / Strength / Genesis / Anthem / Another side / Happened yesterday / Lost / Hypocrisy / Crucified / Censored. *(re-iss. Nov99 on 'Century Media' cd/lp; CM 66002-2/-1)*

— **ALAN PETERS** – vocals; repl. imprisoned MIRET, although the latter still managed to contribute the lyrics. PETERS joined CRAWLPAPPY after its release.

— **MATT HENDERSON** was added

Roadracer — Relativity

Jan 92. (cd/lp) *(RO 9222-2/-1) <88561-3022-2>* **ONE VOICE**
– New Jack / One voice / Infiltrate / The tombs / Your fall / Over the edge / Undertow / Now and then / Crime without sin / Retaliate / Force feed / Bastard. *(re-iss. May95; same) (cd re-iss. Feb99 on 'Century Media'; CM 66004-2)*

— MIRET was now on below album, although they had already disbanded late '92, STIGMA and HENDERSON having moved on to MADBALL (see above).

Jun 93. (cd/lp) *(RO 9078-2/-1) <88561-1170-2/-1>* **LAST WARNING (live)**
– Undertow / Your mistake – Victim in pain / One voice / Infiltrate – Strength / United blood / Public assistance – Over the edge / Blind justice – Last warning / Crucified / Toxic shock – United and strong / Fascist attitudes / Anthem – The eliminator / No one rules / Final war / Last warning / Traitor / Friend or foe / United blood / Fight / Discriminate me / In control / Crucial changes. *(re-iss. May95; same) (cd re-iss. May99 on 'Century Media'; CM 66005-2)*

Epitaph — Epitaph

May 98. (cd/lp) *<(E 6536-2/-1)>* **SOMETHING'S GOTTA GIVE**
– Something's gotta give / Believe / Gotta go / Before my eyes / No fear / Blinded / Voices / Do or die / My war / Bloodsucker / The blame / Today, tomorrow, forever / Rage / Pauly the dog / Crucified.

Dec 98. (7") *(0414-7)* **PURO DE MADRE. /** [-]

Sep 99. (cd/lp) *<(E 6567-2/-1)>* **RIOT, RIOT UPSTART**
– Police state / Had enough / Riot riot upstart / Sit and watch / Blood death and taxes / Frustration / Sickness / Shadows / Nowhere to go / Trust / My life / It's time / Rock star / Nothing's free / Price you pay / Jailbreal / Bullet on Mott street.

– compilations, etc. –

1989. (cd) *Combat; <3001>* **LIVE AT CBGB's (live)** [-]
(UK re-iss. Aug99 on 'Century Media' cd/lp; CM 66003-2/-1)

Jul 92. (cd/c/lp) *Rough Justice; (CD/T+/JUST 20M)* **TO BE CONTINUED . . . THE VERY BEST OF AGNOSTIC FRONT** [-]
– Victim in pain / Your mistake / Hypocrisy / New Jack / Liberty and justice / Time will come / Power / Society sucker / Toxic shock / Public assistance / Blind justice / The eliminator / One voice / Crucified / United and strong / Your mistake / Fascist attitudes (live) / Anthem (live) / Last warning (live).

Jul 95. (cd) *Grand Theft Auto; (GTA 002-R051)* **RAW UNRELEASED**
(re-iss. May99 w/free 7"; GTA 002CD)

Apr 00. (cd) *Grand Theft Auto; (GTA 003CD)* **RAW UNLEASHED**

AIRRACE (see under ⇒ BONHAM)

ALABAMA THUNDER PUSSY (see under ⇒ AVAIL)

ALASKA (see under ⇒ MARSDEN, Bernie)

ALCATRAZZ (see under ⇒ BONNET, Graham)

ALEXA

Born: ALEXA ANASTASIA, Switzerland, although she moved to Los Angeles, USA, where she was discovered by PAUL SABU (of ONLY CHILD), who soon produced her 1989 debut album for 'Savage' records. This was typical hook-line heavy-metal, with her glamourous looks rivalling LEE AARON or SARAYA. • **Songwriters:** Outside collaborators.

Album rating: ALEXA (*3)

ALEXA – vocals; with session people

Savage — Savage

Feb 89. (7") *(7VAG 903)* **WE DON'T REMEMBER WHY. / HEART TO HEART**
(3"cd-s+=/cd-s+=) *(3/CD VAG 903)* –

Feb 89. (lp/c/cd) *(CDVAG/CASVAG/LPVAG 911)* **ALEXA**
– I can't shake you / Dance the night away / A cry away / Heart to heart / From now on / We don't remember why / Wanderlust / Cool wind / Spookey.

— whatever happened to her?

ALICE COOPER (see under ⇒ COOPER, Alice)

ALICE DONUT

Formed: New York, USA . . . mid 80's by singer TOMAS ANTONA, MICHAEL JUNG, RICHARD MARSHALL, TED HOUGHTON, STEPHEN MOSES and DAVE GIFFIN. Described as nasty, horrible Americans, who like nothing better than to outrage people with their crazy lyrics and antics, ALICE DONUT found a natural home at JELLO BIAFRA's 'Alternative Tentacles' label. Fronted by a man who looks like GENESIS P. ORRIDGE (Psychic TV) leaving an Oxfam shop and characterised by a fondness for outlandishly juvenile song titles, ALICE DONUT accumulated a (very!) cult fanbase with releases such as 'DONUT COMES ALIVE' (1988) and 'BUCKETFULLS OF SICKNESS AND HORROR IN AN OTHERWISE MEANINGLESS LIFE' (1989). The lads began the 90's in much the same fashion, spinning their sub-JESUS LIZARD/DEAD KENNEDYS punk squall over a series of critically lambasted sets, their "unique" sense of humour one of their few saving graces. Having bulldozed through Black Sabbath's 'WAR PIGS' on the 'REVENGE FANTASIES OF THE IMPOTENT' album in '91, they virtually demolished The Beatles' 'HELTER SKELTER' on 1994's 'DRY HUMPING THE CASH COW'. The latter remains something of an oddity, featuring as it does a number of bonafide live tracks (at the CBGB's) alongside their best known songs dubbed over with a mock stadium crowd roar. A year later it seemed all over bar the shouting when they delivered their final set, 'PURE ACID PARK'. • **Covered:** SUNSHINE SUPERMAN (Donovan) / I WALKED WITH A ZOMBIE (Roky Erickson).

Album rating: DONUT COMES ALIVE (*4) / BUCKETFULLS OF SICKNESS AND HORROR IN AN OTHERWISE MEANINGLESS LIFE (*3) / MULE (*3) / REVENGE FANTASIES OF THE IMPOTENT (*2) / THE UNTIDY SUICIDES OF YOUR DEGENERATE CHILDREN (*2) / DRY HUMPING THE CASH COW part compilation (*5) / PURE ACID PARK (*4)

TOMAS ANTONA – vocals / **MICHAEL JUNG** – guitar, vocals / **RICHARD MARSHALL** – guitar, vocals / **TED HOUGHTON** – bass, vocals / **STEPHEN MOSES** – drums, trombone / **DAVE GIFFIN** – guitar

Alternative Tentacles — Alternative Tentacles

1988. (lp/cd) *<(VIRUS 61/+CD)>* **DONUT COMES ALIVE**
– Green pea soup / World profit / Mason Reece / Great great big big head / Diet cola syringe / New Jersey exit / American lips / Windshield of love / Mad dogs on a bone / Joan of arc / Bedpost / Sunshine superman / Love is a fickle thing / Tipper Gore / Death shield / I want your mother. *(cd re-iss. Apr00; same)*

Jul 89. (lp/cd) *<(VIRUS 73/+CD)>* **BUCKETFULLS OF SICKNESS AND HORROR IN AN OTHERWISE MEANINGLESS LIFE**
– Lydia's black lung / Testosterone gone wild / Sinead O'Connor on T.V. / Dorothy / Sky of bones / Egg / Consumer decency / My life is a mediocre piece of shit / Incinerator heart / Buckets, pock, fork / Demonologist / Lisa's father (waka baby) (live).

Aug 90. (7") *<(VIRUS 83)>* **MY BOYFRIEND'S BACK. / DEMONOLOGIST**

Sep 90. (lp/cd) *<(VIRUS 82/+CD)>* **MULE**
– Mother of Christ / Mrs. Hayes / Roaches in the sink / Crawlpappy / My severed heads / Bottom of the chain / Burlesque / Big ass / Roadkill / Tiny ugly world / J train downtown – A nest of murder / Cow's placenta to armageddon. *(cd+=)* – My boyfriend's back.

May 91. (lp/cd) *<(VIRUS 91/+CD)>* **REVENGE FANTASIES OF THE IMPOTENT**
– Rise to the skin / My best friend's wife / Telebloodprintmeadiadeathwhore / What / Dead river / Sleep / Naked, sharp and perfect / Come up with your hands out / War pigs / Good posture.

Oct 91. (12") *<(VIRUS 101)>* **BIGGEST ASS. / BIGGER ASS / BIG ASS (live)**
(cd-s+=) *<(VIRUS 101CD)>* – Mr Hayes' gimp leg.

— **SISSI SCHULMEISTER** – bass, vocals; repl. HOUGHTON + GIFFIN

Jul 92. (7") *<(VIRUS 114)>* **MAGDALENE. / ONLY THE GOOD DIE YOUNG**
(cd-s+=) *<(VIRUS 114CD)>* –

Sep 92. (lp/cd) *<(VIRUS 115/+CD)>* **THE UNTIDY SUICIDES OF YOUR DEGENERATE CHILDREN**
– Magdalene / Untidy suicides / Loteria / The tingler / Every body is on sale / Hang the dog / Son of a disgruntled x-postal worker . . . / Annie's empty / Loteria / Medication / Things have never looked better / Wire mother / She loves you she wants you it's amazing / Loteria / In my head.

Mar 93. (7") *<(VIRUS 121)>* **MEDICATION. / LADY DI**
(cd-s+=) *<(VIRUS 121CD)>* – The yellow bridge.

Apr 94. (lp/cd) *<(VIRUS 143/+CD)>* **DRY-HUMPING THE CASH COW** (some live at CBGB's 1993)
– Green meat stew / Hose / The tingler / Dorothy / Every body is on sale / My best friend's wife / Mrs. Hayes / The son of a disgruntled x-postal worker reflects on his life while getting stoned in the parking lot of a Winn Dixie listening to Metallica / Dead river / Mother of Christ / Helter skelter / American lips / Egg / Demonologist / Buckets, pock, fork. *(cd re-iss. Nov97; same)*

— In Oct'94, they teamed up with ICE PRINCESS for a single on 'Cargo'; *BEAT 013)*

Nov 94. (7") *<(VIRUS 154)>* **NADINE. / CHICKEN DOOR** [ ] [ ]
(cd-s+=) *<(VIRUS 154CD)>* – Empty streets.

Jul 95. (lp/cd) *<(VIRUS 163/+CD)>* **PURE ACID PARK** [ ] [ ]
– Millennium / Dreaming in Cuban / Freaks in love / Big cars and blow jobs / I walked with a zombie / The senator and the cabin boy / Mummenschantz Pachinko / Insane / Shining path / The unspeakable pleasure of being me / Lost in place / Cain. *(cd re-iss. Nov97; same)*

— ALICE DONUT have since split up

ALICE IN CHAINS

Formed: Seattle, Washington, USA . . . 1987 as glamsters DIAMOND LIE, then FUCK by main songwriters, LAYNE STALEY and JERRY CANTRELL, who soon opted for the more palatable moniker of ALICE N' CHAINS. They altered this name slightly after enlisting SEAN KINNEY and MIKE STARR, subsequently signing to 'Columbia' in 1989 and debuting the following year with promo EP, 'WE DIE YOUNG'. Their debut album, 'FACELIFT' was released to widespread favourable reviews, although it took some time to scale the Billboard Top 100. Later in '91, they finally cracked the Top 50, their cause furthered by the success of new groundbreaking grunge acts like NIRVANA and SOUNDGARDEN giving metal/hard rock a breath of fresh air. A Grammy nomination under their belt (for the track 'MAN IN THE BOX'), the group enjoyed a flurry of activity in '92 with both the release of the easier going 'SAP' EP and a Top 10 follow-up album, 'DIRT', the latter also breaking the band in Britain. In 1993, they lifted no less than four major hits ('WOULD?', 'THEM BONES', 'ANGRY CHAIR' and 'DOWN IN A HOLE') from this critically acclaimed opus. With acoustic sets all the rage, ALICE IN CHAINS then delivered a stripped-down EP, 'JAR OF FLIES', the set being the first mini-cd to top the US charts. When STALEY subsequently formed grunge 'supergroup', The GACY BUNCH (later changing the name to MAD SEASON) alongside PEARL JAM's MIKE McCREADY and BARRETT MARTIN of The SCREAMING TREES, speculation was rife about an ALICE IN CHAINS split. After a one-off album, 'ABOVE' (1995), however, STALEY, CANTRELL & Co. stormed back with the eponymous 'ALICE IN CHAINS' (1995), the record giving the group their second US No.1. The obligatory 'MTV UNPLUGGED' set followed in 1996, ALICE IN CHAINS being only one of a handful of similar acts to be bestowed with such an 'honour'. With AIC out of action for a few years, JERRY CANTRELL decided it was time for a solo piece. 'BOGGY DEPOT' (1998) – which included a track from the earlier made Jim Carrey film, 'The Cable Guy' – hit the US Top 30 for a week and failed miserably to gain much interest in Britain bar Kerrang(!), of course. • **Songwriters:** CANTRELL solo covered, 'I'VE SEEN ALL THIS WORLD I CARE TO SEE' (Willie Nelson; on a tribute album).

Album rating: FACELIFT (*6) / SAP (*5) / DIRT (*8) / JAR OF FLIES (*7) / ALICE IN CHAINS (*5) / MTV UNPLUGGED (*4) / NOTHING SAFE compilation (*6) / Mad Season: ABOVE (*5) / Jerry Cantrell: BOGGY DEPOT (*5)

LAYNE STALEY (b.22 Aug'67, Bellevue, Wash.) – vocals / **JERRY CANTRELL** (b.18 Mar'66, Tacoma, Wash.) – guitar, vocals / **MICHAEL STARR** (b. 4 Apr'66, Honolulu, Hawaii) – bass (ex-SADO) / **SEAN KINNEY** (b.27 May'66, Seattle) – drums, percussion, megaphone

Columbia Columbia

Jun 90. (cd-s) **EP** [-] [ ]
– We die young / etc.

Sep 91. (cd/c/lp) *(467201-2/-4/-1) <46075>* **FACELIFT** [ ] [42] Mar91
– We die young / Man in the box / Sea of sorrow / Bleed the freak / I can't remember / Love, hate, love / It ain't like that / Sunshine / Put you down / Confusion / I know somethin' ('bout you) / Real thing.

Oct 91. (cd-ep) *<73851>* **MAN IN THE BOX / SEA OF SORROW / BLEED THE FREAK / SUNSHINE** [-] [ ]

Feb 92. (c-ep)(cd-ep) *<74182><74305>* **SAP** [-] [ ]
– Brother / Got me wrong / Right turn / Am I inside / Love song.

— **MIKE INEZ** (b.14 May'66, San Fernando, California) – bass; repl. MIKE STARR. He formed MY SISTER'S MACHINE, who released album in May'92 'DIVA' on 'Caroline'.

Oct 92. (cd/c/lp) *(472330-2/-4/-1) <52475>* **DIRT** [42] [6]
– Them bones / Dam that river / Rain when I die / Down in a hole / Sickman / Rooster / Junkhead / Dirt / God smack / Hate to feel / Angry chair / Would?

Jan 93. (7") *(658888-7)* **WOULD?. / MAN IN THE BOX** [19] [ ]
(12"green+=/pic-cd-s+=) *(658888-6/-2)* – Brother / Right Turn.

Mar 93. (7") *(659090-7)* **THEM BONES. / WE DIE YOUNG** [26] [ ]
(cd-s+=) *(659090-2)* – Got me wrong / Am I inside.

May 93. (7") *(659365-7)* **ANGRY CHAIR. / I KNOW SOMETHIN' ('BOUT YOU)** [33] [ ]
(12"+=) *(659365-6)* – Bleed the freak / It ain't like that.
(cd-s+=) *(659365-2)* – It ain't like that / Hate to feel.

Oct 93. (7"pic-d) *(659751-7)* **DOWN IN A HOLE. / ROOSTER** [36] [ ]
(12"+=) *(659751-6)* – A little bitter / Love, hate, love.
(cd-s+=) *(659751-2)* – What the hell I have I / ('A'radio edit).

Dec 93. (cd-s; w-drawn) *(660047-2)* **ROTTEN APPLE /** [-] [-]

Jan 94. (cd/c/lp) *(475713-2/-4/-1) <57628>* **JAR OF FLIES / SAP** [4] [1]
– Rotten apple / Nutshell / I stay away / No excuses / Whale & wasp / Don't follow / Swing on this. (US-version w /out 'SAP')

Oct 95. (7"/c-s) *(662623-7/-4)* **GRIND. / NUTSHELL** [23] [ ]
(cd-s+=) *(662823-2)* – So close / Love, hate, love.

Nov 95. (cd/c/d-lp) *(481114-2/-4/-1) <67248>* **ALICE IN CHAINS** [37] [1]
– Grind / Brush away / Sludge factory / Heaven beside you / Head creeps / Again / Shame in you / God am / So close / Nothin' song / Frogs / Over now.

Jan 96. (7"white) *(662893-7)* **HEAVEN BESIDE YOU. / WOULD? (live)** [35] [ ]
(cd-s+=) *(662893-2)* – Rooster (live) / Junkhead (live).
(cd-s) *(662893-5)* – ('A'side) / Angry chair (live) / Man in a box (live) / Love, hate, love (live).

— added for below only; **SCOTT OLSEN** – guitar

Jul 96. (cd/c/d-lp) *(484300-2/-4/-1) <67703>* **MTV UNPLUGGED (live)** [20] [3]
– Nutshell / Brother / No excuses / Sludge factory / Down in a hole / Angry chair / Rooster / Got me wrong / Heaven beside you / Would? / Frogs / Over now / Killer is me.

Jul 99. (cd/c) *(494005-2/-4) <63649>* **NOTHING SAFE** (compilation) [ ] [20]
– Get born again / We die young / Man in the box / Them bones / Iron gland / Angry chair / Down in a hole / Rooster / Got me wrong / No excuses / I stay away / What the hell have I / Grind / Again / Would?

– compilations, etc. –

Oct 99. (4xcd-box) *Columbia; (CKX 69580)* **MUSIC BANK** [ ] [ ]

Dec 00. (cd) *Columbia; <85274>* **LIVE (live)** [-] [ ]

MAD SEASON

— were originally called GACY BUNCH with **LAYNE STALEY** – vocals / **MIKE McCREADY** – guitar (of PEARL JAM) / **BARRETT MARTIN** – drums (of SCREAMING TREES)

Mar 95. (cd/c/lp) *(478507-2/-4/-1) <67057>* **ABOVE** [41] [24]
– Wake up / X-ray mind / I'm above / River of deceit / Lifeless dead / Artificial red / Long gone day / I don't know anything / November hotel / All alone.

JERRY CANTRELL

with **SEAN KINNEY + MIKE INEZ** / plus bassists **REX BROWN** (PANTERA), **NORWOOD FISHER** (FISHBONE) + **LES CLAYPOOL** (PRIMUS) / guest **ANGELO MOORE** (FISHBONE) – sax

Apr 98. (cd/c/lp) *(488705-2/-4/-1) <68147>* **BOGGY DEPOT** [ ] [28]
– Dickeye / Cut you in / My song / Settling down / Breaks my back / Jesus hands / Devil by his side / Keep the light on / Satisfy / Hurt a long time / Between / Cold piece.

May 98. (cd-s) *<4704>* **CUT YOU IN** [-] [ ]

ALIEN

Formed: New York, USA . . . 1982 by FRANK STARR, RIK KRISTI, DAMIEN 'The Beast' BARDOT, ROXANN HARLOW and BRIAN FAIR. A mini-lp, 'COSMIC FANTASY' fell to earth in '83 but due to internal bickering, the band failed to realise a follow-up. BARDOT was subsequently charged with first-degree murder for his part in an ill-fated burglary. • **Note:** Not to be confused with the Swedish melodic pop band of the same name.

Album rating: COSMIC FANTASY (*5)

FRANK STARR – vocals / **RIKK KRISTI** – guitar / **BRIAN FAIR** – guitars / **DAMIEN 'The Beast' BARDOT** – bass / **ROXANN HARLOW** – drums

Ultra Noise Mongol Horde

1984. (m-lp) *(NOISE 103) <MONGOL 2>* **COSMIC FANTASY** [ ] [ ] 1983
– Space prelude / Cosmic fantasy / Star lover / Headbangin' / Don't say goodbye / Cosmic fantasy.

— split after arguments arose. KRISTI and STARR joined RIK FOX (ex-STEELER) in a new L.A. band.

ALIEN

Formed: Goteberg, Sweden . . . 1987 by TONY BORG and other melodic rock sidemen, JIM JIDHED, ULF "KEN" SANDIN, TOBY TARRACH and JIMMY WANDROPH. They were initially a big attraction in Scandinavia, following their near No.1 cover of 'ONLY ONE WOMAN' (a late 60's chart hit for GRAHAM BONNET's The MARBLES). Early in 1989, after the release of the eponymous debut album, GILHEAD was replaced by PETE SANDBERG, resulting in a new direction for the follow-up, 'SHIFTIN' GEAR'.

Album rating: ALIEN (*5) / SHIFTIN' GEAR (*5) / CRASH (*4)

JIM JIDHED – vocals / **TONY BORG** – guitar (ex-DOLCEVITA) / **JIMMY WANDROPH** – keyboards / **ULF "KEN" SANDIN** – bass / **TOBY TARRACH** – drums

Virgin Virgin

1987. (7") *(108 970)* **HEADSTRONG. / HEADSTRONG (re-mix)** [-] [-] Sweden

1987. (7") *(108 971)* **I'LL SURVIVE. / I'LL SURVIVE (re-mix)** [-] [-] Sweden

1988. (7") *(109 670)* **ONLY ONE WOMAN. / SOMEWHERE OUT THERE** [-] [-] Sweden

1988. (lp/cd) *(209/259 198)* **ALIEN** [-] [-] Sweden
– Brave new love / Tears don't put out the fire / Go easy / I've been waiting / Jaime remember / Feel my love / Only one woman / Wings of fire / Dying by the golden rule / Touch my fire / Dreamer / Mirror.

1988. (7") *(111 564) <991173>* **TEARS DON'T PUT OUT THE FIRE. / DREAMER** [-] [ ]

— **PETER SANDBERG** – vocals (ex-MADISON) repl. JIDHED

1989. (7") *(112 005)* **THE AIR THAT I BREATHE. / NOW LOVE** [-] [-] Sweden

1989. (lp) *<209 775>* **ALIEN** (US remix) [-] [ ]
– Tears don't put out the fire / Go easy / I've been waiting / Jaime remember / Feel my love / Only one woman / Brave new world / The air that I breathe / Touch my love / Now love.

1989. (7") *(111 819)* **GO EASY (US remix). / TOUCH MY FIRE** [-] [-] Sweden
(12"+=)(cd-s+=) *(611 819)(111 819-2)* – Tears don't put out the fire (US remix).

— also **BERT ANDERSSON** – keyboards; repl. WANDROPH

— **IMRE DAUN** – drums (ex-DON PATROL, ex-SNOWSTORM) repl. TARRACH

1989. (7") *(112 370)* **EASY LIVIN'. / HOW LONG** - - Sweden

1990. (7") *(113 041)* **ANGEL EYES. / EAGLE** - - Sweden
(12"+=)(cd-s+=) *(613 041)(113 041-2)* – ('A'extended).

1990. (cd) *(259 775)* **SHIFTIN' GEAR** - - Sweden
– Hold on move on / Give it up / Desperate dreams / Angel eyes / In the dead of night / Intro "midnight jam" / Turn on the radio / Strangers in a no-mans land / Don't turn me away / Neon lights / Hello how are you.

— **BORG** the sole original; re-grouped the band

— **STEFAN RIDDERSTRALE** – drums; repl. DAUN

— **RICHARD ANDRE** – keyboards; repl. ANDERSSON

— **CONNY SUNDQUIST** – bass (ex-MADISON) repl. SANDIN

— **TOMAS PERSSON** – vocals; repl. PETE

— **DANIEL ZANGGER BORCH** – vocals; repl. TOMAS

Eagle not iss.

1993. (cd-s) *(ECDS-10 63)* **NUMBER ONE** - - Sweden

1993. (cd) *(ECD 043)* **ALIEN** - - Sweden

— **STEFFAN SCHARIN** – drums; repl. RIDDERSTRALE

Megarock not iss.

1995. (cd) *(MRRCD 031)* **CRASH** - - Sweden
– We can fly / Crash / Searchin' / Smooth operator / Looking for love / Got this great thing coming / Computerized efficience / Hold on / Winning touch / Where there's a will.

— split soon after above

ALIEN ANT FARM

Formed: Riverside, California . . . 1996 by DRYDEN MITCHELL, TERRY CORSA, TYE ZAMORA and MIKE COSGROVE. After their debut album, 'GREATEST HITS' (1999) scooped Best Independent Album at the 1999 L.A. Music Awards, the PRIMUS/ALICE IN CHAINS/METALLICA-influenced quartet became the first act signed to PAPA ROACH's 'New Noise' label. The two bands had been friends since their mid-90's beginnings on the Californian club circuit although AAF plough a slightly less intense furrow than their more famous brethren. The 'ANThology' (2001) album brought general critical acclaim with many fans warming to an inventive if unlikely cover of Michael Jackson's 'SMOOTH CRIMINAL'.

Album rating: GREATEST HITS (*5) / ANThology (*6)

DRYDEN MITCHELL (b.15 Jun'76) – vocals / **TERENCE CORSO** (b.28 Nov'71) – guitar / **TYE ZAMORA** (b.30 May'77) – bass, vocals / **MIKE COSGROVE** (b. 7 Nov'75) – drums

not iss. own label

Nov 99. (cd) **GREATEST HITS** -
– These days / Pink tea / Movies / Dole roll / Denigrate / Solution time / S.S. recognize / Nova hands / Universe / Sick thief.

Dreamworks Dreamworks

Mar 01. (cd) *<(450293-2)>* **ANThology**
– Courage / Movies / Flesh and bone / Whisper / Summer / Sticks and stones / Attitude / Stranded / Wish / Calico / Happy death day / Smooth criminal / Universe.

Jun 01. (c-s) *(450899-4)* **MOVIES / PINK TEE** 53 -
(cd-s+=) *(450899-2)* – ('A'-acoustic live on KROQ) / ('A'-video).

ALIEN SEX FIEND

Formed: London, England . . . 1982 by NIK WADE, a former DEMON PREACHERS member who enlisted the help of his wife, CHRISTINE (aka MRS. FIEND). The aforementioned band released a couple of 45's towards the end of the decade, recording for such established indie imprints as 'Illegal' and 'Small Wonder'. Adding DAVID JAMES (aka YAXI HIGHRIZER) and JOHNNY 'HA HA' FRESHWATER, the couple adopted the ALIEN SEX FIEND moniker and secured a residency at the infamous 'Batcave' club. Complete with thick ghoulish make-up, NIK led his band of ALICE COOPER devotees through a regular performance of cabaret goth, recording a live demo cassette 'THE LEWD, THE MAD, THE UGLY & OLD NIK' at their famous haunt. Carving out a deal with Cherry Red subsidiary, 'Anagram', the 'FIENDS released two singles, 'IGNORE THE MACHINE' and 'LIPS CAN'T GO', both highlights of their late 1983 debut set, 'WHO'S BEEN SLEEPING IN MY BRAIN?'. An almost permanent fixture in the indie charts from then on ('ACID BATH' – 1984, etc), the band also became massive in Japan, their third set, 'LIQUID HEAD IN TOKYO – LIVE' (1985) documenting this surprise phenomenon. Subsequently continuing as a trio without JOHNNY, they were finally offered the honour of supporting their schlock-rocker idol, ALICE COOPER, on his 1986 "Nightmare Returns" tour. Having contributed to three further mid-80's sets (' . . . MAXIMUM SECURITY', 'IT – THE ALBUM' and 'HERE CUM GERMS'), YAXI was the next to depart, leaving the husband and wife team to record a one-off single, 'WHERE ARE BATMAN AND ROBIN', as The DYNAMIC DUO. ALIEN SEX FIEND returned to terrorize self-respecting indie fans with the likes of 'ANOTHER PLANET' (1988), 'TOO MUCH ACID?' (1989), although their shift to more electronically based territory ALIENated some of their more traditional fans. Later in the 90's, after a couple of patchy sets, including the 'INFERNO' CD-ROM game/album, they initiated their own '13th Moon Records' label. • **Songwriters:** NIK penned most except; SCHOOL'S OUT (Alice Cooper) / I WALK THE LINE (Johnny Cash) / HURRICANE FIGHTER PLANE (Red Crayola) / SILVER MACHINE (Hawkwind).

Album rating: WHO'S BEEN SLEEPING IN MY BRAIN (*4) / ACID BATH (*5) / LIQUID HEAD IN TOKYO – LIVE mini (*5) / (I'M DOIN' TIME IN A) MAXIMUM SECURITY TWILIGHT HOME (*6) / IT – THE ALBUM (*6) / HERE CUM GERMS (*4) / ANOTHER PLANET (*6) / TOO MUCH ACID? (*4) / CURSE (*4) / OPEN HEAD SURGERY (*6) / THE ALTERED STATES OF AMERICA (*5) / INFERNO (*6) / THE SINGLES 1983-1995 compilation (*6) / NOCTURNAL EMISSIONS (*5)

DEMON PREACHERS

NIK FIEND (b. Wales) – vocals, bass (ex-EARWIGS, ex-MR. & MRS. DEMEANOUR) / (+ 3 others)

Illegal not iss.

1978. (7"m) *(SRTS-CUS 78110)* **ROYAL NORTHERN (N7) / LAUGHING AT ME. / STEAL YOUR LOVE / DEAD END KIDZ** -

Small Wonder not iss.

Aug 78. (7") *(SMALL TEN)* **LITTLE MISS PERFECT. / PERFECT DUB** -

Crypt Music not iss.

1980. (7"; as The DEMONS) *(DEM 1)* **ACTION BY EXAMPLE./ I WISH I WAS A DOG** -

ALIEN SEX FIEND

NIK WADE – vocals, bass / **CHRISTINE WADE** – synthesizers / **DAVID JAMES** (aka YAXI HIGHRIZER) – guitar / **JOHNNY 'HA HA' FRESHWATER** – drums

Anagram not iss.

Aug 83. (7") *(ANA 11)* **IGNORE THE MACHINE. / THE GIRL AT THE END OF MY GUN** -
(12"+=) *(12ANA 11)* – I'm not mad.
(12"+=) *(12ANA 11X)* – Under the thunder.
(re-iss. Mar85 7"pic-d; (PANA 11) – ('A'mix) / ('A'dub version). *(pic-cd-s iss.Sep88; CDANA 11)*

Oct 83. (7") *(ANA 15)* **LIPS CAN'T GO. / DRIVE MY ROCKET (UP URANUS)** -
(12"+=) *(12ANA 15)* – Toytown mix / 30 second coma.

Nov 83. (lp) *(GRAM 10)* **WHO'S BEEN SLEEPING IN MY BRAIN?** -
– I wish I woz a dog / Wild women / I'm not mad / New Christian music / Wigwam wipeout / I'm her Frankenstein / I am a product / Ignore the machine / R.I.P. / Lips can't go / Black rabbit. *(cd-iss. Sep98; CDGRAM 10)*

Feb 84. (7"/7"red) *(ANA 18)* **R.I.P. / NEW CHRISTIAN MUSIC** -
(10"+=/12"+=) *(10/12 ANA 18)* – Crazee.

Aug 84. (7"pic-d/7",7"red) *(P+/ANA 23)* **DEAD AND BURIED. / ATTACK** -
(12"+=) *(12ANA 23)* – Ignore the machine.

Oct 84. (lp/c) *(GRAM/CGRAM 18)* **ACID BATH** -
– In God we trust / Dead and re-buried / Smoke my bones / She's a killer / E.S.T. (trip to the Moon) / Breakdown and cry (lay down and say goodbye) / Hee-haw (here come the bone people) / Attack / Boneshaker baby. *(c+=)* – WHO'S BEEN SLEEPING IN MY BRAIN? *(cd-iss. Jun88 & May93 & Jun97 +=; CDMGRAM 18)* – I am a product (live) / 30 second coma. *<US-iss.1999; ASFLPC 2>*

Oct 84. (7") *(ANA 25)* **E.S.T. (TRIP TO THE MOON). / BONESHAKER BABY** -
(11"+=) *(11ANA 25)* – I am a product (live).

Jul 85. (m-lp) *(MGRAM 22)* **LIQUID HEAD IN TOKYO (live)** -
– R.I.P. / E.S.T. / Dead and buried / In God we trust / Back to the egg / Attack / Lips can't go / Wild woman. *(cd-iss. Jan97 on 'Summit'; SUMCD 4087)*

— trimmed to a trio, when JOHNNY departed HA HA (it's not funny – Ed.)

Aug 85. (12"m) *(12ANA 30)* **I'M DOIN' TIME IN A MAXIMUM SECURITY TWILIGHT HOME. / IN AND OUT OF MY MIND / BACKWARD BEAVER** -

Sep 85. (lp) *(GRAM 24)* **(I'M DOIN' TIME IN A) MAXIMUM SECURITY TWILIGHT HOME** -
– I'm doin' time in a maximum security twilight home / Spies / Depravity lane / Seconds to nowhere / The beaver destroys forest / Mine's full of maggots / In and out of my mind / Fly in the ointment / Do you sleep (not of one mind). *(re-iss. Jun88 on 'Antler'; ANT037) (cd-iss. Nov88 & Apr94 as 'THE FIRST ALIEN SEX FIEND CD' =; CDGRAM 25)* – E.S.T. (trip to the Moon) / Boneshaker baby / Ignore the machine / Attack!!!.

Flicknife not iss.

May 86. (7") *(SFLEP 106)* **I WALK THE LINE. / SCHOOL'S OUT** -
(d7"+=/12"+=) *(DL/FL EP 106)* – Here she comes/ Can't stop smoking. *(d7"re-iss. Feb95; SFLEP 106)*

Vat not iss.

Aug 86. (7") **GET INTO IT. / SOMEONE KEEPS ON BUGGIN' ME** -

Anagram not iss.

Oct 86. (7"/12") *(ANA/12ANA 32)* **SMELLS LIKE SHIT. / SOMEOME KEEPS ON BUGGIN' ME** -

Oct 86. (lp/c) *(GRAM/CGRAM 26)* **IT – THE ALBUM** -
– Smells like shit / Manic depression / Believe it or not / Get into it / Wop bop / April showers / Lesson one / Do it right / To be continued . . . *(re-iss. Jun88 on 'Antler' lp/c+=; ANT 048/+C)* – TWILIGHT HOME (lp tracks) *(cd-iss. Dec91 +=; CDGRAM 26)* – Buggin' me / Hurricane fighter pilot / It lives again.

Feb 87. (7") *(ANA 33)* **HURRICANE FIGHTER PLANE. / IT LIVES AGAIN** -
(12"+=) *(12ANA 33)* – ('A'mix).

Jun 87. (7") *(ANA 34)* **THE IMPOSSIBLE MISSION. / MY BRAIN IS IN THE CUPBOARD ABOVE THE KITCHEN SINK** -
(12"+=) *(12ANA 34)* – Put A-Z.

Aug 87. (7") *(ANA 38)* **HERE CUM GERMS. / ('A'-Ravi mix) / ('A'dub)** -
(12"+=) *(12ANA 38)* – Camel camel.

Oct 87. (lp/c) *(GRAM/CGRAM 31)* **HERE CUM GERMS** -
– The mission impossible / Here cum germs (Ravi mix) / Isolation / My brain is in the cupboard above the kitchen / You are soul / Death / Boots on!. *(cd-iss. Jun92 +=; CDGRAM 31)* – Camel, camel / Stuff the turkey / They all call me crazee.

Nov 87. (7",7"red,7"green) *(ANA 40)* **STUFF THE TURKEY. / THEY ALL CALL ME CRAZEE** -

— now as duo when YAXI left

Oct 88. (12"m) *(12ANA 45)* **BUN HO!. / SILVER MACHINE / SATISFACTION**

Oct 88. (cd/c/lp) *(CD/C+/GRAM 38)* **ANOTHER PLANET**
– Bun ho! / Everybody's dream / Radiant city / Spot your lucky warts / Sample my sausage / Outer limits / Instant karma sutra / So much to do – So little time / Alien / Wild green fiendly liquid / Nightmare zone / Bun ho (time after time) / Another planet. *(c+=)* – Silver machine / Satisfaction. *(cd re-iss. Jun97; same)*

Mar 89. (7") *(ANA 46)* **HAUNTED HOUSE. / ('A'dub version)**
(12"+=/cd-s+=) *(12/CD ANA 46)* –

Sep 89. (cd/c/d-lp) *(CD/C+/GRAM 41)* **TOO MUCH ACID? (live)**
– It lives again / I walk the line / Nightmare zone / Get into it / E.S.T. (trip to the Moon) / So much to do, so little time / Bun ho! / Haunted house / Smells like shit / Hurricane fighter plane / Sample my sausage / Boneshaker baby. *(cd re-iss. May93; same)*

Sep 90. (7") **NOW I'M FEELING ZOMBIEFIED. /**
(12"+=/cd-s+=) –

Oct 90. (cd/c/lp) *(CD/C+/GRAM 46)* **CURSE**
– Katch 22 / You – Along cums reality – Hubble bubble / Goodbye to space / Now I'm feeling zombiefied / Stress / Blessings of the state / Eat! eat! eat! (an eye for an eye) / Ain't got time to bleed / Bleeding (reprise) / Dalisms / Burger bar baby / I think I . . . Mad daddy drives a UFO / Wuthering wind / Radio Jimi / Hands of the silken / Blessing in disguise.

Mar 92. (cd/c/lp) *(CD/C+/GRAM 51)* **OPEN HEAD SURGERY**
– Clockwork banana banana – moon / Magic / Class of '69 / Aliensexfiend / Coma / Lickin' ma bone / Stressed out / B-B-Bone boogie.

Feb 93. (cd/c/lp) *(CD/C+/GRAM 60)* **THE ALTERED STATES OF AMERICA**
– Wild women / Now I'm feeling zombiefied / Class of '69 / Ignore the machine / Magic / Coma / Eat! eat! eat! / R.I.P. (blue crumb truck).

Jul 94. (12") *(MFF 007T)* **INFERNO. /**
(above issued on 'Cherry Red')

Oct 94. (cd) *(CDGRAM 80)* <9529> **INFERNO**
– Inferno / Human installation / Take off tune / Space 1 / Happy tune / Planet 1 / Human atmosphere / Happy finale / Alien installation / Aromatic tune / Moon toon / Planet 2 / Bad news / Space 2 / Alien atmosphere / Death tune / Sad finale / Moon ton (lunaphases mix) / Planet 2 (together dreamscape mix) / Inferno.

Mar 95. (cd-ep) *(CDGRAM 56)* **INFERNO / INFERNO (Mix) / PLANET 2 / ECHOES**

13th Moon 13th Moon

Feb 96. (12"/cd-s) *(FULL T/CDS 001)* **EVOLUTION. / ('A'mixes)**

Mar 97. (cd/d-lp) *(FULL CD/DLP 1301)* **NOCTURNAL EMISSIONS** Nov98
– Evolution / On a mission / Warp out / Big blue moon / Room 101 / Soaking wet, mate / Garbage / Tarot / Sticky. *(re-iss. Jul00; FULLCD 1302)* *<US-iss.2001 on 'Resurgence'; 4642>*

Aug 97. (12") *(FULLT 002R)* **ON A MISSION (remix). /** Oct98

Nov 98. (12") *(FULLT 003R)* **TAROT (7 mix). / ('A'-No.6 mix) / ('A'-POD dub mix)**

– compilations, etc. –

Mar 88. (cd/c/lp) *Anagram; (CD/C+GRAM 34)* **ALL OUR YESTERDAZE (The Singles Collection 1983-87)**
– Ignore the machine / Lips can't go / R.I.P. – Blue crumb truck / Dead & buried / E.S.T. – Trip to the Moon / I'm doing time in a maximum security twilight home / I walk the line / Smells like shit / Hurricane fighter pilot. *(<cd re-iss. May93 & Dec99; same>)*

Mar 88. (12"; as DYNAMIC DUO) *Anagram; (12ANA 42)* **WHERE ARE BATMAN AND ROBIN? / BATMAN THEME**

Oct 93. (cd/c) *Anagram; (CD/C GRAM 69)* **THE LEGENDARY BATCAVE TAPES (live)**
(<re-iss. Jun98 as 'BAT CAVE MASTERS' on 'Cleopatra'; CLP 232)>

Aug 94. (cd) *Cleopatra; (<CLEO 9412-2>)* **DRIVE MY ROCKET**

Jun 95. (cd) *Cleopatra; (<CLEO 9508CD>)* **I'M HER FRANKENSTEIN**

Oct 95. (d-cd) *Anagram; (<CDGRAM 99>)* **THE SINGLES 1983-1995** Feb96

Feb 98. (d-cd) *Snapper; (SMDCD 133)* **WARDANCE OF THE ALIEN SEX FIEND**

May 99. (d-cd) *Anagram; (CDGRAM 120) / Cleopatra; <694>* **FIENDS AT THE CONTROLS VOL.1 & 2** Oct98

ALKALINE TRIO

Formed: Chicago, Illinois, USA . . . 1997 by MATT SKIBA, GLENN PORTER and ROB DORAN. Inspired by 70's punk/pop and drinking, the 'TRIO were all the rage in the late 90's. From 1998's 'GODDAMMIT' to the recent 'FROM HERE TO INFIRMARY' (2001), these square-chinned lads from the Windy City finally came of age by supporting BLINK-182 around the US. However, by the dawn of 2000, they had lost PORTER who was was superseded by MIKE FELUMLEE; DAN ANDRIANO had taken DORAN's place a few years earlier (see discography).

Album rating: GODAMMIT (*8) / MAYBE I'LL CATCH FIRE (*6) / ALKALINE TRIO collection (*7) / FROM HERE TO INFIRMARY (*8)

MATT SKIBA – vocals, guitar (ex-JERKWATER drummer) / **GLENN PORTER** – drums, vocals (ex-88 FINGER LOUIE) / **ROB DORAN** – bass, vocals

Asian Man Asian Man

Jun 98. (m-cd) *<(AM 028CD)>* **FOR YOUR LUNGS ONLY** May98
– Snake oil tanker / Southern rock / Cooking wire / For your lungs only.

— **DAN ANDRIANO** – bass (of SLAPSTICK) repl. DORAN

Oct 98. (lp/cd) *<(AM 034/+CD)>* **GODDAMMIT**
– Cringe / Cop / San Francisco / Nose over tail / As you were / Enjoy your day / Clavicle / My little needle / Southern rock / Message from Kathleen / Trouble breathing / Sorry about that.

Feb 00. (lp/cd) *<(AM 055/+CD)>* **MAYBE I'LL CATCH FIRE**
– Keep 'em coming Madam me / You've got so far to go / Fuck you Aurora / Sleepyhead / Maybe I'll catch fire / Tuck me in / She took him to the lake / 5-3-10-4 / Radio.

Apr 00. (lp/cd) *<(AM 058/+CD)>* **ALKALINE TRIO** (collection)
– Goodbye forever / This is getting over you / Bleeder / I lied my face off / My friend Peter / Snake oil tanker / Southern rock / Cooking wine / For your lungs only / Exploding boy / Sun dials / Nose over tail / '97.

— **MIKE FELUMLEE** – drums (ex-SMOKING POPES) repl. PORTER

Lookout Lookout

Apr 01. (7") *<(LK 264)>* **HELL YES. /**

Vagrant Vagrant

Apr 01. (lp/cd) *<(VR 353/+CD)>* **FROM HERE TO INFIRMARY**
– Private eye / Mr chainsaw / Take lots with alcohol / Stupid kid / Another innocent girl / Steamer trunk / You're dead / Armageddon / I'm dying tomorrow / Bloodied up / Trucks and trains / Crawl.

ALKATRAZZ

Formed: Maidstone, Kent, England . . . 1980 by Australian raised CRAIG STEVENS and friend, BOB JENNER. Soon adding the rhythm section of GARY BEVAN and NICK PARSONS, they were snapped up by 'RCA' amid the major label rush to sign NWOBHM bands. Over the course of the next two years, they released two albums, 'YOUNG BLOOD' and 'RADIO 5', their derivative hard-rock sound compared to UFO or melodic US acts.

Album rating: YOUNG BLOOD (*5)

CRAIG STEVENS – vocals / **BOB JENNER** – guitar / **GARY BEVAN** – bass / **NICK PARSONS** – drums

R.C.A. not iss.

Jan 81. (7") *(RCA 29)* **ROCKIN' HIGH. / RUN WILD**

May 81. (7") *(RCA 81)* **YOU AND THE NIGHT. / RUN WILD**

May 81. (lp/c) *(RCA LP/K 5023)* **YOUNG BLOOD**
– Rockin' high / Young blood / Maybe tomorrow / The late news / Deadline / Crazy dancer / Give it all away / Live fast, die hard / You and the night / Run wild.

Feb 82. (7") *(RCA 183)* **THINK IT OVER. / HALF WAY THERE**

May 82. (lp/c) *(RCA LP/K 5066)* **RADIO 5**
– Blinded / Blame it on the night / Long time no love / Half way there / Short change / Think it over / Communication / Save my heart / So hard / Miles away.

— disbanded around 1983

ALL (see under ⇒ DESCENDENTS)

GG ALLIN

Born: KEVIN ALLIN, 29 Aug'56, New Hampshire, USA. The high priest of animalistic, degenerate punk rock, the man used to relieve himself on stage, yes one's AND two's folks (a bit of an asshole, you could say!). Influenced by, and going one (hundred times!) uglier than IGGY POP and MC5, ALLIN went beyond conventional rock'n'roll outrage by indulging in increasingly more explicit acts of on-stage sex, violence, self-mutilation, drug-taking, defecation, masturbation, verbal-abuse and general depravity as his career dragged on. Public enemy No.1, the crazed ALLIN was continually in trouble with the law, the performance (and actual enactment!) of songs such as 'YOU SCUM, EAT MY DIARRHOEA' not exactly the behaviour of an upstanding US citizen. Alternately backed by The JABBERS and The SCUMFUCS, ALLIN recorded a series of sporadic lp's for a number of independent labels, among them 'ALWAYS WAS, IS, AND ALWAYS SHALL BE' (1980), 'EAT MY FUC' (1984) and 'ARTLESS' (1985). In 1987, ALLIN collaborated with 'Homestead' head honcho, GERARD COSLOY (as The HOLY MEN), on an album, 'YOU GIVE LOVE A BAD NAME'. Early in 1990, ALLIN was sent down for four years (Aggravated GBH was the charge), boasting from his Michigan (Jackson State) prison cell that he'd kill himself on stage upon his return to civvy street. In the event, ALLIN died from a drugs overdose (28th June 1993) having run amok, naked in the street after a New York show, indiscriminately attacking stunned passers-by. He had recently completed sessions with new band, The MURDER JUNKIES, these recordings posthumously released as 'BRUTALITY & BLOODSHED FOR ALL'. ALLIN was recently (late in '98) one of the subjects of a Channel 4 (UK) series documenting the history of subversive performers in rock music.

Album rating: ALWAYS WAS, IS, AND ALWAYS SHALL BE (*3) / EAT MY FUC (*3) / GG ALLIN & THE SCUMFUCS/ARTLESS split (*3) / HATED IN THE NATION comp (*5) / YOU GIVE LOVE A BAD NAME (*3) / FREAKS, FAGGOTS, DRUNKS & JUNKIES (*6) / BANNED IN BOSTON (*3) / SUICIDE SESSIONS (*4) / DOCTINE OF MAYHEM (*3) / BRUTALITY AND BLOODSHED FOR ALL (*4) / TERROR IN AMERICA live (*4) / ROCK'N'ROLL TERRORIST compilation (*5)

GG ALLIN & THE JABBERS

GG ALLIN – vocals (ex-MALPRACTICE drummer) / **CHRIS CHAOS** – guitar / **ALLEN CHAPPLE** – bass / **STEVE L** (b. Manchester, England) – drums

not iss. Blood

1979. (7"m) *<903071>* **BORED TO DEATH. / BEAT, BEAT, BEAT / ONE MAN ARMY**

not iss. Destiny

1979. (7") *<911077-59>* **1980's ROCK'N'ROLL. / CHERI LOVE AFFAIR**

not iss. Orange

Sep 80. (lp) *<ORA-777>* **ALWAYS WAS, IS, AND ALWAYS SHALL BE**
– Bored to death / Beat, beat, beat / One man army / Assface / Pussy summit meeting / Cheri love affair / Automatic / I need adventure / Don't talk to me / Unpredictable /

1980's rock'n'roll. *<re-iss. 1987 & 1989 on 'Black & Blue'; 006053X> <cd-iss. 1998 on 'Halcyon'; 6543>*

— guests included on next, WAYNE KRAMER + DENNIS THOMPSON (both ex-MC5)

Aug 81. (7"; as GG ALLIN & THE MOTOR CITY BAD BOYS) *<ORA-69>* **GIMME SOME HEAD. / DEAD OR ALIVE**

— in 1981, ALLIN played drums for The STRIPSEARCH on their 7" 'Jesus Over New York / Galileo' single

1982. (7"ep) *<ORA 70>* **YOU HATE ME AND I HATE YOU. / AUTOMATIC / ASSFACE**

1983. (7"ep) *<ORA 71>* **NO RULES EP**
– No rules / A fuck up / Up against the wall / NYC tonite.

GG ALLIN & THE SCUMFUCS

— **GG ALLIN** with **KILLER KELSIE** – guitar / **RIPP CORO** – bass / **B. TOFF** – drums

not iss. Blood

1983. (7"ep) *<306015>* **HARD CANDY COCK EP**
– Hard candy cock / Out for blood / I don't give a shit / Drink, fight and fuck / Convulsions.

1984. (lp) *<402019>* **EAT MY FUC**
– Hard candy cock / Out for blood / I don't give a shit / Drink, fight and fuck / Convulsions / Fuckin' the dog / Cock on the loose / Clit licker / God of fire in Hell / Blow jobs / Live at A7 club in NYC. *<re-iss. 1987 & 1989 by GG ALLIN as 'E.M.F.' on 'Black & Blue'+=; 402019X>* – I wanna fuck your brains out / I'm gonna rape you / Teacher's pet.

1984. (7"ep) *<410017>* **LIVE FAST, DIE FAST**
– Live fast, die fast / Living like an animal / I need adventure / Loudenbomber. *<cd-ep iss.1998; 3259>*
(above issued on 'Black & Blue')

1985. (7"ep) *<503016X>* **I WANNA FUCK YOUR BRAINS OUT EP**
– I wanna fuck your brains out / Teacher's pet / I'm gonna rape you / Devil's prayer.

Holy War not iss.

1985. (lp; split w/ ARTLESS) *<HWLP 010>* **G.G. ALLIN & THE SCUMFUCS / ARTLESS** — German
– ARTLESS side / I wanna fuck myself / Assfuckin', buttsuckin', cuntlickin, masterbation / You'll never tame me / Bite it you scum / Scumfuc tradition / Abuse myself, I wanna die / Needle up my cock.

— GG did a stint with The CEDAR STREET SLUTS in 1986

GG ALLIN & THE HOLY MEN

— next was a collaboration with 'Homestead' boss, **GERARD COSLOY** – guitar / with others **GREG BULLOCK** – guitar / **MIKE KIRKLAND** – bass / **MIKE 'MACHINE GUN' EDISON** – drums

not iss. Homestead

1987. (lp) *<HMS 069>* **YOU GIVE LOVE A BAD NAME**
– Swank fuckin' / Bloody Mary's bloody cunt / Tough fuckin' shit / I'm a rapist / Suck dog / Teenage twats / Beer picnic / Stick finger clit / Scars on my body – Scabs on my dick / Garbage dump. *(cd-iss. 1992 on 'Awareness'+=; 4)* – Watch me kill the Boston girl / Castration crufixtion / Snakeman's dance / Slaughterhouse deathcamp / Feces and blood / Master daddy / (interview from prison).

1988. (7") *<HMS 099-7>* **GG ALLIN & THE AIDSBRIGADE**
– Expose yourself to kids / I'm a gypsy motherfucker / Hanging out with Jim.

GG ALLIN & THE BULGE

— now with **DORK** – keyboards / **JOHNNY X** – guitar

1988. (lp) *<HMS 107>* **FREAKS, FAGGOTS, DRUNKS & JUNKIES**
– My revenge / Dope money / Be my fuckin' whore / Suck my ass it smells / Dog shit / Wild riding / Sleeping in my piss / Anti social masterbator / Last in line for the gang bang / Die when you die / Commit suicide / Crash & burn / Outlaw scumfuc / Caroline and Sue / Cunt suckin' cannibal / Family / Young little meat / I wanna kill you / My bloody mutilation. *(cd-iss. 1992 on 'Awareness'; 3)*

GG ALLIN

not iss. Black & Blue

1988. (7") *<R 12280>* **THE 12 DAYS OF CHRISTMAS. / (an Algae Afterbirth track)**

1990. (lp) *<BB 101>* **DOCTRINE OF MAYHEM**
– Blood for you / Darkness and a bottle to hold / In this room / Sluts in the city / Blood for you / (interview) / Abuse me, I wanna die / I wanna fuck myself / Needle up my cock / Assfuckin', buttsuckin', cuntlickin, masterbation / You'll never tame me / Torture you / Bite it you scum / Fuck the dead / I wanna piss on you.

not iss. Repo

1990. (7"grey-ep; as GG ALLIN & THE PRIMATES) *<REPO007-3>* **LIVE . . . CAROLINA IN MY ASS (live)**
– Diarrhea blues / Drink, fight & fuck / Cock on the loose / Out for blood.

not iss. Mountain

1990. (7"ep; by GG ALLIN & MARK SHEEHAN) *<NR 18368>* **THE TROUBLED TROUBADOUR EP**
– When I die / Liquor slicked highway / Sitting in this room.

not iss. Bitter Boy

1990. (7"red-ep) *<27957>* **OUTSIDE INSIDE (live)**
– Outlaw scumfuc / Dope money / Die when you die / Caroline & Sue / Dead flowers.

below was not with the MURDER JUNKIES as stated on the sleeve

not iss. Stomach Ache

1991. (7"ep; as GG ALLIN & MARK SHEEHAN) *<SA 05>* **WATCH ME KILL EP**
– Watch me kill / Castration crucifixion / Snakeman's dance / Slaughterhouse deathcamp / Feces & blood, bacteria of my soul / Master daddy.

not iss. Fudgeworthy

1991. (7"m; as GG ALLIN & BULGE) *<FUDGE 2>* **LEGALIZE MURDER. / SUCK MY ASS IT SMELLS / INTERIOR DEPTHS**

GG ALLIN & THE MURDER JUNKIES

— his last band above incl. **WILLIAM WEBER** – guitar, vocals / **MERLE ALLIN** – bass, vocals / **DINO SEX** – drums

New Rose not iss.

1991. (cd) *(ROSE 265>* **MURDER JUNKIES** — French
– Savage blood bath / Murder for the mission-terrorist anarchy / Sidewalk walking / I love nothing / Self absorbed / 99 stab wounds / No limits no laws / War in my head – I'm your enemy / A dead fuck / Sister sodomy – Death and defication / Kill, kill, kill / Violence now – Assassinate the president / Drink from the pissing snakes mouth / Rape, torture, terminate and fuck / Guns and revolution / Kill the police – Destroy the system / Immortal pieces of me / My prison walls – 206045 / Death before life – Bloody cunt slider / I hate people. *(UK cd-iss. May94 on 'New Rose'; 422008)* *<US cd-iss. Oct94 on 'New Rose'; 4265>*

not iss. Jettison

1992. (7"; as GG ALLIN & ANTiSEEN) *<JET 22>* **VIOLENCE NOW – ASSASSINATE THE PRESEDENT. / COCK ON THE LOOSE**

not iss. Railroad

1992. (7"; as GG ALLIN & THE SOUTHERN BAPTISTS) *<RR 995>* **LOOK INTO MY EYES AND HATE ME. / HOTEL CLERMONT**

not iss. Vinyl Retentive

1993. (7"; as GG ALLIN & THE CRIMINAL QUARTET) *<VRP 001>* **SON OF EVIL. / FUCK AUTHORITY**

not iss. T.P.O.S.

1993. (7"; as GG ALLIN & THE CAROLINA SHITKICKERS) *<TPOS 093>* **LAYIN' UP WITH LINDA. / I WANNA FUCK THE SHIT OUT OF YOU / OUTLAW SCUMFUC**

— in the early 90's, ALLIN was sentenced to 4 years imprisonment. He maintained he would commit suicide on stage after his release, although he OD'd (heroin & cocaine) after a gig on the toilet (where else!) on the 28th June '93. He left behind (you could say!) some more releases

Alive Alive

Oct 93. (cd/lp) *<(ALIVE 001 CD/LP)>* **BRUTALITY AND BLOODSHED FOR ALL**
– Highest power / Kill thy father, rape thy mother / Anal cunt / Raw, brutal, rough and bloody / Shoot, knife, strangle, beat & crucify / I kill everything I fuck / Shove that warrant up your ass / My sadistic killing spree *[UK-only]* / I'll slice yer fucking throat / Terror in America / Fuck off, we murder / Take aim and fire / Bastard son of a loaded gun / Legalize murder / Brutality and bloodshed for all. *(lp re-iss. Jan00; same)*

not iss. Sympathy F

1993. (7") *<SFTRI 268>* **KILL THY FATHER, RAPE THY MOTHER. / TAKE AIM AND FIRE**

– compilations, etc. –

1986. (c) *R.O.I.R.; <(A 148)>* **HATED IN THE NATION**
– Intro / Stimulation / I wanna fuck myself / Bite it you scum / You hate me and I hate you / GG's phone machine / Blood for you / Hard candy cock / Eat my shit / Scumfuc tradition / Drink, fight & fuck / Needle up my cock / Sluts in the city / Ten year old fuck / Assfuckin', buttsuckin', cuntlickin', masterbastion / Gimme some head / Tough fuckin' shit / Board's phone machine. *<(lp-iss.1991 on 'Danceteria'; DANLP 064)> (cd-iss. Nov94; RE 148CD) (cd re-iss. Jul98; RUSCD 8242)*

1987. (7"ep) *Black & Blue; <608068X>* **PUBLIC ANIMAL #1**
– You hate me & I hate you / Gimme some head / Drink, fight and fuck / NYC tonite / No rules / Don't talk to me / I wanna rape you. *<re-iss. 1987 as 'BIGGEST TITS 1980-83'> <cd-ep iss.1998; 3280>*

Nov 87. (d-lp) *Fan Club; (FC 032)* **DIRTY LOVE SONGS** — French

1988. (lp; as GG ALLIN & THE TEXAS NAZIS) *Black & Blue; <8X 358>* **BOOZIN' AND PRANKS (live)** *<cd-iss. Jul98; 7>*

1989. (lp; GG ALLIN & THE JABBERS) **BANNED IN BOSTON**

1989. (cd) *Awareness; <2>* **SUICIDE SESSIONS**

1993. (10"; as GG ALLIN & THE DISAPPOINTMENTS) *Occult; <S27845>* **SICKEST OF THE SICK**
– The troubled troubadour of tomorrow / Dogshit.

1993. (cd) *Evergreen; <206045>* **ANTI-SOCIAL PERSONALITY DISORDER: LIVE (live 1989)**

1993. (7"; as GG ALLIN & THE SCUMFUCS) *Fuckin' A Records; <FUK 4>* **NO ROOM FOR NIGGER. / KISS ME IN THE GUTTER**

1994. (10"ep; as GG ALLIN & THE MURDER JUNKIES) *Alive; <ALIVE 0004-10>* **KILL THEM ALL!**
– Anal cunt / My sadistic killing spree / Terror in America / Legalize murder / (live interviews – one with Jerry Springer).

1995. (10"ep) *Alive; <ALIVE 0011>* **MASTERBATION SESSION**
– Sluts in the city / Tough fucking shit / Now I wanna be you dog (live) / Radio commercial '80 (for those who can take it raw).

Apr 95. (cd) *Performance; <6>* **WAR IN MY HEAD**

Dec 95. (cd; as GG ALLIN & THE MURDER JUNKIES) *Overground; (OVER 43CD) / Alive; <ALIVE 12>* **TERROR IN AMERICA** — Feb98
– Bite it you scum / Look into my eyes and hate me / Take aim and fire / Terror in America / Highest power / I'm a gypsy motherfucker / Outlaw scumfuc / Fuck authority (acoustic) / Cunt suckin' cannibal / Outlaw scumfuc (acoustic) / Wendy and Tilla (acoustic) / I live to be hated. *(UK version has added tracks)*

Jan 96. (lp) *Vinyl Retentive; <4>* **CARNIVAL OF EXCESS**

1997. (7"ep; GG ALLIN & THE JABBERS) *T.P.O.S.; <TPOS 114>* **OUT FOR BLOOD EP**
– Out for blood / Sixtynine / Nuke attack / I'm right / Fags in the living room.

Nov 97. (cd) *Mountain; (MCDLP 008)* **TROUBLED TROUBADOUR**

Aug 99. (d-cd) *Wagram; (LC 3051972)* **ROCK'N'ROLL TERRORIST** *(d-lp iss.Feb00 on 'Munster'; MR 175)*

Dec 99. (cd) *R.O.I.R.; <(RUSCD 8258)>* **RE-ERECTED**

2000. (7"ep; by GG ALLIN & THE JABBERS) *Blood; <OCULA>* **OCCUPATION EP**
– Occupation / GG talk / You hate me & I hate you / Pills / GG talk.

ALLMAN BROTHERS BAND

Formed: Jacksonville, Florida, USA ... 1967 by brothers DUANE and GREGG. They became The HOURGLASS, after previously gigging under the ALLMAN JOYS banner with others:- BOB KELLER (bass), BILLY CANELL or MANARD PORTWOOD (drums). HOURGLASS released two albums and nearly a third for 'Liberty' before disbanding in 1968. They then returned to their homeland to augment BUTCH TRUCKS in his outfit, 31st OF FEBRUARY, with DUANE also relying on session work for 'Atlantic'. In 1969, all three formed The ALLMAN BROTHERS BAND and moved to Macon, Georgia. The brothers had already signed to the 'Atlantic' distributed label 'Capricorn', run by one-time OTIS REDDING manager, Phil Walden. With a final line-up of GREGG, DUANE, BUTCH TRUCKS, BERRY OAKLEY (bass) and a second percussionist, JAIMO JOHANSON, the band cut their self-titled debut in 1969, following it up a year later with 'IDLEWILD SOUTH'. All the elements that would make the ALLMAN's a legend were in place; the smooth fluidity of the guitar runs, bible belt country and gospel in abundance, jazz-influenced explorations and dyed in the wool Southern-soaked vocals. During this time, DUANE continued his session work for the likes of LAURA NYRO and DELANEY & BONNIE, as well as lending an unmistakable hand to ERIC CLAPTON on DEREK AND THE DOMINOES' 'LAYLA' project (yes, that most famous of English rock refrains was created by the blonde maned all-American boy). Like their spiritual brothers The GRATEFUL DEAD, it was in a live setting that The ALLMAN BROTHERS BAND could really cook up a soulful gumbo stew and 'THE ALLMAN BROTHERS BAND AT FILLMORE EAST' (1971) was possibly the band's defining moment as well as one of rock's great live albums. A sprawling double set, the free flowing jams often tripped out on their own momentum and despite being spaced out over a whole side of vinyl, 'WHIPPING POST ' (from the debut) lost none of its hypnotic power. Less than three months later, the band were dealt a potentially fatal blow when DUANE was killed in a motorbike accident. Bloodied but unbowed, the band released the 'EAT A PEACH' (1972) album, a mixture of live tracks left over from the Fillmore recordings and new studio material. Another double set, three tracks had been recorded prior to the accident, including DUANE's fragile 'LITTLE MARTHA'. The indulgence of the side-long DONOVAN adaptation, 'MOUNTAIN JAM', was balanced by the pastoral beauty of tracks like BETTS' 'BLUE SKY'. After BERRY OAKLEY was killed later that year in a crash spookily reminiscent of DUANE's, BETTS' influence was even more pronounced as the band struggled bravely on with the triumphant 'BROTHERS AND SISTERS' (1973) album. Replacing OAKLEY with LAMAR WILLIAMS and drafting in pianist CHUCK LEAVELL, the rootsier sounding album gave The ALLMAN BROTHERS BAND their first and only No.1. BETTS' glorious country-flavoured 'RAMBLIN' MAN' provided their biggest hit single to date and 'JESSICA' fuelled countless boy racer fantasies after it was used as the theme for Britain's 'Top Gear' TV show. The band then returned to their natural habitat, the tourbus, playing a landmark gig to a crowd of over half a million people in Watkins Glen, New York, alongside The GRATEFUL DEAD and The BAND. Patchy solo projects followed in the shape of GREG's 'LAID BACK' (1973) and BETTS' 'HIGHWAY CALL' (1974), while the next band effort 'WIN, LOSE OR DRAW' (1975) signalled that The ALLMANS' infamous fast living was beginning to sap their creativity. GREG began a brief, torrid marriage with CHER in 1975, releasing the 'TWO THE HARD WAY' album in 1977 under the moniker of ALLMAN AND WOMAN (no, seriously!). The turning point, however, came when GREG testified against his road manager/pusher, SCOOTER HERRING, who was up on a serious drugs rap. After HERRING was sentenced to 75 years(!) in prison, the rest of the band turned their backs on GREG, the all-brothers together bravado gone, at least until the reunion. Splitting and reforming numerous times throughout the 80's, their studio output trawled a creative nadir on their 'Arista' albums. Nevertheless, they can still put bums on seats in the American heartlands and their Southern fried innovation was given official recognition in 1995 when they were inducted into the Rock 'n' Roll Hall Of Fame. • **Songwriters:** The ALLMANS and BETTS. In the 90's most were written by BETTS, HAYNES and NEEL. Covered; STATESBORO BLUES (Blind Willie McTell) / ONE WAY OUT (Elmore James) / I'M YOUR HOOCHIE COOCHIE MAN (Muddy Waters) / SLIP AWAY (Clarence Carter). • **Trivia:** DUANE sessioned for WILSON PICKETT, BOZ SCAGGS, ARETHA FRANKLIN, KING CURTIS, etc, etc . . .

Album rating: THE ALLMAN BROTHERS BAND (*8) / IDLEWILD SOUTH (*7) / AT FILLMORE EAST (*9) / EAT A PEACH (*9) / BROTHERS AND SISTERS (*8) / WIN, LOSE OR DRAW (*4) / WIPE THE WINDOWS, CHECK THE OIL, DOLLAR GAS (*5) / ENLIGHTENED ROGUES (*5) / REACH FOR THE SKY (*4) / BROTHERS OF THE ROAD (*4) / DREAMS boxed-set (*7) / SEVEN TURNS (*6) / A DECADE OF HITS 1969-1979 (*8) / 2nd SET: AN EVENING WITH THE ALLMAN BROTHERS (*6) / WHERE IT ALL BEGINS (*5) / Gregg Allman: LAID BACK (*5) / GREGG ALLMAN TOUR (*3) / PLAYIN' UP A STORM (*4) / TWO THE HARD WAY as Allman & Woman (*3) / I'M NO ANGEL (*5) / JUST BEFORE THE BULLETS FLY (*4) / SEARCHING FOR SIMPLICITY (*4)

HOURGLASS

GREGG ALLMAN (b. 8 Dec'48, Nashville, Tenn.) – vocals, keyboards, guitar / **DUANE ALLMAN** (b.20 Nov'46, Nashville) – guitars / **PAUL HORNSBY** – keyboards, guitar, vocals / **MABRON McKINNEY** – bass / **JOHN SANDLIN** – drums

Liberty Liberty

Feb 68. (7") *<56002>* **HEARTBEAT. / NOTHING BUT TEARS** [-] [ ]

Aug 68. (lp; mono/stereo) *(LBL/LBS 83219E) <7536>* **THE HOUR GLASS** [ ] [ ] Feb68
– Out of the night / Nothing but tears / Love makes the world 'round / Cast off all my fears / I've been trying / No easy way down / Heartbeat / So much love / Got to get away / Silently / Bells.

— **JESSE WILLARD CARR** – bass, vocals repl. MABRON McKINNEY

Jul 68. (7") *<56029>* **POWER OF LOVE. / I STILL WANT YOUR LOVE** [-] [ ]

Aug 68. (lp) *<7555>* **POWER OF LOVE** [-] [ ]
– Power of love / Changing of the guard / To things before / I'm not afraid / I can stand alone / Down in Texas / I still want your love / Home for the summer / I'm hangin' up my heart for you / Going nowhere / Norwegian wood / Now is the time. *(re-iss. the 1968 lp's; Mar74 on 'United Artists'; USD 303/4)<013G2>*

Sep 68. (7") *<56053>* **CHANGING OF THE GUARD. / D-I-V-O-R-C-E** [-] [ ]

Nov 68. (7") *<56065>* **GOING NOWHERE. / SHE'S MY WOMAN** [-] [ ]

Dec 68. (7") *<56072>* **NOW IS THE TIME. / SHE'S MY WOMAN** [-] [ ]

Feb 69. (7") *<56091>* **I'VE BEEN TRYING. / SILENTLY** [-] [ ]

— 3rd album was withdrawn

31st FEBRUARY

DUANE and **GREGG** with **BUTCH TRUCKS** – drums / **SCOTT BOYER** – guitar, vocals / **DAVID BROWN** – bass

not iss.

Mar 69. (7") **IN THE MORNING WHEN I'M REAL. / PORCELAIN MIRRORS** [-] [ ]

— An album DUANE AND GREGG was released 1973 on 'Polydor UK'/'Bold' US cont. these demos.

The ALLMAN BROTHERS BAND

(**GREGG** and **DUANE**) plus **DICKEY BETTS** (b.RICHARD, 12 Dec'43, West Palm Beach, Florida) – guitar, vocals / **BERRY OAKLEY** (b. 4 Apr'48, Chicago, Illinois) – bass / **BUTCH TRUCKS** (b.Jacksonville, Florida) – drums, timpani / **JAIMOE JOHANSON** (b.JOHN LEE JOHNSON, 8 Jul'44, Ocean Springs, Miss.) – percussion

Atco Atco

Nov 69. (lp) *(228 033) <308>* **THE ALLMAN BROTHERS BAND** [ ] [ ]
– Don't want you no more / It's my cross to bear / Black hearted woman / Trouble no more / Every hungry woman / Dreams / Whipping post. *(cd-iss. 1994 on 'Polydor'; 823 653-2) (cd re-iss. Jun98; 531257-2)*

Mar 70. (7") *(226 013) <8803>* **BLACK HEARTED WOMAN. / EVERY HUNGRY WOMAN** [ ] [ ]

Nov 70. (lp) *(2400 032) <342>* **IDLEWIND SOUTH** [ ] [38]
– Revival (love is everywhere) / Don't keep me wonderin' / Midnight rider / In memory of Elizabeth Reed / I'm your hoochie coochie man / Please call home / Leave my blues at home. *(cd-iss. Mar89 on 'Polydor'; 833 334-2) (cd re-iss. Jun98; 531258-2)*

Nov 70. (7") *(2091 040) <8011>* **REVIVAL (LOVE IS EVERYWHERE). / LEAVE MY BLUES AT HOME** [ ] [92]

Mar 71. (7") *(2091 070) <8014>* **MIDNIGHT RIDER. / WHIPPING POST** [ ] [ ]

Capricorn Capricorn

Jul 71. (d-lp) *(2659 005) <802>* **AT FILLMORE EAST (live)** [ ] [13]
– Statesboro blues / Done somebody wrong / Stormy Monday / You don't love me / Hot 'Lanta / In memory of Elizabeth Reed / Whipping post. *(re-iss. Nov74;) (d-cd-iss. 1986 on 'Polydor'; 823 273-2) (d-cd re-iss. Jun98; 531260-2)*

— On 29 Oct'71, DUANE was killed in a motorcycle accident in Macon. He had already contributed to 3 tracks on below album.

Feb 72. (d-lp) *(67501) <0102>* **EAT A PEACH** [ ] [4]
– Ain't wastin' time no more / Les brers in A minor / Melissa / Mountain jam / One way out / Trouble no more / Stand back / Blue sky / Little Martha / Mountain jam (reprise). *(re-iss. Nov74;) (cd-iss. 1986 on 'Polydor'; 823 654-2) (cd re-iss. Jun98; 531261-2)*

Apr 72. (7") *<0003>* **AIN'T WASTIN' TIME NO MORE. / MELISSA** [-] [77]

Jul 72. (7") *<0007>* **MELISSA. / BLUE SKY** [-] [86]

Nov 72. (7") *<0014>* **ONE WAY OUT. / STAND BACK** [-] [86]

— (Jan'73) **LAMAR WILLIAMS** (b.1947) – bass; repl. BERRY OAKLEY who also died in a motorcyle accident, again in Macon, 11 Nov'72.

Sep 73. (lp/c) *(2429/3129 102) <0111>* **BROTHERS AND SISTERS** [42] [1] Aug73
– Wasted words / Ramblin' man / Come and go blues / Jelly jelly / Southbound / Jessica / Pony boy. *(re-iss. Jun81; 2482 504) (cd-iss. 1986 on 'Polydor'; 825 092-2) (cd re-iss. Jun87 on 'Polydor'; 823 721-2) (cd re-iss. Jun98; 531262-2)*

Oct 73. (7") *(2089 005) <0027>* **RAMBLIN' MAN. / PONY BOY** [ ] [2] Aug73

Jan 74. (7") *<0036>* **JESSICA. / WASTED WORDS** [-] [65]

Oct 74. (7") *(2089 006)* **JESSICA. / COME AND GO BLUES** [ ] [-]

Sep 75. (lp) *(2476 116) <0156>* **WIN, LOSE OR DRAW** [ ] [5]
– Can't lose what you never had / Just another love song / Nevertheless / Win, lose or draw / Louisiana Lou And Three Card Monty John / High falls / Sweet mama. *(cd-iss. Aug87; 827586-2) (cd re-iss. Jun98; 531263-2)*

Sep 75. (7") *<0246>* **NEVERTHELESS. / LOUISIANA LOU AND THREE CARD MONTY JOHN** [-] [67] [78]

— Jul 76 when GREGG was ostracised by others for giving evidence against convicted drug trafficker and road manager Scooter Herring. GREGG formed his own band. BETTS formed GREAT SOUTHERN and others formed SEA LEVEL who hit US No. 31 Mar 78 with lp 'CATS ON THE COAST'. When rifts were settled **The ALLMAN BROTHERS BAND** re-united early '79. GREGG, DICKEY, BUTCH, JAIMO plus newcomers **DAN TOLER** – guitar / **DAVID GOLDFLIES** – bass (both ex-GREAT SOUTHERN)

Polydor Capricorn

Mar 79. (lp) *(2429 185) <0218>* **ENLIGHTENED ROGUES** [ ] [9]
– Crazy love / Can't take it with you / Pegasus / Need your love so bad / Blind love / Try it one more time / Just ain't easy / Sail away. *(cd-iss. 1987 on 'Polydor'; 831 589-2) (cd re-iss. Jun98; 531265-2)*

Apr 79. (7") *(2089 068) <0320>* **CRAZY LOVE. / IT JUST AIN'T EASY** [ ] [29] Mar79

Jun 79. (7") *<0326>* **CAN'T TAKE IT WITH YOU. / SAIL AWAY** [-] [ ]

Arista Arista

Sep 80. (lp) *(SPART 1146) <9535>* **REACH FOR THE SKY** [ ] [27] Aug80
– Hell & high water / Mystery woman / From the madness of the west / I got a right to be wrong / Angeline / Famous last words / Keep on keepin' on / So long. *(cd-iss. Aug97 on 'Razor & Tie'; RE 2131)*

Sep 80. (7") *<0555>* **ANGELINE. / SO LONG** [-] [58]

Jan 81. (7") *<0584>* **MYSTERY WOMAN. / HELL OR HIGH WATER** [-] [ ]

Sep 81. (lp) *<9564>* **BROTHERS OF THE ROAD** [ ] [44] Aug81
– Brothers of the road / Leavin' / Straight from the road / The heat is on / Maybe we can go back to yesterday / The judgement / Two rights / Never knew how much (I needed you) / Things you used to do / I beg of you. *(cd-iss. Aug97 on 'Razor & Tie'; RE 2132)*

Sep 81. (7") *(ARIST 432) <0618>* **STRAIGHT FROM THE HEART. / LEAVING** [ ] [39] Aug81

Nov 81. (7") *<0643>* **TWO RIGHTS. / NEVER KNEW HOW MUCH** [-] [ ]

—— **CHUCK LEAVELL** rejoined but they soon disbanded once again. Past member **LAMAR** died of cancer on 25 Jan'83.

GREGG ALLMAN BAND

went solo again in 1987 with **DAN TOLER** – guitar / **DAVID 'FRANKIE' TOLER** – drums / **TIM HEDING** – keyboards / **BRUCE WAIBEL** – bass, vocals / **CHAZ TRIPPY** – percussion

Epic Epic

May 87. (lp/c/cd) *<(450392-1/-4/-2)>* **I'M NO ANGEL** [ ] [30] Feb87
– I'm no angel / Anything goes / Evidence of love / Yours for the asking / Things that might have been / Can't keep running / Faces without names / Lead me on / Don't want you no more / It's not my cross to bear.

Jul 87. (7") *(6507 517) <06998>* **I'M NO ANGEL. / LEAD ME ON** [ ] [49] Mar87

Jul 87. (7") *<07215>* **CAN'T KEEP RUNNING. / ANYTHING GOES** [-] [ ]

Sep 87. (7") *<07430>* **EVIDENCE OF LOVE. / ANYTHING GOES** [-] [ ]

Apr 89. (lp/c/cd) *(462 477-1/-4/-2) <44033>* **JUST BEFORE THE BULLETS FLY** [ ] [ ] Aug88
– Demons / Before the bullets fly / Slip away / Thorn and a wild rose / Ocean awash the gunwale / Can't get over you / Island / Fear of falling / Night games / Every hungry woman.

Apr 89. (7") *<08041>* **SLIP AWAY. / EVERY HUNGRY WOMAN** [-] [ ]

Jan 98. (cd/c) *(481691-2/-4)* **SEARCHING FOR SIMPLICITY** [ ] [ ]
– Whippin' post / House of blues / Come back and help me / Silence ain't golden no more / Rendezvous with the blues / Wolf's a howlin' / Love the poison / Don't deny me / Dark end of the street / Neighbour neighbour / I've got news for you / Memphis in the meantime / Startin' over.

– other GREGG ALLMAN releases, etc. –

—— with **SCOTT BOYER** – guitar, vocals / **TOMMY TALTON** – slide guitar / **CHUCK LEAVELL** – keyboards / **DAVID BROWN** – bass / **BILL STEWART** – drums / etc.

Capricorn Capricorn

Nov 73. (lp) *(47508) <0116>* **LAID BACK** [ ] [13]
– Will the circle be unbroken / Don't mess up a good thing / Multi-colored lady / Please call home / Queen of hearts / Midnight rider / Don't mess up a good thing / All my friends / These days. *(cd-iss. Aug87 on 'Polydor';)*

Jan 74. (7") *(2089 002) <0035>* **MIDNIGHT RIDER. / MULTI-COLORED LADY** [ ] [19] Dec73

—— (above releases were issued approx.half a year later in UK).

Mar 74. (7") *<0042>* **PLEASE CALL HOME. / DON'T MESS UP A GOOD THING** [-] [ ]

Oct 74. (7") *<0053>* **DON'T MESS WITH A GOOD THING. / MIDNIGHT RIDER** [-] [ ]

Nov 74. (d-lp) *(2659 038) <0141>* **GREGG ALLMAN TOUR (live)** [ ] [50]
– Don't mess up a good thing / Queen of hearts / Feel so bad / Stand back / Time will take us / Where can you go / Double cross / Dreams / Are you lonely for me / Turn on your love light / Oncoming traffic / Will the circle be unbroken?. *(cd-iss. Oct87 on 'Polydor'; 831 940-2)*

—— retained **BILL STEWART** and brought in **STEVE BECKMEIER + JOHN HUG** – guitar / **RICKY HIRSCH** – slide guitar / **NEIL LARSEN** – piano / **WILLIE WEEKS** – bass

Jun 77. (lp) *(2476 131) <0181>* **PLAYIN' UP A STORM** [ ] [42]
– Come and go blues / Let this be a lesson to ya / The brightest smile in town / Bring it on back / Cryin' shame / Sweet feelin' / It ain't no use / Matthew's arrival / One more try.

Aug 77. (7") *<0279>* **CRYIN' SHAME. / ONE MORE TRY** [-] [ ]

ALLMAN AND WOMAN

the (Woman being GREGG's wife and singer CHER) (same line-up)

Warners Warners

Nov 77. (lp) *(K 56436) <3120>* **TWO THE HARD WAY** [ ] [ ]
– Move me / I found you love / Can you fool / You've really got a hold on me / We're gonna make it / Do what you gotta do / In for the night / Shadow dream song / Island / I love makin' love to you / Love me.

Dec 77. (7") *(K 17057) <8504>* **LOVE ME. / MOVE ME** [ ] [ ]

—— they subsequently split and were divorced on 16th of January '79

The ALLMAN BROTHERS BAND

—— re-formed 1989, **GREGG, DICKEY, JAIMO, BUTCH** and newcomers **ALLEN WOODY** – bass / **WARREN HAYES** – guitar / **JOHNNY NEEL** – keyboards

Epic Epic

Jul 90. (7") *<73504>* **GOOD CLEAN FUN. / SEVEN TURNS** [-] [ ]

Jul 90. (cd/c/lp) *(466850-2/-4/-1) <46144>* **SEVEN TURNS** [ ] [53]
– Good clean fun / Let me ride / Low down dirty mean / Shine it on / Loaded dice / Seven turns / Gambler's roll / True gravity / It ain't over yet.

Sep 90. (7") *<73583>* **SEVEN TURNS. / LET ME RIDE** [-] [ ]

Jul 91. (cd/c/lp) *(468525-2/-4/-1) <47877>* **SHADES OF TWO WORLDS** [ ] [85]
– End of the line / Bad rain / Nobody knows / Desert blues / Get on with your life / Midnight man / Kind of bird / Come on in my kitchen.

Jun 92. (cd/c) *<48998-2/-4>* **AN EVENING WITH THE ALLMAN BROTHERS BAND** [-] [ ]
– Southbound / Nobody knows / Revival (love is everywhere) / Midnight blues / Get on with your life / Dreams / End of the line / Blue sky.

—— **MARC QUINONES** – congas, percussion; repl. NEEL

Jul 94. (cd/c) *(476884-2/-4)* **WHERE IT ALL BEGINS** [ ] [ ]
– All night train / Sailin' 'cross the Devil's sea / Back where it all begins / Soulshine / No one to run with / Change my way of living / Mean woman blues / Everybody's got a mountain to climb / What's done is done / Temptation is a gun.

May 95. (cd,c) *<66795>* **2ND SET – AN EVENING WITH THE ALLMAN BROTHERS BAND** [-] [88]
– Sailin' 'cross the Devil's sea / You don't love me / Soul shine / Back where it all begins / In memory of Elizabeth Reed / Same thing / No one to run with / Jessica. *(UK-iss.Apr99; 480606-2)*

– DUANE & GREGG ALLMAN compilations, etc. –

1972. (7") *Bold;* **MORNING DEW. / (pt. 2)** [-] [ ]

1973. (lp) *Polydor; (2310 235) / Bold; <33-301>* **DUANE & GREGG ALLMAN** (rec.'68) [ ] [ ]
– Morning dew / God rest his soul / Nobody knows when you're down and out / Come down and get me / Melissa / I'll change for you / Back down home with you / Well I know too well / In the morning when I'm real.

– ALLMAN BROTHERS compilations, etc. –

Oct 73. (lp; as ALLMAN JOYS) *Mercury; (6398 005) / Dial; <6005>* **EARLY ALLMANS** [ ] [ ]

Nov 74. (d-lp) *Capricorn; (60046) / Atco; <805>* **BEGINNINGS** [ ] [25] Mar73
– (first 2 ALLMAN BROTHERS BAND lp's) *(cd-iss. Oct87 on 'Polydor'; 827 588-2) (cd re-iss. Jun98; 531259-2)*

1974. (7") *Capricorn; <0050>* **AIN'T WASTIN' TIME NO MORE. / BLUE SKY** [-] [ ]

1974. (7") *Capricorn; <0051>* **MELISSA. / RAMBLIN' MAN** [-] [ ]

Feb 76. (d-lp) *Capricorn; (2637 101) <0164>* **THE ROAD GOES ON FOREVER** [54] [43] Dec75
– Black hearted woman / Dreams / Whipping post / Midnight rider / Statesboro blues / Stormy Monday / Hoochie coochie man / Stand back / One way out / Blue sky / Hot 'Lanta / Ain't wastin' time no more / Melissa / Wasted words / Jessica / Ramblin' man / Little Martha.

Dec 76. (d-lp) *Capricorn; (2637 103) <0177>* **WIPE THE WINDOWS, CHECK THE OIL, DOLLAR GAS** (demos, rarities recorded live) [ ] [75]
– (introduction) / Wasted words / Southbound / Ramblin' man / In memory of Elizabeth Reed / Ain't wastin' time no more / Come and go blues / Can't lose what you never had / Don't want you no more / It's not my cross to bear / Jessica. *(cd-iss. Jun98; 531264-2)*

Aug 80. (lp) *Capricorn; <6339>* **THE BEST OF THE ALLMAN BROTHERS BAND** [ ] [ ] Nov81

Jun 81. (d-lp) *Capricorn; (2637 105)* **THE STORY OF THE ALLMAN BROTHERS BAND** [ ] [ ]

Sep 83. (12"ep) *Polydor; (POSP 607)* **JESSICA / SOUTHBOUND. / WHIPPIN' POST / RAMBLIN' MAN** [ ] [-]

Jul 84. (7") *Old Gold; (OG 9437)* **JESSICA. / RAMBLIN' MAN** [ ] [-]

Sep 85. (lp; as HOURGLASS) *C5; (C5-524)* **THE SOUL OF TIME** [ ] [-]

Feb 88. (7") *Old Gold; (OG 4046)* **JESSICA. / (b-side by; Derek & The Dominoes')** [ ] [-]

Jul 88. (lp/c) *Knight; (KNLP/KNMC 10004)* **NIGHTRIDING** [ ] [-]
(cd-iss. Sep89; KNCD 10004)

Apr 89. (6xlp/4xc/4xcd) *Polydor; <(839417-1/-4/-2)>* **DREAMS** [ ] [ ] Jul89

Jul 90. (d-cd) *Polydor; (843260-2)* **LIVE AT LUDLOW GARAGE 1970 (live)** [ ] [-]

May 92. (cd/c) *Polydor; (511156-2/-4)* **A DECADE OF HITS 1969-1979** [ ] [ ] Nov91
– Statesboro blues / Ramblin' man / Midnight rider / Southbound / Melissa / Jessica / Ain't wastin' time no more / Little Martha / Crazy love / Revival / Wasted words / Blue sky / One way out / In memory of Elizabeth Reed / Dreams / Whipping post.

May 92. (cd/c) *Castle; (CCS CD/MC 327)* **THE COLLECTION** [ ] [-]

Sep 94. (cd) *R.C.A.; (0782 218724-2)* **HELL & HIGH WATER (The Best Of The Arista Years)** [ ] [-]

Mar 93. (d-cd) *Polydor; (517 294-2)* **THE FILLMORE CONCERTS (live)** [ ] [-]

Mar 98. (cd) *Camden; (74321 5696124)* **MADNESS OF THE WEST** [ ] [-]

Jun 98. (cd/c) *Epic; (489087-2/-4)* **MYCOLOGY** [ ] [-]

Sep 98. (cd) *Spectrum; (551824-2)* **THE BEST OF THE ALLMAN BROTHERS BAND LIVE (live)** [ ] [-]

Jan 00. (cd) *Universal; (E 543405-2)* **UNIVERSAL MASTERS COLLECTION** [ ] [-]

DUANE ALLMAN

exploitation compilations featuring all his guitar/sessions

Oct 74. (d-lp) *Capricorn; <2CP 0108>* **AN ANTHOLOGY** [ ] [28] Dec72
– B.B. King medley / Hey Jude / The road of love / Goin' down slow / The weight / Games people play / Shake for me / Loan me a dime / Rollin' stone / Livin' on the open road / Down along the cove / lease be with me / Mean old world / Layla / Statesboro blues / Don't keep me wondering / Stand back / Dreams / Little Martha. *(d-cd.iss.Oct87 on 'Polydor'; 831 444-2)*

Jan 75. (d-lp) *Capricorn; <CPN2-0139>* **AN ANTHOLOGY VOL.2** [ ] [49] Jul74
– Happily married man / It ain't fair / The weight / You reap what you sow / Matchbox / Born to be wild / No money down / Been gone too long / Stuff you gotta watch / Push push / Walk on gilded splinters / Waiting for a train / Don't tell me your troubles / Goin' upstairs / Come on in my kitchen / Dimples / Goin' up the country / Done somebody wrong / Leave my blues at home / Midnight rider. *(d-cd.iss.Oct87 on 'Polydor'; 831 445-2)*

Sep 79. (lp) *Capricorn; (242 919-8)* **THE BEST OF DUANE ALLMAN** [ ] [-]

ALL OUT WAR

Formed: New York, USA . . . 1993 by MIKE SCORE, BRAD MAHER, TARAS APUZZO, ERIC CARRILLO and MATT BYRNE. Having been around the NY hardcore toilet circuit for quite some time, they finally found a label via metal/punk imprint 'Gain Ground'. Late in '97, ALL OUT WAR's debut set, 'TRUTH IN THE AGE OF LIES', was finally unleashed to the public, its SLAYER, SICK OF IT ALL and AGNOSTIC FRONT type sound meeting with the approval of metal critics around the globe. Now based with 'Victory' records, AOW supplied their ever-growing following with a fresh batch of US punk in the shape of 'FOR THOSE WHO WERE CRUCIFIED' (1998); definitely not for the uninitiated.

Album rating: TRUTH IN THE AGE OF LIES (*6) / FOR THOSE WHO WERE CRUCIFIED (*4)

MIKE SCORE – vocals / **BRAD MADER** – guitar / **TARAS APUZZO** – guitar / **ERIC CARRILLO** – bass / **MATT BYRNE** – drums

Gain Ground Gain Ground

Jan 98. (lp/cd) *<(GAIN 011/+CD)>* **TRUTH IN THE AGE OF LIES** Dec97
– Resist / Truth in the age of lies / After Autumn / Destined to burn / Redemption for the innocent / Fall from grace / Cross of disbelief / Fight for God / Deceived & the deceivers / Crucial times in existence / Day of judgement.

Victory Victory

Sep 98. (cd) *<(VR 085CD)>* **FOR THOSE WHO WERE CRUCIFIED**
– Soaked in torment / Burning season / For those who were crucified / Resist / Claim your innocence / False salvation / Redemption for the innocent / Witness the end / Into the flames of progression / After Autumn / Enemies of creation / Truth in the age of lies / Apocalyptic terror.

ALMIGHTY

Formed: Glasgow, Scotland . . . 1988 by RICKY WARWICK and STUMP MUNROE, who had evolved from 'FM Revolver' signed band ROUGH CHARM, WARWICK also having served his time in NEW MODEL ARMY. At odds with most of the glam-metal of the day, the ALMIGHTY favoured warts'n'all, balls to the wall hard rock in the grand tradition of MOTORHEAD. Signing to 'Polydor', the band released their debut, 'BLOOD, FIRE AND LOVE', late the following year. In keeping with the rather overblown title it was all very anthemic stuff, at times reminiscent of 'Electric'-era CULT with the likes of 'FULL FORCE LOVIN MACHINE' and 'WILD & WONDERFUL' highlights in their juggernaut of a live show. This was captured on the equally well received 'BLOOD, FIRE & LIVE', a concert set released in late 1990. 'SOUL DESTRUCTION' (1991) consolidated the band's success, the record (which included the sonic assault of the 'FREE'N'EASY' single) almost breaching the UK Top 20. With ex-ALICE COOPER axeman, PETER FRIESEN, replacing the departed TANTRUM, the band began work on 'POWERTRIPPIN'', their most successful and accomplished work to date. The record reached No.5 upon its release in the Spring of 1993, a reflection of the sizable fanbase the band had built up through their relentless touring schedules. Following a split with 'Polydor', the band signed with 'Chrysalis' in 1994, releasing the defiant 'CRANK' album later the same year. Two years on, they struggled to achieve significant sales on their 'JUST ADD LIFE' album, 'Raw Power' records subsequently taking over the reins of a band about to split. With NICK PARSONS coming into the fold to replace FRIESEN, The ALMIGHTY delivered an eponymous comeback set in 2000. • **Songwriters:** Most penned by WARWICK, with some co-written with others. Covered; BODIES (Sex Pistols) / YOU AIN'T SEEN NOTHIN' YET (Bachman-Turner Overdrive) / IN A RUT (Ruts) / DO ANYTHING YOU WANNA DO (Rods) / etc. • **Trivia:** They had meeting with Hell's Angels to discuss!? their similar group emblem/motif. ANDY CAIRNS of THERAPY? provided backing vox on 'CRANK' album.

Album rating: BLOOD, FIRE & LOVE (*7) / BLOOD, FIRE & LIVE (84) / SOUL DESTRUCTION (*5) / POWERTRIPPIN' (*5) / CRANK (*5) / JUST ADD LIFE (*4) / THE ALMIGHTY (*4)

RICKY WARWICK – vocals, rhythm & acoustic guitars / **TANTRUM** (b. McAVOY) – lead & rhythm guitars, vocals / **FLOYD LONDON** (b. JAMES; surname) – bass, acoustic guitar, vocals / **STUMP MUNROE** (b. JULIANS) – drums, percussion, vocals

Polydor M.C.A.

Jul 89. (7") *(PO 60)* **DESTROYED. / LOVE ME TO DEATH** -
(12"+=/12"s+=/cd-s+=) *(PZ/+P/CD 60)* – Blood, fire & love (metal version).

Oct 89. (lp/c/cd) *(841 347-1/-4/-2)* **BLOOD, FIRE & LOVE**
– Resurrection mutha / Destroyed / Wild and wonderful / Blood, fire & love / Gift horse / You've gone wild / Lay down the law / Power / Full force lovin' machine / Detroit. (c/cd+=) – New love sensation.

Jan 90. (7"ep/c-ep) *(PO/+CS 66)* **THE POWER EP**
– Power / Detroit / Wild and wonderful (live).
(12"clear-ep+=/12"pic-d-ep+=) *(PZF/PZP 66)* – ('A'-Killerwatt mix).
(cd-ep+=) *(PZCD 66)* – Lay down the law (live).

Jun 90. (7"/7"pic-d/c-s) *(PO/+P/CS 75)* **WILD & WONDERFUL. / THUNDERBIRD / GOOD GOD ALMIGHTY** 50
(12"+=/12"pic-d+=) *(PZ/+P/CD 75)* – ('A'extended).

Oct 90. (m-cd/m-c/m-lp) *(847 107-2/-4/-1)* **BLOOD, FIRE & LIVE (live)** 62
– Full force lovin' machine / You've gone wild / Lay down the law / Blood, fire & love / Destroyed / Wild and wonderful / Resurrection mutha / You ain't seen nothin' yet.

Feb 91. (7"/c-s) *(PO/+CS 127)* **FREE'N'EASY. / HELL TO PAY** 35
(12"+=/cd-s+=) *(PZ/+CD 127)* – Bodies.

Mar 91. (cd/c/lp) *(847961-2/-4/-1)* **SOUL DESTRUCTION** 22
– Crucify / Free'n'easy / Joy bang one time / Love religion / Bandaged knees / Praying to the red light / Sin against the light / Little lost sometimes / Devil's toy / What more do you want / Hell to pay / Loaded.

Apr 91. (7"/7"pic-d) *(PO/+P 144)* **DEVIL'S TOY. / BAD TEMPTATION** 36
(12"+=/cd-s+=) *(PZ/+CD 144)* – ('A'extended).

Jun 91. (7") *(PO 151)* **LITTLE LOST SOMETIMES. / WILD ROAD TO SATISFACTION** 42
(12"+=) *(PZ 151)* – Curiosity (live).
(pic-cd-s+=) *(PZCD 151)* – Detroit (live).

— (Apr'92) **PETE FRIESEN** – lead guitar (ex-ALICE COOPER) repl. TANTRAM

Mar 93. (12"ep/cd-ep) *(PZ/+CD 261)* **ADDICTION. / ADDICTION (live) / SOUL DESTRUCTION (demo)** 38

Apr 93. (cd/c/lp) *(519226-2/-4/-1)* **POWERTRIPPIN'** 5
– Addiction / Possession / Over the edge / Jesus loves you . . . but I don't / Sick and wired / Powertrippin' / Taking hold / Out of season / Lifeblood / Instinct / Meathook / Eye to eye. *(cd w/ free live cd)* – Crucify / Full force loving machine / Love religion / Addiction / Sin against the light / Free 'n' easy / Wild and wonderful. *(re-iss. cd Apr95; 519104-2)*

May 93. (7"/c-s) *(PO/+P 266)* **OUT OF SEASON. / IN A RUT** 41
(12"+=) *(PZ 266)* – Insomnia / Wild & wonderful (demo).
(cd-s+=) *(PZCD 266)* – Free'n'easy / Keep on rockin' in the free world.
(cd-s) *(PZCDX 266)* – ('A'side) / Fuckin' up / Out of season (demo) / Bodies.

Oct 93. (7"/c-s) *(PO/+CS 298)* **OVER THE EDGE. / TAKING HOLD (live)** 38
(cd-s) *(PZCD 298)* – ('A'side) / Jesus loves you (but I don't) / Powertrippin' (live) / Blind.
(7"colrd) *(POP 298)* – ('A'side) / Lifeblood.

Chrysalis Chrysalis

Sep 94. (7"clear) *(CHS 5014)* **WRENCH. / SHITZOPHRENIC** 26
(12"pic-d) *(12CHSPD 5014)* – ('A'side) / State of emergency / Hellelujah.
(cd-s) *(CDCHS 5014)* – ('A'side) / Do anything you wanna do / Give me fire.
(cd-s) *(CDCHSS 5014)* – ('A'side) / Thanks again, again / Knockin' on Joe.

Oct 94. (cd/c) *(CD/TC CHR 6086)* **CRANK** 15
– Ultraviolent / Wrench / The unreal thing / Jonestown mind / Move right in / Crank and deceit / United state of apathy / Welcome to defiance / Way beyond belief / Crackdown / Sorry for nothing / Cheat. *(other cd+=; CDCHRZ 6086)* – Shitophrenic.

Jan 95. (7"pic-d) *(CHS 5017)* **JONESTOWN MIND. / ADDICTION (live) / CRANK (live) / DECEIT (live)** 26
(12") *(12CHS 5017)* – ('A'side) / Jonestown dub / The unreal thing (live) / United state of apathy (live).
(cd-s) *(CDCHS 5017)* – ('A'side) / Wrench (live) / Move right in (live).
(cd-s) *(CDCHSS 5017)* – ('A'side) / Welcome to defiance (live) / Sorry for nothing (live).

Mar 96. (7"clear) *(CHS 5030)* **ALL SUSSED OUT. / EVERYBODY'S BURNING** 28
(cd-s) *(CDCHS 5030)* – ('A'side) / Superpower / D.S.S. (Desperately Seeking Something).
(cd-s) *(CSCHSS 5030)* – ('A'side) / Tense nervous headshake / Canned Jesus.

Mar 96. (cd/c/lp) *(CD/TC+/CHR 6086)* **JUST ADD LIFE** 34
– Ongoing and total / Do you understand / All sussed out / How real is real for you / Dead happy / Some kind of anything / Coalition star / 8 day depression / Look what happened tomorrow / 360 / Feel the need / Afraid of flying / Independent deterrent. *(cd re-iss. May96 w/ free live-cd 'JUST ADD LIVE'; RAWCD 118)* – Knockin' on Joe / Thanks again, again / Do anything you wanna do / State of emergency / Give me fire / Hellulajah / Jonestown mind (Therapy? & Ruts studio remixes). *(d-cd re-iss. Nov00 on 'Castle'; CMDDD 070)*

Raw Power not iss.

May 96. (cd-ep) *(RAWX 1022)* **DO YOU UNDERSTAND. / UNITED STATE OF APATHY (live) / OVER THE EDGE (live) / WILD & WONDERFUL (live)** 38 -
(cd-ep) *(RAWX 1023)* – ('A'side) / Crucify (live) / Jesus loves you (live) / I fought the law (live).
(cd-ep) *(RAWX 1024)* – ('A'-radio session) / Cheat (live) / Welcome to defiance (live) / Ultraviolent (live).

— had already split by March, although they re-formed in 2000

— **NICK PARSONS** – guitar, vocals; repl. FRIESEN

Sanctuary Sanctuary

Jun 00. (cd) *(SANC 003CD) <4532>* **THE ALMIGHTY**
– Broken machine / I'm in love (with revenge) / La chispa de la muerte / Big black automatic / For fuck's sake / Poison eyes / White anger comedown / TNT / Stop / USAK-47 / Alright / Barfly / Fat chance.

ALTERNATIVE TV

Formed: London, England . . . 1976 by "Sniffin Glue" fanzine editor, MARK PERRY. Completing the initial line-up with ALEX FERGUSSON, TYRONE THOMAS and JOHN TOWE, the band's first recording was given away with an issue of the aforesaid pamphlet in the form of a flexi-disc (the track in question, 'LOVE LIES LIMP' – a subsequent B-side). A debut ATV single proper, 'HOW MUCH LONGER' / 'YOU BASTARD', arrived on the punk scene in late '77 via the local 'Deptford Fun City' indie imprint. A humourously cynical cockney rant against everything and everyone, the track was one of the genre's rawest missives to date and set the tone for what was to come. In the Spring of '78, PERRY and Co. surprised many commentators by taking a diversion into reggae/dub with the less offensive 'LIFE AFTER LIFE/DUB'. PERRY sought out new personnel in the shape of DENNIS BURNS and CHRIS BENNETT, after his previous backing bailed out for pastures new. This line-up recorded the seminal 'IMAGE HAS CRACKED' (1978) album, a commercially overlooked masterpiece containing such powerhouse gems as 'ACTION TIME VISION', 'VIVA LA ROCK'N'ROLL' and 'SPLITTING IN TWO', while even tackling a Frank Zappa number, 'WHY DON'T YOU DO ME RIGHT' with characteristic sarcasm. Contrary to the last, PERRY ended the year with a defiantly experimental and commercially suicidal follow-up, 'VIBING UP THE SENILE MAN (PART 1)', a difficult, intense and paranoid record which nevertheless yielded up a minimalist treat, 'FACING UP TO THE FACTS'. Its release coincided with a split live set, 'WHAT YOU SEE IS WHAT YOU ARE' with commune-dwelling hippies HERE & NOW, PERRY moving even further left of centre as he attempted to distance himself from the increasingly homogenised punk/new wave industry. ATV delivered a final single before PERRY and BURNS formed The GOOD MISSIONARIES (named after an ATV track) with the former's wife GILLIAN HANNA, releasing one 1979 set, 'FIRE FROM HEAVEN'. Ever industrious, PERRY subsequently juggled a solo venture (one album, 'SNAPPY TURNS') with yet more avant-garde knob-twiddling in the form of The DOOR AND THE WINDOW. However, early in 1981, PERRY, BURNS and the returning ALEX FERGUSSON decided to switch their ATV back on, signing to Miles Copeland's burgeoning 'I.R.S.' label and releasing a one-off album, 'STRANGE KICKS'. Splitting in two once more when FERGUSSON went off to join PSYCHIC TV, PERRY floundered for a spell until he inevitably re-formed his beloved project and continued to sporadically release the odd experimental set.

Album rating: THE IMAGE HAS CRACKED (*9) / VIBING UP THE SENILE MAN (PART ONE) (*4) / STRANGE KICKS (*4) / SPLITTING IN 2 compilation (*8) / PEEP SHOW (*4) / DRAGON LOVE (*4) / MY LIFE AS A CHILD STAR (*4) / PUNK LIFE (*4) / APOLLO (*4) / ACTION TIME VISION: THE BEST OF . . . compilation (*8)

MARK PERRY – vocals, guitar / **ALEX FERGUSSON** (b.16 Dec'52, Glasgow) – guitar / **TYRONE THOMAS** – bass / **CHRIS BENNETT** – drums

Deptford Fun City | not iss.

Dec 77. (7") *(DFC 02)* **HOW MUCH LONGER. / YOU BASTARD** [ ] [-]
May 78. (7") *(DFC 04)* **LIFE AFTER LIFE. / LIFE AFTER DUB** [ ] [-]

— FERGUSSON formed CASH PUSSIES. **PERRY** brought in **JOHN TOWE** – drums; repl. BENNETT / **DENNIS BURNS** – bass; repl. THOMAS

Added guests **KIM TURNER** – rhythm guitar / **JOOLS HOLLAND** – piano (on 2)

May 78. (lp) *(DLP 01)* **THE IMAGE HAS CRACKED** [ ] [-]
– Alternatives / Action time vision / Why don't you do me right / Good times / Still life / Viva la rock'n'roll / Nasty little lonely / Red / Splitting in 2.
Jun 78. (7") *(DFC 07)* **ACTION TIME VISION. / ANOTHER COKE** [ ] [-]
Nov 78. (7") *(DFC 06)* **LIFE. / LOVE LIES LIMP** [ ] [-]

— Trim to duo of **PERRY & BURNS** with **GENESIS P.ORRIDGE / MARK LINEHAN** (TOWE joined The ADVERTS)

Dec 78. (lp) *(DLP 03)* **VIBING UP THE SENILE MAN (PART 1)** [ ] [-]
– Release the natives / Serpentine gallery / Poor association / The radio story / Facing up to the facts / The good missionary / Graves of deluxe green / Smile in the day.
Dec 78. (lp; shared with HERE & NOW) *(DLP 02)* **WHAT YOU SEE IS WHAT YOU ARE (live)** [ ] [-]
– Action time lemon / Circles / Fellow sufferer / Splitting in 2.
May 79. (7") *(DFC 10)* **THE FORCE IS BLIND. / LOST IN ROOM** [ ] [-]

— PERRY went on an experimental mission via The GOOD MISSIONARIES, solo material, The DOOR & THE WINDOW plus the REFLECTIONS before ATV were resurrected

ALTERNATIVE TV

— ATV reformed with **PERRY, BURNS** and **FERGUSSON** plus (ex-CASH PUSSIES) / **ALAN GRUNER** – keyboards / **RAY WESTON** – drums

I.R.S. | I.R.S.

Jun 81. (7") *(PFP 1006)* **THE ANCIENT REBELS. / SLEEP IN DUB** [ ] [-]
Jul 81. (lp) *(SP 70023)* **STRANGE KICKS** [ ] [ ]
– The ancient rebels / Strange kicks / Communicate / Mirror boy / Anye is back / My hand is still wet / Fun city / TV operator / There goes my date with Doug / Cold rain / Who are they / Sleep in dub.
Oct 81. (7") *(PFP 1009)* **COMMUNICATE. / OBSESSION** [ ] [-]

— PERRY went into production, and FERGUSSON joined PSYCHIC TV. ATV reformed in 1984 with **PERRY, DAVE GEORGE, PROTAG + NAG**

— by 1985 **MARK and DAVE** were joined by **STEVEN CANDEL** – bass / **ALISON PHILIPS** – drums

Noiseville | not iss.

Feb 86. (12"ep) *(VOO 1T)* **WELCOME TO THE END OF FUN. / ANTI / DEATH TIME** [ ] [-]
Jul 86. (12"ep) *(VOO 2T)* **LOVE / SEX EP** [ ] [-]
– Victory / Repulsion / You never know.

Anagram | not iss.

Aug 87. (12"m) *(ANA 36)* **MY BABY'S LAUGHING (EMPTY SUMMER'S DREAM). / LOOK AT HER EYES / I HAD LOVE IN MY HANDS** [ ] [-]
Nov 87. (lp) *(GRAM 32)* **PEEP SHOW** [ ] [-]
– Chrissie's moom / Let's sleep now / Tumble time / The river / Boy eats girl / My baby's laughing (empty summer dream) / Scandal / White walls / Animal. *(cd-iss. Oct96 on 'Overground'; OVER 54CD)*

— were now **PERRY + JAMES KYLIO**

Chapter 22 | not iss.

Apr 90. (12"ep) *(12CHAP 46)* **THE SOL EP** [ ] [-]
– Everyday / The word / Affecting people / Pain barrier.
Nov 90. (lp) *(CHAPLP 51)* **DRAGON LOVE** [ ] [-]
– Coming of age / Something happened / Last rites / You pushed it a little too far / Captured fantasy / Never gonna give it up / Dragon love / Few feathers fall / (Do you believe) The time / We're through / Don't you leave me.

Overground | Feel Good All Over

Nov 94. (7") *<FGAO 6>* **BEST WISHES. / WESTERN WORLD** [-] [ ]
Nov 94. (cd) *(OVER 39CD) <FGAO 16>* **MY LIFE AS A CHILD STAR** [ ] [ ] 1995
– Child star / Magic / Reflections on a strange existence / Melting pot / Parasite / Don't you lie to me / Reunion / Breakdown / I'll put aside my feelings for awhile / It's over / Give me love / Emotional inner world / Decline and fall / Best wishes (new mix) / Magic (alternative mix).
Oct 95. (7") *<FGAO 22>* **PURPOSE IN MY LIFE. / COMPANY OF LIES** [-] [ ]

— **MARK** re-formed the band with **TYRONE THOMAS, ALEX FERGUSSON**, the latter subsequently being replaced by a guy called CLIVE (1996) / in '97:- **PERRY + MIKE COOK, IAN McKAY, STEVE CONNELL + STEPHEN O'NEIL**

Jan 98. (cd) *(OVER 70CD)* **PUNK LIFE** [ ] [-]
– Unlikely star / Punk life / Guntai wa Moumoku / Give me love / I had my love in my hands / Jane's not at home / Alternative TG / Jesus on the mainline / You never know / God saves! / Purpose in my life / A bold chance / Alternative television.
Jan 99. (cd) *(OVER 82CD)* **APOLLO** [ ] [-]
– Introducing / Apollo / Communication failure / I loked at your face / Hello, I'm Mika . . . / Where? / Propaganda / Return of the crack / Politics in every sausage / A long song / Oh shit, we fell from grace / Slap and tickle / The green hair / Jane's bath / Just a memory / Do you know what time it is?

Sorted | not iss.

Apr 99. (7") *(SRS 017)* **UNLIKELY STAR. /** [ ] [-]

– compilations, others, etc. –

Dec 79. (lp) *Crystal; (CLP 1)* **LIVE AT THE RAT CLUB (live '77)** [ ] [-]
Mar 80. (lp) *Deptford Fun City; (DLP 05)* **ACTION TIME VISION** [ ] [-]
1980. (c; shared with The GOOD MISSIONARIES) *Weird Noise; (WEIRD 001)* **SCARS ON SUNDAY** [ ] [-]
Aug 80. (c; shared with The GOOD MISSIONARIES) *Conventional; (CON 14)* **AN YE AS WELL** [ ] [-]
Feb 89. (lp) *Anagram; (GRAM 40)* **SPLITTING IN 2 – SELECTED VIEWING** [ ] [-]
– Action time vision / Love lies limp / Life / How much longer / Another coke / Still life / You bastard / Nasty little lonely / Why don't you do me right / Facing up to the facts / Lost in room / Force in blind / Splitting in two.
Jul 93. (cd) *Overground; (OVER 29)* **LIVE 1978 (live)** [ ] [-]
Feb 94. (cd) *Anagram; (CDPUNK 24)* **THE IMAGE HAS CRACKED – THE ALTERNATIVE TV COLLECTION** [ ] [-]
(lp-iss.Apr98 on 'Get Back'; GET 26LP)
Oct 95. (cd) *Overground; (OVER 44CD)* **THE RADIO SESSIONS** [ ] [-]
Mar 96. (cd) *Anagram; (<CDMGRAM 102>)* **VIBING UP THE SENILE MAN / WHAT YOU SEE IS WHAT YOU ARE** [ ] [ ]
Apr 96. (cd) *Overground; (OVER 49CD)* **THE INDUSTRIAL SESSIONS 1977** [ ] [-]
Oct 99. (cd) *(CDMRED 163)* **ACTION TIME VISION (THE BEST OF ATV)** [ ] [-]

AMBOY DUKES (see under ⇒ NUGENT, Ted)

AMBROSE SLADE (see under ⇒ SLADE)

AMEN

Formed: Los Angeles, California, USA . . . 1994 by songwriter/frontman CASEY CHAOS and guitarist PAUL FIG, also recruiting former UGLY KID JOE drummer SHANNON LARKIN, ex-SNOT guitarist and bassist SONNY MAYO and JOHN "TUMOR" FAHNESTOCK. This heavy/metal, socially disfunctional ensemble signed to 'Roadrunner' off-shoot label 'I Am' in early 1999. Their hardcore punk/metal album 'AMEN' surfaced at the end of the year, boasting cynicism and torment to its full extent. The group tried to tackle subjects of a disturbing nature (notably the death of SNOT frontman LYNN STRAIT), although they quite literally ended up being caught in a whirlpool of angry white metallers who were, at the time, content with destroying the world (if not our eardrums) with their loud and abrasive music. 'WE HAVE COME FOR YOUR PARENTS' (2000) was CASEY CHAOS and Co's first effort for 'Virgin', although whether or not the band had progressed from their moaning proto-metal was anybody's guess. • **Note:** Not to be confused with the mid-90's Hi-NRG/industrial dance act on 'DeConstruction' records or for that matter the turn of the century AMEN on 'Primal' records.

Album rating: AMEN (*6) / WE HAVE COME FOR YOUR PARENTS (*5)

CASEY CHAOS – vocals / **PAUL FIG** – guitar / **SONNY MAYO** – guitar (ex-SNOT) / **JOHN "TUMOR" FAHNESTOCK** – bass (ex-SNOT) / **SHANNON LARKIN** – drums (ex-UGLY KID JOE)

Roadrunner | Roadrunner

Sep 99. (cd) *<RR 8654-2>* **AMEN** [ ] [ ]
– Coma America / Down human / Drive / No cure for the pure / When a man dies a woman / Unclean / I don't sleep / TV womb / Private / Everything is untrue / The last time / Fevered / Broken design / Resignation – Naked and violent. *(re-iss. Jan01 +=; RR 8656-9)* – Whores of Hollywood / Lovers are killers / Life crime / Black god.
Nov 99. (cd-s) *(RR 2131-5)* **COMA AMERICA / WHORES OF HOLLYWOOD / LOVERS ARE KILLERS / LIFE CRIME / BLACK GOD** [ ] [-]

Virgin | Virgin

Oct 00. (cd) *(CDVUS 179) <49971>* **WE HAVE COME FOR YOUR PARENTS** [ ] [ ]
– CK killer / Refuse Amen / Justified / The price of reality / Mayday / Under the robe / Dead on the bible / Too hard to be free / Ungreatful dead / Piss virus / The waiting 18 / Take my head / In your suit / Here's the poison.
Dec 00. (7") *(VUS 180) <897117>* **THE PRICE OF REALITY. / MOTORCADE HORIZON** [ ] [ ] Jan01
(cd-s) *(VUSDG 180)* – ('A'side) / In these pills / War / 15 and not alive.
Feb 01. (7") *(VUS 191)* **HARD TO BE FREE. / EUROPE (live)** [ ] [-]
(cd-s) *(VUSCD 191)* – ('A'side) / Room of ruin / Nice to be here (live).
Jun 01. (cd-s) **THE WAITING 18** [ ] [-]

AMERICADE

Formed: New York, USA . . . 1981 by the DE MARIGNY BROTHERS, P.J. and GERARD. Taking on board the rhythm section of ex-RACHEL duo, WALT WOODWARD III and NICK SADANO, they subsequently replaced the latter with DAVE SPITZ before recording a debut album. 'AMERICAN METAL' was a typical hard-rock, VAN HALEN-esque effort that failed to stand out in the metal crowd. After a 5-year sabbatical, GERARD resumed live business with the help of new cohorts, MARK WEITZ (vocals, ex-MALICE), GREG O'SMITH (bass, ex-W.O.W.) and PAUL CAMMARATA (drums).

Album rating: AMERICAN METAL (*4)

P.J. DE MARGIGNY – vocals / **GERARD DE MAGIGNY** – guitar / **DAVE SPITZ** – bass; repl. NICK SADANO / **WALT WOODWARD III** – drums

not iss. Adem

1982. (lp) *<FJ 615>* **AMERICAN METAL** [-] [ ]
– On the prowl / Temptress / Love ain't no reason / California rhythm / One step too far / We're an American band / Go for your guns / Rapid fire / Hold on you / Led to the rock / Showdown / Little lady lover / Climax.

— split in 1984, although GERARD and new musicians returned late 80's

AMON AMARTH

Formed: Sweden . . . 1992 out of the ashes of SCUM. By the early 90's the band had adopted the AMON AMARTH moniker while the line-up had coalesced around JOHAN HEGG, OLLI MIKKONEN, ANDERS HANSSON, TED LUNDSTROM and NIKO KAUKINEN. While an initial demo, 'THOR ARISE', was shelved, a second effort, 'ARRIVAL OF THE FIMBUL WINTER' quickly sold out in 1994. Bizarrely enough, the underground death metal network even stretched as far as Singapore, where the 'Pulverised' label signed them up in 1996 for a debut EP, 'SORROW THROUGHOUT THE NINE WORLD'. By the release of 'ONCE SENT FROM THE GOLDEN HALL' (1998), KAUKINEN had been replaced by MARTIN LOPEZ although he was soon to leave along with HANSSON. New members JOHAN SODERBERG and FREDRIK ANDERSSON plugged the gap for 1999's 'THE AVENGER' while 'CRUSHER' followed in 2001.

Album rating: ONCE SENT FROM THE GOLDEN HALL (*5) / THE AVENGER (*5) / THE CRUSHER (*4)

JOHAN HEGG – vocals / **OLLI MIKKONEN** – guitar / **ANDERS HANSSON** – rhythm guitar / **TED LUNDSTROM** – bass / **NIKO KAUKINEN** – drums

demos not iss.

1993. (cd-s) **THOR ARISE** [-] [-] Sweden
1994. (cd-s) **ARRIVAL OF THE FIMBUL WINTER** [-] [-] Sweden

Pulverised not iss.

Jul 96. (cd-ep) **SPRROW THROUGHOUT THE NINE WORLD** [-] [-] Singa

— **MARTIN LOPEZ** – drums; repl. KAUKINEN

Metal Blade Metal Blade

Feb 98. (cd/lp) *(<14133-2/-1>)* **ONCE SENT FROM THE GOLDEN HALL** [ ] [ ]
– Ride for vengeance / The dragons' flight across the water / Without fear / Victorious march / Friends of the suncross / Abandoned / Amon Amarth / Once sent from the golden hall.

— **JOHAN SODERBERG** – guitar; repl. HANSSON

— **FREDRIK ANDERSSON** – drums; repl. LOPEZ

Sep 99. (cd/lp) *(<14133-2/-1>)* **THE AVENGER** [ ] [ ] Nov99
– Bleed for ancient gods / The last will with pagan blood / North Sea storm / The avenger / God, his son and the holy whore / Metalwrath / Legend of a banished man.

Mar 01. (cd/lp) *(<14360-2/-1>)* **THE CRUSHER** [ ] [ ] May01
– Bastards of a lying breed / Master of war / The sound of eight hooves / Risen from the sea (2000) / As long as the raven flies / A fury divine / Annihilation of Hammerfest / The fall through Ginnungagap / Releasing Surtir's fire. *(cd+=)* – Eyes of horror.

AMORPHIS

Formed: Helsinki, Finland . . . 1990 by ESA HOLOPAINEN and JAN RECHBERGER, who soon recruited TOMI KOIVUSAARI and OLI-PEKKA LAINE. Netting a lucrative contract with the native 'Relapse' label on the strength of a demo, they subsequently recorded a split album with INCANTATION (not the Peruvian panpipers!), which remains unreleased. However, two tracks surfaced on an obscure EP, a prelude to the sonic bludgeon of their debut album, 'THE KARELIAN ISTHMUS'. Licensed to 'Nuclear Blast' in the UK, they unleashed the aforesaid opus followed by a mini-cd, 'PRIVILEGE OF EVIL' (the "lost" tracks originally destined for the "split" lp). With the addition of keyboard player, KASPER MARTENSON, they completed a trilogy of albums, the first being a 70's influenced affair, 'TALES FROM THE THOUSAND LAKES' (1994).

Album rating: THE KARELIAN ISTHMUS (*5) / PRIVILEGE OF EVIL mini (*4) / TALES FROM THE THOUSAND LAKES (*6) / ELEGY (*6) / MY KANTELE (*6) / TUONELA (*4) / AM UNIVERSUM (*6)

TOMI KOIVUSAARI – vocals, guitar / **ESA HOLOPAINEN** – guitar / **JAN RECHBERGER** – drums, synthesizers / **OLI-PEKKA LAINE** – bass (ex-ABHORENCE)

Relapse not iss.

1992. (7"ep) *(not known)* **AMORPHIS** [-] [-] Finnish
– Vulgar necrolatry / Misery path.

Nuclear Blast Relapse

Apr 93. (lp/c/cd) *(NB 072/+MC/CD)* **THE KARELIAN ISTHMUS** [ ] [-]
– Karelia / The gathering / Grails mysteries / Warrior's trial / Black embrace / The exile of the sons of Uisliu / The lost name of God / The pilgrimage / Misery path / The sign from the north side. *(cd+=)* – Vulgar necrolatry. *(<cd re-iss. Jun97 on 'Relapse'; RR 6045-2>)*

Dec 93. (m-cd) *<RR 6024-2>* **PRIVILEGE OF EVIL** [ ] [ ]
– Pilgrimage from darkness / Black embrace / Privilege of evil / Misery path / Vulgar necrolatry / Excursing from existence. *(<re-iss. Jun97 on 'Relapse'; same as US>)*

— added **KASPER MARTENSON** – keyboards

Jun 94. (lp/cd) *(NB 097/+CD) <RR 6500-2>* **TALES FROM THE THOUSAND LAKES** [ ] [ ]
– Thousand lakes / Into hiding / The castaway / First doom / Black winter day / Drowned maid / In the beginning / Forgotten sunrise / To father's cabin / Magic and mayhem / Fork of the north / Moon and Sun / Moon and Sun (part 2) / Light my fire. *(also d-cd; NB 097DCD) (UK cd re-iss. Mar01; same as US)*

Mar 95. (cd-ep) *(NB 117CD) <RR 6918>* **BLACK WINTER DAY** [ ] [ ] Jan95
– Black winter day / Folk of the north / Moon and Sun (part 2:- North's son).

— now without MARTENSON who was repl. by **KIM RANTALA**

— **PEKKA KASARI** – drums (ex-STONE) repl. JAN

— **PASI KOSKINEN** – vocals; repl. JAN

May 96. (cd) *(NB 141CD) <RR 6935>* **ELEGY** [ ] [ ]
– Better unborn / Against windows / The oprhan / On rich and poor / My kantele / Cares / Song of the troubled one / Weeper of the shore / Elegy / Relief / My kantele (instrumental reprise).

Relapse Relapse

Jun 97. (m-cd/m-c) *(<RR 6956-2/-4>)* **MY KANTELE** [ ] [ ]
– My kantele (acoustic reprise) / The brother-slayer / Lost son (the brother-slayer part 2) / Leviation / And I hear you call.

— **SANTERI KALLIO** – keyboards (ex-KRYRIA) repl. RANTALA

Nuclear Blast Relapse

May 99. (cd) *(NB 382-2) <RR 6414>* **TUONELA** [ ] [ ]
– The way / Morning star / Nightfall / Tuonela / Greed / Divinity / Shining / Withered / Rusty moon / Summer's end.

Apr 01. (cd) *(NB 535-2) <RR 6488>* **AM UNIVERSUM** [ ] [ ]
– Alone / Goddess (of the sad man) / The night is over / Shatters within / Crimson wave / Drifting memories / Forever more / Veil of sin / Captured state / Grief stricken heart.

ANATHEMA

Formed: Liverpool, England . . . summer 1990 initially as PAGAN ANGEL by DARREN WHITE (nephew of CILLA BLACK!), DANNY CAVANAGH, his brothers VINCENT and JAMIE plus JOHN DOUGLAS. Initially playing rough death-metal, the band released two early demos, 'AN ILIAD OF WOES' and 'ALL FAITH IS LOST', the latter coming to the attention of Swiss label, 'Witchunt'. They subsequently released a debut 45, 'THEY DIE', a track that turned up on their 'Peaceful' debut album, 'SERENADES' (1992). By this juncture the band had recruited DUNCAN PATTERSON (to replace bassman JAMIE), solidifying their distinctive brand of neo-gothic doom metal, female vocalist RUTH tempering the mogadon grind. They lost vocalist DARREN to The BLOOD DIVINE but ploughed on with a further three albums, 'PENTECOST III' (a mini), 'THE SILENT ENIGMA' and 'ETERNITY' (1996), although they have so far failed to achieve the dizzy heights of contemporaries, PARADISE LOST. With VINCENT CAVANAGH having taken over vocal duties from 'THE SILENT . . .' onwards, the band began veering towards a more darkly atmospheric sound utilising orchestration and neo-psychedelic ambience. 'ETERNITY' was often compared to PINK FLOYD's darker moments while lyrically, ANATHEMA delved even further into man's psychic heart of darkness. Prior to the recording of 'ALTERNATIVE 4' (1998), DOUGLAS was replaced by ex-SOLSTICE sticksman SHAUN STEELS. The record itself followed a similar if less intense approach although critically it was eclipsed by the 1999's 'JUDGEMENT' opus, ANATHEMA's first album for new label 'Music For Nations'. By this point, DOUGLAS was back in the fold and DAVE PYBUS had replaced PATTERSON, the former single-handedly contributing a handful of the album's better tracks. • **Covered:** ONE OF THE FEW + GOODBYE CRUEL WORLD (Pink Floyd) / BETTER OFF DEAD (Bad Religion). • **Trivia:** In 1997, CAVANAGH moonlighted with LID (alongside TROUBLE's ERIC WAGNER) on the one-off set, 'In The Mushroom'.

Album rating: SERENADES (*5) / PENTECOST III mini (*5) / THE SILENT ENIGMA (*6) / ETERNITY (*6) / ALTERNATIVE 4 (*7) / JUDGEMENT (*5) / RESONANCE compilation (*7)

DARREN WHITE – vocals / **DANNY CAVANAGH** – guitar / **VINCENT CAVANAGH** – guitar / **JAMIE CAVANAGH** – bass, vocals / **JOHN DOUGLAS** – drums / **RUTH** – (some guest) vocals

Anathema not iss.

Nov 90. (c-ep) *(none)* **AN ILIAD OF WOES** [ ] [-]
– The lord of mortal pestilence / Memento mori / In the name of the father / Echoes of terror.

— **DUNCAN PATTERSON** – bass; repl. JAMIE

Jul 91. (c-ep) *(none)* **ALL FAITH IS LOST** [ ] [-]
– Crestfallen / At one with the earth / All faith is lost / They die.

Witchunt not iss.

1992. (7") **THEY DIE. / CRESTFALLEN** [ ] [-]

Peaceville Fierce

Sep 92. (lp/cd) *(VILE 034/+CD) <11037>* **SERENADES** 1993
– Lovelorn rhapsody / Sweet tears / J'ai fait une prommesse / They (will always) die / Sleepless / Sleep in sanity / Scars of the old scream / Under a veil (of black lace) / Where shadows dance. *(cd+=)* – Dreaming: the romance. *(re-pressed cd+=)* – THE CRESTFALLEN EP tracks *(cd re-iss. Feb01; CDVILEM 34)*

Nov 92. (12"ep) *(VILE 039T)* **THE CRESTFALLEN EP** -
– . . . And I lust / The sweet suffering / Everwake / Crestfallen.
(cd-ep+=) *(VILE 036CD)* – They die.

— now without DARREN who formed the short-lived, The BLOOD DIVINE

Mar 95. (m-cd) *(CDMVILE 51) <11087>* **PENTECOST III**
– Kingdom / Mine is yours to drown in (ours is the new tribe) / We, the gods / Pentecost III / Momento mori. *(cd re-iss. Mar01 +=; CDVILEM 51)* – THE CRESTFALLEN EP

Oct 95. (cd/c/lp) *(CD/T+/VILE 52) <11109>* **THE SILENT ENIGMA**
– Restless oblivion / Shroud of frost / . . .Alone / Sunset of the age / Nocturnal emission / Cerulean twilight / The silent enigma / A dying wish / Black orchid. *(cd re-iss. Jan01; CDVILEM 52)*

— VINCENT now took over vocal duties from DARREN

Nov 96. (cd/c/lp) *(CD/T+/VILE 64) <11110>* **ETERNITY**
– Sentient / Angelica / The beloved / Eternity part I / Eternity part II / Hope / Suicide veil / Radiance / Far away / Eternity part III / Cries on the wind / Ascension. *(cd-digi+=)* – Far away (acoustic) / Eternity part III (acoustic). *(cd re-iss. Nov00; CDVILEM 64)*

— **SHAUN STEELS** – drums (ex-SOLSTICE) repl. DOUGLAS

1998. (promo-cd-ep) *(CDVILE 54)* **ALTERNATIVE FUTURE E.P.** - -
– Fragile dreams / Empty / Alternative 4.

Jun 98. (cd/c/lp) *(CD/T+/VILE 73) <11112>* **ALTERNATIVE 4**
– Shroud of false / Fragile dreams / Empty / Lost control / Re-connect / Inner silence / Alternative 4 / Regret / Feel / Destiny. *(cd re-iss. Nov00; CDVILEM 73)*

— **DAVE PYBUS** – bass; repl. PATTERSON

— **JOHN DOUGLAS** (re-joined) to repl. STEELS

Music For Nations Koch

Jun 99. (cd/lp) *(CD+/MFN 250) <8225>* **JUDGEMENT**
– Deep / Pitiless / Forgotten hopes / Destiny is dead / One last goodbye / Make it right (F.F.S.) / Parisienne moonlight / Don't look too far / Emotional winter / Wings of God / Judgment / Anyone, anywhere/ 2000 and gone. *(special cd+=; CDMFNX 250)* – Transacoustic.

– compilations, etc. –

Jun 01. (cd) *Peaceville; (CDVILE 82)* **RESONANCE** -
– Scars of the old stream / Everwake / J'fait une promesse / Alone / Far away (acoustic) / Eternity pt.II / Eternity pt.III (acoustic) / Better off dead / One of the few / Inner silence / Goodbye cruel world / Destiny / The silent enigma (orchestral) / Angelica (live Budapest 1997) / Horses / Hope (video).

ANCIENT

Formed: Norway . . . 1992 as the brainchild of guitarist/composer APHAZEL, who shortly teamed up with the bands sinisterly named singer/sticksman GRIMM. This coupling fitted snugly into the expanding Scandanavian black metal scene and produced their first full-set 'SVARTALVHEIM' (1994), and hot on its heels the EP, 'TROLLTAAR' (1995). After these brief beginnings GRIMM departed and APHAZEL journeyed with his dark musings to the States. There, ANCIENT were joined by the singer LORD KAIAPHAS and drummer KJETIL. Inking a deal with 'Metal Blade', they released 'THE CAINIAN CHRONICLE' (1996). This album definitely showed a more developed ANCIENT, with high tempo beats and dark thrashy chords that at the same time showed APHAZEL as the force willing to take his brand of black metal to new depths. Yet another band shuffle occured with the entry of vocalist ERICHTE and, in the true spirit of contradiction, JESUS CHRIST joined them on guitar and keyboards. This new combo came out with ANCIENT's third set 'MAD GRANDIOSE BLOODFIENDS' (1997). An aptly titled album as the boys combined dark riffage with ominous orchestration creating a heavy occult soundtrack to back their impious themes. Between this album and their next, APHAZEL relocated to Italy, although ERICHTE and KJETIL didn't make the trip with him; DEADLY KRISTIN and KRIGSE filling their positions respectively. The new line-up delivered 'HALLS OF ETERNITY' (1999), definitely more antagonistic and doom-laden than any of their previous efforts.

Album rating: SVARTALVHEIM (*5) / THE CAINIAN CHRONICLE (*5) / MAD GRANDIOSE BLOODFRIENDS (*5) / THE HALLS OF ETERNITY (*6) / DET GLEMTE RIKET compilation (*4)

APHAZEL – guitar / **GRIMM** – vocals, drums

own demo not iss.

1994. (cd-ep) *(none)* **EERILY HOWLING WINDS** - - Norway

1994. (cd-ep) *(none)* **TROLLTAAR** - - Norway

Osmose not iss.

Jan 95. (cd) *(POSH 006CD)* **SVARTALVHEIM** -

— **APHAZEL** recruited new people **LORD KAIAPHAS** – vocals / **KIMBERLY** – guitar / **KJETIL** – drums

Metal Blade Metal Blade

Jul 96. (cd) *(<3984 14110CD>)* **THE CAINIAN CHRONICLE**
– Ponderous moonlighting / The Cainian chronicle:- pt.I – The curse, pt.II – Lilith's embrace, pts.III & IV – Disciplines of Caine – Zilah and the crone / At the infernal portal (Canto III) / Cry of Marianne / Prophecy of Gehenna / Song of Kaiaphas / Exu / The pagan cycle / Homage to Pan.

— now without KJETIL + KAIAPHAS (repl. by **ERICHTE** – vocals + **JESUS CHRIST** – keyboards)

Nov 97. (cd) *(<3984 14143CD>)* **MAD GRANDIOSE BLOODFIENDS**
– Malkavian twilight / A mad blood scenario / The draining / Um sonho psycodelico / Sleepless princess of the Arges / Her northern majesty / Blackeyes / The emerald tablet / Willowthewisp / Neptune / 5 / Becate, my love and lust / Dampirize Natasha / Black funeral.

— **DEADLY KRISTIN** – vocals; repl. ERICHTE

— **KRIGSE** – drums; repl. KJETIL

Oct 99. (cd/lp) *(<14201-2/-1>)* **THE HALLS OF ETERNITY** Nov99
– Cast into unfathomed deeps / Born in flames / The battle of the ancient warriors / A woeful summoning / Cosmic exile / Spiritual supremacy / The heritage / I, madman / From behind comes the sword / The halls of eternity / Arrival.
(below mini was actually issued earlier in Norway)

Feb 01. (m-cd) *(14352-2)* **GOD LOVES THE DEAD** -
– God loves the dead / Trolltaar (re-recorded) / Powerslave / Draining (remix) / Un sonho psicodelico (remix) / God loves the dead (video) / Um sonho psicodelico (video).

– compilations, etc. –

May 99. (m-lp/m-cd) *Hammerheart; (<HHR 042/+CD>)* **DET GLEMTE RIKET** (demos, rarities, etc) Dec99
– Trolltaar / Nattens skjonnet / Eerily howling winds / Det glemte riket / Huldra dans / Paa evig vandring / Fjellets hemmelighet / Algol / Sweet leaf.

. . .AND YOU WILL KNOW US BY THE TRAIL OF DEAD

Formed: Olympia, Washington, USA . . . 1994 by CONRAD KEELY and former MUKILTEO FAIRIES singer/percussionist JASON REECE. The duo of noisy songsmiths – who had been friends since childhood – detached themselves from the indie circuit in Olympia, subsequently flitting to Austin, Texas. They began performing loud, riotous concerts, which often escalated in violence and/or the destruction of musical equipment. New recruits KEVIN ALLEN and NEIL BUCSH regularly contributed to the mayhem, earning themselves full-time positions in the increasingly popular group. AYWKUBTOD (probably one of the best named bands in ages) could've been pitched somewhere between The WHO and MOGWAI due to their sharp-edged sonic anarchism. Their intense blasts of instumentation were matched with complex quiet/loud sections, fumbling pianos and screeching guitars . . . like SLINT, but without the boring bits. In 1997, the group issued a limited edition live cassette which ultimately lead to their signing to 'Trance Syndicate' in early 1998. It was with 'Trance Syndicate' that the troupe released their eponymous debut album to much critical acclaim. The set was also met by unexpected success, thanks to thousands of dedicated fans who had already recognised the talent before . . .AND YOU WILL KNOW . . . were even signed. 'MADONNA' followed in 1999 on 'Merge', and boasted the single 'MISTAKES AND REGRETS', plus a much feted performance at 'All Tomorrow's Parties' where the group produced an unhealthy wall of feedback after their 30-minute onslaught. The single wasn't too bad either; crashing drums, demonic bass lines, Mach-speed guitars and the lines "If I had to make a list/of my mistakes and regrets/I'd put your name on top/and every line after that", all mixed to complete perfection.

Album rating: . . . AND YOU WILL KNOW US BY THE TRAIL OF DEAD (*7) / MADONNA (*8)

CONRAD KEELY (b. Plano, Texas) – vocals, drums, harpsicord, trumpet, sax / **JASON REECE** – vocals, accordion, violin, harp (ex-MUKILTEO FAIRIES) / **KEVIN ALLEN** (b.23 May'72, Norman, Oklahoma) – guitar, trumpet, ukelele / **NEIL BUSCH** – bass, samples

Trance Syndicate Trance Syndicate

Jan 98. (lp/cd) *<(TR/+CD 66)>* **. . .AND YOU WILL KNOW US BY THE TRAIL OF DEAD**
– Richter scale madness / Novena without faith / Fake fake eyes / Half of what / Gargoyle waiting / Prince with a thousand enemies / Ounce of prevention / When we begin to steal . . . *(cd re-iss. Nov00 on 'Domino'; REWIG 10)*

Merge Merge

Oct 99. (lp/cd) *<(MRG 171/+CD)>* **MADONNA**
– And you will know them . . . / Mistakes & regrets / Totally natural / Blight takes all / Clair de Lune / Flood of red / Children of the hydra's teeth / Mark David Chapman / Up from redemption / Aged dolls / The day the air turned blue / A perfect teenhood / Sigh your children. *(UK re-iss. May00 on 'Domino' cd/d-lp; WIG CD/LP 84)*

ANGEL

Formed: East Coast, USA . . . mid 70's initially as SWEET MAMA FROM HEAVEN, by GREGG GIUFFRIA and FRANK DiMINO. Drafting in PUNKY and MICKEY from DADDY WARBUCKS (aka BUX), they were duly snapped up by GENE SIMMONS (of KISS) to Neil Bogart's 'Casablanca'. ANGEL first spread their commercial wings late in '75, when their eponymous debut entered the US Top 200. Six months later, the follow-up, 'HELLUVA BAND', trod the same pomp-metal path, the band garnering more column inches for their garish attire than the dull music and predictable sexual inferences of their lyrics. Their third set, annoyingly titled, 'ON EARTH AS IT IS IN HEAVEN' (1977), saw them break into the Top 100 for the first time. With FELIX ROBINSON substituting JONES, they fared even better in the pop-metal stakes; the 4th album, WHITE HOT' made it all the way to No.55. However, the band were brought down to earth with a proverbial bump following the mediocre sales of their next two albums. Squeezed between these releases was the film, 'Foxes', in which ANGEL (managed by ADAM

FAITH and backing CHERIE CURRIE, ex-RUNAWAYS) appeared. '20th CENTURY FOXES' was their final 45, before being cast out by 'Casablanca'. • **Songwriters:** GIUFFRIA / MEADOWS / DiMINO; except GOT LOVE IF YOU WANT IT (Slim Harpo) / ALL THE YOUNG DUDES (Mott The Hoople) / etc. • **Trivia:** PUNKY had cut his teeth in late 60's bubblegum band, The CHERRY PEOPLE. They had a few releases on 'Heritage' records.

Album rating: ANGEL (*7) / HELLUVA BAND (*5) / ON EARTH AS IT IS IN HEAVEN (*5) / WHITE HOT (*5) / SINFUL (*6) / LIVE WITHOUT A NET (*4) / CAN YOU FEEL IT compilation (*5) / ANTHOLOGY compilation (*6)

FRANK DiMINO – vocals / **PUNKY MEADOWS** (b. EDWIN) – guitar / **GREGG GIUFFRIA** – keyboards / **MICKEY JONES** – bass / **BARRY BRANDT** – drums, percussion, vocals

Casablanca Casablanca

Dec 75. (7") <853> **ROCK & ROLLERS. / ANGEL (THEME)** [-] [ ]
Dec 75. (lp) *(CBC 4007)* <7021> **ANGEL** [ ] [ ]
– Tower / Long time / Rock & rollers / Broken dreams / Mariner / Sunday morning / On & on / Angel (theme).
Feb 76. (7") *(CBX 514)* **ON AND ON. / ANGEL (THEME)** [ ] [-]
Jun 76. (lp) *(CBC 4010)* <7028> **HELLUVA BAND** [ ] [ ]
– Feelin' right / The fortune / Anyway you want it / Dr. Ice / Mirrors / Feelings / Pressure point / Chicken soup / Angel (theme).
Sep 76. (7") *(CBX 522)* **FEELINGS. / ANGEL (THEME)** [ ] [-]
Mar 77. (lp) *(CAL 2002)* <7043> **ON EARTH AS IT IS IN HEAVEN** [ ] [76]
– Can you feel it / She's a mover / Big boy (let's do it again) / Telephone exchange / White lightning / On the rocks / You're not fooling me / That magic touch / Cast the first stone / Just a dream.
May 77. (7") *(CAN 104)* <878> **THAT MAGIC TOUCH. / BIG BOY (LET'S DO IT AGAIN)** [ ] [77] Apr77

—— **FELIX ROBINSON** – bass, vocals repl. JONES

Nov 77. (7") *(CAN 113)* <903> **THE WINTER SONG. / YOU CAN FEEL IT** [ ] [ ]
Feb 78. (lp) *(CSL 2023)* <7085> **WHITE HOT** [ ] [55]
– Don't leave me lonely / Ain't gonna eat my heart out anymore / Hold me, squeeze me / Over and over / Under suspicion / Got love if you want it / Stick like glue / Flying with broken wings (without you) / You could lose me / The winter song.
May 78. (7") *(CAN 125)* <914> **AIN'T GONNA EAT OUT MY HEART ANYMORE. / FLYING WITH BROKEN WINGS** [ ] [44]
Jul 78. (7") <933> **DON'T LEAVE ME LONELY. / STICK LIKE GLUE** [-] [ ]
Mar 79. (7") <963> **DON'T TAKE YOUR LOVE. / BAD TIME** [-] [ ]
Mar 79. (lp) <7127> **SINFUL** [-] [ ]
– Don't take your love / L.A. lady / Just can't take it / You can't buy love / Bad time / Waited a long time / I'll bring the whole to your door / I'll never fall in love again / Wild and hot / Lovers live on.
Feb 80. (7") *(CAN 193)* <2240> **20th CENTURY FOXES. / CAN YOU FEEL IT (live)** [ ] [ ]
Feb 80. (d-lp) *(CSL 2703)* <7203> **LIVE WITHOUT A NET (live)** [ ] [ ]
– Tower / Can you feel it / Don't leave me lonely / Telephone exchange / I ain't gonna eat my heart out anymore / Over and over / Anyway you want it / On the rocks / Wild & hot / All the young dudes / Rock & rollers / White lightning / Hold me, squeeze me / Got love if you want it / Feelin' right / 20th century foxes.

—— Disbanded soon after being dropped by label. In the mid 80's, GIUFFRIA re-emerged in his own named outfit. Around the same time, ANGEL reformed briefly without him, but nothing was recorded.

– compilations, etc. –

1989. (lp/cd) *Polygram;* <838 584-1/-2> **CAN YOU FEEL IT** [-] [ ]
1992. (cd/c) *Polygram;* <512431-2/-4> **ANTHOLOGY** [-] [ ]
– Angel (theme) / Tower / On and on / Rock & rollers / Feelin' right / Any way you want it / Can you feel it / White lightning / Don't leave me lonely / Ain't gonna eat out my heart anymore / Got love if you want it / Flying without broken wings (without you) / The winter song / Don't take your love / Bad time / Walk away from Renee / I'll never fall in love again / Wild and hot / 20th Century foxes / The Christmas song.

ANGEL CITY (see under ⇒ ANGELS)

ANGELIC UPSTARTS

Formed: Brockley Whim, South Shields, England . . . 1977 by MENSI along with MOND, RONNIE WOODEN and DECCA. Perhaps unsurprisingly for a northern punk band, The ANGELIC UPSTARTS cited the injustice of the class divide as one of their driving motivations and there was certainly no love lost between them and their more intellectual London-centric cousins. The boys in blue were another sitting target for their righteous anger, an independently released 1978 debut single, 'MURDER OF LIDDLE TOWERS', condemning police brutality and winning them both the patronage of SHAM 69 mainman, JIMMY PURSEY and a deal with 'Warners'. The PURSEY-produced 'TEENAGE WARNING' (1979) was a straightahead three-chord assault on all things right wing, including the creeping plague of racism and the menace of the new Thatcher government. Like fellow working class heroes, SHAM 69, The ANGELIC UPSTARTS were beleaguered by fascist skinheads disrupting their gigs and misinterpreting their political stance. Still, it didn't take a genius to work out which side of the fence MENSI was on from the lyrical content of follow-up set, 'WE GOTTA GET OUT OF THIS PLACE' (1980), another tirade aimed at Britain's would-be oppressors. A switch to 'E.M.I.' at the dawn of the 80's was shortlived as the punk revolution filtered out into the mainstream, the band defiantly carrying on with their collectivist crusade over a series of independently released albums inlcuding 'REASON WHY' (1983) and 'POWER OF THE PRESS' (1986). While their musical palate had broadened to include the use of keyboards etc., the message remained the same, if even more vitriolic than ever. The contentious 'BRIGHTON BOMB' single paid tribute to the IRA's failed attempt at killing the whole Conservative cabinet; after almost a decade of Tory rule, MENSI (who found himself taken up on obscenity charges!) was obviously reaching the end of his tether. Most of the band's fans were also giving up the ghost and in 1986, The ANGELIC UPSTARTS finally called it a day. An ill-advised reformation in 1992 saw the group sign to metal/hardcore specialist, 'Roadrunner', hardly a natural home. The resulting album, 'BOMBED OUT' (1992) was met with little enthusiasm, by either old fans or new. • **Songwriters:** MENSI and MOND, except WE GOTTA GET OUT OF THIS PLACE (Animals) / GREEN FIELDS OF FRANCE (Eric Bogle) / WHITE RIOT (Clash).

Album rating: TEENAGE WARNING (*5) / WE GOTTA GET OUT OF THIS PLACE (*5) / 2,000,000 VOICES (*4) / LIVE (*4) / STILL FROM THE HEART (*4) / REASON WHY? (*5) / LAST TANGO IN MOSCOW (*3) / LIVE IN YUGOSLAVIA (*3) / THE POWER OF THE PRESS (*4) / BOMBED OUT (*3) / ANGEL DUST (THE COLLECTED HIGHS) compilation (*6)

MENSI (b. THOMAS MENSFORTH) – vocals / **MOND** (b. COWIE) – guitar / **RONNIE WOODEN** (b. WARRINGTON) – bass; repl. STEVE due to drug problems / **DECCA** (b. TAYLOR) – drums

Dead not iss.

Jun 78. (7") *(IS-AU 1024)* **THE MURDER OF LIDDLE TOWERS. / POLICE OPPRESSION** [ ] [-]
(re-iss. Sep78 on 'Rough Trade/Small Wonder'; RT-SW 001)

Warners not iss.

Apr 79. (7",7"green/12") *(K 17354/+T)* **I'M AN UPSTART. / LEAVE ME ALONE** [31] [-]
Jul 79. (7"/7"red) *(K 17426/+C)* **TEENAGE WARNING. / THE YOUNG ONES** [29] [-]
Aug 79. (lp/c) *(K/K4 56717)* **TEENAGE WARNING** [29] [-]
– Teenage warning / Student power / The yong ones / Never again / We are the people / Liddle Towers / I'm an upstart / Small town, small mind / Youth leader / Do anything / Let's speed / Leave me alone.
Oct 79. (7") *(K 17476)* **NEVER 'AD NOTHING. / NOWHERE LEFT TO HIDE** [52] [-]
Jan 80. (7") *(K 17558)* **OUT OF CONTROL. / SHOTGUN SOLUTION** [58] [-]
Mar 80. (7") *(K 17586)* **WE GOTTA GET OUT OF THIS PLACE. / UNSUNG HEROES PART 2** [65] [-]
Apr 80. (lp/c) *(K/K4 56906)* **WE GOTTA GET OUT OF THIS PLACE** [54] [-]
– Never 'ad nothing / Police oppression / Lonely man of Spandau / Their destiny is coming / Shotgun solution / King Coal / Out of control / Ronnie is a rocker / Listen to the steps / Can't kill a legend / Capital city / We gotta get out of this place.

Zonophone not iss.

Jul 80. (7") *(Z 7)* **LAST NIGHT ANOTHER SOLDIER. / THE MAN WHO CAME IN FROM THE BEANO** [51] [-]
Nov 80. (7") *(Z 12)* **ENGLAND. / STICK'S DIARY** [ ] [-]
Jan 81. (7") *(Z 16)* **KIDS ON THE STREET. / THE SUN NEVER SHINES** [57] [-]
May 81. (7") *(Z 22)* **I UNDERSTAND. / NEVER COME BACK** [ ] [-]
(12"+=) *(12Z 22)* – Heath's lament.
Jun 81. (lp) *(ZONO 104)* **2,000,000 VOICES** [32] [-]
– 2,000,000 voices / Ghost town / You're nicked / England / Heath's lament / Guns for the Afghan rebels / I understand / Mensi's marauders / Mr. Politician / Kids on the street / We're gonna take the world / Last night another soldier / I wish. *(re-iss. May93 on 'Dojo'; DOJOLP 081) (cd-iss. Jan98; DOJOCD 081) (<cd re-iss. Feb01 on 'Captain Oi'; AHOYCD 158>)*
Sep 81. (lp) *(ZEM 102)* **ANGELIC UPSTARTS LIVE (live)** [27] [-]
– Teenage warning / Never 'ad nothing / Four words / Last night another soldier / Guns for the Afghan rebels / Mr. Politician / Shotgun solution / Pride without prejudice / England / Police oppression / Kids on the street / I understand / You're nicked / 2,000,000 voices / I'm an upstart. *(c+=)* – (free live flexi 7"with above) – THE YOUNG ONES / WHITE RIOT. / WE'RE GONNA TAKE THE WORLD / LEAVE ME ALONE *(cd-iss. Feb94 on 'Dojo'; DOJOCD 169)*
Oct 81. (7") *(Z 25)* **DIFFERENT STROKES. / DIFFERENT DUB** [ ] [-]

—— **TONY FEEDBACK** – bass repl. DECCA who went solo

Mar 82. (7") *(Z 28)* **NEVER SAY DIE. / WE DEFY YOU** [ ] [-]
Apr 82. (lp) *(ZONO 106)* **STILL FROM THE HEART** [ ] [-]
– Never say die / Flames of Brixton / Action man / Wasted (loved by none) / Here comes trouble / Theme for lost souls / I stand accused / Black knights of the 80's / Cry wolf / Soldier. *(cd-iss. Nov93 on 'Dojo'; DOJOCD 144)*

—— (MENSI, MOND and FEEDBACK) were joined by **BRYAN HAYES** – rhythm guitar / **PAUL THOMPSON** – drums

Anagram not iss.

Nov 82. (7"/12") *(ANA/12ANA 3)* **WOMAN IN DISGUISE. / LUST FOR GLORY** [ ] [-]
Mar 83. (7"/12") *(ANA/12ANA 7)* **SOLIDARITY. / FIVE FLEW OVER** [ ] [-]
Jul 83. (7"; w-drawn) *(ANA 12)* **THE BURGLAR. /** [-] [-]

—— next 45 with guest vocalist MAX SPLODGE (ex-SPLODGENESSABOUNDS)

Sep 83. (7") *(ANA 13)* **NOT JUST A NAME. / THE LEECH** [ ] [-]
(12"+=) *(12ANA 13)* – Leave me alone / Liddle Towers.
Dec 83. (lp) *(GRAM 04)* **REASON WHY?** [ ] [-]
– Woman in disguise / Never give up / Waiting, hating / Reason why? / Nobody was saved / Geordie's wife / Loneliness of the long distance runner / 42nd Street / The burglar / Solidarity / As the passion / A young punk / Where we started. *(cd-iss. Nov92; CDGRAM 04) (cd re-iss. Jan97 on 'Summit'; SUMCD 4086) (cd re-iss. Mar01 on 'Anagram'; CDPUNK 17)*

Picasso not iss.

Oct 84. (7") *(PIK 001)* **MACHINE GUN KELLY. / PAINT IT IN RED** [ ] [-]
(12"+=) *(PIKT 001)* – There's a drink in it.
Aug 85. (lp) *(PIK 004)* **LAST TANGO IN MOSCOW (live)** [ ] [-]
– One more day / Machine gun Kelly / Progress / Blackleg miner / Who's got the money / Last tango in Moscow / I think it should be free / Never return / Rude boy / No news / Jarrow woman / Nowhere to run / Paint it in red. *(re-iss. Feb88 on 'Razor'; RAZ 004) (cd-iss. Nov93 on 'Great Expectations'; PIPCD 047) (cd re-iss. May98 on 'Captain Oi'+=; AHOYCD 087)* – There's a drink in it / Listen to the silence / She don't cry anymore / I won't pray for liberty / Never return to Hell / When will they learn / No nukes.
Sep 85. (lp) *(HCLP 002M)* **LIVE IN YUGOSLAVIA (live)** [ ] [-]

– Never ad nothing / Leave me alone / Teenage warning / Solidarity / Last night another soldier / Guns for the Afghan rebels / Machine gun Kelly / Police oppression / Kids on the street / Women in disguise / 2,000,000 voices / One more day / Upstart / Who killed Liddle Towers / White riot. *(re-iss. Feb88 on 'Razor'; RAZM 32) (cd-iss. Aug93 on 'Great Expectations'; PIPCD 048) (cd re-iss. Oct95 on 'Punx'; PUNXCD 2)*

Gas / Chameleon

Jun 85. (7") *(GM 1010)* **BRIGHTON BOMB. / SOLDIER** [ ] [-]
(12"+=) *(GM 3010)* – Thin red line.

Jan 86. (m-lp) *(GAS 4012)* **THE POWER OF THE PRESS** [ ] [-]
– I stand accused / Nottingham slag / Joe where are you now? / Empty street / Soldier / Brighton bomb / The power of the press / Stab in the back / Here I come / Thin red line / I'd kill her for six pence / Green fields of France. *(re-iss. Jun90 on 'Streetlink'; CLINK 006) (<cd-iss. Nov00 on 'Step 1'; STEPCD 039>)*

1987. (c) *<CHC 8603>* **BRIGHTON BOMB** [-] [ ]

— disbanded 1986 and little or nothing heard of until 1992

Roadrunner / not iss.

May 92. (cd/lp) **BOMBED OUT** [ ] [-]
– Red till dead / Albert's gotta gun / Victim of deceit / Open your eyes / Still fighting / The writing on the wall / A real rain / Let's build a bomb / Proud and loud / Stone faced killer. *(re-iss. Aug94 on 'Dojo'; DOJOCD 198)*

– compilations, others, etc. –

Apr 81. (c-s) *Warners; (SPZ 2)* **I'M AN UPSTART / NEVER 'AD NOTHING** [ ] [-]

Sep 83. (lp/c) *Anagram; (GRAM/CGRAM 07)* **ANGEL DUST (THE COLLECTED HIGHS)** [ ] [-]
– The murder of Liddel Towers / Police oppression / I'm an upstart / Teenage warning / Never 'ad nothing / Shotgun solution / England / Last night another soldier / 2,000,000 voices / Kids on the street / Never say die / Heath's lament / I understand / Woman's disguise / Solidarity. *(cd-iss. Oct88; CDMGRAM 7)* – REASON WHY. *(<cd re-iss. Sep93 & Oct99; same>)*

Mar 86. (lp) *Dojo; (DOJOLP 7)* **BOOTLEGS AND RARITIES** [ ] [-]
(cd-iss. Nov93 on 'Great Expectations'; PIPCD 049)

Dec 87. (lp) *Link; (LINKLP 019)* **BLOOD ON THE TERRACES** [ ] [-]
(<cd-iss. Jun99 on 'Harry May'; AHOYCD 116>)

Jul 88. (12"ep) *Skunx; (MENSIX 1)* **ENGLAND'S ALIVE (live)** [ ] [-]
– England / We're gonna take the world / Liddle Towers / The young ones.

Jan 92. (cd) *Streetlink; (AOK 102)* **ALTERNATIVE CHARTBUSTERS** [ ] [-]

Jul 92. (cd) *Streetlink; (STRCD 027)* **GREATEST HITS LIVE (live)** [ ] [-]
(re-iss. Mar93 on 'Dojo'; DOJOCD 127)

Aug 92. (cd) *Soundtrack Music; (SLOGCD 1)* **BLOOD ON THE TERRACES / LOST AND FOUND** [ ] [-]
(re-iss. Feb94 on 'Loma'; LOMACD 11)

Jun 95. (cd) *Anagram; (<CDPUNK 59>)* **THE INDEPENDENT PUNK SINGLES COLLECTION** [ ] [ ] 1999

Dec 97. (cd) *Captain Oi; (<AHOYCD 80>)* **RARITIES** [ ] [ ] Oct00

Jun 99. (cd) *Harry May; (<MAYOCD 116>)* **NEVER 'AD NOTHING** [ ] [ ] Apr00

Sep 99. (cd) *Captain Oi; (<AHOYCD 121>)* **THE E.M.I. PUNK YEARS** [ ] [ ] Jan00

May 00. (cd) *Captain Oi; (<AHOYCD 138>)* **THE BBC PUNK SESSIONS** [ ] [ ]

Nov 00. (cd) *Harry May; (MAYOCD 505)* **LOST AND FOUND** [ ] [-]

ANGELS

Formed: Adelaide, Australia ... 1975 by brothers JOHN and RICK BREWSTER, plus manic frontman DOC NEESON, who had been part of The KEYSTONE ANGELS. Under the wing of producers HARRY VANDA and GEORGE YOUNG (ex-EASYBEATS), their eponymous debut album was issued in 1977, the first in a series of massive selling domestic releases. A follow-up, 'NO EXIT' (1979), prompted 'Epic' records to take control, although they insisted the band change their Stateside moniker to ANGEL CITY (similar US group, ANGEL were still flying high). Concentrating on America, they had three albums ('FACE TO FACE', 'DARKROOM' and 'NIGHT ATTACK') that hit the lower regions of the Top 200, moving on to 'MCA' (US) and 'Mushroom' (Australia) for the 'TWO MINUTE WARNING' set in '84. Through sheer hard graft and mid-late 80's associations with The CULT and GUNS N' ROSES, the group eventually won back their Australian fanbase. They were well rewarded in 1990, when their umpteenth album, 'BEYOND SALVATION' hit the top slot in Australia. They had earlier been paid tribute by GREAT WHITE, who covered their 'FACE THE DAY'.

Album rating: THE ANGELS (*5) / FACE TO FACE (*6) / NO EXIT (*5) / DARKROOM (*5) / NIGHT ATTACK (*3) / WATCH THE RED (*4) / TWO MINUTE WARNING (*5) / HOWLING (*5) / LIVELINE (*4) / BEYOND SALVATION (*6) / RED BACK FEVER (*5) / SKIN & BONE (*5)

DOC NEESON – vocals / **JOHN BREWSTER** – guitar, vocals / **RICK BREWSTER** – guitar / **CHRIS BAILEY** – bass, vocals / **BUZZ THROCKMAN** – drums

Albert / not iss.

1977. (lp) *(APLP 025)* **THE ANGELS** [-] [-] Austra
– Take me home / You're a lady now / Goin' down / Shelter from the rain / Can't get lucky / Am I ever gonna see your face again / You got me runnin' / High on you / Hot Lucy / Dreambuilder.

— **GRAHAM BIDSTRUP** – drums; repl. BUZZ

1978. (lp) *(APLP 031)* **FACE TO FACE** [-] [-] Austra
– Straightjacket / After the rain / Love takes care / Take a long line / Marseilles / Live it up / Be with you / Outcast / I ain't the one / Comin' down. *(UK cd-iss. Mar00 on 'Axe Killer'; AXE 305587CD)*

1979. (m-lp) *(AS 37)* **OUT OF THE BLUE** [-] [-] Austra
– Out of the blue / Mr. Damage / Save me / Am I ver gonna see your face again.

1979. (lp) *(APLP 038)* **NO EXIT** [-] [-] Austra
– Waiting for the world / After dark / Save me / Shadow boxer / No exit / Can't shake it / Out of the blue / Dawn is breaking / Mr. Damage / Ivory stairs. *(UK cd-iss. May00 on 'Axe Killer'; AXE 305588CD)*

— now called **ANGEL CITY** (UK + US)

Epic / Epic

Mar 80. (lp) *(84253) <36344>* **FACE TO FACE** (compilation 76-80) [ ] [ ]
– Take a long line / Marseilles / After the rain / Am I ever gonna see your face again / Shadow boxer / Comin' down / Out of the blue / Can't shake it / Waiting for the world / No exit.

Apr 80. (7") *<50881>* **MARSEILLES. / WAITING FOR THE WORLD** [-] [ ]

Oct 80. (lp) *(451066) <36543>* **DARKROOM** [-] [ ]
– No secrets / Poor baby / Wasted sleepless nights – Dark room / Face the day / Night comes early / Alexander / The moment / I'm scared / Devil's gate. *(UK cd-iss. Jun98 on 'Angels'; ANGELS 123)*

Nov 80. (7") *<50927>* **NO SECRETS. / WASTED SLEEPLESS NIGHTS – DARK ROOM** [-] [ ]

— **BRENT ECCLES** – drums; repl. GRAHAM

1981. (m-lp) *(EX 12016)* **NEVER SO LIVE (live)** [-] [-] Austra
– Fashion and fame / Talk about you / Bad dream / Angel.

— **JIM HILBUN** – bass, keyboards, sax; repl. BAILEY

Mar 82. (lp) *(85480) <37702>* **NIGHT ATTACK** [ ] [ ]
– Long night / Living on the outside / Back on you / Fashion and fame / Night attack / City out of control / Talk about you / Running wild / Nothin' to win / Storm to Bastille.

1983. (lp) *(ELPS 4364)* **WATCH THE RED** [-] [-] Austra
– Live lady live / Eat city / Shoot it up / Easy prey / Bow wow / No sleep in hell / Watch the red / The zoo – Name dropping / Stand up / Is that you / Stay away. *(UK cd-iss. Jun98 on 'Angels'; ANGELS 345)*

Mushroom / M.C.A.

1984. (lp/cd) *(D/CD 53154)* **TWO MINUTE WARNING** [-] [ ]
– Small price / Look the other way / Underground / Front page news / Gonna leave you / Between the eyes / Babylon / Sticky little bitch / Razor's edge / Run for the shelter.

1985. (7") *<52559>* **UNDERGROUND. / BE WITH YOU** [-] [ ]

— **BOB SPENCER** – guitar; repl. JOHN who later joined BOMBERS (they included ex-STATUS QUO bassist, ALAN LANCASTER)

1986. (lp/cd) *(D/CD 53226)* **HOWLING** [-] [ ]
– Did you hurry somebody / When the time comes / Don't waste my time / Can't take anymore / Where do you run / Man there / Hide your face / We gotta get out of this place / Standing over / Stonewall / All night for you / Nature of the beast.

1987. (d-cd) *(CD 5900 1-2)* **LIVELINE (live)** [-] [ ]
– Comin' down / No secrets / Did you hurt somebody / Standing over you / Shadow boxer / After the rain / Small price / Fashion and fame / Love takes care / Be with you / Run for the shelter / Save me / Underground / Am I ever gonna see your face again / Stand up / Don't waste my time / Face the day / Back on you / City out of control / Eat city / Small talk / Take a long line / Mr. Damage / Marseilles.

— **JAMES MORLEY** – bass; repl. HILBUN

Chrysalis / Chrysalis

Mar 90. (cd/c/lp) *(<CCD/ZCHR/CHR 1677>)* **BEYOND SALVATION** [ ] [ ]
– Dogs are talking / Rhythm rude girl / Let the night roll on / City out of control / Junk city / Am I ever gonna see your face again / I ain't the one / Who rings the bell / Can't shake it.

Mushroom / not iss.

1992. (cd) **RED BACK FEVER** [-] [-] Austra

— **JOHN BREWSTER + HILBUN** returned to repl. SPENCER + MORLEY

— split after success in the States eluded them . . . re-formed below

Central / not iss.

Jun 98. (cd-s) **CALL THAT LIVIN'** [-] [-] Austra

Nov 98. (cd-s) *(113047)* **MY LIGHT WILL SHINE** [-] [-] Austra

Nov 98. (cd) *(114130)* **SKIN & BONE** [-] [-] Austra
– Northwest highway / Skin & bone / Caught in the night / With or without you / Invisible man / Wasteland / What the hell is going on / The world stops turning / My light will shine / Soul surgeon / Call that livin' / Movin' on.

– compilations, etc. –

Dec 88. (lp) *Telegram; <ACE 001>* **LIVE FROM ANGEL CITY** [-] [ ]

Apr 99. (cd) *;* **LIVELINE** [-] [-] Austra

ANGEL WITCH

Formed: South East, England ... 1979 by main songwriter KEVIN HEYBOURNE, KEVIN RIDDLES and DAVE DUFORT (brother of Girlschool's DENISE). Updating the occult imagery and death-knell riffing of BLACK SABBATH, the band were one of the earliest figureheads for the NWOBHM scene. After a one-off Top 75 single ('SWEET DANGER') for 'EMI' (also home to IRON MAIDEN), they inked a deal with 'Bronze', releasing their eponymous debut set around Xmas 1980. However, when RIDDLES and DUFORT were poached by TYTAN, HEYBOURNE decided to call it a day. With a new line-up, he returned in 1984, the 'SCREAMIN AND BLEEDIN' album appearing the following year. In 1986, they completed another, 'FRONTAL ASSAULT', neither sets cutting much ice with the critics. Recorded in LA, a live album was released at the turn of the decade, new members SPENCER HOLMAN and GRANT DENNIS failing to fill the shoes of RIDDLES and DUFORT.

Album rating: ANGEL WITCH (*7) / SCREAMIN' 'N' BLEEDIN' (*4) / FRONTAL ASSAULT (*4) / LIVE (*4) / SINISTER HISTORY collection (*4) / RESURRECTION compilation (*6)

KEVIN HEYBOURNE – guitar, vocals / **KEVIN RIDDLES** – bass, vocals / **DAVE DUFORT** – drums

E.M.I. / not iss.

May 80. (7") *(EMI 5064)* **SWEET DANGER. / FLIGHT NINETEEN** [75] [ ]
(12"+=) *(12EMI 5064)* – Hades Paradise.

Bronze / not iss.

Oct 80. (7") *(BRO 108)* **ANGEL WITCH. / GORGON** [ ] [-]

Dec 80. (lp/c) *(BRON/+C 532)* **ANGEL WITCH** -
– Angel witch / Atlantis / White witch / Confused / Sorcerers / Gorgon / Sweet danger / Free man / Angel of death / Devil's tower. *(re-iss. Sep86 as 'DOCTOR PHIBES'+=; RAWLP 025)* – Dr Phibes / Loser / Suffer. *(re-iss. May91 on 'Castle' cd/c/lp; CLA CD/MC/LP 239)* *(<cd re-iss. Aug98 on 'Essential'; ESMCD 598>)*

Jun 81. (7"m) *(BRO 121)* **LOSER / SUFFER. / DR PHIBES** -

— disbanded in 1981, when RIDDLES then DUFORT joined TYTAN

— Late in 1984, **HEYBOURNE** reformed them with **PETER GORDELIER** – bass (ex-BLIND FURY) / **DAVE HOGG** – percussion / **DAVE TATTUM** – vocals; who repl. LOU TAYLOR

Killerwatt J.C.I.

Jul 85. (7") *(KIL 3001)* **GOODBYE. / REAWAKENING** -

Jul 85. (lp) *(KILP 4001)* **SCREAMIN' 'N' BLEEDIN'** -
– Whose to blame / Child of the night / Evil games / Afraid of the dark / Screamin' 'n' bleedin' / Reawakening / Waltz the night / Goodbye / Fatal kiss / U.X.V.

— **SPENCER HOLMAN** – drums; repl. HOGG

May 86. (lp) *(KILP 4003)* <9014> **FRONTAL ASSAULT**
– Frontal assault / Dream world / Rendezvous with the blade / Religion (born again) / Straight from Hell / She don't lie / Take to the wing / Something wrong / Undergods. *(cd-iss. Dec88 as 'SCREAMIN' ASSAULT' with 1985 album; KILCD 1001)*

— **HEYBOURNE + GORDELIER** recruited **GRANT (TACO BELL) DENNIS** – rhythm guitar; repl. TATTUM

Metal Blade Enigma

May 90. (cd/c/lp) *(CD/T+/ZORRO 1)* <73443> **LIVE (live)**
– Angel of death / Sweet danger / Confused / Sorceress / Gorgon / Baphamet / Extermination day / Atlantis / Flight 19 / Angel witch / White witch.

— disbanded around the early 90's; they re-formed late 90's with **HEYBOURNE, RIDDLES + HOGG**

Nov 99. (cd) *(<ZCRCD 21>)* **SINISTER HISTORY** (some new live) Nov00
– Baphomet / Sorceress / Extermination day / Flight 19 / Hades paradise / Devil's tower / White witch / Into the dark / Devil's tower (live) / Night is calling (live) / Angel of death (live) / Confused (live) / Evil games (live).

Zoom Club Orchard

Sep 00. (cd) *(ZCRCD 34)* <5235> **RESURRECTION** Nov00
– Psychopathic / Time to die / Violence / Silent but deadly / Twist of the knife / Psychopathic II / Slowly sever / Worm / Scrape the well / Inertia.

Zoom Club Windsor

May 01. (cd) <47> **2000: LIVE AT THE LA2 (live)**
– Atlantis / Confused / Twist of the knife / Gorgon / White witch / Sorceress / Extermination day / Psychopathic / Baphomet / Angel of death / Guitar solo / Angel Witch.

– compilations, etc. –

May 97. (cd) *Thunderbolt; (CDTB 173)* **'82 REVISITED – LIVE AT THE EAST ANGLIA ROCK FESTIVAL (live)** -

ANGRY SAMOANS

Formed: Van Nuys, Los Angeles, California, USA ... August '78 by 'METAL' MIKE (SAUNDERS), GREGG TURNER, TODD HOMER and BILL VOCKEROTH and P.J. GALLIGAN (the latter was replaced by STEVE DROJENSKY after their first lp). One of the prime movers in the emerging L.A. hardcore scene along with the likes of BLACK FLAG and the CIRCLE JERKS, The ANGRY SAMOANS' first release was an EP, 'INSIDE MY BRAIN'. Transmitted via 'Bad Trip' (the label that is!), their next offering upset radio DJ's & the US music press alike due to the EP's content (i.e. the pseudonym, The QUEER PILLS, the label, 'Homophobic' and the explicit song titles, 'TIME TO F***' and 'THEY SAVED HITLER'S C***'), although subsequent copies were rubber stamped with the ANGRY SAMOANS moniker. Their debut, 'BACK FROM SAMOA' (1982), arrived with a little less controversy, their comic-strip punk rock drawing comparisons to The DICKIES and The RAMONES. However, the 80's proved a fairly barren time on the recording front, their short spell with 'Triple X' resulting in their swansong album, 'LIVE AT RHINO RECORDS' (1990). Well it would have been but for a 1999 comeback set, 'THE 90'S SUCK AND SO DO YOU'. • **Covered:** LAUGHING AT ME (Alice Cooper) / TIME HAS COME TODAY (Chambers Brothers) / SOMEBODY TO LOVE (Jefferson Airplane).

Album rating: BACK FROM SAMOA (*6) / STP NOT LSD (*3) / GIMME SAMOA: 31 GARBAGE-PIT HITS compilation (*6) / LIVE AT RHINO RECORDS (*3) / RETURN TO SAMOA collection (*3) / THE UNBOXED SET compilation (*6) / THE 90'S SUCK AND SO DO YOU (*5)

'METAL' MIKE (SAUNDERS) – vocals, guitar / **GREGG TURNER** – guitar, vocals / **P.J. GALLIGAN** – lead guitar / **TODD HOMER** – bass / **BILL VOCKEROTH** – drums

not iss. Bad Trip

1981. (12"ep) <BT 201> **INSIDE MY BRAIN EP** -
– Right side of my mind / Gimme sopor / Hot cars / Inside my brain / You stupid asshole / Get off the air. *(cd-iss. Jul95 & Nov98 on 'Triple X'; TX 51033CD)* *(lp-iss.Feb99 on 'Cargo'; CGO 7117)*

not iss. Homophobic

Feb 82. (7"; as The QUEER PILLS) <HOMO 02> **STUPID JERK / TIME TO FUCK. / THE TODD KILLINGS / THEY SAVED HITLER'S COCK** -

not iss. P.V.C.

1982. (lp) <PVC 8958> **BACK FROM SAMOA** -
– Gas chamber / The Todd killings / Lights out / My old man's a fatso / Time has come today / They saved Hitler's cock / Homo-sexual / Steak knife / Haiz-man's brain is calling / Tuna taco / Coffin chase / You stupid jerk / Ballad of Jerry Curlan / Not of this earth. *<(cd-iss. Jul95 & Nov98 on 'Triple X'; TX 51034CD)> (lp re-iss. Feb99 on 'Cargo';* **CGO 7118)**

— **STEVE DROJENSKY** – guitar; repl. GALLIGAN

1987. (12"ep) **YESTERDAY STARTED TOMORROW** -
– Different world / Electrocution / It's raining today / Unhinged / Psych-out 129 / Somebody to love. *(cd-iss. Jul95 on 'Triple X'+=; TX 51035CD)* – GIMME SAMOA: 31 GARBAGE PIT HITS (compilation)

1988. (lp/c/cd) *<PVC/+C/D 8965>* **STP NOT LSD** -
– I lost (my mind) / Wild hog rhyde / Laughing at me / STP not LSD / Staring at the sun / Death of Beewak / Egyptomania / Attack of the mushroom people / Feet on the ground / Garbage pit / (I'll drink to this) Love song / Lost highway. *(cd-iss. Jul95 on 'Triple X'; TX 51036CD)*

Triple X Triple X

Nov 90. (cd) *<TX 51037CD>* **LIVE AT RHINO RECORDS (live)** -
– Too animalistic / Right side of my mind / Commando / My old man's a fatso / Party games / Todd's not here / You stupid asshole / I'm a pig / I'm in love with your mom.

— split when 'METAL' MIKE went solo, releasing a mini-cd in 1991

— **MIKE + BILL** were joined by **TONY PALMER + ALISON VICTOR** – bass

Apr 99. (cd) *<(TX 51252CD)>* **THE 90'S SUCK AND SO DO YOU** Feb99
– I'd rather do the dog / Letter from Uncle Sam / Suzy's a loser / In and out of luv / Master M.D. / My baby's gone gone gone / Beat your heart out / Don't change my head.

– compilations, etc. –

1987. (lp) *P.V.C.;* **31 GARBAGE PIT HITS** (live & unreleased) -

1990. (lp) *Shakin' Street;* **RETURN TO SAMOA** -
(UK-iss.Jun97 on 'Vermiform'; YUPPY 008CD)

Jul 95. (cd) *Triple X; <(TX 51190CD)>* **THE UNBOXED SET** Jun95
– (INSIDE MY BRAIN / BACK FROM SAMOA / YESTERDAY STARTED TOMORROW / STP NOT LSD)

ANNIE CHRISTIAN

Formed: Leith, Edinburgh, Scotland ... Spring '97 by main songwriter, LARRY LEAN, CHRIS ADAMS, DAVID HUNTER and ANDREW HASTINGS (another member does the floating job!), all possessing a penchant for PRINCE and the late political comedian, BILL HICKS. Managed by Bruce Findlay (Radio DJ, famous for overseeing SIMPLE MINDS' rise to fame), the quartet delivered their debut, 'LOVE THIS LIFE', early the following year. They fitted neatly into the MANICS / STEREOPHONICS brand of rifferama rock, their gothic lyrics overpowering enough to set them apart. • **Covered:** TRANSMISSION (Joy Division).

Album rating: TWILIGHT (*6)

LARRY LEAN – vocals, guitar / **CHRIS ADAMS** – guitar / **DAVID HUNTER** – bass / **ANDREW HASTINGS** – drums

Equipe Ecosse – V2 Orchard

Mar 98. (7") *(EQE 500139-7)* **LOVE THIS LIFE. / THE SHATTERED BURLESQUE** -
(cd-s+=) *(EQE 500139-3)* – Satellites spin.

May 98. (7") *(EQE 500190-7)* **SOMEDAY MY PRINCE WILL COME AGAIN. / WHILE YOU SLEEP** -
(cd-s+=) *(EQE 500190-3)* – This world has no time for lovers.

Sep 98. (7") *(EQE 500253-7)* **THE OTHER WAY. / TRANSMISSION** -
(cd-s+=) *(EQE 500253-3)* – Drugs work.

Feb 99. (7") *(EQE 500516-7)* **KISS THE DAY GOODBYE. / GET IT ON** -
(cd-s+=) *(EQE 500516-3)* – 500 miles low.

Mar 99. (cd/lp) *(EQE 100214-2/-1)* <6435> **TWILIGHT** <US title 'SOFTCORE'> Jul00
– Love this life / Kiss the day goodbye / The other way / Secret and lies / Here is the news / Clearwater goldmine / Nothing is real / Ode to an Indian summer / The boy with the golden arm / Hicks (1961-1994) / Someday my prince will come again / Stupid thoughts / Twilight. *(CD-ROM tracks+=)* – The other way (video) / Kiss the day goodbye (video). *(cd re-iss. Dec00 as 'SOFTCORE' on 'Filthy Mouth'; FM 1)*

V2 not iss.

Apr 99. (7") *(VVR 500674-7)* **LOVE THIS LIFE. / THE BOY WITH THE GOLDEN ARM (live)** -
(cd-s+=) *(VVR 500674-3)* – Clearwater goldmine (live).

ANNIHILATOR

Formed: Ottawa, Canada ... 1985 by classically-trained songwriter, JEFF WATERS, who relocated to Vancouver. The line-up was completed by RANDY RAMPAGE (drinker extroadinaire), ANTHONY GREENHAM, WAYNE DARLEY and RAY HARTMANN, who recorded the demo 'PHANTASMAGORIA'. This paved the way for the widely acclaimed album, 'ALICE IN HELL' (1989), one of the most accomplished thrash debuts ever released. A highlight was the rivetting title track, perfectly showcasing WATERS' highly inventive and complex guitar style. Following a succesful European tour to promote the album, they returned to Canada minus sacked frontman, RAMPAGE, who was subsequently replaced by COBURN PHARR. A second effort, 'NEVER, NEVERLAND' (again on 'Roadrunner'), followed contemporaries like MEGADETH, METALLICA, etc. into the UK charts, although the band again experienced personnel difficulties. Three years in the making (AARON RANDALL and NEIL GOLDBERG replacing PHARR and DAVIS respectively), the 1993 opus, 'SET THE WORLD ON FIRE' saw the band widen their musical horizons beyond thrash. Now signed to 'Music For Nations', WATERS (now on vox), with a completely rejigged line-up, delivered a further couple of albums, 'KING OF THE HILL' (1994) and 'REFRESH THE DEMON' (1996). 'REMAINS' followed in 1997 yet it wasn't until 1999's comeback set 'CRITERIA FOR A BLACK WIDOW' that WATERS managed to achieve a deal for the lucrative US market. The latter album saw a reunion of sorts with both RAMPAGE and HARTMANN back in the fold, the band cranking out an unashamed blast of trad thrash that flew in the face of modern nu-metal trends. Predictably perhaps, RAMPAGE was out on his ear again for 'CARNIVAL DIABLOS' (2001), his replacement being ex-OVERKILL man JOE COMEAU on a record that found WATERS exploring his favourite metal styles from the root base of thrash.

Album rating: ALICE IN HELL (*7) / NEVER, NEVERLAND (*7) / SET THE WORLD ON FIRE (*5) / BAG OF TRICKS compilation (*5) / KING OF THE KILL (*6) / REFRESH THE DEMON (*6) / IN COMMAND live compilation (*5) / REMAINS (*4) / CRITERIA FOR A BLACK WIDOW (*6) / CARNIVAL DIABLOS (*5)

RANDY RAMPAGE – vocals (ex-D.O.A.) / **JEFF WATERS** – guitar / **ANTHONY GREENHAM** – guitar / **WAYNE DARLEY** – bass / **RAY HARTMANN** – drums

Roadrunner Roadrunner

Apr 89. (lp/cd) *(RR 9488-1/-2)* **ALICE IN HELL** [ ] [-]
– Crystal Ann / Alison hell / W.T.Y.D. / Wicked mystic / Burns like a buzzsaw blade / Word salad / Schizos (are never alone) (parts 1 & 2) / Ligeia / Human insecticide. *(cd re-iss. Sep96; same) (cd re-mast.Jun98 & Jun00; RR 8723-2) <US cd-iss. 2001 on 'Roadrunner Int.'; 618723>*

— **DAVE SCOTT DAVIS** – guitar; repl. ANTHONY GREENHAM

— **COBURN PHARR** – vocals (ex-OMEN) repl. sacked RAMPAGE

Jul 90. (cd/c/lp) *(<RR 9374-2/-4/-1>)* **NEVER, NEVERLAND** [48] [ ] Sep90
– The fun palace / Road to ruin / Sixes and sevens / Stonewall / Never, neverland / Imperiled eyes / Kraf dinner / Phantasmagoria / Reduced to ash / I am in command. *(cd re-iss. Sep96; same) (cd re-mast.Jun98 & Jun00; RR 8722-2)*

Feb 91. (12"ep/c-ep/cd-ep) *(RR 2425-6/-4/-3)* **STONEWALL. / W.T.Y.D. (live) / WORD SALAD (live)** [ ] [-]

— DAVIS departed and was repl. by **NEIL GOLDBERG** – guitar

— **AARON RANDALL** – vocals; repl. COBURN

— **MIKE MANGINI** – drums; repl. HARTMAN

Roadrunner Epic

May 93. (12"/cd-s) *(RR 2385-6/-3)* **SET THE WORLD ON FIRE. / HELL BENT FOR LEATHER** [ ] [-]

May 93. (cd/c/lp) *(RR 9200-2/-4/-1) <EK 53790>* **SET THE WORLD ON FIRE** [ ] [ ]
– Set the world on fire / No zone / Bats in the belfry / Snake in the grass / Phoenix rising / Knight jumps Queen / Sounds good to me / The edge / Don't bother me / Brain dance. *(cd re-iss. Mar96; same)*

— **WATERS** (now on vocals) with new members, **RANDY BLACK** – drums / **CAM DIXON** – bass / and the returning **DAVE SCOTT DAVIS**

Music For Nations Hypnotic

Oct 94. (cd/c) *(CD/T MFN 171)* **KING OF THE KILL** [ ] [ ] 1995
– The box / King of the kill / Hell is a war / Bliss / Second to none / Annihilator / 21 / In the blood / Fiasco ("the slate") / Fiasco / Catch the wind / Speed / Bad child. *<US cd re-iss. 2000 on 'C.M.C.'; 86287>*

— basically **WATERS** with **BLACK** + backing vocalists **DAVE STEELES + LARS**

Mar 96. (cd/c) *(CD/T MFN 197)* **REFRESH THE DEMON** [ ] [-]
– Refresh the demon / Syn. kill 1 / Awaken / The pastor of disaster / A man called nothing / Ultraparanoia / City of ice / Anything for money / Hunger / Voices and victims / Innocent eyes. *<US cd-iss. 2000 on 'C.M.C.'; 86288>*

— **WATERS** – vocals, all instruments; plus guests **JOHN BATES** – guitar / **DAVE STEELES** – backing vocals

Jul 97. (cd) *(CDMFN 228)* **REMAINS** [ ] [-]
– Murder / Sexecution / No love / Never / Human remains / Dead wrong / Wind / Tricks and traps / I want / Reaction / Bastiage. *<US-iss.2000 on 'C.M.C.'; 86289>* – It's you / (words from Jeff Waters).

— **RANDY RAMPAGE** – vocals (returned) to join **WATERS** plus **HARTMAN + DAVIS** + new bassist **RUSSELL BERQUIST**

Roadrunner C.M.C.

May 99. (cd) *(RR 8640-2) <86284>* **CRITERIA FOR A BLACK WIDOW** [ ] [ ] Jan00
– Bloodbath / Back to the palace / Punctured / Criteria for a black widow / Schizos (are never alone) / Nothing left / Loving the sinner / Double dare / Sonic homocide / Mending. *(re-iss. Feb91; same)*

— **JOE COMEAU** – bass (ex-OVERKILL) repl. RAMPAGE

S.P.V. C.M.C.

Feb 01. (cd) *(SPV 857214-2) <85203>* **CARNIVAL DIABLOS** [ ] [ ]
– Denied / The perfect virus / Battered / Carnival diablos / Shallow grave / Time bomb / The rush / Insomniac / Liquid oval / Epic war / Hunter killer.

– compilations, etc. –

Jul 94. (cd/c) *Roadrunner; (RR 8997-2/-4)* **BAG OF TRICKS** [ ] [-]
– Alison hell / Phantasmagoria / Back to the crypt / Gallery / Human insecticide / Fun palace / W.T.Y.D. / Word salad / Live wire / Knight jumps queen / Fantastic things / Bats in the belfry / Evil appetite / Gallery '86 / Alison hell '86 / Phantasmagoria '86. *(cd re-iss. Sep96; same)*

Nov 96. (cd) *Roadrunner; (RR 8852-2)* **IN COMMAND LIVE 1989-1990 (live)** [ ] [ ]

ANtESTOR

Formed: Norway . . . 1990 by the self-proclaimed MARTYR (on vocals), VEMOD, GARD and ARMOTH making up the ever-evolving thrash-metal line-up that finally got on LP/record in 1998. 'THE RETURN OF THE BLACK DEATH' showed them interweaving their past allegiences into a new type of gothic melancholy metal that also harked back to the myths and legends of their northern ancestors – what, a black-metal band and no occult!

Album rating: THE RETURN OF THE BLACK DEATH (*6)

MARTYR – vocals / **VEMOD** – guitar, keyboards / **GARD** – bass / **ARMOTH** – drums

Cacophonous Cacophonous

Sep 98. (cd) *(<NIHIL 030CD>)* **THE RETURN OF THE BLACK DEATH** [ ] [ ] Feb00
– Vinterferden / A sovereign fortress / Svartedauens gjenkomst / Sorg / The bridge of death / Gamlelandt / Kilden-lik en endelos elv / Kongsblod / Battlefield / Ancient prophecy / Ildnatten.

ANTHEM

Formed: Japan . . . 1981 by unknown musicians, the line-up evolving into a more stabilized formation of ELIZO SAKAMOTO, HIROYA FUKADA, NAOTO SHIBATA and TAHAMASA OHUCHI on their eponymous 1985 debut. Like many Japanes metal bands, ANTHEM suffered from a lack of originality, taking all their cues from the Western hard-rock scene (i.e. THIN LIZZY and UFO). After a handful of derivative albums, they signed to 'Music For Nations', although only for a brief spell in 1990.

Album rating: ANTHEM (*5) / TIGHTROPE (*5) / BOUND TO BREAK (*5) / THE SHOE CARRIES ON (*5) / GYPSY WAYS (*4) / NO SMOKE WITHOUT FIRE (*4) / HUNTING TIME (*4)

ELIZO SAKAMOTO – vocals / **HIROYA FUKADA** – guitar / **NUOTO SKI BATA** – bass / **TAHAMASA OHUCHI** – drums

Roadrunner Enigma

1985. (lp) *(RR 9729) <72105>* **ANTHEM** [ ] [ ]
– Wild anthem / Red light fever / Lay down / Racin' rock / Warning action! / Turn back to the night / Rock 'n roll stars / Blind city / Star formation / Steeler.

Black Dragon not iss.

1986. (lp) *(BD 019) <72175>* **TIGHTROPE** [-] [ ] French
– Victim in your eyes / Night after night / Death to death / Tightrope dancer / Driving wire / Finger's on the trigger / Light it up / Black eyed tough.

not iss. Medusa

1987. (lp) *<72202-1>* **BOUND TO BREAK** [-] [ ]
– Bound to break / Empty eyes / The show must go on! / Rock'n'roll survivor / Soldiers / Limited lights / Machine made dog / No more night / Headstrong / Fire 'n' the sword.

not iss. Nexus

1987. (cd) *<K 3242100>* **THE SHOE CARRIES ON (live)** [-] [ ]
– Limited lights / Machine made dog / Empty eyes / The show must go on! / Soldiers / Black eyed tough / Bound to break / Lay down / Steeler / Wild anthem / Headstrong.

— **YUKIO MORIKAWA** – vocals; repl. SAKAMOTO

1988. (cd) *<K32Y 2130>* **GYPSY WAYS** [-] [ ]
– Gypsy ways (win, lose or draw) / Love in vain / Bad habits die hard / Legal killing / Cryin' heart / Silent child / Midnight sun / Shoiut it out! / Final risk / Night stalker. *(UK-iss.Aug90 on 'Music For Nations' cd/lp; CD+/MFN 103)*

Aug 90. (cd/c/lp) *(CD/T+/MFN 101)* **NO SMOKE WITHOUT FIRE** [ ] [ ]
– Shadow walk / Blinded pain / Love on the edge / Power and blood / Night we stand / Hungry soul / Do you understand / Voice of thunderstorm / Fever eyes.

Aug 90. (cd/lp) *(CD+/MFN 104)* **HUNTING TIME** [ ] [ ]
– Juggler / Evil touch / Sleepless night / Let your heart beat / Hunting time / Tears for the lovers / Jailbreak / Bottle bottom.

— split after above

ANTHRAX

Formed: Queens, New York, USA . . . mid'81, by NEIL TURBIN and DAN LILKER. SCOTT 'NOT' IAN, CHARLIE BENANTE and the diminutive DAN SPITZ completed the line-up, the band consequently spotted and signed to the 'Megaforce' label (licensed to 'Music For Nations' in Europe) by the legendary JOHNNY Z. The 1984 debut, 'FISTFUL OF METAL' (if you think the title's cheesy, wait till you see the cover!) hardly set the rock world alight, although 'METAL THRASHING MAD' was good for a laugh and the ALICE COOPER cover, 'I'M EIGHTEEN' was passable. By the release of the mini album, 'ARMED AND DANGEROUS', the following year, the more traditional metal tonsils of JOEY BELLADONNA were employed, a canny move that lent the band a modicum of style and sophistication. This was evident on ANTHRAX's first outing for 'Island', 'SPREADING THE DISEASE', a classy thrash metal affair that frequently rose above the narrow confines of the genre. By turns humorous, impassioned, and bloody loud, the likes of 'MADHOUSE' (a must-see video), 'AFTERSHOCK', 'ARMED AND DANGEROUS' and 'MEDUSA' made this one of the key metal releases of the 80's. 'AMONG THE LIVING' (1987) was almost as good and for many aging metallers, 'I AM THE LAW' is the definitive ANTHRAX track, a tribute to the meanest cop in Mega City One, Judge Dredd. 'INDIANS', meanwhile, was a more serious affair, dealing with the plight of their Native American brethren. Yet accomplished as the music was, it was almost overshadowed by the band's image. A case of bullet belts (!) out, skateboards and surf shorts in; for a brief, heady time in the late 80's, ANTHRAX almost made metal (whisper it now) trendy. Proving there was always a hip-hop element to their hardcore, the band released 'I'M THE MAN', a rap/metal pastiche that quite probably pissed off SAXON fans everywhere. At this point, the band were up there with METALLICA as the great white hopes of thrash and fans waited with baited breath for their next album, 'STATE OF EUPHORIA' (1988). Inevitably, perhaps, the record was a letdown; on first listen it sounded dense, promising, on repeated listening it became obvious the songs just weren't there. Equally inevitably, the band's dayglo image prompted a backlash. They retaliated with a considerably darker, more introspective opus, 'PERSISTENCE OF TIME' (1990). While the JOE JACKSON cover, 'GOT THE TIME', was engaging, the songwriting still wasn't up to scratch. A 1991 collaboration with CHUCK D on a storming cover of PUBLIC ENEMY's 'BRING THE NOISE' was the band's most effective effort for years and showed what they were obviously still capable of. The single was included on 'ATTACK OF THE KILLER B's', a compilation of B-sides and rare tracks, while ANTHRAX went on to tour with PUBLIC ENEMY on a genre busting double bill. Signing a new contract with 'Elektra', the band promptly ditched BELLADONNA in favour of ex-ARMOURED SAINT man, JOHN BUSH. These were tough times for ANTHRAX, as every metal band on the planet purchased a distortion pedal, grew a goatee, and insisted they weren't actually metal after all, no, they were GRUNGE!! (of course). All credit to ANTHRAX then, for sticking to their metal guns and releasing 'THE SOUND OF WHITE NOISE' (1993), a barrage of furious riffing that almost topped the work of their mid-80's golden period. 'STOMP 442' (1995) was equally ferocious, and while ANTHRAX mightn't sell as many records as they used to, they remain one of metal's best loved bands. The ever productive IAN had also turned his hand to side project STORMTROOPERS OF DEATH aka S.O.D. back in the mid-80's. A collaboration with BENANTE, LILKER and ANTHRAX roadie BILLY MILANO, the project came to life with the release of 1985's legendary 'SPEAK ENGLISH OR DIE'. Regarded as one of the pivotal records in the cross-fertilisation of punk/hardcore and thrash metal, the album was a riot of 2-minute-wonder noise, fury and irreverent humour which brought charges (not altogether unjustified) of sexism and racism. Incredibly, sales of this cult record eventually topped one million and prompted 'Megaforce' to release a millennial remastered edition complete with new studio tracks and live material. While it was originally intended as a one-off affair – MILANO going off to form M.O.D. – the group reformed in 1992 for the ironically titled 'LIVE AT BUDOKAN' (actually recorded live in New York). From the hilarious IRON MAIDEN pastiche of the cover art to MILANO's crowd baiting, the record was a treat for fans of the original album from which much of the material was used (alongside a few choice covers). Finally, the cult of S.O.D. demanded a follow-up studio album and in 1999, possibly the most belated sophomore effort in recorded history hit the shelves. 'BIGGER THAN THE DEVIL' carried on where their debut had left off all those years ago, showing the young pretenders how to really mosh and how to get a proper sense of humour. No target was too soft for MILANO's caustic gaze with both mealy-mouthed liberals and bigots coming under attack; they mightn't be bigger than the Devil but SOD probably have all the best jokes. • **Songwriters:** SCOTT IAN except; I'M EIGHTEEN (Alice Cooper) / SABBATH BLOODY SABBATH (Black Sabbath) / GOD SAVE THE QUEEN and FRIGGIN' IN THE RIGGIN' (Sex Pistols) / GOT THE TIME (Joe Jackson) / BRING THE NOISE (Public Enemy) / PROTEST AND SURVIVE (Discharge), LOOKING DOWN THE BARREL OF A GUN (Beastie Boys) / SHE (Kiss) / THE BENDS (Radiohead). • **Trivia:** DAN SPITZ's older brother DAVID played bass in the mid'80's with BLACK SABBATH. ANTHRAX an acting/ singing appearance on a 1992 showing of US TV sit-com 'Married With Children'. • **Note:** Not to be confused with UK "oi" band of the same name.

Album rating: FISTFUL OF METAL (*4) / SPREADING THE DISEASE (*8) / AMONG THE LIVING (*8) / STATE OF EUPHORIA (*5) / PERSISTENCE OF TIME (*7) / SOUND OF WHITE NOISE (*6) / STOMP 442 (*6) / S.O.D.: SPEAK ENGLISH OR DIE (*8) / LIVE FROM BUDOKAN (*7) / BIGGER THEN THE DEVIL (*7)

NEIL TURBIN – vocals / **DAN SPITZ** (b.28 Jan'63) – lead guitar / **SCOTT 'Not' IAN** (b.31 Dec'63) – rhythm guitar / **DAN LILKER** (b.18 Oct'64) – bass / **CHARLIE BENANTE** (b.27 Nov'62, The Bronx) – drums

Music For Nations | Megaforce

Nov 83. (7") **SOLDIERS OF DEATH. / HOWLING FURIES** [-] [ ]
Jan 84. (lp) *(MFN 14) <MRS 469>* **FISTFUL OF METAL** [ ] [ ]
– Deathrider / Metal thrashing mad / I'm eighteen / Panic / Subjagator / Death from above / Across the river / Anthrax. *(re-iss. Apr87 lp/pic-lp; MFN 14DM/P) (c+=/cd+=; CD/T MFN 14)* – Soldiers of metal / Howling furies. *<US-cd-iss. 1987 on 'Caroline'; CAROLCD 1383> (re-iss. cd Sep95 on 'Bulletproof'; CDMVEST 56)*
(Mid'84) **MATT FALLON** – vocals repl. TURBIN

— **FRANK BELLO** (b. 7 Sep'65) – bass (ex-roadie) repl. LILKER

— (Aug'84) **MATT** was replaced by **JOEY BELLADONNA** (b.30 Oct'60, Oswego, NY) – vocals (ex-BIBLE BLACK)

Feb 85. (m-lp/pic-m-lp) *<MRS 05/+P>* **ARMED AND DANGEROUS** [-] [ ]
– Armed and dangerous / Raise Hell / God save the Queen / Metal thrashing mad / Panic. *(UK-iss.Aug87 on 'Music For Nations' lp/c; MFN/CMFN 123) (cd-iss. Nov91; CDMFN 123) (cd re-iss. Sep95 on 'Bulletproof'; CDMVEST 55)*

Music For Nations | Megaforce-Island

Feb 86. (lp/c) *(MFN/TMFN 62) <90460>* **SPREADING THE DISEASE** [ ] [ ] Dec85
– A.I.R. / Lone justice / Madhouse / S.S.C – Stand or fall / The enemy / Aftershock / Armed and dangerous / Medusa / Gung ho. *(cd-iss. May86 on 'Island'; CID 9806) (pic-lp Sep87; MFNP 62) (re-iss. Aug91 on 'Island' cd)(c; IMCD 136)(ICM 9806)*

Island | Island

May 86. (12"/12"s/12"pic-d) *(12IS/+B/P 285)* **MADHOUSE. / A.I.R. / GOD SAVE THE QUEEN** [ ] [ ]
Feb 87. (7"pic-d)(12") *(LAWP 1)(12IS 316)* **I AM THE LAW. / BUD E. LUVBOMB AND SATAN'S LOUNGE BAND** [32] [ ]
('A'live-7"red+=) *(ISX 316)* – Madhouse (live).
Apr 87. (lp/pic-lp/c/cd) *(ILPS/PILPS/ICT/CID 9865) <90584>* **AMONG THE LIVING** [18] [62]
– Among the living / Caught in the mosh / I am the law / Efilnikufesin (N.F.L.) / A skeleton in the closet / One world / A.D.I.- horror of it all / Imitation of life. *(cd re-iss. Mar94; IMCD 186)*
Jun 87. (7"orange/7"pic-d) *(IS/+P 325)* **INDIANS. / SABBATH BLOODY SABBATH** [44] [ ]
(12"+=/12"pic-d+=) *(12IS/+P 325)* – Taint.
Nov 87. (7"/7"sha-pic-d) *(IS/+P 338)* **I'M THE MAN. / CAUGHT IN THE MOSH** [20] [-]
(12"+=) *(12IS 338)* – I am the law (live).
Dec 87. (m-lp,c,cd) *<90685>* **I'M THE MAN** [-] [53]
– I'm the man (censored version) / I'm the man (Def uncensored version) / Sabbath bloody sabbath / I'm the man (live & extremely Def II uncensored version) / Caught in a mosh (live) / I am the law (live).
Sep 88. (7"yellow) *(IS 379)* **MAKE ME LAUGH. / ANTI SOCIAL (live)** [26] [ ]
(12"+=/cd-s+=) *(12IS/CIDP 379)* – Friggin' in the riggin'.
Sep 88. (lp/c/cd) *(ILPS/ICT/CID 9916) <91004>* **STATE OF EUPHORIA** [12] [30]
– Be all, end all / Out of sight, out of mind / Make me laugh / Anti-social / Who cares wins / Now it's dark / Schism / Misery loves company / 13 / (finale). *(re-iss. cd Apr94; IMCD 187)*
Mar 89. (7"/7"amber/7"blue/7"red) *(IS/+A/B/R 409)* **ANTI-SOCIAL. / PARASITE** [44] [ ]
(12"+=/12"amber+=/12"blue+=/12"red+=)(3"cd-s+=) *(12IS/+A/B/R 409)(CIDX 409)* – Le sects.

Island | Megaforce

Aug 90. (7") *(IS 470)* **IN MY WORLD. / KEEP IT IN THE FAMILY** [29] [ ]
(10"+=/12"+=/cd-s+=) *(10IS/12IS/CID 470)* – ('A'&'B'extended).
Aug 90. (cd/c/lp) *(CID/ICT/ILPS 9967) <846480>* **PERSISTENCE OF TIME** [13] [24]
– Time / Blood / Keep it in the family / In my world / Gridlock / Intro to reality / Belly of the beast / Got the time / H8 red / One man stands / Discharge. *(pic-lp.Jan91; ILPSP 9967) (re-iss. Apr94 cd)(c; IMCD 178)(ICM 9967)*
Nov 90. (c-s/10"/7") *(C/10+/CIS 476)* **GOT THE TIME. / WHO PUT THIS TOGETHER** [16] [ ]
(12"+=/cd-s+=) *(12IS/CID 476)* – I'm the man (live).
Jun 91. (c-s/7"; ANTHRAX featuring CHUCK D) *(C+/IS 490)* **BRING THE NOISE. / I AM THE LAW '91** [14] [ ]
(10"+=/12"+=/cd-s+=)(10"pic-d+=/12"pic-d+=) *(10IS/12IS/CID 490)(10/12 ISP 490)* – Keep it in the family (live).

— CHUCK D. (of-PUBLIC ENEMY)

Jun 91. (cd/c/lp) *(CID/ICT/ILPS 9980) <848804>* **ATTACK OF THE KILLER B's** (rare studio) [13] [27]
– Milk (ode to Billy) / Bring the noise / Keep it in the family (live) / Startin' up a posse / Protest and survive / Chromatic death / I'm the man '91 / Parasite / Pipeline / Sects / Belly of the beast (live) / N.F.B. (dallabnikufesin). *(re-iss. Apr94 cd)(c; IMCD 179)(ICM 9980)*

— (May92) **JOHN BUSH** (b.24 Aug'63, L.A.) – vocals (ex-ARMOURED SAINT) repl. MARK OSEGUEDA who had replaced BELLADONNA

Elektra | Elektra

Apr 93. (7"/c-s) *(EKR 166/+C)* **ONLY. / ONLY (mix)** [36] [ ]
(cd-s+=) *(EKR 166CD1)* – Cowboy song / Sodium pentaghol.
(cd-s) *(EKR 166CD2)* – ('A'side) / Auf wiedersehen / Noisegate.
May 93. (cd/c/lp) *<(7559 61430-2/-4/-1)>* **SOUND OF WHITE NOISE** [14] [7]
– Potter's field / Only / Room for one more / Packaged rebellion / Hy pro glo / Invisible / 1000 points of hate / C11 H17 N2 O2 SNA / Burst / This is not an exit. *(cd+=)* – Black lodge. *(cd re-iss. Jap version Apr98 on 'Victor'; VICP 80320)*
Sep 93. (7"/c-s) *(EKR 171/+W)* **BLACK LODGE. / ('A'-Black strings mix)** [53] [ ]
(10"+=/12"pic-d+=/cd-s+=) *(EKR 171 TE/TP/CD)* – Pottersfield / Love her all I can.
Nov 93. (7"/c-s) *(EKR 178/+C)* **HY PRO GLO. / LONDON** [ ] [ ]
(12"+=/cd-s+=) *(EKR 178 T/CD)* – Room for one more (live).
Oct 95. (cd/c) *<(7559 61856-2/-4)>* **STOMP 442** [ ] [47]
– Fueled / Nothing / Bare / Random acts of senseless violence / Tester / Drop the ball / American Pompeii / In a zone / Perpetual motion / Riding shotgun / King size.
Jan 96. (c-s) *(EKR 216C)* **NOTHING / FUELLED (remix)** [ ] [ ]
(cd-s+=) *(EKR 216CD1)* – Remember tomorrow / Grunt and click.
(cd-s) *(EKR 216CD2)* – ('A'side) / Dethroned emperor / No time this time.

Ignition – Tommy Boy | Ignition – Tommy Boy

Jul 98. (cd/c) *<(IGN7 4034-3/-4)>* **VOLUME 8 – THE THREAT IS REAL!** [73] [ ]
– Crush / Catharsis / Inside out / Piss n vinegar / 604 / Toast to the extras / Born again idiot / Killing box / Harms way / Hog tied / Big fat / Cupajoe / Alpha male / Stealing from a thief.
Oct 98. (7") *(IGN 740516)* **INSIDE OUT. / GIVING THE HORNS** [ ] [-]
(cd-s+=) *(IGN 740513)* – The bends.

– compilations, others, etc. –

Nov 92. (d-cd) *Island; (ITSCD 6)* **AMONG THE LIVING / PERSISTENCE OF TIME** [ ] [-]
Apr 94. (cd/c/lp) *Island; (CID/ICT/ILPS 8027) <518920>* **ANTHRAX LIVE – THE ISLAND YEARS (live)** [ ] [ ]
Mar 98. (cd) *Connoisseur; (VSOPCD 252)* **MOSHERS 1986-1991** [ ] [-]
Feb 99. (d-cd) *S.P.V.; (SPV 0761818-2)* **FISTFUL OF METAL / ARMED AND DANGEROUS** [ ] [-]
Nov 99. (cd) *Beyond; <(63985 78067-2)>* **RETURN OF THE KILLER A's** [ ] [ ]
(re-iss. Jan00 on 'Spitfire'; SPITCD 057)

S.O.D.

(STORMTROOPERS OF DEATH) (off-shoot band of **SCOTT IAN + CHARLIE BENANTE** plus ex-ANTHRAX man **DAN LILKER** with **BILLY MILANO** – vocals (ex-PSYCHOS)

Roadrunner | Caroline

Dec 85. (lp) *(RR 9725) <CAROL 1384>* **SPEAK ENGLISH OR DIE** [ ] [ ]
– March of the S.O.D. / Sergeant "D" & the S.O.D. / Kill yourself / Milano mosh / Speak English or die / United forces / Chromatic death / Pi Alpha Nu / Anti-procrastination song / What's that noise / Freddy Krueger / Milk / Pre-menstrual princess blues / Pussy whipped / Fist banging mania / No turning back / Fuck the Middle East / Douche chew / Hey Gordy! / The ballad of Jimi Hendrix / Diamonds and rust / Go. *(re-iss. Oct89 c+=/cd+=; RR/+34 9725-4)* – Identity. *<US cd re-iss. 1995 on 'Megaforce'+=; 1955>* – Live:- March of the S.O.D. – Sergeant "D" / Kill yourself / Milano mosh / Speak English or die / Fuck the Middle East –

Douche crew / Not – Momo – Taint – The camel boy – Diamonds and rust / Milk / United forces / Untitled / Untitled. *(cd re-iss. Feb99 on 'S.P.V.'; PSV 0761839-2)*

Music For Nations — Megaforce

Sep 92. (cd/c/lp) *(CD/T+/MFN 144) <20286-6908-2>* **LIVE AT BUDOKAN (live)** [ ] [ ]
– March of the S.O.D. / Sergeant "D" and the S.O.D. / Kill yourself (an anti-suicide song) / Momo / Pi Alpha Nu / Milano mosh / Speak English or die / Chromatic death / Fist banging mania / The came boy / No turning back / Milk / Vitality / Fuck the Middle East / Douche crew / Get a real job / The ballad of Jimi Hendrix / Livin' in the city / Pussy whipped / Stigmata / Thieves / Freddy Krueger / Territorial pissings / United forces.

Nuclear Blast — Nuclear Blast

Jun 99. (cd; as S.O.D. – STORMTROOPERS OF DEATH) *(NB 383-2) <6383>* **BIGGER THAN THE DEVIL** [ ] [ ] May99
– Bigger than the Devil / The crackhead song / Kill the assholes / Monkey's rule / Skool bus / King at the king – Evil is in / Black war / Celtic frosted flakes / Charlie don't cheat / The song that don't go fast / Shenanigans / Dog on the tracks / Xerox / Make room, make room / Free dirty needles / Fugu / Noise, that's what / We all bleed red / Frankenstein and his horse / Every tiny molecule / Aren't you hungry / L.A.T.K.C.H. / Ballad of Michael H. / Ballad of Phil H. / Moment of truth.

– compilations, etc. –

Mar 98. (cd) *Connoisseur; (VSOPCD 252)* **MOSHERS 1986-1991** [ ] [-]

ANTI

Formed: Los Angeles, California, USA . . . early 80's by DANNY PHILLIPS, GARY KAIL (also of MOOD OF DEFIANCE), original vocalist BERT and JOHN McCARTHY. One of the L.A. hardcore scene's most intense acts, ANTI were basically anti-everything, or at least anything conventional (especially war), airing their angry views over a couple of 1982 EP's and a debut album, 'I DON'T WANT TO DIE IN YOUR WAR' (1983). While they kept up the politically correct fury on follow-up set, 'DEFY THE SYSTEM' (1983), new members, STEVE LIND and DOUG CARRION (who replaced McCARTHY and BERT respectively), ensured a more melodic musical approach. KAIL subsequently split the band, taking PHILLIPS with him to his other hardcore project, MOOD OF DEFIANCE. CARRION, meanwhile, found a new lease of life with INCEST CATTLE (the band that is!), ADOLESCENTS and DAG NASTY.

Album rating: I DON'T WANT TO DIE IN YOUR WAR (*4) / DEFY THE SYSTEM (*4)

BERT – vocals / **GAIL KAIL** – guitar (of MOOD OF DEFIANCE) / **DANNY PHILLIPS** – bass / **JOHN McCARTHY** – drums

not iss. — New U'ground

1982. (7"ep's) **unknown** [-] [ ]
Jan 83. (lp) *<NU-22>* **I DON'T WANT TO DIE IN YOUR WAR** [-] [ ]
– I'm going insane / The cycle / Streets / What do you do / Fight war not wars / Acid test / I don't want to die in your war / New underground / Pushed around / I hate you / Poseur.

—— **STEVE LIND** – drums; repl. McCARTHY (he left during sessions)

—— **DOUG CARRION** – bass; repl. BERT (DANNY now vocals, guitar)

Dec 83. (lp) *<NU-77>* **DEFY THE SYSTEM** [-] [ ]
– I try / Lies / Your government's caling you / Working in a factory / Map of the star's homes / Your problems / Five downtown / Nothing new / Club me like a baby seal / Backfire bomber / Be free / Over-throw the government / Parents of punks / Repressed aggresion.

—— split in 1984, KAIL took PHILLIPS with him to MOOD OF DEFIANCE, while the former moonlighted in many projects. CARRION formed INCEST CATTLE before becoming part of the DESCENDENTS and later DAG NASTY.

ANTI-NOWHERE LEAGUE

Formed: Tunbridge Wells, Kent, England . . . 1980 by biker/punks ANIMAL and MAGOO. First came to the attention of the music world, after their gutter-angst cover of Ralph McTell's folkie hit, 'STREETS OF LONDON' hit the Top 50 at the end of '81. However, it was 'SO WHAT', the b-side of the record that caused the most controversy, when around 10,000 copies of the 45 were seized by the police under the obscene publications act. Another independent chart-topper followed in the Spring of '82, 'I HATE PEOPLE', a song, like most of the hardcore/oi tracks on their debut album, 'WE ARE THE LEAGUE', offended everybody but the mohawks and skins. The UK Top 30 album (like earlier 45's, also with WINSTON and PJ), was a barrage of foul-mouthed protest 100 mph punk, fusing "oi" with "metal". A very disappointing live set recorded in Yugoslavia was their next delivery, although this was their last show as out and out punks. In the mid 80's, they were back as biker-clad heavies, The LEAGUE and after only one album, 'THE PERFECT CRIME' (1987) they had returned to ground. It was a case of sporadic reunions from then on, until that is, METALLICA covered 'SO WHAT' and thus the reformation in '93.

Album rating: WE ARE . . . THE LEAGUE (*6) / LIVE IN YUGOSLAVIA (*4) / THE PERFECT CRIME (*4) / LONG LIVE THE LEAGUE – R.I.P. compilation (*6)

ANIMAL (b. NICK KARMER) – vocals / **MAGOO** (b. CHRIS EXALL) – guitar / **WINSTON BLAKE** – bass / **P.J.** – drums

WXYZ — not iss.

Nov 81. (7"/12"w-drawn) *(ABCD 1/+T)* **STREETS OF LONDON. / SO WHAT** [48] [-]
Mar 82. (7") *(ABCD 2)* **I HATE . . . PEOPLE. / LET'S BREAK THE LAW** [46] [-]
Apr 82. (lp/c) *(LMNOP/+C 1)* **WE ARE . . . THE LEAGUE** [24] [-]
– We are the league / Animal / Woman / Can't stand rock'n'roll / (We will not) Remember you / Snowman / Streets of London / I hate . . . people / Wreck-a-nowhere / World War III / Nowhere man / Let's break the law. *(lp re-iss. Nov85 on 'I.D.'; NOSE 6) (cd-iss. Oct92 on 'Streetlink'; STRCD 028) (<cd re-iss. Apr93 on 'Dojo'; DOJOCD 128>) (cd re-iss. Sep97 on 'Snapper'; SMMCD 515)*
Jun 82. (7"pic-d) *(ABCD 4)* **WOMAN. / ROCKER** [72] [-]
Nov 82. (7") *(ABCD 6)* **FOR YOU. / THE BALLAD OF J.J. DECAY** [ ] [-]

—— added **GILLY** – guitar

I.D. — not iss.

Oct 83. (lp) *(NOSE 3)* **LIVE IN YUGOSLAVIA (live)** [88] [-]
– Let's break the law / Streets of London / Let the country feed you / We will survive / I hate . . .people / Snowman / For you / Going down / Woman / Can't stand rock'n'roll / So what / Wreck-a-nowhere / Paint it black / We are the league. *(<cd-iss. Mar00 on 'Harry May'; MAYOCD 504>)*

A.B.C. — not iss.

Dec 84. (7"/7"pic-d) *(ABCS 004/+P)* **OUT ON THE WASTELAND. / WE WILL SURVIVE** [ ] [-]
(12"+=) *(ABCS 004T)* – Queen and country.

—— **MICHAEL BETTELL** – drums; repl. P.J.

—— also added a keyboard player, before reverting to original name.

G.W.R. — G.W.R.

May 87. (lp/c) *(GW LP/TC 12) <PAL 1238>* **THE PERFECT CRIME** [ ] [ ]
– Crime / On the waterfront / Branded / I don't believe this is my England / Johannesburg / Shining / Working for the company / System / Curtain.

—— disbanded although they re-formed the 1985 line-up in 1992

SPV — Pavement

Nov 97. (cd) *(SPV 0845301-2) <32286>* **SCUM** [ ] [ ] Aug98
– Fucked up and wasted / Chocolate soldiers / Get ready / Suicide . . . have you tried / Pig iron / Scum / Burn 'em all / Gypsies tramps and thieves / How does it feel? / Great unwashed / . . . Long live punk. *(lp-iss.Nov97 on 'Knock Out'; KOLP 069) (cd re-iss. Feb00 on 'Impact'; IRC 102CD)*

– compilations, etc. –

Apr 86. (lp) *Dojo; (DOJOLP 15)* **LONG LIVE THE LEAGUE – R.I.P.** [ ] [-]
– For you / We will survive / Out on the wasteland / Queen & country / We are the League / Streets of London / So what / Let's break the law / The ballad of J.J. Decay / Woman / Snowman / Wreck a nowhere / Let the country feed you / Going down / I hate . . . people. *(cd-iss. 1987; DOJOCD 15)*
Feb 89. (d-lp) *I.D.; (NOSE 36)* **WE ARE . . . THE LEAGUE / LIVE IN YUGOSLAVIA** [ ] [-]
(cd-iss. Jan90; CDOSE 36)
Mar 90. (lp) *Link; (LINKLP 120)* **LIVE AND LOUD (live)** [ ] [-]
(cd-iss. Oct90; LINKCD 120)
Oct 92. (cd) *Streetlink; (STRCD 013)* **THE BEST OF THE ANTI-NOWHERE LEAGUE** [ ] [-]
– Streets of London / I hate . . . people / We are the League / Let's break the law / Animal / Woman / Rocker / For you / Ballad of JJ Decay / Out on the wasteland / We will survive / Queen and country / On the waterfront / Let the country feed you (live) / Going down (live) / Snowman (live) / So what (live). *(cd-iss. Mar93 on 'Dojo'; DOJOCD 113) (<cd re-iss. Jan94 on 'Cleopatra'; CLEO 07279CD>) (re-iss. Apr98 on 'Snapper'; SMMCD 514)*
Nov 92. (cd) *Castle; (LOMACD 9)* **THE PERFECT CRIME / LIVE IN YUGOSLAVIA** [ ] [-]
Feb 95. (cd) *Anagram; (<CDPUNK 44>)* **COMPLETE PUNK SINGLES COLLECTION** [ ] [ ] Sep99
May 96. (cd) *Receiver; (<RRCD 219>)* **THE HORSE IS DEAD (THE ANTI-NOWHERE LEAGUE LIVE)** [ ] [ ]
Nov 96. (7") *Visionary Vinyl; (V 713)* **STREETS OF LONDON. /** [ ] [-]
Jul 98. (cd/lp) *Knock Out; (<IRRCD/KOLP 076>)* **RETURN TO YUGOSLAVIA** [ ] [ ] May01
(cd re-iss. Oct98 on 'S.P.V.'; SPV 0765317-2) (cd re-iss. Feb00 on 'Impact'; IRC 119CD)
Nov 99. (d-cd) *Eagle; (EDGCD 110) / Spitfire; <SPIT 082>* **ANTHOLOGY** [ ] [ ] Jan00
Feb 00. (m-cd) *Impact; (IRC 066CD)* **PIG IRON** [ ] [-]
May 00. (cd) *Receiver; (<RRCD 287>)* **OUT OF CONTROL** [ ] [ ] Jul00
Jul 00. (cd) *Harry May; (CANCAN 012CD) / Cleopatra; <425>* **LIVE: SO WHAT?** [ ] [ ] Jan99

—— also a various artists compilation 'SO WHAT' was released in 1997

Nov 00. (cd) *Step 1; (STEPCD 042)* **LIVE ANIMALS (live)** [ ] [-]
Apr 01. (d-cd) *Snapper; (SMDCD 330)* **THE BEST OF THE ANTI-NOWHERE LEAGUE** [ ] [-]
Apr 01. (cd) *Captain Oi; (<AHOYCD 162>)* **PUNK SINGLES AND RARITIES 1981-1984** [ ] [ ] May01

ANTI-PASTI

Formed: Derby, England . . . 1978 as The SCRINCERS by DUGI BELL, EDDIE BARKE and RUSSELL MAW, adopting the ANTI-PASTI moniker following the recruitment of MARTIN ROPER. By the release of a DIY debut EP, 'FOUR SORE POINTS' (1980), the line-up had undergone the first of many changes, STU WINFIELD and STAN SMITH replacing MAW and BARKE. The record nevertheless contained one of their finest moments, the live favourite, 'NO GOVERNMENT', a blistering tirade against Thatcher and her newly elected Tory cronies. With the agenda established, ANTI-PASTI made their first inroads into the newly established independent chart with follow-up single, 'LET THEM FREE', despite more personnel disruption as SMITH and WINFIELD were replaced by KEVIN NIXON and WILL HOON respectively. More recognition followed as the group nearly scraped into the UK Top 30 with debut album, 'THE LAST CALL' (1981) and topped the indie chart with the defiant 'SIX GUNS' single. Despite building up a committed following, however, ANTI-PASTI, along with the likes of ANGELIC UPSTARTS and SHAM 69 were struggling to set themsleves apart from the proliferation of right wing Oi! bands that were splitting punk unity. Although a joint effort with The EXPLOITED, 'DON'T LET 'EM GRIND YOU DOWN', also made No.1 in the indie chart, follow-up album, 'CAUTION TO THE WIND' (1982) saw them lose momentum. Following the departure of original member ROPER, the group struggled on before finally calling it a day in the mid-80's. With an inevitable CD re-issue of their two albums in the mid-90's, the band re-formed for a one-off bout of touring although no new material was forthcoming.

Album rating: THE LAST CALL (*4) / CAUTION IN THE WIND (*3) / NO GOVERNMENT: THE BEST OF ANTI-PASTI compilation (*5)

MARTIN ROPER – vocals / **DUGI BELL** – guitar / **STU WINFIELD** – bass / **STAN SMITH** – drums

Rondelet not iss.

Nov 80. (7"ep) *(ROUND 2)* **FORE SORE POINTS EP** -
– No government / 1980 / Two years too late / Something new.

— **WILL HOON** – bass; repl. STU

— **KEV NIXON** – drums; repl. STAN

Jan 81. (7",7"red) *(ROUND 5)* **LET THEM FREE. / ANOTHER DEAD SOLDIER** -

Jul 81. (lp/c) *(ABOUT/CARB 5)* **THE LAST CALL** 31 -
– No government / Brew your own / Another dead soldier / Call the army (I'm alive) / City below / 24 hours / Night of the war cry / Freedom row / St.George (get's his gun) / The last call / Ain't got me / Truth and justice / Hell / I wanna be your dog. *(<cd-iss. Mar95 & Feb01 on 'Anagram'+=; CDPUNK 48>)* – 1980 / Something new / Two years too late / Let them be free / Hell (version) / Six guns / Now's the time. *(re-iss. Oct96 on 'Get Back'; GET 7)*

Oct 81. (7"m) *(ROUND 10)* **SIX GUNS. / NOW'S THE TIME / CALL THE ARMY** -

— Late in '81, they shared a single EP, with EXPLOITED.

May 82. (7") *(ROUND 18)* **EAST TO THE WEST. / BURN IN YOUR OWN FLAMES** -

— added **OLLIE (HOON)** – guitar

Jun 82. (lp/c) *(ABOUT/CARB 7)* **CAUTION IN THE WIND** -
– Caution in the wind / One Friday night / X affair / Get out now / Mr. Mystery / East to the west / See how they run / Hate circulation / Agent ABC / The best of us / Guinea pigs / Beyond belief. *(<cd-iss. May95 on 'Anagram'; CDPUNK 53>) (lp re-iss. Nov00 on 'Get Back'; GET 70)*

Sep 82. (7") *(ROUND 26)* **CAUTION IN THE WIND. / LAST TRAIN** -

— they split late 1982 and went to the States (ROPER went solo)

– compilations, etc. –

Sep 83. (lp) *Rondelet; (ABOUT 13)* **ANTI-PASTI (SINGLES COLLECTION)** -

Mar 96. (cd) *Dojo; (DOJOCD 230) / Cleopatra; <9686>* **NO GOVERNMENT: THE BEST OF ANTI-PASTI** Feb96
– No government / 1980 / Two years too late / Another dead soldier / Hell / Ain't got me / East to west / Burn in your own flames / Caution in the wind / Last train to nowhere / Blind faith / Call the army (I'm alive) / Night of the warcry / Six guns / Now's the time / Brew your own.

Jun 98. (cd) *Cherry Red; (<CDPUNK 106>)* **THE PUNK SINGLES COLLECTION** Sep99

LINKMEN

— were formed by 2 former ANTI-PASTI's (STU & STAN)?

Kitchenware not iss.

Jun 84. (12"ep) *(SKX 17)* **EVERY INCH A KING / RUIN. / HEAVEN AND BACK AGAIN / JACK BE NIMBLE / STICKS AND STONES** -

Jan 85. (7") *(SK 17)* **EVERY INCH A KING. / MANIC DEPRESSION** -

Spice not iss.

Oct 85. (7") *(HERB 1)* **ILL WIND. / ?** -

— split when STU formed CLINIC P

ANVIL

Formed: Toronto, Canada . . . 1978 as LIPS, after the sex-obsessed chainsaw-wielding frontman of the same name, who completed the line-up with DAVE ALLISON, IAN DICKSON and ROBB REINER. A major influence on the thrash-metal of the mid-late '80's, ANVIL released a handful of pivotal albums on the domestic 'Attic' label. Following a period of personal and professional disputes, the band made a comeback with the 'STRENGTH OF STEEL' (1987) album. They signed to 'Metal Blade' a year later, 'POUND FOR POUND' failing to make much headway wih the group sounding outdated against young guns like TESTAMENT, METALLICA and MEGADETH. The 90's saw the rebirth of ANVIL (SEBASTIAN MARINO replacing ALLISON), five full sets seeing light of day:- 'WORTH THE WEIGHT' (1992), 'PLUGGED IN PERMANENT' (1996), 'ABSOLUTELY NO ALTERNATIVE' (1997), 'SPEED OF SOUND' (1999) and 'PLENTY OF POWER' (2001). • **Covered:** PAINT IT BLACK (Rolling Stones).

Album rating: HARD 'N' HEAVY (*6) / METAL ON METAL (*7) / FORGED IN FIRE (*7) / BACKWAXED compilation (*5) / STRENGTH OF STEEL (*5) / POUND FOR POUND (*5) / PAST & PRESENT – LIVE IN CONCERT (*4) / WORTH THE WEIGHT (*6) / PLUGGED IN PERMANENT (*5) / ABSOLUTELY NO ALTERNATIVE (*3) / SPEED OF SOUND (*3) / PLENTY OF POWER (*4)

LIPS – vocals, lead guitar / **DAVE ALLISON** – rhythm guitar, vocals / **IAN DICKSON** – bass / **ROBB REINER** – drums

Noir Attic

Dec 81. (lp/c) *(LAT/CAT 1100)* **HARD 'N' HEAVY** - - Canada
– School love / AC/DC / At the apartment / I won't you both (with me) / Bedroom game / Ooh baby / Paint it black / Oh Jane / Hot child / Bondage. *(cd-iss. 1990's on 'Attic'; 841870-2)*

Jun 82. (lp/c) *(LAT/CAT 1130)* **METAL ON METAL** - - Canada
– Metal on metal / Mothra / Stop me / March of the crabs / Jackhammer / Heat sink / Tag team / Scenery / Tease me, please me / 666. *(cd-iss. Jun89 on 'Roadrunner'; RR34 9917)*

Aug 82. (7"ep/12"ep) *(MET/+12 001)* **STOP ME / JACKHAMMER. / TEASE ME, PLEASE ME / STEAMIN'** -

May 83. (lp/c) *(LAT/CAT 1170)* **FORGED IN FIRE** -
– Forged in fire / Shadow zone / Free as the wind / Never deceive me / Butter-bust jerky / Future wars / Hard times – Fast ladies / Make it up to you / Motormount / Winged assassins. *(re-iss. 1988 on 'Roadrunner' lp/cd; RR/+34 9927) (cd-iss. May98 on 'Axe Killer'; AXE 302334CD)*

Jun83. (7"/12") *(MET/+12 002)* **MAKE IT UP TO YOU. / METAL ON METAL** -

Roadrunner Viper

Jun 85. (lp) *(RR 9776)* **BACKWAXED** (material 81-83)
– Pussy poison / Back waxed / Steamin' / You're a liar / Fryin' cryin' / Metal on metal / Butter-bust jerky / Scenery / Jackhammer / School love.

Roadrunner Enigma

Jun 87. (lp) *(RR 9618)* *<CDE 73267>* **STRENGTH OF STEEL**
– Strength of steel / Concrete jungle / 9-2-5 / I dreamed it was the end of the world / Flight of the bumble beast / Cut loose / Mad dog / Straight between the eyes / Wild eyes / Kiss of death / Paper general.

not iss. Z.Y.X.

1988. (lp/cd) *<ZM/+CD 1011>* **POUND FOR POUND** -
– Blood on the ice / Corporate preacher / Toe jam / Safe sex / Where does all the money go / Brain burn / Senile king / Machine gun / Fire in the night / Cramps. *<cd re-iss. 1990 on 'Capitol'; 73336>* (UK cd-iss. Jun96 on 'Massacre'; *MASSCD 097)*

Roadracer Metal Blade

Aug 89. (lp/cd) *(RO 9453-1/-2)* *<73412>* **PAST AND PRESENT – LIVE IN CONCERT (live)**
– Concrete jungle / Toe jam / Motormount / Forged in fire / Blood on the ice / March of the crabs / Jackhammer / Metal on metal / Winged assassins / 666 / Mothra.

— disbanded after ALLISON left in 1989, reformed a few years later

— **SEBASTIAN MARINO** – lead guitar; repl. him

Mausoleum not iss.

1992. (cd) *(904.004-2)* **WORTH THE WEIGHT** -
– Infanticide / On the way to hell / Bushpig / Embalmer / Pow wow / Sins of the flesh / A.Z. #85 / Sadness / Love me when I'm dead.

Massacre Metal Blade

Jun 96. (cd) *(MASSDP 098)* *<14122>* **PLUGGED IN PERMANENT** Mar97
– Racial hostility / Dr. Kevorkian / Smokin' green / Destined for doom / Killer hill / Face pull / I'm trying to sleep / 5 knuckle to shuffle / Truth or consequence / Guilty.

Dec 97. (cd) *(MASSCD 134)* **ABSOLUTELY NO ALTERNATIVE** -
– Old school / Green Jesus / Show me your tits / No one to follow / Hair pie / Rubber neck / Piss test / Red light / Black or white / Hero by death.

Massacre Hypnotic

Mar 99. (cd/lp) *(MASS CD/LP 173)* *<1070>* **SPEED OF SOUND** Nov00
– Speed of sound / Blood in the playground / Deadbeat dad / Man overboard / No evil / Bullshit / Mattress mambo / Secret agent / Life to lead / Park that truck. *(special cd; MASSDP 173)*

May 99. (m-cd) *(MASSH 204)* **ANVIL** -

Mar 01. (cd) *(MASSCD 256)* *<1079>* **PLENTY OF POWER** Apr01
– Plenty of power / Groove science / Ball of fire / The creep / Computer drone / Beat the law / Pro wrestling / Siren of the sea / Disgruntled / Real metal / Left behind.

– compilations, etc. –

Nov 00. (cd) *Metal Blade; <14347>* **ANTHOLOGY** -
– Metal on metal / Smokin' green / Winged assassins / Free as the wind / Old school / Bushpig / Blood on the ice / March of the crabs / Jackhammer / Speed of sound 666 / Stolen / Paper general / Forged in fire / School love / Motormount / Dr. Kevorkian / Mothra.

APARTMENT 26

Formed: Warwick, West Midlands, England . . . mid 90's by schoolfriends BIFF BUTLER, JON GREASLEY and LOUIS CRUDEN. Originally following a grunge direction, the band's sound was radically altered with the addition of electronics wunderkid AC HUCKVALE. Where do they get these names, you may well be asking yourself; well, for starters, BIFF was actually the son of another strangely named metal guru, original BLACK SABBATH bassist GEEZER BUTLER, a subject he's infamously (and understandably) loathe to talk about in interviews. Still, such rich rock bloodlines have hardly been a hindrance, bearing in mind that APARTMENT 26 won themselves a spot on both the US Warped and Ozzfest tours. Their line-up completed by JEREMY COLSON, the band – who'd already released an independent EP – subsequently signed to 'Hollywood' and made their major label debut in mid-2000 with 'HALLUCINATING'. Influenced by the likes of FEAR FACTORY (whose mainman BURTON C BELL actually guests on the album, alongside the likes of BIOHAZARD's SEINFELD) and SLIPKNOT, BUTLER and Co's mechanized nu-metal also made an appearance on the 'Heavy Metal' and 'Mission Impossible' soundtrack sequels. Confusingly, for a band who hail from the English midlands, their debut set had to wait until early 2001 for a full UK release.

Album rating: HALLUCINATING (*7)

BIFF BUTLER – vocals / **JON GREASLEY** – guitar / **AC HUCKVALE** – keyboards, programmer / **LOUIS CRUDEN** – bass

Hollywood Hollywood

Jan 01. (cd) *(0124552HWR)* <162748> **HALLUCINATING** May00
– Backwards / Doing it anyway / Sliced beats / Keep you / Apartment 26 / Dusk / Hallucinating / The fear / Basic breakdown / Anymore / Bruised / Evils / Question of reality / Death.

A PERFECT CIRCLE (see under ⇒ TOOL)

APES, PIGS & SPACEMEN

Formed: Kettering, England . . . 1993 by main songwriter/leader PAUL MIRO, BART and KETTLE. Taking their name from a rather fantastical twist on Charles Darwin's theory of evolution (apparently they believe that aliens mated with apes to form humans!?!), they signed to 'Music For Nations', subsequently releasing their debut EP, 'ANTISEPTIC' late in '94. A follow-up single, 'SAFETY NET', also turned up on their debut album, 'TRANSFUSION' (1995). The band then abbrieviated their name to A,P&S for 1997's second long-playing appearance, 'SNAPSHOTS'.

Album rating: TRANSFUSION (*6) / SNAPSHOTS (*6)

PAUL MIRO – vocals, guitar / **KETTLE** – guitar / **BART** – bass / **SAM CARR** – drums

Music For Nations Fierce

Nov 94. (12"ep/cd-ep) *(12/CD KUT 162)* **ANTISEPTIC** -
– Do I need this / Stuffed / P.V.S. / Come around the world with me.

— **LAURIE JENKINS** – drums; repl. CARR

Jun 95. (cd-ep) *(CDKUT 166)* **SAFETY NET EP** -
– Antiseptic / Unwashed and somewhat slightly dazed / Kiss my enemy / Satnack.

Oct 95. (cd/c/lp) *(CD/T+/MFN 192)* <11095> **TRANSFUSION** Nov95
– Great place / Fragments / Do I need this / Come round the world / Safety net / Twice the man / Regurgitate / PVS / Take our sorrow's swimming / Seep / Open season. *(other cd; CDMFNX 192)*

— **NEIL SHEPHERD** – guitar; repl. KETTLE

Jun 97. (cd/c; as AP&S) *(CD/T MFN 219)* **SNAPSHOT** -
– Unknown territories / Beanman / Monster / Blood simple / Ice cream / Virtual / Hollow / Chair / Mother Courage / Nine lives / Humiliation / Trouble / Suits. *(other cd; CDMFNX 219)*

— split after above

APOCALYPSE

Formed: Switzerland . . . mid 80's by CARLOS R. SPRENGER, JULIEN BROCHER, PIERRE ALAIN ZURCHER, JEAN CLAUDE SCHNEIDER and ANDRE DOMENJOZ. Not exactly noted for its metal scene, this small pacifist country nevertheless produced at least two fearsomely aggressive bands in CELTIC FROST and APOCALYPSE. The band were impressive enough to secure a deal with 'Under One Flag', although they only released a solitary eponymous album in '89.

Album rating: APOCALYPSE (*6)

CARLOS R. SPRENGER – vocals / **JULIEN BROCHER** – guitar / **PIERRE ALAIN ZURCHER** – guitar / **CLAUDE SCHNEIDER** – bass / **ANDRE DOMENJOZ** – drums

Under One Flag not iss.

Aug 89. (cd/c/lp) *(CD/T+/FLAG 23)* **APOCALYPSE** -
– Digital life / A tale of a nightmare / Crash! (instrumental) / F**k off and die / The night before / Apocalypse / Back to the fire / Dark sword (instrumental) / Cemetery.

— folded after above

APOCRYPHA

Formed: Las Vegas, USA . . . 1987 by guitar whizz, TONY FREDIANELLI, who recruited STEVE PLOCICA, CHIP CHROVIAN, AL RUMLEY and MIKE POE. Quickly signed to noted metal label, 'Roadrunner', the group delivered a trio of technically brilliant but derivative thrash albums, debuting with the MARTY FRIEDMAN-produced 'THE FORGOTTEN SCROLL' in early '88.

Album rating: THE FORGOTTEN SCROLL (*5) / EYES OF TIME (*5) / AREA 54 (*5)

TONY FREDIANELLI – guitar / **STEVE PLOCICA** – vocals / **CHIP CHROVIAN** – guitar / **AL RUMLEY** – bass / **MIKE POE** – drums

Roadrunner Schrapnel

Feb 88. (lp) *(RR 9568-1)* <SH 1034> **THE FORGOTTEN SCROLL**
– Penance (keep the faith) / Lost children of hope / Holy wars (only lock the doors) / Fall of the crest / Tablet of destiny / Look to the sun / Riding in the night / Distorted reflections / Broken dream.

— added **CHIP CHROVIAN** – rhythm guitar

Jan 89. (lp/cd) *(RR 9507-1/-2)* <SH 1039/+CD> **EYES OF TIME**
– Father Time / West world / Twilight of modern man / Alexander the king / The day time stood still / The hour glass / H.G. Wells / The man who saw tomorrow / Mystic.

— **BRECK SMITH** – bass; repl. RUMLEY + CHIP

— **DAVE SCHILLER** – drums; repl. POE

Nov 90. (cd) *(RR 9345-2)* <SH 1047CD> **AREA 54**
– Terrors holding on to you / A night in fog / Instrubation / Tian'anmen Square / Refuse the offer you can't refuse / Catch 22 / The power elite / Area 54 / The detriment of man / Born to this world.

— split after above

APOLLYON SUN (see under ⇒ CELTIC FROST)

APRIL WINE

Formed: Halifax, Nova Scotia, Canada . . . 1969 by then teenager, MYLES GOODWYN, along with cousins DAVID, RITCHIE and JIMMY HENMAN. This family affair soon built up a large homegrown and Stateside following, where they had signed to 'Big Tree' through Canadian label 'Aquarius'. In 1972, their eponymous debut was issued, a fine hard-rock effort spawning a US Top 40 hit, 'YOU COULD HAVE BEEN A LADY'. Although the band (through an ever-evolving line-up) were one of the biggest domestic draws, their success didn't extend to America and Europe until they secured a deal with 'Capitol' in 1978. The following year, they scored successfully higher positions on the Billboard chart with their ninth and tenth albums, 'FIRST GLANCE' and 'HARDER . . . FASTER'. The group enjoyed their most commercially rewarding period during the early 80's; albums 'THE NATURE OF THE BEAST' and 'POWER PLAY' both achieving Top 40 status. During this heyday, APRIL WINE frequently scored in the US singles charts, 'ROLLER' and 'JUST BETWEEN YOU AND ME', both hitting Top 40. In the mid 80's, GOODWYN dissolved the band, retreating to a brief solo career and a time in the Bahamas. In 1992, GOODWYN resurrected AW for a reunion tour of North America, although a resulting album, 'ATTITUDE' (1993), failed to turn the clock back. • **Songwriters:** Most by GOODWYN except 21st CENTURY SCHIZOID MAN (King Crimson) / etc. • **Trivia:** Supported The ROLLING STONES at the EL MOCAMBO CLUB in Toronto, released as an album in '76.

Album rating: APRIL WINE (*4) / ON RECORD (*5) / ELECTRIC JEWELS (*4) / LIVE (*4) / STAND BACK (*5) / FOREVER, FOR NOW (*4) / LIVE AT THE EL MOCAMBO (*5) / FIRST GLANCE (*5) / HARDER . . . FASTER (*7) / THE NATURE OF THE BEAST (*7) / POWER PLAY (*4) / ANIMAL GRACE (*4) / WALKING THROUGH FIRE (*3) / ATTITUDE (*5) / FRIGATE (*3) / ALL HITS compilation (*6) / Myles Goodwyn: MYLES GOODWYN (*4)

MYLES GOODWYN (b.23 Jun'48, Woodstock, Canada) – vocals, guitar, piano / **DAVID HENMAN** – guitar / **JIMMY HENMAN** – bass, vocals / **RITCHIE HENMAN** – drums

Pye Big Tree

Apr 72. (lp) <AQR 502> **APRIL WINE** -
– Oceana / Can't find the town / Fast train / Listen mister / Page five / Song for Mary / Wench / Time. <cd-iss. 1998 on 'Aquarius'; 26502>

Apr 72. (7") *(7N 45145)* <133> **YOU COULD HAVE BEEN A LADY. / TEACHER** 32 Mar72

— **JIM CLENCH** – bass repl.JIMMY

Dec 72. (7") *(7N 45163)* <142> **BAD SIDE OF THE MOON. / BELIEVE IN ME**

Jan 73. (lp) <AQR 503> **ON RECORD** -
– Farkus / You could have been a lady / Believe in me / Work all day / Drop your guns / Bad side of the Moon / Refugee / Flow river flow / Carry on / Didn't you. *(UK cd-iss. Jul93 on 'Repertoire'; RR 4213)* <cd-iss. 1998; 26503>

— **GARY MOFFAT** (b.22 Jun'49, Ottawa, Canada) – guitar, vocals repl. DAVID / **JERRY MERCER** (b.27 Apr'39, Montreal, Canada) – drums, vocals repl. RITCHIE

Nov 73. (7") *(7N 45265)* <16010> **WEEPING WIDOW. / JUST LIKE THAT**

Nov 73. (lp) <AQR 504> **ELECTRIC JEWELS** -
– Weeping widow / Just like that / Electric jewels / You opened my eyes / Come on along / Lady run, lady hide / I can hear you callin' / Cat's claw / The band has just begun. *(UK cd-iss. Jul93 on 'Repertoire'; RR 4121)* <cd-iss. 1998; 26502>

Oct 74. (7") <15006> **I'M ON FIRE FOR YOU BABY (live). / COME ON ALONG** -

Oct 74. (lp) <AQR 505> **LIVE (live)** -
– (Mama) It's true / Druthers / Cat's claw / I'm on fire for you baby / The band has just begun / Good fibes / Just like that / You could have been a lady.

1975. (lp) <AQR 506> **STAND BACK** -
– Oowantanite / Don't push me around / Cum hear the band / Slow poke / Victim of your love / Baby done got some soul / I wouldn't want to lose your love / Highway hard run / Not for you, not for rock & roll / Wouldn't want your love / Tonite is a wonderful time to fall in love. <US re-iss. 1981 on 'Capitol'; > <cd-iss. 1998; 26506>

1975. (7") <16036> **OOWATANITE. /** -

— **STEVE LANG** (b.24 Mar'49, Montreal) – bass repl. CLENCH who joined 451 DEGREES

1976. (lp) <AQR 511> **FOREVER, FOR NOW** -
– Forever, for now / Child's garden / Lovin' you / Holly would / You won't dance with me / Come away / Mama Laye / I'd rather be strong / Hard times / Marjorie. <cd-iss. 1998; 26511>

London London

Sep 76. (lp) *(SHU 8503)* **THE WHOLE WORLD'S GOIN' CRAZY** -
– Gimme love / Child's garden / Rock'n'roll woman / Wings of love / Marjorie / So bad / Shotdown / Live a lover, like a song / Kick Willy Rd. / The whole world's goin' crazy. <cd-iss. 1998 on 'Aquarius'; 16510>

Oct 76. (7") *(HLU 10544)* **CHILD'S GARDEN. / THE WHOLE WORLD'S GOIN' CRAZY** -

Mar 77. (7") <245> **SHOTDOWN. /** - -

Jul 77. (7") *(HLU 10549)* <255> **YOU WON'T DANCE WITH ME. / SHOTDOWN** -

Dec 77. (lp) *(SHU 8510)* **LIVE AT THE EL MOCAMBO (live)** -
– Teenage love / Tonight is a wonderful time to fall in love / Juvenile delinquent / Don't push me around / Oowatanite / Drop your guns / Slow poke / You won't dance with me / You could have been a lady.

1978. (7") *<265>* **I'M ALIVE. / ROCK AND ROLL IS A VICIOUS GAME** [-] [ ]

— added **BRIAN GREENWAY** (b. 1 Oct'51, Ontario, Canada) – guitar, vocals, keyboards

Capitol Capitol

Mar 79. (lp/c) *<(EST/TC-EST 11852)>* **FIRST GLANCE** [ ] [ ]
– Get ready for love / Hot on the wheels of love / Rock'n'roll is a vicious game / Right down to it / Roller / Comin' right down on top of me / I'm alive / Let yourself go / Silver dollar. *<US re-iss. 1981> <cd-iss. 1998; 48416>*

Apr 79. (7") *(CL 16075) <4660>* **ROLLER. / RIGHT DOWN TO IT** [ ] [34]

Jun 79. (7") *<4728>* **COMIN' RIGHT DOWN ON TOP OF ME. / GET READY FOR LOVE** [-] [ ]

Nov 79. (7") *<4802>* **BEFORE THE DAWN. / SAY HELLO** [-] [ ]

Feb 80. (lp/c) *<(EST/TC-EST 12013)>* **HARDER . . . FASTER** [34] [64] Nov79
– I like to rock / Say hello / Tonite / Ladies man / Before the dawn / Babes in arms / Better do it well / 21st century schizoid man. *(cd-iss. Feb00 on 'Liberty'; 524600-2)*

Feb 80. (7") *<4828>* **I LIKE TO ROCK. / BABES IN ARMS** [-] [86]

Feb 80. (7"ep) *(CL 16121)* **UNRELEASED LIVE (live)** [ ] [-]
– I like to rock / Rock'n'roll is a vicious game / Before the dawn / Roller.

Aug 80. (7") *(CL 16164) <4859>* **LADIES MAN. / OOWATANITE** [ ] [ ] Jun80
(12"+=) *(12CL 16164)* – Get ready for love / I like to rock.

Jan 81. (7") *(CL 16181)* **ALL OVER TOWN. / CRASH AND BURN** [ ] [ ]

Jan 81. (lp/c) *<(EST/TC-EST 12125)>* **THE NATURE OF THE BEAST** [48] [26]
– All over town / Tellin' me lies / Sign of the gypsy queen / Just between you and me / Wanna rock / Caught in the crossfire / Future tense / Big city girls / Crash and burn / Bad boys / One more time. *<cd-iss. 1998; 46067>*

Mar 81. (7") *(CL 16184) <4975>* **JUST BETWEEN YOU AND ME. / BIG CITY GIRLS** [52] [21] Feb81

Jun 81. (7") *(CL 205) <5001>* **SIGN OF THE GYPSY QUEEN. / CRASH AND BURN** [ ] [57] May81

Dec 81. (lp) *<9632>* **SUMMER TOUR '81 (live)** [-] [ ]

Jun 82. (7") *(CL 254) <5133>* **ENOUGH IS ENOUGH. / AIN'T GOT YOUR LOVE** [ ] [50]

Jul 82. (lp/c) *<(EST/TC-EST 12218)>* **POWER PLAY** [ ] [37]
– Anything you want, you got it / Enough is enough / If you see Kay / What if we fall in love / Waiting on a miracle / Doin' it right / Ain't got your love / Blood money / Tell me why / Runners in the night. *<cd-iss. 1998; 48417>*

Sep 82. (7") *<5153>* **IF YOU SEE KAY. / BLOOD MONEY** [-] [ ]

Nov 82. (7") *<5168>* **TELL ME WHY. / RUNNERS IN THE NIGHT** [-] [ ]

Feb 84. (7") *(CL 328) <5319>* **THIS COULD BE THE RIGHT ONE. / REALLY DON'T WANT YOUR LOVE** [ ] [58]

Apr 84. (lp/c) *(EST/TC-EST 240083-1/-4) <12311>* **ANIMAL GRACE** [ ] [62] Mar84
– This could be the right one / Sons of the pioneers / Without your love / Rock tonite / Hard rock kid / Money talks / Gimme that thing called love / Too hot to handle / Last time I'll ever sing the blues. *<cd-iss. 1998; 48415>*

— **GOODWYN** and **GREENWAY** were joined by **DANIEL BARBE** – keyboards who repl. MOFFAT / **JEAN PELLERIN** – bass repl. LANG / **MARTY SIMON** – drums repl. MERCER

Sep 85. (lp/c) *<EST/TC-EST 12433>* **WALKING THROUGH FIRE** [-] [ ]
– Rock myself to sleep / Wanted dead or alive / Beg for your love / Love has remembered me / Anejo / Open soul surgery / You don't have to act that way / Hold on / All it will ever be / Wait any more. *<cd-iss. 1988; 48418>*

Sep 85. (7") *<5506>* **ROCK MYSELF TO SLEEP. / ALL IT WILL EVER BE** [-] [ ]

— disbanded 1985 and GOODWYN relocated to the Bahamas. Re-formed in 1992 (GOODWYN, MERCER, GREENWAY, CLENCH) adding **STEVE SEGAL** – guitar

not iss. Fre-EMI

Oct 93. (cd) *<L2 104>* **ATTITUDE** [-] [-] Canada
– Givin' it, takin' it / Good from far (far from good) / If you believe in me / That's love / It hurts / Hour of need / Here's lookin' at you kid / Better slow down / Strange kind of love / Can't take another nite / Luv your stuff / Emotional dreams / Voice in my heart / Girl in my dreams.

Nov 94. (cd) *<L2 109>* **FRIGATE** [-] [-] Canada
– Look into the sun / Just wanna make love to you / If I was a stranger / Tonite is a wonderful time to fall in love / Nothin' but a kiss / I'm a man / Whatever it takes / Drivin' with my eyes closed / Hard to believe / Keep on rockin' / Mind over matter.

– compilations, others, etc. –

1979. (lp) *Aquarius; <Q 2525>* **GREATEST HITS** [-] [-] Canada

1985. (lp) *Aquarius; <AQR 538>* **ONE FOR THE ROAD (live in '84)** [-] [ ]
– Anything you want / I like to rock / All over town / Just between you and me / Enough is enough / This could be the right one / Sign of the gypsy queen / Medley: Like a lover like a song – Comin' right down on top of me – Rock'n'roll is a vicious game / Roller.

Nov 94. (4xcd-box) *Aquarius; <2-563>* **WINE COLLECTION** [-] [-] Canada

May 98. (cd) *Aquarius; <2-549>* **THE HITS** [-] [ ]

Jun 98. (cd) *Aquarius; <2-550>* **ALL THE ROCKERS** [-] [ ]

Jun 98. (cd) *Disky; <86242>* **CHAMPIONS OF ROCK** [-] [ ]

Sep 98. (cd) *Aquarius; <56401>* **ROCK BALLADS** [-] [-] Canada

Sep 98. (cd) *Aquarius; <56402>* **OOWANANITE (live)** [-] [-] Canada

Sep 98. (cd) *Aquarius;* **THE FIRST DECADE** [-] [-] Canada

Mar 99. (cd) *King Biscuit; <(KBFHCD 026)>* **KING BISCUIT FLOWER HOUR PRESENTS . . . (live)** [ ] [ ] Feb99

MYLES GOODWYN

Atlantic Atlantic

May 88. (7") *<89110>* **CAVIAR. / FRANK SINATRA CAN'T SING** [-] [ ]

Jun 88. (lp/c/cd) *<(K 781821-1/-4/-2)>* **MYLES GOODWYN** [ ] [ ] Apr88
– Veil of tears / Do you know what I mean / Caviar / Sonja / Head on / Face the storm / Frank Sinatra can't sing / Givin' it up (for you love) / Are you still loving me / Mama won't say (it's good).

Aug 88. (7") *<89073>* **DO YOU KNOW WHAT I MEAN. / FRANK SINATRA CAN'T SING** [-] [ ]

ARCADE (see under ⇒ RATT)

ARCH ENEMY

Formed: Sweden . . . 1995 by former CARNAGE/CARCASS guitarist MICHAEL AMOTT (of SPIRITUAL BEGGARS), together with his brother CHRIS, frontman/growler JOHAN LIIVA and others from MERCYFUL FATE and CARNAGE. Debuting with the 'BLACK EARTH' album in 1996, ARCH ENEMY were obviously compared with AMOTT's old compadres. However, by the release of albums two and three ('STIGMATA' and 'BURNING BRIDGES') in '98 and '99, the group's sound had fleshed out to a more melodic grind like that of MY DYING SUN or even METALLICA.

Album rating: BLACK EARTH (*5) / STIGMATA (*6) / BURNING BRIDGES (*7)

JOHAN LIIVA – vocals / **MICHAEL AMOTT** – guitar (ex-CARNAGE, ex-CARCASS) / **CHRIS AMOTT** – bass (of ARMAGEDDON) / **DANIEL ERLANDSSON** – drums (of EUCHARIST)

Wrong Again not iss.

Nov 96. (cd) *(WAR 011CD)* **BLACK EARTH** [ ] [-]
– Bury me an angel / Dark insanity / Eureka / Idolatress / Cosmic retribution / Demoniality / Transmigration macabre / Time capsule / Fields of desolation / Losing faith / The Ides of March.

— **MARTIN BENGTSSON** – vocals (of ARMAGEDDON) repl. LIIVA

— **PETER WILDOER** – drums (of ARMAGEDDON) deputised for ERLANDSSON

Century Media Century Media

May 98. (cd) *(CM 77212CD) <7912>* **STIGMATA** [ ] [ ]
– Beast of man / Stigmata / Sinister Mephisto / Dark of the son / Let the killing begin / Black Earth / Tears of the dead / Vox stellarum / Bridge of destiny.

— added **SHARLEE D'ANGELO** – bass (of MERCYFUL FATE) / **ERLANDSOON** also returned

Nov 99. (cd) *(77276-2) <7976>* **BURNING BRIDGES** [ ] [ ]
– The immortal / Dead inside / Pilgrim / Silverwing / Demonic science / Seed of hate / Angelclaw / Burning bridges.

ARCTURUS

Formed: Norway . . . 1989 as a kind of side project for originators SVERD and HELLHAMMER, both from Norwegian black metallers, MAYHEM. This double-act released several small pieces under the moniker, ARCTURUS, before fleshing out the band with black metal brethren, GARM (from the outfit ULVER) and SAMOTH (from EMPEROR). This new line-up released another offering, but did not last long in this format as SAMOTH was forced to depart the band, leaving his place open for AUGUST (from TRITONUS) at the same time bringing in the bass player SKOLL (from VED BUENS ENDE). This quintet recorded and released the debut album, 'ASPERA HIEMS SYMFONIA' (1996) on the 'Century Media' label. The set was a hugh critical success; rock writers quickly dubbing them already as one of the most important bands of their genre. Unlike many musicians' side-projects, the members of ARCTURUS put full effort into this piece, creating an intelligent and complex set, in both music and lyrics. They followed this up with their epic sophomore album, 'LA MASQUERADE INFERNALE' (1997). The record was a widely respected work, essentially due to its innovation; combining many elements that were not the normal fodder of black metal bands. Some critics compared them to ROTTING CHRIST in that they extended the boundaries of the genre towards that of classical music. However, ARCTURUS were probably closer in spirit to the work of extreme metal innovators, TODAY IS THE DAY, but where this band was colder and more technical – in both subject-matter and music – ARCTURUS lay on the side of romanticism and more folky-pagan offerings. The band's third full-set, 'DISGUISED MASTERS' was an extremely odd piece if it was to be looked at in terms of black metal. The set consisted of remixes of work from their former outing and other curious experiments; using hip-hop/rapping and techno beats. This strange beast linked with its brother albums in creativity, if not sonically. HELLHAMMER, GARM and SKOLL were joined by vocalist SIMEN and guitarist KNUT on the aforementioned set.

Album rating: ASPERA HIEMS SYMFONIA (*6) / LA MASQUERADE INFERNALE (*7) / DISGUISED MASTERS remixes (*4)

SVERD – keyboards / **HELLHAMMER** – drums (of MAYHEM)

Putrifaction not iss.

1993. (7") *(PUT 006)* **MY ANGEL. /** [-] [-] Norway

— added **GARM** – vocals (of ULVER) / **SAMOTH** – guitar (of EMPEROR)

1994. (m-cd) **CONSTELLATION** [-] [-] Norway
– Rodt og svart / Icebound streams and vapours grey / Naar kulda tar (frostnettenes prolog) / Du Nordavind.

— **AUGUST** – guitar (of TRITONUS) repl. SAMOTH who was in prison

— added **SKOLL** – bass (of VED BUENS ENDE)

Misanthropy Century Media

Apr 96. (cd/lp) *(ALC 002 CD/LP)* **ASPERA HIEMS SYMFONIA** [ ] [ ]
– To thou who dwellest in the night / Wintry grey / Whence and whither goest the wind / Raudt og svart / The bodkin and the quietus (. . .to reach the stars) / Du Nordavind / Fall of man / Naar kulda tar (frostnettenes prolog).

Music For Nations not iss.

Nov 97. (cd/lp) *(CD+/MFN 230)* **LA MASQUERADE INFERNALE** [ ] [-]

– Master of disguise / Ad astra / Chaos path / La masquerade / Alone / Of nails and sinners / Throne of tragedy / Painting my honor.

— **SIMEN** – vocals + **KNUT** – guitar; repl. SVERD + AUGUST

Jester Jester

Jun 99. (cd) *(<TRICK 003>)* **DISGUISED MASTERS** (remixes, etc)
– White tie black noise / Deception genesis / Du Nordavind – Interludium / Alone / The throne of tragedy / La masquerade infernale / Master of disguise / Painting my horror / Ad astra – Postludium / Ad astra (ensemble version).

ARMORED SAINT

Formed: Los Angeles, California, USA . . . 1981 by JOHN BUSH, PHIL E. SANDOVAL, DAVE PRICHARD, JOEY VERA and GONZO. Signed to 'Chrysalis' on the strength of their showing on the 'Metal Massacre II' various artists compilation, they released their proto-thrash debut, 'MARCH OF THE SAINT' in 1984. Two more influential albums, 'DELIRIOUS NOMAD' (1985) and 'RAISING FEAR' (1987) bubbled under the US Top 100 before they were surprisingly dropped by the label, subsequently signing to 'Enigma' in 1988. A live set appeared later that year, although it was almost three years before a new studio effort, 'SYMBOL OF SALVATION' surfaced, the group's most acclaimed piece to date. Tragically, DAVE PRICHARD had succumbed to leukemia a year prior (27th February, 1990) to the album's release, the band splitting soon after, BUSH absconding to the more popular ANTHRAX. However, when the aforementioned metal giants gave up the ghost, BUSH returned to ARMORED SAINT for a much-improved metal affair, 'REVELATION' (2000).

Album rating: MARCH OF THE SAINT (*5) / DELIRIOUS NOMAD (*5) / RAISING FEAR (*5) / SAINTS WILL CONQUER (*5) / SYMBOL OF SALVATION (*6) / REVELATION (*6)

JOHN BUSH – vocals / **PHIL E. SANDOVAL** – guitar / **DAVE PRICHARD** – guitar / **JOEY VERA** – bass / **GONZO** – drums, percussion

not iss. Metal Blade

1983. (12"ep) *<MBR 1009>* **LESSON WELL LEARNED / FALSE ALARM. / ON THE WAY** [-]

Chrysalis Chrysalis

Oct 84. (lp/c) *(CHR/ZCHR 1479) <41476>* **MARCH OF THE SAINT**
– March of the saint / Can U deliver / Mad house / Take a turn / Seducer / Mutiny on the world / Glory hunter / Stricken by fate / Envy / False alarm.

— **JEFF DUNCAN** – guitar; repl. SANDOVAL (still feat. on below)

Jan 86. (lp/c) *(CHR/ZCHR 1516) <41516>* **DELIRIOUS NOMAD**
– Long before I die / Nervous man / Over the edge / The laugh / Conquerer / For the sake / Aftermath / In the hole / You're never alone / Released.

Oct 87. (lp/c) *(CHR/ZCHR 1610) <41601>* **RAISING FEAR**
– Raising fear / Saturday night special / Out on a limb / Isolation / Chemical euphoria / Frozen will – Legacy / Human vulture / Book of blood / Terror / Underdogs.

Roadrunner Enigma

Oct 88. (lp/cd) *(RR 9520-1/-2) <72301>* **SAINTS WILL CONQUER (live)**
– Raising fear / Nervous man / Book of blood / Can U deliver / Mad house / No reason to live. *(cd+=)* – Chemical euphoria / Long before I die. *(re-iss. Sep91 on 'Metal Blade' cd/c/lp; CD/T+/ZORRO 28) (cd re-iss. May96 on 'Enigma'; 3984 14055CD)*

— **ALAN BARLAM** – guitar, repl. DUNCAN

— PRICHARD died of leukemia on the 27th February '90.

Metal Blade Enigma

Apr 91. (cd/c/lp) *(CD/T+/ZORRO 20) <26577-2/-4/-1>* **SYMBOL OF SALVATION**
– Reign of fire / Dropping like flies / Last train home / Tribal dance / The truth always hurts / Half drawn bridge / Another day / Symbol of salvation / Hanging judge / Warzone / Burning question / Tainted past / Spineless. *(cd re-iss. May96 on 'Enigma'; 3984 17014CD)*

— disbanded when BUSH joined ANTHRAX, although he returned to the fold (for below set) when ANTHRAX broke-up

Metal Blade Metal Blade

Mar 00. (cd/lp) *<(14288-2/-1)>* **REVELATION**
– After me / Tension / Creepy feelings / Damaged / Den of thieves / Control issues / No me digas / Deep rooted anger / What's your pleasure / Upon my departure.

ART ATTACKS

Formed: London, England . . . 1977 by 'Sounds' cartoonist extrordinaire, SAVAGE PENCIL (aka EDWIN POUNCEY), who turned his talents to "singing" against a 3-chord punk-rock backdrop provided by STEVE SPEAR, MARION FUDGER and JD HANEY (who replaced WIRE bound, ROBERT GOTOBED). Although they only gigged sporadically, they definitely had their moments, two of which ('Frankenstein's Heartbeat' & 'Animal Bondage') were the only classic punk tracks on that year's otherwise dull Various Artists lp, 'Live At The Vortex'. The ART ATTACKS contributed to yet another V/A compilation, 'Streets', the track in question being 'ARABS IN 'ARRADS', another slice of Dalek-voxed DIY. Appropriately titled, 'I AM A DALEK', became their debut 45 in Spring '78, although the scene had moved on leaps and bounds in such a short time span that their amateurism seemed outdated. They were still flogging a dead horse at the turn of the decade when they issued their wannabe final effort, 'PUNK ROCK STARS'. POUNCEY continued to record occasionally under various pseudonyms while keeping an illustrious career as a cartoonist. As SAVAGE PENCIL, he penned an obscure one-off solo album, 'ANGEL DUST' (1988), the soundtrack to the 'Bikers' movie which did nothing.

Album rating: never released one!

EDWIN POUNCEY – vocals / **STEVE SPEAR** – guitar / **M.S.** (MARION FUDGER) – bass (ex-DERELICTS) / **J.D. HANEY** – drums; repl. ROBERT GOTOBED who joined WIRE

Albatross not iss.

Apr 78. (7") *(TIT 1)* **I AM A DALEK. / NEUTRON BOMB** [-]

— had already split. ? replaced HANEY who joined MONOCHROME SET

Fresh not iss.

Dec 79. (7"m) *(FRESH 3)* **PUNK ROCK STARS. / RAT CITY / FIRST AND LAST** [-]

TAGMEMICS

were formed by EDWIN or an ex-member.

Index not iss.

1980. (7"m) *(INDEX 003)* **CHIMNEYS. / (DO THE) BIG BABY / TAKE YOUR BRAIN OUT FOR A WALK** [-]

SAVAGE PENCIL

Furthur not iss.

Apr 88. (lp) *(FU 3)* **ANGEL DUST** (music from the movie, Bikers') [-]

KRAY CHERUBS

formed by EDWIN? or other.

Fierce not iss.

1988. (7"-1 sided) *(FRIGHT 014)* **NO** [-]

Snakeskin not iss.

1989. (7"ltd.) *(SS 002)* **RIOT IN HELL MOM. / "SAUCERMAN":- Motor Drag** [-]

— Split for final time

ARTILLERY

Formed: Denmark . . . 1982 by JORGEN SANDAU and CARSTEN NIELSEN, who were subsequently joined by STUTZER brothers, MICHAEL and MORTEN. Following a succession of unsuitable vocalists, they opted for FLEMMING RODSDORF, signing to 'Roadrunner' in 1985 ('Neat' in Britain). Their debut, 'FEAR OF TOMORROW' showcased a standard issue thrash-metal sound, the band achieving no more than a cult following. The sequel, 'TERROR SQUAD', was much in the same vein, a few years of hibernation preceding their final effort, 'BY INHERITANCE' (1990). Towards the dawn of the 90's, ARTILLERY fired back at the metal world with their appropriately titled return, 'B.A.C.K.' (1999).

Album rating: FEAR OF TOMORROW (*5) / TERROR SQUAD (*5) / BY INHERITANCE (*4) / B.A.C.K. (*4)

FLEMMING RONSDORF – vocals / **MICHAEL STUTZER** – lead guitar / **JORGEN SANDAU** – rhythm guitar / **MORTEN STUTZER** – bass / **CARSTEN NIELSEN** – drums

Neat not iss.

Nov 85. (lp/c) *(NEAT/+C 1030)* **FEAR OF TOMORROW** [-]
– Time has come / The almighty / Show your hate / King, thy name is Slayer / Out of the sky / Into the universe / The eternal war / Deeds of darkness. *(<cd-iss. Jun98 on 'Axe Killer'; 303863-2>)*

— **PETER TORSLUND** – bass; repl. SANDAU (MORTEN now rhythm guitar)

Apr 87. (lp/c) *(NEAT/+C 1038)* **TERROR SQUAD** [-]
– The challenge / In the trash / Terror squad / Let there be sin / Hunger and greed / Therapy / At war with science / Decapitation of deviants. *<US-iss.1990 on 'Roadracer'; RO 9389>*

— MORTEN left for a period in 1988 but returned the following year

Aug 88. (lp/cd) *(NEAT/+CD 1046)* **ARTILLERY 3** [-] [-] shelved

Roadracer Roadracer

May 90. (cd/c/lp) *(<RO 9397-2/-4/-1>)* **BY INHERITANCE**
– 7:00 from Tashkent / Khomaniac / Beneath the clay (R.I.P.) / By inheritance / Bombfood / Don't believe / Life in bondage / Equal at first / Razamanaz / Back in the trash.

— the group split into different regiments after above, until . . .

Diehard not iss.

Nov 99. (cd) *(P-CD 33)* **B.A.C.K.** [-]

A.S.a.P.

Formed: Originally initiated in 1986 by ADRIAN SMITH (of IRON MAIDEN at the time), under the moniker of The ENTIRE POPULATION OF HACKNEY after a gig in London's Marquee. Subsequently adopting the more sensible A.S.a.P. (ADRIAN SMITH AND PROJECT), his band also featured ANDY BARNETT (with whom he'd played in his first outfit, URCHIN) and ZAK STARKEY (son of RINGO STARR). An album, 'SILVER AND GOLD', appeared in late '89, the set a markedly more mainstream affair. IRON MAIDEN were none too happy at this change of direction, duly serving SMITH notice that he was surplus to requirements. With a less than enthusiastic response to the album from the metal press, it was to be A.S.a.P./SMITH's one and only outing, nothing having been heard from the guitarist since.

Album rating: SILVER AND GOLD (*4)

ADRIAN SMITH – vocals, guitar (ex-IRON MAIDEN) / **ANDY BARNETT** – guitar / **DAVE COLWELL** – guitar / **ROBIN CLAYTON** – bass / **RICHARD YOUNG** – keyboards / **ZAK STARKEY** – drums

E.M.I. Enigma

Oct 89. (7"/7"gold/7"silver) *(EM/+G/S 107)* **SILVER AND GOLD. / BLOOD BROTHERS** [ ] [-]
(remixed;12"+=/cd-s+=) *(12/CD EM 107)* – Fighting man.

Oct 89. (cd/c/lp) *(CD/TC+/EMC 3566)* *<73572-2/-4/-1>* **SILVER AND GOLD** [ ] [ ]
– The lion / Silver and gold / Down the wire / You could be a king / After the storm / Misunderstood / Kid gone astray / Fallen heroes / Wishing your life away / Blood on the ocean.

Jan 90. (c-s/7")(7"sha-pic-d) *(TC+/EM 131)(EMPD 131)* **DOWN THE WIRE (crossed line mix). / WHEN SHE'S GONE** [67] [-]
('A'ext.;12"+=/cd-s+=) *(12/CD EM 131)* – School days.

— split the outfit soon after, COLWELL later joining BAD COMPANY

ASH

Formed: N.Ireland . . . 1989 by TIM WHEELER (then 12 years of age) and MARK HAMILTON, relocating to Downpatrick, County Down a few years later where they officially formed the trio with RICK McMURRAY. ASH's precocious talents were quickly spotted by American record moguls eager for more punk-centric guitar music which would also cross over to the pop market. Though they eventually opted to sign with 'Reprise', the trio had already released their debut set, 'TRAILER' on 'Infectious'. Their starry-eyed, bushy-tailed but ultimately derivative blend of indie punk finally became a part of the pop vocabulary when the catchy 'GIRL FROM MARS' sky-rocketed into the UK Top 20 in summer '95. This was pursued by another Top 20 hit later that year in 'ANGEL INTERCEPTOR'. With the hype machine going into overload, the group hit the UK Top 5 in Spring of the following year with 'GOLDFINGER', the single trailing a No.1 album, '1977' (1996). Apparently a reference to the year 'Star Wars' was released rather than any reference to safety-pins and saliva, the record included all their hit singles to date and confirmed their increasingly melodic approach. Keeping their profile high with festival appearances, the band later added another guitarist, CHARLOTTE HATHERLEY in summer '97. She made her debut on ASH's theme for the much lauded Ewan McGregor/Cameron Diaz film, 'A LIFE LESS ORDINARY', another Top 10 in late '97. While the indie scene continues to cry out for something innovative, it remains difficult to envisage any figureheads less ordinary than ASH (songs!). Surprisingly 'Kerrang!-friendly, the quartet lost a little of their indie cred with the release of their third album proper, 'NU-CLEAR SOUNDS' (1998), a record that quickly vacated the Top 10 with the accompanying single, 'JESUS SAYS', only managing to make a Top 20 placing. With sex (group, that is), drugs (abuse) and rock'n'roll (Tim Wheeler in the buff!) all the ingredients were in the latest promo instalment for ASH's single 'NUMBSKULL'. Unfortunately the viewing public, and for that matter the buying public, didn't get much of a look-in, as the EP (like many others at the turn of the century) was ineligible for the charts via a new ruling by those pesky compilers. Older and wiser, the ASH posse returned in 2001 with their first material of the new millennium, 'FREE ALL ANGELS'. Previewed by the hit singles, 'SHINING LIGHT' and 'BURN BABY BURN', the record recaptured some of their mid-period spunk and used it to temper the aural hangover of its predecessor. • **Songwriters:** WHEELER or w/ HAMILTON except covers; PUNKBOY (Helen Love) / GET READY (Temptations) / DOES YOUR MOTHER KNOW (Abba) / LOSE CONTROL (Backwater) / BLEW (Nirvana) / WHO YOU DRIVIN' NOW? (Mudhoney). • **Trivia:** The cover sleeve of their single, 'KUNG FU', had a photo of French former Man U star footballer, ERIC CANTONA, giving his famous throat and neck tackle on an abusive Crystal Palace supporter in 1995.

Album rating: TRAILER mini (*7) / 1977 (*9) / LIVE AT THE WIRELESS live official bootleg (*5) / NU-CLEAR SOUNDS (*7) / FREE ALL ANGELS (*6)

TIM WHEELER – vocals, guitar / **MARK HAMILTON** – bass / **RICK McMURRAY** – drums

La La Land not iss.

Feb 94. (7") *(LA LA 001)* **JACK NAMES THE PLANETS. / DON'T KNOW** [ ] [-]

Infectious Reprise

Aug 94. (7"ep) *(INFECT 13S)* **PETROL. / THE LITTLE POND / A MESSAGE FROM OSCAR WILDE AND PATRICK THE BREWER** [ ] [-]
(cd-s+=) *(INFEVT 13CD)* – Things. *(re-iss. Nov96; same)*

Oct 94. (cd/c/lp) *(INFECT 14 CD/MC/LP)* *<45985>* **TRAILER** [ ] [ ]Oct95
– Season / Message from Oscar Wilde and Patrick the brewer / Jack names the planets / Intense thing / Uncle Pat / Message from Mr. Waterman / Get out / Petrol / Obscure thing. *(lp w/free 7"yellow) (INFECT 14S)* SILVER SURFER. / JAZZ '59 *<diff.tracks US> (re-iss. Jan01 cd/c/lp; INFECT 14 CD/MC/LPX)*

Oct 94. (7") *(INFECT 16S)* **UNCLE PAT. / DIFFERENT TODAY** [ ] [-]
(cd-s+=) *(INFECT 16CD)* – Hulk Hogan bubble bath. *(re-iss. Nov96; same)*

Mar 95. (7") *(INFECT 21J)* *<17706>* **KUNG FU. / DAY OF THE TRIFFIDS** [57] [ ]Nov95
(cd-s+=) *(INFECT 21CD)* – Luther Ingo's star cruiser. *(re-iss. Nov96 & Jan01; same)*

Jul 95. (7"/c-s) *(INFECT 24S/24MC)* **GIRL FROM MARS. / CANTINA BAND** [11] [-]
(cd-s+=) *(INFECT 24CD)* – Astral conversations with Toulouse Lautrec. *(re-iss. Nov96 & Jan01; same)*

Sep 95. (7"colrd-various) *<G26>* **PETROL. / PUNKBOY** [-] [ ]

Oct 95. (7"/c-s/cd-s) *(INFECT 27S/27MC/27CD)* **ANGEL INTERCEPTOR. / 5 A.M. ETERNAL / GIVE ME SOME TRUTH** [14] [-]
(re-iss. cd-s Nov96 & Jan01; same)

Dec 95. (7"red) *(FP 004)* **GET READY. / ZERO ZERO ZERO** [ ] [-]
(above 45 issued on 'Fantastic Plastic')

Apr 96. (7"/c-s) *(INFECT 39 S/MC)* **GOLDFINGER. / I NEED SOMEBODY / SNEAKER** [5] [-]
(cd-s+=) *(INFECT 39CD)* – Get ready. *(re-iss. Nov96 & Jan01; same)*

May 96. (cd/c/lp) *(INFECT 40 CD/MC/LP)* *<46191>* **1977** [1] [ ]
– Lose control / Goldfinger / Girl from Mars / I'd give you anything / Gone the dream / Kung Fu / Oh yeah / Let it flow / Innocent smile / Angel interceptor / Lost in you / Darkside lightside. *(cd+=hidden track)* – Sick of vomiting. *(lp re-iss. Jan01; same)*

Jun 96. (7"yellow/c-s) *(INFECT 41 S/MC)* **OH YEAH / T. REX / EVERYWHERE IS ALL AROUND / OH YEAH (quartet version)** [6] [-]
(cd-s) *(INFECT 41CD)* – (first 3 tracks) / Does your mother know. *(re-iss. Nov96 & Jan01; same)*

— added **CHARLOTTE HATHERLEY** – guitar (ex-NIGHTNURSE)

Infectious Dreamworks

Oct 97. (7"blue/c-s) *(INFECT 50 S/MC)* **A LIFE LESS ORDINARY. / WHERE IS LOVE GOING / WHAT DEANER WAS TALKING ABOUT** [10] [-]
(cd-s+=) *(INFECT 50CD)* – Halloween. *(re-iss. Jan01; same)*

Sep 98. (7") *(INFECT 059S)* **JESUS SAYS. / TAKEN OUT** [15] [-]
(c-s+=/cd-s+=) *(INFECT 059 MCS/CDS)* – Heroin, vodka, white noise.
(cd-s) *(INFECT 059CDSX)* – ('A'side) / Radiation / Dancing on the Moon. *(re-iss. Jan01; same)*

Oct 98. (cd/c/lp) *(INFECT 060 CD/MC/LP)* *<50121>* **NU-CLEAR SOUNDS** [7] [ ]Sep99
– Projects / Low ebb / Jesus says / Wild surf / Death trip 21 / Folk song / Numbskull / Burn out / Aphrodite / Fortune teller / I'm gonna fall. *(re-iss. Jan01; same)*

Nov 98. (7") *(INFECT 061S)* **WILD SURF. / STORMY WATERS** [31] [-]
(c-s+=/cd-s+=) *(INFECT 061 MCS/CDS)* – When I'm tired.
(cd-s) *(INFECT 061CDSX)* – ('A'side) / Lose control / Gonna do it soon. *(re-iss. Jan01; same)*

— added on tour **DJ DICK KURTAINE** – turntables

Apr 99. (d7"red-ep) *(INFECT 62)* **NUMBSKULL EP** [ ] [-]
– Numbskull / Blew / Who you drivin' now? / Jesus says (live).
(cd-ep+=) *(INFECT 62EP)* – Girl from Mars (live) / Fortune teller (live). *(re-iss. Jan01; same)*

Jan 01. (7"/c-s) *(INFECT 98 S/MCS)* **SHINING LIGHT. / WARMER THAN FIRE** [8] [-]
(cd-s+=) *(INFECT 98CDS)* – Gabriel.
(cd-s) *(INFECT 98CDSX)* – ('A'side) / Feel no pain / Jesus says (headrock valley beats lightyear 12"mix) / ('A'-CD-ROM video).

Apr 01. (7") *(INFECT 99S)* **BURN BABY BURN. / THINKING ABOUT YOU** [13] [-]
(cd-s+=) *(INFECT 99CDSX)* – Submission (Arthur Baker remix).
(cd-s) *(INFECT 99CDS)* – ('A'side) / 13th floor (session) / Only in dreams (session).

Apr 01. (cd/c/lp) *(INFECT 100 CD/MC/LP)* **FREE ALL ANGELS** [1] [-]
– Walking barefoot / Shining light / Burn baby burn / Candy / Submission / Someday / Pacific palisades / Shark / Sometimes / Nicole / There's a star / World domination.

– compilations, etc. –

Feb 97. (cd) *Death Star; (DEATH 3)* **LIVE AT THE WIRELESS (live)** [ ] [-]
– Darkside lightside / Girl from Mars / Oh yeah / T.Rex / I'd give you anything / Kung Fu / What Deaner was talking about / Goldfinger / Petrol / A clear invitation to party. *(lp-iss.Jan01; DEATH 3LP)*

ASIA

Formed: London, England . . . early 1981 by seasoned pomp-rockers, JOHN WETTON, STEVE HOWE, CARL PALMER and GEOFREY DOWNES. These supergroup stadium fillers had no trouble finding a record contract with 'Geffen', their eponymous debut soon climbing to No.1 in the States, supplanting them as top dogs over similar challengers, YES. Their smooth FM friendly AOR blend fared particularly well in the US, 'HEAT OF THE MOMENT', 'ONLY TIME WILL TELL' and 'DON'T CRY', all becoming Top 20 hits in 1982. The follow-up, 'ALPHA', didn't live up to the high expectations afforded it, although it still reached the Top 10 on both sides of the Atlantic. For a brief two year period, GREG LAKE filled in for the absent WETTON, the singer returning to record a third album, 'ASTRA' in '85. HOWE was also missing, having returned to YES, his replacement being MANDY MEYER. All this disruption clearly had a knock-on effect on album sales, the record stiffing in the lower regions of the chart. With another experienced campaigner, PAT THRALL, drafted in, the group recorded 'THEN & NOW', a 1990 set of re-worked favourites and a handful of new tracks. In 1992, with only DOWNES and PALMER remaining from the original line-up, they left 'Geffen' and recorded a fifth album, 'AQUA', which was followed by some more unremarkable cd outings, DOWNES having taken on full control when PALMER returned to ELP. • **Trivia:** Their "Asia In Asia" concert at Budokan, Tokyo 6 Dec'83, went live to over 20 million people in US through MTV station.

Album rating: ASIA (*6) / ALPHA (*4) / ASTRA (*3) / THEN & NOW (*5) / AQUA (*3) / ARIA (*3)

JOHN WETTON (b.12 Jul'49, Derby, England) – vocals, bass (ex-URIAH HEEP, ex-ROXY MUSIC, ex-BRYAN FERRY, ex-KING CRIMSON, ex-FAMILY, ex-U.K.) / **STEVE HOWE** (b. 8 Apr'47) – guitar, vocals (ex-YES, ex-BODAST, ex-TOMORROW) / **GEOFFREY DOWNES** – keyboards, vocals (ex-YES, ex-BUGGLES, ex-ISOTOPE) /

CARL PALMER (b.20 Mar'47, Birmingham, England) – drums, percussion (ex-EMERSON, LAKE & PALMER, ex-P.M.)

Geffen Geffen

Apr 82. (lp/pic-lp/c) *(GEF/+11/40 85577) <2008>* **ASIA** [11] [1]
– Heat of the moment / Only time will tell / Sole survivor / One step closer / Time again / Wildest dream / Without you / Cutting it fine / Here comes the feeling. *(cd-iss. Apr83; CDGEF 85577) (re-iss. Sep86 lp/c; 902008-1/-4) (cd-iss. Feb87; 902008-2)* (re-iss. Apr91 cd/c; *GEFD/GEFC 02008) (re-iss. cd Apr92; GFLD 19054)*

Jun 82. (7") *(A 2494) <50040>* **HEAT OF THE MOMENT. / TIME AGAIN** [46] [4] Apr82

Aug 82. (7"/7"pic-d) *(A/+11 2228) <29970>* **ONLY TIME WILL TELL. / RIDE EASY** [54] [17] Jul82

Oct 82. (7") *(A 2884)* **SOLE SURVIVOR. / HERE COMES THE FEELING** [ ] [ ]

Aug 83. (7"/7"sha-pic-d) *(A/WA 3580) <29571>* **DON'T CRY. / DAYLIGHT** [33] [10] Jul83
(12"+=) *(TA 3580)* – True Colours.

Aug 83. (lp/c) *(GEF/GEC 25508) <4008>* **ALPHA** [5] [6]
– Don't cry / The smile has left your eyes / Never in a million years / My own time (I'll do what I want) / The heat goes on / Eye to eye / The last to know / True colours / Midnight Sun / Open your eyes. *(c+=) –* Daylight. *(re-iss. Sep86 lp/c; 940008-1/-4) (cd-iss. Jun89; 94008-2) (re-iss. Apr91 & Aug99 cd/c; GEFD/GEFC 04008)*

Oct 83. (7") *(A 3836) <29475>* **THE SMILE HAS LEFT YOUR EYES. / LYING TO YOURSELF** [ ] [34]
(12"+=,12"red+=) *(TA 3836)* – Midnight Sun.

— (Oct83) **GREG LAKE** (b.10 Nov'48, Bournemouth, England) – vocals, bass (ex-EMERSON, LAKE & PALMER, ex-Solo Artist, ex-KING CRIMSON) repl. WETTON

— (Mar84). **ARMAND 'Mandy' MEYER** – guitar (ex-KROKUS) repl. HOWE who returned to YES and formed G.T.R.

— **JOHN WETTON** returned to replace LAKE (re-joined E.L.P.)

Nov 85. (7") *(A 6737) <28872>* **GO. / AFTER THE WAR** [ ] [46]
(A-remix-12"+=) *(TA 6737)* – ('A'instrumental).

Dec 85. (lp/c/cd) *(GEF/40GEF/CDGEF 26413) <24072>* **ASTRA** [68] [67]
– Go / Voice of America / Hard on me / Wishing / Rock and roll dream / Countdown to zero / Love now till eternity / Too late / Suspicion / After the war.

Jan 86. (7") **WISHING. / TOO LATE** [-] [ ]

— (early 1986, disbanded) **WETTON** teamed up with **PHIL MANZANERA**

— In Sep87, GEOFFREY DOWNES released solo lp/cd 'THE LIGHT PROGRAMME' on 'Geffen'; *K 924156-1/-2)*

— re-formed late 1989 (WETTON, DOWNES, PALMER plus **PAT THRALL** – guitar (ex-AUTOMATIC MAN). He was replaced by session men **STEVE LUKATHER, RON KOMIE, MANDY MEYER** and **SCOTT GORHAM**

Aug 90. (cd/c/lp) *(CD/40+/GEF 24298)* **THEN & NOW** (hits compliation & new songs) [ ] [ ]
– (THEN) Only time will tell / Wildest dreams / The smile has left your eyes / Heat of the moment / Don't cry / (NOW) – Days like these / Prayin' 4 a miracle / Am I in love? / Voice of America / Summer (can't last too long). *(re-iss. Aug91 cd/c; GEF D/C 24298)*

Sep 90. (c-s,cd-s) *<19677>* **DAYS LIKE THESE. / VOICE OF AMERICA** [-] [64]

— **JOHN PAYNE** – vocals, bass; repl. WETTON

— **AL PITRELLI** – guitar (ex-DANGER DANGER) repl. THRALL

— **STEVE HOWE** also made guest appearance

FM Coast To Coast JRS

Jun 92. (cd/c/lp) *(WKFM XD/XC/LP 180)* **AQUA** [ ] [ ] Mar92
– Aqua (part one) / Who will stop the rain / Back in town / Love under fire / Someday / Little rich boy / The voice of reason / Lay down your arms / Crime of the heart / A far cry / Don't call me / Heaven on Earth / Aqua (part two). *(cd re-iss. Feb98 on 'Snapper'; SMMCD 521)*

Musidisc Sony

Aug 92. (7") *(10952-7)* **WHO WILL STOP THE RAIN. / AQUA (part 1)** [ ] [ ]
(10"pic-d+=/12"+=) *(10952-1/-6)* – Heart of gold.
(cd-s++=) *(10952-2)* – Obsessing.

— **MICHAEL STURGIS** – drums; repl. PALMER

Bulletproof M.F.N.

May 94. (cd-ep) *(CDVEST 1001)* **ANYTIME / REALITY / ANYTIME (extended) / FEELS LIKE LOVE** [ ] [ ]

May 94. (cd/c/lp) *(CD/C+/VEST 8)* **ARIA** [ ] [ ]
– Anytime / Are you big enough? / Desire / Summer / Sad situation / Don't cut the wire (brother) / Feels like love / Remembrance day / Enough's enough / Military man / Aria. *(cd re-iss. Feb98 on 'Snapper'; SMMCD 523)*

— **VINNIE BURNS + TREVOR THORNTON** repl. PITRELLI plus injured HOWE

– compilations, etc. –

Jun 92. (cd) *Essential; (ESSCD 174) / Rhino; <R2 70377>* **ASIA LIVE MOCKBA 09-XI-90 (live)** [ ] [ ] Nov90

May 97. (d-cd) *Blueprint; (BP 252CD)* **LIVE IN OSAKA 1992 (live)** [ ] [-]
(re-iss. Feb01 on 'Recognition'; CDREC 507)

Mar 97. (cd) *Blueprint; (BP 253CD)* **ASIA NOW – LIVE IN NOTTINGHAM 1990 (live)** [ ] [-]

Jul 97. (cd) *Blueprint; (BP 254CD)* **LIVE IN KOLN (live)** [ ] [-]
(re-iss. Feb01 on 'Recognition'; CDREC 506)

Nov 97. (d-cd) *Blueprint; (BP 255CD)* **LIVE IN PHILADELPHIA (live)** [ ] [-]
(re-iss. Feb01 on 'Recognition'; CDREC 505)

Feb 98. (cd) *Snapper; (SMMCD 522)* **ARENA** [ ] [-]
<(re-iss. May98 on 'Resurgence'; LV 103CD)>

Mar 98. (cd) *Eagle; (EAMCD 037)* **LIVE IN MOSCOW (live)** [ ] [ ]

Jun 98. (cd) *Resurgence; (LV 104CD)* **ARCHIVA VOL.1** [ ] [ ]
(re-iss. Sep99 on 'Snapper'; SMMCD 596)

Jun 98. (cd) *Resurgence; (LV 105CD)* **ARCHIVA VOL.2** [ ] [ ]
(re-iss. Sep99 on 'Snapper'; SMMCD 597)

Feb 99. (d-cd) *Recall; (SMDCD 217)* **AXIOMS** [ ] [-]
– Bella nova / Who will stop the rain / Heaven on Earth / Words / Turn it around / Summer / Heaven / Far cry / Love under fire / Tell me why / Anytime / Aqua part two / Into the arena / Military man / Hunter / Desire / Sad situation / The day before the war / Feels like love / Different worlds / Remembrance day / U bring me down / Aria.

Jul 99. (cd) *Snapper; (SMMCD 519)* **ANTHOLOGY** [ ] [-]

Oct 99. (cd) *Resurgence; (LV 107CD)* **LIVE AT THE TOWN & COUNTRY CLUB (live)** [ ] [ ]

Nov 99. (cd) *Resurgence; (LV 108CD)* **LIVE ACOUSTIC (live)** [ ] [ ]

Feb 00. (cd) *Brilliant; (BT 33039)* **LIVE IN RUSSIA (live)** [ ] [-]

Apr 00. (cd) *Connoisseur; (VSOPCD 285)* **THE COLLECTION** [ ] [-]

Apr 00. (cd) *Resurgence; (LV 106CD)* **RARE** [ ] [-]

May 00. (3xcd-box) *Snapper; <(SMXCD 101)>* **THE BOX** [ ] [ ] Jul00
– (AQUA / ARIA / ARENA)

Jul 00. (cd) *Interscope; <(490554-2)>* **HEAT OF THE MOMENT 1982-1990 – THE VERY BEST OF ASIA** [ ] [ ] Jun00

Sep 00. (cd) *Music Club; (MCCD 443)* **ARCHIVES (THE BEST OF ASIA)** [ ] [-]

Oct 00. (cd) *Eagle; (EDMCD 110)* **LIVE** [ ] [-]

Mar 01. (cd) *Zoom Club; (ZCRCD 50)* **ALIVE IN THE HALLOWED HALLS (live 1983)** [ ] [-]

Jun 01. (cd) *Burning Airlines; (<PILOT 87)>* **ASIA IN ASIA (live in Tokyo 1983)** [ ] [ ]

ASIAN DUB FOUNDATION

Formed: Farringdon, London, England ... 1993 by DR. DAS, PANDIT G and MASTER D, a tutor, an assistant and a student respectively at an inner city community music programme designed for young aspiring Asian musicians/DJ's/MC's/etc. Initially trading as a sound system, ADF began making their own records the following year. Signed to 'Nation' (home of TRANSGLOBAL UNDERGROUND), the trio issued the 'CONSCIOUS' EP prior to adding unorthodox sitar-influenced guitarist, CHANDRASONIC, synth man SUN-J and stage dancer, BUBBLE-E. Taking up the agit-prop, slash'n'burn politico-musical baton from the ailing SENSER, ADF fought off the neo-Nazis with an infammatory combination of Bengali folk, drum'n'bass and punk that strangely and uniquely recalled the spirit of ALTERNATIVE TV's MARK PERRY. In 1995, this radical troupe unleashed their debut long player, 'FACTS AND FICTIONS', a surprising cohesive set given the amount of disparate musical strands running through each track. Amassing a cult following drawn from both the indie and dance communities (much in the same way that The PRODIGY rose to such giddy heights a few years earlier), ADF soon found themselves under the wing of 'London' offshoot, 'FFRR' in 1997. Gaining more column inches and higher chart placings with each successive release via the incendiary singles, 'NAXALITE', 'BUZZIN', 'FREE SATPAL RAM' and 'BLACK WHITE', the long awaited follow-up set, 'RAFI'S REVENGE' (1998; 1997 in France!) blazed a trail into the UK Top 20. Nominated for a 'Mercury Award', the album didn't win but received some free televised publicity/criticism courtesy of Fantasy Football thingy/ 3 Lions/"comedian", David Baddiel, who obviously prefers the fluffier sounds of the LIGHTNING SEEDS. While working on their follow-up set (scheduled for 2000), ADF were trying to convince the Home Office to "Free SATPAL RAM", the Asian man still in prison after 13 years.

Album rating: FACTS AND FICTIONS (*7) / RAFI'S REVENGE (*9) / COMMUNITY MUSIC (*7)

MASTER D (DEEDER SAIDULLAH ZAMAN) – rapping / **PANDIT G** (JOHN ASHOK PANDIT) – turntables, voice / **DR. DAS** (ANIRUDDHA DAS) – bass, programming, voice

Nation not iss.

Aug 94. (12"ep/cd-ep) *(NR 42 T/CD)* **CONSCIOUS EP.** [ ] [-]
– Debris / Tu meri / Jericho / Witness.

— added **CHANDRASONIC (STEVE CHANDRA SAVALE)** – guitar, programming, vocals (ex-HEADSPACE, ex-The HIGHER INTELLIGENCE AGENCY)

— added **SUN-J** (SANJAY GULABHAI TAILOR) – synths / + dancer **BUBBLE-E**

Apr 95. (12"ep/cd-ep) *(NR 51 T/CD)* **REBEL WARRIOR** [ ] [-]
– Rebel warrior / Nazrul dub / Strong culture / Rivers of dub.

Oct 95. (cd/lp) *(NAT CD/LP 58)* **FACTS AND FICTIONS** [ ] [-]
– Witness / PKNB / Jericho / Rebel warrior / Journey / Strong culture / Th9 / Tu meri / Debris box / Thacid 9 (dub version) / Return to Jericho (dub version). *(cd re-iss. Aug98; NATCDM 058)*

May 96. (12"ep/cd-ep) *(NR 61 T/CD)* **CHANGE A GONNA COME** [ ] [-]
– Change a gonna come / Operation eagle eye / C.A.G.C. (via pirate satellite) / Jerico (CAPA D dub).

Damaged Goods not iss.

Jul 97. (7"; split with ATARI TEENAGE RIOT) *(DAMGOOD 132)* **split** [ ] [-]

Sub Rosa not iss.

Jul 97. (12"; split with EUPHONIC) *(QUANTUM 605)* **TRIBUTE: ... SOUND SYSTEM / WAY OF THE EXPLODING FIST** [ ] [-]

— now as ASIANDUBFOUNDATION

FFRR Polygram

Oct 97. (7") *(F 320)* **NAXALITE. / CHARGE** [ ] [-]
(12"+=/cd-s+=) *(FX/FCD 320)* – ('A'+'B'mixes).

Feb 98. (7") *(F 326)* **FREE SATPAL RAM. / TRIBUTE TO JOHN STEPHENS** [56] [-]
(12"+=/cd-s+=) *(FX/FCD 326)* – ('A'-Primal Scream & Brendan Lynch mix) / ('A'-ADF Sound System mix).

Apr 98. (12"ep/cd-ep) *(FX/FCD 335)* **BUZZIN' (mixes) / DIGITAL UNDERCLASS** [31] [ ]
(cd-ep) *(FCDP 335)* – ('A'extended) / Free Satpal Ram (live) / Charge (live) / Naxalite (live).

May 98. (cd/c/d-lp) *(556 006-2/-4/-1) <556 053>* **RAFI'S REVENGE** 20 □
– Naxalite / Buzzin' / Black white / Assassin / Hypocrite / Charge / Free Satpal Ram / Dub mentality / Culture move / Operation eagle lie / Change / Tribute to John Stevens. *(cd re-iss. Sep99; 3984 28193-2)*
Jun 98. (12"/cd-s) *(FX/FCDP 337)* **BLACK WHITE / BLACK WHITE (maximum roach mix). / NAXALITE (Underdog mix) / NAXALITE (Underdog instrumental)** 52 -
(cd-s) *(FCD 337)* – ('A'side) / Rafi / Assassin (live) / Buzzin' (live).
Sep 98. (12"ep/cd-ep) *(FX/FCD 348) <570289>* **NAXALITE / CULTURE MOVE EP** □ □ Nov98
– Naxalite (main mix) / Culture move (pusher sound mix) / Free Satpal Ram (Russell Simmons mix) / Culture move (urban decay mix) / Culture move (silver haze mix).

FFRR E.M.I.

Mar 00. (12"/cd-s) *(FX/FCD 376)* **REAL GREAT BRITAIN. / ('A'-Freqnasty acid monsta mix & dub)** 41 -
(cd-s) *(FCDP 376)* – ('A'side) / Officer XX (ADF jump up version) / ('A'-Jazzwad real Jamaica mix).
Mar 00. (cd) *(8573 82042-2) <38204-2>* **COMMUNITY MUSIC** 20 □ May00
– Real Great Britain / Memory war / Officer XX / New way, new life / Riddim I like / Collective mode / Crash / Colour line / Taa deem / The judgement / Truth hides / Rebel warrior / Committed to life / Scaling new heights.
May 00. (12"/cd-s) *(FX/FCD 378)* **NEW WAY, NEW LIFE. / ('A'-Dry & Heavy vocal & dub mixes)** 49 -
(cd-s) *(cd-s) (FCDP 378)* – ('A'side) / Real Great Britain (live) / Crash (live).

ASSERT

Formed: Telford, England . . . mid 90's by the man 'The Times' described as one of the most subversive men in Britain, the heavily tattooed singer, BRITT. The line-up was completed by three other equally anarcho-socialists, RYAN, JOHNNY SINISTER and SPEN, who reactivated the hardcore/oi/punk/thrash days of yore (ANGELIC UPSTARTS and CONFLICT come to mind). Two EP's unleashed either end of 1997 announced the band's agenda, while the following year's 'MORE THAN A WITNESS' varied little in its approach.

Album rating: MORE THAN A WITNESS (*5) / LEFT OPPOSITION (*6)

BRITT – vocals / **RYAN** – guitar / **JOHNNY SINISTER** – bass / **SPEN** – drums

Hideous Eye not iss.

Feb 97. (7"ep) **ASSERT YOURSELF EP** □ -
– Straight edge / Four legs good (two legs bad) / Assert yourself / Corporate logo strangulation.

Household Name Household Name

Oct 97. (7"ep) *(HAUS 008)* **FOUR FINGERS AND A THUMB FOLD A FIST EP** □ -
– Something safe in negativity / Violently blue / Assertiveness (should be a way of life) / A collective force.
Jul 98. (cd) *(HAUS 015CD)* **MORE THAN A WITNESS** □ -
Oct 99. (cd) *(HAUS 029CD)* **LEFT OPPOSITION** □ □ Jan00
– Left opposition / Time to seize / Falsification / A.T.V. / United colours / Welcome to the world / Insight (into the situation) / Revolution / Red wipe out the blues / Statement of intent / James Byrd Jr. / K.R.T.D.

ATARIS

Formed: Anderson, Indiana, USA . . . mid 90's by KRIS ROE. Having been handed a deal (on the strength of a demo tape) by JOE ESCALANTE (of VANDALS fame) and his 'Kung-Fu' label, ROE subsequently relocated to California where he recruited MARCO PENA, MIKE DAVENPORT and ex-LAGWAGON man, DERRICK PLOURDE. The latter was soon replaced by CHRIS KNAPP while debut set, ' . . .ANYWHERE BUT HERE' (1997) brought ATARIS to the attention of Cal-punk institution, 'Fat Wreck Chords'. The cheerily titled 'LOOK FORWARD TO FAILURE' EP in '98 was in turn followed by a sophomore album, 'BLUE SKIES, BROKEN HEARTS . . . NEXT 12 EXITS' (1999). With a decidedly more sentimental streak and a more easygoing sound than your average punk act, ATARIS' nice guy reputation preceded them. Further albums, 'LET IT BURN' (2000) and 'END IS FOREVER' (2001) continued in a similar vein, marking them out from the tired posturing of their spike-haired brethren.

Album rating: . . .ANYWHERE BUT HERE (*6) / LOOK FORWARD TO FAILURE mini (*5) / BLUES SKIES BROKEN HEARTS NEXT 12 EXITS (*6) / END IS FOREVER (*6)

KRIS ROE – vocals / **MARCO PENA** – guitar / **MIKE DAVENPORT** – bass / **CHRIS KNAPP** – drums

Kung Fu Kung Fu

Jun 98. (cd/c/lp) *<(78763-2/-4/-1)>* **. . .ANYWHERE BUT HERE** □ □ Apr97
– Four chord wonders / Are we there yet? / Bite my tongue / Perfectly happy / Hey kid / Ray / As we speak / Sleepy / Lately / Let it go / Neilhouse / Make it last / Alone in Santa Cruz / Angry nerd rock / Take me back / Blind and unkind / Clara.
Nov 98. (m-cd) *<(FAT 581CD)>* **LOOK FORWARD TO FAILURE** □ □
– San Dimas high school football rules / Not a worry in the world / My hotel year / Between you and me / That special girl / My so called life.
(above issued on 'Fat Wreck Chords')
Jun 99. (cd/lp) *<(78769-2)>* **BLUE SKIES BROKEN HEARTS NEXT 12 EXITS** □ □
– Losing streak / 1-15-96 / San Dimas high school football rules / Your boyfriend sucks / I won't spend another night alone / Broken promise ring / Angry nerd rock / The last song I will ever write about a girl / Choices / Better way / My hotel year / Life makes no sense / Answer / In spite of the world.
Jun 00. (cd; shared w/ USELESS I.D.) *<(78779-2)>* **LET IT BURN** □ □ Apr00
– The radio still sucks / Song for a mix tape / P.S. the scene is dead / Blue skies, broken hearts . . . next 12 exits / Let it burn / How I spend my summer vacation / On with the show / San Dimas high school football rules / (other tracks by USELESS I.D.).
Sep 00. (7") *(ATOM 016)* **split** □ -
(above issued on 'Speedowax')
Mar 01. (cd/lp) *<(78782-2)>* **END IS FOREVER** □ □
– Giving up on love / Summer wind was always our song / I.O.U. one galaxy / Bad case of broken heart / Up, up, down, down, left, right, left, right, B, A, start / Road signs and rock songs / If you really want to hear about it . . . / Fast times at Drop-out High / Song for a mix tape / You need a hug / How I spent my summer vacation / Teenage riot / Song #13 / Hello & goodbye.

ATARI TEENAGE RIOT

Formed: West Berlin, Germany . . . 1992 by anti-Nazi cyberpunks ALEC EMPIRE, Syrian-born punk goddess HANIN ELIAS and Swiss-born CARL CRACK. With his 'Digital Hardcore' label as the main weapon of attack, EMPIRE has waged war on what he sees as an increasingly corporate, decadently comatose German dance scene. His self proclaimed 'lo-fi' techno owes more to the headfuck onslaught of radical hardcore punk (like X-RAY SPEX or CRASS) than any regular notion of "dance" music and ATARI TEENAGE RIOT's staunch anti-nazi, anti-Ecstasy stance has made EMPIRE a spokesman of sorts for the disillusioned Berlin underground scene. After a trio of fearsome albums, 'DELETE YOURSELF' (1995), 'THE FUTURE OF WAR' and the well-received 'BURN, BERLIN, BURN!' (both 1997), they secured support slots with big guns RAGE AGAINST THE MACHINE and WU-TANG CLAN. More recently, the 'RIOT released the 'DESTROY 2,000 YEARS OF CULTURE EP', though presumably EMPIRE'll make an exception for dodgy 70's punk, having already covered the old SHAM 69 chestnut, 'IF THE KIDS ARE UNITED'. In 1998, with a number of solo releases behind him, EMPIRE worked on the JON SPENCER BLUES EXPLOSION while planning ATR's comeback complete with a second female, the German/Japanese, face-painted, NIC ENDO. She also delivered a solo EP in '98, 'WHITE HEAT', a searing, uncompromising, computerised set of five hardcore sounds that became NME's Single Of The Week!

Album rating: DELETE YOURSELF (*7) / THE FUTURE OF WAR (*4) / BURN, BERLIN, BURN mini (*7) / 60 SECOND WIPE OUT (*7) / LIVE AT BRIXTON ACADEMY 1999 (*7) / Alec Empire: LTD EDITIONS 90-94 compilation (*7) / GENERATION STAR WARS (*7) / HYPERMODERN JAZZ 2000.5 (*8) / THE DESTROYER (*7) / SQUEEZE THE TRIGGER (*6) / INTENDO TEENAGE RIOTS (*7) / MISS BLACK AMERICA mini (*7) / Carl Crack: BLACK ARK (*6)

HANIN ELIAS – vocals / **ALEC EMPIRE** (b. 2 May'72) – programming, shouts / **CARL CRACK** (b. CARL BOHM) – MC

Force Inc not iss.

Nov 92. (12") **HUNTING FOR NAZIS. /** - - German

Raver Bassline not iss.

Aug 94. (7") *(RB 4)* **RAVERBASHING. /** □ -

Digital Hardcore Digital Hardcore

Apr 95. (cd/lp) *<(DHR CD/LP 001)>* **DELETE YOURSELF** □ □ Mar96
– Start the riot / Into the death / Raverbashing / Speed / Sex / Midijunkies / Delete yourself (live) / Hatzjagd aur Nazis (live) / Cyberpunks are dead! / Atari teenage riot / Kids are united / Riot 1995.
1996. (12"ep) **KIDS ARE UNITED EP** - - German
– Kids are united / FFFF / Not your business / Riot sounds produce riots / Strike / Deutschland (has gotta die!) / ATR (live bootleg) / P.O.F.
1996. (12"ep) **SPEED / MIDIJUNKIES EP** - - German
– Speed / Midijunkies / Midijunkies (remix) / Start the riot (live).
Nov 96. (12"ep) *(DHRUS 7.1)* **RIOT 1996 EP** □ -
– Deutschland (hass gotta die!) / Riot 1996 / Riot sounds produce riots.
Jan 97. (12"ep/cd-ep) *(DHR/+MCD 012)* **SICK TO DEATH EP** □ -
– Sick to death / We got the fucking power / Sick to death (remix) / Waves of disaster.
Mar 97. (cd/d-lp) *<(DHR CD/LP 006)>* **THE FUTURE OF WAR** □ □
– Get up while you can / Fuck all / Sick to death / P.R.E.S.S. / Deutschland (has gotta die) / Destroy 2000 years of culture / Not your business / You can't hold us back / Heatwave / Redefine the enemy / Deathstar / The future of war.

Grand Royal Grand Royal

Jun 97. (12"ep) *<(GR 039)>* **NOT YOUR BUSINESS EP** □ □ Apr97
– Not your business / Atari Teenage riot / Into the death / Raverbashing / Midijunkies (gonna fuck you up).
(re-iss. Dec99; same)
Jul 97. (7"; split with ASIAN DUB FOUNDATION) *(DAMGOOD 132)* **split** □ -
(above single on 'Damaged Goods')
Aug 97. (cd) *(<GR 042>)* **BURN, BERLIN, BURN!** (compilation) □ □
– Start the riot / Fuck all! / Sick to death / P.R.E.S.S. / Deutschland (has gotta die!) / Destroy 2000 years of culture / Not your business / Heatwave / Atari Teenage Riot / Delete yourself (live) / Into the death / Death star / Speed / The future of war. *(re-iss. Jan98 lp/cd; same)*

— added **NIC ENDO** – programmer

Digital Hardcore Elektra

Dec 97. (ltd;12"ep/cd-ep) *(DHR/+MCD 015)* **DESTROY 2000 YEARS OF CULTURE EP** □ -
– Destroy 2000 years of culture / Paranoid / Destroy 2000 years of culture (remix) / You can't hold us back.
Apr 99. (cd/d-lp) *(DHR CD/LP 20) <62354>* **60 SECOND WIPE OUT** □ □ May99
– Revolution action / By any means neccessary / Western decay / Atari Teenage Riot II / Ghost chase / Too dead for me / U.S. fade out / The virus has been spread / Digital hardcore / Death of a president D.I.Y.! / Your uniform (does not impress me!) / No success / Anarchy 999 / No remorse (I wanna die). *(re-iss. May99 on 'Digital Hardcore' d-cd+=/d-lp; DHR CD/LP 2021)* – Get up while you can / Deutschland has gotta die / Sick to death / Destroy 2000 years of culture / Not your business / Speed / Into the death / Atari Teenage Riot / Midijunkies.

Apr 99. (12"ep/cd-ep) *(DHR/+MCD 024)* **REVOLUTION ACTION!!!!!!!!!! EP** [ ] [-]
– Revolution action / No success (Digital Hardcore remix) / your uniform (does not impress me) (Digital Hardcore remix) / Hunt down the Nazis! (live in Washington DC).

Oct 99. (12"ep/cd-ep) *(DHR/+MCD 026)* **TOO DEAD FOR ME / REVOLUTION ACTION (live) / ANARCHY 999 (real mix) / DEATH OF A PRESIDENT DIY (acapella) / NO REMORSE (live)** [ ] [-]
(re-iss. Oct00; DHR/+MCD 027)

Jul 00. (cd/d-lp) *(DHR CD/LP 028)* **LIVE AT BRIXTON ACADEMY 1999 (live)** [ ] [ ]
– 26.47.

Oct 00. (cd-ep) *<DHR 32>* **RAGE (mixes – 6)** [-] [ ]

ALEC EMPIRE

Mille Plateau | Mille Plateau

Oct 94. (12"ep) *(DHR 4)* **DEATH EP** [ ] [-]
(above issued on 'Digital Hardcore') (below on 'Force Inc.)

Dec 94. (12"ep) *(FIM 71)* **JAGUAR EP** [ ] [-]

Mar 95. (12"; by ALEC EMPIRE & IAN POOLEY) *(MP 3)* **PULSE CODE EP** [ ] [-]

Mar 95. (cd/lp) *(<EFA 00661-2/-6>)* **GENERATION STAR WARS** [ ] [ ] Jun95
– Lash the 90ties / Stahl & Blausaure / 13465 / Maschinenvolk / Sonyprotitutes / Blutrote nacht uber Berlin / Pussy heroin / New acid / Smack / Konsumfreiheit / N.Y. summer II / Microchipkinder / Sieg uber die mayday – HJ.

Oct 95. (cd/lp) *(<EFA 00688-2/-6>)* **LOW ON ICE (THE ICELAND SESSIONS)** [ ] [ ] Mar95
– 37.2 part 1 / (Untitled 1) / 20 (1) / 20 (2) / 22.24 / (Untitled 2) / Low on ice / Metall dub / 2572 / We were burnt / 37.2 part 2.

Apr 96. (cd/lp) *(<EFA 00673-2/-6>)* **HYPERMODERN JAZZ 2000.5** [ ] [ ]
– Walk the apocalypse / God told me how to kiss / Get some / I'm gonna die if I fall asleep again / The unknown stepdancer / Chilling through the lives / Many bars and no money / My funk is useless / Slowly falling in love / Dreaming is a form of astrotravel.

Digital Hardcore | Digital Hardcore

Jun 96. (cd/d-lp) *<(DHR CD/LP 004)>* **THE DESTROYER** [ ] [ ]
– We all die! (intro) / We all die! / Suicide / Bang your head! / Don't lie, white girl! / Firebombing / I just wanna destroy . . . / Bonus beats / Nobody gets out alive! / My body cannot die / The peak / Heartbeat that isn't there / I don't care what happens / My face would crack / Pleasure is our business (live) / 'Goodbye my friends'.

Dec 96. (12") *(DHR 7.4)* **22.24** [ ] [-]

Nov 97. (cd/d-lp) *<(DHR CD/LP 011)>* **SQUEEZE THE TRIGGER** [ ] [ ]
– Squeeze the trigger / Silver pills / Fuck the shit up / Streets of gold / The king of the street / The brothers crush / The drum and the bass / Generate / Euphoric / The destroyer / Burn Babylob burn / Destruction / I am you (identity). *(cd w/free cd+=)* – Hectic / L.E.A. / Inbetween two girls / Rise of the lion / I want action (demo).

— In June '98, ALEC EMPIRE collaborated with TECHNO ANIMAL on 'The Curse Of The Golden Vampire' for 'Digital Hardcore'

Mar 99. (cd/d-lp) *<(DHRLTD CD/LP 008)>* **INTENDO TEENAGE RIOTS** [ ] [ ]
– No humanity allowed / Get inline / No disease sex / Machines survive / 50 years later / At the party / I don't get the printer / NNW / Condom personality / CD jockey take over / Everything id forbidden / Nothing is allowed / Dollars / Funk was yesterday / Invasion control / Beatles never counted / Fuck me d/a style.

Aug 99. (m-cd/m-lp) *<(DHRLTD CD/LP 009)>* **MISS BLACK AMERICA** [ ] [ ]
– DFo 2 / Black Sabbath / The Nazi comets / It should be you not me! / They landed inside my head while we were driving in the taxi up to 53rd Street and took over / The robot put a voodoo spell on me / I can hear the winds of Saturn / We take the pain away / (untitled) / Blood and snow.

Jun 01. (12"/cd-s; as ALEC EMPIRE & EL-P) *<(DH 35)>* **SHARDS OF POL POTTERY** [ ] [ ]

– compilations, others, etc. –

Sep 95. (cd/lp) *<(EFA 00652-2/-6)>* **LIMITED EDITIONS 1990-94** [ ] [ ]
– Suecide / Sweet / The sun hurts my eyes / The blackside of my brain / Dark woman / Silver box / Chinese takeaway / Civilization virus / When love disappears / Limited 05.

Dec 96. (cd/lp) *Mille Plateau; (efa 680)* **ETOILES DES FILLES MORTES** [-] [-] French
– La ville des filles mortes / Les enfants de la lune / La consequence, c'est la revolt / Le mur noir / J'ai tue les fictions / Le marriage / Les yeux electroniques / Opus 28: pour la liberte de mille plateau / La revolution obligatoire / La guerre d'opium.

Oct 97. (3xcd-box) *Geist; (GEIST 001CD)* **THE GEIST OF ALEC EMPIRE** [ ] [-]

Jun 99. (lp) *El Turco Loco; (ETL 006)* **ALEC EMPIRE VS. ELVIS PRESLEY** [ ] [ ]
– Jailhouse cock rocks the most / You ain't nothing / Something for the pain / Take away / Come on, fight you punk! I am going insane without your love he's dead, that's the way it is / Last message from the soul / Fuck the majors / Blue moon 1 / Blue moon.

ATHEIST

Formed: Sarasota, Florida, USA . . . 1984 as OBLIVION by KELLY SHAEFER and STEVE FLYNN. The following year they recruited talented bass man ROGER PATTERSON while SHAEFER took up vocal duties after a temporary singer failed to work out. By this point they'd also changed their moniker to R.A.V.A.G.E. (that's RAGING ATHEISTS VOWING A GORY END; of course . . .), playing a mixture of covers and originals and cutting a rough five-track demo which spread their name on the underground tape network. In late '86 the trio briefly recruited a second guitarist in the shape of MARK SCZAWTSBERG and recorded the 'ON THEY SLAY' demo. The latter enjoyed rave reviews from both fanzines and established mags such as Kerrang!, leading to the opportunity of contributing a couple of tracks ('ON THEY SLAY' and 'BRAIN DAMAGE') to the 'Raging Death' compilation alongside the likes of SADUS. By 1988 they'd finally adopted the ATHEIST moniker while the line-up had solidified around SHAEFER, FLYNN, PATTERSON and RAND BURKEY. After a further acclaimed demo tape, the band finally recorded their debut album, 'PIECE OF TIME' with Scott Burns at the production helm. Unfortunately their new label, 'Mean Machine', went bankrupt shortly after and the record was only given a belated European release in 1990 on the 'Active' imprint. A brace of shows followed, both in Europe and America, alongside the likes of NAPALM DEATH, OBITUARY and MORBID ANGEL. Yet tragedy was to strike as the band completed their first full US tour, PATTERSON suffering a fatal car accident as they drove back from California. Vowing to carry on they recruited TONY CHOY (of Miami band CYNIC) on a session basis for the recording of a sophomore set, 'UNQUESTIONABLE PRESENCE' (1991). Regarded as ATHEIST's masterpiece, the record illustrated the complex, technical possibilities within the sphere of extreme metal. It was also to be their last bonafide album as summer '92 found SHAEFER working with his new band NEUROTICA. Contractual obligations, however, meant that KELLY had to deliver a third album. He subsequently rounded up a triple guitar line-up of CHOY, BURKEY, FRANK EMMI and JOSH GREENBAUM (the sticksman from the late RIVER PHOENIX's band ALEKA'S ATTIC!) for 'ELEMENTS' (1993). A further new line-up was in place for European dates yet the band finally folded in late '93 amid financial squabbles and the fact that BURKEY was unable to travel to Europe because of a felony charge.

Album rating: PIECE OF TIME (*6) / UNQUESTIONABLE PRESENCE (*8) / ELEMENTS (*7)

KELLY SHAEFER – vocals, lead guitar / **RAND BURKEY** – lead guitar / **ROGER PATTERSON** – bass / **STEVE FLYNN** – drums

Active | Caroline

Jan 90. (cd/lp) *(CD+/ATV 8) <CAROL 2201-2/-1>* **PIECE OF TIME** [ ] [ ] 1989
– Piece of time / Unholy war / Room with a view / On they slay / Beyond / I deny / Why bother? / Life / No truth.

— **TONY CHOY** – bass (ex-CYNIC) repl. PATTERSON who died in a car crash on 12th February 1991

Music For Nations | Metal Blade

Oct 91. (cd/c/lp) *(CD/T+/ATV 20) <26717>* **UNQUESTIONABLE PRESENCE** [ ] [ ]
– Mother man / Unquestionable presence / Your life's retribution / Enthralled in essence / An incarnation's dream / The formative years / Brains / And the psychic saw.

— added **FRANK EMMI** – lead guitar

— **MARCELL DISANTOS** – drums; repl. FLYNN (although **JOSH GREENBAUM** played on the album)

Music For Nations | Warners

Jul 93. (cd/lp) *(CD+/MFN 150) <45370>* **ELEMENTS** [ ] [ ] May93
– Green / Water / Samba Briza / Air / Displacement / Animal / Mineral / Fire / Fractal point / Earth / See you again / Elements.

— disbanded after above; SCHAEFER joined NEUROTICA

ATOMIC ROOSTER

Formed: London, England . . . mid '69 by VINCENT CRANE, CARL PALMER and NICK GRAHAM. The former two had enjoyed No.1 success with ARTHUR BROWN ('Fire') and signed to 'B&C' label for early 1970 eponymous debut. This breached the Top 50, but CRANE was left on his own, when PALMER co-founded EMERSON, LAKE & PALMER, while GRAHAM joined SKIN ALLEY. Their replacements JOHN CANN and PAUL HAMMOND, helped create a new heavy/progressive sound, which led to two massive hits; 'TOMORROW NIGHT' and 'DEVIL'S ANSWER'. This period also produced two Top 20 albums 'DEATH WALKS BEHIND YOU' & 'IN HEARING OF'; the latter adding PETE FRENCH (from LEAFHOUND and CACTUS). They went through yet another split soon after, although CRANE found new but experienced voxman CHRIS FARLOWE (had 1996 hit with 'OUT OF TIME'). Also in this 1972 line-up was RICK PARNELL (son of orchestra leader JACK PARNELL), although fans "flocked-off" to heavier pastures. The albums, 'MADE IN ENGLAND' and 'NICE 'N' GREASY', plummeted badly, CRANE going off to work with ARTHUR BROWN again. He did resurrect the band a few times later in '79 and 1983, but this was put aside when he was invited to boost KEVIN ROWLAND & DEXY'S on 1985's 'Don't Stand Me Down'. Following a long period of depression, CRANE took his own life in 1989.

Album rating: ATOMIC ROOSTER (*5) / DEATH WALKS BEHIND YOU (*5) / IN HEARING OF (*6) / MADE IN ENGLAND (*4) / NICE 'N' GREASY (*3) / ATOMIC ROOSTER (*3) / HEADLINE NEWS (*2) / IN SATAN'S NAME – THE DEFINITIVE COLLECTION compilation (*7)

VINCENT CRANE (b. VINCENT CHEESMAN, 1945) – keyboards, vocals, bass-pedal / **CARL PALMER** (b. 20 Mar'51, Birmingham, England) – drums, percussion (both ex-CRAZY WORLD OF ARTHUR BROWN) / **NICK GRAHAM** – bass, guitar, flute, vocals

B&C | Elektra

Feb 70. (lp) *(CAS 1010)* **ATOMIC ROOSTER** [49] [-]
– Friday the 13th / And so to bed / Broken wings / Before tomorrow / Banstead / S.L.Y. / Winter / Decline & fall. *(re-iss. Oct86 on 'Charisma'; CHC 58) (cd-iss. Aug91 & Jul93 on 'Repertoire' lp/c/cd; REP 4135WZ) (<cd re-iss. Nov99 on 'Receiver'; RRCD 277>)*

Mar 70. (7") *(CB 121)* **FRIDAY THE 13th. / BANSTEAD** [ ] [-]

— **JOHN CANN** – vocals, guitar (ex-ANDROMEDA) repl. NICK joined SKIN ALLEY **PAUL HAMMOND** – drums, percussion repl. CARL who joined EMERSON, LAKE & PALMER

Dec 70. (7") *(CB 131) <45727>* **TOMORROW NIGHT. / PLAY THE GAME** [11] [ ]

Jan 71. (lp) *(CAS 1026) <EKS 74094>* **DEATH WALKS BEHIND YOU** [12] [90]
– Death walks behind you / Vug / Tomorrow night / Seven streets / Sleeping for years / I can't take no more / Nobody else / Gershatzer. *(cd-iss. Aug91 & Jul93 & Oct00 on 'Repertoire'; REP 4069WZ)*

— added **PETE FRENCH** – vocals (ex-LEAF HOUND, CACTUS)

Jul 71. (7") *(CB 157) <45745>* **DEVIL'S ANSWER. / THE ROCK** [4] [ ]
(re-iss. Jun76; same)

Pegasus Elektra

Aug 71. (lp) *(PEG 1) <EKS 74109>* **IN HEARING OF ATOMIC ROOSTER** [18] [ ]
– Breakthrough / Break the ice / Decision – indecision / A spoonful of bromide helps the pulse rate go down / Black snake / Head in the sky / The rock / The price. *(cd-iss. Aug91 & Jul93 & Jul95 on 'Repertoire'; REP 4068WZ)*

— **CRANE** now with newcomers **CHRIS FARLOWE** (b.1940) – vocals (ex-COLOSSEUM, ex-Solo, etc.) replaced FRENCH who joined LEAFHOUND / **STEVE BOLTON** – guitar repl. CANN (to HARD STUFF) as JOHN DU CANN had 1979 hit / **RICK PARNELL** – drums repl. HAMMOND (to HARD STUFF) added / **BILL SMITH** – bass / **LIZA STRIKE** and **DORIS TROY** – backing vocals

Dawn Elektra

Sep 72. (7") *(DNS 1027) <45800>* **STAND BY ME. / NEVER TO LOSE** [ ] [ ] 1973

Oct 72. (lp) *(DNLS 3038) <EKS 75039>* **MADE IN ENGLAND** [ ] [ ]
– Time take my life / Stand by me / Little bit of inner air / Don't know what went wrong / Never to lose / Introduction / Breathless / Space cowboy / People you can't trust / All in Satan's name / Close your eyes. *(cd-iss. May91 on 'Sequel'; NEMCD 610) (cd-iss. 1991 on 'Repertoire' +=; REP 4165WZ)*– Goodbye Planet Earth / Satans wheel.

Nov 72. (7") *(DNS 1029) <45766>* **SAVE ME. / CLOSE YOUR EYES** [ ] [ ]

Jan 73. (7"; VINCENT CRANE & CHRIS FARLOWE) *(DNS 1034)* **CAN'T FIND A REASON. / MOODS** [ ] [-]

— **JOHNNY MANDELA** – guitar repl. STEVE, BILL, LIZA and DORIS

1973. (lp) *(DNLS 3049) <EKS 75074>* **NICE'N'GREASY** <US-title 'ATOMIC ROOSTER IV'> [ ] [ ]
– All across the country / Save me / Voodoo in you / Goodbye Planet Earth / Take one toke / Can't find a reason / Ear in the snow / Satans wheel. *(cd-iss. Jul91 on 'Sequel'; NEMCD 611) (cd-iss. 1991 on 'Repertoire'; RR 4134WZ)* – (track 4 & 8 repl. by) – Moods / What you gonna do.

— now without FARLOWE who returned to a solo career.

Decca not iss.

Mar 74. (7"; as VINCENT CRANE'S ATOMIC ROOSTER) *(FR 13503)* **TELL YOUR STORY (SING YOUR SONG). / O.D.** [ ] [-]

— CRANE teamed up with ARTHUR BROWN and split band.

— re-formed 1980, with **JOHN DU CANN** – guitar / **PRESTON HEYMAN** – drums

E.M.I. not iss.

Jun 80. (7"/ext.12") *(EMI/12EMI 5084)* **DO YOU KNOW WHO'S LOOKING FOR YOU? / THROW YOUR LIFE AWAY** [ ] [-]

Sep 80. (lp) *(EMC 3341)* **ATOMIC ROOSTER** [ ] [ ]
– They took control of you / She's my woman / He did it again / Where's the show? / In the shadows / Do you know who's looking for you? / Don't lose your mind / Watch out / I can't stand it / Lost in space. *(re-iss. Oct86 on 'Charisma')*

— **PAUL HAMMOND** – drums repl. PRESTON

Polydor not iss.

Sep 81. (7") *(POSP 334)* **PLAY IT AGAIN. / START TO LIVE** [ ] [-]
(12"+=) *(POSPX 334)* – Devil's answer (live).

Feb 82. (7") *(POSP 408)* **END OF THE DAY. / LIVING UNDERGROUND** [ ] [-]
(12"+=) *(POSPX 408)* – Tomorrow night (live).

— guests **BERNIE TORME and DAVID GILMOUR** repl. HAMMOND and CANN

Towerbell not iss.

Jun 83. (lp/c) *(TOWLP/ZCTOW 004)* **HEADLINE NEWS** [ ] [-]
– Hold your fire / Headline news / Taking a chance / Metal minds / Land of freedom / Machine / Dance of death / Carnival / Time. *(cd-iss. Nov94 on 'Voiceprint'; VP 171CD) (cd re-iss. Jun97 on 'Blueprint'; BP 171CD) (cd re-iss. May00 on 'Eagle'; EAMCD 108)*

— Finally split 1983. VINCENT CRANE joined/guested for DEXY'S MIDNIGHT RUNNERS in 1985. He committed suicide 20 Feb'89, after suffering recurring depression. In his latter days, he had also written for pop star KIM WILDE.

– compilations, others, etc. –

1974. (lp) *B&C; (CS 9)* **ASSORTMENT** [ ] [-]

1977. (d-lp) *Mooncrest; (CDR 2)* **HOME TO ROOST** [ ] [-]
– Death walks behind you / V.U.G. / Seven streets / Sleeping for years / Can't take no more / Nobody else / Friday 13th / And so to bed / Broken wings / Before tomorrow / Banstead / Winter / Breakthrough / Decision – Indecision / Devil's answer / A spoonful of bromide helps the pulserate go down / Black snake / Head in the sky / Tomorrow night / Break the ice. *(re-iss. 1983; same) (re-iss. Dec86 on 'Raw Power' d-lp/d-c/cd; RAW LP/TC/CD 027)*

Aug 80. (7"m) *B&C; (BCS 21)* **DEVIL'S ANSWER. / TOMORROW NIGHT / CAN'T TAKE NO MORE** [ ] [-]

Jun 84. (7") *Old Gold; (OG 9391)* **DEVIL'S ANSWER. / TOMORROW NIGHT** [ ] [-]

Apr 89. (cd-ep) *Old Gold; (OG 6136)* **DEVIL'S ANSWER / TOMORROW NIGH / ('Natural Born Boogie' by Humble Pie)** [ ] [-]

Jun 89. (lp/cd) *Demi-Monde; (DM LP/CD 1020)* **THE BEST OF ATOMIC ROOSTER** [ ] [-]

Sep 89. (lp/cd) *Receiver; (RR LD/DCD 003)* **DEVIL'S ANSWER** [ ] [-]

Dec 89. (cd/c) *Action Replay; (CDAR/ARLC 100)* **THE BEST AND THE REST OF . . .** [ ] [-]

Feb 90. (cd/lp) *Demi-Monde; (DM CD/LP 1023)* **THE DEVIL HITS BACK** [ ] [-]

Feb 93. (cd) *Sahara; (SARCD 001-2)* **THE BEST OF VOLS 1 & 2** [ ] [-]

Oct 93. (cd) *Windsong; (WINCD 042)* **BBC LIVE IN CONCERT** [ ] [-]

Jul 94. (cd/c) *Success;* **THE BEST OF ATOMIC ROOSTER** [ ] [-]

Apr 96. (cd) *Laserlight; (12666)* **THE BEST OF ATOMIC ROOSTER** [ ] [-]

Jun 97. (d-cd) *Snapper; (SMDCD 128)* **IN SATAN'S NAME – THE DEFINITIVE COLLECTION** [ ] [-]
– Banstead / And so to bed / Friday the 13th / Broken wings / Tomorrow night / Play the game / V.U.G. / Sleeping for years / Death walks behind you / Devil's answer / The rock / Breakthrough / Break the ice / Spoonful of bromide / Stand by me / Never to lose / Don't know what went wrong / Space cowboy / People you can't trust / All in Satan's name / Close your eyes / Save me / Can't find a reason / All across the country / Voodoo in you / Goodbye Planet Earth / Satans wheel.

May 98. (cd) *Hux; (HUX 005)* **DEVIL'S ANSWER** [ ] [-]

Jan 99. (cd) *Angel Air; (<SJPCD 038>)* **THE FIRST TEN EXPLOSIVE YEARS** [ ] [ ]

Jul 99. (d-cd) *Saraja; (SARCD 0012)* **THE BEST OF ATOMIC ROOSTER VOL.1 & 2** [ ] [-]

Mar 00. (cd) *Retrowrek; (<RETRK 107>)* **LIVE IN GERMANY 1983 (live)** [ ] [ ] May00

Mar 00. (cd) *Angel Air; (<SJPCD 060>)* **LIVE AND RAW 1970-1971** [ ] [ ] May00

Mar 00. (d-cd) *Double Classics; (DC 31024)* **ANTHOLOGY** [ ] [-]

Oct 00. (cd) *Angel Air; (<SJPCD 059>)* **RARITIES** [ ] [ ]

Feb 01. (cd) *Burning Airlines; (<PILOT 030>)* **THE DEVIL HITS BACK** [ ] [ ]

ATOMKRAFT

Formed: Newcastle, England . . . early 80's by IAN SWIFT, TONY DOLAN, ROB MATTHEWS, D.C. RAGE and GED WOLF. They supported fellow bad taste merchants, VENOM and signed to the latter group's label, 'Neat' in 1985. Although the band had pioneered the thrash sound in Britain, their debut album, 'FUTURE WARRIORS', fared to live up to the promise of young Stateside upstarts like METALLICA or SLAYER. Two successive albums appeared in '86 and '87, neither making much impression on the metal scene. DOLAN left for VENOM soon after, effectively ending ATOMKRAFT's flight of fancy.

Album rating: FUTURE WARRIORS (*5) / CONDUCTORS OF NOIZE mini (*4)

IAN SWIFT – vocals / **TONY DOLAN** – guitar / **ROB MATTHEWS** – guitar / **D.C. RAGE** – bass / **GED WOLF** – drums

Neat not iss.

Sep 85. (lp) *(NEAT 1028)* **FUTURE WARRIORS** [ ] [-]
– Future warriors / Starchild / Dead man's hand / Total metal / Pour the metal in / Death valley – This planet's burning / Warzones / Burn in Hell / Heat and pain.

Oct 86. (12"ep) *(NEAT 55-12)* **QUEEN OF DEATH** [ ] [-]
– Queen of death / Protectors / Demolition / Funeral pyre / Mode III.

Roadrunner not iss.

Jul 87. (m-lp) *(RR 9600)* **CONDUCTORS OF NOIZE** [ ] [-]
– Requiem / Foliage / The cage / Vision of Belshazzar / Teutonic pain / Rich bitch.

— Disbanded in 1989, when DOLAN joined the re-formed VENOM

ATOM SEED

Formed: South London, England . . . late 80's PAUL CUNNINGHAM, SIMON JAMES, CHRIS DALE and AMIR. Along with the likes of ACID REIGN and LAWNMOWER DETH, ATOM SEED were one of the hardest grafting, and most promising of Britain's young thrash hopefuls. Tending towards the funkier side of things (i.e. RED HOT CHILIS or FAITH NO MORE), the band released a debut EP, 'I DON'T WANT TO TALK ABOUT IT' in 1990. The same year, they were the band on stage at Knebworth, during the filming of ITV's Ruth Rendall's Mysteries. The buzz surrounding them eventually brought the major label interest of 'London' records, ATOM SEED subsequently releasing their first long player, 'GET IN LINE'. Poor sales of the set along with the departure of AMIR, saw the label only managing to squeeze out some EP's, a second album having been shelved in 1992 after their demise.

Album rating: GET IN LINE (*7)

PAUL CUNNINGHAM – vocals / **SIMON JAMES** – guitar / **CHRIS DALE** – bass / **AMIR** – drums

Organ not iss.

Apr 90. (12"ep) *(ORGAN 001)* **I DON'T WANT TO TALK ABOUT IT. / DOGHOUSE SEXBEAT / SHAKE THAT THING WHAT** [ ] [-]

London London

Dec 90. (cd/c/lp) *(<828260-2/-4/-1>)* **GET IN LINE** [ ] [ ]
– What you say / Get in line / Rebel / Shake that thing / Shot down / Forget it Joe / Better day / What?! / Castle in the sky / Bitchin'. *(re-iss. Nov92 on 'Heavy Metal' cd/c/lp; HMR XD/MC/LP 163) (also rel. as no vocal version)*

— **JERRY HAWKINS** – drums; repl. AMIR

May 91. (7") *(LON 299)* **REBEL. / EVERYBODY** [ ] [ ]
(12"+=/cd-s+=) *(LON X/CD 299)* – Fools to fall / Forget it Joe.
(12"remix+=) *(LONXR 299)* – ('A'-Adrenalin mix).

Aug 91. (7") *(LON 307)* **GET IN LINE. / CASTLES IN THE SKY** [ ] [ ]
(12"+=/12"pic-d+=/cd-s+=) *(LON X/XP/CD 307)* – What you say (live) / Burn (live).

Aug 92. (12"ep/cd-ep) *(LON)* **THE DEAD HAPPY EP** [ ] [ ]

— London dropped the band and a second album was withdrawn from sale

ATROPHY

Formed: Tucson, Arizona, USA . . . 1987 initially as HERESY, by BRIAN ZIMMERMAN and CHRIS LYKINS, who soon enlisted the services of RICK SKOWRON, JAMES GULOTTA and TIM KELLY. Along with SACRED REICH, the group formed a two-pronged desert thrash-attack in the late 80's, signing to 'Roadrunner' and unleashing the album, 'SOCIALIZED HATE' in 1988. A second outing, 'VIOLENT BY NATURE' was completed by early 1990, although by just after the album's release they called it a day.

Album rating: SOCIALIZED HATE (*6) / VIOLENT BY NATURE (*5)

BRIAN ZIMMERMAN – vocals / **CHRIS LYKINS** – guitar / **RICK SKOWRON** – guitar / **JAMES GULOTTA** – bass / **TIM KELLY** – drums

Roadrunner Roadrunner

Oct 88. (lp/cd) *(RR 9518-1/-2)* **SOCIALIZED HATE** [ ] [-]
– Chemical dependency / Killing machine / Matter of attitude / Preacher, preacher / Beer bong / Socialized hate / Best defence / Product of the past / Rest in pieces / Urban decay.

Roadracer Roadracer

Mar 90. (cd/c/lp) *<RO 9450-2/-4/-1>* **VIOLENT BY NATURE** [ ] [ ]
– Puppies and friends / Violent by nature / In their eyes / Too late to change / Slipped through the cracks / Forgotten but not gone / Process of elimination / Right to die / Things change.

— folded after above

AT THE DRIVE-IN

Formed: El Paso, Texas, USA . . . 1994 by frontman CEDRIC BIXLER and twin guitarists OMAR RODRIGUEZ and JIM WARD. Recorded between bouts of hard-bitten touring, the band's first two 7" singles, 'HELL PASO' and 'ALFARO VIVE, CARAJO' served notice of a hardcore storm brewing in the Texas badlands. Night after night spent playing to dismal crowds was rewarded when 'Flipside' caught them at an empty L.A. bar and signed them up for a debut album, 'ACROBATIC TENEMENT'. Released in early '97, the record's blistering emotional outpourings and precocious mastery of punk dynamics won over critics across the board while another stint of touring – with new recruits TONY and PALL – cultivated a grassroots fanbase. A subsequent mini-set, 'EL GRAN ORGO' was issued on the 'Offtime' imprint later that year, after which followed a period of insecurity as the band searched in vain for a label willing to take on their sophomore album. 'IN CASINO OUT' (1998) was finally sponsored by the independent 'Fearless' operation, a label more often associated with pop/punk fare. Nevertheless, the album – recorded almost entirely live with only a few overdubs – represented the closest ATDI had yet come to capturing the passionate drive of their live work. Yet more touring ensued as the band played with the likes of FUGAZI and ARCHERS OF LOAF before undertaking their first European jaunt in Spring '99. Later that summer the 'VAYA' EP showed that their relentless road schedule was paying handsome dividends in terms of musical sharpness and songwriting depth, the newly formed 'DEN Records' signing up the Texas troopers for their third and most highly acclaimed album to date, 'RELATIONSHIP OF COMMAND' (2000). Released on the BEASTIE BOYS' 'Grand Royal' (with whom 'DEN' had merged), produced by Ross 'SLIPKNOT' Robinson and mixed by Andy Wallace, the record had critics reaching for the superlatives in an attempt to describe their unflinchingly honest and unrelentingly intense sound.

Album rating: ACROBATIC TENEMENT (*7) / IN/CASINO/OUT (*7) / RELATIONSHIP OF COMMAND (*7)

CEDRIC BIXLER – vocals / **OMAR RODRIGUEZ** – guitar / **JIM WARD** – guitar, vocals

not iss. Western Breed – Offtime

Dec 94. (7"m) **HELL PASO. / EMPTINESS IS A MULE / RED PLANET** [-] [ ]
Jun 95. (7"ep) **ALFARO VIVE, CARAJO!. / BRADLEY SMITH / INSTIGATE THE ROLE** [-] [ ]
<re-iss. 1990's on 'Headquarter'>

not iss. Flipside

Feb 97. (cd) *<FLIP 94CD>* **ACROBATIC TENEMENT** [-] [ ]
– Star flight / Schaffino / Ebroglio / Initiation / Communication drive-in / Skips on the record / Paid vacation time / Ticklish / Blue tag / Coating of arms / Porfirio Diaz. *(UK-iss.Jan00; same as US)*

— added **PALL HINOJOS** – bass / **TONY HAJJAR** – drums

not iss. One Foot – Offtime

Sep 97. (cd-ep) *<62>* **EL GRAN ORGO** [-] [ ]
– Give it a name / Honest to a fault / Winter month novelty / Fahrenheit / Picket fence cartel / Speechless.

Fearless Fearless

Jul 98. (cd) *<F 034CD>* **IN/CASINO/OUT** [-] [ ]
– Alpha Centauri / Chanbara / Hulahoop wounds / Napoleon Solo / Pickpocket / For now . . . we toast / A devil among tailors / Shaking hand incision / Lopsided / Hourglass / Transatlantic foe. *(UK-iss.Aug00; same as US)*
Nov 98. (7") **DOORMAN'S PLACEBO. / (other track by AASSEE LAKE)** [-] [ ]

— <above iss. on 'Nerd' records>

Oct 99. (12"ep) *(F 040-1)* **VAYA** [-] [ ]
– Rascuache / Proxima centauri / Ursa minor / Heliotrope / Metrognome arthritis / 300 MHz / 198d. *(UK-iss.Oct99; same as US) (cd-ep iss.Aug00; FO 40CD)*

Thick Thick

Mar 00. (7"pic-d) *<THK 066)>* **CATACOMBS. / (other by Burning Airlines)** [ ] [ ]
(UK re-iss. Oct00; same)

Big Wheel Big Wheel

May 00. (12"ep/cd-ep) *<(BWR 0223/+CD)>* **BIG WHEEL RECREATION** [ ] [ ]
– Extracurricular / Autorelocator / (two others by Sunshine).

Grand Royal Grand Royal

Aug 00. (7") *<(GR 91)>* **ONE ARMED SCISSOR. / PATTERN AGAINST USER** [64] [ ]
(cd-s+=) *<(GR 91CD)>* – Incetardis.

Virgin Virgin

Sep 00. (cd/lp) *(CDVUS/VUSLP 184) <49999>* **RELATIONSHIP OF COMMAND** [33] [ ]
– Arcarsenal / Pattern against user / One armed scissor / Sleepwalk capsules / Invalid litter dept. / Mannequin republic / Enfilade / Rolodex propaganda / Quarantined / Cosmonaut / Non-zero possibility / Catacombs.
Oct 00. (7"colrd) **BUDDYHEAD. / (other by Murder City Devils)** [-] [ ]
Nov 00. (7") *(VUS 189)* **ROLODEX PROPAGANDA. / EXTRACURRICULAR** [ ] [-]
(cd-s+=) *(VUSCD 189)* – One armed scissor (Lamacq version).
Mar 01. (7") *(VUS 193)* **INVALID LITTER DEPT. / INITIATION (Lamacq version)** [50] [-]
(cd-s+=) *(VUSCD 193)* – Quarantined (Lamacq version).
(cd-s) *(VUSDX 193)* – ('A'side) / Take up thy stethoscope and walk (Lamacq version) / Metrognome arthritis.

AT THE GATES

Formed: Billdal, Goteberg, Sweden . . . 1990 out of the ashes of GROTESQUE, by ALF SVENSSON and TOMAS LINDBERG (also of short-lived, LIERS IN WAIT). They completed the new line-up with ADRIAN ERLANDSON and twin brothers ANDERS and JONAS BJORLER, setting about creating their brand of death-metal in the process. After initially releasing an EP in '91, the signed to 'Deaf' records, who issued two albums, 'THE RED SKY IN THE SKY IS OURS' (1992) and 'WITH FEAR I KISS THE BURNING DARKNESS' (1993); the latter with MARTIN LARSSON, who replaced SVENSSON. In 1994, they switched labels to 'Peaceville' (US), the albums 'TERMINAL SPIRIT DISEASE' (1994) and 'SLAUGHTER OF THE SOUL' (1995 on 'Earache'), marking a slightly more melodic rock approach. TOMAS has since been heard on the track 'SNOTROCKET', which was released on Black Sun's METALLICA tribute album, 'Metal Militia'. Over the latter half of the 90's, AT THE GATES metamorphosed into The HAUNTED as the BJORLER brothers and ERLANDSSON got together with erstwhile MARY BEATS JANE vocalist PETER DOLVING. The new four piece initially set to work on contributing material to the second volume of 'Earache's 'Earplugged' compilation before cutting an eponymous debut album. Released in 1998, the record carried on where AT THE GATES left off with an admirable attempt at reconciling intensity with accessibility. Despite personnel upheavals which saw PER MOLLER JENSEN and MARCO ARO replace ERLANDSSON and DOLVING respectively, the group created their most realised opus to date in the shape of 2000's 'THE HAUNTED MADE ME DO IT'. A masterclass in rendering complex, inventive metal into a – relatively – melodic framework, the album saw The HAUNTED join the cream of Earache's sonic innovators.

Album rating: THE RED IN THE SKY IS OURS (*5) / WITH FEAR I KISS THE BURNING DARKNESS (*6) / TERMINAL SPIRIT DISEASE (*7) / SLAUGHTER OF THE SOUL (*7) / SUICIDAL FINAL ART compilation (*7) / Haunted: THE HAUNTED (*6) / THE HAUNTED MADE ME DO IT (*7)

TOMAS LINDBERG – vocals / **ALF SVENSSON** – guitar / **ANDERS BJORLER** – guitar / **JONAS BJORLER** – bass / **ADRIAN ERLANDSSON** – drums / **JESPER JAROLD** – violin

Dolores not iss.

1991. (m-lp) *(DOL 005MLP)* **GARDENS OF GRIEF** [-] [-] Sweden
– Souls of the evil departed / At the gates / All life ends / City of screaming statues. *(UK-iss.Nov92; same) (re-iss. Aug95 on 'Black Sun' as cd-ep; BS 04)*

Deaf Grindcore

1992. (cd) *(DEAF 10CD) <89810>* **THE RED IN THE SKY IS OURS** [ ] [ ] 1993
– The red in the sky is ours: The season to come / Kingdom come / Through gardens of grief / Within / Windows / Claws of laughter dead / Neverwhere / The scar / City of screaming statues. *(<re-iss. Feb01 on 'Peaceville'; CDVILEM 98>)*

— **MARTIN LARSSON** – guitar; repl. ALF + JESPER

1993. (lp/cd) *(DEAF 14/+CD)* **WITH FEAR I KISS THE BURNING DARKNESS** [ ] [-]
– Beyond good and evil / Raped by the light of Christ / The break of Autumn / Non-divine / Primal breath / The architects / Stardrowned / Blood of the sunsets / The burning darkness / Ever-opening flower / Through the red. *(<cd re-iss. Mar01 on 'Peaceville'; CDVILEM 97>)*

Peaceville Futurist

Jun 94. (cd/lp) *(CD+/VILE 47) <11061>* **TERMINAL SPIRIT DISEASE** [ ] [ ]
– The swarm / Terminal spirit disease / And the world returned / Forever blind / The fevered circle / The beautiful wound / All life ends (live) / The burning darkness (live) / Kingdom come (live). *(cd re-iss. Jan01; same)*

Earache Earache

Oct 95. (lp/cd) *(<MOSH 143/+CD>)* **SLAUGHTER OF THE SOUL** [ ] [ ] Nov95
– Blinded by fear / Slaughter of the soul / Cold / Under a serpent sun / Into the dead sky / Suicide nation / World of lies / Unto others / Nausea / Need / The flames of the end. *(cd re-iss. Sep97; same)*

— ADRIAN later formed H.E.A.L.; the others The HAUNTED

– compilations, etc. –

May 95. (d-cd) *Peaceville; <CDVILE 59>* **THE RED / WITH FEAR** [-] [ ]
– (THE RED IN THE SKY IS OURS / WITH FEAR I KISS THE BURNING DARKNESS)

Apr 01. (cd) *Peaceville; (CDVILE 86)* **SUICIDAL FINAL ART** -
– The red in the sky is ours / Kingdom come / Windows / Ever opening flower (demo) / The architects (demo) / Raped by the light of Christ / Primal breath / Blood of the sunsets / Burning darkness / The swarm / Terminal spirit disease / Forever blind / Beautiful wound / Blinded by fear / Slaughter of the soul / Terminal spirit disease (video) / Burning disease (video).

Jun 01. (cd) *Century Media; <(CM 8040)>* **GARDENS OF GRIEF / Grotesque: IN THE EMBRACE OF EVIL**

HAUNTED

PETER DOLVING – vocals (ex-MARY BEATS JANE) / **ANDERS BJORLER** – guitar / **JONAS BJORLER** – bass / **ADRIAN ERLANDSSON** – drums

Earache Earache

Jun 98. (cd) *(<MOSH 197CD>)* **THE HAUNTED**
– Hate song / Chasm / In vein / Undead / Chokehold / Three times / Bullet hole / Now you know / Shattered / Soul fracture / Blood rust / Forensick.

— **MARCO ARO** – vocals; repl. DOLVING

— **PER MOLLER JENSEN** – drums (ex-SEANCE) repl. ERLANDSSON

Oct 00. (lp/cd) *(<MOSH 241/+CD>)* **THE HAUNTED MADE ME DO IT**
– Dark intentions / Bury your head / Trespass / Leech / Hollow ground / Revelation / The world burns / Human debris / Silencer / Under the surface / Victim iced.

A II Z

Formed: Manchester, England . . . 1980 by brothers DAVE and GARY OWENS, plus CAM CAMPBELL and KARL RETI. Part of the NWOBHM scene, they signed to 'Polydor' records, subsequently supporting SABBATH and GIRLSCHOOL prior to the release of their live debut album, 'THE WITCH OF BERKELEY'. This album failed to make the anticipated impact, largely due to its inferior sound quality. The band folded soon after another desperate attempt to achieve a hit single with 'I'M THE ONE WHO LOVES YOU'.

Album rating: THE WITCH OF BERKELEY (*3)

DAVE OWENS – vocals / **GARY OWENS** – guitar / **CAM CAMPBELL** – bass / **KARL RETI** – drums

Polydor not iss.

Oct 80. (7") *(POSP 243)* **NO FUN AFTER MIDNIGHT. / TREASON** -
(12"red+=) *(POSPX 243)* – Valhalla force.

Oct 80. (lp/c) *(2383/3170 587)* **THE WITCH OF BERKELEY (live)** -
– No fun after midnight / Lay down / Walking the distance / Glastonbury massacre / Danger / U.X.B. / The witch of Berkeley / Last stand / The romp / The king is dead.

Feb 81. (7") *(POSP 314)* **I'M THE ONE WHO LOVES YOU. / RINGSIDE SEAT** -

— Split up after above

AUGUST REDMOON

Formed: California, USA . . . 1980 by DAVID YOUNG, who recruited MICHAEL HENRY and brothers GREG and RAY WINSLOW. Only one album, 'FOOLS ARE NEVER ALONE', surfaced from this bunch of quickfire hard rock merchants who infused their conventional sound with elements of AEROSMITH and VAN HALEN. They changed their name to TERRACUDA in '84, later springing up as EDEN for an eponymous set in '86.

Album rating: FOOLS ARE NEVER ALONE (*5)

MICHAEL HENRY – vocals / **RAY WINSLOW** – guitar, vocals / **GREG WINSLOW** – bass, vocals / **DAVID YOUNG** – drums, vocals

not iss. Metalworks

1982. (m-lp) *<MBR 401>* **FOOLS ARE NEVER ALONE** -
– Fools are never alone / Jeckyl 'n' Hyde / Bump in the night / We know what you want / Don't stop me.

— changed their name to TERRACUDA. Without RAY (and new bassman, RICK SCOTT) they formed, EDEN, who issued an eponymous lp in 1986 for Dutch 'Enigma'; (72079-1).

AUTOGRAPH

Formed: Los Angeles, California, USA . . . 1983 by STEVE PLUNKETT and RANDY RAND, who enlisted seasoned musos, STEVEN ISHAM, STEVE LYNCH and KENI RICHARDS. Securing a deal with 'RCA' in '84, the group signed their name on the rock scene's consciousness almost immediately, scoring a US Top 20 hit with 'TURN UP THE RADIO'. Their highly commercial strain of melodic AOR and hard-rock was showcased on a debut album, 'SIGN IN PLEASE', which also made the Top 30. However, this was their only significant assault on the charts, 'THAT'S THE STUFF' only scraping a Top 100 placing.

Album rating: SIGN IN PLEASE (*5) / THAT'S THE STUFF (*5) / LOUD AND CLEAR (*5)

STEVE PLUNKETT – vocals (ex-SILVER CONDOR) / **STEVE LYNCH** – guitar / **STEVEN ISHAM** – keyboards (ex-HOLLY PENFIELD) / **RANDY RAND** – bass (ex-LITA FORD, ex-MASTERS OF THE AIRWAVES) / **KENI RICHARDS** – drums

R.C.A. R.C.A.

Mar 85. (7") *(RCA 483) <13953>* **TURN UP THE RADIO. / THRILL OF LOVE** 20 Dec84
(12"+=) *(RCAT 483) <13941>* – Fever line.

Mar 85. (lp/c) *(PL/PK 89495) <8040-1/-4>* **SIGN IN PLEASE** 29 Dec84
– Send her to me / Turn up the radio / Night teen & non stop / Cloud 10 / Deep end / My girlfriend's boyfriend isn't me / Thrill of love / Friday / In the night / All I'm gonna take. *<cd-iss. 1989; PCD 15423>*

Mar 85. (12") *<14023>* **MY GIRLFRIEND'S BOYFRIEND ISN'T ME. / ('A'long version)** -

Jun 85. (12") *<14131>* **NIGHT TEEN AND NON-STOP. / TURN UP THE RADIO / SEND HER TO ME** -

Oct 85. (7") *<14231>* **BLONDES IN BLACK CARS. / BUILT FOR SPEED** -
(12"+=) *<14195>* – ('A'extended) / ('A'side).

Nov 85. (lp/c) *<7009-1/-4>* **THAT'S THE STUFF** - 92
– That's the stuff / Take no prisoners / Blondes in black cars / You'll get over it / Crazy world / Six string fever / Changing hands / Hammerhead / Built for speed / Paint this town. *<cd-iss. 1989; PCD 17009>*

Jan 86. (7") *<14278>* **THAT'S THE STUFF. / SIX STRING FEVER** -
(12") *<14279>* – ('A'extended) / ('A'version).

Apr 86. (7") *<14316>* **WE'RE AN AMERICAN BAND. /** -

Feb 87. (7") *<5245>* **SHE NEVER LOOKED THAT GOOD TO ME. / DANCE ALL NIGHT** -

Mar 87. (lp/c) *<5796-1/-4>* **LOUD AND CLEAR** -
– Loud and clear / Dance all night / She never looked that good for me / Bad boy / Everytime I dream / She's a tease / Just got back from Heaven / Down 'n dirty / More than a million times / When the sun goes down. *<cd-iss. 1989; 5796-2>*

— they split early 1989, after ISHAM and RICHARDS departed, the former having teamed up with ex-DIO guitarist CRAIG GOLDIE

– compilations, etc. –

Apr 97. (cd) *U.S.G.; (USG 3765142-2)* **MISSING PIECES**

AUTOMATIC MAN

Formed: San Francisco, California, USA . . . mid 70's, by former SANTANA drummer MICHAEL SHRIEVE and ex-PAT TRAVERS BAND guitarist, PAT THRALL. Continuing in the experimental spirit of SHRIEVE's former outfit, the group played ambitious keyboard-orientated hard-rock, as evidenced on their eponymous 'Island' debut album. Like the follow-up, 'VISITORS' (1977), it bubbled under the US Top 100.

Album rating: AUTOMATIC MAN (*5) / VISITORS (*4)

MICHAEL SHRIEVE – drums, percussion (ex-SANTANA) / **PAT THRALL** – vocals, guitar (ex-PAT TRAVERS BAND) / **BAYETE** – vocals, keyboards, synthesizers / **DONI HARVEY** – bass, vocals

Island Island

Sep 76. (lp) *<(ILPS 9397)>* **AUTOMATIC MAN**
– Atlantis rising fanfare / Comin' through / My pearl / One and one / Newspapers / Geni-Geni / Right back down / There's a way / I.T.D. – Interstellar Tracking Device / Automatic man / Atlantis rising theme – Turning of the axis.

May 77. (7") *(WIP 6301) <063>* **MY PEARL. / WALLFLOWER** 97 Jan77

— **GLENN SYMMONDS** – drums + **JEROME RIMSON** – bass repl. SHRIEVE + HARVEY

Oct 77. (lp) *<(ILPS 9429)>* **VISITORS**
– Give it to me / Live wire / So you wanna be / Y-2-me / Visitors / Here I am now / Daughter of Neptune / What's done.

— Split soon after above. THRALL joined PAT TRAVERS before teaming up with GLENN HUGHES to form HUGHES-THRALL band. He was later part of ASIA

AUTOPSY

Formed: San Francisco, California, USA . . . late 80's by CHRIS REIFERT with DANNY CORALLES and ERIC CUTLER. The former had previously been a part of death-metal act, appropriately named, DEATH. Purveyors of blood-splattered grindcore, the band were picked up by 'Peaceville', who issued their debut album, 'SEVERED SURVIVAL' (1989). The following year, KEN SOVARI replaced STEVE DiGIORGIO, although the former was succeeded in turn by ERIC's brother, STEVE. A second set, 'MENTAL FUNERAL' appeared in '91, before DiGIORGIO returned in place of STEVE. He stayed for only one mini-album, 'FIEND FOR BLOOD', JOSH BAROHN making his debut on Autumn '92's, 'ACTS OF THE UNSPEAKABLE'. However, AUTOPSY encountered difficulties with the authorities over the gory cover art, Australian custom officials taking particular exception. A brief hiatus was interrupted by their 1995 album, the optimistically titled, 'SHITFUN'. Following AUTOPSY's subsequent demise, REIFERT and CORALLES went on to form the equally unpleasant ABSCESS alongside new faces CLINT BOWER, FREEWAY and JOE ALLEN. A series of demos – including 'RAW, SICK & BRUTAL NOIZE' and 'CRAWLED UP FROM THE SEWER', you get the picture . . . – and a limited edition live radio tape, 'FILTHY FUCKING FREAKS', set out their lowlife stall, all the tracks collected together on 1995's 'URINE JUNKIES' (1995). If that was a title the late GG ALLIN would've been proud of then 'SEMINAL VAMPIRES & MAGGOTMEN' (1996) – the debut album proper – and 'THROBBING BLACK WEREBEAST' (1997) could've been ripped straight from the ROKY ERIKSON school of B-movie horror. The latter was actually an EP, their last effort for the 'Relapse' label before being dropped. Another demo, 'OPEN WOUND', led to a new deal with French label, 'Listenable'. An unprecedented burst of millennial creativity saw the release of the 'TORMENTED' (2000) album, split singles with both DERANGED and

MACHETAZO (who, incidentally, covered ABSCESS' 'SUICIDE FUCK', nice . . .) and a couple of tracks recorded for a compilation on the 'Pigeon' label entitled 'Hyperventilation'. • **Note:** REIFORT's ABSCESS are not to be confused with the German industrial outfit featuring IAN BICKER and SUNNY SCHRAMM.

Album rating: SEVERED SURVIVAL (*3) / MENTAL FUNERAL (*3) / ACTS OF THE UNSPEAKABLE (*4) / SHITFUN (*3) / TORN FROM THE GRAVE compilation (*5) / Abscess: URINE JUNKIES (*5) / SEMINAL VAMPIRES AND MAGGOT MEN (*7) / TORMENTED (*5) / Ravenous: ASSEMBLED IN BLASPHEMY (*4)

CHRIS REIFERT – vocals, drums (ex-DEATH) / **DANNY CORALLES** – guitar / **ERIC CUTLER** – guitar / + guest **STEVE DiGIORGIO** – bass (of SADUS)

Peaceville not iss.

Apr 89. (lp/c/cd) *(VILE/+C/CD 012)* **SEVERED SURVIVAL** [] [-]
– Charred remains / Service for a vacant coffin / Disembowel / Gasping for air / Ridden with disease / Pagan saviour / Impending dread / Severed survival / Critical madness / Embalmed / Stillborn. *(pic-lp Jan92; VILE 012P) <US-iss.1994 on 'Futurist'+=; 11036>* – RETRIBUTION FOR THE DEAD tracks. *(cd re-iss. Jul96; CDMVILE 12)*

— **STEVE CUTLER** – bass; repl. KEN SOVARI (who repl. DiGIORGIO)

Feb 91. (12"ep/cd-ep) *(VILE 024 T/CD)* **RETRIBUTION FOR THE DEAD. / DESTINED TO FESTER / IN THE GRIP OF WINTER** [] [-]

Apr 91. (lp/pic-lp/c/cd) *(VILE 025/+P/MC/CD)* **MENTAL FUNERAL** [] [-]
– Twisted mass of burnt decay / In the grip of winter / Fleshcrawl / Torn from the womb / Slaughterday / Dead / Robbing the grave / Hole in the head / Destined to fester / Bonesaw / Dark crusade / Mental funeral. *(cd re-iss. Jul96; CDMVILE 25) (cd re-iss. Aug95 +=; CDVILE 25)* – SEVERED SURVIVAL

— **DiGIORGIO** returned to repl. STEVE CUTLER

Mar 92. (m-lp/m-cd) *(VILE 029T/+CD)* **FIEND FOR BLOOD** [] [-]
– Fiend for blood / Keeper of decay / Squeal like a pig / Ravenous freaks / A different kind of mindfuck / Deadhole.

— **JOSH BAROHN** – bass (ex-SUFFOCATION) repl. DiGIORGIO

Oct 92. (lp/c/cd) *(VILE 033/+MC/CD)* **ACTS OF THE UNSPEAKABLE** [] [-]
– Meat / Necrocannibalistic vomitorium / Your rotting face / Blackness within / Act of the unspeakable / Frozen with fear / Spinal extractions / Death twitch / Skullptures / Pus / Rot / Lobotomised / Funereality / Tortured moans of agony / Ugliness and secretions / Orgy in excrements / Voices / Walls of the coffin. *(cd re-iss. Jul96; CDMVILE 33)*

— **REIFORT** + crew were joined by guests **FREEWAY** – bass (ex-IMMORTAL HATE) + **CHRIS BOWER** – guitar (ex-HEXX)

Jul 95. (cd) *(CDVILE 49)* **SHITFUN** [] [-]
– Deathmask / Humiliate your corpse / FuckDog / Praise the children / The birthing / Shit eater / Formaldehigh / I sodomize your corpse / Geek / Brain damage / Blood orgy / No more hate / Grave violators / Maim rape kill rape / I shit on your grave / An end to the misery / The 24 public mutilations / Bathe in fire / Bowel ripper / Burnt to a fuck / Excremental ecstasy.

— disbanded after above

– compilations, etc. –

Feb 01. (cd) *Peaceville; (CDVILE 84) <61084>* **TORN FROM THE GRAVE** [] [] Apr01
– Charred remains / Disembowel / Gasping for air / Severed survival / Ridden with disease / Service for a vacant coffin / Retribution for the dead / Robbing the grave / Twisted mass of burnt decay / Fleshcrawl / Torn from the womb / Slaughterday / Dark crusade / Mental funeral / Fiend for blood / Squeal like a pig / Funereality / An act of the unspeakable / Frozen with fear / Spinal extraction / Death twitch / Walls of the coffin / Shiteater / Humiliate your corpse / Brain damage / Blood orgy / Bowel ripper.

Mar 01. (lp) *Vinyl Collectors; (VC 026)* **RIDDEN WITH DISEASE** (early recordings) [] [-]
– Human genocide / Embalmed / Stillborn / Mauled to death / Charred remains / Ridden with disease / Critical madness / Severed survival (live) / Service for a vacant coffin (live).

ABSCESS

CHRIS REIFERT – vocals, drums / **DANNY CORALLES** – bass, guitar, vocals / **CLINT BOWER** – guitar, vocals / **FREEWAY** – bass, drums, vocals

Relapse Relapse

Aug 95. (cd) *<RR 6923-2>* **URINE JUNKIES** [-] []
– Aching meat / Urine junkies / Crawled up from the sewer / 29th lobotomy / Horny hag / Depopulation / Zombiefication / Blacktooth beast / The scent of shit / Altar toy / Suicide fuck / Raw sewage / Die pig die / Inbred abomination / Unquenchable thirst / Abscess / Blood sucker / Anally impared.

Feb 97. (cd) *<(RR 6945-2)>* **SEMINAL VAMPIRES AND MAGGOT MEN** [] [-]
– Naked freak show / Freak fuck fest (naked freak show II: Orgy) / Patient zero / Zombie ward / Mud / Stiff and ditched / Fatfire / I don't give a fuck / Burn, die and fucking fry / Global doom / Removing the leech / Pinworms / Gonna mow you down / Disgruntled / Tunnel of horrors / Worm sty infection / Dirty little brats / The scent of shit.

— FREEWAY had already departed in 1996 (**JOE ALLEN** repl. him)

1997. (cd-ep) **THROBBING BLACK WEREBEAST** [-] []

not iss. Listenable

Feb 01. (cd) *<DEATHVOMIT 6>* **TORMENTED** [-] []
– Rusted blood / Filth chamber / Tormented / Madness and parasites / Deathscape in flames / Street trash / Halo of disease / Scratching at the coffin / Ratbag / Death runs red / Wormwind / From bleeding skies / Madhouse at the end of the world.

RAVENOUS

REIFERT, CORALLES + BOWER

Hammerheart Hammerheart

Nov 00. (cd/lp) *(HHR 066/+LP) <72020>* **ASSEMBLED IN BLASPHEMY** [] []
– Shrieks of the mutilated / Dead, cut up, and ready to fuck / Orgy in dog's blood / Feasting from the womb / Keep my grave open / Assembled in blasphemy / Perverted before God / Hallinations of a deranged mind / Ageless existence / Annointing the worms.

AVAIL

Formed: Washington, DC, USA . . . early 90's by TIM BARRY, JOE BANKS, GWOMPER, ERIK LARSON and the talismanic figure of "cheerleader" BEAU BEAU. AVAIL sprung from the East Coast hardcore/punk revival milieu; their output blending both these genres with some elements of speed metal chucked in for good measure. The band inked a contract with 'Lookout' in 1993, who put out the group's debut album, 'SATIATE' (1993), that same year. The album certainly did what it said on the tin quelling the hunger of many fans of hardcore looking for that added ingredient of punk sensibility, and political integrity. They rapidly followed this up with their second full-length set, 'DIXIE' (1994), a record that showed that the boys could match in the studio their much respected intense live sets. The album also included a great high-octane cover of John Cougar Mellencamp's 'PINK HOUSES'. AVAIL's next album, '4AM FRIDAY' (1996), followed in the same vein and infused with the band's frenetic energy on anthems like, 'SIMPLE SONG'. During the promotional touring for this piece a recording was made at a gig at the Bottom of the Hill club in San Francisco, and was released as an album two years later under the lucid title, 'LIVE AT THE BOTTOM OF THE HILL IN SAN FRANCISCO' (1998). This set also included a couple of numbers, like 'SCUFFLE TOWN', from their next studio album, 'OVER THE JAMES' (1998). This album was slightly shunned by the critics for being too similar in style to the rest of their catalogue, but it did not seem to affect AVAIL much as the following year – as treat for the fans – they released another live album, 'LIVE AT THE KINGS HEAD INN' (1999); taped in their early days, with a set comprising tracks from their debut and sophomore albums. The millennium saw the hardcore punksters going strong releasing their fifth studio album, 'ONE WRENCH' (2000). Again similar in style to their erstwhile sets, the high-energy and honest sentiment here seemed refreshing in the face of the contemptuous attitude like-bands of their genre were now displaying. During the late 90's, LARSON turned guitarist and came up with 5-piece ALABAMA THUNDER PUSSY, a grinding, pounding mob based in Richmond, Virginia. Completing the line-up with vocalist JOHNNY THROCKMORTON, guitarist ASECHISH BOGDEN, bassist SAM KRIVANEC and drummer BRYAN COX, they have since delivered three mighty sets including career best 'RIVER CITY REVIVAL' (1999). TV news channel CNN apparently described 'PUSSY as "the current degeneration and immorality of US music and culture today" – good publicity indeed.

Album rating: SATIATE (*7) / DIXIE (*6) / 4 AM FRIDAY (*6) / LIVE AT THE BOTTOM OF THE HILL IN SAN FRANCISCO (*5) / OVER THE JAMES (*5) / LIVE AT THE KINGS HEAD INN (*6) / ONE WRENCH (*6) / Alabama Thunder Pussy: RISE AGAIN (*6) / RIVER CITY REVIVAL (*7) / CONSTELLATION (*6)

TIM BARRY – vocals / **JOE BANKS** – guitar / **GWOMPER!** – bass / **ERIK LARSON** – drums

Lookout! Lookout!

Feb 94. (cd) *<LK 82CD>* **SATIATE** [-] []
– March / All about it / Forgotten / Bob's crew / Observations / Upward grind / Stride / Timeframe / Pinned up / Predictable / Twisted / Hope / Connection / Mr. Morgan. *(UK-iss.Sep99; same as US)*

Sep 94. (cd) *<LK 103CD>* **DIXIE** [-] []
– On the nod / Clone / Tuning / Song / Sidewalk / 25 years / Virus / Belief's pile / Treading on heels / Model / South bound 95 / Pink houses.

— **ROB KELSHIAN** – bass; repl. GWOMPER! (or same guy?)

Jun 96. (lp/cd) *<(LOOKOUT 138/+CD)>* **4 AM FRIDAY** [] [] May96
– Simple song / Order / Tuesday / 92 / McCarthy / Monroe park / Armchair / Fix / Blue ridge / Swing low, sweet chariot / F.C.A. / Hang / Governor / Nameless.

Dec 97. (cd-ep; split w/ YOUNG PIONEERS) *<(LK 189CD)>* **THE FALL OF RICHMOND** [] [] Nov97
– New #2 / Lombardy street / You may be right / (other 5 by the YOUNG PIONEERS).

Feb 98. (cd) *<(LK 192CD)>* **LIVE AT THE BOTTOM OF THE HILL IN SAN FRANCISCO (live)** [] [] Jan98
– South bound 95 / Stride / Order / Tuning / Fix / F.C.A. / Pinned up / Nickel bridge / Simple song / Clone / Nameless / Scuffle town / Blue ridge / Virus / Model.

Apr 98. (cd/lp) *<(LK 195 CD/LP)>* **OVER THE JAMES** [] []
– Deep wood / New #2 / August / Fall apart / Nickel bridge / Scuffle town / Sanctuary / S.R.O. / Mid-town west / Lombardy St. / Vine / Cross tie / Ask / Fifth wheel.

Old Glory not iss.

Feb 99. (10"m-lp/m-cd) *(NGR 011CD)* **LIVE AT THE KINGS HEAD INN (live)** [] [-]
– Sidewalk / Stride / song / Observations / Predictable / Forgotten / Pinned up / Violent femmes / Connection / Untitled.

Fat Wreck Chords Fat wreck Chords

Oct 99. (cd-ep) *<(FAT 598CD)>* **100 TIMES** [] []
– Order / Union / Song / March / Pinned up / Connection.

Jun 00. (lp/cd) *<(FAT 597/+CD)>* **ONE WRENCH** [] []
– Fast one / Taken / N30 / Levelled / New song / High lonesome / Invisible / Union / Heron / Rest / C. days / Bell / Leather / Old dominion.

ALABAMA THUNDER PUSSY

JOHNNY THROCKMORTON – vocals / **ERIK LARSON** – guitar / **ASECHISH BOGDEN** – guitar / **SAM KRIVANEC** – bass / **BRYAN COX** – drums

Man's Ruin Man's Ruin

Jun 98. (cd) *<(MR 102)>* **RISE AGAIN** [] []
– Falling behind / Victory through defeat / Folk lore / The Lord's prayer / Get mad –

Get even / When mercury drops / Ivy / Speaking in tongues / Jackass / Alto vista / Podium / Fever 103 / Dixie. *(re-iss. Aug00; same)*

Feb 99. (cd) *<(MR 154)>* **RIVER CITY REVIVAL**
– Dry spell / Spineless / Heathen / Mosquito / Giving up on living / Own worst enemy / Rockin' is ma' business. *(re-iss. Aug00; same)*

Mar 00. (cd) *<(MR 177)>* **CONSTELLATION**
– Crying out loud / Ambition / 1/4 mile / Middle finger salute 1271 3108 / 6 shooter / Second wind / Obsari / Foul play / Negligence / 155 minute drive / Burden / Keepsake / Country song.

AVATAR (see under ⇒ SAVATAGE)

AVENGER

Formed: Newcastle, England . . . 1983 by BRIAN ROSS and MICK MOORE (both from heavy rock band, BLITZKRIEG). They added GARY YOUNG and LEE CHEETHAM, recording the debut 45, 'TOO WILD TO TAME' later in the year. Trading places with SATAN's IAN SWIFT, ROSS moved on prior to their first long-player, 'BLOOD SPORTS' (1984). The following year, with American GREG REITER finally taking up the guitar position once held by CHEETHAM, they released a second set, 'KILLER ELITE'. The band soon folded following SWIFT's nimble flight to ATOMKRAFT.

Album rating: BLOOD SPORTS (*5) / KILLER ELITE (*4)

BRIAN ROSS – vocals (ex-BLITZKRIEG) / **LEE CHEETHAM** – guitar / **MICK MOORE** – bass (ex-BLITZKRIEG) / **GARY YOUNG** – drums

Neat — not iss.

Oct 83. (7") *(NEAT 31)* **TOO WILD TO TAME. / ON THE ROCKS** [ ] [-]

— **IAN SWIFT** – vocals (from SATAN) repl. ROSS (to SATAN)

1984. (lp) *(NEAT 1018)* **BLOOD SPORTS** [ ] [-]
– Enforcer / You'll never take me (alive) / Matriarch / Warfare / On the rocks / Rough ride / Victims of force / Death race 2000 / Night of the jackal.

— **GREG REITER** (b. USA) – guitar; repl. STEVE BIRD who repl. CHEETHAM

1985. (lp) *(NEAT 1026)* **KILLER ELITE** [ ] [-]
– Revenge attack / Run for your life / Brand of torture / Steel on steel / (Fight for the) Right to rock / Hard times / Under the hammer / Face to the ground / Dangerous games / Yesterdays heroes / M.M. 85 / Sawmill.

— **DARREN KURLAND** (b. USA) – drums; repl. YOUNG

— split after above, when SWIFT joined ATOMKRAFT

AVENGER (see under ⇒ RAGE)

AVENGERS

Formed: San Francisco, California, USA . . . 1977 by PENELOPE HOUSTON, DANNY FURIOUS, JONATHAN POSTAL and GREG WESTERMARK (the latter two were subsequently replaced by JIMMY WILSEY, BRAD KENT and GREG INGRAHAM before any recordings). Their debut release was a maxi-single featuring the lead track, 'CAR CRASH', a head-on collision of raw punk and primitive hardcore for the 'Dangerhouse' imprint that made its mark on the fertile San Fran underground scene. Garnering a minor degree of fame by supporting the SEX PISTOLS at their final gig in December '78 at the city's Winterland Ballroom, The AVENGERS subsequently worked with ex-PISTOL, STEVE JONES on a follow-up release, 'THE AMERICAN IN ME' EP. However, the file was closed on the group shortly after, PENELOPE HOUSTON going on to become a singer/songwriter. • **Covered:** JOKER'S WILD (Ventures; Batman hit) / MONEY (Barrett Strong).

Album rating: THE AVENGERS 1977-1979 compilation (*6) / DIED FOR YOUR SINS compilation (*7)

PENELOPE HOUSTON – vocals / **GREG INGRAHAM** – guitar; repl. GREG WESTERMARK / **JIMMY WILSEY** – bass; repl. JONATHAN POSTAL / **DANNY FURIOUS** – drums / added **BRAD KENT** – second guitar

not iss. — Dangerhouse

Dec 77. (7"m) *<SFD 400>* **CAR CRASH. / WE ARE THE ONE / I BELIEVE IN ME** [-] [ ]

not iss. — White Noise

Jan 79. (7"ep) *<WNR 002>* **THE AMERICAN IN ME / UH-OH. / CORPUS CHRISTI / WHITE NIGGER** [-] [ ]
<re-iss. 1981 with diff.sleeve; same>

— split in 1979, PENELOPE HOUSTON later became a singer/songwriter, releasing one album, 'BIRDBOYS' for 'Subterranean'.

– compilations, etc. –

Aug 86. (cd) *CD Presents; (CD 007)* **THE AVENGERS 1977-1979** [ ] [-]
– We are the one / Car crash / I believe in me / Open your eyes / No martyr / Desperation / Thin white line / Paint it black / The American in me / White nigger / Uh-oh / Second to none / Corpus Christi / Fuck you (live). *(re-iss. Apr90 as 'CADILLACS AND LINCOLNS' on 'Rockhouse'; ROCK 8901)*

Mar 99. (cd/lp) *Lookout; <(LK 217 CD/LP)>* **DIED FOR YOUR SINS** [ ] [ ] Feb99
– Teenage rebel / Friends of mine / White nigger / The good, the bad and the Kowalskis / I want in / Crazy homocide / The end of the world / Fools or hippies / The American in me / Get up / Open your eyes / Car crash / Tiny pink noise / Fuck you / Joker's wild / Somebody's wrong / Wrong town / Desperation / I believe in me / Money (that's what I want) / We are the one.

AXE

Formed: Florida, USA . . . 1978 out of the band, BABYFACE, by BOBBY BARTH, EDGAR RILEY, MIKE TURPIN and TEDDY MUELLER, who were soon joined by MIKE OSBOURNE. Purveying melodic boogie/pomp rock, they signed to 'MCA', who issued their self-titled debut album in '79. Another, 'LIVING ON THE EDGE', appeared the following year, although 'Atco' took over the reins for their third set, 'OFFERING', which claimed a place in the US Top 100. Taken from it, the single, 'NOW OR NEVER' also peaked quite high, 'NEMESIS' in '83 being the band's swansong prior to the untimely death of singer EDGAR RILEY. BARTH moved on to fellow southerners, BLACKFOOT, before resurrecting AXE in the late 80's. In fact, a decade later (1997 to be exact), BARTH and AXE unleashed their long-awaited fifth set, 'V'; a re-recorded best of CD, 'TWENTY YEARS FROM HOME 1977-1997' was hot on its heels. • **Covered:** I CAN'T HELP MYSELF (Holland-Dozier-Holland) / I GOT THE FIRE (Ronnie Montrose).

Album rating: AXE (*6) / LIVING ON THE EDGE (*6) / OFFERING (*6) / NEMESIS (*4) / V (*4) / TWENTY YEARS FROM HOME compilation (*6) / TWENTY YEARS FROM HOME VOL.2 compilation (*4) / THE CROWN (*4)

EDGAR RILEY – vocals / **BOBBY BARTH** – guitar / **MIKE OSBOURNE** – guitar / **MIKE TURPIN** – bass / **TEDDY MUELLER** – drums

M.C.A. — M.C.A.

Oct 79. (7") *<41073>* **HANG ON. / HOW COME I LOVE YOU** [-] [ ]

Nov 79. (lp) *(MFC 3033) <3171>* **AXE** [ ] [ ]
– Life's just an illusion / Hang on / Sympathize / How come I love you / Forever / Back on the streets / Doin' the best that I can / You're out of line / Battles.

Jun 80. (7") *(MCA 611) <41229>* **I CAN'T HELP MYSELF. / LET ME KNOW** [ ] [ ]

Jan 81. (lp) *<(MFC 3224)>* **LIVING ON THE EDGE** [ ] [ ] Nov80
– Living on the edge / Fantasy of love / First time, last time / Carry on / Running the gauntlet / I can't help myself (sugar pie, honey bunch) / Just walk away / Let me know / Save our love / For a little while.

— **WAYNE HANER** – bass; repl. TURPIN

Atco — Atco

Jul 82. (7") *<7408>* **NOW OR NEVER. / VIDEO INSPIRATIONS** [-] [64]

Nov 82. (lp) *(K 50895) <148>* **OFFERING** [ ] [81] Jun82
– Rock'n'roll party in the streets / Video inspiration / Steal another fantasy / Jennifer / I got the fire / Burn the city down / Now or never / Holdin' on / Silent soldiers.

Nov 82. (7") *<99975>* **ROCK'N'ROLL PARTY IN THE STREETS. /** [-] [ ]

Oct 83. (7") *<99823>* **I THINK YOU'LL REMEMBER TONIGHT. / LET THE MUSIC COME BACK** [-] [94]

Nov 83. (7") *(B 9850) <99850>* **HEAT IN THE STREET. / MIDNIGHT DRIVES ME MAD** [ ] [ ] Aug83

Nov 83. (lp) *<(79 0099-1)>* **NEMESIS** [ ] [ ] Sep83
– Heat in the street / Young hearts / All through the night / I'll think you'll remember tonight / She's had the power / Girls, girls, girls / Eagle flies alone / Keep playing that rock'n'roll / Foolin' your mama again / Let the music come back / Masquerade.

— In 1984, RILEY was killed in a car crash. BARTH joined BLACKFOOT and went solo, before re-forming AXE in 1989, with ANDY PARKER (ex-UFO)

— (mid-90's) **BARTH, MUELLER + RILEY** recruited **BOB HARRIS** – keyboards + **BLAKE EBERHARD** – bass

Made To Measure — Fore Reel

Feb 97. (cd) *(MTM 199617) <1223>* **V** [ ] [ ]
– Intro / Magic (in our eyes) / Heroes and legends / Sting of the rain / Life in the furnace / Burn me once (burn me twice) / Where there's smoke there's fire / Holding on to the night / Anyplace on this highway (is home) / Battles.

Sep 97. (cd) *(MTM 199633) <1224>* **TWENTY YEARS FROM HOME 1977-1997** (re-recorded) [ ] [ ] Oct98
– Running the gauntlet / Burn the city down / All through the night / First time, last time / Rock and roll party in the streets / Back on the streets / Life's just an illusion / Forever / Fantasy of love / Eagle flies alone / Now or never / Heat in the street / Living on the edge / Sting of the rain / Heroes and legends.

Feb 99. (cd) *Made To Measure; (MTM 199672)* **TWENTY YEARS FROM HOME VOL.2** (compilation) [ ] [-]
– Let the music come back / Hang on / Young hearts / Jennifer / I don't want to be alone tonight / Midnight drives me mad / Steal another fantasy / Silent soldiers / Holdin' on / Dangerous games / Sympathize / For a little while / Carry on / Masquerade.

— **CHRISTIAN TEELE** – drums; repl. MUELLER

— added **DANNY MASTERS** – guitar

Nov 00. (cd) *(MTM 068124)* **THE CROWN** [ ] [-]
– The crown / Together we fly (together we fall) / Prelude / Fire and water / Restless angel / Children's memory / Torturous game / Sunshine again (Mario's song) / Foolish deception / Love changes everything.

AXE WITCH

Formed: Linkoping, Sweden . . . 1981 by lyricist ANDERS WALLENTOFT, MAGNUS JARLS, TOMMY BRAGE and brothers MATS and MIKAEL JOHANSSON. Initially a hard and heavy metal outfit, the band released two albums in this vein, 'LORD OF THE FLIES' and 'VISIONS OF THE PAST', the latter gaining a UK release in 1985 on 'Neat'. With recognition still temptingly out of reach, the band underwent a fundamental change in image, the album 'HOOKED ON HIGH HEELS' showing an affinity with RATT as opposed to the NWOBHM bands from which they took their early influences.

Album rating: THE LORD OF FLIES mini (*3) / VISIONS OF THE PAST (*5) / HOOKED ON HIGH HEELS (*4)

ANDERS WALLENTOFT – vocals / **MAGNUS JARLS** – guitar / **MIKAEL JOHANSSON** – guitar / **TOMMY BRAGE** – bass / **MATS JOHANSSON** – drums

Axe / not iss.

1982. (blue-12"ep) <MS 001> **PRAY FOR METAL** [-] [-] Sweden
– Born in a hell / Heavy revolution / In the end of the world / Death angel.

Fingerprint / not iss.

Dec 83. (m-lp) *(FINGLP 101)* **THE LORD OF FLIES** [-] [-] Dutch

1984. (12"ep) *(FINGM 404)* **STAND UP. / TIME TRAVELLER (live) / BORN IN HELL** [-] [-] Sweden

May 85. (lp) *(FINGLP 011)* **VISIONS OF THE PAST** [ ] [-]
– Visions of the past / Give them hell / Tonight / Hot lady / Stand up / Heading for a storm / Born in Hell / Time to live.
(above issued UK on 'Neat' records; *NEAT 1025)*

— **KLAS WOLLBERG** – guitar; repl. MIK

— **MAGNUS HEDIN** – bass; repl. TOMMY who later joined HAZE

— **ABBEY** – drums' repl. MATS

Nov 85. (lp) *(FINGLP 012)* **HOOKED ON HIGH HEELS** [-] [-] Sweden
– City's on fire / Evolution / Too much Hollywood / World of illusion / Nightcomers / Tracks of blood / Alpha and Omega / Shadows through the night / Backstage queen / Leather and passion.

— split soon after above

AXIS

Formed: USA ... 1978 by DANNY JOHNSON and VINNIE APPICE, both hard-rockers from the (RICK) DERRINGER stable. The power-trio enlisted bassist JAY DAVIS but only delivered one album, 'IT'S A CIRCUS WORLD', before APPICE joined BLACK SABBATH (and later DIO), while DAVIS joined SILVER CONDOR. JOHNSON took over from STEVE VAI in ALCATRAZZ before reuniting with DAVIS in PRIVATE LIFE.

Album rating: IT'S A CIRCUS WORLD (*5)

DANNY JOHNSON – vocals, guitar (ex-DERRINGER) / **JAY DAVIS** – bass, vocals / **VINNIE APPICE** – drums (ex-DERRINGER, ex-BECK, BOGART & APPICE)

not iss. / R.C.A.

Jan 79. (lp) <APL-1 2950> **IT'S A CIRCUS WORLD** [-] [ ]
– Brown eyes / Bugged love / Juggler / Soldier of love / Train / Armageddon / Ray's electric farm / Stormy weather / Cat's in the alley / Bandits of rock / Circus world.

— split soon after (see above)

AXXIS

Formed: Dortmund, Germany ... late 80's by WALTER PIETSCH alongside BERNHARD WEISS, WERNER KLEINHANS and RICHARD MICHALSKI. Signed to 'E.M.I.' in 1988 on the strength of a solitary demo track, AXXIS released their debut album, 'KINGDOM OF THE NIGHT' the following year. No one was more surprised than the band themselves when the record became the biggest selling hard rock debut in the history of the German music industry. Keyboard player HARRY OELLERS was added for 'AXXIS II' (1990) while the group's love of the live environment manifested itself in 1991's 'ACCESS ALL AREAS'. Rooted in 70's melodic heavy rock, the band's hook-laden sound was further developed on 1993's Joey Balin-produced 'THE BIG THRILL'. For 1995's 'MATTERS OF SURVIVAL', the band hooked up with legendary rock producer Keith Olsen at his Goodnight L.A. studio, their worldwide reputation growing year on year. Having learned studio craft from the masters, AXXIS decided to take the production helm themselves for 1997's heavier, back to basics 'VOODOO VIBES' album. Following the subsequent departure of PIETSCH, the band recruited youngsters GUIDO WEHMEYER and UDO NIEMEYER. The newcomers made their debut on 'BACK TO THE KINGDOM', the band's first effort for new label, 'Massacre' (also home to PINK CREAM 69).

Album rating: KINGDOM OF THE NIGHT (*7) / AXXIS II (*5) / ACCESS ALL AREAS (*4) / THE BIG THRILL (*4) / MATTERS OF SURVIVAL (*4) / VOODOO VIBES (*4) / BACK TO THE KINGDOM (*5)

BERNHARD WEISS – vocals, guitar / **WALTER PIETSCH** – guitar, vocals / **WERNER KLEINHANS** – bass / **RICHARD MICHALSKI** – drums, vocals

Parlophone / Enigma

Aug 89. (7"/7"pic-d) *(R/RPD 6225)* **KINGDOM OF THE NIGHT. / YOUNG SOULS** [ ] [ ]
(12"+=/cd-s+=) *(12R/CDR 6225)* – Kings made of steel.

Sep 89. (cd/c/lp) *(CD/TC+/PCS 7334)* <D21S-73568> **KINGDOM OF THE NIGHT** [ ] [ ]
– Living in a world / Kingdom of the night / Never say never / Fire and ice / Young souls / For a song / Love is like an ocean / The Moon / Tears of the trees / Just one night / Kings made of steel. *(cd+=)* – Living in a world (extended).

— added **HARRY OELLERS** – keyboards

E.M.I. / not iss.

Sep 90. (cd/lp) *(0777 7 95140-2/-1)* **AXXIS II** [-] [-] German
– The world is looking in their eyes / Save me / Touch the rainbow / Rolling like thunder / Hold you / Ships are sailing / Little look back / Face to face / Get down / Gimme back the paradise / Hold you (acoustic).

Harvest / not iss.

Nov 91. (cd/lp) *(0777 7 97950-2/-1)* **ACCESS ALL AREAS (live)** [-] [-] German
– Kingdom of the night / Trash in Tibet (instrumental) / Little look back / Touch the rainbow / Face to face / Tears of the trees / Ships are sailing / Living in a world / Save me / Fire and ice / Back to the wall.

1993. (cd) *(0777 7 81377-2)* **THE BIG THRILL** [-] [-] German
– Better world – Livin' in the dark / Against a brick wall / Stay don't leave me / Little war / No advice / Love doesn't know any distance / Heaven's 7th train / Brother moon / Waterdrop / The wolf / Road to never neverland.

1995. (cd) *(7243 8 32469-2)* **MATTERS OF SURVIVAL** [-] [-] German
– Ecstasy / Idolator / C'est la vie / On my own / Just a story / All my life / Freedom comes / Another day / Fan the flames / Watch out / Hide away / Back in my bones.

1997. (cd) *(7243 8 55395-2)* **VOODOO VIBES** [-] [-] German
– Helena / Voodoo vibes / Fly away / Sarajevo / Desert song / A little mercy / World of mystery / Allright / Love and pain / A life for a life / Spider / The show is over.

— now without PIETSCH; **WEISS, OELLERS + MICHALSKI** recruited **GUIDO WEHMEYER + UDO NIEMEYER** – bass

Massacre / Massacre

Mar 00. (cd) *(MASS 0238CD)* <85> **BACK TO THE KINGDOM** [ ] [ ] May00
– Shadowman / Like a sphinx / Flashback radio / Heaven in black / Only God knows / Sea of love / White nights / Why not?! / My little princess / Without you / Ice on fire / Na, na, hey, hey, say goodbye.

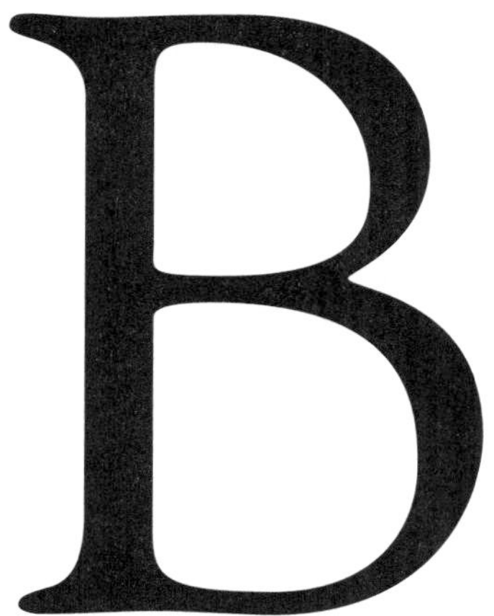

BABE RUTH

Formed: Hatfield, Hertfordshire, England . . . 1971 as SHACKLOCK by namesake ALAN SHACKLOCK, who soon found singer JENNY HAAN. She was raised in the States as a teenager, which probably inspired them to take the new name BABE RUTH (after the legendary baseball player). They were basically a hard-driving progressive-rock act, front-girl HAAN taking most of the plaudits. The debut album, 'FIRST BASE', didn't even hit that mark in the UK, but went gold in Canada, paving the way for a minor success in the States with their third album. However, by 1975, they had lost the two core members SHACKLOCK and HAAN, replacing them with BERNIE MARSDEN and ELLIE HOPE.

Album rating: FIRST BASE (*6) / AMAR CABALERO (*5) / BABE RUTH (*5) / STEALIN' HOME (*4) / KID'S STUFF (*3) / THE BEST OF BABE RUTH compilation (*6)

JANITA 'JENNY' HAAN (b.Edgeware, England) – vocals / **ALAN SHACKLOCK** – guitar, vocals, organ, percussion / **DAVE HEWITT** – bass / **JEFF ALLEN** – drums / **DAVE PUNSHON** – piano

Decca | not iss.

Sep 71. (7") *(F 13234)* **RUPERT'S MAGIC FEATHER. / FLOOD** [ ] [-]

— **DICK POWELL** – drums repl. JEFF ALLEN

Harvest | Harvest

Nov 72. (7") *(HAR 5061) <3553>* **WELLS FARGO. / THEME FROM 'A FEW DOLLARS MORE'** [ ] [ ]

Nov 72. (lp) *(SHSP 4022) <11151>* **FIRST BASE** [ ] [ ]
– Wells Fargo / The runaways / King Kong / Black dog / The mexican / Joker.

Apr 73. (7") *(HAR 5072)* **AIN'T THAT LIVIN'. / WE ARE HOLDING ON** [ ] [-]

— **ED SPEVOCK** – drums (ex-PETE BROWN'S PIBLOKTO) repl. POWELL + PUNSHON

Mar 74. (lp) *(SHVL 812) <1275>* **AMAR CABALERO** [ ] [ ]
– Lady / Broken cloud / Gimme some leg / Baby pride / Cool jerk / We are holding on / Doctor Love / Amar Cabalero: El Cabalero de la reina Isabella – Hombre de la guitarra – El testament de Amelia.

May 74. (7") *(HAR 5082)* **IF HEAVEN'S ON BEAUTY'S SIDE. / DOCTOR LOVE** [ ] [-]

— added **STEVE GURL** – keyboards (ex-WILD TURKEY)

Oct 74. (7") *(HAR 5087)* **WELLS FARGO. / THE MEXICAN** [ ] [-]

Jan 75. (7") *(HAR 5090)* **PRIVATE NUMBER. / SOMEBODY'S NOBODY** [ ] [ ]

Feb 75. (lp) *(SHSP 4039) <11367>* **BABE RUTH** [ ] [75]
– Dancer / Somebody's nobody / Theme from 'A Few Dollars More' / We people darker than blue / Jack O'Lantern / Private number / Turquoise / Sad but rich / The duchess of Orleans.

Oct 75. (7"m) *(SPSR 377)* **THE DUCHESS OF ORLEANS. / THE JACK O'LANTERN / TURQUOISE** [ ] [-]

— **BERNIE MARSDEN** – guitar (ex-WILD TURKEY) repl. SHACKLOCK

Capitol | Capitol

Nov 75. (lp) *<(EST 11451)>* **STEALIN' HOME** [ ] [ ]
– It'll happen in time / Winner takes all / Fascination / 2000 sunsets / Elusive / Can you feel it / Say no more / Caught at the plate / Tomorrow (joining of the day).

Apr 76. (7") *(CL 15689) <4219>* **ELUSIVE. / SAY NO MORE** [ ] [ ]

— **SPEVOCK, MARSDEN + GURL** recruited **ELLIE HOPE** – vocals + **RAY KNOTT** – bass to repl. HAAN + HEWITT who formed JENNY HAAN'S LION

Apr 76. (lp) *(EST 23739) <EST 11515)* **KID'S STUFF** [ ] [ ]
– Oh! dear what a shame / Welcome to the show / Since you went away / Standing in the rain / Sweet, sweet surrender / Oh! doctor / Nickelodeon / Keep your distance / Living a lie.

— **ALLAN ROSS + SID TWINEHAM** – guitar repl.MARSDEN who joined PAICE, ASHTON & LORD. He later formed ALASKA and others, and joined WHITESNAKE. BABE RUTH disbanded in 1977, some members moving on to "dance themselves dizzy" in pop-disco outfit, LIQUID GOLD (aarrgghh!).

– compilations, etc. –

Oct 77. (lp) *Harvest; (SHSM 2019)* **THE BEST OF BABE RUTH** [ ] [ ]
– Wells Fargo / Ain't that livin' / Theme from 'A Few Dollars More' / Private number / Joker / Dancer / The Duchess of Orleans / Black dog / If Heaven's on beauty's side / Lady / Jack O'Lantern. *(re-iss. Aug86 on 'Revolver' lp/c; WKFM LP/MC 81)*

Apr 98. (cd) *Beat Goes On; (BGOCD 382)* **FIRST BASE / AMAR CABALLERO** [ ] [-]

Jun 00. (cd) *Beat Goes On; (BGOCD 491)* **BABE RUTH / STEALIN' HOME** [ ] [-]

BABES IN TOYLAND

Formed: Minneapolis, Minnesota, USA . . . 1987 by KAT BJELLAND, MICHELLE LEON and LORI BARBELO. Signing to influential local label, 'Twintone', the all-girl group released an early proto-grunge classic in the Jack Endino-produced 'SPANKING MACHINE' (1990). Featuring such white hot blasts of feminine subversiveness as 'HE'S MY THING' and 'PAIN IN MY HEART', the album opened the floodgates for a slew of similar angry young women (i.e. L7 and HOLE, whose JENNIFER FINCH and COURTNEY LOVE respectively, LYDIA LUNCH soundalike BJELLAND had previously played with in SUGAR BABY DOLL). Over the course of the next year, they released a mini-album, 'TO MOTHER', replaced MICHELLE with MAUREEN HERMAN and signed to 'Warner Brothers', releasing a second album proper, 'FONTANELLE' in the Spring of '92. Produced by LEE RANALDO of SONIC YOUTH, the record breached the UK Top 30 on the back of rave reviews from both the inkies and the metal press. Following a stop-gap part live set, 'PAINKILLERS', the BABES took a sabbatical, BJELLAND turning up in STUART GRAY (her new husband)'s outfit, LUBRICATED GOAT, while moonlighting with CRUNT. BABES IN TOYLAND returned in 1995 with 'NEMESISTERS', which disappointed many of their more hardcore following by including covers of 'WE ARE FAMILY' (Sister Sledge), 'DEEP SONG' (Billie Holiday) and 'ALL BY MYSELF' (Eric Carmen). • **Other covers:** WATCHING GIRL (Shonen Knife) / THE GIRL CAN'T HELP IT (Little Richard) / CALLING OCCUPANTS OF INTERPLANETARY CRAFT (Carpenters) / HUBBLE BUBBLE TOIL AND TROUBLE (Manfred Mann).

Album rating: SPANKING MACHINE (*7) / TO MOTHER (*7) / FONTANELLE (*8) / PAINKILLERS (*5) / NEMESISTERS (*6)

KAT BJELLAND (b. KATHERINE, 9 Dec'63, Woodburn, Oregon) – vocals, guitar / **MICHELLE LEON** – bass / **LORI BARBERO** (b.27 Nov'60) – drums, vocals

not iss. | Treehouse

Jul 89. (7",7"green) *<TR 017>* **DUST CAKE BOY. / SPIT TO SEE THE SHINE** [-] [ ]

not iss. | Sub Pop

Apr 90. (7",7"gold) *<SP 66>* **HOUSE. / ARRIBA** [-] [ ]

Twin Tone | Twin Tone

Jul 90. (cd/lp/mauve-lp) *<TTR 89183-2/-4/-1>* **SPANKING MACHINE** [-] [ ]
– Swamp pussy / He's my thing / Vomit heart / Never / Boto (w)rap / Dogg / Pain in my heart / Lashes / You're right / Dust cake boy / Fork down throat. *(re-iss. +c Dec91 on purple-lp)*

Jun 91. (m-cd/m-c/m-lp) *<(TTR 89208-2/-4/-1)>* **TO MOTHER** [ ] [ ]
– Catatonic / Mad pilot / Primus / Laugh my head off / Spit to see the shine / Pipe / The quiet room.

— (Mar'92) **MAUREEN HERMAN** (b.25 Jul'66, Philadelphia, Pensylvania) – bass (ex-M+M STIGMATA drummer) repl. MICHELLE whose roadie boyfriend John Cole was killed by a burglar

Strange Fruit | not iss.

Mar 92. (cd/10"m-lp) *(SFPMCD/SFPMA 211)* **THE PEEL SESSIONS (live on John Peel show)** [ ] [-]
– Catatonic / Ripe / Primus / Spit to see the shine / Pearl / Dogg / Laugh my head off / Mad pilot.

Southern | Warners

Aug 92. (cd/c/red-lp) *(18501-2/-4/-1) <2-/4-26998>* **FONTANELLE** [24] [ ]
– Bruise violet / Right now / Blue bell / Handsome & Gretel / Blood / Magick flute / Won't tell / The quiet room / Spun / Short song / Jungle train / Pearl / Real eyes / Mother / Gone.

Nov 92. (7"purple) *(18503-7)* **BRUISE VIOLET. / GONE** [ ] [ ]
(12"+=/cd-s+=) *(18503-6/-2)* – Magick flute.

Jun 93. (cd/c/lp) *(18512-2/-4/-1) <45339>* **PAINKILLERS (part live)** [53] [ ]
– He's my thing / Laredo / Istigkeit / Ragweed / Angel hair / Fontanellette (live at CBGB's): Bruise violet – Bluebell – Angel hair – Pearl – Blood – Magick flute – Won't tell – Real eyes – Spun – Mother – Handsome & Gretel.

— KAT married STUART GRAY and sidelined with bands, CRUNT and KATSTU

CRUNT

— **KAT BJELLAND / STUART GRAY** (of LUBRICATED GOAT) + **RUSSELL SIMINIS** (of JON SPENCER BLUES EXPLOSION)

Insipid | Insipid

1993. (7") *(IV-31)* **SWINE. / SEXY** [ ] [ ]

Trance Syndicate | Trance Syndicate

Mar 94. (lp,blue-lp/cd) *<(TR 19/+CD)>* **CRUNT** [ ] [ ] Feb94
– Theme from Crunt / Swine / Black heart / Unglued / Changing my mind / Snap out of it / Sexy / Punishment / Spam / Elephant.

BABES IN TOYLAND

—— re-formed (see last line-up)

Reprise Reprise

Apr 95. (cd/c/lp) <(9362 45868-2/-4/-1)> **NEMESISTERS**
– Hello / Oh yeah! / Drivin' / Sweet '69 / Surd / 22 / Ariel / Kiler on the road / Middle man / Memory / S.F.W. / All by myself / Deep song / We are family.

May 95. (12"ep/c-ep/cd-ep) *(W 0291 TEX/C/CD)* **SWEET '69 / S.F.W. (live) / SWAMP PUSSY (live)** -

Sep 95. (c-s/cd-s) *(W 0313 C/CD)* **WE ARE FAMILY (Arthur Baker remix) / ('A'-Ben Grosse remix)** -
(12"+=) *(W 0313T)* – (2 other Baker & Grosse mixes).

—— In 1998, KAT's alternative/metal supergroup rock opera, Songs Of The Witchblade: A Soundtrack To The Comic Books', was released on CD (Dreamworks; DRMD 50102) featuring her alongside PETER STEELE (Type O Negative), BUZZ OSBORNE (Melvins), JIM THIRLWELL (Foetus), among others.

– compilations, etc. –

Mar 00. (cd) *Almafame; (ALMACD 11)* **LIVED (live)** -
– Dr. Timothy Leary (intro) / He's my thing / Handsome and Gretel / Blue bell / Sweet 69 / Ripe / Mad pilot / Right now / Dogg / Fork down throat / Ya' know that guy / Hubble bubble toil and trouble / Fair is foul and foul is fair / Big top astroanquility (video) / Bruised violet (video) / Memory (video).

May 00. (d-cd) *Snapper; (SMDCD 299)* **NATURAL BABE KILLERS** -
– Bruised violet / Won't tell / Jungle train / We are family / Big top / Magic flute / Memory / Dogg / Fork down throat / Mad pilot / Ripe / Ya know that guy / Spun / Primus / Sweet 69 / Hubble bubble toil and trouble / Fair is foul and foul is fair / Flesh crawl.

Aug 00. (cd) *Almafame; (ALMACD 12)* **DEVIL** -
– Oh yeah! / Spun / Bruised violet / Primus / Fake fur condo / Won't tell / Magick flute / So fucking what / Jungle train / Knife song / Flesh crawl / Intermentstral / We are family / More, more, more (demo) / Calling occupants of interplanetary craft (demo) / Babes In Toyland photo album.

Apr 01. (cd) *Cherry Red; <(CDMRED 181)>* **MINNEPOLISM: LIVE – THE LAST TOUR** Apr01

Apr 01. (cd) *Almafame; (ALMACD 15)* **VILED** -

BABY ANIMALS

Formed: Perth, Australia . . . 1989 out of DEE DEE & THE ROCKMEN by SUZE DeMARCHI and DAVE LESLIE, who enlisted EDDIE PARISE and FRANK CELENZA. Signed to RCA's new 'Imago' label, they released their eponymous debut album early '92, confounding critics with their diverse melange of influences including SIOUXSIE & THE BANSHEES and INXS. SUZE was the driving force behind the band, flirting between hard rock and smooth ballads, she was the pin-up darling of Kerrang! To promote the album, they supported the likes of BRYAN ADAMS, a further album in '93 not gaining sufficient attention to merit the funding of another. SUZE would subsequently marry NUNO BETTENCOURT of EXTREME and live in the States; he would help her on her debut solo album, 'TELELOVE' (2000).

Album rating: BABY ANIMALS (*6) / SHAVED AND DANGEROUS (*4)

SUZE DeMARCHI – vocals, rhythm guitar / **DAVE LESLIE** – lead guitar / **EDDIE PARISE** – bass / **FRANK CELENZA** – drums

Imago-RCA Imago-RCA

Nov 91. (7") *(PB 49156)* **EARLY WARNING. / BABY ANIMALS**
(12"+=/cd-s+=) *(PT/PD 49156)* – Ain't gonna get / Rush you.

Feb 92. (7"/c-s) *(PB/PK 49135)* **ONE WORD. / WASTE OF TIME (live)**
(12"+=/cd-s+=) *(PT/PD 49136)* –

Feb 92. (cd/c/lp) *(PD/PK/PL 90580)* <21002> **BABY ANIMALS**
– Rush you / Early warning / Painless / Make it end / Big time friends / Working for the enemy / One word / Break my heart / Waste of time / One too many / Ain't gonna get. *(cd re-iss. Aug98; 728723011-2)*

Mar 92. (7") *(PB 49117)* PAINLESS. / DEDICATE
(12"+=) *(PT 49117)* – ('A'extended).
(cd-s+=) *(PD 49118)* – Early warning (live).

Aug 93. (cd/c) *(2787210-192/194)* <21019> **SHAVED AND DANGEROUS**
– Don't tell me what to do / Bupata / Life from a distance / Be my friend / Lovin' lies / Lights out at eleven / Backbone / Nervous at night / Because I can / Stoopid / At the end of the day. *(cd re-iss. Jul98; 728723010-2)*

—— split after above; see above

BABY CHAOS

Formed: Stewarton, Ayrshire, Scotland . . . 1992 by school-mates, CHRIS GORDON, GRANT McFARLANE, BOBBY DUNN and DAVEY GREENWOOD. Discovered by former HAPPY MONDAYS manager turned A&R man, Nathan McGough, after an appearance on BBC2's 'Late Show', BABY CHAOS were promptly signed to 'East West' and initiated a series of singles starting with late 1993's 'SPERM'. 'BUZZ', 'GOLDEN TOOTH' and 'HELLO VICTIM' followed over the course of '94, a year which saw them play at the inaugural 'T In The Park' festival in Scotland and culminated in the release of their debut album, 'SAFE SEX, DESIGNER DRUGS & THE DEATH OF ROCK'N'ROLL'. Described as Britain's answer to post-Seattle grunge rock with similarities to The WILDHEARTS and The MANICS, BABY CHAOS nevertheless had trouble with their musical identity; while the likes of Kerrang! tried to claim them for their own they were always more "Wean's Wild" than "Wayne's World". The band returned in the Spring of '96 with a follow-up, 'LOVE YOUR SELF ABUSE', hardly a departure from the debut but worthy of attention nonetheless.

Album rating: SAFE SEX, DESIGNER DRUGS & THE DEATH OF ROCK'N'ROLL (*5) / LOVE YOUR SELF ABUSE (*6)

CHRIS GORDON – vocals, guitar / **GRANT McFARLANE** – guitar / **BOBBY DUNN** – bass / **DAVEY GREENWOOD** – drums

East West Atlantic

Nov 93. (10"ep/cd-ep) *(YZ 792 TE/CD)* **SPERM. / SUPERPOWERED / TONGUE** -

Feb 94. (7"/c-s) *(YZ 800/+C)* **BUZZ. / ETHER** -
(12"+=/cd-s+=) *(YZ 800 T/CD)* – Coming clean.

May 94. (7"ep/12"ep/cd-ep) *(YZ 822/+T/CD)* **GOLDEN TOOTH E.P.** -
– Golden tooth / Resurrected / No way / The Earth is dying, but never mind.

Oct 94. (7"/c-s) *(YZ 852/+C)* **HELLO VICTIM. / ROTTEN TO THE CORE** -
(12"+=/cd-s+=) *(YZ 852 T/CD)* – Skinny.

Nov 94. (cd/lp) *(<4509 98052-2/-1>)* **SAFE SEX, DESIGNER DRUGS AND THE DEATH OF ROCK'N'ROLL**
– Sperm / Saliva / Go to Hell / Breathe / Hello / Victim / Buzz / A bullet for the end / Camel / Golden tooth / Gazelle boy / Superpowered.

—— (on tour only) **SIMON 'GEN' MATTHEWS** – drums (of JESUS JONES) repl. GREENWOOD due to nervous exhaustion

Apr 96. (7"/c-s) *(EW 036/+C)* **HELLO. / NEGATIVELY YOURS** -
(cd-s+=) *(EW 036CD)* – Consider yourself.

Apr 96. (cd/c) *(<0630 14610-2/-4>)* **LOVE YOUR SELF ABUSE**
– Hello / She's in pain / Mental bruising for beginners / Ignoramus / Sensual art of suffocation / Confessions of a teenage pervert / Penny dropped / Pink / Love your self abuse.

Jun 96. (7"/c-s) *(EW 045/+C)* **IGNORAMUS. / FETCH** -
(cd-s+=) *(EW 045CD)* – I don't want your friend.

—— now without GREENWOOD who had a heart problem; they split soon after

BABYLON A.D.

Formed: San Francisco, California, USA . . . 1987 originally as The PERSUADERS by DEREK DAVIS, RON FRESCHI, ROBB REID and JAMEY PACHECHO. Their eponymous debut album (produced by SIMON HANHART and co-written with JACK PONTI) was released in the States in 1989, a gritty hard-rock affair which impressed many, hitting the US Top 100 in the process. A second 'Arista' album, 'NOTHING SACRED' failed to fulfil the band's initial promise prompting their quick demise in '92.

Album rating: BABYLON A.D. (*6) / NOTHING SACRED (*4)

DEREK DAVIS – vocals / **DANNY DE LA ROSA** – guitar; repl. JOHN MATTHEWS / **RON FRESCHI** – guitar / **ROBB REID** – bass / **JAMEY PACHECO** – drums

Arista Arista

Jun 90. (cd/c/lp) *(260/410/210 313)* <8580> **BABYLON A.D.** 88 Nov89
– Bang go the bells / Hammer swings down / Caught up in the crossfire / Desperate / The kid goes wild / Shot o' love / Maryanne / Back in Babylon / Sweet temptation / Sally danced.

May 92. (c-s) <2434> **SO SAVAGE THE HEART / BAD BLOOD** -

Jun 92. (cd/c) <(07822 18702-2/-4)> **NOTHING SACRED**
– Take the dog of the chain / Bad blood / So savage the heart / Sacrifice your love / Redemption / Down the river of no return / Psychedelic sex reaction / Dream train (Rosalie Allen) / Blind ambition / Slave your body / Of the rose / Pray for the wicked.

—— folded after above

BABYS

Formed: London, England . . . 1976 by JOHN WAITE, MIKE CORBY, TONY BROCK and WALLY STOCKER. As a result of a Mike Mansfield-directed promo video, they signed to 'Chrysalis' records, having subsequently moved to LA to avoid the UK punk explosion. Their move was rewarded early in 1977, when they cracked the American charts with their first single, 'IF YOU'VE GOT THE TIME'. The track was a solitary highlight on their eponymous debut album, which bubbled under the US Top 100. Moving through the airbrushed territory between FOREIGNER and JOURNEY, The BABYS struck gold with their follow-up 45, 'ISN'T IT TIME', a classy piece of mainstream pop/rock that cracked the US Top 20. They continued their late 70's ascendency on the US charts, 'EVERYTIME I THINK OF YOU' another to make the Top 20 in '79. CORBY departed prior to this, having been replaced by JONATHAN CAIN and RICKY PHILLIPS. In 1981, the band folded, BROCK and STOCKER being poached by ROD STEWART, while CAIN progressed to JOURNEY. WAITE, meanwhile struck out on a solo career, achieving his biggest US success to date when 1984's 'MISSING YOU' topped the singles chart (also Top 10 in Britain). After completing a handful of profitable AOR albums, WAITE gave the BABYS a rebirth, albeit in the form of hard-rock outfit, BAD ENGLISH. JONATHAN CAIN and RICKY PHILLIPS were side by side with ex-JOURNEY man, NEAL SCHON and WILD DOGS drummer, DEAN CASTRONOVO. Armed with a more mature, harder-edged style, the band gained considerable Stateside success when their self-titled album (containing the Diane Warren-penned No.1 hit, 'WHEN I SEE YOU SMILE') narrowly missed the Top 20. A few years later, the ironically titled follow-up, 'BACKLASH' suffered just that, although it did manage to hold down a Top 100 placing. WAITE returned to his solo career, although he failed to resurrect past glories. • **Trivia:** In 1984, JOHN WAITE starred as a hairdresser in the US soap 'Paper Dolls'.

Album rating: THE BABYS (*5) / BROKEN HEART (*4) / HEAD FIRST (*4) / UNION JACKS (*3) / ON THE EDGE (*3) / THE BABYS' ANTHOLOGY compilation (*6) / THE BEST OF THE BABYS compilation (*6) / John Waite: IGNITION (*4) / NO BRAKES (*4) / MASK OF SMILES (*4) / ROVERS RETURN (*4) / THE ESSENTIAL JOHN WAITE compilation (*6) / TEMPLE BAR (*4) / WHEN YOU WERE MINE (*4) / Bad English: BAD ENGLISH (*5) / BACKLASH (*3)

JOHN WAITE (b. 4 Jul'54, Lancashire, England) – vocals, bass / **WALLY STOCKER** (b.17 Mar'54) – vocals, guitar / **MIKE CORBY** (b. 3 Jul'54) – vocals, keyboards / **TONY BROCK** (b.31 Mar'54, Bournemouth, England) – drums (ex-SPONTANEOUS COMBUSTION, ex-STRIDER)

Chrysalis Chrysalis

Nov 76. (7"m) *(CXP 1) <2132>* **IF YOU'VE GOT THE TIME. / LAURA / DYING MAN** — 88 Feb77

Jan 77. (lp/c) *(<CHR/ZCHR 1129>)* **THE BABYS**
– Looking for love / If you've got the time / I believe in love / Wild man / Laura / I love how you love me / Rodeo / Over and over / Read my stars / Dying man.

Jan 78. (7") *(CHS <2173>)* **ISN'T IT TIME. / GIVE ME YOUR LOVE** 45 13 Sep77

Jan 78. (lp/c) *(<CHR/ZCHR 1150>)* **BROKEN HEART** — 34 Oct77
– Wrong or right / Give me your love / Isn't it time / And if you see me fly / The golden mile / Broken heart / I'm falling / Rescue me / Silver dreams / A piece of the action. *(re-iss. 1983)*

Jan 78. (7") *<2201>* **SILVER DREAMS. / IF YOU SHOULD SEE ME CRY** - 53

— **JONATHAN CAIN** (b.26 Feb'50, Chicago, Illinois) – keyboards repl. CORBY. (JOHN WAITE now just vocals)

— added **RICKY PHILLIPS** – bass

Jan 79. (7") *<2279>* **EVERY TIME I THINK OF YOU. / PLEASE DON'T LEAVE ME HERE** - 13

Jan 79. (7") *(CHS 2279)* **EVERY TIME I THINK OF YOU. / HEAD FIRST** — -

Feb 79. (lp/c) *(<CHR/ZCHR 1195>)* **HEAD FIRST** — 22 Jan79
– Love don't prove I'm right / Every time I think of you / I was one / White lightning / Run to Mexico / Head first / You (got it) / Please don't leave me here / California. *(re-iss. 1982; same)*

May 79. (7") *<2323>* **HEAD FIRST. / CALIFORNIA** - 77

Jan 80. (7"m) *(<CHS 2398>)* **TRUE LOVE TRUE CONFESSIONS. / BROKEN HEART / MONEY** — Nov79

Jan 80. (lp/c) *(<CHR/ZCHR 1267>)* **UNION JACKS** — 42
– Back on my feet again / True love true confessions / Union Jacks / In your eyes / Anytime / Jesus are you there / Turn around in Tokyo / Love is just a mystery.

Jan 80. (7") *<CHS 2398>* **BACK ON MY FEET AGAIN. / TURN AROUND IN TOKYO** - 33

Apr 80. (7") *<2425>* **MIDNIGHT RENDEZVOUS. / LOVE IS JUST A MEMORY** - 72

— Now a quartet, when CAIN left to join JOURNEY

Nov 81. (7") *<2467>* **TURN AND WALK AWAY. / DARKER SIDE OF TOWN** - 42

Nov 80. (lp/c) *(<CHR/ZCHR 1305>)* **ON THE EDGE** — 71
– Turn and walk away / Sweet 17 / She's my girl / Darker side of town / Too far gone / Rock'n'roll is (alive and well) / Downtown / Postcard / Gonna be somebody / Love don't wait.

— Disbanded late 1981. BROCK and STOCKER joined ROD STEWART tour.

– compilations, others, etc. –

Oct 81. (lp/c) *Chrysalis; (<CHR/ZCHR 1351>)* **THE BABYS' ANTHOLOGY**
– Head first / Isn't it time / Midnight rendezvous / Money / Back on my feet again / Give me your love / Turn and walk away / Everytime I think of you / If you've got the time / Sweet 17.

Jan 98. (cd) *Disky; (<DC 88188-2>)* **ISN'T IT TIME**

May 00. (cd) *Liberty; <(523106-2)>* **ANTHOLOGY**
– If you've got the time / Head above the waves / I love how you love me / Looking for love (live) / Isn't it time / Give me your love / Silver dreams / Money / Every time I think of you / Head first / Love don't prove I'm right / Back on my feet again / Midnight rendezvous / Anytime / Turn and walk away / Sweet 17 / Gonna be somebody.

JOHN WAITE

Chrysalis Chrysalis

Jun 82. (lp/c) *(<CHR/ZCHR 1376>)* **IGNITION** — 68
– White heat / Change / Mr.Wonderful / Going to the top / Desperate love / Temptation / By my baby tonight / Make it happen / Still in love with you / Wild life.

EMI America EMI America

Aug 84. (7"/12") *(EA/12EA 182) <8212>* **MISSING YOU. / FOR YOUR LOVE** 9 1 Jun84

Oct 84. (lp/c) *(WAIT/TC-WAIT 1) <17124>* **NO BRAKES** 64 10 Jul84
– Saturday night / Missing you / Dark side of the Sun / Restless heart / Tears / Euroshima / Dreamtime / Shake it up / For your love / Love collision. *(cd-iss. 1987; CDP 746078-2) (cd re-iss. Jun95 on 'Connoisseur'; NSPCD 514)*

Nov 84. (7") *(EA 186) <8238>* **TEARS. / DREAMTIME** — 37 Oct84
(12"+=) *(12EA 186)* – Shake it up.

Mar 85. (7") *(EA 193) <8252>* **RESTLESS HEART. / EUROSHIMA** — 59 Jan85
(12"+=) *(12EA 193)* – Missing you.

Feb 85. (7") *<42606>* **CHANGE. / WHITE HEAT** - 54
(above from the movie 'Vision Quest' released on Chrysalis records)

Sep 85. (7") *(EA 206) <8282>* **EVERY STEP OF THE WAY. / NO BRAKES** — 26

Oct 85. (lp/c) *(WAITE/TC-WAITE 1) <17164>* **MASK OF SMILES** — 36 Aug85
– Every step of the way / Laydown / Welcome to Paradise / Lust for life / Ain't that peculiar / Just like lovers / The choice / You're the one / No brakes.

Oct 85. (7") *<8278>* **WELCOME TO PARADISE. / YOU'RE THE ONE** - 85

Jan 86. (7") *(EA 211)* **THE CHOICE. / NO BRAKES** — -

Aug 86. (7") *(EA 220) <8315>* **IF ANYBODY HAD A HEART. / JUST LIKE LOVERS** — 76 Jun86

Jul 87. (7") *(EA 236) <43018>* **THESE TIMES ARE HARD FOR LOVERS. / WILD ONE** — 53 Jun87
(12"+=) *(12EA 236)* – Missing you.

Aug 87. (lp/c)(cd) *(AML/TC-AML 3121)(CDP 746332-2) <17227>* **ROVERS' RETURN** — 77 Jul87
– These times are hard for lovers / Act of love / Encircled / Woman's touch / Wild one / Don't lose any sleep / Sometimes / She's the one / Big time for love.

Sep 87. (7") *<43040>* **DON'T LOSE ANY SLEEP. / WILD ONE** - 81

Epic Epic

Dec 90. (7"/7"pic-d/c-s) *(656516-7/-0/-4)* **DEAL FOR LIFE. / ('B'side by 'Terry Reid')**
(12"+=/cd-s+=) *(656516-6/-2)* – (tracks by 'Chicago' & 'Maria McKee').

not iss. Imago

Feb 95. (cd-s) *<25091>* **HOW DID I GET BY WITHOUT YOU? / IN DREAMS / EXTASY** - 89

– (JOHN WAITE) compilations, etc. –

Feb 92. (cd/c) *Chrysalis; (<CD/TC CHR 1864>)* **THE ESSENTIAL JOHN WAITE 1976-1986** (compilation)
– Head above the waves * / A piece of action * / Broken heart * / Love don't prove I'm right * / Love is a rose to me / White lightening / Run to Mexico / World in a bottle / Union Jacks * / Anytime / Jesus are you there? * / Darker side of town * / Rock'n'roll is (alive and well) * / Gonna be somebody * / White heat / Make it happen / Change / Mr.Wonderful / If anybody had a heart / Missing you. *(tracks by BABYS *)*

Feb 93. (c-s/7") *Chrysalis; (TC+/CHS 3938)* **MISSING YOU. / HEAD ABOVE THE WAVES**
(cd-s+=) *(CDCHS 3938)* – Broken heart / Love is a rose to me.

— Virtually all The BABYS were re-united when **WAITE, CAIN & PHILLIPS** formed

BAD ENGLISH

with **NEAL SCHON** – guitar, vocals (ex-JOURNEY) / **DEAN CASTRONOVO** – drums, vocals (ex-WILD DOGS)

Epic Epic

Aug 89. (7") *(655089-7) <68946>* **FORGET ME NOT. / LAY DOWN** — 45 Jul89
(12"+=/cd-s+=) *(655089-6/-2)* – Rockin' horse.

Sep 89. (lp/c/cd) *(463447-1/-4/-2) <45083>* **BAD ENGLISH** 74 21 Jul89
– Best of what I got / Heaven is a 4 letter word / Possession / Forget me not / When I see you smile / Tough times don't last / Ghost in your heart / Price of love / Ready when you are / Lay down / The restless ones / Rockin horse / Don't walk away.

Oct 89. (7"/7"pic-d/c-s) *(655347-7/-0/-4) <69082>* **WHEN I SEE YOU SMILE. / ROCKIN' HORSE** 61 1 Sep89
(12"+=) *(655344-6)* – Tough times don't last.
(cd-s++=) *(655294-2)* – ('A'extended).

Feb 90. (7"/7"pic-d) *(655676-7/-0) <73094>* **PRICE OF LOVE. / THE RESTLESS ONES** — 5 Dec89
(12"+=/cd-s+=) *(655676-6/-3)* – Ready when you are.

Apr 90. (c-s,cd-s) *<73307>* **HEAVEN IS A 4 LETTER WORD. / LAY DOWN** - 66

Jun 90. (c-s,cd-s) *<73398>* **POSSESSION. / TOUGH TIMES DON'T LAST** - 21

Sep 90. (7"/c-s) *(656113-7/-4)* **DON'T WALK AWAY. / TOUGH TIMES DON'T LAST** — -
(12"+=/cd-s+=) *(656113-6/-2)* – Price of love.

Aug 91. (7"/c-s) *(657420-7/-4) <73982>* **STRAIGHT TO YOUR HEART. / MAKE LOVE LAST** — 42
(12"+=) *(657420-8)* – Forget me not.
(cd-s++=) *(657420-9)* – When I see you smile.

Oct 91. (cd/c/lp) *(468569-2/-4/-1) <46935>* **BACKLASH** — 72 Sep91
– So this is Eden / Straight to your heart / Time stood still / The time alone with you / Dancing off the edge of the world / Rebel say a prayer / Savage blue / Pray for rain / Make love last / Life at the top.

Nov 91. (7") *<74091>* **THE TIME ALONE WITH YOU. / MAKE LOVE LAST** -

— They broke-up after above release and SCHON and CASTRONOVO formed HARDLINE (see ⇒ JOURNEY). WAITE released solo album 'TEMPLE BAR' for 'Imago' in 1995 and 'WHEN YOU WERE MINE' for 'Pure' in '97.

BABY TUCKOO

Formed: Barnsley, England . . . late 1982 by ROB ARMITAGE and ANDY BARROTT, who completed the line-up with NEIL SAXTON, PAUL SMITH and TONY SUGDEN. Emerging at the tail-end of the NWOBHM movement, they impressed many with their debut album, 'FIRSTBORN', which featured their version of TOMMY JAMES & THE SHONDELLS' 'MONY MONY'. Two years later in '86, a second set was released by 'Music For Nations', again very vocally reminiscent of DAVID COVERDALE. When they folded soon after, frontman ARMITAGE joined German power-metallers, ACCEPT.

Album rating: FIRSTBORN (*5) / FORCE MAJEURE (*6)

ROB ARMITAGE – vocals / **NEIL SAXTON** – guitar / **ANDY BARROTT** – keyboards / **PAUL SMITH** – bass / **TONY SUGDEN** – drums

Ultra Noise not iss.

Mar 84. (7") *(TUCK 001)* **MONY MONY. / BABY'S ROCKING TONIGHT** — -

Mar 84. (lp) *(ULTRA 2)* **FIRSTBORN** — -
– Hot wheels / Things (ain't always what they seem) / What's it worth / Holdin' on / Mony mony / A.W.O.L. / Baby's rockin' tonight / Broken heart / Sweet rock'n'roll. *(re-iss. 1988 on 'Castle' lp/c; CLA LP/MC 115)*

Music For Nations not iss.

Feb 86. (lp/c) *(MFN/CMFN 56)* **FORCE MAJEURE** — -
– Rock (rock) / Shoot on sight / Over you / Falling star / The lights go down / Keep it together / Maybe / I'm your man / Long way down / Promises.

May 86. (12") *(12KUT 120)* **ROCK (ROCK). /** [ ] [-]

Fun After All — not iss.

Aug 86. (7") *(FAA 105)* **THE TEARS OF A CLOWN. / OVER YOU** [ ] [-]
(12"+=) *(12FAA 105)* – The lights go down.

—— disbanded when ARMITAGE joined ACCEPT

Sebastian BACH (see under ⇒ SKID ROW)

BACHMAN-TURNER OVERDRIVE

Formed: Winnipeg, Canada . . . 1972 by the BACHMAN brothers, RANDY, ROBBIE and TIM. The former had been part of late 60's rock outfit, GUESS WHO, before releasing a 1970 solo album, 'AXE'. He also formed a short-lived country-rock band, BRAVE BELT, who issued two albums for 'RCA' in the early 70's. Together with FRED TURNER, BACHMAN-TURNER OVERDRIVE signed to 'Mercury' in 1973, making steady inroads onto the US airwaves. By late '74, they had a No.1 US hit with the stuttering hard-rock anthem, 'YOU AIN'T SEEN NOTHING YET'. (In the 90's, its intro featured on Harry Enfield's UK TV show DJ creations, Chas Smash and Nicey Nice). The single formed the centrepiece of the album, 'NOT FRAGILE', which also topped the chart. Being of the Mormon persuasion, the BACHMAN's unfortunately couldn't live the rock'n'roll lifestyle to the hilt, their faith forbidding alcohol, drugs, tea or coffee. Nevertheless, they were adopted by the "blue collar" brigade (actually a title of one of their songs), enjoying a brief run of successful albums in the mid 70's. In 1978, without the departed RANDY, the BACHMAN's abbreviated their moniker to BTO, releasing a few more albums while the former formed the similar sounding IRON HORSE. BACHMAN-TURNER OVERDRIVE were re-united in the mid 80's, with RANDY back at the helm.

Album rating: Brave Belt: BRAVE BELT (*3) / BRAVE BELT II (*3) / Bachman-Turner Overdrive: BACHMAN-TURNER OVERDRIVE (*4) / BACHMAN-TURNER OVERDRIVE II (*5) / NOT FRAGILE (*6) / FOUR WHEEL DRIVE (*6) / THE BEST OF BTO (SO FAR) (*6) / HEAD ON (*4) / THE BEST OF B.T.O. compilation (*6) / FREEWAYS (*3) / STREET ACTION (*2) / ROCK'N'ROLL NIGHTS (*2) / GREATEST HITS compilation (*5)

RANDY BACHMAN

with **DAN TROIANO** – guitar / **GARRY PETERSON** – drums / **WES DAKUS** – steel guitar

not iss. — R.C.A.

1970. (lp) **AXE** [-] [ ]
– Zarahemia / Not to return / Pookie's shuffle / Tally's tune / Take the long way home / La Jolla / Tin Lizzie / Suite theam / Noah.

BRAVE BELT

RANDY BACHMAN (b.27 Sep'43) – vocals, guitar (ex-GUESS WHO) / **CHAD ALLAN** – keyboards, vocals (ex-GUESS WHO) / **C.F. (FRED) TURNER** (b.16 Oct'43) – bass, vocals / **ROBBIE BACHMAN** (b.18 Feb'53) – drums, percussion

not iss. — Reprise

1971. (7") **ROCK AND ROLL BAND. / ANY DAY MEANS TOMORROW** [-] [ ]
1971. (lp) *<6447>* **BRAVE BELT** [-] [ ]
– Crazy arms, crazy eyes / Lifetime / Waitin' there for me / I am the man / French kin / It's over / Rock and roll band / Wandering fantasy girl / I wouldn't give up my guitar for a woman / Holy train / Anyday means tomorrow / Scarecrow.
1971. (7") *<1039>* **CRAZY ARMS, CRAZY EYES. / HOLY TRAIN** [-] [ ]
1972. (7") *<1061>* **NEVER COMIN' HOME. / CAN YOU FEEL IT** [-] [ ]
1972. (lp) *<2057>* **BRAVE BELT II** [-] [ ]
– Too far away / Dunrobin's gone / Can you feel it / Put it in a song / Summer soldier / Never comin' home / Be a good man / Long way round / Another way out / Waterloo country.
1972. (7") *<1083>* **ANOTHER WAY OUT. / DUNROBIN'S GONE** [-] [ ]

BACHMAN-TURNER OVERDRIVE

TIM BACHMAN – guitar repl. CHAD

Mercury — Mercury

Aug 73. (7") *<73383>* **GIMME YOUR MONEY PLEASE. / LITTLE GAWDY DANCER** [-] [ ]
Aug 73. (lp) *(6499 509) <SRMI 673>* **BACHMAN-TURNER OVERDRIVE** [ ] [70]
– Gimme your money please / Hold back the water / Blue collar / Little gandy dancer / Stayed awake all night / Down and out man / Don't get yourself in trouble / Thank you for the feelin'. *(cd-iss. Jan93;)*
Sep 73. (7") *(6052 357)* **STAYED AWAKE ALL NIGHT. / DOWN AND OUT MAN** [ ] [-]
Nov 73. (7") *<73417>* **BLUE COLLAR. / HOLD BACK THE WATER** [-] [68]
Feb 74. (7") *<73457>* **LET IT RIDE. / TRAMP** [-] [23]
Mar 74. (7") *(6052 605)* **LET IT RIDE. / BLUE COLLAR** [ ] [-]
Mar 74. (lp) *(6338 482) <SRMI 693>* **BACHMAN-TURNER OVERDRIVE II** [ ] [4] Jan74
– Blown / Welcome home / Stonegates / Let it ride / Give it time / Tramp / I don't have to / Takin' care of business.
Aug 74. (7") *(6052 627) <73487>* **TAKIN' CARE OF BUSINESS. / STONEGATES** [ ] [12] May74

—— **BLAIR THORNTON** (b.23 Jul'50, Vancouver) – guitar repl. TIM who became producer

Oct 74. (7") *(6167 025) <73622>* **YOU AIN'T SEEN NOTHING YET. / FREE WHEELIN'** [2] [1] Sep74
Oct 74. (lp/c) *(9100 007) <SRMI 1004>* **NOT FRAGILE** [12] [1] Aug74
– Not fragile / Rock is my life, and this is my song / Roll on down the highway / You ain't seen nothing yet / Free wheelin' / Sledgehammer / Blue moanin' / Second hand / Givin' it all away. *(cd-iss. Mar91; 830178-2)*
Jan 75. (7") *(6167 071) <73656>* **ROLL ON DOWN THE HIGHWAY. / SLEDGEHAMMER** [22] [14]
May 75. (7") *(6167 173) <73683>* **HEY YOU. / FLAT BROKE LOVE** [ ] [21]
Jun 75. (lp/c) *(9100 012) <SRMI 1027>* **FOUR WHEEL DRIVE** [ ] [5] May75
– Four wheel drive / She's a devil / Hey you / Flat broke love / She's keepin' time / Quick change artist / Lowland fling / Don't let the blues get you down.
Nov 75. (7") *<73724>* **DOWN TO THE LINE. / SHE'S A DEVIL** [-] [43]
Jan 76. (7") *(6167 320)* **AWAY FROM HOME. / DOWN TO THE LINE** [ ] [-]
Feb 76. (lp/c) *(9100 020) <SRMI 1067>* **HEAD ON** [ ] [23] Jan76
– Find out about love / It's over / Average man / Woncha take me for a while / Wild spirit / Take it like a man / Lookin' out for #1 / Away from home / Stay alive.
Feb 76. (7") *<73766>* **TAKE IT LIKE A MAN. / WONCHA TAKE ME FOR A WHILE** [-] [33]
Apr 76. (7") *<73784>* **LOOKING OUT FOR #1. / FIND OUT ABOUT LOVE** [-] [65]
May 77. (7") *<73903>* **MY WHEELS WON'T TURN. / FREE WAYS** [-] [ ]
May 77. (7") *(6167 520)* **MY WHEELS WON'T TURN. / LIFE STILL GOES ON** [ ] [-]
May 77. (lp/c) *(9100 035) <SRMI 3700>* **FREEWAYS** [ ] [70] Mar77
– Can we all come together / Life still goes on (I'm lonely) / Shotgun rider / Just for you / My wheels won't turn / Down, down / Easy groove / Freeways.
Sep 77. (7") *<73926>* **SHOTGUN RIDER. / DOWN, DOWN** [-] [ ]
Sep 77. (7") *(6167 567)* **SHOTGUN RIDER. / JUST FOR YOU** [ ] [-]
Dec 77. (7") *<73951>* **LIFE STILL GOES ON. / JUST FOR YOU** [-] [ ]

B.T.O.

—— **JIM CLENCH** – bass, vocals (ex-APRIL WINE) repl. RANDY who went solo

Mar 78. (lp/c) *(9100 051) <SRMI 3713>* **STREET ACTION** [ ] [ ]
– I'm in love / Down the road / Takes a lot of people / A long time for a little while / Street action / For love / Madison Avenue / You're gonna miss me / The world is waiting for a love song.
Mar 78. (7") *<73987>* **DOWN THE ROAD. / A LONG TIME FOR A LITTLE WHILE** [-] [ ]
Mar 79. (7") *<74046>* **HEARTACHES. / HEAVEN TONIGHT** [-] [60]
Mar 79. (7") *(6167 759)* **HEARTACHES. / ROCK'N'ROLL NIGHTS** [ ] [-]
Apr 79. (lp/c) *<SRMI 3748>* **ROCK'N'ROLL NIGHTS (live)** [-] [ ]
– Jamaica / Heartaches / Heaven tonight / Rock and roll nights / Wastin' time / Here she comes again / End of the line / Rock and roll hell / Amelia Earhart.
Jun 79. (7") *<74062>* **END OF THE LINE (live). / JAMAICA (live)** [-] [ ]

—— Broke-up in 1979

BACHMAN-TURNER OVERDRIVE

Re-united mid-84 with below line-up 1984. **RANDY, TIM, FRED TURNER** and newcomer **GARRY PETERSON** – drums

Compleat — Compleat

Sep 84. (7") *(CLT 6) <127>* **FOR THE WEEKEND. / JUST LOOK AT ME NOW** [ ] [ ]
Nov 84. (lp/c) *(CLTLP/ZCCLT 353) <1010>* **BACHMAN-TURNER OVERDRIVE** [ ] [ ] Sep84
– For the weekend / Just look at me now / My sugaree / City's still growin' / Another fool / Lost in a fantasy / Toledo / Service with a smile.
Jan 85. (7") *<133>* **SERVICE WITH A SMILE. / MY SUGAREE** [-] [ ]
Mar 85. (7") *<137>* **MY SUGAREE. / (part 2)** [-] [ ]

M.C.A. — Curb

Aug 86. (lp/c) *(IMCA/+C 5760)* **LIVE!-LIVE!-LIVE! (live)** [ ] [ ]
– Hey you / Mississippi queen / Sledgehammer / Fragile man / Bad news travels fast / You ain't seen nothin' yet / Roll on down the highway / Takin' care of business.

—— RANDY later joined with (ex-TROOPER), FRANK LUDWIG, in UNION. He also became a songwriter for BEACH BOYS, etc.

– compilations, others, etc. –

Mar 75. (lp) *Warners; (K 54036) <MS 2210>* **BACHMAN-TURNER OVERDRIVE AS BRAVE BELT** [ ] [ ]
Sep 76. (7") *Mercury; <73843>* **GIMME YOUR MONEY PLEASE. / FOUR WHEEL DRIVE** [-] [70]
Sep 76. (7") *Mercury; (6167 425)* **TAKIN' CARE OF BUSINESS. / WON'T CHA TAKE ME FOR A WHILE** [ ] [-]
Nov 76. (lp) *Mercury; (9100 026) <SRMI 1101>* **THE BEST OF B.T.O. (SO FAR)** [ ] [19] Aug76
(cd-iss. Aug98; 558234-2)
1977. (lp) *Mercury;* **JAPAN TOUR (live)** [-] [ ]
Aug 81. (lp)(c) *Mercury; (6430 151)(7420 043)* **GREATEST HITS** [ ] [-]
– Lookin' out for #1 / Hey you / Takin' care of business / You ain't seen nothin' yet / Flat broke love / Rock'n'roll nights / Roll on down the highway / Freeways / Down, down / Let it ride / Can we all come together / Jamaica. *(cd-iss. Jan86; 830039-2)*
Oct 83. (lp/c) *Mercury; (PRICE/PRIMC 46)* **YOU AIN'T SEEN NOTHIN' YET** [ ] [-]
Oct 84. (7") *Mercury; (CUT 109)* **YOU AIN'T SEEN NOTHIN' YET. / ROLL ON DOWN THE HIGHWAY** [ ] [-]
Mar 88. (7") *Old Gold; (OG 9764)* **YOU AIN'T SEEN NOTHIN' YET. / (other track by – Thin Lizzy)** [ ] [-]
Jul 88. (lp/c) *Knight; (KNLP/KNMC 10008)* **NIGHTRIDING** [ ] [-]
Aug 93. (d-cd) *Polygram; (514902-2)* **ANTHOLOGY** [ ] [-]
Aug 94. (cd/c) *Spectrum; (550421-2/-4)* **ROLL ON DOWN THE HIGHWAY** [ ] [-]
Jun 97. (cd) *Go On Deluxe; (1031-2)* **THE VERY BEST OF BACHMAN-TURNER OVERDRIVE** [ ] [-]
Aug 98. (cd) *King Biscuit; (KBFHCD 013)* **KING BISCUIT PRESENTS . . .** [ ] [-]
Apr 00. (m-cd) *Capitol; <24505>* **LIVE** [-] [ ]

Sep 00. (cd) *M.C.A.; <548096>* **THE BEST OF BACHMAN-TURNER OVERDRIVE: THE MILLENNIUM COLLECTION** -
Feb 01. (m-cd) *Madacy; <3530>* **HITS YOU REMEMBER: LIVE** -
Mar 01. (cd) *Spectrum; (544429-2)* **THE COLLECTION** -

RANDY BACHMAN

solo with **BURTON CUMMINGS** – keyboards / **IAN GARDINER** – bass / **JEFF PORCARO** – drums / **TOM SCOTT** – saxophone

Polydor Polydor

Jun 78. (7") *(2066 954)* **JUST A KID. / SURVIVOR**
Jul 78. (lp/c) *(2490 146) <PDI 6141>* **SURVIVOR**
– Just a kid / One hand clappin' / Lost in the shuffle / Is the night too cold for dancin' / You moved me / I am a star / Maybe again / Survivor.

IRONHORSE

was formed by **RANDY** with **TOM SPARKS** – guitar / **JOHN PIERCE** – bass / **MIKE BAIRD** – drums / **BARRY ALLEN** – vocals

Warners Scotti Bros

Mar 79. (7") *(K 11271) <406>* **SWEET LUI-LOUISE. / WATCH ME FLY** 60 36
May 79. (lp/c) *(K 50598) <7103>* **IRONHORSE**
– One and only / Sweet Lui-Louise / Jump back in the light / You gotta let go / Tumbleweed / Stateline blues / Watch me fly / Old fashioned / Dedicated to Slowhand / She's got it / There ain't no clue.
Jul 79. (7") *(K 11319) <408>* **ONE AND ONLY. / SHE'S GOT IT**

— **FRANK LUDWIG** – vocals, keyboards repl. BARRY / **RON FOOS** – bass / **CHRIS LEIGHTON** – drums repl. JOHN + MIKE

Nov 80. (7") *(K 11497) <512>* **WHAT'S YOUR HURRY DARLIN'. / TRY A LITTLE HARDER** 89 Apr80
Nov 80. (lp/c) *(K 50730) <7108>* **EVERYTHING IS GREY**
– Everything is grey / What's your hurry darlin' / Symphony / Only way to fly / Try a little harder / I'm hurting inside / Playin' that same old song / Railroad love / Somewhere sometime / Keep your motor running.

BACHMAN

— **RANDY** with various guests incl. NEIL YOUNG + MARGO TIMMINS

Koch Int. Legend

Sep 93. (cd) *(34108-2) <1>* **ANY ROAD** 1997
– Prairie road / Any road / I wanna shelter you / Overworked & underpaid / 15 minutes of fame / Tailspin / Vanishing heroes / One step ahead of the law / It's only money / One night in Texas / Why am I lonely / Prairie town.

RANDY BACHMAN

True North True North

Sep 97. (cd) *<(TNSD 0117)>* **MERGE**
– Born to ride / There ain't nothin' like it / Bad news travels fast / I play the fool for you / Anthem for the young / Please come to Paris / No reason to cry / Can't go back to Memphis / Burnin' up the floor / Made in Canada.

BACKYARD BABIES

Formed: Nassjo, Sweden . . . 1987 by NICKE BORG, DREGEN, JOHAN BLOMQVIST and PEDER CARLSSON. On a heavy diet of shock-rock troops such as The STOOGES, RAMONES, HANOI ROCKS and even GUNS N' ROSES, the band delivered their dose of apocalyptic mayhem in the shape of 1994's 'DIESEL & POWER'. However, it took all of four years for them to crash out with a follow-up, 'TOTAL 13', a remarkable onslaught of breakneck glam/punk'n'roll that went gold in Scandinavia. • **Covered:** MOMMY'S LITTLE MONSTER (Social Distortion) / BABYLON (Faster Pussycat), which also featured GINGER of The WILDHEARTS.

Album rating: SMELL THE MAGIC (*6) / TOTAL 13 (*7) / MAKING ENEMIES IS GOOD (*6)

NICKE BORG – vocals, guitar / **DREGEN** – guitar (also of The HELLACOPTERS) / **JOHAN BLOMQVIST** – bass / **PEDER CARLSSON** – drums

Opus not iss.

1991. (12"ep) *(OPUS 1)* **SOMETHING TO SWALLOW** - Sweden
– Something to swallow / Strange kind of attitude / Jucy Lucy / Like a child / Kickin' up dust.

Megarock not iss.

1994. (cd-ep) **ELECTRIC SUZY / SHAME / LIES / TAXI DRIVER** - - Sweden
1994. (cd) *(MRRCD 008)* **DIESEL & POWER** - - Sweden
– Smell the magic / Bad to the bone / Strange kind of attitude / Diesel and power / Love / Wild dog / Fly like a little . . . / Electric Suzy / Kickin' up dust / Should I be damned / Fill up this bad machine / Heaven in Hell / Shame. *(UK-iss.Jun98 +=; same)* – Lies.

SR not iss.

Oct 96. (7"colrd) **MOMMY'S LITTLE MONSTER. / (other track by the 69 EYES)** -

M.V.G. not iss.

Nov 97. (cd-ep) *(MVGCDS 47)* **KNOCKOUTS! EP** -
– U.F.O. Romeo / Backstabber / Powderhead / Wireless mind / Ghetto you.
Apr 98. (cd-ep) *(MVGCDS 50)* **LOOK AT YOU EP** - - Sweden
– Look at you / Spotlight the sun / Can't find the door.

Coalition not iss.

Mar 98. (7") *(COLA 046)* **LOOK AT YOU. / POWDERHEAD** -
(cd-s+=) *(COLA 046CD)* – Can't find the door / Wireless mind.
Apr 98. (cd/c/lp) *(3984 22746-2/-4/-1)* **TOTAL 13** -
– Made me madman / U.F.O. Romeo / Get dead / Look at you / Let's go to hell / Spotlight the sun / B-balled / Ghetto you / Subculture hero / Bombed (out of my mind) / Hey, I'm sorry / Robber of life. *(Swedish-issue on Jun98; MVG 135LP) <US-iss.Sep99 on 'Smooch Pooch'+=; 53>* – Babylon / Rocker.
(below 'B' also featured MICHAEL MONROE; ex-HANOI ROCKS)
May 98. (7"orange) *(COLA 051)* **BOMBED (OUT OF MY MIND). / ROCKER** -
Sep 98. (7") *(COLA 058)* **HIGHLIGHTS. / LOOK AT YOU (live)** -
(cd-s) *(COLA 058CD1) <24190>* – ('A'side) / Made me madman (live) / Backstabber (live).
(cd-s) *(COLA 058CD2) <24191>* – ('A'live) / Stars (live) / Fill up this bad machine (live).
Oct 98. (7") *(AFRO 012)* **(IS IT) STILL ALL RIGHT TO SMILE. / BABYLON** -
(above issued on 'Bad Afro')
Dec 98. (m-cd) *(3984 25361-2)* **SAFETY-PIN AND LEOPARD SKIN (live)** -
– Made me madman / Backstabber / Look at you / Highlights / Stars / Fill up this bad machine / Babylon (w/ GINGER & DJ CHAMPAIN) / Backstabber / Gotta go!
Mar 99. (7"red) **BABYLON. / STARS** - - tour

Pastor not iss.

Dec 99. (12") *(BYBS 1)* **BABYLON. / BABYLON (idit for life remix by DJ Champain & Yod)** -

R.C.A. not iss.

Jun 01. (cd-s) **BRAND NEW HATE / BY THE PHONE** - - Sweden
(cd-s+=) – P.O.P.
Jun 01. (cd) **MAKING ENEMIES IS GOOD** - - Sweden
– I love to roll / Payback / Brand new hate / Colours / Star war / The clash / My demonic side / The kids are right / Ex-files / Heaven 2.9 / Too tough to make some friends / Painkiller / Bigger w/a trigger.

BAD BRAINS

Formed: Washington DC, USA . . . 1978 by Afro-Americans, H.R., his brother EARL, DR. KNOW and DARRYL JENNIFER. Prior to the advent of the punk rock movement in 1976/77, they had all played together in a jazz fusion outfit, carrying over the jazz dynamic to their frenetic, dub-wise hardcore. Subsequently relocating to New York, the late 70's saw the release of two classic 45's, 'PAY TO CUM' and 'BIG TAKEOVER'. These virtually went unnoticed, the band's UK profile remaining low after being refused work permits to support The DAMNED on a British tour. In 1983, they finally delivered their debut album, 'ROCK FOR LIGHT' (produced by RIC OCASEK of The CARS), a set that featured one side of hardcore and the other reggae. For three years, H.R. went solo, returning to the fold for 1986's 'I AGAINST I', a more metallic affair which anticipated the funk-rock explosion of the late 80's. H.R. (with EARL) subsequently departed to realise his more reggae orientated ambitions, releasing several albums for 'S.S.T.'. The remainder of BAD BRAINS parted company with this label, eventually reactivating the band for touring purposes with the addition of CHUCK MOSELEY (ex-FAITH NO MORE). H.R. and EARL returned to the fold for the 'QUICKNESS' album in 1989, remaining for the live set, 'THE YOUTH ARE GETTING RESTLESS'. Once again, H.R. and EARL decided to take off, their replacements being ISRAEL JOSEPH-I and the returning MACKIE. This line-up was in place for their major label debut for 'Epic', 'RISE' (1993), although incredibly yet again H.R. and EARL were invited back as BAD BRAINS were offered a place on MADONNA's 'Maverick' label. The resulting 1995 album, 'GOD OF LOVE' (again produced by OCASEK) focused more on dub reggae stylings, proving that the band were as open to experimentation as ever. However, during the accompanying tour, the athletic H.R. left the band for good in controversial circumstances, fighting with his fellow musicians and eventually being pulled up on a drugs charge (BAD BRAINS right enough!). • **Songwriters:** H.R. / DR. KNOW / group, except DAY TRIPPER (Beatles) / SHE'S A RAINBOW (Rolling Stones).

Album rating: BAD BRAINS (*7) / ROCK FOR LIGHT (*8) / I AGAINST I (*8) / LIVE (*5) / QUICKNESS (*4) / RISE (*4) / GOD OF LOVE (*6)

H.R. (b. PAUL HUDSON, 11 Feb'56, London, England) – vocals / **DR. KNOW** (b. GARY WAYNE MILLER, 15 Sep'58, Washington) – guitar, keyboards / **DARRYL AARON JENIFER** (b.22 Oct'60, Washington) – bass, vocals / **EARL HUDSON** (b.17 Dec'57, Alabama) – drums, percussion

not iss. Bad Brains

Jun 80. (7") *<BB 001>* **PAY TO CUM. / STAY CLOSE TO ME** -

Alternative Tentacles Alternative Tentacles

Jun 82. (12"ep) *(VIRUS 13)* **THE BAD BRAINS EP**
– I luv jah / Sailin' on / Big takeover.

R.O.I.R. R.O.I.R.

Dec 82. (c) *(A 106)* **BAD BRAINS**
– Sailin' on / Don't need it / Attitude / The regulator / Banned in D.C. / Jah calling / Supertouch / FVK / Big take over / Pay to cum / Right brigade / I love I jah / Intro / Leaving Babylon. *(cd-iss. Dec89 as 'ATTITUDE – THE ROIR SESSIONS' on 'We Bite' lp/cd; WB 056/+CD) <US re-iss. Nov89 on 'In-Effect'> (re-iss. cd/c/lp 1991 on 'Dutch East Wax'/ re-iss. lp Mar93) (re-iss. cd Apr96; RUDCD 8223) (lp re-iss. Jul98 & Nov99; RUSLP 8223R)*

Food For Thought Important

Mar 83. (12"ep) *(YUMT 101)* **I AND I SURVIVE / DESTROY BABYLON EP**

Abstract P.V.C.

Mar 83. (lp) *(ABT 007) <PVC 8933>* **ROCK FOR LIGHT**
– Coptic times / Attitude / We will not / Sailin' on / Rally around jah throne / Right brigade / F.V.K. (Fearless Vampire Killers) / Riot squad / The meek shall inherit the Earth / Joshua's song / Banned in D.C. / How low can a punk get / Big takeover / I

and I survive / Destroy Babylon / Rock for light / At the movies. *(re-mixed re-iss. Feb91 on 'Caroline' cd/c/lp; CAR CD/MC/LP 4) (re-iss. cd Sep91; same) (cd re-iss. Jun97; CAROLCD 1375)*

S.S.T. S.S.T.

Feb 87. (lp/c) *<(SST 065/+C)>* **I AGAINST I** Nov86
– Intro / I against I / House of suffering / Re-ignition / Secret '77 / Let me help / She's calling you / Sacred love / Hired gun / Return to Heaven. *(cd-iss. Feb88 & May93; SST 065CD)*

—— **CHUCK MOSELEY** – vocals (ex-FAITH NO MORE) repl. H.R.

—— **MACKIE JAYSON** (b.27 May'63, New York City) – drums repl. EARL

Nov 88. (lp/c/cd) *<(SST 160 LP/C/CD)>* **LIVE (live)**
– I cried / At the movies / The regulator / Right brigade / I against I / I and I survive / House of suffering / Re-ignition / Sacred love / She's calling you / Coptic times / F.V.K. (Fearless Vampire Killers) / Secret 77 / Day tripper. *(re-iss. May93; same)*

—— both **H.R. + EARL** returned

Caroline Caroline

Jul 89. (lp/c/cd) *<(CAR LP/C/CD 4)>* **QUICKNESS**
– Soul craft / Voyage into infinity / The messengers / With the quickness / Gene machine – Don't bother me / Don't blow bubbles / Sheba / Yout' juice / No conditions / Silent tears / The prophet's eye / Endtro. *(re-iss. cd Sep91; same) (cd re-iss. Jun97; CAROLCD 1375)*

S.S.T. S.S.T.

Oct 89. (10"m-lp/m-c/m-cd) *<SST 228>* **SPIRIT ELECTRICITY** -
– Return to Heaven / Let me help / Day tripper / She's a rainbow / Banned in D.C. / Attitude / Youth are getting restless.

—— **ISRAEL JOSEPH-I** (b. DEXTER PINTO, 6 Feb'71, Trinidad) – vocals repl. H.R. / **MACKIE** returned EARL

Epic Epic

Sep 93. (cd/c/lp) *<(474265-2/-4/-1)>* **RISE**
– Rise / Miss Freedom / Unidentified / Love is the answer / Free / Hair / Coming in numbers / Yes jah / Take your time / Peace of mind / Without you / Outro.

—— **H.R. + EARL** returned to repl. JOSEPH-I + JAYSON

Maverick Maverick

May 95. (cd/c) *<(9362 45882-2/-4)>* **GOD OF LOVE**
– Cool mountaineer / Justic keepers / Long time / Rights of a child / God of love / Over the water / Tongue tee tie / Darling I need you / To the heavens / Thank jah / Big fun / How I love thee.

—— BAD BRAINS have since split

– compilations, etc. –

May 90. (cd/lp) *Caroline; (CARCD/LP 8) <CAROL 1617>* **THE YOUTH ARE GETTING RESTLESS (live in Amsterdam 1987)**
– I / Rock for light / Right brigade / House of suffering / Day tripper – She's a rainbow / Coptic times / Sacred love / Re-ignition / Let me help / The youth are getting restless / Banned in D.C. / Sailin' on / Fearless vampire killer / At the movies / Revolution / Pay to cum / Big takeover. *(cd re-iss. Jun97; CAROLCD 1617)*

May 92. (d-cd) *Line; (LICD 921176)* **ROCK FOR LIGHT / I AGAINST I** - - German

Oct 96. (cd/lp) *Caroline; (PCAROL 005CD/LP) <7534>* **BLACK DOTS** (rec.1979)
– Don't need it / At the Atlantis / Pay to cum / Supertouch – Shitfit / Regulator / You're a migraine / Don't bother me / Banned in D.C. / Why'd you have to go / Man won't annoy ya / Redbone in the city / Black dots / How low can a punk get / Just another damn song / Attitude / Send you no flowers.

Nov 97. (10"ep/cd-ep) *Victory; <(VR 064/+CD)>* **THE OMEGA SESSIONS**
– I against you / Stay close to me / I love jah / At the movies / Attitude.

BAD COMPANY

Formed: In late Summer 1973, by the English seasoned-pro foursome of PAUL RODGERS and SIMON KIRKE (both ex-FREE), plus MICK RALPHS and BOZ BURRELL. They got together to form this power-rock supergroup, taking their name from a 1972 Western film starring Jeff Bridges. LED ZEPPELIN manager, PETER GRANT, signed the band to his new 'Swan Song' label in 1974 and they hit the big time almost immediately. No.1 in America, No.3 in the UK, their eponymous debut album set the blueprint; driving music par excellence with RODGERS' heavy, soulful vocals set against a rock solid musical backdrop. These were songs that were built to last, and indeed they have, it's just a pity the cock-rock lyrics haven't aged quite so well. Then again, with such timeless melodic fare as 'CAN'T GET ENOUGH OF YOUR LOVE' and 'BAD COMPANY', maybe the lyrics are besides the point (it was the 70's after all). 'STRAIGHT SHOOTER' (1975) was a bit tougher, yet ultimately more of the same. No bad thing, with the classic 'FEEL LIKE MAKIN' LOVE' on a par with FREE's best efforts. Within such a limited framework, however, there was never much room for experimentation and it was probably inevitable that BAD COMPANY would begin to tread water as they waded through the murky tail end of the 70's. Nevertheless, they continued to sell bucketloads of records and put bums on seats right up until their 1983 parting shot, 'ROUGH DIAMONDS'. While RODGERS went on to solo work, BAD CO. reformed three years later with ex-TED NUGENT frontman, BRIAN HOWE, taking RODGERS' place. Their subsequent releases were lukewarm AOR fodder without the saving grace of the latter's voice, although they sold moderately. Come the 90's, RALPHS was the only remaining member from the original line-up, 'COMPANY OF STRANGERS' in '95 being their last effort to date. • **Songwriters:** RALPHS penned most. In the 90's RALPHS and HOWE individually co-wrote with THOMAS. • **Note:** watch out! a dance act going by the name of BAD COMPANY exists.

Album rating: BAD CO. (*7) / STRAIGHT SHOOTER (*8) / RUN WITH THE PACK (*4) / BURNIN' SKY (*4) / DESOLATION ANGELS (*5) / ROUGH DIAMONDS (*4) / 10 FROM 6 compilation (*7) / FAME AND FORTUNE (*3) / DANGEROUS ACE (*3) / HOLY WATER (*4) / HERE COMES TROUBLE (*3) / THE BEST OF BAD COMPANY LIVE . . . WHAT YOU HEAR IS WHAT YOU GET collection (*5) / COMPANY OF STRANGERS (*4) / STORIES TOLD AND UNTOLD (*4)

PAUL RODGERS (b.12 Dec'49) – vocals, piano (ex-FREE) / **MICK RALPHS** (b.31 Mar'48) – guitar, piano (ex-MOTT THE HOOPLE) / **BOZ BURRELL** (b.RAYMOND, 1946) – bass, vocals (ex-KING CRIMSON, ex-SNAFU) / **SIMON KIRKE** (b.28 Jul'49) – drums (ex-FREE)

Island Swan Song

May 74. (7") *(WIP 6191) <70015>* **CAN'T GET ENOUGH. / LITTLE MISS FORTUNE** 15 5

Jun 74. (lp/c) *(ILPS/ICT 9279) <8410>* **BAD CO.** 3 1
– Can't get enough / Rock steady / Ready for love / Don't let me down / Bad company / The way I choose / Movin' on / Seagull. *(cd-iss. Oct94 on 'Atlantic'; 7567 92441-2)*

Jan 75. (7") *<70101>* **MOVIN' ON. / EASY ON MY SOUL** - 19

Mar 75. (7") *(WIP 6223) <70103>* **GOOD LOVIN' GONE BAD. / WHISKEY BOTTLE** 31 36

Apr 75. (lp/c) *(ILPS/ICT 9304) <8413>* **STRAIGHT SHOOTER** 3 3
– Good lovin' gone bad / Feel like makin' love / Weep no more / Shooting star / Deal with the preacher / Wild fire woman / Anna / Call on me. *(cd-iss. Oct88 on 'Swan Song'; SS 8502-2) (cd re-iss. Jul94 on 'Atlantic'; 7567 82637-2)*

Aug 75. (7") *(WIP 6242) <70106>* **FEEL LIKE MAKIN' LOVE. / WILD FIRE WOMEN** 20 10 Jul75

Feb 76. (lp/c) *(ILPS/ICT 9346) <8415>* **RUN WITH THE PACK** 4 5
– Live for the music / Simple man / Honey child / Love me somebody / Run with the pack / Silver, blue & gold / Young blood / Do right by your woman / Sweet lil' sister / Fade away. *(cd-iss. Oct88 on 'Swan Song'; SS 8503-2) (cd re-iss. Jul94 on 'Atlantic'; 7567 92435-2)*

Mar 76. (7") *(WIP 6263)* **RUN WITH THE PACK. / DO RIGHT BY YOUR WOMAN** -

Mar 76. (7") *<70108>* **YOUNG BLOOD. / DO RIGHT BY YOUR WOMAN** - 20

Jul 76. (7") *<70109>* **HONEY CHILD. / FADE AWAY** - 59

Feb 77. (7") *(WIP 6381)* **EVERYTHING I NEED. / TOO BAD**

Mar 77. (lp/c) *(ILPS/ICT 9441) <8500>* **BURNIN' SKY** 17 15
– Burnin' sky / Morning Sun / Leaving you / Like water / Everything I need / Heartbeat / Peace of mind / Passing time / Too bad / Man needs a woman / Master of ceremony. *(cd-iss. Oct94 on 'Atlantic'; 7567 92450-2)*

May 77. (7") *<70112>* **BURNIN' SKY. / EVERYTHING I NEED** - 78

Swan Song Swan Song

Mar 79. (7") *(K 19416) <70119>* **ROCK'N'ROLL FANTASY. / CRAZY CIRCLES** 13

Mar 79. (lp/c) *(SS K/4 59408) <8506>* **DESOLATION ANGELS** 10 3
– Rock'n'roll fantasy / Crazy circles / Gone, gone, gone / Evil wind / Early in the morning / Lonely for your love / Oh, Atlanta / Take the time / Rhythm machine / She brings me love. *(cd-iss. Sep94 on 'Atlantic'; 7567 92451-2)*

Jul 79. (7") *<71000>* **GONE, GONE, GONE. / TAKE THE TIME** - 56

Aug 82. (lp/c) *(SS K/4 59419) <90001>* **ROUGH DIAMONDS** 15 26
– Electricland / Untie the knot / Nuthin' on T.V. / Painted face / Kickdown / Ballad of the band / Cross country boy / Old Mexico / Downhill ryder / Racetrack. *(cd-iss. Oct94 on 'Atlantic'; 7567 92452-2)*

Sep 82. (7") *<99966>* **ELECTRICLAND. / UNTIE THE KNOT** - 74

—— (mid'83) Disbanded. RODGERS went solo before joining The FIRM. KIRKE played with WILDFIRE. BURRELL sessioned for ROGER CHAPMAN.

—— **BAD COMPANY** reformed 1986. **RALPHS, KIRKE, BURRELL** and the incoming **BRIAN HOWE** – vocals (ex-TED NUGENT)

Atlantic Atlantic

Jan 86. (lp/c)(cd) *(WX 31/+C)(781625-2) <81625>* **10 FROM 6** (compilation)
– Can't get enough / Feel like makin' love / Run with the pack / Shooting star / Movin' on / Bad company / Rock'n'roll fantasy / Electricland / Ready for love / Live for the music.

Oct 86. (lp/c)(cd) *(WX 69/+C)(781684-2) <81684>* **FAME AND FORTUNE**
– Burning up / This love / Fame and fortune / That girl / Tell it like it is / Long walk / Hold on my heart / Valerie / When we made love / If I'm sleeping.

Nov 86. (7") *(A 9355) <89355>* **THIS LOVE. / TELL IT LIKE IT IS** 85 Oct86
(12"+=) *(TA 9355)* – Burning up / Fame & fortune.

Feb 87. (7") *(A 9296)* **FAME AND FORTUNE. / WHEN WE MADE LOVE** -

Feb 87. (7") *<89299>* **THAT GIRL. / IF I'M SLEEPING** -

Aug 88. (7") *<89035>* **NO SMOKE WITHOUT FIRE. / LOVE ATTACK** -

Aug 88. (lp/c/cd) *(K 781884-1/-4/-2) <81884>* **DANGEROUS AGE** 58
– One night / Shake it up / No smoke without fire / Bad man / Dangerous age / Dirty boy / Rock of America / Something about you / The way it goes / Love attack. *(cd+=)* – Excited.

Apr 89. (7") *<88939>* **SHAKE IT UP. / DANGEROUS AGE** - 82

Mar 90. (7"/c-s) *(A 7954/+MC)* **CAN'T GET ENOUGH. / BAD COMPANY** -
(12"+=/cd-s+=) *(A 7954 T/CD)* – No smoke without fire / Shake it up.

—— **GEOFF WHITEHORN** – guitar (ex-BACK STREET CRAWLER) repl. RALPHS / **PAUL CULLEN** – bass repl. BURRELL / added **DAVE COLWELL** – keyboards (ex-ASAP)

Atco Atco

Jul 90. (cd/c/lp) *(<7567 91371-2/-4/-1>)* **HOLY WATER** 35 Jun90
– Holy water / Walk through fire / Stranger stranger / If you needed somebody / Fearless / Lay your love on me / Boys cry tough / With you in a heartbeat / I don't care / Never too late / Dead of the night / I can't live without you / 100 miles.

Jul 90. (7") *<98944>* **HOLY WATER. / I CAN'T LIVE WITHOUT YOU** - 89
(12"+=/cd-s+=) – Love attack.

Apr 91. (7") *<98914>* **IF YOU NEEDED SOMEBODY. / DEAD OF THE NIGHT** 16 Nov90
(12"+=/cd-s+=) – Love attack.

Jul 91. (c-s,cd-s) *<98748>* **WALK THROUGH FIRE / LAY YOUR LOVE ON ME** - 28

— (May'91) **STEVE WALSH** – vocals (ex-KANSAS) repl. HOWE / **MICK RALPHS** also returned

Sep 92. (c-s,cd-s) <98509> **HOW ABOUT THAT / BROKENHEARTED** [-] [38]
Sep 92. (7"/c-s) **HOW ABOUT THAT. / HERE COMES TROUBLE** [ ] [-]
(12") – No smoke without a fire (remix) / Stranger stranger.
(cd-s+=) – No smoke without a fire (remix) / If you needed somebody.
Sep 92. (cd/c/lp) *(<7567 91759-2/-4/-1>)* **HERE COMES TROUBLE** [ ] [40]
– How about that / Stranger than fiction / Here comes trouble / This could be the one / Both feet in the water / Take this town / What about you / Little angel / Hold on to my heart / Brokenhearted / My only one.
Nov 92. (c-s,cd-s) <98463> **THIS COULD BE THE ONE / BOTH FEET IN THE WATER** [-] [87]

— **RICK WILLS** – bass (ex-ROXY MUSIC, ex-FOREIGNER, ex-PETER FRAMPTON) repl. WALSH

Dec 93. (cd/c) *(<7567 92307-2/-4>)* **WHAT YOU HEAR IS WHAT YOU GET (The Best Of Bad Company – live)** [ ] [ ]
– How about that / Holy water / Rock'n'roll fantasy / If you needed somebody / Here comes trouble / Ready for love / Shooting star / No smoke without a fire / Feel like makin' love / Take this town / Movin' on / Good lovin' gone bad / Fist full of blisters / Can't get enough / Bad company.

— **RALPHS, KIRKE, COLWELL + WILLS** recruited **ROBERT HART** – vox

Jul 95. (cd/c) *(<7559-61808-2/-4>)* **COMPANY OF STRANGERS** [ ] [ ]
– Company of strangers / Clearwater highway / Judas my brother / Little Martha / Gimme gimme / Where I belong / Down down down / Abandoned and alone / Down and dirty / Pretty woman / You're the only reason / Dance with the Devil / Loving you out loud.
Nov 96. (cd) *(7559 61976-2)* **STORIES TOLD & UNTOLD** (new & old) [-] [-] German
– One on one / Oh Atlanta / You're never alone / I still believe in you / Ready for love / Waiting on love / Can't get enough / Is that all there is to love / Love so strong / Silver, blue and gold / Downpour in Cairo / Shooting star / Simple man / Weep no more. *(UK-iss.Jan98; same)*
Mar 99. (d-cd) *<(7559 62391-2)>* **THE ORIGINAL BAD COMPANY ANTHOLOGY** (compilation) [ ] [ ]
– Can't get enough / Rock steady / Bad company / Seagull / Superstar woman / Little Miss Fortune / Good lovin' gone bad / Shooting star / Deal with the preacher / Wildfire woman / Easy on my soul / Whiskey bottles / Honey child / Run with the pack / Silver, blue and gold / Do right by your woman / Burnin' sky / Heartbeat / Too bad / Smoking / Rock'n'roll fantasy / Evil wind / Oh Atlanta / Rhythm machine / Untie the knot / Downhill rider / Track down a runaway / Ain't it good / Hammer of love / Hey hey.

BAD ENGLISH (see under ⇒ BABYS)

BADLANDS

Formed: 1988, based Los Angeles, USA, by RAY GILLEN, JAKE E. LEE, GREG CHAISSON and ERIC SINGER, all veterans of the heavy rock scene of the 70's & 80's. Their eponymous blues-orientated debut, gave them immediate success in 1989, although a long lay-off curtailed any commercial consolidation. A follow-up appeared two years later, also in the mould of LED ZEPPELIN or BAD COMPANY, seeing only mediocre sales and causing the group to disband. • **Songwriters:** Most by LEE and GILLEN, except FIRE AND RAIN (James Taylor).

Album rating: BADLANDS (*6) / VOODOO HIGHWAY (*4) / DUSK (*4)

RAY GILLEN – vocals, mouth harp (ex-BLACK SABBATH, ex-BLUE MURDER) / **JAKE E. LEE** – guitar, keyboards (ex-OZZY OSBOURNE) / **GREG CHAISSON** – bass (ex-LEGS DIAMOND) / **ERIC SINGER** – drums (ex-GARY MOORE, ex-LITA FORD)

Atlantic Atlantic

Apr 89. (7") <88888> **DREAMS IN THE DARK. / HARD RIVER** [-] [ ]
Jun 89. (lp/c/cd) *(781 966-1/-4/-2)* <81966> **BADLANDS** [39] [57]
– High wire / Dreams in the dark / Jade's song / Winter's call / Dancing on the edge / Streets cry freedom / Hard driver / Rumblin' train / Devil's stomp / Seasons. *(cd+=)* – Ball & chain.
Jul 89. (c-s) <88806> **WINTERS CALL /** [-] [ ]

— ERIC SINGER left for the ALICE COOPER group in 1990

— **JEFF MARTIN** – drums; repl. SINGER

Jun 91. (cd/c/lp) *<(7567 82251-2/-4/-1)>* **VOODOO HIGHWAY** [74] [ ]
– The last time / Show me the way / Shine on / Whiskey dust / Joe's blues / Soul stealer / 3 day funk / Silver horses / Love don't mean a thing / Voodoo highway / Fire and rain / Heaven's train / In a dream.

— split after above . . . GILLEN was to die in March 1995

– others, etc. –

Feb 00. (cd) Z; *(ZR 1997024) / Pony Canyon;* <1334> **DUSK** (their shelved third album) [ ] [ ]
– Healer / Sun red sun / Tribal moon / The river / Walking attitude / The fire lasts forever / Dog / Fat cat / Lord knows / Ride the jack.

BAD RELIGION

Formed: Los Angeles, California, USA . . . 1980 by teenagers, GREG GRAFFIN, BRETT GUREWITZ, JAY BENTLEY and JAY ZISKROUT. To combat disinterest from major labels, the group initiated their own label, 'Epitaph', which has since become a proverbial pillar of the US hardcore/punk fraternity (i.e. OFFSPRING, etc). After one self-titled EP in '81, they unleashed their cheerily-titled debut, 'HOW COULD HELL BE ANY WORSE'. After they withdrew their next album, 'INTO THE UNKNOWN' from sale, BAD RELIGION disappeared for a long spell in the mid 80's. GRAFFIN returned with a new line-up in '87, numbering GREG HETSON, PETE FINESTONE and TIM GALLEGOS. An album, 'SUFFER' was a triumphant comeback effort, defining the new BAD RELIGION sound, a hybrid of melodic punk and machine-gun metal. In 1989, the band consolidated their newfound cult popularity with the follow-up, 'NO CONTROL', although their early 90's output suffered a slight decline. After 'Epitaph' experienced problems with distribution in '93, they signed to 'Columbia', with the result that they cracked the US Top 100 with their album, 'STRANGER THAN FICTION'. Two years later, GUREWITZ having earlier bailed out, they released 'THE GRAY RACE' (produced by RIC OCASEK, ex-CARS), re-establishing them at the forefront of the burgeoning hardcore/metal scene. Following 1997's stop-gap live set, 'TESTED', the band were back with the ironically titled 'NO SUBSTANCE' (1998). If substance is weighed in terms of polemic then BAD RELIGION have it in spades, still railing at American hypocrisy with all guns blazing. However, if substance is weighed in terms of musical innovation then these politico-punks might indeed be found wanting. It took veteran producer TODD RUNDGREN to bring out the latent accessibility within the band's uncompromising grooves, lending his unwaveringly midas touch to 'THE NEW AMERICA' (2000). BAD RELIGION's umpteenth album, the record finally saw them placing their longtime vision in a more musically interesting, melodic framework without losing any of their trademark bite.

Album rating: HOW COULD HELL BE ANY WORSE mini (*5) / INTO THE UNKNOWN (*7) / SUFFER (*7) / NO CONTROL (*8) / AGAINST THE GRAIN (*7) / GENERATOR (*6) / RECIPE FOR HATE (*6) / STRANGER THAN FICTION (*7) / THE GRAY RACE (*6) / ALL AGES compilation (*8) / TESTED (*5) / NO SUBSTANCE (*5) / THE NEW AMERICA (*6)

GREG GRAFFIN – vocals / **BRETT GUREWITZ** – guitar / **JAY BENTLEY** – bass / **JAY ZISKROUT** – drums

Epitaph Epitaph

Sep 81. (7"ep) <EP1> **BAD RELIGION** [-] [ ]
– Bad religion / Politics / Sensory overload / Slaves / Drastic actions / World War III.

— **PETE FINESTONE** – drums; repl. ZISKROUT

Apr 82. (m-lp) <BRLP 1> **HOW COULD HELL GET ANY WORSE** [-] [ ]
– We're only gonna die / Latch key kids / Part III / Faith in God / Fuck armageddon . . . this is hell / Pity / In the night / Damned to be free / White trash (2nd generation) / American dream / Eat your dog / Voice of God is government / Oligarchy / Doing time.

— **PAUL DEDONA** – bass + **DAVY GOLDMAN** – drums; repl. JAY + PETE

Dec 83. (lp) <BR 1> **INTO THE UNKNOWN** [-] [ ]
– It's only over when . . . / Chasing the wild goose / Billy Gnosis / Time and disregard / The dichotomy / Million days / Losing generation / . . .You give up.

— **GRAFFIN** the sole survivor recruited **GREG HETSON** – guitar / **TIM GALLEGOS** – bass / **PETE FINESTONE** – drums (returned) / GUREWITZ joined CIRCLE JERKS

1984. (7"ep) <BREP 2> **BACK TO THE KNOWN** [-] [ ]
– Yesterday / Frogger / Bad religion / Along the way / New leaf.

— **GUREWITZ + BENTLEY** rejoined to repl. GALLEGOS

1988. (lp) <6404-1> **SUFFER** [-] [ ]
– You are (the government) / 1000 more fools / How much is enough / When? / Give you nothing / Land of competition / Forbidden beat / Best for you / Suffer / Delirium of disorder / Part II (the numbers game) / What can you do? / Do what you want / Part IV (the index fossil) / Pessimistic lines. *(UK-iss.cd/lp Mar91 & Jun93; same)*
1989. (lp) <6406-1> **NO CONTROL** [-] [ ]
– Change of ideas / Big bang / No control / Sometimes it feels like *?%+! / Automatic man / I want to conquer the world / Sanity / Henchman / It must look pretty appealing / You / Progress / I want something more / Anxiety / Billy / The world won't stop without you. *(UK-iss.cd/lp Mar91 & Jun93; same)*
Jan 91. (cd/c/lp) *<(6409-2/-4/-1)>* **AGAINST THE GRAIN** [ ] [ ]
– Modern man / Turn on the light / Get off / Blenderhead / Positive aspect of negative thinking / Anesthesia / Flat Earth Society / Faith alone / Entropy / Against the grain / Operation rescue / God song / 21st century digital boy / Misery and famine / Unacceptable / Quality or quantity / Walk away.
Mar 92. (cd/c/lp) *<(6416-2/-4/-1)>* **GENERATOR** [ ] [ ]
– Generator / Too much to ask / No direction / Tomorrow / Two babies in the dark / Heaven is falling / Atomic garden / Answer / Fertile crescent / Chimaera / Only entertainment.
Jun 93. (cd/c/lp) *<(6420-2/-4/-1)>* **RECIPE FOR HATE** [ ] [ ]
– Recipe for hate / Kerosene / American Jesus / Portrait of authority / Man with a mission / All good soldiers / Watch it die / Struck a nerve / My poor friend me / Lookin' in / Don't pray on me / Modern day catastrophists / Skyscraper / Sheath.

— GUREWITZ retired to spend time with his record label 'Epitaph'.

— line-up:- **GRAFFIN / HETSON / BENTLEY / + BRIAN BAKER** – guitar (ex-MINOR THREAT, ex-DAG NASTY) / **BOBBY SCHAYER** – drums

Plastic Head Plastic Head

1993. (7") *(MRR 006)* **NOAM. /** [ ] [ ]

Sympathy F Sympathy F

Aug 94. (7") *(SFTRI 158)* **ATOMIC. /** [ ] [ ]
Aug 94. (7") *(SFTRI 232)* **AMERICAN JESUS. /** [ ] [ ]
Aug 94. (7") *(SFTRI 326)* **STRANGER THAN FICTION. /** [ ] [ ]

Columbia Atlantic

Sep 94. (cd/c/lp) *(477343-2/-4/-1)* <82658> **STRANGER THAN FICTION** [ ] [87]
– Incomplete / Leave mine to me / Stranger than fiction / Tiny voices / The handshake / Better off dead / Infected / Television / Individual / Hooray for me / Slumber / Marked / Inner logic. *(cd re-iss. Jan99; same)*
Jan 95. (10"pic-d-ep) *(661143-0)* **21st CENTURY (DIGITAL BOY) / AMERICAN JESUS (live). / NO CONTROL (live) / WE'RE ONLY GONNA DIE (live)** [41] [ ]
(c-ep/cd-ep) *(661143-8/-2)* – ('A'side) / Leaders and followers (live) / Mediocrity (live) / American Jesus (live).
Mar 96. (cd/c)(grey-lp) *(493524-2/-4)(483652-0)* **THE GRAY RACE** [ ] [ ]
– The gray race / Them and us / Walk / Parallel / Punk rock songs / Empty causes / Nobody listens / Pity the dead / Spirit shine / Streets of America / Ten in

2010 / Victory / Drunk sincerely come join us / Cease / Punk rock song (German version).

Jun 96. (7") *(6628677-7)* **PUNK ROCK SONG. / CEASE** [ ] [ ]
(cd-s+=) *(6628677-5)* – Leave mine to me (live) / Change of ideas (live).
(cd-s) *(6628677-2)* – ('A'-German version) / The universal cynic / The dodo.
(above was shelved when they decided to do some more German gigs)

Apr 97. (cd/lp) *(486986-2/-1)* *<82870-2/-1>* **TESTED (live)** [ ] [56]
– Operation rescue / Punk rock song / Tomorrow / A walk / God song / Pity the dead / One thousand more fool / Drunk sincerity / Generator / Change of ideas / Portrait of authority / What it is / Dream of unity / Sanity / American Jesus / Do what you want / Part III / 10 in 2010 / No direction / Along the way / Recipe for hate / Fuck armageddon / It's reciprocal / Struck a nerve / Leave mine to me / Tested / No control.

May 98. (cd/c) *(489570-2/-4)* *<83094>* **NO SUBSTANCE** [ ] [78]
– Hear it / Shades of truth / All fantastic images / The biggest killer in American history / No substance / Raise your voice / Sowing the seeds of Utopia / The hippy killers / The state of the end of the millennium / The vocacious march of godliness / Mediocre minds / Victims of the revolution / Strange denial / At the mercy of imbeciles / The same person / In so many ways.

May 00. (cd/c/lp) *<83303>* **THE NEW AMERICA** [-] [88]
– You've got a chance / It's a long way to the promise land / A world without melody / The new America / 1000 memories / A streetcar named Desire / Whisper in time / Believe it / I love my computer / The hopeless housewife / There will be a way / Let it burn / Don't sell me short.

– compilations, etc. –

Nov 91. (cd/c) *Epitaph; <(86407-2X/4X)>* **(1980-1985)** [ ] [ ]
– We're all gonna die / Latch key kids / Part III / Faith in God / F*** armageddon . . . this is Hell / Pitty / Into the night / Damned to be free / White trash (2nd generation) / American dream / Eat your dog / Voice of God is government / Oligarchy / Doing time / Politics / Sensory overload / Slaves / Drastic actions / World War III / Yesterday / Frogger. *(w/ free cd)* – HOW COULD HELL BE ANY WORSE

Nov 95. (cd/c/lp) *Epitaph; <(86443-2/-4/-1)>* **ALL AGES** (1988-1992 + 2 from '94) [ ] [ ]
– I want to conquer the world / Do what you want / You are (the government) / Modern man / We're only gonna die / Answer / Flat Earth society / Against the grain / Generator / Anesthesia / Suffer / Faith alone / No control / 21st century digital boy / Atomic garden / No direction / Automatic man / Change of ideas / Sanity / Walk away / Best for you / Fuck armageddon . . . this is Hell.

BAKERLOO

Formed: Tamworth, England . . . March 1968 by DAVE CLEMPSON, TERRY POOLE and KEITH BAKER. They made one self-titled lp for 'Harvest', a heavy blues effort reminiscent of CREAM. Unfortunately, this was to be their sole release, all the band going their fruitful separate ways in the summer of '69.

Album rating: BAKERLOO (*5)

TERRY POOLE – vocals, bass / **DAVE CLEMPSON** – guitar, piano, harmonica, vocals / **KEITH BAKER** – drums

Harvest not iss.

Jul 69. (7") *(HAR 5004)* **DRIVING BACKWARDS. / ONCE UPON A TIME** [ ] [-]

Aug 69. (lp) *(SHVL 762)* **BAKERLOO** [ ] [-]
– Big bear folly / Bring it on home / Drivin' backwards / Last blues / Gang bang / This worried feeling / Son of moonshine.

— Split mid '69. CLEMPSON joined COLOSSEUM, while BAKER went to URIAH HEEP. TERRY POOLE joined GRAHAM BOND then VINEGAR JOE.

BALAAM AND THE ANGEL

Formed: Cannock, Staffordshire, England . . . 1984 by Scottish born brothers JIM, MARK and DES MORRIS. They were encouraged at an early age by their father, who initiated their career by obtaining some cabaret gigs at Motherwell working mens clubs. Along with manager CRAIG JENNINGS, they founded the 'Chapter 22' label and soon found themselves supporting the likes of The CULT. Late in 1985, after releasing three indie hits, they moved onto 'Virgin', their debut for the label, 'SHE KNOWS', breaking them into the Top 75 in March '86. Five months later, the album, 'THE GREATEST STORY EVER TOLD' trod the same post-punk goth path. Two more albums followed until they were dropped by 'Virgin', obviously fans opting for their contemporaries The CULT and SISTERS OF MERCY. They re-emerged in 1990 as the heavier BALAAM, although little happened commercially, MARK nearly joining The CULT that year as the replacement for JAMIE STEWART.

Album rating: THE GREATEST STORY EVER TOLD (*6) / LIVE FREE OR DIE (*7)

MARK MORRIS (b.15 Jan'63, Motherwell) – vocals, bass / **JIM MORRIS** (b.25 Nov'60, Motherwell) – guitar, keyboards, recorder / **DES MORRIS** (b.27 Jun'64, Motherwell) – drums, percussion

Chapter 22 not iss.

Nov 84. (12"ep) *(22-001)* **WORLD OF LIGHT / FOR MORE THAN A DAY. / THE DARKLANDS / A NEW DAWN** [ ] [-]

Mar 85. (12"ep) *(22-002)* **LOVE ME / THE THOUGHT BEHIND IT ALL. / FAMILY AND FRIENDS / 15th FLOOR** [ ] [-]

Sep 85. (7") *(CHAP 3-7)* **DAY AND NIGHT. / ISABELLA'S EYES** [ ] [-]
(12"+=) *(CHAP 3-73)* – Touch / Return again.

Virgin Virgin

Mar 86. (7") *(VS 842)* **SHE KNOWS. / DREAMS WIDE AWAKE** [70] [-]
(d7"+=) *(VSD 842)* – Sister moon / Warm again.
(12"+=) *(VS 842-12)* – 2 into 1 / The darklands.

Jun 86. (7") *(VS 864)* **SLOW DOWN. / WALK AWAY** [ ] [-]
(12"+=) *(VS 864-12)* – Travel on / In the morning.

Aug 86. (lp/c) *(V/TCV 2377)* **THE GREATEST STORY EVER TOLD** [67] [ ]
– New kind of love / Don't look down / She knows / Burn me down / Light of the world / Slow down / The wave / Warm again / Never end / Nothing there at all. *(cd-iss. Jul87+=; CDV 2377)* – Walk away / Day and night. *(re-iss. 1989 lp/c; OVED/+C 250)*

Aug 86. (7") *(VS 890)* **LIGHT OF THE WORLD. / DAY AND NIGHT (live)** [ ] [-]
(12"+=) *(VS 890-12)* – She knows / Love.

Jul 87. (7") *(VS 970)* **(I'LL SHOW YOU) SOMETHING SPECIAL. / I FEEL LOVE** [ ] [-]
(12"+=) *(VS 970-12)* – Let it happen / You took my soul.

Sep 87. (7") *(VS 993)* **I LOVE THE THINGS YOU DO TO ME. / YOU'RE IN THE WAY OF MY DREAMS** [ ] [-]
(12"+=) *(VS 993-12)* – Things you know / As tears go by.

— added **IAN McKEAN** – guitar (ex-20 FLIGHT ROCKERS)

Jul 88. (7") *<99340<* **I LOVE THE THINGS YOU DO TO ME. / WARM AGAIN** [-] [ ]

Jul 88. (lp/c/cd) *(V/TCV/CDV 2476)* *<90869>* **LIVE FREE OR DIE** [ ] [ ] Apr88
– (I'll show you) Something special / I love the things you do to me / Big city fun time girl / On the run / Would I die for you / Live free or die / It goes on / Long time loving you / I won't be afraid / Running out of time. *(c+=)* – I feel love. *(cd++=)* – You took my soul / Let it happen / You're in my way of dreams / As tears go by.

Aug 88. (7") *(VS 1124)* **LIVE FREE OR DIE. / EAGLE** [ ] [-]
(12"+=) *(VST 1124)* – Complete control / ('A'-Texas Redbeard mix).

Sep 89. (7") *(VS 1213)* **I TOOK A LITTLE. / LONG TIME LOVIN' YOU** [ ] [-]
(12"+=/12"pic-d+=) *(VST/VSP 1213)* – Big city fun time girl / Would I die for you.
(12"+=/cd-s+=) *(VSTX/VSCD 1213)* – (remixes).

Nov 89. (lp/c/cd) *(V/TCV/CDV 2598)* **DAYS OF MADNESS** [ ] [ ]
– Don't want your love / I took a little / She really gets to me / Body and soul / Heartbreaker / The tenderloin / Two days of madness / Did you fall (or were you pushed?) / Goodbye forever / I'm the only one / Stop messin' round.

Feb 90. (7") *(VS 1229)* **LITTLE BIT OF LOVE. / DID YOU FALL (OR WERE YOU PUSHED?)** [ ] [-]
(12"+=/cd-s+=) *(VST 1229)* – She really gets to me (acoustic).

— split in the autumn of 1990 and now without McKEAN

Intense not iss.

Oct 91. (m-lp/m-c/m-cd; as BALAAM) *(TENS 001/+MC/CD)* **NO MORE INNOCENCE** [ ] [-]
– Shame on you / Next to me / What love is / She's not you / Mr. Business / Just no good.

— next release took six from last and added five new ones

Bleeding Hearts not iss.

Apr 93. (cd) *(CDBLEED 1)* **PRIME TIME** [ ] [-]
– Shame on you / Prime time / Next to me / What love is / Gathering dust / Eagle / She's not you / Mr. Business / Like a train / Burning / Just no good. *(re-iss. Feb98 on 'Darkend'; DARK 003CD)*

– compilations, etc. –

Oct 86. (lp) *Chapter 22; (CHAPLP 4)* **SUN FAMILY** [ ] [-]

BAL-SAGOTH

Formed: Yorkshire, England . . . 1989 by BYRON ROBERTS. Initially a one-man vision, the idea became more concrete when ROBERTS teamed up with his brother JONNY and guitarist CHRIS MAULDLING in 1993. Additional members JASON PORTER and VINCENT CRABTREE completed the line-up and the band signed to the 'Cacophonous' label on the strength of a demo. By the belated release of debut album, 'A BLACK MOON BROODS OVER LEMURIA' (1995), CRABTREE had been replaced with LEON FORREST. More personnel upheaval overshadowed the release of both 'STARFIRE BURNING UPON THE ICE VEILED THRONE OF ULTIMA THULE' (1996) and 'BATTLE MAGIC' (1998). In fact the line-up had almost completely changed – ROBERTS, MARK GREENWELL and DAVE MACKINTOSH – by the release of 'THE POWER COSMIC' (1999), a record that attempted to translate the intensity and increasing theatricality of Norwegian black metal into a more recognisably English gothic influenced framework.

Album rating: A BLACK MOON BROODS OVER LEMURIA (*6) / STARFIRE BURNING UPON THE ICE-VEILED THRONE OF ULTIMA THULE (*6) / BATTLE MAGIC (*7) / THE POWER COSMIC (*5) / ATLANTIS ASCENDANT (*5)

BYRON ROBERTS – vocals / **CHRIS MAULDLING** – guitar / **JONNY MAULDLING** – drums (+ later keyboards) / **JASON PORTER** – bass / **VINCENT CRABTREE** – keyboards

Cacophonous not iss.

May 95. (lp/cd) *(NIHIL 4/+CD)* **A BLACK MOON BROODS OVER LEMURIA** [ ] [-]
– Batheg kla / Dreaming of Atlantean empires / Spellcraft & moonfire / A black moon broods over Lemuria / Enthroned in the temple of the serpent rings / Shadows 'neath the black pyramid / Bitch-storm / The ravening / Into the silent chambers of the Sapphirean throne. *(cd re-iss. Jun97 +=; same)* – Valley of silent paths. *<US-iss.Feb00; same as UK>*

— **LEON FORREST** – keyboards; repl. CRABTREE

Nov 96. (cd) *(NIHIL 18CD)* **STARFIRE BURNING UPON THE ICE-VEILED THRONE OF ULTIMA THULE** [ ] [-]
– Black dragons soar above the mountain of shadows (prologue) / To dethrone the witch-queen of Mytos K'unn (the legend of the battle of Blackhelm Vale) / As the vortex illumines the crystalline walls of Kor-Avul-Thaa / Starfire burning upon the ice-veiled throne of Ultima Thule / Journey to the isle of Mists (over the moonless depths of night-dark seas) / The splendour of a thousand swords gleaming beneath

the blazon of the Hyperborean empire / And lo, when the imperium marches against Gul-Kothoth, then dark sorceries shall enshroud the citadel of the Obsidian crown / Summoning the guardians of the astral gate / In the raven-haunted forests of Darkenhold, where shadows reign and the hues of sunlight never dance / At the altar of the dreaming gods (epilogue). *<US-iss.Feb00; same as UK>*

— **ALISTAIR MacLATCHY** – bass; repl. PORTER

Mar 98. (cd) *(NIHIL 29CD)* **BATTLE MAGIC** [ ] [-]
– Battle magic / Naked steel (the warrior's saga) / A tale from the deep woods / Return to the Praesidium of Ys / Crystal shards / The dark liege of chaos is unleashed at the ensorcelled shrine of A'zura-Kai / When rides the scion of the storms / Blood slakes the sand at the circus maximus / Twarted by the dark (blade of the vampyre hunter) / And Atlantis falls . . . *<US-iss.Feb00; same as UK>*

— **MARK GREENWELL** – bass; repl. ALISTAIR + LEON

— **DAVE MACKINTOSH** – drums; repl. JONNY

Nuclear Blast / Nuclear Blast

Oct 99. (cd) *(NB 421-2) <6421>* **THE POWER COSMIC** [ ] [ ] Jan00
– The awakening of the stars / The voyagers beneath the mare imbrium / The empyreal lexicon / Of carnage and a gathering of the wolves / Callisto rising / The scourge of the fourth celestial host / Behold, the armies of war descend screaming from the heavens / The thirteen cryptical prophecies of Mu.

Apr 01. (cd) *(NB 584-2) <6584>* **ATLANTIS ASCENDANT** [ ] [ ] May01
– The epsilon exordium / Atlantis ascendant / Draconis albionensis / Star-maps of the ancient cosmographers / The ghosts of Angkor Wat / The splendour of a thousand swords gleaming beneath the blazon of the Hyperborean empire (part III) / The dreamer in the lost cities of Antartica / The chronicle of shadows / Six keys to the onyx pyramid.

BAND OF SUSANS

Formed: Buffalo, New York, USA . . . mid 80's by SUSAN STENGER, SUSAN TALLMAN, SUSAN LYALL and Susan.. no, er . . . ROBERT POSS (the latter rejected a vacant position with PiL, formerly filled by KEITH LEVENE). Adding drummer RON SPITZER and signing to indie imprint, 'Further', The BAND OF SUSANS delivered an EP, 'BLESSING AND CURSE', prior to 1988's debut set, 'HOPE AGAINST HOPE'. Retaining their moniker despite losing two of their Susans (TALLMAN and LYALL), songwriters STENGER and POSS – plus SPITZER – recruited PAGE HAMILTON and KAREN HAGLOF, the latter also formerly a member of RHYS CHATHAM (with messrs., SUSAN and ROBERT). This configuration managed to secure a deal with 'Blast First' and complete another sonic guitar frenzy of an album, 'LOVE AGENDA', before the end of the decade. Yet more personnel upheaval dogged the band as they entered the 90's; PAGE exited to form HELMET while HAGLOF's dislike of touring led to her being temporarily substituted by WIRE's BRUCE GILBERT! – on a more permanent basis they were replaced by MARK LONERGAN and ANNE HUSICK. Inking a fresh deal with 'Restless', BOS unleashed two more sets, 'THE WORD AND THE FLESH' (1991) and 'VEIL' (1993), the second of which featured new drummer JOEY KAYE. Subsequently reuniting with 'Blast First', they issued a retrospective of their work to date entitled 'WIRED FOR SOUND', followed a few months later by new material in the shape of 'HERE COMES SUCCESS' (1995). Unfortunately, success is the one thing that has eluded the BAND OF SUSAN and Co. throughout their decade-plus lifespan.

Album rating: HOPE AGAINST HOPE (*7) / LOVE AGENDA (*7) / THE WORD AND THE FLESH (*6) / VEIL (*5) / HERE COMES SUCCESS (*7) / WIRED FOR SOUND: 1986-1993 compilation) (*7)

ROBERT POSS (b.20 Nov'56) – vocals, guitar / **SUSAN STENGER** (b.11 May'55) – bass, vocals / **SUSAN TALLMAN** – guitar / **SUSAN LYALL** – guitar, vocals / **RON SPITZER** – drums / with also **ALVA ROGERS** – backing vocals (on debut)

Further / Further

1987. (12"ep) *(FU 2T)* **BLESSING AND CURSE EP** [ ] [-]
– Hope against hope / You were an optimist / Sometimes / Where have all the flowers gone.

Apr 88. (lp/c/cd) *(FU 005/+C/CD)* **HOPE AGAINST HOPE** [ ] [ ]
– Not even close / Learning to sin / Throne of blood / Elliott Abrahams in Hell / All the wrong reasons / I, the jury / No God / You were an optimist / Ready to bend / Hope against hope.

— **KAREN HAGLOF** – guitar, vocals (ex-RHYS CHATHAM . . .) repl. LYALL

— **PAGE HAMILTON** – guitar, vocals; repl. TALLMAN

Blast First / Blast First

Apr 89. (lp/c/cd) *<(BFFP 043/+C/CD)>* **LOVE AGENDA** [ ] [ ]
– The pursuit of happiness / It's locked away / Birthmark / Tourniquet / Thorn in my side / Sin embargo / Because of you / Hard light / Which dream came true / Child of the Moon / Take the express.

— **MARK LONERGAN** – guitar; repl. PAGE HAMILTON who formed HELMET

— **ANNE HUSICK** – guitar; repl. KAREN (she had been temp. repl. by BRUCE GILBERT of WIRE)

World Service / Restless

Mar 91. (cd/c) *<72534-2/-4>* **THE WORD AND THE FLESH** [-] [ ]
– Ice age / Now is now / Trouble follows / Plot twist / Estranged / Labor / Sermon on competition (part 2) / Bitter and twisted / Bad timing / Tilt / Silver lining / Guitar trio.

Apr 93. (m-cd/m-cd) *(RTD 1591491-2) <72722-2/-4>* **NOW** [ ] [ ]
– Pearls of wisdom / Following my heart / Trash train / Paint it black / Now is now (remix) / Paint it black (instrumental).

— **JOEY KAYE** – drums; repl. SPITZER

Jun 93. (cd) *(RTD 1571561-2) <72733-2>* **VEIL** [ ] [ ]
– Mood swing / Not in this life / The red and the black / Following my heart / Stained glass / The last temptation of Susan / Truce / Trouble spot / Out of the question / Pearls of wisdom / Troilbinders theme / Blind.

Blast First / World Service

Apr 95. (lp/cd) *(BFFP 114/+CD) <257>* **HERE COMES SUCCESS** [ ] [ ]
– Elizabeth Stride (1843-1888) / Dirge / Hell bent / Pardon my French / As luck would have it / Two Jacks / Stone like a heart / In the eye of the beholder (for Rhys) / Sermon on competition, part 1 (nothing is recoupable).

– compilations, etc. –

Feb 94. (cd) *Strange Fruit; (SFRCD 128) / Dutch East India; <8353>*
THE PEEL SESSIONS [ ] [ ]
– I found that essence rare / Throne of blood / Child of the moon / Hope against hope / Which dream came true / Too late.

Jan 95. (lp/cd) *Blast First; <(BFFP 111/+CD)>* **WIRED FOR SOUND: 1986-1993** [ ] [ ]

BANG

Formed: Florida, USA . . . 1971 by FRANK FERRARA, FRANK GLICKEN and TONY D'LORIO. They immediately signed to 'Capitol', releasing their eardrum splitting self-titled debut in '72, which spawned a minor hit 45, 'QUESTIONS'. Another couple of albums (namely 'MOTHER / BOW TO THE KING' and 'MUSIC') followed over the ensuing two years, although none could replicate the intensity of their debut.

Album rating: BANG (*6) / MOTHER / BOW TO THE KING (*5) / MUSIC (*4)

FRANK FERRARA – vocals, bass / **FRANK GLICKEN** – guitar / **TONY D'LORIO** – drums

Capitol / Capitol

Mar 72. (lp) *<(EST 11015)>* **BANG** [ ] [ ]
– Lions, Christians / The Queen / Last will & testament / Come with me / Our home / Future shock / Questions / Redman. *(cd-iss. Jan99 on 'Lizard'; LR 0706-2)*

Apr 72. (7") *<3304>* **QUESTIONS. / FUTURE SHOCK** [-] [90]

— **BRUCE GARY** – drums; repl. D'LORIO

1973. (lp) *<(EST 11110)>* **MOTHER / BOW TO THE KING** [ ] [ ]
– Mother / Humble / Keep on / Idealist realist / No sugar tonight / Feel the hurt / Tomorrow / Bow to the king. *(cd-iss. Nov99 on 'Lizard'; LR 0709-2)*

1973. (7") *<3386>* **KEEP ON. / REDMAN** [-] [ ]

1973. (7") *<3474>* **IDEALIST REALIST. / NO SUGAR TONIGHT** [-] [ ]

1974. (lp) *<EST 11190>* **MUSIC** [-] [ ]
– Winfair / Glad you're home / Don't need nobody / Page of my life / Love sonnet / Must be love / Exactly who am I / Pearl and her ladies / Little boy blue / Brightness / Another town.

1974. (7") *<3622>* **LOVE SONNET. / MUST BE LOVE** [-] [ ]

1974. (7") *<3816>* **FEELS NICE. / SLOW DOWN** [-] [ ]

— disbanded after above

BANGALORE CHOIR

Formed: USA . . . early 90's by ex-ACCEPT vocalist, DAVID REESE, alongside CURT MITCHELL and JOHN KIRK, plus JACKIE RAMOS and IAN MAYO. Despite a stellar array of hard-rock musicians, the band failed to live up to expectation on their one and only release, 'ON TARGET' (1992). REESE turned out to be yet another DAVID COVERDALE wannabe in an already overly crowded market.

Album rating: ON TARGET (*4)

DAVID REESE – vocals (ex-ACCEPT) / **CURT MITCHELL** – guitar (ex-RAZOR MAID) / **JOHN KIRK** – guitar (ex-RAZOR MAID) / **IAN MAYO** – bass / **JACKIE RAMOS** – drums (ex-HURRICANE ALICE)

Giant / Giant

Apr 92. (cd/c) *<(7599 24433-2/-4)>* **ON TARGET** [ ] [ ]
– Angel in black / Loaded gun / If the good die young (we'll live forever) / Doin' the dance / Hold on to you / All or nothing / Slippin' away / She can't stop / Freight train rollin' / Just one night.

— split after above

BANG TANGO

Formed: Los Angeles, California, USA . . . early '87 by JOE LESTE, who secured the services of MARK KNIGHT, KYLE STEVENS, KYLE KYLE and TIGG KETLER. Feeding on a diet of glam sleaze and gritty hard rock (a la AEROSMITH), they first made waves with their partly self-financed mini-album, 'LIVE INJECTION'. 'MCA' were suitably impressed, picking up the band for a couple of albums, the first of which, 'PSYCHO CAFE', nearly made the US Top 50 in 1989. Despite a marked musical improvement, the second set, 'DANCIN' ON COALS' (1991) seemingly choked on the band's own hype, only managing to sustain a brief sojourn in the Top 200. BANG TANGO continued to record in the 90's, downshifting to 'Music For Nations' for the album, 'LOVE AFTER DEATH' (1995). • **Covered:** 20th CENTURY BOY (T.Rex) / STRUTTER (Kiss) / JUST WHAT I NEEDED (Cars).

Album rating: LIVE INJECTION mini (*5) / PSYCHO CAFE (*6) / DANCIN' ON COALS (*5) / AIN'T NO JIVE . . . LIVE! mini (*4) / LOVE AFTER DEATH (*6) / UNITED AND LIVE (*3) / GREATEST TRICKS compilation (*5)

JOE LESTE – vocals / **MARK KNIGHT** – guitar / **KYLE STEVENS** – guitar, vocals / **KYLE KYLE** – bass, vocals / **TIGG KETLER** – drums

not iss. / World Of Hut

1989. (m-lp) *<WEP 1000>* **LIVE INJECTION** [-] [ ]
– Push to shove / Futurama / Love injection / Do what you're told / Watch her slide / I'm a stranger.

M.C.A. | Mechanic-MCA

May 89. (c-s) *<53744>* **ATTACK OF LIFE. / SOMEONE LIKE YOU** [-] [ ]

Jun 89. (lp/c/cd) *(MCG/MDGC/DMCG 6048) <6300>* **PSYCHO CAFE** [ ] [58]
– Attack of life / Someone like you / Wrap my wings / Breaking up a heart of stone / Shotgun man / Don't stop now / Love injection / Just for you / Do what you're told / Sweet little razor.

Jul 89. (7") *<53753>* **BREAKING UP A HEART OF STONE. / DON'T STOP NOW** [-] [ ]

Jun 91. (lp/c/cd) *<(MCA/+C/D 10196)>* **DANCIN' ON COALS** [ ] [ ]
– Soul to soul / United and true / Emotions in gear / I'm in love / Big line / Midnight struck / Dancin' on coals / My saltine / Dressed up vamp / The last kiss / Cactus juice. *(cd+=)* – Futurama.

Jun 92. (m-lp/m-c/m-cd) *<(MCA/+C/D 10531)>* **AIN'T NO JIVE . . . LIVE! (live)** [ ] [ ]
– Dancin' on coals / 20th century boy / Someone like you / Midnight struck / Attack of life.

Music For Nations | Metal Blade

Nov 94. (cd-s) **NEW GENERATION** [-] [ ]

Feb 95. (cd) *(CDMFN 174) <34470>* **LOVE AFTER DEATH** [ ] [ ]
– New generation / My favourite 9 / Feelin' nothin' / Don't count me out / Live on the Moon / Crazy / The hell I gave / Conversation / So obsessed / Gonna make you feel like / A thousand goodbyes.

— disbanded later in the 90's

– compilations, etc. –

May 99. (cd) *Axe Killer; (AXE 304639CD) / Cleopatra; <423>* **UNITED AND LIVE!!!** <US title 'LIVE'> [ ] [ ] Nov98
– Dressed up vamp / 20th Century boy / Soul to soul / I'm in love / United and true / Do what you're told / Once again / Daddy / Just for you / Midnight struck / Just what I needed / Someone like you. *(UK+=)* – Strutter (remix).

Nov 99. (cd) *Cleopatra; <(CLP 738-2)>* **GREATEST TRICKS** [ ] [ ]
– Daddy / Children of the revolution / Cuts you down / Can you boogie / My favourite 9 / Soul to soul / Dressed up vamp / I'm in love / United and true / Do what you're told / Love injection / Someone like you / Someone like you (the Over-Medium mix).

BANGTWISTER

Formed: Partick, Glasgow . . . 1996 by the trio of ALASDAIR MITCHELL (bass), GORDON 'Go-Go' BRADY (lead guitar) and KEITH BEACOM (drums); all share lead vocal duties. Once established on the local live front, BANGTWISTER released the 'Flotsam & Jetsam' one-off, 'AGONY AUNT', in April 1997. Described as a cross between hard-rock/metal and MC5, the whisky-drinking garage trio recalled the days when vinyl was demo-like and scratchy. This long-haired neo-psyche bunch were all the rage again after a second EP that year, entitled 'GROUNDED'. However, bar a BBC session, very little or nothing was heard from them thereafter, although a split tour 45, 'DOWNWARD SPIRAL' (along with the THANES, the GREASE MONKEYS and FIRESTONE: LEGEND OF THE HAWK) did see light in '98. A planned single for the 'Flycatcher' imprint was having technical difficulties getting released as I write this May 2001.

ALASDAIR MITCHELL – vocals, bass / **GORDON BRADY** – vocals, lead guitar / **KEITH BEACOM** – vocals, drums, percussion

Flotsam & Jetsam | not iss.

Apr 97. (7"m) *(SHaG 011)* **AGONY AUNT. / YOU'RE SO LOOSE / SHAKE IT!** [ ] [-]

BMB Music | not iss.

Dec 97. (cd-ep) *(BMBCD 1)* **GROUNDED e.p.** [ ] [-]
– Grounded / Happening in the back of my mind / Agony aunt / You're so loose / Shake it!

— continued to do the odd session for BBC, etc

— in '98, they also contributed 'DOWNWARD SPIRAL' to a 'Bronx Cheer' 7" EP, which featured The THANES, FIRESTONE: LEGEND OF THE HAWK and the GREASE MONKEYS

Flycatcher | not iss.

May 01. (7") **WE'RE THE REACTION. / SOME KINDA REVOLUTION** [ ] [-]

BANISHED

Formed: Buffalo, USA . . . 1991 as BAPHOMET, who changed their moniker to BANISHED after a German band threatened legal action (therefore a 1990 album 'No Answers' has no relation). After one 1992 album, 'THE DEAD SHALL INHERIT' under their original name, guitarist TOM FROST and co, completed a further effort, 'DELIVER ME UNTO PAIN', for the aptly-named 'Deaf' records.

Album rating: THE DEAD SHALL INHERIT as Baphomet (*5) / DELIVER ME UNTO PAIN (*5)

TOM FROST – guitar / etc. / with others unknown

Peaceville | Deaf

May 92. (lp/c/cd; as BAPHOMET) *(VILE 031/+MC/CD)* **THE DEAD SHALL INHERIT** [ ] [ ]

Deaf | Deaf

Dec 93. (lp/cd) *<(DEAF 013/+CD)>* **DELIVER ME UNTO PAIN** [ ] [ ]
– Diseased chaos / Deliver me unto pain / Cast out the flesh / Skinned / Inherit his soul / Valley of the dead / Succumb to the fear / Altered minds / Scars / Anointing the sick / Enter the confines / Through deviant eyes.

— other BAPHOMET albums 'Trust' (issued Apr'94 on 'Massacre') and 'Tarot Of The Underworld' (issued Jan'96 on 'KK') were the German band

BARKMARKET

Formed: Brooklyn, New York, USA . . . 1987 by lion-maned guitarist DAVE SARDY, the modern day equivalent of STEVE HILLAGE (well, at least his appearance was in '93/'94). After a seedy past delivering hardcore porn to his future employer (allegedly, Howie Weinberg), SARDY hooked up with gothically-bearded bassist JOHN NOWLIN and drummer ROCK SAVAGE (the latter had been "Spinal Tap"-ped in after they lost a few sticksmen – one becoming a grand wizard/master of scientology!) before setting off on a pilgrimage into the studio to vent their anger by recording the industrial '1-899-GODHOUSE' in 1988. Two albums later and their best was yet to come: the engaging, humorous 'GIMMICK' which bizarrely documented some of the most macabre things that would make even RAMMSTEIN flip out. The fifth volume, 'L. RON', appeared in 1996 with exactly the same approach; to make loud noise until our ears bleed! • **Covered:** I DON'T LIVE TODAY (Jimi Hendrix) / BACK STABBERS (O'Jays).

Album rating: 1-899-GODHOUSE (*) / EASY LISTENING RECORD (*) / VEGAS THROAT (*3) / GIMMICK (*7) / L. RON (*6)

DAVE SARDY – vocals, guitar, tapes / **JOHN NOWLIN** – bass, guitar / **ROCK SAVAGE** – drums, objects; repl. a few others / 4th member **GREG GORDON** – live sound

Purge Sound League | not iss.

1988. (lp) *(PURGE 025)* **1-899-GODHOUSE** [ ] [-]

Brake Out | not iss.

Feb 90. (lp/cd) *(OUT 101/+CD)* **EASY LISTENING RECORD** [ ] [-]
– Soul / Happy / Sonny / Buy America / The puppetmaster / The mirror / Condemned bank / Untitled / Foreign places / Pink stainless tail / You'll never fin. *(re-iss. Sep92; same) <(US+re-iss. Aug96 on 'Brake Out'; 03551)>*

not iss. | Triple X

Dec 90. (cd) *<51092>* **VEGAS THROAT** [-] [ ]
– Grinder / Ditty / Nuisance / Patsy / Poverty / Pitbull / Pencil / Fatstamp / Hydrox box / Salvation / I don't live today / Back stabbers / Ten convictions. *<re-iss. 1992 on 'Def American-Warners' cd/c; 2-/4-26893>*

American – Beggars Banquet | American – Warners

Oct 93. (cd/lp) *(DAB CD/LP 4) <45343>* **GIMMICK** [ ] [ ] Jan93
– Easy chair / Whipping boy / Static / Dumbjaw / Gatherer / Hack it off / Curio / Redundant / Radio static / Carjack / Shill /

Jun 94. (c-ep/cd-ep) *<45678>* **LARDROOM EP** [-] [ ]
– I drown / Dig in / Pushin' air / Little white dove / Johnny Shiv.

Aug 94. (7") *(ARB 5)* **I DROWN. /** [ ] [-]
(cd-s+=) *(ARB 5CD)* –

not iss. | Merge

Dec 94. (cd-s) *<MRG 025>* **PEACEKEEPER – THE BRASS RING / THE BRASS RING – CONDEMNED BANK** [-] [ ]

Play It Again Sam | American

Jun 96. (cd) *(BIAS 305CD) <43071>* **L. RON** [ ] [ ]
– Visible cow / Feed me / I don't like you / Undone / How are you? / Let it soak / Is it nice? / Falling / Fresh kills / Shiner / Drain / Lay down / Into the fear / Bootless.

— split after above

Lou BARLOW (see under ⇒ DINOSAUR JR.)

Jimmy BARNES

Born: JAMES SWAN, 28 Apr'56, Cowcaddens, Glasgow – although raised in Adelaide, Australia since the age of four. Subsequently influenced by his older brother John's taste of music (i.e. The ROLLING STONES, The BEATLES and ROD STEWART) the gravel-throated BARNES formed hard rock/radio friendly outfit, COLD CHISEL in 1977, enlisting the help of IAN MOSS, IAN WALKER, PHIL SMALL and STEVEN PRESTWICH. With major label backing from the outset, COLD CHISEL became one of Australia's most consistent homegrown talents. 'BREAKFAST AT SWEETHEARTS' in '79, quickly became regarded as their best work, although a third set, 'EAST' made a minor impact in the States. With several albums under their collective belt, BARNES opted for a solo career, releasing his first album, 'BODY SWERVE' in 1984. Eager to secure a substantial fanbase outside Australia, he signed a worldwide deal with 'Geffen', who in turn issued an eponymous album in 1986. Following the success of a minor US hit single, 'WORKING CLASS MAN', the album enjoyed an extended chart run, hovering on the fringes of the all important US Top 100. Utilizing the cream of the AOR set (i.e. DESMOND CHILD, JIM VALLANCE, NEAL SCHON, JONATHAN CAIN and MICK FLEETWOOD), he achieved similar success with the 'FREIGHT TRAIN HEART' opus in '88. Between these two releases, BARNES had his biggest hit to date, 'GOOD TIMES', although this shared credits with Antipodean allies, INXS. Surprisingly dropped by 'Geffen', BARNES later moved to 'Atlantic' records, releasing the commercially disappointing 1990 set, 'TWO FIRES'. Throughout the 90's, BARNES continued to search for that elusive breakthrough (even re-forming COLD CHISEL in '97), although he remains one of Australian rock's most respected figures. Although Britain as a whole has lost touch, his Scottish fanbase have never wavered; he now lives a bit closer to his roots (due to tax problems), albeit in France.

Album rating: FREIGHT TRAIN HEART (*6)

COLD CHISEL

JIMMY BARNES – vocals / **IAN MOSS** – guitar / **DON WALKER** – keyboards / **PHIL SMALL** – bass / **STEVEN PRESTWICH** – drums

Atlantic not iss.

1978. (lp) *(K 90001)* **COLD CHISEL** - - Austra
– Juliet / Khe Sanh / Home and broken hearted / One long day / Northbound / Rosaline / Das Karzine / Just home many times. *(UK-iss.Aug88 on 'Line'; LILP 400155) (cd-iss. Aug91 as 'COLD CHISEL FIRST' on 'Miles Music';)*

WEA Elektra

1978. (12"ep) *(12-001)* **YOU'RE 13, YOU'RE BEAUTIFUL AND YOU'RE MINE (live)** - - Austra
– Wild thing / Merry-go-round / Mona and the preacher / One long day / Home and broken hearted.

1979. (lp) *(K 90002)* **BREAKFAST AT SWEETHEARTS** - - Austra
– Conversations / Merry-go-round / Dresden / Goodbye (Astrid goodbye) / Plaza / Shipping steel / I'm gonna roll ya / Showtime / Breakfast at sweethearts / The door.

Sep 80. (7") *(K 7007)* **CHEAP WINE. / MY TURN TO CRY** -

May 81. (lp) *(K 90003)* <336> **EAST**
– Cheap wine / Four walls / My turn to cry / Best kept lies / Star hotel / Standing on the outside / Choirgirl / Rising sun / My baby / Tomorrow / Never before. *(cd-iss. Jan96 on 'East West'; 2292 54930-2)*

1981. (7") *<47141>* **CHEAP WINE. / MY BABY** -

1981. (7") *<47194>* **NEVER BEFORE. / KHE SAHN** -

Dec 81. (d-lp) *(K 90025)* **SWINGSHIFT (live Asia 1980)**
– Conversations / Shipping steel / Breakfast at Sweethearts / Rising sun / Choirgirl / Khe Sanh / My turn to cry / Four walls / One long day / Knockin' on Heaven's door / My baby / Star hotel / Don't let go / Long as I can see the light / The party's over / Cheap wine / Goodbye. *(re-iss. Aug88 on 'Line'; LIDLP 500010) (cd-iss. 1989; LICD 900418)*

1982. (7") *<47458>* **FOREVER NOW (ALL MY LOVE). /** -

Polydor Polydor

Jun 82. (7") *(POSP 469)* **YOU GOT NOTHING I WANT. / LETTER TO ALLAN**

Jul 82. (lp) *(POLS 1065)* **CIRCUS ANIMALS** -
– You got nothing I want / Bow river / Forever now / Taipan / Hound dog / Wild colonial boy / No good for you / Numbers fall / When the war is over / Letter to Alan. *(cd-iss. Jan96 on 'East West'; 2292 54931-2)*

Sep 82. (7") *(POLS 514)* **FOREVER NOW. / NO GOOD FOR YOU**

WEA not iss.

1984. (lp) *(250390-1)* **TWENTIETH CENTURY** - - Austra
– Build this love / Twentieth century / Ghost town / Saturday night / Painted doll / No sense / Flame trees / Only one / Hold me tight / Sing to me / The game / Janelle / Temptation. *(UK-iss.May88; same) (cd-iss. Apr96 on 'East West'; 2292 50390-2)*

1985. (lp) *(251525-2)* **THE BARKING SPIDERS LIVE (live)** - - Austra

— disbanded 1985, when BARNES went solo.

– compilations, etc. –

Nov 87. (lp/cd) *WEA; (600148-1/-2)* **RAZOR SONGS** - - Austra
(UK cd-iss. Feb96 on 'East West'; 2292 56827-2)

May 88. (lp/cd) *WEA; (252362-1/-2)* **RADIO SONGS – A BEST OF** -
– Bow river / Cheap wine / Goodbye / No sense / Breakfast at Sweethearts / Saturday night / You got nothing I want / My baby / Forver now / Khe Sanh / Choirgirl / Flame trees.

JIMMY BARNES

— **JIMMY BARNES** – vocals / with numerous session men

Mushroom not iss.

1984. (lp) *(RML 53138)* **BODYSWERVE** - - Austra
– Vision / Daylight / Promise me you'll call / No second prize / Boys cry out for war / Paradise / A change is gonna come / Thick skinner / Piece of my heart / Fire / World's on fire.

1985. (d-lp) *(RML 53196-7)* **FOR THE WORKING CLASS MAN** - - Austra
– I'd die to be with you tonight / Ride the night away / American heartbeat / Working class man / Without your love / No second prize / Vision / Promise me you'll call / Boys cry out for war / Daylight / Thick skinned / Paradise.

— next with guests **JONATHAN CAIN, NEIL SCHON** (both BAD ENGLISH) + **MICK FLEETWOOD + DESMOND CHILD**

Geffen Geffen

May 86. (lp/c) *(924089-1/-4)* *<24089>* **JIMMY BARNES** Mar86
– No second prize / I'd die to be with you tonight / Working class man / Promise me you'll call / Boys cry out for war / Paradise / Without your love / American heartbeat / Thick skinned / Ride the night away / Daylight.

May 86. (7"/12") *(GEF 3/+T)* *<28749>* **WORKING CLASS MAN (remix). / BOYS CRY OUT FOR WAR** 74 Mar86

— In Jun'87, BARNES and INXS hit the Top 50 with the single 'GOOD TIMES' on 'Atlantic' (89237)

May 88. (lp/c/cd) *(924146-1/-4/-2)* *<24146>* **FREIGHT TRAIN HEART**
– Driving wheels / Seven days / Too much ain't enough love / Lessons in love / Waitin' for the heartache / The last frontier / I'm still on your side / Do or die / I wanna get started with you / Walk on.

May 88. (7") *(GEF 38)* *<27920>* **TOO MUCH AIN'T ENOUGH LOVE. / DO OR DIE** 91 Jun88
(12"+=) *(GEF 38T)* – Working class man / Resurrection shuffle.

1988. (cd) *Mushroom; (D 24521-2)* **BARNESTORMING (live)** - - Austra
– Driving wheels / Good times / Too much ain't enough love / Lessons in love / Working class man / Waitin' for the heartache / Do or die / When a man loves a woman / Last frontier / Seven days / Temptation / No second prize / Walk on / Rising sun / Without your love / Paradise. *(UK-iss.May94; same)*

1989. (cd-s) **WAITIN' FOR THE HEARTACHE / SEVEN DAYS – 12" mix / GOING TO MEXICO** - - Austra

Sep 90. (cd/c/lp) *<(7567 82141-2/-4/-1)>* **TWO FIRES**
– Lay down your guns / Let's make it last all night long / Little darlin' / Love is enough / Hardline / One of a kind / Sister mercy / When your love is gone / Caught between two fires / Fade to black. *(cd+=)* – Hold on. *(cd re-iss. May94 on 'Mushroom'; TVD 93318)*

1991. (cd-s) **LAY DOWN YOUR GUNS / BROKEN HEARTS** - - Austra

Mushroom Mushroom

1991. (cd) *(TVD 93344)* **SOUL DEEP** - - Austra
– I gotcha / (Your love keeps lifting me) Higher and higher / When something is wrong with my baby / Show me / Many rivers to cross / Reflections / Ain't no mountain high enough / I found a love / Signed sealed delivered (I'm yours) / Bring it on home to me / Here I am (come and take me) / River deep mountain high. *(UK-iss.Aug94; same)*

1991. (cd-s) **I GOTCHA / I GOTCHA (Tex mix)** - - Austra

1991. (cd-s) **WHEN SOMETHING IS WRONG WITH MY BABY / ALL I GOT** - - Austra

1992. (cd/c/lp) *(TVD/TVC/TVL 93372)* **HEAT**
– Sweat it out / Wheels in motion / Stand up / Burn baby burn / Something's got a hold / Love thing / Talking to you / Stone cold / Wait for me / Tears we cry / Right by your side / A little bit of love / I'd rather be blind / Not the loving kind / Knock me down / Catch your shadow. *(UK-iss.Jun93; same)*

1992. (cd-s) **SWEAT IT OUT / TELL ME THE TRUTH / SITTING AT THE BAR** - - Austra

Nov 93. (c-s/12"/cd-s) **STAND UP. /**

Nov 93. (cd) *(TVD 93390)* **FLESH & WOOD**
– It will be alright / The weight / Ride the night away / Guilty / You can't make love without soul / Hell of a time / Brother of mine / Fade to black / Flame trees / Still got a long way to go / Still on your side / Stone cold / Let it go / We could be gone / Love me tender. *(UK-iss.Dec94; same)*

— (last 2 albums also issued UK Feb94 d-cd/d-c; *D/C 45045)*

Feb 94. (cd-ep) *(D 11504)* **STONE COLD EP**
– Stone cold / Stand up (live) / Stone cold (live) / Catch your shadow (acoustic) / Stone cold (acoustic) / Working class man (acoustic).

1994. (cd-s) **THE WEIGHT / COLD COLD HEART** - - Austra

May 95. (c-s/cd-s) *(C/D 11980)* **CHANGE OF HEART / EDGEWOOD / THE OTHER SIDE** -
(cd-s) *(DX 11980)* – ('A'side) / Lay down your guns (live) / Come undone (acoustic) / You can't always get what you want (acoustic) / Many rivers to cross (acoustic).

Jun 95. (cd/c) *(TVD/TVC 93433)* **PSYCLONE**
– Used to be truth / Spend the night / Change of heart / Every beat / Come undone / Stumbling / Love and devotion / Mirror of your soul / Just a man / Fooling yourself / Tears / Going down alone / Because you wanted it.

1995. (cd-s) **COME UNDONE / BECAUSE YOU WANTED IT** - - Austra

Feb 00. (cd) *(MUSH 67CD)* **LOVE AND FEAR**
– Love and hate / Time will tell / By the grace of God / Thankful for the rain / Temptation / Love song / Do it to me / Love gone cold / Heart cries alone / Radio song / Blind can't lead the blind / Sorry.

2000. (cd-s) **THANKFUL FOR THE RAIN / HERE AND NOW / THANKFUL FOR THE RAIN (instrumental)** - - Austra

Epic not iss.

Sep 00. (cd) *(857386194-2)* **SOUL DEEPER** (covers) - - Austra
– Land of a 1000 dances / Chain of fools / What becomes of the broken hearted / To love somebody / 634-5789 / Ain't too proud to beg / I put a spell on you / Money / Hold on I'm coming / Dancing in the street / All the young dudes / Respect.

Nov 00. (cd-s) *(857385642-2)* **CHAIN OF FOOLS** - - Austra

– compilations, etc. –

May 97. (d-cd) *Mushroom; (TVD 93465)* **THE BEST OF JIMMY BARNES**

1990's. (cd) *Mushroom; (IMPMUSH 32164)* **BARNES HITS ANTHOLOGY** - - Austra

1990's. (3xcd-box) *Mushroom; (MUSH 332742)* **JIMMY BARNES x 3** - - Austra
– (BODYSWERVE, TWO FIRES + CYCLONE)

BARON ROJO

Formed: Madrid, Spain . . . 1981 (pronounced ROCHO), by the guitar-playing DE CASTRO brothers, ARMONDO and CARLOS, who recruited the rhythm section of JOSE LUIS CAMPUZANO and HERMES CALABRIA. One of the few Spanish metal outfits to achieve any recognition outside their homeland and Latin America, they started out on the native 'Chapa Discs' label, releasing a series of retro-esque metal albums distinguished by the at times, incoherent vox of vocalist CARLOS. An English vocal version of one of their albums, 'VOLUMEN BRUTAL', was imported into Britain in 1984, via the European label, 'Mausoleum'. For the latter half of the 80's, they released a further couple of albums for the 'Zafiro' label, 'TIERRA DE NADIE' and 'NO VA MAS!'. In the early 90's, the DE CASTRO brothers were back in town with new BARON ROJO recruits ANGEL ARIAS and JOSE MARTOS – several albums were released in the following years. • **Covered:** GIRLS GOT RHYTHM (Ac/Dc).

Album rating: LARGA VIDA AL ROCK AND ROLL (*5) / VOLUMEN BRUTAL (*7) / METALMORFOSIS (*5) / BARON AL ROJO VIVO (*4) / EN UN LUGAR DE LA MARCHA (*5) / SIEMPRE ESTAIS ALLI (*5) / TIERRA DE NADIE (*4) / NO VA MAS! (*4) / OBSTINADO (*6) / DESAFINO (*4) / ARMA SECRETA (*4) / CUESTE LO QUE CUESTE (*5)

ARMANDO DE CASTRO – vocals, guitar / **CARLOS DE CASTRO** – guitar, vocals / **JOSE LUIS CAMPUZANO** – bass, vocals / **HERMES CALABRIA** – drums, vocals

Chapa Discs not iss.

1981. (lp) *(50612173)* **LARGA VIDA AL ROCK AND ROLL** - - Spain
– Con botas sucias / Anda suelto satanas / El pobre / Los desertores del rock / Efluvios / Larga vida al rock & roll / El Presidente / Chica de la ciudad / Baron Rojo. *(UK-iss.1983 on 'Kamaflage'; KAMLP 5) (UK-iss.1984 on 'Mausoleum'; SKULL 8328) <US cd-iss. 1993 on 'Alex'; 3946>*

Kamaflage not iss.

1982. (lp) *(KAMLP 4)* **VOLUMEN BRUTAL** (English version) - Spain
– Isolation ward / Rockers go to hell / Give me the chance / Termites / Flowers of evil / Stand up / Someone's loving you / Concert for them / You're telling me / The

Baron fly over England. *(UK-iss.1984 on 'Mausoleum'; SKULL 8326)* <*US cd-iss. 1999 on 'BMG'; 25998*>

Chapa Discos / not iss.

1983. (lp) *(HS 35062)* **METALMORFOSIS** [-] [-] Spain
– Casi me mato / Rockero indomable / Tierra de vandalos / Que puedo hacer? / Siempre estas alli / Hiroshima / El malo / Diosa razon / Se escapa el tiempo. *(with free 7")(RS 33.084)* – INVULNERABLE. / HERENCIA LETAL *(UK-iss.1984 on 'Mausoleum'; SKULL 8322)* <*US cd-iss. 1993 on 'Alex'; 3947*>

Mausoleum / not iss.

1984. (d-lp) *(BALLS 834546)* **BARON AL ROJO VIVO (live)** [ ] [-]
– Baron Rojo / Incomunicacion / Campo de concentracion / El mundo puede ser diferente / Flores del mal / Concierto para ellos / Mensajeros de la destruccion / Ataco el hombre blanco / Tierra de vandalos / Solo de Armando / Los rockeros van al infierno / Buenos Aires / Soloo de Hermes / Resistire / Con botas sucias. <*US d-cd-iss. 1993 on 'Alex'; 3949*> <*US d-cd re-iss. Jun98 on 'Imprint'; 29209*>

1985. (lp) **EN UN LUGAR DE LA MARCHA** [-] [-] Spain
– Breakthoven / El baile des los Malditos / Chicos del rock / Caso Perdido / Cuerdos de acero / No ver, no habla, no oir / Tras de ti / Hijos de Cain.

1986. (lp) **SIEMPRE ESTAIS ALLI** [-] [-] Spain
– Larga vida al rock and roll / El malo / El Baron Vuela sobre Inglaterra / El pobre / Diosa razon / Invunerable / Se escapa el tiempo / Que puedo hacer? / Siempre estas Alli. <*US cd-iss. 2001 on 'BMG'; 30023*>

Zafiro / not iss.

1987. (lp) **TIERRA DE NADIE** [-] [-] Spain
– Pico de oro / El pedal / La voz de su amo / Tierra de nadie / Senor inspector / Sombras en el noche / Pobre Madrid / El precio del futuro.

1988. (lp) **NO VA MAS!** [-] [-] Spain
– Travesia urbana / Cansado de Esparar / El gladiador / En tinieblas / Los Domingos son muy aburridos / Kamikaze / Trampa y carton / Carga y Descarga / Celtas cortos / Milanos Luz.

1989. (lp) **OBSTINADO** [-] [-] Spain
– Vampiros y banqueros / Por vez primera / Get on your knees / Tren fantasma / Colapso en ma M-30 / Paraiso terrenal / Dueno de mi destino / Herencia letal / Seguimos vivis / Pura sangre.

—— **ARMANDO + CARLOS** recruited **ANGEL ARIAS** – bass / **JOSE MARTOS** – drums

not iss. / Alex

1993. (cd) <*3952*> **DESAFINO** [-] [ ]
– Te espero en el infierno / Ali-Baba y los cuarenta / Exorcismo / Noches de rock & roll / El enimigo a batir / Rock'stimulacion / Politico / Senor censor / Hijos del blues / Girls got rhythm.

1997. (cd) **ARMA SECRETA** [-] [ ]
– Bajo tierra / Arma secreta / Todo me da Igual / No hay solucion sin rock & roll / Aqui estoy / No odas / Fugitivo / Blues del telefono / Communicacion / Sobre este mundo hostil / Robinsong / Hielo al Rojo.

– compilations, others, etc. –

Mar 01. (cd-s) **CUESTE LO QUE CUESTE / RESISTIRE** [-] [-] Spain
Apr 01. (d-cd) *BMG*; <*70519*> **CUESTE LO QUE CUESTE** [-] [ ]
– Cueste lo que cueste / El trepa / Con bota sucias / Satanico plan / Sr. Inspector / Cuerdas de acero / Invunerable / Chico del rock / Chica de la ciudad / Los rockeros van al infierno / Siemre estas Alli / Vampiros y banqueros / Breakthoven / Rockero indomable / Baron Rojo // Cielo o infierno / Mas de ti / Casi de mato / Larga vida al rock & roll / Campo de concentracion / Celtas cortos / El malo / La voz de su amo / El pobre / Incomunicacioni / Buenos Aires / Concierto para ellos / Pura sangre / Caso perdido / Tierra de vandalos / Resistire nueva (version).

BARREN CROSS

Formed: California, USA . . . 1984 by Christian-rockers, RAY PARRIS and STEVE WHITAKER, who recruited MIKE LEE and JIM LAVERDE. In stark contrast to the bulk of Christian "metal" bands, BARREN CROSS played with a conviction and heaviness missing from most of their fluffy AOR peers. The band initiated their career with a self-financed mini-lp, 'BELIEVER', the record being picked up by the Christian 'Starsong' label a year later. A second, more melodic album, 'ATOMIC ARENA', was given light by 'Enigma' records in '87, the band moving to 'Virgin' soon after. 1989's 'STATE OF CONTROL' preceded an acclaimed live set, 'HOTTER THAN HELL', although this was to be their final offering intil '94's swansong 'RATTLE YOUR CAGE'.

Album rating: ROCK FOR THE KING (*5) / ATOMIC ARENA (*4) / STATE OF CONTROL (*4) / HOTTER THAN HELL (*6) / RATTLE YOUR CAGE (*3)

MIKE LEE – vocals, guitar / **RAY PARRIS** – guitar, vocals / **JIM LA VERDE** – bass, guitar, vocals / **STEVE WHITAKER** – drums

not iss. / Independ.

1985. (lp) <*none*> **BELIEVER** [-] [ ]
– (tracks as below).

not iss. / Starsong

1986. (lp) <*WR 180*> **ROCK FOR THE KING** [-] [ ]
– Dying day / He loves you / It's all come true / Believe / Going nowhere / Rock for the king / Give your life / Just a touch / Light the flame. *(UK cd-iss. 1988 on 'Myrrh'; SSD 8064)* <*US cd-iss. 1990 on 'Medusa'+=; 72329-2*> – (live:-) Killer of the unborn / Dead lock / Cultic regimes / He loves you / Living dead / Heaven or nothing.

Enigma / Enigma

1987. (lp) <*D1-73311*> **ATOMIC ARENA** [-] [ ]
– Imaginary music / Killers of the unborn / In the eye of the fire / Terrorist child / Close to the edge / Dead lock / Cultic regimes / Heaven or nothing / King of kings / Living dead. *(UK-iss.Aug89 on 'Music For Nations'; MFN 84)*

Jun 89. (lp/c/cd) *(ENVLP/TCENV/CDENV 530)* <*73347*> **STATE OF CONTROL** [ ] [ ]
– State of control / Out of time / Cryin' over you / A face in the dark / The stage of intensity / Hard lies / Inner war / Love at full volume / Bigotry man (who are you) / Two thousand years. *(cd+=)* – Escape in the night.

Medusa / Enigma

Jul 90. (cd/lp) *(MD 9383-2/-1)* <*72336-2/-1*> **HOTTER THAN HELL (live)** [ ] [ ]
– Imaginary music / Killers of the unborn / Going nowhere / Opus to the third heaven / In the eye of the fire / Light the flame / King Jesus and blues jam / Dying day / Close to the edge / Dead lock / King of kings / Rock for the king / Terrorist child / Give your life.

—— split for a few years, although they returned to the studio for next

Rugged / Rugged

Nov 94. (cd) <*RGD 4401-2*> **RATTLE YOUR CAGE** [ ] [ ]
– Rattle your cage / Here I am / Unsuspecting / No time to run / Sick / Somewhere far away / Feed the fire / Let it go let it die / Time for love / J.R.M. / Your will / Midnight son.

BASTARD

Formed: Hanover, Germany . . . 1977 by KARL-HEINZ ROTHERT and KEITH KOSSOFF, who enlisted ULI MEISNER and TOTO PETTICOATO. Despite the sensationalist moniker, the group purveyed a relatively safe brand of raunchy AC/DC-esque rock, three nigh on forgettable albums surfacing in the late 70's/early 80's.

Album rating: LIVE AND ALIVE (*5)

KARL-HEINZ ROTHERT – vocals, bass / **KEITH KOSSOFF** (aka GUNTHER GRUSCHKUHN) – guitar / **ULI MEISNER** (aka THEO TREMOLO) – guitar / **TOTO PETTICOATO** (aka THOMAS KORN) – drums

Nova / not iss.

Jan 78. (lp) *(6-23288)* **BACK TO NATURE** [-] [-] German
– Back to nature / Rock & roll lady / Koss / Steamroller / I've got a feeling / Gettin' in a rage / Royal flush / Diana / The way of giving.

Nov 78. (lp) *(6-23619)* **TEARING NIGHTS** [-] [-] German
– Tearing nights / Make my life a dream / Burning heart / Move on / Lovers grief / Rock'n'roll is the winner / Dust on the roof / Faithful love / Daddy was a rock'n'roller / Get up wake up.

Lava / not iss.

Feb 80. (lp) *(TCH 80535)* **LIVE AND ALIVE (live)** [-] [-] German
– We got the power / I'll tell you the lies / Danger of fire / Are you ready / Back to the future / I put you down / I've got the feeling / Can't get enough.

—— split after above

BASTRO (see under ⇒ SQUIRREL BAIT)

BATHORY

Formed: Stockholm, Sweden . . . March '83, by QUORTHON, the sole creator of this pioneering death-metal outfit. Initially recording with KOTHAAR and VVORNTH, he/they laid down a track for a various artists compilation album, 'Scandinavian Metal Attack'. Signed to 'Tyfon' ('Under One Flag' in the UK), the BLACKIE LAWLESS-looking leather-clad QUORTHON established BATHORY as "god" fathers of the now burgeoning Scandinavian satanic metal scene through a series of cult albums. In 1990, BATHORY delivered the 'HAMMERHEART' opus, an epic concept album anticipating his peers' subsequent fixation with Viking mythology and language. QUORTHON as BATHORY (and solo) continuing in a conceptual vein with a string of 90's albums, including 'TWILIGHT OF THE GODS', 'REQUIEM' and 'OCTAGON'. QUORTHON's solo 'ALBUM' in 1994 was a straighter set, fusing heavy metal with a hint of ALICE IN CHAINS grunge.

Album rating: BATHORY (*4) / THE RETURN . . . .. (*4) / UNDER THE SIGN OF THE BLACK MARK (*7) / BLOOD, FIRE, DEATH (*6) / HAMMERHEART (*5) / TWILIGHT OF THE GODS (*6) / JUBILEUM VOLUME 1 compilation (*6) / JUBILEUM VOLUME II compilation (*6) / OCTAGON (*6) / REQUIEM (*6) / BLOOD ON ICE (*6) / JUBILEUM VOLUME III compilation (*6) / Quorthon: ALBUM (*6) / PURITY OF ESSENCE (*6)

QUORTHON – vocals, guitar, multi / with **KOTHAAR** – bass / **VVORNTH** – drums (both left before any of below material) / they were replaced by a plethora of musicians

Under One Flag / New Renaissance

1984. (lp) *(FLAG 8)* **BATHORY** [ ] [-]
– Hades / Reaper / Necromansy / Sacrifice / In conspiracy with Satan / Armageddon / Raise the dead / War. *(<cd-iss. May92 on 'Black Mark'+=; BMCD 666-1>)* – Storm of damnation (intro).

1985. (lp) *(FLAG 9)* **THE RETURN . . . . ..** [ ] [-]
– Total destruction / Born for burning / The wind of mayhem / Beastial lust / Possessed / The rite of darkness / The reap of evil / Son of the damned / Sadist (tormentor) / The return of the darkness and evil. *(<cd-iss. May92 on 'Black Mark'+=; BMCD 666-2>)* – Revelation of doom.

Jun 87. (lp/c) *(FLAG/TFLAG 11)* <*NR/+C 33*> **UNDER THE SIGN OF THE BLACK MARK** [ ] [ ]
– Nocturnal obeisance / Massacre / Woman of dark desires / Call from the grave / Equimanthorn / Enter the eternal fire / Chariots of fire / 13 candles / Of doom . . . *(<cd-iss. May92 on 'Black Mark'; BMCD 666-3>)*

Oct 88. (cd/c/lp) *(CD/C+/FLAG 26)* **BLOOD, FIRE, DEATH** [ ] [-]
– Odens ride over Nordland / A fine day to die / The golden walls of Heaven / Pace 'til death / Holocaust / For all those who died / Dies Irae / Blood fire death. *(also pic-lp; FLAG 26P)* *(<cd re-iss. Oct94 on 'Black Mark'; BMCD 666-4>)*

Noise / S.P.V.

Apr 90. (cd/c/lp) *(CD/ZC+/NUK 153)* <*4092*> **HAMMERHEART** [ ] [ ]
– Shores in flames / Valhalla / Baptised in fire and ice / Father to son / Song to hall up high / Home of once brave / One rode to Asa Bay. *(<cd re-iss. Oct94 on 'Black Mark'; BMCD 666-5>)*

Black Mark / Black Mark

Jun 92. (cd/c/lp) *(<BM CD/CT/LP 666-6>)* **TWILIGHT OF THE GODS**
– (Prologue) / Twilight of the gods / (Epilogue) / Through blood by thunder / Blood and iron / Under the runes / To enter your mountain / Bond of blood / Hammerheart.

Nov 92. (cd/c) *(BMCD/BMCT 666-7)* **JUBILEUM VOLUME I** (compilation) -
– Rider at the gate of dawn / Crawl to the cross / Sacrifice / Dies Irae / Through blood by thunder / You didn't move me (I don't give a fuck) / Odens ride over Nordland / A fine day to die / War / Enter the eternal fire / Song to hall up high / Sadist / Under the runes / Equimanthorn / Blood, fire, death.

May 94. (cd/lp; by QUORTHON) *(<BM CD/LP 666-9>)* **ALBUM** Sep94
– No more and never again / Oh no no / Boy / Major snooze / Too little much too late / Crack in my mirror / Rain / Feather / Relief / Head over heels.

Sep 94. (cd) *(<BMCD 666-8>)* **JUBILEUM VOLUME II** (compilation)
– The return of the darkness and evil / Burnin' leather / One road to Asa Bay / The golden walls of Heaven / Call from the grave / Die in fire / Shores in flames / Possessed / Raise the dead / Total destruction / Bond of blood / Twilight of the gods.

Nov 94. (cd/lp) *(<BM CD/LP 666-10>)* **REQUIEM** Mar95
– Apocalypse / Blood and soil / Crosstitution / Distinguish to kill / Necroticus / Pax vobiscum / Requiem / Suffocate / War machine.

May 95. (cd) *(<BMCD 666-11>)* **OCTAGON** Oct95
– Immaculate pinetreeroad #930 / Born to die / Psychopath / Sociopath / Grey / Century / 33 something / War supply / Schizianity / Judgement of posterity / Deuce.

Jun 96. (cd/lp) *(BM CD/LP 666-12)* **BLOOD ON ICE** - - German
– Intro / Blood on ice / Man of iron / One eyed old man / The sword / The stallion / The woodwoman / The lake / Gods of thunder of wind and of rain / The ravens / The revenge of the blood on ice.

Mar 97. (cd-ep; by QUORTHON) *(<BMCD 666-14>)* **WHEN OUR DAY IS THROUGH**
– When our day is through / An inch above the ground / Cherrybutt & firefly / I've had it coming my way.

Jun 97. (cd; by QUORTHON) *(<BMCD 666-13>)* **PURITY OF ESSENCE**
– Rock and roll / I've had it coming my way / When our day is through / One of those days / Cherrybutt & firefly / Television / Hit my head / Hump for fun / Outta space / Fade away / I want out / Daddy's girl / Coming down in pieces / Roller coaster / It's ok / All in all I know / No life at all / An inch above the ground / The notforgettin' / Deep / Label on the wind / Just the same / You just got to live.

Sep 98. (cd) *(<BMCD 666-16>)* **JULILEUM VOLUME III** (compilation) Jul98
– 33 something / Satan my master / The lake / Crosstitution / In nomine stanas / Immaculate pinetreeroad #930 / War machine / The stallion / Resolution creed / Witchcraft / Valhalla / Sociopath / Pax vobiscum / Genocide / Gods of thunder of wind and of rain.

BATON ROUGE

Formed: New Jersey, USA . . . late 80's out of MERIDIAN, by KELLY KEELING and LANCE BULEN, who recruited CORKY McCLELLAN, DAVID CREMIN and SCOTT BENDER. Relocating to Los Angeles, the group subsequently secured a deal with 'Atlantic', JACK PONTI assigned to songwriting/production duties on their first album, 'SHAKE YOUR SOUL'. Musically reminiscent of early WHITESNAKE and DEF LEPPARD, with a melodic blues-rock sheen, the record hit the Top 200 for over 10 weeks. A second set in '91 (again with PONTI), 'LIGHTS OUT IN THE PLAYGROUND', failed to emulate the promise of their debut.

Album rating: SHAKE YOUR SOUL (*5) / LIGHTS OUT IN THE PLAYGROUND (*4)

KELLY KEELING – vocals / **LANCE BULEN** – guitar / **DAVID CREMIN** – keyboards, guitar, vocals / **SCOTT BENDER** – bass, vocals / **CORKY McCLELLAN** – drums, vocals

not iss. / Atlantic

Apr 90. (12") **WALKS LIKE A WOMAN. /** -

May 90. (cd/c/lp) *<82073-2/-4/-1>* **SHAKE YOUR SOUL** -
– Doctor / Walks like a woman / Big trouble / It's about time / Bad time comin' down / The Midge / Baby's so cool / Young hearts / Melenie / There was a time (the storm) / Hot blood movin' / Spread like fire.

—— **TONY PALMUCCI** – guitar, vocals (ex-KEEL) repl. CREMIN

not iss. / East West

May 91. (12") *<98792>* **THE PRICE OF LOVE** -

Jun 91. (cd/c/lp) *<91661-2/-4/-1>* **LIGHTS OUT IN THE PLAYGROUND** -
– Slave to the rhythm / Full time body / Tie you up / Desperate / Tokyo time / Vampire kiss – The Midge II / The price of love / Dreamin' in black and white / Down by the torchlight / Light at the end of the tunnel / Tear down the walls / Hotter than Hell.

Sep 91. (12") *<98701>* **DESPERATE** -

—— split the following year, but re-formed later

Made To Measure / not iss.

Sep 97. (cd) *(MTM 19963-2>* **BATON ROUGE** -
– Didn't I / Ghost of you / You can jump alone / Shelter / Victims of the night / Hands of time / Love by the numbers / Not in the mood for a heartache / I know better than you do / Love's a loaded gun / Love takes / Back under fire.

Stiv BATORS (see under ⇒ DEAD BOYS)

BATTLEAXE

Formed: Sunderland, England . . . 1983 by DAVE KING, STEVE HARDY, BRIAN SMITH and IAN THOMPSON. Signing to 'Music For Nations' the same year on the strength of a few tracks on the 'Roxcalibur' compilation, they released their debut album, 'BURN THIS TOWN'. Playing a very British blend of heavy metal, the band drew comparisons to MOTORHEAD, more so on their second set, 'POWER FROM THE UNIVERSE' (1984), which featured new drummer IAN McCORMACK.

Album rating: POWER FROM THE UNIVERSE (*6)

DAVE KING – vocals / **STEVE HARDY** – guitar / **BRIAN SMITH** – bass / **IAN THOMPSON** – drums

Music For Nations / not iss.

Jul 83. (lp) *(MFN 8)* **BURN THIS TOWN** -
– Ready to deliver / Her mama told her / Burn this town / Dirty rocker / Overdrive / Running out of time / Battleaxe / Star maker / Thor – thunder angel / Hands off.

—— **IAN McCORMACK** – drums; repl. THOMPSON

Jul 84. (lp) *(MFN 25)* **POWER FROM THE UNIVERSE** -
– Chopper attack / Movin' metal rock / License to rock / Fortune lady / Shout it out / Over the top / Power from the universe / Make it in America.

—— split after above

BAUHAUS

Formed: Northampton, England . . . late 1978, by PETE MURPHY, DANIEL ASH, DAVID J and KEVIN HASKINS, initially calling themselves BAUHAUS 1919. Obtaining a one-off deal with indie label 'Small Wonder', they released an 8-minute epic 'BELA LUGOSI'S DEAD', backed with the infamous 'DARK ENTRIES', the latter track subsequently issued as a follow-up 45. A gender-bending but hard-edged collage of glam and punk influences shrouded in gothic horror posturing, BAUHAUS carved out their own inimitable niche in the early 80's post-new wave wasteland. After an album, 'IN THE FLAT FIELD' (1981) and a couple of singles (one a cover of T.Rex's 'TELEGRAM SAM') on '4 a.d.', the band signed to 'Beggars Banquet', scoring a Top 30 hit with debut set, 'MASK' (1981). Featuring the minor hit singles, 'KICK IN THE EYE' and 'THE PASSION OF LOVERS', the album remains their most consistent set. Still, the underground cred was called into question after MURPHY appeared in a TV ad for Maxell tapes later that year. More appropriate, perhaps, was the band's performance of 'BELA LUGOSI'S DEAD' for 1982 vampire film, 'The Hunger' starring the band's boyhood hero, DAVID BOWIE. In fact, it was one of BOWIE's classics, 'ZIGGY STARDUST', that gave BAUHAUS their commercial breakthrough, the single's Top 20 success seeing the accompanying album, THE SKY'S GONE OUT' make the UK Top 5. The droning affectations of 'SHE'S IN PARTIES' remains one of the band's most recognisable tracks while the swan song album, 'BURNING FROM THE INSIDE' (1983), saw BAUHAUS signing off on an unsettling, if creatively high point. MURPHY soon reappeared with MICK KARN of JAPAN in a new outfit, DALI'S CAR, although only one album, 'THE WAKING HOUR', surfaced in '84. The singer went on to release a string of albums, surprising many in Britain when he had a US Top 50 placing with 'DEEP', which contained the 1990 hit, 'CUTS YOU UP'. Meanwhile, the rest were enjoying success as LOVE AND ROCKETS (from earlier incarnation of TONES ON TAILS and DAVID J solo) and this trio also took America by storm having had a Top 3 smash, 'SO ALIVE' in '89. With current offshoots failing to sparkle during the rest of the 90's, BAUHAUS decided to officially re-form in mid 1998 for two concerts, which enabled their record label to cash-in on an accompanying best-of collection, 'CRACKLE'. • **Covered:** THIRD UNCLE (Eno) / WAITING FOR THE MAN (Velvet Undergound). PETER MURPHY solo, wrote with STREATHAM and covered; FINAL SOLUTION (Pere Ubu) / THE LIGHT POURS OUT OF ME (Magazine) / FUNTIME (Iggy Pop). LOVE AND ROCKETS covered BALL OF CONFUSION (Temptations) / BODY AND SOUL (trad). DAVID J covered 4 HOURS (ClockDva) / SHIP OF FOOLS (John Cale).

Album rating: IN THE FLAT FIELD (*5) / MASK (*6) / THE SKY'S GONE OUT (*6) / BURNING FROM THE INSIDE (*5) / BAUHAUS 1979-1983 compilation (*9) / CRACKLE collection (*6) /

PETER MURPHY (b.11 Jul'57) – vocals / **DANIEL ASH** (b.31 Jul'57) – guitar, vocals / **DAVID J** (b. HASKINS, 24 Apr'57) – bass, vocals / **KEVIN HASKINS** (b.19 Jul'60) – drums, percussion

Small Wonder / not iss.

Aug 79. (12",12"white) *(TEENY 2)* **BELA LUGOSI'S DEAD. / BOYS / DARK ENTRIES** -
(re-dist.Mar81 & Mar82; same) (re-iss. Sep86 in various colours; same) (12"pic-d.1987; TEENY 2P) (re-iss. May88 & Jun98, c-s/cd-s; TEENY 2 C/CD)

Axis / not iss.

Jan 80. (7") *(AXIS 3)* **DARK ENTRIES. / UNTITLED** -
(re-iss. Feb80 on '4.a.d.'; AD 3) (some mispressed on 'Beggars Banquet'; BEG 37)

4.a.d. / not iss.

Jun 80. (7") *(AD 7)* **TERROR COUPLE KILL COLONEL. / SCOPES / TERROR COUPLE KILL COLONEL II** -

Oct 80. (lp) *(CAD 13)* **IN THE FLAT FIELD** 72 -
– Double dare / In the flat field / A god in an alcove / Dive / Spy in the cab / Small talk stinks / St. Vitus dance / Stigmata martyr / Nerves. *(cd-iss. Apr88 +=; CAD 13CD)* – Untitled.

Oct 80. (7") *(AD 17)* **TELEGRAM SAM. / CROWDS** -
(12"+=) *(AD 17T)* – Rosegarden funeral of sores.

Beggars Banquet / A&M

Mar 81. (7"/12") *(BEG 54/+T)* **KICK IN THE EYE. / SATORI** 59 -

Jun 81. (7") *(BEG 59)* **THE PASSION OF LOVERS. / 1: 2: 3: 4:** 56 -

Oct 81. (lp/c) *(BEGA/BEGC 29)* **MASK** 30 -
– Hair of the dog / The passion of lovers / Of lillies and remains / Dancing / Hollow hills / Kick in the eye / Muscle in plastic / In fear of fear / Man with x-ray eyes / Mask. *(re-iss. Feb88 & Jul91 on 'Beggars Banquet-Lowdown' lp/c; BBL/+C 29) (cd-iss. Oct88 & Jul91 +=; BBL 29CD)* – Satori / Harry / Earwax / In fear of dub / Kick in the eye.

Feb 82. (7"ep) *(BEG 74)* **SEARCHING FOR SATORI** [45] [-]
– Kick in the eye / Harry / Earwax.
(12"ep+=) *(BEG 74T)* – In fear of dub.

Jun 82. (7"/7"pic-d) *(BEG 79/+P)* **SPIRIT. / TERROR COUPLE KILL COLONEL (live)** [42] [-]

Sep 82. (7") *(BEG 83)* **ZIGGY STARDUST. / THIRD UNCLE (live)** [15] [-]
(12"+=) *(BEG 83T)* – Party of the first part / Waiting for the man.

Oct 82. (d-lp/d-c) *(BEGA/BEGC 42) / (BEGA/BEGC 38)* *<SP 4918>*
THE SKY'S GONE OUT / PRESS THE EJECT BUTTON AND GIVE ME THE TAPE (live) [4] [ ]
– Third uncle / Silent hedges / In the night / Swing the heartache / Spirit / The three shadows (parts 1, 2, 3) / Silent hedges / All we ever wanted was everything / Exquisite corpse. *(re-iss. Feb88 & Jul91 on 'Beggars Banquet-Lowdown' lp/c; BBL/+C 42) (cd-iss. Oct88 & Jul91 +=; BBL 42CD)* – Ziggy Stardust / Watch that grandad go / Party of the first part / Spirit (extended). **PRESS THE EJECT BUTTON AND GIVE ME THE TAPE** – In the flat field / Rosegarden funeral of sores / Dancing / Man with the x-ray eyes / Bela Lugosi's dead / Spy in the cab / Kick in the eye / In fear of fear / Hollow hills / Stigmata martyr / Dark entries. *(re-iss. Feb88 & Jul91 on 'Beggars Banquet-Lowdown'; BBL/+C 38) (cd-iss. Oct88 & Jul91 +=; BBL 38CD)* – Terror couple kill colonel / Double dare / Waiting for the man / Hair of the dog / Of lillies and remains. *(free 7"ep with above; BH 1)* – SATORI IN PARIS (live)

Jan 83. (7") *(BEG 88)* **LAGARTIJA NICK. / PARANOIA! PARANOIA!** [44] [-]
(12"+=) *(BEG 88T)* – Watch that grandad go / In the flat field (live).

Mar 83. (7") *<2524>* **LAGARTIJA NICK. / ZIGGY STARDUST** [-] [ ]

Apr 83. (7"/7"pic-d) *(BEG 91/+P)* **SHE'S IN PARTIES. / DEPARTURE** [26] [ ]
(12"+=) *(BEG 91T)* – Here's the dub.

Jul 83. (lp/c) *(BEGA/BEGC 45)* **BURNING FROM THE INSIDE** [13] [ ]
– She's in parties / Antonin Artaud / King Volcano / Who killed Mr. Moonlight? / Slice of life / Honeymoon croon / Kingdom's coming / Burning from the inside / Hope. *(re-iss. Feb88 & Jul91 on 'Beggars Banquet-Lowdown' lp/c; BBL/+C 45) (cd-iss. Oct88 & Jul91 +=; BBL 45CD)* – Lagartija Nick / Departure / Here's the dub / The sanity assassin.

—— disbanded mid 1983. DAVID J. continued splinter solo venture before forming LOVE AND ROCKETS with DANIEL and KEVIN who had come from own outfit, TONES ON TAIL. MURPHY went solo (see below).

– compilations, others, etc. –

on 'Beggars Banquet' unless mentioned otherwise

Sep 83. (12"ep) *4 a.d.; (BAD 312)* **THE 4.A.D. SINGLES** [ ] [-]
– Dark entries / Terror couple kill colonel / Telegram Sam / Rosegarden full of sores / Crowds.

Oct 83. (12"ep) *(BEG 100E)* **THE SINGLES 1981-83** [52] [-]
– The passion of lovers / Kick in the eye / Spirit / Ziggy Stardust / Lagartija Nick / She's in parties. *(re-iss. Dec88 as 3"pic-cd; BBP 4CD)*

Nov 85. (d-lp/c) *(BEGA/BEGC 64)* **BAUHAUS 1979-1983** [36] [ ]
(d-cd-iss. Feb88; BEG 64CD) (re-iss. d-cd Sep95)

Jul 89. (d-lp/c)(d-cd) *(BEGA/BEGC 103)(BEGA 103CD) <9804>*
SWING THE HEARTACHE (the BBC sessions) [ ] [ ]
(re-iss. 2xcd Sep95; BBL 64 CD1/CD2)

Aug 98. (cd) *(BEGL 2018CD)* **CRACKLE (live)** [ ] [ ]
– Double dare / In the flat field / Passion of lovers / Bela Lugosi's dead / Sanity assassin / She's in parties / Silent hedges / Hollow hills / Mask / Kick in the eye / Ziggy stardust / Dark entries / Terror couple kill colonel / Spirit / Burning from the inside / Crowds.

Nov 99. (d-lp/d-cd) *KK; (KK 200/+CD)* **GOTHAM (live)** [ ] [ ]

BEASTIE BOYS

Formed: Greenwich Village, New York, USA . . . 1981 by ADAM YAUCH and MIKE DIAMOND. They recruited ADAM HOROWITZ to replace two others (KATE SCHELLENBACH and JOHN BERRY), and after two US indie releases they signed to 'Def Jam', the label run by The BEASTIE's friend and sometime DJ, RICK RUBIN. RUBIN paired with the BEASTIE BOYS was a match made in Heaven (or Hell, if you were unfortunate enough to own a Volkswagen) and the debut album 'LICENSED TO ILL' (1986) was the first real attempt to create a white, rock-centric take on of Afro-American Hip Hop. At turns hilarious and exhilarating, RUBIN and the BEASTIE's shared taste in classic metal was evident with samples from the likes of AC/DC and LED ZEPPELIN along with the theme tune from American TV show 'Mr. Ed'. With snotty rapping and riff-heavy rhymes, tracks like 'FIGHT FOR YOUR RIGHT (TO PARTY) and 'NO SLEEP TILL BROOKLYN' stormed the charts on both sides of the Atlantic, 'LICENSED TO ILL' becoming the fastest selling debut in Columbia's history. The record turned the band into a phenomenon and in 1987 they undertook a riotous headlining tour. Courting controversy wherever they played, the band were savaged by the press, a dispute with 'Def Jam' not helping matters any. Despite all the upheaval, by the release of 'PAUL'S BOUTIQUE' in 1989, the group's profile was negligible and the album was more or less passed over. A tragedy, as it remains one of hip hop's lost gems, a widescreen sampladelic collage produced by the ultra-hip DUST BROTHERS (US). Bypassing the obvious guitar riffs for samples of The BEATLES, CURTIS MAYFIELD and PINK FLOYD along with a kaleidoscopic array of cultural debris and hip references, the album was a funky tour de force. After another extended sabbatical during which the group relocated to California, the BEASTIE BOYS returned in 1992 with 'CHECK YOUR HEAD'. Hipness and attitude were still there in abundance but by now, the group were using live instrumentation. Despite veering from all out thrash to supple funk, the record was a success and only the BEASTIE BOYS could get away with a TED NUGENT collaboration ('THE BIZ VS THE NUGE'). 'ILL COMMUNICATION' (1994) developed this strategy to stunning effect. From the irresistible funk of 'SURE SHOT' and 'ROOT DOWN' to the laid back swing of 'GET IT TOGETHER' and 'FLUTE LOOP', this was the group's most mature and accomplished work to date. The hardcore was still there, 'TOUGH GUY' and 'HEART ATTACK MAN' but it was offset by the sombre strings of 'EUGENE'S LAMENT' and the mellow 'RICKY'S THEME'. A double A-side 'GET IT TOGETHER' and the screechingly brilliant 'SABOTAGE' (complete with entertaining cop-pastiche video) quite rightly returning them into the UK Top 20. From the artwork to the meditative feel of the music (well o.k., maybe not the punk numbers) it was no surprise that YAUCH had become a buddhist and the band subsequently played a high profile benefit for the oppressed nation of Tibet. Ever industrious, the group also started their own label and fanzine 'Grand Royal', signing the likes of LUSCIOUS JACKSON and the now "Big In Japan" BIS. Between development on their magnum-opus comeback (see below), The BEASTIE BOYS dabbled in more electronic/hardcore/instrumental tomfoolery via three mini-albums/EP's, 'ROOT DOWN' (1995), 'AGLIO E OLIO' (1995) and 'THE IN SOUND FROM WAY OUT!' (1996). 1998's 'INTERGALACTIC' single (along with bizarre Power-Rangers-esque video) led the way for the release of the eagerly-awaited 5th set proper, 'HELLO NASTY', an uncompromising, no-holds barred 23-track blinder. With reviews getting near perfect results it was inevitable that The BEASTIE's would have their first transatlantic chart-topper. The band had not lost their tongue-in-cheek attitude despite their recent shifts to a more harmonic religion. Such examples of this would be UK hit singles, 'BODY MOVIN' and 'REMOTE CONTROL', which would also turn up on double-CD anthology 'THE SOUNDS OF SCIENCE' (1999). • **Songwriters:** Although they released few cover versions, they sampled many songs (see above). In 1992, they covered JIMMY JAMES (Jimi Hendrix) + TIME FOR LIVIN' (Stewart Frontline), also collaborating with NISHITA. • **Trivia:** ADAM HOROWITZ is the son of playwrite ISRAEL. HOROWITZ played a cameo role in TV serial 'The Equalizer' (circa '88).

Album rating: LICENSED TO 'ILL (*8) / PAUL'S BOUTIQUE (*7) / CHECK YOUR HEAD (*7) / ILL: COMMUNICATION (*9) / HELLO NASTY (*9) / THE SOUNDS OF SCIENCE compilation (*8)

'MCA' ADAM YAUCH (b. 5 Aug'65, Brooklyn, New York) – vocals / **'MIKE D' MIKE DIAMOND** (b.20 Nov'66, New York) – vocals / **KATE SCHELLENBACH** (b. 5 Jan'66, New York City) – drums / **JOHN BERRY** – guitar

Ratcage Ratcage

Nov 82. (7"ep) *<(MOTR 21)>* **POLLY WOG STEW EP** [ ] [ ]
– B.E.A.S.T.I.E. boys / Transit cop / Jimi / Holy snappers / Riot fight / Ode to . . . / Michelle's farm / Egg raid on mojo. *(UK-iss.Apr88 12"/c-s; same) (re-iss. 12"ep/c-ep/cd-ep Feb93; same)*

—— **KIND AD-ROCK – ADAM HOROWITZ** (b.31 Oct'67, New York City) – vocals, guitar (ex-The YOUNG & THE USELESS) repl.BERRY + SCHELLENBACH (she later joined LUSCIOUS JACKSON)

Aug 83. (7") *<MOTR 26>* **COOKY PUSS. / BEASTIE REVOLUTION** [-] [ ]
(UK-iss.Jan85 + Jul87; MOTR 26 C/CD) (cd-ep-iss.Dec87; same) (re-issues +=) – Bonus batter / Cooky puss (censored version). *(re-iss. 12"ep/c-ep/cd-ep Feb93; same)*

—— added guest RICK RUBIN – scratcher, DJ

Def Jam Def Jam

Dec 85. (12"ep; w-drawn) *<002>* **ROCK HARD / BEASTIE GROOVE. / THE PARTY'S GETTING ROUGH / BEASTIE GROOVE (instrumental)** [-] [-]

Jan 86. (7"/12") *(A/TA 6686) <05683>* **SHE'S ON IT. / SLOW AND LOW** [ ] [ ]

May 86. (7"/12") *(A/TA 7055) <05864>* **HOLD IT NOW, HIT IT. / ACAPULCO (Hold it now, hit it acapella)** [ ] [ ]

Sep 86. (7") *(650 114-7)* **SHE'S ON IT. / SLOW AND LOW** [ ] [-]
(12"+=) *(650 114-6)* – Hold it now, hit it.

Nov 86. (7") *(650 169-7) <06341>* **IT'S THE NEW STYLE. / PAUL REVERE** [ ] [-]
(12"+=) *(650 169-6)* – ('A'&'B'instrumentals).
(d12"+=) *(650 169-8)* – Hold it now, hit it / Hold it now, hit it (Acapulco version) / Hold it now, hit it (instrumental).

Nov 86. (lp/c/cd) *(450 062-1/-4/-2) <40238>* **LICENSED TO 'ILL** [7] [1]
– Rhymin and stealin' / The new style / She's crafty / Posse in effect / Slow ride / Girls / (You gotta) Fight for your right (to party) / No sleep till Brooklyn / Paul Revere / Hold it now, hit it / Brass monkey / Slow and low / Time to get ill. *(re-iss. Nov89 on 'Capitol'; 460 949-1) (re-iss. Jun94 cd/c; 460 949-2/-4) (cd re-iss. Jul95 & Nov99; 527351-2)*

Dec 86. (7") *<06595>* **(YOU GOTTA) FIGHT FOR YOUR RIGHT (TO PARTY). / PAUL REVERE** [-] [7]

Feb 87. (7") *(650 418-7)* **(YOU GOTTA) FIGHT FOR YOUR RIGHT (TO PARTY). / TIME TO GET ILL** [11] [-]
(12"+=) *(650 418-6)* – No sleep till Brooklyn.

Apr 87. (7") *<06675>* **NO SLEEP TILL BROOKLYN. / SHE'S CRAFTY** [-] [ ]

May 87. (7"/7"sha-pic-d) *(BEAST/+P 1)* **NO SLEEP TILL BROOKLYN. / POSSE IN EFFECT** [14] [-]
(12"+=) *(BEASTT 1)* – Hold it now, hit it / Brass monkey.

Jul 87. (7"/7"s/7"s) *(BEAST/+B/D 2)* **SHE'S ON IT. / SLOW AND LOW** [10] [-]
(12"+=) *(BEASTT 2)* – Hold it now, hit it.

Sep 87. (7"/7"s/7"s/7"s/10"sha-pic-d) *(BEAST/+P/S/Q/W 3)* **GIRLS. / SHE'S CRAFTY** [34] [-]
(12"+=/12"s+=) *(BEASTT/+Q 3)* – Rock hard.

Mar 88. (7") *<07020>* **BRASS MONKEY. / POSSE IN EFFECT** [-] [48]

—— no more RICK RUBIN as DJ

Capitol Capitol

Jul 89. (7") *(CL 540) <44454>* **HEY LADIES. / SHAKE YOUR RUMP** [ ] [36]
(12"ep+=/cd-ep+=) *(12/CD CL 540)* **LOVE AMERICAN STYLE** – 33% God / Dis yourself in '89 (just do it). *(re-iss. Jul98 on 'Grand Royal'; GR 064)*

Jul 89. (cd/c/lp) *(DE/TC+/EST 2102) <91743>* **PAUL'S BOUTIQUE** [44] [14]
– To all the girls / Shake your rump / Johnny Ryall / Egg man / High plains drifter / The sound of science / 3-minute rule / Hey ladies / 5-piece chicken dinner / Looking down the barrel of a gun / Car thief / What comes around / Shadrach / Ask for Janice / B-boy bouillabaisse:- (a) 59 Chrystie Street, (b) Get on the mic, (c) Stop that train, (d) A year and a day, (e) Hello Brooklyn, (f) Dropping names, (g) Lay it on me, (h) Mike on the mic, (i) A.W.O.L.

Aug 89. (12"ep) *<Y 15523>* **AN EXCITING EVENING AT HOME WITH SHADRACH, MESHACH AND ABEDNEGO EP** [-] [ ]
– Shadrach / Caught in the middle of a 3-way mix / And what you give is what you get / Car thief / Some dumb cop gave me two tickets already / Your sister's def.

—— Trio now also on instruments; **MCA** – bass / **AD ROCK** – keyboards / **MIKE D** – drums

Apr 92. (c-s/7") *(TC+/CL 653)* **PASS THE MIC. / PROFESSOR BOOTY** [47] [ ]
(etched-12"+=/c-s+=) *(12CL/TCCLX 653)* – Time for livin' / Drunken Praying Mantis style.
(cd-s) *(CDCL 653)* – ('A'side) / Netty's girl / Something's got to give / ('A'-pt.2 – The skills to pay the bills).

May 92. (cd/c/d-lp) *(CD/TC+/EST 2171) <98938>* **CHECK YOUR HEAD** [ ] [10]
– Jimmy James / Funky boss / Pass the mic / Gratitude / Lighten up / Finger lickin' good / So what 'cha want / The biz .vs. the Nuge (with TED NUGENT) / Time for livin' / Something's got to give / The blue nun / Stand together / Pow / The maestro / Groove Holmes / Live at P.J.'s / Mark on the bus / Professor Booty / In 3's / Namaste. *(re-iss. Sep94; CDP 798938-2/-4) (d-lp re-iss. Nov98; GR 066)*

May 92. (12"ep/c-ep/cd-ep) *<Y/4Y/C2 15836>* **JIMMY JAMES / THE MAESTRO / JIMMY JAMES (album version) / BOOMIN' GRANNY / JIMMY JAMES (original) / DRINKIN' WINE** [-] [ ]

Jun 92. (12"ep/12"white-ep/c-ep) *(12CL 665)* **FROZEN METAL HEAD EP** [55] [-]
– Jimmy James / So what'cha want (All the way live freestyle version) / Jimmy James (original) / Drinkin' wine.
(cd-ep) *(CDCL 665)* – The blue nun *[repl. original]*

Jun 92. (cd-ep) *<15847>* **SO WHAT'CHA WANT (3 versions; including pt.2 – The Skills to pay the bills) / GROOVE HOLMES (2 versions)** [-] [93]

Dec 92. (12"ep/cd-ep) *<Y/C2 07777>* **GRATITUDE EP** [-] [ ]
– Gratitude / Stand together (live) / Finger lickin' good (remix) / Gratitude (live) / Honkey rink.

Capitol / Grand Royal

May 94. (cd/c/d-lp) *(CD/TC+/EST 2229) <28599>* **ILL: COMMUNICATION** [10] [1]
– Sure shot / Tough guy / Freak freak / Bobo on the corner / Root down / Sabotage / Get it together / Sabrosa / The update / Futterman's rule / Alright hear this / Eugene's lament / Flute loop / Do it / Rick's theme / Heart attack man / The scoop / Shambala / Bodhisattva vow / Transitions. *(lp re-iss. Apr97 on 'Grand Royal'; GR 006LP)*

Jul 94. (c-s/7"green) *(TC+/CL 716)* **GET IT TOGETHER. / SABOTAGE / DOPE LITTLE SONG** [19] [ ]
(10") *(10CL 716)* – (first 2 tracks) / ('A'-Buck Wild remix) / ('A'instrumental).
(cd-s) *(CDCL 716)* – (first 2 tracks) / ('A'-A.B.A. remix) / Resolution time.

Nov 94. (7"maroon) *(CL 726)* **SURE SHOT. / MULLET HEAD / SURE SHOT (Mario mix)** [27] [ ]
(10"+=) *(10CL 726)* – The vibes.
(cd-s+=) *(CDCLS 726)* – Son of neck bone.
(cd-s) *(CDCL 726)* – ('A'mixes:- Pruins – European B-Boy / Nardone / Large Professor / instrumental).

Jun 95. (m-cd/m-c/m-lp) *(CD/TC+/EST 2262) <33603>* **ROOT DOWN EP** (some live) [23] [50]
– Root down (free zone mix) / Root down / Root down (PP balloon mix) / Time to get ill / Heart attack man / The maestro / Sabrosa / Flute loop / Time for livin' / Something's got to give / So what'cha want. *(m-lp-iss.Apr97 on 'Grand Royal'; GR 018)*

Dec 95. (12"ep/cd-ep) *<GR 026/+CD>* **AGLIO E OLIO** (11 minutes of hardcore) [-] [ ]
– Brand new / Deal with me / Believe me / Nervous assistant / Square wave in unison / You catch a bad one / I can't think straight / I want some. *(UK-iss.Mar98; same)*

—— added guest co-writers **(MONEY) MARK RAMOS NISHITA** – claviers / **ERIC BOBO** – percussion / **EUGENE GORE** – violin

Mar 96. (cd/c) *(CD/TC EST 2281) <7243 8 33590-2/-4>* **THE IN SOUND FROM WAY OUT!** (instrumental) [45] [45]
– Groove Holmes / Sabrosa / Namaste / Pow / Son of neckbone / In 3's / Eugene's lament / Bobo on the corner / Shambala / Lighten up / Ricky's theme / Transitions / Drinkin' wine. *(lp re-iss. Jan99 on 'Grand Royal'; GRA 80013)*

Jun 98. (c-s) *(TCCL 803) <58705>* **INTERGALACTIC / HAIL SAGAN (Special K)** [5] [28] Jul98
(cd-s+=) *(CDCL 803)* – ('A'-Prisoners Of Technology TMSI remix).
(10") *(10CL 803)* – ('A'side) / ('A'-Prisoners Of . . . remix).

Jul 98. (cd/d-lp) *(495723-2/-4/-1) <37716>* **HELLO NASTY** [1] [1]
– Super disco breakin' / The move / Remote control / Song for the man / Just a test / Body movin' / Intergalactic / Sneakin' out of hospital / Putting shame in your game / Flowin' prose / And me / Three MC's and one DJ / Can't, won't, don't stop / Song for Junior / I don't know / The negotiation Limerick file / Electrify / Picture this / Unite / Dedication / Dr. Lee PhD / Instant death.

Oct 98. (cd-s) *(CDCLS 809)* **BODY MOVIN' / (Mickey Finn mix) / DR. LEE phD (dub mix)** [15] [ ]
(cd-s) *(CDCL 809)* – ('A'side) / (Fatboy Slim remix) / (Peanut butter and jelly mix).
(12") *(12CL 809)* – ('A'side) / (Kut Masta Kurt remix) / (Erick Sermon remix) / (instrumental).
(re-iss. /re-mixed May99; GR 069/063)

May 99. (12"/cd-s) *(12CL/CDCLS 812)* **REMOTE CONTROL / THREE MC'S AND ONE DJ / THE NEGOTIATION LIMERICK FILE (Ganja Kru – or – the 41 Small Star remix)** [21] [ ]
(cd-s) *(CDCL 812)* – ('A'side) / Three MC's and one DJ (live video version) / Putting shame in your game (mix) / Three MC's and one DJ (enhanced video).

Aug 99. (12"ep) *<(GR 071)>* **SCIENTIST OF SOUND** [ ] [ ]
– Negotiation Limerick file (mixes) / Intergalactic / Three MC's and one DJ / Body movin' (mixes) / Putting shame in your game.

Nov 99. (d-cd/d-c) *(522940-2/-4) <22940>* **THE SOUNDS OF SCIENCE** (compilation) [36] [19]
– Beastie Boys / Slow and low / Shake your rump / Gratitude / Skills to pay the bills / Root down / Believe me / Sure shot / Body movin' / Boomin' granny / (You gotta) Fight for your right (to party) / Country Mike's theme / Pass the mic / Something's got to give / Bodhisattva vow / Sabrosa / Song for the man / Soba violence / Alive / Jimmy James / Three MC's and one DJ / Biz vs. the Nuge / Sabotage / Shadrach / Brass monkey / Time for livin' / Dub the mic / Benny and the jets / Negotion limerick file / I want some / She's on it / Son of neckbone / Get it together / Twenty questions / Remote control / Railroad blues / Live wire / So what'cha want / Netty's girl / Egg raid on mojo / Hey ladies / Intergalactic.

Dec 99. (10") *(10CL 818)* **ALIVE / START! / ALIVE (B.R.A. remix)** [28] [ ]
(cd-s+=) *(CDCLS 818)* – Start! (video).
(cd-s) *(CDCL 818)* – ('A'side) / You and me together / Big shot (live) / ('A'-video).

– compilations, etc. –

Feb 94. (cd/c) *Honey World; (CD/TC EST 2225) / Grand Royal; <89843>* **SOME OLD BULLSHIT** [ ] [46]
– (compilation of 1st 2 EP's) *(re-iss. Jan99; same)*

Jeff BECK

Born: 24 Jun'44, Surrey, England. His solo career began in earnest at the start of '67, BECK having successfully filled the shoes of ERIC CLAPTON in The YARDBIRDS over the preceding two years. Under the wing of pop maestro MICKIE MOST, he scored an immediate UK hit with the anthemic 'HI HO SILVER LINING'. Two further commercial pop-rock numbers, 'TALLYMAN' and 'LOVE IS BLUE' signalled the end of BECK's brief chart liason, also terminating his period with MOST. With blues-rock back in vogue, the axeman steered a course back into heavier territory, forming The JEFF BECK GROUP alongside old cohorts, ROD STEWART (vocals), RON WOOD (guitar), NICKY HOPKINS (piano) and MICKY WALLER (drums). The resulting two albums, 'TRUTH' (1968) and 'BECK-OLA' (1969), established BECK and co. as a major UK export across the Atlantic, both sets making the US Top 20. With ROD STEWART striking out his own, BECK turned to the unlikely source of hippy-dippy popster DONOVAN, who combined with the group on the summer '69 single, 'GOO GOO BARABAJAGAL'. In the early 70's, The JEFF BECK GROUP was re-modelled around newcomers COZY POWELL (drums) and BOBBY TENCH (vocals), the resulting two albums both making US Top 50 placings. With the country's top guitarist, ERIC CLAPTON, now partially sidelined, BECK took the opportunity to form his own supergroup, BECK, BOGART & APPICE. However, after only one album with the former VANILLA FUDGE heavyweights, BECK resumed a solo career. In the mid 70's he returned to form with the highly successful 'BLOW BY BLOW' opus, regarded by many as his finest hour. Along with many in the rock fraternity, BECK subsequently veered towards jazz-fusion, collaborating with JAN HAMMER on two albums, 'WIRED' (1976) and 'LIVE' (1977). After going to ground for a few years, BECK was 'THERE AND BACK' in the early 80's, although he spent the same amount of time recording his follow-up set, 'FLASH' (1985). This featured a belated reunion with old mucker, ROD STEWART, on the collaborative hit 45, 'PEOPLE GET READY'. After working with MICK JAGGER on his 1987 album, 'Primitive Cool', BECK returned in '89 with his 'GUITAR SHOP' project/album. In the early 90's, he collaborated (yet again!), this time with blues legend, BUDDY GUY, on a superb interpretation of the standard soul/blues classic, 'MUSTANG SALLY'. JEFF showcased yet another dimension to his talent when he recorded a 1993 GENE VINCENT tribute album, 'CRAZY LEGS', with his BIG TOWN PLAYBOYS. A six-year long wait resulted in 1999's 'WHO ELSE!', minor chart positions on both sides of the Atlantic reminding us that in some quarters the man has not been forgotten. Come the new millennium, BECK once again illustrated his instinctive ability to absorb outside influences and adapt his talents to the prevailing musical climate. Thus the digitised beats and bleeps of 'YOU HAD IT COMING' (2001) where the veteran guitarist places his six-string talents in a surprisingly effective contemporary setting. A departure from his familiar sound but an admirable attempt to get to grips with new technology. • **Songwriters:** BECK with covers being; HI HO SILVER LINING (Scott English & Larry Weiss) / TALLYMAN (Graham Gouldman) / ALL SHOOK UP + JAILHOUSE ROCK (Leiber – Stoller) / I'VE BEEN DRINKIN' (D.Tauber & J.Mercer) / I AIN'T SUPERSTITIOUS (Willie Dixon) / MORNING DEW (Tim Rose) / SUPERSTITIOUS + CAUSE WE'VE ENDED AS LOVERS (Stevie Wonder) / GREENSLEEVES (trad.) / OL' MAN RIVER ('Showboat' musical) / GOODBYE PORK PIE HAT (Charlie Mingus) / SHE'S A WOMAN (Beatles) / STAR CYCLE (Jan Hammer) / WILD THING (Troggs) / etc. • **Trivia:** His song 'STAR CYCLE' (written by band members Hymas & Philips), became theme tune for 'The Tube' in 1983.

Album rating: TRUTH (*6) / BECK-OLA (*6) / ROUGH AND READY (*7) / BLOW BY BLOW (*6) / WIRED (*5) / JEFF BECK WITH THE JAN HAMMER GROUP LIVE (*4) / THERE AND BACK (*5) / FLASH (*4) / JEFF BECK'S GUITAR SHOP (*6) / THE BEST OF BECKOLOGY compilation (*7) / CRAZY LEGS (*4) / UP (*4) / WHO ELSE! (*5) / YOU HAD IT COMING (*5)

JEFF BECK (solo) – vocals, lead guitar (ex-YARDBIRDS) with **JET HARRIS** – bass (ex-SHADOWS) / **VIV PRINCE** – drums (ex-PRETTY THINGS)

Columbia / Epic

Mar 67. (7") *(DB 8151) <10157>* **HI-HO SILVER LINING. / BECK'S BOLERO** [14] [ ]

—— **RAY COOK** – drums repl. PRINCE

Jul 67. (7") *(DB 8227)* **TALLYMAN. / ROCK MY PLIMSOUL** [30] [-]
Feb 68. (7") *(DB 8359)* **LOVE IS BLUE. / I'VE BEEN DRINKING** [23] [-]

JEFF BECK GROUP

— with **ROD STEWART** – vocals (also a solo artist, who sang on BECK's last 'B'side) / **RON WOOD** – bass (ex BIRDS) / **MICKY WALLER** (b. 6 Sep'44) – drums / **NICKY HOPKINS** – keyboards

Jul 68. (lp; stereo/mono) *(S+/CX 6293) <26413>* **TRUTH** [ ] [15]
– Shapes of things / Let me love you / Morning dew / You shook me / Ol' man river / Greensleeves / Rock my plimsoul / Beck's bolero / Blues de luxe / I ain't superstitious. *(re-iss. 1985 lp/c; ATAK/TC-ATAK 42) (re-iss. Jun86 on 'Fame' lp/c; FA/TC-FA 3155)*

— **TONY NEWMAN** – drums repl. WALLER

— (mid'69) The JEFF BECK GROUP teamed up with ⇒ DONOVAN, on their joint hit GOO GOO BARABAJAGAL (LOVE IS HOT). (see ⇒ DONOVAN)

Jul 69. (lp) *(SCX 6351) <26478>* **BECK-OLA** [39] [15]
– All shook up / Spanish boots / Girl from Mill Valley / Jailhouse rock / Plynth (water down the drain) / The hangman's knee / Rice pudding. *(re-iss. Jul85 on 'Capitol' lp/c; ED 260600-1/-4)*

Sep 69. (7"; w-drawn) *(DB 8590)* **PLYNTH (WATER DOWN THE DRAIN). / HANGMAN'S KNEE** [-] [-]

— split (Sep'69) when ROD STEWART and RON WOOD joined The FACES.

JEFF BECK GROUP reformed (Apr'71) with **JEFF BECK** – guitar (only) plus **BOBBY TENCH** – vocals / **MAX MIDDLETON** – keyboards / **CLIVE CHAPMAN** – bass / **COZY POWELL** – drums (ex-BIG BERTHA, ex-ACE KEFFORD STAND, ex-SORCERORS)

Epic Epic

Oct 71. (lp/c) *(EPC/40 64619) <30973>* **ROUGH AND READY** [ ] [46]
– Got the feeling / Situation / Short business / Max's tune / I've been used / New ways – Train train / Jody. *(re-iss. Aug84 lp/c; EPC/40 32037) (quad-lp 1974; Q 64619) (cd-iss. 1990; 471047-2)*

Jan 72. (7") *(EPC 7720) <10814>* **GOT THE FEELING. / SITUATION** [ ] [ ]

Jul 72. (lp/c) *(EPC/40 64899) <31331>* **JEFF BECK GROUP** [ ] [19] May72
– Ice cream cakes / Glad all over / Tonight I'll be staying here with you / Sugar cane / I can't give back the love I feel for you / Going down / I got to have a song / Highways / Definitely maybe. *(quad-lp 1974 on 'C.B.S.'; Q 31331) (cd-iss. 1990; 471047-2)*

Aug 72. (7") *<10938>* **DEFINITELY MAYBE. / HI HO SILVER LINING** [-] [ ]

— Broke-up when COZY POWELL went solo & joined BEDLAM. Later to RAINBOW, etc. TENCH joined STREETWALKERS then VAN MORRISON. **JEFF** formed supergroup

BECK, BOGERT, APPICE

— with **TIM BOGERT** – bass, vocals / **CARMINE APPICE** – drums (both ex-VANILLA FUDGE, etc.) plus **DUANE HITCHINS** – keyboards / **JIMMY GREENSPOON** – piano / **DANNY HUTTON** – vox

Mar 73. (7") *(EPC 1251)* **BLACK CAT MOAN. / LIVIN' ALONE** [ ] [-]

Apr 73. (7") *<11027>* **LADY. / OH TO LOVE YOU** [-] [ ]

Jul 73. (7") *<10998>* **I'M SO PROUD. / OH TO LOVE YOU** [-] [ ]

Apr 73. (lp/c) *(EPC/40 65455) <32140>* **BECK, BOGERT, APPICE** [28] [12]
– Black cat moan / Lady / Oh to love you / Superstition / Sweet sweet surrender / Why should I care / Love myself with you / Livin' alone / I'm so proud. *(re-iss. Sep84 lp/c; EPC/40 32491) (re-iss. Nov89 on 'Essential' lp/c/cd; ESS LP/MC/CD 011) (quad-lp 1975 on 'C.B.S.'; Q 65455)*

— This trio, also released widely available (JAP-import Nov74 d-lp) LIVE IN JAPAN

JEFF BECK

— group reformed as instrumental line-up, **BECK + MIDDLETON / PHILIP CHEN** – bass / **RICHARD BAILEY** – drums

Mar 75. (lp/c) *(EPC/40 69117) <33409>* **BLOW BY BLOW** [ ] [4]
– It doesn't really matter / You know what I mean / She's a woman / Constipated duck / Air blower / Scatterbrain / Cause we've ended as lovers / Thelonius / Freeway jam / Diamond dust. *(re-iss. Sep83 lp/c; EPC/40 32367) (re-iss. May94 & Nov95 & Sep99 cd/c; 469012-2/-4)*

May 75. (7") *(EPC 3334)* **SHE'S A WOMAN. / IT DOESN'T REALLY MATTER** [ ] [-]

Jun 75. (7") *<50112>* **CONSTIPATED DUCK. / YOU KNOW WHAT I MEAN** [-] [ ]

— **JAN HAMMER** (b.1950, Prague, Czechoslavakia) – drums, synthesizer / **MICHAEL NARADA WALDEN** – keyboards, drums (both ex-MAHAVISHNU ORCHESTRA) / **WILBUR BASCOMBE** – bass (all 3 replaced CHEN)

Jul 76. (lp/c) *(EPC/40 86012) <33849>* **WIRED** [38] [16] Jun76
– Led boots / Come dancing / Goodbye pork pie hat / Head for backstage pass / Blue wind / Sophie / Play with me / Love is green. *(re-iss. Mar82 lp/c; EPC/40 32067) (cd-iss. 1988; CD 86012)*

Aug 76. (7") *<50276>* **COME DANCING. / HEAD FOR BACKSTAGE PASS** [-] [ ]

— **(BECK, HAMMER)** plus **TONY SMITH** – drums / **FERNANDO SAUNDERS** – bass / **STEVE KINDLER** – violin, synth.

Mar 77. (lp/c) *(EPC/40 86025) <34433>* **LIVE . . . WITH THE JAN HAMMER GROUP (live)** [ ] [23]
– Freeway jam / Earth (still our only home) / She's a woman / Full Moon boogie / Darkness – Earth in search of a sun / Scatterbrain / Blue wind. *(re-iss. Jun85 lp/c; EPC/40 32297)*

— with **TONY HYMAS** – keyboards / **MO FOSTER** – bass / **SIMON PHILLIPS** – drums

Jul 80. (lp/c) *(EPC/40 83288) <35684>* **THERE AND BACK** [38] [21]
– Star cycle / Too much to lose / You never know / The pump / El Becko / The golden road / Space boogie / The final peace. *(re-iss. Aug84 lp/c; EPC/40 32197) (cd-iss. Jan89; CD 83288)*

Jul 80. (7") *(EPC 8806)* **THE FINAL PEACE. / SPACE BOOGIE** [ ] [-]

Aug 80. (7") *<50914>* **THE FINAL PEACE. / TOO MUCH TO LOSE** [-] [ ]

Feb 81. (12"ep) *(EPCA 1009)* **THE FINAL PEACE / SCATTERBRAIN. / TOO MUCH TO LOSE / LED BOOTS** [ ] [-]

— retired from the studio for half a decade, before returning 1985 with **HAMMER, APPICE, HYMAS** and **JIMMY HALL** – vocals

Jun 85. (7") *(EPCA 6387) <05416>* **PEOPLE GET READY. / BACK ON THE STREET** [ ] [48]
(12"+=) *(TA 6387)* – You know, we know.
(above single featured ROD STEWART on vox)

Jul 85. (lp/c) *(EPC/40 26112) <39483>* **FLASH** [83] [39]
– Ambitious / Gets us all in the end / Escape / People get ready / Stop, look and listen / Get workin' / Ecstasy / Night after night / You know, we know. *(re-iss. Jan89; CD 26112) (re-iss. Mar94 on 'Pickwick' cd/c; 982838-2/-4)*

Sep 85. (7") *<05595>* **GETS US ALL IN THE END. / YOU KNOW, WE KNOW** [-] [ ]

Sep 85. (7") *(EPCA 6587)* **STOP, LOOK AND LISTEN. / YOU KNOW, WE KNOW** [ ] [-]
(12"+=) *(TA 6587)* – ('A'remix).

Mar 86. (7"/12") *(EPCA/TA 6981)* **AMBITIOUS. / ESCAPE** [ ] [ ]

Jul 86. (7") *(EPCA 7271)* **WILD THING. / GETS US ALL IN THE END** [ ] [ ]
(12"+=) *(TA 7271)* – Nighthawks.

— In 1987, BECK went to session with MICK JAGGER on his 2nd album.

Oct 89. (lp/c/cd; JEFF BECK with TERRY BOZZIO & TONY HYMAS) *(463472-1/-4/-2) <44313>* **JEFF BECK'S GUITAR SHOP** [ ] [49]
– Guitar shop / Savoy / Behind the veil / Big block / Where were you / Stand on it / Day in the house / Two rivers / Sling shot.

Oct 89. (7") *(BECK 1)* **DAY IN THE HOUSE. / PEOPLE GET READY** [ ] [ ]
(cd-s+=) *(BECK 1CD)* – Cause we've ended as lovers / Blue wind.
(12") *(BECK 1T)* – ('A'side) / Guitar shop (guitar mix) / Cause we've ended as lovers.

— In 1990, sessioned for JON BON JOVI on his BLAZE OF GLORY album.

— In Sep'91 JEFF collaborated with BUDDY GUY on a single 'MUSTANG SALLY' on 'Silvertone'.

— now with **MIKE SANCHEZ** – vocals, piano / **IAN JENNINGS** – bass, vocals / **ADRIAN UTLEY** – rhythm guitar / **CLIVE DENVER** – drums, vocals / **LEO GREEN** – tenor sax / **NICK HUNT** – baritone sax

Jun 93. (cd/c/lp; as JEFF BECK & THE BIG TOWN PLAYBOYS) *(473597-2/-4/-1) <53562>* **CRAZY LEGS** [ ] [ ]
– Race with the devil / Cruisin' / Crazy legs / Double talkin' baby / Woman love / Lotta lovin' / Catman / Pink thunderbird / Baby blue / You better believe / Who slapped John? / Say mama / Red blue jeans and a pony tail / Five feet of lovin' / B-i-bickey-bi-bo-bo-go / Blues stay away from me / Pretty, pretty baby / Hold me, hug me, rock me.
(above was a tribute to GENE VINCENT & HIS BLUE CAPS)

— 1999 with **TONY HYMAS** – keyboards, co-producer / **JENNIFER BATTEN** – guitars / **RANDY HOPE-TAYLOR – bass / STEVE ALEXANDER** – drums

Columbia Epic

Mar 99. (cd/c) *(493041-2/-4) <67987>* **WHO ELSE!** [74] [99]
– What mama said / Psycho Sam / Brush with the blues / Blast from the east / Space for the papa / Angel (footsteps) / THX138 / Hip-notica / Even odds / Declan / Another place. *(cd re-iss. Jan01; same)*

Feb 01. (cd) *(501018-2) <61625>* **YOU HAD IT COMING** [ ] [ ]
– Earthquake / Roy's toy / Dirty mind / Rollin' and tumblin' / Badia / Loose cannon / Rosebud / Left hook / Blackbird / Suspension.

– compilations, others, etc. –

1969. (lp) *Music For Pleasure; (MFP 5219)* **THE MOST OF JEFF BECK** [ ] [-]

Oct 72. (7"m) *RAK; (RR 3)* **HI HO SILVER LINING. / BECK'S BOLERO / ROCK MY PLIMSOUL** [14] [-]
(re-iss. Oct82 7"pic-d/12"; RRP/12RR 3) ; hit No.62.

Apr 73. (7"m; JEFF BECK AND ROD STEWART) *RAK; (RR 4)* **I'VE BEEN DRINKING. / MORNING DEW / GREENSLEEVES** [ ] [-]

Nov 77. (lp) *Embassy-CBS; (31546)* **GOT THE FEELING** [ ] [-]

Feb 83. (d-c) *Epic;* **BLOW BY BLOW / WIRED** [ ] [-]

May 85. (lp/c) *Fame; (FA 413125-1/-4)* **THE BEST OF JEFF BECK featuring ROD STEWART** [ ] [-]
(re-iss. Dec95 on 'Music For Pleasure' cd/c; CD/TC MFP 6202) <US cd-iss. Jul98 on 'E.M.I.'; 53595>

1985. (d-lp) *Epic; (EPC 461009-1)* **WIRED / FLASH** [ ] [-]

Sep 88. (cd) *E.M.I.; (CDP 746710-2)* **LATE 60's WITH ROD STEWART** [ ] [-]

May 89. (d-lp/d-c/d-cd) *That's Original; (TFO LP/MC/CD 19)* **JEFF BECK GROUP / ROUGH & READY** [ ] [-]

Feb 91. (cd)(c) *E.M.I.; (CZ 374)(TCEMS 1379)* **TRUTH / BECK-OLA** [ ] [-]

Feb 92. (7"/c-s; by JEFF BECK & ROD STEWART) *Epic; (657756-7/-4)* **PEOPLE GET READY. / TRAIN KEPT A ROLLIN'** [49] [-]
(cd-s) *(657756-2)* – ('A'side) / Cause we've ended as lovers / Where were you.
(cd-s) *(657756-5)* – ('A'side) / Train train / New ways.

Feb 92. (3xcd/3xc;box) *Epic; (469262-2/-4) <48661>* **BECKOLOGY** [ ] [ ]
(re-iss. May94 & Apr98; same)

Mar 92. (cd/c/lp) *Epic; (471348-2/-4/-1) <64689>* **THE BEST OF BECKOLOGY** [ ] [ ] Aug95
– Heart full of soul (YARDBIRDS) / Shapes of things (YARDBIRDS) / Over under sideways down (YARDBIRDS) / Hi ho silver lining / Tallyman / Jailhouse rock / I've been drinking / I ain't superstitious / Superstition (BECK, BOGART & APPICE) / Cause we've ended as lovers / The pump / Star cycle (theme from 'The Tube') / People get ready (with ROD STEWART) / Wild thing / Where were you (w/ TERRY BOZZIO & TONY HYMAS) / Trouble in mind (TRIDENTS).

Mar 93. (3xcd-box) *Epic; (468802-2) <64808>* **FLASH / BLOW BY BLOW / THERE & BACK** [ ] [ ] Oct95

Jul 94. (cd) *Wisepack; (LECD 080)* **LEGENDS IN MUSIC** [ ] [-]

— ('Wisepack' also issued another collection Aug95, with some tracks by ERIC CLAPTON; *LECDD 639)*

Oct 94. (cd) *Charly; (CDCD 1186)* **SHAPES OF THINGS** [ ] [-]

Oct 96. (cd) *EMI Gold; (CDGOLD 1060)* **THE BEST OF JEFF BECK** [ ] [-]

Apr 98. (cd) *Hallmark; (30858-2)* **GUITAR LEGENDS** [ ] [-]
(re-iss. Feb01 on 'EMI Plus'; 576228-2)

May 98. (cd) *EMI-Capitol; <32983>* **SHAPES OF THINGS** [-] [ ]

Aug 99. (cd) *Dressed To Kill; (RECD 130)* **JEFF BECK** [ ] [-]

Jason BECKER (see under ⇒ CACOPHONY)

BEDLAM

Formed: out of BIG BERTHA, by The BALL's (that is, brothers DAVE and DENNIS BALL). The pair returned late in 1972 as BEAST, alongside COZY POWELL and new singer FRANK AIELLO. This name was discarded in May '73 for the slightly less savage, BEDLAM. An eponymous hard-rock album was soon in the shops, although it was clear COZY wanted to be in the limelight, the drummer subsequently going on to have three solo hit singles over the next year.

Album rating: BEDLAM (*5)

ACE KEFFORD STAND

ACE KEFFORD – vocals (ex-MOVE) / **DAVE BALL** – guitar / **DENNIS BALL** – bass / **COZY POWELL** – drums (ex-SORCERERS)

Atlantic Atlantic

Mar 69. (7") *(584 260)* **FOR YOUR LOVE. / GRAVY BOOBY JAMM** [ ] [ ]

— COZY joined YOUNGBLOOD (aka ex-SORCERERS) after brief spell with below.

BIG BERTHA

DAVE McTAVISH – vocals repl. PETE FRENCH who joined ATOMIC ROOSTER

MAC POOLE – drums repl.COZY

Atlantic Atlantic

Aug 69. (7") *(584 298)* **THIS WORLD'S AN APPLE. / GRAVY BOOBY JAM (w/ ACE KEFFORD)** [ ] [ ]

— split after above. DAVE BALL joined PROCOL HARUM, while DENNIS backed singer LONG JOHN BALDRY.

BEDLAM

FRANK AIELLO – vocals / **DAVE BALL** – guitar / **DENNIS BALL** – bass / **COZY POWELL** – drums

Chrysalis Chrysalis

Aug 73. (lp) *(CHR 1048)* **BEDLAM** [ ] [ ]
– I believe in you (fire in my body) / Hot lips / Sarah / Sweet sister Mary / Seven long years / The beast / Whiskey and wine / Looking through love's eyes (busy dreamin') / Putting on the flesh / Set me free. *(re-iss. Jun85 on 'Metal Masters'; METALP 104) (cd-iss. Jun99 on 'Zoom Club'; ZCRCD 8)*

Sep 73. (7") *(CFB 1)* **I BELIEVE IN YOU (FIRE IN MY BODY). / WHISKEY AND WINE** [ ] [-]

— disbanded after above when COZY had already gone solo

– compilations, etc. –

Nov 99. (d-cd) *Zoom Club; (<ZCRCD 19>)* **ANTHOLOGY** (everything + rare) [ ] [ ] Dec00

BEEFEATER

Formed: Washington DC, USA . . . 1984, most members stemming from various local hardcore acts. The line-up consisted of TOMAS SQUIP JONES, DUG E. BIRD, BRUCE TAYLOR and FRED SMITH, breaking the 'Dischord' norm with an experimental hybrid of avant-jazz, dub, metal and of course hardcore. This soundclash was unleashed on two mid 80's albums, 'PLAYS FOR LOVERS' (1985) and 'HOUSE BURNING DOWN', although their lack of success led to a subsequent break-up (JONES and BIRD formed FIDELITY JONES).

Album rating: PLAYS FOR LOVERS (*6) / HOUSE BURNING DOWN (*6)

TOMAS SQUIP JONES – vocals (ex-RED C) / **FRED SMITH** – guitar / **DUG E. BIRD** (b. BIRDZELL) – bass (ex-UNDERGROUND SOLDIER) / **BRUCE TAYLOR** – drums (ex-CLEAR VISION, ex-HATE FROM IGNORANCE, ex-SUBTLE OPPRESION)

Dischord Dischord

1985. (lp) *<(DISCHORD 17)>* **PLAYS FOR LOVERS** [ ] [ ]

1987. (lp) *<(DISCHORD 23)>* **HOUSE BURNING DOWN** [ ] [ ]

— disbanded when JONES and BIRD formed FIDELITY JONES

– compilations, etc. –

May 92. (cd) *Dischord; (DIS 64CD)* **PLAYS FOR LOVERS / HOUSE BURNING DOWN** (above 2 + extra) [ ] [ ]
– Trash funk / Reaganomix / Song for lucky / 4 3 2 1 / Mr. Silverbird / Manic D / Mourning / Satyagraha / Dog day / Red carpet / Assholes / Beefeater / Fred's song / I miss you / Out of the woods / Wars in space / Just things / Bedlam rainforest / Move me strong / One soul down / Ain't got no time / Sinking me / Dover beach / Insurrection chant / 40 sonnets on plants / With you always / Freditude / Live the life / Blind leads blind.

BEIRUT SLUMP (see under ⇒ LUNCH, Lydia)

Pat BENATAR

Born: PATRICIA ANDRZEJEWSKI, 10 Jan'53, Brooklyn, New York, USA. In her late teens she married long-time boyfriend DENNIS BENATAR and moved to Richmond, Virginia. Returning to New York in the mid-70's, BENATAR turned her hand at the cabaret circuit, adopting a harder edged approach after meeting manager/mentor, RICK NEWMAN. In keeping with her new rock-chick image, PAT retained the (frankly, more rock'n'roll) BENATAR name after divorcing DENNIS in the early 80's. Signing a deal with 'Chrysalis', BENATAR had the soft metal/AOR thing down pat (ouch!) from the off, her debut album, 'IN THE HEAT OF THE NIGHT', eventually going platinum. Her undeniable vocal prowess almost made up for the weakness of the original material, BENATAR only really coming into her own singing other people's songs. She transformed SMOKIE's 'IF YOU THINK YOU KNOW HOW TO LOVE ME', into a sultry mood piece while JOHN MELLENCAMP's 'I NEED A LOVER' benefitted from her scuffed velvet tones. Boasting the likes of 'HIT ME WITH YOUR BEST SHOT' and 'TREAT ME RIGHT', the 'CRIMES OF PASSION' (1980) album was a million seller, establishing BENATAR as a major contender in the American market. Subsequent albums, 'PRECIOUS TIME' (1981) and 'GET NERVOUS' (1982), continued to sell in abundance despite a dearth of decent songs. Things picked up with 'LOVE IS A BATTLEFIELD', a brooding, catchy pop-rock number which gave BENATAR her biggest US hit single to date, the record reaching Top 5 in late '83. A year later, the singer released what was probably her finest moment in 'WE BELONG', a seductively melodic single which secured BENATAR her first substantial UK success. After moderate sales of the 'TROPICO' (1984) and 'SEVEN THE HARD WAY' (1985) albums, BENATAR took an extended break to look after her daughter. During this time, 'Chrysalis' released 'BEST SHOTS' (1987), a compilation that did surprisingly well in Britain (No.6) and saw BENATAR's subsequent 1988 album, 'WIDE AWAKE IN DREAMLAND', make the UK Top 20. That's not to say the record was any good, and it was clear her career was in decline. Subsequent efforts have sold poorly, BENATAR even chancing her arm with an ill-advised album of blues tracks, 'TRUE LOVE' (1991). • **Songwriters:** She collaborated with others, including CHINN / CHAPMAN plus her husband/producer (from 20th Feb'82) NEIL GERALDO. She also covered YOU BETTER RUN (Young Rascals) / PAYIN' THE COST TO BE THE BOSS (B.B. King) / HELTER SKELTER (Beatles) / IF YOU THINK YOU KNOW HOW TO LOVE ME (Smokie) / INVINCIBLE (Simon Climie). • **Trivia:** Her first 7" in US 1976 as "PAT BENETAR" was DAY GIG. / LAST SATURDAY on the 'Trace' label.

Album rating: IN THE HEAT OF THE NIGHT (*6) / CRIMES OF PASSION (*6) / PRECIOUS TIME (*4) / GET NERVOUS (*4) / LIVE FROM EARTH (*3) / TROPICO (*4) / SEVEN THE HARD WAY (*6) / WIDE AWAKE IN DREAMLAND (*4) / BEST SHOTS compilation (*7) / TRUE LOVE (*3) / GRAVITY'S RAINBOW (*3) / ALL FIRED UP: THE VERY BEST OF . . . compilation (*6) / INNAMORATA (*4)

PAT BENATAR – vocals / **NEIL GERALDO** – keyboards (ex-DERRINGER) / **SCOTT ST. CLAIR SHEETS** – guitar / **ROGER CAPPS** – bass / **GLEN ALEXANDER HAMILTON** – drums

Chrysalis Chrysalis

Oct 79. (7") *(CHS 2373)* **IF YOU THINK YOU KNOW HOW TO LOVE ME. / SO SINCERE**

Dec 79. (lp/c) *<(CHR/ZCHR 1236)>* **IN THE HEAT OF THE NIGHT** [ ] [12] Oct79
– Heartbreaker / I need a lover / If you think you know how to love me / In the heat of the night / My clone sleeps alone / We live for love / Rated X / Don't let it show / No you don't / So sincere. *(re-iss. Jun85 lp/c/cd; same/same/ACCD 1236)* – hit UK No.98 *(re-iss. Dec92 on 'Fame' cd/c; CD/TC FA 3286) (cd re-iss. Apr99 on 'DCC'; GZS 1056)*

Jan 80. (7") *<(CHS 2395)>* **HEARTBREAKER. / MY CLONE SLEEPS ALONE** [ ] [23] Dec79

Mar 80. (7") *<2419>* **WE LIVE FOR LOVE. / SO SINCERE** [-] [27]

Apr 80. (7") *(CHS 2403)* **WE LIVE FOR LOVE. / I NEED A LOVER** [ ] [-]
(12"+=) *(CHS12 2403)* – If you think you know how to love me.

— **MYRON GROOMBACHER** – drums; repl. HAMILTON

Jul 80. (7") *<2450>* **YOU BETTER RUN. / OUT-A-TOUCH** [-] [42]

Aug 80. (lp/c) *<(CHR/ZCHR 1275)>* **CRIMES OF PASSION** [ ] [2]
– Treat me right / You better run / Never wanna leave you / Hit me with your best shot / Hell is for children / Little paradise / I'm gonna follow you / Wuthering heights / Prisoner of love / Out-a-touch. *(cd-iss. Jun85; ACCD 1275)*

Sep 80. (7") *<2464>* **HIT ME WITH YOUR BEST SHOT. / PRISONER OF LOVE** [-] [9]

Nov 80. (7") *(CHS 2452)* **HIT ME WITH YOUR BEST SHOT. / YOU BETTER RUN** [ ] [-]
(7"red-ep+=) *(CHS 2474)* – Heartbreaker / We live for love.

Jan 81. (7") *<2487>* **TREAT ME RIGHT. / NEVER WANNA LEAVE YOU** [-] [18]

Jan 81. (7",7"clear) *(CHS 2511)* **TREAT ME RIGHT. / HELL IS FOR CHILDREN** [ ] [-]

Jul 81. (lp/c) *<(CHR/ZCHR 1346)>* **PRECIOUS TIME** [30] [1]
– Promises in the dark / Fire and ice / Just like me / Precious time / It's a tuff life / Take it anyway you want it / Evil genius / Hard to believe / Helter skelter. *(cd-iss. Jun85; ACCD 1346)*

Jul 81. (7"clear/7"pic-d) *<(CHS/+P 2529)>* **FIRE AND ICE. / HARD TO BELIEVE** [ ] [17]

Sep 81. (7") *<2555>* **PROMISES IN THE DARK. / EVIL GENIUS** [-] [38]

— (Feb'82) **NEIL GERALDO** now on guitar / co-production.

Oct 82. (7",7"sha-pic-d/12"blue) *(CHS/+12 2662) <2647><03541>* **SHADOWS OF THE NIGHT. / THE VICTIM** [ ] [13]
(7"ep) *(CHS 2662)* – ('A'side) / Treat me right / Heartbreaker / Anxiety (get nervous).

Nov 82. (lp/pic-lp/c) *(CHR/PCHR/ZCHR 1386) <1396>* **GET NERVOUS** [73] [4]
– Shadows of the night / Looking for a stranger / Anxiety (get nervous) / Fight it out / The victim / Little too late / I'll do it / I want out / Tell it to her / Silent partner. *(cd-iss. Jun85; ACCD 1386)*

— (Nov'82) **CHARLIE GIORDANO** – keyboards; repl. SHEETS

Jan 83. (7") *<03536>* **LITTLE TOO LATE. / FIGHT IT OUT** [-] [20]

Apr 83. (7") *<42688>* **LOOKING FOR A STRANGER. / I'LL DO IT** [-] [39]

Oct 83. (7"/7"pic-d/12") *(CHS/+P/12 2747) <42732>* **LOVE IS A BATTLEFIELD. / HELL IS FOR CHILDREN (live)** [49] [5] Sep83

Oct 83. (lp/pic-lp/c) *(CHR/CHRP/ZCHR 1451) <41444>* **LIVE FROM EARTH (live)** [60] [13]
– Fire and ice / Lookin' for a stranger / I want out / We live for love / Hell is for children / Hit me with your best shot / Promises in the dark / Heartbreaker / Love is a battlefield * / Lipstick lies. *(* studio track) (cd-iss. Jun85; ACCD 1451)*

Oct 84. (7",7"pic-d) *(CHR 2821) <42826>* **WE BELONG. / SUBURBAN KING** [22] [5]
(12"+=) *(CHR12 2821)* – We live for love '85.

Nov 84. (lp/c) *(CHR/ZCHR 1471) <41471>* **TROPICO** [34] [14]
– Diamond field / We belong / Painted desert / Temporary heroes / Love in the ice age / Ooh ooh song / Outlaw blues / Suburban king / A crazy world like this / Takin' it back. *(cd-iss. Apr86; ACCD 1471)*

Jan 85. (7") *<42843>* **OOH OOH SONG. / LA CANCION OOH OOH** [-] [36]

Mar 85. (7"/12") *(PAT/+X 1)* **LOVE IS A BATTLEFIELD. / HERE'S MY HEART** [17] [-]

Jun 85. (7"/7"sha-pic-d) *(PAT/+P 2)* **SHADOWS OF THE NIGHT. / HIT ME WITH YOUR BEST SHOT** [50] [-]
(12"+=) *(PATX 2)* – Fire and ice.

— **DONNIE NOSSOV** – bass repl. CAPPS
(below is the theme from the film 'The Legend Of Billie Jean')

Oct 85. (7") *(PAT 3) <42877>* **INVINCIBLE. / ('A'instrumental)** [53] [10] Jun85
(12"+=) *(PATX 3)* – Promises in the dark / Heartbreaker.

Dec 85. (7"/12") *(PAT/+X 4) <42927>* **SEX AS A WEAPON. / RED VISION** [67] [28] Nov85

Dec 85. (lp/c) *(CHR/ZCHR 1507) <41507>* **SEVEN THE HARD WAY** [69] [26]
– Sex as a weapon / Le bel age / Walking in the underground / Big life / Red vision / 7 rooms of gloom / Run between the raindrops / Invincible (theme from The Legend Of Billie Jean) / The art of letting go. *(cd-iss. Apr86; ACCD 1507)*

Feb 86. (7") *<42968>* **LE BEL AGE. / WALKING IN THE UNDERGROUND** [-] [54]

— **FERNANDO SAUNDERS + FRANK LINX** – bass repl. NOSSOV

Jul 88. (7") *(PAT 5) <43268>* **ALL FIRED UP. / COOL ZERO** [19] [19]
(12"+=) *(PATX 5)* – Hit me with your best shot / Fire and ice / Just like me / Promises in the dark / Precious time.
(12"+=/cd-s+=) *(PAT XD/CD 5)* – ('A'-US version).

Jul 88. (lp/c/cd) *(CDL/ZCDL/CCD 1628) <41628>* **WIDE AWAKE IN DREAMLAND** [11] [28]
– All fired up / One love / Let's stay together / Don't walk away / Too long a soldier / Cool zero / Celebral man / Lift 'em on up / Suffer the little children / Wide awake in Dreamland. *(re-iss. cd Mar94; CD23CR 19)*

Sep 88. (7") *(PAT 6)* **DON'T WALK AWAY. / LIFT 'EM ON UP** [42] [ ]
(12"+=/cd-s+=) *(PAT X/CD 6)* – Hell is for children (live) / We live for love (special mix).

Dec 88. (7") *(PAT 7)* **ONE LOVE. / WIDE AWAKE IN DREAMLAND** [59] [ ]
(12"+=/12"pic-d+=) *(PATX/+P 7)* – Sex as a weapon.
(cd-s+=) *(PATCD 7)* – Love is a battlefield.

Apr 91. (cd/c/lp) *(CCD/ZCHR/CHR 1805) <21805>* **TRUE LOVE** [40] [37]
– Bloodshot eyes / Payin' the cost to be the boss / So long / I've got papers on you / I feel lucky / True love / The good life / Evening / I get evil / Don't happen no more. *(re-iss. Mar94 cd/c; same)*

Jun 91. (c-s/7") **PAYIN' THE COST TO BE THE BOSS. / TRUE LOVE** [ ] [ ]
(12"+=/cd-s+=) – Evening.

Sep 93. (c-s) *(TCCHS 5001)* **SOMEBODY'S BABY. / ('A'- A-C mix)** [48] [ ]
(cd-s+=) *(CDCHS 5001)* – Temptation / Promises in the dark (live).

Nov 93. (cd/c) *(CD/TC CHR 6054) <21982>* **GRAVITY'S RAINBOW** [ ] [85] Jun93
– Pictures of a gone world / Everybody lay down / Somebody's baby / Ties that bind / You and I / Disconnected / Crazy / Everytime I fall back / Sanctuary / Rise (part 2) / Kingdom key / Tradin' down.

C.M.C. C.M.C.

Sep 97. (cd) *<(06076 86216-2)>* **INNAMORATA** [ ] [ ] Jun97
– (guitar intro) / Only love / River of love / I don't want to be your friend / Strawberry wine / Purgatory / At this time / Dirty little secrets / Angry / In these times / Innamorata / Gina's song. *(d-cd-iss. Oct98 as 'INNAMORATA 8/1/80' on 'SPV'; SPV 0852917-2)*

– compilations, others, etc. –

— on 'Chrysalis' unless mentioned othewise

Dec 82. (d-c) *(ZCDP 108)* **IN THE HEAT OF THE NIGHT / CRIMES OF PASSION** [ ] [-]

Nov 87. (cd)(c/lp) *(CCD 1538)(Z+/PATV 1) <21715>* **BEST SHOTS** [6] [67] Nov89
– Hit me with your best shot / Love is a battlefield / We belong / We live for love / Sex as a weapon / Invincible / Shadows of the night / Heartbreaker / Fire and ice / Treat me right / If you think you know how to love me / You better run. *(cd re-iss. Sep97; same)*

Apr 94. (cd/c) *(CD/TC CHR 6070)* **THE VERY BEST OF PAT BENATAR** [ ] [ ]
– Heartbreaker / We live for love / Promises in the dark / Fire and ice / Ooh ooh song / Hit me with your best shot / Shadows of the night / Anxiety (get nervous) / I want out / Lipstick lies / Love is a battlefield / We belong / All fired up / Hell is for children / Invincible / Somebody's baby / Everybody lay down / True love.

Jan 95. (d-cd) *Chrysalis; <31094>* **ALL FIRED UP: THE VERY BEST OF PAT BENATAR** [-] [ ]

Jul 98. (cd) *Ranch Life; <(CRANCH 6)>* **CONCERT CLASSICS** [ ] [ ]

Sep 98. (cd) *Beat Goes On; (BGOCD 418)* **IN THE HEAT OF THE NIGHT / CRIMES OF PASSION** [ ] [-]

Nov 98. (cd) *Beat Goes On; (BGOCD 427)* **PRECIOUS TIME / GET NERVOUS** [ ] [-]

Mar 99. (cd) *Beat Goes On; (BGOCD 433)* **TROPICO / SEVEN THE HARD WAY** [ ] [-]

Mar 99. (cd) *E.M.I.; (CDP 852256-2)* **HEARTBREAKER** [ ] [-]

BENEDICTION

Formed: Birmingham, England ... late 80's out of STILLBORN by DARREN BROOKES, PETER REW, PAUL ADAMS, IAN TREACY and vocalist MARK 'BARNEY' GREENWAY (the latter soon opting to join NAPALM DEATH, his replacement being DAVE INGRAM). After an initial debut, 'SUBCONSCIOUS TERROR' in 1990, they inked a deal with 'Nuclear Blast', who issued a split EP prior to a second set, 'THE GRAND LEVELLER'. Death-metal being more appreciated in Northern Europe, BENEDICTION cultivated a growing fan base outwith the UK with 90's albums, the mini 'DARK IS THE SEASON' (1992), 'TRANSCEND THE RUBICON' (1993), 'THE GROTESQUE – ASHEN EPITAPH' (1994), 'THE DREAMS YOU DREAD' (1995) and 'GRIND BASTARD' (1998).

Album rating: SUBCONSCIOUS TERROR (*5) / THE GRAND LEVELLER (*4) / DARK IS THE SEASON (*4) / TRANSCEND THE RUBICON (*5) / THE GROTESQUE – ASHEN EPITAPH mini (*4) / THE DREAMS YOU DREAD (*5) / GRIND BASTARD (*7)

DAVE INGRAM – vocals; repl. MARK 'BARNEY' INGRAM / **DARREN BROOKES** – guitar / **PETER REW** – guitar / **FRANK HEALY** – bass; repl. PAUL ADAMS / **IAN TREACY** – drums

own label not iss.

Feb 90. (c-ep) *(none)* **THE DREAMS YOU DREAD** [ ] [-]
– Experimental stage / Subconscious terror / Artifacted irreligion / Bonesaw.

Revolver Nuclear Blast

Aug 90. (cd/lp) *(84297-2/-1) <6009>* **SUBCONSCIOUS TERROR** [ ] [ ] 1991
– Intro – Portal to your phobias / Subconscious terror / Artefacted irreligion / Grizzled finale / Eternal eclipse / Experimental stage / Suspended animation / Divine ultimatum / Spit forth the dead / Confess all goodness. *(re-iss. Jul91 on 'Nuclear Blast' pic-lp/c; NB 033 PD/MC) (cd re-iss. Jun96; NB 165CD)*

Nuclear Blast Nuclear Blast

Jun 91. (7"; with other artist) *(NB 031)* **SPLIT E.P.** [ ] [-]

Oct 91. (lp/pic-lp/cd) *(NB 048/+PD/CD) <6017>* **THE GRAND LEVELLER** [ ] [ ] 1992
– Vision in the shroud / Graveworm / Jumping at shadows / Opulence of the absolute / Child of sin / Undirected aggression / Born in a fever / The grand leveller / Senile dementia / Return to the eve.

— now without PAUL ADAMS

Mar 92. (7") *(NB 057)* **EXPERIMENTAL. /** [ ] [-]

Apr 92. (7"pic-d) *(NB 058PDS)* **RETURN TO THE . . .** [ ] [-]

Apr 92. (m-lp/m-cd) *(NB 059/+CD) <6019>* **DARK IS THE SEASON** [ ] [ ]
– Foetus noose / Forged in fire / Dark is the season / Jumping at shadows / Experimental stage.

Jun 93. (lp/c/cd) *(NB 073/+MC/CD) <6465>* **TRANSCEND THE RUBICON** [ ] [ ]
– Unfound mortality / Nightfear / Paradox alley / I bow to none / Painted skulls / Violation domain / Face without soul / Bleakhouse / Blood from stone / Wrong side of the grave / Artefacted – Spit forth. *<US+=>* – Saneless theory / Deadfall.

Jul 93. (7"pic-d) *(NB 073PDS)* **WRONG SIDE OF THE GRAVE. /** [ ] [-]

— **PAUL BROOKES** – drums; repl. IAN

May 94. (cd) *(NB 088-2) <6899>* **THE GROTESQUE – ASHEN EPITAPH** (half live) [ ] [ ] Jul94
– The grotesque / Ashen epitaph / Violation domain (live) / Subconscious terror (live) / Visions in the shroud (live). *(pic-lp Aug94; NB 088PD)*

— **NEIL HUTTON** – drums (ex-WARLORD) repl. PAUL BROOKES

Jun 95. (cd/c/lp) *(<NB 120 CD/MC/LP>)* **THE DREAMS YOU DREAD** [ ] [ ] Aug95
– Down on whores / Certified / Soulstream / Where flies are born / Answer to me / Griefgiver / Denial / Negative growth / Path of the serpent / Saneless theory / The dreams you dread.

Mar 98. (cd) *(<NB 246-2>)* **GRIND BASTARD** [ ] [ ] May98
– Deadfall / Agonised / West of Hell / Magnificat (irenicon) / Nervebomb / Electric eye / Grind bastard / Shadow world / Bodiless / Carcinoma angel / We the freed / Destroyer / I.

BENNET

Formed: Reading, England ... 1993 by JASON APLIN (vocals) and JOHNNY PEER (guitar), who eventually recruited the current line-up of KEVIN MOOREY (drums), ANDY BENNET (bass) and NEIL CURLEY (keyboards). Signing to 'Roadrunner', a label more associated with venom spitting young men with unfeasibly long hair, the NHS-bespectacled BENNET raised the flag for shiny, happy, gawky geek-rock with their late '96 debut album, 'SUPER NATURAL' and the infectious pop parody of 'MUM'S GONE TO ICELAND', a Top 40 hit in early '97. Despite a gruelling trek around the nation's less salubrious music hostelries and another moderately-received album in late '97, 'STREET VS SCIENCE', BENNET have yet to attain the lofty commercial heights of their namesake TONY BENNETT (or, let's face it, even a modicum of his style and sophistication).

Album rating: SUPER NATURAL (*6) / STREET VS SCIENCE (*5)

JASON APLIN – vocals / **JOHNNY PEER** – guitar / **KEVIN MOOREY** – drums / **ANDY BENNET** – bass / **NEIL CURLEY** – keyboards

Roadrunner Roadrunner

Mar 96. (7") *(RR 2316-7)* **IF YOU MET ME THEN YOU'D LIKE ME. / OH YEAH** [ ] [ ]
(cd-s+=) *(RR 2316-3)* – Back to Americaat Bracknell / Jute's theme.

May 96. (7") *(RR 2306-7)* **COLOSSAL MAN. / BIG FAT WIFE** [ ] [-]
(cd-s+=) *(RR 2306-3)* – Club foot angel / Motorbike.

Aug 96. (7"red/c-s) *(RR 2298-7/-4)* **SOMEONE ALWAYS GETS THERE FIRST. / HELLO WE ARE BENNET** [ ] [-]
(cd-s+=) *(RR 2298-3)* – Charity Dave / Congregation de Freitas.

(re-iss. Apr97; same) – hit UK No.69

Sep 96. (cd/c/lp) *(<RR 8866-2/-4/-1>)* **SUPER NATURAL**
– Norway wife / If you met me, then you'd like me / Only thirty / Jordan Bennet / Cha cha Charlie / I hate my family / Wanker / Colossal man / Young, free & snotty / Sandman / Mum's gone to Iceland / Someone always gets there first / Mockney rebel / Kiss the radio / Never ending blue / Secret track.

Feb 97. (7"/c-s) *(RR 2285-7/-4)* **MUM'S GONE TO ICELAND. / BENNET HAVE LEFT THE BUILDING** 34
(cd-s+=) *(RR 2285-3)* – This is a song / Hope you'd like to.

Sep 97. (7"clear) *(RR 2260-7)* **I LIKE ROCK. / TOUCH TOO MUCH**
(cd-s+=) *(RR 2260-3)* – C'mon c'mon / Rock'n'roll all nite.
(cd-s) *(RR 2260-5)* –

Oct 97. (cd/c) *(RR 8761-2/-4)* **STREET VS SCIENCE**
– Unlucky pixie / Hot shot / Be a superstar / My friends are getting fewer / Swap it around / The horse's mouth / I like rock / Built to last / Something's wrong with Mark / Karaoke / Das boot.

Feb 98. (cd-ep) *(RR 2243-3)* **HORSE'S MOUTH / SELF MURDER / DOGS / A.L.I.E.N.D.I.V.O.R.C.E.**
(cd-ep) *(RR 2243-9)* – ('A'side) / Married with children / Polka / Home karaoke.

— BENNET were no more after above

Nuno BETTENCOURT (see under ⇒ EXTREME)

BETTER THAN EZRA

Formed: New Orleans, Louisiana, USA ... 1988 by university pals, KEVIN GRIFFIN (their main songwriter), TOM DRUMMOND and CARY BONNECAZE. Debuting their rather derivative DINOSAUR JR guitar-based sound on a privately distributed cassette at the turn of the decade, the band spent the first half of the 90's rehearsing and touring extensively in their southern domain. In 1993/4, BETTER THAN EZRA self-financed their debut release, 'DELUXE' (on 'Swell'), the album shifting enough copies to attract major label interest. Eventually signing to 'Elektra', the band went back into the studio with producer, Dan Rothchild, the man helping them polish up their aforementioned debut for re-release in '95. Catchy grunge by numbers with a MICHAEL STIPE-esque vocal inflection, the record gradually ascended the US charts helped by the Top 30 success of single, 'GOOD'. The following year, after CARY was replaced by TRAVIS AARON McNABB, the trio returned with a second collection, 'FRICTION BABY', a record that barely reached the shallows of the US chart as the grunge wave subsided. Obviously WEA/Elektra had given up any hope of marketing the band in Britain and like its predecessor, 'HOW DOES YOUR GARDEN GROW?' (1998), was a US-only release.

Album rating: DELUXE (*6) / FRICTION BABY (*5) / HOW DOES YOUR GARDEN GROW? (*6)

KEVIN GRIFFIN – vocals, guitar / **TOM DRUMMOND** – bass / **CARY BONNECAZE** – drums

WEA Int. | Elektra

May 95. (cd/c) *<7559 61784-2/-4>* **DELUXE** 35
– In the blood / Good / Southern girl / The killer inside / Rosealia / Cry in the sun / Teenager / Untitled / Summerhouse / Porcelain / Heaven / This time of year / Coyote.

— <above was initially released on their own 'Swell' imprint>

Jun 95. (c-s) *<64428>* **GOOD / CIRCLE OF FRIENDS (live)** - 30

Jun 95. (c-s) *(EKR 204C)* **GOOD / SUMMERHOUSE** -
(cd-s+=) *(EKR 204CD)* – Know you better (live) / Circle of friends (live).

Nov 95. (c-s,cd-s) *<64352>* **ROSEALIA / IN THE BLOOD (live)** - 71

— **TRAVIS AARON McNABB** – drums; repl. BONNECAZE

Aug 96. (cd/c) *<61944-2/-4>* **FRICTION BABY** - 64
– King of New orleans / Rewind / Long lost / Normal town / Scared are you? / Return of the post moderns / Hung the Moon / Desperately wanting / Still life with Cooley / WWOZ / Happy endings / Speeding up to slow down / At CH, Degaulle, etc.

Dec 96. (c-s,cd-s) *<64228>* **DESPERATELY WANTING / PALACE HOTEL** - 48

Sep 98. (cd/c) *<62247-2>* **HOW DOES YOUR GARDEN GROW?** -
– Je ne m'en souviens pas / One more murder / At the stars / Like it like that / Allison Foley / Under you / Live again / Happy day mama / Pull / Particle / Beautiful mistake / Everything in 2's / New kind of low: a) Low – b) Coma / Waxing or waning?

Mar 99. (-) *<radio cut>* **AT THE STARS** - 78

BEYOND

Formed: Derby, England . . . 1988 by JOHN WHITBY, ANDY GATFORD, JIM KERSEY and NEIL COOPER. Signing to 'E.M.I.'. they were subsequently "loaned out" on a deal to indie-oriented label, 'Big Cat', releasing two EP's in 1990, 'MANIC SOUND PANIC' and 'NO EXCUSE', the latter featuring a cover of The Dead Kennedys' 'CALIFORNIA UBER ALLES'. Their third single, 'ONE STEP TOO FAR' (finally on 'E.M.I.'), failed to capitalise on the band's growing following among the thrash/alternative crowd. In 1991, they delivered their debut album, 'CRAWL', deftly displaying their dense, cerebral strain of intricate prog-rock metal. Despite continued support from the music press, the album failed to take off, The BEYOND subsequently downshifting to 'Music For Nations' for their second and final offering, 'CHASM'. The band became GORILLA for a while and released a couple of sets; please note that The BEYOND who were on 'Volcano' were not the same band. • **Other covers:** BREAK ON THROUGH (Doors) / TOUCH ME I'M SICK (Mudhoney).

Album rating: CRAWL (*6) / CHASM (*6)

JOHN WHITBY – vocals / **ANDY GATFORD** – guitar / **JIM KERSEY** – bass / **NEIL COOPER** – drums

Big Cat | not iss.

Apr 90. (12"ep) *(ABB 15T)* **MANIC SOUND PANIC EP** -

Jul 90. (12"ep/cd-ep) *(ABB 22 T/CD)* **NO EXCUSE. / PORTRAIT (live) / CALIFORNIA UBER ALLES (live)** -

E.M.I. | Continuum

May 91. (7") *(EM 191)* **ONE STEP TOO FAR. / BREAK ON THROUGH** -
(12"+=) *(12EM 191)* – ('A'extended).
(cd-s+=) *(CDEM 191)* – Touch me I'm sick.

Harvest | not iss.

Jun 91. (7") *(HAR 5300)* **EMPIRE. / EVERYBODY WINS** -
(12"+=) *(12HARP 5300)* – ('A'-Cocktail mix).
(cd-s+=) *(CDHAR 5300)* – One step too far (Brain Surgery mix).

Jul 91. (cd/c/lp) *(CD/TC+/SHSP 4128)* *<19204>* **CRAWL** 1992
– Sacred garden / Empire / Sick / The day before tomorrow / One step too far / Second sight / Great indifference / Eve of my release / No more happy ever afters / Lead the blind / Dominoes.

Oct 91. (7"ep) *(HARS 5301)* **RAGING EP** -
– Great indifference / Nail / Eve of my release.
(12"pic-d+=/cd-s+=) *(12HARPD/CDHAR 5301)* – Empire (live) / The day before tomorrow (live).

Oct 92. (12"ep/cd-ep) *(12/CD HAR 5302)* **GOB** -
– Melt / Frog scab / Working man / Throb.

Music For Nations | not iss.

Jul 93. (cd/lp) *(CD+/MFN 147)* **CHASM** -
– Cypress era / Stagnant / Melt / Sentimental vultures / Matter metropolis / Sweat tastes sweeter / Onion / Grey / Vive le republique / Mother my lover. *<US cd-iss. 1999 on 'Imprint'; 31147>*

— split after above; the band became GORILLA (not the US version with albums)

Jello BIAFRA (see under ⇒ DEAD KENNEDYS)

BIF NAKED

Born: 1971, New Delhi, India. BIF's early years read like a rock and roll version of a Mills and Boon heroine. She was the love child of young private school travellers and was then adopted, brought back from India by missionaries to America and raised in Canada. While at the University of Winnipeg, BIF joined a local group named JUNGLE MILK, moving on from there to become lead vocalist for GORILLA GORILLA, at which point she took on the name, BIF NAKED. She moved on from this band to join CHROME DOG, as she felt she would be able to assert her antagonistic leanings better with this hardcore punk mob. Unfortunately though the masculine orientated group would not allow BIF to expand on more feminine subject matter. Thus she moved on to join Canadian punk band, DYING TO BE VIOLENT, but unfortunately the same problems arose as with her former group, leading her to stay on only briefly with DTBV. BIF took the truest route to personal artistic integrity; going solo and releasing an EP, 'FOUR SONGS AND A POEM' in 1994, with the ensuing full-length set, 'BIF NAKED' (1995) – co-written with producer JOHN R DEXTER – following the same year (this album was also re-issued that year on BIF's own label, 'Her Royal Majestys'). This outing gained BIF many new admirers, making her a bit of a feminist icon, with her no-messing punk attitude. 1995 was also a crucial year for BIF as she decided to put an end to years of alcohol and drug abuse, and instead concentrate on her chosen musical path. Following this, BIF spent several years touring and promoting herself, her big break coming in 1998 with a contract for the Atlantic-run 'Lava' imprint, who released her second full-length album, 'I BIFICUS' (1998). The record was a good blend of pop and punk styles, although never selling-out as many so-called punk bands have.

Album rating: BIF NAKED (*6) / I BIFICUS (*5)

BIF NAKED – vocals / with various session people

not iss. | Plum

1994. (cd-ep) **FOUR SONGS AND A POEM** -
– Make like a tree / Tell on you / Never along / Succulent / My Satan poem.

Concrete – Edel | Aquarius

Nov 95. (cd) *(CD 008624-2)* *<6661>* **BIF NAKED**
– Everything / Make like a tree / Daddy's getting married / Tell on you / Never alone / Over you / Succulent / My whole life / The letter / My bike / The gross, gross man.

Nov 95. (cd-s) *(0086265RAD)* **DADDY'S GETTING MARRIED / TELL ON YOU / SUCCULENT** -

1997. (cd-ep) **OKENSPAY ORDWAY I. (aka THINGS I FORGOT TO TELL MOMMY)** (spoken word) - - Canada
– Test / Intro / Infected tattoo / Rock star man / You got the job / Alphabet poem / Dress / We're arseholes / Half a day a week / Alcohol is the root / Zoinks! / Calling all / T.V. baby / Interruption / Metal queen / Alcohol or comedy / Isabelle / Insomnia / Obsessed w/ childhood / No me drink / Canadians / Porno brainwash / 32 fuetes / Ahhhh / I'm yer peer / Factory hot rod / Goodbye / All you ever do / Singin' / Stumpy the mouse / Snowboarding / Poem #357651 / Gig tits / My Satan poem.

Feb 98. (cd) **I BIFICUS** -
– I died / Any day now / Spaceman / Moment of weakness / Lucky / Sophia / Chotee / Violence / The peacock song / Anything / Only the girl / Twitch. *<US re-iss. 1999 on 'Lava-Atlantic'; >*

1998. (cd-s) **SPACEMAN (mixes; Boomtang Boys / radio / I Bificus)** -

not iss. | Atlantic

2000. (cd-ep) **ANOTHER 5 SONGS AND A POEM** - - Canada
– I died / Twitch / Vampire / Lucky (guitar mix) / We're not gonna take it / Eine tasse tee (a poem).

BIG BLACK

Formed: Evanston, Illinois, USA . . . 1982 by mainman STEVE ALBINI (vocals/guitar). The first official release, 'LUNGS' appeared later that year on local independent label, 'Ruthless', a six-track drum-machine driven EP that announced ALBINI's intent to take punk/hardcore into uncharted territory. Now with an expanded line-up numbering SANTIAGO DURANGO on guitar and JEFF PEZZATI on bass, the BIG BLACK trio unleashed two more 12"ep's/mini-lp's in the mid 80's, 'BULLDOZER' (1983) and 'RACER X' (1985), prior to the seminal 'IL DUCE' single in '86. Replacing PEZZATI with DAVE RILEY (aka LOVERING), they created a minor hardcore classic in 'ATOMIZER' (1986), its bleak examinations of small-town American despair a theme which would be echoed countless times by their grunge/industrial successors. With DURANGO off to study law, MERVIN BELLI came in for the inflammatory titled, 'SONGS ABOUT *!?KING', BIG BLACK giving their all on an album which they knew would be their last. However, they did bow out in uncharacteristic style with a double A-sided 45 covering Cheap Trick's 'HE'S A WHORE' and 'Kraftwerk's 'THE MODEL'. Taking his twisted vision to its warped conclusion, ALBINI formed the controversially named RAPEMAN with two former SCRATCH ACID players, DAVID WM. SIMS and REY WASHAM. It wasn't just the name that provoked outrage, tracks such as 'HATED CHINEE', 'SUPERPUSSY' and 'KIM GORDON'S PANTIES' causing a fuss which possibly contributed to ALBINI abandoning the operation early in '89. Having already turned in classic productions for the likes of The PIXIES ('Surfer Rosa'), ALBINI, along with BUTCH VIG became one of the highest profile and most respected/hard working figures of the grunge era (credits include NIRVANA, TAD, PJ HARVEY, etc). ALBINI's other side project, SHELLAC, was first conceived in 1992 along with drummer TODD TRAINER although it only took vinyl form after BOB WESTON began working for STEVE in his Chicago studio. A sporadic string of singles ('URANUS', 'THE ADMIRAL' and 'THE RUDE GESTURE: A PICTORIAL HISTORY') emerged on 'Touch & Go', suggesting a natural progression from BIG BLACK in terms of blackboard-scraping guitar, painfully sardonic lyrics and general sonic terrorism. A debut album, 'AT ACTION PARK', appeared in late '94 although given ALBINI's hectic schedule it'd be a further four years before the slightly disappointing 'TERRAFORM' (1998) hit the shelves. After further singles, haphazard live appearances and the obligatory Peel Session, ALBINI & Co emerged blinking into the new millennium with '1000 HURTS' (2000). As raw, contrary and defiantly unconventional as ever, the record lurched along in the by now well established SHELLAC mould; unlikely to win over new fans but a rich source of perverse treats for diehards.
• **Songwriters:** ALBINI and group compositions except; HEARTBEAT (Wire) / REMA REMA (Rema Rema) / Rapeman: JUST GOT PAID (ZZ Top).

Album rating: ATOMIZER (*7) / SONGS ABOUT *!?KING (*8) / PIGPILE live compilation (*7) / Rapeman: TWO NUNS AND A BLACK MULE (*7) / Shellac: AT ACTION PARK (*6) / TERRAFORM (*7) / 1000 HURTS (*7)

STEVE ALBINI – vocals, guitar

not iss. | Ruthless

1982. (c) <none> **BIG BLACK LIVE (live)**
(UK-iss.Oct89 on 'Blast First' lp/c/cd; BFFP 49/+C/CD)

Nov 82. (12"ep) <RRBB 02> **LUNGS**
– Steelworker / Live in a hole / Dead Billy / I can be killed / Crack / R.I.P. *(UK-iss.Nov92 on 'Touch & Go'; TG 89)*

—— added **SANTIAGO DURANGO** – guitar (ex-NAKED RAYGUN, ex-SILVER ABUSE) / **JEFF PEZZATI** – bass (ex-NAKED RAYGUN) / + on session 4th member **PAT BYRNE** – drums

Nov 83. (12"ep) <RRBB 07> **BULLDOZER**
– Cables / Pigeon kill / I'm a mess / Texas / Seth / Jump the climb. *(UK-iss.Nov92 on 'Touch & Go'; TG 90)*

Homestead | Homestead

Apr 85. (m-lp) <(HMS 007)> **RACER-X** — 1984
– Racer-x / Shotgun / The ugly American / Deep six / Sleep! / Big payback. *(re-iss. Nov92 on 'Touch & Go'; TG 91)*

Sep 86. (7") *(HMS 042)* **IL DUCE. / BIG MONEY** — 1985
(re-iss. Nov92 on 'Touch & Go'; TG 96)

—— **DAVE RILEY** (aka LOVERING) – bass (ex-SAVAGE BELIEFS) repl. PEZZATI / drum machine replaced BYRNE

Sep 86. (lp) <(HMS 43)> **ATOMIZER**
– Jordan, Minnesota / Passing complexion / Big money / Kerosene / Bad houses / Kerosene / Fists of love / Stinking drunk / Bazooka Joe / Strange things. *(re-iss. Nov86 on 'Blast First'; BFFP 11) (re-iss. Nov92 on 'Touch & Go' lp/cd; TG 93/+CD)*

Blast First | Touch&Go

Jun 87. (12"ep/c-ep) *(BFFP 14/+C)* <TG 20> **HEADACHE** — 1986
– My disco / Grinder / Ready men / Pete, king of all detectives.
(free 7"w.a./tracks on c-ep) *(TG 21)* – HEARTBEAT. / THINGS TO DO TODAY / I CAN'T BELIEVE *(UK re-iss. Nov92 on 'Touch & Go'; TG 20)*

—— **MELVYN BELLI** – guitar; repl. DURANGO

Jul 87. (lp/c/cd) *(BFFP 19/+C/CD)* <TG 24/+C/CD> **SONGS ABOUT *!?KING**
– The power of independent trucking / The model / Bad penny / El doper / Precious thing / Columbian neck-tie / Kitty empire / Ergot / Kashmir S. Pulasiday / Fish fry / Pavement saw / Tiny, the king of the Jews / Bombastic intro. *(re-iss. Nov92 on 'Touch & Go' lp/cd +=; TG 24/+CD)* – He's A Whore.

Aug 87. (7") *(BFFP 24)* <TG 23> **HE'S A WHORE. / THE MODEL**
(re-iss. Nov92 on 'Touch & Go'; TG 23)

—— Disbanded in 1988.

– compilations, etc. –

Mar 87. (lp) *Homestead; (HMS 044)* **THE HAMMER PARTY**
– (LUNGS + BULLDOZER) *(re-iss. Nov92 on 'Touch & Go' lp/cd +=; TG 92/+CD)* – RACER-X

Jun 87. (lp) *Not 2; (BUT 1)* **SOUND OF IMPACT (live bootleg)**
(re-iss. 1990)

Jan 88. (cd) *Blast First; (BFFP 23)* **RICH MAN'S EIGHT TRACK TAPE**
– (ATOMIZER + HEADACHE + HEARTBEAT) *(re-iss. Nov92 on 'Touch & Go'; TG 94CD)*

Oct 92. (lp/cd) *Touch & Go; <(TG 81/+CD)>* **PIGPILE (live)**

RAPEMAN

—— were formed by **ALBINI** with **DAVID WM. SIMS** – bass / **REY WASHAM** – drums (both ex-SCRATCH ACID, latter ex-BIG BOYS)

not iss. | Fierce

1988. (7") <none> **HATED CHINEE. / MARMOSET**

Blast First | Touch & Go

Nov 88. (12"ep) *(BFFP 27)* <TG 34> **BUDD (live) / SUPERPUSSY (live). / LOG BASS (live) / DUTCH COURAGE**

Dec 88. (lp/c/cd) *(BFFP 33/+C/CD)* <TG 36/+C/CD> **TWO NUNS AND BLACK MULE**
– Steak and black onions / Monobrow / Up beat / Cotition ignition mission / Kim Gordon's panties / Hated Chinee / Radar love wizard / Marmoset / Just got paid / Trouser minnow. *(cd+=)* – Budd / Superpussy / Log brass / Dutch courage.

Sub Pop | Sub Pop

Aug 89. (7",7"clear) <(SP 40)> **INKI'S BUTT CRACK. / SONG NUMBER ONE**

—— Had to split in Feb'89 due to the backlash against group name. SIMS returned to Austin, where he re-united with ex-SCRATCH ACID members to form JESUS LIZARD. They were produced by ALBINI who continued as a producer, noteably for others The PIXIES, The BREEDERS, NIRVANA, WEDDING PRESENT. ALBINI formed below in '93.

SHELLAC

STEVE ALBINI – guitar, vocals / **BOB WESTON** – bass (ex-VOLCANO SONS) / **TODD TRAINER** – drums (ex-RIFLE SPORT, etc)

Touch & Go | Touch & Go

1993. (7"ep) <TG 123> **THE RUDE GESTURE: A PICTORIAL HISTORY EP**
– The guy who invented fire / Rambler song / Billiard player song.

1993. (7"ep) <TG 124> **URANUS EP**
– Wingwalker / Doris / etc.

1994. (7"ep) **THE BIRD IS THE MOST POPULAR FINGER**
– Pull the cup / The admiral / +6
(above issued on 'Drag City')

Oct 94. (lp/c/cd) <(TG 141/+C/CD)> **AT ACTION PARK** — Sep94
– My black ass / Pull the cup / The admiral / Crow / Song of the minerals / A minute / The idea of north / Dog and pony show / Boche's dick / Il porno star.

1997. (cd) **THE FUTURIST**

May 98. (lp/cd) <(TG 200/+CD)> **TERRAFORM** — Feb98
– Didn't we deserve a look at you the way you really are / This is a picture / Disgrace / Mouthpiece / Canada / Rush job / House full of garbage / Copper.

Jul 00. (lp/cd) <(TG 211/+CD)> **1000 HURTS**
– Prayer to God / Squirrel song / Mama Gina / Q.R.L. / Ghosts / Song against itself / Canaveral / New number order / Shoe song / Watch song.

BIG BOYS

Formed: Austin, Texas, USA . . . 1980 by TIM KERR, CHRIS GATES and singer RANDY 'BISCUITS' TURNER. Completing the line-up with drummer STEVE COLLIER, this not entirely serious skate-punk combo delivered their debut EP later that year, a self-financed 4-song collection that included such "playground standard" gems as 'FRAT CARS' and 'MUTANT ROCK'. The following year, they surfaced on a joint live set with fellow Texans, The DICKS, while their first album proper, 'WHERE'S MY TOWEL / INDUSTRY STANDARD', appeared a few months later. In 1983, now with future RAPEMAN (STEVE ALBINI's outfit) drummer, REY WASHAM, they issued what was to be their final outing, 'LULLABIES HELP THE BRAIN GROW'.
• **Covered:** HOLLYWOOD SWINGING (Kool & The Gang).

Album rating: RECORDED LIVE AT RAUL'S CLUB split (*4) / WHERE'S MY TOWEL – INDUSTRY STANDARD (*5) / FUN, FUN, FUN mini (*4) / LULLABIES HELP THE BRAIN GROW (*6) / NO MATTER HOW LONG THE LINE IS AT THE CAFETERIA, THERE'S ALWAYS A SEAT (*4) / THE SKINNY ELVIS compilation (*6) / THE FAT ELVIS compilation (*6)

RANDY 'BISCUITS' TURNER – vocals / **TIM KERR** – guitar, vocals / **CHRIS GATES** – bass, vocals / **STEVE COLLIER** – drums

not iss. | Big Boys

Nov 80. (7"ep) <BB 42480> **FRAT CARS / HEARTBEAT. / MOVIES / MUTANT ROCK**

not iss. | Rat Race

Jan 81. (m-lp; one side by the DICKS) **RECORDED LIVE AT RAUL'S CLUB (live)**
– Detectives / Out of focus / Psycho / Red/green / In the city / Nightball / After 12.00. *(UK-iss.1990's on 'Plastic Head'; SFLS 010)*

not iss. Wasted Talent

Jun 81. (lp) <*JWT 3405*> **WHERE'S MY TOWEL / INDUSTRY STANDARD** -

– Security / T.V. / I don't wanna / Identity crisis / Thin line / Advice / Complete control / Work without pay / Spit / Act/Reaction / Self contortion / Wise up.

— **REY WASHAM** – drums; repl. FRED SCHULTZ who repl. COLLIER

not iss. Moment

1982. (m-lp) <*MOMBB 001*) **FUN, FUN, FUN** -

– Nervous / Apolitical / Hollywood swinging / Prison / We got soul / Fun, fun, fun.

1983. (lp) <*MOMBB 002*> **LULLABIES HELP THE BRAIN GROW** -

– Brickwall / Jump the fence / Ambivalence . . . I always jump the fence / Assault / Manipulation / Same old blues / Gator fucking / White nigger / Baby let's play God / We got your money / Lesson / Funk off / I'm sorry / We're not in it to lose / Fight back / Sound on sound.

not iss. Enigma

1984. (lp) **NO MATTER HOW LONG THE LINE IS AT THE CAFETERIA, THERE'S ALWAYS A SEAT!** -

– No / Narrow vein / I do care / Listen / What's the word? / Common beat / No love / Which way to go / Killing time / Work.

— split in 1984, KERR joined JUNKYARD, WASHAM joined SCRATCH ACID

– compilations, etc. –

1988. (c) *Unseen Hand;* <*727-C*> **WRECK COLLECTION** -

Aug 93. (cd/c) *Touch & Go;* <*TG 98 CD/C*> **THE SKINNY ELVIS** -

– Frat cars / Heartbeat / Movies / Mutant rock / Detectives / Out of focus / Psycho / Red – Green / In the city / Nightbeat / After 12:00 / Security / T.V. / I don't wanna dance / Identity crisis / Thin line / Advice / Complete control / Work without play / Spit / Act – Reaction / Self contortion / Wise up.

1993. (cd/c) *Touch & Go;* <*TG 99 CD/C*> **THE FAT ELVIS** -

– Nervous / Apolitical / Hollywood swinging / Prison / We got soul / Fun, fun, fun / We got your money / Lesson / Funk off / I'm sorry / We're not in it to lose / Sound on sound / Fight back / Brickwall / Jump the fence / Assault / Manipulation / Same old blues / Gator fuckin' / White nigger / Baby let's play God / No / Narrow view / I do care / Listen / What's the word? / Common beat / No love / Which way to go / Killing time / Work.

BIG CHIEF

Formed: Ann Arbor, Michigan, USA . . . late 80's by singer/growler and head honcho, BARRY HENSSLER, twin-guitarists MARK DANCEY and PHIL DuRR, plus bassist MATT O'BRIEN. Signed to 'Sub Pop', just as grunge was going overground, BIG CHIEF asserted their dominance in the retro stakes with a dirty, leaden guitar sound and a raw soulful edge. Following on from the debut album, 'REPULSION' (1990), the band introduced gritty blues songstress, THORNETTA DAVIS on 1991's 'FACE' outing. She continued to contribute to the BIG CHIEF set-up, advancing to a joint credit on their final 'Sub Pop' set, 'SHOUT OUT (TO THE DUSTHUFFER)', in '94; squeezed inbetween these was 1993's mock soundtrack album, 'MACK AVENUE SKULL GAME'. Contrary as ever, BIG CHIEF brought out 'PLATINUM JIVE' in 1994 (their first for 'Capitol') which was, as they put it, their GREATEST HITS 1969-99 (!) – the first two tracks described the nonsensical proceedings:- 'LION'S MOUTH' from the album, 'Bright Future Behind You', released 1999 and 'TAKEOVER BABY' from the album, 'Titty Twist Whitey', released 1969. Fantasy aside, SCHOOLY D made a guest appearance on the track, 'BONA FIDE'.

Album rating: DRIVE IT OFF compilation (*6) / FACE (*6) / MACK AVENUE SKULLGAME (*6) / PLATINUM JIVE (*5)

BARRY HENSSLER – vocals / **MARK DANCEY** – guitar / **PHIL DuRR** (b. Germany) – guitar / **MATT O'BRIEN** – bass / **MIKE DANNER** – drums, percussion

Sub Pop Sub Pop

Mar 90. (7"white) <*SP 53*> **BLOWOUT KIT. / CHROME HELMET** -

— added **THORNETTA DAVIS** – vocals

Jul 91. (cd/c) <*SP 147 B/A*> **FACE** -

– Fresh vines / Drive it off / Ballad of Dylan Cohl / Desert jam / Honey-legged / 500 reasons / Reduced to tears / Who's gonna do all that / Lie there and be good / Wasted on B.C.

Apr 93. (m-lp/m-cd) <(*SP/+CD 89-260*)> **BIG CHIEF BRAND PRODUCT** (compilation) -

– Fresh vines / Lot lizard / Wasted on B.C. (fresh flavor remix) / Dirty double bottom / Cop kisser (Mack fucks up the scene at the) / Midnight vines.

1993. (7") <(*SFTRI 157*)> **STRANGE NOTES. /**

(above issued on "Sympathy For The Record Industry")

Aug 93. (7") <(*SP 106-282*) **ONE BORN EVERY MINUTE. / LOT LIZARD**

Sep 93. (lp/cd) (*SP/+CD 109-285*) <*SP 218/+B*> **MACK AVENUE SKULLGAME**

– Skullgame No.3, take 3 / My name is Pimp (Mack's theme) / Let's do it again / One born every minute (Doc's theme) / Sonica / No free love on the street (Sonica's theme) / Soul on a roll / 10 karat pinky ring / Have another glass of brandy, baby / Gairty lounge punk / Cop kisser (Mack fucks up the scene) / If I had a nickel for every dime / Mixed jive / He needs to be dead – Ten easy pieces / Cut to the chase / Meet the man day / O woman (Mack's lament) / Skullgame.

Sep 94. (7"ep/cd-ep; as THORNETTA DAVIS and the BIG CHIEF BAND) <(*SP/+CD 135-322*)> **SHOUT OUT**

– Shout out (to the dustshuffer) / No free love on this street (Sonica's theme) / Things have got to get better / Funky dollar bill / Sonica's last stand.

Capitol Capitol

Oct 94. (cd/c) (*CD/TC EST 2239*) <*27302-2/-4*> **PLATINUM JIVE**

– Lion's mouth / Takeover baby / John's scared / M.D. 20-20 / Map of your failure / Bona fide / Armed love / Philly nocturne / Locked out / All downhill from here / The liquor talkin' / Sick to my pants / Your days are numbered / Clown pimp / Simply Barry / Lot lizard.

— they split some time in the mid 90's

– compilations, etc. –

1991. (cd) *Get Hip;* <*1004*> **DRIVE IT OFF** -

– Brake torque / Glare / Blowout kit / Iron pimp / Get down and double check / Crackhore / Chrome helmet / Built like an ordeal / Superstupid.

BIKINI KILL

Formed: Olympia, Washington, USA . . . late 1990 by former stripper KATHLEEN HANNA, TOBI VAIL and KATHI WILCOX, who all met at their local Evergreen College and named themselves after their feminist fanzine. The band released a few low-key albums for the 'Kill Rock Stars' label (one produced by IAN MacKAYE of FUGAZI), adamantly resisting the temptation to sign for a major. Self-styled "Riot-Grrl" spokeswomen and figureheads for a new generation of fearless female punkettes, BIKINI KILL obviously took at least some of their cues from original femme-punks, The SLITS and The RAINCOATS, although musically they combined fragments of SONIC YOUTH and X-RAY SPEX. HANNA was undoubtedly the band's controversial focal point, allegedly appearing T-shirtless on stage in one incident having scrawled "Kill Me" on her chest in lipstick! The feisty frontwoman was also said to have spray-painted "Smells Like Teen Spirit" on KURT COBAIN's house, an action which inspired him to write the legendary song of the same name. In 1993, BIKINI KILL toured and recorded together with UK counterparts, HUGGY BEAR, releasing a split album, 'YEAH YEAH YEAH' (issued by 'Wiiija' in the UK). JOAN JETT produced the subsequent single, 'REBEL GIRL', released around the same time as their first official long-player, appropriately-titled 'PUSSYWHIPPED'. Following the demise of the "Riot Grrl" movement, it was to be two long years before BIKINI KILL re-emerged with what was to be their final statement, 'REJECT ALL AMERICAN' (1996).

Album rating: BIKINI KILL (*6) / PUSSYWHIPPED (*7) REJECT ALL AMERICAN (*6)

KATHLEEN HANNA(-DANDO) (b. 9 Jun'69, Portland, Oregon) – vocals / **KATHI WILCOX** (b.19 Nov'69, Vancouver, Washington) – bass / **TOBI VAIL** (b.20 Jul'69, Auburn, Washington) – drums (ex-SOME VELVET SIDEWALK) / **BILLY BOREDOM** (b. WILLIAM F. KARREN, 10 Mar'65, Memphis, Tenn.) – guitar

not iss. K

1991. (7") <) **BOY/GIRL. / (split w/ Slim Moon)** -

1991. (c) **REVOLUTION GIRL STYLE NOW** -

Kill Rock Stars Kill Rock Stars

Nov 92. (m-lp) <(*KRS 204*)> **BIKINI KILL**

– Double dare ya / Liar / Carnival / Suck my left one / Feels blind / Thurston hearts the who. <(*cd-iss. Mar94 +=; KRS 204CD*)> – YEAH YEAH YEAH

Catcall Kill Rock Stars

Mar 93. (lp; shared with HUGGY BEAR) (*PUSS 001*) **YEAH YEAH YEAH**

– White boy / This is not a test / Don't need you / Jigsaw youth / Resist psychic death / Rebel girl / Outta me.

Wiiija Kill Rock Stars

Oct 93. (cd/lp) (*WIJ 028 CD/V*) <*KRS 218*> **PUSSYWHIPPED**

– Blood one / Alien she / Magnet / Speed heart / Lil red / Tell me so / Sugar / Star bellied boy / Hamster baby / Rebel girl / Star fish / For Tammy Rae.

1994. (7") **NEW RADIO. / REBEL GIRL / DEMIREP** -

1994. (7") **IN ACCORDANCE TO NATURAL LAW. / STRAWBERRY JULIUS / ANTI-PLEASURE DISSERTATION** -

1995. (7") **RAH! RAH! REPLICA. / I LIKE FUCKING / I HATE DANGER** -

Kill Rock Stars Kill Rock Stars

Apr 96. (cd/lp) <(*KRS 260 CD/LP*)> **REJECT ALL AMERICAN**

– Statement of vindication / Capri pants / Jet ski / Distinct complicity / False start / R.I.P. / No backrub / Bloody ice cream / For only / Tony Randall / Reject all American / Finale.

— disbanded around Spring '98, VAIL joined FRUMPIES having already guested on PHRANC's 1995 solo EP, 'Goofyfoot'.

– compilations, etc. –

Jun 98. (cd) *Kill Rock Stars;* <(*KRS 298CD*)> **THE SINGLES** May98

– New radio / Rebel girl / DemiRep / In accordance to natural law / Strawberry Julius / Anti-pleasure dissertation / Rah! rah! replica / I like fucking / I hate danger.

BIOHAZARD

Formed: Brooklyn, New York, USA . . . 1988 by BOBBY HAMBEL, EVAN SEINFELD, BILLY GRAZIADEI and DANNY SCHULER. Emerging out of the NY hardcore/metal scene, they amassed a considerable grassroots following through constant touring and a self-titled indie label debut in 1990. Signed to 'Roadrunner', the band gained further plaudits for their second set, 'URBAN DISCIPLINE', a metal feast that attracted the major label attentions of 'Warner Brothers'. The third album, 'STATE OF THE WORLD ADDRESS', cracked the US Top 50, another savage slab of political aggression, which saw the group incorporating elements of CYPRESS HILL-esque stoner rap. They made their first major UK appearance at Donington's 1994 "Monsters Of Rock" fest, the group causing controversy by indulging in potentially dangerous audience participation (they returned two years later, even higher on the bill!). Although tipped for premier league activity, a fourth album, 'MATA

LEAO' (1996), failed to convince either critics or fans, the band subsequently returning to 'Roadrunner' for a 1997 live set. In 1999, BIOHAZARD were up amongst the big guns again when 'Mercury' unleashed their sixth set, 'NEW WORLD DISORDER'. • **Songwriters:** Group compositions; except AFTER FOREVER (Black Sabbath). • **Trivia:** CYPRESS HILL's SEN DOG guested on the track, 'HOW IT IS'. EVAN aided SEPULTURA's MAX CAVALERA on the lyrics of 'Slave New World'.

Album rating: BIOHAZARD (*4) / URBAN DISCIPLINE (*6) / STATE OF THE WORLD ADDRESS (*6) / MATA LEAO (*4) / NO HOLDS BARRED (*5) / NEW WORLD DISORDER (*5)

BOBBY HAMBEL – guitar / **EVAN SEINFELD** – vocals, bass / **BILLY GRAZIADEI** – vocals, guitar, keyboards / **DANNY SCHULER** – drums

Maze Maze

Dec 90. (cd/lp) *<(MCD/MLP 1067)>* **BIOHAZARD** [ ] [ ]
– Retribution / Victory / Blue blood / Howard Beach / Wrong side of the tracks / Justified violence / Skinny song / Hold my own / Pain / Panic attack / Survival of the fittest / There and back / Scarred for life. *(cd re-iss. Sep94; same) (cd re-iss. Dec96 on 'SPV'; SPV 0764650-2) (cd re-iss. Feb98 on 'Magnetic'; 764650-2)*

Roadrunner Roadrunner

Oct 92. (cd/c/lp) *<(RR 9112-2/-4/-1)>* **URBAN DISCIPLINE** [ ] [ ]
– Chamber spins three / Punishment / Shades of grey / Business / Black and white and red all over / Man with a promise / Disease / Urban discipline / Loss / Wrong side of the tracks / Mistaken identity / We're only gonna die (from our arrogance) / Tears of blood. *(cd+=)* – Hold my own. *(digi-cd+=)* – Shades of grey (live) / Punishment (live). *(re-iss. cd Oct94; same) (cd re-mast.May00; RR 8747-2)*

Warners Warners

May 94. (cd/c/lp) *<(9362 45595-2/-4/-1)>* **STATE OF THE WORLD ADDRESS** [ ] [48]
– State of the world address / Down for life / What makes us tick / Tales from the hard side / How it is / Remember / Five blocks to the subway / Each day / Failed territory / Lack there of / Pride / Human animal / Cornered / Love denied / Ink.

Jun 94. (c-s) *(W 0254C)* **TALES FROM THE HARD SIDE / DOWN FOR LIFE** [47] [ ]
(10"+=/cd-s+=) *(W 0254 TE/CD)* – State of the world address / ('A'video edit).

Jun 94. (cd-s) **FEELING GOOD. /** [-] [ ]
(above single on 'Mercury')

Aug 94. (10"red/c-s/cd-s) *(W 0259 TE/C/CD)* **HOW IT IS. / ('A'-Brooklyn bootleg 2 + 3)** [62] [ ]
(cd-s+=) *(W 0259CDX)* – ('A'-Lethal MOD mix) / ('A'-Lethal instrumental mix).

— now a trio when HAMBEL quit late '95.

May 96. (cd/c) *<(9362 46208-2/-4)>* **MATA LEAO** [72] [ ]
– Authority / These eyes / Stigmatized / Control / Cleansing / Comepetition / Modern democracy / Better days / Gravity / A lot to learn / Waiting to die / Away / True strengths / Thorn / In vain.

— added **ROB ECHEVERRIA** – guitar (ex-HELMET)

Roadrunner Roadrunner

Aug 97. (cd) *<(RR 8803-2)>* **NO HOLDS BARRED (live)** [ ] [ ]
– Shades of grey / What makes us tick / Authority / Urban discipline / Modern democracy / Business / Tales from the hardside / Better days / Victory / Lot to learn / How it is / After forever / Tears of blood / Chamber spins three / Wrong side of the tracks / Waiting to die / These eyes / Punishment / Hold my own. *(re-iss. May00; same)*

Mercury Mercury

May 99. (cd) *<(546032-2)>* **NEW WORLD DISORDER** [ ] [ ]
– Resist / Switchback / Salvation / End of my rope / All for none / Inner fear on / Abandon in place / Skin / Camouflage / Decline / Cycle of abuse / Dogs of war / New world disorder.

BIRTHA

Conception: USA . . . early 70's by all-female hard-rock quartet of SHELE PINIZZOTTO, SHERRY HAGLER, ROSEMARY BUTLER and LIVER FAVELA. Their embryonic days were spent cloning the sounds of URIAH HEEP, the resulting two albums on the 'Probe'(!) label, being a profound influence on the likes of FANNY. The vocal duties were shared by either SHELE, ROSEMARY or LIVER.

Album rating: BIRTHA (*6) / CAN'T STOP THE MADNESS (*5)

SHELE PINIZZOTTO – vocals, guitar / **ROSEMARY BUTLER** – vocals, bass / **SHERRY HAGLER** – keyboards / **OLIVIA 'LIVER' FAVELA** – vocals, drums

Probe Dunhill

Oct 72. (7") *<4328>* **FREE SPIRIT. / WORK ON A DREAM** [-] [ ]

Nov 72. (lp) *(SPBA 6267) <DSK 50127>* **BIRTHA** [ ] [ ]
– Free spirit / Fine talking man / Tuesday / Feeling lonely / She was good to me / Work on a dream / Too much woman (for a hen pecked man) / Judgement day / Forgotten soul.

Aug 73. (7") *<4362>* **DIRTY WORK. / ORIGINAL MIDNIGHT MAMA** [-] [ ]

Sep 73. (lp) *(SPBA 6272)* **CAN'T STOP THE MADNESS** [ ] [-]
– Freedom / My man told me / Don't let it get you down / Sun / Let us sing / Rock me / All this love / (When will ya) Understand / My pants are too short / Can't stop the madness.

— split and it took a decade for BUTLER to start a solo career

BITCH

Formed: Switzerland . . . 1979 by brothers ERIC, JIMMY and GEOFFREY SCHMID. They only managed to squeeze out two mediocre German albums, the band's music hardly as shocking as the name would suggest. BITCH were lambasted by some for their rather derivative Euro-centric take on the NWOBHM.

Album rating: FIRST BITE (*5) / SOME LIKE IT HOT (*4)

ERIC SCHMID – vocals / GEOFFREY SCHMID – guitar, vocals / **MARC PORTMAN** – guitar, vocals / **RODDY LANDOLT** – bass, vocals / **JIMMY SCHMID** – drums, vocals

Bellaphon not iss.

1980. (lp) *(26040001)* **FIRST BITE** [-] [-] German
– First bite / Working for a company / My car / Wheel of time / David (burning desire) / Headlines / Maggie / Hungry eyes / The seashore / She's a rocker / Your love.

1982. (lp) *(26040003)* **SOME LIKE IT HOT** [-] [-] German
– (intro) / Teenage heartache / Babe it's you / Big times / Leaving it all behind / Hollywood dance / Doctor Tricky / C'mon / Start it all over / The end.

— split in 1982

BITCH

Formed: Los Angeles, California, USA . . . early 80's by BETSY WEISS (from a ska band), DAVID CARRUTH, MARK ANTHONY WEBB and ROBBY SETTLES. Big BETSY and the boys first set metal tongues a-wagging in 1982 with the release of their debut EP, 'DAMNATION ALLEY'. Their turbo-charged shlock-rock metal drew comparisons to MOTORHEAD, a debut album, 'BE MY SLAVE', setting out the band's leather-clad S&M agenda. After a 3/4 year hiatus, they returned with the much-improved, 'THE BITCH IS BACK', although the BITCH moniker and attitude were subsequently substituted for an air-brushed AOR image in BETSY. Fortunately, this didn't work and BITCH reverted back to their nasty old ways, releasing the final effort in '89.

Album rating: DAMNATION ALLEY mini (*4) / BE MY SLAVE (*4) / THE BITCH IS BACK (*5) / A ROSE BY ANY OTHER (*3) / Betsy: BETSY (*4)

BETSY WEISS – vocals / **DAVID CARRUTH** – guitar / **MARK ANTHONY WEBB** – bass / **ROBBY SETTLES** – drums

Roadrunner Metal Blade

1982. (m-lp) *<MBR 1002>* **DAMNATION ALLEY** [-] [ ]
– Saturdays / Never come home / Damnation alley He's gone / Live for the whip. *(cd-iss. Jan97; 398414213CD)*

1983. (lp) *<MBR 1007>* **BE MY SLAVE** [-] [ ]
– Right from the start / Be my slave / Leatherbound / Riding in thunder / Save you from the world / Heavy metal breakdown / Gimme a kiss / In heat / Make it real (make it rock) / World War III.

— **RON CORDY** – bass; repl. WEBB

Jun 87. (lp) *(RR 9627) <73256>* **THE BITCH IS BACK** [ ] [ ]
– Do you wanna rock / Hot and heavy / Me and the boys / Storm raging up / The bitch is back / Head banger / Face to face / Turns me on / Skullcrusher. *(cd-iss. Jan97 on 'Metal Blade'; 396414218CD)*

1988. (lp; as BETSY) *(RR 9542-1)* **BETSY** [-] [-] Dutch
– You want it you got it / You'll never get out (of this love alive) / Devil made you do it / Rock 'n roll musician / Cold shot to the heart / Flesh and blood / Turn you inside out / What am I gonna do with you / Stand up for rock / Sunset strut.

— reverted back to the name BITCH, splitting in the late 80's.

1989. (m-lp) *<73418>* **A ROSE BY ANY OTHER** [-] [ ]
– Walls of love / Throw me in / Make it real / Sunset strut / Crashthepartysmashthecake / Skull crusher. *(cd-iss. Jan97; 3984 14214CD)*

BITCHES SIN

Formed: Cumbria, England . . . 1980 by brothers IAN and PETER TOOMEY, alongside BILL KNOWLES, ALAN COCKBURN and PERRY HODDER (the latter two were subsequently replaced by FRANK QUEGAN and MIKE FRAZIER respectively). After a one-off single, 'SIGN OF THE TIMES', for the 'Neat' label, they suffered from more personnel changes before the release of their hard edged heavy rock album, 'PREDATOR' (1982). A few 45's hit the shops before they broke up, their second album, 'INVADERS' finally gaining a belated release in '89.

Album rating: PREDATOR (*4) / INVADERS (*4)

FRANK QUEGAN – vocals; repl. ALAN COCKBURN / **IAN TOOMEY** – guitar / **PETER TOOMEY** – guitar / **MIKE FRAZIER** – bass; repl. PERRY HODDER / **BILL KNOWLES** – drums

Neat not iss.

Apr 81. (7") *(NEAT 09)* **ALWAYS READY. / SIGN OF THE TIMES** [ ] [-]

— **TONY TOMKINSON** – vocals; repl. QUEGAN

— **MARTIN OWEN** – bass; repl. FRAZIER

— **MARK BIDDLESCOMBE** – drums; repl. KNOWLES

Heavy Metal not iss.

Jun 82. (lp) *(HMRLP 4)* **PREDATOR** [ ] [-]
– April fool / Haneka / Runaway / Lady lies / Dirty women / Fallen star / Strangers on the shore / Looser / Riding high / Aardschok.

Terminal not iss.

Aug 83. (c-ep) *(TCAS 21)* **OUT OF MY MIND EP** [ ] [-]

QT not iss.

Dec 83. (7") *(QT 001)* **NO MORE CHANCES. / OVERNIGHT** [ ] [-]
(12"+=) *(QT 001-12)* – Ice angels.

Metalother King Klassic

May 89. (lp) *(OTH 14)* **INVADERS** [ ] [ ] 1986

— In 1988, the TOOMEY's formed FLASH POINT, releasing one album, 'NO POINT OF REFERENCE'.

BIVOUAC

Formed: Derby, England . . . early 90's by songwriter PAUL YEADON, along with GRANVILLE MARSDEN and ANTHONY HODKINSON. Straight outta Derby as the US grunge scene exploded in the UK, BIVOUAC may have seemed unlikely candidates for beating the Americans at their own game. Yet by the mid-90's, the band had been signed to 'Geffen', home to NIRVANA amongst others and a far cry from the band's early days co-headlining with JACOB'S MOUSE. Initially securing a deal with Workers Playtime offshoot, 'Elemental', the band issued a debut single/EP, 'A.B.C.', closely following it up with 'SLACK' and 'GOOD DAY SONG'. Whether by accident or design, BIVOUAC sounded like they'd lived in Seattle all their lives, right down to the choppy, buzz-saw guitar riffs and Americanised vocal style. No bad thing at the time of course, as the band secured themselves support slots with such US alt-rock aristocrats as FUGAZI and The JESUS LIZARD. 1993 also saw the release of their debut album, 'TUBER', a major label bidding war ensuing as the big boys vied for the lads' signatures. Going the whole hog and signing for 'Geffen', the band concentrated their efforts on cracking the American market, KEITH YORK replacing the departing HODKINSON. By the release of 1995's follow-up album, 'FULL SIZE BOY', however, the grunge scene had splintered and BIVOUAC's moment seemed to have passed.

Album rating: TUBER (*7) / FULL SIZE BOY (*7)

PAUL YEADON – vocals, guitar / **GRANVILLE MARSDEN** – bass / **ANTHONY HODKINSON** – drums

El-e-mental | Engine

May 92. (12"ep) *(ELM 002T)* **A.B.C. / FISHES. / STICK STUCK / ME TED AND CHARLES** [ ] [-]

Oct 92. (12"ep/cd-ep) *(ELM 004 T/CD)* **SLACK. / TOWLD / TWO STICKS** [ ] [-]

Jun 93. (c-ep) *<3>* **DERBY & JOAN** (compilation) [-] [ ]

Jun 93. (7") *(ELM 10S)* **GOOD DAY SONG. /** [ ] [ ]
(cd-s+=) *(ELM 10CD)* – Squeaker, Bess, bread, beans and cash / Trepanning.

Jun 93. (cd/c/lp) *(ELM 11 CDX/LP)* **TUBER** [ ] [ ] Mar94
– Good day song / Big question mark / Dragging your weight around / Rue / Deadend friend / Drank / Steel strung / The need / The bell foundry / Bad day song.

Aug 93. (7") *(ELM 12S)* **THE BELL FOUNDRY. / LEAD** [ ] [ ]
(cd-s+=) *(ELM 12CD)* – Saltwater heal.

May 94. (10"ep/7"ep/cd-ep) *(ELM 20/+S/CD)* **MARKED AND TAGGED E.P.** [ ] [ ]
– And then she ate / Spine / Art, science and making things.

—— **KEITH YORK** – drums (ex-DOCTOR PHIBES & THE HOUSE OF WAX EQUATIONS) repl. HODKINSON

Geffen | D.G.C.

May 95. (7") *(GFS 89)* **THINKING. /** [ ] [ ]
(cd-s+=) *(GFSTD 89)* –

Jul 95. (7"/c-s) *(GFS/+C 90)* **MONKEY SANCTUARY (CYNIC). / 45 SEATED STANDING NIL** [ ] [ ]
(cd-s+=) *(GFSTD 90)* – Deadend friend.

Jul 95. (cd/c/lp) *(GED/GEC/GEF 24561)* *<24803>* **FULL SIZE BOY** [ ] [ ]
– Not going back there again / Thinking / Trepanning / Gecko or skink / Monkey sanctuary / My only safe bet / Familiar / Mattress / Bing bong / Lounge lizard / Ray is related to the shark.

—— split after the failure of above

BLACK CROWES

Formed: Atlanta, Georgia, USA . . . 1984 under the name MR CROWE'S GARDEN by the ROBINSON brothers, CHRIS and RICH (sons of STAN ROBINSON, who had a minor US hit in 1959 with 'Boom A Dip Dip'). By 1988, they'd adopted the BLACK CROWES moniker and assembled the line-up that would remain more or less stable throughout their career. Picked up by the ever eclectic RICK RUBIN, for his fledgling 'Def American' label, the band released their debut album in 1990 to almost universal acclaim. Taking its title from an old ELMORE JAMES song, the record was steeped in classic American musical tradition; a seamless mesh of hard-rock, blues, soul, country and R&B that drew inevitable comparisons with The FACES and The ROLLING STONES. Yet the BLACK CROWES were unmistakably American, Southern American in the tradition of The ALLMAN BROTHERS and LYNYRD SKYNYRD. The songwriting was simple but effective, while CHRIS ROBINSON's voice was a revelation, if a little wearing after prolonged exposure. This was feelgood music, genuine rough'n'ready soul music as opposed to the slick, neutered wallpaper that passes for much modern black soul. 'TWICE AS HARD', 'JEALOUS AGAIN', 'COULD'VE BEEN SO BLIND' and a rough hewn cover of OTIS REDDING's 'HARD TO HANDLE' sounded effortless, while ROBINSON put in a spine-tingling vocal performance on the emotive ballad, 'SHE TALKS TO ANGELS'. Live, the BLACK CROWES were naturally in their element and following the album's release, the band embarked on a punishing touring schedule, playing with everyone from DOGS D'AMOUR to ZZ TOP (in a well documented incident, the band were dropped from the ZZ TOP tour following CHRIS ROBINSON's criticisms of corporate sponsorship). With the permanent addition of keyboardist EDDIE HAWRYSCH to flesh out the sound, and replacing guitarist JEFF CEASE with MARC FORD (ex-BURNING TREE), the band cut 'THE SOUTHERN HARMONY AND MUSICAL COMPANION'. Released May 1992 (incredibly, recorded in just over a week), the album built on the solid blueprint of the debut. The band had amassed a sizeable following through their ceaseless live work and the album deservedly hit the top spot in America, No.2 in the UK. With the songwriting more assured and the arrangements more ambitious, The 'CROWES succeeded in carving out a musical identity distinct from their weighty musical influences. The addition of female backing singers added a richness to the sound and the record segued smoothly from the raucous R&B of opener 'STING ME' to the stoned melancholy of 'THORN IN MY PRIDE' and on to the darker, 'Midnight Rambler'-esque 'BLACK MOON CREEPING'. Just to make sure people knew where he was coming from (man), ROBINSON closed the set with a mellow, acoustic reading of BOB MARLEY's 'TIME WILL TELL'. Soon after the album's release, the band hit the road once more, a headlining spot at the 1994 Glastonbury Festival illustrating just how high the 'CROWES had flown. Released later that year amid a storm of controversy over the cover shot (Uncle Sam[antha] in a compromising position, you could say), 'AMORICA' was something of a disappointment. Perhaps the relentless touring was beginning to take its toll, as the record sounded claustrophobic and turgid, the pace rarely rising above a monotonous plod. The songs were also lacking in cohesion and focus, although moments of genius were still evident on the likes of 'A CONSPIRACY' and the single, 'WISER TIME'. The band continued to cut it live, getting further out both musically and image wise. While The 'CROWES had always been defiantly 70's in their choice of apparel, CHRIS ROBINSON, in particular, had graduated from a vaguely glam look to a latter day CHARLES MANSON-alike. This was the revenge of the 70's; oriental rugs, ragged denim flares, bare feet, hell, even a GRATEFUL DEAD t-shirt! Rambling organ solos were also de rigueur of course, but fans lucky enough to catch the band at their low-key London gigs at the tail end of '96/early '97, were treated to a stripped down, largely acoustic set. While completely clueless, mullet headed, rock bores voiced their disapproval, the Christ-like ROBINSON mesmerised the more discerning 'CROWES fans with sterling covers of BOB DYLAN, BYRDS and LITTLE FEAT material. The 1996 album, 'THREE SNAKES AND ONE CHARM' was also a return to form, encompassing a greater diversity of styles and adding a bit of SLY STONE-style funkiness to their ragged retro patchwork. Where the band go from here is anybody's guess although a drum'n'bass remix is unlikely. With bassist JOHNNY COLT and guitarist FORD both leaving within a few months of each other, things didn't look too good. However, all was well again by early '99 with the release of their fifth set, 'BY YOUR SIDE', a typical FACES-meets-'STONES effort that highlighted their best track for some time, 'KICKIN' MY HEART AROUND' (a minor hit from late the previous year). After a much-praised one nighter with 'ZEPPELIN's axe king JIMMY PAGE (an album, 'LIVE AT THE GREEK' was issued in 2000), The BLACK CROWES returned the following year with 'LIONS' on the 'V2' imprint. • **Songwriters:** All written by ROBINSON brothers, except HARD TO HANDLE (Otis Redding) / RAINY DAY WOMAN NOS.12 & 35 + WHEN THE NIGHT COMES FALLING FROM THE SKY (Bob Dylan) / TIME WILL TELL (Bob Marley) / DREAMS (Allman Brothers). • **Trivia:** CHRIS and RICH's father STAN ROBINSON had a minor US hit in '59 with 'BOOM-A-DIP-DIP'. Chuck Leavell (ex-ALLMANS) produced and guested on the 1992 lp.

Album rating: SHAKE YOUR MONEY MAKER (*9) / THE SOUTHERN HARMONY AND MUSICAL COMPANION (*9) / AMORICA (*7) / THREE SNAKES AND ONE CHARM (*7) / BY YOUR SIDE (*7) / LIONS (*5)

CHRIS ROBINSON (b.20 Dec'66) – vocals / **'Young' RICH ROBINSON** (b. RICHARD, 24 May'69) – guitar / **JEFF CEASE** (b.24 Jun'67, Nashville, USA) – guitar / **JOHNNY COLT** (b. 1 May'68, Cherry Point, New Connecticut) – bass (repl. 2 earlier) / **STEVE GORMAN** (b.17 Aug'65, Hopkinsville, Kentucky) – drums (repl. 5 earlier)

Def American | Def American

Mar 90. (cd/c/lp) *(842515-2/-4/-1)* *<24278>* **SHAKE YOUR MONEY MAKER** [ ] [4] Oct89
– Twice as hard / Jealous again / Sister luck / Could I've been so blind / Hard to handle / Seeing things / Thick'n'thin / She talks to angels / Struttin' blues / Stare it cold. *(finally hit UK No.36 Aug91 – re-dist.Sep92) (re-iss. Dec94 on 'American-BMG' cd/c; 74321 24839-2/-4) (cd re-iss. Feb99 on 'Columbia'; 491790-2) (cd re-iss. Aug00; 499653-2)*

May 90. (7") *(DEFA 4)* *<19697>* **JEALOUS AGAIN. / THICK'N'THIN** [ ] [75] Apr90
(12"+=/12"pic-d+=)(cd-s+=) (DEFA/+P 4-12)(DEFAC 4) – Waitin' guilty.

Aug 90. (7"/c-s) *(DEFA/+M 6)* *<19668>* **HARD TO HANDLE. / JEALOUS AGAIN (acoustic)** [45] [45] Oct90
(12"+=/12"sha-pic-d+=) *(DEFA/+P 6-12)* – Twice as hard / Stare it cold (both live).
(cd-s+=) *(DEFAC 6)* – Twice as hard (remix).

Jan 91. (7"/c-s) *(DEFA/+M 7)* **TWICE AS HARD. / JEALOUS AGAIN (live)** [47] [-]
(12"+=)(cd-s+=) *(DEFA 7-12)(DEFAC 7)* – Jealous guy (live).
(12"pic-d+=) *(DEFAP 7-12)* – Could I've been so blind (live).

Mar 91. (c-s/7") *<19403>* **SHE TALKS TO ANGELS. / ('A'live video version)** [-] [30]

Jun 91. (7") *(DEFA 8)* **JEALOUS AGAIN. / SHE TALKS TO ANGELS** [70] [-]
(12"+=) *(DEFA 8-12)* – She talks to angels (live).
(cd-s++=) *(DEFAC 8)* – Could I've been so blind (live).
(12"pic-d) *(DEFAP 8-12)* – ('A'acoustic) / ('B'acoustic) / Waitin' guilty / Struttin' blues.

Jun 91. (7") *<19245>* **HARD TO HANDLE. / WAITIN' GUILTY** [-] [26]

Aug 91. (7") *(DEFA 10)* **HARD TO HANDLE. / SISTER LUCK (live)** [39] [-]
(cd-s+=) *(DEFCD 10)* – Sister Luck (live).
(7"sha-pic-d) *(DEFAP 10)* – Hard to handle / Stare it cold (live).
(12"+=) *(DEFA 10-12)* – Dreams (live).

Oct 91. (7") *(DEFA 13)* **SEEING THINGS. / COULD I'VE BEEN SO BLIND (live)** [72] [-]
(12"+=) *(DEFAG 13-12)* – She talks to angels (live) / Sister luck (live).
(cd-s) *(DEFAC 13)* – ('A'side) / Hard to handle / Jealous again / Twice as hard.

— **MARK FORD** (b.13 Apr'66, Los Angeles, Calif.) – guitar (ex-BURNING TREE) repl. CEASE / added **EDDIE HAWRYSCH** – keyboards

Apr 92. (etched-7") *(DEFA 16)* <18877> **REMEDY / DARLING OF THE UNDERGROUND PRESS** [24] [48] Jun92
(12"+=)(cd-s+=) *(DEFA 16-12)(DEFCD 16)* – Time will tell.

May 92. (cd/c/lp) *(512263-2/-4/-1)* <26916> **THE SOUTHERN HARMONY AND MUSICAL COMPANION** [2] [1]
– Sting me / Remedy / Thorn in my pride / Bad luck blue eyes goodbye / Sometime salvation / Hotel illness / Black moon creeping / No speak, no slave / My morning song / Time will tell. *(re-iss. Dec94 on 'American-BMG' cd/c; 74321 24840-2/-4) (cd re-iss. Feb99 on 'Columbia'; 491791-2)*

Aug 92. (c-s,cd-s) <18803> **THORN IN MY PRIDE. / STING ME** [-] [80]

Sep 92. (7") *(DEFA 21)* **STING ME. / RAINY DAY WOMEN NOS.12 & 35** [42] [-]
(cd-s) *(DEFCD 21)* – ('A'side) / She talks to angels / Thorn in my pride / Darling of the underground press.

Nov 92. (7") *(DEFA 23)* **HOTEL ILLNESS. / NO SPEAK, NO SLAVE** [47] [-]
(12"clear) *(DEFX 23)* – ('A'side) / Words you throw away / Rainy day women Nos.12 & 35.
(cd-s) *(DEFCD 23)* – ('A'side) / Rainy day / (Chris interview).
(cd-s) *(DEFCB 23)* – ('A'side) / Words you throw away / (Rich interview).

Jun 93. (7"/cd-s) *(862202-7/-2)* **REMEDY. / HARD TO HANDLE** [ ] [-]
(12"+=/cd-s+=) *(862203-1/-2)* – Hotel illness / Jealous again.

— added **EDDIE HARSCH** (b.27 May'57, Toronto, Ontario) – keyboards

American-BMG American-BMG

Nov 94. (cd/c/lp) *(74321 23682-2/-4/-1)* <43000> **AMORICA** [8] [11]
– Gone / A conspiracy / High head blues / Cursed diamond / Non-fiction / She gave good sunflower / P.25 London / Ballad in urgency / Wiser time / Downtown money waster / Descending. *(cd+=/c+=)* – Tied up and swallowed. *(cd re-iss. Feb99 on 'Columbia'; 491792-2)*

Jan 95. (7"blue) *(74321 25849-7)* **HIGH HEAD BLUES. / A CONSPIRACY / REMEDY (live)** [25] [-]
(ext'B'live; 12"+=) *(74321 25849-6)* – Thick'n'thin (live).
(cd-s++=) *(74321 25849-2)* – ('A'extended).
('B'live-cd-s+=) *(74321 25849-5)* – P25 London (live).

Jul 95. (7") *(74321 27267-7)* **WISER TIME. / CHEVROLET** [34] [-]
('A'-Rock mix; cd-s+=) (74321 27267-2) – She talks to angels (acoustic).
(cd-s) *(74321 29827-2)* – ('A'acoustic) / Jealous again (acoustic) / Non fiction (acoustic) / Thorn in my pride (acoustic).

Jul 96. (10"pic-d/cd-s) *(74321 39857-1/-2)* **ONE MIRROR TOO MANY. / PIMPERS PARADISE / SOMEBODY'S ON YOUR CASE** [51] [-]

Jul 96. (cd/c) *(74321 38484-2/-4)* <43082> **THREE SNAKES AND ONE CHARM** [17] [15]
– Under a mountain / Good Friday / Nebakanezer / One mirror too many / Blackberry / Girl from a pawnshop / (Only) Halfway to everywhere / Bring on, bring on / How much for your wings? / Let me share the ride / Better when you're not alone / Evil eye. *(cd re-iss. Feb99 on 'Columbia'; 491793-2)*

— COLT + FORD left; repl. by **SVEN PIPPEN** – bass (ex-MARY MY HOPE)

— added touring guitarist **AUDLEY FREED** (ex-CRY OF LOVE)

Columbia Columbia

Oct 98. (c-s) *(666666-4)* **KICKIN' MY HEART AROUND / IT MUST BE OVER** [55] [-]
(cd-s+=) *(666666-2)* – You don't have to go.
(cd-s+=) *(666666-5)* – Diamond ring (version).

Jan 99. (cd/c) *(491669-2/-4)* <69361> **BY YOUR SIDE** [34] [26]
– Go faster / Kickin' my heart around / By your side / Horsehead / Only a fool / Heavy / Welcome to the goodtimes / Go tell the congregation / Diamond ring / Then she said my name / Virtue and vice.

Jul 99. (7"/cd-s) <41902> **ONLY A FOOL. / WHEN THE NIGHT COMES FALLING FROM THE SKY** [-] [ ]

— In Jul'00, The BLACK CROWES were credited with JIMMY PAGE on a special 2CD-set, 'LIVE AT THE GREEK' (recorded late '99)

V2 V2

May 01. (cd) *(VVR 1015678)* <27091> **LIONS** [37] [20]
– Midnight from the inside out / Lickin' / Come on / No use lying / Losing my mind / Ozone mama / Greasy grass river / Soul singing / Miracle to me / Young man, old man / Cosmic friend / Cypress tree / Lay it all on me.

– compilations, etc. –

Aug 98. (5xcd-box) *Columbia; (C5K 65741)* **SHO 'NUFF** [ ] [ ]

Aug 00. (d-cd) *Columbia; (499857-2)* **AMORICA / THREE SNAKES AND ONE CHARM** [ ] [ ]

BLACKEYED SUSAN

Formed: Kentucky, USA ... 1991 by DEAN DAVIDSON, the former BRITNY FOX frontman. The line-up included RICK CRINITI, TONY SANTORO, ERIK VEVY and CHRIS BARNCO, who played their blend of AEROSMITH, 'STONES or BLACK CROWES type blues-based hard rock on their one and only long-player, 'ELECTRIC RATTLEBONE'. • **Note:** not to be confused with Australian outfit, The BLACK EYED SUSANS.

Album rating: ELECTRIC RATTLEBONE (*6)

DEAN DAVIDSON – vocals (ex-BRITNY FOX) / **RICK CRINITI** – guitar / **TONY SANTORO** – guitar / **ERIK LEVY** – bass / **CHRIS BRANCO** – drums

Mercury Mercury

Jul 91. (cd/c/lp) <(848 575-2/-4/-1)> **ELECTRIC RATTLEBONE** [ ] [ ]
– Electric rattlebone / Satisfaction / None of it matters / Sympathy / Ride with me / Old lady snow / Don't bring me down / Indica / She's so fine / How long / Best of friends / Holiday / Heart of the city.

— split after above

BLACK FLAG

Formed: Hermosa Beach, California, USA ... 1976 by GREG GINN and CHUCK DUKOWSKI. In 1977, their demo reached local indielabel 'Bomp', who, after over half a year decided not to release BLACK FLAG's debut 45, 'NERVOUS BREAKDOWN'. Instead, GREG and CHUCK, with sound men MUGGER and SPOT, formed their own label, 'S.S.T.' (Solid State Tuners), issuing the aforesaid single in 1978. By the time BLACK FLAG's debut lp, 'DAMAGED', was released in 1981, the group had suffered label difficulties with 'MCA-Unicorn', who didn't like the outrageous content of the tracks. Numerous personnel changes had also occured, mainly the substitution of KEITH MORRIS, with the harder looking and now legendary HENRY ROLLINS. SST took the major label to court and although the pivotal hardcore group won, they had to pay out a 6-figure sum. The influential label went on to help kickstart the careers of many hardcore/alternative acts such as HUSKER DU, MINUTEMEN, DINOSAUR JR, MEAT PUPPETS, etc. Meanwhile, BLACK FLAG (with GINN and ROLLINS at the helm), completed a series of near brilliant albums, ROLLINS even contributing a spoken word side on the half instrumental album, 'FAMILY MAN' (1984), a thing that he would do more when he took off on a successful solo venture that year. GINN and some new cohorts completed two more mid 80's sets, 'IN MY HEAD' and 'WHO'S GOT THE 10 1/2', before he too pursued a solo sojourn, although at first with instrumental punk-jazz fusion, GONE. BLACK FLAG were one of the first US acts to take DIY punk into hardcore, a hybrid sound that would later be revered by metal fans who had picked up on 90's US hardcore/punk groups like BAD RELIGION and OFFSPRING.

Album rating: DAMAGED (*8) / EVERYTHING WENT BLACK (*5) / THE FIRST FOUR YEARS (*7) compilation / MY WAR (*6) / FAMILY MAN (*4) / SLIP IT IN (*5) / LOOSE NUT (*5) / IN MY HEAD (*6) / WHO'S GOT THE 10 1/2 (*6) / WASTED . . . AGAIN (*7)

KEITH MORRIS – vocals / **GREG GINN** (b. 8 Jun'54) – guitar / **CHUCK DUKOWSKI** – bass / **BRIAN MIGDOL** – drums

not iss. S.S.T.

Oct 78. (7"ep) <SST 001> **NERVOUS BREAKDOWN. / FIX ME / I'VE HAD IT / WASTED** [-] [ ]
<US 10"colrd-ep/12"ep/cd-ep iss.1990; same>

— **CHAVO PEDERAST** (aka RON REYES) – vocals (ex-RED CROSS) repl. KEITH who formed CIRCLE JERKS. **ROBO** – drums repl. MIGDOL

Mar 80. (12"ep) <SST 003> **JEALOUS AGAIN / REVENGE. / WHITE MINORITY / NO VALUES / YOU BET WE'VE GOT SOMETHING PERSONAL AGAINST YOU!** [-] [ ]
(UK-iss.Mar83; same) <US 10"colrd-ep/12"ep/cd-ep iss.1990; same>

— **DEZ CADENA** – vocals, guitar (ex-RED CROSS) repl. REYES

Jan 81. (7"ep) <SST 005> **SIX PACK. / I'VE HEARD IT ALL BEFORE / AMERICAN WASTE** [-] [ ]
(UK-iss.Dec81 on 'Alternative Tentacles'; VIRUS 9) <US 10"colrd-ep/12"/ep/cd-ep iss.1990; same>

— **HENRY ROLLINS** (b. HENRY GARFIELD, 13 Feb '61, Washington, D.C.) – vocals (ex-SOA) repl. CHUCK who formed WURM (with ED DANKY and SIMON SMALLWOOD (vocalist of DEAD HIPPIE) – one lp surfaced in '85, 'FEAST' <SST 041>. CHUCK later formed SWA and was part of OCTOBERFACTION

— group now **ROLLINS, GINN, CADENA** (now rhythm guitar only) + **ROBO**

S.S.T. S.S.T.

Nov 81. (lp) <(SST 007)> **DAMAGED** [ ] [ ]
– Rise above / Spray paint / Six pack / What I see / TV party / Thirsty and miserable / Police story / Gimmie gimmie gimmie / Depression / Room 13 / Damaged II / No more / Padded cell / Life of pain / Damaged I.

— In the US, 'Posh Boy' issued '79 recording LOUIE LOUIE. / DAMAGED 1 *(PBS 13) (This was finally issued 10"coloured 1988 on 'SST' US) (re-iss. cd/c/lp Oct95; same)* LOUIE LOUIE was a KINGSMEN original.

— **BILL STEVENSON** + guest **EMIL** – drums repl. ROBO

1982. (7"ep) <SST 012> **TV PARTY. / I'VE GOT TO RUN / MY RULES** [-] [ ]
<US 12"+cd-ep iss.1990; same>

— guest on half **DALE NIXON** – bass (actually GREG under pseudonym) repl. CADENA who formed DC3

Mar 84. (lp) <(SST 023)> **MY WAR** [ ] [ ]
– My war / Can't decide / Beat my head agaist the wall / I love you / The swinging man / Forever time / Nothing left inside / Three nights / Scream. *(cd-iss. 1990; SST 023CD) (re-iss. cd/c/lp Oct95; same)*

— added **KIRA ROESSLER** – bass

Sep 84. (lp) <(SST 026)> **FAMILY MAN** [ ] [ ]
– Family man / Salt on a slug / The pups are doggin' it / Let your fingers do the walking / Long lost dog of it / I won't stick any of you unless and until I can stick all of you / Hollywood diary / Armageddon man / Account for what? / Shred reading (rattus norvegicus) / No deposit, no return. *(cd-iss. 1990; SST 026CD) (re-iss. cd/c/lp Oct95; same)*

Oct 84. (12") <(SST1 2001)> **FAMILY MAN. / I WON'T STICK ANY OF YOU UNLESS AND UNTIL I CAN STICK ALL OF YOU** [ ] [ ]

Dec 84. (lp) <(SST 029)> **SLIP IT IN** [ ] [ ]
– Slip it in / Black coffee / Wound up / Rat's eyes / Obliteration / The bars / My ghetto / You're not evil. *(cd-iss. 1990; SST 029CD) (re-iss. cd/c/lp Oct95; same)*

Jan 85. (c) <(SST 030)> **LIVE '84 (live)** [ ] [ ]
– The process of weeding out / My ghetto / Jealous again / I love you / Swinging man / Three nights / Nothing left inside / Black coffee. *(cd-iss. 1990; SST 030CD) (re-iss. cd/c/lp Oct95; same)*

Jun 85. (lp) <(SST 035)> **LOOSE NUT** [ ] [ ]
– Loose nut / Bastard in love / Annihilate this week / Best one yet / Modern man / This is good / I'm the one / Sinking / Now she's black. *(cd-iss. 1990; SST 035CD) (re-iss. cd/c/lp Oct95; same)*

— trimmed to **GINN, KIRA + STEVENSON** when ROLLINS went solo

Sep 85. (m-lp) <(SST 037)> **THE PROCESS OF WEEDING OUT**
– Your last affront / Screw the law / The process of weeding out / Southern rise. *(US 10"colrd/m-cd iss.1990)*

Nov 85. (lp) <(SST 045)> **IN MY HEAD**
– Paralyzed / The crazy girl / Black love / Retired at 21 / Drinking and driving / White hot / In my head / Society's tease / It's all up to you / You let me down. *(cd-iss. 1990 +=; SST 045CD)* – Out of this world / I can see you. *(cd re-iss. Oct95; same)*

— **ANTHONY MARTINEZ** – drums; repl. STEVENSON who had already joined OCTOBERFACTION

May 86. (lp) <(SST 060)> **WHO'S GOT THE 10 1/2 (live in Portland 23/8/85)**
– I'm the one / Loose nut / Bastard in love / Slip it in / This is good / Gimmie gimmie gimmie / Drinking and driving / Modern man / My war. *(cd-iss. 1990) (re-iss. cd/c/lp Oct95; same) (cd+=)* – Annihilate / Wasted / Sinking / Jam / Louie Louie / Best one yet.

— had already split earlier in '86. KIRA continued with DOS, alongside MIKE WATT of The MINUTEMEN. After playing bass on a one-off trio project/eponymous album in 1985 with TOM TROCCOLI'S DOG <SST 047> – solo artist GINN had also been part of TOM's own quintet, OCTOBERFACTION – he also teamed up with ANDREW WEISS to form instrumental group, GONE.

– compilations, others, etc. –

on 'S.S.T.' unless mentioned otherwise

Mar 83. (d-lp) <(SST 015)> **EVERYTHING WENT BLACK** (rare 78-81)
(re-iss. Oct95 lp/c/cd; SST 015/+C/CD)

1984. (lp) <SST 021> **THE FIRST FOUR YEARS** -
(UK-iss.Oct95 & Oct99 lp/c/cd; SST 021/+C/CD)

Dec 87. (lp/c/cd) <(SST 166/+C/CD)> **WASTED . . . AGAIN**
– Wasted / TV party / Six pack / I don't care / I've had it / Jealous again / Slip it in / Annihilate this week / Loose nut / Gimme gimme / Louie Louie / Drinking and driving. *(re-iss. Oct95; same)*

Jun 93. (12"/c-s/cd-s) *(SST 226/+C/CD)* **I CAN SEE YOU**

GONE

— **GREG GINN** – guitar / **ANDREW WEISS** – bass

S.S.T. S.S.T.

Jul 86. (lp) <(SST 061)> **LET'S GET REAL, REAL GONE FOR A CHANGE**
– Insideous detraction / Get gone / Peter gone / Rosanne / Climbing Rat's wall / Watch the tractor / Last days of being stepped on / CH 69 / Lawndale Rock City / Hypercharge – the wait (the fifth force suite). *(re-iss. May93 cd/c; SST 061 CD/C)*

Jan 87. (lp) <(SST 086)> **GONE II – BUT NEVER TOO GONE!**
– Jungle law / New vengeance / Unglued / Turned over stone / Drop the hat / Adams / Time of entry / Left holding the bag / GTV / Daisy strut / Cut off / Put it there / Utility hole / Yesterday is teacher / How soon they forget / Cobra XVIII. *(re-iss. May93 cd/c; SST 086 CD/C)*

— In 1993, GREG released 'COLLEGE ROCK' EP as POINDEXTER STEWART

— **GINN** re-formed GONE with **STEVE SHARP** – bass / **GREGORY MOORE** – drums

Jan 94. (lp/cd) <(SST 300/+CD)> **THE CRIMINAL MIND**
– Poor losers / Punch drunk / Pull it out / Pump room / Snagglepuss / PS was wrong / Off the chains / Smoking gun in Waco / Spankin' plank / Piled one higher / Row nine / Toggle / Big check / Ankle strap / Hand out / Freeny / Unknown calibar.

Apr 94. (12"/cd-s) <(SST 303)> **SMOKING GUN IN WACO. /**
(re-iss. Feb96; same)

Aug 94. (lp/c/cd) <(SST 306/+C/CD)> **ALL THE DIRT THAT'S FIT TO PRINT**
– Picket fence asylum / Upward spiral / Mutilated fade / Damage control / Kattiwompus / 39051 / White tail / Crawdad / Meet me in the van / Bosco pit / Huntin w/ a rich man / 4 a.m.

Sep 95. (12") <(SST 303)> **DAMAGE CONTROL. / SMOKING GUN (IN WACO)**

Apr 96. (cd) <(SST 313)> **BEST LEFT UNSAID**
– Bicycle riding assassin / My name is on the masthead but. . . / Hotheaded butchers / Closet courtaholic / Stray bullet / We have pigs / Closeted publishers / Second gunman / Bomb plot case / Mother called Ill / Hostile witness.

Jul 98. (cd) <(SST 344)> **COUNTRY DUMB**
– Dinky cat / (Lost in) Filegate / Big government, small mind / Pentagon expands / Cut your hair, drink Coors / "Punks" in government / Rage against intelligence / Another existential excuse / Paula Jones Clinton / Hip Castro conservative / Woozy news hound / "Punk" and the cash narcotic / Country dumb or city stupid? / Sugar bear.

GREG GINN

— with **GREGORY MOORE** – tom-tom / **DAVID RAVEN** – drums / later added **STEVE SHARP** – bass

Cruz Cruz

Jun 93. (12"/c-s/cd-s) <(CRZ 028/+C/CD)> **PAYDAY. / PAYDAY / PIG MF**

Jun 93. (lp/c/cd) <(CRZ 029/+C/CD)> **GETTING EVEN**
– I've changed / Kill burn fluff / You drive me crazy / Pig MF / Hard thing / Payday / Nightmares / Torn / PF flyer / I can't wait / Short fuse / Not that simple / Yes officer / Crawling inside.

Sep 93. (lp/c/cd) <(CRZ 032/+C/CD)> **DICK**
– Never change baby / I want to believe / You wanted it / I won't give in / Creeps / Strong violent type / Don't tell me / You dirty rat / Disgusting reference / Walking away / Ignorant order / Slow fuse / You're gonna get it.

Mar 94. (12"/cd-s) *(CRZ 033/+CD)* **DON'T TELL ME / DON'T TELL ME (instrumental). / YES OFFICER (remix) / YOU'RE GOING TO GET IT (remix)**

Aug 94. (lp/c/cd) <(CRZ 036/+C/CD)> **LET IT BURN (BECAUSE I DON'T LIVE THERE ANYMORE)**
– On a roll / Taking the other side / Lame Hollywood cop / Lame excuses / In your face motherfucker / Hey, stupid face / Venting / Let it burn / Drifting away / Military destroys mind/body / I don't want it / Destroy my mind / Exiled from Lame Street.

KILLER TWEEKER BEES

GREG GINN + ANDY BATWINAS

S.S.T. S.S.T.

Sep 97. (cd) <(SST 345CD)> **TWEEKER BLUES** Aug97
– Buyer's club / Grounds to indict / Big phoney / Tweeker blues / Erotic edge / Rat zombie / The government protects me / Pure police for now people / Rage against your mother / Now that I've solved society's problem / Junk cool.

BLACKFOOT

Formed: Jacksonville, Florida, USA . . . 1968 by RICKY MEDLOCKE (grandson of 50's bluegrass maestro, SHORTY), who soon cemented the line-up with GREG T. WALKER, CHARLIE HARGRETT and JACKSON SPIRES. They finally found an outlet to release their 1975! debut, 'NO RESERVATIONS' (1975; the title a reference to RICKY's native Indian heritage), the record having surprisingly turned up on the more eclectic UK label, 'Island'. Their second album, 'FLYIN' HIGH' confused many, being released by 'Epic' only in the States! Later in the 70's, they signed to 'Atco', who obviously saw a gap in the market for Southern hard rock'n'boogie, following the tragic LYNYRD SKYNYRD plane crash. BLACKFOOT tracked 'SKYNYRD into the Top 30 with 'HIGHWAY SONG', a number that featured on their breakthrough US Top 50 album, 'STRIKES' (1979). In the same mould, their next two albums, 'TOMCATTIN' (1980) and 'MARAUDER' (1981) both became regulars in the Top 50, the following year's live set, 'HIGHWAY SONG – BLACKFOOT LIVE' a surprise UK Top 20 entry. Much speculation followed the inclusion of keyboard man, KEN HENSLEY, formerly a member of British heavyweights, URIAH HEEP, the resulting sound on '83's 'SIOGO' (stands for 'Suck It Or Get Out'), alienating some of the more traditional elements of their American fan base. With HENSLEY having been substituted by Texan AXE-man, BOBBY BARTH, the band's commercial fortunes declined further with the release of 'VERTICAL SMILES' (1984). In the same year, BARTH was involved in a crash which killed his fellow AXE member MICHAEL OSBOURNE. MEDLOCKE continued to sporadically resurrect BLACKFOOT over the course of the next decade, although their heyday was clearly over. • **Songwriters:** Group compositions, except I GOT A LINE ON YOU (Spirit) / THE STEALER + WISHING WELL (Free) / PAY MY DUES (Blue Image) / etc. • **Trivia:** MEDLOCKE played drums on LYNYRD SKYNYRD's posthumous odds and sods album, 'First & Last'.

Album rating: NO RESERVATIONS (*5) / FLYIN' HIGH (*6) / STRIKES (*6) / TOMCATTIN' (*6) / MARAUDER (*6) / HIGHWAY SONG – BLACKFOOT LIVE (*7) / SIOGO (*4) / VERTICAL SMILES (*4) / RICK MEDLOCKE & BLACKFOOT (*4) / MEDICINE MAN (*4) / AFTER THE REIGN (*4) / RATTLESNAKE ROCK'N'ROLL: THE BEST OF BLACKFOOT compilation (*7)

RICKY MEDLOCKE – vocals, guitar / **CHARLIE HARGRETT** – guitar / **GREG T. WALKER** – bass / **JACKSON SPIRES** – drums, vocals

Island not iss.

1975. (lp) *(ILPS 9326)* **NO RESERVATIONS** -
– Railroad man / Indian world / Stars / Not another maker / Born to rock & roll / Take a train / Big wheels / I stand alone / Railroad man. *(cd-iss. Jan98 on 'Germanofon'; HF 9530)*

not iss. Epic

1976. (lp) <PE 34378> **FLYIN' HIGH** -
– Feelin' good / Flyin' high / Try a little harder / Stranger on the road / Save your time / Dancin' man / Island of life / Junkie's dream / Madness / Mother. *(cd-iss. Jan98 on 'Germanofon'; HF 9547) (cd re-iss. Jul00 on 'Collectables'; COLCD 6452-2)*

M.C.A. M.C.A.

Jul 77. (7") *(MCA 307)* **WHEN WILL I SEE YOU AGAIN. / LAY THE REAL THING ON ME** -

Atco Atco

Aug 79. (lp/c) *(K/K4 50603)* <112> **STRIKES** 42 May79
– Road fever / I got a line on you / Left turn on a red light / Pay my dues / Baby blue / Wishing well / Run and hide / Train train / Highway song.

Sep 79. (7") *(K 11368)* <7104> **HIGHWAY SONG. / ROAD FEVER** 26 Jul79

Feb 80. (7") *(K 11447)* <7207> **TRAIN TRAIN. / BABY BLUE** 38 Oct79

May 80. (7") <7303> **STREET FIGHTER. / MY OWN LOVE** -

Jul 80. (lp/c) *(K/K4 50702)* <101> **TOMCATTIN'** 50 Jun80
– Warped / On the run / Dream on / Street fighter / Gimme, gimme, gimme / Every man should know (Queenie) / In the night / Reckless abandoner / Spendin' cabbage / Fox chase.

Jul 80. (7") *(K 11538)* <7313> **GIMME, GIMME, GIMME. / IN THE NIGHT**

Sep 80. (7") *(K 11610)* **ON THE RUN. / STREET FIGHTER** -

Nov 80. (7") *(K 11636)* **EVERY MAN SHOULD KNOW (QUEENIE). / HIGHWAY SONG** -

Jun 81. (7") <7331> **FLY AWAY. / GOOD MORNING** - 42

Jul 81. (lp/c) *(K/K4 50799)* <107> **MARAUDER** 38 48
– Good morning / Payin' for it / Diary of a workingman / Too hard to handle / Fly away / Dry county / Fire of the dragon / Rattlesnake rock'n'roller / Searchin'. *(cd-iss. Jan93; 7567 90385-2)*

Jul 81. (7") *(K 11673)* **GOOD MORNING. / PAYIN' FOR IT** -

Sep 81. (7") <7338> **SEARCHIN'. / PAYIN' FOR IT** -

Feb 82. (7") *(K 11686)* **DRY COUNTY. / TOO HARD TO HANDLE** 43 -
(w/ free 7") *(SAM 142)* – On the run / Train train.

Aug 82. (lp/c) *(K/K4 50910)* **HIGHWAY SONG – BLACKFOOT LIVE (live)** 14 -
– Gimme, gimme, gimme / Every man should know (Queenie) / Good morning / Dry county / Rollin' and tumblin' / Fly away / Road fever / Trouble in mind / Train train / Highway song / Howay the lads.

Aug 82. (7"m) *(K 11760)* **HIGHWAY SONG (live). / ROLLIN' AND TUMBLIN' (live) / FLY AWAY (live)** [ ] [-]

—— added **KEN HENSLEY** – keyboards (ex-URIAH HEEP)

May 83. (lp/c) *(790 081-1/-4)* <90080> **SIOGO** [28] [82]
– Send me an angel / Crossfire / Heart's grown cold / We're goin' down / Teenage idol / Goin' in circles / Run for cover / White man's land / Sail away / Drivin' fool.

May 83. (7"/7"pic-d) *(B 9880/+P)* **SEND ME AN ANGEL. / DRIVIN' FOOL** [66] [-]
(12"+=) *(B 9880P)* – Wishing well.

Jun 83. (7") <99851> **TEENAGE IDOL. / RUN FOR COVER** [-] [ ]

Jul 83. (7"/12") *(B/BT 9845)* **TEENAGE IDOL. / WE'RE GOIN' DOWN** [ ] [-]

—— **BOBBY BARTH** – keyboards (ex-AXE) repl. HENSLEY

Sep 84. (lp/c) *(790 218-1/-4)* <90218> **VERTICAL SMILES** [82] [ ]
– Morning dew / Living in the limelight / Ride with you / Get it on / Young girl / Summer days / A legend never dies / Heartbeat and heels / In for the kill.

Oct 84. (7"/12") *(B/BT 9690)* <99690> **MORNING DEW. / LIVIN' IN THE LIMELIGHT** [ ] [ ]

—— disbanded March '86, BARTH went solo and released album 'TWO HEARTS – ONE BEAT' for 'Atco'. In the summer of '86, BLACKFOOT were walking again (with **MEDLOCKE, BARTH, WIZZARD** – bass (ex-MOTHER'S FINEST), **DOUG BARE, HAROLD SEAY** (ex-MOTHERS FINEST)

Atlantic Atlantic

Jun 87. (lp/c; RICK MEDLOCKE & BLACKFOOT) <(781743-1/-4)> **RICK MEDLOCKE & BLACKFOOT** [ ] [ ]
– Back on the streets / Saturday night / Closest thing to Heaven / Silent type / Reckless boy / Private life / Liar / Steady rockin' / My wild romance / Rock'n'roll tonight.

Jul 87. (7"; RICK MEDLOCKE & BLACKFOOT) <89223> **BACK ON THE STREETS. / CLOSEST THING TO HEAVEN** [-] [ ]

—— **MEDLOCKE** reformed them again in 1989. Also in new line-up **NEAL CASAL** – guitar; repl. DOUG BARE – keyboards (ex-MOTHER'S FIRST) / **RIKKI MEYER** – bass; repl. MARK 'THE ANIMAL' MENDOZA (ex-TWISTED SISTER) / **GUNNER ROSS** – drums

Music For Nations Nalli

Nov 90. (cd/c/lp) *(CD/T+/MFN 106)* <ANR 1991> **MEDICINE MAN** [ ] [ ] Jun90
– Doin' my job / The stealer / Sleazy world / Not gonna cry anymore / Runnin' runnin' / Chilled to d'bone / Guitar slingers song and dance.

—— **RICK MEDLOCKE** – vocals, guitars, steel guitars, percussion / **MARK WOERPEL** – guitars, vocals / **TIM STUNSON** – bass / **BENNY RAPPA** – drums, percussion, vocals

Bulletproof Wildcat

Jul 94. (cd) *(CDVEST 15)* <9206> **AFTER THE REIGN** [ ] [ ]
– Sittin' on top of the world / Rainbow / It's all over now / Tupelo honey / The road's my middle name / Hang time / Tonight / Nobody rides for free / Bandelero / After the reign.

– compilations, etc. –

Nov 94. (cd) *Rhino-Atlantic;* <71614> **RATTLESNAKE ROCK'N'ROLL: THE BEST OF BLACKFOOT** [-] [ ]
– Feelin' good / Left turn on a red light / Wishing well / Train, train / Highway song / Gimme, gimme, gimme / Every man should know (Queenie) / Spendin' cabbage / Fox chase / Diary of a workin' man / Too hot to handle / Fly away / Rattlesnake rock'n'roller / Good morning (live) / Road fever (live) / Trouble in mind (live) / Doin' my job / Guitar slingers song and dance.

Aug 98. (cd) *King Biscuit;* <(KBFHCD 023)> **KING BISCUIT PRESENTS . . . BLACKFOOT** [ ] [ ]

May 00. (cd) *Capitol;* <24501> **LIVE** [-] [ ]

BLACKFOOT SUE

Formed: Birmingham, England . . . early 70's as GIFT, by twin brothers TOM and DAVE FARMER. The line-up was completed by EDDIE GALGA and ALAN JONES, and it was not long (Spring '72) before they had a UK Top 5 hit with their hard-rock debut, 'STANDING IN THE ROAD'. They suffered a little from comparisons to SLADE, who were to outsell them by millions, after BS only managed to scrape a Top 40 place with their follow-up, 'SING DON'T SPEAK'. They drifted into similar teen-bop territory soon after, their albums being very poor sellers and causing their eventual split in '77. TOM FARMER and GALGA went on to form LINER, a soft-rock AOR outfit (completed by session men) who issued one self-titled album in 1979 and two minor UK hits, 'KEEP REACHING OUT FOR LOVE' and 'YOU AND ME'. After a longer hiatus, the FARMER brothers and GALGA re-united early 1985 in yet another AOR team, OUTSIDE EDGE. They released two albums, the self-titled 'OUTSIDE EDGE' and 'RUNNING HOT'.

Album rating: THE BEST OF BLACKFOOT SUE (*5)

TOM FARMER (b. 2 Mar'52) – vocals, bass, keyboards / **EDDIE GALGA** (b. 4 Sep'51) – lead guitar, keyboards / **ALAN JONES** (b. 5 Jan'50) – bass / **DAVE FARMER** – drums

Jam A&M

May 72. (7") *(JAM 13)* <1386> **STANDING IN THE ROAD. / CELESTIAL PLAIN** [4] [ ]

Nov 72. (7") *(JAM 29)* **SING DON'T SPEAK. / 2 B FREE** [36] [-]

Feb 73. (7") *(JAM 44)* **SUMMER. / MORNING LIGHT** [ ] [-]

1973. (lp) *(JAL 104)* **NOTHING TO HIDE** [ ] [-]
– Messiah / Country home / Cry / My oh my / Now we're three / The Spring of '69 / Glittery obituary / On his own / Too soon / Gypsy.

Sep 73. (7") *(JAM 53)* **GET IT ALL TO ME. / MY OH MY** [ ] [-]

D.J.M. Passport

Mar 74. (7") *(DJS 10296)* **BYE BYE BIRMINGHAM. / MESSIAH** [ ] [-]

Sep 74. (7") *(DJS 10326)* **YOU NEED LOVE. / TOBAGO ROSE** [ ] [-]

1975. (lp) *(DJLPS 455)* **GUN RUNNING** [ ] [ ]

Sep 75. (7") *(DJS 10411)* **MOONSHINE. / CORRIE** [ ] [-]

not iss. Passport

1977. (lp) <1007> **STRANGERS** [-] [ ]

—— Disbanded, TOM + EDDIE formed LINER; others went into session work.

– compilations, etc. –

1979. (7") *Old Gold; (OG 9037)* **STANDING IN THE ROAD. / SUMMER** [ ] [-]

Jul 96. (cd) *Connoisseur; (CSAPCD 123)* **THE BEST OF BLACKFOOT SUE** [ ] [-]

Nov 98. (cd) *H.T.D.; (HTD 68)* **RED ON BLUE** [ ] [-]

BLACK LABEL SOCIETY (see under ⇒ WYLDE, Zakk)

BLACKMORE'S RAINBOW (see under ⇒ RAINBOW)

BLACK 'N BLUE

Formed: Portland, Oregon, USA . . . 1981 originally as BOOGIE STAR, by former drummer turned singer, JAIME ST. JAMES and guitarist TOMMY THAYER, who subsequently added JEFF WARNER, PATRICK YOUNG and PETER HOLMES. B 'N B moved to L.A., where they signed a contract with 'Geffen', releasing their hard-rock, party-metal eponymous DIETER DIERKS-produced debut a couple of years later. This was their first of three albums which bubbled under the Top 100, the others being 'NASTY NASTY' (produced by GENE SIMMONS in 1986) and 'IN HEAT' (1988).

Album rating: BLACK 'N BLUE (*5) / NASTY NASTY (*6) / IN HEAT (*4)

JAIME ST. JAMES – vocals (ex-WILD DOGS) / **TOMMY THAYER** – guitar / **JEFF WARNER** – guitar / **PATRICK YOUNG** – bass / **PETER HOLMES** – drums

Geffen Geffen

Sep 84. (lp/c) *(GEF/40 26020)* <24041> **BLACK 'N BLUE** [ ] [ ]
– The strong will rock / School of hard knocks / Autoblast / Hold on to 18 / Wicked bitch / Action / Show me the night / One for the money / I'm the king / Chains around Heaven.

Oct 86. (lp/c) *(924111-1/-4)* <24111> **NASTY NASTY** [ ] [ ]
– Nasty nasty / I want it all (I want it now) / Does she or doesn't she / Kiss of death / 12 o'clock high / Do what you wanna do / I'll be there for you / Rules / Best in the west.

Apr 88. (lp/c) *(K 924180-1/-4)* <24180> **IN HEAT** [ ] [ ]
– Rock on / Sight for sore eyes / Heat it up! burn it out! / Suspicious / The snake / Live it up / Gimme your love / Get wise to the rise / Stranger / Great guns of fire.

—— split later in the 80's. ST. JAMES joined MADHOUSE, YOUNG to DOKKEN, while THAYER and the other two formed WET ENGINE. THAYER and ST. JAMES teamed up once more in 1992, heading the KISS tribute band, COLD GIN.

BLACK OAK ARKANSAS

Formed: Black Oak, Arkansas, USA . . . 1970 by JIM 'DANDY' MANGRUM (the frontman taking his moniker from a 50's song), having evolved from the 60's band, The KNOWBODY ELSE. Subsequently settling in Los Angeles, DANDY and co. (STAN 'GOOBER' KNIGHT, RICKIE REYNOLDS, PAT DAUGHERTY, HARVEY JETT and WAYNE EVANS) signed to 'Atco', building a solid reputation, mainly in the Southern States. Long-haired, bare-chested JIM DANDY, was the main focal point of this heavy sounding swamp boogie outfit, who made their eponymous debut in '71. The second album, 'KEEP THE FAITH' nearly dented the US Top 100, its successor, 'IF AN ANGEL CAME TO SEE YOU . . .' duly achieving this feat later in '72. BLACK OAK ARKANSAS were nothing if not prolific, with a release schedule of nigh on two albums every year, even managing to hit the Top 30 with their novelty song, 'JIM DANDY' (early '74). The latter track featured on the 'HIGH ON THE HOG' opus, the group subsequently pursuing a more gospel/rock'n'roll orientated direction a few years later. BLACK OAK and JIM DANDY were still going strong (if not commercially) in the late 70's, splitting and reforming intermittently throughout the coming two decades. After more than ten years out of the spotlight, BOA were cookin' once again in 1999 as original members MANGRUM, REYNOLDS and DAUGHERTY came together for a rare reunion. Completing the new line-up were ROCKY ATHOS and JOHNNY BOLIN, the latter being the younger brother of deceased guitar legend TOMMY. Unsurprisingly perhaps, the resulting album, 'THE WILD BUNCH' (1999) boasted a couple of BOLIN classics in the shape of 'POST TOASTEE' and 'SHAKE THE DEVIL' while a brace of BLACK OAK nuggets were dusted down with surprising enthusiasm. Longtime fans even agreed that the new material was up to scratch, making the record BOA's best since the mid-70's. • **Songwriters:** All mostly by MANGRUM, except GREAT BALLS OF FIRE (Jerry Lee Lewis) / SHAKIN' ALL OVER (Johnny Kidd) / RACE WITH THE DEVIL (Gun) / NOT FADE AWAY (Buddy Holly) / SINGING THE BLUES (Guy Mitchell) / DANCING IN THE STREETS (Martha & The Vandellas) / etc.

Album rating: BLACK OAK ARKANSAS (*5) / KEEP THE FAITH (*4) / IF AN ANGEL CAME TO SEE YOU, WOULD YOU MAKE HER FEEL AT HOME? (*5) / RAUNCH'N'ROLL – LIVE (*6) / HIGH ON THE HOG (*4) / STREET PARTY (*4) / AIN'T LIFE GRAND (*4) / X-RATED (*3) / LIVE! MUTHA (*3) / BALLS OF FIRE (*2) / 10 YEAR OVERNIGHT SUCCESS (*2) / RACE WITH THE DEVIL (*3) / I'D RATHER BE SAILING (*2) / READY AS HELL Jim Dandy (*3) / BLACK ATTACK IS BACK (*2) / HOT & NASTY compilation (*6) / THE WILD BUNCH (*4)

JIM 'DANDY' MANGRUM (b. JAMES MANGRUM, 30 Mar'48) – vocals / **HARVEY JETT** – guitar / **RICKIE REYNOLDS** (b.28 Oct'48, Manilla, Arkansas) – guitar, vocals / **STAN 'GOOBER' KNIGHT** (b.12 Feb'49, Little Rock, Arkansas) – guitar, vocals / **PAT DAUGHERTY** (b.11 Nov'47, Jonesboro, Arkansas) – bass, vocals / **WAYNE EVANS** – drums

not iss. Enterprise

1970. (7") *<9010>* **KING'S ROW. / OLDER THAN GRANDPA** [-] [ ]

Atlantic Atco

Jul 71. (lp) *<354>* **BLACK OAK ARKANSAS** [-] [ ]
– Uncle Lijiah / Memories at the window / The hills of Arkansas / I could love you / Hot and nasty / Singing the blues / Lord have mercy on my soul / When electricity came to Arkansas. *(UK-iss.mid-70's; 2400 180) (cd-iss. Jul92 on 'Repertoire';) (cd re-iss. Apr00 on 'Wounded Bird'; WOU 354)*

Sep 71. (7") *<6829>* **LORD HAVE MERCY ON MY SOUL. / UNCLE LIJAH** [-] [ ]

Nov 71. (7") *<6849>* **HOT AND NASTY. / SINGIN' THE BLUES** [-] [ ]

Feb 72. (lp) *<381>* **KEEP THE FAITH** [-] [ ]
– Keep the faith / Revolutionary all American boys / Feet on earth, head in sky / Fever in my mind / The big one's still coming / White-headed woman / We live on day to day / Short life line / Don't confuse what you don't know. *(UK cd-iss. Jun95 on 'Rhino-Sequel'; RSACD 828)*

Mar 72. (7") *<6878>* **KEEP THE FAITH. / THE BIG ONE'S STILL COMING** [-] [ ]

—— **TOMMY ALDRIDGE** (b.15 Aug'50, Nashville) – drums; repl. WAYNE

Aug 72. (lp) *(K 40407) <7008>* **IF AN ANGEL CAME TO SEE YOU, WOULD YOU MAKE HER FEEL AT HOME?** [ ] [93] Jun72
– Gravel roads / Fertile woman / Spring vacation / We help each other / Full Moon ride / Our minds eye / To make us what we are / Our eyes are on you / Mutants of the monster. *(cd-iss. Jun95 on 'Rhino-Sequel'; RSACD 831)*

Aug 72. (7") *<6893>* **FULL BLOWN RIDE. / WE HELP EACH OTHER** [-] [ ]

Mar 73. (lp) *(K 40451) <7019>* **RAUNCH'N'ROLL – LIVE (live)** [ ] [90]
– Gettin' kinda cocky / When electricity came to Arkansas / Gigolo / Hot rod / Mutants of the monster / Hot and nasty / Up. *(cd-iss. Aug93 on 'WEA'; 812271347-2) (cd re-iss. Apr00 on 'Wounded Bird'; WOU 7019)*

Apr 73. (7") *<6925>* **HOT AND NASTY. / HOT ROD** [-] [ ]

Dec 73. (lp) *(K 40538) <7035>* **HIGH ON THE HOG** [ ] [52] Nov73
– Swimmin' in quicksand / Back to the land / Movin' / Happy hooker / Red hot lovin' / I'm Dandy / Moonshine sonata / Why shouldn't I smile / High'n'dry / Mad man. *(cd-iss. Jun95 on 'Rhino-Sequel'; RSACD 832)*

Feb 74. (7") *(K 10405) <6948>* **JIM DANDY (TO THE RESCUE). / RED HOT LOVIN'** [ ] [25] Dec73

—— **RUBY STARR** – vocals; repl. JETT

Jul 74. (lp) *(K 50057) <101>* **STREET PARTY** [ ] [56]
– Dancing in the streets / Sting me / Good good woman / Jail bait / Sure been workin' hard / Son of a gun / Brink of creation / I'm a man / Goin' home / Dixie / Everybody wants to see Heaven / Hey y'all / Brink of creation. *(cd-iss. Jun95 on 'Rhino-Sequel'; RSACD 829)*

Jul 74. (7") *(K 10491)* **DANCING IN THE STREETS. / DIXIE** [ ] [-]

Sep 74. (7") *(K 10504) <7003>* **HEY Y'ALL. / STING ME** [ ] [ ]

Dec 74. (7") *<7015>* **TAXMAN. / DIXIE** [-] [ ]

—— **JIMMY HENDERSON** (b.20 May'54, Jackson, Missouri) – guitar; repl. STARR

Mar 75. (7") *(K 10569)* **TAXMAN. / JAILBAIT** [ ] [-]

May 75. (lp) *(K 50150) <111>* **AIN'T LIFE GRAND** [ ] [ ]
– Taxman / Fancy Nancy / Keep on / Good stuff / Rebel / Back door man / Love can be found / Diggin' for gold / Cryin' shame / Let life be good to you. *(cd-iss. Jun95 on 'Rhino-Sequel'; RSACD 830)*

Apr 75. (7") *<7019>* **BACK DOOR MAN. / GOOD STUFF** [-] [ ]

Jun 75. (7") *(K 10621)* **FANCY NANCY. / KEEP ON** [ ] [-]

—— added 4 backing singers incl. **RUBY STARR** again.

M.C.A. M.C.A.

Oct 75. (lp) *(MCF 2734) <2155>* **X-RATED** [ ] [99]
– Bump'n'grind / Fightin' cock / Highway pirate / Strong enough to be gentle / Flesh needs flesh / Wild men from the mountains / High flyer / Ace in the hole / Too hot to stop.

Dec 75. (7") *<40496>* **STRONG ENOUGH TO BE GENTLE. / ACE IN THE HOLE** [-] [89]

May 76. (7") *(MCA 242) <40536>* **GREAT BALLS OF FIRE. / HIGHWAY PIRATE** [ ] [ ]

Aug 76. (lp) *(MCF 2762) <2199>* **BALLS OF FIRE** [ ] [ ] Jun76
– Ramblin' gamblin' man / Fistful of love / Make that scene / I can feel forever / Rock'n'roll / Great balls of fire / Just to fall in love / Leather angel / Storm of passion / All my troubles. *(cd-iss. Jun95 on 'Repertoire'; RR 4551)*

Aug 76. (7") *(MCA 247) <40586>* **FISTFUL OF LOVE. / STORM OF PASSION** [ ] [ ]

Sep 76. (7") *(MCA 256)* **RAMBLIN' GAMBLIN' MAN. / STORM OF PASSION** [ ] [-]

—— **JIM DANDY** + **JIMMY HENDERSON** recruited new members **ANDY TANAS** – bass repl. PAT / **JACK HOLDER** – guitar, etc. repl. STAN, RICKIE + RUBY / **JOEL WILLIAMS** – drums repl. TOMMY who joined PAT TRAVERS then OZZY OSBOURNE

Feb 77. (lp) *(MCF 2784) <2224>* **10 YEARS OVERNIGHT SUCCESS** [ ] [ ]
– When the band was singin' "Shakin' all over" / Pretty, pretty / Can't blame it on me / Television indecision / Back it up / Bad boy's back in school / Love comes easy / You can't keep a good man down / Fireball.

Feb 77. (7") *<40621>* **WHEN THE BAND WAS SINGIN' "SHAKIN' ALL OVER". / BAD BOY'S BACK IN SCHOOL** [-] [ ]

BLACK OAK

GREG REDDING – guitar, keyboards; repl. PAT

Capricorn Capricorn

Dec 77. (lp) *<(2429 156)>* **RACE WITH THE DEVIL** [ ] [ ]
– Race with the Devil / Freedom / One night stand / Daisy / Rainbow / Feels so good / Stand by your own kind / Not fade away.

Jan 78. (7") *<0284>* **NOT FADE AWAY. / FEELS SO GOOD** [-] [ ]

Dec 78. (lp) *<CP 0207>* **I'D RATHER BE SAILING** [-] [ ]
– I'll take care of you / You keep me waiting / Ride with me / Made of stone / You can count on me / God bless the children / Innocent eyes / Daydreams / Wind in our sails.

Dec 78. (7") *<0305>* **RIDE WITH ME. / WIND IN OUR SAILS** [-] [ ]

—— disbanded in 1978

JIM DANDY

reformed 1984, with **DANDY** and **REYNOLDS** plus **STEVE NUNENMACHER** – guitar / **WILLIAM LEMUEL** – bass, vocals / **JON WELLS** – drums / **BILLY BATTLE** – keyboards

Heavy Metal Heavy Metal

Nov 84. (lp) *<(HMUSA 5)>* **READY AS HELL** [ ] [ ]
– Ready as Hell / Here comes the wind / The liberty rebellion / Don't tempt the Devil / Get ahead of your time / Black cat woman / Rude and crude / Space cadet / Fascination alley / Denouncement. *(pic-lp.Aug85; HMPD 5)*

Aug 85. (7") *(VHF 15)* **READY AS HELL. / BLACK CAT WOMAN** [ ] [ ]
(above on 'FM-Revolver')

JIM DANDY & BLACK OAK ARKANSAS

Apr 86. (lp/c) *<(HM USA/MC 63)>* **BLACK ATTACK IS BACK** [ ] [ ]
– Long distance runner / I'm on your side / The wanderer / I don't want much out of life / (I want a woman with) Big titties / etc.

—— re-formed in 1994; **MANGRUM, REYNOLDS, JOHNNY ROTH** – guitar / **BUDDY CHURCH** – guitar / **ARTIE WILSON** bass / **JOHNNY COURVILLE III** – drums

—— another reformation took place a little later, **JIM DANDY** + **REYNOLDS** with **PAT 'DIRTY' DOUGHERTY** – bass / **JOHNNIE BOLIN** – drums

Cleopatra Cleopatra

Nov 99. (cd; as BLACK OAK ARKANSAS & JIM DANDY) *Cleopatra; <(CLP 705)>* **THE WILD BUNCH** [ ] [ ]
– Forgive and forget / Post toastee / Dark purple blues – Shake the Devil / Jim Dandy to the rescue '99 / The truth be known / Mutants of the monster '99 / This is our time / Hot rod '99 / No time / Happy hooker '99 / To heavy Dallas / Hot'n'nasty '99 / The wild bunch / Talk to the hand.

– compilations, others, etc. –

1974. (lp; when as KNOWBODY ELSE) *Stax; <5504>* **EARLY TIMES** [-] [ ]
(UK cd-iss. Nov92 by BLACK OAK ARKANSAS; CDSXE 067)

Oct 74. (lp) *Atlantic; (K 20083)* **HOT AND NASTY** [ ] [-]
– Jim Dandy / Hey y'all / Memories at the window / Full moon ride / Back to the land / Hot rod / Mutants of the monster / Singing the blues / Fever in my mind / Dancing in the streets / Keep the faith / Hot and nasty.

Feb 76. (lp) *Atlantic; (K 50220) / Atco; <128>* **LIVE! MUTHA (live 74-75)** [ ] [ ]
– Jim Dandy / Fancy Nancy / Lord have mercy on my soul / Cryin' shame / Fever in my mind / Hey y'all / Rebel / Taxman / Hot and nasty.

Mar 93. (cd) *Rhino-Atlantic; <(8122 71146-2)>* **HOT & NASTY: THE BEST OF BLACK OAK ARKANSAS** [ ] [ ]
– Mean woman / Uncle Lijiah / Hot and nasty / Lord have mercy on my soul / When electricity came to Arkansas / Keep the faith / Fever in my mind / Hot rod / Gravel roads / Mutants of the monster / Jim Dandy / Happy hooker / Son of a gun / Dixie / Everybody wants to see Heaven (nobody wants to die) / Diggin' for gold / Taxman / So you want to be a rock'n'roll star.

Aug 98. (cd) *King Biscuit; <(KBFHCD 022)>* **KING BISCUIT PRESENTS . . . BLACK OAK ARKANSAS** [ ] [ ]

Mar 01. (cd) *Cleopatra; <(CLP 995)>* **GREATEST HITS** [ ] [ ]

BLACK RANDY & THE METRO SQUAD

Formed: Los Angeles, California, USA . . . 1977 by caucasian punk rocker, BLACK RANDY. With a free'n'easy attitude to recruitment, The METRO SQUAD were probably the genuine definition of the punk DIY philosophy and the line-up varied accordingly. Tagged after the punk club of the same name, the 'Dangerhouse' label was home to the band's debut single, 'TROUBLE AT THE CUP', featuring such classic B-side material as 'LONER WITH A BONER' and 'SPERM BANK BABY'. Clearly untroubled by the American work ethic, RANDY and co. released a single a year through '78 and '79 – 'IDI AMIN' and 'I SLEPT IN AN ARCADE' respectively – before bowing out with a solitary album, 'PASS THE DUST, I THINK I'M BOWIE' (1980). No prizes for guessing what the dust in the title referred to, RANDY's alleged fondness for PCP no doubt contributing to the chaos surrounding the band. The 'SQUAD's subsequent demise was followed by RANDY's mysterious death while GARRETT went on to play with The DILS. • **Covered:** GIVE IT UP OR TURNIT A LOOSE + I'M BLACK AND PROUD (James Brown).

Album rating: PASS THE DUST, I THINK I'M BOWIE (*4)

BLACK RANDY – vocals / **DAVID BROWN** – keyboards, vocals / **BOB DEADWYLER** – guitar, vocals / **PAT GARRETT** – bass, guitar, vocals / **KK BARRETT** – guitar / **JOE RAMIREZ** – bass / **TOM HUGHES** – guitar, bass / **JOE NANINI** – drums, percussion

not iss. Dangerhouse

Dec 77. (7"m) *<MO 721>* **TROUBLE AT THE CUP. / LONER WITH A BONER / SPERM BANK BABY** [-] [ ]

1978. (7"ep) *<IDI 722>* **IDI AMIN / I'M BLACK AND PROUD PART 3. / I'M BLACK AND PROUD PART 14 / I WANNA BE A NARK** [-] [ ]

Jul 79. (7") *<KY 724>* **I SLEPT IN AN ARCADE. / GIVE IT UP** [-] [ ]

Jan 80. (lp) *<PCP 725>* **PASS THE DUST, I THINK I'M BOWIE** [-] [ ]
– I slept in an arcade / Marlon Brando / Down at the laundromat / I tell lies every day / San Francisco / Give it up or turn it a loose / Idi Amin / Barefootin' on the wicked picket / Shaft / I wanna be a nark / Sperm bank baby / Tellin' lies / I'm black and proud.

— split early 1980 when RANDY died of drug related causes. PAT GARRETT later joined The DILS. RAMIREZ, BROWN, NANINI + bassist JIMMY LEACH were also part of The EYES, who had a few releases in the late 70's.

BLACK ROSE

Formed: Newcastle, England . . . 1982 by STEVE BARDSLEY and CHRIS WATSON, who recruited MICK THOMPSON and MALLA SMITH. The chaff in amongst the wheat of the NWOBHM, BLACK ROSE (nothing to do with CHER's backing band!) failed to gain any substantial following outside Teesside. After one album, 'BOYS WILL BE BOYS', they signed to 'Neat' records (also home to VENOM), where they delivered a second and final effort, 'WALK IT, HOW YOU TALK IT'.

Album rating: BOYS WILL BE BOYS (*4) / WALK IT, HOW YOU TALK IT (*3)

STEVE BARDSLEY – vocals, guitar / **CHRIS WATSON** – guitar, vocals / **MICK THOMPSON** – bass, vocals / **MALLA SMITH** – drums, percussion, vocals

Teesbeat — not iss.

Aug 82. (7") *(TB 5)* **NO POINT RUNNIN'. /** [ ] [-]

Bullet — not iss.

Sep 83. (12"ep) *(BOLT 6)* **WE GONNA ROCK YOU** [ ] [-]

Apr 84. (lp) *(BULP 3)* **BOYS WILL BE BOYS** [ ] [-]
– Boys will be boys / We're gonna be your lover / Just wanna be your lover / Baby believe me / No point runnin' / Fun and games / First light / Burn me blind / Stand your ground / Knocked out.

May 84. (7") *(BOL 9)* **BOYS WILL BE BOYS. / LIAR** [ ] [-]

— **GRAHAM HUNTER** – guitar; repl. WATSON

Neat — not iss.

Mar 85. (12"ep) *(NEAT 48-12)* **ROCK ME HARD / NEED A LOT OF LOVIN'. / NIGHTMARE / BREAKAWAY** [ ] [-]

Apr 87. (lp/c) *(NEAT/+C 1034)* **WALK IT, HOW YOU TALK IT** [ ] [-]
– California USA / Ezly / Don't fall in love / Bright lights burnin' / Walk it how you talk it / Shout it out / I honesty love you / Part animal / Want you love.

— split after above

BLACK SABBATH

Formed: Aston, Birmingham, England . . . early 1969 by TONY IOMMI, OZZY OSBOURNE, TERRY 'GEEZER' BUTLER and BILL WARD, out of the jazz fusion combo, EARTH (IOMMI had also filled in as JETHRO TULL guitarist for a few weeks). Taking the name, BLACK SABBATH from a horror film adapted from a Dennis Wheatley novel of the same name, they signed to 'Fontana' in late '69. After a flop single, 'EVIL WOMAN (DON'T PLAY YOUR GAMES WITH ME)', they were shunted to the more progressive 'Vertigo' label in early 1970. The inimitable SABBATH sound was stunningly defined on the opening title cut from the self-titled debut album, the record storming into the UK Top 10. Occult influenced, BLACK SABBATH fused IOMMI's deceptively basic, doom-laden guitar riffs with OZZY's (much-mimicked since) banshee shriek. Lyrically morbid, with futuristic/medieval themes, tracks like 'THE WIZARD' highlighting their tongue-in-cheek protest against God! The band then branded their name on the nation's musical consciousness with a Top 5 hit single!!! 'PARANOID', a skullcrushing but strangely melodic track which remains one of the most (in)famous metal songs of all time. Not surprisingly, the album of the same name (also in 1970!) bludgeoned its way straight to No.1, a metal classic rammed full of blinding tracks, not least the stop-start dynamics of 'WAR PIGS', the spiralling melancholy of 'IRON MAN' and the doom-driven 'FAIRIES WEAR BOOTS' ("and you gotta believe me!"). Their third set, 'MASTER OF REALITY' (1971), was another dark jewel in the SABBATH legend, softer tracks like 'EMBRYO' and 'ORCHID' sledgehammered into oblivion by mogadon monsters, 'CHILDREN OF THE GRAVE' and 'SWEET LEAF'. The last two years had witnessed SABBATH taking America by the throat, 'VOL. 4' in '72 loosening the grip somewhat, although it did boast a classic rock ballad, 'CHANGES'. Returning to more pseudo-satanic territory, 'SABBATH BLOODY SABBATH' was another milestone, its demonic credibility nevertheless diminished somewhat by the fact that the instrumental, 'FLUFF', was subsequently adopted by namesake Radio One DJ ALAN FREEMAN on his Saturday afternoon prog-rock show! Returning from a year-long sabbatical, the release of the largely disappointing sixth album, 'SABOTAGE', was indicative of the cracks appearing in the IOMMI/OSBOURNE relationship. However, the album did contain two brilliant opening salvos, 'HOLE IN THE SKY' and 'SYMPTOM OF THE UNIVERSE'. The beginning of the end came with the ill-advised experimentation of 'TECHNICAL ECSTASY' (1976), an album which led to OZZY's brief departure (his supernatural consumption of the demon drink was also a factor). However, a newly rehabilited OSBOURNE was back at the helm for 1978's 'NEVER SAY DIE', sales of which were boosted by a near UK Top 20 title track. In 1979, OZZY took off on a solo career, leaving behind IOMMI, BUTLER and WARD to pick up the pieces in LA (where the band had relocated). With a new manager, Don Arden, in tow, they finally recruited American, RONNIE JAMES DIO (from RAINBOW), after auditioning many would-be OZZY clones. This proved to be SABBATH's blackest period, pitch in fact, with the release of two mediocre albums in the early 80's, 'HEAVEN AND HELL' and 'MOB RULES'. Things went from bad to ridiculous in 1983, when DIO was substituted by another hard-rock frontman celebrity, IAN GILLAN, taken straight from the proverbial heart of DEEP PURPLE. The resulting, ironically-titled album, 'BORN AGAIN', was an exercise in heavy-metal cliche, although it still managed to hit the UK Top 5. The original SABBATH reunited on the 13th of July '85 for a rather disapointing one-off performance at the 'Live Aid' concert in Philadelphia. In 1986, IOMMI was in full control once more, even giving his name co-billing on the appalling, 'SEVENTH STAR' set. Astonishingly, SABBATH were given another chance by Miles Copeland's 'I.R.S.' records, IOMMI having found a new vocalist, TONY MARTIN, also securing the services of veteran drummer, COZY POWELL (ex-everyband) to boost the sales of their comeback album, 'HEADLESS CROSS' (1989). The 1990's saw IOMMI and group trying to relive past glories, the 1995 album 'FORBIDDEN' even including a vocal piece from US rapper, ICE-T. At the turn of 1997/8, IOMMI and OZZY had finally settled their differences, coming together in a much heralded SABBATH reunion, which will apparently result in a comeback album, 20 years too late for some! IOMMI finally released his first – eponymous – solo album in 2000, an all-star project that had the cream of the rock/metal world queuing up to work with the legendary riffmeister. Alongside OZZY himself, guest vocalists included HENRY ROLLINS, SKIN (of SKUNK ANANSIE), DAVE GROHL (NIRVANA/FOO FIGHTERS), PHIL ANSELMO (PANTERA), BILLY CORGAN – again! – (SMASHING PUMPKINS), IAN ASTBURY (CULT), PETER STEELE (TYPE O NEGATIVE), SERJ TANKIAN (SYSTEM OF A DOWN) and even BILLY IDOL while the likes of MATT CAMERON (PEARL JAM), BEN SHEPHERD (SOUNDGARDEN) and even BRIAN MAY (!!) lent their musical talents. If not exactly a classic in the BLACK SABBATH mould, the record was certainly diverse enough to offer most fans some value for money. • **Footnote:** Not a band for the easily-led and weak-minded, as the blame for teenage suicide attempts was always laid at their darkended door. Nevertheless, their influence on the worldwide metal scene is inestimable; as well as playing grunge before it was even invented, the likes of METALLICA et al, owe SABBATH a massive debt. • **Songwriters:** Mainly group compositions. Covered EVIL WOMAN (DON'T PLAY YOUR GAMES WITH ME) (Crow) / WARNING (Aynsley Dunbar).

Album rating: BLACK SABBATH (*8) / PARANOID (*9) / MASTER OF REALITY (*9) / VOLUME 4 (*8) / SABBATH BLOODY SABBATH (*8) / SABOTAGE (*7) / WE SOLD OUR SOULS FOR ROCK'N'ROLL compilation (*8) / TECHNICAL ECSTASY (*5) / NEVER SAY DIE (*5) / HEAVEN AND HELL (*7) / LIVE AT LAST (*4) / MOB RULES (*6) / LIVE EVIL (*7) / BORN AGAIN (*5) / SEVENTH STAR (*4) / THE ETERNAL IDOL (*4) / HEADLESS CROSS (*6) / BLACKEST SABBATH compliation (*7) / TYR (*5) / DEHUMANIZER (*5) / CROSS PURPOSES (*5) / FORBIDDEN (*4) / REUNION (*6) / THE BEST OF BLACK SABBATH compilation (*8) / Tony Iommi: IOMMI (*6)

OZZY OSBOURNE (b. JOHN, 3 Dec'48) – vocals / **TONY IOMMI** (b.19 Feb'48) – guitars / **TERRY 'GEEZER' BUTLER** (b.17 Jul'49) – bass / **BILL WARD** (b. 5 May'48) – drums

Fontana — Warners

Jan 70. (7") *(TF 1067)* **EVIL WOMAN, DON'T PLAY YOUR GAMES WITH ME. / WICKED WORLD** [ ] [-]

Vertigo — Warners

Feb 70. (lp) *(VO 6) <1871>* **BLACK SABBATH** [8] [23] Jul70
– Black Sabbath / The wizard / Behind the wall of sleep / N.I.B. / Evil woman, don't play your games with me / Sleeping village / Warning. *(re-iss. Jan74 on 'W.W.A.'; WWA 006) (re-iss. Jun80 + Nov85 on 'NEMS'; NEL 6002) (cd-iss. Dec86+=; NELCD 6002)* – Wicked world. *(cd/c re-iss. Oct96/Oct97 on 'Essential'; ESM CD/MC 301) (lp re-iss. Jan97 on 'Original Recordings'; ORRLP 004) (cd re-iss. Sep00 on 'Essential'; CMTCD 003)*

Mar 70. (7") *(V2)* **EVIL WOMAN (DON'T PLAY YOUR GAMES WITH ME). / WICKED WORLD** [ ] [-]

Aug 70. (7") *(6059 010) <7437>* **PARANOID. / THE WIZARD** [4] [61] Nov70

Sep 70. (lp) *(6360 011) <1887>* **PARANOID** [1] [12] Feb71
– War pigs / Paranoid / Planet Caravan / Iron man / Electric funeral / Hand of doom / Rat salad / Fairies wear boots. *(re-iss. Jan74 on 'W.W.A.'; WWA 007) (re-iss. Jun80 on 'NEMS'; NEL 6003); hit UK 54. (re-iss. Nov85 on 'NEMS' lp/pic-lp/c/cd; NEL/NEP/NELMC/NELCD 6003) (re-iss. Jun89 on 'Vertigo' lp/c/cd+=; 832701-1/-4/-2)* – Tomorrow's world (live). *(cd/c re-iss. Feb96/Oct97 on 'Essential'; ESM CD/MC 302) (cd re-iss. Sep00 on 'Essential'; CMTCD 004)*

Aug 71. (lp) *(6360 050) <2562>* **MASTER OF REALITY** [5] [8]
– Sweet leaf / After forever / Embryo / Children of the grave / Orchid / Lord of this world / Solitude / Into the void. *(re-iss. Jan74 on 'W.W.A.'; WWA 008) (re-iss. Nov80 on 'NEMS'; NEL 6004) (re-iss. Nov85 on 'NEMS' lp/c/cd; NEL/+MC/CD 6004) (re-iss. cd Jun89 on 'Vertigo' lp/c/cd+=; 832707-1/-4/-2)* – Killing yourself to live (live). *(cd/c re-iss. Feb96/Oct97 on 'Essential'; ESM CD/MC 303) (cd re-iss. Sep00 on 'Essential'; CMTCD 005)*

Jan 72. (7") *<7530>* **IRON MAN. / ELECTRIC FUNERAL** [-] [52]
<re-iss. 1974; 7802>

Sep 72. (7") *(6059 061) <7625>* **TOMORROW'S DREAM. / LAGUNA SUNRISE** [ ] [ ]

Sep 72. (lp) *(6360 071) <2602>* **BLACK SABBATH VOL.4** [8] [13] Oct72
– Wheels of confusion / Tomorrow's dream / Changes / FX / Supernaut / Snowblind / Cornucopia / Laguna sunrise / St. Vitus' dance / Under the sun. *(re-iss. Jan74 on 'W.W.A.'; WWA 009) (re-iss. Jun80 on 'NEMS'; NEL 6005) (c/cd-iss. 1988+=; NEL MC/CD 6005)* – Children of the grave (live). *(cd/c re-iss. Feb96/Oct97 on 'Essential'; ESM CD/MC 304) (cd re-iss. Sep00 on 'Essential'; MCTCD 006)*

W.W.A. — Warners

Oct 73. (7") *(WWS 002) <7764>* **SABBATH BLOODY SABBATH. / CHANGES** [ ] [ ]

Dec 73. (lp) *(WWA 005) <2695>* **SABBATH BLOODY SABBATH** [4] [11] Jan74
– Sabbath bloody sabbath / A national acrobat / Fluff / Sabbra cadabra / Killing yourself to live / Who are you? / Looking for today / Spiral architect. *(w-drawn copies were on 'Vertigo'; 6360 115) (re-iss. Jun80 on 'NEMS'; NEL 6017) (re-iss. Nov85 c/cd; NEL MC/CD 6017) (re-iss. Jun89 on 'Vertigo' lp/c/cd+=; 832700-1/-4/-2)* – Cornucopia (live). *(cd/c re-iss. Feb96/Oct97 on 'Essential'; ESM CD/MC 305)*

N.E.M.S. Warners

Sep 75. (lp) *(9119 001)* <2822> **SABOTAGE** [7] [28]
– Hole in the sky / Don't start (too late) / Symptom of the universe / Megalomania / Thrill of it all / Supertzar / Am I going insane (radio) / The writ. *(re-iss. Nov80 on 'NEMS'; NEL 6018) (re-iss. Nov85 c/cd; NEL MC/CD 6018) (re-iss. Jun89 on 'Vertigo' lp/c/cd+=; 832706-1/-4/-2)* – Sweat leaf (live). *(cd/c re-iss. Feb96/Oct97 on 'Essential'; ESM CD/MC 306)*

Feb 76. (d-lp) *(6641 335)* <2923> **WE SOLD OUR SOULS FOR ROCK'N'ROLL** (compilation) [35] [48]
– Black sabbath / The wizard / Warning / Paranoid / Wicked world / Tomorrow's dream / Fairies wear boots / Changes / Sweet leaf / Children of the grave / Sabbath bloody sabbath / Am I going insane (radio) / Laguna sunrise / Snowblind / N.I.B. *(re-iss. Nov80; NELD 101) (re-iss. Apr86 on 'Raw Power' d-lp/c/cd; RAW LP/TC/CD 017) (re-iss. Dec90 on 'Castle' cd/c/d-lp; CCS CD/MC/LP 249) (cd re-iss. Jan98 on 'Essential'; ESDCD 605)*

Feb 76. (7") *(6165 300)* **AM I GOING INSANE (RADIO). / HOLE IN THE SKY** [ ] [ ]

Vertigo Warners

Oct 76. (lp) *(9102 750)* <2969> **TECHNICAL ECSTASY** [13] [51]
– Back street kids / You won't change me / It's alright / Gypsy / All moving parts (stand still) / Rock'n'roll doctor / She's gone / Dirty women. *(re-iss. Aug83 lp/c; PRICE/PRIMC 40) (cd-iss. Jun89; 838224-2) (cd/c re-iss. Jan96/Oct97 on 'Essential'; ESM CD/MC 328)*

Nov 76. (7") <8315> **IT'S ALRIGHT. / ROCK'N'ROLL DOCTOR** [-] [ ]

— Late '77 OZZY leaves and is briefly repl. by **DAVE WALKER** (ex-SAVOY BROWN) Early 1978 **OZZY** returned.

May 78. (7") *(SAB 001)* **NEVER SAY DIE. / SHE'S GONE** [21] [-]

Sep 78. (7",7"purple) *(SAB 002)* **HARD ROAD. / SYMPTOM OF THE UNIVERSE** [33] [-]

Oct 78. (lp) *(9102 751)* <3186> **NEVER SAY DIE!** [12] [69]
– Never say die / Johnny Blade / Juniors eyes / Hard road / Shock wave / Air dance / Over to you / Breakout / Swinging the chain. *(re-iss. May83 lp/c; PRICE/PRIMC 9) (re-iss. Sep93 on 'Spectrum' cd/c;) (cd/c re-iss. Jan96/Oct97 on 'Essential'; ESM CD/MC 329)*

— **RONNIE JAMES DIO** (b.1950, Cortland, N.J.) – vocals (ex-(RITCHIE BLACKMORE'S) RAINBOW, ex-ELF etc.) repl.OZZY who went solo.

Apr 80. (lp)(c) *(9102 752)(7231 402)* <3372> **HEAVEN AND HELL** [9] [28] Jun80
– Neon knights / Children of the sea / Lady evil / Heaven and Hell / Wishing well / Die young / Walk away / Lonely is the word. *(re-iss. May83 lp/c; PRICE/PRIMC 10) (cd-iss. 1987; 830171-2) (re-iss. May93 on 'Spectrum' cd/c;) (cd/c re-iss. Jan96/Oct97 on 'Essential'; ESM CD/MC 330) (cd/c re-iss. Apr96 on 'Raw Power'; RAW CD/MC 104)*

Jun 80. (7") *(SAB 3)* **NEON KNIGHTS. / CHILDREN OF THE SEA** [22] [-]

Jul 80. (7") <49549> **LADY EVIL. / CHILDREN OF THE SEA** [-] [ ]

Nov 80. (7"/ext.12") *(SAB 4/+12)* **DIE YOUNG. / HEAVEN AND HELL (live)** [41] [-]

— **VINNIE APPICE** (b.Staten Island, N.Y.) – drums, percussion repl. WARD

Oct 81. (7"/12") *(SAB 5/+12)* **MOB RULES. / DIE YOUNG** [46] [-]

Nov 81. (lp/c) *(6302/7144 119)* <3605> **MOB RULES** [12] [29]
– Turn up the night / Voodoo / The sign of the southern cross / E5150 / The mob rules / Country girl / Slippin' away / Falling off the edge of the world / Over and over. *(re-iss. Jan85 lp/c; PRICE/PRIMC 77) (cd/c re-iss. Jan96/Oct97 on 'Essential'; ESM CD/MC 332)*

Feb 82. (7")(12"/12"pic-d) *(SAB 6)(SABP 6/+12)* **TURN UP THE NIGHT. / LONELY IS THE WORD** [37] [-]

Jan 83. (d-lp/d-c) *(SAB/+M 10)* <23742> **LIVE EVIL (live)** [13] [37]
– E5150 / Neon knights / N.I.B. / Children of the sea / Voodoo / Black sabbath / War pigs / Iron man / Mob rules / Heaven and Hell / The sign of the southern cross / Heaven and Hell (continued) / Paranoid / Children of the grave / Fluff. *(re-iss. Apr86 lp/c; PRID/+C 11) (cd/c re-iss. Apr96/Oct97 on 'Essential'; ESM CD/MC 333)*

— **IAN GILLAN** (b.19 Aug'45, Hounslow, England) – vocals (ex-DEEP PURPLE, ex-GILLAN) repl. RONNIE who formed DIO. **BILL WARD** – drums returned replacing VINNIE who also joined DIO. **BEV BEVAN** – drums (ex-ELECTRIC LIGHT ORCHESTRA) repl. BILL, only originals in band were IOMMI and BUTLER

Sep 83. (lp/c) *(VERL/+C 8)* <23978> **BORN AGAIN** [4] [39]
– Trashed / Stonehenge / Disturbing the priest / The dark / Zero the hero / Digital bitch / Born again / Hot line / Keep it warm. *(cd/c re-iss. Apr96/Oct97 on 'Essential'; ESM CD/MC 334)*

Oct 83. (7") <29434> **STONEHENGE. / THRASHED** [-] [ ]

— **DAVE DONATO** – vocals repl. GILLAN who rejoined DEEP PURPLE

— **TONY IOMMI** recruited **GLENN HUGHES** – vocals (ex-DEEP PURPLE, etc.) repl. DONATO / **DAVE SPITZ** (b. New York City) – bass repl. BUTLER / **ERIC SINGER** (b.Cleveland, Ohio) – drums repl. BEVAN / added **GEOFF NICHOLLS** (b.Birmingham) – keyboards (ex-QUARTZ) had toured '79.

Feb 86. (lp/c)(cd; as BLACK SABBATH featuring TONY IOMMI) *(VERH/+C 29)(826704-2)* <25337> **SEVENTH STAR** [27] [78]
– In for the kill / No stranger to love / Turn to stone / Sphinx (the guardian) / Seventh star / Danger zone / Heart like a wheel / Angry heart / In memory. *(cd/c re-iss. Apr96/Oct97 on 'Essential'; ESM CD/MC 335)*

— **TONY IOMMI** again added **BOB DAISLEY** – bass / **BEV BEVAN** – percussion / **TONY MARTIN** – vocals repl. HUGHES

Nov 87. (lp/c)(cd) *(VERH/+C 51)(832708-2)* <25548> **THE ETERNAL IDOL** [66] [ ]
– The shining / Ancient warrior / Hard life to love / Glory ride / Born to lose / Scarlet Pimpernel / Lost forever / The eternal idol. *(cd+=)* – Nightmare. *(cd/c re-iss. Apr96/Oct97 on 'Essential'; ESM CD/MC 336)*

— **IOMMI + MARTIN** recruited **COZY POWELL** – drums (ex-RAINBOW, ex-ELP) **LAURENCE COTTLE** – bass (on session)

I.R.S. I.R.S.

Apr 89. (7"/7"s) *(EIRS/+CB 107)* **HEADLESS CROSS. / CLOAK AND DAGGER** [62] [ ]
(12"+=/12"w-poster+=) *(EIRST/+PB 107)* – ('A'extended).

Apr 89. (lp/pic-lp/c/cd) *(EIRSA/+PD/C/CD 1002)* <82002> **HEADLESS CROSS** [31] [ ]
– The gates of Hell / Headless cross / Devil & daughter / When death calls / Kill in the spirit world / Call of the wild / Black moon / Nightwing. *(pic-lp+=)* – Cloak and dagger. *(re-iss. cd Apr94;) (cd re-iss. Aug99 on 'E.M.I.'; 521299-2)*

Jun 89. (one-sided; 7"/7"s/7"pic-d) *(EIRS/+B/PD 115)* **DEVIL AND DAUGHTER** [ ] [ ]
(12"+=) *(EIRST 115)* – (15 minute interview).

— **NEIL MURRAY** – bass (ex-VOW WOW, etc.) joined mid'89 repl.COTTLE

Aug 90. (lp/pic-lp/c/cd) *(EIRSA/+PD/C/CD 1038)* <X2-13049> **TYR** [24] [ ]
– Anno Mundi / The law maker / Jerusalem / The sabbath stones / The battle of Tyr / Odin's court / Valhalla / Feels good to me / Heaven in black. *(pic-lp+=)* – Paranoid (live) / Heaven and Hell (live). *(re-iss. cd Apr94) (cd re-iss. Aug99 on 'E.M.I.'; 521298-2)*

Sep 90. (7"/c-s) *(EIRS/C 148)* **FEELS GOOD TO ME. / PARANOID (live)** [ ] [ ]
(12"+=/cd-s+=) *(EIRS T/CD 148)* – Heaven and Hell (live).

— the 1981-83 line-up re-formed Oct91, **IOMMI, GEEZER, VINNIE** and **R.JAMES DIO**

I.R.S. Reprise

Jun 92. (lp/c/cd) *(EIRS A/C/CD 1064)* <26965> **DEHUMANIZER** [28] [44]
– Computer god / After all (the dead) / TV crimes / Letters from Earth / Masters of insanity / Time machine / Sins of the father / Too late / I / Buried alive. *(re-iss. cd Apr94 & Feb99; same)*

Jun 92. (7"pic-d) *(EIRSP 178)* **TV CRIMES. / LETTERS FROM EARTH** [33] [-]
(12"pic-d+=) *(12EIRSPD 178)* – Mob rules (live).
(cd-s+=) *(CDEIRS 178)* – Paranoid (live).
(cd-s+=) *(CDEIRSS 178)* – Heaven and Hell (live).

— **TONY MARTIN** returned on vocals to repl. DIO

— **BOBBY RONDINELLI** – drums (ex-RAINBOW) repl. APPICE

Feb 94. (cd/c/lp) *(EIRS CD/TC/LP 1067)* <13222> **CROSS PURPOSES** [41] [ ]
– I witness / Cross of thorns / Psychophobia / Virtual death / Immaculate deception / Dying for love / Back to Eden / The hand that rocks the cradle / Cardinal sin / Evil eye.

— The 1990 line-up was once again in force although COZY departed once again after below to be repl. by the returning RONDINELLI

I.R.S. Capitol

Jun 95. (cd/c) *(EIRS CD/TC 1072)* <30620> **FORBIDDEN** [71] [ ]
– The illusion of power / Get a grip / Can't get close enough / Shaking off the chains / I won't cry for you / Guilty as hell / Sick and tired / Rusty angels / Forbidden / Kiss of death.

— the original BLACK SABBATH reformed for live gigs

Epic Epic

Oct 98. (d-cd/d-c) *(491954-2/-4)* <69115> **REUNION (live late '97)** [41] [11]
– War pigs / Beyond the wall of sleep / N.I.B. / Fairies wear boots / Electric funeral / Sweet leaf / Spiral architect / Into the void / Snowblind / Sabbath bloody sabbath / Orchid – Lord of this world / Dirty women / Black sabbath / Iron man / Children of the grave / Paranoid / Psycho man (studio) / Selling my soul (studio). *(also d-cd; 491954-9)*

N.M.C. not iss.

Dec 99. (cd-ep) *(PILOT 49)* **BLACK MASS** [ ] [-]
– Paranoid / Black sabbath / Iron man / Blue suede shoes.

– compilations etc. –

on 'NEMS' / 'Warners' unless otherwise stated

Dec 77. (lp) *(NEL 6009)* **BLACK SABBATH'S GREATEST HITS** [ ] [ ]
(re-iss. Nov90 on 'Castle' lp/c/cd+=; CLA LP/MC/CD 200)

Aug 78. (7") *(NES 121)* **PARANOID. / SNOWBLIND** [ ] [-]

Jun 80. (lp) *(BS 001)* **LIVE AT LAST (live)** [5] [ ]
– Tomorrows dream / Sweet leaf / Killing yourself to live / Cornucopia / Snowblind / Children of the grave / War pigs / Wicked world / Paranoid. *(cd-iss. Aug96 on 'Essential'; ESMCD 331)*

Aug 80. (7") *(BSS 101)* **PARANOID. / SABBATH BLOODY SABBATH** [14] [-]

Aug 82. (7"pic-d) *(NEP 1)* **PARANOID. / IRON MAN** [ ] [ ]
(12"+=) *(12NEX 01)* – Fairies wear boots / War pigs.

Aug 85. (d-lp/c) *Castle; (CCS LP/MC 109)* **THE COLLECTION** [ ] [-]
(cd-iss. 1986; CCSCD 109)

Dec 85. (7xlp-box) *Castle; (BSBOX 01)* **BOXED SET** [ ] [-]
– (all albums with OZZY)

Jun 86. (12"ep) *That's Original; (TOF 101)* **CLASSIC CUTS FROM THE VAULTS** [ ] [-]
– Paranoid / War pigs / Iron man / Black sabbath.

Jun 88. (d-lp/d-c/d-cd) *That's Original; (TFO LP/MC/CD 10)* **SABBATH BLOODY SABBATH / BLACK SABBATH** [ ] [-]

Nov 88. (3"cd-ep) *Castle; (CD 3-5)* **BLACK SABBATH LIMITED EDITION** [ ] [-]
– Paranoid / Iron man / War pigs.

Dec 88. (6xcd-box) *Castle; (BSBCD 001)* **THE BLACK SABBATH CD COLLECTION** [ ] [-]

Mar 89. (cd-ep) *Old Gold; (OG 6129)* **PARANOID / ELECTRIC FUNERAL / SABBATH BLOODY SABBATH** [ ] [-]

Nov 89. (d-lp/c/cd) *Vertigo; (838 818-1/-4/-2)* **BLACKEST SABBATH** [ ] [ ]

Dec 89. (d-lp/d-c/cd) *Masterpiece; (TRK LP/MC/CD 103)* **BACKTRACKIN' (20th ANNIVERSARY EDITION)** [ ] [-]

Mar 90. (7") *Old Gold; (OG 9467)* **PARANOID. / IRON MAN** [ ] [-]

Oct 90. (cd/c/lp) *Castle; (CCS CD/MC/LP 199)* **THE BLACK SABBATH COLLECTION VOL.II** [ ] [-]

May 91. (3xcd/5xlp-box) *Essential; (ESB CD/LP 142)* **THE OZZY OSBOURNE YEARS** [ ] [-]
– (features first 6 albums)

Sep 94. (cd/c) *Spectrum; (550720-2/-4)* **IRON MAN** [ ] [-]

1995. (cd-box with video) *P.M.I.; (7243-8-30069-2)* **CROSS PURPOSES LIVE (live 1994)** [ ] [-]

Sep 95. (cd/c) *Raw Power; (RAW CD/MC 104)* **BETWEEN HEAVEN AND HELL (THE BEST OF BLACK SABBATH)** [ ] [-]

Nov 95. (3xcd-box) *E.M.I.; (CDOMB 014)* **THE ORIGINALS** [ ] [-]
– (HEADLESS CROSS / TYR / DEHUMANISER)

Apr 96. (cd/c) *Essential; (EIRS CD/TC 1076)* **THE SABBATH STONES** [ ] [-]

Nov 96. (4xcd-box) *Essential; (ESFCD 419)* **UNDER THE WHEELS OF CONFUSION** [ ] [-]

Oct 98. (3xcd-box) *Essential; (ESMBX 300)* **BLACK SABBATH / PARANOID / MASTER OF REALITY** [ ] [-]

Oct 98. (3xcd-box) *Essential; (ESMBX 301)* **TECHNICAL ECSTASY / NEVER SAY DIE / HEAVEN AND HELL** [ ] [-]
Jun 00. (d-cd/q-lp) *Raw Power; (RAW DD/LP 145)* **THE BEST OF BLACK SABBATH** [24] [-]
Sep 00. (6xcd-s-box) *Essential; (CMKBX 002)* **THE SINGLES BOX SET** [ ] [-]

TONY IOMMI

with **BILL WARD** plus guests vocalists (see below) + **MATT CAMERON** + **JOHN TEMPESTA** + **KENNY ARONOFF** – drums / **BEN SHEPHERD** + **LAURENCE COTTLE** – bass / **BRIAN MAY** – guitar

Priority Priority

Oct 00. (cd) *(CDPTY 207) <27857>* **IOMMI** [ ] [ ]
– Laughing man (in the devil mask) (with HENRY ROLLINS) / Meat (with SKIN) / Goodbye lament (with DAVE GROHL) / Time is mine (with PHIL ANSELMO) / Patterns (with SERJ TANKIAN) / Black oblivion (with BILLY CORGAN) / Flame on (with IAN ASTBURY) / Just say no to love (with PETER STEELE) / Who's fooling who (with OZZY OSBOURNE) / Into the night (with BILLY IDOL).

BLACK SHEEP (see under ⇒ GRAMM, Lou)

BLACKTHORNE (see under ⇒ BONNET, Graham)

BLACK TRAIN JACK

Formed: Astoria, Queens, New York, USA . . . early 90's by guitarist ERNIE (a former drummer with seminal hardcore outfit, TOKEN ENTRY). This band's line-up included former TOKEN ENTRY roadies, BRIAN and the classically-trained voxman/songsmith, ROB VITALE (they subsequently added drummer NICK). The group took their moniker from a HENRY ROLLINS track entitled 'Wreckage' which blasted the lyrics, "You've got a ticket on the black train, Jack", as their tour van careered off the side of the road. Having signed to 'Roadrunner', they released their debut, 'NO REWARD' in 1993, a collection of melodic punk/hard core! Their follow-up, 'YOU'RE NOT ALONE', was not too much of a departure, the band then consigning themselves to the depot in the mid 90's. • **Covered:** ONE LOVE (Bob Marley) / DOESN'T MATTER (Dwarves).

Album rating: NO REWARD (*5) / YOU'RE NOT ALONE (*5)

ROB VITALE – vocals / **ERNIE** – guitar / **BRIAN** – bass / **NICK** – drums

Roadrunner not iss.

Jun 93. (cd/lp) *(RR 9070-2/-1)* **NO REWARD** [ ] [-]
– Time / This is the way / A guy like me / Who's that man / Mad doll / My discipline / No reward / Leapfrog / Someday / The newest one / One love / Doesn't matter.
May 94. (cd/lp) *(RR 9017-2/-1)* **YOU'RE NOT ALONE** [ ] [-]
– Handouts / Not alone / The joker / What's the deal / The struggle / Alright then / Lottery / Regrets / Back up / The reason / Mr. Walsh blues / That reminds me. *(cd re-iss. Sep96; same)*
Mar 95. (cd-s) *(RR 2362)* **HANDOUTS / NO USE / GUY LIKE ME** [ ] [-]
— disbanded some time in 1995

BLACK WIDOW

Formed: Leicester, England . . . 1969 out of white soul outfit PESKY GEE, by JIM GANNON, ZOOT TAYLOR, CLIVE JONES, CLIVE BOX, BOB BOND and KIP TREVOR. With the occult as their inspiration, the group were exposed to their first major crowd at The Isle Of Wight's 1969 festival. Around this time they "treated" their audiences to mock sacrifices that put fellow demonic hopefuls, BLACK SABBATH in the shade (not for long though!). Securing a deal with 'C.B.S.', they delivered their debut opus, aptly entitled, 'SACRIFICE', in early 1970. With SABBATH already riding high in the UK Top 10, this riff heavy, progressive rock fusion only managed to gain a slight foothold in the Top 40. Moving into more fantasy-based lyrical territory, the group lost their initial momentum, albums 'BLACK WIDOW' and 'THREE' poor cousins of their darker first effort. They virtually vanished without trace, all but ROMEO, who continued to scare God-fearing citizens in the rock'n'roll outfit SHOWADDYWADDY. During the late 90's – and with every other rock band re-forming – BLACK WIDOW shouted out their blend of dark rock releasing a couple of 'lost' albums in the process, namely 'IV' and 'RETURN TO THE SABBAT'.

Album rating: SACRIFICE (*6) / BLACK WIDOW (*5) / BLACK WIDOW III (*5) / IV (*4) / RETURN TO THE SABBAT (*4)

KIP TREVOR – vocals, guitar / **JIM GANNON** – guitar / **ZOOT TAYLOR** – keyboards / **CLIVE JONES** – saxophone / **BOB BOND** – bass / **CLIVE BOX** – drums

C.B.S. Columbia

Mar 70. (lp) *(CBS 63948) <6786>* **SACRIFICE** [32] [ ]
– In ancient days / Way to power / Come to the sabbat / Conjuration / Seduction / Attack of the demon / Sacrifice. *(cd-iss. Oct91 on 'Castle'; CLACD 262) (cd re-iss. Aug91 on 'Repertoire'; RR 4067) (lp re-iss. Sep98 on 'Get Back'; GET 531) (cd re-iss. Apr99 on 'Essential'; ESMCD 531)*
May 70. (7") *(CBS 5031)* **COME TO THE SABBAT. / WAY TO POWER** [ ] [ ]
— **ROMEO CHALLENGER** – drums, percussion; repl. BOX
— **GEOFF GRIFFITHS** – bass; repl. BOND
Apr 71. (lp) *(CBS 64133)* **BLACK WIDOW** [ ] [-]
– Tears and wine / The gypsy / Bridge passage / When my mind was young / The journey / Poser / Mary Clark / Wait until tomorrow / An afterthought / Legend of creation. *(cd-iss. Oct91 on 'Castle'; CLACD 263) (cd re-iss. Aug91 on 'Repertoire'; RR 4031CC)*
Nov 71. (7") *(CBS 7596)* **WISH YOU WOULD. / ACCIDENT** [ ] [-]
— **JOHN CULLEY** – guitar, vocals repl. GANNON
Jan 72. (lp) *(CBS 64562)* **BLACK WIDOW III** [ ] [-]
– (a) The battle, (b) The onslaught, (c) If a man should die / Survival / Accident / Lonely man / The Sun / King of hearts / Old man. *(cd-iss. Oct91 on 'Castle'; CLACD 264) (cd re-iss. 1992 & Dec97 on 'Repertoire'; REP 4241WZ) (<lp re-iss. Feb01 on 'Get Back'; GET 571>)*
— disbanded 1972, ROMEO helped form SHOWADDYWADDY!; BLACK WIDOW unearthed some early material below

Mystic Blueprint

Jul 99. (cd) *(MYSCD 117) <BP 4197>* **IV** [ ] [ ]
– Sleigh ride / More than a day / You're so wrong / The waves / Part of a new day / When will you know / Floating / Pictures in my head / I see you.
Aug 00. (cd) *(MYSCD 129) <BP 4397>* **RETURN TO THE SABBAT** [ ] [-]
– In ancient days / Way to power / Come to the sabbat / Conjuration / Seduction / Attack of the demon / Sacrifice.

BLANKS (see under ⇒ DESTRUCTORS)

BLIND FURY (see under ⇒ SATAN)

BLIND ILLUSION

Formed: Richmond, California, USA . . . late 70's by MIKE BIEDERMAN and LES CLAYPOOL, who enlisted a number of personnel over the next decade. Having released nothing so far, they became virtually a secondary outfit in the mid 80's, when CLAYPOOL and BIEDERMAN took off to join PRIMUS and BLUE OYSTER CULT respectively. However, they finally got around to some studio time after they enlisted the help of (JOE SATRIANI pupil) LARRY LALONDE and MIKE MINER. In 1988, an album, 'THE SANE ASYLUM' was completed, although its techno-thrash sound was overshadowed by more established acts like METALLICA.

Album rating: THE SANE ASYLUM (*5)

MIKE BIEDERMAN – vocals, guitar (ex-BLUE OYSTER CULT) / **LES CLAYPOOL** – bass (of PRIMUS) / **LARRY LALONDE** – guitar (ex-POSSESSED) / **MIKE MINER** – drums

Under One Flag Intercord

Mar 88. (cd/lp) *(CD+/FLAG 18) <970418>* **THE SANE ASYLUM** [ ] [ ]
– The sane asylum / Bloodshower / Vengeance is mine / Death noise / Kamakazi / Smash the crystal / Vicious vision / Metamorphosis of a monster.
— CLAYPOOL took LALONDE to his other, more popular act, PRIMUS

BLIND MELON

Formed: Newport Beach, Los Angeles, California, USA . . . 1989 by West Point, Mississippi born BRAD SMITH and ROGER STEVENS. In the early 90's, they were joined by SHANNON HOON, CHRISTOPHER THORN and a little later, GLEN GRAHAM. After recording a widely circulated demo, the band were eventually picked up by 'Capitol'. While awaiting release of their self-titled debut, SHANNON (cousin of AXL ROSE) guested on the GUNS N' ROSES set, 'Use Your Illusion'. With MTV heralding their excellent 'NO RAIN' track, their debut album finally shot into the US Top 3 in 1993. A laid back 70's/GRATEFUL DEAD influenced affair, alternately jangly and funky, HOON's vocals weren't too dissimilar to AXL's. Following a disappointing second set, 'SOUP' (1995), HOON died of a drug overdose on the 21st October '95. Three years on and the sad death now behind them, THORN and SMITH re-united in the outfit LUMA, frontman CHRIS SHINN and veteran ex-PEARL JAM drummer DAVE KRUSEN were also part of the set-up on an internet-only EP in '99. Adding new singer CHRIS SHINN on vocals and guitar, the quartet became UNIFIED THEORY (an unsolved problem Einstein worked on before his death), releasing the eponymous 'UNIFIED THEORY', to sound reviews in August 2000. • **Covered:** JOHN SINCLAIR (John Lennon) / THE PUSHER (Steppenwolf).

Album rating: BLIND MELON (*6) / SOUP (*5) / NICO posthumous (*4) / Unified Theory: UNIFIED THEORY (*7)

SHANNON HOON (b. RICHARD SHANNON HOON, 26 Sep'67, Lafayette, Indiana) – vocals / **ROGER STEVENS** (b.31 Oct'70, West Point, Mis.) – guitar / **CHRISTOPHER THORN** (b.16 Dec'68, Dover, Pennsylvania) – guitar / **BRAD SMITH** (b.29 Sep'68, West Point) – bass / **GLEN GRAHAM** (b. 5 Dec'68, Columbus, Miss.) – drums

Capitol Capitol

Jun 93. (12"pic-d-ep/12"ep/cd-ep) *(12P/12/CD CL 687)* **TONES OF HOME / NO RAIN (live). / DRIVE (live) / SOAK THE SIN (live)** [62] [-]
Aug 93. (cd/c) *(CD/TC EST 2188) <96585>* **BLIND MELON** [53] [3]
– Soak the sin / Tones of home / I wonder / Paper scratcher / Dear ol' dad / Change / No rain / Deserted / Sleepy house / Holyman / Seed to a tree / Drive / Time. *(re-dist.Jul94 w/free cd, hit UK 53)*
Aug 93. (c-s) *<44939>* **NO RAIN / NO RAIN (live) / SOAK THE SIN** [-] [20]
Dec 93. (c-s/7"yellow) *(TC+/CL 699)* **NO RAIN. / NO BIDNESS (live)** [17] [-]
(12"+=/cd-s+=) *(12/CD CL 699)* – I wonder.
(12"pic-d/pic-cd-s) *(12P/CDP CL 699)* – ('A'live) / Soak the sin / Paper scratcher / Deserted.
Jun 94. (c-s/7"green) *(TC+/CL 717)* **CHANGE. / PAPER SCRATCHER (acoustic)** [35] [-]

(12"pic-d/pic-cd-s) *(12/CDS CL 717)* – ('A'side) / No rain (live) / Candy says (live) / Time (live).

Jul 95. (cd-s) *(CDCL 755)* **GALAXIE / WILT / CAR SEAT (GOD'S PRESENTS)** [37] [-]
(12"+=) *(12CL 755)* – 2 x 4.
(cd-s) *(CDCLS 755)* – (first 2 tracks) / 2 x 4 / Change.

Aug 95. (cd/c) *(CD/TC EST 2261)* <28732> **SOUP** [48] [28]
– Galaxie / 2 x 4 / Vernie / Skinned / Toes across the floor / Walk / Dumptruck / Car seat (God's presents) / Wilt / The duke / St.Andrew's fall / New life / Mouthful of cavities / Lemonade.

— On October 21st, '95, frontman SHANNON HOON died of drug overdose.

– compilations, etc. –

Feb 97. (cd) *Capitol; (CDEST 2291)* <37451> **NICO** [ ] [ ]
– Pusher / Hell / Soup / No rain / Soul one / John Sinclair / All that I need / Glitch / Life ain't so shitty / Swallowed / Oull / St. Andrew's hall / Letters from a porcupine.

UNIFIED THEORY

HOON + SMITH along with **CHRIS SHINN** – vocals, guitar / **DAVE KRUSEN** – guitar (ex-PEARL JAM, etc)

Universal Universal

Aug 00. (cd) <*(AA12 159275-2)*> **UNIFIED THEORY** [ ] [ ]
– Cessna / California / Instead of running / Wither / The sun will come / A.M. radio / Fin / Self medicate / Passive / Full flavor / Not dead / Keep on.

BLINK-182

Formed: Poway, nr. San Diego, California, USA . . . 1992 by vocalist/guitarist TOM DELONGE, bassist MARK HOPPUS and drummer SCOTT RAYNOR. This post new cartoon punk outfit began when DELONGE and BARKER met in college. Soon, they were distributing their collection of demos (all which would later appear on 'BUDDHA' debut set) to A&R upstarts. Unfortunately their quest did not succeed, forcing our mangled, spiky-haired heroes to issue their second, self-financed set 'CHESHIRE CAT' (1995), whilst still under the name of BLINK. However, with pressures from an Irish group of the same name, the band re-emerged as BLINK-182 – the 182 in question, being the number of times Al Pacino said "fuck" in the movie, 'Scarface' – and issued the more successful 'DUDE RANCH' (1997). The album boasted college anthem 'DICK LIPS' which sent the boys quite literally on the road to semi-stardom via a little help from supportive peers GREEN DAY and NOFX. Major labels began to show interest, BLINK-182 (with new drummer TRAVIS BARKER) finally signing on the dotted line with 'M.C.A.' at the beginning of 1999. 'ENEMA OF THE STATE' (which featured porn actress Janine scantily clad in a nurse's uniform) surfaced in that summer and went on to achieve double platinum sales throughout America and Europe. Memorable single, 'WHAT'S MY AGE AGAIN?' (a catchy two minute punk/pop rant), saw the trio run naked through L.A. (in the video at least!) and earned them a cameo performance in "ironic" teen sex movie, 'American Pie'. No underlying message, it seemed that BLINK-182 were just out to drink, party and get nekid!

Album rating: BUDDHA (*5) / CHESHIRE CAT (*6) / DUDE RANCH (*7) / ENEMA OF THE STATE (*6) / THE MARK, TOM & TRAVIS SHOW (*4) / TAKE OFF YOUR PANTS AND JACKET (*6)

TOM DELONGE (b.13 Dec'75) – vocals, guitar / **MARK HOPPUS** (b.15 Mar'72) – bass / **SCOTT RAYNOR** – drums

not iss. unknown

1993. (7"ep; as BLINK) **FLY SWATTER EP** [-] [ ]

not iss. Kung Fu

1994. (cd/lp) <78765-2/-1> **BUDDHA** [-] [ ]
– Carousel / T.V. / Strings / Fentoozler / Time / Romeo & Rebecca / 21 days / Sometimes / Degenerate / Point of view / My pet Sally / Reebok commercial / Toast and bananas / The girls next door / Don't. *(re-iss. Jan99 & Jul99; same)*

not iss. Rapido

Jun 96. (cd-ep) <*RAP 14*> **WASTING TIME – 1996 AUSTRALIAN TOUR EP** [-] [ ]
– Wasting time / Wrecked him / Lemmings / Enthused. *(UK-iss.Apr98; RAP 30)*

Grilled Cheese Grilled Cheese

Nov 96. (cd) <*(GRL 001)*> **CHESHIRE CAT** [ ] [ ] May95
– Carousel / M+M's / Fentoozler / Touchdown boy / Strings / Peggy Sue / Sometimes / Does my breath smell? / Cacophony / T.V. / Toast and bananas / Wasting time / Romeo and Rebecca / Ben wah balls / Just about done / Depends. *(re-iss. Nov00 on 'M.C.A.'; 488136-2)*

Nov 96. (cd-s) <*(GRL 701)*> **THEY CAME TO CONQUER . . . URANUS** [ ] [ ] Dec95
– Waggy / Wrecked him / Zulu.

May 97. (cd-ep) <*(CSGRL 004)*> **DICK LIPS EP** [ ] [ ]
– Dick lips / Apple shampoo / Wrecked him / Zulu.

Jul 97. (cd/lp) <*(CRGD/LPGRL 4)*> **DUDE RANCH** [ ] [67]
– Pathetic / Voyeur / Dammit / Boring / Dick lips / Waggy / Enthused / Untitled / Apple shampoo / Emo / Josie / A new hope / Degenerate / Lemmings / I'm sorry. <*(cd re-iss. Nov97 on 'M.C.A.'; MCD 11624)*>

Dec 97. (7") **DAMMIT. / DAMMIT (Growing Up edit)** [-] [ ]

— **TRAVIS BARKER** (b.14 Nov'75) – drums (ex-AQUABATS, ex-PSYCHO BUTTERFLY) repl. SCOTT

Nov 98. (cd-ep) <55513> **JOSIE / WASTING TIME / CAROUSEL / I WON'T BE HOME FOR CHRISTMAS** [-] [ ]

Dec 98. (7") **I WON'T BE HOME FOR CHRISTMAS** [-] [-]

M.C.A. M.C.A.

Sep 99. (c-s) *(MCSC 40219)* <*radio cut*> **WHAT'S MY AGE AGAIN? / PATHETIC (live)** [38] [59] Jul99
(cd-s+=) <*(MCSTD 40219)*> – Untitled (live).
(cd-s) <*(MCSXD 40219)*> – ('A'side) / Josie (live) / Aliens exist (live).

Oct 99. (cd) *(MCD 11950)* <*111950*> **ENEMA OF THE STATE** [15] [9] Jun99
– Don't leave me / Adam's song / The party song / Wendy clear / Going away to college / Dysentery Gary / Aliens exist / All the small things / Mutt / Anthem / What's my age again? / Dumpweed.

Mar 00. (c-s) *(MCSC 40223)* <*155606*> **ALL THE SMALL THINGS DAMMIT (live)** [2] [6] Nov99
(cd-s+=) *(MCSXD 40223)* – ('A'live) / ('A'-CD-Rom video).
(cd-s) *(MCSTD 40223)* – ('A'side) / Dumpweed (live) / What's my age again? (live).

Jun 00. (c-s) *(MCSC 40219)* **WHAT'S MY AGE AGAIN? / PATHETIC (live)** [17] [-]
(cd-s+=) *(MCSZD 40219)* – Untitled (live) / ('A'-CD-Rom).
(cd-s) *(MCSYD 40219)* – ('A'side) / Josie (live) / (interview on CD-Rom).

Nov 00. (cd) <*(112379-2)*> **THE MARK, TOM AND TRAVIS SHOW – THE ENEMA STRIKES BACK! (live)** [69] [8]
– Dumpweed / Don't leave me / Alines exist / Family reunion / Going away to college / What's my age again? / Dick lips / Blow job / Untitled / Voyeur / Pathetic / Adam's song / Peggy Sue / Wendy clear / Carousel / All the small things / Mutt / The country song / Dammit / Man overboard / (plus a whole bunch of funny shit in between).

Jun 01. (cd) <*(112627-2)*> **TAKE OFF YOUR PANTS AND JACKET** [4] [1]
– Anthem (part 2) / Online songs / First date / Happy holidays you bastard / Story of a lonely guy / Rock show / Stay together for the kids / Roller coaster / Reckless abandon / Everytime I look for you / Give me one good reason / Shut up / Please take me home / What went wrong / Time to break up / Fuck a dog / Man overboard (video).

BLITZ

Formed: New Mills, Derbyshire, England . . . 1978 by CARL, NIDGE, MACKIE and CHARLIE. One of the main players in the second generation "oi" movement, BLITZ made their belated debut (after making an early appearance on the V/A compilation, 'Live At The Roxy') in early '82 with the EP, 'ALL OUT ATTACK'. Anarcho-punk yob anthem, 'SOMEONE'S GONNA DIE TONIGHT', introduced their vicious sound and paved the way for a further couple of indie chartbusters, 'NEVER SURRENDER' and 'WARRIORS'. Incredibly, the band scored a bonafide Top 30 album entry with 'VOICE OF A GENERATION', an ambitiously titled collection that scraped the barrel of punk's aftermath. Thankfully, it was their only chart appearance as the follow-up, 'SECOND EMPIRE JUSTICE' (1983), failed to ignite the same spark as its predecessor. MACKIE and MILLER subsequently formed the short-lived ROSE OF VICTORY, although BLITZ were on the attack once more with a final directionless 45, 'SOLAR'. The turn of the decade saw a brief reformation, an album, 'THE KILLING DREAM' (1990), not exactly hitting any new targets.

Album rating: VOICE OF A GENERATION (*6) / SECOND EMPIRE JUSTICE (*5) / THE KILLING DREAM (*3) / THE COMPLETE BLITZ SINGLES COLLECTION compilation (*6)

CARL FISHER – vocals / **NIDGE MILLER** – guitar / **MACKIE** (b. NEIL McLENNAN) – bass / **CHARLIE HOWE** – drums

No Future not iss.

Jan 82. (7"ep) *(OI 1)* **ALL OUT ATTACK** [ ] [-]
– Someone's gonna die / Attack / Fight to live / Revolutions 45. *(re-iss. Nov94 as 12"ep on 'Retch'; RR 12003)*

Mar 82. (7") *(OI 6)* **NEVER SURRENDER. / RAZOR IN THE NIGHT** [ ] [-]

Jul 82. (7") *(OI 16)* **WARRIORS. / YOUTH** [ ] [-]

Oct 82. (lp) *(PUNK 1)* **VOICE OF A GENERATION** [27] [-]
– We are the boys / Time bomb / Voice of a generation / Bleed / I don't need you / T.O. / Propaganda / Criminal damage / Vicious / Warriors / Nation on fire / Your revolution / Scream / 4.Q. / Escape / Moscow / Closedown. *(cd-iss. Jul89 + May92 on 'Cherry Red'+=; CDPUNK 1)* – Someone's gonna die / Attack / Fight to live / 45 revolutions / Never surrender.

— **TIM HARRIS** – guitar, keyboards repl. NIDGE (briefly)

Future not iss.

Jan 83. (7") *(FS 1)* **NEW AGE. / FATIGUE** [ ] [-]
(12"+=) *(FSL 1)* – Bleed (remix).

Apr 83. (7") *(FS 3)* **TELECOMMUNICATION. / TELETRON** [ ] [-]
(12"+=) *(12FS 3)* –

May 83. (lp) *(FL-1)* **SECOND EMPIRE JUSTICE** [ ] [-]
– Flowers & fire / Underground / Acolyte / Into the daylight / Telecommunication / White man / For you / Skin / H.M.K. Grey.

— were finally blitzed themselves, when MILLER and MACKIE formed ROSE OF VICTORY. Released one single in July '83 'OVERDRIVE. / SUFFRAGETTE CITY' for 'No Future'; *(OI 24)*.

Oct 83. (7") *(FS 6)* **SOLAR. / HUSK** [ ] [-]
(12") *(12FS 6)* – ('A'extended remix) / ('B'dance mix).

— re-formed in the late 80's, although below release was their last

Skunx not iss.

Mar 90. (lp) *(SKUNKLP 002)* **THE KILLING DREAM** [ ] [-]
– The killing dream / Overdrive / Intermission 1 / Intermission 2 / Thrown away / Lady Anne / Fade / All you want / Empire fall / Those days / Final hour / Don't care / Walkaway. *(cd-iss. Nov97 on 'Step 1'+=; STEPCD 111)* – RARE INTERVIEWS

– compilations, etc. –

Apr 88. (lp) *Link; (LINKLP 029)* **ALL OUT ATTACK** [ ] [-]
– All out attack / 4.Q. / Time bomb / Criminal damage / Razor in the night / Attack / Escape / Never surrender / Nation on fire / Warriors / Someone's gonna die / 45 revolutions / Fight to live / Youth / I don't need you / Propaganda / Closedown. *(cd-iss. Aug92 on 'Dojo'; DOJOCD 93) (re-iss. May97 on 'Get Back'; GET 14) (cd re-iss. Jun99 on 'Snapper'; SMMCD 579)*

Mar 93. (cd) *Dojo; (DOJOCD 123)* **THE BEST OF BLITZ** [ ] [-]
(*<re-iss. Jun98 as 'THE VERY BEST OF BLITZ' on 'Anagram'; CDPUNK 104>)*
Dec 93. (cd) *Anagram; (CDPUNK 25)* **THE COMPLETE BLITZ SINGLES COLLECTION** [ ] [-]
(lp-iss.Nov00 on 'Get Back'; GET 71)
Mar 99. (cd) *Harry May; (<MAYOCD 101>)* **WARRIORS** [ ] [ ] Jul99
Apr 00. (d-cd) *Anagram; (<CDPUNK 114>)* **VOICE OF A GENERATION: THE NO FUTURE YEARS** [ ] [ ]
Mar 01. (cd) *Captain Oi; (<AHOYCD 161>)* **PUNK SINGLES AND RARITIES 1980-1983** [ ] [ ]

BLOOD

Formed: London, England . . . 1982 originally as COMING BLOOD by The CARDINAL (aka BILL SYKES) and J.J. MANSON, with also FRANKIE BOY, MUTTZ and NAPOLEON EVO. Often compared to MOTORHEAD, BLOOD straddled a similar punk/metal divide albeit in a decidedly "oi" fashion, releasing a one-off debut EP, 'MEGLOMANIA', for the 'No Future' imprint. Moving on to the German-based thrash label, 'Noise, the band cut their first long-player, 'FALSE GESTURES FOR A DEVIOUS PUBLIC', in 1983. However, personnel problems prevailed with FRANKIE, MUTTZ and NAPOLEON severing links with the outfit, necessitating a transfusion in the shape of new members THE SNAKE, MARK BRABBS and PHIL BUTCHER. In 1985, this line-up completed one of their last albums to secure a UK release, 'SICK KICKS FOR SHOCK ROCKERS'.

Album rating: FALSE GESTURES FOR A DEVIOUS PUBLIC (*5)

THE CARDINAL (aka BILL SYKES) – vocals / **J.J. MANSON** – guitar, vocals / with **FRANKIE BOY** – keyboards / **MUTTZ** – bass / **NAPOLEON EVO** – drums

No Future / not iss.
Mar 83. (12"ep) *(OI12 2)* **MEGLOMANIA. / PARASITE IN PARADISE / CALLING THE SHOTS** [ ] [-]

Noise / not iss.
Oct 83. (7") *(NOY 1)* **STARK RAVING NORMAL. / MESRINE** [ ] [-]
Nov 83. (lp) *(NOYZLP 1)* **FALSE GESTURES FOR A DEVIOUS PUBLIC** [ ] [-]
– Done some brain cells last night / Degenerate / Gestapo khazi / Well sick / Sewer brain / Sucker / Mesrine / Rule 43 / Joys of noise / Waste of flesh and bones / Throttle you blue.

—— FRANKIE, MUTTZ + NAPOLEON were repl. by **SNAKE** – guitar / **PHIL BUTCHER** – keyboards / **MARK BRABBS** – drums

Conquest / not iss.
Jun 85. (lp) *(QUEST 3)* **SICK KICKS FOR SHOCK ROCKERS** [ ] [-]

Last Chance / not iss.
1988. (12"ep) *(LCR 011)* **MOODOO DRUGS** [-] [-] German
– Moodoo / Drugs / Heart of stone / Torment of saints.

Wild Rags / not iss.
1990. (lp) *(WRR 014)* **IMPULSE TO DESTROY** [ ] [-]

Magic / not iss.
Dec 92. (lp/cd) *(3770029/+CD)* **CHRISTBAIT** [-] [-] German

SPV / not iss.
Apr 95. (cd) *(SPV 0841241-2)* **METAL CONFLICT** [ ] [-]

– compilations, etc. –

Feb 88. (lp; shared with GONADS) *Link; (LINKLP 024)* **FULL TIME RESULT** [ ] [-]

BLOODGOOD

Formed: Washington DC, USA . . . 1985 by MICHAEL BLOODGOOD and DAVID ZAFFIRO, who recruited LES CARLSEN and MARK WELLING. In contrast to their Christian peers, BLOODGOOD were inspired by the heavier Brit-rock sounds of the early 80's NWOBHM scene. A series of mid-late 80's albums met with favourable reviews, the group fighting the "dark side" with the same lyrical ferocity the satanic metallists usually reserved for God. Their approach backed off somewhat on the later albums, 'OUT OF DARKNESS' (1989) and 'ALL STAND TOGETHER' (1991), BLOODGOOD clearly aiming at the more commercial end of the market.

Album rating: BLOODGOOD (*4) / DETONATION (*5) / ROCK IN A HARD PLACE (*6) / OUT OF DARKNESS (*5) / HOTTER THAN HELL (*5) / THE COLLECTION compilation (*5)

LES CARLSEN – vocals / **DAVID ZAFFIRO** – guitar, vocals / **MICHAEL BLOODGOOD** – bass, vocals / **MARK WELLING** – drums

Frontline / Frontline
1986. (lp) *<FR 9002>* **BLOODGOOD** [-] [ ]
– Accept the lamb / Stand in the light / Demon on the run / Anguish and pain / Awake / Soldier of peace / You lose / What's following the grave / Killing the beast / Black snake.
Jul 88. (lp/c/cd) *<FR/C/CD 9019>* **DETONATION** [ ] [ ] 1987
– Battle of the flesh / Vagrant people / Self-destruction / Alone in suicide / Heartbeat (of the city) / Eat the flesh / Holy fire / Crucify / The messiah / Live wire.
Nov 88. (lp/c/cd) *<FR/CO/CD 9036>* **ROCK IN A HARD PLACE** [ ] [ ]
– Shakin' it / Never be the same / The presence / What have I done / Heaven on Earth / Do or die / She's gone / The world / Seven.

—— **KEVIN WHISTLER** – drums; repl. WELLING

—— ZAFFIRO went off to record a solo album and was replaced by session guitarists **PAUL JACKSON + TERRY B. SHELTON**

not iss. / Intense
1989. (cd) *<CD 09063>* **OUT OF THE DARKNESS** [-] [ ]
– Out of the darkness / Let my people go / America / It's alright / Top of the mountain / Hey! you / Mad dog world / Changing me / New age illusion.

Broken / Broken
Jan 92. (cd/c) *(CD/C 08793)* **ALL STAND TOGETHER** [ ] [ ]
– S.O.S. / All stand together / Escape from the fire / Say goodbye / Out of love / Kingdom come / Fear no evil / Help me / Rounded are the rocks / Lies in the dark / Streetflight dance / I want to live in your heart.

—— split after above

– compilations, etc. –

Nov 91. (cd/c) *Frontline; <(FLD/FLC 9091)>* **THE COLLECTION** [ ] [ ] Sep91
– Anguish and pain / Battle of the flesh / Eat the flesh / Never be the same / New age illusion / Crucify / The messiah / What's following in the grave / Shakin' it / Killing the beast / Alone in suicide / Out of the darkness / Do or die / The presence / Top of the mountain / Black snake.

BLOODHOUND GANG

Formed: King Of Prussia, Pennsylvania, USA . . . 1994 by JIMMY ALI POP and DADDY LONG LEGS, along with LUPUS, SKIP O' POT2MUS and M.S.G. in tow. Not much can be said for these cheeky US punks who have so obviously ripped off quality comedic acts such as JERKY BOYS and BEASTIE BOYS (latter strictly 80's period only!). The BLOODHOUND GANG quite literally stamped on their peers names, attempting to crush their credibility with sexual innuendos with nasty, juvenile rock. A topsy turvy blend of hip hop, metal, rap, quirky funk and a galaxy of fart jokes, the er . . . BG's signed to 'Columbia' after the minor success of the 'DINGLEBERRY HAZE' EP. The group issued the seminal classic 'USE YOUR FINGERS' (1995) and were subsequently dropped due to an abundance of irate listeners who even disliked their manic version of 'KIDS IN AMERICA'. However, once these pesky youths were knocked down, they arose to their feet once more, rebelling with the 'ONE FIERCE BEER COSTER' album (which was originally delivered through the small 'Republic' label). In 1996, David Geffen and his associates found some relative humour within the group, signing them and re-releasing the aforementioned set. The US hit album was heavily promoted with tongue-in-cheek single, 'KISS ME WHERE IT SMELLS FUNNY', it's video apparently featured a bowler-hatted guy sprinting off to somewhere with a fish(!). This single sent giggling American teens ballistic in campuses everywhere and became the most alternative party tune since '(Y~ou've Gotta) Fight For Your Right (To Party)'. Echoes of KING MISSILE's frank and subtle-as-a-sledgehammer humour could be heard within the realms of the groups madness, although vaguely comparing such acts who were so diverse would be in itself insane. Later (in 1999), the band respectfully (not!) celebrated the female form with another long-player, 'HOORAY FOR BOOBIES', ahhem. To much critical laudering, it went on to win five Grammys and a whole host of international music awards, the best track being the hit single, 'THE BAD TOUCH'.

Album rating: USE YOUR FINGERS (*4) / ONE FIERCE BEER COASTER (*3) / HOORAY FOR BOOBIES (*8)

JIMMY POP ALI (b. M. BOWE) – vocals / **LUPUS** – guitar / **DADDY LONG LEGS** (b. JAMES FRANKS) – vocals / **M.S.G.** – vocals / **SKIP O' POT2MUS** – vocals

not iss. / Cheese Factory
Oct 94. (cd-ep) *<9401>* **DINGLEBERRY HAZE EP** [-] [ ]
– Go down / Cheese tidbit / Legend in my spare time / Neighbor invasion / Mama say / Rang dang / Earlameyer the butt pirate / One way / Record offer / Coo coo ca choo / Live at the Apollo. *<re-iss. 1999 on 'Interscope'; 90455>*

not iss. / TVT-Sony
May 95. (c-s/cd-s) *<7792-9/-8>* **MAMA SAY (mixes; original mess / hip hop / devil's food cake / I didn't get paid shit for this)** [-] [ ]
Jun 95. (cd/c) *<67225>* **USE YOUR FINGERS** [-] [ ]
– Rip Taylor is God / We are the knuckleheads / Legend in my spare time / B.H.G.P.S.A. / Mama say / Kids in America / You're pretty when I'm drunk / The evils of placenta hustling / One way / Shitty record offer / Go down / Earlameyer the butt pirate / No rest for the wicked / She ain't got no legs / We like meat / Coo coo ca choo / Rang dang / Nightmare at the Apollo – K.I.D.S. Incorporated. *(UK-iss.Feb98 on 'TVT-Sony'; same as US) (UK re-iss. Apr00 on 'Columbia'; 480703-2)*

—— **EVIL JARED** – bass / **SPANKY G** – drums / **Q-BALL** – DJ; repl. DADDY, M.S.G. + POT2MUS

not iss. / Republic
Dec 96. (lp) *<REP 26903-1>* **ONE FIERCE BEER COASTER** [-] [57]
– Kiss me where it smells funny / Lift your head up high (and blow your. . . .) / Fire water burn / I wish I was queer so I could get . . . . / Why's everybody always pickin' on me? / It's tricky / Asleep at the wheel / Shut up / Your only friends are make believe / Boom / Going nowhere slow / Reflections of Remoh. *<cd-iss. Sep97 on 'Geffen'; GED 25124>) (UK lp-iss.Oct97 on 'Republic'; same as US)*

Geffen / Geffen
Aug 97. (c-s/12"/cd-s) *(GFS C/V/TD 22252)* **WHY'S EVERYBODY ALWAYS PICKIN' ON ME? (mixes; Honkus Maximus / Hemlock / Greek salad)** [56] [-]
Nov 97. (12") *<REP 9603-1>* **FIRE WATER BURN (Rudimental Jammy Jam). / FIRE WATER BURN (Jim Makin' Jamaican mix)** [ ] [ ]
(above on 'Republic', below on 'Bloodhound Gang')
Dec 97. (7") *<BHG 002>* **ONE CENSORED BEER COASTER** [ ] [ ]
– Yellow fever / The hidden track *[23 minutes long]*
Oct 99. (cd/c) *<(490455-2/-4)>* **HOORAY FOR BOOBIES** [ ] [14] Sep99
– I hope you die / The inevitable return of the great white dope / Mama's boy /

Three point one four / Mope / Yummy down on this / The ballad of Chasey Lain / R.S.V.P. / Magna cum nada / The bad touch / That cough came with a prize / Take the long way home / Hell yeah / Right turn Klyde / This is stupid / A lap dance is so much better when the stripper is crying / 10 coolest things about New Jersey / Along comes Mary. *(re-iss. Apr00 +=; 490457-2)* – (extra CD). – hit UK No.37

Mar 00. (c-s) *(497267-4)* **THE BAD TOUCH / WHY'S EVERYBODY KEEP PICKIN' ON ME** [4] [52]
(cd-s+=) *(497267-2)* – Boom / ('A'-CD-Rom video).
(cd-s) *(497268-2)* – ('A'side) / ('A'-The Eiffel 65 mix) / ('A'-The Rollergirl mix) / ('A'-God Lives Underwater mix).

Aug 00. (c-s) *(497380-4)* **THE BALLAD OF CHASEY LAIN / THE BALLAD OF CHASEY LAIN (Hot Snax mix)** [15] [ ]
(cd-s) *(497381-2)* – ('A'side) / Mope (Pet Shop Boys mix) / The bad touch / The bad touch (uncensored video).
(cd-s) *(497382-2)* – ('A'version) / Mope (Pet Shop Boys mix) / The bad touch (Eiffel 65 extended) / ('A'-CD-Rom).

BLOODROCK

Formed: Fort Worth, Texas, USA ... late 60's by WARREN HAM, ED GRUNDY, STEVE HILL, NICK TAYLOR and RICK COBB. Signed to 'Capitol' records, their eponymous debut album chalked up reasonable sales to obtain a Top 200 placing. TERRY KNIGHT, manager of fellow heavy rock'n'rollers, GRAND FUNK RAILROAD, took them under his wing, enlisting new frontman, JIM RUTLEDGE and guitarist LEE PICKENS to replace HAM. KNIGHT's production on the 1970 single, 'D.O.A.', boosted the band's commercial fortunes, the record and its parent album, 'BLOODROCK 2', both hitting the US Top 40. Six months later, in the Spring of '71, their third set also cracked the Top 30, although a sharp decline in sales for successive efforts (JOHN NITZINGER wrote several tracks for their fourth album 'U.S.A.' released later in '71) led to the group's subsequent demise. Their "lost" album, 'UNSPOKEN WORDS' (shelved in 1974) was finally issued on a double-CD 2000 collection, 'TRIPTYCH'; apparently their best work. RUTLEDGE went on to produce MERI WILSON's 'Telephone Man' 45. • **Covered:** ELEANOR RIGBY (Beatles).

Album rating: BLOODROCK (*4) / BLOODROCK 2 (*5) / BLOODROCK 3 (*4) / BLOODROCK U.S.A. (*4) / BLOODROCK LIVE (*3) / BLOODROCK PASSAGE early work (*2) / WHIRLWIND TONGUES (*2) / BLOODROCK'N'ROLL compilation (*4) / TRIPTYCH collection (*5)

WARREN HAM – vocals, flute, sax / **NICK TAYLOR** – guitar, vocals / **STEVE HILL** – keyboards, vocals / **ED GRUNDY** – bass, vocals / **RICK COBB** – drums

Capitol Capitol

Apr 70. (lp) *<EST 435>* **BLOODROCK** [-] [ ]
– Gotta find a way / Castle of thoughts / Fatback / Double cross / Timepiece / Wicked truth / Gimme your head / Fantastic piece of architecture / Melvin laid an egg. *<cd-iss. 1995 on 'One Way'; OW 18404>*

— **JIM RUTLEDGE** – vocals + **LEE PICKENS** – guitar repl. WARREN

Jan 71. (7") *(CL 15670) <3009>* **D.O.A. / CHILDREN'S HERITAGE** [ ] [36] Dec70

Jan 71. (lp) *(ST 491) <491>* **BLOODROCK 2** [ ] [21] Nov70
– Lucky in the morning / Cheater / Sable and Pearl / Fallin' / Children's heritage / Dier not a lover / D.O.A. / Fancy space odyssey. *<cd-iss. 1995 on 'One Way'; OW 18404>*

Apr 71. (lp) *(ST 765) <765>* **BLOODROCK 3** [ ] [27]
– Jessica / Whiskey vengeance / Song for a brother / You gotta roll / Breach of lease / Kool-aid-kids / A certain kind / America, America. *<cd-iss. Nov98 on 'One Way'; OW 19479>*

Nov 71. (lp) *<SM 645>* **BLOODROCK U.S.A.** [-] [88]
– It's a sad world / Don't eat the children / Promises / Crazy 'bout you baby / Hangman's dance / America burn / Rock and roll candy man / Abracadaver / Magic man. *(<cd-iss. Nov98 on 'One Way'; OW 19478>)*

May 72. (d-lp) *<11038>* **BLOODROCK LIVE (live)** [-] [67]
– Castle of thoughts / Breach of lease / Lucky in the morning / Kool-aid-kids / D.O.A. / You gotta roll / Cheater / Jessica / Gotta find a way. *(<cd-iss. Nov98 on 'One Way'; 19480>)*

Sep 72. (lp) *<SW 11109>* **BLOODROCK PASSAGE** (early material & line-up) [-] [ ]
– Help is on the way / Scottsman / Juice / The power / Life blood / Days and nights / Lost fame / Thank you Daniel Ellsberg / Fantasy.

1974. (lp) *<EST 11259>* **WHIRLWIND TONGUES** [-] [ ]
– It's gonna be love / Sunday song / Parallax / Voices / Eleanor Rigby / Stilled by whirlwind tongues / Guess what I am / Lady of love / Jungle.

1974. (7") *<3770>* **VOICES. / THANK YOU DANIEL ELLSBERG** [-] [ ]

1974. (lp) *<SM 11417>* **BLOODROCK'N'ROLL** (compilation) [-] [ ]
– D.O.A. / Gotta find a way / Cheater / Jessica / Lucky in the morning / You gotta roll / Kool-aid-kids.

— disbanded in the mid-70's; RUTLEDGE + PICKENS both went solo

- compilations, etc. -

Sep 00. (d-cd) *One Way; <25437>* **TRIPTYCH** [-] [ ]
– (PASSAGE + WHIRLWIND TONGUES + shelved UNSPOKEN WORDS):- Gonna help you / The right time / Unspoken words / Afternoon / Chicken fried / Pogo stivk / For the ladies / Cerberus / Follow.

b.l.o.w. (see under ⇒ LITTLE ANGELS)

BLUE CHEER

Formed: San Francisco, California, USA ... early 1967 originally as a 6-piece, The SAN FRANCISCO BLUES BAND. They trimmed down to a trio (DICKIE PETERSON, LEIGH STEPHENS and PAUL WHALEY) soon after witnessing The JIMI HENDRIX EXPERIENCE at the Monterey Pop Festival, signing to 'Philips' that year and later moving to Boston. In 1968, they had a resounding US Top 20 smash with a souped-up version of EDDIE COCHRAN's 'SUMMERTIME BLUES'. Although its parent lp nearly made the Top 10, they failed to consolidate their success with further releases. However, they did claim to be the loudest band in the world and their CREAM similarities gained them a cult Hell's Angels following. In fact, they were actually managed by a fully paid-up member of the gang and were part of the late 60's drug scene, having taken their name from a particularly mindbending brand of LSD. They reformed in the late 80's, although this failed to win them any new converts, most heavy-metal kids opting for their higher octane descendants (i.e. METALLICA, SLAYER, ANTHRAX, etc.) • **Songwriters:** PETERSON and group, except other covers, PARCHMENT FARM (Mose Allison) / (I CAN'T GET NO) SATISFACTION (Rolling Stones) / THE HUNTER (Booker T) / HOOCHIE COOCHIE MAN (Muddy Waters).

Album rating: VINCEBUS ERUPTUM (*7) / OUTSIDEINSIDE (*6) / NEW! IMPROVED! BLUE CHEER (*4) / BLUE CHEER (*4) / B.C.#5 THE ORIGINAL HUMAN BEINGS (*5) / OH! PLEASANT HOPE (*3) / THE BEST OF BLUE CHEER compilation (*7) / THE BEAST IS BACK (*3) / GOOD TIMES ARE SO HARD TO FIND compilation (*7) / BLITZKRIEG OVER NUREMBERG (*3) / HIGHLIGHTS AND LOWLIVES compilation (*4) / DINING WITH SHARKS (*3)

DICKIE PETERSON (b.1948, Grand Forks, N.Dakota) – vocals, bass (ex-GROUP 'B')/ **LEIGH STEPHENS** – guitar, vocals/ **PAUL WHALEY** – drums (ex-OXFORD CIRCLE)

Philips Philips

Mar 68. (7") *(BF 1646) <40516>* **SUMMERTIME BLUES. / OUT OF FOCUS** [ ] [14] Jan68

Jul 68. (lp; stereo/mono) *(S+/BL 7839) <600/200 264>* **VINCEBUS ERUPTUM** [ ] [11] Mar68
– Summertime blues / Rock me baby / Doctor please / Out of focus / Parchment farm / Second time around. *(German cd-iss. Aug92 on 'Line'; LMCD 9.51075 Z) <US cd-iss. 1994 on 'Polygram'; 514685> (cd-iss. Nov94 on 'Repertoire';) (lp re-iss. Aug98 on 'Akarma'; AK 011) (pic-lp-iss.Jun00; AK 011LPP)*

Jul 68. (7") *(BF 1684) <40541>* **JUST A LITTLE BIT. / GYPSY BALL** [ ] [92] Jun68

— added on some **RALPH BURNS KELLOGG** – keyboards

Oct 68. (7") *(BF 1711) <40561>* **FEATHERS FROM YOUR TREE. / SUN CYCLE** [ ] [ ]

Oct 68. (lp) *(SBL 7860) <600 278>* **OUTSIDEINSIDE** [ ] [90] Sep68
– Feathers from your tree / Sun cycle / Just a little bit / Gypsy ball / Come and get it / (I can't get no) Satisfaction / The hunter / Magnolia caboose babyfinger / Babylon. *(German cd-iss. Aug92 on 'Line'; LMCD 9.51076 Z) <US cd-iss. 1994 on 'Polygram'; 514683> (cd-iss. Nov94 on 'Repertoire';) (lp re-iss. Aug98 on 'Akarma'; AK 012) (pic-lp-iss.Jun00; AK 012LPP)*

— **RANDY HOLDEN** – guitar (ex-OTHER HALF, ex-SONS OF ADAM) repl. LEIGH due to his deafness. He went solo before joining SILVER METRE and then PILOT (U.S.). Solo single; 1969 'RED WEATHER / SAKI ZWADOO' *Philips <40628>* / albums; 1969 'RED WEATHER' *Philips (SBL 7897) <PHS-600 294>* / Sep71 'LEIGH STEPHENS & A CAST OF THOUSANDS' *Charisma <CAS 1040>*

May 69. (7") *<40602>* **WHEN IT ALL GETS OLD. / WEST COAST CHILD OF SUNSHINE** [-] [ ]

Jul 69. (lp) *(SBL 7896) <600 305>* **NEW! IMPROVED! BLUE CHEER** [ ] [84] Apr69
– When it all gets old / West Coast child of sunshine / I want my baby back / Aces'n eights / As long as I live / It takes a lot of love, it takes a train to cry / Peace of mind / Fruit & icebergs / Honey butter love. *(cd-iss. Nov94 on 'Repertoire' +=; IMS-7025)* – All night long / Fortunes. *(re-iss. Aug98 on 'Akarma' lp/cd; AK 016/+CD) (pic-lp-iss.Jul00; AK 016PICT)*

— **NORMAN MAYELL** (b.1942, Chicago, Illinois) – drums repl. WHALEY

— **GARY YODER** – guitar, vocals (ex-OXFORD CIRCLE) repl. HOLDEN

Nov 69. (7") *<40651>* **ALL NIGHT LONG. / FORTUNES** [-] [ ]

Feb 70. (lp) *(6336 001) <600 333>* **BLUE CHEER** [ ] [ ]
– Fool / You're gonna need someone / Hello L.A., bye bye Birmingham / Saturday freedom / Ain't that the way (love's supposed to be) / Rock and roll queens / Better when we try / Natural man / Lovin' you's easy / The same old story. *(German cd-iss. Aug92 on 'Line'; LMCD 9.51078 Z) (lp re-iss. Aug98 on 'Akarma'; AK 017) (pic-lp-iss.Jul00; AK 017PICT)*

Feb 70. (7") *<40664>* **HELLO, L.A., BYE BYE, BIRMINGHAM. / NATURAL MEN** [-] [ ]

Jun 70. (7") *<40682>* **FOOL. / AIN'T THAT THE WAY (LOVE'S SUPPOSED TO BE)** [-] [ ]

— **BRUCE STEPHENS** (b.1946) – guitar + **RALPH** repl.YODER

Nov 70. (lp) *(6336 004) <600 347>* **B.C. #5 THE ORIGINAL HUMAN BEINGS** [ ] [ ]
– Good times are hard to find / Love of a woman / Make me laugh / Pilot / Babaji (twilight raga) / Preacher / Black Sun / Tears by my bed / Man on the run / Sandwich / Rest at ease. *(German cd-iss. Aug92 on 'Line'; LMCD 9.51079 Z)*

Apr 71. (7") *(6051 010) <40691>* **PILOT. / BABAJI (TWILIGHT RAGA)** [ ] [ ] Oct70

Nov 71. (lp) *<600 350>* **OH! PLEASANT HOPE** [-] [ ]
– Highway man / Believer / Money troubles / Traveling man / Oh! pleasant hope / I'm the light / Ecological blues / Lester the arrester / Heart full of soul. *(German cd-iss. Aug92 on 'Line'; LMCD 9.51080 Z) (re-iss. Aug98 on 'Akarma' lp/cd; AK 018/+CD)*

— Disbanded 1971, but briefly did reunions 1975 & 1979. In 1984 they returned to studio. (WHALEY and PETERSON, + TONY RAINIER – guitar)

not iss. Megaforce

1985. (lp) *<MRI 1069>* **THE BEAST IS BACK** [-] [ ]
– Nightmares / Summertime blues / Ride with me / Girl next door / Babylon / Heart of the city / Out of focus / Parchment farm. *<US cd-iss. Feb96; 1970> (cd-iss. 1996 on 'Bulletproof'; CDMVEST 72) (cd re-iss. Mar99 on 'S.P.V.'; SPV 0761864-2)*

— toured again in the late 80's/early 90's

— now **PETERSON** plus **ANDREW DUCK McDONALD** – guitar / **DAVID SALCE** – drums

Thunderbolt not iss.

Sep 90. (cd/lp) *(CDTB/THBL 091)* **BLITZKRIEG OVER NUREMBERG (live)** [ ] [-]
– Babylon – Girl next door / Ride with me / Just a little bit / Summertime blues / Out of focus / Doctor please / The hunter / Red house. *(lp re-iss. Aug00 on 'Nibelung'; 13547413)*

Nibelung / not iss.

Nov 90. (lp) *(23010-413)* **HIGHLIGHTS AND LOWLIVES** [-] [-] German
– Urban soldiers / Hunter of love / Girl from London / Blue steel dues / Big trouble in Paradise / Flight of the Enola Gay / Hoochie coochie man / Down and dirty. *(cd-iss. 1991 on 'Thunderbolt'; CDTB 125) <(cd re-iss. Jan00 on 'MagMid'; MM 046)>*

1991. (cd) **DINING WITH THE SHARKS** [-] [-] German
– Big noise / Outrider / Sweet child of the Reeperbahn / Gunflight / Audio whore / Cut the costs / Sex soldier / When two spirits touch / Pull the trigger / Foxy lady.

Captain Trip / not iss.

Nov 99. (cd) *(CTCD 190)* **HELLO TOKYO BYE BYE OSAKA (live 1999)** [ ] [-]

– compilations, others, etc. –

Oct 82. (lp/c) *Philips; (6463/7145 142)* **THE BEST OF BLUE CHEER** [-] [-] Europe

1986. (lp) *Rhino; <RNLP 70130>* **LOUDER THAN GOD: THE BEST OF BLUE CHEER** [-] [ ]

Oct 90. (cd) *Mercury; <834030>* **GOOD TIMES ARE SO HARD TO FIND: THE BEST OF BLUE CHEER** [-] [ ]
– Summertime blues / Out of focus / Parchmen farm / Feathers from your tree / The hunter / Babylon / Peace of mind / Fruit and icebergs / Fool / Hello L.A., bye bye Birmingham / Saturday freedom / Good times are so hard to find / Pilot / Preacher / Hiway man / I'm the light.

Jul 97. (cd) *Captain Trip; (CTCD 023)* **LIVE AND UNLEASHED 1968-1974 (live)** [ ] [-]

Jul 97. (cd) *Captain Trip; (CTCD 026)* **LIVE AND UNLEASHED VOL.2** [ ] [-]

BLUE MURDER

Formed: London, England . . . 1987 by seasoned campaigners JOHN SYKES, TONY FRANKLIN and COZY POWELL, the latter being replaced by CARMINE APPICE during recording of their eponymous debut in '89. Released by 'Geffen', the album met with mixed reviews; as is so often the case, this hard-rock supergroup failed to live up to its potential. Four years in the making, BLUE MURDER returned with another overly indulgent long player, 'NOTHING BUT TROUBLE', an ill-advised cover of The Small Faces' 'ITCHYCOO PARK' glaringly out of place (M-People were even better, lads!).

Album rating: BLUE MURDER (*5) / NOTHING BUT TROUBLE (*4)

JOHN SYKES – vocals, guitar (ex-THIN LIZZY, ex-TYGERS OF PAN TANG, ex-WHITESNAKE) / **TONY FRANKLIN** – bass (ex-FIRM) / **CARMINE APPICE** – drums (ex-VANILLA FUDGE, ex-CACTUS, BECK, ex-KGB, ex-ROD STEWART)

Geffen / Geffen

Apr 89. (lp/c)(cd) *(WX 245/+C)(924212-2) <24212>* **BLUE MURDER** [45] [69]
– Riot / Sex child / Valley of the kings / Jellyroll / Blue murder / Billy / Out of love / Billy / Ptolemy / Black-hearted woman. *(re-iss. Aug93 cd/c; GFL D/C 19225)*

Apr 89. (7") *<22885>* **BLACK HEARTED WOMAN. / JELLYROLL** [-] [ ]

—— FRANKLIN was repl. by unknown

Aug 93. (cd/c) *(GED/GEC 24419)* **NOTHING BUT TROUBLE** [ ] [ ]
– We all fall down / Itchycoo park / Cry for love / Runaway / Dance / I'm on fire / Save my love / Love child / Shouldn't have let you go / I need an angel / She knows.

—— don't think they'll chance another bout in the studio

BLUE OYSTER CULT

Formed: Long Island, New York, USA . . . 1970 as SOFT WHITE UNDERBELLY by BUCK DHARMA, ALLEN LANIER and AL BOUCHARD. They became STALK-FORREST GROUP and signed to 'Elektra', where they released one 45, 'WHAT IS QUICKSAND' / 'ARTHUR COMICS' <45693> but had an album rejected. In late 1971 they renamed themselves The BLUE OYSTER CULT, their manager/guru SANDY PEARLMAN securing them a recording contract with 'Columbia'. The first two albums, 'BLUE OYSTER CULT' (1972) and 'TYRANNY AND MEDITATION' (1973 and containing lyrics by producer Richard Meltzer) were sophisticated proto-metal classics, infusing the crunching guitar and rhythm with a keen sense of melody and keeping tight enough a rein on proceedings to avoid the hoary bombast that characterised other bands of their ilk. Lyrically the band peddled fairly cliched, if more intelligent than average, dark musings and with 1974's 'SECRET TREATIES', the music began to sound similarly predictable. Throughout the remainder of the 70's, the band gravitated to a cleaner cut hard rock sound, although the darkly shimmering 'DON'T FEAR THE REAPER' was a one-off return to their 60's psychedelic roots. The song gave the band a surprise Top 20 UK hit, and while they continued to enjoy minor chart successes with their subsequent releases, the quality of their output struggled to rise above stale cliche. • **Songwriters:** Group compositions, except CAREER OF EVIL (written by LANIER's one-time girlfriend PATTI SMITH) / BLACK BLADE (co-written with Michael Moorcock; ex-Hawkwind) / KICK OUT THE JAMS (MC5) / WE GOTTA GET OUT OF THIS PLACE (Animals) / BORN TO BE WILD (Steppenwolf). • **Trivia:** AL BOUCHARD claimed he was the inspiration for the 1988 album, 'IMAGINOS'.

Album rating: BLUE OYSTER CULT (*6) / TYRANNY & MUTATION (*5) / SECRET TREATIES (*8) / ON YOUR FEET ON YOUR KNEES (*7) / AGENTS OF FORTUNE (*8) / SPECTRES (*5) / SOME ENCHANTED EVENING (*8) / MIRRORS (*5) / CULTOSAURUS ERECTUS (*4) / FIRE OF UNKNOWN ORIGIN (*6) / EXTRATERRESTRIAL LIVE (*3) / THE REVOLUTION BY NIGHT (*5) / CLUB NINJA (*4) / IMAGINOS (*6) / WORKSHOP OF THE TELESCOPES compilation (*7) / CULT CLASSICS (*3) / HEAVEN FORBID (*4) / BAD CHANNELS (*4) / CURSE OF THE HIDDEN MIRROR (*4)

ERIC BLOOM – vocals, "stun" guitar / **BUCK DHARMA** (b.DONALD ROSIER) – lead guitar, vocals / **ALLEN LANIER** – rhythm guitar, keyboards / **JOE BOUCHARD** (b. 9 Nov'48, Watertown, N.Y.) – bass, vocals / **ALBERT BOUCHARD** (b.24 May'47, Watertown) – drums, vocals

not iss. / Reichstag

1972. (7"ep) *<1106>* **LIVE BOOTLEG (live)** [-] [ ]
– In my mouth or on the ground / etc.

C.B.S. / Columbia

1973. (lp) *(64904) <31063>* **BLUE OYSTER CULT** [ ] [ ] May72
– Transmaniacon MC / I'm on the lamb but I ain't no sheep / Then came the last days of May / Stairway to the stars / Before the kiss, a redcap / Screams / She's as beautiful as a foot / Cities on flame with rock and roll / Workshop of the telescopes / Redeemed. *(re-iss. Mar81; 32025)*

1973. (7") *<45598>* **CITIES ON FLAME WITH ROCK AND ROLL. / BEFORE THE KISS, A REDCAP** [-] [ ]

1973. (7") *<45879>* **SCREAMING DIZ-BUSTERS. / HOT RAILS TO HELL** [-] [ ]

1974. (lp) *(65331) <32107>* **TYRANNY AND MUTATION** [ ] [ ] Mar74
– The red & the black / O.D.'d on life itself / Hot rails to Hell / 7 screaming diz-busters / Baby ice dog / Wings wetted down / Teen archer / Mistress of the salmon salt (quicklime girl). *(re-iss. 1981; 32056)*

1974. (7") *<10046>* **CAREER OF EVIL. / DOMINANCE AND SUBMISSION** [-] [ ]

Sep 74. (lp) *(80103) <32858>* **SECRET TREATIES** [ ] [53] Apr74
– Career of evil / Subhuman / Dominance and submission / ME 262 / Cagey cretins / Harvester of eyes / Flaming telepaths / Astronomy. *(re-iss. Mar82; 32055)*

Nov 75. (d-lp) *(88116) <33317>* **ON YOUR FEET OR ON YOUR KNEES (live)** [ ] [22] Mar75
– Subhuman / Harvester of eyes / Hot rails to Hell / The red and the black / 7 screaming diz-busters / Buck's boogie / Then came the last days of May / Cities on flame / ME 262 / Before the kiss (a redcap) / I ain't got you / Born to be wild. *(re-iss. Sep87 lp/c; 460113-1/-4)*

Nov 75. (7") *<10169>* **BORN TO BE WILD (live). / (part 2)** [-] [ ]

Jun 76. (lp/c) *(CBS/40 81835) <34164>* **AGENTS OF FORTUNE** [26] [29]
– This ain't the summer of love / True confessions / (Don't fear) The reaper / E.T.I. (Extra Terrestrial Intelligence) / The revenge of Vera Gemini / Sinful love / Tattoo vampire / Morning final / Tenderloin / Debbie Denise. *(re-iss. Jul89; CDCBS 32221) (cd-iss. Jun94 on 'Sony'; 982732-2) (cd-iss. May95 & Jul99 on 'Columbia'; 468019-2) (lp re-iss. Oct97 on 'Simple Vinyl'; SVLP 2)*

Jul 76. (7") *<10384>* **(DON'T FEAR) THE REAPER. / TATTOO VAMPIRE** [-] [12]

Jul 76. (7") *(4483)* **(DON'T FEAR) THE REAPER. / R.U. READY 2 ROCK** [ ] [-]

Jan 77. (7") *<10560>* **DEBBIE DENISE. / THIS AIN'T THE SUMMER OF LOVE** [-] [ ]

Dec 77. (lp/c) *(CBS/40 86050) <35019>* **SPECTRES** [60] [43] Nov77
– Godzilla / Golden age of leather / Death valley nights / Searchin' for Celine / Fireworks / R.U. ready 2 rock / Celestial the queen / Goin' through the motions / I love the night / Nosferatu. *(re-iss. Feb86 lp/c; CBS/40 32715) (cd-iss. Dec88; CDCBS 82371)*

Dec 77. (7") *(5689) <10659>* **GOING THROUGH THE MOTIONS. / SEARCHIN' FOR CELINE** [ ] [ ]

Feb 78. (7") *<10697>* **GODZILLA. / NOSFERATU** [-] [ ]

May 78. (7"/12") *(7/12 6333)* **(DON'T FEAR) THE REAPER. / R U READY 2 ROCK** [16] [-]
(re-iss. Jun84 on 'Old Gold'; OG 9398)

Jun 78. (7") *<10725>* **GODZILLA. / GODZILLA (live)** [-] [ ]

Aug 78. (7") *(6514)* **I LOVE THE NIGHT. / NOSFERATU** [ ] [-]

Sep 78. (lp) *(CBS/40 86074) <35563>* **SOME ENCHANTED EVENING (live)** [18] [44]
– R.U. ready 2 rock / E.T.I. (Extra Terrestrial Intelligence) / Astronomy / Kick out the jams / Godzilla / (Don't fear) The reaper / We gotta get out of this place. *(cd-iss. Jul97 on 'Columbia'; 487931-2)*

Oct 78. (7") *<10841>* **WE GOTTA GET OUT OF THIS PLACE. / E.T.I. (EXTRA TERRESTRIAL INTELLIGENCE)** [-] [ ]

Nov 78. (7") *(6909)* **WE GOTTA GET OUT OF THIS PLACE (live). / STAIRWAY TO THE STARS** [ ] [-]

Aug 79. (lp/c) *(CBS/40 86087) <36009>* **MIRRORS** [46] [44] Jul79
– Dr. Music / The great sun jester / In thee / Mirrors / Moon crazy / The vigil / I am the storm / You're not the one (I was looking for) / Lonely teardrops.

Aug 79. (7"clear) *(7763)* **MIRRORS. / LONELY TEARDROPS** [ ] [-]

Sep 79. (7") *<11055>* **IN THEE. / LONELY TEARDROPS** [-] [74]

Oct 79. (7") *(8003)* **IN THEE. / THE VIGIL** [ ] [-]

Feb 80. (7") *<11145>* **YOU'RE NOT THE ONE (I WAS LOOKING FOR). / MOON CRAZY** [-] [ ]

Jul 80. (lp) *(86120) <36550>* **CULTOSAURUS ERECTUS** [12] [34]
– Black blade / Monsters / Divine wind / Deadline / Here's Johnny / The Marshall plan / Hungry boys / Fallen angel / Lips in the hills / Unknown tongue. *(cd-iss. Feb99 on 'Columbia'; 493420-2)*

Jul 80. (7") *<11401>* **HERE'S JOHNNY (THE MARSHALL PLAN). / DIVINE WIND** [-] [ ]

Jul 80. (7") *(8790)* **FALLEN ANGEL. / LIPS IN THE HILLS** [ ] [-]

Oct 80. (7") *(8986)* **DEADLINES. / MONSTERS** [ ] [-]

Jul 81. (lp) *(CBS 85137) <37389>* **FIRE OF UNKNOWN ORIGIN** [29] [24]
– Fire of unknown origin / Burnin' for you / Veteran of the psychic wars / Sole survivor / Heaven metal: the black and silver / Vengeance (the pact) / After dark / Joan Crawford / Don't turn your back. *<cd-iss. 1987; CK 85137>*

Aug 81. (7") *<02415>* **BURNIN' FOR YOU. / VENGEANCE (THE PACT)** [-] [40]

Sep 81. (7") *(A 1453)* **BURNIN' FOR YOU. / HEAVY METAL** [ ] [-]
(12"+=) *(A13 1453)* – The black & silver.

May 82. (d-lp) *(CBS 22203) <KF 37946>* **EXTRATERRESTRIAL LIVE (live)** [39] [29]
– Dominance and submission / Cities on flame / Dr. Music / The red and the black / Joan Crawford / Burnin' for you / Roadhouse blues / Black blade / Hot rails to Hell / Godzilla / Veteran of the psychic wars / E.T.I. (Extra Terrestrial Intelligence) / (Don't fear) the reaper.

Jun 82. (7") *<03137>* **BURNIN' FOR YOU (live). / (DON'T FEAR) THE REAPER (live)** [-] [ ]

— (late 1981) **RICK DOWNEY** – drums repl. ALBERT

Nov 83. (lp/c) *(CBS/40 25686)* *<38947>* **THE REVOLUTION BY NIGHT** 95 93
– Take me away / Eyes on fire / Shooting shark / Veins / Shadows of California / Feel the thunder / Let go / Dragon lady / Light years of love. *<cd-iss. Dec88; CK 38947>*

Nov 83. (7") *(A 3937)* **TAKE ME AWAY. / FEEL THE THUNDER** -
(12"+=) *(TA 3937)* – Burnin' for you / Dr. Music.

Feb 84. (7"/12") *(A/TA 4117)* *<04298>* **SHOOTING SHARK. / DRAGON LADY** 83

May 84. (7") *<04436>* **TAKE ME AWAY. / LET GO** -

— **TONY ZVONCHEK** – keyboards (ex-ALDO NOVA) repl. LANIER

— **TOMMY PRICE** – drums repl. DOWNEY.

Oct 85. (7") *<05845>* **DANCIN' IN THE RUINS. / SHADOW WARRIOR** -

Dec 85. (lp/c/cd) *(CBS/40/CD 26775)* *<39979>* **CLUB NINJA** 63
– White flags / Dancin' in the ruins / Rock not war / Perfect water / Spy in the house of the night / Beat 'em up / When the war comes / Shadow warrior / Madness to the method. *(cd-iss. Jun97 on 'Koch Int.'; 37943-2)*

Dec 85. (7") *(A 6779)* **WHITE FLAGS. / ROCK NOT WAR** -
(12"+=) *(TA 6779)* – Shooting shark.

Feb 86. (7") *<06199>* **PERFECT WATER. / SPY IN THE HOUSE OF NIGHT** -

— added **ALBERT BOUCHARD** – guitar, percussion, vocals
ALLEN LANIER – keyboards, returned to repl. TONY

Sep 88. (lp/c/cd) *(460036-1/-4/-2)* *<40618>* **IMAGINOS** Aug88
– I am the one you warned me of / Les invisibles / In the presence of another world / Del Rio's song / The siege and investiture of Baron Von Frankenstein's castle at Weisseria / Astronomy (new version) / Magna of illusion. *(pic-lp Mar89; 460036-0)*

Oct 88. (7") *(652 985)* **ASTRONOMY. / MAGNA OF ILLUSION** -
(12"+=) *(652 985-8)* – ('A'-wild mix).
(12"+=/cd-s+=) *(652 985-6/-2)* – (Don't fear) The reaper.

— (early '89 tour) **JON ROGERS** – bass repl. JOE BOUCHARD / **CHUCK BURGI** – drums repl. RON RIDDLE who repl. RICK DOWNEY

Fragile Herald

Jun 94. (cd/c) *(CD/C FRL 003)* *<HER 008>* **CULT CLASSICS** (re-recorded best of)
– (Don't fear) The reaper / E.T.I. (Extra Terrestrial Intelligence) / Me 262 / This ain't the summer of love / Burnin' for you / O.D.'d on life itself / Flaming telepaths / Godzilla / Astronomy / Cities on fire with rock and roll / Harvester of eyes / Buck's boogie / (Don't fear) The reaper / Godzilla.

Jul 94. (c-s/7") *(TC+/FRS 1001)* **(DON'T FEAR) THE REAPER. / BURNIN' FOR YOU** -
(cd-s+=) *(CDFRS 1001)* – ('A'extended).
above were re-recordings of best known material.

— re-formed in '96 with **BLOOM, DHARMA + LANIER**

C.M.C. C.M.C.

Mar 98. (cd) *<(6076 86241-2)>* **HEAVEN FORBID**
– See you in black / Harvest moon / Power underneath despair / X-ray eyes / Hammer back / Damaged / Cold gay light of dawn / Real world / Live for me / Still burnin' / In thee.

Angel Air Angel Air

Nov 99. (cd) *<(SJPCD 046)>* **BAD CHANNELS (original soundtrack)**
– Demon kiss / Horsemen arrive / Joker: That's how it is – Jane Jane (the hurricane) / Fair game: Somewhere in the night – Blind faith / Synkotik sinfoney: Manic depresso – Mr. Cool / DMT: Myth of freedom – Touching myself again / Little old lady polka / Ukelaliens / Bad channels overture / Power station / Shadow / VU / Cosmos rules but lump controls / Battering ram / This dude is fucked / Pick up her feed / Spray that scumbag / Out of station / Tree full of owls / Cookie in bottle / Corky gets it / Eulogy for Corky / Spore bomb / Remodelling / Ginger snaps / The moon gets it. *(re-iss. Jun01; same)*

Sanctuary C.M.C.

Jun 01. (cd) *(SANCD 089)* *<86304>* **CURSE OF THE HIDDEN MIRROR**
– Dance on stilts / Showtime / Old gods return / Pocket / One step ahead of the Devil / I just like to be bad / Here comes that feeling / Out of the darkness / Stone of love / Eye of the hurricane / Good to feel hungry.

– compilations, others, etc. –

below on 'CBS'/ 'Columbia' unless otherwise mentioned

1984. (7") *(A 4584)* **(DON'T FEAR) THE REAPER. / I LOVE THE NIGHT** -

Apr 90. (cd/c/lp) *(465929-2/-4/-1)* *<44300>* **CAREER OF EVIL: THE METAL YEARS**
– Cities on flame / The red and the black / Hot rails to Hell / Dominance and submission / Seven screaming Diz-busters / M.E. 262 / E.T.I. (Extra Terrestrial Intelligence) / Beat 'em up / Black blade / The harvester of eyes / Flaming telepaths / Godzilla / (Don't fear) The reaper.

Jan 92. (cd/c) *Castle; (CLA CD/MC 269) / Gopaco; <149>* **LIVE 1976 (live)** 1994

Jan 96. (d-cd) *Columbia; (480949-2)* *<64163>* **WORKSHOP OF THE TELESCOPES** Sep95
– Cities in flames with rock'n'roll / Transmaniacon MC / Before the kiss / Redcap / Stairway to the stairs / Buck's boogie / Workshop of the telescopes / Red and the black / 7 screaming dizbusters / Career of evil / Flaming telepaths / Astronomy / Subhuman / Harvester of eyes / M.E. 262 / Born to be wild / (Don't fear) The reaper / This ain't the summer of love / E.T.I. (Extra Terrestial Intelligence) / Godzilla / Goin' through the motions / Golden age of leather / Kick out the jams / We gotta get out of this place / In thee / Marshall plane / Veteran of the psychic wars / Burnin' for you / Domninance and submission / Take me away / Shooting shark / Dancin' in the ruins / Perfect water.

Jun 99. (cd) *Mobile Fidelity; (UDCD 738)* **BLUE OYSTER CULT / TYRANNY AND MUTATION** -

Feb 00. (cd) *Epic; (495243-2) / Columbia; <65918>* **THE BEST OF BLUE OYSTER CULT (DON'T FEAR THE REAPER)**

Jul 00. (cd) *Epic; (498791-2) / Sony; <65638>* **SUPER HITS** Jul98

Aug 00. (d-cd) *S.P.V.; (SPV 31021910)* **HEAVEN FORBID / CULT CLASSICS** -

Jan 01. (d-cd) *Axe Killer; (AXE 306332CD)* **TYRANNY AND MUTATION / SECRET TREATIES** -

BLUETIP

Formed: Washington DC, USA ... mid-90's out of SWIZ by JASON FARRELL and DAVE STERN. Recruiting JAKE KLUMP and ZAC ELLER, the band began gigging around the local hardcore scene while FARRELL's graphic art skills eventually brought BLUETIP to the attention of FUGAZI hardcore guru IAN MacKAYE. Signing them to his legendary 'Dischord' label and guiding them through the stresses of writing and recording, MacKAYE also handled production duties on debut album, 'DISCHORD No.101' (1996). While this was firmly in the bile-filled, noisy DC post-punk tradition, 'JOIN US' (1998) took its cue from a wider sonic palate, its rhythmic attack driven by new sticksman DAVE BRYSON. The shock departure of founding member STERN spurred on FARRELL to hone his songwriting skills for the 'HOT(-)FAST(+)UNION' EP and 'POLYMER' (2000) album, the JAMES DEAN-alike taking a leaner, more direct approach.

Album rating: DISCHORD No.101 (*6) / JOIN US (*5) / POLYMER (*7)

JASON FARRELL – vocals, guitar / **DAVE STERN** – guitar / **JAKE KUMP** – bass / **ZAC ELLER** – drums

Dischord Dischord

Jun 96. (cd/lp) *<(DIS 101 CD/V)>* **DISCHORD No.101**
– Nickelback / Past tense / Precious / If I ever sleep again / 3x2 slow / Sacred heart of the highway / Texas to west / Sweet superior / L.M.N.O.P. / Mapped out / Gainer / Tangle.

— **DAVE BRYSON** – drums; repl. ZAC + other temps

Nov 98. (cd/lp) *<(DIS 116 CD/V)>* **JOIN US**
– Yellow light / Cheap rip / Join us / Castanet / Carbon copy / Salinas / F- / I even drive like a jerk / Bad flat / Jersey blessed / Cold start / Slovakian.

Jul 00. (cd-ep) *<(SLOWDIME 29)>* **HOT(-)FAST(+)UNION**
– Hot fast union / Split up kid / Persistent / Compliment the negative / Anti-Pope. (above issued on 'Slowdime')

— now without STERN

Oct 00. (cd/lp) *<(DIS 121 CD/V)>* **POLYMER** Sep00
– Polymer / New young residents / New shoe premonition / Stereo tinnitus / Getting in / Magnetified / Astigmatic / Don't punch your friend (for being slow) / Anti-bloom / Broke the lease / (untitled).

BODY COUNT (see under ⇒ ICE-T)

Tommy BOLIN

Born: 1 Aug'51, Sioux City, Iowa, USA. Of Native American descent, BOLIN's first forays into the music world came with amateur outfits, DENNY & THE TRIUMPHS and AMERICAN STANDARD, leading to session work for LONNIE MACK. A recording contract with 'Probe' finally arrived in 1968 after BOLIN formed hard-rock act, ZEPHYR. The following year, this band (who included the GIVENS siblings, CANDY and DAVID) had a US Top 50 album, although a second for 'Warners', failed to make the grade. Taking a jazz-fusion departure, BOLIN formed ENERGY, although this too was short-lived, after he was asked to join The JAMES GANG. He stayed for two albums, 'BANG' (1973) and 'MIAMI' (1974), before taking up his most high profile task to date, replacing the esteemed RITCHIE BLACKMORE in DEEP PURPLE. He featured on one studio album, 'COME TASTE THE BAND' (last '75), which coincidentally shared the new release racks with his first solo outing, 'TEASER', a well-received album which nevertheless only managed to scrape into the US Top 100. By this point BOLIN had already bailed out of the sinking DEEP PURPLE ship, beginning work on his second solo set, 'PRIVATE EYES'. Despite BOLIN's worsening drug habit and the attendant studio difficulties, the album finally surfaced in November '76. Ironically, however, BOLIN succumbed to an overdose just weeks after its release, dying on the 4th December, aged only 25.

Album rating: Zephyr: ZEPHYR (*6) / GOING BACK TO COLORADO (*6) / Tommy Bolin: TEASER (*8) / PRIVATE EYES (*7) / THE ULTIMATE TOMMY BOLIN compilation (*7)

ZEPHYR

TOMMY BOLIN – guitar, vocals / **CANDY GIVENS** – vocals / **DAVID GIVENS** – bass, vocals / **JOHN FARRIS** – keyboards, saxophone, vocals / **ROBBIE CHAMBERLAIN** – drums

Probe Probe

1970. (lp) *(SPB 1006)* *<CP 4510>* **ZEPHYR** 48 Dec69
– Sail on / Sun's a-risin' / Raindrops / Boom-da-boom / Somebody listen / Cross the river / St. James Infirmary / Huna buna / Hard chargin' woman. *(cd-iss. Oct89 on 'Beat Goes On'; BGOCD 41) (cd re-iss. Nov99 on 'One Way-MCA'; MCAD 22032)*

1970. (7") *<475>* **SAIL ON. / CROSS THE RIVER** -

— **BOBBY BERGE** – drums repl. CHAMBERLAIN

not iss. Warners

1971. (lp) *<WS 1897>* **GOING BACK TO COLORADO** -
– Going back to Colorado / Miss Libertine / Fades softly / Radio song / See my people come together / Showbizzy / Keep me / Take my love / It'll be right here / At this very moment.

— BOLIN departed from ZEPHYR, leaving GIVENS + GIVENS to recruit new members (JOCK BARTLEY – guitar / P.M. WOOTEN – drums / DAN SMITH – keyboards) and release one more US 'Warners' lp in 1972 'SUNSET RIDE'; *<WS 2603>*. The GIVENS' re-formed ZEPHYR early in 1977. BOLIN guested for BILLY COBHAM on 73's 'SPECTRUM' album. He then replaced DOMENIC TROIANO in The JAMES GANG for two 1974 albums 'BANG' and 'MIAMI'. The following year, he joined British heavyweights DEEP PURPLE (replacing RITCHIE BLACKMORE) and stayed for two albums; 'COME TASTE THE

BAND' and 'MADE IN EUROPE'. Also recorded solo work while a PURPLE member.

TOMMY BOLIN

— + piano with **JAN HAMMER + DAVID FOSTER** – keyboards / **PRAIRIE PRINCE + JEFF PORCARO + BOBBY BERGE** – drums / **STANLEY SHELDON + PAUL STALLWORTH** – bass / etc.

Atlantic Nemperor

Dec 75. (lp) *(50208) <436>* **TEASER** [ ] [96]
– The grind / Homeward strut / Dreamer / Savannah woman / Teaser / People, people / Marching powder / Wild dogs / Lotus. *(cd-iss. Aug93 on 'Epic'; 468016-2)*

Mar 76. (7") *(K 10730) <004>* **THE GRIND. / HOMEWARD STRUT** [ ] [ ]

May 76. (7") *<005>* **SAVANNAH WOMAN. / MARCHING POWER** [-] [ ]

— now w/ **MARK STEIN** – keyboards (ex-VANILLA FUDGE) / **REGGIE McBRIDE** – bass (ex-RARE EARTH) / **NARADA MICHAEL WALDEN** – drums (ex-MAHAVISHNU ORCHESTRA) / **NORMA JEAN BELL** – saxophone, vocals, percussion (ex-FRANK ZAPPA, ex-STEVIE WONDER)

C.B.S. Columbia

Nov 76. (lp) *(81612) <34329>* **PRIVATE EYES** [ ] [98] Sep76
– Bustin' out for Rosey / Sweet burgundy / Post toastee / Shake the Devil / Gypsy soul / Someday will bring our love home / Hello, again / You told me that you loved me. *(re-iss. Aug91 on 'Essential' cd/c; ESS CD/MC 950)*

— TOMMY died of a heart attack on 4th Dec'76 due to a drug overdose.

– compilations, others, etc. –

Mar 90. (cd/c/lp) *Geffen; <(924248-2/-4/-1)>* **THE ULTIMATE TOMMY BOLIN** (all his work) [ ] [ ] Dec89
– Sail on (ZEPHYR) / Cross the river (ZEPHYR) / See my people come together (ZEPHYR) / Showbizzy (ZEPHYR) / Alexis (JAMES GANG) / Standing in the rain (JAMES GANG) / Spanish lover (JAMES GANG) / Do it (JAMES GANG) / Quadrant 4 (BILLY COBHAM) / Train (ENERGY)/ Time to move on (ENERGY) / Golden rainbows (ENERGY) / Nitroglycerin / Gettin' tighter (DEEP PURPLE) / Owed to 'G' (DEEP PURPLE) / You keep on moving (DEEP PURPLE) / Wild dogs / Dreamer / People, people / Teaser / Sweet burgundy / Shake the Devil / Brother, brother.

Jan 96. (cd) *R.P.M.; (RPM 158)* **FROM THE ARCHIVES** [ ] [-]
(re-iss. Mar99 on 'Purple'; PUR 315)

Apr 97. (cd) *Tommy Bolin Archives; <(TBACD 1)>* **BOLIN ARCHIVES VOL.1: EBBETS FIELD '74 (live)** [ ] [ ]

Apr 97. (cd) *Tommy Bolin Archives; <(TBACD 2)>* **BOLIN ARCHIVES VOL.2: EBBETS FIELD '76 (live)** [ ] [ ]

Apr 97. (cd) *Tommy Bolin Archives; <(TBACD 3)>* **BOLIN ARCHIVES VOL.3: THE BOTTOM SHELF – VOLUME ONE** [ ] [ ]

Apr 97. (cd) *Tommy Bolin Archives; <(TBACD 4)>* **BOLIN ARCHIVES VOL.4: NORTHERN LIGHTS** [ ] [ ]

Sep 97. (cd; by ZEPHYR) *Tommy Bolin Archives; <(TBACD 6)>* **LIVE** [ ] [ ] May97

Aug 98. (cd) *Zebra; <(6330 144301-2)>* **FROM THE ARCHIVES VOL.2** [ ] [ ]

Jan 00. (cd) *Cleopatra; <(CLP 8072)>* **SNAPSHOT** [ ] [ ]
– Savannah woman / Standing in the rain / Cat's cradle / Oh Carol ? Gotta dance / Spanish lover / Cucumber jam / Devil is singing our song / Homeward strut / Summer breezes. *<(re-iss. May00 on 'Angel Air'; SJPCD 066)>*

Aug 00. (cd) *Tommy Bolin Archives; <TBACD 13>* **ENERGY** [-] [ ]

BOLLOCK BROTHERS

Formed: London, England . . . 1980 as a punk satirist outfit headed by chief mouthpiece, JOCK McDONALD. Gathering together fellow jesters, RICHARD COLLINS, KEITH LEWIS, KEITH BRADSHAW, DAVID REAGAN and PAUL SHIRLEY, McDONALD incredibly netted a deal with re-issue specialist, 'Charly', releasing a slew of 12"ers that were generally regarded as being er, bollocks. Their debut long-player, 'THE LAST SUPPER' (1983), contained many of the aforementioned 45's, could possibly be termed piss-tiche, a cross between piss-taking and pastiche. An uninspired run through of the SEX PISTOLS' album 'NEVER MIND THE BOLLOCKS' in its entirety brought cheap publicity for the inclusion of guest vocals by MICHAEL FAGIN, the man infamous for getting past the Buckingham Palace security and into the Queen's bedroom. Excepting the first of many official live bootleg albums, The BOLLOCKS BROTHERS finally released their follow-up set in '85, 'THE FOUR HORSEMEN OF THE APOCALYPSE', McDONALD this time around opting for covers of Alex Harvey's 'FAITH HEALER' and Aphrodite Child's 'SEVENTH SEAL'. Following a one-off cover of Brigette Bardot's 'HARLEY DAVIDSON' on Belgium's top indie 'Play It Again Sam', McDONALD recruited an entire new force to record his next album project, 'THE PROPHECIES OF NOSTRADAMUS' (1988). The SEX PISTOLS connection continued as the singer(!?) managed to rope in ex-PISTOLS (McDONALD was also behind a questionable outfit of the same name!), COOK and JONES alongside guests BILLY IDOL, GEORDIE and YOUTH, on the 'MYTHOLOGY' set in '89. Released under the moniker THE FAMOUS B. BROTHERS, McDONALD's final project was another biblical examination going under the title of 'THE DEAD SEA SCROLLS' (1991).

Album rating: THE LAST SUPPER (*3) / NEVER MIND THE BOLLOCKS '83 (*3) / LIVE PERFORMANCES – THE OFFICIAL BOOTLEG (*2) / 77, 78, 79 compilation (*3) / THE FOUR HORSEMEN OF THE APOCALYPSE (*1) / ROCK'N'ROLL SUICIDE (*2) / LIVE – IN PUBLIC IN PRIVATE (*1) / THE PROPHECIES OF NOSTRADAMUS (*3) / MYTHOLOGY (*3) / THE DEAD SEA SCROLLS (*3) / THE BEST OF THE BOLLOCKS compilation (*3)

JOCK McDONALD – vocals / **RICHARD COLLINS** – guitar, french horn / **KEITH LEWIS** – guitar, violin / **KEITH BRADSHAW** – bass / **DAVID REAGAN** – drums, percussion / **PAUL SHIRLEY** – synthesizer

Charly not iss.

Jan 81. (12") *(BOLL 1)* **THE BUNKER. / BOOTLEG MAN** [ ] [-]
(re-iss. Apr83 as 7"; BOLL 4)

Mar 81. (12") *(BOLL 2)* **THE ACT BECAME REAL. / THE ACTORS (DUB-LE)** [ ] [-]

Oct 82. (12") *(BOLL 3)* **SLOW REMOVAL OF VINCENT VAN GOGH'S LEFT EAR. / ROCK & ROLL PART 2 (1 & 2)** [ ] [-]

Jan 83. (12") *(BOLL 5)* **HORROR MOVIES. / ENCHANTMENT** [ ] [-]

Feb 83. (lp) *(BOLL 100)* **THE LAST SUPPER** [ ] [-]
– Horror movies / Enchantment / Reincarnation of / Save our souls / Face in the mirror / The last supper / The act became real / The gift 2. *(cd-iss. Feb89; CDCHARLY 175) (cd re-iss. Feb97; CDCRH 103)*

Jul 83. (lp) *(BOLL 101)* **NEVER MIND THE BOLLOCKS '83** [ ] [-]
– Holidays in the sun / Problems / No feelings / God save the Queen / Pretty vacant / Submission / New York / Seventeen / Anarchy in the UK / Liar / Bodies / E.M.I. *(cd-iss. Dec89; CDCHARLY 178) (cd re-iss. Feb97; CDCRH 104)*

Dec 83. (d-lp) *(BOLL 102)* **LIVE PERFORMANCES – THE OFFICIAL BOOTLEG (live)** [ ] [-]
– Slow removal of Vincent Van Gogh's left ear / Loose / Horror movies / The bunker / The last supper / Reincarnation of / New York / Problems / Holidays in the sun / Vincent / Pretty vacant / God save the Queen. *(cd-iss. Feb89; CDCHARLY 174) (cd re-iss. Feb97; CDCRH 102)*

Aug 84. (12") *(DID 127700)* **PRINCE AND THE SHOWGIRL. / SHOWGIRLS** [ ] [-]
(above issued on Belgium label, 'Disc')

Jul 85. (lp) *(BOLL 103)* **THE FOUR HORSEMEN OF THE APOCALYPSE** [ ] [-]
– Legend of the snake / Mistress of the macabre / Woke up this morning found myself dead / Faith healer / King rat / The four horsemen of the apocalypse / Loud, loud, loud / The seventh seal / Return to the Garden of Eden. *(cd-iss. Mar87; CDCHARLY 72) (cd re-iss. Feb97; CDCRH 109)*

Apr 86. (12") *(BOLL 6)* **DRAC'S BACK. / HORROR MOVIES** [ ] [-]

Oct 86. (12") *(BOLL 7)* **FAITH HEALER. / RETURN TO THE GARDEN OF EDEN** [ ] [-]

Jan 87. (lp) *(BOLL 104)* **LIVE – IN PUBLIC IN PRIVATE (live)** [ ] [-]
– Woke up this morning / Drac's back / The four horsemen of the apocalypse / Midnight Moses / Rock and roll / Count Dracula where's yar troosers / King rat / Faith healer. *(cd-iss. Nov89; CDCHARLY 179) (cd re-iss. Feb97; CDCRH 105)*

Play It Again Sam not iss.

Sep 86. (12") *(BIAS 036)* **HARLEY DAVIDSON. /** [ ] [-]

— **McDONALD** had now recruited **BORIS DOMMENGET** – guitar / **SERGE FEYS** – keyboards / **SEAN PETTIT** – bass / **PATRIK PATTYN** – drums / **GENEVIEVE FRENCH** – vocals

M.B.C. not iss.

Jan 88. (lp) *(85-3527)* **THE PROPHECIES OF NOSTRADAMUS** [ ] [-]
– Magic carpet ride / Calendar of visions / Brigitte Bardot / Ceremony / Heartbreaker / The prophecies of Nostradamus / God created woman / The beast is calling / Harley Davidson.

— **McDONALD** with guests **BILLY IDOL + PAUL YOUNGIE** – vocals / **STEVE JONES + GEORDIE** – guitar / **YOUTH + KEITH BRADSHAW** – bass / **PAUL COOK + PATRICK PATTYN** – drums

Blue Turtle – SPV not iss.

May 89. (lp)(cd) *(08-3543)(853544)* **MYTHOLOGY** [ ] [-]
– G.D.M. / Spooky / Beats of love / Dinner with Dracula / My fair daughter / Monster mash / Wiped out / For your blood / Wilde mythology / Legend piano mix.

— **JOCK, RICHARD, BORIS + PATRIK**

S.P.V. not iss.

Oct 91. (cd/lp; FAMOUS B. BROTHERS) *(084/008 8846-2/-1)* **THE DEAD SEA SCROLLS** [ ] [-]
– Blood meets flood / Nimrod – Tower of Babel / Abraham – Sodom & Gomorrha / Into the night / Joseph (dream interceptor) / The virgin birth / Revelations of St. John / Babylon the great has fallen / The Dead Sea scrolls / In holiness, in honour.

— finally, McDONALD retired

– compilations, etc. –

Apr 85. (lp) *Mausoleum; (KOMA 788011)* ***77, 78, 79*** [ ] [-]

Feb 86. (lp) *Konnexion; (JUNK 788010)* **ROCK'N'ROLL SUICIDE** [ ] [-]

Jul 93. (cd) *Charly; (CDCRM 1011)* **THE BEST OF THE BOLLOCKS** [ ] [-]

Jan 00. (cd) *Metrodome; (METRO 287)* **WHAT A LOAD OF BOLLOCKS** [ ] [-]

BOLT THROWER

Formed: Birmingham, England . . . 1987 by AL WEST, GAVIN WARD, BARRY THOMPSON, JO BENCH and ANDY WHALE (taking the moniker from a fantasy game book). Gaining a recording contract with 'Vinyl Solution' after an early '88 John Peel Radio One session, they released a demo for the label, 'IN BATTLE THERE IS NO LAW'. The Peel Sessions were liberated that year, a subsequent contract with 'Earache' resulting in the 'REALM OF CHAOS' set in '89. Drawing comparisons with grindcore peers, NAPALM DEATH and CARCASS, BOLT THROWER took pride of place on the legendary "Grindcrusher" tour, pitting their indecipherable noise against the likes of American death-metallers, MORBID ANGEL. The second outing for new "vocalist" KARL WILLETS, 'WAR MASTER' deviated little from the band's trademark, skullcrushing sound, although the Colin Richardson-produced 'THE IVth CRUSADE' exhibited some melodic cracks in their reinforced metal armour. In 1994, they released their fifth set, ' . . . FOR VICTORY', this marking the exit of WILLETS and WHALE, who were replaced by MARTIN VAN DRUNEN and MARTIN KEARNS respectively. However, their three-year absence from the metal scene was put aside when they signed a new contract with US-based 'Metal Blade' for their 'MERCENARY' set in '98.

Album rating: IN BATTLE THERE IS NO LAW (*5) / REALM OF CHAOS (*6) / WAR MASTER (*7) / THE IVth CRUSADE (*7) / . . . FOR VICTORY (*5) / MERCENARY (*6) / WHO DARES WINS collection (*5)

AL WEST – vocals / **GAVIN WARD** – guitar / **BARRY THOMPSON** – guitar / **JO BENCH** – bass / **ANDY WHALE** – drums

Vinyl Solution | Future Shock

Aug 88. (lp/cd) *(SOL 11/+CD) <8001>* **IN BATTLE THERE IS NO LAW**
– In battle there is no law / Challenge for power / Forgotten existence / Denial of destiny / Blind to defeat / Concession of pain / Attack in the aftermath / Psychological warfare / Nuclear annihilation. *(re-iss. Aug91 & Nov93; same)*

Strange Fruit | not iss.

Oct 88. (12"ep) *(SFPS 056)* **THE PEEL SESSIONS** (31.1.88) | -
– Forgotten existence / Attack in the aftermath / Psychological warfare / In battle there is no law.

— **KARL WILLETS** – vocals; repl. WEST

Earache | Combat

Sep 89. (pic-lp/cd) *(MOSH 013/+CD) <2034>* **REALM OF CHAOS**
– Eternal war / Through the eye of terror / Dark millenium / All that remains / Lost souls domaine / Plague bearer / World eater / Drowned in torment / Realm of chaos / Prophet * / Outro. *(cd+= *) (re-iss. cd Nov94 & Sep97; same)*

Jan 91. (12"ep/cd-ep) *(MOSH 028 T/CD)* **CENOPATH / DESTRUCTIVE INFINITY. / PROPHET OF HATRED / REALM OF CHAOS (live)** | -

Feb 91. (lp/cd) *(MOSH 029/+CD) <2028>* **WAR MASTER**
– Unleashed (upon mankind) (intro) / What dwells within / The shreds of sanity / Profane creation / Destructive infinity * / Final revelation / Cenopath / War master / Rebirth of humanity / Afterlife. *(cd+= *) (re-iss. cd Nov94 & Sep97; same)*

Nov 92. (lp/cd) *(MOSH 070/+CD) <1157>* **THE IVth CRUSADE** | Feb93
– The IV crusade / Icon / Embers / Where next to conquer / As the world burns / This time its war / Ritual / Spearhead / Celestial sanctuary / Dying creed / Through the ages (outro) / Crown of life / Lament. *(re-iss. cd Nov94 & Sep97; same)*

Jan 93. (12"ep/cd-ep) *(MOSH 073 T/CD)* **SPEARHEAD (extended) / CROWN OF LIFE. / DYING CREED / LAMENT** | -

Earache | Earache

Dec 94. (cd/c) *(<MOSH 120 CD/MC>)* **. . . FOR VICTORY** | Jan95
– War / Remembrance / When glory beckins / . . . For victory / Graven image / Lest we forget / Silent demise / Forever fallen / Tank (Mk.1) / Armageddon bound. *(cd re-iss. Sep97; same)*

— **MARTIN VAN DRUNEN** – vocals (ex-PESTILENCE, ex-ASPHYX) repl. WILLETS / **MARTIN KEARNS** – drums; repl. WHALE

Metal Blade | Metal Blade

Sep 98. (cd) *(<3984 14147-2>)* **MERCENARY** | Nov98
– Zeroed / Laid to waste / Return from chaos / Mercenary / To the last . . . / Powder burns / Behind enemy lines / No guts, no glory / Sixth chapter.

– compilations, etc. –

Aug 91. (cd/lp) *Strange Fruit; (SFR CD/LP 116) / Dutch East India; <8118>* **THE PEEL SESSIONS**

Sep 98. (cd) *Earache; (<MOSH 208CD>)* **WHO DARES WINS** (the EP's)
– Cenotaph / Destructive infinity / Prophet of hatred / Realm of chaos / Spearhead / Crown of life / Dying creed / Lament / World eater '94 / Overlord.

BOMB PARTY

Formed: Leicester, England . . . early 80's initially as FARMLIFE, by SARAH CORINA, STEVE GERRARD, ANDY 'JESUS' MOSQUERA and MARK THOMPSON. Under this moniker they issued only one single, 'SUSIE'S PARTY', early in '82, although it might have been two but for the abandonment of a follow-up, 'BIG COUNTRY, a year later. BOMB PARTY were a different kind of proposition, taking an anti-American stance while treating us to a molotov cocktail of hardcore grebo gothabilly lying somewhere between The CRAMPS or BAUHAUS. Signing to the up and coming indie-punk label, 'Abstract' early in '85, the band blasted out with the 'RAY GUN' EP. Over the course of the next year, the BOMB PARTY unleashed two more, 'THE NEW MESSIAH' and 'LIFE'S A BITCH', before getting around to delivering their debut album, 'DRUGS' (1986). A slight shake up in the band's personnel resulted in the addition of LESZEK RATAJ and he was in place for their first album for 'Worker's Playtime', 'LIBERACE RISING' (1987). Around the same time, SARAH moonlighted with The JANITORS offshoot outfit, BIG ZAP. Augmented by the girls from VOICE OF THE BEEHIVE, The BOMB PARTY released what was to be their most commercial record to date, a cover of The Archies' 'SUGAR SUGAR'. Issued on Germany's 'Normal' label at the back end of '88, it was trailed by their third album, 'FISH' (1989); 'NATIVITY #3' followed a few years later.

Album rating: DRUGS (*5) / THE LAST SUPPER compilation (*5) / LIBERACE RISING (*5) / FISH (*4) / NATIVITY #3 (*4)

JESUS MOSQUERA (b. ANDY) – vocals / **STEVE GERRARD** – guitar / **SARAH CORINA** – bass / **MARK THOMPSON** – drums

Dining Out | not iss.

Feb 82. (7"; as FARMLIFE) *(TUX 19)* **SUSIE'S PARTY. / SIMPLE MEN** | -

Whaam! | not iss.

Sep 83. (7"; as FARMLIFE) *(WHAAM 13)* **BIG COUNTRY. / (part 2)** - | - w/drawn

Abstract | not iss.

May 85. (12"ep) *(12ABS 032)* **RAY GUN EP** | -
– Harry the babysitter / Ray gun / Get lost my love / Knocking.

Aug 85. (12"ep) *(12ABS 035)* **THE NEW MESSIAH EP** | -

Dec 85. (7"ep) *(ABS 038)* **LIFE'S A BITCH. / GET SO DOWN / THE NEW MESSIAH** | -

Jun 86. (lp) **DRUGS** | -
– Kill your wife / Don't die Keith / Johnny took her breath away / Jesus was a pinko / Gas / Johnny Nero / Susie's party / Our love is pushing up daisies / Slide / Zombie head / Refugee.

May 87. (lp) *(ABT 016)* **THE LAST SUPPER** (compilation) | -

— added **LESZEK RATAJ** – guitar

Workers Playtime | not iss.

Oct 87. (m-lp) *(PLAYLP 2)* **LIBERACE RISING** | -
– Crawl / Don't talk just kiss / Come on and get closer / Evil eye / El savor del amor / Metropolis.

Dec 87. (7") *(WPCS 1)* **PRETTY FACE. / THESE ARE YOUR RIGHTS / I WANNA BE ABUSED** | -

Normal | not iss.

Oct 88. (7") *(NORMAL 93)* **SUGAR SUGAR. / DO THE RIGHT THING** | -
(12"+=/cd-s+=) *(NORMAL 93 T/CD)* – Some people settle for less.

May 89. (lp/cd) *(NORMAL 103/+CD)* **FISH** | -
– Praise the Lord / L.S.D. / Some bodies / Venus in dirt / The last waltz / Do the right thing / Theme from "God Bless America" / Mephistopleles (a million worth of pillion) / Shakespeare / Why don't we talk / Love at any price / The only rule (there is no rule) / Car crash (on the highway of love) / Nobody's.

Artlos | not iss.

Apr 91. (lp/cd) *(efa 01819/+CD)* **NATIVITY #3** | -
– The beginning and the end / Ship of fools / Hey Joe / 31st of September / Lucy gas / Unavoidably detained / Dreaming / Gimme summat to love / Use it / In this land / Touched / Tonight / The beginning and the end.

— split soon after above

Beki BONDAGE (see under ⇒ LIGOTAGE)

BONE ORCHARD

Formed: Brighton, England . . . 1983 by female singer CHRISSIE McGEE, MARK HORSE, TROY TYRO, MICK FINCH and PAUL HENDRICKSON. Led by CHRISSIE, a grunting banshee with gothic psychobilly overtones and described by music mags as "Nick Cave with tits~", these post-punk crypt creepers signed to the 'Jungle' label following their fifteen minutes worth of fame on a John Peel session. Hot on the heels of their debut EP 'STUFFED TO THE GILLS', the band made an appearance at that year's Futurama festival, drummer RIM TIM CHEESE subsequently replacing MICK. 'SWALLOWING HAVOC' was the title of their follow-up EP, while BEN TISDALL became their new drummer on 1984's mini-set, 'JACK'. Given short shrift by the music press, BONE ORCHARD faded from view following the release of a low-key album, 'PENTHOUSE POULTRY' (1985).

Album rating: JACK (*4) / PENTHOUSE POULTRY (*3)

CHRISSIE McGEE – vocals / **MARK HORSE** – guitar / **TROY TYRO** – guitar / **PAUL HENDRICKSON** – bass / **MICK FINCH** – drums

Jungle | not iss.

Nov 83. (12"ep) *(JUNG 8)* **STUFFED TO THE GILLS** | -
– Fats terminal / Shall I carry the budgie woman? / etc

— **RIM TIM CHEESE** – drums; repl. MICK

Apr 84. (12"ep) *(JUNG 15)* **SWALLOWING HAVOC** | -

— **BEN TISDALL** – drums; repl. TIM who joined SKELETAL FAMILY

Sep 84. (7") *(JUNG 18)* **JACK. /** | -

Nov 84. (lp) *(FREUD 06)* **JACK** | -
– Jack / Lynched / Marianne / Touched / Five days in the neighbourhood / Girl with a gun / Tongue / Scarlett ropes.

— had a new drummer; unknown to repl. BEN

Jun 85. (12"ep) *(JUNG 22T)* **PRINCESS EPILEPSY. / SAME OLD BALL AND CHAIN / YOU DON'T PRESS MY PANTS** | -

Vax | not iss.

Nov 85. (lp) *(VAXLP 1)* **PENTHOUSE POULTRY** | -

— split some time in the mid 80's

BONFIRE

Formed: Ingolstadt, Germany . . . 1985 out of CACUMEN, by CLAUS LESSMANN and HANS ZILLER, who enlisted HORST MAIER-THORN. Signing a deal with 'R.C.A.' almost immediately, BONFIRE sparked off their career with 'DON'T TOUCH THE LIGHT', before setting the German hard-rock scene alight with the 1988 follow-up, 'FIRE WORKS'. Their third album, 'POINT BLACK', fared even better, although their final effort, 'KNOCKOUT' (1991; with new guitarist MICHAEL VOSS) proved to be something of a damp squib. In 1998, BONFIRE were back on the musical pyre when delivering a comeback set, 'REBEL SOUL', which featured(?) a cover of Cat Stevens' 'THE FIRST CUT IS THE DEEPEST'; the album 'STRIKE X' followed in 2001.

Album rating: DON'T TOUCH THAT LIGHT (*4) / FIRE WORKS (*5) / POINT BLANK (*5) / KNOCKOUT (*5) / REBEL SOUL (*3) / FEELS LIKE COMING HOME (*3) / STRIKE X (*4)

CLAUS LESSMANN – vocals / **HANS ZILLER** – guitar, vocals / **HORST MAIER-THORN** – guitar, vocals / **JORG DEISINGER** – bass / **DOMINIC HULSHORST** – drums

R.C.A. R.C.A.

1986. (lp) *(ZL 71046) <6223>* **DON'T TOUCH THE LIGHT** [-] [ ]
– Intro / Starin' eyes / Hot to rock / You make me feel / Longing for you / Don't touch the light / SDI / No more / L.A.

— DOMINIC replaced by guests **KEN MARY** – drums, percussion (ex-HOUSE OF LORDS) / **MARTIN ERNST** – keyboards

Feb 88. (lp/c/cd) *(ZL/ZK/ZD 71518) <6942>* **FIRE WORKS** [ ] [ ]
– Ready 4 reaction / Never mind / Sleeping all alone / Champion / Don't get me wrong / Sweet obsession / Rock me now / American nights / Fantasy / Give it a try. *(cd+=)* – Cold days.

Jun 88. (7") *(ZB 41569)* **SWEET OBSESSION. / DON'T GET ME WRONG** [ ] [-]
(12"+=) *(ZT 41570)* – Angel in white.

— **ANGEL SCHAEFFER** – guitar, vocals (ex-PRETTY MAIDS, ex-SINNER); repl. THORN

— **EDGAR PATRIK** – drums, percussion, vocals (ex-SINNER, ex-TYRAN PACE, ex-PAUL SAMSON); repl. KEN MARY

Sep 89. (7") *(ZB 43175)* **HARD ON ME. / FREEDOM IS MY BELIEF** [ ] [-]
(12"+=) *(ZT 43176)* – You're back.
(cd-s++=) *(ZD 43194)* – Ready 4 reaction.

Oct 89. (lp/c/cd) *(ZL/ZK/ZD 74249) <75118>* **POINT BLANK** [ ] [ ]
– Bang down the door / Waste no time / Hard on me / Why is it never enough / Tony's roulette / Minestrone / You're back / Look of love / Freedom is my belief / Gimme some / Never surrender / (20th century) Youth patrol / Jungle call / Know right now / Who's foolin' who.

Apr 90. (7") *(ZB 43505)* **WHO'S FOOLIN' WHO. / WHO'S FOOLIN' WHO (1989 live)** [ ] [-]
(12"+=/cd-s+=) *(ZT/ZD 43506)* – ('A'version).

— **MICHAEL VOSS** – guitar; repl. ZILLER, although he soon departed

Oct 91. (cd/c/lp) *(PD/PK/PL 75093) <15886>* **KNOCK OUT** [ ] [ ]
– Streets of freedom / The stroke / Dirty love / Rivers of glory / Home babe / Shake down / Hold you / Down and out / Take my heart and run / All we got / Fight for love.

— folded after above; **LESSMAN + ZILLER** re-formed BONFIRE and recruited **ARMIN WOODS + JUHA VARPIO** – keyboards + **JURGEN WIEHLER** – drums, percussion

unknown not iss.

1990's. (cd) **FUEL TO THE FLAMES** [-] [-] German
– Daytona nights / Don't go changing me / Proud of my country / Sweet home Alabama / Rebel pride / Goodnight Amanda / Ode an die Freude / Thumbs up for Europe / Bandit of love / Break down the walls / Heat in the glow / Life after love / If it wasn't for you / Can't stop rocking / Proud of my country (acoustic) / Goodnight Amanda (extended).

not iss. Saraya

Nov 98. (cd) *<43102-2>* **REBEL SOUL** [-] [ ]
– Wake up / Just to say we did / Before we say goodbye / Somebody's waiting / Lay your heart on the line / Hearts bleed their own blood / Rock me 'til I die / Desire / Good or bad / The first cut is the deepest / You'll be alright / Dixie / Wild Dixie / Back to you.

Apr 00. (cd) *(80001)* **FEELS LIKE COMIN' HOME** [-] [-] German

B.M.G. not iss.

May 01. (cd) *(74321 84038-2)* **STRIKE X** [ ] [-]
– Revelation day / Under blue skies / Strike back / Down to Atlanta / Southern winds / Good time rock'n'roll / Until the last goodbye / Diamonds in the rough / Damn you / Anytime you cry / Too much Hollywood / I need you.

– compilations, etc. –

Apr 95. (cd) *R.C.A.; <72892>* **LIVE . . . THE BEST** [-] [ ]

May 97. (cd) *R.C.A.; <79422>* **THE BEST OF THE BALLADS: HOT AND SLOW** [-] [ ]

Jun 00. (d-cd) *Collectables; <2751>* **DON'T TOUCH THE LIGHT / FIRE WORKS** [-] [ ]

BONHAM

Formed: Birmingham, England . . . mid'88 by JASON BONHAM, son of the late LED ZEPPELIN drummer, JOHN BONHAM. The young sticksman had cut his teeth with melodic hard-rockers, AIRRACE, who released a solitary album, 'SHAFT OF LIGHT' for 'Atco' in late '84. He then beat the skins for the similarly American-influenced VIRGINIA WOLF, issuing two albums for 'Atlantic' in 1986/87. The following year, JASON guested for his father's old LED ZEPPELIN colleague, JIMMY PAGE, on his 'Outrider' album. Soon after, the drummer formed the eponymous BONHAM, alongside DANIEL McMASTER, JOHN SMITHSON and IAN HATTON, releasing the well-received debut set, 'THE DISREGARD OF TIMEKEEPING' in 1989. Three years later, the second set, 'MADHATTER', surfaced to minimal fuss. With a new band intact, JASON BONHAM returned in 1997, although the abysmal 'IN THE NAME OF MY FATHER', a live 'ZEPPELIN tribute/covers album was hardly worth the wait.

Album rating: THE DISREGARD OF TIMEKEEPING (*6) / MADHATTER (*3) / The Jason Bonham Band: IN THE NAME OF THE FATHER (*3) / WHEN YOU SEE THE SUN (*3)

AIRRACE

KEITH MURRELL – vocals / **LAURIE MANSWORTH** – guitar / **TOBY SADLER** – keyboards / **JIM REID** – bass / **JASON BONHAM** (b.1967) – drums

Atco Atco

Dec 84. (7") *(B 9702) <99702>* **I DON'T CARE. / CAUGHT IN THE GAME** [ ] [ ]

Dec 84. (lp) *(790 219-1)* **SHAFT OF LIGHT** [ ] [ ]
– I don't care / Promise to call / First one over the line / Open your eyes / Not really me / Brief encounter / Caught in the game / Do you want my love again / Didn't want to lose ya / All I'm asking.

— disbanded in 1985, although MANSWORTH briefly reformed them with new members a year later

VIRGINIA WOLF

CHRIS OUSEY – vocals / **NICK BOLD** – guitar / **JO BURT** – bass / **JASON BONHAM** – drums

Atlantic Atlantic

Feb 86. (7") *(A 9459) <89459>* **WAITING FOR YOUR LOVE. / TAKE A CHANCE** [ ] [ ]

Apr 86. (lp/c) *(K 781756-1/-4)* **VIRGINIA WOLF** [ ] [ ]
– Are we playing with fire? / Make it tonight / Only love / It's in your eyes / Waiting for your love / Living on a knife edge / For all we know / Don't run away / Take a chance / Goodbye don't mean forever.

Aug 87. (7") *(A 9199) <89201>* **DON'T BREAK AWAY. / OPEN DOOR** [ ] [ ]
(12"+=) *(TA 9199)* – Tearing me down / Matter of time.

Sep 87. (lp/c) *(K 781756-1/-4)* **PUSH** [ ] [ ]
– Don't break away / One night / Standing on the edge of time / Open door / The man in the moon / Let it go / You don't know what you've got / Can you feel the fire / Tables have turned / The strangest thing.

BONHAM

JASON BONHAM (b.1966, Dudley, England) – drums / **DANIEL McMASTER** – vocals / **JOHN SMITHSON** – bass, keyboards / **IAN HATTON** – guitar (ex-HONEYDRIPPERS)

Epic W.T.G.

Oct 89. (lp/c/cd) *(465693-1/-4/-2) <45009>* **THE DISREGARD OF TIMEKEEPING** [39] [38]
– The disregard of timekeeping / Wait for you / Bringing me down / Guilty / Holding on forever / Dreams / Don't walk away / Playing to win / Cross me and see / Just another day / Room for us all.

May 90. (7") *(656024-7) <73034>* **WAIT FOR YOU. / THE DISREGARD OF TIMEKEEPING** [ ] [55] Nov89
(12"+=) *(656024-6)* – Cross me and see.
(7"ep++=/cd-ep++=) *(656024-0/-2)* – ('A'version).

Jun 90. (c-s) *<73248>* **GUILTY. / THE DISREGARD OF TIMEKEEPING** [-] [ ]

1992. (cd/c/lp) *<(469455-2/-4/-1)>* **MADHATTER** [ ] [ ]
– Bing / Madhatter / Change of a season / Hold on / The storm / Ride a dream / Good with the bad / Backdoor / Secrets / Los locos / Chimes.

— split after above

JASON BONHAM BAND

— with **CHARLES WEST** – vocals / **TONY CATANIA** – guitar / **JOHN SMITHSON** – bass, keyboards

Apr 97. (cd) *(<487443-2>)* **IN THE NAME OF MY FATHER – THE ZEPSET (live)** [ ] [ ]
– In the evening / Ramble on / The song remains the same / What is and what should never be / Ocean / Since I've been loving you / Communication breakdown / Ten years gone / Rain song / Whole lotta love.

Oct 97. (cd) *(<68182-2>)* **WHEN YOU SEE THE SUN** [ ] [ ]
– When you see the sun / Drown in me / Out on the prey / Searching / Ordinary black and white / Kiss the world goodbye / Your day will come / Rain / Can't go on / Turning back the time / The unknown / Shagkabob.

BON JOVI

Formed: Sayreville, New Jersey, USA . . . Spring '83, by JON BON JOVI and DAVID BRYAN, who duly recruited RICHIE SAMBORA, ALEC SUCH and TICO TORRES. Gaining a toehold on the music business ladder by helping out at his cousin's recording studio, JON found time to cut a rough demo of 'RUNAWAY', which subsequently gained radio play after being featured on a local various artists compilation. A line-up that would remain stable throughout BON JOVI's career was soon established and by the summer of 1983, the band had signed to a worldwide deal with 'Polygram'. The first two albums, 'BON JOVI' (1984) and '7800 DEGREES FAHRENHEIT' (1985) were generally derided by critics for their formulaic, glossy pop-metal content, yet the latter sold respectably, 'Polygram's marketing muscle and JON's pretty boy looks certainly not doing the band any harm. At this point, BON JOVI were just another name in an endless sea of wet-permed 'hair' bands on the hard-rock circuit and no one was quite expecting the splash that 'SLIPPERY WHEN WET' would make upon its release in 1986. Preceded by the squalling riff and anthemic chorus of 'YOU GIVE LOVE A BAD NAME', the album was heavy metal (in the broadest possible sense) for people who didn't like heavy metal (housewives, junior schoolgirls, construction workers, etc.). The next single taken from it was 'LIVIN' ON A PRAYER', a hard bitten tale of love on the breadline (rather ironic considering the moolah rolling into BON JOVI's coffers) that featured what must rank as one of the most bombastic choruses in the history of rock. Elsewhere on the record, the production loomed equally large and the songs were relentlessly hook-laden, with just enough edge to convince "real" rock fans that the band hadn't sold out. 'WANTED DEAD OR ALIVE' marked the beginning of JON's cowboy fantasies while 'I'D DIE FOR YOU' and 'NEVER SAY GOODBYE' were the obligatory 'sensitive' numbers. The album's success was partly down to the band hiring soft rock songsmith extrordinaire, DESMOND CHILD, whose unerringly catchy way with a tune saw the album going on to sell millions. BON JOVI were at the top of their career already, headlining the Monsters Of Rock shows in Britain and Europe. No doubt feeling more confident about his songwriting abilities, JON BON JOVI followed a more SPRINGSTEEN-esque direction on 'NEW JERSEY' (1988); more rock, less metal, while still retaining the spotless production and impeccable hooks. 'LIVING IN SIN', 'BLOOD ON BLOOD' (title taken from SPRINGSTEEN's 'HIGHAY PATROLMAN', perchance?) and 'WILD IS THE WIND' were all reassuringly strident, the album again selling in mindboggling quantities. In many ways, JON BON JOVI is BON JOVI, so when JON-boy released his 'BLAZE OF GLORY' solo effort (a result of his acting role in 'YOUNG GUNS II'), it was a case of more of the same. When the band re-emerged in 1992 with 'KEEP THE FAITH', there was no question of the album failing to scale the heights of its predecessors. The songs were intact although the likes of 'I'LL SLEEP WHEN I'M DEAD' were verging on self-parody. Needless to say, a compilation, 'CROSSROADS', sold phenomenally with the subsequent studio album, 'THESE DAYS' also hitting No.1 in Britain. While the band continue to win the hearts of coffee table browsers the world over, most metal fans probably lost interest years ago. Something of a celeb these days with his short(er) hair, pseudo-trendy image and acting career, JON recently completed his own short film and accompanying soundtrack (he'd previously made his acting debut proper, in the 1996 film, 'Moonlight And Valentino'). In fact the man could do no wrong, going on to have further major chart success with his 'DESTINATION ANYWHERE' (1997) solo set and its UK Top 5 single, 'MIDNIGHT IN CHELSEA'. He even turned up on Chris Evans' TFI Friday with a rough'n'ready cover of Simon & Garfunkel's 'MRS. ROBINSON'. BON JOVI the band, meanwhile, returned in spring '99 with a one-off single, 'REAL LIFE', followed a year later by the 'CRUSH' album. The only surprises on offer – apart from the fact that JON BON seems immune to the ageing process – were that if anything, the band's sound was even more mainstream than before while previously undetectable influences of British 60's/70's pop/glam were apparent. As if to prove they could still rock it like a proverbial mother, the veterans released the 'ONE WILD NIGHT' live set in 2001. • **Covered:** IT'S ONLY ROCK'N'ROLL (Rolling Stones) / WITH A LITTLE HELP FROM MY FRIENDS + HELTER SKELTER (Beatles) / I DON'T LIKE MONDAYS (Boomtown Rats) / ROCKIN' IN THE FREE WORLD (Neil Young) / HOUSE OF THE RISING SUN (trad). • **Miscellaneous:** April 1988 saw their manager DOC McGEE convicted for drug offences. He was sentenced to five years suspended, although he ended up doing community work. JON married his childhood sweetheart Dorothea Hurley on the 29th April '89. SAMBORA is married to actress Heather Locklear, while TORRES tied the knot with supermodel Eva Herzigova on the 7th of September '96.

Album rating: BON JOVI (*6) / 7800° FAHRENHEIT (*5) / SLIPPERY WHEN WET (*9) / NEW JERSEY (*7) / BLAZE OF GLORY solo (*5) / STRANGER IN THIS TOWN; Sambora solo (*6) / KEEP THE FAITH (*8) / CROSS ROAD – THE BEST OF BON JOVI compilation (*8) / (THESE DAYS) (*6) / DESTINATION ANYWHERE solo (*6) / CRUSH (*5) / ONE WILD NIGHT (*5)

JON BON JOVI (b. JOHN BONGIOVI, 2 Mar'62) – vocals, guitar / **RICHIE SAMBORA** (b.11 Jul'59, Woodbridge, N.J.) – lead guitar / **DAVID BRYAN** (b. DAVID BRYAN RASHBAUM, 7 Feb'62, New York City) – keyboards / **ALEC JOHN SUCH** (b.14 Nov'56, Yonkers, N.Y.) – bass (ex-PHANTON'S OPERA) / **TICO 'Tar Monster' TORRES** (b. HECTOR TORRES, 7 Oct'53, New York City) – drums (ex-FRANKIE & THE KNOCKOUTS)

Vertigo / Mercury

Feb 84. (7") *<818309>* **RUNAWAY. / LOVE LIES** [-] [39]

Apr 84. (lp/c) *(VERL/+C 14) <814982>* **BON JOVI** [71] [43] Feb84
– Runaway / Roulette / She don't know me / Shot through the heart / Love lies / Breakout / Burning for love / Come back / Get ready. *(cd-iss. Jul86; 814 982-2) (cd-enhanced.Oct98 & Sep00 on 'Jambco'; 538023-2)*

May 84. (7"/12") *(VER/+X 11)* **SHE DON'T KNOW ME. / BREAKOUT** [ ] [-]

May 84. (7") *<818958>* **SHE DON'T KNOW ME. / BURNING FOR LOVE** [-] [48]

Oct 84. (7") *(VER 14)* **RUNAWAY. / BREAKOUT (live)** [ ] [-]
(12"+=) *(VERX 14)* – Runaway (live).

Apr 85. (7") *<880736>* **ONLY LONELY. / ALWAYS RUN TO YOU** [-] [54]

May 85. (lp/c) *(VERL/+H 24) <824509>* **7800° FAHRENHEIT** [28] [37]
– In and out of love / The price of love / Only lonely / King of the mountain / Silent night / Tokyo road / The hardest part is the night / Always run to you / To the fire / Secret dreams. *(cd-iss. Jul86; 824 509-2) (cd-enhanced.Oct98 & Sep00 on 'Jambco'; 538026-2)*

May 85. (7"/7"pic-d) *(VER/+P 19)* **IN AND OUT OF LOVE. / ROULETTE (live)** [ ] [-]
(12"+=) *(VERX 19)* – Shot through the heart (live).

Jul 85. (7") *<880951>* **IN AND OUT OF LOVE. / BREAKOUT (Japanese live version)** [-] [69]

Jul 85. (7") *(VER 22)* **THE HARDEST PART IS THE NIGHT. / ALWAYS RUN TO YOU** [68] [-]
(12"+=) *(VERX 22)* – Tokyo Road (live).
(d7"++=) *(VERDP 22)* – Shot through the heart (live).
(12"red) *(VERXR 22)* – ('A'side) / Tokyo Road (live) / In and out of love (live).

Aug 86. (7"/10"sha-pic-d) *(VER/+P 26)* **YOU GIVE LOVE A BAD NAME. / LET IT ROCK** [14] [-]
(12"+=) *(VERX 26)* – Borderline.
(12"blue+=) *(VERXR 26)* – The hardest part is the night (live) / Burning for love (live).

Aug 86. (7") *<884953>* **YOU GIVE LOVE A BAD NAME. / RAISE YOUR HANDS** [-] [1]

Sep 86. (lp/c)(cd) *(VERH/+C 38)(<830 264-2>)* **SLIPPERY WHEN WET** [6] [1]
– Let it rock / You give love a bad name / Livin' on a prayer / Social disease / Wanted dead or alive / Raise your hands / Without love / I'd die for you / Never say goodbye / Wild in the streets. *(pic-lp Aug88; VERHP 38) (re-iss. Dec90; same); hit 46) (re-charted.Jun91 No.42, Sep92 re-issue) (cd-enhanced.Oct98 & Sep00 on 'Jambco'; 538025-2) (lp re-iss. Jun99 & Mar00 on 'Simply Vinyl'; SVLP 93)*

Oct 86. (7"/7"pic-d/7"w-patch) *(VER/+P/PA 28) <888184>* **LIVIN' ON A PRAYER. / WILD IN THE STREETS** [4] [1] Dec86
(12"+=/12"green+=) *(VERX/+P 28)* – Edge of a broken heart.
(d12"+=) *(VERXG 28)* – Only lonely (live) / Runaway (live).

Mar 87. (7"/7"s) *(JOV/+S 1)* **WANTED DEAD OR ALIVE. / SHOT THROUGH THE HEART** [13] [-]
(12"+=) *(JOV 1-12)* – Social disease.
(12"silver++=) – *(JOVR 1-12)* – Get ready (live).

Mar 87. (7") *<888467>* **WANTED DEAD OR ALIVE. / I#D DIE FOR YOU** [-] [7]

Aug 87. (7") *(JOV 2)* **NEVER SAY GOODBYE. / RAISE YOUR HANDS** [21] [-]
(c-s+=) *(JOVC 2)* – ('A'acoustic).
(12"+=/12"yellow+=) *(JOV/+R 2-12)* – Wanted dead or alive (acoustic).

Sep 88. (7") *(JOV 3)* **BAD MEDICINE. / 99 IN THE SHADE** [17] [1]
(12"+=/cd-s+=) *(JOV 3-12/CD3)* – Lay your hands on me.
(12") *(JOVR 3-12)* – ('A'side) / You give love a bad name / Livin' on a prayer (live).

Sep 88. (lp/c)(cd) *(VERH/+C 62)(<836 345-2>)* **NEW JERSEY** [1] [1]
– Lay your hands on me / Bad medicine / Born to be my baby / Living in sin / Blood on blood / Stick to your guns / Homebound train / I'll be there for you / 99 in the shade / Love for sale / Wild is the wind / Ride cowboy ride. *(re-iss. Mar93 cd/c; same) (cd-enhanced.Oct98 & SEp00 on 'Jambco'; 538024-2)*

Nov 88. (7"/7"s) *(JOV/+S 4) <872156>* **BORN TO MY BABY. / LOVE FOR SALE** [22] [3]
(12"+=/12"g-f+=/12"pic-d+=) *(JOV/+R/P 4-12)* – Wanted dead or alive.
(cd-s+=) *(JOVCD 4)* – Runaway / Livin' on a prayer.

Apr 89. (7"/7"w-poster) *(JOV/+PB 5) <872564>* **I'LL BE THERE FOR YOU. / HOMEBOUND TRAIN** [18] [1] Feb89
(12"+=) *(JOV 5-12)* – Wild in the streets (live).
(cd-s+=) *(JOVCD 5)* – Borderline / Edge of a broken heart.

May 89. (7") *<874452>* **LAY YOUR HANDS ON ME. / RUNAWAY (live)** [-] [7]

Aug 89. (7"/c-s)(7"red/7"white/7"blue) *(JOV/+MC 6)(JOVS 6 61/62/63)* **LAY YOUR HANDS ON ME. / BAD MEDICINE** [18] [-]
(10"pic-d+=) *(JOV 6-10)* – Blood on blood.
(12") *(JOVG 6-12)* – ('A'side) / Blood on blood (live) / Born to be my baby (acoustic).
(cd-s) *(JOVCD 6)* – ('A'side) / You give love a bad name / Let it rock.

Nov 89. (7"/c-s) *(JOV/+MC 7) <876070>* **LIVING IN SIN. / LOVE IS WAR** [35] [9] Oct89
(12"+=/box-cd-s+=) *(JOV 7-12/CD7)* – Ride cowboy ride / Stick to your guns.
(12"white+=) *(JOVR 7-12)* **The boys are back in town.**

JON BON JOVI

Jul 90. (7") *(JBJ 1) <875896>* **BLAZE OF GLORY. / YOU REALLY GOT ME NOW (with LITTLE RICHARD)** [13] [1]
(12"+=/cd-s+=) *(JBJ T/CD 1)* – Blood money.

Aug 90. (cd/c/lp) *<(846473-2/-4/-1)>* **BLAZE OF GLORY – YOUNG GUNS II** [2] [3]
– Billy get your guns / Miracle / Blaze of glory / Blood money / Santa Fe / Justice in the barrel / Never say die / You really got me now / Bang a drum / Dyin' ain't much of a livin' / Guano City. *(re-iss. Apr95 cd/c;)*

Oct 90. (c-s) *<878392>* **MIRACLE / BLOOD MONEY** [-] [12]

Nov 90. (7"/c-s) *(JBJ/+C 2)* **MIRACLE. / BANG A DRUM** [29] [-]
(12"+=/cd-s+=) *(JBJ T/CD 2)* – Dyin' ain't much of a livin' / (interview).

BON JOVI

Jambco / Jambco

Oct 92. (7"/c-s) *(JOV/+MC 8) <864432>* **KEEP THE FAITH. / I WISH EVERYDAY COULD BE CHRISTMAS** [5] [29]
(cd-s+=) *(JOVCB 8)* – Living in sin.
(cd-s+=) *(JOVCA 8)* – Little bit of soul.

Nov 92. (cd/c/lp) *(514197-2/-4/-1) <514045>* **KEEP THE FAITH** [1] [5]
– I believe / Keep the faith / I'll sleep when I'm dead / In these arms / Bed of roses / If I was your mother / Dry country / Woman in love / Fear / I want you / Blame it on the love of rock'n'roll / Little bit of soul. *(d-cd-iss. Aug93; 518 019-2)* – (live versions). *(cd-enhanced.Oct98 & Sep00; 538034-2)*

Jan 93. (c-s) *<864852>* **BED OF ROSES / LAY YOUR HANDS ON ME (live)** [-] [10]

Jan 93. (7"/c-s) *(JOV/+MC 9)* **BED OF ROSES. / STARTING ALL OVER AGAIN** [13] [-]
(12"+=) *(JOVT 9)* – Lay your hands on me (live).
(cd-s) *(JOVCD 9)* – ('A'side) / Lay your hands on me (live) / I'll be there for you (live) / Tokyo road (live).

May 93. (cd-s) *<862088>* **IN THESE ARMS / SAVE A PRAYER / IN THESE ARMS (live)** [-] [27]

May 93. (7") *(JOV 10)* **IN THESE ARMS. / BED OF ROSES (acoustic)** [9] [-]
(cd-s) *(JOVCD 10)* – ('A'side) / Keep the faith (live) / In these arms (live).
(c-s) *(JOVMC 10)* – ('A'side) / Blaze of glory (acoustic).

Jul 93. (7"/c-s) *(JOV/+MC 11) <862428>* **I'LL SLEEP WHEN I'M DEAD. / NEVER SAY GOODBYE (live acoustic)** [17] [97]
(cd-s) *(JOVCD 11)* – ('A'side) / Blaze of glory / Wild in the streets (both live).
(cd-ep) **HITS LIVE EP** *(JOVD 11)* – ('A'side) / Blaze of glory / You give love a bad name / Bad medicine.

Sep 93. (7"/c-s) *(JOV/+MC 12)* **I BELIEVE (Clearmountain mix). / ('A'live)** [11] [-]
(cd-s) *(JOVCD 12)* – ('A'side) / Runaway (live) / Livin' on the prayer (live) / Wanted dead or alive ('HITS LIVE PART 2 EP').
(cd-s) *(JOVCB 12)* – ('A'side) / You give love a bad name (live) / Born to be my baby (live) / I'll sleep when I'm dead (live).

Mar 94. (7"/c-s) *(JOV/+MC 13)* **DRY COUNTY. / STRANGER IN THIS TOWN (live)** [9] [-]
(gold-cd-s+=) *(JOVBX 13)* – Blood money (live).
(cd-s) *(JOVCD 13)* – ('A'side) / It's only rock'n'roll (live) / Waltzing Matilda (live).

Sep 94. (c-s) *(JOVMC 14)* **ALWAYS. / THE BOYS ARE BACK IN TOWN** [2] [-]
(12"colrd) *(JOVT 14)* – ('A'side) / Prayer '94.
(cd-s) *(JOVCD)* – ('A'side) / ('A'mix) / Edge of a broken heart.

Sep 94. (cd-s) *<856227>* **ALWAYS / NEVER SAY GOODBYE / EDGE OF A BROKEN HEART** [-] [4]

Oct 94. (cd/c/lp) *(522 936-2/-4/-1)* <526013> **CROSS ROAD – THE BEST OF BON JOVI** (compilation) [1] [8]
– Livin' on a prayer / Keep the faith / Someday I'll be Saturday night / Always / Wanted dead or alive / Lay your hands on me / You give love a bad name / Bed of roses / Blaze of glory / In these arms / Bad medicine / I'll be there for you / In and out of love / Runaway / Never say goodbye. *(cd-enhanced.Oct98; same)*

Dec 94. (7"pic-d/c-s) *(JOV P/MC 16)* **PLEASE COME HOME FOR CHRISTMAS / BACK DOOR SANTA** [7] [-]
(cd-s+=) *(JOVCD 16)* – I wish every day could be like Christmas.

Feb 95. (7"pic-d/c-s) *(JOV P/MC 15)* **SOMEDAY I'LL BE SATURDAY NIGHT. / GOOD GUYS DON'T ALWAYS WEAR WHITE (live)** [7] [-]
(cd-s+=) *(JOVCD 15)* – With a little help from my friends (live).
(cd-s+=) *(JOVDD 15)* – Always (live).

May 95. (c-s) *(JOVMC 17)* **THIS AIN'T A LOVE SONG. / LONELY AT THE TOP** [6] [-]
(cd-s+=) *(JOVCX 17)* – The end.
(cd-s) *(JOVCD 17)* – ('A'side) / When she comes / Wedding day / Prostitute.

May 95. (c-s) *<856227>* **THIS AIN'T A LOVE SONG / ALWAYS (live) / PROSTITUTE** [-] [14]

Jun 95. (cd/c/d-lp) *(528 248-2/-4/-1)* <528181> **(THESE DAYS)** [1] [9]
– Hey God / Something for the pain / This ain't a love song / These days / Lie to me / Damned / My guitar lies bleeding in my arms / (It's hard) Letting you go / Hearts breaking even / Something to believe in / If that's what it takes / Diamond ring / All I want is everything / Bitter wine. *(re-iss. w/ free cd+=)* – (8 tracks). *(iss.w/ tour pack Jun96; 532 644-2) (cd-enhanced.Oct98; 538036-2)*

Sep 95. (c-s) *(JOVMC 18)* **SOMETHING FOR THE PAIN / THIS AIN'T A LOVE SONG** [8] [-]
(cd-s+=) *(JOVCX 18)* – I don't like Mondays.
(cd-s) *(JOVCD 18)* – ('A'side) / Living on a prayer / You give love a bad name / Wild in the streets.

Nov 95. (c-s) *(JOVMC 19)* <852296> **LIE TO ME / SOMETHING FOR THE PAIN (live)** [10] [88] [76]
(cd-s+=) *(JOVCX 19)* – Always (live) / Keep the faith (live).
(cd-s) *(JOVCD 19)* – ('A'side) / Something for the pain / Hey God (live) / I'll sleep when I'm dead (live).

Feb 96. (c-s) *(JOVMC 20)* **THESE DAYS / 634-5789** [7] [-]
(cd-s+=) *(JOVCX 20)* – Rockin' in the free world (live) / (It's hard) Letting you go (live).
(cd-s) *(JOVCD 20)* – ('A'side) / Someday I'll be Saturday night / These days (live) / Helter skelter (live).

Jun 96. (c-s) *(JOVMC 21)* **HEY GOD / LIE TO ME (remix)** [13] [-]
(cd-s+=) *(JOVCX 21)* – House of the rising sun / Livin' on a prayer.
(cd-s) *(JOVCD 21)* – ('A'side) / The end / When she comes / ('A'live).

JON BON JOVI

— with **DAVID BRYAN** – keyboards / **KENNY ARONOFF** – drums / **ERIC BAZILIAN + DAVE STEWART**

Mercury Mercury

Jun 97. (c-s) *(MERMC 488)* **MIDNIGHT IN CHELSEA / MIDNIGHT IN CHELSEA (album version)** [4] [-]
(cd-s+=) *(MERCD 488)* – Sad song tonight / August 7th (acoustic).
(cd-s+=) *(MERCX 488)* – Drive / Every word was a piece of my heart.

Jun 97. (cd/c) *(536 011-2/-4)* <534903> **DESTINATION ANYWHERE** [2] [31]
– Queen of New Orleans / Janie, don't take your love to town / Midnight in Chelsea / Ugly / Staring at your window with a suitcase in my hand / Every word was a piece of my heart / It's just me / Destination anywhere / Learning how to fall / Naked / Little city / August 4, 4:15 / Cold hard heart. *(cd re-iss. Dec97 with bonus cd of live tracks; 536 758-2)* – Queen of New Orleans / Midnight in Chelsea / Destination anywhere / Ugly / It's just me / August 7, 4:15 / Jailbreak / Not fade away / Janie, don't take your love to town.

Aug 97. (c-s) *(MERMC 493)* **QUEEN OF NEW ORLEANS / MIDNIGHT IN CHELSEA (live)** [10] [-]
(cd-s+=) *(MERCD 493)* – ('A'album version) / Destination anywhere (live).
(cd-s) *(MERCX 493)* – ('A'side) / ('A'album version) / Every piece of my heart (acoustic) / Jailbreak (live).

Nov 97. (c-s) *(574986-4)* **JANIE, DON'T TAKE YOUR LOVE TO TOWN / TALK TO JESUS (demo)** [13] [-]
(cd-s+=) *(574987-2)* – Billy get your guns (live).
(cd-s) *(574989-2)* – ('A'album version) / Destination anywhere (MTV acoustic) / It's just me (MTV acoustic) / ('A'-MTV acoustic).

BON JOVI

Warners Reprise

Mar 99. (c-s) *(W 479C)* **REAL LIFE / KEEP THE FAITH (live)** [21] [-]
(cd-s+=) *(W 479CD)* – Real life (instrumental).

May 00. (c-s) *(562753-4)* **IT'S MY LIFE / HUSH** [3] [33]
(cd-s+=) *(562752-2)* – You can't lose at love.
(cd-s) *(562768-2)* – ('A'side) / Temptation / I don't want to live forever / ('A'-CD-Rom).

May 00. (cd/c) *(54256-22/-14)* <542474> **CRUSH** [1] [9]
– It's my life / Say it isn't so / Thank you for loving me / Two storey town / Next 100 years / Just older / Mystery train / Save the world / Captain Crash and the beauty queen from Mars / She's a mystery / I got the girl / One wild night.

Aug 00. (c-s) *(568898-4)* **SAY IT ISN'T SO / AIN'T NO CURE FOR LOVE (demo)** [10] [-]
(cd-s+=) *(568897-2)* – Stay (demo).
(cd-s) *(568898-2)* – ('A'side) / Ordinary people (demo) / Welcome to the good times (demo).

Nov 00. (c-s) *(572730-4)* *<radio play>* **THANK YOU FOR LOVING ME / CAPTAIN CRASH AND THE BEAUTY QUEEN FROM MARS (live)** [12] [57]
(cd-s+=) *(572730-2)* – Runaway (acoustic live).
(cd-s) *(572731-2)* – ('A'side) / Just older (live) / Born to be my baby (live).

May 01. (c-s) *(572949-4)* **ONE WILD NIGHT (2001 version) / LAY YOUR HANDS ON ME (live)** [10] [-]
(cd-s+=) *(572949-2)* – I believe (live).
(cd-s) *(572950-2)* – ('A'side) / Hey God (live) / Tokyo road (live).

May 01. (cd) *<(548865-2)>* **ONE WILD NIGHT (live 1985-2001)** [5] [20]
– It's my life / Livin' on a prayer / You give love a bad name / Keep the faith / Saturday night / Rockin' in the free world / Something to believe in / Wanted dead or alive / Runaway / In and out of love / I don't like Mondays / Just older / Something for the pain / Bad medicine / One wild night.

– (JOHN BONGIOVI) compilations, etc. –

Jul 97. (cd/c) *Masquerade; (MASQ CD/MC 1011)* **THE POWER STATION YEARS** (rec.1980-1983; remixed 1997) [ ] [ ]
(re-iss. Feb99; same)

Aug 97. (cd-ep) *Masquerade; (MASSCD 1001)* **MORE THAN WE BARGAINED FOR** [ ] [ ]

Nov 99. (cd) *Laserlight; (21490)* **JOHN BONGIOVI** [ ] [-]

RICHIE SAMBORA

(solo with **BRYAN + TORRES + TONY LEVIN** – bass)

Mercury Mercury

Aug 91. (7") *(MER 350)* <868790> **BALLAD OF YOUTH. / REST IN PEACE** [59] [63]
(12"+=/cd-s+=) *(MER X/CD 350)* – The wind cries Mary.

Sep 91. (cd/c/lp) *<(848895-2/-4/-1>)* **STRANGER IN THIS TOWN** [20] [36]
– Rest in peace / Church of desire / Stranger in this town / Ballad of youth / One light burning / Mr.Bluesman / Rosie / River of love / Father time / The answer. *(re-iss. Apr95 cd/c;)*

— DAVID BRYAN also had solo album 'NETHERWORLD' (1992) for 'Moonstone'.

Feb 98. (cd-s) *(568503-2)* **HARD TIMES COME EASY / MIDNIGHT RIDER – WANTED DEAD OR ALIVE (live) / WE ALL SLEEP ALONE (live) / BAD MEDICINE (live)** [37] [ ]
(cd-s) *(568503-5)* – ('A'side) / Little help from my friends (live) / Stranger in this town (live) / I'll be there for you (live).

Mar 98. (cd/c) *<(536972-2/-4)>* **UNDISCOVERED SOUL** [24] [ ]
– Made in America / Hard times come easy / Fallen from Graceland / If God was a woman / All that really matters / You're not alone / In it for love / Chained / Harlem rain / Who am I / Downside of love / Undiscovered soul.

Jul 98. (cd-s) *(566063-2)* **IN IT FOR LOVE / MADE IN AMERICA (German acoustic) / IN IT FOR LOVE (German acoustic)** [58] [ ]
(cd-s) *(568825-2)* – ('A'side) / Livin' on a prayer (live at Ronnie Scott's) / I'll be there for you (live '91).

Graham BONNET

Born: 12 Dec'47, Skegness, Lincolnshire, England. As part of pop group The MARBLES, he had a Top 5 hit in 1968 with 'ONLY ONE WOMAN'. This outfit had one more chart appearance, 'THE WALLS FELL DOWN' in '69, before BONNET took off for a solo and acting career (he starred in the film, 'Three For All'). In 1977, he recorded a self-titled album for RINGO STARR's ill-fated, 'Ring O' label; a major hit in Australia, the record plummeted in the UK. BONNET's big break came in 1977, when RITCHIE BLACKMORE decided to substitute RONNIE JAMES DIO in his heavy-rock icons, RAINBOW. In 1979, the neatly-attired BONNET graced RAINBOW's first UK Top 10 hit, 'SINCE YOU'VE BEEN GONE' (penned by RUSS BALLARD) as well as writing another hard-rock/pop classic, 'ALL NIGHT LONG' (both appearing on the album, 'DOWN TO EARTH'). However, this brief association with the band ended as BONNET took the opportunity to revive his own solo career. Initially this proved to be a more fruitful venture than his ill-fated 70's sojourn, 'NIGHT GAMES' giving him his first and only Top 10 solo hit in 1981. An album, 'LINE UP' was issued at the end of the year, although this lacked the hard-edged approach he utilised in RAINBOW. The following year he returned to a group format, joining hard-rockers, The MICHAEL SCHENKER GROUP for their album, 'ASSAULT ATTACK'. Despite the record's success, BONNET relocated to the American West Coast and formed the group, ALCATRAZZ (a training ground for both YNGWIE MALMSTEEN and STEVE VAI). They released a few albums, before he joined JAN AKKERMAN's FORCEFIELD III in 1988. More recently, BONNET has turned back to hard-rock in the shape of BLACKTHORNE, who were signed by 'Music For Nations' for one album in '93.

Album rating: GRAHAM BONNET (*5) / LINE UP (*4) / Alcatrazz: NO PAROLE FROM ROCK'N'ROLL (*6) / LIVE SENTENCE (*4) / DISTURBING THE PEACE (*4) / DANGEROUS GAMES (*3) / Blackthorne: AFTERLIFE (*5)

GRAHAM BONNET

R.C.A. not iss.

Jun 72. (7") *(RCA 2230)* **RARE SPECIMEN. / WHISPER IN THE NIGHT** [ ] [-]

Jun 73. (7") *(RCA 2380)* **TRYING TO SAY GOODBYE. / CASTLES IN THE AIR** [ ] [-]

E.M.I. not iss.

Jan 75. (7") *(EMI 2250)* **SUPERGIRL. / HILL OF LOVIN'** [ ] [-]

Ring O not iss.

May 77. (7") *(2017 105)* **IT'S ALL OVER NOW, BABY BLUE. / HEROES ON MY PICTURE WALL** [ ] [-]

Aug 77. (7") *(2017 106)* **DANNY. / ROCK ISLAND LINE** [ ] [-]

Nov 77. (7") *(2017 110)* **GOODNIGHT & GOODMORNING. / WINO SONG** [ ] [-]

Nov 77. (lp) *(2320 103)* **GRAHAM BONNET** [ ] [-]
– It's all over now, baby blue / Will you love me tomorrow / Tired of being alone / Wino song / It ain't easy / Goodnight and goodmorning / Danny / Sunday 16th / Rock island line / Soul seeker.

		Polydor	not iss.
Jan 78.	(7") *(2017 114)* **WARM RIDE. /**		-
Mar 78.	(7") *(POSP 2)* **WARM RIDE. / 10-12 OBSERVATION**		-

— BONNET joined RAINBOW . . . solo again below

— next with **JON LORD** – keyboards / **MICK MOODY** – guitars / **GARY TWIGG** – bass / **COZY POWELL** – drums

		Vertigo	not iss.
Mar 81.	(7") *(VER 1)* **NIGHT GAMES. / OUT ON THE WATER**	6	
Jun 81.	(7") *(VER 2)* **LIAR. / BAD DAYS ARE GONE**	51	
Oct 81.	(7") *(VER 4)* **THAT'S THE WAY THAT IT IS. / DON'T TELL ME TO GO**		-
Oct 81.	(lp) *(6302151)* **LINE-UP**	62	-

– Night games / S.O.S. / I'm a lover / Be my baby / That's the way that it is / Liar / Anthony boy / Dirty hand / Out on the water / Don't stand in the open / Set me free.

— BONNET then joined The MICHAEL SCHENKER GROUP for the 1982 album, 'ASSAULT ATTACK', before moving to US West Coast and joining

ALCATRAZZ

GRAHAM BONNET – vocals (ex-RAINBOW, ex-MICHAEL SCHENKER GROUP, ex-Solo Artist)
/ YNGWIE MALMSTEEN – guitar / **JIMMY WALDO** – keyboards (ex-NEW ENGLAND) / **GARY SHEA** – bass (ex-NEW ENGLAND) / **JAN UVENA** – drums (ex-ALICE COOPER)

		Rocshire-RCA	Grand Slamm
Aug 84.	(lp/c) *(PL/PK 83263) <SLAMM 11>* **NO PAROLE FROM ROCK'N'ROLL**		

– Island in the sun / General hospital / Jet to jet / Hiroshima mon amour / Kree Nakoorie / Incubus / Too young to die, too drunk to live / Big foot / Starcarr Lane / Suffer me. *<US-iss.1988 on 'Grand Slam'; SLAM 11> (UK cd-iss. Jun92 on 'Music For Nations'; CDMFN 133)*

Aug 84.	(7"/12") *(RCA/+T 434)* **ISLAND IN THE SUN. / GENERAL HOSPITAL**		

— **STEVE VAI** – guitar, vocals (ex-FRANK ZAPPA); repl. MALMSTEEN who went solo

		Capitol	Capitol
Aug 85.	(lp/c) *(EJ 420299-1/-4) <12385>* **DISTURBING THE PEACE**		

– God blessed video / Mercy / Will you be home tonight / Wire and wood / Desert diamond /
The stripper / Painted lover / Lighter shade of green / Sons and lovers / Skyfire / Breaking the heart of the city.

Aug 85.	(7") *(CL 366)* **GOD BLESS VIDEO. / WIRE AND WOOD**		

— **DANNY JOHNSON** – guitar (ex-AXIS); repl. VAI who joined DAVID LEE ROTH (+ solo)

Sep 86.	(lp) *<12477>* **DANGEROUS GAMES**	-	

– It's my life / Undercover / That ain't nothin' / No imagination / Ohayo Tokyo / Dangerous games / Blue boar / Only one woman / Witchwood / Double man / Night of the shooting star.

— disbanded in 1987

- compilations, etc. -

Nov 89.	(lp) *Grand Slamm; <(SLAM 12)>* **LIVE SENTENCE (live '84)**		

– Too young to die, too drunk to live / Hiroshima mon amour / Night games / Island in the sun / Kree Nakoorie / Coming Bach / Since you've been gone / Evil eye / All night long. *(cd-iss. Jun92 on 'Music For Nations'; CDMFN 134)*

— BONNET teamed up with JAN AKKERMAN (ex-FOCUS), COZY POWELL and RAY FENWICK, joining FORCEFIELD III set-up.

BLACKTHORNE

were fronted by **BONNET** plus **BOB KULICK** – guitar (ex-ALICE COOPER, ex-MEAT LOAF, ex-BALANCE) / **JIMMY WALDO** – keyboards (see above) / **CHUCK WRIGHT** – bass (ex-HOUSE OF LORDS) / **FRANKIE BANALI** – drums (ex-W.A.S.P.)

		Music For Nations	C.M.C.
May 93.	(cd/c/lp) *(CD/T+/MFN 148) <6403>* **AFTERLIFE**		May94

– Cradle of the grave / Afterlife / We won't be forgotten / Breaking the chains / Over and over / Hard feelings / Baby you're the blood / Sex crime / Love from the ashes / All night long.

— split after one-off above

BOREDOMS

Formed: Osaka, Japan . . . 1983 by vocalist/frontman, YAMATSUKA EYE and percussionist, TABATA. This pairing released the first BOREDOMS product, the 'ANAL BY ANAL' EP in '85. There was a similarly worrying anal fixation on 'ONAMIE BOMB MEETS THE SEX PISTOLS', a cacophonous blast of musical anarchy akin to a cross between the post-hardcore US noise of JESUS LIZARD and BIG BLACK and the experimental torture of the REVOLUTIONARY PEKING ORCHESTRA. Following TABATA's departure to ZEVI GEVA, YAMATSUKA met HIRA HAYASHI while working in a gay bar, the pair subsequently recruiting second vocalist, TOYOHITO YOSHIKAWA. By the late 80's, the line-up had expanded to include YAMAMOTO, YOSHIMI P-WE and ATARI, the crew finding a natural home at ~KRAMER's 'Shimmy Disc', for 1990's 'SOUL DISCHARGE '89' album. By this point, the band's crazed stage antics (usually resulting in injury for YAMATSUKA) preceded them and partly due to their increasingly infamous reputation, netted a major label deal with 'Reprise'. From the label that once gifted the world FRANK SINATRA came such schizophrenic, subversively unfathomable albums as 'POP TATARI' (1993), 'CHOCOLATE SYNTHESIZER' (1994) and 'SUPER ROOTS VI' (1996), the latter consisting solely of songs titled after cardinal numbers; even the band themselves admit that their lyrics mean absolutely nothing!

Album rating (selective): ONANIE BOMB MEETS THE SEX PISTOLS (*5) / SOUL DISCHARGE 99 (*6) / POP TATARI (*4) / SUPER ROOTS series (*5) / CHOCOLATE SYNTHESIZER (*6)

YAMATSUKA EYE – vocals / **TABATA** – percussion

		not iss.	Reprise
1985.	(7"ep) **ANAL BY ANAL EP**	-	
1985.	(lp) **ONANIE BOMB MEETS THE SEX PISTOLS**	-	

– Wipe out shock shoppers / Boredoms vs. SDI / We never sleep / Bite my bollocks / Young assouls / Call me God / No core punk / Lick'n cock boatpeople / Melt down boogie / Feedbackfuck / Anal eater / God from anal / Born to anal. *(cd-iss. Sep94 on 'Earthnoise'; EN 001) <cd-iss. Nov94 on 'Reprise'; 45636>*

— TABATA left to join as ZEVI GEVA guitarist and was repl. by **TOYOHITO YOSHIKAWA** (aka HUMAN RICH VOX Y) – vocals / **HIRA HAYASHI** (aka HYLA Y) – bass, vocals / **YAMAMOTO** (aka YY) – guitar, vocals / **ATARI** (aka GOD MANA) – synthesizer, drums + **YOSHIMI P-WE** – drums, vocals / and 7th member **KING KAZOO EYE** – kazoo, sound effects

		Shimmy Disc	Shimmy Disc
Aug 90.	(lp) *(<SHIMMY 035>)* **SOUL DISCHARGE 99**		Dec89

– Your name is limitless / Bubblepop shot / 52 boredom (club mix) / Sun, gun, run / Z & U & T & A / TV scorpion / Pow wow now / J.B. Dick and Tina Turner pussy / G.I.L. '77 / Jup-na-keeeeeel / Catastro mix '99 / Milky Way / Songs without electric guitars / Hamaiin disco bollocks / Hamaiin disco without bollocks. *(cd-iss. Sep94 on 'Earthnoise'; EN 002)*

		not iss.	Reprise
1993.	(cd/c) *<45416-2/-4>* **POP TATARI**	-	

– Noise Ramones / Nice B-O-R-E guy & Boyoyo touch / Hey bore hey / Bo go / Bore now bore / Okinawa rasta beef (mockin' fuzz 2) / Which dooyoo like / Molecicco / Telehorse Uma / Hoy / Bocabola / Heeba / Poy (mockin' fuzz 1) / Bod / Cheba / Pop tatari / Cory & the mandara suicide pyramid.

Nov 93.	(cd) *<(AVANT 026)>* **WOW 2**		Oct92

– Doomsbore / Jet net / Rat soup / Pop can / Rydeen!! / Herps / VV rule / Domdoms / 100 dom / Mogo? / Ok / Do / On / Up.
(above released on 'Avant')

Jun 94.	(cd-ep) *<41559>* **SUPER ROOTS**	-	

– Pop kiss / Budokan tape try (500 tapes high) / Finger action No.5 / 4 (chocolate *ut) / Pitch at bunch on itch / Machine 3 / Monster Rex & S*und 'a' R*undus / Nuts room / Ear?wig?web? / 96 teenage bondage / Super frake 009.

1994.	(cd) *<45814>* **CHOCOLATE SYNTHESIZER**	-	

– Acid police / Chocolate synthesizer / Synthesizer guide book on fire / Shock city / Tomato synthesizer / Anarchy in the UKK / Voredoms / B for Boredoms / Eedoms / Smoke 7 / Turn table Boredoms / I'm not synthesizer (YP?) / Now dom go synthesizer way (why?).

Aug 96.	(cd) *<46163>* **SUPER ROOTS VI**	-	

– 01 / 0 (X12) / 6 / 2 / 3 / 9 / 4 / 7 / 8 / 5 / 10 / 11 / 12 / 13v / 14 / 15 / 1.

— in 1996, EYE also worked with JOHN ZORN on the album, 'Nani Nani', while moonlighting with other act . . .

		Birdman	Birdman
Apr 99.	(cd) *(<BMR 019>)* **SUPER ARE**		Oct98

– Super you / Super are / Super going / Super coming / Super are you / Super shine.

HANATARASH

		not iss.	Mom'n'Dad
1993.	(cd) *<MOM 002>* **LIVE!! 1984 Dec.16: ZABO-KYOTO (live)**	-	
		Public Bath	Public Bath
Jun 97.	(cd) *(<PBCD 3>)* **4: AIDS-A-DELIC**		Jan96

BORKNAGAR

Formed: Norway . . . 1995 by OYSTEIN GARNES BRUN, former guitarist of Norwegian death metallers, MOLESTED. BRUN decided to get together a metal band which would be able to manifest his conception of the directions in which the genre could move. For this momentous task he recruited a pack of veteran metallers; GARM (from ARCTURUS and owner of the label 'Jester') on vocals, GRIM (from GORGOROTH and ANCIENT fame) on drums, IVAR BJORNSON (from ENSLAVED and INFERNUS, who also played with GORGOROTH) on bass. Due to the overload of hard metal talent on board, 'Malicious' records took the wise choice of signing and releasing the bands eponymous debut in '96. Following this, INFERNUS took his leave, making room for his replacement, KAI K LIE. Creating a stir in the world of death metal with this first set, BRUN quickly put paid to any critics believing this was an all-star band one-off by releasing a sophomore set, 'THE OLDEN DOMAIN' (1997) – this time on 'Century Media'. With this studio outing, the band showed their determination not to be pigeonholed as black metal. As with progressive black metal bands such as ROTTING CHRIST, the group used a variety of techniques and instrumentation to complement their studio sound. BRUN, himself, prefered the less than modest title, epic metal. BORKNAGAR then commenced a large touring circuit recruiting a second guitarist, JENS F RYLANDS, and replacing singer GARM with SIMEN HESTNAES. Shortly after releasing a third boundary-pushing full-length album, 'THE ARCHAIC COURSE' (1998), they went on to huge national and international acclaim. Tours with death metal legends CRADLE OF FILTH and NAPALM DEATH however, were without the help of departed members GRIM, KAI and BJORNSON. For their fourth full-length release, 'QUINTESSENCE' (2000), the band brought on ASGEIR MICKELSON on drums and LARS A NEDLAND on keyboards. Once again this set was well appreciated, BRUN leading the group yet further into dark uncharted waters.

Album rating: BORKNAGAR (*5) / THE OLDEN DOMAIN (*7) / THE ARCHAIC COURSE (*6) / QUINTESSENCE (*6)

GARM – vocals (of ULVER, of ARCTURUS) / **OYSTEIN GARNES BRUN** – guitar / **IVAR BJORNSON** – synthesizer (ex-ENSLAVED) / **INFERNAL** – bass (of GORGOROTH) / **GRIM** – drums (ex-IMMORTAL, of ANCIENT, of GORGOROTH)

Malicious | not iss.

Oct 96. (cd) *(MR 012CD)* **BORKNAGAR** [ ] [-]
– Vintervredets sjelesagn / Tanker mot tind (kvelding) / Svartskogs glide / Ved steingard / Kridsstev / Dauden / Grimskalle trell / Hord Haagauk / Fandens alheim / Tanker mot tind (gryning). *<US-iss.Feb97 on 'Century Media'; 7967>*

— **KAI K. LEE** – bass; repl. INFERNAL

Century Media | Century Media

Sep 97. (cd/pic-lp) *(CM 77175 CD/PD) <7895>* **THE OLDEN DOMAIN** [ ] [ ] Oct97
– The eye of Oden / The winterway / Om hundredeaareralting glemt / A tale of pagan tongue / The mountains rove / Grimland domain / Ascension of our fathers / The dawn of the end.

— **I.C.S. VORTEX** (b. SIMEN HESTNAAS) – vocals; repl. GARM

— added **JENS F. RYLANDS** – guitar

Nov 98. (cd) *(CM 77236CD) <7936>* **THE ARCHAIC COURSE** [ ] [ ]
– Oceans rise / Universal / The witching hour / The black token / Nocturnal vision / Ad noctum / Winter millennium / Fields of long gone presence.

— added **ASGEIR MICKELSON** – drums; repl. temp. NICK BARKER (of CRADLE OF FILTH) who repl. GRIM (**VORTEX** now vocals + bass)

— **LAZARE** (b. LARS A NEDLAND) – synthesizer (of SOLEFAID) repl. BJORNSON + LEE

May 00. (cd) *(77289-2) <7989>* **QUINTESSENCE** [ ] [ ]
– Rivalry of phantoms / The presence is ominous / Ruins of the future / Colossus / Inner landscape / Invincible / Icon dreams / Genesis torn / Embers / Revolt.

— now without VORTEX who was repl. by **VINTERSORG** – vocals (ex-OTYG, ex-VINTERSORG) + **TYR** – bass (ex-SATYRICON session)

BOSS HOG (see under ⇒ PUSSY GALORE)

BOSTON

Formed: 1975 by technical whizz and sometime musical genius, TOM SCHOLZ, who had set-up his own basement studio in Boston, Massachusetts, USA. Signed to 'Epic' on the strength of some home-crafted demos, SCHOLZ assembled a crew of musician friends (BRAD DELP, BARRY GOUDREAU, FRAN SHEEHAN and JIM MASDEA) and set about creating his first opus. Quintessentially 70's yet one of the most enduring AOR tracks ever recorded, BOSTON's debut single, 'MORE THAN A FEELING', gave the band instant UK and US success upon its release in Christmas 1976. With its powerful twin lead guitar attack, softened with flawless harmonies, the song set a blueprint for the eponymous debut album. While the record contained nothing else quite as affecting, it was all well written stuff and highly listenable if you ignored the cliched lyrics. Inevitably, the album sold in its millions and the pressure was on to record a follow-up. Notoriously perfectionist in the studio, SCHOLZ was unhappy with a mere two years to craft 'DON'T LOOK BACK' (1978). While the title track was top drawer car-stereo material, the formula was sounding tired and the bulk of the album didn't lend itself to repeated listening. While SCHOLZ complained that its relatively disappointing sales (still in the millions!) were down to the record being released prematurely, it was, after all, the height of the punk explosion, when sleeve designs of intergalactic guitars wern't particularly appreciated by the kids (in Britain, at least). It was to be another seven years before BOSTON returned with a follow-up and during this period, SCHOLZ signed with 'M.C.A.', a legal battle with 'C.B.S.' ensuing. The boffin-like SCHOLZ also found time to invent the 'Rockman', a device that amplified guitar sound at low volume for home recording. 'THIRD STAGE' (1986) boasted another airbrushed space fantasy cover and another set of reliable melodic rock songs, 'AMANDA' reaching No.1 in the US singles chart, the album itself achieving a similar feat. Yet again it quickly sold over a million but the BOSTON concept reeked of staleness and after another interminably long lay-off, SCHOLZ/BOSTON came up with 'WALK ON' in 1994. Unsurprisingly, the album only made it to No.51 in the US chart; SCHOLZ had clearly tested his fans' patience once too often.

Album rating: BOSTON (*7) / DON'T LOOK BACK (*5) / THIRD STAGE (*5) / WALK ON (*4) / GREATEST HITS compilation (*7)

BRAD DELP (b.12 Jun'51) – vocals, guitar / **TOM SCHOLZ** (b.10 Mar'47, Toledo, Ohio) – guitar, keyboards, vocals / **BARRY GOUDREAU** (b.29 Nov'51) – guitar / **FRAN SHEENAN** (b.26 Mar'49) – bass / **SIB HASHIAN** (b.17 Aug'49) – drums repl. debut lp session drummer JIM MASDEA

Epic | Epic

Jan 77. (7") *(EPC 4658) <50266>* **MORE THAN A FEELING. / SMOKIN'** [22] [5] Sep76

Jan 77. (lp/c) *(EPC/40 81611) <34188>* **BOSTON** [11] [3] Sep76
– More than a feeling / Peace of mind / Foreplay – Long time / Rock & roll band / Smokin' / Hitch a ride / Something about you / Let me take you home tonight. *(re-iss. Mar81 lp/c; EPC/40 32038)* – hit UK 58) *(cd-iss. Mar87; CD 81611) (cd re-iss. Jul95; 480413-2) (lp re-iss. Oct97 on 'Simply Vinyl'; SVLP 4) (cd re-iss. Dec98; 4894129)*

Mar 77. (7") *(EPC 5043) <50329>* **LONG TIME. / LET ME TAKE YOU HOME TONIGHT** [ ] [22] Jan77

Jun 77. (7") *(EPC 5288) <50381>* **PEACE OF MIND. / FOREPLAY** [ ] [38] May77

Sep 78. (lp/c)<US-pic-lp> *(EPC/40 86057) <35050>* **DON'T LOOK BACK** [9] [1] Aug78
– Don't look back / The journey / It's easy / A man I'll never be / Feelin' satisfied / Party / Used to bad news / Don't be afraid. *(re-iss. Jun81 lp/c; EPC/40 32048) (cd-iss. Mar87; CD 86057)*

Oct 78. (7") *(EPC 6653) <50590>* **DON'T LOOK BACK. / THE JOURNEY** [43] [4] Aug78

Jan 79. (7") *(EPC 6837) <50638>* **A MAN I'LL NEVER BE. / DON'T BE AFRAID** [ ] [31] Nov78

May 79. (7") *(EPC 7295) <50677>* **FEELIN' SATISFIED. / USED TO BAD NEWS** [ ] [46] Mar79

— (broke up for a while, after 3rd album was shelved / not completed) BARRY GOUDREAU made solo album late '80 before in '82 forming ORION THE HUNTER. He was augmented by SCHOLZ and DELP. HASHIAN joined SAMMY HAGAR band.

— **BOSTON** re-grouped around **SCHOLZ** and **DELP** plus **GARY PHIL** – guitar and the returning **JIM MASDEA** – drums

M.C.A. | M.C.A.

Oct 86. (7"/12") *(MCA/+S 1091) <52756>* **AMANDA. / MY DESTINATION** [ ] [1] Sep86

Oct 86. (lp/c/cd) *(MCG/MCGC/DMCG 6017) <6188>* **THIRD STAGE** [37] [1]
– Amanda / We're ready / The launch: Countdown – Ignition – Third stage separation / Cool the engines / My Destination / A new world / To be a man / I think I like it / Can'tcha say (you believe in me) / Still in love / Hollyann. *(cd re-iss. Jun92; MCLD 19066)*

Nov 86. (7") *<52985>* **WE'RE READY. / THE LAUNCH: COUNTDOWN – IGNITION – THIRD STAGE SEPARATION** [-] [9]

Apr 87. (7") *(MCA 1150) <53029>* **CAN'TCHA SAY (YOU BELIEVE IN ME). / STILL IN LOVE** [ ] [20] Mar87
(12"+=) *(MCAT 1150)* – Cool the engines.
(cd-s+=) *(DMCA 1150)* – The launch: Countdown – Ignition – Third stage separation.

— Early in '90 SCHOLZ (aka BOSTON) won $million lawsuit against CBS.

RTZ

— (RETURN TO ZERO) were formed by **BRAD + BARRY** with **BRIAN MAES** – keyboards / **TIM ARCHIBALD** – bass / **DAVID STEFANELLI** – drums

Giant | Giant

Aug 91. (c-s,cd-s) *<19273>* **FACE THE MUSIC / RETURN TO ZERO** [-] [49]

Apr 92. (7") *(543918955-7) <19051>* **UNTIL YOUR LOVE COMES BACK AROUND. / EVERY DOOR IS OPEN** [ ] [26] Jan92
(c-s+=)(12"+=/cd-s+=) *(543918955-4)(93624040-30/-42)* – Return to zero / ('A'extended).

Apr 92. (cd/c) *<(7599 24422-2/-4)>* **RETURN TO ZERO** [ ] [ ] Feb92
– Face the music / There's another side / All you've got / This is my life / Rain down on me / Every door is open / Devil to pay / Until your love comes back around / Livin' for the rock'n'roll / Hard time (in the big house) / Return to zero.

May 92. (c-s,cd-s) *<19112>* **ALL YOU'VE GOT / LIVIN' FOR THE ROCK'N'ROLL** [-] [56]

BOSTON

— another comeback album with; **TOM SHOLTZ** – guitar, keyboards, bass, drums / **GARY 'PIHL'** – keyboards / **DAVID SIKES** – vocals, bass / **DOUG HOFFMAN** – drums / **FRAN COSMO + TOMMY FUNDERBURK** – vocals

M.C.A. | M.C.A.

Jun 94. (cd/c) *<(MCD/MCC 10973)>* **WALK ON** [56] [7]
– I need your love / Surrender to me / Livin' for you / Walkin' at night / Walk on / Get organ-ized / Get reorgan-ized / Walk on (some more) / What's your name / Magdalene / We can make it.

Jul 94. (c-s) *(MCSC 1983) <54803>* **I NEED YOUR LOVE / WE CAN MAKE IT** [ ] [51] Jun94
(cd-s+=) *(MCSTD 1983)* – The launch: The countdown – Ignition – Third stage separation.

– compilations etc. –

Sep 79. (7"m) *Epic; (EPC 7888)* **DON'T LOOK BACK. / MORE THAN A FEELING / SMOKIN'** [ ] [-]

Apr 83. (7") *Old Gold; (OG 9299)* **MORE THAN A FEELING. / DON'T LOOK BACK** [ ] [-]

Aug 83. (d-c) *C.B.S.; (4022155)* **BOSTON / DON'T LOOK BACK** [ ] [-]

Aug 88. (3"cd-ep) *Epic; <34K 02355>* **MORE THAN A FEELING / FOREPLAY / LONG TIME** [-] [ ]

Jun 97. (cd/c) *<(484333-2/-4)>* **GREATEST HITS** [ ] [47]
– Tell me / Higher power / More than a feeling / Peace of mind / Don't look back / Cool the engines / Livin' for you / Feelin' satisfied / Party / Foreplay / Long time / Amanda / Rock/n'roll band / Smokin' / A man I'll never be / Star spangled banner / 4th of July reprise / Higher power.

BOUNCING SOULS

Formed: New Jersey, USA . . . 1987 by JOHNNY X (GREG ATTONITO), THE PETE (PETE STEINKOPF), PAPILLON (BRIAN KIENLEN) and drummer SHAL KHICHI, when the four decided to start a band while still in school. Post-graduation saw the band's endeavors to get themselves signed. Without any label interest they set up their own 'Chunksaah' records in late 1993, where they released two EP's ('ARGYLE' and 'NEUROTIC'), subsequently contained on their debut ~long player 'THE GOOD, THE BAD, AND THE ARGYLE' for label 'Better Youth Organisation'. The ghoulish foursome delivered their second 3-chorded loud'n'proud punk album 'MANIACAL LAUGHTER' early in '96, a more polished effort that included their gruesome version of Johnny Cash's 'BORN TO LOSE'. The lads soon received much attention from the likes of top punk acts NOFX and The DESCENDENTS (whom they supported), which led to them finally signing with 'Epitaph' in 1997. The same year the punk-pop outfit released their self-titled album (which sold a healthy amount of copies around the globe) following that with 1998's live EP, 'TIE ONE ON' and their more recent hardcore punk set, 'HOPELESS ROMANTIC' (1999). With new drummer MICHAEL McDERMOTT in tow, The BOUNCING SOULS released yet another punk album, 'HOW I SPENT MY SUMMER VACATION' (2001). • **Covered:** CANDY (Strangeloves).

Album rating: THE GOOD, THE BAD, AND THE ARGYLE. (*5) / MANIACAL LAUGHTER (*6) / BOUNCING SOULS (*5) / HOPELESS ROMANTIC (*5) / HOW I SPENT MY SUMMER VACATION (*5)

JOHNNY X (b. GREG ATTONITO) – vocals, guitar / **THE PETE** (b. PETE STEINKOPF) – guitar / **PAPILLION (b. BRIAN KIENLEN) – bass / SHAL KHICHI** – drums

not iss. Complex

1992. (7"ep) **UGLY BILL** [-] [ ]
– Ball of confusion / Mad Fillipo's massacre / In your face / PMRC.

not iss. Chunksaah

1992. (cd-ep) **THE GREEN BALL CREW EP** [-] [ ]
8- Wig / Dirt / Kicked / Spank / PMRC / Trapped / Hate.

1992. (7"ep) **KIDS IN AMERICA. / Weston: VIDEO KILLED THE RADIO STAR / Bouncing Souls & Weston: DO THEY KNOW IT'S CHRISTMAS** [-] [ ]

1993. (cd-ep) **THE ARGYLE e.p.** [-] [ ]
– Old school / These are the quotes from out favourite 80's movies / Joe lies (when he cries).

1993. (cd-ep) **NEUROTIC EP** [-] [ ]
– Neurotic / The guest / Some kind of wonderful / I like your mom.

not iss. Creep

1994. (cd-ep) <8> **TALES OF DOOMED ROMANCE BY . . .** [-] [ ]
– Quick check girl / Born to lose / BUGLITE:- She loves me / Just a dream.

Better Youth Org Better Youth Org

Jan 95. (lp/cd) *<(BYO 31/+CD)>* **THE GOOD, THE BAD, AND THE ARGYLE.** [ ] [ ] Nov94
– I like your mom / The guest / These are the quotes from our favourite 80's movies / Joe lies (when he cries) / Some kind of wonderful / Lay 'em down and smack 'em yack 'em / Oldschool / Candy / Neurotic / Inspection station / Deadbeats / I know what boys like.

Jan 97. (7") *<(BYO 36)>* **THE BALLAD OF JOHNNY X. / HERE WE GO / HEADLIGHT DITCH** [ ] [ ] Jan96

Jan 97. (lp/cd) *<(BYO 37/+CD)>* **MANIACAL LAUGHTER** [ ] [ ] Jan96
– Lamar vannoy / No rules / The nerds, the freaks and the romantics / Argyle / All of this and nothing / The BMX song / Quick check girl / Headlights . . . ditch! / Here we go / Born to lose / Moon over Asbury / The ballad of Johnny X.

Epitaph Epitaph

Oct 97. (cd/c/lp) *<(6510-2/-4/-1)>* **BOUNCING SOULS** [ ] [ ] Sep96
– Cracked / Say anything / K8 is great / Low life / Chunksong / East side mags / The toilet song / Single successful guy / Whatever I want (whatever that is) / Serenity / Party at 174 / Holiday cocktail lounge / The screamer / Eastcoast! fuck you! / I like your eyes / Shark attack.

Nov 98. (m-cd) *<(6549-2)>* **TIE, ONE ON! (live)** [ ] [ ]
– Say anything / Lamar Vannoy / K8 is great / Chunksong / Argyle / Born to lose / Here we go / Kid (studio track).

May 99. (cd/lp) *<(6550-2/-1)>* **HOPELESS ROMANTIC** [ ] [ ]
– Hopeless romantic / '87 / Kid / Fight to live / Bullying the jukebox / You're so rad / Night on earth / Monday morning ant brigade / Ole! / Undeniable / Wish me well (go to hell) / It's not the heat, it's the humanity / The whole thing.

Oct 99. (7"/cd-s) *(1024-7/-2)* **FIGHT TO LIVE / HERE WE GO (live) / NEUROTIC (live)** [ ] [-]

Jun 00. (cd-s) **!OLE! / 15 SECOND SNIPPET / 10 SECOND SNIPPET** [ ] [-]

—— **MICHAEL McDERMOTT** – drums; repl. SHALL

May 01. (cd/lp) *<(6606-2/-1)>* **HOW I SPENT MY SUMMER VACATION** [ ] [ ]
– That song / Private radio / True believers / Better life / The something special / Broken record / Lifetime / Manthem / Breakup song / Streetlife serenade (to no one) / Late bloomer / No comply / Gone.

– compilations, etc. –

2000. (cd) *Chunksaah;* **THE BAD, THE WORSE AND THE OUT OF PRINT** [-] [-] Europe
– The ballad of Johnny X / Mommy, can I go out and kill tonight? / Quick check girl / Kids in America / P.M.R.C. / Slave to fashion / Code blue / Lamar Vannoy / Punk uprisings theme / Kicked in the head / St. Jude's day / Pervert / Don't you (forget about me) / Spank / Like a fish in water / Born to lose / Dirt / East Coast! fuck you! / I started drinking again / Instrumental / Here we go / Neurotic.

BOW WOW

Formed: Japan . . . 1976 by KYOJI YAMAMOTO, MITSHHIRO SAITO, KENJI SANO and TOSHIRI NIIMI. Quintessentially Japanese, this hard-rock/metal outfit had clearly soaked up the music of classic western bands such as KISS and DEEP PURPLE, attempting to translate it for the domestic market. Staggeringly prolific, they released over ten albums in six years, each becoming steadily more derivative. In the early 80's, the band switched to funny Engrish-ranguage (sorry!) vocals as well as slightly altering their name to avoid confusion with UK pop/punk outfit, BOW WOW WOW. Now operating under the revised moniker of VOW WOW, they enlisted GENKI HITOMI and REI ATSUMI to replace the outgoing SAITO, 'BEAT OF METAL MOTION' (1984) being the first studio outing for the new look band. Despite a concerted effort to pursue a more commercial direction, VOW WOW remained little more than a cult act outside their native Japan. A surprise addition to the line-up came in the shape of British keyboard veteran, NEIL MURRAY, who appeared on two 'Arista' albums, 'VOW WOW V' (1987) and 'HELTER SKELTER' (1989).

Album rating: BOW WOW (*6) / SIGNAL FIRE (*5) / CHARGE (*5) / SUPER LIVE (*5) / GUARANTEE (*6) / THE BOW WOW compilation (*6) / GLORIOUS ROAD (*6) / TELEPHONE (*6) / X BOMBER (*6) / HARD DOG (*6) / ASIAN VOLCANO (*4) / WARNING FROM STARDUST (*5) / HOLY EXPEDITION (*4) / Vow Wow: BEAT OF METAL MOTION (*5) / CYCLONE (*5) / LIVE: VOW WOW (*5) / VOW WOW V (*4) / HELTER SKELTER (*5)

KYOJI YAMAMOTO – vocals, guitar / **MITSUHIRO SAITO** – vocals, guitar / **KENJI SANO** – bass / **TOSHIRI NIIMI** – drums

Invitation not iss.

1976. (lp) *(VIH 6005)* **SIGNAL FIRE** [-] [-] Japan
– Get on your train / Silver lightning / Rock'n'roll drive / Tell me tell me / Just one more night / Electric power up / Rainbow of sabbath / Still.

1976. (lp) *(VIH 6009)* **BOW WOW** [-] [-] Japan
– Hearts on fire / Brown house / Foxy lady / Volume on / A life in the dark / James in my casket / Withered sun / Theme of Bow Wow.

1977. (lp) *(VIH 6013)* **CHARGE** [-] [-] Japan
– Jet jive / Must say adieu / Blue eyed lady / The clown / Rock and roll kid / Fallen leaves / Heavy / Sister soul / Behind the mask.

1978. (lp) *(VIH 6022)* **SUPER LIVE (live)** [-] [-] Japan
– Heart's on fire / Jet jive / Still / Get on your train / Just one more night / Theme of Bow Wow / Summertime blues.

1978. (lp) *(VIH 6035)* **GUARENTEE** [-] [-] Japan
– (Japanese titles).

1979. (lp) *(VIH 6049)* **THE BOW WOW** (compilation) [-] [-] Japan
– Prelude / Get on your train / Just one more night / Tell me tell me / Signal fire / The clown / Heart's on fire / Jet jive / A life in the dark / Rock'n'roll drive / Theme of Bow Wow / Summertime blues.

S.M.S. not iss.

1979. (lp) **GLORIOUS ROAD** [-] [-] Japan

1980. (lp) *(SM 28-5059)* **TELEPHONE** [-] [-] Japan
– Hot rod tornado / Good times rock'n'roll / Lullaby of Jenny / Carnival / Keep on rockin' / Lonesome way / Rolling night / Tomorrow in your life / Short piece.

1980. (lp) **X BOMBER** [-] [-] Japan

1981. (lp) **HARD DOG** [-] [-] Japan

—— YAMAMOTO released 2 solo albums, 'HORIZONS' (1980) and 'ELECTRIC CINEMA' (1982)

V.A.P. not iss.

1982. (lp) **ASIAN VOLCANO** [-] [-] Japan

Heavy Metal not iss.

Apr 83. (lp) *(HMILP 5)* **WARNING FROM STARDUST** [ ] [-]
– You're mine / Jets / Clean machine / Can't get back to you / Heels of the wind / Poor man's Eden / 20th century child / Abnormal weather / Welcome to the monster city / Breakout the trick / Warning from stardust.

Nov 83. (7") *(HMINT 2)* **YOU'RE MINE. / DON'T CRY BABY** [ ] [-]

Roadrunner not iss.

1983. (lp) *(RR 9881)* **HOLY EXPEDITION** [-] [-] Japan
– Getting back on the road / You're mine / Touch me, I'm on fire / Can't get back to you / Don't cry baby / 20th century child / Devil woman / Theme of Bow Wow.

VOW WOW

—— **GENKI HITOMI** – vocals + **REI ATSUMI** – keyboards, vocals; repl. SAITO

V.A.P. not iss.

1984. (lp) **BEAT OF METAL MOTION** [-] [-] Japan
– Break down / Too late to turn back / Mask of flesh (masquerade) / Diamond night / Feel alright / Baby it's alright / Lonely fairy / Sleeping in a dream house / Rock me / Beat of metal motion. *(re-iss. 1986 on 'East World'; CA 32-1255)*

East Rock not iss.

Jul 86. (lp/c) *(ERLP/ERMC 50)* **CYCLONE** [ ] [-]
– Premonition / Hurricane / Hellraisers wanted / Love walks / U.S.A. / Need your love / Eclipse / Siren song / Shake your body / Rock your cradle / You know what I mean. *(Jap-iss.1985 on 'East World'; CA 32-1149)*

East World not iss.

1986. (lp) *(CA 32-1211)* **III** [-] [-] Japan
– Go insane / Shot in the dark / Running wild / Shock waves / Doncha wanna cum (hangar 15) / Nightless city / Sign of the times / Stay close tonight / You got it made / Pains of love.

Passport not iss.

Feb 87. (lp) *(PBL/+T 102)* **LIVE: VOW WOW (live)** [-] [-] Japan
– Introduction – Beat of metal motion / Doncha wanna come (hangar 15) / Too late to turn back / Mask of flesh (masquerade) / Pains of love / Love walks / Premonition / Hurricane / Shot in the dark / Nightless city. *(Jap-iss.1986 as 'HARD ROCK NIGHT' +=; CA 32-1274)* – (extra tracks).

—— **NEIL MURRAY** – bass (ex-COLOSSEUM, ex-GARY MOORE, WHITESNAKE) repl. SANO

Arista Arista

Sep 87. (7") *(RIS 38)* **DON'T LEAVE ME NOW. / NIGHTLESS CITY** [ ] [ ]
(12"+=) *(RIST 38)* – Shot in the dark.

Oct 87. (lp/c/cd) *(208/408/258 678)* **VOW WOW V** [ ] [ ]
– Don't tell lies / Somewhere in the night / The girl in red / Break out / Cry no more / Same town / Born to die / Waited for a lifetime / Don't leave me now / War man. *(cd+=)* – Don't leave me now (extended).

Nov 87. (7") *(RIS 46)* **CRY NO MORE. / SIGN OF THE TIMES** [ ] [ ]
(12"+=) *(RIST 46)* – Shockwaves.

Feb 88. (12"pic-d) *(609805)* **DON'T TELL ME LIES. / SIREN SONG (live)** [ ] [-]

Jul 88. (7"/7"pic-d) *(VWW/+PK 1)* **ROCK ME NOW. / DON'T WANNA COME** [ ] [ ]
(12"+=/cd-s+=) *(12VWW/VWWCD 1)* – Girl in red / Somewhere in the night / Don't leave me now.

Feb 89. (7"/7"g-f/7"pic-d) *(VWW/+G/PD 2)* **HELTER SKELTER. / KEEP ON MOVING**
(12"+=) *(12VWW 2)* – Sign of the times.
(3"cd-s+=) *(662013)* – Fade away.
Feb 89. (lp/c/cd) *(209/409/259 691)* **HELTER SKELTER**
– I feel the power / Talking 'bout you / Spellbound / Helter skelter / The boy / Rock me now / Turn on the night / Never let you go / Night by night / You're the one for me. *(cd+=)* – Sign of the times.
Apr 89. (7") *(VWW 3)* **I FEEL THE POWER. / SHOT IN THE DARK**
(10"+=) *(10VWW 3)* – Hurricane / You know what I mean.
(12"+=) *(12VWW 3)* – Hurricane / Nightless city.
— split in 1990.

- compilations, etc. -

Mar 88. (d-lp/d-c) *Heavy Metal; (HMI LP/MC 109)* **VOW WOW** –
– (2 earlier albums).

BOY HITS CAR

Formed: Los Angeles, California, USA . . . 1993 by CRegg, LOUIS, SCOTT and MICHAEL. Hailing from the same scene that spawned the nu-metal likes of KORN, PAPA ROACH and SYSTEM OF A DOWN, the strangely named BOY HITS CAR could only look on in envy as their compadres all hit the major label big time. They had to make do with Texas indie imprint, 'Seismic', who issued their debut album, 'MY ANIMAL', in 1998. Conjuring a more expansive, spiritual sound than most of their erstwhile scenesters, the band's perseverance was finally vindicated when they signed to 'Epic' subsidiary, 'Wind-Up' (home to CREED) for 2000's eponymous set.

Album rating: MY ANIMAL (*5) / BOY HITS CAR (*7)

CRegg – vocals / **LOUIS** – guitar / **SCOTT** – bass / **MICHAEL** – drums

not iss. Seismic
May 98. (cd) **MY ANIMAL** –
– Hope / Clear / I'm a cloud / La playa / Happy / Mr. Loh / Make me pure / A letter from prison / Fury 'n' I / Benkei / In the lateness of a day / My animal.
Wind-Up Wind-Up
Apr 01. (cd) *<(501964-2)>* **BOY HITS CAR**
– The rebirth / Lovecore (welcome to) / As I watch the sun fuck the ocean / I'm a cloud / Man without skin / A letter from prison / Unheard / Going to India / Turning inward / Benkel / Before we die.

BOY SETS FIRE

Formed: Delaware, USA . . . 1994 by NATHAN GRAY, JOSH LATSHAW, CHAD ISTVAN, DARRELL HYDE and MATT KRUPANSKI. Playing militant yet emotionally fraught agit-prop hardcore in the traditional sense of the term, BOY SETS FIRE first blazed a trail across the scene in 1995 with a self financed debut single, 'Consider'. This was followed by a split single and finally, on the 'Initial' label, a debut album, 'THE DAY THE SUN WENT OUT' (1997). A second split was in turn followed by a sophomore album, 'IN CHRYSALIS' (1999), after which HYDE was replaced by ROB AVERY. Despite the reservations of some fans, a move to the larger 'Victory' label for 'AFTER THE EULOGY' (2000) found them as politically uncompromising as ever. The mini-set, 'THIS CRYING, THIS SCREAMING, MY VOICE IS BEING BORN' was released later the same year. • **Covered:** LIVE WIRE (Motley Crue).

Album rating: THE DAY THE SUN WENT OUT (*6) / AFTER THE EULOGY (*6)

NATHAN GRAY – vocals / **CHAD ISTVAN** – guitar / **JOSH LATSHAW** – guitar / **DARRELL HYDE** – bass / **MATT KRUPANSKI** – drums

not iss. own label
1995. (7"; split w/ JAZZ MAN'S NEEDLE) **CONSIDER. /** –
Initial Initial
Oct 97. (lp/cd) *<(IR 19/+CD)>* **THE DAY THE SUN WENT OUT**
– Pure / Cringe / The fine art of falling / Another badge of courage / Swingset / The power remains the same / In hope / Toy gun anthem / Cadence / 65 factory outlets / Hometown report card / Live wire.
Jan 99. (m-cd) **IN CHRYSALIS** –
not iss. Equal Vision
Aug 99. (cd-ep; shared with SNAPCASE) *<EQV 51>* **SNAPCASE vs BOY SETS FIRE** –
– (two by SNAPCASE) / Unspoken request / Channel.
— BOY SETS FIRE also split an EP with COALESCE around the late 90's
— **ROB AVERY** – bass; repl. HYDE
Victory Victory
Apr 00. (lp/cd) *<(VR 119/+CD)>* **AFTER THE EULOGY**
– After the eulogy / Rookie / Pariah under glass / When rhetoric dies / Still waiting for the punchline / The abominations of those virtuous / Our time honorer tradition of cannibalism / (Compassion) As skull fragments on the wall / My life in the knife trade / Across five years / Twelve step hammer program / Unspoken request / The force majeure.
not iss. Magic Bullet
Nov 00. (m-cd) **THIS CRYING, THIS SCREAMING, MY VOICE IS BEING BORN** –
– Vehicle / In the wilderness . . . no one can hear you scream / Endorsement / Blame (live at eleven) / My own restraints / Resection.

BOYZZ

Formed: USA . . . 1977 by DIRTY DAN BUCK, ANATOLE HALINKOVITCH, GIL PINI, MIKE TAFOYA, DAVID ANGEL and KENT COOPER. Starting out as a leather-clad biker band, they played a blend of Southern-style hard rock, once the ground of their peers, LYNYRD SKYNYRD and BLACK OAK ARKANSAS. Following a solitary album, 'TOO WILD TO TAME' in 1978, the band split up, some of the members reappearing in 1982 as the abysmally titled, B'ZZ.

Album rating: TOO WILD TO TAME (*4) / B'zz: GET UP (*4)

DIRTY DAN BUCK – vocals, harmonica, percussion, guitar / **MIKE TAFOYA** – guitar / **GIL PINI** – guitar, vocals / **ANATOLE HALINKOVITCH** – keyboards / **DAVID ANGEL** – bass, vocals / **KENT COOPER** – percussion, drums

Epic Epic
Nov 78. (7") *<50610>* **HOOCHIE COOCHIE. / WAKE IT UP, SHAKE IT UP** –
Feb 79. (lp) *(EPC 82995) <35440>* **TOO WILD TO TAME** Nov78
– Too wild to tame / Hoochie koochie / Wake it up, shake it up / Shady lady / Back to Kansas / Destined to die / Lean 'n' mean / Dianne (part 2) / Good life shuffle.
Mar 79. (7") *<50685>* **SHADY LADY. / DIANNE (part 2)** –

B'ZZ

TAFOYA, HALINKOVITCH + ANGEL subsequently became this bunch, alongside **TOM HOLLAND** – vocals / **STEVE RILEY** – drums

Oct 82. (lp) *(25080) <38230>* **GET UP**
– Get up get angry / Too much to ask for / Caught in the middle / Steal my love / When you love / Make it through the night / I love the way / Take your time / Not my girl / Runaway love affair.
Nov 82. (7") *<03819>* **RUNAWAY LOVE AFFAIR. / TOO MUCH TO ASK FOR** –
— folded in 1983, RILEY later joined W.A.S.P, while HOLLAND formed his own named outfit

B-PEOPLE

Formed: Los Angeles, California, USA . . . March 1979 out of various punk outfits by PAT DELANEY (ex-DEADBEATS; one mid'78 EP exists, 'KILL THE HIPPIES' for 'Dangerhouse' IQ 29), ALEX GIBSON, FREDRIK NILSEN and TOM RECCHION (the latter both ex-DOO DOOETTES; some recordings exist from 1976). The early 80's saw B-PEOPLE release their only two EP's, 'YOU AT EIGHT' and the eponymous 'B-PEOPLE', the band's provocatively experimental material later collected together for posterity on the 1986 compilation, 'PETRIFIED CONDITIONS 1979-1981'. Before their split they did manage to appear on V/A compilation, 'Let Them Eat Jellybeans', with the track 'PERSECUTION – THAT'S MY SONG'. MICHAEL GIRA (later SWANS) and PAUL CUTLER were said to have been part of the band prior to their demise.

Album rating: PETRIFIED CONDITIONS 1979-1981 compilation (*6)

PAT DELANEY – synthesizer, saxophone (ex-DEADBEATS) / **ALEX GIBSON** – guitar, vocals / **FREDRIK NILSEN** – bass, vocals, saxophone (ex-DOO DOOETTES) / **TOM RECCHION** – drums (ex-DOO DOOETTES)

not iss. Faulty
May 81. (7"m) *<FP 03>* **YOU AT EIGHT. / WEATHER TO WORRY / M.C.P.D.** –
Feb 82. (12"ep) *<FEP 1300>* **B-PEOPLE** –
— MICHAEL GIRA and PAUL CUTLER could well have been members before they split. In 1984, ALEX GIBSON scored the soundtrack for the film, 'SUBURBIA', which was released by 'Enigma' in the US-only.

- compilations, etc. -

1986. (lp) *Restless; <72029-1>* **PETRIFIED CONDITIONS 1979-1981** –

BRACKET

Formed: Forestville, California, USA . . . early 90's (although they had been playing together since their schooldays in the mid 80's) by MARTY GREGORI, LARRY TINNEY, ZACK CHARLOS and RAY CARLOS. After a series of low-key independently released singles, the band finally delivered their debut album for 'Caroline', '924 FORESTVILLE ST.' in 1994. Another Virgin offshoot, 'Hi-Rise' handled them in the UK, the one-time ardent AC/DC fans now trading in a Power-punk sound closer to GREEN DAY. The following year, BRACKET consolidated their rise with a DON FLEMING-produced second set, '4-WHEEL VIBE', a series of previously recorded 45's flooding onto the UK market courtesy of FAT MIKE's (NOFX) 'Fat Wreck Chords'. This label also masterminded their following two sets, 'E IS FOR EVERYTHING' (1996) and 'NOVELTY FOREVER' (1997). The millennium got underway for BRACKET with the release of their fourth full set, 'WHEN ALL ELSE FAILS' (2000).

Album rating: 924 FORESTVILLE ST. (*6) / 4-WHEEL VIBE (*6) / E IS FOR EVERYTHING (*5) / NOVELTY FOREVER (*5) / WHEN ALL ELSE FAILS (*5)

MARTY GREGORI – vocals, guitar / **LARRY TINNEY** – guitar / **ZACK CHARLOS** – bass / **RAY CARLOS** – drums

Hi-Rise Hut

Jan 95. (12"ep) *(FLAT 13)* <5045> **PRESENTS . . . "5.35"**
– Huge balloon / Why should eye.
(cd-ep+=) *(FLATSCD 13)* – Mother to blame.

Hi-Rise Caroline

Mar 95. (cd/c/lp) *(FLAT CD/MC/LP 15)* <CAROLCD 1754> **924 FORESTVILLE ST.** 1994
– Get it rite / Dodge ball / Missing link / Sleep / Huge balloon / Stalking stuffer / Why should eye / Warren's song (pt.1) / Warren's song (pt.2) / Can't make me / Skanky love song / J. Weed / Rod's post. *(cd re-iss. Jun97 on 'Caroline'; same as US)*

May 95. (cd/c/lp) *(FLAT CD/MC/LP 17)* <CAROLCD 1787> **4-WHEEL VIBE**
– Circus act / Cool aid / Happy to be sad / John Wilkes isolation booth / Tractor / Green apples / Closed caption / Trailer park / Fresh air / PC / G-vibe / Warren's song (pt.4) / 2 hotdogs for 99c / The metal one / Pesimist / Lazy / My stepson. *(cd re-iss. Jun97 on 'Caroline'; same as US)*

Fat Wreck Chords Fat Wreck Chords

May 95. (7") *<(FAT 516-7)>* **STINKY FINGERS. /**
Oct 95. (7") *<(FAT 530-7)>* **FOR THOSE ABOUT TO MOCK. /**
Nov 95. (cd-s) *(FLATSCD 23)* **TRAILER PARK / STYLIN' / WARREN'S SONG PART 5** -
(above issued on 'Hi-Rise')
Nov 96. (m-cd) *<(FAT 548CD)>* **E IS FOR EVERYTHING**
– Hermit / 2RAK005 / Speed bump / WWF / Talk show / Flea market / Eating pie / My stepson / Envy / Warren's song (part 3).
Nov 96. (d7"ep) *<(FAT 549)>* **F IS FOR FAT**
Sep 97. (cd) *<FAT 559>* **NOVELTY FOREVER** -
– Last day Sunday / Three gardens / Exit bean / Don't tell Miss Fenley / Sour / Back to Allentown / Little Q & A / One more hangover day / I won't mind / Optimism / Drama queen / Little Q & A.
May 00. (lp/cd) *<(FAT 607/+CD)>* **WHEN ALL ELSE FAILS**
– Everyone is telling me I'll never win if I fall in love with a girl from Marin / Parade / No brainer / Spazz / Cynically depressed / Warren's song part 9 / Me Vs. the world / You/me / SOB story / A happy song / Suicide note / Yoko oh-no / A place in time.

BRAD

Formed: Seattle, Washington, USA . . . 1992 by SHAWN SMITH, who had spread his soulful vocal talent around groups like PIGEONHED and SATCHEL. He teamed up with PEARL JAM guitarist STONE GOSSARD and two others, JEREMY TOBACK and REGAN HAGAR, to complete a debut album, 'SHAME', in 1993. An evocative, free-form affair, the album utilised influences from an eclectic array of musical styles, garnering rave reviews and notching up respectable sales. They returned four years later with the follow-up, 'INTERIORS', SMITH and REGAN having recorded two albums in the interim, 'E.D.C.' and 'FAMILY', both under the moniker of SATCHEL. Meanwhile, PIGEONHED (SMITH and producer, STEVE FISK again) were delivering their second set for 'Sub Pop', 'THE FULL SENTENCE' (1997), having given us an eponymous headtrippin' set in '93.

Album rating: SHAME (*7) / INTERIORS (*6) / Satchel: E.D.C. (*7) / THE FAMILY (*7) / Pigeonhed: PIGEONHED (*6) / THE FULL SENTENCE (*7)

SHAWN SMITH – vocals, piano / **STONE GOSSARD** – guitar (of PEARL JAM) / **JEREMY TOBACK** – bass / **REGAN HAGAR** – drums (of MALFUNKSHUN)

Epic Epic

May 93. (cd/c/lp) *<(473596-2/-4/-1)>* **SHAME** 72
– Buttercup / My fingers / Nadine / Screen / 20th century / Raise love / Bad for the soul / Down / Rock star / We. *(re-iss. Aug95; same)*
Jun 93. (7") *(659248-7)* **20TH CENTURY. / SKIN** 64
(cd-s+=) *(659248-2)* – ('A'mixes).
Jun 97. (cd/c) *<(487921-2/-4)>* **INTERIORS**
– Secret girl / The day brings / Lift / I don't know / Upon my shoulders / Sweet Al George / The funeral song / Circle and line / Some never come home / Candles / Those three words.

SATCHEL

SMITH + HAGAR plus **JOHN HOAG** – guitar / **CORY KANE** – bass

Epic Epic

Sep 94. (cd/c/lp) *<(477314-2/-4/-1)>* **E.D.C.**
– Mr. Brown / Equilibrium / Taste it / Trouble come down / More ways than 3 / Hollywood / O / Mr. Pink / Built 4 it / Mr. Blue / Willow / Roof almighty / Suffering.
Sep 96. (cd/c) *<(484428-2/-4)>* **THE FAMILY**
– Isn't that right / Without love / Not too late / Criminal justice / Breathe deep / Time "O" the year / For so long / Some more trouble / Tomorrow / Roll on / Breathe deep (instrumental dub).

PIGEONHED

SHAWN SMITH – vocals, guitars, keyboards, drums / **STEVE FISK** – keyboards, loops, producer (of PELL MELL and a solo artist)

Sub Pop Sub Pop

Jun 93. (cd-ep) **THEME FROM PIGEONHED EP**
– Theme from Pigeonhed / Trial by sex / Ain't it so / Theme from Pigeonhed (Overbaked & Lonely X 1000 salvation remix).
Jul 93. (lp/cd) *<(SP/+CD 101/273)>* **PIGEONHED**
– Theme from Pigeonhed / Ain't it so / Special way / Her / Lovely lines / Cadillac / Trial by sex / Salome / Brothers / Buzz / Grace. *(cd re-iss. Oct98; SP 224B)*

—— next added guests JERRY CANTRELL + KIM THAYIL

Feb 97. (lp/cd) *<(SP/+CD 373)>* **THE FULL SENTENCE**
– It's like the man said / The full sentence / Marry me / Keep on keepin' on / Battle flag / Glory bound / P-street / Phunpurephun / Who's to blame / 31st of July / More than just a girl / Fire's coming down / For those gone on / Honor. *(cd re-iss. Aug97 on 'Warners'; 9878 70224-2)*

Warners Sub Pop

Jun 97. (7") *<SP 405>* **GLORY BOUND. /** -
Oct 97. (12"/cd-s) *(W 0420 T/CD)* **IT'S LIKE THE MAN SAID (remixes) / BATTLEFLAG (Lo Fidelity Allstars remix) / MARRY ME**
Mar 98. (cd) *(9878 70408-2)* *<SP 408>* **PIGEONHED'S FLASHBULB EMERGENCY** Oct97
– Full sentence / Phunperephun / Glory bound / Battle flag / Marry me / It's like the man said / Keep on keepin' on / Marry me / Full sentence.

Brian BRAIN

Born: MARTYN ATKINS, 3 Aug'59, Coventry, Midlands, England. The drummer had cut his teeth in an outfit caled MYND before being snapped up by JOHN LYDON (ex-JOHNNY ROTTEN of the SEX PISTOLS) for his avant-garde punks, PUBLIC IMAGE LTD. While contributing on their live set, 'Paris Au Printemps' in 1980, ATKINS departed only to return the following year. Meanwhile, ATKINS (under the guise of BRIAN BRAIN) issued a handful of releases on the 'Secret' imprint, although these were initially of novelty/experimental value. His backing band at the time consisted of BOBBY SURGEONER and PETE JONES, the latter another to join ATKINS on his second expedition to PiL. Having left PiL for the last time, BRIAN BRAIN delivered a few low key disasters before ATKINS was invited to join KILLING JOKE at the turn of the decade. This led to ATKINS collaborating with a plethora of musicians (including CHRIS CONNELLY) on the PIGFACE project, releasing several dark experimental noise albums in the process. • **Covered:** AT HOME HE'S A TOURIST (Gang Of Four) / CAREERING (PiL).

Album rating: UNEXPECTED NOISES (*4) / Pigface: GUB (*4) / WELCOME TO MEXICO (*5) / FOOK (*7) / NOTES FROM THE UNDERGROUND (*5) / FEELS LIKE HEAVEN . . . SOUNDS LIKE SHIT (*5) / A NEW HIGH IN LOW (*4) / BELOW THE BELT (*4) / EAT SHIT, YOU FUCKING REDNECK (*6)

MARTYN ATKINS – drums, vocals / **PETE JONES** (b.22 Sep'57) – bass / **BOBBY SURGEONER** – vocals, guitar

Secret not iss.

Apr 80. (7") *(SHH 101)* **THEY'VE GOT ME IN THE BOTTLE. / I GET PAIN** -
Aug 80. (7") *(SHH 105)* **ANOTHER MILLION MILES. / PERSONALITY COUNTS** -
Nov 80. (lp) *(BRAIN 1)* **UNEXPECTED NOISES** -
– Another million miles / Our man in Hong Kong / I get pain / The hots for you / The asthma game / Brainstorm / Unexpected noises / They've got me in the bottle / Dirty dealing in the lone star state / Turn it into noise / I'm suffocating / Jet boats up the Ganges.
Jan 81. (12"ep) *(12SHH 109)* **CULTURE** -
– Fun people / Working in a farmyard in a white suit / At home he's a tourist / Careering.
Dec 81. (7") *(SHH 119)* **JIVE JIVE. / HELLO TO THE WORKING CLASS** 7-
Oct 82. (7"/12") *(SHH 142/+12)* **FUNKY ZOO. / FLIES** -

—— left PiL and retired for a while. **MARGOT OLAVARRIA** – bass (ex-GO-GO'S) repl. PETE who joined PiL

Wide Angle not iss.

Jul 86. (7") **FUN WITH MUSIC. /** -

—— ATKINS joined KILLING JOKE and then PIGFACE in the 90's

PIGFACE

—— **MARTIN ATKINS** with **TRENT REZNOR** (Nine Inch Nails) / **BILL RIEFLIN** (Ministry / Revolting Cocks) / **OGRE** (Skinny Puppy) / **EN ESCH** (K.M.F.D.M.) / **DAVID YOW** (Jesus Lizard) / **CHRIS CONNELLY** (Revolting Cocks / solo) **WILLIAM TUCKER** (Ministry / Scornflakes) / **MATT SCHULTZ** (A.T.G.) / producer **STEVE ALBINI** (ex-Big Black)

Anagram not iss.

Feb 91. (cd/lp) *(CD+/GRAM 47)* **GUB** -
– Tapeworm / The bushmaster / Cylinder head world / Point blank / Suck / Symphony for taps / The greenhouse / Little sisters / Tailor made / War ich nicht immer ein guter junge? (remix) / Blood and sand / Weightless. *(re-iss. Sep91 on 'Devotion' cd/c/lp; CD/T+/DVN 2) (cd re-iss. Mar96 on 'Invisible'+=; INV 009CD)* – Tonight's the night (little sisters) (remix) / Winnebago induced tapeworm (remix) / Bushmaster bushmaster (remix) / War ich nicht immer.

—— **PAUL RAVEN** (Killing Joke) + **PAUL BARKER** (Ministry) + **MARY BYKER** (Gaye Bykers On Acid) repl. ESCH

Devotion Devotion

Nov 91. (cd/c/d-lp) *(<CD/T+/DVN 3>)* **WELCOME TO MEXICO**
– The love serenade (I hate you?) / Blood and sand / Peaking too early (William) / Little sisters / Twice removed / Beneath my feet / Point blank / Stowaway / Suck / Weightless / T.F.W.O. / Lash – Herb – Taxi / Tapeworm / The breakfast conspiracy. *(cd re-iss. Mar96 on 'Invisible'; INV 011CD)*
Oct 92. (cd/c/lp) *(<CD/T+/DVN 18>)* **FOOK**
– Alles ist mein / Ten ground & down / Seven words / Insemination / Hips, tits, lips, power / Satellite / I'm still alive / Auto hag / Go / I can do no wrong. *(cd re-iss. Mar96 on 'Invisible'; INV 018CD)*
Nov 93. (d-cd) *(<CDDVN 25>)* **TRUTH WILL OUT / WASHINGMACHINE MOUTH**
– TRUTH WILL OUT:- Can you feel pain? / War ich nicht / Point blank / Do no wrong / Weightless / White trash reggae – Pigface in your area / Alle ist mein / Hips tits lips power / 7 words / Henry / Jungle bells / Suck // WASHINGMACHINE MOUTH:- Flowers are evil / Cutting face / Satan on the inside looking in / H.T.L. a) Red around the eye, b) The calm before the storm, c) The return of wet brain 2000 / Cutting face-gas mash mix / Satellite – Needle in the groove / No damage done / Prepare to die go! go! go! / The last word. *(re-iss. Mar96 on 'Invisible'; INV 026CD & INV 021CD)*

Nov 94. (cd) (<CDDVN 29>) **NOTES FROM THE UNDERGROUND**
– Asshole / Dive bomber / Your own your own / Fuck it up / Hagseed / Chicksaw / Empathy / Magazine / Think / Trivial scene / Slut / Blood / Pain / Psalm springs eternal / Steamroller / Your music is garbage.

Invisible Invisible

Nov 95. (cd) (<INV 034CD>) **FEELS LIKE HEAVEN . . . SOUNDS LIKE SHIT**
– (Dialogue) / Think / Steamroller / Hagseed / (Dialogue) / Fuck it up / Chikasaw / Suck / Asphole / Steamroller / Sick asp fuck / (Dialogue) / Empathy / Divebomber / Chikasaw / Chikasaw.

Sep 97. (cd) <(INV 063CD)> **A NEW HIGH IN LOW** Aug97
– Radio bagpipe / Kiss king (high high high) / Burundi / Bring unto me / More / Nutopia / Methylated: . . . / Aboriginal / Metal tangerine / First taken third found / Warzone / You know – you know – you know / Howler: an English breakfast / Train / Howler: an English breakfast.

Jun 98. (cd) <(INV 099CD)> **BELOW THE BELT**
– Radio bagpipe / Kiss king / Burundi / More / Nutopia / More methylated / Metal tangerine / First taken third found / Burundi / Nutopia / More / Warzone / You know . . .

Oct 98. (cd) <(INV 122CD)> **EAT SHIT YOU FUCKIN' REDNECK**

– compilations, etc. –

Jul 93. (12") *Invisible; (INV 008T)* **SPOON BREAKFAST. /** -

Jul 93. (lp/cd) *Invisible; (INV 012/+2)* **LEAN JUICY PARK** (interviews) -

Aug 93. (12"/c-s; BRIAN BRAIN) *(INV 005 T/C)* **EP**

BRICK LAYER CAKE

Formed: Chicago, Illinois, USA . . . early 90's by STEVE ALBINI cohort and SHELLAC drummer, TODD TRAINER, initially as a diversion from his main occupation. Roping in GERARD BOISSY from RIFLE SPORT and producer BRIAN 'EXPENSIVE' PAULSON, TRAINER signed to 'Touch & Go' and released a debut mini album, 'CALL IT A DAY' (1991) – containing their first EP release 'EYE FOR AN EYE, TOOTH FOR A TOOTH'. Hypnotic, noisy and occasionally dreamy, the record's guitar swirls brought to mind the likes of J&MC and LOOP. A full three years passed before their follow-up, 'TRAGEDY – TRAGEDY' hit the shops, an equally intense offering that would serve as a swansong.

Album rating: CALL IT A DAY + EYE FOR AN EYE, TOOTH FOR A TOOTH (*5) / TRAGEDY – TRAGEDY (*6)

TODD TRAINER – drums (of SHELLAC) / **GERARD BOISSY** (ex-RIFLE SPORT) / **BRIAN 'EXPENSIVE' PAULSON** – producer, etc

not iss. Restless

1990. (12"ep) **EYE FOR AN EYE, TOOTH FOR A TOOTH** -

Touch & Go Touch & Go

Nov 91. (lp/cd; BRICK LAYER CAKE featuring TODD TRAINER) <(TG 75/+CD)> **CALL IT A DAY**
– Night / Sitting pretty / Call it a day / Show stopper / Kiss of death / Killer / Execution / Boissy flour Paulson trainer / Happy hour / Curtains / Clockwork / Eye for an eye / Going to go / Winter park. *<(cd+=)>* – EYE FOR AN EYE, TOOTH FOR A TOOTH

Oct 94. (lp/cd) <(TG 127/+CD)> **TRAGEDY – TRAGEDY**
– Christ / Gone today / Thin ice / Precious / Thirteenth drink / Cold day in Hell / Reach me now / Doomsday / Cakewalkmusic / Elevenovens / Boissy Paulson / Trainer / Icing Inc.

—— nothing heard from them after above; TODD's still with SHELLAC

BRIGHTON ROCK

Formed: Toronto, Canada . . . 1984 by GREDD FRASER, GERRY McGHEE, STEVIE SKREEBS, MARK CAVARZAN and MARTIN VICTOR (the latter was replaced by JOHNNY ROGERS after their first release). Kickstarting their career by financing a debut EP, the group soon attracted the attention of 'Warner Brothers', who immediately re-pressed the record. They finally released their first album proper in early '87, 'YOUNG, WILD AND FREE', winning many fans in rock press. A second set, 'TAKE A DEEP BREATH', was another for the production connoisseur, although the songwriting quality was questionable.

Album rating: TAKE A DEEP BREATH (*5) / YOUNG, WILD AND FREE (*5) / LOVE MACHINE (*4)

GERRY McGHEE – vocals / **GREDD FRASER** – guitar, vocals / **MARTIN VICTOR** – keyboards / **STEVIE SKREEBS** – bass, vocals / **MARK CAVARZAN** – drums

not iss. Flying Fist

1986. (12"ep) <252934-1> **BRIGHTON ROCK** - - Canada
– Young, wild & free / Assault attack / Barricade / The fool's waltz. *<re-iss. 1986 by 'Warners'; >*

—— **JOHNNY ROGERS** – keyboards, vocals; repl. VICTOR

Atlantic Warners

Feb 87. (lp/c) <(K 253055-1/-4)> **YOUNG, WILD AND FREE**
– We came to rock / Game of love / Change of heart / Can't wait for the night / Assault attack / Jack is back / Save me / Nobody's hero / Barricade / Rock'n'roll.

WEA WEA

May 89. (lp/c)(cd) *(WX 272/+C)*<(255969-2)> **TAKE A DEEP BREATH**
– Can't stop the earth from shaking / Outlaw / Hangin' high n' dry / One more try / Unleash the rage / Power overload / Shootin' for love / Love slips away / Ride the rainbow / Rebels with a cause.

1991. (cd) <CD 74987> **LOVE MACHINE** -
– Bulletproof / Hollywood shuffle / Love machine / Still the one / Mr. Mistreater / Nightstalker / Love in a bottle / Nothin' to lose / Heart of steel / Cocaine / The magic is back.

—— disbanded in 1992

BRITISH LIONS (see under ⇒ MOTT THE HOOPLE)

BRITNY FOX

Formed: Philadelphia, Pennsylvania, USA . . . 1987 by "DIZZY" DEAN DAVIDSON (former drummer of WORLD WAR III) and MICHAEL KELLY SMITH (ex-CINDERELLA), who subsequently added the rhythm section of BILLY CHILDS and JOHNNY DEE. Having built up a local following, they circulated a cassette-only set entitled, 'IN AMERICA', laying the groundwork for a deal with 'Columbia'. Released at the height of the US glam revival, their eponymous debut soared into the Top 40, the highlight being a rousing version of Slade's 'GUDBUY T' JANE'. Largely indistinguishable from the mascara'ed pack, the only notable factor was DIZZY's cat-scratch vocal gymnastics. A second album, 'BOYS IN HEAT', sold only moderately despite being easier on the ear, while a third, 'BITE DOWN HARD' (1991; with new frontman, TOMMY PARIS) failed to realise renewed expectations.

Album rating: BRITNY FOX (*5)

"DIZZY" DEAN DAVIDSON – vocals, guitar (ex-WORLD WAR III) / **MICHAEL KELLY SMITH** – guitar, vocals (ex-CINDERELLA) / **BILLY CHILDS** – bass, vocals / **JOHNNY DEE** – drums, percussion, vocals (ex-WAYSTED)

not iss.

1987. (c) **IN AMERICA** -

C.B.S. Columbia

Jul 88. (7") *<08016>* **GIRLSCHOOL. / DON'T HIDE** -

Sep 88. (lp/c/cd) *(461111-1/-4/-2) <44140>* **BRITNY FOX** 39 Jul88
– Girlschool / Long way to love / Kick 'n' fight / Save the weak / Fun in Texas / Rock revolution / Don't hide / Gudbuy t' Jane / In America / Hold on.

Sep 88. (7"/7"pic-d) *(653018-7/-0) <07926>* **LONG WAY TO LOVE. / LIVIN' ON THE EDGE** 100
(12"+=) *(653018-6)* – ('A'extended) / Save the weak.

Oct 88. (7"/7"pic-d) *(653144-7/-0)* **GIRLSCHOOL. / KICK 'N' FIGHT**
(ext;12"+=/cd-s+=) *(653144-6/-2)* – Fun in Texas.

Nov 88. (7") *<68561>* **SAVE THE WEAK. / DON'T HIDE** -

Dec 89. (7") *(655499-7)* **STANDING IN THE SHADOWS. / LIVIN' ON A DREAM**
(12"+=/cd-s+=) *(65499-6/-2)* – Girlschool / Long way to love.

Dec 89. (lp/c/cd) *(465954-1/-4/-2) <45300>* **BOYS IN HEAT** 79 Nov89
– In motion / Standing in the shadows / Hair of the dog / Livin' on a dream / She's so lonely / Dream on / Long way from home / Plenty of love / Stevie / Shine on / Angel in my heart / Left me stray / Longroad.

Mar 90. (c-s) *<73220>* **DREAM ON / GIRLSCHOOL** -

—— **TOMMY PARIS** – vocals; repl. DAVIDSON who formed BLACKEYED SUSAN

East West East West

Nov 91. (cd/c/lp) *<(7567 91790-2/-4/-1)>* **BITE DOWN HARD**
– Six guns loaded / Louder / Liar / Closer to your love / Over and out / Shot from my gun / Black and white / Look my way / Lonely too long / Midnight Moses.

—— split in 1993

BROKEN BONES

Formed: Stoke-On-Trent, England . . . 1983 by TONY 'BONES' ROBERTS (ex-DISCHARGE), who recruited his brother TERRY, frontman NOBBY and sticksman CLIFF. Initially operating as a hardcore/punk outfit, BROKEN BONES released a series of albums on the 'Fall Out' label, none of which sparked the interest of heavy metal fans. However, after a two-year sabbatical, the band blasted back in 1989 with the uncompromising 'LOSING CONTROL', released on the 'Heavy Metal' label. Retaining their punk ideals, the band courted a hardcore/metal audience on 1990's 'TRADER IN DEATH' album. Securing a deal with 'Rough Justice' the following year, they finally signed off with 'STITCHED UP'. A re-formed BROKEN BONES were back in 1999/2000 with another set of metal/punk tunes, entitled 'WITHOUT CONSCIENCE'.

Album rating: DEM BONES (*6) / F.O.A.D. (*5) / BONECRUSHER (*4) / LOSING CONTROL (*4) / TRADER IN DEATH (*4) / STITCHED UP (*4) / BRAIN DEAD compilation (*5) / WITHOUT CONSCIENCE (*4)

BONES (b. TONY ROBERTS) – guitar (ex-DISCHARGE) / **NOBBY** – vocals / **TEZZ ROBERTS** – bass / **CLIFF** – drums

Fall Out not iss.

Jan 84. (7"m) *(FALL 020)* **DECAPITATED. / PROBLEM / LIQUIDATED BRAINS** -

May 84. (7"m) *(FALL 025)* **CRUCIFIX. / FIGHT THE GOOD FIGHT / I.O.U.** -

Jul 84. (lp/pic-lp) *(FALLLP 028/+P)* **DEM BONES** -
– Wealth rules / Who's to blame / Iron maiden / Their living is my deeath / Big hard man / Terrorist attack / Stand up / Civil war / Secret agent / City fodder / Intro / Annihilation No.3 / Dem bones. *(<cd-iss. Dec90 & Feb01 +=; FALLCD 028>)* – DECAPITATED 1983-86

Oct 85. (7"/7"pic-d) *(FALL 034/+P)* **SEEING THROUGH MY EYES. / THE POINT OF AGONY / IT'S LIKE** -
(10"+=) *(FALL10 034)* – Decapitated (part 2) / Death is imminent.

Jul 86. (12") *(FALL12 039)* **NEVER SAY DIE. / 10, 5 OR A DIME** -

—— **BAZ** – drums; repl. CLIFF

Feb 87. (lp) *(FALLLP 041)* **F.O.A.D.** -
– F.O.A.D. / Kick down the doors / Teenage kamikaze / Programme control / S.O.T.O. / Missing link / Best of both worlds / Never say die / Decapitated 1 + 2 / Problem / Secret agent / Liquidated brains / Gotta get out of here / I.O.U. nothing /

Seeing through my eyes / Annihilation No.3. *(cd-iss. May93 +=; FALLCD 041)* – BONECRUSHER

Aug 87. (lp/pic-lp) *(FALLLP 043/+P)* **BONECRUSHER**
– Treading underfoot / Bonecrusher / Delusion and anger / Choose death / Untamed power / It's like / Death is imminent.

R.F.B. | not iss.

Jun 87. (12"ep) *(RFBSIN 4)* **TRADER IN DEATH**

—— **QUIV** – vocals + **D.L. HARRIS** – bass; repl. NOBBY + TEZZ

Heavy Metal | Half Moon

Aug 89. (lp/c/cd) *(HMR LP/MC/XD 133)* <665548> **LOSING CONTROL**
– Killing fields / Nowhere to run (alt.mix) / Losing control / Jump / Going down / Shutdown / Brain dead / Life's too fast / Bitching / Mercy / Maniac / Lesson.

Mar 90. (cd/c/lp) *(HMR CD/MC/LP 141)* **TRADER IN DEATH**
– Traders in death / Money, pleasure & pain / Who cares about the cost? / Stabbed in the back (still bleeding) / Booze for free / Crack attack / Trader in death / Blue life.

May 90. (12"ep/cd-ep) *(12HM/HEAVYXD 56)* **RELIGION'S RESPONSIBLE**
– Brain dead / + 3

Rough Justice | not iss.

Oct 91. (cd/c/lp) *(CD/T+/JUST 18)* **STITCHED UP**
– Stitched up / The fix / Propaganda / Wasted nation / Forget it / In fear / Gotta get away / Bring 'em down / Limited greed / Sick world.

—— broke up around 1992

Oct 92. (cd/lp) *(CD+/JUST 19)* **BRAIN DEAD** (compilation)
– Killing fields / Last breath / Losing control / Jump / Going down / Shutdown / Brain dead / Life's too fast / Bitching / Mercy / Maniac / Lesson / Money, pleasure & pain / Who cares about the cost? / Stabbed in the back (still bleeding) / Booze for free / Crack attack / Trader in death / Blue life / Religion is responsible / The madness / Last breath (live).

—— re-formed towards the end of '99

Rhythm Vicar | High Speed

Jul 00. (cd) *(PREACH 026CD)* <HSR 3> **WITHOUT CONSCIENCE** Mar01
– 8 second seizure / Cleansing / Random / Misfit / State of mind / Co.uk / Take / Entut / The pat / Jacob's ladder / Descend / Hedden corner / Without conscience.

– compilations, etc. –

1985. (lp) *Subversive;* **LIVE 100 CLUB (live)**
Dec 93. (cd) *Cleopatra; (<CLEO 9309-2>)* **DEATH IS IMMINENT**
Jan 97. (cd) *Cleopatra; (CLP 9687-2)* **THE COMPLETE SINGLES**

BROKEN HOPE

Formed: Illinois, USA . . . 1989 by JOE PTACEK, JEREMY WAGNER, ED HUGHES and RYAN STANEK. Adding a second guitarist, BRIAN GRIFFIN, they recorded a demo in 1990, which led to a plethora of indie labels knocking on their proverbial door. 'Grindcore International' came up trumps, netting the band for a debut album, 'SWAMPED IN GORE' (1992). Subsequently signed to 'Metal Blade' on the strength of an appearance at Milwaukee's annual Metalfest, BROKEN HOPE recorded the album, 'BOWELS OF REPUGNANCE' (possibly as a result of enduring festival toilet facilities?). What came out next, 'REPULSIVE CONCEPTION' (1995), was another death-metal assault on the eardrums, although after a few years of nursing they were ready again for the fourth set, 'LOATHING'. With RYAN and GLASS being respectively superseded by DUANE TIMLIN and SEAN BAXTER, BROKEN HOPE made another gory stab at cracking the metal market via 5th album, 'GROTESQUE BLESSINGS' (2000); they subsequently added new vocalist SCOTT CREEKMORE.

Album rating: SWAMPED IN GORE (*6) / THE BOWELS OF REPUGNANCE (*5) / REPULSIVE CONCEPTION (*5) / LOATHING (*6) / GROTESQUE BLESSINGS (*5)

JOE PTACEK – vocals / **JEREMY WAGNER** – guitar / **ED HUGHES** – bass / **RYAN STANEK** – drums

Grindcore | Grindcore

Jul 92. (cd) *<(GC 189801)>* **SWAMPED IN GORE** Feb92
– Borvoj's demise / Incinerated / Swamped in gore / Bag of parts / Dismembered carcass / Devourer of souls / Awakened by stench / Gorehog / Gobblin' the guts / Cannibal crave / Claustrophic agnostic dead. *(<re-iss. Nov95 on 'Metal Blade'; 3984-14096-2>)*

—— **SHAUN GLASS** – bass (ex-SINDROME) repl. HUGHES

Metal Blade | Metal Blade

Sep 93. (cd) *(CDZORRO 64)* *<14018>* **BOWELS OF REPUGNANCE**
– Repugnance (intro) / The dead half / Coprophagia / She came out in chunks / Peeled / Hobo stew / Decimated genitalia / Preacher of sodomy / Remember my members / Waterlogged / Embryonic tri-clops / Drinking the Ichor / Felching vampires.

Apr 95. (cd) *(CDZORRO 85)* *<14081>* **REPULSIVE CONCEPTION**
– Dilation and extraction / Grind box / Chewed to stubs / Engorged with impiety / Swallowed whole / Erotic zoophilism / Pitbull grin / Into the negrosphere / Essence of human pain / The eternal twin / Penis envy / For only the sick / Freezer burnt / Imprimis obscurity / Captain Howdy.

Mar 97. (cd) *<(3984-14120CD)>* **LOATHING**
– Siamese screams / Translucence / The cloning / Reunited / High on formaldahyde / A window to hell / Skin is in / Auction of the dead / He was raped / I am God / Deadly embrace.

—— **DUANE TIMLIN** – drums; repl. RYAN

—— **SEAN BAXTER** – bass; repl. GLASS

Plague | Martyr

Nov 00. (cd) *(PLAGUE 010CD)* *<4>* **GROTESQUE BLESSINGS** Dec99
– Wolf among sheep / Chemically castrated / Necro-fellatio / Christ consumed / War-maggot / Earth burner / Internal inferno / Razor #%$and / Hate machine.

—— added **SCOTT CREEKMORE** – vocals

BRUJERIA (see under ⇒ FEAR FACTORY)

BRUTALITY

Formed: Florida, USA . . . late 80's by SCOTT REIGEL and his metal chums JAY FERNANDEZ, DON GATES, JEFF ACRES and JIM COKER. After releasing two independent singles, the band subsequently signed to 'Nuclear Blast', for whom they have so far issued three death-metal albums, 'SCREAMS OF ANGUISH' (1993), 'WHEN THE SKY TURNS BLACK' (1994) – featuring a mighty cover of Black Sabbath's 'ELECTRIC FUNERAL' – and 'IN MOURNING' (1996).

Album rating: SCREAMS OF ANGUISH (*6) / WHEN THE SKY TURNS BLACK (*6) / IN MOURNING (*6)

SCOTT REIGEL – vocals / **JAY FERNANDEZ** – guitar / **DON GATES** – guitar / **JEFF ACRES** – bass, vocals / **JIM COKER** – drums

Gore | not iss.

1990's. (7") *(GORE 007)* **HELL ON EARTH. /**
1990's. (7") **SADISTIC. /**

Nuclear Blast | Nuclear Blast

Jul 93. (lp/cd) *(<NB 075/+CD>)* **SCREAMS OF ANGUISH** Sep93
– These walls shall be your grave / Ceremonial unearthing / Sympathy / Septicemic plague / Crushed / Spirit world / Exposed to the elements / Cries for the forsaken / Cryptorium / Spawned illusion.

—— **BRIAN HIP** – guitar; repl. FERNANDEZ

Dec 94. (cd/c) *(NB 115-2/-4)* *<6883>* **WHEN THE SKY TURNS BLACK** Jan95
– When the sky turns black / Race defects / Awakening / Electric funeral / Foul lair / Screams of anguish / Esoteric / Artistic butchery / Violent generation / Shrine of the master.

—— **DANA WALSH** – guitar; repl. BRIAN

—— **PETE SYKES** – guitar; repl. DON

Aug 96. (cd) *(NB 146CD)* *<6146>* **IN MOURNING** Jan97
– Obsessed / The past / Destroyed by society / Waiting to be destroyed / Died with open eyes / In mourning / Subjected to torture / Calculated bloodshed / Extinction.

—— have been a little conspicuous by their absence

BRUTAL TRUTH

Formed: New York, USA . . . 1992 by ex-ANTHRAX bassist DAN LILKER. He initiated BRUTAL TRUTH while still a fully fledged member of respected thrash merchants, NUCLEAR ASSAULT. Enlisting the services of KEVIN SHARP, BRENT McCARTY and SCOTT LEWIS, his new group signed to 'Relapse' records ('Earache' UK), purveying a more extreme hardcore/metal sound. They released their debut, 'EXTREME CONDITIONS DEMAND EXTREME RESPONSES' in 1992, having earlier opened their musical account with a 7" single!, 'ILL NEGLECT'. Newcomer, RICH HOAK was in place in time for 1993's 'PERPETUAL CONVERSION' EP, having replaced LEWIS, who joined LILKER's other offshoot group, EXIT-13. Both outfits delivered product virtually simultaneously late in '94, BRUTAL TRUTH with 'NEED TO CONTROL' and EXIT-13 with 'ETHOS MUSICK'. LILKER has since successfully juggled the two projects side by side, BRUTAL TRUTH's aforementioned 'NEED . . .' featuring a boxed set with the cover versions as follows:- LORD OF THIS WORLD (Black Sabbath) / DETHRONED EMPEROR (Celtic Frost) / WISH YOU WERE HERE (Pink Floyd).

Album rating: EXTREME CONDITIONS DEMAND EXTREME RESPONSES (*6) / NEED TO CONTROL (*7) / KILL TREND SUICIDE mini (*4) / SOUNDS OF THE ANIMAL KINGDOM (*6) / GOODBYE CRUEL WORLD live finale (*5) / Exit-13: DON'T SPARE THE GREEN LOVE (*5) / ETHOS MUSICK (*6) / JUST A FEW MORE HITS (*5) / SMOKING SONGS (*5)

DAN LILKER – bass (ex-ANTHRAX, ex-S.O.D., ex-NUCLEAR ASSAULT) / **BRENT McCARTY** – guitar / **KEVIN SHARP** – vocals / **SCOTT LEWIS** – drums

Earache | Combat

Aug 92. (7") *(7MOSH 080)* **ILL NEGLECT. /**

Sep 92. (cd/c) *(MOSH 069 CD/MC)* *<1142>* **EXTREME CONDITIONS DEMAND EXTREME RESPONSES**
– P.S.P.I. / Birth of ignorance / Stench of profit / Ill-neglect / Denial of existence / Regression – Progression / Collateral damage / Time / Walking corpse / Monetary gain / Wilt / H.O.P.E. / Blockhead / Anti-homophobe / Unjust compromise. *(cd re-iss. Sep97; same)*

—— **RICH HOAK** – drums; repl. LEWIS

Mar 93. (12"ep/cd-ep) *(MOSH 084 T/CD)* *<1188>* **PERPETUAL CONVERSION EP** May93
– Perpetual conversion / Perpetual larceny / Walking corpse / Lord of this world / Bedsheet.

Earache | Earache

Nov 94. (lp/cd) *(<MOSH 110/+CD>)* **NEED TO CONTROL**
– Collapse / Black door mine / Turn face / Godplayer / I see red / Iron lung / Bite the hand / Ordinary madness / Media blitz / Judgement / Brain trust / Choice of a new generation / Mainliner / Displacement / Crawlspace. *(also in box-set 5"/6"/7"/8"/9"; MOSH 110B)* – B.T.I.T.B. / Dethroned emperor / Painted clowns / Wish you were here. *(cd re-iss. Sep97; same)*

Relapse Relapse

Feb 97. (cd/c) <(RR 6948-2/-4)> **KILL TREND SUICIDE** Oct96
– Blind leading the blind / Pass some down / Let's go to war / Hypocrite invasion / Everflow / Zombie / Homesick / Humanity's folly / I killed my family / Kill trend suicide.

Nov 97. (cd/c/d-lp) <(RR 6968-2/-4/-1)> **SOUNDS OF THE ANIMAL KINGDOM** Sep97
– Dementia / K.A.P. (Kill All Politicians) / Vision / Fucktoy / Jemenez Cricket / Soft mind / Average people (fiend) / Blue world / Callous / Fisting / Die laughing / Dead smart / Sympathy kiss / Pork farm / Promise / Foolish bastard / Postulate then liberate / It's after the end of the world / Machine parts / Unbaptised / Prey. *(d-lp+=)* – Cybergod.

Feb 98. (7"ep) **KINDBUD**
– Vision / I see red / Stench of profit / RUPTURE:- The chosen one / Foot in my grave / Erasor evasor / Vatican City / A breath of cyanide / The annihilator. (above issued on 'Deaf American' and shared with RUPTURE)

— BRUTAL TRUTH split in 1998

– compilations, etc. –

Nov 99. (d-cd) *Relapse;* <(RR 6425-2)> **GOODBYE CRUEL WORLD (live & rare)** Sep99
– Intro / Dementia / K.A.P. / Choice of a new generation / Birth of ignorance / Stench of profit / Walking corpse / Sympathy kiss / Pork farm / Jemenez Cricket / Repeat at length / Media blitz / Fucktoy / Ill-neglect / Kill trend suicide / Cornucopia / Godplayer / I killed my family / Time / Denial of existance / Hippie cult / Callous / Zodiac / No sleep / Hippie cult / Cybergod / Cornupcopia / Born to die / Spare change / Machine parts / Collateral damage x 5 / Fucktoy / Kill trend suicide / Bubblebop shop / Boredoms cover #2 / Telly (with Bucky) / Blind leading the blind / Pass some down / Vision / Fisting / Die laughing / Let's go to war / Zombie / Homesick / Everflow / Dead smart / Soft mind / Dethroned emperor / It's after the end of the world / Callous / Average people / Black door mine / Promise / Foolish bastard / Bite the hand / Collateral damage.

EXIT-13

DAN LILKER – bass / **BILL YURKIEWICZ** – vocals, samples / **STEVE O'DONNELL** – guitar / **SCOTT LEWIS** – drums (of BRUTAL TRUTH)

Relapse Relapse

Dec 93. (cd) <RR 6606> **DON'T SPARE THE GREEN LOVE** [-]
– Spare the wrench surrender the Earth / Only hypocrisy prohibits legality / Only protest gives a hope of life! / Societally provoked genocidal contemplation / My minds mine! / Anthropocentric ecocidal conundrum / Reevaluate life! / Gala / Unintended lyrical befuddlement / An outline of intellectual annoyance / Imbreeding populations / Sell-misunderstood cerebral masturbation / The funk song / Get high on life / Disembowling party / Shatterspackle / Termination habitation / Fingernails / Conclusions on various religious frauds / Political dismay / Impaled / Disembowling party.

Dec 94. (cd) <(RR 6913-2)> **ETHOS MUSICK**
– Societally provoked genocidal contemplation / Ethos musick / Facilitate the emancipation of your mummified mentality / Diet for a new America / Anthropocentric ecocidal conumdrum / Reevaluate life! / Legalize hemp now! – A warm wave of euphoria / Open season (the story of Hunter Slaughter) / My minds mine! / Earth first! / Only protest gives a hope of life! / Disembowling party / An electronic fugue for the imminent demise of planet Earth. *(re-iss. May00; same)*

Dec 95. (cd) <(RR 6966CD)> **JUST A FEW MORE** Aug95
– Legalise hemp now! (edit) / A man and his lawnmower / Oral fixation / Constant persistance of annoyance / Wake up and change / Snakes and alligators.

— added female **BLISS BLOOD** – vocals

Feb 97. (cd) <(RR 6934-2)> **SMOKING SONGS** Oct96
– Light up! / Jack, I'm mellow / If you're a viper (blissful mix) / Stoney Monday / When I get low I get high / Lotis blossom (sweet marijuana) / Willie the record releaser / 1'1 (thirteen inches of fun) / Weed / If you're a viper (Viper mad Lilker mix) / Knockin' myself out / Hempcake / Sweet marijuana brown.

B.T.O. (see under ⇒ BACHMAN-TURNER OVERDRIVE)

BUCKCHERRY

Formed: Los Angeles, California, USA . . . July 1995 by JOSHUA TODD and KEITH NELSON. Swaggering in the footsteps of L.A.'s great tattooed cock-rock tradition, these guys swig from the same half-finished cheap wine bottle as spiritual forebears like GUNS N' ROSES, JUNKYARD and of course AEROSMITH. Featuring a rhythm section of JONATHAN BRIGHTMAN and DEVON GLENN, their much raved over eponymous debut album – co-produced by ex-SEX PISTOL, STEVE JONES – was released by Hollywood label, 'Dreamworks', in 1999. As an antidote to the angst-ridden claustrophobia of the rap-metal brigade, BUCKCHERRY's 100% proof, good-time blues-rock struck a resonating chord and brought endless comparisons with the GNR's punk-fuelled heyday. The perennial rock'n'roll trinity of drugs, sex and booze again provided fertile subject matter for follow-up set, 'TIME BOMB' (2001), giving heart to metal fans who'd rather party than pick a fight.

Album rating: BUCKCHERRY (*7) / TIME BOMB (*6)

JOSHUA TODD – vocals / **KEITH NELSON** – guitar / **YOGI** – guitar, mandolin, keyboards / **JONATHAN (J.B.) BRIGHTMAN** – bass / **DEVON GLENN** – drums

Dreamworks Dreamworks

Apr 99. (cd) <(DRD 50044)> **BUCKCHERRY**
– Lit it up / Crushed / Dead again / Check your head / Dirty mind / For the movies / Lawless and Lulu / Related / Borderline / Get back / Baby / Drink the water.

Apr 01. (cd) <(450287-2)> **TIME BOMB** [64] Mar01
– Frontside / Ridin; / Time bomb / Porno star / Place in the sun / (segue) Helpless / Underneath / Slit my wrists / Whiskey in the morning / You / Slammin' / Fall. *(bonus track+=)* – untitled.

BUDGIE

Formed: Cardiff, Wales . . . 1968 by BURKE SHELLEY and RAY PHILLIPS, who recruited TONY BOURGE. After some local gigs, they signed to 'M.C.A.', where they released their eponymous debut album in '71 and a semi-legendary 45, 'CRASH COURSE IN BRAIN SURGERY' (later made infamous by thrash-kings, METALLICA, who acknowledged BUDGIE as a pivotal influence). Songwriters SHELLEY and BOURGE, delivered two more heavy-riffing power-metal albums, 'SQUAWK' and 'NEVER TURN YOUR BACK ON A FRIEND' (containing their excellent cover of 'BABY PLEASE DON'T GO'), before PHILLIPS gave way to new drummer, PETE BOOT. Commercial success finally followed critical acclaim, when 1974's 'IN FOR THE KILL' hit the UK Top 30. A bludgeoning guitar feast, the record highlighted SHELLEY's high-octane vocals on the title track alongside the first album appearance of 'CRASH COURSE . . .'. BOOT was then succeeded by STEVE WILLIAMS just in time for their classy fifth album, 'BANDOLIER', the record containing some hard-rock gems 'NAPOLEON BONA-PART 1 & 2', 'I AIN'T NO MOUNTAIN' and the rousing 'BREAKING ALL THE HOUSE RULES'. BUDGIE then signed to 'A&M', releasing the wittily titled. 'IF I WAS BRITTANIA I'D WAIVE THE RULES' in 1976, although this was a huge disappointment to many fans outside America, where they had decided to concentrate their efforts. However, they flew back to their native land, possibly due to another failure, 'IMPECKABLE' (1978). Founder member, BOURGE subsequently departed, the band resurfacing in 1980 on RCA's new 'Active' label. This resulted in some minor success with the commercially viable early 80's sets, 'NIGHT FLIGHT' and 'DELIVER US FROM EVIL', the band sticking around for another five years without a contract.

Album rating: BUDGIE (*6) / SQUAWK (*6) / NEVER TURN YOUR BACK ON A FRIEND (*6) / IN FOR THE KILL (*7) / BANDOLIER (*7) / IF I WERE BRITTANIA I'D WAIVE THE RULES (*4) / IMPECKABLE (*3) / POWER SUPPLY (*3) / NIGHTFLIGHT (*4) / DELIVER US FROM EVIL (*5) / THE BEST OF BUDGIE compilation (*9)

BURKE SHELLEY – vocals, bass / **TONY BOURGE** – guitar, vocals / **RAY PHILLIPS** – drums

M.C.A. Kapp

Aug 71. (lp) *(MKPS 2018)* **BUDGIE** [-]
– Guts / Everything in my heart / The author / Nude disintegrating parachutist woman / Rape of the locks / All night petrol / You and I / Homicidal suicidal. *(re-iss. 1974; MCF 2506) (cd-iss. Jul91 on 'Repertoire'; RR 4012) <US cd-iss. 1991 on 'Roadrunner'; RR 9309>*

Sep 71. (7") *(MKS 5072) <2152>* **CRASH COURSE IN BRAIN SURGERY. / NUDE DISINTEGRATING PARACHUTIST WOMAN**

Mar 72. (7") *(MKS 5085)* **WHISKEY RIVER. / GUTS** [-]

Apr 72. (lp) *(MKPS 2023) <3669>* **SQUAWK**
– Whisky river / Rocking man / Rolling home again / Make me happy / Hot as a docker's armpit / Drugstore woman / Bottled / Young is a world / Stranded. *(re-iss. 1974; MCF 2502) (cd-iss. May90; DMCL 1901) (cd-iss. Jul91 on 'Repertoire'; RR 4026) <US cd-iss. 1991 on 'Roadrunner'; RR 9308>*

Jun 72. (7") *<2185>* **WHISKEY RIVER. / STRANDED** [-]

M.C.A. M.C.A.

1973. (lp) *(MDKS 8010)* **NEVER TURN YOUR BACK ON A FRIEND**
– Breadfan / Baby please don't go / You know I'll always love you / You're the biggest thing since powdered milk / In the grip of a tyre fitters hand / Riding my nightmare / Parents. *(re-iss. Jun87 lp/c; MCL/+C 1855) (cd-iss. Jul91 on 'Repertoire'; RR 4013)*

— **PETE BOOT** – drums repl. PHILLIPS (later to TREDEGAR)

May 74. (7") *(MCA 133)* **ZOOM CLUB. / WONDERING WHAT EVERYONE KNOWS** [-]

Jun 74. (lp/c) *(MCF/+C 2546) <429>* **IN FOR THE KILL** [29]
– In for the kill / Crash course in brain surgery / Wondering what everyone knows / Zoom club / Hammer and tongs / Running from my soul / Living on your own. *(cd-iss. Aug91 on 'Repertoire'; REP 4027)*

— **STEVE WILLIAMS** – drums repl. BOOT

Feb 75. (7") *(MCA 175) <40367>* **I AIN'T NO MOUNTAIN. / HONEY**

Sep 75. (lp/c) *(MCF/+C 2723) <4618>* **BANDOLIER** [36]
– Breaking all the house rules / Slipaway / Who do you want for your love? / I can't see my feelings / I ain't no mountain / Napoleon Bona-part one & two. *(cd-iss. Jul91 on 'Repertoire'; RR 4100)*

A&M A&M

Apr 76. (lp/c) *(AMLH/AMC 68377) <4593>* **IF I WERE BRITTANIA I'D WAIVE THE RULES**
– Anne Neggan / If I were Brittania I'd waive the rules / You're opening doors / Quacktors and bureaucats / Sky high percentage / Heaven knows our name / Black velvet stallion. *(cd-iss. Jan94 & Jun00 on 'Repertoire'; RR 4372)*

— added **MYF ISAACS** – 2nd guitar

Feb 78. (lp/c) *(AMLH/AMC 64675) <4675>* **IMPECKABLE**
– Melt the ice away / Love for you and me / All at sea / Dish it up / Pyramids / Smile boy smile / I'm a faker too / Don't go away / Don't dilute the water. *(cd-iss. Jun00 on 'Repertoire'; REP 4371)*

Mar 78. (7") *(AMS 7342)* **SMILE BOY SMILE. / ALL AT SEA**

— **JOHN THOMAS** – guitar, slide, vocals (ex-GEORGE HATCHER BAND) repl. ROB KENDRICK (ex-TRAPEZE) who had repl. BOURGE. (He formed TREDEGAR). (ISAACS had also departed)

Active not iss.

Jul 80. (12"ep) *(BUDGE 1)* **IF SWALLOWED DO NOT INDUCE VOMITING** [-]
– Wildfire / High school girls / Panzer Division destroyed / Lies of Jim (the E-Type lover).

Oct 80. (lp) *(ACTLP 1)* **POWER SUPPLY** [-]
– Forearm smash / Hellbender / Heavy revolution / Gunslinger / Power supply / Secrets in my head / Time to remember / Crime against the world. *(re-iss. Sep81 on 'R.C.A.' lp/c; RCA LP/K 3046) (cd-iss. Jan94 on 'Repertoire'+=; REP 4336WZ)* –

Wildfire / High school girls / Panzer Divsion destroyed / Lies of Jim (the E-Type lover).

Nov 80. (7") *(BUDGE 2)* **CRIME AGAINST THE WORLD. / HELLBENDER** [ ] [-]

R.C.A. not iss.

Sep 81. (7"pic-d) *(BUDGE 3)* **KEEPING A RENDEZVOUS. / APPARATUS** 71 [ ]

Oct 81. (lp/c) *(RCA LP/K 6003)* **NIGHTFLIGHT** 68 [-]
– I turned the stone / Keeping a rendezvous / Reaper of the glory / She used me up / Don't lay down and die / Apparatus / Superstar / Change your ways / Untitled lullaby.

Nov 81. (7",7"orange) *(BUDGE 4)* **I TURNED TO STONE. / ('A'instrumental)** [ ] [ ]

— added **DUNCAN MACKAY** – keyboards (ex-COCKNEY REBEL, ex-10CC)

Sep 82. (7") *(RCA 271)* **BORED WITH RUSSIA. / DON'T CRY** [ ] [-]
(7"pic-d+=) *(RCAP 271)* – Truth drug.

Oct 82. (lp/c) *(RCA LP/K 6054)* **DELIVER US FROM EVIL** 62 [-]
– Bored with Russia / Don't cry / Truth drug / Young girl / Flowers in the attic / N.O.R.A.D. (Doomsday city) / Give me the truth / Alison / Finger on the button / Hold on to love.

— disbanded late '82, although PHILLIPS reformed a sort of BUDGIE (SIX TON BUDGIE) briefly in the mid-90's. They released two cd sets, 'UNPLUCKED!' early '96 (AXEL/VINTAP 1) and mid-97, 'ORNITHOLOGY VOL.1' (AXEL/VINYL TAP 2).

– compilations etc. –

Sep 76. (lp/c) *M.C.A.; (MCF/+C 2766)* **THE BEST OF BUDGIE** [ ] [ ]
– Breadfan / In the grip of a tyre fitter's hand / I ain't no mountain / In for the kill / I can't see my feelings / Napoleon Bona part I & II / Parents / Hammer and tongs / Breaking all the house rules / Zoom club. *(re-iss. Feb82; MCL 1637) (cd-iss. Aug89; DMCL 1637)* – (with extra tracks). *(cd re-iss. Oct92; MCLD 19067) (cd-iss. Nov97 on 'Half Moon'; HMNCD 017)*

1981. (lp) *Cube; (HI-FLY 36)* **THE BEST OF "BUDGIE"** (early material) [ ] [-]
– Whiskey river / Guts / Rolling home again / Homocidal suicide / Hot as a docker's armpit / Drugstore woman / Rocking man / You and I / Stranded / Breadfan / I ain't no mountain / I can't see my feelings / Baby please don't go / Zoom club / Breaking all the house rules / Parents / In for the kill / In the grip of a tyrefitter's hand.

1994. (cd) *Vicious Sloth; (VSC 002)* **BUDGIE & BEYOND** (tracks by associated groups) [ ] [-]

Jul 97. (d-cd) *Burning Airlines; (<PILOT 014>)* **PANZER DIVISION DESTROYED (live at the Reading Festival 1980-1982)** [ ] [ ] Aug98

Jul 00. (d-cd) *Burning Airlines; (<PILOT 042>)* **HEAVIER THAN AIR (THE BBC SESSIONS)** [ ] [ ] Aug98

BUFFALO

Formed: Sydney, Australia . . . 1970 by DAVID TICE, etc. Due to their growing popularity in Europe, the group managed to secure a deal with the German wing of the British label, 'Vertigo'. A blend of heavy rock and blues, they borrowed their style from UK cousins such as BLACK SABBATH and DEEP PURPLE, delivering a series of albums starting with a European top seller, 'DEAD FOREVER' (1972).

Album rating: DEAD FOREVER (*5) / VOLCANIC ROCK (*5) / ONLY WANT YOU FOR YOUR BODY (*4) / MOTHER'S CHOICE (*4) / AVARAGE ROCK AND ROLLER (*3) / BEST OF compilation (*5)

DAVID TICE – vocals / **ALAN MILANO** – guitar / **JOHN BAXTER** – guitar / **PETE WELLS** – bass / **PAUL BALBI** – drums

Vertigo not iss.

1972. (lp) *(6357 100)* **DEAD FOREVER** [-] [-] German
– Leader / Suzie sunshine / Pay my dues / I'm a mover / Ballad of Irving Fink / Bean stew / Forest rain / Dead forever. *(cd-iss. 1990's on 'Some Punkins Music'; UPSC 1) (cd-iss. Aug91 on 'Repertoire'; REP 4141)*

1973. (lp) *(SPM 016)* **VOLCANIC ROCK** [-] [-] German
– Sunrise / Freedom / Till my death / The prophet / Pound of flesh / Shylock. *(cd-iss. 1990's on Some Punkins Music'; SPMC 16) (cd re-iss. Jan99 on 'Second Battle'; SB 060)*

1974. (lp) *(SPM 008)* **ONLY WANT YOU FOR YOUR BODY** [-] [-] German
– I'm a skirt lifter not a shirt raiser / I'm coming on / Dune messiah / Stay with me / What's going on / Kings Cross ladies / United nations. *(cd-iss. 1990's on 'Some Punkins Music'; SPMCD 9)*

1975. (lp) *(SPM 011)* **MOTHER'S CHOICE** [-] [-] German
– Long time gone / Honey babe / Taste it don't waste it / Little Queenie / Lucky / Essukay / Sweet little sixteen / Be alright. *(cd-iss. 1990's on 'Some Punkins Music'; UPSC 6)*

1977. (lp) **AVERAGE ROCK AND ROLLER** [-] [-] German

— split soon after above, WELLS guested for ROSE TATTOO, while TICE and original drummer BALBI, joined The COUNT BISHOPS (of England).

– compilations, etc. –

1980. (lp) *Vertigo;* **BEST OF** [-] [-] German

BULLDOZER

Formed: Milan, Italy . . . 1984 by the classically-trained ANDY PANIGADA and frontman/bassist A.C. WILD, who enlisted the help of drummer DON ANDRAS. Inspired by the satanic warblings of Brit acts like VENOM, BULLDOZER bludgeoned their way through a couple of thrash-metal albums for 'Roadrunner', 'THE DAY OF WRATH' (1985) and 'THE FINAL SEPARATION' (1986). Unable to expand their following beyond cult status, the group downshifted to the small 'Shark' label, who issued two further run-of-the-mill efforts.

Album rating: THE DAY OF WRATH (*4) / THE FINAL SEPARATION (*5) / IX (*4) / NEURODELIRI (*4)

A.C. WILD (b. A. CONTINI) – vocals, bass / **ANDY PANIGADA** – guitar / **"DON" ANDRAS** – drums

Roadrunner not iss.

Jun 85. (lp) *(RR 9779)* **THE DAY OF WRATH** [ ] [-]
– The exorcism / Cut-throat / Insurrection of the living damned / Fallen angel / The great deceiver / Mad man / Whisky time / Welcome death / Endless funeral. *(cd-iss. Feb99 on 'Soundclave'; SC 001CD)*

Jul 86. (lp) *(RR 9711)* **THE FINAL SEPARATION** [ ] [-]
– The final separation / Ride hard – die fast / The cave / Sex symbols' bullshit / "Don" Andras / Never relax / Don't trust the 'saint' / The death of gods. *(cd-iss. Feb99 on 'Soundclave'; SC 002CD)*

Shark not iss.

Apr 89. (lp) *(SHARK 10)* **IX** [ ] [-]
– IX / Desert! / Ilona the very best / Misogynists / Heaven's jail / Rob Klister / The derby / No way / The vision never fades. *(cd-iss. Feb99 on 'Soundclave'; SC 003CD)*

1990. (lp) **NEURODELIRI** [ ] [-]
– Overture / Neurodeliri / Minkions / We are . . . Italians / Art of deception / Ilona has been elected / Impotence / Willful death. *(cd-iss. Feb99 on 'Soundclave'; SC 004CD)*

— WILD became top guy in 'Metal Masters' label and group now defunct

– compilations, etc. –

Feb 99. (4xcd-box) *Soundclave; (SCBOXSET)* **BULLDOZER BOX SET** [ ] [-]
– (THE DAY OF WRATH / THE FINAL SEPARATION / IX / NEURODERELI)

Aug 99. (cd) *Hitland; (SET 1003A)* **GREETINGS FROM POLAND (live)** [ ] [-]
– IX / Desert / Ilona the very best / Impotence / Derby / Heaven's jail / Minkion's / Mors tua vita mea / Overkill / Wilful death / Heaven's jail / Rob Klister / Derby / No ways / Vision never fades.

BULLETBOYS

Formed: Los Angeles, California, USA . . . mid '87 by MICK SWEDA and MARQ TORIEN, who were subsequently joined by LONNIE VINCENT and JIMMY D'ANDA. Signing to 'Warner Brothers' and paired up with seasoned producer, Ted Templeman, the group discharged their self-titled debut the following year. Comparisons with VAN HALEN were inevitable, from TORIEN's ROTH-like blonde mane and stage swagger to their wide boy LA sound, although an interesting cover of The O'Jays' 'FOR THE LOVE OF MONEY', revealed a subtle funk/R&B influence. Released as a single, the track shot into the US Top 100, boosting sales of its parent album, which hit the Top 40. In '91, their second set, 'FREAKSHOW', was unsuccessful in emulating its predecessor's chart performance, a final album, 'ZA-ZA' in 1993 failing to fire up the group's flagging career.

Album rating: BULLETBOYS (*6) / FREAKSHOW (*6) / ZA-ZA (*4)

MARQ TORIEN – vocals (ex-RATT) / **MIKE SWEDA** – guitar (ex-KING KOBRA) / **LONNIE VINCENT** – bass / **JIMMY D'ANDA** – drums

WEA Warners

Jan 89. (lp/c)(cd) *(WX 213/+C)(925782-2) <25782>* **BULLETBOYS** [ ] 34 Oct88
– Hard as a rock / Smooth up in ya / Owed to Joe / Shoot the preacher down / For the love of money / Kissin' Kitty / Hell on my heels / Crank me up / Badlands / F#9.

Apr 89. (7") *<27554>* **FOR THE LOVE OF MONEY. / CRANK ME UP** [-] 78

Sep 89. (7") *(W 2876) <22876>* **SMOOTH UP. / BADLANDS** [ ] 71 Jul89

Warners Warners

Apr 91. (cd/c/lp) *<(7599 26168-2/-4/-1)>* **FREAKSHOW** [ ] 69 Mar91
– Hell yeah! / THC Groove / Thrill that kills / Hang on St. Christopher / Talk to your daughter / Freakshow / Goodgirl / Do me raw / Ripping me / Say your prayers / O me o my / Huge.

Jun 93. (cd/c) *<(9362 45095-2/-4)>* **ZA-ZA** [ ] [ ]
– When pigs fly / Slow and easy / Rising / Sing a song / Mine / 1-800-Goodbye / Show / For the damned / Laughing with the dead / Fess / Crosstop.

— split soon after above

– compilations, etc. –

Jul 00. (cd) *Deadline; (CLP 0837-2)* **GREATEST HITS** [ ] [ ]

BULLYRAG

Formed: Toxteth, Liverpool, England . . . 1994 by ROBBIE AWORK, STEWART BOYLE, MICHAEL CUSICK, STEVE BARNEY and DAVE GOLDRING as a 5-piece crossover, bass-heavy rap/rock and reggae/hardcore, techno/soul outfit similar to DUB WAR. Anything goes for these guys of strange headgear and the lads have been known to get into trouble through the exchange of the weed. The first band to sign for a rehabilitated 'Vertigo', BULLYRAG issued a trio of aggro-vating singles in 1997/98, preceding their promising debut set, 'SONGS OF PRAISE'.

Album rating: SONGS OF PRAISE (*7)

ROBBIE AWORK (b.1967) – vocals / **STEWART BOYLE** – guitars / **MICHAEL CUSICK** (b.1969) – bass / **STEVE BARNEY** (b.1970) – drums / **DAVE GOLDRING** – samples, percussion

Vertigo | unknown

Oct 97. (cd-s) *(BYRCD 1)* **FRANTIC / DIE / FUNKIFIED** [ ] [-]
Feb 98. (cd-s) *(BYRCD 2)* **LEARN TO LIVE / CONTACT / THUGS' PRAYER / LEARN TO LIVE (mellow)** [ ] [-]
(12") *(BYRX 4)* – ('A'side) / ('A'-Dirty Beatniks remix) / ('A'-Sparky Lightbourne mix).
May 98. (7") *(BYR 3)* **JUMP UP IN A FASHION. / FRUSTRATION** [ ] [-]
(cd-s+=) *(BYRCD 3)* – No, we don't give a fuck / ('A'album mix).
(cd-s) *(BYRDD 3)* – ('A'side) / ('A'-Overseer it's obvious mix) / ('A'-Fuzz Townshend almost instrumental mix) / ('A'-Fuzz Townshend mix).
Jun 98. (cd/c) *(568329-2/-4)* **SONGS OF PRAISE** [ ] [ ]
– Jump up in a fashion / Learn to live / You can have me / This / Summer daze / The plague / Frantic / It makes me laff / Wishing / I will learn.
Aug 98. (cd-s) *(BYRCD 4)* **SUMMER DAZE / 'TINGS RUFF (demo) / LOONATIC (live demo)** [ ] [-]
(cd-s) *(BYRDD 4)* – ('A'side) / Boom (short) / Frantic (Cut La Roc remix).

BURNING AIRLINES (see under ⇒ JAWBOX)

Glen BURTNICK

Born: New Jersey, USA. After a spell with HELMET BOY, JAN HAMMER & NEAL SCHON, he turned down an offer to join BON JOVI, BURTNICK instead going into session work for the likes of MARSHALL CRENSHAW and CYNDI LAUPER. He subsequently embarked on a solo career and duly signed to 'A&M', where he delivered two anthemic hard rock albums. In 1990, GLEN took the opportunity to join STYX, replacing TOMMY SHAW.

Album rating: TALKING IN CODES (*5) / HEROES AND ZEROS (*4)

GLEN BURTNICK – vocals, guitar, keyboards / with many on session

A&M | A&M

1986. (7") *<2842>* **CRANK IT UP. / PERFECT WORLD** [-] [ ]
1986. (lp) *<3036>* **TALKING IN CODE** [-] [ ]
– Crank it up / Talking in code / Little red house / Perfect world / Hole in my pocket / Brave hearts / Hold back the night / Talk that talk / Heart on the line / We're alright.
Dec 87. (7") *(AM 421) <2968>* **FOLLOW YOU. / WALLS COME DOWN** [ ] [65] Sep87
(12"+=) *(AMY 421)* – Abalene.
Feb 88. (7") *(AM 437) <3005>* **HEARD IT ON THE RADIO. / WALLS COME DOWN** [ ] [ ]
(12"+=) *(AMY 437)* –
Mar 88. (lp/c) *<(AMA/AMC 5166)>* **HEROES & ZEROS** [ ] [ ] Oct87
– Follow you / Spinning my wheel / Walls come down / Stupid boys (suckers for love) / Love goes on / Heard it on the radio / Abalene / Here comes Sally / Scattered / Day your ship gets thru.

— joined STYX in 1990 for the album, 'EDGE OF THE CENTURY'.

JAKE BURNS & THE WHEEL (see under ⇒ STIFF LITTLE FINGERS)

BURZUM

Formed: Oslo, Norway . . . 1991 initially as URUK HAI, by COUNT GRISHNACKH (aka VARG VIKERNES). A Satanist in every sense of the word, the COUNT took his lyrical inspiration from J.R.R. Tolkien's seminal mythical novel 'Lord Of The Rings', of course, identifying himself with the darker forces of the book. Joining the 'Deathlike Silence' stable (run by MAYHEM's EURONYMOUS (aka OYSTEIN AARSETH), a leading light in the Scandinavian black-metal scene), the dark one unleashed the 'BURZUM' debut, an intriguing combination of eerie death-metal and gothic atmospherics. The same year (1993), saw the release of a second set, the mini 'ASKE' (aka 'ASHES'), the album sleeves featuring a church on fire! (several real ones had mysteriously done so around the same time, arsonists or satanists were said to be behind such acts). Like a demonic MIKE OLDFIELD, GRISHNACKH singlehandedly masterminded each stage of the recording process from writing to execution, unfortunately taking the latter rather literally when on the 10th of August that year, he viciously knifed to death the aforementioned EURONYMOUS. VIKERNES was subsequently convicted and sentenced to the maximum 21 years in a "cushy" jail, although STRYPER fans couldn't breathe easy just yet, as the evil one incredibly continuing his prolific recording schedule apace from behind prison walls (not on the same label though!). He adopted a more atmospheric yet no less menacing style with subsequent releases, obviously restricted to the prison facilities of computer and keyboards. In 1997, the overtly-racist, pro-Aryan VIKERNES, abandoned his satanic ways in favour of the God, Odin, which didn't go down too well with his neo-Nazi fanbase tuned into the internet.

Album rating: BURZUM (*5) / ASKE mini (*5) / HVIS LYSET TAR OSS (*6) / DET SOM ENGANG VAR (*5) / FILOSOFEM (*4) / DAUDI BALDRS (*5)

COUNT GRISHNACKH (b. VARG VIKERNES) – vocals, keyboards, everything

Deathlike Silence | not iss.

May 93. (m-cd/m-lp) *(ANTIMOSH 002 CD/LP)* **BURZUM** [ ] [-]
Dec 93. (m-cd) *(ANTIMOSH 5CD)* **ASKE** [ ] [-]
– Feeble screams from forests unknown / Ea, lord of the depths / Spell of destruction / Channeling the power of souls into a new god / War / The crying Orc / My journey into the stars / Dungeons of darkness / Stemmen fra taarnet / Dominus sathanas / A lost forgotten sad spirit. *(above re-iss. May95 on 'Misanthropy' cd/d-lp; AMAZON 003 CD/LP)* – BURZUM (see above for tracks)

— In the summer of '93, GRISHNACKH murdered MAYHEM black-metalist, EURONYMOUS (see above)

Misanthropy | Misanthropy

Apr 94. (cd/lp) *(<AMAZON 001/+LP>)* **HVIS LYSET TAR OST** [ ] [ ] May94
– Det som en gang var / Hvis lyset tar oss / Inn I slottet fra droemmen / Comhet.
Oct 94. (lp/cd) *(<AMAZON 002/+CD>)* **DET SOMEGAG VAR** [ ] [ ]
– Den onde kysten / Key to the gate / En ring til AA Herske / Lost wisdom / Han som reiste / Naar himmelen klarner / Snu mikrokosmos tegn / Svart troner.
Jan 96. (d-lp/cd) *(AMAZON 009 CDA/B) <602>* **FILOSOFEM** [ ] [ ]
– Dunkelheit / Jesus' tod / Erblicket de tochter des firmaments / Gebrechlichkeit I / Rundgang um die transzendentale saule der singularitat / Gebrechlichkeit II. (above issued on 'Feral House' in the US)
Sep 97. (cd) *(<AMAZON 013>)* **DAUDI BALDRS** [ ] [ ] Oct97
– Duthi baldrs /Hermothr & Helferth / Balferth baldrs / I heimr heljar / Illa tithandi / Moti ragnarokum.
May 98. (lp/cd) *(<AMAZON 021/+CD>)* **HLIDHSKJALF** [ ] [ ]
– Tuistos lierz / Der tod muotans / Ansuzgardaraiwo / Die liebe nerpus' / Das einsame trauern von arija / Die kraft des mitgefuhls / Arijos goldene tranen / Der weinende liadnur.

BUSH

Formed: Kilburn, London, England . . . 1992, as FUTURE PRIMITIVE, by the seasoned Brit team of singer and lyricist GAVIN ROSSDALE, guitarist NIGEL PULSFORD, bassist DAVE PARSONS (from TRANSVISION VAMP!) and drummer ROBIN GOODRIDGE. Virtually ignored outright in the capital, BUSH's luck changed after American label 'Trauma' got hold of a demo, their signature obviously worth its weight in gold to US A&R men looking for the British answer to the recently defunct grungesters, NIRVANA. They relocated to the States early '95, a highlight at this point playing New York's CBGB's. The following year, they issued their debut, 'SIXTEEN STONE', an album that garnered critical acclaim from more rockcentric quarters and massive US sales from all quarters. Finally hitting the Top 5, the set contained a handful of impressive NIRVANA-esque numbers, among them 'EVERYTHING ZEN', 'COMEDOWN' and 'TESTOSTERONE', tracks that were to break the band in the UK a year later. By the end of 1996, BUSH were burning a proverbial trail with their chart-topping follow-up, 'RAZORBLADE SUITCASE', an album that made the UK Top 5 early the next year. A string of British hit singles completed their rise to transatlantic fame, the Top 10 'SWALLOWED' being one of their more memorable efforts. • **Covers:** REVOLUTION BLUES (Neil Young).

Album rating: SIXTEEN STONE (*7) / RAZORBLADE SUITCASE (*6) / THE SCIENCE OF THINGS (*6)

GAVIN ROSSDALE (b.30 Oct'67, London) – vocals, guitar (ex-MIDNIGHT) / **NIGEL PULSFORD** (b.11 Apr'65, Newport, Wales) – guitar (ex-KING BLANK) / **DAVE PARSONS** (b. 2 Jul'66, Uxbridge, England) – bass (ex-TRANSVISION VAMP) / **ROBIN GOODRIDGE** (b.10 Sep'66, Crawley, England) – drums (ex-BEAUTIFUL PEOPLE)

Atlantic | Trauma

Apr 95. (c-s) *(A 8196C)* **EVERYTHING ZEN / BUD** [ ] [-]
(12"+=/cd-s+=) *(A 8196 T/CD)* – Monkey.
May 95. (cd/c/lp) *(<6544-92531-2/-4/-1>)* **SIXTEEN STONE** [ ] [4]
– Everything zen / Swim / Bomb / Little things / Comedown / Body / Machinehead / Testosterone / Monkey / Glycerine / Alien / X-girlfriend. *(re-iss. Jun96 on 'Interscope' cd/c; IND/INC 92531)* – w/ bonus cd; hit UK 42)
Jul 95. (5"ltd/c-s) *(A 8160/+C)* **LITTLE THINGS. / X-GIRLFRIEND** [ ] [-]
(cd-s+=) *(A 8160CD)* – Swim.
Aug 95. (c-s) *<98134>* **COMEDOWN / TESTOSTERONE** [-] [30]
Dec 95. (c-s) *(A 8152C)* **COMEDOWN / REVOLUTION BLUES** [ ] [-]
(cd-s+=) *(A 8152CD)* – Testosterone.
Jan 96. (c-s) *<98088>* **GLYCERINE / SOLOMON'S BONES** [-] [28]

Interscope | Trauma

Apr 96. (c-s) *<98079>* **MACHINEHEAD / ALIEN (live)** [-] [43]
May 96. (10"ep) *(INV 95505)* **MACHINEHEAD. / COMEDOWN / SOLOMON'S BONES** [48] [-]
(cd-s) *(IND 95505)* – (first & third track) / Bud.
(cd-s) *(INDX 95505)* – (first & second track) / X-girlfriend.
Jan 97. (cd/c) *(<IND/INC 90091>)* **RAZORBLADE SUITCASE** [4] [1] Nov96
– Personal Holloway / Greedy fly / Swallowed / Insect kin / Cold contagious / Tendency to start fires / Mouth / Straight no chaser / History / Synapse / Communicator / Bonedriven / Distant voices. *(d-lp-iss.Sep99 on 'Simply Vinyl'; SVLP 120)*
Feb 97. (c-ep/cd-ep) *(INC/IND 95528)* **SWALLOWED / BROKEN TV. / GLYCERINE / IN A LONELY PLACE** [7] [-]
(cd-ep) *(INDX 95528)* – ('A'side) / ('A'-Toasted both sides) / Insect kin (live) / Cold contagious (16oz demo).
May 97. (c-s) *(INC 95536)* **GREEDY FLY / GREEDY FLY (album version)** [22] [-]
(cd-s+=) *(IND 95536)* – ('A'-16 oz demo).
(cd-s) *(INDX 95536)* – ('A'side) / Old / Insect kin (live) / Personal Holloway (live).
Nov 97. (c-s) *(INC 95553)* **BONEDRIVEN / SYNAPSE (Philip Steir remix)** [49] [-]
(cd-s+=) *(IND 95553)* – Personal Holloway (Soundclash Republic remix) / Straight no chaser.
(cd-s) *(INDX 95553)* – ('A'version) / ('A'-Beat Me Clever mix) / Everything zen (Derek DeLarge mix) / ('A'-Video cd-rom).
Nov 97. (cd) *(<IND 90161>)* **DECONSTRUCTED** [ ] [36]
– Everything zen (The lhasa fever mix) / Mouth (the stingray mix) / Swallowed (toasted both sides please – Goldie remix) / Synapse (my ghost in the bush of life remix) / History (Dub Pistols mix) / etc
Oct 99. (cd/c/lp) *<(490483-2/-4/-1)>* **THE SCIENCE OF THINGS** [28] [11]
– Warm machine / Jesus online / The chemicals between us / English fire / Spacetravel / 40 miles from the sun / Prizefighter / Disease of the dancing cat / Altered states / Dead meat / Letting the cables sleep / Mindchanger.

Nov 99. (7"clear) *(497222-7)* <*album cut*> **THE CHEMICALS BETWEEN US. / HOMEBODY** 46 67 Sep99
(cd-s+=) *(497223-2)* – Letting the cables sleep (original demo).
(cd-s) *(497222-2)* – ('A'side) / ('A'-Supercollider remix) / ('A'-video).
Mar 00. (cd-s) *(497275-2)* **WARM MACHINE / SWALLOWED (live) / IN A LONELY PLACE (Tricky mix)** 45
(cd-s) *(497276-2)* – ('A'side) / Greedy fly (live) / The chemicals between us (original demo).
May 00. (7") *(497336-7)* **LETTING THE CABLES SLEEP. / MOUTH (Stingray remix)** 51
(cd-s+=) *(497336-2)* – ('A'-Apocalyptic version).
(cd-s) *(497335-2)* – ('A'side) / ('A'-Nightmares On Wax remix) / ('A'-original demo).

BUSINESS

Formed: South London, England . . . late 1979 by MICKEY FITZ, STEVE WHALE, STUART WILLIAMS and PRYOR. Described as the SLADE of the "oi" movement, The BUSINESS set up shop on the 'Secret' label, debuting in late '81 with the classic Cock-er-nee gangster anthem, 'HARRY MAY'. Almost immediately throwing away any credibility they might have earned, The BUSINESS went artistically bankrupt with a yuletide cover of Elton John's 'STEP INTO CHRISTMAS', released as part of a V/A EP. The lads' love of glitzy nightlife shone through on 'SMASH THE DISCOS', while another proto-TOY DOLLS job, 'DAYO (THE BANANA BOAT SONG)', was thown in for 'bad' measure on the B-side. PRYOR and STUART subsequently clocked out, their replacements, MARK BRENNAN and KEV BOYCE making their inagural appearance on the band's debut lp, 'SUBURBAN REBELS' (1983). Later in the year, the 'OUT OF BUSINESS' EP was shelved and should have contained a cover of Crass' 'DO THEY OWE US A LIVING'. Back in business and on a new label, 'Word Of Warning', the boys returned in 1985 with a single, 'GET OUT OF MY HOUSE'. A cover of Sham 69's 'HURRY UP HARRY', meanwhile, turned up as the extra track on the 12" of the 'DRINKING 'N' DRIVING' single, the accompanying album, 'SATURDAY'S HEROES' (1986) being released on their own 'Harry May' imprint. Over the course of the next decade or so, The BUSINESS continued to set out their stall for hardcore fans every few years, their most recent album being 1997's 'THE WHOLE TRUTH AND NOTHING BUT THE TRUTH!'.
• **Note:** Not to be confused with The BUSINESS who released 'GET UP' for 'M.C.A.' early in 1981.

Album rating: SUBURBAN REBELS (*5) / OFFICIAL BOOTLEG w/ Loud (*4) / SATURDAY'S HEROES (*4) / WELCOME TO THE REAL WORLD (*3) / IN AND OUT OF BUSINESS (*3) / THE BEST OF THE BUSINESS compilation (*4) / KEEP THE FAITH (*3) / THE WHOLE TRUTH AND NOTHING BUT THE TRUTH! (*4)

MICKEY FITZ (b. MICHAEL FITZSIMONS) – vocals / **STEVE WHALE** (b. STEVE KENT) – guitar / **STUART WILLIAMS** – bass / **PRYOR** – drums

Secret not iss.

Oct 81. (7") *(SHH 123)* **HARRY MAY. / NATIONAL INSURANCE BLACKLIST** -
Dec 81. (7"ep; various) *(SHH 126)* **STEP INTO CHRISTMAS** -
Apr 82. (7") *(SHH 132)* **SMASH THE DISCOS. / DISCO GIRLS / THE BANANA BOAT SONG (DAY-O)** -

—— **KEV BOYCE** – drums; repl. PRYOR

—— **MARK BRENNAN** – bass; repl. STUART who joined BANDITS AT 4 O'CLOCK

Mar 83. (lp) *(SEC 11)* **SUBURBAN REBELS** -
– Get out while you can / Blind justice / Work or riot / The employer's blacklist / Nobody listened / Suburban rebels / Mortgage mentality / Guttersnipe / Real enemy / Another rebel dead / Sabotage the hunt / Harry May / Drinking and driving. *(<cd-iss. Sep93 & Dec98 on 'Captain Oi'+=; AHOYCD 7)* – Smash the disco / Disco girls / The banana boat song (day-o) / Loud, proud and punk. *(<lp re-iss. Feb97 on 'Taang!'; TAANG 121>)*
Dec 83. (12"ep; w-drawn) *(SHH 150)* **OUT OF BUSINESS** - -
– Last train to Clapham Junction / Law and order / Do they owe us a living / Tell us the truth.

Wonderful World Of . . . not iss.

Aug 85. (12"ep) *(WOW 121)* **GET OUT OF MY HOUSE / ALL OUT TONIGHT. / FOREIGN GIRL / OUTLAW** -
Sep 85. (lp; shared with LOUD) *(WOWDLP 4)* **THE OFFICIAL BOOTLEG** -

Diamond not iss.

Dec 85. (7") *(DIA 001)* **DRINKING 'N' DRIVING. / H-BOMB (live)** -
(12"+=) *(DIA 001T)* – Hurry up Harry / ('A'original).

Harry May not iss.

Jan 86. (lp) *(SE 13)* **SATURDAY'S HEROES** -
– Spanish jails / All out tonight / Never been taken / Harder life / Freedom / Frontline / Foreign girl / Shout it out / Nothing can stop us / Saturday heroes / Drinking 'n' driving. *(re-iss. Mar90 on 'Street Link'; LINKLP 115) (<re-iss. Feb97 on 'Taang!'+=; TAANG 122>) (<cd-iss. Nov97 on 'Captain Oi'+=; AHOYCD 013>)* – Hurry up Harry / Get out of my house / Outlaw / Coventry. *(cd re-iss. Mar01 on 'Harry May'; MAYDP 005)*

Link not iss.

Apr 88. (12"ep) *(LINK12 01)* **DO A RUNNER / COVENTRY. / WELCOME TO THE REAL WORLD / ANYWHERE BUT HERE / ALL OUT / (YOU'RE) GOING DOWN IN HISTORY** -
Jul 88. (lp) *(LINKLP 035)* **WELCOME TO THE REAL WORLD** -
– Mouth an' trousers / Do a runner / Ten years / We'll take 'em on / Fear in your heart / Welcome to the real world / Never say never / Hand ball / Living in daydreams / Look at him now / We gotta go / Never say never (reprise) / Coventry / No emotions / Tina Turner / Welcome to the real world (12). *(<cd-iss. Apr93 & Mar98 on 'Captain Oi'; AHOYCD 2>) (<re-iss. Feb96 & Nov00 on 'Taang!' cd/lp; TAANG 123 CD/LP>) (cd re-iss. Mar01 on 'Harry May'; MAYDP 008)*
1990. (lp) *(LRMO 1)* **IN AND OUT OF BUSINESS** - - mail-o
(cd-iss. Mar98 on 'Mog'; MOGCD 001)

—— shut up shop at the turn of the decade (opened up again in '94)

Century Media Century Media

Oct 94. (cd/lp) *(<CM 77083-2/-1>)* **KEEP THE FAITH**
– Maradona / Keep the faith / Holiday in Seattle / Divide & rule / Backstreet Billy / Can't take much more / (You're) Going down in history / Breaking the law / All out / Future / Should've known better / Paranoia.

Taang! Taang!

Feb 96. (7"ep/cd-ep) *(<T 114/+CD>)* **DEATH II DANCE EP**
– Death to dance / Hang the DJ (Panic) / Skaghead / N.H.S. (National Health Service) / Out in the cold (unpubbed) / Drinking and driving (unpubbed).

Burning Heart Taang!

Sep 97. (cd/lp) *(BHR 067 CD/LP) <TAANG 115>* **THE TRUTH, THE WHOLE TRUTH AND NOTHING BUT THE TRUTH!**
– Spirit of the street / Blood ties / The truth, the whole truth and nothing but the truth / One common voice / What's the story / Justice not politics / One thing left to say / Death to dance / No time 4U / S.E. 12 / Crime of the century / Informer / Southgate / Hardcore hooligan.

Taang! not iss.

Nov 00. (7") *(TAANG 134)* **ONE THING LEFT TO SAY. / ONE COMMON VOICE** -

– compilations, etc. –

Dec 83. (lp) *Syndicate; (SYNLP 2)* **1980-81 OFFICIAL BOOTLEGS** -
(cd-iss. Mar98 on 'Mog'; MOGCD 002)
1984. (lp) *Syndicate; (SYNLP 6)* **LOUD, PROUD 'N' PUNK, LIVE (live)** -
(tracks originally from a 'TOTAL NOISE' EP released June '82)
Aug 86. (lp) *Dojo; (DOJOLP 35)* **SINGALONG-A-BUSINESS: THE BEST OF THE BUSINESS** -
– Suburban rebels / Blind justice / Loud, proud & punk / The real enemy / Spanish jails / Product / National insurance blacklist / Get out of my house / Saturday heroes / Out in the cold / Smash the discos / Harry May / Drinking 'n' driving / Hurry up Harry. *(<cd-iss. Nov94 & Sep98 on 'Captain Oi'; AHOY 19>)*
Feb 92. (cd/c/lp) *Blackout; <BL 009 CD/MC/LP>* **1979-1989** -
Aug 92. (cd) *Street Link; (LINKCD 156)* **LOUD, PROUD 'N' OI: THE BEST OF THE BUSINESS** -
(<re-iss. Apr93 on 'Dojo'; DOJOCD 124>) (<re-iss. Apr98 on 'Snapper'; SMMCD 539>)
Aug 94. (cd) *Loma; (LOMACD 32)* **SUBURBAN REBELS / WELCOME TO THE REAL WORLD** -
Jun 95. (cd) *Anagram; (<CDPUNK 57>)* **THE COMPLETE BUSINESS SINGLES COLLECTION**
Dec 96. (d-lp/cd) *Taang!; (<TAANG 124 LP/CD>)* **HARRY MAY: THE SINGLES** Mar97
(re-iss. Jul00 on 'Harry May'; CANCAN 011CD)
May 98. (cd) *Step-1; (<STEPCD 024>)* **SMASH THE DISCOS / LOUD, PROUD 'N' PUNK** Jan01
Sep 98. (cd) *PinHead; (PINCD 106) / Original Masters; <576>* **THE BUSINESS LIVE (live)** May99
Jun 99. (cd) *Snapper; (<SMMCD 576>)* **LIVE**
Aug 00. (cd) *T.K.O.; <57>* **DOWN WITH THE PUB** -
Jan 01. (cd) *Past & Present; (AFUNCD 03)* **ARCHIVE LIVE: LIVE AT THE MAIN EVENT** -
Apr 01. (d-cd) *Snapper; (SMDCD 328)* **THE BEST OF THE BUSINESS** -

BUTTHOLE SURFERS

Formed: San Antonio, Texas, USA . . . 1980 originally as The ASHTRAY BABY HEELS by ex-accountant GIBBY (son of US children's TV presenter "Mr. Peppermint") and PAUL LEARY, who met at Trinity College, San Antonio. By 1983, they had signed to JELLO BIAFRA's (Dead Kennedys) label, 'Alternative Tentacles'. Around the mid-80's, they gigged heavily in Britain due to lack of Stateside interest, and this, together with radio play from John Peel, helped them make it into the UK indie charts. Heavy psychedelia mixing noise, confusion and futuristic art-punk, the manic GIBBY, (complete with loudspeaker, etc), was always offensive and disturbing while their weird stage act included the nude dancer, KATHLEEN. She covered herself in green jello, while GIBBY simulated sex with her! GIBBY was well-known for other stage antics; pissing in plastic baseball bats ('piss wands') and annointing the audience at the front. There were other obscenities, too rude to print here (no need to mention President Carter's creamy briefcase). In 1987, they unleashed the brilliantly crazed 'LOCUST ABORTION TECHNICIAN', complete with a parody of BLACK SABBATH's 'SWEET LEAF', the humourously titled 'SWEAT LOAF'. Also deep inside its nightmarish musical grooves was their gem, 'TWENTY TWO GOING ON TWENTY THREE', a track that made John Peel's Festive 50. A longer sojourn in Britain culminated in some riotous, oversubscribed London gigs. The follow-up, 'HAIRWAY TO STEVEN' (another piss-take; this time of LED ZEPPELIN – Stairway To Heaven), deliberately left the tracks nameless (instead using obscene looking symbols) as a twisted tribute to ZEPPELIN's "untitled" symbols album. 1990 saw them shift to a more commercial sound with 'PIOUGHD' (which means "pissed-off" in Red Indian), which featured a re-working of DONOVAN's 'HURDY GURDY MAN'. Having signed to 'Capitol' in 1992, they were back to their abrasive sound of old with the JOHN PAUL JONES-produced album, 'INDEPENDENT WORM SALOON'. This, together with their previous effort, had given them their first taste of chart success in Britain, this being well surpassed in 1996 when 'ELECTRICLARRYLAND' hit the US Top 30. It was due, no doubt, to a surprise domestic hit with 'PEPPER', and probably their "fiery" guest appearance on American mock talk show, The LARRY Sanders Show' in '97. • **Songwriters:** GIBBY and co., except AMERICAN WOMAN (Guess Who) / THE ONE I LOVE (R.E.M.). P covered DANCING QUEEN (Abba).

Album rating: BROWN REASONS TO LIVE mini (*6) / PSYCHIC ... POWERLESS ... ANOTHER MAN'S SAC (*7) / REMBRANDT PUSSYHORSE (*7) / LOCUST ABORTION TECHNICIAN (*8) / HAIRWAY TO STEVEN (*7) / DOUBLE LIVE (*4) / PHIOGHD (*6) / INDEPENDENT WORM SALOON (*7) / ELECTRICLARRYLAND (*7)

GIBBY HAYNES (b. GIBSON JEROME HAYNES, 1957) – vocals / **PAUL LEARY** (b.1958) – guitar / **KING COFFEY** – drums repl. ? / **ALAN ?** – bass

Alternative Tentacles / Alternative Tentacles

Apr 84. (m-lp) *(VIRUS 32)* **BUTTHOLE SURFERS** <'BROWN REASONS TO LIVE; US-title> ☐ ☐ 1983
– The Shah sleeps in Lee Harvey's grave / Hey / Something / Bar-b-que / Pope / Wichita cathedral / Suicide / The legend of Anus Presley. *(re-iss. Sep93 as 'BROWN REASONS TO LIVE' brown-lp; same)*

Jan 85. (12"ep) *(VIRUS 39)* **LIVE PCPPEP (live)** ☐ ☐
– Cowboy Bob / Bar-b-q pope / Dance of the cobras / The Shah sleeps in Lee Harvey's grave / Wichita cathedral / Hey / Something.

— **TERENCE** – bass repl. ALAN (?)

Fundam. / Touch&Go

Apr 85. (7") **LADY SNIFF. /** [-] ☐

Jul 85. (lp) *(SAVE 5)* **PSYCHIC . . . POWERLESS . . . ANOTHER MAN'S SAC** ☐ ☐
– Concubine / Eye of the chicken / Dum dum / Woly boly / Negro observer / Butthole surfer / Lady sniff / Cherub / Mexican caravan / Cowboy Bob / Gary Floyd. *(cd-iss. Jan88+=)* – CREAM CORN FROM THE SOCKET OF DAVIS *(cd re-iss. Jul99 on 'Latino Bugger'; LBV 003)*

— **MARK KRAMER** – bass (of SHOCKABILLY) repl. TREVOR who had repl. TERENCE

Oct 85. (12"ep) *(PRAY 69)* **CREAM CORN FROM THE SOCKET OF DAVIS** ☐ ☐
– Moving to Florida / Comb – Lou Reed (two parter) / Tornados.

Red Rhino Europe / Touch&Go

Apr 86. (lp) *(RRELP 2)* <TGLP 8> **REMBRANDT PUSSYHORSE** ☐ ☐
– Creep in the cellar / Sea ferring / American woman / Waiting for Jimmy to kick / Strangers die / Perry / Whirling hall of knives / Mark says alright / In the cellar. *(cd-iss. May88; RRECD 2) (cd re-iss. Jul99 on 'Latino Bugger'; LBV 004)*

— **JEFF 'TOOTER' PINKUS** – bass repl. KRAMER who formed BONGWATER

Blast First / Blast First

Mar 87. (lp/c/cd) *(BFFP 15/+C/CD)* **LOCUST ABORTION TECHNICIAN** ☐ ☐
– Sweat loaf / Graveyard 1 / Pittsburgh to Lebanon / Weber / Hay / Human cannonball / U.S.S.A. / Theoman / Kintz / Graveyard 2 / 22 going on 23 / The G-men. *(cd re-iss. Jul99 on 'Latino Bugger'; LBV 05)*

— added **THERESA NERVOSA (NAYLOR)** – 2nd drummer / **KATHLEEN** – naked dancer (above with GIBBY, PAUL, COFFEY and PINKUS)

Apr 88. (lp/cd) *(BFFP 29/+CD)* **HAIRWAY TO STEVEN** ☐ ☐
– Hairway part 1 / Hairway part 2 / Hairway part 3 / Hairway part 4 / Hairway part 5 / Hairway part 6 / Hairway part 7 / Hairway part 8 / Hairway part 9. *(9 tracks marked rude symbols as titles) (cd re-iss. Jul99 on 'Latino Bugger'; LBV 06CD)*

Aug 89. (12"ep/10"ep/cd-ep) *(BFFP 41/+T/CD)* **WIDOWERMAKER** ☐ ☐
– Bong song / 1401 / Booze tobacco / Helicopter.

— now without THERESA

Rough Trade / Rough Trade

Nov 90. (7") *(RT 240)* **THE HURDY GURDY MAN. / BARKING DOGS** ☐ ☐
(12"+=/cd-s+=) *(RTT 240/+CD)* – ('A'-Paul Leary remix).

Feb 91. (cd/c/lp) *(R 2081260-2/-4/-1)* <RTE R2601> **PIOUGHD** [68] ☐
– Revolution pt.1 & 2 / Lonesome bulldog pt.1 & 2 / The hurdy gurdy man / Golden showers / Lonesome bulldog pt.3 / Blindman / No, I'm iron man / Something / P.S.Y. / Lonesome bulldog pt.IV. *(cd+=)* – Barking dogs. <*(cd-iss. Dec94 on 'Danceteria'; DAN 069CD)*>

— In Apr'92, GIBBY guested for MINISTRY on single 'Jesus Built My Hotrod'. PAUL LEARY had earlier issued a solo set, while DRAIN (COFFEY's outfit) delivered a further two albums.

Capitol / Capitol

Mar 93. (cd/c/lp) *(CD/TC+/EST 2192)* <98798> **INDEPENDENT WORM SALOON** [73] ☐
– Who was in my room last night / The wooden song / Tongue / Chewin' George Lucas' chocolate / Goofy's concern / Alcohol / Dog inside your body / Strawberry / Some dispute over T-shirt sales / Dancing fool / You don't know me / The annoying song / Dust devil / Leave me alone / Edgar / The ballad of a naked man / Clean it up.

May 96. (cd/c/d-lp) *(CD/TC+/EST 2285)* <29842> **ELECTRICLARRYLAND** ☐ [31]
– Birds / Cough syrup / Pepper / Thermador / Ulcer breakout / Jingle of a dog's collar / TV star / My brother's wife / Ah ha / The Lord is a monkey / Let's talk about cars / L.A. / Space.

Sep 96. (7") *(CL 778)* **PEPPER. / HYBRID** [59] ☐
(cd-s+=) *(CDCL 778)* – Pepper (Butcha' Bros remix) / The Lord is a monkey.

– compilations, others, etc. –

Jun 89. (d-lp/cd) *Latino Bugger; (LBV 01)* **DOUBLE LIVE (live)** ☐ [-]

Nov 94. (7"/7"pic-d) *Trance Syndicate; (TR 30/+PD)* **GOOD KING WENCENSLAUS. / THE LORD IS A MONKEY** ☐ [-]

Apr 95. (cd) *Trance Syndicate; (TR 35CD)* **THE HOLE TRUTH & NOTHING BUTT!** (early demos) ☐ [-]

JACKOFFICERS

off-shoot with **GIBBY, JEFF & KATHLEEN**

Naked Brain / Rough Trade

Dec 90. (lp/c/cd) *(NBX 003/+C/CD)* <ROUGHUS 100> **DIGITAL DUMP** ☐ ☐
– Love-o-maniac / Time machine pt.1 & 2 / L.A.name peanut butter / Do it / Swingers club / Ventricular retribution / 6 / Don't touch that / An Hawaiian Christmas song / Flush.

P

— formed 1993 by **GIBBY + JOHNNY DEPP** – bass, guitar (yes! the actor & beau of supermodel Kate Moss) / **BILL CARTER** – bass / **SAL JENCO** – drums

Capitol / Capitol

Feb 96. (cd/c/lp) *(CD/TC PCS 7379)* <7243 8 32942-2/-4/-1> **P** ☐ ☐
– I save cigarette butts / Zing Splash / Michael Stipe / Oklahoma / Dancing queen / Jon Glenn (megamix) / Mr Officer / White man sings the blues / Die Anne / Scrapings from ring / The deal.

PAUL LEARY

Rough Trade / Rough Trade

Apr 91. (cd/c/lp) <*(R 2081263-2/-4/-1)*> **THE HISTORY OF DOGS** ☐ ☐
– The birds are dying / Apollo one / Dalhart down the road / How much longer / He's working overtime / Indians storm the government / Is it milky / Too many people / The city / Fine home.

DRAIN

aka **KING COFFEY + DAVID McCREETH** (ex-SQUID)

Trance Syndicate / Trance Syndicate

Apr 91. (7") <*(TR 04)*> **A BLACK FIST. / FLOWER MOUND** ☐ ☐

Mar 92. (lp/cd) <*(TR 11/+CD)*> **PICK UP HEAVEN** ☐ ☐
– National anthem / Crawfish / Martyr's road / Non compis mentis / Funeral pyre / Ozark monkey chant / Instant hippie / Flower mound / Every secret thing / The ballad of Miss Toni Fisher.

Apr 96. (cd) <*(TR 49CD)*> **OFFSPEED & IN THERE** ☐ ☐
– Playground twist / Burma slowdrive / Return to Rosedale / Marrakesh: 3 a.m. / Bunch of guys about to turn blue / Helicopters are burning / Saipan murder mystery / Stop six / Wendy will win / Nitrous shuffle / In the Spring we eat cucumbers / Upright and in love.

BUZZOV.EN

Formed: North Carolina, USA . . . early 90's out of SEWER PUPPET, by KIRK FISHER, BRIAN HILL and ASHLEY WILLIAMSON. Taking their cue from the GG ALLIN school of profanity, the oddly named BUZZOV.EN got their first break via the independently issued EP, 'WOUND' (1991). A handful of very rare releases surfaced over the next few years, 'Roadrunner' homing in on their brutal noise terror for the 'SORE' album. A long-awaited long-player follow-up came in the shape of 'AT A LOSS' (1998) – now if this had been released in the early 80's?

Album rating: TO A FROWN (*4) / MUSIC FOR THE PROLETAREAT compilation (*5) / VINYL RETENTIVE compilation (*5) / SORE (*6) / THE GOSPEL ACCORDING . . . II mini (*5) / AT A LOSS (*6)

KIRK FISHER – vocals, guitar / **BRIAN HILL** – bass / **ASHLEY WILLIAMSON** – drums

not iss. / Allied

1991. (7"ep) <*(ALLIEDNO 11)*> **WOUND EP** [-] ☐

1992. (cd) <*ALLIED 21CD*> **TO A FROWN** [-] ☐
– To a frown / Shove / Drained / Forget it / Frayed / Splinter my eye / Wound / Toe fry / Aching improv / Weeding.

Apr 94. (cd-ep) <*ALLIED 35*> **UNWILLING TO EXPLAIN** [-] ☐
– Behave / Done / Hollow / Aching improv #13.

— added **BUDDY APOSTOLIS** – guitar

Plastic Head / Plastic Head

1990's. (7") <*(KD 005)*> **HATE BOX. /** ☐ ☐

Roadrunner / Roadrunner

Sep 94. (cd/lp) <*(RR 8998-2/-1)*> **SORE** ☐ ☐
– Sore / Hawiking to explain / Hollow / Dome / I don't like you / Broken / Pathetic / Should I / Behaved / Blinded / Grit / This is not . . .

Allied / Allied

Mar 97. (m-cd) *(<ALLIED 84CD>)* **THE GOSPEL ACCORDING . . . II** ☐ ☐
– Vagabond / Mainline / Red – Green / Crawl away / Chokehold.

Reptilian / not iss.

Mar 97. (7") *(REP 013)* **USELESS. /** ☐ [-]

Off The Record / Conquest

Feb 99. (cd) *(OFFREC 003)* <*103*> **AT A LOSS** ☐ ☐ May98
– At a loss / A lack of / Kakkila / Loracei / Flow / Crawl away / Whiskey fit / Don't bring me down / Dirtkickers / Red – Green / Useless / Heal / Left behind.

– compilations, etc. –

1993. (lp) *Very Small;* **MUSIC FOR THE PROLETARIAT** [-] ☐

1993. (d-lp) *Very Small;* **VINYL RETENTIVE** [-] ☐

David BYRON (see under ⇒ URIAH HEEP)

B'ZZ (see under ⇒ BOYZZ)

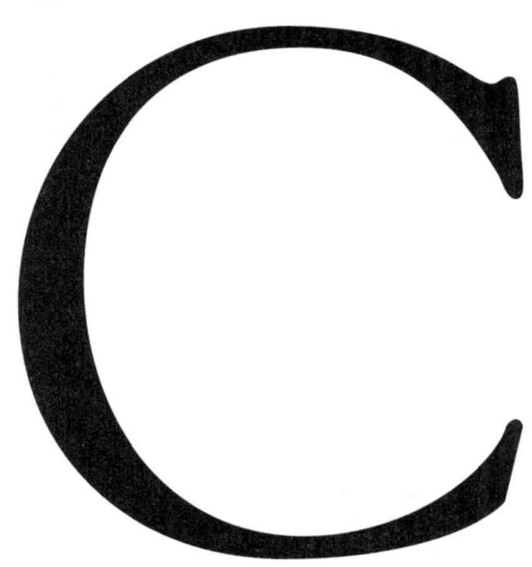

CABLE

Formed: Derby, England . . . 1994 by art-school lads, MATT BAGGULEY, DARIUS HINKS, PETER DARRINGTON and NEIL COOPER. After honing their skills at small venues around the nearby Nottingham locale, they released a couple of early limited edition 7"ers for 'Krunch!', namely 'SALE OF THE CENTURY' and 'OUBLIETTE'. Taking their wired, discordant indie-rock down south to the capital, CABLE were picked up by 'Infectious', who almost immediately delivered their first widely distributed effort, 'BLINDMAN'. With former MEMBRANES man JOHN ROBB at the production helm, they powered their way into '96 with the release of 'SEVENTY', their fourth single and a highlight of the accompanying debut mini-set, 'DOWN-LIFT THE UP-TRODDEN'. Despite being packaged in BLUESBREAKERS pastiche artwork with sleevenotes depicting the band as modern day blues saviours, the actual sound was closer to a relentless, hard-driving PAVEMENT. Over the course of the next year (by which time COOPER had been replaced by RICHIE MILLS – apparently recruited from an Exchange & Mart ad!), they laid the ground work for their first long-player, 'WHEN ANIMALS ATTACK' (1997), with two singles, 'WHISPER FIRING LINE' and 'BLUEBIRDS ARE BLUE'. The album also installed CABLE in the UK Top 50 for the first time via the single, 'FREEZE THE ATLANTIC', although a further track, 'GOD GAVE ME GRAVITY', failed to spark the same interest. After an electrifying EP, 'LIVE AT THE BRIXTON PRISON', in the tradition of JOHNNY CASH (whose 'RING OF FIRE' they actually covered), CABLE began working with ex-BUGGLES, YES & ASIA man, GEOFF DOWNES. A new single, 'ARTHUR WALKER', appeared in late 1998, a taster from the following year's second full-set, 'SUB-LINGUAL'.

Album rating: DOWN-LIFT THE UP-TRODDEN (*6) / WHEN ANIMALS ATTACK (*6) / SUB-LINGUAL (*7)

MATT BAGGULEY – vocals, guitar / **DARIUS HINKS** – guitar / **PETE DARRINGTON** – bass / **NEIL COOPER** – drums

Krunch! / not iss.

Jan 95. (ltd-7") *(KRUNCH 2)* **SALE OF THE CENTURY. / HYDRA** [ ] [-]

Jun 95. (ltd-7") *(KRUNCH 3)* **OUBLIETTE. /** [ ] [-]

Infectious / not iss.

Sep 95. (7") *(INFECT 25S)* **BLINDMAN. /** [ ] [-]
(cd-s+=) *(INFECT 25CD)* –

Feb 96. (7") *(INFECT 29W)* **SEVENTY. / SPORTS CARS AND DEVIL WORSHIP** [ ] [-]
(cd-s+=) *(INFECT 29CD)* – Dead wood for green.

Mar 96. (m-cd/m-lp) *(INFECT 32 CD/LP)* **DOWN-LIFT THE UP-TRODDEN** [ ] [-]
– New set of bruises / Choice / Blindman / Hydra / Seventy / Murdering spree / Sale of the century / Oubliette.

— (after above recording) **RICHIE MILLS** – drums; repl. NEIL

Sep 96. (7") *(INFECT 33S)* **WHISPER FIRING LINE. / MURDERING SPREE ELEVATED** [ ] [-]
(cd-s+=) *(INFECT 33CD)* – Can't find my way home.

Apr 97. (7") *(INFECT 36S)* **BLUEBIRDS ARE BLUE. / HORSE DRAWN AND QUARTERED** [ ] [-]
(cd-s+=) *(INFECT 36CD)* – Action replay replay / Clairvoyant.

May 97. (cd/lp) *(INFECT 35 CD/LP)* **WHEN ANIMALS ATTACK** [ ] [-]
– Souvenir / Bluebirds are blue / Signature tune / Freeze the Atlantic / Ultra violet / I'm always right / Colder climate / Whisper firing line / God gave me gravity / From here you can see yourself / Do the tube.

Jun 97. (7") *(INFECT 38S)* **FREEZE THE ATLANTIC. / (WE DID THE MUSIC FOR THE SPRITE AD) BLUES** [44] [-]
(7") *(INFECT 38SX)* – ('A'side) / Ring of fire.
(cd-s) *(INFECT 38CD)* – (all 3 tracks).

Aug 97. (7"m) *(INFECT 45S)* **GOD GAVE ME GRAVITY. / DINKEY / ELECTRO GAZELLE** [ ] [-]
(cd-s+=) *(INFECT 45CD)* – Let's merengue.

Sep 97. (cd-ep) *(INFECT 48CD)* **LIVE AT THE BRIXTON PRISON EP** [ ] [-]
– Ultraviolet / Bluebirds are blue / Ring of fire / Seventy / San Quentin / Oubilette.

Oct 98. (7") *(INFECT 066S)* **ARTHUR WALKER. / VERTIGO** [ ] [-]
(cd-s) *(INFECT 066CDS)* – ('A'side) / Tick tock alarm clock / ('A'-CD-rom video).

May 99. (cd) *(INFECT 058CD)* **SUB-LINGUAL** [ ] [ ]
– Song 1 / Arthur Walker / Pocket promise / Hexagon eye / Honolulu / Brothers and sisters / Widower / Land speed record / Yesterday on the horizon / Autobahn head / Commprendez.

CACOPHONY

Formed: USA . . . 1986 by axegrinders MARTY FRIEDMAN and JASON BECKER, with PETER MARRINO and ATMA ANUR completing the line-up. MARTY had played guitar in the band, VIXEN (obviously not the girl group!) who released one album, 'MADE IN HAWAII' for 'Azra' US 1983. Signing to 'Roadrunner' records, these six-string virtuosos that were CACOPHONY attempted to fuse classical stylings with fast and furious metal on their 1987 debut, 'SPEED METAL SYMPHONY'. Like many similar projects, it failed to realise in practice what looked fairly promising on paper. Both FRIEDMAN and BECKER subsequently proceeded to work on their own solo assignments, FRIEDMAN on 'DRAGON'S KISS' and BECKER on 'PERPETUAL BURN' (both issued almost simultaneously in the Autumn of '88). The former continued in the instrumental vein, although enhanced by exotic atmospherics, the latter also substituting vocals for dextrous, flying-fingered instrumental intensity. With a completely new rhythm section, FRIEDMAN and BECKER came together again to record a second and final CACOPHONY album, 'GO OFF!', released early in '89 to a less than enthusiast reception. Both guitarists went on to higher profile acts, FRIEDMAN to MEGADETH (making his debut on the acclaimed 'Rust In Peace' set) and BECKER to DAVID LEE ROTH's band. While still a member of MEGADETH, FRIEDMAN released his second solo set, 'SCENES' in 1992.

Album rating: SPEED METAL SYMPHONY (*6) / GO OFF! (*4) / Marty Friedman: DRAGON'S KISS (*5) / SCENES (*4) / INTRODUCTION (*5) / TRUE OBSESSIONS (*6) / Jason Becker: PERPETUAL BURN (*6) / PERSPECTIVE (*5) / THE RASPBERRY JAMS demos (*4)

MARTY FRIEDMAN – guitars, bass (ex-VIXEN) / **JASON BECKER** – guitars / with **PETER MARRINO** – vocals (ex-LE MANS) / **ATMA ANUR** – drums

Roadrunner / Shrapnel

Nov 87. (lp/cd) *(RR/+34 9577)* <*SH 1031/+CD*> **SPEED METAL SYMPHONY** [ ] [ ]
– Savage / Where my fortune lies / The Ninja / Concerto / Burn the ground / Desert island / Speed metal symphony. *(re-iss. Feb91; same)*

— **JIMMY O'SHEA** – bass + **KENNY STAVROPOULOS** – drums; repl. MARRINO + ANUR

Feb 89. (lp/cd) *(RR 9499-1/-2)* <*SH 1040/+CD*> **GO OFF!** [ ] [ ]
– X-ray eyes / Stranger / Black cat / The floating world / E.S.P. / Go off / Sword of the warrior / Images. *(re-iss. Feb91; same)*

— disbanded in 1990, BECKER joined DAVID LEE ROTH, FRIEDMAN went to MEGADETH and STAV teamed up with STARSHIP (!).

MARTY FRIEDMAN

— with various session people

Roadrunner / Shrapnel

Sep 88. (lp/cd) *(RR 9529-1/-2)* <*SH 1035/+CD*> **DRAGON'S KISS** [ ] [ ]
– Saturation point / Dragon mistress / Evil thrill / Namida / Anvils / Jewel / Forbidden city / Thunder march. *(cd re-iss. Dec94; same)*

Nov 92. (cd) *(RR 9104-2)* <*SH 1061CD*> **SCENES** [ ] [ ]
– Tibet / Angel / Valley of eternity / Night / Realm of the senses / West / Trance / Triumph. *(re-iss. Sep96; same)*

Dec 94. (cd) *(RR 8950-2)* **INTRODUCTION** [ ] [ ]
– Arrival / Bittersweet / Be / Escapism / Luna / Mama / Loneliness / Siberia. *(re-iss. May99; same)*

Metal Blade / Shrapnel

Oct 96. (cd) *(14219-2)* <*SH 1100CD*> **TRUE OBSESSIONS** [ ] [ ] Sep96
– Rio / Espionage / Last September / Rock box / The yearning / Live and learn / Glowing path / Intoxicated / Farewell / Thunder march (demo).

JASON BECKER

Roadrunner / Shrapnel

Sep 88. (lp/c/cd) *(RR 9528-1/-4/-2)* <*SH 1036CD*> **PERPETUAL BURN** [ ] [ ]
– Attitudes / Perpetual blues / Mabel's fatal fable / Temple of the absurd / Eleven blue Egyptians / Dweller in the cellar / Opus pocus. *(cd re-iss. Apr91; same)*

— next with various session people

not iss. / Jason Becker

May 96. (cd) <*/*> **PERSPECTIVE** [-] [ ]
– Primal / Rain / End of the beginning / Higher / Blue / Life and death / Empire / Serrana / Meet me in the morning. <*re-iss. 2001 on 'Warners'; 46951*>

– compilations, etc. –

Nov 99. (cd) *Shrapnel;* <*(SH 1134CD)*> **THE RASPBERRY JAMS: A COLLECTION OF DEMOS . . .** [ ] [ ] Oct99
– Becker-ola / Mandy's throbbing heart / Amma / When you wish upon a star / Jasin Street / Beatle grubs / Grilled peeps / If you have to shoot, shoot – don't talk / Purple chewable fern / Black stallion jam / Amamath / Angel eyes / Throat hole / Dang sea of Samsara / Umila / Thousand million suns / Clean solo / Too fast, no good for you! / Sweet baboon / Shock tea / Ghost to the post / Blood on the traches / Oddly enough / Crush / Vocal silliness.

CACTUS (see under ⇒ VANILLA FUDGE)

CANCER

Formed: Telford, Shropshire, England . . . late 80's by JOHN WALKER, IAN BUCHANAN and CARL STOKES. Initially a derivative death-metal outfit, CANCER debuted in 1991 with 'TO THE GORY END', the material as morbidly provocative as their moniker. Adding the ex-DEATH/OBITUARY guitarist JAMES MURPHY, the group developed their musical palate on a second release, 'DEATH SHALL RISE' (1993), the record benefitting from a Scott Burns production. BARRY SAVAGE subsequently replaced MURPHY for their next album, 'THE SINS OF MANKIND', the group at last beginning to fashion their own individual sound. 'East West' were sufficiently impressed to offer the band a worldwide deal, the first act of their ilk to be furnished with this dubious privilege. However only one album, 'BLACK FAITH' (1995) has surfaced since, the record at times very reminiscent of mid-period METALLICA. CANCER were also obviously fans of DEEP PURPLE, though their re-hashed thrash cover of 'SPACE TRUCKIN' would no doubt horrify purists.

Album rating: TO THE GORY END (*5) / DEATH SHALL RISE (*6) / THE SINS OF MANKIND (*7) / BLACK FAITH (*4)

JOHN WALKER – vocals, guitar / **IAN BUCHANAN** – bass / **CARL STOKES** – drums

Vinyl Solution / Restless

Mar 91. (lp) *(SOL 22)* **TO THE GORY END** [ ] [-]
– Blood bath / C.F.C. / Witch hunt / Into the acid / Imminent catastrophy / To the gory end / Body count / Sentenced / Die die. *<US cd-iss. Apr92; 72597>*

— added **JAMES MURPHY** (b. USA) – guitar (ex-DEATH, ex-OBITUARY)

Apr 92. (lp/cd) *(SOL 28/+CD) <72587>* **DEATH SHALL RISE** [ ] [ ]
– Hung, drawn and quartered / Tasteless incest / Burning casket / Death shall rise / Back from the drop / Gruesome tasks / Corpse fire / Internal decay.

— **BARRY SAVAGE** – guitar; repl. MURPHY

Jul 93. (cd) *(SOL 35CD) <72734>* **THE SINS OF MANKIND** [ ] [ ]
– Cloak of darkness / Electro convulsive therapy / Patchwork destiny / Meat train / Suffer our sins / Pasture of delights – At the end / Tribal bloodshed part 1 / The conquest / Under the flag / Tribal bloodshed part II.

East West / East West

Jul 95. (cd/c/lp) *(<0630 10752-2/-4/-1>)* **BLACK FAITH** [ ] [ ]
– Ants (nemesis ride) / Who do you think you are / Face to face / Without clause / White desire / Kill date / Temple song / Black faith / Highest orders / Space truckin' / Sunburnt / Save me from myself.

— disbanded soon after above set

CANDLEBOX

Formed: Beverly Hills, California, USA . . . 1992 by KEVIN MARTIN, PETER KLETT, BARDI MARTIN and SCOTT MERCADO. The band's career got off to a promising start, when MADONNA procured them for her eclectic, high-profile 'Maverick' label. Virtually guaranteed press coverage, then, the group delivered their eponymous debut album the following year to widespread critical acclaim. The record scaled the American charts slowly but surely over the course of a year, finally securing a Top 10 spot and selling a good few million in the process. Combining elements of melodic rock and post-grunge, the album spawned two hit singles, including the Top 20 hit, 'FAR BEHIND'. Unfortunately, this musical recipe for success had obviously been mislaid by the release of 'LUCY' (1995), an album which let down fans and critics alike despite its initial high chart placing. Further post-grunge misery was to beset the CANDLEBOX makers when MERCADO departed during the sessions of their third set. However, former PEARL JAM sticksman, DAVE KRUSEN, stepped in just in time to save the day, although the pundits and critics alike gave the LED ZEPPELIN-esque 'HAPPY PILLS' (1998) the proverbial thumbs down. • **Covered:** VOODOO CHILE (Jimi Hendrix).

Album rating: CANDLEBOX (*6) / LUCY (*4) / HAPPY PILLS (*4)

KEVIN MARTIN – vocals / **PETER KLETT** – guitar / **BARDI MARTIN** – bass / **SCOTT MERCADO** – drums

Maverick-Sire / Maverick-Sire

Jul 93. (cd/c) *<(9362 45313-2/-4)>* **CANDLEBOX** [ ] [7]
– Don't you / Change / You / No sense / Far behind / Blossom / Arrow / Rain / Mothers dream / Cover me / He calls home.

Mar 94. (c-s) *<18304>* **YOU / PULL AWAY** [-] [78]

Aug 94. (7"/c-s) *(W 0258/+C) <18118>* **FAR BEHIND. / YOU (live)** [ ] [18]
(cd-s+=) *(W 0258CD)* – Live medley: Far behind – Voodoo chile (slight return).

Oct 95. (cd/c) *<(9362 45962-2/-4)>* **LUCY** [ ] [11]
– Simple lessons / Drowned / Lucy / Best friend / Become (to tell) / Understanding / Crooked halo / Bothered / Butterfly / It's amazing / Vulgar before me / Butterfly (reprise).

— **DAVE KRUSEN** – drums (ex-PEARL JAM) repl. MERCADO

Jul 98. (cd-s) **IT'S ALRIGHT /** [-] [ ]

Jul 98. (cd/c) *<9362 46975-2/-4>* **HAPPY PILLS** [-] [65]
– 10,000 horses / Happy pills / Blinders / It's alright / Stone's throw away / So real / Offerings / Sometimes / Step back / Belmore place / Breakaway / Look what you've done.

CANDLEMASS

Formed; Stockholm, Sweden . . . 1985 by main writer LEIF EDLING (ex-NEMESIS), who enlisted the services of MATS "MAPPE" BJORKMAN, MATS EKSTROM and early member KLAS BERGWALL. Purveyors of doom-laden rock combining elements of classic British metal including BLACK SABBATH, URIAH HEEP and (BRUCE DICKINSON-era) IRON MAIDEN, the English-singing group successfully updated the style for the 90's when most bands went for speed over content. The band made their vinyl debut in 1986 with the po-faced 'EPICUS, DOOMICUS, METALLICUS' album, a competent start that boasted some of the most foreboding snail-paced riffs since SABBATH's first effort. A follow-up, 'NIGHTFALL' saw the band (now EDLING, BJORKMAN, massive frontman MESSIAH MARCOLIN, LASSE JOHANSSON and JAN LINDH) reach a creative peak, the record featuring highly in many end of year polls and establishing the band as the foremost practioners of the new doom movement. Their third set, 'ANCIENT DREAMS' (also in 1988) consolidated their approach, leading to a deal with top metal merchants, 'Music For Nations'. 'TALES OF CREATION' followed soon after, although there were criticisms that the group were beginning to tread water. After a live set, MARCOLIN (previously a live focal point with his on-stage monk's habit regalia) took a permanent sabbatical, perhaps taking the vow of silence . . . erm . . . too literally. He was replaced by TOMAS VICKSTROM on their swan song, 'CHAPTER VI', an album which saw CANDLEMASS abandoning, to a certain extent, their doom trappings for a faster-paced approach.

Album rating: EPICUS, DOOMICUS, METALLICUS (*4) / NIGHTFALL (*7) / ANCIENT DREAMS (*6) / TALES OF CREATION (*4) / LIVE (*4) / CHAPTER IV (*4) / AS IT IS, AS IT WAS – THE BEST OF CANDLEMASS compilation (*7) / DACTYLIS GLOMERATA (*6) / FROM THE 13th SUN (*5)

LASSE JOHANSSON – guitar / **MATS "MAPPE" BJORKMAN** – guitar / **LEIF EDLING** – bass (ex-NEMESIS) / **MATS EKSTROM** – drums / plus **JOHAN LANGOVIST** – vocals

Black Dragon / Leviathan

1986. (lp) *(BD 013) <LA 19882-1>* **EPICUS, DOOMICUS, METALLICUS** [ ] [-] French
– Solitude / Demons gate / Crystal ball / Black stone wielder / Under the oak / A sorcerer's pledge. *(UK cd-iss. Jun88 & Apr95; BDCD 013)*

— **EDLING + BJORKMAN** recruited new members **MESSIAH MARCOLIN** – vocals / **LARS JOHANSSON** – guitar / **JAN LINDH** – drums

Axis / not iss.

Mar 88. (7"red) *(7AX 1)* **SAMARITHAN. / SOLITUDE (re-recording)** [ ] [-]
(12"+=) *(12AX 1)* – Crystal ball.

— **MARCOLIN, JOHANSSON + LINDH**

Active / Metal Blade

Jun 88. (lp) *(ATVLP 3)* **NIGHTFALL** [ ] [-]
– Gothic stone / Well of souls / Codex gigas / At the gallows end / Samarithan / Marche funebre / Dark are the veils of death / Mourners lament / Bewitched / Black candles. *(cd-iss. Feb90; CDATV 3)*

Jul 88. (12"ep) *<72295-0>* **AT THE GALLOWS END. / CRSTAL BALL / SOLITUDE** [-] [ ]

Dec 88. (lp) *(ACTLP 7) <73340-1>* **ANCIENT DREAMS** [ ] [ ]
– Mirror mirror / A cry from the crypt / Darkness in paradise / Incarnation of evil / Bearer of pain / Ancient dreams / The bells of Acheron / Epistle No.81 / Black Sabbath medley. *(cd-iss. Feb90; ACTCD 7)*

Music For Nations / Metal Blade

Sep 89. (lp/c/cd) *(MFN/+T/CD 95) <73417-1/-4/-2>* **TALES OF CREATION** [ ] [ ]
– The prophecy / Dark reflections / Voices in the wind / Under the oak / Tears / Into the unfathomed tower; pt I:- Dance of the Fay, pt II:- Magic – Entering the tower, pt III:- Dance of the Fay (reprise), pt IV:- Souls flight, pt V:- Towards the unknown, pt VI:- Choir of angels, pt VIII:- Outside the gates of Heaven / At the edge of Heaven / Somewhere in nowhere / Through the infinitive halls of death / Dawn / A tale of creation.

Nov 90. (cd/c/lp) *(CD/T+/MFN 109) <26444-2>* **LIVE** (live in Stockholm 9th June 1990) [ ] [ ] 1991
– Well of souls / Dark are the veils / Bewitched / Solitude / Dark reflections / Under the oak / Demons gate / Bells of Acheron / Through the infinitive halls of death / Samarithan / Mirror mirror / Gallow's end / Sorcerer's pledge.

— **TOMAS VIKSTROM** – vocals (ex-TALK OF THE TOWN) repl. MARCOLIN

May 92. (cd/c/lp) *(CD/T+/MFN 128) <7282>* **CHAPTER VI** [ ] [ ] Apr95
– The dying illusion / Julie laughs no more / Where the runes still speak / Ebony throne / Temple of the dead / Aftermath / Black eyes. *(cd+=)* – The end of pain.

— split in 1993, EDLING formed ABSTRAKT ALGEBRA; CANDLEMASS returned . . .

Apr 98. (cd) *(CDMFN 237)* **DACTYLIS GLOMERATA** [ ] [-]
– Wiz / I still see the black / Dust flow / Cylinder / Karthago / Abstrakt sun / Apathy / Lidocain god / Molotov.

Sep 99. (cd) *(CDMFN 253)* **FROM THE 13th SUN** [ ] [-]
– Droid / Tot / Elephant star / Blumma apt / ARX/NG 891 / Zog / Galatea / Cyclo-F / Mythos.

– compilations, etc. –

Oct 94. (d-cd) *Music For Nations; (CDMFN 166)* **THE BEST OF CANDLEMASS – AS IT IS, AS IT WAS** [ ] [ ]
– Solitude / Bewitched / Dying illusion / Demons gate / Mirror mirror (live) / Samarithan / Into the unfathomed tower / Bearer of pain / Where the runes still speak / At the gallows end / Mourners lament // A tale of creation / Ebony throne / Under the oak / Well of souls (live) / Dark are the veils of death / Darkness in paradise / The end of pain / Sorcerer's pledge / Solitude ('87 12" version) / Crystal ball ('87 12"version) / Bullfest ('93 Swedish party single).

Mar 99. (cd) *Powerage; (PRAGE 012CD)* **EPICUS, DOOMICUS, METALLICUS / CANDLEMASS LIVE** [ ] [-]

CANNIBAL CORPSE

Formed: Buffalo, New York, USA . . . late 80's by CHRIS BARNES, BOB RUSAY, JACK OWEN, ALEX WEBSTER and PAUL MAZURKIEWICZ. Possibly the most offensive band in the history of music, a prison psychiatric report would probably be more apt in this case than a biography. That's if they take themselves seriously, let's hope for the good people of Buffalo that they don't. 'Metal Blade' records stuck their necks out, delivering their death-metal debut, 'EATEN BACK TO LIFE' in 1990. More gruesomely-titled offerings followed with each passing year, namely 'BUTCHERED AT BIRTH', 'TOMB OF THE MUTILATED', 'HAMMER SMASHED FACE' (a mini) and 'THE BLEEDING', the latter featuring new guitarist, ROB BARRETT. Just a cursory glance at the severely twisted sexual brutality inherent in the song titles, surely suggest that this band have their tongues planted firmly in their proverbial cheek. Incredibly, the band made it onto celluloid, featuring in the 1993 film, 'Ace Ventura: Pet Detective'. BARNES was subsequently replaced by new vocalist GEORGE "Corpsegrinder" FISHER (ex-MONSTROSITY), who got his first shot at grinding some lyrical corpses – or at least his gnashers – on 1996's 'VILE' opus. Maybe they were mellowing with age but 'GALLERY OF SUICIDE' (1998) had slightly less sick titles if not exactly toning down the brutal death metal assault. Then again, the lads were back in fine lyrical form once again for 1999's 'BLOODTHIRST', featuring song titles that would have Mary Whitehouse suffering a seizure. Having kept up the flood of gore for almost a decade, CANNIBAL CORPSE must surely have to ask themselves just how much of this stuff any one person can take.

Album rating: EATEN BACK TO LIFE (*5) / BUTCHERED AT BIRTH (*7) / TOMB OF THE MUTILATED (*6) / HAMMER SMASHED FACE mini (*4) / THE BLEEDING (*6) / VILE (*5) / GALLERY OF SUICIDE (*5) / BLOODTHIRST (*4) / LIVE CANNIBALISM (*4)

CHRIS BARNES – vocals / **BOB RUSAY** – guitar / **JACK OWEN** – guitar / **ALEX WEBSTER** – bass / **PAUL MAZURKIEWICZ** – drums

Metal Blade | Caroline

Sep 90. (cd/c/lp) *(CD/T+/ZORRO 12)* *<CAROL 1900-2>* **EATEN BACK TO LIFE** [ ] [ ]
– Shredded humans / Put them to death / Scattered remains, splattered brains / Rotting head / Bloody chunks / Buried in the backyard / Edible autopsy / Mangled / Born in a casket / The undead will feast / A skull full of maggots. *(cd re-iss. Mar96; 3984 14024CD)*

Aug 91. (cd/c/lp) *(CD/T+/ZORRO 26)* *<CAROL 2204-2>* **BUTCHERED AT BIRTH** [ ] [ ]
– Meat hook sodomy / Gutted / Living dissection / Under the rotted flesh / Covered with sores / Vomit the soul / Butchered at birth / Rancid amputation / Innards decay. *(cd re-iss. Mar96; 3984 14072CD)*

Metal Blade | Metal Blade

Sep 92. (cd/c/lp) *(CD/T+/ZORRO 49)* *<14002>* **TOMB OF THE MUTILATED** [ ] [ ]
– Hammer smashed face / I cum blood / Addicted to vaginal skin / Split wide open / Necropedophile / The cryptic stench / Post mortem ejaculation / Beyond the cemetry / Entrails ripped from a virgin's cunt. *(cd re-iss. Mar96; 3984 14010CD)*

Apr 93. (m-cd/m-lp) *(CD+/MZORRO 57)* *<14014>* **HAMMER SMASHED FACE** [ ] [ ]
– Hammer smashed face / Exorcist / Zero the hero / Meat hook sodomy / Shredded humans.

—— **ROB BARRETT** – guitar; repl. RUSAY

Mar 94. (cd/c/lp) *(CD/T+/ZORRO 67)* *<14037>* **THE BLEEDING** [ ] [ ]
– Staring through the eyes of the dead / Fucked with a knife / Stripped, raped and strangled / Pulverized / Return to flesh / The pick-axe murders / She was asking for it / The bleeding / Force fed broken glass / An experiment in homocide. *(cd re-iss. Feb97; 3984 14137CD)*

—— **GEORGE FISHER** – vocals (ex-MONSTROSITY) repl. BARNES who had already formed SIX FEET UNDER (a group, that is)

Apr 96. (cd) *<(3984 14104CD)>* **VILE** [ ] [ ] May96
– Devoured by vermin / Mummified in barbed wire / Perverse suffering / Disfigured / Bloodlands / Puncture wound massacre / Relentless beating / Absolute hatred / Eaten from inside / Orgasm through torture / Monolith. *(uncensored version Aug96; same)*

Apr 98. (cd/lp) *<(3984 14151-2/-1)>* **GALLERY OF SUICIDE** [ ] [ ]
– I will kill you / Disposal of the body / Sentenced to burn / Blood drenched execution / Gallery of suicide / Dismembered and molested / From skin to liquid / Unite the dead / Stabbed in the throat / Chambers of blood / Headless / Every bone broken / Centuries of torment / Crushing the despised.

Nov 99. (cd/lp) *<(14274-2/-1)>* **BLOODTHIRST** [ ] [ ] Oct99
– Pounded into dust / Dead human collection / Unleashing the bloodthirsty / The spine splitter / Ecstasy in decay / Raped by the beast / Coffinfeeder / Hacksaw decapitation / Blowtorch slaughter / Sickening metamorphosis / Condemned to agony. *(also uncensored+=; 14277-2)* – Sentenced to burn.

Oct 00. (cd/lp) *<(14303-2/-1)>* **LIVE CANNIBALISM (live)** [ ] [ ] Sep00
– Staring through the eyes of the dead / Blowtorch slaughter / Stripped, raped and strangled / I cum blood / Covered with sores / Fucked with a knife / Unleashing the bloodthirsty / Dead human collection / Gallery of suicide / Meat hook sodomy / Perverse suffering / The spine splitter / Gutted / I will kill you / Devoured by vermin / Disposal of the body / A skull full of maggots / Hammer smashed face.

Jerry CANTRELL (see under ⇒ ALICE IN CHAINS)

CAPDOWN

Formed: Milton Keynes, England . . . mid 90's as SOAP by schoolfriends JAKE SIMMS-FIELDING, KEITH MINTER, BOOB aka ROBIN GOULD and TIM McDONALD. After a couple of years, the crusty punks changed their name to CAPDOWN (as in Capitalist Downfall), leaving no doubt as to their activist-centred approach. Eventually signed to indie label, 'Household Name', the band released the 'TIME FOR CHANGE' EP in 1999 and also contributed their skanking hardcore to punk compilation, 'Deck Cheese'. A long awaited debut album, 'CIVIL DISOBEDIENTS' (2000) was aural proof of the band's open minded musical policy, chucking in bits of dub reggae and drum'n'bass alongside the politically-charged riffing. Having clawed their way up the hard way, the band were naturally wary of the hordes of yankophile English wannabes, instead praising the self-sufficient ethos behind the free party/rave scene.

Album rating: CIVIL DISOBEDIENTS (*6)

JAKE SIMMS-FIELDING – vocals, saxophone / **KEITH MINTER** – guitar / **BOOB** – bass / **TIM McDONALD** – drums

Household Name | not iss.

Apr 99. (cd-ep) *(HAUS 024CD)* **TIME FOR CHANGE EP** [ ] [–]
– Time for change / Stand my ground / Yourself, your whole self & nothing but yourself / If money's your life / If we don't last very long.

May 00. (cd) *(HAUS 032CD)* **CIVIL DISOBEDIENTS** [ ] [–]
– Unite to progress / Kained but Able / Ska wars / Jnr NBC / Dub No.1 / Positivity / Cousin Cleotis / The neverlution / Civil disobedients / Headstrong / Deal real / Bitches and Nike shoes.

Dec 00. (7"m) *(HAUS 040)* **GREEN. / (others by Southport & Hard Skin)** [ ] [–]

CAPTAIN BEYOND

Formed: Los Angeles, California, USA – based . . . 1972 as yet another supergroup, by ex-DEEP PURPLE singer, ROD EVANS, seasoned blues drummer BOBBY CALDWELL and IRON BUTTERFLY troopers LARRY 'RHINO' RHEINHART and LEE DORMAN. They were duly signed to 'Capricorn' records (home of The ALLMANS), with the moderately successful eponymous album providing a taste of Americanised neo-psychedelic hard-rock. A few personnel changes ensued, CALDWELL departing prior to their second album, 'SUFFICIENTLY BREATHLESS', the record grazing the Top 100 for a couple of weeks. A mid 70's hiatus was finally broken when the band resurfaced on 'Warners' with 'DAWN EXPLOSION', WILLY DAFFERN (EVANS' replacement) now on vocals and CALDWELL back on the drumstool.

Album rating: CAPTAIN BEYOND (*5) / SUFFICIENTLY BREATHLESS (*6) / DAWN EXPLOSION (*4)

ROD EVANS (b.19 Jan'47, Slough, England) – vocals (ex-DEEP PURPLE) / **LARRY 'Rhino' RHEINHART** (b. 7 Jul'48, Florida) – guitar (ex-IRON BUTTERFLY) / **LEE DORMAN** (b.15 Sep'45, St.Louis) – bass, piano, vocals (ex-IRON BUTTERFLY) / **BOBBY CALDWELL** – drums, percussion (ex-JOHNNY WINTER, ex-RICK DERRINGER)

Capricorn | Capricorn

Aug 72. (lp) *(K 47503)* *<CP 0105>* **CAPTAIN BEYOND** [ ] [ ]
– Dancing madly backwards (on a sea of air) / Armworth / Myopic void / Mesmerization eclipse / Raging river of fear / Frozen over / Thousand days of yesterdays (time since come and gone) / I can't feel nothin' / As the Moon speaks (to the waves of the seal) / Astral lady / As the Moon speaks / I can't feel nothin' (part 2). *<US cd-iss. 1989 on 'Polygram'; P33P 25051>*

Sep 72. (7") *<0013>* **AS THE MOON SPEAKS (RETURN). / THOUSAND DAYS OF YESTERDAYS (TIME SINCE COME AND GONE)** [–] [ ]

—— **MARTY RODRIGUEZ** – drums / **REESE WYNANS** – piano / **GUILLE GARCIA** – percussion, repl. CALDWELL

Aug 73. (lp) *<CP 0115>* **SUFFICIENTLY BREATHLESS** [–] [90]
– Sufficiently breathless / Bright blue tango / Drifting in space / Evil men / Starglow energy / Distant Sun / Voyages of past travelers / Everything's a circle. *<US cd-iss. 1989 on 'Polygram'; P28P 25086>*

Sep 73. (7") *<0029>* **DRIFTING IN SPACE. / SUFFICIENTLY BREATHLESS** [–] [ ]

—— (1976) **WILLY DAFFERN** – vocals, repl. EVANS

—— **BOBBY CALDWELL** – drums, returned to repl. RODRIGUEZ, GARCIA + WYNANS

Warners | Warners

Jun 77. (lp) *<BS 3047>* **DAWN EXPLOSION** [–] [ ]
– Do or die / Icarus / Sweet dreams / Fantasy / Breath of fire (part 1 & 2) / If you please / Midnight memories / Oblivion – Space (medley).

—— disbanded after above

Keith CAPUTO (see under ⇒ LIFE OF AGONY)

CARCASS

Formed: Liverpool, England . . . 1985/6 by BILL STEER as a gory sideline to the more politically inclined NAPALM DEATH. Eventually taking the project on full-time, the line-up was completed by ex-ELECTRO HIPPIES frontman JEFF WALKER and KEN OWEN. Long-haired veggie hardcore death-metal grindcrushers (phew!), the band signed to 'Earache' (who else?!) and released their controversial debut album, 'REEK OF PUTREFACTION' in 1988. Radical for the time, the group's lyrical preoccupation with physical decay and medical dissection (which extended to their live slide shows and cover artwork) together with their ferocious musical onslaught pre-empting the subsequent death-metal explosion. Though the band were hounded by the tabloids, an early supporter was the ever eclectic Radio One DJ,

John Peel. In 1989, they gained further notoriety with their second post-mortem, 'SYMPHONIES OF SICKNESS', the group being one of the main attractions on that year's legendary 'Grindcrusher' European tour (a stage-divers paradise). In March '91, their first two albums were seized by police under obscenity laws, although the charges were dropped later that year. In the meantime, MICHAEL AMOTT had been added, the guitarist making his debut on the album, 'NECROTICISM – DESCANTING THE INSALUBRIOUS'. In 1993, the fourth album, the less tongue-twistingly titled 'HEARTWORK' (enjoying extra controversy due to an HR GIGER – famous for getting The DEAD KENNEDYS in trouble – designed sleeve) fractured the UK Top 75, leading to a groundbreaking deal with 'Columbia'. Predictably, major label expectations didn't match the band's own and they were soon back in the 'Earache' stable. Around these wilderness years, they toured alongside BODY COUNT (ICE-T's metal band) and PITCH SHIFTER, although by the release of the lame MEGADETH-sounding 'SWANSONG' album in '96, the musical rot had set in. This was perhaps due to yet another personnel change, CARLOS REGEDAS coming in for AMOTT, although the record again sold respectably (Top 75). Astonishly, the rest of the band mutinied, sacking their founder BILL STEER. They subsequently went on to form BLACK STAR, enlisting ex-CATHEDRAL man, GRIFF.

Album rating: REEK OF PUTREFACTION (*5) / SYMPHONIES OF SICKNESS (*6) / NECROTICISM – DESCANTING THE INSALUBRIOUS (*7) / HEARTWORK (*7) / SWANSONG (*4) / WAKE UP AND SMELL THE . . . compilation (*6)

JEFF WALKER – vocals, bass (ex-ELECTRO HIPPIES) / **BILL STEER** – guitar (also of NAPALM DEATH until 1989) / **KEN OWENS** – drums

Earache Relativity

Jun 88. (lp) *(MOSH 6) <2025>* **REEK OF PUTREFACTION** [ ] [ ] 1991
– Genital grinder / Regurgitation of giblets / Maggot colony / Pyosisified (rotten to the core) / Carbonized eyesockets / Frenzied detruncation / Vomited anal tract / Festerday / Fermenting innards / Excreted alive / Suppuration / Foeticide / Microwaved uterogestation / Feast on dismembered carnage / Splattered cavities / Psychopathologist / Burnt to a crisp / Pungent excruciation / Manifestation of verrucose uretura / Oxidised razor masticator / Mucopurulence excretor / Malignant defecation. *(re-iss. Jan90 cd/c; MOSH 006 CD/MC) (re-iss. cd Sep94 & Sep97; same)*

Nov 89. (pic-lp/c/cd) *(MOSH 18/+MC/CD) <2017>* **SYMPHONIES OF SICKNESS** [ ] [ ] 1990
– Reek of putrefaction / Exhume to consume / Excoriating abdominal examination / Ruptured in purulence / Empathological necroticism / Embryonic necropsy and devourment / Swarming vulgar mass of infected virulency / Cadaveric incubator of Endoparasites / Slash dementia / Creitating bowel erosion. *(re-iss. cd Sep94; same)*

—— added **MICHAEL AMOTT** – guitar (ex-CARNAGE)

Earache Combat

Nov 91. (lp/cd) *(MOSH 042/+CD) <1096>* **NECROTICISM – DESCANTING THE INSALUBRIOUS** [ ] [ ]
– Inpropagation / Corporal jigsore quandary / Symposium of sickness / Pedigree butchery / Incarnated solvent abuse / Carneous cacoffiny / Lavaging expectorate of lysergide compostion / Forensic clinicism – The Sanguine article. *(re-iss. cd Sep94 & Sep97; same)*

Aug 92. (12"ep/cd-ep) *(MOSH 049 T/CD)* **TOOLS OF THE TRADE / PYSISIFIED (STILL ROTTEN TO THE GORE). / INCARNATED SOLVENT ABUSE / HEPATIC TISSUE FERMENTATION II** [ ] [-]

Earache Epic

Oct 93. (lp/c/cd) *(MOSH 097/+MC/CD) <57525>* **HEARTWORK** [67] [ ]
– Buried dreams / Carnal forge / No love lost / Heartwork / Embodiment / This mortal coil / Arbeit macht fleish / Blind bleeding the blind / Doctrinal expletives / Death certificate. *(re-iss. cd Sep94 & Sep97; same)*

Feb 94. (12"ep/cd-ep) *(MOSH 108 T/CD)* **HEARTWORK. / THIS IS YOUR LIFE / ROT'N'ROLL** [ ] [-]

—— **CARLOS REGEDAS** – guitar (ex-DEVOID) repl. AMOTT

Earache Earache

Jun 96. (lp/c/cd) *(<MOSH 160/+MC/CD>)* **SWANSONG** [68] [ ]
– Keep on rotting in the free world / Tomorrow belongs to nobody / Black star / Cross my heart / Childs play / Room 101 / Polarized / Generation hexed / Firm hand / R**k the vote / Don't believe a word / Go to Hell. *(ltd-brain-sha-pic-cd w/ cd+=)*– Emotional flatline. *(cd re-iss. Sep97; same)*

—— finally laid to rest just as they fired BILL STEER

Nov 96. (lp/c/cd) *(<MOSH 161/+MC/CD>)* **WAKE UP AND SMELL THE . . .** (compilation) [ ] [ ]
– Edge of darkness / Emotional flatine / Ever increasing circles / Blood splattered banner / I told you so (corporate rock really does suck) / Buried dreams (radio version) / No love lost (radio version) / Rot'n'roll (radio version) / Edge of darkness (radio version) / This is your life / Rot'n'roll / Tools of the trade / Pyosisified (still rotten to the gore) / Hepatic tissue fermentation II / Genital grinder II / Hepatic tissue fermentation / Exhume to consume.

—— now called BLACK STAR, they recruited GRIFF (ex-CATHEDRAL)

—— split just prior to above album

– other compilations, etc. –

Aug 89. (12"ep) *Strange Fruit; (SFPS 073) / Dutch East India; <8338>*
THE PEEL SESSIONS [ ] [ ]
– Pathological / Genital grinder II / Hepatic tissue fermentation.

CARNAGE

Formed: Sweden . . . late 80's by JOHAN LIIVA AXELSSON, MICHAEL AMOTT (ex-CARCASS), JOHNNY DORDEVIC and JEPPE LARSSON; some stemming from DISMEMBER and CARBONIZED. Spawned from the same grass roots death metal scene which saw the likes of ENTOMBED hailed as conquering heroes, CARNAGE distributed their first two demos via the thriving underground tape swapping network. A bonafide debut album, 'DARK RECOLLECTIONS' was finally released in 1990 – recorded with a revised line-up of AMOTT, MATT KARKI, DAVID BLOMKUIST and FRED ESTBY – by which time the band's constant personnel upheaval had led to its virtual demise. Regarded by extreme metal afficionados as an early classic of the genre, the record took its cue from Brit grindcore acts such as CARCASS with whom AMOTT later hooked up (he subsequently played in both ARCH ENEMY and the SPIRITUAL BEGGARS). DORDEVIC, meanwhile, enjoyed a short stint with ENTOMBED while KARKI and ESTBY went on to court controversy with their own act DISMEMBER. • **Note:** not to be confused with mid 80's outfit.

Album rating: DARK RECOLLECTIONS (*6)

JOHAN LIIVA AXELSSON – vocals, bass / **MICHAEL AMOTT** – guitar / **FRED ESTBY** – drums; repl. JEPPE LARSSON / also early members MATT KARKI – vocals + DAVID BLOMKUIST – guitar

Neurosis Combat

Dec 90. (lp/c/cd) *(NECRO 3/+MC/CD) <88561-1105-2/-4>* **DARK RECOLLECTIONS** [ ] [ ] Feb90
– Dark collections / Torn apart / Blasphemies of the flesh / Infestation of evil / Gentle exhuming / Deranged from blood / Malignant epitaph / Self dissection / Death evocation / Outro / Crime against humanity / Aftermath / The day man lost / Torn apart. *(cd includes a CADAVER album) (<cd re-iss. Jun00 on 'Earache'; MOSH 232CD>)*

—— split when AMOTT moved to CARCASS (he was later in ARCH ENEMY + SPIRITUAL BEGGARS), DORDEVIC joined ENTOMBED while most of the others formed DISMEMBER

CARNIVORE

Formed: New York, USA . . . 1983 by LOUIE BATTREAUX and PETER STEELE (ex-FALLOUT), who enlisted the help of KEITH ALEXANDER. Signing to 'Roadrunner' in Europe, CARNIVORE attempted to claw their way into the metal scene with an eponymous debut album of unremarkable thrash. Nevertheless the band gained some press attention due to their cod-futuristic image. A follow-up, 'RETALIATION' was released in 1987, although it failed to raise them above Vauxhall Conference league status.

Album rating: CARNIVORE (*4) / RETALIATION (*5)

PETER STEELE – vocals, bass / **LOUIE BATTEAUX** (alias LORD PETRUS T) – drums / **KEITH ALEXANDER** – guitar

Roadrunner New Renaissance

Apr 86. (lp) *(RR 9754) <GWC 90534>* **CARNIVORE** [ ] [ ]
– Predator / Male supremacy / Legion of doom / Thermonuclear warrior / Carnivore / Armageddon / God is dead / World Wars III & IV. *(cd-iss. Mar90 on 'Roadracer'; RO 9754-2) (<cd re-mast.Jan01 +=; RR 8746-2>)* – USA for USA (demo) / SMD (demo) / Sex and violence (demo).

—— **MARC PIOVANETTI** – guitar; repl. ALEXANDER

Apr 87. (lp) *(RR 9597)* **RETALIATION** [ ] [-]
– Jack Daniel's sand pizza / Angry neurotic Catholics / S.M.D. / Ground zero Brooklyn / Race war / Inner conflict / Jesus Hitler / Technophobia / Manic depression / U.S.A. for U.S.A. / Five billion dead / Sex and violence. *(cd-iss. Apr89 on 'Roadracer'; RO 9597-2) (<cd re-mast.Jan01 +=; RR 8745-2>)* – World war III & IV (demo) / Carnivore (demo) / Subhuman (demo).

—— folded in 1988; PIOVANETTI joined CRUMBSUCKERS while STEELE formed TYPE O NEGATIVE

CARSON (see under ⇒ JAGUAR)

CATHEDRAL

Formed: Coventry, England . . . 1990 by ex-NAPALM DEATH grunter LEE DORRIAN, his best friend MARK GRIFFITHS, BEN MOCHRIE and two former ACID REIGN members, GARRY JENNINGS and ADAM LEHAN. They released a four-track demo 'IN MEMORIUM', the 12"ep including a version of Pentagram's 'ALL YOUR SINS' and preceding a powerful debut for 'Earache', entitled 'FOREST OF EQUILIBRIUM' (MOCKRIE having been relaced by sticksman MIKE SMAIL). With DORRIAN's vox now notably more accessible, the group followed in the much-trodden (CANDLEMASS, TROUBLE, etc.) footsteps of OZZY-era BLACK SABBATH. In 1992, SMAIL had been succeeded in turn by MARK RAMSEY WHARTON, who was in place for the EP, 'SOUL SACRIFICE'. A year later, now without GRIFF, the grind-merchants became part of Columbia's dubious drive to carve out a piece of the death/grind market, although 'Earache' continued to release the band's material in Britain. 'THE ETHEREAL MIRROR' became the band's most lauded set to date, although they were subsequently dogged by a series of line-up changes. In 1994, the EP 'STATIK MAJIK' contained the 22 minute epic, 'THE VOYAGE OF THE HOMELESS SAPIEN'. By the release of their 1995 'THE CARNIVAL BIZARRE' opus, they had turned into a flares and purple-shirted retro-metal act. Another album, 'SUPERNATURAL BIRTH MACHINE' (1996) was well-received by CATHEDRAL's loyal congregation. With the ghost of BLACK SABBATH ever hovering in the wings like a gloomy guardian angel, DORRIAN and his cohorts waded through a sea of sonic sludge graced by the best classically heavy metal titles this side of MONSTER MAGNET ('CYCLOPS REVOLUTION', 'SUICIDE ASTEROID' etc.). 1998's 'CARAVAN BEYOND REDEMPTION' was another exercise in 70's-style space-rock meltdown, the band even flirting with elements of wah-wah funk and usually managing a fairly supple groove to supplement the ominous lyrics and harbinger-of-doom vocals. Having taken the hippie schtick about as far as inhumanly possible, CATHEDRAL welcomed the new millennium with an album billed as a return to their roots. 'ENDTYME' (2001) attempted to put the grind back into their doom, slowing things down although not quite shaking off the more colourful elements and experimentation of their stoner-rock golden period. • **Covered:** FIRE (Crazy World Of Arthur Brown).

Album rating: FOREST OF EQUILIBRIUM (*4) / THE ETHEREAL MIRROR (*7) / THE CARNIVAL BIZARRE (*6) / SUPERNATURAL BIRTH MACHINE (*6) / CARAVAN BEYOND REDEMPTION (*6) / ENDTYME (*5)

LEE DORRIAN – vocals (ex- NAPALM DEATH) / **GARRY JENNINGS** – guitar (ex-ACID REIGN) / **ADAM LEHAN** – guitar (ex-ACID REIGN) / **MARK 'GRIFF' GRIFFITHS** – bass / **BEN MOCHRIE** – drums

Rise Above / not iss.

Jan 91. (12"purple-ep) *(RISE 008)* **IN MEMORIUM** [ ] [-]
– Mourning of a new day / All your sins / Ebony tears / March. *(cd-ep iss.May94; RISE 008CD)*

— **MIKE SMAIL** – drums (ex-PENANCE, ex-DREAM DEATH) repl. MOCKRIE

Earache / Combat

Sep 91. (lp/c/cd) *(MOSH 043/+MC/CD) <1093>* **FOREST OF EQUILIBRIUM** [ ] [ ]
– Picture of beauty and innocence (intro) / Compromising the celebration / Ebony tears / Serpent eve / A funeral request / Equilibrium / Reaching happiness, touching pain. *(re-iss. cd Sep94 & Sep97; same)*

— **MARK RAMSEY WHARTON** – drums; repl. SMAIL

Earache / Columbia

Aug 92. (12"ep/cd-ep) *(MOSH 040 T/CD) <53149>* **SOUL SACRIFICE** [ ] [ ]
– Soul sacrifice / Autumn twilight / Frozen rapture / Golden blood (flooding).

— now without GRIFF, who later joined CARCASS re-incarnation BLACK STAR

May 93. (lp/blue-lp/c/cd) *(MOSH 077/+C/MC/CD) <53633>* **THE ETHEREAL MIRROR** [ ] [ ] Feb93
– Violent vortex (intro) / Ride / Enter the worms / Midnight mountain / Fountain of innocence / Grim luxuria / Jaded entity / Ashes you leave / Phantasmagoria / Imprisoned in flesh. *(re-iss. cd Sep94; same)*

— guest bassist **MIKE HICKEY** (of CRONOS)

Apr 94. (12"ep) *(MOSH 106 T/CD)* **STATIK MAJIK EP** [ ] [ ]
– Hypnos 164 / Cosmic funeral / The voyage of the homeless sapien.
(cd-ep+=) *(MOSH 106CD)* – Midnight mountain.

Jun 94. (cd-ep) *<64326>* **COSMIC REQUIEM** [-] [ ]
– Cosmic funeral / Hypnos 164 / Funeral request – Rebirth / The voyage of the homeless sapien.

— **JOE HASSELVANDER** – guitar (ex-PENTAGRAM) + **VICTOR GRIFFIN** – drums (ex-PENTAGRAM) to repl. LEHAN + WHARTON

— they were repl. late '94 by **SCOTT HARLSON** – bass (ex-REPULSION) / **DAVE HORNYAK** – drums

— **DORRIAN + JENNINGS** recruited **LEO SMEE** – bass / **BRIAN DIXON** – drums to repl. above

Earache / Earache

Sep 95. (2x10"lp/c/cd) *(<MOSH 130/+MC/CD>)* **THE CARNIVAL BIZARRE** [ ] [ ] Oct95
– Vampire sun / Hopkins (The Witchfinder General) / Utopian blaster (featuring TONY IOMMI) / Night of the seagulls / Carnival bizarre / Inertias cave / Fangalactic supergoria / Blue light / Palace of fallen majesty / Electric grave. *(cd re-iss. Sep97; same)*

Oct 95. (10"ep/cd-ep) *(<MOSH 152/+CD>)* **HOPKINS (THE WITCHFINDER GENERAL) / FIRE / COPPER SUNSET / PURPLE WONDERLAND / THE DEVILS SUMMIT** [ ] [ ] Apr96

Oct 96. (cd) *(<MOSH 156CD>)* **SUPERNATURAL BIRTH MACHINE** [ ] [ ]
– Cybertron 71 – Eternal countdown (intro) / Urko's conquest / Stained glass horizons / Cyclops revolution / Birth machine 2000 / Nightmare castle / Fireball demon / Phaser quest / Suicide asteroid / Dragon ryder 13 / Magnetic hole.

Jan 99. (cd) *(<MOSH 211CD>)* **CARAVAN BEYOND REDEMPTION** [ ] [ ]
– Voodoo fire / The unnatural world / Satanikus Robertikus / Freedom / Captain Clegg / Earth messiah / The caravan / Revolution / Kaleidoscope of desire / Heavy load / The Omega man / Dust of paradise.

Feb 01. (cd) *(<MOSH 236CD>)* **ENDTYME** [ ] [ ] Apr01
– Cathedral flames / Melancholy emperor / Requiem for the sun / Whores to oblivion / Alchemist of sorrows / Ultra earth / Astral queen / Sea serpent / Templar's arise! (the return).

– compilations, etc. –

Oct 99. (cd) *Rise Above; (CDRISE 21)* **IN MEMORIUM** [ ] [-]
– IN MEMORIUM EP tracks / Commissioning the celebration (live) / Ebony tears (live) / Neophytes for the serpent eve (live) / All your sins (live) / Mourning of the day (live).

Oct 99. (cd) *(<MOSH 234CD>)* **SOUL SACRIFICE / STATIK MAJIK** [ ] [ ] Jan00

CATHERINE WHEEL

Formed: Great Yarmouth, England . . . April 1990 by ROB DICKINSON and BRIAN FUTTER, completing the line-up with DAVE HAWES and NEIL SIMS and taking their moniker from a type of firework. The quartet recorded a demo on their own 8-track bedroom studio, the results released early the following year by independent imprint, 'Wilde Club', as debut single/EP, 'SHE'S MY FRIEND'. A second rough sounding EP, 'PAINFUL THING', also found its way into the indie charts resulting in them securing a contract with recently re-activated major label, 'Fontana' (recently home to a TEARDROP EXPLODES compilation, who incidentally, CATHERINE WHEEL bear more than a musical passing resemblance to). Becoming an integral part of the early 90's "shoegazing" scene, the CATHERINE WHEEL steadily built up a fanbase through committed gigging and a couple of minor UK hit singles, namely the 7-minute epic, 'BLACK METALLIC' and 'BALLOON'. Both featured on their TIME FRIESE-GREENE (TALK TALK)-produced debut set, 'FERMENT' (early '92), a Top 40 entrant with enough guitar bashing to hint at their future incarnation as a fully-fledged Rock band. In the meantime, ROB and Co finally cracked the Top 40 with 'I WANT TO TOUCH YOU' and subsequently revealed their eclectic musical tastes with a covers EP, running through versions of Scott Walker's '30th CENTURY MAN', Husker Du's 'DON'T WANT TO KNOW IF YOU ARE LONELY' and Mission Of Burma's 'THAT'S WHEN I REACH FOR MY REVOLVER' (they also did a version of Pink Floyd's 'WISH YOU WERE HERE'). 1993 hardly went off with a bang, however, as the GIL NORTON-produced follow-up set, 'CHROME', suffered at the hands of fickle critics, although steadfast fans did push it into the Top 60. Turning their attention to the States, CATHERINE WHEEL began to ferment a heavier, more rhythmic rock sound, finally laying to rest the "shoegazing" soundscapes of old on, er . . . "comeback" album, 'HAPPY DAYS' (1995). Despite featuring a duet, 'JUDY STARING AT THE SUN', with the BREEDERS' leading lady, TANYA DONELLY, the record went down like a damp squib in Britain. Nevertheless, burgeoning Stateside interest led to a deal with 'Chrysalis' and in 1998, they returned with an ever more Kerrang!-friendly sound on their fourth set, ADAM & EVE', a surprise success in the States after a gruelling coast to coast BUSH-like tour. Longtime bassist HAWES was subsequently given his marching orders prior to the recording of fifth album, 'WISHVILLE'. This may in part explain the poor reviews afforded the record upon its 2000 release, although the blame also seems to lie in the halfhearted songwriting, certainly well below the standard set by DICKINSON on previous outings.

Album rating: FERMENT (*7) / CHROME (*7) / HAPPY DAYS (*5) / LIKE CATS AND DOGS collection (*5) / ADAM AND EVE (*6) / WISHVILLE (*5)

ROB DICKINSON (b.23 Jul'65, Norwich, England) – vocals, guitar / **BRIAN FUTTER** (b. 7 Dec'65, London) – guitar, vocals / **DAVE HAWES** (b.10 Nov'65) – bass / **NEIL SIMS** (b. 4 Oct'65, Norwich) – percussion, drums

Wilde Club / not iss.

Jan 91. (12"ep) *(WILDE 4)* **SHE'S MY FRIEND / UPSIDE DOWN. / WISH / SALT** [ ] [-]

May 91. (12"ep/cd-ep) *(WILDE 5)* **PAINFUL THING / SHALLOW / SPIN / I WANT TO TOUCH YOU** [ ] [-]

Fontana / Fontana

Nov 91. (7") *(CW 1)* **BLACK METALLIC. / LET ME DOWN AGAIN** [68] [-]
(12"+=/cd-s+=) *(CW X/CD 1)* – Crawling over me / Saccharin.

Jan 92. (7") *(CW 2)* **BALLOON. / INTRAVENOUS** [59] [-]
(12"+=/cd-s+=) *(CW X/CD 2)* – Painful thing (live) / Let me down again (live).

Feb 92. (cd/c/lp) *(510903-2/-4/-1) <512510>* **FERMENT** [36] [ ] Jun92
– Texture / I want to touch you / Black metallic / Indigo is blue / She's my friend / Shallow / Ferment / Flower to hide / Tumbledown / Bill and Ben / Salt. *(incl.free 7"ep)*

Apr 92. (d7"/12"ep/cd-ep) *(CW/+X/CD 3)* **I WANT TO TOUCH YOU. / URSA MAJOR SPACE STATION/ / OUR FRIEND JOEY. / COLLIDEOSCOPE** [35] [-]
(12") *(CWT 3)* – (first 7") / Half life.
(cd-s) *(CWCDX 3)* – (first 7") / Wish / Black metallic.

Nov 92. (12"ep/cd-ep) *(CW X/CD 4)* **30th CENTURY MAN. / DON'T WANT TO KNOW IF YOU ARE LONELY / THAT'S WHEN I REACH FOR MY REVOLVER** [47] [-]

Jul 93. (7"/c-s) *(CW/+MC 5)* **CRANK. / COME BACK AGAIN** [66] [-]
(12") *(CWT 5)* – ('A'side) / Black metallic / Painful ting.
(cd-s) *(CWCD 5)* – ('A'side) / La la la-la la / Something strange.
(cd-s) *(CWCDX 5)* – ('A'side) / Pleasure / Tongue twisted.

Sep 93. (7") *(CW 6)* **SHOW ME MARY. / FLOWER TO HIDE (live)** [62] [-]
(cd-s+=) *(CWCDA 6)* – Car / Girl stand still.
(cd-s) *(CWCDB 6)* – ('A'side) / These four wheels / Smother.
(12") *(CWT 6)* – ('A'side) / High heels / Mouth full of air.

Sep 93. (cd/c/lp) *(<518039-2/-4/-1>)* **CHROME** [58] [ ] Jun93
– Kill rhythm / I confess / Crank / Broken head / Pain / Strange fruit / Chrome / The nude / Ursa Major space station / Fripp / Half life / Show me Mary.

— guests on above album:- TIM FRIESE-GREENE and AUDREY RILEY.

Jul 95. (10") *(<CW 7>)* **WAYDOWN. / CRANK / WISH YOU WERE HERE (XFM session)** [67] [-]
(cd-s) *(CWCD 7)* – ('A'side) / Show me Mary (XFM sessions) / Kill rhythm.
(cd-s) *(CWDD 7)* – ('A'side) / Chrome / Broken head (XFM sessions).

Sep 95. (10"ep) *(CW 8)* **JUDY STARING AT THE SUN / GOD INSIDE MY HEAD. / CRANK (live) / WAYDOWN (live)** [ ] [-]
(cd-ep) *(CWCD 8)* – (first 2 tracks) / Glitter.
(cd-ep) *(CWDD 8)* – (first 2 tracks) / Backwards guitar / Angelo Nero.
(above 'A'side featured TANYA DONELLY of BREEDERS)

Nov 95. (cd/c)(d-lp) *(<514717-2/-4>)(526850-1)* **HAPPY DAYS** [ ] [ ] May95
– God inside my head / Waydown / Little muscle / Heal / Empty head / Receive / My exhibition / Eat my dust you insensitive fuck / Shocking / Love tips up / Judy staring at the sun / Hole / Fizzy love / Glitter / Kill my soul.

Chrysalis / Polygram

Dec 97. (10"ep) *(10CHS 5071)* **THE DELICIOUS EP** [53] [-]
– Delicious / Eat my dust you insensitive f**k / Crank (live) / Texture (live).
(cd-ep) *(CDCHS 5071)* – ('A'side) / Future boy / Judy staring at the sun (with TANYA DONELLY) / Heal.

Feb 98. (7"colrd) *(CHS 5077)* **MA SOLITUDA. / KILL RHYTHM (live)** [53] [-]
(cd-s) *(CDCHSS 5077)* – ('A'side) / Delicious / Descending babe / Paranoia.
(cd-s) *(CDCHS 5077)* – ('A'-Tim Friese-Greene mix) / Delicious (live) / Willing to wait / Lucifer.

Apr 98. (7") *(CHS 5086)* **BROKEN NOSE. / LITTLE MUSCLE (live)** [48] [-]
(cd-s) *(CDCHS 5086)* – ('A'side) / Crank (live) / Texture (live) / Black metallic (live).
(cd-s) *(CDCHSS 5086)* – ('A'side) / Flower to hide (live) / Heal (live) / I want to touch you (live).

May 98. (cd/c/d-lp) *(493099-2/-4/-1)* *<534864>* **ADAM AND EVE** 53 Jul98
– Future boy / Delicious / Broken nose / Phantom of the American mother / Ma solituda / Satellite / Thunderbird / Here comes the fat controller / Goodbye / For dreaming.

Chrysalis Columbia

Sep 00. (cd/lp) *(526664-2/-1)* *<69515>* **WISHVILLE**
– Sparks are gonna fly / Gasoline / Lifeline / What we want to believe in / All of that / Idle life / Mad dog / Ballad of a running man / Creme caramel. *(special d-cd+=; 528664-2)* – live:- Lifeline / Crank / Fripp / Ma solituda / Heal / Future boy / Intravenus / Little muscle.

- compilations, etc. -

Sep 96. (cd) *Polygram; (<532456-2>)* **LIKE CATS AND DOGS** (B-sides, rarities, etc)
– Heal 2 / Wish you were here / Mouthful of air / Car / Girl stand still / Saccharine / Backwards guitar / Tongue twisted / These four walls / High heels / Harder than I am / La-la-la.

CATS IN BOOTS

Formed: Tokyo, Japan ... 1987 by former SEIKI MATSU members TAKASHI 'JAM' OHASHI and YASUHIRO 'BUTCH' HATAE, who enlisted Americans JOEL ELLIS and RANDY MEERS. The Japanese contribution to the US glam-rock explosion of the mid to late 80's, CATS IN BOOTS signed to 'E.M.I.' on the strength of their top independent debut, 'DEMONSTRATION – EAST MEETS WEST' (1988). Despite some critical acclaim for their debut album proper, 'KICKED AND KLAWED' (1989), this MTV-friendly sleaze rock outfit failed to make much headway outside their native Japan.

Album rating: DEMONSTRATION – EAST MEETS WEST mini (*4) / KICKED AND KLAWED (*5)

JOEL ELLIS (b. Cleveland, Ohio) – vocals / **TAKASHI 'JAM' OHASHI** – guitar / **YASUHIRO 'BUTCH' HATAE** – bass / **RANDY MEERS** (b. Houston, Texas) – drums (ex-MERRY HOAX)

not iss. Bronze

1988. (m-cd) **DEMONSTRATION – EAST MEETS WEST** -
– Girls all right, tonight / Judas kiss / Bad boys / 9 lives (save me) / The bayou fool / Her monkey / Heaven on a heartbeat.

Manhattan EMI-USA

Nov 89. (cd/c/lp) *(CD/TC+/MTL 1049)* *<E2/E4/E1 91172>* **KICKED AND KLAWED**
– Shotgun Sally / 9 lives (save me) / Her monkey / Whip it out / Long, long way from home / Coast to coast / Every sunrise / Evil angel / Bad boys are back / Judas kiss / Heaven on a heartbeat.

— folded in 1990

CAUSE FOR ALARM

Formed: New York, USA . . . early 80's by KEITH BURKHARDT, JASON BANKS and JOE ORGERA (drummer unknown). In the old hardcore tradition of fellow NY punk-noise merchants, AGNOSTIC FRONT and CRO-MAGS, the quartet plundered this territory until their untimely demise in '84. A decade later, CFA were once again, this time with a new drummer, RAEPH, and a contract with 'Victory'. An eponymous angst-ridden debut in '95 was quickly pursued by a split set with WARZONE, melodic punk was truly fighting back. A 1997 album, 'CHEATERS AND THE CHEATED', was warmly received, although it was with the following year's 'BENEATH THE WHEEL' that Kerrang! people took note.

Album rating: CAUSE FOR ALARM mini (*4) / BEYOND BIRTH AND DEATH split (*6) / CHEATERS AND THE CHEATED (*5) / BENEATH THE WHEEL (*6) / NOTHING EVER DIES (*5)

KEITH BURKHARDT – vocals / **JASON BANKS** – guitar / **JOE ORGERA** – bass / **RAEPH** – drums

Victory Victory

Mar 95. (m-cd) *<(VE 19CD)>* **CAUSE FOR ALARM** (anthology of singles) Feb95
– Parasite / Second chance / Time to try / United races / I search of / Poison in the machine / True colors / Stand as one / Time will tell.

Dec 95. (m-cd; split with WARZONE) *<(VR 026)>* **BEYOND BIRTH AND DEATH** Oct95
– Reflection / Beyond birth and death / Eyes of war / Prison life / (other tracks by WARZONE).

Apr 97. (lp/cd) *<(VR 049/+CD)>* **CHEATERS AND THE CHEATED** Jan97
– Plastic cylinder express / Lies / Shattered faith / Cheaters and the cheated / True believers / Fish on a hook / Still searching / Creation / Eternal life / Quest for reality / Burden.

Oct 97. (d7"ep/c-ep/cd-ep) *<(VR 059/+MC/CD)>* **BIRTH AFTER BIRTH** Sep97
– Cold / Birth after birth / Summer on Avenue A / Animal rights / Rite of passage / Killing children.

Sep 98. (lp/cd) *<(VR 088/CD)>* **BENEATH THE WHEEL**
– Homeless / Hole we live in / Clear / Cleanser / Put it down / Future war / Rich get richer / Nothing ever dies / Serve / Prabupada.

— **ALEX KINON** – guitar; repl. BANKS

Jan 00. (7") *(GOW 001)* **split w/ MIOZAN** -
(above issued on 'Grapes Of Wrath')

Dec 00. (cd) *(<VR 141CD>)* **NOTHING EVER DIES**
– Life is beautiful / Lost in the USA / Homeless / United races / Summer on Avenue A / Lies / Reflection / Cheaters and the cheated / Parasite / Prison life / Cleanser / Birth after birth / Time to try / Killing children / Beyond birth and death / Fish on a hook / Future war / Time will tell / Still searching.

CAVE IN

Formed: Methuen, Boston, Massachusetts, USA . . . 1995 by STEPHEN BRODSKY and JAY FRECHETTE. With ADAM McGRATH, JUSTIN MATTHES and JOHN-ROBERT CONNERS completing the line-up, CAVE IN cut a clutch of early EP's with semi-legendary hardcore producer, Brian McTernan at the helm. While a deal was subsequently inked with the 'Hydra Head' label, personnel upheavals saw MATTHES and then FRECHETTE replaced by ANDY KYTE and DAVE SCROD respectively. Both men were to leave prior to the recording of debut album, 'UNTIL YOUR HEART STOPS' (1999), obliging guitarist BRODSKY to take up the vacant vocal spot while CALEB SCOFIELD became a permanent fixture on bass. The album itself reflected the visceral savagery of their live shows, although by the time of its release, CAVE IN were already becoming bored with their heavy duty sound. The 'CREATIVE ECLIPSES' EP (1999) signalled as much, while 'JUPITER' (2000) literally reinvented the band in nu-prog, noisescape stylee with critics lurching for the collective thesauras and namechecking the likes of RADIOHEAD, FAILURE, PINK FLOYD, hell even RUSH! While many older fans were unpleasantly dismayed, a whole new batch of admirers were turned on to CAVE IN's broodingly therapeutic delights.

Album rating: UNTIL YOUR HEART STOPS (*7) / JUPITER (*7) / BEYOND HYPOTHERMIA collection (*6)

DAVE SCROD – vocals; repl. JAY FRECHETTE / **STEPHEN BRODSKY** – guitar, vocals / **CALEB SCOFIELD** – bass / **JOHN-ROBERT "JR" CONNORS** – drums

not iss. Relapse

May 99. (cd) *<(RR 6439-2)>* **UNTIL YOUR HEART STOPS**
– Moral eclipse / Terminal deity / Juggernaut / The end of our rope is a noose / Segue 1 / Until your heart stops / Segue 2 / Halo of flies / Bottom feeder / Segue 3 / Ebola / Controlled mayhem then erupts / Luminance / Sonata McGrath / Magnified / Burned down / Billboards / Sonata Brodsky. *(UK-iss.Nov00; same)*

— **ADAM McGRATH** – guitar; repl. SCROD (BRODSKY now on vocals)

Hydrahead Hydrahead

Jul 99. (cd-ep) *<(HH666 38CD)>* **CREATIVE ECLIPSES** May99
– Luminance / Sonata McGrath / Magnified / Burning down the billboards / Sonata Brodsky.

Oct 00. (cd) *<(HH666 52CD)>* **JUPITER**
– Jupiter / In the stream of commerce / Big riff / Innuendo and out the other / Brain candle / Requiem / Decay of the delay / New Moon.
(lp-iss.Mar01; HH666 52)

Magic Bullet Magic Bullet

Mar 01. (cd) *(MB 011CD)* **MOONS ON JUPITER**

- compilations, etc. -

Feb 01. (cd) *Hydrahead; (HH666 25CD)* **BEYOND HYPOTHERMIA** (sessions, etc.) May99
– Crossbearer / Chameleon / Capsize / Stoic / Programmed behind / Flypaper / Mitigate / Pivotal / Ritual famine / Crambone.

CECIL

Formed: Liverpool, England . . . 1993 by ageing teenagers, STE WILLIAMS, ANTONY HUGHES, PATRICK HARRISON, JAY BENNETT and ALLY LAMBERT. After taking part in a 'Battle Of The Bands', competition they found themselves on the roster of EMI's 'Parlophone' imprint. Subsequent tours supporting SKUNK ANANSIE, BLAMELESS and The LEVELLERS, helped raise their profile, although critics found it difficult to pigeonhole the band in either the hard-rock or alternative categories. Fusing crunching, hard-driving riffs with WILLIAMS' emotive vocals, CECIL released a trio of competent if hardly groundbreaking singles prior to their first full set, 'BOMBAR DIDDLAH' (1996). Late the following year, with support from the likes of Kerrang!, the 5-piece scored their first of two minor hits with 'HOSTAGE IN A FROCK', the singer a bit overdressed in the accompanying video. The second of these, 'THE MOST TIRING DAY', previewed the follow-up album, 'SUBTITLES' (1998), although a bonafide breakthrough seemed as distant as ever.

Album rating: BOMBAR DIDDLAH (*5) / SUBTITLES (*5)

STE WILLIAMS – vocals / **ANTONY HUGHES** – guitar / **PATRICK HARRISON** – guitar / **JAY BENNETT** – bass / **ALLY LAMBERT** – drums

Parlophone Parlophone

Oct 95. (7") *(R 6418)* **NO EXCUSES. / UPSIDE DOWN SMILE** -
(cd-s+=) *(CDR 6418)* – Friend (demo).

Mar 96. (7") *(R 6427)* **MY NECK. / WALLOW IN FUSION** -
(cd-s+=) *(CDR 6427)* – Revealing symptom / My piano neck.

Jun 96. (7") *(R 6435)* **MEASURED. / SPIRIT LEVEL** -
(cd-s+=) *(CDR 6435)* – The plastics keep coming.

Nov 96. (cd/c/lp) *(CD/TC+/PCS 7384)* *<854162>* **BOMBAR DIDDLAH** Mar97
– Dream awake / Plastics keep coming / Spirit level / Upside down smile / Fishes / My neck / No excuses / Poshinalagweedy.

May 97. (7") *(R 6467)* **RED WINE AT DEAD TIME. / BOMBAR DIDDLAH** -
(cd-s+=) *(CDR 6467)* – So Long Marianne.
(cd-s) *(CDRS 6467)* – ('A'side) / Look out for my love / Friend.

Oct 97. (7"green) *(R 6471)* **HOSTAGE IN A FROCK. / STUBBORN FEATHER** 68 -
(Dave Bascombe mix; cd-s+=) *(CDRS 6471)* – Upside down smile (live).
(cd-s) *(CDR 6471)* – ('A'-Tim Palmer mix) / Antique / Dream awake (live).

Mar 98. (7"colrd) *(R 6490)* **THE MOST TIRING DAY. / SLIPHILLCLIMB** 69 -

(cd-s+=) *(CDRS 6490)* – On the inside.
(cd-s) *(CDR 6490)* – ('A'side) / Tinsel scar / When you're in love with a beautiful woman.

Mar 98. (cd/c/lp) *(859821-2/-4/-1)* **SUBTITLES** [ ] [-]
– Larger than a mountain to the ant / Zips for lips / The most tiring day / Red wine at dead time / Fullstop / Acres / Hostage in a frock / Measured / Lovetooth 14 / Charm wrestling / In the day and aged.

— split after above

CELL

Formed: Hoboken, New Jersey, USA . . . early 90's by New York underground veterans, JERRY DiRIENZO (ex-VIA), IAN JAMES (ex-FLOWER), DAVID MOTAMED (ex-DAS DAMEN) and KEITH NEALY (ex-SWINEDIVE). Mates with SONIC YOUTH (KEITH had been a technician for STEVE SHELLEY), CELL used their contacts to secure an initial deal with THURSTON MOORE's 'Ecstatic Peace' label, releasing their debut single, 'NEVER TOO HIGH', in 1991. The SONIC YOUTH connection also helped them net a Stateside deal with the David Geffen Company (DGC), a debut album, 'SLO*BLO', surfacing the following year. Scraping the mutoid sludge from the Grunge barrel, CELL specialised in layers of mesmerising monster riffing with occasional forays into noise abandon, naming their album after a slow action fuse. Following a solitary single in '93, 'CROSS THE RIVER', CELL broke out for one more stab at cult fame, unlocking the door to more mind-numbing guitar abuse via the album, 'LIVING ROOM' (1994).

Album rating: SLO*BLO (*5) / LIVING ROOM (*5)

JERRY DiRIENZO – vocals, guitar (of VIA; w/ THALIA of COME) / **IAN JAMES** – guitar, vocals (of FLOWER) / **DAVID MOTAMED** – bass (of DAS DAMEN) / **KEITH NEALY** – drums (of SWINEDIVE)

not iss. | Ecstatic Peace

1991. (12") *<E# 14>* **NEVER TOO HIGH. / STRATOSPHERE** [-] [ ]

City Slang | D.G.C.

Sep 92. (7"blue) *(EFA 04905-03)* **FALL. / CIRCLES** [ ] [-]

Oct 92. (lp/c/cd) *(E 04909/+C/CD)* *<24506>* **SLO*BLO** [ ] [ ]
– Fall / Wild / Cross the river / Dig deep / Stratosphere / Two / Everything turns / Tundra / Bad day / Hills.

Nov 92. (7") *<E# 23>* **WILD. / AUF WIEDERSEHEN** [-] [ ]
(above issued on 'Ecstatic Peace/ D.G.C.')

Apr 93. (7"blue) *(EFA 04921-45)* **CROSS THE RIVER. / CHINA LATINA** [ ] [-]
(cd-s+=) *(EFA 04921-03)* – So cool / Free money.

Jan 94. (7") *(EFA 04928-7)* **MILKY. / TWO WEEKS** [ ] [ ]
(cd-s+=) *(EFA 04928-2)* – Deranged.

Feb 94. (cd/lp) *(EFA 04933-2/-1)* *<24633>* **LIVING ROOM** [ ] [ ]
– Milky / China Latina / Sad & beautiful / Goodbye / Chained / Come around / Living room / Fly / Halo / Soft ground / Camera / Blue star.

— disbanded after above

CELTIC FROST

Formed: Zurich, Switzerland . . . 1984 by THOMAS GABRIEL FISCHER (TOM G WARRIOR) and MARTIN ERIC AIN, who had evolved from Satanic-metal outfit, HELLHAMMER. Signed to the German label 'Noise', CELTIC FROST unleashed the pivotal proto death-metal set, 'MORBID TALES' that year. Prior to the follow-up, 'EMPEROR'S RETURN', PRIESTLY was replaced by REED ST. MARK, while more personnel changes (DOMINIC STEINER substituting AIN) preceded their third release, 'TO MEGA THERION'. With AIN back playing bass, CELTIC FROST flirted with the avant-garde on the critically acclaimed 'INTO THE PANDEMONIUM' (1987), almost making the step up to the major league alongside SLAYER and MEGADETH. Astonishingly, TOM G declined to build upon this near breakthrough, choosing instead to hire a completely new cast of musicians for an ill-advised glam/thrash album, 'COLD LAKE' (1988). Retaining only CURT VICTOR BRYANT from the last line-up, TOM G brought back AIN and signed to 'E.M.I.', reclaiming some of their lost ground with their 1990 album, 'VANITY/NEMESIS'. However, this proved to be their final outing, as TOM G returned to the glacial landscapes of Switzerland. However, the man was back with a vengeance in 1998. His new group, APOLLYON SUN, was his most adventurous and experimental to date and although feeding off recent acts like The PRODIGY or NINE INCH NAILS, this sinister 5-piece made the grade.

Album rating: MORBID TALES (*6) / EMPEROR'S RETURN (*6) / TO MEGA THERION (*6) / INTO THE PANDEMONIUM (*7) / COLD LAKE (*4) / VANITY/NEMESIS (*5) / PARCHED WITH THIRST I AM, AND DYING compilation (*7) / Apollyon Sun: GOD LEAVES (AND DIES) mini (*6) / SUB (*6)

HELLHAMMER

TOM G. WARRIOR (b. THOMAS GABRIEL FISCHER) – vocals, guitar / **MARTIN AIN** – bass, vocals / **BRUCE DAY** – drums

Noise Int. | not iss.

1983. (m-lp) *(N 0008)* **APOCALYPTIC RAIDS 1990 A.D.** [-] [-] German
– The third of the storms / (Evoked damnation) / Massacra / Triumph of death / Horus – Aggressor. *(re-iss. Apr90 cd/lp; CD+/NUK 008)*

CELTIC FROST

STEPHEN PRIESTLY – drums, percussion; repl. ISAAC DARSO

Noise Int. | Combat

1984. (m-lp) *(N 0017)* *<60-1684>* **MORBID TALES** [-] [ ]
– Into the crypts of rays / Visions of mortality / Procreation (of the wicked) / Return to the Eve / Danse macabre / Nocturnal fear. *(UK-iss.May87; same) (re-iss. Oct89 cd+=/lp; CD+/NUK 017) (cd re-mast.Feb00; N 0325-2)*

— **REED ST. MARK** – drums; repl. PRIESTLY

1985. (m-lp) *(N 0024)* *<60-1684>* **EMPEROR'S RETURN** [ ] [ ]
– Circle of the tyrants / Morbid tales / Dethroned emperor / Visual aggression / Suicidal winds. *(re-iss. Nov86 pic-lp; NUKP 024) (cd-iss. 1988 +=; NCD 003)<86-1692>* – MORBID TALES *(re-is.Oct89; NUK 024)*

— **DOMINIC STEINER** – bass; repl. MARTIN

Noise Int. | Combat

Dec 85. (lp) *(N 0031)* *<85-4741>* **TO MEGA THERION** [ ] [ ]
– Innocence and wrath / The usurper / Jewel throne / Dawn of Megiddo / Eternal summer / Circle of the tyrants / (Beyond the) North winds / Fainted eyes / Tears in a prophet's dream / Necromantical screams. *(re-iss. Oct89 cd/lp; CD+/NUK 031) (cd re-mast.Feb00 N 0326-2)*

1986. (12"ep) *<MXT 8107>* **TRAGIC SERENADES** [ ] [-]
– The usurper / Jewel throne / Return to the throne.

— **MARTIN AIN** – drums; returned to repl. STEINER

Jun 87. (lp/c/cd) *(N 0065/0066/0067)* *<08-4438><09-4429><85-4430>* **INTO THE PANDEMONIUM** [ ] [ ]
– Mexican radio / Mesmerized / Inner sanctum / Sorrows of the Moon / Babylon fell / Caress into oblivion / One in their pride / I won't dance / Rex Irae (requiem) / Oriental masquerade. *(re-iss. Nov89 cd+=/lp; CD+/NUK 065)* – Tristesses de la lune. *(re-iss. Jun90 cd/c/lp; CD/ZC+/NUK 065) (cd re-mast.Feb00; N 0327-2)*

Oct 87. (12") *(N 0094)* *<50-4454>* **I WON'T DANCE. / ONE IN THEIR PRIDE / TRISTESSES DE LA L UNE** [ ] [-]

— **THOMAS GABRIEL** with brand new line-up **CURT VICTOR BRYANT** – bass / OLIVER AMBERG – guitar + **STEPHEN PRIESTLY** – drums

Nov 88. (lp/c/cd) *(N 0125-1/-2/-3)* *<08-4721><10-4722><85-4723>* **COLD LAKE** [ ] [ ]
– Human (intro) / Seduce me tonight / Petty obsession / (Once) They were eagles / Cherry orchards / Juices like wine / Little velvet / Blood on kisses / Downtown Hanoi / Dance sleazy / Roses without thorns. *(re-iss. Oct89 cd+=/c/lp; CD/ZC+/NUK 125)* – Tease me / Mexican radio.

— **THOMAS + CURT** brought back original line-up; **MARTIN AIN**

E.M.I. | R.C.A.

May 90. (cd/c/lp) *(CD/TC+/EMC 3576)* *<2403>* **VANITY / NEMESIS** [ ] [ ] Nov89
– The heart beneath / Wine in my hand (third from the Sun) / Wings of solitude / The name of my bride / This island Earth / The restless seas / Phallic tantrum / A kiss or a whisper / Vanity / Nemesis. *(cd+=)* – Heroes. *(cd re-iss. Sep92 on 'Noise'; NO 199-2) (cd re-mast.Feb00; N 0328-2)*

— REED ST. MARK rejoined the band from MIND FUNK, although this was only a stopgap before CELTIC FROST disbanded. After several years in the wilderness, THOMAS heralded the arrival of his new outfit, APOLLYON SUN

– compilations, etc. –

Jan 92. (cd/c/lp) *Noise Int.; (N 0191-2/-4/-2)* *<44852>* **PARCHED WITH THIRST AM I AND DYING (1984-1992)** [ ] [ ]
– Idols of Chagrin / A descent to Babylon (Babylon asleep) / Return to the eve / Juices like wine / The inevitable factor / The heart beneath / Cherry orchards / Tristesses de la lune / Wings of solitude / The usurper / Journey into fear / Downtown Hanoi / Circle of the tyrants / In the chapel in the moonlight / I won't dance (the elder's Orient) / The name of my bride / Mexican radio / Under Apollyon's sun. *<US cd re-iss. 1994 on 'Futurist'; 11053>* (cd re-mast.Feb00; *N 0329-2)*

APOLLYON SUN

THOMAS GABRIEL FISCHER – vocals, guitar / **ERROL UNALA** – guitar / **DANY ZINGG** – bass / **MARKY EDELMAN** – drums / **ROGER MULLER** – synthesizers

Mayhem | not iss.

Jun 98. (m-cd) *(MYNCD 1)* **GOD LEAVES (AND DIES)** [ ] [-]
– God leaves / Reefer boy / The cane / Concrete Satan / Bedlam and blind.

Jun 00. (cd) *(<MYNCD 2>)* **SUB** [ ] [ ]
– Dweller (Subhuman remix) / Reefer boy (John Fryer remix) / Feeder / Messiah (second coming) / Naked underground / Slender / Human III / R.U.M. / Mother misplaced / Concrete SAtan.

CEMENT

Formed: Los Angeles, California, USA . . . 1993 by ex-FAITH NO MORE frontman CHUCK MOSELEY, who had also been part of BAD BRAINS and HAIRCUTS THAT KILL. He enlisted the help of SEAN MAYTUM (on guitfiddle!), SENON WILLIAMS and DOUG DUFFY, who appeared on their groundbreaking eponymous hard-rock set (no pun intended!). The following year, 'Rough Trade' in Germany released the brilliantly titled, 'THE MAN WITH THE ACTION HAIR' (1994), although nothing has been heard from them since.

Album rating: CEMENT (*5) / THE MAN WITH THE ACTION HAIR (*5)

CHUCK MOSELEY – vocals (ex-FAITH NO MORE, ex-BAD BRAINS) / **SEAN MAYTUM** – guitar (ex-BEER NUTS) / **SENON WILLIAMS** – bass / **DOUG DUFFY** – drums (ex-PYGMY LOVE CIRCUS)

World Service | Dutch East India

Jun 93. (cd/lp) *(RTD 1571573-2/-1)* *<DEI 2026>* **CEMENT** [ ] [ ]
– Living sound delay / Shout / I feel / Four / Prison love / Six / Blue / Too beat / Take it easy / Old days / Reputation shot / Chip away / KCMT.

Aug 94. (cd/lp) *(RTD 1571745-2/-1)* *<DEI 2038>* **THE MAN WITH THE ACTION HAIR** [ ] [ ]

– The man with the action hair / Killing an angel / Pile driver / Crying / Dancing from the depths of the fire / Life in the sun / Sleep / Train / King Arthur / Hotel Aiablo / Bonnie brae / Magic number / The power and the magic.

— split after above

CEMETARY

Formed: Boras, Sweden . . . 1989 by MATTHIAS LODMALM. Two demos in the early 90's, 'INCARNATION OF MORBIDITY' and 'ARTICULUS MORTIS' were enough to attract the attention of the 'Black Mark' label (home to BATHORY). Emerging from their proverbial crypt, CEMETARY finally came to life in 1992 on a debut album, 'AN EVIL SHADE OF GREY', a rather derivative death-metal affair. The group were re-animated on their next release, 'GODLESS BEAUTY', incorporating gothic atmospherics and horror soundtrack snippets. A third set, 'BLACK VANITY' continued in much the same vein while their final two albums, 'SUNDOWN' (1996) and 'LAST CONFESSIONS' (1997), the group moved increasingly towards a more experimental goth/industrial-influenced metal sound. This was explored more fully by LODMALMS new outfit, also confusingly titled SUNDOWN, wherein the CEMETARY frontman hooked up with TIAMAT bassist JOHNNY HAGEL. Featuring a line-up completed by ANDREAS JOHANSSON and CHRISTIAN SILVER, the group made their debut with 'DESIGN 19' (1997). The record's haunting synth-metal textures garnered significant critical praise and persuaded LODMALMS and Co to make the group a permanent concern. While this success meant the final demise of CEMETARY, fans could console themselves with a SUNDOWN follow-up entitled 'GLIMMER' (1999). Yet the ever restless MATHIAS subsequently changed tack again, re-inventing the band as CEMETARY 1213 and releasing an underwhelming techno-goth set, 'THE BEAST DIVINE' (2000).

Album rating: AN EVIL SHADE OF GREY (*5) / GODLESS BEAUTY (*5) / BLACK VANITY (*4) / SUNDOWN (*4) / LAST CONFESSIONS (*5) / SWEETEST TRAGEDIES compilation (*7) / Sundown: DESIGN 19 (*6) / GLIMMER (*5) / Cemetary 1213: THE BEAST DIVINE (*4)

MATHIAS LODMALM – vocals, guitar / **CHRISTIAN SAARINEN** – guitar / **ZRINKO CULJAK** – bass / **JUHA SIEVERS** – drums

Black Mark / Black Mark

Jun 92. (cd/c/lp) (<BM CD/CT/LP 20>) **AN EVIL SHADE OF GREY** ☐ ☐ 1994
– Dead red / Where the rivers of madness stream / Dark illusions / An evil shade of grey / Sidereal passing / Scars / Nightmare lake / Souldrain.

— **ANTON HEDBERG** – guitar; repl. CHRISTAN

Jul 93. (cd/c) (<BM CD/CT 33>) **GODLESS BEAUTY** ☐ ☐ Oct93
– Now she walks the shadows / The serpent's kiss / And Julie is no more / By my own hand / Chain / Adrift in scarlet twilight / In black / Sunrise (never again) / Where the fire forever burns.

— **ANDERS IWERS** – guitar; repl. ANTON

— **THOMAS JOSEFSSON** – bass; repl. ZRINKO

— **MARKUS NORDBERG** – drums; repl. JUHA

Oct 94. (cd) (<BMCD 59>) **BLACK VANITY** ☐ ☐ Mar95
– Bitter seed / Ebony rain / Hunger of the innocent / Scarecrow / Black flowers of passion / Last departure – Serpentine parade / Sweet tragedy / Pale Autumn fire / Out in sand / Rosemary taste the sky.

Feb 96. (cd/lp) (<BM CD/LP 70>) **SUNDOWN** ☐ ☐
– Elysia / Closer to the pain / Last transmission / Sundown / Ophidian / Primal / New dawn coming / The embrace / Morningstar / The wake.

Feb 97. (cd/lp) (<BM CD/LP 111>) **LAST CONFESSIONS** ☐ ☐
– Forever / Caress the damned / So sad your sorrow / 1213 – Trancegalactica / Twin reactor / Fields of fire / One burning night / Carbon heart.

– compilations, etc. –

Jul 98. (cd) *Black Mark;* (<BMCD 136>) **SWEETEST TRAGEDIES** ☐ ☐ Feb99
– Last transmission / Scarecrow / Caress the damned / By my own hand / Ophidian / Where the rivers of madness stream / Pale Autumn fire / And Julie is no more / So sad your sorrow / Elysia / Sweet tragedy / Where the fire forever burns / Sundown.

SUNDOWN

MATHIS LODMALM – vocals / JOHNNY HAGEL – bass (of TIAMAT) / **HERMAN ENGSTROM** – guitar / **ANDREAS JOHANSSON** – bass / **CHRISTIAN SILVER** – drums

Century Media / Century Media

Jun 97. (cd/lp) (<CM 77161-2/-1>) **DESIGN 19** ☐ ☐
– Aluminium / 19 / Judgement ground / Voyager / Synergy / As time burns / Don't like to live today / Slither / Emotional / 112 – Ghost in the machine.

May 99. (cd) (77250-2) **GLIMMER** ☐ -
– Lifetime / Divine / Halo / Prey / Star / Glimmer / Stab / [22] / Wired / Silencer.

CEMETARY 1213

— the new **LODMALM** project

Century Media / not iss.

Jun 00. (cd) (77287-2) **THE BEAST DIVINE** ☐ -
– The lightning – Firework / Union of the rats / Silicon karma (it just can't be the same) / AntiChrist 3000 / The carrier / Linking shadows / Sunset grace (let me die alone) / Dead boy wonder / Empire of the devine / Anthem apocalypse.

CHAIN REACTION

Formed: Canada . . . 1981 by guitarist WARREN BARVOUR and singer PHIL NARO, who enlisted the rhythm section of RAY LESSARD and JOHN LIVINGSTON. The group released a solitary album in '82, 'X-RATED DREAM', in reality more of an AOR nightmare, redeemed only by the razor-sharp guitar fireworks of BERVOUR.

Album rating: X-RATED DREAM (*4)

PHIL NARO – vocals / **WARREN BARVOUR** – guitar, vocals / **RAY LESSARD** – bass, vocals / **JOHN LIVINGSTON** – drums

Noir / Attic

Jul 82. (lp) <(LAT 1135)> **X-RATED DREAM** ☐ - Canada
– X-rated dream / One night love affair / Sea of flames / Baby let me go all night / You've got the cure / I'd rather be a bore / Looks like I'm in love / Keep our love alive / You have gone too far / Can't give me money.

— when NARO left to join TALAS, the group folded in '83

CHAINSAW KITTENS

Formed: Bartlesville, Oklahoma, USA . . . late 80's by main writer, TYSON MEADE, along with conspirators TRENT BELL, MARK METZGER, KEVIN McELHANEY and TOM LEADER. The 'KITTENS are frequently spoken of as the most overlooked American alternative rock band of their era. They certainly have the talent and a catalogue of sound material to boot, so it seems a mystery to many why prodigious record sales and fame have not come their way. The group were signed up, fairly quickly after their formation, by 'Mammoth', who put out the band's first full-length set, 'VIOLENT RELIGION' (1990). This album unfortunately charteristically did not bring the band immediate notice, although it was an above par debut with some truly worthwhile tracks such as 'SHE'S GONE MAD'. However through a combination of touring, and the massively increased interest in the American alternative rock scene, the boys started to get some deserved acknowledgement. Their subsequent album, 'FLIPPED OUT IN SINGAPORE' (1992) had all the makings of a near-classic; primarily they had BUTCH VIG behind the production desk, who had recently been showered with adulation for his work on NIRVANA's 'Nevermind' (1991). CK had also added guitarist TRENT BELL and swapped their rhythm section; replacing LEADER for AARON PRESTON and MCELHANEY for CLINT McBAY. Following this piece the McBAY and PRESTON pairing took their leave, to be replaced by MATT JOHNSON and ERIC HARMON respectively. The release of the EP 'ANGEL ON THE RANGE' (1993), further proved the band's technical ability, the eponymously titled track being one of the stand-outs of KITTEN's output as a whole. The boys moved on swiftly sending off another full-length set, 'POP HEIRESS' (1994), which in subject matter and style has been compared much to DAVID BOWIE's 'Ziggy Stardust' era and IGGY POP, both artists that CK frontman, MEADE confesses to being a huge fan of. The sound of this set is also enhanced by the work of experienced British producer, JOHN AGNELLO. SMASHING PUMPKINS who had gigged with CK in the early years of the decade decided shortly after this release to sign the boys to their label, 'Scratchie', releasing their next album, the self-titled, 'CHAINSAW KITTENS', two years later in '96. This set which is also known as 'Oklahoma Speedway', was another highly accomplished work with some high-energy pop-rock tunes combined with some inspired string arrangements. For anyone who looked at the sleevenotes and thought that the drummer had again changed, it is in fact still HARMON, but trading under the new title ERIC EDWARD BONES. A long break was had by CK after this set, only resurfacing at the turn of the century with 'THE ALL AMERICAN' (2000); a full-set that equalled any of their former output, and ending on a double cover; a rather dark interpretation of the Go-Go's 'WE GOT THE BEAT' segued onto Iggy Pop's 'NIGHTCLUBBING'. • **Trivia:** CK's promo video for the single from EP 'HIGH IN HIGHSCHOOL' was made by a young Spike Jonze, who was later to become famed for his work on the promo videos for the BEASTIE BOYS ('Sabotage') and FATBOY SLIM ('Praise You') which he also starred in as the head of the dance troupe.

Album rating: VIOLENT RELIGION (*4) / FLIPPED OUT IN SINGAPORE (*4) / ANGEL ON THE RANGE (*3) / POP HEIRESS (*6) / CHAINSAW KITTENS (*5) / THE ALL AMERICAN (*7)

TYSON MEADE – vocals, guitar / **TRENT BELL** – guitar / **MARK METZGER** – guitar / **KEVIN McELHANEY** – bass / **TOM LEADER** – drums

Mammoth / Mammoth

Jan 92. (cd/c/lp) <(MR 0021-2/-4/-1)> **VIOLENT RELIGION** ☐ ☐ Nov90
– Bloodstorm / Skinned knees (kitten theme) / Boyfriend song / Mother (of the ancient birth) / I'm waiting (Leanne's song) / Here at the end / Bliss (we're small) / Feel like a drugstore / Savior boyfriend collides / Violent religion / Death-out at party central / She's gone mad.

— **CLINT McBAY** – bass; repl. KEVIN

— **AARON PRESTON** – drums; repl. TOM

May 92. (cd/c) <(MR 0034-2/-4)> **FLIPPED OUT IN SINGAPORE** ☐ ☐
– Connie I've found the door / High in high school / 2nd theme – Flipped out in Singapore / My friend delirium / She gets / Never to be found / Shannon's Fellini movie / When you shoot / Hold / Ezekial walks through Sodom & Gomorrah / Angels self destruct.

Dec 92. (cd-ep) <(MR 0042-2)> **HIGH IN HIGH SCHOOL EP** ☐ ☐
– High in high school / Connie I've found the door / Couple No.23 / Stuck / One / Walk softly (for D.M.).

Nov 93. (cd/c/lp) *<(MR 0062-2/-4/-1)>* **ANGEL ON THE RANGE** Oct93
– Kick kid / Angel on the range / John Wayne dream / Mary's belated wedding present / Lazy little dove / Sgt. Whore / Little fishes.

— **MATTHEW JOHNSON** – bass; repl. CLINT

— **ERIC EDWARD BONES** – drums; repl. AARON

— **MIKE HOSTY** – lap steel guitar; repl. METZGER

Atlantic Atlantic

Feb 95. (cd/c) *<(7567 92318-2/-4)>* **POP HEIRESS** Nov94
– Sore on the floor / Loneliest China place / Pop heiress dies / Closet song / Dive into the sea / Burn you down / I ride free / Silver millionaire / Media star hymn / Soldier on my shoulder / Justine find Heaven / We're like . . .

not iss. Polygram

Oct 96. (cd/c) *<534002>* **CHAINSAW KITTENS**
– Dorothy's last fling / Heart catch thump / Tongue trick / King monkey smoke / Bones in my teeth / Waltz across debris / Ballad of newsman 5 / Mouthful of glass / Leash / Bicycle head / All (no surprise) / Sounder / Madhatter's blues / Speedway Oklahoma.

Four Alarm Four Alarm

Oct 00. (cd) *<(FAR 450CD)>* **THE ALL AMERICAN**
– Light / All American wiggle wiggle / International me / Calling from space / How many light bulbs / Shutdown / Hedonist / John Wayne / Wedding / Gleaming soft white teens / The treasure is love / We got the beat – Nightclubbing.

Ken CHAMBERS (see under ⇒ MOVING TARGETS)

CHANNEL 3

Formed: Cerritos, Los Angeles, California, USA . . . 1980 by MIKE MAGRANN, alongside fellow punk-rock afficionados, KIMM GARDENER, LARRY KELLEY and MIKE BURTON, the latter surviving three other drummers. Having released a solitary EP in Spring '82 for the influential 'Posh Boy' imprint, CHANNEL 3 became one of the few US hardcore acts to sign a UK deal, securing a licensing agreement with 'No Future'. The latter EP was subsequently released a few months later, while the debut album, 'FEAR OF LIFE' (1982), appeared in Britain as 'I'VE GOT A GUN'. Prior to the recording of the follow-up set, 'AFTER THE LIGHTS GO OUT' (1983), JACK DEBAUN replaced BURTON, further personnel reshuffles coming in the shape of GARDENER making way for JAY LANSFORD. His inaugural appearance arrived with the 'AIRBORNE' EP in '84, the former STEPMOTHERS guitarist sticking around for what was to become their swansong set, 'THE LAST TIME I DRANK . . .' (1985).

Album rating: FEAR OF LIFE – (or)- I'VE GOT A GUN (*4) / AFTER THE LIGHTS GO OUT (*6) / THE LAST TIME I DRANK . . . (*5)

MIKE MAGRANN – vocals, guitar / **KIMM GARDENER** – guitar / **LARRY KELLEY** – bass / **MIKE BURTON** – drums

No Future Posh Boy

Jul 82. (7"ep) *(OI 11)* **I'VE GOT A GUN. / MANZANAR / MANNEQUIN** May82

Sep 82. (lp) *(PUNK 2)* **I'VE GOT A GUN** <US-title 'FEAR OF LIFE'>
(UK)- Fear of life / Out of control / I've got a gun / Wetspots / Accident / You make me feel cheap / You lie / Catholic boy / Waiting in the wings / Strength in numbers / Double standard boys / Life goes on. *(cd-iss. Oct91 on 'Anagram'+=; CDMGRAM 50) <(cd re-iss. Jun94 & May00 +=; CDPUNK 2)>* – AFTER THE LIGHTS GO OUT

— **JACK DEBAUN** – drums; repl. BURTON

Aug 83. (lp) *(PUNK 7)* **AFTER THE LIGHTS GO OUT**
– What about me? / Separate peace / No love / After the lights go out / Truth and trust / I'll take my chances / All my dreams / Can't afford it / Didn't know / Manzanar / Mannequin. *(cd-iss. Jun93; CDPUNK 7)*

— **JAY LANSFORD** – guitar (ex-STEPMOTHERS) repl. KIMM

not iss. Enigma

1984. (12"ep) **AIRBORNE**

1985. (lp/c) *<72008-1/-4>* **THE LAST TIME I DRANK . . .**

— split not long after above

– compilations, etc. –

May 94. (cd) *Lost & Found; (LF 098)* **HOW DO YOU OPEN THE DAMN THING (live)**

1995. (cd) *Poshboy; <88156>* **THE SKINHEAD YEARS**

CHAOS UK

Formed: Bristol, England . . . 1979 by SIMON, ANDY, KAOS and POTTS aka SPOT. One of the very first bands – alongside the likes of CRASS – to turn punk into seething politicised hardcore, this infamous quartet started as they meant to go on with 1982's debut 7" on the 'Riot City' label, 'BURNING BRITAIN'. Follow-up 'LOUD, POLITICAL AND UNCOMPROMISING' could've pretty much been their manifesto while an eponymous debut album hit the shelves in 1983, featuring new member NIGE and KAOS on lead vocals. Both the title and artwork of sophomore set, 'SHORT SHARP SHOCK' (1984) would subsequently be appropriated by MICHELLE SHOCKED. Amusingly, CHAOS UK's answer was to release 'CHIPPING SODBURY BONFIRE TAPES' (1989) as a take-off of SHOCKED's 'Texas Campfire Tapes'. Prior to this the band – now consisting of MOWER, KAOS, GABBA and CHUCK – released a Japan-only live 12", 'JUST MERE SLAVES', as well as a split album with fellow up and coming noiseniks EXTREME NOISE TERROR entitled 'RADIOACTIVE SLAUGHTER' (1986). The subsequent recording gap was due to an enforced lay-off although the group – again featuring a slightly revamped line-up of KAOS, GABBA, CHUCK and new female addition BEKI – were back in 1991 with the 'LIVE IN JAPAN' set. Studio set, 'ENOUGH TO MAKE YOU SICK' (1991) was another JAPANESE import job, featuring second guitarist VIC and new drummer DEVILMAN. That year also saw the release of the 'MAKING A KILLING' 12", originally a split with RAW NOISE (ENT side project) which consisted largely of cover versions. Another extremely rare Japanese artefact was 1993's split album with oriental punk outfit DEATHSIDE. More readily available was '100% TWO FINGERS IN THE AIR PUNK ROCK' (1993), the last to feature BEKI who went on to join SPITE. A new line-up of KAOS, GABBA, J., and PHIL THUDD cut 1996's 'KING FOR A DAY' 12" while 'HEARD IT, SEEN IT, DONE IT' (1997) was an album consisting entirely of cover versions (P.I.L., ELVIS COSTELLO, ALTERNATIVE TV etc). Original material followed in the shape of 1997's 'THE MORNING AFTER THE NIGHT BEFORE' (1997). Various CHAOS UK alumni formed AD RICE & THE WUZZUKS in 1999, a cover project inspired by legendary chart bumpkins The WURZELS . . . • **Note:** Because of pseudonyms, etc, I'm not sure which of them were in The SEERS (if any?).

Album rating: LAWLESS BRITAIN (*4) / Seers: PSYCH OUT (*5) / PEACE CRAZIES (*4) / Chaos UK: 100% TWO FINGERS IN THE AIR PUNK ROCK (*5) / HEARD IT, SEEN IT, DONE IT (*5) / THE BEST OF CHAOS UK compilation (*6)

SIMON – vocals / **ANDY FARRIER** – guitar / **KAOS** (b. ADRIAN RICE) – bass / **SPOT** (aka POTTS) – drums

Riot City not iss.

Mar 82. (7"ep) *(RIOT 6)* **BURNING BRITAIN**
– 4 minute warning / Kill you baby / Army / Victimize. *(re-iss. Jul96 on 'Visionary Vinyl'; V7 08)*

Jul 82. (7"ep) *(RIOT 12)* **LOUD, POLTICAL AND UNCOMPROMISING**
– No security / Hypocrite / What about the future.

Sep 84. (12"ep) *(RIOT12 32)* **THE SINGLES** (tracks above)

— **NIGE GREENHAM** – repl. SIMON

Children Of The Revolution not iss.

Nov 84. (lp) *(GURT 1)* **LAWLESS BRITAIN**
– Lawless Britain / Living in fear / Detention centre / Support / Control / People at the top / Global domination / No one seems to really care / Farmyard stomp (again). *(re-iss. Jul86; same) (cd-iss. Feb96 as 'SHORT SHARP SHOCK' on 'Anagram'; CDPUNK 71)*

— late in '86, they shared an lp, 'EAR SLAUGHTER', with EXTREME NOISE TERROR, which was released on 'Manic Ears' (ACHE 1) – the cd was issued in Jun95 as 'RADIOACTIVE' on 'Receiver' (RRCD 201)

— most of the group drastically changed their names and their moniker

SEERS

— **SPIDER (MUTOID SPAM)** – vocals / **RHYTHM MONSTER BLACK & DECKER** – guitar / **KAT BIKEBITCH** – guitar / **LEISH ALEXANDER WILDMAN** – guitar / **JASON WEIRD BEARD ARGONAUT TUBBY ROUND** – bass / **ADGE** – drums

Rough Trade not iss.

Feb 88. (7") *(RT 182)* **LIGHTNING STRIKES. / GRAVEYARD OF LOVE**
(12"+=) *(RTT 182)* – Don't get hit.

Skull not iss.

Sep 88. (7") *(SKULL 1)* **FREEDOM TRIPS. / DON'T BRING ME DOWN / I'LL SAY NOTHING**
(12"+=) *(SKULL 1T)* – ('A'-Garage mix) / Pittsburgh.

Virgin not iss.

Feb 89. (7") *(HEDD 5)* **SUN IS IN THE SKY. / MAGIC POTION**
(12"+=) *(HEDD 5-12)* – ('A'extended).

Cherry Red Combat

Feb 90. (7") *(CHERRY 106)* **WELCOME TO DEADTOWN. / RUB ME OUT**
(12"+=) *(12CHERRY 106)* – ('A'extended).

Feb 90. (cd/c/lp) *(CD/C+/BRED 86) <1043>* **PSYCH OUT** 1991
– Wildman / Rub me out / One summer / Welcome to praying / Walk / Sun is in the sky / Fly away / Breathless / Freedom trip / (All late nite) Tequila drinking blues. *(lp w/free 7", c+=/cd+=)* – LIGHTNING STRIKES. / MAGIC POTION

May 90. (7") *(CHERRY 110)* **PSYCH OUT. / SPLITTING THE ATOM**
(12"+=/cd-s+=) *(12/CD CHERRY 110)* – Don't get hit (live).
(12") *(RCHERRY 110)* – ('A'remix) / Don't get hit (live) / Magic potion (live).

Mar 92. (cd/c/lp) *(CD/C+/BRED 99)* **PEACE CRAZIES**
– Second time around / Turn me on about now / Earthmover / Reaching in my brain / Liar / Touchstone / Psych out / Girl in action / Safe / Apocalypse yesterday / Looking for tomorrow / It's alright / Splitting the atom / Don't get hit.

CHAOS UK

— re-activated themselves in '92

Slap Up not iss.

Apr 93. (cd) *(SLAPCD 002)* **100% TWO FINGERS IN THE AIR PUNK ROCK**
– Happy spaztic / A swindle / Wall Street crash / Ronnie I / Ronnie II / The alcoholic / No security / Kill your baby / Head on a pole / Kill / Red sky at night / Drink thudd / Victimized / Selfish fever / Police story / 4 minute warning / Too kool for skool / Brain bomb / Cider I up landlord / More songs about cider / Bitch, bitch, bitch. *(re-iss. Jan94 on 'Century Media'; CM 77053-2)*

Apr 94. (7") *(CIDER 001)* **SECRET MEN. / MORE CIDER**

Anagram Cleopatra

Jan 97. (cd) *(CDMGRAM 109) <CLP 9982>* **THE MORNING AFTER THE NIGHT BEFORE** [ ] [ ]
– Fuck the neighbours / No mass panic / Morning after / Take me back to SAn Clemente / Disgruntled / Finger up bum / Another punk rock bastard / Wishful thinking / Advert / Masturbator / Collateral damage / Vegetable soup / Farmyard boogie.

Vinyl Japan Vinyl Japan

Jul 96. (7"ep)(cd-ep) *(FIST 3)(DISC 5X)* **KING FOR A DAY EP** [ ] [-]
Jan 98. (cd/lp) *(<DISC CD/LP 14>)* **HEARD IT, SEEN IT, DONE IT** [ ] [ ] Mar99
– Gob on you / You bastard / Public image / Butcher baby / Pump it up / Don't talk to me / New religion / Sick of you / Fuck all y'all / Handle with care / Witch hunt / Plaistow Patricia / Blackmail man / Belsen was a gas.
Aug 00. (12"ep/cd-ep) *(DISCX/+T 8)* **KANPAI EP** [ ] [-]
– Chunderer / 2000 lives / This song has been genetically modified / TPF-P / Travisty.

– compilations, others, etc. –

Nov 89. (lp) *Slap Up; (SLAPLP 1)* **THE CHIPPING SODBURY BONFIRE TAPES** [ ] [-]
– Intro / World stock market / Indecision / Kill / Uniform choice / No taxo / Think / Rise from the bubble II / Brain bomb / Too cool for school, too stupid for the real world (let's form a band) / Courier / Farmyard (cider house mix).
Nov 91. (cd) *Anagram; (CDGRAM 48)* **CHAOS UK** [ ] [-]
– Selfish few / Fashion change / You'll never own me / The end is nigh / Victimised / Parental love / Leech / Chaos / Mentally insane / Urban guerilla / Farmyard boogie / Four minute warning / Kill your baby / Army / Victimised / No security / What about a future / Hypocrite / Senseless conflict.
Jul 92. (lp/cd) *Vinyl Japan; (DISC 6/+CD)* **RAW NOISE** [ ] [-]
May 93. (cd) *No Future; (CDPUNK 12)* **ENOUGH TO MAKE YOU SICK / THE CHIPPING SODBURY BONFIRE TAPES** [ ] [-]
– Head on a pole / Vicious cabaret / Kettlehead / Midas touch / Loser / Drink thudd / 2010 (the day they made contact) / Urban nightmare / Cider I up landlord / Down on the farm / C-rap. // (see above).
Oct 93. (cd) *Dojo; (DOJOCD 114)* **LIVE IN JAPAN (live)** [ ] [-]
(<re-iss. Mar01 as 'CHAOS IN JAPAN' on 'Anagram'; CDPUNK 119)>
Feb 94. (cd) *Anagram; (<CDPUNK 26>)* **TOTAL CHAOS** [ ] [ ] Sep99
(lp-iss.Aug99 on 'Get Back'; GET 48)
Jun 95. (cd; w/ EXTREME NOISE TERROR) *Receiver; (RRCD 201)* **RADIOACTIVE** [ ] [-]
Oct 95. (cd) *Anagram; (CDPUNK 65) / Cleopatra; <9654>* **FLOGGIN' THE CORPSE; plus unreleased studio tracks** [ ] [ ]
Feb 98. (cd) *Anagram; (CDPUNK 103)* **RADIOACTIVE EAR SLAUGHTER / 100% TWO FINGERS IN THE AIR PUNK ROCK** [ ] [-]
Oct 98. (cd) *Anagram; (<CDPUNK 108>)* **THE BEST OF CHAOS UK** [ ] [ ] Sep99

David T. CHASTAIN

Born: Cincinnati, Ohio, USA. Having left the band SPIKE in 1984, he and bassist MIKE SKIMMERHORN formed two outfits, CHASTAIN and CJSS. These showcased CHASTAIN's virtuoso guitar-playing and introduced female shrieker, LEATHER LEONE. CHASTAIN's first album, 'MYSTERY OF ILLUSION' (also featuring a young FRED COURY, before he moved to CINDERELLA), was released to generally positive reviews, leading to a deal with 'Roadrunner'. Under the CHASTAIN moniker, he then proceeded to deliver several albums in the same vein, none of them earth shattering. DAVID T also devoted part of his recording life to solo outings, although these were issued on another label. In the mid 90's, CHASTAIN's incredibly prolific recording schedule continued apace with a one-off for Music For Nations 'Bulletproof' stable on the more experimental 'NEXT PLANET PLEASE'. He and his band extended their shelf-life with a couple more releases for the 'Massacre' label. • **Covered:** LOCOMOTIVE BREATH (Jethro Tull).

Album rating: Chastain: MYSTERY OF ILLUSION (*6) / RULER OF THE WASTELAND (*5) / THE VOICE OF THE CULT (*5) / WITHIN THE HEAT (*4) / FOR THOSE WHO DARE (*4) / CJSS: WORLD GONE MAD (*5) / PRAISE THE LOUD (*5) / David T. Chastain: THE 7th OF NEVER (*6) / INSTRUMENTAL VARIATIONS (*3) / RETROSPECT compilation (*5) / ELEGANT SEDUCTION (*7) / LIVE! WILD & TRULY DIMINISHED!! with Counterpoint (*3) / MOVEMENTS THRU TIME (*6) / NEXT PLANET PLEASE (*6) / ACOUSTIC VISIONS (*5) / Chastain: SICK SOCIETY (*5) / IN DEMENTIA (*5) / CJSS: Kings Of The World (*4)

CHASTAIN

DAVID T. CHASTAIN – guitar / **LEATHER (LEONE)** – vocals (ex-RUDE GIRL) / **MIKE SKIMMERHORN** – bass / **FRED COURY** – drums

Roadrunner Shrapnel

Oct 85. (lp) *(RR 9742) <SH 1018>* **MYSTERY OF ILLUSION** [ ] [ ]
– Black knight / When the battle's over / Mystery of illusion / I've seen tomorrow / Endlessly / Fear of evil / Night of the gods / We shall overcome / The winds of change. *(cd-iss. Mar90 on 'Roadracer'; RO 9742-2)*

— **KEN MARY** – drums (ex-ALICE COOPER) repl. COURY to CINDERELLA

Oct 86. (lp) *(RR 9689) <SH 1024>* **RULER OF THE WASTELAND** [ ] [ ]
– Ruler of the wasteland / One day to live / The king has the power / Fighting to stay alive / Angel of mercy / There will be justice / The battle of Nevermore / Living in a dreamworld / Children of Eden.

Roadrunner Leviathan

Jul 88. (lp/cd) *(RR 9548-1/-2) <19881-1/-2>* **THE VOICE OF THE CULT** [ ] [ ]
– The voice of the cult / Live hard / Chains of love / Share yourself with me / Fortune teller / Child of evermore / Soldiers of the flame / Evil for evil / Take me home.

— now with bass player, **DAVID HARBOUR**

Roadracer Roadracer

Jan 89. (lp/c/cd) *<(RC 9484-1/-4/-2)>* **WITHIN THE HEAT** [ ] [ ]
– Excursions into reality / Dangerzone F107 / The visionary / The return of the 6 / Nightmares / Within the heat / Zfunknc / It's still in your eyes / In your face / Pantheon / Desert nights.

— added **JOHN LUKE HE'BERT** – drums

Aug 90. (cd/c/lp) *<(RC 9398-2/-4/-1)>* **FOR THOSE WHO DARE** [ ] [ ]
– The mountain whispers / For those who dare / Please set us free / I am the rain / Night of anger / Barracuda / Light in the dark / Secrets of the damned / Not much breathing / Once before.

CJSS

DAVID T. CHASTAIN – guitar / **RUSSELL JINKINS** – vocals / **MIKE SKIMMERHORN** – bass / **LES SHARP** – drums

Black Dragon not iss.

Feb 86. (lp) *(BD 007)* **WORLD GONE MAD** [-] [-] French
– Hell on earth / No-man's-land / Communication breakdown / World gone mad / Run to another day / The gates of eternity / Destiny / Welcome to damnation / Purgatory – Living in exile.
Oct 86. (lp) *(BD 016)* **PRAISE THE LOUD** [-] [-] French
– Out of control / Land of the free / Don't play with fire / Praise the loud / Citizen of Hell / Danger / Metal forever / Thunder and lighting / The bargain.

DAVID T. CHASTAIN

— with **KEN MARY** – drums

Black Dragon Leviathan

Jul 87. (lp) *(BD 025)* **THE 7th OF NEVER** [-] [-] French
– We must carry on / Paradise / It's too late for yesterday / 827 / The wicked are restless / The 7th of never / Take me back in time / Feel his magic / Forevermore. *(cd-iss. Oct95 on 'Massacre'; MASSCD 077)*

— retained only **KEN MARY** (from his CHASTAIN group)

Oct 87. (lp/cd) *<19872>* **INSTRUMENTAL VARIATIONS** [-] [ ]
– Now or never / Capriccio in E minor / 18th century inamorata / Wild and truly diminished / Horizons / Spontaneous combustion / It doesn't have to be / Project 107: Code 3X / The oracle within.
1990. (cd/c) *(BD 044 CD/MC)* **RETROSPECT** (compilation) [-] [-] French
1991. (cd/c) *(BD 049 CD/MC) <19911>* **ELEGANT SEDUCTION** [-] [ ]
– Schizophrenia / Elegant seduction / Trapped in the void / 7 hills groove / Pompous rompous / Blitzkrieg / Menage a trois + 1 / Fortunate happenstance / No repeat disclosure / Images / Postional strategy.
1992. (cd; as DAVID T. CHASTAIN, MICHAEL HARRIS & COUNTERPOINT) *<19921>* **LIVE! WILD & TRULY DIMINISHED!! (live)** [-] [ ]
– Menage a trois + 1 / 827 / Psychotic biorhythms / Collision course / Horizons / Schizophrenia / Mind or heart / Flashattaxe / Trapped in the void / Eminent domain / Dynamo / Elegant seduction / B.O.F. / Wild and truly diminished.

Killerwatt Leviathan

Oct 93. (cd) *(KCLCD 1002) <19925>* **MOVEMENTS THRU TIME** [ ] [ ] Nov92
– Thunder and lightning / 827 / Fortunate and happenstance / Citizen of Hell / Blitzkrieg / The oracle within / New York rush / We must carry on / Cappricco / In E minor / No man's land / 7 hills groove / Now or never / Trapped in the void (live) / Zoned in danger (live) / The bargain.

— LEATHER also released her solo album in 1989, on 'Roadracer' (RO 9463-1), it was produced by CHASTAIN, and included HARBOUR + HE'BERT

— next with **DAVID HARBOUR** – guitar, bass + **MIKE HAID** – drums

Bulletproof Leviathan

May 94. (cd) *(CDVEST 9) <19941>* **NEXT PLANET PLEASE** [ ] [ ]
– Project transformation / Next planet please / Realization / Fusion delusion / Forever searching / Sophisticated deburchery / Dunk the funk / Blame it on the Rio / Homage to an unknown hero / Watching the time go by.

CHASTAIN

— **DAVID** with **KATE FRENCH** – vocals, rhythm guitar

Massacre Leviathan

Nov 95. (cd) *(MASSCD 076) <19952>* **SICK SOCIETY** [ ] [ ]
– I know the darkness / Sick society / Violence in blame / Those were the daze / Destructive ground / To the edge / The price of war / Every emotion / The vampire / Sugarcaine / Love and hate / Angel falls.

— added **KEVIN KEKES** – bass

May 97. (cd) *(MASSCD 122) <19971>* **IN DEMENTIA** [ ] [ ] Apr97
– Human sacrifice / Blackening / Seven / Sick puppy / Tongue / In dementia / House of stone / Conformity / Desperately.

DAVID T. CHASTAIN

not iss. Leviathan

Feb 98. (cd) *<19981-2>* **ACOUSTIC VISIONS** [-] [ ]
– Set / Pyramid of the sun / Appassionata minore / Cadenza in a harmonic minor / Inner journeys / Dirge for yesterday / Evening with Julliard / Lifetime / Time and time again / S.T.C. / Escape from Thera.

CJSS

— **CHASTAIN + SKIMMERHORN**

Pavement Pavement

Aug 00. (cd) *<(32352CD)>* **KINGS OF THE WORLD** [ ] [ ] Jul00
– Kings of the world / The final frontier / The executioner's song / Wild in the streets / Thief of hearts / I 4 I / The fall of Babylon / All is fire / Locomotive breath / The end of the rainbow / Cries of the dawn.

CHEAP AND NASTY (see under ⇒ HANOI ROCKS)

CHEAP TRICK

Formed: Rockford, Illinois, USA . . . 1972 by main writer RICK NIELSEN and TOM PETERSSON, who were part of The GRIM REAPERS prior to becoming FUSE. This brief early period only produced one self-titled album, before they enlisted the help of THOM MOONEY and ROBERT 'STEWKEY' ANTONI, fresh from (TODD RUNDGREN's) NAZZ. In 1972, they changed their moniker yet again, this time to The SICK MAN OF EUROPE, recruiting BUN E. CARLOS in place of the departing MOONEY. This primitive incarnation of CHEAP TRICK also saw the inclusion new vocalist RANDY 'XENO' HOGAN, although after two years of steady touring he was replaced by ROBIN ZANDER. With the classic line-up now in place, the band secured a deal with 'Epic', releasing their eponymous debut album early in '77. Coming at a time of musical turbulence (new wave/punk had just arrived), the album failed to excite an interest from either critics or rock fans. More marketable was the band's highly original image, ZANDER and PETERSSEN the good-lookers, while CARLOS was the joker in the pack with his Tweedle-Dee/Dum attire (i.e. baseball cap, bow-tie and all-round eccentricity). Tours supporting KISS and QUEEN helped promote the band's off-the-wall appeal to a wider audience, the follow-up, 'IN COLOR' (also in '77) gaining healthy sales and a US Top 75 placing. The album featured the excellent 45, 'I WANT YOU TO WANT ME', a flop first time around, although a live equivalent subsequently made the US Top 10 in 1979. Following on from the success of their third studio album, 'HEAVEN TONIGHT' (1978), their harder-edged live set, 'AT BUDOKAN' turned their popularity in Japan into even greater commercial heights in America. The record struck platinum, hitting Top 5 in the process and making them virtual overnight international stars over the ensuing decade. Another Top 10'er, 'DREAM POLICE' (1979), consolidated their newfound fame, although this was nearly wrecked when The BEATLES influenced CHEAP TRICK worked with the legendary GEORGE MARTIN on the album, 'ALL SHOOK UP'. PETERSSEN felt the strain and bailed out before their next album, 'ONE ON ONE' (1982), which had seen JON BRANDT come in as a replacement for the temporary PETE COMITA. In 1983, they employed the services of TODD RUNDGREN (who didn't!?) on their album of that year, 'NEXT POSITION PLEASE', which was a relative flop compared to the lofty chart heights of its predecessors. After a near return to form with the 1985 album, 'STANDING ON THE EDGE', they trawled a creative and commercial trough with 'THE DOCTOR'. Drastic measures were needed; PETERSSEN returned and the group drafted in outside writers to make 1988's 'LAP OF LUXURY' their most successful album of the decade. Of course, this was due in no small part to CHEAP TRICK achieving their first singles chart topper, 'THE FLAME'. Their AOR formula was utilised once more on their 1990 'BUSTED', although this was to be their last taste of major chart action for some time. The 1994 'Warner Brothers' set, 'WOKE UP WITH A MONSTER' saw the band attempting to recapture their heady 70's sound. Three years later, after a one-off for the seminal cult-indie label, 'Sub Pop', CHEAP TRICK released an eponymous set which dented the US Top 100. Come the end of the decade the band were in retrospective mood for a small series of residencies in various US cities, airing one of their first three albums in whole each night. A novel idea, and one which provided the material for 1999's 'MUSIC FOR HANGOVERS', a spirited live effort which offered few surprises but revealed an enthusiasm undimmed by the passing years. Longtime fans also lapped up 'SILVER' (2001), another live affair recorded at a special 25th anniversary homecoming show. In contrast to its predecessor, the record featured more obscure treats while the likes of SMASHING PUMPKINS' BILLY CORGAN and SLASH added a dash of celebrity appeal. • **Covered:** AIN'T THAT A SHAME (Fats Domino) / DON'T BE CRUEL (Elvis Presley) / DANCING THE NIGHT AWAY (Motors) / SPEAK NOW (Terry Reid) / MONEY (Barrett Strong) / MAGICAL MYSTERY TOUR (Beatles).

Album rating: CHEAP TRICK (*7) / IN COLOR (*6) / HEAVEN TONIGHT (*7) / AT BUDOKAN (*7) / DREAM POLICE (*5) / ALL SHOOK UP (*4) / ONE ON ONE (*5) / NEXT POSITION PLEASE (*4) / STANDING ON THE EDGE (*5) / THE DOCTOR (*3) / LAP OF LUXURY (*5) / BUSTED (*4) / THE GREATEST HITS compilation (*6) / BUDOKAN II early live (*5) / WOKE UP WITH A MONSTER (*4) / CHEAP TRICK on 'Red Ant' 1997 (*4) / Robin Zander: ROBIN ZANDER (*6)

FUSE

RICK NIELSEN (b.22 Dec'46, Rockford)– guitar / **JOE SUNBERG** – vocals / **CRAIG MYERS** – guitar / **TOM PETERSSON** (b. 9 May'50) – bass / **CHIP GREENMAN** – drums

not iss. Epic

Jul 68. (7") <5-10514> **HOUND DOG. / CRUISIN' FOR BURGERS** [-] [ ]
<originally-iss.Jun68 as GRIM REAPERS on 'Smack'; >

Jul 69. (lp) **FUSE** [-] [ ]

—— split soon after above **NIELSEN** and **PETERSSON** teamed up invariably as NAZZ and FUSE with ex-NAZZ members **ROBERT 'STEWKEY' ANTONI** – vocals / **THOM MOONEY** – drums

—— In '72 they became **The SICK MAN OF EUROPE** and moved to Philadelphia / **BUN E. CARLOS** (b.BRAD CARLSON, 12 Jun'51) – drums (ex-PAGANS) repl. MOONEY / **XENO** (r.n. RANDY HOGAN) – vocals repl. STEWKEY / **RICK SZELUGA** – bass repl. PETERSSON for a short while, until they became in '73 . . .

CHEAP TRICK

NIELSEN, PETERSSON, CARLOS and **XENO)**

—— Oct74 **ROBIN ZANDER** (b.23 Jan'53, Loves Park, Illinois) – vocals, guitar (ex-TOONS) repl. XENO who joined STRAIGHT UP

Epic Epic

Mar 77. (7") *<50375>* **OH CANDY. / DADDY SHOULD HAVE STAYED IN HIGH SCHOOL** [-] [ ]

Mar 77. (lp) *(EPC 81917) <34400>* **CHEAP TRICK** [ ] [ ] Jan77
– Hot love / Speak now or forever hold your peace / He's a whore / Mandocello / The ballad of T.V. violence (I'm not the only boy) / Elo kiddies / Daddy should have stayed in high school / Taxman, Mr Thief / Cry cry / Oh Candy. *(re-iss. Nov81 lp/c; EPC/40 32070) <cd-iss. Jun88 on 'Collector's Choice'; EK 34400> (cd re-iss. Jul97; 487933-2) (cd re-iss. Oct98 on 'Columbia'; 491229-2)*

Nov 77. (7") *(EPC 5701) <50435>* **I WANT YOU TO WANT ME. / OH BOY (instrumental)** [ ] [ ]
(re-iss. Mar78; same)

Nov 77. (lp/c) *(EPC/40 82214) <34884>* **IN COLOR** [ ] 73 Aug77
– Hello there / Big eyes / Downed / I want you to want me / You're all talk / Oh Caroline / Clock strikes ten / Southern girls / Come on, come on / So good to see you. *<cd-iss. Jun88 on 'Collector's Choice'; EK 34844> (cd-iss. Oct93 on 'Sony Europe'; 982833-2) (cd re-iss. Oct98 on 'Columbia'; 491230-2)*

Nov 77. (7") *<50485>* **SOUTHERN GIRLS. / YOU'RE ALL TALK** [-] [ ]

Mar 78. (7") *(EPC 6199)* **SO GOOD TO SEE YOU. / YOU'RE ALL TALK** [ ] [-]

May 78. (7") *(EPC 6394) <50570>* **SURRENDER. / AUF WIEDERSEHEN** [ ] 62

May 78. (lp/c) *(EPC/40 82679) <35312>* **HEAVEN TONIGHT** [ ] 48
– Surrender / On top of the world / California man / High roller / Auf wiedersehen / Takin' me back / On the radio / Heaven tonight / Stiff competition / How are you / Oh Claire. *(cd-iss. Sep93 on 'Sony Europe'; 982993-2) (cd re-iss. Oct98; 491231-2)*

Jul 78. (7") *(EPC 6427)* **CALIFORNIA MAN. / STIFF COMPETITION** [ ] [-]

Aug 78. (7") *<50625>* **CALIFORNIA MAN. / I WANT YOU TO WANT ME** [-] [ ]

Feb 79. (lp,yellow-lp/c) *(EPC/40 86083) <35795>* **AT BUDOKAN (live)** 29 4
– Hello there / Come on, come on / Look out / Big eyes / Need your love / Ain't that a shame / I want you to want me / Surrender / Goodnight now / Clock strikes ten. *(re-iss. as d-lp.Nov81' EPC 32595) (cd-iss. Feb86; CDEPC 86083) (re-iss. Jul91 on 'Essential' cd/c; ESS CD/MC 949)*

Feb 79. (7"; w-drawn) *(EPC 7144) <50814>* **VOICES (live). / SURRENDER (live)** [ ] 32 Nov79

Mar 79. (7",7"orange) *(EPC 7258) <50680>* **I WANT YOU TO WANT ME (live). / CLOCK STRIKES TEN (live)** 29 7

Jul 79. (7") *(EPC 7724)* **SURRENDER (live). / AUF WIEDERSEHEN (live)** [ ] [-]

Sep 79. (7") *(EPC 7839) <50743>* **AIN'T THAT A SHAME (live). / ELO KIDDIES** [ ] 35 Jul79

Sep 79. (lp/pic-lp/c) *(EPC/11/40 83522) <35773>* **DREAM POLICE** 41 6
– Dream police / Way of the world / The house is rockin' (with domestic problems) / Gonna raise Hell / I'll be with you tonight / Voices / Writing on the wall / I know what I want / Need your love.

Oct 79. (7") *(EPC 7880) <50744>* **DREAM POLICE. / HEAVEN TONIGHT** [ ] 26 Sep79

Jan 80. (7") *(EPC 8114)* **WAY OF THE WORLD. / OH CANDY** 73 [-]

Mar 80. (7"ep) *(EPC 8335)* **I'LL BE WITH YOU TONIGHT. / HE'S A WHORE / SO GOOD TO SEE YOU** [ ] [-]

Apr 80. (7") *<50887>* **EVERYTHING WORKS IF YOU LET IT. / WAY OF THE WORLD** [-] 44

Jul 80. (7") *(EPC 8755)* **EVERYTHING WORKS IF YOU LET IT. / HEAVEN TONIGHT** [ ] [-]

Oct 80. (7") *(EPC 9071) <50942>* **STOP THIS GAME. / WHO D'KING** [ ] 48

Oct 80. (lp/c) *(EPC/40 86124) <36498>* **ALL SHOOK UP** [ ] 24
– Stop this game / Just got back / Baby loves to rock / Can't stop it but I'm gonna try / World's greatest lover / High Priest of rhythmic noise / Love comes a-tumblin' down / I love you honey but I hate your friends / Go for the throat (use your own imagination) / Who d'king. *<cd-iss. Jun88 on 'Collector's Choice'; EK 36498>*

Jan 81. (7") *(EPC 9502)* **WORLD'S GREATEST LOVER. / HIGH PRIEST OF RHYTHMIC NOISE** [ ] [ ]

—— **PETE COMITA** (b. Italy) – bass repl. PETERSSON who formed own group with his wife

Aug 81. (7") *<47187>* **REACH OUT. / I MUST BE DREAMING** [-] [ ]

—— (above single from the film 'Heavy Metal'. issued on 'Full Moon-Asylum') now alongside **NIELSEN** (some bass), **ZANDER + CARLOS**

—— (late '81) **JON BRANT** (b.20 Feb'54) – bass (on three songs) repl. COMITA

May 82. (7") *(EPCA 2406) <02968>* **IF YOU WANT MY LOVE. / FOUR LETTER WORD** 57 45

May 82. (lp,red-lp/pic-lp/c) *(EPC/11/40 85740) <38021>* **ONE ON ONE** 95 39
– I want you / One on one / If you want my love / Oo la la la / Lookin' out for number one / She's tight / Time is runnin' / Saturday at midnight / Love's got a hold on me / I want be man / Four letter word. *(re-iss. Jun85; EPC 32654)*

Sep 82. (7") *<03233>* **SHE'S TIGHT. / ALL I REALLY WANT TO DO** [-] 65

Aug 83. (7") *<04078>* **DANCING THE NIGHT AWAY. / DON'T MAKE OUR LOVE A CRIME** [-] [ ]

Sep 83. (lp/c) *(EPC/40 25490) <38794>* **NEXT POSITION PLEASE** [ ] 61
– I can't take it / Borderline / I don't love her anymore / Next position please / Younger girls / Dancing the night away / 3-D / You say jump / Y.O.Y.O.Y. / Won't take no for an answer / Heaven's falling / Invaders of the heart. *<US c+=/cd+=>* – You take too much / Don't make our love a crime.

Sep 83. (12"ep) *(EPCTA 3743)* **DANCING THE NIGHT AWAY / AIN'T THAT A SHAME. / I WANT YOU TO WANT ME / SURRENDER** [ ] [-]

Nov 83. (7") *<04216>* **I CAN'T TAKE IT. / YOU TALK TOO MUCH** [-] [ ]

Feb 84. (7") *<29723>* **SPRING BREAK. / GET READY** [-] [ ]
(above from the film 'Spring Break', issued on 'Warner Bros')
(below issued on 'Pasha' US)

1984. (7") *<04392>* **UP THE CREEK. / (other artist)** [-] [ ]

Sep 85. (7") *(A 6390)* <05431> **TONIGHT IT'S YOU. / WILD WILD WOMEN** [ ] [44] Jul85
(12"+=) *(EPCTX 6390)* – I want you to want me / If you want my love.
Oct 85. (lp/c) *(EPC/40 26374)* <39592> **STANDING ON THE EDGE** [ ] [35] Aug85
– Little sister / Tonight it's you / She's got motion / Love comes / How about you / Standing on the edge / This time around / Rock all night / Cover girl / Wild wild women.
Jun 86. (7") <06137> **MIGHTY WINGS. / (other artist)** [-] [ ]
Nov 86. (lp/c) *(EPC/40 57087)* <40405> **THE DOCTOR** [ ] [ ] Oct86
– It's up to you / Rearview mirror romance / The doctor / Are you lonely tonight / Name of the game / Kiss me red / Take me to the top / Good girls go to heaven (bad girls go everywhere) / Man-u-lip-u-later / It's only love. *(cd-iss. May87; CDEPC 57087)*
Nov 86. (7") <06540> **IT'S ONLY LOVE. / NAME OF THE GAME** [-] [ ]

— **TOM PETERSSON** – bass, vocals returned to repl. BRANT

May 88. (7"/7"sha-pic-d) *(651466-7/-0)* <07745> **THE FLAME. / THROUGH THE NIGHT** [ ] [1] Apr88
(12"+=/cd-s+=) *(EPC 651466-6/-2)* – I want you to want me / If you want my love. *<re-iss. Dec88; 73792>*
May 88. (lp/c/cd) *(460782-1/-4/-2)* <40922> **LAP OF LUXURY** [ ] [18]
– Let go / No mercy/ The flame / Space / Never had a lot to lose / Don't be cruel / Wrong side of love / All we need is a dream / Ghost town / All wound up. *(re-iss. cd Oct93 on 'Sony Europe'; 982839-2)*
Aug 88. (7"/7"sha-pic-d) *(652896-7/-0)* <07965> **DON'T BE CRUEL. / I KNOW WHAT I WANT** [ ] [4] Jul88
(12"+=/cd-s+=) *(652896-6/-2)* – California man / Ain't that a shame.
(3"cd-s+=) *(653005-3)* – Dream police / Way of the world.
Oct 88. (7"/c-s) <08097> **GHOST TOWN. / WRONG SIDE OF LOVE** [-] [33]
Jan 89. (7"/c-s) <68563> **NEVER HAD A LOT TO LOSE. / ALL WE NEED IS A DREAM** [-] [75]

— In Feb89, ZANDER dueted with Heart's ANN WILSON on US Top 10 single 'SURRENDER TO ME'.

Aug 90. (7"/c-s) *(656148-7/-4)* <73444> **CAN'T STOP FALLIN' INTO LOVE. / YOU DRIVE, I'LL STEER** [ ] [12] Jul90
(12"+=/cd-s+=) *(656148-6/-2)* – The flame.
Sep 90. (cd/c/lp) *(466876-2/-4/-1)* <46013> **BUSTED** [ ] [48] Jul90
– Back 'n blue / I can't understand it / Wherever would I be / If you need me / Can't stop falling into love / Busted / Walk away / You drive, I'll steer / When you need someone / Had to make you mine / Rock'n'roll tonight.
Sep 90. (7"/c-s; w-drawn) <73566> **IF YOU NEED ME. / BIG BANG** [-] [ ]
Oct 90. (7"/c-s) <73580> **WHEREVER WOULD I BE. / BUSTED** [-] [50]
Oct 91. (cd/c) *(469086-2/-4)* <48681> **THE GREATEST HITS** (compilation) [ ] [ ]
– Magical mystery tour / Dream police / Don't be cruel / Tonight it's you / She's tight / I want you to want me (live) / If you want my love / Ain't that a shame / Surrender / The flame / I can't take it / Can't stop fallin' into love / Voices *(re-iss. May94; same)*

— ROBIN ZANDER issued an eponymous solo set in '93

Warners / Warners
Mar 94. (cd/c) <*(9362 45425-2/-4)*> **WOKE UP WITH A MONSTER** [ ] [ ]
– My gang / Woke up with a monster / You're all I wanna do / Never run out of love / Didn't know I had it / Ride the pony / Girlfriends / Let her go / Tell me everything / Cry baby / Love me for a minute.

Sub Pop / Sub Pop
Mar 97. (7") <*(SP 393)*> **BABY TALK. / BRONTOSAURUS** [ ] [ ]

Red Ant / Red Ant
Jun 97. (cd-ep) <*(RAAX 1001)*> **SAY GOODBYE / YEAH YEAH / VOICES (live) / SURRENDER (live)** [ ] [ ]
Jun 97. (cd) <*(RAACD 002)*> **CHEAP TRICK** [ ] [99] Apr97
– Anytime / Hard to tell / Carnival game / Shelter / You let a lotta people down / Baby no more / Yeah yeah / Say goodbye / Wrong all along / Eight miles low / It all comes back to you.

Cheap Trick / Cheap Trick
Jul 99. (cd) <*(CTU 20001)*> **MUSIC FOR HANGOVERS (live)** [ ] [ ] Jun99
– Oh Claire / Surrender / Hot love / I can't take it / I want you to want me / Taxman, Mr. Thief / Mandocello / Oh Caroline / How are you? / If you want my love / Dream police / So good to see you / The ballad of TV violence (I'm not the . . .) / Gonna raise hell.
Feb 01. (d-cd) <*2001*> **SILVER (live August 28, 1999)** [-] [ ]
– Ain't that a shame / I want you to want me / Oh, Candy / That 70's song / Voices / If you want my love / She's tight / Can't stop fallin' into love / Gonna raise hell / I can't take it / It all comes back to you / Tonight it's you / Time will let you know / World's greatest lover / The flame / Stop this game / Dream police / I know what I want / Woke up with a monster / Never had a lot to lose / You're all talk / I'm losin' you / Hard to tell / Oh Claire / Surrender / Just got back / Day tripper / Who d'king.

– compilations etc. –

Apr 80. (10"m-lp) *Epic;* <36453> **FOUND ALL THE PARTS (rare '76-'79)** [-] [39]
– Day tripper (live) / Can't hold on / Such a good girl / Take me I'm yours.
Oct 91. (cd/c) *Castle; (CCS CD/MC 309)* **THE COLLECTION** [ ] [-]
Feb 94. (cd) *Epic;* <*EK 53308*> **BUDOKAN II (live)** [-] [ ]
Aug 96. (cd-box) *Elektra; (E4K 649384)* **SEX, AMERICA, CHEAP TRICK** [ ] [ ]
May 98. (d-cd) *Columbia; (489650-2)* <65527> **AT THE BUDOKAN – THE COMPLETE CONCERT** [ ] [ ] Apr98
Nov 98. (cd) *Sony;* <*2820*> **DON'T BE CRUEL** [-] [ ]
Sep 00. (cd) *Epic; (499660-2)* **CHEAP TRICK / IN COLOR** [ ] [-]
Oct 00. (cd) *Epic; (499677-2)* <66015> **THE AUTHORISED GREATEST HITS** [ ] [ ]

CHELSEA

Formed: London, England . . . October '76 initially as LSD by GENE OCTOBER. He was soon left to take up the reins when other members, BILLY IDOL, TONY JAMES and JOHN TOWE went off to form the more successful GENERATION X. Early the following year, GENE founded CHELSEA along with JAMES STEVENSON, CAREY FORTUNE and SIMON VITESSE, the latter a replacement for short-lived member, HENRY BADOWSKI. Signed to Miles Copeland's new independent imprint, 'Step Forward', CHELSEA released the political protest, 'RIGHT TO WORK' as their debut single in the summer of '77. The people's punks followed up with another anthemic dig at government complacency in the shape of 'HIGH RISE LIVING', a heavy touring schedule taking in the country's more deprived areas as well as the normal city dates. Around this period (Autumn '77), GENE had a bit part in Derek Jarman's controversial punk film, 'Jubilee', alongside the likes of ADAM ANT, TOYAH and WAYNE COUNTY; a couple of CHELSEA songs were to feature on its soundtrack. A new line-up of OCTOBER, STEVENSON, GEOFF MYLES and CHRIS BASHFORD re-emerged in late summer '78 (with 'URBAN KIDS') after a lengthy absence and it was to be a further year before the belated release of their eponymous first album. By this point in time, GENE and Co had been overtaken by the musical experimentation of their now post-punk peers, the band relegated to the Vauxhall Conference Division of straggling punk diehards. Through varying line-ups, CHELSEA continued to fight the punk wars over the course of the 80's and some of the 90's, GENE's last effort to date being 1995's appropriately titled solo set, 'LIFE AND STRUGGLE'. • **Songwriters:** OCTOBER penned, except STREET FIGHTING MAN (Rolling Stones), and his solo SUFFERING IN THE LAND (Jimmy Cliff). • **Trivia:** In 1985, OCTOBER made an appearance on LWT's rock programme alongside JOOLS HOLLAND and MEAT LOAF!

Album rating: CHELSEA (*4) / ALTERNATIVE HITS compilation (*5) / EVACUATE (*3) / LIVE AND WELL (*4) / JUST FOR THE RECORD compilation (*5) / ROCKS OFF (*3) / UNDERWRAPS (*3) / THE ALTERNATIVE (*3) / TRAITOR'S GATE (*3) / Gene October: LIFE AND STRUGGLE (*3)

GENE OCTOBER – vocals / **JAMES STEVENSON** – lead guitar / **CAREY FORTUNE** – drums / **SIMON VITESSE** – bass; repl. HENRY BADOWSKI who joined WRECKLESS ERIC, The DAMNED, and later HELLIONS, before UK SUBS.

Step Forward / I.R.S.
Jun 77. (7") *(SF 2)* **RIGHT TO WORK. / THE LONER** [ ] [-]
Oct 77. (7") *(SF 5)* **HIGH RISE LIVING. / NO ADMISSION** [ ] [-]

— **OCTOBER + STEVENSON** were joined by **DAVE MARTIN** – guitar / **GEOFF MYLES** – bass / **CHRIS BASHFORD** – drums (CAREY later guested on JJ BURNEL's solo album)

Aug 78. (7") *(SF 8)* **URBAN KIDS. / NO FLOWERS** [ ] [-]
Jul 79. (lp) *(SFLP 2)* **CHELSEA** [ ] [-]
– I'm on fire / Decide / Free the fighters / Your toy / Fools and soldiers / All the downs / Government / Twelve men / Many rivers / Trouble is the day. *(cd-iss. Oct98 on 'Captain Oi'; AHOYCD 91) (lp re-iss. Sep99 on 'Get Back'; GET 38)*
Feb 80. (7") *(SF 14)* **NO ONE'S COMING OUTSIDE. / WHAT WOULD YOU DO?** [ ] [-]
Apr 80. (7") *(SF 15)* **LOOK AT THE OUTSIDE. / DON'T GET ME WRONG** [ ] [-]
Jul 80. (7") *(SF 16)* **NO ESCAPE. / DECIDE** [ ] [-]
Nov 80. (lp) *(SFLP 5)* <*SP 70010*> **ALTERNATIVE HITS** <US-title 'NO ESCAPE'> (compilation) [ ] [ ]
– No escape / Urban kids / No flowers / All the downs / Right to work / Look at the outside / What would you do / No one's coming outside / The loner / Don't get me wrong / Decide / Come on. *(<cd-iss. Oct98 on 'Captain Oi'+=; AYOYCD 92>)* – High rise living / No admission.

— disbanded again when DAVE MARTIN joined PINK MILITARY, and STEVENSON was poached by GENE's favourite group GENERATION X

— **OCTOBER** — recruited **NIC AUSTIN** – guitar / **TIM GRIFFIN** – bass / **SOL MINTZ** – drums

May 81. (7") *(SF 17)* **ROCKIN' HORSE. / YEARS AWAY** [ ] [-]
Sep 81. (7"m) *(SF 18)* **FREEMANS. / I.D. PARADE / HOW DO YOU KNOW?** [ ] [-]
Nov 81. (7") *(SF 20)* **EVACUATE. / NEW ERA** [ ] [-]

— **SOL MINTZ** – drums; repl. JONES

Mar 82. (7") *(SF 21)* **WAR ACROSS THE NATION. / HIGH RISE LIVING (remix)** [ ] [-]
Apr 82. (lp) *(SFLP 7)* <*SP 70603*> **EVACUATE** [ ] [ ]
– Evacuate / How do you know? / Cover up / Looks right / Tribal song / War across the nation / Forty people / Running free / Last drink / Only thinking. *(cd-iss. Nov98 on 'Captain Oi'+=; AHOYCD 94)* – Years away / Freemans / I.D. parade / How do you know? / New era / War across the nation / Stand out.
Oct 82. (7",7"pic-d) *(SF 22)* **STAND OUT. / LAST DRINK** [ ] [-]

— disbanded again early in 1983. AUSTIN joined BANDITS AT 4 O'CLOCK, and LINC joined LIGOTAGE.

GENE OCTOBER

Illegal / not iss.
Jan 83. (7") *(ILS 034)* **SUFFERING IN THE LAND. / SUFFERING DUB** [ ] [-]

Slipped Discs / not iss.
Jan 84. (7") *(SPLAT 001)* **DON'T QUIT. / BURNING SOUNDS** [ ] [-]

CHELSEA

— were back for mid-83, with **GENE** plus **PETER DIMMOCK** – bass (ex-CHRON GEN) / **DAVEY JONES** (b. Scotland) – guitar / **GEOFF SEWELL** (or) **COLVILLE** – drums

Picasso / not iss.

May 84. (lp) *(PIK 003)* **LIVE AND WELL (live)** [ ] [-]
(cd re-iss. Oct95 on 'Razor'; PUNXCD 1)

— **PHOENIX + TIM BRIFFA** – guitar; repl. DAVEY

Communique / not iss.

Jun 85. (7") *(LITTLE 1)* **VALIUM MOTHER. / MONICA, MONICA** [ ] [-]
(12"+=) *(12LITTLE 1)* – Break this town.
Aug 85. (lp) *(LARGE 1)* **ORIGINAL SINNERS** [ ] [-]
Mar 86. (7") **SHINE THE LIGHT. / BELIEVE ME** [ ] [-]

Jungle / not iss.

Nov 86. (lp) *(FREUD 14)* **ROCKS OFF** [ ] [-]
– Fool's Paradise / Revolution No.9 / Hard-up baby / Memory fades / Give me more / Inside out / You and me / Street fighting man / Little princess / Sidewinder.

Chelsea / not iss.

May 88. (7") *(CH 001)* **GIVE ME MORE. / SYMPATHY FOR THE DEVIL** [ ] [-]

— next featured **TOPPER HEADON** – drums (ex-CLASH); on 2 tracks / plus **STEVE TANNETT** – guitar (ex-MENACE) / **NIC AUSTIN**

I.R.S. / not iss.

Jun 89. (lp/c/cd) *(EIRSA/+C/CD 1011)* **UNDERWRAPS** [ ] [-]
– Somebody got murdered / Cheat / Give me mercy / Nice girls / No respect / Life of crime / Switchblade / Fool / Time after time / Come on.

Alter-Ego / not iss.

Apr 93. (cd) *(ALTGOCD 002)* **THE ALTERNATIVE** [ ] [-]
– The alternative / Weirdos in wonderland / More than a giro / Wasting time / Ever wonder / Where is everything / You can be there too / What's wrong with you / Oh no / Too late / Dreams of dreams / Ode to the travellers. *(re-iss. Oct94 on 'Weser'; WL 2466-2)*

Weser / not iss.

Aug 94. (cd) *(WL 2480-2)* **TRAITORS GATE** [ ] [-]
– Streets of anarchy / Be what you want to be / Traitors gate / Power for a day / Fireworks / S.A.D. / My hotel room / Guns in paradise / We dare / Floating in the dark / This is now / Nightmares.
May 95. (7") *(WL 2482-7)* **WE DARE. / WHAT'S WRONG WITH YOU (live) / RIGHT TO WORK (live)** [ ] [-]

— CHELSEA finally split in 1995

- compilations, etc. -

May 85. (lp) *Step Forward; (SFLP 10)* **JUST FOR THE RECORD** [ ] [-]
Sep 88. (lp) *Illegal; (ILP 024)* **BACKTRAX** [ ] [-]
Aug 89. (lp) *Clay; (CLAYLP 101)* **UNRELEASED STUFF** [ ] [-]
– I'm on fire / Come on / No flowers / Urban kids / 12 men / Trouble is the day / Young toy / Decide / Curfew / Look at the outside / Don't get me wrong / Fools and soldiers. *(<cd-iss. May93 & Jul94 lp/cd; CLAY/+CD 101>)*
Mar 92. (cd) *Released Emotions; (REM 016CD)* **LIVE AT THE MUSIC MACHINE 1978 (live)** [ ] [-]
Jul 97. (cd) *Receiver; (<RRCD 242>)* **FOOLS AND SOLDIERS** [ ] [ ] Aug97
Dec 98. (cd) *Captain Oi; (AHOYCD 98)* **THE PUNK SINGLES COLLECTION 1977-1982** [ ] [-]
Apr 99. (cd) *Captain Oi; (<AHOYCD 106>)* **PUNK ROCK RARITIES** [ ] [ ]

GENE OCTOBER

— with **JAMES STEVENSON** – guitar / **EMILE LOBO** – guitar / **JAMES HALLAWELL** – organ / **GLEN MATLOCK** – bass /

Receiver / Receiver

Mar 95. (cd) *(<RRCD 196>)* **LIFE AND STRUGGLE** [ ] [ ]
– Born to keep on running / Count to ten / Watch out / Welcome home / Butterfly / Life and struggle / It hurts / I owe you nothing / Big tears / Curfew / Everytime I see you I know I just gotta go.

CHEMICAL PEOPLE

Formed: Los Angeles, California, USA ... mid-80's by DAVE NAZWORTHY, ED ULRIK, JAIME PINA and BLAIR JOBE, the latter bailing out prior to the recording of their 1988 debut set, 'SO SEXIST!'; he however, did contribute several of the songs. These porn-obsessed alternative/pop rockers had the output and background to compete with other stalwarts of their genre, although they unfortunately took a sabbatical just when the mainstream record-buying public begun to take an interest in skatepark-favoured punk-pop music. CP's aforementioned debut release established their musical kudos, as well as forefronting a major theme in their work-porn; of the hardcore variety. With NAZWORTHY now on vocals, the trio released their second full-length outing, 'TEN-FOLD HATE' (1989), which again showed them wearing their skin-flick passions on their sleeves, or more accurately, album sleeve, which featured a photo of famed blue-movie star, Taija Rae. The following year saw the release of a third set, 'THE RIGHT THING', notable for the fact that although the boys may not have matured, their music certainly had. Though it must be said CP's interest in porn was not just voyeuristic, as they lent their artistic help to several movies of the genre in the form of musical accompaniment. Luckily for any puritans in their fanbase there was no need to search out the offending films as CP's movie material was released on the aptly-titled album, 'SOUNDTRACKS' (1992). The same year also saw the release of the 'CHEMICAL PEOPLE' album, which was made with new recruit ROBERT HECKER, from REDD KROSS, who had replaced the recently departed PINA. This release also marked a break for the band which was to last five years. An unfortunate time to take a long holiday as it coincided with the huge rise in popularity of this genre of music exemplified by similar acts like GREEN DAY and OFFSPRING. CP did bounce back though – although arguably half a decade late – with another long-player 'ARPEGGIO MOTORCADE' (1997). • **Covered:** SHOCK ME (Kiss) / VACATION (Go-Go's) / ASK THE ANGELS (Patti Smith) / etc.

Album rating: SO SEXIST! (*2) / TEN-FOLD HATE (*3) / THE RIGHT THING compilation (*6) / OVERDOSED ON . . . compilation (*6) / ANGELS 'N' DEVILS mini (*3) / SOUNDTRACKS (*4) / CHEMICAL PEOPLE (*4) / ARPEGGIO MOTORCADE (*5)

DAVE NAZWORTHY – vocals, drums, guitar / **JAIME PINA** – guitar / **ED URLIK** – bass / (vocalist/guitarist BLAIR JOBE left after contributing half the debut's songs)

Cruz / Cruz

1988. (lp/c/cd) *<CRZ 002/+C/CD>* **SO SEXIST!** [-] [ ]
– Don't tell me / Human fear / Submarine dream / The good, the bad and the ugly / Times will change / Henry Whitpenn / Find out / Donut-run / Shock me / Diet koke / Funky time / Those young girls. *(UK-iss.Jan90; same as US) <(re-iss. Sep95; same)*
Jan 90. (lp/c/cd) *<(CRZ 007/+C/CD)>* **TEN-FOLD HATE** [ ] [ ] 1989
– New food / Aquaman / Old habits / Strange taste / She's got a bad case / Ed intro / Cherry / Intro / All the best things / Nudist camp / Metallica / Cop a feel / Moodchanger / Vacation / Outrage / Black throat.
Aug 90. (lp/c/cd) *(CRZ 013/+C/CD)* **THE RIGHT THING** (compilation) [ ] [-]
– Captain / The right thing / A pornography / Duck song / A different scene / Some other time / Unanswered question / Aqua II / Overdosed / Nutro / Cheri love affair / The jam / Ultramental.
Dec 90. (m-lp/m-c/m-cd) *<CRZ 019/+C/CD>* **ANGELS 'N' DEVILS** [-] [ ]
– Ask the angels / Been here / Faust / Rap / Blo me fatti / 1490. *(UK-iss.May93; same as US)*
Apr 91. (lp/c/cd) *<CRZ 020/+C/CD>* **SOUNDTRACKS** [-] [ ]
– Seventy six / Funk-K / Miami blues / Way we die now / Cockfighter / Noize jam / New wave theme / Sideswipe / Woman chaser / Black mass of Brother Springer / Baptismal / New wave reprise. *(UK-iss.May93 & Sep95; same as US)*

— **ROBERT HECKER** – guitar (of REDD KROSS) repl. PINA

May 92. (lp/c/cd) *<CRZ 023/+C/CD>* **CHEMICAL PEOPLE** [-] [ ]
– Never was / When they're gone / Let it go / Two years / Mid air / Following / I don't mind / Won't do / I gotta know / Drift away. *(UK-iss.May93 & Sep95; same as US)*
Jul 92. (12"/c-s/cd-s) *<(CRZ 025/+C/CD)>* **LET IT GO. / MID AIR** [ ] [ ]

— DAVE NAZ and co took a long break (he now added tenor sax!)

Oct 97. (cd) *<(CRZ 040CD)>* **ARPEGGIO MOTORCADE** [ ] [ ] Aug97
– Counting days / Last one / I hope you're there / Can't see your face / Tables turn / No reason why / No hope / Waiting / It's up to you / Forgot about.

- compilations, etc. -

issued on 'Vinyl Solution' unless stated otherwise

Sep 90. (lp/cd) *(SOL 24/+CD)* **OVERDOSED ON . . .** [ ] [-]
– All the best things / Aquaman / Who killed Marilyn / Hate / Overdosed / X-feminist / Automatic / Tonight I'm gonna rock you / Midnight madness / Shit on my dick / My tattoo / Walking down the street / Bye bye girl / Aqua II / Overdosed / Assface / Ultramental / Henry Whitpenn / All the best things / Find out / Cheri love affair / Aquaman / Old habits / Rip it out.
Apr 93. (7") *(VS 13)* **ASK THE ANGELS. /** [ ] [-]
1990's. (cd) *Two Inch Pecker; <1>* **SINGLES** [-] [ ]

CHEQUERED PAST (see under ⇒ SILVERHEAD)

CHERRY BOMBZ (see under ⇒ HANOI ROCKS)

Desmond CHILD

Born: JOHN CHARLES BARRETT Jr, 28 Oct'53, Miami, Florida, USA; to a Cuban mother and Hungarian father. In 1974/75, CHILD formed his own band, ROUGE, with female singers and fellow university students, DIANE GRASSELLI, MARIA VIDAL and MYRIAM VALE. Signing with 'Capitol' records in 1978, the group's self-titled debut album was a minor success, hitting the US Top 200. The set incorporated a wide cross-section of AOR stylings from hard-edged rock to white funk, even boasting a track written with PAUL STANLEY of KISS (this connection proving extremely profitable a year later when KISS had a near US Top hit with the CHILD-penned 'I WAS MADE FOR LOVING YOU'). A second, harder-rocking group set, 'RUNNERS IN THE NIGHT' failed to attract much interest and CHILD rather wisely decided to concentrate on writing. In the 80's he became one of the most prolific and successful songwriters in the world, his AOR/pop-metal credentials second to none. Artists who've benefitted from the golden pen of CHILD include BON JOVI, CHER, MICHAEL BOLTON, ALICE COOPER and AEROSMITH.

Album rating: DESMOND CHILD & ROUGE (*4) / RUNNERS IN THE NIGHT (*5) / DISCIPLINE (*5)

DESMOND CHILD & ROUGE

DESMOND CHILD – vocals, keyboards; with singers **MYRIAM VALE, MARIA VIDAL + DIANA GRASSELLI** plus many on session including **JOHN SIEGLER** – bass

Capitol / Capitol

Feb 79. (7"/12") *(CL/12CL 16038) <4669>* **OUR LOVE IS INSANE. / CITY IN HEAT** [ ] [51] Jan79
Apr 79. (lp) *<(EST 11908)>* **DESMOND CHILD & ROUGE** [ ] [ ] Mar79
– Westside pow wow / Our love is insane / Lovin' your love / The fight / Main man / City in heat / Lazy love / Otti / Givin' in to my love.
May 79. (7") *<4710>* **GIVIN' IN TO MY LOVE. / MAIN MAN** [-] [ ]
Jan 80. (7") *(CL 16115) <4791>* **GOODBYE BABY. / IMITATION OF LOVE** [ ] [ ]

Jan 80. (lp) *<(EST 11999)>* **RUNNERS IN THE NIGHT**
– Truth comes out / My heart's on fire / Night was not / Goodbye baby / Runners in the night / Tumble in the night / Scared to live / Feeling like this / Imitation of love / Rosa.

Apr 80. (7") *<4815>* **ROSA. / TUMBLE IN THE NIGHT** [-]

— DESMOND returned to songwriting for others (see above)

DESMOND CHILD

— with session people once more

not iss. | Epic

Nov 82. (7") *<03278>* **LET'S MAKE IT RIGHT. / LITTLE ROMANCE** [-]

Elektra | Elektra

Jun 91. (c-s) *<64883>* **LOVE ON A ROOFTOP / A RAY OF HOPE** [-] [40]

Aug 91. (cd)(lp/c) *<(7559 61048-2)(EKT 92/+C)>* **DISCIPLINE**
– Price of lovin' you / Discipline / I don't want to be your friend / Love on a rooftop / You're the story of my life / According to the gospel of love / Do me right / Obsession / Gift of life / A ray of hope.

Sep 91. (c-s) *<64850>* **YOU'RE THE STORY OF MY LIFE / DO ME RIGHT** [-] [74]

— DESMOND returned to songwriting once again

CHILDREN OF BODOM

Formed: Espoo, nr. Helsinki, Finland . . . 1993 by ALEXI LAIHO, ALEXANDER KUOPPALA, JANNE WIRMAN, HENKKA SMITH and JASKA RAATIKAINEN. Originally grouping together under the moniker, INEARTHED, they recorded several demos that did not really produce much attention, and so after a few roster adjustments they settled on the line-up above and the name, CHILDREN OF BODOM. A rather macabre title relating to one of their native countries' most infamous unsolved murder cases – in the 1960's four teenagers camping at Lake Bodom were attacked by an unknown assailant with an axe; killing three of the youngsters. COB debut album, 'SOMETHING WILD' (1997) – released on 'Spinefarm' – came four years after their formation, but this is unsurprising as the majority of the band were still around the ages of 14 and 15 when they first came together. Yet this large gap in time gave the band much time to hone their skills. Thus the debut outing was manifestly more mature in sound than would be expected of a group's embryonic work. This development was seen especially in the STEVE VAI-influenced fretboard fiddlings of ALEXI "Wild Child" LAIHO. COB's output in sound has the power, crunch, and tempo of many of their Scandinavian death metal peers, but with a more heavy metal 80's melodious feel, in tune with bands such as W.A.S.P. and JUDAS PRIEST. Their second full-set, 'HATEBREEDER' (1999) came out two years later, installing them as one of the more important bands of the genre, and again raising LAIHO's status as a bit of a guitar-wizard, gaining him many other offers of work (i.e. playing with the outfit SINERGY and performing off and on for Finnish death metal band, IMPALED NAZARENE). The 'BODOM also showed off their live work, releasing, 'TOKYO WARHEARTS' (1999), taken from a gig in Japan at Tokyo's Club Citta. Another full-set of COB's death metal rocking, 'FOLLOW THE REAPER' (2001) further established their generic credentials.
• **Covered:** MASS HYPNOSIS (Sepultura).

Album rating: SOMETHING WILD (*6) / HATEBREEDER (*5) / TOKYO NIGHTS (*6) / FOLLOW THE REAPER (*5)

ALEXI LAIHO (b.1979) – vocals, guitar (also of IMPALED NAZARENE and SINERGY) / **ALEXANDER KUOPPALA** (b. 1974) – guitar / **JANNE VILJAMI WIRMAN** (b.1979) – keyboards / **HENKKA T. SEPPALA** – bass / **JASKA RAATIKAINEN** (b.1979) – drums

Nuclear Blast | Nuclear Blast

Mar 98. (cd) *(NB 308CD) <6308>* **SOMETHING WILD** Apr98
– Deadnight warrior / In the shadow / Red light in my eyes (part I) / Red light in my eyes (part II) / Lake Bodom / The nail / Touch like angel of death. *(re-iss. Mar98 on 'Spinefarm'; SPI 49CD) (re-iss. Jul99; SPI 64CD)*

May 99. (cd) *(NB 387-2) <6387>* **HATEBREEDER**
– Warheart / Silent night, Bodom night / Hatebreeder / Bed of razors / Towards dead end / Black widow / Wrath within / Children of Bodom / Downfall. *(re-iss. Jul99 on 'Spinefarm'; SPI 69CD)*

Oct 99. (cd) **TOKYO NIGHTS (live)** [-] [-] Finnish
– Intro / Silent night, Bodom night / Lake Bodom / Warheart / Bed of razors / War of razors (solo battles) / Deadnight warrior / Hatebreeder / Touch like angel of death / Downfall / Toeards dead end.

Jan 01. (cd) *(NB 560-2) <6560>* **FOLLOW THE REAPER** Feb01
– Follow the reaper / Bodom after midnight / Children of decadence / Everytime I die / Mask of sanity / Taste of my scythe / Hate me! / Northern comfort / Kissing the shadows. *(hidden track+=)* – Hellion.

CHINA

Formed: Switzerland . . . 1987 by CLAUDIO MATTEO and FREDDY LAURENCE, who enlisted the help of MATH SHIVEROW, MARC LYNN and JOHN DOMMEN. Signing to 'Phonogram' the group released an eponymous debut in '88, displaying a typically European sound (i.e. The SCORPIONS, UFO, etc.), although it was promising enough to warrant an encouraging press reaction. A series of line-up changes saw ex-KROKUS axeman, PATRICK MASON replace the talented SHIVEROW on vocals and bassman BRIAN KOFMEHL substituting LYNN. A second set, 'SIGN IN THE SKY' (1990) seemed to bode well for the future, although their final two albums with new frontman, ERIC ST. MICHAELS, only found takers in Germany.

Album rating: CHINA (*5) / SIGN IN THE SKY (*6) / LIVE mini (*4) / GO ALL THE WAY (*4)

MATH SHIVEROW – vocals / **FREDDY LAURENCE** – guitar / **CLAUDIO MATTEO** – guitar / **MARC LYNN** – bass / **JOHN DOMMEN** – drums

Vertigo | not iss.

May 88. (lp/c)(cd) *(VERH/+C 57)(834 451-2)* **CHINA** [-]
– Intro / Shout it out / Back to you / The fight is on / Wild jealousy / Rock city / Hot lovin' night / Living on the stage / I need your love / One shot to the heart / Staying alive.

— **PATRICK MASON** – vocals (ex-KROKUS) repl. SHIVEROW

— **BRIAN KOFMEHL** – bass; repl. LYNN

Mar 90. (cd/c/lp) *(847 247-2/-4/-1)* **SIGN IN THE SKY** [-]
– Great wall / Dead lights / Animal victim / In the middle of the night / Won't give it up / Sign in the sky / Don't ever say goodbye / Broken dream / Second chance / Bitter cold / Take your time / Harder than Hell / So long.

— **ERIC ST. MICHAELS** – vocals; repl. MASON

Feb 91. (m-cd/m-lp) *(848227-2/-1)* **LIVE (live)** [-] [-] German
– Rock city / Sign in the sky / So long / In the middle of the night / Shout it out / Proud Mary.

Dec 91. (cd) *(848715-2)* **GO ALL THE WAY** [-] [-] German
– Pictures of you / Medicine man / Slow dancing in Hell / She did a real good job / So damn easy / Lost gardens / Shake your cages / Go all the way / Don't let in the night / In love again / Face to the wind / In trouble with angels / Like keep moving on / You've got to me.

— split after above

CHINA DRUM

Formed: Ovingham-upon-Tyne, Northumbria, England . . . 1989 by singing drummer ADAM LEE, bassist DAVE McQUEEN and his guitar-playing brother BILL McQUEEN; drummer JAN ALKELMA was subsequently added. Paying their dues by gigging hard around the toilet circuit of Northern England, the trio finally got round to self-financing a debut single, 'SIMPLE', in 1993. In addition to their full-on power-punk flurry, the record showcased their "sensitive" side with an acoustic track, 'MEANING'. They also pared things down with 'BISCUIT BARREL', a newly softened-up version of a stompalong live favourite that sat alongside 'GREAT FIRE' on their summer '94 GREEN DAY/THERAPY?-esque EP, the first of two releases for 'Fluffy Bunny'. The following year's 'BARRIER' EP was also released in the States, although most of the material had been previously issued in the UK. A one-off cover of Kate Bush's 'WUTHERING HEIGHTS' (a split 7" with the FLYING MEDALLIONS on 'Fierce Panda') preceded a major record deal with Beggars Banquet off-shoot, 'Mantra', through whom they issued a series of singles: 'FALL INTO PLACE', 'PICTURES', 'CAN'T STOP THESE THINGS' and 'LAST CHANCE'. The latter two scored minor chart placings while their long-awaited debut set, 'GOOSEFAIR' (1996), nearly hit the UK Top 50. Around the same time, the trio toured Bosnia to raise money for charities working in the war-torn region while their aforementioned album elbowed for chart position in America with Stateside competitors like OFFSPRING and GREEN DAY (again!). The challenge from across the water eventually proved too much and despite a further couple of minor hits, CHINA DRUM's second album, 'SELF MADE MANIAC' (1997), failed to impress the public.

Album rating: GOOSEFAIR (*6) / SELF MADE MANIAC (*6)

ADAM LEE – vocals (+ some drums) / **DAVE McQUEEN** – bass / **BILL McQUEEN** – guitar / **JAN ALKELMA** – drums

China Drum | Bitzcore

Apr 93. (cd-s) *(CC 193) <1696>* **SIMPLE / ON MY WAY / MEANING (acoustic)**

Fluffy Bunny | M.C.A.

Jul 94. (10"ep/cd-ep) *(FLUFF 6/+CD)* **GREAT FIRE / BISCUIT BARREL (acoustic). / MEANING / DOWN BY THE RIVER (live)** [-]

Mar 95. (10"ep/cd-ep) *(FLUFF 8/+CD) <11293>* **BARRIER EP** Jun95
– Barrier / Simple / Biscuit barrel / One way down / Great fire / The meaning.

Fierce Panda | not iss.

Jul 95. (7") *(NING 06)* **WUTHERING HEIGHTS. / (B-side by The Flying Medallions)** [-]

Mantra | M.C.A.

Sep 95. (10"ep/cd-ep) *(MNT 2 TT/CD)* **FALL INTO PLACE / SIMPLE (original version). / ON MY WAY / BARRIER (live)** [-]

Dec 95. (7"green) *(MNT 4)* **PICTURES. / LAST CHANCE (acoustic)** [-]

Jan 96. (cd-ep) **ROLLING HILLS AND SOAKING GILLS** [-]
– Fall into place / Simple / Barrier / Biscuit barrel / One way down / Great fire / Meaning.

Feb 96. (7"/c-s) *(MNT 8/+C)* **CAN'T STOP THESE THINGS. / WUTHERING HEIGHTS** [65] [-]
(cd-s+=) *(MNT 8CD)* – Drown it.

Apr 96. (7"/c-s) *(MNT 10/+C)* **LAST CHANCE. / WALK** [60] [-]
(cd-s+=) *(MNT 10CD)* – Cut them out / Careful with that chieftain, Adam.

Apr 96. (cd/c/lp) *(MNT CD/MC/LP 1002) <11438>* **GOOSEFAIR** [53]
– Can't stop these things / Cloud 9 / Fall into place / Situation / Simple / Biscuit barrel F.M.R. / God bets / Pictures / Find the time / (Had a good idea on) Monday / Last chance / Take it back / The meaning / Better than me.

Jul 96. (7") *(MNT 12)* **WIPEOUT. / BASEBALL IN THE DARK** [-]
(cd-s+=) *(MNT 12CD)* – Biscuit barrel / Sleazeball (Empirion mix).

Aug 97. (7") *(MNT 21)* **FICTION OF LIFE. / PULL** [65] [-]
(cd-s+=) *(MNT 21CD)* – Bubblegum buzz / Baseball in the dark (acoustic).
(cd-s) *(MNT 21CD2)* – ('A'side) / Fall at your feet / Jack / Down by the river (acoustic).

Sep 97. (7") *(MNT 22)* **SOMEWHERE ELSE. / LOSER** [74] [-]
(cd-s+=) *(MNT 22CD)* – Wrong again / Bothered (acoustic).
(cd-s) *(MNT 22CD2)* – ('A'side) / Sleazeball / Don't throw it / ('A'acoustic).

Oct 97. (cd/c/lp) *(MNT CD/MC/LP 1009)* <81009> **SELF MADE MANIAC** [ ] [ ] Feb98
– One thing / Guilty deafness / Somewhere else / Fiction of life / All I wanna be / Down by the river / Another toy / 60 seconds / Foxhole / Control / Stop it all adding up / Bothered.

Apr 98. (7") *(MNT 30)* **STOP IT ALL ADDING UP. / GUILTY DEAFNESS (live)** [ ] [-]
(cd-s+=) *(MNT 30CD)* – Wipe out (live) / Baseball in the dark (live).

Jun 00. (7"; as The DRUM) *(MNT 57)* **HORNS FRONT. / WATER** [ ] [-]
(cd-s+=) *(MNT 57CD)* – Bullbar.

CHIXDIGGIT!

Formed: Calgary, Canada . . . early 90's by school mates MIKE, MARK and KJ (in '93 they added bass player turned drummer, JASON HIRSCH). Initially a ruse to sell T-shirts with the CHIXDIGGIT! moniker, the idea turned into a real band as the lads decided to actually learn to play their instruments. An unusual signing for 'Sub Pop', CHIXDIGGIT! were compared to the RAMONES and modern day pop-punks, GREEN DAY, summer 96's eponymous debut album fitting right in with the prevailing mood of the US alternative scene. The following year, having amicably split from Sub Pop over musical differences, the comic strip punks found a new home at 'Honest Don's' where they unleashed 'BORN ON THE FIRST OF JULY', another happy-go-lucky collection of hook-laden toons. Dismissing a BOOMTOWN RATS covers EP, 'CHRONIC FOR THE TROOPS' (shared with The GROOVIE GHOULIES) in 1998, CHIXDIGGIT! finally delivered their difficult third set, 'BEST HUNG CARROT IN THE FRIDGE' (1999); their fourth 'FROM SCENE TO SHINING SCENE' appeared the following year on 'Honest Dons'.

Album rating: CHIXDIGGIT! (*5) / BORN ON THE FIRST OF JULY (*6) / BEST HUNG CARROT IN THE FRIDGE (*5) / FROM SCENE TO SHINING SCENE (*5)

K.J. JANSEN – vocals, guitar / **MARK O'FLAHERTY** – guitar / **MIKE EGGERMONT** – bass / **JASON HIRSCH** – drums

Sub Pop Sub Pop

Jun 96. (lp/cd) <(SP/+CD 355)> **CHIXDIGGIT!** [ ] [ ] May96
– Dolphins love kids / Great legs / Where's your mom? / Henry Rollins is no fun / I wanna hump you / Song for "R" / Stacked like that / Hemp hemp hooray / 323 / The angriest young men (we're the) / Toilet seat's coming down / Shadow bangers from a shadowy duplex / Van Horne / I drove the coquihalla / (I feel like) Gerry Cleevers . . .

Honest Don's Honest Don's

Nov 97. (7") *(DON 012)* **CHUPA CABRAS. /** [ ] [-]

May 98. (lp/cd) <*(DON 016/+CD)*> **BORN ON THE FIRST OF JULY** [ ] [ ] Apr98
– Gettin' air / My girl's retro / Sikome beach / Chupacabras / Quit your job / Restaurant / Julianne / 20 times / O-H-I-O / Haven't got time / 2000 flushes / Brunette summer.

—— **DAVE ALCOCK** – drums; repl. HIRSCH

Delmonico Delmonico

Nov 88. (cd-ep; shared w/ Groovie Ghoulies) <*DEL 001*> **CHRONIC FOR THE TROOPS** [-] [ ]
– Someone's looking at you / Don't believe what you read / I don't like Mondays / A tonic for the troops / My girl's retro / She gets all the girls.

Nov 99. (cd) <*(DEL 002)*> **BEST HUNG CARROT ON THE FRIDGE** [ ] [ ]
– CD-ROM track / Best hung carrot in the fridge / Grungebaby / Faith / I should have played football in high school / Mila, Caroline and me / King of Kensington / Church / My debutante.

not iss. Honest Don's

Aug 00. (cd) <*DON 28CD*> **FROM SCENE TO SHINING SCENE** [-] [ ]
– My dad vs. P.M. / Spanish fever / Thursday night / Melissa Louise / Aromatherapy / Folks are gone / Moro foxe / Sweaty and hairless / Going to the peelers? / Summer please / Born to Toulouse.

CHRISTIAN DEATH

Formed: Los Angeles, California, USA . . . 1979 by ROZZ WILLIAMS, who enlisted the help of former ADOLESCENTS guitarist, RIKK AGNEW, JAMES McGEARLY and GEORGE BELANGER. One of the few, if not the only American post-punk outfits to be influenced by the European "Goth" scene, CHRISTIAN DEATH found it difficult to secure a record deal, although two obscure releases – an EP for 'Bemis Brain' and the album, 'ONLY THEATRE OF PAIN' – did surface in '82. Relocating to the more sympathetic climes of Europe where a French-only mini-set (featuring selected tracks from their first two releases), 'DEATHWISH' (1984) was already available, ROZZ found a new bunch of musical disciples GITANE DEMONE, DAVID GLASS and Australian songwriter, VALOR KAND. This line-up played their inaugural UK gig in mid '84 promoting that year's album, 'CATASTROPHE BALLET', continuing in their established style and examining the interface between religious imagery and erotica. Musically, the band relied on funereal paced doom-metal riffing and sinister synth flourishes, not everyone's cup of tea but sufficiently pompous to attract obsessive post-Goths. KAND's influence was increasingly felt as he established himself as the band's chief singer and songwriter, accusations of blasphemy accompanying every other release as he persisted in criticising Christ and organised religion in general. With founding member, ROZZ departing after the recording of 1985's Italian-only mini-set, 'THE WIND KISSED PICTURES', CHRISTIAN DEATH became an even more Euro-centric affair, VALOR KAND subsequently recruiting various backing personnel including his brother and mainstay, SVEN. Signing to 'Jungle' records, CHRISTIAN DEATH Mk.II released a solitary 12" in 1986 before finally getting around to completing their first UK-available set for three and a half years, 'THE SCRIPTURES' (1987). The following year, the band released what was possibly their most commercial track to date, 'CHURCH OF NO RETURN', a very SISTERS OF MERCY/MISSION-esque anthem complete with typical goth-diva backing. While their sleeve artwork had always courted controversy, the image of Jesus jacking-up that (un)graced the cover of 1988's 'SEX AND DRUGS AND JESUS CHRIST' surely represented a nadir of bad taste. VALOR and Co continued on their "merry" way into the 90's without ever troubling the cutting edge of the alternative/metal scene, although doubtless they didn't bank on ROZZ returning to the fray with his own version of the original CHRISTIAN DEATH. The two parties battled it out on the record front while the lawyers argued over the finer legal points, while ROZZ simultaneously combined a solo career. Sadly, however, CHRISTIAN DEATH's founder hanged himself at his Hollywood home in April 1998.
• **Covered:** KILL YOUR SONS (Velvet Underground).

Album rating: ONLY THEATRE OF PAIN (*6) / CATASTROPHE BALLET (*4) / THE DECOMPOSITION OF VIOLETS (*5) / THE SCRIPTURES (*6) / SEX AND DRUGS AND JESUS CHRIST (*6) / ASHES (*5) / ATROCITIES (*4) / THE WIND KISSED PICTURES (*5) / THE HERETICS ALIVE (*4) / ALL THE LOVE ALL THE HATE (*5) / INSANUS, ULTIO, PRODITIO, MISERICORDIAQUE (*4) / SEXY DEATH GOD (*5) / THE RAGE OF ANGELS (*4) / DEATH IN DETROIT (*4) / JESUS POINTS THE BONE AT YOU compilation (*7) / etc, etc.

ROZZ WILLIAMS – vocals / **RIKK AGNEW** – guitar (ex-ADOLESCENTS) / **JAMES McGEARLY** – bass / **GEORGE BELANGER** – drums

not iss. Bemis Brain

1982. (12"ep) <*BB 127-128*> **DESPERATE HELL / CAVITY. / SPIRITUAL CRAMP / ROMEO'S DISTRESS / DEATH WISH** [-] [ ]

No Future Frontier

Aug 83. (lp) *(FL 2)* <*FLP 1997*> **ONLY THEATRE OF PAIN** [ ] [-] Nov82
– Cavity – First communuion / Figurative theatre / Burnt offerings / Mysterium iniquitatis / Dream for mother / Dogs / Stairs – Uncertain journey / Spiritual cramp / Romeo's distress / Resurrection – Sixth communion / Prayer. *(re-iss. Feb85 on 'L'Invitation Au Suicide'; SD 1)* <*(cd-iss. Aug93 on 'Frontier'; FCD 1007)*> <*cd re-iss. 1997 on 'Epitaph'; E 80103*>

L'Invitation Au Suicide not iss.

Feb 84. (m-lp) *(SD 4)* **DEATHWISH** [-] [-] France
– Deathwish / Romeo's distress / Dogs / Desperate hell / Spiritual cramp / Cavity. *(re-iss. 1990 on 'Contempo' c/cd; CONTAE/ECD 137) (cd re-iss. May94 on 'Normal'; N 84CD)*

—— **ROZZ** relocated group to Europe and recruited new band; **VALOR KAND** (b. Australia) – vocals, guitar / **GITANE DEMONE** – vocals, keyboards / **DAVID GLASS** – drums

May 84. (lp) *(SD 5)* **CATASTROPHE BALLET** [-] [-] France
– Awake at the wall / Sleepwalk / The drowning / The blue hour / Evening falls / Andro gynous noise hand permeates / Electra descending. *(re-iss. Nov88 on 'Contempo' lp/cd; CONTE/+CD 105) (cd re-iss. Jan96 on 'Normal'; N 181CD) (cd re-iss. May99 on 'Candlelight'; CANDLE 039CD)* <*US cd-iss. 1999 on 'Cleopatra'; 546*>

R.O.I.R. R.O.I.R.

Sep 85. (c) *(A 138)* **THE DECOMPOSITION OF VIOLETS** [ ] [ ]
– Awake the wall / Sleepwalk / The drowning / Theatre of pain / Cavity / The blue hour / Electra descending / As evening falls / Face / Cervix couch / This glass house / Romeo's distress. <*(re-iss. 1991 & Apr98; RUSCD 8240)*>

—— now without ROZZ, their only remaining founder member

Jungle Nostradamus

Feb 86. (12") *(JUNG 24T)* **BELIEVERS OF THE UNPURE. / ?** [ ] [-]

—— added **JAMES BEAM** – guitar, etc / **SVEN KAND** – flute / **CONSTANCE (KOTA)** – bass

Sep 87. (7"/12") *(JUNG 35/+T)* **SICK OF LOVE. / ?** [ ] [-]

Dec 87. (lp/cd) *(FREUD/+CD 18)* <*1052*> **THE SCRIPTURES** [ ] [ ]
– Prelude / Song of songs / Vanity / Four horsemen / 1983 / Omega dawn / A ringing in their ears / Golden age / Alpha sunset / Split blood / Raw war / Reflections / Jezebel's tribulation / Wraeththu. *(cd re-iss. May94 on 'Normal'; NORMAL 65) (cd re-iss. May99 on 'Candlelight'; CANDLE 043CD)* <*US cd-iss. 1997; same*>

Normal Nostradamus

May 88. (lp/cd) *(NORMAL/+CD 15)* <*1055*> **ASHES** (rec.1985) [ ] [ ] 1992
– Ashes (part 1 & 2) / When I was bed / Lament (over the shadows) / Face / The luxury of tears / Of the wound. *(cd re-iss. May94; same) (cd re-iss. May99 on 'Candlelight'; CANDLE 040)* <*US cd re-iss. 1999 on 'Cleopatra'; 545*>

May 88. (lp/cd) *(NORMAL/+CD 18)* **ATROCITIES** (rec.1986) [ ] [-]
– Bastinado silhouettes / Foaming dogs with whips sharp teeth / Polished buttons / Pelting cadavernous flesh / Belladonna for you now blue eyes / Shuddering following the slice / Orgasmic flush with scalpelin hand / O the soothing / Is such heedless deliverance / Worship ye nearing quietus. *(cd re-iss. May94; same) (cd re-iss. May99 on 'Candlelight'; CANDLE 042)*

Aug 88. (lp/cd) *Supporti Fonografici; (SF 003/+CD)* **THE WIND KISSED PICTURES (PAST AND PRESENT)** [-] [-] Italy
– Believers of the unpure / Ouverture / The wind kisses pictures / The lake of fire / Blast of Bough / Amaterasu / The absolute / Lacrima Christi / Lacrima Christi (Italian version). *(pic-lp Jan92) (cd re-iss. Apr91 Jan96 on 'Normal'; NORMAL 76CD)* <*US cd-iss. 1990's on 'Dali-Chameleon'; 74789*> *(cd re-iss. May99 on 'Candlelight'; CANDLE 041CD)*

Jungle not iss.

May 88. (7"/12") *(JUNG 40/+T)* **THE CHURCH OF NO RETURN. /** [ ] [-]

—— guest **BARRY GALVIN** – guitar, keyboards; repl. BEAM

—— guest **JOHANN SCHUMANN** – bass; repl. KOTA

Nov 88. (7"/12") *(JUNG 45/+T)* **WHAT'S THE VERDICT. / THIS IS NOT BLASPHEMY** [ ] [-]

Nov 88. (lp/c/cd) *(FREUD/+C/CD 25)* **SEX AND DRUGS AND JESUS CHRIST** ☐ ☐
– This is heresy / Jesus where's the sugar / Wretched mankind / Tragedy / The third antichrist / Erection / Ten thousand hundred times / Incendiary lover / Window pain. *(re-iss. Jun91 on 'Normal'; NORMAL 96) (cd re-iss. Oct92; same) (cd re-iss. Jul98; FREUDCD 50) <cd re-iss. 1999 on 'Cleopatra'; 617>*

Jun 89. (7") *(JUNG 50)* **ZERO SEX. / ?** ☐ ☐
(12"+=/cd-s+=) *(JUNG 50 T/CD)* –

Jul 89. (lp/c/cd) *(FREUD/+C/CD 29)* **THE HERETICS ALIVE (live)** ☐ ☐
– This is heresy / Wretched mankind / Sick of love / The nascent virion / Golden age / Erection / Chimere de.si.de.la / Four horsemen / Church of no return.

— **VALOR + SVEN** brought in new members **NICK THE BASTARD** – guitar, keyboards, bass / **MARK BUCHANAN** – soprano sax / **IAN THOMPSON** – drums

Nov 89. (cd-s) *(JUNG 55CD)* **I HATE YOU / WE FALL LIKE LOVE** ☐ ☐

Nov 89. (lp/c/cd) *(FREUD/+C/CD 33)* **ALL THE LOVE ALL THE HATE (PART 1: ALL THE LOVE)** ☐ ☐
– Live love together / We fall in love / Love don't let me down / Suivre la trace de quelqu'un / Love is like a (b)itchin' in my heart / I'm using you (for love) / Deviate love / Angel / Woman to Mother Earth.

Nov 89. (lp/c/cd) *(FREUD/+C/CD 34)* **ALL THE LOVE ALL THE HATE (PART 2: ALL THE HATE)** ☐ ☐
– Born in a womb, died in a tomb / Baptised in fire / I hate you / Children of the valley / Kneel down / Climate of violence: part 1 – The relinquishment, part 2 – The satanic verses (Rushdie's lament), part 3 – A malice of prejudice / The final solution / Nazi killer / Man to father fire.

Jan 91. (pic-lp/cd) *(FREUD/+CD 48)* **INSANUS, ULTIO, PRODITIO, MISERICORDIAQUE** ☐ ☐
– Sevan-us-rex / Malus amor / Tragicus conatus / Infans vexatio / Somnium / Venenum / Mors voluntaria / Vita voluntaria. *(lp-iss.Aug93;)*

Contempo / not iss.

Aug 93. (lp) *(CONTE 138)* **LIVE IN HOLLYWOOD (live)** ☐ ☐

— line-up now with **VALOR** – vocals, violin, guitar / **CULLEN** – violin, cello / **MATRI** – bass / **STREAMER** – percussion, drums / **MARCEL TRUSSEL** – violin, cello

Bulletproof / Nostradamus

Aug 94. (cd) *(CDVEST 26) <1061>* **SEXY DEATH GOD** ☐ ☐
– At the threshold / Kingdom of the tainted kiss / Heresy act two / Damn you / Into dust / Eternal love / Serpent's tail / Kingdom of the solemn kiss / Temples of desire / Deeply deeply / Drilling the hole / Upon the sea of blood / Eyelids down / Invitation au suicide. *(re-iss. May99 on 'Candlelight'; CANDLE 044CD)*

— **VALOR** now with **FLICK** – guitar / **MATRI** – bass, vocals / **STEVE** – drums

Century Media / Century Media

Oct 95. (d-cd) *<(CM 7807)>* **AMEN** ☐ ☐
– Prelude / Prologomenon / Nascent virion / Damn you / Into dust / Sick of love / Drilling the hole / Serpent's tail / Wretched mankind / Kingdom of the tainted kiss / Children of the volley / Eternal love / emples of desire / Untitled / Deeply deeply / Androginous noise hand permeates / Invitation au suicide / Zero sex / Heresy act two / Untitled / Sleepwalk / Ashes.

CHRISTIAN DEATH

— original goths re-formed **WILLIAMS + RIKK + FRANK AGNEW** (guitar) + **GEORGE BELANGER** (drums) + **CASEY** (bass)

Triple X / Triple X

1994. (cd/c) *<(51164-2/-4)>* **ICONOLOGIA** ☐ ☐
– Excommunicamus / Cavity – First communion / Figurative theatre / Cry baby / Dream for mother / Deathwish / Some men – The other / Mysterium iniquitatis / Kill your sons / Stairs (uncertain journey) / Spiritual camp / Ressurection – 6th communion / Sleepwalk / Romeo's distress / Dogs.

— ROZZ committed suicide on the 1st of April '98

– compilations, etc. –

May 88. (lp,pink-lp) *Nostradamus; (NOS 006)* **OFFICIAL ANTHOLOGY OF LIVE BOOTLEGS (live)** ☐ ☐
– Awake at the wall / Sleepwalk / Theatre of pain / Cavity (first communion) / The blue hour / When I was bed / Birth / Coming forth by day / This glass house / The drowning / Cervix couch / Figura five theatre / Untitled – (followed by crowd chaos). *(re-iss. Jul91 lp/cd; NOS/CD 1006)*

Mar 92. (lp/c/cd) *Jungle; (FREUD/+C/CD 39)* **JESUS POINTS THE BONE AT YOU** (singles collection from 1986-90) ☐ ☐
– Believers of the unpure / After the rain / Sick of love / The loving face / Church of no return / Church of no return (endured version) / What's the verdict / This is heresy / Zero sex / The nascent virion (new version) / We fall in love / I hate you.

Nov 92. (d-cd) *Jungle; (FREUDBX 334)* **LOVE AND HATE (ALL THE LOVE, ALL THE HATE parts 1 & 2)** ☐ ☐
(re-iss. Oct99; FREUDCD 64)

Jun 93. (lp/cd; by ROZZ WILLIAMS) *Apollyon; (EFA 11906/+CD)* **PATH OF SORROWS** ☐ ☐
(cd re-iss. Mar94 on 'Cleopatra'; CLEO 39932)

Dec 93. (cd) *Cleopatra; (CLEO 91092)* **TALES OF INNOCENCE: A CONTINUED ANTHOLOGY** ☐ ☐

May 94. (cd) *Cleopatra; (CLEO 81252)* **THE RAGE OF ANGELS** ☐ ☐

Jun 94. (cd) *Cleopatra; (CLEO 62082)* **THE DOLL'S THEATRE (live)** ☐ ☐

Dec 94. (cd) *Apollo; (APOL 001)* **MANDYLION** ☐ ☐

Feb 96. (lp/cd) *Jungle; (FREUD/+CD 053)* **THE PROPHECIES** ☐ ☐

Jul 96. (cd) *Cleopatra; (CLEO 9591CD)* **DEATH IN DETROIT** (remixes) ☐ ☐

Jun 98. (cd) *Trinity; (TRI 006CD)* **PORNOGRAPHIC MESSIAH** ☐ ☐

Oct 99. (cd) *Candlelight; (CANDLE 027CD)* **THE BIBLE** (rarities, etc.) ☐ ☐

Oct 00. (cd) *Candlelight; (CANDLE 045CD)* **BORN AGAIN ANTI-CHRISTIAN** ☐ ☐

ROZZ WILLIAMS

Paragoric / not iss.

Jun 95. (cd; ROZZ WILLIAMS & GITANE DEMONE) *(PA 014CD)* **DREAM HOME HEARTACHE** ☐ ☐
– In every dream home a heartache / These vulnerable eyes / The pope's egg hat / Manic depression / Flowers / World apart / Moon without a tear / Dream home hartache (reprise). *<(re-iss. Sep95 on 'Triple X'; TX 51026CD)> (re-iss. Sep00; PA 014CD)*

Triple X / Triple X

Aug 95. (cd; ROZZ WILLIAMS & DAUCUS KAROTA) *(TX 51172CD)* **SHRINE** ☐ ☐

Aug 95. (cd; ROZZ WILLIAMS & HELTIR) *<(TX 51187CD)>* **NEUE SACH LICH KEIT** ☐ ☐ Feb95
– Neue schlichkeit / Gleichschaltung / Doubtful origins / The enemy / Faith & separation / Frozen roads / Firestorm / Blut und ehre / Flusterwitze / Schane dich / Gotterdammerrung / The great king / Stille nacht / . . .And not look back.

Triple X / Hollow Hill

Nov 95. (cd) *(TX 512002CD) <1>* **THE WHORE'S MOUTH** ☐ ☐ Jun97
– Temptation / Life is but a dream / Raped / Who's in charge here? (beneath the triumph) / A fire of uncommon velocity / Her only sin / Interlude / A brother of low degree / Dear skin / Maggot drain / Dec 30, 1334 / Best of the breed.

– ROZZ posthumous, etc. –

Aug 98. (d-cd; with PREMATURE EJACULATION) *Triple X; <(TX 60004CD)>* **WOUND OF EXIT** ☐ ☐
– Alone with the Devil / Head / At the end of every day / Rope trick / Two thirteen / Wound of exit / Alone with the Devil II / Ruptured walls (7700 volts) / Sick swing / Purged and destroyed / Flesh and blood (you are my) / The end is here – Exit.

May 00. (cd) *Triple X; <(TX 60008CD)>* **LIVE IN BERLIN (live)** ☐ ☐
– Love lies / Sunken rags / Red handed / 2 steps / Nothing / Lord of the flies / World inside / Working on beyond / The stranger / Days of glory.

Sep 00. (cd) *Triple X; <60021>* **PIG** ☐ ☐

CHROME

Formed: San Francisco, California, USA ... 1975 by DAMON EDGE, JOHN LAMBDIN and GARY SPAIN. CHROME interpreted the wigged-out psychedelic heritage of their hometown in bizarre sequences of sci-fi obsessed mechanical noise and their two late 70's albums, 'ALIEN SOUNDTRACKS' and 'HALF MACHINE LIP MOVES' were a significant influence on the industrial and grunge scenes of the 80's and 90's. The wonderfully named HELIOS CREED (having joined their ranks by the release of the former) steered the band towards their experimental techno-goth sound. Signing to British indie, 'Beggars Banquet', the group were reduced to the duo of EDGE and CREED and subsequently moved to a more technology-based style. HELIOS departed in 1983, going on to record a string of suitably nasty grunge albums for the American 'Amphetamine Reptile' label. Meanwhile, DAMON EDGE, along with various collaborators maintained a highly prolific recording schedule under the CHROME moniker, releasing more than 20 albums. • **Songwriters:** EDGE mainly, with others contributing.

Album rating: THE VISITATION (*5) / ALIEN SOUNDTRACKS (*6) / HALF MACHINE LIP MOVES (*7) / RED EXPOSURE (*6) / BLOOD ON THE MOON (*6) / 3RD FROM THE SUN (*6) / RAINING MILK (*5) / INTO THE EYES OF THE ZOMBIE KING (*4) / CHRONICLES (*4) / ANOTHER WORLD (*4) / ALIEN SOUNDTRACKS II (*4) / NO HUMANS ALLOWED compilation (*7) / CHROME BOX boxed set (*7) / Helios Creed: X-RATED FAIRY TALES (*4) / SUPERIOR CATHOLIC FINGER (*5) / THE LAST LAUGH (*5) / BOXING THE CLOWN (*5) / Damon Edge: ALLIANCE (*4) / THE WIND IS TALKING (*4) / GRAND VISIONS (*4) / THE SURREAL ROCK (*3)

DAMON EDGE – vocals, guitar, keyboards, drums, Moog / **JOHN LAMBDIN** – guitar / **GARY SPAIN** – bass, violin

not iss. / Siren

Feb 77. (lp) *<DE 1000>* **THE VISITATION** ☐ ☐
– How many years too soon / Raider / Return to Zanzibar / Caroline / Riding you / Kinky lover / Sun control / My time to live / Memory chords over the body.

— **HELIOS CREED** – guitar, vocals repl. LAMBDIN

Feb 78. (lp) *<DE 2200>* **ALIEN SOUNDTRACKS** ☐ ☐
– Chromosome damage / The monitors / All data lost / S.S. Lygni / Nova feedback / Pygmies in Zee Park / Slip it to the android / Pharoah chromium / St. 31 / Re pt.II.

Beggars Banquet / Siren

Mar 80. (lp) *(BEGA 15)* **RED EXPOSURE** ☐ ☐ 1979
– New age / Rm 10 / Eyes on Mars / Jonestown / Animal / Static gravity / Eyes in the center / Electric chair / Night of the Earth / Isolation.

Apr 80. (7") *(BEG 36)* **NEW AGE. / INFORMATION** ☐ ☐ 1979

— now down to duo **DAMON EDGE + HELIOS CREED**

Aug 80. (lp) *(BEGA 18) <DE 333>* **HALF MACHINE LIP MOVES** ☐ ☐ 1979
– TV as eyes / Zombie warfare (can't let you down) / March of the Chrome police (a cold clamey bombing) / You've been duplicated / Mondo anthem / Half machine lip moves / Abstract nympho / Turned around / Zero time / Creature eternal / Critical mass. *<cd-iss. 1990's on 'Dossier'; 2607496)*

Red-Siren / Siren

May 80. (12"ep) *(RS 12007)* **READ ONLY MEMORY** ☐ ☐ 1979
– You can't see them – They can't touch you / Inacontract / Read only memory / In front of the crowd / I am the jaw.

— added **JOHN STENCH** – drums + **HILARY STENCH** – bass

Don't Fall / Don't Fall

Jan 81. (12"ep) *(Y 3)* **INWORLDS. / DANGER ZONE / IN A DREAM** ☐ ☐

Jun 81. (lp) *(X 6)* **BLOOD ON THE MOON** ☐ ☐
– The need / Inner vacuum / Perfumed metal / Planet strike / The strangers / Insect human / Out of reach / Brain on scan / Blood on the Moon. *(re-iss. Apr87 on 'Dossier'; DOSSIER 001)*

— added guest **FABIENNE SHINE** – vocals

Apr 82. (7") *(Z 17)* **FIREBOMB. / SHADOW OF A THOUSAND YEARS** ☐ ☐

Apr 82. (lp) *(X 18)* **3RD FROM THE SUN**
– Firebomb / Future ghosts / Armageddon / Heartbeat / Off the line / 3rd from the Sun / Shadows of a thousand years.

not iss. Expanded

1983. (lp) *<EX 40>* **NO HUMANS ALLOWED** [-]
– Danger zone / The manifestation (of the idea) / In a dream / Information / Read only memory.

— added guest **BETSY HILL** – vocals

Mosquito not iss.

1983. (lp) *(MOS 001)* **RAINING MILK** [-] [-] France
– Wings born in the night / Tribes (ultra) / Gehenna to Canaan / La legende des sentences du futur / Beacons to the eye / Raining milk / Anorexic sacrifice / Gehenna lion.

— HELIOS CREED went on to sign for 'Subterranean', releasing two albums, 'X-RATED FAIRY TALES' and 'SUPERIOR CATHOLIC FINGER' in 1985 and 1986 respectively. 'Amphetamine Reptile' also issued three sets, 'THE LAST LAUGH' (1989), 'BOXING THE CLOWN' (1990) and 'KISS TO THE BRAIN' (1992). Later albums included 'NUGG THE TRANSPORT' and 'CHROMAGNUM MAN' for 'Dossier' and 'ACTIVATED CONDITION' for 'Man's Ruin' (1998).

DAMON EDGE / CHROME

— with **FABIENNE SHINE** – vocals / **REMY DeVILLA** – guitar / **RENAUD THOREZ** – bass / **PATRICK IMBERT** – drums

1984. (lp) *(MOS 003) <260 5318>* **INTO THE EYES OF THE ZOMBIE KING** [-] France
– And then the red sun / You can't do anything / Walking and looking for you / Into the eyes of the Zombie King / Trip the switch / It wasn't real / Humans in the rain / Don't move like that. *(UK-iss.Apr87 on 'Dossier'; ST 7513) <US-iss.Aug88 on 'Dossier'; DCD 9004>*

DAMON EDGE

New Rose not iss.

Mar 85. (7") *(NEW 51)* **I'M A GENTLEMAN. /** [-]
Mar 85. (lp) *(ROSE 51)* **ALLIANCE** [-] France
Jun 85. (lp) *(ROSE 64)* **THE WIND IS TALKING** [-] France
Jun 86. (lp) *(ROSE 90)* **GRAND VISIONS** [-] France

Dossier not iss.

1987. (lp) **THE SURREAL ROCK** [-]

CHROME

DAMON EDGE + FABIENNE etc.

Dossier Dossier

Apr 86. (lp) *(ST 7503)* **ANOTHER WORLD**
– If you come around / I found out today / Our good dreams / Stranger from another world / Moon glow / The sky said / Loving lovely lover.
Feb 87. (lp) *(ST 7527)* **DREAMING IN SEQUENCE**
– Everyone's the same / Seeing everything / Touching you / Windows in the wind / The Venusian dance / White magic / Love to my rock (cause of me) / She is here.
Apr 87. (lp) *(ST 3004)* **THE LYON CONCERT (live)** [-]
– We are connected / Sanity / As we stand here in time / March of the rubber people / Ghosts of the long forgotten future / Version 2 (Raining milk) / The service improves / Frankenstein's party.
Oct 87. (lp) *(DOSSIER 002)* **THE CHRONICLES**
– The chronicles of the sacrifice / The chronicles of the tribes / The chronicles of the open door / The chronicles of born in the night.
Jul 88. (lp) *(ST 003)* **THE CHRONICLES II**
– The chronicles of the beacons / The chronicles of Gehenna / The chronicles of Canaan. *(cd-iss. Jun89 'CHRONICLES I & II'; 260 7499)*
Feb 89. (lp) *(EFA 5853)* **ALIEN SOUNDTRACKS II** [-]
Sep 89. (lp) *(EFA 5859)* **LIVE IN GERMANY (live)**
Sep 90. (cd/lp) **LIQUID FOREST**
Feb 91. (cd/lp) **MISSION OF THE ENTRANCED**
Jul 94. (cd) *(EFA 06456-2)* **THE CLAIRAUDIENT SYNDROME**
Feb 95. (cd) *(EFA 08461-2)* **CHROME SAMPLER VOL.1 (HAVING A WONDERFUL TIME WITH THE TRIPODS)** [-]
Mar 95. (cd) *(EFA 08462-2)* **HAVING A WONDERFUL TIME IN THE JUICE BOX** [-]

Consolidated unknown

May 95. (cd-s) *(CSD 22003)* **BUMPER /** [-]
Sep 95. (12") *(CSD 22006)* **I WANT YOU. /** [-]

Man's Ruin Man's Ruin

Sep 96. (10") *<(MR 035)>* **CHROME EP**
Feb 98. (cd) *<(MR 061CD)>* **TIDAL FORCES**

– compilations, others, etc. –

Jun 89. (cd) *Dossier; (260 7490CD)* **BLOOD ON THE MOON / ETERNITY**
Jun 89. (cd) *Dossier; (260 7709CD)* **THE LYON CONCERT / ANOTHER WORLD**
Aug 95. (cd) *Cleopatra; (CLEO 9533-2)* **3RD FROM THE SUN / INTO THE EYES OF THE ZOMBIE KING** [-]
Jan 98. (c-cd-box) *Cleopatra; <(CLP 97702)>* **CHROME BOX 1978-1983**
Jan 98. (cd) *Cleopatra; (CLP 0080-2)* **RETRO TRANSMISSION** [-]
Feb 99. (cd) *Cleopatra; <472>* **CHROME FLASHBACK: THE BEST OF CHROME LIVE** [-]
Sep 00. (d-cd) *Cleopatra; <919>* **CHROME AND FRIENDS** [-]

CHROME MOLLY

Formed: Leicester, England . . . 1984 by STEVE HAWKINS and JOHN ANTCLIFFE, who added NIC WASTELL and CHRIS GREEN. In the mid 80's, they released a couple of unremarkable Americanised metal albums for 'Powerstation', before surprisingly signing to the normally astute 'I.R.S.' label. In the Spring of '88, they covered an old SQUEEZE hit, 'TAKE ME I'M YOURS', a dubious but rare highlight on the resulting 'ANGST' album. A few personnel changes had occured prior to this, MARK GODFREY replacing GREEN, TIM READ replacing ANTCLIFFE. In 1989, they added former BABY TUCKOO guitarist, ANDY BARROTT, although a further set in 1990 on 'Music For Nations', 'SLAPHEAD', predictably sinking without trace (a case of hair today, gone tomorrow!).

Album rating: YOU CAN'T HAVE IT ALL . . . (*6) / STICK IT OUT (*4) / ANGST (*5) / SLAPHEAD (*4)

STEVE HAWKINS – vocals / **JOHN ANTCLIFFE** – guitar / **NIC WASTELL** – bass / **CHRIS GREEN** – drums

Bullet not iss.

May 84. (12") *(BOLT 10)* **WHEN THE LIGHTS. /** [-]

Powerstation not iss.

Aug 85. (12"m) *(OHM 11T)* **TAKE IT OR LEAVE IT. / LONELY / DON'T LET GO** [-]
1985. (lp) *(AMP 6)* **YOU CAN'T HAVE IT ALL . . . OR CAN YOU?** [-]
– Thanks for the angst / Cut loose / Too far gone / Set me free / Living a lie / Don't fight dirty / Lose again / Take it or leave it / One at a time / Come back.
Mar 86. (7") *(OHM 12)* **I WANT TO FIND OUT. /** [-]
(cd-s+=) *(OHM 12T)* –

— **MARK GODFREY** – drums; repl. GREEN

May 87. (lp/c) *(AMP 12/+C)* **STICK IT OUT** [-]
– CMA / Breakdown / Something special / That's the way it is / Steel against the sky / Bob Geldof (every egg a bod) / Stand proud / Before you go / Look out for No.1. *(c+=)* – Let go.

— **TIM READ** – vocals; repl. ANTCLIFFE

I.R.S. I.R.S.

Apr 88. (7"/7"pic-d) *(IRM/+P 152)* **TAKE ME I'M YOURS. / DON'T FIGHT DIRTY**
(12"+=) *(IRMT 152)* – Lose again.
Apr 88. (lp/c/cd) *(MIRF/MIRFC/DMIRF 1033) <42199>* **ANGST**
– Thanx for the angst / Take me I'm yours / Don't let go / Come back / I want to find out / Take it or leave it / Living a lie / Cut loose / Too far gone / Set me free.
May 88. (7") *(IRM 158)* **THANX FOR THE ANGST. / LIVING A LIE** [-]
(12"+=) *(IRMT 158)* – One at a time.
Nov 88. (7") *(IRM 176)* **SHOOTING ME DOWN. /** [-]
(12"+=) *(12IRM 176)* –

— added **ANDY BARROTT** – guitar (ex-BABY TUCKOO)

Music For Nations not iss.

May 90. (cd/c/lp) *(CD/T+/MFN 98)* **SLAPHEAD** [-]
– Out of our minds / Gimme that line again / Red hot red rock / Shotgun / Loosen up / Caught with the bottle again / Suffer the children / Assinine nation / Pray with me / Now / A little voodoo magic. *(cd+=/c+=)* – Barking up the wrong tree / She ain't got rhythm.

— disbanded around 1991

CHRON GEN

Formed: Hitchin, Herts, England . . . early 1978 out of the CONDEMNED by schoolmates, GLYNN BARBER and JOHN JOHNSON, the pair drafting in ADAM, who was in turn replaced by PETE DIMMOCK while adding JON THURLOW in the process. CHRON GEN (actually short for CHRONIC GENERATION) really got off the ground in 1981 with an EP, 'PUPPETS OF WAR', followed a few months later by a solitary 45 for 'Step Forward' (then home of CHELSEA, CORTINAS and The FALL!), 'REALITY'. Translating the early spirit of '77 into the yobbish charge of "oi", the band won column inches in the pages of Sounds and toured with the likes of The EXPLOITED. Also in common with the latter band, CHRON GEN signed to the 'Secret' label for a cover of The New York Dolls' 'JET BOY, JET GIRL'. In March '82, they had their one and only chart entry with debut album, 'CHRONIC GENERATION' (containing a savaging of Smokie's 'LIVING NEXT DOOR TO ALICE'), although this would be the last recording to feature THURLOW as guitarist, FLOYD filled his shoes. With DIMMOCK bailing out to join CHELSEA, the band virtually fell apart, only to resurface once more for a low-key comeback set, 'NOWHERE TO RUN', in '85.

Album rating: CHRONIC GENERATION (*5) / NOWHERE TO RUN (*3) / THE BEST OF CHRON GEN compilation (*5)

GLYNN BARBER – vocals, guitar / **JON THURLOW** – rhythm guitar / **PETE DIMMOCK** – bass / **JOHN JOHNSON** – drums

Gargoyle not iss.

Jun 81. (7"ep) *(GRGL 780)* **PUPPETS OF WAR EP** [-]
– Puppets of war / Lies / Mindless few / Chronic generation. *(re-iss. Sep81 by 'Fresh'; FRESH 36)*

Step Forward not iss.

Sep 81. (7") *(SF 19)* **REALITY. / SUBWAY SADIST** [-]

Secret not iss.

Feb 82. (7"m) *(SHH 129)* **JET BOY, JET GIRL. / ABORTIONS / SUBWAY SADIST** [-]
Mar 82. (lp) *(SEC 3)* **CHRONIC GENERATION** [53] [-]

– Lies / Jet boy, jet girl / Hounds of the night / L.S.D. / You make me spew / Chronic generation / Mindless / You'll never change me / Rocka'Bill / Friends tell me lies / Reality / Living next door to Alice. *(with free live-7")* – LIVING NEXT DOOR TO ALICE. / RIPPER / PUPPETS OF WAR *(re-iss. Jul86 as 'CHRON GEN' on 'Razor'; RAZS 20) (re-iss. Feb97 on 'Get Back'; GET 9)*

— **FLOYD** – guitar; repl. THURLOW

Oct 82. (7"m) *(SHH 139)* **OUTLAW. / BEHIND CLOSED DOORS / DISCO** [ ] [-]

— DIMMOCK joined CHELSEA before moving to BANDITS AT 4 O'CLOCK

Picasso / not iss.

Sep 85. (lp) *(PIK 002)* **NOWHERE TO RUN** [ ] [-]

— split for the final time in the mid 80's

– compilations, etc. –

1982. (c) *Chaos; (004)* **APOCALYPSE LIVE TOUR '81 (live)** *(lp-is.Apr84; APOCA 1)* [ ] [-]

Nov 94. (cd) *Captain Oi; (AHOY 18)* **THE BEST OF CHRON GEN** [ ] [-]

Oct 95. (cd) *Punx; (PUNXCD 3)* **LIVE AT THE WALDORF IN SAN FRANCISCO (live)** [ ] [-]

CIANIDE

Formed: Chicago, Illinois, USA ... 1990 by MIKE PERUN, SCOTT CARROLL and JEFF KABELLA. Two demos, 'FUNERAL' and 'SECOND LIFE', secured the band a release for their debut album proper, 'THE DYING TRUTH' (1992). Drawing on a variety of extreme metal styles, CIANIDE issued a further set, 'A DESCENT INTO HELL' in 1994 for 'Bulletproof' in the UK.

Album rating: THE DYING TRUTH (*5) / A DESCENT INTO HELL (*5)

MIKE PERUN – vocals, bass / **SCOTT CARROLL** – guitar / **JEFF KABELLA** – drums

Grind Core / Grind Core

Jul 92. (cd) *<(GCI 89806)>* **THE DYING TRUTH** [ ] [ ]
– Mindscape / Human cesspool / The suffering / Scourging at the pillow / Crawling chaos / The dying truth / Funeral / Second life.

Bulletproof / Red Lightnin'

Aug 94. (cd) *(CDVEST 17) <88367>* **A DESCENT INTO HELL** [ ] [ ]
– Gates of slumber / Eulogy / The undead march / The Luciferian twilight / Beyond the fallen horizon / Darkness / Death dealer / Mountain in thunder.

— split soon after above

CINDERELLA

Formed: Philadelphia, Pennsylvania, USA . . . 1983 by TOM KEIFER, JEFF LaBAR and ERIC BRITTINGHAM. On the recommendation of one JON BON JOVI, the band were signed worldwide to 'Phonogram' records in 1985 and soon added FRED COURY. Surprisingly, their 1986 debut album, 'NIGHT SONGS', reached No.3 in the US album charts at the height of the mid-80's glam-metal scene. KEIFER's whiskey throated shrill took a bit of getting used to (while the original Cinderella of old lost her shoe and was late for the ball, this lot, well KEIFER at least, sounded as if they'd lost their balls to a particularly pointed shoe) but the songs were competent enough, raunchy blues rock heavily influenced by AC/DC and AEROSMITH but coming over like a cross between NAZARETH and LED ZEPPELIN. 'LONG COLD WINTER' (1988) was an accomplished follow-up; more blues, less rock with a number of engaging acoustic-based tracks. 'HEARTBREAK STATION' (1990) upped the R&B ante, drawing inevitable ROLLING STONES comparisons. It was listenable stuff but obviously The 'STONES did it better. After a four year hiatus, CINDERELLA returned with 'STILL CLIMBING' (1994). While it was a more original effort, much had changed in the band's absence and their vaguely glam posturing seemed out of time. • **Songwriters:** All KIEFER compositions, except MOVE OVER (Janis Joplin) / JUMPIN' JACK FLASH (Rolling Stones).

Album rating: NIGHT SONGS (*5) / LONG COLD WINTER (*6) / HEARTBREAK STATION (*5) / STILL CLIMBING (*4) / LOOKING BACK compilation (*7) / BAD ATTITUDE 1986-1994 compilation (*7)

TOM KEIFER (b.26 Jan'??) – vocals, guitar, piano / **JEFF LaBAR** (b.18 Mar'??) – guitar / **ERIC BRITTINGHAM** (b. 8 May'60) – bass / **JODY CORTEZ**– drums repl. TONY DESTRA

Vertigo / Mercury

Aug 86. (lp/c) *(VERH/+C 37) <830076>* **NIGHT SONGS** [ ] [3] Jul86
– Night songs / Shake me / Nobody's fool / Nothin' for nothin' / Once around the ride / Hell on wheels / Somebody save me / In from the outside / Push, push / Back home again. *(cd-iss. Jan87; 830076-2)*

Oct 86. (7") *<884851>* **NOBODY'S FOOL. / PUSH, PUSH** [-] [13]

Feb 87. (7") *(VER 29)* **SHAKE ME. / NIGHT SONGS** [ ] [-]
(12"+=) *(VERX 29)* – Hell on wheels.

Apr 87. (7") *<888483>* **SOMEBODY SAVE ME. / HELL ON WHEELS** [-] [66]

May 87. (7") *(VER 32)* **NOBODY'S FOOL. / SHAKE ME (live)** [ ] [-]
(12"+=) *(VERX 32)* – The galaxy blues.

— **FRED COURY** (b.20 Oct'65) – drums; repl. JODY

Jul 88. (lp/c)(cd) *(VERH/+C 59) <(834612-2)>* **LONG COLD WINTER** [30] [10]
– Bad seamstress blues – Fallin' apart at the seams / Gypsy road / Don't know what you got (till it's gone) / The last mile / Second wind / Long cold winter / If you don't like it / Coming home / Fire and ice / Take me back.

Jul 88. (7") *(VER 40)* **GYPSY ROAD. / SECOND WIND** [54] [-]
(12"+=/12"white+=) *(VERX/+G 40)* – Somebody save me.
(cd-s+=) *(VERCD 40)* – Nobody's fool / Shake me.

Jan 89. (7"/7"pic-d) *(VER/+P 43) <870644>* **DON'T KNOW WHAT YOU GOT (TILL IT'S GONE). / FIRE AND ICE** [54] [12] Aug88
(12"+=/12"g-f+=) *(VERX/+G 43)* – Push, push (live) / Once around the ride.

Jan 89. (7") *<872148>* **THE LAST MILE. / LONG COLD WINTER** [-] [36]
(cd-s+=) *(VERCD 43)* – Push, push (live) / Long cold winter.

Mar 89. (7") *<872982>* **COMING HOME. / TAKE ME BACK** [-] [20]

Jul 89. (7") *<874578>* **GYPSY ROAD. / JUMPIN' JACK FLASH (live)** [-] [51]

Nov 90. (7"/c-s) *(VER/+MC 51)* **SHELTER ME. / LOVE GONE BAD** [55] [-]
(12"+=/cd-s+=) *(VER X/CD 51)* – Electric love.
(12"colrd+=) *(VERXG 51)* – Rock me baby / Bring it on love / Second wind (live).

Nov 90. (c-s) *<878700>* **SHELTER ME / ELECTRIC LOVE** [-] [36]

Nov 90. (cd/c/lp) *<(848018-2/-4/-1)>* **HEARTBREAK STATION** [36] [19]
– The more things change / Love's got me doin' time / Shelter me / Sick for the cure / Heartbreak station / One for rock and roll / Dead man's road / Make your own way / Electric love / Love gone bad / Winds of change.

Mar 91. (c-s) *<878796>* **HEARTBREAK STATION. / LOVE GONE BAD** [-] [44]

Apr 91. (7") *(VER 53)* **HEARTBREAK STATION. / SICK FOR THE CURE** [63] [-]
(12"+=) *(VERX 53)* – Falling apart at the seams.
(10"sha-pic-d+=) *(VERSP 53)* – Move over.
(pic-cd-s+=) *(VERCD 53)* – Gypsy road / Shake me / Somebody save me.

— (1992) **KEVIN VALENTINE** – drums (ex-SHADOW KING) repl. COURY who helped form ARCADE with STEPHEN PEARCY (ex-RATT)

Vertigo / Vertigo

Nov 94. (cd/c) *<(522947-2/-4)>* **STILL CLIMBING** [ ] [ ]
– Bad attitude shuffle / All comes down / Talk is cheap / Hard to find the words / Blood from a stone / Still climbing / Freewheelin' / Through the rain / Easy come easy go / The road's still long / Hot and bothered.

— folded after above

– compilations, etc. –

May 97. (cd) *Polygram; <534775>* **LOOKING BACK** [-] [ ]
– Shake me / Nodody's fool / Somebody save me / Gypsy road / Don't know what you got (till it's gone) / The last mile / Coming home / Shelter me / Heartbreak station / The more things change / Love's got me doin' time / Hot and bothered / Through the rain / War stories / Move over.

Mar 98. (cd) *Connoisseur; (VSOPCD 251)* **BAD ATTITUDE 1986-1994** [ ] [-]
– Shake me / Night songs / Nobody's fool / Somebody save me / Push, push / Nothin' for nothin' / Don't know what you got (till it's gone) / Gypsy road / Bad seamstress blues – Falling apart at the seams / Long cold winter / If you don't like it / Love's got me doin' time / Shelter me / The more things change / Heartbreak station / Hard to find the words / Bad attitude shuffle.

Jul 99. (cd) *Cleopatra; <(CLEO 593-2)>* **LIVE GREATEST HITS** [ ] [ ]

Jul 99. (cd) *Axe Killer; (AXE 3051041CD)* **LIVE AT THE KEY CLUB** [ ] [-]
<(re-iss. Aug99 on 'Cleopatra'; CLP 5932)>

Aug 00. (cd) *Universal; <(AA 314-542850-2)>* **THE MILLENNIUM COLLECTION** [ ] [ ]

CIRCLE JERKS

Formed: Los Angeles, California, USA . . . 1980 by former BLACK FLAG frontman, KEITH MORRIS along with ex-REDD KROSS guitarist, GREG HUTSON, who recruited ROGER ROGERSON and LUCKY LEHRER. Holed up in their Hawthorne, California garage, they set the tone for the rest of their career by recording their debut album, 'GROUP SEX' (1981), a frenetic burst of primal hardcore and adolescent humour. After appearing in that year's docu-film 'Decline Of Western Civilization', the guys were brought to the attention of POLICE manager, Miles Copeland, his 'Faulty' label (licensed to 'Step Forward' in the UK) issuing the follow-up 'WILD IN THE STREETS' (1982). By this point, ex-DOA drummer, CHUCK BISCUITS replaced LEHRER; he was in turn replaced by JOHN INGRAM prior to the mini compilation album, 'GOLDEN SHOWER OF HITS', featuring the title track medley of crooning standards by PAUL ANKA, BACHARACH & DAVID, etc. Other notable tracks included 'COUP D'ETAT' and 'WHEN THE SHIT HITS THE FAN', both surprise inclusions on the soundtrack to cult 1984 movie, 'Repo Man'. Like many of their hardcore/punk peers, The CIRCLE JERKS changed direction into heavy TWISTED SISTER/DICTATORS-like metal as the thrash and speed scene began to gather momentum in the mid to late 80's. With ZANDER SCHLOSS and KEITH CLARK now coming in as the new rhythm section, the 'JERKS made two further albums, 'WONDERFUL' (1985) and 'VI' (1987) for metal labels 'Combat' and 'Roadrunner' respectively. While they continued to tour the States, they virtually abandoned studio work, that is, until 1995's major label debut, 'ODDITIES, ABNORMALITIES AND CURIOSITIES', infamous for its cover of the Soft Boys' 'I WANNA DESTROY YOU' featuring pop starlet DEBBIE GIBSON on lead vocals.

Album rating: GROUP SEX (*6) / WILD IN THE STREETS (*7) / GOLDEN SHOWER OF HITS compilation (*8) / WONDERFUL (*3) / VI (*6) / GIG (*5) / ODDITIES, ABNORMALITIES AND CURIOSITIES (*4)

KEITH MORRIS – vocals (ex-BLACK FLAG) / **GREG HUTSON** – guitar (ex-RED CROSS) / **ROGER ROGERSON** (b. DOWDING) – bass / **LUCKY LEHRER** – drums

not iss. / Frontier

Feb 81. (lp) *<FLP 1002>* **GROUP SEX** [ ] [ ]
– Deny everything / I just want some skank / Beverly Hills / Operation / Back against the wall / Wasted / Behind the door / World up my ass / Paid vacation / Don't care / Live fast die young / What's your problem / Group sex / Red tape. *(UK-iss.Aug88 on 'Weird Systems' lp/cd; WS 031/+YZ) <(re-iss. May92 cd/c/lp; 4600-2L/4L/1L)> <(cd re-iss. Aug92 & Apr97 +=; FCD 1002)>* – WILD IN THE STREETS *<(re-iss. Jun97 cd/c/lp; 0101-2/-4/-1)>*

— **CHUCK BISCUITS** – drums (ex-DOA) repl. LEHRER

Step Forward / Faulty

Jul 82. (lp) *(SFLP 8)* <COPE 3> **WILD IN THE STREETS**
– Wild in the streets / Leave me alone / Stars and stripes / 86' D (good as gone) / Meet the press / Trapped / Murder the disturbed / Letter bomb / Question authority / Defamation innuendo / Moral majority / Forced labor / Political Stu / Just like me / Put a little love in your heart. <*(re-iss. May92 on 'Frontier' cd/c/lp; 4617-2L/4L/1L)*> <*(re-iss. Jun97 on 'Frontier' cd/c/lp; 0105-2/-4/-1)*>

— **JOHN INGRAM** – drums repl. BISCUITS who later joined DANZIG

not iss. / Alleigence

1983. (lp) <72874> **GOLDEN SHOWER OF HITS** [-]
– In your eyes / Parade of the horribles / Under the gun / When the shit hits the fan / Bad words / Red blanket room / High price on our heads / Coup d'etat / Product of my environment / Rats of reality / Junk mail / Golden shower of hits.

— **ZANDER 'Snake' SCHLOSS** – bass repl. ROGERSON

— **KEITH 'Adolph' CLARK** – drums repl. INGRAM

Rough Justice / Combat

Dec 85. (lp) *(JUST 1)* <8048> **WONDERFUL**
– Wonderful / Firebaugh / Making the bombs / Mrs. Jones / Dude / American heavy metal weekend / I & I / Crowd / Killing for Jesus / Karma stew / 15 minutes / Rook house / Another broken heart for Snake. <*(cd-iss. Nov99 on 'Century Media'; 66061-2)*>

Roadrunner / Combat

Nov 87. (lp) *(RR 9584)* **VI**
– Beat me senseless / Patty's killing me / Casualty vampire / Tell me why / Protection / I'm alive / Status clinger / Living / American way / Fortunate son / Love kills / All wound up / I don't. *(cd-iss. Mar90 on 'Roadracer'; RO 9584-2)* <*(re-iss. cd Nov99 on 'Century Media'; 66062-2)*>

— now without ZANDER who joined The WEIRDOS and JOE STRUMMER (ex-Clash). The CIRCLE JERKS subsequently split until 1995

not iss. / Mercury

Jun 95. (cd/c/lp) <526948> **ODDITIES, ABNORMALITIES AND CURIOSITIES** [-]
– Teenage electric / Anxious boy / 22 / Shining through the door / I wanna destroy you / Sinking SHP / Brick / Fable / Dog / Grey life / Exhaust breath / Career day.

– compilations, etc. –

1992. (cd/c) *Combat;* <*88561 1069-2/-4*> **GIG (live)** [-]
– Beat me senseless / High price on our heads / Letter bomb / In your eyes / Making the bombs / All wound up / Coup d'etat / Mrs. Jones / Back against the wall / Casualty vampire / I don't / Making time / Junk mail / I, I and I / World up my ass / I just want some skank / The crowd / When the shit hits the fan / Deny everything / Wonderful / Wild in the streets.

CIRCUS OF POWER

Formed: New York, USA . . . 1987 by Canadian ALEX MITCHELL and RICKY BECK-MAHLER, who enlisted the help of GARY SUNSHINE and RYAN MAHER. With their hard-bitten NY environment reflected in their music, this powerful blues/punk-metal outfit unleashed their eponymous 'R.C.A.' debut in 1988. Drawing comparisons to The CULT or The SEX PISTOLS, the album ranked among the cream of that year's metal releases and spent time in the US Top 200. The blistering combination of MITCHELL's Ian Astbury-esque growl and MAHLER's dirty guitar bludgeon was witnessed to best effect on tracks like the opening 'CALL OF THE WILD' and the evocative 'IN THE WIND'. A stopgap live mini-album followed a year later, the record capturing the raw excitement of their stage set and featuring a raucous run-through of MC5's 'KICK OUT THE JAMS'. Although big things were expected of the band's impressive follow-up, 'VICES' (1990), the record sales weren't enough to prevent RCA pulling the plug. However, the CIRCUS OF POWER's undeniable talent was vindicated when 'Columbia' signed them for a third and final album, 'MAGIC & MADNESS' (1993).

Album rating: CIRCUS OF POWER (*7) / STILL ALIVE (*4) / VICES (*5) / MAGIC & MADNESS (*5)

ALEX MITCHELL (b. Toronto, Canada) – vocals / **RICKY BECK-MAHLER** – guitar / **GARY SUNSHINE** – bass / **RYAN MAHER** – drums

R.C.A. / R.C.A.

Dec 88. (lp/c/cd) *(PL/PK/PD 88464)* <8464> **CIRCUS OF POWER** Nov88
– Call of the wild / Motor / Heart attack / In the wind / Machine / White trash mama / Needles / Crazy / Letters home / Backseat mama. *(cd+=/c+=)* – Turn up the jams.

Jul 89. (m-lp/m-c/m-cd) *(PL/PK/PD 90377)* <72417> **STILL ALIVE (live)**
– Still alive and well / Motor / Letters home / White trash queen / Heart attack / Kick out the jams.

Apr 90. (cd/c/lp) *(PD/PK/PL 90461)* <*2022-2/-4/-1*> **VICES**
– Gates of love / Two river highway / Don't drag me down / Dr. Potion / Got hard / Junkie girl / Desire / Fire in the night / Vices / Last call Rosie / Los Angeles / Temptation / Simple man – simple woman.

Columbia / Columbia

Jul 93. (cd/c) *(472170-2/-4)* <48871> **MAGIC & MADNESS**
– Swamp devil / Evil woman / Heaven and Hell / Circles / Poison girl / Shine / Dreams tonight / Mama tequila / Black roses / Waitin' for the wizard / Outta my head / Slip away.

— folded soon after above

CIRITH UNGOL

Formed: Ventura, California, USA . . . 1980 by ex-TITANIC duo, JERRY FOGLE and ROBERT GARVEN, who checked in former roadie TIM BAKER and GREG LINDSTROM, the latter being subsequently substituted by MICHAEL FLINT. Inspired by J.R.R. Tolkien's 'Lord Of The Rings', the group self-financed their hopelessly pretentious debut, 'FROST AND FIRE', an album that ranks as possibly the most derided in the history of heavy-metal. Taking a few years to recover from the critical backlash, they returned in 1984 with their first 'Roadrunner' set, 'KING OF THE DEAD'. Slightly improved, it was nevertheless another instalment of tedious fantasy naval gazing. A final album, 'ONE FOOT IN HELL' (1985), should've been retitled, 'Two Ears In Hell'. In 1991, the group were resurrected via a one-off return set, 'PARADISE LOST'.

Album rating: FROST AND FIRE (*4) / KING OF THE DEAD (*4) / ONE FOOT IN HELL (*5) / PARADISE LOST (*6)

TIM BAKER – vocals / **JERRY FOGLE** – guitar / **GREG LINDSTROM** – guitar, bass (appeared on lp, but repl. by) **MICHAEL FLINT** – bass / **ROBERT GARVEN** – drums

not iss. / Liquid Flames

1981. (lp) <*LF 001*> **FROST AND FIRE** [-]
– Frost and fire / I'm alive / A little fire / What does it take / Edge of a knife / Better off dead / Maybe that's why. *(cd-iss. Nov99 on 'Metal Blade'+=; 14252-2)* – Cirith Ungol.

Roadrunner / Metal Blade

Aug 84. (lp) *(RR 9832)* **KING OF THE DEAD**
– Atom shasher / Black machine / Master of the pit / King of the dead / Death of the sun / Finger of scorn / Toccata in D-minor / Cirith Ungol. *(cd-iss. Nov99 on 'Metal Blade'+=; 14253-2)* – Last laugh.

Aug 86. (lp) *(RR 9681)* **ONE FOOT IN HELL**
– Blood & iron / Chaos descends / The fire / Nadsokor / 100 m.p.h. / War eternal / Doomed planet / One foot in Hell. *(cd-iss. Apr99 on 'Metal Blade'; 14203-2)*

— split in 1986 and 1991

not iss. / Enigma

Aug 91. (cd/c) <72518> **PARADISE LOST** [-]
– Join the legion / The troll / Fire / Heaven help us / Before the lash / Go it alone / Chaos rising / Fallen idols / Paradise lost.

CITIZEN FISH (see under ⇒ SUBHUMANS)

CIV

Formed: New York, USA . . . 1993 out of GORILLA BISCUITS – a band of several years who released two albums in the late 80's – by frontman, ANTHONY CIVARELLI (proprietor of a tattoo parlour in Long Island), ARTHUR and SAMMY. Recruiting former OUTFACE member, CHARLIE, CIV (pronounced 'Sieve') began making a name for themselves around the city prior to the release of their debut album, 'SET YOUR GOALS' (1995). Produced by CIVARELLI's former QUICKSAND mucker, WALTER SCHREIFELS (who would also contribute songs), the record showcased the band's hardcore rockabilly behind the frontman's straight-talking streetwise lyrics. The band were also infamous for wearing garish lamé suits on stage, the sharp image doing them no harm in securing a record deal with Atlantic subsidiary, 'Lava'. An enhanced version of their first set added a handful of previously unreleased tracks, the major label backing making sure both the album and re-issued single, CAN'T WAIT ONE MORE MINUTE', reached a wider audience. However, it would be three years before a bonafide follow-up, 'THIRTEEN DAY GETAWAY' (1998), featuring an unlikely cover of the Small Faces' 'ITCHYCOO PARK'.

Album rating: Gorilla Biscuits: GORILLA BISCUITS (*6) / START TODAY (*7) / CIV: SET YOUR GOALS (*7) / THIRTEEN DAY GETAWAY (*6)

GORILLA BISCUITS

CIV (b. ANTHONY CIVARELLI) – vocals / **WALLY** – guitar / **ARTHUR** – bass / **LUTHER CAMPBELL** – drums

We Bite / Revelation

1988. (lp/c/cd) <*REV 4 1/4/2*> **GORILLA BISCUITS** [-]
– High hopes / Big mouth / No reason why / Gm2 / Hold your ground / Breaking free / Finish what you started / Sitting aroiund at home / Gorilla biscuits / Short end of the stick / Hold your ground 1 / Gm2 1.

— added **ALEX** – guitar

Nov 89. (lp/c/cd) *(086-103)* <*REV 12 1/4/2*> **START TODAY**
– New direction / Stand still / Degradation / Good intentions / Forgotten / The things we say / Start today / Two sides / First failure / Competition / Time flies / Cats and dogs. *(lp re-iss. Jan96; same as US)*

— ARTHUR subsequently joined TOKEN ENTRY before reunited with CIV

CIV

— **CIV** – vocals / **CHARLIE** – guitar (ex-OUTFACE) / **ARTHUR** – bass / **SAMMY** – drums (ex-YOUTH OF TODAY, ex-SHELTER)

Revelation / not iss.

Apr 95. (lp) *(REV 041LP)* **SET YOUR GOALS** [-]
– Set your goals / Do something / Social climber / Don't gotta prove it / Soundtrack for violence / Et tu brute? / Gang opinion / So far, so good . . . so what? / Trust slips through your hands.

May 95. (7") *(REV 41)* **ALL TWISTED. / PUNK HAIRCUTS** [-] (cd-s+=) *(REV 41-2)* – Can't wait one more minute.

		Lava – Atlantic	Lava – Atlantic
Oct 95.	(cd/c) *<(7567 92603-2/-4)>* **SET YOUR GOALS**	[ ]	[ ]

– Set your goals / So far, so good . . . so what / State of grace / Can't wait one more minute / Trust slips through your hands / Gang opinion / Choices made / Solid bond / Marching goals / United kids / Soundtrack for violence / Boring summer / Et tu brute? / All twisted / Don't got to prove it.

Dec 95.	(7"/c-s) *(A 8154/+C)* **CAN'T WAIT ONE MORE MINUTE. / CLUE**	[ ]	[ ]

(cd-s+=) *(A 8154CD)* – Et tu brute?

Jan 96.	(cd-s) *(A 8127C)* **CHOICES MADE / UNITED TRACKS – SOUNDTRACK FOR VIOLENCE**	[ ]	[-]

(cd-s+=) *(A 8127CD)* – ('A'side) / Trust slips through your hands (live) / Can't wait one more minute (live) / Don't got to prove it (live).

Apr 96.	(7"/c-s) *(A 5682/+C)* **SO FAR, SO GOOD . . .SO WHAT. / CHOICES MADE**	[ ]	[ ]

(cd-s+=) *(A 5682CD)* – Soundtrack for violence / United kids / All twisted.

Aug 96.	(7") *(REV 55)* **SOCIAL CLIMBER. / SAUSAGES?**	[ ]	[-]

(above issued on 'Revelation') (below issued on 'Some Record')

Apr 98.	(7") *(SOM 05)* **SECONDHAND SUPERSTAR. /**	[ ]	[-]
Aug 98.	(cd) *<(7567 83073-2)>* **THIRTEEN DAY GETAWAY**	[ ]	[ ]

– Secondhand superstar / Big girl / Itchycoo park / Haven't been myself in a while / Everyday / Shout it / Owner's manual / Something special / Using something else / It's not your fault / Living life / Ordinary / Little men.

CJSS (see under ⇒ CHASTAIN, David T)

CLAM ABUSE (see under ⇒ WILDHEARTS)

Fast Eddie CLARKE (see under ⇒ FASTWAY)

Gilby CLARKE

Born: 17 Aug'62, Cleveland, Ohio, USA. Coming to the attention of the public by way of joining GUNS N' ROSES (replacing IZZY STRADLIN), the guitarist made his debut for the metal giants on the 'November Rain' video/single. In 1994, he left GN'R and ventured out on his own. 'PAWNSHOP GUITARS' – also in '94 – saw the man enter the UK Top 40 and set his own Bluesy-rock agenda from then on. 'THE HANGOVER' (1997), 'RUBBER' (1998) and '99 LIVE' have followed suit. • **Covered:** DEAD FLOWERS (Rolling Stones) / JAIL GUITAR DOORS (Clash) / HAPPINESS IS A WARM GUN (Beatles) / HANG ON TO YOURSELF (David Bowie) / MERCEDES BENZ (Janis Joplin) / TRASH (New York Dolls).

Album rating: PAWNSHOP GUITARS (*5) / THE HANGOVER (*4) / RUBBER (*4) / 99 ALIVE (*4)

GILBY CLARKE – / plus various session people/band

		Virgin America	Virgin
Jul 94.	(cd/c) *(CDVUS/VUSMC 76)* **PAWNSHOP GUITARS**	39	[ ]

– Cure me . . . or kill me . . . / Black / Tijuana jail / Skin and bones / Johanna's chopper / Let's get lost / Pawn shop guitar / Dead flowers / Jail guitar doors / Hunting dogs / Shut up.

—— after he left GUNS N' ROSES he continued solo

		S.P.V.	Paradigm
Aug 97.	(cd) *(085-1873-2) <PME 0019CD>* **THE HANGOVER**	[ ]	[ ] Sep97

– Wasn't yesterday great / It's good enough for rock'n'roll / Zip gun / Higher / Mickey marmalade / Blue grass mosquito / Happiness is a warm gun / Hang on to yourself / The worst / Captain Chaos / Punk rock pollution. *(lp-iss.Sep97 on 'Paradigm'; PME 0019)*

		S.P.V.	Pavement
Jun 98.	(cd) *(085-1813-2)* **RUBBER**	[ ]	[ ] Sep98

– Kilroy was here / The haunting / Something's wrong with you / Sorry I can't write a song about you / Mercedes Benz / The Hell's Angels / Saturday disaster / Trash / Technicolor stars / Superstar / Bourbon street blues / Frankie's planet.

		R.M.R.	R.M.R.
Oct 99.	(cd) *<(RM 707)>* **99 LIVE (live)**	[ ]	[ ]

– Wasn't yesterday great / Monkey chow / Black / Kilroy was here / Motorcycle cowboys / It's good enough for rock'n'roll / Cure me or kill me / Tijuana jail.

CLASH

Formed: London, England . . . early '76, by MICK JONES, PAUL SIMONON, JOE STRUMMER (ex-101'ers) and TERRY CHIMES (future PIL member, KEITH LEVENE, also had a brief spell). After a riotous tour supporting the SEX PISTOLS, their manager, BERNIE RHODES, attained a deal with major label big boys 'C.B.S.' in early '77 and subsequently unleashed the two minute classic, 'WHITE RIOT'. A driving chantalong stomp, the record smashed into the UK Top 40 and announced the arrival of a band whose influence and impact was second only to the 'PISTOLS. In contrast to LYDON and Co., The CLASH manipulated the energy of punk as a means of political protest and musical experimentation. 'THE CLASH' (1977) was a blinding statement of intent, a finely balanced masterwork of infectious hooklines and raging conviction. 'I'M SO BORED WITH THE U.S.A.' and 'CAREER OPPORTUNITIES' railed against injustice, while a cover of Junior Murvin's 'POLICE AND THIEVES' was the first of many sporadic forays into dub reggae. The album went Top 20, lauded by many critics as the definitive punk set, while a further two classic singles (not on the album), 'CLASH CITY ROCKERS' and 'WHITE MAN IN HAMMERSMITH PALAIS' made the Top 40 (the latter addressing the issue of racism, a subject never far from the band's agenda). CBS (and no doubt the band themselves) were keen to break America, subsequently enlisting the production services of BLUE OYSTER CULT guru, SANDY PERLMAN for follow-up set, 'GIVE 'EM ENOUGH ROPE' (1978). The album's more rock-based, less frenetic approach met with some criticism and despite the label's best efforts, the record just failed to crack the American Top 100. It had, however, made No.2 in Britain and spawned the band's first Top 20 hit in 'TOMMY GUN'. The CLASH subsequently set out to tour the States, while British fans lapped up 'THE COST OF LIVING' EP and its incendiary cover of Sonny Curtis's 'I FOUGHT THE LAW'. Finally, in late '79, The CLASH delivered their marathon masterwork, 'LONDON CALLING'. Overseen by seasoned producer, Guy Stevens, the double set showed The CLASH at an assured creative peak, from the anthemic echo of the title track to the brooding 'GUNS OF BRIXTON'. A UK Top 10'er, it finally cracked the States (Top 30), its universal acclaim spurred them on to ever more ambitious endeavours. After the plangent dub of the 'BANKROBBER' and 'THE CALL-UP' singles, the band unleashed the sprawling, triple vinyl set, 'SANDINISTA!' in December 1980. The record's wildly experimental material met with critical pasting, the bulk of the album's tracks failing to withstand repeated listening. Its relatively poor sales (still at single vinyl price!) forced a back to basics rethink for 'COMBAT ROCK' (1982). Although the record was a healthy seller, it sounded laboured; ironically, it became The CLASH's biggest selling album in America, where the 'ROCK THE CASBAH' single made the Top 10. Drummer TOPPER HEADON was already long gone by this point and was replaced by CHIMES, who had left after the 1977 debut; JONES too, was kicked out the following year. The band stumbled on for a further album, 'CUT THE CRAP' in 1985, before finally disbanding the following month. While JONES enjoyed mid-80's success with BIG AUDIO DYNAMITE, STRUMMER embarked on a low key solo career before working with his pal SHANE MacGOWAN in The POGUES. The CLASH fever gripped the nation again in 1991 when 'SHOULD I STAY OR SHOULD I GO' (a Top 20 hit in 1983), hit the top of the charts after being used in a Levi jeans advert (what else!?). A best of double set, 'THE STORY OF THE CLASH VOL.1', flew off the shelves and rumours were rife of a CLASH reunion (unceremoniously quashed by STRUMMER). • **Songwriters:** Either STRUMMER / – JONES until 1980 group penned, except PRESSURE DROP (Maytals) / POLICE ON MY BACK (Equals) / ARMAGIDEON TIME (Willie Williams) / JUNCO PARTNER + ENGLISH CIVIL WAR (unknown trad) / EVERY LITTLE BIT HURTS (Ed Cobb) / BRAND NEW CADILLAC (Vince Taylor). • **Trivia:** Early in 1980, the band featured live in the docu-film 'Rude Boy' about a fictionalised CLASH roadie. JOE STRUMMER went into acting 1986 (Straight To Hell) / 1989 (Lost In Space).

Album rating: THE CLASH (*10) / GIVE 'EM ENOUGH ROPE (*8) / LONDON CALLING (*9) / SANDINISTA! (*7) / COMBAT ROCK (*6) / CUT THE CRAP (*4) / THE STORY OF THE CLASH, VOL.1 compilation (*9) / CLASH ON BROADWAY (*7) / SUPER BLACK MARKET CLASH (*7) / FROM HERE TO ETERNITY live collection (*8) / Joe Strummer: EARTHQUAKE WEATHER (*5) / ROCK ART AND THE X-RAY STYLE (*5)

JOE STRUMMER (b. JOHN GRAHAM MELLOR, 21 Aug'52, Ankara, Turkey / raised London) – vocals, guitar (ex-101'ers) / **PAUL SIMONON** (b.15 Dec'55, Brixton, England) – bass, vocals / **MICK JONES** (b. MICHAEL JONES, 26 Jun'55) – guitar, vocals / **TORY CRIMES** (b. TERRY CHIMES, 25 Jan'55) – drums

		C.B.S.	Epic
Mar 77.	(7") *(S-CBS 5058)* **WHITE RIOT. / 1977**	38	-
Apr 77.	(lp/c) *(CBS/40 82000)* **THE CLASH**	12	-

– Janie Jones / Remote control / I'm so bored with the U.S.A. / White riot / Hate and war / What's my name / Deny / London's burning / Career oportunities / Cheat / Protex blue / Police and thieves / 48 hours / Garage land. *<US-iss.Aug79 on 'Epic'; 36060> (tracks differed & contained free 7")* – GROOVY TIMES. / GATES OF THE WEST *(this lp version UK-iss.Jan91 on cd) (re-iss. Nov82 lp/c; CBS/40 32232) (cd-iss. Apr89 on 'Columbia'; CD 32232) (cd re-iss. Aug91 on 'Columbia'; 468783-2)*

—— (Jan'77) (NICKY) **TOPPER HEADON** (b.30 May'55, Bromley, Kent, England) – drums; repl. CHIMES who later joined COWBOYS INTERNATIONAL and GENERATION X

May 77.	(7") *(S-CBS 5293)* **REMOTE CONTROL. / LONDON'S BURNING (live)**	[ ]	-
Sep 77.	(7") *(S-CBS 5664)* **COMPLETE CONTROL. / THE CITY OF THE DEAD**	28	-
Feb 78.	(7") *(S-CBS 5834)* **CLASH CITY ROCKERS. / JAIL GUITAR DOORS**	35	-
Jun 78.	(7") *(S-CBS 6383)* **(WHITE MAN) IN HAMMERSMITH PALAIS. / THE PRISONER**	32	-
Nov 78.	(lp/c) *(CBS/40 82431) <35543>* **GIVE 'EM ENOUGH ROPE**	2	[ ] Feb79

– Safe European home / English civil war / Tommy gun / Julie's been working for the drug squad / Guns on the roof / Drug-stabbing time / Stay free / Cheapstakes / All the young punks (new boots and contracts). *(re-iss. 1984 lp/c; CBS/40 32444) (cd-iss. Jan91; CD 32444)*

Nov 78.	(7") *(S-CBS 6788)* **TOMMY GUN. / 1, 2, CRUSH ON YOU**	19	-
Feb 79.	(7") *(S-CBS 7082)* **ENGLISH CIVIL WAR. / PRESSURE DROP**	25	-
May 79.	(7"ep) *(S-CBS 7324)* **THE COST OF LIVING**	22	-

– I fought the law / Groovy times / Gates of the west / Capital radio.

Jul 79.	(7") *<50738>* **I FOUGHT THE LAW. / (WHITE MAN) IN HAMMERSMITH PALAIS**	-	[ ]

—— added on tour MICKEY GALLAGHER – keyboards (ex-IAN DURY)

Dec 79.	(7") *(S-CBS 8087)* **LONDON CALLING. / ARMAGIDEON TIME**	11	-

(12"+=) *(CBS12 8087)* – Justice tonight (version) / Kick it over (version).

Dec 79.	(d-lp/c) *(CLASH/+C 3) <36328>* **LONDON CALLING**	9	27 Jan80

– London calling / Brand new Cadillac / Jimmy Jazz / Hateful / Rudie can't fail / Wrong 'em boyo / Death or glory / Koka Kola / The card cheat / Spanish bombs / The right profile / Lost in the supermarket / The guns of Brixton / Lover's rock /

Four horsemen / I'm not down / Revolution rock / Train in vain. *(re-iss. Feb88 on 'Columbia' d-lp/c; 460114-1/-4) (cd-iss. Apr89 on 'Columbia'; 460114-2)*

Mar 80. (7") *<50851>* **TRAIN IN VAIN (STAND BY ME). / LONDON CALLING** [-] [27]

Aug 80. (7") *(S-CBS 8323)* **BANKROBBER. / Mickey Dread: ROCKERS GALORE . . . UK TOUR** [12] [-]

Nov 80. (7") *(S-CBS 9339)* **THE CALL-UP. / STOP THE WORLD** [40] [-]

Nov 80. (10"m-lp) *<36846>* **BLACK MARKET CLASH** [-] [74]
– Time is tight / Capital radio / Bankrobber / Pressure drop / The prisoner / City of the dead / Justice tonight – kick it over (version). *(UK-iss.Sep91 on 'Columbia' cd/c; 468763-2/-4)*

Dec 80. (t-lp/d-c) *(CBS/40 FSLN 1) <37037>* **SANDINISTA!** [19] [24]
– The magnificent seven / Hitsville U.K. / Junco partner / Ivan meets G.I. Joe / The leader / Something about England / Rebel waltz / Look here / The crooked beat / Somebody got murdered / One more time / One more dub / Lightning strikes (not once but twice) / Up in Heaven (not only here) / Corner soul / Let's go crazy / If music could talk / The sound of the sinners / Police on my back / Midnight log / The equaliser / The call up / Washington bullets / Broadway / Lose this skin / Charlie don't surf / Mensforth Hill / Junkie slip / Kingston advice / The street parade / Version city / Living in fame / Silicone on sapphire / Version pardner / Career opportunites (version) / Shepherds delight. *(d-cd-iss. Apr89 on 'Columbia'; 463364-2)*

Jan 81. (7") *(S-CBS 9480)* **HITSVILLE U.K. / RADIO ONE** [56] [-]

Feb 81. (7") *<51013>* **HITSVILLE U.K. / POLICE ON MY BACK** [-] [ ]

Apr 81. (12"ep) *<02036>* **THE CALL-UP. / THE COOL-OUT. / THE MAGNIFICENT SEVEN / THE MAGNIFICENT DANCE** [-] [ ]

Apr 81. (7"/12") *(A/+12 1133)* **THE MAGNIFICENT SEVEN. / THE MAGNIFICENT DANCE** [34] [-]

Nov 81. (7") *(A 1797)* **THIS IS RADIO CLASH. / RADIO CLASH** [47] [-]
(12"+=) *(A12 1797)* – Outside broadcast / Radio 5.

— **TERRY CHIMES** returned to repl. HEADON who later went solo (signed to 'Mercury', released a couple of singles – 'DRUMMIN' MAN', LEAVE IT TO LUCK' and 'I'LL GIVE YOU EVERYTHING' – all from the 1986 album, 'WAKING UP', which featured 60's soul singer, JIMMY HELMS)

Apr 82. (7") *(A 2309)* **KNOW YOUR RIGHTS. / FIRST NIGHT BACK IN LONDON** [43] [-]

May 82. (lp/c) *(CBS/40 FMLN 2) <37689>* **COMBAT ROCK** [2] [7]
– Know your rights / Car jamming / Should I stay or should I go / Rock the Casbah / Red angel dragnet / Straight to Hell / Overpowered by funk / Atom tan / Sean Flynn / Ghetto defendant / Inoculated city / Death is a star. *(re-iss. Nov86 lp/c; CBS/40 32787) (cd-iss. Jan91 on 'Columbia'; CD 32787)*

May 82. (7") *<03006>* **SHOULD I STAY OR SHOULD I GO. / INNOCULATED CITY** [-] [ ]

Jun 82. (7"/7"pic-d) *(A/+11 2479) <03245>* **ROCK THE CASBAH. / LONG TIME JERK** [30] [8] Sep82
(12") *(A12 2479)* – ('A'side) / Mustapha dance.

Jul 82. (7") *<03061>* **SHOULD I STAY OR SHOULD I GO. / FIRST NIGHT BACK IN LONDON** [-] [45]

Sep 82. (7"/7"pic-d/12") *(A/+11/12 2646)* **SHOULD I STAY OR SHOULD I GO. / STRAIGHT TO HELL** [17] [-]

Feb 83. (7") *<03547>* **SHOULD I STAY OR SHOULD I GO? / COOL CONFUSION** [-] [50]

— (Feb83-Jan84) **STRUMMER & SIMONON** brought in new musicians **PETE HOWARD** – drums (ex-COLD FISH),repl. CHIMES who later joined HANOI ROCKS / **NICK SHEPHERD** – guitar (ex-CORTINAS) + **VINCE WHITE** – guitar; repl. JONES who formed BIG AUDIO DYNAMITE

Sep 85. (7") *(A 6122)* **THIS IS ENGLAND. / DO IT NOW** [24] [-]
(12"+=) *(A12 6122)* – Sex mad roar.

Nov 85. (lp/c) *(CBS/40 26601) <40017>* **CUT THE CRAP** [16] [88]
– Dictator / Dirty punk / We are The Clash / Are you red.. Y / Cool under heat / Movers and shakers / This is England / Three card trick / Play to win / Fingerpoppin' / North and south / Life is wild. *(cd-iss. Apr89 on 'Columbia'; CD 465110-2) (cd-iss. Dec92 on 'Columbia';)*

— disbanded Dec'85 and STRUMMER went solo (see below). SHEPHERD formed HEAD. In the early 90's, SIMONON formed HAVANA 3 A.M. who comprised NIGEL DIXON (ex-WHIRLWIND), GARY MYRICK and TRAVIS WILLIAMS. Signing to 'I.R.S.', they released only one 50's style eponymous rock album in 1991 before splitting their quiffs.

– compilations, others, etc. –

on 'C.B.S.' unless mentioned otherwise

Nov 82. (c-ep) *(A40 2907)* **COMPLETE CONTROL / LONDON CALLING / BANKROBBER / CLASH CITY ROCKERS** [ ] [-]

Sep 86. (c-ep) *(450 123-4)* **THE 12" TAPE** [ ] [-]
– London calling / The magnificent dance / This is Radio Clash / Rock the Casbah / This is England. *(cd-iss. Nov92 on 'Columbia'; 450123-2)*

Mar 88. (7") *(CLASH 1)* **I FOUGHT THE LAW. / THE CITY OF THE DEAD / 1977** [29] [-]
(12"+=/cd-s+=) *(CLASH T/C 1)* – Police on my back / 48 hours.

Mar 88. (d-lp/c/cd) *(460244-1/-4/-2) <44035>* **THE STORY OF THE CLASH** [7] [ ]
– The magnificent seven / Rock the Casbah / This is Radio Clash / Should I stay or should I go / Straight to Hell / Armagideon time / Clampdown / Train in vain / Guns of Brixton / I fought the law / Somebody got murdered / Lost in the supermarket / Bank robber / White man in Hammersmith Palais / London's burning / Janie Jones / Tommy gun / Complete control / Capital radio / White riot / Career opportunities / Clash city rockers / Safe European home / Stay free / London calling / Spanish bombs / English civil war / Police and thieves. *(re-iss. Mar91 as THE STORY OF THE CLASH VOL.1, on 'Columbia'; same)* – (hit UK 13) *(re-iss. Oct95 on 'Columbia'; same)*

Apr 88. (7"/7"box) *(CLASH/+B 2)* **LONDON CALLING. / BRAND NEW CADILLAC** [46] [ ]
(12"+=) *(CLASHT 2)* – Rudie can't fail.
(cd-s+=) *(CLASHC 2)* – The street parade.

Jul 90. (7"/c-s) *(656072-7/-4)* **RETURN TO BRIXTON (remix). / ('A'-SW2 mix)** [57] [-]
(12"+=/cd-s+=) *(656072-6/-2)* – The guns of Brixton.

Feb 91. (7"/c-s) *Columbia; (656667-7/-4)* **SHOULD I STAY OR SHOULD I GO. / B.A.D. II: Rush** [1] [ ]
(12"+=/cd-s+=) *(656667-6/-2)* – ('B'dance mix) / Protex blue.
(cd-s) *(656667-5)* – ('A'side) / London calling / Train in vain / I fought the law.

Apr 91. (7"/c-s) *Columbia; (656814-7/-4)* **ROCK THE CASBAH. / MUSTAPHA DANCE** [15] [ ]
(12"+=/cd-s+=) *(656814-6/-2)* – The magnificent dance / This is Radio Clash.
(cd-s) *(656814-5)* – ('A'side) / Tommy gun / (White man) In Hammersmith Palais / Straight to Hell.

Jun 91. (7"/c-s) *Columbia; (656946-7/-4)* **LONDON CALLING. / BRAND NEW CADILLAC** [64] [ ]
(12"+=) *(656946-6)* – Return to Brixton (remix).
(cd-s++=) *(656946-2)* – The call-up.

Oct 91. (7"/c-s) *Columbia; (656-7/-4)* **TRAIN IN VAIN (STAND BY ME). / THE RIGHT PROFILE** [ ] [-]
(cd-s+=) *(656-2)* – Groovy times / Gates to the west.
(pic-cd-s+=) *(656-5)* – ('A'remix) / Death or glory.

Nov 91. (cd/c) *Columbia; (468946-2/-4)* **THE SINGLES COLLECTION** [68] [ ]

Nov 93. (cd) *Columbia; (474546-2)* **SUPER BLACK MARKET CLASH** [ ] [-]

May 94. (3xcd-box/3xc-box) *Columbia; (469308-2/-4)* **ON BROADWAY** [ ] [ ]

Oct 99. (cd/c/d-lp) *Columbia; (496183-2/-4/-1)* **FROM HERE TO ETERNITY (live)** [13] [ ]
– Complete control / London's burning / What's my name / Clash city rockers / Career opportunities / White man in Hammersmith Palais / Capitol radio / City of the dead / I fought the law / London calling / Armagideon time / Train in vain / Guns of Brixton / The magnificent seven / Should I stay or should I go / Straight to Hell.

— The CLASH also appeared under different guises for singles below

May 83. (12"; FUTURA 2000 with The Clash) *Celluloid; (CYZ 104)* **ESCAPADES OF FUTURA 2000** [ ] [-]

Dec 83. (7"; JANIE JONES & THE LASH) *Big Beat; (NS 91)* **HOUSE OF THE JU-JU QUEEN. / SEX MACHINE** [ ] [-]

— They can also be heard on TYMON DOGG's 45; 'Lose This Skin' (May80)

JOE STRUMMER

C.B.S. Epic

Oct 86. (7"/12") *(A/TA 7244)* **LOVE KILLS. / DUM DUM CLUB** [69] [-]

Virgin Virgin

Feb 88. (cd/c/lp) *(CD/TC+/V 2497)* **WALKER (Soundtrack)** [ ] [ ]
– Filibustero / Omotepe / Sandstorm / Machete / Viperland / Nica libre / Latin romance / The brooding side of madness / Tennessee rain / Smash everything / Tropic of no return / The unknown immortal / Musket waltz.

Epic Epic

Jun 88. (7"/7"s) *(TRASH/+P 1)* **TRASH CITY. / THEME FROM A PERMANENT RECORD** [ ] [-]
(12"+=/pic-cd-s+=) *(TRASH T/C 1)* – Nerfititi rock.

— STRUMMER was augmented by new band **JACK IRONS** – drums (of RED HOT CHILI PEPPERS) **ZANDON SCHLOSS** – guitar (ex-CIRCLE JERKS) / **RONNIE MARSHALL** – bass (of TONE LOC)

Aug 89. (7"/c-s) *(STRUM/+M 1)* **GANGSTERVILLE. / JEWELLERS AND BUMS** [ ] [-]
(7"ep+=) *(STRUME 1)* – Passport to Detroit / Punk rock blues.
(12"+=/cd-s+=) *(STRUM T/C 1)* – Don't tango with my django.

Sep 89. (lp/c/cd) *(465347-1/-4/-2)* **EARTHQUAKE WEATHER** [58] [ ]
– Gangsterville / King of the bayou / Island hopping / Slant six / Dizzy's goatee / Shouting street / Boogie with your children / Leopardskin limousines / Sikorsky parts / Jewellers and bums / Highway on zero street / Ride your donkey / Passport to Detroit / Sleepwalk.

Oct 89. (7") *(STRUM 2)* **ISLAND HOPPING. / CHOLO VEST** [ ] [ ]
(12"+=/cd-s+=/7"ep+=) *(STRUM T/C/E 2)* – Mango street / Baby o' boogie.

— STRUMMER joined The POGUES on tour, deputising when SHANE McGOWAN was under the bottle. At the start of 1992, he had begun writing with them, so who knows? At least it will quell the dogged persistent rumours of a CLASH reformation.

JOE STRUMMER & THE MESCALEROS

— **STRUMMER** with **. . . NORRIS / . . . DYSON / . . . GENN**

Mercury Mercury

Aug 99. (12"/cd-s) *(MER/+CD 523)* **YALLA YALLA. / X-RAY STYLE / TIME AND THE TIDE** [ ] [-]

Oct 99. (cd/c/lp) *(546654-2/-4/-1) <80424>* **ROCK ART & THE X-RAY STYLE** [71] [ ]
– Tony Adams / Sandpaper blues / X-ray style / Techno D-day / Road to rock'n'roll / Diggin' the new / Nitcomb / Forbidden city / Yalla yalla / Willesden to Cricklewood.

CLAWFINGER

Formed: Stockholm, Sweden . . . 1990 by former hospital orderlies ZAK TELL (he was initially in Bristol, England), JOCKE SKOOG and Norwegians ERLAND OTTERN and BARD TORSTENSEN. They actually saw their vinyl debut on JUST D'S MCD's single 'Klafinger'. CLAWFINGER then recorded a demo, 'NIGGER' (actually anti-racist), the subsequent single, a hit after being playlisted by a local radio station. This exposure helped secure a deal with 'East West' records, their 1994 debut album, 'DEAF, DUMB, BLIND', becoming the toast of the Kerrang magazine critics. Heavy duty metal-rap falling somewhere between RAGE AGAINST THE MACHINE and FAITH NO MORE, the record was distinguished by its innovative use of studio technology. A follow-up, 'USE YOUR BRAIN' (1995), failed to garner any further support, the band struggling to achieve the same crossover success enjoyed by many of their peers. Although not as popular as their mid-90's period, CLAWFINGER have continued to despatch the odd album, namely 1998's eponymous 'CLAWFINGER' and 2000's 'TWO SIDES'.

Album rating: DEAF, DUMB, BLIND (*7) / USE YOUR BRAIN (*5) / CLAWFINGER (*5) / TWO SIDES (*5)

ZAK TELL – vocals / **BRAD TORTENSEN** – guitar / **ERLAND OTTERN** – guitar / **JOCKE SKOG** – keyboards, programmer, vocals

M.V.G. / not iss.

1993. (cd-s) *(MVGS 7)* **NIGGER / GET IT / LOVE** - - Sweden
1993. (cd-s) *(MVGCDS 9)* **ROSEGROVE / STARS & STRIPES** - - Sweden

East West / Metal Blade

Nov 93. (7"pic-d/c-s) *(YZ 786 P/C)* **THE TRUTH. / DON'T GET ME WRONG** -
(12"+=/cd-s+=) *(YZ 786 T/CD)* – Love / ('A'-Cyborg law mix).
Mar 94. (7"pic-d/c-s) *(YZ 804/+C)* **WARFAIR (cybersank mix). / STARS AND STRIPES** 54 -
(12") *(YZ 804T)* – ('A'side) / The truth (live) (cyberg law mix) / Nigger (Zorbact mix) / Don't get me wrong (Zorbact-techno mix).
(cd-s) *(YZ 804CD)* – ('A'side) / Profit, preacher / The truth / ('A'mix).
Mar 94. (cd/c) *(4509 93321-2/-4)* <14073> **DEAF, DUMB, BLIND** Oct94
– Nigger / The truth / Rosegrove / Don't get me wrong / I need you / Catch me / Warfair / Wonderful world / Sad to see your sorrow / I don't care.
Mar 95. (7"colrd/c-s/cd-s) *(YZ 921 X/C/CD1)* **PIN ME DOWN. / GET IT (U.S. version)** -
(cd-s) *((YZ 921CD2)* – ('A'side) / What are you afraid of / Better than this.
Apr 95. (cd/c) *(4509 99631-2/-4)* **USE YOUR BRAIN**
– Power / Pay the bill / Pin me down / Waste my time / Die high / It / Do what I say / Undone / What are you afraid of? / Back to the basics / Easy way out / Tomorrow.
Oct 95. (cd-ep) *(EW 012CD)* **TOMORROW / I DON'T WANT TO / DO WHAT I SAY** -

Coalition / not iss.

Dec 97. (7") *(COLA 031)* **BIGGEST AND THE BEST. / RUNNER BOY** -
(cd-s+=) *(COLA 031CD)* – ('A'-Godhead mix) / ('A'-Pitchshifter mix).
Feb 98. (7"clear) *(COLA 038)* **TWO SIDES. / WHAT GIVES US THE RIGHT** -
(cd-s+=) *(COLA 038CD)* – ('A'-Witchman's accelerator remix) / Two sides of every vibe.
(one-sided 10") *(COLA 038T)* – ('A'-Witchman's accelerator remix).
Mar 98. (cd/c) *(3984 22639-2/-4)* **CLAWFINGER** -
– Wrong side of the mind / Biggest and the best / Two sides / Not even you / I can see them coming / I guess I'll never know. *(lp-iss.Feb00 on 'Loquacious'; SHOOSH 001)*

The Music Cartel / The Music Cartel

Mar 00. (cd) *<(TMC 33CD)>* **TWO SIDES**
– Two sides / Two sides (Witchman's accelerator mix) / Two sides of every vibe / Reality / Biggest & the best / Biggest & the best (Godhead remix) / Biggest & the best (Pitchshifter de-mix) / Runner boy / Don't wake me up / Don't wake me up (yoga remix) / What gives us the right / Biggest & the best (US radio remix).

CLAW HAMMER

Formed: Long Beach, California, USA . . . mid 80's by former PONTIAC BROTHERS frontman, JON WAHL, along with ROB WALTHER and RICK SORTWELL. Strangely enough, CLAW HAMMER debuted on vinyl in Australia, the 'POOR ROBERT' EP hitting the shops at the turn of the decade. Pounding out a deal with the incredibly prolific US imprint, 'Sympathy For The Record Industry', the trio delivered their eponymous debut set in 1990, featuring weird and wonderful versions of Gordon Lightfoot's 'SUNDOWN', Pere Ubu's 'FINAL SOLUTION' and Hampton-Kelling's 'HEY OLD LADY AND BERT'S SONG'. A creative, punk-like update of QUICKSILVER MESSENGER SERVICE, WAHL, WALTHER and newcomers CHRIS BAGAROZZI and BOB LEE armed themselves with the CLAW HAMMER sound and set about deconstructing DEVO's 'Q: ARE WE NOT MEN, A: WE ARE DEVO' in its entirety. Around the same time they issued a covers EP, 'DOUBLE PACK WHACK ATTACK'; artists chosen this time were Patti Smith, Eno, Pere Ubu and Devo again(!), while original material surfaced on the early '92 album, 'RAMWHALE'. At this junction of the band's career, WAHL also moonlighted with the RED AUNTS as BAGAROZZI augmented DOWN BY LAW. Picked up by BRETT GUREWITZ's 'Epitaph' label, CLAW HAMMER released the acclaimed 'PABLUM' (1993), in turn attracting the attentions of big wigs 'Interscope'. A couple of years in the making, 1995's major label debut, 'THANK THE HOLDER UPPERS', was as uncompromising as ever, while 1997's JIM DICKINSON-produced, 'HOLD YOUR TONGUE (AND SAY APPLE)', revelled in its hard-nosed Memphis sleaze/punk.

Album rating: CLAW HAMMER (*5) / Q: ARE WE NOT MEN? – A: WE ARE DEVO (*4) / RAMWHALE (*5) / PABLUM (*6) / THANK THE HOLDER UPPERS (*6) / HOLD YOUR TONGUE (AND SAY APPLE) (*5)

JON WAHL – vocals, guitar (ex-PONTIAC BROTHERS) / **ROB WALTHER** – bass / **RICK SORTWELL** – drums

Grown Up Wrong / not iss.

1989. (12"ep) **POOR ROBERT EP** - - Austra

Sympathy F / Sympathy F

Oct 89. (7"ep) *<SFTRI 37>* **F.U.B.A.R.** -
Mar 90. (cd/lp) *<SFTRI 57>* **CLAW HAMMER** -
– Shell shocked / Warm Spring night / Brother Brick says / Drop II / Sundown / Hey old lady and Bert's song / Papa's got us all tied in knots / Mr. Pizzazz / Petri dish / Poor Robert / Three fifteen / Final solution / Candle opera / Drop. *(UK-iss.1993; same as US)*

— **CHRIS BAGAROZZI** – guitar + **BOB LEE** – drums; repl. SORTWELL

1991. (cd-ep) **DOUBLE PACK WHACK ATTACK** -
Oct 91. (lp) *<SFTRI 119>* **Q: ARE WE NOT MEN? A: WE ARE DEVO (the DEVO album live in studio)** -
Jan 92. (cd) *<SFTRI 120>* **RAMWHALE** -
– Naked / Succotash / Maheney bus ride / Beat rice / Sticky thing / Crave / People in my peephole / Three fifteen / Don't walk away / Stough.
1993. (7") *<SFTRI 229>* **MALTHUSIAN BLUES. / THE DAY OF THE TRIFFIDS** -

Epitaph / Epitaph

Apr 93. (cd/c/lp) *<(86425 CD/MC/LP)>* **PABLUM**
– Vigil smile / William Tell / Montezuma's hands / Speak softly / Nick / Nut powder / Shitting gold bricks / Malthusian blues / Pablum of my mind.

Interscope / Interscope

May 95. (cd/c) *<92515>* **THANK THE HOLDER UPPERS** -
– Superthings / When Dan's in town / Sweaty palms / Five filths dead / Bums on the flow / Hollow legs / Bedside coffee table roses / Blind pig / Each hit / Lazy brains / Ol' factory blues – Nose hair.
Apr 97. (cd) *<90105>* **HOLD YOUR TONGUE (AND SAY APPLE)** -
– The day it rained pigeon shit / Valley so high / Black eyed blues / Queen's lead helmet / Sugar breath / Gnashville / Hind sight / Ass kisser's union / Water / Air plant / Formaldehyde / Caravan.

Medfly / Medfly

Jun 97. (12") *<(MEDFLY 001)>* **KILOWATT. / FLYSPRAY**
Feb 98. (12") *<(12MED 003)>* **PEOPLE LOVE. /**

– compilations, etc. –

Aug 96. (m-cd) *Sympathy For The Record Industry; <(SFTRI 447CD)>* **'SCUSE THE EXCURSION**
– Caravan / Nightmare / All blues / Sick fish belly up.

CLAY PEOPLE

Formed: Albany, New York, USA . . . 1990 by DANIEL NEET, DAN McGARVEY, et all. Signed to the 'Reconstriction' label, the band's early albums such as 'FIRETRIBE' (1994) and 'THE IRON ICON' (1995) relied heavily on electronic beats and effects to create their belligerent heavy rock sound. Following 1997's 'STONE TEN STITCHES', the band inked a deal with 'Mercury' subsidiary, 'Slipdisc', through whom they issued their 1998 evolutionary eponymous set. Recorded with a real live drummer, DAN DINSMORE (and also featuring new members MIKE GUZZARDI and DAN WALSH), the record took a markedly more organic approach. With production duties handled by Neil Kernon, critical comparisons to QUEENSRYCHE were hardly surprising.

Album rating: FIRETRIBE (*5) / THE IRON ICON (*5) / STONE TEN STITCHES (*5) / THE CLAY PEOPLE (*6)

DANIEL NEET – vocals / **BRIAN McGARVEY** – guitar / **KEVIN BAKERIAN + ALEX ELLER**

Reconstriction / Reconstruction

Sep 94. (cd) *<CDRED 6>* **FIRETRIBE** -
– Deadman / Crudsong / In chaos / Close my eye / Godsick / Nothing / Scripture / Shroud / Skin / Void / Fire eyes / Teeth to grind.

— **WILL NIVENS** – repl. BAKERIAN

Nov 95. (cd) *<CDRED 15>* **IRON ICON** -
– Lethargic / We are all sick / Palegod / Victims / Rusted iron turning wheel / Spit.
Jan 97. (cd) *<(CDRED 26)>* **STONE TEN STITCHES**
– Intro / Stone / Bloodsuckers / Pariah / Spider's bride / Pandora complex / Mechanized mind / T.M.S. / Little Jack / Strange day / Stone.

— **NEET + McGARVEY** recruited **MIKE GUZZARDI** – guitar / **DAN WALSH** – bass / **DAN DINSMORE** – drums

not iss. / Slipdisc

May 98. (cd) *<633127>* **THE CLAY PEOPLE** -
– Awake / Plug / Mechanized mind / Calling spaceship: Damien Grief / Car bomb (am I human?) / Fade away / Raygun girls / Dying to be you / Thread / Ghostwishing / Who am I?

Les CLAYPOOL & The HOLY MACKEREL
(see under ⇒ PRIMUS)

CLEAR LIGHT

Formed: Los Angeles, California, USA . . . 1967 by CLIFF DE YOUNG, BOB SEAL, RALPH SCHUCKETT, DOUG LABAHN, MICHAEL NEY and DALLAS TAYLOR. A basic heavy-rock outfit, their eponymous album only reached the lower regions of the American Top 200. The single, 'BLACK ROSES,' was definitely the highlight of the album, its flip side, 'SHE'S READY TO BE FREE', subsequently used in the film, 'The President's Analyst'. Individually, the group members went on to more profitable pastures.

Album rating: CLEAR LIGHT (*6)

CLIFF DE YOUNG – vocals / **BOB SEAL** – guitar, vocals / **RALPH SCHUCKETT** – organ, piano, celeste / **DOUG LUBAHN** – bass / **MICHAEL NEY** – drums, percussion / **DALLAS TAYLOR** – drums

Elektra / Elektra

Nov 67. (lp) *<(EKS 74011)>* **CLEAR LIGHT**
– Black roses / Sand / Child's smile / Street singer / Ballad of Freddie & Larry / With all in mind / Mr. Blue / Think again / They who have nothing / How many days have passed / Night sounds loud.
1967. (7") *(EKSN 45019)* <45622> **BLACK ROSES. / SHE'S READY TO BE FREE**
Apr 68. (7") *(EKSN 45027)* **NIGHT SOUNDS LOUD. / HOW MANY DAYS HAVE PASSED** -

— **DANNY KORTCHMAR** – lead guitar; repl. SEAL who joined the PEANUT BUTTER CONSPIRACY

— Split after above. DE YOUNG later went solo, releasing two albums for 'MCA'. LABAHN went onto session for The DOORS, while DALLAS TAYLOR augmented CROSBY, STILLS & NASH. KORTCHMAR later played in The CITY alongside CAROLE KING.

CLOVEN HOOF

Formed: England . . . 1979 by DAVID POTTER, STEVE ROUNDS, LES PAYNE and KEVIN POUNTNEY. With a garish glam/tongue-in-cheek Satanic KISS-like image, the band independently unleashed their debut offering, 'THE OPENING RITUAL' EP (1982). They finally released their first album, the eponymous 'CLOVEN HOOF', on 'Neat'. In 1985, POTTER was replaced by ROB HENDRICK (i.e. WATER, the rest taking the individual aliases of FIRE, AIR and EARTH). By 1985/86, PAYNE was the sole remaining member, revamping the band in 1987 around RUSSELL NORTH, ANDY WOOD and JON BROWN. Abandoning the glam trappings, CLOVEN HOOF took a heavier, more serious approach for the 1988 comeback album, 'DOMINATOR'. Following in the record's footsteps, 'A SULTAN'S RANSOM' (1989), was a slightly more frenetic effort, although its complete lack of originality saw the band given short shrift by the metal press.

Album rating: CLOVEN HOOF (*5) / DOMINATOR (*4)

DAVID POTTER – vocals / **STEVE ROUNDS** – guitar / **LES PAYNE** – bass / **KEVIN POUNTNEY** – drums

Cloven Hoof / not iss.

Oct 82. (7"ep) *(TOA 1402)* **THE OPENING RITUAL** ☐ [-]

Neat / not iss.

Jan 85. (lp/c) *(NEAT/+C 1013)* **CLOVEN HOOF** ☐ [-]
– Cloven hoof / Nightstalker / March of the damned / The gates of Gehemna / Crack the whip / Laying down the law / Return of the passover.

— **ROB HENDRICK ('WATER')** – vocals; repl. POTTER

Moondancer / not iss.

Feb 87. (lp) *(CH 002)* **FIGHTING BACK (live)** ☐ [-]
– Reach for the sky / The fugitive / Daughter of darkness / Heavy metal men of steel / Raised on rock / Break it up / Could this be love? / Eye of the sun.

— split around the mid 80's, although LES PAYNE reformed the band in '87 with **RUSSELL NORTH** – vocals / **ANDREW WOOD** – guitar / **JON BROWN (J.B.)** – drums

Heavy Metal / not iss.

Jul 88. (lp/c/cd) *(HMR LP/MC/XD 113)* **DOMINATOR** ☐ [-]
– Rising up / Nova battlestar / Reach for the sky / Warrior of the wasteland / Invaders / Fugitive / Dominator / Road of eagles.

Aug 89. (lp/c/cd) *(HMR LP/MC/XD 129)* **A SULTANS RANSOM** ☐ [-]
– Astral rider / Forgotten heroes / D.V.R. / Jekyll and Hyde / 1001 nights / Silver surfer / Notre dame / Mad, mad world / Highlander / Mistress of the forest.

— split in the early 90's

CLUTCH

Formed: Germantown, Maryland, USA . . . 1991 by NEIL FALLON, TIM SULT, DAN MAINES and JEAN-PAUL GASTER. Initially signed to 'Earache' records for a one-off EP, 'IMPETUS', they were quickly snapped up by 'East West'. The same year (1993), the group recorded a full album's worth of their punishing doom metallic noise in the shape of 'TRANSNATIONAL SPEEDWAY LEAGUE: ANTHEMS, ANECDOTES AND UNDENIABLE TRUTHS'. Despite a heavy touring commitment with the likes of fellow newcomers FEAR FACTORY and an eponymous follow-up album, CLUTCH never really got into commercial gear. They did, however, hone an engaging Southern stoner-rock sound through the late 90's and into the new millennium with the likes of 'THE ELEPHANT RIDERS' (1998) and 'JAM ROOM' (2000). Flying squarely in the face of musical fashion, CLUTCH's free spirited monster boogie injected a bit of good-time swagger into a chronically angst-ridden metal scene. 'PURE ROCK FURY' (2001), meanwhile, laced the loping riffs with even more oblique lyrical musings although when the music is this fired-up, do words really matter?

Album rating: TRANSNATIONAL SPEEDWAY LEAGUE . . . (*7) / CLUTCH (*7) / THE ELEPHANT RIDERS (*8) / JAM ROOM (*6) / PURE ROCK FURY (*6)

NEIL FALLON – vocals / **TIM SULT** – guitar / **DAN MAINES** – bass / **JEAN-PAUL GASTER** – drums

Earache / not iss.

Apr 93. (12"ep) *(MOSH 074T)* **IMPETUS EP** ☐ [-]
– Passive restraints / Impetus / High caliber consecrator.
(cd-ep+=) *(MOSH 074CD)* – Impetus (demo) / Pile driver.

East West / East West

Oct 93. (cd/c/lp) *<7567 92281-2/-4/-1>* **TRANSNATIONAL SPEEDWAY LEAGUE: ANTHEMS, ANECDOTES AND UNDENIABLE TRUTHS** ☐ ☐
– A shotgun named Marcus / El Jefe speaks / Binge and purge / 12 ounce epilogue / Bacchanal / Milk of human kindness / Rats / Earthworm / Heirloom 13 / Walking in the great shining path of monster trucks / Effigy.

Jun 95. (cd/c/lp) *<7559 61755-2/-4/-1>* **CLUTCH** ☐ ☐
– Big news 1 & 2 / Texan book of the dead / Space grass / Tight like that / Droid / 7 jam / The house that Peter built / Tim Sult vs The Greys / Animal farm / I have the body of John Wilkes Booth / Escape from the prison planet / Rock'n'roll outlaw.

Columbia / Columbia

Nov 98. (cd) *<69113-2>* **THE ELEPHANT RIDERS** ☐ ☐ Apr98
– The elephant riders / Ship of gold / Eight times over Miss October / The soapmakers / Yeti / Muchas veces / Green buckets / Wishbone / Crackerjack / The dragonfly.

Spitfire / Spitfire

Apr 00. (cd) *(SPITCD 061) <3346>* **JAM ROOM** ☐ ☐
– Who wants to rock? / Big fat pig / Going to market / One eye dollar / Raised by horses / "Bertha's big back yard" / Gnomes enthusiast / Swamp boot upside down / Basket of eggs / Release the kraken / Super duper / Release the dub.

Atlantic / Atlantic

Mar 01. (cd) *<(7567 83433-2)>* **PURE ROCK FURY** ☐ ☐
– American sleep / Pure rock fury / Open up the border / Careful with that mic / Red horse rainbow / The great outdoors! / Smike banshee / Frankenstein / Sinkemlow / Immortal / Brazenhead / Drink to the dead / Spacegrass (live).

– compilations, etc. –

Dec 97. (cd-ep) *Earache; (MOSH 192CD)* **IMPETUS** ☐ [-]
– Impetus (demo) / Pile driver / Passive restraints / Impetus / High caliber consecrator.

COAL CHAMBER

Formed: Los Angeles, California, USA . . . mid 90's by vocalist DEZ FAFARA, guitarist MIGUEL "MEEGS" RASCON, bassist RAYNA FOSS and drummer MIKE "BUG" COX. Despite initially splitting soon after their inception, the facial-piercing group quickly re-formed and signed a deal with 'Roadrunner'. In 1996/97, they unleashed their eponymous debut set, a very KORN-like affair (the intro of 'LOCO' virtually a clone of 'Daddy') which saw them become the darlings of the metal press. Wielding a powerful, RATM-esque bass groove overlaid with FAFARA's tongue-twistingly distinctive death growl, COAL CHAMBER boasted one of the most exciting sound blueprints in the current metal scene. Around the middle of '97, they were rumoured to be working on a version of Peter Gabriel's 'SHOCK THE MONKEY'!!!, most people (even myself!) questioning this until its inclusion (and release as single) on their sophomore set, 'CHAMBER MUSIC' (1999). Harking back to the days of industrial-goth rock (ALIEN SEX FIEND their new mentors!?), the "spook-core" album lacked the bite of their debut although it nearly hit the Top 20 on both sides of the Atlantic. Now married to SEVENDUST's drummer MORGAN ROSE, pregnant RAYNA FOSS-ROSE (who had been temp'd by the stunning NADJA POROMBKA) was absent from tour and promotion duties.

Album rating: COAL CHAMBER (*7) / CHAMBER MUSIC (*5)

DEZ FAFARA – vocals / **MIGUEL "MEEGS" RASCON** – guitar, vocals / **RAYNA FOSS** – bass / **MIKE "BUG" COX** – drums

Roadrunner / I.R.S.

Mar 97. (cd/c) *(RR 8863-2/-4) <983.063>* **COAL CHAMBER** ☐ ☐
– Loco / Bradley / Oddity / Unspoiled / Big truck / Sway / First / Maricon puto / I / Clock / My frustration / Amir of the desert / Dreamtime / Pig. *(cd re-iss. Dec97; RR 8863-5)*

Jun 98. (cd-ep) *(RR 2229-3)* **LOCO / BLISTERS / SWAY (remix) / LOCO (remastered)** ☐ [-]

— temp **NADJA POROMBKA** – bass; repl. RAYNA (see above)

Roadrunner / Roadrunner

Sep 99. (cd) *<(RR 8659-2)>* **CHAMBER MUSIC** [21] [22]
– Tragedy / El cu cuy / Untrue / Tyler's song / What's in your mind / Not living / Shock the monkey / Burgundy / Anahstasia / Feed my dreams / My mercy / No home / Shari Vegas / Notion / Anything but you. *(special-cd+=; RR 8659-5)* – Apparation / Wishes.

Nov 99. (cd-s) *(RR 2134-3)* **SHOCK THE MONKEY / SHOCK THE MONKEY (Gorilla mix) / EL CU CUY (remix)** ☐ ☐

COBRA

Formed: USA . . . 1982 by MANDY MEYER (ex-KROKUS) and JIMI JAMISON (ex-TARGET), who completed the line-up with JACK HOLDER, TOMMY KEISER and JEFF KLAVEN. Signed to 'Epic', they were introduced to the hard/blues rock world with a BAD COMPANY / IRON MAIDEN style debut, 'FIRST STRIKE'. Contractual difficulties led to the band folding, nearly every member finding fame in other acts, JAMISON (to SURVIVOR), MEYER (to ASIA) and KLAVEN (to KROKUS).

Album rating: FIRST STRIKE (*5)

JIMI JAMISON – vocals (ex-TARGET) / **MANDY MEYER** – guitar, vocals (ex-KROKUS) / **JACK HOLDER** – guitar, vocals / **TOMMY KEISER** – bass, vocals / **JEFF KLAVEN** – drums, vocals

Epic / Epic

1983. (lp) *(EPC 25536) <38790>* **FIRST STRIKE** ☐ ☐
– Blood on your money / Only you can rock me / Travelin' man / I've been a fool before / First strike / Danger zone / Looking at you / Fallen angel / What love is / Thorn in your flesh.

— split (see above for details)

COCKNEY REJECTS

Formed: London, England . . . 1978, by JEFFERSON TURNER, VINCE RIORDAN, KEITH WARRINGTON and ex-amateur boxer MIKE GEGGUS. After a one-off single in '79, 'FLARES 'N' SLIPPERS' for the indie label 'Small Wonder', they caught the attention of SHAM 69's JIMMY PURSEY. They immediately signed to 'E.M.I.', subsequently enjoying two minor hits,

'I'M NOT A FOOL' and 'BADMAN'. Akin to a more primitive SHAM 69 and taking on that band's rowdy mantle, the average COCKNEY REJECTS gig attracting the less desirable element of the right-wing political spectrum (i.e. NF skinheads and the like). The band were obviously pivotal in the burgeoning "oi" (new punk) movement, their predictable, cartoon-like pro-British (actually pro-South of the Watford Gap) football yob anthems getting an airing on their prophetically-titled first lp, 'GREATEST HITS VOLUME 1'. The album secured them Top 30 success, as did their successive sets, 'VOLUME 2' and the live 'VOLUME 3'. One of their hit singles, 'I'M FOREVER BLOWING BUBBLES', had always been a favourite terrace chant for West Ham United supporters, of which the band could count themselves members. The COCKNEY REJECTS live experience never reached the States, due to the country's crazy work permit rule that didn't allow in musicians without proven musical ability (NEW MODEL ARMY later suffered the same fate). In 1984, casting off the cockney prefix, The REJECTS astonishingly turned their backs on the "oi" scene, opting instead for a full-blown heavy metal approach, hinted at on their previous CR release, 'THE WILD ONES'. Now signed to the 'Heavy Metal' label, the band unleashed their 'ROCK THE WILD SIDE' set, although after one further single they broke up. In 1989, The COCKNEY REJECTS reformed for one more studio outing, 'LETHAL', an unremarkable swansong that soon found its way into the bargain bins. • **Songwriters:** All group compositions, except MOTORHEAD (Motorhead) / MAYBE IT'S BECAUSE I'M A LONDONER (. . . Gregg) / TILL THE END OF THE DAY (Kinks) / BLOCKBUSTER (Sweet) / etc.

Album rating: GREATEST HITS VOL.1 (*5) / GREATEST HITS VOL.2 (*5) / GREATEST HITS VOL.3 (*4) / POWER & THE GLORY (*4) / THE WILD ONES (*5) / ROCK THE WILD SIDE (*4) / LETHAL (*4) / THE BEST OF THE COCKNEY REJECTS compilation (*6)

JEFFERSON TURNER – vocals / **MICK GEGGUS** – guitar, vocals / **VINCE RIORDAN** – bass, vocals / **KEITH WARRINGTON** – drums

Small Wonder — not iss.

Jul 79. (7"m) *(SMALL 19)* **FLARES 'N' SLIPPERS. / POLICE CAR / I WANNA BE A STAR** [ ] [-]

E.M.I. — not iss.

Nov 79. (7") *(EMI 5008)* **I'M NOT A FOOL. / EAST END** [65] [-]
Feb 80. (7") *(EMI 5035)* **BAD MAN. / THE NEW SONG** [65] [-]

Zonophone — not iss.

Mar 80. (lp/c) *(ZONO/TC-ZONO 101)* **GREATEST HITS VOL.1** [22] [-]
– I'm not a fool / Headbanger / Bad man / Fighting in the street / Here they come again / Join the Rejects / East End / The new song / Police car / Someone like you / (They're gonna) Put me away / Are you ready to rock / Where the hell is Babylon?. *(cd-iss. Mar94 on 'Dojo'+=; DOJOCD 136)* – Shitter / I'm forever blowing bubbles / West Side boys. *(cd re-iss. May99 on 'Rhythm Vicar'; PREACH 011CD)*
Apr 80. (7"yellow) *(Z 2)* **THE GREATEST COCKNEY RIPOFF. / HATE OF THE CITY** [21] [-]
May 80. (7") *(Z 4)* **I'M FOREVER BLOWING BUBBLES. / WEST SIDE BOYS** [35] [-]
Jul 80. (7") *(Z 6)* **WE CAN DO ANYTHING. / 15 NIGHTS** [ ] [-]
Oct 80. (7") *(Z 10)* **WE ARE THE FIRM. / WAR ON THE TERRACES** [ ] [-]
Oct 80. (lp/c) *(ZONO/TC-ZONO 102)* **GREATEST HITS VOL.2** [23] [-]
– War on the terraces / In the underworld / Oi, oi, oi / Hate of the city / With the boys / Urban guerilla / The rocker / The greatest Cockney rip-off / Sitting in a cell / On the waterfront / We can do anything / It's alright / Subculture / Blockbuster. *(cd-iss. Mar94 on 'Dojo'+=; DOJOCD 138)* – 15 nights / We are the firm. *(lp re-iss. Jan98; DOJOLP 138)*
Mar 81. (7"m) *(Z 20)* **EASY LIFE. / MOTORHEAD / HANG 'EM HIGH** [ ] [-]
Apr 81. (lp) *(ZEM 101)* **GREATEST HITS VOL.3 (LIVE AND LOUD) (live)** [27] [-]
– The rocker / Bad man / I'm not a fool / On the waterfront / On the run / Hate of the city / Easy life / War on the terraces / Fighting in the streets / Greatest Cockney rip-off / Join the Rejects / Police car / East End / Motorhead / Hang 'em high. *(re-iss. Dec87 as 'LIVE AND LOUD' on 'Link'; LINKLP 09) (cd-iss. Nov94 on 'Dojo'; DOJOCD 168)*
Jun 81. (7") *(Z 21)* **ON THE STREETS AGAIN. / LONDON** [ ] [-]
Jul 81. (lp) *(ZONO 105)* **POWER AND THE GLORY** [ ] [-]
– Power and the glory / Because I'm in love / On the run / Lumon / Friends / Van bollocks / Teenage fantasy / It's over / On the streets again / B.Y.C. / The greatest story ever told. *(<cd-iss. Nov94 on 'Dojo'; DOJOCD 174>) (<cd re-iss. Oct99 on 'Captain Oi'; AHOYCD 122>)*

A.K.A. — not iss.

Nov 82. (lp) *(AKA 1)* **THE WILD ONES** [ ] [-]
– Way of the rocker / City of lights / Rock'n'roll dream / Till the end of the day / Some play dirty / Satellite city / Let me rock you / Victim of the cheap wine / Hell's a long way to go / Heat of the night.
Nov 82. (7") *(AKS 102)* **TILL THE END OF THE DAY. / ROCK & ROLL DREAM** [ ] [-]

Heavy Metal — not iss.

Nov 84. (lp/c; as The REJECTS) *(HMR LP/MC 22)* **ROCK THE WILD SIDE** [ ] [-]
– I ain't nothin' / I saw the light / Back to the start / I can't forget / Quiet storm / Feeling my way / Leave it / Fourth summer / Jog on.

FM Revolver — not iss.

Mar 85. (7"; as The REJECTS) *(VHF 7)* **BACK TO THE START. / LEAVE IT** [ ] [-]

— disbanded 1985; all retired to other work; re-formed in 1990

Neat — not iss.

Jul 90. (lp/cd) *(NEAT/+CD 1049)* **LETHAL** [ ] [-]
– Bad man down / Penitentiary / Struttin' my stuff / Lethal weapon / Rough diamond / Go get it / Down'n'out / One way ticket / Once a rocker / Take me higher. *(cd+=)* – Down the line / Mean city / See you later. *(re-iss. Dec95; same)*

– compilations, others, etc. –

Aug 85. (lp) *Wonderful World; (WOWLP 2)* **UNHEARD REJECTS 1979-1981** [ ] [-]
(cd-iss. Mar95 & Mar99 on 'Step 1'+=; STEPCD 020) – FLARES 'N' SLIPPERS
Aug 86. (lp) *Dojo; (DOJOLP 32)* **WE ARE THE FIRM** [ ] [-]
May 93. (cd) *Dojo; (DOJOCD 82)* **THE BEST OF THE COCKNEY REJECTS** [ ] [-]
– Flares 'n' slippers / Police car / I'm not a fool / East end / Bad man / Headbanger / Join the rejects / Where the hell is Babylon / War on the terraces / Oi oi oi / Hate of the city / Rocker / The greatest Cockney rip-off / We can do anything / We are the firm / I'm forever blowing bubbles / Here we go again / Motorhead (live) / Easy life (live) / On the streets again / Power and the glory / Teenage fantasy.
Nov 94. (cd) *Loma; (LOMACD 38)* **THE WILD ONES / LETHAL** [ ] [-]
Mar 97. (cd) *Anagram; (<CDPUNK 90>)* **THE PUNK SINGLES COLLECTION** [ ] [ ] Sep99
Nov 97. (cd) *Can Can; (CANCAN 005CD)* **OI OI OI** [ ] [-]
May 99. (cd) *Harry May; (<MAYO 102>)* **THE GREATEST COCKNEY RIP-OFF** [ ] [ ] Jul99
Aug 99. (cd) *Anagram; (<CDPUNK 113>)* **THE VERY BEST OF THE COCKNEY REJECTS** [ ] [ ] Sep99
Feb 00. (cd) *Rhythm Vicar; (PREACH 021CD)* **GREATEST HITS VOL.4** [ ] [-]
Aug 00. (cd) *Victory; <VE 133>* **BACK ON THE STREET** [-] [ ]

COCK SPARRER

Formed: London, England . . . 1977 by 'Shock Troops', STEVE BURGESS and STEVE BRUCE. Having originally sold out having to 'Decca', these bovver boy punk rockers released two singles before the fall of '77. 'RUNNIN' RIOT' and a cover of the Rolling Stones' 'WE LOVE YOU', didn't exactly set the music world alight, although it did manage to give the band a foothold into the emerging "oi" scene; they're still pumping out the volume in 2000/1.

Album rating: SHOCK TROOPS mini (*4) / RUNNIN' RIOT IN '84 (*4) / TRUE GRIT (*4) / THE BEST OF COCK SPARRER compilation (*5)

STEVE BURGESS – bass / **STEVE BRUCE** – drums (+ LAMMIN, McFAULL + BEAUFOY)

Decca — not iss.

Jul 77. (7") *(FR 13710)* **RUNNIN' RIOT. / SISTER SUZIE** [ ] [-]
(re-iss. Jun89 on 'Damaged Goods'; FNARR 5)
Oct 77. (7"/12") *(FR/LFR 13732)* **WE LOVE YOU. / CHIP ON MY SHOULDER** [ ] [-]

— one of them joined The LITTLE ROOSTERS who released a few singles

Carrere — not iss.

Nov 82. (7") *(CAR 255)* **ENGLAND BELONGS TO ME. / ARGY BARGY** [ ] [-]

Razor — not iss.

Nov 83. (m-lp) *(RAZ 9)* **SHOCK TROOPS** [ ] [-]
– Where are they now / Riot squad / Working / Take 'em all / We're coming back / England belongs to me / Watch your back / I got your number / Secret army / Droogs don't run / Out on an island / Argy bargy / Colonel Bogey. *(cd-iss. Oct90; RAZCD 9) (<cd re-iss. Aug93 & Nov97 on 'Captain Oi'; AHOYCD 4>) (<re-iss. Nov00 on 'Taang!' lp/cd; TAANG 152/+CD>) (cd re-iss. Mar01 on 'Harry May'; MAYDP 006)*

Syndicate — not iss.

Oct 84. (lp) *(SYNLP 7)* **RUNNING RIOT IN '84** [ ] [-]
(re-iss. 1988 on 'Link'; LINKLP 032) (re-iss. May00 on 'Bitzcore'; BC 1724) (cd-iss. Nov00 on 'Captain Oi'; AHOYCD 057) (cd-iss. Mar01 on 'Harry May'; MAYDP 009)

— the two STEVE's were joined by DARYL SMITH on rhythm guitar

Bitzcore — not iss.

Jun 96. (cd) *<1692>* **GUILTY AS CHARGED** [ ] [-]
Jun 96. (cd-ep) *<1697>* **RUN AWAY EP** [ ] [-]
Nov 97. (cd/lp) *<(BC 1710 CD/LP)>* **TWO MONKEYS** [ ] [ ] Jul98
– A.U. / Before the flame dies / Tart / Lies? / East End girl / Anthem / Time to be me / I live in Marbella / Bats out / Battersea Bardot / I feel a death coming on / Back home / Goodbye.

T.K.O. — T.K.O.

Sep 00. (lp/cd) *(<TKOROUND 055/+CD>)* **RUNNING RIOT ACROSS THE USA** [ ] [ ]
– Riot squad / Watch your back / Working / Teenage heart / Argy bargy / Runaway Johnny / Take 'em all / A.U. / I got your number / Because you're young / We love you / Secret army / Where are they now? / Runnin' riot / Sunday stripper / Chip on your shoulder / England belongs to me / We're coming back / England belongs to me (reprise).

– compilations, etc. –

Mar 87. (lp) *Razor; (RAZ 26)* **TRUE GRIT** [ ] [-]
– We love you / Sister Suzie / Platinum blonde / Taken for a ride / Again again / Runnin' riot / Chip on my shoulder / Watcha gonna do about it / Teenage heart / I need a witness.
Dec 87. (lp) *Link; (LINKLP 05)* **LIVE AND LOUD (live)** [ ] [-]
(cd-iss. Jul98 on 'Pinhead'; PINCD 103)
Aug 92. (cd) *Slogan; (SLOGCD 4)* **SHOCK TROOPS / RUNNIN' RIOT IN '84** [ ] [-]
(<re-iss. Jun98 on 'Step 1'; STEPCD 028>)
Nov 97. (cd) *CanCan; (CANCAN 007CD)* **ENGLAND BELONGS TO ME** [ ] [ ]
Feb 98. (cd; shared with The BUSINESS) *Step 1; (STEPCD 004)* **LIVE AND LOUD** [ ] [-]
Jun 98. (cd/lp) *Step 1; (<STEP CD/LP 014>)* **RUMOURS CARRY MORE WEIGHT THAN FACT: BEST OF COCK SPARRER** [ ] [ ] Mar01
Oct 98. (cd) *Captain Oi; (<AHOYCD 036>)* **RARITIES** [ ] [ ] Jan00
Jun 99. (cd) *Harry May; (<MAYOCD 012>)* **CHIP ON MY SHOULDER** [ ] [ ] Apr00
Apr 00. (cd) *Dr.Strange; (<DSR 73CD>)* **BLOODY MINDED: THE BEST OF COCK SPARRER** [ ] [ ] Sep97

May 00. (m-lp/m-cd) *D.S.S.; (<DSS 004/+CD>)* **DIAMONDS & PEARLS**

COLD

Formed: Jacksonville, Florida, USA . . . 1997 originally as GRUNDIG by frontman SCOOTER WARD, KELLY HAYES, JEREMY MARSHALL and SAM McCANDLESS; guitarist TERRY BALSAMO was added much later. The metallic frenzy that is COLD were apparently discovered by LIMP BIZKIT's singer FRED DURST and, he in turn found them a producer, Ross Robinson, who had also worked with SEPULTURA and KORN. The band looked set for a healthy career following the release of their excellent eponymous early 1998 debut set for 'A&M'; unfortunately the climate turned chilly when their label went under later that year. COLD were back on a new label ('Interscope') for their long-awaited follow-up, '13 WAYS TO BLEED ONSTAGE' (2000), another skull-breaking set that should have done better commercially.

Album rating: COLD (*8) / 13 WAYS TO BLEED ON STAGE (*7)

SCOOTER WARD – vocals, guitar / **KELLY HAYES** – guitar / **JEREMY MARSHALL** – bass / **SAM McCANDLESS** – drums

A&M A&M

Feb 98. (cd/c) *<(540829-2/-4)>* **COLD**
– Go away / Give / Ugly / Everyone dies / Strip her down / Insane / Goodbye cruel world / Serial killer / Superstar / Switch / Make her sick.

Mar 98. (7") *(582570-7)* **GIVE. / MAKES HER SICK**
(cd-s+=) *(582571-2)* – Blame / ('A'-alternative mix).

May 98. (7") *(582672-7)* **GO AWAY. / SPACE ODDITY**
(cd-s+=) *(582673-2)* – ('A'-Eye Socket remix) / ('A'-DJ Lethal remix).

—— added **TERRY BALSAMO** – guitar

Interscope Interscope

Sep 00. (cd) *<(490726-2)>* **13 WAYS TO BLEED ON STAGE** 98
– Just got wicked / She said / No one / End of the world / Confession / It's all good / Send in the clowns / Same drugs / Anti love song / The witch / Sick of man / Outerspace / Bleed.

COLD CHISEL (see under ⇒ BARNES, Jimmy)

Allen COLLINS BAND (see under ⇒ LYNYRD SKYNYRD)

COME

Formed: (based) Boston, Massachusetts, USA . . . 1989 by former LIVE SKULL and UZI mainwoman, THALIA ZEDEK, along with former CODEINE man, CHRIS BROKAW and a rhythm section of ARTHUR JOHNSON and SEAN O'BRIEN. Quite possibly the most convincing exponent of brooding feminine intensity since PATTI SMITH (an obvious influence alongside HOLE's COURTNEY LOVE), ZEDEK first stamped her tortured personality over the emerging grunge scene in summer '91 with the 'CAR' single. Hailed by the critics, the track introduced the trademark COME sound, crushing fragments of SONIC YOUTH, NIRVANA and even BLACK SABBATH into painful emotional wounds. A follow-up single, 'FAST PISS BLUES', further raised expectations for debut album, 'ELEVEN: ELEVEN' (1992) and cemented COME's growing reputation as true guardians of the blues' dark flame. The album itself was met with almost universal acclaim, from the broken-down desolation of 'SUBMERGE' onwards a seriously heavy going trip through COME's often despairing world. Switching from 'Matador' to 'Beggars Banquet', they previewed follow-up set, 'DON'T ASK, DON'T TELL' (1994), with the slo-mo frustration of 'WRONG SIDE', a flavour of the album's mogadon-pace vegetation. Some fresh blood was injected with 1996's 'NEAR LIFE EXPERIENCE' album, however, O'BRIEN and JOHNSON replaced initially by BUNDY K BROWN and MAC McNEILLY and then TARA JANE O'NEILL and KEVIN COULTAS. Guests BETH HEINBERG and ED YAZIJIAN's piano and violin flourishes also added a bit of melancholy colour and subtlety to proceedings. Around the same time the band also backed STEVE WYNN on his solo set, 'Melting In The Dark', while BUNDY and BROKAW hooked up with each other once more as part of the acclaimed PULLMAN project. COME returned in 1998 with another new rhythm section, WINSTON BRAMEN and DANIEL COUGHLIN taking the band back to basics on 'GENTLY DOWN THE STREAM'. • **Covered:** I GOT THE BLUES (Rolling Stones).

Album rating: ELEVEN: ELEVEN (*6) / DON'T ASK, DON'T TELL (*7) / NEAR LIFE EXPERIENCE (*7) / GENTLY DOWN THE STREAM (*6)

THALIA ZEDEK – vocals, guitar, harmonica (ex-LIVE SKULL, ex-UZI) / **CHRIS BROKAW** – guitar, vocals, keyboards (ex-CODEINE) / **ARTHUR JOHNSON** – drums (ex-BAR B Q KILLERS) / **SEAN O'BRIEN** – bass (ex-KILKENNY CATS)

Glitterhouse unknown

Aug 91. (7"white) **CAR. / LAST MISTAKE** -

Apr 92. (12"ep/cd-ep) **CAR. / LAST MISTAKE / SUBMERGE** -

Placebo Matador

Dec 92. (lp/cd) *(PILL A/CD 1) <OLE 045>* **ELEVEN: ELEVEN**
– Submerge / Dead Molly / Brand new vein / Off to one side / Bell / William / Sad eyes / Power failure / Orbit. *(cd+=)* – Car / Last mistake.

Jan 93. (10"m) *(PILL 3) <OLE 027>* **FAST PISS BLUES. / I GOT THE BLUES / BRAND NEW VEIN** Nov92

Beggars Banquet Matador

Apr 94. (7"/12"/cd-s) *(BBQ 34/+T/CD) <OLE 086>* **WRONG SIDE. / LOIN OF THE SURF / SVK** Mar94

Oct 94. (cd/c/lp) *(BBQ CD/MC/LP 160) <OLE 108>* **DON'T ASK, DON'T TELL**
– Finish line / Mercury falls / Yr reign / Poison / Let's get lost / String / German song / In/Out / Wrong side / Arrive.

Feb 95. (10"ep/cd-ep) *(BBQ 48 TT/CD)* **STRING / WHO JUMPED ON MY GRAVE. / GERMAN SONG / ANGELHEAD** -

—— **THALIA + CHRIS** were joined by **BUNDY K BROWN** – bass (ex-ELEVENTH DREAM DAY) / **MAC McNEILLY** – drums (then) **TARA JANE O'NEIL** – bass / **KEVIN COULTAS** – drums / guests **BETH HEINBERG** – piano / **ED YAZIJIAN** – violin

Domino Matador

Apr 96. (cd-s) *(RUG 43CD)* **SECRET NUMBER / PRIZE / HURRICANE II** -

May 96. (m-cd/m-lp) *(WIG CD/LP 25) <OLE 192>* **NEAR LIFE EXPERIENCE**
– Hurricane / Weak as the moon / Secret number / Bitten / Shoot me first / Walk on's / Half life / Slow-eyed.

—— around this period, they worked with STEVE WYNN (ex-DREAM SYNDICATE) on his 1996 set, 'Melting In The Dark'.

—— BUNDY became part of DIRECTIONS IN MUSIC and side-project, PULLMAN, the latter also featuring BROKAW

—— **ZEDEK + BROKAW** recruited **WINSTON BRAMEN** – bass / **DANIEL COUGHLIN** – drums, percussion

Feb 98. (cd/d-lp) *(WIG CD/LP 43) <OLE 254>* **GENTLY DOWN THE STREAM**
– One piece / Recidivist / Stomp / Sorry too late / Saints around my neck / Silk city / Middle of nowhere / The fade-outs / A jam blues / New coat / The former model / March.

– compilations, etc. –

1990's. (lp) *Come; <88203>* **RAMPTON** -
– Submerge / Dead Molly / Brand new vein / Off to one side / Bell / William / Sad eyes / Power failure / Orbit / Fast piss blues / I got the blues.

COMMON RIDER

Formed: California, USA . . . 1998 by Buddhist monk! and former OPERATION IVY frontman, JESSE MICHAELS, who had quite literally come out of hiding. Surrounding himself with like-minded ska-punks, bassist MAS GIORGINI (producer of a multitude of 'Lookout!' acts) and former SCREECHING WEASEL drummer DAN LUMLEY (also like the aforementioned MAS, a one-time member of SQUIRTGUN). The following year, CR released their debut set, 'LAST WAVE ROCKERS', a record that also fused reggae/dub, dancehall punk and melodic pop-punk.

Album rating: LAST WAVE ROCKERS (*6)

JESSE MICHAELS – vocals, guitar (ex-OPERATION IVY) / **MAS GIORGINI** – bass (ex-SQUIRTGUN) / **DAN LUMLEY** – drums (ex-SQUIRTGUN, ex-SCREECHING WEASEL) / also **MARK ARDITO** – guitar

Lookout! Lookout!

Jun 99. (cd/lp) *<(LK 226 CD/LP)>* **LAST WAVE ROCKERS**
– Classics of love / Castaways / Signal signal / Carry on / Rise or fall / True rulers / Conscious burning / On Broadway / Heatseekers / A place where we can stay / Walk down the river / Rough redemption / Deep spring / Angels at play.

COMPANY OF WOLVES

Formed: New York, USA . . . 1989 by brothers STEVE and JOHN CONTE, plus KYF BREWER and FRANKIE LAROCKA. Influenced by AEROSMITH, BAD COMPANY and the like, COMPANY OF WOLVES were initially a studio bound outfit, although they soon got underway live following a breezy, eponymous JEFF GLIXMAN-produced debut album in 1990.

Album rating: COMPANY OF WOLVES (*5) / SHAKERS AND TAMBOURINES (*4)

KYF BREWER (b. KEITH) – vocals / **STEVE CONTE** – guitar / **JOHN CONTE** – bass / **FRANKIE LAROCKA** – drums (ex-BRYAN ADAMS, ex-JOHN WAITE)

Mercury Mercury

Feb 90. (cd/c/lp) *<(842184-2/-4/-1)>* **COMPANY OF WOLVES**
– Call of the wild / Hangin' by a thread / Jilted / Distance / Romance on the rocks / Can't love ya, can't leave ya / Hell's kitchen / St. James infirmary / My ship / I don't wanna be loved / Girl / Everybody's baby.

—— split after they were dropped by their record label – recently re-formed

R.Y.F. R.Y.F.

Sep 99. (cd) *<(RYFC 004)>* **SHAKERS AND TAMBOURINES**
– Labor of love / Words you say / Miles away / Dear life / Can't stand to crawl / The distance / Simon screams / Everybody's baby / In my blood / Rocks in yo' head (demo).

COMPULSION

Formed: King's Cross, North London . . . early 1992 by Irish exiles JOSEPHMARY, GARRET LEE, SID RAINEY and JAN-WILLEM ALKEMA, all veterans of the alternative music scene. JOSEPHMARY and LEE, as members of THEE AMAZING COLOSSAL MEN, had even been signed to 'Virgin' at one point although the deal fell through and the band split halfway through the recording of their second album. COMPULSION had no such headaches, forming their own label, 'Fabulon', after a year of twiddling their thumbs and fruitlessly seeking out pub gigs. An eponymous debut EP arrived in early '93, taking no prisoners with a razorwire guitar attack and vicious, strangulated vocals. The lyrical themes were equally uncompromising, the NIRVANA-esque 'RAPEJACKET' putting forward the idea that everyone is raped by life's hardships in one way or another. 'NINE FOURTH', meanwhile, recalled with disgust yet another Conservative electoral victory. With airplay from Radio One DJ, Mark Goodier, and support from the music press, COMPULSION already had a healthy buzz going by the release of follow-up EP, 'CASSEROLE'. Tours with CREDIT TO THE NATION and SHED SEVEN as well as an appearance at that year's Phoenix festival prompted interest from 'One Little Indian', through whom they released mini-set, 'SAFETY' and full-length debut album, 'COMFORTER' (1994). Drawing praise from both the indie and rock communities, the album carried on where the EP's left off, mixing sonic guitar barrages with more melancholy reflections and combining bitter realism with flights of surreal fancy and black humour. The record even nudged into the Top 60 although spin-off single, 'BASKETCASE', failed to chart. After a prolonged absence, COMPULSION returned in 1996 with follow-up album, 'THE FUTURE IS MEDIUM', apparently recorded in one session.

Album rating: COMFORTER (*6) / THE FUTURE IS MEDIUM (*6)

JOSEPHMARY – vocals / **GARRET LEE** – guitar / **SID RAINEY** – bass / **JAN-WILLEM ALKEMA** (b. Holland) – drums

Fabulon | not iss.

Feb 93. (12"ep) *(FLON 12-01)* **COMPULSION EP** [ ] [-]
– Find time / Rapejacket / Easterman / Ninefourth / Purring not laughing / Accident ahead.

Apr 93. (12"ep) *(FLON 12-02)* **CASSEROLE EP** [ ] [-]
– Yabba yabba yes yes yes / Crying / How do I breathe? / Here comes Ambrose Beasley / Security.

One Little Indian | Elektra

Oct 93. (m-lp/m-c/m-cd) *(TPLP 49M/+C/CD)* **SAFETY** [ ] [-]

Mar 94. (cd-ep) *<66228>* **BOOGIE WOOGIE** [-] [ ]
– Accident ahead / Ninefourth / Yabba yabba yes yes yes / Why do we care? / Find time.

One Little Indian | Interscope

Mar 94. (lp/c/cd) *(TPLP 59/+C/CD) <92456>* **COMFORTER** [59] [ ] Jun94
– Rapejacket / Basketcase / Mall monarchy / Ariadne / Late again / Air-raid for the neighbours / Yancy Dangerfield's delusions / Lovers / I am John's brain / Bad cooking / Dick, Dale, Rick and Ricky / Domestique / Oh my fool life / Jean could be wrong. *(cd+=)***EPs** – COMPULSION + CASSEROLE

Jun 94. (c-s) *(95 TP7C)* **BASKETCASE /** [ ] [-]
(12"+=/cd-s+=) *(95 TP12/TP7CD)* –

Feb 96. (7") *(105 TP7)* **QUESTION TIME FOR THE PROLES. / SPOTLIGHT INTO SPACE** [ ] [-]
(cd-s) *(105 TP7CD)* – ('A'side) / Millions / Drop / Burst.

May 96. (lp/c/cd) *(TPLP 79/+C/CD)* **THE FUTURE IS MEDIUM** [ ] [-]
– All we heard was a dull thud / Question time for the proles / Juvenile scene detective / It's great / They're breeding the grey things again / Fast songs / Western culture collector / Happy monsters / Belly laugh / Is this efficient living? / Down the edifice / Happy ending / Burst / Lost on Abbey Road / Spotlight into space / Me.

Jun 96. (7"/c-s) *(115 TP7/+C)* **JUVENILE SCENE DETECTIVE. /** [ ] [-]
(cd-s+=) *(115 TP7CD)* –

—— disbanded after above

CONEY HATCH

Formed: Toronto, Ontario, Canada ... early 80's by CARL DIXON, ANDY CURRAN, STEVE SHELSKI and DAVE KETCHUM. Signed to the 'Phonogram' stable, they released a stylistically diverse eponymous set in 1982/83, KIM MITCHELL (of the group MAX WEBSTER) taking up the production reins on this heavyweight, jazz-inflected debut. 'OUTA HAND' was next up, making the US Top 200 despite its widely criticised production. A final effort, 'FRICTION' in 1985, saw the band utilise a new drummer, NORMAN CONNORS, too late to save the band from an inevitable split.

Album rating: CONEY HATCH (*6) / OUTA HAND (*3) / FRICTION (*4) / BEST OF THREE compilation (*5)

CARL DIXON – vocals, guitar / **ANDY CURRAN** – bass, vocals / **STEVE SHELSKI** – lead guitar, vocals / **DAVE KETCHUM** – drums, percussion

Mercury | Mercury

Mar 83. (7"/12") *(HATCH 1/12)* **HEY OPERATOR. / DEVILS BACK** [ ] [-]

Apr 83. (lp/c) *(MERS/+C 15) <SRM1 4056>* **CONEY HATCH** [ ] [ ] Nov82
– Devil's back / You ain't got me / Stand up / No sleep tonight / Love poison / We've got the night / Hey operator / I'll do the talkin' / Victim of rock / Monkey bars.

Vertigo | Mercury

Aug 83. (lp) *(VERL 7) <812869-1>* **OUTA HAND** [ ] [ ]
– Don't say make me / Shake it / First time for everything / Some like it hot / To feel the feeling again / Too far gone / Love games / Fallen angel / Music of the night.

—— **BARRY CONNORS** – drums; repl. KETCHUM

Apr 85. (7"/12") *(VER/+X 18)* **THIS AIN'T LOVE. / HE'S A CHAMPION** [ ] [ ]

Apr 85. (lp) *(VERL 23) <824307-1>* **FRICTION** [ ] [ ]
– This ain't love / She's gone / Wrong side of town / Girl from last night's dream / Coming to get you / Fantasy / He's a champion / State line / Burning love. *(cd-iss. Jan98 on 'Anthem'; ANK 1070)*

—— split in 1986

– compilations, etc. –

Nov 97. (cd) *Anthem; <1065>* **BEST OF THREE** [-] [ ]
– Devil's deck / You ain't got me / Stand up / Hey operator / Monkey bars / Where I draw the line / Don't say make me / Shake it / First time for everything / Some like it hot / To feel the feeling again / This ain't love / Wrong side of town / Girl from last night's dreams / Fantasy / He's a champion / Fuel for the fire.

CONFLICT

Formed: Eltham, England ... 1979 by COLIN JERWOOD, JOHN CLIFFORD, GRAHAM and KEN. Debut EP, 'THE HOUSE THAT MAN BUILT', was unleashed by the 'Crass' label in 1982 although the bulk of their output surfaced on their own 'Mortarhate' imprint. CONFLICT's first bonafide long player came in the shape of 1982's 'IT'S TIME TO SEE WHO'S WHO', a savage set of hardcore/Oi!-style punk which substituted any discernible tune ('YOUNG PARASITES' being the exception) for a barrage of abuse aimed mainly at centralised Government but also taking in meat eaters, the media, fame-hungry musicians and big business. 1983's 'SERENADE IS DEAD' single was the first release on their own label, the band adamantly standing by their anarchist agenda over subsequent albums 'INCREASE THE PRESSURE' (1984) and 'THE UNGOVERNABLE FORCE' (1985). Floating member STEVE IGNORANT was drafted in after JERWOOD was assaulted in a pub fight in his home town, the former CRASS man helping out on 1987's 'TURNING REBELLION INTO MONEY' and staying for last gasp albums, 'THE FINAL CONFLICT' (1988) and 'AGAINST ALL ODDS' (1989). As with many bands of their ilk, the message usually took precedence over the music, CONFLICT's hardline stance over a wide range of political issues often seeing them in direct confrontation with the authorities. After an uncharacteristic silence of almost four years, the band attended to unfinished business with 1993's 'CONCLUSION', reworking their debut album the following year and releasing the defiant 'WE WON'T TAKE NO MORE' in 1995.

Album rating: IT'S TIME TO SEE WHO'S WHO (*4) / INCREASE THE PRESSURE (*5) / THE UNGOVERNABLE FORCE (*5) / ONLY STUPID BASTARDS USE EMI (*4) / STANDARD ISSUE compilation (*6) / TURNING REBELLION INTO MONEY (*4) / THE FINAL CONFLICT (*4) / AGAINST ALL ODDS (*4) / CONCLUSION (*4)

COLIN JERWOOD (b. 6 May'62) – vocals / **GRAHAM** – guitar / **JOHN CLIFFORD** – bass / **KEN** – drums

Crass | not iss.

May 82. (7"ep) *(221984-1)* **THE HOUSE THAT MAN BUILT** [ ] [-]
– Conflict / Wargames / I've had enough / Blind attack.
above with **PAULINE BECK** – vocals

Xntrix | not iss.

Oct 82. (7"ep) *(XN 2001)* **LIVE AT THE CENTRE IBERICO (live)** [ ] [-]
– Kings + punks / Meat means murder / Exploitation / Bullshit broadcast / Vietnam serenade / No island of dreams. *(re-iss. 1987 on 'Mortarhate'; MORT 7)*

—— **PACO** – drums + **PAUL FRYDAY** – visuals, tapes repl. KEN

—— **STEVE IGNORANT** – guitar (of CRASS) repl. GRAHAM

Corpus Christi | not iss.

Dec 82. (lp) *(CHRIST IT'S 3)* **IT'S TIME TO SEE WHO'S WHO** [ ] [-]
– Young parasites / Kids and punks / Meat means murder / No island of dreams / Great what? / The guilt & the glory / 1824 overture / Bullshit broadcast / One nation under the bomb / Blind attack / Vietnam serenade / Blood morons / Exploitation / Crazy governments.

Aug 83. (7") *(CHRIST IT'S 4)* **A NATION OF ANIMAL LOVERS. / LIBERATE** [ ] [-]

—— STEVE returned to CRASS

Mortarhate | not iss.

Nov 83. (7"ep) *(MORT 001)* **SERENADE IS DEAD** [ ] [-]

Jun 84. (lp) *(MORT 006)* **INCREASE THE PRESSURE** [ ] [-]
– Increase the pressure / Law and order (throughout the land) / From protest to resistance / Tough shit Mickey / Punk inn it / As others see us / Cruise / The positive junk / The systems maintains / The guilt and the glory / Stop the city / One nation under a bomb / Blind attack / Vietnam serenade / Blood morons / Exploitation / Whichever way you want it. *(<re-iss. Dec96 lp/cd; MORT/+CD 006>)*

Mar 85. (7") *(MORT 008)* **THIS IS NOT ENOUGH. /** [ ] [-]

Oct 85. (7") *(MORT 015)* **THE BATTLE CONTINUES. / (same track)** [ ] [-]
(re-iss. May94; same)

Aug 86. (lp) *(MORT 020)* **THE UNGOVERNABLE FORCE** [ ] [-]
– You cannot win / The ungovernable farce / A piss in the ocean / Crass / Custom rock / 1986 the battle continues / Mental mania / The ungovernable force / They said that / Force or service / The arrest / Statement / The day before / This is the A.L.F. / To be continued. *(<re-iss. Dec96 lp/cd; MORT/+CD 020>)*

Nov 86. (12") *(MORT 22)* **THE FINAL CONFLICT** [ ] [-]

—— **STEVE** returned when JERWOOD was assaulted in a pub fight.

Jun 87. (d-lp/c) *(MORT/+C 030)* **TURNING REBELLION INTO MONEY (live)** [ ] [-]
– Banned in the UK / The piss in the ocean / Increased pressure / Serenade is dead / They said that / From protest to resistance / Big hand / G song / I ain't thick it's a trick / So what / Punk is dead / Rival tribal / Statement. *(re-iss. Dec96 lp/cd; MORT/+CD 030)*

May 88. (lp) *(FUND 1)* **FROM PROTEST TO RESISTANCE** [-] [-] mail-o

Jul 88. (lp/c) *(MORT/+C 040)* **STANDARD ISSUE** (compilation) [ ] [-]
– Conflict / The guilt and the glory / From protest to resistence – Tough s*** Mickey / Reality whitewash / Whichever way you want it / The serenade is dead – The positive junk – The system maintains / This is not enough – Neither is this / Mighty and superior – To whom it may concern. *(<re-iss. Dec96 cd/c; MORT CD/C 040>) (c+=)* – INCREASE THE PRESSURE

Nov 88. (lp) *(MORT 050)* **THE FINAL CONFLICT** [ ] [-]
– Countdown to confrontation / Let the battle commence / I heard a rumour / The

cord is cut / Barricades and broken dreams / Do you get the picture / The 'A' team / These things take time / Radio trash / The final conflict. *(<re-iss. Dec96 lp/cd; MORT/+CD 050>)*

Jul 89. (lp/c) *(MORT/+C 060)* **AGAINST ALL ODDS**
– Against all odds / Slaughter of innocence / Assured mutual destruction / The greatest show on Earth / A message to who / A state of mind. *(<re-iss. May98 lp/cd; MORT LP/CD 060>)*

—— split but re-formed in 1993 on same label

Mortarhate Cleopatra

Oct 93. (7") *(MORT 080)* **THESE COLOURS DON'T RUN. /**
(cd-s+=) *(MORT 080CD)* –

Nov 93. (cd/lp) *(MORT CD/LP 100)* *<9486>* **CONCLUSION** May94
– To live on in hearts / The right to reply / Someday soon / No more excuses / A declaration of independence / The institute of dreams / Climbing the stairs / A question of priorities / Is never to die. *(cd+=)* – These colours don't run.

Apr 94. (cd/lp) *(MORT CD/LP 110)* **IT'S TIME TO SEE WHO'S WHO NOW** (re-workings)
– Berkshire c*** / No island of dreams / Conflict / Great what? / The guilt and the glory / One nation under a bomb / Blind attack / Vietnam serenade / Blood morons / Exploitation / Meat means murder / Whichever way you want it. *(<cd re-iss. Jul00 on 'Rhythm Vicar'; PREACH 027CD>)*

Jul 95. (cd; by CONFLICT & FRIENDS) *(MORJCD 150)* **WE WON'T TAKE NO MORE**

– compilations, others, etc. –

Oct 87. (12") *Konnexion; (KOMA 788029)* **FROM PROTEST TO RESISTANCE**

May 88. (lp) *Model Army; (THIS NOT 599)* **ONLY STUPID BASTARDS USE EMI**
(cd-iss. Jan95 on 'Mortarhate'; MORTCD 130)

1990's. (lp) *Corpus Christi; (CHRIST 16)* **HOUSE THAT MAN BUILT / TO A NATION OF ANIMAL LOVERS**

Jul 94. (cd) *Cleopatra; (<CLEO 1023CD>)* **DEPLOYING ALL MEANS NECESSARY** Oct93

Jan 96. (cd/lp) *Mortarhate; (MORT CD/LP 170)* **STANDARD ISSUE 2** (1988-1994)

Feb 97. (cd/lp) *Mortarhate; (MORT CD/LP 120)* **IN THE VENUE**

Chris CONNELLY

Born: Edinburgh, Scotland. The one-time mainman of FINITRIBE and a stalwart of The REVOLTING COCKS and PIGFACE, he left the latter band for solo pastures in 1991. Enlisting the help of friends, musicians and co-writers, MARTIN ATKINS, CHRIS BRUCE, WILLIAM TUCKER and STUART ZECHMAN, he began work on his debut UK solo outing ('WHIPLASH BOYCHILD' had already been released by 'Wax Trax!' in the States), 'PHENOBARB BAMBALAM' (1992). The record saw CONNELLY shift dramatically from his dance/industrial roots, the Scotsman – whose girlfriend had just recently committed suicide – adopting a different persona (i.e. SCOTT WALKER, BOWIE!, etc) on each track although the cover of Tom Verlaine's 'SOUVENIR FROM A DREAM', added little to the original. 'WHIPLASH BOYCHILD' was issued officially in Britain a few months later while CONNELLY moonlighted with KILLING JOKE off-shoot industrial metal-rap outfit, MURDER INC. Now living in America, CONNELLY delivered two futher US-only albums, 'SHIPWRECK' (1994) and 'THE ULTIMATE SEASIDE COMPANION' (1997). At the beginning of the millennium, CONNELLY reunited with some of his old chums (GEORDIE WALKER, JAH WOBBLE, MARTIN ATKINS and effects man LEE FRASER) via The DAMAGE MANUAL. This heavy/industrial supergroup of sorts turned up the volume on two efforts in 2000, the mini '1' and 'THE DAMAGE MANUAL'.

Album rating: PHENOBARB BAMBALAM (*6) / WHIPLASH BOYCHILD (*5) / SHIPWRECK (*5) / THE ULTIMATE SEASIDE COMPANION (*5) / BLONDE EXODUS (*6) / Damage Manual: 1 mini (*6) / THE DAMAGE MANUAL (*7)

CHRIS CONNELLY – vocals, pianoforte, keyboards, tapes / **CHRIS BRUCE** – guitars / **MARTIN ATKINS** – drums, percussion / **STUART ZECHMAN** – bass / **WILLIAM TUCKER** – guitar, tapes

Devotion Wax Trax!

Dec 90. (12"/cd-s) *<WAX/+CDS 9141>* **STOWAWAY (Downward Spiral remix) / STOWAWAY (Waking Dream mix). / DAREDEVIL (Third Eye mix)**

Nov 91. (cd/c/lp) *<WAXCD 7134>* **WHIPLASH BOYCHILD**
– Daredevil / Ghost of a saint / This edge of midnight / The last of joy / The amorous Humphrey Plugg / Stowaway / The hawk, the butcher, the killer of beauties / The game is all yours. *(UK-iss.Oct92; CD/T+/DVN 14)(cd+=)* – Confessions of the highest bidder / Stowaway (Daydream mix) / This edge of midnight (sparse).

Feb 92. (cd-ep) *<WAXCDS 9190>* **JULY**
– July / July (version) / This edge of midnight (sparse) / The last of joy (secret mix) / Trash (live – spoken word).

Aug 92. (12") *(12DVN 108)* *<WAX 9190>* **COME DOWN HERE (Swollen fruit cocktail). / COME DOWN HERE (instrumental) / SOUVENIR FROM A DREAM** Jun92
(cd-s+=) *(CDDVN 108)* – ('A'version).

Sep 92. (cd/c/lp) *(CD/T+/DVN 13)* *<WAX 7189>* **PHENOBARB BAMBALAM**
– The whistle blower / July / Souvenir from a dream / Come down here / Too good to be true / Heartburn / No lesser of two evils / Ignition times four / Dirtbox Tennessee. *(cd+=)* – Heartburn (twister mix).

—— retained **TUCKER + BRUCE**

not iss. TVT

1994. (7"blue; as CONNELLY & TUCKER) *<8710-7>* **HEARTBURN. / THE HAWK, THE BUTCHER, THE KILLER OF BEAUTIES**
(cd-s+=) **SONGS FOR SWINGING JUNKIES** *<8710-2>* – July.

1994. (cd/c) *<TVT 7214-2/-4>* **SHIPWRECK**
– Candyman collapse / Spoonfed celeste / What's left but solid gold? / Detestimony III / Anyone's mistake / Drench / The early nighters (for River Phoenix) / Swimming / Model murmur / Meridian afterburn / Shipwreck.

—— next with his band the BELLS:- **RIEFLIN + CHRIS BRUCE + JIM O'ROURKE**

not iss. Hit It!

Oct 97. (cd) *<22>* **THE ULTIMATE SEASIDE COMPANION**
– The fortune / Mississippi palisades / My east is your west / Stray / Empty Sam / No more changing of the guard / Island head / Toledo steel / Caravan / To play a slow game / The ultimate seaside companion / The fortune II. *(UK-iss.Oct00 as '. . .REVISITED' on 'Invisible'+=; INV 174CD)* – Chorus of eyes / Thunderland reel / No more changing of the guard (live) / The fortune (live).

Dream Catcher not iss.

Mar 01. (d-cd) *(CRIDE 40)* **BLONDE EXODUS**
– Generique / London fields / Diamonds eat diamonds / Blonde exodus (part 1) / Twilight shiner / Blue hooray / Magnificent wing / The Long weekend / Julie Delpy / Blonde exodus (part 2) / Closing titles / Blonde strings / Moonlight feels right. *(UK-iss.+=)* – THE ULTIMATE SEASIDE COMPANION

—— CONNELLY was also part of cosmopolitan industrial group, MURDER INC.

MURDER INC.

CONNELLY – vocals / **GEORDIE WALKER** – guitar (ex-KILLING JOKE) / **PAUL RAVEN** – bass (ex-KILLING JOKE) / **JOHN BECHDEL** – guitar, keyboards / **MARTIN ATKINS** (ex-PUBLIC IMAGE LTD) + **PAUL FERGUSON** – drums (ex-KILLING JOKE)

Devotion Touch & Go

May 92. (cd/c/lp) *(CD/T+/DVN 9)* *<TG 13>* **MURDER INC.**
– Supergrass / Murder Inc. / Mania / Hole in the wall / Uninvited guest / Gambit / Red black / Last of the urgents / Mrs. Whiskey name. *(re-iss. Feb94 on 'Invisible' lp/cd; INV 016/+CD)*

Jun 92. (12"ep/cd-ep) *(12/CD DVN 106)* **CORPUSCLE EP**
– Murder Inc. (busted corpsicle mix) / Mania (righteous mix 1 & 2) / Motion sickness. *(c-ep-iss.Jul93 on 'Invisible'; INV 016CS)*

Invisible not iss.

Jun 93. (12"ltd.) *(INV 014)* **MANIA**

Jun 00. (cd) *<(INV 158)>* **LOCATE SUBVERT TERMINATE: THE COMPLETE MURDER INC.** (compilation) Nov99

DAMAGE MANUAL

CHRIS CONNELLY – vocals / **GEORDIE WALKER** – guitar / **JAH WOBBLE** – bass (solo artist, ex-PiL) / **MARTIN ATKINS** – drums / **LEE FRASER** – sampler/effects

Invisible Invisible

Apr 00. (m-cd) *(INV 143CD)* **1**
– Sunset gun / Damage addict / Scissor quickstep / Blame and demand / Leave the ground / Bagman damage / M60 dub.

Dream Catcher

Sep 00. (cd) *(CRIDE 31)* **THE DAMAGE MANUAL**
– King mob / Age of urges / Top ten severed / Peepshow ghosts / Sunset gun / Stateless / Expand / Denial / Broadcasting / Sunset gun (Full Monty sunny Orb up mix) / Blame and demand / Damage addict / Stateless (Laswell mix).

CONTRABAND (see under ⇒ SCHENKER, Michael)

Alice COOPER

Formed: Initially as a group by VINCENT FURNIER (son of a preacher), Phoenix, Arizona . . . 1965 as The EARWIGS. Together with his partners in musical crime, GLEN BUXTON, MICHAEL BRUCE, DENNIS DUNAWAY and NEAL SMITH, FURNIER relocated to L.A., becoming The SPIDERS and enjoying healthy airplay for their debut single, 'DON"T BLOW YOUR MIND', released on the local 'Santa Cruz' label. After another low key single and a brief name change to NAZZ, the band adopted the improbable moniker of ALICE COOPER (a 17th Century witch, apparently), signing to FRANK ZAPPA's 'Straight' records. Turgid, clumsy cod-psychedelia, the debut album, 'PRETTIES FOR YOU' (1969) didn't bode well, while 'EASY ACTION' (1970) fared little better. Moving to Detroit in 1970, the band were inspired by the Motor City madness of MC5 and The STOOGES, tightening up their sound and developing their theatrical shock tactics. FURNIER simultaneously used the band name for his ghoulish, androgynous alter-ego, infamously embellishing the band's stage show with all manner of sick trickery: simulated hangings, mangled baby dolls, a live snake, mmm . . . nice. Signing to 'Warners' and drafting in BOB EZRIN on production, the band actually started writing material to match the effectiveness of their live shows. This wasn't gloomy, horror soundtrack minimalism, however, it was freewheeling, revved-up rock'n'roll, often with more than a touch of tongue-in-cheek humour. While 'KILLER' probably stands as COOPER's peak achievement, with the hilarious 'UNDER MY WHEELS' and the classic 'BE MY LOVER', the band really hit big with 'SCHOOL'S OUT' (1972). The title track was an irrepressible blast of adolescent-style attitude that made the UK No.1 spot and propelled the album to the upper reaches of the charts on both sides of the Atlantic. The 'ELECTED' single was another hit and the accompanying 'BILLION DOLLAR BABIES' (1973) album made UK and US No.1. 'MUSCLE OF LOVE' (1974) didn't fare quite so well and cracks were beginning to show in the songwriting armoury. COOPER subsequently sacked the rest of the band in the Summer of '74, hiring a cast of musicians that had previously backed up LOU REED. 'WELCOME TO MY NIGHTMARE' (1975; complete with eerie narration by the legendary VINCENT PRICE) was the last great vintage COOPER effort, a macabre concept album that spawned the hit single, 'ONLY

WOMEN BLEED'. In contrast to his superfreak, anti-hero stage character, offstage COOPER was becoming something of a celebrity, hobnobbing with the Hollywood elite and even hosting his own TV show, wherein the band shamelessly retrod past glories. By the end of the decade, his musical output had degenerated into AOR mush and he spent time in rehab for alcohol addiction. His early 80's work was hardly inspiring and even after a new deal with 'M.C.A.', the subsequent albums, 'CONSTRICTOR' and 'RAISE YOUR FIST AND YELL' failed to resurrect the (unclean) spirit of old. The latter did contain the anthemic 'FREEDOM' and the records were an attempt at the heady rock'n'roll of yore, COOPER even resuming the schlock shock for the subsequent tour. However, it was only with the help of hair-rock writer, DESMOND CHILD, that ALICE once again became a major player on the metal scene, the 'POISON' single seeing COOPER return to the Top 10 for the first time since his 70's heyday. The accompanying album, 'TRASH', fared almost as well, although it sounded about as menacing as BON JOVI. 'HEY STOOPID' (1989) consolidated COOPER's newfound success, as did 'THE LAST TEMPTATION' (1994). Things went quiet on the recording for a while, although the pro-am golfer COOPER continued to pop up in places where you'd least expect him, 'Wayne's World' (1992 movie), US chat shows etc. With appearances from the likes of ROB ZOMBIE and SLASH, 1997's 'A FISTFUL OF ALICE' album was one of the man's better live efforts while 'BRUTAL PLANET' (2000) finally found the grandaddy of gore back in the studio. More streetwise than schlock, the album delivered a sharp poke in the eye to those who'd already written him off for the umpteenth time. • **Songwriters:** ALICE wrote / co-wrote with band most of material, also using producer BOB EZRIN. DICK WAGNER to BERNIE TAUPIN also contributed in the 70's. On 'CONSTRICTOR' album, ALICE co-wrote with ROBERTS, some with KELLY and WEGENER. Collaborated with DESMOND CHILD in '89 and JACK PONTI, VIC PEPE, BOB PFEIFER in 1991. Covered:- SUN ARISE (trad.; a Rolf Harris hit) / SEVEN AND SEVEN IS (Love) / FIRE (Jimi Hendrix). • **Trivia:** Film cameo appearances have been:- DIARY OF A HOUSEWIFE (1970) / SGT. PEPPER'S LONELY HEARTS CLUB BAND (1978) / ROADIE (1980) / PRINCE OF DARKNESS (1987) / FREDDIE'S DEAD: THE FINAL NIGHTMARE (1991' he also acted!). In 1975 he sang 'I'M FLASH' on the Various Artists concept album 'FLASH FEARLESS VS.THE ZORG WOMEN Pts.5 & 6'.

Album rating: PRETTIES FOR YOU (*5) / EASY ACTION (*5) / LOVE IT TO DEATH (*8) / KILLER (*8) / SCHOOL'S OUT (*7) / BILLION DOLLAR BABIES (*8) / MUSCLE OF LOVE (*6) / WELCOME TO MY NIGHTMARE (*8) / ALICE COOPER GOES TO HELL (*6) / LACE AND WHISKEY (*5) / THE ALICE COOPER SHOW (*6) / FROM THE INSIDE (*6) / FLUSH THE FASHION (*6) / SPECIAL FORCES (*6) / ZIPPER CATCHES SKIN (*6) / DA DA (*6) / CONSTRICTOR (*5) / RAISE YOUR FIST AND YELL (*5) / TRASH (*5) / HEY STOOPID (*5) / BEAST OF ALICE COOPER compilation (*8) / THE LAST TEMPTATION (*5) / CLASSICKS compilation (*8) / A FISTFUL OF ALICE (*5) / BRUTAL PLANET (*6) / THE DEFINITIVE compilation (*8)

The SPIDERS

ALICE COOPER (b.VINCENT DAMON FURNIER, 4 Feb'48, Detroit) – vocals / **GLEN BUXTON** (b.17 Jun'47, Washington DC) – lead guitar / **MICHAEL BRUCE** (b.21 Nov'48, California) – rhythm guitar, keyboards / **DENNIS DUNAWAY** (b.15 Mar'46, California) – bass / **NEAL SMITH** (b.10 Jan'48, Washington DC) – drums

not iss. Santa Cruz

1967. (7") *<SCR 10.003>* **DON'T BLOW YOUR MIND. / NO PRICE TAG** -

not iss. Very

1967. (7") *<001>* **WONDER WHO'S LOVING HER NOW. / LAY DOWN AND DIE, GOODBYE** -

ALICE COOPER

Straight Straight

Dec 69. (lp) *<(STS 1051)>* **PRETTIES FOR YOU** Jun69
– Titanic overture / 10 minutes before the worm / Sing low sweet cheerio / Today Mueller / Living / Fields of regret / No longer umpire / Levity ball / B.B. on Mars / Reflected / Apple bush / Earwigs to eternity / Changing, arranging.

Jan 70. (7") *<101>* **LIVING. / REFLECTED** -
Jun 70. (lp) *<(STS 1061)>* **EASY ACTION**
– Mr. and Misdemeanor / Shoe salesman / Still no air / Below your means / Return of the spiders / Laughing at me / Refridgerator heaven / Beautiful flyaway / Lay down and die, goodbye.

Jun 70. (7") *<7141>* **CAUGHT IN A DREAM. / EIGHTEEN** -
Nov 70. (7") *<7398>* **RETURN OF THE SPIDERS. / SHOE SALESMAN** -

Straight Warners

Apr 71. (7") *(S 7209) <7499>* **EIGHTEEN. / IS IT MY BODY** 21 Feb71
Jun 71. (lp) *(STS 1065) <1883>* **LOVE IT TO DEATH** 35 Mar71
– Caught in a dream / Eighteen / Long way to go / Black Juju / Is it my body / Hallowed be my name / Second coming / Ballad of Dwight Fry / Sun arise. *(re-iss. Dec71 on 'Warners' lp/c; K/K4 46177)* – hit UK No.28 in Sep'72.

Warners Warners

Jun 71. (7") *(7490>* **CAUGHT IN A DREAM. / HALLOWED BE THY NAME** - 94
Dec 71. (7") *(K 16127) <7529>* **UNDER MY WHEELS. / DESPERADO** 59
(re-iss. Aug74; same)
Dec 71. (lp/c) *(K/K4 56005) <2567>* **KILLER** 27 21 Nov71
– Under my wheels / Be my lover / Halo of flies / Desperado / You drive me nervous / Yeah yeah yeah / Dead babies / Killer. *(cd-iss. Sep89 on 'WEA'; 927255-2)*

Jan 72. (7") *<7568>* **BE MY LOVER. / YEAH YEAH YEAH** - 49
Feb 72. (7") *(K 16154)* **BE MY LOVER. / YOU DRIVE ME NERVOUS** -
Jul 72. (7") *(K 16188) <7596>* **SCHOOL'S OUT. / GUTTER CAT** 1 7 May72
Jul 72. (lp/c) *(K/K4 56007) <2623>* **SCHOOL'S OUT** 4 2 Jun72
– School's out / Luney tune / Gutter cat vs. the jets / Street fight / Blue Turk / My stars / Public animal No.9 / Alma mater / Grande finale. *(cd-iss. Sep89 on 'WEA'; 927260-2)*

Oct 72. (7") *(K 16214) <7631>* **ELECTED. / LUNEY TUNE** 4 26
Feb 73. (7") *(K 16248) <7673>* **HELLO HURRAY. / GENERATION LANDSLIDE** 6 35 Jan73
Mar 73. (lp/c) *(K/K4 56013) <2685>* **BILLION DOLLAR BABIES** 1 1
– Hello hurray / Raped and freezin' / Elected / Billion dollar babies / Unfinished sweet / No more Mr. Nice guy / Generation landslide / Sick things / Mary Ann / I love the dead. *(cd-iss. Jan93 on 'WEA'; 7599 27269-2) (d-cd-iss. Mar01; 8122 79791-2)* – (with extra tracks).

Apr 73. (7") *(K 16262) <7691>* **NO MORE MR. NICE GUY. / RAPED AND FREEZIN'** 10 25
Jul 73. (7") *<7724>* **BILLION DOLLAR BABIES. / MARY ANN** - 57
Jan 74. (lp/c) *(K/K4 56018) <2748>* **MUSCLE OF LOVE** 34 10 Dec73
– Muscle of love / Woman machine / Hard hearted Alice / Man with the golden gun / Big apple dreamin' (hippo) / Never been sold before / Working up a sweat / Crazy little child / Teenage lament '74. *(cd-iss. Nov99; 7599 26226-2)*

Jan 74. (7") *(K 16345) <7762>* **TEENAGE LAMENT '74. / HARD HEARTED ALICE** 12 48 Dec73
Mar 74. (7") *<7783>* **MUSCLE OF LOVE. / CRAZY LITTLE CHILD** -
Jun 74. (7") *<8023>* **MUSCLE OF LOVE. / I'M EIGHTEEN** -
Sep 74. (lp/c) *(K/K4 56043) <2803>* **ALICE COOPER'S GREATEST HITS** (compilation) 8 Aug74
– I'm eighteen / Is it my body / Desperado / Under my wheels / Be my lover / School's out / Hello hurray / Elected / No more Mr. Nice guy / Billion dollar babies / Teenage lament '74 / Muscle of love. *(cd-iss. Jun89; K2 56045)*

— **ALICE** sacked rest of band, who became BILLION DOLLAR BABIES. He brought in **DICK WAGNER** – guitar, vocals / **STEVE** (DEACON) **HUNTER** – guitars / **PRAKASH JOHN** – bass / **PENTII 'Whitey' GLAN** – drums / **JOSEF CHIROWSKI** – drums (all ex-LOU REED band)

Anchor Atlantic

Feb 75. (7") *(1012) <3280>* **DEPARTMENT OF YOUTH. / COLD ETHYL** -
Mar 75. (lp/c) *(ANC L/K 2011) <18130>* **WELCOME TO MY NIGHTMARE** 19 5
– Welcome to my nightmare / Devil's food / The black widow / Some folks / Only women bleed / Department of youth / Cold Ethyl / Years ago / Steven / The awakening / Escape. *<cd-iss. Sep87 on 'Atlantic'; SD 19157>*

Apr 75. (7") *<3254>* **ONLY WOMEN BLEED. / COLD ETHYL** - 12
Jun 75. (7") *(1018)* **ONLY WOMEN BLEED. / DEVIL'S FOOD** -
Aug 75. (7") *<3280>* **DEPARTMENT OF YOUTH. / SOME FOLKS** - 67
Oct 75. (7") *<3298>* **WELCOME TO MY NIGHTMARE. / COLD ETHYL** - 45
Nov 75. (7") *(1025)* **WELCOME TO MY NIGHTMARE. / BLACK WIDOW** -

Warners Warners

Jun 76. (lp/c) *(K/K4 56171) <2896>* **ALICE COOPER GOES TO HELL** 23 27
– Go to Hell / You gotta dance / I'm the coolest / Didn't we meet / I never cry / Give the kid a break / Guilty / Wake me gently / Wish you were here / I'm always chasing rainbows / Going home. *(cd-iss. May94; 7599 27299-2)*

Jun 76. (7") *(K 16792) <8228>* **I NEVER CRY. / GO TO HELL** 12
Apr 77. (7") *<8349>* **YOU AND ME. / IT'S HOT TONIGHT** - 9
Apr 77. (7") *(K 16935)* **(NO MORE) LOVE AT YOUR CONVENIENCE. / IT'S HOT TONIGHT** 44 -
May 77. (lp/c) *(K/K4 56365) <3027>* **LACE AND WHISKEY** 33 42
– It's hot tonight / Lace and whiskey / Road rats / Damned if you do / You and me / King of the silver screen / Ubangi stomp / (No more) Love at your convenience / I never wrote those songs / My God.

Jul 77. (7") *(K 16984)* **YOU AND ME. / MY GOD** -
Jul 77. (7") *<8448>* **(NO MORE) LOVE AT YOUR CONVENIENCE. / I NEVER WROTE THOSE SONGS** -

— **FRED MANDEL** – keyboards repl. JOSEF

Dec 77. (lp/c) *(K/K4 56439) <3138>* **THE ALICE COOPER SHOW (live)**
– Under my wheels / I'm eighteen / Only women / Sick things / Is it my body / I never cry / Billion dollar babies / Devil's food – The black widow / You and me / a. I love the dead – b. Go to hell – c. Wish you were here / School's out.

— **Alice COOPER** now basically a solo artist with session people, which retaining **MANDEL, DAVEY JOHNSTONE** – guitar (ex-ELTON JOHN) / **MARK VOLMAN + HOWARD KAYLAN** – backing vocals (ex-TURTLES)

Dec 78. (7") *(K 17270) <8695>* **HOW YOU GONNA SEE ME NOW. / NO TRICKS** 61 12 Oct78
Dec 78. (lp/c) *(K/K4 56577) <3263>* **FROM THE INSIDE** 68 60
– From the inside / Wish I were born in Beverly Hills / The quiet room / Nurse Rozetta / Millie and Billie / Serious / How you gonna see me now / For Veronica's sake / Jacknife Johnny / Inmates (we're all crazy). *(cd-iss. Jun99; 7599 26064-2)*

Jan 79. (7") *<8760>* **FROM THE INSIDE. / NURSE ROZETTA** -
above w / **JOHN LO PRESTI** – bass / **DENNIS CONWAY** – drums

May 80. (lp/c) *(K/K4 56805) <3436>* **FLUSH THE FASHION** 56 44
– Talk talk / Clones (we're all) / Pain / Leather boots / Aspirin damage / Nuclear infected / Grim facts / Model citizen / Dance yourself to death / Headlines. *(cd-iss. Jun99; 7599 26229-2)*

Jun 80. (7") *(K 17598) <49204>* **CLONES (WE'RE ALL). / MODEL CITIZEN** 40 May80
Sep 80. (7") *<49526>* **DANCE YOURSELF TO DEATH. / TALK TALK** -

— now w / **MIKE PINERA + DAVEY JOHNSTONE** – guitar / **DUANE HITCHINGS** – keyboards / **ERIC SCOTT** – bass / **CRAIG KRAMPF** – drums

Sep 81. (7") *<49780>* **WHO DO YOU THINK WE ARE. / YOU WANT IT, YOU GOT IT** -
Sep 81. (lp/c) *(K/K4 56927) <3581>* **SPECIAL FORCES** 96
– Who do you think we are / Seven and seven is / Prettiest cop in the block / Don't talk old to me / Generation landslide '81 / Skeletons in the closet / You want it, you got it / You look good in rags / You're a movie / Vicious rumours. *(cd-iss. Jun99; 7599 26230-2)*

Feb 82. (7") *(K 17924) <49848>* **SEVEN AND SEVEN IS (live). / GENERATION LANDSLIDE '81 (live)** 62
May 82. (7"/7"pic-d) *(K 17940/+M)* **FOR BRITAIN ONLY. / UNDER MY WHEELS (live)** 66 -

(12"+=) *(K 17940T)* – Who do you think we are (live) / Model citizen (live).

— now w / **MIKE PINERA + DAVEY JOHNSTONE** – guitar / **DUANE HITCHINGS** – keyboards / **ERIC SCOTT** – bass / **CRAIG KRAMPF** – drums

Oct 82. (7") *<29928>* **I LIKE GIRLS. / ZORRO'S ASCENT** [-] [ ]
Oct 82. (lp/c) *(K/K4 57021) <23719-1/-4>* **ZIPPER CATCHES SKIN** [ ] [ ]
– Zorro's ascent / Make that money (Scrooge's song) / I am the future / No baloney homosapiens / Adaptable (anything for you) / I like girls / Remarkably insincere / Tag, you're it / I better be good / I'm alive (that was the day my dead pet returned to save my life). *(cd-iss. Jun99; 7599 23719-2)*

— **COOPER + WAGNER** re-united w / **EZRIN + PRAKASH** and recruited **GRAHAN SHAW** – synth / **JOHN ANDERSON + RICHARD KOLINGA** – drums

Mar 83. (7") *(K 15004)* **I AM THE FUTURE (remix). / ZORRO'S ASCENT** [ ] [-]
Mar 83. (7") *<29828>* **I AM THE FUTURE (remix). / TAG, YOU'RE IT** [-] [ ]
Nov 83. (lp/c) *(923969-1/-4) <23969-1/-4>* **DA DA** [93] [ ]
– Da da / Enough's enough / Former Lee Warner / No man's land / Dyslexia / Scarlet and Sheba / I love America / Fresh blood / Pass the gun around. *(cd-iss. Jun99; 7599 23969-2)*
Nov 83. (12"m) *(ALICE 1T)* **I LOVE AMERICA. / FRESH BLOOD / PASS THE GUN AROUND** [ ] [ ]

— band now consisted of **KANE ROBERTS** (b.16 Jan'59) – guitar, vocals / **DAVID ROSENBERG** – drums / **PAUL DELPH** – keyboards, vocals / **DONNIE KISSELBACK** – bass, vocals / **KIP WINGER**

M.C.A. M.C.A.

Oct 86. (7") *(MCA 1090) <52904>* **HE'S BACK (THE MAN BEHIND THE MASK). / BILLION DOLLAR BABIES** [61] [ ]
(12"+=) *(MCAT 1090)* – I'm eighteen.
Oct 86. (lp/c) *(MCF/+C 3341) <5761>* **CONSTRICTOR** [41] [59]
– Teenage Frankenstein / Give it up / Thrill my gorilla / Life and death of the party / Simple disobedience / The world needs guts / Trick bag / Crawlin' / The great American success story / He's back (the man behind the mask).
Apr 87. (7") *(MCA 1113)* **TEENAGE FRANKENSTEIN. / SCHOOL'S OUT (live)** [ ] [-]
(12"+=) *(MCAT 1113)* – Only women bleed.

— **KEN K. MARY** – drums repl.ROSENBERG / **PAUL HOROWITZ** – keyboards, repl. DELPH + KISSELBACH.

Oct 87. (lp/pic-lp/c) *(MCF/+P/C 3392) <42091>* **RAISE YOUR FIST AND YELL** [48] [73]
– Freedom / Lock me up / Give the radio back / Step on you / Not that kind of love / Prince of darkness / Time to kill / Chop, chop, chop / Gail / Roses on white lace. *(cd-iss. May88; DMCF 3392)*
Mar 88. (7") *(MCA 1241) <53212>* **FREEDOM. / TIME TO KILL** [50] [ ]
(12"+=/12"s+=) *(MCA T/X 1241)* – School's out (live).

— retained **KIP WINGER** bringing in guests **JON BON JOVI, RICHIE SAMBORA** plus **JOE PERRY, TOM HAMILTON, JOEY KRAMER** etc.

— **COOPER + WAGNER** re-united w / **EZRIN + PRAKASH** and recruited **GRAHAN SHAW** – synth / **JOHN ANDERSON + RICHARD KOLINGA** – drums

Epic Epic

1988. (7") *<08114>* **I GOT A LINE ON YOU. / LIVIN' ON THE EDGE** [-] [ ]
Jul 89. (7") *(655061-7) <68958>* **POISON. / TRASH** [2] [7] Sep89
(12"+=) *(655061-8)* – The ballad of Dwight Fry.
(cd-s++=) *(655061-2)* – I got a line on you (live).
(12"+=) *(655061-9)* – Cold Ethyl (live).
Aug 89. (lp/c/cd) *(465130-1/-4/-2) <45137>* **TRASH** [2] [20]
– Poison / Spark in the dark / House of fire / Why trust you / Only my heart talkin' / Bed of nails / This maniac's in love with you / Trash / Hell is living without you / I'm your gun. *(re-iss. Sep93 cd/c; same)*
Sep 89. (7"/7"green/7"red/7"blue/c-s) *(ALICE/+G/R/B/M 3)* **BED OF NAILS. / I'M YOUR GUN** [38] [-]
(12"+=/12"w-poster/12"pic-d+=) *(ALICE T/Q/P 3)* – Go to Hell (live).
(cd-s++=) *(ALICEC 3)* – Only women bleed (live).
Dec 89. (7"/7"sha-pic-d/c-s) *(ALICE/+P/M 4)* **HOUSE OF FIRE. / THIS MANIAC'S IN LOVE WITH YOU** [65] [-]
(12"+=/cd-s+=) *(ALICE T/C 4)* – Billion dollar babies (live) / Under my wheels (live).
(7"sha-pic-d) *(ALICEX 4)* – ('A'side) / POISON (live).
(12"pic-d+=/12"w-poster+=) *(ALICE S/Q 4)* – Spark in the dark (live) / Under my wheels (live).
Jan 90. (c-s) *<73085>* **HOUSE OF FIRE / BALLAD OF DWIGHT FRY** [-] [56]
Apr 90. (cd-s) *<73268>* **ONLY MY HEART TALKIN'. / UNDER MY WHEELS (live)** [-] [89]

— (Mar'90) touring band **PETE FRIEZZEN** – guitar / **AL PITRELLI** – guitar / **TOMMY CARADONNA** – bass / **DEREK SHERINIAN** – keyboards / **JONATHAN MOVER** – drums

— (1991 sessions) **STEVE VAI, JOE SATRIANI, STEF BURNS** (on tour), **VINNIE MOORE, MICK MARS, SLASH** – guitars / **HUGH McDONALD, NIKKI SIXX** – bass / **MICKEY CURRY** – drums / **ROBERT SALLEY, JOHN WEBSTER** – keyboards / **STEVE CROES** – synclaiver

Jun 91. (7"/c-s) *(656983-7/-4)* **HEY STOOPID. / WIND-UP TOY** [21] [-]
(12"+=/12"pic-d+=/cd-s+=) *(656983-6/-8/-9)* – It rained all night.
Jun 91. (cd/c/lp) *(468416-2/-4/-1) <46786>* **HEY STOOPID** [4] [47]
– Hey stoopid / Love's a loaded gun / Snakebite / Burning our bed / Dangerous tonight / Might as well be on Mars / Feed me Frankenstein / Hurricane years / Little by little / Die for you / Dirty dreams / Wind-up toy. *(cd re-iss. Mar96; same)*
Jul 91. (cd-s) *<73845>* **HEY STOOPID. / IT RAINED ALL NIGHT** [-] [78]
Sep 91. (7"/c-s) *(657438-7/-4)* **LOVE'S A LOADED GUN. / FIRE** [38] [ ]
(12"+=/12"pic-d+=/sha-pic-cd-s+=) *(657438-6/-8/-9)* – Eighteen (live '91).
Jun 92. (7"/c-s) *(658092-7/-4)* **FEED MY FRANKENSTEIN. / BURNING OUR BED** [27] [ ]
(12"pic-d+=/cd-s+=) *(658092-6/-2)* – Poison / Only my heart talkin'.
(cd-s+=) *(658092-5)* – Hey stoopid / Bed of nails.

— w / **STEF BURNS** – guitar, vocals / **GREG SMITH** – bass, vocals / **DEREK SHERINIAN** – keyboards, vocals / **DAVID VOSIKKINEN** – drums

May 94. (c-s) *(660347-4)* **LOST IN AMERICA. / HEY STOOPID (live)** [22] [ ]
(12"pic-d+=/pic-cd-s+=) *(660347-2)* – Billion dollar babies (live) / No more Mr.Nice Guy (live).
Jun 94. (cd/c/lp) *(476594-2/-4/-1) <52771>* **THE LAST TEMPTATION** [6] [68]
(w /free comic)
– Sideshow / Nothing's free / Lost in America / Bad place alone / You're my temptation / Stolen prayer / Unholy war / Lullaby / It's me / Cleansed by fire.
Jul 94. (c-s) *(660563-4)* **IT'S ME. / BAD PLACE ALONE** [34] [ ]
(12"pic-d+=/pic-cd-s+=) *(660563-2)* – Poison / Sick things.
Oct 95. (cd/c) *(480845-2/-4) <67219>* **CLASSICKS** (compilation) [ ] [ ]
– Poison / Hey stoopid / Feed my Frankenstein / Love's a loaded gun / Stolen prayer / House of fire / Lost in America / It's me / Under my wheels (live) / Billion dollar babies (live) / I'm eighteen (live) / No more Mr. Nice guy (live) / Only women bleed (live) / School's out (live) / Fire.

— now with **REB BEACH** – guitar / **RYAN ROXIE** – guitar / **PAUL TAYLOR** – keyboards / **TODD JENSEN** – bass / **JIMMT DeGRASSO** – drums / guests; SAMMY HAGAR, BOB ZOMBIE + SLASH

E.M.I. Capitol

Jun 97. (cd) *(CTM CD/MC 331) <33080>* **A FISTFUL OF ALICE (live)** [ ] [ ]
– School's out / Under my wheels / I'm eighteen / Desperado / Lost in America / Teenage lament '74 / I never cry / Poison / No more Mr. Nice guy / Welcome to my nightmare / Only women bleed / Feed my Frankenstein / Elected / Is anyone home? (studio).

Eagle Spitfire

Jun 00. (cd) *(EAGCD 115) <15038>* **BRUTAL PLANET** [38] [ ]
– Brutal planet / Wicked young man / Sanctuary / Blow me a kiss / Eat some more / Pick up the bones / Pessi-mystic / Gimme / It's the little things / Take it like a woman / Cold machines.
Aug 00. (cd-s) *(EAGXS 157)* **GIMME / BRUTAL PLANET / GIMME (CD-Rom video)** [ ] [-]

– compilations, others, etc. –

on 'Warners' unless otherwise stated

Mar 73. (7") **BE MY LOVER. / UNDER MY WHEELS** [-] [ ]
Jun 73. (d-lp) *(K 66021)* **SCHOOLDAYS** (1st-2 lp's) [ ] [ ]
Feb 75. (7"ep) *(K 16409)* **SCHOOL'S OUT / NO MORE MR.NICE GUY. / BILLION DOLLAR BABIES / ELECTED** [ ] [-]
Feb 76. (7") *(K 16287)* **SCHOOL'S OUT. / ELECTED** [ ] [-]
(re-iss. Dec80; same) (re-iss. Sep85 on 'Old Gold'; OG 9519)
Dec 77. (7"ep/12"ep) *Anchor; (ANE 7/12 001)* **DEPARTMENT OF YOUTH EP** [ ] [-]
– Department of youth / Welcome to my nightmare / Black widow / Only women bleed.
1978. (7") **I'M EIGHTEEN. / SCHOOL'S OUT** [-] [ ]
Apr 84. (pic-lp) *Design; (PXLP 3)* **ROCK'N'ROLL REVIVAL: TORONTO LIVE '69 (live)** [ ] [-]
(re-iss. Apr86 as 'FREAKOUT SONG' on 'Showcase'; SHLP 115)
Apr 87. (m-lp/c) *Thunderbolt; (THBM/+C 005)* **LADIES MAN (live'69)** [ ] [-]
(cd-iss. Aug88; CDTHBM 005) (re-iss cd.Jun91; same) (cd re-iss. Aug98 on 'MagMid'; MM 011)
Dec 89. (lp/c)(cd) *W.E.A.; (WX 331/+C)(241781-2)* **THE BEAST OF ALICE COOPER** [ ] [ ]
– School's out / Under my wheels / Billion dollar babies / Be my lover / Desperado / Is it my body? / Only women bleed / Elected / I'm eighteen / Hello hurray / No more Mr. Nice guy / Teenage lament '74 / Muscle of love / Department of youth.
Jul 90. (cd-box) *Enigma; (773 362-2)* **PRETTIES FOR YOU** [ ] [-]
Jul 90. (cd-box) *Enigma; (773 391-2)* **EASY ACTION** [ ] [-]
May 92. (lp/cd) *Edsel; (NEST/+CD 903)* **LIVE AT THE WHISKEY A GO GO, 1969 (live)** [ ] [-]
Oct 92. (cd) *Pickwick; (SMA 054)* **ROCK LEGENDS VOL.2** [ ] [-]
Apr 93. (cd) *Pulsar; (PULS 010)* **NOBODY LIKES ME** [ ] [-]
Sep 94. (cd) *Wisepack; (LECD 085)* **LEGENDS IN MUSIC** [ ] [-]
Jul 97. (cd) *Going For A Song; (GFS 071)* **ALICE COOPER** [ ] [-]
May 98. (cd) *Dressed To Kill; (DRESS 603)* **SNORTING ANTHRAX** [ ] [-]
Jun 98. (cd) *Raven; (RVCD 69)* **FREEDOM FOR FRANKENSTEIN: HITS AND PIECES 1984-1994** [ ] [ ]
Apr 99. (4xcd-box) *Rhino; <(8122 75680-2)>* **THE LIFE AND CRIMES OF ALICE COOPER** [ ] [ ]
Jul 00. (cd) *Epic; (498788-2)* **SUPER HITS** [ ] [-]
Feb 01. (cd/c) *Warners; <(8122 73534-2/-4)>* **THE DEFINITIVE ALICE COOPER** [33] [ ]
– I'm eighteen / Desperado / Under my wheels / Halo of flies / School's out / Elected / Hello hooray / Generation landslide / No more Mr. Nice Guy / Billion dollar babies / Teenage lament '74 / Muscle of love / Only women bleed / Welcome to my nightmare / Department of love / I never cry / You and me / How you gonna see me now / From the inside / Poison / Hey stoopid.

COP SHOOT COP

Formed: Brooklyn, New York, USA . . . summer '88 by singer/bassist JACK NATZ, second bassist TOD A, DAVE QUIMET, PHIL PULEO and sampler JAMES COLEMAN. Operating from the same seething well of unrelenting negativity as NY "No Wave" pioneers like DNA and MARS, COP SHOOT COP set out to create hateful R&R noise in the most uncompromising, unlistener- friendly style they could muster. Utilising a rhythmic, guitarless sound driven by two bass players, the band made their debut in 1988 with the mini-set, 'HEADKICK FACSIMILE'. Also released on the 'Supernatural Organization' imprint was their 1990 follow-up, 'CONSUMER REVOLT', subsequently unveiled in the UK a few years later on 'Big Cat'. By this time, CSC had already showcased their anti-pop racket on 'WHITE*NOISE' (1991), although surprisingly, given their militant opposition to corporate culture, the band signed a major label deal with 'Interscope'. First up was an EP, 'SUCK CITY', followed by by the slightly more consumer friendly 'ASK QUESTIONS LATER' (1993), an album that found the noisemeisters allowing their claustrophobic sound more room to breathe. Similarly, 1994's

'RELEASE' was easier on the ear with repeated listening, although as far as NY underground kudos is concerned, COP SHOOT COP were still taking no prisoners. However, shortly afterwards the group disbanded (see below).

Album rating: HEADKICK FACSIMILE mini (*4) / CONSUMER REVOLT (*4) / WHITE-NOISE (*5) / ASK QUESTIONS LATER (*7) / RELEASE (*6)

JACK NATZ – vocals, bass / **TOD A.** (b. ASHLEY) – bass, vocals / **DAVE QUIMET** – samples / **PHIL PULEO** – drums, metal / **FILER** (aka JAMES COLEMAN) – samples

not iss. | Supernatural Organization

1988. (m-lp) **HEADKICK FACSIMILE** [-] [ ]

Feb 90. (lp) **CONSUMER REVOLT** [-] [ ]
– Lo. Com. denom / She's like a shot / Waiting for the punchline / Disconnected 666 / Smash retro / Burn your bridges / Consume / Fire in the hole / Pity the bastard / Down come the Mickey / Hurt me baby / System test / Eggs for rib. *(UK + re-iss. Apr92 on 'Big Cat' lp/c/cd; ABB 33/+C/CD)*

Big Cat | Big Cat

Oct 91. (lp/c/cd) *<(ABB 29/+C/CD)>* **WHITE•NOISE** [ ] [ ]
– Discount rebellion / Traitor – Martyr / Coldest day of the year / Feel good / Relief / Empires collapse / Corporate protopop / Heads I win, tails you lose / Chameleon man / Where's the money? / If tomorrow ever comes / Hung again.

Big Cat | Interscope

Aug 92. (12"ep/cd-ep) *(ABB 39 T/SCD) <96116>* **SUCK CITY EP** [ ] [ ] Nov92
– Nowhere / Days will pass / We shall be changed / Suck city (here we come).

Apr 93. (d-lp/d-cd) *(ABB 45/+CD) <92250>* **ASK QUESTIONS LATER** [ ] [ ] Mar93
– Surprise, surprise / Room 429 / No where / Migration / Cut to the chase / $10 bill / Seattle / Furnace / Israeli dig / Cause and effect / Got no soul / Everybody loves you / All the clocks are broken.

Jun 93. (12"green-ep/cd-ep) *(ABB 53 T/SCD)* **$10 BILL. / CAUSE AND EFFECT / SEATTLE** [ ] [ ]

Dec 93. (12"ep/cd-ep) *(ABB 54 T/SCD)* **ROOM 429 E.P.** [ ] [-]
– Room 429 / Ambulance song / Fragment / Shine on Elizabeth (live).

Aug 94. (12"/cd-s) *(ABB 68 T/SCD)* **TWO AT A TIME. /** [ ] [-]

Sep 94. (lp/cd) *(ABB 69/+CD) <92424>* **RELEASE** [ ] [ ]
– Interference / It only hurts when I breathe / Last legs / Two at a time / Slackjaw / Lullaby / Any day now / Swimming in circles / Turning inside out / Ambulance song / Suckerpunch / Divorce / Money drunk.

Jan 95. (12"ep/cd-ep) *(ABB 78 T/SCD)* **ANY DAY NOW / NEW GOD. / QUEEN OF SHINBONE ALLEY / TRANSMISSION** [ ] [-]

Submission | not iss.

Jul 96. (7"/cd-s; with MEATHEAD) *(SUCK 3/+CD)* **KILL A COP FOR CHRIST AND BRING US HIS HEAD** [ ] [-]

— split later in '96 with TOD A forming veteran alt-rock supergroup, FIREWATER – QUIMET followed him in '97 after a spell with MOTHERHEAD BUG

Chris CORNELL (see under ⇒ SOUNDGARDEN)

CORONER

Formed: Switzerland . . . 1985 by RON ROYCE, TOMMY T. BARON and MARQUIS MARKY. They began an association (i.e. roadies) with CELTIC FROST's TOM G WARRIOR, who sang on their early demo, 'DEATH CULT'. CORONER were given a record deal with 'Noise', subsequently releasing their debut, 'R.I.P.' in '87. A second set, 'PUNISHMENT OF DECADENCE' (1988), featured a thrash version of Jimi Hendrix's 'PURPLE HAZE', although this did little to enhance a rather derivative album. A year later, they issued another album of second division thrash, 'NO MORE COLOUR'. Their fourth album, 'MENTAL VORTEX' (1991) found the group once again treading water, the closing track a sacrilegious mangling of The Beatles' 'I WANT YOU (SHE'S SO HEAVY)'. Two further albums appeared in the first half of the 90's, although no inquest was held following the band's demise. • **Songwriters:** music BARON, ROYCE, words MARKY; except DER MUSSOLINI (D.A.F.).

Album rating: R.I.P. (*5) / PUNISHMENT FOR DECADENCE (*4) / NO MORE COLOUR (*7) / MENTAL VORTEX (*5) / GRIN (*4) / THE BEST OF CORONER compilation (*5)

RON ROYCE – vocals, bass / **TOMMY T. BARON** – guitar, vocals / **MARQUIS MARKY** – drums

Noise Int. | Noise Int.

1987. (lp) *(N 0075)* **R.I.P.** [-] [-] German
– Reborn through hate / When angels die / Nosferatu / Suicide command / R.I.P. / Coma / Fried alive / Totentanz. *(UK-iss.Oct89 cd/c/lp; CD/ZC+/NUK 075)*

1988. (cd/c/lp) *(CD/ZC+/NUK 119)* **PUNISHMENT FOR DECADENCE** [ ] [-]
– Intro / Absorbed / Masked jackal / Arc-lite / Skeleton on your shoulder / Sudden fall / Shadow of a lost dream / The new breed / Voyage to eternity. *(UK-iss.Oct89+=; same)* – Purple haze.

Oct 89. (7") *(7HAZE 3)* **PURPLE HAZE. / MASKED JACKAL** [ ] [-]

Oct 89. (cd/c/lp) *(CD/ZC+/NUK 138)* **NO MORE COLOR** [ ] [ ]
– Die by my hand / No need to be human / Read my scars / D.O.A. / Mistress of deception / Tunnel of pain / Why it hurts / Last entertainment.

Aug 91. (cd/c/lp) *(<N 177-2/-4/-1>)* **MENTAL VORTEX** [ ] [ ]
– Divine step (conspectu mortis) / Son of Lilith / Semtex revolution / Sirens / Metamorphosis / Pale sister / About life / I want you (she's so heavy).

May 93. (cd/c/lp) *(<N 0210-2/-4/-1>)* **GRIN** [ ] [ ]
– Dream path / The lethargic age / Internal conflicts / Caveat (to the comming) / Serpent moves / Status: still thinking / Theme for silence / Paralized, mesmerized / Grin (nails hurt) / Host.

Apr 95. (cd) *(<N 0212-2>)* **THE BEST OF CORONER** (part compilation & remixes) [ ] [ ] Mar95
– Benway's world / The favorite game / Shifter / Serpent moves / Snow crystal / Divine step (conspectu mortis) / Gliding above while being below / Der Mussolini / Last entertainment (T.V. bizarre) / Reborn through hate / Golden cashmere sleeper (part 1) / Golden cashmere slipper (part 2) / Masked jackal / I want you (she's so heavy) / Grin (no religion remix) / Purple haze (live).

— went to ground after compilation

CORROSION OF CONFORMITY

Formed: Raleigh, North Carolina, USA . . . 1982 out of NO LABELS by MIKE DEAN, WOODY WEATHERMAN and REED MULLIN, who soon found ERIC EYKE. Debuting with the independently released 'EYE FOR AN EYE' (1984), the group immediately made a name for themselves with their innovative fusion of thrash-core and more traditional power-metal styles. Signed to 'Roadrunner', the group (now without EYKE) developed its approach on a follow-up, 'ANIMOSITY'. SIMON BOB was in place for their third set, 'TECHNOCRACY' (1987), a highly praised effort, which nonetheless marked the end of the first chapter in COC's initial incarnation. In the early 90's, WEATHERMAN and MULLIN resurrected COC with a completely new line-up comprising KARL AGELL, PEPPER KEENAN and PHIL SWISHER. The resulting album, 'BLIND NYC' (1991), saw COC adopt a more accessible yet still uncompromising sound and a more politically-pointed lyrical stance. The critical success of a rare EP, 'VOTE WITH A BULLET' (1992), led to the return of DEAN. With KEENAN now on lead vocals, they signed to 'Columbia', the major label muscle affording them a US Top 200 placing for the first time in their career with 'DELIVERANCE' (1994). Now commanding a wide crossover appeal, COC finally cracked the UK market with a Top 50 album, 'WISEBLOOD' in 1996. While that album anticipated the huge extent to which rap-influenced metal would subsequently infiltrate the millennial rock landscape, 'AMERICA'S VOLUME DEALER' (2000) looked Southwards for inspiration. Southwards as in LYNYRD SKYNYRD and The ALLMAN BROTHERS. Although the likes of RAGING SLAB and even METALLICA had trodden this dusty path before, COC's muscular approach lent itself particularly well to the genre while simultaneously setting them apart from the bulk of metal practitioners. • **Songwriters:** Group with producer J CUSTER.

Album rating: EYE FOR AN EYE (*5) / ANIMOSITY (*6) / TECHNOCRACY mini (*8) / SIX SONGS WITH MIKE SINGING mini (*5) / BLIND, NYC (*5) / DELIVERANCE (*7) / WISEBLOOD (*7)

ERIC EYKE – vocals / **WOODY WEATHERMAN** – guitar / **MIKE DEAN** – bass, vocals / **REED MULLIN** – drums, vocals

No Core | ToxicShock

1984. (lp) *<TXLP 04>* **EYE FOR AN EYE** [ ] [ ]
– Tell me / Minds are controlled / Indiferent / Broken will / Rabid dogs / L.S. / Rednekkk / Coexist / Excluded / Dark thoughts / Poison planet / What? / Negative outlook / Positive outlook / No drunk / College town / Not safe. *<(re-iss. cd/c Feb90 on 'Caroline'; CAROLCD/MC 1356)>*

— now without EYKE

Roadrunner | Combat

Aug 85. (lp) *(RR 9764) <2206>* **ANIMOSITY** [ ] [ ]
– Loss for words / Mad world / Consumed / Holier / Positive outlook / Prayer / Intervention / Kiss of death / Hungry child / Animosity. *(cd-iss. Mar93 & Apr96 on 'Metal Blade'; 398414078 CD)*

— added **SIMON BOB** – vocals (ex-UGLY AMERICANS)

May 87. (12"ep) *(RR12 5477)* **TECHNOCRACY** [ ] [-]
– Technocracy / Hungry child / Happily ever after / Crawling / Ahh blugh / Intervention. *(cd-ep iss.Mar93 on 'Metal Blade'+=; 398417019 CD)* – Technocracy (remix) / Crawling (remix) / Happily ever after (remix).

— (1988) now without SIMON they subsequently disbanded for two years

Caroline | Caroline

Feb 90. (cd/c/lp) *<(CAROLCD/MC/LP 1365)>* **SIX SONGS WITH MIKE SINGING** (rec.1985) [ ] [ ] 1988
– Eye for an eye / Citizen / What / Center of the world / Not for me / Negative outlook. *(re-iss. Jun94 on 'Product Inc'; INCLP 003)*

— **WEATHERMAN + MULLIN** re-formed with new members **KARL AGELL** – vocals (ex-SCHOOL OF VIOLENCE) / **PEPPER KEENAN** – guitar, vocals / **PHIL SWISHER** – bass

Roadracer | Combat

Nov 91. (cd/lp) *(RO 9236-2/-4) <88561-2031-2/-4>* **BLIND, NYC 1991** [ ] [ ]
– Damned for all time / Dance of the dead / Buried / Break the circle / Painted smiling face / Mine are the eyes of God / Vote with a bullet / Great purification / White noise / Echoes in the well.

Roadrunner | Combat

Dec 92. (12"ep/cd-ep) *(RR 2388-6/-3) <1081>* **VOTE WITH A BULLET / CONDITION A – CONDITION B. / FUTURE – NOW / BREAK THE CIRCLE / JIM BEAM AND COON ASS** [ ] [ ]

— **DEAN** returned to repl. SWISHER + AGELL who later formed LEADFOOT (KEENAN now lead vox)

Columbia | Columbia

Oct 94. (cd/c/lp) *(477683-2/-4/-1) <66208>* **DELIVERANCE** [ ] [ ]
– Heaven's not overflowing / Albatross / Clean my wounds / Without wings / Broken man / Senor Limpio / Man de mono / Seven days / No. 2121313 / My grain / Deliverance / Shake like you / Shelter / Pearls before swine.

Sep 96. (cd/cd/c/lp) *(484328-9/-2/-4/-1) <67583>* **WISEBLOOD** [43] [ ]
– King of the rotten / Long whip – Big America / Wiseblood / Goodbye windows / Born again for the last time / Drowning in a daydream / The snake had no head / The door / Man or ash / Redemption city / Wishbone (some tomorrow) / Fuel / Bottom feeder (el que come abajo).

COC

— **WEATHERMAN, KEENAN, DEAN + MULLEN**

not iss. | Sanctuary

Sep 00. (cd) *<84500>* **AMERICA'S VOLUME DEALER** [-] [ ]
– Over me / Congratulations song / Stare too long / Diablo blvd. / Doublewide /

Zippo / Who's got the fire / Sleeping martyr / Take what you want / 13 angels / Gittin' it on.

co.uk

Formed: Lisburn, Northern Ireland . . . 1997 by JOE BRUSH, RAB McNEIL and CHRIS ROBINSON. While the latter pair had been friends since childhood, ROBINSON became the final piece in the jigsaw after being recruited through an ad in the local paper. Inspired by the likes of AC/DC, the mouthy threesome strutted their pop-punk stuff via a series of UK dates and the 'NOT TODAY' single ('BIG GREEN BATH' had already aspired to SOTW in Kerrang!). Signed to 'Mercury', CO.UK delivered their one and only set 'BRAINWASH' late in 1999.

Album rating: BRAINWASH (*6)

JOE BRUSH – vocals, guitar / **CHRIS ROBINSON** – bass / **RAB McNEIL** – drums

Bright Star not iss.

Apr 98. (cd-s) **INFLUENCED / PART OF THE GAME**
Mar 99. (cd-s) **BIG GREEN BATH / BUTTERFLY / HEROES**
Jun 99. (7") *(BSR 5)* **NOT TODAY. / FREAKAZOID**
(cd-s+=) *(BSRCD 5)* – E-time.
Nov 99. (cd-s) *(BSRCD 6)* **SICK OF YOU / BLUE BUDDHA / V.D.U.**

Mercury Mercury

Dec 99. (cd) *(546987-2)* **BRAINWASH**
– Part of the game / Not today / Butterfly / Influenced / Freakazoid / Heroes / Big green bath.

Wayne/Jayne COUNTY

Born: WAYNE COUNTY, c.1950, Georgia, Atlanta, USA. WAYNE left for New York in 1968 where he appeared in a female role alongside PATTI SMITH in an off-Broadway production of 'Femme Fatale' before tackling the role of Florence Nightingale in 'World'. In 1970, the actor/singer encountered ANDY WARHOL, who cast him in his stage show, 'Pork'; the review subsequently arrived in England, impressing DAVID BOWIE and inspiring him to sign COUNTY to his 'Mainman' publishing company. By this point he was already a fully fledged transvestite and began singing in New York band, QUEEN ELIZABETH; their drummer, JERRY NOLAN, was soon to join other cross-dressers, The NEW YORK DOLLS. In 1973, WAYNE found new sidemen, The BACKSTREET BOYS, although BOWIE's manager, Tony DeFries dropped him from Mainman's bulging roster (ooer!). A further setback came a few years later when 'E.S.P.' (former stable of The FUGS) delayed issue of his new group's proposed album, citing it as unsuitable for release, probably due to the fact that it included future singles, 'FUCK OFF' and 'STUCK ON YOU'; it was said the master tapes were lost in an accidental fire. In 1976, the group appeared at Max's Kansas City where three tracks (including one named after the venue itself) were cut for a V/A compilation, John Peel subsequently airing the songs on his night time Radio One show. With punk rock and new wave now dominating the music scene, COUNTY was becoming more accepted and after an infamous gig at another great club, CBGB's (in 1977), Miles Copeland of 'Illegal' records (who had already snapped up brother, STEWART COPELAND and his band The POLICE), signed up the gender-bending punk and his backing band, The ELECTRIC CHAIRS. Based in the less conservative land of Britain, they released their eponymous debut EP which included the tracks 'STUCK ON YOU', 'PARANOIA PARADISE' and The Rolling Stones' 'THE LAST TIME'. Later that year, WAYNE and Co flitted to 'Safari' records (run by DEEP PURPLE's management team), although their controversial second 45, 'FUCK OFF', saw the label issuing it under the pseudonymous guise of the 'Sweet F.A.' imprint. Around the same time, The ELECTRIC CHAIRS re-hashed 'PARANOIA PARADISE' on the punk movie, 'Jubilee', WAYNE kitted out in his trademark blonde wig, pink mini and fish-net stockings. If they were ever to have had a chance to have a hit single, it was surely with 'EDDIE & SHEENA', although its commercial sheen alienated many harder core punks. Hot on the record's heels was the group's eponymous debut album, full of second and occasionally first division sleazy punk rock. WAYNE COUNTY was subsequently given priority billing on their second set that year, 'STORM THE GATES OF HEAVEN' (featuring The Electric Prunes' 'I HAD TOO MUCH TO DREAM LAST NIGHT'), yet The ELECTRIC CHAIRS found it hard to make the big time. Released on either side of the decade, albums 'THINGS YOUR MOTHER NEVER TOLD YOU' (1979) and the live 'ROCK'N'ROLL RESURRECTION' (1980) represented The 'CHAIRS' final sitting as the band had already split. WAYNE was now taking hormone treatment to become his alter-ego, JAYNE, full-time although she never went through with the final operation. After spells in Berlin, JAYNE relocated to London where she released a comeback album, 'PRIVATE OYSTER' (1986); US title 'AMERIKAN CLEOPATRA'. She continues to release the "odd" single and album, although her solo career has been sporadic. WAYNE/JAYNE was the shock formula transvestite turned transexual whose no-holds barred NEW YORK DOLLS meets DUSTY SPRINGFIELD punk'n'roll never survived the "so-called" death of punk rock when the 'PISTOLS split. Her autobiography, 'Man Enough To Be A Woman: The Trials And Tribulations Of An Underground Cult Figure, Wayne County', was published in 1995 and obviously paints a fuller portrait of a bizarre life.

Album rating: THE ELECTRIC CHAIRS (*6) / STORM THE GATES OF HEAVEN (*6) / THINGS YOUR MOTHER NEVER TOLD YOU (*4) / ROCK'N'ROLL RESURRECTION (*5) / THE BEST OF THE ELECTRIC CHAIRS compilation (*7) / ROCK'N'ROLL CLEOPATRA compilation (*7) / PRIVATE OYSTER (*4) / GODDESS OF WET DREAMS (*4) / DEVIATION (*4)

WAYNE COUNTY & THE BACKSTREET BOYS

WAYNE – vocals with **GREG VAN COOK** – guitar / + 3

not iss. Max's Kan.

1976. (7"m) *<MAX 1213>* **MAX'S KANSAS CITY 1976. / FLIP YOUR WIG / CREAM IN MY JEANS**

— all above tracks also on US various artists lp 'MAX'S KANSAS CITY', released 1976 on 'Ram'; *1213) (re-iss. Mar78 as 'NEW YORK NEW WAVE, MAX'S KANSAS CITY' on 'C.B.S.'; CBS 82670)*

ELECTRIC CHAIRS

WAYNE + GREG added **VAL HALLER** – bass / **J.J. JOHNSON** – drums

Illegal not iss.

Jul 77. (7"ep) *(IL 002)* **THE ELECTRIC CHAIRS EP**
– Stuck on you / Paranoia Paradise / The last time.

Sweet F.A. not iss.

Nov 77. (7") *(WC 1)* **FUCK OFF. / ON THE CREST**

— guest on below **JOOLS HOLLAND** – piano (of SQUEEZE)

Safari not iss.

Feb 78. (7") *(SAFE 1)* **EDDIE & SHEENA. / ROCK'N'ROLL CLEOPATRA**
Feb 78. (lp) *(LONG 1)* **THE ELECTRIC CHAIRS**
– Eddie & Sheena / Bad in bed / Hot blood / Worry wart / Twenty eight Model 'T' / Out of control / On the crest / Nazca / Big black window / Max's / Toilet love / Rock & roll resurrection.
May 78. (7";w-drawn) *(SAFE 6)* **I HAD TOO MUCH TO DREAM LAST NIGHT. / FUCK OFF**

WAYNE COUNTY AND THE ELECTRIC CHAIRS

— added **HENRY PADOVANI** – guitar (ex-POLICE)

Jun 78. (7"gold+grey-ep) *(WC 2)* **BLATANTLY OFFENZIVE EP**
– Fuck off / Night time / Toilet love / Mean muthafuckin' man.

— **ELIOT MICHAELS** – guitar repl. COOK who joined The VIBRATORS

Aug 78. (7") *(SAFE 9)* **TRYING TO GET ON THE RADIO. / EVIL MINDED MOMMA**
Aug 78. (lp-grey+multi) *(GOOD 1)* **STORM THE GATES OF HEAVEN**
– Storm the gates of Heaven / Cry of angels / Speed demon / Mr. Normal / Man enough to be a woman / Trying to get on the radio / I had too much to dream last night / Tomorrow is another day.
above album featured MORGAN FISHER keyboards and DARRYL WAY violin
May 79. (lp) *(GOOD 2)* **THINGS YOUR MOTHER NEVER TOLD YOU**
– Wonder woman / Wall city girl / Boy with the stolen face / Un-con-troll-able / Things / Berlin / C3 / Midnight pal / Waiting for the marines / Think straight.

— producer & synth-man on above; DAVID CUNNINGHAM (FLYING LIZARDS)

Jun 79. (7") *(SAFE 13)* **BERLIN. / WAITING FOR THE MARINES**
(ext.12"pink+=) *(SAFELS 13)* – Midnight pal.
Nov 79. (7") *(SAFE 18)* **SO MANY WAYS. / J'ATTENDS LES MARINES**

— **WAYNE + ELIOT** went back to the States and found new members; **PETER JORDAN** – bass / **SAMMY MINELLI** – drums (they replaced HALLER and JOHNSON who joined FLYING LIZARDS after above ELECTRIC CHAIRS credited recording without WAYNE!)

May 80. (lp; as JAYNE COUNTY) *(LIVE 1)* **ROCK'N'ROLL RESURRECTION (live final gig)**
– Night time / Rock'n'roll Cleopatra / Are you a boy / Bad in bed / Hanky panky / Rock'n'roll resurrection / Fucked by the Devil / Cream in my jeans / Stuck on you / Fuck off.

— had already disbanded his/her group at the end of '79. He/she went to Berlin, before relocating to London, England and going solo

JAYNE COUNTY

w/ 1985 band JC5; **MICK ROBINSON** – guitar / STUART 'Dick' CLARKE – lead guitar / **SNIDE** – bass / **BASIL CREECE** – drums

Heighway R not iss.

May 86. (7") *(SAD 002)* **SAN FRANCISCO. / WHEN QUEENS COLLIDE (part 1)**

Revolver not iss.

Oct 86. (lp) *(REVLP 86)* **PRIVATE OYSTER**
– Private oyster / Man enough to be a woman / Fun in America / I feel in love with a Russian soldier / Bad in bed / Are you a boy or are you a girl? / When queens collide (part 1) / Double shot / Xerox that man / That Lady Dye twist / Love lives on lies. *(re-iss. Feb87 as 'AMERIKAN CLEOPATRA' for 'Konnexion'; KOMA 788016)*

Jungle not iss.

Jul 89. (7"ep) *(FREUD 27)* **BETTY GRABLE'S LEGS**
Jul 89. (7") *(JUNG 49)* **TIME MACHINE. / TAKE A DETOUR**

not iss. E.S.P.

Oct 93. (cd) *<ESP 2002-2>* **GODDESS OF WET DREAMS**
– Night time / Cream in my jeans / Paranoia paradise / Looking for a kiss / If you don't want to fuck – fuck off / Johnny gone to Heaven / Private world / Brainwashed / Take a detour / Party till armageddon. *(lp-iss.Oct98 on 'Get Back'; GET 32LP)*

Thunderbird not iss.

Jun 95. (cd) *(CSA 105)* **DEVIATION**

– compilations, etc. –

Feb 79. (7") *Illegal; (IL 005)* **THUNDER WHEN SHE WALKS. / WHAT YOU GOT** [ ] [-]
1981. (lp) *Safari; (NEN 1)* **THE BEST OF THE ELECTRIC CHAIRS** [ ] [-]
Jun 83. (7"pic-d) *Safari; (WCP 3)* **FUCK OFF. / TOILET LOVE** [ ] [-]
Dec 93. (cd) *RPM; (RPM 119)* **ROCK'N'ROLL CLEOPATRA – THE ESSENTIAL . . . VOLUME 1** [ ] [-]
Jul 95. (cd) *RPM; (RPM 145)* **LET YOUR BACKBONE SLIP! – THE ESSENTIAL . . . VOLUME 2** [ ] [-]

COURSE OF EMPIRE

Formed: Dallas, Texas, USA . . . 1988 by VAUGHN STEVENSON, MIKE GRAFF, PAUL SEMRAD and two drummers(!) CHAD LOVELL and MICHAEL JEROME. A rarity in the metal world, COURSE OF EMPIRE's politically aware lyrical slant saw them garner significant acclaim for the two albums – 'COURSE OF EMPIRE' (1992) and 'INITIATION' (1994) – they released on the 'Zoo Entertainment' label in the early 90's. Following Zoo's subsequent financial collapse, the band poured their money into a purpose built studio where they spent an extended period crafting a third album, 'TELEPATHIC LAST WORDS'. 'TVT' eventually took the record on board, releasing it in 1997. From the concept and lyrics right down to the cover art, the album was fashioned in the spirit of QUEENSRYCHE's classic 'Operation Mindcrime'. No bad thing, especially as COE contemporised their tales of new world disorder with experimental textures and inventive sampling.

Album rating: COURSE OF EMPIRE (*3) / INITIATION (*5) / TELEPATHIC LAST WORDS (*6)

VAUGHN STEVENSON – vocals / **MIKE GRAFF** – guitar / **PAUL SEMRAD** – bass / **CHAD LOVELL** – drums / **MICHAEL JEROME** – drums

Zoo – RCA Zoo – RCA

Oct 92. (cd/c) *<72445 11020-2/-4>* **COURSE OF EMPIRE** [-] [ ]
– Ptah / Coming of the century / God's jig / Copious / Cradle calls / Under the skies / Peace child / Sins of the fathers / Thrust / Mountains of the spoken / Dawn of the great eastern sun.
Feb 94. (12"ep/cd-ep) *<72445 14117-1/14109-2>* **INFESTED!** [-] [ ]
– Infested! / Infested! (mix) / Let's have a war / Joy.
Aug 94. (cd/c) *<(72445 11054-2/-4)>* **INITIATION** [ ] [ ] Jan94
– Hiss / White vision blowout / Gear / Breed / Apparition / Infested! / Invertebrate / Sacrifice / Minions / Initiation / The Chihuahuaphile.

not iss. T.V.T.

Jan 98. (cd/c) *<5790>* **TELEPATHIC LAST WORDS** [-] [ ]
– Radio Tehran / Neli maps / Information / Automatic writing #17 / Houdini's blind / Ride the static / Coming of the century / Persian song / 59 minutes / Freaks / Captain control / Respect / Blue moon.
Nov 98. (cd-s) *<113495>* **INFORMATION** [-] [ ]

COVENANT (see under ⇒ KOVENANT)

COVERDALE PAGE (see under ⇒ WHITESNAKE)

CRAAFT

Formed: Germany . . . 1984 by FRANZ KEIL, TOMMY KEISER and KLAUS LULEY, who subsequently recruited REINHARD BESSER and a drummer. Eschewing the typical German metal sound, CRAAFT took off in a more Americanised hard-rock direction. LULEY proved to be the band's greatest asset, his undeniable vocal prowess raising their AOR musings above the average. Signed to 'Epic', CRAAFT's eponymous debut album was roundly praised upon its 1986 release. With the likes of TOTO, STYX and NIGHT RANGER cornering the US market, the band – with MARCUS SCHLEICHER superseding BESSER and TOMMY SCHNEIDER now full-time drummer – found it hard to break through despite a reasonable follow-up album, 'SECOND HONEYMOON' in 1988. Their swansong, German-only 'NO TRICKS – JUST KICKS' was released in '91 without MARCUS who was replaced by DENNY ROTHHARDT and VITEK SPACEK.

Album rating: CRAAFT (*6) / SECOND HONEYMOON (*5) / NO TRICKS – JUST KICKS (*4)

KLAUS LULEY – vocals, guitar / **REINHARD BESSER** – guitar, vocals / **TOMMY KEISER** – bass (ex-KROKUS) / **FRANZ KEIL** – keyboards, vocals / **JURGEN ZOLLER + SANDY GENNARO** – drums

Epic not iss.

Jun 86. (7") *(A 6954)* **I WANNA LOOK IN YOUR EYES. / I GUESS YOU ARE THE NUMBER ONE** [ ] [-]
Jul 86. (lp/c) *(EPC/40 26880)* **CRAAFT** [ ] [-]
– I wanna look in your eyes / Breakin' walls ain't easy / Hold me / You're the best thing in my life / I guess you are the number one / Stranger / Don't wanna wait no more / Now that you're gone / Wasted years / Cool town lovers.

—— **MARCUS SCHLEICHER** – guitar; repl. BESSER

—— **TOMMY SCHNEIDER** – drums; repl. drummers above

R.C.A. not iss.

Dec 88. (lp/c/cd) *(PL/PK/PD 71826)* **SECOND HONEYMOON** [ ] [-]
– Run away / Twisted up all inside / Chance of your life / Jane / Gimme what you got / Running on love / Hey babe / Illusions / Don't you know what love can be / Are you ready to rock. *(cd+=)* – Right to your heart.

—— **DENNY ROTHHARDT** – bass + **VITEK SPACEK** – guitar; repl. MARCUS
1991. (cd/lp) *(PD/PL 74750)* **NO TRICKS – JUST KICKS** [-] [-] German

– No promises / Nothin' we can't take / Rocket / Comong home / Step inside / Bad line / Daytipper / I need a woman / Make it to the top / All 'n' now / Hold on / Break out / Let me love you / Living today / You were there.

—— folded after above

CRADLE OF FILTH

Formed: Suffolk, England . . . 1991 by gothic grave robbers fronted by former journalist, DANI DAVEY. Influenced by the Scandinavian black-metal scene, the group nevertheless carved out their own inimitably gothic-punk-orchestral English sound. Their 1994 debut, 'THE PRINCIPLE OF EVIL MADE FLESH' had distinct gothic overtones, although bludgeoning death-metal was their stock-in-trade. Another set, 'VEMPIRE' (1996), was quickly succeeded by their first for 'Music For Nations', 'DUSK . . . AND HER EMBRACE', although CRADLE OF FILTH garnered more attention for their controversial promo-shoots and "masturbating-nun" T-shirts. 1998 satanism and sex always on the agenda, DANI was the focal point since his awakening from the grave in '96. A TV documentary was made for BBC2, the band a tad uncomfortable when a devoted fan's mum followed them around in her camper van. However, 'CRUELTY AND THE BEAST' (1998), saw COF in the UK Top 50, Europe – especially Scandinavia – having already succumbed to their majesty. Towards the end of the decade, the Suffolk Satan botherers threw yet more filth at our pop kids with the release of home video, 'PANDAEMONAEON', the featured music also released separately as a mini-set, 'FROM THE CRADLE TO ENSLAVE'. Alongside such interestingly titled fare as 'OF DARK BLOOD AND F**KING' was an unlikely rendition of The Misfits' 'DEATH COMES RIPPING'. A new full length album, 'MIDIAN', arrived in late 2000, chock full of the usual tortuous vocals, brain-melting riffs, ridiculously symphonic keyboards and general gothic-tinged heathenry – bliss. On new imprint, 'Abra Cadavar', COF delivered yet another brief UK Top 75 entry, 'BITTER SUITES TO SUCCUMBI' (2001). • **Covered:** DEATH COMES RIPPING (Misfits) / SLEEPLESS (Anathema).

Album rating: THE PRINCIPLE OF EVIL MADE FLESH (*5) / DUSK AND HER VEMPIRE – OR DARK FAIRYTALES IN PHALLUSTEIN (*5) / DUSK . . . AND HER EMBRACE (*6) / CRUELTY AND THE BEAST (*6) / FROM THE CRADLE TO ENSLAVE mini (*4) / MIDIAN (*6) / BITTER SUITES TO SUCCUBI (*6) / December Moon: SOURCE OF ORIGIN (*6)

DANI DAVEY – vocals / **DAMIEN GREGORI** – keyboards / **STUART ANSTIS** – guitar / **GIAN PYRES** – guitar / **ROBIN EAGLESTONE** – bass / **NICHOLAS BARKER** – drums

Cacophonous Cacophonous

Mar 94. (cd/lp,blue-lp) *(<NIHL 1 CD/LP>)* **THE PRINCIPLE OF EVIL MADE FLESH** [ ] [ ]
– Darkness our bride (jugular wedding) / The principle of evil made flesh / The forest whispers my name / Iscariot / The black goddess rises / One final graven kiss / A crescendo of passion bleeding / To Eve the art of witchcraft / Of mist and midnight skies / In secret love we drown / A dream of wolves in the snow / Summer dying fast. *(re-iss. Jul98; same)* *<US re-iss. Feb00; same>*

—— STUART now took the name **JARED DEMETER** for next recording
Apr 96. (cd/lp) *(<NIHL 6/+LP>)* **VEMPIRE – OR DARK FAIRYTALES IN PHALLUSTEIN** [ ] [ ]
– Ebony dressed for sunset / Forest whispers my name / Queen of winter throned / Nocturnal supremacy / She mourns a lengthening shadow / Rape and ruin of angels (hosanas in extremis). *(re-iss. Jul98; same)*

Music For Nations Fierce

Nov 96. (cd/c/lp) *(CD/T+/MFN 208)* *<11096>* **DUSK . . . AND HER EMBRACE** [ ] [ ] Jan97
– Human inspired to nightmare / Heaven from asunder / Funeral in Carpathia / Gothic romance / Malice through the looking glass / Duske and her embrace / Graveyard moonlight / Beauty sleeps in Sodom / Haunted shores. *(sha-cd-iss. Mar97 +=; CDMFNC 208)* – Hell awaits / Camilia's masque. *(other cd; CDMFNX 208)* – Nocturnal supremacy '96.

—— **LES 'LECTOR' SMITH** – keyboards; repl. DAMIEN GREGORI who departed mid-97
May 98. (cd/c/lp) *(CD/T+/MFN 242)* *<11128>* **CRUELTY AND THE BEAST** [48] [ ]
– Once upon atrocity / Thirteen autumns and a widow / Cruelty beneath thee orchids / Beneath the howling stars / Venus in fear / Desire in violent overture / The twisted nails of faith / Bathory aria: Benighted like Usher – A . . . / Portrait of the dead countess / Lustmord and wargasm (the lick of carnivorous winds). *(other cd+=; CDMFNX 242)* – (bonus tracks).

—— **STUART SMITH** – guitar; repl. PYRES

Music For Nations Metal Blade

Nov 99. (m-cd) *(CDMFN 254)* *<14301>* **FROM THE CRADLE TO ENSLAVE** [ ] [ ] Dec99
– From the cradle to enslave / Of dark blood and fucking / Death comes ripping / Sleepless / Perverts church (from the cradle to deprave) / Funeral in Carpathia (be quick or be dead version).

—— STUART had now departed; he subsequently formed APHELION, releasing 'APHELION I-VI' mini-set in March '01

Music For Nations Koch

Oct 00. (cd/lp) *(CD+/MFN 666)* *<8219>* **MIDIAN** [63] [ ] Nov00
– At the gates of Midian / Cthulhu dawn / Saffron's curse / Death magick for adepts / Lord abortion / Amor e morta / Creatures that kissed in cold mirrors / Her ghost in the fog / Satanic mantra / Tearing the veil from grace / Tortured soul asylum.

AbraCadavar AbraCadavar

Jun 01. (cd) *<(CDF 001CD)>* **BITTER SUITES TO SUCCUBI** [63] [ ]
– Dinner at deviant's place / All hope in eclipse / Born in a burial gown / Suicide and other comforts / Black goddess II Ebon Nemesis (2001 version) / Principle of evil made flesh (2001 version) / No time to cry / Born in a burial gown (video).

DECEMBER MOON

— **ROB** with **WAS** – drums (of BLOOD DIVINE)

Spinefarm not iss.

Nov 97. (cd) *(SP 1032CD)* **SOURCE OF ORIGIN** [ ] [-]
– Exaltation of power / You can't bless the damned / Nocturnal transcendency / Winter sunset / Black millennium / The apparition of Mother Earth / Twinned with destiny / An empty gesture.

CRAMPS

Formed: New York City, New York, USA . . . 1975 by LUX INTERIOR and POISON IVY, who recruited fellow weirdos BRYAN GREGORY and PAM 'BALAM' GREGORY (the latter was replaced by MIRIAM LINNA, who in turn was superseded by NICK KNOX). The trashiest, sleaziest 50's throwbacks to ever besmirch the good name of rock'n'roll, The CRAMPS took the genre's inherit debauchery to its thrilling (and often hilarious) conclusion. Crawling from the mire of CBGB's punk scene like the proverbial Swamp Thing in one of their beloved B-movies, The CRAMPS started as they meant to go on, initiating their vinyl career in 1978 with an obscure cover, 'THE WAY I WALK'. The single was backed with a riotous mangling of The Trashmen's 'SURFIN' BIRD', as close to a theme tune as the band came. A follow-up, 'HUMAN FLY', introduced LUX's impressive capacity for disturbing accurate animal (and insect!) noises, its voodoo surf twang and creeping tempo scarier than the frontman's skintight leotard. Subsequently signed to Miles Copeland's 'I.R.S.' label, The CRAMPS set up shop in Sun Studios, Memphis (where else?!) with producer ALEX CHILTON at the production helm, working on the material for their acclaimed debut set, 'SONGS THE LORD TAUGHT US' (1980). Featuring such bad taste gems as 'GARBAGEMAN' (more animal noises!), 'I WAS A TEENAGE WEREWOLF' and 'STRYCHNINE', the record further boosted the band's cult following. The departure of GREGORY after the 'DRUG TRAIN' single was the first in a long series of line-up changes through which IVY (the sexiest thing in stockings!) and INTERIOR were the only constants. With KID CONGO POWERS as a replacement, the band cut the less convincing 'PSYCHEDELIC JUNGLE' (1981), their final release for Copeland who they later sued. A short spell with the French 'New Rose' label and then 'Big Beat' saw the release of the live mini 'SMELL OF FEMALE' (1983). This went at least some way to capturing the cheap thrills of a CRAMPS gig, though readers are advised to experience the real thing; if the primeval spirit of raw rock'n'roll doesn't move you, then the sight of a grown man in a leather thong and and high heels just might! INTERIOR had always modelled himself on a kind of ELVIS-from-the-crypt and in 1986, The CRAMPS met their maker, so to speak, on the classic 'A DATE WITH ELVIS'. The likes of 'THE HOT PEARL SNATCH', 'CAN YOUR PUSSY DO THE DOG?' and 'WHAT'S INSIDE A GIRL?', need no further explanation save that THE KING was no doubt turning in his grave. Though this marked a creative and commercial peak of sorts, The CRAMPS continued to think up the best song titles in the Western World over a string of late 80's/90's albums, including 'STAY SICK' (1990), 'LOOK MOM, NO HEAD' (1991; essential if only for the IGGY POP collaboration, 'MINISKIRT BLUES'), 'FLAME JOB' (1994) and 'BIG BEAT FROM BADSVILLE' (1997). Though they've hardly pushed back the boundaries of music, The CRAMPS are arguably even more essential now than in their heyday, if only to remind he current crop of indie dullards what it REALLY means to play "The Devil's Music". • **Songwriters:** Most written by LUX and IVY except SURFIN' BIRD (Trashmen) / FEVER (Little Willie John) / THE WAY I WALK (Robert Gordon) / GREEN DOOR (Jim Lowe) / JAILHOUSE ROCK (Elvis Presley) / MULESKINNER BLUES (Fendermen) / PSYCHOTIC REACTION (Count Five) / LONESOME TOWN (Ricky Nelson) / HARD WORKIN' MAN (Jack Nitzche) / HITSVILLE 29 B.C. (Turnbow) / WHEN I GET THE BLUES (Larry Mize) / HOW COME YOU DO ME? (. . .Joiner) / STRANGE LOVE (. . .West) / BLUES BLUES BLUES (. . .Thompson) / TRAPPED LOVE (Kohler-Fana) / SINNERS (. . .Aldrich) / ROUTE 66 (. . . Troup) / etc. • **Trivia:** Their fan club was surprisingly based in Grangemouth, Scotland (wee Marty fi the Nash ran it!)

Album rating: SONGS THE LORD TAUGHT US (*7) / PSYCHEDELIC JUNGLE (*7) / OFF THE BONE compilation (*8) / SMELL OF FEMALE (*6) / A DATE WITH ELVIS (*7) / STAY SICK (*6) / LOOK MOM, NO HEAD! (*5) / FLAMEJOB (*6) / BIG BEAT FROM BADSVILLE (*5)

LUX INTERIOR (b. ERICK LEE PURKHISER, 1948, Akron, Ohio) – vocals / **POISON IVY RORSCHACH** (b. KIRSTY MARLANA WALLACE, 1954, Sacramento, Calif.) – guitar / **BRYAN GREGORY** (b. Detroit, Mich.) – guitar / **NICK KNOX** (b. NICHOLAS STEPHANOFF) – drums repl. MIRIAM LINNA (later to The ZANTEES & The A-BONES) who had repl. PAM 'BALAM' GREGORY

not iss. Vengeance

Apr 78. (7") <666> **THE WAY I WALK. / SURFIN' BIRD** [-] [ ]
Nov 78. (7") <668> **HUMAN FLY. / DOMINO** [-] [ ]

Illegal I.R.S.

Jun 79. (12"ep) *(ILS 12-013)* **GRAVEST HITS** [ ] [-]
– Human fly / The way I walk / Domino / Surfin' bird / Lonesome town. *(re-iss. Sep82 – 7"blue-ep / re-iss. Mar83- 7"red-ep; same)*
Mar 80. (7") *(ILS 0017)* **FEVER. / GARBAGEMAN** [ ] [-]
Apr 80. (lp) *(ILP 005)* <SP 007> **SONGS THE LORD TAUGHT US** [ ] [ ]
– TV set / Rock on the Moon / Garbageman / I was a teenage werewolf / Sunglasses after dark / The mad daddy / Mystery plane / Zombie dance / What's behind the mask / Strychnine / I'm cramped / Tear it up / Fever. *(re-iss. Feb90;)*
May 80. (7") <IR 9014> **DRUG TRAIN. / GARAGEMAN** [-] [ ]
Jul 80. (7"m) *(ILS 021)* **DRUG TRAIN. / LOVE ME / I CAN HARDLY STAND IT** [ ] [-]

— **KID CONGO POWERS** (b. BRIAN TRISTAN, 27 Mar'61, La Puente, Calif.) – guitar; repl. JULIEN BOND, who had repl. GREGORY for two months mid 1980.

I.R.S. I.R.S.

May 81. (7"yellow) *(PFS 1003)* <IR 9021> **GOO GOO MUCK. / SHE SAID** [ ] [ ] Aug81
May 81. (lp) <*(SP 70016)*> **PSYCHEDELIC JUNGLE** [ ] [ ] Jul81
– Green fuzz / Goo goo muck / Rockin' bones / Voodoo idol / Primitive / Caveman / The crusher / Don't eat stuff off the sidewalk / Can't find my mind / Jungle hop / The natives are restless / Under the wires / Beautiful gardens / Green door. *(cd-iss. Sep98 on 'E.M.I.'; 496504-2)*
Oct 81. (12"m) *(PFSX 1008)* **THE CRUSHER. / SAVE IT / NEW KIND OF KICK** [ ] [-]

— (LUX, IVY & NICK were joined by **IKE KNOX** (Nick's cousin) – guitar; repl. KID CONGO who returned to GUN CLUB (appeared on live tracks 83-84)

Big Beat not iss.

Nov 83. (red-m-lp) *(NED 6)* **SMELL OF FEMALE (live)** [74] [-]
– Faster pussycat / I ain't nuthin' but a gorehound / Psychotic reaction / The most exhalted potentate of love / You got good taste / Call of the wig hat. *(pic-lp Jun84; NEDP 6) (re-iss. Feb91 cd+=/c+=; CDWIKM/WIKMC 95)* – Beautiful gardens / She said / Surfin' dead.

— (signed to below label in France)

New Rose New Rose

Mar 84. (7"/7"pic-d) *(NEW 28/+P)* **FASTER PUSSYCAT. / YOU GOT GOOD TASTE** [-] [-] French
Mar 84. (7"colrd;various) *(NEW 33)* **I AIN'T NUTHIN' BUT A GOREHOUND. / WEEKEND ON MARS** [-] [-] French

— **CANDY FUR** (DEL-MAR) – guitar; repl. IKE

Big Beat not iss.

Nov 85. (7"orange) *(NS 110)* **CAN YOUR PUSSY DO THE DOG? / BLUE MOON BABY** [68] [-]
(12"blue+=) *(NST 110)* – Georgia Lee Brown.
Feb 86. (blue-lp/c/cd) *(WIKA/WIKC/CDWIK 46)* **A DATE WITH ELVIS** [34] [-]
– How far can too far go / The hot pearl snatch / People ain't too good / What's inside a girl? / Can your pussy do the dog? / Kizmiaz / Cornfed dames / Chicken / (Hot pool of) Woman need / Aloha from Hell / It's just that song. <*US-iss.1994 on 'Capitol'; 73579*>
May 86. (7") *(NS 115)* **WHAT'S INSIDE A GIRL? / GET OFF THE ROAD** [ ] [-]
(12"+=) *(NST 115)* – Give me a woman.
(Mar87; cd-s++=) *(CRAMP 1)* – Scene / Heart of darkness.

Enigma Enigma

Jan 90. (7"/7"sha-pic-d/c-s) *(ENV/+PD/TC 17)* **BIKINI GIRLS WITH MACHINE GUNS. / JACKYARD BACKOFF** [35] [ ]
(12"+=/cd-s+=) *(12ENV/ENVCD 17)* – Her love rubbed off.
Feb 90. (cd/c/lp) *(CDENV/TCENV/ENVLP 1001)* <73543> **STAY SICK** [62] [ ]
– Bop pills / Goddam rock'n'roll / Bikini girls with machine guns / All women are bad / Creature from the black leather lagoon / Shortenini' bread / Daisy's up your butterfly / Everything goes / Journey to the centre of a girl / Mama oo pow pow / Saddle up a buzz buzz / Muleskinner blues. *(cd+=)* – Her love rubbed off. *(pic-lp Nov90; ENVLPPD 101) (re-iss. Feb94 cd/lp; CD+/WIKD 126)*
Apr 90. (7"/c-s) *(ENV/+TC 19)* **ALL WOMEN ARE BAD. / TEENAGE RAGE (live)** [ ] [-]
(12"+=/12"pic-d+=/cd-s+=) *(12ENV/12ENVPD/ENVCD 19)* – King of the drapes (live) / High school hellcats (live).
Aug 90. (7") **CREATURES FROM THE BLACK LEATHER LAGOON. / JAILHOUSE ROCK** [ ] [-]
(12"+=/cd-s+=) – Beat out my love.

— **LUX & IVY** were joined by **SLIM CHANCE** – guitar (ex-PANTHER BURNS) / **JIM SCLAVUNOS** – drums

Big Beat Restless

Sep 91. (7") *(NST 135)* **EYEBALL IN MY MARTINI. / WILDER WILDER FASTER FASTER** [ ] [-]
(12"+=/cd-s+=) *(12/CD NST 135)* – Wilder wilder faster faster.
Sep 91. (cd/c/lp) *(CDWIK/WIKDC/WIKAD 101)* <72586> **LOOK MOM, NO HEAD!** [ ] [ ]
– Dames, booze, chains and boots / Two headed sex change / Blow up your mind / Hard workin' man / Miniskirt blues / Alligator stomp / I wanna get in your pants Bend over, I'll drive / Don't get funny with me / Eyeball in my Martini / Hipsville 29 B.C. / When I get the blues (the strangeness in me). *(also pic-lp/pic-cd; WIKDP/CDWIKD 101)*

— **NICKY ALEXANDER** – drums (ex-WEIRDOS); repl. JIM

Sep 92. (cd-ep) *(CDNST 136)* **BLUES FIX EP** [ ] [-]
– Hard workin' man / It's mighty crazy / Jelly roll rock / Shombalor.

— **HARRY DRUMDINI** – drums; repl. NICKY

Creation Medicine – Warners

Oct 94. (7") *(CRE 180)* **ULTRA TWIST! / CONFESSIONS OF A PSYCHO CAT** [ ] [-]
(12"+=)(cd-s+=) *(CRE 180T)(CRESCD 180)* – No club love wolf.
Oct 94. (cd/c/lp) *(CRECD/C-CRE/CRELP 170)* <24592> **FLAMEJOB** [ ] [ ]
– Mean machine / Ultra twist / Let's get f*cked up / Nest of the cuckoo bird / I'm customized / Sado country auto show / Naked girl falling down the stairs / How come you do me? / Inside out and upside down (with you) / Trapped love / Swing the big eyed rabbit / Strange love / Blues blues blues / Sinners / Route 66 (get your kicks on).
Feb 95. (7") *(CRE 196)* **NAKED GIRL FALLING DOWN THE STAIRS. / LET'S GET F*CKED UP** [ ] [-]
(cd-s+=) *(CRESCD 196)* – Surfin' bird.

Epitaph Epitaph

Oct 97. (cd/c/lp) <*(6516-2/-4/-1)*> **BIG BEAT FROM BADSVILLE** [ ] [ ]
– Cramp stomp / God monster / It thing hard on / Like a bad girl should / Sheena's in a goth gang / Queen of pain / Monkey with your tail / Devil behind that bush / Super goo / Hypno sex ray / Burn she devil, burn / Wet nightmare / Badass bug / Haulass hyena.
Dec 97. (7") *(6527-7)* **LIKE A BAD GIRL SHOULD. / WET NIGHTMARE** [ ] [-]
(cd-s+=) *(6527-2)* – I walked all night.

– compilations, others, etc. –

May 83. (lp) *Illegal; (ILP 012) / I.R.S.; <SP 70042>* **OFF THE BONE** <US-title 'BAD MUSIC FOR BAD PEOPLE'> [44] [ ] Feb84
– Human fly / The way I walk / Domino / Surfin' bird / Lonesome town / Garbageman / Fever / Drug train / Love me / I can't hardly stand it / Goo goo muck / She said / The crusher / Save it / New kind of kick. *(cd-iss. Jan87; ILPCD 012) (cd re-iss. 1992 on 'Castle'+=;)* – Uranium Rock / Good taste (live)

1984. (4x7"box) *New Rose;* **I AIN'T NUTHIN' BUT A GOREHOUND. / WEEKEND ON MARS // FASTER PUSSYCAT. / YOU GOT GOOD TASTE // CALL OF THE WIG HAT. / THE MOST EXHALTED POTENTATE OF LOVE // PSYCHOTIC REACTION. / (one sided)** [-] [-] French
(all 4 either blue/white/black/green)

May 86. (7") *New Rose; (NEW 71)* **KIZMIAZ. / GET OFF THE ROAD** [-] [-]
(12"+=) *(NEW 70)* – Give me a woman.

Nov 87. (lp) *Vengeance;* **ROCKIN' AND REELIN' IN AUCKLAND, NEW ZEALAND (live)** [-] [ ]
(UK cd-iss. Sep94 on 'Big Beat'; CDWIKD 132)

Sep 00. (3xcd-box) *EMI; (528345-2)* **SONGS THE LORD TAUGHT US / OFF THE BONE / PSYCHEDELIC JUNGLE** [ ] [-]

CRASS

Formed: North Weald, Essex, England . . . 1978 by commune dwellers STEVE IGNORANT and PENNY RIMBAUD. With a line-up completed by PHIL FREE, JOY DE VIVRE, N.A. PALMER, PETE WRIGHT and MICK G., the pseudonymous crew unleashed the first instalment of their anarchist manifesto in late '78 on indie label, 'Small Wonder'. 'THE FEEDING OF THE FIVE THOUSAND' EP introduced the raging punk blitzkrieg of CRASS in full flow, an "Oi!-Guv" cockney vocal raging over military-style drumming and shouting down religion and "the system" in all its multifarious guises. Forming their own label (an operation which subsequently released material by a range of protest bands including POISON GIRLS, CONFLICT and RUDIMENTARY PENI) was the logical next step for such an avowedly anti-establishment operation and Autumn '79 saw the release of 'STATIONS OF THE CRASS', a (part-live) double album's worth of bile directed at all the usual subjects and some surprising ones (i.e. The CLASH in 'WHITE PUNKS ON HOPE'), even taking a pot shot at media outrage over Myra Hindley on 'MOTHER EARTH'. Two politically incendiary 45's appeared in the early 80's, the first, 'BLOODY REVOLUTIONS' was a shared affair with The POISON GIRLS, while the peerless epic, 'NAGASAKI NIGHTMARE', represented the pinnacle of punk outrage. The CRASS line-up fluctuated according to whoever was living with them at the time, the band's democratic approach seeing EVE and PENNY take on the vocal chores for feminist tract, 'PENIS ENVY' (1981). Not a band to do things by halves, CRASS released their second double set with 'CHRIST THE ALBUM' (1983), a record that saw them widen their musical horizons and intersperse songs with spoken word poetry. If the band were straying too far into neo-hippy territory for some fans comfort, there was no doubting the strength of feeling behind 'HOW DOES IT FEEL (TO BE THE MOTHER OF 1000 DEAD)?', directed squarely at Margaret Thatcher and taking her to task over the Falklands conflict. As the war raged, CRASS had tapes confiscated by the government and found themselves charged under The Obscene Publications Act. Not surprisingly, no records were ever given a release outside the UK! The album that had spawned such apparently dangerous fare ('SHEEP FARMING IN THE FALKLANDS' being another sarcastic classic) was 'YES SIR, I WILL' (1983), an even more experimental set that divided opinion. It also proved to be the band's swansong, and, staying true to their original vow of breaking up in early '84 (which was the meltdown year according to George Orwell) following a final single, 'YOU'RE ALREADY DEAD'. While EVE and PENNY worked together on a set of poetry, 'ACTS OF LOVE' (1986), IGNORANT subsequently joined fellow anarchists CONFLICT, for whom he'd deputised in the past.

Album rating: THE FEEDING OF THE FIVE THOUSAND (*8) / STATIONS OF THE CRASS (*6) / PENIS ENVY (*6) / CHRIST THE ALBUM (*5) / YES SIR, I WILL (*4) / BEST BEFORE 1984 compilation (*7)

EVE LIBERTINE – vocals / **JOY DE VIVRE** – vocals / **STEVE IGNORANT** – vocals / **PHIL FREE** – lead guitar / **N.A. PALMER** – guitar, vocals / **PENNY RIMBAUD** – drums / **PETE WRIGHT** – bass / **MICK G.** (DUFFIELD) – flute, film-maker /

Small Wonder — not iss.

Dec 78. (12"ep) *(WEENY 2)* **THE FEEDING OF THE FIVE THOUSAND** [ ] [-]
– Asylum / Do they owe us a living? / End result / They've got a bomb / Punk is dead / Reject of society / General Bacardi / Banned from The Roxy's / G's song / Fight war, not wars / Women / Securicor / Sucks / You pay / Angels / What a shame / So what / Well? . . .do they. *(re-iss. Nov80 & Oct81 & Dec87 as 'FEEDING OF THE 5,000 EP (2nd SITTING)' on 'Crass'; 621984) (cd-iss. Oct90 +=; 621984CD)* – Reality asylum.

Crass — not iss.

May 79. (7") *(521984-1)* **REALITY ASYLUM. / SHAVED WOMAN** [ ] [-]
(re-iss. Dec80; CRASS 19454U)

Sep 79. (d-lp) *(CRASS 521984)* **STATIONS OF THE CRASS** [ ] [-]
– Mother Earth / White punks on hope / You've got big hands / Darling / System / Big man, big M.A.N. / Hurry up Garry / Fun going on / Crutch of society / Heard too much about / Chairman of the bored / Tired / Walls / Uptight citizen / Time out / The gasman cometh / Democrats / Contaminational power / I ain't thick it's just a trick. // live:- System / Big man, big M.A.N. / Banned from the Roxy / Hurry up Garry / Time out / They've got a bomb / Fight war, not wars / Women / Shaved women / You pay / Heard too much about / Angels / What a shame / So what / G's song / Do they owe us a living? / Punk is dead. *(re-iss. Oct81 & Dec87; same) (cd-iss. Oct90; 521984CD)*

May 80. (7") *(421984-1)* **BLOODY REVOLUTIONS. / Poison Girls: PERSONS UNKNOWN** [ ] [-]
(re-iss. Dec80 as above on 'Crass/Xntrix' joint label outing)

Feb 81. (7") *(421984-5)* **NAGASAKI NIGHTMARE. / BIG A LITTLE A** [ ] [-]

Oct 81. (lp) *(CRASS 321984-1)* **PENIS ENVY** [ ] [-]
– Bat a motel / Systematic death / Poison in a pretty pill / What the fuck / Where next Columbus / Berkertex bribe / Smother love / Health surface / Dry weather. *(re-iss. Dec87 lp/c; CRASS 321984-1/-4) (cd-iss. Oct90; 321984CD)*

Dec 81. (7") *(COLD TURKEY 1)* **MERRY CRASSMAS. / MERRY CRASSMAS – HAVE FUN** [ ] [-]

Aug 82. (7"promo+flexi) *(421984-6)* **RIVAL TRIBAL REBEL REVEL> / BULLY BOYS GO OUT FIGHTING** [-] [-]

Aug 82. (d-lp) *(BOLLOX 2U2)* **CHRIST THE ALBUM (some live)** [26] [-]
– Have a nice day / Mother love / Nineteen eighty bore / I know there is love / Beg your pardon / Birth control 'n' rock'n'roll / Reality white-wash / It's the greatest working class rip-off / Deadhead / You can be who / Buy no pay as you go / Rival tribal revel rebel part 2 / Bumhooler / Sentiment / Major General despair / Banned from the Roxy / The sound of one hand / Punk is dead / Nagasaki nightmare / Bat a motel blues / Berkertex bribe / Fold it in half / Big hands / Heart-throb of the mortuary / Bumhooler / Big A little A / First woman / Arlington 73 / Bomb plus bomb tape / Contaminational power / I ain't thick / G's song / Securicor / I can't stand it / Shaved women / A part of life / Do they owe us a living? / So what / Salt'n'pepper. *(cd-iss. Oct90; BOLLOX 2U2CD)*

Oct 82. (7") *(221984-6)* **HOW DOES IT FEEL (TO BE THE MOTHER OF 1000 DEAD?). / THE IMMORTAL DEATH / DON'T TELL ME YOU CARE** [ ] [-]

May 83. (lp) *(121984-2)* **YES SIR, I WILL** [ ] [-]
– Yes sir, I will / The pig's head controversy – the aesthetics of anarchy. *(cd-iss. Oct90; 121984-2CD)*

May 83. (7") *(121984-3)* **SHEEP FARMING IN THE FALKLANDS. / GOTCHA! (live)** [ ] [-]
(free-7"brown+=) *(121984-4)* **WHO DUNNIT? / WHO DUNNIT (part 2)**

Jan 84. (7") *(CATNO 4)* **YOU'RE ALREADY DEAD. / DON'T GET CAUGHT / NAGASAKI IS YESTERDAY'S DOG END** [ ] [-]

— broke up 1984. STEVE joined CONFLICT

— note: all albums were issued by CRASS in the States around mid-90's

– compilations, others, etc. –

Jul 86. (d-lp) *Crass; (CATNO 5)* **BEST BEFORE 1984** [ ] [-]
– Intro / Do they owe us a living? / Major general despair / Angela Rippon / Reality asylum / Shaved women / Bloody revolutions / Nagasaki nightmare / Big a little a / Rival tribal rebel revel – Sheep farming in the Falklands (Flexidisc version) / How does it feel / The immortal death / Don't tell me that you care / Sheep farming in the Falklands / Gotcha / Nagasaki is yesterdays dogend / Don't get caught / Smash the mac / Do they owe us a living? (live) *(cd-iss. Oct90; CRASS 5CD)*

Nov 86. (12") *Crass; (CATNO 6)* **TEN NOTES ON A SUMMER'S DAY. / (instrumental mix)** [ ] [-]
(re-iss. Aug98, 12"/cd-s; CATNO 6/+CD)

Dec 93. (cd) *Pomona; (ONA 002CD)* **YOU'LL RUIN IT FOR EVERYONE (live '81)** [ ] [-]

Nov 96. (cd) *Allied; (ALLIED 76CD)* **CHRIST THE BOOTLEG** [ ] [-]
(re-iss. Jun99 on 'No Idea'; NIR 082)

– others, solo, etc. –

on 'Crass; unless mentioned otherwise

May 81. (7"white-flexi; by JOY DE VIVRE) *(CRASS ENVY 1)* **OUR WEDDING** [ ] [-]

Jun 85. (lp; by EVE LIBERTINE) *(1984-4)* **ACT OF LOVE** [ ] [-]
– (short poems written 1968-73 by Joy's deceased friend, WALLY HOPE) *(re-iss. Oct95; same)*

Jul 92. (cd/lp; by PENNY RIMBAUD) **CHRIST'S REALITY ASYLUM** (spoken word) [ ] [-]

Nov 92. (cd; by EVE LIBERTINE) *Red Herring; (RH 2CD)* **SKATING** [ ] [-]

CRAZY GODS OF ENDLESS NOISE

Formed: Bournemouth, England . . . 1992 by ANT HILL, TIM BAKER and GAZ KING. Following on from debut mini-set, 'INFLATABLE GEEK', the trio secured a spot on the Kerrang! Twister Tour and also appeared on the rock mag's free cassette, 'Supersonic Volume 1'. With a buzz already underway, CGOEN pretty much lived up to expectations with their highly anticipated debut album, 'HEAVY PLANET' (1996). Mentioned in the same breath as the likes of RED HOT CHILI PEPPERS and the late, lamented FAITH NO MORE (especially with regards to HILL's voice), the record got jiggy with it in all the right places, proving that truly, in comparison, most metal bands were D'void of the Funk.

Album rating: HEAVY PLANET (*6)

ANT HILL – vocals, bass / **TIM BAKER** – vocals, guitar / **GAZ KING** – drums

Blind — not iss.

1994. (m-cd) **INFLATABLE GEEK** [ ] [-]
– Godloop / Bob's ways / Here comes the split / Mr. Hot dog man / Iron lung / That is correct.

Nov 95. (7") *(CRAZY 73)* **JUGFILL. /** [ ] [-]

Jul 96. (12"/cd-s) *(CRAZY 125/25)* **GODLOOP. /** [ ] [-]

Oct 96. (12"/cd-s) *(CRAZY 127/27)* **TRAPPED WATER. /** [ ] [-]

Nov 96. (cd/c) *(CDCRAZY 26/46)* **HEAVY PLANET** [ ] [-]
– New shoes / Trapped water / Candy calling / Razor baby / The child jumps / Bustenhalter / Jugfill / Coin-op boulevard / Cool propaganda / Treacle tummy fudge – Time treat / My TV told me to do it / Godloop.

— disbanded some time later

CRAZYHEAD

Formed: Leicester, England . . . 1986 by (IAN) ANDERSON, KEV REVERB, FAST DICK, PORK BEAST and ex-DOCTOR & THE MEDICS drummer, VOM. Lumped in with the media created "Grebo" scene along with POP WILL EAT ITSELF, GAYE BYKERS ON ACID and the early WONDER STUFF, CRAZYHEAD signed to EMI offshoot, 'Food', debuting the following year with the 12"er, 'WHAT GIVES YOU THE IDEA YOU'RE SO AMAZING BABY?'. Over the course of the next year or so, the grimy 5-piece released a string of singles, the last of which, 'RAGS', accompanied the 'DESERT ORCHID' album in Autumn '88. Moving upstairs to 'Parlophone', CRAZYHEAD scored their second minor hit single, 'HAVE LOVE, WILL TRAVEL', having previously entered the charts with 'TIME HAS TAKEN ITS TOLL ON YOU'. In March 1990, having played Romania, CRAZYHEAD were the only Western outfit to appear at Namibia's Independence Festival in front of 50,000 people. After failing to cross over into the alternative mainstream, the group were consigned to 'Revolver' where they released their PAT COLLIER-produced follow-up set, 'SOME KIND OF FEVER' (1990). In 1998, CRAZYHEAD made a vain attempt to claw back any sort of respect via the album, 'FUCKED BY ROCK'.

Album rating: DESERT ORCHID (*6) / SOME KIND OF FEVER (*4) / LIVE IN MEMPHIS (*3) / FUCKED BY ROCK (*4)

(IAN) ANDERSON – vocals / **KEV REVERB** (b. KEVIN BAYLISS) – guitar, piano, sitar / **FAST DICK** (b. RICHARD BELL) – guitar / **PORK BEAST** (b. ALEX PEACH) – bass / **VOM** (b. ROB MORRIS) – drums, percussion (ex-DOCTOR & THE MEDICS)

Food / EMI America

Mar 87. (12"ep) *(SNAK 8)* **WHAT GIVES YOU THE IDEA YOU'RE SO AMAZING BABY? / OUT ON A LIMB / SNAKE EYES** [ ] [-]

Jul 87. (7") *(FOOD 10)* **BABY TURPENTINE. / THAT KIND OF LOVE** [ ] [-]
(12"+=) *(SNAK 10)* – Bang bang / That sinking feeling.

Jun 88. (7") *(FOOD 12)* **TIME HAS TAKEN ITS TOLL ON YOU. / DOWN** [65] [-]
(ext-12"+=) *(12FOOD 12)* – The ballad of Baby Turpentine.
(10"+=) *(10FOOD 12)* – Here comes Johnny.
(cd-s+=) *(CDFOOD 12)* – Bang bang.

Sep 88. (7") *(FOOD 14)* **RAGS. / RUB THE BUDDHA** [ ] [-]
(12"+=) *(12FOOD 14)* – Screaming apple.
(12"++=/cd-s++=) *(12FOODS/CDFOOD 14)* – Fortune teller.

Oct 88. (lp/c/cd) *(FOOD LP/TC/CD 1)* <E1/E4 91035> **DESERT ORCHID** [ ] [ ]
– In the sun / Jack the scissorman / Time has taken its toll on you / Have love, will travel / What gives you the idea you're so amazing baby? / I don't want that kind of love / Dragon city / Buy a gun / Rags / Tower of fire / Cardinal Phink. *(c+=)* – Bang bang. *(cd++=)* – Out on a limb / Down / Time has taken its toll on you (extended). *(cd re-iss. Mar89 on 'Parlophone'; CDP 791035-2)*

Parlophone / not iss.

Feb 89. (7"ep/12"ep) *(SGE/12SGE 2025)* **HAVE LOVE, WILL TRAVEL EP** [68] [-]
– Have love will travel / Out on a limb (live) / Baby Turpentine (live) / Snake eyes (live).
(cd-ep++=) *(CDSGE 2025)* – Here comes Johnny (live).

— In Dec'89, CRAZYHEAD also covered Diesel Park West's 'LIKE PRINCES DO' on the Various Artists 'THE FOOD CHRISTMAS EP', which hit No.63.

Revolver / not iss.

Aug 90. (7") **EVERYTHING'S ALRIGHT. /** [ ] [-]

Nov 90. (cd/c/lp) *(REV XD/MC/LP 162)* **SOME KIND OF FEVER** [ ] [-]
– Big sister / Above these things / Everything's alright / Magic eye / I can do anything / Movie theme / Talk about you / Rome / Night train / Some kinda fever.

— disbanded for the rest of the 90's, until . . .

Snatch / not iss.

Dec 98. (cd) *(GASH 3)* **FUCKED BY ROCK** [ ] [-]
– Buy a gun / Every mother's monkey / Time has taken it's toll on you / Baltimore / Movie theme / Golden highway / Out on a limb / Do anything / Bang bang / Sweet sweet life / Pretty sick / Dragon city / Fish / Dragster girl / Long dark daze / The ballad of baby turpentine.

– compilations, etc. –

Jan 89. (12"ep/cd-ep) *Strange Fruit; (SFNT/+CD 018)* **NIGHT TRACKS** [ ] [-]

Sep 95. (cd) *Pearls From The Past; <BOE 3>* **GRIND (live in Memphis)** [-] [ ]

CRAZY TOWN

Formed: Los Angeles, California, USA ... 1998 by SETH BINZER aka SHIFTY SHELLSHOCK and BRET MAZUR aka EPIC. Having hung out with L.A.'s in-crowd for years, the pair began handing out demos to well connected mates and soon had the likes of KORN, SCOTT WEILAND and ORGY all trying to sign them to their respective labels. In the end they plumped for 'Columbia' and duly recorded their major label debut set, 'THE GIFT OF GAME' (1999; UK release, 2000), together with latter day CRAZY TOWN members TROUBLE VALLI, SQUIRREL, FAYDOEDEELAY and JAMES 'JBJ' BRADLEY JR. Featuring cameos by the likes of KRS-1 and MAD LION, the album went for the hip-hop/metal jugular with testosterone-fuelled grooves piledriving seedy tales of Hollywood lowlife. True to their belligerent reputation, the band answered Columbia's refusal to print their website on the sleeve by naming a song after the electronic address and tagging it on to the end of the tracklisting. Although their first two singles ('TOXIC' and 'DARKSIDE') bombed and the group almost imploded amid infighting and drug abuse (SHIFTY went into rehab), their saviour came in the shape of 'BUTTERFLY', an uncharacteristically mellow rap built around a sample of the RED HOT CHILI PEPPERS' 'Pretty Little Ditty'. The track was initially picked up by local L.A. radio stations before turning into a sizeable nationwide hit and even hitting the UK chart in spring 2001. Although fairly unrepresentative of CRAZY TOWN's sound, the group were confident they'd pick up a whole new raft of fans on the back of the track's surprise success.

Album rating: THE GIFT OF GAME (*5)

SHIFTY SHELLSHOCK (b. SETH BROOKS BINZER, 23 Aug'74) – vocals / **EPIC MAZUR** (b. BRET MAZUR) – vocals, producer / **TROUBLE VALLI** (b. ANTONIO LORRENZO) – guitar / **SQUIRREL** (b. KRAYGE TYLER) – guitar / **FAYDOEDEELAY** (b. DOUG MILLER) – bass / **JBJ** (b. JAMES BRADLEY JR) – drums (ex-MARY'S DANISH) / **DJ A.M.** (b. ADAM GOLDSTEIN) – turntables / **RUST EPIQUE** – guitar

Columbia / Sony

Jan 99. (cd-s) *<4313>* **WHO THE FUCK IS . . .** [-] [-] promo
– Toxic / Darkside.

1999. (cd-s) *<14047>* **TALES FROM THE DARKSIDE** [-] [-] promo
– Darkside / Revolving door.

1999. (cd-s) *<47135>* **TOXIC (radio) / TOXIC (album)** [-] [-] promo

Feb 00. (cd/c) *(495297-2/-4) <63654>* **THE GIFT OF GAME** [ ] [9]
– Intro / Toxic / Think fast / Darkside / Black cloud / Butterfly / Only when I'm drunk / Hollywood Babylon / Face the music / Lollipop porn / Revolving door / Players (only love you when they're playing) / B-boy 2000 / Outro www.crazytown.com. *(hit UK No.15 in Apr01)*

— now without RUST

Mar 01. (c-s) *(671001-4) <radio play>* **BUTTERFLY / BUTTERFLY (extreme mix)** [3] [1]
(cd-s+=) *(671001-2)* – ('A'-Epic remix) / ('A'-Jazzy Jim mix) / ('A'-instrumental).

CREAM

Formed: London, England . . . mid '66 as the first ever supergroup, by ERIC CLAPTON, GINGER BAKER and JACK BRUCE, who'd all cut their teeth with top-flight R&B outfits earlier in the decade. This fine pedigree led to Robert Stigwood signing them to his newly-founded 'Reaction' label, after their lauded debut at The National Jazz & Blues Festival in Windsor on the 3rd of July '66. Their initial 45, 'WRAPPING PAPER', gave them the first of many Top 40 hits, a track that didn't inspire much critical praise. To end the year, they issued a debut album, 'FRESH CREAM', lifting from it, the breezy psychedelic single, 'I FEEL FREE', a number which united BRUCE and poet/lyricist PETE BROWN in a new songwriting partnership. It also gave CREAM their biggest hit to date, reaching No.11 in the UK. Alongside original material, the album featured updated blues standards, 'SPOONFUL' (Willie Dixon), 'ROLLIN' & TUMBLIN' (Muddy Waters) and 'I'M SO GLAD' (Skip James). Over the course of the next six months, they became increasingly influenced by the pioneering psychedelic blues of JIMI HENDRIX. This was much in evidence on the next 45, 'STRANGE BREW', a slow-burning piece of sinister psych-blues. One of the highlights of their second album, 'DISRAELI GEARS', this record also featured such enduring CREAM classics as, 'SUNSHINE OF YOUR LOVE' (a US-only Top 5 hit), 'TALES OF BRAVE ULYSSES' & 'WORLD OF PAIN'. In fact every track was fantastic and the album remains an essential purchase for any self-respecting record collector. Their third set, 'WHEELS OF FIRE', recorded in San Francisco and New York, consisted of two records, one studio – one live. The former featured an ominous cover of BOOKER T's 'BORN UNDER A BAD SIGN', while the live disc included a definitive re-working of ROBERT JOHNSON's 'CROSSROADS'. However, the album (which was soon split into two single lp's) failed to garner the same critical praise as its predecessor, pandering too heavily to commerciality. They played their farewell tour in November '68, culminating in a legendary sell-out show on the 26th at The Royal Albert Hall. They were already in the US Top 10 with the GEORGE HARRISON and CLAPTON-penned 'WHITE ROOM', the song later becoming a fitting epitaph after it was given a UK release in early '69. All went on to high profile solo careers, the most obvious being ERIC 'God' CLAPTON.

Album rating: FRESH CREAM (*6) / DISRAELI GEARS (*9) / WHEELS OF FIRE (*8) / GOODBYE (*5) / THE BEST OF CREAM compilation (*7) / LIVE CREAM collection (*5) / LIVE CREAM VOL.2 collection (*5) / HEAVY CREAM compilation (*6) / STRANGE BREW – THE VERY BEST OF CREAM compilation (*9)

ERIC CLAPTON (b.ERIC PATRICK CLAPP, 30 May'45, Ripley, Surrey, England) – guitar, vocals (ex-YARDBIRDS, ex-JOHN MAYALL'S BLUESBREAKERS) / **JACK BRUCE** (b.JOHN BRUCE, 14 May'43, Glasgow, Scotland) – vocals, bass (ex-GRAHAM BOND, ex-JOHN MAYALL'S BLUESBREAKERS, ex-MANFRED MANN) / **GINGER BAKER** (b.PETER BAKER, 19 Aug'39, Lewisham, London, England) – drums (ex-GRAHAM BOND ORGANISATION, ex-ALEXIS KORNER'S BLUES INCORPORATED)

Reaction / Atco

Oct 66. (7") *(591 007)* **WRAPPING PAPER. / CAT'S SQUIRREL** [34] [-]

Dec 66. (lp; mono/stereo) *(593/594 001) <33206>* **FRESH CREAM** [6] [39]
– N.S.U. / Sleepy time time / Dreaming / Sweet wine / Spoonful / Cat's squirrel / Four until late / Rollin' and tumblin' / I'm so glad / Toad. *(re-iss. Feb69; stereo); reached No.7 UK. (re-iss Oct70 as 'FULL CREAM'; 2447 010) (re-iss. Mar75 as 'CREAM' on 'Polydor'+=; 2384 067); 2 tracks) (cd-iss. Jan84+=; 827 576-2)* – Wrapping paper / The coffee song. *(cd re-iss. Mar98; 531810-2) (lp re-iss. Aug99 on 'Simply Vinyl'; SVLP 106)*

Dec 66. (7") *(591 011) <6462>* **I FEEL FREE. / N.S.U.** [11] [ ]

Jun 67. (7") *(591 015)* <6488> **STRANGE BREW. / TALES OF BRAVE ULYSSES** [17] [ ]
Nov 67. (7") <6522> **SPOONFUL. / (part 2)** [-] [ ]
Nov 67. (lp; mono/stereo) *(593/594 003)* <33232> **DISRAELI GEARS** [5] [4]
– Strange brew / Sunshine of your love / World of pain / Dance the night away / Blue condition / Tales of brave Ulysses / S.W.L.A.B.R. / We're going wrong / Outside woman blues / Take it back / Mother's lament. *<US re-iss. Feb77 on 'R.S.O.'; 3010> (re-iss. Nov77 on 'R.S.O.'; 239 412-2) (cd-iss. Jan84 on 'Track'; 823 636-2) (cd re-iss. Mar98; 531811-2) (lp re-iss. Jun99 on 'Simply Vinyl'; SVLP 87)*

Polydor Atco

Jan 68. (7") <6544> **SUNSHINE OF YOUR LOVE. / S.W.L.A.B.R.** [-] [5]
(UK-iss.Sep68; 56286); hit No.25)
May 68. (7") *(56258)* <6575> **ANYONE FOR TENNIS. / PRESSED RAT AND WARTHOG** [40] [64]

— **FELIX PAPPALARDI** – producer, instruments guested as 4th p/t member

Aug 68. (d-lp; mono/stereo) *(582/583 031-2)* <2-700> **WHEELS OF FIRE** [3] [1] Jul68
(re-iss. 1972; 2612 001) <US re-iss. Feb77 on 'R.S.O.'; 3802> (re-iss. Jan84 on 'R.S.O.'; 3216 036) (cd-iss. Jan84; 8254 142) (cd re-iss. Feb89; 827 658-2) (cd re-iss. Mar98; 531812-2) (d-lp re-iss. Apr00 on 'Simply Vinyl'; SVLP 202)
Aug 68. (lp; mono/stereo) *(582/583 033)* **WHEELS OF FIRE – IN THE STUDIO** [7] [-]
– White room / Sitting on top of the world / Passing the time / As you said / Pressed rat and warthog / Politician / Those were the days / Born under a bad sign / Deserted cities of the heart. *(re-iss. Nov77 on 'R.S.O.'; 2394 136)*
Aug 68. (lp; mono/stereo) *(582/583 040)* **WHEELS OF FIRE – LIVE AT THE FILLMORE (live)** [ ] [-]
– Crossroads / Spoonful / Traintime / Toad. *(re-iss. Nov77 on 'R.S.O.'; 2394 137)*
Jan 69. (7") *(65300)* <6617> **WHITE ROOM. / THOSE WERE THE DAYS** [28] [6] Sep68

— They split around mid-'68. The rest of their releases were posthumous and CLAPTON went solo after forming BLIND FAITH with BAKER. He also went solo. JACK BRUCE went solo, etc.

– compilations, others, etc. –

either 'Polydor' in UK and 'Atco' in the US.

Jan 69. (7") <6646> **CROSSROADS. / PASSING THE TIME** [-] [28]
Mar 69. (lp) *(583 053)* <7001> **GOODBYE** [1] [2]
– I'm so glad (live) / Politician (live) / Sitting on top of the world (live) / Badge / Doing that scrapyard thing / What a bringdown. *(re-iss. Nov77 & Aug84 on 'R.S.O.'; 2394 178) (cd-iss. Jan84.+=; 823 660-2)* – Anyone for tennis. *(cd re-iss. Mar98; 531815-2) (lp re-iss. May00 on 'Simply Vinyl'; SVLP 211)*
Apr 69. (7") *(56315)* <6668> **BADGE. / WHAT A BRINGDOWN** [18] [60] Mar69
(re-iss. Oct72; 2058 285)
Nov 69. (lp) *(583 060)* <291> **BEST OF CREAM** [6] [3] Jul69
– Sunshine of your love / Badge / Crossroads / White room / Swlabr / Born under a bad sign / Tales of brave Ulysses / Strange brew / I feel free. *(re-iss. Nov77 on 'R.S.O.'; 3216 031) (re-iss. Apr86 on 'Arcade'; ADAH 429)*
Jun 70. (lp) *(2383 016)* <33-328> **LIVE CREAM (live)** [4] [15] Apr70
– N.S.U. / Sleepy time time / Lawdy mama / Sweet wine / Rollin' and tumblin'. *(re-iss. Nov77 & Mar85 on 'R.S.O.' lp/c; SPE LP/MC 93) (cd-iss. May88; 827 577-2) (cd re-iss. Mar98; 531816-2)*
Jul 70. (7") **LAWDY MAMA (live). / SWEET WINE (live)** [-] [ ]
Jul 71. (7") **I FEEL FREE. / WRAPPING PAPER** [ ] [ ]
(re-iss. Jul84 on 'Old Gold'; OG 9423)
Jun 72. (lp) *(2383 119)* <7005> **LIVE CREAM VOL.2** [15] [27] Mar72
– Deserted cities of the heart / White room / Politician / Tales of brave Ulysses / Sunshine of your love / Steppin' out. *(re-iss. Nov77 on 'R.S.O.';) (cd-iss. May88; 823 661-2) (cd re-iss. Mar98; 531817-2)*
Apr 73. (d-lp) *(2659 022)* <3502> **HEAVY CREAM** [ ] [ ] Oct72
1973. (lp) *Polydor;* <PD 5529> **OFF THE TOP** [-] [ ]
Oct 80. (6xlp-box) *(2658 142)* **CREAM BOX SET** [ ] [ ]
Oct 83. (lp)(c) *(2479 212)(3215 038)* **THE STORY OF CREAM VOL.1** [ ] [ ]
Oct 83. (lp)(c) *(2479 213)(3215 039)* **THE STORY OF CREAM VOL.2** [ ] [-]
Apr 78. (lp)(c) *R.S.O.; (3228 005)* **CREAM VOLUME TWO** [ ] [ ]
Feb 83. (lp/c) *R.S.O.; (RSD/TRSD 5021)* **STRANGE BREW – THE VERY BEST OF CREAM** [ ] [ ]
– Badge / Sunshine of your love / Crossroads / White room / Born under a bad sign / Swlabr / Strange brew / Anyone for tennis / I feel free / Tales of brave Ulysses / Politician / Spoonful. *(cd-iss. Nov87 on 'Polydor';)*
Aug 82. (7") *R.S.O.; (RSO 91)* **BADGE. / TALES OF BRAVE ULYSSES** [ ] [ ]
(12"+=) *(RSOX 91)* – White room.
Jul 86. (7") *(POSP 812)* **I FEEL FREE. / BADGE** [ ] [ ]
Jul 84. (7") *Old Gold; (OG 9425)* **WHITE ROOM. / BADGE** [ ] [-]
Jul 84. (7") *Old Gold; (OG 9426)* **SUNSHINE OF YOUR LOVE. / ANYONE FOR TENNIS** [ ] [-]
Feb 89. (cd) *Koine; (K 880803)* **LIVE 1968 (live)** [ ] [-]
Dec 91. (cd; w/booklet) *U.F.O.;* **IN GEAR** [ ] [-]
Nov 92. (cd) *I.T.M.; (ITM 960002)* **THE ALTERNATIVE ALBUM** [ ] [-]
(re-iss. Jan97 & Dec99 on 'Masterplan'; MP 42009)
Dec 92. (cd/c) *Pickwick; (PWK S/MC 4127P)* **DESERTED CITIES: THE CREAM COLLECTION** [ ] [-]
Feb 95. (cd/c) *(523 752-2/-4)* **THE VERY BEST OF CREAM** [ ] [ ]

CREAMING JESUS

Formed: London, England . . . 1987 by ANDY, RICHARD and MARIO, who subsequently enlisted the rhythm section of TALLY and ROY. Blasphemous and irreverent, CREAMING JESUS caused a minor stir over a succession of releases with their tongue-in-cheek political satire. Musically the band were no great shakes, the lyrics far more amusing than their standard issue hard-core metal. The 1990 album, 'TOO FAT TO RUN, TOO STUPID TO HIDE' and 1992's 'GUILT BY ASSOCIATION' were typical of the band's take-no-prisoners approach to topical issues.

Album rating: TOO FAT TO RUN, TOO STUPID TO HIDE (*5) / GUILT BY ASSOCIATION (*5) / CHAOS FOR THE CONVERTED (*5) / END OF AN ERROR (*6)

ANDY – vocals / **RICHARD** – guitar / **MARIO** – guitar / **TALLY** – bass / **ROY** – drums

House Of Dolls not iss.

Jun 89. (12"ep) *(CREAM 1)* **NAILED UP FOR LOVE** [ ] [-]
(re-iss. Jun91; same)

Jungle not iss.

Dec 89. (12"ep) *(JUNG 052T)* **MUG** [ ] [-]
(re-iss. Dec91; same)
Nov 90. (lp/cd) *(FREUD/+CD 036)* **TOO FAT TO RUN, TOO STUPID TO HIDE** [ ] [-]
– Preacher / Eggy rare / Casserole / Neighbours / Smoke / Russell / Bloody collar / Hate you / Filthy pervert meets the listening nun / Charlie / Too fat to run, too stupid to hide / Charlie jumps the bandwagon.
Jun 91. (12"ep/cd-ep) *(JUNG 054 T/CD)* **DEAD TIME** [ ] [-]
Jul 91. (lp/cd) *(FREUD/+CD 037)* **IT'S DANCE MUSIC** [ ] [-]
– Bloody collar / Jessie / Mug / Stomach bleed / Barbeque / Hungerford / A forest / What the Harpy said / This charming man / P.O.B. / Tales of the Riverbank / Casserole (original vegetarian mix).
Dec 91. (12"ep/cd-ep) *(JUNG 057 T/CD)* **DITCHDWELLER 5** [ ] [-]
Feb 92. (lp/cd) *(FREUD/+CD 040)* **GUILT BY ASSOCIATION** [ ] [-]
– Reptile / Squat / Spray toasters / Legacy (tales No.2) / The skinny head f*** / Hooves . . . / Forget it / Hackney (suffer little children) / Song for Ari / Bathtime for Jim (kickdown the Doors) / Crazy little thing called love / Lillies / Skinny head / I lost my faith.
Jul 92. (12"ep) *(JUNG 053T)* **BARK** [ ] [-]
– A forest / What the Harpy said / This charming man / P.O.B.
Nov 92. (12"ep/cd-ep) *(JUNG 058 T/CD)* **HEADRUSH EP** [ ] [-]
– Upside down / Estate / Bathtime too / Reptile – Faith.
Jul 94. (12"ep/cd-ep) *(JUNG 59 T/CD)* **HAMBURG. /** [ ] [-]
Aug 94. (cd) *(FREUDCD 046)* **CHAOS FOR THE CONVERTED** [ ] [-]
– Shape shifting and face dancing / Lighten up / Blind / Celebrity cannibalism (the painted man) / Hamburg / Transcendental maggot (Olympia's story) / River Techa / Dis-ease / Quiet / Roadman – Synaethesia / Geggy moon – Window fighter.

— split after above

– compilations, etc. –

Oct 96. (cd) *Jungle; (FREUDCD 052)* **END OF AN ERROR** [ ] [-]

CREED

Formed: Tallahassee, Florida, USA . . . 1994 by singer SCOTT STAPP and guitarist MARK TREMONTI, who hooked up with rhythm section BRIAN MARSHALL and SCOTT PHILLIPS. Another band to emerge from the post-Grunge scene, although EDDIE VEDDER and LAYNE STALEY have no fears here about their mantle being taken by these lads. A year or two into their career, CREED released a self-financed debut set, 'MY OWN PRISON', which sold its initial batch and made major labels take note. 'Epic' (through subsidiary 'Wind-Up') finally won the battle for their signatures early in '97 and with a new producer, Ron St. Germain, remixed and re-issued the album later in the year. "Grunge was not dead!" was the claim of their teen-metal followers, although CREED themselves denied they were part of that genre and just a basic rock'n'roll band – basic being the key word. 'MY OWN PRISON' started a steady rise up the American charts finally peaking at No.22 a year later, although Britain had to wait until early '99 to get its first taste of million-sellers CREED. By which point, Grunge had certainly been well and truly buried. Meanwhile, back in the States, the glum-rockers were just about to serve up a second helping in the shape of 'HUMAN CLAY' (1999) – a difficult second album indeed that nevertheless topped the chart. • **Covered:** I'M EIGHTEEN (Alice Cooper). • **Note:** not to be confused with mid-90's act who issued 12" singles on 'Rectory'.

Album rating: MY OWN PRISON (*6) / HUMAN CLAY (*5)

SCOTT STAPP – vocals / **MARK TREMONTI** – guitar, vocals / **BRIAN MARSHALL** – bass / **SCOTT PHILLIPS** – drums

Wind Up-Epic Wind Up-Epic

Oct 97. (cd) <13049> **MY OWN PRISON** [-] [22]
– Torn / Ode / My own prison / Pity for a dime / In America / Illusion / Unforgiven / Sister / What's this life for / One. *<US originally iss.1997 on 'Blue Collar'; 5066> (UK-iss.Feb99 on 'Wind-Up – Epic'; 493072)*
Feb 99. (-) *<radio cut>* **ONE** [-] [70]
Sep 99. (cd/c) *(495027-2/-4)* <13053> **HUMAN CLAY** [ ] [1]
– Are you ready / What if / Beautiful / Say I / Wrong way / Faceless man / Never die / With arms wide open / Higher / Wash away those years / Inside us all. *(re-dist.Jan01)* – hit UK No.29
Jan 00. (7"/cd-s) *(668315-7/-2) <radio cut>* **HIGHER / I'M EIGHTEEN / ROADSIDE BLUES (live)** [47] [7] Aug99
Jan 01. (7"claret) *(670695-7) <album cut>* **WITH ARMS WIDE OPEN. / WITH ARMS WIDE OPEN (acoustic)** [13] [1] Mar00
(c-s+=) *(670695-4)* – Wash away those tears.
(cd-s+=) *(670695-2)* – ('A'-new version / Strings / CD-ROM).

CRIME

Formed: San Francisco, California, USA . . . 1976 . . . by FRANKIE FIX, JOHNNY STRIKE, RON THE RIPPER GRECO and RICKY JAMES. Possibly holding the crown of being the first US punk act to release a single, the self-financed double A-side, 'HOT WIRE MY HEART' and 'BABY YOU'RE SO REPULSIVE', appeared as CRIME's debut at the tail end of '76. By the following year's 'MURDER BY GUITAR', The STOOGES influenced crew were minus RICKY who joined FLIPPER and was superseded by BRITTLEY BLACK. He in turn was replaced by the brilliantly named HANK RANK, who stayed around between early '78 and mid '79, studio takes subsequently released as a bootleg, 'SAN FRANCISCO'S DOOMED'. Featuring two raw sessions (the first of which was produced by Elliott Mazer, who'd previously worked on Neil Young's 'Harvest'!), the album included such choice cuts as 'PISS ON YOUR DOG' (not advice that Great British dog trainer, Mrs. Woodhouse would have given readily!). After a brief stint with The FLAMIN' GROOVIES, BLACK was back on the drum stool for one last 7" effort in 1980, 'MASERATI'.

Album rating: SAN FRANCISCO'S DOOMED posthumous bootleg (*4)

JOHNNY STRIKE – vocals, guitar / **FRANKIE FIX** – guitar / **RON THE RIPPER GRECO** – bass (ex-CHOSEN FEW, aka FLAMIN' GROOVIES) / **RICKY JAMES** – drums

not iss. Crime

Dec 76. (7") **HOT WIRE MY HEART. / BABY YOU'RE SO REPULSIVE**

— **BRITTLEY BLACK** – drums; repl. RICKY who joined FLIPPER

Dec 77. (7") **MURDER BY GUITAR. / FRUSTRATION**

— **HANK RANK** – drums; repl. BLACK who briefly joined FLAMIN' GROOVIES before moving to DEATH (he rejoined for below)

not iss. B Square

1980. (7") **MASERATI. / GANGSTER FUNK**

— split in 1980, STRIKE formed REV, while RANK formed OTHER MUSIC. A bootleg, 'SAN FRANCISCO'S DOOMED' appeared in 1983 on US 'Solar Lodge'.

– compilations, etc. –

Feb 94. (cd) *Overground; (OVER 33CD)* **SAN FRANCISCO'S DOOMED**

CRIMSON GLORY

Formed: Florida, USA . . . 1982 out of PIERCED ARROW and BEOWOLF, by vocalist MIDNIGHT, plus co-writer JON DRENNING, BEN JACKSON, JEFF LORDS and DANA BURNELL. Self-financing their eponymous debut, CRIMSON GLORY had fashioned a cerebral fusion of arty prog-metal (i.e. QUEENSRYCHE) and power-riffing. The group also drew attention with their rather ridiculous steel masks, perhaps updating KISS's 70's make-up heyday (even unmasking themselves in the early 90's). Although CRIMSON GLORY (their name taken from the bible) explored religious themes on their 1988 concept album, 'TRANSCENDENCE', the group distanced themselves from the burgeoning Christian-metal scene. Despite personnel upheavals (RAKI JAKHORTA replacing BURNELL and JACKSON), they returned in 1991 with a strong, ZEPPELIN-esque set, 'STRANGE AND BEAUTIFUL'. The band had apparently been inactive until 1999's comeback album, 'ASTRONOMICA'.

Album rating: CRIMSON GLORY (*7) / TRANSCENDENCE (*7) / STRANGE AND BEAUTIFUL (*6) / ASTRONOMICA (*5)

MIDNIGHT – vocals / **JON DRENNING** – guitar / **BEN JACKSON** – guitar / **JEFF LORDS** – bass / **DANA BURNELL** – drums

not iss. P.A.R.

Nov 86. (lp) **CRIMSON GLORY**
– Valhalla / Dragon lady / Heart of steel / Azrael / Mayday / Queen of the masquerade / Angels of war / Lost reflection. *(UK-iss.Dec88 on 'Roadrunner' lp/cd; RR/+34 9655)*

Roadrunner M.C.A.

Apr 88. (12") *(RR 2467-1)* **DREAM DANCER. / LOST REFLECTION**

Nov 88. (lp/c/cd) *(RR 9508-1/-4/-2) <MCA/+C/D 6350>* **TRANSCENDENCE**
– Lady of winter / Red sharks / Painted skies / Masque of the red death / In dark places / Where dragons rule / Lonely / Burning bridges / Eternal world / Transcendence.

Apr 89. (7") *(RR 2448-7)* **LONELY (remix). / IN DARK PLACES**
(12"+=/cd-s+=) *(RR 2448-1/-2)* – Dream dancer.

— **RAVI JAKHORTA** – drums; repl. BURNELL + JACKSON

Roadrunner Atlantic

Aug 91. (cd/c/lp) *(RR 9301-2/-4/-1) <82239>* **STRANGE AND BEAUTIFUL**
– Strange and beautiful / Love and dreams / The chant / Dance on fire / Song for angels / In the mood / Star chamber / Deep inside your heart / Make you love me / Far away.

— split around 1992 . . . re-formed with **JACKSON, LORDS** with **WADE BLACK** – vocals / **STEVE WACHOLZ** – drums

Rising Son Spitfire

Sep 99. (cd) *(RS 007289CD) <15043>* **ASTRONOMICA**
– March to glory (instrumental) / War of the worlds / New world machine / Astronomica / Edge of forever / Touch the sun / Lucifer's hammer / The other side of midnight / Cyberchrist / Cydonia.

Mar 00. (cd-s) *(RS 0082232CD)* **WAR OF THE WORLDS**

Peter CRISS (see under ⇒ KISS)

CROCKETTS

Formed: Aberystwyth, Wales . . . early 1996 by local college teenagers, OWEN CASH, Irish-born DAVEY MacMANUS, DAN BOONE and RICH TURPIN. A mischievous Celtic-punk outfit lying somewhere between RAMONES or The CLASH, The CROCKETTS unleashed their own self-financed mini-set, 'FROG ON A STICK' (1997), before they were snapped up by Virgin V2 offshoot, 'Blue Dog', after being spotted at Dublin's In The City festival. First up for the label was the EP, 'HELLO AND GOOD MORNING'; released in September '97, it was pure unadulterated punk-pop that even GREEN DAY would have been proud of. A series of singles preceded their debut album, 'WE MAY BE SKINNY & WIREY' (1998), an appropriate title as the lads had about as much meat on them as a vegetarian barbeque.
• **Covered:** RHINESTONE COWBOY (Glen Campbell).

Album rating: WE MAY BE SKINNY & WIREY (*7) / THE GREAT BRAIN ROBBERY (*6)

DAVEY MacMANUS – vocals, guitar / **DAN BOONE** – guitar / **RICH TURPIN** – bass / **OWEN CASH** – drums

Crocketts not iss.

1997. (m-lp) **FROG ON A STICK**

Blue Dog – V2 Imprint

Sep 97. (10"ep/cd-ep) *(BDG 500035-8/-3)* **HELLO AND GOOD MORNING EP**
– Will you still care / Cars and footballs / etc.

Mar 98. (7"/cd-s) *(BDG 500156-7/-3)* **LOVED YA ONCE. /**

May 98. (7"/cd-s) *(BDG 500159-7/-3)* **FLOWER GIRL. /**

Sep 98. (cd/lp) *(BDG 100241-2/-1) <120290>* **WE MAY BE SKINNY & WIREY** Nov98
– Flower girl / Love ya once / Explain / Blust boy / Girl next door / Tennessee / Will you still care / Six soon to be seven / Bucket and spade / Autumn afternoon / Strony guy / Blue dog / (untitled).

Oct 98. (7"blue/cd-s) *(BDG 500252-7/-3)* **EXPLAIN. / RHINESTONE COWBOY / INSIDE HEAD ON**

Oct 99. (cd-s) *(BDG 501082-3)* **NINTENDO FALLACY**

Apr 00. (cd-s) *(BDG 501133-3)* **HOST / YOU DON'T KNOW NOTHING (live) / BEAST WITH TWO BACKS (live)**
(cd-s) *(BDG 501133-8)* – ('A'live) / Will you still care? (live) / Strong guy (live).

Apr 00. (cd/lp) *(BDG 101181-2/-1)* **THE GREAT BRAIN ROBBERY**
– 1939 returning / Mrs Playing dead / Host / Chicken vs macho / On something / Lucifer / Survival of the prettiest / Pity youth doesn't last / One shake / Million things / Ella Luciana / Ladykiller.

Jul 00. (cd-s) *(BDG 501320-8)* **ON SOMETHING / HOST (featuring MARY HOPKIN) / OPPOSITE ENDS**
(cd-s) *(BDG 501320-3)* – ('A'live) / Beauty and the beast (acoustic) / Ella Luciana (live).

CRO-MAGS

Formed: New York, USA . . . 1984 by tattooed Hare Krishna disciple HARLEY FLANEGAN, plus JOHN 'Bloodclot' JOSEPH, PARRIS MITCHELL MAYHEW and MACKIE. One of the pivotal bands in the 80's NY hardcore scene, The CRO-MAGS eventually signed to 'Profile' (G.W.R. in the UK), who released their 1987 debut, 'THE AGE OF QUARREL'. Like most bands of their ilk, the group increasingly crossed over to a metal sound and audience as the decade wore on, signing to 'Roadrunner' for their follow-up, 'BEST WISHES' (1989). This set featured the addition of guitarist DOUG HOLLAND, drummer MACKIE departing for BAD BRAINS in the early 90's before they signed to 'Century Media'. They recorded a further couple of metallic hardcore albums for the label prior to their demise in 1994. The CRO-MAGS re-formed in 2000 for another fresh set, 'REVENGE', which was released a few after a collection of early demos, 'BEFORE THE QUARREL'.

Album rating: THE AGE OF QUARREL (*6) / BEST WISHES (*5) / ALPHA-OMEGA (*5) / NEAR DEATH EXPERIENCE (*4) / HARD TIMES . . . compilation (*6)

JOHN 'Bloodclot' JOSEPH – vocals / **HARLEY FLANEGAN** – bass, (some) vocals / **PARRIS MITCHELL MAYHEW** – guitar / **MACKIE** – drums

G.W.R. Profile

May 87. (lp/c)<cd> *(GW LP/TC 9) <PCD 1218>* **THE AGE OF QUARREL**
– We gotta know / World peace / Show you no mercy / Malfunction / Street justice / Survival of the streets / Seekers of the truth / It's the limit / Hard times / By myself / Don't tread on me / Face the facts / Do unto others / Life of my own / Sign of the times / Death of confusion / Only one / Down, but not out / Crush the demoniac fugitive / Then and now / The age of quarrel. *(re-iss. Nov87 on 'Roadrunner'; RR 9613)*

— added **DOUG HOLLAND** – guitar (ex-KRAUT)

Sep 89. (lp/c/cd) *<FIL ER/ECT/CD 274>* **BEST WISHES**
– Death camps / The only one / Crush the demonic / Then and now / Days of confusion / Down but not out / The fugitive / The age of quarrel.

— MACKIE joined BAD BRAINS

Century Media Century Media

Jun 92. (lp/c/cd) *(CM 9730/+MC/CD) <7730>* **ALPHA-OMEGA**
– See the signs / Eyes of tomorrow / Other side of madness (revenge) / Apocalypse now / Paths of perfection / Victims / Kuruksetra / Changes.

Sep 93. (cd/c/lp) *(CM 77050-2/-4/-1) <7750>* **NEAR DEATH EXPERIENCE**
– Say goodbye to Mother Earth / Kali-yuga / War on the streets / Death in the womb / Time I am / Reflections / Near death experience / Other side of madness (rat soup version).

Jun 94. (d-cd) *(CM 77072-2)* **HARD TIMES IN AN AGE OF QUARREL** (compilation)
– Intro / We gotta know / World peace / Show no mercy / Apocalypso mercy / See the signs / Makfunktion / Survival of the streets / Days of confusion / Street justice / The only one / Crush the demoniac / Changes / Down but not out / Seekers of the truth / It's the limit / Life on my own / Signs of the time // See the signs / World peace / Show no mercy / Say goodbye to Mother Earth / Malfunktion / Path to

perfection / Other side of madness / It's the limit / Life of my own / Age of quarrel / Signs in time / Seekers of the truth / Don't tread on me / Death camp / We gotta know / Apocalypse now / Crush the demoniac / Down but not out. *(re-iss. May00; same)*

— split in 1994 until they re-formed once more

Cargo Cro-Mag

Apr 00. (lp) *(10388)* <2> **REVENGE** Jan00
– Premeditated / Jones / Can you feel / My life / Tore up / Without her / Pressure drop / Open letter / Don't forget / Steal my crown / These streets / Fireburn. *(w/ 2 bonus tracks).*

– compilations, etc. –

Jan 00. (cd) *Cro-Mag;* <1> **BEFORE THE QUARREL** (early demos, etc.) [-]

CROSS (see under ⇒ QUEEN)

CROWBAR

Formed: New Orleans, Louisiana, USA . . . 1991 by KIRK WINDSTEIN, KEVIN NOONAN, TODD STRANGE and CRAIG NUNENMACHER. Wielding a skullcrushingly heavy blend of SABBATH-esque riffing and punk attitude, they signed to 'Grindcore International' for their 1992 debut album, 'OBEDIENCE THRU SUFFERING'. With MATT THOMAS replacing NOONAN, they completed their second set (their first for 'Bulletproof'), simply titled 'CROWBAR', which featured a bulldozing cover of Led Zeppelin's 'NO QUARTER'. They continued to pursue an even heavier direction on subsequent releases, 'TIME HEALS NOTHING' (1995) and 'BROKEN GLASS' (1996). 1998's 'ODD FELLOWS REST' set saw them change label to 'Spitfire' while, in almost SPINAL TAP-fashion, yet another new drummer (SID MONTZ) was in place for CROWBAR's millennial effort, 'EQUILIBRIUM'. While the title might well have referred to the musical balance between old and new, riffs and melodies, the record itself varied little from the established formula and even placed Gary Wright's 'DREAM WEAVER' under its dark spell. • **Note:** Not to be confused with the 70's act.

Album rating: OBEDIENCE THRU SUFFERING (*4) / CROWBAR (*6) / CROWBAR LIVE +1 (*4) / TIME HEALS NOTHING (*5) / BROKEN GLASS (*6) / PAST AND PRESENT compilation (*7) / ODD FELLOWS REST (*7) / EQUILIBRIUM (*6)

KIRK WINDSTEIN – vocals, guitar / **KEVIN NOONAN** – guitar / **TODD STRANGE** – bass / **CRAIG NUNENMACHER** – drums

Grindcore Grindcore

Jun 92. (cd) *<(GCI 8980-2)>* **OBEDIENCE THRU SUFFERING**
– Waiting in silence / I despise / A breed apart / Obedience thru suffering / Vacuum / 4 walls / Subversion / Feeding fear / My agony / The innocent. *(re-iss. Feb95 on 'Bulletproof'; CDVEST 42) (re-iss. Aug98 on 'S.P.V.'; SPV 0845322-2)*

— **MATT THOMAS** – guitar; repl. NOONAN

Bulletproof I.R.S.

Nov 93. (cd) *(CDVEST 5) <IRSCD 981200>* **CROWBAR**
– High rate extinction / All I had (I gave) / Will that never dies / Fixation / No quarter / Self-inflicted / Negative pollution / Existence is punishment / Holding nothing / I have failed. *(re-iss. Apr94 + LIVE + 1)* – High rate extinction / Self-inflicted / Fixation / I hate failed / All I had (I gave) / Numb sensitive. *(cd re-iss. Oct97; same as US)*

Bulletproof Pavement

Mar 94. (m-cd) *<15001>* **CROWBAR LIVE +1 (live)** [-]
– High rate extinction / Self-inflicted / Fixation / I have failed / All I had (I gave) / Numb sensitive (studio) / 4 walls.

May 95. (cd) *(CDVEST 51) <15007>* **TIME HEALS NOTHING**
– The only factor / No more we can crawl / Time heals nothing / Leave it behind / Through a wall of tears / Lack of tolerance / Still I reach / Embracing emptiness / A perpetual need / Numb sensitive.

— **JIMMY BOWERS** – drums (ex-EYEHATEGOD) repl. NUNENMACHER

Oct 96. (cd) *(CDVEST 77) <32236>* **BROKEN GLASS**
– Conquering / Like broken glass / (Can't) Turn away from dying / Wrath of time be judgement / Nothing / Burn your world / I am forever / Above, below and in between / You know (I'll live again) / Reborn thru me.

Mayhem Spitfire

Jul 98. (cd) *(MAIM 11116-2) <15005>* **ODD FELLOWS REST**
– Intro / Planets collide / . . .And suffer as one / 1,000 year internal war / To carry the load / December's spawn / It's all the gravity / Behind the black horizon / New man born / Scattered pieces lay / Old fellows rest / On frozen ground. *(re-iss. Jul99 on 'Spitfire'+=; SPITCD 005)* – Remember tomorrow.

Spitfire Spitfire

Mar 00. (cd) *(SPITCD 016) <5016>* **EQUILIBRIUM**
– I feel the burning sun / Equilibrium / Glass full of liquid pain / Command of myself / Down into the rotting earth / To touch the hand of God / Uncovering / Buried once again / Things you can't understand / Euphoria minus one / Dream weaver / (untitled).

– compilations, etc. –

Aug 98. (cd) *S.P.V.; (SPV 0845321-2) / Pavement; <32265>* **PAST AND PRESENT – THE BEST OF CROWBAR** Oct97
– All I had (I gave) / Existence is punishment / The only factor / Still I reach / Vacuum / Subversion / Waiting in silence / High rate extinction / I have failed / Fixation (live) / Four walls (live) / Self-inflicted.

CRUCIFUCKS (see under ⇒ LOUDSPEAKER)

CRUMBSUCKERS

Formed: Long Island, New York, USA . . . 1983 by CHRIS NOTARO and CHUCK LENIHAN, who added GARY MESKILL, DAVE WYNN and DAN RICHARDSON. Signed to 'Combat' ('Rough Justice' in the UK), the group released the impressive 'LIFE OF DREAMS' set in 1986, a collection of defiant, metal-tinged hardcore. RONNIE KOEBLER replaced WYNN for their follow-up, 'BEAT ON MY BACK', a record which saw the band jump on the speed-metal bandwagon. They subsequently changed their moniker to HEAVY RAIN, while MESKILL and RICHARDSON became part of the up and coming PRO-PAIN.

Album rating: LIFE OF DREAMS (*6) / BEAST ON MY BACK (*5)

CHRIS NOTARO – vocals / **CHUCK LENIHAN** – guitar / **DAVE WYNN** – guitar / **GARY MESKILL** – bass / **DAN RICHARDSON** – drums

Rough Justice Combat

Jul 86. (lp) *(JUST 4) <8090>* **LIFE OF DREAMS**
– Sit there / Trapped / Interlude / Super Tuesday / Shits creek / Return to the womb / The longest war / Shit down / Prelude / Life of dreams / Brainwashed / Faces of death / Hub run / Bullshit society / Live to work / Moment of silence / Mr. Hyde. *(cd-iss. Aug91; CDJUST 4) (cd re-iss. Feb99 on 'Century Media'; 66013-2)*

— **RONNIE KOEBLER** – guitar; repl. WYNN

Rough Justice Grindcore

Mar 88. (lp) *(JUST 9) <89802>* **BEAST ON MY BACK (B.O.M.B.)**
– Breakout / Jimmie's dream / Charge / Initial shock / I am he / Connection / Rejuvenate / Remembering tomorrow / Beast on my back. *(cd-iss. May99 on 'Century Media'; CM 66042CD)*

— **JOE HEGARTY** – vocals; repl. NOTARO

— **MARC PIOVANETTI** – guitar; repl. LENIHAN

— changed their name to HEAVY RAIN; MESKILL and RICHARDSON later resurfaced in PRO-PAIN

CRUNT (see under ⇒ BABES IN TOYLAND)

CRY OF LOVE

Formed: North Carolina, USA . . . 1991 by AUDLEY FREED, JASON PATTERSON and ROBERT KEARNS, who, after gigging as a trio, enlisted the services of frontman KELLY HOLLAND. Signed to 'Columbia' in 1992, they were soon achieving minor chart status with the single 'BAD THING'. This was lifted from the accompanying debut album, 'BROTHER' (1993), a highly praised set which fused the soulfulness of JIMI HENDRIX with the bluesy hard-rock of FREE. After a well-received performance at the 1994 Donington festival, HOLLAND departed. The group finally secured a new vocalist, ROBERT MASON, and three years later came up with a belated second album, 'DIAMONDS & DEBRIS' (1997). Despite FREED's guitar virtuosity and their well-honed Southern revivalism, CRY OF LOVE's tendency to blandness saw the record come in for critical flak with commentators bemoaning the lack of memorable material. • **Songwriters:** FREED – HOLLAND, with producer JOHN CUSTER.

Album rating: BROTHER (*6) / DIAMONDS & DEBRIS (*5)

KELLY HOLLAND – vocals / **AUDLEY FREED** – guitar / **ROBERT KEARNS** – bass / **JASON PATTERSON** – drums

Columbia Columbia

Aug 93. (cd/c/lp) *(473767-2/-4/-1) <CK/CT 53404>* **BROTHER** Dec92
– Highway Jones / Pretty as you please / Bad thing / Too cold in the winter / Hand me down / Gotta love me / Carnival / Drive it home / Peace pipe / Saving grace.

Sep 93. (12"ep) *(659746-6)* **PEACE PIPE / DRIVE IT HOME. / SHADE TREE / CARNIVAL** [-]
(cd-ep) *(659746-2)* – (1st 3 tracks) / Deathbed.

Jan 94. (7") *(660046-7)* **BAD THING. / GOTTA LOVE ME** 60 [-]
(12") *(660046-6)* – ('A'side) / ('A'live) / I ain't superstitious.
(cd-s+=) *(660046-2)* – Peace pipe (live).

— (Aug'97) **ROBERT MASON** – vocals; repl. HOLLAND who departed later in '94

Aug 97. (cd/c) *<66881>* **DIAMONDS & DEBRIS** [-]
– Empty castle / Hung out to dry / Sugarcane / Fire in the dry grass / Georgia pine / Warm river pearl / Sweet Mary's gone / Revelations (rattlesnakes & queens) / Bring me my burden / Sunday morning flood / Diamonds & debris / Hung out redux / Garden of memories.

CRYPTIC SLAUGHTER

Formed: California, USA . . . mid 80's by BILL COOK and LES EVANS, who recruited BOB NICHOLSON and SCOTT PETERSON. Signing with 'Metal Blade' (UK 'Roadrunner'), they unleashed their first album, 'CONVICTED' in 1986, a record which secured the band's credentials as thrash-influenced hardcore merchants. They subsequently moved to Portland, Oregon and completed three others in this vein, 'MONEY TALKS' (1987), 'STREAM OF CONSCIOUSNESS' (1988) and 'SPEAK YOUR PEACE', before they wisely called it a day.

Album rating: CONVICTED (*5) / MONEY TALKS (*4) / STREAM OF CONSCIOUSNESS (*4) / SPEAK YOUR PEACE (*4)

BILL COOK – vocals / **LES EVANS** – guitar / **ROB NICHOLSON** – bass / **SCOTT PETERSON** – drums

Roadrunner Death

Aug 86. (lp)<cd> *(RR 9680) <72148>* **CONVICTED**
– M.A.D. / Little world / Sudden death / Lowlife / Rage to kill / Rest in pain / Nuclear future / State control / Hypocrite / War to the knife / Nation of hate / Black and white / Reich of torture / Convicted.

Jun 87. (lp)<cd> *(RR 9607) <72204>* **MONEY TALKS**
– Money talk / Set your own pace / Could be worse / Wake up / Freedom of expression? / Menace to mankind / Too much, too little / Human contrast / Tables are turned / Positively / All wrong / American heroes.

Roadrunner Restless

Nov 88. (lp/cd) *(RR 9521-1/-2) <72320>* **STREAM OF CONSCIOUSNESS**
– Circus of fools / Aggravated / Last laugh / Overcome / Deteriorate / See through you / Just went back / Drift / Altered visions / One last thought / Whisker biscuit / Addicted.

Metal Blade Enigma

Jul 90. (cd/lp) *(CD+/ZORRO 6) <73442>* **SPEAK YOUR PEACE**
– Born too soon / Insanity by the numbers / Deathstyles of the poor and lonely / Divided minds / Killing time / Still born, again / Co-exist / One thing or another / Speak your peace. *<cd re-iss. 1994; 14062>*

— folded later in 1990

CULPRIT

Formed: Seattle, Washington, USA ... 1980 out of ORPHEUS and AMETHYST, by JOHN DeVOL, SCOTT EARL, JEFF L'HEUREUX, KJARTAN KRISTOFFERSEN and BUD BURRILL. A few years later they finally made it onto vinyl via the IRON MAIDEN-esque 'GUILTY AS CHARGED', although this proved to be their one and only effort, the group splitting soon after due to the time-honoured musical differences.

Album rating: GUILTY AS CHARGED (*5)

JEFF L'HEUREUX – vocals / **JOHN DeVOL** – guitar / **KJARTAN KRISTOFFERSEN** – guitar / **SCOTT EARL** – bass / **BUD BURRILL** – drums

not iss. Shrapnel

1983. (lp) *<1008>* **GUILTY AS CHARGED** [-]
– Guilty as charged / Ice in the black / Steel to blood / I am / Ambush / Tears of repentence / Same to you / Fight back / Players.

— split after drug related problems in '85

CULT

Formed: Bradford, England . . . 1982 as the SOUTHERN DEATH CULT for whom IAN ASTBURY (then going under the name IAN LINDSAY) took on vocal duties. Having spent time in Canada as a kid, ASTBURY had been profoundly influenced by Native American culture and problems soon arose when the singer felt his pseudo hippy/Red Indian philosophy was being compromised by the band set-up. The group split the following year, ASTBURY keeping the name but shortening it to DEATH CULT. Relocating to London, ASTBURY duly recruited a new band (all seasoned hands on the post-punk circuit) and released an eponymous, 4-track 12" single. The band released a further solitary single, 'GOD'S ZOO', before trimming the name further to The CULT. While the band's music still betrayed slight indie/goth tendencies, they were eager to lose the 'gothic' tag. 'DREAMTIME' (1984) sounded confused and directionless, and it wasn't until 'LOVE', the following year, that the band fashioned some kind of distinct identity. Veering from the cascading bombast of the classic singles, 'RAIN' and 'SHE SELLS SANCTUARY' to the mystic schtick of 'BROTHER WOLF, SISTER MOON', the album semi-successfully ploughed a deeper retro furrow than the myriad BYRDS clones of the day. ASTBURY's flowing locks were also something of an anomaly for an 'alternative' band in those dark 80's days, and the band were derided in some areas of the music press. The CULT's response was to throw caution to the wind and do what they'd probably always secretly dreamed of doing, writing massive, anthemic heavy rock songs. With metal guru RICK RUBIN at the production helm, DUFFY's guitar was pushed way up in the mix and the sound generally tightened. The result: any fans clinging to gothic pretensions were aghast while Kerrang readers loved it. Possibly The CULT's finest moment, it spawned the booty-shaking singles 'LOVE REMOVAL MACHINE', 'LI'L DEVIL' and 'WILDFLOWER', hell, it even had a cover of 'BORN TO BE WILD'! 'SONIC TEMPLE' (1989) was another heavy rock effort, if a bit more grandiose in its reach, featuring their tribute to doomed 60's child, EDIE SEDGEWICK, 'EDIE (CIAO BABY)'. This album saw The CULT finally gain major success in America, the US 'big rock' sound evident in the record's grooves. Line-up changes had dogged The CULT throughout their career and by 1991, ASTBURY and DUFFY were the only remaining members from the original line-up. That year's album, 'CEREMONY', sounded somewhat listless, although it was a relative success. 1993 saw a No.1 compilation album, 'PURE CULT' selling like hotcakes, although people weren't quite so eager to shell out for '94's 'THE CULT' album. Their glory days were clearly over, the band remaining a cult (!) phenomenon. In 1996, ASTBURY was in full flight again, fronting a new rock outfit, The HOLY BARBARIANS, although the album, 'CREAM' didn't shift many copies. The ageing rock warrior finally released a bonafide solo album in the shape of 1999's 'SPIRIT/LIGHT/SPEED', enlisting former MASTERS OF REALITY man, CHRIS GOSS, on guitar and production duties. While the lyrical sentiments and mystic overtones remained the same – check out the CHE GUEVARA-style sleeve – the music made a concerted effort to get hip with some pre-millennial industrial angst. When the long awaited new CULT album, 'BEYOND GOOD AND EVIL' finally arrived in summer 2001, it came as little surprise that the new noised-up approach remained intact. Save for a few nods to their classic late 80's/early 90's heyday, the band embraced the harsher sonic climate of post-metal with DUFFY giving it laldy on the distortion pedal. Having said that, oldtime CULT fans were placated to a certain degree with the reliable ASTBURY wail and an obvious reluctance to completely forego the killer hooks which made them so compelling in the first place. • **Songwriters:** From '83 onwards, all by ASTBURY / DUFFY. Covered WILD THING (Troggs) / LOUIE LOUIE (Kingsmen) / CONQUISTADOR (Theatre Of Hate) / FAITH HEALER (Alex Harvey).

Album rating: SOUTHERN DEATH CULT (*6; as the Southern Death Cult) / DREAMTIME (*7) / LOVE (*8) / ELECTRIC (*6) / SONIC TEMPLE (*8) / CEREMONY (*6) / PURE CULT compilation (*7) / THE CULT (*5) / BEYOND GOOD AND EVIL (*6) / Holy Barbarians: CREAM (*6) / Ian Astbury: SPIRIT/LIGHT/SPEED (*5)

SOUTHERN DEATH CULT

IAN LINDSAY (b. ASTBURY, 14 May'62, Heswell, Cheshire, England)– vocals / **BUZZ BURROWS** – guitar / **BARRY JEPSON** – bass / **AKY (NAWAZ QUERESHI)** – drums

Situation2 not iss.

Dec 82. (7") *(SIT 19)* **FATMAN. / MOYA** [-]
(12"+=) *(SIT 19T)* – The girl.

Beggars Banquet not iss.

Jun 83. (lp) *(BEGA 46)* **SOUTHERN DEATH CULT** [43] [-]
– All glory / Fatman / Today / False faces / The crypt / Crow / Faith / Vivisection / Apache / Moya. *(re-iss. Jul88 lp/c/cd; BBL/+C 46/+CD) (cd re-iss. Sep96; BBL 2009CD)*

— (Apr'83) (as BUZZ, AKY and BARRY formed GETTING THE FEAR)

DEATH CULT

with now **IAN ASTBURY** recruited new people– BILLY DUFFY (b.12 May'61)– lead guitar (ex-THEATRE OF HATE, ex-NOSEBLEEDS) / **JAMIE STUART** – bass (ex-RITUAL, ex-CRISIS) / **RAY MONDO** (r.n.SMITH)– drums (ex-RITUAL)

Situation2 not iss.

Jul 83. (12"ep) *(SIT 23T)* **BROTHERS GRIMM / HORSE NATION. / GHOST DANCE / CHRISTIANS** [-]

— **NIGEL PRESTON** – drums (ex-SEX GANG CHILDREN) repl. MONDO

Nov 83. (7"/12") *(SIT 29/+T)* **GOD'S ZOO. / GOD'S ZOO (THESE TIMES)**
(re-iss. Nov88)

CULT

— (same line-up)

Situation2 not iss.

May 84. (7") *(SIT 33)* **SPIRITWALKER. / A FLOWER IN THE DESERT** [-]
(12"+=) *(SIT 33T)* – Bone rag.

Beggars Banquet Sire

Aug 84. (lp/c) *(BEG A/C 57)* **DREAMTIME** [21]
– Horse nation / Spiritwalker / 83rd dream / Butterflies / Go west (crazy spinning circles) / Gimmick / A flower in the desert / Dreamtime / Rider in the snow / Bad medicine waltz. *(free live-lp w/ above, also on c)* **DREAMTIME AT THE LYCEUM** *(CULT 1)* – 83rd dream / God's zoo / Bad medicine / A flower in the desert / Dreamtime / Christians / Horse nation / Bone rag / Ghost dance / Moya. *(pic-lp iss.Dec84; BEGA 57P) (re-iss. Oct88 lp/c/cd; BBL/+C 57/+CD)* – Bone rag / Sea and sky / Resurrection Joe.

Sep 84. (7"/7"poster) *(BEG 115/+P)* **GO WEST. / SEA AND SKY** [-]
(12"+=) *(BEG 115T)* – Brothers Grimm (live).

Dec 84. (7") *(BEG 122)* **RESURRECTION JOE. / ('A'-Hep cat mix)** [74] [-]
(12"+=) *(BEG 122T)* – ('A'extended).

May 85. (7") *(BEG 135)* **SHE SELLS SANCTUARY. / NO.13** [15] [-]
(12"+=) *(BEG 135T)* – The snake.
(12") *(BEG 135TP)* – ('A'-Howling mix) / Assault on sanctuary.
(c-s) *(BEG 135C)* – ('A'extended) / ('A'-Howling mix) / The snake / Assault on sanctuary.

Jul 85. (7") *<28820>* **SHE SELLS SANCTUARY. / LITTLE FACE** [-]

— **MARK BRZEZICKI** – drums (of BIG COUNTRY) deputised repl. PRESTON

Sep 85. (7") *(BEG 147)* **RAIN. / LITTLE FACE** [17] [-]
(12"+=) *(BEG 147T)* – (Here comes the) Rain.

Oct 85. (lp/c)(cd) *(BEGA/BEGC 65)(BEGA 65CD) <25359>* **LOVE** [4] [87]
– Nirvana / Big neon gliter / Love / Brother Wolf, Sister Moon / Rain / The phoenix / The hollow man / Revolution / She sells sanctuary / Black angel. *(cd+=)* – Judith / Little face. *(cd re-iss. Apr97; BBL 65)*

— **LES WARNER** (b.13 Feb'61) – drums (ex-JOHNNY THUNDERS, etc) repl. MARK

Nov 85. (7") *(BEG 152)* **REVOLUTION. / ALL SOULS AVENUE** [30] [-]
(d7"+=/c-s+=/12"+=) *(BEG D/C/T 152)* – Judith / Sunrise.

Feb 87. (7") *(BEG 182)* **LOVE REMOVAL MACHINE. / WOLF CHILD'S BLUES** [18] [-]
(12"+=) *(BEG 182T)* – ('A'extended).
(d7"+=) *(BEG 182D)* – Conquistador / Groove Co.
(c-s++=) *(BEG 182C)* – (all above).

Apr 87. (lp/c)(cd) *(BEGA/BEGC 80)(BEGA 80CD) <25555>* **ELECTRIC** [4] [38]
– Wild flower / Peace dog / Lil' devil / Aphrodisiac jacket / Electric ocean / Bad fun / King contrary man / Love removal machine / Born to be wild / Outlaw / Memphis hip shake. *(gold-pic-lp Aug87; BEGA 80G) (cd re-iss. Apr97; BBL 80CD)*

Apr 87. (7") *(BEG 188)* **LIL' DEVIL. / ZAP CITY** [11] [-]
(12"+=) *(BEG 188T)* – She sells sanctuary (live) / Bonebag (live).
(d12"+=/c-s+=) *(BEG 188 TD/C)* – She sells sanctuary (live) / The phoenix (live) / Wild thing . . .Louie Louie (live).

(cd-s+=) *(BEG 188CD)* – Love removal machine (live) / The phoenix (live) / She sells sanctuary (live).

May 87. (7") *<29290>* **LIL' DEVIL. / MEMPHIS HIPSHAKE** [-] [ ]

Aug 87. (7"/7"pic-d) *(BEG 195/+P) <28213>* **WILD FLOWER. / LOVE TROOPER** [24] [ ]
(12"+=) *(BEG 195T)* – ('A'extended rock mix).
(c-s++=) *(BEG 195C)* – Horse nation (live).
(d7"+=) *(BEG 195D)* – Outlaw (live) / Horse nation (live).
(cd-s+=) *(BEG 195CD)* – (all 5 above) / She sells sanctuary (live).
(12") *(BEG 195TR)* – ('A'ext.) / ('A'-Guitar dub) / ('B'side).

— **MICKEY CURRY** – (on session) drums repl. WARNER + KID CHAOS

Mar 89. (7"/c-s) *(BEG 228/+C) <27543>* **FIRE WOMAN. / AUTOMATIC BLUES** [15] [46] May89
(12"+=/3"cd-s+=) *(BEG 228 T/CD)* – Messin' up the blues.
(12") *(BEG 228TR)* – ('A'-L.A. rock mix) / ('A'-N.Y.C. rock mix).

Apr 89. (lp/c)(cd) *(BEGA/BEGC 98)(BEGA 98CD) <25871>* **SONIC TEMPLE** [3] [10]
– Sun king / Fire woman / American horse / Edie (ciao baby) / Sweet soul sister / Soul asylum / New York City / Automatic blues / Soldier blue / Wake up time for freedom. *(c+=/cd+=)* – Medicine train. *(cd re-iss. Apr97; BBL 98CD)*

— **ASTBURY, DUFFY + STUART** were joined by **MATT SORUM** – drums / **MARK TAYLOR** – keyboards (on tour)

Jun 89. (7"/7"gf/c-s) *(BEG 230/+G/C)* **EDIE (CIAO BABY). / BLEEDING HEART GRAFFITI** [32] [-]
(pic-cd+=) *(BEG 230CP)* – Lil' devil (live) / Love removal machine (live).
(12"/12"poster) *(BEG 230 T/TP)* – ('A'side) / Medicine train / Love removal machine (live).
(3"cd-s) *(BEG 230CD)* – ('A'side) / Love removal machine (live) / Revolution (live).

Sep 89. (7") *<22873>* **EDIE (CIAO BABY). / LOVE REMOVAL MACHINE** [-] [93]

Nov 89. (7"/c-s) *(BEG 235/+C)* **SUN KING. / EDIE (CIAO BABY)** [39] [-]
(12"+=/12"hologram+=) *(BEG 235T/+H)* – She sells sanctuary.
(cd-s++=) *(BEG 235CD)* – ('A'extended).

Feb 90. (7"/c-s) *(BEG 241/+C)* **SWEET SOUL SISTER. / THE RIVER** [42] [-]
(12"gf+=) *(BEG 241TG)* – American horse (live).
(cd-s+=) *(BEG 241CG)* – Soul asylum (live).
(cd-s) *(BEG 241CD)* – ('A'rock mix) / American horse (live) / ('A'live).
(12") *(BEG 241TR)* – ('A'rock's mix) / Soul asylum (live).
(12") *(BEG 241TP)* – ('A'rock's mix) / ('A'side) / ('A'live).

Mar 90. (c-s) *<19926>* **SWEET SOUL SISTER. / SOLDIER BLUE** [-] [ ]

— (Apr-Oct90) **MARK MORRIS** – bass (ex-BALAAM AND THE ANGEL) repl. STUART

— (1991) **ASTBURY and DUFFY** brought in **CHARLIE DRAYTON** – bass / **MICKEY CURRY** – drums / **RICHIE ZITO** – keyboards, producer / **BELMONT TENCH** – piano, mellotron / **TOMMY FUNDERBUCK** – backing vocals

Sep 91. (7"/c-s) *(BEG 255/+C)* **WILD HEARTED SON. / INDIAN** [40] [-]
('A'ext.12"+=) *(BEG 255T)* – Red Jesus.
(cd-s++=) *(BEG 255CD)* – ('A'extended version).

Sep 91. (cd)(c/lp) *(BEGA 122CD)(BEGC/BEGA 122) <26673>* **CEREMONY** [9] [25]
– Ceremony / Wild hearted son / Earth mofo / White / If / Full tilt / Heart of soul / Bangkok rain / Indian / Sweet salvation / Wonderland.

Feb 92. (7"/c-s) *(BEG 260/+C)* **HEART OF SOUL. / EARTH MOFO** [51] [-]
(12"+=/cd-s+=) *(BEG 260 T/CD)* – Edie (ciao baby) (acoustic) / Heart of soul (acoustic).

Beggars Banquet | Alex

Jan 93. (12"ep) *(BEG 263T)* **SANCTUARY 1993 MIXES** [15] [-]
– She sells sanctuary / ('A'-Dog Star Rising) / ('A'-Slutnostic mix) / ('A'-Sundance mix).
(cd-ep) *(BEG 263CD2)* – ('A'live) repl. above original.
(cd-ep) *(BEG 263CD1)* – (first 2 tracks) / ('A'-Phlegmatic mix) / ('A'-Flusteresqueish mix).

Feb 93. (d-lp/c)(cd/4x12") *(BEGA/BEGC 130)(BEGA 130 CD/B) <3246>* **PURE CULT** compilation) [1] [ ]
– She sells sanctuary / Fire woman / Lil' devil / Spiritwalker / The witch / Revolution / Wild hearted Sun / Love removal machine / Rain / Edie (ciao baby) / Heart of soul / Love / Wildflower / Go west / Ressurection Joe / Sun king / Sweet soul ister / Earth mofo. *(d-lp w/ other d-lp)* LIVE AT THE MARQUEE '91 *(cd re-iss. Jun00; BEGA 2026CD)*

— **ASTBURY + DUFFY** now with **CRAIG ADAMS** (b. 4 Apr'62, Otley, England) – bass (ex-MISSION, ex-SISTERS OF MERCY) + **SCOTT GARRETT** (b.14 Mar'66, Washington, D.C.) – drums

Sep 94. (c-s) *(BBQ 40C)* **COMING DOWN. / ('A'remix)** [50] [-]
(12"+=/cd-s+=) *(BBQ 40 T/CD)* – Gone.

Oct 94. (cd/c/lp) *(BBQ CD/MC/LP 164) <45673>* **THE CULT** [21] [69]
– Gone / Coming down / Real grrrl / Black Sun / Naturally high / Joy / Star / Sacred life / Be free / Universal you / Emperor's new horse / Saints are down. *(cd re-iss. Apr97; BBL 164CD)*

Dec 94. (c-s) *(BBQ 45C)* **STAR. / BREATHING OUT** [65] [-]
(12"+=/cd-s+=) *(BBQ 45 T/CD)* – The witch (extended).

— In Apr'95, they cancelled tour, due to new guitarist JAMES STEVENSON returning to the re-formed GENE LOVES JEZEBEL.

HOLY BARBARIANS

— **IAN ASTBURY** plus **PATRICK SUGG** – guitar, vocals (ex-LUCIFER WONG) / **SCOTT GARRETT** – drums / **MATT GARRETT** – bass

Beggars Banquet | Warners

Apr 96. (7") *(BBQ 65)* **SPACE JUNKIE. / DOLLY BIRD** [ ] [-]
(cd-s+=) *(BBQ 65CD)* – Hate you.

May 96. (cd/c/lp) *(BBQ CD/MC/LP 182) <46223>* **CREAM** [ ] [ ]
– Brothers fights / Dolly bird / Cream / Blind / Opium / Space junkie / She / You are there / Magick Christian / Bodhisattva.

IAN ASTBURY

— with **WITCHMAN (JOHN ROOME) + CHRIS GOSS**

Jun 00. (7") *(BBQ 344)* **HIGH TIME AMPLIFIER. / TYGER** [ ] [-]
(cd-s+=) *(BBQ 344CD)* – ('A'-Witchman mix).

Jul 00. (cd/lp) *(BBQ CD/LP 208) <80208>* **SPIRIT/LIGHT/SPEED** [ ] [ ]
– Back on Earth / High time amplifier / Devil's mouth / Tonight (illuminated) / Metaphysical pistol / The witch (SLT return) / It's over / El che – Wild like a horse / Tyger / Shambala (R.F.L.).

CULT

— re-formed with **ASTBURY + DUFFY + SORUM**

Atlantic | Atlantic

Jun 01. (cd/c) *(<7567 83440-2/-4>)* **BEYOND GOOD AND EVIL** [69] [37]
– War (the process) / The saint / Rise / Take the power / Breathe / Nico / American gothic / Ashes and ghosts / Shape the sky / Speed of light / True believers / My bridges burn.

– compilations, others, etc. –

all on 'Beggars Banquet'

Dec 88. (pic-cd-ep) *(BBP 1CD)* **THE MANOR SESSIONS** [ ] [-]

Dec 89. (pic-cd-ep) *(BBP 2CD)* **THE LOVE MIXES** [ ] [-]

Dec 89. (pic-cd-ep) *(BBP 3CD)* **THE ELECTRIC MIXES** [ ] [ ]

Aug 91. (pic-cd-ep) *(BBP 6CD)* **SPIRITWALKER / A FLOWER IN THE DESERT / BONE BAG / GO WEST / SEA AND SKY / BROTHERS GRIMM (live)** [-] [-]

Aug 91. (pic-cd-ep) *(BBP 7CD)* **RESURRECTION JOE / SHE SELLS SANCTUARY / THE SNAKE / NO.13 / ASSAULT ON SANCTUARY / RESURRECTION JOE (Hep Cat mix)** [-] [-]

Aug 91. (pic-cd-ep) *(BBP 8CD)* **RAIN / LITTLE FACE / REVOLUTION / ALL SOULS AVENUE / JUDITH / SUNRISE** [-] [-]

Aug 91. (pic-cd-ep) *(BBP 9CD)* **LOVE REMOVAL MACHINE / CONQUISTADOR / GROOVE CO. / ZAP CITY / LOVE TROOPER / WOLF CHILD'S BLUES / LIL' DEVIL** [-] [-]

Aug 91. (pic-cd-ep) *(BBP 10CD)* **WILD FLOWER / WILD FLOWER (guitar dub) / HORSE NATION (live) / OUTLAW (live) / SHE SELLS SANCTUARY (live) / BONE BAG (live) / PHOENIX (live) / WILD THING . . . LOUIE LOUIE** [-] [-]

Aug 91. (pic-cd-ep) *(BBP 11CD)* **FIRE WOMAN / AUTOMATIC BLUES / MESSIN' UP THE BLUES / EDIE)CIAO BABY) / BLEEDING HEART GRAFFITI / SUN KING / FIRE WOMAN (L.A. rock mix) / FIRE WOMAN (N.Y.C. rock mix)** [-] [-]

Aug 91. (pic-cd-ep) *(BBP 12CD)* **SWEET SOUL SISTER / THE RIVER / LOVE REMOVAL MACHINE (live) / LIL' DEVIL (live) / REVOLUTION (live) / SWEET SOUL SISTER (live) / AMERICAN HORSE (live) / SOUL ASYLUM (live) / SWEET SOUL SISTER (Rock's mix)** [-] [-]

Aug 91. (10x pic-cd-ep) *(CBOX 1)* **SINGLES COLLECTION 1984-1990** [ ] [-]
– (all above)

Jun 92. (video w/free cd-ep) **FAITH HEALER / FULL TILT (live) / LOVE REMOVAL MACHINE (live)** [ ] [ ]

Sep 96. (cd; as DEATH CULT) *(BBL 2008CD)* **GHOST DANCE** [ ] [ ]

Nov 00. (6xcd-box) *(RCBOX 1CD) <82030>* **RARE CULT** [ ] [ ]

Nov 00. (cd) *(BBL 2029CD) <82029>* **THE BEST OF RARE CULT** [ ] [ ]

CULTURE SHOCK (see under ⇒ SUBHUMANS)

Cherie CURRIE

Born: c.1959, USA. A founding member of the all-girl punk band The RUNAWAYS, CURRIE left the group for a solo career following the release of the 'Queens Of Noise' (1977) album. She enlisted the help of her sister, MARIE CURRIE, and guitarist STEVIE T to augment her on a solo debut, 'BEAUTY'S ONLY SKIN DEEP' (1978). The following year, the sisters completed a dual album, 'MESSIN' WITH THE BOYS', and although this included TOTO, it subsequently bombed. Cutting her loses, CHERIE decided to try her hand at acting, although her celluloid career was brief (a lone appearance alongside Jodie Foster in the 1980 film, 'Foxes'). • **Covered:** SINCE YOU'VE BEEN GONE (Russ Ballard; hit- Rainbow) / OVERNIGHT SENSATION (Raspberries) / WISHING WELL (Free).

Album rating: BEAUTY'S ONLY SKIN DEEP (*4)

CHERIE CURRIE – vocals; with session people plus her sister MARIE on extra vocals / also STEVIE T – guitar

Mercury | Mercury

Apr 78. (7") *(6167 640)* **CALL ME AT MIDNIGHT. / YOUNG AND WILD** [ ] [ ]

Apr 78. (lp) *(6338 867)* **BEAUTY'S ONLY SKIN DEEP** [ ] [-]
– Call me at midnight / I surrender / Beauty's only skin deep / I will still love you / Science fiction faze / I like the way you dance / That's the kind of guy I like / Love at first sight / The only one / Young and wild.

CHERIE & MARIE CURRIE

— session men incl. TOTO

Capitol | Capitol

Feb 80. (7") *(CL 16119) <4754>* **SINCE YOU'VE BEEN GONE. / MESSIN' WITH THE BOYS** [ ] [95] Oct79

Jun 80. (7") *<4841>* **THIS TIME. / SECRETS** [-] [ ]

Jul 80. (lp) *<(EST 12022)>* **MESSIN' WITH THE BOYS** [ ] [ ]

– Messin' with the boys / Since you've been gone / I just love the feeling / All I want / Overnight sensation (hit record) / Elaine / This time / Wishing well / Secrets / We're through. *(cd-iss. Jan98 on 'Renaissance'; RME 0189CD)*

Aug 80. (7") *<4861>* **MESSIN' WITH THE BOYS. / ALL I WANT** [-] [ ]

— she retired from music, becoming an actress in 'Foxes' with Jodie Foster, before she disappeared

CYCLEFLY

Formed: Aghada, Ireland . . . 1997 by brothers DECLAN and CIERAN O'SHEA, who teamed up with the French/Italian band, SEVENTEEN (soon to be DOGABONE), an outfit that numbered NONO PRESTA, CHRISTIAN MONTAGNE and JEAN MICHEL CAVALLO. The story goes that the latter trio saw the wild DECLAN singing in his local pub and remembering his antics, decided to get in touch with him and his brother. Unfortunately, this took a little more time than anticipated as the pair were helping to build rollercoasters at Disneyland, Paris! Although their sound called to mind such alt-rock luminaries as JANE'S ADDICTION, PLACEBO and KYUSS, DECLAN's orange PVC attire might challenge more conservative audiences outside the bohemian confines of London or Paris. Finding a sympathetic home at the appropriately named 'RadioActive' label, CYCLEFLY took wing to the States in the Spring of '98. There, they worked with TOOL producer, SYLVIA MASSEY on their forthcoming debut 'Universal' album, 'GENERATION SAP'. Meanwhile, 'CRAWL DOWN' was awarded Kerrang! single of the week later that November. It was followed by 'SUPERGOD', while the aforementioned set was released in August '99.

Album rating: GENERATION SAP (*5)

DECLAN O'SHEA (b.18 May'72) – vocals / **CIERAN O'SHEA** – guitar / **NONO PESTA** – guitar / **CHRISTIAN MONTAGNE** – bass / **JEAN MICHEL CAVALLO** – drums

		RadioActive	RadioActive
Mar 98.	(ltd-cd-s) *(demo)* **SUMP / EVERGREEN**	-	-
Nov 98.	(cd-s) *(RAXTD 35)* **CRAWL DOWN / SELOTAPE / STAR**		-
Mar 99.	(cd-s) *<55537>* **SUPERGOD / VIOLET HIGH**	-	
May 99.	(cd-s) *(RAXTD 37)* **SUPERGOD / PANIC / LOCATE**		-
Aug 99.	(cd) *(<RARD 11930>)* **GENERATION SAP**		May99

– Violet high / Crawl down / Supergod / Whore / Following yesterday / Better than you / Plastic coated man / The hive / Generation sap / Sump / Slaves.

CYNIC

Formed: Florida, USA . . . 1987 by PAUL MASVIDAL, JASON GOBEL, SEAN REINERT and TONY CHOY (the latter being replaced by SHAWN MALONE, before their debut). While the band awaited a recording contract of their own, MASVIDAL and REINERT helped out DEATH on their 'Human' album. CYNIC finally found a home with 'Roadrunner', releasing their much-anticipated debut, 'FOCUS' in '93. By the time of the record's release, CHOY had decamped to the ATHEIST fold, having previously moonlighted with the band. A highly ambitious hybrid of death-metal and 70's style prog/jazz, the band incredibly managed to carry it off, carving out a unique musical identity in the process.

Album rating: FOCUS (*6)

PAUL MASVIDAL – vocals / **JASON GOBEL** – guitar / **SHAWN MALONE** – bass; repl. TONY CHOY who joined ATHEIST / **SEAN REINERT** – drums

		Roadrunner	Roadrunner
Sep 93.	(cd/lp) *<(RR 9169-2/-1)>* **FOCUS**		

– Veil of Maya / Celestial voyage / The eagle nature / Sentiment / I'm but a wave to . . . / Uroboric forms / Textures / How could I.

— disbanded some time later

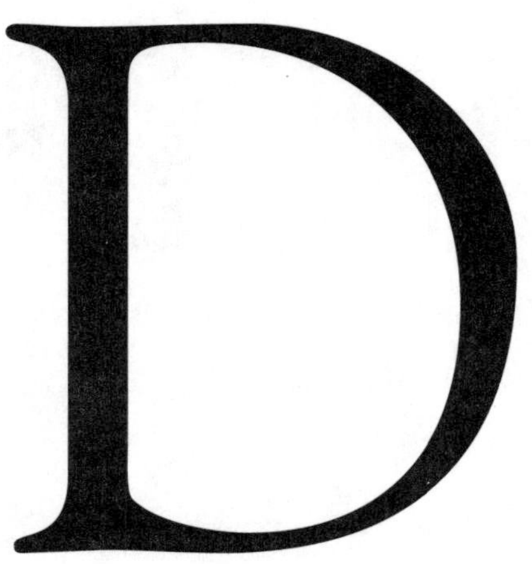

D.A.D.

Formed: Copenhagen, Denmark ... 1985 (originally known as DISNEYLAND AFTER DARK) by brothers JESPER and JACOB A. BINZER, plus STIG PEDERSEN and PETER L. JENSEN. Having initially surfaced in 1986/87 with two independently released albums, D.A.D. signed a reputed 7-figure deal with 'Warner Brothers', issuing their major label debut, 'NO FUEL LEFT FOR THE PILGRIMS' in '89. Despite, or possibly as a result of, a typically "wacky" European sense of humour (i.e. covered AMERICA's 'A HORSE WITH NO NAME'), the group failed to live up to their high-flying expectations. A further attempt, 'RISKIN' IT ALL', flew in the face of metal press criticism with its defiant stab at original power-rock. 1995's 'HELPYOURSELFISH', meanwhile, packed an even harder punch, if – as the title might suggest – not quite abandoning their unique wit. Although many of the choruses were as big and chunky as you'd expect from men who refuse to cut their hair, a hitherto unwitnessed drive towards experimentation helped increase their 90's street cred. Come the end of the decade, D.A.D. were still keeping the faith for straight-up heavy metal with 'SIMPATICO' (1997), the live 'PSYCHO PATICO' (1998) – those puns just keep on coming – and 'EVERYTHING GLOWS' (2000), the latter recorded with new drummer LAUST SONNE.

Album rating: CALL OF THE WILD (*5) / D.A.D. DRAWS A CIRCLE (*5) / NO FUEL LEFT FOR THE PILGRIMS (*7) / RISKIN' IT ALL (*6) / HELPYOURSELFISH (*5) / GOOD CLEAN FAMILY ENTERTAINMENT YOU CAN TRUST . . . compilation (*6) / SIMPATICO (*4) / PSYCHOPATICO (*4) / EVERYTHING GLOWS (*3) / THE EARLY YEARS double compilation (*7)

DISNEYLAND AFTER DARK

JESPER BINZER – vocals, guitar / **JACOB A. BINZER** – guitar / **STIG PEDERSEN** – bass, vocals / **PETER L. JENSEN** – drums

Megadisc | not iss.

Dec 85. (12"ep) **STANDING ON THE NEVER NEVER** [-] [-] Danish
– Up up, over the mountain top / Marlboro man / Never never.

Jan 86. (lp) **CALL OF THE WILD** [-] [-] Danish
– Land of their choice / Call of the wild / Riding with Sue / Marlboro man / Counting the cattle / Jackie 'O' / Trucker / Rock river / Jonnie / Son of a gun / It's after dark.

Dec 86. (7") **IT'S AFTER DARK (SAD SAD XMAS)** [-] [-] Danish

D.A.D.

Aug 87. (7") **ISN'T THAT WILD** [-] [-] Danish

Sep 87. (lp) *(MRLP 3057)* **D.A.D. DRAWS A CIRCLE** [ ] [-]
– Isn't that wild / A horse with no name / Mighty mighty high / I won't cut my hair / Black crickets / There's a ship / God's favorite / 10 knots / Ride my train / I'd rather live than die.

Nov 87. (7") **A HORSE WITH NO NAME** [-] [-] Danish

WEA | Warners

Sep 89. (7"/c-s) *(W 2775/+C)* **SLEEPING MY DAY AWAY. / ILL WILL** [ ] [ ]
(12"+=/cd-s+=) *(W 2775 T/CD)* –

Sep 89. (lp/c)(cd) *(WX 288/+C)(925999-2)* **NO FUEL LEFT FOR THE PILGRIMS** [ ] [ ]
– Sleeping my day away / Jihad / Point of view / Rim of hell / ZCMI / True believer / Girl nation / Lords of the atlas / Overmuch / Siamese twin / Wild talk / Ill will.

Nov 89. (cd-s) **GIRL NATION** [-] [-] Danish

Mar 00. (cd-s) **JIHAD** [-] [-] Danish

Sep 91. (cd-s) **BAD CRAZINESS** [-] [-] Danish

Oct 91. (cd/c/lp) *(<7599 26772-2/-4/-1>)* **RISKIN' IT ALL** [ ] [ ]
– Bad craziness / D-law / Day of wrong moves / I won't cut my hair / Drown that dusty 3rd world road / Makin' fun of money / Grow or pay / Smart boy can't tell ya' / Riskin' it all / Laugh 'n' a 1/2.

Mar 92. (7"/c-s) **GROW OR PAY. / I WON'T CUT MY HAIR** [ ] [ ]
(12"+=/cd-s+=) – Rock'n'roll radar.

—— in the mid-90's, D:A:D released a series of Danish-only singles, 'RECONSTRUCKDEAD', 'HELPYOURSELFISH', 'UNOWNED', 'I WON'T CUT MY HAIR (live)'.

Chrysalis | EMI Medley

Apr 95. (cd/c) *<(CD/TC CHR 6101)>* **HELPYOURSELFISH** [ ] [ ]
– Reconstruckdead / Written in water / Helpyourselfish / Soulbender / Unowned / Candid / Blood in / Out / Prayin' to a god / Naked (but still stripping) / We are alive here / It'swhenit'swrongit'sright / Flat.

Nov 97. (cd) *<823653-2>* **SIMPATICO** [-] [ ]
– Empty heads / Simpatico / Home alone 4 / Cloudy hours / Hate to say I told you so / No one answers / Mad days / Don't tell me anything / You do what I've just done / Life right now / Now or forever / A hand without strength.

Jan 98. (cd-s) **HOME ALONE 4 / FAVOURS** [-] [-] Danish

Nov 98. (d-cd) *<498065-2>* **PSYCHOPATICO (live)** [-] [ ]
– Simpatico / Empty heads / Bad craziness / Grow or pay / Riding with Sue / Hate to say . . . / I won't cut my hair / Cloudy hours // Reconstrucktead / Black crickets / Home alone 5 / Sleeping my day away / Jihad / Written in water / It's after dark / Laugh 'n' A half / Jacketless in December. *(CD-rom bonus track).*

—— **LAUST SONNE** – drums; repl. JENSEN

Mar 00. (cd-s) **EVERYTHING GLOWS / SUMMER ME SOON / I'M A LITTLE CLOUD** [-] [-] Danish

Apr 00. (cd) *<526021-2>* **EVERYTHING GLOWS** [-] [ ]
– Everything glows / Nineteenhundredandyesterday / The road below me / Something good / Sunstar / Evil twin / Candybar / A kiss between the legs / I'm not the same / Summer me soon / As common as.

Sep 00. (cd-s) **NINETEENHUNDREDANDYESTERDAY (radio) / NINETEENHUNDREDANDYESTERDAY (album) / LAST MANGO IN PARIS / EVERYTHING GLOWS** [-] [-] Danish

– compilations, etc. –

Nov 95. (cd) *EMI Medley; <838421-2>* **GOOD CLEAN FAMILY ENTERTAINMENT YOU CAN TRUST – MILESTONE MATERIAL 1985-1995** [-] [ ]

Jun 00. (d-cd) *Mega; <MEG 011331-2>* **THE EARLY YEARS** [-] [-] Danish
– (the first two LP's, + rare stuff + videos)

DAEMON (see under ⇒ KONKHRA)

DAEMONARCH (see under ⇒ MOONSPELL)

DAG NASTY

Formed: Washington DC, USA ... 1985 by BRIAN BAKER, a hardcore veteran of sorts having been a member of MINOR THREAT, GOVERNMENT ISSUE and The MEATMEAN. Guitarist BAKER and vocalist DAVE SMALLEY became part of the DC folklore alongside their aforementioned counterparts and top act, FUGAZI (they almost immediately signed to IAN MacKAYE's 'Dischord' label); the band made their debut in 1986 with the 'CAN I SAY' album. SMALLEY was subsequently replaced by PETER CORTNER for the live set, 'WIG OUT AT DENKOS' (1987) while DAG NASTY's more pop-friendly approach to an infamously uncompromising genre earned them a deal with 'Giant'. The label released 'FIELD DAY' in 1988, generally regarded as a high-water mark in the band's career but also a record which served as their epitaph. BAKER went on to form the highly underrated scuzz-metal band JUNKYARD, along with ex-BIG BOY, CHRIS GATES. • **Covered:** STARING AT THE RUDE BOYS (Ruts) / 12XU (Wire) / LIE DOWN TIME (UK Subs).

Album rating: CAN I SAY? (*5) / WIG OUT AT DENKO'S (*5) / FIELD DAY (*7) / 85-86 compilation (*5) / FOUR ON THE FLOOR (*4)

DAVE SMALLEY – vocals (ex-DYS) / **BRIAN BAKER** – guitar (ex-MINOR THREAT, ex-GOVERNMENT ISSUE, ex-MEATMEN) / **ROGER MARBURY** – bass / **COLIN SEARS** – drums

Dischord | Dischord

1986. (lp/c) *<(DISCHORD 19/+C)>* **CAN I SAY?** [ ] [ ]
– Values here / One to two / Circles / Thin line / Justification / What now? / I've heard / Under your influence / Can I say? / Never go back.

—— (late '86) **PETER CORTNER** – vocals; repl. SHAWN BROWN who had repl. SMALLEY

Sep 87. (lp/c) *<(DISCHORD 26/+C)>* **WIG OUT AT DENKO'S** [ ] [ ]
– The godfather / Trying / Space / Fall / When I love / Simple minds / Wig out at Denko's / Exercise / Dag nasty / Crucial three.

—— **DOUG CARRION** – bass; repl. MARBURY

—— **SCOTT GARRETT** – drums; repl. SEARS

We Bite | Giant

1988. (lp) *(WB 040) <GRI 6013-1>* **FIELD DAY** [ ] [ ]
– Trouble is / Field day / Things that made no sense / The ambulance song / Staring at the rude boys / 13 seconds under water / Penita / Dear Mrs. Touma / Matt / I've heard / Under your influence / Typical / Here's to you / (16 count) / Never green lane / You're mine / All ages show / 12XU. *(cd-iss. Sep93; WB 3040CD)*

—— split in 1989 when BAKER formed turn of the decade raunch'n'rollers, JUNKYARD. **SMALLEY** revived the group name and enlisted **MARBURY, SEARS** (from original line-up) and new guitarist **DALE NIXON**

Epitaph | Epitaph

Mar 92. (cd/lp) *<(E 86415-2/-1)>* **FOUR ON THE FLOOR** [ ] [ ]
– Still waiting / Going down / Turn it down / Million days / Roger / S.F.S. / We went wrong / Down time / Lie down and die / Mango.

– compilations, etc. –

Dec 90. (lp/cd) *Bitzcore; (BC 1674/+CD) / Selfless; <SFLS 5-2>* **85/86** [ ] [ ] Nov92
– Another wrong / Circles / Can I say? / I've heard / Never go back / Justification / Under your influence / Trying / Moni-Q / Fall / Trying / All ages show / Safe / Mule / My dog is a cat / Another wrong LL.

Nov 91. (cd) *Dischord; <DISCHORD 53CD>* **CAN I SAY? / WIG OUT AT DENKO'S** [-] [ ]

Jeff DAHL

Born: Stuttgart, Germany. Brought up in Hawaii, JEFF subsequently joined the army and found himself posted to Washington DC. There, just as Britain's punk scene was beginning to filter through to the States, DAHL cut a debut single, 'ROCK'N'ROLL CRITIC' for a local indie label. Relocating to Los Angeles after his army discharge, he formed VOX POP in 1979 alongside various members of America's burgeoning alternative/underground scene. After an early 80's stint at the helm of ANGRY SAMOANS, DAHL formed the short-lived POWERTRIP, a band blighted by drug problems. The singer/guitarist eventually got his proverbial shit together for a debut solo set, 'VOMIT WET KISS' (1987). Although he once again had a brief dalliance with a band, a new deal with the L.A.-based 'Triple X' imprint initiated a long and prolific 90's solo career. The man's slipshod, buzzsaw punk – as sampled on albums such has 'I KILL ME' (1990), 'WICKED' (1992), 'WASTED REMAINS OF A DISTURBED CHILDHOOD', 'LEATHER FRANKENSTEIN' and 'HEART FULL OF SNOT' (1997) – stood apart from the new breed of so-called American punk acts by dint of its sheer contrariness and worldly-wise/weary lyrics. • **Covered:** GIMME DANGER (Iggy Pop).

Album rating: VOMIT WET KISS (*4) / SCRATCH UP SOME ACTION (*6) / I KILL ME (*4) / HAVE FAITH (*4) / ULTRA UNDER (*4) / WICKED (*5) / WASTED REMAINS OF A DISTURBED CHILDHOOD (*5) / MOONCHILD (*4) / LEATHER FRANKENSTEIN (*6) / BLISS (*4) / FRENCH COUGH SYRUP (*6) / HEART FULL OF SNOT (*4) / ALL TRASHED UP (*5)

JEFF DAHL – vocals, guitar

not iss. Doodley Squat

1977. (7") <2> **ROCK'N'ROLL CRITIC. / JANINE / I HEARD** [-] [ ]

—— DAHL formed VOX POP (not US band of the same name)

VOX POP

JEFF DAHL with **DON BOLES, DINAH CANCER, PAUL B. CUTLER, DEL HOPKINS + MIKI OCHOA**

not iss. Bad Trip

1980. (7") **CAB DRIVER. / JUST LIKE YOUR MOM** [-] [ ]

not iss. Genlyd

1980. (lp) *<GENLP 121>* **VOX POP** [-] [ ]

not iss. Mystic

1981. (12"ep) *<M12 452>* **THE BAND, THE MYTH, THE VOLUME** [-] [ ]
– Become a pagan / Production / Procession.

Hollywood Hollywood

Mar 82. (7") *<(HWD 1)>* **SLEEPING IN A STRANGER'S BED. / LOOKING AT THE WORLD THROUGH TINTED GLASSES** [ ] [ ]

—— when DAHL joined The ANGRY SAMOANS (and later POWERTRIP), BOLES joined The GERMS and 45 GRAVE, the latter group featured CUTLER (later of The DREAM SYNDICATE), NERVOUS GENDER was set up with others

JEFF DAHL

—— with various musicians incl. **RIKK AGNEW, DAVE NAZWORTHY, JAIME PINA, JOHN DUFFY, AMY WICHMANN, MELANIE VAMMEN + JOHN MANIKOFF** / etc

not iss. Sympathy F

1987. (lp) **VOMIT WET KISS** [-] [ ]

Shakin' Street Dog Meat

Jul 90. (lp; by JEFF DAHL GROUP) *(YEAH HUP 007)* **SCRATCH UP SOME ACTION** [ ] [ ] 1989
<(cd-iss. 1995 on 'Triple X'; TX 51141CD)>

Roadrunner Triple X

1990. (cd) *<TX 51041-2>* **I KILL ME** [-] [ ]
(UK-iss.1994; same as US)

Apr 91. (cd/lp) *(RR 9317-2/-1) <TX 51049-2/-1>* **ULTRA UNDER** [ ] [ ]
– Touchy, touch baby / Cherry bomb / Chemical eyeballs / Somebody / Just amazin' / Junkies deserve to die / Pretty blonde hair / Elks Lodge riot / You're a drag / God don't care / Mick and Keith killed Brian / Dirt / Nobody loves you. *(UK cd-iss. 1995 on 'Triple X'; same as US)*

Triple X Triple X

1991. (cd) *<(TX 51110CD)>* **HAVE FAITH** [ ] [ ]

Feb 92. (cd) *<(TX 51091CD)>* **WICKED** [ ] [ ]
– Lisa's world / Look at you / The face of an angel / Just like they should / Radio Babylon / Tonight / Forever (with BOBBY WOMACK) / Arizona / Just a little bit more / Real high school romance / Moon upstairs / Wicked.

Jun 93. (cd) *<(TX 51127CD)>* **WASTED REMAINS OF A DISTURBED CHILDHOOD** [ ] [ ]

Dec 93. (cd; as JEFF DAHL & POISON IDEA) *<(TX 51137CD)>* **JEFF DAHL & POISON IDEA** [ ] [ ]

Apr 94. (cd) *<(TX 51152CD)>* **MOONCHILD** [ ] [ ]

Sep 94. (cd; JEFF DAHL and the SPIDERS FROM URANUS) *<(TX 51176CD)>* **LEATHER FRANKENSTEIN** [ ] [ ]
– Leather Frankenstein / Can't keep from cryin' / Surf TV / Only lovers left alive / Stars and moons / European vacation / Dead heroes / Marianne / Hotrods to Hell / I think I lost my mind / Waitin' for you.

Apr 95. (cd) *<(TX 51191CD)>* **BLISS** [ ] [ ]
– No apologies / Boom boom Willie / Let's talk about sex / Gimme danger / Just a girl / Pissing on your flowers / Sugar O'Dee / Sinville / No fun forever / Methchild / Raunchy raunchy / No reaction / All I own.

May 96. (cd) *<TX 51209CD>* **FRENCH COUGH SYRUP** [-] [ ]

Apr 98. (cd) *<(TX 51240CD)>* **HEART FULL OF SNOT** [ ] [ ] Oct97
– All American overdose / Turn me on / Little girl smile / She's breakin' my heart again / Rosita / Diablo verde / (I wanna be your) Main man / Hung on you / Can ya walk on water / Yesterdaze / People that I hate / More good news / Can't be bothered / Love DTK / Down on you.

May 99. (cd) *<(TX 51247CD)>* **ALL THRASHED UP** [ ] [ ]
– Miss Thing / Kingdom of kicks / There she goes / Goin' down in flames / San Francisco / Silver star / Ravaged Jeff / Some of us / Desert roses / Ain't life a bitch.

– compilations, etc. –

Jun 98. (cd) *Fan Club; (UUCD 502)* **I WAS A TEENAGE GLAM FAG** [ ] [-]

DAMAGE MANUAL (see under ⇒ CONNELLY, Chris)

DAMIEN THORNE

Formed: Chicago, Illinois, USA ... 1985 by JUSTIN FATE and KEN STARR, who recruited extra members, MICHAEL MONROE, SANDERS PATE and PETE PAGONIS. Obviously profoundly influenced by seminal horror book/film, 'The Omen' (in which the DAMIEN THORNE character spine-chillingly portrays the Devil in human form), from the name of their band to the title of their debut album, 'THE SIGN OF THE JACKAL', the group played stereotypical power-metal to match. Terminally derivative, it came as no surprise when 'Roadrunner' declined to renew their contract.

Album rating: THE SIGN OF THE JACKAL (*5)

JUSTIN FATE – vocals / **KEN STARR** – guitar / **MICHAEL MONROE** – guitar / **SANDERS PATE** – bass / **PETE PAGONIS** – drums

Roadrunner Roadrunner

Aug 86. (lp) *(RR 9691)* **THE SIGN OF THE JACKAL** [ ] [ ]
– The sign of the jackal / Fear of the dark / The ritual / Gream reaper / Hell's reign / Escape or die / Siren's call / Damien's procession (march of the undead).

—— split (see above)

DAMNED

Formed: London, England ... May 1976 by BRIAN JAMES and RAT SCABIES who soon found The CAPTAIN and former undertaker, DAVE VANIAN. Signed to new UK indie label, 'Stiff', by JAKE RIVERA, they released the classic track, 'NEW ROSE', produced by stablemate, NICK LOWE. The DAMNED became the first "New Wave Punks" to release and chart with an album, namely the enduring 'DAMNED DAMNED DAMNED' (1977). One of the classic punk debuts, the album pogo'd and thrashed its way through a frenetic set of three-chord wonders, LOWE's garden shed production underlining the riotous pandemonium. The band had also broken into the Top 40, although ironically enough, prolonged chart success would come later in the 80's when The DAMNED had changed almost beyond recognition. Live, the band were also one of the major attractions on the London scene; with VANIAN's proto-goth affectations, SENSIBLE's beret-topped antics and SCABIES' demented-drummer persona all competing against each other, The DAMNED were indeed a motley crew. Their musical assault was bolstered later that year by a second guitarist, LU EDMONDS, who debuted on the flaccid 'MUSIC FOR PLEASURE' (1977). The album was universally derided and SCABIES soon left for pastures new. Although future CULTURE CLUB man, JOHN MOSS was drafted in briefly as a replacement, the band splintered early the following year. After a period of solo work, VANIAN, SENSIBLE and SCABIES regrouped as The DAMNED early in '79 and emerged rejuvenated into the UK Top 20 via the impressive 'LOVE SONG'. With ALGY WARD completing the line-up, the band scored a second chart hit with 'SMASH IT UP', releasing their lauded 'MACHINE GUN ETIQUETTE' album later that year. Sure, they were still as swift and deadly as the title might suggest, but somehow they'd acquired a mastery of pop dynamics; a third single, 'I JUST CAN'T BE HAPPY TODAY', was the closest they'd yet come to a rock-solid tune. PAUL GRAY replaced WARD for 1980's 'UNTITLED (THE BLACK ALBUM)', an even more surprising, ambitious double set which flew in the face of punk convention with its rampant experimentalism. The poppy 'STRAWBERRIES' (1982) marked the last stand of CAPTAIN SENSIBLE, who'd scored with the annoying 'HAPPY TALK' earlier that summer, the first fuits of his solo deal with 'A&M'. VANIAN and SCABIES lumbered on with new members ROMAN JUGG and BRYAN GUNN, suprisingly enough enjoying major chart success with a string of overtly commercial, pseudo-goth rockers, the biggest of which, a cover of BARRY RYAN's 'ELOISE', made the Top 3. 'PHANTASMAGORIA' (1985) became their biggest selling album to date, catering to a whole new generation of fans. Most critics were agreed, however, that it paled in comparison to their earlier work, the DAMNED finally fading in the late 80's. For any interested parties, the band periodically get together with an amorphous line-up for all-dayers and one-off gigs; old punks never die, they just tour with The DAMNED. • **Songwriters:** Most written by JAMES, until he left, when group took over. Covered:- HELP! (Beatles) / I FEEL ALRIGHT (Stooges / Iggy Pop) / JET BOY JET GIRL (New York Dolls) / CITADEL (Rolling Stones) / ELOISE (Paul & Barry Ryan) / WHITE RABBIT (Jefferson Airplane) / ALONE AGAIN OR (Love) / WILD THING (Troggs) / LET THERE BE RATS (aka DRUMS) (Sandy Nelson). • **Trivia:** NICK MASON (Pink Floyd drummer) produced disappointing 2nd album MUSIC FOR PLEASURE.

CAPTAIN SENSIBLE had UK-No.1 in 1982 with (Rogers-Hammerstein's) HAPPY TALK, and although briefly, became a top disco/pop act abroad.

Album rating: DAMNED DAMNED DAMNED (*8) / MUSIC FOR PLEASURE (*5) / MACHINE GUN ETIQUETTE (*7) / BLACK ALBUM (*6) / BEST OF THE DAMNED compilation (*8) / STRAWBERRIES (*5) / PHANTASMAGORIA (*5) / ANYTHING (*3) THE LIGHT AT THE END OF THE TUNNEL compilation (*7) / FINAL DAMNATION exploitation (*4)

DAVE VANIAN (b. DAVE LETTS) – vocals / **BRIAN JAMES** (b. BRIAN ROBERTSON) – guitar (ex-LONDON S.S.) / **CAPTAIN SENSIBLE** (b. RAY BURNS, 23 Apr'55) – bass, vocals / **RAT SCABIES** (b. CHRIS MILLER, 30 Jul'57) – drums (ex-LONDON S.S.)

Stiff Frontier

Nov 76. (7") *(BUY 6)* **NEW ROSE. / HELP!** [ ] [-]

Feb 77. (7") *(BUY 10)* **NEAT NEAT NEAT. / STAB YOR BACK / SINGALONGASCABIES** [ ] [-]

Feb 77. (lp) *(SEEZ 1)* **DAMNED DAMNED DAMNED** [36] [ ] Apr77
– Neat neat neat / Fan club / I fall / Born to kill / Stab yor back / Feel the pain / New rose / Fish / See her tonite / 1 of the 2 / So messed up / I feel alright. *(re-iss. Apr87 on 'Demon' lp/c/cd; FIEND/+CASS/CD 91) (pic-lp 1988; PFIEND 91) (<cd re-iss. Nov97 on 'Frontier'; 31033-2>) (cd re-iss. Aug00 on 'Edsel'; EDCD 677)*

— added (ROBERT) **LU EDMUNDS** – guitar

Sep 77. (7") *(BUY 18)* **PROBLEM CHILD. / YOU TAKE MY MONEY** [ ] [-]

Nov 77. (lp) *(SEEZ 5)* **MUSIC FOR PLEASURE** [ ] [ ]
– Problem child / Don't cry wolf / One way love / Politics / Stretcher case / Idiot box / You take my money / Alone / Your eyes / Creep (you can't fool me) / You know. *(re-iss. Apr88 on 'Demon' lp/c/cd; FIEND/+CASS/CD 108)*

Dec 77. (7",7"purple) *(BUY 24)* **DON'T CRY WOLF. / ONE WAY LOVE** [ ] [-]

— **DAVE BERK** – drums (ex-JOHNNY MOPED) repl. SCABIES who formed various bands

— **JOHN MOSS** – drums replaced BERK. They split Feb 78. VANIAN joined DOCTORS OF MADNESS. SENSIBLE formed SOFTIES then KING. EDMUNDS & MOSS formed THE EDGE. MOSS later joined ADAM & THE ANTS then CULTURE CLUB. EDMUNDS became part of ATHLETICO SPIZZ 80, The MEKONS, SHRIEKBACK, PIL. etc. BRIAN JAMES formed TANZ DER YOUTH, who released one single, 'I'M SORRY I'M SORRY' for 'Radar', before going solo the following year (1979) to issue his version of 'AIN'T THAT A SHAME'. He subsequently formed another punk supergroup, The HELLIONS, issuing one 1981 single for 'Illegal', 'WHY WHY WHY', before he jointly formed The LORDS OF THE NEW CHURCH. The DAMNED re-formed in Autumn '78 as The **DOOMED** with LEMMY of MOTORHEAD on bass. (1 gig) **HENRY BADOWSKI** – bass (ex-CHELSEA) replaced LEMMY. The group reverted to name The **DAMNED** with originals VANIAN, SENSIBLE (now guitar & keyboards) and **SCABIES**

— **ALGY WARD** – bass (ex-SAINTS) replaced BADOWSKI who went solo

Chiswick Roadrunner

Apr 79. (7",7"red) *(CHIS 112)* **LOVE SONG. / NOISE NOISE NOISE / SUICIDE** [20] [-]
(re-iss. 7"blue Feb82 on 'Big Beat'; NS 75)

Oct 79. (7") *(CHIS 116)* **SMASH IT UP. / BURGLAR** [35] [-]
(re-iss. 7"red Mar82 on 'Big Beat'; NS 76)

Nov 79. (lp) *(CWK 3011)* **MACHINE GUN ETIQUETTE** [31] [ ] Dec79
– Love song / Machine gun etiquette / I just can't be happy today / Melody Lee / Anti-Pope / These hands / Plan 9 channel 7 / Noise noise noise / Looking at you / Smash it up (parts 1 & 2). *(re-iss. Jun85 on 'Ace' lp/c; DAM/+MC 3) (cd-iss. 1986 +=; CDWIK 905)* – Ballroom blitz / Suicide / Rabid (over you) / White rabbit.

Nov 79. (7") *(CHIS 120)* **I JUST CAN'T BE HAPPY TODAY. / BALLROOM BLITZ / TURKEY SONG** [46] [-]

— **PAUL GRAY** – bass, vocals (ex-EDDIE AND THE HOT RODS) repl. WARD who formed TANK

Jun 80. (7";w-drawn) *(CHIS 130)* **WHITE RABBIT. / RABID (OVER YOU) / SEAGULLS** [ ] [-]

Sep 80. (7"m/12"m) *(CHIS/+12 135)* **THE HISTORY OF THE WORLD (part 1). / I BELIEVE THE IMPOSSIBLE / SUGAR AND SPITE** [ ] [-]

Nov 80. (d-lp) *(CWK 3015)* **UNTITLED** (THE BLACK ALBUM) (1/2 studio, 1/4 live, 1/4 concept) [29] [-]
– Wait for the blackout / Lively arts / Silly kids games / Drinking about my baby / Hit and miss / Doctor Jekyll and Mr. Hyde / 13th floor vendetta / Twisted nerve / Sick of this and that / History of the world (part 1) / Therapy // Curtain call / live side:- Love song / Second time around / Smash it up (parts 1 & 2) / New rose / I just can't be happy today / Plan 9 Channel 7. *(re-iss. Aug82 on 'Ace' as one-lp/d-c; DAM/+MC 3) (c-iss.Jun85; TCWIK 3015) (cd-iss. Mar90; CDWIK 906)* – (omits live tracks)

Nov 80. (7"m) *(CHIS 139)* **THERE AINT NO SANITY CLAUS. / HIT OR MISS / LOOKING AT YOU (live)** [ ] [-]

N.E.M.S. not iss.

Nov 81. (d7"ep) *(TRY 1)* **FRIDAY THE 13th** [50] [-]
– Disco man / The limit club / Citadel / Billy bad breaks.

Bronze not iss.

Jul 82. (7"m/7"pic-d) *(BRO/+P 149)* **LOVELY MONEY. / LOVELY MONEY (disco) / I THINK I'M WONDERFUL** [42] [-]

Sep 82. (7"ep) *(BRO 156)* **DOZEN GIRLS. / TAKE THAT / MINE'S A LARGE ONE, LANDLORD / TORTURE ME** [ ] [-]

Oct 82. (lp/c) *(BRON 542)* **STRAWBERRIES** [15] [-]
– Ignite / Generals / Stranger on the town / Dozen girls / The dog / Gun fury / Pleasure and the pain / Life goes on / Bad time for Bonzo / Under the floor again / Don't bother me. *(re-iss. Mar86 on 'Legacy' red-lp/c; LLM/+K 3000) (re-iss. Dec86 on 'Dojo' lp/cd; DOJO LP/CD 46) (cd re-iss. Nov92 on 'Dojo'; DOJOCD 46) (cd-iss. Apr94 on 'Cleopatra'; CLEO 1029-2) (cd re-iss. Mar97 on 'Essential'; ESMCD 473)*

Nov 82. (7"m) *(BRO 159)* **GENERALS. / DISGUISE / CITADEL ZOMBIES** [ ] [-]

Damned not iss.

Nov 83. (pic-lp/lp) *(P+/DAMU 2)* **LIVE IN NEWCASTLE (live)** [-] [-] mail-o
(cd-iss. Jan94 on 'Receiver'; RRCD 181)

Plus One not iss.

May 84. (7"colrd/7"pic-d) *(DAMNED 1/+P)* **THANKS FOR THE NIGHT. / NASTY** [ ] [-]
(re-iss. 12"-ltd.1985 +=; DAMNED 1T) – Do the blitz.

— **VANIAN** and **SCABIES** recruited new guys **ROMAN JUGG** – guitar, keyboards / who replaced the CAPTAIN who carried on with solo career. **BRYN GUNN** – bass repl. GRAY

M.C.A. Off Beat

Mar 85. (7"/7"pic-d/'A'-Spic'n'Spec mix-12") *(GRIM/+P/T 1)* **GRIMLY FIENDISH. / EDWARD THE BEAR** [21] [-]
(12"white+=) *(GRIMX 1)* – ('A'-Bad Trip mix).

Jun 85. (7") *(GRIM 2)* **SHADOW OF LOVE. / NIGHTSHIFT** [25] [ ]
('A'-Ten Inches Of Hell mix-10"+=) *(GRIMX 2)* – Would you.
(12"+=) *(GRIMT 2)* – Would you.
(d7"+=) *(GRIMY 2)* – Let there be Rats / Wiped out.

Jul 85. (lp/c/pic-lp/white-lp/blue-lp) *(MCF/+C/P/W/B 3275)* **PHANTASMAGORIA** [11] [ ]
– Street of dreams / Shadow of love / There'll come a day / Sanctum sanctorium / Is it a dream / Grimly fiendish / Edward the bear / The eighth day / Trojans. *(free 7" w.a.)* I JUST CAN'T BE HAPPY TODAY *(re-iss. 1986; same)* – (contains free 12"blue ELOISE) *(cd-iss. Aug89; DMCL 1887)*

Sep 85. (7") *(GRIM 3)* **IS IT A DREAM (Wild West End mix) / STREET OF DREAMS (live)** [34] [ ]
(12"+=) *(GRIMT 3)* – Curtain call (live) / Pretty vacant (live) / Wild thing (live).

Jan 86. (7") *(GRIM 4)* **ELOISE. / TEMPTATION** [3] [ ]
(12"blue+=/'A'-No Sleep Until Wednesday mix-12") *(GRIM T/X 4)* – Beat girl.

Nov 86. (7") *(GRIM 5)* **ANYTHING. / THE YEAR OF THE JACKAL** [32] [ ]
(10"blue+=,10"yellow+=) *(GRIMX 5)* – ('A'mixes).
(12"+=) *(GRIMT 5)* – Thanks for the night.

Nov 86. (lp/c/cd) *(MCG/MCGC/DMCG 6015) <5966>* **ANYTHING** [40] [ ]
– Anything / Alone again or / The portrait / Restless / In dulce decorum / Gigolo / The girl goes down / Tightrope walk / Psychomania.

Feb 87. (7"colrd/12"clear) *(GRIM/+T 6)* **GIGOLO. / THE PORTRAIT** [29] [-]

Apr 87. (7") *(GRIM 7)* **ALONE AGAIN OR. / IN DULCE DECORUM** [27] [-]
(12"+=) *(GRIMT 7)* – Psychomania.
(d7"++=) *(DGRIM 7)* – Eloise.

Nov 87. (7") *(GRIM 8)* **IN DULCE DECORUM. / PSYCHOMANIA** [72] [-]
(12"+=) *(GRIMT 8)* – ('A'dub).

— disbanded in the late 80's, although re-union gigs were forthcoming

Essential Restless

Aug 89. (green-lp) *(ESCLP 008) <72385>* **FINAL DAMNATION** (live '88 reunion) [ ] [ ]
– See her tonite / Neat neat neat / Born to kill / I fall / Fan club / Fish / Help / New rose / I feel alright / I just can't be happy today / Wait for the blackout / Melody Lee / Noise noise noise / Love song / Smash it up (parts 1 & 2) / Looking at you / The last time. *(cd-iss. Apr94 on 'Castle'; CLACD 338)*

– compilations, etc. –

1981. (4x7"box) *Stiff; (GRAB 2)* **FOUR PACK** [ ] [-]
– (NEW ROSE / NEAT NEAT NEAT / PROBLEM CHILD / DON'T CRY WOLF)

Nov 81. (lp/c) *Ace; (DAM/+C 1)* **THE BEST OF THE DAMNED** [43] [-]
– New rose / Neat neat neat / I just can't be happy today / Jet boy jet girl / Hit or miss / There ain't no sanity claus / Smash it up (parts 1 & 2) / Plan 9 channel 7 / Rabid (over you) / Wait for the blackout / History of the world (part 1). *(cd-iss. Oct87; CDDAM 1)*

May 82. (7"/7"pic-d) *Big Beat; (NS/+P 77)* **WAIT FOR THE BLACKOUT. / Captain Sensible & The Softies: JET BOY, JET GIRL** [ ] [-]

Oct 82. (7"green) *Big Beat; (NS 80)* **LIVELY ARTS. / TEENAGE DREAM** [ ] [-]
(10"+=) *(NST 80)* – I'm so bored.

Nov 82. (lp) *Ace; (NED 1)* **LIVE SHEPPERTON 1980 (live)** [ ] [-]
– Love song / Second time around / I just can't be happy today / Melody Lee / Help / Neat neat neat / Looking at you / Smash it up (parts 1 & 2) / New rose / Plan 9 channel 7. *(also iss.Nov82 on 'Big Beat'; WIKM 27) (c-iss.Jun85; WIKC 27) (cd-iss. Jun88; CDWIKM 27)*

Nov 85. (12"ep) *Stiff; (BUYIT 238)* **NEW ROSE / NEAT NEAT NEAT. / STRETCHER CASE / SICK OF BEING SICK** [ ] [-]

Jan 86. (lp/c/cd) *Dojo; (DOJO LP/TC/CD 21)* **DAMNED BUT NOT FORGOTTEN** [ ] [-]
(cd re-iss. Nov92; same) (cd re-iss. Feb97 on 'Essential'; ESMCD 472)

Jun 86. (12"ep) *Strange Fruit; (SFPS 002)* **THE PEEL SESSIONS** (10.5.77) [ ] [-]
– Sick of being sick / Stretcher case / Feel the pain / Fan club. *(c-ep.1987; SFPSC 002) (cd-ep.May88; SFPSCD 002)*

Jul 86. (blue-m-lp) *Stiff; (GET 4)* **THE CAPTAIN'S BIRTHDAY PARTY – LIVE AT THE ROUNDHOUSE** [ ] [-]
(cd-iss. Nov91 on 'Demon'; VEXCD 7)

Jul 87. (12"ep) *Strange Fruit; (SFPS 040)* **THE PEEL SESSIONS (30.11.76)** [ ] [-]
– Stab yor back / Neat neat neat / New rose / So messed up / I fall.

Oct 87. (cd/lp) *I.D.; (C+/NOSE 18)* **MINDLESS, DIRECTIONLESS, ENEMY (live)** [ ] [-]
(re-iss. Jun89 cd/c/lp; CDOSE/KOSE/NOSE 18X)

Dec 87. (d-lp) *M.C.A.; (MCSP 312)* **THE LIGHT AT THE END OF THE TUNNEL** [87] [-]

Jun 88. (lp/c) *Big Beat; (WIK/+C 80)* **THE LONG LOST WEEKEND: BEST OF VOL.1/2** [ ] [-]

1990. (cd) *Marble Arch; (cd)* **THE DAMNED LIVE (live)** [ ] [-]

Dec 90. (cd/c/d-lp) *Castle; (CCS CD/MC/LP 278)* **THE COLLECTION** [ ] [-]

Jan 91. (12"blue-ep) *Deltic; (DELT 7T)* **FUN FACTORY ('82). / Captain Sensible: FREEDOM / PASTIES / A RIOT ON EASTBOURNE PIER** [ ] [-]

Jun 91. (cd/colrd-lp) *Receiver; (RR CD/LP 159)* **BALLROOM BLITZ – LIVE AT THE LYCEUM (live)** [ ] [-]

Dec 91. (cd) *Dojo; (DOJOCD 65)* **TOTALLY DAMNED (live + rare)** [ ] [-]

Jan 92. (cd) *Street Link; (AOK 101)* **ALTERNATIVE CHARTBUSTERS** [ ] [-]

Feb 92. (clear-lp) *Receiver; (RRLP 159)* **LIVE AT THE LYCEUM (live)** [ ] [-]

Aug 92. (cd) *Connoisseur; (VSOPCD 174)* **THE MCA SINGLES A'S & B'S** [ ] [-]
Sep 92. (cd) *Demon; (VEXCD 12)* **SKIP OFF SCHOOL TO SEE THE DAMNED (THE STIFF SINGLES A'S & B'S)** [ ] [-]
May 93. (cd) *Receiver; (RRCD 179)* **SCHOOL BULLIES** [ ] [-]
Jul 93. (cd) *Success; (550 747-2)* **THE DAMNED: FROM THE BEGINNING** [ ] [-]
Nov 93. (cd) *Strange Fruit; (SFRSCD 070)* **SESSIONS OF THE DAMNED** [ ] [-]
Jun 94. (cd/c) *M.C.I.; (MUS CD/MC 017)* **ETERNALLY DAMNED – THE VERY BEST OF THE DAMNED** [ ] [-]
Dec 94. (cd) *Cleopatra; (CLEO 7139-2)* **TALES FROM THE DAMNED** [ ] [-]
May 95. (cd) *Spectrum; (550 747-2)* **FROM THE BEGINNING** [ ] [-]
Sep 95. (cd/c) *Emporio; (EMPR CD/MC 592)* **NOISE – THE BEST OF: LIVE** [ ] [-]
Jun 96. (cd) *Nighttracks; (CDNT 011)* **RADIO 1 SESSIONS** [ ] [-]
Oct 96. (cd) *Cleopatra; (CLP 9804)* **FIENDISH SHADOWS** [ ] [-]
Feb 97. (3xcd-box) *Demon; (FBOOK 14)* **NEAT NEAT NEAT** [ ] [-]
Mar 97. (cd) *Cleopatra; (CLP 9960)* **THE CHAOS YEARS** [ ] [-]
Apr 97. (cd/c) *The Record Label; (MOCDR/MOMC 1)* **I'M ALRIGHT JACK AND THE BEANSTALK** [ ] [-]
May 97. (d-cd) *Snapper; (SMDCD 143)* **BORN TO KILL** [ ] [-]
Jun 97. (lp) *Cleopatra; (CLP 9782)* **SHUT IT** [ ] [-]
Nov 97. (7") *Skinnies Cut; (AVL 1077)* **PROKOFIEV. /** [ ] [-]
Nov 97. (7") *Marble Orchard; (MOS 2)* **TOUR SINGLE. /** [ ] [-]
Jul 98. (cd) *Strange Fruit; (SFRSCD 070)* **THE SESSIONS OF THE DAMNED** [ ] [-]
Oct 98. (7") *Musical Tragedy; (MT 418)* **PRETTY VACANT. / DISCO MAN** [ ] [-]
Jun 99. (t-cd) *Cleopatra; (CLP 542)* **THE DAMNED BOX SET** [ ] [-]
Dec 99. (cd) *Chiswick; (CDWIKK 198)* **MARVELLOUS** [ ] [-]
Dec 99. (cd) *Musical Tragedies; (efa 12354-2)* **MOLTEN LAGER** [ ] [-]
Jun 00. (d-cd) *Essential; (ESACD 901)* **ANTHOLOGY** [ ] [ ]

DAVE VANIAN & THE PHANTOM CHORDS

Camden Town — not iss.

Dec 92. (7") **TOWN WITHOUT PITY. /** [ ] [-]

Big Beat — not iss.

Mar 95. (cd) *(CDWIKD 140)* **BIG BEAT PRESENTS . . .** [ ] [-]
– Voodoo doll / Screamin' kid / Big town / This house is haunted / You and I / Whiskey and me / Fever in my blood / Frenzy / Shooting Jones / Jezebel / Tonight we ride / Johnny Guitar / Chase the wild wind / Swamp thing.

DAMN THE MACHINE (see under ⇒ POLAND, Chris)

DAMN YANKEES (see under ⇒ NUGENT, Ted)

Jim DANDY (see under ⇒ BLACK OAK ARKANSAS)

DANGER DANGER

Formed: Queens, New York, USA . . . 1988 by BRUNO RAVEL (ex-MICHAEL BOLTON), who recruited TED POLEY, KASEY SMITH and STEVE WEST. During the recording of their eponymous 1989 debut, ANDY TIMMONS replacing TONY REY, who went full-time with SARAYA. Securing a deal with the CBS offshoot 'Imagine' records, the band's first album subsequently hit the US Top 100, boosted by the success of the Top 50 'BANG BANG' single'. Melodic cock-rock in the style of WHITE LION and MOTLEY CRUE, the group's sound was rather outdated by the release of their 1992 set, 'SCREW IT!'. Nevertheless, British rockers seemingly took a shine to them, placing a few singles ('MONKEY BUSINESS' and 'I STILL THINK ABOUT YOU') in the UK Top 50. Between the mid-90's and 2000 (and with new vocalist PAUL LAINE), DANGER DANGER released a handful of comeback sets aimed at the pop-metal market.

Album rating: DANGER DANGER (*5) / SCREW IT! (*6) / DAWN (*4) / FOUR THE HARD WAY (*4) / THE RETURN OF GREAT GILDERSLEEVES (*4) / COCKROACH (*5)

TED POLEY – vocals (ex-PROPHET) / **ANDY TIMMONS** – guitar; repl. TONY REY (also on debut) who repl. AL PITRELLI (to ASIA) / **KASEY SMITH** – keyboards / **BRUNO RAVEL** – bass (ex-MICHAEL BOLTON) / **STEVE WEST** – drums

not iss. — Imagine

Jul 89. (c-s) <73050> **NAUGHTY NAUGHTY / SATURDAY NITE** [-] [ ]
Aug 89. (cd) <44342> **DANGER DANGER** [-] [88]
– Naughty naughty / Under the gun / Saturday nite / Don't walk away / Bang bang / Rock America / Boys will be boys / One step from Paradise / Feels like love / Turn it on / Live it up. *(re-iss. Apr98 on 'Imagine'; ZK 44342)*
May 90. (c-s) <73380> **BANG BANG / BOYS WILL BE BOYS** [-] [49]
Aug 90. (c-s) <73606> **DON'T WALK AWAY / BOYS WILL BE BOYS** [-] [ ]

Epic — Epic

Jan 92. (7") *(657751-7)* <73949> **MONKEY BUSINESS. / BOYS WILL BE BOYS** [42] [ ] Nov91
(12"pic-d+=) *(657751-6)* – Naughty naughty.
(cd-s++=) *(657751-2)* – Bang bang.
Feb 92. (cd/c/lp) *(468661-2/-4/-1)* <46977> **SCREW IT!** [ ] [ ]
– (Ginger snaps intro) / Monkey business / Slipped her the big one / C'est loupe (prelude) / Beat the bullet / I still think about you / Get you shit together / Crazy nites / Puppet show / Everybody wants some / Don't blame it on love / Comin' home / Horny S.O.B. / Find your way back home / Yeah, you want it! / D.F.N.S. *(cd re-iss. Apr98 on 'Imagine'; ZK 46977)*
Mar 92. (7") *(657838-7)* <74231> **I STILL THINK ABOUT YOU. / JUST WHAT THE DOCTOR ORDERED** [46] [ ]
(cd-s+=) *(657838-2)* – Rock'n'roll hoochie koo (live).
(7") *(657838-8)* – ('A'side) / Under the gun.
(12"+=) *(657838-6)* – Rock America.
May 92. (7"/7"s) *(658133-7/-0)* **COMIN' HOME. / CRAZY NITES** [75] [ ]
(12"+=) *(658133-6)* – Live it up / Turn it on.
(cd-s+=) *(658133-2)* – Don't walk away.

— split in 1993, although they reformed a few years later

— **PAUL LAINE** (b. Vancouver, Canada) – vocals, acoustic guitar; repl. POLEY

M.T.M. — Lowdice

Nov 95. (cd) <LOWD 41693> **DAWN** [-] [ ]
– Hellicopter / Crawl / Punching bag / Mother mercy / Sorry / Drivin' sideways / Goodbye / Wide awake and dead / Nobody cares / Heaven's fallin' / Hard.
Oct 97. (cd) *(199634)* <LOWD 44697> **FOUR THE HARD WAY** [ ] [ ] May98
– Still kickin' / Sick little twisted mind / Jaded / Captain bring me down / Girl ain't built to sleep alone / Goin' goin' gone / Afraid of love / Heartbreak suicide / I don't need you. <US+=> – Comin' home '98.
Feb 00. (cd) *(068108)* <LD 0303> **THE RETURN OF GREAT GILDERSLEEVES** [ ] [ ]
– Grind / When she's good she's good / Six million dollar man / She's gone / Dead drunk and wasted / Dead dog / I do / My secret / Cherry cherry / Get it the ring / Walk it like you talk it.

not iss. — Sony

May 01. (cd) <A2 52159> **COCKROACH (live)** [-] [ ]
– Still kickin' / Sick little twisted mind / Good time / Don't break my heart again / Tip of my tongue / Walk it like you talk it / Goin' goin' gone / Afraid of love / When she's good she's good (when she's bad she's even better) / Shot o' love / Don't pull the plug / Time in a bottle.

DANGEROUS TOYS

Formed: Texas, USA . . . 1987 by former ONYX members SCOTT DALHOVER, MIKE WATSON and MARK GEARY, who added frontman JASON McMASTER. Fashioning a distinctive sound lying somewhere between the sleaze and thrash genres, the group signed to 'Columbia' in 1989, delivering an eponymous debut set into the US Top 75 soon after. Favourites of the MTV brigade, the band co-penned the track 'DEMON BELL' with the much-in-demand DESMOND CHILD for a horror-flick, 'Shocker'. Their 1991 follow-up, 'HELLACIOUS ACRES' (also with 2nd guitarist DANNY AARON), trod a similar chart path, although PAUL LIDEL was soon in place for a third album, 'PISSED' (1994) released on 'Music For Nations'.

Album rating: DANGEROUS TOYS (*6) / HELLACIOUS ACRES (*4) / PISSED (*5) / THE R-TIST FORMERLY KNOWN AS DANGEROUS TOYS (*4)

JASON McMASTER – vocals (ex-WATCHTOWER) / **SCOTT DALHOVER** – guitar / **MIKE WATSON** – bass / **MARK GEARY** – drums

— added **DANNY AARON** – guitar

C.B.S. — Columbia

Dec 89. (lp/c/cd) *(465423-1/-4/-2)* <45031> **DANGEROUS TOYS** [ ] [65] Jun89
– Teas'n pleas'n / Scared / Bones in the gutter / Take me drunk / Feels like a hammer / Sport'n a woody / Queen of the Nile / Outlaw / Here comes trouble / Ten boots (stompin') / That dog.
Jan 90. (7") <73082> **SCARED. / BONES IN THE GUTTER** [-] [ ]
Jun 91. (cd) <46754> **HELLACIOUS ACRES** [-] [67]
– Gunfighter / Gimme no lip / Sticks & stones / Best of friends / On top / Sugar, leather & the nail / Angel N U / Feel like makin' love / Line 'em up / Gypsy (black-n-blue valentine) / Bad guy.

— **PAUL LIDEL** – guitar (ex-DIRTY LOOKS) repl. AARON

Bulletproof — Dos

Aug 94. (cd) *(CDVEST 30)* <7008> **PISSED** [ ] [ ]
– Pissed / Paintrain / The law is mine / Promise the moon / Strange / Loser / Hard luck champion / Screamin' for more / Oh well, so what? / Illustrated man. *(re-iss. Mar99 on 'Cleopatra'; CLP 5022)*

not iss. — D.M.Z.

Oct 95. (cd) <6004> **THE R-TIST 4-MERLY KNOWN AS DANGEROUS TOYS** [-] [ ]
– Share the kill / Cure the lane / The numb / Take me swiftly / Heard it all / Transmission / Words on the wall / Better to die / Down inside / New anger / Monster man / To live the lie / Mom and dad. *<(re-iss. +UK.Mar99 on 'Cleopatra'; CLP 5032)>*

— split the same year

– compilations, etc. –

Nov 99. (cd) *Cleopatra;* <(CLP 743-2)> **GREATEST HITS LIVE: VITAMINS AND CRASH HELMETS TOUR (live)** [ ] [ ]
– Outlaw / Take me drunk / Queen of the Nile / Bones in the gutter / Sport'n a woody / Scared / Peas'n pleas'n / Best of friends / Angel N.U. / Ten boots / Line 'em up / Gimme no lip / Gunfighter for love / Promise the moon / Pissed / Share the kill / Transmission / Dangerous toys.

DANZIG

Formed: Los Angeles, California, USA . . . 1987 out of SAMHAIN, by ex-MISFITS (70's/80's hardcore/punk group) frontman GLENN DANZIG. In 1981, GLENN released his solo debut 45, 'WHO KILLED MARILYN', while still providing the muscle behind The MISFITS. Retaining bassist EERIE VON, GLENN recruited JOHN CHRIST and CHUCK BISCUITS, both seasoned campaigners of the US hardcore scene. Signed by Rick Rubin in 1988 to boost his newly created 'Def American' label, DANZIG (the group) released their eponymous debut the same year. Subtly powerful, DANZIG were essentially a unique combination of primal blues, gothic-metal and darkly rich melody. Akin to a satanic ELVIS PRESLEY (well, he did cover 'TROUBLE'), (GLENN) DANZIG was a constant, brooding presence, his sinister croon/howl and musclebound frame casting a demonic shadow over proceedings. Highlights of the debut included 'TWIST OF CAIN', the Morrison-esque 'SHE RIDES' and the darkly raging 'MOTHER', a transatlantic hit five years later following MTV exposure. 1990 saw the release of their much-anticipated follow-up, 'LUCIFUGE', a more consistent set which garnered sufficient critical plaudits to give it a Top 75 placing. However, it was only with their third set, 'HOW THE GODS KILL' (1992), that DANZIG achieved the commercial success which had long been their due. In 1994, hot on the heels of 'MOTHER's chart action, they scored their second Top 30 album, 'DANZIG IV', the record's more accessible approach bringing accusations of selling out from the group's more hardcore fans. After losing CHUCK and EERIE, their final album to date, 'DANZIG 5: BLACKACIDEVIL' (1996), saw them lose some commercial and critical ground; it also featured a cover of Black Sabbath's 'HAND OF DOOM' – what else?! The man in black was back in 1999, howling at the moon with another set of evil ditties imaginatively titled 'SATAN'S CHILD'. While lyrically, DANZIG's song remained the same, musically the group further pursued the grinding industrial path they'd initially explored on the album's predecessor.

Album rating: Samhain: INITIUM mini (*5) / UNHOLY PASSION mini (*5) / NOVEMBER-COMING-FIRE (*6) / Danzig: DANZIG (*7) / LUCIFUGE (*8) / DANZIG III – HOW THE GODS KILL (*7) / DANZIG IV (*6) / DANZIG 5: BLACKACIDEVIL (*4) / SATAN'S CHILD (*4)

SAMHAIN

GLENN DANZIG (b.23 Jun'59, Lodi, New Jersey) – vocals (ex-MISFITS) / **EERIE VON** (b.25 Aug'64, Lodi) – bass (ex-MISFITS) / **PETER 'DAMIEN' MARSHALL** – guitars / a series of drummers; **STEVE ZING, LYLE PRESLAR + LONDON MAY**

Revolver / Plan 9

1984. (m-lp) *<PL9 04>* **INITIUM** [-] [ ]
– Initium / Samhain / Black dream / All murder, all guts, all fun / Macabre / He-who-can-not-be-named / Horror biz / The shift / The howl arcangel. *(cd-iss. 2001 on 'Phonographic'; 1056>)*

1985. (12"ep) **UNHOLY PASSION** [-] [ ]
– Unholy passion / All hell / Moribund / The hungry end / I am misery.

Aug 86. (lp) *(REVLP 82)* **NOVEMBER-COMING-FIRE** [-] [ ]
– Diabolos '88 / In my grip / Mother of mercy / Birthright / To walk the night / Let the day begin / Halloween II / November's fire / Kiss of steel / Unbridled / Human pony girl.

—— **JOHN CHRIST** (b.19 Feb'65, Baltimore, Maryland) – guitar; repl. MARSHALL

– compilations, etc. –

1990. (cd/lp) *Plan 9; <PL9 10-2/-1>* **FINAL DESCENT** [-] [ ]
– Night chill / Descent / Death . . . in its arms / Lords of the left hand / The birthing / Unholy passion / All hell / Moribund / The hungry end / Misery tomb / I am misery.

DANZIG

DANZIG, VON + CHRIST plus **CHUCK BISCUITS** (b.17 Apr'??, Calif.) – drums (ex-BLACK FLAG, ex-D.O.A., ex-CIRCLE JERKS)

Mercury / Def American

Dec 88. (lp/c/cd) *(828124-1/-4/-2) <DEF 24208-1/-4/-2>* **DANZIG** [ ] [ ] Sep88
– Twist of Cain / Not of this world / She rides / Soul on fire / Am I demon / Mother / Possession / End of time / The hunter / Evil thing. *(re-iss. Dec89 lp/c/cd; 838487-1/-4/-2) (cd re-iss. Apr95 on 'American'; 74321 24841-2) (cd re-iss. Jan99 on 'American'; 491904-2)*

Def American / Def American

Jun 90. (cd/c/lp) *(846375-2/-4/-1) <DEF 24281-2/-4/-1>* **DANZIG II – LUCIFUGE** [ ] [74]
– Long way back from Hell / Snakes of Christ / Killer wolf / Tired of being alive / I'm the one / Her black wings / Devil's plaything / 777 / Blood and tears / Girl / Pain in the world. *(cd re-iss. Apr95 on 'American'; 74321 24842-2) (cd re-iss. Jan99 on 'American'; 491784-2)*

Sep 90. (c-s) *<19692>* **HER BLACK WINGS /** [-] [ ]

May 92. (7") *(DEFA 17)* **DIRTY BLACK SUMMER. / WHEN DEATH HAD NO NAME** [ ] [ ]
(12"+=)(cd-s+=) *(DEFA 17-12)(DEFCD 17)* – Bodies.

Jul 92. (cd/c/lp) *(512270-2/-4/-1) <DEF 26914-2/-4/-1>* **DANZIG III – HOW THE GODS KILL** [ ] [24] Jun92
– Godless / Anything / Bodies / How the gods kill / Dirty black summer / Left hand black / Heart of the Devil / Sistines / Do you wear the mark / When the dying calls. *(cd re-iss. Apr95 on 'American'; 74321 24843-2) (cd re-iss. Jan99 on 'American'; 491785-2)*

May 93. (m-cd/m-c/m-lp) *(514876-2/-4/-1) <45286>* **THRALL / DEMONSWEATLIVE (live)** [ ] [54]
– It's coming soon / The violent fire / Trouble / Snakes of Christ / Am I demon / Sistines / Mother. *(cd re-iss. Apr95 on 'American'; 74321 24844-2) (cd re-iss. Jan99 on 'American'; 491786-2)*

American / American

May 94. (10"sha-pic-d) *(MOM 1) <18256>* **MOTHER. / MOTHER (live)** [62] [43] Jan94
(12"+=) *(MOMX 1)* – When death had no name.
(cd-s++=) *(MOMCD 1)* – How the gods kill.

Oct 94. (cd/c/lp) *(74321 23681-2/-4/-1) <45647>* **DANZIG IV** [ ] [29]
– Brand new god / Little whip / Cantspeak / Going down to die / Until you call on the dark / Dominion / Bringer of death / Sadistikal / Son of the morning star / I don't mind the pain / Stalker song / Let it be captured. *(cd re-iss. Jan99; 491787-2)*

—— **JOEY CASTILLO** (b.30 Mar'66, Gardenia, Calif.) – drums; repl. BISCUITS (guest on 3 tracks JERRY CANTRELL)

—— **JOSH LAZIE** – bass; repl. EERIE VON

Hollywood / Hollywood

Oct 96. (cd/c) *<(162084-2/-4)>* **DANZIG 5: BLACKACIDEVIL** [ ] [41]
– 7th house / Blackacidevil / See all you were / Sacrifice / Hint of her blood / Serpentia / Come to silver / Hand of doom: version / Power of darkness / Ashes.

—— **TOMMY VICTOR** – guitar (ex-PRONG) was added on tour

Nuclear Blast / Phonographie

Nov 99. (cd) *(NB 449-2) <1005>* **SATAN'S CHILD** [ ] [ ]
– Five finger crawl / Belly of the beast / Lilin / Unspeakable / Cult w/out a name / East Indian devil (Kali's song) / Firemass / Cold eternal / Satan's child / Into the mouth of abandonment / Apokalips / Thirteen.

DARE

Formed: Manchester, England . . . 1985 by DARREN WHARTON (ex-THIN LIZZY). Emerging from the wreckage of a disastrous solo sojourn with 'Phonogram', WHARTON subsequently brought together VINNY BURNS, SHELLEY, JAMES ROSS and BRIAN COX under the DARE banner, signing to 'A&M' in the process. A debut album, 'OUT OF THE SILENCE' (1988), showed off the impressive vocal talents of WHARTON, while the group's striking AOR stylings earned them a fair amount of critical praise. DARE's second album, 'BLOOD FROM THE STONE' (1991), adopted a tougher approach in comparison, the record lifting them from the second division and into the UK Top 50. However, this minor success just wasn't enough to satisfy major label expectations and the group split soon after.

Album rating: OUT OF THE SILENCE (*6) / BLOOD FROM THE STONE (*6) / CALM BEFORE THE STORM (*5)

DARREN WHARTON – vocals, keyboards / **VINNY BURNS** – guitar / **SHELLEY** – bass / **JAMES ROSS** – bass / **BRIAN COX** – keyboards

A&M / not iss.

Sep 88. (7") *(AM 470) <1251>* **ABANDON. / THE LAST TIME** [ ] [-]
(12"+=/cd-s+=) *(AMY/AMCD 470)* – Precious / Love is the price.

Oct 88. (lp/c/cd) *(AMA/AMC/CDA 5221)* **OUT OF THE SILENCE** [ ] [-]
– Abandon / Into the fire / Nothing is stronger than love / Runaway / Under the sun / The raindance / King of spades / Heartbreaker / Return the heart / Don't let go.

Feb 89. (7") *(AM 493)* **NOTHING IS STRONGER THAN LOVE. / VALENTINO** [ ] [-]
(12"+=) *(AMY 493)* – ('A'extended).
(cd-s+=) *(CDEE 493)* – If looks could kill.

Apr 89. (7") *(AM 483)* **THE RAINDANCE. / RETURN THE HEART** [62] [-]
(12"+=/12"pic-d+=/cd-s+=) *(AMY/AMP/CDEE 483)* – No strings attached.

Jul 89. (7"7"pic-d) *(AM/+P 519)* **ABANDON (remix). / LAST TIME** [71] [-]
(12"+=/cd-s+=) *(AMY/CDEE 519)* –

Sep 89. (7") *(AM 525)* **HEARTBREAKER. / KING OF SPADES** [ ] [-]
(ext.12"+=) *(AMY 525)* – Runaway (live).
(cd-s+=) *(CDEE 525)* – ('A'extended).

—— **NIGEL + GREG** respectively repl. SHELLEY + ROSS

Aug 91. (7"/c-s) *(AM/+MC 775)* **WE DON'T NEED A REASON. /** [52] [-]
(12"+=/12"pic-d+=/cd-s+=) *(AM Y/P/CD 775)* –

Sep 91. (cd/c/lp) *(395360-2/-4/-1)* **BLOOD FROM A STONE** [48] [-]
– Wings of fire / We don't need a reason / Surrender / Chains / Lies / Live to fight another day / Cry wolf / Breakout / Wild heart / Real love.

Oct 91. (7") *(AM 824)* **REAL LOVE. /** [67] [-]
(12"+=/12"pic-d+=/cd-s+=) *(AM Y/P/CD 824)* –

—— folded after above . . . until

Made To Measure / not iss.

Jun 98. (cd) *(199649)* **CALM BEFORE THE STORM** [ ] [-]
– Walk on the water / Some day / Calm before the storm / Rescue me / Silence in your head / Rising sun / Ashes / Crown of thorns / Deliverance / Still in love with you. *(re-iss. Jan99 on 'Legend'; DARECD 1)*

DARK ANGEL

Formed: Los Angeles, California, USA . . . 1983 by DON DOTY, JIM DURKIN, ERIC MEYER, ROB YAHN and JACK SCHWARZ. Emerging from the early proto-thrash scene, DARK ANGEL released two albums in the mid 80's, 'WE HAVE ARRIVED' and 'MERCILESS DEATH', before signing to 'Combat' ('Under One Flag' in the UK). Around the same time, their rhythm section of YAHN and SCHWARZ were replaced by MIKE GONZALES and lyricist GENE HOGLAN respectively. Unleashing 'DARKNESS DESCENDS', the group proved their extreme-metal credentials with a savage set of bulldozer riffing and thoroughly nasty vocals/lyrical themes. Frontman RON RINEHART was in place for their fourth set, 'LEAVE SCARS' (1989), a record which boasted a brutal cover of Led Zeppelin's 'IMMIGRANT SONG'. Possibly even more uncompromising than its predecessor, the album nevertheless hit the US Top 200. BRETT ERICKSON stepped into the shoes of the departing DURKIN prior to the final studio effort, 'TIME DOES NOT HEAL' (1991).

Album rating: WE HAVE ARRIVED (*5) / DARKNESS DESCENDS (*5) / LEAVE SCARS (*5) / TIME DOES NOT HEAL (*6) / DECADE OF CHAOS compilation (*6)

DON DOTY – vocals / **JIM DURKIN** – guitar / **ERIC MEYER** – guitar / **ROB YAHN** – bass / **JACK SCHWARZ** – drums

not iss. / Axe Killer

1984. (lp) *<8501>* **WE HAVE ARRIVED** [-] [ ]
– We have arrived / Merciless death / Falling from the sky / Welcome to the slaughter house / No tomorrow / Hell's in its heels / Vendetta. *(UK-iss.Jan88 on 'Metalstorm'; MS 8501)*

1985. (m-lp) **MERCILESS DEATH**
(UK-iss.Jun88 on 'Metalstorm'; MS 8602)

—— **MIKE GONZALES** – bass; repl. YAHN

—— **GENE HOGLAN** – drums, lyrics; repl. SCHWARZ

Under One Flag / Combat

Nov 86. (lp) *(FLAG 6) <8114>* **DARKNESS DESCENDS**
– Darkness descends / The burning of Sodom / Hunger of the undead / Merciless death / Death is certain (life is not) / Black prophecies / Perish in flames. *(cd-iss. 1989; CDFLAG 6) (cd re-iss. Feb99 on 'Century Media'; CM 66014CD)*

—— **RON RINEHART** – vocals; repl. DOTY

Jan 89. (cd/c/lp) *(CD/T+/FLAG 30) <8264>* **LEAVE SCARS**
– The death of innocence / Never to rise again / Cauterization / No more answers / Immigrant song / Older than time itself / Worms / The promise of agony / Leave scars.

Jul 89. (m-cd/m-c/m-lp) *(CD/T+/FLAG 42) <2013>* **LIVE SCARS (live)**
– Leave scars / The burning of Sodom / Never to rise again / Death is certain (life is not) / The promise of agony / We have arrived / The death of innocence / I don't care about you. *(cd re-iss. Oct99 on 'Century Media'; 660222)*

—— **BRETT ERIKSEN** – guitar; repl. DURKIN

Feb 91. (cd/c/lp) *(CD/T+/FLAG 54) <2018>* **TIME DOES NOT HEAL**
– Time does not heal / Pain's invention, madness / Act of contrition / The new priesthood / Psychosexuality / An ancient inherited shame / Trauma and catharsis / Sensory deprivation / A subtle induction. *(cd re-iss. Mar00 on 'Century Media'; 66046-2)*

—— split in 1991, HOGLAN joined DEATH

– compilations, etc. –

Jul 92. (cd/c/lp) *Under One Flag; (CD/T+/FLAG 70) / Combat; <1115>*
DECADE OF CHAOS – THE BEST OF DARK ANGEL
– Darkness descends / Never to rise again / Pain's invention, madness / Merciless death / The promise of agony / Death is certain / Leave scars / Act of contrition / The burning of Sodom / We have arrived.

DARK STAR

Formed: Midlands, England . . . 1980 originally as BERLIN, by RICK STAINES, DAVID HARRISON, ROBERT KEY, MARK OSELAND and STEVE ATKINS. Having appeared on the various artists 'Metal For Muthas 2' compilation, DARK STAR recorded an eponymous debut album for 'Avatar'. Straying from the stereotypical Brit-metal sound, the group found it difficult to attract a grassroots fanbase. Subsequently taking a five-year break, the group returned in 1987 with a similarly hopeless attempt to carve out their own niche in the hard-rock market.

Album rating: DARK STAR (*4) / REAL TO REEL (*3)

RICK STAINES – vocals, synthesizer / **DAVID HARRISON** – guitar, vocals / **ROBERT KEY** – guitar / **MARK OSELAND** – bass, vocals / **STEVE ATKINS** – drums, percussion, vocals

Avatar / not iss.

Aug 81. (7") *(AAA 195)* **LADY OF MARS. / ROCK'N'ROMANCIN'**

Nov 81. (lp/c) *(AALP/ZCAAA 5003)* **DARK STAR**
– Kaptain America / Backstreet killer / The musician / Lady of Mars / Louisa / Rockbringer / Lady love / Green peace.

—— split for over five years, **STAINES, HARRISON + KEY** reforming in '86. Used session people including **ATKINS / + DAVID KEATES** – bass

FM Revolver / not iss.

Jul 87. (lp/c) *(WKFM LP/MC 97)* **REAL TO REEL**
– Voice of America / Rock'n'roll heroes / Only time will tell / Spy zone / Homocide on first & last / Stadium of tears / Sad day in London town / One way love / Going nowhere / Two songs don't make a right.

—— their reunion was very brief

DARKTHRONE

Formed: Oslo, Norway . . . 1986 as BLACK DEATH by GYLVE NAGELL, TED SKJELLUM, IVAR ENGER and DAG NILSEN. At the suggestion of their black- metal compatriot, the late EURONYMOUS (see MAYHEM entry), the quartet changed their moniker to DARKTHRONE, assumed scary individual aliases (FENRIZ, NOCTURNO CULTO and ZEPHYROUS respectively; NILSEN was to subsequently depart) and generally became more evil dudes. Following on from their 'Peaceville' debut set, 'SOULSIDE JOURNEY' (1991), the band earned a place alongside the likes of MAYHEM and EMPEROR with their second album, 'ABLAZE IN THE NORTHERN SKY' (1993). More dastardly musical deeds were afoot with 'UNDER A FUNERAL MOON' (1994) and 'TRANSYLVANIAN HUNGER' (1994) while a deal with SATYR's new 'Moonfog' label resulted in the CELTIC FROST tribute, 'PANZERFAUST' (1994). In another sinister twist to the ongoing Norwegian black-metal soap opera, ZEPHRYOUS allegedly disappeared off the face of the planet, leaving the duo of FENRIZ and NOCTURNO CULTO to complete the 'TOTAL DEATH' (1996) set. Despite the strange turn of events, DARKTHRONE releases continued to flood the market in the shape of 1996's 'GOAT LORD' (c'mon . . .) and RAVISHING GRIMNESS (1999).

Album rating: SOULSIDE JOURNEY (*5) / A BLAZE IN THE NORTHERN SKY (*4) / UNDER A FUNERAL MOON (*8) / TRANSYLVANIAN HUNGER (*4) / PANZERFAUST (*5) / TOTAL DEATH (*5) / GOATLORD (*5) / RAVISHING GRIMNESS (*5) / PREPARING FOR WAR compilation (*6)

GYLVE NAGELL, IVAR ENGER, TED SKJELLUM + DAG NILSEN

Peaceville / Peaceville

Feb 91. (lp/cd) *(<VILE 22/+CD>)* **SOULSIDE JOURNEY**
– Cromelech / Sunrise over Locus Mortis / Soulside journey / Accumulation of generalization / Neptune towers / Sempiternal past – Presense view sepulcharality / Grave with a view / Iconoclasm sweeps Cappadocia / Nor the silent whispers / The watchtower / Eon.

—— changed their names as follows:- NAGELL to **FENRIZ**, ENGER to **ZEPHYROUS**, SKJELLUM to **NOCTURNO CULTO**

Feb 92. (lp/cd) *(<VILE 28/+CD>)* **A BLAZE IN THE NORTHERN SKY**
– Kathaarian life code / In the shadow of the horns / Paragon belial / Where cold winds blow / A blaze in the northern sky / The pagan winter. *(cd re-iss. Jan01; CDVILEM 28)*

—— DAG departed just prior to above release

Feb 93. (lp/cd) *(<VILE 35/+CD>)* **UNDER A FUNERAL MOON**
– Natassja in eternal sleep / Summer of the diabolical holocaust / The dance of the eternal shadows / Unholy black metal / To walk the infernal fields / Under a funeral moon / Inn I de dype Skogers Favn / Crossing the triangle of flames. *(cd re-iss. Feb01; CDVILEM 35)*

Peaceville / Futurist

Feb 94. (cd) *(CDVILE 43) <11060>* **TRANSILVANIAN HUNGER** Feb95
– Transilvanian hunger / Over fjell og gjennom torner / Skald av Satans sol / Slottet I det fjerne / Graven takeheimens saler / I en hall med flesk og Mjod / As flittermice as Satans spys / En as I dype skogen. *(re-iss. Apr01; CDVILEM 43)*

Moonfog / not iss.

May 95. (cd) *(FOG 005CD)* **PANZERFAUST**
– En vind av Sorg / Triumphant gleam / The hordes of Nebulah / Hans siste vinter / Beholding the throne of might / Quintessence / Snv og Granskog (Utferd). *(lp-iss.Apr96; FOGLP 005)*

—— now without ZEPHYROUS

Mar 96. (cd) *(FOG 011CD)* **TOTAL DEATH**
– Earth's last picture / Blackwinged / Gather for attack on the pearly gates / Black victory of death / Majestic desolate eye / Blasphemer / Ravnajuv / The serpents harvest.

Nov 96. (cd) *(FOG 013CD)* **GOATLORD**
– Rex / Pure demoniac blessing / The grimness of which shepherds mourn / Sadomasochistic rites / As desertshadows / In his lovely kingdom / Black Daimon / Towards the thornfields / (Birth of evil) Virgin skin / Green cave float.

Oct 99. (cd) *(FOG 023CD)* **RAVISHING GRIMNESS**
– Lifeless / The beast / The claws of time / Across the vacuum / Ravishing grimness / To the death (under the king).

– compilations, etc. –

Nov 00. (cd) *Peaceville; (CDVILE 83) <61083>* **PREPARING FOR WAR** Feb01
– Transilvanian hunger / Snowfall / Archipelago / I en hall med flesk og Mjod / The pagan winter / Grave with a view / Con – Thulcandra / Soria Moria / Natassja in eternal sleep / Cromlech / In the shadow of the horns / Neptune towers / Under a funeral moon / Skald au Satans so / Iconoclasm sweeps Cappadoria.

DAS DAMEN

Formed: New York – from Arizona – USA . . . mid 80's by JIM WALTERS, ALEX TOTINO, PHIL LEOPOLD VON TRAPP and LYLE HYSEN. After an initial eponymous release on 'Ecstatic Peace', they signed to 'SST', former home of HUSKER DU, MEAT PUPPETS and fIREHOSE. In 1987, they unleashed the sublime 'JUPITER EYE' album, a record of quasi-hardcore that touched on MC5-like garage psychedelia. This sound was even more pronounced on the follow-up album, 'TRISKAIDEKAPHOBE' and the EP 'MARSHMALLOW CONSPIRACY'. On the latter, the band ploughed through a manic re-working of The BEATLES' 'MAGICAL MYSTERY TOUR'. However, this was their last decent effort before signing to 'What Goes On', followed by 'City Slang' in the early 90's.

Album rating: JUPITER EYE (*6) / TRISKAIDEKAPHOBE (*6) / MOUSETRAP (*6) / HIGH ANXIETY (*5)

JIM WALTERS – vocals, guitar / **ALEX TOTINO** – guitar, vocals / **PHIL LEOPOLD VON TRAPP** – bass, vocals / **LYLE HYSEN** – drums, electronics

not iss. / Ecstatic Peace

1986. (lp) *<004>* **DAS DAMEN**
– Tsava / Trick question / Slave bird / House of mirrors / How do you measure / Behind my eyes. *<US re-iss. 1988 on 'SST' lp/c; SST 040/+C)*

S.S.T. / S.S.T.

1987. (lp/c) *<(SST 095/+C)>* **JUPITER EYE**
– Gray isn't black / Quarter after eight / Trap door / Where they all went / Name your poison / Impasse / Raindance / Do / Girl with the hair.

Aug 88. (lp) *<(SST 190)>* **TRISKAIDEKAPHOBE**
– Spiderbirds / Reverse into tomorrow / Pendant / Seven / Five five five / Firejoke / Bug / Siren plugs / Up for the ride / Ruby Woodpecker / Candy korn.

Dec 88. (m-lp/c/cd) *<(SST/+C/CD 218)>* **MARSHMALLOW CONSPIRACY EP**

What Goes On / Twin/Tone

1989. (cd) *<89170>* **MOUSETRAP**
– Noon daylight / Mirror leaks / Twenty four to zero / Somewhere, sometime / Demagnetized / Hey, angel / Sad mile / Please, please me / Click!

1989. (7") *(GOES ON 16)* **NOON DAYLIGHT. / GIVE ME EVERYTHING**

—— **DAVID MOTAMED** – bass; repl. VON TRAPP

City Slang / Sub Pop

Jul 91. (m-cd) *(SLANG 10) <SP 111B>* **HIGH ANXIETY**
– The promise / Chaindrive (a slight return) / The outsider / Thrilled to the marrow / Silence.

—— disbanded after above; DAVID joined CELL

the DAWN

Formed: Sweden . . . 1990 by former OBDURACY mainman FREDRIK SODERBERG. With HENKE FORSS, ANDREAS FULLMESTAD, DENNIS and KARSTEN LARSSON completing the line-up, the band cut its first demo tape in 1992. LARS TANGMARK replaced DENNIS for a second demo while a split single with PYPHOMGERTUM appeared on the Mexican imprint, 'Bellphegot'. A further demo finally secured DAWN a deal with the American 'Necropolis' label and a debut album, 'NAER SOLEN GAR NIPER FOR EVOGHER', appeared in 1994. Mini-set, 'SORGH PA SVARTE VINGAR FLOGH', followed in 1996 while the melodic black metallers excelled themselves on the millennial 'SLAUGHTERSUN (CROWN OF THE TRIARCHY)'. Despite the rave reviews, a wholesale personnel exodus subsequently left SODERBERG and FORSS as the only surviving original members.

Album rating: NAER SOLEN GAR NIPER FUR EVOGHER (*6) / SLAUGHTERSUN (CROWN OF THE TRIARCHY) (*7)

HENKE FORSS – vocals / **FREDRIK SODERBERG** – guitar (ex-OBDURACY) / **ANDREAS FULLMESTAD** – guitar / **DENNIS** – bass / **KARSTEN LARSSON** – drums

own label — not iss.

Jul 92. (cd-ep) *(demo)* **THE DAWN** — - — - Sweden

— **LARS TANGMARK** – bass; repl. DENNIS

1993. (cd-ep) *(demo)* **APPARATIONS** — - — - Sweden

not iss. — Bellphegot

1994. (cd-s; split with PYPHOMGERTUM) **split** — - — - Sweden

Necropolis — Necropolis

Apr 95. (cd) *(NR 006CD)* **NAER SOLEN GAR NIPER FUR EVOGHER** — — -
– Eyesland / The ethereal forest / Diabolical beauty / In the depths of my soul / Binom rinande lughier / As the tears fall / Soater skiner solen / Everflaming. *<US-iss.Feb00; same as UK>*

Oct 96. (cd-ep) *(NR 6664CD)* **SORGH PA SVARTE VINGAR FLOGH** — — -
– Vva kal / Sorrow flew on black wings / Soil of dead earth / Night of the living dead.

— **JOCKE PETTERSON** – drums; repl. LARSSON

May 98. (cd) *(<NR 021CD>)* **SLAUGHTERSUN (CROWN OF THE TRIARCHY)** — — Feb00
– The knell and the world / Falcula / To achieve the ancestral powers / Ride the wings of pestilence / The Aphelion deserts / The stalker's blessing / Malediction murder.

— when SODERBERG + FORSS were only originals remaining (+ **TOMAS ASKLUND** – drums), it looked like it was the end

DAYS OF THE NEW

Formed: Louisville, Kentucky, USA . . . 1996 by TRAVIS MEEKS who sacked his original band before recruiting new members TODD WHITENER, JESSE VEST and MATT TAUL. Described as the new ALICE IN CHAINS or PEARL JAM with the DOORS thrown in for good measure, they carried on the bleak and outdated grunge tradition. Almost immediately signed to Geffen's new 'Outpost' imprint, MEEKS and Co delivered their eponymous set in 1997. Climbing into the US Top 60, the brooding outfit quickly became part of Grunge Mk.II alongside CREED, etc. Two years on, album No.2 fared even better, although it stayed only one week in the Top 40.

Album rating: DAYS OF THE NEW (*7) / DAYS OF THE NEW 2 (*5)

TRAVIS MEEKS – vocals, guitar / **TODD WHITENER** – guitar / **JESSE VEST** – bass / **MATT TAUL** – drums

Outpost — Outpost

Feb 98. (7"/c-s) *(OPR S/MC 22299)* **TOUCH, PEEL & STAND. / GOT TO BE YOU**
(cd-s+=) *(OPRCD 22299)* – Independent slave.

Mar 98. (cd) *<(OPD 30004)>* **DAYS OF THE NEW** — — 54 Oct97
– Shelf in the room / Touch, peel & stand / Face of the earth / Solitude / The down town / What's left for me? / Freak / Now / Whimsical / Where I stand / How do I know you? / Cling.

Jan 99. (cd-s) *<22352>* **THE DOWN TOWN / ('A'version)** — - —

Aug 99. (cd) *<OPD 30037>* **DAYS OF THE NEW 2** — - — 40
– Flight response / Real / Enemy / Weapon and the wounded / Skeleton key / Take me back then / Bring yourself / I think / Longfellow / Phobics of tragedy / Not the same / Provider / Last one.

dBh

Formed: Liverpool, England . . . mid 90's by ANDY McMAHON, ALEX BALLARD, MARTIN HARRIS, SAM AVERY and PAUL SANDERSON. Basically a post-hardcore/aggro-metal outfit, they released a cd-single, 'WHITE GODSENT', before signing to 'Dedicated' (home of SPIRITUALIZED!). An album, 'UNWILLING TO EXPLAIN' was unleashed in the Spring of '97, a brutal, uncompromising set that was described as KORN on punk pills.

Album rating: UNWILLING TO EXPLAIN (*5)

ANDY McMAHON – vocals / **ALEX BALLARD** – guitar / **MARTIN HARRIS** – guitar / **SAM AVERY** – bass / **PAUL SANDERSON** – drums

dBh — not iss.

Nov 96. (cd-s) *(dBh 002CD)* **WHITE GODSENT / FILS / STAND** — — -
(cd-s) *(dBh 002ECD)* –

Dedicated — not iss.

May 97. (cd) *(DEDCD 028S)* **UNWILLING TO EXPLAIN** — — -
– Sense of hatred / White godsent / My great country / Out of control / Face / Reduced / Assimilation / Misogynist / No coalesce / Shooter / Obedience / Two people. *(re-iss. Oct98; same)*

Mar 98. (cd-ep) *(dBh 004CD)* **MY GREAT COUNTRY / REDUCED (live) / MY GREAT COUNTRY (uncensored) / ZEBRA LOVE** — — -

DEAD BOYS

Formed: Cleveland, Ohio, USA . . . mid '76 by CHEETAH CHROME and JOHNNY BLITZ, both ex-ROCKET FROM THE TOMBS (same band as DAVID THOMAS and PETER LAUGHNER of PERE UBU), who relocated to New York with frontman STIV BATORS (also a short-lived RFTT member), JIMMY ZERO and JEFF MAGNUM. Under The DEAD BOYS moniker, they played the infamous CBGB's, a nightclub owned at the time by their manager, Hilly Kristal. America's answer to The DAMNED, they signed to 'Sire' in 1977, finally unleashing their brash HEARTBREAKERS meets STOOGES debut set, 'YOUNG, LOUD & SNOTTY'. Featuring at least two seminal punk classics in 'SONIC REDUCER' and 'ALL THIS AND MORE' (also available on the V/A album, 'New Wave'), it sold moderately enough to make the US Top 200 for a month. The FELIX PAPPALARDI-produced follow-up, 'WE HAVE COME FOR YOUR CHILDREN' (1978), was everything that punk's critics railed against (i.e. brutally nihilistic, musically limited and sheer bloodied minded), although it did feature 'AIN'T IT FUN' (later covered by GUNS 'N ROSES) and was also graced by the presence of two RAMONES, JOEY and DEE DEE. The DEAD BOYS were finally laid to rest when STIV went solo in 1979, recording a handful of singles (including a version of The Choirs' 'IT'S COLD OUTSIDE') and an album for Greg Shaw's 'Bomp', 'DISCONNECTED' (1980). After putting in a brief stint as an actor in John Waters' 'Polyester', BATORS teamed up with ex-SHAM 69 Brits, DAVE TREGANNA, DAVE PARSONS and MARK GOLDSTEIN to form the short-lived WANDERERS. A solitary album, 'THE ONLY LOVERS LEFT ALIVE' (1981), appeared on UK 'Polydor', before he and TREGANNA hooked up with old DAMNED friend, BRIAN JAMES as The LORDS OF THE NEW CHURCH. With ex-BARRACUDAS' drummer NICKY TURNER in tow, the punk supergroup were inaugurated via a live gig in Paris towards the end of 1981. Signed to Miles Copeland's 'Illegal/I.R.S.' imprint, the LORDS delivered their first vinyl sermon in the shape of an eponymous 1982 debut album, a lacklustre sub-metal affair dabbling in pseudo gothic imagery and religious doom-mongering. This set the tone for the remainder of the band's career, two further studio albums, 'IS NOTHING SACRED?' (1983) and 'METHOD TO OUR MADNESS' (1984) hardly adding to their legacy; bizarrely enough, ex-MANFRED MANN'S EARTH BAND keyboard player/bassist, MATT IRVING joined for the latter. As the band's studio output dwindled to almost nothing, BATORS finally sacked his whole band in 1989 and took flight to London where he gathered together a bunch of old punk friends (DEE DEE RAMONE, NEIL X and JOHNNY THUNDERS) for a one-off gig billed as 'Return Of The Living Boys'. Although this loose aggregation actually laid down around half a dozen studio tracks, BATORS was to die in his sleep on the 4th of June, 1990, after he was run over by an automobile in Paris the previous day.

Album rating: YOUNG, LOUD & SNOTTY (*7) / WE HAVE COME FOR YOUR CHILDREN (*5) / Stiv Bators: DISCONNECTED (*5) / Lords Of The New Church: LORDS OF THE NEW CHURCH (*5) / IS NOTHING SACRED? (*4) / THE METHODS TO OUR MADNESS (*4) / KILLER LORDS compilation (*5) / LIVE AT THE SPIT (*3)

STIV BATORS (b. STEVEN BATOR, 22 Oct'56, Cleveland) – vocals / **CHEETAH CROME** (b. GENE CONNOR) – guitar, vocals / **JIMMY ZERO** – guitar / **JEFF MAGNUM** – bass / **JOHNNY BLITZ** – drums

Sire — Sire

Oct 77. (lp) *(9103 329) <SR 6038>* **YOUNG, LOUD & SNOTTY**
– Ain't nothin' to do / All this and more / Caught with the meat in your mouth / Down in flames / Hey little girl / High tension wire / I need lunch / Not anymore / Sonic reducer / What love is. *<cd-iss. Feb00; 7599 26038-2>*

Dec 77. (7"m)(12"m) *(SRE 1004)(6078 609)* **SONIC REDUCER. / LITTLE GIRL / DOWN IN FLAMES**

Aug 78. (7"m) *(SRE 1029)* **TELL ME. / NOT ANYMORE / AIN'T NOTHIN' TO DO**

Aug 78. (lp) *<(SRK 6054)>* **WE HAVE COME FOR YOUR CHILDREN** — — Jun78
– Third generation nation / I won't look back / Catholic boy / Flame thrower love / Son of Sam / Tell me / Big city / Calling on you / Dead and alive / Ain't it fun. *<(cd-iss. Feb00; 7599 26054-2)>*

— now without MAGNUM, they disbanded in 1979. BATORS went solo

– compilations, etc. –

May 81. (lp) *Bomp; (BLP 4017)* **NIGHT OF THE LIVING DEAD BOYS (live)** — — -
– Detention home / Caught with the meat in your mouth / All this and more / 3rd generation nation / Tell me / Catholic boy / Won't look back / Ain't it fun / What love is / Ain't nothin' to do / Need lunch / Sonic reducer / Route 66 / Hang on Sloopy / It's all over now / Ain't it fun / Sonic reducer. *(cd-iss. Apr94 & Mar99; BCD 4017) (lp re-iss. Jul97; same)*

1989. (lp/cd) *Bomp; <BLP/BCD 4064>* **YOUNGER, LOUDER AND SNOTTIER** — - —
(UK-iss.Jul97; same)

Nov 97. (cd/lp) *Bacchus Archives; (BA 1121 CD/LP)* **TWISTIN' ON THE DEVIL'S FORK** -

Aug 98. (d-cd) *Bomp; (BCD 4066)* **ALL THIS AND MORE**

May 99. (cd/lp) *Bad Boy; (RUDE CD/LP 00010)* **3rd GENERATION NATION** -

STIV BATORS

— with band; **GEORGE HARRISON** – guitar (no not that one!) / **FRANK SELICH** – bass / **DAVID QUINTON** – drums

London Bomp

Sep 79. (7") *(HLZ 10575) <BMP 124>* **IT'S COLD OUTSIDE. / THE LAST YEAR**

Bomp Bomp

May 80. (7") *<BMP 128>* **NOT THAT WAY ANYMORE. / CIRCUMSTANTIAL EVIDENCE** -

May 80. (lp) *<BLP 4015>* **DISCONNECTED**
– Evil boy / Bad luck charm / A million miles away / Make up your mind / Swingin' a g-go / Too much to dream / Ready anytime / The last year / I wanna forget you (just the way you are). *(re-iss. Oct87 on 'Line' lp/cd; LILP4/LICD9 00174) (cd re-iss. Feb94; BCD 4043)*

1980. (12"ep) *<BEP 1202>* **TOO MUCH TO DREAM. / MAKE UP YOUR MIND** -

— In Aug'87, BATORS released mini-lp, 'HAVE LOVE WILL TRAVEL' *BMP 12-136*

— BATORS joined The WANDERERS (with ex-SHAM 69 members). They released a few singles and an album in 1981; 'THE ONLY LOVERS LEFT ALIVE'. He then was part of punk supergroup . . .

LORDS OF THE NEW CHURCH

STIV BATOR plus **BRIAN JAMES** – guitar, vocals (ex-DAMNED, ex-TANZ DER YOUTH, ex-HELLIONS) / **DAVE TREGANNA** – bass, vocals (ex-WANDERERS, ex-SHAM 69) / **NICKY TURNER** – drums (ex-BARRACUDAS)

Illegal I.R.S.

Apr 82. (7") *(ILS 0028)* **NEW CHURCH. / LIVIN' ON LIVIN'**

Jul 82. (7") *(ILS 0030)* **OPEN YOUR EYES. / GIRLS GIRLS GIRLS**

Jul 82. (lp) *(ILP 009)* **LORDS OF THE NEW CHURCH**
– New church / Russian roulette / Question of temperature / Eat your heart out / Portobello / Open your eyes / Livin' on livin' / Li'l boys play with dolls / Apocalypso / Holy war. *(cd-iss. Apr87; ILPCD 009)*

Nov 82. (7"/7"pic-d) *(ILS/+P 0033)* **RUSSIAN ROULETTE. / YOUNG DON'T CRY**

I.R.S. I.R.S.

Jun 83. (7") *(PFP 1015)* **LIVE FOR TODAY. / OPENING**

Aug 83. (lp/c) *(SP/CS 70039)* **IS NOTHING SACRED?**
– Dance with me / Bad timing / Johnny too bad / Don't worry children / The night is calling / Black – white girl / Goin' downtown / Tales of two cities / World without end / Partners in crime / Live for today.

Sep 83. (7"/12"colrd-pic-d) *(PFP/PFSX 1022)* **DANCE WITH ME. / I'M NOT RUNNING HARD ENUFF**

— added guest **MATT IRVING** – bass, keyboards (ex-MANFRED MANN'S EARTH BAND)

Oct 84. (7") *(IRS 113)* **M STYLE. / SORRY FOR THE MAN**
(d7"+=) *(IRSY 113)* – Dance with me / I'm not running hard enuff.

Nov 84. (lp) *(IRSA 7049)* **THE METHOD TO OUR MADNESS**
– Method to my madness / I never believed / Pretty baby scream / Fresh flesh / When blood runs cold / M style / The seducer / Kiss of death / Do what thou wilt / My kingdom come.

Illegal not iss.

Apr 85. (7"pic-d) *(LORDSP 1)* **LIKE A VIRGIN. / METHOD TO MY MADNESS** -
(12"+=) *(LORDS 1)* – Gun called Justice.

Nov 85. (lp/c) *(ILP 016)* **KILLER LORDS** (compilation)
– Dance with me / Hey tonight / Russian roulette / M style / Lord's prayer / Live for today / Method to my madness / Open your eyes / I never believed / Black girl – white girl / New church / Like a virgin. *(re-iss. Aug90 cd/lp; ILP 016)*

— trimmed to quartet again, when IRVING joined PAUL YOUNG BAND

BondageInt not iss.

Aug 87. (7") *(B 11)* **REAL BAD TIME. / THINGS GO BAD** -

New Rose not iss.

Sep 87. (7"/12") *(B 100-1/-2)* **PSYCHO SEX. /** -

Illegal not iss.

May 88. (lp/c) *(ILP/+C 021)* **LIVE AT THE SPIT (live)** -
– Method to my madness / Partners in crime / Kiss of death / Bad timing / Dance with me / M style / Livin' on livin' / The seducer / Open your eyes / Gun caled Justice / When blood runs cold / Pretty baby scream / Live for today / Holy war / Black girl – white girl / New church. *(w/free 45)* – Gun called Justice / Johnny too bad / Light and shade / All or nothing.
(re-iss. Aug90 cd; ILPCD 021)

Perfect B. not iss.

May 89. (d-lp; as STIV BATORS & HIS EVIL BOYS) *(PB 003)* **SCENE OF THE CRIME (live at the Limelight 1985)** - - German
– Introduction / Evil boy / It's cold outside / Have love, will travel / Not that way anymore / The last year / Story in your eyes / It's trash / Ready to snap / Do you believe in magic / Dreams & desires / Sonic reducer / 3rd generation nation.

— split, when BATORS sacked the rest, because they were going to sack him. He started to work with ex-members of SIGUE SIGUE SPUTNIK and HANOI ROCKS, but he died in his sleep in 1990 after being knocked down by a car in Paris.

– STIV BATORS compilations, others, etc. –

May 94. (cd) *New Rose; (64200-2)* **THE DEAD BOYS** -

Apr 98. (cd) *Bond Age; (BRCD 96129)* **THE LAST RACE**

DEAD KENNEDYS

Formed: San Francisco, California, USA . . . early 1978 by JELLO BIAFRA and EAST BAY RAY, who recruited KLAUS FLOURIDE, TED and briefly, the mysterious 6025. Inspired by British punk rock, BIAFRA formed The DEAD KENNEDYS primarily as a vehicle for his raging, razor-sharp satire of America and everything it stood for. Public enemy #1 from the off, major labels steered well clear of the band, BIAFRA and Co. subsequently forming their own label, the legendary 'Alternative Tentacles', releasing 'CALIFORNIA UBER ALLES' as their debut 45 in late '79. A scathing critique of California governor, Jerry Brown, the record introduced the singer's near-hysterical vocal undulations set against a pulverising punk/hardcore musical backdrop. Released on the independent 'Fast' imprint in Britain, the record's initial batch of copies sold like proverbial hotcakes. The 1980 follow-up, 'HOLIDAY IN CAMBODIA' (released on Miles Copeland's 'Faulty' label; 'Cherry Red' in the UK), remains The DEAD KENNEDYS' most viciously realised moment, a dark, twisting diatribe on American middle-class liberal trendies. Later in the year, the group kept up their aural assault with a debut album, 'FRESH FRUIT FOR ROTTING VEGETABLES', an unexpected Top 40 entry in the seemingly "Punk Is Dead" Britain, which contained the aforesaid 45's plus perennial favourites, 'LET'S LYNCH THE LANDLORD', 'DRUG ME' and the forthcoming UK hit, 'KILL THE POOR'. The record also offered a glimpse of BIAFRA'S reassuringly twisted sense of humour in such surreal cuts as 'STEALING PEOPLE'S MAIL' and 'VIVA LAS VEGAS' (the latter was a hit for Elvis!). In 1981, drummer D.H. PELIGRO replaced TED, making his debut on the bluntly-titled 'TOO DRUNK TO FUCK', the only UK Top 40 charting single in musical history (up to that point!) to utilise the "f***" word. Once again mocking the inherent hypocrisy of corporate America, The DEAD KENNEDYS released a frenetic 10" mini-set, 'IN GOD WE TRUST INC.' (1981), highlights being the self-explanatory 'NAZI PUNKS FUCK OFF' (a US-only single) and a deadpan version of 'RAWHIDE'. The band then took a brief hiatus, busying themselves with an 'Alternative Tentacles' compilation of promising unsigned American bands, entitled 'Let Them Eat Jellybeans'. That same year (1982), the group released their second album proper, 'PLASTIC SURGERY DISASTERS'; issued on 'Statik' in the UK, it featured the singles 'BLEED FOR ME' and 'HALLOWEEN'. Spending the ensuing few years touring, the band resurfaced in 1985 with 'FRANKENCHRIST', an album that finally saw BIAFRA's upstanding enemies closing in (ie. the PMRC, the US government, etc) due to the album's free "penis landscape" poster by Swiss artist H.R. Giger. Although BIAFRA and Co. (including some senior label staff) were tried in court for distributing harmful material to minors (a revised obscenity law), the case was subsequently thrown out after a hung jury. Nevertheless, the cost of the trial effectively put the band out of business, The DEAD KENNEDYS poignantly-titled finale, 'BEDTIME FOR DEMOCRACY' being issued late in 1986. Although KLAUS and RAY followed low-key solo careers, the ever-prolific BIAFRA vociferously protested against his treatment on spoken-word sets, 'NO MORE COCOONS' (1987) and 'THE HIGH PRIEST OF HARMFUL MATTER' (1989). He subsequently collaborated with a wide range of hardcore/industrial acts such as D.O.A., NO MEANS NO and TUMOR CIRCUS, although it was with LARD (a project with MINISTRY mainmen, AL JOURGENSEN and PAUL BARKER) that BIAFRA really came into his own. A late 80's mini-set, 'THE POWER OF LARD' preceded a full-length album, 'THE LAST TEMPTATION OF LARD', a minor UK hit early in 1990. This demented set included such hilarious BIAFRA monologues as 'CAN GOD FILL TEETH?' and even a rendition of Napolean XIV's 'THEY'RE COMING TO TAKE ME AWAY'. In 1994, he hooked up with another likeminded soul in hillbilly punk, MOJO NIXON, releasing one album, 'PRAIRIE HOME INVASION' (the title possibly a parody of an ICE-T album). BIAFRA continues to work at 'Alternative Tentacles', supplying the country with suitably deranged hardcore and occasionally taking time out for other projects, most recently a second LARD set, 'PURE CHEWING SATISFACTION' (1997). • **Trivia:** In 1979, BIAFRA stood in the elections for Mayor of San Francisco (he came 4th!).

Album rating: FRESH FRUIT FOR ROTTING VEGETABLES (*9) / IN GOD WE TRUST INC. mini (*5) / PLASTIC SURGERY DISASTERS (*6) / FRANKENCHRIST (*6) / BEDTIME FOR DEMOCRACY (*5) / GIVE ME CONVENIENCE OR GIVE ME DEATH compilation (*8) / Jello Biafra: NO MORE COCOONS spoken (*5) / HIGH PRIEST OF HARMFUL MATTER spoken (*5) / THE LAST TEMPTATION OF LARD with Lard (*6) / THE LAST SCREAM OF THE MISSING NEIGHBORS with D.O.A. (*6) / THE SKY IS FALLING AND I WANT MY MOMMY with No Means No (*5) / I BLOW MINDS FOR A LIVING (*6) / HIGH VOLTAGE CONSPIRACY FOR RADICAL FREEDOM with Tumor Circus (*5) / PRAIRIE HOME INVASION with Mojo Nixon (*6) / BEYOND THE VALLEY OF THE GIFT POLICE (*5) / PURE CHEWING SATISFACTION with Lard (*5)

JELLO BIAFRA (b. ERIC BOUCHER, 17 Jun'58, Boulder, Colorado) – vocals / **EAST BAY RAY** (b. RAY GLASSER, Castro Valley, California) – guitar, (synthesisers-later 80's) / **KLAUS FLUORIDE** (b. Detroit, Michigan) – bass, vocals / **BRUCE SLESINGER** (aka TED) – drums

Fast Alternative Tentacles

Oct 79. (7") *(FAST 12) <AT 95-41>* **CALIFORNIA UBER ALLES. / MAN WITH THE DOGS**

Cherry Red Faulty-IRS

Jun 80. (7")12" *(CHERRY/12CHERRY 13) <IR 9016>* **HOLIDAY IN CAMBODIA. / POLICE TRUCK**
(re-iss. 7"/cd-s Jun88 & Mar95; same)

Sep 80. (lp) *(B-RED 10)* *<SP 70014>* **FRESH FRUIT FOR ROTTING VEGETABLES** [33] [ ] Nov80
– Kill the poor / Forward to death / When ya get drafted / Let's lynch the landlord / Drug me / Your emotions / Chemical warfare / Calilfornia uber alles / I kill children / Stealing people's mail / Funland at the beach / Ill in my head / Holiday in Cambodia / Viva Las Vegas. *(cd-iss. Nov87 & Mar95; CDBRED 10)*

Oct 80. (7") *(CHERRY 16)* **KILL THE POOR. / IN SIGHT** [49] [-]
(re-iss. Nov87 & Mar95; CDCHERRY 16)

— **D.H. PELIGRO** (b. DARREN, East St.Louis, Illinois) – drums; repl. BRUCE/TED

Cherry Red / Alternative Tentacles

May 81. (7"/12") *(CHERRY/12CHERRY 24)* *<VIRUS 2>* **TOO DRUNK TO FUCK. / THE PREY** [36] [ ]
(re-iss. May88 & Mar95 cd-s; CDCHERRY 24)

Statik / Alternative Tentacles

Nov 81. (10"ep) *(STATEP 2)* *<VIRUS 5>* **IN GOD WE TRUST INC.** [ ] [ ]
– Religious vomit / Moral majority / Kepone factory / Dog bite / Nazi punks fuck off / We've got a bigger problem now / Rawhide. *<US c-ep+=; VIRUS 5C>* – Too drunk to fuck / The prey / Holiday in Cambodia. *(re-iss. Jun92 cd-ep; STATEP 2CD)*

Dec 81. (7") *<VIRUS 6>* **NAZI PUNKS FUCK OFF. / MORAL MAJORITY** [-] [ ]

Jul 82. (7"/12") *(STAT/+12 22)* *<VIRUS 23>* **BLEED FOR ME. / LIFE SENTENCE** [ ] [ ]
(cd-s Jun92; STAT 22CD)

Nov 82. (lp) *(STATLP 11)* **PLASTIC SURGERY DISASTERS** [ ] [-]
– Government flu / Terminal preppie / Trust your mechanic / Well paid scientist / Buzzbomb / Forest fire / Halloween / Winnebago warrior / Riot / Bleed for me / I am the owl / Dead end / Moon over Marin. *(re-iss. Oct85; same)* *(cd-iss. Nov86 & Jun92 & Jun98 +=; same)* – IN GOD WE TRUST INC. (ep)

Nov 82. (7"/12") *(STAT/+12 27)* *<VIRUS 28>* **HALLOWEEN. / SATURDAY NIGHT HOLOCAUST** [ ] [ ]
(cd-s Jun92; STAT 27CD)

— meanwhile KLAUS and EAST BAY released solo singles (see below)

Alternative Tentacles / Alternative Tentacles

May 82. (12"; KLAUS FLUORIDE) *<(VIRUS 12)>* **SHORTNING BREAD. / DROWNING COWBOY** [ ] [ ]

Jun 84. (7"; EAST BAY RAY) *<(VIRUS 34)>* **TROUBLE IN TOWN. / POISON HEART** [ ] [ ]
(12 re-iss. Apr89 on 'New Rose' France; GMO 40)

Aug 84. (12"ep; KLAUS FLUORIDE) **CHA CHA CHA WITH MR. FLUORIDE** [ ] [-]
– Ghost riders / etc.

Dec 85. (lp) *<(VIRUS 45)>* **FRANKENCHRIST** [ ] [ ]
– Soup is good food / Hellnation / This could be anywhere (this could be everywhere) / A growing boy needs his lunch / Chicken farm / Macho-rama (invasion of the beef-patrol) / Goons of Hazzard / At my job / M.T.V. – Get off the air / Stars and stripes of corruption. *(cd-iss. 1986 & Jun98; VIRUS 45CD)*

Dec 86. (lp/c/cd) *<(VIRUS 50/+C/CD)>* **BEDTIME FOR DEMOCRACY** [ ] [ ]
– Take this job and shove it / Hop with the jet set / Dear Abby / Rambozo the clown / Fleshdunce / The great wall / Shrink / Triumph of the swill / I spy / Macho insecurity / Cesspools in Eden / One-way ticket to Pluto / Do the slag / Gone with the wind / A commercial / Anarchy for sale / Chickenshit conformist / Where do ya draw the line / Potshot heard round the world / D.M.S.O. / Lie detector. *(re-iss. Jun98; same)*

— split Dec'86 when RAY departed (he subsequently turned up in SKRAPYARD). KLAUS FLUORIDE went solo, releasing albums 'BECAUSE I SAY SO' (1988) and 'THE LIGHT IS FLICKERING' (1991) and forming acoustic outfit FIVE YEAR PLAN

– compilations, etc. –

on 'Alternative Tentacles' unless mentioned otherwise

Jun 87. (lp/cd) *<(VIRUS 57/+CD)>* **GIVE ME CONVENIENCE OR GIVE ME DEATH** [84] [ ]
– Police truck / Too drunk to f*** / California uber alles / Man with the dogs / In sight / Life sentence / A child and his lawnmower / Holiday in Cambodia / Night of the living rednecks / I fought the law / Saturday night holocaust / Pull my strings / Short songs / Straight A's / Kinky sex makes the world go round / The prey. *(cd+=/free flexi-disc)* – BUZZBOMB FROM PASADENA

Jun 93. (7"ep) *Subterranean; (SUB 24)* **NAZI PUNKS **** OFF / ARYANISMS. / ('A'live) / CONTEMPTUOUS** [ ] [-]
(re-iss. Dec97 & Jul00; same)

JELLO BIAFRA

Nov 87. (lp) *<(VIRUS 59)>* **NO MORE COCOONS** (spoken word) [ ] [ ]
(cd-iss. Mar93; VIRUS 59CD)

Jul 89. (d-lp) *<(VIRUS 66)>* **HIGH PRIEST OF HARMFUL MATTER (TALES OF THE TRIALS, LIVE)** (spoken word) [ ] [ ]
(cd-iss. Mar93; VIRUS 66CD)

LARD

BIAFRA, AL JOURGENSEN + PAUL BARKER (Ministry) / **JEFF WARD** – drums

Nov 89. (12"ep/c-ep/cd-ep) *<(VIRUS 72 T/C/CD)>* **THE POWER OF LARD / HELL FUDGE. / TIME TO MELT (31 mins.)** [ ] [ ]

Jul 90. (lp/cd) *<(VIRUS 84/+CD)>* **THE LAST TEMPTATION OF LARD** [69] [ ]
– Forkboy / Pineapple face / Hate, spawn and die / Drug raid at 4a.m. / Can God fill teeth? / Bozo skeleton / Sylvestre Matuschka / They're coming to take me away / I am your clock.

JELLO BIAFRA & D.O.A.

— w/ **JOE KEITHLEY + CHRIS PROHOM** – guitar, vocals / **BRIAN GOBLE** – bass, vocals / **JON CARD** – drums

May 90. (lp/cd) *<(VIRUS 78/+CD)>* **THE LAST SCREAM OF THE MISSING NEIGHBORS** [ ] [ ]
– That's progress / Attack of the peacekeepers / Wish I was in El Salvador / Power is boring / We gotta get out of this place / Full metal jackoff.

JELLO BIAFRA & NO MEANS NO

with **TIPPER GORE BOB WRIGHT** – guitar / **JOHN WRIGHT** – drums / **JON CARD** – percussion

Mar 91. (lp/c/cd) *<(VIRUS 85/+C/CD)>* **THE SKY IS FALLING AND I WANT MY MOMMY** [ ] [ ]
– The sky is falling and I want my mommy (falling space junk) / Jesus was a terrorist / Bruce's diary / Sad / Ride the flume / Chew / Sparks in the Gene pool / The myth is real – let's eat.

JELLO BIAFRA

Jun 91. (d-lp/c/cd) *<(VIRUS 94/+C/CD)>* **I BLOW MINDS FOR A LIVING** [ ] [ ]
– Pledge of allegience / Talk on censorship – let us prey / Die for oil, sucker – higher octane version / I was a teenage pacifist / If voting changed anything . . . / Running for mayor / Grow more pot / Lost orgasm / Talk on censorship-Better living through new world orders + Fear of a free planet.

TUMOR CIRCUS

— **DARREN MOR-X / DALE FLAT-UM + MIKE MDRASKOID** (of STEEL POLE BATH TUB) / **KING GRONG CHARLIE (TOLNAY)** (of LUBRICATED GOAT) + **J. BIAFRA**

Nov 91. (lp/c/cd) *<(VIRUS 087/+C/CD)>* **TUMOR CIRCUS – HIGH VOLTAGE CONSPIRACY FOR RADICAL FREEDOM** [ ] [ ]
– Hazing for success / Human cyst / The man with the corkscrew eyes / Fireball / Calcutta a-go-go / Turn off the respirator. (cd+=) Swine flu / Take me back or I'll drown our dog / Meathook up my rectum.

Feb 92. (7") *<(VIRUS 102)>* **MEATHOOK UP MY RECTUM. / (etched side)** [ ] [ ]
(12"+=/cd-s+=) *<(VIRUS 102 T/CD)>* – Take me back or I'll drown the dog / Swine flu / Fireball.

JELLO BIAFRA & MOJO NIXON

Nov 93. (7") *(VIRUS 136)* **WILL THE FETUS BE ABORTED? / THE LOST WORLD** [ ] [-]
(cd-s+=) *(VIRUS 136CD)* – Drinkin' with Jesus / Achey raky heart.

Feb 94. (lp/cd) *<(VIRUS 137/+CD)>* **PRAIRIE HOME INVASION** [ ] [ ]
– Buy my snake oil / Where are we gonna work (when the trees are gone) / Convoy in the sky / Atomic power / Are you drinkin' with me Jesus / Love me, I'm a liberal / Burgers of wrath / Nostalgia for an angel that never existed / Hammer chicken plant disaster / Mascot mania / Let's go burn de Nashville down / Will the fetus be aborted? / Plastic Jesus. *(cd re-iss. Apr00; same)*

JELLO BIAFRA

Oct 94. (d-lp) *<(VIRUS 150)>* **BEYOND THE VALLEY OF THE GIFT POLICE** (spoken word) [ ] [-]
– Message to our sponsor / Experts / Ban everything / I have a dream / Talk on censorship / What we are not being told / President McMuffin tightens the belt / Talk on censorship / What we are not being told / In the belly of the wrong beast / Talk on censorship / Eric meets the moose diarrhea / Virturcrats unreality.

LARD

— see last line-up + add **BILL RIEFLIN** – drums

May 97. (lp/c/cd) *<(VIRUS 199/+MC/CD)>* **PURE CHEWING SATISFACTION** [ ] [ ]
– War pimp renaissance / I wanna be a drug sniffing dog / Moths / Generation execute / Faith hope and treachery / Peeling back the foreskin of liberty / Mangoat / Sidewinder.

Jan 00. (12"ep/cd-ep) *<(VIRUS 235/+CD)>* **70'S ROCK MUST DIE. / VULCANS 2000 / BALLAD OF MARSHALL LEDBETTER** [ ] [ ]

JELLO BIAFRA

Oct 98. (t-lp/d-cd) *<(VIRUS 201/+CD)>* **IF EVOLUTION IS OUTLAWED ONLY OUTLAWS WILL EVOLVE** (spoken word) [ ] [ ]
– Depends on the drug / Wake up and smell the coffee / The murder of Mumia Abu Jemal / Clinton comes to Long Beach / Half time / Hex flies space shuttle sequel / New Soviet Union / Talk on censorship.

– others, etc. –

Jul 00. (12"; by JELLO BIAFRA, EAST BAY RAY & CHRISTIAN LUNCH) *Subterranean; <(SUB 017)>* **THE WITCH TRIALS** [ ] [ ]

DEADLIGHTS

Formed: Huntington Beach, California, USA . . . late 90's as SUCTION by DUKE and JIM FALCONE. With BILLY ROAN and JERRY MONTANO completing the line-up, The DEADLIGHTS (a moniker inspired by Stephen King's truly scary novel, 'It') became an integral part of L.A.'s thriving nu-metal scene alongside the likes of STATIC X and SYSTEM OF A DOWN. A major label deal with 'Elektra' resulted in 'THE DEADLIGHTS' (2000), a hard-nosed affair which avoided the contrived rapping of many nu-metal acts. Despite a stint on the millennial Ozzfest tour, the band were subsequently dropped by their label and split amid bitter infighting. MONTANO went on to join metal outfit NOTHINGFACE.

Album rating: DEADLIGHTS (*7)

DUKE – vocals, guitar / **BILLY ROAN** – guitar / **JERRY MONTANO** – bass / **JIM FALCONE** – drums

Elektra Elektra

Mar 00. (cd) *<(7559 62365-2)>* **THE DEADLIGHTS** ☐ ☐ Feb00
– Bitter / Amplifier / Nothing / Sweet oblivion / Junk / Sado / Foolish pride / Whores / Pox eclipse / Distant sun / Time / Falling down.

DEAF DEALER

Formed: Jonquiere, Canada . . . 1980 by ANDY LA ROCHE, IAN PENN, MARC HAYWARD, J.P. FORSYTH and DAN McGREGOR. Their first vinyl outing was a track on 'Metal Massacre IV', leading to a deal in 1985 with UK label, 'Neat'. The same year, the group replaced LA ROCHE with MICHAEL FLYNN, releasing their debut album, KEEPER OF THE FLAMES' (1986). However, their unremarkable brand of hard-hitting metal failed to garner sufficient interest for a second release.

Album rating: KEEPER OF THE FLAMES (*4)

MICHAEL FLYNN – vocals; repl. ANDY LA ROCHE / **IAN PENN** – guitar / **MARC HAYWARD** – guitar / **J.P. FORSYTH** – bass / **DAN McGREGOR** – drums

Neat Metal Blade

1986. (lp) *(NEAT 1035) <72153>* **KEEPER OF THE FLAMES** ☐ ☐
– Don't get it in my way / Deaf dealer / On the wings of a foxbat / The fugitive / Dead zone / Sadist / Free and easy / Getting ready to go / Caution to kill.

—— folded the following year

DEARLY BEHEADED

Formed: Stockport, England . . . late 1992 by ALEX CREAMER, PHIL STEVENS, STEVE OWENS, TIM PRESTON and ROB RYAN. Brutal, grinding and downright uncompromising, the fivesome delivered their first demo release, 'WE, THE UNWILLING', in '94. Subsequently signing a deal with 'East West' (very briefly) and then 'Music For Nations', DEARLY BEHEADED cut their first proper disc, the EP 'IN A DARKENED ROOM'. The Colin Richardson-produced 'TEMPTATION' set in '96 (with SIMON DAWSON replacing RYAN) received some rave reviews, although many critics cited them as much too SABBATH or PANTERA. With the departing STEVENS now out of the way, the 'BEHEADED delivered one more set, 'CHAMBER OF ONE' (1997), before they er, cut themselves off completely (ouch!).

Album rating: TEMPTATION (*6) / CHAMBER OF ONE (*6)

ALEX CREAMER (b.14 Jul'67) – vocals / **PHIL STEVENS** (b.30 Oct'71) – lead guitar / **STEVE OWENS** (b.20 Apr'69) – rhythm guitar / **TIM PRESTON** (b. 8 Sep'68) – bass / **ROB RYAN** – drums

Music For Nations Fierce

Oct 95. (cd-ep) *(CDKUT 168)* **IN A DARKENED ROOM / BREAK MY BONES / NEVER / THE SEASON OF LIES** ☐ [-]

—— **SIMON DAWSON** – drums; repl. RYAN

Jun 96. (cd/c/lp) *(CD/T+/MFN 203) <11099>* **TEMPTATION** ☐ ☐ Oct96
– Behind the sun / Witness / Temptation / Between night and day / Leaving them behind / We are your family / Fuel my hatred / Break my bones / Break the restraint / No rest.

—— STEVENS departed after above

Oct 97. (cd) *(CDMFN 232)* **CHAMBER OF ONE** ☐ [-]
– Thankless task / Generations / Dead issue / Moment of clarity / Escape / Chamber of one / Giving up the lies / Faceless / Tribal convictions / Haunting your horizons.

DEATH

Formed: Florida, USA . . . 1983 initially as MANTAS, by CHUCK SCHULDINER, who recruited local musicians KAM LEE and RICK ROZZ. They quickly signed for 'Combat' on the understanding their product would be leased to Music For Nations subsidiary 'Under One Flag' in Europe. DEATH were born (so to speak!), when CHUCK moved to California and left the other two behind with their group, MASSACRE. He employed the services of drummer CHRIS REIFERT to augment him/DEATH on a 1987 thrash-metal debut, 'SCREAM BLOODY GORE'. However, by the following year's 'LEPROSY', CHUCK had brought back RICK ROZZ together with two of his MASSACRE stable, TERRY BUTLER and BILL ANDREWS. In a remarkable 1990, he took on JAMES MURPHY to replace ROZZ, and nearing a European tour supporting KREATOR, CHUCK announced his departure. They had to carry on without him (!), bringing in former DEATH roadcrew guys LOUIE CARRISALEZ (actually ex-drummer with DEVASTATION!) on vox and WALTER THRASHLER (ex-ROTTING CORPSE) on guitar. When this near-nightmare was over, BUTLER and ANDREWS thought it best to leave and re-form MASSACRE. CHUCK then resurrected DEATH with an entire new crew, releasing 'HUMAN' in the process. Needless to say, CHUCK lived up to his name yet again and again, and brought in replacement members throughout the 90's over such albums as 'INDIVIDUAL THOUGHT PATTERNS' (1993) and 'SYMBOLIC' (1995). In 1998, SCHULDINER brought in a cast of unknowns – SHANNON HAMM, SCOTT CLENDENIN and RICHARD CHRISTY – for a record which many fans hailed as the pinnacle of his career. 'SOUND OF PERSEVERANCE' melded the bone-splintering aggression and technical skill of old with a new – albeit relative – melodicism, laying down a bloodstained sonic gauntlet for the new generation of metal pretenders and tipping a hat to the old giants with a cover of Judas Priest's 'PAINKILLER'. The brainchild and pioneer of "death-metal", CHUCK remains one of the foremost purveyors of extreme sacrilegious musical assaults.

Album rating: SCREAM BLOODY GORE (*8) / LEPROSY (*8) / SPIRITUAL HEALING (*6) / HUMAN (*6) / FATE: THE BEST OF DEATH (*8) / INDIVIDUAL THOUGHT PATTERNS (*7) / SYMBOLIC (*5) / SOUND OF PERSEVERANCE (*7)

CHUCK SCHULDINER – vocals, guitar / **CHRIS REIFERT** – drums

Under One Flag Combat

Jun 87. (cd/lp) *(CD+/FLAG 12) <8146>* **SCREAM BLOODY GORE** ☐ ☐
– Infernal death / Zombie ritual / Denial of life / Sacrificial / Mutilation / Regurgitated guts / Baptized in blood / Torn to pieces / Evil dead / Scream bloody gore. *(cd re-iss. Oct99 on 'Century Media'; CM 660192)*

—— **CHUCK** now with **RICK ROZZ** – guitar / **TERRY BUTLER** – bass / **BILL ANDREWS** – drums (all of MASSACRE)

Oct 88. (cd/c/lp) *(CD/C+/FLAG 24) <8248>* **LEPROSY** ☐ ☐
– Leprosy / Born dead / Forgotten past / Left to die / Pull the plug / Open casket / Primitive ways / Choke on it. *(pic-lp May89; FLAG 26P) (cd re-iss. May99 on 'Century Media'; CM 660012)*

—— **JAMES MURPHY** – guitar repl. ROZZ who returned to MASSACRE

Jan 90. (cd/c/lp) *(CD/T+/FLAG 38) <2011>* **SPIRITUAL HEALING** ☐ ☐
– Living monstrosity / Altering the future / Defensive personality / Within the mind / Spiritual healing / Low life / Genetic reconstruction / Killing spree. *(cd re-iss. Nov99 on 'Century Media'; CM 660302)*

—— **CHUCK** returned after briefly leaving tour (see above). He recruited **PAUL MASVIDAL** – guitar (ex-CYNIC) / **STEVE DiGIORGIO** – bass (ex-SADUS) / **SEAN REINERT** – drums (ex-CYNIC)

Roadracer Combat

Nov 91. (cd/c/lp) *(RC 9238-2/-4/-1) <2036>* **HUMAN** ☐ ☐
– Flattening of emotions / Suicide machine / Together as one / Secret face / Lack of comprehension / See through dreams / Cosmic sea / Vacant planets. *(cd re-iss. Aug99 on 'Century Media'; 660182)*

—— **ANDY LAROCQUE** – guitar (ex-KING DIAMOND) repl. SKOTT KARINO who had repl. MASVIDAL

—— **GENE HOGLAN** – drums (ex-DARK ANGEL) repl. REINERT

Roadrunner Combat

Jul 93. (cd/c/lp) *(RR 9079-2/-4/-1) <1168-2>* **INDIVIDUAL THOUGHT PATTERNS** ☐ ☐
– Overactive imagination / Jealousy / Trapped in a corner / Nothing is everything / Mentally blind / Individual thought patterns / Destiny / Out of touch / Philosopher / In human form. *(cd re-iss. Nov99 on 'Century Media'; CM 660282)*

Roadrunner Roadrunner

Mar 95. (cd/c/lp) *<(RR 8957-2/-4/-1)>* **SYMBOLIC** ☐ ☐
– Symbolic / Zero tolerance / Empty words / Sacred serenity / 1000 eyes / Without judgement / Crystal mountain / Misanthrope / Perennial quest. *(cd re-iss. Nov96; same)*

—— **SHANNON HAMM** – guitar; repl. LaROCHE

—— **SCOTT CLENDENIN** – bass; repl. DiGIORGIO

—— **RICHARD CHRISTY** – drums; repl. HOGLAN

Nuclear Blast Nuclear Blast

Sep 98. (cd) *<(NB 337-2)>* **SOUND OF PERSEVERANCE** ☐ ☐
– Scavenger of human sorrow / Bite the pain / Spirit crusher / Story to tell / Flesh and the power it holds / Voice of the soul / To forgive is to suffer / A moment of clarity / Painkiller.

– compilations, etc. –

Jun 92. (cd/c/lp) *Under One Flag; (CD/T+/FLAG 71) / Combat; <1199>*
FATE: THE BEST OF DEATH ☐ ☐ Nov91
– Zombie ritual / Together as one / Open casket / Spiritual healing / Mutilation / Suicide machine / Altering the future / Baptized in blood / Left to die / Pull the plug.

DEATH ANGEL

Formed: San Francisco, California, USA . . . 1982 by MARK OSEGUEDA, ROB CAVESTANY, DENNIS PEPA, GUS PEPA and ANDY GALEON. Among the cream of the second wave of thrash acts to emerge from the Bay Area, the group eventually made it on to vinyl in 1987 with 'THE ULTRA-VIOLENCE'. From the frenzied 'THRASHERS' onwards, the album was a full-force frontal assault on the earlobes, buzzing with the group's youthful energy. A second set, 'FROLIC THROUGH THE PARK', was released the following year, its more complex structures showing a band in transition. 'Geffen' were impressed enough to offer the band a deal, DEATH ANGEL becoming the first act of their ilk to appear on the major label's roster. The brilliant 'ACT III' (1990) vindicated 'Geffen's foresight and then some. One of the most innovative, consistent and accomplished thrash albums ever released, the record reached beyond the usually restrictive confines of the genre to create something truly unique. Displaying a masterful grasp of dynamics for such a young band, tracks like 'THE ORGANIZATION' and 'ROOM WITH A VIEW' are up there with the best of METALLICA's work. Tragically, however, the group's vast potential failed to be realised further, drummer ANDY GALEON critically injured after the band's tour bus crashed in the Arizona desert. By the time his wounds had healed more than a year later, MARK OSEGUEDA had departed and DEATH ANGEL had lost its momentum. The remaining members regrouped under The ORGANIZATION banner, releasing two albums for the 'MFN' subsidiary, 'Bulletproof', in the mid-90's, 'THE ORGANIZATION' (1993) and 'SAVOR THE FLAVOR' (1995).

Album rating: THE ULTRA-VIOLENCE (*6) / FROLIC THROUGH THE PARK (*5) / FALL FROM GRACE: LIVE (*5) / ACT III (*7) / Organization: THE ORGANIZATION (*5) /

MARK OSEGUEDA – vocals / **ROB CAVESTANY** – guitar / **GUS PEPA** – guitar **DENNIS PEPA** – bass / **ANDY GALEON** – drums

Under One Flag / Enigma

May 87. (lp) *(FLAG 14) <72353>* **THE ULTRA-VIOLENCE**
– Thrashers / Evil priest / Voracious souls / Kill as one / The ultra-violence / Mistress of pain / Final death / I.F.P.S. *(cd-iss. Jul94 on 'Restless'; 772548-2)*

Enigma / Enigma

Aug 88. (lp) *(ENVLP/TCENV/CDENV 502) <73332>* **FROLIC THROUGH THE PARK**
– 3rd floor / Road mutants / Why you do this / Bored / Confused / Guilty of innocence / Open up / Shores of sin / Cold gin / Mind rape. *(cd re-iss. Jul94 on 'Restless'; 772549-2)*

Geffen / Geffen

Apr 90. (cd/c/lp) *<(7599 24280-2/-4/-1)>* **ACT III**
– Seemingly endless time / Stop / Veil of deception / The organization / Discontinued / A room with a view / Stagnant / Ex-TC / Disturbing the peace / Falling asleep.

— split after above, GALEON was inactive due to an accident, while OSEGUEDA departed; they became The ORGANIZATION

– compilations, etc. –

Dec 90. (cd/c/lp) *Roadracer; (RO 9333-2/-4/-1) / Enigma; <73585>* **FALL FROM GRACE (live 1988)**
– Evil priest / Why you do this / Mistress of pain / Road mutants / Voracious souls / Confused / Bored / Kill as one / Guilty of innocence / Shores of sin / Final death.

ORGANIZATION

ROB CAVESTANY – vocals, guitar / **ANDY GALEON** – drums, vocals / **D. PEPA** – bass / **GUS PEPA** – guitar

Bulletproof / Metal Blade

Jul 94. (cd) *(CDVEST 23) <14023>* **THE ORGANIZATION** Nov93
– Free burning / Policy / Lit / Bringer / Brainstorm / Bottom dog / Wonder / Withdrawal / Past / Been nice.

May 95. (cd) *(CDVEST 50) <14086>* **SAVOR THE FLAVOR**
– Savor the flavor / So full of lies / Doomsday eve / A way today / Had a long today / The chase / War 25 / Begin a life / The drought / Insomnia / Stupid mood / By the time.

DEATH CULT (see under ⇒ CULT)

DEATH FOLK (see under ⇒ GERMS)

DEATH MASK

Formed: New York, USA ... 1985 by STEVEN MICHAELS, BENNY RANSOM, CHRIS EICHHORN and LEE NELSON. Hailing from a gang background, the various members of DEATH MASK unfortunately failed to translate their hard-bitten experience into vital, visceral music. Their one and only album (produced by JON-MIKL THOR), 'SPLIT THE ATOM' (1986) was a cliched set of heavy metal posturing, the group unsurprisingly fading back into obsurity soon after the record's release.

Album rating: SPLIT THE ATOM (*4)

STEVEN MICHAELS – vocals / **BENNY RANSOM** – guitar / **CHRIS EICHHORN** – bass / **LEE NELSON** – drums

Killerwatt / not iss.

Oct 86. (lp) *(KILP 4004)* **SPLIT THE ATOM**
– Split the atom / I'm dangerous / Reign / Lust for fire / Tortured mind / Nightmare (a lesson for the innocent) / Hell rider / Walk alone / Death has no boundaries / Commando.

— disappeared after above

DECEMBER MOON (see under ⇒ CRADLE OF FILTH)

DEDRINGER

Formed: Leeds, England . . . late 1977 by JOHN HOYLE, NEIL HUDSON, AL SCOTT, LEE FLAXINGTON and KENNY JONES. Building up a core grassroots following, the group eventually signed with 'Dindisc', releasing debut single and album in early '81, 'DIRECT LINE'. After the release of an EP, 'MAXINE', later that year, the band decided to call it a day. SCOTT, HUDSON and JONES subsequently reformed the group along with new members, NEIL GARFITT and CHRIS GRAHAM. Abandoning their earlier heavy rock approach for a more metallic sound in keeping with the burgeoning NWOBHM, DEDRINGER recorded a belated follow-up album, 'SECOND ARISING' (1983), for the 'Neat' label. The record failed to impress, however, and the group split shortly after.

Album rating: DIRECT LINE (*6) / SECOND ARISING (*4)

JOHN HOYLE – vocals / **NEIL HUDSON** – guitar / **AL SCOTT** – rhythm guitar / **LEE FLAXINGTON** – bass / **KENNY JONES** – drums

Dindisc / not iss.

Jan 81. (7") *(DIN 12)* **DIRECT LINE. / SHE'S NOT READY** -

Feb 81. (lp) *(DID 7)* **DIRECT LINE** -
– Direct line / She's not ready / So still / Maxine / High stool / Sunday drivers / First class tonight runaway.

Apr 81. (7"ep) *(DIN 11)* **MAXINE EP** -
– Maxine / Innocent till proven guilty / Took a long time / We don't mind.

— split in '81, **SCOTT, HUDSON + JONES** reformed the band with **NEIL GARFITT** – vocals / **CHRIS GRAHAM** – bass

Neat / not iss.

Nov 82. (7") *(NEAT 18)* **HOT LADY. / HOT LICKS / ROCK'N'ROLL** -

Jan 83. (lp) *(NEAT 1009)* **SECOND ARISING** -
– Rock night / Going to the movies / Sold me lonely / I'm on the outside / Donna / Comin' out fightin' / Throw me the line / Never gonna lose it / The eagle never waits.

— disbanded soon after above

DEEP PURPLE

Formed: London, England . . . 1968 intially as ROUNDABOUT, by former Searchers sticksman, CHRIS CURTIS. He duly recruited classically-trained organist, JON LORD and guitar maestro, RITCHIE BLACKMORE, who was living in Germany at the time. By Spring of that year, the band had become DEEP PURPLE with NICK SIMPER on bass and ROD EVANS on vocals. Their debut single, a cover of JOE SOUTH's 'HUSH', reached the US Top 5 and the band were subsequently furnished with a three album contract, signing with 'Tentagramme' in America (a label run by US comedian Bill Cosby!), 'Parlophone'in Britain. This line-up (known as Mk.I in DEEP PURPLE parlance) recorded three albums, 'SHADES OF DEEP PURPLE' (1968), 'BOOK OF TALIESYN' (1969) and the eponymous 'DEEP PURPLE' (1969), littered with chugging, proto-metal covers of the era's pop hits a la VANILLA FUDGE. Following the collapse of 'Tentagramme', the band signed with 'Warners', drafting in IAN GILLAN and ROGER GLOVER (both ex-EPISODE SIX) to replace EVANS and SIMPER respectively. The revamped line-up's first release was the pseudo-classical drivel of the live 'CONCERTO FOR GROUP AND ORCHESTRA WITH THE ROYAL PHILHARMONIC ORCHESTRA' (1970). Thankfully, after the record failed to sell in any great quantity, common sense prevailed and BLACKMORE steered the group in a heavier direction. 'IN ROCK', released later the same year, announced the arrival of a major contender in the heavyweight arena alongside the likes of BLACK SABBATH and LED ZEPPELIN. Preceded by the lumbering 'BLACK NIGHT' (No.2 in the UK) single, the album was dinosaur rock before the phrase was even coined; the pummelling rhythm section of GLOVER and PAICE driving the beast ever onward while BLACKMORE's razor sharp guitar solos clawed mercilessly at LORD's shuddering organ. 'CHILD IN TIME' was the ballad, the full range of GILLAN's talent on show as he progressed from mellow musings to his trademark glass-shattering shriek. While 'FIREBALL' (1971) was competent, if lacking in the songs department, 'MACHINE HEAD' (1972) was the DEEP PURPLE tour de force, the classic album from the classic Mk.II line-up. Cuts like 'HIGHWAY STAR' and 'SPACE TRUCKIN' were relentless, high-octane metal riff-athons which became staples in the DP live set for years to come. 'SMOKE ON THE WATER' probably stands as the band's most famous track, its classic three chord bludgeon and tale of disaster averted, reaching No.4 in America upon its release as a single a year later. This further boosted 'MACHINE HEAD's sales into the millions, DEEP PURPLE now firmly established as a world class act. The band also had a stellar live reputation, the concert double set, 'MADE IN JAPAN' (1972), going on to achieve cult status among metal afficiondos and earning the group a place in the Guiness Book Of Records as loudest band, woaargh!! As the heavy touring and recording schedule ground on, the beast began to stumble, however, recording a further, fairly lacklustre album, 'WHO DO WE THINK WE ARE' (1973), before disintegrating later that summer among constant in-fighting and personality clashes. BLACKMORE, LORD and PAICE remained, enlisting future WHITESNAKE vocalist DAVID COVERDALE on vocals and GLENN HUGHES (ex-TRAPEZE) in place of GLOVER to create DEEP PURPLE Mk.III. 'BURN' (1974) and 'STORMBRINGER' (1974) were characterised by COVERDALE's bluesy voice, although the new boy and BLACKMORE were not exactly fond of each other, the latter eventually quitting in 1975. His replacement was semi-legendary guitarist TOMMY BOLIN, who graced 'COME TASTE THE BAND' (1975). Less than a year later, however, DEEP PURPLE were no more, the behemoth finally going belly up after the perils of rock'n'roll had finally taken their toll. While BOLIN overdosed on heroin, of the remaining members, GLENN HUGHES reformed TRAPEZE while COVERDALE formed WHITESNAKE. BLACKMORE, meanwhile, had not been simply sitting around stuffing cucumbers down his pants and turning his amp up to 11, he had formed the rather grandiose-sounding RITCHIE BLACKMORE'S RAINBOW. The other key member of DEEP PURPLE, IAN GILLAN, had also been equally prolific during the 70's, initially with the IAN GILLAN BAND. A revamped DEEP PURPLE is where the paths of messrs. BLACKMORE, GILLAN, GLOVER, LORD and PAICE (the latter two had dabbled in solo and group work throughout the 70's – see discography) crossed once more. While the comeback album, 'PERFECT STRANGERS' (1984), was welcomed by fans, it became clear that the ever-dominant BLACKMORE was being as dominant as ever. After another relatively successful studio effort, 'HOUSE OF BLUE LIGHT' (1987), and a live album, GILLAN was given the order of the boot. Typically incestuous, DEEP PURPLE then recruited ex-RAINBOW man, JOE LYNN TURNER, for the awful 'SLAVES AND MASTERS' (1990) album. In an increasingly absurd round of musical

chairs, GILLAN was then reinstated, consequently clashing once more with BLACKMORE who eventually stomped off to reform RAINBOW. DEEP PURPLE lumbered on, recruiting STEVE MORSE for their 1996 album, 'PURPENDICULAR'. 'ABANDON' (1998) was another to disappoint their ever faithful support who were literally growing old and grey waiting for them to retire. If The ROLLING STONES are still rolling, some might say, what's to stop DEEP PURPLE? Well, considering The 'STONES have had around three line-up changes in their whole career while DEEP PURPLE have almost managed the same number for each album, the future doesn't look particularly promising. Then again, is anyone still listening? (my mate Russell, apparently!)
• **Songwriters:** Mk.I:-Mostly BLACKMORE / EVANS / LORD. Mk.II:- Group. Mk.III:- BLACKMORE / COVERDALE, adding at times LORD and PAICE. Mk.IV:- Permutate any two of COVERDALE, BOLIN or HUGHES. Covered HUSH (Joe South) / WE CAN WORK IT OUT + HELP (Beatles) / KENTUCKY WOMAN (Neil Diamond) / RIVER DEEP MOUNTAIN HIGH (Ike & Tina Turner) / HEY JOE (Jimi Hendrix) / I'M SO GLAD (Cream).
• **Trivia:** To obtain charity monies for the Armenian earthquake disaster late 1989, BLACKMORE, GILLAN and others (i.e. BRUCE DICKINSON, ROBERT PLANT, BRIAN MAY etc.) contributed to Top 40 new version of SMOKE ON THE WATER.

Album rating: SHADES OF DEEP PURPLE (*5) / THE BOOK OF TALIESYN (*4) / DEEP PURPLE (*4) / CONCERTO FOR GROUP AND ORCHESTRA (*1) / IN ROCK (*8) / FIREBALL (*7) / MACHINE HEAD (*9) / MADE IN JAPAN (*8) / WHO DO WE THINK WE ARE (*6) / BURN (*7) / STORMBRINGER (*5) / COME TASTE THE BAND (*6) / DEEPEST PURPLE compilation (*9) / PERFECT STRANGERS (*6) / HOUSE OF BLUE LIGHT (*5) / NOBODY'S PERFECT (*5) / SLAVES AND MASTERS (*4) / COME HELL OR HIGH WATER (*7) / PURPENDICULAR (*5) / ABANDON (*4)

RITCHIE BLACKMORE (b.14 Apr'45, Weston-Super-Mare, Avon, England) – guitar (ex-MANDRAKE ROOT, ex-OUTLAWS, ex-SCREAMING LORD SUTCH, etc.) / **JON LORD** (b.9 Jun'41, Leicester, England) – keyboards (ex-FLOWERPOT MEN) / **NICK SIMPER** (b. 1946, Southall, London) – bass (ex-JOHNNY KIDD & PIRATES) / **ROD EVANS** (b. 1945, Edinburgh, Scotland) – vocals (ex-MAZE, ex-MI5) / **IAN PAICE** (b.29 Jun'48, Nottingham, England) – drums (ex-MAZE, ex-MI5)

Parlophone Tetragramme

Jun 68. (7") *(R 5708) <1503>* **HUSH. / ONE MORE RAINY DAY** [ ] [4]
Sep 68. (lp) *(PCS 7055) <102>* **SHADES OF DEEP PURPLE** [ ] [24]
– And the address / Hush / One more rainy day / (prelude) Happiness – I'm so glad / Mandrake root / Help / Love help me / Hey Joe. *(re-iss. Feb77 on 'EMI Harvest'; SHSM 2016) (cd-iss. Mar89; CZ 170) (cd-iss. Feb95 on 'Fame'; CDFA 3314) (lp re-iss. Nov97 on 'E.M.I.'; LPCENT 25) (cd re-mast.Feb00 on 'Liberty'; 498336-2)*
Nov 68. (7") *<1508>* **KENTUCKY WOMAN. / HARD ROAD** [-] [38]
Nov 68. (7") *(R 5745)* **KENTUCKY WOMAN. / WRING THAT NECK** [ ] [-]
Jan 69. (7") *<1514>* **RIVER DEEP – MOUNTAIN HIGH. / LISTEN, LEARN, READ ON** [-] [53]
Feb 69. (7") *(R 5763)* **EMMARETTA. / WRING THAT NECK** [ ] [-]
Apr 69. (7") *<1519>* **EMMARETTA. / THE BIRD HAS FLOWN** [-] [ ]

Harvest Tetragramme

Jun 69. (lp/c) *(SHVL/TC-SHVL 751) <107>* **BOOK OF TALIESYN** [ ] [54] Jan69
– Listen, learn, read on / Wring that neck / Kentucky woman / Shield / a) Exposition – b) We can work it out / The shield / Anthem / River deep, mountain high. *(re-iss. Jun85 on 'EMI';) (cd-iss. Aug89; CDP 792408-2) (cd re-iss. Feb96 on 'Premier'; CZ 171) (cd re-mast.Feb00 on 'Liberty'; 521608-2)*
Nov 69. (lp) *(SHVL 759) <119>* **DEEP PURPLE** [ ] [ ] Jul69
– Chasing shadows / Blind / Lalena: (a) Faultline, (b) The painter / Why didn't Rosemary? / The bird has flown / April. *(re-iss. Jun85 on 'EMI';) (cd-iss. Mar89; CZ 172) (re-iss. cd May95 on 'Fame'; CDFA 3317) (cd re-mast.Feb00 on 'Liberty'; 521597-2)*

—— (In Jun'69 below two were used on session for 'HALLELUJAH'. They became regular members after the recording of 'DEEP PURPLE' album.) / **IAN GILLAN** (b.19 Aug'45, Hounslow, London) – vocals (ex-EPISODE SIX) replaced EVANS who joined CAPTAIN BEYOND. / **ROGER GLOVER** (b.30 Nov'45, Brecon, Wales) – bass (ex-EPISODE SIX) replaced SIMPER who later formed WARHORSE

Jul 69. (7") *(HAR 5006) <1537>* **HALLELUJAH (I AM THE PREACHER). / APRIL (part 1)** [ ] [ ]

Harvest Warners

Jan 70. (lp/c) *(SHVL/TC-SHVL 767) <1860>* **CONCERTO FOR GROUP AND ORCHESTRA WITH THE ROYAL PHILHARMONIC ORCHESTRA (live)** [26] [ ] May70
– First Movement: Moderato – Allegro / Second Movement: Andante (part 1) – Andante conclusion / Third Movement: Vivace – Presto. *(cd-iss. Aug90 on 'E.M.I.'+=; CZ 342)* – Wring that neck / Child in time.
Jun 70. (7") *(HAR 5020)* **BLACK NIGHT. / SPEED KING** [2] [-]
Jun 70. (lp/c) *(SHVL/TC-SHVL 777) <1877>* **DEEP PURPLE IN ROCK** [4] [ ] Sep70
– Speed king / Blood sucker / Child in time / Flight of the rat / Into the fire / Living wreck / Hard lovin' man. *(re-iss. May82 on 'Fame' lp/c; FA/TC-FA 3011) (cd-iss. Apr88; CDFA 3011) (pic-lp.Jun85; EJ 2603430) (purple-lp iss.1995 on 'E.M.I.'; 7243-8-34019-8) (with free-lp)* – Black night / Speed king (piano version) / Cry free (Roger Glover remix) / Jam stew / Flight of the rat (Roger Glover remix) / Speed king (Roger Glover remix) / Black night (Roger Glover remix).
Jul 70. (7") *<7405>* **BLACK NIGHT. / INTO THE FIRE** [-] [66]
Feb 71. (7") *(HAR 5033) <7493>* **STRANGE KIND OF WOMAN. / I'M ALONE** [6] [ ]
Sep 71. (lp/c) *(SHVL/TC-SHVL 793) <2564>* **FIREBALL** [1] [32] Aug71
– Fireball / No no no / Demon's eye / Anyone's daughter / The mule / Fools / No one came. *(re-iss. Mar84 on 'Fame' lp/c; FA/TC-FA 41-3093-1/-4) (re-iss. Aug87 lp/c; ATAK/TC-ATAK 105) (re-iss. Oct87 on 'E.M.I.' lp/c; EMS/TC-EMS 1255) (cd-iss. Jan88 on 'E.M.I.'; CZ 30) (pic-lp.Jun85 on 'E.M.I.'; EJ 2403440) (lp re-iss. 1996 on 'E.M.I.'; 7243-8-53711-0) (with free lp)* – Strange kind of woman (remix '96) / I'm alone / Freedom (session out-take) / Slow train (session out-take) / Midnight in Moscow – Robin Hood – William Tell – Fireball (the noise abatement) / Backwards piano / No one came (remix '96).
Oct 71. (7") *(HAR 5045)* **FIREBALL. / DEMON'S EYE** [15] [-]
Nov 71. (7") *<7528>* **FIREBALL. / I'M ALONE** [-] [ ]

Purple Warners

Mar 72. (7") *(PUR 102) <7572>* **NEVER BEFORE. / WHEN A BLIND MAN CRIES** [35] [ ]
Apr 72. (lp/c) *(TPSA/TC-TPSA 7504) <2607>* **MACHINE HEAD** [1] [7]
– Highway star / Maybe I'm a Leo / Pictures of home / Never before / Smoke on the water / Lazy / Space truckin'. *(re-iss. Jun85 on 'E.M.I.' lp/c; ATAK/TC-ATAK 39) (re-iss. Oct86 on 'Fame' lp/c; FA/TC-FA 3158) (cd-iss. Mar87 on 'E.M.I.'; CZ 83) (cd re-iss. Mar89; CDFA 3158) (re-iss. Sep97 on 'E.M.I.' d-cd/d-lp; CD+/DEEPP 3)*
Jun 72. (7") *<7595>* **LAZY. / WHEN A BLIND MAN CRIES** [-] [ ]
Oct 72. (7") *<7634>* **HIGHWAY STAR. / (part 2)** [-] [ ]
Dec 72. (d-lp/d-c) *(TPSP/TC2-TPSP 351) <2701>* **MADE IN JAPAN (live)** [16] [6] Apr73
– Highway star / Child in time / Smoke on the water / The mule / Strange kind of woman / Lazy / Space truckin'. *(cd-iss. Sep88 on 'E.M.I.'; CDTPS 351) (re-iss. Oct92 on 'Fame' cd/c; CD/TC FA 3268) (re-iss. Jan98 on 'E.M.I.' cd/lp; 857864-2/-4)* – hit No.73
Feb 73. (lp/c) *(TPSA/TC-TPSA 7508) <2678>* **WHO DO YOU THINK WE ARE!** [4] [15] Jan73
– Woman from Tokyo / Mary Long / Super trouper / Smooth dancer / Rat bat blue / Place in line / Our lady. *(re-iss. Jun85 on 'E.M.I.' lp/c; ATAK/TC-ATAK 127) (cd-iss. Oct87 on 'E.M.I.'; CZ 6) (cd re-iss. Dec94 on 'Fame'; CDFA 3311) (cd re-iss. Jul00 on 'E.M.I.'+=; 521607-2)* – (the 1999 remixes).
Apr 73. (7") *<7672>* **WOMAN FROM TOKYO. / SUPER TROUPER** [-] [80]
May 73. (7") *<7710>* **SMOKE ON THE WATER. / (part 2)** [-] [4]
Sep 73. (7") *<7737>* **WOMAN FROM TOKYO. / SUPER TROOPER** [-] [60]

—— **BLACKMORE, LORD** and **PAICE** brought in new members / **DAVID COVERDALE** (b.22 Sep'49, Saltburn-by-the-sea, Cleveland, England) – vocals replaced GILLAN who later formed own band. / **GLENN HUGHES** (b.Penkridge, England) – bass (ex-TRAPEZE) repl. GLOVER who became top producer.

Feb 74. (lp/c) *(TPS/TC-TPS 3505) <2766>* **BURN** [3] [9]
– Burn / Might just take your life / Lay down stay down / Sail away / You fool no one / What's goin' on here / Mistreated / "A" 200. *(re-iss. Mar84 on 'E.M.I.' lp/c; ATAK/TC-ATAK 11) (cd-iss. Jul89; CZ 203)*
Mar 74. (7") *(PUR 117) <7784>* **MIGHT JUST TAKE YOUR LIFE. / CORONARIAS REDIG** [ ] [91]
May 74. (7") *<7809>* **BURN. / CORONARIAS REDIG** [-] [ ]
Nov 74. (lp/c) *(TPS/TC-TPS 3508) <2832>* **STORMBRINGER** [6] [20]
– Stormbringer / Love don't mean a thing / Holy man / Hold on / Lady double dealer / You can't do it right (with the one you love) / High ball shooter / The gypsy / Soldier of fortune. *(re-iss. Jun85 on 'E.M.I.' lp/c; ATAK/TC-ATAK 70) (cd-iss. Oct88 on 'E.M.I.'; CZ 142)*
Nov 74. (7") *<8049>* **HIGH BALL SHOOTER. / YOU CAN'T DO IT RIGHT** [-] [ ]
Jan 75. (7") *<8069>* **STORMBRINGER. / LOVE DON'T MEAN A THING** [-] [ ]

—— **TOMMY BOLIN** (b.1951, Sioux City, Iowa, USA) – guitar (ex-JAMES GANG, ex-ZEPHYR) repl. BLACKMORE who formed RAINBOW. (see further below)

Oct 75. (lp/c) *(TPSA/TC-TPSA 7515) <2895>* **COME TASTE THE BAND** [19] [43]
– Comin' home / Lady luck / Gettin' together / Dealer / I need love / Drifter / Love child / This time around – Owed to the 'G' / You keep on moving. *(re-iss. Jun85 on 'E.M.I.' lp/c;) (cd-iss. Jul90 on 'E.M.I.'; CZ 343) (cd re-iss. Jul95 on 'Fame'; CDFA 3318)*
Mar 76. (7") *(PUR 130)* **YOU KEEP ON MOVING. / LOVE CHILD** [ ] [-]
Mar 76. (7") *<8182>* **GETTIN' TIGHTER. / LOVE CHILD** [-] [ ]
Nov 76. (lp/c) *(TPSA/TC-TPSA 7517) <2995>* **MADE IN EUROPE (live)** [12] [ ]
<US title 'DEEP PURPLE LIVE'>
– Burn / Mistreated (interpolating 'Rock me baby') / Lady double dealer / You fool no one / Stormbringer. *(cd-iss. Jul90 on 'E.M.I.'; CZ 344)*

—— split Spring 76, TOMMY BOLIN went solo. He died (of an overdose) 4th Dec'76. HUGHES reformed TRAPEZE. COVERDALE formed WHITESNAKE, he was later joined by LORD and PAICE, after they had been in PAICE, ASHTON and LORD. Remarkably **DEEP PURPLE** reformed 8 years later with early 70's line-up. **GILLAN, BLACKMORE, LORD, PAICE** and **GLOVER.**

Polydor Mercury

Nov 84. (lp/pic-lp/c) *(POLH/+P/C 16) <824003>* **PERFECT STRANGERS** [5] [17]
– Knocking at your back door / Under the gun / Nobody's home / Mean streak / Perfect strangers / A gypsy's kiss / Wasted sunsets / Hungry daze. *(c+=)* – Not responsible. *(re-iss. Mar91 cd/c/lp; 823777-2/-4/-1) (cd re-mast.Aug99; 546045-2)*
Jan 85. (7"/7"pic-d) *(POSP/+P 719)* **PERFECT STRANGERS. / SON OF ALERIK** [48] [ ] Mar85
(12"+=) *(POSPX 719)* – Wasted sunsets / Hungry daze.
Jun 85. (7"/12") *(POSP/+X 749) <880477>* **KNOCKING AT YOUR BACK DOOR. / PERFECT STRANGERS** [68] [61] Jan85
Jan 87. (lp/c)(cd) *(POLH/+C 32)(<831318-2>)* **THE HOUSE OF BLUE LIGHT** [10] [34]
– Bad attitude / The unwritten law / Call of the wild / Mad dog / Black and white / Hard lovin' woman / The Spanish archer / Strangeways / Mitzi Dupree / Dead or alive. *(re-iss. Mar91 lp/c; 831318-1/-4) (cd re-mast.Aug99; 546162-2)*
Jan 87. (7"/7"pic-d) *(POSP/+P 843)* **CALL OF THE WILD. / STRANGEWAYS** [ ] [ ]
(12") *(POSPX 843)* – ('A'side) / ('B'-long version).
Jun 88. (7") *(PO 4)* **HUSH (live). / DEAD OR ALIVE (live)** [62] [ ]
(12"+=/cd-s+=) *(PZ/+CD 4)* – Bad attitude (live).
Jun 88. (d-lp/d-c)(cd) *(PODV/+C 10)(<835897-2>)* **NOBODY'S PERFECT (live)** [38] [ ]
– Highway star / Strange kind of woman / Perfect strangers / Hard lovin' woman / Knocking at your back door / Child in time / Lazy / Black night / Woman from Tokyo / Smoke on the water / Hush. *(d-lp has extra tracks) (re-iss. Mar91 d-lp/d-c; 835897-1/-4) (cd re-mast.Aug99; 546128-2)*

—— **JOE LYNN TURNER** – vocals (ex-RAINBOW, ex-YNGWIE MALMSTEEN'S RISING FORCE) repl. GILLAN who continued solo.

R.C.A. R.C.A.

Oct 90. (7") <c-s> *(PB 49247) <2703>* **KING OF DREAMS. / FIRE IN THE BASEMENT** [70] [ ]
(12"+=/cd-s+=) *(PT/PD 49248)* – ('A'-album version).
Nov 90. (cd/c/lp) *(PD/PK/PL 90535) <2421>* **SLAVES AND MASTERS** [45] [87]
– King of dreams / The cut runs deep / Fire in the basement / Truth hurts / Breakfast

in bed / Love conquers all / Fortuneteller / Too much is not enough / Wicked ways. *(re-iss. cd Apr94; 74321 18719-2)*

Feb 91. (7"/c-s) *(PB/PK 49225)* **LOVE CONQUERS ALL. / TRUTH HURTS** [57] [ ]
(12"+=)(12"pic-d+=)(cd-s+=) *(PT 49212)(PT 49224)(PD 49226)* – Slow down sister.

— early 70s line-up again after TURNER was sacked.

R.C.A. Giant

Jul 93. (cd/c/lp) *(74321 15240-2/-4/-1) <24517>* **THE BATTLE RAGES ON** [21] [ ]
– The battle rages on / Lick it up / Anya / Talk about love / Time to kill / Ramshackle man / A twist in the tale / Nasty piece of work / Solitaire / One man's meat. *(re-iss. cd Oct95; same)*

Arista Arista

Nov 94. (cd/c/d-lp) *(<74321 23416-2/-4/-1>)* **COME HELL OR HIGH WATER (live mid-93)** [ ] [ ]
– Highway star / Black night / Twist in the tail / Perfect strangers / Anyone's daughter / Child in time / Anya / Speed king / Smoke on the water.

— **STEVE MORSE** – guitar (ex-DIXIE DREGS) repl. JOE SATRIANI who repl. BLACKMORE on European tour late '93-mid '94

R.C.A. C.M.C.

Feb 96. (cd/c) *(74321 33802-2/-4) <86201>* **PURPENDICULAR** [58] [ ]
– Vavoom: Ted the mechanic / Loosen my strings / Soon forgotten / Sometimes I feel like screaming / Cascades: I'm not your lover / The aviator / Rosa's cantina / A castle full of rascals / A touch away / Hey Cisco / Somebody stole my guitar / The purpendicular waltz.

May 98. (cd) *(495306-2) <86250>* **ABANDON** [ ] [ ]
– Any fule kno that / Almost human / Don't make me happy / Seventh heaven / Watching the sky / Fingers to the bone / Jack Ruby / She was / Whatsername / 69 / Evil Louie / Bludsucker.

– compilations, exploitation releases, etc. –

Sep 72. (d-lp) *Warners; <2644>* **PURPLE PASSAGES** [-] [57]

Oct 72. (7") *Warners;* **HUSH. / KENTUCKY WOMAN** [-] [ ]

1972. (lp) *Citation; <CTN 18010>* **THE BEST OF DEEP PURPLE** [-] [ ]

Jun 75. (lp/c) *Purple; (TPSM/TC-TPSM 2002)* **24 CARAT PURPLE (1970-73)** [14] [-]
– Woman from Tokyo / Fireball / Strange kind of woman / Never before / Black night / Speed king / Smoke on the water / Child in time. *(re-iss. Sep85 on 'Fame' lp/c; FA41 3132-1/-4) (cd-iss. Oct87; CDFA 3132)*

Mar 77. (7"m,7"purple) *Purple; (PUR 132)* **SMOKE ON THE WATER. / CHILD IN TIME / WOMAN FROM TOKYO** [21] [ ]

Sep 77. (7"ep) *Purple; (PUR 135)* **NEW LIVE & RARE** [31] [ ]
– Black night (live) / Painted horse / When a blind man cries.

Jan 78. (lp/c) *Purple; (TPS 3510)* **POWERHOUSE** (early 70's line-up) [ ] [-]

Sep 78. (7"ep) *Purple; (PUR 137)* **NEW LIVE & RARE VOL.2** [45] [ ]
– Burn (edit) / Coronarias redig / Mistreated (live).

Oct 78. (lp/c) *Harvest; (SHSM 2026)* **THE SINGLES A's & B's** [ ] [-]
(re-iss. Nov88 on 'Fame' cd/c/lp; CD/TC+/FA 3212) (cd-iss. Jan93 on 'E.M.I.'; TCEMC 3658)

Apr 79. (lp/c) *Purple; (TPS/TC-TPS 3514)* **THE MARK II PURPLE SINGLES** [24] [ ]

Apr 79. (7"/12") *Harvest; (HAR 5178)* **BLACK NIGHT. / STRANGE KIND OF WOMAN** [ ] [ ]

Jul 80. (lp/c) *E.M.I.; (EMTV/TC-EMTV 25) / Warners; <3486>* **DEEPEST PURPLE** [1] [ ] Oct80
– Black night / Speed king / Fireball / Strange kind of woman / Child in time / Woman from Tokyo / Highway star / Space truckin' / Burn / Demon's eye / Stormbringer / Smoke on the water. *(cd-iss. Aug84; CDP 746032-2) (re-iss. 1989 lp/c; ATAK/TC-ATAK 138) (re-iss. Jul90 on 'Fame' cd/c/lp; CD/TC+/FA 3239) (cd re-iss. Aug00 on 'Harvest'; CDP 746032-2)*

Jul 80. (7") *Harvest; (HAR 5210)* **BLACK NIGHT. / SPEED KING (live)** [43] [-]

Oct 80. (7"ep) *Harvest; (SHEP 101)* **NEW LIVE & RARE VOL.3** [48] [ ]
– Smoke on the water (live) / The bird has flown / Grabsplatter.

Dec 80. (lp/c) *Harvest; (SHDW 412)* **IN CONCERT 1970-1972 (live)** [30] [ ]
– Speed king / Wring that neck / Child in time / Mandrake root / Highway star / Strange kind of woman / Lazy / Never before / Space truckin' / Lucille. *(cd-iss. May92;)*

Aug 82. (lp/c) *Harvest; (SHSP/TC-SHSP 4124)* **DEEP PURPLE LIVE IN LONDON (live '74)** [23] [ ]
– Burn / Might just take your life / Lay down, stay down / Mistreated / Smoke on the water / You fool no one.

Jun 85. (d-lp/d-c) *Harvest; (PUR/TC-PUR 1)* **THE ANTHOLOGY** [50] [ ]
(d-cd iss.Mar91 on 'E.M.I.'; CDEM 1374)

Nov 87. (lp/c/cd) *Telstar; (STAR/STAC/TCD 2312)* **THE BEST OF DEEP PURPLE** [ ] [-]

Oct 88. (d-lp/d-c/d-cd) *Connoisseur; (DPVSOP LP/MC/CD 125)* **SCANDINAVIAN NIGHTS (live)** [ ] [-]
(d-cd re-iss. Aug99; same)

Mar 91. (d-cd/d-c/t-lp) *E.M.I.; (CD/TC+/EM 5013)* **THE ANTHOLOGY** [ ] [ ]

Aug 91. (d-cd/d-c/d-lp) *Connoisseur; (DPVSOP CD/MC/LP 163)* **IN THE ABSENCE OF PINK (KNEBWORTH '85 live)** [ ] [-]

Sep 91. (cd/c/lp) *Polgram TV; (845534-2/-4/-1)* **PURPLE RAINBOWS** [ ] [-]
– (all work including RAINBOW, GILLAN, WHITESNAKE, etc.)

Apr 92. (cd/c) *Polygram; (511438-2/-4)* **KNOCKING AT YOUR BACK DOOR** [ ] [-]

May 93. (cd/c) *Spectrum; (550027-2/-4)* **PROGRESSION** [ ] [-]

Jul 93. (cd) *Connoisseur; (VSOPCD 187)* **THE DEEP PURPLE FAMILY ALBUM** (associated releases) [ ] [-]

Nov 93. (3xcd-box) *E.M.I.; (CDEM 1510)* **LIVE IN JAPAN (live)** [ ] [-]

May 95. (d-cd) *Connoisseur; (DPVSOPCD 217)* **ON THE WINGS OF A RUSSIAN FOXBAT – LIVE IN CALIFORNIA 1976** [ ] [-]

Jun 95. (12"/cd-s) *E.M.I.; (CD/12 EM 382)* **BLACK NIGHT (remix). / SPEED KING (remix)** [66] [-]

Sep 95. (cd) *Spectrum; (551339-2)* **CHILD IN TIME** [ ] [-]

Nov 95. (3xcd-box) *E.M.I.; (CDOMB 002)* **BOOK OF TALIESYN / SHADES OF DEEP PURPLE / DEEP PURPLE IN CONCERT** [ ] [-]

May 96. (cd) *Premier; (PRMUCD 2)* **CALIFORNIA JAMMING** [ ] [-]

Jul 96. (3xcd-box) *Connoisseur; (DPVSOPCD 230)* **THE FINAL CONCERTS (live)** [ ] [-]

Feb 97. (cd) *EMI Gold; (CDGOLD 1060) / Disky; <DC 878642>* **THE COLLECTION** [ ] [ ] Mar97

Jun 97. (d-cd) *E.M.I.; (CDEM 1615)* **LIVE AT THE OLYMPIA (live)** [ ] [ ]

Jul 98. (cd) *Camden; (74321 59737-2)* **PURPLEXED** [ ] [-]

Oct 98. (cd/c/d-lp) *E.M.I.; (496807-2/-4/-1)* **THE VERY BEST OF** [39] [ ]
– Hush / Black night / Speed king / Child in time / Strange kind of woman / Fireball / Demon's eye / Smoke on the water / Highway star / When a blind man cries / Never before / Woman from Tokyo / Burn / Stormbringer / You keep on moving / Perfect strangers / Ted the mechanic / Any fule know that. *(d-cd-iss. ; 496808-2)*

Nov 98. (4xcd-box) *Connoisseur; (DPBOX 400)* **ON THE ROAD (live)** [ ] [-]

Jan 00. (d-cd) *Eagle; (EDGCD 124) / Spitfire; <15068>* **LIVE AT THE ROYAL ALBERT HALL with The London Symphony Orchestra** [ ] [ ]

Feb 00. (cd) *Liberty; (495635-2)* **IN PROFILE** [ ] [-]

Apr 00. (cd) *Spectrum; (544204-2)* **UNDER THE GUN** [7-] [ ]

Apr 00. (cd) *Purple; (PUR 303)* **DAYS MAY COME AND DAYS MAY GO (THE CALIFORNIA REHEARSALS JUNE 1975)** [ ] [ ]

Sep 00. (3xcd-box) *E.M.I.; 528344-2)* **SHADES OF / BOOK OF TALIESYN / DEEP PURPLE** [ ] [-]

Sep 00. (cd) *EMI Gold; (528512-2)* **ANTHEMS** [ ] [-]

JON LORD

solo (first 3 albums while still a **DEEP PURPLE** member) with the **LONDON SYMPHONY ORCHESTRA** and guests.

Purple not iss.

Apr 72. (lp) *(TPSA 7501)* **GEMINI SUITE** [ ] [-]
– Guitar / Piano / Drums / Vocals / Bass guitar / Organ. *(re-iss. Nov84 on 'Safari' lp/c; LONG/+C 10) (cd-iss. Jul93 as 'THE GEMINI SUITE LIVE 1970' on 'R.P.M.'; RPM 114) (cd re-iss. May99 on 'Purple'; PUR 304) (cd re-iss. May99 on 'Cleopatra'; CLEO 2342)*

— now with the MUNICH CHAMBER OPERA ORCHESTRA and guests

Apr 74. (lp) *(TPSA 7513)* **WINDOWS** [ ] [-]
– Continuo on B.A.C.H. / Windows: Renga – Gemini – Alla Marcia – Allegro.

ASHTON & LORD

ASHTON – keyboards, vocals (ex-ASHTON GARDNER and DYKE, ex-FAMILY, ex-REMO FOUR, ex-CHRIS FARLOWE)

Purple Warners

Apr 74. (lp) *(TPSA 3507) <2778>* **FIRST OF THE BIG BANDS** [ ] [ ]
– We're gonna make it / I've been lonely / Silly boy / The jam / Downside upside down / Shut up / Ballad of Mr.Giver / Celebration / The resurrection shuffle. *(cd-iss. Jun93 on 'Windsong'; WINCD 033) (cd re-iss. Oct94 on 'Line'; 900119)*

May 74. (7") *(PUR 121)* **WE'RE GONNA MAKE IT. / BAND OF THE SALVATION ARMY BAND** [ ] [-]

JON LORD

solo again, plus guests.

Sep 76. (7") *(PUR 131)* **BOUREE. / ARIA** [ ] [-]

Nov 76. (lp) *(TPSA 7516)* **SARABANDE (live)** [ ] [-]
– Fantasia / Sarabande / Aria / Gigue / Bouree / Pavane / Caprice / Finale. *(cd-iss. 1989 & Sep94 on 'Line'; LICD 900124)*

PAICE, ASHTON and LORD

formed Aug76 and recruited **BERNIE MARSDEN** – guitar (ex-BABE RUTH) / **PAUL MARTINEZ** – bass (ex-STRETCH)

Oyster Warners

Feb 77. (lp) *(2391 269) <BS 3088>* **MALICE IN WONDERLAND** [ ] [ ]
– Ghost story / Remember the good times / Arabella / Silas and Jerome / Dance with me baby / On the road again, again / Sneaky Private Lee / I'm gonna stop drinking / Malice in Wonderland. *(re-iss. Nov80 on 'Polydor'; 2482 485) (cd-iss. Jul95 on 'Repertoire';)*

– other recording, etc. –

Sep 92. (cd) *Windsong; (WINCD 025)* **BBC RADIO 1 IN CONCERT (live)** [ ] [-]
(re-iss. Jul97 on 'Strange Fruit'; SFRSCD 030)

— When this bunch split up MARTINEZ joined JOHN OTWAY and more sessions. ASHTON became noted producer. MARSDEN was followed by LORD and then PAICE into WHITESNAKE.

JON LORD

and more solo work. (with **MARSDEN, PAICE, NEIL MUNRO, COZY POWELL** and **BAD COMPANY** most of group.

Harvest not iss.

May 82. (7") *(JAR 5220)* **BACH INTO THIS. / GOING HOME** [ ] [-]

Jul 82. (lp) *(SHSP 4123)* **BEFORE I FORGET** [ ] [-]
– Chance on a feeling / Tender babes / Hollywood rock and roll / Bach onto this / Before I forget / Say it's alright / Burntwood / Where are you. *(cd-iss. Mar93 on 'R.P.M.'; RPM 126)*

Safari not iss.

Mar 84. (lp/c) *(DIARY/+C 1)* **COUNTRY DIARY OF AN EDWARDIAN LADY** [ ] [-]

Mar 84. (7") *(SAFE 60)* **COUNTRY DIARY OF AN EDWARDIAN LADY. /** [ ] [-]

DEF LEPPARD

Formed: Sheffield, England . . . 1977 as ATOMIC MASS by RICK SAVAGE, PETE WILLIS and TONY KENNING. Frontman JOE ELLIOT came into the picture not long after and the band adopted the name DEAF LEOPARD, soon altering it to the more rock'n'roll DEF LEPPARD. Additional guitarist STEVE CLARK joined in time for the band's first gigs in July 1978, while FRANK NOON replaced KENNING on drums prior to the band recording their first single. With finance provided by ELLIOT's father, the group issued a debut EP on their own label, 'Bludgeon Riffola', entitled 'GETCHA ROCKS OFF' (was the young BOBBY GILLESPIE a fan, perchance?). Later that year (1979), with RICK ALLEN taking up permanent residence on the drum stool, and following tours supporting AC/DC etc., the band were signed to 'Vertigo'. This prompted a move to London and in 1980, their debut album, 'ON THROUGH THE NIGHT', broke the UK Top 20 although it would be America that would initially embrace the band. They were certainly metal, albeit metal of the most easy listening variety and while the critics hated them, their growing army of fans lapped up their every release. Although 'HIGH 'N' DRY' (1981) marked the beginning of their association with MUTT LANGE and was far more assured in terms of songwriting, DEF LEPPARD's big break came with 1983's 'PYROMANIA'. Legendary for its use of all manner of studio special effects and state-of-the-art technology, the record revolutionised heavy metal and became the benchmark by which subsequent 80's albums were measured. Yet it wasn't a case (as it so often is) of studio flash masking a dearth of genuine talent, DEF LEPPARD were actually capable of turning out finely crafted songs over the course of a whole album. Highly melodic and relentlessly hook-laden, the Americans loved 'PYROMANIA' and its attendant singles, 'PHOTOGRAPH', and 'ROCK OF AGES', the album selling over 7 million copies. Tragedy struck, however, when RICK ALLEN lost his arm in a car crash on New Year's Eve 1984. A true metal warrior, ALLEN soldiered bravely on using a customised drum kit with programmable drum pads and foot pedals. Bearing in mind ALLEN's accident and the band's perfectionist nature, four years wasn't too long to wait for a new album, and for the majority of fans the delay was well worth it. A melodic rock tour de force, the album finally broke the band in their home country with three of its attendant singles reaching the UK Top 10, 'LOVE BITES' giving the band their first No.1. Similarly successful across the Atlantic and worldwide, the album sold a staggering amount, DEF LEPPARD staking their claim as the biggest heavy metal act on the planet. Ironically, just as the group were entering the big league, tragedy struck again as STEVE CLARK was found dead in January 1991 after a prolonged drink/drugs binge. The band recruited elder statesman of rock, VIVIAN CAMPBELL, as a replacement and began work on the 'ADRENALIZE' (1992) album. While the likes of single, 'LET'S GET ROCKED' bordered on the cringeworthy (if only for the awful title), the album's glossy pop-metal once again pulled in the punters in their millions. The next few years saw the release of a B-sides/rareties affair, 'RETRO ACTIVE' (1993) and greatest hits collection, 'VAULT' (1995). A new studio set, 'SLANG', eventually graced the racks in 1996, showcasing a more modern sound (ELLIOT had even traded in his poodle mane for a relatively trendy bobbed haircut). A record executive's wet dream, DEF LEPPARD remain radio friendly unit shifters in the true sense of the phrase. • **Songwriters:** Group compositions, except ONLY AFTER DARK (Mick Ronson) / ACTION (Sweet) / YOU CAN'T ALWAYS GET WHAT YOU WANT (Rolling Stones) / LITTLE WING (Jimi Hendrix) / ELECTED (Alice Cooper) / ZIGGY STARDUST (David Bowie). Roadie STUMPUS MAXIMUS sung; PLEASE RELEASE ME (Engelbert Humperdinck).

Album rating: ON THROUGH THE NIGHT (*5) / HIGH 'N' DRY (*6) / PYROMANIA (*7) / HYSTERIA (*7) / ADRENALIZE (*6) / RETROACTIVE compilation (*5) / VAULT 1980-1995 – DEF LEPPARD'S GREATEST HITS compilation (*8) / SLANG (*5) / EUPHORIA (*5)

JOE ELLIOT (b. 1 Aug'59) – vocals / **PETE WILLIS** – lead guitar / **STEVE CLARK** (b.23 Apr'60) – guitar / **RICK SAVAGE** (b. 2 Dec'60) – bass / **FRANK NOON** – drums

Bludgeon Riffola | not iss.

Jan 79. (7"ep) *(SRT-CUS 232)* **THE DEF LEPPARD EP** [ ] [-]
– Ride into the sun / Getcha rocks off / The overture.

Feb 79. (7"m) *(MSB 001)* **RIDE INTO THE SUN / GETCHA ROCKS OFF / THE OVERTURE** [ ] [-]

—— **RICK ALLEN** (b. 1 Nov'63) – drums; repl. FRANK who later joined LIONHEART, then WAYSTED

Vertigo | Mercury

Aug 79. (7"m) *(6059 240)* **GETCHA ROCKS OFF. / RIDE INTO THE SUN / THE OVERTURE** [ ] [-]

Nov 79. (7") *(6059 247)* **WASTED. / HELLO AMERICA** [61] [ ]

Feb 80. (7") *(LEPP 1)* **HELLO AMERICA. / GOOD MORNING FREEDOM** [45] [ ]

Mar 80. (lp)(c) *(9102 040)(7231 028)* <3828> **ON THROUGH THE NIGHT** [15] [51]
– Rock brigade / Hello America / Sorrow is a woman / It could be you / Satellite / When the walls come tumblin' down / Wasted / Rocks off / It don't matter / Answer to the master / Overture. *(re-iss. Jan89 lp/c/cd; 822533-1/-4/-2)*

Jun 80. (7") <76064> **ROCK BRIGADE. / WHEN THE WALLS COME TUMBLIN' DOWN** [-] [ ]

Jul 81. (lp/c) *(6359/7150 045)* <4021> **HIGH 'N' DRY** [26] [38]
– High 'n' dry (Saturday night) / You got me runnin' / Let it go / Another hit and run / Lady Strange / Mirror, mirror (look into my eyes) / No no no / Bringin' on the heartbreak / Switch 625. *<US re-iss. May84 +=; 818836>* – Bringin' on the heartbreak (remix) / Me and my wine. *(re-iss. Jan89 lp/c/cd+=; 818836-1/-4/-2)* – You got me runnin' (remix) / Me and my wine.

Aug 81. (7") *(LEPP 2)* <76120> **LET IT GO. / SWITCH 625** [ ] [ ]

Jan 82. (7") *(LEPP 3)* **BRINGIN' ON THE HEARTACHE (remix). / ME AND MY WINE** [ ] [-]
(12"+=) *(LEPP 3-12)* – You got me runnin'.

—— **PHIL COLLEN** (b. 8 Dec'57) – lead guitar (ex-GIRL) repl. PETE

Jan 83. (7") *(VER 5)* <811215> **PHOTOGRAPH. / BRINGIN' ON THE HEARTBREAK** [66] [-]
(12"+=) *(VERX 5)* – Mirror, Mirror (look into my eyes).

Feb 83. (7") <811215> **PHOTOGRAPH. / ACTION! NOT WORDS** [-] [12]

Mar 83. (lp/c) *(VERS/+C 2)* <810308> **PYROMANIA** [18] [2] Jan83
– Rock! rock! (till you drop) / Photograph / Stagefright / Too late for love / Die hard the hunter / Foolin around / Rock of ages / Comin' under fire / Action! not words / Billy's got a gun. *(cd-iss. 1988; 810308-2)*

Jun 83. (7") <812604> **ROCK OF AGES. / BILLY'S GOT A GUN** [-] [16]

Aug 83. (7"/7"s/7"sha-pic-d/12") *(VER/+Q/P/X 6)* **ROCK OF AGES. / ACTION! NOT WORDS** [41] [-]

Aug 83. (7") <814178> **FOOLIN'. / COMIN' UNDER FIRE** [-] [28]

Nov 83. (7") *(VER 8)* <814178> **FOOLIN'. / TOO LATE FOR LOVE** [ ] [-]
(12"+=) *(VERX 8)* – High'n'dry.

Jun 84. (7") <818779> **BRINGIN' ON THE HEARTBREAK (remix). / ME AND MY WINE** [-] [61]

Aug 85. (7"/7"g-f) *(VER/+G 9)* **PHOTOGRAPH. / BRINGIN' ON THE HEARTBREAK** [ ] [-]
(12"+=) *(VERX 9)* – Mirror, mirror.

—— Remained a 5-piece although RICK ALLEN lost an arm in a car crash (31st December '84). He now used a specially adapted programmable drum pads and foot pedals.

Jul 87. (7") *(LEP 1)* **ANIMAL. / TEAR IT DOWN** [6] [-]
(12"+=/12"red+=) *(LEP X/C 1)* – ('A'extended).
(cd-s++=) *(LEPCD 1)* – Women.

Aug 87. (lp/pic-lp/c)(cd) *(HYS LP/PD/MC 1)(<830675>)* **HYSTERIA** [2] [1]
– Women / Rocket / Animal / Love bites / Pour some sugar on me / Armageddon it / Gods of war / Don't shoot shotgun / Run riot / Hysteria / Excitable / Love and affection. *(cd+=)* – I can't let you be a memory.

Aug 87. (7") <888757> **WOMEN. / TEAR IT DOWN** [-] [80]

Sep 87. (7"/7"sha-pic-d/c-s) *(LEP/+S/MC 2)* **POUR SOME SUGAR ON ME. / I WANNA BE YOUR HERO** [18] [-]
(12"+=) *(LEPX 2)* – ('A'extended mix).

Oct 87. (7") <888832> **ANIMAL. / I WANNA BE YOUR HERO** [-] [19]

Nov 87. (7"/7"s/c-s) *(LEP/+S/MC 3)* <870004> **HYSTERIA. / RIDE INTO THE SUN ('87 version)** [26] [10] Jan88
(12"+=/12"s+=) *(LEPX 3/+13)* – Love and affection (live).
(cd-s++=) *(LEPCD 3)* – I wanna be your hero.

Apr 88. (7") <870298> **POUR SOME SUGAR ON ME. / RING OF FIRE** [-] [2]

Apr 88. (7"/7"s) *(LEP/+P 4)* **ARMAGEDDON IT! (The Atomic mix). / RING OF FIRE** [20] [-]
(12"+=/12"s+=) *(LEPX/+B 4)* – ('A'version).
(pic-cd-s++=) *(LEPCD 4)* – Animal / Pour some sugar on me.

Jul 88. (7"g-f) *(LEPG 5)* <870402> **LOVE BITES. / BILLY'S GOT A GUN (live)** [11] [1]
(12"+=/12"box+=/cd-s+=) *(LEP X/XB/CD 5)* – Excitable (orgasmic mix).

Nov 88. (7") <870692> **ARMAGEDDON IT. / RELEASE ME (STUMPUS MAXIMUS & THE GOOD OL' BOYS)** [-] [3]

Jan 89. (7"/7"s) *(LEP/+C 6)* **ROCKET. / RELEASE ME (STUMPUS MAXIMUS & THE GOOD OL' BOYS)** [15] [-]
('A'-Lunar mix; 12"+=/12"s+=/12"pic-d+=/cd-s+=) *(LEP X/XC/XP/CD 6)* – Rock of ages (live).

Feb 89. (7") <872614> **ROCKET. / WOMEN (live)** [-] [12]

—— STEVE CLARK was found dead on the 8th of January '91 after drinking/drugs session. Replaced by **VIVIAN CAMPBELL** (b.25 Aug'62, Belfast, N.Ireland) – guitar (ex-DIO, ex-WHITESNAKE, ex-SHADOWKING)

Mar 92. (7"/c-s) *(DEF/+MC 7)* <866568> **LET'S GET ROCKED. / ONLY AFTER DARK** [2] [15]
(12"pic-d+=) *(DEFXP 7)* – Too late for love (live).
(pic-cd-s+=) *(DEFCD 7)* – Women (live).

Apr 92. (cd/c/lp) *(510978-2/-4/-1)* <512185> **ADRENALIZE** [1] [1]
– Let's get rocked / Heaven is / Make love like a man / Tonight / White lightning / Stand up (kick love into motion) / Personal property / Have you ever needed someone so bad / I wanna touch you / Tear it down. *(pic-lp iss.Dec92, w / 2 extra tracks; 510978-0) (lp re-iss. Nov99 on 'Simply Vinyl'; SVLP 148)*

Jun 92. (7"/c-s) *(LEP/+MC 7)* <864038> **MAKE LOVE LIKE A MAN. / MISS YOU IN A HEARTBEAT** [12] [36]
(12"+=) *(LEPXP 7)* – Two steps behind (acoustic).
(cd-s++=) *(LEPCD 5)* – Action.

Aug 92. (c-s) <864136> **HAVE YOU EVER NEEDED SOMEONE SO BAD / ELECTED (live)** [-] [12]

Sep 92. (7"/c-s) *(LEP/+MC 8)* **HAVE YOU EVER NEEDED SOMEONE SO BAD. / FROM THE INSIDE** [16] [-]
(12"pic-d+=) *(LEPXP 8)* – You can't always get what you want.
(cd-s++=) *(LEPCD 8)* – Little wing.

Dec 92. (c-s) <864604> **STAND UP (KICK LOVE INTO MOTION) / FROM THE INSIDE (THE ACOUSTIC HIPPIES FROM HELL)** [-] [34]

Jan 93. (7"etched/c-s) *(LEP/+MC 9)* **HEAVEN IS. / SHE'S TOO TOUGH** [13] [-]
(pic-cd-s+=) *(LEPCD 9)* – Let's get rocked (live) / Elected (live).
(12"pic-d) *(LEPX 9)* – ('A'side) / Let's get rocked (live) / Tokyo road (live).

Mar 93. (c-s) <862016> **TONIGHT / SHE'S TOO TOUGH** [-] [62]

Apr 93. (7"/c-s) *(LEP/+MC 10)* **TONIGHT. / NOW I'M HERE (live)** [34] [-]
(12"pic-d+=) *(LEPX 10)* – Hysteria (live).
(cd-s+=) *(LEPCD 10)* – Photograph (live).
(cd-s) *(LEPCB 10)* – ('A'side) / Pour some sugar on me / ('A'demo).

Sep 93. (7"/c-s) *(LEP/+MC 12)* <77116> **TWO STEPS BEHIND. / TONIGHT (acoustic demo)** [32] [12]
(cd-s+=) *(LEPCD 12)* – S.M.C.

—— <above single from the film 'Last Action Hero' on 'Columbia' US>

Oct 93. (cd/c/lp) *(<518305-2/-4/-1>)* **RETRO ACTIVE** [6] [9]

– Desert song / Fractured love / Two steps behind (acoustic) / Only after dark / Action / She's too tough / Miss you in a heartbeat (acoustic) / Only after dark (acoustic) / Ride into the sun / From the inside / Ring of fire / I wanna be your hero / Miss you in a heartbeat / Two steps behind.

Nov 93. (c-s,cd-s) *<858080>* **MISS YOU IN A HEARTBEAT (acoustic version) / LET'S GET ROCKED (live)** [-] [39]

Jan 94. (7"/c-s) *(LEP/+MC 13)* **ACTION. / MISS YOU IN A HEARTBEAT (demo)** [14] [-]
(cd-s+=) *(LEPCD 13)* – She's too tough (demo).
(cd-s+=) *(LEPCX 13)* – Two steps behind (demo) / Love bites (live).

Oct 95. (c-s) *(LEPMC 14)* **WHEN LOVE & HATE COLLIDE / POUR SOME SUGAR ON ME (remix)** [2] [-]
(cd-s+=) *(LEPCD 14)* – Armageddon it! (remix).
(cd-s++=) *(LEPDD 14)* – ('A'demo).
(cd-s) *(LEP 14)* – ('A'side) / Rocket (remix) / Excitable (remix).
(cd-s) *(LEP 14)* – ('A'side) / Excitable (remix) / ('A'demo).

Oct 95. (cd/c/lp) *(528656-2/-4/-1)* *<528815>* **VAULT 1980-1995 DEF LEPPARD GREATEST HITS** (compilation) [3] [15]
– Pour some sugar on me / Photograph / Love bites / Let's get rocked / Two steps behind / Animal / Heaven is / Rocket / When love & hate collide / Action / Make love like a man / Armageddon it / Have you ever needed someone / So bad / Rock of ages / Hysteria / Bringin' on the heartbreak. *(cd w/free cd)* – LIVE AT DON VALLEY, SHEFFIELD

Nov 95. (c-s) *<852424>* **WHEN LOVE AND HATE COLLIDE / CAN'T KEEP AWAY FROM THE FLAME** [-] [58]

Apr 96. (c-s) *(LEPMC 15)* **SLANG / ANIMAL (live acoustic)** [17] [-]
(cd-s+=) *(LEPCD 15)* – Ziggy Stardust (live acoustic) / Pour some sugar on me (live acoustic).
(cd-s) *(LEPDD 15)* – ('A'side) / Can't keep the flame away / When love and hate collide (strings and piano version).

May 96. (cd/c/lp) *(<532486-2/-4/-1>)* **SLANG** [5] [14]
– Truth / Turn to dust / Slang / All I want is everything / Work it out / Breathe a sigh / Deliver me / Gift of flesh / Blood runs cold / Where does love go when it dies / Pearl of euphoria. *(cd w/ free cd rec. live in Singapore)* – Armageddon it / Two steps behind / From the inside / Animal / When love & hate collide / Pour some sugar on me.

Jun 96. (c-s) *(LEPMC 16)* **WORK IT OUT / TWO STEPS BEHIND** [22] [-]
(cd-s+=) *(LEPCD 16)* – Move with me slowly.
(cd-s) *(LEPDD 16)* – ('A'side) / ('A'demo) / Truth?

Sep 96. (c-s) *(LEPMC 17)* **ALL I WANT IS EVERYTHING / WHEN SATURDAY COMES** [38] [-]
(cd-s+=) *(LEPCD 17)* – Jimmy's theme / ('A'radio edit).
(cd-s) *(LEPDD 17)* – ('A'side) / 'Cause we ended as lovers / Led boots / ('A'radio edit).

Nov 96. (c-s) *(578838-4)* **BREATHE A SIGH / ROCK! ROCK! (TILL YOU DROP)** [43] [-]
(cd-s+=) *(578839-2)* – Deliver me (live) / Slang (live).
(cd-s) *(578841-2)* – ('A'side) / Another hit and run (live) / All I want is everything (live) / Work it out (live).

Jun 99. (cd/c) *(<546 244-2/212-4>)* **EUPHORIA** [11] [11]
– Demolition man / Promises / Back in your face / Goodbye / All night / Paper sun / It's only love / 21st century sha la la girl / To be alive / Disintigrate / Guilty / Day after day / Kings of oblivion.

Jul 99. (c-s) *(562136-4)* **PROMISES / BACK IN YOUR FACE – GOODBYE – ALL NIGHT (excerpts)** [41] [ ]
(cd-s+=) *(562137-2)* – Under my wheels.
(cd-s) *(562136-2)* – ('A'side) / World's collide / Immortal.

Sep 99. (c-s) *(562288-4)* **GOODBYE / IMMORTAL** [ ] [ ]
(cd-s+=) *(562288-2)* – Burnout.
(cd-s) *(562289-2)* – ('A'side) / Who do you love? / When love and hate collide.

DEFTONES

Formed: Sacramento, California, USA . . . 1989, by magnetic frontman CHINO MORENO, plus STEPHEN CARPENTER, CHI CHENG and ABE CUNNINGHAM. One of the more promising acts to have signed to MADONNA's 'Maverick' label (through 'Warners'), DEFTONES released their debut album, 'ADRENALINE' in 1995. Like a gonzoid cross between JONATHAN DAVIS (KORN) and ZACK DE LA ROCHA, CHINO's incendiary live presence helped the group build up a loyal following. By the release of their next set, 'AROUND THE FUR' (1997), their post-metal noise had reached fruition, from the sonic assault of the album's opener, 'MY OWN SUMMER (SHOVE IT)' to 'HEADUP' (a collaboration with Sepultura's MAX CAVALERA). After much soul searching and turmoil, the veteran – at least in terms of today's high turnover music scene – Cali noise abusers returned with that difficult third album, 'WHITE PONY' (2000). Older and wiser if no more content with his lot, the perennially pissed off MORENO reflects on his lost youth in 'TEENAGER' while TOOL frontman MAYNARD JAMES KEENAN joins the fray on the poignant 'PASSENGER'. Leaving the rap-metal posturing to the young pretenders, DEFTONES took their foot off the gas while still maintaining a head of steam. • **Covered:** THE CHAUFFEUR (Duran Duran) / TO HAVE AND TO HOLD (Depeche Mode). • **Trivia:** CHINO formed side project, TEAM SLEEP, in 1998.

Album rating: ADRENALINE (*9) / AROUND THE FUR (*8) / WHITE PONY (*6) / BACK TO SCHOOL (MINI MAGGIT) (*6)

CHINO MORENO – vocals / **STEPHEN CARPENTER** – guitar / **CHI CHENG** – bass, vocals / **ABE CUNNINGHAM** – drums

Maverick Maverick

Oct 95. (cd/c) *<(9362 46054-2/-4)>* **ADRENALINE** [ ] [ ]
– Bored / Minus blindfold / One weak / Nosebleed / Lifter / Root / 7 words / Birthmark / Engine No.9 / Fireal.

Nov 97. (cd/c) *<(9362 46810-2/-4)>* **AROUND THE FUR** [56] [29]
– My own summer (shove it) / Lhabia / Mascara / Around the fur / Be quiet and drive / Lotion / Dai the flu / Headup / MX.

Mar 98. (7"/c-s) *(W 0432/+C)* **MY OWN SUMMER (SHOVE IT). / ROOT (live)** [29] [ ]
(cd-s+=) *(W 0432CD)* – Nosebleed (live) / Lifter (live).
(cd-s) *(W 0432CDX)* – ('A'side) / Lotion (live) / Fireal swords (live) / Bored (live).

Jun 98. (7") *(W 0445)* **BE QUIET AND DRIVE (FAR AWAY). / ('A'acoustic)** [50] [ ]
(cd-s+=) *(W 0445CD)* – Birthmark (live).
(cd-s) *(W 0445CDX)* – ('A'side) / Engine No.9 (live) / Teething (live).

Jun 00. (cd/lp) *<(9362 47799-2/-1)>* **WHITE PONY** [13] [3]
– Fleticeria / Digital bath / Elite / RX queen / Street carp / Teenager / Knife party / Korea / Passenger / Change (in the house of flies) / Pink maggit. *<US-iss.+=>* – The boy's republic.

Aug 00. (cd-s) *(W 531CDX)* **CHANGE (IN THE HOUSE OF FLIES) / (+ 2 similar versions)** [53] [-]

Mar 01. (m-cd) *<(9362 48082-2)>* **BACK TO SCHOOL (MINI MAGGIT)** [35] [ ]
– Back to school (mini maggit) / Falticeira (live) / Back to school (live) / Nosebleed (live) / Teething (live) / Change (in the house of flies) (live acoustic) / Pink maggit / White pony EPK (short version).

DEICIDE

Formed: Florida, USA . . . 1987 initially as AMON by GLEN BENTON, brothers ERIC and BRIAN HOFFMAN and STEVE ASHEIM. Signing to 'Roadracer', the group released their self-titled debut in the summer of 1990. Hardly groundbreaking stuff, the group earned more column inches for their aggressively satanic beliefs. Predictably, this brought the band into direct confrontation, initially with Christian bible-thumpers, then more seriously with animal rights activists outraged by BENTON's disturbingly candid comments on how he spent his leisure time (i.e. mutilating God's creatures). One particular group, the Animal Militia, subsequently furnished DEICIDE with death threats and allegedly bombed a gig in Stockholm. Amid all this carry on, DEICIDE released a follow-up album, 'LEGION' (1992), the record a distinct improvement on the death- metal drudgery of the debut. While many supposedly satanic metal bands no doubt still get their mum to do their washing, BENTON at least appeared to be the real thing, even branding an inverted cross into his forehead! Jesus Christ!!! God almighty!!! That's just going a bit too far, don't you think? Then again, he won't have to go through the embarrassment of explaining it to his grandchildren as he's reputedly entered into a suicide pact which won't see the lad reach 40 (certainly gives new meaning to The Who's 'My Generation'). Meanwhile, the albums have come thick and fast from 1995's 'ONCE UPON THE CROSS' to their most recent 'INSINERATEHYMN' (2000).

Album rating: DEICIDE (*6) / LEGION (*7) / AMON: FEASTING THE BEAST (*4) / ONCE UPON THE CROSS (*5) / SERPENTS OF THE LIGHT (*8) / WHEN SATAN LIVES (*7) / INSINERATEHYMN (*5)

GLEN BENTON – vocals, bass / **ERIC HOFFMAN** – guitar / **BRIAN HOFFMAN** – guitar / **STEVE ASHEIM** – drums

Roadracer R.C.

Jun 90. (cd) *(9381-2)* **DEICIDE** [ ] [ ]
– Lunatic of God's creation / Sacrificial suicide / Oblivious to evil / Dead by dawn / Blasphererein / Deicide / Carnage in the temple of the damned / Mephistopheles / Crucifixation. *(cd re-mast.Jun00 on 'Roadrunner'; RR 8744-2)*

R.C. R.C.

Jun 92. (cd) *(RC 9192-2)* **LEGION** [ ] [ ]
– Satan spawn, the Caco-daemon / Dead but dreaming / Repent to die / Trifixion / Behead the prophet (no Lord shall live) / Holy deception / In Hell I burn / Revocate the agitator. *(re-iss. Mar96; same)*

Roadrunner Roadrunner

Feb 93. (cd/c) *<(RR 9112-2/-4)>* **AMON: FEASTING THE BEAST** (Amon demos) [ ] [ ]
– Lunatic of God's creation / acrificial suicide / Crucifixation / Carnage in the temple of the damned / Dead by dawn / Blasphererein / Feasting of the beast (intro) / Sacrificial suicide / Day of darkness / Oblivious to nothing.

May 95. (cd/c/lp) *<(RR 8949-2/-4/-1)>* **ONCE UPON THE CROSS** [66] [ ]
– Once upon the cross / Christ denied / When Satan rules his world / Kill the Christian / Trick or betrayed / They are the children of the underworld / Behind the light thou shall rise / To be dead / Confessional rape. *(cd re-iss. Jun00; same)*

Oct 97. (cd) *<(RR 8811-2)>* **SERPENTS OF THE LIGHT** [ ] [ ]
– Serpents of the light / Bastard of Christ / Blame it on God / This is hell we're in / I am no one / Slave to the cross / Creatures of habit / Believe the lie / The truth above / Father Baker's. *(re-iss. Jun00; same)*

Nov 98. (cd) *<(RR 8704-2)>* **WHEN SATAN LIVES (live)** [ ] [ ]
– When Satan rules his world / Blame it on God / Bastard of Christ / Children of the underworld / Serpents of the light / Dead but dreaming / Slave to the cross / Lunatic of God's creation / Oblivious to evil / Once upon the cross / Believe the lie / Trick or be betrayed / Behind the light thou shall rise / Deicide / Father Baker's / Dead by dawn / Sacrificial suicide. *(re-iss. Jun00; same)*

Jun 00. (cd) *<(RR 8570-2)>* **INSINERATEHYMN** [ ] [ ]
– Bible basher / Forever hate you / Standing in the flames / Remnant of a hopeless path / The gift that keeps on giving / Halls of warship / Suffer again / Worst enemy / Apocalyptic fear / Refusal of penance.

DEMOLITION 23 (see under ⇒ HANOI ROCKS)

DEMON

Formed: Midlands, England ... early 80's by DAVE HILL and MAL SPOONER. Enlisting LES HUNT, CHRIS ELLIS and JOHN WRIGHT, the group were initially part of the NWOBHM movement, headed by the likes of IRON MAIDEN and DEF LEPPARD. After an independently released debut single, 'LIAR', the group signed with the French-based 'Carrere' label, issuing an album, 'NIGHT OF THE DEMON', in the summer of '81. This was followed by another unremarkable effort a year later, 'THE UNEXPECTED GUEST'. By the release of 'THE PLAGUE' (1983), a futuristic concept effort, the group had toned down the pseudo-Satanic trappings for a more intelligent, ambitious approach and melodic hard rock style. Days after recording a fourth set, 'BRITISH STANDARD APPROVED' (1985), tragedy struck, with the death of founding member SPOONER. Electing to carry on, HILL recruited a new line-up of STEVEN BROOKES, SCOT CRAWFORD and JOHN WATERHOUSE, releasing a further string of consistent albums for 'Clay' including 'HEART OF OUR TIME' (1985), 'BREAKOUT' (1987) and 'TAKING THE WORLD BY STORM' (1989), the latter featuring new member NICK BUSHELL. The turn of the decade saw DEMON sign to the 'Sonic' label, releasing a live double set, 'ONE HELLUVA NIGHT' (1990). The album was recorded in Germany, a metal heartland where the more traditional style of bands like DEMON still commands an audience. It wasn't enough, however, and after a final effort in 1992, 'BLOW OUT', they called it a day.

Album rating: NIGHT OF THE DEMON (*5) / THE UNEXPECTED GUEST (*6) / THE PLAGUE (*6) / BRITISH STANDARD APPROVED (*5) / HEART OF OUR TIME (*5) / HEART OF OUR TIME (*5) / TAKING THE WORLD BY STORM (*6) / ONE HELLUVA NIGHT – LIVE (*4) / ANTHOLOGY compilation (*6) / HOLD ON TO THE DREAM (*6) / BLOW-OUT (*5)

DAVE HILL – vocals / **MAL SPOONER** – guitar / **LES HUNT** – guitar / **CHRIS ELLIS** – bass / **JOHN WRIGHT** – drums

Clay | not iss.

Aug 80. (7"red) *(CLAY 4)* **LIAR. / WILD WOMAN** [ ] [-]

Carrere | not iss.

Jun 81. (7") *(CAR 185)* **RIDE THE WIND. / ON THE ROAD** [ ] [-]

Jul 81. (lp/c) *(CAL/CAC 126)* **NIGHT OF THE DEMON** [ ] [-]
– Full moon (instrumental) / Night of the demon / Into the nightmare / Father of time / Decisions / Liar / Big love / Ride the wind / Fool to play the hard way / One helluva night. *(re-iss. Apr88 on 'Clay'; CLAYLP 25) (re-iss. Jun90 on 'Sonic' cd/lp; SONIC CD/LP 1)*

Mar 82. (7") *(CAR 226)* **ONE HELLUVA NIGHT. / INTO THE NIGHTMARE** [ ] [-]

Jul 82. (7") *(CAR 249)* **HAVE WE BEEN HERE BEFORE? / VICTIM OF FORTUNE** [ ] [-]

Aug 82. (lp/c) *(CAL/CAC 139)* **THE UNEXPECTED GUEST** [47] [-]
– Intro: An observation / Don't break the circle / The spell / Total possession / Sign of a madman / Victim of fortune / Have we been here before? / Strange institution / The grand illusion / Beyond the gates / Deliver us from evil. *(re-iss. Jan87 on 'Clay'; CLAYLP 22) (re-iss. Sep90 on 'Sonic' cd/lp; SONIC CD/LP 2)*

Clay | not iss.

Jun 83. (lp/pic-lp) *(CLAY 6/+P)* **THE PLAGUE** [73] [-]
– The plague / Nowhere to run / Fever in the city / Blackheath / Blackheath intro / The writings on the wall / The only sane man / A step too far. *(cd-iss. Sug88; CLAY 6CD) (re-iss. Sep90 on 'Sonic' cd/lp; SONIC CD/LP 3) (cd re-iss. Jul95 on 'H.T.D.'; HTDCD 36)*

Aug 83. (7") *(CLAY 25)* **THE PLAGUE. / THE ONLY SANE MAN** [ ] [-]

Nov 84. (7") *(CLAY 41)* **WONDERLAND. / BLACKHEATH** [ ] [-]
(12"+=) *(12CLAY 41)* – Nowhere to run.

— **STEVEN WATTS** – keyboards, synthesizer; repl. HUNT + ELLIS

Mar 85. (lp) *(CLAYLP 15)* **BRITISH STANDARD APPROVED** [ ] [-]
– First class / Cold in the air / Touching the ice / Second stage / Proxima / The link (part 1) / The link (part 2) / New ground / From the outside / Wonderland / Hemispheres (British standard approved). *(re-iss. Sep90 on 'Sonic' cd/lp; SONIC CD/LP 4)*

— after the death of MAL SPOONER in '85, **HILL + WATTS** enlisted **STEVEN BROOKES** – guitar (ex-DISCHARGE) + **JOHN WATERHOUSE** – guitar / **SCOTT CRAWFORD** – drums

Nov 85. (lp/c) *(CLAY/+C LP 18)* **HEART OF OUR TIME** [ ] [-]
– Heart of our time / In your own light / Genius / Expressing the heart / High climber / Crossfire / Grown-ups / Summit / One small step / Computer code. *(re-iss. Sep90 on 'Sonic' cd/lp; SONIC CD/LP 5)*

Mar 86. (12"ep) *(PLATE 8)* **DEMON E.P.** [ ] [-]
– Heart of our time / Blackheath parts 1 & 2) / High climber / The lague / The link (parts 1 & 2).

Jun 87. (lp) *(CLAYLP 23)* **BREAKOUT** [ ] [-]
– Life on the wire / Hurricane / Breakout / Living in the shadow / England's glory / Standing in the shadow / Hollywood / Big chance / Through these eyes / Finale. *(re-iss. Sep90 on 'Sonic' cd/lp; SONIC CD/LP 6)*

— added **NICK BUSHELL** – bass (ex-DISCHARGE)

Apr 88. (d7") *(CLAY 48D)* **TONIGHT (THE HERO IS BACK). / HURRICANE // NIGHT OF THE DEMON. / DON'T BREAK THE CIRCLE** [ ] [-]

May 89. (lp/cd) *(CLAY LP/CD 27)* **TAKING THE WORLD BY STORM** [ ] [-]
– Commercial dynamite / Taking the world by storm / The life brigade / Remembrance day (a song for peace) / What do you think about Hell / Blue skies in Red Square / Time has come. *(re-iss. Sep90 on 'Sonic' cd/lp; SONIC CD/LP 8) (cd re-iss. Mar95 on 'H.T.D.'; HTDCD 32)*

— **ANDY DALE** – bass; repl. BUSHELL

Total | Flametrader

Aug 90. (d-cd/d-lp) *(DEMON CD/LP 1)* **ONE HELLUVA NIGHT (live in Germany)** [ ] [ ]
– Blue skies in Red Square / Blackheath / Commercial dynamite / Living in the shadow / The plague / Don't break the circle / The life brigade / Remembrance day / Hurricane / Sign of a madman / One helluva night / Night of the demon / Life on the wire / Wonderland / Big chance.

Sonic | not iss.

May 91. (cd/lp) *(SONIC CD/LP 10)* **HOLD ON TO THE DREAM** [ ] [-]
– No more hell on earth / New frontiers / Hold on to the dream / The lion's share / Eastern sunset / Barons of darkness / Ivory towers / Nothing turned out right / Out of the shadows / Shoot for the city / Coming home.

— **MIKE THOMAS** – bass; repl. DALE + WATTS

— **PAUL ROSSCROW** – drums; rel. CRAWFORD

Jun 92. (cd) *(SONICCD 11)* **BLOW-OUT** [ ] [-]
– Still worth fighting for / Everything has changed / Visions of the future / Tell me what you're looking for / Sacred heart / Crazy town / Victim of his time (God bless Freddie) / Million dollar ride / ar games / Soldier of fortune / Visions of the future II / Stop the fire. *(lp-iss.Nov92 on 'Flametrader'; FT 30019LP)*

— finally gave up in 1992.

– compilations, etc. –

Oct 91. (cd/c) *Clay; (CLAY CD/C 108)* **THE ANTHOLOGY** [ ] [-]
– Night of the demon (remix) / Into the nightmare / Fathr of time / Don't break the circle (remix) / The spell / Sign of the madman / The plague / Nowhere to run / Blackheath (alt.mix) / Touching the ice / From the outside / Hear of the time / Crossfire / Life on the wire / Breakout / Hollywood / England's glory. *(cd re-iss. Apr93; same)*

Nov 99. (cd) *Spaced Out; (<SPMCD 001>)* **THE BEST OF DEMON VOL.1** [ ] [ ] Feb00

DENISON / KIMBALL TRIO

(see under ⇒ JESUS LIZARD)

Rick DERRINGER

Born: RICHARD ZEHRINGER, 5 Aug'47, Union City, Indiana, USA. In 1962, together with brother RANDY, he formed the Indiana-based teenage bubblegum pop band, The McCOYS. After many gigs, supporting the likes of The FOUR SEASONS, The BEACH BOYS and CHUCK BERRY, they were spotted by Bert Berns, who wrote their 1965 chart-topper, 'HANG ON SLOOPY'. After more mid-60's success, and an early 70's back-up career with JOHNNY & EDGAR WINTER (he subsequently produced EDGAR's chart-topping album, 'They Only Come Out At Night'), RICK DERRINGER went solo. Keeping this connection going, RICK signed to the brother's 'Blue Sky' label, having major success with the single, 'ROCK'N'ROLL HOOCHIE KOO' (1974). Featuring EDGAR on keyboards and sax, its parent album, 'ALL AMERICAN BOY' also hit the US Top 30. A second hard-rocking solo set, 'SPRING FEVER', failed to emulate the success of its predecessor, the guitarist enlisting the help of VINNY APPICE, KENNY AARONSON and DANNY JOHNSON to form the group, DERRINGER. In 1976, they released an eponymous set, which also failed to find a sizeable audience. They released a few more unremarkable albums before the aforementioned trio departed to form AXIS. Far from being down and out, RICK earned his crust by sessioning for such 70's alumni as STEELY DAN, TODD RUNDGREN, MEAT LOAF and ALICE COOPER. He continued to surface as a low-key solo artist, only re-appearing commercially as the live guitarist with CYNDI LAUPER! In the 80's, he worked with the likes of BONNIE TYLER and WEIRD AL YANKOVIC ('Eat It!'), before he returned to a more mature blues-based sound.

Album rating: ALL AMERICAN BOY (*6) / SPRING FEVER (*4) / DERRINGER (*4) / SWEET EVIL (*4) / RICK DERRINGER LIVE (*5) / IF YOU WEREN'T SO ROMANTIC, I'D SHOOT YOU (*4) / GUITARS AND WOMEN (*4) / FACE TO FACE (*4) / GOOD DIRTY FUN (*3) / BACK TO THE BLUES (*5) / ELECTRA BLUES (*5) / TEND THE FIRE (*5) / BLUES DELUXE (*4) / ROCK & ROLL HOOCHIE COO: THE BEST OF RICK DERRINGER compilation (*6) / JACKHAMMER BLUES (*4)

RICK DERRINGER

— (solo) **RICK DERRINGER** – vocals, guitar; with **BOBBY CALDWELL** – drums / **EDGAR WINTER** – keyboards / **KENNY PASSARELLI** – bass / plus other guests

Epic | Blue Sky

Feb 74. (lp/c) *(EPC 65831)* *<32481>* **ALL AMERICAN BOY** [ ] [25] Nov73
– Rock and roll hoochie koo / Joy ride / Teenage queen / Cheap tequila / Uncomplicated / Hold / The airport giveth (the airport taketh away) / Teenage love affair / It's raining / Time warp / Slide on over slinky / Jump, jump, jump.

Feb 74. (7") *(EPC 1984)* **TEENAGE LOVE AFFAIR. / JOY RIDE** [ ] [-]

Apr 74. (7") *(EPC 2062)* *<2751>* **ROCK AND ROLL HOOCHIE KOO. / TIME WARP** [ ] [23] Jan74

Apr 74. (7") *<2752>* **TEENAGE LOVE AFFAIR. / SLIDE ON OVER SLINKY** [-] [80]

Jul 74. (7") *<2753>* **CHEAP TEQUILA. / IT'S RAINING** [-] [ ]

— **JOHHNY SIEGLER** – bass repl. KENNY

Blue Sky | Blue Sky

Apr 75. (7") *(SKY 3219)* *<2755>* **HANG ON SLOOPY. / SKYSCRAPER BLUES** [ ] [94]

Apr 75. (lp) *(SKY 80733)* *<33423>* **SPRING FEVER** [ ] [ ]
– Gimme more / Tomorrow / Don't ever say goodbye / Still alive and well / Rock / Hang on Sloopy / Roll with me / Walkin' the dog / He needs some answers / Skyscraper blues.

Aug 75. (7") *(SKY 3511)* *<2757>* **DON'T EVER SAY GOODBYE. / GIMME MORE** [ ] [ ]

— In Dec'75, RICK featured on the album, 'THE EDGAR WINTER GROUP WITH RICK DERRINGER'.

DERRINGER

formed by **RICK** plus **DANNY JOHNSON** – guitar / **KENNY AARONSON** – bass / **VINNY APPICE** – drums

Aug 76. (lp) *(SKY 81458)* <34181> **DERRINGER** Jul76
– Let me in / You can have it / Loosen up your grip / Envy / Comes a woman / Sailor / Beyond the universe / Goodbye again *(cd-iss. Jul93 on 'Sony Europe';)*

Oct 76. (7") *(SKY 4661)* <2765> **LET ME IN. / YOU CAN HAVE ME** 86 Aug76

Mar 77. (lp) *(SKY 81847)* <34470> **SWEET EVIL** Feb 77
– Don't stop loving me / Sittin' by the pool / Keep on makin' love / One-eyed Jack / Let's make it / Sweet evil / Drivin' sideways / I didn't ask to be born.

Mar 77. (7") <2767> **DON'T STOP LOVING ME. / LET'S MAKE IT** -

Aug 77. (lp) *(SKY 82130)* <34848> **DERRINGER LIVE (live)** Jul77
– Let me in / Teenage love affair / Sailor / Beyond the universe / Sittin' by the fool / Uncomplicated / Still alive and well / Rock and roll hoochie koo.

RICK DERRINGER

(solo) retained AARONSON and brought in newcomers / **MARK CUNNINGHAM** – guitar to repl. JOHNSON who later formed AXIS / **MYRON GROOMBACHER** – drums repl. APPICE who also formed AXIS. (with KENNY also)

Sep 78. (7") <2770> **LAWYERS, GUNS AND MONEY. / SLEEPLESS** -

Sep 78. (lp) *(SKY 82464)* <35075> **IF I WEREN'T SO ROMANTIC, I'D SHOOT YOU**
– It ain't funny / Midnight road / If I weren't so romantic, I'd shoot you / EZ action / Lawyers, Guns and money / Power of love / Sleepless / Tonight / Rocka rolla / Attitude / Monomania.

Nov 78. (7") <2774> **MIDNIGHT ROAD. / ROCKA ROLLA** -

— session players from **TODD RUNDGREN / UTOPIA** repl. CUNNINGHAM

Oct 79. (lp) *(SKY 83746)* <36092> **GUITARS & WOMEN**
– Something warm / Guitars & women / Everything / Man in the middle / It must be love / Desires of the heart / Timeless / Hopeless romantic / Need a little girl (just like you) / Don't ever say goodbye. *(cd-iss. Jun98 on 'Razor & Tie'; RE 821702)*

Oct 79. (7") <2783> **SOMETHING WARM. / NEED A LITTLE GIRL (JUST LIKE YOU)** -

Apr 80. (7") *(SKY 8326)* <2788> **TIMELESS. / DON'T EVER SAY GOODBYE**

— **RICK** with **BENJY KING** – keys / **DON KISSELBACH** – bass / **JIMMY WILCOX** – drums

Dec 80. (lp) *(SKY 84462)* <36551> **FACE TO FACE**
– Runaway / You'll get yours / Big city loneliness / Burn the midnight oil / Let the music play / Jump jump / I want a lover / My my, hey hey (out of the blue).

Dec 80. (7") <2793> **RUNAWAY. / TEENAGE LOVE AFFAIR** -

Feb 81. (7") <2794> **LET THE MUSIC PLAY. / YOU'LL GET YOURS** -

— RICK returned to production work in the early 80's.

Polydor Passport

1983. (lp) *(311235)* <6025> **GOOD DIRTY FUN**
– Shake me / Party at the hotel / White heat / Just wanna dance / Doo wah diddy / When love attacks / I play guitar / Take it like a man / Numb / Hardball. *(cd-iss. 1988; 311235)*

DNA

were formed by **RICK DERRINGER & CARMINE APPICE** – drums (ex-VANILLA FUDGE, ex-CACTUS, etc) **DUANE HITCHINGS** – keyboards / **JIMMY JOHNSON** – bass

Polydor Passport

Dec 83. (lp/c) *(POLD/+C 5129)* **PARTY TESTED**
– Doctors of the universe / Intellectual freedom for the masses / Rock'n'roll (part 2) / The song that wrote itself / Party tested / The recipe for life / What about.

Jan 84. (7") *(POSP 669)* **DOCTORS OF THE UNIVERSE. / RECIPE OF LIFE**
(12"+=) *(POSPX 669)* – Intellectual freedom for the masses.

— RICK became producer for WEIRD AL JANKOVIC (Eat It) and BONNIE TYLER. He also became live guitarist for CYNDI LAUPER in 1986.

RICK DERRINGER

not iss. Epic

1985. (7") <05830> **REAL AMERICA. / GRAB THEM CAKES** -

Roadrunner Blues Bureau

Aug 93. (cd) *(RR 9048-2)* <SH 2008> **BACK TO THE BLUES**
– Trouble in Paradise / Blue suede shoes / Blues all night long / Meantown blues / Sorry for your heartache / Sink or swim / Diamond / Crybaby / Unsolved mystery / Blue velvet / Time to go. *(re-iss. Sep96; same)*

Oct 94. (cd) *(RR 8968-2)* <SH 2023> **ELECTRA BLUES** Aug94
– I got something to say / Unsung hero of the blues / Electra blues / If it's the blues / Firebrand rebel / Blue boogie / You can't be everywhere at once / All I want to do is cry / Deeper in the blues / You don't miss what you never had.

East West East West

Aug 96. (cd) <(0630 15341-2)> **TEND THE FIRE**
– I'm set on you / Wound up tight / Who do you love? / Big time love / Talk to me / Too sorry / Wrong side of paradise / Tough on me, tough on you / I'm in love / I'm doin' fine / I'll be lovin' you.

Blues Bureau Blues Bureau

Sep 99. (cd) <(BB 2039-2)> **BLUES DELUXE** Jun98
– Let the good times roll / Runnin' blue / Blues power / Key to the highway / Blues deluxe / Hide away 1962 / Killing floor / Funky music / Something inside of me / Still alive and well / Bright lights, big city / Checking up on my baby.

Jun 00. (cd) <(BB 2043-2)> **JACKHAMMER BLUES** May00
– Shake your money maker / Wrapped up in love again / You've got to love her with feeling / Street corner talking / Somebody loan me a dime / Just a little bit / All your love (I miss loving) / Red hot / Crying won't help you now / Parchman farm / Texas.

– others, compilations, etc. –

Mar 96. (cd) *Sony;* <26748> **REQUIRED ROCKING** -

Sep 97. (cd) *Archive; (ACHV 80012)* **ARCHIVE ALIVE** -

Apr 98. (cd) *K.N.B.; (88036)* **RICK DERRINGER AND FRIENDS** -

Aug 98. (cd) *King Biscuit; (KBFHCD 021)* **KING BISCUIT PRESENTS . . .**

Jun 00. (cd) *Akarma; (LK 001)* **LIVE AT THE PARADISE THEATRE (live)** -

Michael DES BARRES (see under ⇒ SILVERHEAD)

DESCENDENTS

Formed: South Bay, California, USA . . . early 80's by FRANK NAVETTA, TONY LOMBARDO and BILL STEVENSON. Following the release of debut single, 'RIDE THE WILD', the band recruited the short-lived CECILIA as lead vocalist, her tenure lasting only six months. A more permanent replacement was found in MILO AUCKERMAN, who made his debut on 1981's seminal 'FAT' EP, a warpspeed blast of angst-ridden but self-deprecatingly humorous hardcore that took in such favoured teenage obsessions as junk food and parent hating. The following year's debut album, 'MILO GOES TO COLLEGE', is widely regarded as a milestone of the genre, its blitzkrieg hardcore bop equal parts hormonal fury, pop genius and teenage humour, bypassing much of the macho posturing favoured by the DESCENDENTS' peers. MILO did indeed go to college, however, while NAVETTA and STEVENSON also departed, the former replaced by RAY COOPER upon MILO's return and the band's re-emergence in the mid-80's. 'I DON'T WANT TO GROW UP' (1985) was the sound of a band in transition, the full- pelt chaos of old making way for a more streamlined power-pop/punk direction. With DOUG CARRION coming in for the outgoing LOMBARDO, subsequent albums put the emphasis on louder, heavier guitars and pop hooks while the band's last remaining founder member, MILO, left prior to 1989's swansong, 'HALLRAKER'. His short-lived replacement, SMALLEY, was also a member of the band, ALL, who, along with BILL STEVENSON, KARL ALVEREZ and STEPHEN EGERTON, carried the DESCENDENTS' patented brand of fun-time punk-pop into the 90's on such albums as 'ALLROY SEZ . . .' (1988), 'ALLROY'S REVENGE' (1990) and 'ALLROY SAVES' (1990), all released on 'Cruz' records. The band took on even more of a DESCENDENTS hue in the early 90's with the addition of TONY LOMBARDO, subsequently signing with hardcore stalwart, 'Epitaph', for 1988's 'MASS NERDER' set. With a whole new generation of bands (i.e. GREEN DAY, OFFSPRING etc.) citing the DESCENDENTS as a guiding influence, the original L.A. ne'er- do-wells were persuaded to reform in the mid-90's, releasing an album, 'EVERYTHING SUCKS' (1996) and a string of singles for who else but 'Epitaph'.

Album rating: MILO GOES TO COLLEGE (*6) / BONUS FAT compilation (*5) / I DON'T WANT TO GROW UP (*6) / ENJOY (*5) / ALL (*6) / LIVEAGE (*5) / HALLRAKER (*4) / SOMERY compilation (*7) / EVERYTHING SUCKS (*6) / All: ALLROY SEZ (*6) / ALLROY'S REVENGE (*6) / TRAILBLAZER (*6) / ALLROY SAVES (*6) / BREAKING THINGS mini (*5) / PUMMEL (*5) / MASS NERDER (*5) / PROBLEMATIC (*3)

MILO AUCKERMAN – vocals / **FRANK NAVETTA** – guitar / **TONY LOMBARDO** – bass / **BILL STEVENSON** – drums

not iss. A.O.M.

1979. (7") **RIDE THE WILD. / IT'S A HECTIC WORLD** -

1980. (7") <AOM 445> **UNNATIONAL ANTHEM. / FACELIFT** -

not iss. New Alliance

1981. (7"ep) <NAR 005> **FAT EP** -
– My dad sucks / Mr. Bass / I like food / Hey hey / Der weinerschnitzel. *(UK-iss.Mar89 on 'S.S.T.' 12"ep/c-ep/cd-ep; SST 212/+C/CD)*

1982. (lp) <NAR 012> **MILO GOES TO COLLEGE** -
– My age / I wanna be a bear / I'm not a loser / Parents / Tonyage / M 16 / I'm not a punk / Catalina / Suburban home / Statue of liberty / Kabuki girl / Marriage / Hope / Bikage / Jean is dead. *(re-iss. Nov87 & May93 on 'SST' lp/cd; SST 142/+CD)*

— **RAY COOPER** – guitar; repl. NAVETTA (BILL joined BLACK FLAG and NIG HEIST)

1985. (lp) **I DON'T WANT TO GROW UP** -
– Descendents / I don't want to grow up / Pervert / Rockstar / No FB / Can't go back / GCF / My world / Theme / Silly girl / In love this way / Christmas vacation / Good good things / Ace. *(re-iss. Nov87 & Nov90 on 'SST' lp/c/cd; SST 143/+C/CD)*

1985. (m-lp) **BONUS FAT** (compilation) -
– My dad sucks / Mr. Bass / I like food / Hey hey / Wienerschnitzel / Global probing / Ride the wild / It's a hectic world. *(re-iss. Nov87 on 'SST' lp/cd; SST 144/+CD) (cd re-iss. May93; same)*

— **DOUG CARRION** – bass (ex-ANTI, ex-INCEST CATTLE) repl. LOMBARDO

1986. (m-lp) **ENJOY** -
– Enjoy / Floater / 50-50 / Sausage / Barnacle / Loaf / Carbunkle / Choda / Half pipe / Cable service / Lockout. *(re-iss. Sep90 on 'SST' lp/c/cd; SST 242/+C/CD)*

S.S.T. S.S.T.

Jun 87. (lp/c/cd) <(SST 112/+C/CD)> **ALL**
– All / Coolidge / No all / Van / Carneage / Impressions / Iceman / Uranus / Jealous of the world / Clean sheets / Pep talk / All-o-gistics / Schizophrenia. *(cd re-iss. May93; same)*

Feb 88. (lp/c/cd) <(SST 163/+C/CD)> **LIVEAGE (live)**
– All / I'm not a loser / Silly girl / I wanna be a bear / Coolidge / Wienerschnitzel / I don't want to grow up / Kids / Wendy / Get the time / Descendents / Sour grapes / All-o-gistics / My age / My dad sucks / Van / Suburban home / Hope / Clean sheets / Pervert.

— **DAVE SMALLEY** – vocals (ex-DYS, ex-DAG NASTY) repl. MILO

Feb 89. (lp/c/cd) <(SST 205/+C/CD)> **HALLRAKER (live)**
– Global probing / My world / Hurtin' crue / Hey hey / Kabuki girl – All / Pep talk / Jealous of the world / Christmas vacation / I like food / Iceman / Good good things / Cheer / Rockstar / No FB / Cameage. *(re-iss. May93 cd/c; SST 205 CD/C)*

- compilations, etc. -

Nov 87. (lp/c/cd) *S.S.T.; <(SST 145/+C/CD)>* **TWO THINGS AT ONCE** ☐ ☐
– (MILO GOES TO COLLEGE / BONUS FAT)
Sep 90. (d-lp/c/cd) *S.S.T.; <(SST 259/+C/CD)>* **SOMERY** ☐ ☐
(re-iss. May93 & Sep95; same)

ALL

— had already been formed by **BILL STEVENSON** – drums / **DAVE SMALLEY** – vocals / **KARL ALVEREZ** – bass / **STEPHEN EGERTON** – guitar

Cruz Cruz-SST

Jan 88. (lp/c/cd) *<CRZ 001/+CA/CD)>* **ALLROY SEZ . . .** ☐ ☐
– Pretty little girl / Hooidge / Sex in the way / Alfredo's / Sugar and spice / Allthymn / Just perfect / Paper tiger / Auto wreck / A muse / Don Quixote. *(UK-iss.Jan90; same) (re-iss. Sep95; same)*

— **SCOTT REYNOLDS** – vocals; repl. SMALLEY

Jan 90. (12"ep/c-ep/cd-ep) *<CRZ 004/+C/CD)>* **ALLROY FOR PREZ** ☐ ☐ 1988
– Just perfect / Skin deep / Wrong again / I hate to love / Wishing well / Son-o-qua / Postage / Daveage.
Jan 90. (7") *(CRZ 005/+C)* **SHE'S MY EX. / CRAZY?** ☐ ☐ 1989
(re-iss. 10"ep; CRZ 703) (re-iss. Jun96; same)
Jan 90. (lp/c/cd) *<CRZ 006/+C/CD)>* **ALLROY'S REVENGE** ☐ ☐ 1989
– Gnutheme / Fool / Scary sad / Man-o-steel / Box / Copping Z / Hot rod Lincoln / She's my ex / Bubblegum / Mary / Net / No traffic / Carnage.
Jun 90. (lp/c/cd) *<CRZ 010/+C/CD)>* **TRAILBLAZER (live)** ☐ ☐
– Carnage / Fool / Box / Skin deep / Just perfect / Postage / Copping Z / She's my ex / Man-o-steel / Paper tiger / Sex in the way / Check one / Hate to love / Gnutheme.
Oct 90. (lp/c/cd) *<CRZ 011/+C/CD)>* **ALLROY SAVES** ☐ ☐
– Educated idiot / Just like them / Prison / Just living / Freaky / Frog / Simple things / Cyclops / Ratchet / Sum / Crawdad / Explorator.
May 93. (lp/c/cd; as TONYALL) *<(CRZ 016/+C/CD)>* **NEW GIRL, OLD STORY** ☐ ☐ 1992
above added **TONY LOMBARDO** – bass (ex-DESCENDENTS)
May 93. (12"ep/c-ep/cd-ep) *<(CRZ 022/+C/CD)>* **PERCOLATOR** ☐ ☐ May92
– Charligan / Nothin' / Dot / Nobody's / Wonder / Minute / Birds / Empty / Mo. 63 / Egg timer / Gnugear (hot) / Hotplate / Hey bug / Breathe. *(re-iss. Sep95; same)*
May 93. (12"ep/c-ep/cd-ep) *<(CRZ 024/+C/CD)>* **DOT. / A BOY NAMED SUE / CAN'T SAY** ☐ ☐ 1992
Aug 93. (10"ep/cd-ep) *<(CRZ 030/+CD)>* **SHREEN. / ORIGINAL ME / CRUCIFIED** ☐ ☐
Sep 93. (lp/c/cd) *<(CRZ 031/+C/CD)>* **BREATHING THINGS** ☐ ☐
– Original me / Right / Shreen / 'Cause / Bail / Excuses / Strip bar / Horizontal / Guilty / Birthday I.O.U. / Rosco / Stick / Crucified / Politics.
Feb 94. (10"ep/cd-ep) *<(CRZ 033/+CD)>* **GUILTY. / ALL'S FAIR / MAN'S WORLD** ☐ ☐

— not without SCOTT; repl. by **CHAD PRICE**

not iss. Interscope

1995. (cd) *<92528>* **PUMMEL** [-] ☐
– Self-righteous / Million bucks / Uncle critic / Miranda / Not easy / Long distance / Stalker / Button it / This world / Gettin' there / Breakin' up / On foot / Broken / Hetero / Black sky.

Epitaph Epitaph

May 98. (cd/c/lp) *<(6531-2/-4/-1)>* **MASS NERDER** ☐ ☐
– World's on heroin / I'll get there / Life on the road / Fairweather friend / Perfection / Greedy / Until I say so / Think the world / Honey peeps / Refrain / Silly me / Romantic junkie / Vida blue / Until then / Good as my word / Silence.
May 00. (cd/lp) *<(6585-2/-1)>* **PROBLEMATIC** ☐ ☐
– Carry you / She broke my dick / Better than that / www.sara / Roir / What are you for? / Stupid kind of love / Alive / Real people / Lock 'em away / Teresa / I want out / Crucifiction / The skin / Nothin' to live for / Never too / Make believe / Drive away.

- compilations, etc. -

Apr 99. (cd) *Owned & Operated; <(O&O 007CD)>* **ALL** ☐ ☐ Feb99

DESCENDENTS

— re-formed **AUCKERMAN, EGERTON** / + **KARL ALVAREZ** – bass / **BILL STEVENSON** – drums, co-producer

Epitaph Epitaph

Sep 96. (cd/c/lp) *<(6481-2/-4/-1)>* **EVERYTHING SUCKS** ☐ ☐
– Everything sux / I'm the one / Coffee mug / Rotting out / Sick-o-me / Caught / When I get old / Doghouse / She loves me / Hateful notebook / We / Eunuch boy / This place / I won't let me / Thank you.
Jan 97. (7"colrd-ep/cd-ep) *(6490-7/-2)* **I'M THE ONE / EVERYTHING SUX. / LUCKY / SHATTERED MILO** ☐ ☐
Jun 97. (7"ep/cd-ep) *(6506-7/-2)* **WHEN I GET OLD. / GOTTA / SICK-O-ME** ☐ [-]

Sessions unknown

Jun 97. (7") *(7SMS 12)* **GRAND THEME. / GOTTA** ☐ ☐

DESTINY

Formed: Gothenberg, Sweden . . . 1984 by STEFAN BJORNSHOG, who finally evolved the line-up of HAKAN RING, JOHN PRODEN, MAGNUS OSTERMAN and PETER LUNDGREN. Disillusioned by the direction of their debut, 'BEYOND THE SENSE' (1985), RING, PRODEN and OSTERMAN departed, leaving behind STEFAN and PETER to recruit three new members JORGEN PETTERSSON, FLOYD KONSTATIN and ZENNY HANSON. This new improved line-up recorded the 'ATOMIC WINTER' (1989) set, a harder-edged affair which met with the same disinterest as the debut. Annoyed with this state of affairs, PETTERSSON and KONSTANTIN promptly bailed out leaving the remaining three members to recruit GUNNAR KINDBERG and record a final album for 'Music For Nations', 'NOTHING LEFT TO FEAR' (1991), before splitting soon after.

Album rating: BEYOND ALL SENSE (*4) / ATOMIC WINTER (*5) / DESTINY (*6) / NOTHING LEFT TO FEAR (*5) / THE UNDISCOVERED COUNTRY (*4)

HAKAN RING – vocals / **MAGNUS OSTERMAN** – guitar / **JOHN PRODEN** – guitar / **STEFAN BJORNSHOG** – bass / **PETER LUNDGREN** – drums

not iss. Mars

1985. (lp) **BEYOND ALL SENSE** [-] ☐
– Intro – Destiny / Rest in peace / Spellbreaker / Hang them high / Sirens in the dark / Kill the witch / Lost to Heaven / More evil than evil / Power by birth / Sacrilege.

— **FLOYD KONSTATIN** (ex-KING DIAMOND) / **JORGEN PETTERSSEN + ZENNY HANSON** ; repl. RING, OSTERMAN + PRODEN

US Metal US Metal

Mar 89. (lp/cd) *<(US 014/+CD)>* **ATOMIC WINTER** ☐ ☐
– Bermuda / Who am I / Spellbreaker / Beware / Religion / The extreme junction / Dark heroes / Living dead / Atomic winter.

— **GUNNAR KINDBERG** ; repl. KONSTATIN + PETTERSSEN

Active Active

May 91. (cd/lp) *(<CD+/ATV 18>)* **NOTHING LEFT TO FEAR** ☐ ☐
– Nothing left to fear / Medieval rendezvous / The evil trinity / Sirens in the dark / Sheer death / F.O.S. / Beyond all sense / No reservation / The raven / Rest in peace / Du gamla du fria.

— split after above, **STEFAN** re-formed the band with **ZENNY GRAM** – vocals / **KNUT HASSEL** – guitars / **HAKAN SVANTESSON** – drums

G.N.W. not iss.

May 98. (cd) *(GNW 01CD)* **THE UNDISCOVERED COUNTRY** [-] [-] Sweden
– Devil in the dark / Wink of an eye / The undiscovered country / A taste of armageddon / By any other way / Balance of terror / Tomorrow is yesterday / Danger of the mind.

DESTROY ALL MONSTERS

Formed: Detroit, Michigan, USA . . . 1973 by former model and visual artist NIAGARA, who was to be joined by veterans of the garage-punk era MIKE DAVIS (ex-MC5) and RON ASHETON (ex-STOOGES). In 1977, they played a handful of experimental gigs by which time the line-up had expanded to include LARRY and BEN MILLER. The following year, DESTROY ALL MONSTERS released a debut single, 'BORED', a record licensed to UK indie label, 'Cherry Red'. Punk-ish rock'n'roll characterised by NIAGARA's sexual monotone, the band's sound was developed over a further couple of singles, namely 'MEET THE CREEPER' and 'NOBODY KNOWS'. A disappointing tour of Britain led to them disbanding a year later, although two further US-only EP's did surface around the turn of the decade.

Album rating: BORED compilation (*7)

NIAGARA (b. LYNN ROVNER) – vocals, violin / **RON ASHETON** – guitar (ex-STOOGES) repl. CARY LOREN / **LARRY MILLER** – guitar repl. MIKE KELLY / **MIKE DAVIS** – bass (ex-MC5) / **RON KING** – drums repl. JIM SHAW / **BEN MILLER** – saxophone

Cherry Red Idibi

Jan 79. (7"red) *(CHERRY 3)* **BORED. / YOU'RE GONNA DIE** ☐ ☐ 1978
Jun 79. (7") *(CHERRY 7)* **MEET THE CREEPER. / NOVEMBER 22nd, 1963** ☐ ☐ 1978
Sep 79. (7") *(CHERRY 9)* **NOBODY KNOWS. / WHAT DO I GET** ☐ [-]

not iss. Black Hole

1979. (7"ep) *<18551>* **LIVE (live)** [-] ☐
– Assassination photograph / Dream snug / Destroy all monsters / There is no end.
1980. (7"ep) **BLACK OUT IN THE CITY** [-] ☐
– No change / Switch the topic / Time bomb 1977.

— disbanded; ASHETON formed NEW RACE

- compilations, etc. -

1989. (lp) *Fan Club; (FC 050)* **LIVE (live)** ☐ [-]
– Anyone can fuck her / Bored / Party girl / Fast city / Go away / Having it all / Boots / Little boyfriend / November 22nd, 1963 / Right stuff / Ground zero.
1989. (cd) *Revenge; (MIG 11)* **NOVEMBER 22nd, 1963 - SINGLES AND RARITIES** ☐ [-]
– Bored / You're gonna die / Meet the creeper / November 22nd, 1963 / Jesus is a shotgun / Nobody knows / What do I get / These boots are made for walking / Anybody can / Party girl / A/D (angel in the daytime, Devil at night.
Oct 91. (cd) *Cherry Red; (CDMRED 94)* **BORED** ☐ [-]
– Bored / You're gonna die / November 22nd 1963 / Meet the creeper / Nobody knows / What do I get? / Goin' to lose. *(re-iss. Apr97; same)*
Oct 96. (cd) *Sympathy For The Record Industry; (SFTRI 444)* **SILVER WEDDING** ☐ [-]
Apr 98. (lp) *Get Back; (GET 31LP)* **AMAZING . . .** ☐ [-]

DESTRUCTION

Formed: Germany . . . 1983 by SCHMIER, MIKE and TOMMY. Signing to 'S.P.V.', the group debuted in early '85 with the perfunctory 'SENTENCE OF DEATH' mini-album. A full length effort, 'INFERNAL OVERKILL' appeared later the same year, a slightly improved effort which focused some of their gonzoid thrash aggression. 'ETERNAL DEVASTATION' (1986) cemented the band's growing stature in Germany's thrash scene alongside the likes of KREATOR although, in common with many German acts, the strangulated vocals sometimes worked against the band. 'RELEASE FROM AGONY'

(1987) saw the addition of guitarist HARRY, while OLLY replaced SENMAN on the drum stool, the extra guitar allowing the group to explore more complex arrangements. Highlights included the epic 'SIGN OF FEAR', with its exotic, Spanish-style intro. The same year, the band undertook a European jaunt in support of MOTORHEAD, subsequently going on to the States. Following the release of concert set, 'LIVE – WITHOUT SENSE' (1989), however, SCHMIER departed, leaving ex-POLTERGEIST vocalist, ANDRE, to fill in on subsequent studio outing, 'CRACKED BRAIN' (1990). The album saw DESTRUCTION moving away somewhat from their thrash roots, bringing criticism from fans and critics alike. It came as little surprise, then, when they finally self-destructed after the record's release.

Album rating: SENTENCE OF DEATH mini (*4) / INFERNAL OVERKILL (*5) / RELEASE FROM AGONY (*5) / ETERNAL DEVASTATION (*6) / LIVE WITHOUT SENSE (*4) / CRACKED BRAIN (*1) / THE BEST OF DESTRUCTION compilation (*6) / ALL HELL BREAKS LOOSE (*5)

SCHMIER (b. MARCUS SCHIRMER) – vocals, bass / **MIKE** (b. MICHAEL SIFFRINGER) – guitars / **TOMMY** (b. THOMAS SENMANN) – drums

S.P.V. not iss.

Jan 85. (m-lp) *(60-1838)* **SENTENCE OF DEATH** [-] [-] German
– Intro / Total disaster / Black mass / Mad butcher / Satan's revenge / Devil's soldiers.

Nov 85. (lp) *(08-1086)* **INFERNAL OVERKILL** [-] [-] German
– Invincible force / Death trap / The ritual / Tormentor / Bestial invasion / Thrash attack / Antichrist / Black death.

Jul 86. (lp) *(08-1885)* **ETERNAL DEVASTATION** [-] [-] German
– Curse the gods / Confound games / Life without sense / United by hatred / Eternal ban / Upcoming devastation / Confused mind. *(UK cd-iss. Mar98 on 'Axe Killer'; AXE 303503CD)*

— added **HARRY** (b. HARALD WILKENS) – guitar

— **(OLLY)** (b. OLIVER KAISER) – drums; repl. SENMANN

Feb 87. (lp/cd) *(08-/85-7503)* **RELEASE FROM AGONY** [-] [-] German
– Beyond eternity / Release from agony / Dissatisfied existence / Sign of fear / Unconscious ruins / Incriminated / Our oppression / Survive to die.

Nov 87. (m-lp) *(601 897)* **MAD BUTCHER** [-] [-] German
– Mad butcher / The damned / Reject emotions / The last judgement.

Noise Int. S.P.V.

Feb 89. (cd/c/lp) *(CD/ZC+/NUK 126) <08-7568>* **LIVE – WITHOUT SENSE (live)** □ □
– Curse the gods / Unconscious ruins / Invincible force / Dissatisfied existence / Reject emotions / Eternal ban / Mad butcher / Pink panther / Life without sense / In the mood / Release from agony / Bestial invasion.

— **ANDRE GRIEDER** – vocals (ex-POLTERGEIST) repl. guest ENGLER, who repl. SCHMIER

Jun 90. (cd/c/lp) *(CD/ZC+/NUK 136) <SPV 76192>* **CRACKED BRAIN** □ □
– Cracked brain / Frustrated / S E D / Time must end / My Sharona / Rippin' you off blind / Die a day before you're born / No need to justify / When your mind was free.

Brain Butcher not iss.

Oct 95. (m-cd) *(UAM 0447)* **DESTRUCTION** □ [-]

Nuclear Blast Nuclear Blast

May 00. (cd) *(<NB 494-2>)* **ALL HELL BREAKS LOOSE** □ □
– Intro / The final curtain / Machinery of lies / Tears of blood / Devastation of your soul / The butcher strikes back / World domination of pain / X-treme measures / All hell breaks loose / Total disaster 2000 / Visual prostitution / Kingdom of damnation / (untitled).

– compilations, etc. –

1989. (cd) *S.P.V.; (851 860)* **ETERNAL DEVASTATION / MAD BUTCHER** □ □

1989. (cd) *S.P.V.; (857 529)* **INFERNAL OVERKILL / SENTENCE OF DEATH** □ □

Apr 93. (d-cd) *S.P.V.; (SPV 084-7648CD)* **BEST OF DESTRUCTION** □ [-]

Jul 00. (cd) *S.P.V.; (SPV 31021960)* **MAD BUTCHER / INFERNAL OVERKILL** □ [-]

DESTRUCTORS

Formed: Peterborough, England ... 1977 by ALAN ADAMS and PHIL ATTERSON, although they soon adopted The BLANKS moniker upon entering the studio. Notorious for their controversial one and only single, 'THE NORTHERN RIPPER' (released at the same time as the Yorkshire Ripper was on the loose), the punk outfit later resurrected The DESTRUCTORS name. However, it would be only singer turned bass player, ADAMS, who would remain in the line-up, ATTERSON departing after the recruitment of frontman NEIL SINGLETON, DAVE ITHERMEE (who replaced ANDY JACKSON) and GRAHAM BUTTS. Well-meaning but cliched political punk, The DESTRUCTORS' sound was first heard on the 1982 EP, 'SENSELESS VIOLENCE'. A series of anti-everything EP's were released at regular intervals, culminating in the debut long-player, 'BOMB HANOI, BOMB SAIGON, BOMB DISNEYLAND' (1984).

Album rating: BOMB HANOI, BOMB SAIGON, BOMB DISNEYLAND (*3)

BLANKS

ALAN ADAMS – vocals / **PHIL ATTERSON** – guitar / **ANDY JACKSON** – rhythm guitar, bass; repl. DIP / **ANDY BUTLER** – drums

Void not iss.

1979. (7") *(SRTS 79-CUS-560)* **THE NORTHERN RIPPER. / UNDERSTAND / BREAK DOWN** □ [-]

DESTRUCTORS

— **ALAN ADAMS** – (now) bass / **NEIL SINGLETON** – vocals / **ANDY McDONALD** – drums / **DAVE ITHERMEE** – rhythm guitar; repl. JACKSON / **GRAHAM BUTTS** – lead guitar; repl. DAVE (diff.)

Paperback not iss.

Apr 82. (7"ep) *(BOOK 2)* **SENSELESS VIOLENCE EP** □ [-]
– Meaningless names / AK 47 / Police state / Dachau / Death squad.

Carnage not iss.

Jul 82. (7"ep) *(KILL 2)* **RELIGION THERE IS NO RELIGION EP** □ [-]
– Religion / Soldier boy / Agent orange / Corpse gas.

Illuminated not iss.

Oct 82. (7"ep) *(ILL 14)* **JAILBAIT EP** □ [-]
– Jailbait / Kalgsnocov / Sewage worker / Image.

Apr 83. (7"ep) *(ILL 19)* **FORCES OF LAW EP** □ [-]
– Forces of law / Wild thing / Neutron bomb.

Criminal Damage not iss.

Nov 83. (12"ep) *(CRI12 104)* **CRY HAVOC AND UNLEASH THE DOGS** □ [-]

Feb 84. (7"ep; as DESTRUCTORS V) *(CRI 108)* **TV EYE** □ [-]
– TV eye / The fatal kiss / Love like glass.

Carnage Benelux not iss.

Aug 84. (lp) *(KILL 666)* **BOMB HANOI, BOMB SAIGON, BOMB DISNEYLAND** □ [-]
– Northern Ripper / Orders / Class war / Breakdown / Overdose / Jailbait / Cocieties morons / Superstars / Control / Prostitute / Son of Sam / Hillside strangler / Sewage worker / Born too late / Urban terrorist / Deathsquad 2 / Out of control / Modern medicine.

— split in 1984

– compilations, etc. –

1980's. (lp) *Radical Change; (RCLP 2)* **ARMAGEDDON IN ACTION** □ [-]
– Soldier boy / AK 47 / Neutron bomb / Bullshit / European sacrifice / Urban terrorist / Forces of law / Duty unto death / Electronic church / Khmer rouge boogie / Nerve gas / Death squad / Wild thing / Northern ripper / Dachau.

DETECTIVE (see under ⇒ SILVERHEAD)

DEVIANTS (see under ⇒ PINK FAIRIES)

Dennis DeYOUNG (see under ⇒ STYX)

D GENERATION

Formed: New York City, New York, USA ... 1993 by frontman JESSE MALIN, DANNY SAGE and RICK BACCHUS, the latter two twin-guitarists. Almost immediately, the sleazy metal-punk 5-piece (including rhythm men HOWIE PYRO and MICHAEL WILDWOOD) landed a deal with 'Capitol', who set to work polishing up their strait-laced sound. The largely over-produced and therefore disappointing eponymous offering in '94 went astray somewhat with the buying public; their label duly dropped them. Over the course of the next few years, D GENERATION promoted their glitzy hard-rocking vision all over the place and were soon rewarded with another lucrative record contract via 'Sony'. In 1996, a smashing RIC OCASEK-produced sophomore set, 'NO LUNCH', hit all the right buttons (well, critically at least), although this would be the swansong for BACCHUS. A replacement was found in the shape of former MURPHY'S LAW man TODD YOUTH, the darker results evidenced on the quintet's third long-player, the TONY VISCONTI-produced 'THROUGH THE DARKNESS' (1999). If you liked your punk between NY DOLLS, RAMONES and The CLASH, well D GENERATION were obviously your metal.

Album rating: D GENERATION (*4) / NO LUNCH (*7) / THROUGH THE DARKNESS (*5)

JESSE MALIN – vocals / **DANNY SAGE** – guitar, vocals / **RICK BACCHUS** – guitar, vocals / **HOWIE PYRO** – bass / **MICHAEL WILDWOOD** – drums

Chrysalis Capitol

Oct 94. (cd) *(CDCHR 6092) <30050>* **D GENERATION** □ □
– No way out / Sins of America / Guitar mafia / Feel like suicide / Waiting for the next big parade / Falling / Wasted years / Stealing time / Ghosts / Frankie / Working on the avenue / Vampire nation / Degenerated.

not iss. Sony

Jul 96. (cd) *<67588>* **NO LUNCH** [-] □
– Scorch / She stands there / Frankie / Capital offender / No way out / Major / Disclaimer / Waiting for the next big parade / Not dreaming / Too loose / 1981 / Degenerated.

— **TODD YOUTH** – guitar (ex-MURPHY'S LAW) repl. BACCHUS

Feb 99. (cd/c) *<68782>* **THROUGH THE DARKNESS** [-] □
– Helpless / Every mother's son / Hatred / Rise & fall / Only a ghost / Lonely / Good ship down / Sick on the radio / Chinatown / So messed up / Sunday secret saints / Cornered / Don't be denied.

Munster Munster

Mar 00. (7") *<(MR7 132)>* **PROHIBITION. /** □ □

DIAMOND HEAD

Formed: Stourbridge, Midlands, England ... 1976 by schoolmates SEAN HARRIS and BRIAN TATLER, who recruited COLIN KIMBERLEY and DUNCAN SCOTT. One of the leading lights in the NWOBHM and certainly one of the most influential, DIAMOND HEAD released a series of self-financed 45's in the early 80's. An obscure German album on 'Woolfe' also surfaced before the band signed to 'M.C.A.'. Following on from the release of an EP 'FOUR CUTS', the band finally delivered their debut album proper, 'BORROWED TIME' (1982). Acclaimed as the new LED ZEPPELIN by the now-defunct Sounds music broadsheet, DIAMOND HEAD quickly found themselves in the UK Top 30. The following year, nearing the completion of their next album, the more ambitious 'CANTERBURY', the group suffered their first split (KIMBERLEY and SCOTT being replaced by MERV GOLDSWORTHY and ROBBIE FRANCE respectively). Although the record hit the UK Top 40, its poor reception prompted an eventual split in 1985 after they found themselves minus a record contract. Save for a farewell appearance at "The Monsters Of Rock" festival, their heavy-metal dream was over. Cited as a guiding inspiration by METALLICA (they recorded 'AM I EVIL'), DIAMOND HEAD were suffiently encouraged to reform in the early 90's. Releasing a track ('WILD IN THE STREETS') that was actually written in 1978, they subsequently secured a deal with 'Essential' records for whom they recorded a couple of competent, if hardly groundbreaking albums. • **Songwriters:** HARRIS-TATLER compositions.

Album rating: LIGHTNING TO THE NATIONS (*8) / BORROWED TIME (*7) / CANTERBURY (*7) / DEATH & PROGRESS (*6)

SEAN HARRIS – vocals, guitar / **BRIAN TATLER** – guitar / **COLIN KIMBERLEY** – bass / **DUNCAN SCOTT** – drums

Happy Face / not iss.

Mar 80. (7") *(MMDH 120)* **SHOOT OUT THE LIGHTS. / HELPLESS** [ ] [-]

Media / not iss.

Aug 80. (7") *(SCREEN 1)* **SWEET AND INNOCENT. / STREETS OF GOLD** [ ] [-]

D.H.M. / not iss.

1980. (lp; mail-order) *(MMDHLP 105)* **LIGHTNING TO THE NATIONS** [ ] [-]
– Lightning to the nations / The prince / Sucking my love / Am I evil / Sweet and innocent / It's electric / Helpless.

Mar 81. (7") *(DHM 004)* **PLAY IT LOUD. / WAITED TOO LONG** [ ] [-]

Aug 81. (12"ep) *(DHM 005)* **DIAMOND LIGHTS EP** [ ] [-]
– Diamond lights / We won't be back / I don't got / It's electric.

M.C.A. / M.C.A.

Apr 82. (7"ep/12"ep) *(DHM/+T 101)* **FOUR CUTS** [ ] [-]
– Call me / Trick or treat / Dead reckoning / Shoot out the lights.

Sep 82. (7"/ext-12") *(DHM 102)* **IN THE HEAT OF THE NIGHT. / PLAY IT LOUD (live)** [67] [-]
(7"w-free-7") *(MSAM 23)* – Sweet and innocent (live) / (interview with Tommy Vance).

Oct 82. (lp) *(DH 1001)* **BORROWED TIME** [24] [-]
– In the heat of the night / To Heaven from Hell / Call me / Lightning to the nations / Borrowed time / Don't you ever leave me / Am I evil. *(re-iss. Feb84 lp/c; MCL/+C 1783)*

Feb 83. (7") *<52161>* **CALL ME. / LIGHTNING TO THE NATIONS** [-] [ ]

Aug 83. (7"/12") *(DHM/+T 103)* **MAKING MUSIC. / (Andy Peebles interview)** [ ] [-]

Sep 83. (lp) *(DH 1002)* **CANTERBURY** [32] [-]
– Making music / Out of phase / The kingmaker / One more night / To the Devil his due / Knight of the swords / Ishmael / I need your love / Canterbury.

Oct 83. (7"/7"pic-d) *(DHM/+P 104)* **OUT OF PHASE. / THE KINGMAKER** [ ] [-]
(12"+=) *(DHMT 104)* – Sucking my love (live).

— (Dec'83) **DAVID WILLIAMSON** – bass repl. MERVYN GOLDSWORTHY who had repl. KIMBERLEY / **ROBBIE FRANCE** – drums repl. SCOTT

FM-Revolver / not iss.

May 87. (lp/c/cd) *(WKFM LP/MC/CD 92)* **AM I EVIL** (compilation) [ ] [-]
– Am I evil / Heat of the night / Don't you ever leave me / Borrowed time / To Heaven from Hell / Dead reckoning / Lightning to the nations / Sucking my love. *(pic-lp.May88; WKFMPD 92) (cd re-iss. Oct94 on 'Heavy Metal'; WKFMXD 92)*

— In 1990, HARRIS formed a new band NOTORIOUS with guitarist ROBIN GEORGE. They released the quickly deleted eponymous album that year on 'Bronze' (US 'Geffen'). A single, 'THE SWALK' was backed with 'EYES OF THE WORLD' late in 1990 (Bronze; BYZ 1). Meanwhile TATLER worked with RADIO MOSCOW, who issued one lp WORLD SERVICE.

— re-formed mid'91, when **TATLER** and **HARRIS** changed from new adopted group name MAGNETIC AKA to DIAMOND HEAD, brought in newcomers **EDDIE CHAOS** – bass / **CARL WILCOX** – drums

Bronze / not iss.

Nov 91. (7")(1-sided 12") **WILD ON THE STREETS. /** [ ] [ ]

Jan 92. (m-lp) **RISING UP** [ ] [-]
– Feels good / Can't help myself / Rising up / Kiss of fire / Calling your name / Wild on the streets.

Esssential / Blackheart

Jun 93. (cd/c/lp) *(ESS CD/MC/LP 192) <668>* **DEATH & PROGRESS** [ ] [ ] Mar96
– Star crossed (lovers of the night) / Truckin' / Calling your name (the light) / I can't help myself / Paradise (featuring BILLY & SARAH GAINES) / Dust / Run / Wild on the streets / Damnation Street / Home. *(cd re-iss. Sep96; ESMCD 387)*

Sep 94. (d-cd) *(ESDCD 219)* **EVIL LIVE (live)** [ ] [-]
– Am I evil? / Dust / Truckin' / To the Devil his due / Sucking my love / Run / To Heaven from Hell / Helpless.

– compilations, others, etc. –

Apr 86. (lp) *Metal Masters; (METALP 110)* **BEHOLD THE BEGINNING** [ ] [-]
– It's electric / The prince / Sweet and innocent / Sucking my love / Streets of gold / Play it loud / Shoot out the lights / Waited too long / Helpless. *(re-iss. May91 on 'Heavy Metal' cd/c/lp; HMR XD/MC/LP 165)*

1988. (m-cd) *Metal Masters; (METALMCD 122)* **SWEET AND INNOCENT** [ ] [-]

Feb 91. (cd/c/lp) *FM-Revolver; (WKFM CD/MC/LP 165)* **IN THE BEGINNING** [ ] [-]

Feb 92. (cd) *Raw Fruit; (FRSCD 006)* **FRIDAY ROCK SHOW SESSIONS (live '86)** [ ] [-]

Jun 99. (cd) *Half Moon; (HMNCD 046)* **THE BEST OF DIAMOND HEAD** [ ] [ ]

Aug 00. (d-cd) *Zoom Club; (ZCRCD 27)* **LIVE IN THE HEAT OF THE NIGHT (live)** [ ] [ ]

Paul DI'ANNO

Born: 17 May'59, Chingford, London, England. After the vocalist's sacking from IRON MAIDEN in 1981, DI'ANNO put together his own outfit, initially calling it LONEWOLF, before opting for the simpler DI'ANNO following objections from a similarly named group. He brought together the line-up of JOHN WIGGINS, PETER J. WARD, MARK VENABLES, KEVIN BROWNE and MARK STEWART, engendering a complete musical about face as DIANNO concentrated on tight, American-sounding AOR. Around 1983, before the recording of the group's eponymous debut album, guitarist LEE SLATER replaced the outgoing WIGGINS and drummer STEWART, the record subsequently being lambasted by the music press. DI'ANNO took the hint and eventually resurfaced with PAUL DI'ANNO'S BATTLEZONE, a return to his power-metal roots and in reality, a more appropriate vehicle for the singer's impressive vocal abilities. Hooking up once more with JOHN WIGGINS and recruiting PETE WEST, JOHN HURLEY and BOB FALCK, the outfit signed to the 'Raw Power' label and released a solitary eponymous album in summer '86. Following a European tour, FALCK and HURLEY both departed, their replacements being STEVE HOPGOOD and GRAHAM BATH respectively. Released on the 'Powerstation' label, the 'CHILDREN OF MADNESS' (1987) set saw DI'ANNO once again veer towards a more American sound. Perhaps as a result, the record failed to take off and the group splintered. DI'ANNO drafted in a new set of musicians before disbanding the project altogether and eventually forming PAUL DI'ANNO'S KILLERS with a crew of NWOBHM stalwarts. The outfit released a clutch of albums, the first and second of which were 'MURDER ONE' (1992) and 'SOUTH AMERICAN ASSAULT' (1994).

Album rating: FIGHTING BACK (*5) / CHILDREN OF MADNESS (*4) / Killers: MURDER ONE (*5) / SOUTH AMERICAN ASSAULT: LIVE (*4)

DIANNO

PAUL DI'ANNO – vocals (ex-IRON MAIDEN) / **PETER J. WARD** – guitar, vocals / **LEE SLATER** – guitar; repl. JOHN WIGGINS / **MARK VENABLES** – keyboards, vocals / **KEVIN BROWNE** – bass, vocals / **DAVE IRVING** – drums (session) repl. MARK STEWART

FM Revolver / not iss.

1984. (lp/pic-lp) *(WKFM LP/PD 1)* **DIANNO** [ ] [-]
– Flaming heart / Heartuser / Here to stay / The runner / Tales of the unexpected / Razor edge / Bright lights / Lady heartbreak / Antigua / Road rat.

PAUL DI'ANNO'S BATTLEZONE

— with **JOHN WIGGINS** – guitar / **GRAHAM BATH** – guitar / **PETE WEST** – bass / **STEVE HOPGOOD** – drums

Raw Power / Profile

Jul 86. (lp/c) *(RAW LP/TC 020) <PAC 1222>* **FIGHTING BACK** [ ] [ ]
– Fighting back / Welcome to the battlezone / War child / In the darkness / The land God gave to Caine / Running blind / Too much to heart / Voice on the radio / Welfare warriors / Feel the rock. *(cd-iss. 1988 as 'WARCHILD' on 'Powerstation'; AMPCD 15) (cd re-iss. Jun99 on 'Zoom Club'; ZCRCD 2)*

Powerstation / Profile

Jun 87. (lp) *(AMP 13) <PAC 1234>* **CHILDREN OF MADNESS** [ ] [ ]
– Rip it up / I don't wanna know / Nuclear breakdown / Torch of hate / Whispered rage / Children of madness / Metal tears / It's love / Overloaded / The promise. *(cd-iss. Jun99 on 'Zoom Club'; ZCRCD 3)*

KILLERS

— **PAUL DI'ANNO** with **NICK BURR** – guitar / **CLIFF EVANS** – guitars / **GAVIN COOPER** – bass / **STEVE HOPGOOD** – drums

R.C.A. / R.C.A.

May 92. (cd/c/lp) *(PD/PK/PL 90643)* **MURDER ONE** [ ] [ ]
– Impaler / The beast arises / Children of the revolution / S&M / Takin' no prisoners / Marshall Lockjaw / Protector / Dream keeper / Awakening / Remember tomorrow.

S.P.V. / Magnetic Air

Aug 94. (cd; as PAUL DI'ANNO & KILLERS) *(SPV 084-38952) <4007>* **SOUTH AMERICAN ASSAULT: LIVE** [ ] [ ]
– Overloaded / Murders in the Rue Morgue / Wrathchild / Remember tomorrow / Children of madness / Phantom of the opera / Metal tears / Strange world / Sanctuary / Running free / The promise / We will rock you – Smoke on the water.

Bleeding Hearts / not iss.

Nov 94. (cd) *(CDBLEED 11)* **MENACE TO SOCIETY** [ ] [-]
– Advance for the recognised / Die by the gun / Menace to society / Missing track / Think brutal / Past due / Faith healer / Chemical imbalance / A song for you / Three words / Conscience / City of fools.

not iss. / Spitfire

Nov 00. (cd; as PAUL DI'ANNO KILLERS) *<15173>* **LIVE AT THE WHISKEY (live)** [-] [ ]
– Impaler / Wrathchild / A song for you / Marshall Lockjaw / Children of the revolution / Three words / Protector / Die by the gun / Remember tomorrow / Phantom of the opera / Sanctuary.

Jan 01. (cd; as PAUL DI'ANNO) <15178> **THE BEAST - LIVE** [-] [ ]
– Wrathchild / Killers / Prowler / Murders in the Rue Morgue / Women in uniform / Remember tomorrow / Sanctuary / Running free / Phantom of the opera / Iron maiden.

– compilations, etc. –

Jul 95. (cd) *Scratch; (ASBCD 004)* **THE IRON MEN** [ ] [-]
Jun 96. (cd; PAUL DI'ANNO & DENNIS STRATTON) *Thunderbolt; (CDTB 176)* **HARD AS IRON** [ ] [-]
Dec 96. (cd) *Scratch; (ABSCD 008)* **THE ORIGINAL IRON MAN** [ ] [-]
Mar 97. (cd) *Hardware; (HR 001CD)* **LIVE (live)** [ ] [-]
Jan 99. (d-cd) *Cleopatra;* <CL 446> **BEYOND THE MAIDEN** [-] [ ]
Jun 99. (cd; as PAUL DI'ANNO BATTLEZONE) *Zoom Club; (ZCRCD 10)* **FEEL MY PAIN** [ ] [-]
Jun 99. (cd) *Eagle; (EDMCD 040)* **THE MASTERS** [ ] [-]

DICKIES

Formed: San Fernando Valley, California, USA ... 1977 by CHUCK WAGON, STAN LEE, BILLY CLUB, LEONARD PHILLIPS and KARLOS KABALLERO. Forebears to the likes of GREEN DAY and a poppier prototype of English cover fiends, SNUFF, the DICKIES initially made a name for themselves on the L.A. punk scene through their rabid, tongue-in-cheek versions of rock's sacred cows. Signed to 'A&M', the band's eponymous debut three-tracker surfaced in Spring '78, leading with a frantic reading of Black Sabbath's 'PARANOID'. This was subsequently released as a single in its own right, followed up by a trashing of the Barry McGuire protest classic, 'EVE OF DESTRUCTION'. Christmas '78, meanwhile, saw what else but a rendition of 'SILENT NIGHT', DICKIES style (backed with a none too quiet cover of Simon & Garfunkel's 'SOUNDS OF SILENCE'), a track that gave them an early Top 50 hit. While not featured on debut album, 'THE INCREDIBLE SHRINKING DICKIES' (1979), early '79's version of The Moody Blues' 'NIGHTS IN WHITE SATIN' was a stage favourite and a hit second time around later that year. The DICKIES' defining moment, however, came with their punked-up pilgrimage to classic 70's kids TV, a cover of the theme tune to 'Banana Splits'. A Top 10 UK hit, it cemented the band's reputation as a punk novelty act although the DICKIES' self-penned good-time three-chord anthems won them respect among the safety-pin crew on both sides of the Atlantic. A prolific year came to a close with the release of a follow-up album, 'DAWN OF THE DICKIES', again drawing inspiration from B-movies and assorted American cultural debris. Sadly, CHUCK committed suicide in summer '81, effectively halting the band's career. Although 1983's 'STUKAS OVERT DISNEYLAND' comprised of recordings made before CHUCK's death, the band didn't re-emerge with new material until the late 80's. With a line-up of PHILLIPS, LEE, LORENZO BUNHE, JEROME ANGEL, ENOCH HAIN and CLIFF MARTINEZ, the DICKIES inked a deal with 'Enigma' and released the 'KILLER KLOWNS FROM OUTER SPACE' EP in late '88. An album, 'SECOND COMING', followed in '89, replete with the usual helping of cover versions including Gene Pitney's 'TOWN WITHOUT PITY'. The early 90's saw future SMASHING PUMPKINS keyboard player, JONATHON MELVOIN, come on board while a new deal with L.A.'s 'Triple X' label was inaugurated with 'ROADKILL' (1993). Come 1998, the DICKIES were still chasing their proverbial tail with 'DOGS FROM THE HARE THAT BIT US', basically a covers set ripping into Iron Butterfly's 'UNCONSCIOUS POWER', Uriah Heep's 'EASY LIVIN', Beatles' 'THERE'S A PLACE', etc.

Album rating: THE INCREDIBLE SHRINKING DICKIES (*7) / DAWN OF THE DICKIES (*7)/ STUKAS OVER DISNEYLAND (*6) / WE AREN'T THE WORLD (*5) / SECOND COMING (*4) / GREAT DICTATIONS (THE DEFINITIVE DICKIES COLLECTION) compilation (*6) / IDJIT SAVANT (*5) / DOGS FROM THE HARE THAT BIT US (*5)

LEONARD GRAVES PHILLIPS – vocals, keyboards / **STAN LEE** (b.24 Sep'56) – guitar, vocals / **CHUCK WAGON** (b. BOB DAVIS) – keyboards, guitar / **BILLY CLUB** – bass, vocals / **KARLOS KABALLERO** – drums

A&M A&M

May 78. (12"m) <12-008> **THE DICKIES** [-] [ ]
– Paranoid / Hideous / You drive me ape (you big gorilla).
Jun 78. (7",7"clear) *(AMS 7368)* **PARANOID. / I'M OK, YOU'RE OK** [ ] [ ]
(re-iss. Jul79; same) – hit UK No.45
Aug 78. (7",7"pink) *(AMS 7373)* **EVE OF DESTRUCTION. / DOGGIE DO** [ ] [-]
Oct 78. (7",7"white) *(AMS 7391)* **GIVE IT BACK. / YOU DRIVE ME APE (YOU BIG GORILLA)** [ ] [-]
Dec 78. (7",7"white) *(AMS 7403)* **SILENT NIGHT. / THE SOUNDS OF SILENCE** [47] [-]
Jan 79. (7") <2225> **NIGHTS IN WHITE SATIN. / MANNY, MOE & JACK** [-] [ ]
Feb 79. (lp,yellow-lp,blue-lp,orange-lp) *(AMLE 64742)* **THE INCREDIBLE SHRINKING DICKIES** [ ] [ ]
– Give it back / Poodle party / Paranoid / She / Shadow man / Mental ward / Eve of destruction / You drive me ape (you big gorilla) / Waterslide / Walk like an egg / Curb job / Shake and bake / Rondo. *<cd-iss. Sep00 on 'Captain Oi' cd/lp; AHOY CD/LP 149>*
Apr 79. (7",7"clear) *(AMS 7431)* **BANANA SPLITS (TRA LA LA SONG). / HIDEOUS / GOT IT AT THE STORE** [7] [-]
May 79. (7") <2241> **BANANA SPLITS (TRA LA LA SONG). / THE SOUNDS OF SILENCE** [-] [ ]
Jun 79. (7",7"purple; by CHUCK WAGON) *(AMS 7450)* **ROCK'N'ROLL WON'T GO AWAY. / THE SPY IN MY FACE** [ ] [-]
Aug 79. (7"white) *(AMS 7469)* **NIGHTS IN WHITE SATIN. / WATERSLIDE** [39] [ ]
Oct 79. (lp,blue-lp) *(AMLH 68510)* **DAWN OF THE DICKIES** [ ] [ ]
– Where did his eye go / Fan mail / Manny, Moe & Jack / Infedil zombie / I'm a chollo / Nights in white satin / (I'm stuck in a pagoda) With Tricia Toyota / I've got a splitting headache / Attack of the mole men / She loves me not. *<cd-iss. Sep00 on 'Captain Oi' cd/lp; AHOY CD/LP 150>*
Nov 79. (7") *(AMS 7491)* **MANNY, MOE & JACK. / SHE LOVES ME NOT** [ ] [-]
Jan 80. (7"red) *(AMS 7504)* **FAN MAIL. / (I'M STUCK IN A PAGODA) WITH TRICIA TOYOTA** [ ] [-]
Jul 80. (7"yellow) *(AMS 7544)* **GIGANTOR. / BOWLING WITH BEDROCK BARNEY** [ ] [-]

— CHUCK WAGON committed suicide in June '81 as the band continued in a lower profile (below recordings between 1980-83 with CHUCK)

— other people used incl. **SCOTT SINDON + STEVE HUFSTETER** – guitar / **LORENZO BUHNE** – bass / **JEROME ANGEL** – drums, percussion

not iss. P.V.C.

1983. (lp) <6903> **STUKAS OVER DISNEYLAND** [-] [ ]
– Rosemary / She's a hunch back / Out of sight, out of mind / Communication breakdown / Pretty please me / Wagon train / If Stuart could talk / Stukas over Disneyland. *(UK cd-iss. Jul95 on 'Restless'; 772247-2) (re-iss. Jul98 on 'Overground' 10"lp/cd; OVER 76/+CD) <(cd re-iss. May00 on 'Triple X'; TX 51265CD)>*

— **PHILLIPS, LEE, ANGEL + BUHNE** plus newcomers **ENOCH HAIN** – guitar / **CLIFF MARTINEZ** – drums

Enigma-Virgin Enigma

Nov 88. (12"ep) <D2 73322> **KILLER KLOWNS FROM OUTER SPACE** [-] [ ]
– Killer klowns / Booby trap / Jim Bowie / Magoomba / Eep oop ork (uh uh). *(UK cd-iss. Jul95 on 'Restless'; 772554-2)*
May 89. (lp/c/cd) *(ENVLP/TCENV/CDENV 526)* <73289> **SECOND COMING** [ ] [ ] Feb89
– Hair / Monster island / Town without pity / Cross-eyed Tammy / Going homo / Dummy up / Booby trap / Magoomba / Caligula / I'm Stan / Monkey see, monkey do. *(cd re-iss. Jul95 on 'Restless'; 772553-2)*

Overground unknown

Jul 90. (7"white,7"mauve,7"blue) *(OVER 12)* **JUST SAY YES. / AYATOLLAH YOU SO** [ ] [-]
Oct 90. (7"flexi-tour) *(OVER 17)* **ROADKILL** [ ] [-]

Receiver not iss.

Apr 91. (cd/c/lp) *(RR CD/LC/LP 137)* **LIVE IN LONDON - LOCKED 'N' LOADED 1990 (live)** [ ] [-]
– Attack of the killer clowns from Outer Space / Eve of destruction / Nights in white satin / Pretty please me / You drive me ape (you big gorilla) / Give it back / Just say yes / (Stuck in a pagoda) With Tricia Toyota / Curb job / Cross-eyed Tammy / Going homo / She's a hunch back / If Stuart could talk / Manny, Moe & Jack / Paranoid / Gigantor / Communication breakdown / Banana splits / Fan mail.

— now with **JONATHAN MELVOIN** – keyboards (of SMASHING PUMPKINS)

Triple X Relativity

May 93. (m-cd) *<(TX 51149CD)>* **ROADKILL**
Sep 94. (cd/c) *<(51168-2/-4)>* **IDJIT SAVANT** [ ] [ ] Jan95
– Welcome to the diamond mine / Golden boys / Pretty ballerina / Elevator / Oh baby / Make it so / I'm on crack / I'm stuck in a condo (with Marlon Brando) / Zeppelina / Roadkill / Just say yes / House of Raoul / Song of the dawn. *(cd re-iss. Mar95 & Aug99 on 'Golf'; CDHOLE 002)*
1995. (7") *(HOLE 008)* **MAKE IT SO. / OH BABY** [ ] [-]
(above issued on 'Golf' records)
Jun 98. (lp/cd) *<(TX 51232/+CD)>* **DOGS FROM THE HARE THAT BIT US** [ ] [ ]
– Intro / Solitary confinement / Easy livin' / Unconscious power / There's a place / Nobody but me / Can't let go / Let me out / Epistle to Dippy.

– compilations, etc. –

Apr 86. (c) *R.O.I.R.; <A 140>* **WE AREN'T THE WORLD (live '78-'85)** [-] [ ]
(cd-iss. Nov94; RE 140CD)
Mar 89. (lp/c/cd) *A&M; (CDA/AMC/AMA 5236)* **GREAT DICTATIONS (THE DEFINITIVE DICKIES COLLECTION)** [ ] [-]
– Hideous / You drive me ape (you big gorilla) / Give it back / Paranoid / I'm ok, you're ok / Got it at the store / The sounds of silence / Banana splits (tra la la song) / Nights in white satin / (Stuck in a pagoda) With Tricia Toyota / Manny, Moe & Jack / Fan mail / Attack of the mole men / Gigantor / Eve of destruction / Silent night.
Jun 99. (cd) *R.O.I.R.; <(RUSCD 8252)>* **STILL LIVE EVEN IF YOU DON'T WANT IT** [ ] [ ]

Bruce DICKINSON

Born: 7 Aug'58, Sheffield, England. As BRUCE BRUCE, DICKINSON cut his teeth in heavyweights, SAMSON, between 1978-1981. This outfit released two albums, 'HEAD ON' (1980) and 'SHOCK TACTICS', before he opted to join IRON MAIDEN. Now using his real surname, he became Britain's top heavy voxman, his inimitable growl/warble seeing MAIDEN through the most suuccessful period of their career. In fact, every single album made the UK Top 3 over the course of the subsequent eleven years. Early in 1990 while still an IRON MAIDEN member, he unleashed his debut solo outing, 'TATTOOED MILLIONAIRE'. While a little lighter and more commercial, it still gathered enough hard-rock support, even when re-hashing the classic MOTT THE HOOPLE number, 'ALL THE YOUNG DUDES'. Surprisingly, he opted to leave IRON MAIDEN in 1993 and released a second hit album, 'BALLS TO PICASSO' the following year. This more cultured of heavy metal troopers has also diversified into writing, penning two tongue-in-cheek novels, 'The Adventures Of Lord Iffy Boatrace' and 'The Missionary Position'. In 1996, his third studio album, 'SKUNKWORKS' was produced by grungemeister,

JACK ENDINO. The man's solo career continued apace with 'ACCIDENT OF BIRTH' (1997) meanwhile, an album which saw BRUCE reunited with his old 'MAIDEN sparring partner ADRIAN SMITH. As well as contributing his distinctive guitar work, SMITH was also involved in the songwriting alongside DICKINSON's chief co-writer/producer ROY Z. Unsurprisingly, both this record and its successor, 'THE CHEMICAL WEDDING' (1998) conjured up more of the old IRON MAIDEN magic than even the band themselves could muster during this period, foregoing the more whimsical elements of BRUCE's initial solo output for a finely wrought metallic edge. Hardly surprising then, that both DICKINSON and SMITH returned to IRON MAIDEN at the close of the decade following on from their '98/'99 tour. The latter was documented on the 'SCREAM FOR ME BRAZIL' (1999) set, the first release on BRUCE's newly inaugurated 'Air Raid' label.

Album rating: TATTOOED MILLIONAIRE (*5) / BALLS TO PICASSO (*5) / ALIVE IN STUDIO A (*4) / SKUNKWORKS (*5) / ACCIDENT OF BIRTH (*6) / THE CHEMICAL WEDDING (*6) / SCREAM FOR ME BRAZIL (*5)

solo, with **JANICK GERS** – guitar, co-composer / **FABIO DEL RIO** – drums (ex-JAGGED EDGE)

E.M.I. Columbia

Apr 90. (7"/7"sha-pic-d/c-s) *(EM/EMPD/TCEM 138) <73338>* **TATTOOED MILLIONAIRE. / BALLAD OF MUTT** [18] [ ]
(12"+=/12"w-poster+=/cd-s+=) *(12EM/12EMP/CDEM 138)* – Winds of change.

May 90. (cd/c/lp) *(CD/TC+/EMC 3574) <46139>* **TATTOOED MILLIONAIRE** [14] [100]
– Son of a gun / Tattooed millionaire / Born in 58 / Hell on wheels / Gypsy road / Dive! dive! dive! / All the young dudes / Lickin' the gun / Zulu Lulu / No lies. *(cd re-iss. May99 on 'Air Raid'; AIRCD 2)*

Jun 90. (7"/7"sha-pic-d/c-s) *(EM/EMPD/TCEM 142)* **ALL THE YOUNG DUDES. / DARKNESS BE MY FRIEND** [23] [-]
(12"+=/cd-s+=) *(12EMG/CDEM 142)* – Sin city.

Aug 90. (c-s/7") *(TC+/EM 151)* **DIVE! DIVE! DIVE!. / RIDING WITH THE ANGELS (live)** [45] [-]
(12"+=/12"sha-pic-d+=/cd-s+=) *(12EM/EMPD/CDEM 151)* – Sin city / Black night.

Mar 91. (c-s/7") *(TC+/EM 185)* **BORN IN 58. / TATTOOED MILLIONAIRE (live)** [ ] [-]
(12"+=/cd-s+=) *(12/CD EM 185)* – Son of a gun (live).

— In Apr'92, he was credited on the charity UK Top 10 hit 'ELECTED' by MR. BEAN and SMEAR CAMPAIGN for 'London'; *LON 319)*
(below featured backing from gangstas TRIBE OF GYPSIES)

E.M.I. Polygram

May 94. (7"clear) *(EM 322)* **TEARS OF THE DRAGON. / FIRE CHILD** [28] [-]
(7"pic-d) *(EMPD 322)* – ('A'side) / Elvis has left the building.
(cd-s+=) *(CDEMS 322)* – Breeding house / No way out . . . to be continued.
(cd-s+=) *(CDEM 322)* – Winds of change / Spirit of joy.

Jun 94. (cd/c/lp) *(CD/TC+/EMCD 1057) <522491>* **BALLS TO PICASSO** [21] [ ]
– Cyclops / Hell no / Gods of war / 1000 points of light / Laughing in the hiding bush / Change of heart / Shoot all the clowns / Fire / Sacred cowboy / Tears of the dragon. *(cd re-iss. May99 on 'Air Raid'; AIRCD 3)*

Sep 94. (7") *(EM 341)* **SHOOT ALL THE CLOWNS. / OVER AND OUT** [37] [-]
(cd-s) *(CDEMS 341)* – ('A'side) / Tibet / Tears of the dragon: The first bit . . .
(cd-s) *(CDEM 341)* – ('A'side) / Cadillac gas mask / No way out – continued.
(12") *(12EM 341)* – ('A'side) / Laughing in the hiding bush (live) / The post alternative Seattle fallout (live).

Raw Power not iss.

Mar 95. (d-cd/c/d-lp) *(RAW DD/DC/DV 102)* **ALIVE IN STUDIO A (live)** [ ] [-]
– Cyclops / Shoot all the clowns / Son of a gun / Tears of the dragon / 1000 points of light / Sacred cowboys / Tattooed millionaire / Born in '58 / Fire / Change of heart / Hell no / Laughing in the hiding bush // Cyclops / 1000 points of light / Born in '58 / Gods of war / Change of heart / Laughing in the hiding bush / Hell no / Tears of the dragon / Shoot all the clowns / Sacred cowboys / Son of a gun / Tattooed millionaire. *(re-iss. Apr96 on 'Raw Power'; same) <US-iss.1998 on 'C.M.C.'; 86227> (d-cd re-iss. Aug99 on 'Essential'; ESDCD 764)*

— now w/ **ALEX DICKSON** – guitar / **CHRIS DALE** – bass / **ALESSANDRO ELENA** – drums

Raw Power Raw Power

Mar 96. (cd/c/lp) *(<RAW CD/MC/LP 106>)* **SKUNKWORKS** [41] [ ]
– Space race / Back from the edge / Inertia / Faith / Solar confinement / Dreamstate / I will not accept the truth / Inside the truth / Headswitch / Meltdown / Octavia / Innerspace / Strange death in Paradise. *(cd re-iss. Aug99 on 'Essential'; ESMCD 766)*

Apr 96. (7"pic-d) *(RAW 1012)* **BACK FROM THE EDGE. / I'M IN A BAND WITH AN ITALIAN DRUMMER** [68] [-]
(cd-s) *(RAWX 1012)* – ('A'side) / R-101 / Re-entry / Americans are behind.
(cd-s) *(RAWX 1013)* – ('A'side) / Rescue day / God's not coming back / Armchair hero.

— now with **ROY Z** – guitar / **ADRIAN SMITH** – guitar / **EDDIE CASILLAS** – bass / **DAVE INGRAM** – drums

Apr 97. (pic-cd-s) *(RAWX 1042)* **ACCIDENT OF BIRTH / GHOST OF CAIN / ACCIDENT OF BIRTH (demo)** [54] [-]
(pic-cd-s) *(RAWX 1045)* – ('A'side) / Star children (demo) / Taking the queen (demo).
(12"red) *(RAWT 1042)* –

Raw Power C.M.C.

May 97. (cd/c/lp) *(RAW CD/MC/LP 124) <86217>* **ACCIDENT OF BIRTH** [53] [ ] Jun97
– Freak / Toltec 7 arrival / Starchildren / Taking the queen / Darkside of Aquarius / Road to Hell / Man of sorrows / Accident of birth / Magician / Welcome to the pit / Omega / Arc of space. *(cd re-iss. Aug99 on 'Essential'; ESMCD 767)*

Air Raid C.M.C.

Sep 98. (cd) *(AIRCD 1) <86259>* **THE CHEMICAL WEDDING** [55] [ ]
– King in crimson / The chemical wedding / The tower / Killing floor / Book of Thel / Gates of Urizen / Jerusalem / Trumpets of Jericho / Machine men / The alchemist.

Air Raid Never

Oct 99. (cd) *(AIRCD 4) <4502>* **SCREAM FOR ME BRAZIL (live)** [ ] [ ]
– Trumpets of Jericho / King in crimson / The chemical wedding / Gates of Urizen / Killing floor / Book of Thel / Tears of the dragon / Laughing in the hiding bush / Accident of birth / Dark side of Aquarius / The road to Hell.

DICKS (see under ⇒ SISTER DOUBLE HAPPINESS)

DICTATORS

Formed: The Bronx, New York, USA . . . 1974 by ROSS THE BOSS FUNICELLO, MARK "The Animal" MENDOZA, main songwriter ADNY (ANDY) SHERNOFF, SCOTT KEMPNER and STU BOY KING, who were soon joined by "Handsome" DICK MANITOBA. Exploding onto the embryonic NY punk scene at the same time as bands like The RAMONES and The HEARTBREAKERS, the group harnessed the energy of garage-rock to a raucous pre-MOTORHEAD metallic bludgeon. Signed to the 'Epic' label, they nevertheless delivered a rather poorly-received debut album in 1975, 'GO GIRL CRAZY!', which included a few covers including Sonny & Cher's 'I GOT YOU BABE'. 'Asylum' subsequently took up the reins, releasing the much-improved 'MANIFEST DESTINY' (1977), a hard-rocking set that featured their version of Iggy (Pop) & The Stooges' 'SEARCH & DESTROY' (one of the first ever tracks to be released on the 12" format). The single, which also featured new drummer RITCHIE TEETER, surprisingly hit the UK Top 50, although a third album, 'BLOOD BROTHERS' failed to garner any wider support from the evolving punk scene, The DICTATORS were also misunderstood by purist metal fans. ROSS THE BOSS and MENDOZA finally found some degree of recognition with MANOWAR and TWISTED SISTER respectively.

Album rating: GO GIRL CRAZY (*7) / MANIFEST DESTINY (*6) / BLOODBROTHERS (*6) / FUCK 'EM IF THEY CAN'T TAKE A JOKE (*6)

'HANDSOME' DICK MANITOBA (b. RICHARD BLUM, 29 Jan'54) – vocals / **ROSS THE BOSS FUNICELLO** (b. 3 Jan'54) – guitar, vocals / **ADNY SHERNOFF** (b. ANDY, 19 Apr'52) – vocals, bass / **SCOTT KEMPNER** (b. 6 Feb'54) – guitar, vocals / **STU BOY KING** – drums, percussion

Epic Epic

Dec 75. (lp) *(EPC 80767) <33348>* **GO GIRL CRAZY!** [ ] [ ]
– The next big thing / I got you babe / Back to Africa / Master race rock / Teengenerate / California sun / Two tub man / Weekend / (I live for) Cars and girls. *(cd-iss. Jul93 on 'Sony Europe';)*

— **RITCHIE TEETER** (b.16 Mar'51, Long Island, N.Y.) – drums repl. STU / added **MARK MENDOZA** (b.13 Jul'56, Long Island) – bass

Asylum Asylum

Jun 77. (7") *<45420>* **DISEASE. / HEY BOYS** [-] [ ]
Jun 77. (lp) *(K 53061) <7E 1109>* **MANIFEST DESTINY** [ ] [ ]
– Exposed / Heartache / Sleepin' with the T.V. on / Disease / Hey boys / Steppin' out / Science gone too far! / Young, fast, scientific / Search & destroy.

Aug 77. (7") *<45470>* **SLEEPIN' WITH THE T.V. ON. / SCIENCE GONE TOO FAR** [-] [ ]

Sep 77. (7"/12") *(K 13091/+T))* **SEARCH & DESTROY. / SLEEPIN' WITH THE T.V. ON** [49] [ ]

— now without MENDOZA who later joined TWISTED SISTER

Aug 78. (lp) *(K 53083) <147>* **BLOODBROTHERS** [ ] [ ]
– Faster & louder / Baby let's twist / No tomorrow / The Minnesota strip / Stay with me / I stand tall / Borneo Jimmy / What is it / Slow death.

Aug 78. (7") *<45523>* **I STAND TALL. / TOO MUCH FUN** [-] [ ]

not iss. PrTempore

1980. (lp) *<10017>* **DICTATORS** [-] [ ]
– The next big thing / Disease / Hey boys / Two tub man / The moon upstairs / Weekend / New York, New York / I stand tall / Slow death.

— disbanded 1980. ROSS formed SHAKIN' STREET and later MANOWAR. DICK and SHERNOFF later formed MANITOBA'S WILD KINGDOM. In 1990, they were joined by FUNICELLO. In 1994, he, MANITOBA, KEMPNER (ex-DEL-LORDS), SHERNOFF and FRANK FUNARO – drums, reformed The DICTATORS

– compilations, others, etc. –

1981. (c) *R.O.I.R.; <A 102>* **FUCK 'EM IF THEY CAN'T TAKE A JOKE** [-] [ ]
(cd-iss. Nov94 on 'Danceteria'; DANCD 052)

Jan 97. (cd-s) *White Jazz; (JAZZ 003CD)* **I AM RIGHT** [ ] [-]

Nov 97. (7"; split with The NOMADS) *Next Big Thing; (NBT 4527)* [ ] [-]

Dec 98. (cd) *ROIR; <(RUSCD 8247)>* **NEW YORK NEW YORK – THE DICTATORS LIVE (live)** [ ] [ ]

— (there is also two tribute albums out there on 'Roto' RTI 205/206)

DIE CHEERLEADER

Formed: London, England . . . early 90's by RITA BLAZYCA, SAM IRELAND, DEBBIE QUARGNOLO and ANDY SEMPLE. A dominantly female outfit, DIE CHEERLEADER served up a cocktail of spiky indie-metal with lashings of girlie angst. Three promising EP's were released in the space of a year between '92-'93, the tracks collected on their debut album, 'FILTH BY ASSOCIATION' (1993). One particularly high profile fan was HENRY ROLLINS who signed them up to his American publishing company and subsequently helped secure a deal with 'London' records. The US-only

HENRY ROLLINS-produced release, 'SON OF FILTH' (1995), again featured some of their early work, although there was some new material on offer.

Album rating: FILTH BY ASSOCIATION compilation (*6) / SON OF FILTH (*5)

SAM IRELAND – vocals / **RITA BLAZYCA** – guitar / **DEBBIE QUARGNOLO** – bass / **ANDY SEMPLE** – drums

Abstract | not iss.

Oct 92. (12"ep) *(12ABS 097)* **D.C. EP** [ ] [-]

Feb 93. (12"ep/cd-ep) *(12ABS/ABSCD 098)* **SATURATION EP** [ ] [-]

Jun 93. (7") *(ABS 099)* **CHRIST WITH TEETH. / REMEMBER ZELDA** [ ] [-]
(12"ep+=/cd-s+=) **69 HAYLOFT ACTION E.P.** *(12ABS/CDABS 099)* – Massive tangled muscle / Disease or accident / Smothered.

Oct 93. (cd/lp) *(ABT 097 CD/LP)* **FILTH BY ASSOCIATION** (compilation) [ ] [-]
– Smothered / Remember Zelda / Christ with teeth / Gargoyle son / E.C.T. / Act like a dumshit and they'll treat you as an equal / Saturation / Massive tangled muscle / Sticky flower / Evil poppin' eye / Disease or accident / Washington D.C.

not iss. | Human Pitbull – London

1995. (cd) *<828591-2>* **SON OF FILTH** [-] [ ]
– Massive tangled muscle / Pigskin parade / Saturation / Smothered / Chokecherry / Starsucker / A case of bad face / Remember Zelda / Disease or accident / Washington D.C.

— disbanded after above

DIMMU BORGIR

Formed: Norway ... 1993 by the interestingly named SHAGRATH, ERKEKJETTER SILENOZ and TJODALV. Taking their moniker from an Icelandic lava field, these happy-go-lucky lads set about combining their love of vintage black metal with classical influences such as Wagner. A scary combination, granted, and one which DIMMU BORGIR seem to have perfected over the last decade. Their recording career got off the ground in 1994 with an independently released debut EP, 'INN I EVIGHETENS' ('INTO THE ETERNITY OF DARKNESS'). The record promptly sold out its initial print run and hastened the release of debut album, 'FOR ALL TID' (1994), by which point the original trio had been joined by STIAN AARSTAD and BRYNJARD TRISTAN. 1996 saw the release of a follow-up set, 'STORMBLAST', on the 'Cacophonous' label, a record which the band's official website claims as one of the most important in the history of black metal, hmmm .... This was trailed later in the year by a mini-CD, 'DEVIL'S PATH', issued by the 'Hot Records' label with whom SHAGRATH was employed. The latter release signalled a move into English language lyrics although SHAGRATH's TCP-gargling vocal style means you still won't have a clue what the guy's on about. A shame really, as 1997's 'ENTHRONE DARKNESS TRIUMPHANT' album is apparently one of the top black metal albums of the last century although for the life of us we can't think of any black metal albums released pre-1980. Trivia fans and satanists will no doubt be interested to learn that the lyrics from 'TORMENTOR OF CHRISTIAN SOULS' were omitted from the CD booklet at the behest of the band's new label, 'Nuclear Blast'; presumably they're available on written request from the boys themselves. A period of personnel upheaval ensued during which time the band recorded stopgap set, 'GODLESS SAVAGE GARDEN' (1998), subsequently nominated for a Norwegian Grammy award. A temporary line-up of SHAGRATH, SILENOZ, ASTENNU, TJODALV, NAGASH and MUSTIS played on 1999's 'SPIRITUAL BLACK DIMENSIONS' album although TJODALV was to leave for good (due to family commitments!!!) shortly before its release and was replaced by CRADLE OF FILTH sticksman NICHOLAS BARKER. The ever prolific BORGIR boys duly cut a split album with OLD MAN'S CHILD entitled 'SONS OF SATAN GATHER FOR ATTACK' (no sniggering at the back) while their mission of musical darkness gathered strength into the new millennium with the release of 'PURITANICAL EUPHORIC MISANTHROPIA' (2000). Featuring contributions from the Gothenburg Symphony Orchestra (no, really), the record thrashed and flailed in all the right places with the requisite chugging guitar, hyperspeed snares, swirling keyboard interludes and ludicrously demonic vocals. If nothing else, the album's title would surely make a perfect subheading for the next Tory manifesto ... • **Covers:** NOCTURNAL FEAR (Celtic Frost) / METAL HEART (Accept) / BURN IN HELL (Twisted Sister).

Album rating: FOR ALL TID (*5) / STORMBLAST (*5) / ENTHRONE DARKNESS TRIUMPHANT (*7) / GODLESS SAVAGE GARDEN collection (*4) / SPIRITUAL BLACK DIMENSIONS (*6) / PURITANICAL EUPHORIC MISANTHROPIA (*6)

SHAGRATH – drums, vocals / **ERKEKJETTER SILENOZ** – guitar, vocals / **TJODALV** – guitar / **BRYNJARD TRISTAN** – bass / **STIAN AARSTAD** – synthesizers, piano, effects

Necromantic Gallery | not iss.

1994. (7"ep) **INN I EVIGHETENS MORKE (part I). / INN I EVIGHETENS MORKE (part II) / RAABJORN SPEILER DRAUGHEIMS SKODDE** [-] [-] Norway

— it was around this time that TJODALV + BRYNJARD moonlighted with the outfit OLD MAN'S CHILD on their demo set, 'In The Shades Of Life'

No Colours | not iss.

Mar 95. (cd) **FOR ALL TID** [-] [-] Norway
– Det nye riket / Under korpens vinger / Over bieknede blaner till dommedag / Stien / Glittertind / For all tid / Hunnerkongens sorgsvarte ferd over steppene / Raabjorn speiler draugheims skodde / Den gjemte sannhets herskar. *(<UK/US re-iss. Aug97 on 'Nuclear Blast'; NB 279CD>)*

— **SHAGRATH + TJODALV** swapped instruments (**SILENOZ**) was still a member / added **NVAGASH** – bass (of KOVENANT + TROLL)

Hot | not iss.

Oct 96. (cd-ep) *(SHAGRATH 006CD)* **DEVIL'S PATH** [ ] [-]
– Master of disharmony / Devil's path / Nocturnal fear / Nocturnal fear (Celtically processed). *(re-iss. Apr99; same)*

— **STIAN** returned after a spell in the army

Cacophonous | Cacophonous

1996. (cd) *(<NIHIL 12CD>)* **STORMBLAST** [ ] [ ]
– Alt lys er svunnet hen / Broderskapets ring / Nar sjelen hentes til helvete / Sorgens kammer / Da den kristne satte livet til / Stormblast / Dodsferd / Antikrist / Vinder fra en ensom gray / Guds fortapelse – Apenbaring av dommedag. *(lp-iss.Jul98; NIHIL 12LP)*

— **ASTENNU** (b. Australia) – lead guitar (ex-LORD KAOS) repl. STIAN

Nuclear Blast | Nuclear Blast

May 97. (cd/lp) *(<NB 247 CD/LP>)* **ENTHRONE DARKNESS TRIUMPHANT** [ ] [ ]
– Mourning palace / Spellbound (by the Devil) / In death's embrace / Relinquishment of spirit and flesh / The night masquerade / Tormentor of Christian souls / Entrance / Master of disharmony / Prudence's fall / A succubus in rapture / Raabjorn speiler draugheimens skodde.

— (SHAGRATH now vocals only)

Aug 98. (cd/lp) *(<NB 300-2/-1>)* **GODLESS SAVAGE GARDEN** (collection) [ ] [ ]
– Moonchild domain / Hunnerkongens sorgsvarte ferd over steppene / Chaos without prophecy / Raabjorn speiler draugheimens skodde / Metal heart / Stormblast (live) / Master of disharmony (live) / In death's embrace (live). *(lp+=)* – Mourning place.

— added **MUSTIS** – synthesizers, piano

Mar 99. (cd) *(<NB 349-2>)* **SPIRITUAL BLACK DIMENSIONS** [ ] [ ]
– Reptile / Behind the curtains of night – Phantasmagoria / Dreamside dominions / United in unhallowed grace / The promised future aeons / The blazing monoliths of defiance / The insight & the catharsis / Grotesquery conceiled / Arcane life force mysteria.

— **ICS VORTEX** (b. SIMEN HESTNAES) – bass (of BORKNAGAR, ex-ARCTURUS) repl. NVAGASH

— **NICK BARKER** – drums, percussion (ex-CRADLE OF FILTH) repl. TJODALV who joined SEVEN SINS

— **GALDER** (aka GRUSOM) – lead guitar (of OLD MAN'S CHILD) repl. ASTENNU who joined CARPE TENEBRUM

Mar 01. (cd/lp) *(<NB 527-2/-1>)* **PURITANICAL EUPHORIC MISANTHROPIA** [ ] [ ]
– Fear and wonder (intro) / Blessings upon the throne of tyranny / Kings of the carnival creation / Hybrid stigmata – The apostasy / Architecture of a genocidal nature / Puritania / IndoctriNation / The maelstrom Mephisto / Absolute sole right / Sympozium / Perfection or vanity / Devil's path (re-recording feat. ANDY LA ROQUE) / Burn in Hell.

– compilations, etc. –

May 99. (cd) *Hammerheart; (HHR 044CD)* **DIMMU BORGIR – DEVIL'S PATH / Old Man's Child: IN THE SHADES OF LIFE demo** [ ] [-]

DINOSAUR JR.

Formed: Amherst, Massachusetts, USA ... 1983 by J. MASCIS. Initially recording hardcore punk under the DEEP WOUND moniker, the band recruited PATRICK MURPHY and metamorphosed into DINOSAUR. Their self-titled debut album appeared in 1985, a raw blueprint for their distinctive candy-coated noise rock that was good enough to secure an American tour support slot with SONIC YOUTH. After protestations from aging West Coast rockers DINOSAUR, J.MASCIS' crew added the JR. to part of their name. Subsequently recording one album for 'SST', 'YOU'RE LIVING ALL OVER ME' (1987), the band further developed their melodic distortion although it was the 'FREAK SCENE' (1988) single, their debut for 'Blast First', which saw DINOSAUR JR. pressed to the cardigan-clad bosoms of the nation's pre-baggy indie kids. A wildly exhilarating piece of pristine pop replete with copious amounts of intoxicating noise pollution, MASCIS' go-on-impress-me vocals epitomised the word slacker when that dubious cliche was still gestating in some hack's subconscious. The follow-up album, 'BUG' (1988) was arguably the band's finest moment, perfectly crafted pop spiked with scathing slivers of guitar squall. BARLOW departed soon after the album's release, going off to form SEBADOH while MASCIS' mob came up with a wonderfully skewed cover of The CURE's 'JUST LIKE HEAVEN'. DON FLEMING (of GUMBALL fame) and JAY SPIEGEL featured on DINOSAUR JR.'s major label debut for 'WEA' subsidiary 'Blanco Y Negro', 'THE WAGON' (1991). Another slice of cascading noise-pop, the single raised expectations for the follow-up album 'GREEN MIND' (1991). More or less a MASCIS solo album, it failed to live up to its promise although by the release of 1993's 'WHERE YOU BEEN', MASCIS had found a permanent bassist in MIKE JOHNSON. Their most successful album to date, DINOSAUR JR. at last reaped some rewards from the grunge scene they'd played a major role in creating. With both JOHNSON and MASCIS releasing solo albums in 1996, DINOSAUR JR. have been conspicuous by their absence of late. MASCIS finally re-emerged in late 2000 with the KEVIN SHIELDS-produced 'MORE LIGHT', issued under J.MASCIS & THE FOG. Anyone expecting some kind of artistic rebirth or millennial rejuvenation was to be sorely disappointed as J delivered another set of ragged, tumbledown fuzz-pop. The slacker's slacker, MASCIS makes music that seemingly hangs together by only the seared threads of his own beleaguered vocal chords and he isn't likely to change anytime soon.

• **Songwriters:** MASCIS wrote all, except LOTTA LOVE (Neil Young) / QUICKSAND (David Bowie) / I FEEL A WHOLE LOT BETTER (Byrds) / GOIN' BLIND (Kiss) / HOT BURRITO 2 (Gram Parsons). J. MASCIS solo:- EVERY MOTHER'S SON (Lynyrd Skynyrd) / THE BOY WITH THE THORN IN HIS SIDE (Smiths) / ON THE RUN (Wipers) / ANTICIPATION (Carly Simon) / LEAVING ON A JET PLANE (John Denver). MIKE JOHNSON solo:- SECOND LOVERS SONG (Lynyrd Skynyrd) / LOVE AND OTHER CRIMES (Lee Hazlewood) / IF YOU'RE GONE (Gene Clark). • **Trivia:** In Jun'91, MASCIS moonlighted as a drummer with Boston satanic hard-core group UPSIDE DOWN CROSS, who made one self-titled album Autumn '91 on 'Taang!'. He also wrote songs and made a cameo appearance in the 1992 film, 'Gas, Food, Lodging'.

Album rating: DINOSAUR (*6) / YOU'RE LIVING ALL OVER ME mini (*7) / BUG (*8) / GREEN MIND (*7) / WHERE YOU BEEN (*8) / WITHOUT A SOUND (*5) / HAND IT OVER (*7) / J. Mascis: MARTIN AND ME (*6) / Mike Johnson: WHERE AM I? (*5) / YEAR OF MONDAYS (*5) / I FEEL ALRIGHT (*6) / J. Mascis & The Fog: MORE LIGHT (*6)

LOU BARLOW (b.17 Jul'66, Northampton, Mass.) – guitar / **J. MASCIS** (b. JOSEPH, 10 Dec'65) – drums / **CHARLIE NAKAJIMA** – vocals / **SCOTT HELLAND** – bass

not iss. Radiobeat

Dec 83. (7"ep; as DEEP WOUND) <RB 002> **I SAW IT** [-] [ ]
– I saw it / Sisters / In my room / Don't need / Lou's anxiety song / Video prick / Sick of fun / Deep wound / Dead babies.

— **J. MASCIS** – vocals, guitar, percussion / **LOU BARLOW** – bass, ukelele, vocals / added **MURPH** (b. EMMETT "PATRICK" MURPHY, 21 Dec'64) – drums (ex-ALL WHITE JURY)

not iss. Homestead

Jun 85. (lp; as DINOSAUR) <HMS 015> **DINOSAUR** [-] [ ]
– Forget the swan / Cats in a bowl / The leper / Does it float / Pointless / Repulsion / Gargoyle / Several lips / Mountain man / Quest / Bulbs of passion.

Mar 86. (7"; as DINOSAUR) <HMS 032> **REPULSION. / BULBS OF PASSION** [-] [ ]
(UK-iss.Apr97; same)

S.S.T. S.S.T.

Mar 87. (12"ep) <SST 152> **DINOSAUR JR.** [-] [ ]
– Little fury things / In a jar / Show me the way. *(cd-ep iss.Dec88; SSTCD 152)*

Jul 87. (m-lp/c) <(SST/+C 130)> **YOU'RE LIVING ALL OVER ME** [ ] [ ]
– Little fury things / Kracked / Sludgefeast / The lung / Raisans / Tarpit / In a jar / Lose / Poledo / Show me the way. *(cd-iss. Oct95; same)*

Blast First S.S.T.

Sep 88. (7") *(BFFP 30)* **FREAK SCENE. / KEEP THE GLOVE** [ ] [ ]
(US-iss.7",7"green; SST 220)

Oct 88. (lp/c/cd) *(BFFP 31/+C/CD)* <SST/+C/CD 216> **BUG** [ ] [ ]
– Freak scene / No bones / They always come / Yeah we know / Let it ride / Pond song / Budge / The post / Don't. *(cd re-iss. Feb99; SST 216CD)*

— **DONNA BIDDELL** – bass (ex-SCREAMING TREES) repl. BARLOW who formed SEBADOH

Apr 89. (7"/etched-12"/cd-s) *(BFFP 47 S/T/CD)* <SST 244> **JUST LIKE HEAVEN. / THROW DOWN / CHUNKS (A Last Rights Tune)** [78] [ ] Feb 90
(US version 12"ep+=/c-ep+=/cd-ep+=) (SST/+C/CD 244) – Freak scene / Keep the glove.

— DONNA left and was repl. by **DON FLEMING** – guitar + **JAY SPIEGEL** – drums (both B.A.L.L.)

Glitterhouse Sub Pop

Jun 90. (7"/7"white) *(GR 0097)* <SP 68> **THE WAGON. / BETTER THAN GONE** [ ] [ ]

— In Oct 90, J.MASCIS and other ex-DINOSAUR JR member FLEMING + SPIEGEL, made an album 'RAKE' as VELVET MONKEYS (aka B.A.L.L. + friends).

Blanco Y Negro Sire

Jan 91. (7"/c-s) *(NEG 48/+C)* **THE WAGON. / THE LITTLE BABY** [49] [-]
(12"+=/cd-s+=) *(NEG 48 T/CD)* – Pebbles + weeds / Quicksand.

Feb 91. (lp/c/cd) *(BYN 24/+C/CD)* <26479> **GREEN MIND** [36] [ ]
– The wagon / Puke + cry / Blowing it / I live for that look / Flying cloud / How'd you pin that one on me / Water / Muck / Thumb / Green mind.

Aug 91. (7"/c-s) *(NEG 52/+C)* **WHATEVER'S COOL WITH ME. / SIDEWAYS** [ ] [-]
(12"+=/cd-s+=) *(NEG 52 T/CD)* – Thumb (live) / Keep the glove (live).

— **MASCIS + MURPH** introduced new member **MIKE JOHNSON** (b.27 Aug'65, Grant's Pass, Oregon, USA) – bass (ex-MARK LANEGAN, ex-GEORGE LANE, ex-SNAKEPIT)

Nov 92. (7") *(NEG 60)* **GET ME. / HOT BURRITO #2** [44] [-]
(c-s+=/12"+=/cd-s+=) *(NEG 60 C/T/CD)* – Qwest (live).

Jan 93. (7") *(NEG 61)* **START CHOPPIN'. / TURNIP FARM** [20] [-]
(10"+=/12"+=/cd-s+=) *(NEG 61 TEP/T/CD)* – Forget it.

Feb 93. (lp/c/cd) *(BYN 28/+C/CD)* <45108> **WHERE YOU BEEN?** [10] [50]
– Out there / Start choppin' / What else is new? / On the way / Not the same / Get me / Drawerings / Hide / Goin' home / I ain't sayin'.

Jun 93. (7"/c-s/12") *(NEG 63/+C/T)* **OUT THERE. / KEEBLIN' (live) / KRACKED (live)** [44] [ ]
(10"+=) *(NEG 63TE)* – Post.
(cd-s++=) *(NEG 63CD)* – Quest (live).
(cd-s) *(NEG 63CDX)* – ('A'side) / Get me / Severed lips / Thumb (radio sessions).

— now without MURPH

Aug 94. (7"/c-s) *(NEG 74/+C)* **FEEL THE PAIN. / GET OUT OF THIS** [25] [ ]
(10"etched+=/cd-s+=) *(NEG 74 TE/CD)* – Repulsion (acoustic).

Sep 94. (cd/c/lp) *(4509 96933-2/-4/-1)* <45719> **WITHOUT A SOUND** [24] [44]
– Feel the pain / I don't think so / Yeah right / Outta hand / Grab it / Even you / Mind glow / Get out of this / On the brink / Seemed like the thing to do / Over your shoulder.

Feb 95. (7"green/c-s) *(NEG 77 X/C)* **I DON'T THINK SO. / GET ME (live)** [67] [ ]
(cd-s+=) *(NEG 77CD)* – What else is new? / Sludge.

Mar 97. (c-s/12"/cd-s) *(NEG 103 C/T/CD)* **TAKE A RUN AT THE SUN. / DON'T YOU THINK IT'S TIME / THE PICKLE SONG** [53] [ ]

Mar 97. (cd/c/lp) *(0630 18312-2/-4/-1)* <46506> **HAND IT OVER** [ ] [ ]
– Take a run at the sun / Never bought it / Nothin's goin' on / I'm insane / Can't we move this alone / Sure not over you / Loaded / Mick / I know yer insane / Gettin' rough / Gotta know.

Trade 2 not iss.

Sep 97. (7") *(TRDSC 009)* **I'M INSANE. / I MISUNDERSTOOD** [ ] [-]

– compilations, etc. –

Aug 91. (10"m-lp) *S.S.T.; (SST 275)* **FOSSILS** [-] [ ]
– Little fury things / In a jar / Show me the way / Freak scene / Keep the glove / Just like heaven / Throw down / Chunks. *<(cd-iss. +UK May93 & Oct96; SST 276CD)>*

Feb 99. (cd) *Strange Fruit; (SFRSCD 078)* **THE BBC SESSIONS** [ ] [-]
– Raisins / Does it float / Leper / Bulbs of passion / Keep the glove / In a jar / Get me / Keeblin / Budge / No bones.

MIKE JOHNSON

— with **BARRETT MARTIN, AL LARSEN + DAVID KRUEGER**

not iss. Up

Nov 94. (cd) <8> **WHERE AM I?** [-] [ ]
– Overland – Turn back alone / Save today / Separation / Untitled / Second lovers song / Down the line / Love and other crimes / See through / If you're gone / Carry on / 100% off / Atrophy.

— now with his wife **LESLIE HARDY** – bass (of JUNED, who he produced) / **J. MASCIS, BARRETT MARTIN + MARK LANEGAN**

Atlantic Atlantic

Apr 96. (cd/c) <(7567 92669-2/-4)> **YEAR OF MONDAYS** [ ] [ ] Feb96
– Where am I? / One way out / The way it will be – Too far / Another side / Circle / Eclipse / Left in the dark / Hold the reins / Say it's so / Overdrive.

— now with **KRUEGER, JOHN ATKINS, ELI BRADEN, DAN PETERS, TIFFANY ANDERS, CLAUDIA GROOM + BRETT ARNOLD**

not iss. Up

Aug 98. (cd) <UP 057> **I FEEL ALRIGHT** [-] [ ]
– All there is / Turn around / I don't love you / Minor aversion / Not over yet / Leaving Greensleeves / I've got to have you / One liner / Message to pretty / Impatient and unwilling / Performer / Tradewinds.

J. MASCIS

WEA Warners

May 96. (cd/c) <(46177)> **MARTIN + ME** [ ] [ ] Apr96
– Thumb / So what else is new / Get me / Blowin' it / Repulsion / Goin' home / The boy with the thorn in his side / Not you again / On the run / Keeblin / Flying cloud / Anticipation / Drawerings / Every mother's son.

J. MASCIS & THE FOG

— with **KEVIN SHIELDS**

City Slang Artemis

Sep 00. (cd-s) *(20171-2)* **WHERE'D YOU GO / CAN I TELL U STORIES / TOO HARD** [ ] [-]

Oct 00. (cd/lp) *(20168-2/-1)* <76665> **MORE LIGHT** [ ] [ ]
– Same day / Waistin' / Where'd you go / Back before you go / Grand me to you / Anmaring / All the girls / I not fine / Can I take this on / Does the kiss fit / More light.

Jun 01. (cd-s) **WAISTIN' / LEAVING ON A JET PLANE** [ ] [-]

DIO

Formed: Autumn '82 . . . by American RONNIE JAMES DIO after basing himself in London and recruiting Irishman VIVIAN CAMPBELL along with two Englishmen, JIMMY BAIN and VINNY APPICE (brother of CARMINE). DIO's previous experience stretched back to 1962, when he ran his own school group RONNIE & THE PROPHETS. The group managed to issue a number of singles starting with 'LOVE PAINS' / 'OOH POO PAH DOO' for 'Atlantic'. In 1967, RONNIE and his cousin DAVID FEINSTEIN formed The ELECTRIC ELVES, who in the early 70's, became ELF. In 1972, they signed to 'Purple' records, soon supporting label bosses DEEP PURPLE. They made a couple of well-received albums, before he and most of others took off in April 1975, to join RITCHIE BLACKMORE'S RAINBOW. In May '79, RONNIE took the place of OZZY OSBOURNE in BLACK SABBATH, staying with them until he formed DIO. Building up a live reputation, the group signed to 'Vertigo', releasing their debut set, 'HOLY DIVER' the following year. With his dynamic vocal range, wee RONNIE obviously carried on where he left off with RAINBOW, setting his anthemic tunes to cliched mystical/fantasy lyrical themes. 'THE LAST IN LINE' (1984) fared even better commercially, a transatlantic smash hitting both the UK Top 5 and American Top 30. Their third album, 'SACRED HEART' (1985) followed a similar chart pattern, making them/him major league metal stars. Guitarist CRAIG GOLDIE replaced CAMPBELL for the 1987 'DREAM EVIL' set, although this proved to be a brief alliance as DIO found 17-year old unknown, ROWAN ROBERTSON to fill his shoes. RONNIE proceeded to replace the rest of the band, a completely new line-up in place by the release of 1990's 'LOCK UP THE WOLVES'. With the DIO style of metal warbling not exactly in vogue, the album saw the group faltering both critically and eventually commercially. The time was right then, for RONNIE to hook up once more with BLACK SABBATH, although ego battles ensured the reunion was brief (one album, 'Dehumanizer'). When he inevitably returned to solo pastures, his fanbase had seemingly deserted him, 'STRANGE HIGHWAYS' dismal failure proving commercially, at least, that DIO had had his day. Yet while gothic-fantasy metal no longer whetted the appetites of rock tastemakers, the genre's core fanbase – as well as RONNIE's semi-legendary pedigree – ensured that 'ANGRY MACHINES' (1996) found at least a few sympathetic ears, even if the man's attempt at casting both his lyrical and musical net a bit wider were only partially successful. 'INFERNO: LAST IN LIVE' (1998) found DIO back at his bombastic best, sweeping through his sumptuous back catalogue with a grace and muster less seasoned campaigners could only dream of. 'MAGICA' (2000), meanwhile, was an unashamed return to the conceptual dungeons'n'dragons fare the man made his name with, JIMMY BAIN and CRAIG GOLDIE enhancing the golden era appeal.

Album rating: HOLY DIVER (*7) / THE LAST IN LINE (*6) / SACRED HEART (*6) / INTERMISSION mini (*5) / DREAM EVIL (*6) / LOCK UP THE WOLVES (*6) / STRANGE HIGHWAYS (*4) / DIAMONDS – THE BEST OF DIO compilation (*7) / ANGRY MACHINES (*4) / DIO'S INFERNO: LAST IN LIVE (*6) / ANTHOLOGY compilation (*6) / MAGICA (*6)

RONNIE JAMES DIO (b.RONALD PADAVONA, 10 Jul'47, Portsmouth, New Hampshire, USA, raised Portland, NY) – vocals (ex-ELF, ex-RAINBOW, ex-BLACK SABBATH) / **VIVIAN CAMPBELL** – guitar (ex-SWEET SAVAGE) / **JIMMY BAIN** – bass (ex-RAINBOW, ex-WILD HORSES) / **VINNIE APPICE** – drums (ex-BLACK SABBATH) / **CLAUDE SCHNELL** – keyboards

Vertigo Warners

Jun 83. (lp/c) *(VERS/+C 5) <23836>* **HOLY DIVER** 13 56
– Stand up and shout / Holy diver / Gypsy / Caught in the middle / Don't talk to strangers / Straight through the heart / Invisible / Rainbow in the dark / Shame on the night. *(cd-iss. 1986; 811021-2) (re-iss. Mar88 lp/c; PRICE/PRIMC 117)*

Aug 83. (7") *(DIO 1)* **HOLY DIVER. / EVIL EYES** 72 -
(12"+=) *(DIO 1-12)* – Don't talk to strangers.

Oct 83. (7") *(DIO 2)* **RAINBOW IN THE DARK. / STAND UP AND SHOUT (live)** 46 -
(12"+=) *(DIO 2-12)* – Straight through the heart (live).

Nov 83. (7") *<29527>* **RAINBOW IN THE DARK. / GYPSY** -

Jul 84. (lp/c) *(VERL/+C 16) <25100>* **THE LAST IN LINE** 4 23
– We rock / The last in line / Breathless / I speed at night / One night in the city / Evil eyes / Mystery / Eat your heart out / Egypt (the chains are on). *(cd-iss. 1986; 822366-2) (re-iss. cd Mar93 on 'Polygram';)*

Jul 84. (7") *(DIO 3)* **WE ROCK. / HOLY DIVER (live)** 42 -
(12"+=) *(DIO 3-12)* – Shame on the night / Rainbow in the dark.

Sep 84. (7"/7"pic-d) *(DIO/+P 4)* **MYSTERY. / EAT YOUR HEART OUT (live)** 34 -
(12"+=) *(DIO 4-12)* – Don't talk to strangers (live).

Oct 84. (7") *<29183>* **MYSTERY. / I SPEED AT NIGHT** -

Aug 85. (7") *(DIO 5)* **ROCK'N'ROLL CHILDREN. / SACRED HEART**
(12"+=) *(DIO 5-12)* – The last in line (live) / We rock (live).
(12"white) *(DIOW 5-12)* – ('A'side) / We rock (live) / The last in line (live).

Aug 85. (lp/c)(cd) *(VERH/+C 30)(834848-2) <25292>* **SACRED HEART** 4 29
– King of rock and roll / Sacred heart / Another lie / Rock'n 'roll children / Hungry for heaven / Like the beat of a heart / Just another day / Fallen angels / Shoot shoot. *(re-iss. cd Mar93 on 'Polygram';)*

Oct 85. (7"/7"sha-pic-d) *(DIO/+P 6)* **HUNGRY FOR HEAVEN. / KING OF ROCK AND ROLL** 72
(12"+=) *(DIO 6-12)* – Like the beat of a heart (live).
(12"white) *(DIOW 6-12)* – ('A'side) / The message.

May 86. (d7"ep/10"pic-d-ep/12"ep) **THE DIO EP** 56 -
– Hungry for Heaven / Hiding in the rainbow / Shame on the night / Egypt (the chains are on).

— **CRAIG GOLDIE** – guitar (in the studio); repl. CAMPBELL

Jun 86. (m-lp/m-c) *(VERB/+C 40) <25443>* **INTERMISSION (live except *)** 22 70
– King of rock and roll / Rainbow in the dark / Sacred heart / Time to burn* / Rock'n'roll children / We rock. *(re-iss. cd Mar93 on 'Polygram';)*

Jul 87. (7") *(DIO 8)* **I COULD HAVE BEEN A DREAMER. / NIGHT PEOPLE** 69
(12"+=) *(DIO 8-12)* – Sunset superman.

Aug 87. (lp/c)(cd) *(VERH/+C 46)(832530-2) <25612>* **DREAM EVIL** 8 43
– Night people / Dream evil / Sunset superman / All the fools sailed away / Naked in the rain / Overlove / I could have been a dreamer / Faces in the window / When a woman cries.

Aug 87. (7") **I COULD HAVE BEEN A DREAMER. / OVER LOVE** -

— **DIO** recruited entire new line-up; **ROWAN ROBERTSON** (b.1971, Cambridge, England) – guitar repl. GOLDIE / **JENS JOHANSSON** (b.Sweden) – keyboards repl. SCHNELL / **TEDDY COOK** (b.New York, USA) – bass repl. BAIN / **SIMON WRIGHT** (b.19 Jun'63, England) – drums (ex-AC/DC) repl. APPICE

May 90. (cd/c/lp) *(846033-2/-4/-1) <26212>* **LOCK UP THE WOLVES** 28 61
– Wild one / Born on the sun / Hey angel / Between two heats / Night music / Lock up the wolves / Evil on Queen street / Walk on water / Twisted / My eyes. *(cd+=)* – Why are they watching me.

Jun 90. (7") *(DIO 9)* **HEY ANGEL. / WALK ON WATER**
(12"+=) *(DIO 9-12)* – Rock'n'roll children / Mystery.
(cd-s++=) *(DIOCD 9)* – We rock.
(12"+=) *(DIOP 9-12)* – We rock / Why are they watching me.

— RONNIE subsequently rejoined BLACK SABBATH for one album, 'Dehumanizer' (1992)

Jun 92. (cd/c/lp) *(512206-2/-4/-1) <8032>* **DIAMONDS – THE BEST OF DIO** (compilation)
– Holy diver / Rainbow in the dark / Don't talk to strangers / We rock / The last in line / Rock'n'roll children / Sacred heart / Hungry for Heaven / Hide in the rainbow / Dream evil / Wild one / Lock up the wolves.

Vertigo Reprise

Oct 93. (cd/c/lp) *(518486-2/-4/-1) <45527>* **STRANGE HIGHWAYS** Jan94
– Jesus, Mary & the holy ghost / Firehead / Strange highways / Hollywood black / Evilution / Pain / One foot in the grave / Give her the gun / Blood from a stone / Here's to you / Bring down the rain. *(re-iss. cd Apr95; same)*

S.P.V. Mayhem

Oct 96. (cd) *(SPV 08518292) <11104>* **ANGRY MACHINES**
– Institutional man / Don't tell the kids / Black / Hunter of the heart / Stay out of my mind / Big sister / Double Monday / Golden rules / Dying in America / This is your life.

Mayhem Mayhem

Mar 98. (d-cd) *Mayhem; <(9086-11115CD)>* **INFERNO – LIVE IN LINE (live)**
– Intro / Jesus, Mary and the holy ghost / Don't talk to strangers / Holy diver / Drum solo / Heaven and Hell / Double Monday / Stand up and shout / Hunter of the heart / Mistreated / Guitar solo / The last in line / Rainbow in the dark / The mob rules / Man on the silver mountain / Long live rock & roll / We rock.

Spitfire Spitfire

Apr 00. (cd) *(SPITCD 020) <15020>* **MAGICA** Mar00
– Discovery / Magica theme / Lord of the last day / Fever dreams / Turn to stone / Feed my head / Ebeil / Challis / As long as it's not about love / Losing my insanity / Otherworld / Magica (reprise) / Lord of the last day (reprise) / Magica story.

– compilations, etc. –

Nov 97. (cd) *Connoisseur; (VSOPCD 245)* **ANTHOLOGY** -
Oct 00. (cd) *Rhino; <79983>* **THE VERY BEAST OF DIO** -
Mar 01. (cd) *Connoisseur; (VSOPCD 338)* **ANTHOLOGY VOL.2** -

– early material below –

ELECTRIC ELVES

RONNIE JAMES DIO – vocals, bass / **DAVE FEINSTEIN** – guitar / **DOUG THALER** – keyboards / **GARY DRISCOLL** – drums / **NICK PANTAS** – guitar

not iss. M.G.M.

Dec 67. (7") **HEY LOOK ME OVER. / IT PAYS TO ADVERTISE** -

The ELVES

Decca

Sep 69. (7") **IN DIFFERENT CIRCLES. / SHE'S NOT THE SAME**

M.C.A. M.C.A.

Feb 70. (7") *(MU 1114)* **AMBER VELVET. / WEST VIRGINIA**

— Mid'70, all were involved in a car crash, PANTAS was killed and THALER hospitalised for a year.

ELF

were formed mid'71, by DIO, THALER (now guitar), **FEINSTEIN, DRISCOLL** and **MICKEY LEE SOULE** – keyboards, guitar

not iss. Epic

Aug 72. (lp) *<31789>* **ELF** -
– Hoochie coochie lady / First avenue never more / I'm coming back for you / Sit down honey / Dixie Lee junction / Love me like a woman / Gambler gambler. *(UK-iss.Sep86 on 'CBS' lp/c; CBS/40 26910)*

— In Jul'93, 'ELF' was issued on cd, by 'Sony Europe'.

Sep 72. (7") *<10933>* **HOOCHIE KOOCHIE LADY. / FIRST AVENUE** -

— Early'73, moved to England. Added **CRAIG GRUBER** – bass / **STEVE EDWARDS** – guitar repl. FEINSTEIN

Purple M.G.M.

Mar 74. (lp) *(TPSA 3506) <M3G 4974>* **CAROLINA COUNTRY BALL** <US-title 'L.A. 59'>
– Carolina country ball / L.A. 59 / Ain't it all amusing / Happy / Annie New Orleans / Rocking chair rock'n'roll blues / Rainbow / Do the same thing / Blanche. *(re-iss. Aug84 on 'Safari' lp/c; LONG/+C 7)*

Apr 74. (7") *(PUR 118) <14752>* **L.A. 59. / AIN'T IT ALL AMUSING**

1975. (7"; by RONNIE DIO featuring ROGER GLOVER & GUESTS) *(PUR 128)* **SITTING IN A DREAM / (b-side by JOHN LAWTON)** -

— added **MARK NAUSEEF** – percussion (ex-VELVET UNDERGROUND)

Jun 75. (lp) *<M3G 4994>* **TRYING TO BURN THE SUN** -
– Black swan water / Prentice wood / When she smiles / Good time music / Liberty road / Shotgun boogie / Wonderworld / Streetwalker. *(UK-iss.Aug84 on 'Safari' lp/c; LONG/+C 8)*

— Apr'75. NAUSEEF joined GILLAN then THIN LIZZY. The rest with DIO joined (RITCHIE BLACKMORE'S) RAINBOW. DIO joined BLACK SABBATH in 1979.

– compilations, others, etc. –

May 87. (cd) *Safari; (LONGCD 78)* **THE GARGANTIAN ELF ALBUM** -
– (1974 + 1975 albums, minus a few tracks)

Sep 91. (cd) *Connoisseur; (VSOPCD 167)* **THE ELF ALBUMS** -
– (CAROLINA COUNTY BALL / TRYING TO BURN THE SUN)

DIRTY LOOKS

Formed: Pennsylvania, USA ... early 80's by Danish-born HENRIK OSTERGAARD, who enlisted PAUL LIDEL, JACK PYERS and GENE BARNETT. Having released a number of albums on various labels throughout the US and Europe, DIRTY LOOKS finally managed to get their AC/DC-esque boogie-metal across to a wider audience via a major label deal with 'Atlantic'. In 1988, they scored their first piece of chart action with the near US Top 100 album, 'COOL FROM THE WIRE'. A second set, 'TURN OF THE SCREW' (1989), failed to capitalise on its critical acclaim, the band subsequently downscaling once more. After a one-off 'BOOTLEGS' album for 'Roadrunner' in '91, DIRTY LOOKS released a few more, 'CHEWING ON THE BIT' (1994), 'ONE BAD LEG' (1995) and 'SLAVE TO THE MACHINE' (1996). • **Note:** Not the same group as the early 80's outfit.

Album rating: DIRTY LOOKS (*4) / I WANT MORE (*5) / IN YOUR FACE (*5) / COOL FROM THE WIRE (*6) / BOOTLEGS (*3) / TURN OF THE SCREW (*5) / CHEWING ON THE BIT (*4) / ONE BAD LEG (*5) / SLAVE TO THE MACHINE (*3)

HENRIK OSTERGAARD – vocals / **PAUL LIDEL** – guitar / **JACK PYERS** – bass / **GENE BARNETT** – drums

not iss. Axekiller

1985. (lp) **DIRTY LOOKS** -

not iss. Storm

1986. (lp) **I WANT MORE** -

not iss. Mirror

1987. (lp) **IN YOUR FACE** -
<cd-iss. Dec95 as 'RIP IT OUT'; 021>

Atlantic Atlantic

Apr 88. (lp/c/cd) *(<K 781836-1/-4/-2>)* **COOL FROM THE WIRE**
– Cool from the wire / It's not the way you rock / Can't take my eyes off of you / Oh Ruby / Tokyo / Wastin' my time / Put a spell on you / No brains child / Get it right / It's a bitch / Get off.

Jul 89. (lp/c/cd) *(<781992-1/-4/-2>)* **TURN OF THE SCREW**
– Turn of the screw (who's screwing who) / Nobody rides for free / C'mon Frenchie / Take what ya get / Hot flash jelly roll / Always a loser / L.A. Anna / Slammin' to the big beat / Love screams / Go away / Have some balls.

Roadrunner Shrapnel

Nov 91. (cd) *(RR 9306-2) <SH 1051>* **BOOTLEGS**
– Speed queen / Dude, where's the money? / Fade away / In black & white / Loveless / Only tomorrow / The last forever / Fool for you / Fang and the love pig.

Music For Nations Rockworld

Jan 94. (cd) *<64253>* **CHEWING ON THE BIT** -
– This way / Love train / Chewing on the bit / Falling down / You can't take it back / Trip the light / Dead, white and blue / Killing time / My shallow grave / Last cigarette / Encore.

Jan 95. (cd) *(CDMFN 178) <66886>* **ONE BAD LEG** Nov94
– One bad leg / Hello it's me / Point of view / Loveless / Lamb's breath / YMI / Anyway you want / Raining in the sun / Oh Ruby (live) / Cool from the wire (live).

not iss. B.H.

Dec 96. (cd) *<0001>* **SLAVE TO THE MACHINE** -
– Slave to the machine / The hole / The rotten kind / A better way / Quite so high / Better off dead / Murder for money / Droperindol / Jaw breaker / Anesthesia / Getting even / Feelings of dread / Last crack.

— disbanded soon after above

DIRTY TRICKS

Formed: England . . . 1974 by KENNY STEWART, JOHN FRASER BINNIE, TERRY HORBURY and JOHN LEE. Taking BAD COMPANY and DEEP PURPLE as their inspiration, the group attempted to infuse the former's easy-going blues-rock with the latter's hard-edged assault. The group managed to release three average albums between 1975-1977, ANDY BEIRNE replacing LEE on their third, 'HIT AND RUN'.

Album rating: DIRTY TRICKS (*5) / NIGHT MAN (*4) / HIT AND RUN (*4)

KENNY STEWART – vocals / **JOHN FRASER BINNIE** – guitar, keyboards / **TERRY HORBURY** – bass / **JOHN LEE** – drums

Polydor Polydor

Sep 75. (7") *(2058 640)* **CALL ME UP FOR LOVE. / HIRE CAR** -

Sep 75. (lp) *(2383 351)* **DIRTY TRICKS** -
– Wait till Saturday / Back off evil / Sunshine days / If you believe in me / Too much wine / Call me up for love / Marcella / High life.

Jun 76. (7") *(2058 739)* **NIGHT MAN. / I'M GONNA GET ME A GUN** -

Aug 76. (lp) *(2383 398) <1-6082>* **NIGHT MAN**
– Night man / Weekend raver / Armageddon (song for a rainbow) / Fun brigade / Play dirty / Now you're gone / You got my soul / Black diamond.

Feb 77. (7") *(2058 833)* **TOO MUCH WINE. / WAIT TILL SATURDAY** -

— **ANDY BEIRNE** – drums, percussion; repl. LEE

Sep 77. (lp) *(2383 446) <1-6104>* **HIT AND RUN**
– Hit and run / Get out on the street / The gambler / Road to Deriabah / I've had these dreams before / Walkin' tall / Last night of freedom / Lost in the past.

— split when HORBURY joined VARDIS. Later BEIRNE joined GRAND PRIX and BINNIE joined ROGUE MALE

DISCHARGE

Formed: Birmingham, England . . . late 1978 by CAL (KELVIN MORRIS), BONES (TONY ROBERTS), RAINY WAINWRIGHT and original drummer TEZ, who was replaced by BAMBI then GARRY MALONEY. Signing to the newly-formed Stoke-On-Trent based indie label, 'Clay', they initiated their bruising musical assault with the release of the debut EP, 'REALITIES OF WAR' in 1980. Aggressively anti-war and pro-vegetarian, they were unfairly branded as one of the many up and coming "oi" bands by the now defunct Sounds music magazine (notably journalist and future Sun critic, Gary Bushell, who hated them profusely). They nevertheless marched on in their own inimitable style, releasing a series of deliberately inexpensive EP's upon which they innovated the incomprehensible "death-grunt", later adopted by mid 80's grindcore outfits like NAPALM DEATH, EXTREME NOISE TERROR, etc. By mid '81, they progressed to the 12 inch format, releasing an EP, 'WHY', another barrage of sound that did well in the indie charts. This minor success was consolidated when the group had their first real chart hit, 'NEVER AGAIN' denting the Top 75 for 3 weeks (the DHSS had previously fined them for collecting dole money while on tour, perhaps the time had come to sign off?!). Further recognition followed when their 1982 debut album, 'HEAR NOTHING, SEE NOTHING, SAY NOTHING' scraped into the Top 40. Bassist BROKEN BONES subsequently left the band to explore a punk/metal fusion with a solo career, POOCH PURTILL taking his place in time for a disappointing semi-live set, 'NEVER AGAIN' (1983). DISCHARGE concentrated on single/EP's over the next few years, the album, 'GRAVE NEW WORLD' breaking the sequence in 1986. However, frontman CAL was to leave the following year, his replacement coming in the shape of ROB BERKELEY, although no new material was forthcoming. In the early 90's, DISCHARGE were back once more, CAL back in the fold with other members ANDY GREEN, ANTHONY MORGAN and GARRY MALONEY. Embracing the metal genre more explicitly than ever before, they emerged with the album, 'MASSACRE DIVINE' (1991), followed two years later by 'SHOOTIN' UP THE WORLD'.

Album rating: HEAR NOTHING, SEE NOTHING, SAY NOTHING (*7) / NEVER AGAIN (*5) / GRAVE NEW WORLD (*6) / DISCHARGE 1980-1986 compilation (*6) / THE NIGHTMARE CONTINUES comilation (*6) / MASSACRE DIVINE (*4) / SHOOTIN' UP THE WORLD (*5)

CAL (b. KELVIN MORRIS) – vocals / **BONES** (b. ANTHONY ROBERTS) – guitar (gutarist changed often) / **RAINY WAINWRIGHT** – bass / **GARRY MALONEY** – drums

Clay not iss.

Apr 80. (7"ep) *(CLAY 1)* **REALITIES OF WAR / THEY DECLARE IT / BUT AFTER THE GIG / SOCIETY'S VICTIM** -
(re-iss. Feb87; same)

Jul 80. (7"ep) *(CLAY 3)* **FIGHT BACK / WAR'S NO FAIRY TALE / ALWAYS RESTRICTIONS / YOU TAKE PART IN CREATING THIS SYSTEM / RELIGIOUS INSTIGATES** -

Dec 80. (7"ep) *(CLAY 5)* **DECONTROL / IT'S NO TV SKETCH / TOMORROW BELONGS TO US** -

May 81. (12"ep) *(PLATE 2)* **WHY** -
– Visions of war / Does the system work / A look at tomorrow / Why / Maimed and slaughtered / Mania for conquest / Ain't no feeble bastard / Is this to be / Massacre of innocents (air attack). *(re-iss. Jan90 & Apr93 lp/cd+=; PLATE 002/+CD)* – State violence – state control / Doomsday. *(<cd re-iss. Aug98 on 'Receiver'; RRCD 259>)*

Oct 81. (7") *(CLAY 6)* **NEVER AGAIN. / DEATH DEALERS / TWO MONSTROUS NUCLEAR STOCK-PILES** 64 -

May 82. (lp) *(CLAYLP 3)* **HEAR NOTHING, SEE NOTHING, SAY NOTHING** 40 -
– Hear nothing, see nothing, say nothing / The nightmare continues / The final blood bath / Protest and survive / I won't subscribe / Drunk with power / Meanwhile / A hell on earth / Cries of help / The possibility of life's destruction / Q – and children?, A – and children / The blood runs red / Free speech for the dumb / The end. *(re-iss. Jan90 & Mar95 lp/cd; CLAY LP/CD 3) (<cd re-iss. May98 on 'Receiver'; RRCD 255>)*

Oct 82. (7") *(CLAY 14)* **STATE VIOLENCE – STATE CONTROL. / DOOMSDAY** -

— (Nov'82) **POOCH PURTILL** – guitar repl. BONES who formed BROKEN BONES

Feb 83. (red-lp) *(CLAYLP 12)* **NEVER AGAIN (1/2 live)** -
– Warning / Never again / Hear nothing, see nothing, say nothing / The nightmare continues / The final bloodbath / Drunk with power / Where there's a will / Anger burning / Two monstrous nuclear stockpiles / The price of silence / Protest and survive / Born to die in the gutter / Doomsday / The more I see / State violence – state control / Decontrol / In defence of our future. *(re-iss. Jan90 lp/cd; CLAY LP/CD 12) (<cd re-iss. Jul98 on 'Receiver'; RRCD 256>)*

Mar 83. (7") *(CLAY 29)* **PRIDE OF SILENCE. / BORN TO DIE IN THE GUTTER** -

Sep 83. (12"ep) *(PLATE 5)* **WARNING – H.M. GOVERNMENT: WARNING / WHERE THERE'S A WILL / IN DEFENCE OF OUR FUTURE / ANGER BURNING** -

May 84. (7"/ext.12") *(CLAY/12CLAY 34)* **THE MORE I SEE. / PROTEST AND SURVIVE** -

May 85. (7") *(CLAY 43)* **IGNORANCE. / NO COMPROMISE** -
(12"+=) *(12CLAY 43)* – ('A'extended).

Jul 86. (lp) *(CLAYLP 19)* **GRAVE NEW WORLD** -
– Grave new world / In love believe / DTY/AYF / Time is kind / We dare speak (a moment only) / Sleep in hope / The downward spiral

— (Feb'87) **ROB BERKELEY** – guitar; repl. CAL

— (note:- DAVE ELLESMERE an early member later joined FLUX and DR.& CRIPPENS)

— **DISCHARGE** reformed 1991, with **CAL** and long-standing **GERRY MALONEY** – drums Newcomers were **ANTHONY MORGAN** – bass / **ANDY GREEN** – guitar

Nov 91. (lp/c/cd) *(CLAY/+MC/CD 110)* **MASSACRE DIVINE** -
– City of fear / F.E.D. / Lost tribe rising / Challenge the terrior / White knuckle ride / New age / Terror police / Kiss tomorrow goodbye / Sexplosion / Dying time / E 2.30 / F.E.D. (F2 mix) / Terror police (F2 mix). *<US cd-iss. Oct96; same as UK>*

Oct 93. (cd) *(CLAYCD 118)* **SHOOTIN' UP THE WORLD** -
– Manson child / Lost in you / Shootin' up the world / Psycho active / Leaders – Deceivers / Fantasy overload / Down and dirty / Never came to care / Real life snuff / Exiled in Hell / Manson's child (reprise). *<US-iss.May95; same>*

— a tribute album, 'DISCHARGED' was issued by 'Rhythm Vicar' in 1992 and included tracks by EXTREME NOISE TERROR, CONCRETE SOX, etc

– compilations etc. –

on 'Clay' unless mentioned otherwise

Jul 87. (lp) *(CLAYLP 24)* **DISCHARGE THE SINGLES COLLECTION 1980-1986** -
(cd-iss. Aug95; same)

Feb 90. (lp/cd) *(CLAY/+CD 103)* **LIVE AT CITY GARDEN NEW JERSEY (live)** -

Mar 91. (lp/c/cd) *(CLAY/+MC/CD 107)* **THE NIGHTMARE CONTINUES (live)** — 1996
Nov 92. (7") *Finn; (FINNRECC 006)* **EXCREMENT OF WAR. /** — -
Jan 94. (lp/c/cd) *Nuclear Blast; (NB/+MC/CD 085)* **SEEING, FEELING, BLEEDING** — -
Jun 94. (cd) *(<CLAYCD 113>)* **PROTEST & SURVIVE**
Jul 95. (cd) *(<CLAYCD 120>)* **THE SINGLES COLLECTION**
May 97. (d-cd) *Snapper; (SMDCD 131)* **PROTEST AND SURVIVE** — -
May 99. (cd) *Cleopatra; (<CLP 540>)* **HARDCORE HITS**
Oct 99. (d-cd) *Essential; (ESACD 798)* **ANTHOLOGY – FREE SPEECH FOR THE DUMB**

DISGUST (see under ⇒ EXTREME NOISE TERROR)

DISMEMBER

Formed: Stockholm, Sweden . . . early 90's by frontman MATTI KARKI and his death-metal cohorts, drummer FRED ESTBY, bassist RICHARD CABENZA and guitarists ROBERT SENNEBACK and DAVID BLOMQUIST. Signed to 'Nuclear Blast' (who else!), DISMEMBER promptly carved out a gory reputation amongst the ever controversial Scandinavian/Viking metal fraternity upon the release of their debut, 'LIKE AN EVER FLOWING STREAM' (1991). Clearly not a band with "new man" credentials, their charmingly titled 'SKIN HER ALIVE' met with predictable outrage at Her Majesty's ever vigilant Customs department. Spared the delights of Wormwood Scrubs hospitality, the group were subsequently cleared to go on their blasphemous way. In 1993, following the previous year's 'PIECES' mini-set, they cut their second album, 'INDECENT AND OBSCENE', a calculated two-fingered salute to their would-be censors. Possibly a sequel to 'SKIN . . .', the track 'EVISCERATED (BITCH)' continued in the same blood-soaked vein. In 1995, they returned to mutilate the minds of unsuspecting metal fans with 'CASKET GARDEN', while the rather worryingly-titled 'MASSIVE KILLING CAPACITY' had Scandinavian police on full alert (possibly). 'MISANTHROPIC' (defined in the dictionary as "hating or distrusting mankind") summed up the DISMEMBER approach, not a record to play at your neighbour's barbeque.

Album rating: LIKE AN EVERFLOWING STREAM (*6) / PIECES mini (*5) / INDECENT AND OBSCENE (*5) / MASSIVE KILLING CAPACITY (*6) / DEATH METAL (*7) / HATE CAMPAIGN (*6)

MATTI KARKI – vocals / **DAVID BLOMQUIST** – lead guitar / **ROBERT SENNEBACK** – rhythm guitar / **RICHARD CABEZA** – bass / **FRED ESTBY** – drums

Nuclear Blast — Nuclear Blast

1991. (cd-ep) *(demo)* **SKIN HER ALIVE** — - — - Sweden
Aug 91. (lp/pic-lp/c/cd) *(NB 047/+PD/MC/CD) <6018>* **LIKE AN EVERFLOWING STREAM**
– Override of the overture / Soon to be dead / Bleed for me / And so is life / Dismembered / Skin her alive / Sickening art / In death's sleep / Deathevocation / Defective decay. *(cd re-iss. Jun96; NB 163CD)*
Apr 92. (m-lp/pic-lp/cd) *(NB 060/+PD/CD)* **PIECES** — -
– Intro / Pieces / I wish you hell / Carnal tomb / Soon to be dead / Torn apart.
Jul 93. (lp/pic-lp/c/cd) *(NB 077/+PD/MC/CD) <6077>* **INDECENT AND OBSCENE** — Sep93
– Fleshless / Skinfather / Sorrowfilled / Case # obscene / Souldevourer / Reborn in blashemy / Eviscerated (bitch) / 9th circle / Dreaming in red. *(cd re-iss. Jul00 +=; NB 468-2)* – PIECES
Mar 95. (cd-ep) *(NB 130-2)* **CASKET GARDEN / WARDEAD / JUSTIFIABLE HOMOCIDE** — -
Sep 95. (cd/c/lp) *(NB 123-2/-4/-1) <6123>* **MASSIVE KILLING CAPACITY**
– I saw them die / Massive killing capacity / On frozen fields / Crime divine / To the bone / Wardead / Hallucigenia / Collection by blood / Casket garden / Menia / Life – Another shape of sorrow.
Jun 97. (cd) *(NB 250CD) <6250>* **DEATH METAL** — Aug97
– On fire / Trendkiller / Misanthropic / Let the napalm rain / Live for the fear of pain / Stillborn ways / Killing compassion / Bred for war / When hatred killed the light / Ceremonial comedy / Silent are the watchers / Mistweaver.
Jun 97. (cd-ep) *(NB 254CD) <6254>* **MISANTHROPIC** — Jul97
– Misanthropic / Pagan saviour / Shadowlands / Afterimage / Shapeshifter.

—— **SHARLEE D'ANGELO** – bass; repl. RICHARD

Feb 00. (cd) *(NB 419-2) <6419>* **HATE CAMPAIGN**
– Suicidal revelations / Questionable ethics / Beyond good and evil / Retaliate / Enslaved to bitterness / Mutual animosity / Patrol / Thanatology / Bleeding over / In death's cold embrace / Hate campaign.

DISORDER

Formed: Bristol, England . . . 1980 by STEVE ALLEN, DEAN CURTIS, MICK and a drummer named VIRUS. Another one of the "Punk's Not Dead" crew, DISORDER showcased their nihilistic, barely listenable yob-noise on the following year's debut EP, 'THE COMPLETE DISORDER'. Rejected by their local 'Riot City' label, the band were forced to self-finance all their releases and concentrated on EP's for the first three years of their career. During this period the one-chord wonder Mohawk-punks suffered an almost constant personnel turnover, the most serious of which occurred when BOOBS (their roadie!) substituted for frontman DEAN. In the summer of '84, DISORDER finally delivered a debut LP, 'UNDER THE SCALPEL BLADE', the first in a series of occasional album releases that would be coveted by hardcore fans and ignored by everyone else. With the mid-90's going through a mini-punk renaissance, DISORDER were surprisingly still causing a musical breach of the peace via 1998's 'SLICED PUNX ON MEATHOOKS'.

Album rating: UNDER THE SCALPEL BLADE (*3) / LIVE IN OSLO (*3) / ONE DAY SON ALL THIS WILL BE YOURS shared with Kaska Process (*3) / VIOLENT WORLD (*4) / THE COMPLETE DISORDER compilation (*5) / SLICED PUNX ON MEATHOOKS (*4)

DEAN CURTIS – vocals / **STEVE ALLEN** – guitar / **MICK** – bass / **VIRUS** – drums

Disorder — not iss.

Jun 81. (7"ep) *(ORDER 1)* **THE COMPLETE DISORDER EP** — -
– Today's world / Violent crime / Complete disorder / Insane youth.

—— **STEVE ROBINSON** – bass; repl. MICK

Dec 81. (7"ep) *(ORDER 2)* **DISTORTION TO DEAFNESS / MORE THAN FIGHTS / DAILY LIFE / YOU'VE GOT TO BE SOMEONE** — -

—— **TAFF** – bass (ex-X-CERTS REVIEW) repl. ROBINSON

—— **BOOBS** – vocals (their roadie) repl. DEAN

Sep 82. (12"ep) *(12ORDER 3)* **PERDITION** — -

—— **GLENN** – drums (ex-DEAD POPSTARS) repl. VIRUS

Mar 83. (7"ep) *(ORDER 4)* **MENTAL DISORDER** — -
Jun 84. (lp) *(AARGH 1)* **UNDER THE SCALPEL BLADE** — -
– Driller killer / Education // Security guard / The g-song / Transparency / Victim of the NHS / Bent edge / The rhino song / God nose / Overproduction / Other side of the fence / Fuck your nationality / Men make frontiers / Prisoner of conscience / After.
Nov 85. (lp) *(AARGH 2)* **LIVE IN OSLO (live)** — -
– Complete disorder / Daily life / More than fights / Remembrance day / Maternal obsession / Bent edge / Provocated wars / God nose / Education / Driller killer / Prisoners of conscience / Stagnation / Life / Rampton / After / Fuck your nationality / Out of order / Rhino song.
Nov 86. (m-lp; shared with KASKA PROCESS) *(AARGH 3)* **ONE DAY SON, ALL THIS WILL BE YOURS** — -
– Double standards / Be bad be glad / Marriage story / Love and flowers / Togetherness.
Oct 89. (lp) *(AARGH 4)* **VIOLENT WORLD** — -
– Driller killer / Into / Every ate seconds / Another fight another gig / Gods are born in the U.S.A. / I don't like war / Joleen / Fur Elise / Health hazard (live) / Todays world (live) / Violent world / Dope not Pope / Distortion till U vmoit / Take what you need.

—— split after above, although they did surface again from time to time

Desperate Attempt — not iss.

Nov 94. (lp/cd; with MUSHROOM ATTACK) *(DAR 010/+CD)* **MASTERS OF THE GLUENIVERSE** — -

Anagram — Anagram

Feb 98. (cd) *(<CDMGRAM 118>)* **SLICED PUNX ON MEATHOOKS** — Sep99
– Fight the right / Fast food / Free society / Therefore we shout / Giro song / Boring / Insane war / Coz of death / Tied down / Pass the gluebag (to the right hand side) / To be continued / Intro / Army of aggressors / Warfear / Drop the bomb / Rumours and lies / Brutal attack / Anti-social reject / Jack hammer / Fight the right (live) / Fuck your nationality (live).

Position Chrome — not iss.

Sep 98. (2x12") *(EFA 060816)* **GLOBAL DISORDER EP** — -

– compilations, etc. –

Jan 84. (12"ep) *Disorder; (12ORDER 5)* **THE SINGLES COLLECTION** — -
Dec 91. (cd) *Anagram; (CDPUNK 46)* **THE COMPLETE DISORDER** — -
– Today's world / Violent crime / Dirorder / Insane youth / You've got to be someone / More than fights / Daily life / RAmpton / Provocated war / Bullshit everyone / 3 blind mice / Buy I gurt pint / Stagnation / Life / Out of order / Condemned / Media / Suicide children / Preachers / Remembrance day. *(re-iss. Oct96; same) (lp-iss.Oct98 on 'Get Back'; GET 37LP)*
Nov 93. (cd) *Anagram; (CDPUNK 19)* **UNDER THE SCALPEL BLADE / ONE DAY SON ALL THIS WILL BE YOURS** — -
Oct 94. (cd) *Anagram; (CDPUNK 39)* **LIVE IN OSLO / VIOLENT WORLD** — -
Jul 96. (cd) *Cleopatra; (<CLEO 9704CD>)* **DRILLER KILLER COLLECTION**
– Driller killer / Prisoners of conscience / Remembrance day / Complete disorder / Rampton / I don't like war / Out of order / Double standards / Love & flowers / Togetherness & unity / More than fights / Provocated wars / Life / Education / Bent edge / God nose / The other side of the fence / Security guard / Transparency.
Feb 97. (cd) *Anagram; (<CDPUNK 88>)* **THE REST HOME FOR SENILE OLD PUNKS PROUDLY PRESENTS . . .** — Sep99
Oct 98. (cd) *Anagram; (CDPUNK 109)* **THE BEST OF DISORDER** — -

DISSECTION

Formed: Gothenburg, Sweden . . . 1989 by JON NODTVEIDT and PETER PALMDAHL. With OLE OHMAN completing the trio, DISSECTION cut 'THE GRIEF PROPHECY' as their first demo, followed closely by a debut 7", 'INTO INFINITE OBSCURITY'. NODTVEIDT was subsequently handed an eight year sentence for the murder of an Algerian gay man, although this didn't curtail the group's activities, instead recording a second demo, 'The SOMBERLAIN'. This resulted in an album deal with the 'No Fashion' label through whom they issued a debut of the same name in 1993, the guitar attack bolstered by JOHN ZWETSLOOT. The latter was replaced by JOHAN NORMAN for sophomore set, 'STORM OF THE LIGHT'S BANE' (1996) while 1997's 'THE PAST IS ALIVE' collected together various DISSECTION rarities from the early 90's including material from NODTVEIDT's side project, SATANIZED. The chillingly titled 'WHERE DEAD ANGELS LIE' – a 1997 mini-set which served as their epitaph – took on a new resonance when NODTVEIDT was sentenced in summer '97 along with a friend.

Album rating: THE SOMBERLAIN (*5) / STORM OF THE LIGHT'S BANE (*6) / WHERE DEAD ANGELS LIE mini (*4) / THE PAST IS ALIVE collection (*4)

JON NODTVEIDT – vocals, guitar / **PETER PALMDAHL** – bass / **OLE OHMAN** – drums

—— added **JOHN ZWETSLOOT** – guitar

No Fashion | not iss.

1994. (cd) *(NFR 006)* **THE SOMBERLAIN** [ ] [-]
– Black horizons / The somberlain / Crimson towers / A land forlorn / Heaven's damnation / Frozen / Into infinite obscurity / In the cold winds of nowhere / The grief prophecy – Shadows over a lost kingdom / Mistress of the bleeding sorrow / Feathers fell.

Nuclear Blast | Nuclear Blast

Jan 96. (cd/c/lp) *(NB 129 CD/MC/LP)* <6129> **STORM OF THE LIGHT'S BANE** [ ] [ ]
– At the fathomless depths / Night's blood / Unhallowed / Where dead angels lie / Retribution – Storm of the light's bane / Thorns of crimson death / Soulreaper / No dreams breed in breathless sleep.

May 96. (m-cd) *(NB 167CD)* <6167> **WHERE DEAD ANGELS LIE** [ ] [ ] Feb97
– Where dead angels lie (demo) / Elisabeth Bathori / Antichrist / Feather's fell / Son of the morning / Where dead angels lie.

—— In 1997, NODTVEIDT was convicted of murder (see above)

—— after they obviously split, OHMAN formed REAPER

– compilations, etc. –

Mar 98. (lp/cd) *Necropolis; (NR 017/+DP)* **THE PAST IS ALIVE** (demos 1990-92) [ ] [-]
– Shadows over a lost kingdom / Frozen / Feather's fell / Sun of the mourning / Mistress of the bleeding sorrow / In the cold winds of nowhere / Into infinite obscurity / The call of the mist / Severed into shreds / Satanized / Born in fire. *(cd re-iss. Mar98; NR 017CD)*

DISTURBED

Formed: Chicago, Illinois, USA . . . early 90's by DAN DONEGAN, MIKE WENGREN and FUZZ. With the addition of severely angry young man DAVID DRAIMAN in 1997, the DISTURBED bandwagon began rolling with a vengeance as they built up a grassroots following from Chicago's mean streets. Subsequently signed to 'Giant' on the strength of a demo, the band joined the nu-metal melee in 2000 with debut album, 'THE SICKNESS'. Equal parts Big Rock chorus and itchy, rap-metal chops, naggingly addictive opening track 'VOICES' was as good a place as any to enter the unforgiving world of DISTURBED. The track was subsequently released as a single while the album itself made the US Top 75.

Album rating: SICKNESS (*5)

DAVID DRAIMAN – vocals / **DAN DONEGAN** – guitar / **THE FUZZ** – bass / **MIKE WENGREN** – drums

R.C.A. | Giant – Warners

Jul 00. (cd) *(74321 70267-2)* <24738> **THE SICKNESS** [ ] [29] Mar00
– Voices / The game / Stupify / Down with the sickness / Violence fetish / Fear / Numb / Want / Conflict / Shout 2000 / Droppin' plates / Meaning of life.

Mar 01. (7"red) *(74321 84896-7)* <100410> **VOICES. / VOICES (live)** [52] [ ] 2000
(cd-s) *(74321 84641-2)* – ('A'side) / Stupify (live) / The games (live).
(cd-s) *(74321 84896-2)* – ('A'side) / Down with the sickness (live) / ('A'-CD-ROM).

DIVINE HORSEMEN (see under ⇒ FLESH EATERS)

D'MOLLS

Formed: Chicago, Illinois, USA . . . 1987 by DESI REXX, S.S. PRIEST, NIGEL ITSON, LIZZY VALENTINE and BILLY DIOR. Coming at the height of the late 80's glam-metal craze and taking their pseudonyms from the POISON school of cheesiness, D'MOLLS managed to secure a deal with 'Atlantic'. Releasing an eponymous debut in late '88, the group garnered favourable reviews for their ballsy take on the genre although a 1990 follow-up, 'WARPED', sank without trace. Inevitably, the band split the following year with ITSON joining The MILLIONAIRE BOYS CLUB.

Album rating: D'MOLLS ((*5)

DESI REXX – vocals, guitar / **NIGEL ITSON** – vocals / **S.S. PRIEST** – guitar / **LIZZY VALENTINE** – bass / **BILLY DIOR** – drums

Atlantic | Atlantic

Sep 88. (lp/c/cd) <(781 791-1/-4/-2)> **D'MOLLS** [ ] [ ]
– All I want / 777 / Rally baby / Dressed to thrill / Supersonic / D'stroll / All night long / French quarter / Hi'n'lo / Crimes of fashion / A-C-T-I-O-N.

1990. (cd/c/lp) <(820 070-2/-4/-1)> **WARPED** [-] [ ]
– My life / Down t'nothing / Backstage bombers / This time it's love / Real love / On 'n' on / The answer / Centerfold girl / Passion / Father time.

—— split in 1991, ITSON joined The MILLIONAIRE BOYS CLUB

DNA (see under ⇒ DERRINGER, Rick)

D.O.A.

Formed: Vancouver, Canada . . . 1978 with an initial line-up of JOEY 'SHITHEAD' KEITHLEY, RANDY RAMPAGE and CHUCK BISCUITS, their moniker an acronym for DEAD ON ARRIVAL. The name reflected their no-messing approach, D.O.A.'s unceasingly radical stance and uncompromising musical approach doing much to shape the early 80's American hardcore scene. Following a clutch of early 7"/12" EP's and an album 'HARDCORE '81', the group signed to JELLO BIAFRA's 'Alternative Tentacles' and released the influential 'POSITIVELY D.O.A.' EP, such raging political barbs as 'FUCKED UP RONNIE' underlining the band's agit-punk approach. The lean three-chord attack which formed the basis of much of their material was much in evidence on 1984's top compilation 'BLOODIED BUT UNBOWED'. This included the 'WAR ON 45' EP, which introduced new members DAVE GREGG (actually around since 1980), GREGG JAMES and BRIAN GOBLE, recruited as replacements for RAMPAGE and BISCUITS, the latter moving on to CIRCLE JERKS, then BLACK FLAG and later DANZIG. These punk lumberjacks of the North American scene finally released an album's worth of new material, 'LET'S WRECK THE PARTY' in 1985, a set that saw the band's deceptively simple approach reach fruition. JAMES subsequently departed, JON CARD taking up the post prior to the release of their next hardcore delivery, 'TRUE (NORTH) STRONG AND FREE' (1987). More personnel changes were to follow, when DAVE GREGG split to form GROOVAHOLICS, CHRIS PROHOM coming in for the 1990 album, 'MURDER'. This was released around the same time as a collaboration set with JELLO BIAFRA (ex-DEAD KENNEDYS) entitled 'LAST SCREAM OF THE MISSING NEIGHBORS'. The band stuck by their hardcore principles into the 90's with albums like 'TALK – ACTION = 0' (1991), '13 FLAVOURS OF DOOM' (1992) and 'LOGGERHEADS' (1993), the latter two finding D.O.A. back with 'Alternative Tentacles'. • **Covers:** WE GOTTA GET OUT OF THIS PLACE (Animals) / FOLSOM PRISON BLUES (Johnny Cash) / COMMUNICATION BREAKDOWN (Led Zeppelin). • **Note:** To the Canadian guy who wrote to me a few years ago and pointed out a certain error, I've intentionally retained this original uncorrected biography – I think I threw out your "nice" letter.

Album rating: HARDCORE '81 (*6) / BLOODED BUT UNBOWED compilation (*8) / LET'S WRECK THE PARTY (*7) / TRUE (NORTH) STRONG AND FREE (*5) / MURDER (*6) / TALK – ACTION = 0 (*6) / 13 FLAVOURS OF DOOM (*6) / LOGGERHEADS (*5)

JOEY "SHITHEAD" KEITHLEY – vocals, guitar / **RANDY RAMPAGE** – bass / **CHUCK BISCUITS** – drums

not iss. | Sudden Death

May 78. (7"ep) <SD 001> **DISCO SUCKS EP** [-] [ ]
– Royal police / Woke up screaming / Disco sucks / Nazi training camp. *(re-iss. Apr79 on 'Quintessence'; QEP 002)*

not iss. | Quintessence

1978. (7") <QS 102> **THE PRISONER. / 13** [-] [ ]

1979. (12"ep) **TRIUMPH OF THE IGNOROIDS EP** [-] [ ]
– Nazi training camp / Want some bondage / Let's fuck / Rich bitch.

Dec 79. (7") <QD 206> **WHATCHA GONNA DO?. / WORLD WAR 3** [-] [ ]

not iss. | Friends

Sep 80. (7"ep) <FR 003> **SOMETHING BETTER CHANGE EP** [-] [ ]

Jun 81. (lp) <FR 010> **HARDCORE '81** [-] [ ]

not iss. | Sudden Death

1983. (7") <SD 003> **BURN IT DOWN. / FUCK YOU** [-] [ ]

1983. (7") *(SD 004)* **GENERAL STRIKE. / THAT'S LIFE** [-] [ ]

Alternative Tentacles | Alternative Tentacles

Jan 82. (7"ep) <(VIRUS 7)> **POSITIVELY D.O.A.** [ ] [ ]
– Fucked up Ronnie / World War Three / The enemy / My old man's a bum / New wave sucks. *(re-iss. Jul93' same)*

—— **KEITHLEY** was now joined by **DAVE GREGG** – guitar, vocals / **GREGG JAMES** – drums / **BRIAN "SUNNY BOY ROY" GOBLE** – bass, vocals (they repl. RAMPAGE + BISCUITS; latter to CIRCLE JERKS, BLACK FLAG then DANZIG)

Nov 82. (7"ep) <(VIRUS 24)> **WAR ON 45** [ ] [ ]
– America the beautiful / Unknown / Rich bitch / Let's fuck war / I hate you / War in the east / Class war.

Feb 84. (lp) <(VIRUS 31)> **BLOODED BUT UNBOWED** (compilation 1978-83) [ ] [ ]
– Liar for hire / Fuck you / The prisoner / I'm right, you're wrong / Smash the state / Slumlord / New age / I don't give a shit / Waiting for you / Whatcha gonna do / World War 3 / 2 + 2 / The enemy / Fucked up Ronnie / Woke up screaming / 001 Loser's club / 13 / Get out of my life / D.O.A. *(cd-iss. Mar92 w/ 'WAR ON 45' on 'Restless'; LS 91852)*

Dec 84. (12"ep) <(VIRUS 42)> **DON'T TURN YER BACK (ON DESPERATE TIMES)** (The John Peel session) [ ] [ ]
– General strike / Race riot / A season in Hell / Burn it down.

Sep 85. (lp) <(VIRUS 44)> **LET'S WRECK THE PARTY** [ ] [ ]
– Our world / Dangerman / Race riot / Singin' in the rain / Dance o'death / General strike / Let's wreck the party / Shout out / Murder in Hollywood / The warrior ain't no more / No way out / Trial by media.

—— split for a while, reformed in '87

—— **JON CARD** – drums (ex-PERSONALITY CRISIS, ex-SNFU) repl. JAMES

not iss. | Profile

Mar 87. (cd) <1228> **TRUE (NORTH) STRONG AND FREE** [-] [ ]

—— **CHRIS PROHOM** – guitar (ex-RED TIDE) repl. GREGG

not iss. | Philo

1988. (m-lp) <9000> **ORNAMENT OF HOPE** [-] [ ]

1988. (m-lp) <9004> **ANCIENT BEAUTY** [-] [ ]

Restless | Restless

Mar 90. (cd/lp) <(72376-2/-4)> **MURDER** [ ] [ ]
– We know what you you want / Guns, booze & sex / Boomtown / Afrikana security / Waiting for you / No productivity / The agony and the ecstasy / The midnight special / Bananaland / The warrior lives again / Concrete beach / Suicidal. *(re-iss. cd Jul95; same)*

— In May'90, teamed up w/ JELLO BIAFRA (ex-DEAD KENNEDYS) to release 'Alternative Tentacles' album 'LAST SCREAM OF THE MISSING NEIGHBORS' (Soundtrack to 'Terminal City Ricochet')

Dec 91. (cd/lp) <(72506-2/-1)> **TALK – ACTION = 0**
– America the beautiful / 13 / Burn it down / Murder in Hollywood / Lumberjack city / Waiting for you (part 2) / F*** you / Woke up screaming / Liar for hire / 2 + 2 / Let's wreck the party / The prisoner / Do or die / F*** that shit / General strike / Race riot. *(re-iss. cd Jul95; same)*

Alternative Tentacles / Alternative Tentacles

Feb 92. (cd) <(VIRUS 106CD)> **THE DAWNING OF A NEW ERROR**
(compilation of EP's, etc.)

Oct 92. (lp/c/cd) <(VIRUS 117/+MC/CD)> **13 FLAVOURS OF DOOM**
– Already dead / Death machine / Bombs away / The living dead / I played the fool / Too f***in' heavy / Hole in the sky / Hey sister / Use your raincoat / Legalized theft / Rosemary's baby / Beatin' rock'n'roll to death / Time of illusion. *(c+=/cd+=)* – Phantom zone.

Mar 93. (7") <(VIRUS 120)> **IT'S NOT UNUSUAL . . . BUT IT'S UGLY!. / DEAD MEN TELL NO TALES**
(cd-s) <(VIRUS 120CD)> – ('A'side) / Blue to brown / Help me get out of here / Runaway world.

Oct 93. (lp/c/cd) <(VIRUS 130/+MC/CD)> **LOGGERHEADS**
– Logjam / I see you cross / You little weiner / Overpowering urges / That turbulent uneasy feeling / The only green thing / Overtime / Cocktail time in Hell / Cut and dried / Burning in anger / Liberation and execution / Witch hunt / Knots / I can't take much more. *(c+=/cd+=)* – Fulsom prison dirge.

Oct 93. (7") <(VIRUS 131)> **THE ONLY THING GREEN. / FOLSOM PRISON BLUES**
(above a benefit single for the "Friends Of Clayoquot Sound" to save the region of Tofino, British Columbia, Canada from commercial logging)

Jan 94. (7") <(VIRUS 133)> **DISCO SUCKS. /**

Essential Noise / Essential Noise

Dec 96. (cd) <(35299-2)> **THE BLACK SPOT** — Oct95
– Blind men / Kill ya later / Order / Marijuana motherfuckers / You're playing for your body now / Worries / Road hill / Get away / More / Je declare / Big guys like D.O.A. / I know who you are / 1 bound for glory / Unchained melody / Cut time / Running out of time.

Earache / not iss.

Jan 97. (cd; various artists) *(MOSH 164CD)* **NEW YORK CITY SPEEDCORE** — [-]
– Total annihilation / Ya mutha / Brooklyn mob / NYC speedcore / Wanna be a gangsta / Zu leiten / Uncle Bill's message / Pound down on your brain / Kill / Uncle Bill's message / Minute madness / Extreme gangsta / Our father / Our father / Ya mutha III / Noize core / I'll give you hard / Ya mutha II / You're dead / This is D.O.A.

– compilations, etc. –

Mar 98. (cd) *Golf; (CDHOLE 015)* **THE LOST TAPES**
May 98. (cd) *Golf; (CDHOLE 014)* **A FESTIVAL OF ATHEISTS**

DOC HOLLIDAY

Formed: USA . . . 1980 by BRUCE BOOKSHIRE, RICK SKELTON, EDDIE STONE, JOHN SAMUELSON and ROBERT LIGGIO (the latter replaced by HERMAN NIXON). Clearly raised on a backwoods diet of classic LYNYRD SKYNYRD / ALLMAN BROTHERS, the group laced their southern boogie with a harder-edged Jack Daniels-sluggin' metal poison. Signed to 'A&M', they released two highly praised albums, the second of which, 'RIDES AGAIN' (1982), should have propelled them to greater commercial heights. A third album, 'MODERN MEDICINE' took a rather ill-advised AOR approach, ultimately resulting in the band temporarily breaking up. However, DOC HOLLIDAY, complete with new drummer JAMIE DECUARD, resurfaced in 1986 on a UK label with the album, 'DANGER ZONE'. BOOKSHIRE subsequently recruited an entire new line-up for a live set, 'SONG FOR THE OUTLAW' in 1989. Four years in the making, the DOC were back on song with the comeback album, 'SON OF THE MORNING STAR' (1993).

Album rating: DOC HOLLIDAY (*6) / RIDES AGAIN (*6) / MODERN MEDICINE (*4) / DANGER ZONE (*5) / SONG FOR THE OUTLAW LIVE (*5) / LEGACY compilation (*6)

BRUCE BOOKSHIRE – vocals, guitar / **RICK SKELTON** – guitar, vocals / **EDDIE STONE** – keyboards, vocals / **JOHN SAMUELSON** – bass, vocals / **HERMAN NIXON** – drums, vocals; repl. ROBERT LIGGIO

A&M / A&M

1981. (lp) <(AMLH 64847)> **DOC HOLLIDAY**
– Ain't no fool / Magic midnight / A good woman's hard to find / Round and round / Moonshine runner / Keep on running / Never another night / The way you do / Somebody help me / I'm a rocker.

1981. (7") <2328> **MAGIC MIDNIGHT. / NEVER ANOTHER NIGHT** [-]

May 82. (7") <2403> **DON'T STOP LOVING ME. / HOT ROD** [-]

Jun 82. (lp) <(AMLH 64882)> **DOC HOLLIDAY RIDES AGAIN**
– The last ride / Good boy gone bad / Don't go talkin' / Southern man / Let me be your lover / Doin' it again / Don't stop loving me / Hot rod / Lonesome guitar.

1983. (lp) <SP 6-4947> **MODERN MEDICINE** [-]
– City night / Dreamin' / Gimme some / You don't have to cry / Rock city / Hell to pay / No relation to love / You turn me on / We are not alone / You like to rock.

— **JAMIE DECUARD** – drums; repl. NIXON + SKELTON (on some)

Metal Masters / not iss.

Jul 86. (lp) *(METALP 113)* **DANGER ZONE** — [-]
– Danger zone / Ready to burn / Redneck rock & roll band / Run to me / Southern girls / Automatic girl / Tijuana motel / Thunder and lightning – Into the night / All the right moves / Easy goin' up. *(cd-iss. Jan90; METALMCDL 8) (cd re-iss. Jan00 on 'NSJ'; NSJ 316)*

— **BOOKSHIRE** recruited entire new line-up; **BILLY YATES** – guitar / **DANIEL BUDFORD** – bass / **JOHN VAUGHN** – drums

Loop / S.P.V.

May 89. (lp/c/cd) *(LOP L/C/CD 504)* <844643> **SONG FOR THE OUTLAW LIVE (live)**
– The last ride / Southern man – Doin' it again / Hometown sweetheart / Song for the outlaw / Ain't no fool / Magic midnight lady – Moonshine runner / Lonesome guitar / Bad love. *(cd re-iss. Jan00 on 'N.S.'; NSROM 58)*

Interchord / not iss.

Aug 93. (cd) *(CDIRS 972190)* **SON OF THE MORNING STAR** — [-]
– Let it ride / Rebel girl / Rock attack / All of my life / I got an angel / Son of the morning star / Workin' man / That girl (is mine tonite) / Red hot and ready / On the run. *<(re-iss. Jan00 on 'New South'; NS 11679)>*

— folded after above

– compilations, etc. –

Jan 00. (cd) *New South; <(NS 113054)>* **LEGACY**
– Hoodoo man / Redneck rock & roll band / Through with you / Song for the outlaw / Keep on running / Southern girls / Renegade / Dead man's road / Damn Yankees / Lonesome guitar.

May 00. (cd) *Orchard; <5979>* **THROUGH THE YEARS** [-]
Jul 00. (cd) *Orchard; <6579>* **PAY BACK'S A BITCH** [-]

DOG EAT DOG

Formed: New York City, New York, USA . . . August '90 by DAVE NEABORE, SEAN KILKENNY and DAN NASTASI, initially as a splinter group of MUCKY PUP. Their roadie, JOHN CONNOR, was subsequently asked to be their vocalist, the mini-lp 'WARRANT' being issued in 1992. One of countless bands attempting to cross-fertilize thrash, hip-hop and hardcore, DOG EAT DOG were found snapping at the heels of more able contemporaries like RED HOT CHILI PEPPERS, RAGE AGAINST THE MACHINE and BIOHAZARD. Their first full set for 'Roadrunner', 'ALL BORO KINGS' (1994), continued in the same vein, although it sounded more cohesive than its predecessor. In August '95, they briefly charted in Britain with the catchy 'NO FRONTS' single, although when re-issued five months later, it crashed into the Top 10. Coming on like a rather tame cross between EXTREME ('Get The Funk Out'-era) and REEF, 'ISMS' gave them another Top 50 hit, boosting sales of the accompanying UK Top 40 parent album, 'PLAY GAMES'. Despite dubious street cred, DOG EAT DOG continue to chase their musical tail all the way up their proverbial backside.

Album rating: WARRANT mini (*5) / ALL BORO KINGS (*6) / PLAY GAMES (*5) / AMPED (*5) / IN THE DOGHOUSE – THE BEST OF . . . compilation (*6)

JOHN CONNOR – vocals / **DAN NASTASI** – guitar, vocals / **SEAN KILKENNY** – guitar / **DAVE NEABORE** – bass, vocals / **DAVID MALTBY** – drums

Roadrunner / Roadrunner

1992. (m-lp) <(RR 9071-1)> **WARRANT**
– It's like that / Dog eat dog / World keeps spinnin' / In the dog house / Psychorama / In the dog house (dog pound remix). *(cd-iss. Aug93; RR 9071-2)*

Jun 94. (cd/c) <(RR 9020-2/-4)> **ALL BORO KINGS**
– If these are good times / Think / No fronts / Pull my finger / Who's the king / Strip song / Queen / In the dog house / Funnel king / What comes around / It's like that / Dog eat dog / World keeps spinnin'. *(cd re-iss. May00; RR 90208)*

Sep 94. (cd-ep) *(RR 2361-2)* **IF THESE ARE THE GOOD TIMES / NO FRONTS / MORE BEER / WHY DOES IT HURT WHEN I PEE?** — [-]

Mar 95. (cd-s) *(RR 2341-2)* **WHO'S THE KING / PULL MY FINGER OUT (live)** — [-]
(cd-s) *(RR 2341-3)* – ('A'side) / Think (live) / Dog eat dog (live).

Aug 95 (c-s/cd-s) *(RR 2331-4/-2)* **NO FRONTS: THE REMIXES** 64 [-]
– (Jam Master Jay's main mix) / (Clean Greene mix) / (Psycho Les Pass mix) / (Jam Master Jay's TV mix).
(12") *(RR 2331-6)* – (first 2 tracks) / (Not Pearl Jam mix) / (Jam Master Jay's TV mix).
(re-iss. Jan96, hit UK No.9)

— **BRANDON FINLEY** – drums; repl. MALTBY

— **MARK DeBACKER** – guitar + **SCOTT MUELLER** – sax; repl. NASTASI

Jul 96. (7"pic-d/c-s) *(RR 2308-7/-4)* **ISMS. / GETTING LIVE (featuring Roguish Armament)** 43 [-]
(cd-s+=) *(RR 2308-2)* – Isms (Royale with cheese remix) / Isms (instrumental with cheese remix).

Jul 96. (cd/c/lp) <(RR 8876-2/-4/-1)> **PLAY GAMES** 40
– Bullet proof / Isms / Hi-lo / Rocky / Step right in / Rise above / Games / Getting live / Buggin' / Numb / Sore loser. *(cd re-iss. Aug97; RR 8876-5) (cd re-iss. May00; same)*

Sep 96. (7"/c-s) *(RR 2296-7/-4)* **ROCKY. / H-LO / ROCKY (mix)** — [-]
(cd-s+=) *(RR 2296-2)* – (band interview).

Jul 97. (12"ep; with THE R.Z.A.) *(2286-6)* **STEP RIGHT IN (Wisedog mix) / AND YPSILON STEPS IN (club). / STEP RIGHT IN (Fantastic Plastic Machine entertainment mix – instrumental) / STEP RIGHT IN (Junkie XL mix)** — [-]
(cd-ep+=) *(2286-2)* – ('A'-SEDA mix) / ('A'lp version).

Jun 99. (cd) *(RR 8726-2)* **AMPED** — [-]
– Gangbusters / Expect the unexpected / Whateverman / Modern day devils / Get up / Always the same big wheel / In the city / Right out / One day / True colour / In time (growing game).

– compilations, etc. –

Sep 00. (cd) *Roadrunner; <(RR 8527-2)>* **IN THE DOGHOUSE – THE BEST OF DOG EAT DOG** — May01
– No fronts (Jam Master Jay's edit) / Who's the king (slight remix) / If these are good

times (remix) / Isms / Rocky (radio version) / Step right in (fantastic plastic machine entertainment mix) / Expect the unexpected / One day / Dog eat dog / More beer / Why does it hurt when I pee / Step right in (Junkie XL mix) / Expect the unexpected (rockin' Rio mix) / Isms (royale with cheese remix) / No fronts (not Pearl Jam mix). *(cd-bonus videos).*

DOG FASHION DISCO

Formed: Washington DC, USA . . . late 1999 by TODD SMITH, GREG COMBS, JEFF SIEGEL, STEVE MEARS and JOHN ENSMINGER. Taking their cue from the likes of TOOL, CLUTCH and MR. BUNGLE, the band made their independent debut with the 'EMBRYOS IN BLOOM' mini-set. Subsequently signing with the 'Spitfire' label, the DC noise terrorists caused a minor stir with debut album proper, 'ANARCHISTS OF GOOD TASTE' (2001). Instantly recognisable by their dinky DOORS-style carnival organ – which unsurprisingly sits rather incongruously beside the requisite crunching guitar, manic tub thumping and death growl – these avant-garde nu-metallers occasionally shower sparks of genius on the unsuspecting listener. With a knack for a bizarre, cerebral lyric or two and a laudable attempt at experimental dynamics, DOG FASHION DISCO could yet be canine kings of the left-field catwalk.

Album rating: ANARCHISTS OF GOOD TASTE (*5)

TODD SMITH – vocals / **GREG COMBS** – guitar / **JEFF SIEGEL** – keyboards / **STEVE MEARS** – bass / **JOHN ENSMINGER** – drums

not iss. own label

2000. (m-cd) **EMBRYOS IN BLOOM** [-] [ ]

Spitfire Spitfire

Mar 01. (cd) <(SPITCD 170)> **ANARCHISTS OF GOOD TASTE** [ ] [ ]
– Leper friend / 9 to 5 at the morgue / Mushroom cult / Antiquity's small rewards / Headless / Corpse is corpse / Pour some urine on me / Vertigo motel / Cartoon autopsy / Pink riots.

DOGS D'AMOUR

Formed: Birmingham, England . . . early 1983 by TYLA, NICK HALLS, NED CHRISTIE, CARL and BAM-BAM. Due to peronnel reshuffles, TYLA was soon in place as frontman, the tousle-haired singer also penning all the lyrics and even the comic sleeve artwork of their subsequent albums. Initially spending time in Finland (home of glam/sleaze legends, HANOI ROCKS, to whom DOGS D'AMOUR owed something of a musical debt), they recorded a debut album, 'THE STATE WE'RE IN' (1984), for a small domestic label, 'Kumibeat', before they were briefly contracted to Japanese label, 'Watanabe'. Following yet more personnel changes (with a line-up now consisting of TYLA, CARL, JO-DOG and STEVE JAMES), they secured a deal with semi-major label, 'China', releasing the 'HOW COME IT NEVER RAINS' single in early '88. This was closely followed by another single, 'THE KID FROM KENSINGTON' and a limited album, 'THE (UN)AUTHORISED BOOTLEG' (1988), before the group released 'IN THE DYNAMITE JET SALOON' (1988), for many people the band's first real album and certainly the one which garnered most column inches in the music press. A British answer to the countless hordes of mascara'd hopefuls of the burgeoning US sleaze-rock scene, The DOGS D'AMOUR were nevertheless a rootsier proposition, primarily influenced by the likes of The ROLLING STONES and The FACES alongside usual suspects like The NEW YORK DOLLS, AEROSMITH etc. With TYLA's red-wine-scarred tonsils and hard-bitten tales of boozers, losers and abusers, the group were tipped for greatness. Certainly, their lengthy musical apprenticeship was obvious in the quality of tracks like 'THE LAST BANDIT', although DOGS D'AMOUR's endearingly ramshackle approach could hardly be called professional. A remixed and re-released 'HOW COME IT NEVER RAINS' almost clipped the UK Top 40 early the following year while a mini-album, 'A GRAVEYARD OF EMPTY BOTTLES' (1989), crashed into the Top 20 a few months later. A largely acoustic affair, the record included a tribute to TYLA's hard-drinking hero, the late great Charles Bukowski, entitled 'THE BULLETPROOF POET'. Another single, 'THE SATELLITE KID' hit the Top 30 later that summer while The DOGS D'AMOUR recording schedule continued apace with 'ERROL FLYNN' (1989; US title 'KING OF THIEVES'). A tribute to another bad boy icon, the record was a fine collection of good-time bar-room rock that narrowly missed the Top 20. Despite constant touring, however, the group failed to build on this success, a subsequent album, 'STRAIGHT' (1990) failing to make the Top 30 while peers The QUIREBOYS almost made No.1. DOGS D'AMOUR eventually ground to a halt when the ever controversial TYLA slashed himself onstage with a broken bottle, requiring over 30 stitches to an open chest wound. BAM BAM subsequently went on to bigger and better things, joining The WILDHEARTS, while STEVE JAMES formed The LAST BANDITS. The members regrouped in late '92 for a further Top 30 effort, 'THE MORE UNCHARTED HEIGHTS OF DISGRACE' (1993), although the reunion proved to be short-lived. In the latter half of the 90's, TYLA was quite prolific via a clutch of somewhat derivative sets beginning with 1995's 'LIFE AND TIMES OF A BALLAD MONGER'.

Album rating: IN THE DYNAMITE JET SALOON (*7) / A GRAVEYARD OF EMPTY BOTTLES (*7) / ERROL FLYNN (*6) / STRAIGHT (*5) / DOG HITS AND BOOTLEG ALBUM compilation (*6) / MORE UNCHARTED HEIGHTS OF DISGRACE (*5) / Tyla: LIFE AND TIMES OF A BALLAD MONGER (*5) / LIBERTINE (*5) / GOTHIC (FLOWERS OF A BRUTAL CALLING) mini (*5) / NOCTURNAL NOMAD (*5) / ILIAD OF A WOLVERHAMPTON WANDERER (*5) / PIECE FOR THE WICKED VOL.1 (*4)

TYLA – vocals, guitar / **CARL** – bass / **DAVE KUSWORTH** – guitar repl. NICK HALLS + NED CHRISTIE – vocals (Sep'83) / **PAUL HORNBY** – drums repl. BAM-BAM

Kumibeat not iss.

Apr 84. (7") *(JOM 3)* **HOW DO YOU FALL IN LOVE. / THE STATE I'M IN** [-] [-] Finn

Sep 84. (lp) **THE STATE WE'RE IN** [-] [-] Fin

— **BAM-BAM** – drums returned to repl. HORNBY

— **JO-DOG** – guitar repl. DAVE KUSWORTH who with NIKKI SUDDEN became JACOBITES. (above later went solo in 1987, at this time TYLA, while having no contract, also joined JACOBITES)

— (Aug85) **MARK DRAX** – bass repl. MARK DUNCAN (ex-DOLL BY DOLL) who repl. CARL

— (Jan87) **STEVE JAMES** – bass repl. DRAX in new line-up – **STEVE, TYLA, BAM-BAM & JO DOG.**

Supertrack not iss.

Dec 87. (7"m) *(DOGS 1)* **HOW COME IT NEVER RAINS. / SOMETIMES / LAST BANDIT** [ ] [-]

China China

Feb 88. (7"m/12"m) *(CHINA/CHINX 1)* **HOW COME IT NEVER RAINS. / SOMETIMES / LAST BANDIT** [ ] [-]

May 88. (7"/7"w-poster) *(CHINA/CHING 5)* **THE KID FROM KENSINGTON. / EVERYTHING I WANT** [ ] [-]
(12"+=/12"yellow+=) *(CHINX/CHIXP 5)* – The state I'm in.

Jul 88. (lp-ltd) *(WOL 7)* **THE (UN)AUTHORISED BOOTLEG** [ ] [-]
– Firework girl / Chains / Gold / Pourin' out my heart / Wait until I'm dead / How do you fall in love again? / Kiss this joint / Heroine / Tales of destruction / Dynamite jet saloon / Swingin' the bottle.

Sep 88. (7"/7"w-poster) *(CHINA/CHING 10)* **I DON'T WANT YOU TO GO. / HEROINE** [ ] [-]
(12"+=/12"pink+=) *(CHINX/CHIXP 10)* – Ugly.

Sep 88. (lp/c)(cd) *(WOL/ZWOL 8)(837 368-2)* **IN THE DYNAMITE JET SALOON** [97] [-]
– Debauchery / I don't want you to go / How come it never rains / Last bandit / Medicine man / Gonna get it right / Everything I want / Heatbreak / Billy Two rivers / Wait until I'm dead. *(cd+=)* – The kid from Kensington / Sometimes / The state I'm in. *(re-iss. cd Apr91; WOLCD 1004)*

Jan 89. (7"/7"g-f) *(CHINA/CHING 13)* **HOW COME IT NEVER RAINS (Dynamite remix). / BABY GLASS (live)** [44] [-]
(12"+=/12"pic-d+=) *(CHINX/CHIXP 13)* – Kirsten jet (live).
(cd-s++=) *(CHICD 13)* – ('A'extended).

Mar 89. (10"m-lp)(lp/c) *(WOL 11)(839 074-1/-4)* **A GRAVEYARD OF EMPTY BOTTLES** [16] [-]
– I think it's (love again) / So once I was / Comfort of the Devil / Saviour / Errol Flynn / The bullet proof poet / When the dream has come / Angel. *(cd-iss. Mar91; WOLCD 1005)*

Jun 89. (7"/7"pic-d) *(CHINA/CHING 17)* **SATELLITE KID. / SHE THINKS TOO MUCH OF ME / DRUNK LIKE ME** [26] [-]
(12"+=/12"pic-d+=) *(CHINX/CHIXP 17)* – Things he'd do.
(cd-s+=) *(CHICD 17)* – As I see the poppies fall.

Sep 89. (lp/c/cd) *(839 700-1/-4/-2)* *<841168>* **ERROL FLYNN** <US-title 'KING OF THIEVES'> [22] [ ]
– Drunk like me / Goddess from the gutter / Hurricane / Satellite kid / Errol Flynn / Planetary Pied Piper / Princess Valium / Dogs hair / Trail of tears / Ballad of Jack / The prettiest girl in the world / Girl behind the glass. *(cd+=)* – Things seem to go wrong / Baby glass.

Oct 89. (7"/7"w-poster/c-s) *(CHINA/CHING/CHICS 20)* **TRAIL OF TEARS. / POURIN' OUT MY HEART** [24] [-]
(cd-s+=) *(CHICD 20)* – In the dynamite set saloon / Swingin' the bottle.
(12"++=/12"pic-d++=) *(CHINX/CHIXP 20)* – As I see the poppies fall.

Jun 90. (7"/7"s/c-s) *(CHINA/CHINS/CHICS 24)* *<877375>* **VICTIMS OF SUCCESS. / BILLY TWO RIVERS** [36] [ ]
(12"+=/cd-s+=) *(CHINX/CHICD 24)* – ('A'extended) / Ballad of Jack (live).

Sep 90. (7"/c-s) *(CHINA/CHICS 27)* **EMPTY WORLD. / LADY NICOTINE** [61] [-]
(12"+=/cd-s+=) *(CHINX/CHICD 27)* – Chiva / Heading for the target of insanity.

China Polygram

Sep 90. (cd/c/lp) *(843796-2/-4/-1)* *<1007>* **STRAIGHT** [32] [ ]
– Cardboard town / Kiss my heart goodbye / Lie in this land / You can't beat the Devil / Gypsy blood / Empty world / Back on the juice / Evil / Flyin' solo / Victims of success / Heroine. *(cd+=/c+=)* – Chiva / Lady Nicotine. *(re-iss. cd Mar91; WOLCD 1007)*

Nov 90. (7"/c-s) *(CHINA/CHICS 30)* *<879121>* **BACK ON THE JUICE. / VICTIMS OF SUCCESS (live)** [ ] [ ]
(12"+=/12"pic-d++/) *(CHINX/CHIXP 30)* – Bullet proof poet (live).
(cd-s+=) *(CHICD 30)* – Lie in this land.

Aug 91. (cd/c/d-lp) *(WOL/+C/CD 1020)* **DOGS HITS AND BOOTLEG ALBUM** (compilation) [58] [-]
– How come it never rains / The kid from Kensington / I don't want you to go (extended) / Satellite kid / Trail of tears / Victims of success / Empty world / Back on the juice / I think it's (love again) / (BOOTLEG ALBUM tracks).

— Disbanded Jul'91 after TYLA had slashed himself on stage. BAM BAM joined The WILDHEARTS and STEVE JAMES formed The LAST BANDITS. Re-formed again late 1992.

Mar 93. (c-ep/12"ep/cd-ep) *(WOK MC/T/CD 2033)* **ALL OR NOTHING EP** [53] [-]
– All or nothing / When nobody loves you / What's happening here (acoustic) / Hard to leave this world. *(remixed.Jun93;)*

May 93. (cd/c/lp) *(WOL/+C/CD 1032)* **. . . MORE UNCHARTERED HEIGHTS OF DISGRACE** [30] [-]
– What's happening here? / What you do / Pretty, pretty once / World's different now (an ode to Drug Hill) / Mr.Addiction / Johnny Silvers / Cach / More uncharted heights of disgrace / Scared of dying / Mr.Barfly / Put it in her arm.

Aug 93. (7"m) *(WOKA 2038)* **PRETTY PRETTY ONCE. / EVERYTHING I WANT (live) / HEARTBREAK (live)** [ ] [-]
(7"m) *(WOKB 2038)* – ('A'side) / Trail of tears (live) / Medicine man (live).
(7"m) *(WOKC 2038)* – ('A'side) / Drunk like me (live) / I don't want to go (live).
(cd-s) *(WOKCD 2038)* – ('A'side) / Mr.Addiction (live) / Last bandit (live) / How come it never rains (live).

—— disbanded after above

– compilations, etc. –

Jun 93. (5xcd-box/5xc-box) *China; (DOGSBOX CD/MC)* **DOGS BOLLOX** (compilation; all) [ ] [-]
Nov 98. (cd) *Edsel; (EDCD 588)* **DYNAMITE JET SALOON / GRAVEYARD OF EMPTY BOTTLES** [ ] [-]
Dec 98. (cd) *Edsel; (EDCD 589)* **ERROL FLYNN / STRAIGHT** [ ] [-]

TYLA

—— his solo venture with various people

Revolver Polydor

Nov 95. (cd) *(REVXD 197) <1440>* **LIFE AND TIMES OF A BALLAD MONGER** [ ] [ ] 1994
– Ballad of no-one in particular / All you had / Bloody Mary / Where were you / Little thing / The adultra / Throw it all away / Hard to leave this world / The town . . . / Damnation / Daddie's dead / Spirit of the Jag / The whisper / Kings of the street.
Dec 96. (cd) *(REVXD 208)* **LIBERTINE** [ ] [-]
– Here forever / Ballad of a broken heart / Angelina / Lament of night / Woman of my dreams / Low / Break the spell / Growin' up / What if / Hotel life / Hate pain / Thunder rolls / Rosary mozaic / Libertine blues.
Aug 97. (m-cd) *(REVXD 218)* **GOTHIC (FLOWERS OF A BRUTAL CALLING)** [ ] [-]
– Passenger of time / Mad bad Jack / Ghost lover / Best regards / Those days / Gods of dogs / Gracie.

King Outlaw not iss.

Feb 99. (cd) *(KOCD 2)* **NOCTURNAL NOMAD** [ ] [-]
– Unidentified / Lovers / Animal / Untitled / Legend of the thief / Powder / How did you sleep last night / Only girl I ever loved / Error of my ways / If only . . . / Another night in the life of a day / Seems like yesterday / Most hated man in town / Hour of need / North of darkness.
Jun 99. (cd) *(KOCD 3)* **ILIAD OF A WOLVERHAMPTON WANDERER** (compilation) [ ] [-]
– Mad bad Jack / All you had / Angelina / Beautifully insane / Ghost lover / Lament of night / Bloody Mary / Only girl / Best regards / The town . . . / Hate pain / If only / Seems like yesterday / Animal / Kings of the streets.
Nov 99. (cd) *(KOCD 4)* **PIECE FOR THE WICKED VOL.1** [ ] [-]

DOGSTAR

Formed: Los Angeles, California, USA ... 1993 by actor/Hollywood heart-throb turned bass player, KEANU REEVES, actor/drummer ROB MAILHOUSE, ex-NUNS frontman/songwriter, BRET DOMROSE and GREGG MILLER, the latter leaving after playing a handful of gigs. Apparently formed out of a chance meeting in a supermarket rather than being a planned strategy for KEANU to move into music, the DOGSTAR trio played their inaugural gigs as low-key affairs in local bars. Selling out an American tour almost immediately on the strength of KEANU's sex appeal/fame factor, it was obvious the band's music was always going to take a back seat to the sensationalism. Eventually signing with RCA outlet, 'Zoo', DOGSTAR debuted with the 'QUATTRO FORMAGGI' EP in summer '96, coinciding with a UK tour that took in Scotland's 'T In The Park'. A few months later, the trio released their debut album, 'OUR LITTLE VISIONARY', a run-of-the-mill sub-Grunge affair that contained an ill-advised cover of Badfinger's 'NO MATTER WHAT'. A second set, 'HAPPY ENDING', was issued in the summer of 2000 – the cover this time being Leon Russell's 'SUPERSTAR'. • **KEANU's filmography:** included 'River's Edge' and 'Bill And Ted's Big Adventure' to mention but a few. • **Note:** Another DOGSTAR released an EP, 'ILLUMINATI FABRICATION', for 'La La Land', in 1994.

Album rating: OUR LITTLE VISIONARY (*5) / HAPPY ENDING (*4)

BRET DOMROSE – vocals, guitar (ex-NUNS) / **KEANU REEVES** (b.1965) – bass, vocals / **BOB MAILHOUSE** – drums

American Zoo

Jul 96. (c-ep/cd-ep) *(74321 40142-4/-2) <11128>* **QUATTRO FORMAGGI EP** [ ] [ ]
– Honest anyway / Behind her / Return / 32 stories.
Sep 96. (cd) *<11133>* **OUR LITTLE VISIONARY** [-] [ ]
– Forgive / Our little visionary / No matter what / Breathe tonight / Nobody home / History light / Honest anyway / And I pray / Enchanted / Bleeding soul / Goodbye / Denial.

Ultimatum Ultimatum

Jul 00. (cd) *<(ULT 005)>* **HAPPY ENDING** [ ] [ ]
– Halo / Slipping down / Enemies / Superstar / Cornerstore / A dreamtime / Stagger / Washington / Alarming / Swim / Blown away.

DOKKEN

Formed: Los Angeles, California, USA ... 1981 by DON DOKKEN alongside GEORGE LYNCH, JUAN CROUCIER and MICK BROWN. Together with future members of DOKKEN, he had a solo album, 'BACK IN THE STREETS', withdrawn around the early 80's. After he'd contributed backing vocals for The SCORPIONS on their 'BLACKOUT' album, the singer/guitarist signed to the French-based label, 'Carrere', in 1982, forming DOKKEN. Following a promising debut set, 'BREAKING THE CHAINS' (1983), JEFF PILSON replaced the departing CROUCIER who went on to form RATT. Signing with 'Elektra', DOKKEN made the US Top 50 with the 'TOOTH AND NAIL' set in 1984, although they finally broke through in the mid-80's with the massive-selling 'UNDER LOCK AND KEY' opus. Streamlining the band's melodic power-rock sound, the album almost made the US Top 30, spawning the minor hit, 'IN MY DREAMS'. Although DOKKEN were never a glam-metal act as such, the group benefitted from the thriving US scene and the success of acts like MOTLEY CRUE and RATT, the 'BACK FOR THE ATTACK' (1987) opus making the Top 20. Despite their growing stature, however, there was increasing friction between DON and LYNCH, eventually coming to a head in 1988 and leading to the group's demise. By the release of the live 'BEAST FROM THE EAST' (1988), DOKKEN had already split. While LYNCH formed The LYNCH MOB, DON went solo, enlisting seasoned veterans MIKKEY DEE, PETER BALTES, BILLY WHITE and JOHN NORUM and recording a lone Top 50 album for 'Geffen', 'UP FROM THE ASHES' (1990). DOKKEN eventually reformed in 1995, signing with 'Columbia' and releasing the 'DYSFUNCTIONAL' album, its Top 50 placing proving the group could still command an audience after an absence of almost seven years.

Album rating: BREAKING THE CHAINS (*5) / TOOTH AND NAIL (*6) / UNDER LOCK AND KEY (*6) / BEAST FROM THE EAST (*6) / BACK FOR THE ATTACK (*6) / UP FROM THE ASHES solo (*4) / ONE LIVE NIGHT (*5) / DYSFUNCTIONAL (*4) / SHADOWLIFE (*4) / ERASE THE SLATE (*4)

DON DOKKEN (b.29 Jun'53) – vocals, guitar / **GEORGE LYNCH** (b.28 Sep'54) – guitar / **JUAN CROUCIER** – bass / **MICK BROWN** – drums

Carrere Elektra

Apr 82. (7") *(CAR 229)* **WE'RE ILLEGAL. / PARIS** [ ] [ ]
May 82. (lp) *(CAL 136) <60290>* **BREAKIN' THE CHAINS** [ ] [ ] Oct83
– Breakin' the chains / Seven thunders / I can see you / In the middle / We're illegal / Paris / Stick to your guns / Young girl / Felony / Night rider.

—— **JEFF PILSON** – bass repl. JUAN CROUCIER who later formed RATT.

Elektra Elektra

Oct 83. (7") *<69778>* **BREAKING THE CHAINS. / FELONY** [-] [ ]
Oct 84. (7") *<69687>* **BULLETS TO SPARE. / INTO THE FIRE** [-] [ ]
Oct 84. (lp) *(960376-1) <60376>* **TOOTH AND NAIL** [ ] [49]
– Without warning / Tooth and nail / Just got lucky / Heartless heart / Don't close your eyes / When Heaven comes down / Into the fire / Bullets to spare / Alone again / Turn on the action.
Jan 85. (7") *<69664>* **JUST FOR LUCKY. / DON'T CLOSE YOUR EYES** [-] [ ]
Apr 85. (7") *<69650>* **ALONE AGAIN. / TOOTH AND NAIL** [-] [64]
Mar 86. (7") *(EKR 37) <69563>* **IN MY DREAMS. / TELL THE LIVING END** [ ] [77] Feb86
(12"+=) *(EKR 37T)* – Alone again.
Mar 86. (lp/c)(cd) *(EKT 28/+C)(960458-2) <60458>* **UNDER LOCK AND KEY** [ ] [32] Dec85
– Unchain the night / The hunter / In my dreams / Lightnin' strikes again / Slippin' away / It's not love / Jaded heart / Don't lie to me / Will the sun rise / Til the livin' end.
Jun 86. (7") *<69533>* **LIGHTNING STRIKES AGAIN. / IT'S NOT LOVE** [-] [ ]
May 87. (7") *<69483>* **BACK FOR THE ATTACK. / DREAM WARRIORS** [-] [ ]
Nov 87. (lp/c)(cd) *(EKT 43/+C)(960735-2) <60735>* **BACK FOR THE ATTACK** [96] [13]
– Kiss of death / Prisoner / Night by night / Standing in the shadows / Heaven sent / Mr. Scary / So many tears / Burning like a flame / Lost behind the wall / Stop fighting love / Cry of the gypsy / Sleepless nights / Dream warriors.
Feb 88. (7") *(EKR 67) <69435>* **BURNING LIKE A FLAME. / LOST BEHIND THE WALL** [ ] [72] Dec87
(12"+=/12"pic-d+=) *(EKR 67T/+P)* – Back for the attack.
Apr 88. (7") *<69405>* **HEAVEN SENT. / MR. SCARY** [-] [ ]
Jun 88. (7") *<69379>* **SO MANY TEARS. / MR. SCARY** [-] [ ]
Dec 88. (d-lp/c)(cd) *(EKT 55/+C)(960823) <60823>* **BEAST FROM THE EAST (live)** [ ] [33] Nov88
– Unchain the night / Tooth and nail / Dream warriors / Kiss of death / When heaven comes down / Into the fire / Mr. Scary / Heaven sent / It's not love / Alone again / Just got lucky / Breaking the chains / In my dreams / Walk away. *(d-lp+=/c+=)* – Standing in the shadows / Sleepless nights / Turn on the action.
Dec 88. (7") *<69353>* **ALONE AGAIN (live). / IT'S NOT LOVE (live)** [-] [ ]
Feb 89. (7") *<6969324>* **WALK AWAY (live). / UNCHAIN THE NIGHT (live)** [-] [ ]

—— (DOKKEN had split earlier in the year) LYNCH + BROWN formed LYNCH MOB

DON DOKKEN

went solo, augmented by **JOHN NORUM** – guitar (ex-EUROPE) / **BILLY WHITE** – guitar (ex-WATCHTOWER) / **PETER BALTES** – bass (of ACCEPT) / **MIKKEY DEE** – drums (ex-KING DIAMOND)

Geffen Geffen

Sep 90. (cd/c/lp) *<(7599 24301-2/-4/-1)>* **UP FROM THE ASHES** [ ] [50]
– Crash 'n' burn / 1000 miles away / Whern some nights / Forever / Living a lie / When love finds a fool / Give it up / Mirror mirror / Stay / Down in flames / The hunger. *(re-iss. Aug91 cd/c; GEFD/GEFC 24301) (cd re-iss. Jun97; GED 24301)*

DOKKEN

—— re-formed **DOKKEN, PILSON, BROWN + LYNCH**

not iss. Columbia

May 95. (cd) *<CK 67075>* **DYSFUNCTIONAL** [-] [47]
– Inside looking out / Hole in my head / The maze / Too high to fly / Nothing left to

say / Shadows of life / Long way home / Sweet chains / Lesser of two evils / What price / From the beginning.

S.P.V. C.M.C.

Apr 97. (cd) <86210> **SHADOWLIFE** [-] [ ]
– Puppet on a string / Cracks in the ground / Sky beneath my feet / Until I know / Hello / Convenience store messiah / I feel / Hard to believe / Sweet life / Bitter regret / I don't mind / Until I know (slight return).

—— **REB BEACH** – guitar (ex-WINGER) repl. GEORGE who re-formed LYNCH MOB

Aug 99. (cd) *(SPV 0858112)* <607686274-2> **ERASE THE SLATE** [ ] [ ] Jun99
– Erase the slate / Change the world / Maddest hatter / Drown / Shattered / One / Who believes / Voice of the soul / Crazy Mary goes round / Haunted lullabye / In your honor.

– compilations, etc. –

Aug 91. (lp/c)(cd) *Repertoire; (REP 2005/+TO)(REP 4005WG)* **BACK IN THE STREETS** (rec.1979) [ ] [-]
– Back in the streets / Felony / Day after day / We're going wrong / Liar / Prisoner.

Apr 97. (cd) *C.M.C.; (0607 686206-2)* **ONE NIGHT LIVE (live)** [ ] [ ]

Aug 99. (d-cd) *S.P.V.; (SPV 0851808-2)* **ONE LIVE NIGHT / SHADOWLIFE** [ ] [ ]

Apr 00. (cd) *S.P.V.; (SPV 0852174-2)* **LIVE FROM THE SUN / BEST FROM THE WEST – LIVE** [ ] [ ]

DONE LYING DOWN

Formed: London, England . . . 1992 by Boston, Massachusetts, (USA)-born JACK PLUG (aka JEREMY PARKER), alongside ALI MAC, GLEN YOUNG and JAMES SHERRY. Scoring an NME Single Of The Week award with their debut EP, 'HEART OF DIRT' (1993), DONE LYING DOWN immediately drew comparisons with NIRVANA, if only for their decidedly 'Bleach'-era rhythm sound. Like most bands of the day, they also had the quiet part/loud part formula down pat, attempting to break into the American-dominated grunge market with a further three EP's (produced by JOHN ROBB, former MEMBRANES) the following year: 'FAMILY VALUES', 'NEGATIVE ONE FRIENDS' and 'JUST A MISDEMEANOUR'. 1994 also saw the release of a debut album, 'JOHN AUSTIN RUTLEDGE', apparently named after one of PARKER's friends who co-wrote some of the material (he also featured on the cover shot). Despite praise from John Peel, DONE LYING DOWN found it difficult to break the American stranglehold on the genre, their 1995 US tour not exactly doing much to raise their profile in a UK which was in the grip of Brit-pop madness. Nevertheless, they weren't going to take this lack of mainstream success erm, lying down (aarrgh!) and soldiered on with a further EP, 'CHRONIC OFFENDER', and a second album, 'KONTRAPUNKT' (1996) – on their new 'Immaterial' label. This set moved away somewhat from the NIRVANA comparisons and was acclaimed in the heavy music press.

Album rating: JOHN AUSTIN RUTLEDGE (*6) / KONTRAPUNKT (*8)

JEREMY PARKER – vocals, guitar / **GLEN YOUNG** – guitar / **ALI MAC** – bass / **JAMES SHERRY** – drums

Abstract B&W-Indians

Oct 93. (7"ep/cd-ep) *(ABS 101)* **HEART OF DIRT** [ ] [ ]

Mar 94. (7"clear-ep/cd-ep) *(ABS/+CD 102) (ABS/ABCD 102)* **FAMILY VALUES EP** [ ] [-]
– Septic / Quit smacking the baby / Divorcee / Preservatives.

Jul 94. (7"ep/cd-ep) *(ABS/+CD 105)* **NEGATIVE ONE FRIENDS EP** [ ] [-]
– Throughout / Punktune / Cheat on me.

Aug 94. (7"ep/cd-ep)(12"ep) *(ABS/+CD 106)(12ABS 106)* **JUST A MISDEMEANOUR EP** [ ] [-]
– Just a misdemeanor / Fictional woman / Do what you sell / Factory.

Oct 94. (cd/c/lp) *(ABT 099 CD/MC/LP)* **JOHN AUSTIN RUTLEDGE** [ ] [-]
– Choose / !$%OX? (or something) / If I only had listened / Too fast (I thought . . .) / Pasadina / Just a misdemeanor / Christmas shoplifting / Pennyhead / Student III / Music habit / Before she changed / Fun / Dissent / Heroes let themselves be killed / That makes 1 of us / Trenchmouth / Purple seeds. *(lp w/ free lp) (ABT 099LPX)*

Org not iss.

Jul 95. (7") *(ORGAN 017)* **ANGEL CAGE. /** [ ] [-]

Immaterial Immaterial

Aug 95. (7") *(DLD 001)* **CHRONIC OFFENDER. / MY BIRTHDAY AND ME ARE NOT FRIENDS (live)** [ ] [-]
(cd-s+=) *(DLD 001CD)* – Defence mechanisms / 73 measures of acoustic (imaterial).

Nov 95. (7") *(DLD 002)* **SO YOU DRIVE. /** [ ] [-]
(cd-s+=) *(DLD 002CD)* –

Apr 96. (cd/c) *(DLD 100 CD/MC)* **KONTRAPUNKT** [ ] [-]
– Chronic offender / Columbus day / Shut the door / Scared too stiff / So you drive / Back to where I'm king / Seemed like a good idea at the time / Backseat driver's license / Song for freeloaders / Nirvana ripoff / Star search / Insignificant other / Not my friend / Producer / Can't be too certain.

Jun 96. (7") *(DLD 003)* **CAN'T BE TOO CERTAIN. / STAR SEARCH** [ ] [-]
(cd-s+=) *(DLD 003CD)* – Columbus Day / Back seat drivers licence / Not my friend.

—— disbanded soon afterwards

DONNAS

Formed: Palo Alta, California, USA . . . 1996 initially as speed-metal outfit ELECTROCUTE by eighth graders, DONNA A (aka BRETT), DONNA R (aka ALLISON), DONNA F (aka MAYA) and DONNA C (aka TORRY). Retreading the blitzkrieg bop pioneered by the RAMONES twenty years earlier, the four Donnas came on like a latter day RUNAWAYS minus the pop glamour. Unrelenting punk-rock with a capital P, the girls' eponymous debut album (written and produced by their svengali, DARRIN RAFFAELLI) surfaced on the tiny 'Superteem' imprint in '97, a frantic document of teen rebellion revelling in the usual US high school cliches. Subsequently becoming part of the 'Lookout' stable (which launched GREEN DAY and others), The DONNAS toured the States and Japan promoting a follow-up set, 'AMERICAN TEENAGE ROCK'N'ROLL' (1998). Now writing themselves, the DONNAS delivered their third set, 'GET SKINTIGHT', the following year. The girls came of age with 'DONNAS TURN 21' (2001) although musically and lyrically they were still fumbling around behind the proverbial bike shed looking for cheap thrills. If they could only translate the sexual ambition of '40 BOYS IN 40 NIGHTS' into some form of musical ambition then they wouldn't have to rely on a Judas Priest cover ('LIVING AFTER MIDNIGHT') to bolster their now cliche'd sound. • **Covered:** DRIVE IN (Beach Boys) / DA DOO RON RON (Crystals) / WIG WAM BAM (Sweet) / SCHOOL'S OUT (Alice Cooper).

Album rating: THE DONNAS (*5) / AMERICAN TEENAGE ROCK'N'ROLL MACHINE (*6) / TURN 21 (*7)

DONNA A. (b. BRETT ANDERSON) – vocals / **DONNA R.** (b. ALLISON ROBERTSON) – guitar / **DONNA F.** (b. MAYA FORD, 8 Jan'79) – bass / **DONNA C.** (b. TORRY CANSTELLANO, 8 Jan'79) – drums

not iss. Superteem

1997. (lp) **THE DONNAS** [-] [ ]
– Hey, I'm gonna be your girl / Let's go Mano! / Teenage runaway / Lana and Stevie / I'm gonna make him mine (tonight) / Huff all night / I don't wanna go / We don't go / Friday fun / Everybody's smoking cheeba / Get rid of that girl / Drive in / Do you wanna go out with me / Rock'n'roll boy / High school yum yum / A boy like you / Let's rab. *<cd-iss. Aug98 on 'Lookout'+=singles tracks; LK 201CD>* – Let's go Mano! / Last chance dance / I wanna be a unabomber / Da doo ron ron / I don't wanna go to school / I don't wanna rock'n'roll tonight.

Lookout Lookout

Jan 98. (7") *<LK 196>* **ROCK'N'ROLL MACHINE. / SPEEDIN' BACK TO MY BABY** [ ] [ ]

Feb 98. (cd/lp) *<LK 191 CD/LP>* **AMERICAN TEENAGE ROCK'N'ROLL MACHINE** [ ] [ ] Jan98
– Rock'n'roll machine / You make me hot / Checkin' it out / Gimmie my radio / Outta my mind / Looking for blood / Leather on leather / Wanna get some stuff / Speed demon / Shake in the action.

Feb 99. (7") *<LK 214>* **split w/ TOILET BOYS** [ ] [ ]

Jun 99. (cd/lp) *<LK 225 CD/LP>* **GET SKINTIGHT** [ ] [ ] May99
– Skintight / Hyperactive / You don't wanna call / Hook it up / Doin' donuts / Searchin' the streets / Party action / I didn't like you anyway / Get outta my room / Well done / Get U alone / Hot boxin' / Too fast for love / Zero.

Epitaph Epitaph

Jan 01. (cd) *<6611-2>* **TURN 21** [ ] [ ]
– Are you gonna move it for me? / Do you wanna it? / 40 boys in 40 nights / Play my game / Midnite snack / Drivin' thru' my heart / You've got a crush on me / Little boy / Don't get me busted / Police blitz / Hot pants / Gimme a ride / Livin' after midnight / Nothing to do.

Apr 01. (cd-s) *(1045-7/-2)* **40 BOYS IN 40 NIGHTS. / WIG WAM BAM / SCHOOL'S OUT** [ ] [-]

DORO (see under ⇒ WARLOCK)

DOS (see under ⇒ MINUTEMEN)

DOWN (see under ⇒ PANTERA)

DOWN BY LAW

Formed: Los Angeles, California, USA . . . early 90's by seasoned hardcore belter, DAVE SMALLEY. Finding a home at BRETT GUREWITZ's (BAD RELIGION) 'Epitaph' stable, they unleashed the take-no-prisoners punk-metal assault of their eponymous debut. They carried on in much the same vein with a fairly prolific recording schedule over the first half of the 90's. The line-up evolved into a more stabilized affair, SMALLEY enlisting the help of SAM WILLIAMS III, ANGRY JOHN and DANNY WESTMAN. Their mid 90's period was overshadowed by labelmates OFFSPRING, although they did manage to squeeze out some competent hardcore on the albums, 'ALL SCRATCHED UP!' (1996) and 'LAST OF THE SHARPSHOOTERS' (1997).

Album rating: DOWN BY LAW (*6) / BLUE (*5) / PUNKROCKACADEMYFIGHTSONG (*7) / ALL SCRATCHED UP! (*5) / LAST OF THE SHARPSHOOTERS (*5) / FLY THE FLAG (*5)

DAVE SMALLEY – vocals (ex-DYS, ex-ALL, ex-DAG NASTY) / + members of CHEMICAL PEOPLE + CLAW HAMMER:- **CHRIS BAGAROZZI** – guitar / **DAVE NAZ** – drums / **ED URIK** – bass, vocals

Epitaph Epitaph

Jul 91. (cd/lp) *<(E 86411-2/-1)>* **DOWN BY LAW** [ ] [ ]
– Right or wrong / Vision / Dreams away / Down the drain / American dream / The truth / Best friends / Mat Gleason is God / The one / Can't see it still / Surf punk / Too much grey.

Oct 92. (cd/c/lp) *<(E 86419-2/-4/-1)>* **BLUE** [ ] [ ]
– Last brigade / Looking for something / Break the wall / At home in the wasteland / Rain / Turn away / Air conditioner / Greenest field / Straw / Finally here / Our own way / Dead end. *<actually a re-issue of their eponymous set in '91>*

—— **SMALLEY** recruited **MARK PHILIPS** – guitar / **PAT HOED** – bass / **COLIN SEARS** – drums

Aug 93. (cd) *<(LF 064CD)>* **SPLIT** (with GIGANTOR) [ ] [ ] Jun95
(above cd issued on German 'Lost & Found' label)

— **SMALLEY** with **SAM WILLIAMS III** (b.Tampa Bay, Florida) – guitar (ex-SLAP OF REALITY, ex-BALANCE) / **ANGRY JOHN** – bass (ex-CLAY IDOLS, ex-LEONARDS) / **DANNY WESTMAN** – drums (ex-SPINDLE, ex-FLORECENE)

Jul 94. (cd/c/lp) *<(86431-2/-4/-1)>* **PUNKROCKACADEMYFIGHTSONG**
– Punk won / Hit or miss / Flower tattoo / Sympathy for the world / 500 miles / Brief Tommy / Bright green globe / Minn same / Drummin' Dave / Hunter up / Punk as funk / 1944 / The king and I / Haircut / Chocolate jerk / Sam I / Heroes & hooligans / Soldier boy / Goodnight song / Sam II.

Nov 95. (7"/cd-s) *(WOOS 9 S/CDS)* **500 MILES. /**
(above released on 'Out Of Step')

Mar 96. (cd/c/lp) *<(86456-2/-4/-1)>* **ALL SCRATCHED UP!**
– Independence day / Cheap thrill / All American / Hell song / True believers / Giving it all away / Gruesome Gary / Radio ragga / Attention: anyone / Superman / Post office lament / Ivory girl / No has beens / Kevin's song / True music / Far and away / Punks and drunks.

Oct 96. (7"ep) *(BEP 930715)* **YELLOW RAT BASTARD**
(above issued on 'Break Even Point')

Aug 97. (cd/c/lp) *<(6501-2/-4/-1)>* **LAST OF THE SHARPSHOOTERS**
– USA today / No equalizer / Call to arms / Gun of '96 / Get out / Burning heart / Question marks and periods / Urban napalm / DJG / Concrete times / No one gets away / The last goodbye / Factory day / Cool crowd / Self destruction.

Sep 97. (7"m) *(SDR 005)* **NO EQUALIZER. / CONCRETE TIMES / SUPERFUCKED**
(above issued on 'Suspect Device')

Nov 97. (7") *(6523-7)* **QUESTION MARKS AND PERIODS. / THE SUPERHEROES**
(cd-s+=) *(6523-2)* – Self-destruction.

Go Kart Go Kart

Aug 99. (lp/cd) *<(GOKART 053/+CD)>* **FLY THE FLAG**
– Fly the flag / Nothing good on the radio / Automatic / Breakout / Sorry sometimes / Steel and concrete / Man on the street / This is the new breed / Revolution compromised / Fiery shade of blue / Find it / Greenwich mean time / Promises / Fight song.

Theologian Theologian

Nov 00. (cd; split w/ PSEUDO HEROES) *<(T 078CD)>* **split**
– Pseudo heroes / Fickle fate / New #2 / Down and out / T.V. people / (others by PSEUDO HEROES).

DOWNER

Formed: Los Angeles, California, USA . . . 1993 by frontman JOHN SCOTT (a veteran from several Orange County hardcore combos), guitarist AARON SILBERMAN, bassist JED HATHAWAY and drummer TRACY SLEDGE. Having played the Whiskey A Go-Go (with KORN as support act!), the heavy quartet were hoping to take their mogadon-Rock to the masses. A low-key self-financed debut LP whetted the fans' appetite (for destruction) and things looked on the up towards the end of the decade/century when DOWNER signed a worldwide deal with 'Roadrunner'. Unleashed in the Spring of 2001, the eponymous 'DOWNER' was a large disappointment compared to their up-to-date metal contemporaries. Heavy to the point of feeding from most apocalyptic metal sources from the 70's to the 90's (SABBATH to PANTERA and TOOL, to name but a few), the much-hyped DOWNER were in for a proverbial pasting from the critics. Over-emphasised vocals, effects and clumsy instrumental work, meant that the album was not just a downer, but a complete bummer.

Album rating: DOWNER (*3)

JOHN SCOTT – vocals / **AARON SILBERMAN** – guitar / **JED HATHAWAY** – bass / **TRACY SLEDGE** – drums

Roadrunner Roadrunner

Apr 01. (cd) *<(RR 8584-2)>* **DOWNER**
– Flex / Bi-furious / Last time / Savior / Weed eater / Mud bath / Born again / Speed teet / Punching bag / Ventilation / Curbed.

DOWNSET.

Formed: Los Angeles, California, USA . . . 1986 as SOCIAL JUSTICE (any recordings?), by REY OROPEZA, JAMES MORRIS, ARES and CHRIS LEE. They changed their style and name to DOWNSET in 1993, unveiling their eponymous debut the following year. Brash power-metal rap quartet likened to RAGE AGAINST THE MACHINE, they signed to 'Mercury' for the 1996 second set, 'DO WE SPEAK A DEAD LANGUAGE?'. Late in 2000, they finally resurrected their flagging careers by delivering a new third album, 'CHECK YOUR PEOPLE'.

Album rating: DOWNSET. (*6) / DO WE SPEAK A DEAD LANGUAGE? (*7) / CHECK YOUR PEOPLE (*5)

REY OROPEZA – vocals / **ARES** (b. B.SCHWAGER) – guitar / **JAMES MORRIS** – bass / **CHRIS LEE** – drums

Abstract not iss.

May 94. (7"ep) *(ABS 104)* **ABOUT TO BLAST EP**

Oct 94. (7"ep/cd-ep) *(ABS/+CD 108)* **DOWNSET EP**
– Empower / Bring meaning / Keep on breathing / Horrifying.

Mar 95. (7"ep/cd-ep) *(ABS/+CD 110)* **GENERATION OF HOPE** (other side by Shootyz Groove)

Mercury Polygram

Apr 95. (cd/c) *<(518 880-2/-4)>* **DOWNSET.** Nov94
– Anger / Ritual / Take 'em out / Prostitutionalized / Downset / My American prayer / Holding hands / About to blast / Breed the killer / Dying of thirst.

Jun 96. (cd/c) *<(532 416-2/-4)>* **DO WE SPEAK A DEAD LANGUAGE?**
– Intro / Empower / Eyes shut tight / Keep on breathing / Hurl a stone / Fire / Touch / Against the spirits / Sickness / Pocket full of fatcaps / Sangre de mis manos / Horrifying / Sickness (reprise) / Permanent days unmoving / Ashes in hand.

Epitaph Epitaph

Dec 00. (cd/lp) *<(6601-2/-1)>* **CHECK YOUR PEOPLE**
– Fallen off / Coming back / Together / Play big / Check your people / No home (steady!) / Which way / Chemical strange / Tear us apart / 2000 / En el aire / Test of my heart / Pure trauma.

DRAIN (see under ⇒ BUTTHOLE SURFERS)

DRAIN

Formed: Stockholm, Sweden . . . 1994 by MARIA SJOHOLM, FLAVIA CANEL, ANNA KJELBERG and MARTINA AXEN. Touted as the all-female ALICE IN CHAINS, DRAIN (not to be confused with BUTTHOLE SURFERS 'Trance Syndicate' off-shoot group), secured a major label deal with 'Atlantic'. In 1996, after a couple of 45's, they released their one and only album to date, 'HORROR WRESTLING'. Stop press:- there has since been a new addition to their discography – see below.

Album rating: HORROR WRESTLING (*5)

MARIA SJOHOLM – vocals / **FLAVIA CANEL** – guitar / **ANNA KJELBERG** – bass / **MARTINA AXEN** – drums

East West not iss.

Mar 96. (cd-s) *(EW 033CD)* **I DON'T MIND / MIRROR'S EYES / CRACK THE LIAR'S SMILE**

May 96. (cd/c) *(0630 13774-2/-4)* **HORROR WRESTLING**
– Stench / Smile / Mirrors eyes / Serve the shame / Unforgiving hours / Mind over body / Crucified / Don't mind / Crack in the liars smile / Unreal.

Jul 96. (cd-s) *(EW 057CD)* **CRACK THE LIAR'S SMILE / KLOTERA**

Dec 99. (cd) *(3984 27719-2)* **FREAKS OF NATURE**
– Enter my mind / Alive / Simon says / I wish . . . / Black crave / Bubble song / Right through you / Leech / Get inside / I will follow.

DREAD ZEPPELIN

Formed: California, USA . . . early '89 by ELVIS-lookalike, TORTELVIS, plus JAH PAUL JO, CARL JAH, PUT-MON, ED ZEPPELIN and FRESH CHEESE. Coming up with the bizarre concept of merging two of the greatest icons in rock history, ELVIS PRESLEY and LED ZEPPELIN, in a cod-reggae stylee, DREAD ZEPPELIN were nothing if not imaginative, as well as being off their respective rockers. They were also highly marketable, at least until the novelty wore off. Signing to 'I.R.S.', DREAD ZEPPELIN debuted in 1990 with what else, a highly amusing cover of ELVIS' 'HEARTBREAK HOTEL', backed, of course, with a LED ZEP track, 'YOUR TIME IS GONNA COME'. As the title might suggest, 'UN-LED-ED' (1990) was an album of erm . . .'unique' LED ZEPPELIN covers sung with a PRESLEY swagger, the fact that TORTELVIS modelled himself on the latter- day, burger-eating version rather than the hip swivelling sex-God of yore only upping the tongue-in-cheek factor. The record broke the US Top 75 and Graceland Estate were reportedly none too happy although PLANT and Co saw the funny side. A second effort, '5,000,000', followed in May '91, the DREADs' extending their homage to BOB MARLEY with a cover of 'STIR IT UP'. The album also spawned the group's final piece of chart action with the 'STAIRWAY TO HEAVEN' / 'JAILHOUSE ROCK' single, the track again almost making the UK Top 40. Thankfully, the group disbanded in 1992 before they'd delved into ZEPPELIN's later work; a cover of 'KASHMIR' really would have been too much to take!

Album rating: UN-LED-ED (*1 or *8 depending on your sense of humour) / 5,000,000 (*3)

TORTELVIS – vocals / **JAH PAUL JO** – guitar / **CARL JAH** – guitar / **PUT-MON** – bass / **ED ZEPPELIN** – bongos / **FRESH CHEESE** (b. BRUCE FERNANDEZ) – drums

I.R.S. I.R.S.

Aug 90. (7") *(EIRS 146)* **HEARTBREAK HOTEL. / YOUR TIME IS GONNA COME**
(12"+=/12"s+=/cd-s+=) *(EIRS T/TX/CD 146)* –

Aug 90. (lp/c/cd) *(EIRSA/+C/CD 1042) <82048>* **UN-LED-ED** 71
– Black dog / Living loving maid / Bring it on home / Black mountain side / Heartbreaker (at the end of lonely street) / Your time is gonna come / Whole lotta love / I can't suit you baby / Immigrant song / Moby Dick. *(cd re-iss. Jan99 on 'E.M.I.'; 713048-2)*

Nov 90. (7"/c-s) *(DREAD/+C 1)* **YOUR TIME IS GONNA COME. / WOODSTOCK** 59
(12"+=) *(DREADT 1)* – All I want for Xmas is my two front teeth / Hey, hey, what can I do.
(cd-s+=) *(DREADCD 1)* – All I want for Xmas is my two front teeth / Viva Las Vegas.

May 91. (lp/c/cd) *(EIRSA/+C/CD 1057) <13092>* **5,000,000**
– F.A.B. (Forgetting About Business) (part 1) / Stir it up / Do the claw / When the levee breaks / Misty mountain hop / Train kept a-rollin' / Nobody's fault (butt-man) / Big ol' gold belt / F.A.B. (part 2) / Stairway to Heaven. *(cd re-iss. Jan99 on 'E.M.I.'; 713092-2)*

Jun 91. (7"/c-s) *(DREAD/+C 2)* **STAIRWAY TO HEAVEN. / JAILHOUSE ROCK** 62
(12"+=/12"pic-d+=/cd-s+=) *(DREAD T/PD/CD 2)* – A quiet moment with Tortelvis / Rock'n'roll medley:- Rock'n'roll / The ocean / Dazed and confused – Moby Dick.

— split when TORTELVIS was repl. by GARRY BIBB in '92, FERNANDEZ joined HO CAKE

1992. (m-cd) *<13161>* **IT'S NOT UNUSUAL** [-] [ ]
– Disco inferno / You should be dancing / Night fever / Shaft / Jungle boogie / Ramble on / More than a woman / Jive talkin' / Dancing on the killing floor / Takin' care of business.

not iss. Bird Cage

Sep 95. (m-cd) *<11005>* **HOT AND SPICY BEANBURGER** [-] [ ]
– Good times, bad times / Goin' to California / Good rockin' tonight / Ballad of Charlie Haj / Unchained melody / Stairway to heaven / Hot and spicy beanburger / Hot dog / All of my love / Wot happened (the sloppy shuffle) / Rock & roll / Communication breakdown. *(UK-iss.Mar99 on 'Musical Tragedies'; efa 12411-2)*

Sep 95. (cd) *<11006>* **NO QUARTER POUNDER** [-] [ ]
– Un-Led-Ed (in 3D) / Ramble on / Viva Las Vegas / What is and what should never be / Lil' baby Elvis action / How many more times / No quarter / The last resort / 1-800 psychic pal / American trilogy / Brick houses (of the holy) / Lil baby E.J. goes to college (the "son" sessions).

Nov 95. (cd-s) *<3>* **THE FIRST NO-ELVIS** (festive) [-] [ ]

– compilations, etc. –

1997. (cd-s) *Birdcage; <0077>* **RUINS** [-] [ ]

Jul 98. (cd) *Imago; <(7287 23004-2)>* **THE FUN SESSIONS: TORTELVIS SINGS THE CLASSICS** [ ] [ ] Feb96

Nov 00. (cd) *Anagram; (CDMGRAM 135) / Deadline; <CLP 7662>* **DEJAH VOODOO – THE BEST OF DREAD ZEPPELIN** [ ] [ ] Sep00

DREAM THEATER

Formed: Berkeley, California, USA . . . 1988 by local music students JOHN PETRUCCI, MIKE PORTNOY and JOHN MYUNG. They recruited former schoolchum KEVIN MOORE, plus frontman CHARLIE DOMINICI and signed to 'M.C.A.'. Their blend of techno-rock was much in the mould of the English progressive scene of the 70's, although they subsequently hardened up their sound to a more QUEENSRYCHE / RUSH-esque approach. One poor selling album, 'WHEN DREAM AND DAY UNITE', led to DOMINICI departing, the band quitting their label soon after. In the early 90's, they drafted in Canadian JAMES LaBRIE and signed to 'Atco', where they finally broke through in 1993 with 'IMAGES AND WORDS'. The success of more recent albums, 'AWAKE' (1994), 'A CHANGE OF SEASONS' (1995) and 'FALLING INTO INFINITY' (1997), proved there was still a market (well, in America at least) for cerebral art-rock.

Album rating: WHEN DREAM AND DAY UNITE (*4) / IMAGES AND WORDS (*7) / LIVE AT THE MARQUEE (*5) / AWAKE (*6) / A CHANGE OF SEASONS (*6) / FALLING INTO INFINITY (*6) / ONCE IN A LIVETIME (*5) / METROPOLIS PT.2: SCENES FROM A MEMORY (*6)

CHARLIE DOMINICI – vocals / **JOHN PETRUCCI** – guitar / **KEVIN MOORE** – keyboards / **JOHN MYUNG** – bass / **MIKE PORTNOY** – drums

M.C.A. M.C.A.

Mar 89. (lp/c/cd) *(MCF/MCFC/DMCF 3445) <42259>* **WHEN DREAM AND DAY UNITE** [ ] [ ]
– A fortune in lies / Status seeker / The Ytse jam / The killing hand / Light fuse and get away / Afterlife / The ones who help to set the sun / Only a matter of time.

— **JAMES LaBRIE** (b. Canada) – vocals (ex-WINTER ROSE, ex-CONEY HATCH) repl. DOMINICI

East West Atco

Jul 92. (cd/c) *<7567 92148-2/-4>* **IMAGES AND WORDS** [ ] [61]
– Pull me under / Another day / Take the time / Surrounded / Metropolis – part 1 / Under a glass moon / Wait for sleep / Learning to live.

1993. (c-s) *<4-98415>* **ANOTHER DAY / UNDER A GLASS MOON** [-] [ ]

Sep 93. (cd/c) *(7567 92286-2/-4)* **LIVE AT THE MARQUEE (live)** [ ] [-]
– Metropolis / Fortune in lies / Bombay vindaloo / Surrounded / Another hand – The killing hand / Pull me under.

East West East West

Oct 94. (cd/c) *<7567 90126-2/-4>* **AWAKE** [65] [32]
– 6:00 / Caught in a web / Innocence faded / Erotomania / Voices / The silent man / The mirror / Lie / Lifting shadows off a dream / Scarred / Space-dye vest.

Dec 94. (12"/c-s) *(A 5835 T/C)* **LIE / TAKE THE TIME (demo) / SPACE-DYE VEST** [ ] [-]
(7"/cd-s) *(A 5835/+CD)* – (first & third tracks) / To live forever / Another day (live).

— (Jun'94) now without MOORE (to CHROMAKEY) who was repl. by **JORDAN RUDESS** (ex-VINNIE MOORE, ex-JAN HAMMER)

East West East West

Sep 95. (cd/c) *(7559 61830-2/-4) <61642>* **A CHANGE OF SEASONS** [ ] [58]
– A change of seasons / Funeral for a friend / Perfect strangers / The rover – Achilees last stand – The song remains the same / The big medley.

— **DEREK SHERINAN** – guitar (ex-ALICE COOPER, etc) repl. RUDESS

Oct 97. (cd) *<(7559 62060-2)>* **FALLING INTO INFINITY** [ ] [52]
– New millennium / You not me / Peruvian skies / Hollow years / Burning my soul / Hell's kitchen / Lines in the sand / Take away my pain / Just let me breathe / Anna Lee / Trial of tears.

Nov 98. (d-cd) *<(7559 62308-2)>* **ONCE IN A LIVETIME (live)** [ ] [ ]
– A change of seasons I – The crimson sunrise / A change of seasons II – Innocence / Puppies on acid / Just let me breathe / Voices / Take the time / Derek Sherinan keyboard solo / Lines in the sand / Scarred / A change of seasons IV – The darkest of winters / Ytse jam / Mike Portnoy drum solo // Trial of tears / Hollow years / Take away my pain / Caught in a web / Lie / Peruvian skies / John Petrucci guitar solo / Pull me under / Metropolis / Learning to live / A change of seasons VII – The crimson sunset.

— **RUDESS** was back in the line-up with **LaBRIE, MYUNG, PETRUCCI + PORTNOY**

Oct 99. (cd/c) *<(7559 62448-2/-4)>* **SCENES FROM A MEMORY: METROPOLIS PART 2** [ ] [ ]
– Regression / Overture 1928 / Strange deja vu / Through my words / Fatal tragedy / Beyond this life / Through her eyes / Home / The dance of eternity / One last time / The spirit carries on / Finally free.

D.R.I.

Formed: Houston, Texas, USA . . . 1982 as DIRTY ROTTEN IMBECILES, by brothers KURT and ERIC BRECHT, SPIKE CASSIDY and DENNIS JOHNSON. With their roots firmly entrenched in punk, both British and American, this group nevertheless increasingly found an audience within the metal fraternity as the thrash scene began to kick in around the early 80's. Their self-financed debut album, 'DIRTY ROTTEN' (1984), set out the D.R.I. agenda of blistering metallic hardcore, the band appropriately enough moving to the Bay Area of San Francisco soon after. With ERIC subsequently replaced by FELIX GRIFFIN, the group signed with 'Metal Blade' for the 'DEALING WITH IT' (1986) album before 'Roadrunner' picked them up for Europe with the release of the self-explanatory 'CROSSOVER' set in 1988. As the speed metal craze reached its height towards the end of the decade, so the group became progressively heavier, releasing the 'FOUR OF A KIND' (1988) set later that year. 1989's 'THRASH ZONE' saw D.R.I. reach a creative peak, the group bowing out on a high soon after its release.

Album rating: DIRTY ROTTEN (*5) / DEALING WITH IT! (*6) / CROSSOVER (*6) / 4 OF A KIND (*5) / THRASH ZONE (*5) / DEFINITION (*3) / FULL SPEED AHEAD (*5)

KURT BRECHT – vocals / **SPIKE CASSIDY** – guitar / **DENNIS JOHNSON** – bass / **ERIC BRECHT** – drums

not iss. Rotten

1984. (7"ep) **VIOLENT PACIFICATION** [-] [ ]
– Violent pacification / Snap / The explorer.

1984. (lp) *<ROT 001>* **DIRTY ROTTEN** [-] [ ]
– I don't need society / Commuter man / Plastique / Why (with DON BYAS) / Balance of terror / My fate to hate / Who am I / Money stinks / Human waste / Yes ma'am / Dennis' problem / Closet punk / Reaganomics / Running around / Couch slouch / To open closed doors / Sad to be / War crimes / Busted / Draft me / F.R.D.C. / Capitalist suck / Misery loves company / No sense / Blockhead. *(UK-iss.remixed-May88 on 'Roadrunner' lp/cd+=; RR 9555-1/-2)* – VIOLENT PACIFICATION *(cd-iss. Nov95 on 'Rotten'; ROTCD 001)*

— **FELIX GRIFFIN** – drums; repl. ERIC

Armageddon Metal Blade

Sep 86. (lp)<cd> *(ARM 2) <73401-2>* **DEALING WITH IT** [ ] [ ] 1985
– Snap / Marriage / Counter attack / Nursing home blues / Give my taxes back / Equal people / Bail out / Evil minds / I'd rather be sleeping / Yes ma'am / God is broke / I don't need society / Explorer / On my way home / Argument the war / Slit my wrist. *<US re-iss. Sep87 on 'Death'; 72069-1> (re-iss. Feb89 on 'Roadrunner' lp/cd; RR 9898-1/-2) (cd re-iss. Nov95 on 'Rotten'; ROTCD 2091)*

not iss. Radical

Aug 87. (lp) *<DRR 1983>* **22 SONGS** [-] [ ]

Roadrunner Metal Blade

Jun 88. (lp/cd) *(RR/+34 9620) <73402>* **CROSSOVER** [ ] [ ] 1987
– Five year plan / Tear it out / A coffin / Probation / I.D.K.Y. / Decisions / Hooked / Go die / Redline / No religion / Fun and games / Oblivion. *(cd re-iss. Nov95 on 'Rotten'; ROTCD 2092)*

— **JOSH PAPPE** – bass; repl. JOHNSON

Aug 88. (lp/cd) *(RR 9538-1/-2) <77304>* **4 OF A KIND** [ ] [ ]
– All for nothing / Manifest destiny / Gone too long / Do the dream / Shut-up! / Modern world / Think for yourself / Slum lord / Dead in a ditch / Suit and tie guy / Man unkind. *(re-iss. Aug92 on 'Metal Blade' cd/c/lp; CD/TC+/ZORRO 46) (cd re-iss. May96 on 'Metal Blade'; 3984 17012CD)*

— **JOHN MENOR** – bass; repl. PAPPE

Roadracer Metal Blade

Oct 89. (lp/cd) *(RO 9429-1/-2) <73407>* **THRASH ZONE** [ ] [ ]
– Thrashard / Beneath the wheel / Enemy within / Strategy / Labeled uncurable / You say I'm scum / Gun control / Kill the words / Drown you out / The trade / Standing in line / Give a hoot / Worker bee / Abduction. *(cd re-iss. Oct95 on 'Metal Blade'; 3981 47002CD)*

— folded after above

– others, compilations, etc. –

Nov 92. (lp/cd) *Rotten; <(ROT 2093/+CD)>* **DEFINITION** [ ] [ ]

Nov 95. (cd) *Rotten; <ROTCD 2096>* **LIVE** [-] [ ]

Nov 95. (cd) *Rotten; <(ROTCD 2099)>* **FULL SPEED AHEAD** [ ] [ ]

DRIVE LIKE JEHU

(see under ⇒ ROCKET FROM THE CRYPT)

DRIVIN' N' CRYIN'

Formed: Atlanta, Georgia, USA . . . mid 80's, by Milwaukee-born KEVN KINNEY and TIM NIELSEN, who subsequently borrowed JEFF SULLIVAN from MR CROWE'S GARDEN (later The BLACK CROWES) to work on their 'Island' debut, 'SCARRED BUT SMARTER' (1986). Employing the services of a clutch of highly notable session people (i.e. ANTON FIER and BERNIE WORRELL), they eventually surfaced from the studio with a fine second set, 'WHISPER TAMES THE LION', which hovered below the Top 100 in '88. A third effort, 'MYSTERY ROAD', saw the addition of a fourth member, ex-R.E.M. roadie, BUREN FOWLER. Two years later in '91, 'FLY

ME COURAGEOUS' (which was also their first release in the UK), dented the US Top 100, although this met with mixed fortunes in the music tabloids. A further album in 1993, 'SMOKE', led to their fans losing interest, although there was more to come via 1995's 'WRAPPED IN SKY' and '97's self-titled set. KEVN KINNEY also released a handful of albums ('MACDOUGAL BLUES' – 1990, 'DOWN OUT LAW' – 1994 and the more recent 'THE FLOWER & THE KNIFE' 2000), but these were of the laid-back rootsy variety.

Album rating: SCARRED BUT SMARTER (*6) / WHISPER TAMES THE LION (*6) / MYSTERY ROAD (*5) / FLY ME COURAGEOUS (*6) / SMOKE (*6) / WRAPPED IN SKY (*6) / DRIVIN' N' CRYIN' (*4) / THE ESSENTIAL LIVE (*7) / THE ULTIMATE COLLECTION compilation (*7)

KEVN KINNEY – vocals, guitar (ex-PROSECUTORS) / **TIM NIELSEN** – bass / **JEFF SULLIVAN** – drums

Island Island

1986. (lp,cd) *<885037>* **SCARRED BUT SMARTER** [-] [ ]
– Scarred but smarter / Keys to me / Another scarlet butterfly / You mean everything / Saddle on the side of the road / Danger stranger / Count the flowers / Gotta move on / Bring home the bacon / Watch the fire – To coin a phrase / Stand up and fight for it.

—— added session people; ANTON FIER – drums / BERNIE WORRELL – keyboards / IRWIN FISCH – piano, strings / LARRY SALTZMAN – guitar / FATS KAPLIN – guitars

Mar 88. (lp,cd) *<90699>* **WHISPER TAMES THE LION** [-] [ ]
– The whiper tames the lion / Catch the wind / Powerhouse / The friend song / On a clear daze / Ridin' on the soul road / Can't promise you the world / Livin' by the book / Good day every day / Legal gun / Check your tears at the door / Blue ridge way.

—— added **BUREN FOWLER** – guitar (ex-REM roadie)

Mar 89. (cd) *<422-842661-2>* **MYSTERY ROAD** [-] [ ]
– Ain't it strange / Toy never played with / Honeysuckle blue / With the people / Wild dog moon / House for sale / Peacemaker / You don't know me / Malfunction junction / Straight to Hell / Syllables.

Mar 92. (c-s/7") *(C+/IS 523)* **FLY ME COURAGEOUS. / LIVIN' BY THE BOOK** [ ] [ ]
(10"+=) *(10IS 523)* – Toy never played with (demo).
(cd-s++=) *(CID 523)* – Scarred but smarter (live) / With the people.

May 92. (cd/c/lp) *(CID/ICT/ILPS 9991) <848000>* **FLY ME COURAGEOUS** [ ] [90] Jan91
– Around the block again / Chain reaction / Fly me courageous / Look what you've done to your brother / For you / Let's go dancing / The innocent / Together / Lost in the shuffle / Build a fire / Rush hour.

May 92. (7"ep/10"ep/12"ep/cd-ep) *(IS/10IS/12IS/CID 531)* **THE HISTORY EP** [ ] [ ]
– Build a fire / House for sale / Can't promise you the world / addle on the side of the road.

Feb 93. (cd/c) *(CID/ICT 8008) <514319>* **SMOKE** [ ] [ ]
– Back against the wall / She doesn't wanna go / Smoke / When you come back / Patron lady beautiful / 100 swings / 1988 / Whiskey soul woman / What's the difference / Eastern European Carny man / All around the world / Turn it up or turn it off.

not iss. Geffen

Aug 95. (cd) *<24826>* **WRAPPED IN SKY** [-] [ ]
– Indian song / Telling stories / Leader the follow / Saving grace / Underground umbrella / Right side of town / Senorita Louise / Pura vida / Light / Silence of me / Wrapped in sky.

not iss. Ichiban

Aug 97. (cd) *<24921>* **DRIVIN' 'N' CRYIN'** [-] [ ]
– Keepin' it close to my heart / Roof garden / I've got a message / Drivin' 'n' cryin' / Around the long way / Let Lenny B / Paid in full / Everything's gonna be alright / Beneath the undertow / Passing through / Leaving on a jet plane / Nothin' to lose.

– compilations, etc. –

Jun 00. (cd) *Intersound; <(15095 9580-2)>* **THE ESSENTIAL LIVE** [ ] [ ] Sep99
– Build a fire / Scarred but smarter / Let's go dancing / Honeysuckle blue / Indian song / Dirty angles / The innocent / Peacemaker / Check your tears at the door / House for sale / For you / Fly me courageous / Sometimes I wish I didn't care / Hello son, where are you going? / Straight to hell / Rush hour.

Aug 00. (cd) *Hightone; <(314 542792-2)>* **THE ULTIMATE COLLECTION** [ ] [ ]
– Scarred but smarter / Count the flowers / Powerhouse / Catch the wind / Can't promise you the world / Honeysuckle blue / House for sale / Wild dog moon / Straight to hell / Fly me courageous / Build a fire / Let's go dancing / For you / The innocent / Toy never played with (live) / Turn it up or turn it off / When you come back / Indian song / Telling stories / Passing through.

DRONES

Formed: Manchester, England ... late 1976 by M.J. DRONE, GUS GANGRENE, STEVE 'WHISPER' CUNDALL and PETE PURFECT. Bonafide DIY three- chord wonders, The DRONES were there at punk's inception; while their fuzzy guitar anthems mightn't have been in the same league as The SEX PISTOLS or even The DAMNED, the pogo-tastic likes of 'BONE IDOL' and 'LOOKALIKES' were loud, dumb and a hell of a lot more fun than the latest REO SPEEDWAGON offering. Making their vinyl debut on the 'Ohm' label in 1977 with the 'TEMPTATIONS OF A WHITE COLLAR WORKER' EP, the band followed up with the aforementioned 'BONE IDOL' (a double A-side with 'I JUST WANNA BE MYSELF') on their self-financed 'Valer' imprint later that year. The DRONES' one and only album, 'FURTHER TEMPTATIONS', also surfaced late in 1977, their two-minute formula not exactly suited to a long playing format (probably in the same way as The SUBURBAN STUDS and The LURKERS). Prior to their inevitable demise in the early 80's, they did manage to have material included on two various artists compilations – the 'Beggars Banquet' compilation, 'Streets' and live punk effort, 'Short Circuit: Live At The Electric Circus' – as well as releasing a final single, 'CAN'T SEE' on the 'Fabulous' label.

Album rating: FURTHER TEMPTATIONS (*5)

M.J. DRONE (b. HOWELLS) – vocals, rhythm guitar / **GUS GANGRENE** (b. CALLENDAR) – lead guitar, vocals / **WHISPER** (b. STEVE CUNDELL) – bass / **PETE PURFECT** (b. LAMBERT) – drums

O.H.M.S. not iss.

May 77. (7"ep) *(GOOD MIX 1)* **TEMPTATIONS OF A WHITE COLLAR WORKER** [ ] [-]
– Lookalikes / Corgi crap / Hard on me / You'll lose.

Valer not iss.

Oct 77. (7") *(VRS 1)* **BONE IDOL. / I JUST WANNA BE MYSELF** [ ] [-]

Dec 77. (lp) *(VRLP 1)* **FURTHER TEMPTATIONS** [ ] [-]
– Persecution complex / Bone idol / Movement / Be my baby / Corgi crap / Lookalikes / The underdog / No more time / City drones / I just wanna be myself / Lift off the bans. *(cd-iss. Oct93 on 'Anagram'+=; CDPUNK 20)* – TEMPTATIONS OF A WHITE COLLAR WORKER (tracks) / (other 2 singles). *(lp re-iss. Oct96 on 'Get Back'; GET 6)*

Jan 78. (12"; w-drawn) *(VRSP 1)* **BE MY BABY. / LIFT OFF THE BANS** [ ] [-]

—— continued to work sporadically until final single below

Fabulous not iss.

Mar 80. (7") *(JC 4)* **CAN'T SEE. / FOOLED TODAY** [ ] [-]

– compilations, etc. –

Apr 97. (cd) *Overground; (OVER 60CD)* **TAPES FROM THE ATTIC 1975-1982** [ ] [-]
(lp-iss.Oct97 on 'Get Back'; GET 25)

May 99. (cd) *Captain Oi; (<AHOYCD 111>)* **SORTED** [ ] [ ] May00

DROPKICK MURPHYS

Formed: Boston, Massachusetts, USA ... 1996 by Irish-American guys, MIKE McCOGLAN, KEN CASEY, RICK BARTON and MATT KELLY. Hellraising pub-brawling punk rockers, their sound was STIFF LITTLE FINGERS shaken-not-stirred with the more traditional POGUES – adding bagpipes for good measure (a double of course!). Touring with The MIGHTY MIGHTY BOSSTONES, they duly signed to TIM ARMSTRONG's (of RANCID) label, 'Hellcat'. The 'MURPHY's finally fought their way out of the studio, the results being the highly entertaining, 'DO OR DIE', in 1998. Scotsman AL BARR subsequently joined as lead growler for 1998's mini-set, 'BOYS ON THE DOCKS', a record which preceded a slew of 7" singles over the latter half of the year. The Celtic connection remained as strong as ever on 1999's 'GANG'S ALL HERE', an album which even featured a bagpipe-enhanced cover of 'AMAZING GRACE' alongside the roughneck punk and hard-bitten social comment. Bizarrely enough, 'MOB MENTALITY' (1999) saw The DROPKICK MURPHYS teaming up with veteran English Oi! band The BUSINESS – they of classic 'Harry May' fame – after an inital 7" collaboration, the transatlantic shenanigans resulting in raucous covers of both The Who's 'THE KIDS ARE ALRIGHT' and The Faces' 'BORSTAL BOY' alongside mutual appreciation of the respective bands' back catalogues. A more appropriate guest turned up on 'SING LOUD, SING PROUD' (2001); who else but SHANE MAcGOWAN? The legendary London-Irish rapscallion added an aura of authenticity to a cover of 'THE WILD ROVER', a new line-up CASEY, JAMES LYNCH, SPICY McHAGGIS (aye, right) and RYAN FOLTZ kicking out the jigs in time-honoured, beer-stained fashion.

Album rating: DO OR DIE (*6) / THE GANG'S ALL HERE (*5) / SING LOUD SING PROUD (*5)

MIKE McCOGLAN – vocals / **KEN CASEY** – bass, vocals / **RICK BARTON** – guitar, vocals / **MATT KELLY** – drums

Flat Flat

Mar 97. (7") *(U 44257M)* **split with The DUCKY BOYS** [ ] [ ]

Gimmie My Money not iss.

Jul 97. (7") *(GMM 124)* **TATTOOS AND SCALLY CAPS. /** [ ] [ ]

Epitaph Hellcat

Mar 98. (cd/c/lp) *<(80407-2/-4/-1)>* **DO OR DIE** [ ] [ ]
– Cadence to arms / Do or die / Get up / Never alone / Caught in a jar / Memories remain / Road of the righteous / Far away coast / Fighstarter Karanke / Barroom hero / 3rd man in / Tenant enemy #1 / Finnegan's wake / Noble / Boys in the docks / Skinhead on the MTBA.

—— **AL BARR** (b. Scotland) – vocals (ex-BRUISERS) repl. McCOGLAN

Cyclone Cyclone

Mar 98. (m-cd) *(CYCD 105)* **BOYS ON THE DOCKS** [ ] [ ] Jul98
– Boys on the docks / Never alone / In the streets of Boston / Caps and bottles / Euro trash / Front seat.

Hellcat-TKO Hellcat-TKO

Sep 98. (d7") *(TKOROUND 005)* **split with ANTI HEROES** [ ] [ ]

Oct 98. (7"ep) *(TKOROUND 014)* **CURSE OF A FALLEN SOUL / GOING STRONG. / THE LEGEND OF FINN MacCUMHALL / ON THE ATTACK** [ ] [ ]

Knock Out Knock Out

Dec 98. (7") *(KOEP 082)* **WATCH YOUR BACK. / Weirdoz: Oxymoron** [ ] [ ]

Dec 98. (7") *(KOEP 083)* **CURSE OF THE FALLEN SOUL. / YOU'RE A REBEL** [ ] [ ]

Hellcat Hellcat

Mar 99. (cd/c/lp) <(8 0413-2/-4/-1)> **THE GANG'S ALL HERE**
– Riot call / Blood and whiskey / Pipebomb and Landsdowne / Perfect stranger / 10 years of service / Upstairs and broken hearts / Devil's brigade / Curse of a fallen soul / Homeward bound / Going strong / The fighting 69th / Boston asphalt / Wheel of misfortune / The only road / Amazing grace / The gang's all here.

Taang! Taang!

May 99. (cd/lp; split w/ The BUSINESS) <(T 143)> **MOB MENTALITY**
– Mob mentality / In the streets of London / Going strong / Boys on the dock / etc + others by the BUSINESS. *(pic-lp iss.Nov00; TAANG 143PD)*

Nov 99. (7"ep) <(TAANG 143)> **INFORMER. / Business: IN THE STREETS OF BOSTON**

Hellcat Hellcat

Feb 91. (cd/c) <(0430-2/-1)> **SING LOUD SING PROUD**
– For Boston / The legend of Finn Mac / Which side are you on? / The rocky road to Dublin / Heroes from out past / Forever / The gauntlet / Good rats / The new American way / The torch / The fortunes of war / A few good men / Ramble and roll / Caps and bottles / The wild rover / The spicy McHaggis jig.

– compilations, etc. –

Feb 99. (cd) *Sidekicks; <(JABSCO 017CD)>* **THE EARLY YEARS – UNDERPAID & OUT OF TUNE** Sep98

DROWN

Formed: Los Angeles, California, USA . . . 1987 initially as YESTERDAY'S TEAR by tattooed frontman LAUREN BOQUETTE, with drummer MARCO FORCONE and two others. Changing their moniker to DROWN at the turn of the decade, the quartet began to make inroads into the metallic ears of the LA underground sect (LAPD aka KORN and HUMAN WASTE PROJECT, among them). Finally, they achieved the recognition they richly deserved by inking a deal with 'Elektra'. However, this partnership turned sour when the label dropped them after their 1994 album, 'HOLD ON TO THE HOLLOW', did not sell particularly well. Disillusioned by this betrayal, two members left and, although they found replacements (PATRICK SPRAWL and SEAN E DERMOTT), a stint with 'Geffen' in '96 was also cut short. DROWN's follow-up album, 'PRODUCT OF A TWO FACED WORLD' (recorded that year), looked like being shelved for good, their careers put into an underwater limbo, until, that is, Mercury offshoot, 'Slipdisc', came to their rescue. Late in 1998, DROWN's forgotten album resurfaced, the much-maligned BOQUETTE and Co., finally finding a platform for their blend of DEFTONES-esque nu-metal. • **Covered:** KEROSENE (Big Black).

Album rating: HOLD ON TO THE HOLLOW (*6) / PRODUCT OF A TWO FACED WORLD (*7)

LAUREN BOQUETTE – vocals / **unknown** – guitar / **unknown** – bass / **MARCO FORCONE** – drums

not iss. Elektra

1994. (cd) **HOLD ON TO THE HOLLOW** [-]

Mercury Mercury

Dec 98. (cd) <()> **PRODUCT OF A TWO FACED WORLD**

DUB WAR

Formed: Newport, Wales . . . 1993 by JEFF ROSE, MARTIN 'GINGE' FORD, RICHIE GLOVER and vocalist BENJI. GINGE had once drummed for Page 3 cum pop star, SAMANTHA FOX, while the man previously gained experience with reggae dubmeister The MAD PROFESSOR, before finding a home with the more rock-orientated DUB WAR. His LENNY KRAVITZ-esque voice lent a certain rhythmic lilt to their Nu-metal/metallic dub fusion (a combination of metal, punk and ragga). A surprise signing to 'Earache' records (home of NAPALM DEATH, CARCASS, GODFLESH, etc), the group made inroads to the unsuspecting ears of the public with albums, 'PAIN', (1995) 'WRONG SIDE OF BEAUTIFUL' (1996). The latter of these included three minor UK singles, the first of them, 'ENEMY MAKER', being disturbingly reminiscent of The Police's "white-reggae" hit, 'MESSAGE IN A BOTTLE'.

Album rating: DUB WAR mini (*5) / PAIN (*7) / WRONG SIDE OF BEAUTIFUL (*6)

BENJI – vocals / **JEFF ROSE** – guitar / **RICHIE GLOVER** – bass / **MARTIN 'GINGE' FORD** – drums

Words Of Warning not iss.

Nov 93. (12"ep/cd-ep) *(WOW TV/CD 34)* **DUB WAR** [-]
– Respected / Dub over now / Nar-say-a-ting / Over now / Dub war (live). *(re-iss. Dec95 12" on 'Earache'; BEASTWAX 002)*

1994. (cd/c/lp) *(WOW CD/CS/LP 47)* **DUB WARNING** [-]
– Original murder / Crack / Psycho system / Words of warning / Crack D dub / Dub war. *(re-iss. Dec95; same)*

Earache Earache

Oct 94. (7") *(7MOSH 118)* **MENTAL. / DOWIT** [-]
(12"/cd-s) *(MOSH 118 T/CD)* – ('A'side) / ('A'-Senser mix) / ('A'-Brand New Heavies mix) / ('A'-Jamiroquai mix).

Jan 95. (7") *(7MOSH 126)* **GORRIT. / BLACK ANADIN TOXIC WASTE** [-]
(12"+=) *(MOSH 126T)* – Mad zone (live).
(cd-s+=) *(MOSH 126CD)* – Respected (live).
(cd-s+=) *(MOSH 126CDD)* – Respected (live) / Gorrit (live).

Feb 95. (lp/c/cd) *(<MOSH 121/+MC/CD>)* **PAIN**
– Why / Mental / Nar say a thing / Mad zone / Strike it / Respected / Pain / Nations / Gorrit / Spiritual warfare / Fool's gold / Over now. *(special cd+=; GMOSH 121CD)* – Anadin. *(special lp+=; MOSH 121L) (cd re-iss. as 'XTRA PAIN'+=; MOSH 121CDF)* – Psycho system / Words of warning / Original murder. *(cd re-iss. Sep97; GMOSH 121CD)*

May 95. (7") *(7MOSH 138)* **STRIKE IT. / THE FAX** [70] [-]
(cd-s+=) *(MOSH 138CD)* – ('A'version) / ('A'live).
(cd-s) *(MOSH 138CDD)* – ('A'side) / Nothing to say / Over now (Bonobo's tea party mix).

Jan 96. (7") *(<7MOSH 147>)* **ENEMY MAKER. / MONEY IN THE BANK** [41]
(cd-s+=) *(<MOSH 147CD-1>)* – Peace maker / Nations (Aphrodite mix).
(cd-s) *(<MOSH 147CD-2>)* – ('A'side) / Silencer (demo) / Dublic enemy / Pain (Ninj "manic" mix).

Aug 96. (7") *(7MOSH 163)* **CRY DIGNITY. / GLOVER'S WEIRD** [59] [-]
(cd-s) *(MOSH 163CD)* – ('A'side) / Word association / Cry dubnatty / The show.
(cd-s) *(MOSH 163CDD)* – ('A'side) / Strike it (nine to six mix) / Cry dignity (acoustic) / Problem.

Sep 96. (lp/c/cd) *(<MOSH 159/+MC/CD>)* **WRONG SIDE OF BEAUTIFUL**
– Control / Armchair thriller / Greedee / Bassballbat / One chill / Enemy maker / Million dollar love / Silencer / Cry dignity / Can't stop / Prisoner / Love is / Mission / Universal jam. *(cd re-iss. Nov97+=; MOSH 159CDL)* – RIGHT SIDE OF BEAUTIFUL

Oct 96. (12"ep/cd-ep) *(MOSH 166 T/CD)* **SOUNDCLASH EP** [-]
– Soundclash (one chill Aphrodite smash up the place mix) / Million dollar love (DJ rap mix) / Armchair thriller (Dub War dub) / Nar say a ting (Rootsman dub).

Mar 97. (7") *(7MOSH 170)* **MILLION DOLLAR LOVE. / WAY OF THE RIVER** [73] [-]
(cd-s) *(MOSH 170CD)* – ('A'side) / Prisoner (Nico dub) / Woman possessed / Dreams & illusions (dub).
(cd-s) *(MOSH 170CDD)* – ('A'side) / Universal jam (dub) / Step / Can't stop (tv mix).

Jul 97. (cd-s) *(MOSH)* **ENEMY MAKER / PEACE MAKER / CRY DIGNITY (acoustic)** [-]

Dec 97. (7") *(MOSH)* **DREAMS AND ILLUSIONS. / SILENCER** [-]

Nov 98. (cd) *(MOSH 216)* **STEP TA DIS** (remixes)
– One chill / Million dollar love / Nations / Over now / Strike it / Silencer / Mental / Strike it / Nay say a ting / Mental / Gerrit / Prisoner / Strike it / Prisoner / Strike it / Pain.

—— they split during 1998/99; BENJI formed MASS MENTAL with ROB TRUJILLO (of INFECTIOUS GROOVES) although they only played several gigs

DWARVES

Formed: Chicago, Illinois, USA . . . 1985 out of The SUBURBAN NIGHTMARE (one album, 'A HARD DAY'S NIGHTMARE' for 'Midnight') by SIGH MOAN, SALT PETER, JULIUS SEIZURE, PETE VIETNAMACHEQUE and WHITE SLAMBEAU. Following in the filth encrusted wake of GG ALLIN, this grossly offensive hardcore punk outfit make local bad boys The JESUS LIZARD look like HANSON! Debuting in 1986 with 'HORROR STORIES', the pseudonymous jokers caused outrage wherever they deemed to inflict their music on the local populace, indulging freely in such time honoured rock'n'roll pastimes as self-mutilation, on-stage sex and hard drugs. After a second set, 'TOOLIN' FOR A WARM TEABAG' (1988), SALT PETER recruited an entire new band of merry pranksters in the shape of guitarist, HEWHOCANNOTBENAMED, BLAG DAHLIA and VADGE MOORE (although it was unclear if they were in fact the same people; the band were notorious for their hoaxes, read on . . .). The DWARVES career reaching a climax of sorts with their outrageously titled 'Sub Pop' debut, 'BLOOD GUTS & PUSSY' (1990) – featuring an equally disgusting sleeve pic that again found them coming under severe flak from feminists. After a further two albums, 'THANK HEAVEN FOR LITTLE GIRLS' (1991) and 'SUGAR FIX' (1993), the grunge bastion finally cracked when the band falsely announced the death of HEWHOCANNOTBENAMED. Just when parents were breathing a sigh of relief, the dreaded DWARVES re-emerged in 1997 with a belated sixth album, 'THE DWARVES ARE YOUNG AND GOOD LOOKING' (on 'Epitaph'); if you believe that you'll believe anything!

Album rating: HORROR STORIES (*5) / TOOLIN' FOR A WARM TEABAG (*3) / BLOOD GUTS AND PUSSY (*7) / THANK HEAVEN FOR LITTLE GIRLS (*5) / SUGAR FIX (*5) / THE DWARVES ARE YOUNG AND GOOD LOOKING (*4) / COME CLEAN mini (*5)

SIGH MOAN – vocals / **SALT PETER** – bass / **JULIUS SEIZURE** – guitar, vocals / **PETE VIETNAMACHEQUE** – keyboards / **WHITE SLAMBEAU** – drums

not iss. Voxx

Aug 86. (lp) <VOXX 200037> **HORROR STORIES** [-]
– In & out / Oozie / Don't love me / Monday blues / Mind expanders / I'm a living sickness / College town / Be a caveman / Get outta my life / Sometimes gay boys don't wear pink / Stop & listen / Love gestapo. *(UK cd-iss. Dec90 & Jul92; VOXXCD 2037)*

not iss. Ubik

Sep 88. (7"ep) *(CRASH 001)* **LICK IT EP** [-]

not iss. Nasty Gash

Dec 88. (lp) **TOOLIN' FOR A WARM TEABAG** [-]

—— **SALT PETER** recruited **BLAG DAHLIA** – vocals / **HEWHOCANNOTBENAMED** – guitar / **VADGE MOORE** – drums

Sub Pop Sub Pop

Apr 90. (7",7"white) <(SP 50)> **SHE'S DEAD. / FUCKHEAD**

Jul 90. (lp,red-lp,pic-lp/c/cd) <(SP 67/+A/B)> **BLOOD, GUTS AND PUSSY**

– Back seat of my car / Detention girl / Let's fuck / Drug store / Skin poppin' slut / Fuck you up and get high / Insect whore / Flesh tantrum / SFVD / What hit you / Astro boy / Motherfucker / Fuckhead. *(cd/c+=)* – (5 tracks). *(lp re-iss. Aug00; same)*

Oct 90. (7",7"purple) <*(SP 81)*> **DRUG STORE / MOTHERFUCKER. / ASTRO BOY / DETENTION GIRL**

1991. (12"ep) **LUCIFER'S CRANK EP** [-]

— <above issued on 'No.6'>

Feb 92. (lp/cd) <*(SP 166/+CD)*> **THANK HEAVENS FOR LITTLE GIRLS**
– Fuck 'em all / Anybody but me / Blood brothers revenge / Three seconds / Dairy queen / Fuck around / Lucky tonight / Blag the ripper / Satan / Speed demon / Who's fucking who.

Jun 93. (12"ep)(cd-ep) <*(SP 83-254)*><*(SPCD 63-230)*> **ANYBODY OUT THERE**

Jul 93. (lp/cd) <*(SP/+CD 76-243)*> **SUGAR FIX**
– Anybody out there / Evil primeval / Reputation / Lies / Saturday night / New Orleans / Action man / Smack city / Cain novacaine / Underworld / Wish that I was dead.

Jan 94. (c-ep/cd-ep) <*SP 183*> **UNDERWORLD. / LIES / DOWN BY THE RIVER** [-]

— was NICK OLIVERI (REX EVERYTHING) (ex-KYUSS) a member at this point?

Sympathy F / not iss.

1990's. (7") *(SFTRI 132)* **I WANNA KILL YOUR . . . /** [-]

not iss. / Man's Ruin

1990's. (7") <*MR 005*> **DRUG STORE – DAIRY QUEEN. / GOODNIGHT TACOMA / RADIO 2** [-]

Mar 97. (7") <*MR 051*> **WE MUST HAVE BLOOD. / SURFING THE INTERCOURSE BARN** [-]

Epitaph / Theologian

Nov 97. (cd/c/lp) *(6512-2/-4/-1)* <*TH 53*> **THE DWARVES ARE YOUNG AND GOOD LOOKING** Mar97
– Unrepentent / We must have blood / I will deny / Demonica / Everybodies girl / Throw that world away / Ballad of Vadge Moore / One time only / Pimp / Crucifixion is now / You gotta burn.

— bassist at the time **STEVE BORGERDING** subsequently joined GRAND MAL (BILL WHITTEN formerly of ST*JOHNNY mid-late 90's outfit)

Epitaph / Epitaph

Feb 00. (m-cd/m-lp) <*(6575-2/-1)*> **COME CLEAN**
– How's it done / River city / Over you / Way out / Come where the favour is / Deadly eye / Better be women / I want you to die / Johnny on the spot / Accelerator / Act like you know / Production value. *(pic-lp on 'Jul00 on 'Cold Front'; CF 046)*

Reptilian / Reptilian

Mar 01. (7") <*(REP 018)*> **I WILL DENY YOU. /**

– compilations, etc. –

Feb 97. (lp/cd) *Recess;* <*(RECESS 32/+CD)*> *TOOLIN' FOR LUCIFER'S CRANK*

Feb 99. (m-cd) *Recess;* <*(RECESS 51)*> **FREE COCAINE** (early bites) Mar99

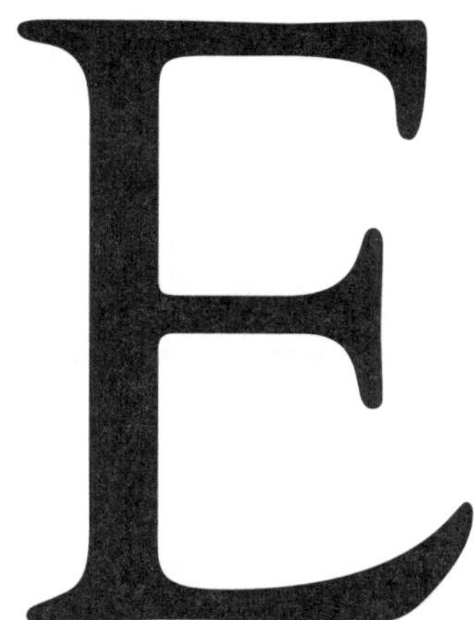

EARL BRUTUS

Formed: London, England . . . 1992 by ex-WORLD OF TWIST keyboard-player, NICK ANDERSON, JAMIE FRY (none other than the brother of ABC's MARTIN FRY), ROB MARCHE and GORDON KING. An unlikely but surprisingly effective combination of KILLING JOKE/FALL-like intensity and GLITTER BAND stomp!, EARL BRUTUS self-financed a debut single, 'LIFE'S TOO LONG', on their own 'Icerink' label. After a long-awaited follow-up in '95!, 'BONJOUR MONSIEUR' (for the 'Royal Mint' imprint), they almost immediately signed to Radio One/Music Week journo, Steve Lamacq's 'Deceptive' label and proceeded to churn out a series of sleazy singles prior to their debut album, 'YOUR MAJESTY . . . WE ARE HERE' (1996). The EARL's bolstered their claim to indie high society by being tipped for the top by none other than soft-porn mag, Club International (don't ask me how I found this out!?). Moving on to 'Fruition' records, the band treated their ever-growing cult following with a further string of near excellent singles beginning late in '97 with 'THE S.A.S. AND THE GLAM THAT GOES WITH IT'. It was a highlight from the following year's much talked about second long-player, 'TONIGHT YOU ARE THE SPECIAL ONE'.

Album rating: YOUR MAJESTY . . . WE ARE HERE (*8) / TONIGHT YOU ARE THE SPECIAL ONE (*7)

NICK SANDERSON – vocals, keyboards (ex-WORLD OF TWIST) / **JAMIE FRY** – keyboards, vocals / **ROB MARCHE** – guitar / **GORDON KING** – keyboards, drum machine

Icerink / not iss.

Jun 93. (12"/cd-s) *(DAVO 7 12/CD)* **LIFE'S TOO LONG. /** — -

Royal Mint / not iss.

Sep 95. (7") *(MINT 001)* **BONJOUR MONSIEUR. / ON ME, NOT IN ME** — -

Deceptive / not iss.

Dec 95. (7"etched) *(BLUFF 020)* **SINGLE SEATER XMAS** — -

Mar 96. (7"m) *(BLUFF 025)* **NAVYHEAD. / NORTH SEA BASTARD / 48 TRASH** — -
(cd-s+=) *(BLUFF 025CD)* – Navyhead (Union Street).

Jun 96. (7"m) *(BLUFF 030)* **LIFE'S TOO LONG. / MOTOROLA / I LOVE EARL BRUTUS** — -
(cd-s+=) *(BLUFF 030CD)* – Life's too long (Flash Vs Tarkus).

Sep 96. (7"m/cd-s) *(BLUFF 032/+CD)* **I'M NEW. / LIKE QUEER DAVID / MONDO ROTUNDA** — -

Sep 96. (cd/lp) *(BLUFF 036 CD/LP)* **YOUR MAJESTY . . . WE ARE HERE** — -
– Navyhead / I'm new / Male milk / On me, not in me / Don't leave me behind mate (Thelemix TM) / Black speedway / Motarola / Shrunken head (curtsy) / Blind date / Life's too long / Karl Brutus. *(cd+=)* – Singer seater Xmas.

Mar 97. (7"one-sided) *(BLUFF 039)* **PURCHASING POWER** — -

Fruition / not iss.

Oct 97. (7"clear) *(FRU 5)* **THE S.A.S. AND THE GLAM THAT GOES WITH IT. / MIDLAND RED** — -
(cd-s+=) *(FRUCD 5)* – The Scottish.

Jan 98. (7") *(FRU 6)* **COME TASTE MY MIND. / SUPERSTAR** — -
(cd-s+=) *(FRUCD 6)* – Nice man in a bubble / William.

May 98. (7") *(FRU 7)* **UNIVERSAL PLAN. / GYPSY CAMP BATTLE** — -
(cd-s+=) *(FRUCD 7)* – TV tower / Bonjour monsieur.
(cd-s) *(FRUDX 7)* – ('A'live) / The S.A.S. and the glam that goes with it (live) / Come taste my mind (live) / Nicotine stains (live).

Jun 98. (cd/lp) *(FRU CD/LP 1003)* **TONIGHT YOU ARE THE SPECIAL ONE** — -
– The S.A.S. and the glam that goes with it / Universal plan / Midland red / God, let me be kind (bitterfeld) / Come taste my mind (live) / Second class war / Your majesty, we are here / Don't die Jim / 99p (take me away) / East / Edelweiss (blown away) / Male wife.

May 99. (7"/cd-s) *(FRUT 5 S/CD)* **LARKY. / TEENAGE OPERA** — -

EARTH CRISIS

Formed: Syracuse, New York, USA . . . early 90's by straight-edgers KARL BUECHNER, SCOTT CROUSE, ERIC KRIS, IAN EDWARDS and DENNIS MERRICK. Straight-Edge meaning:- non-drinking, non-smoking, non-drug taking, non-sexual promiscuity, or by God you will be punished, er sort of thing. In fact, these animal rights sympathisers were a powerhouse hardcore metal quintet of some repute, living off the territory that MINOR THREAT (FUGAZI's IAN MacKAYE's first influential band) once inhabited. A number of worthy albums appeared around the mid 90's, although it wasn't until 1998's 'BREED THE KILLERS' (featuring a guest spot from MACHINE HEAD's ROBB FLYNN) that they gained some overdue musical recognition. The new millennium saw their 6th set, 'SLITHER' (2000), a truly grinding set that gave the band bigger recognition. The following year's, 'LAST OF THE SANE', was basically a covers sets of odds'n'ends, the highlight being a version of the Dead Kennedys 'HOLIDAY IN CAMBODIA'. • **Other covers:** CHILDREN OF THE GRAVE (Black Sabbath) / EARTH A.D. (Danzig) / THE WANTON SONG (Led Zeppelin) / HELL AWAITS (Slayer).

Album rating: DESTROY THE MACHINE (*6) / GOMORRAH'S SEASON ENDS (*6) / BREED THE KILLERS (*6) / SLITHER (*5) / LAST OF THE SANE (*5)

KARL BUECHNER – vocals / **SCOTT CROUSE** – guitar / **ERIC KRIS** – guitar / **IAN EDWARDS** – bass / **DENNIS MERRICK** – drums

not iss. / Conviction

1992. (cd-ep) **ALL OUT WAR EP** -
– All out war / Ecocide / Stand by / No allegience. *<(UK + re-iss. May95 on 'Victory'; VR 20-3CD)>*

We Bite / Victory

Apr 94. (m-cd) *<(VR 12-2)>* **FIRESTORM**
– Firestorm / Forged in the flames / Unseen holocaust / Eden's demise.

Victory / Victory

Aug 95. (cd/lp) *<(VE 022 CD/LP)>* **DESTROY THE MACHINE** — May95
– Forced march / Born from pain / Destroy the machines / New ethic / The discipline / Fortress / Inherit the wasteland / Asphyxiate / The wrath of sanity.

Sep 96. (pic-lp/cd; shared with SNAPCASE and STRIFE) *<(VR 042/+CD)>* **LIVE CALIFORNIA TAKEOVER (live)**

Dec 96. (cd/lp) *<(VR 044 CD/LP)>* **GOMORRAH'S SEASON ENDS** — Oct96
– Broken foundation / Cease to exist / Gomorrah's season ends / Constrict / Names carved into granite / Situation degenerates / Morality dictates / Cling to the edge / Forgiveness denied.

Mar 98. (lp/cd) *<(VR 066/+CD)>* **LIVE (live)** — Feb98
– Sunshine / Born from pain / Situation degenerates / Smash or be smashed / Deliverance / Unseen holocaust / Constrict / Fate of the neo-gods / All out war / Gomorrah's season / Wrath of sanity / Firestorm.

Roadrunner / Roadrunner

Sep 98. (cd) *<(RR 8706-2)>* **BREED THE KILLERS**
– The end begins / Filthy hands to famished mouths / Breed the killers / Wither / Ultramilitance / Into the fray / One against all / Drug related homicide / Overseers / Death rate solution / Unvanquished / Ecocide. *(lp-iss.Oct98 on 'Equal Vision'; EVR 046)*

Victory / Victory

May 00. (lp/cd) *<(VR 121/+CD)>* **SLITHER**
– Loss of humanity / Slither / Provoke / Nemesis / Agress / Biomachines / Killing brain cells / Arc of descent / Mechanism / Behind the wire / Mass arrest / Hairtrigger / Escape.

Feb 01. (cd) *<(VR 140CD)>* **LAST OF THE SANE** — Jan01
– Hell awaits (intro) / The wanton song / City to city / Children of the grave / Holiday in Cambodia / Paint it black / Earth A.D. / The order / Broken foundation / Gomorrah's season ends / Panic floods.

EARTHSHAKER

Formed: Japan . . . 1981 by guitarist SHINICHIRO ISHIHARA, who took the name from a Y&T album. He enlisted the services of MASAFUMI NISHIDA, TAKAYUKI KAI and YOSHIHIRO KUDO, subsequently moving to San Francisco in the process. An eponymous ADRIAN SMITH-produced debut appeared in late '83, closely followed by the 'FUGITIVE' set early in '84. Very much in the guitar solo orientated, classic hard-rock/metal vein, EARTHSHAKER's consistently derivative take on the genre has precluded any significant recognition outside of Japan, despite an attempt at a more accessible approach on subsequent albums.

Album rating: EARTHSHAKER (*4) / FUGITIVE (*5) / MIDNIGHT FLIGHT (*6) / LIVE (*4) / OVER THE RUN (*5) / TREACHERY (*6) / LIVE BEST (*5)

MASAFUMI "MARCY" NISHIDA – vocals / **SHINICHIRO "SHARA" ISHIHARA** – guitar / **TAKAYUKI KAI** – bass / **YOSHIHIRO KUDO** – drums

Music For Nations / not iss.

Nov 83. (12") *(12KUT 107)* **BLONDIE GIRL. /** — -

Nov 83. (lp) *(MFN 13)* **EARTHSHAKER** — -
– Earthshaker / Wall / 412 / I feel all sadness / Dark angel (animals) / Marionette / Children's dream / Time is going / Yume no hate o. *<cd-iss. 1990's on 'Nexus'; K32Y-2048>*

—— added guest (on below only) **MITCHELL FROOM** – keyboards

Apr 84. (lp) *(MFN 21)* **FUGITIVE** — -
– Kioku no naka / Young girls / Shiny day / Love destiny / More / 22:00 / Drive me crazy / Fugitive. *(c-iss.Jan85; TMFN 21) <cd-is.1990's on 'Nexus'; K32Y-2049>*

Dec 85. (12"ep) *(MFN 35)* **T-O-K-Y-O / LOST 7224. / Live: MORE / YOUNG GIRLS / WALL** — -

Feb 86. (lp) *(MFN 37)* **MIDNIGHT FLIGHT** — -
– T-O-K-Y-O / Midnight flight / Radio magic / Family / Zawameku Tokieto / Ushinawareta 7224 / Money / Tada kanashiku.

		not iss.	Nexus
1986.	(lp) <K32Y-2025> **LIVE IN BUDOHKAN (live)** – More / Kioku no naka / Zawameku Tokieto / Whiskey and woman / Midnight flight / Yume no hate o / The night we had / Take my heart / T-O-K-Y-O / Radio magic / Come on.	-	
		Eastworld	**not iss.**
1987.	(lp) **OVER THE RUN**		- Japan
1989.	(lp) **TREACHERY**		- Japan
1990.	(lp) **LIVE BEST (live)**		- Japan
1992.	(cd) *(TOCT 6646)* **BEST OF 87-92** (compilation) – Earthshaker / Wall / Blondie girl / More / Fugitive / T-O-K-Y-O / Midnight flight / Radio magic / Come on / Whisky and women / Arigato kimini / Don't need to surrender.		- Japan

— went to ground after above

EARTHTONE9

Formed: Nottingham, England ... 1997 by KARL MIDDLETON, JOE ROBERTS, OWEN PACKARD, DAVE ANDERSON and SIMON HUTCHBY. This bruising five-piece initially came to the notice of metal fans with the release of the 'LO DEF(INITION) DISCORD' album in 1998, a hugely promising effort recorded on a paltry budget of just 500 quid. Although the band were initially known as vegetarians who also steered pretty much clear of the demon drink, the press lapped up tales of renewed interest in alcohol and drugs while MIDDLETON's appearance at the Lost Weekend festival clad in cling-film pants generated more than a few column inches. EARTHTONE9 themselves prefer to the let the music do the talking with the pulverising, dynamic riffing of 2000's 'ARC'TAN'GENT' album speaking volumes.

Album rating: OFF KILTER ENHANCEMENT (*6) / LO-DEF(INITION) DISCORD (*6) / ARC'TAN'GENT (*6)

KARL MIDDLETON – vocals / **OWEN PACKARD** – guitar / **JOE ROBERTS** – guitar / **DAVE ANDERSON** – bass / **SIMON HUTCHBY** – drums

		Copro	Copro
Aug 98.	(cd) *(<COP 07CD>)* **LO-DEF(INITION) DISCORD** – Withered / Sand (spiral/prophet) / 2:00:00 / Intonegrateattached / 3rd ripple in (wave) / Leadfoot / Ever you say / Cracked hands, dry face / Lo-def(inition) discord / Vitriolie hsf / Sand.		Dec99
Jul 99.	(cd) *(<COP 010CD>)* **OFF KILTER ENHANCEMENT** – Grind & click / Zechariah rush (Uru shalom har meggidon) / Offkilter / O . . .O . . .O . . . / I nagual eye / Enertia 65800 / Moe=ra (t-talk) / Serpentine placement / Nameless (the 4th and the 10th) / Simon says.		Nov99
Apr 00.	(m-cd) *(COP 015CD)* **HI-POINT** – Tat twam asi / Alpha-hi / You again / Vitriolic HSF2000.		-
Sep 00.	(cd) *(COP 017CD)* **ARC'TAN'GENT** – Tat twam asi / Evil crawling / P.R.D. chaos / Aprrox. purified / Walking day / Star damage (for beginners) / Ni9e / Yellow fever / Alpha-hi / Binary 101.		-

Damon EDGE (see under ⇒ CHROME)

ED GEIN'S CAR

Formed: New York, USA . . . 1982 by ERIC HEDIN and TIM CARROLL who found SCOTT WEISS and filled the drumstool with a succession of temp sticksmen (the group moniker came via a character in the cult horror movie, 'Texas Chainsaw Massacre'). Poo-pooing the po-faced sincerity of the hardcore scene, the smart-arsed quartet joked their way onto vinyl with 1984's debut single, 'BRAIN DEAD', following it up with a full-length album, 'MAKING DICK DANCE' (1985). Blessed/cursed with the same un-PC adolescent humour as The BEASTIE BOYS would later make their name with, ED GEIN'S CAR were a regular fixture at the infamous CBGB's where their sarcastic stage antics went down a storm; the highlights of this period were captured for posterity on the swansong 1987 set, 'YOU LIGHT UP MY LIVER'. The same year saw WEISS continue his bad taste comedy crusade with the short-lived IRON PROSTATE.

Album rating: MAKING DICK DANCE (*5) / YOU LIGHT UP MY LIVER (*6)

ERIC HEDIN – guitar / **TIM CARROLL** – bass / **SCOTT WEISS** – vocals

		not iss.	Ed Gein's Car
1984.	(7") **BRAIN DEAD. /**	-	
1985.	(lp) **MAKING DICK DANCE**	-	
		not iss.	**Celluloid**
1987.	(lp/cd) <97295-1/-2> **YOU LIGHT UP MY LIVER (live at CBGB'S 1986)** – R.A.P.E. / My choice / Too old to die young / Take me to the petting zoo / Middle (r)age / My life's a game / Selby / Last caress / A girl just like you / Anette / Boo fuckin' hoo / Bars and brick / Surf Nazis / We're not you're world / Brain dead baby / Wait till your father gets home / Progress.	-	

— disbanded after above

EDGE OF SANITY

Formed: Sweden . . . early 90's by DAN SWANO, ANDREAS AXELSSON (aka DREAD), SAMI NERBERG, ANDERS LINDBERG and BENNY LARSSON. Signed to the 'Black Mark' label, these Scandinavian death/black metallers initiated an industrious recording schedule with 1992 debut set, 'NOTHING BUT DEATH REMAINS'. 'UNORTHODOX' followed later that year while 'SPECTRAL SORROWS' (1993), 'PURGATORY AFTERGLOW' (1994) and 'UNTIL ETERNITY ENDS' (1994) took them up to the mid-90's. Taking the idea of the concept album to its deathly conclusion, the band recorded 'CRIMSON' as one long neo-classically inspired track. 'CRYPTIC' was unambitious in comparison, featuring new frontman ROBBEN KARLSSON in place of the departed SWANO. • **Covered:** BLOOD OF MY ENEMIES (Manowar) / INVISIBLE SUN (Police).

Album rating: NOTHING BUT DEATH REMAINS mini (*5) / UNORTHODOX (*5) / SPECTRAL SORROWS (*6) / PURGATORY AFTERGLOW (*7) / CRIMSON mini (*5) / INFERNAL (*5) / CRYPTIC (*5) / EVOLUTION compilation (*6)

DAN SWANO – vocals, guitar / **DREAD** (b. ANDERS AXELSON) – guitar / **SAMI NERBERG** – guitar / **ANDERS LUNDBERG** – bass / **BENNY LARSSON** – drums

		Black Mark	Black Mark
Jan 92.	(m-cd/m-c/m-lp) *(BM CD/CT/LP 10)* **NOTHING BUT DEATH REMAINS** – Tales / Human aberration / Maze of existence / Dead / Decepted by the cross / Angel of distress / Impulsive necroplasma / Immortal souls. *<US cd-iss. Oct95; same as UK>*		
Jun 92.	(cd/c/lp) *(<BM CD/CT/LP 18>)* **UNORTHODOX** – Unorthodox / Enigma / Incidence to the butchery / In the veins – Darker than black / Human aberration / Everlasting / After afterlife / Beyond the unknown * / Nocturnal / Curfew for the damned / Cold sun / Day of maturity * / Requiscon by pace / Dead but dreaming / When all is said. *(cd+= */ c+= **)*		
Nov 93.	(cd/c) *(<BM CD/CT 37>)* **SPECTRAL SORROWS** – Spectral sorrows / Darkday / Livin' hell / Lost / The masque / Blood of my enemies / Jesus cries / Across the fields of forever / On the other side / Sacrificed / Waiting to die / Feedin' the charlatan / Serenade for the dead.		Mar94
Aug 94.	(m-cd) *(<BMCD 58>)* **UNTIL ETERNITY ENDS** – Until eternity ends / Eternal eclipse / Bleed / Invisible sun.		Apr95
Oct 94.	(cd) *(<BMCD 61>)* **PURGATORY AFTERGLOW** – Twilight / Of darksome origin / Blood-covered / Silent / Black tears / Elegy / Velvet dreams / Enter chaos / Sinner and the sadness / Song of sirens.		Mar95
Apr 96.	(cd) *<BMCD 68>* **CRIMSON** – Crimson.	-	
Mar 97.	(cd/c) *<BM CD/CT 108>* **INFERNAL** – Hell is where the heart is / Helter skelter / 15:36 / Bleakness of it all / Damned (by the damned) / Forever together forever / Losing myself / Hollow / Inferno / Burn the sun / Last song.	-	

— **ROBBEN KARLSSEN** – vocals; repl. SWANO

Oct 97.	(cd) *(<BMCD 125>)* **CRYPTIC** – Hell written / Uncontroll me / Demon I / Not of this world / Dead I walk / Born, breed, bleeding / Bleed you dry.		

– compilations, etc. –

Nov 99.	(d-cd) *S.P.V.; (085-13367-2) / Black Mark; <BM 140CD>* **EVOLUTION** – Pernicious anguish / Immortal souls / Maze of existence / The dead / Angel of distress / Everlasting / After afterlife / Human aberation / Kill the police / When all is said / Blood of the enemies / Elegy // The masque / Pernicious anguish / Until eternity ends / Criminally insane / Murder dividead / I wanna go home / Damned by the damned / Moonshine / Bleed you dry / Mother / Epidemic reign.		Sep00

8 EYED SPY (see under ⇒ LUNCH, Lydia)

EINSTÜRZENDE NEUBAUTEN

Formed: Berlin, Germany . . . 1st April 1980, when this arty industrial conglomerate played their first live gig. They issued a few singles for Germany's 'Zick Zack', before unleashing 'KOLLAPS' at the end of '81. A few more arrived (signed to UK label 'Some Bizzare'), before they settled with the line-up of BLIXA BARGELD, N.U. UNRUH, MUFTI and new mid-80's members ALEX HACKE and MARC CHUNG. By this time, most of them were finding moonlighting work, mainly BARGELD who had joined NICK CAVE & THE BAD SEEDS. HACKE joined CRIME & THE CITY SOLUTION, while FM EINHEIT went solo (backed by STEIN ('STONE') for the early 90's. EINSTÜRZENDE NEUBAUTEN subsequently released the album, 'STEIN', in 1990 and three years later, 'PROMETHEUS LEAR', although always intending to split during this period. Pioneers of experimental industrial power-metal, picking up any object to make a barrage of sound (from either power tools, metal piping, large hammers, steel girders and anything that could cut metal). The band were prone to just basically strip to the waist, wear hard hats and get on with the job. Incredibly for such an avant-garde outfit, EINSTÜRZENDE NEUBAUTEN were still going strong come the new millennium, twenty years on from their first blast of cochlea-collapsing noise. As the title might suggest, 'SILENCE IS SEXY' (2000) tended to forego the gratuitous sonic excess which characterises much of the band's work, instead opting for a more subtle yet just as disturbing line in musical subversion. • **Trivia:** BARGELD featured alongside The BAD SEEDS in the 1988 Wim Wenders film 'Angels Uber Berlin'.

Album rating: KOLLAPS (*4) / PORTRAIT OF PATIENT O.T. (*5) / STRATEGIES AGAINST ARCHITECTURE compilation (*6) / 2x4 (*5) / HALBER MENSCHE (*5) / HANS DER LUEGE (*4) / STRATEGIES AGAINST ARCHITECTURE, VOL.2 compilation (*7) / TABULA RASA (*7) / ENDE NEU (*5) / SILENCE IS SEXY (*6)

BLIXA BARGELD (b.12 Jan'59) – vocals, guitar, percussion / **N.U. UNRUH** (b. ANDREW, 9 Jun'57, New York City) – vocals, bass, percussion / **BEATE BARTEL** – also industrial percussion / **GODRUN GUT** – industrial percussion / soon added **ALEXANDER VAN BORSIG** – percussion

Mongam not iss.

Nov 80. (7") *(005)* **FUR DEN UNTERGANG. / STAHLVERSION** – – German

— **(STUART) MUFTI** (aka F.M. EINHEIT) (b.18 Dec'58, Dortmund, Germany) – industrial percussion (ex-ABWARTS) repl. BARTEL and GUT, who formed MANIA D and MATADOR

Zick Zack not iss.

Aug 81. (d7"ep) *(ZZ 40)* **DURSTIGES TIER** – – German
– Kalte sterne / Aufrecht gehen / Erlicher stein & pygmaen / Schwarz.
above featured BIRTHDAY PARTY and LYDIA LUNCH

Dec 81. (lp) *(ZZ 65)* **KOLLAPS** – – German
– Kollaps / Sehnsucht / Vorm krieg / Hirnsaege / Abstieg & zerfall / Helga / Tanz debil / Steh auf Berlin / Negativ nein / U-haft muzak / Draussen ist feindlich / Horen mit schmerzen / Jet'm. *(re-iss. Dec88 lp/cd; EFA 2517/+CD) (UK-iss.Oct96 on 'Strange Ways' cd/lp; INDIGO 2517-2/-1) (cd re-iss. Mar98 on 'Spalax'; 14537)*

— added **MARC CHUNG** (b. 3 Jun'57, Leeds, England) – bass (ex-ABWARTS)

Some Bizarre Ze-PVC

Nov 83. (lp) *(SBVART 2) <PVC 9902>* **PORTRAIT OF PATIENT O.T.**
– Vanadium-I-Ching / Hospitalistische kinder-engel der vernichtung / Abfackeln / Neun arme / Herde / Merle / Zeichnungen des patienten O.T. / Finger und zaehne / Falschgeld / Styropor / Armenia / Die genaue zeit. *<cd-iss. 1195 on 'Thirsty Ear'; 57011>*

— added **ALEXANDER HACKE** (b.11 Oct'65) – guitar, electronics

Mar 85. (12") *(BART 12)* **YU-GUNG. / SEELEBRENNT / SAND** –

Oct 85. (lp) *(BART 331)* **HALBER MENSCH** (HALF MEN) –
– Halber mensch / Yu-gung (futter mein ego) / Trinklied / Z.N.S. / Seelebrennt / Sehnsucht / Der tod ist ein dandy / Letztes biest / Das schaben / Sand. *(cd-iss. Jan87; BART 331CD) (re-iss. Oct96 on 'Strange Ways'; INDIGO 26141) <cd-iss. 1995 on'Thirst EAr'; TE 57010>*

Jul 87. (lp/c/cd) *(BART 332/+C/CD)* **FUNF AUF DER NACH OBEN OFFENEN RICHTERSKALA** (means 'FIVE ON THE OPEN-ENDED RICHTER SCALE') –
– Zerstorte zell / Morning dew / Ich bin's / Modimidofraso / Zwolf stadte / Keine schonheit ohne gefahr / Kein bestandteil sein. *<cd-iss. 1995 on 'Thirsty Ear'; TE 57016>*

Some Bizzare Rough Trade

Sep 89. (lp/c/cd) *(BART 333/+C/CD) <ROUGHUS 71/+C/CD>* **HANS DER LUEGE**
– Prolog / Feurio / Ein stuhl in der Holle / Haus der luge / Epilog / Fiat lux / Maifestspiele / Himlego / Schwindel / Der kuss. *<cd re-iss. 1995 on 'Thirsty Ear'; TE 57017>*

Beton-Mute Mute-Elektra

Jan 93. (12"ep/cd-ep) *(BETON 205/+CD) <61509>* **INTERIM**
– Interimlovers / Salamandrina / 3 thoughts / Ring my bell / Rausch – Die interimsliebenden.

Feb 93. (lp/c/cd) *(BETON 106/+MC/CD) <61458>* **TABULA RASA**
– Die interimsliebenden / Zebulon / Blume / 12305 (te nacht) / Sie / Wuste / Headcleaner.

Apr 93. (lp/cd) *(BETON 206/+CD)* **MALADICTION** –
– Blume (French version) / Blume (English version) / Blume (Japanese version) / Ubique media version / 3 thoughts / Ein gansz kleines loch in einem / Diapositiv / Ring my bell.

Rough Trade Revolver

Mar 94. (cd) *(1971208) <1208-2>* **HEINER MULLER: HAMLETMASCHINE**
– Soll ich / Weils brauch ist ein stuck eisen stecken in / Das nachste Fleisch oder ins uberachste / Mich dran zu halten weil die welt sich dreht / Herr brich mir das Genick im sturz von einer / Bierbank. *<re-iss. 1996 on 'Grey Area-Ego'; EGO 111>*

Ego-Grey Area Elektra

Feb 96. (cd) *(EGO 501) <69021>* **FAUSTMUSIK** May96
– Tische / Monolog / Besetzt / Burokratie / Burleske / Walpurgisnachtfestchen / Orchestrion / Still am abend / Letztes bild.

— next featured JON SPENCER + ALEC EMPIRE (+ now without CHUNG)

Jul 96. (cd-ep) *(BETON 503CD) <EGO 503>* **STELLA MARIS (mixes)**

Beton-Mute Beton-Mute

Jul 96. (lp/cd) *(<BETON 504/+CD>)* **ENDE NEU**
– Was ist ist (What is it) / Stella maris / Die explosion im festspielhaus / Installation No.1 / Nnnaaammm / Ende neu (Ending new) / The garden / Der schacht von babel (shaft of . . .).

Jul 97. (12"ep) *(<BETON 601>)* **THE DARK WELCOME / SIDE GRINDER. / AMBIENT GUILLOTONE / STRAIGHT TO THE PLAIN**
(cd-ep) *(<BETON 601CD>)* – Nnnaaammm remixes (by DARKUS) / (Trilogy & Side Grinder).

Sep 97. (d-lp/cd) *(BETON 602/+CD)* **ENDE NEU REMIXED** –

Aug 99. (cd-s) **TOTAL ECLIPSE OF THE SUN / SONNENBARKE / HELIUM / TOTAL ECLIPSE OF THE SUN**

Mute Orchard

Apr 00. (d-cd) *(CDSTUMM 182) <2>* **SILENCE IS SEXY** May00
– Sabrina / Silence is sexy / In circles / Newton's gravitalichkeit / Zampano / Heaven is of honey / Beauty / Die befindlichkeit des landes / Sonnebarke / Musentango / Alles / Redukt / Dingsaller / Total eclipse of the sun / Pelikanol.

– compilations, etc. –

Jan 84. (lp) *Mute; (Stumm 14) / Homestead; <HMS 063>* **80-83 STRATEGIES AGAINST ARCHITECTURE**
– Tanz debil / Schmerzen hoeren / Mikroben / Krieg in den staedten / Zum tier machen / Draussen ist feindlich / Stahlversion / Schwarz / Negativ nein / Kalte sterne / Spaltung / U-haft muzak / Gestohlenes band (ORF) / Schwarz (mutiert). *(cd-iss. Apr88 + Nov92; CDStumm 14) <US cd-iss. 1995 on 'Elektra'; 61677>*

Dec 84. (c) *R.O.I.R.; (<A 133>)* **2 x 4**
– Fleisch "Blutihaut" knochen / Sehnsucht (nie mehr) / Womb / Krach der schlegenden herzen / Armenisch bitter / Zum tier machen / Sehnsucht (still stehend) / Durstige tiere. *(cd-iss. Nov97; RUSCD 8235)*

May 91. (d-cd/d-c) *Mute; / Mute-Elektra; <61100-2/-4>* **STRATEGIES AGAINST ARCHITECTURE II**

– Abfackeln! / Partynummer (live) / Z.N.S. / Die elektrik (Merle) / Intermezzo – Yu-gung (live) / Seelebrennt / Blutvergiftung / Sand / Kangolicht / Armenia (live) / Ein stuhl in der holle / Vanadium I-Ching / Leid und elend (live) / DNS wasserturm / Armenia II (live) / Fackeln! / Ich bin's / Hirnlego / Wardrobe / Bildbeschreibung / Haus der luege (live) / Jordache / Kein bestandteil sein (alternative ending).

Dec 94. (3xcd-box) *Beton-Mute; (BETONBOX 1)* **TRI SET** –

EJECTED

Formed: Dagenham, Essex, England . . . late '81 by ex-DAWN PATROL (who issued a solitary eponymous 12" EP) members BIG JIM BROOKS and GARY SANDBROOK, along with drummer PAUL GRIFFITHS. Another second division "oi/punk" band signed to 'Riot City', The EJECTED nevertheless debuted on vinyl that year via a 'Secret' V/A compilation, 'Carry On Oi'. The following year, the Essex lads released an EP in their own right, 'HAVE YOU GOT 10p?', proof that two-bit bands were ten a penny in the early 80's. Around six months later the trio issued a second EP, 'NOISE FOR THE BOYS', closely pursued by an ambitiously titled debut album, 'A TOUCH OF CLASS' (1983). Such nauseating nationalist yob mentality numbers as 'YOUNG TRIBES OF ENGLAND', 'ENGLAND AIN'T DEAD' and 'GANG WARFARE' just about summed this band up and made sure they were ignored by the more discerning music papers. They finally pressed the eject button in '84 after a final an"oi"ing album, 'THE SPIRIT OF REBELLION'.

Album rating: A TOUCH OF CLASS (*3) / THE SPIRIT OF REBELLION (*3) / THE BEST OF THE EJECTED compilation (*5)

BIG JIM BROOKS – vocals, guitar / **GARY SANDBROOK** – bass, vocals / **PAUL GRIFFITHS** – drums, vocals

Riot City not iss.

Sep 82. (7"ep) *(RIOT 14)* **HAVE YOU GOT 10p?** –
– Have you got 10p? / Class of '82 / One of the boys.

Feb 83. (7"ep) *(RIOT 19)* **NOISE FOR THE BOYS** –
– Fast 'n' loud / Don't care / What happened in Brighton.

May 83. (lp) *(CITY 003)* **A TOUCH OF CLASS** –
– Young tribes of England / Fast 'n' loud / Gang warfare / Class of '82 / England ain't dead / Carnival / Football song / Man of war / Fifteen / Have you got 10p? / Mr. Muggins / East End kids / I'm gonna get me a gun / Dressed to kill / Karnal dub / The sky's in love. *(<cd-iss. Jul98 on 'Captain Oi'+=; AHOYCD 024>)* – HAVE YOU GOT 10p? + NOISE FOR THE BOYS (EP tracks).

Dec 83. (7"ep) *(RIOT 28)* **PRESS THE BUTTON** –
– Russians / 24 years / In the city.

Aug 84. (lp) *(CITY 007)* **THE SPIRIT OF REBELLION** –
– Afghan rebels / Army dog / Greenham woman / Young punks go for it / Dirty schoolgirls / Mental case / Look, stop & listen / Warcry / The enemy awaits / Hang 'em high / Mary-go-round / Go buddy go / What am I gonna do? *(<cd-iss. Nov98 on 'Captain Oi'+=; AHOYCD 034)* – PRESS THE BUTTON EP tracks / Public animals No.1 / Generation landslide / Rock star.

— disbanded after above album

– compilations, etc. –

Jun 99. (cd) *Captain Oi; (AHOYCD 112)* **THE BEST OF THE EJECTED** –
– East End kids / Have you got 10p / Fast 'n' loud / Football song / Man o' war / Mr Muggins / I'm gonna get a gun / What happened in Brighton / Gang warfare / Army song / Greenham woman / Dirty schoolgirls / Hang 'em high / Go buddy go / Russians / Public animal No.1 / 24 hours / Road rage / I think I just saw Elvis / Violence breeds violence / Factory song / All my loving.

ELECTRIC BOYS

Formed: Stockholm, Sweden . . . 1988 by CONNY BLOOM and ANDY CHRISTELL. The duo first came to the attention of the European metal press when their 1989 single, 'ALL LIPS 'N' HIPS' became a large hit in their native Sweden. Encouraged by this interest, they recruited FRANCO SANTUNIONE and NICLAS SIGEVALL, recording an acclaimed debut album, 'FUNK-O-METAL CARPET RIDE' (1989) for 'Polygram' Sweden. The record's compelling fusion of wigged-out, grinding funk and hard rock had the critics in rapture and The ELECTRIC BOYS were tipped for world domination on the back of the funk-metal zeitgeist. Signing to 'Atco' in America (sticking with 'Polygram' for Europe, with their UK work appearing on the 'Vertigo' imprint), the group revamped their debut with some new Bob Rock-produced tracks, the record breaking the US Top 100. More of the DAN REED NETWORK/PRINCE school of funk-rock than the FAITH NO MORE/CHILI PEPPERS assault, The ELECTRIC BOYS spiced their grooves with a distinct retro feel which also manifested itself in the band's 'lively' choice of apparel. A follow-up album, 'GROOVUS MAXIMUS' (1992) went even further down the late 60's/early 70's route, although by the time of the record's release, the music press had new fish to fry and the album sank without trace. Disillusioned with this state of affairs, SANTUNIONE and SIGEVALL subsequently departed with MARTIN THOMANDER and THOMAS BROMAN drafted in as respective replacements. Despite a revised strategy of more straightahead classic rock on 1994's 'FREEWHEELIN', the band failed to reverse their ailing fortunes and split soon after.

Album rating: FUNK-O-METAL CARPET RIDE (*7) / GROOVUS MAXIMUS (*6) / FREEWHEELIN' (*5)

CONNY BLOOM (b. BLOMQUIST) – vocals, guitar / **FRANCO SANTUNIONE** – guitar / **ANDY CHRISTELL** – bass / **NICLAS SIGEVALL** – drums

Mercury / not iss.

1987. (7") *(888 885-7)* **ALL LIPS 'N HIPS. / CHEESECAKE FUNK** [-] [-] Sweden
1988. (7") *(870 586-7)* **GET NASTY. / IN THE DITCH** [-] [-] Sweden
(12") *(870 586-1)* – ('A'side) / Get stoopid / ('A'version).
1989. (7") *(872 618-7)* **ELECTRIFIED. / DO THE DIRTY DOG** [-] [-] Sweden
1989. (7") *(7") (874 498-7)* **HALLELUJAH! I'M ON FIRE. / FREAKY FUNKSTERS** [-] [-] Sweden
(cd-s+=) *(874 499-2)* – Into the ditch / Do the dirty dog.

— the group backed comedian SVULLO on his single 'For Fet For Ett Fuck'

Vertigo / Atco

Apr 90. (7") *(VER 48) <98973>* **ALL LIPS 'N HIPS. / HALLELUJAH** [ ] [76]
(12"+=/12"pic-d+=/cd-s+=) *(VER X/XP/CD 48)* – Funk-o-metal carpet ride.
May 90. (cd/c/lp) *(846 055-2/-4/-1) <91337>* **FUNK-O-METAL CARPET RIDE** [ ] [90]
– Psychedelic eyes / All lips 'n hips / Change / If I had a car / Captain of my soul / Rags to riches / Cheek to cheek / Electrified / Who are you / Into the woods.

— (originally released in Sweden 1989 on 'Mercury'; *836 913)*

Nov 90. (7") *(VER 50)* **ELECTRIFIED. / WHO ARE YOU** [ ] [-]
(12"+=/cd-s+=) *(VER X/CD 50)* – All lips 'n' hips / Into the ditch.
May 92. (7") *(VER 65)* **MARY IN THE MYSTERY WORLD. / WHY DON'T WE DO IT IN THE ROAD** [ ] [-]
(12"+=/cd-s+=) *(VER X/CD 65)* – All lips 'n hips.
(12"pic-d++=) *(VERXP 65)* – Knee deep in you.
Jun 92. (cd/c/lp) *(512 255-2/-4/-1) <92143>* **GROOVUS MAXIMUS** [ ] [ ]
– Groovus maximus / Knee deep in you / Mary in the mystery world / Fire in the house / The sky is crying / Bed of roses / She's into something heavy / Dying to be loved / Bad motherfunker / When love explodes / Tambourine / Tear it up / March of the spirits.

— **MARTIN THOMANDER** – guitar; repl. FRANCO

— **THOMAS BROMAN** – drums (ex-GREAT KING RAT) repl. SIGEVALL

Polydor / Music For Nations

Mar 94. (cd/c) *(521 722-2/-4) <CDMFN 164>* **FREEWHEELIN'** [ ] [ ]
– Are you ready to believe / Straight no chaser / Groover / Mountains and sunsets / Sad day / Nothing for nothing / Sleeping in the world's smallest bed / My knuckles your face / Not my cross to bear / Sharpshooter / Some kind of voodoo / Freewheelin' / Black Betty.

Polar / not iss.

1994. (cd-s) *(855 296-2)* **ARE YOU READY TO BELIEVE** [-] [-] Sweden
1994. (cd-s) *(855 402-2)* **MOUNTAINS AND SUNSETS / SOME KIND OF VOODOO** [-] [-] Sweden
1994. (cd-ep) *(855 405-2)* **GROOVER / SOME KIND OF VOODOO / BLACK BETTY / FREEWHEELIN'** [-] [-] Sweden

— split up after above

ELECTRIC CHAIRS

(see under ⇒ COUNTY, Wayne/Jayne)

ELECTRIC FRANKENSTEIN

Formed: New York, USA . . . 1992 by SAL CANZONIERI, DAN CANZONIERI, JIM FOSTER and ROB SEFCIK; STEVE MILLER (no, not THAT Steve Miller) was added later. Inspired by the primal punch of The STOOGES, MC5, ALICE COOPER and The NEW YORK DOLLS (what more inspiration do you need!!??) as well as the latter day hardcore scene, these veteran punk rockers decided to inject a bit of authenticity into the Big Apple's jaded scene. Promoting themselves as the sonic equivalent of Mary Shelley's mythic monster, ELECTRIC FRANKENSTEIN kicked out the 7" jams for a slew of indie labels before cutting their 1996 full length debut, 'ELECTRIC FRANKENSTEIN CONQUERS THE WORLD'. Their prolific recording schedule continued apace in 1997 with no less than three albums: 'SICK SONGS', 'THE TIME IS NOW!' and 'FRACTURED'. 1998 resulted in an even larger haul of EF garage-style booty including 'SPARE PARTS', 'I WAS A TEENAGE SHUTDOWN' and 'ROCK'N'ROLL MONSTER'. The late 90's saw the departure of longtime drummer SEFCIK, his replacement being JOHN STEELE. A more concrete deal with the 'Victory' label was initiated with 'HOW TO MAKE A MONSTER' (1999) while 'DAWN OF ELECTRIC FRANKENSTEIN' (2000) paid homage to the band's founding influences. While UK audiences were hard pressed to find these records on import, Scottish indie label, 'Twenty Stone Blatt' released a live set, 'DON'T TOUCH ME, I'M ELECTRIC' in 2000. • **Covered:** YOUR EMOTIONS (Dead Kennedys) / BORNEO JIMMY (Dictators) / WE ARE THE ROAD CREW (Motorhead) / 1977 (Clash) / THIRD GENERATION (Dead Boys) / etc.

Album rating: ROCK'N'ROLL MONSTER (*7) / HOW TO MAKE A MONSTER (*7) / LIVE, LOUD AND ANGRY! (*8) / DON'T TOUCH ME, I'M ELECTRIC! (*5) / THE DAWN OF THE ELECTRIC FRANKENSTEIN (*5)

STEVE MILLER – vocals / **JIM FOSTER** – lead guitar / **SAL CANZONIERI** – guitar / **DAN CANZONIERI** – bass / **ROB SEFCIK** – drums

Demolition Derby / Demolition Derby

Jan 97. (cd) *(NITR 005)* **THE TIME IS NOW!** [ ] [ ]
– Teenage shutdown / The time is now! / Superstar / Right on target / I want more / Demolition joyride / E.F. theme / Fast & furious / Rise and crash / We are the dangerous / Too much for you / A sweet sickness. *(lp-iss.Nov97; DD 5) (re-iss. Jan01 on 'One Foot'; OFR 047CD)*

One Louder / One Louder

Jun 97. (cd/lp) *<(LOUD EST/ER 24)>* **ACTION HIGH** [ ] [ ]
– Action high / I'll be standing (on my own) / Not with U / Pure & simple / Born wild / I wish I could / Learn to burn / Back at you / Clock-wise / Out there / Frustration.

Nesak / Nesak

Jun 97. (cd) *<(19819-2)>* **ELECTRIC FRANKENSTEIN CONQUERS THE WORLD!** [ ] [ ] Jan96
– It's all moving faster / Electrify me / Just like your mom / New rage / Deal with it / Home of the brave / Monster demolisher / Face at the edge of the crowd / Get off my back / Coolest little monster. *(re-iss. Jan01 on 'One Foot'; OFR 046CD)*

not iss.

Nov 97. (cd-ep) **MONSTER** [-] [ ]
– Naked heat / Blackout (Christy's song) / Savage / Imperial world / Used to know / Queen Wasp. *<(re-iss. May99 as 'ROCK'N'ROLL MONSTER' on 'Au Go Go' lp/cd+=; ANDA 245/+CD)>* – I got power / Meat house / Do the nihil / Out there.

V&V / V&V

Nov 97. (m-cd/m-lp) *<(41286/+0)>* **FRACTURED** [ ] [ ]
– Devil dust / Right now / Your emotions / Fractured / Man's ruin / Borneo Jimmy.

Man's Ruin / Man's Ruin

Jul 98. (10"lp) *<(MR 107)>* **LISTEN UP, BABY!** [ ] [ ]
– Listen up, baby! / Neurotic pleasures / Hostage situation / Social infections / Hammered / Takin' it all.
Sep 98. (cd-ep; shared w/ Hookers) *<(MR 108)>* **split** [ ] [ ]
(re-iss. Aug00; same)

Estrus / Estrus

Oct 98. (lp/cd) *<(ES 1249/+CD)>* **I WAS A TEENAGE SHUTDOWN!** [ ] [ ]
– Teenage shutdown / It's all moving faster / Superstar / Rise & crash / New rage / I wish I could / E.F. theme / Right on target / Demotion joyride. *(lp re-iss. Jun00; ESD 125-1)*

Coldfront / Coldfront

Oct 98. (7") *<(CF 010)>* **UP FROM THE STREETS** [ ] [ ]

One Foot / One Foot

Nov 98. (cd) *<(OFR 30035CD)>* **HOW I ROSE FROM THE DEAD . . .** [ ] [ ]
– Devil dust / Black out / Action high / Rocket in my veins / Right now / Deal w' it / Neurotic pleasures / Time is now / Get off my back / E.F. theme.

Get Hip / Get Hip

Jan 99. (cd/lp) *(IGOR 001/+LP)* **IT'S MOVING IT'S ALIVE** [ ] [ ]

20 Stone Blatt / 20 Stone Blatt

Feb 99. (cd) *20 Stone Blatt; (BAMF 001CD)* **LIVE, LOUD AND ANGRY! (live Autumn '98)** [ ] [ ]
(w/ bonus-CD; 'RECHARGED FROM THE VAULTS')

— **JOHN STEELE** – drums; repl. ROB

Victory / Victory

Feb 99. (cd-ep) *<(VR 093CD)>* **I'M NOT YOUR (NOTHING) / I WAS A PUNK BEFORE YOU WAS A PUNK / RIGHT ON TARGET (live)** [ ] [ ]
May 99. (lp/cd) *<(VR 095/+CD)>* **HOW TO MAKE A MONSTER** [ ] [ ]
– I was a modern Prometheus / Cut from the inside / Speed girl / Use me / Friction / Feel the burn (chronic) / My world / Don't know how to stop you / Up from the streets / Pretty deadly / Something for the pain / I'm not your (nothing) / Phatty boom batty.

Akarma / Akarma

Aug 99. (lp/cd) *<(AK 1005/+CD)>* **ELECTRIC FRANKENSTEIN** [ ] [ ]

— (mid-'99) **CARL** – guitar; repl. JIM

Safety-Pin / Safety-Pin

Jul 00. (7") *(SP 019)* **TATTOO VAMPIRE. / CHAIN** [ ] [ ]

Sub Pop / Sub Pop

Nov 00. (7") *<(SP 532)>* **PERFECT CRIME. /** [ ] [ ]

20 Stone Blatt / 20 Stone Blatt

Nov 00. (cd) *<(BAMF 21)>* **DON'T TOUCH ME, I'M ELECTRIC!** (covers) [ ] [ ] Apr01
– Already dead / Fistful of rock / Hate machine / Third generation nation / I just can't kick it / Annie's grave / My father's son / Not for sale / Get off / Graveyard drag race / 1977 / Takin' you down / Backs against the wall / Don't touch me, I'm electric! / We are the road crew. *(lp-iss.Mar01; BAMF 21LP)*

Scooch Pooch / Scooch Pooch

Dec 00. (7") *(PO 48)* **GET OFF. / THIS GENERATION NATION** [ ] [ ]
Feb 01. (cd) **ANNIE'S GRAVE** [-] [ ]
– Already dead / Get off / Just can't kick / Hate machine / Third generation nation / Graveyard dragrace / Takin' you down / Fistful of rock / Annie's grave / My father's son / Backs against the wall / The perfect crime (live).

– compilations, others, etc. –

Jun 97. (m-cd) *Kado; (19829-2)* **SICK SONGS** [ ] [ ]
– Action high / I'll be standing (on my own) / Now with you / Pure and simple / I wish I could / Learn to burn / Back at you / Clockwise / Out there. *(re-iss. Jan01 on 'One Foot'; OFR 045CD)*
Sep 98. (cd/lp) *Get Hip; <(GH 1076 CD/LP)>* **SPARE PARTS** [ ] [ ]
– Devil dust / Right now / Fractured / Your emotions / Man's ruin / Borneo Jimmy / Ef stomp / All moving faster (live) / Rise & crash (live) / Superstar (live).
Oct 99. (m-cd/10"m-lp) *20 Stone Blatt; (BAMP 11 CD/TEN)* **SOD THE ODDS** [ ] [-]
Jul 00. (cd) *Triple X; <(TX 51264CD)>* **THE DAWN OF THE ELECTRIC FRANKENSTEIN** (1992 demos) [ ] [ ]
– Live for it all / Never gonna get it / Lie to me / One last show / Ruin you / Subway suicide boy / Not my sin / Nowhere / 21 dead / Kiss the sun / Austere precautions / How I rose from the dead in my spare time / Blu 4 U / Mistress / Desperado / Evening fear / Descending wish.

ELECTRIC SUN

Formed: Germany . . . 1977 by ex-SCORPIONS guitarist ULI JON ROTH, initially together with ULE RITGEN and CLIVE EDWARDS. Signed to 'Brain' records, the group debuted with 'EARTHQUAKE' in 1979. Largely instrumental and experimental, the record's quasi-mystical jazz-rock explorations were further developed on the Eastern-influenced 'Firewind'

(1981), SIDHATTA GAUTAMA having replaced EDWARDS. It was four years before another release, 'BEYOND THE ASTRAL SKIES' finally surfaced under the moniker, ULI ROTH & ELECTRIC SUN in 1985.

Album rating: EARTHQUAKE (*5) / FIRE WIND (*6) / ELECTRIC SUN compilation (*7) / Uli Roth & Electric Sun: BEYOND THE ASTRAL SKIES (*6)

ULI ROTH – guitars, vocals (ex-SCORPIONS) / **ULE RITGEN** – bass / **CLIVE EDWARDS** – drums

Brain not iss.

Dec 79. (lp) *(0060.196)* **EARTHQUAKE**
– Electric sun / Lilac / Burning wheels turning / Japanese dream / Sundown / Winterdays / Still so many lives away / Earthquake. *(cd-iss. Apr98 as 'RETROSPECTIVE VOL.1' on 'Event'; 992215)*

— EDWARDS joined WILD HORSES and was repl. by **SIDHATTA GAUTAMA**

Mar 82. (lp) *(0060.378)* **FIRE WIND**
– Cast away your chains / Indian dawn / I'll be loving you always / Fire wind / Prelude in space minor / Just another rainbow / Children of the sea / Chaplin and I / Hiroshima: a) Enola Gay, b) Tune of Japan, c) Attack, d) Lament. *(cd-iss. Apr98 as 'RETROSPECTIVE VOL.2' on 'Event'; 922216)*

ULI ROTH & ELECTRIC SUN

— SIDHATTA was repl. by a plethora of musicians and singers; **CLIVE BUNKER** – drums, percussion / **ROBERT CURTIS** – violin, viola / **ELIZABETH MacKENZIE** – saxophones / vocalists; **MICHAEL FLECHSICH, RAINER PRZYWARA, ZENO ROTH, JENNI EVANS, NICKY MOORE + DOROTHY PATTERSON**

E.M.I. not iss.

Jan 85. (7") *(EMI 5511)* **THE NIGHT THE MASTER COMES. / RETURN**

Jan 85. (lp/c) *(ROTH/TC-ROTH 1)* **BEYOND THE ASTRAL SKIES**
– The night the master comes / What is love / Why / I'll be there / Return (chant of angels) / Icebreaker / I'm a river / Angel of peace / Eleison / Son of sky.

— seems to have taken a back seat for the next decade or so . . .

– compilations, etc. –

Jul 88. (d-cd) *Razor; (METALCD 123)* **ELECTRIC SUN**
(re-iss. May91 d-cd/d-lp; MET CD/LP 123)

Oct 94. (d-cd) *Essential; (ESDCD 216)* **EARTH QUAKE / FIRE WIND**

Jun 98. (3xcd-box) *Dressed To Kill; (DTKBOX 71)* **ULI JOHN ROTH**

Sep 00. (cd) *S.P.V.; (SPV 0897203-2)* **TRANSCENDENTAL SKY GUITAR VOL.1 & 2**

ELECTRIC WIZARD

Formed: Dorset, England . . . 1994 by JUS OSBORNE, TIM BAGSHAW and MARK GREENING. A stoner's stoner metal band, ELECTRIC WIZARD released their eponymous debut album in 1995. A record to nod out to rather than chill, the trio's monolithic sludge riffing sounded like they'd collectively ingested a whole greenhouse worth of gear before entering the studio. Combine that with some seriously medieval lyrics and you've got a recipe for almost SPINAL TAP-style metal, served up heavier than a proverbial lead balloon over albums such as 'COME MY FANATICS' (1995), 'CHRONO.NAUT' (1997), 'SUPERCOVEN' (1998) and 'DOPETHRONE' (2000). Watch out for that bad acid maaan . . .

Album rating: ELECTRIC WIZARD (*7) / COME MY FANATICS . . . (*7) / SUPERCOVEN mini (*5) / DOPETHRONE (*5)

JUS OSBORNE – vocals, guitar / **TIM BAGSHAW** – bass / **MARK GREENING** – drums

Rise Above not iss.

Feb 95. (lp/cd) *(RISE 009/+CD)* **ELECTRIC WIZARD**
– Stone magnet / Mourning prayer / Mountains of Mars / Behemoth / Devil's bride / Black butterfly / Electric wizard / Wooden Pipe.

Apr 95. (7"; split) *(RISE 011)* **DEMON LUNG. / (other by Our Haunted Kingdom)**

Dec 95. (cd) *(RISE 014CD)* **COME MY FANATICS . . .**
– Return trip / Wizard in black / Doom-mantia / Ivixor B-phase / Inducer / Son of nothing / Solarian 13. *(re-iss. Apr99 +=; CDRISE 020)* – ELECTRIC WIZARD

Man's Ruin Man's Ruin

Feb 97. (cd; split w/ ORANGE GOBLIN) *<MR 071>*
CHRONO.NAUT (Phase I) / CHRONO.NAUT (Phase II – CHAOS REVEALED) / (others by ORANGE GOBLIN)
(re-iss. Aug00; same)

Jul 97. (cd-s) *<MR 083>* **CHRONO.NAUT (Phase 1) / CHRONO.NAUT (Phase II – CHAOS REVEALED)**

Bad Acid Mia

Aug 98. (cd/lp) *(TRIP 001/+LP)* *<1021>* **SUPERCOVEN** — Apr99
– Supercoven / Burnout. *(cd re-iss. Jan00 on 'Southern'+=; SUNN 04)* – Grimly / Wizards of love.

Rise Above The Music Cartel

Oct 00. (cd) *(CDRISE 27)* *<TMC 44>* **DOPETHRONE** — Nov00
– Vinium sabbathi – Funeropolis / Weird tales: a) Electric frost – b) Golgotha – c) Altar of Melektau / I, witchfinder / We hate you / Untitled / Dopethrone.

ELECTRO HIPPIES

Formed: Liverpool + Lancashire, England . . . 1986 by ANDY, DOM and SIMON. Wilfully extreme grindcore punk/metal which utilised a similar sub-human-grunting-over-death-bass-barrage to NAPALM DEATH, the 'HIPPIES 'music' was initially given exposure by late night Radio One DJ John Peel, who actually released an EP of sessions on Clive Selwood's 'Strange Fruit' in 1987. Following this early exposure, the group recorded a further handful of albums for 'Peaceville' before dropping out of the scene.

Album rating: PLAY LOUD OR DIE mini (*4) / THE ONLY GOOD PUNK IS A DEAD ONE (*6) / ELECTRO HIPPIES LIVE (*5)

ANDY – vocals, guitar / **DOM** – vocals, bass / **SIMON** – drums, vocals

Necrosis not iss.

1986. (m-lp) *(NECRO 1)* **PLAY LOUD OR DIE**
– Acid rain / Wings of death / Theme toon / The reaper / Profit from death / Run Ronald / Terror eyes / Am I punk yet? / Vivisection / The horns of Hades. *(re-iss. May89 on 'Earache';)*

Strange Fruit not iss.

Jul 87. (12"ep) *(SFSP 042)* **PEEL SESSION** (12/7/87)
– Sheep / Starve the city (to feed the poor) / Meltdown / Escape / Dead end / Thought / Chickens / Mother / Mega-armageddon death.

Peaceville not iss.

Feb 88. (lp) *(VILE 002)* **THE ONLY GOOD PUNK IS A DEAD ONE**
– Faith / Acid rain / Run Ronald / Scum / B.P. / Unity / Terror eyes / So wicked / Profit / Freddy's revenge / Mistake / Things of beauty / Protest / Gas Joe Pearce / Lies / Tortured tears / Turkeys / D.I.Y. (not D.R.I.) / Suck / Deception. *(cd-iss. Jun89; VILE 002CD)*

May 89. (m-lp) *(VILE 013)* **ELECTRO HIPPIES LIVE (live)**
– Could you look me in the eyes / Sometimes I'm so glad / Reject / Escape / Mega-armageddon death (pt.3 & pt.2) / Mother / Faith / Unity / Sheep / City / Acid rain / Run Ronald / Chickens / So wicked / Profit / Meltdown / Mega-armageddon death / Mega-armageddon death (extended) / Silver machine.

— split after above

ELF / (ELECTRIC) ELVES) (see under ⇒ DIO)

ELIXIR

Formed: England . . . 1986 by PAUL TAYLOR, PHIL DENTON, NORMAN GORDON and brothers KEVIN and NIGEL DOBBS. A NWOBHM-esque band well out of time, ELIXIR's only claim to fame was having ex-IRON MAIDEN drummer, CLIVE BURR, in place for their second set, 'LETHAL POTION' (1990). This followed an equally hackneyed eponymous debut in 1988. Suffice to say, their brand of tired trad metal went down like a particularly weighty lead balloon. • **Note:** The ELIXIR of the 90's was not of the same.

Album rating: THE SON OF ODIN (*3) / LETHAL POTION (*2)

PAUL TAYLOR – vocals / **PHIL DENTON** – guitar / **NORMAN GORDON** – guitar / **KEVIN DOBBS** – bass / **NIGEL DOBBS** – drums

Elixir not iss.

1986. (lp) *(ELIXIR 2)* **THE SON OF ODIN**
– The star of Beshaan / Pandora's box / Hold high the flame / Children of tomorrow / Trial by fire / Starflight / Dead man's gold / Treachery (ride like the wind) / Son of Odin. *(re-iss. Feb88 as 'ELIXIR' on 'Goasco'; GM 003)*

— **CLIVE BURR** – drums (ex-IRON MAIDEN) repl. NIGEL

— **MARK WHITE** – bass; repl. KEVIN

Sonic not iss.

Apr 90. (cd/lp) *(SONIC CD/LP 9)* **LETHAL POTION**
– She's got it / Sovereign remedy / Llagaeran / Louise / Shadows of the night * / Elixir / All together again * / Light in your heart / (Metal trance intro) Visions of darkness / Edge of eternity / Last rays of the sun. *(cd+= *)*

— folded after the failure of above. The ELIXIR of the mid-late 90's was not the same group

ELOY

Formed: Hanover, Germany . . . early '69 by FRANK BORNEMANN, who took the name from the futuristic race in HG Wells' 'The Time Machine'. BORNEMANN and the rest (ERICH SCHRIEVER, MANFRED WIECZORKE, WOLFGANG STOCKER and HELMUTH DRAHT) won a talent contest, resulting in a record deal with 'Philips'. Their eponymous debut in 1971 (written mostly by SCHRIEVER and WIECZORKE), was basically bloated, over-weight progressive rock and its relative failure led to BORNEMANN taking over control. They returned in 1973 on 'Harvest' records with a markedly improved second set, 'INSIDE', which contained the spaced-out 17-minute 'LAND OF NO BODY'. Their next, 'FLOATING' (1974) was a lot heavier than its predecessor, leading to a tour of the States. In 1975, BORNEMANN again changed direction, this time to a full-blown HG Wells-type concept piece, 'POWER AND THE PASSION', but it was lambasted for being over-produced and self-indulgent. ELOY continued in this vein for the next few albums until 1979's 'SILENT CRIES AND MIGHTY ECHOES' took on a more mid-70's PINK FLOYD or HAWKWIND approach. The sci-fi biased 80's albums were outdated slices of symphonic rock, although synthesizers were always present. They were finally rewarded with a UK contract in 1982 for the release of the album, 'PLANETS'. Another change of direction, this time to an even heavier progressive sound, won them a new audience, although this didn't improve their critical standing. • **Trivia:** All their 70's German lp's were issued on cd by 'Harvest' in the 90's.

Album rating: ELOY (*6) / INSIDE (*7) / FLOATING (*6) / POWER AND THE PASSION (*7) / DAWN (*6) / OCEAN (*6) / SILENT CRIES AND MIGHT ECHOES (*6) / LIVE (*4) / COLOURS (*5) / PLANETS (*6) / TIME TO BURN (*5) / PERFORMANCE (*4) / METROMANIA (*7) / RA (*4) / DESTINATION (*5) / THE

TIDES RETURN FOREVER (*5) / OCEAN 2 (*5) / CHRONICLES I & II compilation (*7)

FRANK BORNEMANN – lead guitar, vocals, percussion / **MANFRED WIECZORKE** – keyboards, vocals / **E. SCHRIEVER** – / **H. DRAHT** –

Philips not iss.

1971. (lp) *(6305 089)* **ELOY** - - German
– Today / Something yellow / Eloy / Song of a paranoid soldier / Voice of revolution / Isle of Sun / Dillus roady. *(re-iss. Jan98 on 'Second Battle'; SB 010)*

— **WOLFGANG STOECKER** – bass / **FRITZ RANDOW** – drums, percussion, flute, guitar, repl. SCHRIEVER + DRAHT

Electrola Janus

1973. (lp) *(IC 062-29479) <3062>* **INSIDE** - German
– Land of nobody / Inside / Future city / Up and down.

— **LUITJEN JANSSEN** – bass repl. STOECKER

1974. (lp) *(IC 062-29521) <7018>* **FLOATING** - German
– Floating / The light from deep darkness / Castle in the air / Plastic girl / Madhouse.

— added **DETLEV SCHWAAR** – guitar

1975. (lp) *(IC 062-29602)* **POWER AND THE PASSION** - - German
– Introduction / Journey into / Lover over six centuries / Mutiny / Imprisonment / Daylight / Thoughts of home / The zany magician / Back into the present / Notre Dame.

— **BORNEMANN** with complete new line-up **DETLEV SCHMIDTCHEN** – keyboards, guitar / **KLAUS-PETER MATZIOL** – bass, vocals / **JUERGEN ROSENTHAL** – drums, percussion

1976. (lp) *(IC 062-31787)* **DAWN** - - German
– Awakening / Between the times: Memory – Flash – Appearance of the voice – Return to the voice / The Sun-song / The dance in doubt and fear / Lost (introduction) / Lost (the decision) / The midnight fight / The victory of mental force / Gliding into light and knowledge / Le reveil du soleil / The dawn.

1977. (lp) *(IC 064-32596)* **OCEAN** - - German
– Poseidon's creation / Incarnation of Logos / Decay of Logos / Atlantis agony at June 5th, 8498, 13 p.m. Gregorian Earthtime.

1978. (lp) *(IC 064-45269)* **SILENT CRIES AND MIGHTY ECHOES** - - German
– Astral entrance / Master of sensation / The apocaypse: Silent cries divide the nights – The vision – Burning – Force majeure / Pilot to Paradise / De labore solis / Mighty echoes.

1979. (d-lp) *(IC 164-32934/5)* **LIVE (live)** - - German
– Poseidon's creation / Incarnation of Logos / The Sun-song / The dance in doubt and fear / Mutiny / Gliding into light and knowledge / Inside / Atlantis agony at June 5th, 8498, 13 p.m., Gregorian Earthtime.

— **FRANK + KLAUS-PETER** added **HANNES ARKONA** – guitar / **HANNES FOLBERTH** – keyboards / **JIM McGILLIVRAY** – drums, percussion

1980. (lp) *(IC 064-45936)* **COLOURS** - - German
– Horizons / Illuminations / Giant / Impressions / Child migration / Galery / Silhouette / Sunset.

Heavy Metal not iss.

Jul 82. (lp/pic-lp/c) *(HMI LP/PD/MC 1) (IC 064-46483)* **PLANETS** -
– On the verge of darkening lights / Point of no return / Mysterious monolith / Queen of the night / At the gates of dawn / Sphinx / Carried by cosmic winds.

— **FRITZ RANDOW** – drums, percussion, returned to repl. McGILLIVRAY

Jan 83. (clear-lp/c) *(HMI LP/MC 3) (IC 064-46548)* **TIME TO TURN** -
– Through a somber galaxy / Behind the walls of imagination / Magic mirrors / Time to turn / End of an odyssey / The flash / Say, is it really true.

Apr 83. (lp/pic-lp/c) *(HMI LP/PD/MC 12) (IC 064-46714)* **PERFORMANCE** -
– In disguise / Shadow and light / Mirador / Surrender / Heartbeat / Fools / A broken frame.

Nov 83. (7"/7"pic-d) *(HM INT/PD 1)* **FOOLS. / HEARTBEAT** -

— (In 1984, they moved to 'E.M.I.' label in Germany only)

Sep 84. (lp/pic-lp/c/cd) *(HMI LP/PD/MC/XD 21) (792502-1)* **METROMANIA** -
– Escape to the heights / Follow the light / All life is one / Nightriders / Seeds of creation / Metromania / The stranger.

— **BORNEMANN** added **MICHAEL GERLACH** – keyboards, synthesizers + sessioners

— (Moved to 'S.P.V.' label in Germany only)

FM Revolver not iss.

Aug 89. (lp/pic-lp/c/cd) *(REV LP/PD/MC/XD 120)* **RA** -
– Voyager of the future race / Sensations / Dreams / Invasion of a megaforce / Rainbow / Hero. *(cd re-iss. Jan95 & Jan97 on 'SPV'; SPV 085-48022)*

— the basic duo added **MATZIOL** plus **NICO BARETTA** – drums

S.P.V. not iss.

Dec 92. (cd) *(SPV 085-48082)* **DESTINATION** -
– Call of the wild / Racing shadows / Destination / Prisoner in mind / Silent revolution / Fire and ice / Eclipse of mankind / Jeanne d'Arc. *(re-iss. Jan97; same)*

Dec 94. (cd) *(SPV 084-48202)* **THE TIDES RETURN FOREVER** -
– The day of crimson tides / Fatal illusions / Childhood memories / Generation of innocence / The tides return forever / The last in line / The company of angels. *(re-iss. Jan97; same)*

— next incl. **BODO SCHOPF** – percussion, drums + **STEVE MANN** – guitar / + others

Gun B.M.G.

Nov 98. (cd) *(GUN 167CD) <61259>* **OCEAN 2**
– Between future and past / Ro setau / Paralysed civilization / Serenity / Awakening of consciousness / Reflections from the spheres beyond / Waves of intuition / The answer.

– compilations, etc. –

Oct 91. (cd) *Alex; <2196>* **RARITIES** -
– Daybreak / On the road / Child migration / Let the sun rise in your brain / Silhouette / Horizons / Wings of vision / Sunset / Time to turn / Through a sombre galaxy / The stranger / Wings of vision (12"version).

Jul 93. (cd) *S.P.V.; (<SPV 084-48182>)* **CHRONICLES 1** (re-produced in '93)
– Poseidons creation '93 / The apocalypse '93 / Silhouette '93 / Mysterious monolith '93 / Sphinx '93 / Illuminations '93 / End of an odyssey '93 / Time to turn '93 / Spirit in chains '93 / Say it is really true '93.

Jul 94. (cd) *S.P.V.; (<SPV 084-48192>)* **CHRONICLES II** (re-produced in '94)
– Escape to the heights '94 / All life is one '94 / Nightriders '94 / Follow the light '94 / Rainbow / Voyager of the future race / Fire & ice / Call of the wild / Prisoner in mind / Eclipse of mankind.

Apr 96. (cd) *Griffin; <587>* **THE BEST OF ELOY: VOLUME ONE – THE EARLY DAYS 1972-1975** -

Jul 00. (cd) *S.P.V.; (<SPV 31048220>)* **CHRONICLES VOL.I & II**

EMPEROR

Formed: Norway … 1992 by mostly unknown members of the Black Metal Circle, run by the late EURONYMOUS (once leader of black metal outfit MAYHEM, he was subsequently murdered by fellow Satanist, COUNT GRISHNAKH). The group made their death-rattle debut in 1993 with 'IN THE NIGHTSHADE ECLIPSE', a record stalked early 1994 by a split CD with fellow Norwegian metallers, ENSLAVED. While guitarist SAMOTH wasn't serving a jail sentence for setting fire to churches, the group returned to the studio with similarly controversal, FAUST, taking his place in the drumstool. He walked it like he talked it by murdering a homosexual (he was also convicted of arson). EMPEROR kept right on the proverbial highway to hell with a second set, 'ANTHEMS TO THE WELKIN AT DUSK' (1997), presumably a collection of worksongs for Scandinavian whelk pickers. The satanic gangstas were back to terrorise the Norwegian hood in 1999 with 'IX EQUILIBRIUM', another brutal sonic assault no doubt designed to put the fear of death-metal into anyone observing the niceties of decent music taste. Bizarrely enough, Norway was recently voted the world's most desirable place to live in a UN Human Development Report; hmmm . . ..

Album rating: IN THE NIGHTSHADE ECLIPSE (*5) / HORDANES LAND split with Enslaved (*5) / ANTHEMS TO THE WELKIN AT DUSK (*5) / IX EQUILIBRIUM (*8) / EMPERIAL LIVE CEREMONY (*4) /

IHSAHN – vocals, guitar, keyboards / **SAMOTH** – drums (then guitar) / **ALVER** – bass / **FAUST** (b. BARD G. EITHUN) – drums / **MORTIIS** – bass

Candlelight Century Media

Jan 93. (cd/c/lp) *(CANDLE 008 CD/MC/LP) <7759>* **IN THE NIGHTSIDE ECLIPSE** Jan94
– Introduction / Into the infinity of thoughts / The burning shadows of silence / Cosmic keys to my creations and times / Beyond the great vast forest / Towards the pantheon / The majesty of the night sky / I am the black wizards / Inno a satana. *(re-iss. Jan95; same) (cd re-iss. Sep98; CANDLE 030) (pic-lp iss.Oct00; CANDLE 030PLP)*

Jan 94. (cd; shared with ENSLAVED) *(CANDLE 12CD) <7774>* **HORDANES LAND** Jul94
– I am the black wizards / Wrath of the tyrant / Night of the graveless souls / Cosmic keys to my creations and times / (others by ENSLAVED). *(re-iss. Sep98; CANDLE 029CD)*

— **TCHORT** – bass; repl. MORTIIS who went solo

— **TRYM** – drums (ex-ENSLAVED) repl. FAUST who was sentenced to 14 years in prison

Mar 97. (7"ep/12"ep/cd-ep) *(CANDLE 018/+12/CDS)<100>* **THE LOSS AND CURSE OF REVERENCE. / IN LONGING SPIRIT / OPUS A SATANA** Dec99

May 97. (lp/cd) *(CANDLE 023/+CD) <7848>* **ANTHEMS TO THE WELKIN AT DUSK** Jul97
– Alsvartr (the oath) / Ye entrancempirium / Thus spake the nightspirit / Ensorcelled by khaos / The loss and curse of reverance / The acclamation of bonds / With strength I burn / The wanderer / In longing spirit / Opus a satana. *(cd re-mast.Sep98 +=; same)* – loss and curse of reverance (live). *(pic-lp iss.Oct00; CANDLE 031PLP)*

— **IHSAHN + SAMOTH** recruited **TRYM** – bass (session) + **CHARMAND GRIMLOCH** – keyboards

Mar 99. (cd/lp) *(CANDLE 035 CD/LP) <7870>* **IX EQUILIBRIUM**
– Curse you all men / Decrystallizing reason / Elegy of Icarus / Source of Icon E / Sworn / Nonus aequilibrium / Warriors of modern death / Of blindness / Subsequent seers. *(pic-cd-iss. Oct99 +=; CANDLE 050DP)* – Sworn (Ulver remix) / Curse all you men (live). *(pic-lp iss.Oct00; CANDLE 035PLP)*

Oct 00. (dvd)(pic-lp) *(<CANDLE 060DVD>)<(CANDLE 048PLP)>* **EMPERIAL LIVE CEREMONY (live)** Jun00
– I am the black wizards / Curse you all men! / Thus spake the nightspirit / I am the black wizards / An elegy of Icaros / With strength I burn / Sworn / Night of the graveless souls / Inni a satana / Ye entrancempirium.

– compilations, etc. –

Sep 98. (cd) *Candlelight; (CANDLE 029CD) / Century Media; <7879>* **WRATH OF THE TYRANT** (all MORTIIS material) Nov98

Mar 99. (cd/d-cd) *Moonfog; (FOG 019 CD/BX)* **THORNS / EMPEROR**
– Exordium / AErie descent / I am / AErie descent / (others by THORNS).

Apr 00. (5xlp-box) *Candlelight; (CANDLE 053BOX)* **EMPERIAL VINYL PRESENTATION**

Alec EMPIRE (see under ⇒ ATARI TEENAGE RIOT)

ENGLISH DOGS (see under ⇒ JANUS STARK)

Jeremy ENIGK (see under ⇒ SUNNY DAY REAL ESTATE)

ENSIGN

Formed: New Jersey, USA . . . mid 90's by former SICK OF IT ALL roadie, TIM SHAW. Recruiting JOHN FRAUBERGER, NATE GLUCK and RYAN MURPHY, SHAW set about creating the kind of hardcore he felt was missing from the contemporary scene. A couple of EP's preceded an acclaimed debut album, 'DIRECTION OF THINGS TO COME' (1997), subsequently resulting in a deal with DEXTER HOLLAND's 'Nitro' label. RYAN DONOGHUE replaced FRAUBERGER for the recording of 'CAST THE FIRST STONE' (1999), another uncompromisingly aggressive effort which featured a guest spot from LOU KOLLER (of SHAW's previous employers SOIA). The line-up had changed yet again – SHAW, GLUCK and new faces CHRIS BYRNES and CHRIS OLIVER – by 'THE PRICE OF PROGRESSION' (2001), a record featuring another guest appearance in the shape of GOOD RIDDANCE's RUSS RANKIN.

Album rating: DIRECTION OF THINGS TO COME (*6) / CAST THE FIRST STONE (*6) / THE PRICE OF PROGRESSION (*6)

TIM SHAW – vocals / **RYAN DONOGHUE** – guitar / **NATE GLUCK** – bass / **RYAN MURPHY** – drums

Revelation Revelation

Nov 97. (lp/cd) *<IND 012/+CD)>* **DIRECTION OF THINGS TO COME**
– Page 32 / Foundation / Day by day / Direction of things to come / Blueprint / Furthest from the middle / Where did we go wrong / Revolutions end / Tomorrow's shadow / Tourniquet / First, last, only / Hold / Image.

Nitro Nitro

Apr 99. (cd/lp) *<(15823-2/-1)>* **CAST THE FIRST STONE**
– Silent weapons for quiet wars / #22 / 15 years / Wash away / Fade into years / Waiting for the breakdown / Absent / For the record / The winner takes all / Never give in / Pale horse / Unanswered / D.B.C. / Cornered / The road less travelled / Fallen.

Oct 00. (cd-s) *<(15834-2)>* **FOR WHAT IT'S WORTH / CAST IN SHADOWS / NINE-ONE-ZERO-ZERO / LEFT HAND SYNDROME**

Jan 01. (7") *(RFL 016)* **split w/ Reaching Forward** -
(above issued on 'Reflections')

Apr 01. (cd/lp) *<(15842-2/-1)>* **THE PRICE OF PROGRESSION**
– The spark / Black clouds vs. silver linings / While the iron is hot / Lesser of two / Absolute zero / Grasping at straws / Foot in mouth as an art form / Everything you ever love / Slow burn / Never go home again / How to bleed / The May conspiracy / 33 1/3 / Cast in shadows / Stay warm / Sworntosecrecy / File under misunderstood.

– compilations, others, etc. –

Apr 00. (cd) *Indecision; <(IND 025CD)>* **THREE YEARS TWO MONTHS ELEVEN DAYS**
– Alzheimer's / Pale horse / Trying again / Enemy of my enemy / Standing / M.P.S.R. / Blue skies / Fall from grace / Uncommon bond / M.P.S.R. #2 / We'll make a difference / Hold / Say it to my face / Tourniquet / Where did we go wrong / Fade into years / Target.

ENTHRONED

Formed: Belgium . . . . at the fall of '93 by LORD SABATHAN and his drumming sidekick CERNUNNOS, the unusually located death-metallers arose from MORBID DEATH . . . the group that is. Supplementing their act with guitarist TSEBAOTH, ENTHRONED issued a demo plus a shared EP with likeminded ANCIENT RITES. These helped give the band a platform to unleash their debut set, 'PROPHECIES OF PAGAN FIRE' (1995). However, a series of line-up changes – via the addition of NORNAGEST and the replacement of TSEBAOTH with NEBIROS – and the tragic suicide of CERNUNNOS in Spring '97, nearly found ENTHRONED give up. After a rush-released but much improved second set, 'TOWARDS THE SKULLTHRONE OF SATAN' (1997) – a tribute set to CERNUNNOS came out by way of mini-set, 'REGIE SATHANAS' and, not long after new drummer NAMROTH BLACKTHORN was in place for the following year's third effort, 'THE APOCALYPSE MANIFESTO'.

Album rating: PROPHECIES OF PAGAN FIRE (*5) / TOWARDS THE SKULLTHRONE OF SATAN (*6) / REGIE SATHANAS (*4) / THE APOCALYPSE MANIFESTO (*4)

LORD SABATHAN – vocals, bass / **CERNUNNOS** – drums / **TSEBAOTH** – guitar (ex-SLANESH)

Osmose not iss.

May 96. (cd) *(EORCD 004)* **PROPHECIES OF PAGAN FIRE** -
– Intro: Prophecies of pagan fire / Deny the holy book of lies / Under the holocaust / Scared by darkwinds / Tales from A'blackened horde / At dawn of a funeral winter / Rites of the northern fullmoon / Skjeldenland / At the sound of the millennium black bells / As the wolves howl again. *<US cd-iss. Feb00 on 'Cleopatra'+=; CL 1111>* – Evil church (live) / At the sound of the millennium black bells (live) / The conqueror (live) / Ha Shaitan (live) / Legend of the coldest breeze / Tales from a blackened horde (demo) / Deny the holy book of lies (demo) / Rites of the northern full moon (demo) / Scared by darkwinds (demo) / At the sound of the millennium black bells (demo) / Postmortem penetrations.

— added **NORNAGEST** – guitar

— **NEBIROS** – guitar; repl. TSEBAOTH

— CERNUNNOS was to commit suicide in April '97

Blackend Blackend

Oct 97. (cd) *(<BLACK 008CD>)* **TOWARDS THE SKULLTHRONE OF SATAN** May98
– Satan's realm / The ultimate horse fights / Ha Shaitan / Evil church / The antichrist summons the black flame / The forest of Nathrath / Dusk of the regin darkness / Throne to Purgatory / When horny flames begin to rise / Hertogenwald / Final armageddon.

— **NAMROTH BLACKTHORN** – drums; finally repl. CERNUNNON

Apr 98. (m-cd) *(<BLACK 009MCD>)* **REGIE SATHANAS** Jul99
– Prelude to Satan's avengers / By dark glorious thoughts / Walpurgis night / Satan never sleeps / The conqueror / Deny the holy book of lies / Outro.

May 99. (cd) *(<BLACK 018CD>)* **THE APOCALYPSE MANIFESTO** Dec99
– Whisperings of terror (intro) / The apocalypse manifesto / Death faceless chaos / Retribution of the holy trinity / Post mortem penetration (messe de sanites mortes) / Genocide (concerto No.35 for razors) / Volkermord, der antigott / Alastor Rex perpetuus Doloris / The scourge of God / The scourge of God (reprise).

ENTOMBED

Formed: Stockholm, Sweden . . . 1987 as NIHILIST, a teenage SLAYER-esque outfit who released four titled demos, ('DROWNED', 'PREMATURE AUTOPSY', 'BUT LIFE GOES ON' and 'ONLY SHREDS REMAIN'), before they became ENTOMBED. The line-up consisted of LARS GOREN PETROV, ALEX HELLID, UFFE CEDERLUND and NICKE ANDERSSON (added LARS ROSENBERG), the group subsequently signing to UK label, 'Earache', and recording their acclaimed debut, 'LEFT HAND PATH' (1990). A highly distinctive take on death-metal, the record avoided much of the bluster and cheesiness which too often characterises the genre. PETROV was then replaced, initially with ORVAR SAFSTROM (for the 'CRAWL' single) then JOHNNY DOREDEVIC for the follow-up album, 'CLANDESTINE' (1991). Moving ever further away from their death-metal roots, the record employed a slightly more accessible aproach which was developed over each successive release to form the full-on punk/metal assault of 'WOLVERINE BLUES' (1993) and 1997's 'TO RIDE, SHOOT STRAIGHT AND SPEAK THE TRUTH'. In the interim, this hardiest of metal outfits have seen the return of LG PETROV (for 1993's EP 'HOLLOWMAN'), undergone label hassles with 'East West' (they're now signed to 'Music For Nations') and even found time to record a spook-core cover of ROKY ERICKSON's (reclusive genius who once tested the limits of sanity with The 13th FLOOR ELEVATORS) 'NIGHT OF THE VAMPIRE'. The ever adept and adaptable Swedes even managed to carry off Bob Dylan's 'BALLAD OF HOLLIS BROWN' on a 1997 EP, while 'SAME DIFFERENCE' (1998) ranked as their most "alternative" metal release to date. The album steered away slightly from the uber-guitar assault of its predecessor for a more measured, distorted sound which saw grumblings from some sections of their fiercely loyal fanbase. More in tune with the diehard metalheads was 'UPRISING' (2000), a return to diesel-powered guitar meltdown combining the extremity of their death metal roots with biker-style scuzz. • **Covers:** KICK OUT THE JAMES (MC5) / 21st CENTURY SCHIZOID MAN (King Crimson) / BURSTING OUT (Jethro Tull) / AMAZING GRACE (hymn).

Album rating: LEFT HAND PATH (*6) / CLANDESTINE (*5) / WOLVERINE BLUES (*6) / TO RIDE, SHOOT STRAIGHT AND SPEAK THE TRUTH (*7) / SAME DIFFERENCE (*6) / UPRISING (*6)

LG PETROV (b. LARS GORAN PETROV, 1972) – vocals / **ALEX HELLID** (b. LOFO TWANGAKA KALLE ALEXANDER HELLID, 1973) – guitar / **UFFE CEDERLUND** (b.1971) – guitar / **LARS ROSENBERG** – bass / **NICKE ANDERSSON** – drums

Earache Earache

May 90. (lp/pic-lp/c/cd) *(MOSH 21/+P/C/CD) <2021>* **LEFT HAND PATH** 1991
– Left hand path / Drowned / Revel in flesh / When life has ceased / Supposed to rot / But life goes on / Bitter loss / Morbid devourment / Abnormally deceased / The truth beyond. *(cd+=)* – Carnal leftovers / Premature autopsy. *(cd re-iss. Aug99; MOSH 021CDL)*

— **DEVOR SAFSTROM** – vocals, guitar; repl. the sacked PETROV

Apr 91. (7") *(MOSH 038) <1075>* **CRAWL. / FORSAKEN**
(12"+=) *(MOSH 038T)* – Bitter loss.

— **JOHNNY DORDEVIC** – vocals (ex-CARNAGE) repl. SAFSTROM (although it was ANDERSSON's vocal chords that were recorded on below album)

Earache Relativity

Sep 91. (lp/cd) *(MOSH 037/+CD) <1095>* **CLANDESTINE** 1992
– Living dead / Sinners bleed / Evilyn / Blessed be / Stranger aeons / Chaos breed / Crawl / Severe burns / Through the collonades. *(cd re-iss. Aug99; MOSH 037CDL)*

Apr 92. (12"ep/cd-ep) *(MOSH 052 T/CD) <1111>* **STRANGER AEONS. / DUSK / SHREDS OF FLESH**

— **PETROV** returned to repl. DORDEVIC

Earache Columbia

Apr 93. (12"ep/cd-ep) *(MOSH 094 T/CD) <57504>* **HOLLOWMAN EP**
– Hollowman / Serpent speech / Wolverine blues / Bonehouse / Put off the scent / Hellraiser.

Sep 93. (lp/c/cd) *(MOSH 082/+C/CD) <57593>* **WOLVERINE BLUES** Jan94
– Eyemaster / Rotten soil / Wolverine blues / Demon / Contempt / Full of Hell / Blood song / Hollowman / Heavens die / Out of hand. *(cd re-iss. Aug99; MOSH 082CDL)*

Jul 94. (7"ep/12"ep/cd-ep) *(MOSH 114/+T/CD)* **OUT OF HAND. / GOD OF THUNDER / BLACK BREATH**

Jun 95. (7") *(7MOSH 132)* **NIGHT OF THE VAMPIRE. / New Bomb Turks: I HATE PEOPLE** -

— (mid'95) **JORGEN SANDSTROM** – bass (ex-GRAVE); repl. ROSENBERG

Music For Nations — Jive

Mar 97. (cd/c/lp) *(CD/T+/MFN 216)* *<41625>* **RIDE, SHOOT STRAIGHT AND SPEAK THE TRUTH** 75
– To ride, shoot straight and speak the truth / Lights out / Wound / They / DCLXVI / Parasight / Somewhat vulgar / Put me out / Just as sad / Damn deal done / Wreckage / Like this with the Devil / Boats / Mr. Uffe's horrorshow.

Oct 97. (cd-ep) *(CDMFNM 233)* **WRECKAGE (Larceny mix) / TEAR IT LOOSE / LOST / THE BALLAD OF HOLLIS BROWN / SATAN** -
(re-iss. Jun98; same)

— **PETER STJARNWIND** (b.1973) – drums (ex-FACE DOWN) repl. ANDERSSON who had already formed the HELLACOPTERS

Music For Nations — Roadrunner

Nov 98. (cd/lp) *(CD+/MFN 244)* *<RR 8616>* **SAME DIFFERENCE** Sep99
– Addiction king / The supreme good / Clauses / Kick in the head / Same difference / Close but nowhere near / What you need / High waters / 20-20 vision / The day, the Earth / Smart Aleck / Jack worm / Wolf tickets. *(cd+=)* – Kick out the jams / 21st Century schizoid man / Bursting out / Under the sun / Vices by proxy / Dagger.

Music For Nations — Sanctuary

Mar 00. (cd) *(CDMFN 257)* *<4534>* **UPRISING** Jul00
– Seeing red / Say it in slugs / Won't back down / Insanity's contagious / Something out of nothing / Scottish hell (original dead horse) / Time out / The itch / Year in year out / Return to madness / Come clean / In the flesh. *<US cd+=>* – Superior / The only ones / Words.

- compilations, etc. -

Mar 97. (m-cd) *Earache; <(MOSH 125CD)>* **ENTOMBED**
– (the EP tracks).

Sep 98. (cd) *Earache; <(MOSH 213CD)>* **MONKEY PUSS** (live in London)

Aug 00. (m-cd) *Man's Ruin; (<MR 119>)* **BLACK JU JU** (B-sides, etc) Dec99

ENUFF Z'NUFF

Formed: Chicago, Illinois, USA . . . 1988 by CHIP Z'NUFF, DONNIE VIE, DEREK FRIGO and VIKKI FOXX. Signed by DEREK SHULMAN (ex-Gentle Giant) to 'Atco' records, ENUFF Z'NUFF immediately made the grade with their eponymous debut album in 1989. Breezing in on a harmony-laden, pop-metal magic carpet, the CHEAP TRICK comparisons were rife. In addition to summoning up the musical ghost of ZANDER & Co, ENUFF Z'NUFF also shared a similar taste in flamboyant clothes, sporting defiantly retro, psychedelic finery, but please, those star-shaped glasses?! Deservedly, the album broke the US Top 75 while a subsequent single, the trippy 'FLY HIGH MICHELLE', went Top 50. A slightly more rocking follow-up album, 'STRENGTH' (1991), almost made the US Top 50 and for a moment, it looked as if ENUFF Z'NUFF might achieve substantial crossover success. It wasn't to be though, and the group subsequently languished in the margins, matters not helped any by the departure of FOXX (to VINCE NEIL's band) and record company hassles which resulted in a move to 'Arista' for 1993's 'ANIMALS WITH HUMAN INTELLIGENCE'. Further lack of sales resulted in a move to 'Music For Nations' where they released 'TWEAKED' and the impressive 'SEVEN' (1997) to little interest. 1998's imaginatively titled 'LIVE' album concentrated on the older material with a cover of The Beatles' 'REVOLUTION' thrown in for good measure yet ENUFF Z'NUFF's finely crafted hard rock arguably benefits from the comforting womb of a studio. 'PARAPHERNALIA' (1999) seemed to confirm this with a clutch of breezy yet sophisticated power-pop/metal tracks finding the band at their most relaxed and generous since the mid-90's. Again the most obvious influences were the Fab Four and Cheap Trick, a cover of the latter act's 'EVERYTHING WORKS IF YOU LET IT' featuring the ubiquitous guest talents of BILLY CORGAN. Content to go with the flow and do what they do best, regardless of fashion, ENUFF Z'NUFF satisfied retro fans once again with '10' (2000). • **Covered:** TEARS OF A CLOWN (Smokey Robinson) / JEALOUS GUY (John Lennon) / REVOLUTION (Beatles) / EVERYTHING WORKS IF YOU LET IT (Cheap Trick) / THE JEAN GENIE (David Bowie).

Album rating: ENUFF Z'NUFF (*7) / STRENGTH (*5) / ANIMALS WITH HUMAN INTELLIGENCE (*7) / TWEAKED (*5) / SEVEN (*6) / LIVE (*4) / PARAPHENALIA (*5) / 10 (*5)

DONNIE VIE – vocals / **DEREK FRIGO** – guitar (ex-LE MANS) / **CHIP Z'ENUFF** – bass / **VIKKI FOXX** – drums

Atco — Atco

Sep 89. (lp/c/cd) *(K 791262-1/-4/-2)* *<91262>* **ENUFF Z'NUFF** 74
– New thing / She wants more / Fly high Michelle / Hot little summer girl / In the groove / Indian angel / For now / Kiss the clown / I could never be without you / Finger on the trigger.

Apr 90. (7") *(B 8990)* *<99207>* **NEW THING. / KISS THE CLOWN** 67 Oct89
(12"+=/cd-s+=) *(B 8990 T/CD)* – ('A'versions).

Jul 90. (7") *(B 9135)* *<99135>* **FLY HIGH MICHELLE. / FINGER ON THE TRIGGER** 47 Jan90
(12"+=/cd-s+=) *(B 9135 T/CD)* – Hot little summer girl.

Apr 91. (cd/c/lp) *<(7567 91638-2/-4/-1)>* **STRENGTH** 56
– Heaven or Hell / Missing you / Strength / In crowd / Hollywood ya / The world is a gutter / Goodbye / Long way to go / Mother's eyes / Baby loves you / Blue island / The way home – Coming home / Something for free / Time to let you go.

May 91. (7"/7"pic-d/7"green) **MOTHER'S EYES. / LET IT GO**
(12"+=/cd-s+=) – Kitty / Little Indian angel.

Aug 91. (7") **BABY LOVES YOU. / NEW THING (live)**
(10"+=/cd-s+=) – Fly high Michelle (live) / Revolution (live).

— FRIGO departed for a month late 1991. FOXX now joined VINCE NEIL.

Arista — Arista

Mar 93. (cd/c) *<(7822 18587-2/-4)>* **ANIMALS WITH HUMAN INTELLIGENCE** Nov92
– Superstitious / Black rain / Right by your side / These daze / Master of pain / Innocence / One step closer to you / Bring it on home / Takin' a ride / The love train / Mary Anne lost her baby / Rock'n'world.

Apr 93. (7"/c-s) *(74321 14592-7/-4)* **RIGHT BY YOUR SIDE. / BRING IT ON HOME**
(12"+=/cd-s+=) *(74321 14592-1/-2)* – ('A'versions).

Music For Nations — Mayhem

Oct 95. (cd) *(CDMFN 190)* *<11077>* **TWEAKED**
– Stoned / Bullet from a gun / Mr. Jones / My dear dream / Life is strange / Without your love / We're all right / It's too late / If I can't have you / Has Jesus closed his eyes / Style / My heroin / How am I supposed to write a love song? *<(re-iss. Mar00 on 'Spitfire'; SPITCD 010)>*

Feb 97. (cd) *(CDMFN 212)* *<11082>* **SEVEN**
– Wheels / Still have tonight / 5 miles away / L.A. burning / New kind of motion / Clown on the town / U & I / On my way back home / We don't have to be / So sad to see you / Jealous guy / For you girl / I won't let you go. *(re-iss. Mar00 on 'Spitfire'; SPITMCD 009)*

Pony Canyon — Mayhem

Feb 98. (cd) *(PCCY 01193-2)* *<11125>* **LIVE (live 1997)** Jul98
– Kiss the clown / Indian angel / She wants more / Baby loves you / In the groove / Piano vie / The "in" crowd / Takin' a ride / Social disease / Runaway / Way home / Fly high Michelle / New thing / Revolution / Bring it on home. *(re-iss. Jul98 on 'Mayhem'; MAIM 111252) (re-iss. Mar00 on 'Spitfire'; SPITMCD 008)*

Mayhem — Spitfire

Oct 98. (cd) *(MAIM 11144-2)* *<15007>* **PARAPHERNALIA** May99
– Freak / Top of the hill / Ain't it funny / Believe in love / Habit / Baby you're the greatest / Someday / Unemotional / Invisible / All alone / Everything works if you let it / Loser of the world.

Z — Pony Canyon

Sep 00. (cd) *(ZR 1997034)* *<1445>* **10** Apr00
– There goes my heart / Fly away / The beast / Your heart's no good . . . / Wake up / What can I do? / Suicide / All right / Holiday / Bang on / The jean genie / Everything works if you let it.

- compilations, etc. -

Mar 99. (cd) *Big Deal; <(BGD 9007)>* **1985** (demos) Apr94
– Tears of a clown / Catholic girls / Day by day / No second time / Hollywood squares / Fingers on it / Aroused / Marie / I'll B the 1 2 luv U / Goodbye, goodbye. *(cd+=)* – (hidden track). *<(re-iss. Mar00 on 'Spitfire'; SPITMCD 012)>*

Mar 99. (cd) *Big Deal; <(BGD 9028)>* **PEACH FUZZ** (demos) Feb96
– You're not me / Let it go / Who's got you now / Rainy day / Message of love / Happy holiday / Make believe / So long / Long enough for me / Vacant love. *<(re-iss. Mar00 on 'Spitfire'; SPITMCD 011)>*

EPITAPH

Formed: Dortmund, Germany . . . 1969 by CLIFF JACKSON. Comprising an Anglo-Germanic blend of musicians, and drawing on early 70's English heavy rock, the band's self-titled debut was released in 1971 on Polydor. Both this album and 1972's 'STOP, LOOK AND LISTEN' were heavily progressive in style while 'OUTSIDE THE LAW' (1974) saw the band adopting a more basic heavy rock sound. Signed to American label 'Billinsgate', the band were primed to break into the lucrative U.S. market when disaster struck and the company went bankrupt. This effectively finished off the band although CLIFF JACKSON recruited a new cast of musicians, finally emerging with the 'RETURN TO REALITY' album in 1979 after inking a deal with 'Brain' records. Neither this album nor any subsequent efforts matched the quality of the band's earlier output and even a reformation of the original EPITAPH line-up in the early 80's failed to repeat past glories.

Album rating: EPITAPH (*6) / STOP, LOOK AND LISTEN (*7) / OUTSIDE THE LAW (*6) / RETURN TO REALITY (*5) / SEE YOU IN ALASKA (*4) / HANDICAP compilation (*7) / LIVE (*6) / DANGER MAN (*6)

CLIFF JACKSON (b. England) – vocals, guitar / **BERND KOLBE** – bass, vocals / **KLAUS WALZ** – guitar, vocals / **JIM McGILLIVRAY** – drums

Polydor — not iss.

1971. (lp) *(2371 225)* **EPITAPH** - - German
– Moving to the country / Visions / Hopelessly / Little Maggie / Early morning / London girl / Visions / I'm trying / Changing world. *(cd-iss. Apr98 on 'Repertoire'; RR 7084)*

1972. (7") **LONDON GIRL. /** - - German

1972. (7") **I'M TRYING. / CHANGING WORLD** - - German

1972. (lp) *(2371 274)* **STOP, LOOK AND LISTEN** - - German
– Crossroads / Nightingale / Uptight / Fly / Stop, look and listen. *(cd-iss. Apr98 on 'Repertoire'+=; RR 7083)* – Autumn / Are you ready / We love you Alice / Paradise for sale.

Zebra-Polydor — not iss.

Jan 73. (7") *(2047 003)* **AUTUMN '71. / ARE YOU READY** - - German

Apr 73. (7") *(2047 005)* **WE LOVE YOU ALICE. / PARADISE FOR SALE** - - German

— **ACHIM WIELERT** – drums, percussion; repl. McGILLIVRAY

Membran — Billingsgate

1974. (lp) *(22-131-1)* *<BG 1009>* **OUTSIDE THE LAW** -
– Reflexion / Woman / Big city / In your eyes / Outside the law / Tequila shuffle / Fresh air. *(re-iss. 1979 on 'Babylon'; 80.001) (cd-iss. Aug00 on 'Repertoire'; REP 4885)*

— **NORBERT LEHMANN** – drums (ex-KARTHAGO) repl. ACHIM

— split **JACKSON** but re-formed new line-up in 1977; **HEINZ GLASS** – guitar /

MICHAEL KARCH – keyboards / **HARVEY JANSSEN** – bass / **FRITZ RANDOW** – drums

Brain / not iss.

1979. (lp) *(60.185)* **RETURN TO REALITY** [-] [-] German
– Set your spirit free / Strangers / We can get together / Summer sky / On the road / Return to reality / Spread your wings.

— KARSCH departed during recording of below

1980. (lp) *(60.274)* **SEE YOU IN ALASKA** [-] [-] German
– Do you believe in love / Hold on / Bad feeling / Fantasy / See you in Alaska / When I lose your love / Keep on moving / Tonight / Telephone line.

1981. (lp) *(60.385)* **LIVE (live)** [-] [-] German
– Still alive / Hard life / Kamikaze / Tequila Fritz / Goin' to Chicago / Die high / On the road / What about me / Do you feel right.

— **JACKSON** re-united original members; *KLAUS WALZ* – guitar, vocals / **BERNIE KOLBE** – bass, vocals / **NORBERT LEHMANN** – drums, vocals

Rockport / not iss.

1982. (lp) *(RO 14)* **DANGER MAN** [-] [-] German
– Long live the children / Heartless / High wire / Snake charmer / Small town girl / Ain't no liar / Let me know / The daughter.

— split after aboves attempt

– compilations, etc. –

1979. (d-lp) *Babylon; (80.002)* **HANDICAP** [-] [-] German

EUROPE

Formed: Upplands-Vasby, Stockholm, Sweden . . . 1980 by JOEY TEMPEST, JOHN NORUM and JOHN LEVEN as FORCE. In 1982, they changed their name to EUROPE, and after a number of homeland triumphs on 'Hot', they signed to 'Epic' in 1986. Their first 45, 'THE FINAL COUNTDOWN', gave them an international breakthrough, peaking at No.1 in the UK. An epic slice of 80's pop-metal, its clarion call of a synth riff heralded equally cheesy lyrics about blasting off to Venus, or something. Storming the charts at the same time as BON JOVI's 'Livin' on a prayer', it seemed, for one heady moment, that poodle rock was taking over. It wasn't to be though, not for EUROPE anyhow, and after a further couple of hits (the hilarious 'ROCK THE NIGHT' and the obligatory ballad, 'CARRIE'), the band were consigned to the metal ghetto. Still, with a name like TEMPEST, this was a man who wasn't going out without a fight, and the band released a further two albums, 'OUT OF THIS WORLD' (1988) and 'PRISONERS IN PARADISE' (1991), before JOEY went on to clinch a solo deal with 'Polygram' in 1994. Rumours that TEMPEST is planning a pomp-metal cover of 'DANCING QUEEN' have proved unfounded. • **Songwriters:** TEMPEST wrote English lyrics. • **Trivia:** Producers were KEVIN ELSON (1st album) / RON NEVISON (2nd) / BEAU HILL (3rd).

Album rating: EUROPE (*5) / WINGS OF TOMORROW (*5) / THE FINAL COUNTDOWN (*6) / OUT OF THIS WORLD (*3) / PRISONERS IN PARADISE (*4) / 1982-92 compilation (*6)

JOEY TEMPEST (b. JOAKIM LARSSON, 19 Aug'63) – vocals / **JOHN NORUM** – guitar / **JOHN LEVEN** – bass / **JOHN RENO** – drums

Hot / not iss.

Mar 83. (lp) *(HOTLP 83001)* **EUROPE** [-] [-] Swedish
– In the future to come / Female / Seven doors hotel / The king will return / Boyazant / Children of the time / Memories / Words of wisdom / Paradise beach. *(German-iss.1985 on 'Epic'; 25365) (UK-iss.Jan87 on 'Chord' lp/c; CHORD/+TC 008) (cd-iss. Feb97 on 'Columbia'; 477786-2)*

Apr 84. (lp) *(HOTLP 84004)* **WINGS OF TOMORROW** [-] [-] Swedish
– Stormwind / Scream of anger / Open your heart / Treated bad again / Aphasia / Wings of tomorrow / Wasted time / Lyin' eyes / Dreamer / Dance the night away. *(German-iss.1985 on 'Epic'; 26384) (UK-iss.Mar88 on 'Epic' lp/c; 460213-1/-4) (cd-iss. Nov91 on 'Sony Collectors'; 982650-2)*

— **IAN HAUGHLAND** – drums, vocals repl. RENO / **KEE MARCELLO** – guitar (ex-EASY ACTION) repl. NORUM / added **MIC MICHAELI** – keyboards

Epic / Epic

Oct 86. (7"/12") *(A/TA 7127) <06416>* **THE FINAL COUNTDOWN. / ON BROKEN WINGS** [1] [8] Jan87
(3"cd-s+=) *(CD 7127)* – Heart of stone.

Nov 86. (lp/c/cd) *(EPC/40/CD 26808) <40241>* **THE FINAL COUNTDOWN** [9] [8] Oct86
– The final countdown / Rock the night / Carrie / Danger on the track / Ninja / Cherokee / Time has come / Heart of stone / On the loose / Love chaser. *(re-iss. Mar90 & Jul98 cd/c/lp; 466328-2/-4/-1)*

Jan 87. (7"/7"colrd) *(EUR/+Q 1) <07091>* **ROCK THE NIGHT. / SEVEN DOORS HOTEL** [12] [30] Apr87
(12"+=) *(EURT 1)* – Storm wind / Wings of tomorrow.

Apr 87. (7"/7"colrd) *(EUR/+Q 2) <07282>* **CARRIE. / LOVE CHASER** [22] [3] Jul87
(12"+=) *(EURT 2)* – Danger on the track.
(d7"+=) *(EURD 2)* – Open your heart / Dance the night away.

Nov 87. (7") *<07638>* **CHEROKEE. / HEART OF STONE** [-] [72]

Aug 88. (7"/7"colrd/7"s) *(EUR/+Q/C 3) <07979>* **SUPERSTITIOUS. / LIGHTS AND SHADOWS** [34] [31]
(12"+=/cd-s+=) *(EURT/CDEUR 3)* – Towers calling / The final countdown.

Aug 88. (lp/c/cd) *(462449-1/-4/-2) <44185>* **OUT OF THIS WORLD** [12] [19]
– Superstitious / Let the good times rock / Open your heart / More than meets the eye / Coast to coast / Ready or not / Sign of the times / Just the beginning / Never say die / Lights and shadows / Towers callin' / Tomorrow.

Oct 88. (7") *<08102>* **OPEN UP YOUR HEART. / TOWER'S CALLING** [-] [ ]

Oct 88. (7"/7"colrd/7"s) *(EUR/+Q/B 4)* **OPEN YOUR HEART. / JUST THE BEGINNING** [ ] [-]
(12"+=/cd-s+=) *(EURT/CDEUR 4)* – Rock the night / Lyin' eyes.

Mar 89. (7") *(EUR 5)* **LET THE GOOD TIMES ROCK. / NEVER SAY DIE** [ ] [ ]
(12"+=/cd-s+=) *(EURT/CDEUR 5)* – Carrie / Seven doors hotel.

Oct 91. (cd/c/lp) *(468755-2/-4/-1) <45328>* **PRISONERS IN PARADISE** [61] [ ]
– All or nothing / Halfway to Heaven / I'll cry for you / Little bit of lovin' / Talk to me / Seventh sign / Prisoners in Paradise / Bad blood / Homeland / Get your mind in the gutter / 'Til my heart beats down your door / Girl from Lebanon. *(pic-cd.Feb92; 468755-9)*

Jan 92. (7"/c-s) *(657697-7/-4)* **I'LL CRY FOR YOU. / BREAK FREE** [28] [ ]
(12"+=) *(657697-6)* – ('A'acoustic).
(cd-s++=) *(657697-2)* Prisoners in Paradise.

Mar 92. (7"/c-s) *(657851-7/-4)* **HALFWAY TO HEAVEN. / YESTERDAY'S NEWS** [42] [ ]
(12"+=) *(657851-6)* – Superstitious / Got your mind in the gutter.
(cd-s+=) *(657851-2)* – The final countdown / Open your heart (acoustic mix).

— folded after above

– compilations, others, etc. –

— on 'Epic' unless mentioned otherwise

Sep 90. (7") *Old Gold; (OG 9946)* **THE FINAL COUNTDOWN. / CARRIE** [ ] [-]

Dec 90. (3xcd-box) *(467393-2)* **THE FINAL COUNTDOWN / WINGS OF TOMORROW / OUT OF THIS WORLD** [ ] [-]

Jun 92. (12") *Old Gold; (OG 4228)* **ROCK THE NIGHT. / CARRIE** [ ] [-]

Apr 93. (cd/c/lp) *(473589-2/-4/-1) <57445>* **EUROPE 1982-1992** [ ] [ ]
– In the future to come / Seven doors hotel / Stormwind / Open your heart / Scream of anger / Dreamer / The final countdown / On broken wings / Rock the night / Carrie / Cherokee / Superstitious / Ready or not / Prisoners in Paradise / I'l cry for you / Sweet love child / Yesterday's news.

Jul 98. (cd) *(486576-2)* **THE DEFINITIVE COLLECTION** [ ] [-]

Dec 99. (c-s/cd-s) *(668504-4/-2)* **THE FINAL COUNTDOWN 2000 (mixes)** [39] [-]

Jan 00. (cd) *(4735899)* **GREATEST HITS 1978-2000** [ ] [-]

Jul 00. (cd) *(498633-2) <65440>* **SUPER HITS** [ ] [ ] Jan98

EVERCLEAR

Formed: Portland, Oregon, USA . . . 1991 by former teenage junkie, ART ALEXAKIS (he gave up alcohol, drugs and nicotine in June '84). Coming from a broken home, he was also dogged by the drug deaths of his girlfriend and older brother, George. Another founder member, CRAIG MONTOYA (other two, STEVEN BIRCH and SCOTT CUTHBERT) helped produce their debut indie album, 'WORLD OF NOISE', in 1994 and after rave reviews they were whisked away by 'Capitol' A&R man PERRY WATTS-RUSSELL. It was alleged that they were released from the indie, only when the gun-totting ALEXAKIS convinced the boss to let them go. By Spring '96 (and now with GREG EKLUND who had replaced CUTHBERT and BIRCH), their second album, 'SPARKLE AND FADE', had climbed into the US Top 30. A stylish anti-drug affair, it was described as ELVIS COSTELLO fused with LED ZEPPELIN, HUSKER DU or NIRVANA! ALEXAKIS and Co. returned in 1998 with a third set proper (the previous year's 'WHITE TRASH HELL' consisted of outtakes), 'SO MUCH FOR THE AFTERGLOW', the US Top 40 album almost spawning another UK Top 40 single, 'EVERYTHING TO EVERYONE'. While many of the tail-end grunge acts imploded before the 90's were through, EVERCLEAR entered the new millennium with their most ambitious project to date, a two-volume concept set exporing ALEXAKIS' divorce. 'SONGS FROM AN AMERICAN MOVIE, VOL.1: LEARNING HOW TO SMILE' (2000) covered the dating years with a peppy soundtrack inspired by the A.M. pop/rock of the frontman's youth (including a cover of Van Morrison's timeless 'BROWN EYED GIRL'). 'SONGS FROM AN AMERICAN MOVIE, VOL.2: GOOD TIME FOR A BAD ATTITUDE' (2000), meanwhile, hit the shelves a few months later and documented the dream turning sour. Unsurprisingly, the music was harder and the subject matter heavier as ALEXAKIS exorcised the pain of lost love and broken friendship. • **Covered:** HOW SOON IS NOW (Smiths).

Album rating: WORLD OF NOISE (*8) / SPARKLE AND FADE (*7) / SO MUCH FOR THE AFTERGLOW (*6) / SONGS FROM AN AMERICAN MOVIE VOL.1: LEARNING HOW TO SMILE (*7) / SONGS FROM AN AMERICAN MOVIE VOL.2: GOOD TIME FOR A BAD ATTITUDE (*5)

ART ALEXAKIS (b.12 Apr'62) – vocals, guitar / **STEVEN BIRCH** – guitar / **CRAIG MONTOYA** (b.14 Sep'70) – bass, vocals / **SCOTT CUTHBERT** – drums, vocals

not iss. / Tim/Kerr

Oct 93. (7") **NERVOUS AND WEIRD. / ELECTRA MADE ME BLIND** [-] [ ]
(cd-ep+=) – Drunk again / Lame / Connection / Slow motion genius (instrumental).

Nov 93. (cd/lp) *(FIRE CD/LP 46) <TK 59>* **WORLD OF NOISE** [-] [ ]
– Your genius hands / Sick & tired / The laughing world / Fire maple song / Pennsylvania is . . . / Nervous and weird / Malevolent / Sparkle / Trust fund / Loser makes good / Invisible / Evergleam. *<US re-iss. Nov94 on 'Capitol' cd/c; 30562-2/-4> (UK-iss.Feb95 on 'Fire' cd/lp; FIRE CD/LP 46)*

Fire / Capitol

Nov 94. (cd-ep) *<58255>* **FIRE MAPLE SONG EP** [-] [ ]
– Fire maple song / Detroit / 1975 / Blondes / Pacific wonderland (instrumental) / Fire maple song (acoustic version).

Feb 95. (cd-ep) *(BLAZE 77CD)* **FIRE MAPLE SONG EP** [ ] [-]
– Fire maple song / Loser makes good / Lame / Connection.

— **GREG EKLUND** (b.18 Apr'70) – drums, vocals; repl. CUTHBERT + BIRCH

Nov 95. (7") *<23261-7>* **HEROIN GIRL. / AMERICAN GIRL** [-] [ ]
(cd-s+=) *<23261-2>* – Annabella's song / Nahalem (alt. mix).

Capitol Capitol

Mar 96. (cd/c/lp) *(CD/TC+/EST 2257) <30929>* **SPARKLE AND FADE** [ ] [25] May95
– Electra made me blind / Heroin girl / You make me feel like a whore / Santa Monica / Summerland / Strawberry / Heartspark dollar / The twistinside / Her brand new skin / Nehalem / Queen of the air / Pale green stars / Chemical smile / My sexual life. *(d-cd re-iss. Jun98; CDESTX 2257)* – (extra tracks).

Apr 96. (cd-ep) *<58538>* **HEARTSPARK DOLLARSIGN / HEROIN GIRL (acoustic) / SIN CITY / HAPPY HOUR** [-] [85]

May 96. (7"clear) *(CL 773)* **HEARTSPARK DOLLARSIGN. / LOSER MAKES GOOD (live)** [48] [-]
(cd-s+=) *(CDCL 773)* – Sparkle (live).
(cd-s) *(CDCLS 773)* – ('A'side) / Pennsylvania is . . . (live) / Nervous & weird (live).

Aug 96. (7") *(CL 775)* **SANTA MONICA (WATCH THE WORLD DIE). / AMERICAN GIRL (KDGE version)** [40] [-]
(cd-s+=) *(CDCL 775)* – Strawberry (KDGE version) / Fire maple song (KDGE version).
(cd-s) *(CDCLS 775)* – ('A'side) / Heroin girl (KDGE version) / Summerland (KDGE version) / Sin city.

Sep 96. (cd-s) **YOU MAKE ME FEEL LIKE A WHORE / AMERICAN GIRL (live) / LIKE BRANDON DOES (by Klinger)** [-] [ ]

—— added **CHRIS BIRCH** – guitar

Mar 98. (cd/c) *<(36503-2/-4/-1)>* **SO MUCH FOR THE AFTERGLOW** [63] [33] Oct97
– So much for the afterglow / Everything to everyone / Ataraxia / Normal like you / I will buy you a new life / Father of mine / One hit wonder / El distorto de melodica / Amphetamine / White men in black suits / Sunflower / Why don't I believe in God / Like a California king.

Apr 98. (7") *(CL 799)* **EVERYTHING TO EVERYONE. / OUR LIPS ARE SEALED** [41] [ ]
(cd-s+=) *(CDCL 799)* – What do I get / ('A'-CD-Rom video).
(cd-s) *(CDCLS 799)* – ('A'side) / Walk don't run / Search and destroy / Santa Monica heroin (CD-Rom video).

Jul 98. (cd-s) *<85592>* **I WILL BUY YOU A NEW LIFE** [-] [ ]

Nov 98. (cd-s) *<86181>* **FATHER OF MINE** [-] [70]

Aug 00. (cd) *(527864-2) <97061>* **SONGS FROM AN AMERICAN MOVIE VOL.1 - LEARNING HOW TO SMILE** [51] [9] Jul00
– Songs from an American movie (part 1) / Here we go again / AM radio / Brown eyed girl / Learning how to smile / The honeymoon song / Now that it's over / Thrift store chair / Otis Redding / Unemployed boyfriend / Wonderful / Annabella's song.

Oct 00. (c-s) *(TCCL 824) <album cut>* **WONDERFUL / FATHER OF MINE (remix) / I'M ON YOUR TIME** [36] [11] Apr00
(cd-s+=) *(CDCLS 824)* – ('A'-CD-ROM video)>

Mar 01. (cd-s) *(CDCL 827)* **AM RADIO / I'M ON YOUR TIME / SANTA MONICA (live from Woodstock)** [ ] [-]

Apr 01. (cd) *(530419-2) <95873>* **SONGS FROM AN AMERICAN MOVIE VOL.2 - GOOD TIME FOR A BAD ATTITUDE** [69] [ ] Nov00
– When it all goes wrong again / Slide / Babytalk / Rock star / Short blonde hair / Misery whip / Out of my depth / The good witch of the north / Halloween Americana / All f**ked up / Overwhelming / Song from an American movie (part 2).

– compilations, etc. –

Aug 95. (cd) *Imprint; <97633>* **LIVE FROM TORONTO (live)** [-] [ ]

Apr 97. (m-cd) *Fire; (MCD 45)* **WHITE TRASH HELL** [ ] [-]
– Heroin girl (demo) / Detroit / 1975 / Blondes / Pacific wonderland (instrumental) / For Pete's sake / Fire maple song (acoustic).

EVERY MOTHER'S NIGHTMARE

Formed: Nashville, Tennessee, USA . . . 1989 by RICK RUHL and STEVE MALONE, who soon enlisted the help of MARK McMURTRY and JIM PHIPPS. Signed to 'Arista', the group eschewed the country music trappings of their hometown for a classy, hard-rock sound, showcased on their eponymous 1990 debut album. Although EMN gained some favourable reviews in the music press and were flavour of the month for erm . . . a month, they subsequently faded into obscurity.

Album rating: EVERY MOTHER'S NIGHTMARE (*6)

RICK RUHL – vocals / **STEVE MALONE** – guitar / **MARK McMURTRY** – bass / **JIM PHIPPS** – drums

Arista Arista

Jun 90. (c-s) *<2078>* **LOVE CAN MAKE YOU BLIND / EASY COME, EASY GO** [-] [ ]

Jul 90. (cd/c/lp) *(260/410/210 921) <ARCD/ARC/ARL 8633>* **EVERY MOTHER'S NIGHTMARE** [ ] [ ]
– Hard to hold / Bad on love / Love can make you blind / Dues to pay / Lord willin' / EZ come, EZ go / Walls come down / Listen up / Long haired country boy / Nobody knows.

—— disbanded in '91

EVILDEAD

Formed: Los Angeles, California, USA . . . 1988 by ex-AGENT STEEL guitarist, JUAN GARCIA, who recruited PHIL FLORES, ALBERT GONZALES and ROB AILINZ. Signing to the German 'Steamhammer' label, the group made their debut in 1988 with 'RISE ABOVE'. A derivative old-school thrash-metal act, EVILDEAD now appear rather tame in comparison with the blood-soaked death-metal hordes from Florida, Sweden etc., and subsequent albums, 'ANNIHILATION OF CIVILISATION' (1990) and 'THE UNDERWORLD' failed to adequately update their sound, despite an almost completely new line-up on the latter.

Album rating: ANNIHILATION OF CIVILIZATION (*5) / THE UNDERWORLD (*4)

PHIL FLORES – vocals / **JUAN GARCIA** – guitar (ex-AGENT STEEL, ex-ABATTOIR) / **ALBERT GONZALES** – guitar / **ROB AILINZ** – drums (ex-NECROPHILIA)

Steamhammer Roadracer

1988. (12"ep/cd-ep) *(5075 77/90) <RC/+C 9466>* **RISE ABOVE / RUN AGAIN. / SLOE-DEATH / S.T. RIFF** [ ] [ ]

1990. (cd)(lp) *(847603)(087602)* **ANNIHILATION OF CIVILIZATION** [ ] [ ]
– F.C.I. / The awakening / Annihilation of civilization / Living good / Future shock / Holy trails / Gone shooting / Parricide / Unauthorized exploitation / B.O.H.I.C.A.

—— **GARCIA + FLORES** recruited new line-up; **DAN FLORES** – guitar / **KARLOS MEDINA** – bass / **DOUG "The Claw" CLAWSON** – drums

1991. (cd) *(084-76362)* **THE UNDERWORLD** [ ] [ ]
– Intro (comshell) / Global warning / Welcome to Kuwait / Critic – Cynic / The hood / The underworld / He's a woman – she's a man / Process elimination / Labyrinth of the mind / Reap what you sow.

—— split around 1991

EVIL SUPERSTARS

Formed: Antwerp, Belgium . . . 1993 by former school mates, MAURO PAWLOWSKI, TIM VANHAMEL, MARC REQUILE, BART VANDEBROEK and DAVE SCHROYEN. One of a growing number of North European bands to make inroads into the influential British market, the evil ones debuted late in 1995 with the EP, 'HAIRFACTS'. Presumably the band were also capable of breaking an ill wind with the best of them, given the title of their follow-up single, 'SATAN IS IN MY ASS'. (F)Art-rockers on a mission to twist our minds with their sexy, sleazy sounds (think of GIRLS AGAINST BOYS meeting The FLAMING LIPS influenced by Euro-rock), the evil ones finally delivered the surprisingly titled 'LOVE IS OKAY' (1996). The group subsequently released a couple of stop gap singles prior to the issue of a second set, 'BOOGIE CHILDREN-R-US' (1998), proving boys and their toys can never be parted.

Album rating: LOVE IS OKAY (*5) / BOOGIE CHILDREN-R-US (*6)

MAURO PAWLOWSKI – vocals, guitar / **TIM VANHAMEL** – guitar / **MARC REQUILE** – keyboards / **BART VANDEBROEK** – bass / **DAVE SCHROYEN** – drums

Paradox not iss.

Nov 95. (7"ep) *(PDOX 007)* **HAIRFACTS EP** [ ] [-]
– Must be mystery puke / Stay angry / (Nothing but a) Sluthead / Nice feelings now.

Feb 96. (7") *(PDOX 009)* **SATAN IS IN MY ASS. / SCRATCH** [ ] [-]
(cd-s+=) *(PDOXD 009)* – Worse than Kafka / Fucking love.

Feb 96. (cd/lp) *(PDOX CD/LP 002)* **LOVE IS OKAY** [ ] [-]
– No more bad people / Power of Haha / Go home for lunch / Parasol / Your dump or mine / Rocking all over / Pantomiming with her parents / Oh funlump / We need your head / 1,000,000 demons can't be wrong / Satan is in my ass / Death by summer. *(cd+=)* – Miss your disease.

Jun 96. (7") *(PDOX 010)* **PANTOMIMING WITH HER PARENTS. / HOLY PEOPLE'S BONER** [ ] [-]
(cd-s+=) *(PDOXD 010)* – March of the losers' families / A higher ugliness.

Mar 97. (7"ep) *(PDOX 016)* **REMIX APOCALYPSE EP** [ ] [-]
– I will always remember lust / It's a sad sad planet / Darkage disco / Waiting for Elvis.
(cd-ep+=) *(PDOX/+D 016)* – Rock against romance / A few screams for the teens / Last children.

Mar 98. (7") *(PDOX 017)* **B.A.B.Y. / X-MASLESS FOREVER / (WE WANT) THE NEW PAIN** [ ] [-]
(cd-s+=) *(PDOXD 017)* – Failure machine.

May 98. (7") *(PDOX 019)* **IT'S A SAD SAD PLANET. / GOOD NEWS FOR WOMEN** [ ] [-]
(cd-s+=) *(PDOXD 019)* – Years of science.

Jun 98. (cd/lp) *(PDOX 018 CD/LP)* **BOOGIE CHILDREN-R-US** [ ] [-]
– B.A.B.Y. / If you cry (I'll go to hell) / I've been wrong before / Can't seem to fuck things up / Gimme animal rights / Just a princess / Oh girl / It's a sad sad planet / Holy spirit come home / First comes farewell / Song off the record / My little dead one / Laserblack / Love happened.

—— looks like the EVIL ones are no more

the EX

Formed: Amsterdam, Netherlands . . . 1977 by G.W. SOK and TERRIE HESSELS. Over the years, The EX brought in a sizeable cast of musicians and singers to complement each release. The first of these, 'DISTURBING DOMESTIC PEACE' (1980), found its way to British shores via import where it was playlisted by Radio One DJ, John Peel. This agit-prop punk collective were finally let loose on a UK label in 1984 courtesy of a shared EP, 'RED DANCE PACKAGE' with ALERTA. A brief stint on the 'Ron Johnson' imprint (with the double 7" EP, 'THE SPANISH REVOLUTION – 1936'), paved the way for the EX to set up their own self-titled indie late in 1987. Always ready to experiment with various musical genres, the left-wing musical activists subsequently worked with SONIC YOUTH's LEE RANALDO and THURSTON MOORE, while on 1990's 'DEAD FISH' set, they were produced by JON LANGFORD of The MEKONS. That year's 'STONE STAMPERS SONG' was adapted from composer, KURT TUCHOLSKY, the band also working with avant-garde violinist, TOM CORA on subsequent collaborative albums, 'SCRABBLING AT THE DOCK' (1991) and 'SHRUG THEIR SHOULDERS' (1993).

Album rating: DISTURBING DOMESTIC PEACE (*5) / HISTORY IS WHAT'S HAPPENING (*5) / TUMULT (*5) / BLUEPRINTS FOR A BLACKOUT (*5) / POKKEHERRIE (*6) / THE SPANISH REVOLUTION 1936 double-7"EP (*7) / TOO MANY COWBOYS (*5) / HANDS UP YOU'RE FREE (*5) / AURAL GUERILLA (*5) /

JOGGERS AND SMOGGERS (*4) / DEAD FISH (*4) / SCRABBLING AT THE LOCK (*5) / SHRUG THEIR SHOULDERS (*4) / MUDBIRD SHIVERS (*4) / INSTANT (*5)

G.W. SOK – vocals / **TERRIE HESSELS** – guitar / **BASZ** – bass / **OME GUERT** – drums

Verrecords — not iss.

1980. (7"ep) *(EX 001)* **ALL CORPSES SMELL THE SAME EP** [-] [-] Dutch
1980. (7"flexi) *(EX 002)* **NEW HORIZONS IN RETAILING** [-] [-] Dutch
1980. (lp) *(EX 005)* **DISTURBING DOMESTIC PEACE** [-] [-] Dutch
– The sky is blue again / Map / Outlook-army / Sucking pig / Sense of tumour / Meanwhile / Rules / Squatalong / Warning-shot / New wars / Introduction / Human car / Punk / Horse. *(with free live-7") (UK cd-iss. Jun94 on 'Konkurrent'; EX 004-005D)*
Apr 81. (7") *(EX 006)* **WAR IS OVER (WEAPONS FOR EL SALVADOR). / DUST / NEW WARS II** [-] [-] Dutch
Jun 81. (7"flexi) *(EX 007)* **CONSTITUTIONAL STATE** [-] [-] Dutch

— **WIM** – drums; repl. OME

More DPM — not iss.

1982. (lp) **HISTORY IS WHAT'S HAPPENING** [ ] [-] Dutch
– Six of one and half a dozen of the other / Barricades / Life line / Machinery / E.M. why / Moving pictures / Shoes / Watch-dogs / Dutch disease / Blessed box at the back-seat / Who pays / Strong & muscled / Grey / Equals only / H'wood – W'ton / Sports / $ / Pep talk / Attacked / 148.

— over the next decade or so, **G.W. SOK + HESSELS** added **KARTIN BORNFELD + SABIEN WITTEMAN** – drums / **JOS KLEY** – vocals / **JOKE LAARMAN + LUC KLASSEN** – bass / **DOLF PLANTEYDT + TOM GREENE** – guitar / **WINEKE T. HART** – violin / **KEES VANDEN HAAK** – saxophone

Sneeleeer — not iss.

Jun 83. (7"ep) **GONNA ROB THE SPERMBANK** [-] [-] Dutch
– Soldier toy / etc.

C.N.T. — not iss.

Feb 84. (12"ep) *(CNT 017)* **RED DANCE PACKAGE** (shared w/ ALERTA) [ ] [-]
– EX:- Crap rap / Long live the aged / ALERTA:- Perk avenue / Violet days.

V.G.Z. — not iss.

Feb 84. (7"box) *(EX 010-013)* **DIGNITY OF LABOUR** [ ] [-]
– Sucked out Cnucked out (parts 1-8). *(cd-iss. Aug95 on 'Konkurrent'; EX 010-013D)*

F.A.I. — not iss.

Nov 83. (lp) *(EX 014)* **TUMULT** [-] [-] Dutch
– Bouquet of barbed wire / Fear / Hunt the hunters / Survival of the fattest / Red musak / Happy thoughts / Well-known soldier / Black and white statements / Squat! / Same old news / F.U.N.E.I.D.Y. / O.S.L. (new schvienhunt league) / Island race. *(UK-iss.May93 on 'Konkurrent'; EX 14D) <US cd-iss. 1994 on 'Fist Puppet'; 19>*

Pig Brother — not iss.

Apr 84. (lp) *(EX 019)* **BLUEPRINTS FOR A BLACKOUT** [ ] [-]
– Streetcars named DEsire – Animal harmonies / Blueprints for a blackout / Rabble with a cause / Requiem for a rip-off / Pleased to meet you / Goodbuy to you / Swim / Boo hoo / U.S. hole / (Not) 2B continued / Grimm stories / Plague to survive / Rise of the Dutch republic / Kidnap connection / Fire and ice / Jack Frost is innocent / Love you till eh / Food on 45 / Scrub that scum. *(cd-iss. May93 on 'Konkurrel-Ex'; EX 19D) <US cd-iss. 1994 on 'Fist Puppet'; 13>*

Pockabilly — not iss.

Nov 85. (d-lp) *(EX 024)* **POKKEHERRIE** [ ] [-]
– Nurse / Soviet threat / Mmm crisis / 1,000,000 ashtrays / Rock / White liberals / Everything we never wanted / Friendly neighbors / Hit the headlines / Rumours of music (the original soundtrack). *(cd-iss. Aug95 on 'Konkurrel'; EX 024D)*

Ron Johnson — not iss.

Jul 86. (d7"ep) *(ZRON 11)* **THE SPANISH REVOLUTION – 1936** [ ] [-]
– They shall not pass / Al Carmela / People again / E tron Bundano. *(re-iss. Jan89 & Nov97 on 'Ex'; EX 028-029)*

Mordam — not iss.

Jul 87. (d-lp) *(5)* **TOO MANY COWBOYS** [ ] [-]
– Red and black / White shirts / Adversity / People again / Knock / Hands up! you're free / Ignorance / Butter or bombs / Dumbo / How can one sell the air / Business as usual / Olympigs / Choice / Job / Stupid / Oops / No fear / Vivisection / Piece of paper / They shal not pass. *<US cd-iss. 1994 on 'Fist Puppet'; 19>*

Red — not iss.

1987. (c) **LIVE IN WROCLAW (live)** [-] [-] Dutch

Ex — Homestead

Apr 88. (lp) *(EX 035)* *<HMS 116>* **HANDS UP! YOU'RE FREE** (compilation of John Peel sessions) [ ] [ ] Sep88
Jul 88. (lp) *(EX 036)* *<HMS 115>* **AURAL GUERRILLA** [ ] [ ]
– Headache by numbers / Fashionation / 2.2 / Carcass / Welcome to the asylum / Meanwhile at McDonna's / Shooting party / Evolution(?) / A motorbike in Afrika / Godgloeiendeteringklootzat. *<cd-iss. 1994 on 'Fist Puppet'; 21>*

Ex — Fist Puppet

Oct 89. (d-lp/d-cd) *(EX 040/041)* *<05>* **JOGGERS & SMOGGERS** [ ] [ ] 1990
– Humm (the full house mumble) / At the gate / Pigs and scales / Coughing / Morning star / The wall has ears / Invitation to the dance / Tightly stretched / Ask the prisoner / To be clear / Gentlemen / Make that call / Buzzword medley / Shopping street / Crackle engines vrop vrop / Greetings from Urbania / Wired / Got everything? / Waarom niet / Courtyard / Burst! crack! split! / Brickbat / Hieronymus / Nosey Parker / People who venture / Watch the driver / Let's get sceptical / Tin gods / State of freedom / Provisionally untitled / Kachun-K pschuh / Early bird's worm / Catkin / Upstairs with Picasso.
May 90. (7") *(EX 043)* **STONE STAMPERS SONG. /** [ ] [-]
Jun 90. (12"ep/cd-ep) *(EX 044/+CD)* **DEAD FISH EP** [ ] [-]
– Elvis & I / White liberals / Blah blah / Mousetrap / Dead fish / No more cigars.

— In 1990, the EX also collaborated with the DOG FACED HERMANS on a cassette-only release, 'TREAT'.

Mar 91. (7") *(EX)* **SLIMY TOAD JAKE'S CAFE. /** [ ] [-]
Mar 92. (lp/cd; The EX / TOM CORA) *(EX 051/+CD)* **SCRABBLING AT THE LOCK** [ ] [-]
– State of shock / Hidegen fujnak a szelek / King commie / Crusoe / The flute's tale / A door / Propadada / Batium / Total preparation / 1993 / Fire and ice / Sukaina.
above was a collaboration with violin player **TOM CORA**
May 92. (7") **THIS SONG IS IN ENGLISH. /** [ ] [-]
(above issued on 'Palber')
Jul 92. (12") *(EX 066)* **EUROCONFUSION. /** [ ] [-]
Sep 93. (cd; The EX / TOM CORA) *(EX 57CD)* **SHRUG THEIR SHOULDERS** [ ] [-]
– Dere gellyor dere / The big black / What's the story / Lamp lady / One-liner from China / Everything & me / New clear daze / Oh puckerlips now / Empty V / Okinawa mon amour / Dear house / Conviction going gaga / Stupid competitions / Hickwall / War OD / Untitled. *(re-iss. Feb94 as 'AND THE WEATHERMEN SHRUG THEIR SHOULDERS' on 'Fist Puppet'; 15)*
Aug 95. (cd) *(EX 060D)* **MUDBIRD SHIVERS** [ ] [-]
– Thunderstruck blues / Only if you want 3 / Ret Roper / Embarrassment / House carpenter / Newsense / Former reporter / Shore thing / Things most people think / Audible bacillus / Hunt hat.
Nov 95. (d-cd; The EX & GUESTS) *(EX 063-064D)* **INSTANT** [ ] [-]
– If the hat fits the suit / Duo rumpus / Kloptimog twist / Baars vs. Karakeit / Keng lil surf / Duo triptych too / Lip up, stump / So low, solex? / Skoplje bop / Buildance / Bratunac / Horsemeal / Expoobident / Slow sleeper / Duo loom / Te-au-o-tonga // Travel on, poor Bob / What inflexibility?! / Bon-go tell you git-la-la / Duo variola / Meanwhile back in Ozone street / Smuiger / Rusticles / Atoll / Exile o'phonics / Danse maudit / Knit, knack & zoom / Oh muted foghorn / Duo tonebone & hitgit / The turtle the hare / Karreman's last measure / Thereweresonicbangsinthesong . . .

Touch & Go — Touch & Go

Oct 98. (cd) *(<TG 198>)* **STARTERS & ALTERNATORS** [ ] [ ]
– Frenzy / Let's panic later / I.O.U. (nought) / Art of losing / It's a sin / Two struck by the moon / Mother / Bee coz / Lump sum insomnia / Wildebeast / Nem ugy van most.

– others, etc. –

Aug 95. (12"ep) *Moonroof; <50015>* **WE MUST GO FREE** [ ] [-]
Nov 00. (3xcd-box) *Alternative Tentacles; <(VIRUS 253)> ⇒SPANISH REVOLUTION* [ ] [ ]

EXCALIBUR

Formed: Yorkshire, England . . . 1981 by schoolboys PAUL McBRIDE, PAUL SOLYNSKYJ, MARTIN HAWTHORN and MICK DOBSON. Signing to the small 'Conquest' label, the group debuted in Autumn '85 with 'THE BITTER END', a promising if hardly original slab of melodic brit-metal. With the addition of Scot, STEVE BLADES, the group recorded a session for Radio 1's Tommy Vance in 1986, the tracks subsequently released as the 'HOT FOR LOVE' EP (1988). A number of personnel changes ensued with DAVE SYKES and GEOFF LIVERMORE replacing DOBSON and HAWTHORNE respectively prior to the release of their much praised 'ONE STRANGE NIGHT' (1990) opus. Just when it looked as if the band were poised for greater things, McBRIDE took his leave, the band splitting soon after.

Album rating: THE BITTER END mini (*5) / ONE STRANGE NIGHT (*6)

PAUL McBRIDE – vocals / **PAUL SOLYNSKYJ** – guitar / **MARTIN HAWTHORN** – bass / **MICK DOBSON** – drums

Conquest — not iss.

Sep 85. (m-lp) *(QUEST 5)* **THE BITTER END** [ ] [-]
– I'm telling you / Devil in disguise / The bitter end / Only time can tell / Come on and rock / Haunted by the shadows.

— added **STEVE BLADES** (b. Scotland) – guitar, keyboards

Clay — not iss.

Aug 88. (12"ep) *(PLATE 9)* **HOT FOR LOVE** [ ] [-]
– Hot for love / Early in the morning / Come on and rock / Deaths door.

— **DAVE SYKES** – drums; repl. DOBSON

— (1989) **GEOFF LIVERMORE** – bass; repl. HAWTHORN

Active — not iss.

Feb 90. (12"ep) *(12ATV 101)* **CAROLE ANN. / EARLY IN THE MORNING / SICK AND TIRED** [ ] [-]
Mar 90. (cd/lp) *(CD+/ATV 10)* **ONE STRANGE NIGHT** [ ] [-]
– Una notte strana / Fight / Waiting / Lights go down / Round and round / Frozen promises / Early in the morning / Carole Ann / Running scared / Death's door. *(cd+=)* – Sick and tired.

— **DEAN WILSON** – bass; repl. LIVERMORE

— band split in 1991 when McBRIDE departed

EX-CATHEDRA

Formed: Glasgow (or nearby) . . . 1994 by guitarist ALEX and his motley crew of Ska-punks (MACHINE GUN ETIQUETTE drummer, PARKER, was also a member). Influenced by RANCID and G.B.H. (remember them!), EX-CATHEDRA were part of the old skool hardcore punk brigade (with Ska being top of the class). A few releases on their own 'Tartan' label, helped the band build up their profile as tours and V/A demos (alongside MACHINE GUN ETIQUETTE and Germany's NUTCASE) filled their time. Inking a deal with 'Damaged Goods', EX-CATHEDRA released their 'TARTAN MATERIAL' set in '96, while Scandic tours with their 'ETIQUETTE chums ensured more notoriety; both ALEX and PARKER filled in for this band while personnel changes were rife. A split EP with MGE was subsequently scheduled (with benefits going to a squat in the Czech Republic town of Ladronka), although this was postponed while a sophomore album, 'FORCED KNOWLEDGE' (2000), hit some retail shops. • **Note:** don't get mixed up with Michael Lautenschlaeger's 'Ex-Cathedra' New Age set for 'Terra Nova' in the mid-90's and even more so, the 'Sir Christmas' festive offering around the same time.

ALEX – guitar / **PARKER** – drums / + others

Tartan / not iss.

Sep 94. (7") *(TARTAN 1)* **STICK TOGETHER. /** -
Jun 95. (7"ep) *(TAR 002)* **WATCH OUT EP** -

Damaged Goods / not iss.

Dec 95. (7") *(DAMGOOD 83)* **TRESPASS. /** -
Sep 96. (lp/cd) *(DAMGOOD 106/+CD)* **TARTAN MATERIAL** -
– Directions / Watch-out / Buckfast happy / Something coming down / Reasons / Dirty ol' town / Stick together / Waiting game / Stop yer running / Buckfast (reprise) / Hooligans in suits / Shock wi' surprise.
Jul 97. (7"m) *(DAMGOOD 131)* **KARMA CHAMELEON. / +2** -

Moon Ska / not iss.

Jul 00. (cd) *(MOONCD 048)* **FORCED KNOWLEDGE** -
– Breakdown / Just begun / Trapped / Truth in flight / Down to fate / Give me tomorrow / Anaesthetised / Something new / Your time / Needles / Just another war song / Geno.

EXCITER

Formed: Ottawa, Canada . . . 1979 by DAN BEEHLER, JOHN RICCI and ALLAN JOHNSON. Taking their name from a JUDAS PRIEST track, EXCITER traded in high-octane metal of a distinctly 80's hue. Signed to Mike Varney's 'Shrapnel' label on the strength of their 'HEAVY METAL MANIAC' demo, the cassette was soon given a proper domestic release in 1983. The set was strong enough to interest 'Music For Nations' and the band released a more polished follow-up for the label, 'VIOLENCE AND FORCE', in early '84. Taking their uncompromising stage show to Europe, the group toured with German metallers ACCEPT in support of a third set, 'LONG LIVE THE LOUD' (1985). There were criticisms from some quarters that the group were moving away from the ferocity of their earlier recordings, this chorus of dissent growing even louder with the release of 'UNVEILING THE WICKED' (1986), a set which featured the talents of new guitarist BRIAN McPHEE (a replacement for JOHN RICCI). In a desperate effort to shake themsleves out of terminal decline, the group subsequently recruited frontman ROB MALNATI. Despite a harder-edged approach, further albums 'OVER THE TOP' (1989) and 'KILL AFTER KILL' (1992) failed to improve the group's ailing fortunes and EXCITER eventually faded from view.

Album rating: HEAVY METAL MANIAC (*6) / VIOLENCE AND FORCE (*6) / LONG LIVE THE LOUD (*5) / UNVEILING THE WICKED (*4) / EXCITER (*4) / KILL AFTER KILL (*4) / BETTER LIVE THAN DEAD (*4) / THE DARK COMMAND (*4) / BLOOD OF TYRANTS (*4)

DAN BEEHLER – vocals, drums / **JOHN RICCI** – guitar, vocals / **ALLAN JOHNSON** – bass, vocals

not iss. / Shrapnel

1983. (lp) *<1004>* **HEAVY METAL MANIAC** - Canada
– The holocaust / Stand up and fight / Heavy metal maniac / Iron dogs / Mistress of evil / Under attack / Rising of the dead / Blackwitch / Cry of the banshee. *(UK-iss.Apr86 on 'Roadrunner'; RR 9710) (cd-iss. Apr89 on 'Roadracer'; RO 9710-2)*

Music For Nations / not iss.

Feb 84. (lp) *(MFN 17)* **VIOLENCE & FORCE** -
– Oblivion / Violence & force / Scream in the night / Pounding metal / Evil sinner / Destructor / Swords of darkness / Delivering to the master / Saxons of the fire / War is hell.
May 85. (lp) *(MFN 47)* **LONG LIVE THE LOUD** -
– Fall out / Long live the loud / I am the beast / Victims of sacrifice / Beyond the gates of doom / Sudden impact / Born to die / Wake up screaming.
Jun 85. (12") *(12KUT 113)* **FEEL THE KNIFE. / VIOLENCE AND FORCE** -

— **BRIAN McPHEE** – guitar, vocals; repl. RICCI

Aug 86. (cd/c/lp) *(CD/T+/MFN 61)* **UNVEILING THE WICKED** -
– Break down the walls / Brainstorm / Die in the night / (I hate) School rules / Shout it out / Invasion – Waiting in the dark / Living vile / Live fast die young / Mission destroy.

— added **ROB MALNATI** – vocals

Maze / Maze

1989. (lp)(cd) *(MML 1040)* **EXCITER** Canada
– Scream bloody murder / Back in the light / Ready to rock / O.T.T. / I wanna be king / Enemy lines / Dying to live / Playin' with fire / Eyes in the sky / Termination.

Noise / Spy

Apr 92. (cd/c/lp) *(N 0192-2/-4/-1)* **KILL AFTER KILL**
– Rain of terror / No life no future / Cold blooded murder / Smashin' 'em down / Shadow of the cross / Dog eat dog / Anger, hate and destruction / Second coming / Born to kill (live).

Bleeding Hearts / Bleeding Hearts

Mar 93. (cd) *(CDBLEED 5)* **BETTER LIVE THAN DEAD (live)**
– Stand up and fight / Heavy metal maniac / Victims of sacrifice / Under attack / Sudden impacts / Delivering to the master / I am the beast / Black witch / Long live the loud / Rising of the dead / Cry of the banshee / Pounding metal / Violence and force. *(<re-iss. +US Sep99; same)>*

— **RIK CHARRON** – drums; repl. temp

Osmose / S.P.V.

Nov 97. (cd/lp) *(OSCD/OSLP 059)* *<72005>* **THE DARK COMMAND** Mar98
– The dark command / Burn at the stake / Aggressor / Assassins in rage / Ritual death / Sacred war / Let us prey / Executioner / Suicide overdose / Screams from the gallows.

Osmose / Osmose

Jul 00. (cd/lp) *(<OSCD/OSLP 089>)* **BLOOD OF TYRANTS** May01
– Metal crusaders / Rule with an iron fist / Intruders / Predator / Martial law / War cry / Brutal warning / Weapons of mass destruction / Blood of tyrants / Violator.

EXIT-13 (see under ⇒ BRUTAL TRUTH)

EXODUS

Formed: San Francisco, California, USA . . . 1982 by TOM HUNTING alongside GARY HOLT, PAUL BALOFF and KIRK HAMMETT, the latter subsequently being poached by METALLICA with RICK HUNOLT coming in as a replacement. Premier exponents of second division thrash, EXODUS made a career out of workmanlike metal, despite the fact they're often cited as kickstarting the Bay Area scene. Signed to 'Combat' records (licensed to 'Music For Nations' in Britain), the group finally released a debut set in 1985, 'BONDED IN BLOOD'. On the strength of this set it was clear EXODUS hadn't named themselves after the BOB MARLEY album, a prototype piece of guitar savagery which was admittedly exciting for the time if not quite matching up to METALLICA's 'Kill 'Em All' for example. With STEVE SOUSA replacing BALOFF, the group recorded a follow-up, 'PLEASURES OF THE FLESH' (1987). Almost as brutal with equally strangulated vocals, the set began with what sounded like a mental patient gibbering away to his psychiatrist. All cliches present and correct, then, in addition to lyrics which lent new meaning to cheesiness, 'BRAIN DEAD', 'DERANGED', etc. Still, to give them their due, there was an anti-pollution track, 'CHEMI-KILL', raging incoherently at all manner of targets. With JOHN TEMPESTA replacing HUNTING on drums, the group recorded a third set, 'FABULOUS DISASTER' (1989) which predictably failed to give them the much heralded breakthrough. EXODUS even attracted the attentions of 'Capitol' who attempted to jump on the (by now ailing) thrash bandwagon with subsequent releases, 'IMPACT IS IMMINENT' (1990) and 'FORCE OF HABIT' (1992). Unfortunately for EXODUS, success was always imminent but never quite came, the band finally splitting after the latter set. In 1997, they resurfaced once more with a live set, 'ANOTHER LESSON IN VIOLENCE'.

Album rating: BONDED BY BLOOD (*6) / PLEASURES OF THE FLESH (*6) / FABULOUS DISASTER (*5) / IMPACT IS IMMINENT (*6) / GOOD FRIENDLY VIOLENT FUN collection (*4) / THE BEST OF EXODUS: LESSONS IN VIOLENCE compilation (*7) / FORCE OF HABIT (*5) / ANOTHER LESSON IN VIOLENCE (*5)

PAUL BALOFF – vocals / **RICK HUNOLT** – guitars / **GARY HOLT** – guitars / **ROB McKILLOP** – bass / **TOM HUNTING** – drums

Music For Nations / Combat

Apr 85. (lp) *(MFN 44)* *<8019>* **BONDED BY BLOOD**
– Bonded by blood / Exodus / And then there were none / A lesson in love / Metal command / Piranha / No love / Deliver us to evil / Strike of the beast. *(cd-iss. Feb90+=; CDMFN 44)* – And then there were none (live) / Lesson in violence (live). *(cd re-iss. Nov99 on 'Century Media'; CM 66024-2)*

— **STEVE SOUZA** – vocals; repl. BALOFF who formed PIRAHNA

Nov 87. (lp) *(MFN 77)* *<8169>* **PLEASURES OF THE FLESH** 82
– Deranged / 'Till death do us part / Parasite / Brain dead / Faster than you'll ever live to be / Pleasures of the flesh / 30 seconds / Seeds of hate / Chemi-kill / Choose your weapon. *(pic-lp Jan88; MFN 77P) (cd-iss. Aug89; CDMFN 77) (cd re-iss. Nov99 on 'Century Media'; CM 66044-2)*

— **JOHN TEMPESTA** – drums; repl. HUNTING

Feb 89. (cd/c/lp)(pic-lp) *(CD/T+/MFN 90)(MFN 90P) <2001>* **FABULOUS DISASTER** 82
– The last act of defiance / Fabulous disaster / The toxic waltz / Low rider / Cajun hell / Like father like son / Corruptions / Verbal razors / Open season. *(cd+=)* – Overdose. *(cd re-iss. Nov99 on 'Century Media'; CM 66033-2)*

Capitol / Capitol

Jul 90. (cd/c/lp) *(CD/TC+/EST 2125)* *<90379>* **IMPACT IS IMMINENT**
– Impact is imminent / A.W.O.L. / Lunatic parade / Within the walls of chaos / Objection overruled / Only death decides / Heads they win (tails you lose) / Changing of the guard / Thrash under pressure.
Nov 90. (7") *(CL 597)* *<44561>* **OBJECTION OVERRULED. / CHANGING OF THE GUARD**
(12"+=/12"pic-d+=) *(12CL/+PD 597)* – Free for all.
Sep 92. (cd/lp) *(CD/TC+/EST 2179)* *<96676>* **FORCE OF HABIT** Aug92
– Thorn in my side / Me, myself and I / Force of habit / Bitch / Fuel for the fire / One foot in the grave / Count your blessings / Climb before the fall / Architect of pain / When it rains it pours / Good day to die / Pump it up / Feeding time at the zoo.

— they split after above

Century Media / Century Media

Jun 97. (lp/c/cd) *<(CM 77173/+MC/CD)>* **ANOTHER LESSON IN VIOLENCE (live 1997 reunion)**
– Bonded by blood / Exodus / Pleasures of the flesh / And then there were none / Piranha / Seeds of hate / Deliver us to evil / Brain dead / No love / A lesson in violence / Impaler / Strike of the beast.

– compilations, etc. –

Nov 91. (cd/c/lp) *Roadracer; (RO 9235-2/-4/-1) / Combat; <2026>* **GOOD FRIENDLY VIOLENT FUN**
(cd re-iss. Nov99 on 'Century Media'; 66035-2)
Jul 92. (cd/c/lp) *Music For Nations; (CD/T+/MFN 138M)* **THE BEST OF EXODUS – LESSONS IN VIOLENCE**

EXPLODING WHITE MICE

Formed: Adelaide, Australia . . . January 1985 by PAUL GILCHRIST, JEFF STEPHENS and GILES BARROW, the trio subsequently being joined by ANDY McQUEEN and CRAIG RODDA (the latter replaced by DAVID BUNNEY during initial recordings). Taking their musical cue from such veteran US punk icons as MC5, The STOOGES and the RAMONES, The EXPLODING WHITE MICE played muscular trash-rock in the best Australian tradition, debuting with that year's 'A NEST OF VIPERS', a mini-set of half covers/half original material that was given a UK release the following year. Preceding the HAPPY MONDAYS by a few years, the EWM dusted down John Kongos' 'HE'S GONNA STEP ON YOU AGAIN' for release as a single. In 1988, they delivered their first full-set, 'BRUTE FORCE & IGNORANCE', JACK JACOMOS subsequently coming in for BARROW shortly after. Despite a limited audience in the homeland and virtually no interest in Britain, the 'MICE received a sympathetic reaction in Germany where they released two further sets, an eponymous(e) partly live affair in 1990 and 'COLLATERAL DAMAGE' in '92.

Album rating: A NEST OF VIPERS (*5) / BRUTE FORCE & IGNORANCE (*6) / EXPLODING WHITE MICE (*6) / COLLATERAL DAMAGE (*5)

PAUL GILCHRIST – vocals / **JEFF STEPHENS** – guitar, vocals / **GILES BARROW** – guitar, vocals / **ANDY McQUEEN** – bass, vocals / **DAVID BUNNEY** – drums; repl. RODDA

Big Time | not iss.

May 86. (m-lp) *(BTA 010)* **A NEST OF VIPERS** [ ] [-]
– Burning red / Bad little woman / Let the kids dance / Pipeline / Your claws / Dangerous. *(Australian-release 1985 on 'Greasy Pop'; GPR 115) (German-iss.1987 on 'Normal'+=; 87)* – He's gonna step on you again / Blaze of glory.

1986. (7") **HE'S GONNA STEP ON YOU AGAIN. / BLAZE OF GLORY** [-] [-] Austra

Festival | not iss.

1988. (lp) **BRUTE FORCE & IGNORANCE** [-] [-] Austra
– Fear (late at night) / Goodbye gravity / Worry about nothing / Verbal abuse / The wheel / Surfing in a dust storm / Breakdown No.2 / Bury me / Uninvited / Sea of justice / Hit in the face / When I get off / Without warning. *(German-iss.+=; 88)* – A NEST OF VIPERS

—— **JACK JACOMOS** – guitar; repl. BARROW

Normal | not iss.

Jul 90. (lp/cd) *(NORMAL 119/+CD)* **EXPLODING WHITE MICE** (some live) [ ] [-]
– Sleepwalk / Intuition / Real tough guy / Do the crunch / You're losing me / I just want my fun / Misunderstood / Ain't it sad / Verbal abuse / Meet the creeper / Univited / Bangkok / King of the surf / Dangerous / First time is the best time. *(cd+=)* – Do the crunch.

—— now a trio of **STEPHENS, McQUEEN + BUNNEY**

1992. (lp/cd) *(NORMAL 144/+CD)* **COLLATERAL DAMAGE** [-] [-] German
– And stay out / Enemies / In your eyes / Imaginary world / Human garbage / Frozen alive / Shadow in the sky / Everybody's waiting / Empty T.V. / This is the news / When she walks / Falling on all sides / Tooth and nail / Hate mail.

—— split after above

EXPLOITED

Formed: East Kilbride, Scotland . . . 1979 by 'BIG JOHN' DUNCAN, WATTIE BUCHAN, GARY McCORMICK AND DRU STIX. Subsequently moving to the capital, they issued three independently released maxi-singles in 1980, 'ARMY LIFE', 'EXPLOITED BARMY ARMY' and 'EXTRACTS FROM AN EDINBURGH NITE CLUB EP', a barrage of three-chord 100 mph punk/oi anthems with BUCHAN spitting out raging anti-establishment diatribes (Maggie Thatcher was a favourite lyrical punchbag). In 1981, after a minor hit, 'DOGS OF WAR' (on 'Secret' records), they unleashed a whole album's worth of two-minute wonders, 'PUNK'S NOT DEAD' (a battlecry of the dyed mohawk hairdo brigade!) which incredibly hit the Top 20. It was quickly pursued by 'DEAD CITIES' (a near Top 30 hit), an abysmal live set, a shared EP with fellow oi-stars ANTI-PASTI, and a Top 50 hit single, 'ATTACK'. A second album proper, 'TROOPS OF TOMORROW' (1982) followed their debut into the Top 20, featuring their infamous tribute to punk's greatest dead hero, 'SID VICIOUS WAS INNOCENT'. When BIG JOHN left at the end of '82 (he formed The BLOOD UNCLES before joining GOODBYE MR MACKENZIE!), the rot set in after the Falklands Conflict-inspired set, 'LET'S START A WAR (SAID MAGGIE ONE DAY)' (1983). A further series of personnel changes marred their subsequent releases, 'HORROR EPICS' in '85 relying on substandard heavy metal to get their still raging points across. WATTIE and his ever changing cast of ageing punk/metal diehards continued, if intermittently, to release predictable albums, while former member BIG JOHN found brief fame when he deputised in 1993 for an A.W.O.L. KURT COBAIN in NIRVANA.

Album rating: PUNK'S NOT DEAD (*5) / ON STAGE (*3) / TROOPS OF TOMORROW (*5) / LET'S START A WAR (SAID MAGGIE ONE DAY) (*5) / HORROR EPICS (*5) / DEATH BEFORE DISHONOUR (*4) / THE MASSACRE (*4) / BEAT THE BASTARDS (*3) / THE SINGLES COLLECTION compilation (*6)

WATTIE BUCHAN – vocals / **'BIG JOHN' DUNCAN** – guitar, vocals / **GARY McCORMICK** – bass, vocals (ex-JOSEF K) / **DRU STIX** (b. DREW CAMPBELL) – drums, vocals

Exploited | not iss.

Aug 80. (7"m) *(EXP 001)* **ARMY LIFE. / FUCK THE MODS / CRASHED OUT** [ ] [-]
(re-iss. May81 on 'Secret'; SHH 112)

Nov 80. (7"m) *(EXP 002)* **EXPLOITED BARMY ARMY. / I BELIEVE IN ANARCHY / WHAT YOU WANNA DO?** [ ] [-]
(re-iss. May81 on 'Secret'; SHH 113)

1981. (7"ep) *(EXP 003)* **EXTRACTS FROM EDINBURGH NITE CLUB (live)** [ ] [-]

Secret | not iss.

Apr 81. (7") *(SHH 110)* **DOGS OF WAR. / BLOWN TO BITS (live)** [63] [-]

May 81. (lp) *(EXP 1001)* **PUNK'S NOT DEAD** [20] [-]
– Punk's not dead / Mucky pup / Exploited barmy army / S.P.G. / Cop cars / Free flight / Army life (Pt.2) / Dole q / Out of control / Ripper / Blown to bits / Son of a copper / Sex and violence / Royalty / I believe in anarchy. *(re-iss. Feb89 on 'Link'; LINK 065) (cd-iss. Oct92 on 'Streetlink'; STRCD 006) (cd re-iss. Mar93 on 'Dojo'; DOJOCD 106) (re-iss. Mar98 on 'Harry May'; MAYLP 701) (cd re-iss. Aug98 on 'Snapper'; SMMCD 530)*
(above original released on 'Exploited' records)

Oct 81. (7"m) *(SHH 120)* **DEAD CITIES. / HITLER'S IN THE CHARTS AGAIN / CLASS WAR** [31] [-]

Superville | not iss.

Nov 81. (lp) *(EXP 1002)* **EXPLOITED LIVE-ON STAGE (live)** [52] [-]
– Cop cars / Crashed out / Dole Q / Dogs of war / Army life / Out of control / Ripper / F*** the mods / Exploited barmy army / Royalty / Sex & violence / Punks not dead / I believe in anarchy. *(re-iss. 1987 on 'Dojo' lp/c; DOJO LP/TC 9) <US cd-iss. Oct92 on 'Continium'; 10001-2> (UK cd-iss. Mar00 on 'Mayo-Harry May'; MAYOCD 500)*

Nov 81. (12"ep; shared with ANTI-PASTI) *(EXP 1003)* **DON'T LET 'EM GRIND YOU DOWN** [70] [-]

Secret | not iss.

Apr 82. (7") *(SHH 130)* **ATTACK. / ALTERNATIVES** [50] [-]

Jun 82. (lp) *(SEC 8)* **TROOPS OF TOMORROW** [17] [-]
– Jimmy Boyle / Daily news / Disorder / Alternatives (remix) / Germs / Rapist / UK '82 / War / Troops of tomorrow / Sid Vicious was innocent / They won't stop / So tragic. *(re-iss. Feb89 on 'Link'; LINK 066) (cd-iss. Oct92 on 'Streetlink'; STRCD 007) (cd re-iss. Mar93 on 'Dojo'; DOJOCD 107) (re-iss. Mar98 on 'Harry May'; MAYLP 702) (cd re-iss. Aug98 on 'Snapper'; SMMCD 529)*

Oct 82. (7") *(SHH 140)* **COMPUTERS DON'T BLUNDER. / ADDICTION** [ ] [-]

—— **BILLY DUNN** – guitar (ex-SKROTEEZ) repl. BIG JOHN who joined the SQUARE PEG. DUNCAN subsequently formed The BLOOD UNCLES before he hooked up with GOODBYE MR MACKENZIE.

Blurg-Pax | not iss.

Oct 83. (7"m) *(PAX 15)* **RIVAL LEADERS. / ARMY STYLE / SINGALONGABUSHELL** [ ] [-]

Pax | Combat

Dec 83. (lp) *(PAX 18)* **LET'S START A WAR (SAID MAGGIE ONE DAY)** [ ] [ ]
– Let's start a war / Insanity / Safe below / Eyes of the vulture / Should we can't we / Rival leaders (remix) / God save the Queen / Psycho / Kidology / False hopes / Another day to go nowhere / Wankers. *(re-iss. 1987 on 'Dojo' lp/c; DOJO LP/TC 10) (cd-iss. Mar94 on 'Dojo'; DOJOCD 010) (cd re-iss. Aug98 on 'Snapper'; SMMCD 531)*

—— **DEPTFORD JOHN** repl. WAYNE / **MAD MICK** repl. EGGHEAD / **also with WATTIE, KARL, WILLIE BUCHAN** – drums / **CAPTAIN SCARLETT** – guitar

—— McCORMICK formed ZULU SYNDICATE, while STIX struggled with a drug addiction and then was sentenced to seven years for armed robbery.

Konnexion | not iss.

Mar 85. (lp/c) *(KOMA/AMOK 788012)* **HORROR EPICS** [ ] [-]
– Horror epics / Don't forget the chaos / Law and order / I hate you / No more idols / Maggie / Dangerous vision / Down below / Treat you like shit / Forty odd years ago / My life. *(re-iss. Aug86 on 'Dojo' lp/c; DOJO LP/TC 37) (cd-iss. Mar94; DOJOCD 184) (cd re-iss. Aug98 on 'Snapper'; SMMCD 532)*

Rough Justice | not iss.

Apr 86. (12"ep) *(12KORE 102)* **JESUS IS DEAD / POLITICIANS. / DRUG SQUAD / PRIVACY INVASION** [ ] [-]

Nov 88. (12"ep) *(12KORE 103)* **WAR NOW. / UNITED CHAOS AND ANARCHY / SEXUAL FAVOURS** [ ] [-]

Aug 89. (lp/cd) *(JUST/+CD 6)* **DEATH BEFORE DISHONOUR** [ ] [-]
– Anti UK / Power struggle / Scaling the Derry wall / Barry Prossitt / Don't really care / No forgiveness / Death before dishonour / Adding to their fears / Police informer / Drive me insane / Pulling us down / Sexual favours. *(cd+=)* – Drug squad man / Privacy invasion / Jesus is dead / Politicians / War now / United chaos and anarchy / Sexual favours (dub version). *(cd re-iss. Jun00 on 'Dream Catcher'; CRIDE 37)*

—— **WATTIE** – vocals / **SMEGS** – bass, vocals / **GOGS** – guitar / **TONY** – drums

Sep 90. (cd/c/lp) *(CD/T+/JUST 15)* **THE MASSACRE** [ ] [-]
– The massacre / Sick bastard / Porno slut / Now I'm dead / Boys in blue / Dog soldier / Don't pay the poll tax / F. . . religion / About to die / Blown out of the city / Police shit / Stop the slaughter. *(cd re-iss. Jun00 on 'Dream Catcher'; CRIDE 36)*

—— new line-up mid-90's; **WATTIE** – vocals / **ARTHUR** – guitar / **BILLY** – bass / **WULLIE** – drums

Mar 96. (cd/c/lp) *(CD/T+/JUST 22)* **BEAT THE BASTARDS** [ ] [-]
– Beat the bastards / Affected by them / Law for the rich / System fucked up / They lie / If you're sad / Fightback / Massacre of innocents / Police TV / Sea of blood / Dont blame me / 15 years / Serial killer.

– compilations, etc. –

Dec 84. (lp) *Dojo; (DOJOLP 1)* **TOTALLY EXPLOITED** [ ] [-]
– Punk's not dead / Army life / F**k a mod / Barmy army / Dogs of war / Dead cities / Sex and violence / Yops / Daily news / Dole Q / Believe in anarchy / God save the Queen / Psycho / Blown to bits / Insanity / S.P.G. / Jimmy Boyle / U.S.A. / Attack / Rival leaders. *(re-iss. Apr86 lp/c/cd; DOJO LP/TC/CD 1)*

Jan 85. (c) *Chaos; (APOCA 2)* **LIVE ON THE APOCALYPSE TOUR '81 (live)** [ ] [-]
(lp-iss.Feb87; APOCA 2)

Feb 86. (lp) *Suck; (SDLP 2)* **LIVE AT THE WHITE HOUSE (live)** [ ] [-]
(cd-iss. Jul98 on 'PinHead'; PINCD 104) (cd re-iss. Jun99 on 'Snapper'; SMMCD 574)

Aug 86. (12"ep) *Archive 4; (TOF 107)* **DEAD CITIES / PUNK'S NOT DEAD. / ARMY LIFE / EXPLOITED BARMY LIFE** [ ] [-]

Mar 87. (lp) *Snow; (WAT 1)* **INNER CITY DECAY** [ ] [-]

Dec 87. (lp) *Link; (LINKLP 018)* **LIVE AND LOUD (live)** [ ] [-]
(cd-iss. Oct93; LINKCD 018) (cd re-iss. Apr96 on 'Anagram'; CDPUNK 18)

Jul 88. (12"ep) *Skunx; (EXPX 1)* **PUNK'S ALIVE** [ ] [-]
– Alternative / Let's start a war / Horror epics / Troops of tomorrow / Dogs of war.
1989. (d-lp) *Roadrunner; (RR 4965-1)* **PUNK'S NOT DEAD / TROOPS OF TOMORROW** [ ] [-]
1989. (lp) *Grand Slam; <SLAM 7>* **LIVE, LEWD, LUST (live)** [-] [ ]
– Law and order / Let's start a war / Horror epics / Blown to bits / Hitler's in the charts again / Troops of tomorrow / Sex and violence / Alternative / Cop cars / Dole Q / Dead cities / SPG / I believe in anarchy / Warhead / Daily news / Dogs of war. *(UK cd-iss. Nov00 on 'Step 1'; STEPCD 035)*
Dec 91. (cd) *Streetlink; (STRCD 018)* **THE SINGLES COLLECTION** [ ] [-]
(re-iss. Apr93 & Jan98 on 'Dojo'; DOJOCD 118)
Feb 94. (cd) *Loma; (LOMACD 2)* **LIVE ON STAGE 1981 / LIVE AT THE WHITE HOUSE 1985** [ ] [-]
Feb 94. (cd) *Loma; (LOMACD 3)* **LET'S START A WAR . . . / HORROR EPICS** [ ] [-]
Mar 94. (cd) *Dojo; (DOJOCD 20109)* **LIVE IN JAPAN (live)** [ ] [-]
Apr 94. (cd) *Cleopatra; (CLEO 5000CD)* **THE SINGLES** [ ] [-]
(re-iss. Jun99 on 'Eagle'; EAGCD 094)
Sep 97. (d-cd) *Snapper; (SMDCD 136)* **TOTALLY EXPLOITED / LIVE IN JAPAN** [ ] [-]
May 00. (3xcd-box) *Snapper; (SMXCD 103)* **THE BOX** [ ] [-]
– (LET'S START A WAR / HORROR EPICS / LIVE AT THE WHITE HOUSE)
Jul 00. (cd) *Harry May; (CANCAN 008CD)* **DEAD CITIES** [ ] [-]
Mar 01. (cd) *Captain Oi; (AHOYCD 180)* **PUNK SINGLES AND RARITIES** [ ] [-]

EXTREME

Formed: Boston, Massachusetts, USA . . . 1988 initially as The DREAM, by GARY CHERONE and PAUL GEARY. After the band split, CHERONE began collaborating with Portuguese-born axe wizard, NUNO BETTENCOURT (the main songwriter), who recruited bassist PAT BADGER. Naming themselves EXTREME (a self-deprecating jape, perhaps?) they were picked up by A&M in 1987, releasing their eponymous debut two years later. Drawing its influences from QUEEN, KISS and CHEAP TRICK, it was a fairly unremarkable affair although it did give an indication of where they were headed. Coming on like a neutered CHILI PEPPERS, 'GET THE FUNK OUT' surprisingly made the UK Top 20, but it was the acoustic ballad, 'MORE THAN WORDS', which propelled the band to stadium status. No.1 in America, No.2 in Britain, the single boosted sales of the album, 'PORNOGRAFFITTI' (1991), which eventually went double platinum. Another ballad, 'HOLE HEARTED', made Top 5 in the States and the band toured with big guns like ZZ TOP. 'III SIDES TO EVERY STORY' (1992) was a wildly ambitious affair, echoes of dodgy 70's prog-rock concepts evident in their use of musical 'suites'. The album was a relative success nevertheless, although by the release of 'WAITING FOR THE PUNCHLINE' (1995), interest in the band was dwindling. BETTENCOURT delivered a solo album, 'SCHIZOPHONIC', early in '97, an improvement on the aforesaid EXTREME finale, although nothing startling. • **Covers:** LOVE OF MY LIFE (Queen) / STRUTTER (Kiss).

Album rating: EXTREME (*5) / PORNOGRAFFITTI (*7) / III SIDES TO EVERY STORY (*6) / WAITING FOR THE PUNCHLINE (*4) / THE BEST OF EXTREME compilation (*6) / Nuno Bettencourt: SCHIZOPHONIC (*5) / MOURNING WIDOWS (*4) / FURNISHED SOULS FOR RENT (*5)

GARY CHERONE (b.26 Jul'61, Malden, Mass.) – vocals / **NUNO BETTENCOURT** (b.20 Sep'66, Azores, Portugal) – guitar, keyboards, vocals / **PAT BADGER** (b.22 Jul'67, Boston) – bass, vocals / **PAUL GEARY** (b.24 Jul'61, Medford, Mass.) – drums, percussion

not iss. Toppe
1985. (lp; as The DREAM) **THE DREAM** [-] [ ]
– Take your time / The tender touch / Makes no sense / All over again / Tipsy on the brink of love / You / Here is the love / Desires / Suzanne / Wonderful world / Last Monday.

A&M A&M
Mar 89. (lp/c/cd) *(<AMA/AMC/CDA 5238>)* **EXTREME** [ ] [80]
– Little girls / Wind me up / Kid ego / Watching, waiting / Mutha (don't wanna go to school today) / Teachers pet / Big boys don't cry / Smoke signals / Flesh 'n' blood / Rock a bye bye. *(cd+=)* – (1 track).
Apr 89. (7") *<1415>* **KID EGO. / SMOKE SIGNALS** [-] [ ]
Apr 89. (7";w-drawn) *(AM 504)* **KID EGO. / FLESH 'N' BLOOD** [ ] [-]
(12"+=) *(AMY 504)* – Smoke signals.
Jun 89. (7") *<1438>* **LITTLE GIRLS. / NICE PLACE TO STAY** [-] [ ]
Aug 89. (7") *<1444>* **TEACHER'S PET. / MUTHA (DON'T WANNA GO TO SCHOOL TODAY)** [-] [ ]
Mar 91. (7") *<1552>* **MORE THAN WORDS. / ('A'remix)** [-] [1]
May 91. (7"/c-s) *(AM/+MC 737)* **GET THE FUNK OUT. / LI'L JACK HORNY** [19] [-]
(12"+=) *(AMX 737)* – Little girls (edit).
(12"pic-d+=) *(AMP 737)* – Nice place to visit.
(cd-s+=) *(AMCD 737)* – Mutha (don't wanna go to school) (remix).
May 91. (cd/c/lp) *(395313-2/-4/-1) <5313>* **PORNOGRAFFITTI** [12] [10] Aug90
– Decadence dance / Li'l Jack Horny / When I'm president / Get the funk out / More than words / Money (in God we trust) / It ('s a monster) / Pornograffitti / When I first missed you / Suzi (wants her all day what?) / He-man woman hater / Song for love. *(originally released UK Sep90)*
Jul 91. (7"/c-s) *(AM/+MC 792)* **MORE THAN WORDS. / NICE PLACE TO VISIT** [2] [-]
(cd-s+=) *(AMCD 792)* – Little girls.
(12"++=) *(AMX 792)* – Mutha (don't wanna go to school) (remix).
Jul 91. (c-s) *<1564>* **HOLE HEARTED. / SUZI (WANTS HER ALL DAY WHAT?)** [-] [4]
Sep 91. (7"/c-s) *(AM/+MC 773)* **DECADENCE DANCE. / MONEY (IN GOD WE TRUST)** [36] [ ] Mar91
(12"+=/cd-s+=) *(AM Y/CD 773)* – ('A'version) / More than words (acappella with congas).
Nov 91. (7"/c-s) *(AM/+MC 839)* **HOLE HEARTED. / GET THE FUNK OUT (remix)** [12] [-]
(12"box+=/cd-s+=) *(AM Y/CD 839)* – Suzi (wants her all day what?) / Sex and love.
Apr 92. (7"/c-s/12"/cd-s) *(AM/+MC/Y/CD 698)* **SONG FOR LOVE. / LOVE OF MY LIFE (featuring BRIAN MAY)** [12] [ ]
Aug 92. (7"/c-s) *(AM/+MC 0055) <0055>* **REST IN PEACE. / PEACEMAKER DIE** [13] [96] Oct92
(etched-12"+=) *(AMY 0055)* – ('A'-lp version).
(cd-s++=) *(AMCD 0055)* – Monica.
Sep 92. (cd/c/d-lp) *(540006-2/-4/-1) <40006>* **III SIDES TO EVERY STORY** [2] [10]
– Warheads / Rest in peace / Politicalamity / Color me blind / Cupid's dead / Peacemaker die/ / Seven Sundays / Tragic comic / Our father / Stop the world / God isn't dead/ / Everything under the Sun (I) Rise'n shine / (II) Am I ever gonna change / (III) Who cares?
Nov 92. (7"/c-s) *(AM/+MC 0096)* **STOP THE WORLD. / CHRISTMAS TIME AGAIN** [22] [-]
(12"+=) *(AMY 0096)* – Warheads / ('A'version).
(cd-s++=) *(AMCD 0096)* – Don't leave me alone.
Jan 93. (7"etched/c-s) *(AM/+MC 0156)* **TRAGIC COMIC. / HOLEHEARTED (horn mix)** [15] [ ]
(12"pic-d+=/cd-s+=) *(AM Y/CD 0156)* – ('A'version) / Rise'n'shine (acoustic).
(cd-s) *(AMCDR 0156)* – ('A'side) / Help! / When I'm president (live).
Feb 93. (c-s) *<0120>* **STOP THE WORLD / WARHEADS** [-] [95]
Feb 95. (cd/c) *(540305-2/-4) <0327>* **WAITING FOR THE PUNCHLINE** [10] [40]
– There is no God / Cynical / Tell me something I don't know / Hip today / Naked / Midnight express / Leave me alone / No respect / Evilangelist / Shadow boxing / Unconditionally / Fair-weather friend.
Mar 95. (7"sha-pic-d) *(580099-7)* **HIP TODAY. / THERE IS NO GOD** [44] [ ]
(cd-s+=) *(580099-2)* – Better off dead / Kid ego (live).
(cd-s+=) *(580099-5)* – Never been funked / When I'm president (live) / Strutter.
(12") *(580099-6)* – ('A'side) / Wind me up (1987 demo).
Jul 95. (cd-s; w-drawn) **UNCONDITIONALLY /** [ ] [ ]

— Disbanded after above. CHERONE joined VAN HALEN late '96 while BETTENCOURT released a solo album, 'SCHIZOPHONIC', in '97.

– compilations, etc. –

Oct 93. (cd) *A&M; (CDA 24117)* **EXTREME / PORNOGRAFFITTI** [ ] [-]
Mar 98. (cd) *A&M; (540836-2)* **THE BEST OF EXTREME** [ ] [ ]
– Decadance dance / Rest in peace / Kid ego / Get the funk out / Tragic comic / Hip today / Stop the world / More than words / Cupid's dead / Leave me alone / Play with me / Hole hearted / Am I ever gonna change.

NUNO BETTENCOURT

— with also GARY CHERONE

A&M A&M
Feb 97. (cd) *<(540 593-2)>* **SCHIZOPHONIC** [ ] [ ]
– Gravity / Swollen princess / Crave / What do you want / Fallen angels / Two weeks in Dizkneelande / Pursuit of happiness / Fine by me / Karmalaa / Confrontation / Note on the screen door / I wonder / Got to have you / Severed.

not iss. Polygram
Mar 99. (cd) *<7294>* **MOURNING WIDOWS** [-] [ ]
– All automatic / Paint the town red / The temp / The air that you breathe / I wanna be your friend / Hotel asylum / Over & out / Love is a cigarette / Too late / True love in the galaxy. *(+=)* – Sex in a jar (demo) / And the winner is . . . (demo).
Oct 00. (cd) *<7478>* **FURNISHED SOULS FOR RENT** [-] [ ]
– Furnished souls for rent / No regrets / Upsidedownside / Monkey paw / 667 / Space / The swing / Fuck you / War paint / Angerexia.

EXTREME NOISE TERROR

Formed: Ipswich, England . . . early 1985 by DEAN JONES, PHIL VANE, PETE HURLEY and JERRY CLAY. Another group to enjoy indie success through the playlisting of DJ John Peel, who, alongside Clive Selwood, released a PEEL SESSIONS album in 1988. Preceding this, they had unleashed a split debut album, 'EAR SLAUGHTER', alongside CHAOS UK. Appropriately titled, the record was tinnitus-inducing testament to ENT's mission of melding punk and metallic influences into savage thrash-core. In 1992, after numerous personnel changes, ENT's five minutes of fame came when they performed with The KLF on an 'enlivened' version of '3am Eternal' at the normally staid Brit Awards. One of the all-time highlights in the event's history, the performance no doubt had many industry bigwigs spluttering into their champagne and has deservedly gone down in music biz legend. The following year, ENT found their natural home at 'Earache', the group subsequently revamping a number of old tracks for the 'RETRO-BUTION (TEN YEARS OF TERROR)' (1995) collection. New material finally surfaced in the form of 'DAMAGE 381' (1997), although VANE had departed by this point for a stint in NAPALM DEATH, the frontman later returning soon after the album's release. During this period, DEAN JONES teamed up with LEE BARRETT (of Candlelight records) to form two-album project, DISGUST. On the same Candlelight imprint, ENT were on form once again with a fresh set of tunes courtesy of 2001's 'BEING AND NOTHING'. This featured dual vocalist ADAM CATCHPOLE (alongside the ever-present DEAN) plus CRADLE OF FILTH axeman GIAN PYRES. • **Trivia:** PHIL was frontman in group FILTHKICK (with members of DOOM), and they released late '89 lp 'IN IT FOR LIFE' on 'Sink Below'.

Album rating: HOLOCAUST IN YOUR HEAD (*6) / PHONOPHOBIA (*8) / RETRO-BUTION (TEN YEARS OF TERROR) remixes (*5) / DAMAGE 381 (*5) / BEING AND

NOTHING (*6) / Disgust: BRUTALITY OF WAR (*5) / A WORLD OF NO BEAUTY (*6)

DEAN JONES – vocals / **PHIL VANE** – vocals / **PETE HURLEY** – guitar / **JERRY CLAY** – bass / **PIG KILLER** – drums

Manic Ears not iss.

Nov 86. (lp) *(ACHE 01)* **EAR SLAUGHTER** (with CHAOS UK on side one) [ ] [-]

— **MICK HARRIS** – drums repl. PIG KILLER

Strange Fruit not iss.

Apr 88. (12"ep) *(SFPS 048)* **THE PEEL SESSION** (10.11.87) [ ] [-]
– False profit / Another nail in the coffin / Use your mind / Carry on screaming / Human error / Conned through life / Only in it for the music part two.

— **TONY DICKENS** – drums repl. HARRIS who joined NAPALM DEATH

— **MARK BAILEY** – bass repl. MARK GARDINER who had repl. CLAY

Hurt not iss.

Mar 89. (lp) *(HURT 1)* **HOLOCAUST IN YOUR HEAD** [ ] [-]
– Statement / Deceived / We the helpless / Bullshit propaganda / Fucked up system / No threat / Show us you care / Use your mind / Innocence to ignorance / Conned thru life Murder / Take the strain / Another nail in the coffin / Raping the earth / If your only in it for the music (S.O.D. off). *(<cd-iss. May99 on 'Rhythm Vicar'; PREACH 016CD>) (lp re-iss. Feb00 on 'Distortion'; DISTLP 054)*

Discipline not iss.

Feb 92. (12"/cd-s) *(DISC 001X/+CD)* **PHONOPHONE** [ ] [-]
Feb 92. (cd) *(DISC 17)* **PHONOPHOBIA** [ ] [-]
Nov 93. (12"; by EXTREME NOISE TERROR / THE KLF) *(DISC 2T)* **3 A.M. ETERNAL. / ('A'-1991 Christmas Top Of The Pops mix)** [ ] [-]

— **LEE BARRETT** – bass (of DISGUST) repl. BAILEY

— added **ALI FIROUZBAKHT** – lead guitar + returning **PIG KILLER** – drums

Earache Earache

Jan 95. (lp/cd) *(<MOSH 083/+CD>)* **RETRO-BUTION (TEN YEARS OF TERROR)** (re-mixes) [ ] [ ] Mar95
– Raping the earth / Bullshit propaganda / Love brain / Work for never / We the helpless / Invisible war / Subliminal music / Human error / Murder / Think about it / Pray to be saved / Conned thru life / Deceived / Third world genocide.

— late in 1996, PHIL VANE replaced GREENWAY in NAPALM DEATH, although he returned a few months later after below recording

Jul 97. (cd) *(<MOSH 173CD>)* **DAMAGE 381** [ ] [ ]
– Utopia burns / Punishment solitude / Icon of guilt / Jesus on my side / Cold world / Damage 381 (instrumental) / Shallow existence / Chaos perverse / Crawl / Downside.

— line-up now **DEAN, ADAM, ALI** plus **GIAN PYRES** – guitar (of CRADLE OF FILTH) + **MANNY** – bass / **ZAC O'NEIL** – drums

Candlelight Candlelight

Mar 01. (cd) *(<CANDLE 057CD>)* **BEING AND NOTHING** [ ] [ ]
– Being and nothing / Through mayhem / When gods burn / Man made hell / Damage limitation / No longer as slaves / One truth one hate / Awkening /

– compilations, etc. –

Sep 90. (lp) *Strange Fruit; (SFPMA 208) / Dutch East India; <8403>* **THE PEEL SESSIONS** (10.11.97 + 16.2.90) [ ] [ ]
– False profit / Another nail in the coffin / Use your mind / Carry on screaming / Human error / Conned thru life / Only in it for the music (part 2) / Work for never / Subliminal music / Third world genocide / Punk: fact or fiction? / I am a bloody fool – In it for life / Deceived / Shock treatment.

Jan 99. (cd/lp) *Discipline; (DISC CD/LP 19)* **THE PEEL SESSIONS** (different) [ ] [-]

May 99. (cd; split w/ FILTHKICK) *Rhythm Vicar; (<PREACH 017CD>)* **IN IT FOR LIFE** [ ] [ ]
(lp-iss.Feb00 on 'Distortion'; DISTLP 055)

DISGUST

DEAN JONES – vocals / **LEE BARRETT** – bass / + various

Earache Earache

Nov 93. (lp/c/cd) *(<MOSH 104/+MC/CD>)* **BRUTALITY OF WAR** [ ] [ ] Apr94
– Intro / Mother Earth / As millions suffer / An horrific end / Thrown into oblivion / Civilization decoys / Relentless slaughter / And still . . . / The light of death / What kind of mind / You have no right / Sea of tears / The anguished cry / Life erased / Outro. *(cd re-iss. Apr99; same)*

— now with guest **WORZEL** – drums

Nuclear Blast not iss.

Mar 97. (cd) *(NB 232CD)* **A WORLD OF NO BEAUTY** [ ] [-]
– Intro / The result of war / Remember / Eden / The last embrace / A mother's bleeding heart / Can your eyes see / Just another war crime / Evil trade / Blood soaked soul / The wounds are never healed / Hymn for a dying planet.

EYEHATEGOD

Formed: New Orleans, Louisiana, USA . . . early 90's by ex-CRAWLSPACE frontman, MICHAEL WILLIAMS and JIMMY BOWER, the pair bringing onboard MICHAEL D WILLIAMS, BRIAN PATTON, and STEVE DALE. Southerners EYEHATEGOD were an integral part of the rather fittingly coined 'sludgecore' scene, epitomised by bands like CROWBAR and DOWN. Their sound was heavily influenced by the MELVINS, BLACK FLAG (the band which launched the career of big man HENRY ROLLINS), and of course BLACK SABBATH. These angry church-dodgers created a dirty mesh of mostly slow tempo hardcore riffing penetrated by feedback galore, with a distraught edge created by WILLIAMS' croaky shrieking vocals. Needless to say, they are one of the darker, heavier branches of the Southern Rock tradition. EYEHATEGOD's first studio outing was 'IN THE NAME OF SUFFERING' (1992) which probably captures their sound in its most primitive and pure state, largely due to the lo-fidelity recording techniques used. MARK SCHULTZ replaced DALE on bass (a position which virtually changed with each album) and the band recorded their second set 'TAKE AS NEEDED FOR PAIN' (1993). Though with a slightly more polished sound, the boys again managed to show their unprententious love of dirty, downtrodden hardcore. After this EYEHATEGOD took a long break; BOWER played with DOWN, and drummed for CROWBAR; PATTON played with death metallers SOILENT GREEN, and WILLIAMS opted for pen rather than mic, writing for 'Metal Maniacs' magazine. After exploring these other avenues the band came together again, this time with bassist VINCE LeBLANC, to record what is regarded as their masterpiece thus far, 'DOPESICK' (1996). Created with seasoned producer Billy Anderson (who had worked with the band's mentors the MELVINS) EYEHATEGOD managed to reach new depths of depressive anxiety, but in the best possible sense, and managed at the same time to put their musicianship to the fore to raise it above the noise of their previous output. After this the band took another departure with BOWER once more rocking and recording with CROWBAR. They did, however, record a handful of singles on several independent labels during this period. The turn of the century saw these hard-to-find tracks collected onto the aptly titled 'SOUTHERN DISCOMFORT' (2000), plus other tracks made during the recording sessions for 'DOPESICK' (1996). Not to be outdone by rumours of 'that was that', the band reformed, this time with DANIEL NICK on bass, to record 'CONFEDERACY OF RUINED LIVES' (2000), torturing their instruments one more time for another apocalyptic metal set, although here the formula begins to look a little tired.

Album rating: IN THE NAME OF SUFFERING (*5) / TAKE AS NEED FOR PAIN (*6) / DOPESICK (*7) / SOUTHERN DISCOMFORT collection (*4) / CONFEDERACY OF RUINED LIVES (*5)

MICHAEL WILLIAMS – vocals (ex-CRAWLSPACE) / **BRIAN PATTON** – lead guitar / **JIMMY BOWER** – guitar / **STEVE DALE** – bass / **JOE LaCAZE** – drums (of STRESSBALL)

C/Z Century Media

Sep 91. (lp/cd) *(SPASM 003/+CD) <7738>* **IN THE NAME OF SUFFERING** [ ] [ ] 1992
– Depress / Man is too ignorant to exist / Shinobi / Pigs / Run it into the ground / Godsong / Children of God / Left to starve / Hostility dose / Hit a girl.

— **MARK SCHULTZ** – bass (of BOTH LEGS BROKEN) repl. DALE

Century Media Century Media

Sep 93. (cd/lp) *<(CM 7752-2/-4)>* **TAKE AS NEEDED FOR PAIN** [ ] [ ] Nov93
– Blank / Sister fucker (part 1) / Shop lift / White nigger / 30$ bag / Disturbance / Take as needed for pain / Sister fucker (part 2) / Crimes against skin / Kiss your boss / Who gave her the roses / Laugh it off.

— members moonlighted – BOWER to CROWBAR (as drummer) and DOWN, PATTON to SOILENT GREEN

— **VINCE LeBLANC** – bass; repl. SCHULTZ

Apr 96. (cd/c/lp) *(CM 77114 CD/MC/LP) <7814>* **DOPESICK** [ ] [ ]
– My name is God (I hate you) / Dogs holy life / Masters of legalized confusion / Dixie whiskey / Ruptured heart theory / Non conductive negative reasoning / Lack of almost everything / Zero nowhere / Methamphetamine / Peace thru war (thru peace and war) / Broken down but not locked up / Anxiety hangover.

— split but re-formed to promote the release of a rarities collection

Mar 00. (cd) *Century Media; (CM 77252-2) <7952>* **SOUTHERN DISCOMFORT** (recent singles & outtakes) [ ] [ ] Jan00
– Ruptured heart theory / Story of the eye / Blank – Shoplift / Southern discomfort / Serving time in the middle of nowhere / Lack of almost everything / Peace thru war (thru peace and war) / Depress / Dopesick jam.

Nov 00. (cd/lp) *(77308-2/-1) <8008>* **CONFEDERACY OF RUINED LIVES** [ ] [ ] Sep00
– Revelation – Revolution / Blood money / Jack ass in the will of God / Self medication blues / The concussion machine process / Inferior and full of anxiety / .001% / 99 miles of bad road / Last year (she wanted a doll house) / Corruption scheme. *(cd+=)* – Sabbath jam. *(lp re-iss. Feb01 on 'Pessimiser'; PESS 035LP)*

– compilations, etc. –

May 01. (cd) *Century Media; <(CM 8048)>* **TEN YEARS OF ABUSE AND STILL BROKE** [ ] [ ]

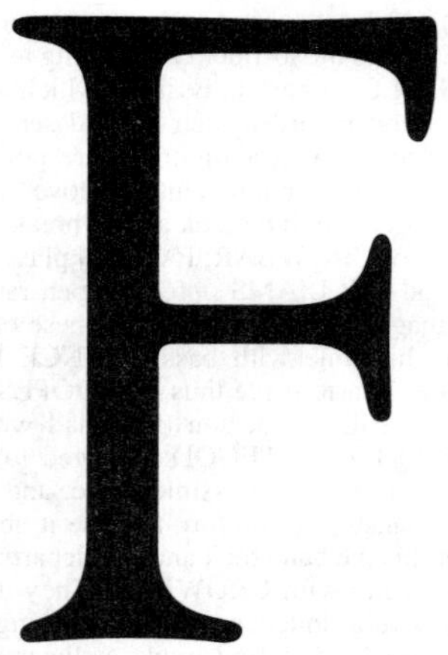

FAITHFUL BREATH

Formed: Germany . . . 1974 by HEINRICH MIKUS, HORST STABENOW, MANFRED VON BUTTLAR and JURGEN WERITZ. Initially one of Germany's many keyboard-dominated prog-rock outfits, FAITHFUL BREATH abandoned this approach after their first album, 'FADING BEAUTY' (1974). By the time the group re-emerged an incredible six years later, the rock scene had changed immeasurably. Wisely perhaps, FAITHFUL BREATH had now opted for a more straightforward guitar attack, introducing their new sound on 1980's 'BACK ON MY HILL'. Vocals aside, the group's pile-driving hard-rock was reminiscent of traditional English bands like URIAH HEEP, a strategy they maintained on further albums, 'ROCK LIONS' (1981) and 'HARD BREATH' (1983). Despite a series of line-up changes, the band recorded what is generally regarded as their best work in the form of 1984's 'GOLD 'N' GLORY'. No major success was forthcoming however, and although the group subsequently adopted a harder sound in keeping with the direction of the metal scene in general, they bowed out after a final live effort in 1987. MIKUS subsequently went on to form RISK.

Album rating: FADING BEAUTY (*5) / BACK ON MY HILL (*5) / ROCK LIONS (*4) / HARD BREATH (*5) / GOLD 'N' GLORY (*6) / SKOL (*5) / LIVE (*4)

HEINRICH MIKUS – vocals, guitar / **HORST STABENOW** – bass, guitar / **MANFRED VON BUTTLAR** – keyboards, synthesizers, guitar, vocals / **JURGEN WERITZ** – drums, percussion

Kopec / Cade

Jan 74. (lp) *(AA 6963233)* <10002> **FADING BEAUTY** [-] [ ] German
– Autumn fantasia: 1st movement – Fading beauty – 2nd movement – Lingering cold / Tharsis. *(cd-iss. Nov98 on 'Laser's Edge'; LE 1011)*

Sky / not iss.

1980. (lp) *(SKY 038)* **BACK ON MY HILL** [-] [-] German
– Back on my hill / Keep me away / This is my love song / Stick in your eyes / Judgement day.

— **UWE OTTO** – drums; repl. BUTTLAR + WERITZ

1981. (lp) *(SKY 055)* **ROCK LIONS** [-] [-] German
– Hurricane / Better times / Rock city / Rollin' into our lives / Down, down / Never be like you / No time / Rock'n'roll women.

— **JURGEN DUSTERLOH** – drums; repl. OTTO

1983. (lp) *(SKY 079)* **HARD BREATH** [-] [-] German
– Killers on the loose / Give me what I need / Always too late / Dark angel / Under my wheels / Kids, we want the world / Illusions / Like an eagle in the sky / Warriors / Riding to Mongolis / Fly to another star / Night comes again.

— added **ANDY HONIG** – guitar

Mausoleum / not iss.

Nov 84. (lp/c) *(SKULL/TAPE7 8335)* **GOLD 'N' GLORY** [ ] [-]
– Don't feel hate / King of the rock / Jailbreaker / A million hearts / Gold 'n' glory / Play the game / Princess in disguise / Don't drive me mad.

— **THILO HERRMANN** – guitar; repl. HONIG

— **PETER DELLENOW** – bass; repl. STABENOW

Ambush / not iss.

Jan 86. (lp) *(HI 401001)* **SKOL** [-] [-] German
– Start it up / Double dealer / Lady M. / Rock rebels / We want you / Inside out / Crazy in metal / Backstreet heroes / S.K.O.L.

Noise / not iss.

Dec 86. (lp) *(N 0051)* **LIVE (live)** [-] [-] German
– Bacchu ber (intro) / Gold 'n' glory / Warriors / Like an eagle in the sky / Princess disguise / A million hearts / Herrmann Feature / Jailbreaker / Play the game / King of the rock.

— in 1987, MIKUS subsequently formed RISK

FAITH NO MORE

Formed: Los Angeles & San Francisco, California, USA . . . 1980 by BILL GOULD and MIKE BORDIN, although they only started gigging in 1982. With CHUCK MOSELEY and JIM MARTIN completing the line-up, the band began to carve out their innovative fusion of funk, rap, hardcore and metal. In 1985, they issued their eponymous debut album on local indie label, 'Mordam', the single, 'WE CARE A LOT' drawing the attention of 'Slash' records, who unleashed 'INTRODUCE YOURSELF' the same year. In 1988, due to musical differences and off-beat stage humour, MOSELEY was discharged from the band. His replacement was magnetic, Kyle Mclachlan-like, MIKE PATTON who immediately became a focal point, his impressive vocal theatrics and commanding stage presence transforming FAITH NO MORE into a formidable live act. PATTON also penned the bizarre, enigmatic lyrics for the band's breakthrough record, 'THE REAL THING' (1989). Arguably the best metal album of the decade, if you could call it metal, it veered from the stuttering rap-rock of 'EPIC' to the sublimely aquatic 'UNDERWATER LOVE' and on to a searing cover of BLACK SABBATH's 'WAR PIGS'. The record went on to sell over a million copies, gave a tired heavy metal scene a much needed boot up the arse and more importantly, gave FAITH NO MORE the convenience of a bigger budget for their next album. 'ANGEL DUST' (1992) wreaked aural havoc, a mish-mash of styles even more diverse than its predecessor. By turns defiantly inaccessible ('MALPRACTICE') and pop-friendly ('MIDLIFE CRISIS'), the record was characterised by a fractured, schizophrenic sound that seemed to tally with PATTON's increasingly outrageous antics. Following on from their live TECHNOTRONIC/NEW KIDS ON THE BLOCK (ironic? Americans? nah) medley, the band released their rather uninspired cover of The COMMODORES' 'I'M EASY'. It became their biggest selling UK single to date, while the album also sold by the truckload following a world tour with GUNS N' ROSES. By the release of 'KING FOR A DAY . . . FOOL FOR A LIFETIME' (1995), MARTIN had been replaced with TREY SPRUANCE, who played alongside PATTON in his part-time side project, MR. BUNGLE. The record was as uncompromising as ever, venom-spewing hardcore rage sitting side by side with wilful weirdness. A blistering headlining set at that year's Phoenix festival (almost topping PUBLIC ENEMY's poignant farewell slot earlier that day) proved once more that live, FAITH NO MORE have few peers and even less scruples. While the group maintain they're simply a rock band and nothing more, they remain one of the genre's quintessential outsiders, image-unfriendly and maverick to the last, as evidenced on their last studio set, 'ALBUM OF THE YEAR' (1997). If not quite living up to the rather presumptious title, the record illustrated that FAITH NO MORE still have their collective finger in more than one pie, 'LAST CUP OF SORROW' being their most affecting single for years. Unfortunately, it would also be their epitaph as the band split up the following April. • **Covered:** THE RIGHT STUFF (Edwin Starr) / MIDNIGHT COWBOY (John Barry) / MALPRACTICE (sampled: Kronos Quartet No.8) / LET'S LYNCH THE LANDLORD (Dead Kennedys) / I'M EASY (Commodores) / I STARTED A JOKE (Bee Gees) / GREENFIELDS (Gilykson-Dehr-Miller) / SPANISH EYES (hit; Al Martino) / THIS GUY'S IN LOVE WITH YOU (Burt Bacharach) / HIGHWAY STAR (Deep Purple). IMPERIAL TEEN covered SHAYLA (Blondie).

Album rating: FAITH NO MORE (*5) / INTRODUCE YOURSELF (*8) / THE REAL THING (*8) / LIVE AT BRIXTON ACADEMY (*6) / ANGEL DUST (*8) / KING FOR A DAY – FOOL FOR A LIFETIME (*7) / ALBUM OF THE YEAR (*6) / WHO CARES A LOT? compilation (*9) / Mr. Bungle: MR. BUNGLE (*4) / DISCO VOLANTE (*4) / CALIFORNIA (*6) / Imperial Teen: SEASICK (*4) / WHAT IS NOT TO LOVE (*5)

CHUCK MOSELEY – vocals / **BILLY GOULD** (b.24 Apr'63, L.A.) – bass / **RODDY BOTTUM** (b. 1 Jul'63, L.A.) – keyboards / **JIM MARTIN** (b.JAMES, 21 Jul'61, Oakland, Calif.) – guitar / **MIKE BORDIN** (b.27 Nov'62) – drums

not iss. / Mordan

1985. (lp) <*MDR 1*> **FAITH NO MORE** [-] [ ]
– We care a lot / The jungle / Mark Bowen / Jim / Why do you bother / Greed / Pills for breakfast / As the worm turns / Arabian disco / New beginnings. *(imported into UK.Feb88 as 'WE CARE A LOT'; same)*

Slash / Slash

Oct 87. (lp/c)(cd) *(SLAP/SMAC 21)*<*(828051-2)*> **INTRODUCE YOURSELF** [ ] [ ]
– Faster disco / Anne's song / Introduce yourself / Chinese arithmetic / Death march / We care a lot / R'n'r / Crab song / Blood / Spirit.

Jan 88. (7") *(LASH 17)* <*28287*> **WE CARE A LOT. / SPIRIT** [53] [ ]
(12"+=) *(LASHX 17)* – Chinese Arithmetic (radio mix).

Apr 88. (7"/7"pic-d/12") *(LASH/+P/X 18)* **ANNE'S SONG (remix). / GREED** [ ] [ ]

— **MIKE PATTON** (b.27 Jan'68, Eureka, Calif.) – vocals (of-MR. BUNGLE) repl. CHUCK who later (1991) joined BAD BRAINS

Jul 89. (lp/c/cd) *(828154-1/-4/-2)* <*25878*> **THE REAL THING** [30] [11]
– From out of nowhere / Epic / Falling to pieces / Surprise, you're dead / Zombie eaters / The real thing / Underwater love / The morning after / Woodpecker from Mars. *(cd+=)* – Edge of the world / War pigs. *(actually hit charts early 1990) (re-iss. Sep92 cd/c; same)*

Oct 89. (7") *(LASH 19)* **FROM OUT OF NOWHERE. / COWBOY SONG** [ ] [ ]
(12"+=) *(LASHX 19)* – The grave.

Jan 90. (7"/7"sha-pic-d) *(LASH/LASPD 21)* **EPIC. / WAR PIGS (live)** [37] [-]
(7"m+=) *(LASHG 21)* – Surprise you're dead (live).
(12"++=/cd-s++=) *(LASHX/LASCD 21)* – Chinese arithmetic.

Apr 90. (c-s) *(LASCS 24)* **FROM OUT OF NOWHERE. / WOODPECKER FROM MARS (live)** [23] [ ]
(7"m+=) *(LASHG 24)* – Epic (live).
(12"++=/12"pic-d++=/cd-s++=) *(LASHX/LASPX/LASCD 24)* – The real thing (live).

Jun 90. (c-s) <*19813*> **EPIC / EDGE OF THE WORLD** [-] [9]

Jul 90. (7") *(LASHP 25)* **FALLING TO PIECES. / WE CARE A LOT (live)** [41] [-]
(7"m+=)(c-s+=) *(LASHG/LASCS 25)* – Underwater love (live).
(12"++=/12"w-poster++=/cd-s++=) *(LASHX/LASPX/LASCD 25)* – From out of nowhere (live).

Sep 90. (7"sha-pic-d) *(LASPD 26)* **EPIC. / FALLING TO PIECES (live)** 25 -
(7"m+=/c-s+=) *(LASH/LASCS 26)* – Epic (live).
(12"++=/cd-s++=) *(LASHX/LASCD 26)* – As the worm turns.
Oct 90. (c-s) *<19563>* **FALLING TO PIECES / ZOMBIE EATERS** - 92
Feb 91. (cd/c/lp) *(828238-2/-4/-1)* **LIVE AT BRIXTON ACADEMY (live)** 20 -
– Falling to pieces / The real thing / Pump up the jam / Epic / War pigs / From out of nowhere / We care a lot / The right stuff / Zombie eaters / Edge of the world. *(cd+=/c+=)* – The grade / Cowboy song.
May 92. (7"/7"colrd/c-s) *(LASH//LASCS 37)* **MIDLIFE CRISIS. / JIZZLOBER / CRACK HITLER** 10
(12"pic-d+=/pic-cd-s+=) *(LASHX/LASCD 37)* – Midnight cowboy.
Jun 92. (cd/c/lp) *(828321-2/-4/-1) <26785>* **ANGEL DUST** 2 10
– Land of sunshine / Caffeine / Midlife crisis / RV / Smaller and smaller / Everything's ruined / Malpractise / Kindergarten / Be aggressive / A small victory / Crack Hitler / Jizzlober / Midnight cowboy. *(lp w/free-12"ep)* – MIDLIFE CRISIS (remix) / (2). *(re-iss. Feb93) (+=)* – I'm easy.
Aug 92. (7"/c-s) *(LASH/LASCS 39)* **A SMALL VICTORY. / LET'S LYNCH THE LANDLORD** 29
(12"+=)(12"pic-d+=) *(LASHX 39)* – Malpractise.
(cd-s++=) *(LASCD 39)* – ('A'extended).
Sep 92. (12"ep/cd-ep) *(LASHX/LASCD 40)* **A SMALL VICTORY (Youth remix) / R-EVOLUTION 23 (Full Moon mix) / SUNDOWN (mix) / SUNDOWN (instrumental)** 55 -
Nov 92. (7"/c-s) *(LASH/LASCS 43)* **EVERYTHING'S RUINED. / MIDLIFE CRISIS (live)** 28
(cd-s+=) *(LASCD 43)* – Land of sunshine (live).
(cd-s) *(LASHCD 43)* – ('A'side) / Edge of the world (live) / RV (live).
Jan 93. (7"/c-s/12"/cd-s) *(LASH/LASCS/LASHX/LACDP 44)* **I'M EASY. / BE AGGRESSIVE** 3 -
Mar 93. (c-s) *<18569>* **EASY / DAS SCHUTENFEST** - 58
Oct 93. (12"ep/c-ep/cd-ep; by FAITH NO MORE & BOO-YAA TRIBE) *(659794-6/-4/-2)* **ANOTHER BODY MURDERED. / Just Another Victim (by "HELMET / HOUSE OF PAIN")** 26

— (above from the film 'Judgement Day', released on 'Epic')

— **DEAN MENTA** – guitar; repl. JIM MARTIN (TREY SPRUANCE played on below album) – JIM MARTIN released a solo album, 'MILK AND BLOOD' for 'S.P.V.' in 1997

Mar 95. (7"/c-s) *(LASH/LASCS 51)* **DIGGING THE GRAVE. / UGLY IN THE MORNING** 16
(12"blue+=) *(LASHX 51)* – Absolute zero / Get out.
(cd-s+=) *(LASCD 51)* – Absolute zero / Cuckoo for Caca.
(cd-s) *(LASHCD 51)* – ('A'side) / I started a joke / Greenfields.
Mar 95. (cd/c/lp) *(828 560-2/-4/-1) <45723>* **KING FOR A DAY – FOOL FOR A LIFETIME** 5 31
– Get out / Ricochet / Evidence / The great art of making enemies / Star A.D. / Cuckoo for Caca / Caralho Voador / Ugly in the morning / Digging the grave / Take this bottle / King for a day / What a day / The last to know / Just a man. *(7"box-set)* – (interviews). *(re-iss. Sep97 cd/c; same)*
May 95. (c-s) *(LASCS 53)* **RICOCHET / SPANISH EYES** 27
(cd-s+=) *(LASCD 53)* – I wanna f**k myself.
(cd-s) *(LACDP 53)* – ('A'side) / Midlife crisis (live) / Epic (live) / We care a lot (live).
Jul 95. (c-s) *(LASCS 54)* **EVIDENCE / EASY (live)** 32
(cd-s+=) *(LASCD 54)* – Digging the grave (live) / From out of nowhere (live).
(cd-s) *(LACDP 54)* – ('A'side) / Das schutzenfest / (interview).

— **JON HUDSON** – guitar; repl. MENTA

May 97. (cd-ep) *(LASCD 61) <5915>* **ASHES TO ASHES / LIGHT UP AND LET GO / COLLISION / ASHES TO ASHES (DJ Icey & Mystero mix)** 15
(cd-ep) *(LASCDP 61) <5909>* – ('A'side) / The big Kahuna / Mouth to mouth / ('A'-Hard Knox alternative mix).
(12"ep) *(LASX 61)* – ('A'side) / ('A'-Hard Knox alternative mix) / ('A'-DJ Icey & Mystero mix) / ('A';-DJ & Mystero dub mix).
Jun 97. (cd/c/lp) *(828 901-2/-4/-1) <46629>* **ALBUM OF THE YEAR** 7 41
– Collision / Strip search / Last cup of sorrow / Naked in front of the computer / Helpless / Mouth to mouth / Ashes to ashes / She loves me not / Got that feeling / Paths of glory / Home sick home / Pristina. *(cd with free cd Jan98; 828902-2)*
Jul 97. (cd-ep) *(LASCD 62)* **LAST CUP OF SORROW / LAST CUP OF SORROW (Bonehead mix) / SHE LOVES ME NOT (Spinna main mix) / SHE LOVES ME NOT (Spinna crazy dub)** -
(cd-ep) *(LASDP 62)* – ('A'side) / Pristina (Billy Gould mix) / Last cup of sorrow (Roli Mosimann mix) / Ashes to ashes (Dillinja remix).

— In Nov'97, they teamed up with 70's popsters SPARKS on a combined version of 'THIS TOWN AIN'T BIG ENOUGH FOR BOTH OF US'.

Jan 98. (cd-s) *(LASCD 63)* **ASHES TO ASHES / LAST CUP OF SORROW (Rammstein mix) / LAST CUP OF SORROW (Sharam Vs FNM club mix)** 29 -
(cd-s) *(LASCX 63)* – ('A'side) / ('A'-Dillinja remix) / The gentle art of making enemies / ('A'live).
(12") *(LASHX 63)* – ('A'-Dillinja mix) / ('A'-Hardknox mix).

— the band had already split in April '98

Oct 98. (cd-s) *(LONCD 65) <570331>* **I STARTED A JOKE / THE WORLD IS YOURS / THEME FROM MIDNIGHT COWBOY** 49 Nov98
(cd-s) *(LASCX 65) <570333>* – ('A'side) / This guy's in love with you / We care a lot (CD-rom).
Nov 98. (d-cd/d-c) *(556 057-2/-4) <47149>* **WHO CARES A LOT? – THE GREATEST HITS** (compilation) 37
– We care a lot (original) / Introduce yourself / From out of nowhere / Epic / Falling to pieces / Midlife crisis / A small victory / Easy / Digging the grave / The gentle art of making enemies / Evidence / I started a joke / Last cup of sorrow / Ashes to ashes / Stripsearch // The world is yours / Hippie jam song / Instrumental / I won't forget you / Introduce yourself (4-track demos) / Highway star / Theme from Midnight Cowboy / This guy's in love with you.

MR. BUNGLE

PATTON + **TREY DUNN** – bass / **WILLIAM WINANT** – percussion, etc

Slash Warners

Sep 91. (cd/c/lp) *(828267-2/-4/-1) <26640>* **MR. BUNGLE** 57
– Quote unquote / Slowly growing deaf / Squeeze me macaroni / Carousel / Egg / Stubb (a dub) / The girls of porn / Love is a fist / Dead goon.

— **PATTON, TREY, THEO, UNCOOKED MEAT PRIOR TO STATE VECTOR COLLAPSE / CLINTON McKINNON + I QUIT**

Jan 96. (cd/c) *(828 694-2/-4) <45963>* **DISCO VOLANTE** Oct95
– Everyone I went to high school with is dead / Chemical marriage / Sleep / Desert search for techno Allah / Violenza domestica / After school special / Sleep / Ma meeshka mow skwoz / Bends / Backstrokin' / Platypus / Merry go bye bye – Nothing.
Nov 99. (cd) *(3984 29829-2) <47447>* **CALIFORNIA** Jul99
– Sweet charity / None of them knew they were robots / Retrovertigo / Air conditioned nightmare / Ars moriendi / Pink cigarette / Golem II: the bionic vapour boy / Holy filament / Vanity fair / Goodbye sober day.

IMPERIAL TEEN

RODDY BOTTUM – vocals, guitar, etc / **WILL SCHWARTZ** – vocals, etc / **JONE STEBBINGS** – bass (ex-WRECKS) / **LYNN PERKO** – drums (ex-DICKS, ex-SISTER DOUBLE HAPPINESS)

Custom Custom

Jun 96. (7") *<(CUSTOM 001)>* **IMPERIAL TEEN. /**

Slash Slash

Aug 96. (7") *(LASH 57)* **YOU'RE ONE. / SHAYLA** 69 -
(12"/c-s/cd-s) *(LAST/LASCS/LASCD 57)* – ('A'side) / Waterboy / Pretty.
Sep 96. (cd/c) *(828 728-2/-4)* **SEASICK**
– Imperial / Water boy / Butch / Pig Latin / Blaming the baby / You're one / Balloon / Tippy tap / Copafeelia / Luxury / Eternity.
Oct 96. (7") *(LASH 59)* **BUTCH. / HELPFUL** -
(cd-s+=) *(LASCD 59)* – Pig Latin.
Sep 98. (cd) *<556014>* **WHAT IS NOT TO LOVE** -
– Open season / Birthday girl / Yoo hoo / Lipstick / Alone in the grass / Crucible / The beginning / Year of the tan / Seven / Hooray (live) / Beauty.

FALSE PROPHETS

Formed: New York City, New York, USA . . . June 1980 by frontman STEPHAN IELPI, who surrounded himself with like-minded hardcore punks, PETER CAMPBELL, STEVE WISHNIA and MATTY SUPERTY. One of the first wave US hardcore acts, the FALSE PROPHETS eschewed the hard-man approach favoured by BLACK FLAG etc, choosing instead an intellectually-based manifesto that sought to oppose injustice in all its multifarious guises. Yet like many bands of their ilk, the line-up was in almost constant flux and by the mid-80's – by which point the band's vinyl output amounted to a solitary 7" single, 'BLIND OBEDIENCE' – IELPI was the only remaining founder member (newcomers being DEBRA DeSALVO, STEVEN TAYLOR, NICK MARDEN and BILLY ATWELL III). Securing a deal with the San Francisco-based 'Alternative Tentacles' label, the band re-emerged in 1986 with a long awaited eponymous debut album. This was followed up by 'IMPLOSION' just over a year later although a second extended sabbatical from the recording front meant that fans had to wait until 1990 for further new material. Featuring brass courtesy of new addition JAMES WHITE, 'INVISIBLE PEOPLE' was a much more adventurous affair combining the adrenaline rush of hardcore with the visceral thrill of Latin rhythms.

Album rating: FALSE PROPHETS (*5) / IMPLOSION (*5) / INVISIBLE PEOPLE (*6) / BLIND ROACHES AND FAT VULTURES compilation (*6)

STEPHAN IELPI – vocals / **PETER CAMPBELL** – guitar / **STEVE WISHNIA** – bass / **MATTY SUPERTY** – drums

not iss. Worn Out Brothers

1981. (7") *<WOB 001>* **BLIND OBEDIENCE. / OVERKILL / ROYAL SLIME** -

— **IELPI** was the solo survivor, the quartet having involved others **DEBRA DE SALVO** – guitar, vocals / **STEVEN TAYLOR** – guitar, vocals / **NICK MARDEN** – bass, vocals / **BILLY ATWELL III** – drums, vocals

Alternative Tentacles Alternative Tentacles

Jul 86. (lp) *<(VIRUS 48)>* **FALSE PROPHETS**
Sep 87. (lp) *<(VIRUS 58)>* **IMPLOSION**

— added **JAMES WHITE** – horns (ex-CONTORTIONS)

— **BENJAMIN ORICK** – drums; repl. ATTWELL

Konkurrel Patois

1990. (m-lp) *<003>* **INVISIBLE PEOPLE**
– Never again, again / Plenty of death for all / Shadow government / Invisible people / No deposit, no return / Limit of the limitless.

— folded in the early 90's after a decade as a unit

– compilations, etc. –

Jun 00. (cd) *Alternative Tentacles; <(VIRUS 244CD)>* **BLIND ROACHES AND FAT VULTURES: PHANTASMAGORICAL BEASTS OF THE REAGAN ERA** (virtually the debut + others)
– Overkill / Blind obedience / Good clean fun / Royal slime / Suburbanites / 7 deadly sins / Somebody react / Scorched earth / Mental ghetto / Functional / Marat – Sade / Taxidermist / Baghdad stomp / Helplessly screaming / Faith / Banana split republic / Decade of decay / Creatures of the woodwork / Premediated suicide / Dear mom I'm dead / Pounding raw burgers.

FAMOUS MONSTERS (see under ⇒ WHITE ZOMBIE)

FANDANGO

Formed: USA . . . 1976 by JOE LYNN TURNER and RICK BLAKEMORE. With the addition of DENNIS LA RUE, BOB DANYLS and LOU MONDELLI, the group signed to 'R.C.A.', releasing an eponymous debut album in 1977. Highly stylised, the group combined the more accessible elements of British and US hard-rock with AOR to produce a melodic blueprint for all their subsequent releases. Improving with each album, the group introduced an extra keyboard player, LARRY DAWSON, to flesh out the sound on 1978's 'LAST KISS' while ABE SPELLER filled the drum stool for their final and probably best set, 'CADILLAC' (1980). TURNER was then thrust into the limelight with RAINBOW, performing on their biggest hit, 'I SURRENDER'. He subsequently struck out on a solo career, his debut, 'RESCUE YOU' (1985), breaking the US Top 200. While TURNER never quite scaled those chart heights again, he enjoyed reasonable success with YNGWIE MALMSTEEN and DEEP PURPLE. • **Note:** Not to be confused with the UK FANDANGO, who included NICK SIMPER.

Album rating: FANDANGO (*4) / ONE NIGHT STAND (*5) / CADILLAC (*5) / Joe Lynn Turner: RESCUE YOU (*6) / NOTHING'S CHANGED (*6)

JOE LYNN TURNER – vocals / **RICK BLAKEMORE** – guitar / **DENNIS LA RUE** – keyboards / **BOB DANYLS** – bass / **LOU MONDELLI** – drums

		not iss.	R.C.A.
Nov 77.	(lp) *<AFL1 2306>* **FANDANGO**	-	
	– Headliner / Down, down, down / Jesse and Will / San Joaquin / Life of the party / Shadow boxing / Helpless heart / Devil rain / Misery road / Goin' down for the last time.		
Mar 78.	(7") *<11194>* **HEADLINER. / GOIN' DOWN FOR THE LAST TIME**	-	
——	added **LARRY DAWSON** – keyboards		
Jun 78.	(7") *<11357>* **LAST KISS. / SAN JOAQUIN**	-	
Jul 78.	(lp) *<AFL1 2696>* **LAST KISS**	-	
	– Last kiss / Sure got the power / Mexico / Losin' kind of love / Hotel La Rue / Feel the pain / City of angels / The mill's on fire / I keep going / Hard bargain.		
Jul 79.	(7") *<11639>* **HARD HEADED WOMAN. / LATE NIGHTS**	-	
Aug 79.	(lp) *<AFL1 3245>* **ONE NIGHT STAND**	-	
	– One night stand / Thief in the night / Hard man (bless my soul) / Hard headed woman / I would never leave / Dancer / Little Cherie / Late nights / Two time loser / Ain't no way.		
	ABE SPELLER – drums; repl. MONDELLI + LA RUE		
Nov 79.	(7") *<11761>* **BLAME IT ON THE NIGHT. / HARD HEADED WOMAN**	-	
Jun 80.	(7") *<12000>* **STRANGER (IN A STRANGE LAND). / CADILLAC**	-	
Jun 80.	(lp) *<AFL1 3591>* **CADILLAC**	-	
	– Blame it on the night / Rock and roll you / Hypnotized / Don't waste my time / Stranger (in a strange land) / Cadillac / Fortune teller / Getaway / Headliner.		

—— when they split, TURNER joined RAINBOW for their biggest hit, 'I SURRENDER'. He subsequently went solo before joining YNGWIE MALMSTEEN'S RISING FORCE, then DEEP PURPLE in 1990

JOE LYNN TURNER

		Elektra	Elektra
Oct 85.	(7") *(EKR 25) <69593>* **ENDLESSLY. / THE RACE IS ON**		
Nov 85.	(lp/c) *(EKT 20/+C) <60449>* **RESCUE YOU**		
	– Losing you / Young hearts / Prelude – Endlessly / Rescue you / Feel the fire / Get tough / Eyes of love / On the run / Soul searcher / The race is on.		
Jan 86.	(7") *<69553>* **DON'T COME TO ME. / EYES OF LOVE**	-	

FANNY

Formed: Sacramento, California . . . 1969 originally as WILD HONEY, by sisters JUNE and JEAN MILLINGTON. With NICOLE BARCLAY and ALICE DeBUHR completing the line-up, the group signed to 'Reprise' through the help of producer RICHARD PERRY. Following a name change to FANNY, the group released an eponymous debut in early '71 (having previously guested on BARBRA STREISAND's 'Stoney End' album). Though the record company made full use of the marketing possibilities inherent in such a controversial moniker, the group themselves denied there were any sexual connotations (the fact that even in sexual terms, FANNY meant something completely different in Britain than it did in America, perhaps accounted for the band's lack of UK success!) Nevertheless, the group were afforded considerable interest in the States, not only for their name but for the fact that they were one of the first ever all-female hard-rock combos. Chart success came later that year with the title track from the 'CHARITY BALL' (1971) opus, the single just making the US Top 40. A third set, 'FANNY HILL', was released in Spring '72, the record marking a creative peak of sorts. For 'MOTHER'S PRIDE' (1973), TODD RUDGREN replaced PERRY in the producer's chair, resulting in the hardest-edged set of FANNY's career. It was to be the last album the sisters recorded together, however, JUNE subsequently being replaced with PATTI QUATRO (SUZI's older sister). ALICE also left, her replacement being the rather cheesily named BRIE BRANDT-HOWARD. For their swansong set, the ambitious quasi-concept album, 'ROCK'N'ROLL SURVIVORS' (1975), the group added a keyboard player, JAMES NEWTON-HOWARD, to embellish their basic sound. Although the album spawned FANNY's biggest hit (Top 30) in 'BUTTER BOY', they splintered later that year.

Album rating: FANNY (*6) / CHARITY BALL (*6) / FANNY HILL (*6) / MOTHER'S PRIDE (*5) / ROCK'N'ROLL SURVIVORS (*4) / Millington: LADIES ON THE STAGE (*4)

JUNE MILLINGTON (b.1949, Manila, Philippines) – vocals, lead guitar/ **JEAN MILLINGTON** (b.1950, Manila, Philippines) – bass, vocals/ **NICOLE BARCLAY** (b.21 Apr'51, Washington DC) – keyboards (ex-JOE COCKER) / **ALICE DeBUHR** (b.Mason City, Iowa) – drums

		Reprise	Reprise
1970.	(7") *<0901>* **LADIES' CHOICE. / NEW DAY**	-	
1970.	(7") *<0938>* **ONE STEP AT A TIME. / NOWHERE TO RUN**	-	
Jan 71.	(lp) *<(6416)>* **FANNY**		
	– Come and hold me / I just realized / Candlelighter man / Conversation with a cop / Badge / Changing horses / Bitter wine / Take a message to the captain / It takes a lot of lovin' / Shade me / Seven roads.		
Jan 71.	(7") *(K 14086) <0963>* **CHANGING HORSES. / CONVERSATION WITH A COP**		
Nov 71.	(7") *(K 14109) <1033>* **CHARITY BALL. / PLACE IN THE COUNTRY**		40 Sep71
Nov 71.	(lp) *(K 44144) <6456>* **CHARITY BALL**		
	– Charity ball / What kind of lover / Cat fever / A person like you / Special care / What's wrong with me / Soul child / You're the one / Thinking of you / Place in the country / A little while later.		
Apr 72.	(lp) *(K 44174) <2058>* **FANNY HILL**		Mar72
	– Ain't that peculiar / Knock on my door / Blind alley / You've got a home / Wonderful feeling / Borrowed time / Hey bulldog / Think about the children / Rock bottom blues / Sound and the fury / The first time.		
Apr 72.	(7") *(K 14165) <1080>* **AIN'T THAT PECULIAR. / THINK ABOUT THE CHILDREN**		85
Jul 72.	(7") *<1097>* **ROCK BOTTOM BLUES. / WONDERFUL FEELING**	-	
Oct 72.	(7") *(K 14207) <1119>* **YOUNG AND DUMB. / KNOCK ON MY DOOR**		
Jan 73.	(7") *<1148>* **I NEED YOU NEED ME. / ALL MINE**	-	
Jan 73.	(7") *(K 14220)* **SUMMER SONG. / BORROWED TIME**		-
Feb 73.	(lp) *(K 44233) <2137>* **MOTHER'S PRIDE**		
	– Last night I had a dream / Long road home / Old hat / Solid gold / Is it really you? / All mine / Summer song / Polecat blues / Beside myself / Regular guy / I need you need me / Feelings / I'm satisfied.		
Apr 73.	(7") *(K 14250)* **I NEED YOU NEED ME. / BESIDE MYSELF**		-
Apr 73.	(7") *<1162>* **LAST NIGHT I HAD A DREAM. / BESIDE MYSELF**	-	
——	**PATTI QUATRO** (SUZI's sister) – bass, repl. JUNE who joined ISIS		
——	**BRIE BRANDT-HOWARD** – drums + **JAMES NEWTON-HOWARD** – keyboards, repl. ALICE		

		Casablanca	Casablanca
Nov 74.	(7") *(CBX 502) <0009>* **I'VE HAD IT. / FROM WHERE I STAND**		79 Jun74
Jan 75.	(lp) *(4001) <7007>* **ROCK'N'ROLL SURVIVORS**		
	– Rock'n'roll survivors / Butter boy / Long distance lover / Let's spend the night together / Rockin' (all nite long) / Get out of my jungle / Beggar man / Sally go 'round the roses / I've had it / From where I stand.		
Mar 75.	(7") *(CBX 508) <814>* **BUTTER BOY. / BEGGAR MAN**		29 Jan75

—— disbanded after above, when CAIT DAVIS had replaced BRIE. After their last hit, JUNE returned for a short spell. NICKY BARCLAY went solo in 1976, and released an album; 'DIAMOND IN A JUNKYARD' for 'Ariola'.

MILLINGTON

were formed by **JUNE + JEAN**, with loads of session people incl. **LEO ADAMIAN** – drums, vocals

		U.A.	U.A.
Mar 78.	(7") *(UP 36367)* **LADIES ON THE STAGE. / FANTASY**		
Mar 78.	(lp) *(UAG 30158) <LA 821>* **LADIES ON THE STAGE**		
	– Ladies on the stage / Love brought us together / How can I make it better / dream desire / Heaven is in your mind / Young and in love / You need this woman / Fantasy / Bird in flight / So good to be home.		

—— They split again, and JEAN married EARL SLICK, who sessioned on above album.

FAR

Formed: Sacramento, California, USA . . . 1991 by JONAH SONZ MATRANGA, SHAUN LOPEZ, JOHN GUTENBERGER and CHRIS ROBYN. Describing themselves as "emo-core" (i.e. hardcore with emotion), they issued a batch of 7" singles, demo cassettes and CD's, the latter two released on independent imprints, 'Rusty Nail' and 'Our Own Records'. During this period they built up a loyal groundswell of support through constant touring before finally delivering their first official set, the quirkily titled 'TIN CANS WITH STRINGS TO YOU' (1996), via a deal with Epic subsidiary 'Immortal'. Early in 1998, FAR unleashed their second set, 'WATER & SOLUTIONS', although they seem no nearer Kerrang! domination two years on.

Album rating: TIN CAN WITH STRINGS TO YOU (*6) / WATER & SOLUTIONS (*7)

JONAH SONZ MATRANGA – vocals, guitar / **SHAUN LOPEZ** – guitar / **JOHN GUTENBERGER** – bass / **CHRIS ROBYN** – drums

—— released a series of singles, etc.

		Immortal – Epic	Immortal – Epic
Apr 96.	(cd) *<67491>* **TIN CANS WITH STRINGS TO YOU**	-	

– What I've wanted to say / Love, American style / In the aisle, yelling / Girl / Seasick / Job's eyes / Punch drunk / Celebrate her / Boring life / Joining the circus / Cut iut / Sorrow's end.

Mar 98. (cd/c) *(489233-2/-4)* <68718> **WATER & SOLUTIONS** [ ] [ ]
– Bury white / Realy here / Water & solutions / Mother Mary / I like it / The system / Nestle / In 2 again / Wear it so well / Man overboard / Another way out / Waiting for Sunday.

Mick FARREN (see under ⇒ PINK FAIRIES)

Perry FARRELL (see under ⇒ JANE'S ADDICTION)

FASTER PUSSYCAT

Formed: Los Angeles, California, USA . . . 1986 by TAIME DOWNE and MICK CRIPPS, although the latter subsequently departed for L.A. GUNS with DOWNE enlisting GREG STEELE, BRENT MUSCAT, ERIC STACY and MARK MICHAELS. One of the leading lights of the L.A. sleaze-rock scene alongside GUNS N' ROSES etc., they quickly signed to 'Elektra', unleashing the Ric Browde-produced eponymous debut album in 1987. A classic of the genre, the album covered all the right reference points, HANOI ROCKS, AEROSMITH, KISS, The ROLLING STONES etc., DOWNE's debauched innuendo of a vocal backed by the scuzziest riffs and most infectious bubbleglam choruses this side of The NEW YORK DOLLS. One of the best tracks on the album, as well as the debut single, 'DON'T CHANGE THAT SONG' illustrated Russ Meyer (creator of cult film, 'Faster Pussycat Kill! Kill!') had inspired more than the group's name, with its lurid video of large-breasted rock chicks bouncing around a jukebox. While the album never achieved quite the same commercial success as GUNS N' ROSES' 'Appetite For Destruction', it nevertheless broke the US Top 100, while a follow-up, 'WAKE ME WHEN IT'S OVER' (1989) made the UK Top 40. Though this second effort benefitted from a more professional, conventional hard rock approach, some of the earlier sleazy charm was lost in the transition. Predictably, then, they even made the UK Top 30 with the obligatory ballad, 'HOUSE OF PAIN'. A well-received European tour with The ALMIGHTY and DANGEROUS TOYS followed although sticksman MICHAELS was out on his ear after being arrested on drugs charges. With the rock landscape changed dramatically by the release of 1992's 'WHIPPED', FASTER PUSSYCAT were subsequently dropped by their label despite continuing critical praise from certain sections of the rock press, the group disbanding soon after. • **Songwriters:** TOWNE-STEELE, + some with MUSCAT and others.

Album rating: FASTER PUSSYCAT (*7) / WAKE ME WHEN IT'S OVER (*6) / WHIPPED (*6)

TAIME DOWNE – vocals / **GREGG STEELE** – guitars / **BRENT MUSCAT** – guitar / **ERIC STACY** – bass / **MARK MICHAELS** – drums

Elektra Elektra

Jul 87. (lp/c) *(980730-1/-4)* <60730> **FASTER PUSSYCAT** [ ] [97]
– Don't change that song / Bathroom wall / No room for emotion / Cathouse / Babylon / Smash alley / Shooting you down / The city has no heart / Ship rolls in / Bottle in front of me.

Sep 87. (7"/12") *(EKR 62/+T)* **DON'T CHANGE THAT SONG. / CAT HOUSE** [ ] [ ]

Nov 87. (7") *<69437>* **CATHOUSE. / BATHROOM** [-] [ ]

Feb 88. (7") *<69413>* **BABYLON. / SMASH ALLEY** [-] [ ]

Sep 89. (lp/c)(cd) *(EKT 110/+C)(7559 61124-2)* <60883> **WAKE ME WHEN IT'S OVER** [35] [48]
– Where there's a whip there's a way / Crying shame / Little dove / House of pain / Pulling the weeds / Poison ivy / Gonna walk / Slip of the tongue / Tattoo / Ain't no way. *(cd re-iss. Nov93; same)*

Dec 89. (7"/12") *(EKR 103/+T)* <69274> **POISON IVY. / TATTOO** [ ] [ ]

Feb 90. (7") *<64995>* **HOUSE OF PAIN. / SLIP OF THE TONGUE** [-] [28]

Jul 90. (7") *(EKR 112)* **HOUSE OF PAIN. / LITTLE DOVE (live)** [ ] [-]
(12"+=/cd-s+=) *(EKR 112 T/CD)* – Smash alley (live) / Pulling weeds (live).

Aug 92. (cd)(lp/c) *<(7559 61124-2)>* *(EKT 110/+C)* **WHIPPED!** [58] [90]
– Nonstop to nowhere / Body thief / Jack the bastard / Big dictionary / Madam Ruby's love boutique / Only way out / Maid in Wonderland / Friends / Cat bash / Loose booty / Mr.Lovedog / Out with a bang.

Sep 92. (7"ep/12"ep/cd-ep) **NONSTOP TO NOWHERE / CHARGE ME UP / TOO TIGHT / YOU'RE SO VAIN** [-] [ ]

— split after above; DOWNE subsequently appeared with PIGFACE

FASTWAY

Formed: London, England . . . mid '82 by ex-MOTORHEAD guitarist, "FAST" EDDIE CLARKE and PETE WAY together with Irishman DAVE KING and ex-HUMBLE PIE sticksman, JERRY SHIRLEY. Signing to 'C.B.S.', the group nudged into the UK Top 75 with their debut single, 'EASY LIVIN' in Spring '83, an eponymous album almost breaking the US Top 30. Comparisons with the mainlining scuzz-rock of MOTORHEAD were inevitable and FASTWAY's rather unadventurous Brit-rock approach emerged looking pretty lame. The fact that WAY had left just prior to the album's release (he subsequently formed WAYSTED) didn't help matters, although FASTWAY put their faith in their encouraging US reception and began work on another album. With CHARLIE McCRACKEN replacing WAY, the group recorded 'ALL FIRED UP'. Sticking to the same basic formula as the debut, the record struggled to make it into the US Top 60, while in Britain and Europe, FASTWAY found it difficult to make any significant headway at all. Disillusioned with this state of affairs, McCRACKEN and SHIRLEY departed, their replacements being SHANE CARROLL and ALAN CONNOR respectively. Following another listless album in 1986, 'WAITING FOR THE ROAR', FASTWAY enjoyed a bit of belated success with their soundtrack for cheesy metal/horror flick, 'Trick Or Treat'. Despite this surprise exposure, the band subsequently broke up with EDDIE heading back to Britain and enlisting a complete new line-up headed by ex-JOAN JETT man, LEA HART along with PAUL GRAY and STEVE CLARKE. Now signed to 'G.W.R.' (also home to MOTORHEAD), this revamped FASTWAY took another shot at rock fame with 'ON TARGET' (1988), although predictably their aim was poor and the album missed by a mile. Surely flogging the proverbial dead horse, EDDIE and HART lined-up yet another variation on the FASTWAY theme (including members of GIRLSCHOOL) for a final effort, 'BAD BAD GIRLS' (1990), before finally calling it a day. CLARKE subsequently pursued a low-key solo career.

Album rating: FASTWAY (*6) / ALL FIRED UP (*6) / WAITING FOR THE ROAR (*5) / TRICK OR TREAT soundtrack (*6) / ON TARGET (*4) / BAD BAD GIRLS (*4)

"FAST" EDDIE CLARKE (b. 5 Oct'50, Isleworth, Middlesex, England) – guitar (ex-MOTORHEAD, exBLUE GOOSE, ex-CURTIS KNIGHT'S ZEUS) / **PETE WAY** – bass (ex-UFO) / **DAVE KING** – vocals / **JERRY SHIRLEY** – drums (ex-HUMBLE PIE)

C.B.S. Columbia

Mar 83. (7") *(A 3196)* **EASY LIVIN'. / SAY WHAT YOU WILL** [74] [ ]
(12"+=) *(A13 3196)* – Far far from home.

Apr 83. (lp/c) *(CBS/40 25359)* <38662> **FASTWAY** [43] [31]
– Easy livin' / Feel me, touch me (do anything you want) / All I need is your love / Another day / Heft! / We become one / Give it all you got / Say what you will / You got me runnin' / Give it some action.

Jun 83. (7"/12") *(A/TA 3480)* **WE BECOME ONE. / CRAZY DREAM** [ ] [-]

Aug 83. (7") *<04112>* **WE BECOME ONE. / BACK IN THE GAME** [-] [ ]

— PETE WAY left to form WAYSTED just prior to above album

— **CHARLIE McCRACKEN** – bass (replaced him)

May 84. (7") *(A 4370)* **THE STRANGER. / HURTIN' ME** [ ] [ ]

Jul 84. (7"/12") *(A/TA 4503)* **ALL FIRED UP. / HURTIN' ME** [ ] [-]

Jul 84. (7") *<04591>* **ALL FIRED UP. / STATION** [-] [ ]

Jul 84. (lp/c) *(CBS/40 25958)* <39373> **ALL FIRED UP** [ ] [59]
– All fired up / Misunderstood / Steal the show / Station / Non-stop love / Hurtin' me / Tell me / Hung up on love / The stranger / Telephone / If you could see.

— **SHANE CARROLL** – guitar, keyboards; repl. McCRACKEN

— **ALAN CONNOR** – drums; repl. SHIRLEY

Jan 86. (7"/12") *(A/TA 6804)* **THE WORLD WAITS FOR YOU. / GIRL** [ ] [ ]

Feb 86. (lp/c) *(CBS/40 26654)* <40268> **WAITING FOR THE ROAR** [ ] [ ]
– The world waits for you / Kill me with your heart / Tired of your love / Change / Move over / Little by little / Rock on / Waiting for the roar / Girl / Back door man. *(cd-iss. May87+=; CD 26654)* – Doin' just fine.

— added **PAUL REID** – bass

Nov 86. (lp,cd) *<40549>* **TRICK OR TREAT (soundtrack)** [-] [ ]
– Trick or treat / After midnight / Don't stop the fight / Get tough / Stand up / Tear down the walls / Hold on to the night / Heft! / If you could see.

— **CLARKE** enlisted a complete new line-up

— **LEA HART** – vocals, guitar (ex-JOAN JETT) repl. KING

— **PAUL GRAY** – bass (ex-UFO, ex-EDDIE & THE HOT RODS, ex-DAMNED) repl. CARROLL + REID

— **STEVE CLARKE** – drums; repl. CONNOR

G.W.R. G.W.R.

Feb 88. (7") *(GWR 8)* **A FINE LINE. / CHANGE OF HEART** [ ] [ ]

Mar 88. (lp/c/cd) *(GW LP/TC/CD 22)* <75411> **ON TARGET** [ ] [ ]
– Dead or alive / Change of heart / A fine line / Two hearts / You / Let him rock / She is danger / Show some emotion / These dreams / Close your eyes. *(<cd re-iss. Nov98 on 'Receiver'; RRCD 261>)*

— **K.B. BREN** (b. California, USA) – bass; repl. GRAY

— **RIFF RAFF** – drums; repl. CLARKE

Legacy Enigma

Mar 90. (cd/c/lp) *(LLCD/LLK/LLP 130)* <73582> **BAD BAD GIRLS** [ ] [ ]
– I've had enough / Bad bad girls / All shook up / Body rock / Miles away / She won't rock / No repair / Death of me / Cut loose / Lucky to lose / Big beat no heart.

May 90. (7") *(LGY 104)* **BAD BAD GIRLS. /** [ ] [ ]
(cd-s+=) *(LSYC 104)* –

Aug 90. (7") *(LGY 105)* **I'VE HAD ENOUGH. / ALL SHOOK UP** [ ] [-]

— split when EDDIE went solo

– compilations, etc. –

Oct 91. (cd/c/lp) *Receiver; (RR CD/MC/LP 147)* **SAY WHAT YOU WILL – LIVE (live)** [ ] [-]

Feb 94. (cd) *Loma; (LOMCD 6)* **ON TARGET / BAD BAD GIRLS** [ ] [-]

Mar 00. (cd) *Beat Goes On; (BGOCD 484)* **FASTWAY / ALL FIRED UP** [ ] [-]

Aug 00. (cd) *Connoiseur; (VSOPCD 318)* **THE COLLECTION** [ ] [-]

— CLARKE also appeared on PHIL TAYLORS's 'Naughty Old Santas Xmas Classics' in '89 and The MUGGERS 'Muggers Tapes' in '93. In the same year, CLARKE released a solo album, 'IT AIN'T OVER TILL IT'S OVER' on 'Chequered Flag' records.

FATES WARNING

Formed: Cincinatti, Ohio, USA . . . 1982 as MISFIT, by JOHN ARCH, JIM MATHEOS, VICTOR ARDUINI, JOE DiBIASE and STEVE ZIMMERMAN. The band's break came when they were asked to contribute a track to 'Metal Blade's 'METAL MASSACRE V' compilation, the label subsequently signing them to a long-term deal. A debut album, 'NIGHT ON BROCKEN' (1984), was a competent heavy metal affair owing something of a debt to the NWOBHM style which influenced many American acts around this time. A further two albums, 'THE SPECTRE WITHIN' (1985) and 'AWAKEN THE GUARDIAN' (1986), built on this approach to create a much more cerebral, intricately structured sound. The transformation was complete with the addition of new vocalist RAY ALDER, ARCH disillusioned with the more progressive direction. With Max Norman producing, the group's finest release to date, 'NO EXIT' (1988) brought inevitable comparisons with the epic concept-metal of QUEENSRYCHE. Although the record almost cracked the US Top 100, the group nevertheless failed to achieve the same degree of success as the latter act. 'PERFECT SYMMETRY' (1989) boasted the keyboard skills of DREAM THEATER's KEVIN MOORE, adding even more of a progressive feel to proceedings. While certain sections of the metal press have praised subsequent releases like 'PARALLELS' (1991) and 'INSIDE OUT' (1994), the group's pomp-rock approach, more than ever, remains a specialised taste. Their last outing to date, 1997's 'A PLEASANT SHADE OF GREY', was a concept affair numbering a single (albeit album length) 'song' and proving that the ideas and concepts of the 70's are alive and kicking today, if not exactly relevant. A live follow-up also featured the track and it looked as if FATES WARNING were treading water. However, the band were back to their Prog-metal best with their well-acclaimed umpteenth set, 'DISCONNECTED', in mid-2000.

Album rating: NIGHT ON BROCKEN (*6) / THE SPECTRE WITHIN (*5) / AWAKEN THE GUARDIAN (*6) / NO EXIT (*7) / PERFECT SYMMETRY (*4) / PARALLELS (*5) / A PLEASANT SHADE OF GREY (*4) / STILL LIVE (*4) / DISCONNECTED (*6)

JOHN ARCH – vocals / **JIM MATHEOS** – guitar / **VICTOR ARDUINI** – guitar / **JOE DiBIASE** – bass / **STEVE ZIMMERMAN** – drums

Roadrunner / Metal Blade

1984. (lp) *(RR 9823)* *<MBR 1025>* **NIGHT ON BROCKEN** [ ] [ ]
– Buried alive / The calling / Kiss of death / Night on Brocken / S.E.K. / Misfit / Shadowfax / Damnation / Soldier boy. *(cd-iss. May96 on 'Metal Blade'; 398414053CD)*

—— **FRANK ARESTI** – guitar; repl. ARDUINI

Nov 85. (lp) *(RR 9737)* *<14054>* **THE SPECTRE WITHIN** [ ] [ ]
– Traveler in time / Without a trace / Orphan gypsy / Pirates of the underground / The apparition / Kyrie eleison / Epitaph. *(cd-iss. May96 on 'Metal Blade'; 398414054CD)*

Jan 87. (lp) *(RR 9660)* *<73231>* **AWAKEN THE GUARDIAN** [ ] [ ]
– The sorceress / Valley of the dolls / Fata morgana / Guardian / Prelude to ruin / Giant's lore (heart of winter) / Time long past / Exodus.

—— **RAY ALDER** – vocals; repl. ARCH

Apr 88. (lp/cd) *(RR 9558-1/-2)* *<73330>* **NO EXIT** [ ] [ ]
– No exit / Anarchy divine / Silent cries / In a word / Shades of heavenly death / The ivory gate of dreams (parts 1-8). *(cd-iss. Apr96 on 'Metal Blade'; 398414047CD)*

—— **MARK ZONDER** – drums; repl. ZIMMERMAN

—— guest KEVIN MOORE – keyboards (of DREAM THEATER)

Sep 89. (lp/cd) *(RR 9451-1/-2)* *<73408>* **PERFECT SYMMETRY** [ ] [ ]
– Part of the machine / Through different eyes / Static acts / A world apart / At fates hands / The arena / Chasing time / Nothing left to say. *(cd re-iss. May94; CDMZORRO 73)*

Nov 91. (cd/c/lp) *(CD/T+/ZORRO 31)* *<26698>* **PARALLELS** [ ] [ ]
– Leave the past behind / Life in still water / Eye to eye / The eleventh hour / Point of view / We only say goodbye / Don't follow me / The road goes on forever.

Massacre / Priority

Jun 94. (cd/c/lp) *(MASS CD/MC/LP 037)* *<53915>* **INSIDE OUT** [ ] [ ]
– Outside looking in / Pale fire / The strand / Shelter me / Island in the stream / Down to the wire / Face the fear / Inward bound / Monument / Afterglow. *<re-iss. 1994 on 'Priority'; 53918>*

Massacre / Metal Blade

Jun 97. (cd) *(MASSCD 125)* *<14129>* **A PLEASANT SHADE OF GREY** [ ] [ ] Apr97
– A pleasant shade of grey (parts 1-12).

Oct 98. (d-cd) *(MASSCD 147)* *<14188>* **STILL LIVE (live)** [ ] [ ]
– A pleasant shade of grey (parts 1-12) / The ivory gate of dreams / The eleventh hour / Point of view / Monument / At fate's hands / Prelude to ruin / We only say goodbye.

Jul 00. (cd) *(MASSCD 242)* *<14324>* **DISCONNECTED** [ ] [ ]
– Disconnected (part 1) / One / So / Pieces of me / Something from nothing / Still remains / Disconnected (part 2).

– compilations, etc. –

Jul 90. (cd) *Metal Blade; (CDZORRO 38)* **NIGHTS ON BROCKEN / THE SPECTRE WITHIN** [ ] [-]

Jul 90. (cd) *Metal Blade; (CDZORRO 39)* **AWAKEN THE GUARDIAN / NO EXIT** [ ] [-]

Feb 95. (cd) *Metal Blade; (CDZORRO 84)* **CHASING TIME** [ ] [-]
(re-iss. Apr97; 398414085CD)

FEAR

Formed: San Francisco, California, USA . . . 1978 by LEE VING, PHILO CRAMER, DERF SCRATCH and SPIT STIX. One of the first bands to emerge from the US West Coast punk/proto-hardcore scene, The FEAR had already become infamous for their raucous stage show by the time they made their vinyl debut on the soundtrack (released in the States on 'Slash') to Penelope Spheeris' acclaimed punkumentary, 'Decline Of Western Civilization'. Subsequently signing a full deal with 'Slash', these defiantly un-PC reprobates eventually issued a single in their own right via 1982's 'THE RECORD', a mini-set rammed with brief bursts of full-throttle hardcore-punk that even stretched to a fine trashing of The Animals' 'WE GOT TO GET OUT OF THIS PLACE'. By the time of the record's release, STIX had already been replaced by JOHNNY BACKBEAT while a certain FLEA (of subsequent hyperactive CHILI PEPPERS fame) honed his bass playing on 1983's yuletide extravaganza, the 'FUCK CHRISTMAS' EP. With FLEA going on to better things, ex-DICKIES sticksman, LORENZO, was in place for 1985's 'MORE BEER' album, FEAR's first release for new label, 'Restless'. Save for a 1991 live album, the ensuing decade saw FEAR keep a low profile, most fans having long forgotten about them by the release of 1995's belated 'HAVE ANOTHER BEER WITH FEAR'.

Album rating: THE RECORD (*6) / MORE BEER (*4) / LIVE . . . FOR THE RECORD (*4) / HAVE ANOTHER BEER WITH FEAR (*4)

LEE VING – vocals, guitar, harmonica / **PHILO CRAMER** – guitar / **DERF SCRATCH** – bass / **SPIT STIX** – drums

not iss. / Slash

Feb 82. (m-lp) *<SR 111>* **THE RECORD** [-] [ ]
– Let's have a war / Beef bologna / Camarillo / I don't care about you / New York's alright if you like.., / Gimme some action / Foreign policy / We destroy the family / I love living in the city / Disconnected / We got to get out of this place / Fresh fresh / Getting the brush / No more nothing. *<cd-iss. 1990 on 'Warners'; 828806>*

—— STIX had already been repl. by **JOHNNY BACKBEAT** – drums

—— **FLEA** – bass; repl. SCRATCH

1983. (7"ep) **FUCK CHRISTMAS EP** [-] [ ]

—— **LORENZO** – bass (ex-DICKIES) repl. FLEA who joined RED HOT CHILI PEPPERS

Restless / Restless

1985. (lp) *<772039-1>* **MORE BEER** [-] [ ]
– Mouth don't stop (the trouble with . . .) / Responsibility / More beer / Hey / I am a doctor / Have a beer with fear / Bomb the Russians / Welcome to the dust ward / Null detector / Waiting for the meat / I love iving in the city / Now you're dead. *(UK cd-iss. Jul95; same as US)*

—— **SPIT STIX** was back in the fray after joining NINA HAGEN

Oct 91. (cd) *<772391-2>* **LIVE . . . FOR THE RECORD (live)** [-] [ ]
– Null detector / I love livin' in the city / New York's all right / Beef bologna / More beer / What are friends for / Welcome to the dust war / I am a doctor / We gotta get out of this place / F*** Christmas / Responsibility / Hey / Waiting for the meat / Camarillo / Foreign policy / Give me some action / We destroy the destroy / I don't care about you / Let's have a war. *(re-iss. Jul95; same)*

—— had already gave up the ghost . . . until . . .

Sector 2 / Sector 2

Jan 96. (cd) *<(SECT2 10020)>* **HAVE ANOTHER BEER WITH FEAR** [ ] [ ] Oct95
– Back into battle again / Demons stickin' pitchforks in my . . . / Ugly as you / Bad day / Everybody needs to believe in something / Chaos / U.S.A. / Legalize drugs / Drink some beer / Fuck you let's rodeo / Honor and obey / Meat and potatoes / Beer fight / Untermenschen / Publuc hangings / Free beer. *(cd re-iss. Jun98 on 'Fear'; HR 005-2)*

– compilations, etc. –

Mar 95. (cd) *Solar; <1003>* **AS FAR AS THE I CAN C** [-] [ ]

FEAR FACTORY

Formed: Los Angeles, California, USA . . . 1991 by BURTON C. BELL, the very-large DINO CAZARES and RAYMOND HERRERA. The group completed two BILL GOULD (Faith No More)-produced tracks for compilation album, 'L.A. Death Metal' before being snapped up by 'Roadrunner'. Instrumental in ushering in the current era of fertile cross-breeding between extreme metal and extreme techno, FEAR FACTORY debuted with the COLIN RICHARDSON-produced album, 'SOUL OF A NEW MACHINE' (1992), the record indicating expansive new possibilities for a flagging death-metal scene. Following US live work with BIOHAZARD and SICK OF IT ALL, they teamed up with veteran Canadian industrialists, FRONT LINE ASSEMBLY, who remixed their debut as 'FEAR IS THE MINDKILLER', NIN style. 1995 saw them grow into frontrunners of the new electronic-industrial death-metal brigade with the groundbreaking 'DEMANUFACTURE' set, a brutallly uncompromising album which continued their obsession with technology and the darker side of the human psyche. The record broke the UK Top 30, while another follow-up remix project, 'REMANUFACTURE (CLONING TECHNOLOGY)' (1997), made an even bigger dent in the UK charts. Featuring rhythmic (ranging from the funky to the synapse-shattering) reworkings from the likes of JUNKIE XL and DJ DANO, the album further blurred the fine line between organic and electronic music. CAZARES, with the help of BELL and FAITH NO MORE's BILL GOULD, were the mysterious members (although they denied this) behind BRUJERIA, a mock death-metal (pseudo-Mexican) septet, who released two albums, 'MATANDO GUEROS' (1993) and 'RAZA ODLADA' (1995). In 1998, FEAR FACTORY released another set, 'OBSOLETE', while the following year they took on Gary Numan's 'CARS' and released it as a single. The Angeleno doom-mongers were back on the production line in 2001 with 'DIGIMORTAL', a reliably menacing album concerning itself with portents of computer-aided oblivion and man's electronic heart of darkness. As ever, digitally-enhanced jackhammer rhythms, relentless riffing and grim soundscapes drove the message home as the FEAR FACTORY team took their militant industrial action to new extremes. • **Songwriters:** BELL / CAZARES / HERRERA, except DOG DAY SUNRISE (Head Of David).

Album rating: SOUL OF A NEW MACHINE (*6) / FEAR IS THE MINDKILLER mini (*5) / DEMANUFACTURE (*6) / REMANUFACTURE (CLONING TECHNOLOGY)

(*8) / OBSOLETE (*7) / DIGIMORTAL (*6) / Brujeria: MATANDOS GUEROS (*5) / RAZA ODIADA (*5) / BRUJERIZMO (*5)

BURTON C. BELL – vocals / **DINO CAZARES** – guitar (also of BRUJERIA) / **ANDREW SHIVES** – bass / **RAYMOND HERRERA** – drums

Roadrunner Roadrunner

Sep 92. (cd) *<(RR 9160-2)>* **SOUL OF A NEW MACHINE**
– Martyr / Leechmaster / Scapegoat / Crisis / Crash test / Flesh hold / Lifeblind / Scumgrief / Natividad / Big god – Raped souls / Arise above oppression / Self immolation / Suffer age / W.O.E. / Desecrate / Escape confusion / Manipulation. *(re-iss. Feb01; same)*

Apr 93. (m-cd) *<(RR 9082-2)>* **FEAR IS THE MINDKILLER**
– Martyr (suffer bastard mix) / Self immolation (vein tap mix) / Scapegoat (pigf*** mix) / Scumgrief (deep dub trauma mix) / Self immolation (liquid sky mix) / Self immolation (album version).

— **CHRISTIAN OLDE WOLBERS** – bass; repl. SHIVES

Jun 95. (cd/c/lp) *<(RR 8956-2/-4/-1)>* **DEMANUFACTURE** 27
– Demanufacture / Self bias resistor / Zero signal / Replica / New breed / Dog day sunrise / Body hammer / H-K (Hunter-Killer) / A therapy for pain / Flashpoint / Pisschrist. *(d-lp+=)* – Resistancial! / New breed (revolutionary designed mix).

Nov 95. (12"ep/cd-ep) *(RR 2330-6/-3)* **DOG DAY SUNRISE / ('A'version) / CONCRETO / REPLICA (electric sheep mix)** -
(12"/cd-s) *(NRR 2330-6/-3)* – ('A'remixes).

Jun 97. (cd/c/lp) *<(RR 8834-2/-4)>* **REMANUFACTURE (CLONING TECHNOLOGY)** 22
– Remanufacture / National panel beating / Genetic blueprint / Faithless / Bionic chronic / Cloning technology / Burn / T-1000 / Machines of hate / 21st century Jesus / Bound for forgiveness / Refinery / Remanufacture (edit).

Jul 97. (12"ep) **THE BABBER MIXES** -
– New breed (Steel gun mix) / Flashpoint (Chosen few mix) / T-1000 (DJ Dano mix) / Manic cure.

Oct 97. (cd-ep) *(RR 2271-3)* **BURN / CYBERDYNE / TRANSGENIC / REFUELLED** -

Jul 98. (cd/c) *<(RR 8752-2/-4)>* **OBSOLETE** 20 77
– Shock / Edgecrusher / Smasher – Devourer / Securiton / (Police state 2000) Descent / Hi-tech hate / Freedom or fire / Obsolete / Resurrection / Timelessness.

Dec 98. (cd-ep) *(RR 2232-5)* **RESURRECTION / 0-0 (WHERE EVIL DWELLS) / SOULWOUND** -

Sep 99. (cd-s) *(RR 2189-3)* **CARS / DESCENT (Falling Deeper mix) / EDGECRUSHER (Urban Assault mix)** -

Apr 01. (cd) *<(RR 8561-2)>* **DIGIMORTAL** 24 32
– What will become? / Damaged / Digimortal / No one / Linchpin / Invisible wounds (dark bodies) / Acres of skin / Back the f*** up / Byte block / Hurt conveyor / (Memory imprints) Never end. *(other cd+=; RR 8561-5)* – Dead man walking / Strain vs resistance / Repentance / Full metal contact.

BRUJERIA

JUAN BRUJO – vocals / **GUERO SIN FE + FANTASMA + HONGO** – bass / **ASESINO** – guitar / **GRENUDO** – drums / **JR HOZICON/DIRECTOR DIABOLICO** (aka CAZARES, BELL + BILL GOULD, etc.)

Roadrunner Roadrunner

Jul 93. (cd) *<(RR 9061-2)>* **MATANDO GUEROS**
– Pura de venta / Leves narcos / Sacrificio / Santa Lucia / Matando gueros / Seis seis seis / Cruza la frontera / Grenudos locos / Chingo de mecos / Narcos – Satanicos / Desperado / Culeros / Misas negras (sacrifico lo) / Chinga tu madre / Verga del Brujo – Estan chingados / Moestando ninos muertos / Machetazos (sacrifico II) / Castigo del Brujo / Cristo de la Roca. *(re-iss. Sep96; same)*

Sep 95. (cd) *<(RR 8923-2)>* **RAZA ODLADA**
– Raza odiado (Pito Wilson) / Colas de rata / Hechando chingasos (grenudo locos II) / La migra (cruza la frontera II) / Revolucion / Consejos narcos / Almas de venta / La ley de plomo / Los tengo colgando (chingo de mecos II) / Sesos humanos (sacrificio IV) / Primer meco / El patron / Hemanos Menendez / Radre nuestro / Ritmos santanicos. *(re-iss. Sep96; same)*

Mar 99. (cd-ep) *<(TRCD 071)>* **MARIJUANA** Oct00
– Marijuana / Matando gueros / Pito Wilson / Echando chingazos / Motando gueros / (untitled).
(above issued on 'Tralla')

Nov 00. (cd) *<(RR 8504-2)>* **BRUJERIZMO**
– Brujerizmo / Vayan sin miedo / La tracion / Pitits te invoco / Laboratorio cristalitos / Division del norte / Margha de odio / Adti-Castro / Guided a los ninos / El bajon / Mecosario / El Desmadre / Sida de la mente. *(lp-iss.Dec00 on 'Beat Generation'; BEAT 005LP)*

FEEDER

Formed: London, England . . . 1993 by Newport-born frontman GRANT NICHOLAS, fellow Welshman JON HENRY LEE on bass and through many auditions, Japanese bassist TAKA HIROSE, the group now set out to become the British answer to The SMASHING PUMPKINS. After slogging around the toilet circuit, the band signed to 'Echo' (home of JULIAN COPE and BABYBIRD), releasing their debut single 'TWO COLOURS' at the end of '95. The mini-album, 'SWIM' (mid '96), consolidated their pop-metal/grunge credentials, while an appearance at the CMJ music business conference in New York, led them to sign for 'Elektra'. Following on from the glistening dynamics and sonic confetti of their well-received debut album, 'POLYTHENE' (1997), they scored a number of minor UK chart successes culminating in the Top 30 single 'HIGH'. Never far from the pages of the Kerrang! or the NME, FEEDER continued to scale the charts via two equally enterprising hard rock-meets-indie sets, 'YESTERDAY WENT TOO SOON' (1999) and 'ECHO PARK' (2001).

Album rating: POLYTHENE (*6) / YESTERDAY WENT TOO SOON (*6) / ECHO PARK (*6)

GRANT NICHOLAS (b.1967) – vocals, guitar / **TAKA HIROSE** – bass / **JON HENRY LEE** – drums

Echo Elektra

Oct 95. (7"/cd-s) *(ecs/+cd 13)* **TWO COLOURS** -
– Chicken on a bone / Pictures of pain.

May 96. (m-cd/m-c/m-lp) *(ech cd/mc/lp 9)* **SWIM** -
– Sweet 16 / Stereo world / W.I.T. / Descend / World asleep / Swim. *(m-cd re-iss. Oct98; same)*

Oct 96. (7") *(ecs 27)* **STEREO WORLD. / MY PERFECT DAY** -
(cd-s+=) *(ecscd 27)* – World asleep / Change.

Feb 97. (7") *(ecs 32)* **TANGERINE. / RHUBARB** 60 -
(cd-s+=) *(ecscd 32)* – Rain.
(cd-s+=) *(ecscx 32)* – ('A'side) / TV me / Elegy.

Apr 97. (7") *(ecs 36)* **CEMENT. / PICTURES OF PAIN** 53 -
(cd-s+=) *(ecscd 36)* – Undivided.
(cd-s) *(ecscx 36)* – ('A'live) / Tangerine (live) / Shade (live) / Stereo world (live).

May 97. (cd/c/lp) *(ech cd/mc/lp 15)* *<62085>* **POLYTHENE** 65
– Polythene girl / My perfect day / Cement / Crash / Radiation / Suffocate / Descend / Stereo world / Tangerine / Waterfall / Forgive / Twentieth century trip. *(re-iss. Oct97 & Oct99 cd/c; ech cd/mc 19)*

Aug 97. (7") *(ecs 42)* **CRASH. / HERE IN THE BUBBLE** 48 -
(cd-s+=) *(ecscd 42)* – Forgive (acoustic) / Stereo world (video).
(cd-s) *(ecscx 42)* – ('A'side) / Undivided / Swim (version) / Tangerine (video).

Oct 97. (7"colrd) *(ecs 44)* **HIGH. / WHEN THE MORNING COMES** 24 -
(cd-s+=) *(ecscd 44)* – Women in towels / Cement (video cd-rom).
(cd-s) *(ecscx 44)* – ('A'side) / ('A'acoustic) / Sweet 16 / Crash (video cd-rom).

Feb 98. (7"purple) *(ecs 52)* **SUFFOCATE. / ECLIPSE** 37 -
(cd-s+=) *(ecscd 52)* – Cockroach / High (video – live).
(cd-s) *(ecscx 52)* – ('A'side) / Dry (acoustic) / Teddy bear / Descend (live).

Mar 99. (7") *(ecs 75)* **DAY IN DAY OUT. / CAN'T DANCE TO DISCO / HONEYFUZZ** 31 -
(cd-s) *(ecscd 75)* – ('A'side) / I need a buzz / Fly.
(cd-s) *(ecscx 75)* – ('A'side) / Can't dance to disco / Don't bring me down.

May 99. (c-s/cd-s) *(ecs mc/cd 77)* **INSOMNIA / SPACE AGE HERO / LIVING IN PARANOID** 22 -
(cd-s) *(ecscx 77)* – ('A'side) / Divebomb / Fly.

Aug 99. (c-s) *(ecsmc 79)* **YESTERDAY WENT TOO SOON / OXIDISE / TOMORROW SHINE** 20 -
(cd-s) *(ecscd 79)* – ('A'side) / Getting to know you well / Tomorrow shine.
(cd-s) *(ecscx 79)* – ('A'side) / Rubberband / Slide.

Aug 99. (cd/c/lp) *(ech cd/mc/lp 28)* *<62400>* **YESTERDAY WENT TOO SOON** 8 Oct99
– Anaesthetic / Insomnia / Picture of perfect youth / Yesterday went too soon / Waiting for changes / Radioman / Day in day out / Tinsel town / You're my evergreen / Dry / Hole in my head / So well / Paperfaces. *(d-cd; echcx 28)* – Bubble head.

Nov 99. (c-s) *(ecsmc 85)* **PAPERFACES / WHOOEY / WAITING FOR CHANGES (session)** 41 -
(cd-s) *(ecscd 85)* – (first two tracks) / Tinsel town (session).
(cd-s) *(ecscx 85)* – ('A'side) / Crash mat / You're my evergreen (session).

Jan 01. (7"orange) *(ecs 106)* **BUCK ROGERS. / SEX TYPE DRUG** 5 -
(cd-s) *(ecscd106)* – ('A'side) / Purple / Heads.
(cd-s) *(ecscx 106)* – ('A'side) / We the electronic / 21st Century meltdown / ('A'-CD-Rom).

Apr 01. (7") *(ecs 107)* **SEVEN DAYS IN THE SUN. / JUST A DAY** 14 -
(c-s+=/cd-s+=) *(esc mc/cd 107)* – Home for the summer.
(cd-s) *(ecscx 107)* – ('A'side) / Reminders / Forever glow / ('A'-CD-Rom).

Apr 01. (cd/c/lp) *(ech cd/mc/lp 34)* **ECHO PARK** 5 -
– Standing on the edge / Buck Rogers / Piece by piece / Seven days in the sun / We can't rewind / Turn / Choka / Oxygen / Tell all your friends / Under the weather / Satellite news / Bug / Just a day.

FEMME FATALE

Formed: Albuquerque, New Mexico . . . 1987 by LORRAINE LEWIS, MAZZI RAWD, BILL D'ANGELO, RICK RAEL and BOBBY MURRAY. Relocating to L.A., this glammy pop-metal outfit quickly secured a deal with 'M.C.A.', releasing their eponymous debut in late '88. Frontwoman LEWIS wasn't exactly one to hide her light under a bushel, playing on her womanly charms to market the band and proving that she was indeed, er . . . 'WAITING FOR THE BIG ONE'. While the album was a competent enough affair with melodies and big choruses in all the right places, the band couldn't compete with the big boys in the genre and promptly faded from view. • **Covers:** IT'S A LONG WAY TO THE TOP . . . (Ac-Dc).

Album rating: FEMME FATALE (*5)

LORRAINE LEWIS – vocals / **BIL D'ANGELO** – guitar / **MAZZI RAWD** – guitar / **RICK RAEL** – bass / **BOBBY MURRAY** – drums

M.C.A. M.C.A.

Oct 88. (7") *(MCA 1286)* **WAITING FOR THE BIG ONE. /** -
(12"+=) *(MCATR 1286)* –

Nov 88. (lp/c/cd) *(MCF/MCFC/DMCF 3433)* *<4215>* **FEMME FATALE**
– Waiting for the big one / Falling in & out of love / My baby's gun / Back in your arms again / Rebel / Fortune & fame / Touch and go / If / Heat the fire / Cradle's rockin'.

Jan 89. (7") *(MCA 1309)* *<53445>* **FALLING IN AND OUT OF LOVE. / FORTUNE & FAME**
(12"+=/12"w-poster/cd-s+=) *(MCAT/MCATR/DMCA 1309)* – It's a long way to the top (if you wanna rock'n'roll).

— LORRAINE teamed up with ROXY PETRUCCI (ex-VIXEN) and GINA STILE (ex-POISON DOLLYS)

FIELDS OF THE NEPHILIM

Formed: Stevenage, Hertfordshire, England . . . 1985 by CARL McCOY, TONY PETTITT, PETER YATES and brothers PAUL and NOD WRIGHT. Eternally popular among flour-faced goths and much ridiculed by the indie/rock press, FIELDS OF THE NEPHILIM were a sort of poorer cousin to darklords, SISTERS OF MERCY and The MISSION. Unlike those two bands, however, The 'NEPHILIM were never likely to cross over for mainstream rock consumption, if only for their steadfast adherence to goth cliches. To be fair, they did have a slightly different slant, at least image wise, kitted out in a kind of faux-Western garb, stetsons and all (black of course). Following on from an independently released debut EP, 'BURNING THE FIELDS', the band signed to 'Beggars Banquet' subsidiary, 'Situation Two' and unveiled their debut album, 'DAWNRAZOR'. OTT apocalyptic vocals and anthemic guitar doom was the order of the day, 'PREACHER MAN' becoming the band's calling card despite boasting a hilariously amateurish video. Attracting a fanatical fanbase, the band even managed to crack the UK Top 20 with the more accomplished follow-up set, 'THE NEPHILIM' (1988) and topped the indie charts with the 'MOONCHILD' single. Yet time-honoured "musical differences" would eventually prove the straw that broke the bat's back, third set 'ELYZIUM' (1990) displaying a much more toned-down approach in contrast to its predecessor. It was the last album McCOY would record with the band, bailing out in 1991 and taking the name with him while his former pardners in musical crime carried on under the name RUBICON. • **Songwriters:** Group compositions except; IN EVERY DREAM HOME A HEARTACHE (Roxy Music).

Album rating: DAWNRAZOR (*6) / THE NEPHILIM (*6) / ELYZIUM (*4) / EARTH INFERNO (*5) / REVELATIONS compilation (*6)

CARL McCOY – vocals / **PAUL WRIGHT** – guitar / **PETER YATES** – guitar / **TONY PETTITT** – bass / **NOD WRIGHT** – drums

Tower | not iss.

Aug 85. (12"ep) *(N 1)* **BURNING THE FIELDS** [ ] [-]
– Back in the Gehenna / Trees come down / Dark cell / Laura. *(re-iss. Jul87 on 'Jungle'; JUNG 28T)*

Situation 2 | Beggars Banquet

Aug 86. (12"m) *(SIT 42T)* **POWER. / SECRETS / THE TOWER** [ ] [-]
(above 2 re-iss. cd Dec91 as 'LAURA' on 'Contempo'; CONTECD 196)

Mar 87. (7") *(SIT 46)* **PREACHER MAN. / LAURA II** [ ] [-]
(12"+=) *(SIT 46T)* – ('A'-Contaminated version).

May 87. (lp/c)(cd) *(SIT UP/CP 18)(SITU 18CD) <6599>* **DAWNRAZOR** [62] [ ]
– Intro (The harmonica man) / Slow kill / Volcane (Mr. Jealousy has returned) / Vet for the insane / Dust / Reanimator / Dawnrazor / The sequel. *(c+=)* – Preacher man / Power. *(cd++=)* – Laura II / Secrets / The Tower. *(re-iss. 1988 lp/c/cd; SITL/+C 18/+CD) (cd-iss. Sep95 on 'Beggars Banquet-Lowdown'; BBL 18CD)*

Oct 87. (7") *(SIT 48)* **BLUE WATER. / IN EVERY DREAM HOME A HEARTACHE** [75] [-]
(12") *(SIT 48T)* – ('A'-Electrostatic mix) / ('A'-Hot wire version).

May 88. (7") *(SIT 52)* **MOONCHILD (first seal). / SHIVA** [28] [-]
(12"+=) *(SIT 52T)* – ('A'-Longevity version).
(12"+=) *(SIT 52TR)* – Power (live) / Vet for the insane (live).

Sep 88. (lp/c)(cd) *(SIT U/C 22)(SITU 22CD) <8511>* **THE NEPHILIM** [14] [ ]
– Endemoniada / The watchman / Phobia / Moonchild / Chord of souls / Shiva / Celebrate / Love under will / Last exit for the lost. *(re-iss. Jun89 as 2x12"; SITU 22L) (cd re-iss. Sep95 on 'Beggars Banquet-Lowdown'; BBL 22CD)*

May 89. (7"/12") *(SIT 57/+T)* **PSYCHONAUT (Lib.II). / CELEBRATE (second seal)** [35] [-]
(cd-s+=) *(SIT 57CD)* – Psychonaut (Lib.IV).
(12") *(SIT 57T)* – Psychonaut (Lib.III) / Psychonaut (Lib.I) / Psychonaut (Lib.IV).

Beggars Banquet | Polydor

Jul 90. (7") *(BEG 244)* **FOR HER LIGHT. / SUBMISSION** [54] [-]
(12"+=/cd-s+=) *(BEG 244 T/CD)* – ('A'&'B'extended).

Sep 90. (cd)(c/lp) *(BEGA 115CD)(BEGC/BEGA 115) <849488>* **ELIZIUM** [22] [ ]
– (Dead but dreaming) For her light (At the gates of silent memory) Paradise regained / Submission / Sumerland (what dreams may come) / Wail of summer / And there will your heart be also. *(re-iss. cd Sep95 on 'Beggars Banquet-Lowdown'; BBL 115CD)*

Nov 90. (7") *(BEG 250)* **SUMERLAND (DREAMED). / THE WATCHMAN (live)** [37] [-]
(12"+=/cd-s+=) *(BEG 250 T/CD)* – Blue water (live) / Phobia (live).

—— In 1990, for live work they added **PAUL CHOWSER** – keyboards

Mar 91. (cd)(c/d-lp) *(BEGA 120CD)(BEGC/BEGA 120)* **EARTH INFERNO (live)** [39] [-]
– Intro (Dead but dreaming) For her light (at the gates of silent memory) Paradise regained / Moonchild / Submission / Preacher man / Love under will / Sumerland / Last exit for the lost / Psychonaut / Dawnrazor. *(cd re-iss. Sep95 on 'Beggars Banquet-Lowdown'; BBL 120CD)*

—— CARL McCOY departed Oct'91

– compilations, etc. –

Aug 88. (m-lp) *Supporti Fonograph; (SF 008)* **RETURN TO GEHENNA** [ ] [-]
– Power (new version) / Laura (new version) / Secrets / The tower / Returning to Gehenna new version). *(cd-ep iss.Nov93; SF 008CV)*

Jun 92. (cd) *Windsong; (<WINCD 023>)* **BBC RADIO 1 IN CONCERT (live)** [ ] [ ] 1993

Jul 93. (cd)(c/lp) *Beggars Banquet; (BEGA 137CD)(BEGC/BEGA 137) / Atlantic; <82475>* **REVELATIONS** [ ] [ ] 1994
– Moonchild / Chord of souls / Last exit for the lost / Preacher man / Love under will / Power / Psychonaut lib III / For her light / Blue water / Vet for the insane / The watchman / Dawnrazor. *(cd-iss. Sep95 on 'Beggars Banquet-Lowdown'; BBL 137CD)*

Dec 93. (cd) *Nostradamus; (MOO 1CD)* **BURNING THE FIELDS** [ ] [-]

RUBICON

—— (aka FIELDS OF THE NEPHILIM)

—— with new vocalist **ANDY DELANEY** replacing McCOY

Beggars Banquet | Atlantic

Aug 92. (12"ep/cd-ep) *(BBQ T/CD)* **WATCH WITHOUT PAIN. / WATCH WITHOUT PAIN (full version) / KILLING TIME (demo version)** [ ] [-]

Oct 92. (12"ep/cd-ep) *(BBQ 4 T/CD)* **CRAZED. / CHAINS ARE GONE / BRAVE HEARTS (CELLAR TAPE)** [ ] [-]

Oct 92. (cd/c/lp) *(BBQ CD/MC/LP 128) <92495>* **WHAT STARTS, ENDS** [ ] [ ]
– Before my eyes / Crazed / Watch without pain / Brave hearts / Killing time / Inside your head / Unspoken / Hand for you / Rivers / What starts, ends. *(re-iss. Apr93 cd/c; same)*

Mar 93. (12"ep/cd-ep) *(BBQ 10 TP/CD)* **BEFORE MY EYES / STANDING ALONE. / ON YOUR SIDE / HARD FOR YOU** [ ] [-]

Apr 95. (cd-ep) *(BBQ 47CD)* **INSATIABLE / BURY MY GOLD / PRIME** [ ] [-]

Apr 95. (cd/c/lp) *(BBQ CD/MC/LP 170)* **ROOM 101** [ ] [-]
– Ageless / Rest a while / Doubt all / Insatiable / Cut down / On your side / This drenching night / Bury my gold / Empty hands / Eat with me.

NEPHILIM

—— **McCOY** + **PAUL MILES** – guitar / **CIAN HOUCHIN** – bass, programming / **SIMON RIPPIN** – drums

Beggars Banquet | Beggars Banquet

Mar 96. (12"ep/cd-ep) *(BEG 265 T/CD)* **PENETRATION. / XODUS / 24th MOMENT** [ ] [-]

Mar 96. (cd)(c/lp) *(BEGA 172CD)(BEGC/BEGA 172) <80172>* **ZOON** [ ] [ ] Oct96
– Still life / Xodus / Shine / Penetration / Melt (the catching of the butterfly) / Venus decomposing / Pazuzu (black rain) / Zoon / Zoon / Coma. *<US re-iss. 1997 on 'Metal Blade'; 14116>*

FIELDS OF THE NEPHILIM

—— re-formed the originals

Jungle | not iss.

Jul 00. (10"/cd-s) *(JUNG 64 T/CD)* **ONE MORE NIGHTMARE (TREES COME DOWN AD). / DARKCELL AD** [ ] [-]

FIFTEEN

Formed: Bay Area, San Francisco, California, USA . . . early 90's by JEFF OTT, who was the only original member by the time of the band's 7th album release. 1991 heralded the debut ('SWAIN'S FIRST BIKE') from this 'Lookout'-signed punk rock outfit whose songs declared war on the nasty corporate individual and outlasted that standard 3-minute punk song terrain. Their second LP, 'THE CHOICE OF A NEW GENERATION' (1993), offered little to the emergence of US punk since GREEN DAY, who, at the time, were at the helm of that genre. It wasn't really until 'BUZZ' was issued the following year that the band were beginning to make a name for themselves. Although shifting labels to 'Grass' for albums 'BUZZ' and its follow-up, 'SURPRISE!', GREEN DAY's BILLIE JOE ARMSTRONG still admitted a strong liking for the group. This forced FIFTEEN to return to 'Lookout' for a one-off EP, 'THERE'S NO PLACE LIKE HOME (GOOD NIGHT)'. The untimely suicide of their bassist, LUCKY, didn't stop JEFF OTT and his umpteenth line-up delivering two further studio sets for 'Cool Guy' and 'Sub City' respectively, 'EXTRA MEDIUM KICKBALL ALL-STAR' (1998) and 'LUCKY' (1999). If the "Over The Top!" OTT wasn't singing about summer love and world peace, he certainly showed venom for the average American man, the protagonist spending his career screaming through a haze of excellent pop-punk riffs. The latter set was incidentally devoted to their departed bassist, with all of the man's earnings going towards 'The Redwood Justice Project'.

Album rating: SWAIN'S FIRST BIKE (*3) / THE CHOICE OF A NEW GENERATION (*4) / BUZZ (*6) / SURPRISE! (*5) / ALLEGRA (*4) / EXTRA MEDIUM KICKBALL ALL-STAR (*4) / LUCKY (*5)

JEFF OTT – vocals, guitar / **MARK A. MORENO** – drums; repl. MICKEY MISCHIEF

not iss. | Lookout

1991. (cd) *<LOOKOUT 40>* **SWAIN'S FIRST BIKE** [-] [ ]
– Intentions / Definition / C#(tion) / Someday / Alienation / Implications / Resolution / Inclination / Subdivision / End / Liberation / Sweet valentine / Devotion / Imagination.

1993. (cd) *<LOOKOUT 65>* **CHOICE OF A NEW GENERATION** [-] [ ]
– Petroleum distillation / End of the summer / Separation 2 / Communication / Domination = destruction / Lookin' for trouble / Separation 1 / Perfection / Fation / Rejection / Sweet distraction / End of the century.
JOHN – bass / **CHRIS FLANAGAN** – drums; repl. MARK

Grass | Grass

Nov 94. (cd/lp) *(GROW 15-2/-1) <13006>* **BUZZ** [ ] [ ] Aug94
– World starvation / Helter smelter / No tion / Situations / I keep on trying / Question / Violation / Fifteen / Flood not bombs / Predisposition / Abel's song / In our world.

Aug 95. (cd-s) *<61>* **I'D RATHER KISS A WOOKIE** [-] [ ]

Apr 96. (cd/c/lp) *<13031>* **SURPRISE!** [-] [ ]
– Middle / Armed gang / Whore / Famous / No / Nancy's song / Circles / Parking lots / Stolen smiles / Song #14 / Back / My friend II / End II.

Lookout Lookout

Nov 96. (7") <(LOOKOUT 150)> **THERE'S NO PLACE LIKE HOME (GOOD NIGHT). / OOZE**
(cd-ep) <(LOOKOUT 150CD)> – ('A'side) / Sun song / Land mine / 924 / Ain't life a drag . . . / All the good times / Hey Joe / My world audio fanzine #4.

Cool Guy Cool Guy

Sep 97. (d-lp) <(CG 04)> **ALLEGRA (live)**
(cd-iss. Nov99 on 'Sub City'; SC 008CD)

Sep 98. (cd/c/lp) <CG 12> **EXTRA MEDIUM KICKBALL ALL-STAR** [-]
– Front / Chris' song / Eun II / Deal / Grow up / Emancipation proclamation / Over and over / Intelligence / Jesus / Rainbow connection / Violation II / Here by the shore / Algebra / Windfall / Johnny come lately / Trust fund junkie / Termaline / Booty shake / Lightning top / Favorite suit / Scared militia / Nando / Civilization.

Sub City Sub City

Apr 99. (cd/d-lp) <(SC 002 CD/LP)> **LUCKY**
– Family values / Lucky / My congressman / I am a man / Man against man / Stolen life / Evolve / Welcome to Berkeley / Mount shrink wrap / Land / War on drugs / We will win / Sinseriously / Payback is beautiful / When is he going to fucking shut up . . ..

FIFTH ANGEL

Formed: Bellevue, Washington, USA . . . 1984 by TED PILOT, JAMES BYRD, ED ARCHER, JOHN MACKO and KEN MARY. Taking their name from The Book Of Revelations, the group promptly came to the attention of metal guru MIKE VARNEY, who signed them to his 'Shrapnel' label. An eponymous debut surfaced in 1986, its uncompromising riffing impressing 'Epic' to the tune of a major label deal, the company subsequently re-issuing the record in remixed form a couple of years after its initial appearance. A follow-up, 'TIME WILL TELL' (1989), was another competent set although the group subsequently folded when MARY hooked up with ALICE COOPER.

Album rating: FIFTH ANGEL (*6) / TIME WILL TELL (*4)

TED PILOT – vocals / **JAMES BYRD** – guitar / **ED ARCHER** – guitar / **JOHN MACKO** – bass / **KEN MARY** – drums

not iss. Shrapnel

Jan 86. (lp) <SH 1022> **FIFTH ANGEL** [-]
– The night / Shout it out / Call out the warning / Fifth angel / Wings of destiny / In the fallout / Cry out the fools / Only the strong survive / Fade to flames.

— **KENDALL BECHTEL** – guitar, vocals; repl. BYRD

Roadrunner Epic

Jul 88. (lp) (RR 9688-1) <EK 44201> **FIFTH ANGEL** (remixed) Apr88
– In the fallout / Shout it out / Call out the warning / Fifth angel / Wings of destiny / The night / Only the strong survive / Cry out the fools / Fade to flames. *(cd-iss. Mar90 on 'Roadracer'; RO 9688-2)*

Nov 89. (lp/c/cd) <EK 45021-1/-4/-2> **TIME WILL TELL** [-]
– Cathedral / Midnight love / Seven hours / Broken dreams / Time will tell / Lights out / Wait for me / Angel of mercy / We rule / So long / Feel the heat.

— split after KEN MARY joined ALICE COOPER

59 TIMES THE PAIN

Formed: Fagersta, Sweden . . . 1992 by MICHAEL CONRADSSON, TONI VIRTANEN, MAGNUS LARNHED, and KAI KALLIOMAKI. Named after a song by American classic hardcore band HUSKER DU, these boys became a prominent feature of the Swedish punk revival scene in the '90s alongside bands like the anarcho-punk band REFUSED. Though unlike many bands of the international retro-punk movement who were weened in large part on the American hardcore style, 59xTP were raised also on much of the late 70's British punk output; the early material of The CLASH certainly influencing their work. Early days saw the departure of KALLIOMAKI, his replacement on guitar being NIKLAS LUNDGREN. 1993 brought about their first demo and the subsequent interest of the 'Burning Heart' label, who released the band's debut full-length 'MORE OUT OF TODAY' (1995). This first outing certainly pleased the ears of the rapidly emerging Swedish underground metal/punk scene. 59xTP capitalised on this success by delivering their second album, '20 PERCENT OF MY HAND' (1996). The turn of the century saw these Swedes release their aptly-titled third full offering, 'END OF THE MILLENNIUM' (1999). Unfortunately, this set was a little formulaic in sound, although there was no loss of the trademark punk spirit and passion. Luckily for the group, the new century did not see the end of 59xTP as they released their fourth LP, 'CALLING THE PUBLIC' (2000), to far greater critical praise than its predecessor.

Album rating: BLIND ANGER & HATE mini (*5) / MORE OUT OF TODAY (*5) / TWENTY PERCENT OF MY HAND (*6) / MUSIC FOR HARDCORE PUNK mini (*5) / END OF THE MILLENNIUM (*6) / CALLING THE PUBLIC (*6)

MAGNUS LARNHED – vocals, guitar / **NIKLAS LUNDGREN** – guitar; repl. KAI LALLIOMAKI / **MICHAEL CONRADSSON** – bass / **TONI VIRTANEN** – drums

Burning Heart Burning Heart

Oct 94. (m-cd) (BHR 13CD) **BLIND ANGER & HATE** [-]
– Leave me alone / Lost our trust / Our approach / Blind anger & hate / Sense of right and wrong / Let me in / Beliefs / Give us a break / Nothing left / Together we're stronger.

May 95. (m-cd) (BHR 24CD) **MORE OUT OF TODAY** [-]
– Stay / More out of today / Something you're not / Leaders & followers / Gotta be ready / So blind / As things were before / When it all comes down / One after another / To me you're dead / Is this it / All you got / We're in, now what / 2min remaining in the 3rd / For now / Time to chill.

Oct 95. (cd-ep) (BHR 029) **EVEN MORE OUT OF TODAY** [-]

Dec 96. (cd) (<BHR 52CD>) **TWENTY PERCENT OF MY HAND** Jul97
– With instead of against / Can't change me / Start the song / Don't belong here / Once proud to be / Keeping the dream alive / Face the truth / Gutfeeling / Today is the day / When ends never meet / Too late / Neither question nor disagree / We're still around.

Burning Heart Epitaph

Jan 98. (m-cd) (BHR 69CD) **MUSIC FOR HARDCORE PUNK** [-]
– Can't change me / Burned / Against it / Flares n' slippers / Small man, big mouth / Police on my back.

Feb 99. (cd-s) (BHR 84CD) **TURN AT 25th /** [-]

Mar 99. (cd) (BHR 85CD) <82085> **END OF THE MILLENNIUM** Aug99
– Working man hero / Me against the world / Turn at 25th / Priority II / Need no alibi / Weakend revolution / Found home / Broken unity / Got it all in sight / Make it go away / Daily mind distrortion / Clear enough? / Punkrock college (on with the show).

Jun 99. (12"ep/cd-ep; shared with The SUBTERRANEANS) (TR EP/CDS 75) **SPLIT EP** [-]
– Make it go away / Old news / Walk together, rock together / (others by SUBTERRANEANS).
(above issued on 'Tralla')

Apr 01. (cd/lp) (BHR 130-2/-1) **CALLING THE PUBLIC**
– Rock the city / Classaction / Calling the public / Welcome to the 21st century / Freedom station / Cash on delivery / Room with a view / Dead on a day like this / Upgraded system / My life my choice my call / Addicted / The emergency.

FIGHT (see under ⇒ HALFORD, Rob)

FILTER

Formed: Cleveland, Ohio, USA . . . 1995 by RICHARD PATRICK and BRIAN LIESEGANG (once both of NINE INCH NAILS). With the addition of GENO LENARDO, FRANK CAVANAGH and MATT WALKER, the group scraped into the lower regions of the US chart with their debut album, 'SHORT BUS' (1995). A basement industrial outfit utilising dense Euro-rock sounds, the group eventually secured some widespread exposure when they hit the UK Top 40 via a collaboration with The CRYSTAL METHOD, '(CAN'T YOU) TRIP LIKE I DO', featured on the soundtrack to 'The Spawn'. Mixing a cocktail of metal and goth once again (the kids just loved it, didn't they!), FILTER resurfaced with that difficult second album. Entitled confusingly enough, 'TITLE OF RECORD' (1999), the set made it all the way into the US Top 30 (UK Top 75), 'WELCOME TO THE FOLD' and 'TAKE A PICTURE' were worthy specimens. • **Note:** Don't let yourself buy the different house/club act, FILTER, who released a single, 'RUNNING AWAY', in '97.

Album rating: SHORT BUS (*8) / TITLE OF RECORD (*6)

RICHARD PATRICK (b.1967) – vocals, guitar, bass / **BRIAN LIESEGANG** (b.1970) – keyboards, drums / with **KEVIN HANLEY** – guitars / **SCOTT KERN + MIKE PEFFER** – drums

Warners Reprise

May 95. (cd/c) <(9362 45864-2/-4)> **SHORT BUS** [59]
– Hey man, nice shot / Dose / Under / Spent / Take another / Stuck in here / It's over / Gerbil / White like that / Consider this / So cool.

— basic duo now with **GENO LENARDO** – guitar / **FRANK CAVANAGH** – bass / **MATT WALKER** – drums

Aug 95. (12"/cd-s) (W 0299 T/CD1) <43531> **HEY MAN NICE SHOT (sober mix) / ('A'-1/2oz mix) / ('A'-1/4lb mix) / ('A'-Big Mac mix)** [76] Jul95
(cd-s) (W 0299 CD2) <43531> – ('A'-Bud gets the lead out mix) / ('A'-Sawed off edit) / ('A'-Nickel bag mix) / White like that.
(re-iss. May96; same)

— WALKER joined the SMASHING PUMPKINS in '96

— In Sep'97, FILTER & The CRYSTAL METHOD hit UK Top 40 with '(CAN'T YOU) TRIP LIKE I DO' from the film 'The Spawn'.

Aug 99. (9362 47519-2/-4) <47388> **TITLE OF RECORD** [75] [30]
– Sand / Welcome to the fold / Captain Bleigh / It's gonna kill me / The best things / Take a picture / Skinny / I will lead you / Cancer / I'm not the only one / Miss Blue.

Sep 99. (cd-s) (W 502CD) **WELCOME TO THE FOLD / ONE (IS THE LONELIEST NUMBER) / (CAN'T YOU) TRIP LIKE I DO** [-]
(cd-s) (W 502CDX) – ('A'-Freaq Nasty remix) / ('A'-Militant Moving Fusion remix) / ('A'-video).

Mar 00. (c-s) (W 515C) <44788> **TAKE A PICTURE (Letterman edit) / TAKE A PICTURE (live)** [25] [12] Nov99
(cd-s) (W 515CD) – ('A'side) / ('A'-Hybrid mix) / ('A'-Rennie Pilgrem mix).
(cd-s) (W 515CDX) – ('A'side) / Welcome to the fold (live) / Hey man, nice shot (live).

FINAL (see under ⇒ GODFLESH)

FIONA

Born: FIONA FLANAGAN, 13 Sep'61, New York City, New York, USA. After playing in a number of bands in the Big Apple, FIONA finally got a break when 'Atlantic' signed her to a solo deal in 1985. Alongside STARZ guitarist BOBBY MESSANO and session players BENJIE KING, DONNIE KISSELBACH and JOE FRANCO, she cut an eponymous debut set, released to encouraging reviews and an eventual Top 75 chart position later that summer. Moving away somewhat from the lightwieght pop-metal sound of the debut, a BEAU HILL-produced second set, 'BEYOND THE PALE' (1986), failed to break the Top 100 despite its more considered approach and guest appearances by glam/hair crew, WINGER. KIP WINGER was also credited on the risque hit, 'EVERYTHING YOU DO (YOU'RE SEXING ME)', a track which furnished FIONA with her biggest hit single to date, almost reaching the Top

50 in late '89. Despite co-starring in the musical, 'Hearts Of Fire', with BOB DYLAN amongst others, further chart success continued to elude the singer. After a final effort for 'Atlantic', 'HEART LIKE A GUN', and a one-off set for 'Geffen', 'SQUEEZE' (1992), she retired from the rock scene.

Album rating: FIONA (*4) / BEYOND THE PALE (*4) / HEART LIKE A GUN (*3) / SQUEEZE (*3)

FIONA – vocals / with **BOBBY MESSANO** – guitar / **BENJIE KING** – keyboards / **DONNIE KISSELBACH** – bass / **JOE FRANCO** – drums

Atlantic Atlantic

Jan 85. (7") *<89610>* **ITCHIN' FOR A FIGHT. / LOVE MAKES YOU BLIND** [-] [ ]
May 85. (7") *(A 9572) <89572>* **TALK TO ME. / JAMES** [ ] [64] Mar85
Jun 85. (lp/c) *(781242-1/-4) <81242>* **FIONA** [ ] [71] Mar85
– Hang your heart on mine / Talk to me / You're no angel / Rescue you / James / Love makes you blind / Over now / Na na song.
Jul 85. (7") *<89543>* **OVER NOW. / LOVE MAKES YOU BLIND** [-] [ ]
May 86. (7") *(A 9432) <89432>* **LIVING IN A BOY'S WORLD. / KEEPER OF THE FLAME** [ ] [ ]
May 86. (lp/c) *(781639-1/-4) <81639>* **BEYOND THE PALE** [ ] [ ]
– Tragedy / Hopelessly love you / Living in a boy's world / Thunder and lightning / Tender is the heart / Running out of night / In my blood / He's on my side / You better wait / Keeper of the flame.
Nov 87. (7") *<07596>* **HEARTS OF FIRE. / CARRY ON** [-] [ ]
(above from the film of the same name, released on 'Columbia')

— **MIKE SLAMMER** – guitar; repl. MESSANO

Nov 89. (7") *<88823>* **EVERYTHING YOU DO (YOU'RE SEXING ME). / CALLING ON YOU** [-] [52]
above credited KIP WINGER
Nov 89. (lp/c/cd) *(781903-1/-4/-2) <81903>* **HEART LIKE A GUN** [ ] [ ]
– Little Jeannie (got the look of love) / Everything you do (you're sexing me) / Where the cowboys go / Mariel / Draw the line / Here it comes again / Bringing in the beast / Victoria cross / Look at me now / When pink turns to blue.

Geffen Geffen

Mar 92. (lp/c/cd) *<(GEF/+C/D 24429)>* **SQUEEZE** [ ] [ ]
– Kiss the boys goodbye / Ain't that just like love / Treat me right / All over now / The best is yet to come / Squeeze / Don't come cryin' / Nobody dies of a broken heart / Mystery of love / Life on the Moon.

— she retired from the biz after above

fIREHOSE (see under ⇒ MINUTEMEN)

FIRE PARTY

Formed: Washington DC, USA ... 1986 by the all-girl foursome of AMY PICKERING, NATALIE AVERY, KATE SAMWORTH and NICKY THOMAS. Charged up by European support slots to SCREAM then THAT PETROL EMOTION, FIRE PARTY unleashed their eponymous debut mini-set in 1988 for 'Dischord' (base of FUGAZI). The album showed an astonishingly fresh grunge sound fusing elements of NIRVANA, WIRE and SONIC YOUTH, although the following year's, 'NEW ORLEANS OPERA', lacked the debut's bite and the girls split.

Album rating: FIRE PARTY (*6) / NEW ORLEANS OPERA (*4)

AMY PICKERING – vocals / **NATALIE AVERY** – guitar / **KATE SAMWORTH** – bass / **NICKY THOMAS** – drums

Dischord Dischord

May 88. (m-lp) *<(DISCHORD 28)>* **FIRE PARTY** [ ] [ ]
Oct 89. (m-lp/m-c) *<(DISCHORD 37/+C)>* **NEW ORLEANS OPERA** [ ] [ ]

— fizzled out after above

– compilations, etc. –

Oct 96. (cd) *Dischord; <DIS 103>* **FIRE PARTY** (first two sets) [-] [ ]
– Jerk / Basis / Cake / Drowning intentions / Walls of mind / Engine / Pilate / Make it quick / Bite / First course / Gethsemane / Prisoner / Fire / Only nine mottos / New Orleans opera / Basis / Are you on? / How to / Stray bullet.

FIRM (see under ⇒ LED ZEPPELIN)

FISH

Born: DEREK WILLIAM DICK, 25 Apr'58, Dalkeith, Lothian, Scotland. After leaving top progsters, MARILLION, in less than agreeable circumstances in September '88, he finally released a debut single, 'STATE OF MIND', a year later. This hit the UK Top 40, as did his early 1990 follow-up, 'BIG WEDGE'. A Top 5 album, 'VIGIL IN A WILDERNESS OF MIRRORS' was soon in the charts, FISH solo following a more commercial yet ambitiously diverse guitar-based sound while retaining the PETER GABRIEL-esque vocal theatrics. Through an ever changing cast of backing musicians, FISH recorded another two major label albums for 'Polydor, 'INTERNAL EXILE' (1991) and a covers set, 'SONGS FROM THE MIRROR' (1993), the latter of which stalled outside the Top 40. Moving back to Scotland after living in London, the singer then set up his own label, 'Dick Bros.', proceeding to maintain a prolific recording schedule over the ensuing four years as well as producing and releasing other low-key Scottish-based projects. Much of the material consisted of concert recordings, FISH retaining a loyal live following, especially in Europe. Studio wise, he released the 'SUITS' set in 1994, another Top 20 hit despite crticisms from the usual quarters. The Caledonian maverick even recorded a duet with forgotten 80's starlet SAM BROWN although predictably it failed to make the chart. 1995 saw the release of two complementary best of/live affairs, 'YIN' and 'YANG', while the singer returned in 1997 with 'SUNSETS ON EMPIRE'. The aquatic one subsequently became an unusual signing for 'Roadrunner' after a series of legal hassles with previous labels. The resulting Elliot Ness-produced 'RAINGODS WITH ZIPPOS' (1999) was hailed by many critics and fans as his most complete effort since splitting from MARILLION more than a decade previously. The new 'Roadrunner' deal also resulted in a veritable avalanche of live sets and oddity collections in late '98, among them 'KETTLE OF FISH 88-98', 'UNCLE FISH AND THE CRYPT CREEPERS' and 'TALES FROM THE BIG BUS'. • **Songwriters:** FISH co-wrote most of material with MICKEY SIMMONDS. He covered; THE FAITH HEALER (Sensational Alex Harvey Band). In early 1993, he released full covers album with tracks: QUESTION (Moody Blues) / BOSTON TEA PARTY (Sensational Alex Harvey Band) / FEARLESS (Pink Floyd) / APEMAN (Kinks) / HOLD YOUR HEAD UP (Argent) / SOLD (Sandy Denny) / I KNOW WHAT I LIKE (Genesis) / JEEPSTER (T.Rex) / FIVE YEARS (David Bowie) / ROADHOUSE BLUES (Doors). • **Trivia:** October '86, FISH was credited on TONY BANKS (Genesis) single 'Short Cut To Nowhere'.

Album rating: VIGIL IN A WILDERNESS OF MIRRORS (*6) / INTERNAL EXILE (*5) / SONGS FROM THE MIRROR (*3) / SUSHI (*5) / ACOUSTIC SESSION (*5) / SUITS (*4) / YIN collection (*6) / YANG collection (*6) / SUNSETS ON EMPIRE (*6) / RAINGODS WITH ZIPPOS (*4)

FISH – vocals (ex-MARILLION) with guest musicians on debut album **FRANK USHER** – guitar / **HAL LINDES** – guitar / **MICKEY SIMMONDS** – keyboards / **JOHN GIBLIN** – bass / **MARK BRZEZICKI** – drums / **CAROL KENYON** – backing vocals / plus **LUIS JARDIM** – percussion / **JANICK GERS** – guitar

E.M.I. E.M.I.

Oct 89. (c-s/7") *(TC+/EM 109)* **STATE OF MIND. / THE VOYEUR (I LIKE TO WATCH)** [32] [-]
(12"+=/cd-s+=) *(12/CD EM 109)* – ('A'-Presidential mix).
Dec 89. (7"/7"s)(c-s) *(EM/+S 125)(TC 125)* **BIG WEDGE. / JACK AND JILL** [25] [-]
(12"+=/12"pic-d)(cd-s+=) *(12EM/+PD 125)(CDEM 125)* – Faith healer (live).
Feb 90. (lp/c/cd)(pic-lp) *(CD/C+/EMD 1015)(EMPD 1015) <2202>* **VIGIL IN A WILDERNESS OF MIRRORS** [5] [ ]
– Vigil / Big wedge / State of mind / The company / A gentleman's excuse me / The voyeur (I like to watch) / Family business / View from the hill / Cliche. *(cd re-iss. Nov98 on 'Roadrunner'+=; RR 8687-2)* – Jack and Jill / Internal exile / A gentleman's excuse me / Whiplash.
Mar 90. (7"/7"red/7"sha-pic-d)(c-s) *(EM/+S/PD 135)(TCEM 135)* **A GENTLEMAN'S EXCUSE ME. / WHIPLASH** [30] [-]
(12"+=/12"pic-d+=)(cd-s+=) *(12EM/+PD 135)(CDEM 135)* – ('A'demo version).

— retained SIMMONDS and USHER, and brought in **ROBIN BOULT** – lead guitar, vocals / **DAVID PATON** – bass / **ETHAN JOHNS** – drums, percussion / guest drummer **TED McKENNA**

Polydor Polydor

Sep 91. (7") *(FISH Y/C 1)* **INTERNAL EXILE. / CARNIVAL MAN** [37] [-]
(12"+=) *(FISHS 1)* – ('A'-Karaoke mix).
(cd-s++=) *(FISCD 1)* – ('A'remix).
Oct 91. (cd/c/lp) *(511049-2/-4/-1) <513765>* **INTERNAL EXILE** [21] [ ]
– Shadowplay / Credo / Just good friends (close) / Favourite stranger / Lucky / Dear friend / Tongues / Internal exile. *(re-iss. cd Apr95; same) (cd re-iss. Nov98 on 'Roadrunner'+=; RR 8683-2)* – Poet's moon / Something in the air / Carnival man.
Dec 91. (7"/c-s) *(FISH Y/C 2)* **CREDO. / POET'S MOON** [38] [-]
(12"box+=/cd-s+=) *(FISHS/FISCD 2)* – ('A'mix).
(12"+=) *(FISHX 2)* – (the 2 'A'versions) / Tongues (demo).
Jun 92. (7"/c-s) *(FISH Y/C 3)* **SOMETHING IN THE AIR. / DEAR FRIEND** [51] [-]
(12"+=) *(FISHX 3)* – ('A'-Teddy bear mix).
(cd-s++=) *(FISHP 3)* – ('A'radio mix).
(cd-s) *(FISHL 3)* – ('A'side) ('A'-Christopher Robin mix) / Credo / Shadowplay.

— **FOSTER PATTERSON** – keyboards, vocals repl. SIMMONS / **KEVIN WILKINSON** – drums, percussion repl. JOHNS.

Jan 93. (cd/c/lp) *(517499-2/-4/-1)* **SONGS FROM THE MIRROR** [46] [-]
– Question / Boston tea party / Fearless / Apeman / Hold your head up / Solo / I know what I like (in your wardrobe) / Jeepster / Five years. *(re-iss. cd Apr95; same) (cd re-iss. Nov98 on 'Roadrunner'; RR 8682-2)*

Dick Bros Griffin

Mar 94. (d-cd) *(DDICK 002CD) <158>* **SUSHI (live)** [ ] [ ]
– Fearless / Big wedge / Boston tea party / Credo / Family business / View from a hill / He knows you know / She chameleon / Kayleigh / White Russian / The company / / Just good friends / Jeepster / Hold your head up / Lucky / Internal exile / Cliche / Last straw / Poet's Moon / Five years. *(re-iss. Sep96 on 'Blueprint'; DDICK 2CD) (re-iss. Nov98 on 'Roadrunner'; RR 8680-2)*
Apr 94. (c-s/ext-12"pic-d/cd-s) *(DDICK 3 CAS/PIC/CD1)* **LADY LET IT LIE / OUT OF MY LIFE. / BLACK CANAL** [46] [-]
(cd-s) *(DDICK 3CD2)* – ('A'extended) / ('B'live) / Emperors song (live) / Just good friends.
May 94. (cd/c/lp/pic-lp) *(DDICK 004 CD/MC/LP/PIC)* **SUITS** [18] [-]
– 1470 / Lady let it lie / Emperor's song / Fortunes of war / Somebody special / No dummy / Pipeline / Jumpsuit city / Bandwagon / Raw meat. *(cd re-iss. Sep96 on 'Blueprint'; DDICK 4CD) (cd re-iss. Nov98 on 'Roadrunner'; RR 8686-2)*
Sep 94. (cd-ep) *(DDICK 008CD1)* **FORTUNES OF WAR (edit) / SOMEBODY SPECIAL (live) / STATE OF MIND (live) / LUCKY (live)** [67] [-]
(cd-ep) *(DDICK 008CD2)* – ('A'live) / Warm wet circles / Jumpsuit city / The company (all live).
(cd-ep) *(DDICK 008CD3)* – ('A'acoustic) / Kayleigh (live) / Internal exile (live) / Just good friends (acoustic).
(cd-ep) *(DDICK 008CD4)* – ('A'acoustic) / Sugar mice (live) / Dear friend (live) / Lady let it lie (acoustic).

— Above 4-cd single (nearly 90 mins.) (can be fitted in together as 1 package.

Aug 95. (c-s; FISH featuring SAM BROWN) *(DDICK 014MC)* **JUST GOOD FRIENDS / SOMEBODY SPECIAL** 63 -
(cd-s+=) *(DDICK 014CD1)* – State of mind.
(cd-s) *(DDICK 014CD2)* – ('A'side) / Raw meat (live) / Roadhouse blues (live).

Sep 95. (cd/c) *(DDICK 011 CD/MC)* **YIN** (THE BEST OF FISH & '95 remixes) 58 -
– Incommunicado / Family business / Just good friends / Pipeline / Institution waltz / Tongues / Favourite stranger / Boston tea party / Raw meat / Time & a word / Company / Incubus / Solo. *(cd re-iss. Sep96 on 'Blueprint'; DDICK 11CD) (cd re-iss. Sep00 on 'Chocolate Frog – Voiceprint'; CFVP 004CD)*

Sep 95. (cd/c) *(DDICK 012 CD/MC)* **YANG** (THE BEST OF FISH & '95 remixes) 52 -
– Lucky / Big wedge / Lady let it lie / Lavender / Credo / A gentleman's excuse me / Kayleigh / State of mind / Somebody special / Sugar mice / Punch & Judy / Internal exile / Fortunes of war. *(cd re-iss. Sep96 on 'Blueprint'; DDICK 12CD)*

Dick Bros. Lightyear

May 97. (cd-s) *(DDICK 24CD1)* **BROTHER 52 / BROTHER 52 (Stateline mix) / DO NOT WALK OUTSIDE THIS AREA / BROTHER 52 (album version)** -
(cd-s) *(DDICK 24CD2)* – (first 2 tracks) / ('A'-4 am dub mix).

May 97. (cd) *(DDICK 25CD)* *<54197>* **SUNSETS ON EMPIRE** 42 Jun97
– Perception of Johnny punter / Goldfish and clowns / Change of heart / What colour is God / Tara / Jungle ride / Worm in a bottle / Brother 52 / Sunsets on empire / Say it with flowers / Do not walk outside this area. *(other cd; DDICK 26CD) (re-iss. Nov98 on 'Roadrunner'; RR 8679-2)*

Aug 97. (cd-s) *(DDICK 27CD)* **CHANGE OF HEART / GOLDFISH AND CLOWNS / THE PERCEPTION OF JOHNNY PUNTER** -

Roadrunner Roadrunner

Apr 99. (7"pic-d/cd-s; as FISH with ELIZABETH ANTWI) *(RR 2185-7/-3)* **INCOMPLETE. / MAKE IT HAPPEN (acoustic mix) / INCOMPLETE (castle demo)** -

Apr 99. (cd) *(<RR 8677-2>)* **RAINGODS WITH ZIPPOS** 57
– Tumbledown / Mission statement / Incomplete / Tilted cross / Faith healer / Rites of passage / Plague of ghosts – (i) Old haunts, (ii) Digging deep, (iii) Chocolate frogs, (iv) Waving at stars, (v) Raingods dancing, (vi) Wake-up call (make it happen).

– compilations, others, etc. –

Sep 94. (cd) *Blueprint; (DDICK 6CD)* **ACOUSTIC SESSIONS (live)** -
– Lucky / Internal exile / Kayleigh / Fortunes of war / Dear friend / Sugar mice / Somebody special / Jumpsuit city / Lady let it lie. *(re-iss. Jan01 on 'Chocolate Frog – Voiceprint'+=; CFVP 006CD)* – KRAKOW

Sep 96. (d-cd) *Blueprint; (DDICK 16CD)* **PIGPENS BIRTHDAY** -
(re-iss. Nov98 on 'Roadrunner'; RR 8684-2)

Nov 98. (cd) *Roadrunner; (<RR 8678-2>)* **KETTLE OF FISH 88-98**
– Big wedge / Just good friends (with SAM BROWN) / Brother 52 / Chasing Miss Pretty / Credo / A gentleman's excuse me / Goldfish and clowns / Lady let it lie / Lucky / State of mind / Mr Buttons / Fortunes of war / Internal exile. *(also w/ CD-ROM; RR 8678-8)*

Nov 98. (d-cd) *Roadrunner; (RR 8681-2)* **KRAKOW (live acoustic 1995)** -
– Somebody special / Jumpsuit city / Lady let it lie / Out of my life / State of mind / Kayleigh / Solo / Company / Giz a bun / Lavender.

Nov 98. (d-cd) *Roadrunner; (RR 8685-2)* **UNCLE FISH AND THE CRYPT CREEPERS**

Nov 98. (d-cd) *Roadrunner; (RR 8688-2)* **TALES FROM THE BIG BUS (live)** -

Nov 98. (cd) *Roadrunner; (RR 8689-2)* **FORTUNES OF WAR** -

May 99. (cd) *Blueprint; (BP 297CD)* **THE BBC SESSIONS** -

Jan 01. (d-cd) *Chocolate Frog – Voiceprint; (CFVP 001CD)* **TOILING IN THE REEPERBAHN** -

FISHBONE

Formed: Los Angeles, California, USA . . . 1980 by school friends ANGELO MOORE, KENDALL JONES, WALTER KIBBY, CHRIS DOWD, JOHN NORWOOD FISHER, PHILIP 'FISH' FISHER and CHARLIE DOWN. Fusing a variety of music styles including funk, jazz, ska and hard rock, FISHBONE initially showcased their eclectic and energetic stylee on stage supporting the likes of the DEAD KENNEDYS (one gig resulted in NORWOOD getting stabbed!). Influenced by BAD BRAINS, SEX PISTOLS and DUKE ELLINGTON!, these sets were noted for the wacky rooster-haired ANGELO playing saxophone while doing backflips (later in their career he was to play completely naked although at times his sax hid his essentials). Helped along by the production of DAVID KAHANE, their self-titled debut mini-lp for 'Columbia' in 1985 should have brought them commercial fruits, as yet similar groups such as LIVING COLOUR and RED HOT CHILI PEPPERS were gaining much wider attention. 'IN YOUR FACE' (1986) was next up, an improvement on their first effort, it nevertheless failed to achieve its goal. In the Autumn of '88, their third set, 'TRUTH AND SOUL' dented the US Top 200. Two classy singles were lifted from it, their version of Curtis Mayfield's 'FREDDIE'S DEAD' and 'MA & PA', the latter backed incidentally by another risque gem, 'BONIN' IN THE BONEYARD'. After concentrating on getting their manic message to the world on stage, FISHBONE returned with a new guitarist, JOHN BIGHAM, who played on their long-awaited follow-up, 'THE REALITY OF MY SURROUNDINGS' (1991). This SLY STONE-influenced set finally awoke the buying public and gave them a US Top 50 placing, the track 'EVERYDAY SUNSHINE' one of its highlights. However, the band were blighted when the bible-thumping KENDALL took off to join a religious cult, all the members were subsequently ending up in court having tried to kidnap him from his new found "family". The impetus was certainly lost on their next album, the strangely titled 'GIVE A MONKEY A BRAIN AND HE'LL SWEAR HE'S THE CENTRE OF THE UNIVERSE' (1993), although they did have a minor UK hit with 'SWIM'. It took them three years to get back in the studio, although the resulting album, 'CHIM CHIM'S BADASS REVENGE' (1996) was over indulgent and disappointing. • **Trivia:** FISHBONE have also appeared in the films 'Back To The Beach', 'Tape Heads', 'Far Out, Man' and 'I'm Gonna Git You'.

Album rating: FISHBONE (*6) / IN YOUR FACE (*7) / TRUTH AND SOUL (*7) / THE REALITY OF MY SURROUNDINGS (*8) / GIVE A MONKEY A BRAIN AND HE'LL SWEAR HE'S THE CENTER OF THE UNIVERSE (*4) / CHIM CHIM'S BAD ASS REVENGE (*4) / FISHBONE 101: NUTTASAURUSMEG FOSSIL FUELIN part compilation (*7)

ANGELO MOORE (b. 5 Nov'65) – vocals, saxophone / **KENDALL JONES** – guitar, vocals / **WALTER A. KIBBY II** (b.13 Nov'64) – vocals / **JOHN NORWOOD FISHER** (b. 9 Dec'65) – bass, vocals / **CHRIS 'MAVERICK MEAT' DOWD** (b.20 Sep'65) – trombone, keyboards / **PHILIP 'FISH' FISHER** – drums, percussion / **CHARLIE DOWN** – guitars

C.B.S. Columbia

Sep 85. (lp/c) *(CBS/40 20529)* *<40032>* **FISHBONE**
– Ugly / Another generation / ? (Modern industry) / Party at Ground Zero / V.T.T.L.O.T.F.D.G.F. / Lyin' ass bitch.

Sep 85. (7") *<04922>* **MUSIC INDUSTRY. / V.T.T.L.O.T.F.D.G.F.** -

Sep 85. (7"/12") *(A/TA 6544)* **PARTY AT GROUND ZERO. / V.T.T.L.O.T.F.D.G.F.**

Nov 86. (cd/c/lp) *<CK/BCT+/40333>* **IN YOUR FACE** -
– When problems arise / A selection / Cholly / I wish I had a date / Movement in the light / Give it up / In the air / Turn the other way / Knock it / "Simon says" The kingpin / Post cold war politics / It's a wonderful life (gonna have a good time) / Slick Nick, you devil you / Iration / Just call me Scrooge.

Nov 87. (12"ep) **IT'S A WONDERFUL LIFE EP** -

Epic Epic

Sep 88. (7") *(FSH 1)* **FREDDIE'S DEAD. / IT'S A WONDERFUL LIFE (GONNA HAVE A GOOD TIME)** -
(12"+=/12"pic-d+=) *(FSH T/P 1)* – ('A'versions).
(cd-s++=) *(CDFSH 1)* – I like to hide behind my glasses.

Oct 88. (lp/c/cd) *(461173-1/-4/-2)* *<40891>* **TRUTH AND SOUL** Sep88
– Freddie's dead / Ma and pa / Mighty long way / Pouring rain / Deep inside / Question of life / Bonin' in the boneyard / One day / Subliminal fascism / Slow bus movin' (Howard beach party) / Ghetto soundwave / Change.

Jan 89. (7") *<08500>* **FREDDIE'S DEAD. / QUESTION OF LIFE** -

Mar 89. (7"/7"pic-d) *(FSH/+P 2)* **MA AND PA. / BONIN' IN THE BONEYARD**
(12"+=) *(FSHT 2)* – I like to hide behind my glasses.
(cd-s++=) *(CPFSH 2)* – In the name of swing.

— **'BIG' JOHN BIGHAM** – guitar; repl. DOWN

Columbia Columbia

Apr 91. (c-ep) *<73549>* **NEW AND IMPROVED BONIN' / IN THE NAME OF SWING / LOVE AND BULLSHIT / HIDE BEHIND MY GLASSES / BONIN' IN THE JUNGLE** -

Jun 91. (cd/c/lp) *(467615-2/-4/-1)* *<46142>* **THE REALITY OF MY SURROUNDINGS** 75 49 Apr91
– Fight the youth / If I were a . . . I'd / So many millions / Asswhippin' / Housework / Deathmarch / Behavoir control technician / If I were a . . . I'd / Pressure / Junkies prayer / Prayer to the junkiemaker / Everyday sunshine / If I were a . . . I'd / Naz-tee may'en / Babyhead / If I were a . . . I'd / Those days are gone / Sunless Saturday.

Jun 91. (cd-ep) *<73668>* **SUNLESS SATURDAY / UNDERSTAND ME / FIGHT SWA SKA** -

Nov 91. (c-ep) *<73859>* **EVERYDAY SUNSHINE / SO MANY MILLIONS / PRAYING TO THE JUNKIEMAKER / BEHAVIOR CONTROL TECHNICIAN** -

Jul 92. (7") *(658193-7)* **EVERYDAY SUNSHINE. / FIGHT THE YOUTH** 60 -
(12"+=/cd-s+=) *(658193-6/-2)* – Fight the youth (extended) / Freddie's dead (Zeoniq mix).

— now without KENDALL who joined a religious cult!

Jun 93. (cd/c/lp) *(473875-2/-4/-1)* *<52764>* **GIVE A MONKEY A BRAIN AND HE'LL SWEAR HE'S THE CENTRE OF THE UNIVERSE** 99 May93
– Swim / Servitude / Black flowers / Unyielding conditioning / Properties of propaganda (f**k this shit on up) / The warmth of your breath / Lemon meringue / They all have abandoned their hopes / End the reign / Drunk skitzo / No fear / Nutt megalomaniac.

Aug 93. (12"/cd-s) *(659625-6/-2)* **SWIM. / ('A'-ofishal extended) / ('A'-JB dub) / ('A'stroke mix)** 54

not iss. Rowdy-Arista

Apr 96. (cd) *<37010>* **CHIM CHIM'S BADASS REVENGE** -
– Alcoholic / In the cube / Sourpuss / Psychologically overcast / Beergut / Love . . . hate / Nutmeg / Monkey Dick / Pre nut / Rock star / Chim Chim's badass revenge.

– compilations, etc. –

Sep 96. (d-cd) *Sony; <65009>* **FISHBONE 101: NUTTASAURUSMEG FOSSIL FUELIN** (hits & rarities) -

FIST

Formed: Canada . . . 1978 by brothers RON and JOHN CHENIER. Recruiting EDMUND EAGAN and JEFF NYSTROM, the group released a domestic debut in 1979 on their own 'Fist' label, 'ROUND ONE'. Picked up by 'A&M', FIST made their major label debut in late 1980 with 'HOT SPIKES', another competent yet unremarkable hard-rock affair which showed little progression from the debut. 1983's 'IN THE RED' saw DAVE McDONALD replace CHENIER on vocals, while RON was the only remaining member by the release of 'DANGER ZONE' (1985), the group's final release.

Album rating: ROUND ONE (*5) / HOT SPIKES (*6) / THUNDER IN ROCK (*5) / IN THE RED (*6) / DANGER ZONE (*5)

RON CHENIER – vocals, guitar / **EDMUND EAGAN** – keyboards / **JEFF NYSTROM** – bass, vocals / **JOHN CHENIER** – drums

— as **MYOFIST** in Europe only

not iss. Fist

1979. (lp) <WRC1 562> **ROUND ONE** Canada
– Too late / Who did you love / Anyway you want / Memories / Fall / Madness / Fly.

A&M A&M

Oct 80. (7") *(AMS 7565)* **HOT SPIKES. / IT'S A SIN**
Nov 80. (lp) *(AMLH 64823)* <SP 4823> **HOT SPIKES**
– Money / Teenage love affair / What am I to do / Hot spikes / Are you crying / Rock'n'roll suicide / Alimony / Never come back / It's a sin / Lord I miss you.

— **IVAN TESSIER** – keyboards; repl. ED
BOB PATTERSON – drums

Jul 82. (lp) *(AMLH 64893)* <SP 4893> **THUNDER IN ROCK**
– Double or nothin' / Thunder in rock / Leather 'n' lace / On the radio / It's late / Better way to go / Evil gold / Fleet Street / Open the gates.

— **DAVE McDONALD** – vocals; repl. CHENIER

1983. (lp) <SP 9089> **IN THE RED** -
– When I'm bad I'm better / Crazy on you / It ain't good / Undercover lover / If I'm not loved / Over the line / Street fighting heroes / Day by day / Gimme love / Dirty girl / New York City.
LAURIE CURRY – keyboards; repl. TESSIER

— **BOB MOFFAT** – bass; repl. NYSTROM

not iss. Cobra

1985. (lp) <CL 1003> **DANGER ZONE** -
– Danger zone / Muscle gun / I will remember / Voices / Killer / Starlight / Rock city / Raise hell / Rebels / Streets of fire.

— split after above

FIST

Formed: Newcastle-upon-Tyne, England . . . 1978 initially as AXE, by KEITH SATCHFIELD, DAVE IRWIN, JOHN WYLIE and HARRY HILL (not THAT one!). After a debut single on 'Neat' records the group were snapped up as potentially lucrative NWOBHM fodder by 'M.C.A.'. One lacklustre and cringeworthy-titled album later ('TURN THE HELL ON'), the group found themselves minus a vocalist and a record deal. With an almost completely different line-up, boasting new recruits, GLENN COATES, JOHN ROACH and POP APPLEBY, the group returned to 'Neat' and proceeded to release the ambitiously titled 'BACK WITH A VENGEANCE' (1982). Sensibly, the group split soon after.

Album rating: TURN THE HELL ON (*4) / BACK WITH A VENGEANCE (*5)

KEITH SATCHFIELD – vocals, guitar / **DAVE IRWIN** – guitar / **JOHN WYLIE** – bass / **HARRY HILL** – drums

Neat not iss.

Apr 80. (7") *(NEAT 04)* **NAME RANK AND SERIAL NUMBER. / YOU'LL NEVER GET ME UP ON ONE OF THOSE** -
(re-iss. Jul80 on 'M.C.A.' MCA 615)

M.C.A. not iss.

Aug 80. (7") *(MCA 640)* **FOREVER AMBER. / TURN OUT THE LIGHT** -
Nov 80. (lp) *(MCF 3082)* **TURN ON THE HELL** -
– Hole in the wall gang / The watcher / Collision course / You'll never get me up (in one of those) / Forever amber / Axeman / The vamp / Terminus / One percenter (1%) / Name, rank and serial number.

Jan 81. (7") *(MCA 663)* **COLLISION COURSE. / LAW OF THE JUNGLE** -

— **GLENN COATES** – vocals / **JOHN ROACH** – guitar / **POP APPLEBY** – bass; repl. SATCHFIELD

Neat not iss.

1982. (lp) *(NEAT 1003)* **BACK WITH A VENGEANCE** -
– Turn the hell on / S.S. giro / Too hot / Lost and found / The feeling's right / Dog soldier / All I can do / Devil rise / Going wild tonight.

Nov 82. (7") *(NEAT 21)* **WANDERER. / TOO HOT** -

— split soon after above

FLAMINGOES

Formed: Hitchin, Hertfordshire, England . . . Spring 1993 by identical twin brothers, JUDE and JAMES COOK, who completed the line-up with off-kilter drummer KEVIN. Taking flight to the capital, the lads won a talent competition run by DJ, Gary Crowley, stirring up even more publicity when they played the celebrated New Art Riot gig alongside THESE ANIMAL MEN and S*M*A*S*H towards the end of the year. The following February, The FLAMINGOES unleashed their vinyl debut in the shape of 7" single, 'THE CHOSEN FEW', already being tipped for the top by such unlikely organs as the News Of The World. Yet another band harking back to the year of 1977 when The CLASH and The JAM ruled the pop charts, the feathered ones had no reservations about airing their suitability to wipe the floor with the New Wave of neo-Mod Brit-pop acts. Signed to 'Pandemonium', the trio released the 'TEENAGE EMERGENCY' EP (the title track having already netted them the aforementioned award) and a further single, 'DISAPPOINTED', both highlights from their forthcoming debut album, 'PLASTIC JEWELS' (1995). However, just as things looked promising for the hell-raising lads, they rather mysteriously disappeared from view. • **Note:** Not to be confused with another outfit of the same name who had a few singles released on dance label, Rob's, either end of '93.

Album rating: PLASTIC JEWELS (*6)

JUDE COOK (b.1970) – vocals, guitar / **JAMES COOK** (b.1970) – bass, vocals / **KEVIN** – drums

La La Land not iss.

Feb 94. (7") *(LALA 002)* **THE CHOSEN FEW. /** -

Pandemonium not iss.

Jul 94. (12"ep/cd-ep) *(PANN/+CD 005)* **TEENAGE EMERGENCY** -
– Teenage emergency / Running away / Six burning seven / Everyone makes mistakes.

Oct 94. (7") *(PANN 006)* **DISAPPOINTED. / DISTORT** -
(cd-s+=) *(PANNCD 006)* – London's laughing.

Feb 95. (cd/c/lp) *(PANN CD/MC/LP 007)* **PLASTIC JEWELS** -
– Disappointed / Teenage emergency / Safe / Try it on / Absent fathers, violent sons / Winter / Scenester / The chosen few / Unstable / Suicide bridge / Last of the big spenders / It's been a thrill.

Mar 95. (12"ep/cd-ep) *(PANN/+CD 008)* **SCENESTER. / SUBURBAN SINNERS / TOUGH AGAIN** -

— split after above single

FLESH EATERS

Formed: Los Angeles, California, USA . . . 1977 by CHRIS 'D' DESJARDINS, who has been the only constant fixture in the band's line-up over its decade and a half lifespan. A cast of DAVE ALVIN, JOHN DOE, BILL BATEMAN, DON BONEBRAKE and STEVE BERLIN were present on their debut album, 'NO QUESTIONS ASKED', at the turn of the decade, although the revolving door personnel policy led them on to better things. CHRIS D and Co delivered a series of average post-punk albums that verged on alternative heavy-metal, although lack of interest led the singer to change direction in the mid 80's via the rootsier DIVINE HORSEMEN. While their music might have less intensity, a sinister lyrical edge was never far from the surface, 'S.S.T.' albums such as 'DEVIL'S RIVER' (1986) and 'SNAKE HANDLER' (1987) finding DESJARDINS splitting the vocals with his partner, JULIE C(HRISTENSEN). Towards the end of the decade, CHRIS D founded yet another vehicle for his dark talent, issuing 'I PASS FOR HUMAN' as STONE BY STONE in 1989. The 90's, meanwhile, saw The FLESH EATERS return with a convincing comeback album, 'DRAGSTRIP RIOT' (1991), although the following year's 'SEX DIARY OF MR VAMPIRE' would be their final offering.

Album rating: NO QUESTIONS ASKED (*6) / A MINUTE TO PRAY, A SECOND TO DIE (*6) / FOREVER CAME TODAY (*6) / DRAGSTRIP RIOT (*5) / SEX DIARY OF MR VAMPIRE (*5) / GREATEST HITS – DESTROYED BY FIRE compilation (*6) / PREHISTORIC FITS compilation (*6) / Divine Horsemen: TIME STANDS STILL (*5) / DEVIL'S RIVER (*5) / SNAKE HANDLER (*5) / Stone By Stone: I PASS FOR HUMAN (*5)

CHRIS 'D' DESJARDINS – vocals / **DAVE ALVIN** – guitar / **JOHN DOE** – bass / **BILL BATEMAN** – drums / **DON BONEBRAKE** – marimbas, percussion / **STEVE BERLIN** – saxophone

not iss. Upsetter

1980. (lp) <UPCD 34> **NO QUESTIONS ASKED** -

Initial Ruby

Sep 81. (lp) *(IRC 007)* <JRR 101> **A MINUTE TO PRAY, A SECOND TO DIE**
– Digging my grave / Pray til you sweat / River of fever / Satan's stomp / See you in the boneyard / So long / Cyrano de Berger's back / Divine horsemen.

— **DON KIRK** – guitar; repl. ALVIN who was already part of The BASTERS / **ROBYN JAMESON** – bass; repl. DOE + BONEBRAKE who were part of X / **CHRIS WAHL** – drums; repl. BATEMAN (also of BLASTERS)

1982. (lp) **FOREVER CAME TODAY** -
– My life to live / A minute to pray, a second to die / Secret life / Shallow water / The rosy hours / The wedding dice / Hand of glory / Drag my name in the mud / Because of you / Tightrope of fire.

1983. (lp) **A HARD ROAD TO FOLLOW** -

— split after above

DIVINE HORSEMEN

CHRIS D – vocals / members of BLASTERS, X and GUN CLUB

not iss. Enigma

1984. (lp) **TIME STANDS STILL** -

— added **JULIE C** (b. CHRISTENSEN) – vocals

New Rose S.S.T.

Nov 86. (12"ep) *(NEW 87)* <SST 090> **MIDDLE OF THE NIGHT**
Dec 86. (lp/cd) *(ROSE 102/+CD)* <SST 091/+CD> **DEVIL'S RIVER**
(re-iss. May93 on 'S.S.T.' lp/cd; same as US)

— now with **PETE ANDRUS** – guitar

Oct 87. (lp/cd) *(ROSE 134/+CD)* <SST 140/+CD> **SNAKE HANDLER**
– Snake handler / Kiss tomorrow goodbye / Stone by stone (fire is my home) / Curse of the crying woman / Someone like you / Fire kiss / What is red / The blind leading the blind / That's no way to live / Superlungs / Frankie Silver / Past all dishonour / Sanctuary. *(re-iss. May93 on 'S.S.T.' lp/cd; same as US)*

1988. (12"ep) *(NEW 110)* <SST 176> **HANDFUL OF SAND**

— broke up the partnership, although CHRIS D formed below solo project with **JOHN NAPIER, ERIC MARTIN + CHRIS HASKETT**

Jul 89. (lp/c/cd; as STONE BY STONE with CHRIS D) <(SST 247/+C/CD)> **I PASS FOR HUMAN**

FLESH EATERS

— reformed with of course **CHRIS D** at the helm / + **WAYNE JAMES** – guitar / **GLENN HAYS** – bass / **RAY TORRES** – drums, percussion / **TERRI LAIRD** – backing vocals

S.S.T. S.S.T.

Nov 90. (lp/c/cd) *<(SST 264/+C/CD)>* **PREHISTORIC FITS** (compilation)
(re-iss. May93; same)

Mar 91. (d-lp/c/cd) *<(SST 273/+C/CD)>* **DRAGSTRIP RIOT**
– Tomorrow never comes / Youngest profession / Soul kiss / Dragstrip riot / Bedful of knives / My baby's done her best / Sugarhead and panther breath / Out of nowhere / Dove's blood ink / Take my hand / Agony shorthand / Agony sorehead / The moon upstairs / Slipped, tripped, fell in love / Fur magnet. *(re-iss. May93; same)*

— **CHRISTIAN FREE** – drums, percussion; repl. TORRES

May 93. (cd/c) *<(SST 292 CD/C)>* **THE SEX DIARY OF MR. VAMPIRE** Nov92
– Death installment plan / Cemetery without crosses / Better tomorrow / Soft knife and a brick pillow / Covert counter-insurgency man / Five dolls for an August moon / I love you so / Car named Ego / Diary of a psycho / Diamond in my eye / Eyes of lightning / Kill, baby, kill.

Dec 92. (12"ep/cd-ep) *<SST/+CD 297)* **CRUCIFIED LOVERS IN WOMAN HELL** -

— disbanded after above; CHRIS D subsequently released a solo album, 'LOVE CANNOT DIE' for 'Sympathy For The Record Industry'

– compilations, etc. –

May 87. (lp) *Fan Club; (FC 025) / S.S.T.; <SST 094>* **DESTROYED BY FIRE – GREATEST HITS** 1986
– See you in the boneyard / Cyrano / Dominoes / Impossible crime / Secret life / Hard road to follow / The wedding dice / Pony dress / We'll never die / Digging my grave / Lake of burning fire. *(re-iss. May93 on 'S.S.T.'; same as US)*

Mar 89. (lp) *Homestead; <(HMS 124-1)>* **LIVE (live 1979-83)**
– Version nation / Digging my grave / So long / Divine horsemen / Cinderella / A minute to pray, a second to die / Because of you / My destiny / Poison arrow / My life to live / I take what I want / Shallow water / Buried treasure / Digging my grave.

FLIPPER

Formed: San Francisco, California, USA . . . 1979 out of NEGATIVE TREND by WILL SHATTER and STEVE DePACE. Following the departure of the latter act's original singer, ROZZ, the pair recruited RICKIE WILLIAMS, who in turn thought up the FLIPPER moniker. He was soon replaced himself with the wonderfully named BRUCE LOOSE alongside fourth member, TED FALCONI, the raggedy-assed punk renegades attracting a cult following in the Bay Area with their painfully slow, monolithically rhythmic noise-grind. Signed to the newly inaugurated 'Subterranean', the FLIPPER crew made their vinyl debut with a track on the 1979 label sampler, 'SF Underground', while they also popped up on a local v/a album, 'Live At Target'. A belated debut single, 'LOVE CANAL', eventually appeared in 1980 on the tiny 'Thermidor' label while a first single for 'Subterranean', the marathon one (two at a push!) chord screamathon, 'SEX BOMB BABY', previewed the definitive debut set, 'ALBUM-GENERIC FLIPPER' (1982). Seemingly dredged up from the blackest studio murk, this lumbering, deceptively basic collection of inspired hardcore sloppiness set the scene for all manner of SF weirdness to come (i.e. PRIMUS etc.), its malign influence winding its way right up the coast to Seattle where the likes of TAD and NIRVANA would later incorporate at least the spirit of FLIPPER into their work. Yet by the release of the cleaned-up but demented follow-up, 'GONE FISHIN' (1984), FLIPPER had done just that, posthumous live releases following in the shape of 'BLOWING CHUNKS' (1984) and double set, 'PUBLIC FLIPPER LTD.' (1987). Tragically, any possiblilites of a full reunion were cut short when WILL SHATTER died of an accidental heroin overdose in late '87. Nevertheless, the patronage of many leading figures in the 90's grunge scene (and KURT COBAIN in particular) led to a belated re-formation with new member, JOHN DOUGHERTY. A surprise signing to Rick Rubin's 'Def American' label, the band were afloat once again with comeback album, 'AMERICAN GRAFISHY' (1993). Despite being given a cautious thumbs up by FLIPPER commentators, many mourned the noisy abandon of old as it became clear the guys had actually been practicing in their absence!
• **Songwriters:** SHATTER – LOOSE.

Album rating: GENERIC FLIPPER (*8) / GONE FISHIN' (*7) / BLOW'N'CHUNKS: LIVE (*4) / PUBLIC FLIPPER LIMITED (*5) / SEX BOMB BABY (*6) / AMERICAN GRAFISHY (*4)

WILL SHATTER (b. RUSSELL WILKINSON, 1956) – vocals, bass (ex-NEGATIVE TREND) / **TED FALCONI** (b. LAURENCE FALCONI, 2 Sep'47, Bryn Mawr, Penns.) – guitar (ex-RAD COMMAND) / **BRUCE LOOSE** (b. BRUCE CALDERWOOD, 6 Jun'59, Fresno, Calif.) – bass, vocals / **STEVE DePACE** (b.29 Jan'57) – drums

not iss. Thermidor

1980. (7") *<T 1>* **LOVE CANAL. / HA HA HA** -
<re-iss. 1981 on 'Subterranean'; SUB 7> (UK-iss.Jan82 on 'Alternative Tentacles'; VIRUS 8)

Alternative Tentacles Subterranean

Apr 82. (7"red) *(VIRUS 18) <SUB 23>* **SEX BOMB. / BRAINWASH** Nov81

Apr 82. (lp) *<SUB 25>* **ALBUM-GENERIC FLIPPER** -
– Ever / Life is cheap / Shed no tears / (I saw you) Shine / Way of the world / Life / Nothing / Living for the depression / Sex bomb. *(UK-iss.Aug93 on 'Def American' cd/lp; DAB CD/LP 3)*

1984. (lp) **GONE FISHIN'** -
(UK-iss.Mar87 on 'Fundamental'; SAVE 017)

— On the 9th Dec'87, SHATTER died of an accidental heroin overdose. They decided to split, although they re-formed early '91 with new member **JOHN DOUGHERTY** (b.20 Apr'61, Oakland, Calif.) – bass

not iss. Matador

Dec 92. (7") *<OLE 048>* **FLIPPER TWIST. /** -

American American

Jun 93. (cd/lp) *(DABCD/LP 1) <45120>* **AMERICAN GRAFISHY** Jan93
– Someday / Flipper twist / May the truth be known / We're not crazy / Fucked up once again / Exist or else / Distant illusion / Telephone / It pays to know / Full speed ahead.

Fuel unknown

Mar 98. (12"ep/cd-ep) *(FUEL 004/+CD)* **TWISTED EP**

– compilations, etc. –

Feb 84. (c) *R.O.I.R.; <A 126>* **BLOW'N CHUNKS (live)** -
– Way of the world / The light, the sound, the rhythm, the . . . / Shed no tears / Love canal / Ha ha ha / In your arms / Life is cheap / In life my friend / Get away. *(UK cd-iss. Nov94; RE 126CD)*

Feb 87. (d-lp) *Fundamental; (SAVE 015/016) / Subterranean;* **PUBLIC FLIPPER LTD. (live 1980-82)** Nov86
– Nuru nuru / Hard cold world / I'm fighting / The game's gotta price / Love canal / Oh oh ay oh / We don't understand / If I can be drunk / Sex bomb / Brainwash / Shy / Southern California / Life / The whel / Flipper blues.

1988. (lp) *Subterranean; <SAVE 059>* **SEX BOMB BABY** -
– Sex bomb / Love canal / Ha ha ha / Sacrifice / Falling / Ever get away / Earthworm / The games got a price / The old lady who swallowed a fly / Brainwash / Lowrider / End the game. *(UK cd-iss. Oct95 on 'Infinite Zero-BMG'; 74321 29898-2)*

Jul 97. (cd) *Overground; (OVER 63CD)* **LIVE AT CBGB'S 1983 (live)** -

FLOODGATE

Formed: New Orleans, USA . . . 1994 by former EXHORDER mainman and songwriter, KYLE THOMAS alongside STEVEN FISHER, KEVIN THOMAS and NEIL MONTGOMERY. Signed to 'Roadrunner', the band's belated debut set, 'PENALTY', arrived in late '96, revealing them to be fans of the heavy retro/Southern rock axis favoured at the time by the likes of C.O.C. Nevertheless, they rarely sounded as menacing as the latter outfit, assuming a more accessible sound which occasionally toughened itself up. A sophomore effort seems unlikely given that THOMAS has been linked with a number of other projects.

Album rating: PENALTY (*6)

KYLE THOMAS – vocals, guitar (ex-RAID, ex-ARMAGEDDON) / **STEVEN FISHER** – guitar, vocals / **KEVIN THOMAS** – bass, vocals (ex-ACID BATH, ex-MOON CRICKETS) / **NEIL MONTGOMERY** – drums

Roadrunner Roadrunner

Oct 96. (cd/c) *<(RR 8890-2/-4)>* **PENALTY**
– Shivering / Through my days into my nights / Before the line divides / Those days / Till my soil / Whole / Second guesser / Running with sodden legs / Imitation salvation / Feel you burn / Black with sin.

— split after above

FLOTSAM AND JETSAM

Formed: Phoenix, Arizona, USA . . . 1984 by DAVID KELLY and JASON NEWSTED. Recruiting frontman ERIC A.K. and guitarists MIKE GILBERT and ED CARLSON, the group recorded tracks for a couple of compilation albums before signing to 'Roadrunner'. Their debut set, 'DOOMSDAY FOR THE DECEIVER' (1986), was warmly received by the thrash factions of the metal press, FLOTSAM AND JETSAM initially tipped for great things alongside contemporaries like TESTAMENT and EXODUS. The beginning of their troubles came, however, with the departure of NEWSTED to METALLICA (as a replacement for the late CLIFF BURTON) later that year. When a second set, 'NO PLACE FOR DISGRACE', eventually surfaced in 1988 (with TROY GREGORY filling NEWSTED's shoes), it became clear that the group were destined to dally in the second division, their speed-metal chops beginning to sound derivative next to the innovations being made by, yes, METALLICA et al. Despite releasing a rather ill-advised cover of Elton John's 'SATURDAY NIGHT'S ALRIGHT FOR FIGHTING' and subsequently being dropped by 'Roadrunner' (come on, it wasn't that bad!), the group were caught up in the predictable major label rush to cash in on the thrash scene. Obviously, most of the really talented acts had already moved on, although 'M.C.A.' funded two albums, 'WHEN THE STORM COMES DOWN' (1990) and 'CUATRO' (1993), both failing to come up with anything new or even coming anywhere near the company's commercial expectations. When they were unceremoniously dropped, FLOTSAM AND JETSAM just downscaled, moving to 'Metal Blade' where they continue to produce old-school thrash for the diehards, 'HIGH' (1997), 'UNNATURAL SELECTION' (1999) and 'MY GOD' (2001), being their last releases to date.

Album rating: DOOMSDAY FOR THE DECEIVER (*6) / NO PLACE FOR DISGRACE (*4) / WHEN THE STORM COMES DOWN (*4) / CUATRO (*5) / DRIFT (*5) / HIGH (*6) / UNNATURAL SELECTION (*5) / MY GOD (*4)

ERIC A.K. – vocals / **MIKE GILBERT** – guitar / **ED CARLSON** – guitar / **JASON NEWSTEAD** – bass / **DAVID KELLY** – drums

Roadrunner Elektra

Jun 87. (lp) *(RR 9683) <722081>* **DOOMSDAY FOR THE DECEIVER**
– Iron tears / Desecrator / Fade to black / Hammerhead / Doomsday for the deceiver / Metalshock / She took an axe / U.L.S.W. / Der fuhrer. *(re-iss. Oct89 lp/cd; RR/+34 9683) (re-iss. Sep91 on 'Music For Nations' lp/c/cd; ZORRO 36/T/CD) (cd re-iss. Mar96 on 'Metal Blade'; 398414077CD)*

Dec 87. (12") *(RR12 5471)* **FLOTZILLA. / I LIVE YOU DIE** [ ] [-]

— **TROY GREGORY** – bass; repl. NEWSTEAD who joined METALLICA

May 88. (lp/c) *(RR 9549-1/-4) <60777>* **NO PLACE FOR DISGRACE** [ ] [ ]
– No place for disgrace / Dreams of death / N.E. terror / Escape from within / Saturday nights alright for fighting / Hard on you / I live you die / Misguided fortune / P.A.A.B. / The Jones. *(cd-iss. Jan94; RR 9549-2)*

Dec 88. (12"ep/cd-ep) *(RR 2453-1/-2)* **SATURDAY NIGHT'S ALRIGHT FOR FIGHTING / HARD ON YOU. / MISGUIDED FORTUNE / DREAMS OF DEATH** [ ] [-]

M.C.A. M.C.A.

Apr 90. (cd/c/lp) *(DMCG/MCGC/MCG 6084) <6382>* **WHEN THE STORM COMES DOWN** [ ] [ ]
– The master sleeps / Burned device / Deviation / October thorns / No more fun / Suffer the masses / Six VI / Greed / E.M.T.E.K. / Scars / K.A.B.

Feb 93. (cd/c) *<(MCD/MCC 10678)>* **CUATRO** [ ] [ ] Nov92
– Natural enemies / Swatting at flies / The message / Cradle me now / Wading through the darkness / Double zero / Never to reveal / Forget about Heaven / Secret square / Hypodermic midnight snack / Are you willing / (Ain't nothing gonna) Save this world.

Apr 95. (cd) *<MCD 11212>* **DRIFT** [-] [ ]
– Me / Empty air / Pick a window / 12 year old with a gun / Missing / Blindside / Remember / Destructive signs / Smoked out / Poet's tell.

— **JASON WARD** – bass; repl. GREGORY who joined PRONG

Metal Blade Metal Blade

Jun 97. (cd) *<(14126-2)>* **HIGH** [ ] [ ]
– Final step / Hallucinational / It's on me / Highnoon / Your hands / Monster / Lucky day / Toast / High / Everything / Forkboy.

— **MARK SIMPSON** – guitar; repl. GILBERT

— **CRAIG NELSON** – drums; repl. KELLY

Feb 99. (cd) *<(14184-2)>* **UNNATURAL SELECTION** [ ] [ ]
– Dreamscape / Chemical noose / Promise keepers / Liquid noose / Falling / F**kers / Brain dead / Way to go / Win, lose or dead / Welcome to the bottom.

Jun 01. (cd) *<(14370-2)>* **MY GOD** [ ] [ ] May01
– Dig me up to bury me / Keep breathing / Nothing to say / Weather to do / Camera eye / Trash / Praise / My god / Learn to dance / Frustrate / Killing time / I.A.M.H.

Gary FLOYD

(see under ⇒ SISTER DOUBLE HAPPINESS)

FLUFFY

Formed: London, England . . . 1994 by AMANDA E. ROOTES, BRIDGET JONES, ANGIE ADAMS and PANDORA ORMSBY-GORE, the latter making way for new bassist HELEN STORES. The latest bunch of tough-nut girlies to pick up guitars and take on the boys at their own game, FLUFFY were initially accused of being talentless posh birds on the musical make. Dressing down in provocative mini-skirted grunge chic, the lassies had NME journos frothing at the mouth, especially when they proved their working class credentials. Taking their musical cue from ELASTICA, HOLE or even the GERMS, the feisty punkettes released their debut single, 'HYPERSONIC', in the Autumn of '95. With the hype machine still in overdrive, they released a second single, 'HUSBAND', scraping into the Top 60 the following February; the label, 'Tim/Kerr' subsequently issued it in America, where the girls recorded the '5 LIVE' EP shortly after. Landing themselves a lucrative contract with 'Virgin', they finally made it onto Top Of The Pops with single, 'NOTHING', a minor hit which previewed the accompanying debut album, 'BLACK EYE' (1996). Despite featuring a guest spot from the FOO FIGHTERS' PAT SMEAR, the record failed to live up to the publicity they'd already generated and with a final flop single, 'I WANNA BE YOUR LUSH', FLUFFY became yesterday's bunnies. • **Covered:** I'M A BOY (Who).

Album rating: BLACK EYE (*6)

AMANDA E. ROOTES – vocals, guitar / **BRIDGET JONES** – guitar / **HELEN STORES** – bass; who repl. PANDORA ORMSBY-GORE / **ANGIE ADAMS** – drums

Parkway Tim/Kerr

Sep 95. (7") *(PARK 003)* **HYPERSONIC. / CROSSDRESSER** [ ] [-]
(cd-s+=) *(PARK 003CD)* – Psychofudge.

Feb 96. (7") *(PARK 006) <135>* **HUSBAND. / DENY EVERYTHING** [58] [ ] May96
(cd-s+=) *(PARK 006CD)* – Cheap.

Enclave not iss.

Jul 96. (10"ep/cd-ep) *(58571-1/-2)* **5 LIVE (live in New York)** [ ] [-]
– I wanna be your lush / Deny everything / Psychofudge / Bed of vomit / Scream.

Virgin Capitol

Sep 96. (7") *(VS 1614)* **NOTHING. / SCREAM (live)** [52] [-]
(cd-s+=) *(VSCDT 1614)* – Laphog.
(7") *(VSX 1614)* – ('A'side) / I'm a boy.

Oct 96. (cd/c) *(CDV/TCV 2817) <53020>* **BLACK EYE** [ ] [ ]
– Nothing / Hypersonic / Black eye / Scream / I wanna be your lush / Crossdresser / Psychofudge / Too famous / Technicolour yawn / Cosmetic dog / Crawl / Husband / Dirty old bird / Cheap. *(lp on 'Enclave'; ENC 53020-1)*

Jun 97. (7") *(VS 1631)* **I WANNA BE YOUR LUSH. / BED OF VOMIT (live)** [ ] [-]
(cd-s) *(VSCDT 1631)* – ('A'side) / Reanimator / ('A'live).
(cd-s) *(VSCDX 1631)* – ('A'side) / Sick things / Deny everything.

— looked to have split after above

FLUID

Formed: Denver, Colorado, USA . . . 1986 by JOHN "JR" ROBINSON, JAMES CLOWER, RICK KULWICKI, MATT BISCHOFF and GARRETT SHAVLIK. Yet another outfit to base their sound on the proto-punk blueprint of The STOOGES and MC5, the FLUID first made it on to vinyl via a self-financed album, 'PUNCH N JUDY' (1986). Picked up by the fledgling 'Sub Pop' label, the grungey retro-rockers subsequently toured with labelmates, TAD, while promoting their second set, 'CLEAR BLACK PAPER' (1988), issued in the UK a year later as 'FREAK MAGNET'. 'ROADMOUTH' (1989) was another transitional set, honing their chops for 1990's mini-album, 'GLUE'. Next on the agenda was a shared 7" with the soon-to-be massive NIRVANA, the FLUID's 'CANDY' back to back with COBAIN and Co's cover of The VASELINES 'Molly's Lips'. One of the original grunge pioneers, the FLUID had evaporated by the time the Seattle scene really took off, ROBINSON, CLOWER, etc (having now signed to 'Hollywood') quitting while on top after recording the best album of their career, 'PURPLEMETALFLAKEMUSIC'.

Album rating: PUNCH N JUDY (*4) / CLEAR BLACK PAPER (*5) / ROADMOUTH (*5) / GLUE mini (*6) / PURPLEMETALFLAKEMUSIC (*7)

JOHN "JR" ROBINSON – vocals / **JAMES CLOWER** – guitar / **RICK KULWICKI** – guitar / **MATT BISCHOFF** – bass / **GARRETT SHAVLIK** – drums, vocals

not iss. Rayon

1986. (lp) **PUNCH N JUDY** [-] [ ]

Glitterhouse Sub Pop

May 88. (lp/c) *<SP 16/+A>* **CLEAR BLACK PAPER** [-] [ ]
(UK-iss.May89 as 'FREAK MAGNET'; efa 4476)

Oct 89. (lp/cd) *(efa 4489) <SP 36/+B>* **ROADMOUTH** [ ] [ ] Jun89
– Hooked / Human mill / Big brother / Girl bomb / Leave it / Fools rule / Cop a plea / Ode to Miss Lodge / Twisted & pissed / Is it day / What man / Saccharin rejection.

Mar 90. (7"orange,7"yellow) *<SP 57>* **TIN TOP TOY. / TOMORROW** [-] [ ]

Apr 90. (m-lp/m-c/m-cd) *<SP 64/+B/A>* **GLUE** [-] [ ]
– Our love will still be there / Black glove / Closet case / Candy / Pretty mouse / Wasted time. *<cd+=/c+=>* – ROADMOUTH

Jan 91. (7"/7"green) *<SP 97>* **CANDY (live). / (B-side by Nirvana)** [-] [ ]

not iss. Hollywood

Apr 93. (c/cd) *<1+/61445>* **PURPLEMETALFLAKEMUSIC** [-] [ ]
– My kind / One eye out / She don't understand / 7/14 / Pill / Wasn't my idea / On my feet / Lies / Mister Blameshifter / Said that I'm through / Change / Hand in hand.

— disbanded some time in 1993; SHAVLIK formed SPELL

FLUX OF PINK INDIANS

Formed: Bishop Stortford, England . . . 1978 as The EPILEPTICS by DEREK BIRKETT and COLIN LATTER. Unsurprisingly, complaints from The British Epilepsy Association led to them changing their moniker to EPI-X or The LICKS. It would be the latter incarnation under which their debut EP, '1970s' would surface at the turn of the decade. An EPILEPTICS single, meanwhile, 'LAST BUS TO DEBDEN', surfaced a few years later although its release was overshadowed by the new line-up of FLUX OF PINK INDIANS, who unleashed the 'NEU SMELL' EP (featuring the definitive 'TUBE DISASTERS'); the record was actually issued by the in-house label of fellow anarcho subversives, CRASS, whom FOPI had recently supported on tour. In 1982, they set up their own independent label, 'Spiderleg', notching up a small victory in early 1983 with the non-tunes and militant politicism of debut album, 'STRIVE TO SURVIVE'. Eighteen months later, in a follow-up, the uncompromising troopers issued what must surely be a contender for the most bluntly (to put it lightly!) titled album in the history of rock, 'THE FUCKING CUNTS TREAT US LIKE PRICKS'. Predictably, this piece of fractured, barely listenable noise caused uproar among retailers such as HMV who immediately banned it. The Eastern Bloc record shop in Manchester was even charged for daring to display the album sleeve, seeing their stock seized by the Greater Manchester police under the obscene articles for publication law. 1987's more subdued 'UNCARVED BLOCK', meanwhile, was released on BIRKETT's new label project, 'One Little Indian', replacing the seething mess of noise with a caustic brand of free-funk influenced by the likes of ACR and 23 SKIDOO and produced by dubmeister, ADRIAN SHERWOOD. BIRKETT's label went on to become one of the main players in the indie scene, signing The SUGARCUBES, The HEART THROBS and The SHAMEN while 1990 saw the man return in his own right with new project, HOTALACIO. • **Songwriters:** BIRKETT (+ COLIN).

Album rating: STRIVE TO SURVIVE (*7) / THE FUCKING CUNTS . . . (*2) / UNCARVED BLOCK (*6)

LICKS

COLIN 'Colsk The Terrible' LATTER – vocals / **KEVIN HUNTER** – guitar / **DEREK BIRKETT** (b.18 Feb'61, London, England) – bass / **MARTIN WILSON** – drums

Stormbeat not iss.

Nov 79. (7"ep) *(BEAT 8)* **1970'S E.P.** [ ] [-]
– 1970's have been made in Japan / System rejects / Hitler's still a Nazi / War crimes. *(re-iss. Jan82 by EPILEPTICS on 'Spiderleg'; SDL 1)*

EPILEPTICS

(same line-up)

Spiderleg | not iss.

Oct 81. (7"ep) *(SDL 2)* **LAST BUS TO DEBDEN** | | -
– Tube disasters / Two years too late / Target on my back / What've you got.

FLUX OF PINK INDIANS

COLIN + DEREK / + ANDY – guitar / **SID ATTION** (b.18 Apr'60, Sutton Coalfield, England) – drums

Crass | not iss.

Oct 81. (7"ep) *(321984-2)* **NEU SMELL EP** | | -
– Neu smell / Tube disasters / Poem: Sick butchers / Background of malfunction. *(re-iss. Aug87 on 'One Little Indian' 12"ep; 12T PEP 1)*

—— **DAVE 'BAMBI'** – drums (ex-DISCHARGE) repl. SID who joined RUBELLA BALLET / **SIMON** – guitar repl. ANDY repl. NEIL PINCHER

—— **KEVIN HUNTER + MARTIN WILSON** returned to repl. SIMON + BAMBI who went back to INSANE

Spiderleg | not iss.

Jan 83. (lp) *(SDL 8)* **STRIVE TO SURVIVE CAUSING THE LEAST SUFFERING POSSIBLE** | 79 | -
– Song for them / Charity hilarity / Some of us scream, some of us shout / Take heed / TV dinners / Tapioca surprise / Progress / They lie, we die / Blinded by justice / Myxamatosis / Is there anybody there? / The fun is over. *(re-iss. Jun87 on 'One Little Indian'; TPLP 2) (cd-iss. Jun88 & Oct98; TPLP 2CD)*

Sep 84. (d-lp) *(SDL 13)* **THE FUCKING CUNTS TREAT US LIKE PRICKS** | | -
– Punk / Mind fuckers fucking minds / Hard sell / Love song / Mickey Tuneoil / Desire / Blood lust rite / The Falklands war / Punk / Life we make / Trouble at the heart / The sun / Shadow of abuse / Very funny / Cure for the coprlite. *(re-iss. Jun87 on 'One Little Indian'; TPLP 3) (cd-iss. Jan89 & Oct98; TPLP 3CD)* (+=) – TAKING A LIBERTY EP

FLUX

Mar 85. (7"ep) *(SDL 16)* **TAKING A LIBERTY EP** | | -
– Taking a liberty / Pass me another issue / For the love of beauty.

One Little Indian | not iss.

Jan 87. (lp) *(TP 1)* **UNCARVED BLOCK** | | -
– Value of nothing / Youthful immortal / Just is / Children who know / Back word / Footprints in the snow / Nothing is not done / The stonecutter. *(re-press.Aug87; TPLP 1) (cd-iss. Jun88 & Oct98; TPLP 1CD)*

Mar 87. (12") *(12TP 6)* **NEU SMELL. / TAKING A LIBERTY** | | -

May 87. (12") *(12TP 9)* **VISION. /** | | -

– compilations, etc. –

Nov 97. (lp/cd) *Overground; (OVER 67/+CD)* **NOT SO BRAVE** | | -

Sep 00. (cd/lp) *Overground-Voiceprint; (<OVER 87 VPCD/VPLP>)* **LIVE STATEMENT** | |

HOTALACIO

BIRKETT / TIM KELLY / COAL (ex-FLUX) / **LYDIE** (b. France) – drums / **KEITH LeBLANC** – producer (of TACKHEAD)

Big Kiss | not iss.

Mar 90. (7") **TALKIN' OUT THE SIDE OF YOUR NECK** | | -

Sep 90. (lp) *(KISS 5)* **SURVEILLANCE** | | -
– Talkin' out the side of your neck / Take me for a ride / How ya livin / Bass hell / Why d'ya lie? / Big boss boys / Don't kick me / Why July / Imagination / Deconstruction.

—— DEREK now concentrated on his record company

FLYS

Formed: Hollywood, California, USA . . . 1997 by ADAM PASKOWITZ, PETER PERDISCHIZZI, JAMES BOOK and NICKY LUCERO. With ADAM's brother, JOSHUA, completing the line-up in a rapping capacity, The FLYS signed to the 'Trauma' label and proceeded to buzz their way into the nation's (the USA, that is) consciousness via debut single, 'GOT YOU (WHERE I WANT YOU)'. MASTERS OF REALITY mainman and general retro maverick CHRIS GOSS was at the production helm for 'HOLIDAY MAN' (1998), a much acclaimed amalgam of pop, metal, funk/rap and psychedelia shot through with the healthy glow of L.A. sunshine. The fast talking, adrenaline sport junkies – JACK HOLDER replacing LUCERO – were back in 2000 with 'OUTTA MY WAY', a slightly harder take on their inimitably Californian hybrid.

Album rating: HOLIDAY MAN (*7) / OUTTA MY WAY (*6)

ADAM PASKOWITZ – vocals / **JOSHUA PASKOWITZ** – vocals/rapper / **PETER PERDISCHIZZI** – guitar / **JAMES BOOK** – bass / **NICKY LUCERO** – drums

R.C.A. | Delicious Vinyl – Trauma

May 99. (cd) *(74321 62150-2)* *<74006>* **HOLIDAY MAN** | | Aug98
– She's so huge / Got you (where I want you) / Take U there / Afraid / Holiday man / Groove is where you find it / The gods of basketball / Girls are the cruelest / Give you my car / Family / Superfly / Sexual sandwich.

—— **JACK HOLDER** – drums; repl. LUCERO

Apr 00. (cd) *<74017>* **OUTTA MY WAY** | - |
– No sad story / Losin' it / Fire in the pit damn! / Hellva time / Outta my way / Pakistani man says / T.V. song / Ain't no stoppin' U / Hawaiian dreams.

FM

Formed: England . . . 1979 as WILDLIFE by the OVERLAND brothers (STEVE and CHRIS) together with MARK BOOTY, BOB SKEAT and PETE JUPP. After two albums (ex-FREE man, SIMON KIRKE, briefly replacing JUPP who'd departed for a stint with SAMSON on the eponymous 1983 set, WILDLIFE) they became FM, BOOTY and SKEAT replaced with DIDGE DIGITAL and MERV GOLDSWORTHY. Signed to CBS outlet 'Portrait' in 1985, the first album from the revamped group, 'INDISCREET', appeared in 1986, selling moderately enough for a UK Top 75 place. Although the set was praised by critics, the lightweight AOR on offer was hardly enough to distinguish them from the countless bands peddling similar material, and besides, the yanks undeniably did it better. Reshuffling their masterplan, the group adopted a more metallic approach on 1989's 'TOUGH IT OUT', while still staying firmly within the hard-rock camp. Despite continuing live success and critical support, the album again failed to take off and there were accusations that 'Epic' hadn't been giving the release their full support. The group finally split in 1990, although they subsequently reformed the following year with ANDY BARNETT in place of the absent CHRIS OVERLAND. Signing to 'Music For Nations', the group chose a cover of MARVIN GAYE's 'I HEARD IT THROUGH THE GRAPEVINE' as their comeback single in late '91. An album, 'TAKING IT TO THE STREETS' (1991) followed soon after, the group going back to their roots. FM recorded their own version of MTV Unplugged with the 'NO ELECTRICITY REQUIRED' (1994) set, reprising many old blues and soul numbers along with acoustic versions of their own material. Though it seems highly unlikely the band will ever break out of the Brit-rock ghetto, they retain a loyal audience, releasing their last effort to date, 'DEAD MAN'S SHOES' in 1996 on 'Raw Power'. • **Covered:** ADDICTED TO LOVE (Robert Palmer) / HOT LEGS (Rod Stewart) / LITTLE BIT OF LOVE (Free) / NO ELECTRICITY REQUIRED (covers album; obvious), etc (see below). • **Note:** Not to be confused with the late 70's group of the same name.

Album rating: INDISCREET (*7) / TOUGH IT OUT (*4) / TAKIN' IT TO THE STREETS (*4) / APHRODISIAC (*7) / LIVE – NO ELECTRICITY REQUIRED (*5) / DEAD MAN'S SHOES (*4)

WILDLIFE

STEVE OVERLAND – vocals, guitar / **CHRIS OVERLAND** – guitar / **MARK BOOTY** – keyboards / **BOB SKEAT** – bass / **PETE JUPP** – drums

Chrysalis | Chrysalis

May 80. (lp) *(<CHR 1288>)* **BURNING** | |
– Burning / Playing it too close to the heart / Alena / Misplaced love / If the night / Incredible shrinking love / I'm winning / That diamond / Too late / Only a fool.

May 80. (7") *(CHS 2430)* **BURNING. / TOO LATE** | |

—— **SIMON KIRKE** – drums (ex-BAD COMPANY) repl. JUPP who joined SAMSON

Swan Song | Swan Song

Jul 83. (lp) *(B 0078)* **WILDLIFE** | |
– Somewhere in the night / Just a friend / Surrender / Charity / One last chance / Taking a chance / Haven't you heard the news / Midnight stranger / Rock and roll dreams / Downtown heartbreak.

Oct 83. (7") *(B 9842)* *<99842>* **SOMEWHERE IN THE NIGHT. / THE SUN DON'T SHINE** | |

FM

STEVE + CHRIS OVERLAND brought back **JUPP** + newcomers **DIDGE DIGITAL** – keyboards / **MERV GOLDSWORTHY** – bass (ex-DIAMOND HEAD)

Portrait | Portrait

Oct 85. (7"/12") *(A/TA 6613)* **FROZEN HEART. / DANGEROUS (live)** | |

Mar 86. (7") *(A 7005)* **THAT GIRL. / AMERICAN GIRLS** | |

Jun 86. (7"/12") *(A/TA 7233)* **LOVE WAS DYING. / CAPTURED** | |

Aug 86. (7") *(650036-7)* **AMERICAN GIRLS. / THAT GIRL** | |
(12"+=) *(650036-6)* – ('A'remix).

Sep 86. (lp/c/cd) *(PRT/40/CD 26827)* *<40460>* **INDISCREET** | 76 |
– That girl / The other side of midnight / Love lies dying / I believe to the night / American girls / Hot wire / Face to face / Frozen heart / Heart of the matter. *(re-iss. Mar90 on 'Epic' cd/c/lp; 466339-2/-4/-1) (cd re-iss. May93 on 'Beat Goes On'; BGOCD 184)*

Jan 87. (7") *(DIDGE 1)* **FROZEN HEART. / LOVE LASTS FOREVER** | 64 | -
(12"+=) *(DIDGET 1)* – The other side of midnight.
(d7"+=) *(DIDGED 1)* – Addicted to love / Hot legs.

Jun 87. (7"/7"pic-d) *(MERV/+P 1)* **LET LOVE ME THE LEADER. / ('A'live)** | 71 | -
(12"+=/12"+=) *(MERV B/T 1)* – I belong to the night ('87 version).

Epic | Epic

Jun 89. (7"/7"pic-d) *(655031-7/-9)* **BAD LUCK. / THIS COULD BE THE LAST TIME** | 54 | -
(12"+=) *(655031-6)* – Hurt is where the heart is.
(cd-s++=/c-s++=/7"ep++=) *(655031-2/-0)* – ('A'extended).

Sep 89. (lp/c/cd) *(465589-1/-4/-2)* *<45308>* **TOUGH IT OUT** | 34 |
– Tough it out / Don't stop / Bad luck / Someday (you'll come running) / Everytime I think of you / Burning my heart down / The dream that died / Obsession / Can you hear me calling? / Does it feel like love / Feels so good.

Sep 89. (7"/7"pic-d) *(DINK/+P 1)* **SOMEDAY (YOU'LL COME RUNNING). / ALIBI** | 64 | -
(12"+=/c-s+=/cd-s+=) *(DINK T/B/CD 1)* – ('A'extended).
(7"ep+=) *(DINKG 1)* – Obsession / Everytime we touch.

Feb 90. (7"/c-s) *(DINK/+M 2)* **EVERYTIME I THINK OF YOU. / FROZEN HEART (live)** | 73 | -
(10"+=/12"+=/3"cd-s+=) *(DINK QT/T/C 2)* – Face to face (live) / Other side of midnight (live).

—— (split but re-formed May'91) **ANDY BARNETT** – guitar repl. OVERLAND

Music For Nations — not iss.

Nov 91. (c-s/7") *(T+/KUT 142)* **I HEARD IT THROUGH THE GRAPEVINE. / HOT LOVE**
(ext-12"+=) *(12KUT 142)* – Fuel to the fire.
(cd-s++=) *(CDKUT 142)* – ('A'side again).

Nov 91. (cd/c/lp) *(CD/T+/MFN 119)* **TAKIN' IT TO THE STREETS**
– I'm ready / I heard it through the grapevine / Only the strong survive / Just can't leave her alone / She's no angel / Dangerous ground / Bad blood / Crack alley / If it feels good (do it) / The girl's gone bad.

Feb 92. (7") *(KUT 145)* **ONLY THE STRONG SURVIVE. / LITTLE BIT OF LOVE**
(12"+=/cd-s+=) *(12/CD KUT 145)* – Primitive touch.

Aug 92. (7") *(KUT 147)* **BLOOD AND GASOLINE. / CHINESE WHISPERS**
(12"+=/cd-s+=) *(12KUT 147)* – Some kind of wonderful / I'll be creepin'.

Oct 92. (cd/c/lp) *(CD/T+/MFN 141)* **APHRODISIAC**
– Closer to heaven / Blood and gasoline / All or nothing / Aphrodisiac / Inside out / Run no more / Play dirty / Rivers run dry.

Feb 93. (12"ep/cd-ep) *(12/CD KUT 151)* **BLUES & SOUL EP**
– Closer to Heaven / I heard it through the grapevine / Need your love so bad / Medley / Rocky mountain way (with Black velvet).

Nov 93. (d-cd) *(CDMFN 155)* **LIVE – NO ELECTRICITY REQUIRED (live)**
– Burning my heart down – Don't stop – Get back (medley) / Face to face – Enter sandman – American girls (medley) / Seagull / Need your love so bad / Rocky mountain way (with BLACK VELVET) / Blood and gasoline / Superstition / I heard it through the grapevine / Some kind of wonderful / Midnight hour – Dancing in the street (medley) / Closer to Heaven / Only the strong survive / Little bit of love / Rockin' me / Tush / Long way to go / Burning my heart down ('93 version) / Flesh and blood / Don't stop ('93 version) / All or nothing (racket mix).

Raw Power — not iss.

Mar 96. (cd-ep) *(RAWX 1015)* **TATTOO NEEDLE / LOCOMOTIVE LOVE / DON'T WANNA PLAY THESE GAMES**

Apr 96. (cd) *(RAWCD 107)* **DEAD MAN'S SHOES**
– Nobody's fool / Ain't no cure for love / Get ready / Don't say / Mona / Sister / You're the one / Tattoo needle / Misery / Dead man's shoes.

—— disbanded after above; BARNET and DAVIS became The BARNSTORMERS while JUPP and OVERLAND formed SO

– compilations, etc. –

Aug 94. (cd) *Connoisseur; (VSOPCD 203)* **ONLY THE STRONG – THE BEST OF FM 1984-1994**
– That girl / Other side of midnight / American girls / Face to face / Frozen heart / Tough it out / Don't stop / Bad luck / Burning my heart down / Let love be the leader / Heard it through the grapevine / Only the strong survive / Dangerous ground / Breathe fire / Blood & gasoline / All or nothing / Closer to Heaven.

FOETUS

Formed: London, England . . . 1980 as a vehicle for Australian emigre and all round musical extremist JIM THIRLWELL (once a guest for PRAG VEC in '79). Despite being released under various FOET-al incarnations (i.e FOETUS UBER FRISCO, YOU'VE GOT FOETUS ON YOUR BREATH, FOETUS Inc., THE FOETUS ALL-NUDE REVUE etc.), almost all THIRLWELL's excursions have a common trait of ear grinding nihilism, all done in the best possible taste of course and not without a scraping of black-(board, as in nails) humour. After failing to secure a deal, JIM boy started up his own label, 'Self Immolation', releasing his first abortive attempts at industrial noise via 'OKFM' (1981; as FOETUS UNDER GLASS) and as the inimitable YOU'VE GOT FOETUS ON YOUR BREATH, 'DEAF' (1981) and 'ACHE' (1982). One his few early admirers was 'Some Bizzare' head honcho, STEVO, who was sufficiently impressed to offer added financial backing for 1984's 'HOLE' album. Released under the guise of SCRAPING FOETUS OFF THE WHEEL, the record saw THIRLWELL adopt the persona of CLINT RUIN – a parody of bloated rock star excess – for a "musical" blitzkrieg skewering snippets of film dialogue, WWII chaos and assorted surreal/apocalyptic samples with sheets of clattering metallic noise, distorted guitar and pulverising percussion. Under the guise of RUIN, THIRLWELL also played a handful of anarchic shows with NICK CAVE, MARC ALMOND and LYDIA LUNCH as The IMMACULATE CONSUMPTIVE. The mid-80's proved a busy time as the growing cult of FOETUS found THIRLWELL working his black magic alongside everyone from the VIRGIN PRUNES to ORANGE JUICE (!), even finding time for a follow-up SCRAPING . . . record, 'NAIL' (1985). Subsequently relocating to noise mecca New York, he formed WISEBLOOD with SWANS man, ROLI MOSSIMANN, pooling their capacity for ear-bleeding noise on 1986's 'DIRTDISH'. While still beavering away at his own work – including FOETUS INTERRUPTUS' 'THAW' (1988) – and composing soundtracks for NY avant-garde filmaker, Richard Kern (he also co-starred with LYDIA LUNCH in a famous "blow your mind if it's under your belt" scene from one of Kern's sex flicks, 'Right Side Of My Brain') – THIRLWELL's pioneering influence could be heard in the work of up and coming industrial acts such as MINISTRY, REVOLTING COCKS, NINE INCH NAILS etc. Ironically, these were the very bands who took the genre to the masses in the early to mid-90's, THIRLWELL having to content himself with releases on indie label 'Big Cat'. 1995's 'GASH' found him in as lyrically and musically uncompromising form as ever, putting the boot in to such time honoured targets as religion and white Western smugness to a musical backdrop embellished with the alternately screaming/grooving brass of The HERESY HORNS. • **Covered:** LITTLE JOHNNY JEWEL (Television) / I AM THE WALRUS (Beatles) / SONIC REDUCER (Dead Boys) / ELECTED (Alice Cooper) / HELLO THERE (Cheap Trick).

Album rating: DEAF (*6) / ACHE (*6) / HOLE (*8) / NAIL (*6) / BEDROCK mini (*5) / THAW (*6) / SINK compilation (*6) / RIFE (*5) / QUILOMBO (*5) / MALE (*5) / GONDWANALAND (*5) / GASH (*7) / BOIL (*6) / YORK (*5) / NULL AND VOID (*5) / Wiseblood: DIRTDISH (*6) / PEDDLE TO THE METAL (*5)

JIM FOETUS – synthesizers, keyboards

Self Immolation — not iss.

Jan 81. (7"; as FOETUS UNDER GLASS) *(WOMB S201)* **OKFM. / SPITE YOUR FACE**

Apr 81. (7"; as YOU'VE GOT FOETUS ON YOUR BREATH) *(WOMB ALL007)* **WASH IT ALL OFF. / 333**

Sep 81. (lp; as YOU'VE GOT FOETUS ON YOUR BREATH) *(OYBL-1)* **DEAF**
– New York or bust / Is that a line / Why can't it happen to me / I am surrounded by incompetence / What have you been doing / Today I started slogging again / Harold McMillan / Thank heavens for push button phones / Flashback / Negative energy. *(cd-iss. Mar98 by FOETUS on 'Thirsty Ear'; THI 57034-2)*

Jan 82. (7"; as PHILIP & HIS FOETUS VIBRATIONS) *(WOMB KX 07)* **TELL ME, WHAT IS THE BANE OF YOUR LIFE. / MOTHER I'VE KILLED THE CAT**

Apr 82. (12"m; as FOETUS UBER FRISCO) *(WOMB 125-SUSC 12)* **CUSTOM BUILT FOR CAPITALISM. / 1.0.4.5. / BIRTHDAY**

Aug 82. (lp; as YOU'VE GOT FOETUS ON YOUR BREATH) *(OYBL-2)* **ACHE**
– Dying with my boots on / J.Q. murder / Gums bleed / Mark of the ostracizor / Exit the man with nine lives / Get out of my house / Wholesome town / Whole wheat rolls / Kid hate kid / Instead . . . I became anenome. *(cd-iss. Mar98 by FOETUS on 'Thirsty Ear'; THI 57035-2)*

Sep 84. (lp; as SCRAPING FOETUS OFF THE WHEEL) *(WOMB FDL 3)* **HOLE**
– I'll meet you in Poland baby / Hot horse / Sickman / Suck this, sickman, eat hot led . . . he's grinding-shaking-daning dead / Street of shame / Satan place / White knuckles / Water torture / Cold day in Hell. *(cd-iss. Jan89; WOMB FDL 3CD)*

Oct 84. (12"; as FOETUS ART TERRORISM) *(WOMB FAT 11.12)* **CALAMITY CRUSH. / CATASTROPHE CRUNCH**

Feb 85. (12"; as YOU'VE GOT FOETUS ON YOUR BREATH) *(FGH 12.8)* **WASH IT ALL OFF. / TODAY I STARTED SLOGGING AGAIN**

Mar 85. (12"; as FOETUS UBER FRISCO) *(WOMB UNC 7.12)* **FINELY HONED MACHINE. / SICK MINUTES**

Oct 85. (lp/c; as SCRAPING FOETUS OFF THE WHEEL) *(WOMBFIP/WOMBCFIP 4)* **NAIL**
– Theme from pigdom come / The throne of agony / Pigswill / Descent into the inferno / Enter the exterminator / DI-1-9026 / The overture from pigdom come / Private war / Anything. *(cd-iss. Apr86; WOMBCDFIP 4)*

Nov 85. (box for lp's; as FOETUS) *(FOE 1)* **THE FOETUS OF EXCELLENCE**

Jun 87. (m-lp; as The FOETUS ALL NUDE REVUE) *(WOMBFAN 13)* **BEDROCK**
– Diabolus in musica / Shut / Rattlesnake insurance / Bedrock ship.

Oct 87. (12"; as SCRAPING FOETUS OFF THE WHEEL) *(WOMD PIG 12.1)* **RAMROD. / BOXHEAD / SMUT**

below was a collaboration with MARC ALMOND

Feb 88. (12"; as FLESH VOLCANO) *(SLUT 001)* **SLUT. / THE UNIVERSAL CESSPOOL / BRUISIN' CHAIN**

Sep 88. (lp/c/cd; as FOETUS INTERRUPTUS) *(WOMBFIP 5/+C/CD)* **THAW**
– Don't hide it provide it / Asbestos / Fin / English faggot – Nothin man / Hauss-on-fah / Fratricide pastorale / Dipsomaniac / Barbedwire tumbleweed / Chingada / Prayer for my death. *<US cd-iss. 1995 on 'Thirsty Ear'; THI 57013>*

—— toured with **NORMAN WESTBERG** – guitar / **AL KYZYS** – bass / **BOB BERT** – drums / **NAINZ WATTS** – guitar, effects

Oct 88. (12"; as CLINT RUIN & LYDIA LUNCH) *(WSP 14)* **STINKFIST. / THE MELTDOWN ORATORIO 1,2,3 / SON OF STINK**

Big Cat — Wax Trax!

Apr 90. (d-lp/c/cd; as FOETUS INC) *(WOMBINC 6/+C/CD)* *<WAX 7110>* **SINK** (compilation)
– Bedrock / Ramrod / Boxhead / Lilith / Shut / Diabolus in musica / Smut / Sick minutes / Rattlesnake insurance / Himmelfahrtstransport – Primordial industry / Spit on the griddle / Anxiety attack / Baphomet / Dead Christian / Halo flamin lead / OKFM / Catastrophe crunch / Wash it all off / Slog / Calamity crush. *(w/ free booklet 'THE FOETUS OF EXCELLENCE 2')*

May 90. (12")(cd-s; as FOETUS INC) *(ABB 16T)(ABBCD 16)* **BUTTERFLY POTION. / FREE JAMES BROWN**

Rifle — not iss.

Dec 90. (d-lp; as FOETUS CORRUPTUS) *(RIFLE 1)* **RIFE**
– Fin / Honey I'm home / The dipsomatic kiss / English faggot / Grab yr ankles / Slut / A prayer for my death / Chingada / Hate feeler / The fudge punch / Clothes hoist / Private war – Anything (viva). *(re-iss. pic-d-lp Jul91; RIFLEPIC 001) (d-cd-iss. Dec94 & Jun96; RIFLECD 001)*

Big Cat — Atavistic

Nov 91. (cd; as STEROID MAXIMUS) *(ABBCD 028)* **QUILOMBO**
– Life in the greenhouse effect / The Heidnik manoeuvre / No joy in Pudville / Fighteous / Big Hedda meets little Napoleon / Quilombo / Phantom miscarriage / Ogro / The smother brother / Transcendental moonshine.

Mar 92. (d-cd/d-c; as FOETUS IN EXCELSIS CORRUPTUS) *(ABB 31-2/+C)* *<24>* **MALE** — Jan94
– Free James Brown / Fin / Hot horse / English faggot / Faith healer / Honey I'm home / Butterfly potion / I'll meet you in Poland / Anything (viva) / Death rape 2000 / Puppet dude / Stumbo / Someone drowned in my pool / Behemoth / Salvation.

Nov 92. (cd; as STEROID MAXIMUS) *(ABBCD 037)* **GONDWANALAND**
– Quilombo / Radio Raheem / The Trojan hearse (1st movement) / The auctioneer of souls (2nd movement) / Crawling Goliath (3rd movement) / Erupture (4th movement) / Life in the greenhouse effect / I will love you always (wild Irish rose) /

Destino matar / Cross double cross / Volgarity / Ol (kwik lube) / Powerhouse / Homeo.

— with **TOD ASHLEY** – bass / **VINNIE SIGNORELLI** – drums / **MARC RIBOT** – guitar / **STEVE BERNSTEIN** – trumpet / etc

Aug 94. (7"pic-d; as FOETUS & CHROME CRANKS) *(PCP 011-7)* **VICE SQUAD DICK. / LITTLE JOHNNY JEWEL** [ ] [-]
(cd-s+=) *(PCP 011-2)* – Outside of time.
(above issued on 'PCP')

Big Cat Columbia

May 95. (cd) *(ABB 88CD)* *<66461>* **GASH** [ ] [ ]
– Mortgage / Mighty Whity / Friend or foe / Hammer falls / Downfall / Take it outside godboy / Verklemmt / They are not so true / Slung / Steal your life away / Mutapump / See ya later.

Oct 95. (12"ep/cd-ep) *(ABB 87 T/CD)* **NULL EP** [ ] [-]

Big Cat Cleopatra

Aug 96. (cd) *(ABB 119CD)* *<9789>* **BOIL (live)** [ ] [ ]
– Take it outside Godboy / Clothes hoist / Verklemmt / I'll meet you in Poland baby / I am the walrus / They are not so true / Hot horse / Mortgage / Mighty whity / Elected / Sonic reducer / Hello there.

Oct 97. (cd) *(ABB 149CD)* *<9931>* **NULL AND VOID** [ ] [ ] Feb97
– Verklemmt / Be thankful / Verklemmt / Butter / Into the light / Verklemmt / Friend or foe / Incesticide / See Dick run / Flux / Friend or foe / Iris evergreen.

Big Cat Thirsty Ear

Oct 97. (cd; as the FOETUS symphony orchestra featuring Lydia Lunch) *(ABB 148XCD)* *<57031>* **YORK** [ ] [ ] Mar97
– Black adonis / Crumpled city / Puddlin' doorway / Egomaniacs with insecurity problems / Arschficken.

WISEBLOOD

CLINT RUIN + ROLI MOSIMANN

Some Bizzare/K422 WaxTrax!

May 85. (12") *(WISE 1-12)* *<TRAX 012>* **MOTORSLUG. / DEATH RAPE 2000** [ ] [ ] Oct90

Nov 86. (12") *(WISE 2-12)* **STUMBO (remix). / SOMEONE DROWNED IN MY POOL** [ ] [-]

Nov 86. (lp/c) *(WISE/+C 003)* **DIRTDISH** [ ] [-]
– Prime Gonzola / O-O (where evil dwells) / Stumbo / Someone drowned in my pool / Godbrain / The fudge punch. *(cd-iss. May89; WISECD 3)(+=)* – Stumbo (extended) / Motorslug / Death race 2000. *<US cd-iss. 1995 on 'Thirsty Ear'; 57015>*

Big Cat Big Cat

Nov 91. (m-lp/cd) *(ABB/+CD 030X)* **PEDAL TO THE METAL** [ ] [-]
– Stop trying to tie me / Hey bop a ree bop / Grease nipples / Pedal to the metal.

FOIL

Formed: Fauldhouse, West Lothian ... 1995 out of guitar-rockers The NAKED SEE (who issued two singles for 'Human Condition', 'NOTHING'S LOST' and 'FACELESS') and MUTINY STRINGS by frontman/guitarist HUGH DUGGIE, guitar-man COLIN McINALLY, bassist SHUG ANDERSON and drummer JIM ANDERSON. Spreading their word via a gig at London's Underground venue early the following year, the band were picked up by Paul Taylor, who signed them to Mute-backed imprint '13th Hour'. That summer, their debut single, 'REVIVING GENE', hit the shops and was noted for its unmistakable STEREOPHONICS-meets-SUGAR hooklines. Over the course of the next 18 months, FOIL giftwrapped a string of other, equally impressive 45's which previewed their first long-player, 'SPREAD IT ALL AROUND' (1998). Witty, barbed and exquisitely catchy, the set highlighted the aforementioned singles, 'ARE YOU ENEMY?', 'A PLACE TO HIDE' and a remixed 'REVIVER GENE', plus the comical 'ACID KEWPIE'. With new drummer ALAN LINDLAY on board, FOIL returned in 2000, although follow-up album, 'NEVER GOT HIP', did exactly as its title suggested.

Album rating: SPREAD IT ALL AROUND (*7) / NEVER GOT HIP (*6)

NAKED SEE

PADDY – vocals, guitar / **COLIN McINALLY** – guitar / **MOONEY** – bass / **JIM ANDERSON** – drums

Human Condition not iss.

Aug 93. (7") *(HC 004)* **NOTHING'S LOST. / NEVER SO NEAR** [ ] [-]

Sep 94. (cd-ep) *(HC 006)* **FACELESS EP** [ ] [-]
– Faceless / Endgames / Night-town / The journey.

FOIL

— **HUGH DUGGIE** – vocals, guitar; repl. PADDY

— **SHUG ANDERSON** – bass; repl. MOONEY

13th Hour 13th Hour

Jul 96. (7") *(HOUR 8)* **REVIVER GENE. / SNECK** [ ] [-]
(cd-s+=) *(CDHOUR 8)* – In the ground.

Oct 96. (7") *(HOUR 9)* **LET IT GO BLACK. / MAN OVERBOARD** [ ] [-]
(cd-s+=) *(CDHOUR 9)* – Spleen / Voodoo autograph.

May 97. (7") *(HOUR 10)* **ARE YOU ENEMY? / GOIN' DOWN** [ ] [-]
(cd-s+=) *(CDHOUR 10)* – Denny.

Sep 97. (7"blue) *(HOUR 11)* **A PLACE TO HIDE. / DON'T COME AROUND** [ ] [-]
(cd-s+=) *(CDHOUR 11)* –

Nov 97. (7"green) *(HOUR 13)* **REVIVER GENE. / SEDATE ME** [ ] [-]
(cd-s+=) *(CDHOUR 13)* – Hey you / Play dead.

Jan 98. (cd/lp) *(<13TH CD/LP 5>)* **SPREAD IT ALL AROUND** [ ] [ ] Mar98
– A.C. rocker / High wire / Acid kewpie / Control freak / Penicillin / A place to hide / Soup / Don't come around / Are you enemy? / Coup d'etat / Reviver gene / Carstairs.

— **ALAN LINDLAY** – drums; repl. JIM

May 00. (7") *(HOUR 14)* **I'LL TAKE MY CHANCES. / UNDERTOW** [ ] [-]
(cd-s+=) *(CDHOUR 14)* – Careering / Reviving gene (CD-Rom).

Jun 00. (cd/lp) *(<13TH CD/LP 6>)* **NEVER GOT HIP** [ ] [ ]
– Never got hip / Easy life and ignominy / Superhero No.1 / End of the world / Groundwork / Half life bunker / British East India Co. trafficker / Weird kid / I'll take my chances / The ghost of Vernon Howell / Claremont junction optimist.

Oct 00. (7") *(HOUR 15)* **SUPERHERO NO.1. / BAD GIRLFRIEND / HONESTY FIT** [ ] [-]
(cd-s) *(CDHOUR 15)* – ('A'side) / World is weird / Curse of me / Forget to breathe / Stranger's almanac.

FOO FIGHTERS

Formed: Seattle, Washington, USA ... April/May '94, after the death of KURT COBAIN (Nirvana), by drummer turned singer/guitarist DAVE GROHL. He subsequently brought in COBAIN stand-in, PAT SMEAR, along with NATE MANDEL and WILLIAM GOLDSMITH, taking the group name from the mysterious lights reported by pilots during World War II. Continuing the UFO concept, the group founded their own 'Roswell' label, (funded by 'Capitol') and debuted in the summer of '95 with UK Top 5 single, 'THIS IS A CALL'. More harmonic and positively life-affirming than NIRVANA (comparisons were inevitable), The FOO FIGHTERS' offered up one of the most exciting debuts of the year; while the lyrics may have been somewhat cryptic, the obvious grunge influences were tempered with an infectious, pop-hardcore rush that was impossible to resist. The album sold well on both sides of the Atlantic, with GROHL & Co heading out on a successful series of festival dates. Work on the Gil Norton-produced follow-up, 'THE COLOUR AND THE SHAPE', got off to a difficult start with initial sessions in Seattle being scrapped. Further problems arose with the departure of sticksman GOLDSMITH halfway through recording, although GROHL subsequently completed the drum parts and the record was finally released in Spring '97 to rave reviews. Outpacing even the debut, The FOO FIGHTERS had come on leaps and bounds in the songwriting department, their rich post-grunge tapestry markedly more diverse. With good old romantic love as the driving theme of the record, the likes of the heart-rending (UK Top 20) 'EVERLONG' took starry-eyed, melodic distortion-pop to new (neck) hair-raising limits (complete with 'Evil Dead'-style video for that true-love atmosphere!), while more mellow musings like 'WALKING AFTER YOU' (used on the movie 'X-Files: Fight The Future') and 'DOLL' suggested GROHL was gaining enough confidence in his writing to chill out and reflect rather than continually going for the jugular. The group's growing self-belief was confirmed by some storming festival sets, while the album later came out top in rock 'bible', 'Kerrang!'s yearly critic's poll. After GROHL's brief expedition into film score work (with soundtrack 'TOUCH' being issued mid-'98), the band inked a deal with 'R.C.A.' and were ready to unleash a third album. 'THERE IS NOTHING LEFT TO LOSE' (1999), which disappointed no one with its melodic, HUSKER DU/PIXIES-inspired rock tunes, especially the hit 'LEARN TO FLY' (although I hear RUSH's 'Finding My Way' every time). • **Covers:** OZONE (Kiss) / GAS CHAMBER (Angry Samoans) / BAKER STREET (Gerry Rafferty). • **Trivia:** GREG DULLI (Afghan Whigs) played guitar on 'X-static'.

Album rating: FOO FIGHTERS (*8) / THE COLOUR AND THE SHAPE (*9) / TOUCH soundtrack by Dave Grohl (*6) / THERE IS NOTHING LEFT TO LOSE (*8)

DAVE GROHL (b.14 Jan'69, Warren, Ohio) – vocals, guitar / **PAT SMEAR** – guitar (ex-GERMS) / **NATE MANDEL** – bass / **WILLIAM GOLDSMITH** – drums (both of SUNNY DAY REAL ESTATE)

Roswell Roswell

Jun 95. (7",7"red) *(CL 753)* **THIS IS A CALL. / WINNEBAGO** [5] [-]
(12"luminous+=/cd-s+=) *(12/CD CL 753)* – Podunk.

Jun 95. (cd/c/lp) *(CD/TC+/EST 2266)* *<34027>* **FOO FIGHTERS** [3] [23]
– This is a call / I'll stick around / Big me / Alone + easy target / Good grief / Floaty / Weenie beenie / Oh, George / For all the cows / X-static / Wattershed / Exhausted.

Sep 95. (c-s/7"red) *(TC+/CL 757)* **I'LL STICK AROUND. / HOW I MISS YOU** [18] [-]
(12"+=/cd-s+=) *(12/CD CL 757)* – Ozone.

Nov 95. (c-s/7"blue) *(TC+/CL 762)* **FOR ALL THE COWS. / WATTERSHED (live at Reading)** [28] [-]
(cd-s+=) *(CDCL 762)* – ('A'-live at Reading).

Mar 96. (c-s/7"white) *(TC+CL 768)* **BIG ME. / FLOATY (BBC session) / GAS CHAMBER (BBC session)** [19] [-]
(cd-s+=) *(CDCL 768)* – Alone + easy target (BBC session).

— **TAYLOR HAWKINS** – drums (of-ALANIS MORISSETTE) repl. GOLDSMITH

Apr 97. (7") *(CL 788)* **MONKEY WRENCH. / THE COLOUR AND THE SHAPE** [12] [-]
(cd-s+=) *(CDCLS 788)* – Up in arms (slow version).
(cd-s) *(CDCL 788)* – ('A'side) / Down in the park / See you (acoustic).

May 97. (cd/c/lp) *(CD/TC+/EST 2295)* *<58530>* **THE COLOUR AND THE SHAPE** [3] [10]
– Doll / Monkey wrench / Hey Johnny Park / My poor brain / Wind up / Up in arms / My hero / See you / Enough space / February stars / Everlong / Walking after you / New way home.

Aug 97. (7"blue) *(CL 792)* **EVERLONG. / DRIVE ME WILD** [18] [-]
(cd-s+=) *(CDCL 792)* – See you (live).
(cd-s) *(CDCLS 792)* – ('A'side) / Requiem / I'll stick around (live).

— now without SMEAR who was repl. by **FRANZ STAHL** (ex-SCREAM)

Jan 98. (7"red) *(CL 796)* **MY HERO. / DEAR LOVER** [21] [-]
(cd-s+=) *(CDCL 796)* – Baker Street (BBC session). *(with enhanced cd+=)* – Everlong (video) / Monkey wrench (video).

Jun 98. (cd; by DAVE GROHL) *<(7243 855632-25)>* **TOUCH** (music from the motion picture)
– Bill Hill theme / August Murray theme / How do you do / Richie Baker's miracle / Making popcorn / Outrage / Saints in love / Spinning newspapers / Remission my ass / Scene 6 / This loving thing / Final miracle / Touch.
above featured guests LOUISE POST + JOHN DOE plus BARRETT JONES keyboards + ERIC RICHARDS slide guitar

Aug 98. (7"/c-s/cd-s) *(E 4100/+C/CD)* **WALKING AFTER YOU (remix). / (Ween: Beacon Light)** [20] [-]
(above from the movie, 'X-Files: Fight The Future' on 'Elektra')

— now trio of **GROHL, MENDEL + HAWKINS**/ added on tour **CHRIS SHIFLETT** – guitar (ex-NO USE FOR A NAME)

R.C.A. R.C.A.

Oct 99. (c-s) *(74321 71308-4) <album cut>* **LEARN TO FLY / HAVE A CIGAR** [21] [19]
(cd-s+=) *(74321 71308-2)* – Iron and stone.
(cd-s+=) *(74321 71310-2)* – Make a bet.

Nov 99. (cd/c/lp) *<(07863 67892-2/-4/-1)>* **THERE IS NOTHING LEFT TO LOSE** [10] [10]
– Stacked actors / Breakout / Learn to fly / Gimme stitches / Generator / Aurora / Live-in skin / Next year / Headwires / Ain't it the life / M.I.A.

Mar 00. (cd-ep) *(74321 74958-2)* **GENERATOR EP**
– Generator / Ain't it the life (two meter Dutch session) / Floaty (two meter Dutch session) / Fraternity / Breakout (live)

Sep 00. (7") *(74321 79012-7)* **BREAKOUT. / STACKED ACTORS (live)** [29] [-]
(cd-s+=) *(74321 79011-2)* – Monkey wrench.
(cd-s) *(74321 79010-2)* – ('A'side) / Iron and stone / Learn to fly (live).

Dec 00. (7"/c-s) *(74321 80926-7/-4)* **NEXT YEAR. / BIG ME (live/session)** [42] [-]
(cd-s+=) *(74321 80926-2)* – Next year (live/session).
(cd-s) *(74321 80927-2)* – ('A'side) / Baker street (live/session) / ('A'-CD-ROM).

FORBIDDEN

Formed: San Francisco, California, USA . . . 1985 initially as FORBIDDEN EVIL by RUSS ANDERSON, GLEN ALVELAIS, CRAIG LOCIERO, MATT CAMACHO and PAUL BOSTAPH. This respected Bay Area thrash quintet were one of the many San Fran acts to be snapped up in the wake of METALLICA's growing success, the group signing to 'Metal Blade' and trimming their moniker to The FORBIDDEN. Their original group name was reserved for the debut album, released in 1988 to widespread acclaim. Like TESTAMENT, The FORBIDDEN played at the legendary Dynamo metal-fest in Holland, taping the show for posterity and releasing it as a mini-set (the record featured a particularly frenetic take on Judas Priest's 'VICTIM OF CHANGES'). A follow-up album proper, 'TWISTED INTO FORM' represented a career best and the group looked like they might move up to the major league. However, record label hassles left FORBIDDEN without any new product on the shelves for the bulk of the early 90's. They eventually emerged in 1994 on German indie label, 'Gun' with 'DISTORTION', the record paying heed to the changing times with more than a passing nod at the grunge scene.

Album rating: FORBIDDEN EVIL (*5) / TWISTED INTO FORM (*7) / POINT OF NO RETURN – THE BEST OF FORBIDDEN compilation (*6) / DISTORTION (*5) / GREEN (*5)

RUSS ANDERSON – vocals / **GLEN ALVELAIS** – guitar / **CRAIG LOCIERO** – guitar / **MATT CAMACHO** – bass / **PAUL BOSTAPH** – drums

Under One Flag Combat

1988. (cd/c/lp) *(CD/T+/FLAG 27) <8257>* **FORBIDDEN EVIL**
– Chalice of blood / Off the edge / Through the eyes of glass / Forbidden evil / March into fire / Feel no pain / As good as dead / Follow me. *(cd re-iss. Nov99 on 'Century Media'; CM 66029-2)*

— **TIM CALVERT** – guitar (ex-MILITIA) repl. ALVELAIS

Jul 89. (cd/c/lp) *(CD/T+/FLAG 43) <2014>* **TWISTED INTO FORM**
– Parting of the ways / Instrumental / Infinite / Out of body (out of mind) / Step by step / Twisted into form / R.I.P. / Spiral depression (instrumental) / Tossed away / One foot in Hell. *(cd re-iss. Feb99 on 'Century Media'; CM 66026CD)*

Sep 89. (12"ep) *(12FLAG 108) <2009>* **RAW EVIL – LIVE AT THE DYNAMO (live)**
– Victim of changes / Forbidden evil / Chalice of blood / Through eyes of glass. *(cd-iss. Jun99 on 'Century Media'; CM 66012-2)*

Jul 92. (cd/c/lp) *(CD/T+/FLAG 73) <88561-1118-2>* **POINT OF NO RETURN – THE BEST OF FORBIDDEN** (compilation)
– Chalice of blood / Out of body (out of mind) / Feel no pain / Step by step / Off the edge / One foot in hell / Through the eyes the eyes of glass / Tossed away / March into fire / Victim of changes.

— **STEVE JACOBS** – drums; repl. BOSTAPH + CAMACHO

Gun-RCA Pavement

Mar 97. (cd) *(74321 44249-2) <32256>* **GREEN**
– What is the last time? / Green / Phat / Turns to rage / Face down heroes / Over the middle / Kanaworms / Noncents / Blank / Focus.

not iss. Fierce

Sep 97. (cd) *<11091>* **DISTORTION** (rec. 1994) [-]
– Distortion / Hypnotized by the rhythm / Rape / No reason / Feed the hand / Wake up! / Mind's "I" / All that is / Under taker / 21st century schizoid man.

— disbanded some time after above

Lita FORD

Born: ROSANNA FORD, 23 Sep'59, London, England. After leaving California band The RUNAWAYS in 1979, she went solo, signing to 'Mercury' in 1982. The following year, she and her band issued a debut album, 'OUT FOR BLOOD'. A fairly unremarkable, if ballsy affair, by the release of her next effort, 'DANCIN' ON THE EDGE' (1984), FORD was a fully fledged solo artiste. A lone female in the predatory territory of hard rock was (and is) something of an anomaly, although, against all the odds, Ms FORD won herself a fair bit of respect. Of course, this was nothing to do with the fact that she looked like Ulrika Jonsson in leather trousers, all flowing blonde locks and pouting attitude. No, what the cod-piece commandos really admired was her axe spanking, rated the best in the world, apparently. Whatever, she eventually hit the Top 20 (US) in Summer '88 with the catchy glam-metal of 'KISS ME DEADLY', going even higher with the spooky but cheesy vampire ballad collaboration with OZZY OSBOURNE, 'CLOSE MY EYES FOREVER'. The album, 'LITA', just nosed into the US Top 30 and that, basically, was about the size of her proverbial 15 minutes of fame. A further two major label sets of nondescript AOR follwed, RCA dropping her after 1992's 'DANGEROUS CURVES'. • **Songwriters:** Mostly written by LITA, with many collaborations (mid-80's with LEIB and LACHOON, 1988 with MIKE CHAPMAN & HOLLY KNIGHT, and latterly with GROMBACHER and KISSELBACH, plus DAVID EZRIN) except covers; ONLY WOMEN BLEED (Alice Cooper). FALLING IN AND OUT OF LOVE was co-written with NIKKI SIXX of MOTLEY CRUE. • **Trivia:** In June '89, LITA married WASP guitarist CHRIS HOLMES.

Album rating: OUT FOR BLOOD (*5) / DANCIN' ON THE EDGE (*5) / LITA (*6) / STILETTO (*4) / DANGEROUS CURVES (*4) / THE BEST OF LITA FORD compilation (*6) / BLACK (*3)

LITA FORD – vocals, lead guitar (ex-RUNAWAYS)with **BRIAN MERRYWEATHER** – bass, vocals, producer / **DUSTY WATSON** – drums, vocals

Mercury Mercury

Jul 83. (lp/c; as LITA FORD BAND) *(MERL/+C 26) <810 331-1/-4>* **OUT FOR BLOOD**
– Out for blood / Stay with me baby / Just a feeling / Die foe me only (black widow) / Ready willing and able / Rock'n'roll made me what I am today / If you can't live with it / On the run / Any way that you want me / I can't stand it.

— now with **HUGH McDONALD** – bass / **RANDY CASTILLO** – drums

Vertigo Mercury

Apr 84. (7"/7"w-poster) *(VER/+P 10)* **GOTTA LET GO. / RUN WITH THE MONEY** [-]
(12"+=) *(VERX 10)* – Lady killer.

May 84. (lp/c) *(VERL/+C 13) <818864>* **DANCIN' ON THE EDGE** [96] [66]
– Gotta let go / Dancin' on the edge / Dressed to kill / Hit 'n run / Lady killer / Still waitin' / Five in my heart / Don't let me down tonight / Run with the $.

— **ERIC SINGER** – drums repl. CASTILLO who joined OZZY OSBOURNE / **TOMMY CALABONNA** – bass repl. McDONALD

R.C.A. R.C.A.

Apr 88. (lp/c/cd) *(PL/PK/PD 86397) <6397>* **LITA** [29] Feb88
– Back to the cave / Can't catch me / Blueberry / Kiss me deadly / Falling in and out of love / Fatal passion / Under the gun / Broken dreams / Close my eyes forever. *(re-iss. cd Mar94; 74321 13887-2)*

May 88. (7"/7"pic-d) *(PB/PA 49501) <6866>* **KISS ME DEADLY. / BROKEN DREAMS** [12] Mar88

Nov 88. (7"/7"pic-d) *(PB 49575/+P)* **KISS ME DEADLY. / BROKEN DREAMS** [75] [-]
(12"+=) *(PT 49576)* – ('A'instrumental).

Nov 88. (7") *<8640>* **BACK TO THE CAVE (remix). / UNDER THE GUN** [-]

May 89. (7"/7"pic-d; by LITA FORD with OZZY OSBOURNE) *(PB 49049) <8899>* **CLOSE MY EYES FOREVER. / UNDER THE GUN** [47] [8] Feb89
(12"+=/cd-s+=) *(PT/PD 49409)* – Blueberry.

Jul 90. (7") *<c-s> (PB 49265) <2607>* **HUNGRY. / BIG GUN** [98]
(12"+=/cd-s+=) *(PT/PD 49266)* – Aces and eights.

Jul 90. (cd/c/lp) *(PL/PK/PD 82090) <2090>* **STILETTO** [66] [52] Jun90
– Your wake up call / Hungry / Dedication / Stiletto / Lisa / The ripper / Big gun / Only women bleed / Bad boy / Aces & eights / Cherry red / Outro.

Oct 91. (c-s) *<62074>* **SHOT OF POISON / (excerpts)** [-] [45]

Dec 91. (7") *(PB 49145)* **SHOT OF POISON. / LARGER THAN LIFE** [63] [-]
(12"+=/12"pic-d+=)(cd-s+=) *(PT 4913 2/0)(PD 49146)* – ('A'remixed).

Jan 92. (cd/c/lp) *(PD/PK/PL 90592) <61025>* **DANGEROUS CURVES** [51] Nov91
– Larger than life / What do you know about love / Shot of poison / Bad love / Playin' with fire / Hellbound train / Black widow / Little too early / Holy man / Tambourine dream / Little black spider. *(re-iss. cd Mar94; 74321 16000-2)*

BMG-RCA BMG-RCA

Aug 92. (cd/c/lp) *<(7863 66047-2/-4/-1)>* **THE BEST OF LITA FORD** (compilation) Jul92
– What do you know about love / Kiss me deadly / Shot of poison / Hungry / Gotta let go / Close my eyes forever / Larger than life / Only women bleed / Playin' with fire / Back to the cave / Lisa.

not iss. ZYX

Feb 95. (cd) *<ZYX 20330-2>* **BLACK** [-]
– Black / Fall / Loverman / Killin' kind / Hammerhead / Boilin' point / Where will I find my heart tonight / War of the angels / Joe / White lightnin' / Smokin' toads / Spider monkeys.

— In Apr'95, LITA collaborated on a single, 'A FUTURE TO HIS LIFE' with JOE WALSH

– compilations, etc. –

Aug 96. (cd) *R.C.A.; (7863 66037-2)* **GREATEST HITS** [ ] [-]
Sep 97. (cd) *Camden-RCA; (74321 51200-2)* **KISS ME DEADLY** [ ] [-]
Jun 00. (cd) *Cleopatra; <(CLP 0804-2)>* **GREATEST HITS LIVE** [ ] [ ] May00

FOREIGNER

Formed: New York, USA . . . early 1976 by English expatriot MICK JONES, who was already the owner of a rather chequered music biz CV. After beginning his career in England with 60's outfit NERO & THE GLADIATORS, he later worked with French singer JOHNNY HALLIDAY as well as undergoing a stint in SPOOKY TOOTH before moving to New York and securing a job as an A&R man. Eventually hooking up with Englishmen, IAN McDONALD and DENNIS ELLIOTT alongside New Yorkers, LOU GRAMM, AL GREENWOOD and ED GAGLIARI, JONES formed FOREIGNER. After a year in the studio, the group unleashed an eponymous debut album for 'Atlantic'. Although the record failed to chart in the UK, it hit Top 5 in the States, becoming a multi-million seller and staying in the chart for a year. Its success boosted by two hit singles, 'FEELS LIKE THE FIRST TIME' and 'COLD AS ICE', FOREIGNER rapidly became established as prime staples for American FM radio. Though their material was harder-edged than the likes of REO SPEEDWAGON etc., FOREIGNER captured the middle ground perfectly, their AOR/hard rock-straddling sound gaining them massive sales for subsequent releases such as 'DOUBLE VISION' (1978) and 'HEAD GAMES' (1979), the former's title track narrowly missing the US top spot. Despite the group headlining the 1978 Reading Festival, the latter album (which saw another seasoned player, RICK WILLS, replacing GREENWOOD) failed to chart in the UK. FOREIGNER would have to wait until the release of the huge, Mutt Lange-produced '4' (1981) album, before they enjoyed transatlantic success. This was secured on the back of the UK/US Top 10, 'WAITING FOR A GIRL LIKE YOU'. It would be another histrionic AOR ballad, 'I WANT TO KNOW WHAT LOVE IS' (featuring the gospel talents of the New Jersey Mass Choir), that would become the group's best known song, its success even furnishing the band with a UK No.1 album. Released after a lengthy sabbatical, 'AGENT PROVOCATEUR' (1984), gave FOREIGNER yet another multi-million selling set, the success of the single making the band a household name. While LOU GRAMM cut a successful solo set in 1987, 'READY OR NOT', MICK JONES flopped with an eponymous set in '89, GRAMM eventually leaving the band for a time at the beginning of the 90's. While FOREIGNER had enjoyed reasonable success with the 1987 set, 'INSIDE INFORMATION', their first GRAMM-less set (with JOHNNY EDWARDS on vocals) was a relative commercial failure. GRAMM finally returned in 1994 although it was clear FOREIGNER's glory days were over. • **Songwriters:** JONES penned some with GRAMM, until his 1987 departure.

Album rating: FOREIGNER (*5) / DOUBLE VISION (*6) / HEAD GAMES (*6) / 4 (*7) / RECORDS compilation (*8) / AGENT PROVOCATEUR (*6) / INSIDE INFORMATION (*5) / UNUSUAL HEAT (*5) / THE VERY BEST OF FOREIGNER or THE VERY BEST . . . AND BEYOND compilations (*7) / MR MOONLIGHT (*4)

LOU GRAMM (b. 2 May'50, Rochester, New York) – vocals (ex-BLACK SHEEP) / **MICK JONES** (b.27 Dec'47, London, England) – guitar (ex-SPOOKY TOOTH) / **IAN McDONALD** (b.25 Jun'46, London) – guitar, keyboards (ex-KING CRIMSON) / **AL GREENWOOD** (b. New York) – keyboards / **ED GAGLIARI** (b.13 Feb'52, New York) – bass (ex-STORM) / **DENNIS ELLIOTT** (b.18 Aug'50, London) – drums (ex-IAN HUNTER BAND)

Atlantic Atlantic

Apr 77. (7") *(K 10917) <3394>* **FEELS LIKE THE FIRST TIME. / WOMAN OH WOMAN** [ ] [4] Mar77
Apr 77. (lp/c) *(K/K4 50356) <18215>* **FOREIGNER** [ ] [4] Mar77
– Feels like the first time / Cold as ice / Starrider / Headknocker / The damage is done / Long, long way from home / Woman oh woman / At war with the world / Fool for the anyway / I need you. *(cd-iss. Apr85; 250356) (re-iss. cd Oct95;)*
Jul 77. (7",7"clear) *(K 10986) <3410>* **COLD AS ICE. / I NEED YOU** [ ] [6]
(hit UK No.24 in Jul'78)
Dec 77. (7") *<3439>* **LONG, LONG WAY FROM HOME. / THE DAMAGE IS DONE** [-] [20]
Apr 78. (7"m) *(K 11086)* **FEELS LIKE THE FIRST TIME. / LONG, LONG WAY FROM HOME / COLD AS ICE** [39] [-]
Aug 78. (lp/c) *(K/K4 50476) <19999>* **DOUBLE VISION** [32] [3] Jul78
– Back where you belong / Blue morning, blue day / Double vision / Hot blooded / I have waited so long / Lonely children / Spellbinder / Tramontane / You're all I am. *(cd-iss. 1988 & Oct95)*
Oct 78. (7",7"red) *(K 11167) <3488>* **HOT BLOODED. / TRAMONTANE** [42] [3] Jun78
Dec 78. (7") *(K 11199) <3514>* **DOUBLE VISION. / LONELY CHILDREN** [ ] [2] Sep78
Feb 79. (7",7"pic-d) *(K 11236) <3543>* **BLUE MORNING, BLUE DAY. / I HAVE WAITED SO LONG** [45] [15] Dec78

—— **RICK WILLS** – bass (ex-ROXY MUSIC, ex-SMALL FACES) repl. AL (he joined The SPYS)

Sep 79. (7") *(K 11373) <3618>* **DIRTY WHITE BOY. / REV ON THE RED LINE** [ ] [12]
Sep 79. (lp/c) *(K/K4 50651) <29999>* **HEAD GAMES** [ ] [5]
– Dirty white boy / Love on the telephone / Women / I'll get even with you / Seventeen / Head games / The modern day / Blinded by science / Do what you like / Rev on the red line. *(cd-iss. Feb93 on 'Atco'; 7567 81598-2) (re-iss. cd Nov95; 250651)*
Feb 80. (7") *(K 11417) <3633>* **HEAD GAMES. / DO WHAT YOU LIKE** [ ] [14] Nov79
Apr 80. (7") *(K 11456) <3651>* **WOMEN. / THE MODERN DAY** [ ] [41] Feb80
Sep 80. (7") *(K 11602)* **I'LL GET EVEN WITH YOU. / BLINDED BY SCIENCE** [ ] [-]

—— Trimmed to quartet, when GAGLIARI and McDONALD left

Jul 81. (7") *(K 11665) <3831>* **URGENT. / GIRL ON THE MOON** [54] [4] Jun81
Jul 81. (lp/c) *(K/K4 50796) <16999>* **4** [5] [1]
– Night life / Juke box hero / Break it up / Waiting for a girl like you / Luanne / Urgent / I'm gonna win / Woman in black / Urgent / Girl on the Moon / Don't let go. *(cd-iss. Aug85; 250796) (re-iss. cd Feb91; 7567 82795-2)*
Sep 81. (7") *(K 11678) <4017>* **JUKE BOX HERO. / I'M GONNA WIN** [48] [26] Feb82
Oct 81. (7") *<3868>* **WAITING FOR A GIRL LIKE YOU. / I'M GONNA WIN** [-] [2]
Nov 81. (7"m) *(K 11696)* **WAITING FOR A GIRL LIKE YOU. / FEELS LIKE THE FIRST TIME / COLD AS ICE** [8] [-]
Mar 82. (7") *(K 11718)* **DON'T LET GO. / FOOL FOR YOU ANYWAY** [ ] [-]
Apr 82. (7") *<4044>* **BREAK IT UP. / LUANNE** [-] [26]
Apr 82. (7") *(K 11728)* **URGENT. / HEAD GAMES (live)** [45] [-]
(12") *(K 11728T)* – ('A'side) / Hot blooded (live).
Jul 82. (7") *<4072>* **LUANNE. / FOOL FOR YOU ANYWAY** [-] [75]
Dec 82. (lp/c)(cd) *(A 0999/+4)(780 999-2) <80999>* **RECORDS (THE BEST OF . . .)** (compilation) [58] [10]
– Cold as ice / Double vision / Head games / Waiting for a girl like you / Feels like the first time / Urgent / Dirty white boy / Jukebox hero / Long, long way from home / Hot blooded. *(re-iss. cd Oct95; 7567 82800-2)*
Nov 84. (7",7"sha-pic-d) *(A 9596) <89596>* **I WANT TO KNOW WHAT LOVE IS. / STREET THUNDER** [1] [1]
(12"+=) *(A 9596T)* – Urgent.
Dec 84. (lp/c/cd) *(781999-1/-4/-2) <81999>* **AGENT PROVOCATEUR** [1] [4] Nov84
– Tooth and nail / That was yesterday / I want to know what love is / Growing up the hard way / Reaction to action / Stranger in my own house / A love in vain / Down on love / Two different worlds / She's too tough. *(re-iss. cd Oct95;)*
Mar 85. (7") *(A 9571) <89571>* **THAT WAS YESTERDAY (remix). / TWO DIFFERENT WORLDS** [28] [12]
(12"+=) *(A 9571T)* – ('A'-orchestral version).
May 85. (7") *<89542>* **REACTION TO ACTION. / SHE'S TOO TOUGH** [-] [54]
Jun 85. (7") *(A 9539)* **COLD AS ICE (remix). / REACTION TO ACTION** [64] [-]
(12"+=) *(A 9539T)* – Head games (live).
(d7"++=) *(A 9539/SAM 247)* – Hot blooded (live).
Aug 85. (7") *<89493>* **DOWN ON LOVE. / GROWING UP THE HARD WAY** [-] [54]

—— LOU GRAMM left to go solo

Jul 87. (7") *(A 9169) <89169>* **SAY YOU WILL. / A NIGHT TO REMEMBER** [71] [6] Nov87
(7"box+=/12"+=/cd-s+=) *(A 9169 B/T/CD)* – Hot blooded (live).
Dec 87. (lp/c)(cd) *(WX 143/+C)(781808-2) <81808>* **INSIDE INFORMATION** [64] [15]
– Heart turns to stone / Can't wait / Say you will / I don't want to live without you / Counting every minute / Inside information / The beat of my heart / Face to face / Out of the blue / A night to remember.
May 88. (7") *(A 9101) <89101>* **I DON'T WANT TO LIVE WITHOUT YOU. / FACE TO FACE** [ ] [5] Mar88
(12"+=/cd-s+=) *(A 9101 T/CD)* – Urgent.
Jul 88. (7") *<89046>* **HEART TURNS TO STONE. / COUNTING EVERY MINUTE** [-] [56]

—— (1990) added **JOHNNY EDWARDS** – vocals to join **JONES + THOMAS**

Jun 91. (7"/c-s) **LOWDOWN AND DIRTY. / FLESH WOUND** [ ] [ ]
(12"+=/cd-s+=) – No hiding place.
Jul 91. (cd)(lp/c) *<(7567 82299-2)>(WX 424/+C)* **UNUSUAL HEAT** [56] [ ]
– Only Heaven knows / Lowdown and dirty / I'll fight for you / Moment of truth / Mountain of love / Ready for the rain / When the night comes down / Safe in my heart / No hiding place / Flesh wound / Unusual heat. *(cd-iss. Nov93;)*
Aug 91. (7"/c-s) *(A 7608/+MC)* **I'LL FIGHT FOR YOU / MOMENT OF TRUTH** [ ] [ ]
(12"+=/cd-s+=) *(A 7608 T/CD)* – Dirty white boy (live).
Apr 92. (cd)(lp/c) *(7597 80511-2)(WX 469/+C) <89999>* **THE VERY BEST OF FOREIGNER** (compilation) [19] [ ]
– Feels like the first time / Cold as ice / Starrider / Hot blooded / Blue morning, blue day / Double vision / Dirty white boy / Women / Head games / Juke Box hero / Waiting for a girl like you / Urgent / That was yesterday / I want to know what love is / Say you will / I don't want to live without you. *(re-iss. Dec92 as 'THE VERY BEST. . . AND BEYOND' cd; 7567 89999-2)(+=)* – (3 extra tracks).
Apr 92. (7"/c-s) **WAITING FOR A GIRL LIKE YOU. / COLD AS ICE** [ ] [ ]
(12"+=/cd-s+=) – That was yesterday / Feels like the first time.
Dec 93. (cd/c) *<(7567 82525-2/-4)>* **CLASSIC HITS LIVE (live)** [ ] [ ]
– Double vision / Cold as ice / Damage is done / Women / Dirty white boy / Fool for you anyway / Head games / Not fade away – Mona / Waiting for a girl like you / Juke box hero / Urgent / Love maker / I want to know what love is / Feels like the first time.

—— **JONES + GRAMM** recruited **MARK SCHULMAN** – drums / **JEFF JACOBS** – keyboards / **BRUCE TURGON** – bass

B.M.G. Rhythm Safari

Oct 94. (7"/c-s) *(74321 23286-7/-4)* **WHITE LIE. / UNDER THE GUN** [58] [ ]
(cd-s+=) *(74321 23286-2)* – ('A'-alternate version).
Nov 94. (cd/c) *(74321 23285-2/-4)* **MR. MOONLIGHT** [59] [ ]
Mar 95. (c-s) *<53183>* **UNTIL THE END OF TIME / UNDER THE GUN** [-] [42]
Mar 95. (c-s) *(74321 25457-4)* **UNTIL THE END OF TIME / HAND ON MY HEART** [ ] [-]
(cd-s+=) *(74321 25457-2)* – ('A'mix).

– compilations, etc. –

Oct 00. (d-cd) *Atlantic; <(8122 79884-2)>* **JUKEBOX HEROES – THE FOREIGNER ANTHOLOGY** [ ] [ ]

MICK JONES

Atlantic Atlantic

Nov 88. (7") *<88954>* **JUST WANNA HOLD. / YOU ARE MY FRIEND** [-] [ ]

Jun 89. (7") *(A 8954) <88787>* **EVERYTHING THAT COMES AROUND. / THE WRONG SIDE OF THE LAW** [ ] [ ]
(12"+=) *(A 8954T)* – ('A'extended).

Aug 89. (lp/c/cd)(cd) *(WX 290/+C/CED)(K 781991-2) <81991>* **MICK JONES** [ ] [ ]
– Just wanna hold / Save me tonight / That's the way my love is / The wrong side of the law / 4 wheels turnin' / Everything that comes around / You are my friend / Danielle / Write tonight / Johnny (part 1).

FOR LOVE NOT LISA

Formed: Oklahoma, USA . . . 1990 by MILES, MIKE LEWIS, DOUG CARRION and AARON PRESTON. Relocating to L.A., the group secured a deal with 'East West' in the post-NIRVANA rush to sign up any band with the elusive 'grunge' factor, in fact any band with one check shirt between them. A debut album followed in late '93, showcasing the group's interesting fusion of alternative rock and metal. Although they also built up something of a live reputation, FOR LOVE NOT LISA's recording silence indicates that they've since packed it in.

Album rating: MERGE (*6)

MIKE LEWIS – vocals, guitar / **MILES** – guitar / **DOUG CARRION** – bass / **AARON PRESTON** – drums

East West East West

Oct 93. (cd/c) *<(7567 92283-2/-4)>* **MERGE** [ ] [ ]
– Softhand / Slip slide melting / Lucifer for now / Daring to pick up / Simple line of decline / Travis Hoffman / Just a phase / Traces / Mother's faith / Swallow / More than a girl / Merge.

—— disbanded soon after above

FOUR HORSEMEN

Formed: London, England . . . 1990 by HAGGIS, formerly known as KID CHAOS when he had been a member of ZODIAC MINDWARP and The CULT. He completed the line-up with FRANK C. STARR, DAVE ZIZMI, BEN PAPE and KEN 'DIMWIT' MONTGOMERY. Furnished with a prestigious 'Def American' deal via Rick Rubin, the group ploughed the same earthy furrow as BLACK CROWES, DAN BAIRD, etc., albeit with a scuzzy rock'n'roll undertow. Their one and only album, 'NOBODY SAID IT WOULD BE EASY' (1991), brought inevitable CULT comparisons which missed the point entirely.

Album rating: NOBODY SAID IT WOULD BE EASY (*5) / GETTIN' PRETTY GOOD AY BARELY GETTIN' BY (*5)

FRANK C. STARR – vocals / **HAGGIS** (b. MARK MANNING) – guitar, slide, vocals (ex-CULT, ex-ZODIAC MINDWARP & THE LOVE REACTION) / **DAVE LIZMI** – guitar, vocals / **BEN PAPE** – bass, vocals / **KEN 'DIMWIT' MONTGOMERY** – drums (ex-D.O.A.)

PhonogramPhonogram

Jul 90. (12"ep)(cd-ep) *(SICK 1-12)(SICCD 1)* **WELFARE BOOGIE / SHELLEY. / HIGH SCHOOL ROCK'N'ROLLER / HARD LOVIN' MAN** [ ] [-]
above might not be same group

Def American Def American

Sep 91. (7"/7"pic-d) *(DEFA/P 12)* **NOBODY SAID IT WAS EASY. / HOMESICK BLUES** [ ] [ ]
(12"+=/cd-s+=) *(DEF X/CD 12)* – Can't stop rockin'.

Sep 91. (cd/c/lp) *(510047-2/-4/-1) <26561>* **NOBODY SAID IT WAS EASY** [ ] [ ]
– Nobody said it was easy / Rockin' is ma business / Tired wings / Can't stop rockin' / Wanted man / Let it rock / Hot head / Moonshine / Homesick blues / 75 again / Looking for trouble / I need a thrill – Somethin' good.

Mar 92. (7"/c-s) *(DEFA/+C 15)* **ROCKIN' IS MA BUSINESS. / MOONSHINE** [ ] [ ]
(12"pic-d+=) *(DEFAP 15-12)* – 75 again.

—— folded in '92, but re-formed for a one-off below

S.P.V. Magnetic Air

Apr 96. (cd) *(4701 44025-2)* **GETTIN' PRETTY GOOD AT BARELY GETTIN' BY** [ ] [ ]
– Still alive and well / Gettin' pretty good at barely gettin' by / Drunk again / Livin' these blues / Song for absent friends / Keep your life / Hot rod / Rock my universe / Back in business again / Hit the road / Keep on keepin' on / My song / What the hell went wrong.

4-SKINS

Formed: Southall, London, England . . . early 80's by er, 4 SKINS (i.e. four skinheads), namely PANTHER, HOXTON TOM and JOHNNY JACOBS together with a mysterious sticksman. This cheesily monikered bunch of Oi! upstarts followed in the wake of working class hero punk acts like SHAM 69, combining a seething but simplistic lyrical manifesto and punk-by-numbers riffs with an archetypal boot-boy image. After a one-off debut single, 'ONE LAW FOR THEM', on the tiny 'Clockwork Fun' label, the band signed to "Oi!" sanctuary, 'Secret', where they released a second single, 'YESTERDAY'S HEROES' (initially withdrawn) and a part-live debut album, 'THE GOOD, THE BAD AND THE 4-SKINS' (1982). More line-up changes followed as TOM recruited PAUL SWAIN on guitar, the new look 4 SKINS subsequently cutting a pseudonymous one-off single as The PLASTIC GANGSTERS in Spring '83. Later that year came the cringeingly titled 'A FISTFUL OF . . . 4-SKINS' album, their parting shot save for a live album, 'FROM CHAOS TO 1984'. • **Covered:** MERRY XMAS EVERYBODY (Slade). • **Note:** Not to be confused with another turn of the decade hardcore outfit from New York.

Album rating: THE GOOD, THE BAD AND THE 4-SKINS (*4) / A FISTFUL OF 4-SKINS (*3) / FROM CHAOS TO 1984 (*3) / THE BEST OF THE 4 SKINS compilation (*4)

PANTHER – vocals / **HOXTON TOM** – bass, vocals / **JOHNNY JACOBS** – guitar, vocals / **TONE** – drums

Clockwork Fun not iss.

Jul 81. (7") *(CF 101)* **ONE LAW FOR THEM. / BRAVE NEW WORLD** [ ] [-]

Secret not iss.

Oct 81. (7"; w-drawn) *(SHH 118)* **YESTERDAY'S HEROES. / ONE LAW FOR THEM** [ ] [-]

Dec 81. (7"m) *(SHH 125)* **YESTERDAY'S HEROES. / JUSTICE / GET OUT OF MY LIFE** [ ] [-]

Apr 82. (lp) *(SEC 4)* **THE GOOD, THE BAD AND THE 4-SKINS** (some live) [80] [-]
– Plastic gangsters / Jealousy / Yesterday's heroes / Justice / Jack the lad / Remembrance day / Manifesto / Wonderful world / Sorry / Evil / I don't wanna be / A.C.A.B. / Chaos / One law for them. *(cd-iss. Jul93 & Mar98 on 'Captain Oi'; AHOYCD 3) (cd re-iss. Mar01; MAYDP 007)*

—— (mid '82) **TOM** recruited **PAUL SWAIN** – guitar; repl. JACOBS

Oct 82. (7") *(SHH 141)* **LOW LIFE. / BREAD OR BLOOD** [ ] [-]

Apr 83. (7"; as PLASTIC GANGSTERS) *(SHH 144)* **PLASTIC GANGSTERS. / SRETSGNAG CITSALP** [-] [-] promo

Syndicate not iss.

Oct 83. (lp) *(SYN 1)* **A FISTFUL OF . . . 4-SKINS** [ ] [-]
– Five more years / Waiting for a friend / Johnny go home / The gambler / I'll stick to my guns / On file / Forgotten hero / Spy from Alaska / H.M.P. / No excuse / Betrayed / City boy / New war / One the streets / Saturday. *(cd-iss. Nov93 & May98 on 'Captain Oi'; AHOYCD 8) (cd re-iss. Mar01; MAYDP 011)*

Jun 84. (lp) *(SYNLP 5)* **FROM CHAOS TO 1984 (live)** [ ] [-]
– Wonderful world / Jealousy / On the streets / Johnny go home / 1984 / Bread or blood / Saturday / A.C.A.B. / City boy / 5 more years / Evil / On file / Clockwork skinhead / Chaos. *(re-iss. Apr99 on 'Get Back'; GET 44) (cd-iss. Mar99 on 'Harry May'; MAYOCD 503)*
above was HOXTON and Co's final release; might re-form or will he?

– compilations, etc. –

on 'Street Link' unless mentioned otherwise

Feb 87. (lp) *(LINKLP 02)* **WONDERFUL WORLD OF 4 SKINS** [ ] [-]
(cd-iss. May98 on 'Step 1'; STEPCD 027)

Sep 87. (lp) *(LINKLP 15)* **A FEW 4 SKINS MORE, VOL.1** [ ] [-]
(cd-iss. Oct92; LINKCD 15) (cd re-iss. Nov00 on 'Step 1'; STEPCD 047)

Dec 87. (lp) *(LINKLP 21)* **A FEW 4 SKINS MORE, VOL.2** [ ] [-]
(cd-iss. Feb98 on 'Step 1'; STEPCD 016)

Jun 89. (lp) *(LINKLP 90)* **LIVE AND LOUD! (live)** [ ] [-]

Aug 92. (cd) *(LINKCD 154)* **THE BEST OF THE 4-SKINS** [ ] [-]
– One law for them / Yesterday's heroes / Clockwork skinhead / Brave new world / Chaos / Wonderful world / Evil / Sorry / 1984 / A.C.A.B. / I don't wanna die / Plastic gangsters / Yesterday's heroes (7"version) / Get out of my life / Justice / Jack the lad / Low life / Bread or blood / Seems to me / Norman / On the streets / Five more years / Betrayed / Saturday (live) / Dambusters. *(<re-iss. Jun93/Oct94 on 'Dojo'; DOJOCD 140>) (lp re-iss. Mar98 on 'Harry May'; MAYLP 705) (cd re-iss. Jun99 on 'Snapper'; SMMCD 520)*

Nov 97. (cd) *CanCan; (CANCAN 006CD)* **ONE LAW FOR THEM** [ ] [-]
(<re-iss. +US Nov00; same>)

Jul 98. (cd) *Pinhead; (PINCD 102)* **SINGALONG-A-4-SKINS** [ ] [-]

Mar 99. (cd) *Harry May; (<MAYOCD 103>)* **CLOCKWORK SKINHEAD** [ ] [ ] Jul99

Nov 99. (cd) *Captain Oi; (<AHOYCD 128>)* **SINGLES AND RARITIES** [ ] [ ] Jan00

Sep 00. (lp) *Get Back; (<GET 43>)* **LOW LIFE** [ ] [ ]

Apr 01. (d-cd) *Snapper; (<SMDCD 329>)* **THE BEST OF THE 4-SKINS** [ ] [ ]

FREAK OF NATURE

Formed: USA . . . 1992 by ex-WHITE LION frontman MIKE TRAMP, plus KENNY KORADE, JERRY BEST, JOHNNY HARO and OLIVER STEFFENSON, the latter being subsequently replaced by DENNIS CHICK. Taking a harder edged approach than TRAMP's previous musical incarnation, FON signed to 'Music For Nations', releasing their eponymous set in '93. With the lyrics also taking a more uncompromising stance, TRAMP and his group found it hard to tame the lucrative US market as WHITE LION had done before them. A second album, 'GATHERING OF FREAKS' (1994), was their last to feature KORADE who was replaced by MARCUS MAND.

Album rating: FREAK OF NATURE (*6) / GATHERING OF FREAKS (*5) / OUTCASTS collection (*4) / Mike Tramp: CAPRICORN (*5)

MIKE TRAMP (b.14 Jan'61, Denmark) – vocals (ex-WHITE LION) / **KENNY KORADE** – guitar / **DENNIS CHICK** – guitar (ex-HOUSE OF LORDS) repl. OLIVER STEFFENSON / **JERRY BEST** – bass / **JOHNNY HARO** – drums

Music For Nations not iss.

Mar 93. (cd/c/lp) *(CD/T+/MFN 146)* **FREAK OF NATURE** [ ] [-]
– Turn the other way / What am I / Rescue me / '92 / People / World doesn't mind / Possessed / Where can I go / If I leave / Love was here.

Jul 93. (12"ep/cd-ep) *(12/CD KUT 153)* **RESCUE ME. / TURN THE OTHER WAY / WHAT AM I** [ ] [-]

Sep 94. (cd/c/lp) *(CD/T+/MFN 169)* **GATHERING OF FREAKS** [ ] [-]
– The gathering / Enemy / Stand back / Raping the cradle / Big black hole / The tree / Candle / Need / Open space / Get it yourself / Powerless / The parting.

—— **MARCUS MAND** – guitar; repl. KORADE (before their split)

– compilations, etc. –

Nov 98. (cd) *Dream Catcher; (CRIDE 9)* **OUTCASTS** [ ] [-]
– Blame it on the fool / One love / Where you belong / Wartime / Dead and gone / What am I / I regret / Can't find my way / Turn the other way / Ready to go / Possessed / Disturbin' the peace.

MIKE TRAMP

—— with **KIM BULLARD, JERRY WEST + DORIAN CROZIER**

Music For Nations — C.M.C.

Oct 97. (cd) *(CDSINE 001) <86222>* **CAPRICORN** [ ] [ ] Feb98
– Already gone / Have you ever / Better off / Wait for me / Love will come and go / If I live tomorrow / Here I don't belong / Heart of every woman / Had I not complained / Running out of life.

FREE

Formed: London, England . . . Spring 1968 by PAUL RODGERS (vocals), PAUL KOSSOFF (guitar) and SIMON KIRKE (drums). The latter two had been members of blues combo BLACK CAT BONES before poaching RODGERS from another blues outfit, BROWN SUGAR. With the addition of young ex-BLUESBREAKER, ANDY FRASER, on bass, this precocious line-up was complete, adopting the name FREE at the suggestion of blues grandaddy ALEXIS KORNER. KORNER also tipped off 'Island' supremo CHRIS BLACKWELL, and after resisting an extremely misguided BLACKWELL attempt to rename them The HEAVY METAL KIDS, FREE duly signed to his label and began work on their debut album, TONS OF SOBS (1968). Emerging from the shadow of CREAM, the album was an impressive set of heavy, organic blues, KOSSOFF stealing the show with his emotionally charged, liquid gold guitar style, in full effect on BOOKER T's 'THE HUNTER'. By the release of 'FREE' (1969), RODGERS soulful voice was developing into one of the best in rock, while FRASER had taken on joint songwriting duties with RODGERS. The band also had a blistering live reputation and had already built up a sizeable following by the time 'ALL RIGHT NOW' was a massive worldwide hit. It's gritty R&B stomp paved the way for FREE's magnum opus, 'FIRE AND WATER' (1970), a No.3 UK album that boasted such enduring fare as the introspective ballads, 'OH I WEPT' and 'HEAVY LOAD' while RODGERS' wonderfully evocative vocals lent 'REMEMBER' a mellow resonance. That summer, cresting the wave of their popularity, the band played to over half a million people at the Isle Of Wight festival. With pressure to come up with a successful follow-up to 'ALL RIGHT NOW', FREE were confident that the 'THE STEALER' would do the business. When it stiffed completely things started to go seriously awry, the 'HIGHWAY' (1970) album receiving a similarly lukewarm reception. This relative commercial failure increased tensions in what was already a perilously fraught inter-band relationship, the group deciding to call it a day after fulfilling touring commitments in Japan and Australia. The split eventually came in May '71, ironically almost coinciding with their biggest hit since 'ALL RIGHT NOW', a FACES-style romp entitled 'MY BROTHER JAKE'. Solo projects by RODGERS (PEACE) and FRASER (TOBY) came to little, although KOSSOFF and KIRKE's eponymous collaboration with Texan keyboard player, JOHN 'RABBIT' BUNDRICK, and Japanese bassist TETSU YAMAUCHI, was released to relative critical and commercial success, KOSSOFF relishing the opportunity to realise his ideas outwith the confines of FREE. The band subsequently regrouped in early 1972 and recorded the 'FREE AT LAST' album, a reasonable effort which spawned a Top 20 hit with the 'LITTLE BIT OF LOVE' single, a highly melodic slice of rock, the sort of thing RODGERS would go on to perfect with BAD COMPANY. While the album made the Top 10, KOSSOFF was spiralling into serious drug dependence, and following a disastrous American tour, the band's stability received a further blow when FRASER departed for the group SHARKS (he subsequently released a few melodic rock albums in the mid 70's). With TETSU and RABBIT filling in, FREE undertook a Japanese tour prior to recording a final album, 'HEARTBREAKER' (1973). Although KOSSOFF was too ill to make much of a contribution, the album stands among FREE's best, boasting RODGER's desperate plea to KOSSOFF, 'WISHING WELL', and the superb, BEATLES-esque 'COME TOGETHER IN THE MORNING'. Following a final tour of America with TRAFFIC, FREE finally split in summer '73, RODGERS and KIRKE going on to form BAD COMPANY. KOSSOFF, meanwhile, had already begun his ill-fated solo career, forming BACK STREET CRAWLER. After a handful of relatively well-received albums, KOSSOFF finally succumbed to heroin addiction, dying in his sleep on the 19th March '76. It was a tragic end for a guitarist who was once destined to be remembered in the same breath as the likes of ERIC CLAPTON and JIMI HENDRIX.

Album rating: TONS OF SOBS (*5) / FREE (*6) / FIRE AND WATER (*8) / HIGHWAY (*6) / FREE LIVE (*4) / FREE AT LAST (*5) / HEARTBREAKER (*5) / THE FREE STORY compilation (*8) / COMPLETELY FREE compilation (*7) / THE BEST OF FREE – ALL RIGHT NOW compilation (*8) / MOLTEN GOLD: THE ANTHOLOGY compilation (*8) / KOSSOFF, KIRKE, TETSU & RABBIT (*4) / Back Street Crawler: BACK STREET CRAWLER (*6) / AND THE BAND PLAYS ON (*5) / postumous:- KOSS (*6) / THE COLLECTION (*6) / STONE FREE (*6)

PAUL RODGERS (b.12 Dec'49, Middlesbrough, England) – vocals (ex-BROWN SUGAR) / **PAUL KOSSOFF** (b.14 Sep'50, Hampstead, London, England) – guitar (ex-BLACK CAT BONES) / **SIMON KIRKE** (b.28 Jul'49, Shrewsbury, England) – drums (ex-BLACK CAT BONES) / **ANDY FRASER** (b. 7 Aug'52, Shropshire, England) – bass (ex-JOHN MAYALL'S BLUESBREAKERS)

Island — A&M

Nov 68. (lp) *(ILPS 9089) <4198>* **TONS OF SOBS** [ ] [ ] Aug69
– Over the green hills (part 1) / Worry / Walk in my shadow / Wild Indian woman / Goin' down slow / I'm a mover / The hunter / Moonshine / Sweet tooth / Over the green hills (part 2). *(cd-iss. Jun88; CID 9089) (cd re-iss. 1989; IMCD 62)*

Mar 69. (7") *<1099>* **I'M A MOVER. / WORRY** [-] [ ]

Mar 69. (7") *(WIP 6054)* **BROAD DAYLIGHT. / THE WORM** [ ] [-]

Jul 69. (7") *(WIP 6062)* **I'LL BE CREEPIN'. / SUGAR FOR MR. MORRISON** [ ] [-]

Aug 69. (7") *<1172>* **I'LL BE CREEPIN'. / MOUTHFUL OF GRASS** [-] [ ]

Oct 69. (lp) *(ILPS 9104) <4204>* **FREE** [22] [ ]
– I'll be creepin' / Songs of yesterday / Lying in the sunshine / Trouble on double time / Mouthful of grass / Woman / Free me / Broad daylight / Mourning sad morning. *(cd-iss. Jun88; CID 9104) (lp re-iss. Jan00 on 'Simply Vinyl'; SVLP 165)*

May 70. (7") *(WIP 6082) <1206>* **ALL RIGHT NOW. / MOUTHFUL OF GRASS** [2] [4] Jul70
(re-iss. Jul73 hit UK No.15)

Jun 70. (lp) *(ILPS 9120) <4268>* **FIRE AND WATER** [2] [17] Aug70
– Fire and water / Oh I wept / Remember / Heavy load / Mr. Big / Don't say you love me / All right now. *(re-iss. Sep86 lp/c/cd; ILPM/ICM/CID 9120) (cd-iss. Apr90; IMCD 80) (re-iss. lp Jan94 + May94; ILPS 9120) (lp re-iss. Jul99 on 'Simply Vinyl'; SVLP 97)*

Nov 70. (7") *(WIP 6093)* **THE STEALER. / LYING IN THE SUNSHINE** [ ] [-]

Nov 70. (7") *<1230>* **THE STEALER. / BROAD DAYLIGHT** [-] [49]

Dec 70. (lp) *(ILPS 9138) <4287>* **HIGHWAY** [41] [ ] Feb71
– The highway song / The stealer / On my way / Be my friend / Sunny day / Ride on pony / Love you so / Bodie / Soon I will be gone. *(cd-iss. Jun88; CID 9138) (cd re-iss. 1989; (IMCD 63)*

Jan 71. (7") *<1248>* **THE HIGHWAY SONG. / LOVE YOU SO** [-] [ ]

Mar 71. (7") *<1266>* **I'LL BE CREEPIN'. / MR. BIG** [-] [ ]

Apr 71. (7") *(WIP 6100) <1276>* **MY BROTHER JAKE. / ONLY MY SOUL** [4] [ ]

Jun 71. (lp) *(ILPS 9160) <4306>* **FREE LIVE! (live)** [4] [89] Aug71
– All right now / I'm a mover / Be my friend / Fire and water / Ride on pony / Mr. Big / The hunter / Get where I belong (studio). *(cd-iss. Jun88; CID 9160) (cd re-iss. 1989; IMCD 73)*

—— They had already split May'71. FRASER formed TOBY, while RODGERS formed the short-lived PEACE.

KOSSOFF, KIRKE, TETSU & RABBIT

were formed by the other two plus **TETSU YAMAUCHI** (b.21 Oct'47, Fukuoka, Japan) – bass / **JOHN 'RABBIT' BUNDRICK** – keyboards, vocals / and guest **B.J. COLE** – steel guitar

Nov 71. (lp) *(<ILPS 9188>)* **KOSSOFF, KIRKE, TETSU & RABBIT** [ ] [-]
– Blue grass / Sammy's alright / Just for the box / Colours / Hold on / Yellow house / Dying fire / Fool's life / Anna / I'm on the run. *(re-iss. Aug91 cd)(c; IMCD 139)(ICM 9188)*

FREE

—— re-formed originals Feb'72 (**RODGERS, KOSSOFF, FRASER + KIRKE**)

May 72. (7") *(WIP 6129) <1352>* **LITTLE BIT OF LOVE. / SAIL ON** [13] [ ]

Jun 72. (lp/c) *(ILPS/ICT 9192) <4349>* **FREE AT LAST** [9] [69]
– Catch a train / Soldier boy / Magic ship / Sail on / Travelling man / Little bit of love / Guardian of the universe / Child / Goodbye. *(cd-iss. Jun88; CID 9192) (cd re-iss. Feb90; IMCD 82)*

—— **TETSU YAMAUCHI** – bass (see above); repl. FRASER who joined SHARKS / added **JOHN 'RABBIT' BUNDRICK** – keyboards (see above) / **RODGERS** – also added guitar

Dec 72. (7") *(WIP 6146)* **WISHING WELL. / LET ME SHOW YOU** [7] [-]

Jan 73. (lp/c) *(ILPS 9217) <9324>* **HEARTBREAKER** [9] [47]
– Wishing well / Come together in the morning / Travellin' in style / Heartbreaker / Muddy water / Common mortal man / Easy on my soul / Seven angels. *(cd-iss. Jun88; CID 9217) (cd re-iss. Feb90; IMCD 81)*

Mar 73. (7") *(WIP 6160)* **TRAVELLIN' IN STYLE. / EASY ON MY SOUL** [ ] [-]
(re-iss. Mar74; WIP 6223)

—— **WENDELL RICHARDSON** – guitar of OSIBISA, on UK & US tour early '73) repl. KOSSOFF who formed BACK STREET CRAWLER. He died in his sleep 19 Mar'76 after years of drug abuse. FREE split early '73. RABBIT went solo before joining (KOSSOFF's) CRAWLER. TETSU joined The FACES. RODGERS and KIRKE formed BAD COMPANY.

– compilations, etc. –

on 'Island' UK / 'A&M' US unless mentioned otherwise

Mar 74. (d-lp) *(ISL D4)* **THE FREE STORY** [2] [ ]
– I'm a mover / I'll be creepin' / Mourning sad morning / All right now / Heavy load / Fire and water / Be my friend / The stealer / Soon I will be gone / Mr. Big / The hunter / Get where I belong / Travelling man / Just for the box / Lady / My brother Jake / Little bit of love / Sail on / Come together in the morning. *(re-iss. Oct89 lp/c/cd; ILPS/ICT/CID 9945) (cd re-iss. Sep96; IMCD 226)*

1974. (7") *<1629>* **LITTLE BIT OF LOVE. / THE STEALER** [-] [ ]

1974. (7") *<1720>* **ALL RIGHT NOW. / THE STEALER** [-] [ ]

Apr 75. (lp) *<3663>* **THE BEST OF FREE** [-] [ ]

Nov 76. (lp) *(ILPS 9453)* **FREE AND EASY, ROUGH AND READY** [ ] [-]

Nov 76. (7") *(WIP 6351)* **THE HUNTER. / WORRY** [ ] [-]

Feb 78. (7"ep) *(IEP 6)* **THE FREE EP** [11] [-]
– All right now / My brother Jake / Wishing well. *(re-iss. Oct82 as 12"pic-d; PIEP 6)* – hit UK No.57.

Oct 82. (lp/c) *(ILPS/ICT 9719)* **COMPLETELY FREE** [ ] [-]

May 85. (7") *(IS 221)* **WISHING WELL. / WOMAN** [ ] [-]
(12"+=) *(12IS 221)* – Walk in my shadow.

Feb 91. (c-s/7") *(C+/IS 486)* **ALL RIGHT NOW. / I'M A MOVER** [8] [ ]
(12"+=/cd-s+=) *(12IS/CID 486)* – Get where I belong.

Feb 91. (cd/c/lp) *(CID/IC/ILP TV 2)* **ALL RIGHT NOW – THE BEST OF FREE** [9] [ ]
– Wishing well / All right now / Little bit of love / Come together in the morning / The stealer / Sail on / Mr. Big / My brother Jake / The hunter / Be my friend / Travellin' in style / Fire and water / Travelling man / Don't say you love me.
Apr 91. (c-s/7") *(C+/IS 495)* **MY BROTHER JAKE (remix). / WISHING WELL (remix)** [ ] [ ]
(12"+=/cd-s+=) *(12IS/CID 495)* – The stealer (extended) / Only my soul (extended).
Nov 92. (d-cd) *(ITSCD 3)* **FIRE AND WATER / HEARTBREAKER** [ ] [-]
May 94. (d-cd) *(CRNCD 2) <518456>* **MOLTEN GOLD: THE ANTHOLOGY** [ ] [-]
Nov 98. (cd) *(IMCD 255)* **WALK IN MY SHADOW – AN INTRODUCTION TO FREE** [ ] [-]
Oct 99. (cd) *Spectrum; (544167-2)* **ALL RIGHT NOW** [ ] [-]
May 00. (5xcd-box) *(IBXCD 3)* **SONGS OF YESTERDAY** [ ] [-]

PAUL KOSSOFF

with all of FREE as guests; plus **TREVOR BURTON** – bass / **ALAN WHITE** – drums

Island Island

Dec 73. (lp) *(ILPS 9264)* **BACK STREET CRAWLER** [ ] [-]
– Tuesday morning / I'm ready / Time away / Molten gold / Back street crawler. *(re-iss. Apr87, lp/c; ILPM/ICM 9264) (cd-iss. Feb90; IMCD 84) (cd-iss. Jul92; IMCD 144)*

BACK STREET CRAWLER

KOSSOFF – lead guitar with **TERRY WILSON-SLESSER** – vocals / **TERRY WILSON** – bass / **TONY BRAUNAGEL** – drums / **MIKE MONTGOMERY** – keyboards / plus **PETER VAN DER PUIJE** – sax / **EDDIE QUANSAH** – horns / **GEORGE LEE LARNYOH** – flute, saxes

Atlantic Atco

Aug 75. (lp) *(K 50173) <36125>* **THE BAND PLAYS ON** [ ] [ ]
– Who do women / New York, New York stealing my way / Survivor / It's a long way down to the top / All the girls are crazy / Jason blue / Train song / Rock & roll junkie / The band plays on.

— **GEOFF WHITEHORN** – guitar repl. wind section

May 76. (lp) *(K 50267)* **2ND STREET** [ ] [-]
– Selfish lover / Blue soul / Stop doing what you're doing / Raging river / Some kind of happy / Sweet beauty / Just for you / On your life / Leaves the wind.

— Tragedy had already struck when on the 19th March '76, KOSSOFF died in his sleep, suffering from drug abuse.

— The rest carried on as CRAWLER and released 4 singles as well as 2 albums on 'Epic'; 'CRAWLER' (1977) & 'SNAKE, RATTLE & ROLL' (1978).

– his compilations, etc. –

Oct 77. (d-lp) *D.J.M.; (29002) <300>* **KOSS** (1974/75) [ ] [ ]
(re-iss. Aug83 on 'Street Tunes'; SDLP 1001) (cd-iss. Jul87 on 'Castle' lp/c/cd; CLA LP/MC/CD 127)
May 83. (lp) *Street Tunes; (STLP 001)* **THE HUNTER** (1969-75) [ ] [-]
Aug 83. (lp) *Street Tunes; (STLP 002)* **LEAVES IN THE WIND** (1975 /76) [ ] [-]
Sep 83. (d-lp) *Street Tunes; (SDLP 1002)* **CROYDON – JUNE 15th 1975 (live)** [ ] [-]
Nov 83. (c) *Street Tunes; (STC 0012)* **MR. BIG** [ ] [-]
Apr 86. (lp/c) *Island; (PKSP/PKC 100)* **BLUE SOUL** [ ] [-]
May 95. (cd) *The Hit Label; (AHLCD 31)* **THE COLLECTION** [ ] [-]
Mar 97. (cd/c) *Carlton; (303600095-2/-4)* **STONE FREE** [ ] [-]
Mar 98. (cd) *Eeagle; (EAMCD 035)* **LIVE AT FAIRFIELD HALLS** [ ] [-]

FREHLEY'S COMET

Formed: New York, USA . . . 1987 by former KISS guitarist ACE FREHLEY, who enlisted the services of TOD HOWARTH, JOHN REGAN and ANTON FIG. While still a member of KISS in 1978, ACE released an eponymous solo debut, a record that hit the US Top 30 and spawned a Top 20 Russ Ballard-penned 45, 'NEW YORK GROOVE'. Having departed from KISS in '83 with a problematic drug habit, FREHLEY eventually got his act together for a 1987 album, named after his new group, FREHLEY'S COMET. The record was surprisingly well-received, peaking inside the US Top 50. While this set was a natural progression from his KISS days, a follow-up studio effort, 'SECOND SIGHTING' (1988), rather ill-advisedly took a turn towards airbrushed AOR. His final album for 'Megaforce', 'TROUBLE WALKIN' (1989) attempted to recover lost ground, although unlike its predecessors it just failed to crack the US Top 100. With FREHLEY's band deserting him halfway through the subsequent tour, he went to ground and has yet to make a reappearance.

Album rating: FREHLEY'S COMET (*5) / LIVE +1 mini (*4) / SECOND SIGHTING (*5) / TROUBLE WALKIN' (*4)

ACE FREHLEY (b. PAUL FREHLEY, 27 Apr'51, The Bronx, NY) – guitar, vocals (ex-KISS) / **TOD HOWARTH** – vocals, guitar / **JOHN REGAN** – bass / **ANTON FIG** – drums

Atlantic Megaforce-Atlantic

Jun 87. (7") *(A 9255) <89255>* **INTO THE NIGHT. / FRACTURE TOO** [ ] [ ]
(12"+=) *(A 9255T)* – Breakout.
Jun 87. (lp/c) *(781 749-1/-4) <81749>* **FREHLEY'S COMET** [ ] [43] May87
– Rock soldiers / Breakout / Into the night / Something moved / We got your rock / Love me right / Calling to you / Dolls / Stranger in a strange land / Fractured too.
Feb 88. (m-lp/m-c/m-cd) *(781 826-1/-4/-2) <81826>* **LIVE + 1 (live)** [ ] [84]
– Rip-it-out / Breakout / Something moved / Rocket ride / Words are not enough.
May 88. (7") *<89072>* **INSANE. / THE ACORN IS SPINNING** [-] [ ]
Jun 88. (lp/c/cd) *(781 862-1/-4/-2) <81862>* **SECOND SIGHTING** [ ] [81]
– Insane / Time ain't runnin' out / Dancin' with danger / It's over now / Loser in a fight / Juvenile delinquent / Fallen angel / Separate / New kind of lover / The acorn is spinning.
Sep 89. (c-s) *<88788>* **DO YA. / FRACTURED III** [-] [ ]
Oct 89. (lp/c/cd) *(782 042-1/-4/-2) <82042>* **TROUBLE WALKIN'** [ ] [ ]
– Shot full of rock / Do ya / Five card stud / Hide your heart / Lost in limbo / Trouble walkin' / 2 young 2 die / Back to school / Remember me / Fractured III.

— split after above

Marty FRIEDMAN (see under ⇒ CACOPHONY)

FRONT 242

Formed: Belgium . . . 1981 by DANIEL B., recruiting JEAN-LUC DE MEYER and PATRICK CODENYS shortly after. Pioneers of the 80's Belgian 'New Beat' scene, the band's avant-garde industrial dance was shaped by its founders' design background; a cut 'n' paste collage of sound that incorporated loops, samples and repetitive, minimal rythms. While their initial recordings were vaguely similar to the synth hits of early 80's British acts, by the release of 'OFFICIAL VERSION' (1987), the band were well on the way to crystallising their dark JOY DIVISION/TEST DEPT. fusion. With an ever expanding cult following and increasing critical acclaim, along with the underground success of the 'HEADHUNTER (V1.0)' single, FRONT 242 finally dented the lower regions of the UK charts with 'TYRANNY FOR YOU' (1991). The album was preceded by the doom-laden electro of the 'TRAGEDY FOR YOU' single, proffering a slightly more sinister take on the indie-dance sound of the day. As well as influencing the likes of MINISTRY and NINE INCH NAILS, FRONT 242 were favourites with Braintree's finest, The PRODIGY, who worked their voodoo magic on the 'RELIGION' single in 1993. The band were given another boost later that summer when they were invited to play on the American Lollapalooza Tour. • **Songwriters:** DANIEL and PATRICK. • **Trivia:** JEAN-LUC and RICHARD were also part of REVOLTING COCKS with AL JOURGENSEN of MINISTRY.

Album rating: BACK CATALOGUE compilation (*6) / OFFICIAL VERSION (*8) / FRONT BY FRONT (*8) / TYRANNY FOR YOU (*7) / 06:21:03:11 UP EVIL (*6) / 05:22:09:12 OFF (*6) / MUT@GE MIX@GE (*6)

DANIEL B. PROTHESE – keyboards / **RICHARD K. 23** – vocals, drum programmes / **JEAN-LUC DE MEYER** – vocals, drum machine / **PATRICK CODENYS** – keyboards

New Dance not iss.

Nov 81. (7") *(ND 002)* **PRINCIPLES. / BODY TO BODY** [ ] [-]
May 82. (7") *(ND 005)* **U-MEN. / ETHICS** [ ] [-]
(12"of above 4 tracks; issued Jan86; ND 009) (cd-ep Oct88; ND 009CD)

— DANIEL B. had now departed in 1984

Himalaya not iss.

Feb 86. (7"/12") *(OPS/12OPA 13)* **NO SHUFFLE. / BODY TO BODY** [ ] [-]
below releases on 'Mask' were issued much earlier in Belgium

Mask not iss.

Nov 86. (lp) *(MK 001/+MC)* **GEOGRAPHY (1981-83)** [ ] [-]
– Operating tracks / With your cries / Art & strategy / Geography II / U-men / Dialogues / Least inkling / G.V.D.T. / Geography I / Black, white blues / Kinetics / Kampfbereit. *(cd-iss. 1988; CDMK 1) (cd-iss. Jun92 +=; MK 001CD)* – Rthics / Principles / Body to body.
Nov 86. (lp/c) *(MK 002)* **NO COMMENT (1984-85)** [ ] [-]
– Commando (mix) / S.Fr. no menklatura (pt.1 & 2) / Deceit / Lonely day / No shuffle / Special forces (demo). *(cd-iss. Jan87 on 'Mask'; CDMK 2) (cd-iss. Jun92 +=; MK 002CD)* – See the futire (live) / In November (live) / Special forces (demo) / Body to body.
Nov 86. (12"ep) *(MK 003)* **ENDLESS RIDDANCE** [ ] [-]
– Take one / Controversy / Between / Sample D. *(cd-ep.Aug88; MK 003CD)*
Nov 86. (12"ep) *(MK 004)* **POLITICS OF PRESSURE** [ ] [-]
– Commando (remix) / No shuffle / Don't crash / Funkahdafi.

Red Rhino Europe Epic

Nov 86. (7"/ext.12") *(RRE/+T 003)* **INTERCEPTION: QUITE UNUSUAL. / AGGRESIVA** [ ] [-]
(cd-ep.Aug88; RRET 003CD)
Jan 87. (cd) *(RRECD 004)* **BACK CATALOGUE** (compilation 1982-85) [ ] [-]
(re-iss. Jun92 +=; RRE 004CD) – (extra tracks).
Jun 87. (lp/c/cd) *(RRE LP/MC/CD 005) <52405>* **OFFICIAL VERSION** [ ] [ ]
– What you have is what you get / Re-run / Television station / Aggressive due / Masterhits 1 & 2 / Slaughter / Quite unusual / Red team / Aggressive angst. *(cd re-iss. Jun92 +=; RRE 005CD)* – Quite unusual / Aggresiva / Masterblaster / Hypnomix.
Nov 87. (12"ep) *(WAX 036)* **MASTER HIT (pt.1 masterblaster mix). / MASTER HIT (pt.2 hypno mix) / MASTER HIT (pt.3 lp edited version)** [ ] [-]
(above on 'Waxtrax') (re-iss. Jan90 on 'Red Rhino Europe' 12"ep/c-ep/cd-ep; RRE T/C/CD 009)
Sep 88. (7"/12") *(RRE/+T 006)* **HEADHUNTER (V1.0). / WELCOME TO PARADISE (V1.0)** [ ] [-]
(cd-s+=) *(RRECD 006)* – Headhunter (V2.0).
Oct 88. (lp/c/cd) *(RRE LP/MC/CD 007) <52406>* **FRONT BY FRONT** [ ] [ ]
– Until death (do us part) / Circling overland / Im rhythmus bleiben / Felines / First in – first out / Blend the strengths / Headhunter V 3.0 / Work 01 / Terminal state. *(cd re-iss. Jun92 +=; RRE 007CD)* – Welcome to paradise / Head hunter / Never stop! / Work 242 N.off is N.off / Agony (until death) / Never stop! / Work 242.
Mar 89. (7") *(RRE 008)* **NEVER STOP (V1.1). / WORK 242** [ ] [-]
(12"+=/3"cd-s+=) *(RRE T/CD 008)* – Never stop (V1.0) / Work 242 N.off is N.off / Agony (until death).

— RICHARD was now only a live performer

Red Rhino Europe Epic

Oct 90. (7") *(RRE 10)* **TRAGEDY FOR YOU. / ('A'short version)** [ ] [-]
(12"/cd-s) *(RRE T/CD 10)* – ('A'side) / ('A'long version) / ('A'slow-mo mix).

(12"/cd-s) *(RRE TX/CDX 10)* – ('A'neurodancer mix) / ('A'instrumental) / Trigger 3.

Jan 91. (cd/c/lp) *(RRE CD/MC/LP 11) <46998>* **TYRANNY FOR YOU** [49] [95]
– Sacrifice / Rhythm of time / Moldavia / Trigger 2 (anatomy of a shot) / Gripped by fear / Tragedy for you / The untold / Neurobashing / Leitmotiv 136 / Soul manager.

1991. (12") *<73767>* **RHYTHM OF TIME (Anti-G mix) / ('A'-Victor The Cleaner mix)** [-] [ ]

Apr 93. (12"ep/cd-ep) *(RRE 16 T/CD)* **RELIGION (7"mix) / RELIGION (pussy whipped mix) / RELIGION (the Prodigy bass under siege mix) / RELIGION (bitch slapper mix) / RELIGION (the Prodigy trance U down mix)** [46] [ ]
(12"ep/cd-ep) *(RRE 16 R/CDR)* – Crapage (never hurry a Murray mix) / Crapage (the turd mix) / Religion (lovelace a go-go mix).
(cd-ep re-iss. Dec93; RRECDX 16)

May 93. (lp/c/cd) *(RRE 21/+MC/CD) <53433>* **06:21:03:11 UP EVIL** [44] [ ]
– Crapage / Waste / Skin / Motion / Religion / Stratoscape / Hymn / Fuel / Melt / Flag / Mutilate. *(cd+=)* – (S)Crapage / Religion (pussy whipped mix).

Sep 93. (lp/c/cd) *(RRE 22/+MC/CD) <53902>* **05:22:09:12 OFF** [46] [ ]
– Animal – Cage – Gate – Guide / Modern angel / Junkdrome / Serial killers don't kill their girlfriend / Skin – Fur coat / Genecide / Crushed / Offend / Animal zoo / Serial killers don't kill their boyfriend / Happiness – More angels / Crushed – Obscene / Melt – Again / Speed angels.

Nov 93. (12") *(RRE 18T)* **ANIMAL. / ('A'version)** [ ] [ ]

Nov 93. (m-cd) *(RRE 18CD)* **ANGELS VERSUS ANIMALS** (re-workings) [ ] [-]
– Animal (radio) / Angel (wipe out) / Serial killers don't kill their dog either / Modern angel (KMFDM remix) / Animal (extended) / Break me / Der verfluchte engel / L'ange modern / Born to breathe.

Mar 96. (12") *(RRE 20T)* **HAPPINESS (dance mix by UNDERWORLD). / RELIGION (trance u down mix by THE PRODIGY) / RHYTHM OF LIFE (victor the cleaner mix by THE ORB)** [ ] [ ]

Mar 96. (cd) *(RRE 20CD)* **MUT@GE.MIX@GE** [ ] [-]
– Rhythm of time / Happiness / Gripped by fear / Crapage / Junkdrome / Religion / Break me / Dancesoundtrackmusic.

Zoth Ommog — Metropolis

Jul 98. (d-lp/cd) *<ZOT 242/+CD) <MET 100>* **RE-BOOT: LIVE '98 (live)** [ ] [ ]
– Happiness / Master hit / Moldavia / Melt / Soul manager / No shuffle / In rhythmus bleiben / Crapage / Body to body / Religion / Headhunter / Welcome to Paradise / First in first out / Punish your machine. *(cd re-iss. Jul00 on 'Iris Light'; ILIGHT 016CD)*

Dec 98. (cd) *<MET 121>* **HEADHUNTER (17 various mixes)** [-] [ ]

– compilations, others, etc. –

Dec 92. (cd) *Guzzi; (GUZZ 1888)* **LIVE TARGET (live)** [ ] [-]

Nov 94. (cd) *Play It Again Sam; (<BIAS 242CD>)* **LIVE CODE 6413356-424225** [ ] [ ]
– Der verfluchte engel / Motion / Masterhit / Flag / Tragedy for you / Im rhythmus bleiben / Skin / Headhunter / Welcome to Paradise / Crapage / Soul manager / Punish your machine / Religion.

FUDGE TUNNEL

Formed: Nottingham, England ... 1989 by main songwriter ALEX NEWPORT, with DAVE RYLEY and ADRIAN PARKIN. Their debut single in 1990, 'SEX MAMMOTH', made an immediate impact on the UK indie scene, NME (New Musical Express) awarding it their prestigious Single Of The Week. Brutally uncompromising noise merchants, FUDGE TUNNEL were also up and coming favourites of the metal press. A second EP, 'THE SWEET SOUND OF EXCESS' was also lauded and a home was found with 'Earache' records for the classic Colin Richardson-produced debut album, 'HATE SONGS IN E MINOR' (1991). Featuring a drawing of a headless body on the cover (from the John Minnery book 'How To Kill'), the record was subsequently seized by vice police, doing FUDGE TUNNEL's infamous reputation no harm whatsoever. Released at the height of grunge, 'CREEP DIETS' (1993), was tarred with the Seattle brush despite FUDGE TUNNEL's vicious onslaught, more reminiscent of BIG BLACK than PEARL JAM. The same year, ALEX hooked up with SEPULTURA's MAX CAVALERA, releasing the 'NAILBOMB' collaboration. In between another NAILBOMB album, FUDGE TUNNEL released a further bruising noise assault in the shape of 1994's 'THE COMPLICATED FUTILITY OF IGNORANCE'. • **Covered:** SUNSHINE OF YOUR LOVE (Cream).

Album rating: HATE SONGS IN E MINOR (*8) / CREEP DIETS (*6) / IN A WORD compilation (*6) / THE COMPLICATED FUTILITY OF IGNORANCE (*7) / FUDGE CAKE (*8)

ALEX NEWPORT – vocals, guitar / **DAVE RYLEY** – bass / **ADRIAN PARKIN** – drums

Pigboy — not iss.

Jan 90. (12"ep) **SEX MAMMOTH EP** [ ] [-]
– Sex mammoth / Leprosy / Persecuted / Fudge.

Jun 90. (12"ep) **THE SWEET SOUND OF EXCESS EP** [ ] [-]
– Best friends wife / No money / Like Jeff / Shit for brains.

Earache — Combat

May 91. (lp/c/cd) *(MOSH 036/+MC/CD) <2037>* **HATE SONGS IN E MINOR** [ ] [ ]
– Hate song / Bed crumbs / Spanish fly / itchen belt / Hate song (version) / Boston baby / Gut rot / Soap and water / Tweezers / Sunshine of your love / Cat scratch fever. *(w/free 7")* – CATCH SCRATCH FEVER. / JOINED AT THE DICK

Apr 92. (12"ep/cd-ep) *(MOSH 057 T/CD)* **TEETH EP** [ ] [-]
– Teeth / S.R.T. / Shit for brains / Like Jeff / Sunshine of your love / Joined at the dick.

Sep 92. (12"ep/cd-ep) *(MOSH T/CD)* **FAT BOBBED CHISELLER** [ ] [-]

Earache — Columbia

May 93. (lp/c/cd) *(MOSH 064/+MC/CD) <57502>* **CREEP DIETS** [ ] [ ]
– Grey / Tipper Gore / Ten percent / Face down / Grit / Don't have time for you / Good kicking / Hot salad / Creep diets / Stuck / Always.

Earache — Earache

Aug 94. (cd/lp) *(<MOSH 099 CD/LP>)* **IN A WORD** (compilation) [ ] [ ]
– Sex mammoth / Bed crumbs / Boston baby / Sweet meat / Grey / Spanish fly / Ten percent / Good kicking / Stuck / Tipper Gore / Gut rot / SRT / Kitchen belt / For madmen only / Changes.

Sep 94. (lp/cd) *(<MOSH 119/+CD>)* **THE COMPLICATED FUTILITY OF IGNORANCE** [ ] [ ] Oct94
– Random acts of cruelty / The joy of irony / Backed down / Cover up / Six eight / Long day / Excuse / Find your fortune / Suffering makes great stories / Circle of friends, circle of trends / Grudge with a G.

Nov 94. (7") *(7MOSH 124)* **THE JOY OF IRONY. / ROTTWEILER** [ ] [-]

— disbanded after above

– compilations, etc. –

Apr 92. (lp/c/cd) *Pigboy; (<OINK 11/+MC/CD>)* **FUDGE CAKE** [ ] [ ]
– (SEX MAMMOTH EP / THE SWEET SOUND OF EXCESS EP)

FUEL (238)

Formed: Harrisburg, Pennsylvania, USA ... mid-90's by Tennessee lads BRETT SCALLIONS and JEFF ABERCROMBIE. Picking up songwriter CARL BELL and KEVIN MILLER along the way, the group were called FUEL 238 in the UK to distinguish them from JIM ALLISON's other punk band of the same name who had issued 'Monuments To Excess' for 'Allied' records in '95. Having grown up in the American wilderness with only his brother's extensive record collection for inspiration, BELL's development as a songwriter was relatively free from the vagaries of changing tastes and fashion. This perhaps explains why the band's solid hard rock/metal sound struck such a chord with the American populace. After a demo cassette had sold nigh on 5000 copies at gigs and local record stores, the group relocated to Harrisburg, where they amassed a rabid following. A self-financed EP, 'PORCELAIN', subsequently caught the attention of local radio programmers who playlisted the track 'SHIMMER' and set the music industry ball rolling. After a gig in Philadelphia, the group were signed to Sony's '550' label and made their major label debut with the 'HAZELTON' EP. The 'SUNBURN' album followed in 1998, garnering widespread critical acclaim, making No.1 on Billboard's Heatseekers chart and eventually going platinum. A revamped version of 'SHIMMER' narrowly missed the US Top 40 with its accompanying video nominated for two Billboard awards. Although a session sticksman was used on the album, permanent drummer KEVIN MILLER joined the band soon after its release and played on sophomore effort, 'SOMETHING LIKE HUMAN' (2000).

Album rating: SUNBURN (*6) / SOMETHING LIKE HUMAN (*5)

BRETT SCALLIONS – vocals, rhythm guitar / **CARL BELL** – lead guitar / **JEFF ABERCROMBIE** – bass / **KEVIN MILLER** – drums

not iss. — own label

1996. (cd-ep) *<none>* **PORCELAIN** [-] [ ]

Epic — 550 – Sony

Jan 98. (cd-ep) **HAZLETON** [-] [ ]

Nov 98. (cd-ep) *(111508) <79019>* **SHIMMER / WALK THE SKY / SUNDAY GIRL** [ ] [ ] Aug98

Feb 99. (cd) *(493223-2) <68554>* **SUNBURN** [ ] [77] Mar98
– Untitled / Bittersweet / Shimmer / Jesus or a gun / Sunburn / New thing / It's come to this / Song for you / Mary pretends / Ozone / Hideaway.

Oct 00. (-) *<radio play>* **HEMORRHAGE (IN MY HANDS)** [-] [30]

Apr 01. (cd) *(498095-2) <69436>* **SOMETHING LIKE HUMAN** [ ] [17] Sep00
– Last time / Hemorrhage (in my hands) / Empty spaces / Scar / Bad day / Prove / Easy / Down / Solace / Knives / Innocent / Slow.

FUGAZI

Formed: Arlington, Virginia, USA ... 1987 by IAN MacKAYE (now of Washington DC), who had the previous year featured on an album by EMBRACE (not the more recent outfit!). MacKAYE and drummer JEFF NELSON subsequently founded the 'Dischord' label, a bedrock of the Washington DC hardcore scene and an outlet for the pair's new band, MINOR THREAT. Completing the line-up with LYLE PRESLAR and BRIAN BAKER, this highly influential outfit released two singles in 1981, before they added STEVE HANSEN to boost their minimalist sound on the album, 'OUT OF STEP' (1983). A further album, the eponymous 'MINOR THREAT', contained the track 'STRAIGHT EDGE', a term which would be adopted by a generation of fans who followed MacKAYE and Co.'s example of abstinence and individual responsibility. Following their split, mainman MacKAYE formed FUGAZI, sharing vocal and songwriting duties with GUY PICCOTTO (ex-leader of RITES OF SPRING and INSURRECTION – the latter outfit having released a self-titled effort for 'Peaceville'). With the FUGAZI line-up crystallising around BRENDAN CANTY and JOE LALLY, they released two HENRY ROLLINS-produced mini-sets, the eponymous 'FUGAZI' and 'MARGIN WALKER' (1989), before fully realising their aggressively economical sound on the acclaimed 'REPEATER' (1990) album. Bringing to mind the once wilfully obscure vocals of DAVID THOMAS (PERE UBU) backed by the hardcore of NO MEANS NO, FUGAZI delivered a fourth set, 'STEADY DIET OF NOTHING' (1991), their perseverance paying off with a minor placing in the UK charts. Two years later, 'IN ON THE KILLTAKER' scored a deserved UK Top 30 and dominated the indie charts for months; despite persistent major label interest, FUGAZI have admirably refused to play the corporate game (how many bands can you say that about?). The mid 90's saw the release of 'RED MEDICINE', the album taking the staunchly independent hardcore crusaders into previously uncharted territory, i.e. the UK Top 20 (appropriately enough, the commercial behemoth that is the American music industry has so far prohibited the band's domestic success). MacKAYE, PICCIOTTO and crew were back in '98, although 'END HITS' (not a compilation) suffered a little commercially due to their long absence. Unperturbed, FUGAZI worked on a soundtrack album. Jem Cohen's docu-film, 'INSTRUMENT', was delivered the following Spring, the music (with sparse vocals!) a return of sorts to their abrasive best. • **Covered:** 12XU (Wire). • **Trivia:** MacKAYE produced the early '89 BEEFEATER single, 'House Burning Down'.

Album rating: 13 SONGS compilation (*8) / REPEATER (*8) / STEADY DIET OF NOTHING (*7) / IN ON THE KILLTAKER (*7) / RED MEDICINE (*6) / END HITS (*6) / INSTRUMENT soundtrack (*7) / Minor Threat: COMPLETE DISCOGRAPHY compilation (*8)

MINOR THREAT

IAN MacKAYE (b.1963) – vocals, guitar / **LYLE PRESLAR** – guitar / **BRIAN BAKER** – bass (ex-GOVERNMENT ISSUE) / **JEFF NELSON** – drums

Dischord Dischord

Jun 81. (7"ep) *<Dischord 3>* **MINOR THREAT EP** [-] [ ]
Dec 81. (7",7"red) *<Dischord 5-Limp 41>* **IN MY EYES** [-] [ ]

— added **STEVE HANSEN** – bass (BAKER now on second guitar)

1983. (lp/c) *<(DISCHORD 10/+C)>* **OUT OF STEP** [ ] [ ]
– Betray / It follows / Think again / Look back and laugh / Sob story / No reason / Little friend / Out of step / Stand up / 12XU.

1984. (lp/c) *<(DISCHORD 12/+C)>* **MINOR THREAT** [ ] [ ]
– Filler / I don't wanna hear it / Seeing red / Straight edge / Small man, big mouth / Screaming at a wall / Bottled violence / Minor threat / In my eyes / Out of step (with the world) / Guilty of being white / Steppin' stone.

Aug 85. (7"ep) *<(DISCHORD 15)>* **SALAD DAYS / GOOD GUYS. / STUMPED / CASHING IN** [ ] [ ]

Mar 90. (cd) *<(DISCHORD 40)>* **COMPLETE DISCOGRAPHY** (compilation) [ ] [ ]

FUGAZI

IAN MacKAYE – vocals, guitar (ex-MINOR THREAT, ex-TEEN IDES, ex-EMBRACE) / **GUY PICCIOTTO** (b.1966) – vocals (ex-INSURRECTION, ex-RITES OF SPRING, ex-ONE LAST WISH) / **JOE LALLY** (b.1964, Rockville, Maryland) – bass / **BRENDAN CANTY** (b.1967) – drums

Dischord Dischord

Dec 88. (m-lp/m-c) *<(DISCHORD 30/+C)>* **FUGAZI** [ ] [ ]
– Waiting room / Bulldog front / Bad mouth / Burning / Give me the cure / Suggestion / Glue man. *(re-iss. Apr98; same)*

Jul 89. (m-lp/m-c) *<(DISCHORD 35/+C)>* **MARGIN WALKER** [ ] [ ]
– Margin walker / And the same / Burning too / Provisional / Lockdown / Promises. *(cd-iss. Oct89 as '13 SONGS'+=; DIS 36)* – FUGAZI *(re-iss. Apr98; same)*

Feb 90. (7",7"green) *<(DISCHORD 43)>* **JOE #1. / BREAK IN / SONG #1** [ ] [ ]

Mar 90. (lp/c/cd) *<(DISCHORD 44/+C/CD)>* **REPEATER** [ ] [ ]
– Turnover / Repeater / Brendan /1 / Merchandise / Blueprint / Sieve-fisted grind / Greed / Two beats off / Styrofoam / Reprovisional / Shut the door. *(cd+=)* – Song #1 / Joe /1 / Break in. *(re-iss. Apr98; same)*

Aug 91. (lp/c/cd) *<(DISCHORD 60/+C/CD)>* **STEADY DIET OF NOTHING** [63] [ ]
– Exit only / Reclamation / Nice new outfits / Stacks / Latin roots / Steady diet / Long division / Runaway return / Polish / Dear justice letter / K.Y.E.O. *(re-iss. Apr98; same)*

Jun 93. (m-lp/m-c/m-cd) *<(DIS 70/+C/D)>* **IN ON THE KILLTAKER** [24] [ ]
– Facet squared / Public witness program / Returning the screw / Smallpox champion / Rend it / 23 beats off / Sweet and low / Cassavetes / Great cop / Walken's syndrome / Instrument / Last chance for a slow dance. *(re-iss. Apr98; same)*

May 95. (lp/cd) *(DIS 90/+CD)* *<EFA 17990-2>* **RED MEDICINE** [18] [ ]
– Do you like me / Bed for the scraping / Latest disgrace / Birthday pony / Forensic scene / Combination lock / Fell, destroyed / By you / Version / Target / Back to base / Downed city / Long distance runner. *(re-iss. Apr98; same)*

— FUGAZI were put in backburner until their return below

Apr 98. (cd/c/lp) *<(DIS 110 CD/C/V)>* **END HITS** [47] [ ]
– Break / Place position / Recap modotti / No surprise / Five corporations / Caustic acrostic / Closed captioned / Floating boy / Foreman's dog / Arpeggiation / Guilford fall / Pink frosty / F/D.

Apr 99. (cd/c/lp) *<(DIS 120 CD/C/V)>* **INSTRUMENT** (soundtrack) [ ] [ ]
– Pink frosty (demo) / Lusty scripps / Arpeggiator (demo) / Afterthought / Trio's / Turkish disco / Me and Thumbelina / Floating boy (demo) / Link track / Little Debbie / H.B. / I'm so tired / Rend it (demo) / Closed caption (demo) / Guildford fall (demo) / Swingset / Shaken all over / Slo crostic.

FU MANCHU

Formed: San Clemente, California, USA ... 1990 by main songwriter/guitarist SCOTT HILL, plus RUBEN ROMANO, GREG McCAUGHEY and vocalist GLEN CHIVENS. It wouldn't be long until the arrival of the debut 45, 'KEPT BETWEEN TREES', although this would be the only single to include GREG and GLEN who were replaced by SCOTT VOTAW and MARK ABSHIRE on the sophomore 7", 'SENORITIS'. Fusing their blend of noisy garage metal (STOOGES to BLUE CHEER to MONSTER MAGNET), they initially released singles for 'Elastic' and a couple of long players for 'Bongload', 'NO ONE RODES FOR FREE' (1994) and 'DAREDEVIL', before signing to 'Man's Ruin'. With sole original HILL now recruiting bassist BRAD DAVIS, former KYUSS drummer BRANT BJORK and EDDIE GLASS (the latter having come in on their prior set), FU MANCHU's third album, 'IN SEARCH OF . . .' (1996), showed them taking a retro fixation to a wider market. In 1997, another newcomer to the fold, lead guitarist BOB BALCH, took over from the departing GLASS; this man would soon turn up with former FU MANCHU's ABSHIRE and ROMANO in the stoner-rock trio, NEBULA. The following year, a limited edition cover of Blue Oyster Cult's 'GODZILLA', gave the FU's Kerrang! street cred, while WHITE ZOMBIE's Y YUENGER produced yet another splendid set, 'THE ACTION IS GO' (1998). Two further sets, the mini for 'Man's Ruin', 'EATIN' DUST' (1999) and Mammoth's 'KING OF THE ROAD' (1999/2000) – containing a cover of Devo's 'FREEDOM OF CHOICE' – showed the band weren't exactly slacking from their recording duties, while a subsequent tour of North America and Australasia kept up their heavy metal/stoner profile. • **Covers:** NOTHING DONE (. . . Barile) / JAILBREAK (Thin Lizzy).

Album rating: NO ONE RIDES FOR FREE (*6) / DAREDEVIL (*6) / IN SEARCH OF. . . (*7) / THE ACTION IS GO (*7) / RETURN TO EARTH 91-93 compilation (*7) / EATIN' DUST mini (*6) / KING OF THE ROAD (*7)

GLEN CHIVENS – vocals / **SCOTT HILL** – guitar / **GREG McCAUGHEY** – bass / **RUBEN ROMANO** – drums, vocals

not iss. Slap-A-Ham

Nov 90. (7"m) **KEPT BETWEEN TREES. / BOULLINABAISSE / JR. HIGH SCHOOL RING (7 KARAT)** [-] [ ]

— **SCOTT VOTAW** – lead guitar; repl. CHIVENS (HILL now vocals)

— **MARK ABSHIRE** – bass; repl. McCAUGHEY

not iss. Elastic

Dec 91. (7"ep) *<ELS >* **SENIORITIS / PINBUSTER. / EL DON / SIMCO** [-] [ ]

May 92. (7") *<ELS 005>* **PICK-UP SUMMER. / VANKHANA (ROLLIN' ROOMS)** [-] [ ]
(UK-iss.Oct96; same)

— now without VOTAW

Nov 92. (7"m) *<ELS 007>* **DON'T BOTHER KNOCKIN' (IF THIS VAN'S ROCKIN'). / SPACE SUCKER** [-] [ ]
(UK-iss.Oct96; same)

Bongload Bongload

1994. (cd) *<BL 10>* **NO ONE RIDES FOR FREE** [-] [ ]
– Time to fly / Ojo rojo / Show and shine / Mega-bumpers / Free and easy (summer girls) / Superbird / Shine it on / Snakebellies. *(UK-iss.Feb97; same)*

— added **EDDIE GLASS** – lead guitar

Mar 95. (cd/lp) *<(BL 19 CD/LP)>* **DAREDEVIL** [ ] [ ] Jan95
– Trapeze freak / Tilt / Gathering speed / Coyote duster / Travel agent / Sleestak / Space farm / Lug / Egor / Wurkin' / Push button magic. *(re-iss. Feb97; same)*

— **BRAD DAVIS** – bass; repl. ABSHIRE who formed NEBULA

— **BRANT BJORK** – drums (ex-KYUSS) repl. ROMANO (also to NEBULA)

Man's Ruin Man's Ruin

Mar 96. (cd/lp) *<(MR 0134-2/-1)>* **IN SEARCH OF . . .** [ ] [ ]
– Regal begal / Missing link / Asphalt risin' / Neptune's convoy / Redline / Cyclone launch / Strato-streak / Solid hex / The falcon has landed / Seahag / The bargain / Supershooter.

May 96. (7"red) *<(MR 139-7)>* **ASPHALT RISIN'. / CHEVY VAN** [ ] [ ]
Aug 96. (7"white) *<(MR 157-7)>* **MISSING LINK. / OJO ROJO** [ ] [-]
Apr 97. (10"green-ep) *(<MR 048>)* **GODZILLA. / MODULE OVERLOAD / LIVING LEGEND** [ ] [ ]

— **BOB BALCH** – guitars; repl. GLASS

Feb 98. (cd-ep) **EVIL EYE / MODULE OVERLOAD / SWAMI'S LAST COMMAND** [ ] [ ]

Sessions not iss.

Mar 98. (7") *(SES7 14)* **JAILBREAK. / (other track by Fatso Jetson)** [ ] [-]

Mammoth Mammoth

Mar 98. (cd) *(557070-2)* *<3549 80173-2>* **THE ACTION IS GO** [ ] [ ] Nov97
– Evil eye / Urethene / Action is go / Burning road / Guardrail / Anodizer / Trackside hoax / Unknown world / Laserblast! / Hogwash / Grendel, snowman / Strolling astronomer / Saturn III / Nothing done.

Sep 98. (7") *(567750-7)* **JAILBREAK. / URETHANE** [ ] [-]
(cd-s+=) *(567686-2)* – Coyote duster (live).

Man's Ruin Man's Ruin

Feb 99. (10"lp/m-cd) *<(MR 158/+CD)>* **EATIN' DUST** [ ] [ ]
– Godzilla / Module overload / Living legend / Eatin' dust / Shift kicker / Orbiter / Mongoose / Pigeon toe. *<(12"lp-iss.Apr99; MR 163LP)>*

Mammoth Mammoth

Oct 99. (cd) *(0103352MAM)* *<980207>* **KING OF THE ROAD** [ ] [ ] Feb00
– Hell on wheels / Over the edge / Boogie van / King of the road / No dice / Blue tile fever / Grasschopper / Weird beard / Drive / Hotdoggin' / Freedom of choice.

– compilations, etc. –

Nov 98. (cd/lp) *Elastic; (ELS 001 CD/LP)* **RETURN TO EARTH 91-93** [ ] [ ] May97
– (the early singles)

FURY OF FIVE

Formed: New Jersey, USA ... 1994 by JAMES ISMEAN, CHICO, JAY and CHRIS. Combining shades of nu-metal and Knuckled-dusted hardcore in the tradition of nearby New York, FURY OF FIVE contributed to a clutch of compilations and issued a couple of 7" EP's prior to the release of their full length debut, 'NO REASON TO SMILE' (1996). The appropriately titled

'AT WAR WITH THE WORLD' served as the angry young men's sophomore effort in 1998 while with 'THIS TIME IT'S PERSONAL', they bowed out on a bum note in 2000. According to the album's sleevenote boast, the group were banned from playing in certain clubs because they'd beaten up the bouncers . . .

Album rating: NO REASON TO SMILE (*4) / AT WAR WITH THE WORLD (*6) / THIS TIME IT'S PERSONAL (*4)

JAMES ISMEAN – vocals, bass / **CHICO VIOLENCE** – guitar / **JAY FURY** – guitar / **CHRIS** – drums / +1

		Gain Ground	Gain Ground
Dec 96.	(lp/cd) <*(GAIN 007/+CD)*> **NO REASON TO SMILE**	☐	☐

– Everlasting memories / Street edge / Unreal / Every man for himself / Want it all / Loved by none / Running in fear / Decades of hatred / Deadhead / Our dying mother.

		Century Media	Victory
Feb 98.	(cd) *(CM 77159CD)* <*VR 69CD*> **AT WAR WITH THE WORLD**	☐	☐ Jun98

– Mission 1: Come and get it / Mission 2: Wake up America / Mission 3: No time for love / Mission 4: Once upon a time / Mission 5: Takin' respect / Mission 6: Last price / Mission 7: Follow the tracks / Mission 8: Do or die / Mission 9: Inbred hate / Mission 10: Just go quietly.

Apr 00.	(cd) *(77264-2)* <*VR 117CD*> **THIS TIME IT'S PERSONAL**	☐	☐ Mar00

– This time it's personal / Can't escape / Never / Forever down / It's over / Hundred percent real / Seasons change / One foot in the grave / Two sides to every story / Suckers wish / Hold my own / Wigga in da hood.

FUSE (see under ⇒ CHEAP TRICK)

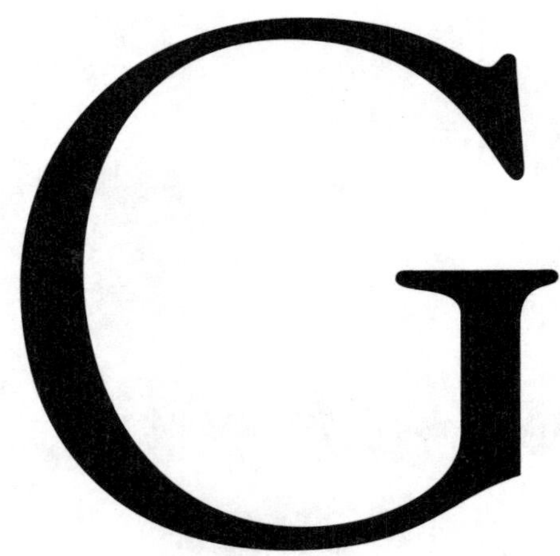

GALACTIC COWBOYS

Formed: Houston, Texas, USA . . . 1990 by vocalist BEN HUGGINS and guitarist DANE SONNIER, who teamed up with bassist MONTY COLVIN and drummer ALAN DOSS (the latter two piecing the band together from the ashes of the AWFUL TRUTH). Signed to 'Geffen' in 1991, The GALACTIC COWBOYS released their widely acclaimed eponymous debut later that year. Working on the same intelligent eclecticism premise as fellow cerebro-metallers KINGS X (they also share the latter band's Christian/spiritual outlook), these stellar music pioneers explored the frontiers of rock, mixing and matching everything from blues to melodic grunge. Two years later, 'SPACE IN YOUR FACE' continued their mission, although unfortunately critical praise wasn't translated into sales and 'Geffen' gave them their P.45. After a couple of years lost in the cosmos, the spaceage ranchers returned on 'Metal Blade' with 'MACHINE FISH' (1996). Like its two successors, 'FEEL THE RAGE' (actually a mini-set featuring two covers:- Kiss' 'I WANT YOU' and Paul McCartney/Wings' 'JUNIOR'S FARM') and 'THE HORSE THAT BUD BOUGHT' (1997), the record was a finely honed mesh of post-grunge metal pop, often sublime but lacking the x-factor which makes the band such a compelling live proposition. At the turn of the millennium, the GALACTIC COWBOYS were doing the rounds and making hard-rock albums, namely 1999's 'AT THE END OF THE DAY' (1998) and 'LET IT GO' (2000).

Album rating: GALACTIC COWBOYS (*7) / SPACE IN YOUR FACE (*5) / MACHINE FISH (*6) / FEEL THE RAGE mini (*4) / THE HORSE THAT BUD BOUGHT (*5) / AT THE END OF THE DAY (*5) / LET IT GO (*4)

BEN HUGGINS – vocals, acoustic guitar / **DANE SONNIER** – guitar, vocals / **MONTY COLVIN** – bass, vocals / **ALAN DOSS** – drums, vocals

Geffen Geffen

Aug 91. (lp/c/cd) *<(DGC/+C/D 24234)>* **GALACTIC COWBOYS** [ ] [ ]
– I'm not amused / My school / Why can't you believe in me / Kaptain Krude / Someone for everyone / Sea of tranquility / Kill floor / Pump up the space suit / Ranch on Mars reprise / Speak to me. *(re-iss. Jun93 cd/c; GFLD/GFLC 19202)*

Jun 93. (cd/c) *<(GED/GEC 24524)>* **SPACE IN YOUR FACE** [ ] [ ]
– Space in your face / You make me smile / I do what I do / Circles in the fields / If I were a killer / Blind / No problems / About Mrs. Leslie / Where are you now? *(cd+=)* – Ranch on Mars / Still life of peace.

— **WALLY FARKAS** – guitar, keyboards; repl. DANE

Metal Blade Metal Blade

Jan 96. (cd) *<(3984 11410-2)>* **MACHINE FISH** [ ] [ ]
– Feel the rage / The struggle / Fear not / Stress / Psychotic companion / In this life / Easy to love / Red sun / Idle minds / The lens / Puttin' yourself on the block / In a lonely room / 9th of June (do you believe) / Arrow.

Oct 96. (m-cd) *<(3984 14117-2)>* **FEEL THE RAGE** [ ] [ ]
– Feel the rage / Parodigm shift / I want you / Junior's farm / Idle minds (live) / 9th of June (live).

Jul 97. (cd) *<(3984 14127-2)>* **THE HORSE THAT BUD BOUGHT** [ ] [ ]
– Tilt-a-whirl / Evil twin / Oregon / The buzz / Tomorrow / Ribbon / Breakthrough / Bound / Media slant / Mona Lisa / I can't wait / Trip on love / You've changed / My life.

— **JERRY GASKILL** – drums (of KINGS X) repl. DOSS

Feb 99. (cd) *<(14183-2)>* **AT THE END OF THE DAY** [ ] [ ] Sep98
– Nothing to say / Ants / Just like me / The machine fish suite:- a) Where do I sign? – b) Bright horizons – c) Puppet show – d) Mr. Magnet – e) Never understand – f) Ranch on Mars pt.2 (set me free) – g) How does it feel? / Young man's dream / Shine / The shape / It's not over / Through / At the end of the day.

Aug 00. (cd) *<(14299-2)>* **LET IT GO** [ ] [ ] Jun00
– Intro / T.I.M. / A different way / Life and times / Flag / Disney's spinnin' / Her Mr. / Another hill / Dirty hands / Boom! / Ordinary / Internalize / Swimming in December / Song for Sybo / Future / Bucket of chicken / The record ends.

— the band split some time in 2000

Rory GALLAGHER

Born: 2 Mar'49, Ballyshannon, Donegal, Ireland. After playing in various school bands in Cork, RORY formed The FONTANA SHOWBAND, who subsequently became The IMPACT. By 1965, they'd secured residencies in Hamburg, mostly playing CHUCK BERRY songs to post-BEATLES audiences. A year later, just as the British blues revival was gathering steam, he formed TASTE with NORMAN DAMERY and ERIC KITTERINGHAM, although the latter two were eventually replaced by CHARLIE McCRACKEN and JOHN WILSON. After an eponymous debut album failed to break through, TASTE hit the UK Top 20 in 1970 with the follow-up set, 'ON THE BOARDS'. The album established GALLAGHER as Ireland's ambassador of the blues guitar, setting the stage for his forthcoming solo career. A self-titled debut appeared in 1971, the record selling enough initial copies to give it a Top 40 placing. Worshipping at the altar of blues KING-s; B.B., FREDDIE and ALBERT that is, GALLAGHER was revered by loyal fans for his musical integrity and down-to-earth approach (described as the working man's guitarist, due to his unconformist attire – i.e. lumberjack shirt, jeans and ruffled hair – GALLAGHER could also drink many a rock star under the table, eventually into the grave). After another blistering studio set in 1971, 'DEUCE', he scored a massive UK Top 10 with the concert album, 'LIVE IN EUROPE' (1972). Recorded at the peak of GALLAGHER's powers, 'BLUEPRINT' (1972) and 'TATTOO' (1973) stand among the Irishman's most overlooked albums, although the former nearly hit the UK Top 10. To coincide with the projected release of an in-concert rockumentary, GALLAGHER released yet another live set, the electrifying double set, 'IRISH TOUR '74'. Moving to 'Chrysalis' records soon after, GALLAGHER's form slumped slightly just as the new, leaner breed of guitar acts were up and coming, his commercial appeal subsiding under this pressure with each successive release. Nevertheless he continued to record some worthwhile material and perform live for a hardcore following, persevering with the rock industry well into the 90's. Death was the only thing that could prise GALLAGHER away from his guitar, the Irishman passing away on the 14th June '95 after suffering complications with a liver transplant. • **Covers:** SUGAR MAMA + DON'T START ME TALKING (Sonny Boy Williamson) / I'M MOVING ON (Hank Snow) / I TAKE WHAT I WANT (Hayes-Porter-Hedges) / ALL AROUND MAN (Davenport) / OUT ON THE WESTERN PLAINS (Leadbelly) / RIDE ON RED, RIDE ON (Levy-Glover-Reid) / I WONDER WHO (. . . Boyle) / AS THE CROW FLIES (Josh White) / JUST A LITTLE BIT (Dexter Gordon) / MESSING WITH THE KID (Julie London) / PISTOL SLAPPER BLUES (. . . Allen) / etc. • **Trivia:** VINCENT CRANE of ATOMIC ROOSTER guested on RORY's debut lp in '71. GALLAGHER also sessioned on albums by MUDDY WATERS (London Sessions) / JERRY LEE LEWIS (London Sessions) / LONNIE DONEGAN (Putting On The Style) / etc.

Album rating: Taste: TASTE (*6) / ON THE BOARDS (*7) / LIVE TASTE (*4) / LIVE AT THE ISLE OF WIGHT exploitation (*4) / Rory Gallagher: RORY GALLAGHER (*6) / DEUCE (*5) / LIVE IN EUROPE (*6) / BLUEPRINT (*7) / TATTOO (*7) / IRISH TOUR '74 (*8) / SINNER . . . AND SAINT early stuff (*5) / AGAINST THE GRAIN (*5) / THE STORY SO FAR compilation (*6) / CALLING CARD (*7) / PHOTO FINISH (*5) / TOP PRIORITY (*5) / STAGE STRUCK (*5) / JINX (*5) / DEFENDER (*4) / THE BEST OF RORY GALLAGHER & TASTE compilation (*6) / EDGED IN BLUE (*7)

TASTE

RORY GALLAGHER – vocals, guitar / **CHARLIE McCRACKEN** (b.26 Jun'48) – bass repl. ERIC KITTERINGHAM / **JOHN WILSON** (b. 3 Dec'47) – drums (ex-THEM) repl. NORMAN DAMERY

Major Minor not iss.

Apr 68. (7") *(MM 560)* **BLISTER ON THE MOON. / BORN ON THE WRONG SIDE OF TIME** [ ] [-]
(re-iss. Jul70; MM 718)

Polydor Atco

Mar 69. (7") *(56313)* **BORN ON THE WRONG SIDE OF TIME. / SAME OLD STORY** [ ] [-]

Apr 69. (lp) *(583 042)* **TASTE** [ ] [ ]
– Blister on the moon / Leaving blues / Sugar mama / Hail / Born on the wrong side of time / Dual carriageway pain / Same old story / Catfish / I'm moving on. *(re-iss. 1977; 2384 076) (cd-iss. Aug92; 841 600-2)*

Jan 70. (lp) *(583 083)* **ON THE BOARDS** [18] [ ]
– What's going on / Railway and gun / It's happened before, it'll happen again / If the day was any longer / Morning sun / Eat my words / On the boards / If I don't sing I'll cry / See here / I'll remember. *(cd-iss. Apr94; 841 599-2)*

Feb 71. (lp) *(2310 082)* **LIVE TASTE (live)** [ ] [-]
– Sugar mama / Gamblin' blues / Feel so good (part 1) / Feel so good (part 2) / Catfish / Same old story.

— GALLAGHER went solo. The other two formed STUD. McCRACKEN also joined SPENCER DAVIS GROUP

RORY GALLAGHER

solo – vocals, guitar with **GERRY MacAVOY** – bass (ex-DEEP JOY) / **WILGAR CAMPBELL** – drums (ex-METHOD)

Polydor Atlantic

May 71. (lp) *(2383 044)* *<33368>* **RORY GALLAGHER** [32] [ ]
– Laundromat / Just the smile / I fall apart / Wave myself goodbye / Hands up / Sinner boy / For the last time / It's you / I'm not surprised / Can't believe it's true. *(re-iss. 1979 on 'Chrysalis' lp/c; CHR/ZCHR 1258) (cd-iss. Sep98 on 'Capo'; CAPO 101)*

Jun 71. (7"m) *(2814 004)* **IT'S YOU. / JUST THE SMILE / SINNER BOY** [ ] [ ]

Nov 71. (lp) *(2383 076) <7004>* **DEUCE** 39
– Used to be / I'm not awake yet / Don't know where I'm going / Maybe I will / Whole lot of people / In your town / Should've learn't my lesson / There's a light / Out of my mind / Crest of a wave. *(re-iss. 1979 on 'Chrysalis' lp/c; CHR/ZCHR 1254) (cd-iss. Sep98 on 'Capo'; CAPO 102)*

Polydor Polydor

May 72. (lp) *(2383 112) <5513>* **LIVE! IN EUROPE (live)** 9
– Messin' with the kid / Laundromat / I could've had religion / Pistol slapper blues / Going to my home town / In your town / Bullfrog blues. *(re-iss. 1979 on 'Chrysalis' lp/c; CHR/ZCHR 1257) (cd-iss. Mar95 on 'Castle'; CLACD 406) (cd re-iss. Feb99 on 'Capo'; CAPO 103)*

— **ROD DE'ATH** – drums (ex-KILLING FLOOR) repl. CAMPBELL / added **LOU MARTIN** – keyboards, mandolin (ex-KILLING FLOOR)

Feb 73. (lp) *(2383 189) <5522>* **BLUEPRINT** 12
– Walk on hot coals / Daughter of the Everglades / Banker's blues / Hands off / Race the breeze / The seventh son of a seventh son / Unmilitary two-step / If I had a reason. *(re-iss. 1979 on 'Chrysalis' lp/c; CHR/ZCHR 1253) (cd-iss. Feb94 on 'Castle; CLACD 316) (cd re-iss. Feb00 on 'Capo'; CAPO 104)*

Aug 73. (lp) *(2383 230) <5539>* **TATTOO** 32
– Tattoo'd lady / Cradle rock / 20:20 vision / They don't make them like you anymore / Livin' like a trucker / Sleep on a clothes-line / Who's that coming / A million miles away / Admit it. *(re-iss. 1979 on 'Chrysalis' lp/c; CHR/ZCHR 1259) (cd-iss. Jan94 on 'Castle'; CLACD 315) (cd re-iss. Feb00 on 'Capo'; CAPO 105)*

Jul 74. (d-lp) *(2659 031) <9501>* **IRISH TOUR '74 (live)** 36
– Cradle rock / I wonder who (who's gonna be your sweet man) / Tattoo'd lady / Too much alcohol / As the crow flies / A million miles away / Walk on hot coals / Who's that coming / Back on my (stompin' ground) / Just a little bit. *(re-iss. 1979 on 'Chrysalis' lp/c; CTY/ZCTY 1256) (re-iss. May88 on 'Demon' d-lp)(d-c/d-cd; DFIEND 120)(FIEND CASS/CD 120) (cd re-iss. Sep98 on 'Capo'; CAPO 106)*

Chrysalis Chrysalis

Oct 75. (lp/c) *(<CHR/ZCHR 1098>)* **AGAINST THE GRAIN**
– Let me in / Cross me off your list / Ain't too good / Souped-up Ford / Bought and sold / I take what I want / Lost at sea / All around man / Out on the western plain / At the bottom. *(re-iss. May91 on 'Castle' cd/c/lp; CLA CD/MC/LP 223) (cd re-iss. Feb99 on 'Capo'; CAPO 107)*

Nov 75. (7") *(CDV 102)* **SOUPED-UP FORD. / I TAKE WHAT I WANT** -

Oct 76. (lp/c) *(<CHR/ZCHR 1124>)* **CALLING CARD** 32
– Do you read me / Country mile / Moonchild / Calling card / I'll admit you're gone / Secret agent / Jack-knife beat / Edged in blue / Barley and grape rag. *(re-iss. Apr91 on 'Essential' cd/c/lp; ESS CD/MC/LP 143) (re-iss. cd Mar94 on 'Castle'; CLACD 352) (cd re-iss. Sep98 on 'Capo'; CAPO 108)*

— **TED McKENNA** – drums (ex-SENSATIONAL ALEX HARVEY BAND) repl.DE'ATH and MARTIN (to RAMROD)

Oct 76. (lp/c) *(<CHR/ZCHR 1170>)* **PHOTO FINISH**
– Shin kicker / Brute force and ignorance / Cruise on out / Cloak and dagger / Overnight bag / Shadow play / The Mississippi sheiks / The last of the independents / Fuel to the fire. *(cd-iss. Sep98 on 'Capo'; CAPO 109)*

Jan 79. (7"m) *(CHS 2281)* **SHADOW PLAY. / SOUPED UP FORD / BRUTE FORCE AND IGNORANCE** -
(10"+=) *(CXP 2281)* – Moonchild

Aug 79. (7",7"colrd) *(CHS 2364)* **PHILBY. / HELLCAT / COUNTRY MILE**

Sep 79. (lp/c) *(<CHR/ZCHR 1235>)* **TOP PRIORITY** 56
– Follow me / Philby / Wayward child / Keychain / At the depot / Bad penny / Just hit town / Off the handle / Public enemy No.1. *(re-iss. May88 on 'Demon' lp/c/cd; FIEND/+CASS/CD 123) (cd re-iss. Feb99 on 'Capo'; CAPO 110)*

Aug 80. (7",7"colrd) *(CHS 2453)* **WAYWARD CHILD (live). / KEYCHAIN** -

Sep 80. (lp/c) *(<CHR/ZCHR 1280>)* **STAGE STRUCK (live)** 40
– Shin kicker / Wayward child / Brute force and ignorance / Moonchild / Follow me / Bought and sold / The last of the independents / Shadow play. *(cd-iss. Mar95 on 'Castle'; CLACD 407) (cd re-iss. Feb00 on 'Capo'; CAPO 111)*

Dec 80. (7") *(CHS 2466)* **HELLCAT. / NOTHIN' BUT THE DEVIL**

— (May'81) **GALLAGHER** with **McAVOY** brought in **BRENDAN O'NEILL** – drums; repl. McKENNA who joined GREG LAKE BAND then MSG

Chrysalis Mercury

Apr 82. (lp/c) *(CHR/ZCHR 1359) <SRMI 4051>* **JINX** 68
– Signals / The Devil made me do it / Double vision / Easy come, easy go / Big guns / Jinxed / Bourbon / Ride on Red, ride on / Loose talk. *(re-iss. May88 on 'Demon' lp/c/cd; FIEND/+CASS/CD 126) (cd re-iss. Feb00 on 'Capo'; CAPO 112)*

Jun 82. (7") *(CHS 2612)* **BIG GUNS. / THE DEVIL MADE ME DO IT**

1983. (10"ep) *(CXP 2281)* **SHADOW PLAY / BRUTE FORCE AND IGNORANCE. / MOONCHILD / SOUPED UP FORD** -

Capo-Demon Intercord

Jul 87. (lp)(c/cd) *(XFIEND 98)(FIEND CASS/CD 98)* **DEFENDER** -
– Kickback city / Loanshark blues / Continental op / I ain't no saint / Failsafe day / Road to Hell / Doing time / Smear campaign / Don't start me talkin' / Seven days. *(c+=/cd+=) (free-7")* – SEEMS TO ME. / NO PEACE FOR THE WICKED *(cd-iss. Feb99 on 'Capo'+=; CAPO 113)* – Seems to me / No peace for the wicked.

— guests **MARK FELTHAM** – harmonica / **LOU MARTIN** – piano / **JOHN EARL** – saxophones / **GERAINT WATKINS** – accordion / **JOHN COOKE** – keyboards / **RAY BEAVIS** – tenor sax / **DICK HANSON** – trumpet

Capo Intercord

Jun 90. (cd/c/lp) *(CAPO CD/MC/LP 14)* **FRESH EVIDENCE**
– 'Kid' gloves / The king of Zydeco (to: Clifton Chenier) / Middle name / Alexis / Empire state express / Ghost blues / Heaven's gate / The loop / Walkin' wounded / Slumming angel. *(re-iss. cd Oct92 on 'Essential'; ESSCD 155) (cd re-iss. Sep98 on 'Capo'; CAPO 114)*

— on the 14th June 1995, RORY died after complications from a liver transplant operation

– compilations etc. –

1974. (c) *Emerald-Gem; (GES 1110) / Springboard; <SPB 4056>* **IN THE BEGINNING (VOCAL AND GUITAR)** (rec.'67) <US-title 'TAKE IT EASY BABY'> 1976

Aug 72. (lp; by TASTE) *Polydor; (2383 120)* **TASTE – LIVE AT THE ISLE OF WIGHT (live)** 41 -

(cd-iss. Apr94; 841 601-2)

Feb 75. (lp) *Polydor; (2383 315) <6510>* **SINNER . . . AND SAINT** (1971 material)

Oct 82. (7"ep/12"ep) *Polydor; (POSP/+X 609)* **BLISTER ON THE MOON / SUGAR MAMA. / CATFISH / ON THE BOARDS** -

Feb 76. (lp) *Polydor; (2383 376) <6519>* **THE STORY SO FAR**

1977. (lp) *Polydor; (2384 079)* **LIVE** -

May 80. (lp) *Hallmark; (HSC 3041)* **RORY GALLAGHER** -

Feb 88. (cd) *Razor; (MACH 10D)* **THE BEST OF RORY GALLAGHER & TASTE** -
– Blister on the moon / Hail / Born on the wrong side of time / Dual carriageway pain / Same old story / On the boards / See here / I'll remember / Sugar mama (live) / Sinner boy (live) / I feel so good (live) / Catfish / I'm movin' on / What's going on / Ralway and gun / Morning Sun / Eat my words.

May 89. (d-lp/d-c/d-cd) *That's Original; (TFO LP/MC/CD 20)* **LIVE! IN EUROPE / STAGE STRUCK** -

Jul 89. (d-lp/d-c/d-cd) *That's Original; (TFO LP/MC/CD 21)* **TATTOO / BLUEPRINT** -

May 91. (4xcd-box) *Demon; (RORY G1)* **RORY GALLAGHER** -
– (IRISH TOUR '74 / DEFENDER / TOP PRIORITY / JINX)

Jun 92. (lp/c/cd) *Demon; (FIEND/+C/CD 719)* **EDGED IN BLUE** -

Nov 92. (3xcd-box) *Essential; (ESBCD 187)* **G-MEN: BOOTLEG SERIES VOLUME ONE** -

Nov 98. (cd) *I.R.S.; (35783)* **A BLUE DAY FOR THE BLUES** -

Nov 98. (cd) *Camden; (74321 62797-2)* **ETCHED IN BLUE** -

Aug 99. (d-cd) *Capo; (CAPO 701)* **THE BBC SESSIONS**

GAMMA (see under ⇒ MONTROSE)

GAMMA RAY

Formed: Germany . . . 1989 by ex-HELLOWEEN guitarist KAI HANSEN and TYRAN PACE frontman RALF SCHEEPERS. Enlisting the rhythm section of UWE WESSEL and MATHIAS BURCHARDT, HANSEN came to the recording studio armed with songs left over from his HELLOWEEN period. Consequently, then, a debut set, 'HEADING FOR TOMORROW', was released on 'Noise' the following year, its melodic pomp-metal drawing critical praise and inevitable comparisons with HANSEN's old band. Initiated as a studio project, HANSEN was persuaded to take the show on the road, the group perfecting their sound for a second, sharper set entitled 'SIGH NO MORE' (1991). A third full length set, 'INSANITY & GENIUS', appeared in summer '93, although GAMMA RAY's rather trad Euro-metal was beginning to sound a bit dated. Nevertheless, GAMMA RAY continued in their trademark style, 'LAND OF THE FREE' (1995), struggling to compete in an overly crowded metal marketplace; SCHEEPERS had already formed PRIMAL FEAR with the help of KAI. The subsequent GAMMA RAY European tour was recorded for posterity as 'ALIVE 1995' (1996) while 1997's sixth studio set, 'SOMEWHERE OUT IN SPACE', heralded the formation of a stable line-up featuring HANSEN and SCHLACHTER alongside newcomers HENJO RICHTER and DANIEL ZIMMERMANN. The 'POWERPLANT' album followed in 1999 while GAMMA RAY saw in the new millennium with 'BLAST FROM THE PAST', a double-set retrospective with a twist; the tracklisting was chosen via an internet poll and the songs were re-recorded by the original line-up. This illustrates the hardcore pool of fans still eager for the kind of strident, uniquely Germanic metal GAMMA RAY specialise in, oblivious to trends in the brave nu-metal world. Thus 'NO WORLD ORDER' (2001), a record firmly in the established mould which avoids style over content at every turn.

Album rating: HEADING FOR TOMORROW (*6) / HEAVEN CAN WAIT mini (*5) / SIGH NO MORE (*6) / INSANITY GENIUS (*5) / LAND OF THE FREE (*4) / ALIVE 1995 (*4) / SOMEWHERE OUT IN SPACE (*5) / POWER PLANT (*5) / BLAST FROM THE PAST compilation (*7)

RALF SCHEEPERS – vocals (ex-TYRAN PACE) / **KAI HANSEN** – guitar, vocals (ex-HELLOWEEN) / with **DIRK SCHLACHTER** – guitar, keyboards / **UWE WESSEL** – bass, vocals / **ULI KUSCH** – drums; repl. MATHIS BURCHARDT

Noise R.C.A.

Mar 90. (cd/c/lp) *(N 0151-2/-4/-1) <2253>* **HEADING FOR TOMORROW**
– Welcome / Lust for life / Heaven can wait / Space eater / Money / The silence / Hold your ground / Free time / Heading for tomorrow. *(cd+=)* – Look at yourself.

Sep 90. (m-cd/m-lp) *(CD+/NUK 151-5)* **HEAVEN CAN WAIT** -
– Heaven can wait / Who do you think you are? / Sail on / Mr. Outlaw / Lonesome stranger.

Oct 91. (cd/c/lp) *(N 0178-2/-4/-1) <44853>* **SIGH NO MORE**
– Changes / Rich & famous / As time goes by / (We won't) Stop the war / Father and son / One with the world / Start running / Countdown * / The spirit / Dream healer. *(cd+= *)*

Noise Futurist

Jun 93. (cd/c/lp) *(N 0203-2/-4/-1) <11034>* **INSANITY AND GENIUS** Dec93
– Tribute to the past / No return / Insanity and genius / 18 years / The cave principle / Future madhouse / Your turn is over / Heal me / Gamma ray. *(cd+=)* – Brothers.

Jun 93. (cd-s) *(N 0203-3)* **FUTURE MADHOUSE / GAMMA RAY (version) / DREAM HEALER (preproduction 'Sigh No More' version)** -

— **JAN RUBACH** – bass; repl. WESSEL

— **THOMAS T. NACK** – drums; repl. KUSCH

— SCHEEPERS also departed (see PRIMAL FEAR below); HANSEN now + vox

Noise Noise

May 95. (lp/cd) *(<N 0227-1/-2>)* **LAND OF THE FREE**
– Rebellion in dreamland / Man on a mission / Fairytale / All of the damned / Rising

of the damned / Gods of deliverance / Farewell / Salvation's calling / Land of the free / The saviour / Abyss of the void / Time to break free / Afterlife. *(cd+=)* – Heavy metal mania / As time goes by / Miracle.

Feb 96. (cd-ep) *(N 0262-3)* **SILENT MIRACLES** [ ] [-]
– Miracle / Farewell / The silence ('95 version) / A while in dreamland.

Jun 96. (cd) *(<N 0265-2>)* **ALIVE 1995 (live)** [ ] [ ] Jul98
– Land of the free / Man on a mission / Rebellion in dreamland / Space eater / Fairytale / Tribute to the past / Heal me / The saviour / Abyss of the void / Ride the sky / Future world / Heavy metal mania / Lust for life / No return / Changes / Insanity and genius / Last before the storm / Future madhouse / Heading for tomorrow.

— **HANSEN + SCHLACHTER** recruited **HENJO RICHTER** – guitar, keyboards / **DAN ZIMMERMANN** – drums

Jun 97. (cd-ep) *(<N 0283-3>)* **VALLEY OF THE KINGS** [ ] [ ] Jun98
– Valley of the kings / Somewhere out in space / Watcher in the sky / Victim of changes.

Sep 97. (cd) *(<N 083-2>)* **SOMEWHERE OUT IN SPACE** [ ] [ ]
– Beyond the black hole / Men, Martians and machines / No stranger (another day in life) / Somewhere out in space / The guardians of mankind / The landing / Valley of the kings / Pray / The winged horse / Cosmic chaos / Lost in the future / Watcher in the sky / Rising star / Shine on / Return to fantasy.

May 99. (cd) *(N 0310-2)* **POWER PLANT** [-] [-] German
– Anywhere in the galaxy / Razorblade sigh / Send me a sign / Strangers in the night / Gardens of the sinner / Short as hell / It's a sin / Heavy metal universe / Wings of destiny / Hand of fate / Armageddon.

Jun 01. (cd) **NO WORLD ORDER** [-] [-] German

– compilations, etc. –

Jul 00. (d-cd) *Noise; (N 0332-2)* **BLAST FROM THE PAST** [ ] [-]
– Welcome / Lust for life / Heaven can wait / Heading for tomorrow / Changes / One with the world / Dream healer / Tribute to the past / Last before the storm / Heal me / Rebellion in dreamland / Man on a mission / Land of the free / The silence / Beyond the black hole / Somewhere out in space / Valley of the kings / Anywhere in the galaxy / Send me a sign / Armageddon.

GANG GREEN

Formed: Boston, Massachusetts, USA . . . 1982 by main songwriter CHRIS DOHERTY, who was sole survivor by 1985, when he recruited FRITZ ERICKSON (who replaced CHUCK STILPHEN), JOE GITTLEMAN and BRIAN BERTZGER. After securing the honour of being the first band to release a record on the influential indie label, 'Taang!', GANG GREEN delivered their debut album, 'ANOTHER WASTED NIGHT' (1986). Firmly committed to drinking beer and riding their skateboards, the group's ramshackle line in thrash/funcore drew in fans from both sides of the metal/punk divide. Ex-DRI man, JOSH PAPP, was recruited to replace GITTLEMAN, the sticksman debuting on the band's first release for 'Roadrunner', 'YOU GOT IT' (1987). GANG GREEN were at their best when wielding their cutting brand of subversive humour, in full effect with the VAN HALEN send-up, 'I81B4U' (1988). Another "hilarious" album title was unearthed on 'OLDER . . . BUDWEISER' (1989), although GANG GREEN proved they were anything but with their terminally adolescent musical antics. A final live set, 'CAN'T LIVE WITHOUT IT', signalled the end of the line, the corpse of GANG GREEN left to rot in the annals of hardcore history. • **Covered:** SUSPECT DEVICE (Stiff Little Fingers).

Album rating: ANOTHER WASTED NIGHT (*5) / YOU GOT IT (*5) / I81B4U mini (*6) / OLDER . . . (BUDWEISER) (*4) / CAN'T LIVE WITHOUT IT (*4) / KING OF BANDS compilation (*5)

CHRIS DOHERTY – vocals, guitar / **FRITZ ERICKSON** – guitar; repl. CHUCK STILPHEN / **JOE GITTLEMAN** – bass / **BRIAN BERTZGER** – drums

not iss. Deluxe

1986. (12"ep) **DRUNK AND DISORDERLY, BOSTON MA** [-] [ ]

Funhouse Taang!

1987. (12"ep) *<TAANG! 1>* **P.M.R.C. SUCKS** [-] [ ]

Oct 87. (lp) *(FH 12-002) <856418>* **ANOTHER WASTED NIGHT** [ ] [ ] 1986
– Another wasted night / Skate to Hell / Last chance / Alcohol / Have fun / 19th hole / Skate hate / Let's drink some beer / Protect and serve / Another bomb / Voices carry / Sold out Alabama. *(re-iss. May89; 086 401) (cd-iss. Jan90; FH 039) (re-iss. Nov92 & Aug97 on 'Taang!' lp/cd; TAANG 131 LP/CD)*

— **JOSH PAPP** – bass (ex-DRI), repl. JOE

Roadrunner Roadrunner

Nov 87. (lp) *<RR 9591-1>* **YOU GOT IT** [ ] [ ]
– Haunted house / We'll give it to you / Sheetrock / Ballerina massacre / Born to rock / Bomb / L.S.D.B. / Whoever said / Party with the Devil / Some things / The climb / Sick sex six. *(re-iss. 1989 cd/c; RR 9591-2/-4)*

Jul 88. (12") *<RR 24631>* **LIVING LOVING MAID. /** [ ] [ ]

Jan 89. (m-lp/m-c/m-cd) *<RR 9500-1/-4/-2>* **I81B4U** [ ] [ ]
– Bartender / Lost chapter / Rent / Put her on top / Cum in u.

Sep 89. (lp/c/cd) *(EM 9464-1/-4/-2)* **OLDER . . . (BUDWEISER)** [ ] [ ]
– Church of fun / Just one bullet / We can go / Tear down the walls / Flight 911 / Bedroom of doom / Casio jungle / Why should you care / I'm still young / The ballad. (above was co-issued with 'Emergo')

Jul 90. (cd/lp) *<RR 9380-2/-1>* **CAN'T LIVE WITHOUT IT (live at the Marquee)** [ ] [ ]
– Let's drink some beer / Bartender / Lost chapter / We'll give it to you / We can go / Have fun / Last chance / Just one bullet / Born to rock / Rabies / Voices carry / Sold out / Bedroom of doom / Bomb / Alcohol.

Nov 91. (cd/c/lp) *<RR 9254-2/-4/-1>* **KING OF BANDS** (compilation) [ ] [ ]
– Thunder / Alcohol / We'll give it to you / Bartender / Ballad / Fuck in A / Just one bullet / Another wasted night / Put her on top / Church of fun / Rub it in your face.

— disbanded late in 1991 when DOHERTY quit to raise his family; he subsequently re-formed the group in '97 with **GUSTAFSON, SWEET + MARK WEISS**

Taang! Taang!

Aug 97. (12"/cd-s) *<(TAANG 133/+CD)>* **BACK AND CRACKED** [ ] [ ]

Oct 97. (lp/c/cd) *<(TAANG 135/+MC/CD)>* **ANOTHER CASE OF BREWTALITY** [ ] [ ]
– Eviction party / Wash the blood / Break the bottle / Hole (in the road) / Death of the party / I missed it / Beach whistle / Don't you know / Tricked into bed . . . again / Denied / This job sucks / Out on the couch / Weekend millionaire / I'll woryy about it Monday / Time to pay / Say good buy / Livin' in oblivion / Accidental overdose / 6,000 crucified slaves / Suspect device / Penalty box / To the point / Here to saty.

– compilations, etc. –

Sep 97. (cd) *Taang!; <1>* **PRE SCHOOL** [-] [ ]
– Sold out / Terrorize / Snob / Lie lie / Don't know / Rabies / Narrow mind / Kill a Commie / Have fun / Selfish.

GARBAGE

Formed: Madison, Wisconsin, USA . . . 1994 by BUTCH VIG, DUKE ERIKSON and STEVE MARKER, out of the ashes of FIRE TOWN and SPOONER. BUTCH's latter ham-pop/rock act, had been on the go since early 1978 and released their debut ep 'CRUEL SCHOOL' a year later <Boat; SP 4001>. Another soon followed, 'WHERE YOU GONNA RUN?' <Boat; SP 3001>, before an album, 'EVERY CORNER DANCE' surfaced in '82; <Mountain Railroad; HR 8005>. BUTCH then set up his own studio and produced KILLDOZER, before giving SPOONER another outing with the album 'WILDEST DREAMS' <Boat; SP 1004>. In 1986, their final flop 45, 'MEAN OLD WORLD' <Boat; SP 1018>, made BUTCH form FIRE TOWN, with old buddy STEVE MARKER and co-songwriter DOUG ERIKSON. A few singles, 'CARRY THE TORCH' <7-89242> and 'RAIN ON YOU' <7-89204>, appeared from the 'Atlantic' stable alongside albums 'IN THE HEART OF THE HEART COUNTRY' <Boat; 1013 / re-iss. Atlantic; 81754> & 'THE GOOD LIFE' cd/lp; <781945-2/-1>. In 1989/90, BUTCH re-formed with the original line-up of SPOONER, DUKE ERIKSON, DAVE BENTON, JEFF WALKER and JOEL TAPPERO, to release one-off comeback cd 'THE FUGITIVE DANCE' <Dali-Chameleon; 89026>. He was then to find fame in production work for greats like NIRVANA, SONIC YOUTH, SMASHING PUMPKINS, NINE INCH NAILS and U2, before coming across Edinburgh-born vixen SHIRLEY MANSON fronting the band ANGELFISH on MTV. The new-look GARBAGE contributed the electro-goth of 'VOW' to a 'Volume' various artists compilation and this ended up as their limited edition debut 45 in 1995. By that year's summer, they had signed to Geffen's 'Almo Sounds' (UK 'Mushroom') records, which helped them break into the UK Top 50 with 'SUBHUMAN'. Success finally came with the 'ONLY HAPPY WHEN IT RAINS' single, a grungey, more tuneful affair that retained the goth overtones, MANSON weaving her deep throat vocals around the melody like a spider's web. She was an obvious focal point for the group; on their Top Of The Pops debut the singer made like a brooding, 90's incarnation of CHRISSIE HYNDE while the rest of the band remained comfortably anonymous in uniform black. The eponymous debut album, released later that year, was a mixed bag of styles that worked fairly effectively. Subsequent single, 'QUEER', kind of summed up the GARBAGE ethos, a deceptively poppy number featuring a MANSON vocal positively dripping with loathing, self or otherwise. GARBAGE continued their rise to the top of the pile with a UK chart-topping second set, 'VERSION 2.0', masterfully treading the finest of lines between alternative credibility and outright mainstream success; the hits kept on coming with 'PUSH IT', 'I THINK I'M PARANOID' and 'SPECIAL' all making the UK Top 20. • **Covered:** KISS MY ASS (Vic Chesnutt) / sampled the CLASH's 'Train In Vain' on 'STUPID GIRL'.

Album rating: GARBAGE (*8) / VERSION 2.0 (*7)

SHIRLEY MANSON (b. 3 Aug'66, Edinburgh, Scotland) – vocals, guitar (ex-GOODBYE MR MACKENZIE) / **STEVE MARKER** – guitar, samples, loops / **DUKE ERIKSON** (b. DOUG) – guitar, keyboards, bass / **BUTCH VIG** (b. BRYAN VIG, Viroqua, Wisconsin) – drums, loops, efx

Discordant AlmoSounds

Mar 95. (7") *(CORD 001) <89000>* **VOW. / VOW (Torn Apart version)** [ ] [97] Jul95

Mushroom AlmoSounds

Aug 95. (s7"/7") *(SX/S 1138) <89001>* **SUBHUMAN. / £1 CRUSH** [50] [ ]
(cd-s+=) *(D 1138)* – Vow.

Sep 95. (7"/c-s/cd-s) *(SX/C/D 1199) <89002>* **ONLY HAPPY WHEN IT RAINS. / GIRL DON'T COME / SLEEP** [29] [55] Feb96

Oct 95. (cd/c/2x45rpm-lp/6x7"box) *(D/C/L/LX 31450) <80004>* **GARBAGE** [6] [20] Aug95
– Supervixen / Queer / Only happy when it rains / As Heaven is wide / Not my idea / A stroke of luck / Vow / Stupid girl / Dog new tricks / My lover's box / Fix me now / Milk. *(d-lp re-iss. Sep99 on 'Simply Vinyl'+=; SVLP 123)* – Dumb (live) / Stupid girl (live) / Temptation waits (live) / Vow (live).

— on above **MIKE KASHAN** – bass / **PAULI RYAN** – percussion

Nov 95. (7") *(SX 1237) <89003>* **QUEER. / QUEER (Adrian Sherwood remix)** [13] [ ] Mar96
(silver-cd-s) *(D 1237)* – ('A'side) / Trip my wire / ('A'-The very queer dub-bin mix) / ('A'-The most beautiful girl in town mix).
(gold-cd-s) *(DX 1237)* – ('A'side) / Butterfly collector / ('A'-Rabbit in the Moon remix) / ('A'-Danny Saber remix).

Mar 96. (7") *(SX 1271)* **STUPID GIRL. / DOG NEW TRICKS (pal mix)** [4] [-]
(red-cd-s+=) *(D 1271)* – Driving lesson / ('A'-Red Snapper mix).
(blue-cd-s) *(DX 1271)* – ('A'side) / Alien sex fiend / ('A'-Dreadzone dub) / ('A'-Dreadzone vox).

Jul 96. (c-s) <89004> **STUPID GIRL / DRIVING LESSON** [-] [24]
Nov 96. (7") *(SX 1494) <89007>* **MILK (The wicked mix). / MILK (the Tricky remix)** [10] [ ]
(cd-s) *(D 1494)* – Milk (the wicked mix featuring TRICKY) / ('A'-Goldie's completely trashed remix) / ('A'-original version) / Stupid girl (Tees radio mix by TODD TERRY).
(cd-s) *(DX 1494)* – Milk (the wicked mix featuring TRICKY) / ('A'-Massive Attack classic remix) / ('A'-Rabbit in the moon udder remix) / Stupid girl (the Danny Saber remix).
May 98. (c-s) *(MUSH 28MCS) <89014>* **PUSH IT / LICK THE PAVEMENT** [9] [52]
(cd-s+=) *(MUSH 28CDS)* – ('A'-Boom Boom Satellites remix).
(3"cd-s) *(MUSH 28CDSX)* – ('A'side) / Thirteen.
May 98. (cd/c/lp) *(74321 55410-2/-4/-1) <80018>* **VERSION 2.0** [1] [13]
– Temptation waits / I think I'm paranoid / When I grow up / Medication / Special / Hammering in my head / Push it / The trick is to keep breathing / Dumb / Sleep together / Wicked ways / You look so fine. *(d-cd-iss. Jun99; MUSH 29CDX)*
Jul 98. (c-s) *(MUSH 35MCS) <40035>* **I THINK I'M PARANOID / DEADWOOD** [9] [ ]
(cd-s+=) *(MUSH 35CDS)* – Afterglow.
(cd-s) *(MUSH 35CDX)* – ('A'side) / ('A'extended) / ('A'-Purity mix).
(3"cd-ep+=) *(MUSH 35CDXXX)* – (all of the above).
Oct 98. (c-s) *(MUSH 39MCS) <827>* **SPECIAL / THIRTEEN X FOREVER** [15] [52] Nov98
(cd-s+=) *(MUSH 39CDS)* – ('A'-Brothers In Rhythm mix).
(cd-s) *(MUSH 39CDSX)* – ('A'side) / Medication (acoustic) / Push it (Victor Calderone remix).
(3"cd-s) *(MUSH 39CDSXXX)* – (all 5 above).
Jan 99. (c-s) *(MUSH 43MCS)* **WHEN I GROW UP / CAN'T SEEM TO MAKE YOU MINE** [9] [ ]
(cd-s+=) *(MUSH 43CDS)* – ('A'-Danny Tenaglia club mix).
(cd-s+=) *(MUSH 43CDSXXX)* – Tornado / ('A'-Danny Tenaglia club).
(cd-s) *(MUSH 43CDSX)* – ('A'side) / Tornado / Special (Rickidy raw mix).
May 99. (c-s) *(MUSH 49MCS)* **YOU LOOK SO FINE / SOLDIER THROUGH THIS** [19] [ ]
(cd-s+=) *(MUSH 49CDS)* – ('A'-Fine Young Cannibals remix).
(cd-s) *(MUSH 49CDSX)* – ('A'side) / Get busy with the fizzy / ('A'-Eric Kupper mix).
(3"cd-s) *(MUSH 49CDSXXX)* – ('A'side) / ('A'-Fine Young Cannibals mix) / ('A'-Eric Kupper mix) / ('A'-Plaid mix).
Nov 99. (c-s/cd-s) *(RAX C/TD 40)* **THE WORLD IS NEVER ENOUGH (mixes; original / UNKLE / Ice Bandits)** [11] [ ]
(above from the Bond movie of the same name – isued on 'Radioactive')

GATHERING

Formed: Netherlands . . . early 90's by BART SMITS, RENE RUTTEN, FRANK BOEIJEN, HUGO PRINSEN GEERLIGS and HANS RUTTEN. Following on from the fairly rote death metal of their debut album, 'ALWAYS' (1993), the band began experimenting with different vocalists and a more atmospheric style. For 'ALMOST A DANCE' (1994), NIELS DUFFHUES replaced SMITS' death grunting although more interesting in terms of the band's future direction were the contributions of MARTINE VAN LOON. Struck by the compatibility of their music with female vocals, the band headhunted BAD BREATH frontwoman/songwriter ANNEKE VAN GIERSBERGEN after seeing her perform a gig in their hometown of Oss. To many fans and critics a musical marriage made in heaven, the partnership was developed over the 'MANDYLION' (1995) and 'NIGHTTIME BIRDS' (1997) albums. Having abandoned their deathly roots, The GATHERING now favoured mournfully symphonic prog-metal accompanied by ANNEKE's lyrical flights of fancy and ethereal, otherworldly vocals acrobatics. The quasi concept set, 'HOW TO MEASURE A PLANET?' followed in 1999 while 'SUPERHEAT' (2000) documented the subsequent tour. Massive on the continent, it seems only a matter of time before Britain succumbs to the band's spacey charms. • **Covered:** LIFE'S WHAT YOU MAKE IT (Talk Talk).

Album rating: ALWAYS (*3) / ALMOST A DANCE (*4) / MANDYLION (*5) / NIGHTTIME BIRDS (*7) / HOW TO MEASURE A PLANET? (*7) / SUPERHEAT (*6) / IF . . . THEN . . . ELSE (*5)

BART SMITS – vocals / **FRANK BOEIJEN** – keyboards / other **RUTTEN** (were a 6-piece at some time)

Foundation 2000 | Pavement

Jul 92. (lp/cd) *(FDN 2004/+CD) <76962 32203-2>* **ALWAYS** [ ] [ ]
– Mirror wiers / Subzero / In sickness and health / King for a day / Second sunrise / Stonegarden / Always . . . / Gaya's dream. *(d-lp re-iss. Dec00 on 'Vinyl Collectors'; VC 025)*

—— **NIELS DUFFHUES** – vocals; repl. BART

—— added **MARTINE VAN LOON** – vocals (some)

Dec 93. (cd) *(FDN 2008-2)* **ALMOST A DANCE** [ ] [-]
– On a wave / The blue vessel / Her last flight / The sky people / Nobody dares / Like fountains / Proof / Heartbeat amplifier / A passage to desire.

—— added **ANNEKE VAN GIERSBERGEN** – vocal

Century Media | Century Media

Sep 95. (cd/c) *(<CM 77098 CD/MC>)* **MANDYLION** [ ] [ ]
– Strange machines / Eleanor / In motion #1 / Leaves / Fear the sea / Mandylion / Sand and mercury / In motion #2.
May 96. (cd-ep) *(CM 77135CD)* **ADRENALINE / LEAVES (edit) / THIRD CHANCE / LEAVES (album version)** [ ] [-]
Jun 97. (cd-ep) *(CM 77164CD)* **THE MAY SONG / THE EARTH IS MY WITNESS / STRANGE MACHINES (live) / THE MAY SONG (extended)** [ ] [-]
Jun 97. (lp/c/cd) *(<CM 77168/+MC/CD>)* **NIGHTTIME BIRDS** [ ] [ ]
– On most surfaces / Confusion / May song / The Earth is my witness / New moon different day / Third chance / Kevin's telescope / Nighttime birds / Shrink.
Oct 97. (cd-ep) *(CM 77192CD)* **KEVIN'S TELESCOPE / IN POWER WE ENTRUST THE LOVE ADVOCATED / WHEN THE SUN HITS / CONFUSION (demo/Eroc mix)** [ ] [-]
Nov 98. (cd-ep) *(CM 77267CD)* **LIBERTY BELL / SHRINK / FRAIL (live) / HOW TO MEASURE A PLANET?** [ ] [-]
Nov 98. (d-lp/d-cd) *(CM 77268/+CD) <7968>* **HOW TO MEASURE A PLANET?** [ ] [ ] Jan99
– Frail (you might as well be me) / Great ocean road / Rescue me / My electricity / Liberty bell / Red is a slow colour / Big sleep / Marooned / Travel / South American ghost ride / Illuminating / Locked away / Probably built in the fifties / How to measure a planet?
Feb 00. (cd) *(77278-2) <7978>* **SUPERHEAT** (a live album) [ ] [ ]
– The big sleep / On most surfaces / Probably built in the fifties / Liberty bell / Marooned / Rescue me / Strange machines / Nighttime birds / My electricity / Sand and mercury. *(video+=)* – Eleanor.
Jun 00. (cd-ep) *(77296-3)* **ROLLERCOASTER** [ ] [-]
– Rollercoaster / Theme from The Cyclist / Leaves (live from the Metropole Orchestra) / Liberty bell (CD-ROM excerpt).
Jul 00. (cd/lp) *(77298-2/-1)* **IF . . . THEN . . . ELSE** [ ] [ ]
– Rollercoaster / Shot to pieces / Amity / Bad movie scene / Colorado incident / Beautiful war / Analog park / Herbal movement / Saturnine / Morphia's waltz / Pathfinder.
Feb 01. (cd-ep) *(77358-3)* **AMITY / LIFE'S WHAT YOU MAKE IT / AMITY (mixes; Trip-pop radio / Timecode audio / extended trip / Three people / live at "Isabelle")** [ ] [-]

– compilations, etc. –

May 01. (cd) *Martyr; <18>* **DOWNFALL: THE EARLY YEARS** [-] [ ]

GAYE BYKERS ON ACID

Formed: Leicester, England . . . mid 80's by IAN GARFIELD HOXLEY (aka MARY MARY or MARY GOLIGHTLY) and TONE, along with KEVIN HYDE, ROBBER, and subsequently DJ, WILLIAM SAMUEL RONALD MONROE. A bizarre troupe of dayglo, grebo pseudo-bikers led by the cross-dressing, MARY MARY, GBOA made their album debut in 1987 with the 'Virgin' album (who else!), 'DRILL YOUR OWN HOLE'. Fans had to do just that as the record came minus a centre-punch, rendering it impossible to play. Though some might argue that was actually a blessing in disguise, the band atracted a cult following, gaining coverage mainly in the indie press. After a further major label set, 'STEWED TO THE GILLS' (1989), the band subsequently completed the independently issued 'GROOVEDIVESOAPDISH' the same year, before starting up their own label, 'Naked Brain'. The group folded after a few albums, various members going on to new projects, most notably MARY MARY, who surfaced in industrial "supergroup", PIGFACE, before co-forming HYPERHEAD. • **Trivia:** The band were at times complemented/augmented on stage by "drag-queen" DJ, ROCKET RONNIE, winner of 'The Alternative Miss Universe'.

Album rating: DRILL YOUR OWN HOLE (*6) / STEWED TO THE GILLS (*5) / GROOVEDIVESOAPDISH (*5) / CANCER PLANET MISSION (*4) / FROM THE TOMB OF THE YEAR (*4) / EVERYTHING'S GROOVY compilation (*6)

MARY MARY (b. IAN GARFIELD HOXLEY) – vocals / **TONE** (b. RICHARD ANTHONY HORSFALL) – guitar / **ROBBER** (b. IAN MICHAEL REYNOLDS) – bass / **KEVIN HYDE** (aka DR. JECKYL) – drums / plus **ROCKET RONNIE** (b. WILLIAM SAMUEL RONALD MONROE) – DJ

In-Tape | not iss.

Nov 86. (7"/12") *(IT/+TI 040)* **EVERYTHING'S GROOVY. / T.V. CABBAGE** [ ] [-]
May 87. (7") *(IT 046)* **NOSEDIVE KARMA. / DON'T BE HUMAN ERIC** [ ] [-]
(10"+=) *(IT 46-10)* – Golf trek.
(12"+=) *(ITTO 46)* – Delirium.

Virgin | Caroline

Oct 87. (7") *(VS 1008)* **GIT DOWN (SHAKE YOUR THANG). / TOLCHOCKED BY KENNY PRIDE** [54] [-]
(12"+=/12"s+=) *(VS T/X 1008)* – Go go in out, in out Garotschka.
Nov 87. (cd/c/lp) *(CD/TC+/V 2478) <CAROL 1347>* **DRILL YOUR OWN HOLE** [95] [ ]
– Motorvate / Call me a liar / All hung up / Zen express / World War 7 blues / Git down / After suck there's blow / So far out / Drive-in salvation / T.V. cabbage.
Dec 87. (7") *(VS 1027)* **ALL HUNG UP. / AFTERNOON TEA WITH DAVE GREENFIELD** [ ] [-]
(12"+=/12"pic-d+=) *(VS T/X 1027)* – ('A'-Rough Rider mix) / ('A'-Reprisal mix).
Jan 89. (7") *(VS 1165)* **HOT THING. / RAD DUDE** [ ] [-]
(10"+=/12"+=) *(VSA/VST 1165)* – After there's blow there's suck.
Feb 89. (cd/c/lp) *(CD/TC+/V 2579) <CAROL 1376>* **STEWED TO THE GILLS** [ ] [ ]
– It is are you? / Better of dead / M.A.D. / Hot thing / Testicle of God (and was it good) / Ill / Mass gyrate / Harmonious murder / Shoulders / Hair of dog / Rad dude / Teeth / Floydrix / Bedlam a g-go / Fairway to Heaven / It is are you? (concept reprise).

Naked Brain | not iss.

Mar 90. (lp/c) *(NBX 001/+MC)* **CANCER PLANET MISSION** [ ] [-]
– Welcome cancer planet mission / Face at the window / Hope ans psyche / Satyr naked / Catalytic converter / Advertise / Alive oh! / Mr. Muggeridge / Got is the kink / Demon seed / Bleed / Candle / Insomnia / Heavenly body. *(cd-iss. Oct90; NBXCD 001)*
Dec 90. (lp/c/cd; as PFX) *(NBX 2/+C/CD)* **PERNICIOUS NONSENSE** [ ] [-]

—— when they split during this period, KEVIN formed G.R.O.W.T.H. with JEFF from The JANITORS. TONE formed The CAMP COLLECTION with BRAD BRADBURY.

– compilations, etc. –

Jan 89. (12"ep) *Nighttracks; (SFNT 010)* **THE JANICE LONG SESSIONS** [ ] [-]

Nov 89. (m-lp/c/cd) *Dry Communications; (MLP/DRY/DRYCD 002)* **GROOVEDIVESOAPDISH** [ ] [-]

Apr 93. (cd/lp) *Receiver; (<RRCD/RRLP 160>)* **G.B.O.A.** [ ] [ ] May99
– Killer teens in New Orleans / S.P.A.C.E. / Radiation / John Wayne's a fag / Iguana trifle / What happened to Malcolm / Disinformation rise & shine / T.V. cabbage / Face at the window / Don't be human Eric – Let's be frank / Delirium / Everythings groovy baby.

May 93. (cd) *Receiver; (<RRCD 162>)* **FROM THE TOMB OF THE NEAR LEGENDARY** [ ] [ ] Dec94
– Watch that roundabout Ben / Shit happens / Killer teens in New Orleans (a joy toy remix) / Why? / Space cadet / Nero fiddles / Animal farm / No justice, just us / S.P.A.C.E. (a joy toy remix).

Jun 01. (cd) *Cherry Red; (<CDMRED 188>)* **EVERYTHING'S GROOVY** [ ] [ ]
– Everything's groovy / TV cabbage / Space rape / Nosedive karma / Don't be humam let's be frank / Delerium / Golf trek / All hanging up / Motorvate / Save your soul / Don't take me there / Leave your head alone / 007 / Getting down / Toytown / Toytown revisited.

GBH

Formed: Stoke-On-Trent, England . . . 1980 as CHARGED GBH, by CAL, JOCK, ROSS and WILF. Taking their name from the criminal offence GBH (Grevious Bodily Harm), these uncompromising Mohican-sporting oi/punks followed in the mould of EXPLOITED, BLITZ or DISCHARGE, releasing the violent debut EP, 'LEATHER BRISTLES . . .' in 1981. A year later, after a minor hit single, 'NO SURVIVORS', they found themselves smashing into the UK Top 20 with debut album, 'CITY BABY ATTACKED BY RATS'. Brutally basic three-chord punk assaults bolstered with a metallic edge and mob-rule vocals, the record was in tune with the prevailing zeitgeist, although they never again matched this success as the scene gave way for NWOBHM and proto-thrash acts. As the 80's wore on, GBH subsequently turned their backs on the punk/hardcore movement, taking an overtly metallic/speed approach on albums such as 'A FRIDGE TOO FAR' (1989) and 'FROM HERE TO REALITY' (1990).

Album rating: CITY BABY ATTACKED BY RATS (*6) / CITY BABIES REVENGE (*5) / MIDNIGHT MADNESS AND BEYOND . . . (*5) / NO NEED TO PANIC (*4) / A FRIDGE TOO FAR (*4) / FROM HERE TO ETERNITY (*4) / CHURCH OF THE TRULY WARPED (*4) / THE CLAY YEARS 1981-84 compilation (*6)

CAL (b. COLIN ABRAHALI) – vocals / **JOCK BLYTH** – guitar / **ROSS LOMAS** – bass / **WILF WILLIAMS** – drums

Clay — not iss.

Aug 81. (12"ep) *(PLATE 3)* **LEATHER BRISTLES, STUDS AND ACNE** [ ] [-]
– Race against time / Knife edge / Lycanthropy / Necrophilia / State executioner / D.O.A. / Generals / Freaks. *(re-iss. May90 lp/c/cd; PLATE/+MC/CD 3)*

Jan 82. (7"m) *(CLAY 8)* **NO SURVIVORS. / SELF DESTRUCT / BIG WOMEN** [63] [-]

Jun 82. (7"m) *(CLAY 11)* **SICK BOY. / SLIT YOUR OWN THROAT / AM I DEAD YET?** [ ] [-]

Aug 82. (lp/c; as CHARGE GBH) *(CLAY/+MC 4)* **CITY BABY ATTACKED BY RATS** [17] [-]
– City baby attacked by rats / The prayer of a realist / Passenger on the menu / Heavy discipline / Boston babies / Bellend bop / Time bomb / Sick boy / Willie Whitelaw's willie / No survivors / Self destruct / Big women / Slit your own throat. *(re-iss. Jul90 cd/c/lp; CLAY CD/MC/LP 4) (cd re-iss. Jul98 on 'Receiver'; RRCD 257) <US-iss.1990 on 'Combat'; 8217>*

Nov 82. (7"/7"pic-d) *(CLAY 16/+P)* **GIVE ME FIRE. / MANTRAP** [69] [-]

Dec 82. (lp) **LIVE AT THE CITY GARDEN (live)** [ ] [-]

Apr 83. (7") *(CLAY 22)* **CATCH 23. / HELLHOLE** [ ] [-]

Dec 83. (lp/c) *(CLAY/+MC 8)* **CITY BABYS REVENGE** [ ] [-]
– Diplomatic immunity / Drugs party in 526 / See the man run / Vietnames blues / Womb with a view / The forbidden zone / Valley of death / City babies revenge / Pins and needles / Christianised cannibals / Faster faster / High octane fuel / I feel alright / Skanga (herby weed). *(re-iss. May90 cd/c/lp; CLAY CD/MC/LP 8) <US-iss.1990 on 'Combat' lp,cd; 8004> (cd re-iss. Aug98 on 'Receiver'; RRCD 258)*

Aug 84. (7") *(CLAY 36)* **DO WHAT YOU DO. / FOUR MEN** [ ] [-]
(12"+=) *(12CLAY 36)* – Children of dust.

Rough Justice — Combat

Feb 86. (lp/c) *(JUST/TJUST 2) <8067>* **MIDNIGHT MADNESS AND BEYOND . . .** [ ] [ ]
– Limpwristed / Future fugitives / Too much / Iroquis / Guns and guitars / Horror story / Midnight madness / Chance for living / Seed of madness / Sam is your leader / How come? / Blood. *(cd-iss. Aug87; CDJUST 2)*

Sep 86. (12"ep) *(12KORE 101)* **OH NO IT'S GBH AGAIN** [ ] [-]
– [then take from below]

Jul 87. (lp) *(JUST 7)* **NO NEED TO PANIC** [ ] [-]
– Transylvanian perfume / Hearing screams (for the last time) / To unerstand / Makin' whips / I shot the marshall / Electricity through space / Hit the deck / Rumblin' underground / Desperate times / Gunning for the president / Avenues and alleyways / Unanswered prayers. *(cd-iss. 1989+=; CDJUST 7)* – OH NO IT'S GBH AGAIN / WOT A BARGAIN

Mar 88. (12"ep) *(12KORE 104) <8232>* **WOT A BARGIN** [ ] [ ]

—— **KAI LUIGI REDER** – drums; repl. WILF

Mar 89. (cd/c/lp) *(CD/T+/JUST 13)* **A FRIDGE TOO FAR** [ ] [-]
– Pass the axe / Captain Chaos / Go home / Checkin' out / See you bleed / When will it end? / A fridge too far / Fist of regret / Needle in the haystack / Twenty floors below / Nocturnal journal / Crossfire.

Rough Justice — Restless

Oct 90. (cd/c/lp) *(CD/T+/JUST 16) <72525-2/-4>* **FROM HERE TO REALITY** [ ] [ ]
– New decade / Trust me, I'm a doctor / B.M.T. / Mass production / The old school of self destruction / You don't do enough / From here to reality / Dirty too long / Destroy / Just in time for the epilogue / Don't leave your honey down the pits / Moonshine song. *(cd re-iss. Oct96 on 'Powerage'; PRAGE 007CD)*

—— **ANTHONY MORGAN** – bass; repl. ROSS

Oct 92. (c/lp) *(T+/JUST 21) <11015>* **CHURCH OF THE TRULY WARPED** [ ] [ ] 1993
– Pure greed / Not enough hate / Leather coffin / Candy man / Lords of discipline / Where the wild things are / Church of the truly warped / Back / I need energy / Evil ever / All for the cause. *(cd-iss. Oct96 on 'Powerage'; PRAGE 008CD)*

—— **JOSEPH MONTANARO** – drums; repl. KAI

We Bite — Triple X

Sep 96. (cd) *(WB 1151CD) <TX 51211>* **PUNK JUNKIES** [ ] [ ] Jun97
– Intro / Junkies / Impounded / Harmony / Tokyo after dark / Shakin' hands with the machine / Don't drag me down / Break the chains / Kangaroo court / Stormchaser / Hole / Damn good time / Cryin (on the hard shoulder) / Civilized / Lowering the standard / Enzo / Outro.

– compilations, etc. –

on 'Clay' unless mentioned otherwise

1982. (lp) *(CLAYLP 5)* **LEATHER, BRISTLES, NO SURVIVORS AND SICK BOYS** [ ] [-]
– Race against time / Knife edge / Lycanthropy / Necrophilia / State executioner / Dead on arrival / Generals / No survivors / Self destruct / Big women / Slit your own throat / Sick boy / Am I dead yet / Freak. *(re-iss. Jul90 cd/c/lp; CLAY CD/MC/LP 5) <US-iss.1990 on 'Combat'; 8218>*

Jul 86. (lp/cd) *(CLAY LP/CD 21) / Combat; <8216>* **THE CLAY YEARS 1981-84** [ ] [ ] 1990
(re-iss. cd Jul92; same)

Aug 89. (lp/cd) *(CLAY LP/CD 102)* **NO SURVIVORS** [ ] [-]

1989. (c) *Roadrunner; (RR 49643)* **CITY BABY ATTACKED BY RATS / LEATHER BRISTLES etc** [ ] [-]

1989. (cd) *Roadrunner; (RR 349678)* **ATTACK AND REVENGE** [ ] [-]

Apr 90. (lp/c/cd) *(<CLAY/+MC/CD 106>)* **DIPLOMATIC IMMUNITY** [ ] [ ]
– No survivors / Self destruct / Give me fire / Catch 23 / City baby attacked by rats / Time bomb / Maniac / I am the hunted / Sick boy / Boston babies / I feel alright / Slut / Diplomatic immunity / Pins and needles / Faster faster / City babies revenge / Necrophilia / Generals / Womb with a view / Christianised cannibals / Four men.

Jul 93. (d-cd) *(<CLAYDCD 112>)* **CHAGED G.B.H.: THE CLAY RECORDINGS** [ ] [ ]

Oct 93. (cd) *Dojo; (DOJOCD 112) / Creative Man; <5>* **LIVE IN JAPAN (live)** [ ] [ ] Oct94

May 95. (cd) *Clay; (<CLAYCD 119>)* **THE CLAY PUNK SINGLES COLLECTION** [ ] [ ]

Jun 96. (cd) *Cleopatra; <9744>* **GBH CELEBRITY LIVE STYLE (live)** [-] [ ]

Sep 96. (cd) *Anagram; (CDPUNK 82)* **LIVE IN LOS ANGELES (live)** [ ] [-]

Jun 99. (cd) *Cleopatra; (<CLP 5322>)* **THE PUNK ROCK HITS** [ ] [ ]

GEHENNAH

Formed: Sweden . . . 1992 by MR. VIOLENCE, STRINGBURNER, RONNIE REAPER and HELLCOP; their parents obviously prophecising their future work as purveyors of metal. A retro-fied NWOBHM combo with a penchant for everything black, these loud, brash and drunken black-metal punks were all the rage back in Scandinavia. After a couple of well-received demos and a debut set, 'HARDROCKER' (1995), the gruesome quartet inked a deal with 'Osmose' records (who else) and cracked open the skulls of many a young listener by way of two blistering long-players, 'KING OF THE SIDEWALK' (1996) and 'DECIBEL REBEL' (1998). • **Note:** not to be confused with the similarly monikered metal outfit, GEHENNA, who also released a number of albums in the 90's.

Album rating: HARDROCKER (*5) / KING OF THE SIDEWALK (*6) / DECIBEL REBEL (*7)

MR. VIOLENCE – vocals / **STRINGBURNER** – guitar / **RONNIE REAPER** – bass / **HELLCOP** – drums

1993. (cd-ep) **KILL** [-] [-] demo

1994. (cd-ep) **BRILLIANT OVERLORDS OF DESTRUCTION** [-] [-] demo

1995. (cd) **HARDROCKER** [-] [-]
– Hardrocker / Skeletons in leather / Say hello to Mr Fist / Brilliant loud overlords of destruction / Winter of war / Beezerk / I am the wolf / Bloodmetal / Crucifucked / Bombraid over paradise / The house / Gehennah / Piss off, I'm drinking / Psycho slut.

Osmose — Osmose

Nov 96. (cd) *(OPCD 046)* **KING OF THE SIDEWALK** [ ] [-]
– Rock'n'roll patrol / Hellstorm / Bitch with a bulletbelt / King of the sidewalk / (You're the) Devil in disguise / Bang your heads for Satan / Chickenrace / Tough guys don't look good / Saturday night blasphemer / Bulldozer / Demolition team. *<US-iss.Apr99; same as UK>*

Mar 98. (cd/lp) *(<OSCD/OSLP 065>)* **DECIBEL REBEL** [ ] [ ] Aug98
– Beat that poser down / Six pack queen / Hungover / Decibel rebel / Hellhole bar / Get out of my way / Under the table again / Street metal gangfighters / Rocking through the kill / 666, drunks and rock'n'roll / I fucked your mom / We love alcohol.

GEORDIE

Formed: Newcastle, England . . . 1971 by Geordie lads, BRIAN JOHNSON (vocals), VIC MALCOLM (guitarist and songwriter), TOM HILL (bass) and BRIAN GIBSON (drums). Capitalising on the success of similar good-time rockers, SLADE, MUNGO JERRY and STATUS QUO, GEORDIE hit the Top 40 in 1972 with their debut single, 'DON'T DO THAT'. Moving upstairs to 'E.M.I.', they scored a Top 10 hit with the follow-up, 'ALL BECAUSE

OF YOU', JOHNSON's sandpaper larynx their forte. Two more hits were to register in '73, GEORDIE stubbornly refusing to follow the glam-conscious fashion of their erstwhile peers. With further success eluding them, they gave up, although JOHNSON was to be given a second shot at flat-capped glory when Australian rockers, AC/DC needed a replacement for the deceased BON SCOTT. GEORDIE returned in 1982, a cover of IKE & TINA TURNER's 'NUTBUSH CITY LIMITS' not exactly engendering a revival in their flagging fortunes.

Album rating: HOPE YOU LIKE IT (*5) / DON'T BE FOOLED BY THE NAME (*4) / SAVE THE WORLD (*3) / ROCKIN' WITH THE BOYS compilation (*5)

BRIAN JOHNSON (b. 5 Oct'47, Dunstan, England) – vocals / **VIC MALCOLM** – guitar, vocals / **TOM HILL** – bass / **BRIAN GIBSON** – drums

Regal Zonophone / not iss.

Sep 72. (7") *(RZ 3067)* **DON'T DO THAT. / FRANCIS WAS A ROCKER** 32 -

E.M.I. / Capitol

Feb 73. (7") *(EMI 2008)* **ALL BECAUSE OF YOU. / AIN'T IT JUST LIKE A WOMAN** 6

Apr 73. (lp) *(EMC 3001)* **HOPE YOU LIKE IT** -
– Keep on rockin' / Give you till Monday / Hope you like it / Don't do that / All because of you / Old time rocker / Oh Lord / Natural born loser / Strange man / Ain't it just like a woman / Geordie's lost his liggie. *(cd-iss. 1990's on 'Repertoire'+=; (REP 4033)* – Can you do it / Electric lady / Geordie stomp / Black cat woman.

Jun 73. (7") *(EMI 2031)* **CAN YOU DO IT. / RED EYED LADY** 13

Aug 73. (7") *(EMI 2048)* **ELECTRIC LADY. / GEORDIE STOMP** 32 -

Nov 73. (7") *(EMI 2100)* **ROCK'N'ROLLER. / GEORDIE'S LOST HIS LIGGIE**

Apr 74. (lp) *(EMA 764)* **DON'T BE FOOLED BY THE NAME**
– Goin' down / House of the rising Sun / So what / Mercenary man / Ten feet tall / Got to know / Little boy / Look at me. *(cd-iss. 1990's on 'Repertoire'+=; (REP 4124)* – Treat her like a lady / Rockin' with the boys tonite / Francis was a rocker / Red eyed lady.

Aug 74. (7") *(EMI 2197)* **SHE'S A TEASER. / WE'RE ALL RIGHT NOW**

Oct 74. (7") *(EMI 2226)* **RIDE ON BABY. / GOT TO KNOW**

Jun 75. (7") *(EMI 2314)* **GOODBYE LOVE. / SHE'S A LADY**

1976. (lp) *(EMC 3134)* **SAVE THE WORLD** -
– Mama's going to take you home / She's a teaser / Goodbye love / I cried today / You do this to me / Save the world / Rocking horse / Fire queen / She's a lady / Light in my window / Ride on baby / We're all right now.

— Disbanded in 1976. Four years later, JOHNSON replaced the deceased BON SCOTT in Australian heavy rock band AC/DC. GEORDIE re-formed in the early 80's.

— **MALCOLM, HILL, GIBSON / + ROB TURNBULL** – vocals / **DAVID STEPHENSON** – guitar

Armageddon / not iss.

Apr 82. (7") *(AS 034)* **NUTBUSH CITY LIMITS. / NO SWEAT** -

Neat / not iss.

Sep 83. (lp) *(NEAT 1008)* **NO SWEAT** -
– No sweat / This time / Move away / Time to run / So you lose again / Rock and roll / Oh no! / Hungry / We make it rock.

— Split again after above, the group releasing one more self-titled album under the POWERHOUSE moniker.

compilations, others

Jan 81. (lp) *Red Bus; (RBMP 5001)* **FEATURING BRIAN JOHNSON** -
– All because of you / Keep on rocking / Natural born loser / Rocking with the boys / Going down / Black cat woman / Electric lady / Can you do it / Ain't it just like a woman / Hope you like it / Fire queen / Mercenary man / Treat her like a lady.

Feb 81. (7") *Red Bus; (RBUS 58)* **DON'T DO THAT. / KEEP ON ROCKING** -

Aug 92. (cd; GEORDIE featuring BRIAN JOHNSON) *Raven-Topic;* **ROCKIN' WITH THE BOYS** -

GEORGIA SATELLITES

Formed: Atlanta, Georgia, USA . . . 1979 as KEITH & THE SATELLITES by DAN BAIRD and RICK RICHARDS. During the early 80's, they included KEITH CHRISTOPHER (ex-BRAINS). After a well-received debut, 'KEEP THE FAITH', in 1985 on independent UK label, 'Making Waves', the band recruited drummer MAURO MAGELLAN and bassist RICK PRICE (both ex-BRAINS), eventually securing a deal with 'Elektra'. Boosted by the No.2 US success of the 'KEEP YOUR HANDS TO YOURSELF' single, their eponymous major label debut went Top 5 in early 1987. Basically, this band dealt in unreconstructed, Southern fried boogie, more ROLLING STONES than LYNYRD SKYNYRD, but commercial enough to hook pop fans. 'OPEN ALL NIGHT' (1988) was more of the same really, but despite a minor hit with 'HIPPY HIPPY SHAKE' (from the 'Cocktail' soundtrack), the album lingered in the lower reaches of the chart. After a final, more introspective effort, 'IN THE LAND OF SALVATION AND SIN' (1989, the band split with BAIRD going off to 'Def American' for a solo career. • **Songwriters:** All BAIRD compositions except; HIPPY HIPPY SHAKE (Swinging Blue Jeans) / GAMES PEOPLE PLAY (Joe South) / I'M WAITING FOR THE MAN (Velvet Underground) / EVERY PICTURE TELLS A STORY (Rod Stewart) / ALMOST SATURDAY NIGHT – ROCKIN' ALL OVER THE WORLD (John Fogerty).

Album rating: KEEP THE FAITH mini (*4) / GEORGIA SATELLITES (*7) / OPEN ALL NIGHT (*5) / IN THE LAND OF SALVATION AND SIN (*5) / LET IT ROCK (BEST OF GEORGIA SATELLITES) compilation (*6) / SHAKEN NOT STIRRED (*4)

DAN BAIRD (b.12 Dec'53, San Diego, Calif.) – vocals, guitar / **RICK RICHARDS** (b.30 Mar'54, Jasper, Georgia) – guitar, vocals / **RICK PRICE** (b.15 Aug'51) – bass (ex-BRAINS) / **MAURO MAGELLAN** – drums (ex-BRAINS)

Making Waves / not iss.

Mar 85. (m-lp/m-c) *(SPRAY/CSPRAY 301)* **KEEP THE FAITH** -
– Tell my fortune / Red light / Six years gone / Keep your hands to yourself / Crazy / The race is on. *(cd-iss. Jul87; CDSPRAY 301)*

Elektra / Elektra

Nov 86. (lp/c/cd) *(960496-1/-4/-2)* *<60496>* **GEORGIA SATELLITES** 52 5 Oct86
– Keep your hands to yourself / Railroad steel / Battleship chains / Red light / The myth of love / Can't stand the pain / Golden light / Over and over / Nights of mystery / Every picture tells a story. *(re-iss. Mar93 on 'Pickwick' cd/c; 7559 60496-2/-4)*

Jan 87. (7") *(EKR 50)* *<69502>* **KEEP YOUR HANDS TO YOURSELF. / CAN'T STAND THE PAIN** 69 2 Nov86
(12"+=) *(EKR 50T)* – Nights of mystery / I'm waiting for the man. *(re-iss. Aug87; same)*

Mar 87. (7") *<69497>* **BATTLESHIP CHAINS. / GOLDEN LIGHT** - 86

Apr 87. (7"/12") *(EKR 58/+T)* **BATTLESHIP CHAINS (remix). / HARD LUCK BOY** 44 -

Jun 88. (7") *<69393>* **OPEN ALL NIGHT. / DUNK 'N' DIME** -

Jun 88. (lp/c)(cd) *(EKT 47/+C)(960793-2)* *<60793>* **OPEN ALL NIGHT** 39 77
– Open all night / Sheila / Whole lotta shakin' / Cool inside / Don't pass me by / My baby / Mon cheri / Down and down / Dunk 'n' dine / Baby so fine / Hand to mouth.

Jan 89. (7") *(EKR 86)* *<69366>* **HIPPY HIPPY SHAKE (from film 'Cocktail'). / HAND TO MOUTH** 63 45 Oct88
(12"+=) *(EKR 86T)* – Powerful stuff.

May 89. (7") *(EKR 89)* *<69328>* **SHEILA. / HIPPY HIPPY SHAKE**
(12"+=) *(EKR 89T)* – Battleship chains (live) / Railroad steel (live).

Oct 89. (7") *<69267>* **ANOTHER CHANCE. / SADDLE UP** -

Oct 89. (7") *(EKR 102)* **ANOTHER CHANCE. / OPEN ALL NIGHT** -
(12"+=) *(EKR 102T)* – Saddle up / That woman.
(re-iss. Mar90; same)

Oct 89. (lp/c)(cd) *(EKT 62/+C)(960887-2)* *<60887>* **IN THE LAND OF SALVATION AND SIN**
– I dunno / Bottle o'tears / All over but the cryin' / Shake that thing / Six years gone / Games people play / Another chance / Bring down the hammer / Slaughterhouse / Stellazine blues / Days gone by / Sweet blue midnight / Crazy / Dan takes five.

— disbanded Feb'92, although **RICHARDS + PRICE** re-formed in 1993 (without solo bound DAN BAIRD) alongside **JOEY HUFFMAN** – keyboards / **BILLY PITTS** – drums

3 N.M. / 3 N.M.

Feb 97. (c-s/cd-s) *(3NMS 301-4/-2)* **GAMES PEOPLE PLAY /**

– compilations, etc. –

Jan 93. (cd/c) *WEA; <(7559 61336-2/-4)>* **LET IT ROCK (THE BEST OF THE GEORGIA SATELLITES)**

Jun 97. (cd) *C.M.C.; (10322)* **THE VERY BEST OF GEORGIA SATELLITES** -

DAN BAIRD

— with various session people incl. **TERRY ANDERSON** – drums

American / Atlantic

Nov 92. (cd/c/lp) *<(74321 28758-2-4/-1)>* **LOVE SONGS FOR THE HEARING IMPAIRED**
– The one I am / Julie and Lucky / I love you period / Look what you started / Seriously gone / Pick up the knife / Knocked up / Baby talk / Lost highway / Dixie beauxderaunt.

Feb 93. (7"/c-s) *(DEFA/MC 22)* *<18724>* **I LOVE YOU PERIOD. / LOST HIGHWAY** 26 Nov92
(cd-s+=) *(DEFCD 22)* – Rocket in my pocket.

May 93. (c-s) *<18526>* **LOOK WHAT YOU STARTED /** -

American / Warners

Jan 96. (cd) *(74321 29517-2)* *<43037>* **BUFFALO NICKEL**
– Younger face / Cumberland river / I want you bad / On my way / Lil' bit / Hell to pay / Woke up Jake / Birthday / Hush / Trivial as the truth / Hit me like a train / Frozen head state park.

GERMS

Formed: Los Angeles, California, USA . . . April '77 by DARBY CRASH, PAT SMEAR, LORNA DOOM and BELINDA CARLISLE. The latter soon departed before groundbreaking debut 45, 'FORMING' (she later helped to form The GO-GO'S). The GERMS signed to the (then) indie, 'Slash', finally issuing a debut album, 'GI', in '79, this highly influential (KURT COBAIN was a massive fan!) outfit doing more than their fair share to define the boundaries of American punk/hardcore. In keeping with their incendiary nature, the band burned out in early 1980, only to reform approximately a year later. This incarnation was even more short-lived, CRASH dying of a heroin overdose a week after their reunion on the 12th July '80, aged only 22. Pioneers of hardcore punk, The GERMS made way for The DEAD KENNEDYS, BLACK FLAG and a host of grunge devotees including NIRVANA, HOLE, etc. • **Covered:** ROUND AND ROUND (Chuck Berry) / DEATHFOLK covered AUTOMATIC (Go-Go's). • **Trivia:** They were given tribute from many of the aforementioned bands on 1996 album, 'GERMS (TRIBUTE) – A SMALL CIRCLE OF FRIENDS' on 'Grass Grow' label; (10042). In March '95, PAT SMEAR, now a member of DAVE GROHL's post-Nirvana outfit, FOO FIGHTERS, was part of HOLEZ (aka COURTNEY LOVE, PATTY & ERIC) on their 7" tribute to The GERMS, 'CIRCLE 1' (released by 'Dutch East India'; (9037-7); The B-side was by MONKEYWRENCH)

Album rating: GI (*8) / GERMICIDE: LIVE AT THE WHISKY live (*4) /

ROCK'N'RULE rare (*4) / THE COMPLETE ANTHOLOGY compilation (*7) / Pat RuthenSmear: RUTHENSMEAR (*4) / Deathfolk: DEATHFOLK (*6) / DEATHFOLK II (*3) / Pat Smear: SO YOU FELL IN LOVE WITH A MUSICIAN (*4)

DARBY CRASH (b. JAN PAUL BEAHM) – vocals / **PAT SMEAR** (b. GEORGE RUTHENBERG) – guitar / **LORNA DOOM** – bass / **D.J. BONEBRAKE** (b. DON BOLES) – drums; repl. BELINDA CARLISLE who later joined GO-GO'S and is currently top solo chanteuse

not iss. — What?

Nov 77. (7") *(WHAT 01)* **FORMING. / SEXBOY (live)** [-] [ ]

not iss. — Slash Scam

Nov 78. (7"m) *<101>* **LEXICON DEVIL. / CIRCLE ONE / NO GOD** [-] [ ]

—— **DON BOLLES** – drums (of 45 GRAVE) repl. BONEBRAKE who joined X

Nov 80. (lp) *<SR 103>* **GI** (rec.1979> [-] [ ]
<US re-iss. 1990's on 'Warners'; 23932>

—— split early in 1980, but featured on various artists lp 'THE DECLINE' for 'Slash'; <SR 105>. Had to split once more, when on 6th December '80, CRASH died of heroin overdose.

Sep 81. (12"ep) *<SREP 108>* **WHAT WE DO IS SECRET** [-] [ ]
– Round and round / Lexicon devil / Circle one / Caught in my eye / No god / The other newest one / My love.

—— PAT SMEAR later went solo, initially as PAT RUTHENSMEAR

– compilations, etc. –

May 83. (c) *R.O.I.R.; <A 108>* **GERMICIDE – LIVE AT THE WHISKY (live)** [-] [ ]
– Forming / Sex boy / Victim / Street dreams / Let's pretend / Get a grip / Suicide machine / Sugar sugar / Teenage clone (wild baby) / Grand old flag. *(cd-iss. Nov94; RE 108CD)*

1985. (lp) *Gasatanka;* **LET THE CIRCLE BE UNBROKEN** [-] [ ]

1988. (lp) *Ghost O' Darb;* **LION'S SHARE** (live first show) [-] [ ]

1986. (lp) *X.E.S.;* **ROCK AND RULE (live at the Whisky, December 1979)** [-] [ ]

Nov 92. (7") *Crash;* **MANIMAL. / DRAGON LADY / STRANGE NOTES** [-] [ ]

Apr 93. (7") *Rockville; (ROCK 6094) / Gasatanka;* **COMMUNIST EYES. / FORMING / WHAT WE DO IS SECRET** [ ] [ ] Nov92

Aug 93. (cd) *Slash; <45239-2>* **GERMS (M.I.A.) THE COMPLETE ANTHOLOGY** [-] [ ]
– Forming / Sexboy / Lexicon devil / Circle one / No God / What we do is secret / Communist eyes / Land of treason / Richie Dagger's crime / Strange notes / American leather / Lexicon devil / Manimal / Our way / We must bleed / Media blitz / Other newest one / Let's pretend / Dragon lady / Slave / Shut down (annihilation man) / Caught in my eye / Round and round / My tunnel / Throw it away / Not all right / No I hear the laughter / Going down / Lion's share / Forming 2.

Jan 94. (cd) *Cleopatra; <(CLEO 3731CD)>* **MEDIA BLITZ** [ ] [ ] Jun93
– Forming / Round 'n' round / Sex boy / Strange notes / Caught in my eye / Let's pretend / Lexicon devil / Manimal / Our way / Shut down / What we do is secret / Art / Communist eyes / Lion's share / Media blitz / What we do is secret 2 / Lion's share / Throw it away.

1990's. (cd-ep) *Munster; <MR 25>* **CAT'S CLAUSE** [-] [ ]

PAT RUTHENSMEAR

—— with **PAUL ROESSLER** – keyboards (of DC3)

S.S.T. — S.S.T.

Jan 88. (lp/c) *<(SST 154/+C)>* **RUTHENSMEAR** [ ] [ ]
– Sahara hotel / Golden boys / Odenora / Princes / Magic candle tragic canary / The area of the circle / Xmas song / I heart / A gentle axe. *<(re-iss. May93; same)*

DEATHFOLK

PAT SMEAR + GARY JACOBY (also of CELEBRITY SKINS)

not iss. — New Alliance

1990. (lp/c/cd) *<NAR 047/+C/CD>* **DEATHFOLK** [-] [ ]
(UK-iss.May93; same as US)

Apr 92. (lp/c/cd) *<NAR 076/+C/CD>* **DEATHFOLK II** [-] [ ]
– Freedom / Scary girl / Romeo Bob / Regina boxing party / Jojo luv / Azreal / Adream / Motherfucker / Medeley / Baby Hugh / Lulu bell / Automatic. *(UK-iss.May93; same as US)*

PAT SMEAR

—— with **WALTER SPENCER** – bass / **GARY JACOBY** – drums / **MICHELE GREGG** – voices

May 93. (cd/c) *<(SST 294 CD/C)>* **SO YOU FELL IN LOVE WITH A MUSICIAN** [ ] [ ] Nov92
– I'll find you / Lulu Belle / Creep street / Holy Bulsara / Ever alone with thee / All my cheating / Innocent X / Cold towne / Yummy yuck / Love your friends / Lazy.

—— he joined NIRVANA in '93 and helped form FOO FIGHTERS with DAVE GROHL

G-FORCE (see under ⇒ MOORE, Gary)

GIANT

Formed: Nashville, Tennessee, USA . . . 1988 by DANN HUFF, who brought in his younger brother DAVID (who had also been part of Christian rock act, WHITE HEART), plus ALAN PASQUA and MIKE BRIGNARDELLO. DANN and DAVID had cut their proverbial teeth as L.A. session players, the elder HUFF and ALAN PASQUA meeting while working with DAVID COVERDALE (i.e. WHITESNAKE) the previous year. Signed to 'A&M', they released their impressive debut album, 'LAST OF THE RUNAWAYS', which cracked the US Top 100 in 1989. The following year, they dented the US Top 20 with the single, 'I'LL SEE YOU IN MY DREAMS', although this failed to create the same stir in Britain. A change of record label (to 'Epic') proved to be a mistake, the group's second album, 'TIME TO BURN' failing commercially despite a consumate performance.

Album rating: LAST OF THE RUNAWAYS (*6) / TIME TO BURN (*5)

DANN HUFF – vocals, guitar / **ALAN PASQUA** – keyboards, vocals / **DAVID HUFF** – drums / **MIKE BRIGNARDELLO** – bass

A&M — A&M

Jan 90. (7") *<1467>* **INNOCENT DAYS. / THE BIG PITCH** [-] [ ]

Mar 90. (7") *(AM 546) <1454>* **I'M A BELIEVER. / THE BIG PITCH** [ ] [56] Sep89
(12"+=/cd-s+=) *(AM Y/CD 546)* – No way out.

Apr 90. (cd/c/lp) *<(CDA/AMC/AMA 5272)>* **LAST OF THE RUNAWAYS** [ ] [80] Oct89
– I'm a believer / Innocent days / I can't get close enough / I'll see you in my dreams / No way out / Shake me up / It takes two / Stranger to me / Hold back the night / Love welcome home / The big pitch.

May 90. (7") *(AM 564) <1495>* **I'LL SEE YOU IN MY DREAMS. / STRANGER TO ME** [ ] [20] Mar90
(12"+=/cd-s+=) *(AM Y/CD 564)* – Hold back the night.

Aug 90. (7") *(AM 571)* **IT TAKES TWO. / I'LL SEE YOU IN MY DREAMS** [ ] [ ]
(12"+=/cd-s+=) *(AM Y/CD 571)* – Innocent days / I'm a believer / It takes two (live) / I can't get close enough (live) / Shake me up (live).

—— **BLAIR MASTERS** – keyboards; repl. PASQUA

Epic — Epic

May 92. (c-s) *<74324>* **STAY / STAY (acoustic)** [-] [ ]

May 92. (7") *(658098-7)* **STAY. / GET USED TO IT** [ ] [-]
(12"pic-d+=/cd-s+=) *(658098-6/-2)* – Time to burn.

May 92. (cd/c/lp) *(469457-2/-4/-1) <48509>* **TIME TO BURN** [ ] [ ] Dec91
– Thunder and lightning / Chained / Lay it on the line / Stay / Lost in Paradise / Smoulder / Time to burn / I'll be there (when it's over) / Save me tonight / Where would I be without you / Now until forever / Get used to it.

—— split after above

GIFT (see under ⇒ POISON IDEA)

Paul GILBERT (see under ⇒ MR. BIG)

GILDED LIL

Formed: Edinburgh, Scotland . . . mid-90's by GERRY HILLMAN and KERRY McDONALD, along with MALCY DUFF (ex-MONGERS, + PIZZA BOY DELIVERY), ROSS ROBERTSON and MARK BAILLIE. If you can imagine POLLY HARVEY fronting the MAGIC BAND or JON SPENCER BLUES EXPLOSION backing JANIS JOPLIN, in fact a blitzkrieg onslaught of all four, you'd be getting some way towards this quintet's abrasive sound. Shockingly fresh-faced for such noisy youngsters, the GILDED LIL crew courted controversy from day one when they veered perilously close to the bone with their debut single, 'MOTHERFUCKER OF CALCUTTA'. Released on 'Bosque' in summer '97, the track preceded a follow-up EP entitled 'WANG', although the brilliantly titled 'LAST TANGO IN TOLLCROSS' appeared on 'Butcher's Wig'. Having trod the indie treadmill with a few Peel sessions, the group cast convention to the wind by performing in porn cinemas and young offenders institutes. Between 1998/99, GILDED LIL issued a one-off single for 'Guided Missile' as well as making a contribution to the label's 'Hits & Missiles' V/A collection via the track, 'LANDS RIGHT'. Back to 'Bosque' for the new millennium, the ear-crushing KERRY and her pals delivered their belated debut album, 'CORPUS DELICTI' (2000).

Album rating: CORPUS DELICTI (*6)

KERRY McDONALD – vocals / **MALCY DUFF** – guitar, vocals (ex-MONGERS) / **ROSS ROBERTSON** – slide, guitar / **GERRY HILLMAN** – bass / **MARK BAILLIE** – drums

Bosque — not iss.

Jun 97. (7") *(bosc 023)* **MOTHERFUCKER OF CALCUTTA. /** [ ] [-]

Mar 98. (7"ep) *(bosc 026)* **WANG EP** [ ] [-]

Butcher's Wig — not iss.

Aug 98. (7") *(SYRUP 005)* **LAST TANGO IN TOLLCROSS. /** [ ] [-]

Guided Missile — not iss.

Sep 98. (7") *(GUIDE 31)* **WHEN I WAS YOUNG. / ROUGHIE** [ ] [-]

Stupidcat — not iss.

Apr 00. (7") *(SCAT 05)* **DEPARTURE LOUNGE. / (other track by THE MALE NURSE)** [ ] [-]

Bosque — not iss.

Nov 00. (cd/lp) *(bosc 028 CD/LP)* **CORPUS DELICTI** [ ] [-]
– Departure lounge / Stunt cock / Teaparty / Doctor / Klang/BingBong / Bee / Lands right / Last tango in Tollcross / Sick men.

GILLAN

Formed: London, England . . . mid 70's by veteran rocker, IAN GILLAN (b. 19 Aug'45, Hounslow, Middlesex, England), who had just been sacked from DEEP PURPLE in June '73. Surrounding himself with seasoned hands, he cut the well-received 'CHILD IN TIME' (1976) album, before recording another couple of more experimental "rock" albums for 'Island'. After recruiting a completely new line-up, including guitarist BERNIE TORME, the singer almost hit the UK Top 10 with 'MR. UNIVERSE' (1979), a tougher

affair, trading under the trimmed down moniker of GILLAN. At the turn of the decade, as the 'New Wave Of British Heavy Metal' was at its peak, GILLAN scored two UK Top 5 albums in a row with 'GLORY ROAD' and 'FUTURE SHOCK'. By the release of 'MAGIC' (1982), however, the tonsil torturer was losing interest, joining BLACK SABBATH, then the revamped DEEP PURPLE (re-Mk.II) soon after. When this predictably fell apart once again, GILLAN reshaped his band for a 1990 comeback album, 'NAKED THUNDER'. 'TOOLBOX' was hot on its heels, an acclaimed hard-rock set that preceded a return to his old compadres, yes you guessed it, DEEP PURPLE.
• **Covered:** LUCILLE (Little Richard) / LIVING FOR THE CITY (Stevie Wonder) / SOUTH AFRICA (Bernie Marsden).

Album rating: CHILD IN TIME (*6) / CLEAR AIR TURBULENCE (*4) / SCARABUS (*4) / LIVE AT THE BUDOKAN (*4) / MR. UNIVERSE (*4) / GLORY ROAD (*7) / FUTURE SHOCK (*5) / DOUBLE TROUBLE (*5) / MAGIC (*5) / ACCIDENTALLY ON PURPOSE (*4) / TROUBLE – THE BEST OF GILLAN compilation (*6) / Ian Gillan: NAKED THUNDER (*6) / TOOLBOX (*5) / DREAMCATCHER (*4)

IAN GILLAN BAND

IAN GILLAN – vocals (ex-DEEP PURPLE, ex-EPISODE SIX) / **RAY FENWICK** – guitar (ex-SPENCER DAVIS GROUP, ex-AFTER TEA) / **MIKE MORAN** – keyboards / **JOHN GUSTAFSON** – bass (ex-BIG THREE, ex-EPISODE SIX, ex-QUATERMASS) / **MARK NAUSEEF** – drums (ex-ELF)

Polydor Oyster

Jul 76. (lp) *(2490 136)* <1602> **CHILD IN TIME** 55
– Lay me down / You make me feel so good / Shame / My baby loves me / Down the road / Child in time / Let it slide. *(cd-iss. Apr90 on 'Virgin'; CDVM 2606)*

— **COLIN TOWNS** – keyboards repl. MICKEY LEE SOULE who had briefly repl. MIKE TOWNS also contributed some songs.

Island Antilles

Apr 77. (lp) *(ILPS 9500)* **CLEAR AIR TURBULENCE** -
– Clean air turbulance / Five moons / Money lender / Over the hill / Goodhand Liza / Angel Manchenio. *(re-iss. Jun82 on 'Virgin' lp/c; VM/+C 4) (re-iss. Aug88 on 'Virgin'; OVED 76) (cd-iss. Jan90; CDVM 4) (cd re-iss. Jun98 on 'Eagle'; EAMCD 047)*

Oct 77. (lp) *(ILPS 9511)* <7066> **SCARABUS**
– Scarabus / Twin exhausted / Poor boy hero / Mercury high / Pre release / Slags to bitches / Apathy / Mad Elaine / Country lights / Fool's mate. *(re-iss. Jun82 on 'Virgin' lp/c; VM/+C 3) (reiss.Aug88 on 'Virgin'; OVED 77) (cd-iss. Jan90 +=; CDVM 4)* – My baby loves me. *(cd re-iss. Jun98 on 'Eagle'; EAMCD 048)*

Jan 78. (7") *(WIP 6423)* **MAD ELAINE. / MERCURY HIGH**
This band also recorded LIVE AT BUDOKAN VOL 1 & 2, only released in Japan. – Clear air turbulence / My baby loves me / Scarabus / Money lender / Twin exhausted / Over the hill / Child in time / Smoke on the water / Mercury high / Woman from Tokyo. *(UK-issue 1987 on 'Virgin'; VGD 3507) (cd-iss. Nov89; CDCM 3507)*

GILLAN

— he only retained TOWNS and brought in **STEVE BYRD** – guitar / **JOHN McCOY** – bass / **PETE BARNACLE** – drums. An album GILLAN was released in Japan (only May78). *(re-iss. cd Sep93 as 'GILLAN – THE JAPANESE ALBUM' on 'R.P.M.'; RPM 113)*

— (May79) **BERNIE TORME** – guitar (ex-solo artist) repl. BYRD / **MICK UNDERWOOD** – drums (ex-EPISODE SIX, ex-QUATERMASS, ex-STRAPPS, etc.) repl. BARNACLE

Acrobat Warners

Sep 79. (lp/c) *(ACRO 3)* <81254> **MR. UNIVERSE** 11
– Second sight / Secret of the dance / She tears me down / Roller / Mr. Universe / Vengeance / Puget sound / Dead of night / Message in a bottle / Fighting man. *(re-iss. Jan83 on 'Fame' lp/c; FA/TCFA 3507) (cd-iss. 1990 +=; CDVM 2589)* – Bite the bullet / Mr. Universe (version) / Smoke on the water / Lucille. *(cd re-iss. Jun99 on 'Caramba'; CRMCD 005) (cd re-iss. Sep99 on 'Repertoire'; RR 4790)*

Oct 79. (7") *(BAT 12)* **VENGEANCE. / SMOKE ON THE WATER**

Virgin Virgin-RSO

Jun 80. (7") *(VS 355)* **SLEEPING ON THE JOB. / HIGHER AND HIGHER** 55

Jul 80. (7"m) *(VS 362)* **NO EASY WAY. / HANDLES ON HER HIPS / I MIGHT AS WELL GO HOME**

Aug 80. (lp/c) *(V/TCV 2171)* <1001> **GLORY ROAD** 3
– Unchain your brain / Are you sure? / Time and again / No easy way / Sleeping on the job / On the rocks / If you believe me / Running, white face, city boy / Nervous / Your mother was right. *(free ltd-lp w/a)* **FOR GILLAN FANS ONLY** *(re-iss. Mar84 lp/c; OVED 49) (cd-iss. Nov89; CDVM 2171)* – Redwatch / Abbey of Thelema / Trying to get to you / Come tomorrow / Dragon's tongue / Post fade brain damage / Egg timer / Harry Lime theme. *(cd re-iss. Jun99 on 'Caramba'; CRMCD 006) (cd re-mast.Sep99 on 'Repertoire'; RR 4791)*

Sep 80. (7") *(VS 377)* **TROUBLE. / YOUR SISTER'S ON MY LIST** 14
(free live-7"w.a.) **MR. UNIVERSE. / VENGEANCE / SMOKE ON THE WATER**

Virgin Warners

Feb 81. (7") *(VSK 103)* **MUTUALLY ASSURED DESTRUCTION. / THE MAELSTROM** 32

Mar 81. (7") *(VS 406)* **NEW ORLEANS. / TAKE A HOLD OF YOURSELF** 2

Apr 81. (lp/c) *(V/TCV 2196)* <26331> **FUTURE SHOCK** 2
– Future shock / Nightride out of Phoenix / (The ballad of) Lucitania Express / No laughing in Heaven / Sacre bleu / New Orleans / Bite the bullet / If I sing softly / Don't want the truth / For your dreams. *(re-iss. Aug88 lp/c; OVED/+C 74) (cd-iss. 1990 +=; CDVM 2196)* – One for the road / Bad news / Take a hold of yourself / M.A.D. / The maelstrom / Trouble / Your sisters on my list / Handles on her hips / Higher and higher / I might as well go home (mystic). *(re-iss. May95 on 'Virgin-VIP' cd/c; CD/TC VIP 131) (cd re-iss. Jun99 on 'Caramba'; CRMCD 007) (cd re-mast.Sep99 on 'Repertoire'; RR 4793)*

Jun 81. (7"ep) *(VS 425)* **NO LAUGHING IN HEAVEN / ONE FOR THE ROAD. / LUCILLE / BAD NEWS** 31

— **JANICK GERS** – guitar (ex-WHITE SPIRIT) repl. TORME (later to DESPERADO)

Oct 81. (7") *(VS 441)* **NIGHTMARE. / BITE THE BULLET (live)** 36

Nov 81. (d-lp/d-c) *(VGD/TCVGD 3506)* <26330> **DOUBLE TROUBLE (live)** 12
– I'll rip your spine out / Restless / Men of war / Sunbeam / Nightmare / Hadely bop bop / Life goes on / Born to kill / No laughing in Heaven / No easy way / Trouble / Mutally assured destruction / If you believe me / New Orleans. *(cd-iss. Nov89; CDVM 3506) (cd re-iss. Jun99 on 'Caramba'; CRMCD 008) (cd re-mast.Sep99 on 'Repertoire'; RR 4792)*

Jan 82. (7"/7"pic-d) *(VS/+Y 465)* **RESTLESS. / ON THE ROCKS (live)** 25

Aug 82. (7") *(VS 519)* **LIVING FOR THE CITY. / BREAKING CHAINS** 50
(with free 7"pic-d) *(VSY 519)* – ('A'side) / PURPLE SKY

Sep 82. (lp/pic-lp/c) *(V/VP/TCV 2238)* <26332> **MAGIC** 17
– What's the matter / Bluesy blue sea / Caught in a trap / Long gone / Driving me wild / Demon driver / Living a lie / You're so right / Living for the city / Demon driver (reprise). *(re-iss. Aug88; OVED 75) (cd-iss. Nov89 +=; CDVM 2238)* – Breaking chains / Fiji / Purple sky / South Africa / John / South Africa (extended) / Helter skelter / Smokestack lightning. *(cd re-iss. Mar94;) (cd re-iss. Jun99 on 'Caramba'; CRMCD 009) (cd re-mast.Sep99 on 'Repertoire'; RR 4794)*

Oct 82. (7") *(VS 537)* **LONG GONE. / FIJI**

— IAN GILLAN, then joined BLACK SABBATH, before the reformation of DEEP PURPLE in Nov84. GILLAN left PURPLE again to team up with ROGER GLOVER.

GILLAN / GLOVER

10-Virgin not iss.

Jul 87. (7") *(TEN 193)* **DISLOCATED. / CHET** -
(12"+=) *(TENT 193)* – Purple people eater.

Virgin not iss.

Jan 88. (7"/12") *(VS/+T 1041)* **SHE TOOK MY BREATH AWAY. / CAYMAN ISLAND** -

Feb 88. (lp/c/cd) *(V/TCV/CDV 2498)* **ACCIDENTALLY ON PURPOSE** -
– Clouds and rain / Evil eye / She took my breath away / Dislocated / Via Miami / I can't dance to that / Can't believe you wanna leave / Lonely avenue / Telephone box / I thought no. *(cd+=)* – Cayman Island / Purple people eater / Chet. *(cd re-iss. Jun98 on 'Eagle'; EAMCD 049)*

IAN GILLAN

Jun 88. (7") *(VS 1088)* **SOUTH AFRICA. / JOHN (live)** -
(12"+=) *(VST 1088)* – ('A'extended).

— GILLAN left DEEP PURPLE in late 80's. He formed a new band with **STEVE MORRIS** – guitar / **CHRIS GLEN** – bass (ex-MICHAEL SCHENKER GROUP, ex-SAHB) / **TED McKENNA** – drums (ex-MICHAEL SCHENKER GROUP, ex-SAHB) / **TOMMY EYRE** – keyboards (ex-SAHB) / **MICK O'DONAGHUE** – rhythm guitar / **DAVE LLOYD** – vocals, percussion

East West Atco

Jul 90. (cd/c/lp) *(9031 71899-2/-4/-1)* **NAKED THUNDER**
– Gut reaction / Talking to you / No good luck / Nothing but the best / Loving on borrowed time / Sweet Lolita / Nothing to lose / Moonshine / Long and lonely ride / Love gun / No more can on the Brazos. *(cd re-iss. Jun98 on 'Eagle'; EAMCD 050)*

Aug 90. (7") *(YZ 513)* **NO GOOD LUCK. / LOVE GUN** -
(12"+=/cd-s+=) *(YZ 513/+TW/CD)* – Rock'n'roll girls.

— with **STEVE MORRIS** – guitar / **BRETT BLOOMFIELD** – bass (ex-STARSHIP) / **LEONARD HAZE** – drums (ex-Y&T)

Oct 91. (cd/c/lp) *(9031 75641-2/-4/-1)* **TOOLBOX**
– Hang me out to dry / Toolbox / Dirty dog / Candy horizon / Don't hold me back / Pictures of Hell / Dancing nylon shirt (part 1) / Bed of nails / Gassed up / Everything I need / Dancing nylon shirt (part 2). *(cd re-iss. Apr98 on 'Voiceprint'; GILVP 102CD) (cd re-iss. Jun98 on 'Eagle'; EAMCD 051)*

— GILLAN also re-joined DEEP PURPLE late '92 . . . + below

Caramba Forbidden

Nov 97. (cd) *(CRMCD 001)* <7237> **DREAMCATCHER** 1998
– Hard on you / You sold my love for a song / Sugar plum / A day late and a dollar short / Chandra's coriander / All in my mind / Prima donna / Sleepy warm / Country mile / That's why God is singing the blues / Gunga din / Any way you want me.

– compilations etc. –

Jun 86. (d-lp/c/cd) *10-Virgin; (DIXD/+C/CD 39)* **WHAT I DID ON MY VACATION** -
– On the rocks / Scarabus / Puget sound / No easy way / If I sing softly / I'll rip your spine out / New Orleans / Mutally assured destruction / You're so right / Long gone / If you believe in me / Bluesy blue sea / Lucille. *(d-lp+=)* – Mad Elaine / Time and again / Vengeance / Unchain your brain / No laughing in Heaven. *(cd re-iss. Jun99 on 'Caramba'; CRMCD 010) (cd re-iss. Sep99 on 'Repertoire'; RR 4796)*

Feb 90. (cd/c/lp; by GARTH ROCKETT & THE MOONSHINERS) *Rock Hard; (ROHA CD/MC/LP 3)* **GARTH ROCKETT & THE MOONSHINERS** -

Feb 90. (12"/cd-s) **I'LL RIP YOUR SPINE OUT / NO LAUGHING IN HEAVEN. / (Ian Gillan interview)** -

Dec 90. (cd/c/lp) *Raw Fruit; (FRS CD/MC/LP 002)* **LIVE AT READING (live)** -

May 91. (cd/c) *Virgin-VIP; (VVIP D/C 113)* **TROUBLE – (THE BEST OF GILLAN)** -
– Trouble / New Orleans / Fighting man / Living for the city / Helter skelter / Mr.Universe / Telephone box / Dislocated (GILLAN-GLOVER) / Sleeping on the job / MAD (Mutally Assured Destruction) / No laughing in Heaven / Nightmare / Restless / Purple sky / Born to kill (live) / Smoke on the water (live). *(re-iss. Dec93 cd/c; CD/TC VIP 108)*

Sep 91. (cd/c) *Music Club; (MCCD/MCTC 032)* **THE VERY BEST OF GILLAN** -

Apr 92. (cd) *R.P.M.; (RPM 104)* **CHERKAZOO AND OTHER STORIES** -

(re-iss. Jun98 on 'Eagle'; EAMCD 052) <US-iss.Jun99 on 'Spitfire'; 5031>

Aug 94. (cd; by IAN GILLAN & THE JAVELINS) *R.P.M.; (RPM 132)* **SOLE AGENCY & REPRESENTATION** [ ] [-]
Jul 95. (cd; Various Artists) *Connoisseur; (VSOPCD 214)* **ROCK PROFILE** [ ] [-]
Mar 97. (cd) *Angel Air; (SJPCD 007) / Resurgent; <4133>* **THE ROCKFIELD MIXES** [ ] [ ] May97
Jan 98. (cd) *R.P.M.; (RPM 185)* **THE BBC SESSIONS VOL.1 1979: DEAD OF NIGHT** [ ] [-]
Jan 98. (cd) *R.P.M.; (RPM 186)* **THE BBC SESSIONS VOL.2 1980: UNCHAIN YOUR BRAIN** [ ] [-]
Apr 98. (cd) *Angel Air; (SJPCD 004) / Resurgent; <4089>* **GILLAN TAPES VOL.1** [ ] [ ] May98
Apr 98. (cd) *Angel Air; (<SJPCD 017>)* **LIVE AT THE RAINBOW** [ ] [ ]
Jun 99. (cd) *Caramba; (CRMCD 004)* **LIVE AT THE BUDOKAN** [ ] [-]
(re-iss. Sep99 on 'Repertoire'; RR 4795)
Jun 99. (cd) *Angel Air; (<SJPCD 023>)* **GILLAN TAPES VOL.2** [ ] [ ] Aug99
Jul 99. (cd) *Purple; (PUR 306) / Cleopatra; <CL 314>* **THE JAPANESE ALBUM** [ ] [ ] 1994
Sep 99. (cd) *Delta; (47006)* **RESTLESS** [ ] [-]
Dec 99. (d-cd) *Angel Air; (<SJPCD 055>)* **LIVE AT THE BBC 1979-1980** [ ] [ ]
Apr 00. (cd; as IAN GILLAN & THE JAVELINS) *Purple; (PUR 311)* **RAVING WITH IAN GILLAN & THE JAVELINS** [ ] [-]
Jul 00. (cd) *Angel Air; (<SJPCD 051>)* **GILLAN TAPES VOL.3** [ ] [ ]
Jul 00. (cd) *Connoisseur; (VSOPCD 307)* **THE GILLAN FAMILY ALBUM** [ ] [-]
Sep 00. (cd) *Purple; (PUR 324)* **MOONSHINERS LIVE** [ ] [-]

Greg GINN / GONE (see under ⇒ BLACK FLAG)

GIRL

Formed: London, England . . . 1979 by PHILIP LEWIS, PHIL COLLEN, DAVE GAYNOR, plus brothers GERRY and SIMON LAFFY. This influential proto-glam/sleaze act stood in stark contrast to the bullet belts and leather brigade which populated the NWOBHM, GIRL's mascara'd image fairly unique for its day. Securing a deal with 'Jet' records (home of ELO), the group debuted with 'SHEER GREED' in 1980, this album nearly cracking the UK Top 30. A few years went by before their next long-player, 'WASTED YOUTH', a sitting-duck for the critics with its third-rate glam-metal posturing. After an extensive tour of the Far East, the band fell apart with COLLEN joining DEF LEPPARD and LEWIS biding his time before relocating to America and experiencing another period of also-ran success with L.A. GUNS.

Album rating: SHEER GREED (*6) / WASTED YOUTH (*4)

PHILIP LEWIS – vocals / **PHIL COLLEN** (b. 8 Dec'57) – guitar / **GERRY LAFFY** – guitar / **SIMON LAFFY** – bass / **DAVE GAYNOR** – drums

Jet Jet

Oct 79. (7"clear) *(JET 159)* **MY NUMBER. / MY NUMBER (version)** [ ] [-]
Jan 80. (7") *(JET 169)* **DO YOU LOVE ME? / STRAWBERRIES** [ ] [ ]
Jan 80. (lp/c) *(JET LP/CA 224) <36490>* **SHEER GREED** [33] [ ]
– Hollywood tease / The things you say / Lovely Lorraine / Strawberries / Little Miss Ann / Doctor doctor / Do you love me / Take me dancing / What's up / Passing clouds / My number / Heartbreak America. *(<cd-iss. Oct94 & Feb98; JETCD 1009>) (cd re-iss. Jun99 on 'Receiver'; RRCD 269)*
Apr 80. (7"m) *(JET 176)* **HOLLYWOOD TEASE (remix). / YOU REALLY GOT ME / MY NUMBER** [50] [ ]
Aug 80. (7"white/10"white) *(JET/+10 191)* **LOVE IS A GAME. / LITTLE MISS ANN** [ ] [ ]

—— **PETE BARNACLE** – drums (ex-GILLAN, ex-BROKEN HOME) repl. GAYNOR

Sep 81. (7"/7"pic-d) *(JET/+P 7014)* **THRU THE TWILIGHT. / McKITTY'S BACK** [ ] [-]
Jan 82. (7") *(JET 7019)* **OLD DOGS. / PASSING CLOUDS** [ ] [-]
Jan 82. (lp/c) *(JET LP/CA 238)* **WASTED YOUTH** [92] [-]
– Thru the twilite / Old dogs / Ice in the blood / Wasted youth / Standard romance / Nice 'n' nasty / McKitty's back / 19 / Overnight angels / Sweet kids. *(<cd-iss. Oct94 & Feb98; JETCD 1010>) (cd re-iss. Jun99 on 'Receiver'; RRCD 268)*

—— folded when COLLEN joined DEF LEPPARD. LEWIS joined The LONDON COWBOYS, then AIRRACE and later fronted American band, L.A. GUNS. In 1992, GERRY LAFFY released his 2nd solo album, 'SUBLIME . . . TO THE RIDICULOUS' (COLLEN, LEWIS + his brother SIMON guested on it).

GIRLS AGAINST BOYS

Formed: Washington DC, USA . . . 1988 out of LUNCHMEAT, then SOULSIDE (2/3 albums for 'Dischord') by SCOTT McCLOUD, ALEXIS FLEISIG and JOHNNY TEMPLE. ELI JANNEY, who had been the latter act's soundman joined as the band evolved into GIRLS AGAINST BOYS (drummer BRENDAN CANTY was also part of the part-time band before he joined FUGAZI, while AMY PICKERING was also involved). Their brand of hardcore industrial rock was first sampled on the 'Adult Swim' debut, 'NINETIES Vs. EIGHTIES' (1990), although it was their second set a few years later, 'TROPIC OF SCORPIO', that tested the waters. SCOTT subsequently moved to New York to try out film school, the others joining as they signed with 'Touch & Go'. Three albums of considerable European success were delivered during the mid 90's, 'VENUS LUXURE NO 1 BABY' (1993), 'CRUISE YOURSELF' (1994) and 'HOUSE OF GVSB' (1996), before their bass-heavy gutter sound was wanted by major 'Geffen'. In 1998, the 'BOYS were on the threshold of mini-stardom with their sixth set, 'FREAK*ON*ICA', an album full of sexual sleaze and of course, noise.
• **Covered:** SHE'S LOST CONTROL (Joy Division).

Album rating: NINETIES VS. EIGHTIES mini (*5) / TROPIC OF SCORPIO (*6) / VENUS LUXURE NO.1 BABY (*7) / CRUISE YOURSELF (*6) / HOUSE OF GVSB (*7) / FREAK*ON*ICA (*6) / Soulside: SOON COME HAPPY compilation (*6)

SOULSIDE

SCOTT McCLOUD (b.1968) – vocals, guitar / **JOHNNY TEMPLE** (b.1968) – bass / **ALEXIS FLEISIG** (b.1967) – drums

Dischord Dischord

Aug 88. (lp) *<(DISCHORD 29)>* **TRIGGER** [ ] [ ] Dec87
Jun 89. (7") *<(DISCHORD 34)>* **BASS. / 103** [ ] [ ]
Jan 90. (m-lp) *<(DISCHORD 38)>* **HOT BODI-GRAM** [ ] [ ]
Feb 91. (cd) *<(DISCHORD 51)>* **SOON COME HAPPY** (compilation of all work) [ ] [ ]
– Baby / Trigger / Name is mind / Problems faced with traveling / War / K.T.T.K. / Pocket hurts / Forgiveness / Bass / 103 / The other side / God city / What / Punch the geek / Clifton wall / New slow fucky / Pembroke / Hate music / New fast fucky / Kill / Bad show / Love supreme / Crazy.

—— had already evolved into . . .

GIRLS AGAINST BOYS

McCLOUD, TEMPLE, FLEISIG + ELI JANNEY (b.1967) – sampler bass (keyboards) / plus **AMY PICKERING** (angel vocals) + **BRENDAN CANTY** (drums, organ) also on debut, CANTY joined FUGAZI

Adult Swim Adult Swim

Nov 90. (m-cd) *<AS 3CD>* **NINETIES vs. EIGHTIES** [-] [ ]
– Stay in the car / Jamie / Kitty-yo / Move / Angels / Skind.
Jun 92. (cd/c/lp) *<(AS 4 CD/C/V)>* **TROPIC OF SCORPIO** [ ] [ ]
– My night of pleasure (with the mudjacking . . .) / Wow wow wow / Matching wits with flaming Frank / Can't do anything but I love you, babe / Wasting away / Plush / Everything I do seems to cost me $20 / Taste all the fruit / Little buccaneer / Everywhere I go I seem to spend $20.

Touch & Go Touch & Go

May 93. (7") *<(TG 115)>* **BULLETPROOF CUPID. /** [ ] [ ]
Jun 93. (lp/c/cd) *<(TG 117/+C/CD)>* **VENUS LUXURE NO.1 BABY** [ ] [ ]
– In like Flynn / Go be delighted / Rockets are red / Satin down / Let me come back / Learned it / et down / Bullet proof Cupid / Seven seas / Billy's one stop / Bug house.
May 94. (7") *<(TG 129)>* **SEXY SAM. / I'M FROM FRANCE** [ ] [ ]
(cd-s+=) *<(TG 129CD)>* – Stay in the car / My night of pleasure / Rockets are red.
Sep 94. (7") *<(TG 137)>* **I DON'T GOT A PLACE. / MAN RAY OF LOVE** [ ] [ ]
Oct 94. (lp/c/cd) *<(TG 134/+C/CD)>* **CRUISE YOURSELF** [ ] [ ]
– Tucked-in / Cruise your new baby fly self / Kill the sexplayer / I don't got a place / Psychic know-how / Explicitly yours / From now on / Raindrop / The royal lowdown / My martini / Glazed eye.
Feb 95. (cd-ep) *<(TG 140CD)>* **KILL THE SEXPLAYER / SEXY SAM (live) / LEARNED IT (live) / LET ME COME BACK (live)** [ ] [ ]
Sep 95. (7"white/cd-s) *(HUT 61/+CD)* **SHE'S LOST CONTROL. / Miranda: LOVE WILL TEAR US APART** [ ] [ ]
(above issued on 'Hut')
Feb 96. (7"etched) *<(TG 160)>* **SUPER-FIRE** [ ] [ ]
(10"+=) *<(TG 160-10)>* – Viva Roma Star / Cashmachine.
(cd-s+=) *<(TG 160CD)>* – If glamour is dead / Cashmachine.
Mar 96. (lp/c/cd) *<(TG 149/+C/CD)>* **HOUSE OF GVSB** [ ] [ ]
– Super-fire / Click click / Crash 17 (X-rated car) / Disco six six six / Life in pink / The kinda mzk you like / Vera Cruz / Another drone in my head / Cashmachine / Wilmington / Zodiac love team. *(re-iss. Jun98; same)*
Nov 96. (cd-ep) *<(TG 166CD)>* **DISCO SIX SIX SIX / DISTRACTED (RVS7) / DO IT LIKE DIAMONDS / BLACK LEATHER / KEEP YER PANTS ON** [ ] [ ]

Radiopaque Radiopaque

Mar 97. (cd; shared with GUIDED BY VOICES) *<(RR 13CD)>* **8 ROUNDS** [ ] [ ] Jul97
– Learned it / Vera Cruz / Disco six six six / Kill the sexplayer / (others by GUIDED BY VOICES).

Geffen Geffen

May 98. (cd/d-lp) *<(GED/GEF 25156)>* **FREAK*ON*ICA** [ ] [ ]
– Park avenue / Pleasurized / Psycho-future / Black hole / Roxy / One firecracker / Speedway / Exorcisto / Vogue thing / Push the fader / Exile / Cowboy's orbit.
Jun 98. (7"/cd-s) *(GFS/+TD 22335)* **PARK AVENUE. / AMERICAN WHITE DWARF (Miami Bassomatic remix) / EPR** [ ] [ ]
Dec 98. (7") *(AKR 07)* **ROXY (WHATEVER). /** [ ] [-]
(above issued on 'Akashic')

GIRLSCHOOL

Formed: South London, England . . . March '78 by ex-PAINTED LADY members KIM McAULIFFE and ENID WILLIAMS. With the addition of fellow rock chicks, KELLY JOHNSON and DENISE DUFORT, this all-female gang set about taking the male-dominated bastion of heavy metal by the balls and squeezing till it hurt. After a debut indie 45, 'TAKE IT ALL AWAY', for 'City', they moved to 'Bronze' in late '79, subsequently snapped up by MOTORHEAD manager, Doug Smith. Later that year, they clawed their way into the UK Top 30 album charts with debut set, 'DEMOLITION', a punchy hard-rock/metal affair influenced by glam and RUNAWAYS-esque punk. The record even spawned a Top 50 hit single in their high octane cover of the old Gun/Adrian Gurvitz track, 'RACE WITH THE DEVIL'. This minor success set the scene for their hugely successful collaboration with mates MOTORHEAD on Top 5 EP, 'ST. VALENTINE'S DAY MASSACRE'. Credited to HEADGIRL, the record's A-side was a tongue-in-cheek cover of

Johnny Kidd's 'PLEASE DON'T TOUCH', while the rabble rousing continued on the flip with run throughs of established GIRLSCHOOL/MOTORHEAD favourites, 'EMERGENCY' and 'BOMBER'. On the back of this exposure, the group scored a Top 5 placing with the 'HIT AND RUN' album, although this wasn't enough to hold a frustrated WILLIAMS. The bassist was subsequently replaced with GILL WESTON for the 'SCREAMING BLUE MURDER' (1982) set, their last major chart success. As the NWOBHM scene began to dissipate, GIRLSCHOOL opted for a more accessible, hook-laden approach on the NODDY HOLDER-produced 'PLAY DIRTY' (1983), although the album duly failed to break the Top 40. JOHNSON departed soon after for an unsuccessful solo career, the group bringing in Antipodean guitarist CHRIS BONACCI and providing a focal point with the addition of a frontwoman, JACQUI BODIMEAD. She lasted only one album, the US-only 'RUNNING WILD' (1985), 'Mercury' releasing the record in the States as the girls struggled to find a UK home. 'G.W.R.' finally picked them up, trying in vain for another big-name collaborative chart strike, this time with GARY GLITTER on a version of his platform-shaking classic, 'I'M THE LEADER OF THE GANG (I AM)'. Following a further couple of unremarkable albums, 'NIGHTMARE AT MAPLE CROSS' (1986) and 'TAKE A BITE' (1988), the group called it a day in the late 80's. A few years on the girls (a line-up of McAULIFFE, BONACCI, DUFORT and JACKIE CARRERA) were back in class for an eponymous set on the 'Communique' label. • **Songwriters:** McAULIFFE and JOHNSON penned most, and used covers; 20th CENTURY BOY (T.Rex) / TUSH (ZZ Top) / FOX ON THE RUN (Sweet) / C'MON LET'S GO (McCoys) / LIVE WITH ME + PLAY WITH FIRE (Rolling Stones) / TIGER FEET (Mud) / etc. • **Trivia:** DENISE was the sister of DAVE DUFORT; drummer of ANGELWITCH.

Album rating: DEMOLITION (*6) / HIT AND RUN (*5) / SCREAMING BLUE MURDER (*5) / PLAY DIRTY (*4) / RUNNING WILD (*4) / NIGHTMARE AT MAPLE CROSS (*4) / TAKE A BITE (*4) / GIRLSCHOOL (*4) / LIVE (*4) / THE COLLECTION compilation (*6)

KIM McAULIFFE – vocals, guitar / **KELLY JOHNSON** – lead guitar, vocals / **ENID WILLIAMS** – bass, vocals / **DENISE DUFORT** – drums

City | not iss.

Nov 79. (7",7"red) *(NIK 6)* **TAKE IT ALL AWAY. / IT COULD BE BETTER** | | -

Bronze | Stiff

Jan 80. (7") *(BRO 89)* **EMERGENCY. / FURNITURE FIRE** | | -

May 80. (7") *(BRO 95)* **NOTHING TO LOSE. / BABY DOLL** | | -

Jun 80. (lp) *(BRONX 525)* **DEMOLITION** | 28 | -
– Demolition boys / Not for sale / Race with the Devil / Take it all away / Nothing to lose / Breakdown / Midnight ride / Emergency / Baby doll / Deadline.

Jul 80. (7") *(BRO 100)* **RACE WITH THE DEVIL. / TAKE IT ALL AWAY** | 49 | -

Nov 80. (7") *(BRO 110)* **YEAH RIGHT. / THE HUNTER** | | -
(below EP with labelmates MOTORHEAD)

Feb 81. (7"ep/10"ep; as HEADGIRL) *(BRO/+X 116)* **ST. VALENTINE'S DAY MASSACRE** | 5 | -
– Please don't touch / Emergency / Bomber.

Apr 81. (7") *(BRO 118)* **HIT AND RUN. / TONIGHT** | 32 | -
(10"+=) *(BROX 118)* – Tush.

Apr 81. (red-lp) *(BRON 534)* *<18>* **HIT AND RUN** | 5 | Apr82
– C'mon let's go / The hunter / (I'm your) Victim / Kick it down / Following the crowd / Tush / Hit and run / Watch your step / Back to start / Yeah right / Future flash.

Jul 81. (7") *(BRO 126)* **C'MON LET'S GO. / TONIGHT (live)** | 42 | -
(10"+=) *(BROX 126)* – Demolition (live).

—— **GIL WESTON** – bass, vocals (ex-KILLJOYS) repl. ENID who joined FRAMED

Mar 82. (7"red-ep) *(BRO 144)* **THE WILDLIFE EP** | 58 | -
– Don't call it love / Wildlife / Don't stop.

Jun 82. (lp) *(BRON 541)* **SCREAMING BLUE MURDER** | 27 | -
– Screaming blue murder / Live with me / Take it from me / Wildlife / It turns your head around / Don't call it love / Hell razor / When your blood runs cold / You got me / Flesh and blood.

Aug 83. (7") *(BRO 169)* **1-2-3-4 ROCK AND ROLL. / TUSH (new version)** | | -
(ext.12"+=) *(BROX 169)* – Don't call it love (new version) / Emergency.

Oct 83. (lp) *(BRON 548)* **PLAY DIRTY** | 66 | -
– Going under / High and dry / Play dirty / 20th century boy / Breaking all the rules / Burning in the heat / Surrender / Rock me shock me / Running for cover / Breakout (knob in the media).

Oct 83. (7") *(BRO 171)* **20th CENTURY BOY. / BREAKING ALL THE RULES** | | -
(12"+=) *(BROX 171)* – Like it like that.

Jan 84. (7"/12") *(BRO/+X 176)* **BURNING IN THE NIGHT. / SURRENDER** | | -

—— added **JACKIE BONIMEAD** – vocals, guitar (ex-SHE) / **CHRIS BONACCI** – guitar (ex-SHE) repl. KELLY

not iss. | Mercury

1985. (lp) *<824611-1>* **RUNNING WILD** | - |
– Let me go / Running wild / Do you love me? / Something for nothing / Are you ready? / Nowhere to run / I want you back / Nasty nasty / Love is a lie / Can't you see.

—— trimmed when BODIMEAD departed

G.W.R. | Enigma

May 86. (7"; with GARY GLITTER) *(GWR 1)* **I'M THE LEADER OF THE GANG (I AM). / NEVER TOO LATE** | | -
(12"+=) *(GWT 1)* – ('A'extended).

Jul 86. (lp/c) *(GW LP/TC 2)* **NIGHTMARE AT MAPLE CROSS** | | -
– All day all nite / Play with fire / Danger sign / Never too late / Tiger feet / Back for more / Let's go crazy / You got me (under your skin) / Let's break out / Turn it up.

Oct 88. (lp/c/cd) *(GW LP/TC/CD 21)* *<75406>* **TAKE A BITE** | |
– Action / Fox on the run / Girls on top / Tear it up / Love at first bite / Head over heels / Up all night / This time / Don't walk away / Too hot to handle. *(re-iss. 1989 on 'Roadrunner'; RR 9513-2)*

—— re-formed 1992 with **KIM, CRIS, DENISE / + JACKIE CARRERA** – bass

Communique | Communique

Nov 92. (cd) *(CMGCD 006)* **GIRLSCHOOL** | | -
– My ambition / One more / Can't say more / Wild at heart / You can't do that / We came / Can't keep a good girl down / Sitting pretty / On my way / Take me I'm yours.

Nov 95. (cd) *(<CMGCD 013>)* **LIVE (live)** | | Jun96
– Screaming blue murder / Hit and run / We came / Action / Future flash / On my way / Knife / Not for sale / Little green men / Kick it down / Demolition boys / C'mon let's go / Emergency / Take it all the way.

—— GIRLSCHOOL disbanded (from the studio at least)

– compilations, others, etc. –

Apr 86. (lp/c) *Raw Power; (RAW LP/TC 013)* **RACE WITH THE DEVIL** | | -
(<cd-iss. Apr98 on 'Receiver'; RRCD 254>)

Sep 89. (m-lp) *Razor; (METALPM 127)* **CHEERS YOU LOT** | | -
(cd-iss. Jul91 on 'Metal Masters'; METALMCD 127)

Jul 91. (cd) *Dojo Lama; (LOMACD 1)* **DEMOLITION / HIT AND RUN** | | -

Dec 91. (cd) *Castle; (CCSCD 314)* **THE COLLECTION** | | -
– 1-2-3-4 rock'n'roll / Furniture fire / Take it all away / Kick it down / Midnight ride / Race with the Devil / Play dirty / Yeah right / Emergency / Breakout / Victim / Flesh and blood / Tush / Don't stop / Future flash / Rock me shock me / Screaming blue murder / Wild life / Bomber / Nothing to lose / Live with me / Like it like that / Tonight / Take it from me.

Jan 92. (cd) *Dojo Lama; (LOMACD 4)* **SCREAMING BLUE MURDER / PLAY DIRTY** | | -

Feb 94. (cd) *Dojo Lama; (LOMACD 8)* **NIGHTMARE AT MAPLE CROSS / TAKE A BITE** | | -

Feb 94. (cd) *Dojo; (DOJOCD 103)* **THE BEST OF GIRLSCHOOL** | | -

Apr 94. (cd) *Sequel; (NEMCD 642)* **FROM THE VAULTS** | | -

Jul 94. (cd/c) *Success;* **C'MON LET'S GO** | | -

Jul 97. (cd) *King Biscuit; (<88032-2>)* **IN CONCERT 1984 (live)** | | -

Nov 99. (cd) *Delta; (47005)* **CAN'T KEEP A GOOD GIRL DOWN** | | -

Sep 00. (d-cd) *Essential; (<CMDDD 014>)* **THE COLLECTION** | |

GIUFFRIA

Formed: California, USA . . . 1981 by former ANGEL keyboard star, GREG GIUFFRIA. He gathered together CRAIG GOLDY, CHUCK WRIGHT, ALAN KRIGGER and vocalist DAVID GLEN EISLEY, who augmented him on the eponymous GIUFFRIA debut in 1984. The group's luxurious, expansive sound was lapped up by AOR fans, GIUFFRIA's keyboard swathes cutting their way effortlessly through the lacklustre competition. Despite the record's critical and commercial (US) success, GOLDY and WRIGHT both departed soon after, their replacements being LANNY CORDOLA and DAVID SIKES respectively. By the time a follow-up, 'SILK AND STEEL', reached the shelves in summer '86, the early momentum had been lost and the group were subsequently dropped by their label. Undaunted, the same line-up (with new drummer, ex-ALICE COOPER man, KEN MARY) resurfaced as HOUSE OF LORDS on GENE SIMMONS' new 'R.C.A.'-backed label. Frontman JAMES CHRISTIAN was soon installed in place of EISLEY and the new-look band scored immediate success with the eponymous 'HOUSE OF LORDS' in 1988. Epic, keyboard-dominated pomp-rock, the album was well received in both the States and Europe, although the group were reluctant to take their arena-rock into the actual arena. Despite this lack of tour promotion, the group enjoyed further critical and commercial success with 'SAHARA' (1990), connoisseurs of their lush, melodic sound ensuring healthy sales. Again the band declined to tour, surprisingly splitting shortly after.

Album rating: GIUFFRIA (*6) / SILK AND STEEL (*4) / House Of Lords: HOUSE OF LORDS (*6) / SAHARA (*6) / DEMONS DOWN (*5)

GREG GIUFFRIA – keyboards (ex-ANGEL) **DAVID GLEN EISLEY** – vocals / **CRAIG GOLDY** – guitar / **CHUCK WRIGHT** – bass / **ALAN KRIGGER** – drums

M.C.A. | M.C.A.

Feb 85. (lp/c) *(MCF/+C 3244)* *<5524>* **GIUFFRIA** | | 26 Nov84
– Do me right / Call to the heart / Don't tear me down / Dance / Lonely in love / Trouble again / Turn me on / Line of fire / The awakening / Out of the blue. *(re-iss. Mar87 lp/c; MCL/+C 1844) (cd-iss. Jun89; DMCL 1844) (cd re-iss. Sep99 on 'Axe Killer'; AXE 305217CD)*

Mar 85. (7") *(MCA 935)* *<52497>* **CALL TO THE HEART. / OUT OF THE BLUE (TOO FAR GONE)** | | 15 Oct84
(12"+=/d7"+=) *(MCA T/S 935)* –

Mar 85. (7") *<52558>* **LONELY IN LOVE. / DO ME RIGHT** | - | 57

—— **LANNY CORDOLA** – guitar, vocals; repl. GOLDY (later to DIO)

—— **DAVID SIKES** – bass, vocals; repl. WRIGHT (to QUIET RIOT; briefly)

Apr 86. (7") *<52794>* **I MUST BE DREAMING. / TELL IT LIKE IT IS** | - | 52

Aug 86. (lp/c) *<(MCA/+C 5742)>* **SILK + STEEL** | | 60 May86
– No escape / Love you forever / I must be dreaming / Girl / Change of heart / Radio / Heartache / Lethal lover / Tell it like it is / Dirty secrets. *(cd-iss. 1988; MCAD 5742)*

Aug 86. (7") *<52882>* **HEARTACHE. / LOVE YOU FOREVER** | - |

—— folded although **GIUFFRIA, CORDOLA, EISLEY, WRIGHT / + KEN MARY** – drums (ex-ALICE COOPER); reformed although they changed name to . . .

HOUSE OF LORDS

— **JAMES CHRISTIAN** – vocals (ex-CANATA) repl. EISLEY

R.C.A. | RCA-Simmons

Nov 88. (lp/c/cd) *(PL/PK/PD 88530)* <8530> **HOUSE OF LORDS** [ ] [78]
– Pleasure palace / I wanna be loved / Edge of your life / Lookin' for strange / Love don't lie / Slip of the tongue / Hearts of the world / Under blue skies / Call my name / Jealous heart. *(cd re-iss. Jul00 on 'Axe Killer'; AXE 306077CD)*

Mar 89. (7") *(PB 49485)* <8805> **I WANNA BE LOVED. / CALL MY NAME** [ ] [58] Dec88
(12"+=) *(PT 49485)* – Slip of the tongue.

May 89. (cd-s) <8900> **LOVE DON'T LIE (remix) / LOOKING FOR STRANGE / HEARTS OF THE WORLD** [-] [ ]

— **MICHAEL GUY** – guitar (ex-FIRE) repl. CORDOLA (to Christian rock bands)

Sep 90. (c-ep,cd-ep) <2658> **HOUSE OF LORDS EP** [-] [ ]

Oct 90. (cd/c/lp) *(PD/PK/PL 82170)* <2170> **SAHARA** [ ] [ ]
– Shoot / Chains of love / Can't find my way home / Heart on the line / Laydown staydown / Sahara / It ain't love / Remember my name / American Babylon / Kiss of fire.

Dec 90. (c-ep,cd-ep) <2736> **REMEMBER MY NAME /** [-] [72]

not iss. | Victory

Jun 92. (cd/c) <383-420002-2/-4> **DEMONS DOWN** [-] [ ]
– O father / Demons down / What's forever for / Talkin' 'bout love / Spirit of love / Down, down, down / Metallic blue / Inside you / Johnny's got a mind of his own / Can't fight love.

Sep 92. (cd-s) <483002> **WHAT'S FOREVER FOR** [-] [ ]

— **DAVID GLEN EISLEY** – vocals; repl. CHRISTIAN who went solo with 1995 set, 'Rude Awakening'

GLASSJAW

Formed: Long Island, New York, USA . . . 1994 by schoolboys DARYL PALUMBO and JUSTIN BECK. Fermenting their uncompromising post-hardcore sound through the pre-millennium tension of the late 90's, GLASSJAW finally unleashed their debut album, 'EVERYTHING YOU EVER WANTED TO KNOW ABOUT SILENCE' in spring 2000. By this point their ever evolving personnel situation had coalesced around PALUMBO, BECK, TODD WEINSTOCK, MANUEL CARRERO and NYHC veteran skins wizard SAMMY SIEGLER with DARYL's personal trials providing the record's driving force. A sufferer of the rare Crohn's Disease and an advocate of the clean living Straight Edge lifestyle, the frontman's inner demons were exorcised on disc with the help of producer of the moment Ross Robinson. Baptised in the fire of the traditional NY hardcore sound but brandishing a fearsome heretical streak, the record's pulverising nu-metal proved painful yet rewarding listening with PALUMBO's primal screaming pushed way up in the mix. A subsequent summer tour with spiritual cadres The DEFTONES saw SIEGLER replaced by ex-ORANGE 9MM sticksman, LARRY GORMAN.

Album rating: EVERYTHING YOU EVER WANTED TO KNOW ABOUT SILENCE (*5)

DARYL PALUMBO – vocals / **JUSTIN BECK** – guitar / **TODD N. WEISTOCK** – guitar / **MANUEL CARRERO** – bass / **SAMMY SIEGLER** – drums (ex-CIV, ex-GORILLA BISCUITS)

Roadrunner | Roadrunner

May 00. (cd) <*(RR 8578-2)*> **EVERYTHING YOU EVER WANTED TO KNOW ABOUT SILENCE** [ ] [ ]
– Pretty lush / Siberian kiss / When one eight becomes two zeros / Ry Ry's song / Lovebites and razorlines / Hurting and shoving (she should have let me sleep) / Majour / Her middle name was Boom / Piano / Babe / Eveything you ever wanted to know about silence / Hotel of the white locust.

— **LARRY GORMAN** – drums (ex-ORANGE 9mm) repl. SIEGLER

Nov 00. (cd-ep) *(RR 2060-3)* **RY RY'S SONG / SIBERIAN KISS / MODERN LOVE STORY / CONVECTUOSO** [ ] [-]

GLITTERBOX

Formed: London, England . . . late 1993 by JONNY GREEN, MILES HESELTINE and MARK SERVAS, who met at a college in Norwich, deciding there and then to start a band without the knowledge of how to play an instrument (who said punk was dead!). Early the following year, the three recruited TONY HOLLAND and subsequently played a disastrous solitary gig at a pub in London before retreating to their day jobs. Resurfacing with some of their own material early in '95, JONNY, MILES and TONY came up with the group name, SHE, eventually coaxing MARK to return from his new home in Barcelona. Annoyed by UK record labels who could not pigeonhole them between rock and indie, they sent demos to the States, the result being that A&R men quickly flew over to size them up; 'Atlantic' won the battle. However, luck was not on their side, when, in 1996, 'Death Row' all-female R&B act, SHE, threatened legal action (sleeping and fishes are two words that come to mind!?). Having already finished off the recording of their debut album, the release was delayed while the band came up with a new moniker, GLITTERBOX. However, yet more problems ensued as JONNY was hit by a throat virus which kept him out of the game for half a year. In August '97, the quartet finally released a single, 'YOU CAN'T LIVE ON MARS', its lack of appeal seeing the band downshift to Atlantic's subsidiary, 'Radar' for subsequent releases. Early the following year, the first of these, 'SCARED OF ALL THE WORLD', hit the shops and another, 'HOUDINI' preceded the long-awaited and nearly cancelled album, 'TIED AND TANGLED'. This was an overdue piece of Britrock-pop taking a whole list of influences including The MANICS, AFGHAN WHIGS and even TALKING HEADS!

Album rating: TIED & TANGLED (*7)

JONNY GREEN – vocals, guitar / **MILES HESELTINE** – guitar, vocals / **TONY HOLLAND** – bass / **MARK SERVAS** – drums

Atlantic | Atlantic

Aug 97. (7") *(AT 005)* **YOU CAN'T LIVE ON MARS. / MOTORCYCLE SONG** [ ] [ ]
(cd-s+=) *(AT 005CD)* – Roller skates.

Radar | Atlantic

Feb 98. (7") *(SCAN 28)* **SCARED OF ALL THE WORLD. / I'M YOUR MONSTER** [ ] [-]
(cd-s+=) *(SCANCS 28)* – Your ghost.

Apr 98. (7") *(SCAN 29)* **HOUDINI. / SUNK** [ ] [-]
(cd-s) *(SCANCS 29)* – ('A'side) / Still breathing / Illuminate you / Promises.

May 98. (cd) *(SCANCD 30)* <83021> **TIED & TANGLED** [ ] [ ] Oct97
– Houdini / Scared of all the world / Woody Allen / Superman / I can wait / You can't live on Mars / Jesus song / Summer song / Step inside / Sit back and watch her fly / Tonight to Hell.

Roger GLOVER

Born: 30 Nov'45, Brecon, Powys, Wales. A long time mate of IAN GILLAN, whom he played bass with initially in 60's R&B outfit, EPISODE SIX and more recently DEEP PURPLE (Mk.2). Sacked by 'PURPLE in '73, he concentrated more on production work, while also acting as the brains behind the 'BUTTERFLY BALL' project. A concept piece which was later developed into a film and a book, the project included such future luminaries as DAVID COVERDALE, RONNIE JAMES DIO, GLENN HUGHES, MICKEY LEE SOULE and RAY FENWICK. GLOVER eventually released a solo album proper in 1978, 'ELEMENTS', although this received scant shrift from critics and public alike. Perhaps disillusioned with his solo career, he opted to rejoin BLACKMORE, this time around in RAINBOW. The bassist finally offered up another studio solo album, 'MASK' in 1984, the same year he rejoined DEEP PURPLE (Mk.2, once again!). Surprisingly, GLOVER's tenure with the band stretched to more than one album, during which time he simultaneously resumed production work and subsequently undertook a one-off collaboration with GILLAN for the album, 'ACCIDENTALLY ON PURPOSE' (1988). At the time of going to press, GLOVER remains an integral part of the STEVE MORSE fronted DEEP PURPLE.

Album rating: THE BUTTERFLY BALL (*6) / ELEMENTS (*4) / MASK (*4)

GLOVER with a host of top musicians (see above)

Purple | UK

Nov 74. (7") *(PUR 125)* **LOVE IS ALL. / OLD BLIND MOLE** [ ] [-]

Dec 74. (lp) *(TPSA 7514)* <1605> **THE BUTTERFLY BALL (Soundtrack)** [ ] [ ]
– Dawn / Get ready / Saffron doormouse and Lizzy bee / Harlequin hare / Old blind mole / Magician moth / No solution / Behind the smile / Fly away / Arena / Sitting in a dream / Waiting / Sir Maximus mouse / Dreams of Sir Bedivere / Together again / Watch out for the bat / Little chalk blue / The feast / Love is all / Homeward. *<US re-iss. Jan76 on 'UK'; 56000>* – with THE GRASSHOPPER'S FEAST. *(re-iss. Nov84 on 'Safari' lp/c; LONG/+C 9) (cd-iss. 1989 on 'Line'; LICD 900013) (re-iss. cd Jul95 on 'Repertoire';) (cd re-iss. Mar99 on 'Connoisseur'; EVSOPCD 265)*

1975. (7") <2800> **LOVE IS ALL. / WAITING** [-] [ ]

Polydor | Oyster

Apr 78. (lp) *(2391 306)* <1637> **ELEMENTS** [ ] [ ]
– The first ring made of clay / The next a ring of fire / The third ring's watery flow / The fourth ring's with the wind / Finale.

Polydor | 21 Records

May 84. (lp/c) *(POLD/+C 5139)* **MASK** [ ] [ ]
– Divided world / Getting stranger / The mask / Fake it / Dancin' again / (You're so) Remote / Hip level / Don't look down. *(cd-iss. Apr93 w/ ELEMENTS on 'Connoisseur' d-lp/c/cd; VSOP LP/MC/CD 139)*

Jun 84. (7") *(POSP 678)* **THE MASK. / (YOU'RE SO) REMOTE** [ ] [-]

— GLOVER rejoined DEEP PURPLE (late '84) and collaborated with IAN GILLAN on the album, 'ACCIDENTALLY ON PURPOSE' (1988)

GLUECIFER

Formed: Oslo, Norway . . . 1994 by BIFF MALIBU, CAPTAIN POON, SINDURU KHAN, JON AVERAGE and GLUEROS HELLFIRE. Yet another Scandinavian band hell-bent on bringing back the metal world's sex, drugs and rock'n'roll formula, these vikings summoned up the ghosts of MC5, TED NUGENT and VAN HALEN in a bid to rid the scene of limp-wristed pseuds and navel-gazing aesthetes. 1995's 'GOD'S CHOSEN DEALER' EP and 1996's 'DICK DISGUISED AS PUSSY' mini-album, set – or rather lowered – the tone while a bonafide long player, 'RIDIN' THE TIGER' surfaced in 1997 on the 'White Jazz' label. A rash of 7" singles peppered their release schedule over the ensuing two years bearing such endearing titles as 'SHITTY CITY', 'LARD ASS HAGAN' and 'THE YEAR OF MANLY LIVING'. 'SOARING WITH EAGLES AT NIGHT TO RISE WITH PIGS IN THE MORNING' (1998) served as the band's sophomore album while they even managed an EP on veteran Seattle indie, 'Sub Pop' entitled 'GET THE HORN'. Stepping up their party-rock campaign, GLUECIFER subsequently released 'TENDER IS THE SAVAGE' (2000) and 'GENERAL SAYS HELL YEAH' (2000) in an unprecedented bout of millennial recording activity. • **Covered:** MAX'S

KANSAS CITY (Electric Chairs) / CAT SCRATCH FEVER + JUST WHAT THE DOCTOR ORDERED (Ted Nugent) / SON OF A GOOD FAMILY (Leather Nun) / REMEDY (Rose Tattoo) / THUNDER & LIGHTNING (Thin Lizzy) / DRIFTING AWAY (Status Quo) / WHAM BAM THANK YOU MAM (Small Faces).

Album rating: NINETEEN INCHES OF ROCK mini compilation (*5) / RIDIN' THE TIGER (*6) / SOARING WITH EAGLES AT NIGHT . . . (*6) / TENDER IS THE SAVAGE (*7)

BIFF MALIBU – vocals / **SINDURU KHAN** – guitar / **CAPTAIN POON (#1 KING OF ROCK)** – guitar / **JON AVERAGE** – bass / **GLUEROS HELLFIRE** – drums

Hit Me! / not iss.

Feb 95. (7"ep) **GOD'S CHOSEN DEALER** – Norway
– God's chosen dealer / 1994 / Monoman.

May 96. (m-lp) **DICK DISGUISED AS PUSSY** – Norway
– Head to head boredom / Stuck to the floor / Dogburner / Dick disguised as pussy / Under my hood / Phonebooth creep / Suck city / Ace wheels.

Sep 96. (m-cd) **NINETEEN INCHES OF ROCK** (above compilation) – Norway
(UK-iss.Jun98 on 'Voices Of Wonder'; BLUE 001CD) (<re-iss. + US Jul99 on 'Devil Doll'+=; DDR 010>) – live 1997:- Rock & roll asshole / Evil matcher / Rock throne.

Feb 97. (7") **SHITTY CITY. / MAX'S KANSAS CITY** – Norway

— **RALDO USELESS** – guitar; repl. SINDURU

— **DANNY YOUNG** – drums; repl. HELLFIRE

White Jazz / not iss.

Jun 97. (cd) *(JAZZ 005CD)* **RIDIN' THE TIGER**
– Leather chair / Rock'n'roll asshole / Bounced checks / Evil matcher / Rock throne / Burnin' white / Titanium sunset / We're out loud / Obi damned Kenobi / Under my hood / Prime mover.

— In Aug'97, they split a single with HELLACOPTERS, 'RESPECT THE ROCK'

Oct 97. (7") *(BA 04)* **DAMBUSTER. / CAT SCRATCH FEVER**
(above single issued on 'Bad Afro')

Feb 98. (7") *(7JAZZ 007)* **LEATHER CHAIR. / HOT SEAT**
(cd-s) *(JAZZ 007CD)* – (as above).

May 98. (7") **LARD ASS HAGEN. / SON OF A GOOD FAMILY**
(above issued on '007' records, below on 'Frank' & 'Safety-Pin')

Aug 98. (7") **BOILER TRIP. / (other by Electric Frankenstein)**

Sep 98. (7") **MANO-A-MANO. / REMEDY** – Spain

Sep 98. (7"/cd-s) **GET THE HORN. / THUNDER & LIGHTNING** – Sweden

Oct 98. (lp/cd) *(JAZZ 012/+CD)* **SOARING WITH EAGLES AT NIGHT . . . (. . .TO RISE WITH PIGS IN THE MORNING)**
– Bossheaded / Go away man / The year of manly living / Get the horn / Critical minute / Silver wings / Lord of the dusk / Deadend beat / Clean gone man / Heart of a bad machine / Gimme solid gold.

Feb 99. (7") **GET THAT PSYCHO OUT OF MY FACE. / DRIFTING AWAY**
(above issued on 'Munster')

Mar 99. (7") *(7JAZZ 017)* **YEAR OF MANLY LIVING. / WHAM BAM THANK YOU MAM**
(cd-s+=) *(JAZZ 017CD)* –

Mar 99. (10"ep) *<(MR 106)>* **GARY O'KANE**
– Gary O'Kane / Shitty city / My card says / No goddamn phones / Going down. *<(re-iss. Mar99 as 'RESPECT THE ROCK AMERICA' a split with HELLACOPTERS' MR 117)>*
(above issued on 'Man's Ruin')

Aug 99. (7"ep) **ROCK'N'ROLL**
– Just what the doctor ordered / (other 2 by Murder City Devils)

May 00. (cd/lp) *(JAZZ 029 CD/LP) <SP 495>* **TENDER IS THE SAVAGE** Aug00
– I got a war / Chewin' fingers / Ducktail heat / The general says: "hell yeah" / Red noses, shit poses / Drunk and pompous / Rip-off strasse / Dog day, dog night / Sputnik Monroe / Exit at gate zero / Rock & roll / Rat down to the bone / Get that psycho out of my face.

Sep 00. (7") *(7JAZZ 031)* **THE GENERAL SAYS: "HELL YEAH". / GET THAT PSYCHO OUT OF MY FACE**
(cd-s+=) *(JAZZ 031CD)* – I gotta war (video).

– compilations, etc. –

Mar 00. (10"m-lp/m-cd) *Sub Pop; <(SP/+CD 508)>* **GET THE HORN**
– Get the horn / The year of manly living / Go away man / Leather chair / Bounced checks / Titanium sunset.

GOATSNAKE

Formed: Los Angeles, California, USA . . . 1998 by former OBSESSED bassist and drummer GUY PINHAS and GREG ROGERS and one-time WOOL and SCREAM frontman PETER STAHL. Their heavy influence could sometimes be a bad thing as proved on GOATSNAKE's first release, 'GOATSNAKE VOL 1' (1999), which borrowed largely from BLACK SABBATH and early MUDHONEY. STAHL's whining vocals, however, had much improved since his days with DAVE GROHL's former self-confessed fold SCREAM, although it's PINHAS who takes on the riffs with almighty glory before turning them on their heads like a horrible car crash. Nothing short of boring, ' . . . VOL 1' lacked adequate prodution techniques that ultimately credited early WOOL albums, and songs on this debut set fell into the cracks of raw '90s grunge. By the same token, it may be essential listening for OZZY fans across the globe, or alternatively, the soundtrack to a rough, pissed-up weekend.

Album rating: GOATSNAKE (*5)

PETER STAHL – vocals (ex-WOOL, ex-SCREAM) / **GREG ANDERSON** – guitar / **GUY PINHAS** – bass (ex-OBSESSED) / **GREG ROGERS** – drums (ex-OBSESSED)

Prosthetic / not iss.

Mar 99. (7") *(PRV 301)* **THE INNOCENT. / IV**

Rise Above / Man's Ruin

May 99. (cd) *(CDRISE 22) <MR 174CD>* **GOATSNAKE**
– Slippin' the stealth / The innocent / What love remains / IV / Lower / Dog catcher / Lord of Los Feliz / Trower. *(lp-iss.Jun99 on 'Man's Ruin'; same as US)*

— at the turn of the century, they issued the 'DOG DAYS' EP

GOD BULLIES

Formed: Kalamazoo, Michigan, USA . . . 1986 by vocalist MIKE HARD and three other angry young men, DAVID LIVINGSTONE, MIKE CORSO and ADAM BERG. Similar in some respects to The CRAMPS, The BUTTHOLE SURFERS and The STOOGES, the band gained a deal with US label, 'Amphetamine Reptile' (home of HALO OF FLIES, THROWN UPS and subsequently, HELMET), for whom they released a handful of releases from 1987's 'FEAR AND PAIN' single to 1991's double-7", 'JOIN SATAN'S ARMY'. Three years on, 'Alternative Tentacles' took up the reins for what was to become their swansong set, 'KILL THE KING' (1994).

Album rating: PLASTIC EYE MIRACLE (*5) / MAMAWOMBWOMB (*5) / DOG SHOW (*5) / WAR ON EVERYBODY (*5) / KILL THE KING (*4)

MIKE HARD – vocals / **DAVID LIVINGSTONE** – guitar / **MIKE CORSO** – bass / **ADAM BERG** – drums

not iss. / Mad Queen

1988. (7") **ALL I WANT IS MY MAMMA. /**
1988. (c) **PLASTIC EYE MIRACLE** (half studio/half live)

Amphetam. Reptile / Amphetam. Reptile

1989. (7") *<Scale 10>* **FEAR AND PAIN. /**
1989. (lp) **MAMAWOMBWOMB**

— added **MARY KATE MURRAY + TABATHA PREDOVICH** – backing vocals

1990. (m-cd) *<ARR 181>* **DOG SHOW**
– Let's go the hell / Monster Jesus / Cemetary / I am invisible / Buddha / The godfather goes to hell (pt.2) / 2 + 2 / Do it again / Shallow grave / Like it like that / Abigail.

— **TONY OLIVERI** – drums (ex-COWS) repl. BERG

1990. (d7") *(Scale 31)* **JOIN SATAN'S ARMY. /**

Dec 91. (lp/cd) *(ARR 180/+CD)* **WAR ON EVERYBODY**
– Book report time / I want to kill you / Ordinary man / Automaker / Long way home / Peace and love / Senojmot / Magical butterfly / Pet monkey / Andre / Safety zone / Saw you dead.

— <they also featured one track on Various EP, 'Ugly American Overkill'; Scale 34>

— split for a time in the early 90's

Sympathy F / Sympathy F

1990's. (7") *<(SFTRI 130)>* **HOW LOW. /**

Alternative Tentacles / Alternative Tentacles

Oct 94. (cd) *<(VIRUS 152CD)>* **KILL THE KING**
– Neighborhood kid / King of sling / How many times / Detain my brain / She's wild / Pretty on the inside / Space kid zoom / You have been warned / It's him / Artificial insemination by Aliens / Hate. *(re-iss. Nov97; VIRUSUK 152)*

Radical / Radical

Nov 95. (7") *(RDL 0087)* **MILLENNIUM. / I FORGOT WHERE I LIVE**

— disbanded after above

GODFLESH

Formed: Birmingham, England . . . 1988 by JUSTIN BROADRICK and G. CHRISTIAN ('Benny') GREEN. Scary purveyors of brutally uncompromising, drum-machine driven industrial noise, GODFLESH debuted in late '88 with an eponymous mini-album on the small 'Swordfish' label. Moving to 'Earache' for the 'STREETCLEANER' (1989) set, the group toured with labelmates NAPALM DEATH, BROADRICK having previously played on the band's legendary 'Scum' album. 1991's 'SLAVESTATE' was a collection of previously released singles, the acclaimed 'PURE' (1992) being their second "proper" album. A relentlessly bleak set featuring LOOP's ROBERT HAMPSON, tracks like 'MOTHRA' and 'LOVE, HATE (SLUGBAITING)' trawled new depths of grinding claustrophobia. The following year, the ubiquitous BROADRICK guested for SCORN on their debut set, 'VAE SOLIS', before remixing PANTERA's 'WALK', a new GODFLESH album finally surfacing in 1994 as 'SELFLESS'. This was the first full-length set to feature a real drummer, namely BRIAN MANTIA, though the clinical savagery of the GODFLESH sound remained intact. Like most 'Earache' acts, GODFLESH remain a cult attraction, content to push the boundaries of extreme music and enjoy regular critical acclaim. Their most recent claims to the avant-noise throne were 'SONGS OF LOVE AND HATE' (1996) and a remixed version, 'LOVE AND HATE IN DUB' (1997), MANTIA subsequently leaving for PRIMUS and being replaced by ex-PRONG sticksman TED PARSONS. After another moonlighting episode as FINAL ('SOLARIS' in 1998), BROADRICK and his ever-faithful partner in crime, GREEN, were back to their industrial/grind roots courtesy of their 5th full-set, 'US AND THEM' (1999) • **Songwriters:** BROADRICK – GREEN except MERCILESS (Fall Of Because; i.e. GREEN). • **Trivia:** Note that BROADRICK was also part of ICE and TECHNO ANIMAL.

Album rating: STREETCLEANER (*8) / SLAVESTATE mini (*5) / PURE (*7) / SELFLESS (*6) / SONGS OF LOVE AND HATE (*7) / US AND THEM (*6) / Final: ONE (*5) / 2 (*5) / THE FIRST MILLIONTH OF A SECOND (*6) / SOLARIS (*6)

JUSTIN BROADRICK – vocals, guitar, samples (ex-HEAD OF DAVID) / **G. CHRISTIAN ('Benny') GREEN** – bass, samples (ex-FALL OF BECAUSE) / + drum machine

Swordfish / Silent Scream

Nov 88. (m-lp) *(FLESHLP 1) <8003>* **GODFLESH** [ ] [ ] 1990
– Avalanche master song / Veins godhead / Spinebender weak flesh / Ice nerveshatter wounds / Streetcleaner 2. *(cd-iss. Feb90 on 'Earache'; MOSH 020CD)*

Jan 89. (12"ep) *(12FLESH 002)* **TINY TEARS / WOUND. / DEAD HEAD / SUCTION** [ ] [-]

— added **PAUL NEVILLE** – guitar (ex-FALL OF BECAUSE)

Earache / Combat

Sep 89. (lp/c/cd) *(MOSH 015/+C/CD) <2023>* **STREETCLEANER** [ ] [ ] 1990
– Like rats / Christbait rising / Pulp / Dream long dead / Head dirt / Devastator – Mighty trust krusher / Life is easy / Streetcleaner / Locust furnace. *(cd+=)* – Tiny tears / Wound / Dead head / Suction.

Oct 90. (12"ep) *(MOSH 030T)* **SLAVESTATE / PERFECT SKIN. / SOMEONE SOMEWHERE SCORNED / MELTDOWN** [ ] [-]
(12"ep) *(MOSH 030TR)* – ('A'radio slave mix) / Perfect skin / ('A'-total state mix).

Apr 91. (lp/cd) *(MOSH 030/+CD) <1073>* **SLAVESTATE** [ ] [ ]
– Slavestate / Perfect skin / Someone somewhere scorned / Meltdown / Slavestate (radio slave) / Slavestate (total state mix) / Perfect skin (dub) / Slate man / Wound '91. *(cd re-iss. Mar99; same)*

Apr 91. (12"ep/cd-ep) *(MOSH 47 T/CD)* **SLATEMAN / WOUND '91 / COLD WORLD. / NIHIL / NIHIL / NIHIL** [ ] [ ] Mar96

— **ROBERT HAMPSON** – guitar (ex-LOOP) repl. NEVILLE to CABEL REGIME

Feb 92. (lp/c/cd) *(MOSH 032/+MC/CD) <1087>* **PURE** [ ] [ ]
– Spite / Mothra / I wasn't born to follow / Predominance / Pure / Monotremanta / Baby blue eyes / Don't bring me flowers / Love, hate (slugbaiting) / Pure II.

Aug 92. (12"ep/cd-ep) *(MOSH 056 T/CD) <1153>* **COLD WORLD** [ ] [ ]

— duo added to repl. HAMPSON on tour **BRIAN MANTIA** – drums

Earache / Columbia

Apr 94. (12"ep/cd-ep) *(MOSH 116 T/CD) <64360>* **MERCILESS / BLIND (BIOCHEMICAL 01). / UNWORTHY (BIOCHEMICAL 02) / FLOWERS** [ ] [ ]

Oct 94. (lp/cd) *(MOSH 085/+CD) <66157>* **SELFLESS** [ ] [ ]
– Xnoybis / Bigot / Black bored angel / Anything is mine / Empyreal / Crush my soul / Body dome light / Toll / Heartless / Mantra. *(cd+=)* – Go spread your wings. *<US cd-iss. Oct96 on 'Earache'+=; same as UK>* – MERCILESS

Apr 95. (12"ep/cd-ep) *(MOSH 127 T/CD)* **CRUSH MY SOUL (mixes). / XNOYBIS** [ ] [-]

Earache / Earache

Aug 96. (lp/cd) *(<MOSH 157/+CD>)* **SONGS OF LOVE AND HATE** [ ] [ ]
– Wake / Sterile prophet / Circle of shit / The hunter / Gift from Heaven / Amoral / Angel domain / Kingdom come / Time death and wastefulness / Frail / Almost Heaven.

— now without MANTIA who joined PRIMUS. He was repl. by **TED PARSONS** – drums (ex-PRONG)

— now duo of **JUSTIN + BENNY**

Jun 97. (cd) *(<MOSH 178CD>)* **LOVE AND HATE IN DUB** (remixes) [ ] [ ]
– Circle of shit / Wake / Almost Heaven / Gift from Heaven / Frail / Sterile prophet / Almost Heaven / Kingdom come / Time, death and wastefulness / Sterile prophet / Domain / Gift from Heaven.

May 99. (cd) *(<MOSH 179CD>)* **US AND THEM** [ ] [ ] Jun99
– I me mine / Us and them / Endgames / Witchhunt / Whose truth is your truth / Defiled / Bittersweet / Nail / Descent / Control freal / The internal / Live to lose.

FINAL

BROADRICK with various others

Subharmonic / not iss.

Dec 93. (cd) *(7014)* **ONE** [ ] [-]
– Fall / Light underground – Dark overground / Awake but numb / Despotic / Round our bodies / Hold me / Death-Love dealer / 1983-1987 (edits).

Sentrax / Royalty

May 96. (cd) *(SNTX 3001CD) <1114>* **FINAL 2** [ ] [ ] Jun96

not iss. / Manifold

Aug 97. (cd) *<16>* **THE FIRST MILLIONTH OF A SECOND** [-] [ ]
– Critical thresholds / Electron / Quark / New species / Subatomic (live) / Foundations / Pathway.

Invisible / Invisible

Sep 98. (cd) *(<INV 9016CD>)* **SOLARIS** [ ] [ ]
– Arise / Light / Solaris / Dying star.

GOD MACHINE

Formed: San Diego, California, USA . . . early 1990 after ROBYN PROPER-SHEPPARD, JIMMY FERNANDEZ and RONALD AUSTIN uprooted themselves over the water to England. Choosing Camden Town (London) as their home/squat, they found menial jobs to provide them with the necessary cash to buy instruments; a year after formation they had sufficiently mastered their instruments to enable them to begin recording. The trio debuted with the 'PURITY' EP on the small 'Eve' label, immediately garnering press feedback with their mesmerising hybrid of gothic psychedelia taking in elements of The CURE, SWANS and BLACK SABBATH. Signed to Polydor's 'Fiction' offshoot label (home to The CURE), GOD MACHINE delivered a further three EP's before their debut album, 'SCENES FROM THE SECOND STOREY', a surprise Top 60 entry early in '93. Temporarily setting up home in Prague to record their follow-up, tragedy struck immediately after the record's completion as FERNANDEZ was diagnosed with brain cancer. He was to die within a matter of weeks (23rd of May 1994), the GOD MACHINE grinding to a halt prior to posthumous release of the morbidly titled 'LAST LAUGH IN A PLACE OF DYING' later that year.

Album rating: SCENES FROM THE SECOND STOREY (*6) / LAST LAUGH IN A PLACE OF DYING (*6)

ROBYN PROPER-SHEPPARD – vocals, guitar / **JIMMY FERNANDEZ** – bass / **RONALD AUSTIN** – drums

Eve / not iss.

Nov 91. (12"ep/cd-ep) **PURITY** [ ] [-]

Fiction / Polygram

May 92. (12"ep/cd-ep) **THE DESERT SONG / PROSTITUTE. / COMMITMENT / PICTURES OF A BLEEDING BOY** [ ] [-]

Oct 92. (12"/cd-s) **EGO. / TEMPTATION / PIANO SONG** [ ] [-]

Jan 93. (12"ep/cd-ep) *(FIC SX/CD 47)* **HOME / ALL MY COLOURS. / TRAIN / FEVER** [ ] [-]

Feb 93. (cd/c/lp) *<(517 156-2/-4/-1)>* **SCENES FROM THE SECOND STOREY** [55] [ ]
– Dream machine / She said / Blind man / I've seen the man / Desert song / Home / It's all over / Temptation / Out / Ego / Seven / Purity / Piano song.

Sep 94. (cd/c/lp) *<(523 685-2/-4/-1)>* **LAST LAUGH IN A PLACE OF DYING** [ ] [ ] Feb95
– Tremelo song / Mama / Alone / In bad dreams / Painless / Love song / Life song / Devil song / Hunter / Evol / Train song / Flower song / Boy by the roadside / Sunday song.

— chose to disband after the untimely death of FERNANDEZ on 23 May'94

GODSMACK

Formed: Boston, Massachusetts, USA . . . 1996 by frontman SALLY ERNA and his musical mates, TONY ROMBOLO, ROBBIE MERRILL and TOMMY STEWART, who named themselves after an ALICE IN CHAINS track. If you were to put the aforementioned ALICE IN CHAINS, METALLICA and the rest of the Grunge crew together – and without getting too sarcy – you would probably come up with GODSMACK. This dour 4-piece got their break from noneother than PAUL GEARY (former sticksman with EXTREME), who sorted out a contract with 'Universal' in 1998. By the following year, their self-titled debut album was high in the US Top 30, with an invite to Woodstock and Ozzfest to boot. Heralded by young trendy Americans into "that sort of thing", the band also had a surprise alternative rock hit with probably their finest five minutes, 'WHATEVER'. By late 2000, the lads thought we'd enjoy a second set. 'AWAKE' was not an appropriate title.

Album rating: GODSMACK (*3) / AWAKE (*4)

SULLY ERNA – vocals / **TONY ROMBOLO** – guitar / **ROBBIE MERRILL** – bass / **TOMMY STEWART** – drums; repl. JOE D'ARCO (although he did return)

Universal / Universal

Aug 99. (cd) *(UND 53190) <153190>* **GODSMACK** [ ] [22] Aug98
– Moon baby / Whatever / Keep away / Time bomb / Bad religion / Immune / Someone in London / Get up, get out! / Now or never / Stress / Situation / Voodoo. *<clean version as 'ALL WOUND UP'; UND 53183>*

Oct 00. (cd) *<(159688-2)>* **AWAKE** [ ] [5]
– Sick of life / Awake / Greed / Bad magick / Goin' down / Mistakes / Trippin' / Forgive me / Vampires / The journey / Spiral.

GODZ

Formed: Columbus/Cleveland, Ohio, USA . . . 1977 by ERIC MOORE, MARK CHATFIELD, BOB HILL and GLEN CATALINE. Catering for the leather-clad biker crowd, the group's down'n'dirty hard-rock'n'roll took its cue from early GRAND FUNK RAILROAD. In fact their eponymous debut album was produced by the latter's DON BREWER, a rough-shod gem which nudged into the US Top 200. With CATALINE now taking on vocal duties, the group's second set, 'NOTHING IS SACRED' (1979), was a relative failure and the band folded shortly after. MOORE and CHATFIELD reformed The GODZ in the mid 80's, releasing a generally ignored comeback album, 'I'LL GET YOU ROCKIN'' in 1985. The band made a last-ditch attempt to revive their earlier promise, re-recording and mixing their last set under a new title of 'MONGOLIANS' (1987).

Album rating: THE GODZ (*5) / NOTHING IS SACRED (*4) / I'LL GET YOU ROCKIN' (*4) /

ERIC MOORE – vocals, bass / **MARK CHATFIELD** – guitar / **BOB HILL** – guitar, keyboards / **GLEN CATALINE** – drums

R.C.A. / Millenium

1978. (lp) *(XL 13051) <8003>* **THE GODZ** [ ] [ ]
– Go away / Baby I love you / Guarenteed / Gotta keep a runnin' / Under the table / Cross country / Candy's going bad. *(re-iss. 1983 as 'POWER ROCK FROM U.S.A.' lp/c; XL/XK 13051)*

— CATALINE now on lead vocals

R.C.A. / Casablanca

Jan 79. (lp) *(XL 13072) <7134>* **NOTHING IS SACRED** [ ] [ ]
– Gotta muv / Festyvul seasun / Rock yer sox auf / I'll bi yer luv / Luv kage / He's a fool / 714 / Hey mama / Snakin' / I don't wanna go home.

— folded, but reformed in 1985 with **MOORE + CHATFIELD** plus **FREDDY SALEM** – guitar (ex-OUTLAWS) / **KEITH VALENTINE** – drums

Heavy Metal / Mongolians

Nov 85. (lp) *(HMUSA 48) <0962>* **I'LL GET YOU ROCKIN'** [ ] [ ]
– Timeless / Chest fever / I'll get you rockin' / Foolin' yourself / Hey you / Fool for you / Fire / Love cage / Mississippi / We're all crazy. *<US re-iss. & remixed 1987 as 'MONGOLIANS' on 'Grudge'; 0962>*

— folded after above

GOLDEN EARRING

Formed: The Hague, Netherlands . . . 1961 as The TORNADO'S by RINUS GERRITSEN and GEORGE KOOYMANS, who subsequently added JAAP EGGERMONT, FRANS KRASSENBURG and PETER DE RONDE. In August '65, as EARRING (as they were known then) they scored a domestic Top 10 hit with the single, 'PLEASE GO'. Throughout the latter half of the 60's, the group continued to hit the Dutch charts with a string of quasi-bubblegum psychedelic pop ditties. At the turn of the decade they followed the nascent trend towards hard and heavy rock, a support tour in '72 with newfound friends The WHO, resulting in a deal with Kit Lambert & Chris Stamp's 'Track'. By this juncture, several changes had taken place, the most notable being in 1967, when the enigmatic BARRY HAY took over the vocals. Though their first release for the label, 'HEARRING EARRING' was a compilation of their previous two Dutch lp's, a new single, 'RADAR LOVE', finally gave the band a deserved breakthrough in 1973. This highly distinctive tarmac-scorching classic virtually came to define the band's hard-drivin' sound and they found it difficult to create a worthy successor. The accompanying album, 'MOONTAN' also sold by the barrow-load, the group enjoying a brief honeymoon period of success in the States in addition to their European standing. Not exactly one-hit wonders, the band nevertheless enjoyed only minimal success (outside Holland) with subsequent albums, 'SWITCH' (1975), 'TO THE HILT' (1976), 'MAD LOVE' (1977), etc, etc. The albatross round their necks was briefly lifted late '82/early '83 with the freak US success of the single, 'TWILIGHT ZONE', which engendered a return to the album charts with 'CUT'. GOLDEN EARRING continued to chip away at the American market throughout the 80's, WHITE LION's successful cover of 'RADAR LOVE' in 1991 generating renewed interest in the group. • **Songwriters:** KOOYMANS, GERRITSEN and HAY. • **Trivia:** Early member JAAP EGGERMONT, went on to become man behind the fruitful 80's pop STARSOUND medleys.

Album rating: JUST EARRINGS (*6) / WINTER HARVEST (*6) / MIRACLE MIRROR (*6) / EIGHT MILES HIGH (*6) / GOLDEN EARRING (WALL OF DOLLS) (*6) / SEVEN TEARS (*6) / TOGETHER (*6) / HEARING EARRING collection (*6) / MOONTAN (*7) / SWITCH (*6) / TO THE HILT (*6) / CONTRABAND (*5) / MAD LOVE (*5) / GOLDEN EARRING LIVE (*6) / GRAB IT FOR A SECOND (*5) / PRISONER OF THE NIGHT <US= LONG BLOND ANIMAL> (*5) / SECOND LIVE (*4) / CUT (*7) / N.E.W.S. (*6) / SOMETHING HEAVY GOING DOWN – LIVE FROM THE TWILIGHT ZONE (*4) / THE HOLE (*3) / THE CONTINUING STORY OF RADAR LOVE compilation (*8) / KEEPER OF THE FLAME (*5) / BLOODY BUCCANEERS (*5) / THE NAKED TRUTH (*3) / FACE IT (*4) / NAKED II (*3) / LAST BLAST OF THE CENTURY compilation (*7)

GOLDEN EARRINGS

GEORGE KOOYMANS (b.11 Mar'48) – vocals, guitar / **RINUS GERRITSEN** (b.9 Aug'46) – bass, keyboards / **FRANS KRASSENBURG** (b.24 Feb'44) – vocals / **PETER DE RONDE** (b.11 Jul'48) – guitar / **JAAP EGGERMONT** (b.31 Oct'46) – drums (early TORNADO'S members also included HANS VAN HERWERDEN + FREDDIE VAN DER HILST)

Polydor / not iss.

Aug 65. (7") *(S 1181)* **PLEASE GO. / CHUNK OF STEEL** [-] [-] Dutch

Nov 65. (7"; w-drawn) *(S 1185)* **LONELY EVERYDAY. / NOT TO FIND** [-] [-] Dutch

Nov 65. (lp) *(736 007)* **JUST EARRINGS** [-] [-] Dutch
– Nobody but you / I hate saying these words / She may be / Holy witness / No need to worry / Please go / Sticks and stones / I am a fool / Don't stay away / Lonely everyday / When people talk / Now I have.

Jan 66. (7") *(421 023)* **THAT DAY. / THE WORDS I NEED** [-] [-] Dutch
(above imported into UK in 1970; BM 56514)

—— trim slightly when PETER departed

1966. (lp) *(736 068)* **WINTER HARVEST** [-] [-] Dutch
– Another man in town / Smoking cigarettes / In my house / Don't wanna lose that girl / Impecable / Tears and lies / There will be a tomorrow / You've got the intention to hurt me / You break my heart / Baby don't make me nervous / Call me / Happy and young together / Lionel the mission. *<US-iss.1967 as 'THE GOLDEN EARRINGS' on 'Capitol'; ST 2823>*

Jun 66. (7") *(421 036)* **IF YOU LEAVE ME. / WAITING FOR YOU** [-] [-] Dutch

Aug 66. (7") *(SL 3004)* **THINGS GO BETTER. / RUM AND COCA COLA** [-] [-] Dutch
(above issued for the Coca Cola company!)

Oct 66. (7") *(421 050)* **DADDY BUY ME A GIRL. / WHAT YOU GONNA TELL** [-] [-] Dutch

Dec 66. (7") *(421 056)* **DON'T RUN TOO FAR. / WINGS** [-] [-] Dutch

Apr 67. (7") *(S 1223)* **IN MY HOUSE. / SMOKING CIGARETTES** [-] [-] Dutch

Jul 67. (7") *(S 1244)* **SOUND OF THE SCREAMING DAY. / SHE WON'T COME TO ME** [-] [-] Dutch

Oct 67. (7") *(S 1250)* **TOGETHER WE LIVE, TOGETHER WE LOVE. / I WONDER** [-] [-] Dutch

Capitol / Capitol

May 68. (lp) *<ST 164>* **MIRACLE MIRROR** [-] [ ]
– Truth about Arthur / Circus will be in town in time / Crystal heaven / Sam & Sue / I've just lost somebody / Mr. Fortune's wife / Who cares / Born a second time / Magnificent magistral / Nothing can change this world of mine / Gipsy rhapsody.

Jun 68. (7") *(CL 15552)* **I'VE JUST LOST SOMEBODY. / THE TRUTH ABOUT ARTHUR** [ ] [ ]

—— (late 1967) added **BARRY HAY** (b.16 Aug'48, Faizabad) – vocals, occasional guitar flute, saxophone

Nov 68. (7") *(CL 15567)* **DONG-DONG-DIKI-DIGI-DONG. / WAKE UP BREAKFAST!** [ ] [-]

—— (were still signed to 'Polydor' in Holland)

—— **SIEB WARNER** – drums; repl. JAAP; he re-emerged in medley outfit STARSOUND

Major Minor / Polydor

Mar 69. (7") *(MM 601)* **JUST A LITTLE BIT OF PEACE IN MY HEART. / REMEMBER MY FRIEND** [ ] [-]

Aug 69. (7") *(MM 633)* **IT'S ALRIGHT BUT I ADMIT IT COULD BE BETTER. / WHERE WILL I BE** [ ] [-]

Sep 69. (7") *<2-14001>* **IT'S ALRIGHT I ADMIT IT COULD BE BETTER. / SONG OF A DEVIL'S SERVANT** [-] [ ]

GOLDEN EARRING

Major Minor / Atlantic

Jan 70. (lp) *(SMLP 65) <SD 8244>* **EIGHT MILES HIGH** [ ] [ ]
– Landing / Song of a Devil's servant / One high road / Everyday's torture / Eight miles high. *(cd-iss. 1987; 825 371-2)*

Feb 70. (7") *(MM 679)* **ANOTHER FORTY-FIVE MILES. / I CAN'T GET HOLD OF HER** [ ] [-]

Feb 70. (7") *<45-2710>* **EIGHT MILES HIGH. / ONE HIGH ROAD** [-] [ ]

—— **CESAR ZUIDERWIJK** (b.18 Jul'48) – drums; repl. SIEB

Polydor / Perception

1970. (lp) *(2310 049) <PDLP 2000>* **GOLDEN EARRING (WALL OF DOLLS)** [ ] [ ]
– Yellow and blue / The loner / This is the time of the year / As long as the wind blows / Wall of dolls / Back home / See see / I'm going to send my pigeons to the sky / Big tree blue sea.

Sep 70. (7") *(2001 073)* **BACK HOME. / THIS IS THE TIME OF THE YEAR** [ ] [-]

Feb 71. (7") *(2001 135)* **HOLY HOLY LIFE. / JESSICA** [-] [-] Dutch

Oct 71. (7") *(2001 237)* **SHE FLIES ON STRANGE WINGS. / (part 2)** [ ] [-]

Oct 71. (lp) *(2310 135)* **SEVEN TEARS** [ ] [-]
– Silver ships / The road / Swallowed her name / Hope / Don't worry / She flies on strange wings / This is the other side of fire / You're better off free.

May 72. (7") *(2050 184)* **BUDDY JOE. / AVALANCHE OF LOVE** [-] [-] Dutch

Jun 72. (lp) *(2310 210)* **TOGETHER** [ ] [-]
– All day watcher / Avalanche of love / Cruising Southern Germany / Brother wind / Buddy Joe / Jangalene / From Heaven to Hell / Thousand feet below.

Sep 72. (7") *(2050 216)* **STAND BY ME. / ALL DAY WATCHER** [-] [-] Dutch

Track / Track

1973. (lp) *(2406 109)* **HEARING EARRING** (compilation of last 2 lp's) [ ] [-]
– Jangeline / All day watcher / She flies on strange wings / Avalanche of love / Silver ships / Brother wind / Hope / Thousand feet below.

Aug 73. (7") *(2050 262)* **RADAR LOVE. / THE SONG IS OVER** [-] [-] Dutch

Nov 73. (7") *(2094 116) <40202>* **RADAR LOVE. / JUST LIKE VINCE TAYLOR** [7] [13] Apr74

Dec 73. (lp) *(2406 112) <396>* **MOONTAN** [24] [12] Apr74
– Radar love / Candy's going bad / Vanilla queen / Big tree, blue sea / Are you receiving me. *<US cd-iss. Jun88 on 'M.C.A.'; 31014>*

May 74. (7") *(2094 121)* **INSTANT POETRY. / FROM HEAVEN, FROM HELL** [ ] [ ]

Nov 74. (7") *(2094 126) <40309>* **CANDY'S GOING BAD. / SHE FLIES ON STRANGE WINGS** [ ] [91] Oct74

—— added **ROBERT-JAN STIPS** (b.4 Feb'50) – keyboards

Track / M.C.A.

Mar 75. (7") *(2094 130) <40369>* **CE SOIR. / LUCKY NUMBERS** [ ] [ ]

Apr 75. (lp) *(2406 117) <2139>* **SWITCH** [ ] [ ]
– (intro) / Plus minus absurdio / Love is a rodeo / Switch / Kill me, ce soir / Tons of times / Daddy's gonna save my soul / Troubles and hassles / Lonesome D.J.

Jun 75. (7") *<40412>* **SWITCH. / LONESOME D.J.** [-] [ ]

Polydor / M.C.A.

Jan 76. (7") *(2001 626) <40513>* **SLEEP WALKIN'. / BABYLON** [ ] [ ]

Mar 76. (lp) *(2430 330) <2183>* **TO THE HILT** [ ] [ ] Feb76
– Why me / Facedancer / To the hilt / Nomad / Sleep walkin' / Latin lightnin' / Violins.

—— **EELCO GELLING** – guitar (ex-guest) repl. STIPS (remained guest)

Feb 77. (7") *(2121 312)* **BOMBAY. / FADED JEANS** [ ] [-]

Mar 77. (lp)(c) *(2310 491)(3100 340) <2254>* **CONTRABAND** <US-title 'MAD LOVE'> [ ] [ ] May77
– Bombay / Sueleen (Sweden) / Con man / Mad love's comin' / Fightin' windmills / Faded jeans / Time's up.

Sep 77. (d-lp) *(2625 034)* **GOLDEN EARRING LIVE (live)** [ ] [-]
– Candy's going bad / She flies on strange wings / Mad love's comin' / Eight miles high / The vanilla queen / To the hilt / Fightin' windmills / Con man / Radar love / Just like Vince Taylor. *(re-iss. Oct93; SPELP 44)*

Sep 77. (12") *(2121 335)* **RADAR LOVE (live). / JUST LIKE VINCE TAYLOR (live)** [44] [-]

Oct 77. (7") *<40802>* **RADAR LOVE (live). / RADAR LOVE (studio)** [-] [ ]

Polydor / Polydor

Jan 79. (lp) *(2310 639) <1-6223>* **GRAB IT FOR A SECOND** <US-title 'NO PROMISES'> [ ] [ ]
– Movin' down life / Against the grain / Grab it for a second / Cell 29 / Roxanne / Leather / Temptin' / U-turn time.

1980. (lp) *(2344 161) <1-6303>* **PRISONER OF THE NIGHT** <US-title 'LONG BLOND ANIMAL'> [-] [ ] Dutch
– Long blond animal / No for an answer / My town / Prisoner of the night / I don't wanna be nobody else / Cut 'em down to size / Will & Mercy / Come in Outerspace / Going crazy again.

Sep 81. (7") *<14581>* **WEEKEND LOVE. / TIGER BAY** [-] [ ]

Sep 81. (d-lp)(c) *(2625 042)(3500 130)* **SECOND LIVE (live)** [-] [-] Dutch
– Don't stop the show / My town / No for an answer / Heartbeat / Save your skin / I don't wanna be nobody else / Long blond animal / Prisoner of the night / Weekend love / Sleepwalkin' / I do rock'n'roll / Slow down / Buddy Joe / Back home.

Mercury / 21 Records

Jan 83. (7"/12") *(MER/+X 122) <103>* **TWILIGHT ZONE. / KING DARK** [ ] [10] Nov82

Philips 21 Records

Apr 83. (lp/c) *(6302/7144 224) <9004>* **CUT** [ ] [24] Nov82
– The Devil made me do it / Future / Baby dynamite / Last of the Mohicans / Lost and found / Twilight zone / Chargin' up my batteries / Secrets.

Apr 83. (7") *<108>* **THE DEVIL MADE ME DO IT. / CHARGIN' UP MY BATTERIES** [-] [79]

Carrere 21 Records

Apr 84. (7"/12") *(CAR/+T 321) <112>* **WHEN THE LADY SMILES. / ORWELL'S YEAR** [ ] [76] Mar84

Apr 84. (lp/c) *(CAL/CAC 204) <9008>* **N.E.W.S.** [ ] [ ] Mar84
– Clear night moonlight / When the lady smiles / Enough is enough / Fist in love / N.E.W.S. / I'll make it all up to you / Mission impossible / It's over now. *(cd-iss. 1988;)*

21 Records 21 Records

Feb 85. (lp) *(21-0022) <823717>* **SOMETHING HEAVY GOING DOWN – LIVE FROM THE TWILIGHT ZONE (live)** [ ] [ ] Nov84
– Long blond animal / Twilight zone / When the lady smiles / Future / Something heavy going down / Enough is enough / Mission impossible / Clear night moonlight.

Apr 86. (7") *(21-043)* **QUIET EYES. / GIMME A BREAK** [-] [-] Dutch

Jun 86. (lp) *(21-0022) <90514>* **THE HOLE** [-] [ ] German
– They dance / Quiet eyes / Save the best for later / Have a heart / Love in motion / Jane Jane / Jump and run / Why do I / Shout in the dark.

Jun 86. (7") *<7-99533>* **QUIET EYES. / LOVE IN MOTION** [-] [ ]

Nov 86. (7") *<7-99515>* **WHY DO I. / LOVE IN MOTION** [-] [ ]

Dec 86. (7") *(21-049)* **THEY DANCE. / LOVE IN MOTION** [-] [-] Dutch

GEORGE KOOYMANS

— Note:- GEORGE was first to moonlight solo with the 7", 'LOVIN' AND HURTIN' / 'FOR GAIL' on 'Polydor' (2050 156); both from the Dutch-only LP, 'JOJO' (2925 004)

Ring not iss.

1987. (7") *(108 814)* **LOST FOR LOVE. / THE DEVIL RIDES AGAIN TONIGHT** [-] [-] Dutch

1987. (lp) *(258 167)* **SOLO** [-] [-] Dutch
– Lost for love, give it all you got / World of our own / I'll never give in / To you / The Devil rides again tonight / The beat goes on / Shoot the man down / Lonely hearts / Again.

1987. (7") *(108 814)* **LOST FOR LOVE. / THE DEVIL RIDES AGAIN TONIGHT** [-] [-] Dutch

1987. (7") *(109 095)* **THE BEAT GOES ON. / AGAIN** [-] [-] Dutch

1988. (7") *(109 260)* **WORLD OF OUR OWN. / ALL THINGS ARE LIGHT** [-] [-] Dutch

— Also:- GERRITSEN delivered a one-off US-only single in 1980 for 'Atco', 'ROCK AND BEAST' / 'SUZY'S SONG' <7213> (from the set 'DE G.V.D. BAND' with MICHEL VAN DIK), while ZUIDERWIJK issued two in the mid-80's, 'GIVE ME BACK MY FEELINGS' / 'BETWEEN DUSK AND DAYLIGHT' (21 Records; 039) and 'HELP ME OUT' / 'GRIMACE' (041); taken from the LP, 'LABYRINTH' <90477-1>

BARRY HAY

— Note:- BARRY had issued a single in '72, 'DID YOU REALLY MEAN IT' / 'ROLL ANOTHER ROCK' for 'Polydor' (2050 193); taken from the Dutch-only LP, 'ONLY PARROTS, FROGS AND ANGELS' (2925 006).

Nov 87. (7") *(109 460)* **DRAGGIN' THE LINE. / WHAT KINDA LOVE** [-] [-] Dutch

Dec 87. (lp) *(208 498)* **VICTORY OF BAD TASTE** [-] [-] Dutch
– Draggin' the line / I'd lie to you for your love / Jezebel / My favourite spot / Firewater / Did you really mean it / She's here / Girl / Going blind.

Feb 88. (7") *(109 672)* **JEZEBEL. / GOING BLIND** [-] [-] Dutch

GOLDEN EARRING

— re-formed in the late 80's, with **HAY, GERRITSEN, KOOYMANS + ZUIDERWIJK**

Feb 88. (7") *(21-055)* **MY KILLER, MY SHADOW. / (version)** [-] [-]
(12"+=)(cd-s+=) *(2-155)(100.142)* – ('A'extended).

Music Box not iss.

Apr 89. (7") *(559-7)* **TURN THE WORLD AROUND. / YOU GUN MY LOVE** [-] [-] Dutch
(cd-s+=) *(559-3)* – Say my prayer.

Apr 89. (lp) *(40402) (Dutch; JAWS 5542)* **KEEPER OF THE FLAME** [ ] [-]
– Can do that / Too much woman / One word / Keeper of the flame / Turn the world around / Circles / My killer, my shadow / Distant love.

Jun 89. (7") *(5512-7)* **DISTANT LOVE. / NIGHTHAWKS** [-] [-] Dutch
(cd-s+=) *(5512-3)* – Can't do that.

— (basically same line-up for over 20 years)

Columbia First Quake

Apr 91. (7"/3"cd-s) *(656802-7/-1)* **GOING TO THE RUN. / TIME WARP** [-] [-] Dutch
(12"+=/cd-s+=) *(656802-6/-2)* – Steam roller.

Jun 91. (7"/3"cd-s) *(657283-7/-1)* **TEMPORARY MADNESS. / ONE SHOT AWAY FROM PARADISE** [-] [-] Dutch
(12"+=/cd-s+=) *(657283-6/-2)* – Madame Zou Zou.

Aug 91. (cd/c/lp) *(468093-2/-4/-1) <FQCD 4482-2>* **BLOODY BUCHANEERS** [ ] [ ]
– Making love to yourself / Temporary madness / When love turns to pain / Joe / Planet blue / Going to the run / Bloody buchaneers / One shot away from Paradise / In a bad mood / Pouring my heart out again.

Dec 91. (7") *(657545-7)* **POURING MY HEART OUT AGAIN. / PLANET BLUE** [-] [-] Dutch
(d7"+=/cd-s+=) *(657545-0/-2)* – When the lady smiles (live) / Back home (live).

Feb 92. (7") *(657809-7)* **MAKING LOVE TO YOURSELF. / IN A BAD MOOD** [-] [-] Dutch
(cd-s+=) *(657809-2)* – When love turns to pain.

Apr 92. (7") *(658025-7)* **RADAR LOVE. / BLOODY BUCCANEERS** [-] [-] Dutch
(cd-s+=) *(658025-2)* – Joe.

1993. (12") *(658952-1)* **ANOTHER 45 MILES (live-acoustic). / WHEN THE LADY SMILES (live-acoustic)** [-] [-] Dutch
(cd-s+=) *(658952-2)* – Going to the run (live-acoustic).

1993. (d-cd) *(472619-2) <4481>* **THE NAKED TRUTH** (live-acoustic) [-] [ ] Dutch
– (introduction) / Jangalene / Another 45 miles / Mad love's comin' / Why do I / I can't sleep with you / Weekend love / Vanilla queen / Twilight zone / One shot away from paradise / Long blond animal / Pouring my heart out again / Radar love / Eight miles high / The naked truth. *(UK-iss.Jan99 on 'Epic'; 472619-2)*

1993. (cd-ep's) *(659333-2'5)* **LONG BLOND ANIMAL (live-acoustic) / TWILIGHT ZONE (live-acoustic) / JANGALENE (live-acoustic) / DON'T STOP THE SHOW (live-acoustic)** [-] [-] Dutch

1993. (cd-s) *(659719-1)* **AS LONG AS THE WIND BLOWS (live-acoustic) / PLEASE GO (live-acoustic) / SOUND OF THE SCREAMING DAY (live-acoustic)** [-] [-] Dutch
(cd-s+=) *(659719-2)* – Murdock 9-6182 (live-acoustic).

1994. (cd-s) *(660761-1)* **HOLD ME NOW / LIVIN' WITH ME (AIN'T THAT EASY)** [-] [-] Dutch
(cd-s+=) *(660761-2)* – Freedom don't last forever.

1994. (cd-s) *(661150-1)* **JOHNNY MAKE BELIEVE / MINUTE BY MINUTE** [-] [-] Dutch
(cd-s+=) *(661150-2)* – Spaceship (remix) / Hold me now (remix).

1995. (cd-s) *(661380-1)* **ANGEL / THE UNFORGETTABLE DREAM** [-] [-] Dutch
(cd-s+=) *(661380-2)* – Yellow and blue (live-acoustic) / The Devil made me do it (live-acoustic).

Jun 95. (cd/c) *(477650-2/-4)* **FACE IT** [ ] [ ]
– Angel / Hold me now / Liquid soul / Minute by minute / Johnny make believe / Spaceship / The unforgettable dream / I can't do without your kiss / Freedom don't last forever / Maximum make up / Legalize telepathy.

Nov 95. (cd) *(481122-2)* **LOVESWEAT** (covers) [-] [-] Dutch

1996. (cd-s) *(662831-1)* **THIS WHEEL'S ON FIRE / MY LITTLE RED BOOK** [-] [-] Dutch
(cd-s+=) *(662831-2)* – So you want to be a rock'n'roll star – L.A. woman.

1996. (cd-s) *(663224-1)* **GOTTA SEE JANE / TRY A LITTLE TENDERNESS** [-] [-] Dutch

C.N.R. not iss.

1997. (c-s) *(200340-4)* **BURNING STUNTMAN / BOMBAY** [-] [-] Dutch
(cd-s+=) *(200340-5)* – When I was young (live) / This wheel's on fire (live).

1997. (cd) *(2003 447)* **NAKED II** (live-acoustic([-] [-] Dutch

1998. (cd-s) *(2003 607)* **THE DEVIL MADE ME DO IT / MOOD INDIGO** [-] [-] Dutch
(cd-s) *(200360-8)* – ('A'side) / Holy holy life / Kill me (ce soir) / ('A'version).

Mar 99. (cd-ep) *(48003)* **PARADISE IN DISTRESS EP** [-] [-] Dutch
– Paradise in distress / Fluid conduction / Leather / Are you receiving me.

– compilations, others, etc. –

on Polydor' unless mentioned otherwise

Oct 76. (lp) *(2482 329)* **GOLDEN EARRING** [ ] [-]

Nov 80. (d-lp)(c) *(2664 440)(3578 487)* **GREATEST HITS** [ ] [-]

Mar 86. (7") *Old Gold; (OG 9582)* **RADAR LOVE. / TWILIGHT ZONE** [ ] [-]

May 88. (cd) *Arcade; (01290161)* **THE VERY BEST OF GOLDEN EARRING VOLUME 1** [ ] [-]

May 88. (cd) *Arcade; (01290261)* **THE VERY BEST OF GOLDEN EARRING VOLUME 2** [ ] [-]

1989. (cd) *M.C.A.; <MCAD 6355>* **THE CONTINUING STORY OF RADAR LOVE** [-] [ ]

Jul 92. (cd) *Connoisseur; (VSOPCD 171)* **THE BEST OF GOLDEN EARRING** [ ] [-]
– Radar love / She flies on strange wings / Kill me / Mission impossible / Vanilla queen / Sleepwalkin' / Long blonde animal / Weekend love / When the lady smiles / Quiet eyes / Twilight zone / Turn the world around / Eight miles high.

Aug 00. (d-cd) *C.N.R.; (2004480)* **LAST BLAST OF THE CENTURY** [ ] [-]

GOLDFINGER

Formed: Los Angeles, California, USA ... 1994 by leader JOHN FELDMANN and his skatalistic punk mates CHARLIE PAULSON, SIMON WILLIAMS and DARRIN PFEIFFER. Signed to 'Universal' subsidiary, 'Uptown' on the strength of the 'FREAKY NASTY' single, GOLDFINGER released their eponymous debut album in 1996 amidst a considerable press buzz and a US radio hit with 'HERE IN YOUR BEDROOM'. Despite a punishing tour schedule, the group managed to find time to record a sophomore effort, 'HANG-UPS' (1997). While this attempted to broaden their ska-punk musical canvas with more contemporary brush strokes, the live mini-set, 'DARRIN'S COCONUT ASS' (1999), unashamedly revealed their new wave roots with covers of everyone from Joe Jackson ('IS SHE REALLY GOING OUT WITH HIM') to The Cure ('JUST LIKE HEAVEN'). Come the new millennium, the band were still in cover mode courtesy of a reading Nena's 80's classic, '99 RED BALLOONS' tucked away at the end of 'STOMPING GROUND' (2000). • **Covered:** FEEL LIKE MAKING LOVE (Bad Company) / NITE CLUB (Specials) / THE KIDS ARE ALRIGHT (Who) / etc. • **Note:** Not to be confused with the GOLDFINGER that issued the 12"ep, 'Season To Season', in September '94; add to the '8.5%' 12" with LOCHIL in '97.

Album rating: THIS BEAT IS FOR FREAKS mini (*4) / GOLDFINGER (*6) / HANG-UPS (*6) / DARRIN'S COCONUT ASS: LIVE mini (*4) / STOMPING GROUND (*6)

JOHN FELDMANN – vocals, guitar / **CHARLIE PAULSON** – guitar / **SIMON WILLIAMS** – bass / **DARRIN PFEIFFER** – drums / + a versatile horn section

not iss. Ultrax

1994. (12"/c-s) *<2001-1/-4>* **THIS BEAT IS FOR FREAKS** [-] [ ] not iss. Jazzmind

Feb 95. (cd-s) *<4001>* **FREAKY NASTY /** [-] [ ]

Universal Universal

Nov 96. (cd) *<(UND 53007)>* **GOLDFINGER** [ ] [ ] Feb96
– Mind's eye / Stay / Here in your bedroom / Only a day / KIng for a day / Anxiety / Answers / Anything / Mable / The city with two faces / My girlfriend's shower sucks / Miles away / Nothing to prove / Pictures. *<originally issued in US on 'Mojo'; 17>*

Sep 97. (cd) *<UND 53079>* **HANG-UPS** [-] [85]
– Superman / My head / If only / This lonely place / 20c goodbye / Question / Disorder / Carlita / Too late / I need to know / Authority / S.M.P. / Last time / Chris Cayton.

Dec 97. (cd-s) *<1188>* **MY HEAD** [-] [ ]

— **KELLY LEMIEUX** – bass; repl. WILLIAMS

Nov 99. (m-cd) *<UND 153270>* **DARRIN'S COCONUT ASS: LIVE (live)** [-] [ ]
– Just like heaven / Is she really going out with him? / Feel like making love / Nite club / The kids are alright / Downpressor man / You say you don't love me / Man in the suitcase.

2000. (cd) *<157531>* **STOMPING GROUND** [-] [ ]
– I'm down / Pick a fight / Carry on / The end of the day / Don't say goodbye / Counting the days / Bro / San Simeon / You think it's a joke / Forgiveness / Margaret Ann / Get away / 99 red balloons / Donut Dan.

GOOBER PATROL

Formed: Norwich, England . . . 1989 by SIMON ROBERT SANDALL, his brother STUART SANDALL and TOM BLYTH. Taking their cue from the likes of SENSELESS THINGS and SNUFF and taking their moniker from Goober peas – a term for peanuts eaten by poor people – the fresh-faced pop-punks made their debut in 1991 with the cheekily-titled 'TRUCK OFF'. By the release of 1992's 'DUTCH OVENS' (apparently a euphemism for breaking wind under the bed sheets!), the lads' irrepressible enthusiasm was being at least partially matched by musical expertise, their growing reputation leading to high-profile support slots with such up and coming US luminaries as GREEN DAY and NOFX. By this point, a fourth member, TIM SNELSON, had been added, the guitarist making his debut on the first of a batch of singles, 'BAD COMEDY'. Despite never achieving quite the same level of success as their US peers, GOOBER PATROL subsequently signed to FAT MIKE's 'Fat Wreck Chords' in the States ('Them's Good' in Britain), through whom they've since released two sets, 'VACATION' (1996) and 'UNBEARABLE LIGHTNESS OF BEING DRUNK' (1998).

Album rating: TRUCK OFF (*4) / DUTCH OVENS (*5) / VACATION (*5) / EXTENDED VACATION (*5)

SIMON ROBERT SANDALL – vocals, guitar / **TOM BLYTH** – bass / **STUART SANDALL** – vocals, drums

Boss Tuneage not iss.

1991. (lp) *(BOSTAGE 004)* **TRUCK OFF** [ ] [-]
– Timothy / Do it right / She knows / What's the point / I think it's time / Stop me / Hand in hand / Shadows and reflections / Playing with fire / 20 minute song / You can't repeat / Small gain / Wasn't it you. *(cd-iss. Aug98 on 'Them's Good'; GOOD 004CD)*

Oct 92. (lp/cd) *(BOSTAGE 009/+CD)* **DUTCH OVENS** [ ] [-]
– Hay, hay and thrice hay / Paddington bear / Don't give up your day job / I can hear / Far below you / Northwest / Waterfront / Tailor made / Here she comes / Part of me / Easy life / Good times, bad times / Piss off. *(cd re-iss. Aug98 on 'Them's Good'; GOOD 001CD)*

— added **TIM SNELSON** – guitar

Lost & Found not iss.

1993. (7") **BAD COMEDY. /** [-] [-] German

Them's Good Fat Wreck Chords

Mar 96. (7") *(GOOD 003S)* **THE BIGGEST JOKE. / SMELL THE COFFEE** [ ] [-]

Apr 96. (cd) *(GOOD 002CD)* *<FAT 541>* **VACATION** [ ] [ ]
– Easy life / I'll do without / Empty / Crammin' / Egghead / The biggest joke / One more time / Happy tunes / Grabbers / 1000 ways / Duvet rising / Painless way / I'm not home / Piss off.
(re-iss. Aug98; same) (lp-iss.Oct96; as US)

Aug 98. (cd) *(GOOD 005CD)* **EXTENDED VACATION** [ ] [-]
– Dollar creed / It's OK / Downward nobility / Tow the line / Overboards / Worse things happen at C / We deal you choose / In at the deep end / Years behind. *(cd+=)* – (hidden track).

Fat Wreck Chords Fat Wreck Chords

Oct 98. (cd) *(<FAT 577>)* **UNBEARABLE LIGHTNESS OF BEING DRUNK** [ ] [ ]
– 1000th beer / Not that shrewd / Easy answers / Unbearable lightness of being drunk / Part-time SF ecologist / Stereophonic nutter / Don't you let nobody / High time / Watch us drown / Nothing can go wrong / Different window / I forget your name.

— disbanded after above

GOOD RIDDANCE

Formed: Santa Cruz, California, USA . . . 1986 as a straight-edged, political hardcore/punk outfit. Frontman RUSS RANKIN and his musical buddies LUKE PABICH, CHUCK PLATT and SEAN "SC" SELLERS were in there right from the start, keeping the punk spirit alive. A one-off 7" in 1990, 'GIDGET', took a long time to follow. However in 1995, they finally hit out on the album front via 'FOR GOD AND COUNTRY', their first of a handful on 'Fat Wreck Chords'. A second set a year later, 'A COMPREHENSIVE GUIDE TO MODERNE REBELLION' (1996), was much of the same and if you liked your punk with attitude then GOOD RIDDANCE were there for the taking. Tours supporting the likes of NO USE FOR A NAME and SICK OF IT ALL put paid to any releases, although they were soon back with album No.3 'BALLADS FROM THE REVOLUTION' (1998). A year later, the album 'OPERATION PHOENIX' (1999), picked up the tempo once again. However, SELLERS was to depart soon after, his temporary replacement being LAGWAGON's DAVE RAUN. An EP, the BILL STEVENSON-produced 'THE PHENOMENON OF CRAVING' (2000) was promoted by a Warped Tour 2000 series of gigs while SELLERS' more permanent replacement came in the shape of DAVE WAGENSCHUTZ.

Album rating: FOR GOD AND COUNTRY (*5) / A COMPREHENSIVE GUIDE TO MODERNE REBELLION (*5) / BALLADS FROM THE REVOLUTION (*5) / OPERATION PHOENIX (*4)

RUSS RANKIN – vocals / **LUKE PABICH** – guitar / **CHUCK PLATT** – bass / **SEAN "SC" SELLERS** – drums

not iss. Little Deputy

1990. (7") **GIDGET. /** [-] [ ]

Fat Wreck Chords Fat Wreck Chords

Mar 95. (lp/c/cd) *<(FAT 523/+MC/CD)>* **FOR GOD AND COUNTRY** [ ] [ ] Feb95
– Flies first class / Better / All fall down / United cigar / Decoy / Boys and girls / Mother Superior / Twelve year circus / Man of God / Lisa / Wrong again / October.

Jun 96. (lp/c/cd) *<(FAT 539/+MC/CD)>* **A COMPREHENSIVE GUIDE TO MODERNE REBELLION** [ ] [ ]
– Weight of the world / Steps / A credit to his gender / Trophy / Up and away / Last believer / Static / Favorite son / West End memorial / This is the light / Bittersweet / Token idiot / Come dancing / Lampshade / Think of me / Sky is falling / Sometimes.

Mar 98. (lp/c/cd) *<(FAT 565/+MC/CD)>* **BALLADS FROM THE REVOLUTION** [ ] [ ] Feb98
– Fertile fields / Sacrifice / State control / Jeannie / Salt / Choices made / Not with him / Understood / Waste / Slowly / Without anger / Holding on / Eversmile / I.S.Y.L. / Years from now.

May 99. (lp/cd) *<(FAT 587/+CD)>* **OPERATION PHOENIX** [ ] [ ]
– Shadows of defeat / Blueliner / The hardest part / Eighteen seconds / Heresy, hypocrisy and revenge / Self-fulfilling catastrophe / Article IV / Indoctrination / Shit-talking capitalists / Letters home / 30 day wonder / Dear Cammi / Yesterday died – Tomorrow won't be born / Winning the hearts and minds / A time and a place / Second coming / After the nightmare.

— **DAVE RAUN** – drums (of LAGWAGON) repl. SELLERS

May 00. (10"ep/cd-ep) *<(FAT 611/+CD)>* **THE PHENOMENON OF CRAVING** [ ] [ ]
– Cages / One for the braves / Uniontown / Calendar / Start at zero / Undefeated.

— **DAVE WAGENSCHUTZ** – drums (ex-KID DYNAMITE) repl. RAUN

Miles GOODWYN (see under ⇒ APRIL WINE)

GOO GOO DOLLS

Formed: Buffalo, New York, USA . . . 1986 by ROBBY TAKAC (a former DJ), JOHNNY RZEZNIK and GEORGE TUTUSKA. Like a grunge-punk fusion of CHEAP TRICK, The LEMONHEADS and The DESCENDENTS, they debuted the following year with a low-rent eponymous debut album thankfully not given a release in Britain. A follow-up, 'JED' (1989), was also sprinkled with the odd cover version, a reading of Creedence Clearwater Revival's 'DOWN ON THE CORNER' presided over by guest crooner, LANCE DIAMOND. In the early 90's, 'Metal Blade' took over the reins, their powerful metal-punk winning new audiences after the release of their third set, 'HOLD ME UP' (1990). Three years on, the GOO GOO DOLLS returned with 'SUPERSTAR CARWASH', a transitional set preceding their break for the big time. GEORGE had now been replaced by MIKE MALININ, the sticksman coming in for the band's LOU GIORDANO-produced set, 'A BOY NAMED GOO' (1995), a US Top 30 success that featured Top 5 smash, 'NAME'. However, unlike many of their peers (GREEN DAY, OFFSPRING, etc), the 'DOLLS didn't really translate to the saturated British market despite having another two radio airplay hits in the States, both taken from 1998 album, 'DIZZY UP THE GIRL'. • **Covered:** I WANNA DESTROY YOU (Soft Boys) / DON'T FEAR THE REAPER (Blue Oyster Cult) / SUNSHINE OF YOUR LOVE (Cream) / I COULD NEVER TAKE THE PLACE OF YOUR MAN (Prince) / GIMME SHELTER (Rolling Stones) / I DON'T WANNA KNOW (Fleetwood Mac) / etc.

Album rating: GOO GOO DOLLS (*4) / JED (*4) / HOLD ME UP (*5) / SUPERSTAR CARWASH (*5) / A BOY NAMED GOO (*7) / DIZZY UP THE GIRL (*5)

JOHNNY RZEZNIK (b. 5 Dec'65) – vocals, guitar / **ROBBY TAKAC** (b.30 Sep'64) – bass, vocals / **GEORGE TUTUSKA** – drums

Celluloid Mercenary

1987. (lp) *(2211)* *<97292-2>* **GOO GOO DOLLS** [-] [ ] French
– Torn apart / Messed up / Livin' in a hut / I'm addicted / Sunshine of your love / Hardsores / Hammering eggs (the metal song) / (Don't fear) The reaper / Beat me / Scream / Slaughterhouse / Different light / Come on / Don't beat my ass (with a baseball bat). *(re-iss. Nov95 on 'Metal Blade'; 14079-2)*

Roadracer Death-Enigma

Apr 89. (lp/cd) *(RO 9477-1/-2)* *<847859>* **JED** [ ] [ ]
– Out of sight / Up yours / No way out / 7th of last month / Love dolls / Sex maggot / Down on the corner / Had enough / Road to Salinas / Em Elbmuh / Misfortune / Artie / Gimme shelter / James Dean. *(cd re-iss. Feb94 on 'Metal Blade'; CDZORRO 70)*

Fun After All / Metal Blade

Nov 90. (lp/cd) *(AFTER 8/+CD)* <26259-1/-2> **HOLD ME UP** [ ] [ ]
– Laughing / Just the way you are / So outta line / There you are / You know what I man / Out of the red / I could never take the place of your man / Hey / On your side / 22 seconds / Kevin's song / Know my name / Million miles away / Two days in February. *(cd re-iss. May96 on 'Metal Blade'; 3984 17018CD)*

Warners / Warners

1993. (cd/c) *<9362 45206-2/-4>* **SUPERSTAR CARWASH** [-] [ ]
– Fallin' down / Lucky star / Cuz you're gone / Don't worry / Girl right next to me / Domino / We are the normal / String of lies / Another second time around / Stop the world / Already there / On the lie / Close your eyes / So far away. *(UK-iss.Aug99 on 'Edel'; 0102702HWR)*

— **MIKE MALININ** (b.10 Oct'67, Washington, DC) – drums, vocals; repl. GEORGE

Apr 95. (cd/c) *<(9362 45750-2/-4)>* **A BOY NAMED GOO** [ ] [27]
– Long way down / Burnin' up / Naked / Flat top / Impersonality / Name / Only one / Somethin' bad / Ain't that unusual / So long / Eyes wide open / Disconnected / Slave girl. *(cd re-iss. Aug99 on 'Edel'; 0103122HWR)*

May 95. (c-s) *(W 0293C)* **ONLY ONE / IMPERSONALITY** [ ] [ ]
(cd-s+=) *(W 0293CD)* – Hit or miss.

Sep 95. (c-s) *<17758>* **NAME / BURNIN' UP / HIT OR MISS** [-] [5]

Feb 96. (c-s) *(W 0333C)* **NAME / NOTHING CAN CHANGE YOU** [ ] [-]
(cd-s+=) *(W 0333CD)* – I wanna destroy you.

Jul 96. (c-s) *(W 0362C)* **LONG WAY DOWN / NAME (live)** [ ] [-]
(cd-s+=) *(W 0362CD)* – Don't change (live).

Jul 98. (c-s) *(W 0449C)* *<44525>* **IRIS / LAZY EYE** [50] [9] Sep98
(cd-s+=) *(W 0449CD)* – I don't want to know.

Hollywood / Imprint-Warners

Mar 99. (c-s) *(010239HWR)* *<1763>* **SLIDE / ACOUSTIC #3** [43] [8] Nov98
(cd-s+=) *(010205HWR)* – Nothing can change you.

Jul 99. (c-s/cd-s) *(01024 89/42 HWR)* **IRIS / IRIS (acoustic)** [26] [-]

Jul 99. (cd/c) *(0102042HWR)* *<47058-2/-4>* **DIZZY UP THE GIRL** [47] [15] Sep98
– Dizzy / Slide / Broadway / January friend / Black balloon / Bullet proof / Amigone / All eyes on me / Full forever / Acoustic #3 / Iris / Extra pale / Hate this place.

Nov 99. (c-s/cd-s) *(010535 9/5 HWR)* **DIZZY / SLIDE (acoustic)** [ ] [-]

Feb 00. (c-s/cd-s) *(010311 9/5 HWR)* *<16946>* **BLACK BALLOON / BLACK BALLOON (album version) / NAKED** [ ] [16] Jul99

Apr 00. (-) *<album cut>* **BROADWAY** [-] [24]

GOREFEST

Formed: Netherlands . . . 1989 by JAN-CHRIS DE KOEIJER and FRANK HARTHOORN. With MARK and ALEX completing the line-up, the group released their 'MINDLOSS' (1991) album in 1991 although the latter two were soon replaced by ED WARBY and BOUDEWIJN BONEBAKKER respectively. The first fruits of a new deal with 'Nuclear Blast' arrived in the shape of 1992's 'FALSE', a record which quickly became a must-have in underground death metal circles. The band's growing fanbase was out in force for their appearance at the annual Dynamo Festival in Eindhoven, a performance recorded for posterity and released as 'THE EINDHOVEN INSANITY' in 1994. Subsequent albums, 'ERASE' (1995) and 'SOUL SURVIVOR' (1996) found GOREFEST tempering their more extreme instincts with elements of 70's stoner rock in line with contemporaries like ENTOMBED. Yet 'CHAPTER 13' (1998), released on the 'Steamhammer/SPV' label, proved to be the band's epitaph as they announced their split a matter of months after the record's release.

Album rating: MINDLOSS (*4) / FALSE (*7) / THE EINDHOVEN INSANITY (*5) / ERASE (*6) / SOUL SURVIVOR (*7) / CHAPTER 13 (*6)

JAN-CHRIS DE KOEIJER – vocals, bass / **BOUDEWIJN BONEBAKKER** – guitars / **FRANK HARTHOORN** – rhythm guitar / **ED WARBY** – drums

F 2000 / Pavement

Jan 92. (lp/cd) *(FDN 8244/+CD)* *<32201>* **MINDLOSS** [ ] [ ]
– Intro / Mental misery / Putrid stench of human remains / Foetal carnage / Tangled in gore / Confessions of a serial killer / Horrors in a retarded mind / Loss of flesh / Decomposed / Gorefest. *(re-iss. Aug93 on 'Nuclear Blast' cd/c/lp; NB 086-2/-4/-1)* *<re-iss. 1996 on 'Volcano'; 35020>*

Nuclear Blast / Nuclear Blast

Dec 92. (lp/pic-lp/c/cd) *(NB 069/+PD/MC/CD)* *<6056>* **FALSE** [ ] [ ]
– The glorious dead / State of mind / Reality – When you die / Get-a-life / False / Second face / Infamous existence / From ignorance to oblivion / Mass insanity.

Aug 93. (cd/c/lp) *(NB 091-2/-4/-1)* *<6087>* **THE EINDHOVEN INSANITY (live)** [ ] [ ] Jan94
– The glorious dead / State of mind / Get-a-life / Mental misery / From ignorance to oblivion / Reality – When you die / The mass insanity / Confessions of a serial killer / (Eindhoven roar).

Jul 94. (lp/c/cd) *(NB/+MC/CD 110)* *<6921>* **ERASE** [ ] [ ]
–
May95
– Low / Erase / I walk my way / Fear / Seeds of hate / Peace of paper / Goddess in black / To Hell and back. *(cd+=)* – Raven / Horrors 94. *(cd-tin-box Jan95; NB 110BOX) (cd re-iss. Apr97; NB 231CD)*

Dec 94. (cd-ep) *(NB 122-2)* **FEAR E.P.** [ ] [-]
– Fear / Raven / Horrors '94 / Fear (live).

Apr 96. (cd/c/lp) *(NB 143 CD/MC/LP)* *<6143>* **SOUL SURVIVOR** [ ] [ ] Jun96
– Freedom / Fourty shades / River / Electric poet / Soul survivor / Blood is thick / Dog day / Demon seed / Chameleon / Dragon man.

Apr 97. (cd-ep) *(NB 172CD)* **FREEDOM E.P.** [ ] [-]

S.P.V. / S.P.V.

Mar 98. (cd) *(<SPV 085-1886-2>)* **CHAPTER 13** [ ] [ ]
– Chapter 13 / Broken wing / Nothingness / Smile / The idiot / Repentance / Bordello / F.S. 2000 / All is well / Unsung / Burn out / Super reality / Serve the masses.

— disbanded in 1999

GORGOROTH

Formed: Norway . . . 1993 by guitarists INFERNUS and TORMENTOR, HAT (of the black variety presumably), KJETTAR and GOAT PERVERTOR (did VENOM really have any idea what they were starting way back when ??!!). The band's cunningly titled debut album, 'PENTAGRAM', appeared on the tiny 'Embassy' label the following year, bass duties kindly handled by EMPEROR guitarist, SAMOTH. Personnel upheaval during the recording of mini-set, 'ANTICHRIST' (1995), eventually threw up a revised line-up which included new vocalist PEST and SATYRICON's FROST. 'UNDER THE SIGN OF HELL' (1997), meanwhile, saw a rhythm section of ARES (AETURNUS) and GRIM (BORKNAGAR) pound out the unreconstructed satanic bludgeon. A new deal with 'Nuclear Blast' resulted in the 'DESTROYER' (1998) album wherein FROST again showed up alongside yet another new face, T-REAPER. The die-hard traditionalists even introduced keyboards courtesy of DAIMONION. A whole new line-up of GAAHL, KING OF HELL and SGT. ERICHSEN were in place for GORGOROTH's millennial effort, 'INCIPIT SATAN' (2000).

Album rating: PENTAGRAM (*6) / ANTICHRIST mini (*5) / UNDER THE SIGN OF HELL (*4) / DESTROYER (*7) / INCIPIT SATAN (*5)

INFERNUS – guitar / **TORMENTOR** – guitar / **HAT** – vocals / **SAMOTH** – bass (of EMPEROR) temp. repl. KJETTAR / **GOAT PERVERTOR** – drums

Embassy / Century Media

Oct 94. (cd) *(TE 001CD)* *<7935>* **PENTAGRAM** [ ] [ ]
– Begravelsenatt / Crushing the sceptor (regaining a lost dominion) / Ritual / Drommer om dod / Katharinas Bortgang / Guldrelokk / (Under) The pagan megalith / Mooneskyggens slave. *(re-iss. Apr96 on 'Malicious'; MR 007CD)*

— **PESI** – vocals; repl. HAT

— **FROST** – drums (of SATYRICON) repl. GOAT

Malicious / Century Media

May 96. (m-cd) *(MR 008CD)* *<7944>* **ANTICHRIST** [ ] [ ] Oct97
– En stram lukt av Kristent blod / Bergtrollets revon / Gorgoroth / Possessed (by Satan) / Heavens fall / Sorg.

— **STORM** – bass; joined for live work repl. SAMOTH

— **ARES** – bass (of AETURNUS) repl. STORM

— **GRIM** – drums (of BORKNAGAR) repl. FROST

Oct 97. (cd) *(MR 013CD)* *<7945>* **UNDER THE SIGN OF HELL** [ ] [ ]
– Revelation of doom / Krig / Funeral procession / Projetens upenbaring / Postludium / Odeleggelse og undergang / Blood stains the circle / The rite of infernal invocation / The Devil is calling.

— **INFERNUS + TORMENTOR** brought in new disciples . . .

— **VROLOK** – drums (of AETURNUS) repl. GRIM

— **T-REAPER** – bass; repl. ARES

— guests also incl. FROST + synth man DAIMONION

Nuclear Blast / Nuclear Blast

Jul 98. (cd) *(NB 321-2)* *<6321>* **DESTROYER** [ ] [ ]
– Destroyer / Open the gates / The Devil, the sinner and his journey / Im kristen og Jodisk Cru / Pa slagmark langt mot popr / Blodoffer / The virginborn / Slottet I det fierne.

— **GAAHL** – vocals; repl. PESI

— **KING OF HELL** – bass; repl. T-REAPER

— **SGT. ERICHSEN** – drums; repl. VROLOK

Feb 00. (cd) *(NB 423-2)* *<6423>* **INCIPIT SATAN** [ ] [ ] Mar00
– Incipit Satan / A world to win / Gitani til Satan / Unchain my heart / An excerpt of X / Fin eim au blod og heluetesild / Will to power / When love rages wild in my heart.

GORILLA BISCUITS (see under ⇒ CIV)

Lou GRAMM

Born: LOUIS GRAMMATICO, 2 May'50, Rochester, New York, USA. He formed BLACK SHEEP in 1970 with DONALD MANCUSO, enlisting the help of BRUCE TURGON, LARRY CROZIER and RON ROCCO. Finally signing to 'Capitol' records in '74 (who were probably looking for another BAD COMPANY), BLACK SHEEP released two patchy albums of rather pompous hard-rock. With this experience under his belt, LOU GRAMM, as he was now calling himself, subsequently took up the post of frontman for the new Anglo-American AOR campaigners, FOREIGNER. Over the course of the next decade or so, GRAMM developed his distintive, highly emotive vocal chords which he employed with impressive results on such FOREIGNER epics as 'FEELS LIKE THE FIRST TIME', 'WAITING FOR A GIRL LIKE YOU' and 'I WANT TO KNOW WHAT LOVE IS'. Eager to try out material unsuitable for the established FOREIGNER format, GRAMM (still with FOREIGNER) teamed up once more with TURGON to pen a US Top 30 debut solo album, 'READY OR NOT' (1987). The record proved that GRAMM could still cut the mustard, spawning the Top 5 hit, 'MIDNIGHT BLUE'. Two years later, after leaving FOREIGNER, he completed a second solo album, 'LONG HARD LOOK', which delivered another major hit, 'JUST BETWEEN YOU AND ME'. In need of a band once more, GRAMM and TURGON formed the one-off SHADOW KING project, bringing into the fold, VIVIAN CAMPBELL and KEVIN VALENTINE. It was another AOR affair, GRAMM re-joining FOREIGNER and taking TURGON with him.

Album rating: Black Sheep: BLACK SHEEP (*5) / ENCOURAGING WORDS (*5) / Lou Gramm: READY OR NOT (*5) / LONG HARD LOOK (*5) / Shadow King: SHADOW KING (*6)

BLACK SHEEP

LOUIS GRAMMATICO – vocals / **DONALD MANCUSO** – guitar / **LARRY CROZIER** – keyboards / **BRUCE TURGON** – bass / **RON ROCCO** – drums

not iss. Capitol

1975. (lp) *<11369>* **BLACK SHEEP** –

1976. (lp) *<11447>* **ENCOURAGING WORDS** –

— LOUIS became LOU GRAMM and joined FOREIGNER.

LOU GRAMM

with **BRUCE TURGON** – bass, guitar, keyboards / **PHILIP ASHLEY** – keyboards / **NILS LOFGREN** – guitar / **BEN GRAMM** – drums

Atlantic Atlantic

Feb 87. (lp/c/cd) *(K 781728-1/-4/-2) <81728>* **READY OR NOT** 27
– Ready or not / Heartache / Midnight blue / Time / Not if I don't have you / She's got to know / Arrow thru your heart / Until I make you mine / Chain of love / Lover come back.

Mar 87. (7") *(A 9034) <89304>* **MIDNIGHT BLUE. / CHAIN OF LOVE** 5 Jan87
(12"+=) *(A 9034T)* – ('A'extended).

Apr 87. (7") *<89269>* **READY OR NOT. / LOVER COME BACK** – 54

Jul 87. (7") *<89236>* **LOST IN THE SHADOWS. / POWER PLAY** –

— ASHLEY repl. by **PETER WOLF** – keyboards / **DANN HUFF** – guitar / **VIVIAN CAMPBELL** – guitar / + session people

WEA Atlantic

Oct 89. (7") *<88781>* **JUST BETWEEN YOU AND ME. / TIN SOLDIER** – 6

Jan 90. (lp/c)(cd) *(WX 228/+C)(781915-2) <81915>* **LONG HARD LOOK** 85 Nov89
– I'll come running / Heart and soul / One dream / Warmest rising sun / Hangin' on my hip / Word gets around / I'll know when it's over / Lightnin' strikes again / Angel with a dirty face / Just between you and me / Broken dreams / True blue love / Tin soldier / Day one.

Jan 90. (7") *(A 8755)* **JUST BETWEEN YOU AND ME. / DAY ONE** –
(12"+=/cd-s+=) *(A 8755 T/CD)* – Midnight blue.

Aug 90. (7")<c-s> *(A 7957) <88768>* **TRUE BLUE LOVE. / DAY ONE** 40 Feb90

– compilations, etc. –

Nov 88. (lp/cd) *Thunderbolt; (THBL/CDTB 065)* **FOREIGNER IN A STRANGE LAND** –
– Won't somebody take her home / Don't you know me, my friend / Better know your heart / I can't make it alone / How do you tell someone / Society's child / I wish I was yesterday / My baby / Headin' home / Watch you walk away.

SHADOW KING

GRAMM + TURGON / + VIVIAN CAMPBELL – guitar (ex-DIO, ex-WHITESNAKE) / **KEVIN VALENTINE** – drums

EastWest East West

Sep 91. (cd/c/lp) *<(7567 82324-2/-4/-1)>* **SHADOW KING**
– What would it take / Anytime anywhere / Once upon a time / Don't even know I'm alive / Boy / I want you / This heart of stone / Danger in the dance of love / No man's land / Russia.

— CAMPBELL joined DEF LEPPARD, GRAMM re-joined FOREIGNER with TURGON

GRAND FUNK RAILROAD

Formed: Flint, Michigan, USA . . . 1964 as TERRY KNIGHT & THE PACK, by RICHARD KNAPP, MARK FARNER and DON BREWER. A few years into their career, the soulful rock trio scored a US Top 50 hit with 'I (WHO HAVE NOTHING)'. KNIGHT subsequently became their manager in 1969, FARNER (now on vocals and guitar) and BREWER (drums) recruiting bass player MEL SCHACHER, the revamped threesome adopting the GRAND FUNK RAILROAD moniker. Along with STEPPENWOLF, MOUNTAIN, etc, they formulated their own brand of populist proto-heavy metal/rock with an emphasis on extreme volume. Having signed to 'Capitol' around the same time as their Atlanta Pop Festival appearance (mid '69), they immediately hit the US Top 50 with the single, 'TIME MACHINE', a track from their debut Top 30 album, 'ON TIME'. From that point on, the group proceeded to enjoy increasing and extremely profitable popularity with each successive release despite regular critical derision. Highly prolific, GFR delivered an album approximately every six months, the American public seemingly never tiring of their formulaic approach (in June '71, they broke The BEATLES' box-office record, selling out New York's Shea Stadium). By Spring '72, the group had split from the management of TERRY KNIGHT, hiring John Eastman (brother-in-law of PAUL McCARTNEY) to control their finances. The following year, with their moniker clipped to GRAND FUNK, the group enjoyed their finest three minutes with the US chart-topping, 'WE'RE AN AMERICAN BAND'. The similarly-titled, TODD RUNDGREN-produced parent album also shifted millions of copies, although British rock fans were more interested in prog rock or glam. In 1974, they fleshed out their sound with the brief addition of keyboard player, CRAIG FROST, who graced their second US No.1, a rock version of Little Eva's 'LOCOMOTION'. The group proceeded to churn out the inevitable hard rockin' pop hits and patchy albums, culminating in FRANK ZAPPA's disastrous 1976 attempt to redefine the band's sound with 'GOOD SINGIN', GOOD PLAYIN'. This release finally saw GRAND FUNK RAILROAD hitting the buffers at the end of the commercial line. MARK FARNER subsequently took off on a solo sojourn, returning in 1981 with some more below par GRAND FUNK material. • **Covers:** WE'VE GOTTA GET OUT OF THIS PLACE (Animals) / GIMME SHELTER (Rolling Stones) / etc.

Album rating: ON TIME (*6) / GRAND FUNK (*6) / CLOSER TO HOME (*6) / LIVE ALBUM (*6) / SURVIVAL (*6) / E PLURIBUS FUNK (*5) / PHOENIX (*5) / WE'RE AN AMERICAN BAND (*6) / SHININ' (*5) / ALL THE GIRLS IN THE WORLD BEWARE!!! (*5) / CAUGHT IN THE ACT (*4) / BORN TO DIE (*4) / GOOD SINGIN' GOOD PLAYIN' (*6) / GRAND FUNK HITS compilation (86) / GRAND FUNK LIVES (*3) / WHAT'S FUNK? (*3) / CAPITOL COLLECTORS SERIES compilation (*7) / MORE OF THE BEST compilation (*6)

TERRY KNIGHT & THE PACK

TERRY KNIGHT (b. RICHARD KNAPP) – vocals / **MARK FARNER** (b. 29 Sep'48) – vocals, bass (guitar from 1969) / **DONALD BREWER** (b. 3 Sep'48) – drums (ex-JAZZ MASTERS)

not iss. A&M

1965. (7") *<769>* **YOU LIE. / THE KIDS WILL BE THE SAME** –

Cameo Parkway Lucky 11

1966. (7") *<225>* **I'VE BEEN TOLD. / HOW MUCH MORE?** –

1966. (7") *<226>* **BETTER MAN THAN I. / I GOT LOVE** –

1966. (7") *<228>* **LOVIN' KIND. / LADY JANE** –

1966. (7") *<229>* **WHAT'S ON YOUR MIND? / A CHANGE ON THE WAY** –

Nov 66. (lp) *<S-8000>* **TERRY KNIGHT & THE PACK** –
– Numbers / What's on your mind / Where do you go / Better man than I / Lovin' kind / The shut-in / Got love / A change on the way / Lady Jane / Sleep talkin' / I've been told / I (who have nothing).

Jan 67. (7") *(C 102) <230>* **I (WHO HAVE NOTHING). / NUMBERS** 46

Apr 67. (7") *<235>* **THIS PRECIOUS TIME. / LOVE, LOVE, LOVE, LOVE, LOVE** –

Jul 67. (7") *<236>* **ONE MONKEY DON'T STOP NO SHOW. / THE TRAIN** –

1968. (7"; as MARK FARNER & DON BREWER) **WE GOTTA HAVE LOVE. / DOES IT MATTER TO YOU GIRL** –

GRAND FUNK RAILROAD

KNIGHT became their manager. Added **MEL SCHACHER** (b. 3 Apr'51, Owosso, Michigan) – bass (ex-? AND THE MYSTERIANS)

Capitol Capitol

Sep 69. (7") *<2567>* **TIME MACHINE. / HIGH ON A HORSE** – 48

Sep 69. (lp) *<(E-ST 307)>* **ON TIME** 27
– Are you ready / Anybody's answer / Time machine / High on a horse / T.N.U.C. / Into the sun / Heartbreaker / Call yourself a man / Can't be too long / Ups and down.

Nov 69. (7") *<2691>* **MR. LIMOUSINE DRIVER. / HIGH FALOOTIN' WOMAN** – 97

Jan 70. (lp) *<(E-ST 406)>* **GRAND FUNK** 11
– Got this thing on the move / Please don't worry / High falootin' woman / Mr. Limousine driver / In need / Winter and my soul / Paranoid / Inside looking out.

Mar 70. (7") *(CL 15632) <2732>* **HEARTBREAKER. / PLEASE DON'T WORRY** 72 Jan70

Jun 70. (7") *<2816>* **NOTHING IS THE SAME. / SIN'S A GOOD MAN'S BROTHER** –

Jul 70. (lp) *<(E-ST 471)>* **CLOSER TO HOME** 6
– Sin's a good man's brother / Aimless lady / Nothing is the same / Mean mistreater / Get it together / I don't have to sing the blues / Hooked on love / I'm your captain.

Oct 70. (7") *(CL 15661) <2877>* **CLOSER TO HOME. / AIMLESS LADY** 22 Aug70

Dec 70. (7") *<2996>* **MEAN MISTREATER. / MARK SAYS ALRIGHT** – 47

Jan 71. (d-lp) *(E-STDW 1-2) <633>* **LIVE ALBUM (live)** 5 Nov70
– (introduction) / Are you ready / Paranoid / In need / Heartbreaker / Inside looking out / Words of wisdom / Meam mistreater / Mark says alright / T.N.U.C. / Into the sun.

Jan 71. (7";33rpm) *(CL 15668)* **INSIDE LOOKING OUT. / PARANOID** 40 –

Apr 71. (7") *(CL 15683) <3095>* **FEELIN' ALRIGHT. / I WANT FREEDOM** 54

Apr 71. (lp) *<(E-SW 764)>* **SURVIVAL** 6
– Country road / All you've got is money / Comfort me / Feelin' alright / I want freedom / I can feel him in the morning / Gimme shelter.

Jul 71. (7"m;B-33rpm) *(CL 15689)* **I CAN FEEL HIM IN THE MORNING. / ARE YOU READY / MEAN MISTREATER** –

Aug 71. (7") *<3160>* **GIMME SHELTER. / I CAN FEEL HIM IN THE MORNING** – 61

Sep 71. (7") *(CL 15694)* **GIMME SHELTER. / COUNTRY ROAD** –

Dec 71. (7") *(CL 15705)* **PEOPLE, LET'S STOP THE WAR. / SAVE THE LAND**

Jan 72. (lp) *(EA-SW 853) <E-AS 853>* **E PLURIBUS FUNK** 5 Nov71
– Footstompin' music / People, let's stop the war / Upsetter / I come tumblin' / Save the land / No lies / Loneliness.

Mar 72. (7") *(CL 15709) <3255>* **FOOTSTOMPIN' MUSIC. / I COME TUMBLIN'** 29 Dec71

May 72. (7") *(CL 15720) <3316>* **UPSETTER. / NO LIES** 73 Apr72

Nov 72. (7") *(CL 15738) <3363>* **ROCK'N'ROLL SOUL. / FLIGHT OF THE PHOENIX** 29 Sep72

Jan 73. (lp) *<(E-AST 11099)>* **PHOENIX** 7 Oct72
– Flight of the Phoenix / Trying to get away / Someone / She got to move me / Rain keeps fallin' / I just gotta know / So you won't have to die / Freedom is for children / Gotta find me a better day / Rock'n roll soul.

GRAND FUNK

Aug 73. (7")<7"US-pic-d> *(CL 15760)* <3660> **WE'RE AN AMERICAN BAND. / CREEPIN'** [ ] [1] Jul73

Aug 73. (lp) <*(E-AST 11027)*> **WE'RE AN AMERICAN BAND** [ ] [2]
– We're an American band / Stop lookin' back / Creepin' / Black licorice / The railroad / Ain't got nobody / Walk like a man / Loneliest rider.

Nov 73. (7") *(CL 15771)* <3760> **WALK LIKE A MAN. / RAILROAD** [ ] [19]

added **CRAIG FROST** (b.20 Apr'48) – keyboards

May 74. (7") *(CL 15780)* <3840> **THE LOCO-MOTION. / DESTITUTE & LOSIN'** [ ] [1] Mar74

Jun 74. (lp) <*(SWAE 11278)*> **SHININ' ON** [ ] [5] Mar74
– Shinin' on / To get back in / The loco-motion / Carry me through / Please me / Mr. Pretty boy / Gettin' over you / Little Johnny Hooker.

Jul 74. (7") *(CL 15789)* <3917> **SHININ' ON. / MR. PRETTY BOY** [ ] [11]

— reverted back to trio.

Dec 74. (lp) *(E-ST 11356)* <*SO 11356*> **ALL THE GIRLS IN THE WORLD BEWARE!!!** [ ] [10]
– Responsibility / Runnin' / Life / Look at granny run run / Memories / All the girls in the world beware / Wild / Good & evil / Bad time / Some kind of wonderful.

Feb 75. (7") *(CL 15805)* <4002> **SOME KIND OF WONDERFUL. / WILD** [ ] [3] Dec74

Apr 75. (7") *(CL 15816)* <4046> **BAD TIME. / GOOD AND EVIL** [ ] [4] Mar75

GRAND FUNK RAILROAD

Dec 75. (d-lp) *(E-STSP 15)* <*11445*> **CAUGHT IN THE ACT (live)** [ ] [21] Sep75
– Footstompin' music / Rock'n'roll soul / Closer to home / Some kind of wonderful / Heartbreaker / Shinin' on / The locomotion / Black licorice / The railroad / We're an American band / T.N.U.C. / Inside looking out / Gimme shelter.

Dec 75. (7") <*4199*> **TAKE ME. / GENEVIEVE** [-] [53]

Mar 76. (7") <*4235*> **SALLY. / LOVE IS DYIN'** [-] [69]

Apr 76. (lp) <*(E-ST 11482)*> **BORN TO DIE** [ ] [47] Jan76
– Born to die / Duss / Sally / I fell for your love / Talk to the people / Take me / Genevieve / Love is dying / Politician / Good things.

EMI Inter. M.C.A.

Aug 76. (7") *(INT 523)* <*40590*> **CAN YOU DO IT. / 1976** [ ] [45]

Aug 76. (lp) *(EMC 1503)* <*2216*> **GOOD SINGIN' GOOD PLAYIN'** [ ] [52]
– Just couldn't wait / Can you do it / Pass it around / Don't let 'em take your gun / Miss my baby / Big buns / Out to get you / Crossfire / 1976 / Release your love / Goin' for the pastor. *(cd-iss. Jan99 on 'Hippo'; HIPCD 40144)*

Jan 77. (7") *(INT 528)* **PASS IT AROUND. / DON'T LET 'EM TAKE YOUR GUN** [ ] [-]

Jan 77. (7") <*40641*> **JUST COULDN'T WAIT. / OUT TO GET YOU** [-] [ ]

— Disbanded when the rest formed FLINT. FARNER went solo for a while.

GRAND FUNK

re-formed with **FARNER, BREWER + DENNIS BELLINGER** – bass, vocals / (FROST had joined BOB SEGER)

Full Moon Full Moon

Nov 81. (7") <*49823*> **Y-O-U. / TESTIFY** [-] [ ]

Jan 82. (lp) *(K 99251)* <*3625*> **GRAND FUNK LIVES** [ ] [ ] Oct81
– Good times / Queen bee / Testify / Can't be with you tonight / No reason why / We gotta get out of this place / Y.O.U. / Stuck in the middle / Greed of man / Wait for me.

Feb 82. (7") <*49866*> **STUCK IN THE MIDDLE. / NO REASON WHY** [-] [ ]

Jan 83. (lp) *(K 99251)* <*923750-1*> **WHAT'S FUNK?** [-] [ ] German
– Rock & roll American style / Nowhere to run / Innocent / Still waitin' / Borderline / El Salvador / It's a man's world / I'm so true / Don't lie to me / Life in Outer Space.

— Disbanded again after appearing on 'Heavy Metal' soundtrack. BREWER joined BOB SEGER'S SILVER BULLET BAND. FARNER went solo again in 1988, releasing an album 'JUST ANOTHER INJUSTICE' for 'Frontline'.

– compilations, others, etc. –

on 'Capitol' unless mentioned otherwise

May 72. (d-lp) *(E-STSP 10)* <*11042*> **MARK, DON & MEL 1969-1971** [ ] [17]

Oct 72. (lp) **MARK, DON AND TERRY 1966-67** [-] [ ]

Nov 76. (lp) <*11579*> **GRAND FUNK HITS** [-] [ ]

May 89. (c-s) <*44394*> **WE'RE AN AMERICAN BAND. / THE LOCO-MOTION** [-] [ ]

Mar 91. (cd) *(CDP 790608-2)* **CAPITOL COLLECTORS** [ ] [-]
– Time machine / Heartbreaker / Inside looking out / Medley / Closer to home / I'm your captain / Mean mistreater / Feelin' alright / Gimme shelter / Footstompin' music / Rock & roll soul / We're an American band / Walk like a man / The Loco-motion / Shinin' on / Some kind of wonderful / Bad time.

Sep 91. (cd) *Rhino;* **MORE OF THE BEST** [-] [ ]

May 92. (cd/c) *Castle; (CCS CD/MC 332)* **THE COLLECTION** [ ] [-]
– The loco-motion / Gimme shelter / Inside looking out / Closer to home / I'm your captain / We're an American band / Into the Sun / Loneliness / Paranoid / Walk like a man / Shinin' on / Creepin' / Sally.

GRAND PRIX

Formed: London, England . . . late 70's by BERNIE SHAW, PHIL LANZON, MICHAEL O'DONOGHUE, RALPH HOOD and ANDY BEIRNE. Signed to 'R.C.A.', they made their bid to corner the melodic pomp end of the rock market with the self-explanatory 'GRAND PRIX – THE FIRST ALBUM' in 1980. Prior to the follow-up set, 'THERE FOR NONE TO SEE' (1982), they replaced frontman SHAW with ROBIN McAULEY, although commercial success still proved elusive. A further album for 'Chrysalis', 'SAMURAI' (1983), passed without much notice, McAULEY venturing onwards to The FAR CORPORATION, before making the big time with The McAULEY / SCHENKER GROUP.

Album rating: GRAND PRIX (*5) / THERE FOR NO ONE TO SEE (*6) / SAMURAI (*5)

BERNIE SHAW – vocals (ex-DIRTY LOOKS) / **MICHAEL O'DONOGHUE** – guitar / **PHIL LANZON** – keyboards, vocals (ex-CHRIS SPEDDING) / **RALPH HOOD** – bass, vocals / **ANDY BEIRNE** – drums

R.C.A. not iss.

Oct 80. (7") *(RCA 7)* **THINKING OF YOU. / FEELS GOOD** [ ] [-]

Oct 80. (lp/c) *(PL/PK 25321)* **GRAND PRIX** [ ] [-]
– Waiting for the night / Day in the life / Thinking of you / Mama sayes / Which way did the wind blow / Westwind / Next to you / You know it can be / Feel like I do / The very best time (dreamer).

Jan 81. (7") *(RCA 18)* **WHICH WAY DID THE WIND BLOW. / FEELS GOOD** [ ] [-]

— **ROBIN McAULEY** – vocals; repl. SHAW who joined PRAYING MANTIS, then STRATUS

Nov 81. (7") *(RCA 162)* **KEEP ON BELIEVING. / LIFE ON THE LINE** [75] [-]

Mar 82. (lp/c) *(RCA LP/K 6027)* **THERE FOR NONE TO SEE** [ ] [-]
– Heaven to Hell / Troubadour / Take a chance / Runaway / Tough of the track / Paradise / Keep on believing / Taking your life away / Atlantis / Relay.

Chrysalis Chrysalis

May 83. (7") *(PRIX 1)* **GIVE ME WHAT'S MINE. / ONE FIVE JIVE** [ ] [ ]

Jun 83. (lp/c) *(<CHR/ZCHR 1430>)* **SAMURAI** [ ] [ ]
– Give me what's mine / Shout / 50-50 / Here we go again / Countdown to zero / Somewhere tonight / High time / Never before / Freedom / Samurai.

Jul 83. (7"/12") *(PRIX 2/+T)* **SHOUT. / KEEP ON BELIEVING** [ ] [ ]

— folded early in 1984, McAULEY joined FAR CORPORATION, before spreading himself further in The McAULEY SCHENKER GROUP

GRAND THEFT AUDIO (see under ⇒ 3 COLOURS RED)

GRAVITY KILLS

Formed: Jefferson City, Missouri, USA . . . 1994 by JEFF SCHEEL, MATT DUDENHOEFFER, DOUGLAS FIRLEY and KURT KERNS. Signed to 'TVT' (home of NINE INCH NAILS), they scored a minor US hit in 1996 with 'GUILTY', this techno-rock track enjoying heavy rotation after being used in movie, 'Seven'. An eponymous album was released to coincide with a major US tour, the group's mainstream industrial style borrowing heavily from NIN. Brushing aside a remix album in '97 ('MANIPULATED'), GRAVITY KILLS were back at the grind with what's turned out to be their swansong set, 'PERVERSION' (1998).

Album rating: GRAVITY KILLS (*5) / MANIPULATED remixes (*4) / PERVERSION (*5)

JEFF SCHEEL – vocals / **MATT DUDENHOEFFER** – guitar / **DOUGLAS FIRLEY** – keyboards / **KURT KERNS** – bass, drums

Virgin T.V.T.

Mar 96. (cd-ep) <*5912*> **GUILTY (9 versions) / GOODBYE (2 versions)** [-] [86]

Jan 97. (cd-ep) *(VSCDT 1630)* **ENOUGH / ('A'-Critters Carnal mix). / ('A'-Martin Atkins White Light mix) / ('A'-Scott Burns metal mix)** [ ] [ ]
(12"ep) *(VST 1630)* – ('A'side) / ('A'-Undulate mix) / ('A'-Hindustan mix) / ('A'-PM Dawn I Feel Love mix).

Feb 97. (cd/c) *(CD/TC+/V 2819)* <*TVT 5910*> **GRAVITY KILLS** [ ] [89] Mar96
– Forward / Guilty / Blame / Down / Here / Enough / Inside / Goodbye / Never / Last / Hold.

Mar 97. (cd-ep) *(VSCDT 1621)* **GUILTY (2 mixes) / ENOUGH (2 mixes)** [ ] [ ]
(12"ep) *(VST 1621)* – ('A'-3 mixes) / Enough.

Jun 97. (cd) <*(TVT 59162)*> **MANIPULATED** (remixes) [ ] [ ] Apr97

May 98. (cd) <*(TVT 5920-2)*> **PERVERSION** [ ] [ ]
– Falling / If / Crashing / Drown / Alive / Wanted / Always / One / Disintigrate / Belief (to rust).

GREAT WHITE

Formed: Los Angeles, California, USA . . . as DANTE FOX in 1981, becoming GREAT WHITE by mid '82. Presumably named after a shark, they could hardly be classified in the 'Jaws' category, their workmanlike blues metal about as dangerous as a can of sardines. Nevertheless, they were professional if nothing else, 'E.M.I.' picking them up for one album after hearing their self-financed, DAN DOKKEN-produced debut, 'OUT OF THE NIGHT'. The major label effort, the aptly named 'STICK IT' (1984), failed to make any headway and the band were promptly dropped. As tirelessly determined as their music, GREAT WHITE recorded 'SHOT IN THE DARK' (1986) for the 'Capitol'-affiliated indie, 'Enigma', eventually leading to a deal with the major and some long awaited success. The more commercial sounding 'ONCE BITTEN' (1987) gave the band their first (US) Top 30 album, while their highly enjoyable romp-along cover of IAN HUNTER's 'ONCE BITTEN, TWICE SHY' went Top 5 in the States. 'TWICE SHY' (1989) was another massive seller and saw the band gaining worldwide recognition, their ballsy sound perfect for stadium rocking. By the release of 'HOOKED' (1991), however, the band were beginning to fray at the edges, KENDALL suffering alcohol related problems and MONTANA departing soon after the album's release. After a final effort for 'Capitol', 'PSYCHO CITY' (1992), the band signed with BMG subsidiary, (the appropriately titled) 'Zoo', although by this point it was clear the band were as good as washed up. • **Songwriters:**

Group compositions with fan/manager ALAN NIVEN contributing. Covered; IMMIGRANT SONG + ROCK AND ROLL + a whole album's worth by:- (Led Zeppelin) / GIMME SOME LOVIN' (Spencer Davis Group) / BITCH + IT'S ONLY ROCK'N'ROLL (Rolling Stones) / I DON'T NEED NO DOCTOR (Ashford & Simpson) / BABY'S ON FIRE (Eno) / MONEY (Barrett Strong) / etc. • **Trivia:** MARK KENDALL married long-time girlfriend Sharon Schsol.

Album rating: OUT OF THE NIGHT (*4) / GREAT WHITE (*5) / SHOT IN THE DARK mini (84) / ONCE BITTEN (*6) / TWICE SHY (*5) / RECOVERY: LIVE (*4) / LIVE IN LONDON (*4) / HOOKED (*5) / PSYCHO CITY (*5) / THE BEST OF GREAT WHITE compilation (*6) / SAIL AWAY (*5) / LET IT ROCK (*4) / CAN'T GET THERE FROM HERE (*4)

JACK RUSSELL (b. 5 Dec'60) – vocals / **MARK KENDALL** (b.29 Apr'59) – lead guitar / **LORNE BLACK** – bass / **GARY HOLLAND** – drums other **ALAN NIVEN** – percussion, co-writer

not iss. Aegian

1982. (m-lp) <*AR 001*> **OUT OF THE NIGHT** [-] [ ]
– Out of the night / Last time / On your knees / No way / Dead end. <*re-iss. '90 as 'ON YOUR KNEES – THE FIRST LP' on 'Enigma'*>

EMI America EMI America

Mar 84. (lp) *(AML 240087-1)* <*17111*> **GREAT WHITE** [ ] [ ]
– Out of the night / Stick it / Substitute / Bad boys / On your knees / Streetkiller / No better than hell / Hold on / Dead end / Nightmares. *(cd-iss. Sep99 on 'Axe Killer'; AXE 304677CD)*

Apr 84. (7") *(EA 167)* **SUBSTITUTE. / NO BETTER THAN HELL** [ ] [ ]
(12"+=) *(12EA 167)* – Bad boys.

Apr 86. (7"m) **FACE THE DAY. / HARD AND COLD / NO WAY** [-] [ ]

Capitol Capitol

Aug 86. (m-lp) <*12525*> **SHOT IN THE DARK** [-] [82]
– She shakes me / What do you do / Face the day / Gimme some lovin' / Shot in the dark / Is anybody there / Run away / Waiting for love. *(cd-iss. Jul96 on 'Razor & Tie'; RE 2110-2)*

—— **AUDIE DESBROW** (b.17 May'57) – drums repl. GARY / added **MICHAEL LARDIE** (b. 8 Sep'58, Alaska) – keyboards, guitar (later became a producer)

Jan 87. (7") *(CL 424)* **FACE THE DAY. / RED HOUSE** [ ] [ ]
(12"+=) *(12CL 424)* – ('A'-Blues version).

Aug 87. (7") *(CL 455)* <*44042*> **ROCK ME. / THIS FAST ROAD** [ ] [60]
(12"+=) *(12CL 455)* – Immigrant song / Rock and roll.

Nov 87. (lp/c) *(EST/TC-EST 2039)* <*12565*> **ONCE BITTEN** [ ] [23] Jul87
– Lady red light / Gonna getcha / Rock me / All over now / Mistreater / Never change heart / Fast road / On the edge / Save my love. *(cd-iss. Apr90; CDEST 2039) (re-iss. Oct90 on 'Fame' cd/c/lp; CD/TC+/FA 3252) (cd re-iss. Jun95 on 'Connoisseur') (cd re-iss. Feb00 on 'Liberty'; 524576-2)*

Jan 88. (c-s,cd-s) <*44104*> **SAVE YOUR LOVE. / ALL OVER NOW** [-] [57]

—— **TONY MONTANA** – bass repl. LORNE BLACK

Apr 89. (cd/c/lp) *(CD/TC+/EST 2096)* <*90640*> **TWICE SHY** [ ] [9]
– Move it / Heart the hunter / Hiway nights / The angel song / Bitches and other women: a) Bitch, b) It's only rock n' roll, c) Women / Mista bone / Baby's on fire / House of broken love / She only / Once bitten twice shy / Wasted rock ranger. *(UK re-iss. Dec89 d-cd/d-c/d-lp; CD/TC+/ESTS 2096)* **LIVE AT THE MARQUEE** (live) – Shot in the dark / What do you do / Gonna getcha / Money / All over now / Is anybody there / Face the day / Rock me.

Jul 89. (7") *(CL 532)* <*44366*> **ONCE BITTEN TWICE SHY. / WASTED ROCK RANGER** [ ] [5] May89
(12"+=/cd-s+=)(12"pic-d+=) *(12/CD CL 532)(12CLPD 532)* – Slow ride.

Sep 89. (7") <*44449*> **THE ANGEL SONG. /** [-] [30]

Nov 89. (7"/7"pic-d) *(CL/+PD 555)* **HEART THE HUNTER. / ALL OVER NOW** [ ] [ ]
(12"+=/cd-s+=) *(12/CD CL 555)* – She shakes me.

Feb 90. (7"/7"pic-d) *(CL/+PD 562)* <*44491*> **HOUSE OF BROKEN LOVE. / BITCHES AND OTHER WOMEN (Medley:- BITCH – IT'S ONLY ROCK'N'ROLL – WOMAN)** [44] [83]
(12"+=/cd-s+=) *(12/CD CL 562)* – Red house (live).

Aug 90. (m-cd) *(TOCP 6147)* **LIVE IN LONDON (live)** [ ] [-]
– Move it / Heart the hunter / On your knees / House of broken love / Face the day / All over now / Once bitten twice shy.

Feb 91. (c-s/7") *(TC+/CL 605)* **CONGO SQUARE. / SOUTH BAY CITIES** [62] [-]
(12"+=/cd-s+=)(12"pic-d+=) *(12/CD CL 605)(12CLPD 605)* – ('A'version) / House of broken love (live).

Feb 91. (c-s) <*44676*> **CALL IT ROCK N' ROLL / NEED YOUR LOVE TONIGHT / DOWN AT THE DOCTOR** [-] [53]

Mar 91. (cd/c/lp) *(CD/TC+/EST 2138)* <*95330*> **HOOKED** [43] [18]
– Call it rock n 'roll / The original Queen of Sheba / Cold hearted lovin' / Can't shake it / Lovin' kind / Heartbreaker / South Bay cities / Desert Moon / Afterglow.

Aug 91. (c-s/7") *(TC+/CL 625)* <*44676*> **CALL IT ROCK N' ROLL. / HEART THE HUNTER** [67] [-]
(12"+=/cd-s+=)(12"pic-d+=) *(12/CD CL 625)(12CLPD 625)* – Train to nowhere.

—— now without MONTANA, and employing **DAVE SPITZ** – guitar (ex-WHITE LION)

Nov 92. (cd/c/lp) *(CD/TC+/ESTU 2182)* <*98835*> **PSYCHO CITY** [ ] [ ] Oct92
– Psycho city / Step on you / Old Rose hotel / Maybe someday / Big goodbye / Doctor me / I want you / Never trust a pretty face / Love is a lie / Get on home. *(cd re-iss. Dec99 on 'Axe Killer'; AXE 305332CD)*

Nov 93. (cd/c) <*(CD/TC EST 2219)*> **THE BEST OF GREAT WHITE** (compilation) [ ] [ ]
– Step on you / All over now / Save your love / House of broken love / Big goodbye / Rock me / Face the day (blues mix) / Old Rose motel / Once bitten twice shy / Afterglow (of your love).

—— **TEDDY COOK** (b. 5 Aug'65, Long Island, N.Y.) – bass; repl. SPITZ

Zoo Zoo

May 94. (cd/c) <*(72445 11080-2/-4)*> **SAIL AWAY** [ ] [ ]
– Short overture / Mother's eyes / Cryin' / Momma don't stop / Alone / All right / Sail away / Gone with the wind / Livin' in the U.S.A. / If I ever saw a good thing. *(free live-cd w/cd+=)* – Call it rock'n'roll / All over now / Love is a lie / Old rose metal / Babe (I'm gonna leave you) / Rock me / Once bitten twice shy.

—— **DESBROW + LARDIE** returned to repl. HOLLAND + COOK

not iss. Imago

May 96. (cd) <*72787 23005-27*> **LET IT ROCK** [-] [ ]
– My world / Lil mama / Where is the love / Hand on the trigger / Easy / Pain overload / Lives in chains / Anyway I can / Man in the sky / Ain't no way to treat a lady / Miles away. *(UK-iss.Jun99; same as US)*

Axe Killer Portrait

Feb 00. (cd) *(AXE 305282CD)* <*69547*> **CAN'T GET THERE FROM HERE** [ ] [ ] Jun99
– Rolling stoned / Gone to the dogs / Ain't no shame / Wooden Jesus / Silent night / Sister Mary / Saint Lorraine / Loveless age / In the tradition / Psychedelic hurricane / Freedom song / Hey mister.

– others, etc. –

Jul 88. (lp/c) *Capitol; (EMS/TC-EMS 1302) / Enigma;* <*D2 73295*> **RECOVERY: LIVE! (live 1983 & jam side from early 1986)** [ ] [99] Feb88
– Out of the night / On your knees / Last time / No way / Dead end / Hard and cold / Substitute / Streetkiller / Bad boys / Stick it / Immigrant song / Rock n roll / Money (that's what I want) / Red house / I don't need no doctor.

Aug 97. (cd) *Disky; (DC 88186-2)* **ROCK ME** [ ] [ ]

Feb 99. (cd) *Axe Killer; (AXE 304137CD) / Cleopatra;* <*CLP 504-2*> **GREAT ZEPPELIN: A TRIBUTE TO LED ZEPPELIN** [ ] [ ] Mar99

May 99. (cd) *Axe Killer; (AXE 305006CD)* **GALLERY** [ ] [-]

GREEN DAY

Formed: Rodeo, nr. Berkeley, California, USA . . . early 90's out of The SWEET CHILDREN by BILLY JOE and MIKE. When TRE COOL replaced BILLY JOE's sister ANA on drums, they became GREEN DAY, this line-up releasing their debut LP, '39 / SMOOTH', which was recorded in under 24 hours. Their third album, 'DOOKIE' (their first for 'Reprise'), was a surprise US smash in 1994 due to its college/MTV favourite, 'BASKET CASE'. Retro punk-rock for young Americans (and now older Brits) who missed out on BUZZCOCKS, DICKIES, RAMONES (and even earlier 60's pop outfit, the MONKEES), GREEN DAY became a phenomenon in the States; like the SEX PISTOLS' revolution all over again, without the danger, unpredictability and raw excitement. Instead we got formulaic, annoyingly and yes, inanely catchy punk retreads that took you way back to '77. Still, the multi-millions who bought the record ensured that GREEN DAY were indeed radio-friendly unit shifters. A follow-up set, 'INSOMNIAC' (1995), was another massive seller, although it had to compete with the hordes of equally faceless acts clogging up the charts with similar material. A fifth set, 'NIMROD' (1997), made sure they were still in touch with their fanbase, the tried and tested formula again getting them into the Top 10. The album also spawned a surprise hit single in the shape of a rare ballad, 'TIME OF YOUR LIFE (GOOD RIDDANCE)', geeing the band on to er, express their more feminine side, or at least their less frantic side. With 'WARNING' (2000), GREEN DAY went ahead and exorcised those pop demons which had clearly been haunting them since way back when. By investing their punk-pop formula with a measure of melodic sparkle and a hint of vintage 60's flavour, the 3-chord thumpers had come up with their most consistently listenable album to date. • **Songwriters:** Lyrics; BILLY JOE, group songs except TIRED OF WAITING FOR YOU (Kinks). • **Trivia:** DIRNT guested on The SCREAMING WEASEL album, 'How to Make Enemies And Irritate People'. BILLIE JOE was also a member of PINHEAD GUNPOWDER, who released an album, 'Jump Salty', plus a few EP's (also for 'Lookout').

Album rating: 39/SMOOTHED OUT SLAPPY HOUR compilation (*5) / KERPLUNK! (*5) / DOOKIE (*7) / INSOMNIAC (*6) / NIMROD (*6) / WARNING (*6)

BILLY JOE ARMSTRONG (b.17 Feb'72, San Pablo, Calif.) – vocals, guitar / **MIKE DIRNT** (b. PRITCHARD, 4 May'72) – bass, vocals / **TRE COOL** (b. FRANK EDWIN WRIGHT III, 9 Dec'72, Germany) – drums repl. JOHN KIFTMEYER who had repl. AL SOBRANTE

not iss. Lookout

1989. (7"ep) <*LOOKOUT 17*> **1000 HOURS EP** [-] [ ]
– 1000 hours / Dry ice / Only of you / The one I want. *(UK-iss.Dec94; as above)*

1990. (lp) <*LOOKOUT 22*> **39 / SMOOTH** [-] [ ]
– At the library / Don't leave me / I was there / Disappearing boy / Green day / Going to Pasalacgua / 16 / Road to exceptance / Rest / The judge's daughter / Paper lanterns / Why do you want him? / 409 in your coffeemaker / Knowledge / 1000 hours / Dry ice / Only of you / The one I want / I want to be alone. *(re-iss. Nov91 lp/cd; LOOKOUT 22/+CD) (UK-iss.Sep94 as '1,039 / SMOOTHED OUT SLAPPY HOURS'; as above) (cd re-iss. Aug97 on 'Epitaph'; 6522-2)*

1991. (7"ep) <*LOOKOUT 35*> **SLAPPY EP** [-] [ ]
– Paper lanterns / Why do you want him? / 409 in your coffeemaker / Knowledge. *(UK-iss.Sep94; as above)*

Dec 91. (lp) <*LOOKOUT 46*> **KERPLUNK!** [-] [ ]
– 2000 light years away / One for the razorbacks / Welcome to Paradise / Christie Road / Private ale / Dominated love slave / One of my lies / 80 / Android / No one knows / Who wrote Holden Caulfield? / Words I might have ate. *(UK-iss.Sep94 on 'Lookout' lp/cd+=; LOOKOUT 46/+CD)* – Sweet children / Best thing in town / Strangeland / My generation. *(by SWEET CHILDREN and released US 1990 on 'Skene') (cd re-iss. Aug97 on 'Epitaph'; 6517-2)*

Reprise Reprise

Feb 94. (cd/c) <*(9362 45529-2/-4)*> **DOOKIE** [ ] [2]
– Burnout / Having a blast / Chump / Longview / Welcome to Paradise / Pulling teeth / Basket case / She / Sassafras roots / When I come around / Coming clean / Emenius sleepus / In the end / F.O.D. *(cd+=)* – (hidden track). *(re-dist.Jun94) (re-iss. Oct94 on green-lp soon hit UK No.13; 9362 45795-2/-4)*

Jun 94. (7") *(W 0247)* **LONGVIEW. / ON THE WAGON** [ ] [-]
(10"/cd-s) *(W 0247 T/CD)* – ('A'side) / Going to Pasalaqua / F.O.D. (live) / Christy Road (live).

Aug 94. (7"green/c-s) *(W 0257/+C)* **BASKET CASE. / TIRED OF WAITING FOR YOU** [55] [-]
(cd-s+=) *(W 0257CD)* – On the wagon / 409 in your coffeemaker.

Oct 94. (12"green/c-s/cd-s) *(W 0269 T/C/CDX)* **WELCOME TO PARADISE. / CHUMP (live) / EMENIUS SLEEPUS** [20] [-]

Jan 95. (7"green/c-s) *(W 0279/+C)* **BASKET CASE. / 2,000 LIGHT YEARS AWAY (live)** [7] [-]
(cd-s+=) *(W 0279CD)* – Burnout (live) / Longview (live).

Mar 95. (7"/c-s) *(W 0278/+C)* **LONGVIEW. / WELCOME TO PARADISE (live)** [30] [ ]
(cd-s+=) *(W 0278CD)* – One of my lies (live).

May 95. (7"pic-d/c-s) *(W 0294/+C)* **WHEN I COME AROUND. / SHE (live)** [27] [-]
(cd-s+=) *(W 0294CD)* – Coming clean (live).

Sep 95. (7"red/c-s) *(W 0320/+C)* **GEEK STINK BREATH. / I WANNA BE ON T.V.** [16] [-]
(cd-s+=) *(W 0320CD)* – Don't wanna fall in love.

Oct 95. (cd/c/lp) *<(9362 46046-2/-4/-1)>* **INSOMNIAC** [8] [2]
– Armatage Shanks / Brat / Stuck with me / Geek stink breath / No pride / Bab's Uvula who? / 86 / Panic song / Stuart and the Ave. / Brain stew / Jaded / Westbound sign / Tight wad hill / Walking contradiction.

Dec 95. (7") *(W 0327X)* **STUCK WITH ME. / WHEN I COME AROUND (live)** [24] [-]
(c-s+=) *(W 0327C)* – Jaded (live).
(cd-s) *(W 0327CD)* – ('A'side) / Dominated love slave (live) / Chump (live).

Jun 96. (c-s) *(W 0339C)* **BRAIN STEW / JADED / GOOD RIDDANCE** [28] [-]
(cd-s+=) *(W 0339CD)* – Do da da.
(brain-shaped cd-s++=) *(W 0339CDX)* – Brain stew (radio).

Sep 97. (c-s) *(W 0424C)* *<43945>* **HITCHIN' A RIDE / SICK** [25] [ ] Jun98
(cd-s+=) *(W 0424CD)* – Espionage.

Oct 97. (cd/c) *<(9362 46794-2/-4)>* **NIMROD** [11] [10]
– Nice guys finish last / Hitchin' a ride / The grouch / Reduntant / Scattered / Worry rock / Desensitized / All the time / Platypus (I hate you) / Last ride in / Jinx / Haushinka / Walking alone / Suffocate / Uptight / Take back / King for a day / Good riddance / Prosthetic head.

Jan 98. (c-s) *(W 0430C)* *<43974>* **TIME OF YOUR LIFE (GOOD RIDDANCE) / DESENSITIZED** [11] [ ] Jun98
(cd-s+=) *(W 0430CD1)* – Rotting.
(cd-s) *(W 0430CD2)* – ('A'side) / Suffocate / You lied.

Apr 98. (7"/cd-s) *(W 0438/+CD1)* **REDUNDANT. / THE GROUCH (live) / PAPER LANTERN (live)** [27] [ ]
(cd-s) *(W 0438CD2)* – ('A'side) / Reject all American (live) / She (live).

Sep 00. (c-s) *(W 532C)* **MINORITY / BRAT (live)** [18] [-]
(cd-s+=) *(W 532CD)* – 86 (live).
(7"ep iss.Nov00 on 'Adeline'+=; ADELINE 013) – Jackass.

Oct 00. (cd/c) *<(9362 48030-2/-4)>* **WARNING** [4] [4]
– Warning / Blood, sex and booze / Church on Sunday / Fashion victim / Castaway / Misery / Deadbeat holiday / Hold on / Jackass / Waiting / Minority / Macy's day parade. *<US version+=; 47857>* – Brat (live) / 86 (live). *<(lp; 9362 47613-1)>* *<US lp-iss.Oct00 on 'Adeline'; ADELINE 012>*

Dec 00. (7") *(W 548)* **WARNING. / SUFFOCATE** [27] [-]
(cd-s+=) *(W 548CD2)* – Outsider. *(7"iss.Feb01 on 'Adeline'; ADELINE 014)*
(cd-s) *(W 548CD1)* – ('A'side) / Scumbag / I don't want to know if you are lonely.

GREEN JELLY

Formed: Kenmore, New York, USA ... 1981 as GREEN JELLO, by BILL MANSPEAKER (aka MARSHALL "DUH" STAXX or MORONIC DIKTATOR), who concentrated on releasing videos only. With a plethora of musicians, singers, etc, this veteran bunch of parodic punksters eventually made a breakthrough on the back of the grunge explosion in 1993, when they infiltrated the US (& UK) charts with comical renditions of 'THREE LITTLE PIGS' and 'ANARCHY IN THE UK'. However, due to an objection by Kraft Foods, they had to slightly adjust the group moniker to GREEN JELLY. The accompanying album, 'CEREAL KILLER', shockingly sold over a million in the States, this irreverent fun-core snapped up by the young and the not-so-young. Predictably, their jelly set in 1995 with the commercially dead-in-the-water, '333', only half the beast it could've been.

Album rating: CEREAL KILLER (*4) / 333 (er, *3)

BILL MANSPEAKER (MARSHALL "DUH" STAXX) – guitar, vocals / **PINATA HEAD / COWGOD / ROCK'N'ROLL PUMPKIHN / JOE SUBPOPPY** – instruments / 12 members

Zoo / Zoo

May 93. (7") *(74321 15142-7)* *<14088>* **THREE LITTLE PIGS. / OBEY THE COWGOD** [5] [17] Mar93
(12"+=/cd-s+=) *(74321 15142-1/-2)* – ('A'extended).

Jun 93. (cd-s) *<14098>* **ELECTRIC HARLEY HOUSE (OF LOVE) / TRIPPIN' ON XTC / ELECTRIC HARLEY HOUSE (OF LOVE) version** [-] [ ]

Jun 93. (cd/c) *<(72445 11038-2/-4)>* **CEREAL KILLER SOUNDTRACK** [18] [23] Apr93
– Obey the cowgod / Three little pigs / Cereal killer / Rock'n'roll pumpkihn / Anarchy in the UK / Electric Harley house (of love) / Trippin' on XTC / Misadventures of Shitman / House me teenage rave / Flight of the Skajaquada / Green Jelly theme song.

Aug 93. (7"/c-s) *(74321 15905-7/-4)* **ANARCHY IN THE UK. / GREEN JELLY THEME SONG** [27] [ ]
(12"+=/cd-s+=) *(74321 15905-1/-2)* – Three little pigs (blowin' down the house mix).

— In Dec'93, they were credited on wrestler HULK HOGAN's 'Arista' single 'I'M THE LEADER OF THE GANG'. An old GARY GLITTER No.1, it made UK No.29.

Jul 94. (cd-s) *<14148>* **SLAVE BOY** [-] [ ]

May 95. (cd) *<(74321 23536-2)>* **333** [ ] [ ] Nov94
– Carnage blues / Orange krunch / Pinta head / Fixation / Bear song / Fight / Super elastic / Jump jerk / Anthem / Slave boy.

— disbanded after above

GREEN RIVER (see under ⇒ PEARL JAM)

GRIM REAPER

Formed: Droitwich, England ... 1979 by STEVE GRIMMET, NICK BOWCROFT, DAVE WANKLIN and LEE HAMS. Signed in 1983 to 'Ebony' ('R.C.A.' in the States), the group turned from purveyors of NWOBHM to fringe players in the US heavy metal scene. Like a more accessible 'SABBATH or 'PRIEST, GRIM REAPER's cliche-ridden, tonsil-terrorising material went down well in America, all three albums (beginning with 'SEE YOU IN HELL') hitting the US Top 200.

Album rating: SEE YOU IN HELL (*6) / FEAR NO EVIL (*4) / ROCK YOU TO HELL (*4)

STEVE GRIMMET – vocals / **NICK BOWCROFT** – guitars / **DAVE WANKLIN** – bass / **LEE HAMS** – drums

Ebony / R.C.A.

Nov 83. (lp) *(EBON 16)* *<8038>* **SEE YOU IN HELL** [ ] [73] Jul84
– Dead on arrival / Liar / Wrath of the ripper / All hell let loose / Now or never / Run for your life / The show must go on / See you in Hell.

Jun 85. (lp) *(EBON 32)* *<5431>* **FEAR NO EVIL** [ ] [ ]
– Fear no evil / Never coming back / Lord of darkness (your living hell) / A matter of time / Rock and roll tonight / Let the thunder roar / Lay it on the line / Fight to the last / Final scream.

Jul 87. (lp) *<6250-1>* **ROCK YOU TO HELL** [-] [93]
– Rock you to Hell / Night of the vampire / Lust for freedom / When Heaven comes down / Suck it and see / Rock me 'til I die / You'll wish that you were never born / Waysted love / I want more.

— split when GRIMMET joined ONSLAUGHT (he later went to LIONSHEART)

GROOP DOGDRILL

Formed: Doncaster, England ... early 1996 by tattooed "hard" lads, PETE SPIBY, DAMO FOWKES and HUG, who got together through ads put in American Army mag, 'Guns And Ammo'. Manic grinding, metallic punk like JON SPENCER BLUES EXPLOSION or THERAPY? on testosterone, GROOP DOGDRILL began their career in fine fettle with two independently issued 45's, 'GENTLEMEN'S SOIREE' and 'GRACELANDS'. The following year saw them sign to Beggars Banquet offshoot, 'Mantra', where they delivered a trio of greasy, Kerrang!-friendly singles prior to the release of their heavily touted debut set, 'HALF NELSON'. The group's sophomore album, 'EVERY SIX SECONDS' (2000), was a little disappointing – compare their first effort – however, there was yet again no compromise to their sound.

Album rating: HALF NELSON (*8) / EVERY SIX SECONDS (er, *6)

PETE SPIBY – vocals, guitar / **DAMO FOWKES** – bass / **HUG (KELLY)** – drums / 4th member **BOX** – lyrics, roadie

EXP Limited / not iss.

Aug 96. (7") *(GDD 7010)* **GENTLEMEN'S SOIREE. / SILVER BOOTS** [ ] [-]

Nov 96. (7") *(EXP 7011)* **GRACELANDS. / SPOILER** [ ] [-]
(cd-s) *(EXPCD 7011)* – Eyelash trauma.

Mantra / Imprint

Sep 97. (7") *(MNT 023)* **LOVELY SKIN. / ROCKABILLY WORKOUT** [ ] [-]
(cd-s+=) *(MNT 023CD)* – Shrub.

Feb 98. (7") *(MNT 028)* **OILY RAG. / PACKMULE** [ ] [-]
(cd-s+=) *(MNT 028CD)* – Feeding frenzy.

Apr 98. (7") *(MNT 033)* **JACKIE O. / SPORT OF KINGS** [ ] [-]
(cd-s+=) *(MNT 033CD)* – New York sushi / Speedball.

Apr 98. (cd/c/lp) *(MNT CD/MC/LP 1010)* *<58844>* **HALF NELSON** [ ] [ ] Aug98
– Lovely skin / Cocksuker blues / Gentleman's soiree / Lifestyle / Oily rag / Southbound tuxedo / Jackie O / Gracelands / Hessus / (That) Texaco feeling / Salt Peter / Personal / Silver boots.

Nov 98. (7"colrd) *(MNT 035)* **PERSONAL. / HOBOKEN THING / HEDLEY HADLEY (ODE TO LILLEY)** [ ] [-]

Oct 99. (7"/cd-s) *(MNT 048/+CD)* **ANGEL WINGS. / SHIPWRECKED / QUEEN OF THE STRIP** [ ] [-]

Feb 00. (7"/c-s) *(MNT 051/+CD)* **HEAD OF SAFETY. / SIMIAN KIND / INDIAN ROPE BURN** [ ] [-]

Mar 00. (cd/lp) *(MNT CD/LP 1016)* *<81016>* **EVERY SIX SECONDS** [ ] [ ] Sep00
– Simian kind / Head of safety / On me not in me / Clown smash everything / Komet / Low sperm count / Angel wings / Spek and spell / Bob 'n' Laura / Best sex in Texas / Smaller target / Mummy's little soldier / Sour milk.

GROUNDHOGS

Formed: New Cross, London, England ... 1963 by TONY McPHEE, who named them after a JOHN LEE HOOKER track. In 1964, they signed with Mickie Most's Anglo-American agency, soon having their debut 45, 'SHAKE IT', issued on 'Interphon'. Around the same time, they recorded an lp, 'LIVE AT THE AU-GO CLUB, NEW YORK', with their hero, HOOKER. They returned to England in 1965 and subsequently went through a series of false starts before finally stablising their line-up in 1968. Just prior to this, McPHEE had teamed up with The JOHN DUMMER BLUES BAND, who released two singles for 'Mercury'. However, with advice from Andrew Lauder of 'United Artists', the new GROUNDHOGS took-off with (their) debut, 'SCRATCHING THE SURFACE'. In 1969, the single 'BDD' (Blind

Deaf Dumb) flopped in the UK, although it bizarrely hit the top spot in Lebanon! In the early 70's, they scored with two UK Top 10 lp's, 'THANK CHRIST FOR THE BOMB' (which caused controversy with its sarcastic praise of the nuclear deterrent) and 'SPLIT' (which they always seemed to do, from then on). One of the tracks from the latter, 'CHERRY RED', featured on Top Of The Pops (22nd of April '71). Although they had lost none of their white-boy Chicago blues elements, the aforementioned couple of albums moved towards a more mellotron-based prog-rock sound. Two albums in 1972, 'WHO WILL SAVE THE WORLD?' and 'HOGWASH', revisited their blues roots. 1974's 'SOLID' album, meanwhile, saw a return to the charts, a feat TONY McPHEE & his GROUNDHOGS couldn't emulate with further releases. They were still going strong well into the 90's, releasing albums for the diserning blues connoisseur. • **Songwriters:** McPHEE penned except; EARLY IN THE MORNING (Sonny Boy Williamson) / STILL A FOOL (Muddy Waters) / MISTREATED (Tommy Johnson) / etc. • **Trivia:** TONY McPHEE appeared on JOHN DUMMER BAND releases between 1968-69. Around the same time he guested on BIG JOE WILLIAMS recordings.

Album rating: SCRATCHING THE SURFACE (*5) / BLUES OBITUARY (*6) / THANK CHRIST FOR THE BOMB (*8) / SPLIT (*7) / WHO WILL SAVE THE WORLD? THE MIGHTY GROUNDHOGS? (*6) / HOGWASH (*5) / SOLID (*4) / CROSSCUT SAW (*4) / BLACK DIAMOND (*4) / RAZOR'S EDGE (*4) / BACK AGAINST THE WALL (*4) / HOGS ON THE ROAD (*4) / NO SURRENDER (*4) / FOOLISH PRIDE (*4) / DOCUMENT SERIES PRESENTS . . . THE GROUNDHOGS (*8)

TONY McPHEE (b.22 Mar'44, Lincolnshire, England) – guitar, vocals, keyboards / **JOHN CRUIKSHANK** – vocals, mouth harp / **PETE CRUIKSHANK** (b. 2 Jul'45) – bass / **DAVID BOORMAN** – drums / on session **TOM PARKER** – piano repl. BOB HALL

not iss. Interphon

Jan 65. (7") *<7715>* **SHAKE IT. / ROCK ME** [-] [ ]

JOHN LEE'S GROUNDHOGS

HOOKER – solo blues guitarist **TERRY SLADE** – drums repl. BOORMAN + added 3-piece brass section

Planet Planet

Jan 66. (7") *(<PLF 104>)* **I'LL NEVER FALL IN LOVE AGAIN. / OVER YOU BABY** [ ] [ ]

— TONY McPHEE joined The TRUTH for a short stint before sessioning for CHAMPION JACK DUPREE on his '66 single 'Get Your Head Happy'

T.S. McPHEE

– solo with **PETE CRUICKSHANK / BOB HALL /** and **VAUGHN REES** – drums / **NEIL SLAVEN** – guitar

Purdah not iss.

Aug 66. (7") *(45-3501)* **SOMEONE TO LOVE ME. / AIN'T GONNA CRY NO MO'** [ ] [-]

— This band also backed JO-ANN KELLY. In summer McPHEE formed HERBAL MIXTURE around the same time he joined JOHN DUMMER BLUES BAND on two 1966 singles.

GROUNDHOGS

re-formed (**TONY McPHEE** and **PETE CRUICKSHANK**) recruited **STEVE RYE** – vocals, mouth harp / **KEN PUSTELNIK** – drums

Liberty World Pacific

Nov 68. (lp; mono/stereo) *(LBL/LBS 83199E) <21892>* **SCRATCHING THE SURFACE (live in the studio)** [ ] [ ]
– Man trouble / Married men / Early in the morning / Come back baby / You don't love me / Rocking chair / Walkin' blues / No more daggin' / Still a fool. *(re-iss. Sep88 & Apr97 on 'Beat Goes On' lp/cd+=; BGO LP/CD 15)* – Oh death / Gasoline / Rock me / Don't pass the hat around. *(cd-iss. Jan99 on 'Akarma'; AKCD 038CD)*

Dec 68. (7") *(LBF 15174)* **YOU DON'T LOVE ME. / STILL A FOOL** [ ] [ ]

— trimmed to a trio when RYE left due to illness

Liberty Imperial

Jul 69. (lp) *(LBS 83253) <12452>* **BLUES OBITUARY** [ ] [ ]
– B.D.D. / Daze of the weak / Times / Mistreated / Express man / Natchez burning / Light was the day. *(re-iss. Jan89 on 'Beat Goes On' lp/cd; BGO LP/CD 6) (cd re-iss. Jan99 on 'Akarma'; AK 039CD)*

Aug 69. (7") *(LBF 15263)* **BDD. / Tony McPhee: GASOLINE** [ ] [ ]

Liberty Liberty

May 70. (lp) *(LBS 83295) <7644>* **THANK CHRIST FOR THE BOMB** [9] [ ]
– Strange town / Darkness is no friend / Soldier / Thank Christ for the bomb / Ship on the ocean / Garden / Status people / Rich man, poor man / Eccentric man. *(re-iss. 1975 on 'Sunset'; 50376) (re-iss. May86 on 'Fame' lp/c; FA41/TCFA 3152) (re-iss. Dec89 on 'Beat Goes On' lp/cd; BGO LP/CD 67) (cd re-iss. Jan99 on 'Akarma'; AK 040CD)*

1970. (7") *(LBF 15346)* **ECCENTRIC MAN. / STATUS PEOPLE** [ ] [-]

1970. (7") *<56205>* **SHIP ON THE OCEAN. / SOLDIER** [-] [ ]

Liberty U.A.

Mar 71. (lp) *(LBS 83401) <UA 5513>* **SPLIT** [5] [ ]
– Split (parts 1-4) / Cherry red / A year in the life / Junkman / Groundhog. *(re-iss. Aug80; LBR 1017) (re-iss. Mar86 on 'E.M.I.' lp/c; ATAK/TC-ATAK 73) (re-iss. Dec89 on 'Beat Goes On'; BGO LP/CD 76) (cd re-iss. Jan99 on 'Akarma'; AK 041CD)*

U.A. U.A.

Mar 72. (lp) *(UAG 29237) <UA 5570>* **WHO WILL SAVE THE WORLD? THE MIGHTY GROUNDHOGS** [ ] [ ]
– Earth is not room enough / Wages of peace / Body in mind / Music is the food of thought / Bog roll blues / Death of the sun / Amazing Grace / The grey maze. *(re-iss. Dec89 & Apr91 on 'Beat Goes On' lp/cd; BGO LP/CD 77)*

— **CLIVE BROOKS** – drums (ex-EGG) repl. PUSTELNIK

Oct 72. (lp) *(UAG 29419) <UA 008>* **HOGWASH** [ ] [ ]
– I love Miss Ogyny / You had a lesson / The ringmaster / 3744 James Road / Sad is the hunter / S'one song / Earth shanty / Mr. Hooker, Sir John. *(re-iss. Apr89 on 'Beat Goes On' lp/cd; BGO LP/CD 44) (cd re-iss. May91;)*

W.W.A. W.W.A.

Oct 73. (lp; T.S. McPHEE; solo) *(WWA 1)* **THE TWO SIDES OF TONY (T.S.) McPHEE** [ ] [-]
– Three times seven / All my money, alimoney / Morning's eyes / Dog me, bitch / Take it out / The hunt. *(cd-iss. Dec92 on 'Castle';)*

Nov 73. (7") *(WWS 006)* **SAD GO ROUND. / OVER BLUE** [ ] [ ]

Jun 74. (lp) *(WWA 004)* **SOLID** [31] [ ]
– Light my light / Free from all alarm / Sins of the father / Sad go round / Corn cob / Plea sing plea song / Snowstorm / Jokers grave. *(cd-iss. Oct91 on 'Castle'; CLACD 266)*

Aug 74. (7") *(WWS 012)* **PLEA SING – PLEA SONG. / Tony McPhee: DOG ME BITCH** [ ] [ ]

— **McPHEE** brought back **PETE CRUIKSHANK** – rhythm guitar, / plus new members **DAVE WELLBELOVE** – guitar / **MARTIN KENT** – bass / **MICK COOK** – drums

U.A. U.A.

Feb 76. (lp) *(UAG 29917) <LA 603>* **CROSSCUT SAW** [ ] [ ]
– Crosscut saw / Promiscuity / Boogie withus / Fulfilment / Live a little lady / Three way split / Mean mistreater / Eleventh hour.

Mar 76. (7") *(UP 36095)* **LIVE A LITTLE LADY. / BOOGIE WITHUS** [ ] [ ]

— **RICK ADAMS** – rhythm guitar repl. PETE

Oct 76. (lp) *(UAG 29994) <LA 680>* **BLACK DIAMOND** [ ] [ ]
– Body talk / Fantasy partner / Live right / Country blues / Your love keeps me alive / Friendzy / Pastoral future / Black diamond.

Oct 76. (7"; as TONY McPHEE & GROUNDHOGS) *(UP 36177)* **PASTORAL FUTURE. / LIVE RIGHT** [ ] [ ]

— split '77. **McPHEE** formed **TERRAPLANE,** with **ALAN FISH** – bass / **WILGUR CAMPBELL** – drums. They appeared on album CHECKIN' IT OUT by 'BILLY BOY ARNOLD'. (1979 split) **TONY** formed TURBO ('79-'83) with **CLIVE BROOKS** – drums / **PAUL RAVEN**

TONY McPHEE BAND

with **MICK MIRTON** – drums / **STEVE TOWNER** – bass

T.S. not iss.

May 83. (7"; sold at gigs) *(TS 001)* **TIME OF ACTION. / BORN TO BE WITH YOU** [ ] [-]

GROUNDHOGS

McPHEE with **ALAN FISH** – bass / **MICK MIRTON** – drums

Conquest not iss.

May 85. (lp) *(QUEST 1)* **RAZOR'S EDGE** [ ] [-]
– Razor's edge / I confess / Born to be with you / One more chance / The protector / Superseded / Moving fast, standing still / I want you to love me. *(re-iss. Nov89 on 'Landslide'; BUTLP 005) (cd-iss. Oct92; BUTCD 005) (cd re-iss. Nov97 on 'Blueprint'; BP 270CD)*

— (Early'86) **DAVE THOMPSON** – bass repl. FISH who joined DUMPY'S RUSTY NUTS / **KEN PUSTELNIK** – drums returned to repl. MIRTON who joined DUMPY'S RUSTY NUTS. They gigged several times and appeared on Radio 2's 'Rhythm and Blues'.

— **DAVE ANDERSON** – bass (ex-AMON DUUL II, ex-HAWKWIND) repl. THOMPSON / **MIKE JONES** – drums repl. PUSTELNIK

Demi-Monde not iss.

May 87. (lp) *(DMLP 1014)* **BACK AGAINST THE WALL** [ ] [-]
– Back against the wall / No to submission / Blue boar blues / Waiting in shadows / Ain't no slaver / Stick to your guns / In the meantime / 54156. *(cd-iss. Jul87 on 'The CD Label'; CDTL 005)*

— ANDERSON re-formed AMON DUUL II, taking with him McPHEE as guest

TONY McPHEE and the GROUNDHOGS

recorded album below

Apr 88. (d-lp) *(DMLP 1016)* **HOGS ON THE ROAD (live)** [ ] [-]
– Express man / Strange town / Eccentric man / 3744 James Road / I want you to love me / Split IV / Soldier / Back against the wall / Garden / Split I / Waiting in shadows / Light my light / Me and the Devil / Mistreated / Groundhogs blues / Split II / Cherry red. *(cd-iss. Aug88 on 'The CD Label'; CDTL 008) (cd re-iss. Mar94 on 'Thunderbolt'; CDTB 114)*

H.T.D. Gopaco

Aug 89. (lp/cd) *(HTD LP/CD 2)* **NO SURRENDER** [ ] [-]
– Razor's edge / 3744 James Road / Superseeded / Light my light / One more chance / Garden. *(cd+=)* – Split (pt.2) / Eccentric man / Strange town / Cherry red. *(re-iss. Dec90 cd/lp; same) <US cd-iss. Oct95 on 'Magnum'; 8> (cd re-iss. Feb00 on 'Transatlantic'; TRACD 328)*

Feb 93. (cd; TONY McPHEE) *(HTDCD 10)* **FOOLISH PRIDE** [ ] [-]
– Foolish pride / Every minute / Devil you know / Masqueradin' / Time after time / On the run / Took me by surprise / Whatever it takes / Been there done that / I'm gonna win. *(re-iss. Sep96; same)*

Jul 93. (d-cd) *(HTDCD 12) <169>* **GROUNDHOG NIGHT – GROUNDHOGS LIVE (live)** [ ] [ ] 1994
– Shake for me / No more doggin' / Eccentric man / 3744 James Road / I want you to love me / Garden / Split pt.1 / Split pt.2 / Still a fool / I love you Miss Ogyny / Thank Christ for the bomb / Soldier / Mistreated / Me and the Devil blues / Cherry red / Groundhog blues / Been there, done that / Down in the bottom. *(re-iss. Feb00; same)*

Dec 94. (cd; as TONY (T.S.) McPHEE) *(HTDCD 26)* **SLIDE T.S. SLIDE** [ ] [-]
– Reformed man / Mean dispostion / Slide to slide / From a pawn to a king / Tell me baby / Hooker & the hogs / Someday, baby / Driving duck / No place to go / Me & the Devil / Death letter / Can't be satisfied / Still a fool / Write me a few short lines / Down in the bottom. *(re-iss. Sep96; same)*

Apr 97. (cd) *(HTDCD 72)* **BLEACHING THE BLUES** [ ] [-]
– When you're down / All your women / There's a light / Went in like a lamb / When your man has gone / Many times / All last night / When you're walking down the street / Meeting of the minds / Bleaching the blues / If I had possession / Love in vain / Floatin' bridge / Terraplane blues / Little red rooster.

H.T.D. Transatla.

Jan 98. (cd) *(HTDCD 81)* <314> **HOGS IN WOLF'S CLOTHING** [ ] [ ] Apr99
– Smokestack lightnimg / Baby how long / Commit a crime / Forty-four / No place to go / I ain't superstitious / Evil / So glad / My life / Sittin' on top of the world / Shake for me / Wang dang doodle / How many more years / Nature / Down in the bottom.

– compilations etc. –

Sep 74. (d-lp) *United Artists; (UDF 31)* <60063-4> **GROUNDHOGS' BEST 1969-1972** [ ] [ ]
– Groundhog / Strange town / Bog roll blues / You had a lesson / Express man / Eccentric man / Earth is not room enough / BDD / Split part 1 / Cherry red / Mistreated / 3744 James Road / Soldier / Sad is the hunter / Garden / Split part 4 / Amazing grace. *(re-iss. Mar88 on 'Beat Goes On' d-lp/cd; BGO DLP/MC 1) (cd-iss. Mar90 on 'E.M.I.'; CDP 7-90434-2)*

Apr 84. (d-lp) *Psycho; (PSYCHO 24)* **HOGGIN' THE STAGE** [ ] [-]
(with free 7") (cd-iss. Nov95 on 'Receiver'; RRCD 207)

May 86. (d-lp/c) *Raw Power; (RAW LP/TC 021)* **MOVING FAST, STANDING STILL** [ ] [-]
– RAZOR'S EDGE' & 'THE TWO SIDES OF T.S. McPHEE', incl. 4 extra 'Immediate' 45's)

Jun 92. (cd) *Beat Goes On; (BGOCD 131)* **CROSSCUT SAW / BLACK DIAMOND** [ ] [-]

Dec 92. (cd/c) *Connoisseur; (CSAP CD/MC 112)* **DOCUMENT SERIES PRESENTS (CLASSIC ALBUM CUTS 1968-1976)** [ ] [-]
– Still a fool / Walking blues / Mistreated / Express man / Eccentric man / Status people / Cherry red / Split (part IV) / Wages of peace / Amazing Grace / Love you Miss Ogyny / Earth shanty / Live a little lady / Boogie with us / Pastoral future / Live right.

Sep 94. (cd) *Windsong; (WINCD 064)* **BBC RADIO 1 LIVE IN CONCERT** [ ] [-]

Feb 96. (4xcd-box) *E.M.I.; (CDHOGS 1)* **FOUR GROUNDHOGS ORIGINALS** [ ] [-]
– (SCRATCHING THE SURFACE / BLUES OBITUARY / THANK CHRIST FOR THE BOMB / SPLIT)

Oct 96. (cd; as TONY McPHEE'S GROUNDHOGS) *Indigo; (IGOCD 2058)* **WHO SAID CHERRY RED?** [ ] [-]

Feb 97. (cd) *EMI Gold; (CDGOLD 1074)* **THE BEST OF** [ ] [-]

Jun 97. (cd; with HERBAL MIXTURE) *Distortions; (D 1012)* **PLEASE LEAVE MY MIND** [ ] [-]

Feb 98. (cd) *Strange Fruit; (SFRSCD 053)* **ON AIR 1970-72** [ ] [-]

Aug 98. (lp) *Akarma; (AK 010)* **LIVE AT LEEDS** [ ] [-]

Mar 98. (cd) *Eagle; (EABCD 087)* **THE MASTERS** [ ] [-]
(re-iss. Sep98 on 'Cleopatra'; CLEO 370)

Sep 98. (cd) *H.T.D.; (HTDCD 68)* **NO SURRENDER / RAZOR'S EDGE TOUR** [ ] [-]

Apr 99. (cd) *H.T.D.; (HTDCD 91) / Castle;* <548> **MUDDY WATERS SONGBOOK** [ ] [-]

May 99. (cd) *Music; (CD 6189)* **GROUNDHOG BLUES** [ ] [-]

Sep 99. (lp/cd) *Akarma; (AK/+CD 073)* **US TOUR** [ ] [-]

Aug 00. (cd) *Mooncrest; (CRESTCD 049Z)* **BOOGIE WITH US** [ ] [-]

TONY McPHEE

also released other solo work.

1968. (lp) *Liberty; (LBS 83190)* **ME AND THE DEVIL** [ ] [-]
(contributed some tracks to below compilation)

1969. (lp) *Liberty; (LBS 83252)* **I ASKED FOR WATER, SHE GAVE ME GASOLINE** [ ] [-]

— Next credited with **JO-ANN KELLY**

1971. (lp) *Sunset; (SLS 50209)* **SAME THING ON THEIR MINDS** [ ] [-]

Apr 98. (cd) *Beat Goes On; (BGOCD 332)* **ME AND THE DEVIL / I ASKED FOR WATER SHE GAVE ME GASOLINE** [ ] [-]

GUN

Formed: Glasgow, Scotland . . . 1986 by BABY STAFFORD and MARK RANKIN. Originally called HAIRSPRAY TO HEAVEN then PHOBIA, before opting simply for GUN, the band's line-up was completed by guitarist GUILIANO GIZZI, his brother DANTE on bass and SCOTT SHIELDS on drums. In late 1987, they signed to 'A&M', soon making the UK Top 50 lists with their debut 1989 album, 'TAKING ON THE WORLD'. Along with TEXAS (whose SHARLEEN SPITERI guested on their debut) and SLIDE (anyone remember them?), the band were hailed as the saviours of the Scottish rock scene although in truth, if any group was up to that mammoth task then it was PRIMAL SCREAM, GUN essentially another bunch of workmanlike grafters in the mode of DEL AMITRI or DEACON BLUE, if a bit heavier. Their debut single, the pop/rock of 'BETTER DAYS', was a minor Top 40 hit, the album lingering on the fringes of the chart. The songwriting was competent enough and the band did have a certain cocksure swagger that caught the eye of MICK JAGGER and KEITH RICHARDS who duly invited GUN to support them on the UK leg of their 'Urban Jungle' tour. STAFFORD quickly became disillusioned, however, departing soon after. Replacing him with ALEX DICKSON, the band began work on a new album, 'GALLUS' (1992), a more organic, harder hitting affair that almost made the Top 10 and spawned the group's first Top 30 single, 'STEAL YOUR FIRE'. By 1994's 'SWAGGER', DICKSON had left and MARK KERR had replaced SHIELDS on the drum stool. The first single from the album was a horrendous, club-footed re-hash of CAMEO's funk classic, 'WORD UP', although ironically/predictably, the song gave them a Top 10 hit at long last. Buoyed by the single's success (and to be fair, it wasn't wholly representative of the album), the album went Top 5. In 1997, G.U.N. (as they were now called) disappointed many of their fans with their new pop/rock-orientated material, which sounded more like a poor man's INXS. • **Songwriters:** RANKIN-GIZZI-GIZZI except; LET'S GO CRAZY (Prince) / DON'T BELIEVE A WORD (Thin Lizzy) / CHILDREN OF THE REVOLUTION (T.Rex) / SUFFRAGETTE CITY (David Bowie) / PANIC (Smiths) / KILLING IN THE NAME (Rage Against The Machine) / SO LONELY (Police) / ARE YOU GONNA GO MY WAY (Lenny Kravitz).

Album rating: TAKING ON THE WORLD (*6) / GALLUS (*5) / SWAGGER (*5) / 0141 632 6326 (*5)

MARK RANKIN – vocals / **BABY STAFFORD** (b. STEVE) – guitar / **GUILIANO GIZZI** – guitar / **DANTE GIZZI** – bass / **SCOTT SHIELDS** – drums

A&M A&M

May 89. (lp/c/cd) *(AMA/AMC/CDA 7007)* <5285> **TAKING ON THE WORLD** [44] [ ]
– Better days / The feeling within / Inside out / Shame on you / Money (everybody loves her) / Taking on the world / Shame / Can't get any lower / Something to believe in / Girls in love / I will be waiting. *(re-iss. Mar95 cd/c; 397007-2/-4)*

Jun 89. (7") *(AM 505)* <1482> **BETTER DAYS. / WHEN YOU LOVE SOMEBODY** [33] [ ]
(12"+=/cd-s+=) *(AMY/CDEE 505)* – Coming home.

Aug 89. (7") *(AM 520)* **MONEY (EVERYBODY LOVES HER). / PRIME TIME** [73] [-]
(12"+=/12"pic-d+=/cd-s+=) *(AMY/AMP/CDEE 520)* – Dance.

Oct 89. (7"/7"s/7"pic-d) *(AM/+S/P 531)* **INSIDE OUT. / BACK TO WHERE WE STARTED** [57] [-]
(12"+=/cd-s+=/d7"+=) *(AMY/CDEE/AMB 531)* – Where do we go?

Jan 90. (7"/7"s) *(AM/+S 541)* **TAKING ON THE WORLD. / DON'T BELIEVE A WORD** [50] [-]
(12"+=/cd-s+=) *(AMY/CDEE 541)* – Better days (extended).

Jun 90. (7"/c-s) *(AM/+MC 573)* **SHAME ON YOU. / BETTER DAYS (live)** [33] [-]
(12"+=/12"s+=/cd-s+=) *(AM X/T/CD 573)* – Money (everybody loves her).
(12") *(AMY 573)* – ('A'remixes).

— **ALEX DICKSON** – guitar; repl. BABY STAFFORD (to own band)

Mar 92. (7"/c-s) *(AM/+MC 851)* **STEAL YOUR FIRE. / DON'T BLAME ME** [24] [-]
(12"+=/cd-s+=) *(AM Y/CD 851)* – Burning down the house / Reach out for love.

Apr 92. (7"/c-s) *(AM/+MC 869)* **HIGHER GROUND. / RUN** [48] [-]
(12"+=/pic-cd-s+=) *(AM Y/CD 869)* – One desire.

Apr 92. (cd/c/lp) *(395383-2/-4/-1)* <75021-5383-2/-4> **GALLUS** [14] [ ]
– Steal your fire / Money to burn / Long road / Welcome to the real world / Higher ground / Borrowed time / Freedom / Won't break down / Reach out for love / Watching the world go by. *(re-iss. Mar95 cd/c; 395383-2/-4)*

Jun 92. (7"/c-s) *(AM/+MC 885)* **WELCOME TO THE REAL WORLD. / STEAL YOUR FIRE (live)** [43] [-]
(12"pic-d+=) *(AMY 885)* – Standing in your shadow.
(cd-s+=) *(AMCD 885)* – Better days / Shame on you (acoustic).

— **MARK KERR** – drums; repl. SHIELDS + DICKSON

Jul 94. (7"/c-s) *(580 664-7/-4)* **WORD UP. / STAY FOREVER** [8] [-]
(cd-s+=) *(580 665-2)* – The man I used to be / Stranger.
(cd-s) *(580 667-2)* – ('A'mixes).
(12") *(580 665-1)* – ('A'mixes).

Aug 94. (cd/c) *(<540 254-2/-4>)* **SWAGGER** [5] [ ] Feb95
– Stand in line / Find my way / Word up / Don't say it's over / The only one / Something worthwhile / Seems like I'm losing you / Crying over you / One reason / Vicious heart.

Sep 94. (7") *(580 754-7)* **DON'T SAY IT'S OVER. / STEAL YOUR FIRE** [19] [-]
(cd-s+=) *(580 755-2)* – Shame on you.
(cd-s) *(580 757-2)* – ('A'side) / Better days / Money (everybody loves her).

Feb 95. (c-s) *(580 953-4)* **THE ONLY ONE / WORD UP (mix) / WORD UP (Tinman remix)** [29] [-]
(12"+=) *(580 953-1)* – Inside out – So lonely.
(cd-s++=) *(580 953-2)* – Time.
(cd-s) *(580 955-2)* – ('A'side) / Killing in the name / Panic / Are you gonna go my way.

Apr 95. (cd-ep) *(581 043-2)* **SOMETHING WORTHWHILE / SUFFRAGETTE CITY / CHILDREN OF THE REVOLUTION / WORD UP** [39] [-]
(cd-ep) *(581 045-2)* – ('A'side) / One reason / ('A'-Mac attack mix) / ('A'-Priory mix).
(12"pic-d-ep) *(581 043-1)* – ('A'side) / ('A'-Mac attack mix) / ('A'-King Dong mix) / ('A'-Breakdown mix).

G.U.N.

Apr 97. (cd-s) *(582 191-2)* **CRAZY YOU / SOME THINGS NEVER CHANGE / A WOMAN LIKE YOU** [21] [-]
(c-s/cd-s) *(582 193-4/-2)* – ('A'side) / ('A'-K.M. mix) / ('A'instrumental) / ('A'demo).

May 97. (cd/c/lp) *(540 723-2/-4/-1)* **0141 632 6326** [32] [-]
– Rescue you / Crazy you / Seventeen / All my love / My sweet Jane / Come a long way / All I ever wanted / I don't mind / Going down / Always friends.

Jun 97. (c-s) *(582 279-4)* **MY SWEET JANE / GOING DOWN (Mizzy Hog mix)** [51] [-]
(cd-s+=) *(582 279-2)* – Crazy you / Word up (Tinman mix).
(cd-s) *(582 277-2)* – ('A'side) / Don't cry / Sometimes.

— G.U.N. have since split up

GUNS N' ROSES

Formed: Los Angeles, California, USA . . . early 1985 by AXL ROSE, IZZY STRADLIN and moonlighting L.A. GUNS member TRACII GUNS, who was soon to return to said outfit. With the addition of SLASH, DUFF McKAGAN and STEVEN ADLER, the seminal G N' R line-up was complete, the ramshackle collection of petty thieves and drug addicts subsequently embarking on the 'hell' tour of the US. Although this outing was a disaster, the band created a major buzz with their residency at L.A.'s Troubadour club and in the summer of '86 unleashed their debut recording, a 7"ep entitled 'LIVE ?!*' LIKE A SUICIDE'. A short, sharp shock of visceral rock'n'raunch, the record struck a major chord with critics and fans alike, quickly selling out of its limited 10,000 pressing. Snapped up by 'Geffen', the band released their debut album, 'APPETITE FOR DESTRUCTION', the following year. A head-on collision of AC/DC, AEROSMITH and The SEX PISTOLS, what the record lacked in originality, it made up for with sheer impact. The opening unholy trinity ('WELCOME TO THE JUNGLE', 'IT'S SO EASY', 'NIGHTRAIN') alone laid the rest of the L.A. hairspray pack to waste, while with 'PARADISE CITY' and 'SWEET CHILD O' MINE', the band staked their claim to chart domination and stadium stardom. In spite of its controversial cover art featuring a robot raping a woman (later withdrawn), the record went on to sell a staggering 20 million copies worldwide and remains one of metal's defining moments. It also remains one of the most vivid portrayals of the claustrophobic seediness of the L.A. metal scene in much the same way as N.W.A. captured the fuck-you nihilism of the city's black ghetto with 'Straight Outta Compton'. Live, GUNS N' ROSES were caustic and volatile, as likely to produce tabloid headlines as blistering performances. Image wise, they had SLASH as an unmistakable focal point; his trademark top hat perched on a nest of thick curls that all but obscured his face, fag constantly hanging from his lips a la KEITH RICHARDS. Controversy turned into tragedy the following summer, however, when two fans were crushed to death during a G N' R set at the 1988 Castle Donington Monsters Of Rock festival. Later that year, the band released 'G N' R LIES', a half live/ half studio affair that combined their earlier EP with four new acoustic numbers. On the lovely 'PATIENCE', ROSE was transformed from sneering vocal acrobat to mellow songsmith, although by 'ONE IN A MILLION', he was back to his old ways with a vengeance. While the song was performed with undeniable passion, it was all the more worrying given the subjects he was railing against. The track was basically an unforgivable tirade of abuse aimed at 'niggers', 'faggots' and 'immigrants', hmmm.. ironic? Yeah, right. Still, the good citizens of America snapped up the record and it peaked at No.2. in the US, No.22 in Britain. Come 1990, the band were supporting The ROLLING STONES on a world tour, their star status rapidly assuming the same magnitude as their drug habits. ADLER's heroin problems eventually saw him kicked out later that summer, CULT drummer MATT SORUM taking his place on the drum stool. The band also recruited a keyboard player, DIZZY REED, a sure sign they were beginning to lose the plot. A terminally dull cover of DYLAN's 'KNOCKIN' ON HEAVEN'S DOOR' (included on the 'Days Of Thunder' soundtrack) seemed to confirm this although 'CIVIL WAR', their contribution to Romanian orphan project, 'Nobody's Child', was more encouraging. When it eventually surfaced, the band's next studio project, 'USE YOUR ILLUSION' (1991), was a resounding disappointment. The very fact they released the disc in 2 volumes showed a severe lack of objectivity and needless to say, the quality control was non-existent. A sprawling, unfocused jumble, the collection nevertheless included a few inspired moments (notably the classic 'NOVEMBER RAIN') and both albums reached No.1 and 2 respectively in both Britain and America. During the subsequent world tour, STRADLIN walked out, finally leaving the band soon after for a solo career (his replacement was GILBY CLARKE). Among the dates on the record-breaking 28 month world tour was a performance at AIDS benefit concert, The Freddie Mercury Tribute, rather ironic in light of ROSE's lyrical homophobic tendencies. The bandana'ed one courted further outrage when the group included a CHARLES MANSON song on their 1993 covers album, 'THE SPAGHETTI INCIDENT', a record that also saw the band rework their faves from NAZARETH to The UK SUBS. They also massacred 'SYMPATHY FOR THE DEVIL' for the 'Interview With The Vampire' soundtrack, their last outing to date. CLARKE has subsequently left the band following a solo release, 'PAWNSHOP GUITARS', while SLASH also released a side project, 'IT'S FIVE O'CLOCK SOMEWHERE', in 1995 under the moniker SLASH'S SNAKEPIT. • **Songwriters:** All written by AXL except; MAMA KIN (Aerosmith) / NICE BOYS DON'T PLAY ROCK'N'ROLL (Rose Tattoo) / WHOLE LOTTA ROSIE (Ac-Dc) / LIVE AND LET DIE (Paul McCartney & Wings). Punk covers album; SINCE I DON'T HAVE YOU (Skyliners) / NEW ROSE (Damned) / DOWN ON THE FARM (UK Subs) / HUMAN BEING (New York Dolls) / RAW POWER (Iggy & The Stooges) / AIN'T IT FUN (Dead Boys) / BUICK MAKANE (T.Rex) / HAIR OF THE DOG (Nazareth) / ATTITUDE (Misfits) / BLACK LEATHER (Sex Pistols) / YOU CAN'T PUT YOUR ARMS AROUND A MEMORY (Johnny Thunders) / I DON'T CARE ABOUT YOU (Fear) / WHAT'S YOUR GAME! (Charles Manson). McKAGAN covered CRACKED ACTOR (David Bowie) • **Trivia:** On 28 Apr'90, AXL was married to ERIN, daughter of DON EVERLY (Brothers), but a couple of months later, they counterfiled for divorce. BAILEY was AXL's step-father's surname, and he found out real surname ROSE in the 80's.

Album rating: APPETITE FOR DESTRUCTION (*9) / G N' R LIES (*7) / USE YOUR ILLUSION I (*7) / USE YOUR ILLUSION II (*6) / THE SPAGHETTI INCIDENT (*5) / LIVE ERA – 1987-1993 exploitation (*6)

W. AXL ROSE (b. WILLIAM BAILEY, 6 Feb'62, Lafayette, Indiana, USA) – vocals / **SLASH** (b. SAUL HUDSON, 23 Jul'65, Stoke-On-Trent, England) – lead guitar / **IZZY STRADLIN** (b.JEFFREY ISBELL, 8 Apr'62, Lafayette) – guitar / **DUFF McKAGAN** (b. MICHAEL, 5 Feb'64, Seattle, Wash.) – bass (ex-10 MINUTE WARNING, ex-FASTBACKS) / **STEVE ADLER** (b.22 Jan'65, Ohio) – drums repl. ROB to L.A. GUNS again.

not iss. — Uzi Suicide

Aug 86. (7"ep) *<USR 001>* **LIVE ?!*' LIKE A SUICIDE** [-] [ ]
– Mama kin / Reckless life / Move to the city / Nice boys (don't play rock'n'roll). *<re-iss. Jan87 on 'Geffen'; >*

Geffen — Geffen

Jun 87. (7") *(GEF 22)* **IT'S SO EASY. / MR. BROWNSTONE** [ ] [ ]
(12"+=/12"pic-d+=) *(GEF 22T/+P)* – Shadow of your love / Move to the city.

Aug 87. (lp/c)(cd) *(WX 125/+C)(924148-2) <24148>* **APPETITE FOR DESTRUCTION** [5] [1]
– Welcome to the jungle / It's so easy / Nightrain / Out ta get me / Mr. Brownstone / Paradise city / My Michelle / Think about you / Sweet child o' mine / You're crazy / Anything goes / Rocket queen. *(peaked UK-No.5 in 1989) (re-iss. Nov90 lp/c/cd; GEF/+C/D 24148) (re-iss. Oct95 cd/c;)*

Sep 87. (7") *(GEF 30)* **WELCOME TO THE JUNGLE. / WHOLE LOTTA ROSIE (live)** [67] [ ]
(12"+=/12"w-poster/12"pic-d+=) *(GEF 30 T/TW/P)* – It's so easy (live) / Knockin' on Heaven's door (live).

Aug 88. (7") *(GEF 43) <27963>* **SWEET CHILD O' MINE. / OUT TA GET ME** [24] [1] Jun88
(12"+=/12"s+=/10"+=) *(GEF 43T/+V/E)* – Rocket queen.

Oct 88. (7") *(GEF 47) <27759>* **WELCOME TO THE JUNGLE. / NIGHTRAIN** [24] [7]
(12"+=/12"w-poster+=/12"w-patch+=/12"pic-d+=/cd-s+=) *(GEF 47 T/TW/TV/TP/CD)* – You're crazy.

Dec 88. (lp/c)(cd) *(WX 218/+C)(924198-2) <24198>* **G N' R LIES (live)** [22] [2]
– Reckless life / Nice boys (don't play rock'n'roll) / Move to the city / Mama kin / Patience / I used to love her / You're crazy / One in a million. *(re-iss. Nov90 lp/c/cd; GEF/+C/D 24198) (re-iss. Oct95 cd/c;)*

Mar 89. (7"/7"sha-clear/7"white-pic-d) *(GEF 50/+P/X) <27570>* **PARADISE CITY. / I USED TO LOVE HER** [6] [5] Jan89
(c-s+=)(12"+=) *(9275 704)(GEF 50T)* – Anything goes.
(cd-s++=) *(GEF 50CD)* – Sweet child o' mine.

May 89. (7"/7"s/c-s) *(GEF 55/+W/C)* **SWEET CHILD O' MINE (remix). / OUT TA GET ME** [6] [-]
(7"sha-pic-d+=) *(GEF 55P)* – Rocket queen.
(12"/3"cd-s) *(GEF 55 T/CD)* – ('A'side) / Move to the city / Whole lotta Rosie (live) / It's so easy (live).

Jun 89. (7"/c-s) *(GEF 56/+C) <22996>* **PATIENCE. / ROCKET QUEEN** [10] [4] Apr89
(12"+=/3"cd-s+=) *(GEF 56 T/CD)* – (W. Axl Rose interview).

Aug 89. (7"/7"sha-pic-d/c-s) *(GEF 60/+P/C) <22869>* **NIGHTRAIN. / RECKLESS LIFE** [17] [93] Jul89
(12"+=/3"cd-s+=) *(GEF 60 T/CD)* – Knockin' on Heaven's door (live '87).

—— (Aug90) **MATT SORUM** (b.19 Nov'60, Long Beach, Calif.) – drums (ex-CULT) repl. ADAM MARPLES (ex-SEA HAGS) who repl. ADLER due to bouts of drunkeness. added **DIZZY REED** (b. DARREN REED, 18 Jun'63, Hinsdale, Illinois) – keyboards

Jul 91. (7"/c-s/12"clear-pic-d/cd-s) *(GFS/+C/TP/TD 6) <19039>* **YOU COULD BE MINE. / CIVIL WAR** [3] [29]

Sep 91. (d-lp/c/cd) *<(GEF/+C/D 24415)>* **USE YOUR ILLUSION I** [2] [2]
– Right next door to Hell / Dust n' bones / Live and let die / Don't cry (original) / Perfect crime / You ain't the first / Bad obsession / Back off bitch / Double talkin' jive / November rain / The garden / Garden of Eden / Don't damn me / Bad apples / Dead horse / Coma.

Sep 91. (d-lp/c/cd) *<(GEF/+C/D 24420)>* **USE YOUR ILLUSION II** [1] [1]
– Civil war / 14 years / Yesterdays / Knockin' on Heaven's door / Get in the ring / Shotgun blues / Breakdown / Pretty tied up / Locomotive / So fine / Estranged / You could be mine / Don't cry (alt.lyrics) / My world.

Sep 91. (7"/c-s) *(GFS/+C 9) <19027>* **DON'T CRY (original). / DON'T CRY (alternate lyrics)** [8] [10]
(12"+=/cd-s+=) *(GFST/+D 9)* – ('A'demo).

Dec 91. (7"/c-s/12") *(GFS/+C/X 17) <19114>* **LIVE AND LET DIE. / ('A'live)** [5] [33]
(cd-s+=) *(GFSTD 17)* – Shadow of your love.

—— (Sep'91) **DAVID NAVARRO** – guitar (of JANE'S ADDICTION) repl. IZZY who walked out on tour. **GILBY CLARKE** (b.17 Aug'62, Cleveland, Ohio) – guitar finally repl. IZZY who formed IZZY STRADLIN & THE JU JU HOUNDS

Feb 92. (7"/c-s) *(GFS/+C 18) <19067>* **NOVEMBER RAIN. / SWEET CHILD O' MINE (live)** [4] [3] Jun92
(12"+=/pic-cd-s+=) *(GFST/+D 18)* – Patience.

May 92. (7"/c-s/12"/cd-s) *(GFS/+C/T/TD 21)* **KNOCKIN' ON HEAVEN'S DOOR (live '92 at Freddie Mercury tribute). / ('A'studio)** [2] [-]

Oct 92. (7"/c-s) *(GFS/+C 27)* **YESTERDAYS. / NOVEMBER RAIN** [8] [-]
(12"pic-d+=/cd-s+=) *(GFST/+D 27)* – ('A'live) / Knockin' on Heaven's door (live '87).

Nov 92. (c-s) *<19142>* **YESTERDAYS / ('A'live)** [-] [72]

May 93. (cd-ep) *(GFSTD 43)* **CIVIL WAR EP** [11] [-]
– Civil war / Garden of Eden / Dead horse / (interview with Slash).

Nov 93. (c-s) *(GFSC 62)* **AIN'T IT FUN. / DOWN ON THE FARM** [9] [-]
(cd-s+=) *(GFSTD 62)* – Attitude.

Nov 93. (cd/c/lp) *<(GED/GEC/GEF 24617)>* **THE SPAGHETTI INCIDENT** [2] [4]
– Since I don't have you / New rose / Down on the farm / Human being / Raw power / Ain't it fun / Buick Makane / Hair of the dog / Attitude / Black leather / You can't put your arms around a memory / I don't care about you / What's your game!.

May 94. (7"colrd/c-s) *(GFS/+C 70) <19266>* **SINCE I DON'T HAVE YOU. / YOU CAN'T PUT YOUR ARMS AROUND A MEMORY** [10] [69] Feb94
(cd-s+=) *(GFSTD 70)* – Human being.
(cd-s) *(GFSXD 70)* – ('A'side) / Sweet child o' mine / Estranged.

—— **PAUL HUGE** – guitar; repl. the sacked and solo bound GILBY
(below from the movie 'Interview With A Vampire')

Jan 95. (c-s) *(GFSC 86)* **SYMPATHY FOR THE DEVIL / LIVE AND LET DIE** [9] [55] Dec94
(cd-s) *(GFSTD 86) <19381>* – ('A'side) / (track by Elliot Goldenthal).

— DUFF and MATT teamed up with STEVE JONES (Sex Pistols) and JOHN TAYLOR (Duran Duran) to form mid '96 supergroup, The NEUROTIC OUTSIDERS; released an eponymous album and single, 'JERK', for 'Maverick' records. In early November, SLASH quit, citing ill feeling between him and AXL.

– compilations, etc. –

Nov 99. (d-cd/d-c) *Geffen; <(490514-2/-4)>* **LIVE ERA 87-93 (live)** [45] [45]
– Nightrain / Mr. Brownstone / It's so easy / Welcome to the jungle / Dust n' bones / My Michelle / You're crazy / Used to love her / Patience / It's alright / November rain / Out to get me / Yesterdays / Move to the city / Rocket queen / Sweet child o' mine / Knockin' on Heaven's door / Don't cry / Estranged / Paradise city.

GUTTERMOUTH

Formed: Los Angeles, California, USA . . . 1989 by MARK ADKINS, ERIC DAVIS, SCOTT SHELDON, STEVE RAPP and JAMES NUNN. Veterans of the Huntington Beach punk scene, GUTTERMOUTH lived up to their name from the off. Casually laying in to a range of soft targets at will, the band nevertheless claim to avoid offending anyone deliberately. Nope, only those who take life too seriously will likely take umbrage according to ADKINS and Co. Following their debut single, 'PUKE', the irreverent quintet's first album, 'FULL LENGTH LP', arrived in 1992. Subsequently signed to DEXTER HOLLAND's 'Nitro' label, the foul-mouthed Californians released their sophomore effort, 'FRIENDLY PEOPLE', in 1994. 'TERI YAKIMOTO' and the satirically titled collection 'THE ALBUM FORMERLY KNOWN AS A FULL LENGTH LP' followed in 1996, 'MUSICAL MONKEY' in 1997. GUTTERMOUTH's infamously expletive-filled stage show was captured for posterity on 1998's 'LIVE FROM THE PHARMACY' while the artwork for 'GORGEOUS' (1999) left little to the imagination. After nearly a decade with 'Nitro', the lads signed to rival West Coast punk bastion, 'Epitaph', for 'COVERED WITH ANTS' (2001).

Album rating: FULL LENGTH LP (*5) / FRIENDLY PEOPLE (*5) / TERI YAKIMOTO (*6) / MUSICAL MONKEY (*6) / LIVE FROM THE PHARMACY (*6) / GORGEOUS (*7) / COVERED WITH ANTS (*6)

MARK ADKINS – vocals / **SCOTT SHELDON** – guitar / **ERIC DAVIS** – guitar / **JAMES NUNN** – bass / **TY SMITH** – drums

not iss. Dr.Strange

Feb 94. (cd) *<DSR 09CD>* **FULL LENGTH LP** [-] [ ]
– Racetrack / No more / Jack la Lanne / Where was I? / Old glory / I'm punk / Mr. Barbeque / Bruce Lee vs. the Kiss army / Chicken box / Carp / Toilet / Oats / 1,2,3 . . . slam! / I used to be 20 / Reggae man / *(UK-iss.Sep95; same as US) <(US re-iss. Jul96 as 'THE ALBUM FORMERLY KNOWN AS FULL LENGTH LP' on 'Nitro'+=; 15807-2/-1)>* – Chicken box (again) / Just a fuck / Hypocrite / Marco Polo / Under my skin / Gas out / No such thing / Malted vomit / Ghost.

Nitro Nitro

Mar 95. (cd/c/lp) *<(15801-2/-4/-1)>* **FRIENDLY PEOPLE** [ ] [ ]
– End of 9 / Derek / Jamie's petting zoo / Bullshit / P.C. / Disneyland / Can't we all just get along at the dinner table / Veggicide / Chaps my hide / What's gone wrong / Your late / Summer's over / Asshole. *(re-iss. Oct96; same)*

Sep 96. (cd/c/lp) *<(15804-2/-4/-1)>* **TERI YAKIMOTO** [ ] [ ] May96
– Use your mind / Trinket trading, tick toting, toothless and / Generous portions / A day at the office / Teri Yakimoto / Whiskey / Lock down / God's kingdom / Mark's ark / Room for improvement / Casserole of life / Thought provoking sonic device / I saw the light / 1-2-3-4 / Under the sea (Barney "get your hand off my child" the dinosaur).

Jul 97. (cd/c/lp) *<(15812-2/-4/-1)>* **MUSICAL MONKEY** [ ] [ ]
– What's the big deal? / Lucky the donkey / Big pink dress / Do the hustle / Good Friday / Baker's dozen / Abort mission / Corpse rotting in Hell / Lipstick / When Hell freezes over / S.D.F.B. / What if? / Perfect world / Gold / Musical monkey.

Jul 98. (cd/c/lp) *<(15819-2/-4/-1)>* **LIVE FROM THE PHARMACY (live + 4 new songs)** [ ] [ ]
– Oats / Just a fuck / Where was I? / Disneyland / Chicken box / Jamie's petting zoo / Marco Polo / Pot / No such thing / Racetrack / Bruce Lee vs. the Kiss army / 1,2,3 . . . slam! / Veggicide / What's gone wrong / Derek / Asshole / American made / This won't hurt a bit / Steak (the underwater version) / Born in the U.S.A.

Jun 99. (cd/lp) *<(15825-2/-1)>* **GORGEOUS** [ ] [ ]
– Hit machine / Enclyclopedia brown / Con especial / Vive America / Diamond studded bumblebee / Date with destiny / Dreaded sea lice have come out / Nice place to visit / Food storage / I have a dream / BBB / High balls / Power up.

Epitaph Epitaph

Mar 01. (cd/lp) *<(6589-2/-1)>* **COVERED WITH ANTS** [ ] [ ]
– That's life / Can I borrow some ambition / Secure horizons / She's got the look / Looking good is all that matters / I'm destroying the world / Chug a lug night / What you like about me / I won't see you in the pit / Black enforcers / Cram it up your ass.

GWAR

Formed: Richmond, Virginia, USA . . . 1987 by the entertainingly monikered posse of ODERUS URUNGUS, BALSAC THE JAWS OF DEATH, FLATTUS MAXIMUS, BEEFCAKE THE MIGHTY and NIPPLEUS ERECTUS. Like SUN RA and LEE PERRY before them, GWAR apparently claim to come from outer space, Uranus via Antarctica to be precise. That said, there's nothing particularly stellar about either their music or their stage show. Updating the schlock tactics of ALICE COOPER and taking them to their ultimate conclusion, the GWAR onstage look combined loincloth primitivism with hideous, quasi-futuristic body armour and grotesque face masks. GWAR is reportedly a pseudonym for 'God What A Racket', a fairly accurate description of their formless sub-thrash from a group who obviously have their collective tongue planted (or more likely, stapled) firmly in cheek. The group released a string of albums including 'HELL-O' (1988; for KRAMER's 'Shimmy Disc'), 'SCUMDOGS OF THE UNIVERSE' (1990) and 'AMERICA MUST BE DESTROYED' (1992), although far more interesting were their infamous live antics. Their moral-majority-baiting show centred upon the reliable topics of sex and death with lashings of blood, dismembered bodies, giant penises etc. (all fake, obviously). Fans who couldn't make it to their shows (probably because they had so many cancelled by shit-scared local councils) or decided they didn't particularly want to be splattered with fake semen, were free to view the debauchery from the comfort of their armchair via GWAR videos such as 'PHALLUS IN WONDERLAND' and 'TOUR DE SCUM'.

Album rating: HELL-O (*6) / SCUMDOGS OF THE UNIVERSE (*4) / AMERICA MUST BE DESTROYED (*5) / THIS TOILET EARTH (*4) / RAGNAROK (*4) / CARNIVAL OF CHAOS (*3) / WE KILL EVERYTHING (*5)

ODEROUS URUNGUS – vocals / **BALSAC THE JAWS OF DEATH** – guitar / **FLATTUS MAXIMUS** – guitar / **BEEFCAKE THE MIGHTY** – bass / **NIPPLEUS ERECTUS** – drums

Shimmy Disc Shimmy Disc

Feb 89. (lp/c) *<(SHIMMY 010/+MC)>* **HELL-O** [ ] [ ] 1988
– Time for death / Americanized / Slutman city / War toy / Pure as the arctic snow / GWAR theme / Ollie North / U ain't shit / Black and huge / A.E.I.O.U. / I'm in love with a dead dog / World o' filth / Captain Crunch / Je m'appelle J. Cousteau / Bone meal / Techno's song / Rock'n'roll party theme. *(re-iss. Sep92 on 'Metal Blade' cd/c; CD/T ZORRO 35) (cd re-iss. May96; 3984 14004CD)*

— others; **JIZ MAC THE GUSHER, SLYMENSTRA HYMEN + THE SEXECUTIONER**

Master Metal Blade

May 90. (cd/c/lp) *(MAS CD/MC/LP 001) <26243-2/-4/-1>* **SCUMDOGS OF THE UNIVERSE** [ ] [ ]
– The salaminizer / Maggots / Sick of you / Slaughterama / The years without light / King queen / Horror of Yig / Vlad the impaler / Black and huge / Love surgery / Death pod / The sexecutioner. *(cd+=)* – Cool place to park. *(cd re-iss. Sep95 on 'Metal Blade'; 3984 17003CD)*

Metal Blade Metal Blade

Mar 92. (cd/c/lp) *(CD/T+/ZORRO 037) <26807>* **AMERICA MUST BE DESTROYED** [ ] [ ] Sep91
– Ham on the bone / Crack the egg / Gor-Gor / Have you seen me / The morality squad / America must be destroyed / Gilded Lily / Poor ole Tom / Rock'n'roll never felt so good / Blimey / The road behind / Pussy planet. *(cd re-iss. Jun96; 3984 17016CD)*

Mar 94. (cd) *(CDZORRO 63) <53889>* **THIS TOILET EARTH** [ ] [ ]
– Saddam a go-go / Penis I see / Eat still / Jack the world / Sonderkommando / Bad bad man / Pepperoni / Insidious soliliquy of skulhedface / B.D.F. / Fight / The issue of the tissue (spacecake) / Pocket pool / Slap U around / Krak-down / Filthy flow / The obliteration of Flab Quarv 7.

Oct 95. (cd) *(3984 17001-2) <50527>* **RAGNAROK** [ ] [ ]
– Meat sandwich / The new plague / Wargoul / Ragnarock / Dirty, filthy / Stalin's organs / Knife in yer guts / Think you oughta know this / Martyr dumb / Nudged / Fire in the loins / Surf of sin / Crush kill destroy / None but the brave.

Nov 95. (m-cd) *(3984 17004CD) <2-45101>* **THE ROAD BEHIND** [ ] [ ] Oct92
– The road behind / Overture in N minor / Krak-down / Voodoo summoning / Captain Crunch / Have you seen me?

Apr 97. (cd) *(3984 17025CD) <14125>* **CARNIVAL OF CHAOS** [ ] [ ]
– Penguin attack / Let's blame the lightman / First rule is / Sammy / Endless apocalypse / Billy bad ass / Hate love songs / Letter from the scallop boat / Pre-skool prostitute / If I could be that / In her fear / Back to Iraq / I suck on my thumb / Private pain of techno destructo / Gonna kill U / Sex cow / Antartican drinking song / Don't need a man.

May 99. (cd) *<(14237-2)>* **WE KILL EVERYTHING** [ ] [ ] Apr99
– Baby raper / Fishfuck / The performer / Short history of the end of the world / Escape from Moose lodge / Tune from da Moon / Jiggle the handle / Nitro burnin' funny bong / Jagermonsta / My girly ways / The master has a butt / We kill everything / Child / Penile drip / Mary Anne / Friend / Fuckin' an animal.

GYPSY QUEEN

Formed: Florida, USA . . . 1986 by twin sisters and former topless Playboy bunnies, PAM and PAULA MATTIOLA, who enlisted musicians PEDRO RIERA, BRYAN LE MAR, MARS COWLING and KEITH DANIEL CRONIN. Kerrang!'s favourite flame-haired beauties, the girls were more noted for their basque'n'roll choreography than their flimsy snatches (er . . . snippets) of melodic hard rock. Renowed 70's producer, JACK DOUGLAS, took the opportunity to twiddle the knobs on their anti-climactic 1987 eponymous debut (no pun intended!?). Thankfully, this was the only effort from the sisters, a subsequent album left on the shelf.

Album rating: GYPSY QUEEN (*3)

PAM MATTIOLA – vocals / **PAULA MATTIOLA** – vocals / **BRYAN LE MAR** – guitar / **PEDRO RIERA** – guitar / **MARS COWLING** – bass (ex-PAT TRAVERS) / **KEITH DANIEL CRONIN** – drums

Loop Loop

Dec 87. (lp/c/cd) *(LOP L/C/CD 500)* **GYPSY QUEEN** [ ] [ ]
– Love is strange / She can't help herself / Radio / (Hey) Are you ever satisfied / Leave us alone / Don't rush me / Love is a shadow / I still don't care / Who are you / She wants to unh. *(cd+=)* – Love is strange (remix) / Where does our love go.

Jan 88. (7"ep/12"ep) *(LOOP/12LOOP 100)* **SNARL 'N STRIPES** [ ] [ ]
– Radio (remix) / The doctor needs a doctor / War and peace / Where does our love go.

— PAM + PAULA brought in entire new line-up; **SCOTT MIGONE** – guitar / **JOEY O'JEDA** – bass, keyboards / **KENNY WENDLAND** – drums

Mar 89. (7"/12") *(LOOP/12LOOP 102)* **TAKE CARE OF YOURSELF. /** [ ] [-]

— After an album was shelved, the sisters became The CELL MATES

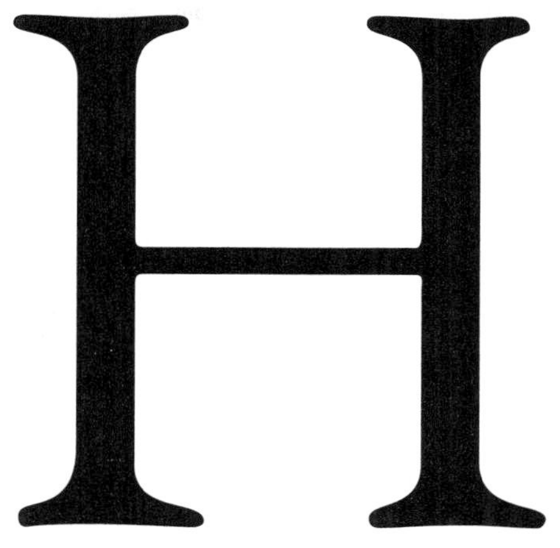

Sammy HAGAR

Born: 13 Oct'47, Monterey, California, USA. Honing his inimitably hoary vocal style in a number of local bands, including FABULOUS CASTILLAS and The JUSTICE BROTHERS, HAGAR subsequently joined MONTROSE in 1973. A prototype 80's hair-metal band, MONTROSE recorded two lauded albums with HAGAR as frontman, 'MONTROSE' (1973) and 'PAPER MONEY' (1974). These sets featured a clutch of classy HAGAR numbers, namely 'SPACE STATION No.5', 'ROCK THE NATION' and 'BAD MOTOR SCOOTER', the singer resurrecting these tracks as the core of his feted stage show. After parting company with MONTROSE, he formed a few short-lived outfits (i.e. DUST COWBOYS and SAMMY WILD), before inking a deal with 'Capitol' records and releasing a solo debut album, 'NINE ON A TEN SCALE' in 1976. Initially he struggled to break through commercially, that is, until 1979's triumphant 'STREET MACHINE', an album that hit the UK! Top 40. Crossover success followed with the more overtly commercial (but hard-rockin' nonetheless) 'DANGER ZONE' (1980) set, although HAGAR only really came into his own in the live arena. Signing to 'Geffen', he delivered a further handful of workmanlike albums, before stunning the rock community by joining VAN HALEN in 1985. Faced with the nigh-on impossible task of replacing the charismatic DAVE LEE ROTH, HAGAR nonetheless won over the fans with his solid and dependable style on such massive 80's albums as '5150' (1986) and 'OU812' (1988). He fulfilled his contractual obligations to 'Geffen', by delivering an eponymous set in 1987. HAGAR continued to enjoy worldwide stardom with VAN HALEN right up until the mid 90's, when he left to resume his solo career. In 1997 and 1999, the man returned to the US Top 30 with two further sets, 'MARCHING TO MARS' and 'RED VOODOO', the latter credited with his new backing band, The WABORITAS. • **Covers:** THE DOCK OF A BAY (Otis Redding) / A WHITER SHADE OF PALE (Procol Harum). • **Trivia:** BETTE MIDLER covered his 'KEEP ON ROCKIN'', in the film 'The Rose'.

Album rating: NINE ON A TEN SCALE (*5) / SAMMY HAGAR (*5) / MUSICAL CHAIRS (*5) / ALL NIGHT LONG (aka LOUD AND CLEAR) (*7) / STREET MACHINE (*5) / DANGER ZONE (*6) / STANDING HAMPTON (*6) / THREE LOCK BOX (*6) / REMATCH compilation (*6) / THROUGH THE FIRE (*5; by HAGAR, SCHON, AARONSON, SHRIEVE) / VOA (*6) / SAMMY HAGAR on 'Geffen' (*5) / THE BEST OF SAMMY HAGAR compilation (*6) / MARCHING TO MARS (*5) / RED VOODOO (*5)

SAMMY HAGAR – vocals (ex-MONTROSE) / with **GARY PHIL** – guitar / **BILL CHURCH** – bass (ex-MONTROSE) / **ALAN FITZGERALD** – keyboards / plus session drummers, etc.

Capitol | Capitol

May 76. (lp) *<(E-ST 11489)>* **NINE ON A TEN SCALE** [ ] [ ]
– Keep on rockin' / Urban guerilla / Flamingos fly / China / Silver lights / All American / Confession / Please come back / Young girl blues / Rock'n'roll Romeo. *(re-iss. Jun81 on 'Greenlight'; GO 2017) (re-iss. May83 on 'Fame' lp/c; FA/TC-FA 3068) (cd-iss. May93 on 'Beat Goes On'; BGOCD 182)*

Jun 76. (7") *(CL 15872)* **FLAMINGOS FLY. / URBAN GUERILLA** [ ] [ ]

— **SCOTT MATTHEWS** – drums (repl. session people)

Mar 77. (red-lp) *<(E-ST 11599)>* **SAMMY HAGAR** [ ] [ ] Feb77
– Red / Catch the wind / Cruisin' and boozin' / Free money / Rock'n'roll weekend / Fillmore shuffle / Hungry / The pits / Love has found me / Little star – Eclipse. *(re-iss. May81 on 'Greenlight'; GO 2007) (cd-iss. May93 as 'RED' on 'Beat Goes On'; BGOCD 181)*

Mar 77. (7") *<4388>* **CATCH THE WIND. / RED** [-] [ ]

Mar 77. (7") *(CL 15913)* **CATCH THE WIND. / ROCK'N'ROLL WEEKEND** [ ] [-]

Jun 77. (7") *<4411>* **CRUISIN' AND BOOZIN'. / LOVE HAS FOUND ME** [-] [ ]

— **DENNY CARMASSI** – drums repl. SCOTT / added **DAVID LEWARK** – guitar

Jan 78. (7") *(CL 15960) <4502>* **YOU MAKE ME CRAZY. / RECKLESS** [ ] [62] Nov77

Jan 78. (lp) *<(E-ST 11706)>* **MUSICAL CHAIRS** [ ] [100]
– Turn up the music / It's gonna be alright / You make me crazy / Reckless / Try (try to fall in love) / Don't stop me now / Straight from the hip kid / Hey boys / Someone out there / Crack in the world. *(re-iss. Jul81 on 'Greenlight'; GO 2021) (cd-iss. May94 on 'Beat Goes On'; BGOCD 201)*

Apr 78. (7") *<4550>* **TURN UP THE MUSIC. / HEY BOYS** [-] [ ]

May 78. (7") *(CL 15983)* **TURN UP THE MUSIC. / STRAIGHT FROM THE HIP KID** [ ] [-]

May 78. (7") *<4596>* **SOMEONE OUT THERE. / I'VE DONE EVERYTHING FOR YOU** [-] [ ]

— **GARY PIHL** – guitar repl. LEWARK

Aug 78. (lp) *<E-ST 11812>* **ALL NIGHT LONG (live)** [-] [89]
– Red / Rock'n'roll weekend / Make it last – Reckless / Turn up the music / I've done everything for you / Young girl blues / Bad motor scooter. *(UK-iss.Mar80 as 'LOUD & CLEAR' red-lp +=; E-ST 25330)* – Space station No.5. *(hit No.12) (cd-iss. Aug92 as 'LOUD & CLEAR' on 'Beat Goes On'; BGOCD 149)*

Sep 78. (7") *(CL 160010)* **I'VE DONE EVERYTHING FOR YOU (live). / BAD MOTOR SCOOTER (live)** [ ] [-]

Jun 79. (7") *(CL 16083) <4699>* **(SITTIN' ON) THE DOCK OF THE BAY. / I'VE DONE EVERYTHING FOR YOU** [ ] [65] Mar79

— **CHUCK RUFF** – drums repl. DENNY / **NEAL SCHON** – guitar (of JOURNEY) repl. FITZGERALD

Sep 79. (7") *(CL 16101) <4757>* **PLAIN JANE. / WOUNDED IN LOVE** [ ] [77]

Sep 79. (lp) *<(E-ST 11983)>* **STREET MACHINE** [38] [71]
– Growing pains / Child to man / Trans am (highway wonderland) / Feels like love / Plain Jane / Never say die / This planet's on fire (burn to hell) / Wounded in love / Falling in love / Straight to the top. *(re-iss. Jun86 on 'Revolver'; REVLP 72) (cd-iss. Dec92 on 'Beat Goes On'; BGOCD 150)*

Nov 79. (7") *<4825>* **GROWING PAINS. / STRAIGHT TO THE TOP** [-] [ ]

Nov 79. (7") *(CL 16114)* **THIS PLANET'S ON FIRE (BURN IN HELL). / SPACE STATION No.5 (live)** [52] [-]

Jan 80. (7") *(CL 16120)* **I'VE DONE EVERYTHING FOR YOU. / RED** [36] [-]

— added **GEOFF WORKMAN** – keyboards

May 80. (lp) *<(E-ST 12069)>* **DANGER ZONE** [25] [85]
– Love or money / 20th century man / Miles from boredom / Mommy says, daddy says / In the night (entering the danger zone) / The iceman / Bad reputation / Heartbeat / Run for your life / Danger zone. *(cd-iss. Jul95 on 'Beat Goes On'; BGOCD 261)*

May 80. (7") *(RED 1)* **HEARTBEAT. / LOVE OR MONEY** [67] [-]

May 80. (7") *<4893>* **HEARTBEAT. / MILES FROM BOREDOM** [-] [ ]

— **DAVID LAUSER** – drums repl. CHUCK

Epic | Epic

Sep 81. (7"/12") *(EPCA/+13 1600)* **HEAVY METAL. / SATISFIED** [ ] [ ]
(above from film 'Heavy Metal')

Geffen | Geffen

Dec 81. (7"/7"pic-d) *(GEFA/+11 1884)* **PIECE OF MY HEART. / BABY'S ON FIRE** [67] [-]

Dec 81. (7") *<49881>* **I'LL FALL IN LOVE AGAIN. / SATISFIED (by Journey)** [-] [43]
(also issued on 'B'side of CRAZY FOR YOU by 'Madonna' Jun85 hit)

Jan 82. (lp) *(GEF 85456) <GHS 2006>* **STANDING HAMPTON** [84] [28]
– There's only one way to rock / Baby's on fire / Can't get loose / I'll fall in love again / Heavy metal / Baby it's you / Surrender / Inside looking in / Sweet hitchhiker / Piece of my heart. *(re-iss. Sep86 lp/c; 902006-1/-4)*

May 82. (7") *<50059>* **PIECE OF MY HEART. / SWEET HITCHHIKER** [-] [73]

Jan 83. (lp)(c) *(GEF 25454)(402425-4) <GHS 2021>* **THREE LOCK BOX** [ ] [17] Dec82
– Three lock box / Remote love / Remember the heroes / Your love is driving me crazy / In the room / Rise of the animal / I wouldn't change a thing / Growing up / Never give up / I don't need love. *(re-iss. Sep96 lp/c; 902021-1/-4)*

Jan 83. (7") *(GEF 3043) <29816>* **YOUR LOVE IS DRIVING ME CRAZY. / I DON'T NEED LOVE** [ ] [13] Dec82

Mar 83. (7") *<29718>* **NEVER GIVE UP. / FAST TIMES AT RIDGEMONT HIGH** [-] [46]

— **SCHON** – guitar / **AARONSON** – bass / **SHRIEVE** – drums

May 84. (lp/c; by HAGAR, SCHON, AARONSON, SHRIEVE) *(GEF/GEC 25893) <4023>* **THROUGH THE FIRE** [92] [42] Mar84
– Top of the rock / Missing you / Animation / Valley of the kings / Giza / Whiter shade of pale / Hot and dirty / He will understand / My home town. *(cd-iss. Jan96 on 'Retroactive'; RETRO 50059CD)*

May 84. (7"; by HAGAR, SCHON, AARONSON, SHRIEVE) *<29280>* **A WHITER SHADE OF PALE. / HOT AND DIRTY** [-] [94]

— added to 1982 line-up **JESSE HARMS** – keyboards, vocals

Aug 84. (7") *(GEF 4696) <29246>* **TWO SIDES OF LOVE. / BURNING DOWN THE CITY** [ ] [38] Jul84

Sep 84. (7") *<29173>* **I CAN'T DRIVE 55. / PICK IN THE DIRT** [-] [26]

Sep 84. (lp/c) *(GEF/GEC 26054) <24043>* **VOA** (Voice Of America) [ ] [32] Aug84
– I can't drive 55 / Swept away / Rock is in my blood / Two sides of love / Dick in the dirt / VOA / Don't make me wait / Burnin' down the city. *(re-iss. Sep86 lp/c/cd; GEF/GEC/GED 924043-1/-4/-2)*

— It was around this time he replaced DAVE LEE ROTH in VAN HALEN

Apr 87. (7") *(650407-7) / Columbia; <06647>* **WINNER TAKES ALL. / THE FIGHT (by Giorgio Moroder)** [ ] [54] Feb87
(above from the 'Columbia' movie, 'Over The Top')

— **EDDIE VAN HALEN** – bass, vocals repl. CHURCH + PIHL

Jul 87. (lp/c)(cd) *(WX 114/+C)(924144-2) <24144>* **SAMMY HAGAR** [86] [14]
– When the hammer falls / Hands and knees / Give to live / Boy's night out / Returning home / Standin' at the same old crossroads / Privacy / Back into you / Eagles fly / What they gonna say now. *(some w/free conversation disc)*

Aug 87. (7") *(GEF 23) <28314>* **GIVE TO LIVE. / WHEN THE HAMMER FALLS** [ ] [23] Jun87
(12"+=) *(GEF 23T)* – Standing at the same old crossroads.

Oct 87. (7") *<28185>* **EAGLES FLY. / HANDS AND KNEES** [-] [82]

Mar 94. (cd/c) *<(GED/GEC 24702)>* **UNBOXED** (compilation) [ ] [51]
– High hopes / Buying my way into Heaven / I'll fall in love again / There's only one way to rock / Heavy metal / Eagles fly / Baby's on fire / Three lock box / Two sides of love / I can't drive / Give to live / I don't need to love.

Track Factory / Track Factory

May 97. (cd) *<(TRD 11627)>* **MARCHING TO MARS** [ ] [18]
– Little white lie / Salvation on Sand Hill / Who has the right / Would you do it for free / Leaving the warmth of the womb / Kama / On the other hand / Both sides now / Yogi's so high (I'm stoned) / Amnesty is granted / Marching to Mars.

Mar 99. (cd/c; as SAMMY HAGAR AND THE WABORITAS)
<TRD 11872> **RED VOODOO** [-] [22]
– Mas tequila / Shag / Sympathy for the human / Red voodoo / Lay your hand on me / High and dry again? / Revival / Don't fight it (feel it) / Love / Right on right / Returning of the wish.

– compilations, etc. –

1979. (7"m) *Capitol; (SPSR 441)* **TURN UP THE MUSIC. / RED / BAD MOTOR SCOOTER** [ ] [-]

Oct 82. (lp/c) *Capitol; (EST/TC-EST 26882)* **RED ALERT – DIAL NINE (THE VERY BEST OF SAMMY HAGAR)** [ ] [ ]

Jan 83. (lp) *Capitol; <12238>* **REMATCH (some live)** [-] [ ]
– Trans am (highway wonderland) / Love or money / Plain Jane / 20th century man / This planet's on fire (burn in Hell) / In the night / Danger zone / Space Station No.5.

Jan 87. (lp/c) *Geffen; (924127-1/-4)* **LOOKING BACK** [ ] [-]

Aug 89. (lp/c)(cd) *Warners; (WX 291/+C)<(K 924255-2)>* **THE BEST OF SAMMY HAGAR** [ ] [ ]
– Red / (Sittin' on) The dock of the bay / I've done everything for you / Rock'n'roll weekend / Cruisin' and boozin' / Turn up the music / Reckless / Trans am (highway wonderland) / Love or money / This planet's on fire (burn in Hell) / Plain Jane / Bad reputation / Bad motor scooter / You make me crazy.

Nov 94. (cd) *Connoisseur; (VSOPCD 207)* **THE ANTHOLOGY** [ ] [-]

Jun 97. (cd) *EMI Gold; (CPD 780262-2)* **THE BEST OF SAMMY HAGAR** [ ] [-]

HA LELA

Formed: Lithuania . . . 1994 by RAMUNAS, LAURAS, AURIUS, VAIDAS, DONATAS, VADIMAS, LAURA and KILMA. Following on from a well received demo, 'RAUDA', the band attracted the attention of the 'Edelthorn' label with the 'PABUDIMAS' four-track. A subsidiary of 'Neat' records, the imprint furnished them with the finances to re-record the four songs along with a further three new tracks. The resulting album – which retained the 'PABUDIMAS' title – was issued in '98 and has been described by the band themselves as "ambient black metal", inspired by the bleak landscapes of their Eastern European homeland. What's more, the lyrics are sung in the band's native tongue so you might just need that Lithuanian Mini Collins dictionary to hand. Don't say we didn't warn you . . .

Album rating: PABUDIMAS (*7)

VAIDAS – vocals / **KILMA** – vocals / **RAMUNAS** – guitar, keyboards, bass, vocals / **LAURAS** – guitar, keyboards, vocals / **AURIUS** – drums / **DONATAS** – wind instruments / **VADIMAS** – tambourine, vocals / **LAURA** – backing vocals

Eldethorn / not iss.

Mar 98. (cd) *(ELD 003)* **PABUDIMAS** [ ] [-]
– Pabudimas / Sidabrines saules simbolis / Audros sirdis ir kraujas / Isjojo bernelis / Prakeittas troskimas / Sokis . . . septyni ratai / Reikejo zengi tris zingsnius.

Rob HALFORD

Born: 25 Aug'51, Birmingham, England. The focal point of heavy-rock specialists JUDAS PRIEST, ROB decided it was time to branch out on his ownsome. Forming FIGHT with RUSS PARISH, BRIAN TILSE, JAY JAY and JUDAS PRIEST drummer, SCOTT TRAVIS in tow, HALFORD's intention was to explore more modern sounds incompatible with the J.P. format. Signing to 'Epic' in the early 90's, the group debuted in 1993 with the 'WAR OF WORDS' album, a set which many critics compared with the aggressive power-metal of PANTERA. Through committed live work with such established acts as ANTHRAX and METALLICA, the group built up a sizeable following, obviously including many JUDAS PRIEST diehards. This success didn't come without a price, however, HALFORD subsequently falling out with JUDAS PRIEST and concentrating on FIGHT full-time. A mini-album, 'MUTATIONS', appeared in 1994, a stop-gap part-live affair before the release of the next album, 'A SMALL DEADLY SPACE' (1995). Obviously a huge mistake by HALFORD, the frontman took time out to "come out" as a homosexual and find himself musically in the much improved project, TWO. Augmented by TRENT REZNOR and SKINNY PUPPY's DAVE OGILVIE (whom he had taken demo tapes to in '97), the bald Nosferatu/Manson of rock delivered the '98 set, 'VOYEURS'. In the year 2000, ROB HALFORD was now officially solo with a release of his debut album proper, 'RESURRECTION'.

Album rating: WAR OF WORDS (*6) / MUTATIONS mini (*5) / A SMALL DEADLY SPACE (*6) / Two: VOYEURS (*7) / Rob Halford: RESURRECTION (*6)

FIGHT

ROB HALFORD – vocals / **RUSS PARISH** – guitar (ex-WAR AND PEACE) / **BRIAN TILSE** – guitar / **JAY JAY** – bass (ex-CYANIDE) / **SCOTT TRAVIS** – drums (ex-JUDAS PRIEST)

Epic / Epic

Sep 93. (cd/c/white-lp) *(EPC 474547-2/-4/-1) <57372>* **WAR OF WORDS** [ ] [ ]
– Into the pit / Nailed to the gun / Life in black / Immortal sin / War of words / Laid to rest / For all eternity / Little crazy / Contortion / Kill it / Vicious / Reality, a new beginning.

Nov 93. (cd-ep) *(659612-2)* **NAILED TO THE GUN / KILL IT / NAILED TO THE GUN (Bulletproof mix) / KILL IT (Dutch death mix)** [ ] [-]

—— now without PARISH (temp. ROBBIE LOCKNER)

1994. (m-cd) *<EK 66127>* **MUTATIONS** [-] [ ]
– Into the pit / Nailed to the gun / Freewheel burning / Little crazy / War of words (Bloody Tongue mix) / Kill it (Dutch death mix) / Vicious (Middle Finger mix) / Immortal sin (Tolerance mix) / Little crazy (Straight Jacket mix).

—— added **MARK CHAUSSE** – guitar

Apr 95. (cd/c) *(EPC 478400-2/-4) <66649>* **A SMALL DEADLY SPACE** [ ] [ ]
– I am alive / Mouthpiece / Legacy of hate / Blowout in the radio room / Never again / Small deadly space / Gretna Greene / Beneath the violence / Human crate / In a world of my own making.

TWO

ROB HALFORD – vocals / with **JOHN LOWERY** – guitar / **JAMES WOOLLEY** – keyboards / **RAY REANDEAU** – bass / **SID RIGGS** – drums

East West / Nothing

Mar 98. (cd) *(3984 22089-2) <90155>* **VOYEURS** [ ] [ ]
– I am a pig / Stutter kiss / Water's leaking / My ceiling's low / Leave me alone / If / Deep in the ground / Hey sha la la / Wake up / Gimp / Bed of rust.

HALFORD

with **PATRICK LACHMAN** – guitar / **MIKE CHLASCIAK** – guitar / **RAY RIENDEAU** – bass / **BOBBY JARZOMBEK** – drums

Metal-Is / C.M.C.

Aug 00. (cd/lp) *(MIS CD/LP 001) <85200>* **RESURRECTION** [ ] [ ]
– Resurrection / Made in Hell / Locked and loaded / Nightfall / Silent screams / The one you love to hate / Cyberworld / Slow down / Twist / Temptation / Drive / Saviour.

HALLOWS EVE

Formed: USA . . . 1984 by STACY ANDERSON, TOMMY STEWART and DAVID STUART, who subsequently enlisted the hilariously named SKELLATOR and TYM HELTON. Offering up brutal quasi-thrash, the group debuted with the rather amateurish 'TALES OF TERROR' (1985), ANDERSON's death-grunt vocals complementing the unholy racket perfectly. A further couple of efforts, 'DEATH & INSANITY' (1986) and 'MONUMENT' (1988), the latter complete with a rendition of Queen's 'SHEER HEART ATTACK'), refined their rough-shod sound somewhat, while simultaneously failing to raise the group above cult status.

Album rating: TALES OF TERROR (*4) / DEATH & INSANITY (*6) / MONUMENT (*5)

STACY ANDERSON – vocals / **SKELLATOR** – guitar / **DAVID STUART** – guitar / **TOMMY STEWART** – bass / **TYM HELTON** – drums

Roadrunner / Metal Blade

Jun 85. (lp) *(RR 9772) <72426>* **TALES OF TERROR** [ ] [ ]
– Plunging to megadeath / Outer limits / Horrorshow / The mansion / There are no rules / Valley of the dolls / Metal merchants / Hallows eve (incl. 'Routine'). *(cd-iss. May89 on 'Roadracer'; RO 9772-2)*

Oct 86. (lp) *(RR 9676-1) <72163>* **DEATH & INSANITY** [ ] [ ]
– Death & insanity / Goblet of gore / Lethal tendencies / Obituary / Plea of the aged / Suicide / D.I.E. (Die In Effect) / Attack of the iguana / Nefarious / Nobody lives forever / Death & insanity (reprise).

—— **RONNY APPOLDT** – drums; repl. HELTON

Apr 88. (lp) *(RR 9583) <73290>* **MONUMENT** [ ] [ ] Mar88
– Speed freak / Sheer heart attack / Rot gut / Monument (to nothing) / Painkiller / Mighty decibel / Righteous ones / No sanctuary.

—— disbanded when STACY bailed out

HALO OF FLIES

Formed: Minneapolis, Minnesota, USA . . . 1985 by TOM HAZELMYER, who had previously been frontman for Seattle outfit, the U-MEN, after earlier enlisting for the US Marines. The brains behind the 'Amphetamine Reptile' label, TOM recruited a rhythm section of TIM 'MAC' McLAUGHLIN and JOHN ANGLIM, releasing 'RUBBER ROOM' as a debut single and the second release for that label. The latter track was issued as a strictly limited edition, as were subsequent 7"er's, 'SNAPPING BACK ROSCOE BOTTLES EP', 'CIRCLING THE PILE', 'RICHIE'S DOG', 'NO TIME' and 'LEDERHOSEN' (a collaboration with KILLDOZER's BILL HOBSON under the pseudonym, POGO THE CLOWN). Combining crazed rockabilly-based attitude with head-on crashing noise, HAZELMYER and Co continued to slash'n'burn their way through the alternative jungle, cutting a couple of EP's for 'Twin/Tone' ('GARBAGE ROCK' and 'HEADBURN'). Collected together as 'GARBAGEBURN', the records were licensed to 'What Goes On' for European release in 1988. A further two singles (including one in '91 shared with MUDHONEY) and a couple of compilation sets rounded up the band's career as HAZELMYER devoted more time to his ever growing 'Amphetamine Reptile'.

Album rating: GARBAGEBURN mini (*6) / SINGLES GOING NOWHERE compilation (*6) / MUSIC FOR INSECT MINDS compilation (*6)

TOM HAZELMYER – vocals, guitar / **JOHN ANGLIM** – drums / **TIM 'MAC' McLAUGHLIN** – bass

What Goes On / Amphetam. Reptile

1986. (7") *<Scale 2>* **RUBBER ROOM. / THOUGHTS IN A BOOTH** [-] [ ]
1986. (7") *<Scale 3>* **SNAPPING BLACK ROSCOE BOTTLES EP** [-] [ ]
– Can't touch her / D.D.T. / Fin 13.
1986. (7") *<Scale 4>* **CIRCLING THE PILE EP** [-] [ ]
– Sinner sings / Pipebomb / M.D. 20-20.
1987. (7") *<Scale 6>* **RICHIE'S DOG. / HOW DOES IT FEEL TO FEEL** [-] [ ]
1987. (c) *<Scale 11>* **FOUR FROM THE BOTTOM** [-] [ ]
1988. (7") *<Scale 13>* **NO TIME. / YOU GET NOTHING** [-] [ ]
1988. (7"; as POGO THE CLOWN) *<Scale 15>* **LEDERHOSEN. /** [-] [ ]
(above was TOM's collaboration with KILLDOZER's BILL HOBSON)
1988. (m-lp) *(GOES ON 24)* **GARBAGEBURN** (a compilation of two 'Twin/Tone' EP's, 'GARBAGE ROCK' <TTR 87132> & 'HEADBURN') [ ] [-]
– Garbage rock / D.D.T. beat 69 / One barrel spent / I'm clean // Headburn / Easy or hard / Father paranoia / Drunk (in Detroit).
1990. (7") *<Scale 19>* **DEATH OF A FLY. / CLOWNS** [-] [ ]

not iss. / Forced Exposure

1990. (12"ep) *<FE 019>* **WINGED EP** [-] [ ]

not iss. / Silt Breeze

1991. (12"ep) **LIVE EP (live)** [-] [ ]

—— HAZELMYER split the trio in 1991

– compilations, etc. –

1990. (lp) *Amphetamine Reptile; <001>* **SINGLES GOING NOWHERE** [-] [ ]
1991. (7",7"maroon; shared with MUDHONEY) *<Scale 35/36>* **BIG MOD HATE TRIP EP** [-] [ ]
– Wasted time / Tired & cold / etc.
1991. (cd) *Amphetamine Reptile; <002>* **MUSIC FOR INSECT MINDS** [ ] [ ]

HANDSOME BEASTS

Formed: Wolverhampton, England . . . 1980 by GARY DALLOWAY, along with PAUL ROBINS, STEVE HOUGH and PETE MALBASA. Notorious for the tasteless antics of girthsome frontman DALLOWAY, the group are also noted as originators of 'Heavy Metal Records' along with their manager, the brilliant Paul Birch. With a cover shot of DALLOWAY naked in a pigsty, 'BEASTIALITY' (1981) was fairly standard Brit-metal fare once you got past the sniggering gimmickry. Though the company prospered, The HANDSOME BEASTS split for most of the 80's, eventually resurfacing in 1990 with a one-off album, 'THE BEAST WITHIN'.

Album rating: BEASTIALITY (*4) / THE BEAST WITHIN (*3)

GARY DALLOWAY – vocals / **PAUL ROBINS** – guitar / **STEVE HOUGH** – bass / **PETE MALBASA** – drums

Heavy Metal / not iss.

May 80. (7") *(HEAVY 1)* **ALL RIOT NOW. / MARK OF THE BEAST** [ ] [-]
Mar 81. (7"m) *(HEAVY 2)* **BREAKER. / ONE IN A CROWD / CRAZY** [ ] [-]
Apr 81. (lp) *(HMRLP 2)* **BEASTIALITY** [ ] [-]
– Sweeties / David's song / Breaker / One in a crowd / Local heroes / Another day / Crazy / Tearing me apart / High speed. *(cd-iss. Feb97 on 'British Steel'; CDMETAL 5)*
Feb 82. (7") *(HEAVY 11)* **SWEETIES. / YOU'RE ON YOUR OWN** [ ] [-]

—— split for the rest of the 80's, although DALLOWAY reformed the band for below release

Feb 90. (cd/c/lp) *(HMR XD/MC/LP 132)* **THE BEAST WITHIN** [ ] [-]
– Mr. Mescalito / Hairy legs / The way I am / Chain gang / The beast within / Rough justice / Don't hold on / The sixth day / Let it go.

HANOI ROCKS

Formed: Helsinki, Finland . . . 1980 by ANDY McCOY and MICHAEL MONROE. After releasing a few lp's for 'Joanna' records, and moving to Stockholm, Sweden in Oct'81, they came to London in late '82, signing for the small 'Lick' label. There, the band set to work with DALE GRIFFIN and OVEREND WATTS (both ex-MOTT THE HOOPLE), fashioning the UK Top 100 album, 'BACK TO MYSTERY CITY'. Falling somewhere between The NEW YORK DOLLS and AEROSMITH and fronted by androgynous blond bombshell, MONROE, the band quickly became something of a cult favourite with certain sections of the rock press, for their attitude and trashy aesthetic if nothing else. By the following year, HANOI ROCKS had generated enough interest for 'C.B.S.' to offer the band a three album deal, another ex-MOTT THE HOOPLE dude, frontman IAN HUNTER, enlisted to help out on lyric duties. The result was a UK Top 30 album, 'TWO STEPS FROM HEAVEN' (1984), the band's most accomplished to date. The opening cut, a sleaze-driven re-run of the classic CREEDENCE CLEARWATER REVIVAL track, 'UP AROUND THE BEND', had dented the lower regions of the singles chart earlier that summer. However, tragedy struck on the 3rd December '84, when RAZZLE was killed in a car driven by VINCE NEIL of MOTLEY CRUE. They disbanded soon after, evolving into CHERRY BOMBZ, minus the solo-bound MONROE. It was a sad end for a band who were only just beginning to hit their stride and the way the L.A. glam-pack (FASTER PUSSYCAT, L.A. GUNS, even GUNS N' ROSES) later appropriated HANOI ROCKS' style shows just how far ahead of their time the band were. • **Songwriters:** All written by McCOY except covers; GOOD GOOD LOVING (Link Wray) / AIN'T WHAT YOU DO (Juke Joint Jimmy) / TRAVELLIN' BAND (Creedence Clearwater Revival) / MAGIC CARPET RIDE (Steppenwolf) / UNDER MY WHEELS (Alice Cooper) / WALKIN' WITH MY ANGEL (Goffin-King). • **Trivia:** They were also a big hit in Japan, where they were signed to 'Nippon-Phonogram'.

Album rating: BANGKOK SHOCKS, SAIGON SHAKES (*6) / ORIENTAL BEAT (*6) / SELF DESTRUCTION BLUES (*6) / BACK TO MYSTERY CITY (*7) / TWO STEPS FROM THE MOVE (*7) / ALL THOSE WASTED YEARS compilation (*5) / THE BEST OF HANOI ROCKS double compilation (*7) / Cherry Bombz: COMING DOWN SLOW (*4) / Cheap And Nasty: BEAUTIFUL DISASTERS (*5) / Michael Monroe: NIGHTS ARE SO LONG (*5) / NOT FAKIN' IT (*5) / LIFE GETS YOU DIRTY (*5) / PEACE OF MIND (*5) / Jerusalem Slim: JERUSALEM SLIM (*5) / Demolition 23: DEMOLITION 23 (*5)

MICHAEL MONROE (b. MATTI FAGERHOLM, 17 Jun'62) – vocals / **ANDY McCOY** (b. ANTTI HULKKO, 11 Oct'62) – guitar (ex-BRIARD) repl. STEFAN PIESHACK / **NASTY SUICIDE** (b. JAN STENFORS, 4 Sep'63) – guitar (ex-BRIARD) / **SAM YAFFA** (b. SAMI TAKAHAKI, 4 Aug'63) – bass repl. PASI STI / **GYP CASINO** (b. JESPER SPORE) – drums repl. PEKI SENOLA

Joanna / not iss.

Nov 80. (7") *(JHNS 145)* **I WANT YOU. / KILL CITY KILLS** [-] [-] Fin
Feb 81. (lp) *(JHN 2037)* **BANGKOK SHOCKS, SAIGON SHAKES, HANOI ROCKS** [-] [-] Fin
– Tragedy / Village girl / Stop cryin' / Don't ever leave me / Lost in the city / First timer / Cheyenne / 11th street kidz / Walking with my angel / Pretender. *(UK-iss.Aug83 on 'Lick' lp/c; LIC LP/K 2) (cd-iss. Sep89; LICCD 2) <US-iss.Oct89 on 'Uzi Suicide' yellow-lp; GHS 24262> (<cd-iss. Feb95 on 'Essential'; ESMCD 273>)*
Feb 81. (7") *(JHNS 174)* **TRAGEDY. / CAFE AVENUE** [-] [-] Fin
Oct 81. (7") *(JHNS 199)* **DESPERADOES. / DEVIL WOMAN** [-] [-] Fin
Dec 81. (7") *(JHNS 216)* **DEAD BY XMAS. / NOTHING NEW** [-] [-] Fin
Feb 82. (lp) *(JHN 2063)* **ORIENTAL BEAT** [-] [-] Fin
– Motorvatin' / Don't follow me / Visitor / Teenangels outsiders / Sweet home suburbia / M.C. baby / No law or order / Oriental beat / Devil woman / Lightnin' bar blues / Fallen star. *(UK-iss.Aug83 on 'Lick' lp/c; LIC LP/K 3) (cd-iss. Sep89; LICCD 3) <US-iss.Oct89 on 'Uzi Suicide' red-lp; GHS 24263> (<cd-iss. Apr95 on 'Essential'; ESMCD 274>)*

—— **RAZZLE** (b. NICHOLAS DINGLEY, Isle Of Wight) – drums (ex-DARK) repl. GYP

Sep 82. (7") *(JHNS 244)* **LOVE'S AN INJECTION. / TAXI DRIVER** [-] [-] Finnish
(12"+=) *(JHNS 244)* – Malibu beach / Problem child / In the year '79.
Oct 82. (lp) *(JHN 3008)* **SELF DESTRUCTION BLUES** (early stuff) [-] [-] Finnish
– Love's an injection / I want you / Cafe avenue / Nothing new / Kill city kills / Self destruction blues / Beer and a cigarette / Whispers in the dark / Taxi driver / Desperados / Problem child / Dead by X-mas. *(UK-iss.Aug83 on 'Lick' lp/c; LIC LP/K 4) (re-iss. Apr85 pic-lp; LICLPPD 4) (cd-iss. Sep89; LICCD 4) <US-iss.Oct89 on 'Uzi Suicide' blue-lp; GHS 24264> (<cd-iss. Feb95 on 'Essential'; ESMCD 271>)*

Lick / not iss.

May 83. (7"/7"pic-d) *(LIX/+PD 1)* **MALIBU BEACH NIGHTMARE. / REBEL ON THE RUN** [ ] [-]
(12"+=) *(LIXT 1)* – Taxi driver / Beer and a cigarette.
May 83. (lp/c) *(LIC LP/K 1)* **BACK TO MYSTERY CITY** [87] [-]
– Strange boys play weird openings / Malibu Beach nightmare / Mental beat / Tooting bee wreck / Until I get you / Sailing down the years / Lick summer love / Beating gets faster / Ice cream summer / Back to Mystery City. *(re-iss. Apr85 white-lp; same) (cd-iss. Sep89; LICCD 1) <US-iss.Oct89 on 'Uzi Suicide' green-lp; GHS 24265> (<cd-iss. Feb95 on 'Essential'; ESMCD 272>)*
Aug 83. (7") *(LIX 2)* **UNTIL I GET YOU. / TRAGEDY** [ ] [-]
(12"+=) *(LIXT 2)* – Oriental beat.

C.B.S. / Columbia

Jun 84. (7") *(A 4513)* **UP AROUND THE BEND. / UNTIL I GET YOU** [61] [ ]
(12"+=) *(TA 4513)* – Back to Mystery City / Mental beat.
(d7"+=) *(DA 4513)* – Under my wheels / The train kept a-rollin' / I feel alright.
Sep 84. (7") *(A 4732)* **UNDERWATER WORLD. / SHAKES** [ ] [ ]
(12"+=/12"pic-d+=) *(TA/WA 4732)* – Magic carpet ride.
Oct 84. (lp/c) *(CBS/40 26066)* **TWO STEPS FROM THE MOVE** [28] [ ]
– Up around the bend / High school / I can't get it / Underwater world / Don't you ever leave me / Million miles away / Boulevard of broken dreams / Boiler (me boiler 'n' me) / Futurama / Cutting corners.
Nov 84. (7") *(A 4885)* **DON'T YOU EVER LEAVE ME. / OIL & GASOLINE** [ ] [ ]
(12"+=/12"pic-d+=) *(TA/WA 4885)* – Malibu Beach (calypso).

—— (Feb85) **TERRY CHIMES** – drums (ex-CLASH, ex-GENERATION X, ex-COWBOYS INTERNATIONAL) repl. RAZZLE who was killed in a car crash 3 Dec'84. Later **RENE BERG** – guitar (ex-IDLE FLOWERS) repl. JAFFA

—— Split Jun85. MICHAEL MONROE later went solo. RAZZLE, NASTY and YAFFA had also been part of KNOX's band FALLEN ANGELS

– compilations, etc. –

on 'Lick' unless otherwise mentioned

Apr 85. (d-lp) *(LICDLP 5-6)* **ALL THOSE WASTED YEARS** [ ] [-]
– Pipeline / Oriental beat / Back to Mystery City / Motorvatin' / Intil I get you / Mental beat / Don't never leave me / Tragedy / Malibu beach nightmare / Visitor / Taxi driver / Lost in the city / Lightnin' bar blues / Beer and cigarettes / Under my wheels / I feel alright / Train kept a-rollin'. *(re-iss. Mar87 d-c; LICKCAS 5-6) (d-cd-iss. Sep89; LICCD 5-6)*
Sep 85. (lp) *(BOOTLIC 7)* **ROCK'N'ROLL DIVORCE** [ ] [-]
Dec 85. (lp/c) *(LIC LP/K 8)* **THE BEST OF HANOI ROCKS** [ ] [-]
– Strange boys play weird openings / Malibu Beach / Loves an injection / Lost in the city / Until I get you / 11th Street kids / Motor vatin' / Don't follow me / Back to Mystery City / Taxi driver / Oriental beat / Don't never leave me (live) / Visitor / Tragedy (live) / Under my wheels (live). *(cd-iss. Nov88; LICCD 8)*
Apr 86. (lp/c) *Raw Power; (RAW LP/TC 016)* **DEAD BY CHRISTMAS** *(with free flexi 7")* [ ] [-]
Dec 90. (lp/c/cd) *(LIC LP/K/CD 10) / Caroline; <CAROL 1704-1/-4/-2>* **TRACKS FROM A BROKEN DREAM** [ ] [ ]
– Boulevard of broken dreams / Rebel on the run / Oil & gasoline / Shakes / Malibu calypso / Problem child / I can't get it / Do the duck / Two steps from the move / Magic carpet ride / I love you / Don't you

ever leave me / Underwater world / Willing to cross the ocean / It's too late.

Mar 93. (cd/c) *(LICCD/LICK 11)* **LEAN ON ME** [ ] [-]
– Tragedy / Oriental beat / Motorvatin' / Taxi driver / Back to mystery city / Malibu beach nightmare / Life's been hard / Heart attack / Menaced by nightingales / Fast car / Shame, shame, shame / Rock and roll / Lean on me. *(cd re-iss. Apr95 on 'Essential'; ESMCD 282)*

May 00. (d-cd) *Essential; (<ESDCD 882>)* **THE BEST OF HANOI ROCKS** [ ] [ ]
– Kill city kills / Tragedy / Pretender / Back to Mystery City / Tooting beck wreck / Taxi driver / Love's an injection / Lost in the city / Until I get to you / Motorvatin' / Teenage outsiders / No law or order / Oriental beat / Malibu beach nightmare / Village girl / Fallen star / Dead by Christmas / Beer and a cigarette / Problem child / It's too late / I feel alright / Mental beat / Self destruction blues / Until I get you / Lightnin' bar blues / Don't follow me / 11th Street kids / MC baby / I want you / Rebel on the run / Malibu beach nightmare / Two steps from the move.

CHERRY BOMBZ

— were formed by guitarist **ANDY McCOY** and **NASTY SUICIDE**, plus **ANITA MAHADERLAN** – vocals (ex-TOTO CEOLO, ex-PAN'S PEOPLE) / **DAVE TREGANNA** – bass (ex-SHAM 69, etc.) / **TERRY CHIMES** – drums (ex-CLASH, ex-GEN X, ex-COWBOYS INTERNATIONAL)

Lick | P.V.C.

Feb 86. (12"ep) *(LIXT 3)* **HOT GIRLS IN LOVE / FELINE FEELING. / 100 DEGREES IN THE SHADE / OIL AND GASOLINE** [ ] [-]

May 86. (7") *(LIX 4)* **HOUSE OF ECSTASY. / DECLARATION** [ ] [ ]
(12") *(LIXT 4)* <PVC 5911> – ('A'side) / Running (Back to your lover) / Countryfied inner city blues.

Jul 86. (lp) <PVC 5913> **100 DEGREES IN THE SHADE** [-] [ ]
– (12"singles)

High Dragon | not iss.

Mar 87. (lp/c)(cd) *(HD/+T 021)(HD 021CD)* **COMING DOWN SLOW** [ ] [-]
– Intro / House of ecstasy / 100 degrees in the shade / Pin up boy / Life's been hard / Oil and gasoline / Sweet pretending / Coming down slow / Good good loving / Hot girl's in love / Ain't what you do / Travellin' band.

— ANITA became a SKY TV presenter in '88. NASTY, CHIMES and TREGANNA formed WYLDE THINGS. In 1989, NASTY guested on the MICHAEL MONROE album 'NOT FAKIN IT'. He then relocated to Los Angeles and formed . . .

CHEAP AND NASTY

NASTY with **TIMO CALTIO** – guitar / **LES RIGGS** – drums / **ALVIN GIBBS** – bass (ex-UK SUBS)

China | not iss.

Nov 90. (7"/c-s) *(CHINA/CHICS 31)* **MIND ACROSS THE OCEAN. / MIDNIGHT EMPEROR** [ ] [-]
(ext.12"+=/ext.12"blue+=) *(CHINX/CHIXG 31)* – Queen bee.
(cd-s++=) *(CHICD 31)* – ('A'version).

Feb 91. (7"/c-s) *(CHINA/CHICS 34)* **BEAUTIFUL DISASTERS. / FANTASY** [ ] [-]
(12"+=/cd-s+=) *(CHINX/CHICD 34)* – Electric flag.

Mar 91. (lp/c/cd) *(WOL/+MC/CD 1002)* **BEAUTIFUL DISASTERS** [ ] [-]
– Midnight emeror / Moonlight / Beautiful disasters / Queen bee / Sweet love / Body electric / Stateline / Live in a lie / Retribution / Shot down / Break for the border.

— disbanded early '92

MICHAEL MONROE

– vocals, harmonica / with session men

Yahoo | not iss.

Nov 87. (cd) *(105)* **NIGHTS ARE SO LONG** [-] [-] Danish
– She's no angel / Million miles away / Shake some action / It's a lie / High school / Nights are so long / Can't go home again / Too rich to be good / You can't put your arms around a memory / Keep it up.

— now with **PHIL GRANDE** – guitar / **ED ROYNESDAL** – keyboards / **KENNY AARONSON** – bass / **TOMMY PRICE** – drums

Vertigo | Mercury

Aug 89. (lp/c/cd) *(<838 627-1/-4/-2>)* **NOT FAKIN' IT** [ ] [ ]
– Dead, jail or rock'n'roll / While you were looking at me / She's no ange / All night with the lights on / Not fakin' it / Shakedown / Man with no eyes / Love is thicker than blood / Smoke screen / Thrill me.

Nov 89. (7"/c-s) *(VER/+MC 45)* **DEAD, JAIL OR ROCK'N'ROLL. / SHAKEDOWN** [ ] [ ]
(12"+=/12"s+=/cd-s+=) *(VER X/XP/CD 45)* – Thrill me.

Feb 90. (7"/7"s/c-s) *(VER/+P/MC 46)* **MAN WITH NO EYES. / DEAD, JAIL OR ROCK'N'ROLL** [ ] [ ]
(12"+=/12"s+=/cd-s+=) *(VER X/T/CD 46)* – Love is thicker than blood / She's no angel.

S.P.V. | S.P.V.

Oct 99. (cd) *(<SPV 085-2152-2>)* **LIFE GETS YOU DIRTY** [ ] [ ] Apr00
– Life gets you dirty / Just because you're paranoid / Since when did you care? / Self destruction blues / Always never again / Go hard / I send you back / What's with the world / Love and light / If the world don't want me / Little troublemaker / Not bad for a white boy (shitmuthafucka) / No means no.

not iss. | Cleopatra

Mar 00. (cd) <CLP 830> **PEACE OF MIND** [-] [ ]
– Where's the fire John? / Make it go away / Machine gun etiquette / Always right / Relationship wrecked / Loneliness loves me more / Kick out the jams / Not anymore / Rent free / Peace of mind. *(bonus+=)* – I wanna be with you / It's a lie.

— MONROE also set up his own group

JERUSALEM SLIM

MICHAEL MONROE – vocals / **STEVE STEVENS** – guitar (ex-BILLY IDOL) / **SAM YAFFA** – bass (ex-HANOI ROCKS) / **GREG ELLIS** – drums

not iss. | Mercury

Jan 93. (cd/c) *<514660-2/-4>* **JERUSALEM SLIM** [-] [ ]
– Rock'n'roll degeneration / Deadman / Attitude adjustment / 100 proof / Criminal instinct / Lethal underground / Teenage nervous breakdown / Gotta get a hold / World is watching / Rock'n'roll degeneration 9demo) / Teenage nervous breakdown (demo).

— prior to above's release, STEVENS had took off to join VINCE NEIL

DEMOLITION 23

MONROE + YAFFA plus **NASTY SUICIDE** – guitar (ex-HANOI ROCKS) / **JIMMY CLARK** – drums

Music For Nations | Music For Nations

Nov 94. (cd/c/lp) *(<CD/T+/MFN 176>)* **DEMOLITION 23** [ ] [ ] Jan95
– Nothin's alright / Hammersmith Palais / The scum lives on / Dysfunctional / Ain't nothin' to do / I wanna be loved / You crucified me / Same shit different day / Endangered species / Deadtime stories.

HARDCORE SUPERSTAR

Formed: Gothenburg, Sweden . . . 1997 by SILVER SILVER, JOCKE BERG, MARTIN SANDVIK and MAGNUS ANDREASSON. So called because of their 100% determination rather than porn or shouty music from Washington DC, HARDCORE SUPERSTAR set out to revive the bruised'n'tattooed early spirit of GUNS N' ROSES and their L.A. glam punk ilk. Even SILVER SILVER's name was a reference to NEW YORK DOLLS legend SYLVAIN SYLVAIN. In their native land, the lads got off to flyer when debut single, 'SOMEONE SPECIAL', roared in to the No.1 slot. Follow-up, 'LIBERATION', almost achieved a similar feat while over in Blighty, one of their most famous fans was MOTORHEAD'S LEMMY, citing the Swedes' limited edition, independently released debut album as his record of '98. The more widely available 'BAD SNEAKERS AND A PINA COLADA' (1999) rejuvenated their earlier work, becoming the highest charting rock act in Sweden since JOEY TEMPEST flourished his golden locks.

Album rating: IT'S ONLY ROCK'N'ROLL (*5) / BAD SNEAKERS AND A PINA COLADA (*6)

JOCKE BERG – vocals / **SILVER SILVER** – guitar / **MARTIN SANDVIK** – bass / **MAGNUS ANDREE** – drums

Megarock | not iss.

Jan 99. (cd) *(GPCD 007)* **IT'S ONLY ROCK'N'ROLL** [ ] [-]
– Hello goodbye / Baby come along / Send myself to Hell / Bubblegum ride / Rock'n'roll star / Someone special / Dig a hole / Punk rock song / Right here, right now / So deep inside. *(hidden+=)* – Fly away.

Music For Nations | Koch Int.

Apr 00. (cd-s) *(CDKUT 180)* **SOMEONE SPECIAL / SEND MYSELF TO HELL / SO DEEP INSIDE** [ ] [-]
(cd-s) *(CDXKUT 180)* – ('A'side) / Don't you ever leave me / Fly away.

May 00. (cd/lp) *(CD+/MFN 256)* <8221> **BAD SNEAKERS AND A PINA COLADA** [ ] [ ]
– Hello goodbye / You will never know / Liberation / Have you been around / Punk rock song / Beat you down / Rock'n'roll star / Someone special / Slide song / Hey now!! / Strapped / Bubblegum ride / So deep inside / Don't you ever leave me / Baby come along / Send myself to Hell / Dig a hole / Right here, right now / Fly away.

Jul 00. (cd-s) *(CDKUT 181)* **LIBERATION / COME ALONG / YOU SAY YOU WANT ME** [ ] [-]

HARDLINE (see under ⇒ JOURNEY)

HARD-ONS

Formed: Sydney, Australia . . . 1982 out of The PLEBS and The DEAD RATS, by PETER BLACK, RAY AHN and KEISH DE SILVA, all ex-patriots from Yugoslavia, Korea and Sri Lanka. Fun lovin', if not exactly PC, this bunch of Aussie ne'er do wells initially traded exclusively in the 7" single market, releasing such sniggeringly titled "classics" as 'SURFIN' ON MY FACE' and 'SUCK 'N' SWALLOW' (both from 1985). More toilet humour followed with a debut album, the enticingly named 'SMELL MY FINGER' (no relation to the GEORGE CLINTON album!), their primary school punk RAMONES meets The DEAD KENNEDYS rehashes predictably finding a loyal, largely male audience. The MACC LADS of three-chord hardcore carried on inflicting their "hilarious" compositions on a largely uninterested metal scene throughout the 80's with the likes of 'HOT FOR YOUR LOVE, BABY' (aka 'THE WORST OF THE HARD-ONS') (1987), 'DICKCHEESE' (1988), 'LOVE IS A BATTLEFIELD OF WOUNDED HEARTS' (1989), 'YUMMY!' (1991) and 'TOO FAR GONE' (1993). Apart from a split album with The STUPIDS, their most high profile outing was probably the collaboration with HENRY ROLLINS, a 1991 cover of AC/DC's 'LET THERE BE ROCK'.

Album rating: SMELL MY FINGER (*4) / HOT FOR YOUR LOVE, BABY (*4) / DICKCHEESE (*4) / LOVE IS A BATTLEFIELD OF WOUNDED HEARTS (*5) / YUMMY! (*6) / TOO FAR GONE (*4) / THE HARD-ONS AT THEIR BEST compilation (*6) / THIS TERRIBLE PLACE (*5)

KEISH DE SILVA – vocals, drums / **PETER BLACK** – guitar / **RAY AHN** – bass

Vi-Nil | Big Time

1985. (7"ep) **SURFIN' ON MY FACE EP** [-] [-] Austra
1985. (7") **SUCK 'N' SWALLOW. /** [-] [-] Austra
1986. (7") **GIRL IN A SWEATER. /** [-] [-] Austra
1986. (lp) *<6040>* **SMELL MY FINGER** <US title 'THE HARD-ONS'> [-] [ ] Austra
– Buddies / Squat house / Then I kissed her / Lolipop / I farted / Dancing girls / Wog food / Think about you everyday / I heard her call my name. *(UK-iss.Sep87 on 'Waterfront'; DAMP 37)*

Vinyl Solution | Taang!

Feb 88. (lp) *(SOL 8)* **HOT FOR YOUR LOVE, BABY** (other title 'THE WORST OF THE HARD-ONS') [ ] [ ]
– All set to go / Long song for Cindy / Coffs harbour blues / School days / It's cold outside / Then I kissed her (Arabic version) / By my side / I'll come again / Fifteen / Keish's new song / From my window / Rock'n'roll all nite.
Apr 88. (lp) *(SOL 10) <26>* **DICKCHEESE** [ ] [ ]
– Made to love you / What am I supposed to do? / Oozing for pleasure / Everytime I do a fart / Get away / Pretty face / There was a time / Mickey juice / Figaro / F**k society / Yuppies sick / Something about you / All washed up / Ache to touch you / Why don't you shut up / Nerds / Got a baby / Stairway to punchbowl.
Oct 89. (lp/cd) *(SOL 19/+CD) <35>* **LOVE IS A BATTLEFIELD OF WOUNDED HEARTS** [ ] [ ]
– Don't wanna see you cry / Rejects / Chitty chitty bang bang / Been has before / You're a tease / Who do you wanna fool / Get wet / Rich scrag / Do it with you / Missing you missing me / Throw it in / Kill your mum / Made to love you / What am I 'spose to do / Everytime I do a fart / Get away / Pretty face.

—— in 1989, split an album with The STUPIDS; 'NO CHEESE' on 'Waterfront'

Jan 91. (7") **WHERE DID SHE COME FROM? /** [ ] [-]
Feb 91. (lp/c/cd) *(SOL 26/+C/CD)* **YUMMY!** [ ] [ ]
– Where did she come from? / Raining / Dull / Cool hand Luke / Something I don't want to do / Sit beside you, Jaye's song / On and on / Ain't gonna let you go / Me or you / Spew / Fade away / Little Miss Evil / Wait around / Feast on flash / Stairway to Heaven.
Jul 91. (12"/cd-s/<7">) HENRY ROLLINS & The HARD-ONS) *(VS 30/+CD) <CZ 035>* **LET THERE BE ROCK. / CARRY ME DOWN** [ ] [ ]
Sep 91. (12"ep/cd-ep) **DULL EP** [ ] [-]
– Dull / Sri Lanka / Just being with you / Growing old.

not iss. | Waterfront

1992. (m-cd) *<176>* **DATELESS DUDES CLUB!** [-] [ ]
– She's a dish / Selfish / World / Hate so hard / Test / Raining / What am I supposed to do / Suck'n'swallow.

Survival | Skene

Sep 93. (lp/cd) *(SUR 538/+CD) <29>* **TOO FAR GONE** [ ] [ ]
– Crazy crazy eyes / Notice me / If it makes you happy / Carphone / Test / I do I do I do / Lost / Blade / No one can stop you / Cat scan / If she only knew / It's up to me / Stressed out / Sleepy.
above was their last release, although they shared a single with The CELIBATE RIFLES, 'WHERE THE THINGS ARE' on 'Waterfront'

—— they re-formed after the new millennium

Bad Taste | Bad Taste

Feb 01. (cd) *(<BTR 45>)* **THIS TERRIBLE PLACE** [ ] [ ]
– Fallen star / Strangers / Ice cream / First cut is the weakest / Time won't let me / Trouble trouble / Shark's head / Oyster sauce / Charger / I'm bringing you dead / Nosebleed / Sadly ever after / Birthday / I hate clubbers.

– compilations, etc. –

Apr 99. (d-cd/d-lp) *Citadel; (CITCD 546)* **THE HARD-ONS BEST** [ ] [-]
– Small talk / Raining / She's a dish / Something about you / Think about you everyday / Do it with you / Sorry / Where did she come from / Suck 'n' swallow / Missing you missing me / Get away / It's up to me / Girl in the sweater / Busted / There was a time / On and on / Wishing well / All set to go / Lost / Lose it / Wogfood / Don't wanna see you cry / I do I do I do / Just being with you.

Charlie HARPER (see under ⇒ UK SUBS)

HARRY CREWS (see under ⇒ LUNCH, Lydia)

HATER (see under ⇒ SOUNDGARDEN)

HAUNTED (see under ⇒ AT THE GATES)

HAWKWIND

Formed: London, England . . . mid-69 as GROUP X, by ex-FAMOUS CURE members DAVE BROCK and MICK SLATTERY, who were joined by NIK TURNER, TERRY OLLIS, DIK MIK and JOHN HARRISON. They subsequently became HAWKWIND ZOO, although SLATTERY opted out for a gypsy lifestyle in Ireland after they signed to 'United Artists' in late '69. Now as HAWKWIND and many free concerts later (mostly at open-air festivals), they released their eponymous debut in late summer 1970. While this album was a melange of bluesy, heavy psychedelic rock, the band added more personnel for the follow-up, 'IN SEARCH OF SPACE' (1971), including synth player DEL DETTMAR and vocalist/poet ROBERT CALVERT. His sci-fi musings featured heavily on the album, while the scattered electronic stabs and saxophone honking merged with the driving rhythm section to create their own tripped-out take on space rock. The record saw HAWKWIND break into the Top 20, while the following summer they smashed into the Top 3 with the classic 'SILVER MACHINE' (1972) single, LEMMY KILMISTER's pile driving bass fuelling the beast with a turbo-charged power. The track previously featured on the live various artists 'GREASY TRUCKERS' PARTY' album, as well as appearing on the similar 'GLASTONBURY FAYRE' compilation. The success of the single secured the band Top 20 placings on all four of their future albums for 'United Artists', although come 1975, after the semi-classic 'WARRIOR ON THE EDGE OF TIME' album, LEMMY had departed to form MOTORHEAD, while CALVERT had been replaced by sci-fi writer, MICHAEL MOORCOCK. HAWKWIND signed to 'Charisma' and despite continuing moderate success, were dogged by legal battles over their moniker (HAWKLORDS was used for one album, 1978's '25 YEARS ON'). With a substantially altered line-up, HAWKWIND continued to release albums on their own 'Flicknife' label throughout the 80's. Tragedy struck when CALVERT died from a heart attack on 14 August '88, although yet another line-up saw HAWKWIND into the 90's with the 'SPACE BANDITS' (1990) album. The band continue to attract a loyal following of die-hard hippies and the emergence of the psychedelic/crusty techno scene has done them no harm, many young stoners citing HAWKWIND as a prominent influence.
• **Songwriters:** Mostly by BROCK or CALVERT until the latter's departure, ALAN DAVEY eventually replacing him. Other various personnel over the years also took part in writing.

Album rating (original & group only): HAWKWIND (*6) / IN SEARCH OF SPACE (*8) / DOREMI FASOL LATIDO (*5) / SPACE RITUAL ALIVE (*8) / HALL OF THE MOUNTAIN KING (*6) / WARRIOR ON THE EDGE OF TIME (*7) / ROADHAWKS live collection (*6) / ASTOUNDING SOUNDS AND AMAZING MUSIC (*5) / QUARK, STRANGENESS AND CHARM (*4) / 25 YEARS ON (*4) / PRX 5 (*5) / LIVE 1979 (*4) / LEVITATION (*5) / SONIC ATTACK (*6) / CHURCH OF HAWKWIND (*6) / CHOOSE YOUR MASQUES (*6) / ZONES (*5) / THIS IS HAWKWIND, DO NOT PANIC (*4) / CHRONICLE OF THE BLACK SWORD (*6) / THE XENON CODEX (*6) / STASIS – THE U.A. YEARS 1971-1975 compilation (*8) / SPACE BANDITS (*6) / ELECTRIC TEEPEE (*6) / IT'S THE BUSINESS OF THE FUTURE TO BE DANGEROUS (*6) / THE BUSINESS TRIP (*4) / ALIEN 4 (*5) / LOVE IN SPACE (*5)

DAVE BROCK (b. 20 Aug'41, Isleworth, England) – vocals, guitar / **NIK TURNER** (b. 26 Aug'40, Oxford, England) – vocals, saxophone / **HUW-LLOYD LANGTON** – guitar repl. MICK SLATTERY (Oct69, when as HAWKWIND ZOO) **JOHN HARRISON** – bass / **TERRY OLLIS** – drums / **DIK MIK** (b. S. McMANUS, Richmond, England) – electronics engineer, synthesizers

Liberty | U.A.

Jul 70. (7") *(LBF 15382)* **HURRY ON SUNDOWN. / MIRROR OF ILLUSION** [ ] [ ]
Aug 70. (lp) *(LBS 83348) <5519>* **HAWKWIND** [ ] [ ]
– Hurry on sundown / The reason is? / Be yourself / Paranoia (part 1 & 2) / Seeing it as you really are / Mirror of illusion. *(re-iss. Sep75 on 'Sunset'; SLS 50374) (re-iss. Feb80 as 'ROCKFILE' on 'United Artists'; LBR 1012) (re-iss. Feb84 on 'E.M.I.' lp/pic-lp; SLS/+P 1972921) (hit UK 75) (cd-iss. Feb94 on 'Repertoire';)*

—— (Sep'70) **THOMAS CRIMBLE** – bass repl. JOHN HARRISON / **DEL DETTMAR** – synthesizer repl. LANGTON (partway through next album)

—— (May'71) **DAVE ANDERSON** – bass (ex-AMON DUUL II) repl. CRIMBLE On stage they also added on vocals **ROBERT CALVERT** (b. 9 Mar'45, Pretoria, South Africa) – poet, vocals, **MICHAEL MOORCOCK** – sci-fi writer and **STACIA** – exotic dancer

U.A. | U.A.

Oct 71. (lp) *(UAG 29202) <5567>* **IN SEARCH OF SPACE** [18] [ ]
– You shouldn't do that / You know you're only dreaming / Master of the universe / We took the wrong step years ago / Adjust me / Children of the sun. *(re-iss. Jan81 on 'Liberty'; LBG 29202) (re-iss. Jun85 on 'Liberty-EMI' lp/c; ATAK/TCATAK 9) (re-iss. Oct87 on 'Fame' lp/c; FA/TCFA 3192) (cd-iss. May89 & Dec95 on 'Fame'; CDFA 3192)*

—— (Sep'71) **LEMMY** (b. IAN KILMISTER, 24 Dec'45, Stoke-On-Trent, England) – bass, vocals repl. ANDERSON

—— (Jan'72) **SIMON KING** – drums (ex-OPAL BUTTERFLY) repl. OLLIS (group now **KING, LEMMY, BROCK, TURNER, DIK MIK, DETTMAR, CALVERT, STACIA** and p/t **MOORCOCK**)

Jun 72. (7") *(UP 35381) <50949>* **SILVER MACHINE. / SEVEN BY SEVEN** [3] [ ]
(re-iss. '76) (re-iss. Oct78, hit UK 34) (re-hit 67 when re-iss. Dec82 7"/7"pic-d/12"; UP/UPP/12UP 35381)
Nov 72. (lp) *(UAG 29364) <LA 001>* **DOREMI FASOL LATIDO** [14] [ ]
– Brainstorm / Space is deep / One change / Lord of light / Down through the night / Time we left this world today / The watcher. *(re-iss. 1979) (re-iss. Jun85 on 'Liberty-EMI') (US cd-iss. Jul91 on 'One Way') (cd re-iss. Mar96 on 'E.M.I.'+=; HAWKS 3)* – Urban guerilla / Brainbox pullution / Lord of light / Ejection.
May 73. (d-lp) *(UAD 60037-8) <LA 120>* **SPACE RITUAL – RECORDED LIVE IN LIVERPOOL AND LONDON (live)** [9] [ ]
– Earth calling / Born to go / Down through the night / The awakening / Lord of light / The black corridor / Space is deep / Electronic No.1 / Orgone accumulator / Upside down / 10 seconds of forever / Brainstorm / 7 by 7 / Sonic attack / Time we left this world today / Master of the universe / Welcome to the future. *(re-iss. 1979;)*
Aug 73. (7") *(UP 35566) <314>* **URBAN GUERILLA. / BRAINBOX POLLUTION** [39] [ ]

—— Now a trim sex/septet when DIK MIK and CALVERT departed. The latter going solo. (Apr74) **SIMON HOUSE** – keyboards, synthesizers, violin (ex-THIRD EAR BAND, ex-HIGH TIDE) repl. DETTMAR who emigrated to Canada

Aug 74. (7") *(UP 35715)* **PSYCHEDELIC WARLORDS (DISAPPEAR IN SMOKE). / IT'S SO EASY** [ ] [ ]
Sep 74. (lp/c) *(UAG/UAC 29672) <LA 328>* **HALL OF THE MOUNTAIN GRILL** [16] [ ]
– The psychedelic warlords (disappear in smoke) / Wind of change / D-rider / Web weaver / You'd better believe it / Hall of the Mountain Grill / Lost Johnnie / Goat willow / Paradox. *(re-iss. Jan81 on 'Liberty'; LBG 29672) (re-iss. Jun85 on 'Liberty-EMI';) (re-iss. Sep85 on 'Fame'; FA41 3133-1) (cd-iss. May89 & Dec95; CD-FA 3133)*

—— added **ALAN POWELL** – 2nd drums (ex-STACKRIDGE, ex-CHICKEN SHACK, etc)

Charisma Atco

Mar 75. (7") *(UP 35808)* **KINGS OF SPEED. / MOTORHEAD** [ ] [ ]
May 75. (lp/c) *(UAG/UAC 29766) <35115>* **WARRIOR ON THE EDGE OF TIME** [13] [ ]
– Assault and battery – part one / The golden void – part two / The wizard blew his horn / Opa-Loka / The demented man / Magnu / Standing at the edge / Spiral galaxy 28948 / Warriors / Dying seas / Kings of speed. *(re-iss. 1979; same) (re-iss. Jan81 + Jun85 on 'Liberty-EMI'; TCK 29766) (re-iss. Feb94 on 'Dojo'; DOJOCD 84)*

— **PAUL RUDOLPH** – bass (ex-PINK FAIRIES) repl. LEMMY who formed MOTORHEAD **BOB CALVERT** – vocals returned, STACIA the dancer left to get married. **CALVERT** and **RUDOLPH** now with **BROCK, TURNER, KING, HOUSE** and **POWELL**. note also that MOORCOCK left to form his DEEP FIX

Charisma Sire

Jul 76. (7") *(CB 289)* **KERB CRAWLER. / HONKY DORKY** [ ] [-]
Aug 76. (lp/c) *(CDS 4004)* **ASTOUNDING SOUNDS, AMAZING MUSIC EMPORIUM** [33] [-]
– Reefer madness / Steppenwolf / City of lagoons / The aubergine that ate Rangoon / Kerb crawler / Kadu flyer / Chronoglide skyway. *(re-iss. Mar83; CHC 14) (cd-iss. Apr89 on 'Virgin'; CDSCD 4004)*
Jan 77. (7") *(CB 299)* **BACK ON THE STREETS. / THE DREAM OF ISIS** [ ] [ ]

— **ADRIAN SHAW** – bass TURNER who formed SPHINX then INNER CITY BLUES

Jun 77. (lp/c) *(CDS/CDC 4008) <6047>* **QUARK, STRANGENESS AND CHARM** [30] [ ]
– Spirit of the age / Damnation alley / Fable of a failed race / Quark, strangeness and charm / Hassan I Sahba / The forge of Vulcan / Days of the underground / Iron dream. *(re-iss. Oct86 lp/c; CHC/MC 50) (cd-iss. Apr89 on 'Virgin'; CDSCD 4008)*
Jul 77. (7") *(CB 305)* **QUARK, STRANGENESS AND CHARM. / THE FORGE OF VULCAN** [ ] [-]

— **PAUL HAYLES** – keyboards repl. HOUSE who joined DAVID BOWIE on tour

HAWKLORDS

BROCK and **CALVERT** recruiting new members **STEVE SWINDELLS** – keyboards (ex-STRING DRIVEN THING, ex-PILOT) / **HARVEY BAINBRIDGE** – bass / **MARTIN GRIFFIN** – drums

Charisma Charisma

Oct 78. (lp/c) *(CDS/CDC 4014) <2203>* **25 YEARS ON** [48] [ ]
– PSI power / Free fall / Automoton / 25 years / Flying doctor / The only ones / (only) The dead dreams of the cold war kid / The age of the micro man. *(re-iss. Aug82; CHC 10) (cd-iss. Apr89 on 'Virgin'; CDS4014)*
Oct 78. (7") *(CB 323)* **PSI POWER. / DEATH TRAP** [ ] [-]
Dec 78. (7") *<CAS 701>* **PSI POWER. / ('A'extended)** [-] [ ]
Mar 79. (7") *(CB 332)* **25 YEARS. / (ONLY) THE DEAD DREAMS OF THE COLD WAR KID** [ ] [ ]
(12"grey+=) *(CB 332-12)* – P.X.R. 5.

HAWKWIND

recorded '78 by **BROCK, TURNER, SHAW, KING / + HAYLES**

May 79. (lp/c) *(CDS 4016)* **P.X.R. 5** [59] [-]
– Death trap / Jack of shadows / Uncle Sam's on Mars / Infinity / Life form / Robot / High rise / P.X.R. 5. *(re-iss. Mar84; CHC 25) (cd-iss. Apr89 on 'Virgin'; CDSCD 4016)*

— **HAWKWIND** in 1979 were **SIMON KING** – drums returned from QUASAR, to repl. GRIFFITHS in Dec78 (CALVERT left to go solo). **TIM BLAKE** – keyboards (ex-GONG) repl. SWINDELLS who went solo

— added **HUW-LLOYD LANGTON** – guitar who returned from QUASAR — now:- **BROCK, LANGTON, BAINBRIDGE, KING + BLAKE**

Bronze not iss.

Jul 80. (lp/c) *(BRON/TCBRON 527)* **LIVE 1979 (live)** [15] [-]
– Shot down in the night / Motorway city / Spirit of the age / Brainstorm / Lighthouse / Master of the universe / Silver machine (requiem). *(cd-iss. Feb92 on 'Castle'; CLACD 243) (cd re-iss. Jul99 on 'Essential'; ESMCD 735)*
Jul 80. (7") *(BRO 98)* **SHOT DOWN IN THE NIGHT (live). / URBAN GUERILLA (live)** [59] [-]

— **GINGER BAKER** – drums (ex-CREAM, ex-BLIND FAITH, ex-AIRFORCE etc) repl. KING who teamed up with SWINDELLS

Nov 80. (7") *(BRO 109)* **WHO'S GONNA WIN THE WAR. / NUCLEAR TOYS** [ ] [-]
Nov 80. (blue-lp/c) *(BRON/TCBRON 530)* **LEVITATION** [21] [-]
– Levitation / Motorway city / Psychosis / World of tiers / Prelude / Who's gonna win the war / Space chase / The 5th second forever / Dust of time. *(re-iss. Jul87 on 'Castle' lp/cd; CLA/+CD 129) (cd-iss. Jul99 on 'Essential'; ESMCD 736)*

— **MARTIN GRIFFIN** – drums returned to repl. BAKER / **KEITH HALE** – keyboards repl. BLAKE

RCA Active not iss.

Oct 81. (7") *(RCA 137)* **ANGELS OF DEATH. / TRANS-DIMENSIONAL** [ ] [-]
Oct 81. (lp/c) *(RCA LP/K 6004)* **SONIC ATTACK** [19] [-]
– Sonic attack / Rocky paths / Psychosonia / Virgin of the world / Angels of death / Living on a knife edge / Coded languages / Disintigration / Streets of fear / Lost chances. *(cd-iss. Nov97 on 'Emergency Broadcast'; EBSCD 123)*
May 82. (lp/c) *(RCA LP/K 9004)* **CHURCH OF HAWKWIND** [26] [-]
– Angel voices / Nuclear drive / Star cannibal / The phenomena of luminosity / Fall of Earth city / The church / The joker at the gate / Some people never die / Light specific data / Experiment with destiny / The last Messiah / Looking in the future. *(cd-iss. Jun94 on 'Dojo')*

— **NIK TURNER** – vocals, saxophone returned to repl. HALE

Aug 82. (7"/7"pic-d) *(RCA/+P 267)* **SILVER MACHINE (remix). / PSYCHEDELIC WARLORDS (remix)** [ ] [-]
Oct 82. (lp/c) *(RCA LP/K 6055)* **CHOOSE YOUR MASQUES** [29] [-]
– Choose your masques / Dream worker / Arrival in Utopia / Utopia / Silver machine / Void city / Solitary mind games / Fahrenheit 451 / The scan / Waiting for tomorrow. *(cd-iss. Nov97 on 'Emergency Broadcast'; EBSCD 124)*

Flicknife not iss.

Oct 83. (lp) *(SHARP 014)* **ZONES** (live, with other 80's line-ups) [57] [-]
– Zones / Dangerous vision / Running through the back brain / The island / Motorway city / Utopia 84 / Society alliance / Sonic attack / Dream worker / Brainstorm. *(re-iss. Mar84 on pic-lp; PSHARP 014)*
Oct 83. (7") *(FLS 025)* **MOTORWAY CITY (live). / MASTER OF THE UNIVERSE (live)** [ ] [-]
Jan 84. (7") *(7FLEP 104)* **NIGHT OF THE HAWKS. / GREEN FINNED DEMON** [ ] [-]
(12"ep+=) *(FLEP 104)* **- THE EARTH RITUAL PREVIEW** – Dream dancers / Dragons + fables.
Nov 84. (lp) *(SHARP 022)* **STONEHENGE: THIS IS HAWKWIND, DO NOT PANIC** [ ] [-]
– Psy power / Levitation / Circles / Space chase / Death trap / Angels of death / Shot down in the night / Stonehenge decoded / Watching the grass grow. *(cd-iss. May92 on 'Anagram'; CDM GRAM 54)*

— **ALAN DAVEY** – bass, vocals repl. BAINBRIDGE and TURNER / **CLIVE DEAMER** – drums repl. GRIFFIN

Nov 85. (lp/c/cd) *(SHARP 033/+C/CD)* **CHRONICLE OF THE BLACK SWORD** [65] [-]
– Song of the swords / Shade gate / The sea king / The pulsing cavern / Elric the enchanter / Needle gun / Zarozinia / The demise / Sleep of a thousand tears / Chaos army / Horn of destiny. *(cd-iss. w / 3 extra tracks) (re-iss. cd Aug92 on 'Dojo'; DPJPCD 72)*
Nov 85. (7") *(FLS 032)* **NEEDLE GUN. / ARIOCH** [ ] [-]
(12"+=) *(FLST 032)* – Song of the swords.
Mar 86. (7") *(FLS 033)* **ZAROZINIA. / ASSAULT AND BATTERY** [ ] [-]
(12"+=) *(FLST 033)* – Sleep of a 1000 tears.

— **HAWKWIND** are now **BROCK**, as DR. HASBEEN – vocals, guitar, keyboards, synthesizers, **LANGTON, DAVEY, BAINBRIDGE** now vocals, keyboards, synthesizer and **DANNY THOMPSON** – drums, percussion, vocals

G.W.R. Roadrunner

May 88. (lp/c/cd) *(GW/+C/CD 26)* **THE XENON CODEX** [79] [ ] 1989
– The war I survived / Wastelands of sleep / Neon skyline / Lost chronicles / Tides / Heads / Mutation zone / E.M.C. / Sword of the east / Good evening. *<US-iss. on pic-d> (cd re-iss. Jul99 on 'Essential'; ESMCD 737)*

— **BROCK, BAINBRIDGE, DAVEY** plus **SIMON HOUSE, RICHARD CHADWICK & BRIDGETT WISHART**

Oct 90. (lp/c/cd) *(GW/+C/CD 103)* **SPACE BANDITS** [70] [-]
– Images / Black elk speaks / Wings / Out of the shadows / Realms / Ship of dreams / TV suicide. *(re-iss. cd Feb92 on 'Castle'; CLACD 282) (cd re-iss. Jul99 on 'Essential'; ESMCD 738)*

Essential not iss.

May 92. (cd/c/d-lp) *(ESSCD/ESSMC/ESSD 181)* **ELECTRIC TEPEE** [53] [-]
– LSD / Blue shift / Death of war / The secret agent / Garden pests / Space dust / Snake dance / Mask of the morning / Rites of Netherworld / Don't understand / Sadness runs deep / Right to decide / Going to Hawaii / Electric teepee. *(re-iss. Jul95 on 'Dojo'; DOJOCD 244) (cd re-iss. May00; ESMCD 885)*
Oct 93. (cd/c/lp) *(ESD CD/MC/LP 196)* **IT IS THE BUSINESS OF THE FUTURE TO BE DANGEROUS** [75] [ ]
– It's the business of the future to be dangerous / Space is their (Palestine) / Tibet is not China (pt.1 & 2) / Let barking dogs lie / Wave upon wave / Letting in the past / The camera that could lie / 3 or 4 erections during the course of the night / Technotropic zone exists / Give me shelter / Avante. *(cd re-iss. Jul99; ESMCD 740)*

4 Real not iss.

Jun 93. (12"ep/c-ep/cd-ep) *(4R 1 T/CS/D)* **SPIRIT OF THE AGE (The Solstice remixes)** [ ] [-]
– (Full Vocal / Hard Trance / Cyber Trance / Flesh To Phantasy)
Nov 93. (12"ep/cd-ep) *(4R 2 T/D)* **DECIDE YOUR FUTURE EP** [ ] [-]
– Right to decide / The camera that could lie / Right to decide (radio edit mix) / Assassin (Magick Carpet mix).

Emergency not iss.

Sep 94. (12"ep/cd-ep) *(EBT/+D 110)* **QUARK, STRANGENESS AND CHARM** [ ] [-]
– Uncle Sam's on Mars (Red Planet radio mix) / Quark, strangeness and charm / Black sun / Uncle Sam's on Mars (Martian Conquest mix).
Sep 94. (cd/c/d-lp) *(EBS CD/MC/LP 111)* **THE BUSINESS TRIP (live)** [ ] [-]
– Altair / Quark, strangeness and charm / LSD / The camera that would lie / Green finned demon / Do that / The day a wall came down / Berlin axis / Void of golden light / Right stuff / Wastelands / The dream goes on / Right to decide / The dream has ended / The future / Terra mystica.
Sep 95. (12"ep/cd-ep) *(EB T/CD 107)* **AREA S.4.** [ ] [-]
– Alien / Sputnik Stan / Medley: Death trap – Wastelands of sleep – Dream has . . . .
Oct 95. (cd/lp) *(EB SCD/LP 118)* **ALIEN 4** [ ] [-]
– Abducted / Alien (I am) / Reject your human touch / Blue skin / Beam me up / Vega / Xenomorph / Journey / Sputnik Stan / Kapal / Festivals / Deah trap / Wastelands / Are you losing your mind? / Space sex.
May 96. (cd/lp) *(EBS CD/LP 120)* **LOVE IN SPACE (live October 1995)** [ ] [-]
– Abducted / Death trap / Wastelands / Are you losing your mind? / Photo encounter / Blue skin / Robot / Alien I am / Sputnik Stan / Xenomorph / Vega / Love in space / Kapal / Elfin / Silver machine / Welcome.

– compilations, etc. –

1973. (d7") *United Artists;* **HURRY ON SUNDOWN. / MASTER OF THE UNIVERSE/ / SILVER MACHINE. / ORGONE ACCUMULATOR** [-] [ ]
Apr 76. (lp) *United Artists; (UAK 29919)* **ROADHAWKS** [34] [ ]
– Hurry on sundown / Paranoia (excerpt) / You shouldn't do that (live) / Silver machine (live) / Urban guerilla / Space is deep / Wind of change / The golden void. *(re-iss. Apr84 on 'Fame' lp/c; FA 413096-1/-4)*
Feb 77. (lp) *United Artists; (UAG 30025)* **MASTERS OF THE UNIVERSE** [ ] [-]
– Master of the universe / Brainstorm / Sonic attack / Orgone accumulator / It's so easy / Lost Johnnie. *(re-iss. May82 on 'Fame' lp/c; FA/C 3008) (re-iss. Jun87 & Dec95 on 'Liberty' lp/c; EMS/TCEMS 1258) (re-iss. May89 on 'Fame' lp/c/cd; FA/TCFA/CDFA 3220) (re-iss. Jul90 on 'Marble Arch' c/cd; CMA/+CD 129) (re-iss. Jul94 on 'Success' cd/c;) (cd-iss. Apr97 on 'Spalax'; 14972)*
Sep 80. (lp/c) *Charisma; (BG/+C 2)* **REPEAT PERFORMANCE** [ ] [-]
– Kerb crawler / Back on the streets / Quark strangeness and charm / Spirit of the

age / Steppenwolf / 25 years / PSI power / The only ones / High rise / Uncle Sam's on Mars.

May 81. (12"ep; as HAWKWIND ZOO) *Flicknife; (FLEP 100)* **HURRY ON SUNDOWN. / SWEET MISTRESS OF PAIN / KINGS OF SPEED (live)** -
(re-iss. Dec83)

Jul 81. (7"/12") *Flicknife; (FLS/+EP 205)* **MOTORHEAD. / VALIUM TEN** -
(re-iss. 12" Oct82)

Nov 81. (12"ep; as SONIC ASSASSINS) *Flicknife; (FLEP 101)* **OVER THE TOP. / FREEFALL / DEATH TRAP** -

Mar 82. (lp) *Flicknife; (SHARP 001)* **FRIENDS & RELATIONS** (1/2 live '77-78, 1/2 studio '82) -
(re-iss. Nov83) (re-iss. Nov94 on 'Emporio' cd/c)

Jun 82. (7"; as HAWKLORDS) *Flicknife; (FLS 209)* **WHO'S GONNA WIN THE WAR. / TIME OFF** -

Feb 83. (7") *Flicknife; (FLS 14)* **HURRY ON SUNDOWN. / LORD OF THE HORNETS / DODGEM DUKE** -

Mar 83. (d-c) *Charisma; (CASMC 110)* **QUARK, STRANGENESS & CHARM / PXR 5** -
(re-iss. '88)

1983. (lp) *Flicknife; (SHARP 107)* **TWICE UPON A TIME: HAWKWIND FRIENDS AND RELATIONS VOL.2** -

Jul 83. (d-lp) *Illuminated; (JAMS 29)* **TEXT OF FESTIVAL (live '70-72)** -
(1-lp re-iss. Jul85 as 'IN THE BEGINNING' on 'Demi Monde'; DM 005) (re-iss. cd Mar94 on 'Charly') (re-iss. Dec88 on 'Thunderbolt'; THBL 2.068) (cd-iss. first 3 sides) (cd re-iss. Mar97; CDTB 068)

Jun 84. (10"m-lp) *Flicknife; (SHARP 109)* **INDEPENDENTS DAY** -

Nov 84. (d-lp/d-c) *A.P.K.; (APK/+C 8)* **SPACE RITUAL 2 (live)** -
(cd-iss. 1987 on 'The CD Label'; CDTL 003)

Feb 85. (lp) *Demi-Monde; (DM 002)* **BRING ME THE HEAD OF YURI GAGARIN** (live '73 Empire Pool) -
(cd-iss. Nov86 on 'Charly'; CDCHARLY 40) (cd-iss. Nov92 on 'Thunderbolt'; CDTB 101) (cd re-iss. Apr97 on 'Spalax'; 14846)

Feb 85. (lp) *Flicknife; (SHARP 024)* **HAWKWIND, FRIENDS AND RELATIONS VOL.3** -
(c-iss.Apr84 with VOL.1 on reverse; *SHARP C1024) (other c-iss.Apr84 with VOL.2 on reverse; SHARP C2024)*

Jul 85. (lp) *Dojo; (DOJOLP 11)* **LIVE 70-73 (live)** -

May 85. (lp) *Mausoleum; (SKULL 8333369)* **UTOPIA 1984** -

Nov 85. (lp) *Mausoleum; (SKULL 83103)* **WELCOME TO THE FUTURE** -

Nov 85. (lp) *Obsession; (OBLP 1)* **RIDICULE** -
(re-iss. of disc 2 of 'SPACE RITUAL') (re-iss. 1990 cd/lp; OBSESS CD/LP 1)

Nov 85. (lp/pic-lp)(cd) *Samurai; (SAMR 038/+PD)(SAMRCD 038)* **ANTHOLOGY - HAWKWIND VOL.1** -
(cd+=) – Silver machine. *(re-iss. pic-lp.Nov86 as 'APPROVED HISTORY OF HAWKWIND'; SAMR 046) (re-iss. Apr90 as 'ACID DAZE 1' on 'Receiver'; RR 125)*

Mar 86. (lp/cd)(c) *Samurai; (SAMR/+CD 039)(TCSAMR 039)* **ANTHOLOGY - HAWKWIND VOL. 2** -
(cd-iss. 1986 extra 4 tracks) (re-iss. Apr90 as 'ACID DAZE 2' on 'Receiver'; RR 126)

May 86. (7"/7"sha-pic-d) *Samurai; (HW 7001/001)* **SILVER MACHINE. / MAGNU** -
(12"+=) *(HW12-001)* – Angels of death.

Jul 86. (7") *Flicknife; (FLS 034-A)* **MOTORHEAD. / HURRY ON SUNDOWN** -

Jul 86. (lp/c) *Samurai; (SAMR 040/+TC)* **ANTHOLOGY - HAWKWIND VOL.3** -
(re-iss. Apr90 as 'ACID DAZE 3' on 'Receiver'; RR 127)

Jul 86. (lp) *Hawkfan; (HWFB 2)* **HAWKFAN 12** -

Sep 86. (d-lp/d-c/cd) *Castle; (CCS LP/MC/CD 148)* **THE HAWKWIND COLLECTION (Pts. 1 & 2)** -
(cd-iss. Dec86 omits some tracks)

Nov 86. (lp/c) *Flicknife; (SHARP 036/+C)* **INDEPENDENTS DAY VOL.2** -

Jan 87. (lp/c) *R.C.A.; (NL/NK 71150)* **ANGELS OF DEATH** -

Apr 87. (lp/c/cd) *Flicknife; (SHARP 040/+C/CD)* **OUT AND INTAKE** -
(cd+=) – (2 extra tracks).

Sep 87. (lp/c/cd) *Start; (STF L/C/CD 2)* **BRITISH TRIBAL MUSIC** -

Oct 87. (3xbox-pic-lp) *Flicknife; (HWBOX 1)* **OFFICIAL PICTURE LOGBOOK** -
– ('STONEHENGE' / 'BLACK SWORD' / 'OUT & INTAKE' / '(interview)' lp
(cd-iss. Nov94 on 'Dojo';)

Dec 87. (lp/c) *Thunderbolt; (THBL/THBC 044)* **EARLY DAZE (THE BEST OF HAWKWIND)** -
(cd-iss. Jun88; CDTB CDTB 044)

Sep 88. (cd) *Virgin; (COMCD 8)* **SPIRIT OF THE AGE** -
(re-iss. Oct91 on 'Elite'; ELITE 021CD) (re-iss. Sep 93)

Nov 88. (cd) *Flicknife; (SHARP 1422CD)* **ZONES / STONEHENGE** -

Nov 88. (cd) *Flicknife; (SHARP 1724CD)* **BEST OF HAWKWIND, FRIENDS & RELATIONS** -

Dec 88. (d-lp/cd) *Flicknife; (SHARP 2045/+CD)* **THE TRAVELLERS AID TRUST** -

Dec 88. (d-lp/d-cd) *That's Original; (TFO 17/+CD)* **LEVITATION / HAWKWIND LIVE** -

Mar 89. (cd) *Avanti; (ISTCD 004)* **IRONSTRIKE** -

May 89. (lp) *Legacy; (GWSP 1)* **LIVE CHRONICLES** -
(re-iss. Feb92 cd/c on 'Castle; CCS CD/MC 123) (cd re-iss. Sep00 on 'Essential'; CMDDD 013)

May 89. (lp/c/cd) *Powerhouse; (POW/+C/CD 5502)* **NIGHT OF THE HAWK** -
(cd-iss. has 3 extra tracks)

1990. (cd/c) *Action Replay; (ARLC/CDAR 1018)* **BEST AND THE REST OF HAWKWIND** -

Mar 90. (2xcd-box)(3xlp-box) *Receiver; (RRDCD 1X)(RRBX 1)* **ACID DAZE (re-issue)** -
(3 VOLUMES re-iss. cd Jul93)

May 90. (cd)(c/lp) *E.M.I.; (CDP 746694-2)(TC+/NTS 300)* **STASIS, THE U.A. YEARS 1971-1975** -
– Urban guerilla / Psychedelic warlords (disappear in smoke) / Brainbox pollution / 7 by 7 / Paradox / Silver machine / You'd better believe it / Lord of light / The black corridor (live) / Space is deep (live) / You shouldn't do that (live). *(re-iss. cd Dec95 on 'Fame')*

Dec 90. (12"blue-ep) *Receiver; (REPLAY 3014)* **THE EARLY YEARS LIVE** -
– Silver machine / Spirit of the age / Urban guerilla / Born to go.

1990. (c) *Capitol; <4XLL 57286>* **METAL CLASSICS 2: BEST OF HAWKWIND** -

1990. (cd/c) *Knight; (KN CD/MC 10017)* **NIGHT RIDING** -

Jun 91. (lp/c/cd) *G.W.R.; (GW/+MC/CD 104)* **PALACE SPRINGS** -
– (remixed tracks from 'WARRIORS . . . ' & 'XENON . . .) *(re-iss. cd Jul92 on 'Castle'; CLACD 303) (cd re-iss. Jul99 on 'Essential'; ESMCD 739)*

Oct 91. (cd/c) *Windsong; (WIN CD/MC 007)* **BBC RADIO 1 LIVE IN CONCERT (live)** -

Feb 92. (3xcd-box) *Castle; (CLABX 911)* **3 ORIGINALS** -

Feb 92. (cd) *Raw Fruit; (FRSCD 005)* **THE FRIDAY ROCK SHOW SESSIONS (live '86)** -

Jun 92. (cd) *Anagram; (GRAM 53)* **MIGHTY HAWKWIND CLASSICS 1980-1985** -

Aug 92. (cd) *Dojo; (DOJOCD 71)* **HAWKLORDS LIVE** -

Apr 94. (cd) *Cleopatra; (CLEO 57732)* **LORD OF LIGHT** -

Apr 94. (cd) *Cleopatra; (CLEO 57412)* **PSYCHEDELIC WARLORDS** -

Dec 94. (cd) *Cyclops; (CYCL 021)* **CALIFORNIA BRAINSTORM** -

Feb 95. (cd) *Emergency Broadcast; (EMBSCD 114)* **UNDISCLOSED FILES - ADDENDUM** -

Mar 95. (cd) *Anagram; (CDMGRAM 91)* **THE RARITIES . . .** -

May 95. (cd) *Spectrum; (550764-2)* **SILVER MACHINE** -

Oct 95. (cd) *Anagram; (CDGRAM 94)* **INDEPENDENTS DAY VOLUMES 1 & 2** -

Mar 97. (cd) *Emporio; (EMPRCD 710)* **ONWARD FLIES THE BIRD - LIVE AND RARE** -

Jul 97. (cd-ep) *E.B.S.; (EBCD 106)* **LOVE IN SPACE / LORD OF LIGHT / SONIC ATTACK** -

Sep 97. (cd) *Snapper; (SMDCD 121)* **AMBIENT ANARCHISTS** -

Nov 97. (cd/lp) *Emergency Broadcast; (EBS CD/LP 117)* **RITUAL OF THE SOLSTICE** -

Nov 97. (cd) *Emergency Broadcast; (EBSCD 139)* **DISTANT HORIZONS** -

Nov 97. (d-cd) *E.M.I.; (HAWKS 6)* **1999 PARTY** -

Mar 98. (cd) *Eagle; (EABCD 084)* **THE MASTERS** -

Apr 98. (cd) *Cleopatra; <(CLEO 2202)>* **WELCOME TO THE FUTURE** -

Sep 98. (cd) *Repertoire; (REP 4676)* **SONIC BOOM KILLERS** -

Sep 98. (d-cd) *Essential; (<ESDCD 664>)* **ANTHOLOGY** -

Feb 99. (cd) *Cleopatra; <(CLP 0471-2)>* **GOLDEN VOID 1969-1979** -

Mar 99. (lp) *Black Widow; (BWR/+CD 026)* **THE ELF AND THE HAWK** -

Apr 99. (cd) *Blueprint; (BP 309CD)* **THE DAWN OF HAWKWIND** -

May 99. (cd) *Anagram; (CDMGRAM 61)* **THE BEST OF FRIENDS AND RELATIONS** -

May 99. (4xcd-box) *Dressed To Kill; (REDTK 98)* **ENTIRE AND INFINITE** -
– (MASTERS OF THE UNIVERSE / BRING ME THE HEAD OF URI GAGARIN / SPACE RITUAL / TEXT OF FESTIVAL)

Jun 99. (cd) *Thunderbolt; (CDTB 099)* **SPACE RITUAL VOL.2** -

Aug 99. (cd) *EMI; (521747-2)* **EPOCH - ECLIPSE (THE ULTIMATE BEST OF HAWKWIND)** -

Aug 99. (3xcd-box) *EMI; (521751-2)* **EPOCH - ECLIPSE 30 YEAR ANTHOLOGY** -

Nov 99. (cd) *Hawkwind; (HAWKVP 1CD)* **LIVE AT THE GLASTONBURY FESTIVAL 1990** -

Nov 99. (cd) *Hawkwind; (HAWKVP 2CD)* **GREASY TRUCKERS (live at the Roundhouse 1972)** -

Nov 99. (d-cd) *Hawkwind; (HAWKVP 3CD)* **COLLECTORS SERIES VOL.1** -

Dec 99. (d-cd) *Hawkwind; (HAWKCD 4CD)* **COLLECTORS SERIES VOL.2** -

Apr 00. (cd) *Hawkwind; (HAWKVP 5CD)* **ATOM HENGE** -

Apr 00. (d-cd) *Hawkwind; (HAWKVP 13CD)* **LIVE IN NOTTINGHAM 1990** -

Apr 00. (cd) *Hawkwind; (HAWKVP 17CD)* **IN YOUR AREA** -

Jul 00. (d-cd) *Burning Airlines; (PILOT 033)* **YEAR 2000 - CODENAME HAWKWIND VOL.1 (live)** -

Jul 00. (cd) *Burning Airlines; (PILOT 064)* **LIVE FROM THE DARKSIDE** -

Jul 00. (d-cd) *Cleopatra; <(CLP 850)>* **THE STONEHENGE COLLECTION**

Barry HAY (see under ⇒ GOLDEN EARRING)

HEAD EAST

Formed: St. Louis, Missouri, USA . . . 1974 by JOHN SCHLITT, MIKE SOMERVILLE, ROGER BOYD, DAN BIRNEY and STEVE HUSTON. Signed to 'A&M' the following year, the band showcased their commercial hard rock boogie on their debut set, 'FLAT AS A PANCAKE'. A minor breakthrough, it spawned two hit singles, 'NEVER BEEN ANY REASON' and 'LOVE ME TONIGHT'. They continued to chart regularly, the hooklines of SCHLITT appealing to the burgeoning AOR market. In the early 80's, their songcraft was often enhanced by the pen of RUSS BALLARD (ex-ARGENT), the hopefully-titled, 'U.S. No.1' signalling a more overtly mainstream approach.

Album rating: FLAT AS A PANCAKE (*7) / GET YOURSELF UP (*6) / GETTIN' LUCKY (*4) / HEAD EAST (*5) / LIVE! (*6) / A DIFFERENT KIND OF CRAZY (*5) / U.S. 1 (*4) / ONWARDS AND UPWARDS (*3) / CHOICE OF WEAPONS (*4) / CONCERT CLASSICS (*5)

JOHN SCHLITT – vocals / **MIKE SOMERVILLE** – guitar, vocals / **ROGER BOYD** – keyboards, vocals / **DAN BIRNEY** – bass, guitar, vocals / **STEVE HUSTON** – drums, percussion

A&M A&M

Oct 75. (lp) *(AMLH 64537)* <4537> **FLAT AS A PANCAKE** Aug75
– Never been any reason / One against the other / Love me tonight / City of gold / Fly by night lady / Jefftown Creek / Lovin' me along / Ticket back to Georgia / Brother Jacob.

Jan 76. (7") *(AMS 7208)* <1718> **NEVER BEEN ANY REASON. / ONE AGAINST THE OTHER** 68 Oct75

Feb 76. (7") <1784> **LOVE ME TONIGHT. / FLY BY NIGHT LADY / BROTHER JACOB** - 54

Jun 76. (7") <1872> **SEPARATE WAYS. / FLY BY NIGHT LADY** -

Jul 76. (lp) *(AMLH 64579)* <4579> **GET YOURSELF UP** May76
– When I get ready / Separate ways / This woman's in love / I don't want the chance / Sailor / Monkey shine / Jailer / Love my blues away / The victim / Trouble.

Mar 77. (7") <1930> **GETTIN' LUCKY. / SANDS OF TIME** -

Apr 77. (lp) *(AMLH 64624)* <4624> **GETTIN' LUCKY** Mar77
– Gettin' lucky / Back in my own hands / Show me I'm alive / Take it on home / Dancer road / Don't let me sleep in the morning / Sands of time / Call to arms and legs / Time has a way / Every little bit of my heart.

May 78. (lp) *(AMLH 64680)* <4680> **HEAD EAST** 78 Mar78
– Open up the door / Man I wanna be / Nothing to lose / Since you been gone / Pictures / Get up & enjoy yourself / I'm feelin' fine / Dance away lover / Elijah.

May 78. (7") *(AMS 7359)* <2026> **SINCE YOU BEEN GONE. / PICTURES** 46 Apr78

Apr 79. (7") <2122> **NEVER BEEN ANY REASON (live). / I'M FEELIN' FINE (live)** -

Apr 79. (d-lp) *(AML 6607)* <6007> **LIVE! (live)** 65 Jan79
– Take a hand / Man I wanna be / Gettin' lucky / City of gold / Fly by night lady / Monkey shine / When I get ready / Every little bit of my heart / Get up and enjoy yourself / Since you been gone / It's for you / Never been any reason / Elijah / Prelude to creek / Jefftown Creek / Love me tonight / I'm feelin' fine.

Nov 79. (7") <2208> **GOT TO BE REAL. / MORNING** -

Nov 79. (lp) <4795> **A DIFFERENT KIND OF CRAZY** - 96
– Speciality / Keep a secret / Feelin' is right / Lonelier now / Morning / Got to be real / If you knew me better / Too late / Hard drivin' days.

Apr 80. (7") <2222> **SPECIALITY. /** -

—— **DAN ODUM** – vocals / **TONY GROSS** – guitar, vocals / **MARK BOATMAN** – bass, vocals, repl. SCHLITT, SOMERVILLE + BIRNEY

Nov 80. (lp) <4826> **U.S. 1** -
– Fight for your life / I surrender / Susan / You'll be the one / Love me now / Out of the blue / Babie Ruth / Sister sister / Look to the sky.

—— **ROBBIE ROBINSON** – bass, repl. BOATMAN

not iss. Allegiance

1982. (lp) <AV 432> **ONWARD AND UPWARD** -
– I'm coming home / Don't talk to me / Show me / I make believe I believe her / Ready to go / Onward and upward / Wanted woman / She doesn't mean a thing to me / Wrong time / Take my hand.

—— disbanded for several years until one-off comeback below (originals?)

not iss. Dark Heart

1989. (lp) <2001> **CHOICE OF WEAPONS** -
– Come alive / Time of your life / Girl / Wrong time / End of the avenue / So afraid / Hard to believe / Going under / Forgive and forget / Break your heart.

– compilations, etc. –

Nov 99. (cd) *Ranch Life; <(RRCC 0707)>* **CONCERT CLASSICS**
– Take a hand / Man I wanna be / Keep a secret / Speciality / Monkey shine / Love me now / City of gold / Fly by night / Get up and enjoy yourself / Out of the blue / Ready to go / Jefftown creek / Since you've been gone / Never had any reason / Take my hand.

HEAD OF DAVID

Formed: Dudley, Midlands, England ... mid 80's by RUEBEN BURROUGHS, ERIC JURENOVSKIS and DAVE COCHRAN. A highly influential but often overlooked band, HEAD OF DAVID were one of the earliest British exponents of grating, industrial noise, a sound which would influence not only a host of grindcore acts but many extreme metal/industrial outfits of the 90's. Hardly surprising was the fact that JUSTIN BROADRICK was also an early member of NAPALM DEATH, the frontman presiding over the debut 'DOGBREATH' EP and subsequent albums 'FROM HERE TO ETERNITY' (1986) and 'DUSTBOWL' (1988) before going on to form the equally seminal GODFLESH. HEAD OF DAVID regrouped with a line-up of BURROUGHS, JURENOVSKIS and BIPIN KUMAR to record 'SEED STATE' in 1991 before finally splitting.

Album rating: FROM HERE TO ETERNITY LP (*7) / DUSTBOWL (*5) / WHITE ELEPHANT (*5) / SEED STATE (*4)

STEPHEN RUEBEN BURROUGHS – vocals, guitar / **ERIC JURENOVSKIS** – guitar, drum programming / **DAVE COCHRAN** – bass / **JUSTIN BROADRICK** – drums

Blast First not iss.

Jun 86. (12"ep) *(BFFP 5)* **DOGBREATH** -

Oct 86. (lp) *(BFFP 10)* **FROM HERE TO INFINITY** -
– Dogbreath / Smears / I'll fall at your feet / White bastard / Rocket U.S.A. / Godbreath / Snuff ride M.C. / Joyride burning X / Shadow hills California / Newly shaven saint. *(cd-iss. Apr88; BFFP 10CD)*

Jul 87. (lp) *(NOT 3)* **THE SHIT HITS THE FAN** -

Oct 87. (lp) *(BFFP 18)* **DUSTBOWL** -
– Tequila / El supremo / Dog day sunrise / Bugged / Great white heat / Cult of coats / Ditchwater / 108 / Roadkill / Snake domain / Grand rift faultline / Adrenicide / Pierced all over / Skin drill / Ink vine.
(cd-iss. Apr88; BFFP 18CD)

—— now without BROADRICK who formed GODFLESH

Jan 89. (lp) *(WANT 001)* **WHITE ELEPHANT** - - mail-o

Feb 89. (12") *(BFFP 37)* **SAVANNAH (mixes)** -

—— **BIPIN KUMAR** – bass; repl. COCHRAN

not iss. Mute-Elektra

1991. (cd,c) <61229> **SEED STATE** -
– Three robes, one bowl / How primitive are you? / Human feel / Vulture culture / Girderland / Zen walker / Sweetandlovingthing / Wolf.

—— disbanded after above

HEADS

Formed: Bristol, England ... 1993 by SIMON PRICE, PAUL ALLEN, HUGO MORGAN and WAYNE MASKELL. As their moniker may suggest, these lads are fond of the odd magic cigarette or two which quite possibly explains their laid-back work rate. After finally getting around to releasing a debut single, 'COOGAN'S BLUFF' in '94, the group drew early notices for their psychedelic SONIC YOUTH-meets-MC5 garage-punk jams. An import copy of debut album, 'RELAXING WITH ...' (1996) subsequently caught the attention of artist Frank Kozik who signed the band to his US-based 'Man's Ruin' label. The punningly titled 'EVERYBODY KNOWS WE GOT NOWHERE' finally drew commercial breath in 2000, incredibly only the second long player of their decade-long career. Well, Rome wasn't built in a day ...

Album rating: RELAXING WITH ... (*6) / THE TIME IS NOW mini compilation (*6) / EVERYBODY KNOWS WE GOT NOWHERE (*5)

SIMON PRICE – vocals, guitar / **PAUL ALLEN** – guitar / **HUGO MORGAN** – bass / **WAYNE C. MASKELL** – drums

Rooster not iss.

Oct 94. (7") *(ROOSTER 2)* **COOGAN'S BLUFF. /** -

Headhunter Headhunter

Nov 95. (7") *(HED 718)* **TELEVISION. /** -
(re-iss. Feb97; same)

Oct 96. (lp/cd) *(<HUK 001/+CD>)* **RELAXING WITH ...**
– Quad / Don't know yet / Chipped / Slow down / U33 / Television / Woke up / Widowmaker / Taken too much / Coogan's bluff.

Nov 96. (ltd-7") *(HH 701)* **GNU. / DEMONIZER 48:48**

Man's Ruin Man's Ruin

Feb 97. (10"ep) *(<MR 041>)* **THE HEADS EP**
– Delwyn's conkers / Snake pit / Spliff riff.

Nov 97. (7") **DIRTY WATER. / Magic Dirt: Goofy Gumb** -
(above issued on 'Butcher's Hook' & below on 'Rocket')

Mar 98. (7") *(LAUNCH 001)* **unknown. / Lilydamnwhite: (track)** -

Mar 98. (10") *(<MR 078>)* **MAO TINITUS. / LEGEVAN SATELLITE / YOU CAN LEARN BACK SOMETIMES** Jan98

May 98. (m-cd) *(<MR 097>)* **THE TIME IS NOW** (compilation)
– Delwyn's conkers / Snakepit / Spliff riff (roached out ...) / Dirty water / Mao tinitus / Legevan satellite / You can lean back sometimes. *(re-iss. Aug00; same)*

Sweet Nothing Sweet Nothing

Jul 00. (cd/d-lp) *(SNCD/SNLP 007)* **EVERYBODY KNOWS WE GOT NOWHERE**
– Legevan satellite / Thumbs / Fuego / Kraut Byrds / Could be ... / #'75 / Wobble / Barcoded / Song No.1 / My my / Stab railroad / Chrome plated / Motorjam / Dirty water / Pill jam / Long gone.

– compilations, etc. –

Jun 97. (cd-ep) *Headhunter; (CCSHED 726)* **GNU EP** -
– GNU / Demonizer 48:48 / Looking at you / Jellystoned park.

Jun 00. (7"ep) *Rocket; (LAUNCH 010)* **SESSIONS** -

HEADSWIM

Formed: Essex, England ... 1992 initially as BLINDER by brothers DAN and TOM GLENDINING, plus NICK WATTS and CLOVIS TAYLOR (aka DILLWEED for a wee while). A bass-heavy post-grunge outfit, the group initially surfaced with two well-received EP's, 'TENSE NERVOUS HEAD' (October '93) and 'MOMENTS OF TRUTH' (March '94), collected together a few months later as 'TENSE MOMENTS' for their new label 'Epic'. Akin to an amphetamine-thrash/sludge-metal combination of SOUNDGARDEN, FAITH NO MORE and LED ZEPPELIN (to these ears, 'MY LIFE' being just a tad reminiscent of the latter's 'Black Dog') they played the inaugural 'T In The Park' in the summer of '94. They delivered their first album proper, 'PRECIPITY FLOOD', later that year, a decidedly more introspective affair with similarly subdued sales figures. With PEARL JAM's STONE GOSSARD now a huge fan, HEADSWIM returned from a near four year hiatus with a much improved third set, 'DESPITE YOURSELF' (1998). An album virtually dedicated to DAN and TOM's brother dying of leukaemia in 1994, it also marked a change of direction to more laid back rock sound (RADIOHEADswim, maybe!), resulting in a UK Top 30 placing.

Album rating: PRECIPITY FLOOD (*6) / DESPITE YOURSELF (*7)

DAN GLENDINING (b.1971) – vocals, guitar / **NICK WATTS** (b.1970, York, England) – keyboards / **CLOVIS TAYLOR** (b.1971, Forest Gate, London) – bass / **TOM GLENDINING** (b.1970) – drums

Crush not iss.

Oct 93. (12"ep/cd-ep) *(12HEAD/HEADCD 1)* **TENSE NERVOUS HEAD EP** -
– Violent / My life (is driving me crazy) / One red eye / Chains and nails.

Mar 94. (12"ep/cd-ep) *(12HEAD/HEADCD 2)* **MOMENTS OF UNION EP** [ ] [-]
– Dead / Proud? / Freedom from faith / Inside of us.

Epic Epic

Jun 94. (cd/lp) *(476990-2/-1)* **TENSE MOMENTS** (compilation of 2 EP's) [ ] [-]
Aug 94. (12"ep/cd-ep) *(660657-6/-2)* **GONE TO POT / VIOLENT. / PROUD / LUCILLE** [ ] [-]
Oct 94. (cd-ep) *(660863-2)* **SOUP / DOWN / THE FEAR / FREEDOM FROM FAITH (live)** [ ] [-]
Oct 94. (cd/c/lp) *(477878-2/-4/-1)* *<494>* **PRECIPITY FLOOD** [ ] [ ]
– Gone to pot / Soup / Try disappointed / Crawl / Dead / Years on me / Apple of my eye / Down / Stinkhorn / Safe harvest / Beneath a black moon.
Feb 95. (c-s) *(661225-4)* **CRAWL / APPRENTICED TO PAIN** [64] [-]
(12"+=) *(661225-6)* – Morning song.
(cd-s++=) *(661225-2)* – Rotting tooth.
Jun 95. (7"colrd) *(662153-7)* **YEARS ON ME. /** [-] [-]
(cd-s) *(662153-2/-5)* – (probably shelved)

Epic Sony

Jan 98. (cd-ep) **HYPE /** [-] [ ]
Feb 98. (c-s) *(665044-4)* **TOURNIQUET / BLACK CAR** [30] [-]
(cd-s+=) *(665044-2)* – Last subway coma / Recovery position.
(cd-s) *(665044-5)* – ('A'side) / ('A'-Steve Osbourne remix) / ('A'-Mekon's apocalyptic remix) / ('A'-Mekon's C'mon Feel The Noise mix).
Apr 98. (c-s) *(665840-4)* **BETTER MADE / NO TICKET** [42] [-]
(cd-s+=) *(665840-2)* – Moving on (live) / Tourniquet (live).
(cd-s) *(665840-5)* – ('A'side) / Dead (donedifferent) / Beneath a black moon (live) / Holy ghost (live).
May 98. (cd/c) *(487726-2/-4)* *<68072>* **DESPITE YOURSELF** [24] [ ] Sep98
– Tourniquet / Hype / Years on me / Clinging to the wreckage / Better made / Wishing I was naive / Old angel midnight / Holy ghost / Burnt out shell of bliss / Devil in my palm / Moving on / Brother.

Pet Sounds not iss.

Sep 00. (cd-ep) *(PET 021CDS)* **DUSTY ROAD** [ ] [-]

HEART

Formed: Vancouver, Canada . . . 1975 by sisters ANN and NANCY WILSON, who had graduated from Seattle groups The ARMY and WHITE HEART. In these line-ups were brothers ROGER and MIKE FISHER, the respective boyfriends of ANN and NANCY. The latter had arrived from the solo-folk scene to replace MIKE, who became their sound engineer, the group moving to Vancouver to avoid his draft papers. With bassist STEVE FOSSEN completing the line-up, the group named themselves HEART and were duly signed to the local 'Mushroom' label by owner Shelley Siegal, issuing their well-received debut album, 'DREAMBOAT ANNIE', in 1976. With the help of two US Top 40 singles, 'MAGIC MAN' and 'CRAZY ON YOU', the album made the American Top 10, its JEFFERSON STARSHIP meets LED ZEPPELIN folky pop/rock sound sitting well with FM radio. Following the record's success, HEART returned to Seattle in late '76 and inked a new deal with 'CBS-Portrait', Mushroom promptly sueing them for breach of contract. Despite the legal hassles, the group ploughed on, adding keyboardist HOWARD LEESE and permanent drummer MICHAEL DEROSIER for the 'LITTLE QUEEN' (1977) album. A heavier affair, the record was another critical and commercial success, spawning the hard rocking single, 'BARRACUDA'. While punk precluded any real UK success, the band were consistently popular in the States, the rock babe glamour of the WILSON sisters and impressive vocal acrobatics of younger sibling ANNE marking them out from the AOR pack. In 1978, a Seattle judge gave Mushroom the rights to issue their out-takes album, 'MAGAZINE', but ruled that the group could re-record it. Inevitably, the record was a patchy affair, although it surprised many, even the band themselves, by making the Top 20. Later that year, their fourth album, 'DOG AND BUTTERFLY' was another Top 20 success, their last for 'Portrait' as the band underwent personal upheavals and signed a new deal with 'Epic'. The FLEETWOOD MAC-style inter-band relationship problems resulted in ROGER FISHER departing, and though 'BEBE LE STRANGE' (1980) wasn't quite 'Rumours', it was an improvement on their previous effort. The line-up remained unsettled, however, as the band went through a kind of mid-period slump, MARK ANDES and DENNY CARMASI having replaced FOSSEN and DEROSIER respectively by the release of 'PASSIONWORKS' (1983). This album signalled the end of their tenure with 'Epic', although HEART's fortunes were given a bit of a boost when ANN WILSON duetted with LOVERBOY's MIKE RENO on the Top 10 hit single, 'ALMOST PARADISE' (used in the film 'FOOTLOOSE'). Signing a new deal with 'Capitol', the band rose phoenix-like to top the American charts with the eponymous 'HEART' in 1985. Full of gleaming, MTV-friendly power ballads (i.e.'THESE DREAMS', 'WHAT ABOUT LOVE'), the band had practically re-invented themselves and had the leather'n'lace-style soft-rock market well and truly cornered. 'BAD ANIMALS' was more of the same, ANNE flexing maximum vocal muscle on the 'ALONE' single and duly breaking the band in Britain where the song went Top 3. 'BRIGADE' (1990) was almost as successful though not quite as convincing, the WILSONs taking time out for solo projects after touring the record. HEART returned with an almost original line-up for 1993's 'DESIRE WALKS ON', while 'THE ROAD HOME' showcased a stripped down acoustic sound. • **Songwriters:** ANN WILSON or the group wrote most except; TELL IT LIKE IT IS (Aaron Neville) / I'M DOWN (Beatles) / LONG TALL SALLY (Little Richard) / UNCHAINED MELODY (hit; Righteous Brothers) / I'VE GOT THE MUSIC IN ME (Kiki Dee) / THESE DREAMS (Martin Page & Bernie Taupin) / ALONE (Billy Steinberg & Tom Kelly) / ALL I WANNA DO IS MAKE LOVE TO YOU (Mutt Lange) / etc. • **Trivia:** In 1967, ANN WILSON AND THE DAYBREAKS issued a couple of singles on 'Topaz'; STANDIN' WATCHIN' YOU. / WONDER HOW I MANAGED and THROUGH EYES AND GLASS. / I'M GONNA DRINK MY HURT AWAY.

Album rating: DREAMBOAT ANNIE (*8) / LITTLE QUEEN (*5) / MAGAZINE (*5) / DOG AND BUTTERFLY (*7) / BEBE LE STRANGE (*5) / GREATEST HITS / LIVE live compilation (*5) / PRIVATE AUDITION (*6) / PASSION WORKS (*6) / HEART (*7) / BAD ANIMALS (*7) / BRIGADE (*5) / ROCK THE HOUSE LIVE (*5) / THESE DREAMS – GREATEST HITS compilation (*8)

ANN WILSON (b.19 Jun'51, San Diego, Calif.) – vocals, guitar, flute / **NANCY WILSON** (b.16 Mar'54, San Francisco, Calif.) – guitar, vocals / **ROGER FISHER** (b.1950) – guitar / **STEVE FOSSEN** – bass with session keyboard player and drummer

Arista Mushroom

Apr 76. (7") *<7021>* **CRAZY ON YOU. / DREAMBOAT ANNIE** [-] [35]
<re-hit US No.62 early 1978>
Oct 76. (7") *(ARISTA 71) <7011>* **MAGIC MAN. / HOW DEEP IT GOES** [ ] [ ] Feb76
<finally climbed to No.9 by mid-'76>
Oct 76. (lp/c)<US-pic-lp> *(ARTY/TC-ARTY 139) <5005>* **DREAMBOAT ANNIE** [36] [7] Mar76
– Magic man / Dreamboat Annie (fantasy child) / Crazy on you / Soul of the sea / Dreamboat Annie / White lightning and wine (love me like music) / I'll be your song / Sing child / How deep it goes / Dreamboat Annie (reprise). *(re-iss. Oct87 on 'Capitol' cd/c/lp; CD/TC+/EMS 1277) (<cd re-iss. Jul97 on 'Disky'; DC 88124-2>)*
Feb 77. (7") *(ARISTA 86)* **CRAZY ON YOU. / SOUL OF THE SEA** [ ] [-]
Apr 77. (7") *(ARISTA 104) <7023>* **DREAMBOAT ANNIE. / SING CHILD** [ ] [42] Dec76

— added **HOWARD LEESE** (b.13 Jun'51) – keyboards, synthesizer, guitar (appeared as guest on debut album) / **MICHAEL DEROSIER** – drums

Portrait Portrait

Jul 77. (lp/c) *(PRT 82075) <34799>* **LITTLE QUEEN** [34] [9] May77
– Barracuda / Love alive / Sylvan song / Dream of the archer / Kick it out / Little queen / Treat me well / Say hello / Cry to me / Go on cry. *(re-iss. Aug86; same) (cd-iss. May87; CDPRT 82075) (cd re-iss. Sep93 on 'Sony Collectors';) (cd re-is.Feb97 on 'Columbia'; 474678-2)*
Aug 77. (7") *(PRT 5402) <70004>* **BARRACUDA. / CRY TO ME** [ ] [11] May77
Oct 77. (7") *(PRT 5570)* **LOVE ALIVE. / KICK IT OUT** [ ] [-]
Nov 77. (7") *(PRT 5751) <70008>* **LITTLE QUEEN. / TREAT ME WELL** [ ] [62] Sep77
Nov 77. (7") *<70010>* **KICK IT OUT. / GO ON CRY** [-] [79]
(The following few releases on 'Arista' UK & 'Mushroom' US were contractual)

Arista Mushroom

Sep 77. (7"w-drawn) *(ARISTA 140)* **HEARTLESS. / HERE SONG** [-] [-]
Mar 78. (7") *<7031>* **HEARTLESS. / JUST THE WINE** [-] [24]
Apr 78. (lp)<US-pic-lp> *(SPART 1024) <5008>* **MAGAZINE** [-] [17]
– Heartless / Devil delight / Just the wine / Without you / Magazine / Here song / Mother Earth blues / I've got the music in me (live). *(UK-iss.Oct87 on 'Capitol' cd/c/lp; CD/TC+/EMS 1278)*
May 78. (7") *(ARIST 187)* **HEARTLESS (version II). / HERE SONG** [ ] [-]
May 78. (7") *<7035>* **WITHOUT YOU. / HERE SONG** [-] [ ]
Jul 78. (7") *<7043>* **MAGAZINE. / DEVIL DELIGHT** [-] [ ]
Aug 78. (7") *(ARIST 206)* **MAGAZINE. / JUST THE WINE** [ ] [-]

Portrait Portrait

Oct 78. (7") *(PRT 6704) <70020>* **STRAIGHT ON. / LIGHTER TOUCH** [ ] [15] Sep78
Dec 78. (lp/c) *(PRT 83080) <35555>* **DOG & BUTTERFLY** [ ] [17] Oct78
– Cook with fire / High time / Hijinx / Straight on / Lighter touch / Dog & butterfly / Nada one / Mistral wind. *(re-iss. Aug86; PRT 32803) (cd-iss. May87; CDPRT 32803)*
Jan 79. (7") *<70025>* **DOG & BUTTERFLY. / MISTRAL WIND** [-] [34]

— Now a quartet when Nancy's boyfriend ROGER FISHER left the band

Epic Epic

Mar 80. (7") *(EPC 8270)* **EVEN IT UP. / PILOT** [ ] [34] Feb 80
Mar 80. (lp/c) *(EPC/40 84135) <36371>* **BEBE LE STRANGE** [ ] [5]
– Bebe le strange / Down on me / Silver wheels / Break / Rockin' heaven down / Even it up / Strange night / Raised on you / Pilot / Sweet darlin'. *(cd-iss. 1988; CDEPC 84135) (cd re-iss. May93 on 'Sony Collectors' cd/c;)*
May 80. (7") *<50874>* **DOWN ON ME. / RAISED ON YOU** [-] [ ]
Jul 80. (7") *<50892>* **BEBE LE STRANGE. / SILVER WHEELS** [-] [ ]
Nov 80. (7") *<50950>* **TELL IT LIKE IT IS. / STRANGE EUPHORIA** [-] [8]
Jan 81. (7") *(EPC 9436)* **TELL IT LIKE IT IS. / BARRACUDA (live)** [ ] [-]
Mar 81. (lp/c)<US-d-lp> *(EPC/40 84829) <36888>* **GREATEST HITS / LIVE** (half comp / half live) [ ] [13] Nov80
– Tell it like it is / Barracuda / Straight on / Dog & butterfly / Even it up / Bebe le strange / Sweet darlin' / I'm down – Long tall Sally – Unchained melody / Rock and roll. *(re-iss. +cd Dec88)*
Mar 81. (7") *<51010>* **UNCHAINED MELODY (live). / MISTRAL WIND** [-] [83]
Jun 82. (7") *(EPCA 2436) <02925>* **THIS MAN IS MINE. / AMERICA** [-] [33] May82
Jun 82. (lp/c) *(EPC/40 85792) <38049>* **PRIVATE AUDITION** [77] [25]
– City's burning / Bright light girl / Perfect stranger / Private audition / Angels / This man is mine / The situation / Hey darlin' darlin' / One word / Fast times / America. *(re-iss. Feb88 on 'C.B.S.' lp/c; 460174-1/-4) (cd-iss. 1988; CDEPC 85792) (re-iss. cd May94)*
Sep 82. (7") *<03071>* **PRIVATE AUDITION. / BRIGHT LIGHT GIRL** [-] [ ]

— **MARK ANDES** (b.19 Feb'48, Philadelphia, Pennsylvania) – bass (ex-SPIRIT, ex-JO JO GUNNE, ex-FIREFALL) repl. FOSSEN / **DENNY CARMASSI** – drums (ex-MONTROSE, ex-SAMMY HAGAR, ex-GAMMA) repl. DEROSIER who formed ORION THE HUNTER

Aug 83. (7") *<04047>* **HOW CAN I REFUSE. / JOHNNY MOON** [-] [ ]
Sep 83. (lp/c) *(EPC/40 25491) <38800>* **PASSIONWORKS** [ ] [39]
– How can I refuse / Blue guitar / Johnny Moon / Sleep alone / Together now / Allies / (Beat by) Jealousy / Heavy heart / Love mistake / Language of love / Ambush. *(cd-iss. Feb88; CDEPC 25391)*
Sep 83. (12"m) *(TA 3695)* **HOW CAN I REFUSE. / BARRACUDA / LITTLE QUEEN** [ ] [-]
Oct 83. (7") *<04184>* **ALLIES. / TOGETHER NOW** [-] [83]

— While HEART looked for new contract ANN WILSON teamed up in '84 with MIKE RENO of LOVERBOY on 7" 'ALMOST PARADISE' from the film 'Footloose'.

Capitol Capitol

Jul 85. (7") *(CL 361) <5481>* **WHAT ABOUT LOVE?. / HEART OF DARKNESS** [ ] [10] May85

Oct 85. (lp/c) *(EJ 0372-1/-4) <12410>* **HEART** [50] [1] Jul85
– If looks could kill / What about love? / Never / These dreams / The wolf / All eyes / Nobody home / Nothin' at all / What he don't know / Shell shock. *(cd-iss. Feb86; CDP 746157-2) (re-iss. cd Sep94;)*

Oct 85. (7") *(CL 380) <5512>* **NEVER (remix). / SHELL SHOCK** [ ] [4] Sep85
(12"+=) *(12CL 380)* – ('A'extended remix).

Jan 86. (7") *<5541>* **THESE DREAMS. / SHELL SHOCK** [-] [1]

Mar 86. (7") *(CL 394)* **THESE DREAMS. / IF LOOKS COULD KILL (live)** [62] [-]
(12"+=) *(12CL 394)* – Shell shock.
(d7"+=) *(CLD 394)* – What about love? / Heart of darkness.

May 86. (7"/7"sha-pic-d) *(CL/+P 406) <5572>* **NOTHIN' AT ALL (remix). / THE WOLF** [ ] [1] Apr86
(12"+=) *(12CL 406)* – ('A'extended remix).

Jul 86. (7") *<5605>* **IF LOOKS COULD KILL. / WHAT HE DON'T KNOW** [-] [54]

Dec 86. (7") *<5654>* **THE BEST MAN IN THE WORLD. /** [-] [61]
(above from the film 'The Golden Child' starring Eddie Murphy)

May 87. (7") *(CL 448) <44002>* **ALONE. / BARRACUDA (live)** [3] [1]
(c-s+=/12"+=) *(CCL/12CL 448)* – Magic man (live).

May 87. (cd/c/lp) *(CD/TC+/ESTU 2032) <12546>* **BAD ANIMALS** [7] [5]
– Who will you run to / Alone / There's the girl / I want you so bad / Wait for the answer / Bad animals / You ain't so tough / Strangers of the heart / Easy target / RSVP. *(re-iss. cd Jul94;)*

Aug 87. (7") *<44040>* **WHO WILL YOU RUN TO. / MAGIC MAN** [-] [ ]

Sep 87. (7"/7"pic-d) *(CL/+P 457)* **WHO WILL YOU RUN TO. / NOBODY HOME** [30] [-]
('A'-Rock mix-12"+=) *(12CL 457)* – These dreams.
(cd-s++=) *(CDCL 457)* – ('A'-Rock mix).

Nov 87. (7") *(CL 473) <44089>* **THERE'S THE GIRL (remix). / BAD ANIMALS** [34] [12]
(12"+=) *(12CL 473)* – ('A'extended remix).
(c-s++=/cd-s++=) *(TC/CD CL 473)* – Alone.

Jan 88. (7"/7"g-f/7"pic-d) *(CL/+G/P 482)* **NEVER. / THESE DREAMS** [8] [-]
(12"+=) *(12CL 482)* – ('A'extended remix) / These dreams (version).
(etched-12") *(12CLE 482)* – These dreams (remixes & instrumental) / ('A'extended remix).
(ext-remix.cd-s+=) *(CDCL 482)* – Heart of darkness / If looks could kill (live).

Feb 88. (7") *<44116>* **I WANT YOU SO BAD. / EASY TARGET** [-] [49]

May 88. (7"/7"pic-d) *(CL/+P 487)* **WHAT ABOUT LOVE. / SHELL SHOCK** [14] [-]
(12"+=/12"g-f+=) *(12CL/+G 487)* – ('A'extended remix).
(cd-s+=) *(CDCL 487)* – Crazy on you / Dreamboat Annie.

Oct 88. (7") *(CL 507)* **NOTHIN' AT ALL (remix). / I'VE GOT THE MUSIC IN ME (live)** [38] [-]
(12"+=/12"pic-d+=) *(12CL/+P 507)* – I want you so bad (extended remix).
(cd-s++=) *(CDCL 507)* – ('A'extended).
(below with ZANDER (CHEAP TRICK) and from the film 'Tequila Sunrise')

Feb 89. (7"; ANN WILSON & ROBIN ZANDER) *(CL 525) <44288>* **SURRENDER TO ME. / (B-side by Dave Grusin featuring Lee Ritenour)** [ ] [6]
(12"+=/cd-s+=) *(12/CD CL 525)* – (by Diamond & Cerney).

Dec 89. (7") *<44488>* **HERE IS CHRISTMAS. /** [-] [ ]

Mar 90. (c-s/7") *(TC+/CL 569) <44507>* **ALL I WANNA DO IS MAKE LOVE TO YOU. / CALL OF THE WILD** [8] [2]
(12"+=/12"pic-d+=/12"clear+=/cd-s+=) *(12CL/12CLPD/12CLE/CDCL 569)* – Cruel tears.

Apr 90. (cd/c/lp) *(CD/TC+/ESTU 121) <91820>* **BRIGADE** [2] [3]
– Wild child / All I wanna do is make love to you / Secret / Tall, dark handsome stranger / I didn't want to need you / The night / Fallen from grace / Under the sky / Cruel nights / Stranded / Call of the wild / I want your world to turn / I love you. *(re-iss. Mar94 cd/c; CD/TC ESTU 2121)*

Jul 90. (7") *(CL 580) <44553>* **I DIDN'T WANT TO NEED YOU. / THE NIGHT** [47] [23] Jun90
(c-s+=/12"+=/12"pic-d+=/cd-s+=) *(TCCL/12CL/12CLPD/CDCL 580)* – The will to love.

Nov 90. (c-s/7") *(TC+/CL 595) <44621>* **STRANDED. / UNDER THE SKY** [60] [13] Sep90
(12"+=/12"pic-d+=/cd-s+=) *(12CL/12CLP/CDCL 595)* – I'll never stop loving you.

Feb 91. (c-s/7") *(TC+/CL 603) <44614>* **SECRET. / I LOVE YOU** [ ] [64] Jan91
(12"+=/cd-s+=) *(12/CD CL 603)* – How can I refuse (live).

Sep 91. (cd/c/lp) *(CD/TC+/ESTU 2154) <95797>* **ROCK THE HOUSE (live)** [45] [ ]
– Wild child / Fallen from grace / Call of the wild / How can I refuse / Shell shock / Love alive / Under the sky / The night / Tall, dark, handsome stranger / If looks could kill / Who will you run to / You're the voice / The way back machine / Barracuda.

Sep 91. (c-s/7") *(TC+/CL 624)* **YOU'RE THE VOICE (live). / CALL OF THE WILD (live)** [56] [ ]
(10"colrd+=/cd-s+=) *(10/CD CL 624)* – Barracuda (live).

— In 1992, the WILSONS were in splinter group LOVEMONGERS. The latter (which also included SUE ENNIS + FRANK COX) released a self-titled cd-ep on 'Capitol' w/tracks – Battle of evermore / Love of the common man / Papa was a rollin' stone / Crazy on you.

— **FERNANDO SAUNDERS** (b.17 Jan'54, Detroit, Mich.) – bass repl. ANDES / **DENNY FONGHEISER** (b.21 Apr'59, Almeda, Calif.) – drums repl. CARMASSI

Nov 93. (7"pic-d/c-s) *(CLPD/TCCL 700)* **WILL YOU BE THERE (IN THE MORNING). / THESE DREAMS (live)** [19] [-]
(cd-s) *(CDCLS 700)* – ('A'side) / What about love? / Risin' suspicion / Who will you run to.

Nov 93. (cd/c) *(CD/TC EST 2216) <99627>* **DESIRE WALKS ON** [32] [48]
– Desire / Black on black II / Back to Avalon / The woman in me / Rage / In walks the night / My crazy head / Ring them bells / Will you be there (in the morning) / Voodoo doll / Anything is possible / Avalon (reprise) / Desire walks on *[UK+=]* / La mujer que hay en mi / Te quedaras (en la manana).

Dec 93. (c-s) *<58041>* **WILL YOU BE THERE (IN THE MORNING) / RISIN' SUSPICION** [-] [39]

Mar 94. (cd-s) **BACK TO AVALON / WILL YOU BE THERE (IN THE MORNING) / ALL I WANNA DO IS MAKE LOVE TO YOU** [ ] [ ]

Aug 95. (cd/c) *(CD/TC EST 2258) <30489>* **THE ROAD HOME (live)** [ ] [87]
– Dreamboat Annie (fantasy child) / Dog and butterfly / (Up on) Cherry blossom road / Back to Avalon / Alone / These dreams / Love hurts / Straight on / All I wanna do is make love to you / Crazy on you / Seasons / The river / Barracuda / Dream of the archer. *(re-iss. Sep97; same)*

– compilations etc. –

Sep 87. (d-lp/c) *Epic; (460174-1/-4)* **HEART (THE BEST OF . . .)** [ ] [-]

Nov 88. (d-lp-box/d-c-box/d-cd-box) *Capitol; (CD/TC+/LOVE 2)* **WITH LOVE FROM HEART** (HEART / BAD ANIMALS) [ ] [-]

Nov 90. (t-cd-box)(t-lp-box) *Capitol; (795247-2)(HGIFT 1)* **HEART BOX SET** (HEART / BAD ANIMALS / BRIGADE) [ ] [-]

Nov 91. (d-cd) *Epic; (465222-2)* **DOG & BUTTERFLY / LITTLE QUEEN** [ ] [-]

May 94. (cd/c) *Columbia; (460174-2/-4)* **GREATEST HITS** [ ] [ ]

Apr 97. (cd) *Capitol; (7243 8 53376 2 8)* **THESE DREAMS – HEART'S GREATEST HITS** [35] [ ]
– Crazy on you / All I wanna do is make love to you / If looks could kill / Never / Alone / Who will you run to / Straight on (acoustic) / Magic man / What about love / Dreamboat Annie / Dog and butterfly (acoustic) / Nothin' at all / Heartless / Stranded / Will you be there (in the morning) / These dreams / Barracuda (live).

Jul 98. (cd) *Epic; (480561-2)* **THE DEFINITIVE COLLECTION** [ ] [-]

Jul 00. (cd) *Liberty; (527128-2)* **GREATEST HITS** [ ] [-]

HEARTBREAKERS (see under ⇒ THUNDERS, Johnny)

Reverend Horton HEAT

Born: JIM HEATH, Corpus Christi, Dallas, Texas. Initially conceived as a one-off gospel send-up, the hick REVEREND scoured the proverbial music biz congregation for a rhythm section of JIMBO WALLACE and TAZ BENTLEY. A hard-drinking, pot-smoking, card-gambling, women-chasing, bar-brawling kinda guy, The REVEREND's high-octane, CRAMPS-esque punkabilly sermons presented him as the 'Sub Pop' generation's answer to 50's wildman, JERRY LEE LEWIS. The preacher man's vinyl christening, 'SMOKE 'EM IF YOU GOT 'EM', certainly kicked up an unholy racket upon its release late in '91, whipping his boys into a beer-soaked rock'n'roll frenzy. The musical equivalent of tearing down Route 66 in a stolen Cadillac convertible high on Jack Daniels and Holy Water, 1993's 'THE FULL CUSTOM GOSPEL SOUNDS' even outstripped most of his heathen peers in the alternative/grunge sphere; the trio (with SCOTT CHURILLA replacing TAZ) were to support SOUNDGARDEN in '94. Subsequently making a pact with the Dev.. sorry, 'Interscope', The REV's next ten commandments (well er, thirteen actually!) came in the shape of the AL JOURGENSEN-produced 'LIQUOR IN THE FRONT' (1994), although the title was surely open to interpretation. Finally getting through to the non-believers and sinners among the American public, the REV hit the US Top 200 with his 1996 set, 'IT'S MARTINI TIME' (containing a cover of Bill Haley's 'ROCK THE JOINT'), a record that critically fell on its knees and suggested that the drink-saddled HEAT was in need of a bit of musical "heeeeaaling" himself. Likewise, 1998's 'SPACE HEATER', indicated that the REVEREND's reliable but increasingly predictable brand of metallic rockabilly was closer to anachronism than evangelism – praise the Lord!

Album rating: SMOKE 'EM IF YOU GOT 'EM (*7) / THE FULL CUSTOM GOSPEL SOUNDS (*8) / LIQUOR IN THE FRONT (*6) / IT'S MARTINI TIME (*4) / SPACE HEATER (*5)

REVEREND HORTON HEAT (b. JIM HEATH) – vocals, guitar / **JIMBO WALLACE** – stand-up bass / **TAZ BENTLEY** – drums

Sub Pop Sub Pop

Dec 90. (7",7"blue) *(<SP 96>)* **PSYCHOBILLY FREAKOUT. / BABY YOU-KNOW-WHO** [ ] [ ]

Nov 91. (10"lp,c,cd) *<(SP 25-177)>* **SMOKE 'EM IF YOU GOT 'EM** [ ] [ ]
– Bullet / I'm mad / Bad reputation / Put it to me straight / Marijuana / Baby, you-know-who / Eat steak / Love whip. *(cd+=/c+=)* – It's a dark day / Big dwarf rodeo / Psychobilly freakout / D for Dangerous.

Apr 93. (lp/cd) *(SP/+CD 248) <SP 202/+B>* **THE FULL CUSTOM GOSPEL SOUNDS** [ ] [ ]
– Wiggle stick / 400 bucks / The Devil's chasing me / Livin' on the edge (of Houston) / You can't get away from me / Beer / Big little baby / Lonesome train whistle / Bales of cocaine / Loaded gun / Nurture my pig! / Gin and tonic blues. *(cd re-iss. Sep98; same as US)*

May 94. (7") *<(SP 125-308)>* **CALIENTE. / (other side by SUPERSUCKERS)** [ ] [ ]

— **SCOTT CHURILLA** – drums; repl. TAZ

Interscope Interscope

Jul 94. (cd/c) *<(6544 92364-2/-4)>* **LIQUOR IN THE FRONT** [ ] [ ]
– Big sky / Baddest of the bad / One time for me / Five-o Ford / In your wildest dreams / The entertainer / Rockin' dog / Jezebel / I can't surf / Liquor, beer and wine / I could get used to it / Cruisin' for a bruisin' / Yeah right. *(cd re-iss. Jul96; IND 92364)*

— added guests **TIM ALEXANDER** – keyboards + **DAN PHILLIPS** – steel guitar

Dec 96. (cd/c) *<(INTD 90065-2/-4)>* **IT'S MARTINI TIME** [ ] [ ] Jul96
– Big red rocket of love / Slow / It's martini time / Generation why / Slingshot / Time to pray / Crooked cigarette / Rock the joint / Cowboy love / Now, right now / Spell on me / Or is it just me / Forbidden jungle / That's showbiz.

Sep 98. (cd) <(INTD 90168)> **SPACE HEATER**
– The price of San Jacinto / Lie detector / Hello Mrs. Darkness / Jimbo song / Revolution under foot / Starlight lounge / Goin' manic / Mi amor / For never more / Prophet stomp / Native tongue of love / Couch surfin' / Cinco de Mayo / Texas rock-a-billy rebel / Baby I'm drunk / Space heater.
Sep 98. (cd-s) <(IND 97357)> **LIE DETECTOR / STARLIGHT LOUNGE**

HEAVY METAL KIDS

Formed: London, England ... 1973 by GARY HOLTON, MICKEY WALLER, RON THOMAS and KEITH BOYCE. Taking a name originally suggested to FREE, this group were arguably more suited to such a kitsch moniker, their ragged hard rock sound and knowing lyrics attracting a cult fanbase centred in London. Signed to 'Atlantic', the group released their eponymous debut in summer '74, adding keyboard player DENNY PEYRONNEL and guitarist COSMO for the following year's 'ANVIL CHORUS'. The group (who were then known as The KIDS) were subsequently dropped by the label, taking a final pot shot at rock'n'roll fame with 1977's punk wannabe set, 'KITSCH', released on the 'RAK' label. The record failed to sell and The HEAVY METAL KIDS went their separate ways, HOLT frequenting the fringes of the rock scene until he took up an acting career, most famously as the role of cockney chancer, Wayne, in brickies-abroad series, 'Auf Wiedersehen Pet'. Like many before him, HOLT sadly died from a drugs overdose in the mid-80's.

Album rating: HEAVY METAL KIDS (*4) / ANVIL CHORUS (*4) / KITSCH (*4)

GARY HOLTON – vocals / **MICKEY WALLER** – guitar / **RON THOMAS** – bass / **KEITH BOYCE** – drums / **DENNY PEYRONEL** – keyboards / **COSMO** – guitar (the 6th member)

Atlantic Atlantic

Jul 74. (7") *(K 10465)* **HANGIN' ON. / ROCK'N'ROLL MAN** -
Aug 74. (lp) *(K 50047)* <7047> **HEAVY METAL KIDS**
– Hangin' on / Ain't it hard / It's the shame / Runaround eyes / We gotta go / Always plenty of women / Nature of my game / Kind of woman / Rock'n'roll man / We gotta go (reprise).
Oct 75. (7") *(K 10671)* **AIN'T NOTHING BUT A HOUSEPARTY. / YOU GOT ME ROLLIN'** -
Nov 75. (lp; as The KIDS) *(K 50143)* **ANVIL CHORUS** -
– Hard at the top / You got me rollin' / On the street / Situations outta control / Blue eyed boy / Old time boogie / The Turk (an'wot'e smokes) / Crisis / The cops are coming / The big fire.

— **JOHN SINCLAIR** – keyboards; repl. PEYRONEL

— **BARRY PAUL** – guitar; repl. WALLER

RAK not iss.

May 76. (7") *(RAK 234)* **SHE'S NO ANGEL. / HEY LITTLE GIRL** -
Jul 76. (7") *(RAK 239)* **FROM HEAVEN TO HELL AND BACK AGAIN. / BOOGIE WOOGIE** -
Nov 76. (lp) *(SRAK 523)* **KITSCH** -
– Overture / Chelsea kids / From Heaven to Hell and back again / Cry for me / She's no angel / Jackie the lad / Docking in / Squalliday Inn / Delirious. *(re-iss. Aug87 as 'CHELSEA KIDS' on 'Razor'; METALP 117) (cd-iss. Jun99 on 'Zoom Club'; ZCRCD 4)*
Jun 77. (7") *(RAK 258)* **CHELSEA KIDS. / JACKIE THE LAD** -
Sep 77. (7") *(RAK 262)* **DELIRIOUS. / CHELSEA KIDS** -

— HOLTON went on to a solo career (see above)

HEAVY PETTIN

Formed: Glasgow, Scotland ... 1980 as WEEPER, by drummer GARY MOAT, guitarist GORDON BONNAR and bassist BRIAN WAUGH. They issued one demo single, 'NOTHIN' TO LOSE', before adding frontman HAMIE (STEVE HAYMAN) and lead guitarist PUNKY MENDOZA, subsequently becoming HEAVY PETTIN. Picked up by 'Neat' for a singles deal, the group were soon the subject of major label interest with 'Polydor' eventually securing their signatures. A BRIAN MAY-produced debut set, 'LETTIN LOOSE', eventually appeared in late '83, its fairly tepid melodic hard-rock stylings hardly setting the metal scene alight. Nevertheless, the group were encouraged by a UK rock press eager for more home-grown success and subsequent touring with big guns like OZZY OSBOURNE certainly did HEAVY PETTIN no harm. A follow-up set, 'ROCK AIN'T DEAD' (1985), testified to their growing confidence and the band were tipped for great things. Greater than the Eurovision song contest anyhow, 'Polydor' incredibly entered new song, 'ROMEO', in a failed bid which did much to scupper the group's career. The accompanying album, 'THE BIG BANG', was duly shelved by the label and the group gave up the ghost (the record was given a belated release through 'FM Revolver' in late '89).

Album rating: LETTIN' LOOSE (*6) / ROCK AIN'T DEAD (*6) / THE BIG BANG (*5)

HAMIE (b. STEVE HAYMAN) – vocals / **PUNKY MENDOZA** – lead guitar / **GORDON BONNAR** – lead guitar / **BRIAN WAUGH** – bass / **GARY MOAT** – drums

Neat not iss.

Aug 82. (7") *(NEAT 17)* **ROLL THE DICE. / LOVE X LOVE** -

Polydor not iss.

Sep 83. (7") *(HEP 1)* **IN AND OUT OF LOVE. / LOVE ON THE RUN** -
(12"+=) *(HEPX 1)* – Roll the dice.
Oct 83. (lp) *(HEPLP 1)* **LETTIN LOOSE** 55 -
– In and out of love / Broken heart / Love on the run / Love times love / Victims of the night / Rock me / Shout it out / Devil in her eyes / Hell is beautiful.
Nov 83. (7"/ext.12") *(HEP/+X 2)* **ROCK ME. / SHADOWS OF THE NIGHT** -
Mar 84. (7"/7"sha-pic-d) *(HEP/+P 3)* **LOVE TIMES LOVE. / SHOUT IT OUT** 69 -
(12"+=) *(HEPX 3)* – Hell is beautiful.
Jul 85. (7") *(HEP 4)* **SOLE SURVIVOR. / CRAZY** -
(12"+=) *(HEPX 4)* – Northwinds.
Jul 85. (lp)(cd) *(HEPLP 4)(825 897-2)* **ROCK AIN'T DEAD** 81 -
– Rock ain't dead / Sole survivor / China boy / Lost in love / Northwinds / Angel / Heart attack / Dreamin' time / Walkin' with angels / Throw a party. *(cd+=)* – Crazy.
Apr 87. (7") *(POSP 849)* **ROMEO. / DON'T CALL IT LOVE** -
(12"+=) *(POSPX 849)* – City girl.

— folded early 1987, although they finally got below album released

FM Revolver not iss.

Nov 89. (lp/c/cd) *(WFFM LP/MC/XD 130)* **THE BIG BANG** -
– Born to burn / Romeo / Lonely people / This is America / Looking for love / Madonna on the radio! / Don't call it love / Heaven scent / Two hearts.

HECATE ENTHRONED

Formed: England ... 1993 as DAEMONUM by JON, MARC and NIGEL. A succession of line-up changes ensued, including JON's departure for a brief spell in CRADLE OF FILTH, before the trio began recording a demo tape, 'AN ODE FOR A HAUNTED WOOD'. Having renamed themselves HECATE ENTHRONED, they subsequently signed to US imprint 'Metal Blade' and released a remixed version of the demo entitled 'UPON PROMETHEAN SHORES' (1996). New recruits MICHAEL, PAUL and ROBERT were added for sophomore set, 'THE SLAUGHTER OF INNOCENCE – A REQUIEM FOR THE MIGHTY' (1997) while 'DARK REQUIEMS AND UNSILENT MASSACRE' followed in 1999. HECATE ENTHRONED's sinister blend of death, gothic and black metal was further updated on 'KINGS OF CHAOS' (2000). • **Note:** not to be confused with HECATE, a band on 'Zhark' records.

Album rating: UPON PROMETHEAN SHORES (*5) / THE SLAUGHTER OF INNOCENCE (*6) / DARK REQUIEMS ... AND UNSILENT MASSACRE (*5) / KING OF CHAOS (*5)

JON – vocals / **NIGEL** – guitar / **MARC** – guitar / **MICHAEL** – keyboards / **PAUL** – bass / **ROBERT** – drums

Blackend Metal Blade

Jun 96. (m-cd) *(BLACK 002CD)* *<14139>* **UPON PROMETHEAN SHORES** Aug97
– Promeathea – Thy darkest make of surreality / The crimson thorns (my immortal dreams) / A graven winter / To feed up thy dreams / An ode for a haunted wood / Through spellbinding branches (deepest witchcraft. outro). *(re-mast.Oct98 +=; BLACK 002MCD)* – Danse macabre (new version) / Luciferian death code.
Apr 97. (cd/lp) *(BLACK 004 CD/LP)* *<14144>* **THE SLAUGHTER OF INNOCENCE / A REQUIEM FOR THE DYING** Oct97
– Goetia / Beneath a December twilight / The spell of the winter forest / Aflame in the halls of blasphemy / A monument for eternal martyrdom / The slaughter of innocence – A requiem for the dying / At the haunted / Gallows of dawn / Christfire / Within the ruins of Eden / The dance macabre / Beckoning (an eternity of darkness).
May 98. (cd) *(BLACK 012CD)* *<14198>* **DARK REQUIEMS . . . AND UNSILENT MASSACRE** Mar99
– (untitled) / The pagan swords of legend / Centuries of wolfen hunger / Forever in ebony drowning / Upon the kingdom throne / For thee, in sinful obscurity / Dark requiems and unsilent massacre / Thy sorrow bequeathed / The scarlet forsaken / Ancient graveless dawn.

Blackend Cleopatra

Nov 99. (cd) *(BLACK 020CD)* *<1110>* **KING OF CHAOS** Feb00
– Miasma / Perjurer / Deceiving the deceiver / Malignant entity / Blessing in disguise / I am born / Exalted in depravity / Conquest complete / The downfall / Repent / Witch queen ascending.

(hed)pe

Formed: Orange County, California, USA ... late '93 (pronounced HEAD P.E.) by M.C.U.D. (pronounced 'Em Cee You Dee'), CHIZAD, WESSTYLE, MAWK, BC and DJ PRODUCT. Venomous guitar noise merchants akin to a fusion of The DEFTONES and RAGE AGAINST THE MACHINE, the annoyingly monikered band delivered an equally annoyingly-titled eponymous debut set in the fall of '97. (HED) PLANET EARTH were back crunching metal fine style with a long-awaited, although a tad disappointing follow-up LP, 'BROKE' (2000).

Album rating: (hed)pe (*7) / BROKE (*5)

M.C.U.D. (aka JAHRED SHAINE) – vocals / **CHIZAD** (aka CHAD BENEKOS) – guitar, vocals / **WESSTYLE** (aka WES GEER) – guitar / **MAWK** (aka MARK YOUNG) – bass / **B.C.** (aka BEN VAUGHT) – drums / **DJ PRODUCT** (aka DOUG BOYEE) – turntables

not iss. own label

1995. (cd-ep) **CHURCH OF REALITIES EP** -

Jive Jive

Oct 97. (cd/c) *(CHIP/HIPC 192)* **(hed)pe**
– P.O.S. / Ground / Serpent boy / Firsty / Tired of sleep (T.O.S.) / Darky / Schpamb / Ken 2012 / Circus / 33 / Hill / IFO / Bitches.
May 98. (cd-ep) **SERPENT BOY / SERPENT BOY (Rock da beat mix) / DARKY (machine mix) / EPILOGUE / SERPENT BOY (album mix)** -

Music For Nations Jive

Aug 00. (cd) *(CDMFN 262)* *<41710>* **BROKE** 73 63
– Killing time / Waiting to die / Feel good / Bartender / Crazy legs / Pac Bell / I got you / Boom (how you like that) / Swan dive / Stevie / Jesus / The meadow.

HELIX

Formed: Ontario, Canada . . . 1978 by BRIAN VOLLMER, brothers BRENT and BRIAN DOERNER, PAUL HACKMAN and KEITH ZURBRIGG. Following the release of their domestic debut in 1979, ZURBRIGG and BRENT DOERNER were subsequently replaced with MIKE VZELAC and LEO NIEBUDEK respectively. Again released on an independent label, a follow-up effort, 'WHITE LACE AND BLACK LEATHER' (1982), signalled a marked improvement in sound quality and the group's effervescent party-rock. A major label deal in place with 'Capitol', the group recruited new drummer, GREG NINZ, before recording 'NO REST FOR THE WICKED' (1983). Despite being reduced to a single guitar attack, following the departure of BRENT DOERNER, the group created one of the finest outings of their career. Another line-up change ensued prior to 'WALKIN' THE RAZORS EDGE' (1984), bassist VZELAC being replaced with DARYL GRAY. This was their only set to breach the US Top 100, despite an increasingly commercial approach on successive sets, 'LONG WAY TO HEAVEN' (1985) and 'WILD IN THE STREETS' (1987). Eventually dropped by their label, HELIX returned on 'G.W.R.' at the turn of the decade with 'BACK FOR ANOTHER TASTE', duly splitting in the early 90's after the tragic death of HACKMAN in a road accident ('I.R.S.' belatedly releasing 'IT'S BUSINESS DOING PLEASURE' in 1993).

Album rating: BREAKING LOOSE (*4) / WHITE LACE & BLACK LEATHER (*5) / NO REST FOR THE WICKED (*5) / WALKIN' THE RAZOR'S EDGE (*5) / LONG WAY TO HEAVEN (*5) / WILD IN THE STREETS (*5) / BACK FOR ANOTHER TASTE (*4) / IT'S BUSINESS DOING PLEASURE (*5)

BRIAN VOLLMER – vocals / **BRENT DOERNER** – guitar / **PAUL HACKMAN** – guitar / **KEITH 'Bert' ZURBRIGG** – bass / **BRIAN DOERNER** – drums

not iss. — H&S

1979. (lp) *<HS 101>* **BREAKING LOOSE** [-] [ ] Canada
– I could never leave / Don't hide your love / Down in the city / Crazy women / Billy Oxygen / Here I go again / You're a woman now / Wish I could be there.

— **MIKE VZELAC** – bass; repl. KEITH

— **LEO NIEBUDEK** – guitar; repl. BRENT

Logo — Lark

Jun 82. (lp) *(MOGO 4013) <INL 3534>* **WHITE LACE & BLACK LEATHER** [ ] [ ]
– Breaking loose / It's too late / Long distance heartbreak / Time for a change / Hangman's tree / It's what I wanted / Mainline / Women, whiskey & sin / Thoughts that bleed.

— **GREG HINZ** – drums (ex-STARCHILD) repl. LEO

Capitol — Capitol

Aug 83. (lp/c) *(EST/TC-EST 400185-1/-4) <12281>* **NO REST FOR THE WICKED** [ ] [ ]
– Does a fool ever learn / Let's all do it tonight / Heavy metal love / Check out the love / No rest for the wicked / Don't get mad get even / Ain't no high like rock'n'roll / Dirty dog / Never want to lose you / White lace and black leather.

Oct 83. (7"/7"pic-d) *(CL/+P 314) <5294>* **HEAVY METAL LOVE. / NO REST FOR THE WICKED** [ ] [ ]
(12"+=) *(12CL 314)* – ('A'extended).

— **DARYL GRAY** – bass, vocals; repl. MIKE

Aug 84. (7") *(CL 339) <5391>* **ROCK YOU. / YOU KEEP ME ROCKIN'** [ ] [ ]

Oct 84. (lp/c) *(EJ 240183-1/-4) <12362>* **WALKIN' THE RAZOR'S EDGE** [ ] [69] Aug84
– Rock you / Young & wreckless / Animal house / Feel the fire / When the hammer falls / Gimme gimme good lovin' / My kind of rock / (Make me do) Anything you want / Six strings, nine lives / You keep me rockin'.

Jan 85. (7"/7"pic-d) *(CL/+P 349) <5423>* **GIMME GIMME GOOD LOVIN'. / WHEN THE HAMMER FALLS** [ ] [ ]

Jun 85. (7") *<5490>* **BANGIN' OFF-A-THE BRICKS. / DEEP CUTS THE KNIFE** [-] [ ]

Oct 85. (lp/c) *(EJ 240348-1/-4) <12411>* **LONG WAY TO HEAVEN** [ ] [ ] Jun85
– The kids are shakin' / Deep cuts the knife / Ride the rocket / Long way to Heaven / House on fire / Christine / Without you (Jasmine's song) / School of hard knocks / Don't touch the merchandise / Bangin' off-a-the bricks.

Oct 87. (7") *(CL 468) <44073>* **WILD IN THE STREETS. / KISS IT GOODBYE** [ ] [ ]
(12"+=) *(12CL 468)* –

Dec 87. (lp/c) *(EST/TC-EST 2046) <46920>* **WILD IN THE STREETS** [ ] [ ]
– Wild in the streets / Never gonna stop the rock / Dream on / What ya bringin' to the party / High voltage kids / Give 'em hell / Shot full of love / Love hungry eyes / She's too tough / Kiss it goodbye.

Jan 88. (7") *<44096>* **WHAT YA BRINGIN' TO THE PARTY. / DREAM ON** [-] [ ]

G.W.R. — Grudge

Aug 90. (cd/c/lp) *(GW CD/TC/LP 102) <4521>* **BACK FOR ANOTHER TASTE** [ ] [ ]
– The storm / That's life / Heavy metal cowboys / Back for another taste / Midnight express / Give it to you / Running wild in the 21st century / Breakdown / Wild in the streets / Rockin' rollercoaster / Good to the last drop / Wheels of thunder.

Oct 90. (7") *(GWR 18)* **WILD IN THE STREETS. /** [ ] [ ]
below was their last recording due to HACKMAN tragic death on tour

I.R.S. — Intercord

Aug 93. (cd) *(CDIRS 986969) <Q 2570>* **IT'S BUSINESS DOING PLEASURE** [ ] [ ]
– That day is gonna come / Tug o' war / Wrong side of bed / Can't even afford to die / Misery loves company / Look me straight in the heart / Trust the feeling / Love is a crazy game / Sleepin' in the doghouse again / Mad mad world.

HELLACOPTERS

Formed: Stockholm, Sweden . . . 1994 by drummer/songwriter turned guitarist, NICKE ANDERSON (aka NICK ROYALE), as a stop-gap project while his regular band, The ENTOMBED, tried to obtain a new record deal. NICKE enlisted the help of childhood chum, ROBERT ERIKSSON (bass), ASK DREGEN (guitarist of the BACKYARD BABIES) and drummer KENNY HAKANSSON, indulging his passion for bluesy, anthemic punk/metal in the vein of MC5 or KISS. The mainman subsequently made this bunch a full-time project in '97 after finally leaving his beloved ENTOMBED. It was on the 14th & 15th of June that year that The HELLACOPTERS were to support their heroes KISS in Stockholm. Significantly more prolific than ANDERSON's previous outfit, the airborne metallers have released a plethora of 45's (on various labels, including their own 'White Jazz') alongside three albums to date, 'SUPERSHITTY TO THE MAX!' (1996), 'PAYIN' THE DUES' (1997) and 'DISAPPOINTMENT BLUES' (1998). • **Covered:** THE CREEPS (Social Distortion) / I GOT A RIGHT (Iggy & The Stooges) / LOW DOWN SHAKIN' CHILLS (Nomads) / AIN'T NOTHIN' TO DO (Dead Boys) / AMERICAN RUSE (MC5) / WORKING FOR MCA (Lynyrd Skynyrd) / A MAN AND A HALF (Wilson Pickett) / HER STRUT (Bob Seger) / GIMME SHELTER (Rolling Stones) / I WANT A LIP (April Stevens) / IT'S ALL MOVING FASTER (Electric Frankenstein) / IT'S TOO LATE (New York Dolls) / ANGEL DUST (Venom) / CITY SLANG + HEAVEN (Sonic Rendezvous Band) / SPEED FREAK (Motorhead) / 455 SD + TIME TO FALL (Radio Birdman) / YOU'RE TOO GOOD (TO ME BABY) (Silky Hargreaves) / MASTER RACE ROCK (Dictators) / A HOUSE IS NOT A MOTEL (Love) / BULLET (Misfits) / TELEVISION ADDICT (Victims) / EVIL WOMEN (Black Sabbath) / ALL AMERICAN MAN (Kiss) / UNGROUNDED CONFUSION (Flaming Sideburns) / COLD NIGHT FOR ALLIGATORS (Roky Erickson) / STAB YOR BACK (Damned) / GET READY + WHOLE LOTTA SHAKIN' GOIN' ON IN MY HEART (SINCE I MET YOU) (Smokey Robinson) / YOU LEFT THE WATER RUNNING (Rick Hall, Oscar Franck & Dan Penn).

Album rating: SUPERSHITTY TO THE MAX! (*7) / PAYIN' THE DUES (*7) / DISAPPOINTMENT BLUES mini collection (*5) / GRANDE ROCK (*7) / HIGH VISIBILITY (*8)

NICKE ANDERSON (aka NICK ROYALE) – vocals, guitar (of/ex-ENTOMBED) / **ASK DREGEN** – guitar / **ROBERT ERIKSSON** – bass / **KENNY HAKANSSON** – drums

Psych-out — not iss.

Feb 95. (7") *(Psych 001)* **KILLING ALLAN. / FERRYTALE / THE CREEPS** [ ] [-]

Freak Scene — not iss.

Dec 95. (7"ep) *(Freak 3)* **1995. / TILT CITY / FREESPEEDIN'** [ ] [-]
(re-iss. Jan98 on 'Get Hip'; GH 201)

White Jazz — not iss.

Jun 96. (cd/clear-lp) *(JAZZ 001 CD/LP)* **SUPERSHITTY TO THE MAX!** [ ] [-]
– (Gotta get some action) Now! / 24h hell / Fire fire fire / Born broke / Bore me / It's too late *[lp-only]* / Tab / How could I dare / Didn't stop us / Random riot / Fake baby / Ain't no time / Such a blast / Sprock in my rocket. *(cd re-iss. Jan98; same) (cd re-iss. Apr98 on 'Toy Factory'; TFCK 87143) <US-iss.Nov98 on 'Man's Ruin'; MR 22>*

Oct 96. (7",7"red) *(Pon 007)* **WHAT ARE YOU. / LOWDOWN / ANOTHER PLACE** [-] [-] Sweden
(above issued on 'Planet Of Noise')

Oct 96. (clear-d7"ep/cd-ep) *(WJ 002CD)* **(GOTTA GET SOME ACTION) NOW! / FREEWAY TO HELL / GHOUL SCHOOL / LOW DOWN SHAKIN' CHILLS** [ ] [-]
(re-iss. Dec97; same)

Nov 96. (7") *(BA 001)* **MISANTHROPIC HIGH. / I GOT A RIGHT** [ ] [-]
(above single on 'Bad Afro')

Aug 97. (10"/cd-s; shared with GLUECIFER) *(JAZZ 666/+CD)* **RESPECT THE ROCK** [ ] [-]
– You are nothing / Kick this one slow / Another place.

— in Aug'97, they also collaborated with ELECTRIC FRANKENSTEIN on the 7" EP for 'Frank' records; *Frank 004)*

— added **BOBBY LEE FLETT** – piano

Sep 97. (cd/purple-lp) *(JAZZ 004 CD/LP)* **PAYIN' THE DUES** [ ] [-]
– You are nothin' / Like no ther man / Looking at me / Riot on the rocks / Hey! / Soulseller / Where the action is / Twist action / Colapso nervioso / Psyched out and furious. *(bonus live lp/cd+=)* – Action de grace / You are nothin' / Disappointment blues / Born broke / Alright already now / Down right blue / City slang *[lp-only]* / (Gotta get some action) Now! / Soulseller. *(cd re-iss. Apr98 on 'Toy Factory'; TFCK 87142)*

Nov 97. (7") *(SP 003)* **RIOT ON THE ROCKS. / TELEVISION ADDICT** [-] [-] Sweden
(above issued on 'Safety-Pin')

Apr 98. (7") *(7JAZZ 008)* **SOULSELLER. / AIN'T NOTHIN' TO DO** [ ] [-]
(cd-s) *(JAZZ 008CD)* – (same as above).

Jul 98. (7") *(7JAZZ 010)* **HEY! / HER STRUT** [ ] [-]
(cd-s+=) *(JAZZ 010CD)* – (same as above)

— now without DREGEN who was still in the BACKYARD BABIES

Flapping Jet — not iss.

Jul 98. (7",7"pic-d) *(FJ 007)* **LIKE NO OTHER MAN. / GIMME SHELTER** [ ] [-]

Munster — not iss.

Aug 98. (7"blue) *(7112)* **CITY SLANG. / BORN BROKE** [ ] [-]
(re-iss. Nov99; same)

Estrus — Estrus

Aug 98. (7",7"colrd) *(<ES7 122>)* **LOOKING AT ME. / ROCK HAMMER** [ ] [ ]

Rocketdog not iss.

Nov 98. (7") *(RD-07001)* **ROCK'N'ROLL JIHAD** -
– Times are low / NITWITZ: Jackass.

Bang not iss.

Dec 98. (7"colrd) *(BANG 004)* **DIRTY WOMEN** -
– I got the shakes / Evil woman.

Anyway not iss.

Mar 99. (7") *(AWR 49)* **LOWERED PENTANGLES. / (other by New Bomb Turks)** -

Man's Ruin Sub Pop

Mar 99. (cd; split with GLUECIFER) *(MR 117)* *<SP 476>* **RESPECT THE ROCK AMERICA**
– American ruse / Working for MCA / A man and a half / Her strut / Doggone your bad luck soul / (others by GLUCIFER). *(re-iss. Aug00; same)*

Mar 99. (10"ep) *(MR 155)* **DOGGONE YOUR BAD LUCK SOUL** -
– (same tracks as above).

Butcher's Hook not iss.

Mar 99. (7") *(HOOK 004)* **A HOUSE IS NOT A MOTEL. / (other by the Powder Monkeys)** -

— guests on below were **SCOTT MORGAN** – lead guitar, vocals + **DANIEL REY** – lead guitar

Sub Pop Sub Pop

Apr 99. (7") *<(SP 454)>* **DOWN RIGHT BLUE. / THANKS FOR NOTHING**

White Jazz Sub Pop

May 99. (cd/lp) *(JAZZ 016 CD/LP)* *<SP 474>* **GRANDE ROCK** Jun99
– Action de Grace / Alright already now / Move right out of here / Welcome to Hell / The electric eel index / Paul Stanley / Angel dust *[lp-only]* / The Devil stole the beat from the Lord / Dogday mornings / Venus in force / 5 vs. 7 / Lonely / Renvoyer.

Aug 99. (7"/cd-s)<7"pic-d> *(7JAZZ 021/+CD)* *<SP 477>* **THE DEVIL STOLE THE BEAT FROM THE LORD. / HOLIDAY CRAMPS / BE NOT CONTENT** Aug99

Oct 99. (7"/cd-s) *(7JAZZ 023/+CD)* **MOVE RIGHT OUT OF HERE. / HEART OF THE MATTER** -
(cd-s+=) *(JAZZ 023CDL)* – Makes it alright / The Devil stole the beat from the Lord (live).
(10"++=) *(JAZZ 023)* – Alright already now (live).

Gearhead not iss.

Jun 99. (7") *(none)* **CRIMSON BALLROOM. / (other by Rocket From The Crypt)** - - fanz

Jul 99. (7") *(none)* **DISAPPOINTMENT BLUES. / (split w/ BLA TAGET)** - - Norway

— added **ROBERT 'STRINGS' DAHLQVIST** – guitar
(below was a shared effort with the QUADRAJETS)

not iss. Estrus

Oct 99. (7") *<ES7 144>* **Quadracopters: THINK IT OVER. / Hellajets: I WASN'T BORN IN A HALLWAY** -

Feb 00. (7"; as SCOTT MORGAN & THE HELLACOPTERS) *<SP 483>* **SLOW DOWN TAKE A LOOK. / 16 WITH A BULLET** -

Munster Munster

Nov 99. (7") *(MR 7112)* **CITY SLANG. / BORN BROKE**

Safety Pin Safety Pin

Jun 00. (7") *(SP 017)* **MASTER RACE ROCK. / Powder Monkeys: TWO TUB MAN** -

Universal Polygram

Oct 00. (cd-s) *(158 349-2)* **TOYS AND FLAVORS / A CROSS FOR CAIN** -
(7"-iss. on 'Sweet Nothings'; 7SN 002)

Oct 00. (cd) *(159 737-2)* *<1003>* **HIGH VISIBILITY** Mar01
– Hopeless case of a kid in denial / Baby borderline / Sometimes I don't know / Toys and flavours / You're too good (to me baby) / Throw away heroes / So song unheard / Truckload of nuthin' / A heart without a home / No one is gonna do it for you / I wanna touch / Hurtin' time / Envious. *(d-lp-iss.Oct00 on 'Sweet Nothing'; SNLP 006)*

Jan 01. (10"m-lp)(m-cd) *(<FRO 1003>)(<AFROCD 008>)* **WHITE TRASH SOUL** (split w/ FLAMING SIDEBURNS)
– Whole lotta shakin' goin' on in my heart (since I met you) / Get ready / Ungrounded confusion / (others by the FLAMING SIDEBURNS).
(above issued on 'Bad Afro')

Jan 01. (cd-s) *(158 553-2)* **HOPELESS CASE OF A KID IN DENIAL / COLD NIGHT FOR ALLIGATORS / (I'M A) STEALER** - - Sweden

Mar 01. (cd-ep) *(158801-2)* **FLIGHTCASE** -
– Hopeless case of a kid in denial / A cross for Cain / Cold night for alligators / (I'm a) Stealer / Like no other man (live).

May 01. (cd-s) *(158 782-2)* **NO SONG UNHEARD / HAVE MERCY ON THE CHILDREN / YOU LEFT THE WATER RUNNING** - - Sweden

Fandango not iss.

Mar 01. (7") *(fr-017)* **STAB YOR BACK. / Adam West: NEAT NEAT NEAT** -

– compilations, others, etc. –

Sep 98. (cd) *Au-Go-Go; (<ANDA 246CD>)* **DISAPPOINTMENT BLUES** (B-sides)
– Long gone losers / Freeway to Hell / Heaven / Speed freak / Disappointment blues / Ferrytale / 455 SD. *(lp-iss.Oct98; ANDA 246) (re-iss. Nov98 on 'White Jazz' 10"lp/cd; JAZZ 015 LP/CD)*

Jan 99. (7"pic-d) *007; <#20>* **IT'S NOT A LONG WAY DOWN. / FREEDOM TO HELL (live) / LONG GONE LOSERS (live)** - - mail-o

Feb 99. (7") *Fandango; <fr-015>* **TWIST ACTION. / FAKE BABY** - - tour

HELLANBACH

Formed: Newcastle-upon-Tyne, England . . . 1980 by JIMMY BRASH, DAVE PATTON, KEV CHARLTON and STEVE WALKER. Although the band started out as NWOBHM foot soldiers, their debut long-player, 'NOW HEAR THIS', brought widespread comparisons to VAN HALEN. Though the media reaction was muted, their label, 'Neat', persevered with a second set, 'THE BIG H'.

Album rating: NOW HEAR THIS (*5) / THE BIG H (*4)

JIMMY BRASH – vocals / **DAVE PATTON** – guitar / **KEV CHARLTON** – bass / **STEVE WALKER** – drums

Neat not iss.

Mar 83. (12"ep) *(NEAT 25-12)* **ALL SYSTEMS GO** -
– All systems go / Knocked out / Could have done better / Hot 'n' heavy express.

1983. (lp) *(NEAT 1006)* **NOW HEAR THIS** -
– Dancin' / Times are getting harder / Look at me / All systems go / Maybe tomorrow / Motivated by desire / Taken by surprise / Let's get this show on the road / Kick it out / All the way / Everybody wants to be a cat.

1984. (lp) *(NEAT 1019)* **THE BIG H** -
– Beaten to the bone / Main man / Nobody's fool / Bandits run / S.P.G.C. / Saturday night / Panic state O.D. / Daddy dig those cats / When all is said and done / Urban paranoia.

— split soon after above

HELLHAMMER (see under ⇒ CELTIC FROST)

HELLION

Formed: Los Angeles, California, USA . . . 1982 by vocalist ANN BOLEYN, who, after much personnel changes, completed the line-up with ALAN BARLAM, RAY SCHENCK, BILL SWEET and SEAN KELLY. Though American based, the band's musical strategy owed more to European heavy metal, HELLION subsequently securing a deal with the fledgling London-based label, 'Music For Nations'. Early in '84, they unleashed their eponymous debut, though business difficulties led to the original line-up falling apart. This left BOLEYN to pick up the pieces, the songstress enlisting the services of CHET THOMPSON, ALEX CAMPBELL and GREG PECKA to record a belated follow-up, 'SCREAMS IN THE NIGHT' (1987). However, she subsequently convinced her original band to return, albeit without SWEET, who was replaced by DAVE DUTTON for their third effort, the mini-album, 'POSTCARDS FROM THE ASYLUM' (also 1987). This contained a version of Judas Priest's 'EXCITER', although the bulk of the original material struggled to meet the same standard. In 1989, BOLEYN finished her novel, 'The Black Dragon', which translated into her final vinyl as 'THE BLACK BOOK' (1990).

Album rating: HELLION mini (*4) / SCREAMS IN THE NIGHT (*5) / POSTCARDS FROM THE ASYLUM mini (*4) / THE BLACK BOOK (*4) / LIVE AND WELL IN HELL (*3) / UP FROM THE DEPTHS (*3)

ANN BOLEYN – vocals / **ALAN BARLAM** – guitar / **RAY SCHENCK** – guitar / **BILL SWEET** – bass / **SEAN KELLY** – drums

Music For Nations New Renaissance

Jan 84. (m-lp) *(MFN 15)* **HELLION** -
– Break the spell / Don't take no / Backstabber / Lookin' for a good time / Driving hard / Up from the depths. *<US-iss.Jun87; NRR 28>*

— **BOLEYN** with new line-up, **CHET THOMPSON** – guitar, sitar / **ALEX CAMPBELL** – bass / **GREG PECKA** – drums

Mar 87. (lp) *(MFN 73)* *<NRR 23>* **SCREAMS IN THE NIGHT**
– Screams in the night / Bad attitude / Better off dead / Upside down guitar solo – The hand / Explode / Easy action / Put the hammer down / Stick 'em / Children of the night / The tower of air. *(cd-iss. Aug89; CDMFN 73)*

— originals re-form bar **DAVE DUTTON** – bass; who repl. SWEET

Feb 88. (m-lp/m-c) *(MFN/TMFN 82)* *<NRR/NRC 36>* **POSTCARDS FROM THE ASYLUM** Nov87
– Nevermore! / The evil one / Exciter / Run for your life.

— **BOLEYN** was again on her own using session people

Music For Nations Restless

Oct 90. (cd/c/lp) *(CD/T+/MFN 108)* *<72505>* **THE BLACK BOOK**
– Breakdown / The black book / Stormrider / Living in hell / The discovery / Losing control / Arrest . . . jail . . . bail / Deamon attack / Conspiracy / Amnesty / The warming / The room behind the door / The atonement / Immigrant song.

— ANN retired from music, having earlier written a novel, 'The Black Dragon' to coincide with the above album; however . . .

Sep 98. (cd-ep) *<NRR 101>* **THE WITCHING HOUR** -
– The witching hour / Morning star / The hand / Children of the night.

Nov 98. (cd) *<NRR 103>* **LIVE AND WELL IN HELL** -
– Impromptu sound check / Break the spell / Don't waste your love (on me) / Crowd rap I / Backstabber / Crowd rap II / Run for your life / Crowd rap III / Don't take no for an answer / Crowd rap IV / Fire / Crowd rap V / Driving hard.

Dec 98. (cd) *<NRR 104>* **UP FROM THE DEPTHS** -
– Nightmares in daylight / Backstabber / Fire / Up from the depths / Break the spell / Nevermore / The evil one / Exciter / Run for your life.

HELLOWEEN

Formed: Hamburg, Germany ... 1982 out of local bands IRON FIST and SECOND HELL by MICHAEL WEIKATH, KAI HANSEN, MARKUS GROBKOFF and INGO SCHWICHTENBERG. A few years into their career, they were picked up by native label, 'Noise International', releasing an eponymous mini-LP in early '85. Press interest was gathering momentum by the time of the band's follow-up set, 'WALLS OF JERICHO', issued the same year. With the addition of teenage vocalist MICHAEL KISKE, HELLOWEEN's consumate power-metal assault was in full flight. A cross between ROB HALFORD and BRUCE DICKINSON, KISKE's throbbing larynx was the driving force behind the powerful, yet ingeniously melodic 'KEEPER OF THE SEVEN KEYS' (1987). Critical darlings, the band were equally popular with grassroots metal fans and the album featured highly in many end of year metal polls. HELLOWEEN also matched IRON MAIDEN in terms of live spectacle, the group playing to sell-out crowds all over Europe. In the midst of this whirlwind success, the band found time to record the second instalment of 'KEEPER ...', the record hitting the UK Top 30 in the Autumn of '88. After completing a live set with newcomer JORN ELLERBROOK (which also made the Top 30), HANSEN bailed out to form GAMMA RAY, his replacement being ROLAND GRAPOW. The band finally got it together for a long-awaited studio set, 'PINK BUBBLES GO APE', finally being delivered by 'E.M.I.' in 1991. The record, and its 1993 follow-up, 'CHAMELEON', were a major disappointment to fans and critics alike, HELLOWEEN suffering further trauma when WEIKATH clashed with KISKE and SCHWICHTERBERG. A beleaguered line-up of WEIKATH, GROBKOFF, and new members ANDI DERIS and ULLI KUSCH, completed a new album in 1994 for 'Raw Power', the unfortunately-titled, 'MASTER OF THE RINGS'. Against the odds, HELLOWEEN are still peddling their fantasy-metal to a core audience, releasing two albums in 1996, 'TIME OF THE OATH' (aarrgghh!) and 'HIGH LIVE'. Longtime fans and critics were generally in agreement that 1998's 'BETTER THAN RAW' ranked as the band's most accomplished and fully realised album since HANSEN's departure while 'METAL JUKEBOX' (1999) featured a choice array of 70's covers (including Abba's 'LAY ALL YOUR LOVE ON ME', Focus' 'HOCUS POCUS', Alex Harvey's 'FAITH HEALER' and Bowie's 'SPACE ODDITY'), presumably not all of which their diehard metal fanbase would be familiar with. Come the new millennium, HELLOWEEN had signed a new deal with 'Nuclear Blast', releasing 'THE DARK SIDE' in late 2000. • **Songwriters:** WEIKATH or HANSEN (and later KISKE), except BLUE SUEDE SHOES (Carl Perkins).

Album rating: HELLOWEEN mini (*4) / WALLS OF JERICHO (*4) / JUDAS mini (*4) / KEEPER OF THE SEVEN KEYS (*8) / KEEPER OF THE SEVEN KEYS PART II (*7) / LIVE IN THE UK (*4) / PINK BUBBLES GO APE (*4) / THE BEST, THE REST, THE RARE collection (*6) / CHAMELEON (*4) / MASTER OF THE RINGS (*5) / THE TIME OF THE OATH (*5) / HIGH LIVE (*5) / BETTER THAN RAW (*5) / METAL JUKEBOX (*4) / THE DARK RIDE (*6)

MICHAEL WEIKATH – vocals, guitar / **KAI HANSEN** – guitar / **MARKUS GROBKOFF** – bass / **INGO SCHWICHTENBERG** – drums

Noise Int. — R.C.A.

Feb 85. (m-lp) *(N 0021)* **HELLOWEEN** [-] [-] German
– Starlight / Murderer / Warrior / Victim of fate / Cry for freedom. *(UK-iss.Oct89; NUK 021)*

Dec 85. (lp) *(N 0032)* **WALLS OF JERICHO** [-] [-] German
– Walls of Jericho / Ride the sky / Reptile / Guardians / Phantoms of death / Metal invaders / Gorgar / Heavy metal (is the law) / How many tears. *(UK-iss.Oct89 cd/c/lp; CD/ZC+/NUK 032)*

— added **MICHAEL KISKE** – vocals

Sep 86. (m-lp) *(N 0048)* <88561-8128-1> **JUDAS** [ ] [ ] Sep87
– Judas / Ride the sky / Guardians / Victim of fate (live)* / Cry for freedom (live)*. *(re-iss. as 12" Sep89; 12NUK 022)* ; omits*.

May 87. (lp) *(N 0057)* <6399> **KEEPER OF THE SEVEN KEYS – PART I** [-] [ ]
– Initiation / I'm alive / A little time / Twilight of the gods / A tale that wasn't right / Judas / Future world / Halloween / Follow the sign. *(UK-iss.Oct89 lp/c)(pic-lp; NUK/ZCNUK 057)(CDNUK 057)*

— <below mini-lp released on 'Combat Core'>

Sep 87. (12"/12"pic-d) *(NUK/+PD 083)* **FUTURE WORLD. / STARLIGHT / A LITTLE TIME** [ ] [-]

Aug 88. (7"white) *(N 0116-5)* **DR. STEIN. / SAVAGE / LIVIN' AIN'T NO CRIME** [57] [-]
(12"+=/12"pic-d+=/3"cd-s+=) *(N 0116 1/1P/53)* – Victim of fate.

Sep 88. (cd/c/lp) *(CD/ZC+/NUK 117)* <8529> **KEEPER OF THE SEVEN KEYS – PART II** [24] [ ]
– Invitation / Eagle fly free / You always walk alone / Rise and fall / Dr. Stein / We got the right / March of time / I want out / Keeper of the seven keys. *(pic-lp.Oct89; NUKPD 117) (cd+=)* – Save us.

Oct 88. (7"/7"pic-d) <c-ep> *(7/P HELLO 2)* <8732> **I WANT OUT. / DON'T RUN FOR COVER** [69] [ ]
(12"+=/3"cd-s+=) *(12/3 HELLO 2)* – Save us.

— added **JORN ELLERBROOK** – keyboards

E.M.I. — R.C.A.

Apr 89. (cd/c/lp) *(CD/TC+/EMC 3558)* <9709> **LIVE IN THE UK (live)** [26] [ ]
<US-title 'I WANT OUT – LIVE'>
– A little time / Dr. Stein / Future world / Rise and fall / We got the right / I want out / How many tears.

— (Feb'89) **ROLAND GRAPOW** – guitar repl. HANSEN who joined GAMMA RAY

Feb 91. (c-s/7") *(TC+/EM 178)* **KIDS OF THE CENTURY. / BLUE SUEDE SHOES** [56] [ ]
(10"+) *(10EMS 178)* – (interview).
(12"++=/cd-s++=) *(12EMS/CDEM 178)* – Shit and lobster.

Mar 91. (cd/c/lp) *(CD/TC+/EMC 3588)* **PINK BUBBLES GO APE** [41] [-]
– Pink bubbles go ape / Kids of the century / Back on the streets / Number one / Heavy metal hamsters / Going home / Someone's crying / Mankind / I'm doin' fine – Crazy man / The chance / Your turn. *(<cd re-iss. Aug96 on 'Essential'; ESMCD 411>)*

Jun 93. (cd/c/lp) *(CD/TC+/EMD 1045)* **CHAMELEON** [ ] [-]
– First time / When the sinner / I don't wanna cry no more / Crazy cat / Giants / Windmill / Revolution now / San Francisco (be sure to wear flowers in your hair) / In the night / Music / Step out of Hell / I believe / Longing. *(re-iss. Dec94 on 'Fame' cd/c; CDFA/TCFA 3308) (<cd re-iss. Aug96 on 'Essential'; ESMCD 412>)*

— **ANDI DERIS** – vocals (ex-PINK CREAM 69) repl. KISKE

— **ULI KUSCH** – drums; repl. SCHWICHENBERG

Raw Power — Raw Power

Aug 94. (cd/c/lp) *(<RAW CD/MC/LP 101>)* **MASTER OF THE RINGS** [ ] [ ]
– Irritation / Sole survivor / Where the rain grows / Why? / Mr. Ego / Perfect gentlemen / The game is on / Secret alibi / Take me home / In the middle of a heartbeat / Still we go. *(pic-lp.Apr95; RAWPD 101) (cd re-iss. Jan01 on 'Castle'; CMRCD 118)*

Mar 96. (cd/c/lp) *(<RAW CD/MC/LP 109>)* **THE TIME OF THE OATH** [ ] [ ]
– We burn / Steel tormentor / Wake up the mountain / Power / Forever and one (Neverland) / Before the war / A million to one / Anything my mama don't like / Kings will be kings / Mission motherland / If I knew / The time of the oath. *(cd re-iss. Jan01 on 'Castle'; CMRCD 119)*

Apr 96. (cd-ep) *(RAWX 1001)* **MR. EGO (TAKE ME DOWN)** [ ] [-]
– Mr. Ego (take me down) / Where the rain grows / Can't fight your desire / Star invasion.

Apr 96. (cd-ep) *(RAWX 1002)* **PERFECT GENTLEMAN / COLD SWEAT / SILICON DREAMS / GAPOWSKI'S MALMSUITE 1001 (IN D DOLL)** [ ] [-]

Apr 96. (cd-ep) *(RAWX 1014)* **POWER / WE BURN / RAIN / ON YOUR WAY** [ ] [-]

Sep 96. (d-cd/d-lp) *(<RAW CD/VF 116>)* **HIGH LIVE (live)** [ ] [ ]
– We burn / Wake up the mountain / Sole survivor / The chance / Why / Eagle fly, free / The time of the oath / Future world / Dr. Stein / Before the war / Mr. Ego (take me down) / Power / Where the rain grows / In the middle of a heartbeat / Perfect gentleman / Steel tormentor. *(d-cd re-iss. Jan01 on 'Castle'; CMDDD 121)*

Raw Power — Velvel

Apr 98. (cd/c) *(RAW CD/MC 135)* <79736> **BETTER THAN RAW** [ ] [ ]
– Deliberately limited prelude period in Z / Push / Falling higher / Hey Lord / Don't spit on my mind / Revelation / Time / I can / Handful of pain / Lavdate dominum / Midnight run. *(cd re-iss. Jan01 on 'Castle'; CMRCD 120)*

Raw Power — Never

Sep 99. (cd/c) *(RAWCD 143)* <4504> **METAL JUKEBOX** [ ] [ ] Nov99
– He's a woman she's a man / Locomotive man / Lay all your love on me / Space oddity / From out of nowhere / All my loving / Hocus pocus / The faith healer / Juggernaut / White room / The Mexican.

Nuclear Blast — Nuclear Blast

Oct 00. (cd) *(NB 480-2)* <164800> **THE DARK RIDE** [ ] [ ] Dec00
– Behind the portal / Mr. Torture / All over the nation / Escalation 666 / Mirror mirror / If I could fly / Salvation / The departed / I live for your pain / We damn the night / The dark ride.

Dec 00. (cd-s) *(NB 532-2)* **IF I COULD FLY / DELIVER US from temptATION / IF I COULD FLY (extended)** [ ] [-]

– compilations, etc. –

1987. (cd) *Noise; (NCD 0088)* **HELLOWEEN** [ ] [-]
– (first 2 albums)

Dec 89. (cd) *Noise; (N 0148-2)* **PUMPKIN TRACKS** [-] [-] German
– Savage / Save us / Victim of fate / Livin' ain't no crime / Don't run for cover / Judas / Future world / Murderer / Starlight / Phantoms of death / A tale that wasn't right / I want out / March of time / I'm alive.

Aug 91. (cd/c/lp) *Noise; (N 0176-2/-4/-1)* <44849> **THE BEST, THE REST, THE RARE** [ ] [ ]
– I want out / Dr. Stein / Future world / Judas / Walls of Jericho / Ride the sky / Helloween / Livin' ain't no crime / Save us / Victim of fate / Savage / Don't run for cover / Keeper of the seven keys. (w/ free 12") **HELLOWEEN. / KEEPER OF THE SEVEN SEAS** (both over 13 minutes).

Jan 94. (cd) *Noise; (N 0240-2)* **KEEPER OF THE SEVEN KEYS – THE WHOLE STORY** [ ] [-]

HELMET

Formed: New York City, New York, USA ... 1989 by Oregon raised, jazz-trained guitarist, PAGE HAMILTON, who had briefly played with BAND OF SUSANS. He completed his line-up around 1990, when PETER MENGEDE, HENRY BOGDAN and JOHN STAINER were added. After a one-off release for 'Amphetamine Reptile', they were signed to 'East West', who released their debut album, 'STRAP IT ON' late in 1990. Unconventional non-image anti-fuss hardcore metal, channelling HENRY ROLLINS-like aggression with avant-garde rhythmic structures, HELMET drew influences from BLACK SABBATH to BLACK FLAG. The band's reputation was such that former BIG BLACK mainman STEVE ALBINI, deigned to produce their major label debut, 'MEANTIME', a Top 75 breakthrough in America despite its punishing musical content. MENGEDE departed the following year, his replacement being ROB ECHEVERRIA, who subsequently played on the track, 'JUST ANOTHER VICTIM' (a collaboration with HOUSE OF PAIN recorded for the 'Judgment Night' soundtrack). TODD RAY was at the controls for their third set, 'BETTY', a transatlantic Top 50 success which included a BUTCH VIG-produced number, 'MILQUETOAST' (also used on 'The Crow' film soundtrack). Three years in the making, 'AFTERTASTE' proved to be their most realised and accessible recording to date, if somewhat overlooked.

Album rating: STRAP IT ON (*6) / MEANTIME (*7) / BETTY (*5) / BORN ANNOYING early stuff (*7) / AFTERTASTE (*8)

PAGE HAMILTON (b.18 May'60, Portland, Oregon) – vocals, guitar (ex-BAND OF SUSANS) / **PETER MENGEDE** – guitar / **HENRY BOGDAN** (b. 4 Feb'61, Riverside, Calif.) – bass / **JOHN STANIER** (b. 2 Aug'68, Baltimore, Maryland; lived a time in Australia?) – drums

Amphetam. Reptile / Amphetam. Reptile

Nov 89. (7") *<SCALE 22>* **BORN ANNOYING. / RUMBLE** [-] [ ]

Mar 91. (7"; Various Artists) *<SCALE 34>* **Ugly American Overkill EP** [-] [ ]
– Taken / (other tracks by GOD BULLIES / SURGERY / TAR).

Oct 91. (7") *<SCALE 41>* **UNSUNG. / YOUR HEAD** [-] [ ]

Nov 91. (cd/c/m-lp) *<SCALE 202>* **STRAP IT ON** [-] [ ]
– Repetition / Rude / Bad mood / Sinatra / FBLA / Blacktop / Distracted / Make room / Murder. *(UK-iss.Jul93 on 'East West' cd/c; 7567 92235-2/-4) (re-iss. cd Jul96 on 'Interscope'; IND 92235)*

— early '92, 'Sub Pop' issued d7" 'OVEN' alongside various artists

Apr 92. (7"colrd) *<SCALE 47>* **IN THE MEANTIME. / NO NICKY NO** [-] [ ]

East West / Interscope

Jun 92. (cd/c/lp) *<(7567 92162-2/-4/-1)>* **MEANTIME** [ ] [68]
– In the meantime / Iron head / Give it / Unsung / Turned out / He feels bad / Better / You borrowed / FBLA II / Role model. *(cd re-iss. Jul96; IND 92162)*

Nov 92. (7"/c-s) *(A 8484/+C)* **UNSUNG. / FBLA (live)** [ ] [ ]
(cd-s+=) *(A 8484CD)* – FBLA II (live).
(12") *(A 8484T)* – ('A'side) / Better (live) / Bad mood (live) / Distracted (live).

— **ROB ECHEVERRIA** (b.15 Dec'67) – guitar repl. MENGEDE who joined HANDSOME

not iss. / Sony

Aug 93. (12") *<77037>* **JUST ANOTHER VICTIM** [-] [ ]

Interscope / Interscope

Jun 94. (7"/c-s/12") *(A 8291/+C/T)* **BISCUITS FOR SMUT. / MILQUETOAST** [ ] [ ]
(cd-s+=) *(A 8291CD)* – Flushings.

Jun 94. (cd/c) *<(7567 92404-2/-4)>* **BETTY** [38] [45]
– Wilma's rainbow / I know / Biscuits for smut / Milquetoast / Tie / Rollo / Street crab / Clean / Vaccination / Beautiful love / Speechless / The silver Hawaiian / Overrated / Sam Hell. *(cd re-iss. Jul96; IND 92404)*

Nov 94. (m-cd) *<(6544 92492-2)>* **WILMA'S RAINBOW EP** [ ] [ ]
– Wilma's rainbow / Sam Hell / Sinatra (live) / FBLA 11 (live) / TIC (live) / Just another victim (live) / In the meantime (live).

— In 1996, ECHEVERRIA joined BIOHAZARD and was repl. by **CHRIS TRAYNOR** – guitar

Apr 97. (cd) *<(IND 90073)>* **AFTERTASTE** [ ] [47] Mar97
– Pure / Renovation / Exactly what you wanted / Like I care / Driving nowhere / Birth defect / Broadcast emotion / It's easy to get bored / Diet aftertaste / Harmless / (High) Visibility / Insatiable / Crisis king.

– compilations, etc. –

Mar 93. (7") *Amphetamine Reptile; <SCALE 55>* **PRIMITIVE. / BORN ANNOYING (1993)** [-] [ ]

Apr 95. (lp/cd)(c) *Amphetamine Reptile; (ARR/+CD 60-003)(ARR 13C) <16>* **BORN ANNOYING** [ ] [ ]
– Born annoying (1989) / Rumble / Shirley MacLaine / Geisha to go / Taken / Your head / Oven / No Nicky no / Primitive / Born annoying (1993).

Jimi HENDRIX

Born: JOHNNY ALLEN HENDRIX, 27 Nov'42, Seattle, Washington, USA. He was raised by a part Cherokee Indian mother and black father, who, at age 3, changed his forenames to JAMES MARSHALL and bought him his first guitar. Being left-handed, he turned it upside down and reversed the strings, teaching himself by listening to blues and rock'n'roll artists such as ROBERT JOHNSON, MUDDY WATERS, B.B. KING and CHUCK BERRY. In the early 60's, he enlisted in the paratroopers, thus avoiding the draft into the US army. He was subsequently discharged for medical reasons in 1962, after injuring himself during a jump. Two years later, the young HENDRIX moved to New York and backed acts LITTLE RICHARD, The ISLEY BROTHERS and IKE & TINA TURNER. He soon struck up a partnership with soul singer CURTIS KNIGHT, also obtaining a contract with Ed Chalpin (KNIGHT is said to have written 'The Ballad Of Jimi' in 1965, after JIMI prophesied his own death circa 1970!). Early the following year, HENDRIX's first real band, JIMMY JAMES & THE BLUE FLAMES, were born. With JIMI's reputation now spreading, he was seen by ex-ANIMALS bassman CHAS CHANDLER, who invited him to London. After auditions, they found a rhythm section of NOEL REDDING and MITCH MITCHELL, smashing their way into the UK Top 10 in early '67 with the 'Polydor' one-off 45, 'HEY JOE'. CHANDLER then set up a deal with Kit Lambert's new 'Track' label, and The JIMI HENDRIX EXPERIENCE exploded onto the scene. Their first Hendrix-penned 45, the thundering acid-fever of 'PURPLE HAZE', made the UK Top 3, as did the scintillating debut album, 'ARE YOU EXPERIENCED?'. This was released hot on the heels of their third Top 10 single, 'THE WIND CRIES MARY'. Hendrix was a revelation, a black super-freak whose mastery of the guitar was above and beyond anything previously heard. In fact, he virtually re-invented the instrument, duly illustrating various methods of on-stage abuse (i.e. biting it, playing it with his teeth, shagging it and even setting fire to it!). He was duly booked on the Monterey International Pop Festival bill, where he proceeded to play an orgasmic version of 'WILD THING'. From the sublime to the ridiculous, the following month saw a wholly inappropriate US support tour with The MONKEES, leaving both him and teenybop audiences baffled, but no doubt entertained for seven nights. After another classic UK hit, 'THE BURNING OF THE MIDNIGHT LAMP', he released his second LP, 'AXIS: BOLD AS LOVE', which made the Top 5 early in '68, and was the first to chart and hit the Top 3 in his native America. In the Autumn of '68, JIMI revived and transformed BOB DYLAN's 'ALL ALONG THE WATCHTOWER', a song that broke into the US Top 20 and UK Top 5. It was trailed by a superb British Top 10 (US No.1) double-LP, 'ELECTRIC LADYLAND', the record featuring the now infamous naked women sleeve (much to JIMI's displeasure), which some shops sold in a brown cover! The beginning of the end came in 1969, when he was busted for drugs, leading to his band disintegrating; the trio played together for the last time on the 29th June at the Denver Pop Festival. REDDING had already formed FAT MATTRESS, MITCHELL returning with other musicians BILLY COX and LARRY LEE to make the group a quartet. The new "Experience" played the Woodstock Festival on the 17-18 August '69, performing an excellent version of 'STAR SPANGLED BANNER' that went down in the folklore of rock music. To end the year, JIMI was found not guilty of an earlier charge of heroin and marijuana possession and at the same time, he formed all-black outfit, BAND OF GYPSYS, along with COX and drummer BUDDY MILES. They released the self-titled live set in May '70 (recorded at FILLMORE EAST, New Year's Eve/Day 1969/70). This hit the Top 5 in the States, and, following a court order, he paid ex-manager Ed Chalpin $1m in compensation and a percentage of royalties. Tragically, after a few more open-air festival concerts and some bad drugs trips, he died in London on the 18th of September '70. He was said to have left a phoned message to Chandler saying "I need help bad, man". The official cause of death was an inhalation of vomit, due to barbiturate intoxication, leading to a coroner's decision of an open verdict. To many rock music buffs, he remains the greatest axegrinder of all-time and who knows what he might have become had he survived the heady sixties. • **Songwriters:** HENDRIX except other covers; HEY JOE (William Roberts) / JOHNNY B.GOODE (Chuck Berry) / GLORIA (Them) / SGT. PEPPER (Beatles) / HANG ON SLOOPY (McCoys) / TUTTI FRUTTI + LUCILLE (Little Richard) / BO DIDDLEY (Bo Diddley) / PETER GUNN (Henry Mancini) / HOOCHIE COOCHIE MAN (Muddy Waters) / BLUE SUEDE SHOES (Carl Perkins) / etc. • **Trivia:** In Jan'69, he and band play live tribute of CREAM's 'Sunshine Of Your Love' on The LULU Show, much to annoyance of TV controllers.

Album rating (selective): ARE YOU EXPERIENCED? (*10) / AXIS: BOLD AS LOVE (*9) / SMASH HITS compilation (*8) / ELECTRIC LADYLAND (*10) / BAND OF GYPSYS (*8) / posthumous:- THE CRY OF LOVE (*7) / EXPERIENCE (*3) / AT THE ISLE OF WIGHT (*4) / RAINBOW BRIDGE (*4) / HENDRIX IN THE WEST (*5) / WAR HEROES (*4) / SOUNDTRACK RECORDINGS FROM THE FILM 'JIMI HENDRIX' (*5) / CRASH LANDING (*4) / MIDNIGHT LIGHTNING (*4) / THE JIMI HENDRIX CONCERTS (*5) / THE SINGLES ALBUM (*7) / LIVE AT WINTERLAND (*7) / RADIO ONE (*7) / CORNERSTONES 1967-1970 (*8) / THE ULTIMATE EXPERIENCE (*10) / BLUES (*6) JIMI HENDRIX: WOODSTOCK (*6) / VOODOO SOUP (*5) / FIRST RAYS OF THE NEW RISING SUN (*6)

JIMI HENDRIX – vocals, lead guitar (ex-CURTIS KNIGHT) with **NOEL REDDING** (b.DAVID REDDING, 25 Dec'45, Folkstone, Kent, England) – bass / **MITCH MITCHELL** (b.JOHN MITCHELL, 9 Jun'47, Ealing, London, England) – drums

Polydor / Reprise

Dec 66. (7"; as JIMI HENDRIX) *(56139)* **HEY JOE. / STONE FREE** [6] [-]
(re-iss. Jul84 on 'Old Gold')

Track / Reprise

Mar 67. (7") *(604 001)* **PURPLE HAZE. / 51ST ANNIVERSARY** [3] [-]

Mar 67. (7") *<0572>* **HEY JOE. / 51st ANNIVERSARY** [-] [ ]

May 67. (7") *(604 004)* **THE WIND CRIES MARY. / HIGHWAY CHILE** [6] [-]

May 67. (lp; mono/stereo) *(612/613 001) <6261>* **ARE YOU EXPERIENCED?** [2] [5] Aug67
– Foxy lady / Manic depression / Red house / Can you see me / Love or confusion / I don't live today / May this be love / Fire / Third stone from the sun / Remember / Are you experienced? *(re-iss. Nov70; 2407 010) (re-iss. Nov81; 612 001) (re-iss. Sep85 on 'Polydor' lp/c; SPE LP/MC 97) (cd-iss. Jun91 & Oct93 cd/c; 521036-2/-4) (re-iss. Apr97 on 'MCA' cd/c; MCD/MCC 11608)*

Aug 67. (7") *<0597>* **PURPLE HAZE. / THE WIND CRIES MARY** [-] [65]

Aug 67. (7") *(604 007)* **THE BURNING OF THE MIDNIGHT LAMP. / THE STARS THAT PLAY WITH LAUGHING SAM'S DICE** [18] [-]

Dec 67. (7"; by JIMI HENDRIX) *<0641>* **FOXY LADY. / HEY JOE** [-] [67]

Dec 67. (lp; mono/stereo) *(612/613 003) <6281>* **AXIS: BOLD AS LOVE** [5] [3] Feb68
– Experience / Up from the skies / Spanish castle magic / Wait until tomorrow / Ain't no telling / Little wing / If six was nine / You've got me floating / Castles made of sand / She's so fine / One rainy wish / Little Miss Lover / Bold as love. *(re-iss. Nov70;) (re-iss. Aug83 on 'Polydor' lp/c; (SPE LP/MC 71) (cd-iss. 1987 on 'Polydor'; 813 572-2) (re-iss. Jul91 & Oct93 on 'Polydor' lp/c/cd; 847243-1/-4/-2) (re-iss. Apr97 on 'MCA' cd/c; MCD/MCC 11601)*

Feb 68. (7") *<0665>* **UP FROM THE SKIES. / ONE RAINY WISH** [-] [82]

Apr 68. (lp; mono/stereo) *(612/613 004) <2025>* **SMASH HITS** (compilation) [4] [6] Jul69
– Purple haze / Fire / The wind cries Mary / Can you see me / 51st anniversary / Hey Joe / Stone free / The stars that play with laughing Sam's dice / Manic depression / Highway chile / The burning of the midnight lamp / Foxy lady. *(re-iss. Jun73 on 'Polydor'; 2310 268) (re-iss. Aug83 on 'Polydor' lp/c; SPE LP/MC 3) (cd-iss. Feb85; 813 572-2)*

May 68. (7") *<0728>* **FOXY LADY. / PURPLE HAZE** [-] [ ]

Jul 68. (7") *<0742>* **ALL ALONG THE WATCHTOWER. / CROSSTOWN TRAFFIC** [-] [ ]

— JIMI now brought in old session campaigners **AL KOOPER** and **STEVE WINWOOD** – keyboards plus **JACK CASADY** – bass / **BUDDY MILES** – drums / (to repl. MITCHELL and REDDING)

Sep 68. (7") *<0767>* **ALL ALONG THE WATCHTOWER. / BURNING OF THE MIDNIGHT LAMP** [-] [20]

Oct 68. (7") *(604 025)* **ALL ALONG THE WATCHTOWER. / LONG HOT SUMMER NIGHT** [5] [-]

Nov 68. (d-lp) *(613 008-9) <6307>* **ELECTRIC LADYLAND** [6] [1] Oct68

– And the gods made love / (Have you ever been to) Electric Ladyland / Crosstown traffic / Voodoo chile / Rainy day, dream away / 1983 (a merman I should turn to be) / Moon, turn the tide . . . gently gently away / Little Miss Strange / Long hot summer night / Come on / Gypsy eyes / The burning of the midnight lamp / Still raining still dreaming / House burning down / All along the watchtower / Voodoo chile (slight return). *(also iss.lp/lp; 613 010/017) (re-iss. Jun73 on 'Polydor'; 2657 012) (re-iss. Jan84 on 'Polydor'; 350011-2) (re-iss. Jul91 & Oct93 on 'Polydor' lp/c/cd; 847233-1/-4/-2) (re-iss. Apr97 on 'MCA' cd/c; MCD/MCC 11600) (hit UK No.47 in Aug97)*

Apr 69. (7") *(604 029) <0798>* **CROSSTOWN TRAFFIC. / GYPSY EYES** [37] [52] Nov68
Oct 69. (7") *(604 033)* **(LET ME LIGHT YOUR) FIRE. / THE BURNING OF THE MIDNIGHT LAMP** [-] [ ]
Feb 70. (7") *<0853>* **STONE FREE. / IF 6 WAS 9** [-] [ ]
Apr 70. (7") *<0905>* **STEPPING STONE. / IZABELLA** [-] [ ]

JIMI HENDRIX

retained **BUDDY MILES** + recruited **BILLY COX** – bass

Track Capitol

Jun 70. (lp) *(2406 002) <472>* **BAND OF GYPSYS (live)** [6] [5] Apr70
– Who knows / Machine gun / Changes / Power of soul / Message to love / We gotta live together. *(re-iss. Aug83 on 'Polydor'; SPELP 16) (cd-iss. May88; 821 933-2) (re-iss. Dec89 & Jul91 on 'Polydor' lp/c/cd; 847 237-1/-4/-2) (re-iss. Apr97 on 'MCA' cd/c; MCD/MCC 11607)*

—— On the 18th September '70, HENDRIX died of a drug overdose.

– compilations, etc. –

Feb 68. (lp; with CURTIS KNIGHT) *London; (HA 8349) / Capitol; <2856>* **GET THAT FEELING (live 1964)** [39] [75]
Nov 68. (lp) *London; (HA 8369)* **STRANGE THINGS** [ ] [-]
(re-iss. Apr86 on 'Showcase' lp/c; SHLP/SHTC 101)
Note; All below 'Track' releases were issued on 'Reprise' US.
Sep 67. (7") *Track; (604 009)* **HOW WOULD YOU FEEL. / YOU DON'T WANT ME** [ ] [-]
May 70. (lp; shared with The WHO) *Track; (2407 004)* **BACKTRACK:4** [ ] [-]
May 70. (lp; shared with The WHO) *Track; (2407 008)* **BACKTRACK:8** [ ] [-]

– posthumous releases –

on 'Polydor' unless mentioned otherwise / 'Reprise' US

Oct 70. (7"; JIMI HENDRIX with CURTIS KNIGHT) *London; (HLZ 10321)* **BALLAD OF JIMI. / GLOOMY MONDAY** [ ] [ ]
Sep 70. (lp) *Reprise; <2029>* **MONTEREY INTERNATIONAL POP FESTIVAL (live soundtrack)** [-] [16]
Oct 70. (7"m) *Track; (2095 001)* **VOODOO CHILE (SLIGHT RETURN). / HEY JOE / ALL ALONG THE WATCHTOWER** [1] [-]
Mar 71. (lp) *Track; (2408 101) <2034>* **THE CRY OF LOVE** [2] [3]
– Freedom / Drifting / Ezy rider / Night bird flying / My friend / Straight ahead / Astro man / Angel / In from the storm / Belly button window. *(re-iss. Jun73 on 'Polydor' lp)(c; 2302 023)(3194 025) (re-iss. Sep85 on 'Polydor' lp/c; SPE LP/MC 98) (cd-iss. Mar89; 829 926-2) (re-iss. Jul91 & Mar93 on 'Polydor' cd/c/lp; 847242-2/-4/-1)*
Apr 71. (7") *Track; (2094 007)* **NIGHT BIRD FLYING. / FREEDOM** [ ] [-]
Mar 71. (7") *Reprise; <1000>* **FREEDOM. / ANGEL** [-] [59]
Oct 71. (7") *Reprise; <1044>* **DOLLY DAGGER. / STAR SPANGLED BANNER** [-] [74]
Oct 71. (7"ep) *Track; (2094 010)* **GYPSY EYES. / REMEMBER / PURPLE HAZE / STONE FREE** [35] [ ]
Nov 71. (lp) *(2302 016)* **JIMI HENDRIX AT THE ISLE OF WIGHT (live)** [17] [-]
– Midnight lightning / Foxy lady / Lover man / Freedom / All along the watchtower / In from the storm. *(re-iss. Apr84 lp/c; SPE LP/MC 71) (cd-iss. Mar89; 831 813-2) (re-iss. Jul91 & Mar93 cd/c/lp; 847 236-2/-4/-1)*
Jan 72. (lp) *(2302 018) <2049>* **HENDRIX IN THE WEST (live)** [7] [12]
– Johnny B. Goode / Lover man / Blue suede shoes / Voodoo chile (slight return) / The queen / Sergeant Pepper's lonely hearts club band / Little wing / Red house.
Jan 72. (7") *Reprise; <1082>* **JOHNNY B. GOODE. / LOVERMAN** [-] [ ]
Feb 72. (7") *(2001 277)* **JOHNNY B. GOODE. / LITTLE WING** [35] [-]
May 72. (7") *Reprise;* **LITTLE WING. / THE WIND CRIES MARY** [-] [ ]
Nov 72. (lp) *(2302 020) <2103>* **WAR HEROES** [23] [48]
– Bleeding heart / Highway chile / Tax free / Peter Gunn / Catastrophe / Stepping stone / Midnight / 3 little bears / Beginning / Izabella. *(re-iss. Aug83 on 'Polydor' lp/c; SPE LP/MC 4) (cd-iss. Mar89; 813 573-2) (re-iss. Jul91 cd/c/lp;) (re-iss. cd+c Mar93)*
Oct 73. (d-lp) **ARE YOU EXPERIENCED / AXIS: BOLD AS LOVE** [ ] [-]
Feb 74. (lp) *(2310 301)* **LOOSE ENDS** [ ] [-]
– Come down hard on me baby / Blue suede shoes / Jam 292 / The stars that play with laughing Sam's dice / The drifter's escape / Burning desire / I'm your hoochie coochie man / (Have you ever been) To Electric Ladyland. *(cd-iss. Mar89; 837 574-2)*
Mar 75. (lp) *(2343 080)* **JIMI HENDRIX** [35] [-]
Sep 75. (lp) *(2310 398) <2204>* **CRASH LANDING** [35] [5] Mar75
– Message to love / Somewhere over the rainbow / Crash landing / Coming down hard on me / Peace in Mississippi / With the power / Stone free again / Captain Coconut. *(re-iss. Mar83 lp/c; SPE LP/MC 94) (cd-iss. Mar89;) (cd-iss. Jun91 & Mar93 cd/c/lp; 847263-2/-4/-1)*
Nov 75. (lp) *(2310 415) <2229>* **MIDNIGHT LIGHTNING** [46] [43]
– Trashman / Midnight lightning / Hear my train a coming / Hey baby (new rising sun) / Blue suede shoes / Machine gun / Once I had a woman / Beginnings. *(re-iss. Mar89 lp/c/cd; 825 166-1/-4/-2)*
Oct 76. (lp) *(2343086)* **JIMI HENDRIX VOL.2** [ ] [-]
Jul 78. (d-lp)(d-c) *(261 2034)(350 0122) <2245>* **THE ESSENTIAL JIMI HENDRIX** [ ] [ ]
(with free one-sided 33rpm 7" **GLORIA**
Jun 80. (lp) *<2299>* **NINE TO THE UNIVERSE** [-] [ ]
Jun 80. (lp) *(2343 114)* **STONE FREE** [ ] [ ]
(re-iss. Nov83 lp/c; SPE LP/MC 51)
Sep 80. (7") **VOODOO CHILE. / GLORIA** [ ] [ ]
Sep 80. (6x7"-box) **6 SINGLES BOXED** (1st 6) [ ] [ ]
Sep 80. (12xlp-box) *(2625 038)* **10th ANNIVERSARY BOXED SET** [ ] [ ]
Jan 81. (lp) *(2311 014) <2293>* **THE ESSENTIAL JIMI HENDRIX VOLUME 2** [ ] [ ] Aug79
Nov 81. (12"ep) *(POSPX 401)* **ALL ALONG THE WATCHTOWER. / FOXY LADY / PURPLE HAZE / MANIC DEPRESSION** [ ] [ ]
Jun 82. (lp) *(234 3115)* **VOODOO CHILE** [ ] [ ]
(re-iss. Nov83 lp/c; SPE LP/MC 52)
Sep 82. (12"ep) *(POSPX 608)* **VOODOO CHILE. / GIPSY EYES / HEY JOE / 3RD STONE FROM THE SUN** [ ] [ ]
Feb 83. (lp/c) *(PODV/+C 6)* **SINGLES ALBUM** [77] [-]
Jun 83. (d-c) *(TWOMC 3)* **CRASH LANDING / MIDNIGHT LIGHTNING** [ ] [ ]
Nov 84. (lp/c/cd) *(823 704-1/-4/-2)* **KISS THE SKY** [ ] [ ]
(re-iss. Jun91 cd/c/lp;) (re-iss. Mar93 cd/c)
Feb 86. (lp/c/cd) *(827 990-1/-4/-2)* **JIMI PLAYS MONTEREY (live)** [ ] [ ]
(re-iss. Jun91 & Mar93 cd/c/lp; 847 244-2/-4/-1)
1986. Capitol; (lp,cd) *<SJ 12416>* **BAND OF GYPSYS 2** [-] [ ]
Jul 87. (lp/c/cd) *(833 004-1/-4/-2) / Rykodisc; <RCD 20038>* **LIVE AT WINTERLAND (live)** [ ] [ ]
(re-iss. Jun91 & Mar93 cd/c/lp; 847 238-2/-4/-1)
Jan 89. (7") *(PO 33)* **PURPLE HAZE. / 51ST ANNIVERSARY** [ ] [ ]
(12"+=) *(PZ 33)* – All along the watchtower.
(cd-s+=) *(PZCD 33)* – Hey Joe.
1989. (4xcd-box) **BOXED SET** [ ] [ ]
– ARE YOU EXPERIENCED? / WAR HEROES / IN THE WEST / BAND OF GYPSIES
Nov 89. (cd) *Hal Leonard; <HL 00660036>* **FUZZ, FEEDBACK & WAH-WAH (live)** [-] [ ]
Nov 89. (cd) *Hal Leonard; <HL 00660038>* **WHAMMY BAR & FINGER GREASE (live)** [-] [ ]
Nov 89. (cd) *Hal Leonard; <HL 00660040>* **RED HOUSE: VARIATIONS ON A THEME (live)** [-] [ ]
Nov 89. (cd) *Hal Leonard; <HL 00660041>* **OCTAVIA & UNIVIBE (live)** [-] [ ]
Mar 90. (7"/c-s) *(PO/+CS 71)* **CROSSTOWN TRAFFIC. / PURPLE HAZE** [61] [ ]
(12"+=) *(PZ 71)* – All along the watchtower.
(cd-s++=) *(PZCD 71)* – Have you ever been (to Electric Ladyland).
1990. (cd) **THE JIMI HENDRIX EXPERIENCE** [ ] [ ]
Oct 90. (cd/c/lp) *(847 231-2/-4/-1)* **CORNERSTONES (1967-1970, FOUR YEARS THAT CHANGED THE MUSIC) (live)** [5] [ ]
– Hey Joe / Foxy lady / Purple haze / The wind cries Mary / Have you ever been to (Electric Ladyland) / Crosstown traffic / All along the watchtower / Voodoo chile (slight return) / Star spangled banner / Stepping stone / Room full of mirrors / Ezy rider / Freedom / Drifting / In from the storm / Angel. *(cd+=/c+=)* – Fire (live) / Stone free (live).
Oct 90. (7"ep) *(PO 100)* **ALL ALONG THE WATCHTOWER. / VOODOO CHILE / HEY JOE** [52] [ ]
(12"+=/c-s+=) *(POCS/PZCD 100)* – Crosstown traffic.
Nov 90. (4xcd-box) *<9-26435-2>* **LIFELINES: THE JIMI HENDRIX STORY (live)** [-] [ ]
Feb 91. (4xcd-box) *(847232-2)* **SESSIONS BOX – ARE YOU EXPERIENCED? / AXIS: BOLD AS LOVE / ELECTRIC LADYLAND / CRY OF LOVE** [ ] [ ]
Mar 91. (4xcd-box) *(847 235-2)* **FOOTLIGHTS (live)** [ ] [ ]
– JIMI PLAYS MONTEREY / ISLE OF WIGHT / BAND OF GYPSIES / LIVE AT WINTERLAND
Feb 92. (4xcd-box) *(511 763-2)* **STAGES (live)** [ ] [ ]
– (Stockholm 5 Sep'67 / Paris 29 Jan'68 / San Diego 24 May'69 / Atlanta 4 Jul'70)
Nov 92. (cd/c) *Polygram TV; (517235-2/-4) / M.C.A.; <10829>* **THE ULTIMATE EXPERIENCE** [25] [72] Jul93
– All along the watchtower / Purple haze / Hey Joe / The wind cries Mary / Angel / Voodoo chile (slight return) / Foxy lady / Burning of the midnight lamp / Highway chile / Crosstown traffic / Castles made of sand / Long hot summer night / Red house / Manic depression / Gypsy eyes / Little wing / Fire / Wait until tomorrow / Star spangled banner (live) / Wild thing (live). *(re-iss. Sep95; same)*
Feb 94. (cd) *I.T.M.; (ITM 960004)* **PURPLE HAZE IN WOODSTOCK (live)** [ ] [ ]
Apr 94. (3xcd-box) *Pulsar; (PULSE 301)* **GREATEST HITS** [ ] [-]
'Polydor' (the ones not mentioned), were issued on 'M.C.A.' in US.
Apr 94. (cd/c) *(521037-2/-4) <11060>* **BLUES** [10] [45]
Aug 94. (cd/c) *(523384-2/-4) <11063>* **AT WOODSTOCK (live)** [32] [37]
May 94. (cd) *Ramble Tamble; (RATA 002)* **LIVE AT THE 'SCENE' CLUB N.Y., N.Y. (live)** [ ] [-]
Aug 94. (cd) *Charly; (CDCD 1172)* **BEFORE THE EXPERIENCE** [ ] [-]
Oct 94. (cd) *Charly; (CDCD 1189)* **THE EARLY YEARS** [ ] [-]
Apr 95. (cd/c) *(527 520-2/-4) <11236>* **VOODOO SOUP** [ ] [66]
– The new rising sun / Belly button window / Stepping stone / Freedom / Angel / Room full of mirrors / Midnight / Night bird flying / Drifting / Ezy rider / Pali gap / Message to love / Peace in Mississippi / In from the storm.

– others, etc. –

Oct 70. (7"; with CURTIS KNIGHT) *R.C.A.;* **NO SUCH ANIMAL (part 1). / (part 2)** [ ] [ ]
Apr 71. (lp) *Saga; (6307)* **JIMI HENDRIX** [ ] [ ]
1972. (lp) *Saga; (6313)* **JIMI HENDRIX AT HIS BEST VOL.1** [ ] [ ]
1972. (lp) *Saga; (6314)* **JIMI HENDRIX AT HIS BEST VOL.2** [ ] [ ]
1972. (lp) *Saga; (6315)* **JIMI HENDRIX AT HIS BEST VOL.3** [ ] [ ]
Apr 71. (lp; with CURTIS KNIGHT) *Hallmark;* **THE ETERNAL FIRE OF JIMI HENDRIX** [ ] [-]
1973. (lp; with CURTIS KNIGHT) *Hallmark; (SHM 791)* **THE WILD ONE** [ ] [-]
Aug 71. (lp) *Ember; (NR 5057)* **EXPERIENCE (live)** [9] [-]
– The sunshine of your love / Room full of mirrors / Bleeding heart / Smashing of amps.
(re-iss. Sep79 on 'Bulldog'; BDL 4002) (cd-iss. Jan87 & Nov91; BDCD 40023) (cd-iss. Mar95 on 'Nectar';)
Mar 72. (lp) *Ember; (NR 5061)* **MORE EXPERIENCE (live)** [ ] [-]
(re-iss. Sep79 & Jul82 on 'Bulldog')

Feb 75. (lp) *Ember; (EMB 3428)* **LOOKING BACK WITH JIMI HENDRIX (live)** ☐ -
Oct 73. (lp) *Ember; (NR 5068)* **IN THE BEGINNING (live)** ☐ -
(re-iss. 1984 on 'Everest'; CBR 1031)
1974. (lp) *Ember;* **FRIENDS FROM THE BEGINNING (with 'LITTLE RICHARD')** ☐ -
(re-iss. Jan77)
Nov 71. (lp) *Reprise; (K 44159) <2040>* **RAINBOW BRIDGE (live soundtrack)** 16 15 Oct71
– Dolly dagger / Earth blues / Pali gap / Room full of mirrors / Star spangled banner / Look over yonder / Hear my train a comin' / Hey baby. *(cd-iss. Mar87; K2 44159) (cd re-iss. Apr89; 831 312-2)*
Jun 73. (7") *Reprise;* **HEAR MY TRAIN A-COMIN'. / ROCK ME BABY** ☐ ☐
Jul 73. (d-lp) *Reprise; (K 64017)* **SOUNDTRACK RECORDINGS FROM THE FILM 'JIMI HENDRIX'** 37 ☐
Jun 82. (7") *Reprise;* **FIRE. / LITTLE WING** - ☐
Jul 72. (lp) *Music For Pleasure; (MFP 5278)* **WHAT'D I SAY (live)** ☐ -
Sep 84. (lp) *Music For Pleasure; (MFP 50053)* **THE BIRTH OF SUCCESS (live)** ☐ -
Nov 72. (lp) *Enterprise; (ENTF 3000)* **RARE HENDRIX** ☐ -
Dec 72. (lp) *Enterprise;* **JIMI HENDRIX IN SESSION** ☐ -
1973. (lp) *Enterprise; (ENTF 1030)* **HENDRIX '66** ☐ -
1973. (lp) *Boulevard; (41060)* **JIMI HENDRIX 1964** ☐ -
Nov 75. (lp) *D.J.M.; (DJLMD 8011)* **FOR REAL** ☐ -
(re-iss. Feb82 on 'Audio Fidelity';)
Aug 79. (lp) *Bulldog; (BDL 2010) / Douglas;* **20 GOLDEN PIECES OF JIMI HENDRIX (live)** ☐ ☐
Sep 79. (lp) *Bulldog; (BDL 4003)* **MORE ESSENTIAL** ☐ -
Oct 80. (lp) *Red Lightnin'; (RL 0015)* **WOKE UP THIS MORNING AND FOUND MYSELF DEAD (live)** ☐ -
(cd-iss. Apr00 on 'Stony Plain'; 725320068-2)
(cd-iss. Nov86; RLCD 0068) (pic-lp.Oct88; RLP 0048) (cd-iss. 1992 on 'Point'; 262033-2)
Jun 81. (lp) *Audio Fidelity; (1002) / Nutmeg; <NUT 1002>* **COSMIC TURNAROUND** ☐ -
Oct 81. (4xlp-box) *Audio Fidelity;* **THE GENIUS OF HENDRIX** ☐ -
Mar 82. (lp) *Audio Fidelity;* **HIGH, LIVE AND DIRTY** ☐ -
Dec 82. (cd) *Bulldog; (BDL 2027)* **20 GOLDEN PIECES OF JIMI HENDRIX VOL.2 (live)** ☐ -
Oct 84. (c) *Audio Fidelity; (ZCGAS 703)* **JIMI HENDRIX VOL.1** ☐ -
Oct 84. (c) *Audio Fidelity; (ZCGAS 704)* **JIMI HENDRIX VOL.2** ☐ -
Oct 84. (c) *Audio Fidelity; (ZCGAS 732)* **JIMI HENDRIX VOL.3** ☐ -
Nov 81. (lp) *Phoenix; (PHX 1012)* **FREE SPIRIT** ☐ -
(re-iss. Jun87 on 'Thunderbolt'; THBM 006)
Sep 82. (lp) *Phoenix; (PHX 1020)* **MOODS** ☐ -
Sep 82. (lp) *Phoenix; (PHX 1026)* **ROOTS OF HENDRIX** ☐ -
Aug 82. (d-lp) *C.B.S.; (88592) / Reprise; <22306>* **THE JIMI HENDRIX CONCERTS (live)** 16 79
– Fire / I don't live today / Red house / Stone free / Are you experienced? / Little wing / Voodoo chile (slight return) / Bleeding heart / Hey Joe / Wild thing / Hear my train a-comin'. *(re-iss. Aug89 on 'Media Motion' lp/c/cd; MEDIA/+C/CD 1) (re-iss. Feb90 on 'Castle' lp+=/c+=/cd+=; CCS LP/MC/CD 235)* – Foxy lady.
Aug 82. (7"/12") *C.B.S.; (A/+13 2749)* **FIRE (live). / ARE YOU EXPERIENCED (live)** ☐ -
Oct 82. (lp) *Dakota;* **THE BEST OF JIMI HENDRIX** ☐ -
Nov 83. (lp/c) *Contour; (CN/+4 2067)* **THE JIMI HENDRIX ALBUM** ☐ -
Jul 84. (7") *Old Gold; (OG 9430)* **PURPLE HAZE. / THE WIND CRIES MARY** ☐ -
Jul 84. (7") *Old Gold; (OG 9431)* **VOODOO CHILE (SLIGHT RETURN). / BURNING OF THE MIDNIGHT LAMP** ☐ -
Jul 84. (7") *Old Gold; (OG 9432)* **ALL ALONG THE WATCHTOWER. / FOXY LADY** ☐ -
Jul 85. (lp/c) *Topline; (TOP/KTOP 124)* **GANGSTER OF LOVE** ☐ -
Apr 86. (lp/c) *Arcade; (ADAH/+C 430)* **THE LEGEND** ☐ -
May 86. (lp/c) *Sierra; (FEDB/CFEDB 5032)* **REPLAY OF JIMI HENDRIX** ☐ -
Aug 86. (lp/c) *Fame; (FA/TC-FA 3160)* **JOHNNY B. GOODE (live)** ☐ -
May 87. (cd) *E.M.I.; (CDP 746 485-2)* **THE BEST OF JIMI HENDRIX** ☐ -
May 88. (lp/c/cd) *Big Time; (261 525-1/-4/-2)* **16 GREAT CLASSICS** ☐ -
Jun 88. (cd; shared with TINA TURNER) *Thunderbolt; (CDTBD 001)* **VOICES IN THE WIND** ☐ -
Nov 88. (12"ep/cd-ep) *Strange Fruit; (SFPS/+CD 065)* **THE PEEL SESSIONS** ☐ -
– Radio One theme / Day tripper / Wait until tomorrow / Hear my train a'comin' / Spanish castle magic. *(cd re-iss. Apr96; same)*
Feb 89. (d-lp/c/cd) *Castle; (CCS LP/MC/CD 212) / Rykodisc; <RALP 00782>* **THE RADIO ONE SESSIONS** 30 ☐
– Stone free / Radio one theme / Day tripper / Killing floor / Love or confusion / Catfish blues / Drivin' south / Wait until tomorrow / Hear my train a-comin' / Hound dog / Fire / Hoochie coochie man / Purple haze / Spanish castle magic / Hey Joe / Foxy lady / The burning of the midnight lamp.
Nov 89. (5xlp/3xc/3xcd-box) *Castle; (HB LP/MC/CD 100)* **LIVE AND UNRELEASED – THE RADIO SHOWS (live)** ☐ ☐
Feb 89. (cd) *Koine; (K 880 802)* **JAM SESSIONS** ☐ -
Jan 90. (cd) *Zeta; (ZET 517)* **THE LAST EXPERIENCE CONCERT (live)** ☐ -
Apr 90. (cd/lp) *Thunderbolt; (CDTB/THBL 075)* **NIGHT LIFE** ☐ -
Dec 90. (pic-lp) *Discussion; (IFSIXWAS 9)* **WELL I STAND NEXT TO A MOUNTAIN** ☐ -
Feb 91. (cd/c) *Action Replay; (CDAR/ARLC 1022)* **THE BEST & THE REST OF JIMI HENDRIX** ☐ -
Dec 91. (cd/lp) *U.F.O.;* **IN 1967 (free w/booklet)** ☐ -
Nov 92. (7"/c-s) *East West;* **THE WIND CRIES MARY. / FIRE** ☐ -
(12"+=/cd-s+=) – Foxy lady / May this be love.
Dec 92. (cd) *Univibes;* **CALLING LONG DISTANCE** ☐ -
Apr 93. (d-cd/d-c) *Deja Vu; (R2CD 4003)* **THE GOLD COLLECTION** ☐ -
(re-iss. Jun95; same)
Apr 93. (cd) *Pulsar;* **HIS FINAL LIVE PERFORMANCE (live)** ☐ -
Sep 93. (cd) *I.T.M.; (ITM 960008)* **JIMI HENDRIX AT THE MONTEREY POP FESTIVAL, 1967 (live)** ☐ ☐
Dec 93. (cd) *Entertainers;* **FIRE** ☐ -
Jan 95. (cd) *Collection; (COL 017)* **THE COLLECTION** ☐ -
Mar 95. (cd) *Top Masters; (3179)* **THE EARLY JIMI HENDRIX** ☐ -
Apr 95. (cd/c) *Muskateer; (MU 5/4 018)* **LIVE IN NEW YORK** ☐ -
May 95. (cd) *Thunderbolt; (CDTB 075)* **NIGHT LIFE** ☐ -
Jun 95. (cd) *Receiver; (RRCD 200)* **SUNSHINE OF YOUR LOVE** ☐ -
Aug 95. (cd) *Voiceprint; (844200-2)* **SUPERSESSION** ☐ -
Sep 95. (cd) *Strawberry; (SRCD 115)* **THE LAST EXPERIENCE** ☐ -
Nov 95. (3xcd-box) *Pulsar; (PULS 301)* **GREATEST HITS** ☐ -
— On April 5th 1996, JIMI's girlfriend at the time of his death; MONIKA DANNEMAN, committed suicide (carbon monoxide poisoning). In her book 'The Inner Life Of Jimi Hendrix', she had recently broke an injunction, involving a libellous statement made to JIMI's other one-time girlfriend KATHY ETCHINGHAM.
Apr 96. (cd/c) *Hallmark; (30418-2/-4)* **EARLY DAZE** ☐ -
Aug 96. (d-cd) *Natural Collection; (TNC 96205)* **REAL ROCK STANDARDS** ☐ -
Feb 97. (cd) *S.P.V.; (SPV 0854468-2)* **BALLAD OF JIMI: THE AUTHENTIC PPX RECORDINGS VOLUME 3** ☐ -
Feb 97. (cd) *S.P.V.; (SPV 0854469-2)* **LIVE AT GEORGE'S CLUB: THE AUTHENTIC PPX RECORDINGS VOLUME 4** ☐ -
Apr 97. (cd) *Arcade; (300455-2)* **THE DIAMOND COLLECTION** ☐ -
May 97. (cd/c/d-lp) *M.C.A.; (MCD/MCC/MCA2 11599)* **FIRST RAYS OF THE NEW RISING SUN** 37 49
May 97. (d-cd) *Metro; (OTR 1100030)* **IN WORDS AND MUSIC** ☐ -
Jun 97. (cd) *BR Music; (RM 1536)* **PSYCHO** ☐ -
Sep 97. (cd/c) *Telstar; (TTV CD/MC 2930)* **EXPERIENCE HENDRIX – THE BEST OF** 21 ☐
– Purple haze / Fire / The wind cries Mary / Hey Joe / All along the watchtower / Stone free / Crosstown traffic / Manic depression / Little wing / If six was nine / Foxy lady / Bold as love / Castles made of sand / Red house / Voodoo chile (slight return) / Freedom / Night bird flying / Angel / Dolly dagger / Star spangled banner.
Oct 97. (cd/c/d-lp) *M.C.A.; (MCD/MCC/MCA 11684)* **SOUTH SATURN DELTA** ☐ 51
Dec 97. (cd) *Institute Of Art; (RTD 39700829CD)* **HOT TRIGGER** ☐ -
Mar 98. (cd) *Mo's Music Machine; (ANXCD 001)* **LIVE AT THE SCENE CLUB NEW YORK 1968** ☐ -
May 98. (3xcd-box) *Dressed To Kill; (DTKBOX 81)* **GROOVE MAKER** ☐ -
Jun 98. (cd) *Multimedia; (MIL 610-2)* **NYC 1968** ☐ -
Jun 98. (d-cd/d-c/t-lp) *M.C.A.; <(MCD/MCC/MCA 11742)>* **THE BBC SESSIONS** 42 50
Oct 98. (d-cd) *S.P.V.; (085-2927-2)* **THE BEST OF THE AUTHENTIC PPX STUDIO RECORDINGS** ☐ ☐
Feb 99. (lp) *Get Back; (GET 513)* **THE LOST YOUNGBLOOD TAPES** ☐ ☐
(cd-iss. Dec99 on 'Ugo'; UGO 1)
Feb 99. (d-cd/d-c/t-lp) *M.C.A.; <(MCD/MCC/MCA 11931)>* **LIVE AT FILLMORE EAST** ☐ 65
Jul 99. (d-cd/d-c) *M.C.A.; <(MCD 11987)>* **JIMI HENDRIX LIVE AT WOODSTOCK (live)** ☐ 90
Jul 99. (10x7"box) *M.C.A.; (MCA 55578)* **THE CLASSIC SINGLES COLLECTION** ☐ ☐
Dec 99. (cd) *Traditional Line; (TL 1301)* **NEW YORK SESSION** ☐ -
Apr 00. (6xcd-box) *S.P.V.; (088-2980-2)* **THE COMPLETE PPX STUDIO RECORDINGS** ☐ ☐
Apr 00. (cd) *Dressed To Kill; (FABBY 275)* **RARE AS LOVE** ☐ -
May 00. (lp/cd) *Jungle; (FREUD/+CD 65)* **DRIVIN' SOUTH** ☐ -
Jul 00. (d-cd) *Collection; (KBOX 238)* **JIMI HENDRIX** ☐ -
Sep 00. (4xcd-box/8xlp-box) *Universal TV; (1122316-2/-1) <11671-2/-1>* **EXPERIENCE HENDRIX: THE BEST OF JIMI HENDRIX** 10 ☐ Jun99
Apr 01. (d-cd) *Dressed To Kill; (TOPAK 952)* **THE LEGENDS COLLECTION** ☐ -
May 01. (d-cd) *Universal; <(112603-2)>* **VOODOO CHILD: THE JIMI HENDRIX COLLECTION** ☐ -
May 01. (3xcd-box) *K-Box; (KBOX 3270)* **THE BEST OF JIMI HENDRIX** ☐ -

Ken HENSLEY (see under ⇒ URIAH HEEP)

HERETIC

Formed: Los Angeles, California, USA . . . 1984 by JULIAN MENDEZ, BRIAN KORBAN, BOB MARQUEZ, DENNIS O'HARA and RICK MERICK. Signed to 'Metal Blade' ('Roadrunner' in Europe), they finally released a debut set of strident power-metal in early '87, entitled 'TORTURE KNOWS NO BOUNDARIES'. MENDEZ bailed out soon after, the new frontman MIKE HOWE proving a more suitable candidate for the job as evidenced on their 1988 follow-up, 'BREAKING POINT'. When HOWE abandoned his HERETIC-al credentials after finding faith with METAL CHURCH, the band had indeed reached their breaking point and split soon after. • **Note:** not the same group as the band who issued 12", 'Burnt At The Stake'.

Album rating: TORTURE KNOWS NO BOUNDARIES (*5) / BREAKING POINT (*4)

JULIAN MENDEZ – vocals / **BOB MARQUEZ** – guitar / **BRIAN KORBAN** – guitars / **DENNIS O'HARA** – bass / **RICKY MERICK** – drums

Roadrunner Metal Blade

Feb 87. (m-lp) *(RR 9640) <72170>* **TORTURE KNOWS NO BOUNDARIES** ☐ ☐
– Riding with the angels / Blood will tell / Portrait of faith / Whitechapel / Torture knows no boundaries.
— **MIKE HOWE** – vocals; repl. MENDEZ

Aug 88. (lp/c/cd) *(RR 9534-1/-4/-2) <73415>* **BREAKING POINT** [ ] [ ]
Heretic / And kingdoms fall / The circle / Enemy within / Time runs short / Pale shelter (instrumental) / Shifting fire / Let 'em breed / Evil for evil / The search.

— when HOWE joined METAL CHURCH, the band folded

HOLE

Formed: Los Angeles, California, USA . . . late 1989 by COURTNEY LOVE (bizarrely enough, a two-piece indie band of the same moniker – see under LOIS – surfaced with a few 45's a year later!) and six foot plus guitarist and Capitol records employee, ERIC ERLANDSON. LOVE, who had previously worked as an exotic dancer and an actress (she appeared in the 1986 punk movie, 'Sid & Nancy') and played alongside JENNIFER FINCH (L7) and KAT BJELLAND (Babes In Toyland) in a band called SUGAR BABY DOLL, was also involved in an early incarnation of FAITH NO MORE. Taking the name HOLE from a line in Euripides' Medea, they placed an ad in a local paper, 'Flipside', finding a bassist and drummer, namely JILL EMERY and CAROLINE RUE. In the Spring of 1990, HOLE released the 'RAT BASTARD' EP, subsequently relocating to the burgeoning Seattle area. Early the following year, 'Sub Pop' issued the 'DICKNAIL' EP, the band duly signing to 'Caroline' records for their debut album, 'PRETTY ON THE INSIDE'. Produced by KIM GORDON and DON FLEMING, it hit the lower regions of the US charts, the record being voted album of the year by New York's Village Voice magazine. A harrowing primal howl of a record, LOVE's demons were confronted mercilessly on such psyche-trawling dirges as 'TEENAGE WHORE' and 'GARBAGE MAN'. Around the same time, LOVE's relationship with NIRVANA's KURT COBAIN, was the talk of the alternative rock world, the singer subsequently marrying him in February '92, giving birth to his daughter, Frances Bean, later that summer. The following year, with newcomers PATTY SCHEMEL (drums) and KRISTEN PFAFF (bass), the group secured a deal with the David Geffen Company ('D.G.C.'), much to the dismay of MADONNA who wanted HOLE for her newly formed 'Maverick' label. In Spring 1994, LOVE finally celebrated a UK Top 20 album, 'LIVE THROUGH THIS', although its success was overshadowed by the shocking suicide of KURT on the 8th of April. She subsequently held a memorial two days later, hailing everyone there to call him an asshole. More press coverage followed later that summer, when PFAFF was found dead in her bath on the 16th June (it was believed to be another tragic drug related death). Despite the press circus surrounding LOVE, the band played a rather disappointing Reading Festival stint in August that year, her at times lethargic vox letting some of the more discerning fans down (EVAN DANDO of The LEMONHEADS was rumoured to be her new boyfriend, although a number of lucky people – including DANDO – were privy to her womanly charms – both of them – when she "flashed" at the side of the stage). With a new bassist, MELISSA AUF DER MAUR, the group released two UK hits, 'DOLL PARTS' and 'VIOLET', LOVE certainly back on top form with her incendiary Top Of The Pops performances (LYDIA LUNCH eat your heart out!?). Back in the news again, she was fined for assaulting BIKINI KILL's KATHLEEN HANNA, LOVE and SCHEMEL conversely taking three security guards to court following an alleged assault incident while signing autographs stagefront at a GREEN DAY concert in Lakefront Arena (yet more column inches were devoted to the controversial singer in August '96, when LOVE was acquitted of a stage assault nine months previous on two teenage fans in Florida). More recently, LOVE has played down her wild child character, exchanging the Seattle grunge mantle for a more respectable Hollywood career. This was largely down to her acclaimed roles in the movies, 'Feeling Minnesota' and more so with the controversial, 'The People Vs. Larry Flint'. On the recording front, only a lone version of FLEETWOOD MAC's 'GOLD DUST WOMAN' has surfaced (this was included on the film soundtrack from 'The Crow II: City Of Angels'). In '98, COURTNEY (and HOLE) was once again writing new material, this time with BILLY CORGAN of the SMASHING PUMPKINS, although a dispute over who actually wrote what the public thought were collaborations was subsequent tabloid news. The album in question, 'CELEBRITY SKIN' (1998), was worthy of its Top 10 placing although a little commercialised for some. The following year (in November), MELISSA bailed out of the band and more shocking still was that she joined COURTNEY's old pal CORGAN in The SMASHING PUMPKINS. • **Covers:** STAR BELLY sampled DREAMS (Fleetwood Mac) + INTO THE BLACK (Neil Young) / DO IT CLEAN (Echo & The Bunnymen) / CREDIT IN THE STRAIGHT WORLD (Young Marble Giants) / HUNGRY LIKE THE WOLF (Duran Duran) / SEASON OF THE WITCH (Donovan) / HE HIT ME (IT FELT LIKE A KISS) (Goffin-King) / IT'S ALL OVER NOW, BABY BLUE (Bob Dylan). 'I THINK THAT I WOULD DIE' was co-written w / KAT BJELLAND (Babes In Toyland). • **Note:** Not to be confused with band who released in the late 80's; OTHER TONGUES, OTHER FLESH (LP) and DYSKINSIA (12") both on 'Eyes Media'.

Album rating: PRETTY ON THE INSIDE (*7) / LIVE THROUGH THIS (*9) / MY BODY, THE HAND GRENADE collection (*6) / CELEBRITY SKIN (*7)

COURTNEY LOVE (b. MICHELLE HARRISON, 9 Jul'65, San Francisco, Calif.) – vocals, guitars / **ERIC ERLANDSON** (b. 9 Jan'63) – guitars / **JILL EMERY** – bass, vocals / **CAROLINE RUE** – drums

not iss. / Sympathy F

Jul 90. (7"white-ep) *<SFTRI 53>* **RETARD GIRL. / PHONEBILL SONG / JOHNNIES IN THE BATHROOM** [-] [ ]
(UK-iss.cd-ep Sep97 +=; SFTRI 53CD) – Turpentine.

not iss. / Sub Pop

Apr 91. (7"colrd-various) *(SP 93)* **DICKNAIL. / BURNBLACK** [-] [ ]

City Slang / Caroline

Aug 91. (7"colrd-various) *(EFA 04070-45)* **TEENAGE WHORE. / DROWN SODA** [ ] [ ]
(12"+=/cd-s+=) *(EFA 04070-02/-03)* – Burnblack.

Oct 91. (cd/c/lp-some red) *(EFA 0407-2/-C/-1) <SLANG 012>* **PRETTY ON THE INSIDE** [59] [ ] Jul91
– Teenage whore / Babydoll / Garbage man / Sassy / Goodsister – bad sister / Mrs. Jones / Berry / Loaded / Star belly / Pretty on the inside / Clouds. *(re-iss. Sep95; same)*

— **LESLEY** – bass repl. JILL / **PATTY SCHEMEL** (b.24 Apr'67, Seattle Washington) – drums repl. CAROLINE

City Slang / D.G.C.

Apr 93. (7") *(EFA 04916-45)* **BEAUTIFUL SON. / OLD AGE** [54] [-]
(12"+=/cd-s+=) *(EFA 04916-02/-03)* – 20 years in the Dakota.

— **KRISTEN PFAFF** – bass, piano, vocals repl. LESLEY

Mar 94. (7"some pink) *(EFA 04936-7)* **MISS WORLD. / ROCK STAR (alternate mix)** [64] [ ]
(cd-s+=) *(EFA 04936-2)* – Do it clean (live).

Apr 94. (cd/c/lp;some white) *(EFA 04935-2/-4/-1) <24631>* **LIVE THROUGH THIS** [13] [52]
– Violet / Miss World / Plump / Asking for it / Jennifer's body / Doll parts / Credit in the straight world / Softer, softest / She walks on me / I think that I would die / Gutless / Rock star. *(re-iss. cd/lp Mar95 on 'Geffen'; GED/GEF 24631)*

— KRISTEN was found dead in her bath 16th June 1994. COURTNEY, ERIC + PATTI continued and later recruited **MELISSA AUF DER MAUR** (b.17 Mar'72, Montreal, Canada) – bass. As HOLEZ (HOLE + PAT SMEAR of GERMS) they released tribute GERMS cover 'CIRCLE 1' on 'Dutch East India' Mar95.

Geffen / D.G.C.

Nov 94. (c-s) *<19379>* **DOLL PARTS / PLUMP (live)** [-] [58]

Apr 95. (7") *(GFS 91)* **DOLL PARTS. / THE VOID** [16] [-]
(cd-s+=) *(GFSTD 91)* – Hungry like the wolf (live).
(cd-s) *(GFSXD 91)* – ('A'side) / Plump (live) / I think that I would die (live) / Credit in the straight world (live).

Jul 95. (7") *(GFS 94)* **VIOLET. / OLD AGE** [17] [ ]
(7"colrd) *(GFSP 94)* – ('A'side) / He hit me (it felt like a kiss).
(cd-s++=) *(GFSCD 94)* – Who's porno you burn (black).

Nov 96. (etched-d7") *(573164-7)* **GOLD DUST WOMAN. / (NY LOOSE: Spit)** [ ] [ ]
(above 45 was a limited edition on 'Polydor' UK, 'Hollywood' US)

Sep 98. (7"/c-s) *(GFS/+C 22345) <radio play>* **CELEBRITY SKIN. / BEST SUNDAY DRESS** [19] [85]
(cd-s+=) *(GFSTD 22345)* – Dying (original demo).

Sep 98. (cd/c/lp) *<(GED/GEC/GEF 25164)>* **CELEBRITY SKIN** [11] [9]
– Celebrity skin / Awful / Hit so hard / Malibu / Reasons to be beautiful / Dying / Use once & destroy / Northern star / Boys on the radio / Heaven tonight / Playing your song / Petals. *(special cd w/tour cd Jun99 +=; IND 90385)* – Pretty on the inside / Heaven tonight / Northern star / Awful / Paradise city / Celebrity skin.

Jan 99. (7") *(GFS 22369) <radio cut>* **MALIBU. / DRAG** [22] [81]
(cd-s+=) *(GFSTD 22369)* – It's all over now, baby blue.
(cd-s) *(GFSCX 22369)* – ('A'side) / Celebrity skin (live) / Reasons to be beautiful (live).

Interscope / Interscope

Jun 99. (7") *(INTS7 97098)* **AWFUL. / VIOLET (live)** [42] [ ]
(cd-s) *(INTDE 97099)* – ('A'side) / Miss World (live) / Celebrity skin (CD-Rom video).
(cd-s) *(INTDE 97098)* – ('A'side) / She walks on me (live) / Malibu (CD-Rom video).

– compilations, etc. –

Oct 95. (m-cd) *Caroline; <1470>* **ASK FOR IT** (radio session) [-] [ ]

Sep 97. (cd/c/lp) *City Slang; <(EFA 04995-2/-4/-1)>* **MY BODY, THE HAND GRENADE** [ ] [ ] Oct97
– Turpentine / Phonebill song / Retard girl / Burn black / Dicknail / Beautiful son / 20 years in Dakota / Miss World / Old age / Softer softest / He hit me (it felt like a kiss) / Season of the witch / Drown soda / Asking for it.

HOLOCAUST

Formed: Edinburgh, Scotland . . . 1978 by GARY LETTICE, JOHN MORTIMER, ED DUDLEY, ROBIN BEGG and PAUL COLLINS. Inspired by the NWOBHM, HOLOCAUST released a few singles in 1980 on the obscure independent label, 'Phoenix'. With NICKY ARKLESS replacing COLLINS, the group released the 'GARAGE DAYS REVISITED EP', hardly a massive hit but a record which impressed a young LARS ULRICH, METALLICA later taking the title for an EP of covers (which included a run through of HOLOCAUST's 'THE SMALL HOURS'). A debut album, 'THE NIGHTCOMBERS' surfaced in 1981, an unpretentious, yet influential record that marked them out as one of the unsung heroes of their genre. They split in 1982, ED DUDLEY leaving to form the similarly titled HOLOGRAM. The one album project was short-lived however, with the guitarist returning to the HOLOCAUST fold in '84 for the 'NO MAN'S LAND' set. They split once more, only to reform for the 90's, following METALLICA's well-publicised patronage.

Album rating: THE NIGHTCOMERS (*7) / LIVE, HOT CURRY AND WINE (*6) / NO MANS LAND (*4) / THE SOUND OF SOULS mini (*4) / HYPNOSIS OF BIRDS (*4) / SPIRITS FLY (*4) / THE COURAGE TO BE (*5)

GARY LETTICE – vocals / **ED DUDLEY** – guitar / **JOHN MORTIMER** – guitar / **ROBIN BEGG** – bass / **PAUL COLLINS** – drums

Phoenix not iss.

Jul 80. (7") *(PSP 1)* **HEAVY METAL MANIA. / ONLY AS YOUNG AS YOU FEEL** [ ] [-]

Dec 80. (7"ep) *(PSP 2)* **SMOKIN' VALES** [ ] [-]
– Smokin' valves / Friend or foe / Out my book.

—— **NICKY ARKLESS** – drums; repl. COLLINS

Oct 81. (7") *(PSP 3)* **GARAGE DAYS REVISITED EP** [ ] [-]
– Lovin' feeling / Danger / No nonsense / Death or glory / Forcedown / Breakdown.

1981. (lp) *(PSPLP 1)* **THE NIGHTCOMBERS** [ ] [-]
– Smokin' valves / Death or glory / Come on back / Mavrock / It don't matter to me / Cryin' shame / Heavy metal mania / Push it around / The nightcombers. *(cd-iss. Jul00 on 'Edgy'+=; EDGY 106)* – Heavy metal mania / Love's power / Only as young as you feel.

Apr 82. (12"ep) *(12PSP 4)* **COMING THROUGH. / DON'T WANNA BE (A LOSER) / GOOD THING GOING** [ ] [-]

—— DUDLEY left to form HOLOGRAM, who released one 'Phoenix' album, 'STEAL THE STARS' in 1982. He returned in 1983/84.

May 83. (lp) *(PSPLP 4)* **LIVE (HOT CURRY & WINE)** [ ] [-]
– No nonsense / Smokin' valves / Long the bell will toll / Jirmakenyerut / The small hours / Forcedown breakdown / Heavy metal mania – The nightcombers. *(cd-iss. Jul00 on 'Edgy'+=; EDGY 107)* – Lovin' feeling danger / Death or glory.

Apr 84. (lp) *(PSPLP 5)* **NO MAN'S LAND** [ ] [-]
– No man's land / We will rock and we will roll / No time left / Let's go / On the ropes / Satellite city / Power play / By the waterside / Missing presumed dead / Alone / Here come the good times.

Chrome S.P.V.

Jan 90. (m-lp/m-cd) *(CROM 301/+CD)* <820974> **THE SOUND OF SOULS** [ ] [ ]
– This annihilation / I smash the void / Dance into the vortex / Curious / Three ways to die.

Taurus Moon not iss.

Apr 93. (cd) *(TRMCD 010)* **HYPNOSIS OF BIRDS** [ ] [-]
– Hypnosis of birds / The tower / Book of seasons / Mercier and Camier / Small hours / Into Lebanon / Summer tides / Mortal mother / Cairnpapple hill / In the dark places of the earth / Caledonia.

Neat Metal not iss.

May 96. (cd) *(NM 006CD)* **SPIRITS FLY** [ ] [-]
– Into Lebanon / The small hours / Hypnosis of birds / The tower / Book of seasons / Mercier & camier / Summer tides / Mortal mother / Cairnpapple Hill / In the dark places of the Earth / Caledonia / Heavy metal mania / Death & glory / Master of puppets. *(re-iss. Oct97; same)*

Sound Riot not iss.

Oct 00. (cd-ep) *(SRP 004CD)* **HELLFIRE HOLOCAUST** [ ] [-]

Edgy Edgy

Oct 00. (cd) *(<EDGY 111>)* **THE COURAGE TO BE** [ ] [ ] May01
– The collective / A gentleman's penny / Farthing / Neurosis / When Penelope dreams (part 1 & 2) / From the mine shaft to the bike shed / Fundamentalist / Spanner omelette / Home from home / The age of reason.

HOLY BARBARIANS (see under ⇒ CULT)

HONEYCRACK

Formed: London, England . . . August '94 by WILDHEARTS outcasts, CJ (CHRIS JAGDHAR) and WILLIE DOWLING, along with MARK McRAE. As unadorned and unpretentious as The WILDHEARTS themselves, HONEYCRACK signed to 'Epic' records, scoring the following year with their first UK Top 50 hit, 'SITTING AT HOME'. Multi-racial Brit-rock similar to TERRORVISION and METALLICA fused with the harmony of The BEACH BOYS, the group enjoyed a further two chart encounters, before releasing their GIL NORTON-produced debut set, 'PROZAIC' (1996). This Top 40 album gave 'Epic' another stab at the charts with the re-issued 'SITTING AT HOME', the band subsequently moving to another label before splitting early the following year. CJ recruited new members (JEFF and STIDI) to form The JELLYS. They have since released a clutch of singles and two albums, 'WELCOME TO OUR WORLD' (1998) and 'DOCTORED FOR SUPERSOUND' (2000), the latter with Dumfries-born guitarist DAVIE JARDINE. • **Covered:** HEY BULLDOG (Beatles).

Album rating: PROZAIC (*7) / Jellys: WELCOME TO OUR WORLD (*6) / DOCTORED FOR SUPERSOUND (*5)

CJ (CHRIS JAGDHAR) – vocals, guitar (ex-WILDHEARTS, ex-TATTOOED LOVE BOYS) / **WILLIE DOWLING** – bass / **MARK McRAE** – guitar / **PETE CLARKE** – bass / **HUGO DEGENHARDT** – drums

Epic not iss.

Nov 95. (7"/c-s) *(662538-7/-4)* **SITTING AT HOME / IF I HAD A LIFE** [42] [-]
(cd-s+=) *(662538-2)* – 5 minutes / Hey bulldog.

Feb 96. (7"yellow) *(662864-7)* **GO AWAY. / GUN** [41] [-]
(cd-s+=) *(662864-2)* – Where do you come from?
(cd-s) *(662864-5)* – ('A'side) / Sitting at home (live) / Powerless (live).

May 96. (7"blue) *(663147-7)* **KING OF MISERY. / GO AWAY (live)** [32] [-]
(cd-s+=) *(663147-2)* – Paperman (live) / Hey bulldog (live).
(cd-s) *(663147-5)* – ('A'side) / Mr. Ultra sheen / All gone wrong / Still dead (. . .and then there were three).

May 96. (cd/c/lp/white-lp) *(484230-2/-4/-1/-0)* **PROZAIC** [34] [-]
– King of misery / No – please don't / Go away / Powerless / The genius is loose / Good good feeling / If I had a life / I hate myself and everybody else / Animals / Samantha Pope / Paperman / Sitting at home / Parasite.

Jul 96. (c-s) *(663503-4)* **SITTING AT HOME / ('A'-Renegade Soundwave remix)** [32] [-]
(cd-s+=) *(663503-2)* – Animals (Martin Steib remix).
(cd-s) *(663503-5)* – ('A'side) / Good, good feeling (live) / No – please don't / Samantha Pope (live).

E'G not iss.

Nov 96. (cd-s) *(EGO 52-A)* **ANYWAY / MORE THAN I WAS / ANYWAY (demo)** [67] [-]
(cd-s) *(EGO 52-B)* – ('A'side) / You're not worth it / ('A'-Papa Brittle mix).

—— split early in 1997

JELLYS

—— were formed by **CJ** who recruited **JEFF** – bass, vocals / **STIDI** – drums, vocals

Proud not iss.

Sep 97. (cd-ep) *(PROUDCD 1)* **JELLY BELLY EP** [ ] [-]
– Over you / Fat cat / One way or another / Stupid.

Mission Impossible not iss.

Apr 98. (cd-ep) *(MIRCDS 1)* **HEADS FIRST . . . LEGS LAST EP** [ ] [-]
– Strawberry icecream / Up to me / Be my alien / My little squirt.

Aug 98. (cd-ep) *(MIRCDS 2)* **FEELS LIKE SUNSHINE / LET IT GO / HANG UP** [ ] [-]

Oct 98. (cd/lp) *(MIR CDL/VL 1)* **WELCOME TO OUR WORLD** [ ] [-]
– My little squirt / Just a love song / Lemonade girl / Messed up / Feels like sunshine / A big trip / You've got it all / Strawberry icecream / Hang up / Up to me / Over you / It's going down / Stupid / Jughead / Girl in my pocket / Falling for you / Love me, love us / Had a good time (animal magic).

Feb 99. (cd-s) *(MIRCDS 3)* **LEMONADE GIRL / YOU'RE THE ONE / SO HIGH** [ ] [-]

Aug 99. (cd) *(MIRCDL 2)* **BIG TRIP ON A PANTOMIME HOARSE** [ ] [-]

—— (Dec'99) **DAVIE JARDINE** (b. Dumfries, Scotland) – guitar, vocals; repl.

Feb 00. (cd-s) *(MIRCDS 4)* **MILK'N'HONEY / SONG FOR YOU / FASTER** [ ] [-]
(cd-s) *(MIRCDS 5)* – ('A'side) / In a rut / ('A'live).

Apr 00. (cd-s) *(MIRCDS 6)* **SHIP GOES DOWN / YOU & ME / MY LUCKY DAY** [ ] [-]

May 00. (cd) *(MIRCDL 3)* **DOCTORED FOR SUPERSOUND** [ ] [-]
– Just for 69 / Ship goes down / Don't throw it away / Loser / 90° in the shade / Milk'n'honey / Beta-blocker / Who loves ya baby / Popcorn / Fly / We don't care / 3rd gender classification / Leaving / Kings of garage land / Falling down / Skinny / Drug induced friend / Doctored for supersound / A cotton pickin' time.

HONEYDRIPPERS (see under ⇒ LED ZEPPELIN)

HOUSE OF LORDS (see under ⇒ GIUFFRIA)

Greg HOWE

Born: Easton, Pennsylvania, USA. After cutting his teeth on the local club scene with DUKE (also featuring his brother AL), HOWE became one of the late 80's proteges of eagle-eared Mike Varney and his 'Shrapnel' label. Birthplace of the "shred guitar" movement, 'Shrapnel' was home to hordes of would-be virtuosos eager to demonstrate their flying fingered wizardry and neo-classical genius. Yet 'GREG HOWE' (1988) announced a slightly more organic talent, adept at limbering up with some funk/fusion-influenced licks as well as lightning speed fretwork, the talents of BILLY SHEEHAN and ATMA ANUR oiling the rhythmic wheels. GREG adopted the HOWE II moniker for the release of his second set, 'HIGH GEAR' (1989), a bonafide band set-up involving AL on lead vocals along with a rhythm section of VERN PARSONS and JOE NEVOLO. Cruising the melodic party-rock freeway normally frequented by sun-tanned L.A. acts such as VAN HALEN, the album channelled virtuoso excess into a more accessible song-orientated structure with imnpressive results. 'NOW HEAR THIS' (1990) went even further, succumbing to a polished production and a brazen attempt at commercial acceptance which sold HOWE's talents short. Wisely perhaps, GREG retreated to his home studio where he began crafting a series of imstrumental solo sets oblivious to the new grunge-orientated direction of the metal scene. The likes of 'INTROSPECTION' (1993), 'UNCERTAIN TERMS' (1994), 'PARALLAX' (1995) and 'FIVE' (1996) found him catering squarely to the guitar freak market with dizzying, diverse displays of technical prowess rooted in fusion. The mid-90's also saw him collaborate with fellow Pennsylvanian shredder, RICHIE KOTZEN on the 'TILT' set, a partnership further developed on 1997's 'RICHIE KOTZEN – GREG HOWE PROJECT'. 'ASCEND' (1999) finally marked the end of GREG's long association with 'Shrapnel', the veteran axeman signing to the 'Tone Center' label for the acclaimed 'HYPERACUITY' (2000). A masterclass in the complex possibilities inherent in the genres of jazz, blues and rock, the album deftly demonstrated HOWE's fleet-fingered adaptability and even featured a reading of the Stevie Wonder classic, 'I WISH'.

Album rating: GREG HOWE (*5) / HIGH GEAR (*6) / NOW HEAR THIS (*6) / INTROSPECTION compilation (*6) / UNCERTAIN TERMS (*5) / PARALLAX (*4) / FIVE (*4) / ASCEND (*5) / HYPERCUITY (*6)

GREG HOWE – guitar / with **BILLY SHEEHAN** – bass / **ATMA ANUR** – drums

Roadrunner Shrapnel

Aug 88. (lp/cd) *(RR 9531-1/-2)* <SH 1037/+CD> **GREG HOWE** [ ] [ ]
– Kick it all over / The pepper shake / Bad racket / Super unleaded / Land of ladies / Straight up / Red handed / After hours / Little roses.

HOWE II

GREG HOWE – guitars / **AL HOWE** – vocals / **VERN PARSONS** – bass / **JOE NEVOLO** – drums

Oct 89. (lp/c/cd) *(RR 9467-1/-4/-2)* <SH 1044/+C/CD> **HIGH GEAR** [ ] [ ]
– High gear / Carry the torch / Strat-o-various / Disorderly conduct / Thinking of

you / Standing on the line / Ferocious / Don't let the sloe gin (order the wine) / Party favours / Social fever.

— **KEVIN SOFFREA** – drums; repl. NEVOLO

Sep 91. (cd/c/lp) *(RR 9288-2/-4/-1)* *<SH 1053/+C/CD>* **NOW HEAR THIS**
– Fat cat / The ride / Now hear this / Motherlode / Bigger the bite / Crowd pleaser / A delicacy / Tip of my tongue / Heart of a woman / A few good men.

GREG HOWE

— solo again

Nov 93. (cd) *<SH 1064CD>* **INTROSPECTION** (compilation) [-]
– Jump start / Button up / Come and get it / In step / Desiderata / No place like home / Direct injection / Pay as you go.

Nov 94. (cd) *<SH 1075CD>* **UNCERTAIN TERMS** [-]
– Faulty outlet / 5 mile limit / Run with it / Business conduct / Public and private / Song for Rachelle / Stringed sanity / Solid state / Second thought.

Nov 95. (cd) *<SH 1095CD>* **PARALLAX** [-]
– Howe 'bout it / Found unwound / Dance / Time off / Joker's wild / The portrait / Bottom line / On sail / Roundhouse.

Oct 96. (cd) *<SH 1101CD>* **FIVE** [-]
– Just kiddin' / Sit / Three toed sloth / The terrace / Acute / Quiet hunt / Bach mock / Plush interior / Dusty maid / Skyline.

May 99. (cd) *<SH 1128CD>* **ASCEND** [-]
– Unlocked / Tales told / Garden of harmony / Abrupt terminal / La villa strangiato / Maniacal / Her dance / Full throttle.

not iss. / Tone Center

Jun 00. (cd) *<4009>* **HYPERCUITY** [-]
– Hypercuity / Blindfold drive / Order of dawn / Heat activated / Receptionist / Trinka / I wish.

H2O

Formed: New York, USA ... 1993 initially as SICK OF IT ALL's stage party piece when roadie, TOBY MORSE, picked up a mic and augmented their encores (during a tour he had sung on the hard-rock pastiche, 'MY LOVE IS REAL'). H2O were really born late in '94, when TOBY and ex-SOIA drummer, MAX CAPSHAW, played their first NY gig (he subsequently drafted in new sticksman, TODD FRIEND plus TOBY – his older brother – and RUSTY PISTACHIO). The angst-ridden spirit of the mid to late 80's hardcore scene was resurrected once again with the release of their eponymous debut album in '96. Adding ex-SHELTER bassist, ADAM BLAKE to the fold, H2O released a second set (their first for 'Epitaph'), 'THICKER THAN WATER', the following year. Their love of hardcore punk shone through, although the band always interspersed their tracks with melody. The liquid theme continued with 'F.T.T.W.' (1999), that's 'FINALLY TASTE THE WATER', another blink-and-you-miss-it set of rollicking hardcore jollies. With any form of punk big business these days, H2O were subsequently snapped up by 'M.C.A.', making their major label debut with 'GO' (2001). Backing up the often overly simplistic lyrical fare this time around was an attempt to assimilate 80's influences into their buoyant riffing, a concept which sounded as lame on record as it did on paper.

Album rating: H20 (*6) / THICKER THAN WATER (*6) / F.T.T.W. (*6) / GO (*4)

TOBY MORSE – vocals / **TODD MORSE** – guitar (ex-OUTCROWD) / **RUSTY PISTACHIO** – guitar / **ERIC RICE** – bass / **TODD FRIEND** – drums (ex-OUTCROWD) repl. MAX CAPSHAW

Blackout / Blackout

Jun 96. (cd) *<(BLK 030E-CD)>* **H2O**
– 5 yr. plan / Scene report / Spirit of '84 / I know why / Gen-eric / Surrounded / Here today, gone tomorrow / Family tree / Hi-low / My curse / My love is real. *(lp-iss.Sep96; BLK 030E-LP) (cd re-iss. Sep00; same)*

— **ADAM BLAKE** – bass (ex-SHELTER) repl. RICE

Epitaph / Epitaph

Nov 97. (cd/c/lp) *<(6505-2/-4/-1)>* **THICKER THAN WATER**
– Universal language / Everready / Talk too much / I see it in us / Sacred heart / Innocent kids / Scarred / Go / This time / Friend / Plus / The phone song / Responsible / Wake up / Thicker than water.

Jun 98. (cd-ep) *<(1004-2)>* **EVERREADY / FRIEND / UNIVERSAL LANGUAGE / HERE TODAY, GONE TOMORROW**

May 99. (cd/lp) *<(6556-2/-2)>* **F.T.T.W.**
– Faster than the world / Empty pockets / One life, one chance / Guilty by association / Fading / Bootstraps / Can I overcome / Found the truth within / Old school recess / Helpless not hopeless / On your feet / Day by day / Force field / Ez.2.B anti / M&M / Reputation calls / Liberate / Follow the three way / Not just boys fun.

Side One / not iss.

Jan 01. (7") *(S1 11)* **IT WAS A GOOD DAY. / I WANT I WANT** [-]

M.C.A. / M.C.A.

May 01. (cd) *<112583>* **GO** [-]
– Role model / Self reliable / Well behaved / Out of debt / Memory lane / Ripe or rotting? / I want I want / Songs remain / Forest king / Shine the light / Repair / Underneath the flames.

Glenn HUGHES

Born: 21 Aug'52, Crannock, Staffordshire, England. Initially inspired by soul music, a youthful HUGHES joined R&B act, The NEWS in 1967. A few years later, he and another member of the said outfit, MEL GALLEY, formed TRAPEZE, this hard-rocking formation releasing four albums for 'Threshold', the MOODY BLUES' label. Turning down a chance to join ELO in '73, the singer/guitarist opted instead to join DEEP PURPLE as replacement bassist for the departed ROGER GLOVER. He stuck around for three mid 70's studio albums, 'Burn', 'Stormbringer' and 'Come Taste The Band', although by this point 'PURPLE were already past their prime. He subsequently reformed TRAPEZE, although his tenure with the band was brief and he left to pursue a solo career. This was initiated by 'PLAY ME OUT' in 1978, a mediocre affair that did little to resurrect former glories. The HUGHES-THRALL collaboration met with similarly discouraging reviews early in 1983, although it later came to be regarded as something of a forgotten masterpiece. A few years later, HUGHES surfaced alongside a plethora of musicians under the banner of PHENOMENA. To regain some credibility, he accepted an invitation to become part of BLACK SABBATH, replacing IAN GILLAN as frontman. In the 90's, HUGHES enjoyed a bizarre guest spot with KLF, augmenting the hit single, 'America: What Time Is Love'. This spurred the singer on to resurrect his solo career (after 25 years!), the resulting 'BLUES' (1993) his first album for 'Roadrunner'. The rest of the 90's (and into 2000 . . .) saw HUGHES churn out album after album, although one of them did manage to pay tribute to long-time deceased DEEP PURPLE axeman, TOMMY BOLIN, late in '99.

Album rating: PLAY ME OUT (*5) / Hughes-Thrall: HUGHES-THRALL (*6) / Glenn Hughes: BLUES (*5) / FROM NOW ON (*6) / BURNING JAPAN (*5) / FEEL (*4) / ADDICTION (*6) / GOD OF VOICE – THE BEST BEST OF . . . compilation (*7) / THE WAY IT IS (*4) / A TRIBUTE TO TOMMY BOLIN (*5) / THE RETURN OF THE CRYSTAL KARMA (*4)

GLENN HUGHES – vocals, guitar, bass, keyboards (ex-TRAPEZE, ex-DEEP PURPLE) / with **MEL GALLEY** – guitar (ex-TRAPEZE) / **DAVE HOLLAND** – drums (ex-TRAPEZE) / **BOB BOWMAN** – guitar / **PAT TRAVERS** – guitar / + others on session

Safari / not iss.

Apr 78. (lp/c) *(LONG/+C 2)* **PLAY ME OUT** [-]
– I got it covered / Space high / It's about time / L.A. cut off / Well / Solution / Your love is like a fire / Destiny / I found a woman. *(re-iss. Aug90 on 'Connoisseur' cd/c/lp; += VSOP CD/MC/LP 153)* – Smile / There goes my baby / Gypsy woman / Any day now / Glimmer twins medley. *(cd re-iss. Mar95 on 'R.P.M.' +=; RPM 149)* – Smile / Getting near to you / Fool's condition / Take me with you / She knows. *(<cd re-iss. Jul98 on 'Cleopatra'; CLEO 313>) (cd re-iss. Sep99 on 'Purple'; PUR 312)*

Nov 79. (7") *(SAFE 14)* **I FOUND A WOMAN. / L.A. CUT OFF** [-]

HUGHES-THRALL

GLENN HUGHES – vocals, bass / **PAT THRALL** – guitar (ex-PAT TRAVERS BAND) / **FRANKIE BANALI** – drums (ex-QUIET RIOT)

Epic / Boulevard

Dec 82. (7") *<03355>* **BEG, BORROW OR STEAL. / WHO WILL YOU RUN TO** [-] 79

Jan 83. (lp) *(EPC 25052)* *<ARZ 38116>* **HUGHES-THRALL**
– I got your number / The look in your eye / Beg, borrow or steal / Where did the time go / Muscle and blood / Hold out your life / Who will you run to / Coast to coast / First step of love.

— just a one-off as he subsequently teamed up with old cohort, MEL GALLEY and a plethora of big names to record the concept, 'PHENOMENA' album (1985). GLENN was then off to join BLACK SABBATH before going solo for the 90's.

GLENN HUGHES

— with various session people

Roadrunner / not iss.

Jan 93. (cd/c) *(RR 9088-2/-4)* **BLUES** (L.A. BLUES AUTHORITY VOL.II) [-]
– The boy can sing the blues / I'm the man / Here comes the rebel / What can I do for ya / You don't have to save me anymore / So much love to give / Shake the ground / Hey buddy (you got me wrong) / Have you read the book / Life of misery / Can't take away my pride / Right to live. *(cd re-iss. Sep96; same)*

Feb 94. (cd/c) *(RR 9007-2/-4)* *<34781>* **FROM NOW ON**
– Pickin' up the pieces / Lay my body down / The only one / Why don't you stay / Walking on the water / The liar / Into the void / You were always there / If you don't want me to / Devil in you / Homeland / From now on / Burn. *(cd re-iss. Sep96; same) (cd re-iss. Feb99 on 'Empire'; ERCD 1001)*

S.P.V. / Shrapnel

Jul 95. (cd) *(SPV 0851820-2)* *<SH 1085CD>* **BURNING JAPAN LIVE (live)** Nov95
– Burn / Liar / Muscle and blood / Lay my body down / From now on / Into the void / Still in love with you / Coast to coast / This time around / Owed to G / Gettin' lighter / You keep on moving / Lady double dealer / I got your number / Stormbringer. *(re-iss. Mar99; SPV 1761820-2)*

Nov 95. (cd) *(SPV 085 8976-2)* **FEEL** [-]
– Big time / Livin' for the minute / Does it mean that much to you / Save me tonight (I'll be waiting) / Redline / Coffeee and vanilla / Push / She loves your money / Speak your mind / Talking to messiah / Maybe your baby. *(re-iss. Mar99; SPV 1768976-2) <US-iss.Sep00 on 'E.M.I.'; 50787>*

Nov 97. (cd) *(SPV 0854441-2)* *<SH 1132CD>* **ADDICTION**
– Death of me / Down / Addiction / Madelaine / Talk about it / I'm not your slave / Cover me / Blue jade / Justified man / I don't want to live that way again. *(re-iss. Mar99; same)*

Mar 99. (cd) *(SPV 0852103-2)* *<SH 1130CD>* **THE WAY IT IS**
– The way it is / You kill me / Neverafter / Rain on me / The curse / Freedom / The truth will set me free / Stoned in the temple / Too far gone / Second son / Take you down / Don't look away.

Oct 99. (cd; as GLENN HUGHES & FRIENDS) *(SPV 0856018-2)* **A TRIBUTE TO TOMMY BOLIN**

Jun 00. (cd) *(SPV 0852181-2)* **THE RETURN OF THE CRYSTAL KARMA** [-]
– The state I'm in / Midnight mediated / It's alright / Switch the mojo / Gone / The other side of me / Angela / Owed to "J" / This life / Days of Avalon / You kill me / Neverafter / First step of love / No stranger to love / Coast to coast / Your love is alright.
(re-iss. Aug00 on 'Storm Surge'; 693723218120)

– compilations, etc. –

Nov 96. (cd; all his groups) *(60234)* **THE BEST OF GLENN HUGHES** [ ] [-]
Jun 98. (cd) *Zero; (XRCN 2027)* **GOD OF VOICE: THE VERY BEST OF GLENN HUGHES** [ ] [-]
Aug 98. (cd; by GLENN HUGHES & GEOFF DOWNES) *Blueprint; (<BP 285CD>)* **THE WORK TAPES** [ ] [-]
Feb 99. (cd) *Empire; (ERCD 1030)* **GREATEST HITS** [ ] [-]
Jul 00. (cd) *S.P.V.; (SPV 31029960)* **FEEL / ADDICTION** [ ] [-]

HUM

Formed: Champaign, Illinois, USA ... 1989 by JEFF DIMPSEY, TIM LASH, BRYAN ST. PERE and MATT TALBOTT. Enterprising and self-reliant, HUM built up a grassroots following through heavy touring while initiating their own label, '12 Inch Records', for the release of debut album, 'ELECTRA 2000' (1993). A few years later, a follow-up set, 'YOU'D PREFER AN ASTRONAUT' was bubbling under the US Top 100; released on 'R.C.A.' ('Dedicated' in the US), the record set layers of mid-paced, muscular guitar against TALBOTT's complex, cryptic lyrics to compelling effect. In early '98, HUM were back with a third long-player, 'DOWNWARD IS HEAVENWARD', carrying on in much the same vein.

Album rating: ELECTRA 2000 (*5) / YOU'D PREFER AN ASTRONAUT (*6) / DOWNWARD IS HEAVENWARD (*5)

MATT TALBOTT (b.27 Jun'67, Geneseo, Illinois) – vocals, guitar / **TIM LASH** (b.16 Jun'74) – guitar / **JEFF DIMPSEY** (b.23 May'67) – bass / **BRYAN ST. PERE** (b. 2 Apr'66, Evergreen Park, Illinois) – drums

not iss. / 12-Inch Records

1993. (cd) **ELECTRA 2000** [-] [ ]
– Iron clad Lou / Pinch and roll / Shovel / Pewter / Scraper / Fire head / Sun dress / Double dip / Winder. *(hidden track+=)* – Diffuse. *(UK-iss.Sep97 on 'Martians Go Home'; MGH 001)*

Dedicated / R.C.A.

Feb 96. (7"green) *(HUM 001)* **STARS. / STARS (version)** [ ] [-]
(cd-s) *(HUM 001CD)* – ('A'side) / Boy with stick / Baby, baby.
Mar 96. (cd/lp) *(DED CD/LP 023)* **YOU'D PREFER AN ASTRONAUT** [ ] [ ] Apr95
– Little dipper / The pod / Stars / Suicide machine / The very old man / Why I like the robins / I'd like your hair long / I hate it too / Songs of farewell and departure. *(originally issued in the UK Oct95 as lp on '12 Inch Inch Records'; TIN 012)*
May 96. (7") *(HUM 002)* **THE POD. / MS LAZARUS** [ ] [ ]
(cd-s+=) *(HUM 002CD)* – Firehead.
Jan 98. (cd) *<67446>* **DOWNWARD IS HEAVENWARD** [-] [ ]
– Isle of the cheetah / Comin' home / If you are to bloom / Ms. Lazarus / Afternoon with the Axolotis / Green to me / Dreamboat / The inuit promise / Apollo / The scientists.

HUMAN WASTE PROJECT

Formed: Huntington Beach, California, USA . . . 1993 by bass-player JEFF SCHARTOFF and singer ROMAN MARISAK. The latter went AWOL for a period (returned as live guitarist, but only briefly) and was replaced by the frighteningly peroxide manic blonde mistress, AIMEE ECHO, while enlisting MIKE TEMPESTA on guitar and drummer SCOTT ELLIS. Like KORN, PJ HARVEY on BAUHAUS pills, HWP supported the likes of KORN (becoming friends of JONATHAN DAVIES), although it took some time to get some vinyl into the shops. This came via the 'E:LUX' set released late in '97, an at times remarkable debut, loved by Kerrang! writers and readers alike. However, just as things looked promising, HWP lost their contract with 'Hollywood' and splintered into different segments. JEFF went full-time with HWP original, ROMAN MARISAK, in their industrial/sci-fi inspired side-project, PROFESSIONAL MURDER MUSIC, while AIMEE and SCOTT formed the more indie-biased, HERO, with the Baltimore-raised pair of JAMIE MILLER (ex-SNOT) and MIKE SMITH (the original MIKE joined POWERMAN 5000 with ROB ZOMBIE's kid brother, SPIDER). PMM, who also boasted BRIAN HARRAH (ex-TURA SATANA guitarist), CHRIS BLAIR (second bassist) and JUSTIN BENNET (on drums), premiered an eponymous internet-only debut album late in 1998, while HERO were still looking for a recording contract.

Album rating: E:LUX (*6)

AIMEE ECHO – vocals; repl. ROMAN MARISAK / **MIKE TEMPESTA** – guitar / **JEFF SCHARTOFF** – bass / **SCOTT ELLIS** – drums

Hollywood / Hollywood

Dec 97. (cd-ep) *(569293-2)* **POWERSTRIP / ELECTRA / SHE GIVES / POWERSTRIP (extended)** [ ] [-]
Mar 98. (cd) *<(HOL 162067)>* **E:LUX** [ ] [ ] Jun97
– Grave robbers from Mars / Disease / Drug store / Exit wound / Shine / Hold me down / Electra / Drowned / Interlude / Powerstrip / Spain / Slide / Dog / Get with it.

—— split in the summer of '98 (see above for breakaway details)

HUMBLE PIE

Formed: Essex, England . . . Spring 1969 as a mini-supergroup by STEVE MARRIOT (ex-SMALL FACES, vocals, guitar) and PETER FRAMPTON (ex-HERD, vocals, guitar). Recruiting GREG RIDLEY (bass, ex-SPOOKY TOOTH) and JERRY SHIRLEY (drums, ex-LITTLE WOMEN), the band signed to Andrew Loog Oldham's 'Immediate' label and released their debut album, 'AS SAFE AS YESTERDAY', in the summer of '69. A solid collection of rootsy rock, the record spawned a Top 5 UK single with 'NATURAL BORN BUGIE', MARRIOT ditching the chirpy cockney popster persona he'd developed with the SMALL FACES in favour of an 'authentic' R&B rasp. The more acoustic-based follow-up, 'TOWN AND COUNTRY' (1969) flopped, and HUMBLE PIE returned from an American tour in late '69 to discover that their record label had gone under. Severe financial problems ensued until help came in the form of US lawyer, Dee Anthony, who helped secure the band a new deal with A&M. The eponymous 'HUMBLE PIE' (1970) failed to resurrect their fortunes, as did the harder-edged 'ROCK ON' (1971), Anthony subsequently packing the band off to America on another tour from whence came the US gold-selling live album, 'PERFORMANCE-ROCKIN' THE FILLMORE' (1971). Despite his diminutive size, MARRIOT had a towering stage presence, the singer blazing his way through a fiery set of boogie-based blues-rock, both HUMBLE PIE originals and frenetic covers including Muddy Waters' 'ROLLIN' STONE' and Dr. John's 'I WALK ON GILDED SPLINTERS'. FRAMPTON departed for a solo career later that year, ex-COLOSSEUM man, DAVE CLEMPSON taking his place. While FRAMPTON had proved a melodic acoustic-rock foil to MARRIOT's hard rockin' excess, the new-look 'PIE continued to move in a heavier direction with 'SMOKIN' (1972), the highest charting album in the band's career, reaching No.6 in the States. Augmented by all-girl backing trio, The BLACKBERRIES (CLYDIE KING, BILLIE BARNUM & VANETTA FIELDS), the band attempted a hard rock/soul fusion with the half live/half studio double set, 'EAT IT' (1973). The album was another American Top 20 hit but HUMBLE PIE's popularity was on the wane, a further two efforts, 'THUNDERBOX' (1974) and 'STREET RATS' (1975) barely making the charts and receiving a scathing critical reaction. The group finally split shortly after the release of the latter album, SHIRLEY forming NATURAL GAS with ex-BADFINGER guitarist JOEY MOLLAND while MARRIOT put together the short lived STEVE MARRIOTT ALL-STARS with MICKEY FINN (guitar, ex-T.REX), IAN WALLACE (drums, ex-KING CRIMSON) and DAMON BUTCHER (keyboards). CLEMPSON, meanwhile, joined GREENSLADE. After a brief SMALL FACES reunion in the late 70's, MARRIOT reformed HUMBLE PIE along with SHIRLEY and new members BOBBY TENCH (guitar, ex-STREETWALKERS, ex-JEFF BECK GROUP) and ANTHONY JONES (bass). Signed to 'Atco', the band released two generally ignored albums, 'ON TO VICTORY' (1980) and 'GO FOR THE THROAT' (1981) before disbanding finally in 1981. MARRIOT continued to tour, releasing a low key solo album, 'PACKET OF THREE', in 1986. Hopes of a musical reunion between MARIOTT and FRAMPTON were finally dashed on 20th April '91 when MARIOTT was tragically killed in a fire at his Essex cottage. • **Songwriters:** All took a shot at writing, with MARRIOTT the main contributor. Covered; C'MON EVERYBODY + HALLELUJAH I LOVE HER SO (Eddie Cochran) / ROADRUNNER (Junior Walker) / HONKY TONK WOMAN (Rolling Stones) / ROCK'N'ROLL MUSIC (Chuck Berry) / ALL SHOOK UP (Elvis Presley) / etc.

Album rating: AS SAFE AS YESTERDAY (*6) / TOWN AND COUNTRY (*5) / HUMBLE PIE (*5) / ROCK ON (*6) / PERFORMANCE – ROCKIN' THE FILLMORE (*7) / SMOKIN' (*5) / EAT IT (*5) / THUNDERBOX (*4) / STREET RATS (*3) / ON TO VICTORY (*3) / GO FOR THE THROAT (*2) / HOT N' NASTY – THE ANTHOLOGY compilation (*7) / Steve Marriott: MARRIOTT (*4) / PACKET OF THREE (what else . . . *3) / 30 SECONDS TO MIDNIGHT exploitation (*4)

STEVE MARRIOTT (b.30 Jan'47, London, England) – vocals, guitar, keyboards (ex-SMALL FACES) / **PETER FRAMPTON** (b.22 Apr'50, Beckenham, England) – vocals, guitar (ex-HERD) / **GREG RIDLEY** (b.23 Oct'47, Carlisle, England) – bass (ex-SPOOKY TOOTH) / **JERRY SHIRLEY** (b. 4 Feb'52) – drums (ex-LITTLE WOMEN)

Immediate / Immediate

Jul 69. (lp) *(IMSP 025)* *<101>* **AS SAFE AS YESTERDAY** [32] [ ]
– Desperation / Stick shift / Buttermilk boy / Growing closer / As safe as yesterday / Bang? / Alabama '69 / I'll go alone / A nifty little number like you / What you will. *(cd-iss. Nov89 on 'Line'; LICD 900296) (cd re-iss. Dec92 on 'Repertoire'+=;)* – Natural born bugie / Wrist job. *(lp re-iss. Dec99 on 'Get Back'; GET 549)*
Sep 69. (7") *(IM 082)* **NATURAL BORN BUGIE. / WRIST JOB** [4] [ ]
(re-iss. Feb83; same)
Oct 69. (7") *<101>* **NATURAL BORN BUGIE. / I'LL GO ALONE** [-] [ ]
Dec 69. (lp) *(IMSP 027)* **TOWN AND COUNTRY** [ ] [-]
– Take me back / The sad bag of shaky Jake / The light of love / Cold lady / Down home again / Ollie Ollie / Every mother's son / Heartbeat / Only you can say / Silver tongue / Home and away. *(re-iss. 1978 on 'Charly'; CR 300016) (cd-iss. Nov93; CDIMM 020) (cd-iss. Dec92 on 'Repertoire'+=;)* – Greg's song / 79th Street blues. *(cd re-iss. Feb95 on 'Charly'; CDIMM 020)*

A&M / A&M

Jul 70. (lp) *(AMLS 986)* *<4270>* **HUMBLE PIE** [ ] [ ]
– Live with me / Only a roach / One eyed trouser-snake rumba / Earth and water song / I'm ready / Theme from Skint (see you later liquidator) / Red light mamma / Red hot / Sucking on the sweet vine.
Mar 71. (lp) *(AMLS 203)* *<4301>* **ROCK ON** [ ] [ ]
– Shine on / Sour grain / 79th and sunset / Stone cold fever / Rollin' stone / A song for Jenny / The light / Big George / Strange days / Red neck jump. *(cd-iss. 1988 on 'Mobile Fidelity'; MFCD 847)*
Sep 71. (7") *<1282>* **I DON'T NEED NO DOCTOR (live). / SONG FOR JENNY** [-] [73]
Nov 71. (d-lp/d-c) *(AMLH/CDM 63506)* *<3506>* **PERFORMANCE – ROCKIN' THE FILLMORE (live)** [32] [21]
– Four day creep / I'm ready / Stone cold fever / I walk on guilded splinters / Rollin' stone / Hallelujah (I love her so) / I don't need no doctor. *(re-iss. 1974;)*

—— **DAVE CLEMPSON** (b. 5 Sep'45) – guitar (ex-COLOSSEUM) repl. FRAMPTON who went solo

Mar 72. (lp) *(AMLS 64342) <4342>* **SMOKIN'** [28] [6]
– Hot 'n' nasty / The fixer / You're so good to me / C'mon everybody / Old time feelin' / 30 days in the hole / (I'm a) Road runner / Roadrunner "G" jam / I wonder who / Sweet peace and time.

Apr 72. (7") *<1349>* **HOT 'N' NASTY. / YOU"RE SO GOOD FOR ME** [-] [52]

Sep 72. (7") *<1366>* **30 DAYS IN THE HOLE. / SWEET PEACE AND TIME** [-] [ ]

— now augmented by all-girl backing trio The BLACKBERRIES (**CLYDIE KING / BILLIE BARNUM + VANETTA FIELDS**)

Jan 73. (7") *(AMS 7052) <1406>* **BLACK COFFEE. / SAY NO MORE** [ ] [ ]

Apr 73. (d-lp) *(AMLD 6004) <3701>* **EAT IT** (1-side live) [34] [13] Mar73
– Get down to it / Good booze and bad women / Is it for love / Drugstore cowboy / Black coffee / I believe to my soul / Shut up and don't interrupt me / That's how strong my love is / Say no more / Oh, Bella (all that's hers) / Summer song / Beckton dumps / Up our sleeve / Honky tonk woman / (I'm a) Road runner.

Jun 73. (7") *(AMS 7070) <1440>* **GET DOWN TO IT. / HONKY TONK WOMAN (live)** [ ] [ ]

Oct 73. (7") *(AMS 7090)* **OH LA DE DA. / THE OUTCROWD** [ ] [-]

Feb 74. (lp) *(AMLH 63611) <3611>* **THUNDERBOX** [ ] [52]
– Thunderbox / Groovin' with Jesus / I can't stand the rain / Anna / No way / Rally with Ali / Don't worry, be happy / Ninety-nine pounds / Every single day / No money down / Drift away / Oh la de da.

May 74. (7") *<1530>* **NINETY-NINE POUNDS. / RALLY WITH ALI** [-] [ ]

Feb 75. (lp) *(AMLS 68282) <4514>* **STREET RATS** [ ] [100]
– Street rat / Rock'n'roll music / We can work it out / Scored out / Road hog / Rain / Funky to the bone / Let me be your lovemaker / Countryman / Stomp / Drive my car / Queens and nuns.

Mar 75. (7") *(AMS 7185)* **ROCK'N'ROLL MUSIC. / SCORED OUT** [ ] [-]

Jul 75. (7") *<1711>* **ROCK'N'ROLL MUSIC. / ROAD HOG** [-] [ ]

— Disbanded Spring 1975. JERRY SHIRLEY formed NATURAL GAS, and the others joined

STEVE MARRIOTT ALL-STARS

also included **DAMON BUTCHER** – keyboards / **IAN WALLACE** – drums (ex-KING CRIMSON) / **MICKEY FINN** – guitar (ex-T.REX)

A&M A&M

May 76. (lp) *(AMLH 64572) <4572>* **MARRIOTT** [ ] [ ]
– Star in my life / Are you lonely for me baby / You don't know me / Late night lady / Early evening light / East side struttin' / Lookin' for love / Help me through the day / Midnight rock'n'rollin' / Wam bam thank you ma'am.

Jun 76. (7") *(AMS 7230)* **STAR IN MY LIFE. / MIDNIGHT ROCK'N'ROLLIN'** [ ] [-]

Jun 76. (7") *<1825>* **STAR IN MY LIFE. / EAST SIDE STRUTTIN'** [-] [ ]

— CLEMPSON and BUTCHER joined ROUGH DIAMOND. WALLACE toured with BOB DYLAN. MICKEY FINN joined PHIL MAY'S FALLEN ANGELS. MARRIOTT re-formed The SMALL FACES

HUMBLE PIE

also re-formed in 1979, with **STEVE MARRIOTT** – vocals, guitar / **JERRY SHIRLEY** – drums / **BOBBY TENCH** – guitar (ex-STREETWALKERS, ex-JEFF BECK) / **ANTHONY JONES** – bass

Jet Atco

Apr 80. (7") *(JET 180) <7216>* **FOOL FOR A PRETTY FACE. / YOU SOPPY PRATT** [ ] [52]

Apr 80. (lp) *(JET LP/CA 231) <38122>* **ON TO VICTORY** [ ] [60]
– Fool for a pretty face / You soppy pratt / Get it in the end / Infatuation / Further down the road / My lover's prayer / Take it from here / Baby don't do it.

Jun 81. (lp) *(38131) <131>* **GO FOR THE THROAT** [ ] [ ] May81
– All shook up / Chip away / Driver / Go for the throat / Keep it on the island / Lottie and the charcoal queen / Restless blood / Teenage anxiety / Tin soldier.

— Finally called it a day in '81

– compilations, others –

Sep 72. (d-lp) *A&M; <3513>* **LOST AND FOUND** (1st-2 lp's) [-] [37]
Jul 76. (lp) *Immediate; (IML 1005)* **BACK HOME AGAIN** [ ] [-]
Jan 78. (lp) *Immediate; (IML 2005)* **HUMBLE PIE'S GREATEST HITS** [ ] [-]
Sep 85. (7") *Old Gold; (OG 9529)* **NATURAL BORN BUGIE. / (other artist)** [ ] [-]
Nov 85. (d-lp/c/cd) *Castle; (CCS LP/MC/CD 104)* **THE COLLECTION** [ ] [-]
– Bang? / Natural born bugie / I'll go alone / Buttermilk boy / Desperation / Nifty little number like you / Wrist job / Stick shift / Growing closer / As safe as yesterday / Heartbeat / Down home again / Take me back / Only you can see / Silver tongue / Every mother's son / The sad bag of Shaky Jake / Cold lady / Home and away / Light of love. *(cd-iss. Apr94;)*
1988. (cd) *A&M; (393 208-2)* **THE BEST OF HUMBLE PIE** [ ] [ ]
Nov 92. (cd) *Dojo; (EARLD 4)* **THE EARLY YEARS** [ ] [-]
Feb 95. (cd) *Band Of Joy; (BOJCD 101)* **NATURAL BORN BOOGIE** [ ] [-]
May 95. (cd) *A&M; (540 179-2)* **A PIECE OF THE PIE** [ ] [-]
Nov 95. (d-cd) *Charly; (CDIMMBOX 3)* **THE IMMEDIATE YEARS** [ ] [-]
Jul 98. (cd) *Strange Fruit; (SFRSCD 066)* **NATURAL BORN BOOGIE** [ ] [-]
Aug 98. (cd) *King Biscuit; (<KBFHCD 017>)* **KING BISCUIT PRESENTS . . .** [ ] [ ]
Nov 99. (cd) *Eagle; (EAGCD 114)* **THE SCRUBBERS SESSIONS** [ ] [-]
Jul 00. (cd) *Burning Airlines; (<PILOT 048>)* **RUNNING WITH THE PACK** [ ] [ ]

Ian HUNTER

Born: 3 Jun'46, Shrewsbury, England. After years spent playing clubs in Hamburg, Germany, he joined AT LAST THE 1958 ROCK & ROLL SHOW, who released a one-off 45 for 'CBS' in 1967, 'I CAN'T DRIVE' / 'WORKIN' ON THE RAILROAD'. The following year, he wrote a few songs for the CHARLIE WOLFE demos, which remained unissued until 'Nems' released them in mid-70's ('STAY STAY STAY' / 'HOME'). After answering an ad in the music press, HUNTER successfully auditioned in June '69 for lead singer in MOTT THE HOOPLE. For the next five years, they became one of Britain's best rock acts, until HUNTER decided to opt for solo career in 1975. His debut 45, 'ONCE BITTEN TWICE SHY', took up where 'THE HOOPLE left off, making the UK Top 20 in the process. With help from stalwart supporter and guitarist MICK RONSON, he continued to surface either in England or New York, with credible material, having already toured supporting each other's solo projects, as the HUNTER-RONSON BAND. Following the Top 30 success of the 'ALL AMERICAN ALIEN BOY' (1976) set, the shady (as in dark spectacled) rock'n'roll hero/icon formed touring band, The OVERNIGHT ANGELS featuring EARL SLICK amongst others (RONSON had joined DYLAN's 'Rolling Thunder' tour in mid-'76), the group backing up HUNTER on a one-off eponymous album which the curly locked frontman was allegedly none too happy with. Signing to 'Chrysalis' at the end of the decade, HUNTER teamed up with RONSON once more on 'YOU'RE NEVER ALONE WITH A SCHIZOPHRENIC' (1979), while 1981's 'SHORT BACK 'N' SIDES' featured such esteemed guests as TODD RUNDGREN, MICK JONES and TOPPER HEADON (the latter two both members of The CLASH; HUNTER also proved his punk credentials by producing GENERATION X's 'VALLEY OF THE DOLLS' album the same year). He subsequently went to ground following 1983's 'ALL THE GOOD ONES ARE TAKEN', eventually re-emerging in 1990 with another RONSON collaboration, 'Y U I ORTA', released on 'Mercury' (his old pal was to die of cancer in '94). Though HUNTER has never quite risen above second division status in his post-HOOPLE career, he remains, especially among his peers, one of the most respected figures in the rock world.

Album rating: IAN HUNTER (*7) / ALL AMERICAN ALIEN BOY (*5) / OVERNIGHT ANGELS (*4) / YOU'RE NEVER ALONE WITH A SCHIZOPHRENIC (*7) / SHADES OF IAN HUNTER compilation (*7) / WELCOME TO THE CLUB (*6) / SHORT BACK AND SIDES (*7) / ALL THE GOOD ONES ARE TAKEN (*6) / YUI ORTA (*6; as Hunter-Ronson) / THE VERY BEST OF IAN HUNTER compilation (*6) / IAN HUNTER'S DIRTY LAUNDRY (*4) / THE ARTFUL DODGER (*4)

IAN HUNTER – vocals, guitar (ex-MOTT THE HOOPLE, ex-AT LAST THE 1958 . . .) with **MICK RONSON** – guitar, vocals (ex-MOTT THE HOOPLE, ex-DAVID BOWIE, Solo artist) / **PETE ARNESEN** – keyboards / **JEFF APPLEBY** – bass / **DENNIS ELLIOTT** – drums

C.B.S. Columbia

Mar 75. (7") *(CBS 3194) <10161>* **ONCE BITTEN TWICE SHY. / 3,000 MILES FROM HERE** [14] [ ]

Apr 75. (lp/c) *(CBS/40 80710) <33480>* **IAN HUNTER** [21] [50]
– Once bitten twice shy / Who do you love / Lounge lizard / Boy / 3,000 miles from here / The truth, the whole truth, nuthin' but the truth / It ain't easy when you fall / Shades off / I get so excited. *<US cd-iss. Jul90; CK 33480> (re-iss. cd Sep94 on 'Sony Rewind'; COL 477359-2)*

Jul 75. (7") *(CBS 3486)* **WHO DO YOU LOVE. / BOY** [ ] [-]

— HUNTER with RONSON, brought in mainly session people including **AYNSLEY DUNBAR** – drums / **CORNELL DUPREEE** – guitar / **JACO PASTORUS** – bass / **CHRIS STAINTON** – keyboards / guests **BRIAN MAY + FREDDIE MERCURY** – vocals (QUEEN) All replaced PETE and JEFF who went into sessions + DENNIS who joined FOREIGNER

May 76. (7") *(CBS 4268)* **ALL AMERICAN ALIEN BOY. / RAPE** [ ] [-]

May 76. (lp/c) *(CBS/40 81310) <34142>* **ALL AMERICAN ALIEN BOY** [29] [ ]
– Letter to Brittania from the Union Jack / All American alien boy / Irene Wilde / Restless youth / Rape / You nearly did me in / Apathy 83 / God (take 1). *<US cd-iss. Jan90; CK 34142> (cd-iss. Aug98 on 'Columbia'; 491695-2)*

Aug 76. (7") *(CBS 4479)* **YOU NEARLY DID ME IN. / LETTER TO BRITANNIA FROM THE UNION JACK** [ ] [-]

— HUNTER formed tour band OVERNIGHT ANGELS:- **EARL SLICK** – guitar (ex-BOWIE) / **PETER OXENDALE** – keyboards / **BOB RAWLINSON** – bass / **CURLY SMITH** – drums (MICK RONSON joined BOB DYLAN's Rolling Thunder Tour mid-76)

May 77. (7"; as IAN HUNTER'S OVERNIGHT ANGELS) *(CBS 5229)* **JUSTICE OF THE PEACE. / THE BALLAD OF LITTLE STAR** [ ] [ ]

May 77. (lp/c) *(CBS/40 81993) <34721>* **OVERNIGHT ANGELS** [ ] [ ]
– Golden opportunity / Shallow crystals / Overnight angels / Broadway / Justice of the peace / Silver dime / Wild'n'free / The ballad of little star / To love a woman. *(re-iss. cd Jun94 on 'Sony Europe'; 474 780-2)*

Jul 78. (7"; as IAN HUNTER'S OVERNIGHT ANGELS) *(CBS 5497)* **ENGLAND ROCKS. / WILD'N'FREE** [ ] [-]

— now with **RONSON** plus **ROY BITTAN** – keyboards / **MAX WEINBERG** – drums / **GEORGE YOUNG + LEW DELGATTO** – sax / **GARY TALLENT** – bass / **ELLEN FOLEY** – vocals

Chrysalis Chrysalis

Apr 79. (7"white) *(CHS 2324)* **WHEN THE DAYLIGHT COMES. / LIFE AFTER DEATH** [ ] [-]

Apr 79. (lp/c) *(<CHR/ZCHR 1214>)* **YOU'RE NEVER ALONE WITH A SCHIZOPHRENIC** [49] [35]
– Just another night / Wild east / Cleveland rocks / When the daylight comes / Ships / Life after death / Standin' in my light / Bastard / The outsider. *<cd-iss. Jun94 on 'Razor & Tie'; RE 2011> (re-iss. cd Mar94; CD 25CR 03) (cd re-iss. Aug99 on 'E.M.I.'; 521853-2)*

Jul 79. (7") *(CHS 2346)* **SHIPS. / WILD EAST** [ ] [-]
Aug 79. (7") *<2352>* **JUST ANOTHER NIGHT. / CLEVELAND ROCKS** [-] [68]
Oct 79. (7") *(CHS 2390)* **CLEVELAND ROCKS. / BASTARD** [ ] [-]

— **MARTIN BRILEY** – bass repl. TALLENT / **ERIC PARKER** – drums repl. WEINBERG / **GEORGE MEYER + TOM MANDEL** – keyboards repl. BITTAN also to BRUCE SPRINGSTEEN / **TOMMY MORRONGIELLO** – guitar, bass repl. YOUNG + DELGATTO

Apr 80. (d-lp/c) *(CJT/ZCJT 6) <1269>* **WELCOME TO THE CLUB (live)** [61] [69]
– F.B.I. / Once bitten twice shy / Angelline / Laugh at me / All the way from Memphis / I wish I was your mother / Irene Wilde / Just another night / Cleveland rocks / Standin' in my light / Bastard / Walkin' with a mountain / Rock'n'roll queen / All the young dudes / Slaughter on Tenth Avenue / We gotta get out of here / Silver needles / Man o' war / Sons and daughters. *(re-iss. d-cd May94; CDCHR 6075)*

Jun 80. (d7") *(2434)* **WE GOTTA GET OUT OF HERE (live). / MEDLEY: PNCE BITTEN TWICE SHY – BASTARD – CLEVELAND ROCKS (live) // SONS AND DAUGHTERS (live). / ONE OF THE BOYS (live)** [ ] [-]

— virtualy same band except featured guests **TODD RUNDGREN** – vocals, bass / **MICK JONES** – guitar / **TOPPER HEADON** – drums (both of CLASH) / **TYMON DOGG** – violin

Aug 81. (7"clear) *(CHS 2542)* **LISA LIKES ROCK'N'ROLL. / NOISES** [ ] [-]

Aug 81. (lp/c) *(<CHR/ZCHR 1326>)* **SHORT BACK 'N' SIDES** [79] [62]
– Central Park'n'West / Lisa likes rock'n'roll / I need your love / Old records never die / Noises / Rain / Gun control / Theatre of the absurd / Leave me alone / Keep on burning. *(re-iss. d-cd.May94+=; CDCHR 6074)* – LONG ODDS AND OUT TAKES *(cd re-iss. Feb00 on 'Liberty'; 524625-2)*

— now with **RONSON + ROBBIE ALTER + JIMMY RIP** – guitar / **MARK CLARKE + DAN HARTMAN** – bass / **MANDAL / JEFF BOVA + BOB MAYO** – keyboards / **CLARENCE CLEMONS + LOU CORTLEZZI** – sax / **HILLY MICHAELS** – drums

C.B.S. Columbia

Jul 83. (7") *(A 3855)* **ALL THE GOOD ONES ARE TAKEN. / DEATH 'N' GLORY BOYS** [ ] [-]
(12"+=) *(TA 3855)* – Traitor.

Aug 83. (lp/c) *(CBS/40 25379) <38628>* **ALL THE GOOD ONES ARE TAKEN** [ ] [ ]
– All the good ones are taken / Every step of the way / Fun / Speechless / Death 'n' glory boys / Somethin's goin' on / That girl is rock'n'roll / Captain Void 'n' the video jets / Seeing double / All the good ones are taken (reprise). *(re-iss. cd Jun94 on 'Sony Europe'; 474780-2)*

Oct 83. (7") *(A 3541)* **SOMETHIN'S GOIN' ON. / ALL THE GOOD ONES ARE TAKEN** [ ] [-]

Oct 83. (7") *<04166>* **SEEING DOUBLE. / THAT GIRL IS ROCK'N'ROLL** [-] [ ]

— HUNTER retired from public eye until late '89 he and RONSON re-formed

HUNTER-RONSON

— IAN HUNTER + MICK RONSON's band, with **PAT KILBRIDE** – bass / **MICKEY CURRY** – drums / **TOMMY MANDEL** – keyboards

Mercury Mercury

Jan 90. (cd/c/lp) *(<838 973-2/-4/-1>)* **Y U I ORTA** [ ] [ ] Oct89
– American music / The loner / Women's intuition / Tell it like it is / Livin' in a heart / Big time / Cool / Beg a little love / Following in your footsteps * / Sons 'n' lovers / Pain * / How much more can I take * / Sweet dreamer. *(c+=/cd+= *)*

Feb 90. (7"/c-s) *(MER/+MC 315)* **AMERICAN MUSIC. / TELL IT LIKE IT IS** [ ] [ ]
(12"+=/cd-s+=) *(MER X/CD 315)* – Sweet dreamer.

NorskPlate-produksjon not iss.

Feb 95. (cd-s; as IAN HUNTER'S DIRTY LAUNDRY) *(IDS 44)* **MY REVOLUTION / DANCING ON THE MOON** [-] [-] Norway

Mar 95. (cd; as IAN HUNTER'S DIRTY LAUNDRY) *(IDCD 44)* **IAN HUNTER'S DIRTY LAUNDRY** [-] [-] Norway

Polydor not iss.

Sep 96. (cd) *(531 794-2)* **THE ARTFUL DODGER** [ ] [-]
– Too much / Now is the time / Something to believe in / Resurrection Mary / Walk on water / 23a Swan Hill / Michael Picasso / Open my eyes / Artful dodger / Skeletons in your closet / Still the same. *(UK-iss.Sep97 on 'Citadel' pic-cd; CID 1-CD)*

Citadel not iss.

Apr 97. (cd-s) *(CIT 101)* **THE ARTFUL DODGER / NOW IS THE TIME / FUCK IT UP** [ ] [-]

– compilations, etc. –

Feb 80. (lp/c) *Columbia; (CBS/40 88476)* **SHADES OF IAN HUNTER – THE BALLAD OF IAN HUNTER & MOTT THE HOOPLE** [ ] [ ]
<US cd-iss. Nov88; VK 41670>

Apr 91. (cd/c/lp) *C.B.S.; (467508-2/-4/-1)* **THE VERY BEST OF IAN HUNTER** [ ] [ ]

Jul 91. (cd/c) *Castle; (CCS CD/MC 290)* **THE COLLECTION** [ ] [-]
(Includes tracks by MOTT THE HOOPLE)

Oct 95. (cd) *Windsong; (WINCD 078)* **THE HUNTER-HONSON BAND BBC LIVE IN CONCERT** [ ] [-]

Jul 99. (cd) *Citadel; (CIT 1BOX)* **THE ARTFUL DODGER / THE DIARY OF A ROCK'N'ROLL STAR** [ ] [-]

May 00. (d-cd) *Columbia; (496284-2) <61406>* **ONCE BITTEN TWICE SHY** [ ] [ ] Aug00

Jul 00. (cd; as IAN HUNTER BAND) *Burning Airlines; (<PILOT 052>)* **MISSING IN ACTION** [ ] [ ]

HURRICANE

Formed: Los Angeles, California, USA ... 1983 by ROBERT SARZO (brother of WHITESNAKE's, RUDY), TONY CAVAZO (brother of QUIET RIOT's, CARLOS), KELLY HANSEN and JAY SCHELLEN. Signed to 'Enigma' in 1985, they delivered a promising collection of solid hard rock tunes that went the following year under the banner of 'TAKE WHAT YOU WANT'. Their second set, 'OVER THE EDGE', sold well enough to hit the US Top 100. Surprisingly, despite encouraging reviews the group's third set, 'SLAVE TO THE THRILL' didn't fare so well, although it did initially perform reasonably well.

Album rating: TAKE WHAT YOU WANT mini (*6) / OVER THE EDGE (*4) / SLAVE TO THE THRILL (*6)

KELLY HANSEN – vocals / **ROBERT SARZO** – guitar, vocals / **TONY CAVAZO** – bass, vocals / **JAY SCHELLEN** – drums, vocals

Roadrunner Enigma

Jul 86. (m-lp) *(RR 9723) <73265>* **TAKE WHAT YOU WANT** [ ] [ ]
– Take me in your arms / The girls are out tonight / Take what you want / Hurricane / It's only heaven / Hot and heavy. *<US cd+=)* – Livin' over the edge (7"version) / I'm on to you (na na na na na) (Super stormin' hook mix) / Baby snakes (instrumental).

Enigma Enigma

Apr 88. (lp/cd) *<73320-1/-2>* **OVER THE EDGE** [-] [92]
– Livin' over the edge / I'm eighteen / I'm on to you / Messin' with a hurricane / Insane / We are strong / Spark in my heart / Give me an inch / Shout / Baby snakes.

Feb 89. (7") *(ENV 7)* **I'M ON TO YOU. / BABY SNAKES (instrumental)** [ ] [ ]
(12"+=) *(ENVT 7)* – ('A'radio edit) / Girls are out tonight.

— **DOUG ALDRICH** – guitar, vocals (ex-LION) repl. SARZO

Apr 90. (cd/c/lp) *(CDENV/TCENV/ENVLP 1004) <73511>* **SLAVE TO THE THRILL** [ ] [ ]
– Reign of love / Next to you / Young man / Dance little sister / Don't wanna dream / Temptations / 10,000 years / In the fire / Let it slide / Lock me up / Smiles like a child.

— split after above

HUSKER DU

Formed: St. Paul, Minnesota, USA ... 1978 by MOULD, HART and NORTON. In 1980-82, they issued a few 45's and a live LP 'LAND SPEED RECORD', on their own label, 'New Alliance'. The record typified the band's early uncompromising hardcore which was often tediously workmanlike in its adherence to the steadfast confines of the genre. 'EVERYTHING FALLS APART' (1983) was also unflinching in its intensity and it was all the more surprising when the band showed glimmers of noise-pop greatness on their 1983 debut for 'SST', 'METAL CIRCUS'. They consolidated this by cross-fertilising the previously polarised worlds of psychedelia and hardcore punk on an electrifying cover of The BYRDS' 'EIGHT MILES HIGH' (1984). The follow-up double set, 'ZEN ARCADE' (1984) was a further giant step for hardcore-kind. A concept album no less, the twin songwriting attack of MOULD and HART was becoming sharper and even the sprawling, unfocused feel of the whole affair wasn't enough to blunt the edges of songs like 'WHATEVER' and 'TURN ON THE NEWS'. The songwriting on 'NEW DAY RISING' (1985) was even more trenchant, the band's adrenaline fuelled pop-core hybrid developing at breakneck speed. 'FLIP YOUR WIG' (1985), the band's last indie release, marked a stepping stone to their major label debut for 'Warners', 'CANDY APPLE GREY' (1986). While HART perfected HUSKER DU's melodic dischord on tracks like 'DEAD SET ON DESTRUCTION', MOULD showcased darkly introspective, acoustic elegies 'TOO FAR DOWN' and 'HARDLY GETTING OVER IT'. The more musically-challenged among HUSKER DU's following were none too taken with this new fangled unplugged business although the album was released to unanimous critical acclaim. The band's swansong, 'WAREHOUSE: SONGS AND STORIES' (1987) was the culmination of a decade's experimentation and possessed an unprecedented depth, clarity and consistency. By the time of its release, though, tension in the band was reaching breaking point and HUSKER DU was disbanded in 1987. While GRANT HART and BOB MOULD went on to solo careers, as well as respectively forming NOVA MOB and SUGAR, they were always better together and the magic of HUSKER DU is inestimable in its influence on a generation of alternative guitar bands. • **Songwriters:** MOULD-HART compositions except; SUNSHINE SUPERMAN (Donovan) / TICKET TO RIDE + SHE'S A WOMAN + HELTER SKELTER (Beatles) / EIGHT MILES HIGH (Byrds). NOVA MOB covered I JUST WANT TO MAKE LOVE TO YOU (Willie Dixon) / SHEENA IS A PUNK ROCKER (Ramones). Solo GRANT HART covered SIGNED D.C. (Love). • **Trivia:** HUSKER DU means DO YOU REMEMBER in Swedish.

Album rating: EVERYTHING FALLS APART (*5) / ZEN ARCADE (*9) / NEW DAY RISING (*9) / FLIP YOUR WIG (*9) / CANDY APPLE GREY (*7) / WAREHOUSE: SONGS & STORIES (*9) / THE LIVING END live compilation (*6) / Grant Hart: INTOLERANCE (*6) / Nova Mob: THE DAYS DAYS OF POMPEII (*6) / NOVA MOB (*6) / ECCE HOMO (*5)

BOB MOULD (b.12 Oct'60, Malone, N.Y.) – vocals, guitar, keyboards, percussion / **GRANT HART** (b. GRANTZBERG VERNON HART, 18 Mar'61) – drums, keyboards, percussion, vocals / **GREG NORTON** (b.13 Mar'59, Rock Island, Illinois) – bass

not iss. Reflex

1980. (7") *<38285>* **STATUES. / AMUSEMENT (live)** [-] [ ]

Alternative Tentacles New Alliance

1982. (lp) *(VIRUS 25) <NAR 007>* **LAND SPEED RECORD (live)** [-] [ ]
– All tensed up / Don't try to call / I'm not interested / Big sky / Guns at my school / Push the button / Gilligan's Island / MTC / Don't have a life / Bricklayer / Tired of doing things / You're naive / Strange week / Do the bee / Ultracore / Let's go die / Data control. *(re-iss. Nov88 on 'S.S.T.'; SST 195) (re-iss. cd/c/lp Oct95)*

1982. (7"m) *<NAR 010>* **IN A FREE LAND. / WHAT DO I WANT? / M.I.C.** [-] [ ]

not iss. Reflex

Jul 83. (lp) *<D>* **EVERYTHING FALLS APART** [-] [ ]
– From the gut / Blah, blah, blah / Punch drunk / Bricklayer / Afraid of being wrong / Sunshine Superman / Signals from above / Everything falls apart / Wheels / Obnoxious / Gravity. *(cd-iss. May93 on 'WEA'+=; 8122 71163-2)* – In a free land /

What do I want / M.I.C. / Statues / Let's go die / Amusement (live) / Do you remember?

S.S.T. S.S.T.

Dec 83. (m-lp) <(SST 020)> **METAL CIRCUS**
– Real world / Deadly skies / It's not funny anymore / Diane / First of the last calls / Lifeline / Out on a limb.

Apr 84. (7"colrd) *(SST 025)* **EIGHT MILES HIGH. / MASOCHISM WORLD**
(cd-s iss.Dec88; SST 025CD)

Sep 84. (d-lp) <(SST 027)> **ZEN ARCADE**
– Something I learned today / Broken home, broken heart / Never talking to you again / Chartered trips / Dreams reoccurring / Indecision time / Hare Krishna / Beyond the threshold / Pride / I'll never forget you / The biggest lie / What's going on / Masochism world / Standing by the sea / Somewhere / One step at a time / Pink turns to blue / Newest industry / Monday will never be the same / Whatever / The tooth fairy and the princess / Turn on the news / Reoccurring dreams. *(cd-iss. Oct87; SST 027CD) (re-iss. cd/c/d-lp Oct95 & Jun97; same)*

Feb 85. (lp) <(SST 031)> **NEW DAY RISING**
– New day rising / Girl who lives on Heaven Hill / I apologize / Folklore / If I told you / Celebrated summer / Perfect example / Terms of psychic warfare / 59 times the pain / Powerline / Books about UFO's / I don't know what you're talking about / How to skin a cat / Watcha drinkin' / Plans I make. *(cd-iss. Oct87; SST 031CD) (re-iss. cd/c/lp Oct95; same)*

Aug 85. (7") <(SST 051)> **MAKE NO SENSE AT ALL. / LOVE IS ALL AROUND (MARY'S THEME)**

Oct 85. (lp) <(SST 055)> **FLIP YOUR WIG**
– Flip your wig / Every everything / Makes no sense at all / Hate paper doll / Green eyes / Divide and conquer / Games / Find me / The baby song / Flexible flyer / Private plane / Keep hanging on / The wit and the wisdom / Don't know yet. *(cd-iss. Oct87; SST 055CD) (re-iss. cd/c/lp Oct95; same)*

Warners Warners

Feb 86. (7") *(W 8746)* **DON'T WANT TO KNOW IF YOU ARE LONELY. / ALL WORK NO PLAY**
(12"+=) *(W 8746T)* – Helter skelter (live).

Mar 86. (lp/c) *(WX 40/+C)* <25385> **CANDY APPLE GREY**
– Crystal / Don't want to know if you are lonely / I don't know for sure / Sorry somehow / Too far down / Hardly getting over it / Dead set on destruction / Eiffel Tower high / No promises have I made / All this I've done for you. *(cd-iss. Nov92; 7599 25385-2)*

Sep 86. (7") *(W 8612)* **SORRY SOMEHOW. / ALL THIS I'VE DONE FOR YOU**
(d7+=/12"+=) *(W 8612 F/T)* – Flexible flyer / Celebrated summer.

Jan 87. (7") *(W 8456)* **COULD YOU BE THE ONE. / EVERYTIME**
(12"+=) *(W 8456T)* – Charity, chastity, prudence, hope.

Jan 87. (d-lp/d-c) *(925544-1/-4)* <25544> **WAREHOUSE: SONGS & STORIES** 72
– These important years / Charity, chastity, prudence and hope / Standing in the rain / Back from somewhere / Ice cold ice / You're a soldier / Could you be the one? / Too much spice / Friend, you've got to fall / Visionary / She floated away / Bed of nails / Tell you why tomorrow / It's not peculiar / Actual condition / No reservations / Turn it around / She's a woman (and now he is a man) / Up in the air / You can live at home. *(cd-iss. Oct92; 7599 25544-2)*

Jun 87. (7") *(W 8276)* **ICE COLD ICE. / GOTTA LETTA**
(12"+=) *(W 8276T)* – Medley.

—— Disbanded in 1987 after manager, DAVID SAVOY Jr., committed suicide. GRANT HART went solo in '89, as did BOB MOULD. In 1992 the latter formed SUGAR.

– compilations, etc. –

May 94. (cd/c) *Warners;* <(9362 45582-2/-4)> **THE LIVING END (live)**
– New day rising / Heaven Hill / Standing in the rain / Back from somewhere / Ice cold ice / Everytime / Friend you're gonna fall / She floated away / From the gut / Target / It's not funny anymore / Hardly getting over it / Terms of psychic warfare / Powertime / Books about UFO's / Divide and conquer / Keep hangin' on / Celebrated summer / Now that you know me / Ain't no water in the well / What's goin' on / Data control / In a free land / Sheena is a punk rocker.

HYPERHEAD

Formed: London, England ... early 90's by MARY MARY (aka IAN GARFIELD HOXLEY), a punk/grebo renegade from 80's outfit GAYE BIKERS ON ACID. Taking a more industrial-metal stance, MARY teamed up with KARL LEIKER and some other cohorts from his PIGFACE days. Two EP's were duly followed by 'METAPHASIA' (1993), an unpredictable album that was a confused hybrid of many styles such as indie rock, funk, soul and of course, industrial. However, MARY and his team were never heard of again after establishing themselves as a manic stage act.

Album rating: METAPHASIA (*6)

MARY MARY (b. IAN GARFIELD HOXLEY) – vocals / **KARL LEIKER** – bass / **PAUL DALLOWAY** – guitar / with live temps **OSCAR** – guitar / **CHIN** – drums / KEITH – percussion

Devotion Wax Trax

Oct 92. (12"ep/cd-ep) *(12/CD DVN 109)* **TEENAGE MIND** -

—— live temps repl. by **MARTIN ATKINS** – drums (of PIGFACE, ex-PIL, ex-KILLING JOKE) / **WILLIAM TUCKER** – guitar (of PIGFACE, plus REVOLTING COCKS + MY LIFE WITH THE THRILL KILL KULT)

Feb 93. (12"ep/cd-ep) *(12/CD DVN 110)* **TERMINAL FEAR** -

Devotion Triple X

Mar 93. (cd/c/lp) *(CD/T+/DVN 16)* <51178> **METAPHASIA** Jul94
– Making waves / Teenage mind / Terminal fear / Easy slide / Close to hysteria / Pre-emprive counter attack / Ingnition x 4 / Method one / Trash.

—— seemed to have just been a one-off

HYPOCRISY

Formed: Ludvika, Sweden ... early 90's out of CONQUEST by PETER TAGTGREN and LARS SZOKE. After a time spent in the States, PETER returned to his native land and laid down tracks for their debut with LARS, vocalist MAGNUS 'MASSE' BROBERG and guitarist JONAS OSTERBERG. Exponents of Scandinavian black-metal, the band toured alongside stablemates, BRUTALITY, finally unleashing their blood-curdling debut, 'OSCULUM OBSCENUM' for 'Nuclear Blast' in 1993. The following year, PETER and LARS were back (recruiting MIKAEL HEDLUND), this time with the extremely powerful, 'INFERIOR DEVOTEES' (a mini that included Slayer's 'BLACK MAGIC') and 'THE FOURTH DIMENSION', a skullcrushing, mindblowing affair that sacrificed the senses with every track. The doom-laden group returned in '96 with their third set proper, 'ABDUCTED', It encouraged the band to remix the album, releasing it a few months later as 'MAXIMUM ABDUCTION'. All had changed their instruments by this release, while the record contained a cover of Kiss's 'STRANGE WAYS'. HYPOCRISY was at times put on the proverbial backburner while TAGTGREN and his pal IT of ABRUPTUM collaborated on the first of two side-project albums ('TOTAL WAR' and 'WE ARE WAR') under the banner of WAR; and not a 'Low Rider' in site. Touted as a farewell set, 'THE FINAL CHAPTER' (1997) concluded the lyrical themes of kidnap by little green men initially explored on its predecessor. UFO freaks and death metal afficionados alike were no doubt delighted to subsequently discover that HYPOCRISY had decided to carry on in light of their most successful release to date. Thus the more expansive, accessible textures of 'HYPOCRISY' (1999), an eponymous set which incorporated elements of power-metal into their death-defying musical framework. 'INTO THE ABYSS' – what else! – followed in 2000.

Album rating: PENETRALIA (*5) / OSCULUM OBSCENUM (*6) / THE FOURTH DIMENSION (*7) / ABDUCTED (*7) / THE FINAL CHAPTER (*6) / HYPOCISY DESTROYS WACKEN 1998 (*5) / HYPOCRISY (*6) / INTO THE ABYSS (*5) / War: Total War mini (*7) / WE ARE WAR (*6)

PETER TAGTGREN – vocals, guitar, keyboards (ex-EPITAPH) / **JONAS OSTERBERG** – guitar (ex-EPITAPH) / **LARS SZOKE** – drums / **MAGNUS 'MASSE' BROBERG** – vocals (ex-VOTARY)

Nuclear Blast Nuclear Blast

Oct 92. (lp/cd) *(NB 067/+CD)* <6055> **PENETRALIA**
– Impotent god / Suffering souls / Nightmare / Jesus fall / God is a . . . / Left to rot / Burn the cross / To escape to die / Take the throne / Penetralia. *(cd re-iss. Jun96+=; NB 164CD)* – (1 track).

—— **MIKAEL HEDLUND** – bass; repl. MAGNUS + JONAS

1993. (cd-ep) <RR 6040> **PLEASURE OF MOLESTATION / EXCLAMATION OF A NECROFAG / NECRONOMICON / ATTACHMENT TO THE ANSESTER** -

Aug 93. (lp/c/cd) *(NB 080/+MC/CD)* <6081> **OSCULUM OBSCENUM** Oct93
– Pleasure of molestation / Exclamation of a necrofag / Osculum obscenum / Necronomicon / Black metal / Inferior devotees / Infant sacrifices / Attachment to the ancestor / Althotas / Symbol of Baphomet / Mental emotions / God is a lie / Black magic. *(cd+=)* – PLEASURE OF MOLESTATION demos

Mar 94. (m-cd) *(NB 098CD)* <6104> **INFERIOR DEVOTEES**
– Inferior devoties (re-recorded) / God is a lie / Symbol of baphomet / Mental emotions / Black magic.

Oct 94. (cd/lp) *(NB 112 CD/LP)* <6894> **THE FOURTH DIMENSION**
– Apocalypse / Mind corruption / Reincarnation / Reborn / Black forest / Never to return / Path to Babylon / Slaughtered / Orgy in blood / The north wind / T.E.M.P.T. / The fourth dimension / The arrival of the demons / Request denied / Strange ways. *(d-cd-iss. Dec94+=; NB 112DCD)* – The abyss.

Feb 96. (cd/c/lp) *(NB 133 CD/MC/LP)* <6133> **ABDUCTED**
– The gathering / Roswell 47 / Killing art / The arrival of the demons (part 2) / Buried / Abducted / Paradox / Point of no return / When the candle fades / Carved up / Reflections / Slippin' away / Drained.

May 96. (sha-d-cd-s) *(NB 145CD)* <6145> **MAXIMUM ABDUCTION** Feb97
– Roswell 47 / Carved up / Request denied / Strange ways.

Sep 97. (cd/lp) *(NB 283 CD/LP)* <6283> **THE FINAL CHAPTER**
– Inseminated adoption / A coming race / Dominion / Inquire within / Last vanguard / Request denied / Through the window of time / Shamateur / Adjusting the sun / Lies / Evil invaders / The final chapter.

Feb 99. (cd) *(NB 376-2)* <6376> **HYPOCRISY DESTROYS WACKEN 1998 (live)**
– Roswell 47 / Inseminated adoption / A coming race / Apocalypse / Osculum obscenum / Buried / Left to rot / The fourth dimension / Pleasure of molestation / Killing art / The final chapter / Time warp / Till the end / Fuck U / Beginning of the end.

Jun 99. (cd) *(NB 388-2)* <6388> **HYPOCRISY**
– Fractured millennium / Apocalyptic hybrid / Fusion programmed minds / Elastic inverted visions / Reversed reflections / Until the end / Paranormal mysterie / Time warp / Disconnected magnetic corridors / Paled empty sphere. *(hidden+=)* – Selfinflicted overload.

Sep 00. (cd) *(NB 529-2)* <6529> **INTO THE ABYSS**
– Legions descent / Blinded / Resurrected / Unleash the beast / Digital prophecy / Fire in the sky / Total eclipse / Unfold the sorrow / Sodomized / Death row (no regrets).

– compilations, etc. –

Nov 96. (cd) *Nuclear Blast; (NB 215CD)* **OSCULUM OBSCENUM / INFERIOR DEVOTEES / PLEASURES OF MOLESTATION** -

WAR

PETER TAGTGREN + IT (of ABRUPTUM)

	Necropolis	not iss.
Jan 98. (m-cd) *(NR 019MCD)* **TOTAL WAR** – Satan / I am elite / Total war / The sons of war / Revenge / Reapers of Satan / Satan's millennium.		-
Jun 99. (cd) *(NR 036CD)* **WE ARE WAR** – Soldiers of Satan / Rapture 2 / Ave Satan / Kill God / 666 / Infernal / Hell / Execution / Bombenhagel.		-

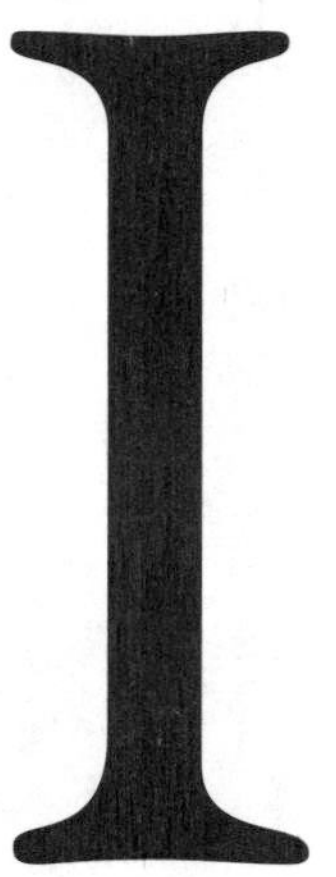

I AGAINST I

Formed: Netherlands . . . mid-90's by school friends RONALD VAN MAREN and JASPER BLAZER. The pair kept themselves from dying of boredom in small-townsville by finding a supply of hardcore/punk via a taping of their heroes-to-be, The DEAD KENNEDYS. Finding a suitable bass player in the shape of BOB HOORWEG, the trio spent just over a year rehearsing, culminating in them gaining the acolade of being the first Europeans to ink a deal with 'Epitaph'. They whetted the appetite of their punk/metal buying public by debuting with a 4-track EP, 'TOP OF THE WORLD'; a B-side track even saw them covering the Beatles' 'I WANNA HOLD YOUR HAND'. Produced by BILL STEVENSON and STEPHEN EGERTON (of the DESCENDENTS/ALL), I AGAINST I showcased more of their material by releasing their first full-set, 'HEADCLEANER', early in '98. A year later, after extensive European and US tours, the youthful three-piece worked with seasoned knob-twiddler THEO VAN ROCK on a more creative follow-up album, 'I'M A FUCKED UP DANCER, BUT MY MOODS ARE SWINGING' (1999).

Album rating: HEADCLEANER (*6) / I'M A FUCKED UP DANCER, BUT MY MOODS ARE SWINGING (*5)

RONALD VAN MAREN – vocals, guitar / **BOB HOORWEG** – bass, vocals / **JASPER BLAZER** – drums

Epitaph Epitaph

Aug 97. (7"ep/cd-ep) *(6520-7/-2)* **TOP OF THE WORLD / CHAOS DAYS. / LOOK INSIDE / I WANNA HOLD YOUR HAND** [ ] [-]

Feb 98. (cd/lp) *<(6525-2/-1)>* **HEADCLEANER** [ ] [ ] Sep98
– Maybe tomorrow / Passed me by / Stumble and stare / Top of the world / Ordinary flight / Look inside / The signs / Nailed to the floor / Time / The bottom / Lesson to be learned / Ideals / Utopia / All by yourself.

Jun 98. (cd-s) *(1002-2)* **TIME** [-] [-] w-drawn

Nov 99. (cd/lp) *(6568-2/-1)* **I'M A FUCKED UP DANCER, BUT MY MOODS ARE SWINGING** [ ] [-]
– – noname- / 1963 / Nothing happened / Who's losing / A love supreme / Only alphabet / Change of address / Seconds away / One last warning / Standard free / Read and weep / Space oddyssey / Best place in the world to leave / Pick up lies.

Jan 00. (cd-s) *(1027-2)* **SPACE ODYSSEY / ARMS TO CALL / THE SIGNS** [ ] [-]

ICE-T

Born: TRACY MORROW, 16 Feb'58, Newark, New Jersey, USA. With a ghetto background that reportedly involved copious amounts of unlawful activity, a name derived from superpimp, ICEBERG SLIM, and a mean line in caustic wit, ICE-T set himself up as the original 'gangsta' rapper. The fact of the matter is he wasn't actually the first gangsta rapper, although he did invent the particularly potent West Coast strain. With backing from AFRIKA ISLAM and DJ ALADDIN, his debut for 'Warners', 'RHYME PAYS' (1987), set out the ICE-T agenda of unashamed criminal glorification over tough, made-to-measure beats. 'POWER' (1988) thankfully laid off the "I'm mental, me" sentiments to a certain degree, allowing room for more objectively intelligent lyrics, although that obviously couldn't be applied to 'GIRLS L.G.B.N.A.F.' (LET'S GET BUTT NAKED AND FUCK, dummy). Hardly the most offensive or potentially damaging lyrics in the ICE-T canon, the song nevertheless upset those nice people at the PMRC (an American institutionalised neighbourhood watch scheme for bad pop stars), not the first time he'd upset the powers that be (or would be). This storm in a teacup informed much of 1989's 'THE ICEBERG: FREEDOM OF SPEECH . . . JUST WATCH WHAT YOU SAY', a more rock-based, anti-censorship rant that laid the ground-work for his subsequent BODY COUNT project. The record that really took ICE-T's dubious message to the masses was the landmark 'O.G. ORIGINAL GANGSTER' (1991), a UK Top 5 album that saw ICE powering his way through a hardcore rap set of unrelenting intensity. As ever, the lyrics were sharp, witty and artfully articulate but ultimately offensive. While ICE-T argues that he tells it like it is, his lame attempts to justify his continual objectification of women are rarely satisfactory. It's one of hip hop's great tragedies that a rapper as charismatic, intelligent and creative as ICE-T continues to reinforce prejudice and stereotyping; for every inch that CHUCK D advances the black cause, ICE-T drags it back two. The next logical step for ICE was a foray into the world of heavy metal, another genre not exactly noted for its tolerance. Recruiting ERNIE-C (guitar), D-ROC (guitar), MOOSEMAN (bass) and BEATMASTER V (drums), ICE-T debuted his hardcore/speed metal band, BODY COUNT, on the 1991 Lollapalooza tour prior to the release of their eponymous debut the following year. While the record addressed racism on the likes of 'MOMMA'S GOTTA DIE TONIGHT', the rapper's trademark misogyny was ever present, notably on 'KKK BITCH'. However, the track that really hit the fan squarely with the shit was 'COP KILLER', a nasty little ditty about "taking out" some lawmen. While the LAPD were hardly in a postion to come over all moral, they perhaps understandibly took offence to such sentiments. As did President George Bush and good ol' Ollie North, ICE-T subsequently being given the honour of the biggest threat to American security since McCARTHY flushed out "those damn commies" in the 50's. The final straw for 'Warners' was when record company personnel started receiving death threats, the label finally giving in and removing the offending song from subsequent pressings. While it's arguably one of the functions of art to question the "norm", to go about it in such a club-footed manner ultimately benefits no-one. ICE-T was as defiant as ever, though, moving to 'Virgin' for 'BORN DEAD' (1994), another accomplished collection that wasn't quite so inflammatory. The rapper's solo career continued, meanwhile, with 'HOME INVASION' (1993) upon which, gasp!, the rapper actually admitted to feelings for his fellow man in 'GOTTA LOTTA LOVE' while remaining as unrepentant about his lifestyle as ever, ('THAT'S HOW I'M LIVIN'). It was to be another three years before the next album and in the interim, ICE-T used his not inconsiderable talent to host a Channel 4 documentary on Blaxploitation movies as well as presenting 'Baadaasss TV', a semi-successful attempt at catering for black culture. He also published a book of his forthright opinions which only served to furnish his opponents with yet more ammunition. ICE-T resumed his recording career in typically bigoted fashion with, 'VI: RETURN OF THE REAL' (1996), a cliched gangsta affair that added anti-semitic sentiment to his litany of hate.

Album rating: RHYME PAYS (*5) / POWER (*5) / THE ICEBERG: FREEDOM OF SPEECH . . . JUST WATCH WHAT YOU SAY (*7) / O.G. ORIGINAL GANGSTER (*8) / BODY COUNT (*8; with Body Count) / HOME INVASION (*6) / BORN DEAD (*5; with Body Count) / IV: RETURN OF THE REAL (*5) / VIOLENT DEMISE (THE LAST DAYS (*4; with Body Count) / THE SEVENTH DEADLY SIN (*5)

BODY COUNT

ICE-T with **ERNIE C** – lead guitar / **D-ROC** – rhythm guitar / **MOOSEMAN** – bass / **BEATMASTER 'V'** – drums

Sire Sire

Jan 92. (12"/cd-s; w-drawn) **COP KILLER. / (withdrawn)** [-] [ ]

Mar 92. (cd/c) *(9362 45139-2/-4) <26876>* **BODY COUNT** [ ] [26]
– Smoked pork / Body Count's in the house / New sports / Body count / A statistic / Bowels of the Devil / The real problem / KKK bitch / C note / Voodoo / The winner loses / There goes the neighborhood / Oprah / Evil Dick / Body Count anthem / Momma's gotta die tonight / Freedom of speech.

Jun 92. (12") **THERE GOES THE NEIGHBORHOOD. / KKK BITCH** [ ] [ ]

Rhyme Syndicate Virgin

Sep 94. (red-lp/c/cd) *(RSYN/+C/D 2) <39802>* **BORN DEAD** [15] [74]
– Body M-F Count / Masters of revenge / Killin' floor / Necessary evil / Drive by / Last breath / Hey Joe / Shallow graves / Surviving the game / Who are you / Sweet lobotomy / Born dead.

Sep 94. (c-s) *(SYNDC 4)* **BORN DEAD / BODY COUNT'S IN THE HOUSE (live)** [28] [ ]
(12"pic-d+=) *(SYNDTP 4)* – ('A'live).
(cd-s+=) *(SYNDD 4)* – Body M-F Count (live) / On with the Body Count (live).

Virgin Virgin

Dec 94. (etched-10"pic-d) *(VSA 1529)* **NECESSARY EVIL / NECESSARY EVIL (live) / BOWELS OF THE DEVIL (live)** [45] [ ]
(cd-s) *(VSCDX 1529)* – ('A'side) / Body Count anthem (live) / Drive by (live) / There goes the neighborhood (live).

—— **GRIZ** – bass + **O.T.** – drums; repl. MOOSEMAN + BEATMASTER V

Mar 97. (cd/c/lp) *(CDTC+/V 2813) <41915>* **VIOLENT DEMISE (THE LAST DAYS)** [ ] [ ]
– (interview) / My way (BODY COUNT & RAW BREED) / Strippers intro / Strippers / Truth or death / Violent demise / Bring it to pain / Music business / I used to love her / Root of all evil / Dead man walking / (interview end) / You're fuckin' with BC / Ernie's intro / Dr. K / Last days.

ICON

Formed: Phoenix, Arizona, USA . . . 1981 as The SCHOOLBOYS, by DAN WEXLER, TRACY WALLACH and STEPHEN CLIFFORD, who enlisted JOHN AQUILINO and PAT DIXON. Through the hard graft of 'Shrapnel' boss, MIKE VARNEY, they inked a deal with 'Capitol' in 1983. An eponymous debut surfaced the following year, the FM-friendly set featuring a guest spot from ALICE COOPER. This no doubt helped the record hit the US Top 200, developing a groundswell of support for the feted follow-up, 'NIGHT OF THE CRIME' (1985). Though acclaimed by some critics, this tough melodic rock collection didn't sell sufficiently to meet 'Capitol's expectations. Going back to their roots, ICON cut a low-key cassette in 1987, although this was with new frontman, JERRY HARRISON, who took the place of CLIFFORD (he became a born-again Christian!). The tape eventually found its way into the hands of 'Megaforce' mainman, JOHNNY Z, who snapped the band up for a third and final set, 'RIGHT BETWEEN THE EYES' in '89.

Album rating: ICON (*6) / NIGHT OF THE CRIME (*7) / A MORE PERFECT UNION cass (*6) / RIGHT BETWEEN THE EYES (*5)

STEPHEN CLIFFORD – vocals / **DAN WEXLER** – guitar / **TRACY WALLACH** – bass, vocals / **JOHN AQUILINO** – guitar / **PAT DIXON** – drums

Capitol Capitol

May 84. (lp) *<ST 12336>* **ICON** [-] [ ]
– (Rock on) Through the night / Killer machine / On your feet / World war / Hot desert night / Under my gun / Iconoclast / Rock'n'roll maniac / I'm alive / It's up to you. *(Euro-iss.1985; 064 7123361) (cd-iss. Mar00 on 'Axe Killer'; AXE 305673CD)*

May 84. (7") *<5342>* **HOT DESERT NIGHT. / ON YOUR FEET** [-] [ ]

Nov 85. (lp) *<ST 12395>* **NIGHT OF THE CRIME** [-] [ ]
– Naked eyes / Missing / Danger calling / Shot at my heart / Out for blood / Raise the hammer / Frozen tears / The whites of their eyes / Hungry for love / Rock my radio. *(UK cd-iss. Jul00 on 'Axe Killer'; AXE 305733CD)*

— **JERRY HARRISON** – vocals; repl. CLIFFORD who became a Christian

not iss. Icon

1987. (c; sold at gigs) **A MORE PERFECT UNION** [-] [ ]
<cd-iss. 1995 on 'Epilogue'>

— **DREW BOLLMANN** – guitar; repl. AQUILINO

Atlantic Atlantic

Sep 89. (lp/c)(cd) *(K 82010-1/-4)<(782 010-2)>* **RIGHT BETWEEN THE EYES** [ ] [ ]
– Right between the eyes / Two for the road / Taking my breath away / A far cry / In your eyes / Holy man's war / Double life / Forever young / Running under fire / Peace & love.

— split after above; the 90's ICON was a different group

– compilations, etc. –

Mar 00. (cd) *Orchard; <2930>* **1984: LIVE BOOTLEG (live)** [-] [ ]

IDLEWILD

Formed: Edinburgh, Scotland . . . late '95 by RODDY WOOMBLE, ROD JONES and COLIN NEWTON, each having a penchant for noise veterans, SONIC YOUTH and FUGAZI. Having met at a party, the erstwhile students whittled away their revision time with ramshackle rehearsals, eventually channelling their frustrations into a debut single, 'QUEEN OF THE TROUBLED TEENS'. Famously financed by a student loan (and issued on their own 'Human Condition' imprint), the track was championed by Radio One DJ Steve Lamacq, duly rescuing the band from eternal toilet gig hell and setting in motion the mechanics of A&R overload. A follow-up single, 'CHANDELIER', appeared on 'Fierce Panda' while an acclaimed mini-album on 'Deceptive', 'CAPTAIN', kickstarted '98 and became their final fully fledged indie release prior to a deal with 'Food'. Somewhere along the way the band also picked up bassist BOB FAIRFOULL and began to coax some melancholic tunefulness from the blizzard of sound and fury that characterised their youthful approach. 'A FILM FOR THE FUTURE' announced their major label arrival in fittingly convulsive style, the first of many minor hits which have cemented the band's reputation as one of Scotland's most talked about and possibly most dedicated sonic abusers. Their highly anticipated first album proper, 'HOPE IS IMPORTANT' (late '98), made the UK Top 60 and the band's steady rise proves that noisy guitars never go out of fashion. '100 BROKEN WINDOWS' (2000) might've been the casualties of noise, perhaps. But surprisingly enough, the four-piece turned the screeching guitars down for this commercially-orientated release. The single, 'THESE WOODEN IDEAS' unveiled another side to the band that used to literally knee-cap themselves on stage. Still, with its edge intact 'LITTLE DISCOURAGE' found IDLEWILD adopting an REM-esque style (circa 1995), and 'THERE'S A GLORY IN YOUR STORY' saw them unplugging their guitars altogether. Still, this set could make ears bleed if played at the correct volume. Idle? – nah. Wild? – definitely.

Album rating: HOPE IS IMPORTANT (*7) / 100 BROKEN WINDOWS (*7)

RODDY WOOMBLE (b.1976) – vocals / **ROD JONES** (b.1976) – guitar / **COLIN NEWTON** (b.1977) – drums / **PAUL TIPLER** (helped out on) bass

Human Condition not iss.

Mar 97. (7") *(HC 0017)* **QUEEN OF THE TROUBLED TEENS. / FASTER / SELF HEALER** [ ] [-]
(re-iss. Jan98; same)

— **BOB FAIRFOULL** (b.1976) – bass; repl. PAUL

Fierce Panda not iss.

Dec 97. (ltd-7") *(NING 42)* **CHANDELIER. / I WANT TO BE A WRITER** [ ] [-]

Deceptive not iss.

Jan 98. (m-cd) *(BLUFF 058CD)* **CAPTAIN** [ ] [-]
– Self healer / Annihilate now / Captain / Last night I missed all the fireworks / Satan polaroid / You just have to be who you are.

Feb 98. (7") *(BLUFF 057)* **SATAN POLAROID. / HOUSE ALONE** [ ] [-]

Food Odeon-EMI

Apr 98. (7") *(FOOD 111)* **A FILM FOR THE FUTURE. / MINCE SHOWERCAP (part I)** [53] [-]
(cd-s+=) *(CDFOOD 111)* – What am I going to do?

Jul 98. (7") *(FOOD 113)* **EVERYONE SAYS YOU'RE SO FRAGILE. / MINCE SHOWERCAP (part II)** [47] [-]
(cd-s+=) *(CDFOOD 113)* – Theory of achievement.

Oct 98. (7") *(FOOD 114)* **I'M A MESSAGE. / MINCE SHOWERCAP (part III)** [41] [-]
(cd-s+=) *(CDFOOD 114)* – This is worse.
(cd-s) **THE SESSIONS EP** *(CDFOODS 114)* – ('A'live) / Satan polaroid (live) / You've lost your way (live).

Oct 98. (cd/c/lp) *(497132-2/-4/-1) <9504>* **HOPE IS IMPORTANT** [53] [ ]
– You've lost your way / A film for the future / Paint nothing / When I argue I see shapes / 4 people do good / I'm happy to be here tonight / Everyone says you're so fragile / I'm a message / You don't have the heart / Close the door / Safe and sound / Low light.

Feb 99. (7") *(FOOD 116)* **WHEN I ARGUE I SEE SHAPES. / (1903-70) / CHANDELIER (10.15 version)** [19] [-]
(cd-s) *(CDFOOD 116)* – (first 2 tracks) / Last night I missed all the fireworks (live).
(cd-s) *(CDFOODS 116)* – (first & third tracks) / Palace flophouse.

Sep 99. (7") *(FOOD 124)* **LITTLE DISCOURAGE. / BROKEN WINDOWS** [24] [-]
(cd-s+=) *(CDFOOD 124)* – A-Tone.
(cd-s) *(CDFOODS 124)* – ('A'side) / You don't have the heart (live) / 1990 – night-time.

Mar 00. (7") *(FOOD 127)* **ACTUALLY IT'S DARKNESS. / MEET ME AT THE HARBOUR** [23] [-]
(cd-s+=) *(CDFOODS 127)* – West Haven.
(cd-s) *(CDFOOD 127)* – ('A'side) / Forgot to follow / It'll take a long time.

Apr 00. (cd/c/lp) *(FOOD CD/TC/LP 32) <65397>* **100 BROKEN WINDOWS** [15] [ ] May00
– Little discourage / I don't have the map / These wooden ideas / Roseability / Idea track / Let me sleep (next to the mirror) / Listen to what you've got / Actually it's darkness / Rusty / Mistake pageant / Quiet crown / The bronze medal.

Jun 00. (7") *(FOOD 132)* **THESE WOODEN IDEAS. / THERE'S GLORY IN YOUR STORY** [32] [-]
(c-s) *(TCFOOD 132)* – ('A'side) / When the ship comes in.
(cd-s+=) *(CDFOODS 132)* – (three tracks above).
(cd-s) *(CDFOOD 132)* – ('A'side) / Actually it's darkness (acoustic) / Rescue.

Oct 00. (7") *(FOOD 134)* **ROSEABILITY. / RUSTY (the poop soldier mix)** [38] [-]
(cd-s+=) *(CDFOOD 134)* – A thousand.
(cd-s) *(CDFOODS 134)* – ('A'side) / I've only just begun / Self healer (live acoustic version) / ('A'-CD-Rom).

IMMORTAL

Formed: Norway . . . early 90's by pseudonymous brothers ABBATH and DEMONAZ DOOM OCCULTA – try and register these names with your local community/poll tax patrons. Along with the equally apocalyptic ARMAGEDDA on drums, this pioneering Black-metal trio were all the rage (quite literally) in their Scandivanian homeland. Their 1993 debut masterpiece, 'PURE HOLOCAUST', was what the metal world had been waiting for, its darker-than-dark gothic rhythms matched with cliched power riffs; it was recently marked as being DANI of CRADLE OF FILTH's essential Black-metal album. However, IMMORTAL (without the departing ARMAGEDDA) couldn't hold on to this Satan-given lifeforce and served up a bummer with their follow-up, 'BLIZZARD BEASTS' (1995); "a bumblebee in a matchbox!" was how the aforementioned DANI described it. A certain dignity was restored with their third and fourth sets, 'BLIZZARD BEASTS' (1997) and 'AT THE HEART OF WINTER' (1999), although IMMORTAL had obviously suffered too many cold and dark nights. Although they plodded on regardless (ABBATH recruited a new rhythm section of ISCARIAH and HORGH), IMMORTAL was indeed a distant memory of what might've been.

Album rating: PURE HOLOCAUST (*8) / BATTLES IN THE NORTH (*3) / BLIZZARD BEASTS (*5) / AT THE HEART OF WINTER (*4) / DAMNED IN BLACK (*4)

ABBATH DOOM OCCULTA – vocals, bass / **DEMONAZ DOOM OCCULTA** – guitar / **ARMAGEDDA** – drums

Osmose not iss.

Dec 91. (7") **DIABOLICAL FULL MOON MYSTICISM. / UNHOLY FORCES OF EVIL / THE COLD WINDS OF FUNERAL FROST** [-] [-] Norway

Dec 93. (cd) *(OPCD 019)* **PURE HOLOCAUST** [ ] [-]
– Unsilent storms in the north abyss / A sign for the Norse hordes to ride / The sun no longer rises / Frozen by icewinds / Storming through red clouds and holocaust winds / Eternal years on the path to the cemetary gates / As the eternity opens / Pure holocaust. *<US-iss.Apr99; same as UK>*

— now without ARMAGEDDA

Apr 95. (cd/lp) *(OP CD/LP 027)* **BATTLES IN THE NORTH** [ ] [-]
– Battle in the north / Grim and frostbitten kingdoms / Descent into eminent silence / Throned by blackstorms / Moonrise fields of sorrow / Cursed realms of the winterdemons / At the stormy gates of mist / Through the halls of eternity / Circling above in time before time / Blashyrkh (mighty raven dark). *(cd+=)* – Diabolical full moon mysticism / Unholy forces of evil / The cold winds of funeral frost. *(pic-lp iss.Jun98; OPPIC 027)*

Mar 97. (cd/lp) *(OP CD/LP 051)* **BLIZZARD BEASTS** [ ] [-]
– Intro / Blizzard beasts / Nebular ravens winter / Suns that sank below / Battlefields / Mountains of might / Noctambulant / Winter of the ages / Frostdemonstorm.

Mar 99. (cd/lp) *(OP CD/LP 079)* **AT THE HEART OF WINTER** [ ] [-]
– Withstand the fall of time / Solarfall / Tragedies blow at horizon / Where dark and light don't differ / At the heart of winter / Years of silent sorrow.

— **ABBATH** recruited new disciples **ISCARIAH** – bass + **HORGH** – drums

Apr 00. (cd/lp) *(OP CD/LP 095)* **DAMNED IN BLACK** [ ] [-]
– Triumph / Wrath from above / Against the tide (in the arctic world) / My dimension / The darkness / In our mystic visions blest / Damned in black.

– compilations, etc. –

1990's. (cd) *JL America; <41075>* **DIABOLICAL FULL MOON MYSTICISM** (early material) -
– Intro / The call of the Wintermoon / Unholy forces of evil / Cryptic winterstorms / Cold winds of funeral dust / Blacker than darkness / A perfect vision of the rising northland.

IMPALED NAZARENE

Formed: Finland ... 1990 with the original line-up of brothers MIKA and KIMMO LUTTINEN, MIKA PAAKKO, ARI HOLAPPA and AUTTI PIHKALA. After recording several demos, consisting of new material and some of the LUTTINEN brothers' former band's (MUTILATION) tracks, PIHKALA made a sharp exit and was replaced by HARI HALONEN. This new bassist was not to last long either, leaving with HOLAPPA shortly after the band released their now hard to get hold of 1991 7" 'GOAT PERVERSION' (although it was later made available on the 'NAZ' compilation, 'DECADE OF DECADENCE' (2000). The aforementioned EP got the Finnish punky death-metallers noticed by 'Osmose Productions', who released their debut album, 'TOL CORMPT NORZ NORZ NORZ' (1993) – here the band were joined by TANELI JARVA on bass while also swapping PAAKKO on guitar for JARNO ANTILLA. The group then toured but were quickly back in the studio to record their second full-length set, 'UGRA KARMA' (1993). The cover-art of this outing offended the Hare Krishna movement who won a court action against the band. This was certainly not the last time 'NAZARENE were to court controversy, as their third full-set, 'SUOMI FINLAND PERKELE' (1994) – initially to be named 'Hail to Finland' – managed to offend a French youth group, with the lyrics of 'TOTAL WAR-WINTER WAR', and so was withdrawn from the shelves of a major French retailer. While in recording sessions in 1995, friction in the studio resulted in the departure of KIMMO LUTTINEN who was replaced by REIMA KELLOKOSKI. The court action was also dropped. The 'NAZ delivered their fourth album, 'LATEX CULT' (1996), JARVA leaving straight after the tracks were cut; JANI LEHTOSAARI superseded him. IMPALED NAZARENE followed the success of this album two years later with the release of 'RAPTURE' (1998). These last two sets could be described as on the punk side of death metal, the band using a gritty, machine-like guitar sound that gained them the unique categorisation of "nuclear metal". Distinct in a way from their less-punk-more-extreme metal sounding sixth release, 'NIHIL' (2000), this was thanks in part to the guitar wizardry of ALEXI LAIHO, who joined part-time after a joint Russian gig with his band, CHILDREN OF BODOM. Also of note was the side project RAISM, masterminded by MIKA LUTTINEN, IN's shaven-headed frontman as MIKA X6X, MW DAOLOTH (of NECROMANTIA) on keyboards, with additional help on guitar by SEPTIC FLESH's SOTIRIS. RAISM, formerly DIABOLOS RISING, was an anarchic mesh of death metal riffage and machine techno beats creating a very extreme sound (MIKA LUTTINEN's favourite descriptive word for hi output). Their releases included the mini-album, 'THE VERY BEST OF PAIN' (1996) and the full-set, 'AESTHETIC TERRORISM' (1998), definitely made for the initiated; even death metal fans finding this exploratory blend too much to cope with.

Album rating: TOL CORMPT NORZ NORZ NORZ (*5) / UGRA-KARMA (*7) SUOMI FINLAND PERKELE (*4) / LATEX CULT (*5) / RAPTURE (*5) / NIHIL (*6) / DECADE OF DECADENCE compilation (*6) / Raism: THE VERY BEST OF PAIN mini (*5) / AESTHETIC TERRORISM (*7)

MIKA LUTTINEN – vocals / **ARI HOLAPPA** – guitar / **MIKA PAAKKO** – guitar / **HARRI HALONEN** – bass / **KIMMO LUTTINEN** – drums

Nosferatu / not iss.

1992. (7") **GHOST RIDERS. /** - - Finnish
1992. (cd-ep) **GOAT PERVERSION EP** - - Finnish

— **JARNO ANTTILA** – guitar; repl. HOLAPPA

— **TANELI JARVA** – bass; repl. HALONEN

Osmose / Osmose

Apr 93. (ltd; lp/cd) *(OP 010/+CD)* **TOL CORMPT NORZ NORZ NORZ** -
– Apolokia I: Al purg vompo / My blessing (the beginning of the end) / Apolokia II: Aikolopa 666 / In the name of Satan / Impure orgies / Goat perversion / The forest (the darkness) / Mortification blood red razor blade / The god (symmetry of penis) / Condemned to Hell / The dog (art of vagina) / The crucified / Apolokia III: Agony / Body-mind-soul / Hoath: Darbs Lucifero / Apolokia finale XXVII A.S. / Damnation (raping the angels).
1993. (cd-ep) **SATANIC MASOWHORE** - - Finnish
Dec 93. (cd/lp) *(OPCD/OPLP 018)* **UGRA KARMA** -
– Goatized / The horny and the horned / Sadhu Satana / Chaosgoat law / Hate / Gott ist tot (Antichrist war mix) / Coraxo / Soul rape / Kali-Yuga / Cyberchrist / False Jehova / Sadistic 666 – Under a golden shower.
Nov 94. (cd/lp) *(OPCD/OPLP 026)* **SUOMI FINLAND PERKELE** -
– Intro / Vitutuksen multihuipennus / Blood is thicker than water / Steelvagina / Total war – Winter war / Quasb – The burning / Kuolema kaikille (paitsi meille) / Let's fucking die! / Genocide / Ghettoblaster / The oath of the goat.

— **REIMA KELLOKOSKI** – drums; repl. KIMMO

Apr 96. (cd/lp) *(OPCD/OPLP 038)* **LATEX CULT** -
– 66.6 S of foreplay / 1999: karmakeddon warriors / Bashing in heads / Motorpenis / Zum Kotzen / Alien militant / Goat war / Punishment is absolute / When all golden turned to shit / Masterbator / The burning of Provinciestrat / I eat pussy for breakfast / Delirium tremens.
Jun 96. (m-cd) *(OPCD 039)* **MOTORPENIS** -
– Motorpenis / Whore / S-M party / Transvestite / Alkohol.

— **JANI LEHTOSAARI** – guitar; repl. JARVA

May 98. (cd/lp) *(<OPCD/OPLP 069>)* **RAPTURE** Aug98
– Penis et circes / 6th degree mindfunk / Iron fist with an iron will / Angel rectums do bleed / We're Satan's generation / Goatvomit and gasmasks / Fallout theory in practice / Healers of the red plague / The pilory / The return of the nuclear gods / Vitulation / JCS / Inbred / Phallus maleficarum.

— in 1999, they split a 7" single with DRILLER KILLER

— **ALEXI LAIHO** – guitar (of CHILDREN OF BODOM) repl. PAAKKO

Mar 00. (cd/lp) *(OPCD/OPLP 093)* **NIHIL** -
– Cogito ergo sum / Human-proof / Wrath of the goat / Angel rectums still bleed – The return / Posteclipse era / Nothing is sacred / Zero tolerance / Assault the weak / How the laughter died / Nihil.
Jan 01. (cd) *(OPCD 108)* **DECADE OF DECADENCE** (compilation) -
– Intro / Condemned to Hell / The crucified / Disgust suite O:P I / Morbid fate / Disgust suite O:P II / Worms in rectum / Conned thru life / Crucifixation / Nuctemeron of necromanteion / Condemned to Hell / Impurity of dawn / The crucified / Infernus / Morbid fate / Ave satanas / In the name of Satan / Fall to fornication / Damnation (raping the angels) / Noisrevrep eht refta / Damnation (raping the angels) / The black vomit / Ghost riders / Sadogoat / I am the killer of trolls / Kill yourself / Burst command 'til war / Nuclear metal retaliation / Instrumental I / Instrumental II / Instrumental III.

RAISM

MIKA X6X – vocals (of IMPALED NAZARENE) / **MW DAOLOTH** – synthesizer (of NECROMANTIA) / with **SOTIRIS** – guitar (of SEPTIC FLESH)

Kronh / not iss.

Jul 96. (m-cd) *(KRONH 004CD)* **THE VERY BEST OF PAIN** -
– Chaosphere / Killing machine / Les 120 journees de sodome (a velvet ballad for De Sade) / Alienation / What kind of hell is this anyway?
Jun 98. (cd) *(KRONH 007CD)* **AESTHETIC TERRORISM** -
– Survival of the fittest scum / S.O.T.F.S. (destructive club version) / Aesthetic terrorism / A.T. (distorted reality cyberspace version) / Gluttony / G (carnivorous commercial version) / Negative / Hate you / Politically incorrect (non P.C.) / P.I. (government approved explicit version) / Nexus / N (multiple personality psychoid version).

Chris IMPELLITTERI

Born: Connecticut, USA. In the vanguard of the new, hi-tech guitar maestros who proliferated during the latter half of the 80's, IMPELLITTERI released an instrumental debut set for 'Relativity' in 1987. A year later he formed his own group, the modestly named IMPELLITTERI alongside ex-RAINBOW frontman GRAHAM BONNET, PHIL WOLFE, CHUCK WRIGHT and PAT TORPEY. The resulting album, 'STAND IN LINE', was a rockier, more palatable affair, although this proved to be a one-off venture as his band moved to take up other posts (TORPEY joined MR. BIG).

Album rating: IMPELLITERRI (*5) / STAND IN LINE (*6) / EYE OF THE HURRICANE (*5) / CRUNCH + SCREAMING SYMPHONY (*5)

IMPELLITTERI

— with **BOB ROCK** – vocals / **LONI SILVA** – drums

Music For Nations / Relativity

1987. (m-lp/m-cd) *<61-8219-1/-2>* **IMPELLITTERI** -
– Lost in the rain / Play with fire / Burning / I'll be searching. *<(UK + re-iss. m-cd-iss. Mar00 on 'Century Media'; 66047-2)>*

— now with **GRAHAM BONNET** – vocals (ex-Solo artist, ex-MICHAEL SCHENKER GROUP, ex-RAINBOW) / **PHIL WOLFE** – keyboards / **CHUCK WRIGHT** – bass (ex-QUIET RIOT) / **PAT TORPEY** – drums (ex-TED TUGENT)

Aug 88. (cd/c/lp) *(CD/T+/MFN 87) <8225>* **STAND IN LINE** 91 Jun88
– Stand in line / Since you've been gone / Secret lover / Somewhere over the rainbow / Tonight I fly / White and perfect / Leviathan / Goodnight and goodbye / Playing with fire. *<(US + re-iss. Nov99 on 'Century Media'; 66032-2)>*

— after above last release, TORPEY joined MR. BIG

not iss. / RCA Victor

1993. (cd) **VICTIM OF THE SYSTEM** -
above/or below **IMPELLITTERI** now with **ROBERT ROCK** – vocals / **MIKE SMITH** – keyboards / **CHUCK WRIGHT + JAMES AMELIO PULLI** – bass / **KEN MARY** – drums
1994. (cd) **ANSWER TO THE MASTER** -
– The future is black / Fly away / Warrior / I'll wait / Warrior / Something's wrong with the world today / Answer to the master / Hungry days / The king is rising.

not iss. / J.V.C.

1995. (cd) *<1689>* **SCREAMING SYMPHONY** -
– (see below for tracks)

Dream Catcher / unknown

Oct 98. (cd) *(CRIDE 4) <33817>* **EYE OF THE HURRICANE**
– Eye of the hurricane / Shed your blood / Fuel for the fire / Race into the light / Bleed in silence / Master of disguise / On and on / Everything is you / Kingdom fighter / Halloween / Paradise / Warrior / Fly away / Hold the line / Victim of the system / Glory.
Aug 00. (d-cd) *(CRIDE 29)* **CRUNCH / SCREAMING SYMPHONY** (Japanese imports) -
– Beware of the Devil / Turn of the century / Speed demon / Wake me up / Spanish fire / Slay the dragon / Wasted earth / Forever yours / Texas nuclear boogie / Fear no evil / Spanish fire // Father forgive me / I'll be with you / Walk away / Kingdom of light / Countdown to the revolution / 17th century chicken pickin' / Rat race / For your love / You are the fire.

IMPERIAL TEEN (see under ⇒ FAITH NO MORE)

IN-BE-TWEENS (see under ⇒ SLADE)

INCA BABIES

Formed: Manchester, England . . . 1982 by BILL BONNEY, HARRY STAFFORD and vocalist/drummer PETE. A whirling, hard-hitting thrash-punk outfit in the grinding mould of LIVING IN TEXAS or a punkabilly BIRTHDAY PARTY, they formed their own 'Black Lagoon' label and proceeded to release a string of well-received (in indie circles at least) 45's beginning with 1983's 'THE INTERIOR'. Two full albums, 'RUMBLE' and 'THIS TRAIN', also surfaced in the mid 80's, although the INCA BABIES would be best remembered for the presence of CLINT BOON (later of The INSPIRAL CARPETS), who played on their final effort, 'EVIL HOUR' (1988).

Album rating: RUMBLE (*5) / THIS TRAIN (*5) / OPIUM DEN mini (*4) / EVIL HOUR (*5)

PETE – vocals, drums / **HARRY STAFFORD** – guitar / **BILL BONNEY** – bass

Black Lagoon | not iss.

Nov 83. (7") *(INC 001)* **THE INTERIOR. / SENSE OF LOSS** [ ] [-]
Mar 84. (7") *(INC 002)* **GRUNT CADILLAC. / NO SACRED SOUND** [ ] [-]
May 84. (12"ep) *(INC 003)* **BIG JUGULAR** [ ] [-]
Aug 84. (7") *(INC 004)* **THE JUDGE. / BUS BREAKER** [ ] [-]
(12"+=) *(INC 004T)* –

—— added **MIKE LOUIS** – vocals, harmonica (PETE no vocals)

Feb 85. (lp) *(INCLP 005)* **RUMBLE** [ ] [-]
– She mercenary / The interior / Blind man (the chiller) / The diseased stranger's waltz / Leucotomy meat boss / Big jugular / 16 tons of fink / Cactus mouth informer / Greaseball mechanic.
Oct 85. (12"ep) *(INC 007)* **SURFIN' IN LOCUSTLAND** [ ] [-]
Mar 86. (7") *(INC 009)* **SPLATTER BALLISTICS COP. / BURY THE SWAGGER** [ ] [-]
(12"+=) *(INC 009T)* – ('A'version).
May 86. (lp) *(INCLP 010)* **THIS TRAIN** [ ] [-]
– Plenty more mutants / Correction stack / Hole in the gulley / Candy mountain / Splatter ballistics cop / The depths / Backyard bones / Daniella / Call me enemy.
Jun 87. (m-lp) *(INCMLP 012)* **OPIUM DEN** [ ] [-]
– Opium den / Thirst / Devil in my room / Ramblin' man / Big Cyprus / A grim thought / Dresden.
Oct 87. (7") *(CON! 00027)* **BUSTER'S ON FIRE. /** [-] [-] German
(above issued for 'Constrictor')

—— **HARRY + BILL** recruited newcomers **TONY CLARKE** – drums / **CLINT BOON** – keyboards / **DIRK BULLOWS + SIMON HINSON**

May 88. (lp) *(INCLP 013)* **EVIL HOUR** [ ] [-]
– Evil hour / Long uphill trek / Partisan's river / A madman's demise / Bad hombre / Artillery switchback / Two rails to nowhere / Volts / Burning town / Young blood. *(re-iss. Oct88 on 'Vinyl Drip'; SUK 002) (cd-iss. Jan89 on 'Communion'; COMM 6CD)*

—— split after above, CLINT joined The INSPIRAL CARPETS

INCUBUS

Formed: Los Angeles, California, USA . . . 1991 by BRANDON BOYD, MIKE EINZIGER, ALEX KATUNICH, GAVIN POPPEL and JOSE ANTONIO PASILLAS II. Taking their moniker from an evil spirit purported to indulge in sexual activities with sleeping women, the band were nevertheless an uptempo funk/metal combo rather than a ghoulish death-metal act. One of the better acts to stay faithful to the spirit of classic RED HOT CHILI PEPPERS and FAITH NO MORE, updating the jack-in-the-box slap bass of the former and the resounding vocal depth of the latter, the group signed to Epic subsidiary 'Immortal' for their debut album, 'ENJOY INCUBUS' (1996) – actually they had self-financed a "real" debut album in '94. Well received in the metal press, 'ENJOY . . .' transcended the barriers of the genre to successfully embrace everything from reggae to laid-back jazz, and still sounded funkin' great! Equally challenging and inventive, their next set, 'S.C.I.E.N.C.E.', was another mish-mash of styles even incorporating BOYD's didgeridoo, although don't let that put you off! In 1999, INCUBUS were back with a second full-set, 'MAKE YOURSELF', an album that finally gave them a US Top 75 success. • **Note:** Not the same group who released records on 'Nuclear Blast'.

Album rating: ENJOY INCUBUS mini (*6) / S.C.I.E.N.C.E. (*6) / MAKE YOURSELF (*6)

BRANDON OF THE JUNGLE (b. BRANDON BOYD) – vocals, percussion / **DYNAMIKE** (b. MIKE EINZIGER) – guitar / **DIRK LANCE** (b. ALEX KATUNICH) – bass / **KID LYFE** (b. GAVIN POPPEL) – scratches / **JOSE ANTONIO PASILLAS II** – drums

Immortal-Epic | Immortal-Epic

Feb 97. (m-cd/m-c) *<(487102-2/-4)>* **ENJOY INCUBUS** [ ] [ ] Nov96
– You will be a hot dancer / Shaft / Take me to your leader / Version / Azwethinkweiz / Hilikus / Hidden bonus. *(check this)*
Oct 97. (cd) *<(4882616)>* **S.C.I.E.N.C.E.** [ ] [ ]
– Redefine / New skin / Idiot box / Glass / Magic medicine / Certain shade of green / Favourite things / Anti-gravity love song / Nebula / Deep inside / Calgon. *(re-iss. Jan01; same)*
Oct 99. (cd/c) *(495040-2/-4) <63652>* **MAKE YOURSELF** [ ] [47]
– Privilege / Nowhere fast / Consequence / Warmth / When it comes / Stellar / Make yourself / Drive / Clean / Battle star / I miss you / Pardon me / Out from under. *(cd re-iss. May01 w/ extra cd)* – Pardon me (acoustic) / Stellar (acoustic) / Make yourself (acoustic) / Drive (live orchestral).
May 00. (7"red) *(669346-7)* **PARDON ME. / PARDON ME (acoustic)** [61] [-]
(cd-s) *(669346-2)* – ('A'side) / I miss you / Crowded elevator / ('A'-CD-Rom).
Nov 00. (m-cd) *<61497>* **FUNGUS AMONGUS** [-] [ ]
Jun 01. (cd-s) *(671378-2) <radio play>* **DRIVE / DRIVE (acoustic) / CLEAN (live)** [40] [14] Feb01
(7"m) *(671378-7)* – ('A'live) / Favourite things (live) / Pardon me (live).

INFA-RIOT

Formed: London, England . . . 1981 by LEE WILSON, BARRY D'AMERY, FLOYD WILSON and MARK REYNOLDS. Another bunch of "oi" hopefuls to emerge on the 'Secret' label, INFA RIOT debuted with a couple of simplistic three minute singles, 'KIDS OF THE 80'S' and 'THE WINNER', before knocking off a surprise Top 50 placing for their 1982 album, 'STILL OUT OF ORDER'. However, with all the (un)healthy competition around in such a crowded scene, the band evolved into The INFAS and inflicted one more album, 'SOUND AND FURY' (1984) upon the post-punk populace.

Album rating: STILL OUT OF ORDER (*4) / Infas: SOUND AND FURY (*2) / IN FOR A RIOT compilation (*5)

LEE WILSON – vocals / **BARRY D'AMERY** – guitar, vocals / **FLOYD WILSON** – bass, vocals / **MARK REYNOLDS** – drums, vocals

Secret | not iss.

Oct 81. (7") *(SHH 117)* **KIDS OF THE 80'S. / STILL OUT OF ORDER** [ ] [-]
Apr 82. (7") *(SHH 133)* **THE WINNER. / SCHOOL'S OUT** [ ] [-]
Jul 82. (lp/c) *(SEC/TSEC 7)* **STILL OUT OF ORDER** [42] [-]
– Emergency / You ain't seen nothing yet / Five minute fashion / Each dawn I die / The drug squad / Still out of order / Catch 22 / Power / Boot boys / The winner / Friday oh Friday / Catalogue kids / In for a riot. *(cd-iss. Jul98 on 'Captain Oi'; AHOYCD 010)*

—— changed their moniker to The INFAS

INFAS

Pancake | not iss.

Feb 84. (lp/c) *(PAN LP/CA 501)* **SOUND AND FURY** [ ] [-]
– Rock all ye faithful / These dangerous days / Sound and fury / Punch the air with glory / There's gotta be a better way / Birds and bees / A spirit wild / Manthing / Don't want to be (in the in-crowd) / Pushers on the rampage / Triffic spiff ya o.k. / Captain England. *(<cd-iss. Jan00 on 'Captain Oi'; AHOYCD 49>)*
Mar 84. (7") *(PAN 101)* **SOUND AND FURY. / TRIFFIC SPIFF YA O.K.** [ ] [-]

—— they split after above

– compilations, etc. –

Mar 99. (cd) *Harry May; (<MAYOCD 104>)* **IN FOR A RIOT** [ ] [ ] Jul99
– Five minute fashion / Riot riot / Kids of the 80's / Each dawn I die / You ain't seen nothing yet / Emergency / The winner / Drug squad / Still out of order / School's out / Friday oh Friday / Catch 22 / Bootboys / In for a riot / Punch the air with glory (live) / Feel the rage (live).

INFECTIOUS GROOVES
(see under ⇒ SUICIDAL TENDENCIES)

INSANE CLOWN POSSE

Formed: Detroit, Michigan, USA . . . 1989 as The INNER CITY POSSE, by SHAGGY 2 DOPE and VIOLENT J, two face-painted rappers with er . . . a wicked sense of fun. They changed their moniker in 1992, releasing their debut album 'CARNIVAL OF CARNAGE' the following year. Championed by the metal press, INSANE CLOWN POSSE are basically nevertheless a dyed-in-the-wool rap duo, albeit an extremely offensive one with a bizarre line in twisted circus trappings. Following a little contretemps with the Walt Disney corporation (and a short-lived spell with 'Jive' records), the gruesome jokers delivered their breakthrough release, 'THE GREAT MILENKO' in 1997, although this initially ran into difficulties with the all-powerful moral majority (the old record company recalling all copies due to its offensive content). Predictably, sales of the album (released by 'Island') soared, culminating in a US Top 75 placing. Just in time for Yuletide festivities, the 'POSSE laid their Christmas gift 45, 'SANTA'S A FAT BITCH' under the tree of hypocritical middle class America. 1998 saw a further couple of minor UK hit singles while 'THE AMAZING JECKEL BROTHERS' (1999) amazingly made the US Top 5. Yet the posse's most ambitious moment was still to come: in the year 2000, the jokers released 'BIZZAR' – accompanied by the US-only 'BIZAAR'. Confused? You might well be, especially by the former's choice of cover material, a reading of the 80's Sly Fox hit, 'LET'S GO ALL THE WAY'.

Album rating: CARNIVAL OF CHANGE (*4) / THE RING MASTER (*4) / RIDDLE BOX (*6) / THE GREAT MILENKO (*5) / THE AMAZING JECKEL BROTHERS (*4) / BIZZAR (*4)

SHAGGY 2 DOPE (b. CLARK) – rapper / **VIOLENT J** (b. BROWN) – rapper; with guests **SLASH + STEVE JONES** – guitars

not iss. | Psychopathic

1993. (12"ep) *<PSY 1005>* **BEVERLY HILLS 50187** [-] [ ]
1993. (cd) **CARNIVAL OF CARNAGE** [-] [ ]
– Intro / Carnival of carnage / Juggla / First day out / Red neck hoe / Wizard of the hood / Guts on the ceiling / Is that you / Night of the axe / Psychopathic / Blackin' your eyes / Never had made it / Your ebel flag / Ghetto freak show / Taste. *(UK-iss.Jun98 on 'Island'; 524514-2)*

1994. (12"ep) <PSY 1007> **THE TERROR WHEEL** -
1994. (cd) **THE RING MASTER** -
– Wax museum / Murder go round / Chicken huntin' / Mr. Johnson's head / Southwest song / Get off me dog / Who asked who / Dead one / For the maggots / Wagon wagon / Loons / Love song / Bugz on my nugz / House of mirrors / Ringmaster's world. *(UK-iss.Jun98 on 'Island'; 524515-2)*

not iss. Battery

Oct 95. (cd) <02141-46001-2> **RIDDLE BOX** -
– Riddle box / The show must go on / Chicken huntin' / Toy box / Cemetery girl / 3 rings / Headless boogie / Joker's wild / Dead body man / Lil' somethin' somethin' / Ol' evil eye / 12 / Killing fields / I'm coming home.

Island Hollywood

Oct 97. (cd/c) *(CID/ICT 8061)* <524442-2> **THE GREAT MILENKO** 63 Jul97
– Intro / The great Milenko / Hokus pokus / Piggy pie / How many times? / Southwest voodoo / Halls of illusion / Under the moon / What is a juggalo? / House of horrors / Boogie woogie wu / Neden game / Hellalujah / Down with the clown / Just like that / Pass me by.
Dec 97. (cd-s) <57219-2> **CARNIVAL CHRISTMAS: SANTA'S A FAT BITCH** - 67
Jan 98. (7") *(IS 685)* **HALLS OF ILLUSION. / SMOG** 56
(cd-s+=) *(CID 685)* – Southwest voodoo / Cotton candy.
May 98. (7"pic-d) *(ISP 705)* **HOKUS POKUS. / PROM QUEEN** 53
('A'-Headhunta'z mix; cd-s+=) *(CID 705)* – My kind of bitch / Skitzofrantic.
(cd-s) *(CIDX 705)* – ('A'-Headhunta'z mix) / ('A'-radio mix) / ('A'-lp version) / ('A'-Headhunta'z instrumental).
May 99. (cd) <(524661-2)> **THE AMAZING JECKEL BROTHERS** 4
– Intro / Jake Jeckel / Bring it on / I want my shit / Bitches! / Terrible / I stab people / Another love song / Everyone rize / Play with me / Jack Jeckel / Fuck the world / The Shaggy show / Mad professor / Assassins / Echo side / Nothing left.
Nov 00. (cd) <(548174-2)> **BIZZAR** 21
– Intro / Take me away / Fearless / Rainbows and stuff / What / Still stabbin' / Tilt-a-whirl / We gives no fuck / Please don't hate me / Behind the paint / My homie baby mama / The pendulum's promise.

– compilations, etc. –

Aug 98. (d-cd,d-c) *Island;* <524552> **FORGOTTEN FRESHNESS VOL.1 & 2** (first two albums) - 46

(INTERNATIONAL) NOISE CONSPIRACY

(see under ⇒ REFUSED)

IN THE WOODS . . .

Formed: Norway . . . 1992 by X BOTTERI, CM BOTTERI, ODDVAR A:M, A. KOBRO, SYNNE DIANA, B. BESERK OVL. SVITHJOD (aka JAN TRANSIT). To call IN THE WOODS black metal would certainly be an erroneous delimiting of their abilities and output. The band certainly came from this strain of metal, but, although not comparable in sound, followed down the same route of experimental, progressive darkness as fellow Scandanavians ARCTURUS. INW saw themselves as more of a collective, only cagily giving information about themselves and what instruments each member played. Their output was heavily influenced by classical music, strings and piano work being integral to their sound. 1993 saw the band record and release a demo which quickly attracted the attention of the label 'Misanthropy', who signed them in 1994 and released their debut album 'HEART OF THE AGES' (1995) the following year. This record introduced the record-buying public to their innovative combination of black metal tempo and classical/ambient keyboards and strings. It was certainly something new, although it had its roots in bands like CELTIC FROST. Unfortunately though, innovation could not always save this debut outing from certain moments of prog-rock mundanity. INW followed this up with their second full-length 'OMNIO' (1997), which featured the mesmerising vocals of new member SYNNE SOPRANA. On this album and the following, 'STRANGE IN STEREO' (1999), the individual talents of the members (ODDVAR being replaced by CHRISTER CEDERBERG) came to the fore with some stunning and complex guitar work. 'THREE TIMES SEVEN ON A PILGRIMAGE' (2000) collected together some of the band's 7"s along with other reworked material. A standout on this collection was the aptly-chosen and interesting take on JEFFERSON AIRPLANE's psychedelic classic 'WHITE RABBIT', originally released by INW as a B-side in 1996. • **Covered:** LET THERE BE MORE LIGHT (Pink Floyd) / EPITAPH (King Crimson).

Album rating: HEART OF THE AGES (*5) / OMNIO (*7) / STRANGE IN STEREO (*5) / THREE TIMES SEVEN ON A PILGRIMAGE (*5)

X-BOTTERI, C.M. BOTTERI, B. BESERK OVL. SVITHJOD, ODDVAR A:M, A. KOBRO + SYNNE DIANA + others play various instruments/vocals

demo not iss.

1993. (m-c) **ISLE OF MEN** - - Norway
– The wings of my dreamland / Tele de Dode / In the woods . . . / Creations of an ancient shape / Wotan's return. *(re-iss. 1996 m-cd as 'A RETURN TO THE ISLE OF MEN' on 'Hammerheart'+=;)* – HEart of the ages / . . .And all this from which was and will never come again . . . (Child of universal tongue).

Misanthropy Misanthropy

May 95. (lp/cd) *(AMAZON 004 LP/CD)* **HEART OF THE AGES** -
– Yearning the seeds of a new dimension / Heart of the ages / In the woods . . . / Mourning the death of Aase (instrumental) / Wotan's return / Pigeon (instrumental) / The divinity of wisdom. *(<US + cd re-iss. Nov97; same>)*
1996. (7") *(OVL 69)* **WHITE RABBIT. / MOURNING THE DEATH OF AASE** - - Norway
Jun 97. (d-lp/cd) *(<AMAZON 011 LP/CD>)* **OMNIO** Oct97
– 299 796 km/s / I am your flesh / Kairos! / Weeping willow / Omnio? / – Pre / – Bardo / – Post.
Jul 98. (7") *(OVL 68)* **LET THERE BE MORE LIGHT. / CHILD OF UNIVERSAL TONGUE** -
Feb 99. (cd) *(<AMAZON 020CD>)* **STRANGE IN STEREO** Apr99
– Closing in / Cell / Vanish in the absence of virtue / Basement corridors / Ion / Generally more worried than married / Path of the righteous / Dead man's creek / Titan transcendence / Shelter / By the banks of pandemonium.

— **CHRISTER CEDERBERG** repl. ODDVAR

Jun 00. (7") *(OVL 67)* **EPITAPH. / KARMAKOSMIK** - - Norway

Prophecy not iss.

Jun 00. (cd) *(PRO 024)* **THREE TIMES SEVEN ON A PILGRIMAGE** -
– Seed of sound / Karmakosmik / Epitaph / Empty room / Let there be more light / Child of universal tongue / Soundtrax for Cycoz (1st ed) / White rabbit / Mourning the death of Aase / If it's in you.

— IN THE WOODS . . . split late 2000

INTO ANOTHER

Formed: New York, USA . . . August 1990 by RICHIE BIRKENHEAD and TONY BONO. The former had been in YOUTH OF TODAY, which featured SAMMY of CIV and vocalist RAY CAPPO of SHELTER. Fusing together elements of indie, hardcore and grunge, the group fashioned a cerebral brand of post-rock developed over a series of releases from the early to mid 90's. Their eponymous debut was met with little response, although 'SEAMLESS' brought in PEARL JAM/SOUNDGARDEN producer, Rick Parashar for a more accessible sound.

Album rating: INTO ANOTHER (*5) / IGNARUS (*6) / SEAMLESS (*6)

RICHIE BIRKENHEAD – vocals (ex-YOUTH OF TODAY) / **PETER MOSES** – guitar / **TONY BONO** – bass (ex-WHIPLASH) / **DREW THOMAS** – drums

We Bite Revelation

Jan 92. (lp/cd) *(WB 083/+CD)* <REV 024/+CD> **INTO ANOTHER** Nov91
– Robot whales / Underlord / Powered / Splinters / Apalindrome / While I die / For lack of a better world / As it were / Dare me. *(re-iss. Jan96 on 'Revelation' lp/cd; REV 024/+CD)*

Revelation Revelation

Apr 92. (12"ep/cd-ep) <REV 026> **CREEPY EPPY EP** -
– I'll be damned / Without a medium / Absolute zero / The other.
May 94. (lp/cd) <(REV 035/+CD)> **IGNAURUS**
– Running into walls / Poison fingers / Ungodly / Two snowflakes / Laughing at oblivion / Maritime murder / William / Drowning / Anxious.

Revelation Hollywood

Jan 96. (lp/cd) *(REV 048/+CD)* <162 008-2> **SEAMLESS**
– Mutate me / Locksmiths & lawyers / T.A.I.L. / Getting nowhere / Seemless / Actual size / For a wounded wren / After birth / Regarding earthlings / May I / The way down. *(re-iss. cd Feb96 on 'Hollywood'; 162 008-2)*
Mar 96. (7") <(REV 042)> **POISON FINGERS. / TO BE FREE** Jun95
(cd-s+=) *(REV 042CD)* – Herbivore.

— disbanded after above

Tony IOMMI (see under ⇒ BLACK SABBATH)

IRON BUTTERFLY

Formed: San Diego, California, USA . . . 1966 by DOUG INGLE, RON BUSHY, DANNY WEIS, JERRY PENROD and DARRYL DeLOACH. They soon moved to Los Angeles and after being spotted at the Whiskey A-Go-Go, they signed to Atlantic subsidiary label, 'Atco'. Early in 1968, they issued the 'HEAVY' album, which bulldozed its way into the lower regions of the US Top 100. Later that summer, WEIS and PENROD departed, superseded by LEE DORMAN and ERIK BRAUN. This line-up subsequently recorded the organ-driven, progressive proto-metal of 'IN-A-GADDA-DA-VIDA' (aka 'The Garden of Life'), a classic album which hit the US Top 5, going on to sell over three million copies. The edited title track (trimmed from 17-minute LP version) gave them additional success in the singles chart. With the aforementioned album still riding high in the charts, their 1969 'BALL' album bounced into the Top 3. In 1970, IRON BUTTERFLY introduced the twin-guitar assault of MIKE PIERA and LARRY REINHARDT, who featured on their Top 20 set, 'METAMORPHOSIS'. They split soon after, only to surface again in 1975 with two poor efforts, 'SCORCHING BEAUTY' and 'SUN AND STEEL'. • **Songwriters:** INGLE and BUSHY were main contributors until the addition/departure of BRAUN and DORMAN. • **Trivia:** In 1968, two tracks, 'OSSESSION' and 'UNCONSCIOUS POWER' were used on the film soundtrack of 'The Savage Seven'.

Album rating: HEAVY (*6) / IN-A-GADDA-DA-VIDA (*9) / BALL (*6) / IRON BUTTERFLY LIVE (*3) / METAMORPHOSIS (*5) / THE BEST OF IRON BUTTERFLY – EVOLUTION compilation (*6) / SCORCHING BEAUTY (*4) / SUN AND STEEL (*3) / LIGHT AND HEAVY – THE BEST OF IRON BUTTERFLY compilation (*7)

DOUG INGLE (b. 9 Sep'46, Omaha, Nebraska) – keyboards, vocals /**JERRY PENROD** – guitar / **DANNY WEIS** – guitar (both ex-DAVID ACKLES band) / **RON BUSHY** (b.23 Sep'45, Washington, D.C.) – drums, vocals / **DARRYL DeLOACH** – bass, vocals

Atco Atco

Feb 68. (lp) *(2465 015)* <33227> **HEAVY** 78
– Possession / Unconscious power / Get out of my life, woman / Gentle as it may seem / You can't win / So-lo / Look for the sun / Fields of sun / Stamped ideas / Iron butterfly theme. *(cd-iss. 1992 on 'Repertoire'+=;)* – I can't help but deceive you little girl / To be alone.

Atlantic | Atco

Jun 68. (7") *(584 188) <6573>* **POSSESSION. / UNCONSCIOUS POWER** [ ] [ ] May68

— **ERIK BRAUN** (b.11 Aug'50, Boston, Mass.) – lead guitar, vocals repl. WEIS and PENROD who formed RHINOCEROS / **LEE DORMAN** (b.19 Sep'45, St.Louis, Missouri) – bass, multi repl. DeLOACH

Jul 68. (lp; mono/stereo) *(587/588 116) <33250>* **IN-A-GADDA-DA-VIDA** [ ] [4]
– Most anything you want / Flowers and beads / My mirage / Termination / Are you happy / In-a-gadda-da-vida. *(re-iss. Jan73; K 40022) (cd-iss. Jul87 & Jun93; K2 40022) (re-iss. cd deluxe version Nov95 on 'Rhino'; 8122 72196-2) (lp re-iss. Oct97 on 'Simply Vinyl'; SVLP 15)*

Aug 68. (7") *<6606>* **IN-A-GADDA-DA-VIDA (edit). / IRON BUTTERFLY THEME** [-] [30]

Feb 69. (lp) *(228 011) <33280>* **BALL** [ ] [3]
– In the time of our lives / Soul experience / Lonely boy / Real fright / In the crowds / It must be love / Her favourite style / Filled with fear / Belda-beast. *(cd-iss. May00 on 'Collector's Choice'; CCM 0088-2)*

Mar 69. (7") *(584 254) <6647>* **SOUL EXPERIENCE. / IN THE CROWDS** [ ] [75] Feb69

Jul 69. (7") *<6676>* **IN THE TIME OF OUR LIVES. / IT MUST BE LOVE** [-] [96]

Nov 69. (7") *<6712>* **I CAN'T HELP BUT DECEIVE YOU LITTLE GIRL. / TO BE ALONE** [-] [ ]

Apr 70. (lp) *(2400 014) <33318>* **IRON BUTTERFLY LIVE (live)** [ ] [20]
– In the time of our lives / Filled with fear / Soul experience / You can't win / Are you happy / In-a-gadda-da-vida. *(re-iss. 1972; K 40086) (re-iss. 1981; K 40088)*

Jul 70. (7") *(2091 024)* **IN-A-GADDA-DA-VIDA (edit). / TERMINATION** [ ] [-]

— **INGLE, BUSHY and DORMAN** recruited new members **MIKE PINERA** (b.29 Sep'48, Tampa, Florida) – guitar, vocals (ex-BLUES IMAGE) repl. BRAUN who later formed FLINTWHISTLE / added **LARRY REINHARDT** (b. 7 Jul'48, Florida) – guitar

Oct 70. (7") *<6782>* **EASY RIDER (LET THE WIND PAY THE WAY). / SOLDIER IN OUR TOWN** [-] [66]

Feb 71. (7") *<6818>* **SILLY SALLY. / STONE BELIEVER** [-] [ ]

Apr 71. (lp) *(2401 003) <33339>* **METAMORPHOSIS** [ ] [16] Aug70
– Free flight / New day / Shady lady / Best years of our lives / Slower than guns / Stone believer / Soldier in our town / Easy rider (let the wind pay the way) / Butterfly bleu. *(re-iss. 1971; K 40294) (cd-iss. Jun92 on 'Repertoire'; RR 4262)*

— Disbanded Spring '71, with DORMAN and REINHARDT forming CAPTAIN BEYOND. PINERA formed RAMATAM before later joining ALICE COOPER (1981-82). Re-formed 1974, as 4-piece with **BUSHY, BRAUN** and newcomers **HOWARD REITZES** (b.22 Mar'51, Southgate, Calif.) – keyboards, vocals / **PHIL KRAMER** (b.12 Jul'52, Youngstown, Ohio) – bass, vocals

M.C.A. | M.C.A.

Feb 75. (lp) *(MCF 2694) <465>* **SCORCHING BEAUTY** [ ] [ ]
– 1975 overture / Hard miseree / High on a mountain top / Am I down / People of the world / Searchin' circles / Pearly Gates / Lonely hearts / Before you go. *(cd-iss. Jun95 on 'Repertoire'; RR 4558)*

Feb 75. (7") *<40379>* **SEARCHIN' CIRCLES. / PEARLY GATES** [-] [ ]

— **BILL DeMARTINES** – keyboards repl. REITZES

Dec 75. (lp) *(MCF 2738) <2164>* **SUN AND STEEL** [ ] [ ]
– Sun and steel / Lightnin' / Beyond the Milky Way / Free / Scion / Get it out / I'm right, I'm wrong / Watch the world goin' by / Scorching beauty. *(cd-iss. Mar95 on 'Edsel'; EDCD 408)*

Jan 76. (7") *(MCA 221) <40494>* **BEYOND THE MILKY WAY. / GET IT OUT** [ ] [ ]

— Broke up again in 1976, BUSHY formed JUICY GROOVE.

— In May'89, IRON BUTTERFLY reformed w/**DORMAN, BRAUN, REINHARDT** and new men **STEVE FELDMANN** – vocals / **DEREK HILLARD** – keyboards / **KENNY SUAREZ** – drums

– compilations, others, etc. –

on 'Atlantic' UK & 'Atco' US unless mentioned otherwise

Jan 72. (lp) *(K 40298) <33369>* **EVOLUTION – THE BEST OF IRON BUTTERFLY** [ ] [ ] Dec71
– Iron Butterfly theme / Possession / Unconscious power / Flowers and beads / Termination / In-a-gadda-da-vida / Soul experience / Stone believer / Belda-beast / Easy rider (let the wind pay the way) / Slower than guns.

1973. (lp) *(30038)* **STAR COLLECTION** [ ] [-]

Oct 75. (d-lp) *(K 80003)* **TWO ORIGINALS OF . . .** [ ] [-]
– (BALL / METAMORPHISIS)

Feb 93. (cd) *Rhino; (8122 71166-2)* **LIGHT AND HEAVY: THE BEST OF IRON BUTTERFLY** [ ] [ ]

IRONHORSE

(see under ⇒ BACHMAN-TURNER OVERDRIVE)

IRON MAIDEN

Formed: Leytonstone, East London, England . . . mid 1976 by STEVE HARRIS, DAVE MURRAY, PAUL DiANNO and DOUG SAMPSON, who played their earliest gigs around mid '77 – an embryonic late '75 IRON MAIDEN included HARRIS, PAUL DAY (vocals), DAVE SULLIVAN (guitar), TERRY RANCE (guitar) and RON MATTHEWS (drums). The band's amphetamine-fuelled trad-metal soon procured them a rabid following around the capital and the following year they released a self-financed debut EP, 'THE SOUNDHOUSE TAPES'. The cassette came to the attention of Rock DJ, Neal Kay, who sent them on a 'Heavy Metal Crusade' tour at London's Music Machine, the resultant publicity and increasing interest in the band leading to a deal with 'E.M.I.' in 1979 (this coincided with personnel changes, CLIVE BURR replacing SAMPSON, while DENNIS STRATTON replaced brief member TONY PARSONS. Their debut single, the 100 horsepower outlaw fantasy, 'RUNNING FREE', hit the shops and UK Top 40 early in 1980, soon followed by a self-titled debut album which made the Top 5. IRON MAIDEN were the leading lights of the New Wave Of British Heavy Metal; carrying on where BLACK SABBATH and URIAH HEEP left off, they helped to create and embody the cartoon caricature that the genre would become. Despite production problems, the debut album remains one the most enduring of their career, the material raw and hungry where later efforts have tended towards flabbiness. Masters of the power chord, tracks like 'IRON MAIDEN' and 'CHARLOTTE THE HARLOT' (Politically Correct this band were not, although the phrase could be interpreted in a different way with regards to the 'KILLERS' album sleeve, a depiction of Thatcher meeting an untimely end) were prime headbanging material, DI'ANNO's vocals more gutteral punk than metal warbling. Yet the band were no musical novices, the stop-start exhilaration of 'PHANTOM OF THE OPERA' sounding considered and spontaneous at the same time. A hasty follow-up, the aforementioned 'KILLERS' (1981), lacked the focus of the debut, something which didn't deter metal fans from buying it in droves. By the release of 'THE NUMBER OF THE BEAST' (1982), DI'ANNO had been replaced by BRUCE DICKINSON, more of a vocal acrobat in the traditional metal sense. More accessible and melodic, if not as exciting, the record was a massive success (No.1 in Britain), packed with songs that would go on to form the backbone of the 'MAIDEN live set. 'RUN TO THE HILLS' was a particular favourite, giving the band their first Top 10 placing in the pop singles chart. 'PIECE OF MIND' (1983) and 'POWERSLAVE' (1984) carried on in much the same anthemic vein, the band capitalising on their staggering worldwide popularity with a mammoth touring schedule. With their trademark ghoulish mascot, 'EDDIE', horror fantasy artwork and readily identifiable sound, the band were arguably the very essence of 'Heavy Metal', a phenomenon which traversed all language boundaries in much the same way as dance music in the 90's. 'SOMEWHERE IN TIME' (1986) marked something of a departure, a more ambitious and musically diverse collection both in terms of songwriting and playing. This avenue was further explored on 'SEVENTH SON OF A SEVENTH SON' (1988), a concept affair that piled on the synth and sharpened the harmonies, resulting in four consecutive Top 10 singles. The steadfast reliability of the band's fanbase was amply illustrated when a series of EP's repackaging the band's singles went Top 10 almost without exception. But there was tension in the ranks with HARRIS favouring a return to their chest beating roots while guitarist ADRIAN SMITH was less than pleased with the prospect. In the event, SMITH was replaced with JANICK GERS and the band released the no-frills 'NO PRAYER FOR THE DYING' (1990), a back to basics effort which spawned IRON MAIDEN's first No.1 single, the side-splittingly titled 'BRING YOUR DAUGHTER . . . TO THE SLAUGHTER'. 'FEAR OF THE DARK' (1992) gave the band yet another No.1 album, the last to feature the tonsils of DICKINSON, who soon departed for a solo career. DICKINSON's eventual replacement was BLAZE BAILEY (ex-WOLFSBANE) who made his debut on 'THE X-FACTOR' (1995), a record that achieved their lowest chart placing since 'KILLERS'. 1998's 'VIRTUAL XI' was another relative disappointment although the MAIDEN hordes took heart when BRUCE DICKINSON returned to the fray in early '99. The resulting tour was a blockbuster and paved the way for a new studio album featuring the classic line-up of DICKINSON, HARRIS, MURRAY, McBRAIN and SMITH alongside JANICK GERS who was retained as a third guitarist. 'BRAVE NEW WORLD' was released in Spring 2000 amid much fanfare and expectation, the album's return to MAIDEN's halcyon mid-80's period – in terms of both gothic fantasy songwriting and crunching powerchord assault – pleasing longtime fans no end and seemingly securing the band's place in the post-metal wilderness.
• **Songwriters:** All mostly HARRIS and group. In the 90's, HARRIS or DICKINSON + GERS. Covered; COMMUNICATION BREAKDOWN (Led Zeppelin) / KILL ME, CE SOIR (Golden Earring) / SPACE STATION No.5 (Montrose). DICKINSON solo re-hashed; ALL THE YOUNG DUDES (hit; Mott The Hoople). • **Trivia:** Derek Riggs became the group's artistic designer and created 'EDDIE', an evil skeleton comic-strip character, who appeared on album sleeves, poster bills & theatrical stage shows. Banned in Chile for being interpreted as 'devils and satanists'. First band to play 'live' on Top Of The Pops since The Who.

Album rating: IRON MAIDEN (*9) / KILLERS (*6) / THE NUMBER OF THE BEAST (*7) / PIECE OF MIND (*6) / POWERSLAVE (*6) / LIVE AFTER DEATH (*8) / SOMEWHERE IN TIME (*6) / SEVENTH SON OF A SEVENTH SON (*7) / NO PRAYER FOR THE DYING (*7) / FEAR OF THE DARK (*7) / A REAL LIVE ONE (*5) / A REAL DEAD ONE (*5) / LIVE AT DONINGTON 1992 (*5) / THE X FACTOR (*6) / THE BEST OF THE BEAST compilation (*9) / VIRTUAL XI (*5) / BRAVE NEW WORLD (*7)

PAUL DI'ANNO (b.17 May'59, Chingford, Essex, England) – vocals / **DAVE MURRAY** (b.23 Dec'58) – guitar / **STEVE HARRIS** (b.12 Mar'57) – bass, vocals / **DOUG SAMPSON** – drums

Rock Hard | not iss.

Jan 79. (7"ep) *(ROK 1)* **THE SOUNDHOUSE TAPES** [ ] [-]
– Invasion / Iron Maiden / Prowler.

— (Nov79) **CLIVE BURR** (b. 8 Mar'57) – drums repl. SAMPSON / **DENNIS STRATTON** (b. 9 Nov'54) – guitar repl. TONY PARSONS (brief stay)

E.M.I. | Harvest

Feb 80. (7") *(EMI 5032)* **RUNNING FREE. / BURNING AMBITION** [34] [-]

Apr 80. (lp/c) *(EMC/TCEMC 3330)* **IRON MAIDEN** [4] [ ]
– Prowler / Remember tomorrow / Running free / Phantom of the opera / Transylvania / Strange world / Charlotte the harlot / Iron maiden. *(re-iss. May85 on 'Fame' lp/c; FA/TCFA 41-3121-1)* – hit 71 *(cd-iss. Oct87 on 'Fame'; CDFA 3121)*

(re-iss. cd Jul94; CDEMS 1538) (re-iss. cd Dec95; CDEM 1570) (cd re-iss. Sep98; 496916-0)

May 80. (7"m) *(EMI 5065)* **SANCTUARY. / DRIFTER / I'VE GOT THE FIRE (live)** 29 -

Oct 80. (7") *(EMI 5105)* **WOMEN IN UNIFORM. / INVASION** 35 -
(12"+=) *(12EMI 5105)* – Phantom of the opera (live).

— **ADRIAN SMITH** (b.27 Feb'57) – guitar (ex-URCHIN) repl. STRATTON who formed LIONHEART

Feb 81. (lp/c) *(EMC/TCEMC 3357)* <12141> **KILLERS** 12 78
– The ides of march / Wrathchild / Murders in the Rue Morgue / Another life / Ghenghis Khan / Innocent exile / KIllers / Prodigal son / Purgatory / Drifter. *(re-iss. May85 on 'Fame' lp/c; FA/TCFA 41-3122-1) (cd-iss. Oct87 on 'Fame'; CDFA 3122) (re-iss. cd Jul94; CDEMS 1539) (re-iss. cd Dec95; CDEM 1571) (cd re-iss. Sep98; 496917-0)*

Mar 81. (7",7"clear,7"red,c-s) *(EMI 5145)* **TWILIGHT ZONE. / WRATH CHILD** 31 -

Jun 81. (7") *(EMI 5184)* **PURGATORY. / GHENGIS KHAN** 52 -

Sep 81. (12"ep)<m-lp> *(12EMI 5219)* <15000> **MAIDEN JAPAN** 43 89
– Remember tomorrow / Killers / Running free / Innocent exile.

— **BRUCE DICKINSON** (b. PAUL BRUCE DICKINSON, 7 Aug'58, Sheffield, England) – vocals (ex-SAMSON) repl. DI'ANNO who formed LONE WOLF

Feb 82. (7"/7"pic-d) *(EMI/+P 5263)* **RUN TO THE HILLS. / TOTAL ECLIPSE** 7 -

Mar 82. (lp/pic-lp)(c) *(EMC/EMCP/TCEMC 3400)* <12202> **THE NUMBER OF THE BEAST** 1 33
– Invaders / Children of the damned / The prisoner / 22, Acacia Avenue / The number of the beast / Run to the hills / Gangland / Hallowed be thy name. *(re-iss. May87 on 'Fame'; FA/TCFA 3178) (cd-iss. Apr88 on 'Fame'; CDFA 3178) (re-iss. cd Jul94; CDEMS 1533) (re-iss. Dec95 on d-cd w/bonus tracks; CDEM 1572) (cd re-iss. Sep98; 496918-0)*

Apr 82. (7"/7"red) *(EMI 5287)* **THE NUMBER OF THE BEAST. / REMEMBER TOMORROW** 18 -

— now **HARRIS, MURRAY, DICKINSON** and **SMITH** were joined by **NICKO McBRAIN** (b. MICHAEL, 5 Jun'54) – drums (ex-PAT TRAVERS, ex-TRUST, ex-STREETWALKERS) repl. BURR who joined STRATUS

E.M.I. Capitol

Apr 83. (7"/12"pic-d)(c-s) *(EMI/12EMIP 5378)(TC IM4)* <5248> **FLIGHT OF ICARUS. / I'VE GOT THE FIRE** 11

May 83. (lp/c) *(EMA/TCEMA 800)* <12274> **PIECE OF MIND** 3 14
– Where eagles dare / Revelations / Flight of Icarus / Die with your boots on / The trooper / Still life / Quest for fire / Sun and steel / To tame a land. *(cd-iss. Dec86; CZ 82) (re-iss. 1989 lp/c; ATAK/CDATAK 139) (re-iss. cd Jun91 on 'Fame'; CDFA 3245) (re-iss. cd Jul94; CDEMS 1540) (re-iss. Dec95 on d-cd w/bonus tracks; CDEM 1573) (cd re-iss. Sep98; 496919-0)*

Jun 83. (7",7"sha-pic-d) *(EMI 5397)* **THE TROOPER. / CROSS-EYED MARY** 12 -

Aug 84. (7") *(EMI 5489)* **2 MINUTES TO MIDNIGHT. / RAINBOW'S GOLD** 11 -
(12"pic-d+=) *(12EMI 5489)* – Mission from 'Arry.

Sep 84. (lp/pic-lp)(c)(cd) *(POWER/+P 1)(TCPOWER 1)(746045-2)* <12321> **POWERSLAVE** 2 21
– Aces high / 2 minutes to midnight / Losfer words (big 'orra) / Flash of the blade / The duellists / Back in the village / Powerslave / Rime of the ancient mariner. *(re-iss. 1989 lp/c; ATAK/TCATAK 140) (re-iss. Jun91 on 'Fame'; FA 3244) (re-iss. cd Jul94; CDEMS 1539) (re-iss. Dec95 d-cd w/bonus tracks; CDEM 1574) (cd re-iss. Sep98; 496920-0)*

Oct 84. (7") *(EMI 5502)* **ACES HIGH. / KING OF TWILIGHT** 20 -
(12"+=/12"pic-d+=) *(12EMI/+P 5502)* – The number of the beast (live).

Sep 85. (7") *(EMI 5532)* **RUNNING FREE (live). / SANCTUARY (live)** 19 -
(12"+=/12"pic-d+=) *(12EMI/+P 5532)* – Murders in the Rue Morgue (live).

Oct 85. (d-lp/c)(cd) *(RIP/TCRIP 1)(746186-2)* <12441> **LIVE AFTER DEATH (live)** 2 19
– Aces high / 2 minutes to midnight / The trooper / Revelations / Flight of Icarus / The rime of the ancient mariner / Powerslave / The number of the beast / Hallowed be thy name / Iron maiden / Run to the hills / Running free. *(d-lp+=/c+=)* – Wrathchild / 22 Acacia Avenue / Children of the damned / Die with your boots on / Phantom of the opera. *(re-iss. 1989 lp/c; ATAK/TCATAK 141) (re-iss. Jun91 on 'Fame' w/ less tracks; CDFA 3248) (re-iss. cd Jul94 w/ fewer tracks; CDEMS 1535) (re-iss. Dec95 d-cd w/ bonus tracks; CDEM 1575) (d-cd re-iss. Sep98; 496921-0)*

Nov 85. (7") *(EMI 5542)* **RUN TO THE HILLS (live). / PHANTOM OF THE OPERA (live)** 26 -
(12"+=/12"pic-d+=) *(12EMI/+P 5542)* – Losfer words (The big 'orra) (live).

Aug 86. (7"/7"sha-pic-d) *(EMI/+P 5583)* **WASTED YEARS. / REACH OUT** 18 -
(12"+=) *(12EMI 5583)* – The sheriff of Huddersfield.

Sep 86. (lp/c)(cd) *(EMC/TCEMC 3512)(746341-2)* <12524> **SOMEWHERE IN TIME** 3 11
– Caught somewhere in time / Wasted years / Sea of madness / Heaven can wait / The loneliness of the long distance runner / Stranger in a strange land / Deja-vu / Alexander the Great. *(re-iss. 1989 lp/c; ATAK/TCATAK 142) (re-iss. Jun91 on 'Fame'; CDFA 3246) (re-iss. cd Jul94; CDEMS 1537) (re-iss. Dec95 d-cd w/bonus tracks; CDEM 1576) (cd re-iss. Sep98; 496924-0)*

Nov 86. (7") *(EMI 5589)* **STRANGER IN A STRANGE LAND. / THAT GIRL** 22 -
(12"+=/12"pic-d+=) *(12EMI/+P 5589)* – Juanita.

Mar 88. (7"/7"w sticker & transfer/7"sha-pic-d) *(EM/+S/P 49)* <44154> **CAN I PLAY WITH MADNESS. / BLACK BART BLUES** 3
(12"+=/cd-s+=) *(12EM/CDEM 49)* – Massacre.

Apr 88. (cd/c/lp)(pic-lp) *(TC/CD+/EMD 1006)(EMDP 1006)* <90258> **SEVENTH SON OF A SEVENTH SON** 1 12
– Moonchild / Infinite dreams / Can I play with madness / The evil that men do / Seventh son of a seventh son / The prophecy / The clairvoyant / Only the good die young. *(re-iss. 1989 lp/c; ATAK/TCATAK 143) (re-iss. Jun91 on 'Fame'; CDFA 3247) (re-iss. cd Jul94; CDEMS 1534) (re-iss. Dec95 d-cd w/bonus tracks; CDEM 1577) (cd re-iss. Sep98; 496864-0)*

Aug 88. (7"/7"g-f/7"sha-pic-d) *(EM/+G/P 64)* **THE EVIL THAT MEN DO. / PROWLER '88** 5
(12"+=/12"poster)(cd-s+=) *(12EM/+S 64)(CDEM 64)* – Charlotte the harlot '88.

Nov 88. (7"/7"clear/7"sha-pic-d) *(EM/+S/P 79)* **THE CLAIRVOYANT (live). / THE PRISONER (live)** 6
(12"+=/12"pic-d+=)(cd-s+=) *(12EM/+P 79)(CDEM 79)* – Heaven can wait (live).

Nov 89. (7"/7"sha-pic-d)(c-s) *(EM/+PD 117)(TCEM 117)* **INFINITE DREAMS (live). / KILLERS (live)** 6
(12"+=/cd-s+=)(12"etched+=) *(12/CD EM 117)* – Still life (live).

— (Feb'90) **JANICK GERS** – guitar (ex-GILLAN, ex-WHITE SPIRIT, etc.) repl. SMITH who formed A.S.A.P.

E.M.I. Epic

Sep 90. (7"/c-s) *(EM/TCEM 158)* **HOLY SMOKE. / ALL IN YOUR MIND** 3
(12"+=/12"pic-d+=)(cd-s+=) *(12EM/+P 158)(CDEM 158)* – Kill me ce soir.

Oct 90. (cd/c/lp)(pic-lp)<red-lp> *(CD/TC+/EMD 1017)(EMPD 1017)* *<E 46905>* **NO PRAYER FOR THE DYING** 2 17
– Tailgunner / Holy smoke / No prayer for the dying / Public enema number one / Fates warning / The assassin / Run silent run deep / Hooks in you / Bring your daughter . . . to the slaughter / Mother Russia. *(re-iss. cd Jul94; CDEMS 1541) (re-iss. Dec95 d-cd w/bonus tracks; CDEM 1578) (cd re-iss. Sep98; 496865-4)*

Dec 90. (7"/7"pic-d)(c-s) *(EM/+PD 171)(TCEM 171)* **BRING YOUR DAUGHTER . . . TO THE SLAUGHTER. / I'M A MOVER** 1
(12"+=/12"pic-d+=)(cd-s+=) *(12EM/+P 171)(CDEM 171)* – Communication breakdown.

— In Summer 1991, HARRIS and McBAIN back up tennis stars McENROE & CASH on their version of LED ZEPPELIN'S 'Rock And Roll'. In Mar'92, BRUCE DICKINSON was to feature on single with Rowan Atkinson's comic character 'MR.BEAN & SMEAR CAMPAIGN' on a version of an Alice Cooper song '(I Want To Be) Elected'.

Apr 92. (7") *(EM 229)* **BE QUICK OR BE DEAD. / NODDING DONKEY BLUES** 2
(12"+=/12"pic-d+=)(cd-s+=) *(12EM/+P 229)(CDEM 229)* – Space station No.5.

May 92. (cd/c/d-lp) *(CD/TC+/EMD 1032)* *<48993>* **FEAR OF THE DARK** 1 12
– Be quick or be dead / From here to eternity / Afraid to shoot strangers / Fear is the key / Childhood's end / Wasting love / The fugitive / Chains of misery / The apparition / Judas be my guide / Weekend warrior / Fear of the dark. *(re-iss. cd Jul94; CDEM 1542) (re-iss. Dec95 d-cd w/bonus tracks +=; CDEM 1579)* – Nodding donkey blues / Space station No.5 / I can't see my feeling / No prayer for the dying (live) / Public enema No.1 (live) / Hook in you (live). *(cd re-iss. Sep98; 496925-0)*

Jul 92. (7"etched) *(EM 240)* **FROM HERE TO ETERNITY. / ROLL OVER VIC VELLA** 21
(12"+=/cd-s+=) *(12/CD EM 240)* – Public enema number one / No prayer for the dying.
(7"sha-pic-d) *(EMPD 240)* – ('A'side) / I can't see my feeling.

E.M.I. Capitol

Mar 93. (7"/7"sha-pic-d) *(EMP/+D 263)* **FEAR OF THE DARK (live). / TAILGUNNER (live)** 8
(cd-s+=) *(CDEM 263)* – Hooks in you (live) *(on some 7"sha-pic-d)* / Bring your daughter . . .to the slaughter (live).

Mar 93. (cd/c/lp) *(CD/TC+/EMD 1042)* *<81456>* **A REAL LIVE ONE (live)** 3
– Be quick or be dead / From here to eternity / Can I play with madness / Wasting love / Tailgunner / The evil that men do / Afraid to shoot strangers / Bring your daughter . . .to the slaughter / Heaven can wait / The clairvoyant / Fear of the dark.

— DICKINSON had already announced he had departed to go solo in '94

Oct 93. (7"red) *(EM 288)* **HALLOWED BE THY NAME (live). / WRATHCHILD (live)** 9
(12"pic-d+=/cd-s+=) *(12EMP/CDEM 288)* – The trooper (live) / Wasted years (live).

Oct 93. (cd/c/lp) *(CD/TC+/EMD 1048)* *<89248>* **A REAL DEAD ONE (live)** 12
– The number of the beast / The trooper / Prowler / Transylvania / Remember tomorrow / Where eagles dare / Sanctuary / Running free / Run to the hills / 2 minutes to midnight / Iron Maiden / Hallowed be thy name. *(this & last "live" set, re-iss. Sep98; 496926-0)*

Nov 93. (d-cd/d-c/t-lp) *(CD/MC+/DON 1)* **LIVE AT DONINGTON 1992 (live)** 23 -
– Be quick or be dead / The number of the beast / Wrathchild / From here to eternity / Can I play with madness / Wasting love / Tailgunner / The evil that men do / Afraid to shoot strangers / Fear of the dark / Bring your daughter . . . to the slaughter / The clairvoyant / Heaven can wait / Run to the hills / 2 minutes to midnight / Iron maiden / Hallowed be thy name / The trooper / Sanctuary / Running free. *(re-iss. Sep98; 496929-0)*

— **BLAZE BAILEY** – vocals (ex-WOLFSBANE) now his replacement

E.M.I. CMC Int.

Sep 95. (c-s) *(TCEM 398)* **MAN ON THE EDGE / THE EDGE OF DARKNESS** 10
(12"pic-d+=) *(12EM 398)* – I live my way.
(cd-s+=) *(CDEMS 398)* – Judgement day / (Blaze Bailey interview part 1).
(cd-s+=) *(CDEM 398)* – Justice of the peace / (Blaze Bailey interview part 2).

Oct 95. (cd/c/clear-d-lp) *(+CD/TC EMD 1087)* *<8003>* **THE X FACTOR** 9
– Sign of the cross / Lord of the flies / Man on the edge / Fortunes of war / Look for the truth / The aftermath / Judgement of Heaven / Blood on the world's hands / The edge of darkness / 2 a.m. / The unbeliever.

Sep 96. (12") *(12EM 443)* **VIRUS. / PROWLER (the Soundhouse tapes) / INVASION (the Soundhouse tapes)** 16
(cd-s) *(CDEM 443)* – ('A'side) / My generation / Doctor, doctor.
(cd-s) *(CDEMS 443)* – ('A'side) / Sanctuary (metal for muthas) / Wrathchild (metal for muthas).

Sep 96. (d-cd/q-lp) *(CDEMDS 1097)* **BEST OF THE BEAST** (compilation with all line-ups) 16
– Virus / Sign of the cross / Afraid to shoot strangers (live) / Man on the edge / Be quick or be dead / Fear of the dark (live) / Holy smoke / Bring your daughter . . . to the slaughter / Seventh son of a seventh son / Can I play with madness / The evil that men do / The clairvoyant / Heaven can wait / Wasted years / / 2 minutes to midnight / Running free (live) / Rime of the ancient mariner (live) / Aces high / Where eagles dare / The trooper * / The number of the beast / Revelations * / The prisoner * / Run to the hills / Hallowed be thy name / Wrathchild / Killers * / Remember tomorrow

* / Phantom of the opera / Sanctuary / Prowler * / Invasion * / Strange world / Iron maiden. *(q-lp+= *)*

Mar 98. (7"pic-d) *(EM 507)* **THE ANGEL AND THE GAMBLER. / BLOOD ON THE WORLD'S HANDS (live) / THE AFTERMATH (live)** [18] [ ]
(cd-s) *(CDEMS 507)* – (first 2 tracks) / Afraid to shoot strangers (CD-Rom video).
(cd-s) *(CDEM 507)* – (first & third tracks) / The aftermath (live) / Man on the edge (CD-Rom video).

Mar 98. (cd/c/d-lp) *(493915-2/-4/-1) <86240>* **VIRTUAL XI** [16] [ ]
– Futureal / The angel and the gambler / Lightning strikes twice / Clansman / When two worlds collide / Educated fool / Don't look to the eyes of a stranger / Como estais amigos.

Sep 98. (7"pic-d) *(EM 525)* **FUTUREAL. / THE EVIL THAT MEN DO (live) / MAN ON THE EDGE (live)** [-] [-]
(cd-s) *(CDEM 525)* – (first 2) / Futureal (CD-rom).
(cd-s) *(CDEMS 525)* – (first & third) / The angel and the gambler (CD-rom).
(above only available through the internet shopping channel)

— early in '99, BRUCE DICKINSON was now back at the helm (as was **ADRIAN SMITH** – guitar (now a six-piece)

May 00. (12"pic-d) *(12EM 568)* **THE WICKER MAN. / POWERSLAVE (live) / Killers (live)** [9] [ ]
(cd-s) *(CDEMS 568)* – (first two tracks) / Man on the edge (live) / ('A'-CD-Rom).
(cd-s) *(CDEM 568)* – (first & third tracks) / Futureal (live) / Futureal (CD-Rom).

May 00. (cd/c/d-lp) *(526605-2/-4/-1) <62208>* **BRAVE NEW WORLD** [7] [39]
– The wicker man / Ghost of the navigator / Brave new world / Blood brothers / The mercenary / Dream of mirrors / The fallen angel / The nomad / Out of the silent planet / The thin line between love and hate.

Oct 00. (7"red) *(EM 576)* **OUT OF THE SILENT PLANET. / ACES HIGH (live)** [20] [-]
(12"pic-d+=) *(12EM 576)* – Wasted years (live).
(cd-s+=) *(CDEM 576)* – ('A'-CD-ROM video).

– compilations, etc. –

on 'E.M.I.' unless otherwise stated

Feb 90. (cd-ep/d12") *(CD+/IRN 1)* **RUNNING FREE / BURNING AMBITION / SANCTUARY / DRIFTER (live) / I'VE GOT THE FIRE (live) / Listen with Nicko (part 1)** [10] [ ]

Feb 90. (cd-ep/d12") *(CD+/IRN 2)* **WOMEN IN UNIFORM / INVASION / PHANTOM OF THE OPERA / TWILIGHT ZONE / WRATHCHILD / Listen with Nicko (part 2)** [10] [ ]

Feb 90. (cd-ep/d12") *(CD+/IRN 3)* **PURGATORY / GENGHIS KHAN / RUNNING FREE / REMEMBER TOMORROW / KILLERS / INNOCENT EXILE / Listen with Nicko (part 3)** [5] [ ]

Mar 90. (cd-ep/d12") *(CD+/IRN 4)* **RUN TO THE HILLS / TOTAL ECLIPSE / THE NUMBER OF THE BEAST / REMEMBER TOMORROW (live) / Listen with Nicko (part 4)** [3] [ ]

Mar 90. (cd-ep/d12") *(CD+/IRN 5)* **FLIGHT OF ICARUS / I'VE GOT THE FIRE / THE TROOPER / CROSS-EYED MARY / Listen with Nicko (part 5)** [7] [ ]

Mar 90. (cd-ep/d12") *(CD+/IRN 6)* **2 MINUTES TO MIDNIGHT / RAINBOW'S GOLD / MISSION FROM 'ARRY / ACES HIGH / KING OF TWILIGHT / THE NUMBER OF THE BEAST (live) / Listen with Nicko (part 6)** [11] [ ]

Apr 90. (cd-ep/d12") *(CD+/IRN 7)* **RUNNING FREE / SANCTUARY / MURDERS IN THE RUE MORGUE / RUN TO THE HILLS / PHANTOM OF THE OPERA / LOSFER WORDS (THE BIG 'ORRA) / Listen with Nicko (part 7)** [9] [ ]

Apr 90. (cd-ep/d12") *(CD+/IRN 8)* **WASTED YEARS / REACH OUT / THE SHERIFF OF HUDDERSFIELD / STRANGER IN A STRANGE LAND / THAT GIRL / JUANITA / Listen with Nicko (part 8)** [9] [ ]

Apr 90. (cd-ep/d12") *(CD+/IRN 9)* **CAN I PLAY WITH MADNESS / BLACK BART BLUES / MASSACRE / THE EVIL THAT MEN DO / PROWLER '88 / CHARLOTTE THE HARLOT '88 / Listen with Nicko (part 9)** [10] [ ]

Apr 90. (cd-ep/d12") *(CD+/IRN 10)* **THE CLAIRVOYANT (live) / THE PRISONER (live) / HEAVEN CAN WAIT (live) / INFINITE DREAMS (live) / KILLERS (live) / STILL LIFE (live) / Listen with Nicko (part 10)** [11] [ ]

— (all 10 singles above, basically hit peak number before crashing out)

Aug 94. (cd,cd-vid) *(SAV 4913103)* **MAIDEN ENGLAND (live)** [ ] [-]
– Moonchild / The evil that men do / Prisoner / Still life / Die with your boots on / Infinite dreams / Killers / Heaven can wait / Wasted years / The clairvoyant / Seventh son of a seventh son / The number of the best / Iron maiden.

Dec 98. (16xcd-box) *(4979990)* **EDDIE'S HEAD** [ ] [ ]

May 99. (3xcd-ROM) *(5205200)* **ED HUNTER** [ ] [-]

NICKO McBRAIN

E.M.I. | not iss.

Jul 91. (7") *(NICKO 1)* **RHYTHM OF THE BEAST. / BEEHIVE BOOGIE** [ ] [-]
(7"pic-d) *(NICKOPD 1)* – ('A'extended) / (McBrain damage interview).

IRON MONKEY

Formed: Nottingham, England . . . 1994 by DOUG DALZIEL, JIM RUSBY, DEAN BERRY, JUSTIN GREAVES, and JOHNNY MORROW. By their own admission this quintet set out to antagonise. This they certainly did, but also in a short space of time, along with bands like Southern America's EYEHATEGOD, they became one of the most prominent purveyors of the lowdown and dirty style known as sludgecore. Soon after emitting their eponymous debut album in 1996, IRON MONKEY garnered a large respect from the underground metal scene, and not just in their native country, but stateside as well. This culminated in the band attracting the attention of the noted metal imprint 'Earache', signing a deal with them in 1997. The following year they released their debut full-length album 'OUR PROBLEM' (1998). This set was certainly a disturbing audio experience; MORROW's pained singing with his almost unintelligible lyrics combined with the band's grimy hardcore sound to produce an aggressive, but at the same time, depressive atmosphere – not a criticism as this seemed to be the alienating key in which the band thrived. Following this short time in the rock limelight it seemed the band did not wish to get tied into the corporate rock deal and recorded their next piece, 'WE'VE LEARNED NOTHING' (1999) for independent 'Man's Ruin'. This record was seemingly IRON MONKEY's coda, and was a three-song split with the exploratory hardcore band CHURCH OF MISERY. Both bands certainly wear their BLACK SABBATH/MELVINS influences on their sleeves for this small set and combine well for a worthy piece of alternative metal.

Album rating: IRON MONKEY mini (*6) / OUR PROBLEM (*6)

JOHNNY MORROW – vocals / **JIM RUSBY** – guitar / **DEAN BERRY** – guitar / **DOUG DALZIEL** – bass / **JUSTIN GREAVES** – drums

Earache | Earache

Sep 97. (m-cd) *(<MOSH 182CD>)* **IRON MONKEY** [ ] [ ]
– Fink dial / Web of piss / Big loader / 666 pack / Black aspirin / Shrimp fist.

Aug 98. (cd) *(<MOSH 207CD>)* **OUR PROBLEM** [ ] [ ] Sep98
– Bad year / Supagorgonizer / Boss keloid / I.R.M.S. / House anxiety / 2 golden rules / 9 joint siritual whip / Omi bozu.

Man's Ruin | Man's Ruin

Jul 99. (10"ep) *<(MR 130)>* **WE'VE LEARNED NOTHING** [ ] [ ]
– Sleep to win / Arsonaut / Kiss of death.

Jul 99. (cd-ep; split w/ CHURCH OF MISERY) *<(MR 132)>* **WE'VE LEARNED NOTHING** [ ] [ ]
– WE'VE LEARNED NOTHING / (others by Church Of Misery).

JACK OFFICERS (see under ⇒ BUTTHOLE SURFERS)

JACK OFF JILL

Formed: South Florida, USA . . . late 1992 by the all-female crew of singer JESSICKA, bassist ROBIN MOULDER, LAURA SIMPSON and HO-HO SPADE. Controversial to say the least (and also loved by TAIRRIE B of TURA SATANA), JOJ, well the cutesy JESSICKA actually, attempted to burn off a fan's testicles on stage! The group finally got around to recording a few singles/EP's and a cassette; the debut album in '97, 'SEXLESS DEMONS AND SCARS', was a DON FLEMING-produced record that attempted to portray their fixation with sex and depravity. Having previously supported MARILYN MANSON on tour, they snatched the band's departing guitarist DAISY BERKOWITZ, who was now dealing under his real name of SCOTT MITCHELL PUTESKY. The new quartet (complete with new drummer, CLAUDIA ROSSI), remixed the album (some with CHRIS VRENNA of NIN), although the patchy product, 'COVETOUS CREATURE', emerged at the same time as the UK release of the aforementioned set late in '98. VRENNA was also at the controls for their second set proper, 'CLEAR HEARTS GREY FLOWERS' (2000).

Album rating: SEXLESS DEMONS AND SCARS (*5) / COVETOUS CREATURE remixes (*4) / CLEAR HEARTS GREY FLOWERS (*5)

JESSICKA – vocals / **HO-HO SPADE** – guitar / **ROBIN MOULDER** – bass / **LAURA SIMPSON** – drums

not iss. own label

1993. (m-c) **CHILDREN 5 AND UP** [-] [ ]
– Choke / Bruises are back in style (dirty panties mix) / Spit and rape / Hypocrite / Lollirot one – rock / Bruises are back in style (clean panties mix) / Lollirot two – extra metal.

1994. (7") **MY CAT. / SWOLLEN** [-] [ ]

1995. (m-c) **CANNIBAL SONGBOOK** [-] [ ]
– Don't wake the baby / Super sadist / Cumdumpster / French kiss the elderly / Media C-section / Swollen / Working with meat / Horrible / Yellow brick road / Cherry scented / My cat.

1996. (m-c) **COCKROACH WALTZ** [-] [ ]
– American made / Cockroach waltz / Everything's brown / Kringle / Chocolate chicken / Confederate fag / Lollirot.

1997. (7") **AMERICAN MADE. / GIRLSCOUT** [-] [ ]

— **SCOTT MITCHELL PUTESKY** – guitar; repl. HO-HO

— **CLAUDIA ROSSI** – drums; repl. LAURA

Risk I.C.B.

Oct 98. (7") *(L 48600)* **AMERICAN MADE. / GIRL SCOUT** [ ] [ ]

404 Music I.C.B.

Nov 98. (cd) *(FOF 4103-2)* <24910> **SEXLESS DEMONS AND SCARS** [ ] [ ] Sep97
– American made / Horrible / My cat / Super sadist / Devil with the black dress / Girlscout / Swollen / Poor impulse control / Lollirot / Covet / Working with meat / Cumdumpster / Everything's brown / Angels fuck.

404 Music 404 Music

Oct 98. (cd) <*(FOF 0402-2)*> **COVETOUS CREATURE** (remixes) [ ] [ ]
– American made (tweaker remix) / My cat (meow mix) / Poor impulse control (no control mix) / Girlscout (Sunday mix) / Cumdumpster (delusional cannibal mix) / My cat (automatic speed mix) / Poor impulse control (750 degrees of separation mix). *(hidden+=)* – American made (Chris Vrenna mix) / Covet (pure psychopath mix).

— **NORM BLOCK** – drums; repl. CLAUDI

Risk Risk

Jul 00. (cd) <*(RSK 4113CD)*> **CLEAR HEARTS GREY FLOWERS** [ ] [ ] Jun00
– When I am queen / Fear of dying / Nazi halo / Rabbiteen / Strawberry gashes / Author unknown / Vivica / Witch hunt / Cinnamon spider / Underjoyed / Sugary / Star no star / Losing his touch / Clear hearts grey flowers.

JACKYL

Formed: Atlanta, Georgia, USA . . . 1990 by JESSE JAMES DUPREE, JIMMY STIFF, TOM BETTINI, brothers JEFF and CHRIS WORLEY. Fronted by the outrageous, chainsaw-wielding DUPREE, the group were signed to 'Geffen' on the strength of their balls-to-the-wall live act. The eponymous debut was released in late '92, a full-frontal assault of unreconstructed, barnstorming boogie that wasn't afraid to speak its mind, especially when baiting feminists on the likes of 'SHE LOVES MY COCK'~! A high profile tour with AEROSMITH (they'd already been chucked off a LYNYRD SKYNYRD jaunt) brought valuable exposure and sales of the debut went through the roof. A follow-up, 'PUSH COMES TO SHOVE', was eventually unleashed in summer '94, although the group have since been silent and it seems as if the day of the JACKYL may actually have passed. No such luck as 1996 saw their infamous live show committed to vinyl/cd in the shape of the disappointing 'NIGHT OF THE LIVING DEAD'. A further studio outing, 'CUT THE CRAP' (1997), sounded laboured as the band struggled to think up any new jokes while 1998's hopefully titled 'STAYIN ALIVE' hardly remedied the situation. • **Covered:** GIMME BACK MY BULLETS (Lynyrd Skynyrd) / LIVE WIRE (Ac/Dc) / NOBODY'S FAULT (Aerosmith).

Album rating: JACKYL (*7) / PUSH COMES TO SHOVE (*6) / NIGHT OF THE LIVING DEAD (*4) / CUT THE CRAP (*4) / STAYIN' ALIVE (*4)

JESSE JAMES DUPREE – vocals / **JEFF WORLEY** – guitar / **JIMMY STIFF** – guitar / **TOM BETTINI** – bass / **CHRIS WORLEY** – drums

Geffen Geffen

Nov 92. (cd/c/lp) <*(GED/GEC/GEF 24489)*> **JACKYL** [ ] [ ]
– I stand alone / Dirty little mind / Down on me / When will it rain / Redneck punk / The lumberjack / Reach for me / Back off brother / Brain drain / Just like a devil / She loves my cock.

Jul 94. (12"/cd-s) *(GFST P/D 76)* **PUSH COMES TO SHOVE. /** [ ] [-]

Aug 94. (cd/c/pic-lp) <*(GED/GEC/GEFA 24710)*> **PUSH COMES TO SHOVE** [ ] [ ]
– Push comes to shove / Headed for destruction / My life / I could never touch you like you do / Dixieland / I want it / Private hell / I am the I am / Secret of the bottle / Rock-a-ho / Back down in the dirt / Chinatown.

Music For Nations Ma

Feb 96. (cd/c) *(CD/T MFN 199)* <11085> **NIGHT OF THE LIVING DEAD** [ ] [ ]
– Intro / Push comes to shove / Mental masturbation / I stand alone / Rock-a-ho / Deeper in darkness / Down on me / Dirty little mind / Redneck punk / The lumberjack.

not iss. Sony

Jul 97. (cd) <67948> **CUT THE CRAP** [-] [ ]
– Dumb ass country boy / Locked and loaded / Open up / Misery loves company / Let's don't go there / Cut the crap / Twice as ugly / God strike me dead / Thanks for the grammy / Speak of the devil / Push pull.

Shimmering Tone Shimmering Tone

Nov 98. (cd) <*(SHMT 1)*> **STAYIN' ALIVE** [ ] [ ]
– Problem / Crush / Can't beat it with a stick / Open for business / Street went ligit / Live wire / Gimme back my bullets / Nobody's fault / Dumb ass country boy / Twice as ugly / Locked and loaded.

JADE

Formed: Winnipeg, Canada . . . 1982 by ROXY LYONS and PAT BELROSE who enlisted LENNY RICHARDSON and BEN MICHAELS. Following the domestic lightweight AOR release, 'TEASING EYES' (1984), BELROSE recruited a whole new line-up, namely SWEET MARIE BLACK, TERRY RUDD and DAVE SAMSON. Signed to 'Roadrunner' on the strength of new demos, the group's revamped, harder-edged style was showcased on the 'IF YOU'RE MAN ENOUGH' (1985) set. Material for a proposed third collection was subsequently turned down and the band faded from view.

Album rating: TEASING EYES (*5) / IF YOU'RE MAN ENOUGH (*5)

ROXY LYONS – vocals / **PAT BELROSE** – guitar, vocals / **LENNY RICHARDSON** – bass / **BEN MICHAELS** – drums

not iss. Zaphia

1984. (lp) <*WRC 1-3101*> **TEASING EYES** [-] [-] Canada
– Heroes and villains / Out of luck / Beyond the kiss / Reflections / Strike back / Musical woman / Let me down easy / Head over heels / Change romance / Nightmares.

— **BELROSE** now with **SWEET MARIE BLACK** – vocals (ex-AGGRESSOR) / **TERRY RUDD** – bass / **DAVE SAMSON** – drums, percussion

Roadrunner not iss.

Nov 85. (lp) *(RR 9755)* **IF YOU'RE MAN ENOUGH** [ ] [-]
– Timeless / We'll show you how to rock / Breakin' away / I'm not yours / We fight together / Seventh heaven / Poison in the chalice / Instruments of the night / If you're man enough.

— folded in 1986 when a third album was turned down

JAGGED EDGE

Formed: England . . . mid 80's by MYKE GRAY, the line-up finally gelling towards the end of the decade around MATTI ALFONZETTI, ANDY ROBBINS and FABIO DEL RIO. With a 'Polydor' deal already in the can, the group debuted in early 1990 with the mini-album 'TROUBLE'. Although the record served to showcase the much touted skills of both ALFONZETTI and GRAY, JAGGED EDGE's classy hard-rock melodica was fully realised on the subsequent 'FUEL FOR YOUR SOUL' (1990) set. Despite the album's promise, the group were to split the following year, with both GRAY and DEL RIO joining BRUCE DICKINSON.

Album rating: TROUBLE mini (*4) / FUEL FOR YOUR SOUL (*6)

MATTI ALFONZETTI (b. Sweden) – vocals (ex-BAM BAM BOYS) / **MYKE GRAY** – guitar / **ANDY ROBBINS** – bass / **FABIO DEL RIO** (b. Italy) – drums

Polydor / not iss.

Feb 90. (m-cd)(m-lp) *(841 983-2)(JAG 1)* **TROUBLE** [ ] [-]
– Trouble / You don't love me / Rosie Rosie / Crash and burn / Good golly Miss Molly.

Sep 90. (7"/c-s) *(PO/+CS 97)* **YOU DON'T LOVE ME. / ALL THROUGH THE NIGHT** [ ] [-]
(12"+=/12"pic-d+=/cd-s+=) *(PZ/+P/CDG 97)* – Fire and water / Resurrect.

Sep 90. (cd/c/lp) *(847 201-2/-4/-1)* **FUEL FOR YOUR SOUL** [ ] [-]
– Liar / Out in the cold / You don't love me / Hell ain't a long way / Smooth operator / Sweet Lorraine / Fuel for your soul / Law of the land / Loving you too long / All through the night.

Nov 90. (7"/7"pic-d/c-s) *(PO/+P/CS 105)* **OUT IN THE COLD. /** [ ] [-]
(12"+=/cd-s+=) *(PZ/+CD 105)* –

Mar 91. (7"/c-s) *(PO/+CS 132)* **HELL AIN'T A LONG WAY. /** [ ] [ ]
(12"+=/cd-s+=) *(PZ/+CD 132)* –

— split when GRAY and DEL RIO joined BRUCE DICKINSON

JAG PANZER

Formed: Colorado, USA . . . 1981 by HARRY CONKLIN, MARK BRIODY, JOHN TETLEY and RICK HILYARD. Following the release of a debut mini-set, 'THE TYRANTS', the band relocated to Los Angeles where they recruited JOEY TAFOLLA. A guitar wunderkid, TAFOLLA bolstered the sound on 'AMPLE DESTRUCTION' (1985) before moving on to play with ALICE COOPER and record a solo album for Mike Varney's six-string-shredding 'Shrapnel' label. CONKLIN was the next to leave, going on to join RIOT before forming his own outfit. Although JAG PANZER had effectively spluttered to a halt, BRIODY and TETLEY rejuvenated the group in 1987 and even signed a new deal. Inevitably perhaps, the original line-up (save new drummer RIKARD STORMQUIST) eventually came together in the mid-90's and released 'THE FOURTH JUDGEMENT' (1997). By the following year's 'AGE OF MASTERY' album, CHRIS BRODERICK had replaced TAFOLLA while 'THANE TO THE THRONE' followed in 2000.

Album rating: AMPLE DESTRUCTION (*5) / CHAIN OF COMMAND bootleg (*3) / DISSIDENT AGGRESSOR (*6) / THE FOURTH JUDGEMENT (*4) / THE AGE OF MASTERY (*4) / THANE TO THE THRONE (*4)

HARRY 'THE TYRANT' CONKLIN – vocals / **MARK BRIODY** – guitar, keyboards, vocals / **JOHN TETLEY** – bass / **RICK HILYARD** – drums

not iss. / Azra

1983. (12"ep) **UNTITLED** (aka 'THE TYRANTS') [-] [ ]
– Battlezones / Death row / Metal melts the ice / Iron shadows.

1983. (7"pic-d) **DEATH ROW** [-] [ ]

— added **JOEY TAFOLLA** – guitar

not iss. / Iron Works

Jul 85. (lp) *<IW 1001>* **AMPLE DESTRUCTION** [-] [ ]
– Licensed to kill / Warfare / Symphony of terror / Harder than steel / Generally hostile / The watching / Reign of the tyrants / Cardiac arrest / The crucifix. *(UK cd-iss. Dec90 on 'Barricade'+=; PRD 7006-2) <US cd-iss. Dec90 on 'Caroline'+=; CAROL 2205>* – Black Sunday / The possession – Suffer unto me – Apostles of the damned – The beast – Armageddon.

— **BUTCH CARLSON** – drums; repl. RICK

— TAFOLLA was to join ALICE COOPER, TYRANT briefly joined RIOT before forming TITAN FORCE

— **BRIODY + TETLEY** recruited **BOB PARDUBA** – vocals / **CHRISTIAN LANGE** – guitar / **RIKARD STJERNQVIST** – drums

not iss. / Auburn

1988. (pic-d-lp) *<bootleg>* **CHAIN OF COMMAND** [-] [ ]
– Eyes of the night / Fallen angel / Viper / Take this pain / Lustful and free / In a gadda da vida / Shadow thief / Lying deceiver / Out of sight, out of mind / Prelude / Chain of command / Shadow thief / She waits / Ride through the storm / In a gadda da vida / Never surrender / Burning heart / Sworn to silence / Dream theme / Gavotte in D.

— the new line-up was the originals except drummer RIKARD + **CHRIS KOSTKA** – guitar (no CARLSON or TAFOLLA)

S.P.V. / Pavement

Aug 94. (cd-ep) *(SPV 050-6230CDS)* **JEFFREY EP** [ ] [-]
– Jeffrey behind the gate / Spirit suicide / Jeffrey behind the gate (remix).

Nov 94. (cd) *(62292CD) <32216>* **DISSIDENT AGGRESSOR** [ ] [ ] Feb95
– Jeffrey behind the gate / The clown / Forsaken child / Edge of blindness / Eye of penance / Last dying breath / Psycho next door / Spirit suicide / GMV-407 / The church / Whisper God.

— **JOEY TAFOLLA** returnmed to repl. KOSTKA

Century Media / Century Media

Aug 97. (cd) *(CM 77172CD) <7872>* **THE FOURTH JUDGEMENT** [ ] [ ] Nov97
– Black / Call of the wild / Despair / Future shock / Recompense / Ready to strike / Tyranny / Shadow thief / Sonet of sorrow / Judgement day.

— **CHRIS BRODERICK** – guitar; repl. TAFOLLA

Oct 98. (cd) *(CM 77225CD) <7925>* **THE AGE OF MASTERY** [ ] [ ] Sep98
– Iron eagle / Lustfull and free / Twilight years / Sworn to silence / False messiah / The age of mastery / Viper / Displacement / Chain of command / Take this pain away / Burning heart / The moors.

Jul 00. (cd/lp) *(77293-2/-1) <7993>* **THANE TO THE THRONE** [ ] [ ] May00
– Thanes of Cawdor / King at a price / Bloody crime / The premonitions / Treachery's stain / Spectres of the past / Banquo's final rest / Three voices of fate / Hell to pay / The prophecies (fugue in D minor) / Insanity's mind / Requiem for Lady Macbeth / Face of fear / Fall of Dunsianne / Fate's triumph / The downward fall / Tragedy of Macbeth.

JAGUAR

Formed: Bristol, England . . . 1979 by ROB REISS, GARRY PEPPERD, JEFF COX and CHRIS LOVELL. Initially gaining momentum via the NWOBHM, the group attracted the attention of 'Heavy Metal' records who issued a one-off single in late '81, 'BACK STREET WOMAN'. With the leather-lunged PAUL MERRELL subsequently replacing REISS, JAGUAR subsequently secured a deal with 'Neat', showcasing their rapid-fire guitar attack to impressive effect on the debut long player, 'POWERGAMES' (1983). Promoting the record with wide-scale touring, the band built up a sizeable following, especially in Europe, where they signed to 'Roadrunner'. The resulting album, 1984's 'THIS TIME', was something of an unwelcome surprise for many fans, its more lightweight approach drawing critical barbs and eventually leading to the group's demise. During the late 90's, the trio reunited under the billing of CARSON, releasing the pop/glum-metal, 'A VISION', early 1999.

Album rating: POWER GAMES (*6) / THIS TIME (*4) / Carson: A VISION (*5)

ROB REISS – vocals / **GARRY PEPPERD** – guitar / **JEFF COX** – bass / **CHRIS LOVELL** – drums

Heavy Metal / not iss.

Nov 81. (7") *(HEAVY 10)* **BACK STREET WOMAN. / CHASING THE DRAGON** [ ] [-]

— **PAUL MERRELL** – vocals; repl. REISS

Neat / not iss.

Aug 82. (7") *(NEAT 16)* **AXE CRAZY. / WAR MACHINE** [ ] [-]

Feb 83. (lp) *(NEAT 1007)* **POWER GAMES** [ ] [-]
– Dutch connection / Out of luck / The fox / Master game / No lies / Run for your life / Prisoner / Ain't no fantasy / Rawdeal / Coldheart.

Roadrunner / not iss.

Jul 84. (lp) *(RR 9851)* **THIS TIME** [ ] [-]
– This time / Last flight / A taste of freedom / Another lost weekend / Stand up (tumble down) / Sleepwalker / Tear the shackles down / Stranger / Driftwood / (Nights of) Long shadows.

— **GARY DAVIES** – drums; repl. LOVELL

— split in 1985; re-formed over a decade later

CARSON

— probably the same line-up

WEA / not iss.

Oct 98. (7") *(W 0457)* **I QUIT. /** [ ] [-]
(cd-s+=) *(W 0457CD)* –

Jan 99. (7") *(W 0470)* **UP AND DOWN. /** [ ] [-]
(cd-s+=) *(W 470CD)* –

Feb 99. (cd) *(9362 24614-2)* **A VISION** [ ] [-]
– Up and down / But tomorrow / I quit / Coming alive / Together / Into yesterday / A vision / Feeling free / Sweet soul music / Better blue / Closer to the end.

JAMES GANG

Formed: Cleveland, Ohio, USA . . . 1967 by JIM FOX, TOM KRISS and GLENN SCHWARTZ, taking the name from the legendary outlaw gang. When the latter left to join the group, PACIFIC GAS & ELECTRIC, he was replaced by guitarist JOE WALSH (future EAGLES strummer). Late in '69, the JAMES GANG debut set, 'YER' ALBUM', was complete, the record breaking into the US Top 100. A wholesome serving of earthy mid-Western hard-rock revered by PETE TOWNSHEND, the "Pinball Wizard" was so impressed by WALSH's PAGE-esque axe-grinding, he invited them to support The WHO on a European tour. On his return to the States, WALSH witnessed the killings of four students on the campus of his old university of Kent State, Ohio (4th of May, 1970 – he was later to campaign vigorously for a memorial). With DALE PETERS replacing KRISS, they released their follow-up album, 'RIDES AGAIN', which boasted a minor hit single, 'FUNK 49', a sequel to 'FUNK NO.48', from the first album. Two more Top 30 gold-selling sets followed in quick succession, before WALSH took his not inconsiderable talents to an extremely fruitful solo career. It took two people to replace him, Canadians DOMENIC TROIANO on guitar and ROY KENNER on vocals. The resulting WALSH-less output was found lacking, two albums 'STRAIGHT SHOOTER' (1972) and 'PASSIN' THRU' (1973) not a patch on their earlier work. Following the subsequent departure of TROIANO, guitar prodigy TOMMY BOLIN was secured as a replacement on the recommendation of WALSH. Despite BOLIN's talent, a further two lacklustre albums continued to disappoint all but the most loyal fans, the guitarist soon poached by the revamped DEEP PURPLE. This finally brought about the 'GANG's demise, although FOX and PETERS resurrected the band with two newcomers, BUBBA KEITH and RICHARD SHACK for a couple of forgettable albums. • **Songwriters:** WALSH – KRISS to WALSH-PETERS to group compositions. Covered; CAST YOUR FATE TO THE WIND (Guaraldi-Werber) / STOP (Ragavoy-Schean) / YOU'RE GONNA NEED ME (B.B. King) / LOST WOMAN (Yardbirds) / BLUEBIRD (Buffalo Springfield) / etc.

Album rating: YER' ALBUM (*6) / THE JAMES GANG RIDES AGAIN (*8) / THIRDS (*6) / JAMES GANG LIVE IN CONCERT (*5) / STRAIGHT SHOOTER (*4) / PASSIN' THRU (*4) / THE BEST OF THE JAMES GANG FEATURING JOE WALSH compilation (*7) / 16 GREATEST HITS compilation (*7) / BANG (*4) / MIAMI (*4) / NEWBORN (*4) / JESSE COME HOME (*3) / THE TRUE STORY OF THE JAMES GANG compilation (*7)

JOE WALSH (b.20 Nov'47, Wichita, Kansas, USA) – guitar, vocals; repl. GLEN SCHWARTZ who joined PACIFIC GAS & ELECTRIC / **TOM KRISS** – bass, vocals / **JIM FOX** – drums, vocals

Stateside | Bluesway

Sep 69. (7") *<61027>* **I DON'T HAVE THE TIME. / FRED** [-] [ ]

Nov 69. (lp) *(SSL 10295) <6034>* **YER' ALBUM** [ ] [83] Oct69
– Tuning part one / Take a look around / Funk #48 / Bluebird / Lost woman / Stone rap / Collage / I don't have the time / a) Wrapcity in English, b) Fred / Stop. *(re-iss. Oct90 on 'Beat Goes On'; BGOCD 60)*

Jan 70. (7") *(SS 2158) <61030>* **FUNK #48. / COLLAGE** [ ] [ ] Nov69

Jun 70. (7") *(SS 2173) <61033>* **STOP. / TAKE A LOOK AROUND** [ ] [ ]

—— **DALE PETERS** – bass, vocals repl. KRISS

Probe | A.B.C.

Aug 70. (7") *(PRO 502) <11272>* **FUNK #49. / THANKS** [ ] [59]

Oct 70. (lp) *(SPBA 6253) <711>* **JAMES GANG RIDES AGAIN** [ ] [20] Jul70
– Funk #49 / Asshtonpark / Woman / The bomber: (a) Closet queen – (b) Cast your fate to the wind / Tend my garden / Garden gate / There I go again / Thanks / Ashes the rain and I. *(re-iss. Oct74; 5009) <cd-iss. Jun88; 31145> (cd-iss. Sep91 on 'Beat Goes On'; BGOCD 121)*

Apr 71. (7") *(PRO 533) <11301>* **WALK AWAY. / YADIG?** [ ] [51]

Jul 71. (lp) *(SPB 1038) <721>* **THIRDS** [ ] [27] Apr71
– Walk away / Yadig? / Things I could be / Dreamin' in the country / It's all the same / Midnight man / Again / White man – black man / Live my life again. *(cd-iss. Sep91 on 'Beat Goes On'; BGOCD 119)*

Oct 71. (7") *<11312>* **MIDNIGHT MAN. / WHITE MAN – BLACK MAN** [-] [80]

Dec 71. (lp) *(SPB 1045) <733>* **JAMES GANG LIVE IN CONCERT (live)** [ ] [24] Sep71
– Stop / You're gonna need me / Take a look around / Tend my garden / Ashes, the rain & I / Walk away / Lost woman. *(cd-iss. Sep91 on 'Beat Goes On'; BGOCD 120)*

—— **DOMENIC TROIANO** (b. Canada) – guitar, vocals repl. WALSH went solo / added **ROY KENNER** – vocals

Apr 72. (7") *<11325>* **LOOKING FOR MY LADY. / HAIRY HYPOCHONDRIAC** [-] [ ]

Jul 72. (lp) *(SPB 1056) <741>* **STRAIGHT SHOOTER** [ ] [58] Mar72
– Madness / Kick back man / Get her back again / Looking for my lady / Getting old / I'll tell you why / Hairy hypochondriac / Let me come home / My door is open.

Jul 72. (7") *<11336>* **KICK BACK MAN. / HAD ENOUGH** [-] [ ]

Oct 72. (lp) *(SPB 1065) <760>* **PASSIN' THRU** [ ] [72]
– Ain't seen nothin' yet / One way street / Had enough / Up to yourself / Every day needs a hero / Run, run, run / Things I want to say to you / Out of control / Drifting girl.

Atlantic | Atco

Dec 73. (lp) *(K 50028) <SD 7039>* **BANG** [ ] [ ]
– Standing in the rain / The Devil is singing our song / Must be love / Alexis / Ride the wind / Got no time for trouble / Rather be alone with you / From another time / Mystery.

Jan 74. (7") *(K 10432) <6953>* **MUST BE LOVE. / GOT NO TIME FOR TROUBLES** [ ] [54]

Apr 74. (7") *<6966>* **STANDING IN THE RAIN. / FROM ANOTHER TIME** [-] [ ]

—— **TOMMY BOLIN** (b.1951, Sioux City, Iowa) – guitar (ex-ENERGY, ex-ZEPHYR) repl. TROIANO (to GUESS WHO)

Aug 74. (7") <7006> **CRUISIN' DOWN THE HIGHWAY. / MIAMI TWO-STEP** [-] [ ]

Sep 74. (lp) *(K 50028) <9739>* **MIAMI** [ ] [97]
– Cruisin' down the highway / Do it / Wildfire / Sleepwalker / Miami two-step / Red skies / Spanish lover / Summer breezes / Head above the water.

—— **PETERS + FOX** recruited **RICHARD SHACK** – guitar repl. KENNER **BUBBA KEITH** – vocals, guitar repl. BOLIN who joined DEEP PURPLE, then went solo (he died on the 4th December '76)

—— added **DAVID BRIGGS** – keyboards

May 75. (7") *<7021>* **MERRY GO ROUND. / RED SATIN LOVER** [-] [ ]

May 75. (lp) *(K 50148) <36112>* **NEWBORN** [ ] [ ]
– Merry-go-round / Gonna get by / Earthshaker / All I have / Watch it / Driftin' dreamer / Shoulda' seen your face / Come with me / Heartbreak Hotel / Red satin lover / Cold wind.

—— **BOB WEBB** – vocals, guitar / **PHIL GIALLOMARDO** – keyboards, vocals / **FLACO PADRON** – percussion repl. BUBBA, RICHARD + DAVID

Feb 76. (7") *<7067>* **I NEED LOVE. / FEELIN' ALRIGHT** [-] [ ]

Feb 76. (lp) *<36141>* **JESSE COME HOME** [-] [ ]
– I need love / Another year / Feelin' alright / Pleasant song / Hollywood dream / Love hurts / Pick up the pizzas / Stealin' the show / When I was a sailor.

—— Disbanded later in 1976.

– compilations, others –

Jan 73. (lp) *Probe; (1070) / A.B.C.; <774>* **THE BEST OF THE JAMES GANG FEATURING JOE WALSH** [ ] [79]
– Walk away / Funk #49 / Midnight man / The bomber: (a) Closet queen – (b) Cast your fate to the wind / Yadig? / Take a look around / Funk No.48 / Woman / Ashes the rain and I / Stop. *(re-iss. Oct74; 5027) (re-iss. Oct81 on 'M.C.A.'; 1615)*

Dec 73. (d-lp) *A.B.C.; <801-2>* **16 GREATEST HITS** [-] [ ]

Mar 87. (lp) *See For Miles; (SEE 88)* **THE TRUE STORY OF THE JAMES GANG** [ ] [-]
(cd-iss. Mar93; SEECD 367) – (with . . . PLUS tracks)

—— (also some JAMES GANG tracks on May'94 release, 'ALL THE BEST' by JOE WALSH & THE JAMES GANG)

JANE'S ADDICTION

Formed: Los Angeles, California, USA . . . 1984 by Miami-raised PERRY FARRELL. The band's debut effort was a self-financed eponymous live album on 'Triple XXX', the record's naked intensity going some way towards capturing FARRELL's skewed musical vision. More successful was the band's debut for 'Warner Brothers', 'NOTHING'S SHOCKING' (1988), a wilfully perverse and eclectic blend of thrash, folk and funk that, musically and lyrically, made L.A.'s cock-rock brigade look like school boys. FARRELL's creepy shrill was something of an acquired taste, although it complemented the abrasive, mantra-like music perfectly, from the juddering 'PIGS IN ZEN' to the bleakly beautiful 'JANE SAYS'. The record courted controversy almost immediately, with its cover art depicting naked siamese twins strapped to an electric chair. Live, the band were just as confrontational, FARRELL stalking the stage like some transexual high priest. 'RITUAL DE LO HABITUAL' (1990) was JANE'S' masterstroke, combining the compelling musical dynamics of the debut with more rhythm and melody. The result was a UK Top 40 hit for 'BEEN CAUGHT STEALING', a funky paeon to the delights of shoplifting. Inevitably, JANE'S ADDICTION incurred, yet again, the wrath of America's moral guardians and the record was banned from several US retail chains. The band replied by re-releasing it in a plain white sleeve with only the First Amendment printed on it. The following year, FARRELL organised the first Lollapalooza tour, a travelling festival of indie, rap and alternative acts. It was while headlining this jaunt that the band reached its messy conclusion, FARRELL eventually coming to blows with guitarist NAVARRO and splitting soon after. While NAVARRO subsequently joined the RED HOT CHILI PEPPERS, FARRELL formed PORNO FOR PYROS with PERKINS and a cast of likeminded musicians. The 1993 eponymous debut was like a more aggressive, less mysterious JANE'S ADDICTION, reaching the Top 5. Following personal problems and a drug bust, the band eventually released a follow-up three years later, 'GOOD GOD'S URGE', a more heavy-lidded, narcotic-centric affair which even featured NAVARRO on one track, 'FREEWAY'. JANE'S ADDICTION have since reformed (with the 'CHILI's FLEA on bass), initially for some live work in 1997, although a handful of new tracks surfaced on the odds'n'sods collection, 'KETTLE WHISTLE'. Towards the end of the millennium, PERRY was back in a solo capacity, the album 'REV' receiving some tender reviews for his er, carnival of sound (see covers below). • **Songwriters:** Group penned, except SYMPATHY FOR THE DEVIL (Rolling Stones). Perry solo covered WHOLE LOTTA LOVE (Led Zeppelin) / TONIGHT (from 'West Side Story') / SATELLITE OF LOVE (Lou Reed) / RIPPLE (Grateful Dead).

Album rating: JANE'S ADDICTION (*7) / NOTHING'S SHOCKING (*8) / RITUAL DE LO HABITUAL (*9) / KETTLE WHISTLE part compilation (*6) / Porno For Pyros: PORNO FOR PYROS (*6) / GOOD GOD'S URGE (*8) / Perry Farrell: REV (*7)

PERRY FARRELL (b. PERRY BERNSTEIN, 29 Mar'59, Queens, N.Y.) – vocals / **DAVE NAVARRO** (b. 6 Jun'67, Santa Monica, Calif.) – guitar / **ERIC AVERY** (b.25 Apr'65) – bass / **STEPHEN PERKINS** (b.13 Sep'67) – drums

not iss. | Triple X

Aug 87. (lp) *<XXX 51004>* **JANE'S ADDICTION (live)** [-] [ ]
– Trip away / Whores / Pigs in Zen / 1% / I would for you / My time / Jane says / Rock'n'roll / Sympathy / Chip away. *<re-iss. Dec88 lp/c/cd; TX 510041 LP/MC/CD> (UK-iss.Dec90 on 'WEA' cd/c/lp; 7599 26599-2/-4/-1)*

Warners | Warners

Sep 88. (lp/c)(cd) *(WX 216/+C)(925727-2) <25727>* **NOTHING'S SHOCKING** [ ] [ ]
– Up the beach / Ocean size / Had a dad / Ted, just admit it . . . / Standing in the shower . . . thinking / Summertime rolls / Mountain song / Idiots rule / Jane says / Thank you boys. *(cd+=)* – Pigs in Zen.

Mar 89. (7") *<27520>* **MOUNTAIN SONG. / STANDING IN THE SHOWER . . . THINKING** [-] [ ]

May 89. (7") *(W 7520)* **MOUNTAIN SONG. / JANE SAYS** [ ] [-]
(12"ep+=) **THE SHOCKING EP** *(W 7520T)* – Had a dad (live).

—— added guest **MORGAN** (a female) – violin

Aug 90. (cd)(lp/c) *(7599 25993-2)(WX 306/+C) <25993>* **RITUAL DE LO HABITUAL** [37] [19]
– Stop / No one's leaving / Ain't no right / Obvious / Been caught stealing / Three days / Then she did . . . / Of course / Classic girl.

Aug 90. (7"/c-s) *(W 9584/+C)* **THREE DAYS. / (part 2)** [ ] [ ]
(12"/cd-s) *(W 9584 T/CD)* – ('A'side) / I would for you (demo) / Jane says (demo).

Mar 91. (7"/c-s) *(W 0011/+C) <19574>* **BEEN CAUGHT STEALING. / HAD A DAD (demo)** [34] [ ]
(12"+=/12"box+=/cd-s+=) *(W 0011 T/TB/CD)* – ('A'remix) / L.A. medley:- L.A. woman / Nausea / Lexicon devil.

May 91. (7"/c-s) *(W 0031/+C)* **CLASSIC GIRL. / NO ONE'S LEAVING** [60] [ ]
(12"pic-d+=/cd-s+=) *(W 0031 TP/CD)* – Ain't no right.

—— Had already disbanded when FARRELL looked liked heading into film acting. NAVARRO had briefly filled in for IZZY STRADLIN in GUNS N' ROSES, before joining RED HOT CHILI PEPPERS.

PORNO FOR PYROS

— **FARRELL + PERKINS** with **PETER DISTEFANO** (b.10 Jul'65) – guitar, samples, vocals / **MARTYN LE NOBLE** (b.14 Apr'69, Vlaardingen, Netherlands) – bass (ex-THELONIUS MONSTER) / and guest **DJ SKATEMASTER TATE** – keyboards, samples

Warners Warners

Apr 93. (cd/c/lp) <(9362 45228-2/-4/-1)> **PORNO FOR PYROS** [13] [3]
– Sadness / Porno for pyros / Meija / Cursed female – cursed male / Pets / Badshit / Packin' / • 25 / Black girlfriend / Blood rag / Orgasm.

Jun 93. (7"/c-s) (W 0177/+C) <18480> **PETS. / TONIGHT (from 'West Side Story')** [53] [67]
(12"pic-d+=/cd-s+=) (W 0177 T/CD) – Cursed female – cursed male (medley).

— **MIKE WATT** – bass (ex-fIREHOSE, ex-MINUTEMEN, ex-CICCONE YOUTH) repl. MARTYN (on most)

— added **THOMAS JOHNSON** – samples, engineer and co-producer

May 96. (cd/c/lp) <(9362 46126-2/-4/-1)> **GOOD GOD'S URGE** [40] [20]
– Porpoise head / 100 ways / Tahitian moon / Kimberly Austin / Thick of it all / Good God's:// Urge! / Wishing well / Dogs rule the night / Freeway / Bali eyes.

JANE'S ADDICTION

— re-formed **PERRY FARRELL / DAVE NAVARRO / STEPHEN PERKINS + FLEA**

Dec 97. (cd/c) <(9362 46752-2/-4)> **KETTLE WHISTLE** (4 new + live, demos & out-takes) [ ] [21] Nov97
– Kettle whistle / Ocean size / Maceo / Hadadad / So what / Jane says / Mountain song / Slow divers / Three days / Ain't no right / Up the beach / Stop / Been caught stealing / Whores / City.

PERRY FARRELL

Nov 99. (cd/c) <(9362 47544-2/-4)> **REV** [ ] [ ]
– Rev / Whole lotta love / Been caught stealing / Jane says / Stop / Mountain song / Summertime rolls / Kimberley Austin / Tonight / Tahitian moon / Pets / Cursed male / 100 ways / Hard charger / Ripple / Satellite of love.

JANUS STARK

Formed: Grantham, England . . . 1983 as young punk act, The ENGLISH DOGS by ex-DESTRUCTORS frontman/guitarist GIZZ BUTT, Muslim bassist SHOP and drummer PINCH. After a number of releases in the mid-80's (most notably the 1986 album, 'ALL THE WORLD'S A RAGE'), the group were another to move from oi/punk to metal, although their mid-90's material went unnoticed. By good fortune, GIZZ (who had taught music therapy to handicapped children) then found employment playing guitar for The PRODIGY on stage. When the three duly came back together in 1994, they added new vocalist SHAUN ATKINS and became metal/punk outfit, DOWN RIVER NATION. The following year, they toured supporting BLAGGERS ITA while trying to find a label for their 'SUBWORLD DISCIPLES' demo. However, ATKINS was to subsequently depart and the trio opted for another change of moniker, this time to JANUS STARK (taken from a 70's comic character). Their direction too, had shifted to a more accessible, spiritual! punk/metal/pop (DESCENDENTS/ALL and FOO FIGHTERS were quoted), although it was with 'Earache' records that they found a home. JANUS STARK's debut, 'GREAT ADVENTURE CIGAR' (1998) received some fine reviews in the all new metal/punk Kerrang!, their constant dedication finally bearing fruits; GREEN DAY eat your heart out! • **Covered:** ENGLISH DOGS covered CRANKED UP REALLY HIGH (Slaughter & The Dogs).

Album rating: GREAT ADVENTURE CIGAR (*7) / English Dogs: INVASION OF THE PORKY MEN (*5) / FORWARD INTO BATTLE (*5) / WHERE LEGEND BEGAN (*6) / BOW TO NONE (*4) / ALL THE WORLD'S A RAGE (*6)

ENGLISH DOGS

GIZZ BUTT – vocals, guitar / **SHOP** – bass / **PINCH** – drums

Clay not iss.

Oct 83. (12"ep) (PLATE 6) **MAD PUNX & ENGLISH DOGS** [ ] [-]
(re-iss. Sep97 on 'Sewage Co.'; EDMP 01)

Jun 84. (lp) (CLAYLP 10) **INVASION OF THE PORKY MEN** [ ] [-]
– The fall of Max / World War 2 / Your country / Blind men / Mercenary / Never die / Astrophs waiting / Newsflash / Ghost of the past / Carol / Spoils of war / Cranked up really high / Invasion of the Porky men / Cavemen brain.

Rot not iss.

Nov 84. (12"ep) (ASS 17) **TO THE ENDS OF THE EARTH** [ ] [-]
– Ambassador of fear / The chase is on / Icisor / Survival of the fittest.

Mar 85. (lp) (ASS 20) **FORWARD INTO BATTLE** [ ] [-]
– Forward into line / The final conquest / Ultimate sacrifice / Ordeal by fire / False prophet / Wall of steel / Nosferatu / He that is bound shall be freed / Five days to death / Brainstorm.

Under One Flag not iss.

Nov 86. (lp) (FLAG 4) **WHERE LEGEND BEGAN** [ ] [-]
– Trauma / The eye of Shamahn / Enter the domain / Premonition / Calm before the storm / Flashback / A tomb of traveller's past / Middle earth / Epilogue. (<cd-iss. Jun97 on 'Powerage'; PRAGE 003CD>)

Dec 86. (12"ep) (12FLAG 101) **METALMORPHOSIS EP** [ ] [-]
– Nightmare of reality / Absolution / Let the killing begin.

— split for a while until their reformation in the mid 90's

Impact Century Media

Jun 94. (cd/lp) (IR-C-021 CD/LP) <7785> **BOW TO NONE** [ ] [ ] Oct94
– Nipper tripper / Amsterdam / Face pollution / Criminal justice / Fun door enlightening / Psycho killer / Bastard / Barnaby Hoofer / The fall of Max / Surgical cocoon / Left me for dead / The hanging wanker / D.N.A. / Balloon. (lp-iss.Aug94; IR-C-023) (re-iss. Mar97; same)

Impact Pavement

Dec 95. (cd) (IMR 22CD) <32285> **ALL THE WORLD'S A RAGE** [ ] [ ] Aug98
– Shoot your own head off / I've got a gun (body guard) / Last one standing / This is not a war / Delete it / Out in the cold / Wrecking spree / Die waiting / Under a privare attack / Fortress Europe / A cog in their machine / Poor air quality / Be what you are / Grass / Reduction lane / Body on the line / Disarm. (re-iss. Jun96 on 'S.P.V.'; 084.5363-2) (re-iss. Jun97 & Feb00 on 'Impact'; IR-C-053)

Retch not iss.

Jun 97. (cd-s) (RRCD 006) **WHAT A WONDERFUL FEELING, TO BE FUCKED BY EVERYONE. / WASTED LIFE** [ ] [-]

– compilations, etc. –

Nov 97. (cd) Step 1; (STEPCD 041) **TO THE ENDS OF THE EARTH / FORWARD INTO BATTLE** [ ] [-]

Sep 98. (cd) Captain Oi; (AHOYCD 048) **INVASION OF THE PORKY MEN / PUNX AND ENGLISH DOGS** [ ] [-]

Jul 00. (d-cd) Retch; (RRCD 017) **I'VE GOT A GUN / WHAT A WONDERFUL FEELING TO BE FUCKED BY EVERYONE** [ ] [ ] jan01

JANUS STARK

— same line-up

Earache Trauma

Dec 97. (ltd-7") **DYNAMO. / FLAG OF DISCONTENT** [ ] [-]

Mar 98. (7") (7MOSH 206) **FLOYD – WHAT ARE YOU ON?. / HYPERMANIA (demo)** [ ] [-]
(cd-s) (MOSH 206CD) – ('A'side) / Black box / No way / Barriers.

May 98. (cd) (MOSH 186CD) <74008> **GREAT ADVENTURE CIGAR** [ ] [ ] Oct98
– Enemy lines / Panic attack / Every little things counts / Floyd, what are you on? / Dynamo / White man speak with fork tongue / Clique / New slant on nothing / 200 duty frees / Barriers.

JAWBOX

Formed: Washington DC, USA . . . summer '89 by ex-GOVERNMENT ISSUE mainman, J. ROBBINS, who, over the course of the next year enlisted BILL BARBOT, KIM COLETTA and ZACHARY BAROCAS. Older than, and untypical of (both lyrically and musically) many 'Dischord' bands, a label for whom they signed during the early 90's and for whom KIM had previously worked, JAWBOX nevertheless won respect from both their peers and the press. After releasing two albums, 'GRIPPE' (1991) and 'NOVELTY' (1992) for IAN MacKAYE's fiercely independent operation, JAWBOX were tempted by the greater opportunities available as a new addition to Atlantic's new sideline, 'Tag' (although they remained independent in the UK via 'City Slang'). Early in '94, the quartet made their major label debut with the acclaimed 'FOR YOUR OWN SPECIAL SWEETHEART', previewed by the laid-back post-grunge reflections of the 'SAVORY' single. Yet by the release of 1996's eponymous fourth set, the buzz had died down and JAWBOX had become yet another casualty of the US major label Grunge goldrush. By the time of the group's final demise in 1997, ROBBINS had already begun working on new material with ex-GOVERNMENT ISSUE (a band ROBBINS had also played in) and WOOL sticksman PETE MOFFETT. JAWBOX stalwart BARBOT completed the trio and they took the name BURNING AIRLINES, their expansive, melodic noise-pop unveiled for public consumption on 1999's acclaimed 'MISSION: CONTROL!' album. BARBOT, in particular, was instrumental in shaping the band's sound, his previously unheard bass-playing talent shoring up a solid, fluid groove behind the infectious lead runs and incisive lyrics. • **Covered:** SOUND ON SOUND (Big Boys) / CORNFLAKE GIRL (Tori Amos).

Album rating: GRIPPE (*5) / NOVELTY (*5) / FOR YOUR OWN SPECIAL SWEETHEART (*7) / JAWBOX (*5) / Burning Airlines: MISSION: CONTROL! (*6)

J. ROBBINS – vocals, guitar, Hammond organ (ex-GOVERNMENT ISSUE) / **(W.C.3db)**
BILL BARBOT – guitar, vocals, sax, Hammond organ / **KIM COLETTA** – bass, vocals / **ZACHARY BAROCAS** – drums

not iss. DeSoto

Apr 90. (7"ep) <JA 2> **JAWBOX** [-] [ ]

not iss. Selfless

Jun 91. (7") **AIRWAVES DREAM** [-] [ ]

Dischord Dischord

May 91. (cd/c/lp) <(DIS 52 CD/C/V)> **GRIPPE** [ ] [ ]
– Freezeburn / Impossible figure / Tools and chrome / Paint out the light / Consolation prize / Grip / Ballast / Something must break / Green-line delayed / Bullet park / Manatee bound. (re-iss. Jun94; same)

Jan 92. (7") <DIS 61> **TONGUES. /** [-] [ ]

May 92. (cd/c/lp) <(DIS 69 CD/C/V)> **NOVELTY** [ ] [ ]
– Cutoff / Tracking / Dreamless / Channel 3 / Spiral fix / Linkwork / Chump / Static / Spit – Bite / Send down / Tongues / Ones and zeros.
(re-iss. Jun94; same)

Feb 93. (7") <(DIS 77V)> **MOTORIST. / JACKPOT PILS!** [ ] [ ]

Touch & Go Touch & Go

Apr 93. (7"; shared w/ TAR) <(TG 113)> **STATIC X2** [ ] [ ]

City Slang DeSoto

Jun 93. (7") <EJ 6> **SAVORY. / Edsel: PENALUMA** [-] [ ]

Sep 93. (7") <WH 9> **FALK. / (other by Crackerbash)** [-] [ ]
(above on 'Simple Machines')

Feb 94. (7") (EFA 04931-7) **SAVORY. / SOUND ON SOUND** [ ] [-]
(cd-d+=) (EFA 04931-2) – Lil' shaver / 68.

City Slang Atlantic

Mar 94. (cd/lp) *(EFA 04932-2/-1) <82555>* **FOR YOUR OWN SPECIAL SWEETHEART** Jan94
– FF=66 / Savory / Breathe / Motorist / LS/MFT / Cooling card / Green glass / Cruel swing / Jackpot lus! / Chicago piano / Reel / U-trau / Whitney walks.

May 95. (7") *<JA 11>* **ABSENTER. / CHINESE FORKTIE** -
(above issued on 'DeSoto')

Jun 96. (cd/lp) *(EFA 04981-2/-1) <92707>* **JAWBOX**
– Mirrorful / Livid / Iodine / His only trade / Chinese fork tie / Won't come off / Excandescent / Spoiler / Desert sea / Empire of one / Mule / Stall / Nickel nickel millionaire / Capillary life / Absenter. *(cd hidden track+=)* – Cornflake girl.

— disbanded the following Spring

- compilations, etc. -

Dec 95. (10"lp/cd; shared with LEATHERFACE) *Your Choice Live; <(YCLS 23/+CD)>* **YOUR CHOICE LIVE** Sep95

Jun 98. (cd) *DeSoto; <JA 23>* **MY SCRAPBOOK OF FATAL ACCIDENTS** -

BURNING AIRLINES

J. ROBBINS – vocals, guitar / **BILL BARBOT** – bass, vocals / **PETE MOFFETT** – drums (ex-GOVERNMENT ISSUE, ex-WOOL)

De Soto De Soto

Aug 98. (7") *<DESOTOBA 24>* **CARNIVAL. / SCISSORING** -

Oct 98. (7") *<DESOTOBB 27>* **BACK OF LOVE. / Braid: ALWAYS SOMETHING THERE TO REMIND ME**

Apr 99. (cd) *<(DESOTOBU 30)>* **MISSION: CONTROL!** Feb99
– Carnival / Wheaton calling / Pacific 231 / Scissoring / Escape engine / My pornograph / Meccano / 3 sisters / Flood of foreign capital / Crowned / Sweet deals on surgery / I sold myself in.

Thick Thick

Mar 00. (7") *<(THK 066)>* **DELUXE WAR BABY. / (a track by At The Drive In)**

JAWBREAKER

Formed: Santa Monica, California, USA . . . 1988 by songwriter BLAKE SCHWARZENBACH and ADAM PFAHLER, the high school mates soon being joined by CHRIS BAUERMEISTER. JAWBREAKER subsequently came into existence with the addition of CHRIS BAUERMEISTER, a fellow student SCHWARZENBACH had met while studying at New York University. Although PFAHLER was attending film school in Los Angeles at the time, the trio managed sporadic recording sessions which resulted in a clutch of singles and EP's. An independently released (on the 'Shredder' label) debut album, 'UNFUN', arrived in 1989, its stark, deeply introspective lyrics and intelligent punk-pop/proto grunge sound heralding the arrival of an exciting new talent. 'BIVOUAC' (1992) and '24-HOUR THERAPY' (1993) garnered the band a sizeable underground following, their muscular chords and literate songwriting attracting the attention of NIRVANA who secured their support services for a number of dates on the 'In Utero' tour. Yet bad luck seemed to stalk JAWBREAKER, both in terms of personal health problems and misdirected criticisms from both inside and outside the grunge scene. A subsequent deal (allegedly of the multi-million dollar variety) with 'Geffen' resulted in 'DEAR YOU' (1995), a record which hardly compromised their principled approach yet failed to break through alongside the likes of GREEN DAY et al. • **Covered:** YOU DON'T KNOW . . . + PACK IT UP (Chrissie Hynde / Joan Jett).

Album rating: UNFUN (*6) / BIVOUAC (*6) / 24 HOUR REVENGE THERAPY (*5) / DEAR YOU (*7) / LIVE 4/30/96 (*6)

BLAKE SCHWARZENBACH – vocals, guitar / **CHRIS BAUERMEISTER** – bass / **ADAM PFAHLER** – drums

— released a handful of other singles (unknown)

not iss. Shredder

Nov 89. (cd) *<7>* **UNFUN** -
– Want / Seethruskin / Fine day / Incomplete / Imaginary war / Busy / Softcore / Driven / Wound / Down / Gutless / Drone / Lawn / Crane / Eye-5.

1991. (7") *<(SHREDFIFTY)>* **BUSY. /**

Tupelo Tupelo

May 92. (m-lp) *<(TUPLP 35-1)>* **CHESTERFIELD KINGS** 1991

Nov 92. (cd/c/lp) *<(TUP 38-2/-4/-1)>* **BIVOUAC** 1991
– Shield your eyes / Big / Chesterfield kings / Sleep / Donatello / Face down / P.S. New York is burning / Like a secret / Tour song / You don't know . . . / Pack it up / Parabola / Bivouac. *(re-iss. Nov99 on 'Communion' lp/cd; COMM 38/+CD)*

Feb 94. (cd/c/lp) *<(TUP 49-2/-4/-1)>* **24 HOUR REVENGE THERAPY** 1993
– The boat dreams from the hill / Indictment / Boxcar / Outpatient / Ashtray monument / Condition Oakland / Ache / Do you still hate me? / West Bay invitational / Jinx removing / In sadding around.

not iss. D.G.C.

Sep 95. (cd/c) *<24831>* **DEAR YOU** -
– Save your generation / I love you so much it's killing us . . . . / Fireman / Accident prone / Chemistry / Oyster / Million / Lurker II: Dark son of night / Jet black / Bad scene, everyone's fault / Sluttering / Basilica / (untitled track).

— disbanded after a final gig in April '96

- compilations, etc. -

Nov 99. (cd) *Blackball; <(BBALL 002)>* **LIVE 4/30/96 (live)**
– Jinx removing / Save your generation / Ashtray monument / Accident prone / Boxcar / Gemini / Parabola / For Esme / Shirt.

JELLYS (see under ⇒ HONEYCRACK)

JERUSALEM SLIM (see under ⇒ HANOI ROCKS)

JESUS LIZARD

Formed: Austin, Texas, USA . . . late 80's by DAVID YOW and DAVID SIMS, who had just folded SCRATCH ACID. This band, who also had in their ranks, BRETT BRADFORD, REY WASHAM and brief frontman STEVE ANDERSON, released a clutch of demented hardcore punk releases including the eponymous 'SCRATCH ACID' (1984), 'JUST KEEP EATING' (1986) and 'BERSERKER' (1986) before WASHAM joined STEVE ALBINI in RAPEMAN. YOW and SIMS subsequently recruited Chicago-born DUANE DENISON and MAC McNEILLY to complete the JESUS LIZARD formation, embarking on extensive US and UK tours. Roping in the ubiquitous ALBINI to produce their debut release, 'PURE' (a 1989 mini-set), YOW delivered a ferocious fusion of howling punk metallic blues that called to mind prime(evil) BIRTHDAY PARTY, IGGY POP and The BUTTHOLE SURFERS. Live, the JESUS LIZARD experience was a psychotic, apocalyptic cabaret with the bare-chested YOW a deranged focal point. He was renowned for launching himself into the audience mid set, at times disappearing from view, other times crowd-surfing while remarkably still managing to sing! In the early 90's, the group released a series of uncompromising, lyrically disturbing albums for 'Touch & Go', the last of these 'LIAR' (1992) omitting possibly their most gross track/single to date, a cover of The Dicks' 'WHEELCHAIR EPIDEMIC'. YOW and Co. enjoyed an unexpected taste of success (UK Top 20) the following year when they shared a split 45 with NIRVANA, JESUS LIZARD contributing the lovely 'PUSS'. The group released an unofficial live affair before leaving their label with a final effort, 'DOWN', an album that witnessed them at their grimy, bass-heavy best. Surprisingly signing a lucrative deal with 'Capitol' records (having earlier rejected 'Atlantic'), they signalled that their twisted musical vision remained resolutely uncommercial with the 1996 'SHOT' album. • **Covered:** SUNDAY YOU NEED LOVE (Remmler – Cralle).

Album rating: Scratch Acid: SCRATCH ACID (*6) / JUST KEEP EATING (*6) / BERSERKER (*6) / Jesus Lizard: PURE mini (*5) / HEAD (*6) / GOAT (*7) / LIAR (*7) / SHOW (*5) / DOWN (*6) / SHOT (*7) / BLUE (*7) / Denison – Kimball Trio: WALLS IN THE CITY (*6) / SOUL MACHINE (*5) / NEUTRONS (*5)

SCRATCH ACID

DAVID YOW – vocals, bass / **BRETT BRADFORD** – guitar, vocals / **DAVID WILLIAM SIMS** – bass, guitar / **REY WASHAM** – drums, piano (ex-BIG BOYS)

Fundam. Rabid Cat

Apr 86. (lp) *(HOLY 1)* **SCRATCH ACID**
– Cannibal / Greatest gift / Monsters / Owners lament / She said / Mess / El spectro / Lay screaming.

Jul 86. (m-lp) *(SAVE 012)* **JUST KEEP EATING**
– Crazy Dan / Eyeball / Big bone lick / Unlike a beast / Damned for all time / Ain't that love / Holes / Albino slug / Spit a kiss / Amicus / Cheese plug.

Mar 87. (lp) *(HOLY 2)* **BERSERKER**
– Mary had a little drug problem / For crying out loud / Moron's moron / Skin drips / Thing is bliss / Flying houses.

— In 1988, YOW joined RAPEMAN alongside STEVE ALBINI (BIG BLACK). WESHAM joined TAD.

- compilations, etc. -

Oct 91. (lp/cd) *Touch & Go; <(TG LP/CD 76)>* **THE GREATEST GIFT**

JESUS LIZARD

— **DAVID YOW** – vocals / **DUANE DENISON** – guitar / **DAVID WILLIAM SIMS** – bass / **MAC McNEILLY** – drums

Touch & Go Touch & Go

Feb 89. (m-lp) *<TGLP 30>* **PURE** -
– Blockbuster / Bloody Mary / Rabid pigs / Starlet / Happy bunny goes fluff fluff along. *(UK-iss.Jul93; same)*

Feb 90. (7") *<(TG 53)>* **CHROME. /**

May 90. (lp) *<(TGLP 54)>* **HEAD**
– One evening / S.D.B.J. / My own urine / If you had lips / 7 vs 8 / Pastoral / Waxeater / Good thing / Tight 'n shiny / Killer McHann. *(cd-iss. Jul93+=; TGCD 54)* – PURE

Nov 90. (7") *<(TG 66)>* **MOUTH BREATHER. / SUNDAY YOU NEED LOVE**

Feb 91. (lp/cd) *<(TG 68/+CD)>* **GOAT**
– Then comes Dudley / Mouthbreaker / Nub / Monkey trick / Karpis / South mouth / Lady shoes / Rodeo in Joliet / Seasick. *(re-iss. Apr94; same)*

— In Apr'91, YOW featured for super techno-punks PIGFACE on their 'GUB' album

May 92. (7") *<(TG 87)>* **WHEELCHAIR EPIDEMIC. / DANCING NAKED LADIES**

Oct 92. (lp/c/cd/pic-lp) *<(TG 100/+C/CD/P)>* **LIAR**
– Boilermaker / Gladiator / The art of self-defence / Slave ship / Puss / Whirl / Rope / Perk / Zachariah / Dancing naked ladies.

Feb 93. (7"/cd-s) *<(TG 83/+CD)>* **PUSS. / (b-side by NIRVANA)** 12

Jun 93. (cd/lp) **SHOW (live)** -
– Glamorous / Deaf as a bat / Sea sick / Bloody Mary / Mistletoe / Nub / Elegy / Killer McHann / Dancing naked ladies / Fly on the wall / Boilermaker / Puss / Gladiator / Wheelchair epidemic / Monkey trick. *(imported into UK Jul94 on 'Collision Arts-Giant')*

Sep 93. (12"ep/cd-ep) *<TG 121/+CD>* **LASH** -
– Glamorous / Deaf as a bat / Ladyshoes (live) / Killer McHaan (live) / Bloody Mary (live) / Monkey trick (live).

Nov 93. (12"/cd-s) *<(TG 128/+CD)>* **FLY ON THE WALL. / WHITE HOLE**

Aug 94. (lp/c/cd) *<(TG 131/+C/CD)>* **DOWN (live)** 64
– Fly on the wall / Mistletoe / Countless backs of sad losers / Queen for a day / The associate / Destroy before reading / Low rider / 50 cents / American BB / Horse / Din / Elegy / The best parts.

Capitol Capitol

May 96. (cd/c/lp) *<(CD/TC+/EST 2284)>* **SHOT**
– Thumper / Blue shot / Thumbscrews / Good riddance / Mailman / Skull of a German / Trephination / More beautiful than Barbie / Too bad about the fire / Churl / Now then / Inamorata / Pervertedly slow.

— **JIM KIMBALL** – drums (ex-MULE, ex-LAUGHING HYENAS) repl. MAC

Feb 98. (ltd-10"/cd-s) *(TWA 10/+CD)* **THE JESUS LIZARD**
– Cold water / Inflicted by hounds / Eyesore / Valentine / Needles for teeth.
(above issued on 'Jet Set'; as was below on lp; *TWA 12LP)*

Mar 98. (cd-s) *(882656-2)* **THUMPER EP** -
– Thumper / Good riddance / Shut up.

Apr 98. (cd) *<(8 59266-2)>* **BLUE**
– I can learn / Horse doctor man / Eucalyptus / A tale of two women / Cold water / And then the rain / Postcoital glow / Until it stopped to die / Soft damage / Happy snakes / Needles for teeth / Terremoto. *(lp-iss.May98 on 'Jetset'; TWA 12LP)*

– compilations, etc. –

Feb 00. (cd) *Touch & Go; <(TG 207CD)>* **BANG** Jan00
– Chrome / 7 vs 8 / Gladiator / Seasick / Wheelchair epidemic / Dancing naked ladies / Mouth breather / Sunday you need love / Glamorous / Deaf as a bat / Lady shoes / Killer McHann / Monkey trick / Uncommonly good / Test / Blockbuster / Fly on the wall / White hole / Anna.

DENISON / KIMBALL TRIO

— aka **DUANE + JAMES** on a soundtrack for a film starring YOW

Skin Graft Skin Graft

Oct 94. (lp/cd) *<(GR 16/+CD)>* **'WALLS IN THE CITY**
– Prelude / Cold light of day / Walk away / Reunion / Harry's theme / One if by land . . . / Romantic interlude / Separate checks / Blue corridor / Postlude / . . . Two if by sea.

May 95. (m-cd) *<(GR 22CD)>* **SOUL MACHINE**

Quarter Stick Quarter Stick

Aug 97. (cd/lp) *<(QS 48 CD/LP)>* **"NEUTRONS"**
– Downriver / Landshark pt.2 / Monte's casino / Heavy water / Traveling salesman / Neutrons / Issa / Lullaby.

— DENISON + KIMBALL became part of TOD A's (COP SHOOT COP) ensemble, FIREWATER

JETHRO TULL

Formed: London, England . . . late 1967 by Scots-born IAN ANDERSON and GLENN CORNICK, who had both been in Blackpool band, JOHN EVANS' SMASH for four years alongside school friends EVANS and JEFFREY HAMMOND-HAMMOND. IAN and GLENN brought in former McGREGORY'S ENGINE members MICK ABRAHAMS plus CLIVE BUNKER, adopting the 18th century name of an English agriculturist/inventor, JETHRO TULL. It was often mistaken by the uninitiated as the name of the lead singer, IAN ANDERSON. Early in 1968, through agents Terry Ellis & Chris Wright, 'M.G.M.' issued their debut single, 'SUNSHINE DAY', mistakenly credited as JETHRO TOE at the pressing plant (it has since changed hands for over £100 at record fairs). On the 29th of June '68, after a residency at the Marquee Club, they supported PINK FLOYD at a free rock concert in Hyde Park, London. Following another enthusiastically received concert at Sunbury's Jazz & Blues Festival in August, they signed to 'Island'. By the end of the year, their debut album, 'THIS WAS', had cracked the UK Top 10, even managing to break into the American Top 75. Early in '69, they hired TONY IOMMI (future BLACK SABBATH) and DAVID O'LIST (of The NICE), for a few gigs following the departure of ABRAHAMS. In May '69, with the addition of MARTIN BARRE, they secured a UK Top 3 placing with the classic 'LIVING IN THE PAST' single. This was quickly followed by the UK No.1 album, 'STAND UP', which also made the Top 20 in the States. They then signed to associate label, 'Chrysalis', scoring two more UK Top 10 singles in 'SWEET DREAM' and 'THE WITCH'S PROMISE'. By this juncture, the band were moving away from their early blues-orientated sound into the murky waters of progressive rock, ANDERSON's songwriting voice becoming more vocal with each successive release. With his fevered, one-legged flute playing and laughably outlandish vagrant garb, ANDERSON gave the group its visual trademark, for many people he was *JETHRO TULL*. After a series of line-up changes and continued success in America, the band released 'AQUALUNG' (1971), a million selling concept album through which ANDERSON expressed his contempt for organised religion. This was nothing, however, compared to the contempt which ANDERSON himself would be subject to from a volatile music press whose patience was wearing thin. If the ambitious 'THICK AS A BRICK' (1972) received a less than enthusiastic response from the press, then 'PASSION PLAY's whimsical self-indulgence was met with a critical mauling. As is often the case, the public ignored the reviews and queued up in droves for a copy, especially in America. 'WAR CHILD' and 'MINSTREL IN THE GALLERY' heralded a return to more traditional song structures but by this time, the critics had it in for the band. 'TULL did little to improve the situation by releasing the execrable 'TOO OLD TO ROCK'N'ROLL, TOO YOUNG TO DIE' (1976). Cast into the ghetto of eternal unhipness with the onslaught of punk, JETHRO TULL carried on unhindered, their live shows attracting hordes of die-hard fans. While their recorded output took on a more folky bent with 'SONGS FROM THE WOOD' and 'HEAVY HORSES', the beast that was the 'TULL live phenomenon was beamed around the world by satellite from a show at New York's Madison Square Garden in 1978. ANDERSON began working on a solo album in 1980 with ex-members of ROXY MUSIC and FAIRPORT CONVENTION, the finished article, "A", eventually being released as an official JETHRO TULL album. While the record was greeted with enthusiasm from fans, the follow-up ANDERSON solo LP, 'WALK INTO THE LIGHT' (1983) and subsequent group project 'UNDER WRAPS' (1984) tested even the most ardent 'TULL devotees with their cod-electronica. After a few years break, the band released 'CREST OF A KNAVE' (1987), a harder rocking affair and a return to form of sorts. 'ROCK ISLAND' (1989) and 'CATFISH RISING' (1991) were disappointing in comparison while the live 1992 album, 'A LITTLE LIGHT MUSIC', saw the band in refreshing semi-acoustic mode. 1995 marked a fair solo effort by ANDERSON and a well received 'TULL album, 'ROOTS TO BRANCHES'. While the band's studio output continues to be inconsistent at best, the prospect of a JETHRO TULL live show still has old prog die-hards parting with their hard-earned cash. • **Songwriters:** ANDERSON lyrics / group compositions, except BOUREE (J.S.Bach) / JOHN BARLEYCORN (trad.) / CAT'S SQUIRREL (Cream). • **Trivia:** ANDERSON still controls his trout-farming business in Northern Scotland. In 1974, he produced STEELEYE SPAN's 'Now We Are Six' album.

Album rating: THIS WAS (*6) / STAND UP (*7) / BENEFIT (*6) / AQUALUNG (*8) / THICK AS A BRICK (*5) / LIVING IN THE PAST part compilation/live (*7) / A PASSION PLAY (*7) / WAR CHILD (*6) / MINSTREL IN THE GALLERY (*6) / M.U. – THE BEST OF JETHRO TULL compilation (*8) / TOO OLD TO ROCK'N'ROLL, TOO YOUNG TO DIE (*4) / SONGS FROM THE WOOD (*7) / REPEAT – THE BEST OF JETHRO TULL, VOL.II compilation (*6) / HEAVY HORSES (*6) / JETHRO TULL LIVE – BURSTING OUT (*5) / STORMWATCH (*4) / "A" (*4) / THE BROADSWORD AND THE BEAST (*4) / UNDER WRAPS (*3) / CREST OF A KNAVE (*6) / 20 YEARS OF JETHRO TULL boxed-set compilation (*8) / ROCK ISLAND (*4) / CATFISH RISING (*5) / A LITTLE LIGHT MUSIC (*3) / THE BEST OF JETHRO TULL: THE ANNIVERSARY COLLECTION compilation (*7) / NIGHTCAP rare material (*4) / ROOTS TO BRANCHES (*4) / J-TULL DOT COM (*3) / Ian Anderson: WALK INTO LIGHT (*3)

IAN ANDERSON (b.10 Aug'47, Edinburgh, Scotland) – vocals, flute / **GLENN CORNICK** (b.24 Apr'47, Barrow-in-Furness, England) – bass / **MICK ABRAHAMS** (b. 7 Apr'43, Luton, England) – guitar, vocals (ex-McGREGORY'S ENGINE) / **CLIVE BUNKER** (b.12 Dec'46) – drums (ex-McGREGORY'S ENGINE)

M.G.M. not iss.

Mar 68. (7"; as JETHRO TOE) *(MGM 1384)* **SUNSHINE DAY. / AEROPLANE** -

Island Reprise

Aug 68. (7") *(WIP 6043)* **A SONG FOR JEFFREY. / ONE FOR JOHN GEE** -

Oct 68. (lp; mono/stereo) *(ILP/+S 9805) <6336>* **THIS WAS** 10 62 Feb69
– My Sunday feeling / Some day the sun won't shine for you / Beggar's farm / Move on alone / Serenade to a cuckoo / Dharma for one / It's breaking me up / Cat's squirrel / A song for Jeffrey / Round. *(re-iss. Jan74 lp/c; CHR/ZCHR 1041) (cd-iss. 1986; CCD 1041) (lp re-iss. Apr99; 499468-1)*

Dec 68. (7") *(WIP 6048)* **LOVE STORY. / A CHRISTMAS SONG** 29 -

Mar 69. (7") *<0815>* **LOVE STORY. / A SONG FOR JEFFREY** -

— **MARTIN BARRIE** (b.17 Nov'46) – guitar repl. MICK ABRAHAMS who formed BLODWYN PIG

May 69. (7") *(WIP 6056)* **LIVING IN THE PAST. / DRIVING SONG** 3 -

Jul 69. (lp) *(ILPS 9103) <6360>* **STAND UP** 1 20 Oct69
– A new day yesterday / Jeffrey goes to Leicester Square / Bouree / Back to the family / Look into the sun / Nothing is easy / Fat man / We used to know / Reasons for waiting / For a thousand mothers. *(re-iss. Nov83 on 'Fame' lp/c; FA/TCFA 413086-1/-4) (cd-iss. Jan89; CCD 1042) (re-iss. Feb97 on 'E.M.I.'; LPCENT 8)*

Chrysalis Reprise

Oct 69. (7") *(WIP 6070)* **SWEET DREAM. / 17** 9 -

Oct 69. (7") *<0886>* **SWEET DREAM. / REASONS FOR WAITING** -

Jan 70. (7") *(WIP 6077) <0899>* **THE WITCH'S PROMISE. / TEACHER** 4

— augmented by **JOHN EVAN** (b.28 Mar'48) – keyboards (he later joined full-time)

Apr 70. (lp) *(ILPS 9123) <6400>* **BENEFIT** 3 11
– With you there to help me / Nothing to say / Alive and well and living in / Son / For Michael Collins, Jeffrey and me / To cry you a song / A time for everything / Inside / Play in time / Sossity; you're a woman. *(re-iss. Jan74 lp/c; CHR/ZCHR 1043) (cd-iss. Jun87; CPCD 1043)*

May 70. (7") *(WIP 6081)* **INSIDE. / ALIVE AND WELL AND LIVING IN** -

Jul 70. (7") *<0927>* **INSIDE. / A TIME FOR EVERYTHING** -

— **JEFFREY HAMMOND-HAMMOND** (b.30 Jul'46) – bass repl. CORNICK who formed WILD TURKEY

Mar 71. (lp) *(ILPS 9145) <2035>* **AQUALUNG** 4 7 Apr 71
– Aqualung / Cross-eyed mary / Cheap day return / Mother goose / Wond'ring aloud / Up to me / My God / Hymn #43 / Slipstream / Locomotive breath / Wind up. *(re-iss. Jan74 lp/c; CHR/ZCHR 1044) (cd-iss. 1988; CCD 933-2) (re-iss. cd Mar94; CD25CR 08) (cd re-iss. Jun96 +=; CD25CR 08)* – (sessions):- Lick your fingers clean / Wind up (quad version) / (Ian Anderson interview) / Song for Jeffrey / Fat man / Bouree.

Jul 71. (7") *<1024>* **HYMN #43. / MOTHER GOOSE** - 91

— **ANDERSON, BARRE, HAMMOND-HAMMOND** and **EVAN** were joined by **BARRIEMORE BARLOW** (b.10 Sep'49) – drums (ex-JOHN EVAN'S SMASH) who repl. BUNKER who joined BLODWYN PIG

Sep 71. (7"ep) *(WIP 6106)* **LIFE IS A LONG SONG / UP THE POOL. / DR. BOGENBROOM / FOR LATER / NURSIE** 11 -

Oct 71. (7") *<1054>* **LOCOMOTIVE BREATH. / WIND** -

Chrysalis Reprise

Mar 72. (lp) *(CHR 1003) <2071>* **THICK AS A BRICK** 5 1 May72
– Thick as a brick (side 1) / Thick as a brick (side 2). *(re-iss. Jan74 lp/c; CHR/ZCHR 1003) (cd-iss. 1986; ACCD 1003) (cd-re-iss. Apr89 on 'Mobile Fidelity'; UDCD 510) (cd re-iss. as part of 25th Anniversary on 'E.M.I.'+=; CDCNTAV 5)* – Thick as a brick (live at Madison Square Gardens 1978) / (interview).

Apr 72. (7") *<1153>* **THICK AS A BRICK (edit #1). / HYMN #43** [-] [ ]

Chrysalis Chrysalis

Jul 72. (d-lp) *(CJT 1) <2106>* **LIVING IN THE PAST** (live / studio compilation) [8] [3] Nov72
– A song for Jeffrey / Love story / Christmas song / Teacher / Living in the past / Driving song / Bouree / Sweet dream / Singing all day / Witches promise / Teacher / Inside / Just trying to be / By kind permission of / Dharma for one / Wond'ring again / Locomotive breath / Life is a long song / Up the pool / Dr. Bogenbroom / For later / Nursie. *(cd-iss. Oct87; CCD 1035) (re-iss. Mar94 cd/c; ZCJTD 1)*

Oct 72. (7") *<2006>* **LIVING IN THE PAST. / CHRISTMAS SONG** [-] [11]

May 73. (7") *<2012>* **A PASSION PLAY (edit #8). / A PASSION PLAY (edit #9)** [-] [80]

Jul 73. (lp) *(<CHR/ZCHR 1040>)* **A PASSION PLAY** [13] [1]
– A passion play (part 1; including 'The story of the hare who lost his spectacles' part 1)- /- (part 2) / A passion play (part 2). *(cd-iss. Jan89; CCD 1040)*

Aug 73. (7") *<2017>* **A PASSION PLAY (edit #6). / A PASSION PLAY (edit #10)** [-] [ ]

Oct 74. (7") *(CHS 2054) <2101>* **BUNGLE IN THE JUNGLE. / BACK-DOOR ANGELS** [ ] [12]

Oct 74. (lp/c) *(<CHR/ZCHR 1067>)* **WAR CHILD** [14] [2]
– Warchild / Queen and country / Ladies / Back-door angels / Sealion / Skating away on the thin ice of a new day / Bungle in the jungle / Only solitaire / The third hooray / Two fingers. *(cd-iss. Apr99 on 'Mobile Fidelity'; UDCD 745) (cd re-iss. Aug00; CCD 1067)*

Jan 74. (7") *<2103>* **SKATING AWAY ON THE THIN ICE OF A NEW DAY. / SEA LION** [-] [ ]

Sep 75. (lp/c) *(<CHR/ZCHR 1082>)* **MINSTREL IN THE GALLERY** [20] [7]
– Minstrel in the gallery / Cold wind to Valhalla / Black satin dancer / Requiem / One white duck / 0x10 = Nothing at all – Baker St. Muse (including Pig-me and the whore – Nice little tune – Crash barrier waltzer – Mother England reverie) / Grace. *(cd-iss. 1986; CCD 1082)*

Oct 75. (7") *(CHS 2075) <2106>* **MINSTREL IN THE GALLERY. / SUMMER DAY SANDS** [ ] [79]

— **JOHN GLASCOCK** (b.1953) – bass (ex-CHICKEN SHACK, ex-TOE FAT) repl. HAMMOND-HAMMOND

Mar 76. (7") *(CHS 2086)* **TOO OLD TO ROCK'N'ROLL, TOO YOUNG TO DIE. / RAINBOW BLUES** [ ] [-]

Apr 76. (7") *<2114>* **TOO OLD TO ROCK'N'ROLL, TOO YOUNG TO DIE. / BAD-EYED AND LOVELESS** [-] [ ]

May 76. (lp/c) *(<CHR/ZCHR 1111>)* **TOO OLD TO ROCK'N'ROLL: TOO YOUNG TO DIE** [25] [14]
– Quizz kid / Crazed institution / Salamander / Taxi grab / From a dead beat to an old greaser / Bad-eyed and loveless / Big dipper / Too old to rock'n'roll: too young to die / Pied piper / The chequered flag (dead or alive). *(cd-iss. Nov86 & Aug00; CCD 1111)*

— added **DAVID PALMER** – keyboards (He had been their past orchestrator)

Nov 76. (7"ep) *(CXP 2)* **RING OUT, SOLSTICE BELLS / MARCH THE MAD SCIENTIST. / A CHRISTMAS SONG / PAN DANCE** [28] [-]

Jan 77. (7") *(CHS <2135>)* **THE WHISTLER. / STRIP CARTOON** [ ] [59] Apr77

Feb 77. (lp/c) *(<CHR/ZCHR 1132>)* **SONGS FROM THE WOOD** [13] [8]
– Songs from the wood / Jack-in-the-green / Cup of wonder / Hunting girl / Ring out, solstice bells / Velvet green / The whistler / Pibroch (cap in hand) / Fire at midnight. *(cd-iss. 1986; ACCD 1132)*

Apr 78. (7") *(CHS 2214)* **MOTHS. / LIFE IS A LONG SONG** [ ] [-]

Apr 78. (lp/c) *(<CHR/ZCHR 1175>)* **HEAVY HORSES** [20] [19]
– . . .And the mouse police never sleeps / Acres wild / No lullaby / Moths / Journeyman / Rover / One brown mouse / Heavy horses / Weathercock. *(cd-iss. 1986; CCD 1175)*

Oct 78. (d-lp/c) *(CJT/ZCJT 4) <1201>* **LIVE – BURSTING OUT (live)** [17] [21]
– No lullaby / Sweet dream / Skating away on the thin ice of a new day / Jack in the green / One brown mouse / A new day yesterday / Flute solo improvisation – God rest ye merry gentlemen – Bouree / Songs from the wood / Thick as a brick / Hunting girl / Too old to rock'n'roll: too young to die / Conundrum / Cross-eyed Mary / Quatrain / Aqualung / Locomotive breath / The dambusters march.

Nov 78. (7",7"white) *(CHS 2260)* **A STITCH IN TIME. / SWEET DREAM (live)** [ ] [-]

Sep 79. (7") *(CHS 2378)* **NORTH SEA OIL. / ELEGY** [ ] [ ]

Sep 79. (lp/c) *(<CDL/ZCDL 1238>)* **STORMWATCH** [27] [22]
– North Sea oil / Orion / Home / Dark ages / Warm sporran / Something's on the move / Old ghosts / Dun Ringill / Flying Dutchman / Elegy. *(cd-iss. Jan89; CCD 1238)*

Nov 79. (7") *<2387>* **HOME. / WARM SPORRAN** [-] [ ]

Nov 79. (7"ep) *(CHS 2394)* **HOME / KING HENRY'S MADRIGAL (THEME FROM MAINSTREAM). / WARM SPORRAN / RING OUT SOLSTICE BELLS** [ ] [-]

— ANDERSON for what was supposed to be a solo album retained **BARRE** / plus new **DAVE PEGG** (b. 2 Nov'47, Birmingham, England) – bass (ex-FAIRPORT CONVENTION) repl. GLASCOCK who died. / **EDDIE JOBSON** (b.28 Apr'55, England) – keyboards (ex-ROXY MUSIC, ex-CURVED AIR, etc) repl. EVANS and PALMER who took up session work / **MARK CRANEY** (b. Los Angeles, Calif.) – drums repl. BARLOW who went solo.

Aug 80. (lp/c) *(<CDL/CDC 1301>)* **"A"** [25] [30] Sep 80
– Crossfire / Fylingdale flyer / Working John, working Joe / Black Sunday / Protect and survive / Batteries not included / 4.W.D. (low ratio) / The Pine Marten's jig / And further on.

Oct 80. (7") *(CHS 2468)* **WORKING JOHN, WORKING JOE. / FYLINGDALE FLYER** [ ] [-]

— **PETER JOHN VITESSE** – keyboards repl. JOBSON who went solo / **GERRY CONWAY** – drums (ex-STEELEYE SPAN) repl. CRANEY

Apr 82. (lp/c) *(<CDL/CDC 1380>)* **THE BROADSWORD AND THE BEAST** [27] [19] May82
– Beastie / Clasp / Fallen on hard times / Flying colours / Slow marching band / Broadsword / Pussy willow / Watching me watching you / Seal driver / Cheerio. *(cd-iss. Apr83; CCD 1380)*

May 82. (7") *<2613>* **PUSSY WILLOW. / FALLEN ON HARD TIMES** [-] [ ]

May 82. (7"/7"pic-d) *(CHS/+P 2616)* **BROADSWORD. / FALLEN ON HARD TIMES** [ ] [-]

— **DOANNE PERRY** – drums repl. CONWAY

Sep 84. (lp/pic-lp/c/cd) *(CDL/CDLP/ZCDL/CCD 1461) <1-/0-/4-/2-1461>* **UNDER WRAPS** [18] [76]
– Lap of luxury / Under wraps #1 / European legacy / Later that same evening / Saboteur / Radio free Moscow / Nobody's car / Heat / Under wraps #2 / Paparazzi / Apogee. *(c+=/cd+=)* – Automatic engineering / Astronomy / Tundra / General crossing.

Sep 84. (7") *(TULL 1)* **LAP OF LUXURY. / ASTRONOMY** [70] [ ]
(d7"+=/12"+=) *(TULL D/X 1)* – Tundra / Automatic engineering.

Jun 86. (7") *(TULL 2)* **CORONIACH. / JACK FROST AND THE HOODED CROW** [ ] [ ]
(12"+=) *(TULLX 2)* – Living in the past / Elegy.

— **ANDERSON, BARRE, PEGG** and **PERRY** recruited new member **MARTIN ALLCOCK** – keyboards (ex-FAIRPORT CONVENTION) repl. VITESSE

Sep 87. (lp/c/cd) *(CDL/ZCDL/CCD 1590) <1-/4-/2-1590>* **CREST OF A KNAVE** [19] [32]
– Steel monkey / Farm on the freeway / Jump start / Said she was a dancer / Dogs in midwinter * / Budapest / Mountain men / The waking edge * / Raising steam. *(cd+= *) (cd re-iss. Aug00; same)*

Oct 87. (7"/7"pic-d) *(TULL/+P 3)* **STEEL MONKEY. / DOWN AT THE END OF YOUR ROAD** [ ] [ ]
(12"+=)(c-s+=) *(TULLX/ZTULL 3)* – Too many too / I'm your gun.

Dec 87. (7"/7"pic-d) *(TULL/+P 4)* **SAID SHE WAS A DANCER. / DOGS IN MIDWINTER** [55] [ ]
(12"+=) *(TULLX 4)* – The waking edge.
(cd-s+=) *(TULLCD 4)* – Down at the end of your road / Too many too.

Aug 89. (lp/pic-lp/c/cd) *(CHR/CHRP/ZCHR/CCD 1708) <1-/0-/4-/2-21708>* **ROCK ISLAND** [18] [56]
– Kissing Willie / The rattlesnake trail / Ears of tin / Undressed to kill / Rock Island / Heavy water / Another Christmas song / The whalers dues / Big Riff and Mando / Strange avenues.

Aug 89. (c-s) **KISSING WILLIE. / EARS OF TIN** [-] [ ]

Nov 89. (7") *(TULL 5)* **ANOTHER CHRISTMAS SONG. / SOLSTICE BELLS** [ ] [ ]
(12"+=) *(TULLX 5)* – Jack Frost.
(12"+=/cd-s) *(TULL EX/CD 5)* – ('A'side) / Intro – A Christmas song (live) / Cheap day return – Mother goose / Outro – Locomotive breath (live).

— **ANDY GIDDINGS** – keyboards (3) / **MATT PEGG** – bass (3) / etc. repl. ALLCOCK

Aug 91. (7"/c-s) *(TULL/+XMC 6)* **THIS IS NOT LOVE. / NIGHT IN THE WILDERNESS** [ ] [ ]
(12"+=/cd-s+=) *(TULL X/CD 6)* – Jump start (live).

Sep 91. (cd/c/lp) *(CCD/ZCHR/DCHR 1886) <2-/4-/1-1863>* **CATFISH RISING** [27] [88]
– This is not love / Occasional demons / Rocks on the road / Thinking round corners / Still loving you tonight / Doctor to my disease / Like a tall thin girl / Sparrow on the schoolyard wall / Roll yer own / Gold-tipped boots, black jacket and tie. *(free 12"ep)* – WHEN JESUS CAME TO PLAY. / SLEEPING WITH THE DOG / WHITE INNOCENCE

— **DAVID MATTACKS** – drums, percussion, keyboards repl. PERRY and guests

Mar 92. (12"pic-d) *(TULLX 7)* **ROCKS ON THE ROAD. / JACK-A-LYNN (demo) / AQUALUNG – LOCOMOTIVE BREATH (live)** [47] [ ]
(c-s) *(TULLMC 7)* – ('A'side) / Bouree (live) / Mother goose – Jack-a-Lyn (live).
(2xbox-cd-s++=) *(TULLCD 7)* – Tall thin girl (live) / Fat man (live).

Sep 92. (cd/c/d-lp) *(CCD/ZCHR/CHR 1954) <2-/4/-1-1954>* **A LITTLE LIGHT MUSIC (live in Europe '92)** [34] [ ]
– Someday the sun won't shine for you / Living in the past / Life is a long song / Rocks on the road / Under wraps / Nursie / Too old to rock and roll, too young to die / One white duck / A new day yesterday / John Barleycorn / Look into the sun / A Christmas song / From a dead beat to an old greaser / This is not love / Bouree / Pussy willow / Locomotive breath.

— **PERRY** returned to repl. MATTACKS; bass playing was provided by **DAVE PEGG / STEVE BAILEY**

Sep 95. (cd/c/d-lp) *(CCD/ZCHR/CHR 6109) <2-/4-/1-6109>* **ROOTS TO BRANCHES** [20] [ ]
– Roots to branches / Rare and precious chain / Out of the noise / This free will / Valley / Dangerous veils / Beside myself / Wounded old and treacherous / At last, forever / Stuck in the August rain / Another Harry's bar.

— **ANDERSON, BARRE, GIDDINGS + PERRY** were joined by **JONATHAN NOYCE** – bass

Papillon unknown

Aug 99. (cd) *(BTFLYCD 0001)* **J-TULL DOT COM** [44] [ ]
– Spiral / Dot com / Awol / Nothing @ all / Wicked windows / Hunt by numbers / Hot mango flush / El Nino / Black mamba / Mango surprise / Bends like a willow / Far Alaska / The dog-ear years / A gift of roses.

Nov 99. (cd-s) *(BTFLYS 0001)* **BENDS LIKE A WILLOW / BENDS LIKE A WILLOW (version) / IT ALL TRICKLES DOWN** [ ] [-]

– compilations, others, etc. –

on 'Chrysalis' unless mentioned otherwise

Jan 76. (7") *(CHS 2081)* **LIVING IN THE PAST. / REQUIEM** [ ] [ ]

Jan 76. (lp/c) *(<CHR/ZCHR 1078>)* **M.U. – THE BEST OF JETHRO TULL** [44] [13]
– Teacher / Aqualung / Thick as a brick (edit #1) / Bungle in the jungle / Locomotive breath / Fat man / Living in the past / A passion play (#8) / Skating away on the thin ice of a new day / Rainbow blues / Nothing is easy. *(cd-iss. Dec85; ACCD 1078)*

Feb 76. (7") *<2110>* **LOCOMOTIVE BREATH. / FAT MAN** [-] [62]

Nov 77. (lp/c) *(<CHR/ZCHR 1135>)* **REPEAT – THE BEST OF JETHRO TULL VOL.2** [ ] [94]
– Minstrel in the gallery / Cross-eyed Mary / A new day yesterday / Bouree / Thick as a brick (edit #1) / War child / A passion play (edit #9) / To cry you a song / Too old to rock'n'roll, too young to die / Glory row. *(cd-iss. Apr86; CCD 1135)*

Dec 82. (d-c) *(ZCDP 105)* **M.U. / REPEAT** [ ] [-]

Oct 85. (lp/c/cd) *(JTTV/ZJTTV/CCD 1515)* **ORIGINAL MASTERS** [63] [ ]

Aug 87. (7") *Old Gold; (OG 9637)* **LIVING IN THE PAST. / THE WITCHES' PROMISE** [ ] [-]

Jun 88. (5xlp-box/3xc-box/3xcd-box) *(T/MC/CD BOX 1) <41653>*
20 YEARS OF JETHRO TULL [78] [97]
– THE RADIO ARCHIVES:- A song for Jeffrey / Love story * / Fat man / Bouree / Stormy Monday blues * / A new day yesterday * / Cold wind to Valhalla / Minstrel in the gallery / Velvet green / Grace * / The clasp / / Pibroch (pee-break) – Black satin dancer (instrumental) * / Fallen on hard times // THE RARE TRACKS:- Jack Frost and the hooded crow / I'm your gun / Down at the end of your road / Coronach * / Summerday sands * / Too many too / March the mad scientist * / Pan dance / Strip cartoon / King Henry's madrigal / A stitch in time / 17 / One for John Gee / Aeroplane / Sunshine day // FLAWED GEMS:- Lick your fingers clean * / The Chateau Disaster Tapes: Scenario – Audition – No reheasal / Beltane / Crossword * / Saturation * / Jack-A-Lynn * / Motoreyes * / Blues instrumental (untitled) / Rhythm in gold // THE OTHER SIDES OF TULL:- Part of the machine * / Mayhem, maybe * / Overhang * / Kelpie * / Living in these hard times / Under wraps II * / Only solitaire / Cheap day return / Wond'ring aloud * / Dun Ringill * / Salamander / Moths / Nursie * / Life is a long song * / One white duck – 0x10 = Nothing at all // THE ESSENTIAL TULL:- Songs from the wood / Living in the past * / Teacher * / Aqualung * / Locomotive breath * / The witches promise * / Bungle in the jungle / Farm on the freeway / Thick as a brick / Sweet dream. *(re-iss. Aug88 as d-lp/d-c/d-cd; tracks *; CHR/ZCHR/CCD 1655)*

Jun 88. (pic-cd) *(TULLPCD 1)* **PART OF THE MACHINE / STORMY MONDAY BLUES (live) / LICK YOUR FINGERS CLEAN (live) / MINSTREL IN THE GALLERY (live) / FARM ON THE FREEWAY (live)** [ ] [-]

Jan 91. (cd/c/lp) *Raw Fruit; (FRS CD/MC/LP 004)* **LIVE AT HAMMERSMITH 1984 (live)** [ ] [-]

Apr 93. (4xcd-box) *(CDCHR 60044)* **25th ANNIVERSARY BOXED SET** [ ] [ ]
– REMIXED (CLASSIC SONGS) / CARNEGIE HALL N.Y. (RECORDED LIVE NEW YORK CITY 1970) / THE BEACON'S BOTTOM (TAPES) / POT POURRI (LIVE ACROSS THE WORLD AND THROUGH THE YEARS)

May 93. (7") *(CHS 3970)* **LIVING IN THE PAST. / HARD LINER** [32] [ ]
(12") *(12CHS 3970)* – ('A'side) / ('A'club)/ ('A'dub ravey master) / ('A'dub N.Y. mix).
(d-cd-s) *(23970-1)* – Living in the (slightly more recent) past (live) / Silver river turning / Rosa on the factory floor / I don't want to be me / ('A'side) / Truck stop runner / Piece of cake / Man of principle.

May 93. (d-cd/d-c) *(CDCHR/ZCHR 6001)* **THE VERY BEST OF JETHRO TULL – THE ANNIVERSARY COLLECTION** [ ] [ ]
– A song for Jeffrey / Beggar's farm / A Christmas song / A new day yesterday / Bouree / Nothing is easy / Living in the past / To cry you a song / Teacher / Sweet dream / Cross-eyed Mary / Mother goose / Aqualung / Locomotive breath / Life is a long song / Thick as a brick (extract) / Skating away on the thin ice of a new day / Bungle in the jungle/ / Minstrel in the gallery / Too old to rock'n'roll / Songs from the wood / Jack in the green / The whistler / Heavy horses / Dun Ringill / Fylingdale flyer / Jack-a-Lynn / Pussy willow / Broadsword / Under wraps II / Steel monkey / Farm on the freeway / Jump start / Kissing Willie / This is not love.

Nov 93. (d-cd) *(CDCHR/ZCHR 6057)* **NIGHTCAP – THE UNRELEASED MASTERS 1973-1991** [ ] [ ]
– CHATEAU D'ISASTER – First post / Animelee / Tiger Moon / Look at the animals / Law of the bungle / Law of the bungle part II / Left right / Solitaire / Critique oblique / Post last / Scenario / Audition / No rehearsal/ / UNRELEASED & RARE TRACKS – Paradise steakhouse / Sealion II / Piece of cake / Quartet / Silver river turning / Crew nights / The curse / Rosa on the factory floor / A small cigar / Man of principle / Commons brawl / No step / Drive on the young side of life / I don't want to be me / Broadford bazaar / Lights out / Truck stop runner / Hard liner.

Apr 95. (cd) *Windsong; (WINCD 070)* **IN CONCERT (live)** [ ] [-]

Feb 97. (cd) *EMI Gold; (CDGOLD 1079)* **THROUGH THE YEARS** [ ] [-]
(re-iss. Apr00 on 'Disky'; SI 99195-2)

Mar 97. (cd) *Disky; (DC 87861-2)* **THE JETHRO TULL COLLECTION** [ ] [-]

Apr 97. (3xcd-box) *(CDOMB 021)* **THE ORIGINALS** [ ] [-]
– (THIS WAS / STAND UP / BENEFIT) *(re-iss. Sep00 on 'EMI'; 528364-2)*

Feb 98. (cd) *Strange Fruit; (SFRSCD 051)* **BBC LIVE IN CONCERT** [ ] [ ]

Joan JETT

Born: 22 Sep'60, Philadelphia, Pennsylvania, USA. Following a baptism by new-wave fire in all-girl act, The RUNAWAYS, JETT relocated to London, where she hooked up with STEVE JONES and PAUL COOK (both ex-SEX PISTOLS). The results were to eventually surface in 1979 on UK indie label 'Cherry Red' as 'AND NOW . . . THE RUNAWAYS'. Back in America, the singer came under the wing of veteran 60's producer/session man Kenny Laguna, who helped finance the independent US release of JETT's eponymous solo debut (issued by 'Ariola' in Europe) in 1980. Intense interest subsequently led to a deal with Neil Bogart's 'Boardwalk' operation, the record remixed and re-released the following year as 'BAD REPUTATION'. With backing by The BLACKHEARTS (RICKY BIRD, GARY RYAN and LEE CRYSTAL), the album was a heady hoedown of post-glitter raunch-pop, cruising on a hefty dose of punk energy and a healthy, two-fingered attitude to music industry convention. Culled from follow-up set, 'I LOVE ROCK'N'ROLL' (1981), the sledgehammer riffing and foot-stomping bravado of the anthemic title track saw JETT and her BLACKHEARTS scale the US charts and stay there for nigh-on two months; the single also made a significant impact in the UK, which JETT would nevertheless find difficult to sustain. Although the album itself narrowly missed the top spot Stateside, the harder hitting set only spawned one other major hit, a cover of Tommy James & The Shondells' 'CRIMSON AND CLOVER', Bogart's surprise death casting a shadow over proceedings. Moving to 'M.C.A.' for third set, the originally titled 'ALBUM' (1983), the record witnessed JETT expanding her musical horizons somewhat, attempting a partially successful run-through of Sly Stone's 'EVERYDAY PEOPLE'. The spunky 'GLORIOUS RESULTS OF A MISSPENT YOUTH' (1984) was another strong set, although by this point, JETT's commercial muscle was flagging. Despite being three years in the making, 'GOOD MUSIC' (1987) did little to rectify matters, its diversions into rock-rap failing to mask a lack of inspiration. With an acting appearance alongside Michael J.Fox in 'Light Of Day' and a US Top 10 hit with 'I HATE MYSELF FOR LOVING YOU', JETT's fortunes took a turn for the better in 1988. With TOMMY PRICE and CASMIN SULTAN replacing CRYSTAL and RYAN respectively, the accompanying album, 'UP YOUR ALLEY' (1988), saw the group benefitting from the golden pen of Desmond Child. No such help was needed on 'THE HIT LIST' (1990), a solid covers set which took in everything from The Sex Pistols ('PRETTY VACANT') to Creedence Clearwater Revival ('HAVE YOU EVER SEEN THE RAIN'). 1992's 'NOTORIOUS' again saw Child (along with Diane Warren) share writing duties, while JETT duetted with The REPLACEMENTS' PAUL WESTERBURG on the poignant 'BACKLASH'. While her raw power may only surface in fits and starts, JOAN JETT remains something of a cult figurehead for female anti-rockers, L7 and BABES IN TOYLAND contributing to the BLACKHEART's 'Warners' debut, 'YEAH, RIGHT' (1994; US title, 'PURE AND SIMPLE'). • **Other covers:** I CAN'T CONTROL MYSELF (Troggs) / BITS AND PIECES (Dave Clark Five) / I'M GONNA RUN AWAY FROM YOU (Tammi Lynn) / I LOVE ROCK'N'ROLL (Arrows) / SHOUT (Isley Brothers) / WOOLY BULLY (Sam The Sham & The Pharoahs) / TOSSIN' AND TURNIN' (Searchers) / DO YOU WANNA TOUCH ME + I LOVE YOU LOVE ME LOVE (Gary Glitter) / TULANE (Chuck Berry) / LITTLE DRUMMER BOY (Harry Simone Chorale) / LIGHT OF DAY (Bruce Springsteen) / FUN FUN FUN (Beach Boys). THE HIT ALBUM was full of covers:- DIRTY DEEDS (Ac-Dc) / LOVE HURTS (Everly Brothers) / PRETTY VACANT (Sex Pistols) / TUSH (ZZ Top) / ROADRUNNER (Jonathan Richman) / HAVE YOU EVER SEEN THE RAIN (Creedence Clearwater Revival) / LOVE ME TWO TIMES (Doors) / CELLULOID HEROES (Kinks) / TIME HAS COME TODAY (Chamber Brothers). • **Trivia:** In 1989, JOAN tried to sue Playboy magazine for publishing nude pics of a lookalike, although the case was allegedly dropped when JOAN failed to turn up in court.

Album rating: JOAN JETT (aka BAD REPUTATION) (*6) / I LOVE ROCK'N'ROLL (*7) / ALBUM (*6) / GLORIOUS RESULTS OF A MISSPENT YOUTH (*6) / GOOD MUSIC (*5) / UP YOUR ALLEY (*5) / THE HIT LIST (*5) / NOTORIOUS (*5) / FLASHBACK collection (*6) / PURE AND SIMPLE (*5)

JOAN JETT – vocals, rhythm guitar (ex-RUNAWAYS) / with **RICKY BIRD** – lead guitar repl. ERIC AMBLE / **GARY RYAN** – bass / **LEE CRYSTAL** – drums (later to become The BLACKHEARTS)

Ariola / not iss.

Apr 80. (7") *(ARO 227)* **MAKE BELIEVE. / CALL ME LIGHTNING** [ ] [-]

Jun 80. (lp) *(ARL 5058)* **JOAN JETT** [ ] [-]
– (Do you wanna) Touch me (oh yeah) / Make believe / You don't know what you've got / You don't own me / Too bad on your birthday / Bad reputation / Shout / Let me go / Doin' all right with the boys / Jezebel / Don't abuse me / Wooly bully.

Jun 80. (7") *(ARO 235)* **YOU DON'T KNOW WHAT YOU GOT. / DON'T ABUSE ME** [ ] [-]

Aug 80. (7") *(ARO 242)* **JEZEBEL. / BAD REPUTATION** [ ] [-]

JOAN JETT & THE BLACKHEARTS

(same line-up)

Epic / Boardwalk

Mar 81. (lp/c) *(EPC/40 25045) <37065>* **BAD REPUTATION** (debut remixed) [ ] [51]
– Bad reputation / Make believe / You don't know what you've got / You don't own me / Too bad on your birthday / Doing all right with the boys / Do you wanna touch me (oh yeah) / Let me go / Jezebel / Shout / Don't abuse me / Wooly bully.

Jan 82. (7") *<135>* **I LOVE ROCK'N'ROLL. / YOU DON'T KNOW WHAT YOU GOT** [-] [1]

Mar 82. (7"/7"pic-d) *(EPCA/+11 2152)* **I LOVE ROCK'N'ROLL. / LOVE IS PAIN** [4] [-]

Mar 82. (lp/c) *(EPC/40 85686) <33245>* **I LOVE ROCK'N'ROLL** [25] [2] Dec81
– I love rock'n'roll / (I'm gonna) Run away / Bits and pieces / Love is pain / Nag / Crimson and clover / Victim of circumstance / Bits and pieces / Be straight / You're too possessive / Little drummer boy. *(pic-lp.1983; EPC11 85686) (cd-iss. Feb97 on 'Columbia'; 486509-2)*

Jun 82. (7"/7"pic-d) *(EPCA/+11 2485) <144>* **CRIMSON AND CLOVER. / OH WOE IS ME** [60] [7] Apr82

Jul 82. (7") *<150>* **DO YOU WANNA TOUCH ME (OH YEAH). / VICTIM OF CIRCUMSTANCE** [-] [20]

Aug 82. (7") *(EPCA 2674)* **DO YOU WANNA TOUCH ME (OH YEAH). / JEZEBEL** [ ] [-]

Oct 82. (7") *(EPCA 2880)* **YOU DON'T KNOW WHAT YOU'VE GOT. / (I'M GONNA) RUN AWAY** [ ] [-]

Nov 82. (7") *<5706>* **YOU DON'T OWN ME. / JEZEBEL** [-] [ ]

Epic / Blackheart-MCA

Jul 83. (7") *<52240>* **FAKE FRIENDS. / NIGHTIME** [-] [35]
(12"+=) *<52256>* – Coney Island whitefish.

Jul 83. (7") *(EPCA 3615)* **FAKE FRIENDS. / CONEY ISLAND WHITEFISH** [ ] [-]
(12"+=) *(TA 3615)* – Nightime.

Jul 83. (lp/c) *(EPC/40 25414) <5437>* **ALBUM** [ ] [20]
– Fake friends / Handyman / Everyday people / A hundred feet away / Secret love / The French song / Tossin' and turnin' / Why can't we be happy / I love playin' with fire / Coney Island whitefish / Had enough. *(c+=)* – Star, star. *(cd-iss. Sep98 on 'BKHE'; 74833 7180926)*

Aug 83. (7") *<52256>* **FAKE FRIENDS. / HANDY MAN** [-] [ ]

Sep 83. (7") *(EPCA 3790) <52272>* **EVERYDAY PEOPLE. / WHY CAN'T WE BE HAPPY** [ ] [37]

May 84. (7") *(EPCA 4391)* **I NEED SOMEONE. / TALKIN' 'BOUT MY BABY** [ ] [-]
(12"+=) *(TA 4391)* – The French song.

Oct 84. (7") *(EPCA 4851)* **I LOVE YOU LOVE ME LOVE. / LONG TIME** [ ] [-]
(12"+=) *(TA 4851)* – Bird dog.

Sep 84. (7") *<52472>* **I LOVE YOU LOVE ME LOVE. / TALKIN' 'BOUT MY BABY** [-] [ ]

Jan 85. (lp) *(EPCA 25993) <5476>* **GLORIOUS RESULTS OF A MISSPENT YOUTH** [ ] [67] Oct84
– Cherry bomb / I love you love me love / Frustrated / Hold me / Long time / Talkin' 'bout my baby / I need someone / Love like mine / New Orleans / Someday / Push and stomp / I got no answers. *(cd-iss. Sep98 on 'BKHE'; 74833 718022)*
(below 45 with others from film and soundtrack of same name)

Feb 87. (7"; as The BARBUSTERS) *<06692>* **LIGHT OF DAY. / ROADRUNNER** [-] [33]

Polydor Blackheart

Jul 87. (7") *(POSP 877) <06336>* **GOOD MUSIC. / FANTASY** [ ] [83] Oct86
(12"+=) *(POSPX 877)* – Fun, fun, fun (with The BEACH BOYS).

Sep 87. (lp/c/cd) *(833 078-1/-4/-2) <40544>* **GOOD MUSIC** [ ] [ ] Oct86
– Good music / This means war / Roadrunner / If ya want my luv / Light of day / Black leather / Outlaw / Just lust / You got me floatin' / Fun, fun, fun / Contact.

— In Jan'88, they featured on 'B' side of BANGLES 45 from the film 'Less Than Zero'. The track SHE'S LOST YOU on 'Def Jam'.

— retained **BIRD,** and recruited **TOMMY PRICE** – drums (ex-BILLY IDOL) / **CASMIN SULTAN** – bass (ex-TODD RUNDGREN / UTOPIA)

London Blackheart-Epic

Aug 88. (7"sha-pic-d) *(LONP 195) <07919>* **I HATE MYSELF FOR LOVING YOU. / LOVE IS PAIN** [46] [8] Jun88
(12"+=) *(LONX 195)* – I can't control myself.
(cd-s++=) *(LONCD 195)* – ('A'live version).

Sep 88. (lp/c)(cd) *(LON LP/C 67)(837 158-2) <44146>* **UP YOUR ALLEY** [ ] [19] May88
– I hate myself for loving you / Ridin' with James Dean / Little liar / Tulane / I wanna be your dog / I still dream about you / You want in I want out / Just like in the movies / Desire / Back it up / Play that song again.

Oct 88. (7") *<08095>* **LITTLE LIAR. / WHAT CAN I DO FOR YOU** [-] [19]

Chrysalis Blackheart-Epic

Jan 90. (c-s,12") *<73267>* **DIRTY DEEDS. / LET IT BLEED** [-] [36]

Mar 90. (7"/c-s) *(CHS/+MC 3518)* **DIRTY DEEDS (DONE DIRT CHEAP). / PRETTY VACANT** [69] [-]
(12"+=/12"pic-d+=/cd-s+=) *(CHS 12/P12/CD 3518)* – ('A'extended).

Apr 90. (cd/c/lp) *(CHR/ZCHR/CCD 1773) <45473>* **THE HIT LIST** [ ] [36] Jan90
– Dirty deeds (done dirt cheap) / Love hurts / Pretty vacant / Celluloid heroes / Tush / Time has come today / Up from the skies / Have you ever seen the rain? / Love me two times / Roadrunner USA (1990 version).

Apr 90. (c-s) *<73314>* **LOVE HURTS. / HANDYMAN** [-] [ ]

Jul 90. (7") *(CHS 3546)* **LOVE HURTS. / UP FROM THE SKIES** [ ] [-]
(12"+=/cd-s+=) *(CHS 12/CD 3546)* – Tush.

Silenz Epic

Feb 92. (c-s) *<74067>* **DON'T SURRENDER. / ('A'-Most Excellent version)** [-] [ ]

Apr 92. (cd-s) **TREADIN' WATER / WAIT FOR ME / MISUNDERSTOOD** [ ] [-]

Apr 92. (cd/c) *(907080-2/-4) <47488>* **NOTORIOUS** [ ] [ ] Aug91
– Backlash / Ashes in the wind / The only good thing (you ever said was goodbye) / Lie to me / Don't surrender / Goodbye / Machismo / Treadin' water / I want you / Wait for me.

Reprise Reprise

Feb 94. (7"/c-s) *(W 0232/+C)* **I LOVE ROCK'N'ROLL. / ACTIVITY GRRRL** [75] [ ] Jan94
(cd-s+=) *(W 0232CD) <18245>* – Wayne's World theme.

Blackheart Warners

Jun 94. (cd/c) *<45567>* **YEAH, RIGHT** <US-title 'PURE AND SIMPLE'> [ ] [ ]
– Go home / Eye to eye / Spinster / Torture / Rubber & glue / as I am / Activity grrrl / Insecure / Wonderin' / Consumed / You got a problem / Brighter day.

J.F.A.

Formed: Phoenix, Arizona, USA . . . 1983 by BRIAN, DON, MICHAEL C and BAM BAM. Originally an out-and-out punk outfit, they slipped into skateboard-punk and surf-punk with two rare, fun-packed albums, 'VALLEY OF THE YAKES' (1986) and 'J.F.A.' (1988), both for 'Fundamental' records. What did happen to them and what did their moniker mean? (one can only guess?).

Album rating: VALLEY OF THE YAKES (*6) / J.F.A. (*5)

BRIAN – vocals / **DON** – guitar / **MICHAEL C** – bass / **BAM BAM** – drums

Fundam. Fundam.

Jul 87. (lp) *<(SAVE 023)>* **VALLEY OF THE YAKES** [ ] [ ] 1986
– Kick you / The great equaliser / Preppie / Little big man / Johnny D / Walk don't run / Skateboard / We know you suck / Too late / Sadistic release / Axed at Howard's / One-ten / Guess what?

Feb 88. (lp) *<(SAVE 044)>* **J.F.A.** [ ] [ ]
– Deltitnu / Tent peg / Aba / It's not right / The day Walt Disney died / Standin' on the verge / I love broads / Ramp song / Pipetruck / Zimbobway / Untitled / I still could not forget you.

— split in the late 80's

JIMMY EAT WORLD

Formed: Tempe, Arizona, USA . . . 1993 by JIM ADKINS, TOM LINTON, RICK BURCH and ZACH LIND. Having begun life as a METALLICA covers band, the quartet soon developed a more lugubrious, melodic post-grunge sound as evidenced on their independently released debut 7". An eponymous album quickly followed as did a slew of split singles with the likes of CHRISTIE FRONT DRIVE and BLUEPRINT. Subsequently signed to 'Capitol', the group released 'STATIC PREVAILS' as their major label debut in 1996. Their contract nevertheless allowed for indie releases and they issued an eponymous five track EP in 1998 as a taster for the acclaimed 'CLARITY' (1999).

Album rating: STATIC PREVAILS (*5) / CLARITY (*6)

JIM ADKINS – vocals, guitar / **TOM LINTON** – vocals, guitar / **RICK BURCH** – bass / **ZACH LIND** – drums

not iss. Wooden Blue

1994. (7") [-] [ ]

1994. (lp) **JIMMY EAT WORLD** [-] [ ]

— split singles with CHRISTIE FRONT DRIVE / BLUEPRINT + EMERY

Capitol Capitol

1996. (cd/c) *<32404>* **STATIC PREVAILS** [-] [ ]
– Thinking, that's all / Rockstar / Claire / Call it in the air / Seventeen / Episode IV / Digits / Caveman / World is static / In the same room / Robot factory / Anderson Mesa.

Feb 99. (cd) *55950>* **CLARITY** [-] [ ]
– Table for glasses / Lucky Denver mint / Your new aesthetic / Believe in what you want / Sunday / Crush / 12.23.95 / Ten / Just watch the fireworks / For me this is Heaven / Blister / Clarity / Goodbye sky harbor.

Fueled By Ramen Fueled By Ramen

Apr 99. (m-cd) *<(FBR 020CD)>* **JIMMY EAT WORLD** [ ] [ ] Oct98
– Lucky Denver mint / For me this is heaven / Your new aesthetic / Softer / Roller queen.

JOHNBOY

Formed: Austin, Texas, USA . . . 1991 by BARRY STONE, TONY BICE and JASON MEADE. Not a band destined for the alt-rock mainstream, JOHNBOY were picked up by local label, 'Trance Syndicate' (also home of CRUNT amongst others), who issued their debut album, 'PISTOLSWING' (1993). A nihilistic blast of mutant R&R, the record caught the ear of both BOB MOULD (who offered them a support slot) and STEVE ALBINI, the latter working on their 1994 follow-up, 'CLAIM DEDICATION'.

Album rating: PISTOLSWING (*6) / CLAIM DEDICATION (*5)

BARRY STONE – guitar, vocals / **TONY BICE** – bass, vocals / **JASON MEADE** – drums

Trance Syndicate Trance Syndicate

Jun 93. (lp/cd) *<(TR 16/+CD)>* **PISTOLSWING** [ ] [ ]
– Admiration / Sourmouth / Sunday two / Pistolswing / Hold / Freestanding / New Jersey roadbase / Yellow / I.

Sep 94. (lp/cd) *<(TR 27/+CD)>* **CLAIM DEDICATION** [ ] [ ] Aug94
– Shortstack / Quick to drain / Driving reservoirs up noses / 10 W 40 / Chair / Genius / Pivotal / Lorac / Flung circles.

— disbanded after above

Mike JOHNSON (see under ⇒ DINOSAUR JR.)

Mick JONES (see under ⇒ FOREIGNER)

JOSHUA

Formed: Los Angeles, California, USA . . . 1981 by namesake JOSHUA PERAHIA, who had played guitar with BLIND ALLEY. An amorphous line-up eventually gelled around STEPHEN FONTAINE, DOUGIE GOUGEON, MAHLON HAWK and TONY ZACCAGLINI, who performed on the debut album, 'THE HAND IS QUICKER THAN THE EYE' (1982). This nimble-finger set of hard-rock histrionics caught the attention of 'Polydor' in America, PERAHIA recruiting a complete new set of musicians (JEFF FENHOLT, KEN TAMLIN, PATRICK BRADLEY, LOREN ROBINSON and JO GALLETTA) for the recording of the follow-up album, 'SURRENDER' (1986). PERAHIA once again found himself having to enlist yet another new cast, this bunch appearing on a final 'R.C.A.' long-player, 'INTENSE DEFENCE' (1989). • **Note:** This JOSHUA not to be confused with Canada's gospel-rock outfit of the early 70's.

Album rating: THE HAND IS QUICKER THAN THE EYE (*5) / SURRENDER (*6) / INTENSE DEFENSE (*5)

JOSHUA PERAHIA – vocals, guitar (ex-BLIND ALLEY) / **STEPHEN FONTAINE** – vocals / **DONNIE GOUGEON** – keyboards, vocals / **MAHLON HAWK** – bass, vocals / **TONY ZACCAGLINI** – drums

not iss. Olympic

1982. (lp) *<E 1013>* **THE HAND IS QUICKER THAN THE EYE** [-] [ ]
– Falling again / November is going away / Sweet lil' hurricane / Let's breakaway / Broken dream / Flying high.

— **PERAHIA** recruited new line-up **JEFF FENHOLT** – vocals / **KEN TAMLIN** – guitar, vocals / **PATRICK BRADLEY** – keyboards, vocals / **LOREN ROBINSON** – bass, vocals / **JO GALLETTA** – drums

FM Revolver not iss.

Mar 86. (lp/c/cd) *(WKFM LP/MC/XD 64)* **SURRENDER** [ ] [-]
– Surrender / Heart full of soul / Your love is gone / Hold on / Back to the rock / Rockin' the world / Stay alive / Loveshock / Reprise.

— again **PERAHIA** brought in new members **ROB ROCK** – vocals / **GREG SHULTZ** – keyboards, vocals / **EMIL LECH** – bass / **TIM GEHRT** – drums

R.C.A. | not iss.

Mar 89. (lp/c/cd) *(PL/PK/PD 71905)* **INTENSE DEFENSE** [ ] [-]
– Reach up / I've been waiting / Only yesterday / Crying out for love / Living on the edge / Tearing at my heart / Remembering you / Look to the sky / Don't you know / Stand alone.

—— split when ROCK, SCHULTZ and LECH formed DRIVER

JOURNEY

Formed: San Francisco, California, USA . . . early 1973, originally as The GOLDEN GATE BRIDGE by NEAL SCHON, GEORGE TICKNER, ROSS VALORY and PRAIRIE PRINCE. Due to manager Walter Herbert auditioning through a radio station for the group name, they settled with JOURNEY. They made their live debut on the 31st of December 1973 in front of over 10,000 people at San Francisco's 'Wonderland' venue. Prior to the recording of their eponymous first album in 1975, (the group had secured a deal with 'Columbia'), another SANTANA veteran, GREGG ROLIE, was added, while English-born AYNSLEY DUNBAR replaced the TUBES-bound PRINCE. The debut, and subsequent releases, 'LOOK INTO THE FUTURE' (1976) and 'NEXT' (1977), focused on jazzy art-rock, although major changes were afoot by 1978's 'INFINITY'. With the addition of ex-ALIEN PROJECT vocalist, STEVE PERRY, the group were transformed from noodling jam-merchants into sleek AOR-pomp exponents set for American FM radio domination. Produced by Roy Thomas Baker (QUEEN), the album saw PERRY's strident, impressively dynamic vocals given free rein over a new improved pop-friendly format, gleaming synths and irresistible hooks now the order of the day. The record also gave JOURNEY a near brush with the Top 20, a feat they'd achieve with 'EVOLUTION' (1979). By this juncture, DUNBAR had departed for JEFFERSON STARSHIP, his replacement being STEVE SMITH on a set which provided JOURNEY with their biggest hit single to date (Top 20) in 'LOVIN', TOUCHIN', SQUEEZIN'. The following year's 'DEPARTURE' album performed even better, JOURNEY finally nearing their ultimate destination, i.e. the top of the US charts. Enhanced by the polished pop instincts of ex-BABYS' frontman JONATHAN CAIN (a replacement for ROLIE, who went solo, later forming The STORM with VALORY and SMITH), JOURNEY scored their first (and only) No.1 album with the massively successful 'ESCAPE' (1981). The record spawned an unprecedented three US Top 10 hits, namely 'WHO'S CRYING NOW', 'OPEN ARMS' and the swooning 'DON'T STOP BELIEVIN'. Despite almost universal critical derision from the more elitist factions of the music press, JOURNEY continued to capture the lucrative middle ground between pop and tasteful metal, even breaking into the previously impenetrable UK Top 10 with 'FRONTIERS' (1983). The same month, SCHON released his second solo collaboration with keyboard wizard, JAN HAMMER, 'HERE TO STAY', while PERRY subsequently launched his solo career to huge success with the melodramatic 'OH SHERRIE' single and 'STREET TALK' (1984) album. JOURNEY eventually regrouped in the mid-80's, the band now comprising the core trio of PERRY, SCHON and CAIN, augmented by RANDY JACKSON and LARRIE LONDIN. The resulting album, 'RAISED ON RADIO' (1986) proved to be JOURNEY's end, the group bowing out on a high point. Following an official split in early '87, CAIN (along with VALORY) joined MICHAEL BOLTON, while SCHON eventually hooked up with JOHN WAITE in BAD ENGLISH, before forming HARDLINE in '92 with ROLIE and SMITH. With reunion fever all the rage in the 90's, JOURNEY finally got back together in 1996 for the successful 'TRIAL BY FIRE' album. Fans were disappointed, however, with the subsequent departure of PERRY and his replacement with STEVE AUGERI. Although a relative soundalike, AUGERI couldn't quite match PERRY's charisma on 'ARRIVAL' (2001), a blatant attempt to capture the spirit of the band's early 80's golden period. • **Trivia:** A couple of JOURNEY tracks, featured on the 1980 & 1981 film soundtracks of 'Caddyshack' & 'Heavy Metal'.

Album rating: JOURNEY (*3) / LOOK INTO THE FUTURE (*4) / NEXT (*3) / IN THE BEGINNING compilation (*4) / INFINITY (*6) / EVOLUTION (*5) / DEPARTURE (*4) / CAPTURED (*7) / ESCAPE (*8) / FRONTIERS (*6) / RAISED ON RADIO (*7) / THE BEST OF JOURNEY compilation (*8) / TIME 3 compilation (*7) / TRIAL BY FIRE (*4) / ARRIVAL (*5)

NEAL SCHON (b.27 Feb'54, San Mateo, Calif.) – lead guitar, vocals (ex-SANTANA) / **GREGG ROLIE** (b.17 Jun'47) – vocals, keyboards (ex-SANTANA) / **GEORGE TICKNER** – guitar, vocals / **ROSS VALORY** (b. 2 Feb'49) – bass, vocals (ex-STEVE MILLER BAND) / **AYNSLEY DUNBAR** (b.1946, Liverpool, England) – drums (ex-FRANK ZAPPA, ex-JOHN MAYALL, ex-JEFF BECK) repl. PRAIRIE PRINCE who joined The TUBES

C.B.S. | Columbia

Apr 75. (lp/c) *(CBS/40 80724) <33388>* **JOURNEY** [ ] [ ]
– Of a lifetime / In the morning day / Kohoutek / To play some music / Topaz / In my lonely feeling – Conversations / Mystery mountain. *(cd-iss. Oct93 on 'Sony Collectors'; 983313-2) (cd re-iss. Oct94 on 'Columbia'; 477854-2)*

Jun 75. (7") *<10137>* **TO PLAY SOME MUSIC. / TOPAZ** [-] [ ]

—— (Apr'75) reverted to a quartet when TICKNER departed

Jan 76. (lp/c) *(CBS/40 69203) <33904>* **LOOK INTO THE FUTURE** [ ] [100]
– On a Saturday nite / It's all too much / Anyway / She makes me (feel alright) / You're on your own / Look into the future / Midnight dreamer / I'm gonna leave you. *(re-iss. Mar82; CBS 32102)*

Mar 76. (7") *<10324>* **ON A SATURDAY NIGHT. / TO PLAY SOME MUSIC** [-] [ ]

Jul 76. (7") *<10370>* **SHE MAKES ME (FEEL ALRIGHT). / IT'S ALL TOO MUCH** [-] [ ]

Feb 77. (7") *<10522>* **SPACEMAN. / NICKEL AND DIME** [-] [ ]

Feb 77. (lp/c) *(CBS/40 81554) <34311>* **NEXT** [ ] [85]
– Spaceman / People / I would find you / Here we are / Hustler / Next / Nickel & dime / Karma.

—— (Jun'77) added **ROBERT FLEISCHMAN** – lead vocals

—— (Oct77) **STEVE PERRY** (b.22 Jan'53, Hanford, Calif.) – lead vocals; repl. FLEISCHMAN

Mar 78. (7") *(CBS 6238) <10700>* **WHEEL IN THE SKY. / CAN DO** [ ] [57]

May 78. (lp/c) *(CBS/40 82244) <34912>* **INFINITY** [ ] [21] Feb78
– Lights / Feeling that way / Anytime / La do da / Patiently / Wheel in the sky / Somethin' to hide / Winds of March / Can do / Opened the door. *(cd-iss. 1988; CD 82244) (cd re-iss. Nov96 on 'Columbia'; 486665-2)*

Jun 78. (7") *<10757>* **ANYTIME. / CAN DO** [-] [83]

Aug 78. (7") *(CBS 6392)* **LIGHTS. / OPEN THE DOOR** [ ] [-]

Aug 78. (7") *<10800>* **LIGHTS. / SOMETHIN' TO HIDE** [-] [68]

—— (Nov'78) **STEVE SMITH** – drums repl. DUNBAR who joined JEFFERSON STARSHIP (above now alongside SCHON, ROLIE, PERRY and VALORY)

Apr 79. (lp/c) *(CBS/40 83566) <35797>* **EVOLUTION** [100] [20]
– Sweet and simple / Just the same way / Do you recall / City of angels / Lovin', touchin', squeezin' / Daydream / When you're alone (it ain't easy) / Lady luck / Too late / Lovin' you is easy / Majestic. *(re-iss. Jul83 lp/c; CBS/40 32342) (cd-iss. Oct93 on 'Sony Collectors'; 982737-2) (cd re-iss. Nov96 on 'Columbia'; 486666-2)*

Apr 79. (7") *<10928>* **JUST THE SAME WAY. / SOMETHIN' TO HIDE** [-] [58]

Sep 79. (7") *(CBS 7890) <11036>* **LOVIN', TOUCHIN', SQUEEZIN'. / DAYDREAM** [ ] [16] Jul79

Dec 79. (7") *<11143>* **TOO LATE. / DO YOU RECALL** [-] [70]

Feb 80. (7") *<11213>* **ANY WAY YOU WANT IT. / WHEN YOU'RE ALONE (IT AIN'T EASY)** [-] [23]

Mar 80. (lp/c) *(CBS/40 84101) <36339>* **DEPARTURE** [ ] [8]
– Any way you want it / Walks like a lady / Someday soon / People and places / Precious time / Where were you / I'm cryin' / Line of fire / Departure / Good morning girl / Stay awhile / Homemade love. *(re-iss. Feb86 lp/c; CBS/40 32714) (cd-iss. 1987; CD 84101) (cd re-iss. Nov96 on 'Columbia'; 486667-2)*

May 80. (7"/12") *(CBS/12 8558)* **ANY WAY YOU WANT IT. / DO YOU RECALL** [ ] [-]

May 80. (7") *<11275>* **WALKS LIKE A LADY. / PEOPLE AND PLACES** [-] [ ]

Aug 80. (7") *<11339>* **GOOD MORNING GIRL. / STAY AWHILE** [-] [55]

Feb 81. (d-lp) *(CBS 88525) <37016>* **CAPTURED (live)** [ ] [9]
– Majestic / Where were you / Just the same way / Line of fire / Lights / Stay awhile / Too late / Dixie highway / Feeling that way / Anytime / Do you recall / Walks like a lady / La do da / Lovin', touchin', squeezin' / Wheel in the sky / Any way you want it / The party's over (hopelessly in love). *(re-iss. Sep87 d-lp/d-c/cd; 451132-1/-4/-2) (cd re-iss. Jun89; CD 88525) (cd re-iss. Nov96 on 'Columbia'; 486661-2)*

Mar 81. (7") *(CBS 9578) <60505>* **THE PARTY'S OVER (HOPELESSLY IN LOVE) (live). / WHEEL IN THE SKY (live)** [ ] [34] Feb81

—— (Apr'81) **JONATHAN CAIN** (b.26 Feb'50, Chicago, Illinois) – keyboards, guitar, vocals (ex-BABYS) repl. ROLIE who went solo, and later formed The STORM with VALORY and SMITH

Aug 81. (lp/c) *(CBS/40 85138) <37408>* **ESCAPE** [32] [1]
– Don't stop believin' / Stone in love / Who's crying now / Keep on runnin' / Still they ride / Escape / Lay it down / Dead or alive / Mother, father / Open arms. *(cd-iss. May87; CD 85138) (re-iss. Feb88 lp/c; 460185-1/-4) (cd re-iss. Apr89; 460285-2) (cd re-iss. Nov96 on 'Columbia'; 486662-2)*

Jul 81. (7") *<02241>* **WHO'S CRYING NOW. / MOTHER, FATHER** [-] [4]

Aug 81. (7"/12") *(A/TA 1467)* **WHO'S CRYING NOW. / ESCAPE** [ ] [-]

Dec 81. (7"/12"/12"pic-d) *(A/+13/11 1728) <02567>* **DON'T STOP BELIEVIN'. / NATURAL THING** [62] [9] Oct81

Apr 82. (7") *(A 2057) <02687>* **OPEN ARMS. / LITTLE GIRL** [ ] [2] Jan82

May 82. (7") *<02883>* **STILL THEY RIDE. / RAZA DEL SOL** [-] [19]

Aug 82. (7") *(A 2725)* **WHO'S CRYING NOW. / DON'T STOP BELIEVIN'** [46] [-]
(12") *(TA 2725)* – ('A'side) / The Journey story (14 best snips).

Oct 82. (7") *(A 2890)* **STONE IN LOVE. / ONLY SOLUTIONS** [ ] [-]

Feb 83. (lp/c) *(CBS/40 25261) <38504>* **FRONTIERS** [6] [2]
– Separate ways (worlds apart) / Send her my love / Chain reaction / After the fall / Faithfully / Edge of the blade / Troubled child / Back talk / Frontiers / Rubicon. *(cd-iss. 1988; CD 25261) (cd re-iss. Nov96 on 'Columbia'; 486663-2)*

Feb 83. (7"/12") *(A/+13 3077) <03513>* **SEPARATE WAYS (WORLDS APART). / FRONTIERS** [ ] [8]

Apr 83. (7") *<03840>* **FAITHFULLY. / FRONTIERS** [-] [12]

Apr 83. (7") *(A 3358)* **FAITHFULLY. / EDGE OF THE BLADE** [ ] [-]

Jul 83. (7") *<04004>* **AFTER THE FALL. / OTHER SOLUTIONS** [-] [23]

Jul 83. (7") *(A 3692)* **AFTER THE FALL. / RUBICON** [ ] [-]
(12"+=) *(TA 3692)* – Any way you want me / Don't stop believin'.

Sep 83. (7") *<04151>* **SEND HER MY LOVE. / CHAIN REACTION** [-] [ ]

—— (the band take on some solo projects, see further below)

Feb 85. (7") *(A 6058) <29090>* **ONLY THE YOUNG. / (B-side by Sammy Hagar)** [ ] [9] Jan85
(above songs from the film 'Vision Quest' on 'Geffen' records)

—— **PERRY, SCHON and CAIN** regrouped and added **RANDY JACKSON** – bass (ex-ZEBRA) / **LARRIE LONDIN** – drums

Apr 86. (7") *(A 7095) <05869>* **BE GOOD TO YOURSELF. / ONLY THE YOUNG** [ ] [9]
(12"+=) *(TA 7095)* – Any way you want it / Stone in love.
(d7"+=) *(DA 7095)* – After the fall / Rubicon.

May 86. (lp/c/cd) *(CBS/40/CD 26902) <39936>* **RAISED ON RADIO** [22] [4]
– Girl can't help it / Positive touch / Suzanne / Be good to yourself / Once you love somebody / Happy to give / Raised on radio / I'll be alright without you / It could have been you / The eyes of a woman / Why can't this night go on forever. *(re-iss. Apr91 on 'Columbia' cd/c; 467992-2/-4) (cd re-iss. Nov96 on 'Columbia'; 486664-2)*

Jul 86. (7") *(A 7265) <06134>* **SUZANNE. / ASK THE LONELY** [ ] [17] Jun86
(12"+=) *(TA 7265)* – Raised on radio.

—— (Aug'86) **MIKE BAIRD** – drums repl. LONDIN

Oct 86. (7") *(650116-7) <06302>* **GIRL CAN'T HELP IT. / IT COULD HAVE BEEN YOU** [ ] [17] Aug86

Dec 86. (7") *<06301>* **I'LL BE ALRIGHT WITHOUT YOU. / THE EYES OF A WOMAN** [-] [14]

Apr 87. (7") *<07043>* **WHY CAN'T THIS NIGHT GO ON FOREVER. / POSITIVE TOUCH** [-] [60]

— split early '87. CAIN and VALORY joined MICHAEL BOLTON. SCHON joined BAD ENGLISH in '89, then HARDLINE in '92 with ROLIE and SMITH.

NEAL SCHON / JAN HAMMER

collaboration with HAMMER – keyboards (solo)

C.B.S. Columbia

Nov 81. (lp/c) *(CBS/40 85355) <37600>* **UNTOLD PASSION** (instrumental) [ ] [ ] Oct81
– Wasting time / I'm talking to you / The ride / I'm down / Arc / It's alright / Hooked on love / On the beach / Untold passion.

Feb 83. (lp/c) *(CBS/40 25229) <38428>* **HERE TO STAY** [ ] [ ]
– No more lies / Don't stay away / (You think you're) So hot / Turnaround / Self defence / Long time / Time again / Sticks and stones / Peace of mind / Covered by midnight.

Mar 83. (7") *<03785>* **NO MORE LIES. / SELF DEFENCE** [-] [ ]

— **NEAL SCHON** collaborated next (May'84) on album 'THROUGH THE FIRE' with **SAMMY HAGAR, KENNY AARONSON & MIKE SHRIEVE.**

STEVE PERRY

C.B.S. Columbia

May 84. (7") *(A 4342) <04391>* **OH SHERRIE. / DON'T TELL ME WHY YOU'RE LEAVING** [ ] [3] Mar84
(12"+=) *(TA 4342)* – I believe.

May 84. (lp/c) *(CBS/40 25967) <39334>* **STREET TALK** [ ] [12] Apr84
– Oh Sherrie / I believe / Go away / Foolish heart / It's only love / She's mine / You should be happy / Running alone / Captured by the moment / Strung out.

Jul 84. (7") *(A 4638) <04496>* **SHE'S MINE. / YOU SHOULD BE HAPPY** [ ] [21] Jun84

Sep 84. (7") *<04598>* **STRUNG OUT. / CAPTURED BY THE MOMENT** [-] [40]

Jan 85. (7") *(A 6017) <04693>* **FOOLISH HEART. / IT'S ONLY LOVE** [ ] [18] Nov84

— STEVE PERRY released solo recordings between 88-89. In Aug'94, 'Columbia' issued his album 'FOR THE LOVE OF STRANGE MEDICINE' (it hit UK No.64), the record included US hits, 'YOU BETTER WAIT' and 'MISSING YOU'.

The STORM

ROLIE – vocals, keyboards / **ROSS VALORY** – bass / **STEVE SMITH** – drums) with **KEVIN CHALFANT** – vocals (ex-707) / **JOSH RAMOS** – guitar (ex-LE MANS)

East West Interscope

Oct 91. (c-s) *<98726>* **I'VE GOT A LOT TO LEARN ABOUT LOVE / GIMME LOVE** [-] [26]

Nov 91. (cd/c/lp) *<(7567 91741-2/-4/-1)>* **THE STORM** [ ] [ ]
– You got me waiting / I've got a lot to learn about love / In the raw / You're gonna miss me / Call me / Show me the way / I want you back / Still loving you / Touch and go / Gimme love / Take me away / Can't live without your love.

— **RON WIKSO** – drums repl. SMITH

not iss. Bulletproof

Jan 96. (cd) **EYE OF THE STORM** [-] [ ]

HARDLINE

NEAL SCHON – lead guitar, vocals / **JOHNNY SCHON** – vocals / **JOEY GIOELLI** – guitar / **TODD JENSEN** – bass (ex-DAVID LEE ROTH) / **DEAN CASTRONOVO** – drums (ex-BAD ENGLISH)

M.C.A. M.C.A.

May 92. (cd) *<(MCAD 10586)>* **DOUBLE ECLIPSE** [ ] [ ]
– Life's a bitch / Dr. love / Red car / Change of heart / Everything / Taking me down / Hot Cheri / Bad taste / Can't find my way / I'll be there / 31-91 / In the hands of time.

Jun 92. (c-s) *<54548>* **CAN'T FIND MY WAY / HOT CHERIE / TAKIN' ME DOWN / I'LL BE THERE** [-] [ ]

JOURNEY

re-formed the quintet in 1996:- **PERRY, SCHON, CAIN, VALORY + SMITH**

Columbia Columbia

Oct 96. (cd/c) *(485264-2/-4) <67514>* **TRIAL BY FIRE** [ ] [3]
– Message of love / One more / When you love a woman / If he should break your heart / Forever in blue / Castles burning / Don't be down on me baby / Still she cries / Colours of the spirit / When I think of you / Easy to fall / Can't tame the lion / It's just the rain / Trial by fire / Baby I'm leaving you. *(cd re-iss. Jan00; same)*

Oct 96. (c-s) *<78428>* **WHEN YOU LOVE A WOMAN / MESSAGE OF LOVE / OPEN ARMS** [-] [12]

— **DEAN CASTRONOVO** – drums; repl. SMITH

Apr 01. (cd) *(498479-2) <69864>* **ARRIVAL** [ ] [ ]
– Higher piece / All the way / Signs of life / All the things / Loved by you / Livin' to do / I got a reason / With your love / Lifetime of dreams / Live and breathe / Kiss me softly / I'm not that way / We will meet again.

– compilations, others, etc. –

on 'CBS' UK / 'Columbia' US, unless mentioned otherwise

Sep 80. (d-lp) *(CBS 22073) <36324>* **IN THE BEGINNING** (from first 3 albums) [ ] [ ] Jan80

Dec 82. (c-ep) *(40 2908)* **CASSETTE EP** [ ] [-]
– Don't stop believin' / Who's crying now / Open arms / Lovin' touchin' squeezin'.

Aug 82. (7") *<03133>* **OPEN ARMS. / THE PARTY'S OVER** [-] [ ]

Aug 82. (7") *<03134>* **DON'T STOP BELIEVIN'. / WHO'S CRYING NOW** [-] [ ]

Feb 83. (d-c) *(EPC-40 22150)* **INFINITY / NEXT** [-] [-]

Aug 87. (d-lp) *(CBSJ 241)* **FRONTIERS / ESCAPE** [ ] [-]

Nov 88. (lp/c/cd) *(463149-1/-4/-2) <44493>* **GREATEST HITS** [ ] [10]
– Only the young / Don't stop believin' / Wheel in the sky / Faithfully / I'll be alright with you / Any way you want it / Ask the lonely / Who's crying now / Separate ways (worlds apart) / Lights / Lovin', touchin', squeezin' / Open arms / Girl can't help it / Send her my love / Be good to yourself. *(cd re-iss. Apr96 & Apr00 on 'Columbia'; 463149-2)*

Jan 89. (7") *(654541-7)* **WHO'S CRYING NOW. / OPEN ARMS** [ ] [-]
(12"+=/cd-s+=) *(654541-6/-2)* – Suzanne / Don't stop believing.

— (now on 'Columbia' unless mentioned otherwise)

Dec 92. (t-cd/t-c) *(472810-2/-4) <48937>* **TIME 3** [ ] [90]
(re-iss. Apr98; C3K 65159)

Jan 93. (c-s) *<74842>* **LIGHTS (live) / (6 album excerpts)** [-] [74]

Apr 98. (cd/c) *(489703-2/-4) <69139>* **GREATEST HITS LIVE (live)** [ ] [ ]

Nov 00. (3xcd-box) *(492658-2)* **INFINITY / ESCAPE / FRONTIERS** [ ] [ ]

Mar 01. (cd) *Sony; <2416>* **THE JOURNEY CONTINUES . . .** [-] [ ]

JOY DIVISION

Formed: Salford, Manchester, England . . . mid'77 initially as The STIFF KITTENS by IAN CURTIS, BERNARD ALBRECHT, PETER HOOK and STEPHEN MORRIS. By the time they were ready to take the stage for the first time, the group were going under the WARSAW moniker, finally settling on JOY DIVISION later that year. A term used by the Nazis for Jewish prostitutes, the band had taken the name from the book, 'House Of Dolls'; unsurprisingly, they ran into a little media trouble, the press subsequently speculating about their supposedly fascistic tendencies and unfairly branding them little Adolfs. Particularly controversial was the track, 'AT A LATER DATE', included on the 'Virgin' various artists punk sampler, 'Short Circuit: Live At The Electric Circus'. A vinyl debut proper came with the limited EP, 'AN IDEAL FOR LIVING', although it was through manager Rob Gretton and a subsequent deal with the emerging 'Factory' records that JOY DIVISION's career really got off the ground. Their first recordings for the label were a couple of tracks, 'GLASS' and 'DIGITAL', featured on a 'Factory' sampler (in mid-'79, a further two tracks, 'AUTO-SUGGESTION' and 'FROM SAFETY TO WHERE', surfaced on the 'Fast' records compilation EP, 'Earcom 2'), while their legendary Martin Hannett-produced debut album, 'UNKNOWN PLEASURES' was finally released later that summer. Groundbreaking in its bass-heavy, skeletal sound and evocation of urban alienation, isolation and despair, the record ensured CURTIS's position as a latter day messiah of existential angst; while his lyrics trawled the underbelly of the human psyche with disturbing clarity, his sub-JIM MORRISON ruminations were a blueprint for every pasty-faced goth pretender of the next decade. Tony Wilson's faith in the band was such that he contributed his life savings of over £8,000 towards the album's cost, t~he 'Factory' supremo's investment rewarded as the record topped the indie charts and JOY DIVISION became the foremost post-punk cult act. Yet even as the hypnotic rhythms of sublime new single, 'TRANSMISSION', hinted at an equally compelling new direction, CURTIS's robotic contortions and trance-like stage presence were giving way to epileptic fits as the singer struggled to cope with the increasing demands of live work. Tragically, on the 18th May, 1980, depressed with the break-up of his marriage and his worsening illness, CURTIS hanged himself. Ironically, JOY DIVISION scored their first chart hit a month later with the seminal 'LOVE WILL TEAR US APART'; the loss of such a fiercely individual talent was underlined as the track suggested a singer (and indeed, band) at the very apex of their creative potential. CURTIS had actually recorded a full album's worth of material before his death, released that summer as 'CLOSER'; even more lyrically unsettling, the record's bleak vision nevertheless pre-empted rock's dancefloor embrace on the synth-laced likes of 'ISOLATION', as well as forming the basis for NEW ORDER's experiments in cross-genre innovation. The latter act were formed later that year from JOY DIVISION's ashes, while further CURTIS-era material was posthumously released in late '81 as 'STILL'. The band remain one of the most revered and certainly one of the most influential outfits to emerge from the punk 'revolution', the best of NEW ORDER's work an indication as to what musical heights JOY DIVISION might have scaled had CURTIS prolonged the battle with his personal demons.

Album rating: UNKNOWN PLEASURES (*10) / CLOSER (*10) / STILL part compilation/live (*8) / SUBSTANCE compilation (*9) / PERMANENT: JOY DIVISION 1995 remixes (*6)

IAN CURTIS (b.15 Jul'56, Macclesfield, England) – vocals / **BERNARD ALBRECHT** (b. BERNARD DICKEN, 4 Jan'56) – guitar, vocals / **PETER HOOK** (b.13 Feb'56, Salford, Manchester) – bass / **STEPHEN MORRIS** (b.28 Oct'57, Macclesfield) – drums

Enigma not iss.

Jun 78. (7"ep) *(PSS 139)* **AN IDEAL FOR LIVING** [ ] [-]
– An ideal for living / Warsaw / Leaders of men / No love lost / Failures. *(re-iss. Jul78 on 'Anonymous' 12"ep; ANON 1)*

Factory not iss.

Aug 79. (lp) *(FACT 10)* **UNKNOWN PLEASURES** [ ] [-]
– Disorder / Day of the lords / Candidate / Insight / New dawn fades / She's lost control / Shadowplay / Wilderness / Interzone / I remember nothing. *(re-dist.Jul80, hit No.71) (re-iss. Jul82; same) (c-iss.Nov84; FACT 10C) (cd-iss. Apr86; FACD 10) (re-iss. Jul93 on 'Centredate-London' cd/c; 520016-2) <US-iss.1989 on 'Qwest' lp/c/cd; 1-/4-/2-25840> (cd re-iss. Jan00; 3984 28223-2)*

Oct 79. (7") *(FAC 13)* **TRANSMISSION. / NOVELTY** [ ] [-]
(re-iss. Oct80 as 12"; FAC 13-12)

Mar 80. (7") *(SS 33-002)* **ATMOSPHERE. / DEAD SOULS** [-] [-] France
(above single released on 'Sordide Sentimentale' & now worth lots)

Jun 80. (7") *(FAC 23)* **LOVE WILL TEAR US APART. / THESE DAYS** [13] [-]
(re-iss. Oct80 as 12"+=; FAC 23-12) – ('A'version). *(re-iss. Oct83; same); hit UK No.19)*

Jul 80. (lp) *(FACT 25)* **CLOSER** [6] [-]
– Heart and soul / 24 hours / The eternal / Decades / Atrocity exhibition / Isolation / Passover / Colony / Means to an end. *(c-iss.Jul82; FACT 25C) (cd-iss. Apr86; FACD 25) (re-iss. Jul93 on 'Centredate-London' cd/c; 520015-2) <US-iss.1989 on 'Qwest' lp/c/cd; 1-/4/-2-25841> (cd re-iss. Sep99 on 'Factory Too'; 3984 28219-2)*

— After another fit of depression, IAN CURTIS hanged himself 18th May 1980. The others became NEW ORDER

– compilations, others, etc. –

Sep 80. (12") *Factory Benelux; (FACTUS 2)* **ATMOSPHERE. / SHE'S LOST CONTROL** [ ] [-]

Apr 81. (free 7"flexi) *Factory; (FAC 28)* **KOMAKINO. / INCUBATION** [-] [-]

May 81. (7"ep/12"ep; as WARSAW) *Enigma; (PSS 138)* **THE IDEAL BEGINNING** [ ] [-]
– Inside the line / Gutz / At a later date.

Oct 81. (d-lp) *Factory; (FACT 40)* **STILL (live & rare)** [5] [-]
– Exercise one / Ice age / The sound of music / Glass / The only mistake / Walked in line / The kill / Something must break / Dead souls / Sister Ray / Ceremony / Shadowplay / Means to an end / Passover / New dawn fades / Transmission / Disorder / Isolation / Decades / Digital. *(c-iss.Dec86; FACT 40C) (cd-iss. Mar90; FACD 40) (re-iss. Jul93 on 'Centredate-London' cd/c; 520014-2/-4) <US-iss.1989 on 'Qwest' lp/c/cd; 26495> (cd re-iss. Jan00 on 'Factory Too'; 3984 28222-2)*

Nov 86. (12"ep) *Strange Fruit; (SFPS 013)* **THE PEEL SESSIONS (31.1.79)** [ ] [-]
– Exercise one / Insight / She's lost control / Transmission. *(re-iss. Jul88 cd-ep; SFPSCD 013)*

Sep 87. (12"ep) *Strange Fruit; (SFPS 033)* **THE PEEL SESSIONS 2 (26.11.79)** [ ] [-]
– Love will tear us apart / 24 hours / Colony / The sound of music. *(re-iss. Jul88 cd-ep; SFPSCD 033)*

1987. (7"ep+book) *Stampa; (SCONIC 001)* **YOU'RE NO GOOD FOR ME / KOMAKINO / INCUBATION / INCUBATION (version)** [-] [-] Italy

Jun 88. (7") *Factory; (FAC 213-7)* **ATMOSPHERE. / THE ONLY MISTAKE** [34] [-]
(12"+=) *(FAC 213)* – The sound of music.
(cd-s) *(FACD 213)* – ('A'side) / Love will tear us apart / Transmission.

Jul 88. (lp/c/dat)(cd) *Factory; (FACT 250/+C/D)(FACD 250) / Qwest; <1-/4-/2-25747>* **SUBSTANCE** (The best of..) [7] [ ]
– She's lost control / Dead souls / Atmosphere / Love will tear us apart / Warsaw / Leaders of men / Digital / Transmission / Auto-suggestion. *(cd+=) – (7 extra tracks). (re-iss. Jul93 on 'Centredate-London' cd/c; 520 014-2/-4) (cd re-iss. Sep99 on 'Factory Too'; 3984 28224-2)*

Sep 90. (cd/c) *Strange Fruit; (SFR CD/MC 111)* **COMPLETE PEEL SESSIONS** [ ] [-]

Jun 95. (c-s) *London; (YOJC 1)* **LOVE WILL TEAR US APART (radio version) / ('A'-original version)** [19] [ ]
(12"+=/cd-s+=) *(YOJ T/CD 1)* – These days / Transmission.

Jun 95. (cd/c/d-lp) *London; (828 624-2/-4/-1) / Warners; <45979>* **PERMANENT: JOY DIVISION 1995** (remixes) [16] [ ] Aug95
– Love will tear us apart / Transmission / She's lost control / Shadow play / Day of the lords / Isolation / Passover / Heart and soul / 24 hours / These days / Novelty / Dead souls / The only mistake / Something must break / Atmosphere / Love will tear us apart (Permanent mix). *(cd re-iss. Sep99; 3984 28221-2)*

Jan 98. (4xcd-box) *London; (<828 968-2>)* **HEART AND SOUL** (all material) [70] [ ]
(re-iss. Sep99; 3984 29040-2)

Feb 98. (cd+book) *Sonic Book; (SB 10)* **ALL THE LYRICS** [ ] [-]

Jul 00. (cd) *Fractured; (FACD 260)* **PRESTON – THE WAREHOUSE 28/2/80 (live)** [ ] [ ]
(lp-iss.Oct00 on 'Get Back'; GET 69)

Aug 00. (cd) *Strange Fruit; (SFRSCD 094)* **THE COMPLETE RADIO ONE RECORDINGS** [ ] [ ]
(lp-iss.Apr01; SFRSCD 084)

Apr 01. (cd) *Fractured; (FACD 261)* **LES BAINS DOUCHES** [ ] [-]

JOYRIDER

Formed: Portadown, N.Ireland ... 1992 by PHIL WOOLSEY, CLIFF MITCHELL, SIMON HADDOCK and BUCK HAMILL. Signed to Dublin-based indie label, 'Blunt', they released a few singles in 1994 produced by ANDY CAIRNS (Therapy?). Akin to a cross between THERAPY? and TERRORVISION, their bouncy/punky hard-rock endeared them to A&M off-shoot 'Paradox' later that year. They released a string of EP's over the course of the next year, before finally unleashing a debut album, 'BE SPECIAL' in the Spring of '96. The record boasted a few hits, the biggest (and most annoying) being the near UK Top 20 cover of Jane Wiedlin's (ex-GO-GO's) 'RUSH HOUR'. Unfortunately the group had more than rush hour traffic to deal with when their tour van (complete with instruments) was blown up in London by the bomb disposal squad. Moving upstairs to 'A&M', they released a second set, 'SKID SOLO' (1997).

Album rating: BE SPECIAL (*6) / SKID SOLO (*6)

PHIL WOOLSEY – vocals, guitar / **CLIFF 'Mitch' MITCHEL** – guitar / **SIMON HADDOCK** – bass / **BUCK HAMILL** – drums

Blunt | not iss.

Apr 94. (7"pink-ep) *(BLUNT 003)* **JOYRIDER EP** [ ] [-]
– Dweeb king / Happy / In a car.

Aug 94. (7"ep) *(BLUNT 004)* **GETTING THAT JOKE. / GONE / ON A MISSION** [ ] [-]

Paradox | not iss.

Feb 95. (7"colrd-ep/cd-ep) *(PDOX/+D 001)* **SEVEN SISTERS EP** [ ] [-]
– Something new / Fear / They all hate me.

Mar 95. (7"colrd-ep) *(PDOX 002)* **IT MOVED. / GONE / E.T.U.** [ ] [-]
(cd-ep+=) *(PDOXD 002)* – Dweeb king.

May 95. (7"colrd-ep/cd-ep) *(PDOX/+D 004)* **SELF INFLICTION / WANTING IT. / THAT TIRED / KINDA LOSING IT** [ ] [-]

Nov 95. (7"ep/cd-ep) *(PDOX/+D 006)* **FABULAE / IN A CAR. / SPECIAL ONE / STICKS AND STONES** [ ] [-]

Feb 96. (7"ep/cd-ep) *(PDOX/+D 008)* **VEGETABLE ANIMAL MINERAL / ALL WE HAVE TO FEAR IS EACH OTHER. / WE'LL JUST DO IT / T&DA IN WHITE SOCKS** [ ] [-]

Mar 96. (cd/c/lp) *(PDOX CD/MC/LP 003)* **BE SPECIAL** [ ] [-]
– Fabulae / Strikes sparks everywhere / That tired / Said she to me / Bible blackbelt / I cursed you / Nobody home / Another skunk song / Vegetable animal mineral / I don't give in / Are you sure you're alright / Imagine dead language / Rush hour / All gone away. *(re-iss. Aug96; PDOX CD/MC 005)*

— (Jan'96) **CARL ALTY** – drums repl. BUC

May 96. (7") *(PDOX 011)* **ANOTHER SKUNK SONG. / LOST IN TIME** [ ] [-]
(cd-s+=) *(PDOXD 011)* – Lost in time / 50 blanks / More about yerself.

Jul 96. (7"ep/cd-ep) *(PDOX/+D 012)* **RUSH HOUR / WHAT YOU GET. / ANOTHER SKUNK SONG (acoustic) / BIBLE BLACK BELT (acoustic)** [22] [-]
(cd-ep) *(PDOXDX 012)* – ('A'side) / Fabulae (live) / Said she to me (live) / Animal vegetable mineral (live).

Sep 96. (7") *(PDOX 013)* **ALL GONE AWAY. / ONE TRICK PONY** [54] [-]
(cd-s+=) *(PDOXD 013)* – Over the edge / I can't decide.

A&M | not iss.

May 97. (cd/c) *(540740-2/-4)* **SKID SOLO** [ ] [-]
– Skid solo / Chop logic / What do you think of me / Learn the ropes / Whole reason / Confession / Mongoose / Tonight is stolen / Day in the sun / Growing pains / Hub of the north / Wise is nice / The devil you know / Hit for fun.

JUDAS FACTOR

Formed: New York, USA ... 1998 by ROB FISH alongside CHAD DZIEWIOR, JUSTIN FULLAM, LITTLE DAVE and JASON LEDERMAN. FISH had previously played in Krishnacore band 108, his disillusionment with the movement almost causing him to leave the business for good. Subsequently putting all his energies into The JUDAS FACTOR, he exorcised his demons on acclaimed debut album, 'BALLADS IN BLUE CHINA' (1999). Cathartic, ferocious and emotionally charged, the record consistently drew comparisons with WILL HAVEN and, by dint of its quieter moments, acoustic shambler ELLIOT SMITH. The 'KISS SUICIDE' mini-set followed in 2000, as did a European tour.

Album rating: BALLADS IN BLUE CHINA (*8) / KISS SUICIDE mini (*5)

ROB FISH – vocals (ex-108) / **CHAD DZIEWIOR** – guitar / **JUSTIN FULLHAM** – guitar / **LITTLE DAVE** – bass / **JASON LEDERMAN** – drums

Revelation | Revelation

May 99. (lp/cd) *<(REV 078/+CD)>* **BALLADS IN BLUE CHINA** [ ] [ ] Apr99
– Beauty mark / That beautiful old Victorian bathtub / As I lie down to die / Essay / Will you wait up for me? / Choose your poison / My favourite stranger / If you are going to kill then murder / Re-invent / Intangibles / Stealing away / The last song.

Apr 00. (m-lp/m/cd) *<(REV 092/+CD)>* **KISS SUICIDE** [ ] [ ]
– Kiss suicide / Safety net / One fine day / Music without person / When we learn to love ourselves / November 20, 1999.

JUDAS PRIEST

Formed: Birmingham, England ... 1969 by KK DOWNING and IAN HILL. In 1971, they completed the line-up with vocalist AL ATKINS – who named the band after a BOB DYLAN track, 'The Ballad Of Frankie Lee And Judas Priest' – and drummer JOHN ELLIS; the latter was replaced by ALAN MOORE then CHRIS CAMPBELL. In 1973, both CAMPBELL and ATKINS bailed out (the latter went solo in the 90's releasing 'Victim Of Changes') as the 'PRIEST recruited singer ROB HALFORD and drummer JOHN HINCH. Three years later, with a few hundred gigs behind them, they brought in second guitarist GLENN TIPTON. Signed to 'Decca' off-shoot label 'Gull', they unleashed a debut album, 'ROCKA ROLLA', the same year. The record made little impact and after replacing HINCH with the returning ALAN MOORE, the band surfaced again in '76 with the excellent 'SAD WINGS OF DESTINY'. Following a resoundingly triumphant appearance at that year's Reading Festival, they signed to 'C.B.S.' in early '77. They soon had a UK Top 30 album with the ROGER GLOVER (Deep Purple)-produced 'SIN AFTER SIN', another metal masterpiece which included an unlikely, but effective cover of Joan Baez's 'DIAMONDS AND RUST'. While the leather clad JUDAS PRIEST weren't exactly original in their steadfast adherence to the leaden riffing and helium overdose of heavy metal, they helped to shape the genre's increasing preoccupation with all things grim 'n' nasty. 'STAINED CLASS' (1978), another Top 30 UK album, proferred such lyrical delights as 'SAINTS IN HELL', 'SAVAGE' and 'BEYOND THE REALMS OF DEATH', plus a cover of SPOOKY TOOTH's 'BETTER BY YOU, BETTER THAN ME', the record later having serious repercussions for the band (see below). Coming at the height of the NWOBHM explosion, 'BRITISH STEEL' (1980) was the band's biggest critical and commercial success to date, the Top 20 success of the 'LIVING AFTER MIDNIGHT' and 'BREAKING THE LAW' singles showing the more accessible, hook-driven face of the band. This was to be one of the most fertile periods of the 'PRIEST's career with a trio of consistent Top 20 albums; 'POINT OF ENTRY' (1981), 'SCREAMING FOR

VENGEANCE' (1982) and 'DEFENDERS OF THE FAITH' (1984) were all testosterone-saturated howlers, the kind of British metal that just doesn't exist anymore. The latter housed the PMRC-baiting 'EAT ME ALIVE', securing the band's position as perceived deviant enemy of the nation's lank-haired youth alongside the equally wholesome W.A.S.P. Late in 1985, two of their fans shot themselves while listening to a track off the 'STAINED CLASS' album, prompting the boys' parents to sue both JUDAS PRIEST and their label, 'Columbia'. They alleged the record contained subliminal satanic messages hidden in the lyrics, thus forcing the boys to commit suicide. This fiasco finally got to court in July '90, the judge ruling against the dead boys' parents, although he did fine the label a 5-figure sum for withholding the master tapes!!? Despite the controversy, fans were less enamoured with 'TURBO' (1986), PRIEST's attempts at guitar synthesized innovation cutting no ice with the band's metal diehards. 'RAM IT DOWN' (1988) was a return to harder fare while the band underwent a critical rebirth of sorts with the thrash-y 'PAINKILLER' (1990), their status acknowledged as grandaddies of heavy metal and a glaring influence on the likes of METALLICA and SLAYER. ROB HALFORD has since left the band after forming side-project, FIGHT, the group soon turning into a full-time affair. 'PRIEST returned in 1997 with a new frontman, the cornily-monikered "RIPPER" OWENS lending his eardrum rupturing shriek over the tuneless assault of the poorly-received comeback set, 'JUGULATOR'. • **Songwriters:** TIPTON, HALFORD & DOWNING on most, except extra covers; THE GREEN MANALISHI (Fleetwood Mac) / JOHNNY B. GOODE (Chuck Berry).

Album rating: ROCKA ROLLA (*2) / SAD WINGS OF DESTINY (*8) / SIN AFTER SIN (*7) / STAINED CLASS (*6; recommended only to those without access to a gun, a bazooka, a tank or any tactical nuclear weapon) / KILLING MACHINE (*6) / UNLEASHED IN THE EAST (*7) / BRITISH STEEL (*8) / POINT OF ENTRY (*4) / SCREAMING FOR VENGEANCE (*8) / DEFENDERS OF THE FAITH (*6) / TURBO (*5) / PRIEST . . . LIVE! (*6) / RAM IT DOWN (*6) / PAINKILLER (*8) / METAL WORKS compilation (*8) / JUGULATOR (*3) / MELTDOWN LIVE '98 (*4)

ROB HALFORD (b.25 Aug'51, Walsall) – vocals; repl. ALAN ATKINS / **KK DOWNING** (b. KENNETH, 27 Oct'51, West Midlands) – guitars / **GLENN TIPTON** (b.25 Oct'48, West Midlands) – guitar, vocals (ex-FLYING HAT BAND) / **IAN HILL** (b.20 Jan'52, West Midlands) – bass / **JOHN HINCH** – drums; repl. CHRIS CAMPBELL who'd repl. ALAN MOORE who'd repl. JOHN ELLIS

Gull Janus

Aug 74. (7") *(GULS 6)* **ROCKA ROLLA. / NEVER SATISFIED** [ ] [-]

Sep 74. (lp) *(GULP 1005)* **ROCKA ROLLA** [ ] [-]
– One for the road / Rocka rolla / Winter / Deep freeze / Winter retreat / Cheater / Never satisfied / Run of the mill / Dying to meet you / Caviar and meths. *(re-iss. Sep77; same)* <US-iss.Oct82 on 'Visa'; 7001> *(re-iss. Nov85 on 'Fame' lp/c; FA41 3137-2/-4) (cd-iss. Nov87 on 'Line'; LICD 900101) (cd-iss. Mar93 on 'Repertoire'; RR 4305) (cd re-iss. Aug98 on 'Snapper'; SMMCD 562)*

— **ALAN MOORE** – drums (who had been 1971 member) returned to repl. HINCH

Mar 76. (7") *(GULS 31)* **THE RIPPER. / ISLAND OF DOMINATION** [ ] [-]

Apr 76. (lp) *(GULP 1015)* <7019> **SAD WINGS OF DESTINY** [ ] [ ]
– Prelude / Tyrant / Genocide / Epitaph / Island of domination / Victim of changes / The ripper / Epitaph / Dreamer deceiver. *(pic-lp.Sep77; PGULP 1015) (re-iss. 1984 on 'Line' white-lp; LILP 4.00112) (cd-iss. Nov87; LICD 9.00112) (re-iss. cd May95 on 'Repertoire';) (cd re-iss. Aug98 on 'Snapper'; SMMCD 562)*

— **SIMON PHILLIPS** – drums repl. MOORE

C.B.S. Columbia

Apr 77. (7") *(CBS 5222)* **DIAMONDS AND RUST. / DISSIDENT AGGRESSOR** [ ] [-]

Apr 77. (lp/c) *(CBS/40 82008)* <34587> **SIN AFTER SIN** [23] [ ]
– Sinner / Diamonds and rust / Starbreaker / Last rose of summer / Let us prey / Call for the priest – Raw deal / Here come the tears / Dissident aggressor. *(re-iss. Mar81; CBS 32005) (re-iss. cd.Nov93 on 'Sony Collectors'; 983286-2) (cd re-iss. Feb97 on 'Epic'; 474684-2)*

— **LES BINKS** – drums repl. PHILLIPS

Jan 78. (7") *(CBS 6077)* **BETTER BY YOU, BETTER BY ME. / INVADER** [ ] [-]

Feb 78. (lp/c) *(CBS/40 82430)* <35296> **STAINED CLASS** [27] [ ]
– Exciter / White heat, red hot / Better by you, better by me / Stained class / Invader / Saints in Hell / Savage / Beyond the realms of death / Heroes end. *(re-iss. Nov81; CBS 32075) (re-iss. May91 on 'Columbia' cd/c; CD/40 32075)*

Sep 78. (7") *(CBS 6719)* **EVENING STAR. / STARBREAKER** [ ] [-]

Nov 78. (red-lp/c) *(CBS/40 83135)* <36179> **KILLING MACHINE** [32] [ ]
<US-title 'HELL BENT FOR LEATHER'>
– Delivering the goods / Rock forever / Evening star / Hell bent for leather / Take on the world / Burnin' up / Killing machine / Running wild / Before the dawn / Evil fantasies. *(re-iss. red-lp.Sep82; CBS 32218)*

Oct 78. (7") *(CBS 6794)* **BEFORE THE DAWN. / ROCK FOREVER** [ ] [ ]

Jan 79. (7") *(CBS 6915)* **TAKE ON THE WORLD. / STARBREAKER (live)** [ ] [14]
(12"+=) *(CBS12 6915)* – White heat red hot (live).

Apr 79. (7") *(CBS 7312)* **EVENING STAR. / BEYOND THE REALMS OF DEATH** [53] [ ]
(12"clear+=) *(CBS12 7312)* – The green Manalishi.

May 78. (7") <11000> **ROCK FOREVER. / THE GREEN MANALISHI (WITH THE TWO-PRONGED CROWN)** [-] [ ]

Sep 79. (lp/c) *(CBS/40 83852)* <36179> **UNLEASHED IN THE EAST (live)** [10] [70]
– Exciter / Running wild / Sinner / The ripper / The green manalishi (with the two-pronged crown) / Diamonds and rust / Victim of changes / Genocide / Tyrant. *(free 7"w.a.)* **ROCK FOREVER / HELL BENT FOR LEATHER. / BEYOND THE REALMS OF DEATH** *(cd-iss. 1988; CD 83852) (re-iss. May94 on 'Columbia' cd/c; 468604-2/-4)*

Dec 79. (7") <11135> **DIAMONDS AND RUST (live). / STARBREAKER (live)** [-] [ ]

— **DAVE HOLLAND** – drums repl. BINKS

Mar 80. (7") *(CBS 8379)* **LIVING AFTER MIDNIGHT. / DELIVERING THE GOODS (live)** [12] [-]
(12"+=) *(CBS12 8379)* – Evil fantasies (live).

Apr 80. (lp/c) *(CBS/40 84160)* <36443> **BRITISH STEEL** [4] [34]
– Rapid fire / Metal gods / Breaking the law / Grinder / United / You don't have to be old to be wise / Living after midnight / The rage / Steeler. *(re-iss. Jan84 lp/c; CBS/40 32412) (cd-iss. 1988; CD 32412) (cd re-iss. Jun94 on 'Sony'; 982725-2)*

May 80. (7") <11308> **LIVING AFTER MIDNIGHT. / METAL GODS** [-] [ ]

May 80. (7") *(CBS 8644)* **BREAKING THE LAW. / METAL GODS** [12] [ ]

Aug 80. (7") *(CBS 8897)* <11396> **UNITED. / GRINDER** [26] [ ]

Feb 81. (7") *(CBS 9520)* **DON'T GO. / SOLAR ANGELS** [51] [-]

Feb 81. (lp/c) *(CBS/40 84834)* <37052> **POINT OF ENTRY** [14] [39]
– Heading out to the highway / Don't go / Hot rockin' / Turning circles / Desert plains / Solar angels / You say yes / All the way / Troubleshooter / On the run. *(cd-iss. Apr01 on 'Columbia'; 502132-2)*

Apr 81. (7") *(A 1153)* **HOT ROCKIN' / BREAKING THE LAW (live)** [60] [-]
(12") *(A12 1153)* – ('A'side) / Steeler / You don't have to be old to be wise.

Apr 81. (7") <02083> **HEADING OUT TO THE HIGHWAY. / ROCK FOREVER** [-] [ ]

Jul 82. (lp/c) *(CBS/40 85941)* <38160> **SCREAMING FOR VENGEANCE** [11] [17]
– The hellion / Electric eye / Riding on the wind / Bloodstone / (Take these) Chains / Pain and pleasure / Screaming for vengeance / You've got another thing comin' / Fever / Devil's child. *(re-iss. Feb86 lp/c; CBS/40 32712)*

Aug 82. (7"/7"pic-d) *(A/+11 2611)* **YOU'VE GOT ANOTHER THING COMIN'. / EXCITER (live)** [66] [-]

Oct 82. (7") <03168> **YOU'VE GOT ANOTHER THING COMIN'. / DIAMONDS AND RUST** [-] [67]

Oct 82. (7") *(A 2822)* **(TAKE THESE) CHAINS. / JUDAS PRIEST AUDIO FILE** [ ] [ ]

Jan 84. (7") *(A 4054)* **FREEWHEEL BURNING. / BREAKING THE LAW** [42] [-]
(12"+=) *(TA 4054)* – You've got another thing comin'.

Jan 84. (lp/c) *(CBS/40 25713)* <39219> **DEFENDERS OF THE FAITH** [19] [18]
– Freewheel burning / Jawbreaker / Rock hard ride free / The sentinel / Love bites / Eat me alive / Some heads are gonna roll / Night comes down / Heavy duty / Defenders of the faith. *(cd-iss. Jul84; CD 25713)*

Feb 84. (7") <04371> **SOME HEADS ARE GONNA ROLL. / BREAKING THE LAW (live)** [-] [ ]

Mar 84. (7") *(A 4298)* **SOME HEADS ARE GONNA ROLL. / THE GREEN MANALISHI (WITH THE TWO-PRONGED CROWN)** [ ] [-]
(12"+=) *(TA 4298)* – Jawbreaker.

Apr 84. (7") <04436> **JAWBREAKER. / LOVE BITES** [-] [ ]

Apr 86. (lp/c/cd) *(CBS/40/CD 26641)* <40158> **TURBO** [33] [17]
– Turbo lover / Locked in / Private property / Parental guidance / Rock you all around the world / Out in the cold / Wild night, hot and crazy days / Hot for love / Reckless. *(re-iss. Feb89 lp/c/cd; 463365-1/-4/-2)*

Apr 86. (7") *(A 7048)* **TURBO LOVER. / HOT FOR LOVE** [ ] [-]

May 86. (7") *(A 7144)* **LOCKED IN. / RECKLESS** [ ] [-]
(ext.12"+=) *(QTA 7144)* – Desert plains (live) / Free wheel burning (live).

May 86. (7") <05856> **LOCKED IN. / HOT FOR LOVE** [-] [ ]

Aug 86. (7") <06142> **TURBO LOVER. / RESTLESS** [-] [ ]

Nov 86. (7") <06281> **PARENTAL GUIDANCE. / ROCK YOU AROUND THE WORLD** [-] [ ]

Jun 87. (d-lp/c/cd) *(450639-1/-4/-2)* <40794> **PRIEST . . . LIVE! (live)** [47] [38]
– Out in the cold / Heading out to the highway / Metal gods / Breaking the law / Love bites / Some heads are gonna roll / The sentinel / Private property / Rock you all around the world / Electric eye / Turbo lover / Free wheel burning / Parental guidance / Living after midnight / You've got another thing comin'. *(cd+=)* – Shout – Oh yeah!

Atlantic Columbia

Apr 88. (7") *(A 9114)* <89114> **JOHNNY B. GOODE. / ROCK YOU ALL AROUND THE WORLD (live)** [64] [ ]
(12"+=) *(AT 9114)* – Turbo lover (live).
(3"cd-s++=) *(A 9114CD)* – Living after midnight (live).

May 88. (lp/c/cd) *(461108-1/-4/-2)* **RAM IT DOWN** [24] [31]
– Ram it down / Heavy metal / Love zone / Come and get it / Hard as iron / Blood red skies / I'm a rocker / Johnny B. Goode / Love you to death / Monsters of rock.

— **SCOTT TRAVIS** – drums (ex-RACER-X) repl. HOLLAND

C.B.S. Columbia

Sep 90. (7"/c-s) *(656273-7/-4)* **PAINKILLER. / UNITED** [74] [ ]
(12"+=/cd-s+=) *(656273-6/-2)* – Better by you, better than me.

Sep 90. (cd/c/lp) *(467290-2/-4/-1)* <46891> **PAINKILLER** [24] [26]
– Painkiller / Hell patrol / All guns blazing / Leather rebel / Metal meltdown / Night crawler / Between the hammer and the anvil / A touch of evil / Battle hymn (instrumental) / One shot at glory.

Columbia Columbia

Mar 91. (7"/7"sha-pic-d/c-s) *(656589-7/-0/-4)* **A TOUCH OF EVIL. / BETWEEN THE HAMMER AND THE ANVIL** [58] [ ]
(12"+=/cd-s+=) *(656589-6/-2)* – You've got another thing comin' (live).

— In Oct'92, HALFORD left after already forming FIGHT in 1991, taking with him SCOTT TRAVIS.

Apr 93. (7"/c-s) *(659097-7/-4)* **NIGHT CRAWLER (Edit) / BREAKING THE LAW** [63] [ ]
(cd-s+=) *(659097-2)* – Living after midnight.

Apr 93. (d-cd/d-c/t-lp) *(473050-2/-4/-1)* <53932> **METAL WORKS '73-'93** (compilation) [37] [ ]
– The hellion / Electric eye / Victim of changes / Painkiller / Eat me alive / Devil's child / Dissident aggressor / Delivering the goods / Exciter / Breaking the law / Hell bent for leather / Blood red skies / Metal gods / Before the dawn / Turbo lover / Ram it down / Metal meltdown/ / Screaming for vengeance / You've got another thing comin' / Beyond the realms of death / Solar angels / Bloodstone / Desert plains / Wild nights, hot & crazy days / Heading out to the highway / Living after midnight / A touch of evil / The rage / Night comes down / Sinner / Freewheel burning / Night crawler.

— **"RIPPER" OWENS** – vocals; completed the line-up

S.P.V. C.M.C.

Nov 97. (cd/c/lp) *(SPV 085 1878-2/-4/-1)* <86224> **JUGULATOR** [ ] [82]
– Jugulator / Blood stained / Dead meat / Death row / Decapitate / Burn in hell / Brain dead / Abductors / Bullet train / Cathedral spires.

Oct 98. (d-cd) *(SPV 0891954-2)* <86261> **MELTDOWN (live '98)** [ ] [ ]

– The hellion / Electric eye / Metal gods / Grinder / Rapid fire / Blood stained / The sentinnel / Touch of evil / Burn in hell / The ripper / Bullet train / Beyond the realms of death / Death row / Metal meltdown / Night crawler / Abductors / Victim of changes / Diamonds and rust / Breaking the law / The green manalishi (with the two-pronged crown) / Painkiller / You've got another thing comin' / Hell bent for leather / Living after midnight.

Jun 01. (cd-s) *(0567245-2)* **MACHINE MAN / SUBTERFUGE / BURN IN HELL (video)** ☐ -

– compilations, etc. –

Feb 78. (pic-lp/lp) *Gull; (P+/GULP 1026)* **THE BEST OF JUDAS PRIEST** (early work) ☐ -
(cd-iss. May87 +=; GUCD 1026) – (2 extra tracks).

Aug 80. (7") *Gull; (GULS 71)* **THE RIPPER. / VICTIMS OF CHANGE** ☐ -
(12"+=) *(GUL 71-12)* – Never satisfied.

Jun 83. (12"white) *Gull; (GULS 76-12)* **TYRANT. / ROCKA ROLLA / GENOCIDE** ☐ -

Jan 83. (c-ep) *C.B.S.; (A40 3067)* **CASSETTE EP** ☐ -
– Breaking the law / Living after midnight / Take on the world / United.

Aug 83. (d-c) *C.B.S.; (22161)* **SIN AFTER SIN / STAINED GLASS** ☐ -

Sep 83. (7"ep/c-ep) *(7SR/ 5018)* **6 TRACK HITS** ☐ -
– Sinner / Exciter / Hell bent for leather / The ripper / Hot rockin' / The green manalishi.

Aug 86. (pic-lp) *Shanghai; (PGLP 1026)* **JUDAS PRIEST** ☐ -

Nov 87. (cd) *Line; (LICD 900414)* **HERO HERO** - - German
(re-iss. 1988 on 'Gull' c/lp; *ZC+/GUD 2005-6) (cd re-iss. Jul95 on 'Connoisseur'; CSAPCD 119)*

Feb 89. (7") *Old Gold; (OG 9864)* **LIVING AFTER MIDNIGHT. / BREAKING THE LAW** ☐ -

May 89. (lp/c/cd) *Castle; (CCS LP/MC/CD 213)* **THE COLLECTION** ☐ -
– (first two albums)

Mar 93. (3xcd-box) *Columbia; (468328-2)* **BRITISH STEEL / SCREAMING FOR VENGEANCE / STAINED GLASS** ☐ -

Apr 97. (cd) *Columbia; (487242-2)* **LIVING AFTER MIDNIGHT** ☐ -

Jun 98. (cd) *Ranch Life; (CRANCH 3)* **CONCERT CLASSICS (live)** ☐ -

Nov 98. (3xcd-box) *Columbia; (492657-2)* **BRITISH STEEL / POINT OF ENTRY / SCREAMING FOR VENGEANCE** ☐ -

Jan 99. (cd) *Columbia; (493008-2) / Sony; <7713>* **LIVE AND RARE** ☐ ☐ Sep99

Jul 99. (cd) *Eureka; (EURCD 401)* **TYRANT (THE ORIGINAL MASTERS)** ☐ -

Feb 00. (d-cd) *Snapper; (<SMDCD 273>)* **GENOCIDE** ☐ ☐

Feb 01. (cd) *Koch; <8071>* **THE BEST OF JUDAS PRIEST** - ☐

JUNKIE XL

Formed: by Dutch DJ, TOM HOLKENBORG, the latest addition to the ever evolving dance-metal scene (alongside The PRODIGY, etc). He had previously played in a plethora of groups including NERVE, an industrial rock outfit best known for their seminal 'CANCER OF CHOICE' (1993) album. Enlisting the awesome talents of FEAR FACTORY guitarist, DINO CAZARES, TOM went into the studio to record JUNKIE XL's 1997 'Roadrunner' debut, 'SATURDAY TEENAGE KICK' (TOM/JUNKIE XL had produced tracks on FEAR FACTORY's 'Remanufacture' set while also working with DOG EAT DOG). Unfortunately, TOM ran into some trouble when BOB MOULD (ex-HUSKER) objected to him sampling a song of his, with 8,000 copies of the album subsequently withdrawn. The techno terrorist subsequently sought out a band for live work including RUDE BOY from URBAN DANCE SQUAD. Released intially on 'Roadrunner' in the Netherlands, their sophomore set, 'BIG SOUNDS OF THE DRAGS', was finally issued in Britain summer 2000.

Album rating: SATURDAY TEENAGE KICK (*7) / BIG SOUNDS OF THE DRAGS (*5)

TOM HOLKENBORG – vocals, samples, etc. / **DINO CAZARES** – guitars (of FEAR FACTORY)

Roadrunner Medcom

Oct 97. (12"/cd-s) *(RR 2263-6/-3)* **BILLY CLUB (mixes; radio / Toxik Twins / Rotten beats / Def beat)** ☐ -
(re-iss. Aug98; same)

Oct 97. (cd/d-lp) *(RR 8792-2/-1) <924>* **SATURDAY TEENAGE KICK** ☐ ☐ Dec97
– Underachievers / Billy Club / No remorse / Metrolike / X-panding limits / War / Saturday teenage kick / Dealing with the roster / Fight / Melange / Def beat / Future in computer hell. *(re-iss. Sep98; same)*

—— added for live work, **RENE** – guitar / **BAS** – drums / **FRANKIE** – DJ / **RUDE BOY** (b. Patrick REMINGTON) – rapper (ex-URBAN DANCE SQUAD)

Mar 98. (12") *(RR 2245-6)* **SATURDAY TEENAGE KICKS. / 100 / BUSTIN' LIKE THIS / FIGHT (live)** ☐ -
(cd-s) *(RR 2245-3)* – (first 2 tracks) / No remorse (live) / ('A'live).
(cd-s) *(RR 2245-9)* – ('A'mixes) / Bustin' like this (live) / Fight (live).

Manifesto not iss.

Jul 00. (c-s/12"/cd-s) *(FES MC/X/CD 71)* **ZEROTONINE (mixes). / DISCO 2000** ☐ -

Jul 00. (cd) *(542799-2)* **BIG SOUNDS OF THE DRAGS** ☐ -
– Check your basic groove / Synasthesia / Power of big slacks / Zerotonine / Love like a razorblade / Legion / Disco 2000 / Future in computer hell (part 2) / Bon voyage / Power of big slacks (reprise) / Gettin' lost / Black Jack / Next plateau.

Mostiko not iss.

Aug 00. (12") *(MO 2081-6)* **ZEROTONINE (slacker remix). / FUTURE IN COMPUTER HELL (part 2)** ☐ -

JUNKYARD

Formed: Los Angeles, California, USA . . . late 80's by Texans DAVID ROACH and CHRIS GATES (ex-BIG BOYS), plus BRIAN BAKER (from D.C. hardcore acts, DAG NASTY, GOVERNMENT ISSUE and MINOR THREAT), PATRICK MUZINGO and CLAY ANTHONY. Their debut album for 'Geffen', the eponymous 'JUNKYARD' (1989), saw the group opt for a sizzling platter of Southern-fried, metallic roots boogie, albeit with a serrated punk edge. From the opening blitz of 'BLOOZE' to the SKYNYRD-esque beauty of 'SIMPLE MAN' (not that one!), the record, which nearly made the US Top 100, proved to be one of the most enjoyable debuts of the year. 'SIXES, SEVENS AND NINES' (1991) carried on in much the same fashion, if anything even more bluesy than the first album. Despite encouraging reviews and considerable press interest, however, there didn't appear to be a market for such fare and the band were unfortunately dropped by 'Geffen'.

Album rating: JUNKYARD (*7) / SIXES, SEVENS AND NINES (*6) / WE'RE TRYING TO PRACTICE demos (*3)

DAVID ROACH – vocals / **CHRIS GATES** – guitar (ex-BIG BOYS) / **BRIAN BAKER** – guitar (ex-DAG NASTY, ex-GOVERNMENT ISSUE, ex-MINOR THREAT) / **CLAY ANTHONY** – bass / **PAT MUZINGO** – drums

Elektra Geffen

Apr 89. (lp/c/cd) *(WX 266/+C)(924227-2) <24227>* **JUNKYARD** ☐ ☐
– Blooze / Hot rod / Simple man / Shot in the dark / Hollywood / Life sentence / Long way home / Can't hold back / Texas / Hands off. *(re-iss. Aug91 on 'Geffen' cd/c; GEF D/C 24227)*

Jun 89. (7") *<22823>* **HOLLYWOOD. / LONG WAY HOME** - ☐

Jan 90. (c-s) *<19949>* **SIMPLE MAN /** - ☐

Geffen Geffen

May 91. (lp/c/cd) *<(GEF/+C/D 24327)>* **SIXES, SEVENS AND NINES** ☐ ☐
– Back on the streets / All the time in the world / Give the devil his due / Slippin' away / Nowhere to go but down / Misery loves company / Throw it all away / Killing time / Clean the dirt / Lost in the city.

—— folded early in 1992

– compilations, etc. –

Jan 00. (cd) *Cleopatra; <CLEO 799>* **WE'RE TRYING TO PRACTICE** - ☐
– Life sentence / Hot rod / Long way home / Can't hold back / Take me home / Simple man / Blooze / Misery / Hollywood / Hallelujah, I love her so / Shot in the dark / Texas.

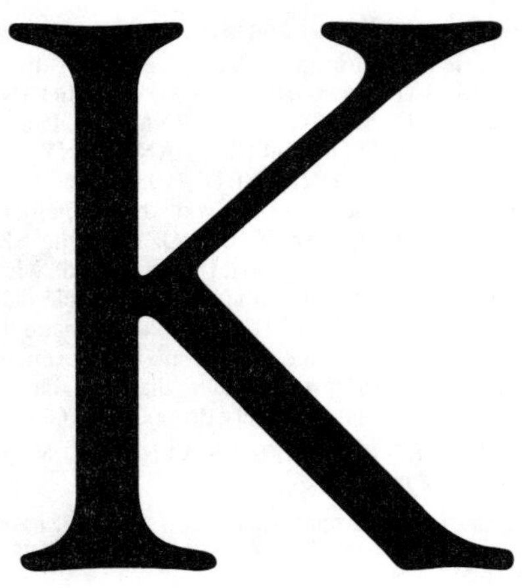

KANSAS

Formed: Topeka, Kansas, USA . . . 1970 initially as WHITE CLOVER, by KERRY LIVGREN, DAVE HOPE and PHIL EHART. With the addition of classically trained ROBBY STEINHARDT, RICH WILLIAMS and frontman STEVE WALSH, the group adopted the KANSAS moniker during 1972. Two years of constant touring later, they signed to 'Kirshner' (the new label set up by industry guru, Don Kirshner) and hit the US Top 200 with their eponymous debut set. A windswept American answer to the British art-rock scene of the early 70's, KANSAS combined progressive, harmony laden muscle (somewhat akin to the likes of BOSTON or STYX) with ambitiously intricate 'suites'. Throughout the 70's, the band enjoyed increasing commercial success, the Jeff Glixman-produced 'LEFTOVERTURE' (1976) taking them into the US Top 5 for the first time on the back of the grandiose Top 10 smash, 'CARRY ON WAYWARD SON. For many fans, the subsequent triple-platinum 'POINT OF KNOW RETURN' (1977) marked the peak of the group's career, its string-laden pseudo-classical pretensions providing another Top 10 hit with 'DUST IN THE WIND'. KANSAS' more indulgent tendencies were glaringly evident on the rambling live set, 'TWO FOR THE SHOW' (1978), although as the 70's turned into the 80's, the group increasingly pursued a more accessible approach. Disillusioned with this direction, WALSH had already recorded a solo debut, 'SCHEMER-DREAMER' in 1980, eventually leaving the band following the 'AUDIO-VISIONS' (1980) set and forming a harder rocking outfit, STREETS. LIVGREN, meanwhile, had become a born-again Christian, the inspiration for his solo debut, 'SEEDS OF CHANGE' (1980). With JOHN ELEFANTE now in place as frontman, KANSAS cut a further couple of albums, 'VINYL CONFESSIONS' (1982) and 'DRASTIC MEASURES' (1983), before splitting in late '83. While LIVGREN and ELEFANTE both went on to successful careers in the Christian music field, EHART and WILLIAMS subsequently reformed KANSAS with former vocalist STEVE WALSH, fellow ex-STREETS man, BILLY GREER, and guitar maestro STEVE MORSE. Now signed to 'M.C.A.', the new improved KANSAS enjoyed middling chart success with 'POWER' (1986), an album which bore the stamp of WALSH's heavier work with STREETS. A follow-up set, 'IN THE SPIRIT OF THINGS' (1988), was a commercial failure, however, and the band found themselves without a record deal. Ploughing on, they re-introduced violin to their sound in 1991 courtesy of DAVID RAGSDALE, MORSE having left by the independently released concert set, 'LIVE AT THE WHISKY' (1993). A belated studio set, 'FREAKS OF NATURE' (1995) finally appeared in summer '95, KANSAS retaining a core fanbase despite their absence from the charts. Things became more interesting in 1998 with the release of 'ALWAYS NEVER THE SAME', an album recorded at Abbey Road and utilising the LONDON SYMPHONY ORCHESTRA. Hardly an original idea but one which breathes new life into KANSAS chestnuts alongside a trio of competent new tracks and a bombastic cover of The Beatles' 'ELEANOR RIGBY'. 'SOMEWHERE TO ELSEWHERE' (2000), meanwhile, heralded a new decade and a new millennium with an album recorded by the original line-up. Based on a WWII concept, the record captured at least some of the band's early flair and dynamism with a clutch of near-10 minute epics tailor made for longtime fans.

Album rating: KANSAS (*6) / SONG FOR AMERICA (*6) / MASQUE (*5) / LEFTOVERTURE (*7) / POINT OF KNOW RETURN (*6) / TWO FOR THE SHOW (*5) / MONOLITH (*6) / AUDIO-VISIONS (*6) / VINYL CONFESSIONS (*5) / DRASTIC MEASURES (*4) / THE BEST OF KANSAS compilation (*7) / POWER (*5) / IN THE SPIRIT OF THINGS (*5) / LIVE AT THE WHISKY (*2) / FREAKS OF NATURE (*3) / ALWAYS NEVER THE SAME (*4) / SOMEWHERE TO ELSEWHERE (*5)

STEVE WALSH (b.1951, St. Joseph, Missouri) – vocals, keyboards, synthesizer / **KERRY LIVGREN** (b.18 Sep'49) – guitar, piano, synthesizer / **ROBBY STEINHARDT** (b.1951, Mississippi) – violin / **RICH WILLIAMS** (b.1951) – guitar / **DAVE HOPE** (b. 7 Oct'49) – bass / **PHIL EHART** (b.1951) – drums

Kirshner Kirshner

Nov 74. (7") *<4253>* **CAN I TELL YOU. / THE PILGRIMAGE** [-] [ ]

Feb 75. (7") *<4256>* **BRINGING IT ALL BACK. / LONELY WIND** [-] [ ]

Apr 75. (lp) *(KIR 80174) <32817>* **KANSAS** [ ] [ ] Jun74
– Can I tell you / Bringing it back / Lonely wind / Belexes / Journey from Mariabronn / The pilgrimage / Apercu / Death of Mother Nature suite. *(cd-iss. Apr92 on 'Sony Collectors'; 982733-2) (cd re-iss. Feb97 on 'Epic'; 468883-2)*

Apr 75. (7") *<4258>* **SONG FOR AMERICA. / (part 2)** [-] [ ]

Aug 75. (lp) *(KIR 80740) <33385>* **SONG FOR AMERICA** [ ] [57] Mar75
– Down the road / Song for America / Lamplight symphony / Lonely street / The Devil game / Incomudro – hymn to the Atman.

Feb 76. (7") *<4259>* **IT TAKES A WOMAN'S LOVE (TO MAKE A MAN). / IT'S YOU** [-] [ ]

May 76. (lp) *(KIR 81180) <33806>* **MASQUE** [ ] [70] Dec75
– It takes a woman's love (to make a man) / Two cents worth / Icarus – borne on wings of steel / All the world / Child of innocence / It's you / Mysteries and mayhem / The pinnacle.

Dec 76. (lp) *(KIR 81728) <34224>* **LEFTOVERTURE** [ ] [5] Nov76
– Carry on wayward son / The wall / What's on my mind / Miracles out of nowhere / Opus insert / Questions of my childhood / Cheyenne anthem / Magnus opus: Father Padilla meets the gnat – Howling at the Moon – Man overboard – Industry on parade – Release the beavers – Gnat attack. *(re-iss. Nov92 on 'Sony Collectors' cd/c; 982837-2/-4)*

Dec 76. (7") *<4267>* **CARRY ON WAYWARD SON. / QUESTIONS OF MY CHILDHOOD** [-] [11]

May 77. (7") *<4270>* **WHAT'S ON MY MIND. / LONELY STREET** [-] [ ]

Nov 77. (lp)<US-pic-lp> *(KIR 82234) <34929>* **POINT OF KNOW RETURN** [ ] [4] Oct77
– Point of know return / Paradox / The spider / Portrait (he knew) / Closet chronicles / Lightning's hand / Dust in the wind / Sparks of the tempest / Nobody's home / Hopelessly human. *(cd-iss. Jul89 on 'C.B.S.'; CD 32361)*

Dec 77. (7") *(S-KIR 5820) <4273>* **POINT OF KNOW RETURN. / CLOSET CHRONICLES** [ ] [28] Oct77

Mar 78. (7") *(S-KIR 6205) <4274>* **DUST IN THE WIND. / PARADOX** [ ] [6] Jan78

Jun 78. (7") *(S-KIR 4932)* **CARRY ON WAYWARD SON. / QUESTIONS OF MY CHILDHOOD** [51] [-]

Jun 78. (7") *<4276>* **PORTRAIT (HE KNEW). / LIGHTNING'S HAND** [-] [64]

Dec 78. (d-lp) *(KIR 88318) <PZ2 35560>* **TWO FOR THE SHOW (live)** [ ] [32] Nov78
– Songs for America / Point of know return / Paradox / Icarus – borne on wings of steel / Portrait (he knew) / Carry on wayward son / Journey from Mariabronn / Dust in the wind / Lonely wind / Mysteries and mayhem / Lamplight symphony / The wall / Closet chronicles / Magnum opus: Father Padilla meets the gnat – Howling at the Moon – Man overboard – Industry on parade / Release the beavers – Gnat attack.

Jan 79. (7") *<4280>* **LONELY WIND (live). / SONG FOR AMERICA (live)** [-] [60]

Jun 79. (7") *(S-KIR 7426) <4284>* **PEOPLE OF THE SOUTH WIND. / STAY OUT OF TROUBLE** [ ] [23]

Jul 79. (lp) *(KIR 83644) <36000>* **MONOLITH** [ ] [10] May79
– On the other side / People of the south wind / Angels have fallen / How my soul cries out for you / A glimpse of home / Away from you / Stay out of trouble / Reason to be.

Sep 79. (7") *<4285>* **REASON TO BE. / HOW MY SOUL CRIES OUT FOR YOU** [-] [52]

Sep 80. (7") *<4291>* **HOLD ON. / DON'T OPEN YOUR EYES** [-] [40]

Oct 80. (lp) *(KIR 84500) <36588>* **AUDIO-VISIONS** [ ] [26] Sep80
– Relentless / Anything for you / Hold on / Loner / Curtain of iron / Got to rock on / Don't open your eyes / No one together / No room for a stranger / Back door. *(cd-iss. Mar96 on 'Epic'; 481161-2)*

Dec 80. (7") *<4292>* **GOT TO ROCK ON. / NO ROOM FOR A STRANGER** [-] [76]

—— **JOHN ELEFANTE** (b.1958, Levittown, N.Y.) – vocals, keyboards repl. WALSH who continued on recent solo work

Jul 82. (7") *(S-KIR 2408) <02903>* **PLAY THE GAME TONIGHT. / PLAY ON** [ ] [17] May82

Jul 82. (lp) *(KIR 85714) <38002>* **VINYL CONFESSIONS** [ ] [16] Jun82
– Play the game tonight / Right away / Fair exchange / Chasing shadows / Diamonds and pearls / Face it / Windows / Borderline / Play on / Crossfire. *(cd-iss. Mar96 on 'Epic'; 481162-2)*

Aug 82. (7") *<03084>* **RIGHT AWAY. / WINDOWS** [-] [73]

—— now w/out STEINHARDT

Epic CBS Assoc.

Aug 83. (7") *<04057>* **FIGHT FIRE WITH FIRE. / INCIDENT ON A BRIDGE** [-] [58]

Sep 83. (lp) *(EPC 25561) <38733>* **DRASTIC MEASURES** [ ] [41]
– Fight fire with fire / Everybody's my friend / Mainstream / Andi / Going through the motions / Get rich / Don't take your love away / End of the age / Incident on a bridge. *(cd-iss. Mar96 on 'Epic'; 481163-2)*

Sep 83. (12"m) *(TA 3696)* **FIGHT FIRE WITH FIRE. / CARRY ON WAYWARD SON / DUST IN THE WIND** [ ] [-]

Nov 83. (7") **EVERYBODY'S MY FRIEND. / END OF THE AGE** [-] [ ]

—— Disbanded late 1983. Re-formed 1986 but without LIVGREN, HOPE & ELEFANTE. Past members **EHART & WILLIAMS** brought back **STEVE WALSH.** They recruited **STEVE MORSE** (b.28 Jul'54, Hamilton, Ohio) – guitar (ex-DIXIE DREGS) / **BILLY GREER** – bass (ex-STREETS)

M.C.A. M.C.A.

Dec 86. (lp/c) *(MCG/+C 6021) <5838>* **POWER** [ ] [35] Nov86
– Silhouettes in disguise / Power / All I wanted / Secret service / We're not alone anymore / Musicatto / Taking in the view / Three pretenders / Tomb 19 / Can't cry anymore.

Jan 87. (7"/12") *(MCA/+S 1116) <52958>* **ALL I WANTED. / WE'RE NOT ALONE ANYMORE** [ ] [19] Oct86

Feb 87. (7") *<53027>* **POWER. / TOMB 19** [-] [84]

Apr 87. (7") *<53070>* **CAN'T CRY ANYMORE. / THREE PRETENDERS** [-] [ ]

Oct 88. (lp/c/cd) *<(MCA/MCAC/DMCA 6254)>* **IN THE SPIRIT OF THINGS** [ ] [ ]
– Ghosts / One big sky / Inside of me / One man, one heart * / House on fire / Once

in a lifetime * / Stand beside me / I counted on love * / The preacher / Rainmaker / T.O. Witcher * / Bells of Saint James. *(cd+= *)*

Nov 88. (7") *<53425>* **STAND BESIDE ME. / HOUSE ON FIRE**

— In 1991, they added **DAVID RAGSDALE** – violin

— **WALSH / LIVGREN / EHART / RAGSDALE**

Essential Intersound

Jul 93. (cd) *<9107>* **LIVE AT THE WHISKY (live)**
– Introduction / Howlin' at the moon from Magnum Opus / Paradox / Point of know return / Song for America / The wall / Hold on / Dust in the wind / Miracles out of nowhere / Mysteries and mayhem / Portrait (he knew) / Carry on wayward son / Down the road. *(hidden track+=)* – Lonely street.

Jul 95. (cd/c) *(ESS CD/MC 299) <9148>* **FREAKS OF NATURE**
– I can fly / Desperate times / Hope once again / Black fathom four / Under the knife / Need / Freaks of nature / Cold grey morning / Peaceful and warm.

— next with the London Symphony Orchestra

not iss. River North

May 98. (cd) *<161384>* **ALWAYS NEVER THE SAME**
– Eleanor Rigby / Dust in the wind / Preamble / Song for America / In your eyes / Miracles out of nowhere / Hold on / The sky is falling / Cheyenne anthem / Prelude & introduction / The wall / Need to know / Nobody's home.

— reverted to the original sextet of **WALSH, WILLIAMS, STEINHARDT, HOPE, LIVGREN + EHART** plus **GREER** (to make seven)

S.P.V. Magna Carta

Jul 00. (cd) *(SPV 0857101-2) <9050>* **SOMEWHERE TO ELSEWHERE**
– Icarus II / When the world was young / Grand fun alley / The coming down (Thanatopsis) / Myriad / Look at the time / Disappearing skin tight blues / Distant vision / Byzantium / Not man bag. *(hidden+=)* – (untitled).

– compilations, others –

Sep 84. (lp/c) *Epic; (EPC/40 26065) / CBS Assoc; <39283>* **THE BEST OF KANSAS**
– Carry on wayward son / The point of know return / Fight fire / No one together / Play the game tonight / The wall. *(cd-iss. Nov85; CD 26065) (cd re-iss. Aug90; 461036-2)*

Jul 94. (d-cd) *Legacy; (CD 47364)* **THE KANSAS BOXED SET**

Jul 98. (cd) *Epic; (487592-2)* **THE DEFINITIVE COLLECTION**

Nov 98. (cd) *King Biscuit; <(KBFHCD 024)>* **KING BISCUIT PRESENTS . . .**

— STEVE WALSH and KERRY LIVGREN both issued solo releases, although they were of the soft-rock/AOR variety.

STEVE WALSH

solo, with some KANSAS members.

not iss. Kirshner

Mar 80. (lp) <36320> **SCHEMER-DREAMER**
– Schemer-dreamer (that's all right) / Get too far / So many nights / You think you got it made / Every step of the way / Just how does it feel / Wait until tomorrow.

Mar 80. (7") *<4287>* **SCHEMER-DREAMER (THAT'S ALL RIGHT). / JUST HOW DOES IT FEEL**

Jun 80. (7") *<4288>* **EVERY STEP OF THE WAY. / YOU THINK YOU GOT IT MADE**

After his KANSAS departure early '81, WALSH formed STREETS with **MIKE SLAMER** – guitar (ex-CITY BOY) / **BILLY GREER** – bass / **TIM GEHRT** – drums. Released 2 albums for 'Atlantic' between 1983 & 1985; STREETS & CRIMES IN MIND.

KERRY LIVGREN

solo, with KANSAS members

Kirshner Kirshner

Oct 80. (lp) *(KIR 84453) <36567>* **SEEDS OF CHANGE**
– Just one way / Mask of the great deceiver / How can you live / Whiskey seed / To live for the king / Down to the core / Ground zero.

Oct 80. (7") *<4290>* **MASK OF THE GREAT DECEIVER. / TO LIVE FOR THE KING**

— After he left KANSAS in 1982, he made 4 more albums, mostly religious. He also formed Christian band AD in 1984.

KARMA TO BURN

Formed: Hicksville, West Virginia, USA . . . 1993 by DICKIE, WILLIAM and NICHOLAS, who invited vocalist JASON JAROSZ when JOHN GARCIA (of KYUSS) turned them down. Their eponymous album (early '97) was well-received at least in heavy quarters. Following in the footsteps of KYUSS, MONSTER MAGNET, etc, KARMA TO BURN summoned up the sludgiest riffs from the back of beyond and on the likes of the brilliant 'BOBBI, BOBBI, BOBBI – I'M NOT GOD' they combined hick-industrial vocals a la MINISTRY/REVOLTING COCKS with female diva-esque backing to compelling effect. They even stretched to a cover of Joy Division's '24 HOURS'. Numbers were also used as tracks (all over the place) on their slightly below par sophomore set, 'WILD WONDERFUL PURGATORY' (1999).

Album rating: KARMA TO BURN (*6) / WILD WONDERFUL PURGATORY (*5)

JASON JAROSZ – vocals / **WILLIAM** – guitar / **DICKIE** – bass / **NICHOLAS** – drums

Roadrunner Roadrunner

Feb 97. (cd) *<(RR 8862-2)>* **KARMA TO BURN**
– Waltz of the Playboy pallbearers / Bobbi, Bobbi, Bobbi – I'm not God / Patty Hearst's closet mantra / Mt. Penetrator / Eight / Apalachian woman / 24 hours / Six-gun sucker punch / Thirten six / Ma petite mort / Twin sisters and a half bottle of bourbon. *(re-iss. May99; same)*

— (Mar'97) **JIM DAVISON** – briefly repl. JAROSZ

— without a frontman two months later when JIM left

— **ROB** was their new drummer

Roadrunner Teepee

Jul 99. (cd) *(RR 8635-2) <MIA 1011>* **WILD WONDERFUL PURGATORY**
– 20 / 28 / 30 / 31 / 29 / 32 / 25 / 26 / 1 / 3 / 7 / 8. *(re-iss. Nov99; same as US)*

Great KAT

Born: New York, USA. Classically trained, KAT (or 'The GREAT KAT' as she rather modestly likes to be known) eventually switched from violin to guitar, rather ill-advisedly attempting to become The VANESSA MAE of thrash. A queasy prospect, granted, and one which was given free rein on KAT's universally derided 'WORSHIP ME OR DIE' (1987). Something of a novelty, KAT could nevertheless talk a good fight and she was certainly sexier than LEMMY but the album was third division speed metal at best. Still, anyone unlucky enough to have actually purchased the record could always console themselves by ringing the KAT hotline in America (rather handily printed on the back of the album sleeve; yep, for the cost of a transatlantic phone call, mere mortals could be privvy to a recorded message along the lines of 'Great Kat is God, I am the Great Kat, etc, etc,'). Despite the critical barbs, KAT continued apace with her grand classical/metal masterplan, inflicting another opus, 'BEETHOVEN ON SPEED' on an unsuspecting rock scene in 1990. The record fared equally badly, KAT finally fading into obscurity. Rumours of an attempt to re-record SLAYER's 'Reign In Blood' with a woodwind orchestra have proved unfounded. • **Note:** A Polish band going by the name of KAT (and nothing to do with her) released an album in 1986, 'Metal And Hell'.

Album rating: WORSHIP ME OR DIE (*2) / BEETHOVEN ON SPEED (*3) /

GREAT KAT – vocals, guitar, violin

Roadrunner Roadrunner

Nov 87. (lp) *<(RR 9589)>* **WORSHIP ME OR DIE**
– Metal messiah / Kat possessed / Death to you / Satan goes to church / Worship me or die / Demons / Speed death / Kill the mothers / Ashes to dust / Satan says / Metal massacre. *(cd-iss. Mar90 on 'Roadracer'; RO 9589-2)*

Roadracer not iss.

Oct 90. (cd/c/lp) *(RO 9373-2/-4/-1)* **BEETHOVEN ON SPEED**
– Beethoven on speed / Flight of the bumblebee / Funeral march / God / Sex and violins / Gripping obsession / Worshipping bodies / Total tyrant / Ultra-dead / Revenge of the mongrel / Kat abuse / Made in Japan / Beethoven mosh (5th symphony) / Paganini's 24th Caprice / Guitar concerto in blood minor / Bach to the future, for geniuses only.

— seemed to have retired from music until below return

not iss. Life

1994. (cd-ep) *<79014>* **DO YOU WANNA GO PARTY**

T.P.R. T.P.R.

Feb 97. (cd-ep) *<(45619)>* **ROSSINI'S THE BARBER OF SEVILLE / DOMINATRIX / FEAST OF THE DEAD / SARASATE'S GYPSY VIOLIN WALTZ ZIGEUNERWEISEN** 2000

not iss. own label

2001. (cd-ep) **BLOODY VIVALDI**
– Vivaldi's "The Four Seasons" / Torture chamber / BLOOD / Sarasati's "Carmen fantasy".

John KAY (see under ⇒ STEPPENWOLF)

KEEL

Formed: Los Angeles, California, USA . . . 1983 by former STEELER frontman RON KEEL. The aforementioned Nashville-based hard-rock act delivered only one eponymous album for MIKE VARNEY's 'Shrapnel' label before they relocated to L.A. The line-up was completed by RIK FOX, MIKE EDWARDS and Swedish guitarist YNGWIE MALMSTEEN, the latter being introduced just prior to the band hitting the studio (he was later to be a star in his own right). RON KEEL brought together his own band, including BRIAN JAY and MARC FERRARI on guitars, KENNY CHAISSON on bass and BOBBY MARKS on drums. Sticking with VARNEY, the group released their debut, 'LAY DOWN THE LAW', an album that caught the attention of one GENE SIMMONS (of KISS). He provided the production on their 1985 follow-up, 'THE RIGHT TO ROCK', an AEROSMITH-inspired affair that just dented the US Top 100. SIMMONS also worked on the third set, 'THE FINAL FRONTIER' (1986), their first for 'M.C.A.' and a record that included a cover of Patti Smith's 'BECAUSE THE NIGHT'.

Album rating: Steeler: STEELER (*6) / Keel: LAY DOWN THE LAW (*4) / THE RIGHT TO ROCK (*6) / THE FINAL FRONTIER (*5) / KEEL (*5) / LARGER THAN LIVE (*5) / KEEL VI: BACK IN ACTION (*4)

STEELER

RON KEEL – vocals, guitar / **YNGWIE MALMSTEEN** – guitar / **RIK FOX** – bass, vocals / **MARL EDWARDS** – drums

not iss. Shrapnel

1983. (lp) *<SM 1007>* **STEELER**
– Cold day in hell / Backseat driver / No way out / Hot on your heels / Abduction / On the rox / Down to the wire / Born to rock / Serenade.

— MALMSTEEN departed nearing the completion of above album. He joined

ALCATRAZZ, before going solo with his own backing band, RISING FORCE (FOX formed SIN).

KEEL

RON KEEL – vocals, guitar / **MARC FERRARI** – guitar, vocals / **BRIAN JAY** – guitar, vocals / **KENNY CHAISSON** – bass, vocals / **BOBBY MARKS** – drums

not iss. / Shrapnel

1984. (lp) <*SH 1014*> **LAY DOWN THE LAW** [-] [ ]
– Thunder and lightning / Lay down the law / Speed demon / Princess of illusion / Born ready / Metal generation / Till Hell freezes over / Tonight you're mine / Let's spend the night together.

— now without MARKS; on session STEPHEN RILEY

Vertigo / Gold Mountain

Apr 85. (lp/c) *(VERL/+C 26)* <*5041*> **THE RIGHT TO ROCK** [ ] [99] Mar85
– The right to rock / Back to the city / Let's spend the night together / Easier said than done / So many girls, so little time / Electric love / Speed demon / Get down / You're the victim (I'm the crime).

— **DWAIN MILLER** – drums; repl. RILEY

Vertigo / M.C.A.

Mar 86. (7"/12") *(KEEL/+X 1)* <*52783*> **BECAUSE THE NIGHT. / ARM AND A LEG** [ ] [ ]
Apr 86. (lp/c) *(VERH/+C 33)(826 815-2)* <*5727*> **THE FINAL FRONTIER** [83] [53] Apr86
– The final frontier / Rock and roll animal / Because the night / Here today, gone tomorrow / Arm and a leg / Raised on rock / Just another girl / Tears of fire / Nightfall / No pain no gain.
Jul 86. (7") <*52861*> **THE FINAL FRONTIER. / TEARS OF FIRE** [-] [ ]

M.C.A. / M.C.A.

Jul 87. (lp/c/cd) *(MCF/MCFC/DMCF 3393)* <*42005*> **KEEL** [ ] [79] Jun87
– United nations / Somebody's waiting / Cherry lane / Calm before the storm / King of the rock / It's a jungle out there / I said the wrong thing to the right girl / Don't say you love me / If love is a crime (I wanna be convicted) / 4th of July.

— **TONY PALMUCCI** – guitar; repl. FERRARI

not iss. / Gold Castle

1989. (cd) <*DZ 71328*> **LARGER THAN LIVE** [-] [ ]
– Evil wicked mean and nasty / Riding high / Die fighting / Dreams are not enough / So many good ways to be bad / Fool for a pretty face / Hard as hell / Rock and roll animal / Private lies / Rock'n'roll outlaw / The right to rock / Cold day in Hell. *(UK cd-iss. Aug95 on 'S.P.V.'; SPV 0851210-2)*

— RON KEEL went into session work until a brief KEEL reformation

Derock / Derock

Apr 98. (cd) <*(DERCD 9003)*> **KEEL VI: BACK IN ACTION** (new, outtakes) [ ] [ ]
– Back in action / Reason to rock / United nations / Friday every night / Reach out and rock somebody / Hold your head up / Proud to be loud / Answers in your eyes / Lay down the law '84 / Speed demon '84.

KEPONE

Formed: Richmond, Virginia, USA . . . early 90's by the imposingly bearded MICHAEL BISHOP, along with TIM HARRISS and SETH HARRIS, taking the group name from a dangerous chemical manufactured by a local firm (previously detailed by musical mentor JELLO BIAFRA on The DEAD KENNEDYS' 'Kepone Factory'). Signed to noted US indie label, 'Quarter Stick', the band premiered their blend of idiosyncratic yet powerful mutant punk-blues on the debut album, 'UGLY DANCE' (1994). Like a downhome JESUS LIZARD, they flavoured their music and especially their lyrics with a Deep South small-town weirdness. Now without SETH – who was replaced by EDWARD JEFFERSON TRASK – KEPONE issued a second set, 'SKIN' (1995), which was followed by 1997's acclaimed eponymous album.

Album rating: UGLY DANCE (*6) / SKIN (*6) / KEPONE (*7)

MICHAEL BISHOP – vocals, bass / **TIM HARRISS** – guitar, vocals / **SETH HARRIS** – drums

Tenderizer / Tenderizer

Jun 93. (7") *(TZR 002)* **HENRY. /** [ ] [-]

not iss. / Alternative Tentacles

Dec 93. (7") <*VIRUS 144*> **295. / PHOBIC** [-] [ ]

Quarter Stick / Quarter Stick

Aug 94. (lp/cd) <*(QS 27/+CD)*> **UGLY DANCE** [ ] [ ]
– Loud / Dickie boys / Leadbreath / Brainflower / Some pig / Henry / Shit talk / Fly bop / Wrong / Eenie meenie / Sick river / Silly Sally / Ugly dance.

— **EDWARD JEFFERSON TRASK** – drums; repl. SETH

Sep 95. (lp/cd) <*(QS 33/+CD)*> **SKIN** [ ] [ ] Aug95
– Knifethrower / Velveteen / Blue-devil / Stay down / Ed's sad party / Idiot ball drop / Superfucker / Prisoners / Left Eskimo / Thin solution.
Sep 96. (7") *(QS 45)* **THE GHOST. / DANGERMANE** [ ] [-]
Apr 97. (cd) <*(QS 46CD)*> **KEPONE** [ ] [ ] Mar97
– Bring it down / Joe / Pointless / Ghost / Liner hymn / Thaw/ Clicking jam / Leave your bones / I am an alien / Slow build / Jimmy Spit / Scrub / Virginia creeper / Dead pop ideal.

— disbanded after above

KERBDOG

Formed: Kilkenny, Ireland . . . 1991 by CORMAC BATTLE, COLIN FENNELLY and DARRAGH BUTLER, who evolved from indie outfit, The CHRISTIAN BROTHERS, adopting a heavier approach with the addition of second guitarist BILLY DALTON. Signed to 'Vertigo', they unleashed the gutteral 'EARTHWORKS' EP prior to their eponymous 1994 debut album. Loaded with lumbering riffs of seismic intensity, the album nevertheless lacked quality songs, although the single 'DUMMY CRUSHER' reached the Top 40. Although a few singles surfaced in the mid 90's (usually with punk cover b-sides!), it would be early 1997 before KERBDOG (now trimmed to original trio) issued their long-playing follow-up, 'ON THE TURN'. A more melodic affair, the album (a minor hit!) opened promisingly with the thrilling 'SALLY', although many tracks came across as rather pedestrian. Despite good reviews and half decent record sales the band were subsequently dropped, splitting soon after. BATTLE duly struggled with personal demons while studying for a degree at Dublin University and DARRAGH got a job in computing. Quickly realising that a sensible life wasn't for them, the pair reunited in new outfit, WILT, alongside old friend MICK MURPHY. Featuring dark, caustic lyrics borne of BATTLE's bitter industry experience, the band's first two singles ('NO WORRIES' and 'IT'S ALL OVER NOW') both netted Kerrang! singles of the week awards while their debut album, 'BASTINADO' (2000) served notice that KERBDOG's bruised spirit had well and truly been laid to rest.
• **Songwriters:** Group except IN A RUT (Ruts) / SUSPECT DEVICE (Stiff Little Fingers) / KENNEDY (Wedding Present) / DEBASER (Pixies) / THIS IS NOT A LOVE SONG (Public Image Ltd).

Album rating: KERBDOG (*5) / ON THE TURN (*5) / Wilt: BASTINADO (*6)

CORMAC BATTLE – vocals, guitars / **COLIN FENNELLY** – bass / **DARRAGH BUTLER** – drums / with **BILLY DALTON** – guitars

Vertigo / Mercury

May 93. (7"ep/cd-ep) *(DOG/+CD 1)* **EARTHWORKS** [ ] [-]
– Earthworks / Cleaver / Scram.
Oct 93. (7"ep/cd-ep) *(VER/+CD 80)* **END OF GREEN. / IN A RUT / KEROSENE** [ ] [-]
Mar 94. (7") *(VER 83)* **DRY RISER. / SOMETHING IN MY HEAD** [ ] [-]
(12"+=/cd-s+=) *(VERCD 83)* – Xenophobia / Self inflicted.
(7"clear) *(VERR 83)* – ('A'side) / Same with the hammer.
(cd-s+=) *(VERXC 83)* – New day rising / Suspect device.
Apr 94. (cd/c/lp) *(<518866-2/-4/-1>)* **KERBDOG** [ ] [ ]
– End of green / Dry riser / Dead anyway / Cleaver / Earthworks / Dummy crusher / The inseminator / Clock / Schism / Scram.
Jul 94. (7"/c-s) *(VER/+MC 86)* **DUMMY CRUSHER. / TOO MUCH TOO YOUNG** [37] [-]
(cd-s) *(VERCD 86)* – ('A'side) / Kennedy / Debaser.
(cd-s) *(VERDD 86)* – ('A'side) / Mildred Pierce / This is not a love song.
(12"pic-d) *(VERT 86)* – ('A'side) / Mr. Clean / Don't stand in line.

— added other guest guitarist **ROY Z**

Fontana / Mercury

Jul 96. (7"ep/cd-ep) *(KER/+CD 1)* **J.J.'S SONG / DIDN'T EVEN TRY. / HARD TO LIVE / GRIDLOCK** [ ] [-]
Sep 96. (cd-ep) *(KERCD 2)* **SALLY / MY ACQUAINTANCE / RETRO READY** [69] [-]
(cd-ep) *(KERCC 2)* – ('A'side) / Dyed in the wool / Spence.
(cd-ep) *(KERDD 2)* – ('A'side) / Dragging through / The fear.

— now original trio

Mar 97. (cd-s) *(KERCD 3)* **MEXICAN WAVE / SALLY (live) / ON THE TURN (live)** [49] [-]
(cd-s) *(KERDD 3)* – ('A'side) / Dry riser (live) / Pledge (live).
(cd-s) *(KERCC 3)* – ('A'side) / End of green (live) / Secure (live).
Mar 97. (cd/c/lp) *(<532999-2/-4/-1>)* **ON THE TURN** [64] [ ]
– Sally / J.J.'s song / Didn't even try / Mexican wave / Severed / Pledge / On the turn / Secure / Lesser shelf / Pointless / Rewind / Sorry for the record.

— the band changed their name to . . .

WILT

CORMAC + DARRAGH with **MICK MURPHY** – bass

Discordant / not iss.

Sep 98. (7") *(CORDS 014)* **NO WORRIES. / WORKING FOR THE MAN** [ ] [-]
(cd-s+=) *(CORDD 014)* – I want it all.

Mushroom / not iss.

Oct 99. (7"/cd-s) *(MUSH 64 S/CDS)* **IT'S ALL OVER NOW. / WORKING FOR THE MAN** [ ] [-]
Mar 00. (7") *(MUSH 71S)* **RADIO DISCO. / HEADLINE NEWS** [ ] [-]
(cd-s+=) *(MUSH 71CDS)* – The party's over.
Jun 00. (7") *(MUSH 75S)* **OPEN ARMS. / RADIO DISCO (XFM session)** [ ] [-]
(cd-s) *(MUSH 75CDS)* – ('A'side) / No worries (XFM session) / Mansion on the hill / ('A'-CD-Rom).
Jul 00. (cd) *(MUSH 65CD)* **BASTINADO** [ ] [-]
Sep 00. (7"/cd-s) *(MUSH 80S)* **NO WORRIES. / RADIO DISCO (evening session)** [ ] [-]
(cd-s) *(MUSH 80CDS)* – ('A'side) / Flutter / Expedestrians (evening session).
(cd-s) *(MUSH 80CDSX)* – ('A'side) / April skies (evening session) / TBC.

KID ROCK

Born: ROBERT RITCHIE, Romeo, Michigan, USA. This white rapper-cum-metalist debuted with the depthless 'GRITS SANDWICHES FOR BREAKFAST' (1990) before his stab at major label success via the even weaker 'THE POLYFUZE METHOD' (1993). The baseball clad, cigar smoking MC shot to notoriety in 1997 – one year after the release of the single 'EARLY MORNING STONED PIMP' – when a leading radio station in Motor City played his infamous 'YODELING IN THE VALLEY' track (from the debut album) and were subsequently fined for obscene broadcasting. KID ROCK signed to 'Atlantic' in 1997 and issued his third set 'DEVIL WITHOUT A CAUSE' the following year. Like the string of white suburban metal bands, ROCK relied heavily on bad language, songs about drugs (and "bitches") and endless references to the degenerate culture, which somehow made this album sound like a bit of a charlatan. The entertainer (who's now going down a storm with WWF mob!) spent much of his time prancing around on stage in a pair of horrible silver MC HAMMER-esque baggy trousers – with a dwarf and two lap dancers in tow – proving he could yet become a novelty act for juvenile teens after all.

Album rating: GRITS SANDWICHES FOR BREAKFAST (*4) / THE POLYFUZE METHOD (*3) / DEVIL WITHOUT A CAUSE (*6)

KID ROCK – rapper, bass, guitar / with various friends

not iss. Novus-Jive

Oct 90. (c-s/12") *<1349/+1>* **YO-DA-LIN IN THE VALLEY** [-] [ ]

Nov 90. (cd/c/lp) *<1409-2/-4/-1>* **GRITS SANDWICHES FOR BREAKFAST** [-] [ ]
– Yo-da-lin in the valley / Genuine article / Cramp ya style / New York's not my home / Super rhyme maker / With a one two / Wax the booty / Pimp of the nation / Abdul Jabar cut / Step in stride / Upside / Style of X pression / Trippin' over a rock.

Continuum Continuum

1992. (c-s/12"/cd-s) *<19255>* **BACK FROM THE DEAD (extended). / ('A'-short) / ('A'-instrumental)** [-] [ ]

Aug 93. (12"/cd-s) *(12/CD CTUM 101) <12205>* **U DON'T KNOW ME /** [ ] [ ] Feb93

Sep 93. (cd/lp) *(CD+/CTUM 2) <19205-2/-4>* **THE POLYFUZE METHOD** [ ] [ ]
– Fred / Killin' brain cells / Prodigal son / Cramper / 3 sheets to the wind / Fuck U blind / Desperate (radio) / Back from the dead / My Oedipus complex / Balls in your mouth / Trippin' with Dick Vitale / TV dinner / Pancake breakfast / Blow me / In so deep / U don't know me.

Dec 93. (m-cd/m-c) *<15205>* **FIRE IT UP** [-] [ ]
– I am the bullgod / My Oedipus complex / Country boy can survive / Balls in your mouth / Cramper / Rollin' on the island.

not iss. Top Dog

Jan 96. (c-ep/cd-ep) *<50001>* **EARLY MORNIN' STONED PIMP** [-] [ ]

— now backed by band, TWISTED BROWN TRUCKER:- **KENNY OLSON** – guitar / **STEFANIE EULINBERG** – drums / **TWEEDS KRACKER** – turntables / **JIMMY BONES** – keyboards / **JASON KRAUSE** – guitar / **MISTY LOVE + SHIRLEY HAYDEN** – backing vocals

Lava – Atlantic Lava – Atlantic

Jun 99. (cd/c) *<(7567 83119-2/-4)>* **DEVIL WITHOUT A CAUSE** [ ] [4] Aug98
– Bawitdaba / Cowboy / Devil without a cause / I am the bullgod / Roving gangster (rollin') / Wasting time / Welcome 2 the party (ode 2 the old skool) / I got one for ya / Somebody's gotta feel this / Fist of rage / Only God knows why / Fuck off (w/ EMINEM) / Where U at Rock (w/ EMINEM) / Black chick, white guy (w/ EMINEM). *<clean version-iss.Oct98; 83152>*

Oct 99. (c-s/cd-s) *(AT 0076 C/CD) <84520>* **COWBOY / COWBOY (album version) / I AM THE BULLGOD (live)** [36] [82]

Feb 00. (-) *<album cut>* **ONLY GOD KNOWS WHY** [-] [19]

May 00. (cd/c) *<(7567 83314-2/-4)>* **THE HISTORY OF ROCK** [73] [2]
– Intro / American bad ass / Prodigal son / Paid / Early mornin' stoned pimp (by KID ROCK & JOE C) / Tino / Dark and grey / 3 sheets to the wind (what's my name) / Abortion / I wanna go back / Ya' keep on / Fuck that / Fuck you blind / Born to be a hick / My oedipus complex (KID ROCK & TWISTED BROKEN TRUCKER).

Aug 00. (c-s) *(AT 0085C)* **AMERICAN BAD ASS (clean version) / 3 SHEETS TO THE WIND (live) / COWBOY (live)** [25] [ ]
(cd-s+=) *(AT 0085CD)* – ('A'-promo video).

Apr 01. (cd-s) *(AT 0098CD1)* **BAWITDADA / MY OEDIPUS COMPLEX (father edit) / MY OEDIPUS COMPLEX (Son edit) / ('A'video)** [41] [-]
(cd-s) *(AT 0098CD2)* – ('A'side) / Cowboy / Prodigal son / Cowboy (video).
(cd-s) *(AT 0098CD3)* – ('A'side) / I am the the bullgod / Paid / I am the bullgod (video).

KILLDOZER

Formed: Madison, Wisconsin, USA . . . 1986 by brothers BILL and DAN HOBSON alongside MICHAEL GERALD. Politically aware punks with an acute sense of humour/observation and a penchant for gritty country, KILLDOZER made their debut in 1984 with the wonderfully titled mini-set, 'INTELLECTUALS ARE THE SHOESHINE BOYS OF THE RULING ELITE'. Subsequently picked up by Chicago's 'Touch & Go' label, the band ran off a series of BUTCH VIG-produced records – 'SNAKEBOY' (1986), 'BURL' (1987) and 'LITTLE BABY BUNTIN' (1988) – exploring the backwoods mentality of rural America from differing narrative perspectives. Occasionally unsettling and often highly amusing, the band's lyrical caricatures were put on hold for 1989's 'FOR LADIES ONLY', wherein the boys KILLDOZER-ed their way through a selection of prime 70's FM rock classics. Following the release of '12 POINT BUCK' later that year, the band entered a period of instability as BILL departed due to family commitments. After periods of sporadic touring, KILLDOZER finally re-emerged – complete with new guitarist, PAUL ZAGORES – in 1994 with 'UNCOMPROMISING WAR ON ART UNDER THE DICTATORSHIP OF THE PROLETARIAT'. While the latter set revisited the political sentiments of the band's debut, 1995's STEVE ALBINI-produced 'GOD HEARS PLEAS OF THE INNOCENT' and 1997's 'THE LAST WALTZ' saw the band bow out with some of the most skull-crushing music of their career. • **Covered:** FUNK #49 (James Gang) / CINNAMON GIRL (Neil Young) / RUN THROUGH THE JUNGLE (John Fogerty) / AMERICAN PIE (Don McLean) / GOOD LOVIN GONE BAD (Bad Company) / TAKE THE MONEY AND RUN (Steve Miller Band) / HUSH (Joe South) / EVERY CHRISTIAN HEARTED MAN WILL (Bee Gees) / CONQUISTADOR (Procol Harum) / AQUARIUS – LET THE SUNSHINE IN (Fifth Dimension) / POUR MAN (Lee Hazlewood) / WHEN THE LEVEE BREAKS + NO QUARTER + HOT DOG (Led Zeppelin) / etc.

Album rating: INTELLECTUALS ARE THE SHOESHINE BOYS OF THE RULING ELITE (*5) / SNAKEBOY (*5) / BURL mini (*5) / LITTLE BABY BUNTIN' (*6) / FOR LADIES ONLY (*7) / 12 POINT BUCK (*7) / UNCOMPROMISING WAR ON ART UNDER THE DICTATORSHIP OF THE PROLETARIAT (*6) / GOD HEARS PLEAS OF THE INNOCENT (*7) / THE LAST WALTZ (*5)

MICHAEL GERALD – vocals, bass / **DAN HOBSON** – guitar / **BILL HOBSON** – drums

not iss. Bone Air

1984. (m-lp) **INTELLECTUALS ARE THE SHOESHINE BOYS OF THE RULING ELITE** [-] [ ]
– Man of meat! / Pile driver! / Parade! / Farmer Johnson! / Ed Gein! / A man's gotta be a man . . .! / Dead folks! / Run through the jungle! *(re-iss. Oct89 on 'Touch & Go' lp/cd+=; T&G LP/CD 47)* – SNAKEBOY

Touch & Go Touch & Go

Aug 86. (lp) *(T&GLP 6)* **SNAKEBOY** [ ] [ ] 1985
– King of sex / Going to the beach / River / L.Y.L.L.Y.D.E. / Don't cry / Cinnamon girl / Gone to Heaven / Revelations / Burning house.

1987. (m-lp) *(T&GLP 17)* **BURL** [ ] [ ] 1986
– Hamburger martyr / Cranberries / Slackjaw / Hot n' tot / One for the people / I'm not Lisa.

Mar 88. (lp) *(T&GLP 26)* **LITTLE BABY BUNTIN'** [ ] [ ] 1987
– Little Baby Buntin' / Cotton bolls / The puppy / Hi there / Ballad of my old man / The rub / 3/4 inch drill bit / I am I said / Cyst / Never gave me a kiss / The noble art of self defence.

Apr 89. (lp-ltd.) *(T&GLP 39)* **FOR LADIES ONLY** [ ] [ ]
– Hush / Good lovin' gone bad / Burnin' love / You've never been this far before / One tin soldier / Take the money and run / American pie / Funk #49 . *(re-iss. Sep90 lp/c/cd/pic-lp/pic-cd; T&GLP 39/+C/CD/PD/CP)*

Sep 89. (12"ep) *<T&G 44>* **YOW EP** [-] [ ]

Nov 89. (lp/cd) *(T&G LP/CD 48)* **TWELVE POINT BUCK** [ ] [ ] 1988
– Twelve point buck / New pants and shirt / Space 1999 / Lupus / Richard / Man versus nature / Gates of Heaven / Pigfoot and bear / Seven thunders / Free love in Amsterdam / Ted Key beef. *(cd+=)* – LITTLE BABY BUNTIN'

— **PAUL ZAGORAS** – guitar; repl. GERALD who took accountancy exams until he returned in '93

Mar 94. (lp/c/cd) *<(TG 82/+C/CD)>* **UNCOMPROMISING WAR ON ART UNDER THE DICTATORSHIP OF THE PROLETARIAT** [ ] [ ]
– Final market / Knuckles the dog (who helps people) / Turkey shoot / Grandma Smith said a curious thing / Hot 'n' nasty / Peach pie / Enemy of the people / Earl Scheib / Das kapital / The pig was cool / Working hard, or hardly working?

Sep 94. (12") *<TG 122>* **THE PIG WAS COOL. /** [-] [ ]

Feb 95. (lp/cd) *<(TG 139/+CD)>* **GOD HEARS PLEAS OF THE INNOCENT** [ ] [ ]
– A mother has a hard road / Porky's dead / Pour man / The buzzard / Paul doesn't understand jazz / Daddy's boy / The Nobbies (a sea chanty) / Big song of Hell / Cannonball run II '95 / I have seen grown men cry / Spork.

May 96. (7"ep/cd-ep; with ALICE DONUT) *<(TG 146/+CD)>* **MICHAEL GERALD'S PARTY MACHINE EP** [ ] [ ] Apr96
– Every Christian lion hearted man will / Conquistador / Medley: Aquarius – Let the sunshine in.

Man's Ruin Man's Ruin

Sep 96. (12"ep) *<(MR 007)>* **WHEN THE LEVEE BREAKS. / NO QUARTER / HOT DOG** [ ] [ ]

Aug 97. (7") *(ISM 27V)* **GO BIG RED. /** [ ] [-]
(above issued on 'Ismist')

Sep 97. (cd) *<(MR 065CD)>* **THE LAST WALTZ** [ ] [ ]
– Porky's dad / The nobbies / Man of meat / I've seen grown men cry / A mother's road / Space: 1999 / Richard / A Xmas song / Knuckles the dog / Cannonball run III '97 / Mama's boy / Way down in old Alabam' / Songs for grand folks. *(re-iss. Aug00; same)*

KILLERS (see under ⇒ DI'ANNO, Paul)

KILLER TWEEKER BEES (see under ⇒ BLACK FLAG)

KILL FOR THRILLS

Formed: Los Angeles, California, USA . . . 1989 by GILBY CLARKE, TODD MUSCAT (brother of FASTER PUSSYCAT's BRENT?), JASON NESMITH and DAVID SCOTT. Standard issue L.A. sleaze-rock, the group cut an independently released debut mini-lp in 1989 entitled 'COMMERCIAL SUICIDE'. A couple of the tracks were re-worked on the group's 'M.C.A.' debut, 'DYNAMITE FROM NIGHTMARE LAND' (1990), Vic Maile's co-production adding a gritty edge to proceedings. The band gained more fame from GILBY joining GUNS N' ROSES than any of their recorded output.

Album rating: COMMERCIAL SUICIDE mini (*4) / DYNAMITE FROM NIGHTMARE LAND (*5)

GILBY CLARKE – vocals, guitar / **JASON NESMITH** – guitar / **TODD MUSCAT** – bass / **DAVID SCOTT** – drums

not iss. World Of Hurt

1989. (m-lp) *<WCD 1001>* **COMMERCIAL SUICIDE** [-] [ ]
– Commercial suicide / Silver bullets / I wanna be your kill / Danger / Pump it up.

not iss. M.C.A.

1990. (cd,c) *<6297>* **DYNAMITE FROM NIGHTMARE LAND** [-] [ ]
– Motorcycle cowboys / Commercial suicide / Brother's eyes / Paisley killers / Something for the suffering / Rockets / Wedding flowers / Ghosts and monsters / My addiction / Misery pills / Silver bullets.

— split when GILBY joined GUNS N' ROSES

KILLING JOKE

Formed: Notting Hill, London, England . . . 1979 by JAZ COLEMAN and PAUL FERGUSON, who subsequently added GEORDIE (K. WALKER) and YOUTH (MARTIN GLOVER). After borrowing money to finance a debut EP (contained three tracks including 'TURN TO RED'), the band were the subject of some interest to DJ John Peel who championed their alternative rock sound. This immediately led to KILLING JOKE signing a deal with 'Island', who virtually re-issued the aforementioned single/EP in abbreviated 7" form (A-side, 'NERVOUS SYSTEM'), adding a fourth track on the 12". While supporting the likes of JOY DIVISION and The RUTS, they released a follow-up double A-sided single, 'WARDANCE' / 'PSYCHE', resurrecting their own 'Malicious Damage' label in the process. The left-field 'E.G.' operation were quick to spot the group's potential, taking on both KILLING JOKE and their label. The first results of this partnership came in the form of 'REQUIEM', the single taken from their pioneering eponymous UK Top 40 album. Replacing the anger of punk with apocalyptic doom mongering, KILLING JOKE were akin to a sonically disturbing, industrialised BLACK SABBATH. Now regarded as a catalystic classic in metal circles, the album also inspired many US hardcore acts, as well as such big guns as METALLICA, MINISTRY, SOUNDGARDEN and NIRVANA. By the release of follow-up set, 'WHAT'S THIS FOR' (1981), KILLING JOKE had taken their occult punk-like chants/anthems to extreme new dimensions. Nevertheless, they retained a strange accessiblity which saw the single, 'FOLLOW THE LEADERS' attaining a minor UK chart placing and incredibly, a hit on the American dancefloors! A third set, 'REVELATIONS' (1982), eased up a little on the intensity factor, although it peaked at No.12 having already spawned another hit single, 'EMPIRE SONG'. Convinced of imminent world destruction, the occult-fixated COLEMAN remained in Iceland after a tour, YOUTH initially returning home but later following his lead to the frozen north. He subsequently flew back to England, teaming up with FERGUSON and newfound friend, PAUL RAVEN to form BRILLIANT. However, both FERGUSON and RAVEN soon departed from YOUTH's group, taking off for Iceland in search of the missing COLEMAN. Eventually locating their frontman, all three returned to UK shores and re-entered the studio (GEORDIE also in tow) with a view to recording new KILLING JOKE material. The resulting album, 'FIRE DANCES' (1983), only managed to scrape into the Top 30, its lack of bite and experimentation possibly a hangover from their northern treks. The following year, KILLING JOKE released only two 45's, although one of them, 'EIGHTIES' (a minor hit), was showcased in all it's eccentric glory on Channel 4's new pop show, 'The Tube'. Having overcome the mental obstacle of 1984 (and all of its apocalyptic implications), COLEMAN and Co. unleashed their most focused work to date in 'NIGHT TIME' (a near Top 10 album), the 'LOVE LIKE BLOOD' single preceding the set and breaking into the Top 20 in early '85. The latter half of the eighties weren't so kind, both critically and commercially, the albums, 'BRIGHTER THAN A THOUSAND SUNS' (1986) and 'OUTSIDE THE GATE' (1988), taking a more self-indulgent keyboard-orientated approach. Following major personnel upheavals, KILLING JOKE decided to take a brief sabbatical, COLEMAN finding time to release a collaborative album with ANNE DUDLEY (ex-ART OF NOISE), 'SONGS FROM THE VICTORIOUS CITY' (1990). The same year, COLEMAN, GEORDIE, RAVEN and newcomer MARTIN ATKINS, returned with the acclaimed 'EXTREMITIES, DIRT AND VARIOUS REPRESSED EMOTIONS' album. Having spent most of the early 90's globetrotting in various exotic locations, KILLING JOKE (now COLEMAN, GEORDIE and the returning YOUTH), were back with a vengeance on 1994's 'PANDEMONIUM'. Their biggest selling album to date, the record and the 'PANDEMONIUM' single from it, both making the Top 30 (the previous 'MILLENIUM' made Top 40), while also seeing an American release on the 'Zoo' label. Another, increasingly metallic/industrial set, 'DEMOCRACY' followed in 1996, although COLEMAN now spends the bulk of his time in New Zealand, where he is composer in residence for the country's Symphony Orchestra.

Album rating: KILLING JOKE (*9) / WHAT'S THIS FOR . . .! (*7) / REVELATIONS (*5) / HA! KILLING JOKE LIVE (*5) / FIRE DANCES (*7) / NIGHT TIME (*7) / BRIGHTER THAN A THOUSAND SUNS (*6) / OUTSIDE THE GATE (*6) / EXTREMITIES, DIRT AND VARIOUS REPRESSED EMOTIONS (*7) / LAUGH? I NEARLY BOUGHT ONE! compilation (*8) / PANDEMONIUM (*8) / DEMOCRACY (*6)

JAZ COLEMAN (b. JEREMY, 26 Feb'60, Cheltenham, England; raised Egypt) – vocals, keyboards / **GEORDIE** (b. K.WALKER, 18 Dec'58, Newcastle-upon-Tyne, England) – guitar, synthesizers / **YOUTH** (b. MARTIN GLOVER, 27 Dec'60, Africa) – bass, vocals (ex-RAGE) / **PAUL FERGUSON** (b.31 Mar'58, High Wycombe, England) – drums

Malicious Damage | not iss.

Oct 79. (10"ep) *(MD 410)* **ARE YOU RECEIVING ME. / TURN TO RED / NERVOUS SYSTEM** [ ] [-]

Island | not iss.

Nov 79. (7") *(WIP 6550)* **NERVOUS SYSTEM. / TURN TO RED** [ ] [-]
(12"+=) *(12WIP 6550)* – Almost red / Are you receiving me.

Malicious Damage | not iss.

Mar 80. (7") *(MD 540)* **WARDANCE. / PSYCHE** [ ] [-]

E.G. – Malicious Damage | Editions

Sep 80. (7") *(EGMD 1.00)* **REQUIEM. / CHANGE** [ ] [-]
(12"+=) *(EGMX 1.00)* – Requiem 434 / Change (version).

Oct 80. (lp/c) *(EGMD/+C 545)* **KILLING JOKE** [39] [-]
– Requiem / Wardance / Tomorrow's world / Bloodsport / The wait / Complications / S.O. 36 / Primitive. *(re-iss. Jan87 lp/c/cd; EG LP/MC/CD 57) <US cd-iss. 1987 on 'Caroline'; 1538>*

May 81. (7") *(EGMDS 1.01)* **FOLLOW THE LEADERS. / TENSION** [55] [-]
(10"+=) *(EGMDX 1.010)* – Follow the leaders – dub.

Jun 81. (lp/c) *(EGMD/+C 550) <111>* **WHAT'S THIS FOR . . .!** [42] [ ]
– The fall of Because / Tension / Unspeakable / Butcher / Follow the leaders / Madness / Who told you how? / Exit. *(re-iss. Jan87 lp/c/cd; EG LP/MC/CD 58) <US cd-iss. 1987 on 'Caroline'; 1539>*

E.G. | Caroline

Mar 82. (7") *(EGO 4)* **EMPIRE SONG. / BRILLIANT** [43] [-]

— **GUY PRATT** – bass; repl. YOUTH who formed BRILLIANT

Apr 82. (lp/c) *(EGMD/+C 3)* **REVELATIONS** [12] [-]
– The hum / Empire song / We have joy / Chop chop / The Pandys are coming / Chapter III / Have a nice day / Land of milk and honey / Good samaritan / Dregs. *(re-iss. Jan87 lp/c/cd; EG LP/MC/CD 59) <US cd-iss. 1987 on 'Caroline'; 1540>*

Jun 82. (7") *(EGO 7)* **CHOP CHOP. / GOOD SAMARITAN** [ ] [-]

Oct 82. (7") *(EGO 10)* **BIRDS OF A FEATHER. / FLOCK THE B-SIDE** [64] [-]
(12"+=) *(EGOX 10)* – Sun goes down.

Nov 82. (10"m-lp/m-c) *(EGMD T/C 4)* **HA – KILLING JOKE LIVE (live)** [66] [-]
– Psyche / Sun goes down / The Pandys are coming / Take take take / Unspeakable / Wardance.

— **PAUL RAVEN** – bass (ex-NEON HEARTS) repl. PRATT who joined ICEHOUSE

Jun 83. (7") *(EGO 11)* **LET'S ALL GO (TO THE FIRE DANCES). / DOMINATOR (version)** [51] [-]
(12"+=) *(EGOX 11)* – The fall of Because (live).

Jul 83. (lp/c) *(EGMD/+C 5)* **FIRE DANCES** [29] [-]
– The gathering / Fun and games / Rejuvenation / Frenzy / Harlequin / Feast of blaze / Song and dance / Dominator / Let's all go (to the fire dances) / Lust almighty. *(re-iss. Jan87 lp/c/cd; EG LP/MC/CD 60) <US cd-iss. 1987 on 'Caroline'; 1541>*

Oct 83. (7") *(EGOD 14)* **ME OR YOU?. / WILFUL DAYS** [57] [-]
(with free 7") *(KILL 1-2)* – ('A'side) / Feast of blaze.
(d12"++=) *(EGOXD 14)* – Let's all go (to the fire dances) / The fall of Because (live) / Dominator (version).

Mar 84. (7") *(EGO 16)* **EIGHTIES. / EIGHTIES (Coming mix)** [60] [-]
(12"+=) *(EGOX 16)* – ('A'-Serious dance mix).

Jun 84. (7") *(EGO 17)* **A NEW DAY. / DANCE DAY** [56] [-]
(12"+=) *(EGOX 17)* – ('A'dub).

Jan 85. (7") *(EGO 20)* **LOVE LIKE BLOOD. / BLUE FEATHER** [16] [-]
(12"+=) *(EGOY 20)* – ('A'-Gestalt mix).
(12"++=) *(EGOX 20)* – ('A'instrumental).

Feb 85. (lp/c) *(EGMD/+C 6) <1531>* **NIGHT TIME** [11] [ ]
– Night time / Darkness before dawn / Love like blood / Kings and queens / Tabazan / Multitudes / Europe / Eighties. *(re-iss. Jan87 lp/c/cd; EG LP/MC/CD 61)*

Mar 85. (7") *(EGO 21)* **KINGS AND QUEENS. / THE MADDING CROWD** [58] [-]
(12"+=) *(EGOX 21)* – ('A'-Right Royal mix).
(12"+=) *(EGOY 21)* – ('A'-Knave mix).

Aug 86. (7") *(EGO 27)* **ADORATIONS. / EXILE** [42] [-]
(d7"+=) *(EGOD 27)* – Ecstacy / ('A'instrumental).

E.G. | Virgin

Oct 86. (7") *(EGO 30)* **SANITY. / GOODBYE TO THE VILLAGE** [70] [-]
(free c-s with-7") *(above tracks)* – Wardance (remix).
(12"+=) *(EGOX 30)* – Victory.

Nov 86. (lp/c/cd) *(EG LP/MC/CD 66) <90568-1/-4/-2>* **BRIGHTER THAN A THOUSAND SUNS** [54] [ ]
– Adorations / Sanity / Chessboards / Twilight of the mortal / Love of the masses / A southern sky / Wintergardens / Rubicon. *(c+=/cd+=)* – Goodbye to the village / Victory.

E.G. | Caroline

Apr 88. (7") *(EGO 40)* **AMERICA. / JIHAD (Beyrouth edit)** [ ] [-]
(12"+=) *(EGOX 40)* – ('A'extended).
(cd-s++=) *(EGOCD 40)* – Change (original 1980 mix).

Jun 88. (lp/c/cd) *(EG LP/MC/CD 73) <1378>* **OUTSIDE THE GATE** [92] [ ]
– America / My love of this land / Stay one jump ahead / Unto the ends of the Earth / The calling / Obsession / Tiahuanaco / Outside the gate. *(cd+=)* – America (extended) / Stay one jump ahead (extended).

Jul 88. (7") *(EGO 43)* **MY LOVE OF THIS LAND. / DARKNESS BEFORE DAWN** [ ] [-]
(12"+=) *(EGOX 43)* – Follow the leaders (dub) / Psyche.
(10"+=) *(EGOT 43)* – Follow the leaders (dub) / Sun goes down.

— **JAZ + GEORDIE** brought in new members **MARTIN ATKINS** (b. 3 Aug'59, Coventry, England) – drums (ex-PUBLIC IMAGE LTD.) repl. FERGUSON / **TAFF** – bass repl. ANDY ROURKE (ex-SMITHS) who had repl. RAVEN. Early 1990, **JAZ COLEMAN** teamed up with ANNE DUDLEY (see; ART OF NOISE)

— **KILLING JOKE** reformed (**COLEMAN, GEORDIE, ATKINS + RAVEN**)

Noise Int. | R.C.A.

Nov 90. (cd/c/lp) *(AGR 054-2/-4/-1) <4828-2/-4>* **EXTREMITIES, DIRT AND VARIOUS REPRESSED EMOTIONS** [ ] [ ]
– Money is not our god / Age of greed / Beautiful dead / Extremities / Inside the termite mound / Intravenus / Solitude / North of the border / Slipstream / Kalijuga struggle. *(cd re-iss. Sep98 on 'F.A.D.'; FAD 5054)*

Jan 91. (12"/cd-s) *(AG 054-6/-3)* **MONEY IS NOT OUR GOD. / NORTH OF THE BORDER** [ ] [-]

Invisible | Invisible

Jul 93. (d-lp) *(<INV 004>)* **THE COURTHOLD TALKS** [ ] [ ]
– (spoken word with JAZ, GEORDIE & JAFF SCANTLEBURY on percussion)

— **YOUTH** returned to repl. RAVEN

— **GEOFF DUGMORE** – drums (ex-ART OF NOISE) repl. ATKINS (to PIGFACE, etc)

Butterfly Volcano-Zoo

Mar 94. (10"ep/cd-ep) *(BFL T/D 11)* **EXORCISM. / ('A'live) / ('A'-German mix) / WHITEOUT (Ugly mix) / ANOTHER CULT GOES DOWN (mix) / ('A'-Bictonic revenge mix)** [ ] [-]
Apr 94. (7"clear/c-s) *(BFL/+C 12)* **MILLENIUM. / ('A'-Cybersank remix)** [34] [-]
(12"+=/cd-s+=) *(BFL T/D 12)* – ('A'-Drum Club remix) / ('A'Juno Reactor remix).
Jul 94. (12"/c-s/cd-s) *(BFL T/C/D 17) <14178>* **PANDEMONIUM. / ('A'mix)** [28] [ ] Oct94
(cd-s) *(BFLD 17)* – ('A'side) / Requiem (Kris Weston & Greg Hunter remix).
Jul 94. (cd/c/d-lp) *(BFL CD/MC/LP 9) <31085>* **PANDEMONIUM** [16] [ ] Aug94
– Pandemonium / Exorcism / Millenium / Communion / Black Moon / Labyrinth / Jana / Whiteout / Pleasures of the flesh / Mathematics of chaos.

— re-united originals **JAZ COLEMAN / GEORDIE + YOUTH**

Jan 95. (cd-ep) *(BFLDA 21)* **JANA (Youth remix) / JANA (Dragonfly mix) / LOVE LIKE BLOOD (live) / WHITEOUT** [54] [-]
(12"ep/cd-ep+=) *(BFL T/DB 21)* – Jana (live) / Wardance (live) / Exorcism (live) / Kings and queens (live).
Mar 96. (cd-s) *(BFLDA 33) <34262>* **DEMOCRACY / DEMOCRACY (Rooster mix by Carcass) / MASS** [39] [ ]
(cd-s) *(BFLDB 33)* – ('A'-United Nations mix) / ('A'-Russian tundra mix) / ('A'-Hallucinogen mix).
Apr 96. (cd/c) *(BFL CD/MC 17) <31127>* **DEMOCRACY** [71] [ ]
– Savage freedom / Democracy / Prozac people / Lanterns / Aeon / Pilgrimage / Intellect / Medicine wheel / Absent friends / Another bloody election. *(cd re-iss. Aug99; same)*

– compilations, etc. –

on 'Virgin' unless mentioned otherwise

Sep 92. (12"/c-s) *(VST/VSC 1432)* **CHANGE. / REQUIEM** [ ] [-]
(cd-s) *(VSCDT 1432)* – ('A'spiral tribe mix). / ('B'trash Greg Hunter mix).
(cd-s) *(VSCDX 1432)* – ('A'-Youth mix). / ('B'-Youth mix).
Oct 92. (cd/c) *(CDV/TCV 2693) / Caroline; <1596>* **LAUGH? I NEARLY BOUGHT ONE!** [ ] [ ]
– Turn to red / Psyche / Requiem / Wardance / Follow the leaders / Unspeakable / Butcher / Exit / The hum / Empire song / Chop-chop / The Sun goes down / Eighties / Darkness before dawn / Love like blood / Wintergardens / Age of greed.
May 95. (cd) *(CDOVD 440) / Caroline; (1884>* **WILFUL DAYS** (remixes) [ ] [ ]
Oct 95. (cd) *Windsong; (WINCD 068)* **BBC LIVE IN CONCERT (live)** [ ] [-]
Apr 98. (12") *Dragonfly; <48>* **LOVE LIKE BLOOD. / INTELLECT** [-] [ ]
Aug 99. (cd) *Butterfly; (BFLCD 9) <114151>* **WAR DANCE** (remix album) [-] [ ] Aug98

KILLJOYS

Formed: Stoke, England . . . 1977 by main writer, KEVIN ROLAND (aka ROWLAND, i.e. future lead singer for DEXY'S MIDNIGHT RUNNERS), alongside HEATHER TONGE, MARK PHILLIPS, GEM STONE (later bass player of GIRLSCHOOL) and JOE 45 (apparently, only half the man of puppet, JOE 90!). The KILLJOYS managed only one blasting raw punk anthem, 'JOHNNY WON'T GET TO HEAVEN' (a prophetic tale for JOHNNY ROTTEN!), before all but KEVIN disappeared from punk's underground limelight. However, an "oi" crew formed another KILLJOYS (not this lot!) for a one-off single, 'THIS IS NOT LOVE', late in 1982. • **Note:** Not to be confused with the Canadian power-pop outfit of the 90's.

Album rating: NAIVE mini compilation (*4)

KEVIN ROLAND – vocals / **GEM (STONE)** – bass / **HEATHER TONGE** – vocals / **MARK PHILLIPS** – guitar / **JOE 45** – drums

Raw not iss.

Nov 77. (7") *(RAW 3)* **JOHNNY WON'T GET TO HEAVEN. / NAIVE** [ ] [-]

— they split for a long period while KEVIN advanced his DEXY's career

— GEM joined RUBELLA BALLET and later GIRLSCHOOL

– compilations, etc. –

May 92. (m-lp) *Damaged Goods; (FNARRLP 10)* **NAIVE** [ ] [-]

— Note: another KILLJOYS (not this one!) issued an album for 'Mushroom'.

KILL II THIS

Formed: Manchester, England . . . 1996 by MARK MYNETT, JEFF SINGER, New Yorker NICK ARLEA and BEN CALVERT. A year later, this queasily titled band unveiled a metal template, 'ANOTHER CROSS II BARE', which shifted between PANTERA and MACHINE HEAD. With newcomers MATT POLLOCK and CAROLINE CAMPBELL replacing ARLEA and SINGER respectively, they released a second set, 'DEVIATE' (1998), while securing slots with the likes of MEGADETH and STUCK MOJO. K2T returned with a third set, 'TRINITY . . .' in Spring 2000, the North of England was certainly alive and well courtesy of tours with EARTHTONE9 and MISERY LOVES CO.

Album rating: ANOTHER CROSS II BARE (*6) / DEVIATE (*6) / TRINITY: VOODOO, VICE AND THE VIRGIN MARY (*6)

NICK ARLEA (b. New York) – vocals / **MARK MYNETT** (b. 7 Apr'69, Preston) – guitar / **JEFF SINGER** – bass / **BEN CALVERT** (b.27 Jan'81, Berwick-Upon-Tweed) – drums

Hardware not iss.

Mar 97. (cd) *(HR 02CD)* **ANOTHER CROSS II BARE** [ ] [-]
– Subversive / The Wicker man / Blessed are the blind / Another cross II bare / Questions / Ascension / Bleeding / Stillborn / My reality / Burn / Brainwash. *(re-iss. Jun00 on 'Visible Noise'; TORMENT 004CD)*

— **MATT POLLOCK** (b.22 Mar'75, Scunthorpe) – vocals (ex-SWAMPDIVA) repl. NICK ARLEA

— **CAROLINE CAMPBELL** (b.10 Nov'79) – bass; repl. JEFF SINGER

Visible Noise not iss.

Nov 98. (cd) *(TORMENTCD 1)* **DEVIATE** [ ] [-]
– Soundtrack to murder / Kill your gods / Freedom of speech / The flood / Generation pain / Funeral around my heart / This world / Mourning sickness / Crucified / Faith rape / Twisted / Spiral of despair.
Apr 00. (cd) *(TORMENT 003CD)* **TRINITY: VOODOO, VICE AND THE VIRGIN MARY** [ ] [-]
– Art emotion religion / Figure of Eight / God on drugs / This is the news / 2 tribes / Spiritual darkness / Way of the flesh / Trinity / Heal the separation / Guided by voices.

KING DIAMOND (see under ⇒ MERCYFUL FATE)

KINGDOM COME

Formed: West Coast, USA . . . 1987 by Hamburg born LENNY WOLF, previously mainman for STONE FURY (released two album for 'M.C.A.', 'BURNS LIKE A STAR' (1984) and 'LET THEM TALK' (1986). Hooking up with DANNY STAG, RICK STEIER, JOHNNY B. FRANK and JAMES KOTTACK, WOLF and co. were signed to 'Polydor' as KINGDOM COME by Derek Shulman (ex-GENTLE GIANT). One of the most controversial debuts of the decade, the group's eponymous 1988 album so closely resembled prime 'ZEPPELIN that it sparked major debate between advocates and doubters in the metal press. Nevertheless it sold half a million copies in the States, reaching Top 20 in the process. Obviously taking the hint, the band made a half-hearted attempt at originality for the second effort, although this time around they came out sounding like a second-hand DEF LEPPARD. Faced with a slightly more favourable critical reaction but average sales figures, WOLF retired for a rethink, only to return in 1991 with a new bunch of recruits for the album, 'HANDS OF TIME'. Once again, WOLF took time out before he resurfaced with a fourth set, 'BAD IMAGE' (1994). For the rest of the 90's, WOLF and his ever-changing KINGDOM COME continued to strike out with a handful of other equally unimpressive albums, namely 'TWILIGHT CRUISER' (1997), 'MASTER SEVEN' (1997), 'LIVE & UNPLUGGED' (1998), 'BALLADESQUE – THE PEARLS' (1998) and 'TOO' (2000). • **Songwriters:** WOLFF (their manager) – WOLF – STEIER collaborations, until 1991 WOLF-TATUM. Covered:- WHO DO YOU LOVE (Bo Diddley) / AND I LOVER HER (Beatles).

Album rating: KINGDOM COME (*5) / IN YOUR FACE (*6) / HANDS OF TIME (*3) / BAD IMAGE (*4) / TWILIGHT CRUISER (*3) / MASTER SEVEN (*3) / LIVE & UNPLUGGED (*4) / BALLADESQUE . . . THE PEARLS (*3) / TOO (*3)

LENNY WOLF – vocals (ex-STONE FURY) / **DANNY STAG** – lead guitar / **RICK STEIER** – rhythm guitar / **JOHNNY B. FRANK** – bass / **JAMES KOTTACK** – drums

Polydor Polydor

Mar 88. (7") *(KCS 1)* **GET IT ON. / 17** [75] [69]
(12"+=/12"pic-d+=/cd-s+=) *(KC X/XP/CD 1)* – Loving you.
Mar 88. (lp/c)(cd) *(KC LP/MC 1)<(835 368-2)>* **KINGDOM COME** [43] [12]
– Living out of touch / Pushin' hard / What love can be / 17 / The shuffle / Get it on / Now "forever after" / Hideaway / Loving you / Shout it out.
Jul 88. (7") *(KCS 2)* **WHAT LOVE CAN BE. / THE SHUFFLE** [ ] [ ]
(12"+=/12"g-f+=/cd-s+=) *(KC X/XG/CD 2)* – Helping hand.
Apr 89. (7"/7"clear) *(KC S/CV 3)* **DO YOU LIKE IT. / HIGHWAY 6** [73] [ ]
(12"+=/12"pic-d+=) *(KC X/PDX 3)* – Slow down.
(cd-s++=) *(KCCDS 3)* – Get it on (the full version).
May 89. (lp/c/cd) *<(839 192-1/-4/-2)>* **IN YOUR FACE** [25] [49]
– Do you like it / Who do you love / The wind / Gotta go (can't wage a war) / Highway 6 / Perfect "O" / Just like a wild rose / Overrated / Mean dirty Joe / Stargazer.
Sep 89. (7"/7"clear) *(KC S/CV 4)* **OVERRATED. / JUST LIKE A WILD ROSE** [ ] [ ]
(12"+=/cd-s+=) *(KC X/CDS 4)* – The perfect "O" (live).
(10"+=) *(KCCVX 4)* – The wind (live).

— Split Aug'89, but WOLF reformed in '91 complete with **BLUES SARACENO** – guitar / **VOEN VAN BAAL** – keyboards / **JIMMY BRALOWER + STEVE BURKE** – drums

Jun 91. (cd/c/lp) *<(849 329-2/-4/-1)>* **HANDS OF TIME** [ ] [ ]
– I've been trying / Should I / You'll never know / Both of us / Stay / Blood on the land / Shot down / You're not the only . . . I know / Do I belong / Can't deny / Hands of time.

W.E.A. W.E.A.

Feb 94. (cd/c/lp) *<(4509 93148-2/-4/-1)>* **BAD IMAGE** [ ] [ ]
– Passion departed / You're the one / Fake believer / Friends / Mad queen / Pardon the difference (but I like it) / Little wild thing / Can't resist / Talked too much / Glove of stone / Outsider.

— now down to **LENNY WOLF** and whoever was available

not iss. Viceroy

Jan 97. (cd) *<11945>* **TWILIGHT CRUISER** [-] [ ]
– Always on the run / Law of emotions / Twilight cruiser / Janine / Hope is on fire / Thank you all / Rather be on my own / Can't put out and not take back / Cold ground / I don't care / Gonna change / Should have known.

Bellaphon not iss.

Dec 97. (cd) *(290.25.002)* **MASTER SEVEN** [-] [-] German
– Only rainbows know / More restrictions / Gonna lose her / Can't let go / Slow down / Seen enough / Can't let go (director's cut) / Gonna try / Can't take affection / Bad I am / High on love / Get up my friend / Roses.
Jun 98. (cd) *(35450-425)* **LIVE & UNPLUGGED (live)** [-] [-] German
– Living out of touch / Blood on the land / I don't care / What love can be / Always

on the run / Do you like it / Thank you all / Hope is on fire / Friends / And I love her / You'll never know / Rather be on my own / Janine / You're not the only / You're not the only.

Dogo Bros | not iss.

Dec 98. (cd) *(39035-023)* **BALLADESQUE . . . THE PEARLS** - | - German
– Should have known / Can't let go / Twilight cruiser / Cold ground / Rather be on my own / Can't take affection / Friends / You'll never know / Janine / What love can be / And I love her.

Nov 00. (cd) *<95124>* **TOO** -
– It ain't so bad / Free your mind / Waiting / Too late / You're my secret / Hey man / Tease / Mighty old man / Tell me what I've done / Should have told you / Joe English.

KING KOBRA

Formed: California, USA . . . 1984 by veteran drummer CARMINE APPICE, who enlisted the help of MARK FREE, MIKE SWEDA, DAVID MICHAEL-PHILLIPS and JOHNNY ROD. Signing to 'Capitol', the group released their debut set in 1985, a sturdy collection of accessible, often flashy US hard-rock. With promising reviews, the future looked bright for the band but, like so many 80's outfits, they subsequently shot themselves in the foot by adopting a more radio-orientated approach. The resulting 'THRILL OF A LIFETIME' (1987) accordingly suffered poor sales as original fans deserted them and their label eventually issued their P45's. ROD then decamped to shock merchants W.A.S.P., leaving APPICE and MICHAELS-PHILLIPS to restructure the group around ex-MONTROSE vocalist JOHNNY EDWARDS, JEFF NORTHRUP and LARRY HART. Securing a new deal with 'Music For Nations', the revamped KING KOBRA attempted a return to the tougher sound of their debut on 'KING KOBRA III' (1989). Praise was in short supply, however, and there weren't many tears shed when APPICE finally disbanded the group following his move to the newly formed BLUE MURDER.

Album rating: READY TO STRIKE (*6) / THRILL OF A LIFETIME (*5) / KING KOBRA III (*5) / THE LOST YEARS demos (*4)

MARK FREE – vocals / **MIKE SWEDA** – guitar / **DAVID MICHAELS-PHILLIPS** – guitar / **JOHNNY ROD** – bass / **CARMINE APPICE** – drums (ex-OZZY OSBOURNE, etc, etc.)

Capitol | Capitol

1985. (lp) *<240312-1>* **READY TO STRIKE** -
– Ready to strike / Hunger / Shadow rider / Shake up / Attention / Breakin' out / Tough guys / Dancing with desire / Second thoughts / Piece of the rock. *(cd-iss. May00 on 'Axe Killer'; AXE 305723CD)*

May 86. (7") *(CL 397) <5559>* **IRON EAGLE (NEVER SAY DIE). / THIS RAGING FIRE** Nov85

FM Revolver | Capitol

Jan 87. (12") *(12VHF 35)* **HOME STREET HOME. / IRON EAGLE (NEVER SAY DIE)** | -

Mar 87. (lp/c) *(WKFM LP/MC 83) <ST/TC-ST 12473>* **THRILL OF A LIFETIME** Nov86
– Second time around / Dream on / Feel the heat / Thrill of a lifetime / Only the strong survive / Iron eagle (never say die) / Home street home / Overnight sensation / Raise your hands to rock / Party animals.

— **JOHNNY EDWARDS** – vocals (ex-MONTROSE) repl. FREE

— **JEFF NORTHRUP** – guitar; repl. SWEDA

— **LARRY HART** – bass; repl. ROD who joined W.A.S.P.

Music For Nations | New Renaissance

Aug 89. (cd/c/lp) *(CD/T+/MFN 86) <NRCD 26>* **KING KOBRA III** Nov88
– Mean St. machine / Take it off / Walls of silence / Legends never die / Redline / Burning in her fire / Perfect crime / It's my life / #1.

— the band split when APPICE joined BLUE MURDER

– compilations, etc. –

Jun 99. (cd) *Cleopatra; <(CLP 585)>* **THE LOST YEARS**
– Mean street machine / Fool in the rain / Young hearts survive / Your love's a sin / #1 / Walls of silence / Lonely nites / Red line / Perfect crime / Overnight love affair / Poor boy (you are my life).

KING PRAWN

Formed: East London, England . . . 1995 by AL-FARABI RUMJEN, ARYAN DEVIL, BABAR LUCK and SLUGBOYE. Their debut album, 'FIRST OFFENCE', was produced by SKUNK ANANSIE's ACE, apparently for free. A manic burst of speedball hardcore with a list of diverse influences as long as your arm (er, DEAD KENNEDYS to RAGE AGAINST THE MACHINE), the KING PRAWN sound was developed over a series of 7" singles culminating with a second long-player, 'FRIED IN LONDON' (1998). Known to dislike each other . . . immensely! • **Covered:** BIG A LITTLE A (Crass).

Album rating: FIRST OFFENCE (*5) / FRIED IN LONDON (*5) / SURRENDER TO THE BLENDER (*5)

AL-FARABI RUMJEN – vocals / **ARYAN DEVIL** – guitar / **BABAR LUCK** – bass / **NICK 'SLUG' SWINDONBOYE** – drums

Word Of Warning | Word Of Warning

Nov 95. (7") *(WOW 45)* **POISON ON THE AIR. /** | -
(cd-s+=) *(WOWCD 45)* –

Jun 96. (cd) *(WOWCD 46)* **FIRST OFFENCE** | -
– Doledrums / Salvation / Boxed & packaged / Immigrant song too / Restart (acts I & II) / Bossman's bleeding / Nobody like you / Alien spawn / First defence.

Jun 97. (7") *(WOW 52)* **DEPTHS OF MY SOUL. / FELLED** | -

Nov 97. (7") *(WOW 53)* **NOT YOUR PUNK. / BIG A LITTLE A** | -
(cd-s+=) *(WOW 53CD)* – Ruthless.

Apr 98. (cd) *(<WOWCD 54>)* **FRIED IN LONDON** Jul98
– Sound of we / Not your punk / Felled / Increase the pressure / Role model / Racist copper / Survive / Depths of my soul / Clocked / Rewards and prizes / Last request.

Spitfire | Spitfire

Nov 99. (cd-ep) *(SPITCD 050)* **YOUR WORST ENEMY** | -
– Poison in the air / No peace / Your worst enemy / War cry.

Mar 00. (cd-s) *(SPITXS 101)* **DAY IN DAY OUT / DAY IN DAY OUT (The Peri Coloso mix – radio edit) / RACIST COPPER (live)** | -

Jul 00. (cd-s) *(SPITXS 122)* **SOMEONE TO HATE / INCREASE THE PRESSURE (live) / SOMEONE TO HATE (Corridors Of Tension mix)** | -

Jul 00. (cd) *(SPITCD 053) <15053>* **SURRENDER TO THE BLENDER**
– Intro / Someone to hate / No peace / Day in day out / London born / Be warned / The postman song / Your worst enemy / American funded genocide / Amuse the young & amaze the old / Espiritu du carnival / Crackhead / The postman song (2nd post) / People taking over / Freedom day.

KING'S X

Formed: Springfield, Missouri, USA . . . 1981, initially as The EDGE by DOUG PINNICK (bass/vocals), TY TABOR (guitar) and JERRY GASKELL (drums). After five years of touring, they signed to US metal label 'Megaforce' in 1987 with the help of manager SAM TAYLOR, changing their name to KING'S X. Their debut album, the C.S. Lewis-inspired 'OUT OF THE SILENT PLANET' (1988), fused strong BEATLES-esque harmonies (dominated by black singer, PINNICK) and heavy blues riffs to create a uniquely spiritual sound reflecting their Christian beliefs. 'SHOT OF LOVE' was the highlight, a rousing piece of pop-rock that vaguely recalled BIG COUNTRY (!) of all people. The record attracted the interest of 'Atlantic', and a year later they made their major label debut with 'GRETCHEN GOES TO NEBRASKA'. The album was more complex and ambitious while still favouring content over style, the likes of 'OVER MY HEAD' possessing both an addictive chorus and a considerable lyrical and devotional depth. 'FAITH HOPE LOVE' (1990) continued to expand the group's unique vision, stressing the value of spirituality in a general sense rather than preaching Christian dogma. Both the eponymous third album and 'DOGMAN' (1994) continued the band's quietly determined efforts to make a difference in a cut throat music business, KING'S X gaining valuable exposure in their quest when they played at the 'Woodstock II' festival in 1994. Two years later, they returned with 'EAR CANDY', an average set that failed to win the band any new fans. A move to independent label, 'Metal Blade', served to free up the band from commercial pressures and the influence of outside writers/producers, resulting in the much improved 'TAPE HEAD' (1998). The fact that the songs were credited to the band as a whole was hardly surprising given the record's sharpened focus and melodic incisiveness, its heavier approach maintained on the bizarrely titled 'PLEASE COME HOME . . . MR.BULBOUS' (2000).

Album rating: OUT OF THE SILENT PLANET (*6) / GRETCHEN GOES TO NEBRASKA (*8) / FAITH HOPE LOVE (*6) / KING'S X (*5) / DOGMAN (*4) / EAR CANDY (*5) / THE BEST OF KING'S X compilation (*7) / TAPE HEAD (*6) / PLEASE COME HOME MR. BULBOUS (*5)

DOUG PINNICK (b. 3 Sep'50, Joliet, Illinois) – vocals, bass / **TY TABOR** (b.17 Sep'61, Jackson, Missouri) – guitar / **JERRY GASKILL** (b.27 Dec'57, Bridgeton, New Jersey) – drums

Megaforce | Megaforce

Mar 88. (lp/c/cd) *(K 781825-1/-4/-2) <81825>* **OUT OF THE SILENT PLANET**
– In the new age / Goldilox / Power of love / Wonder / Sometimes / King / What is this? / Far, far away / Shot of love / Visions.

Jun 89. (lp/c)(cd) *(WX 279/+C)(761 997-2) <81997>* **GRETCHEN GOES TO NEBRASKA** 52
– Out of the silent planet / Over my head / Summerland / Everybody knows a little bit of something / The difference (in the garden of St.Anne's-On-the-Hill) / I'll never be the same / Mission / Fall on me / Pleiades / Don't believe it (it's easier said than done) / Send a message / The burning down. *(re-iss. cd Feb95; same)*

Mar 90. (7"/c-s) *(A 8982/+C) <88868>* **OVER MY HEAD. / SHOT OF LOVE**
(12"+=/cd-s+=) *(A 8982 T/CD)* – I'll never be the same.

May 90. (7") *<88776>* **SUMMERLAND. /** -

Oct 90. (cd/c/lp) *<(7567 82145-2/-4/-1)>* **FAITH HOPE LOVE** 70 | 85
– We are finding who we are / It's love / I'll never get tired of you / Fine art of friendship / Mr. Wilson / Moonjaw / Six broken soldiers / I can't help it / Talk to you / Everywhere I go / We were born to be loved / Faith hope love / Legal kill.

Apr 91. (7"/c-s) *(A 7791/+C)* **IT'S LOVE. / WE WERE BORN TO BE LOVED**
(12"+=/cd-s+=) *(A 7791 T/CD)* – Six broken soldiers.

— The track 'Junior's Gone Wild' appeared on the film 'Bill & Ted's Bogus Journey', & the b-side of ARGENT's 'God Gave Rock'n'roll To You II' single.

Mar 92. (cd/c/lp) *(7567 80506-2/-4/-1) <82372>* **KING'S X** 46
– World around me / Prisoner / The big picture / Lost in Germany / Chariot song / Ooh song / Not just for the dead / What I know about love / Black flag / Dream in my life / Silent wind.

Feb 94. (cd/c/lp) *<(7567 82558-2/-4/-1)>* **DOGMAN** 49
– Dogman / Shoes / Pretend / Flies and blue skies / Black the sky / Fool you / Don't care / Sunshine rain / Complain / Human behavior / Cigarettes / Go to hell / Pillow / Manic depression.

May 96. (cd/c/lp) *<(7567 82880-2/-4/-1)>* **EAR CANDY**
– Train / Mississippi moon / Lies in the sand / Fathers / Picture / American cheese / Life going by / Run / 67 / Looking for love / (Thinking and wondering) What I'm gonna do / Box / Sometime.

Nov 97. (cd) <83066> **THE BEST OF KING'S X** (compilation) [-] [ ]
– King / Goldilox / Summerland / Pleiades / It's love / Mr. Wilson / Black flag / Lost in Germany / Dogman / Cigarettes / The train / Looking for love / Life going by / Sally / April showers / Lover / Over my head (live).

Metal Blade / Metal Blade

Nov 98. (cd) <(3984 14187-2)> **TAPE HEAD** [ ] [ ] Oct98
– Groove machine / Fade / Over and over / Ono / Cupid / Ocean / Little bit of soul / Hate you / Higher than God / Happy / Mr. Evil / World / Walter Bela Farkas (live).

Feb 99. (cd-s) **FADE / OCEAN / FRIENDS / GROOVE MACHINE (live)** [ ] [-]

Jul 00. (cd) <(14298-2)> **PLEASE COME HOME MR. BULBOUS** [ ] [ ] May00
– Fish bowl man / Julia / She's gone away / Marsh mallow field / When you're scared / Charlie Sheen / Smudge / Bitter sweet / Move me / Move me (pt.2).

TY TABOR

Inside Out / Inside Out

Nov 98. (cd) **MOONFLOWER LANE** [ ] [ ]

Nov 98. (cd-s) **I DO / HOLLOW EYES / HAD TO MOVE** [ ] [ ]

KISS

Formed: New York City, New York, USA . . . late '71 by ex-WICKED LESTER members GENE SIMMONS and PAUL STANLEY, who recruited guitarist ACE FREHLEY and drummer PETER CRISS. After a year of touring in '73, they were signed to the new 'Casablanca' label, hitting the US Top 100 with an eponymous debut album in early '74. This, together with subsequent follow-up albums, 'HOTTER THAN HELL' (1974) and 'DRESSED TO KILL' (1975) set the greasepainted scene for what was to follow; low-rent glitter-metal so tacky it almost stuck to the speakers. Though these early albums sound like they were recorded on a cheap walkman in a sawmill, they contained some of KISS' finest groin-straining moments; 'STRUTTER', 'DEUCE' and 'ROCK AND ROLL ALL NITE' were anthemic shout-alongs for white college kids who could pretend to be rebellious for three minutes. But KISS undoubtedly built their reputation on a garish image and the sensory overkill of their live show, ALICE COOPER-style make-up and onstage schlock the order of the day. Accordingly, it was the double live album, 'ALIVE' (1975) that finally powered the band into the US Top 10 and the stadium major league. With 'DESTROYER' (produced by COOPER mentor, BOB EZRIN), the band refined their sound slightly, even recording a ballad, the PETER CRISS-penned/crooned teen heartbreaker, 'BETH' which furnished the band with their biggest ever hit single. This mid-70's career peak also saw a further three releases achieve platinum status, 'ROCK AND ROLL OVER' (1976), 'LOVE GUN' (1977) and 'ALIVE II'. KISS had struck a resounding chord in some back alley of the American consciousness and now boasted a merchandise line almost as long as SIMMONS' grotesque tongue, a perverted, proto-SPICE GIRLS marketing job from the dark side. And you couldn't get a much better marketing coup than releasing four solo albums simultaneously on the same day, which is exactly what KISS did (one by each member), probably because they knew they could get away with it. Unsurprisingly, most of the material was self-indulgent rubbish and, with the threat of punk never far away, the band began to falter. Although the 'DYNASTY' (1979) album went Top 10 and provided a massive hit with 'I WAS MADE FOR LOVIN' YOU', CRISS soon bowed out, the drum stool filled by session man ANTON FIG for the 'UNMASKED' (1980) album. A permanent replacement was found in ERIC CARR who made his debut on the ill-advised concept nonsense of 'THE ELDER' (1981), though the new musical direction was just too much for FREHLEY to take and he wisely departed the following year. His place was filled by VINNIE VINCENT, who played on the back to basics 'CREATURES OF THE NIGHT'. When this album failed to revive their commercial fortunes, the band did the unthinkable, removing their make-up for the 'LICK IT UP' album. Perhaps as a result of the public discovering they weren't blood sucking ghouls after all but (relatively) normal looking people, the album went Top 30. Ironically, the band had just started to re-establish themselves in Britain, where 'LICK IT UP' made the Top 10, no doubt giving them heart in their struggle back to world domination. KISS then went through more line-up changes, with VINCENT being replaced first by MARK ST. JOHN, then BOB KULICK. With the unashamedly commercial 'CRAZY CRAZY NIGHTS' single and 'CRAZY NIGHTS' (1987) album, the band enjoyed their biggest success since their 70's heyday, both releases reaching No.4 in the UK. After another reasonably successful album, 'HOT IN THE SHADE' (1989), tragedy struck the band in the early 90's when CARR died following heart problems and cancer. Shaken but unbowed the band carried on with ERIC SINGER on drums, going back to the hoary sound of old with the 'REVENGE' (1992) opus, an album that saw them showing the young bucks who had patented the moves. It had to happen of course; 1996 marked a money-spinning, full-blown reunion tour with the original line-up and re-applied warpaint, the perfect KISS-off to those who had written them off for dead. Of course, this now meant that KULICK and SINGER were surplus to requirement; the pair were duly given their marching orders and the KISS album they'd just worked on, 'CARNIVAL OF SOULS: THE FINAL SESSIONS' was shelved. With bootleggers having a field day, the album was eventually given a belated release in 1997 although critics were generally agreed that its lacklustre contents should've been kept on the mastertape. Still, KISS were flying high after the runaway success of the reunion tour and even decided to record a full album together. The resulting 'PSYCHO CIRCUS' (1998) made the US Top 3 to incredibly become the highest charting album of their near three decade career! This despite the fact it offered nothing new or even compared to their glory days. Then again, when the mainstream modern alternatives are so bland is it any wonder people consistently cling to retro fantasies? • **Songwriters:** Most by STANLEY or SIMMONS, with some ballads by CRISS. Covered; THEN (S)HE KISSED ME (Crystals) / GOD GAVE ROCK'N'ROLL TO YOU (Argent). MICHAEL BOLTON co-wrote with STANLEY their minor hit ballad 'FOREVER'. GENE SIMMONS solo covered; WHEN YOU WISH UPON A STAR (Judy Garland). • **Trivia:** In 1977, Marvel Comics started a KISS feature series in their monthly mag. In 1984, SIMMONS starred as a villain in the film 'Runaway' alongside Tom Selleck. Two years later 'The Bat-Winged Vampire' featured in films 'Never Too Young To Die', 'Trick Or Treat' & 'Wanted Dead Or Alive'. In 1994, a tribute album 'KISS MY ASS' was released by 'Mercury'. It featured star cover versions by LENNY KRAVITZ, GARTH BROOKS, ANTHRAX, GIN BLOSSOMS, TOAD THE WET SPROCKET, SHANDI's ADDICTION, DINOSAUR JR., EXTREME, LEMONHEADS, etc.

Album rating: KISS (*7) / HOTTER THAN HELL (*7) / DRESSED TO KILL (*7) / ALIVE! (*8) / DESTROYER (*8) / ROCK AND ROLL OVER (*6) / LOVE GUN (*6) / ALIVE II (*7) / DOUBLE PLATINUM compilation (*8) / DYNASTY (*6) / UNMASKED (*5) / (MUSIC FROM) THE ELDER (*4) / KILLERS compilation (*5) / CREATURES OF THE NIGHT (*6) / LICK IT UP (*6) / ANIMALIZE (*5) / ASYLUM (*6) / CRAZY NIGHTS (*5) / SMASHES, THRASHES AND HITS compilation (*7) / HOT IN THE SHADE (*6) / REVENGE (*6) / ALIVE III (*7) / MTV UNPLUGGED (*5) / CARNIVAL OF SOULS (*5) / PSYCHO-CIRCUS (*4) / ALIVE IV (*3)

GENE SIMMONS (b. GENE KLEIN, 25 Aug'49, Haifa, Israel) – vocals, bass / **PAUL STANLEY** (b. STANLEY EISEN, 20 Jan'52, Queens, N.Y.) – guitar, vocals / **ACE FREHLEY** (b. PAUL FREHLEY, 22 Apr'51, Bronx, N.Y.) – lead guitar, vocals / **PETER CRISS** (b. PETER CRISSCOULA, 27 Dec'47, Brooklyn, N.Y.) – drums, vocals

Casablanca / Casablanca

Feb 74. (7") <0004> **NOTHIN' TO LOSE. / LOVE THEME FROM KISS** [-] [ ]

Feb 74. (lp) <9001> **KISS** [-] [87]
– Strutter / Nothin' to lose / Fire house / Cold gin / Let me know / Kissin' time / Deuce / Love theme from Kiss / 100,000 years / Black diamond. *(UK-iss.Feb75; CBC 4003) (re-iss. May77 red-lp; CAL 2006) (re-iss. Feb82 lp/c; 6399/7199 057) (re-iss. Jul84 lp/c; PRICE/PRIMC 68) (cd-iss. Aug88; 824146-2)*

May 74. (7") <0011> **KISSIN' TIME. / NOTHIN' TO LOSE** [-] [83]

Aug 74. (7") <0015> **STRUTTER. / 100,000 YEARS** [-] [ ]

Nov 74. (lp) <7006> **HOTTER THAN HELL** [-] [100]
– Got to choose / Parasite / Goin' blind / Hotter than Hell / Let me go, rock'n roll / All the way / Watchin' you / Mainline / Comin' home / Strange ways. *(UK-iss.May77 red-lp; CAL 2007) (re-iss. Feb82 lp/c; 6399/7199 058) (cd-iss. Aug88; 824147-2)*

Jan 75. (7") *(CBX 503)* **NOTHIN' TO LOSE. / LOVE THEME FROM KISS** [ ] [-]

Mar 75. (7") <823> **LET ME GO ROCK'N'ROLL. / HOTTER THAN HELL** [-] [ ]

Aug 75. (lp) *(CBC 4004)* <7016> **DRESSED TO KILL** [ ] [32] Mar75
– Room service / Two timer / Ladies in waiting / Getaway / Rock bottom / C'mon and love me / Anything for my baby / She / Love her all I can / Rock and roll all nite. *(re-iss. May77 red-lp; CAL 2008) (re-iss. Feb82 lp/c; 6399/7199 059) (cd-iss. Aug88; 824148-2)*

May 75. (7") <829> **ROCK AND ROLL ALL NITE. / GETAWAY** [-] [68]

Jun 75. (7") *(CBX 510)* **ROCK AND ROLL ALL NITE. / ANYTHING FOR MY BABY** [ ] [-]

Oct 75. (7") <841> **C'MON AND LOVE ME. / GETAWAY** [-] [ ]

Nov 75. (7") <850> **ROCK AND ROLL ALL NITE (live). / ('A'studio mix)** [-] [12]

Apr 76. (7") *(CBX 516)* <854> **SHOUT IT OUT LOUD. / SWEET PAIN** [ ] [31] Mar76

May 76. (lp) *(CBC 4008)* <7025> **DESTROYER** [22] [11] Mar76
– Detroit rock city / King of the night time world / God of thunder / Great expectations / Flaming youth / Sweet pain / Shout it out loud / Beth / Do you love me. *(re-iss. May77 red-lp; CAL 2009) (re-iss. Feb82 lp/c; 6399/7199 064) (cd-iss. Apr87; 824149-2)*

Jun 76. (7") <858> **FLAMING YOUTH. / GOD OF THUNDER** [-] [74]

Jun 76. (d-lp) *(CBC 4011+2)* <7020> **ALIVE! (live)** [49] [9] Oct75
– Deuce / Strutter / Got to choose / Hotter than Hell / Firehouse / Nothin' to lose / C'mon and love me / Parasite / She / Watchin' you / 100,000 years / Black diamond / Rock bottom / Cold gin / Rock and roll all nite / Let me go, rock'n'roll. *(re-iss. May77 red-lp; CALD 5001) (re-iss. Feb82; 6640 064) (re-iss. Sep84 d-lp/d-c; PRID/+C 3) (cd-iss. Apr87; 822780-2)*

Aug 76. (7") <863> **BETH. / DETROIT ROCK CITY** [-] [7]

Jul 76. (7") *(CBX 519)* **BETH. / GOD OF THUNDER** [ ] [-]

Feb 77. (red-lp) *(CALH 2001)* <NBLP 7037> **ROCK AND ROLL OVER** [ ] [11] Nov76
– I want you / Take me / Calling Dr. Love / Ladies room / Baby driver / Love 'em and leave 'em / Mr. Speed / See you in your dreams / Hard luck woman / Makin' love. *(re-iss. Feb82 lp/c; 6399/7199 060) (cd-iss. Aug88; 824150-2)*

Dec 76. (7") <873> **HARD LUCK WOMAN. / MR. SPEED** [-] [15]

Mar 77. (7") <880> **CALLING DR. LOVE. / TAKE ME** [-] [16]

May 77. (7"m) *(CAN 102)* **HARD LUCK WOMAN. / CALLING DR. LOVE / BETH** [ ] [-]

Jun 77. (lp) *(CALH 2017)* <7057> **LOVE GUN** [ ] [4]
– I stole your love / Christine sixteen / Got love for sale / Shock me / Tomorrow and tonight / Love gun / Hooligan / Almost human / Plaster caster / The she kised me. *(re-iss. Feb82 lp/c; 6399/7199 063) (re-iss. Jul84 lp/c; PRICE/PRIMC 69) (cd-iss. Aug88; 824151-2)*

Jul 77. (7") <889> **CHRISTINE SIXTEEN. / SHOCK ME** [-] [25]

Aug 77. (7"m/12"m) *(CAN/L 110)* **THEN SHE KISSED ME. / HOOLIGAN / FLAMING YOUTH** [ ] [-]

Sep 77. (7") <895> **LOVE GUN. / HOOLIGAN** [-] [61]

Nov 77. (d-lp/d-c) *(CALD/+C 5004)* <7076> **KISS ALIVE II** [60] [7]
– Detroit rock city / King of the night time world / Ladies room / Makin' love / Love gun / Calling Dr. Love / Christine sixteen / Shock me / Hard luck woman / Tomorrow and tonight / I stole your love / Beth / God of thunder / I want you / Shout it out loud / All American man / Rockin' in the U.S.A. / Larger than life / Rocket ride /

Anyway you want it. *(re-iss. Feb82 d-lp)(d-c; 6685 043)(7599 512) (cd-iss. May89; 822781-2)*

Jan 78. (7") *<906>* **SHOUT IT OUT LOUD (live). / NOTHIN' TO LOSE (live)** [-] [54]

Feb 78. (7") *<915>* **ROCKET RIDE. / TOMORROW AND TONIGHT** [-] [39]

Mar 78. (7") *(CAN 117)* **ROCKET RIDE. / LOVE GUN (live)** [ ] [-]
(12"+=) *(CANL 117)* – Detroit rock city (live).

Jun 78. (7") *(CAN 126)* **ROCK AND ROLL ALL NITE. / C'MON AND LOVE ME** [ ] [-]

— Took time to do solo projects (all same label on below)

GENE SIMMONS

Sep 78. (lp/pic-lp) *<NBLP/NBPIX 7120>* **GENE SIMMONS** [-] [22]
– Radioactive / Burning up with fever / See you tonite / Tunnel of love / True confessions / Living in sin / Always near you – Nowhere to hide / Man of 1000 faces / Mr. Make Believe / See you in your dreams / When you wish upon a star. *<re-iss. 1987 pic-lp; NBLPP 7120>*

Oct 78. (7") *<NB 951>* **RADIOACTIVE. / SEE YOU IN YOUR DREAMS** [-] [ ]

Jan 79. (7",7"red) *(CAN 134)* **RADIOACTIVE. / WHEN YOU WISH UPON A STAR** [41] [-]

ACE FREHLEY

Sep 78. (lp/pic-lp) *<NBLP/NBPIX 7121>* **ACE FREHLEY** [-] [26]
– Rip it out / Speedin' back to my baby / Snow blind / Ozone / What's on your mind / New York groove / I'm in need of love / Wiped-out / Fractured mirror. *<re-iss. 1987 pic-lp; NBLPP 7121> (cd-iss. May88; 826916-2)*

Nov 78. (7"blue) *(CAN 135) <NB 941>* **NEW YORK GROOVE. / SNOW BLIND** [ ] [13] Sep78

PETER CRISS

Sep 78. (lp/pic-lp) *<NBLP/NBPIX 7122>* **PETER CRISS** [-] [43]
– I'm gonna love you / You matter to me / Tossin' and turnin' / Don't you let me down / That's the kind of sugar papa likes / Easy thing / Rock me, baby / Kiss the girl goodbye / Hooked on rock'n'roll / I can't stop the rain. *<re-iss. 1987 pic-lp; NBLPP 7122> (cd-iss. Nov91; 826917-2) (re-iss. Aug94 cd+red-lp+book on 'Megarock')*

Dec 78. (7") *(NB 952>* **DON'T YOU LET ME DOWN. / HOOKED ON ROCK AND ROLL** [-] [ ]

Feb 79. (7"green) *(CAN 139)* **YOU MATTER TO ME. / HOOKED ON ROCK AND ROLL** [ ] [-]

PAUL STANLEY

Sep 78. (lp/pic-lp) *<NBLP/NBPIX 7123>* **PAUL STANLEY** [-] [40]
– Tonight you belong to me / Move on / Ain't quite right / Wouldn't you like to know / Take me away (together as one) / It's alright / Hold me, touch me (think of me when we're apart) / Love in chains / Goodbye. *(re-iss. 1987 pic-lp; NBLPP 7123> (cd-iss. Nov91; 826918-2)*

Feb 79. (7",7"purple) *(CAN 140)* **HOLD ME TOUCH ME. / GOODBYE** [ ] [-]

KISS

— returned to studio

Casablanca Casablanca

Jun 79. (7") *(CAN 152) <983>* **I WAS MADE FOR LOVIN' YOU. / HARD TIMES** [50] [11] May79
(12") *(CANL 152)* – ('A'side) / Charisma.

Jun 79. (lp/c) *(CALH/+C 2051) <7152>* **DYNASTY** [50] [9]
– I was made for lovin' you / 2,000 man / Sure know something / Dirty livin' / Charisma / Magic touch / Hard times / X-ray eyes / Save your love. *(re-iss. Oct83 lp/c; PRICD/PRIMC 42) <cd-iss. 1988; > (cd-iss. Aug88; 812770-2)*

Aug 79. (7") *(CAN 163) <2205>* **SURE KNOW SOMETHING. / DIRTY LIVIN'** [ ] [47]

Feb 80. (7"m/12"m) *(NB/+L 1001)* **2000 MAN. / I WAS MADE FOR LOVIN' YOU / SURE KNOW SOMETHING** [ ] [-]

Mercury Casablanca

Jun 80. (7") *<2282>* **SHANDI. / SHE'S SO EUROPEAN** [-] [47]

Jun 80. (7") *(MER 19)* **TALK TO ME. / SHE'S SO EUROPEAN** [ ] [-]

Jun 80. (lp/c) *(6302 032) <7225>* **UNMASKED** [48] [35]
– Is that you / Shandi / Talk to me / Naked city / What makes the world go 'round / Tomorrow / Two sides of the coin / She's so European / Easy as it seems / Torpedo girl / You're all that I want. *(cd-iss. May83; 800041-2)*

Aug 80. (7") *(KISS 1)* **WHAT MAKES THE WORLD GO 'ROUND. / NAKED CITY** [ ] [-]

Aug 80. (7") *<2299>* **TOMORROW. / NAKED CITY** [-] [ ]

— (May'80) **ERIC CARR** (b.12 Jul'50) – drums, producer repl. CRISS who went solo (early 80's pop albums; 'OUT OF CONTROL' / 'LET ME ROCK YOU')

Nov 81. (lp/c) *(6302/7144 163) <7261>* **MUSIC FROM 'THE ELDER'** [51] [75]
– The oath / Fanfare / Just a boy / Dark light / Only you / Under the rose / A world without heroes / Mr. Blackwell / Escape from the island / Odyssey / I. *(cd-iss. Jun89; 825153-2)*

Nov 81. (7") *<2343>* **A WORLD WITHOUT HEROES. / DARK LIGHT** [-] [56]

Jan 82. (7"/7"pic-d) *(KISS/+P 2)* **A WORLD WITHOUT HEROES. / MR. BLACKWELL** [55] [-]

— **VINNIE VINCENT** (b. VINCENT CUSANO) – guitar repl. BOB KULICK who had repl. FREHLEY (he formed FREHLEY'S COMET)

Casablanca Casablanca

Oct 82. (7") *<2365>* **DANGER. / I LOVE IT LOUD** [-] [ ]

Oct 82. (7") *(KISS 3)* **KILLER. / I LOVE IT LOUD** [ ] [-]
(12"+=) *(KISS 3-12)* – I was made for lovin' you.

Oct 82. (lp/c) *(6302/7144 219) <7270>* **CREATURES OF THE NIGHT** [22] [45]
– Creatures of the night / Saint and sinner / Keep me comin' / Rock and roll Hell / Danger / I love it loud / I still love you / Killer / War machine. *(cd-iss. Aug88; 824154-2)*

Mar 83. (7") *(KISS 4)* **CREATURES OF THE NIGHT. / ROCK AND ROLL ALL NITE (live)** [34] [-]
(12"+=) *(KISS 4-12)* – War machine.

Vertigo Mercury

Oct 83. (7") *<814 671-7>* **LICK IT UP. / DANCE ALL OVER YOUR FACE** [-] [66]

Oct 83. (7"/7"sha-pic-d) *(KISS 5/+P)* **LICK IT UP. / NOT FOR THE INNOCENT** [34] [-]
(12"+=) *(KISS 5-12)* – I still love you.

Oct 83. (lp/c) *(VERL/+C 9) <814 297>* **LICK IT UP** [7] [24]
– Exciter / Not for the innocent / Lick it up / Young and wasted / Gimme more / All Hell's breakin' loose / A million to one / Fits like a glove / Dance all over your face / And on the 8th day. *(cd-iss. Dec89 on 'Mercury'; 814297-2)*

Jan 84. (7") *<818 216-2>* **ALL HELL'S BREAKIN' LOOSE. / YOUNG AND WASTED** [-] [ ]

— **MARK (NORTON) ST. JOHN** – guitar repl. VINCENT who formed VINNIE VINCENT'S INVASION

Sep 84. (7") *(VER 12) <880 205-7>* **HEAVEN'S ON FIRE. / LONELY IS THE HUNTER** [43] [49]
(12"+=) *(VERX 12)* – All hell's breakin' loose.

Sep 84. (lp/c) *(VERL/+C 18) <822 495>* **ANIMALIZE** [11] [19]
– I've had enough (into the fire) / Heaven's on fire / Burn bitch burn / Get all you can take / Lonely is the hunter / Under the gun / Thrills in the night / While the city sleeps / Murder in high-heels. *(cd-iss. Dec89 on 'Mercury'; 822 495-2)*

Nov 84. (7") *<880 535-2>* **THRILLS IN THE NIGHT. / BURN BITCH BURN** [-] [ ]

— **BRUCE KULICK** – guitar repl. MARK who became ill

Oct 85. (lp/c) *(VERH/+C 32) <826 099>* **ASYLUM** [12] [20]
– King of the mountain / Any way you slice it / Who wants to be lonely / Trial by fire / I'm alive / Love's a deadly weapon / Tears are falling / Secretly cruel / Radar for love / Uh! All night. *(cd-iss. May89 on 'Mercury'; 826 303-2)*

Oct 85. (7") *<884 141-7>* **TEARS ARE FALLING. / ANY WAY YOU SLICE IT** [-] [51]

Oct 85. (7") *(KISS 6)* **TEARS ARE FALLING. / HEAVEN'S ON FIRE (live)** [57] [-]
(12"+=) *(KISS 6-12)* – Any way you slice it.

Sep 87. (7"/7"s) *(KISS 7/+P) <888 796-7>* **CRAZY CRAZY NIGHTS. / NO, NO, NO** [4] [65]
(12"+=) *(KISS 7-12)* – Lick it up / Uh! All night.
(12"pic-d+=) *(KISSP 7-12)* – Heaven's on fire / Tears are falling.

Oct 87. (lp/c) *(VERH/+C 49) <832626>* **CRAZY NIGHTS** [4] [18]
– Crazy crazy nights / I'll fight Hell to hold you / Bang bang you / No, no, no / Hell or high water / My way / When your walls come down / Reason to live / Good girl gone bad / Turn on the night / Thief in the night. *(cd-iss. Feb91; 832 626-2)*

Dec 87. (7"/7"s) *(KISS/+P 8) <870 022-7>* **REASON TO LIVE. / THIEF IN THE NIGHT** [33] [64]
(c-s+=) *(KISSMC 8)* – Who wants to be lonely.
(12"++=) *(KISS 8-12)* – Thrills in the night.
(12"pic-d++=) *(KISSP 8-12)* – Secretly cruel.
(cd-s+=) *(KISCD 8)* – Tears are falling / Crazy crazy nights.

Feb 88. (7"/7"s) *(KISS/+P 9) <870 215-7>* **TURN ON THE NIGHT. / HELL OR HIGH WATER** [41] [ ]
(12"+=/12"pic-d+=) *(KISS/+P 9-12)* – King of the mountain / Any way you slice it.
(cd-s+=) *(KISCD 9)* – Heaven's on fire / I love it loud.

Oct 89. (7"/7"red/c-s) *(KIS S/R/MC 10) <876 146-7>* **HIDE YOUR HEART. / BETRAYED** [59] [66]
(12"+=/cd-s+=) *(KIS SX/CD 10)* – Boomerang.
(10"pic-d) *(KISP 10-10)* – ('A'side) / Lick it up / Heaven's on fire.

Oct 89. (lp/c/cd) *<(838 913-2/-4/-1)>* **HOT IN THE SHADE** [35] [29]
– Rise to it / Betrayed / Hide your heart / Prisoner of love / Read my body / Love's a slap in the face / Forever / Silver spoon / Cadillac dreams / King of hearts / The street giveth and the street taketh away / You love me to hate you / Somewhere between Heaven and Hell / Little Caesar / Boomerang.

Mar 90. (7"/7"s) *(KISS/+P 11) <876 716-7>* **FOREVER (remix). / THE STREET GIVETH AND THE STREET TAKETH AWAY** [65] [8] Feb90
(12"white+=) *(KISS 12-12)* – Deuce (demo) / Strutter (demo).
(12"/12"g-f) *(KIS SX/XG 11)* – ('A'side) / All American man / Shandi / The Oath.
(cd-s) *(KISCD 11)* – ('A'side) / Creatures of the night / Lick it up / Heaven's on fire.

Jun 90. (c-s) *<875096>* **RISE TO IT. / SILVER SPOON** [-] [81]

— In May'91, ERIC CARR underwent open heart surgery. He was admitted to hospital again but they found malignant cancer growth. He died on the 24th Nov'91. In Jan'92, KISS hit UK No.4 with 'GOD GAVE ROCK'N'ROLL TO YOU II' from the film 'Bill & Ted's Bogus Journey'. On the same single issued on 'Interscope' were tracks by 'KINGS X' & 'SLAUGHTER'.

— **ERIC SINGER** – drums (ex-BADLANDS, ex-BLACK SABBATH) repl. CARR

May 92. (7"/c-s) *(KISS/KISMC 12)* **UNHOLY. / GOD GAVE ROCK'N'ROLL TO YOU II** [26] [ ]
(12"+=/12"pic-d+=)(cd-s+=) *(KISS/+P 12-12)(KISCD 12)* – Partners in crime / Deva / Strutter (demos).

May 92. (cd/c/lp) *(848 037-2/-4/-1) <48037>* **REVENGE** [10] [6]
– Unholy / Take it off / Tough love / Spit / God gave rock'n'roll to you II / Domino / Heart of chrome / Thou shalt not / Every time I look at you / Paralyzed / I just wanna / Carr jam 1981.

May 93. (cd/c) *<(514 827-2/-4)>* **KISS ALIVE III (live)** [24] [9]
– Creatures of the night / Deuce / I just wanna / Unholy / Heaven's on fire / Watchin' you / Domino / I was made for lovin' you / I still love you / Rock'n'roll all nite / Lick it up (featuring BOBBY WOMACK) / Take it off / I love it loud / Detroit rock city / God gave rock'n'roll to you / Star spangled banner.

Mar 96. (cd/c/lp) *<(528 950-2/-4/-1)>* **MTV UNPLUGGED (live)** [74] [15]
– Comin' home / Plaster caster / Goin' blind / Do you love me / Domino / Sure know something / A world without heroes / Rock bottom / See you tonight / I still love you / Every time I look at you / 2,000 man / Beth / Nothin' to lose / Rock and roll all nite.

Oct 97. (cd/c) *<(536 323-2/-4)>* **CARNIVAL OF SOULS** [ ] [27]
– Hate / Rain / Master and slave / Childhood's end / I will be there / Jungle / In my head / It never goes away / Seduction of the innocent / I confess / In the mirror / I walk alone.

—— originals were back again (**SIMMONS, STANLEY, FREHLEY + CRISS**)

Sep 98. (cd/c) *<(558 992-2/-4)>* **PSYCHO-CIRCUS** [47] [3]
– Psycho-circus / Within / I pledge allegience (to the state of rock & roll) / Into the void / We are one / You wanted the best / Raise your glasses / I finally found my way / Dreamin' / Journey of 1,000 years.

Apr 00. (cd) *<(542 457-2)>* **ALIVE IV (live)** [ ] [ ]
(above was possibly shelved?)

– compilations etc. –

Aug 76. (t-lp) *Casablanca; <7032>* **THE ORIGINALS** (first 3 albums) [-] [ ]

May 78. (d-lp) *Casablanca; (CALD 5005) <7100 1-2>* **DOUBLE PLATINUM** [ ] [24]
(re-iss. Feb82; 6641 907) (re-iss. May85 d-lp/d-c; PRID/+C 8) cd-iss. Jun87; 824 148-2)

Jan 81. (lp) *Casablanca; (6302 060)* **THE BEST OF THE SOLO ALBUMS** [ ] [-]

Jun 82. (lp) *Casablanca; (CANL 1)* **KILLERS** [42] [-]

Nov 88. (7") *Mercury; <872 246-7>* **LET'S PUT THE 'X'. / CALLING DR. LOVE** [-] [97]

Nov 88. (lp/c/cd) *Vertigo / Mercury; <(836 759-1/-4/-2)>* **SMASHES, THRASHES AND HITS** [62] [21]
– Let's put the X in sex / Crazy, crazy nights / (You make me) Rock hard / Love gun / Detroit rock city / I love it loud / Reason to live / Lick it up / Heavens on fire / Strutter / Beth / Tears are falling / I was made for lovin' you / Rock and roll all nite / Shout it out loud.

Oct 88. (5"vid-cd) *Vertigo; (080 232-2)* **CRAZY, CRAZY NIGHTS. / NO, NO, NO / WHEN YOUR WALLS COME DOWN / THIEF IN THE NIGHT** [ ] [-]

1989. (7") *Mercury; <814 303-7>* **BETH. / HARD LUCK WOMAN** [-] [ ]

1989. (7") *Mercury; <814 304-7>* **ROCK AND ROLL ALL NITE. / I WAS MADE FOR LOVIN' YOU** [-] [ ]

Sep 89. (5"vid-cd) *Vertigo; (080 044-2)* **LICK IT UP. / DANCE ALL OVER YOUR FACE / GIMME MORE / FITS LIKE A GLOVE** [ ] [-]

Sep 89. (5"vid-cd) *Vertigo; (080 058-2)* **TEARS ARE FALLING. / ANY WAY YOU SLICE IT / WHO WANTS TO BE LONELY / SECRETLY CRUEL** [ ] [-]

—— (all lp's were released as pic-lp's in Europe)

Jul 96. (cd/c) *Mercury; <(532 741-2/-4)>* **YOU WANTED THE BEST, YOU GOT THE BEST (live compilation)** [ ] [17]

Jul 97. (cd/c) *Polygram TV; <(536 159-2/-4)>* **GREATEST HITS** [58] [77] Apr97

KITTIE

Formed: London, Ontario, Canada . . . 1997 by schoolgirls MORGAN LANDER and FALLON BOWMAN, the line-up completed by LANDER's sister MERCEDES and TANYA CANDLER (subsequently replaced by TALENA ATHELD). Combining feline allure with howling rage, these angry young women started out playing grunge covers before graduating to the 'Artemis' label and releasing a debut album, 'SPIT', in late 1999. Lurching from breathy vocal teasing to hysterical screaming in the space of a few bars, the adolescent fury on offer perhaps reflected the trials of an all-girl band in the hoary old world of rawk. Similarly, by cutting and pasting old metal with nu, the record's schizophrenic/progressive (delete according to taste) approach suggested a band yet to reach musical maturity. Live EP, 'PAPERDOLL' (2000) confirmed the impression of a KITTIE still trying to find its claws or at least the musical wherewithal to scale the heights of spiritual forebears such as BABES IN TOYLAND and HOLE.

Album rating: SPIT (*7)

MORGAN LANDER – vocals, guitar / **FALLON BOWMAN** – guitar, vocals / **TALENA ATFIELD** – bass; repl. TANYA CANDLER / **MERCEDES LANDER** – drums

Artemis-Epic Artemis-Epic

Jan 00. (cd/c) *(497630-2/-4) <751002>* **SPIT** [ ] [79]
– Spit / Charlotte / Suck / Do you think I'm a whore / Brackish / Jonny / Trippin' / Raven / Get off (you can eat a dick) / Choke / Paperdoll / Immortal.

Mar 00. (7") *(669129-7)* **BRACKISH. / DA SHIT YOU CAN'T FUC WIT** [46] [ ]
(cd-s+=) *(669129-2)* – Charlotte (alternative mellow version).

Jul 00. (7") **CHARLOTTE. / SPIT (live)** [60] [ ]
(cd-s+=) – Suck (live) / ('A'-CD-ROM video).

Dec 00. (cd-ep) *<751066>* **PAPERDOLL EP** [-] [ ]
– Paperdoll (remix) / Spit / Brackish / Suck / Do you think I'm a whore / Raven.

KIX

Formed: Hagerstown, Maryland, USA . . . 1980 by DONNIE PURNELL and RONNIE YOUNKINS, who were subsequently joined by STEVE WHITEMAN, BRIAN FORSYTHE and JIMMY CHALFANT. Building up a formidable local live reputation, the band soon secured a contract with 'Atlantic', releasing their self-titled debut in 1981. Raucous, good-time, if hardly original metal/hard-rock, the group's forthright style assimilated a variety of classic influences into an invigorating brew. It wasn't until 1985's 'MIDNITE DYNAMITE', however, that the KIX sound really came into its own, the ubiquitous BEAU HILL lending his midas production touch. Following a period of extensive touring, a belated follow-up, 'BLOW MY FUSE', eventually appeared in 1988. Another impressive slab of raunch'n'roll, the record saw the group breaking into the US Top 50 for the first time. Moving to 'East West' for 'HOT WIRE' (1991), KIX's fortunes began to falter as they attempted to swim against the grunge tide. When they eventually reappeared four years later with 'SHOW BUSINESS', they had downscaled their operation to the independent 'Music For Nations' label. Another band seemingly inextricably linked to the 80's hair-metal heyday, KIX's moment seems to have passed.

Album rating: KIX (*4) / COOL KIDS (*3) / MIDNITE DYNAMITE (*6) / BLOW MY FUSE (*7) / HOT WIRE (*5) / KIX LIVE (*5) / SHOW BUSINESS (*3)

STEVE WHITEMAN – vocals / **RONNIE YOUNKINS** – guitar / **BRIAN FORSYTHE** – guitar / **DONNIE PURCELL** – bass / **JIMMY CHALFANT** – drums

Atlantic Atlantic

1981. (lp) *<50834>* **KIX** [-] [ ]
– Atomic bombs / Love at first sight / Heartache / Poison / The itch / Kix are for kids / Contrary Mary / The kid / Yeah yeah yeah.

1981. (7") *<3859>* **THE ITCH. /** [-] [ ]

1981. (7") *<3885>* **HEARTACHE. /** [-] [ ]

1982. (7") *<4018>* **ATOMIC BOMBS. /** [-] [ ]

—— **BRAD DIVENS** – guitar, vocals; repl. YOUNKINS

May 83. (7") *<89852>* **BODY TALK. /** [-] [ ]

May 83. (lp) *(780056-1) <80056>* **COOL KIDS** [ ] [ ]
– Burning love / Cool kids / Love pollution / Body talk / Loco-emotion / Mighty mouth / Nice on ice / Get your monkeys out / For shame / Restless blood.

Jun 83. (7") *(A 9810)* **COOL KIDS. / MIGHTY MOUTH** [ ] [-]

Aug 83. (7") *<89802>* **LOCO-EMOTION. /** [-] [ ]

—— **YOUNKINS** returned to repl. DIVENS

Oct 85. (lp) *(K 781 267-1) <81267>* **MIDNITE DYNAMITE** [ ] [ ]
– Midnight dynamite / Red hot (black & blue) / Bang bang (balls of fire) / Layin' rubber / Walkin' away / Scarlet fever / Cry baby / Cold shower / Lie like a rug / Sex.

Sep 88. (lp/c/cd) *(K 781 877-1/-4/-2) <81877>* **BLOW MY FUSE** [ ] [46]
– Red lite, green lite, TNT / Get it while it's hot / No ring around Rosie / Don't close your eyes / She dropped me the bomb / Cold blood / Piece of the pie / Boomerang / Blow my fuse / Dirty boys.

Oct 88. (7") *<88940>* **BLOW MY FUSE. / COLD BLOOD** [-] [ ]

Jan 90. (7") *(A 7889) <88902>* **DON'T CLOSE YOUR EYES. / GET IT WHILE IT'S HOT** [ ] [11] Aug89
(12"+=) *(A 7889T)* – She dropped me the bomb.

East West East West

Jul 91. (cd/c/lp) *<(7567 91714-2/-4/-1)>* **HOT WIRE** [ ] [64]
– Hot wire / Girl money / Luv-a-holic / Tear down the walls / Bump the la la / Rock & roll overdose / Cold chills / Same Jane / Pants on fire (liar, liar) / Hee bee jee bee crush.

Jul 91. (c-s) *<98757>* **GIRL MONEY** [-] [ ]

Jan 92. (c-s) *<98691>* **TEAR DOWN THE WALLS** [-] [ ]
below without FORSYTHE

Apr 93. (cd) *<82499>* **KIX LIVE (live)** [-] [ ]
– Hot wire / Same Jane / Rock and roll overdose / Sex / The itch / For shame / Tear down the walls / Blow my fuse / Girl money / Cold blood / Don't close your eyes / Yeah, yeah, yeah.

May 93. (cd-s/c-s) *<84875>* **DON'T CLOSE YOUR EYES** [-] [ ]

Music For Nations C.M.C.

Apr 95. (cd) *(CDMFN 159) <87303>* **SHOW BUSINESS** [ ] [ ]
– Ball baby / 9-1-1 / Fireballs / Baby time bomb / Book to hypnotize / Put my money where your mouth is / She loves me not / Fire boy / I'm bombed / If you run around.

—— KIX decided to get some elsewhere

KMFDM

Formed: Germany . . . 1984 by the trio of EN-ESCH, SASCHA KONIETZKO and NAINZ WATTS. KMFDM (which apparently stands for KEINE MEHRHEIT FUR DIE MITLEID – No Majority For Compassion) were one of the pioneers of the mid-80's hardbeat/industrial revolution that swept Europe and threw up acts like FRONT 242, YOUNG GODS and NITZER EBB. Following an eponymous German-only debut album and its follow-up, 'WHAT DO YOU KNOW, DEUTSCHLAND?', the group became part of the burgeoning 'Wax Trax!' stable, the tastemakers of the US industrial scene and home to MINISTRY, REVOLTING COCKS, etc. The late 80's also saw the appearance of two further sets, 'DON'T BLOW YOUR TOP' (1988) and 'UAIOE' (1989), the band's growing cult popularity based on their uncompromising steamhammer beats 'n distorted guitar/vocals formula. Varying their brutal musical strategy only slightly, the Germans maintained their prolific release schedule throughout the first half of the 90's, the nihilistic minimalism of the music extending to the album titles:- 'NAIVE' (1990), 'MONEY' (1992), 'SUCKS' (1993), 'ANGST' (1993) and 'NIHIL' (1995). Subsequently signing to 'TVT' (home of industrial chart slayers, NINE INCH NAILS), KMFDM continued to take no prisoners with 1996's 'XTORT'. The bade farewell to the music industry via 1999's appropiately-titled 'ADIOS'.

Album rating: KMFDM (*5) / NAIVE (*7) / MONEY (*6) / ANGST (*6) / NIHIL (*4) / XTORT (*5) / SYMBOLS (*5) / RETRO compilation (*7) / ADIOS (*5)

SASCHA KONIETZKO + EN-ESCH + NAINZ WATTS

Zensor not iss.

1986. (lp) *(ZR 2016)* **KMFDM (KEINE MEHRHEIT FUR DIE MITLEID)** [-] [-] German
– Zip / Deutsche schuld / Sieg-Sieg / Positive / Conillon / What do you know / Me I funk.

Skysaw Wax Trax!

Feb 88. (lp/cd) *(SAW/CDSAW 004)* **WHAT DO YOU KNOW, DEUTSCHLAND?** [ ] [-]
– Kickin' ass / Me I funk / What do you know? / Zip / Conillon / Itchy bitchy / Deutsche schuld / Sieg sieg / Positiv / Lufthans / Itchy bitchy (dance version) / The unrestrained use of excessive force.

Nov 88. (lp/cd) *(SAW/CDSAW 006) <WAX 052>* **DON'T BLOW YOUR TOP** [ ] [ ]
– Don't blow your top / No meat no man / Oh look / What a race / King Kong / No news / Oh look.

Dec 88. (12") *(SAW 008)* <*WAX 049*> **DON'T BLOW YOUR TOP. /**

Strikeback Wax Trax!

May 89. (lp/cd) *(SBR 032/+CD)* <*WAX 7083*> **UAIOE**
– Murder / UAIOE / Loving can be an art / More & faster 243 / Rip the system / Thrash up / En Esch / Ganja rock / Thumb thumb / Rot the system / More & faster / Naff off.

1989. (12") <*WAX 9077*> **MORE & FASTER** [-]
(above produced by FM EINHEIT / mixed by ADRIAN SHERWOOD)

Nov 89. (12"/cd-s) *(SBR 034 T/CD)* <*WAX 9108*> **VIRUS. / MURDER / M&F 244 (MORE AND FASTER remix)**
(re-iss. Oct94; same)

Wax Trax! Wax Trax!

Sep 90. (cd/lp) *(WAX CD/LP 148)* <*WAXCD 7148*> **NAIVE**
– Welcome / Naive / Die now – Live later / Piggy bank / Achtung! / Friede (remix) / Liebeslied / Go to hell / Virus (dub) / Disgust (live) / Godlike.

Transglobal Wax Trax!

Feb 92. (cd/c/lp) *(GLOBAL 2 CD/C/LP)* <*WAXCD 7177*> **MONEY**
– Money / Vogue / Help us – save us – take us away / Bargeld / Spiritual house / Sex on the flag (Jezebeelzebuttfunk mix) / I will pray / We must awaken / Under Satan (dub) / Vogue (2000) / Money (Deutschmark mix).

May 92. (12"/cd-s) *(TRAN 07 T/CD)* <*9172*> **MONEY. / ('A'mix) / BARGELD** Jul91

— line-up now **KONIETZKO, ESCH, WATTS + GUNTER SCHULZ** – bass, guitar, piano / **MARK DURANTE** – guitar, slide guitar

Roadrunner T.V.T.

May 93. (cd-ep) <*TVT 8703*> **SUCKS (mixes) / MORE 'N' FASTER** [-]

Jul 94. (cd,c) *(RR 8987-2)* <*TVT 7202*> **ANGST** Oct93
– Light / A drug against war / Blood evil / Lust / Glory / Move on / No peace / A hole in the wall / Sucks / The problem.

Intercord Wax Trax!

Feb 96. (cd) *(IRS 993603CD)* <*7199*> **NIHIL** Apr95
– Ultra / Juke joint Jezebel / Flesh / Beast / Terror / Search and destroy / Disobedience / Revolution / Brute / Trust.

T.V.T. T.V.T.

Mar 95. (12") <*TVT 8730*> **YEAR OF THE PIG (mixes)** [-]

Oct 95. (12",cd-s) <*TVT 8733*> **BRUTE (mixes)** [-]

— **KONIETZKO + SCHULZ + EN ESCH** with **DURANTE, CHRIS CONNELLY, FM EINHEIT + NICOLE BLACKMAN**

Apr 96. (cd-s) <*TVT 8719*> **GLORY (mixes)** [-]

Jun 96. (cd,c) <*TVT 7242*> **XTORT** [-] 92
– Power / Apathy / Rules / Craze / Dogma / Inane / Blame / Son of a gun / Ikons / Wrath.

Aug 96. (12") <*TVT 8740*> **POWER (mixes)** [-]

Nov 96. (12"/cd-s) <*(TVT 8746-0/-2)*> **RULES. / SON OF AS GUN / INANE**

Dragnet-Sony T.V.T.

Oct 97. (cd/lp) *(488971-2/-1)* <*TVT 7245-2*> **SYMBOLS** Sep97
– Meglomaniac / Stray bullet / Leid und elend / Mercy / Torture / Spit sperm / Anarchy / Down and out / Unfit / Waste.

Jan 98. (m-cd) <*TVT 8753*> **MDFMK** [-]
– Megalomaniac / Anarchy / Megalomaniac / Unfit / Anarchy / Megalomaniac.

Apr 99. (cd) <*TVT 7258*> **ADIOS** [-]
– Adios / Syncopant / D.I.Y / Today / Witness / R.U.Ok? / That's all / Full worm garden / Rubicon / Bereit.

— they band had already split in Jan'99

– compilations, etc. –

Nov 98. (cd) *Wax Trax!;* <*8741*> **RETRO** [-]
– Power / Juke-joint Jezebel / Brute / Drug against war / Light / Money / Vogue / Godlike – Doglike / Virus – Pestilence / Liebeslied-Liebeslied / More and faster / Rip the system / What do you know, Deutschland? / Don't blow your top.

Nov 98. (cd) *Wax Tra~x!;* <*8760*> **AGOGO** [-]
– Thank you / Godlike / Virus-dub / Rip the system / Naff off / Mysterious ways / Ooh la la / Hole in the wall / Agogo / Zip.

— note: there were a number of other US promos on 'Wax Trax-TVT'

KONKHRA

Formed: Koge, Denmark . . . 1989 by CLAUS VEDEL, who recruited JON CLAUSEN and ANDERS LUNDEMARK, the latter aged only 16 at the time and who was to become the only member still with the band to this day. They began under the moniker VICIOUS CIRCLE, but within a year had changed this to KONKHRA. Although later becoming one of the big names in the international death metal scene, their beginnings hardly belied this, as they toured as a soundtrack for a stage company. However, after recruiting bassist MARTIN CHRISTENSEN (with LUNDEMARK moving to guitar and second vocal), the group recorded a demo in 1991 that caught the attention of Denmark's more hardcore metal fans and some further afield. Progress, a small Danish metal fanzine, struck up a mutually beneficial arrangement with the group in 1992, whereby they jointly released the EP in order to lure a record contract and simultaneously promote themselves. Around this time CLAUSEN and CHRISTENSEN split from the band and were replaced – in their respective positions – by LARS SCHMIDT and JOHNNY NIELSEN. KONKHRA released their debut album 'SEXUAL AFFECTIVE DISORDER' the following year. This set was a solid piece of death metal from start to finish, and gained them many more fans abroad. At this point the founder VEDEL decided to exit the band and was replaced on guitar by KIM MATHIESEN. With LUNDEMARK taking solo responsibiltity for the vocals the sound of the band's second full set, 'SPIT OR SWALLOW' (1995), was remarkably different, with a more antagonistic feel which built to make this album a classic of its genre. This gained KONKHRA much credibility with their death metal brethren; touring shortly after the albums release with NAPALM DEATH. This also led the band to release a live set, 'LIVE ERASER' (1995), recorded at the Roskilde festival. Unfortunately things went pear-shaped for these dark Danes after all this attention, leaving LUNDEMARK as the only full-time member of KONKHRA. But the man was not going to let it die. He recruited a bit of an all-star metal band in the shape of CHRIS KONTOS (ex-MACHINE HEAD) on drums, JAMES MURPHY (formerly of TESTAMENT) on guitar and THOMAS CHRISTENSEN on bass. They put together the fourth album 'WEED OUT THE WEAK' (1997) – a bit of a departure from a death metal scene they saw as lagging but still stridently hard metal in its approach. Again problems arose in the band, mainly due to touring responsibilities, but KONKHRA managed to leak out another album, 'COME DOWN COLD' (2000). This record saw the return of SCHMIDT on bass, PER M JENSEN on drums and LARS MAYLAND taking over MURPHY's duties except on the title track. LUNDEMARK also found time to moonlight with DAEMON, a death-metal outfit which featured NICKE ANDERSSON (of the HELLACOPTERS) on their first set, 'SEVEN DEADLY SINS' (1996).
• **Covered:** PROWLER (Iron Maiden) / ORGASMATRON (Motorhead).

Album rating: STRANDED mini (*5) / SEXUAL AFFECTIVE DISORDER (*6) / SPIT OR SWALLOW (*6) / LIVE ERASER (*5) / WEED OUT THE WEAK (*7) / COME DOWN COLD (*5)/ Daemon: SEVEN DEADLY SINS (*5) / THE SECOND COMING (*4)

ANDERS LUNDEMARK – vocals, guitar / **CLAUS VEDEL** – guitar, vocals / **MARTIN KRISTENSEN** – bass / **JON CLAUSEN** – drums

Progress Red not iss.

Jun 93. (promo m-cd) *(CD 791300-2)* **STRANDED** [-]
– Time will destroy / Day-break / Stranded / Lustration of the need / Spread around / Death wish.

— **LARS SCHMIDT** – bass; repl. KRISTENSEN

— **JOHNNY NIELSEN** – drums; repl. CLAUSEN

Nuclear Blast not iss.

Mar 94. (lp/cd) *(NB 105/+CD)* **SEXUAL AFFECTIVE DISORDER** [-]
– Center of the flesh / Seasonal affective disorder / The dying art / Visually intact / Evilution / Lucid dreams / Blindfolded / Thoughts abandoned / Chaos to climb / Empty frames.

— **KIM MATHIESEN** – guitar; repl. VEDEL

Progress Pavement

Aug 95. (cd-ep) *(PCD 18)* **THE FACELIFT EP** [-]
– Drowning (dead dreaming) / Facelift / Warzone / Basic facts of life.

Sep 95. (cd) *(PCD 19)* <*32223*> **SPIT OR SWALLOW** Mar96
– Centuries / Spit or swallow / Life eraser / Hail the body, burden the spirit / Hooked / Facelift / Scorn of the earth / Subconscience / Necrosphere / Hold another level. *(re-iss. w/+=)* – THE FACELIFT

Diehard Metal Blade

Jul 96. (cd) *(PCD 31)* **LIVE ERASER (live)** [-]
– Hooked / Warzone / Basic facts of life / S.A.D. / The dying art / Centuries / Drowning, dead dreaming / Facelift / Subconscience / Life eraser / Spit or swallow.

— **LUNDEMARK** enlisted new band **JAMES MURPHY** – guitar / **THOMAS CHRISTENSEN** – bass / **CHRIS KONTOS** – drums

Apr 98. (cd) *(PCD 44)* <*14174*> **WEED OUT THE WEAK** Jul98
– Heavensent / Time will heal / Crown of the empire / Kinshasa highway / Through my veins / The reckoning / Misery / Melting / Inhuman / Pain and sorrow / My belief.

— **LARS SCHMIDT** – bass (returned) to repl. CHRISTENSEN + MURPHY

— **PER M. JENSEN** – drums; repl. KONTOS

Aug 99. (cd-ep) *(PCD 48)* **THE FREAKSHOW EP** [-]
– Sight for sore eyes / Fully defiled / None of these days / Prowler / Orgasmatron.

— added **LARS MAYLAND** – lead guitar

Oct 99. (cd) *(PCD 49)* **COME DOWN COLD** [-]
– Godgiven / White / Lost to the world / Divide & conquer / Truly defiled / Cold / Sight for sore eyes / Back in the day / Convene the freaks / Blessed / Life is fragile / Procreation.

DAEMON

NICKE ANDERSSON + ANDERS LUNDEMARK (of KONKHRA)

Diehard not iss.

Dec 96. (cd) *(RRS 947CD)* **SEVEN DEADLY SINS** [-]
– Sloth / Wrath / Greed / Lust / Gluttony / Pride / Envy / The eighth sin.

— now without NICKE who contined with The HELLACOPTERS

Mar 99. (cd) *(RRS 964CD)* **THE SECOND COMING** [-]
– What if . . . / Come die with me / The truth / My kingdom is a sacred place / Prince of lies / Make me bleed / Way out of hand / Spirit in flames / Symptom of the universe.

KORN

Formed: Bakersfield / Huntington Beach, California, USA . . . 1993 out of CREEP, by JONATHAN DAVIS, J MUNKY SHAFFER, BRIAN 'HEAD' WELCH, FIELDY and DAVID. Signed to 'Epic' the following year, they unleashed to the public their eponymous US Top 75 debut. A barrage of aural psychosis, DAVIS' tortured performance more than lived up to the hype surrounding the record's release. Among its schizophrenic highs and lows were the disturbing but cathartic ten minute (+) emotional minefield, 'DADDY', which cried out from the core of DAVIS' very soul. Bizarrely, DAVIS turned his hand (and elbow) to the bagpipes on the nursery rhyme parody, 'SHOOTS

AND LADDERS', a track that even GAVIN FRIDAY might have disowned in his VIRGIN PRUNES heyday! Consolidating this seminal meisterwork, KORN toured the world, resurfacing in 1996 with another primal scream of sinuous, bass-heavy angst-metal in the shape of 'LIFE IS PEACHY'. The album contained no less than three UK Top 30 hits, 'NO PLACE TO HIDE', 'A.D.I.D.A.S.' (which stands for "All Day I Dream About Sex"; nothing to do with the sports company) and 'GOOD GOD', the set also featuring covers of Oshea Jackson's 'WICKED' and War's 'LOWRIDER'. A US Top 3, the record also cracked the UK Top 40, due largely to the strong Kerrang! support only rivalled in 1997 by DAVIS's more attention-seeking contemporary, MARILYN MANSON. Two further chart-topping albums, 'FOLLOW THE LEADER' (1998) and the concept 'ISSUES' (1999), didn't sell quite so well in Britain, the grim storytelling of KORN's leader beginning to get short shrift from some of his gloomy disciples. • **Covered:** EARACHE MY EYE (Cheech & Chong) / SHOULD I STAY OR SHOULD I GO (Clash).

Album rating: KORN (*9) / LIFE IS PEACHY (*8) / FOLLOW THE LEADER (*5) / ISSUES (*6)

JONATHAN DAVIS – vocals, bagpipes / **J MUNKY SHAFFER** (b. JAMES) – guitar, vocals / **BRIAN 'HEAD' WELCH** – guitar, vocals / **FIELDY** – bass, vocals / **DAVID** – drums, vocals

Epic | Immortal

Jul 95. (cd/c) *(478080-2/-4)* <66633> **KORN** — | 72 Nov94
– Blind / Ball tongue / Need to / Clown / Divine / Faget / Shoots and ladders / Predictable / Fake / Lies / Helmet in the bush / Daddy.

Oct 95. (10"ep) *(KORN 1)* **BLIND**

Oct 96. (7"white) *(663845-0)* **NO PLACE TO HIDE. / PROUD** — 26
(cd-s+=) *(663845-2)* – Sean Olsen.
(cd-s) *(663845-5)* – ('A'side) / Shoots and ladders (Dust Brothers industrial mix) / Shoots and ladders (Dust Brothers hip-hop mix).

Oct 96. (cd/c/lp/cd-rom) *(485369-2/-4/-1/-6)* <67554> **LIFE IS PEACHY** — 32 | 3
– Twist / Chi / Lost / Swallow / Porno creep / Good God / Mr. Rogers / K"£o%! / No place to hide / Wicked / A.D.I.D.A.S. / Lowrider / Ass itch / Kill you.

Feb 97. (10"white-ep) *(664204-0)* **A.D.I.D.A.S. / CHI (live). / LOWRIDER – SHOOTS AND LADDERS (live)** — 22
(cd-ep+=) *(664204-2)* – Ball tongue (live).
(cd-ep) *(664204-5)* – ('A'side) / Faget / Porno creep / Blind.

Jun 97. (cd-ep) *(664658-2)* **GOOD GOD / GOOD GOD (Mekon mix) / GOOD GOD (Dub Pistols mix) / WICKED (Tear The Roof Off mix)** — 25
(cd-ep) *(664658-5)* – ('A'side) / A.D.I.D.A.S. (Synchro dub) / A.D.I.D.A.S. (Under Pressure mix) / A.D.I.D.A.S. (The Wet Dream mix).
(12"ep) *(664658-6)* – ('A'-Mekon mix) / ('A'-Dub Pistols mix) / A.D.I.D.A.S. (Synchro dub) / A.D.I.D.A.S. (Under Pressure mix).

Aug 98. (ltd-cd-s) *(666391-2)* **GOT THE LIFE / (12"mixes by DeeJay Punk-Roc and D.O.S.E.)** — 23
(cd-s) *(666391-5)* – ('A'side) / I can remember / Good god (oomph! vs such a surge mix).

Aug 98. (cd/c/lp) *(491221-2/-4/-1)* <69001> **FOLLOW THE LEADER** — 5 | 1
– It's on / Freak on a leash / Got the life / Dead bodies eveywhere / Children of the korn / B.B.K. / Pretty / All in the family / Reclaim my place / Justin / Seed / Cameltosis / My gift to you.

Apr 99. (cd-s) *(667252-2)* **FREAK ON A LEASH / FREAK ON A LEASH (Dante Ross mix) / FREAK ON A LEASH (Josh A's beast on a leash mix)** — 24
(cd-s) *(667252-5)* – ('A'-Freakin' bitch mix) / ('A'-Josh A's beast on a leash mix) / ('A'-Dante Ross mix).
(12") *(667252-6)* – ('A'mixes; above).

Nov 99. (cd/c/lp) *(496359-2/-4/-1)* <63710> **ISSUES** — 37 | 1
– Dead / Falling away from me / Trash / 4U / Beg for me / Make me bad / It's gonna go away / Wake up / Am I going crazy / Hey daddy / Somebody someone / No way / Let's get the party started / I wish you could be me / Counting / Dirty. *(re-iss. Apr00 cd/cd/cd; 497850-2/-6/-9)*

Jan 00. (7"orange) *(668869-7)* **FALLING AWAY FROM ME. / JINGLE BALLS** — 24
(cd-s+=) *(668869-2)* – ('A'-Krust remix) / ('A'-CD-Rom).
(cd-s) *(668869-5)* – ('A'side) / ('A'-Mantronik Beatdown formula) / Got the life (Josh Abraham remix).

May 00. (7") *(669433-7)* **MAKE ME BAD. / DIRTY (live)** — 25
(cd-s+=) *(669433-2)* – ('A'-live).
(cd-s) *(669433-5)* – ('A'side) / ('A'mixes; Kornography / Sickness In Salvation / Sybil / Danny Saber).

Paul KOSSOFF (see under ⇒ FREE)

KOTTONMOUTH KINGS

Formed: Orange County, California, USA . . . 1994 by frontman BRAD DADDY X (formerly of the HUMBLE GODS), rappers D-LOC and SAINT VICIOUS, DJ BOBBY B, gigantic masked mekanik dancer PAKELIKA and others including drummer LOU DOG and JOHNNY RICHTER (although the latter left then returned after a short-lived solo career and bouts with the authorities). With friends and stablemates such as CORPORATE AVENGER, DOG BOY, GRAND VANACULAR (down at Capitol offshoot 'Suburban Noize'), SEN DOG (of CYPRESS HILL) and The INSANE CLOWN POSSE, who needed enemas (as they say). Seriously though, if one could be looking at this hybrid of trippy hip-hop punks, the tattooed KOTTONMOUTH KINGS were the new hopefuls for a young generation bored with their father's punk-rock LP's. In 1998, the ever-expanding group declared themselves fit to join the ranks of the R&R world via the track, 'SUBURBAN LIFE', which subsequently featured on the 'Scream 2' movie soundtrack. Through 'Capitol', KMK unleashed their debut set, 'ROYAL HIGHNESS' (1998), a slightly disappointing set LP that nevertheless won a loyal support through their riotous gigs; 'STONERS REEKING HAVOC', indeed. For some reason their sophomore effort, 'HIDDEN STASH' (1999), was dismissed by Capitol; legalize marijuana was their cry. With a third album, 'HIGH SOCIETY' (2000), rolling around the US Top 200, it was also unclear why Britain did not take up the option of releasing their white, hardcore malarky; the jury was out for the time being.

Album rating: ROYAL HIGHNESS (*4) / HIDDEN STASH (*5) / HIGH SOCIETY (*5)

BRAD DADDY X (b. BRADFORD LAMBERT) – vocals (ex-HUMBLE GODS) / **SAINT VICIOUS** – rapper / **D-LOC** – rapper / **DJ BOBBY B** – DJ / **PAKELIKA** (b. BILL WADSWORTH) – visuals / **LOU DOG** – drums / and one or two others; also SPIKE XAVIER + ROGER MILLER were real names of two of the above.

not iss. | Capitol

Feb 98. (12"ep) **STONERS REEKING HAVOC** — - |
– Freaks of the industry / Lovesongs / Suburban life / Suburban life (1605 mix) / Bong tokin alcoholics (original).

Feb 98. (cd-ep) <58694> **STONERS REEKING HAVOC** — - |
– Frontline / Suburban life (1605 mix) / Roll it up / 3 horny devils / Bump (Bobby B homegrown mix).

Aug 98. (cd/c) <23857> **ROYAL HIGHNESS** — - |
– Bong tokin' alcoholics / Play on / Suburban life / Life ain't what it seems / So high / Big Hoss / Spies / Bump / Dog's life / What's your trip / High society / Psychedelic funk / Me and my shake / Discombobulated / Planet Budtron.

Sep 98. (12") **DOG'S LIFE (mixes). / PLAY ON (mixes)** — - |

not iss. | Suburban Noize

1999. (cd) <10003> **HIDDEN STASH** — - |
– Frontline / Old (so high) / Roll it up / Everyday / 1605 life / Love songs / Shouts going out / Three horny devils / Freaks / Nightlife / Pimp twist.

— **JOHNNY RICHTER** – vocals; returned to repl. SAINT

not iss. | Capitol

Jun 00. (cd/c) <21480> **HIGH SOCIETY** — - |
– Kona gold greeting / Here we go again / First class / Day dreamin' fazes / The joint / Good as gold / Face facts / Peace not greed / The lottery / Round and round / King's blend / Anarchy through capitolism / We the people / Elevated sounds Unxplanetory / Wickit klowns / Coffee shop / Size of an ant / Crucial / B-Dubb's blend. *(hidden track+=)* – Pimp twist.

Jul 00. (7") **PEACE NOT GREED. / COFFEE SHOP** — - |

Sep 00. (12"ep/cd-ep) **THE LOTTERY (Stackin' chips remix) / THE LOTTERY (E-Swift remix) / LADY KILLER / THE LOTTERY (E-Swift instrumental)** — - |

Richie KOTZEN

Born: c. 1969, USA. Something of a child prodigy, KOTZEN was a veteran of live work by the time he'd reached his late teens, wowing club crowds with his technically brilliant guitar histrionics. Nurtured by metal guru Mike Varney, KOTZEN recorded an eponymous instrumental album for 'Roadrunner' in 1989, alongside fellow new-age virtuoso, MIKE HAMM and ex-JOURNEY man, STEVE SMITH. Extending his talents to vocals, he recruited DANNY THOMPSON and ATMA ANUR for 'FEVER DREAM' (1990), a slightly more accessible offering which nevertheless bore the muso stamp. A final solo set, the more listenable 'ELECTRIC JOY', appeared in 1991 before KOTZEN took up the rather unlikely position of axeman for pop-metal poseurs POISON. In 2000, he released a series of sets (namely 'WAVE OF EMOTION', 'WHAT IS . . .', 'SOMETHING TO SAY' and 'BREAK IT ALL DOWN', the latter ending with a Motown cover!

Album rating: RICHIE KOTZEN (*5) / FEVER DREAM (*6) / ELECTRIC JOY (*5) / MOTHER HEAD'S FAMILY REUNION (*4) / TILT with Greg Howe (*4) / THE INNER GALACTIC FUSION EXPERIENCE (*4) / PROJECT with Greg Howe (*4) / BI-POLAR BLUES (*4) / WAVE OF EMOTION (*4) / WHAT IS . . . (*4) / SOMETHING TO SAY (*4) / BREAK IT ALL DOWN (*4)

RICHIE KOTZEN – guitar / **STUART HAMM** – bass (of JOE SATRIANI) / **STEVE SMITH** – drums (ex-JOURNEY)

Roadrunner | Shrapnel

Jul 89. (lp/c/cd) *(RR 9468-1/-4/-2)* <SH 1042/+C/CD> **RICHIE KOTZEN**
– Squeeze play / Strut it / Unsafe at any speed / Rat trap / Cryptic script / Plaid plesiosaur / Spider legs / Jocose Jenny / Noblesse oblige.

— now with **DANNY THOMPSON** – bass / **ATMA ANUR** – drums

Sep 90. (cd/c/lp) *(RR 9367-2/-4/-1)* <SH 1046 CD/C> **FEVER DREAM**
– She / Fall of a leader / Off the rails / Yvonne / Things remembered never die / Dream of a new day / Money power / Rollercoaster / Wheels can fly / Truth in lies.

— now completely solo

Sep 91. (cd/c/lp) *(RR 9290-2/-4/-1)* <SH 1056 CD/C> **ELECTRIC JOY**
– B-funk / Electric joy / Shufina / Acid lips / Slow blues / High wire / Dr. Glee / Hot rails / The deece song.

— KOTZEN replaced C.C. DEVILLE in POISON, although he remained solo

not iss. | Geffen

1994. (cd) <24712> **MOTHER HEAD'S FAMILY REUNION** — - |
– Socialite / Mother head's family reunion / Where did our love go / Natural thing / Love devine / Soul to soul / Reach out (I'll be there) / Testify / Used / Woman and a man / Livin' easy / Cover me.

— KOTZEN was now no longer with POISON

Shrapnel | Shrapnel

Apr 95. (cd; by RICHIE KOTZEN & GREG HOWE) <SH 1085CD> **TILT** — - |
– Tilt / Chase the dragon / Tarnished with age / Outfit / Confusion / I wanna play / Seventh place / O.D. / Full view.

Nov 95. (cd) <SH 1092CD> **THE INNER GALACTIC FUSION EXPERIENCE** — - |
– Pulse (part 1) / Pulse (part 2) / Dose / Hypnotist / Ultramatic / Trick / Stark / Hype / Tramp / Last words.

— next also with **ANUR** on drums

Nov 97. (cd; by RICHIE KOTZEN & GREG HOWE) *<SHR 1110>*
PROJECT [ ] [ ]
– One fuction / Retro slow / Present moment / Trench / Groove epidemic / Space / Led boots / Crush / Accessed / Noise.

— **KROTZEN** recruited **MATT LUNEAU** – drums

not iss. / Blues Bureau

May 99. (cd) *<2040>* **BI-POLAR BLUES** [-] [ ]
– Gone tomorrow blues / Tied to you / They're red hot / Tobacco road / Broken mam blues / The thrill is gone / From four till late / A step away / Burn it down / No kinda hero / Richie's boogie.

not iss. / Spitfire

May 00. (cd) *<15060>* **WAVE OF EMOTION** [-] [ ]
– Wave of emotion / Times gonna tell / No reason / Breakdown / I'm comin' out / Moonshine / Stoned / Sovereign / World affair / Degeneration / Air.

May 00. (cd) *<15071>* **WHAT IS . . .** [-] [ ]
– What is / Too deep / You got a fire / Locked out / You don't owe me / Angie / Angie / Open your eyes / Strength / Lose again / Cross the line / I'm losing you.

May 00. (cd) *<15095>* **SOMETHING TO SAY** [-] [ ]
– Something to say / What makes a man / The bitter end / Faded / Let me in / Rust / Ready / Aberdine / Holy man / Camouflage / Turned out.

May 00. (cd) *<15096>* **BREAK IT ALL DOWN** [-] [ ]
– Break it all down / Killing time / The feelin's gone / Some voodoo / I would / You don't know / Live a little / I don't belong / My addiction / It burns / I'll be around.

KOVENANT

Formed: Norway . . . 1992 as COVENANT by NAGASH (of DIMMU BORGIR) and BLACKHEART. After a clutch of early demo tapes and the belated release of debut album, 'IN TIMES BEFORE THE LIGHT' (1997), new members ASTENNU (also of DIMMU BORGIR), SVERD and HELLHAMMER (of MAYHEM) joined the fray for the recording of 'NEXUS POLARIS' (1998). The latter album marked the beginning of a new deal with 'Nuclear Blast', the resulting wider exposure leading to impressive European album sales and even a Grammy nomination in their native Norway. The higher profile also resulted in a slight change of name to avoid confusion with a similarly monikered Swedish band. Thus 'ANIMATRONIC' (1999) was released as KOVENANT, a record that had begun life with the working title, 'Prophecies Of Fire'. With ASTENNU having departed due to his commitments in DIMMU BORGIR, CRADLE OF FILTH vocalist SARAH JEZEBEL DIVA was drafted in to provide a bit of airy goth-style atmospherics. Markedly more experimental than KOVENANT's previous efforts, the album expanded its black metal horizons by flirting with scary keyboard ambience, amateur theatrics and industrial grinding.

Album rating: Covenant: IN TIMES BEFORE THE LIGHT (*5) / NEXUS POLARIS (*7) / Kovenant: ANIMATRONIC (*6)

LEX ICON (aka NAGASH) – vocals, bass (of DIMMU BORGIR) / **PSY COMA** (aka BLACKHEART) – guitar

Nuclear Blast / Nuclear Blast

Feb 97. (cd; as COVENANT) **IN TIMES BEFORE THE LIGHT** (rec.1995) [-] [-] Norway
– Towards the crown of nights / Dragonstorms / The dark conquest / From the storm of shadows / Night of the blackwinds / The chasm / Visions of a lost kingdom / Through the eyes of the raven / In times before the light / Monarch of the mighty darkness.

— added **ASTENNU** – guitar (of DIMMU BORGIR) / **SVERD** – keyboards, synthesizer / **VON BLOMBERG** (aka HELLHAMMER) – drums (of MAYHEM, of ARCTURUS)

Mar 98. (cd/lp; as COVENANT) *(NB 301 CD/LP) <6301>* **NEXUS POLARIS** [ ] [ ]
– The suplur feast / Bizarre cosmic industries / Planetarium / The last of dragons / Bringer of the sixth sun / Dragonheart / Planetary black elements / Chariots of thunder.

— (mid'98) added **SARAH JEZEBEL DEVA** – vocals

— (mid'99) now only **LEX, PSY + VON**

Oct 99. (cd) *(NB 406-2) <6406>* **ANIMATRONIC** [ ] [ ]
– Mirrors paradise / New world order / Mannequin / Sindrom / Jihad / The human abstract / Prophecies of fire / In the name of the future / Spaceman / The birth of tragedy.

Wayne KRAMER (see under ⇒ MC5)

Lenny KRAVITZ

Born: 26 May'64, New York City, New York, USA, son of a Russian Jew and black Bahamas-born actress. As a teenager, he moved with his family to Los Angeles, where he joined the local boys' choir and taught himself to play guitar and piano. In 1987, KRAVITZ formed his own one-man band, ROMEO BLUE, marrying girlfriend of two years, 'Cosby Show' actress Lisa Bonet. Over the course of the ensuing two years, he recorded demos which were soon heard by Henry Hirsch, who recommended them to 'Virgin'. In October '89, after many arguments with the record company over production techniques, etc., KRAVITZ finally released a debut album and single, 'LET LOVE RULE'. A back to basics operation of luddite proportions, the record slavishly imitated KRAVITZ's paisley heroes of yesteryear (HENDRIX, CURTIS MAYFIELD, DYLAN) in much the same fashion as The BLACK CROWES paid homage to The FACES and The ALLMAN BROTHERS. Yet, despite charges of plagiarism from critics, much like The 'CROWES debut, 'LET LOVE RULE' was consistently listenable. Unsurprisingly then, the album subsequently notched up sales of half a million copies in the US, eventually reaching Top 60 in the UK. In 1990, the title track became KRAVITZ's first Top 40 success in Britain, tempting MADONNA into requesting his writing skills (along with INGRID CHAVEZ) for her controversial 'Justify My Love' single. Quite a celebrity in his own right, KRAVITZ played up the part of Hollywood socialite to the max, immaculately decked out in nouveau-retro clobber (a la PRINCE) and de rigueur dreadlocks. Later that year, he also appeared in Liverpool at YOKO ONO's tribute to her late husband JOHN LENNON. 'MAMA SAID' (1991) was a more accomplished, soulful affair which fleshed out the sound with brass and strings, songs alternating between introspective mood pieces (he'd recently split with his wife) and gritty funk-rock. Early in '92, LENNY settled out of court over royalties owing to INGRID CHAVEZ from the MADONNA collaboration, although the whole thing seemed a bit of a sham bearing in mind that the main thrust of the song was highly reminiscent of PUBLIC ENEMY's 'Security Of The First World'. Nevertheless, KRAVITZ could well afford to pay, 'MAMA SAID' notching up considerable American and British sales, while the single, 'IT AIN'T OVER 'TIL IT'S OVER' was a US No.2. After writing a passable album for sexy French goddess, VANESSA PARADIS, KRAVITZ re-emerged in thundering rock-God mode (replete with red leather trousers, no less) for 'ARE YOU GONNA GO MY WAY', a HENDRIX-esque song that made the UK Top 5. The album of the same name was KRAVITZ's biggest success to date, scaling the album charts in Britain, although it was clear the singer was running out of fresh ideas (or at least fresh ways of presenting old ideas). 'CIRCUS' (1995) carried on in much the same vein, successful but stale. In 1998, his fifth set, entitled er . . . '5' was much of the same as his last, although it did feature subsequent UK No.1, 'FLY AWAY', a record to feature on his 'GREATEST HITS' in 2000. • **Covered;** COLD TURKEY + GIVE PEACE A CHANCE (John Lennon) / IF SIX WAS NINE (Jimi Hendrix) / DEUCE (Kiss) / AMERICAN WOMAN (Guess Who). • **Trivia:** SLASH of GUNS N' ROSES played guitar on 2 tracks from 'MAMA SAID'.

Album rating: MAMA SAID (*8) / LET LOVE RULE (*7) / ARE YOU GONNA GO MY WAY (*7) / CIRCUS (*5) / 5 (*5) / GREATEST HITS compilation (*8)

LENNY KRAVITZ – vocals, guitar, piano, bass, drums with on session / **HENRY HIRSCH** – keyboards / **KARL DENSON** – sax / + guests

Virgin / Virgin

Oct 89. (7"/7"w-poster) *(VUS/+P 10) <99166>* **LET LOVE RULE. / EMPTY HANDS** [ ] [89]
(12"+=/cd-s+=) *(VUS T/CD 10)* – Blues for Sister Someone / Flower child.

Nov 89. (lp/c/cd) *(VUSLP/VUSMC/CDVUS 10) <91290>* **LET LOVE RULE** [56] [61]
– Sitting on top of the world / Let love rule / Freedom train / My precious love / I build this garden for us / Fear / Does anybody out there even care / Mr. Cab driver / Rosemary / Be. *(c+=)* – Blues for Sister Someone / Flower child. *(cd++=)* – Empty hands.

Jan 90. (7"/c-s) *(VUS/+C 17)* **I BUILT THIS GARDEN FOR US. / FLOWER CHILD** [81] [-]
(12"+=/cd-s+=) *(VUS T/CD 17)* – Fear.

May 90. (7"/c-s) *(VUS/+C 20)* **MR. CAB DRIVER. / BLUES FOR SISTER SOMEONE (live) / DOES ANYBODY OUT THERE EVEN CARE (live)** [58] [ ]
(12"/cd-s) *(VUS T/CD 20)* – (first 2 tracks) / Rosemary (live).
(10") *(VUSA 20)* – ('A'side) / Rosemary (live) / Let love rule (live).

Jul 90. (7"/c-s) *(VUS/+C 26)* **LET LOVE RULE. / COLD TURKEY (live)** [39] [-]
(12"+=) *(VUSTG 26)* – Flower child (live).
(cd-s+=) *(VUSCD 26)* – My precious love (live).
(10") *(VUSA 26)* – ('A'side) / If six was nine (live) / My precious love (live).

Mar 91. (7"/c-s) *(VUS/+C 34)* **ALWAYS ON THE RUN. / ('A'instrumental)** [41] [-]
(12"+=/12"box+=) *(VUST/+X 34)* – Light skin girl from London.
(cd-s++=) *(VUSCD 34)* – Butterfly.

Apr 91. (cd)(c/lp) *(CDVUS 31)(VUS MC/LP 31) <91610>* **MAMA SAID** [8] [39]
– Fields of joy / Always on the run / Stand by my woman / It ain't over 'til it's over / More than anything in this world / What goes around comes around / The difference is why / Stop draggin' around / Flowers for Zoe / Fields of joy (reprise) / All I ever wanted / When the morning turns to night / What the . . .. are we saying? / Butterfly.

May 91. (7"/c-s) *(VUS/+C 43)* **IT AIN'T OVER 'TIL IT'S OVER. / THE DIFFERENCE IS WHY** [11] [-]
(12"+=/cd-s+=) *(VUST 43)* – I'll be around.
(12"pic-d) *(VUSTY 43)* – ('A'side) / (interview).

May 91. (c-s) *<98795>* **IT AIN'T OVER 'TIL IT'S OVER / I'LL BE AROUND** [-] [2]

Sep 91. (7"/c-s) *(VUS/+C 45)* **STAND BY MY WOMAN. / FLOWERS FOR ZOE** [55] [-]
(12"+=) *(VUST 45)* – Stop dragging around (live).
(cd-s+=) *(VUSCD 45)* – What the . . .. are we saying? (live) / Always on the run (live).

Oct 91. (c-s) *<98736>* **STAND BY MY WOMAN / LIGHT SKIN GIRL FROM LONDON** [-] [76]

— now with **CRAIG ROSS** – electric guitar (co-writes some music) / **TONY BRETT** – bass / **MICHAEL HUNTER** – flugel horn

Feb 93. (7"/c-s) *(VUS/+C 65)* **ARE YOU GONNA GO MY WAY. / MY LOVE** [4] [-]
(cd-s) *(VUSCD 65)* – ('A'side) / Always on the run / It ain't over 'til it's over / Let love rule.

Mar 93. (cd)(c/lp) *(CDVUS 60)(VUS MC/LP 60) <86984>* **ARE YOU GONNA GO MY WAY** [1] [12]
– Are you gonna go my way / Believe / Come on and love me / Heaven help / Just be a woman / Is there any love in your heart / Black girl / My love / Sugar / Sister / Eleutheria.

May 93. (7"/c-s) *(VUS/+C 72)* *<12662>* **BELIEVE. / FOR THE FIRST TIME** [30] [60]
(10"pic-d+=/cd-s+=) *(VUS T/CD 72)* – ('A'acoustic) / Sitar (acoustic).

Aug 93. (7"/c-s) *(VUS/+C 73)* **HEAVEN HELP. / ELEUTHERIA** [21] [-]
(cd-s+=) *(VUSDG 73)* – Ascension / Brother.

Nov 93. (7"pic-d/12") *(VUS P/T 76)* **IS THERE ANY LOVE IN YOUR HEART. / ALWAYS ON THE RUN (live)** [52] [ ]
(cd-s+=) *(VUSDG 76)* – What goes around comes around (live) / Freedom train (live).

Mar 94. (c-s) *<38412>* **HEAVEN HELP. / SPINNING AROUND OVER YOU** [-] [80]

Aug 95. (c-s) *(VUSC 93)* **ROCK AND ROLL IS DEAD / ANOTHER LIFE** [22] [-]
(10"+=/cd-s+=) *(VUS AB/CD 93)* – Confused / Is it me or is it you.

Sep 95. (c-s) *<38514>* **ROCK AND ROLL IS DEAD / ANOTHER LIFE / ARE YOU GONNA GO MY WAY (live)** [-] [75]

Sep 95. (cd/c/lp) *(CDVUS/VUSLP/MUSMC 86)* *<40696>* **CIRCUS** [5] [10]
– Rock and roll is dead / Circus / Beyond the 7th sky / Tunnel vision / Can't get you off my mind / Magdalene / God is love / Thin ice / Don't go and put a bullet in your head / In my life today / The resurrection.

Dec 95. (c-s) *(VUSC 96)* **CIRCUS / ('A'acoustic)** [54] [ ]
(10"+=/cd-s+=) *(VUS A/CD 96)* – Tunnel vision (live) / Are you gonna go my way (live).

Feb 96. (7"/c-s) *(VUS A/C 100)* *<38535>* **CAN'T GET YOU OFF MY MIND. / EMPTY HANDS** [54] [62]
(cd-s+=) *(VUSCD 100)* – Stand by my woman.

Sep 96. (10"/cd-s) *(VUS A/CD 107)* **THE RESURRECTION (live). /** [-] [-] w'drawn

May 98. (c-s) *(VUSC 130)* **IF YOU CAN'T SAY NO / WITHOUT YOU** [48] [ ]
(12"+=/cd-s+=) *(VUS T/CD 130)* – ('A'-Zero & BT . . . mixes).

May 98. (cd/c) *(CDVUS/VUSMC 140)* *<47758>* **5** [18] [28]
– Live / Supersoulfighter / I belong to you / Black velveteen / If you can't say no / Thinking of you / Take time / Fly away / It's your life / Straight cold player / Little girl's eyes / You're my flavor / Can we find a reason? *(cd re-iss. Jun99; CDVUSX 140)*

Sep 98. (c-s) *(VUSC 138)* **I BELONG TO YOU / IF YOU CAN'T SAY NO (Flunky in the attic mix)** [75] [ ]
(cd-s+=) *(VUSCD 138)* – If you can't say no (BT twilo dub).

Feb 99. (c-s/cd-s) *(VUSC/+D 141)* *<radio cut>* **FLY AWAY / FLY AWAY (live acoustic) / BELIEVE (live acoustic)** [1] [12] Nov98

Jun 99. (c-s) *(VUSC 146)* **BLACK VELVETEEN / LIVE / FLY AWAY** [ ] [-]
(cd-s) *(VUSCD 146)* – (first 2 tracks) / Supersoulfighter.
(cd-s) *(VUSCDX 146)* – (first & third tracks) / Straight cold player. *(re-iss. Dec99; same)*

Aug 99. (c-s) *(VUSC 153)* *<radio cut>* **AMERICAN WOMAN / THINKING OF YOU (Nick Hexam's dancehall mix)** [ ] [49] Jul99
(cd-s+=) *(VUSCD 153)* – Straight cold player (live) / Fields of joy (live).

Mar 00. (-) *<album cut>* **I BELONG TO YOU** [-] [71]

Oct 00. (cd/c) *(CDVUSX/VUSMCX 183)* *<50316>* **GREATEST HITS** (compilation) [12] [2]
– Are you gonna go my way / Fly away / Rock and roll is dead / Again / It ain't over 'til it's over / Can't get you off my mind / Mr. Cab driver / American woman / Stand by my woman / Always on the run / Heaven help / I belong to you / Believe / Let love rule / Velveteen.

Nov 00. (c-s) *(VUSC 187)* *<radio play>* **AGAIN / FLY AWAY (live) / ARE YOU GONNA GO MY WAY (live)** [ ] [4]
(cd-s) *(VUSCD 187)* – (first two tracks) / Always on the run (live).
(cd-s) *(VUSCDG 187)* – (first & third tracks) / Let love rule (live).

KREATOR

Formed: Essen, Germany . . . 1984 initially as TORMENTOR, by MILLE PETROZA, ROB FIORETTI and VENTOR. Changing their name to KREATOR, the band secured a deal with 'Noise' and unleashed their savage debut album, 'ENDLESS PAIN' (1985). A distinctively European take on the frantic but largely unfocused thrash which was filtering through from America (especially SLAYER), KREATOR had tempered their fearsome assault, albeit very slightly, by the release of follow-up, 'PLEASURE TO KILL' (1986). Along with the likes of CELTIC FROST, KREATOR became one of Europe's most high profile thrash outfits, even if they never really looked like threatening the American giants of the genre. 1989's 'EXTREME AGGRESSION' marked the last stand of their take-no-prisoners approach and as the thrash scene started to splinter, the group diversified into more industrial-style grinding on 1992's 'RENEWAL'. After a four year silence, they eventually resurfaced in 1996 with 'SCENARIOS OF VIOLENCE', although it was clear KREATOR were struggling for fresh ideas. The following year's 'OUTCAST' set even attempted a SEPULTURA-esque ethnic-thrash hybrid with less than sparkling results. • **Covered:** LUCRETIA MY REFLECTION (Sisters Of Mercy).

Album rating: ENDLESS PAIN (*5) / PLEASURE TO KILL (*7) / AFTER THE ATTACK (*4) / TERRIBLE CERTAINTY (*6) / OUT OF THE DARK . . . INTO THE LIGHT mini (*4) / EXTREME AGGRESSION (*5) / COMA OF SOULS (*5) / RENEWAL (*6) / CAUSE FOR CONFLICT (*4) / SCENARIOS OF VIOLENCE (*5) / OUTCAST (*5) / ENDORAMA (*4) / VOICES OF

MILLE PETROZA – vocals, guitar / **ROB FIORETTI** – bass / **VENTOR** – drums

Noise S.P.V.

1985. (lp) *(N 0025)* **ENDLESS PAIN** [ ] [-]
– Endless pain / Total death / Storm of the beast / Tormentor / Son of evil / Flag of hate / Cry war / Bonebreaker / Living in fear / Dying victims. *(re-iss. Oct89 cd+=/lp; CD+/NUK 025)* – Take their lives / Awakening of the gods.

—— added **WULF** – guitar

Apr 86. (lp) *(N 0037)* *<84733>* **PLEASURE TO KILL** [ ] [ ]
– Choir of the damned / Ripping corpse / Death is your saviour / Pleasure to kill / Riot of violence / The pestilence / Carrion / Command of the blade / Under the guillotine. *<US+=>* – FLAG OF HATE *(re-iss. Oct89 cd/lp; CD+/NUK 037)*

—— now without WULF

Noise Combat

Feb 87. (12"ep) *(N 0047)* *<88561-8125-1>* **FLAG OF HATE** [ ] [ ]
– Take their lives / Flag of hate / Awakening of the gods. *(pic-d-iss.Oct89; NUKPD 084)* *<US+=>* – Endless pain / Tormentor / Total death.

May 87. (pic-lp) *(N 0072)* **AFTER THE ATTACK** [ ] [-]
– Choir of the damned / Ripping corpse / Death is your saviour / Pleasure to kill / Riot of violence / After the attack / The pestilence / Carrion / Command of the blade / Under the guillotine.

—— added **JORG TRITZE** – guitar

Oct 87. (12"pic-d) *(NOISE 0084)* **BEHIND THE MIRROR. / GANGLAND** [ ] [-]

Nov 87. (lp) *(N 0086)* *<85-4457>* **TERRIBLE CERTAINTY** [ ] [-]
– Blind faith / Storming with menace / Terrible certainty / As the world burns / Toxic trace / No escape / One of us / Behind the mirror. *(re-iss. Oct89 cd/c/lp; CD/ZC+/NUK 086)*

Aug 88. (m-lp) *(NUK 118)* **OUT OF THE DARK . . . INTO THE LIGHT** [ ] [-]
– Impossible to cure / Lambs to the slaughter / Terrible certainty / Riot of violence / Awakening of the gods. *(cd-iss. Sep92; N 0200-2)*

Feb 89. (cd/c/lp) *(CD/T+/NUK 129)* *<85-4751>* **EXTREME AGGRESSION** [ ] [ ]
– Extreme aggression / No reason to exist / Love us or hate us / Stream of consciousness / Some pain will last / Betrayer / Don't trust / Bringer of torture / Fatal energy. *(pic-lp-iss.Nov89; NUKPD 145)*

—— **FRANK BLACKFIRE** – guitar (ex-SODOM) repl. JORG

Noise Epic

Oct 90. (cd/c/lp) *(CD/T+/NUK 158)* *<EK/E 46971>* **COMA OF SOULS** [ ] [ ]
– When the sun burns red / Coma of souls / People of the lie / World beyond / Terror zone / Agents of brutality / Material world paranoia / Twisted urges / Hidden dictator / Mental slavery.

Noise Futurist

Oct 92. (cd/c/lp) *(N 0193-2/-4/-1)* *<1017>* **RENEWAL** [ ] [ ]
– Winter martyrium / Renewel / Reflection / Brainseed / Karmic wheel / Realitatskontrolle / Zero to none / Europe after the rain / Depression unrest.

Noise Gun

Oct 95. (cd/lp) *(N 0260-2/-1)* *<74321 30001-2/-1>* **CAUSE FOR CONFLICT** [ ] [ ]
– Prevail / Catholic despot / Progressive proletarians / Crisis of disorder / Hate inside your head / Bomb threat / Men without God / Lost / Dogmatic / Sculpture of regret / Celestial deliverance / State oppression / Isolation.

Feb 96. (cd) *(N 0266-2)* **SCENARIOS OF VIOLENCE** (live) [ ] [-]
– Suicide in swamps / Renewal / Extreme aggressions / Brainseed / Lost / Ripping corpse (live) / Tormentor (live) / Some pain will last / Toxic trace / Isolation / Depressive unrest / Agents of brutality / Europe after the rain / Limits of liberty / Temble certainty / Karmic wheel.

Jun 97. (cd) *(N 287CD)* *<GUN 140CD>* **OUTCAST** [ ] [ ]
– Leave this world behind / Phobia / Forever / Black sunshine / Noncomformist / Enemy unseen / Outcast / Stronger than before / Ruin of life / Whatever it may take / Alive again / Against the rest / A better tomorrow.

Drakkar Pavement

Apr 99. (cd) *(DRAKKAR 001CD)* *<65498>* **ENDORAMA** [ ] [ ]
– Golden age / Endorama / Shadowland / Chosen few / Everlasting flame / Passage to Babylon / Future ring / Entry / Soul eraser / Willing spirit / Pandemonium / Tyranny.

– compilations, etc. –

Aug 99. (cd) *Gun; (GUN 182CD) / Pavement; <32343>* **VOICES OF TRANSGRESSION** [ ] [ ] Apr00
– Lucretia my reflection / The chosen few / Isolation / Leave this world behind / Golden age / Bomb threat / Phobia / Whatever it may take / Renewal / Lost / Hate inside your head / Inferno / Outcast / State oppression / Endorama / Black sunrise / As we watch the west.

Die KREUZEN

Formed: Milwaukee, Wisconsin, USA . . . early 80's by DAN KUBINSKI, BRIAN EGENESS, KEITH BRAMMER and ERIC TUNISON. Beginning life as a frantic metallic punk outfit, DIE KREUZEN thrashed their way onto the scene in 1982 with the 'COWS AND BEER' EP, reworking the tracks a couple of years later for their seminal eponymous debut on US indie label, 'Touch & Go'. Subsequent albums such as 'OCTOBER FILE' (1986) and 'CENTURY DAYS' (1988) saw the group attempt to assimilate a greater diversity of styles and influences into their uncompromising yet increasingly accessible sound. BRAMMER departed prior to the release of the Butch Vig-produced 'CEMENT' (1991) set, a record which saw the group explore the grunge sound which they had helped to develop.

Album rating: DIE KREUZEN (*6) / OCTOBER FILE (*7) / CENTURY DAYS (*6) / GONE AWAY mini (*5) / CEMENT (*5)

DAN KUBINSKI – vocals / **BRIAN EGENESS** – guitar / **KEITH BRAMMER** – bass / **ERIC TUNISON** – drums

not iss. Version Sound

1982. (7") **COWS AND BEER. / PINK FLAG** [-] [ ]

Touch & Go Touch & Go

1984. (lp) *<(TGLP 4)>* **DIE KREUZEN** [ ] [ ]
– Rumors / This hope / In school / I'm tired / On the street / Enemies / Get 'em fighting / No time / All white / Pain / Sick people / Hate me / Live wire / Not anymore / Mannequin / Fuck ups / Think for me / Dirt and decay / Don't say please / No name. *<US cd-iss. Aug94; TGCD 4>*

1986. (lp) *<(TGLP 7)>* **OCTOBER FILE** [ ] [ ]

– Man in the trees / Uncontrolled passion / It's been so long / Imagine a light / Cool breeze / Counting cracks / Red to green / Among the ruins / Hear and feel / Hide and seek / Conditioned / There's a place / Open lines / Melt. *<US cd-iss. 1992 +=; TG 07CD>* – DIE KREUZEN

Aug 88. (lp/cd) *<(TGLP 30/+CD)>* **CENTURY DAYS** [ ] [ ]
– Earthquakes / Lean into it / Different ways / So many times / These days / Elizabeth / Stomp / Slow / The bone / Bitch magnet / Number three / Dream sky / Halloween.

Jul 90. (12"ep) *<(TGEP 40)>* **GONE AWAY** (part live compilation) [ ] [ ]
– Cows and beer / Gone away / Seasons of wither / Pink flag / Land of treason / Stomp / Cool breeze / Man in the trees / Bitch magnet / Number three / Different ways / In school / Think for me / Hate me / Pain / Don't say please / Enemies / On the street / All white / Fighting.

1991. (12") *<TG 62>* **PINK FLAG. /** [-] [ ]

— BRAMMER joined WRECK

Oct 91. (12") *<TG 79>* **BIG BAD DAYS. /** [-] [ ]

Nov 91. (lp/cd) *<(TG LP/CD 80)>* **CEMENT** [ ] [ ]
– Wish / Shine / Big bad days / Holes / Downtime / Blue song / Best goodbye / Heaven / Deep space / Shake loose / Over and the edge / Black song.

— split after above

Liv KRISTINE (see under ⇒ THEATRE OF TRAGEDY)

KROKUS

Formed: Soluthurn, Switzerland . . . 1974 by CHRIS VON ROHR (bass, vocals), FERNANDO VON ARB (guitar, bass), TOMMY KIEFER (guitar, vocals), JUERG NAEGELLI (keyboards, vocals), and the cheesily named FREDDY STEADY (drums). After two domestic releases on the 'Schmoritz' label, 'KROKUS' (1976) and 'TO YOU ALL' (1977), they signed to 'Philips', dropping the progressive rock pretensions and opting for a more earthy hard boogie feel in the tradition of AC/DC. The band debuted their new sound on the 'PAINKILLER' album, KROKUS subsequently deciding that VON ROHR (who had taken up vocal duties following the departure of FRIEZ in 1977) was ill- equipped for the job, the singer switching to bass, while Malta-born new boy MARK STORACE was recruited on vocals. Signing to 'Ariola' in late '79, the band soon relocated to London in an attempt to break out of the relative musical isolation of their home country. The move paid off with the heavy duty 'METAL RENDEZ-VOUS' (1980) album attracting a fair bit of interest from the metal press. With the 'New Wave Of British Heavy Metal' in full flow, the genre was enjoying a surge in popularity, KROKUS's brand of no frills hard rock going down particularly well at the Reading Festival later that summer (they also played at Loch Lomond in Scotland). The group followed up with the 'HARDWARE' (1981) album, their most successful to date, the record almost making the UK Top 40. A period of personnel upheaval ensued with RANDY MEIER briefly replacing the departing KEIFER (who later committed suicide on the 24th December '86), before MARK KOEHLER was recruited as MEIER joined ASIA. 'ONE VICE AT A TIME' (1982), though hardly an improvement on their derivative formula, became their most successful UK album to date, going Top 30. Following the departure of FREDDY STEADY, STEVE PACE joined on drums and the band cracked the US Top 30 with 'HEADHUNTER' (1983). Yet more line-up shuffles followed the album's release, PATRICK MASON replacing KOEHLER on tour. The latter eventually returned, filling VON ROHR's vacant bass slot, while JEFF KLAVEN replaced PACE on drums, phew!!. And after all that, they could still only come up with second division rock-by-numbers like 'BLITZ' (1984), a record that featured possibly the worst ever cover version of SWEET's 'BALLROOM BLITZ'. From here on in, the band went downhill, line-up changes continuing to dog them. 1987 saw the return of VON ROHR although by 1990, there were virtually no original members remaining and KROKUS wisely called it a day. With frontman STORACE now back at the helm, the band released comeback set, 'TO ROCK OR NOT TO BE' (1995), while newcomer CARL SENTANCE took over the ever-vacant position for 1999's 'ROUND 13'.

Album rating: KROKUS (*4) / TO YOU ALL (*4) / PAINKILLER (*4) / METAL RENDEZ-VOUS (*5) / HARDWARE (*6) / ONE VICE AT A TIME (*6) / HEADHUNTER (*6) / THE BLITZ (*4) / CHANGE OF ADDRESS (*5) / ALIVE AND SCREAMIN' (*4) / HEART ATTACK (*4) / STAMPEDE (*4) / TO ROCK OR NOT TO BE (*4) / ROUND 13 (*4) / THE DEFINITIVE COLLECTION compilation (*7)

HENRY FRIEZ – vocals / **TOMMY KIEFER** – guitar, vocals / **FERNANDO VON ARB** – guitar, bass / **JUERG NAEGELLI** – keyboards, vocals / **CHRIS VON ROHR** – bass, vocals / **FREDDY STEADY** – drums

Schnoutz / not iss.

1976. (lp) **KROKUS** [-] [-] Swiss

1977. (lp) *<200195>* **TO YOU ALL** [-] [-] Swiss
– Highway song / To you all / Festival / Move it on / Mr. Greedy / Lonesome rider / Protection / Trying hard / Don't stop playing / Take it, don't leave it. *<cd-iss. 1990's>*

— **CHRIS** now lead vocals, percussion; when HENRY left

Philips / not iss.

Oct 78. (lp) *(6326800)* **PAINKILLER** [-] [-] Euro
– Killer / Werewolf / Rock ladies / Bad love / Get out of my mind / Rock me, rock you / Deadline / Susie / Pay it! / Bye by baby. *(imp.Mar81; same) (UK-iss.Aug82 as 'PAY IT IN METAL'; 6326 800)*

— added **MARC STORACE** – vocals (ex-TEA)

Ariola / Ariola

Mar 80. (7"clear) *(ARO 225)* **BEDSIDE RADIO. / BACK SEAT ROCK'N'ROLL** [ ] [-]

May 80. (7") *(ARO 233) <804>* **HEATSTROKES. / SHY KID** [ ] [ ]

Jul 80. (lp) *(ARL 5056)* **METAL RENDEZ-VOUS** [ ] [-]
– Heatstrokes / Bedside radio / Come on / Streamer / Shy kid / Tokyo nights / Lady double dealer / Fire / No way / Back seat rock'n'roll. *(re-iss. Sep82 lp/c; ARL/ZCARL 5056) (cd-iss. Jun88 on 'Arista'; 259048)*

Aug 80. (7") *(ARO 241)* **TOKYO NIGHTS. / BEDSIDE RADIO (live)** [ ] [-]
(ext.12"yellow+=) *(AROD 241)* – Shy kid (live).

— now quintet when NAEGELLI departed (retained on some studio work)

Feb 81. (7"red) *(ARO 254)* **ROCK CITY. / MR. 69 / MAD RACKET (live)** [ ] [-]

Feb 81. (lp/c) *(ARL/ZCARL 5064) <1508>* **HARDWARE** [44] [ ]
– Celebration / Easy rocker / Smelly Nelly / Mr. 69 / She's got everything / Burning bones / Rock city / Winning man / Mad racket.

Apr 81. (7") *<819>* **WINNING MAN. / MAD RACKET** [-] [ ]

— **RANDY MEIER** – guitar repl. KIEFER (He committed suicide 24 Dec'86)

Apr 81. (7"ep) *(ARO 258)* **INDUSTRIAL STRENGTH** [62] [-]
– Bedside radio / Celebration / Easy rocker / Bye bye baby.

— **MARK KOEHLER** – guitar, vocals repl. MEIER who joined ASIA

Arista / Arista

Feb 82. (7") *(ARIST 451)* **BAD BOYS RAG DOLLS. / SAVE ME** [ ] [-]

Feb 82. (lp/c) *(SPART/TCART 1189) <9591>* **ONE VICE AT A TIME** [28] [53]
– Long stick goes boom / Bad boys rag dolls / Playin' the outlaw / To the top / Down the drain / American woman / I'm on the run / Save me / Rock'n'roll.

May 82. (7") *<0683>* **SAVE ME. / LONG STICK GOES BOOM** [-] [ ]

Jul 82. (7") *(ARIST 468) <0693>* **AMERICAN WOMAN. / LONG STICK GOES BOOM** [ ] [ ]

— **STORACE, VON ARB, KOEHLER + VON ROHR** recruited **STEVE PACE** – drums; who repl. FREDDY

Apr 83. (lp/c) *(205/405 255) <9623>* **HEADHUNTER** [74] [25]
– Headhunter / Eat the rich / Screaming in the night / Ready to burn / Night wolf / Stayed awake all night / Stand and be counted / White din / Russian winter. *(re-iss. Apr88 lp/c; 209/409 080) (cd-iss. May88; 255255)*

May 83. (7") *<9017>* **SCREAMING IN THE NIGHT. / RUSSIAN WINTER** [-] [ ]

Sep 83. (7") *<9099>* **STAYED AWAKE ALL NIGHT / ('A'version)** [-] [ ]

— on tour **PATRICK MASON** – guitar repl. KOEHLER / **KOEHLER** returned on – bass repl. VON ROHR / **JEFF KLAVEN** – drums (ex-COBRA) repl. PACE

Aug 84. (7") *(ARIST 579)* **BALLROOM BLITZ. / READY TO ROCK** [ ] [ ]
(12"+=) *(ARIST12 579)* – Out of control.

Aug 84. (lp/c) *(206/406 494) <8243>* **THE BLITZ** [ ] [31]
– Midnite maniac / Out of control / Boys nite out / Our love / Out to lunch / Ballroom blitz / Rock the nation / Hot stuff / Ready to rock. *(cd-iss. 1988; 610 198)*

Sep 84. (7") *<9248>* **MIDNITE MANIAC. / READY TO ROCK** [-] [71]

— now a 4-piece (**STORACE, VON ARB** and **KLAVEN** plus **ANDY TAMAS** – bass (ex-BLACK OAK ARKANSAS) repl. KOEHLER (reverted to guitar)

— Late '85, **TOMMY KESSLER** – bass repl. TAMAS

May 86. (7") *<9468>* **SCHOOL'S OUT. / SCREAMING IN THE NIGHT** [-] [67]

Jun 86. (lp/c/cd) *(407/607/257 647) <8402>* **CHANGE OF ADDRESS** [ ] [45] Apr86
– Now (all through the night) / Hot shot city / School's out / Let this love begin / Burning up the night / Say goodbye / World on fire / Hard luck hero / Long way from home.

Feb 87. (lp/c/cd) *(208/408/258 025) <8445>* **ALIVE AND SCREAMIN' (live)** [ ] [97] Oct86
– Long stick goes boom / Eat the rich / Screaming in the night / Hot shot city / Midnite maniac / Bedside radio / Lay me down / Stayed awake all night / Headhunter.

Feb 87. (7") *<9524>* **LET THE LOVE BEGIN. / HOT SHOT CITY** [-] [ ]

Apr 87. (12") *<9543>* **SCREAMING IN THE NIGHT (live). / HEADHUNTER (live)** [-] [ ]

— **CHRIS VON ROHR** – bass, vocals returned to repl. KESSLER. **DANI CRIVELLI** – drums (ex-KILLER) repl. KLAVEN

M.C.A. / M.C.A.

Mar 88. (lp/c/cd) *(IMCA/UNMCA/MCAD 42087) <42087>* **HEART ATTACK** [ ] [87]
– Everybody rocks / Wild love / Let it go / Winning man / Axx attack / Rock'n'roll tonight / Flyin' high / Shoot down the night / Bad, bad girl / Speed up.

Apr 88. (7") **LET IT GO. / WINNING MAN** [-] [ ]
(12"+=) – Bourbon Street.

— **MANNY MAURER** – guitar repl. VON ARB

— **PETER TANNER** – vocals; repl. STORACE

not iss. / Justin

1991. (cd/c/lp) *<JED 18>* **STAMPEDE** [-] [ ] Canada
– Stampede / Electric man / Rock'n'roll gypsy / Shotgun boogie / Nova zano / Street love / Good times / She drives me crazy / In the heat of the night / Rhythm of love / Wasteland.

— it was no wonder they split with virtually no originals remaining

— **MARC STORACE** – vocals repl. TANNER

S.P.V. / Cass

Jul 95. (cd) *(SPV 0854387-2) <CAS 70098-2>* **TO ROCK OR NOT TO BE** [ ] [ ]
– Lion heart / Flying through the night / To rock or not to be / In the dead of night / Natural blonde / Doggy style / Talking like a shotgun / Soul to soul / Stop the world / You ain't got the guts to do it / Wagon gone / Stormy nights.

— line-up now **VON ARB, LAUPER, MAURER, HAAS** + new frontman **CARL SENTANCE**

Angel Air / Angel Air

Oct 99. (cd) *(<SJPCD 031>)* **ROUND 13** [ ] [ ] Jan00
– Heya / Money back / Break free / Guitar rules / Blood comes easy / Suck my guitar / Gypsy love / Whitchhunt / Backstabber / Wild times.

– compilations, etc. –

1989. (cd) *Arista; <ARCD 8607>* **STAYED AWAKE ALL NIGHT – THE BEST OF KROKUS** [-] [ ]

Dec 93. (cd) *Ariola; (74321 13471-2)* **THE DIRTY DOZEN** [-] [-] German

Jul 99. (d-cd) *Angel Air; (<SJPCD 042>)* **STAMPEDE / TO ROCK OR NOT TO ROCK** [ ] [ ] Oct99

Jun 00. (cd) *B.M.G.; <07822 14638-2>* **THE DEFINITIVE COLLECTION** -
– Ballroom blitz / Long stick goes boom / Bad boys – Rag dolls / Playin' the outlaw / American woman / Midnite maniac / Night wolf / Headhunter / Eat the rich / School's out / Bedside radio / She's got everything / Heatstrokes / Screaming in the night / Syayed awake all night.

Die KRUPPS

Formed: Dusseldorf, Germany . . . 1980 by JURGEN ENGLER (formerly of punk outfit, MALE) and ROLF DORPER. Initially a hard-edged new-beat/industrial act in the vein of FRONT 242, NITZER EBB etc., DIE KRUPPS firmly established themselves in the vanguard of the German independent scene through domestic releases like 'VOLLE KRAFT VORAUS' (1982) and 'ENTERING THE ARENA' (1985). With their churning teutonic rhythms and the growling vox of ENGLER, the group were something of a precursor for bands like MINISTRY, NINE INCH NAILS and FEAR FACTORY. Though the group split during the latter half of the 80's, ENGLER, DORPER and CHRIS LIETZ reformed DIE KRUPPS at the turn of the decade. Inspired by the pioneering work of METALLICA, ENGLER was moved to introduce grinding guitar parts to thrilling effect on 'I' (1992), going the whole hog later that year with a METALLICA tribute set, 'METAL FOR THE MASSES PART II – A TRIBUTE TO METALLICA' (reportedly loved by LARS ULRICH). For their next set, 'THE FINAL OPTION' (1993), DIE KRUPPS even recruited a real drummer, DARREN MINTER, and a guitarist, ex-HEATHEN man, LEE ALTUS, although it was with 'III: ODYSSEY OF THE MIND' (1995) that the group finally allowed heavy guitars free rein in the mix. The album marked their debut for metal label, 'Music For Nations', DIE KRUPPS continuing in an overtly rock vein for 1997's 'PARADISE NOW'.

Album rating: STAHLWERKSINFONIE (*4) / VOLLE KRAFT VORAUS (*4) / METAL MASCHINEN MUSIK 91-81 (*5) / I (*7) / METAL FOR THE MASSES PART II – A TRIBUTE TO METALLICA (*5) / THE FINAL OPTION (*5) / III: ODYSSEY OF THE MIND (*6) / PARADISE NOW (*6)

JURGEN ENGLER – vocals, guitar, electronics / **ROLF DORPER** – synthesizer, vocals / **BERNARD MALAKA** – bass, vocals / **FRANK KOLLGES** – drums, vocals / **EVA GOSSLING** – sax

Zick Zack / not iss.

1981. (lp) *(ZZ 30)* **STAHWERKSYNFONIE** ('STEELWORKS SYMPHONY') - - German

— **TINA SCHNECKENBURGER** – electronic drums; repl. FRANK + EVA

1981. (12") **WAHRE ARBEIT, WAHRER LOHN** - - German

WEA / not iss.

Jun 82. (7") *(K 191390)* **GOLDFINGER. / ZUEI HERZEN** -
Jul 82. (lp) *(K 58463)* **VOLLE KRAFT VORAUS** -
– Volle kraft voraus / Goldfinger / Fur einen Augenblink / Tod und Teufel / Das ende der traume / Neue helden / Wahre arbeit, wahrer lohn / . . . Denn du lebst nur einmal / Zwei herzen, ein rhythmus / Laerm macht spass.

— **CHRIS LIETZ** – drum programming + **WALTER JAGER** – bass; repl. DORPER who went solo and joined PROPAGANDA

Quiet / not iss.

Jun 84. (12") *(PST 03)* **GOLDFINGER. / ZUEI HERZEN**

Statik / Virgin

Jul 85. (lp) *(STAB 2) <207260>* **ENTERING THE ARENA**
– Risk / The rise and fall / Communication breakdown / Risky soul version / Gladiators / Your voice.

— split after above, although **JURGEN, CHRIS + ROLF** did reform in the late 80's.

Mute / Geffen

May 89. (7") *(MUTE 101) <21291>* **MACHINERIES OF JOY. /** -
(12"+=/cd-s+=) *(12/CD MUTE 101)* – ('A'mixes).

Grey Area / Mute

Aug 91. (d-lp/cd) *(KRUPPS 1/+CD) <61128-4/-2>* **METALL MASCHINEN MUSIK 91-81 PAST FORWARD**
– Maniac / The machineries of joy.

Rough Trade / Hollywood

Aug 92. (cd/lp) *(RTD 1951266-2/-1)* **I** -
Dec 92. (m-cd/m-lp) *(1951240-2/-1) <61515-2/-1>* **A TRIBUTE TO METALLICA** Sep93
– Enter sandman / Nothing else matters / Blackened / Battery / For whom the bell tolls.

— added **LEE ALTUS** – guitar (ex-HEATHEN) + **DARREN MINTER** – drums

Equator / Rough Trade

Oct 93. (12"/cd-s) *(AXIS T/CD 002)* **FATHERLAND / FATHERLAND (mixes) / METAL MACHINE MUSIC** -
Oct 93. (cd/c/lp) *(ATLAS CD/MC/LP 004) <1587>* **II: THE FINAL OPTION**
Feb 94. (12") *(AXIST 003) <1662>* **TO THE HILT. / THE DAWNING OF DOOM (live)**
(cd-s) *(AXISCD 003)* – ('A'mixes) / Bloodsuckers (live).
Jul 94. (12"/cd-s) *(AXIS T/CD 008) <19516933>* **CROSSFIRE (mixes)** -
Sep 94. (d-cd/d-lp) *(ATLAS CDD/LPD 006) <1995>* **THE FINAL REMIXES**
– To the hilt / Paradise of sin / Language of reality / Fatherland / Worst case scenario / Shellshocked / Crossfire / Bloodsuckers / Iron man / Inside out / New temptation / Dawning of doom / Ministry of fear / Hi tech low life / Metal machine music / Rings of steel.

— (remixes by:- ANDREW ELDRITCH, JIM MARTIN, GUNSHOT, JULIAN BEESTON)

Nov 94. (12"/cd-s) *(AXIS T/CDD 010) <9579>* **BLOODSUCKERS (mixes; Biohazard / original / Julian Beeston / live)** Aug95
(cd-s) *(AXISCDS 010)* – Dawning of doom (live) / High tech low life (Julian Beeston remix) / Metal machine music (Cassandra Complex remix) / Rings of steel (Pro-pain remix).

— **GEORGE LEWIS** – drums + **RUDIGER ESCH** – bass; repl. MINTER

Music For Nations / Cleopatra

Jul 95. (cd) *(CDMFN 187) <9668>* **III: ODYSSEY OF THE MIND**
– The last flood / Scent / Metamorphasis / Isolation / The final option / Alive / Odyssey / LCD / Eggshell / Jekyll or Hyde.
Oct 95. (cd-ep) *<9578>* **FATHERLAND (the Sisters Of Mercy & original mixes) / GERMANIC (live) / CROSSFIRE (original & Gunshot remixes) / IRON MAN (original & N-factor remixes) / SHELLSHOCKED (Einsturzende Neubauten remix)** -
May 96. (cd-ep) *<9730>* **ISOLATION / ISOLATION (Luc Van Acker mix) / SCENT (club) / ISOLATION (Clawfinger mix) / THE LAST FLOOD (live) / THE FINAL OPTION (S.P.Q.R. mix)** -
Apr 97. (cd) *(CDMFN 218)* **PARADISE NOW** -
– Moving beyond / Gods of void / Paradise now / Black beauty / Reconstruction / Behind taste of taboo / Rise up / Fire / Full circle / Vortex / 30 seconds / Society treaty.

– compilations, etc. –

Sep 93. (3xcd-box) *Rough Trade; (RTD 1951542-2)* **DIE KRUPPS BOX** -
Nov 95. (cd) *Rough Trade; (RTD 19532003)* **SCENT** -
Oct 96. (cd) *Cleopatra; (CLP 9812)* **METAMORPHOSIS 1981-1992** -
Jul 97. (cd) *Captain Trip; (CTCD 057)* **FOUNDATION** -

KYUSS

Formed: Palm Springs, California, USA . . . 1991 by JOHN GARCIA, JOSH HOMME, SCOTT REEDER and ALFREDO HERNANDEZ. Initially playing bluesy punk, the group's rather lacklustre debut, 'WRETCH', was followed up by the blinding intensity of 'BLUES FOR THE RED SUN' (1992). Seemingly coming from out of nowhere, it had taken MASTERS OF REALITY retro guru CHRIS GOSS to develop the band's latent genius. A smouldering slab of frazzled flare-rock, the band had dragged garage-psych stoned and stumbling into the 90's, carving a new benchmark for would-be sonic archivists. Live, most commentators were in agreement that KYUSS were peerless, the group soon finding themsleves playing on the same bill as the likes of DANZIG and METALLICA. 'Elektra' were sufficiently impressed to offer the band a deal when their label went belly-up, KYUSS once again working with GOSS on the fuzzed-up bludgeon of 'WELCOME TO SKY VALLEY' (1994). Despite the critical raving, the group's label were unsure how to market their hippy-rock sound with the result that KYUSS' record sales were less than impressive. So it was then, that after a final masterpiece, 'AND THE CIRCUS LEAVES TOWN' (1995), the group decided to call it a day. The fact that KYUSS were only obviously beginning to reach their full potential was illustrated with the 'QUEENS OF THE STONE AGE' (1997) set. A combination of unreleased KYUSS material and a clutch of new, even more mind-altering tracks from HOMME's similarly titled new outfit (also numbering GOSS, VAN CONNER and VIC THE STICK), the album was a disorientatingly heavy testament (including a suitably trippy cover of Black Sabbath's 'INTO THE VOID') to one of the most criminally ignored bands of the 90's. Meanwhile, KYUSS' former frontman, GARCIA, was making his name with a new outfit, UNIDA. QUEENS OF THE STONE AGE carried the KYUSS flag into the new millennium courtesy of a new major label deal with 'Interscope' and the highly acclaimed 'R' (2000) album. A record that featured highly in many end of year polls and finally saw HOMME, OLIVERI and Co gain the popular rock god homages that their music had always begged, 'R' started as it meant to go on with 'FEEL GOOD HIT OF THE SUMMER' gratuitously reeling off a list of narcotics ad nauseam. While markedly more hallucinogenically swinging than its predecessor with more elaborate instrumentation and arrangements, the California stoners proved their desert-grunge could still scorch at a hundred paces on the likes of the demented 'TENSION HEAD'. 'LEG OF LAMB', meanwhile, recalled MASTERS OF REALITY at their trippy best.

Album rating: WRETCH (*7) / BLUES FOR THE RED SUN (*9) / WELCOME TO SKY VALLEY (*8) / . . .AND THE CIRCUS LEAVES TOWN (*8) / QUEENS OF THE STONE AGE (*8) / MUCHAS GRACIAS compilation (*8) / Queens Of The Stone Age: QUEENS OF THE STONE AGE (*8) / RATED R (*9)

JOHN GARCIA – vocals / **JOSH HOMME** (b.1973) – guitar / **SCOTT REEDER** – bass; repl. NICK OLIVERI (b.1971) who joined the DWARVES / **ALFREDO HERNANDEZ** (b.1966) – drums

Dali-Chameleon / Dali-Chameleon

Nov 91. (cd) *<61256-2>* **WRETCH** -
– HWY 74 (beginning of what's about to happen) / Love has passed me by / Son of a bitch / Black widow / Katzenjammer / Deadly kiss / The law / Isolation / I'm not / Big bikes / Stage III. *(UK-iss.Feb98; same as US)*
Feb 93. (cd/c) *<(3705 61340-2/-4)>* **BLUES FOR THE RED SUN**
– Thumb / Green machine / Molten universe / 50 million years trip / (Downside up) / Thong song / Apothecaries' weight / Catepillar march / Freedom run / 800 / Writhe / Capsized. *(cd+=)* – Allen's wrench / Mondo generator / Yeah.

Elektra / Warners

Jun 94. (cd/c/lp) *<(7559 61571-2/-4/-1)>* **WELCOME TO SKY VALLEY**
– I / Gardenia / Asteroid / Supa scoopa and mighty scoop / II / 100 degrees / Space cadet / Demon cleaner / III / Odyssey / Conan troutman / N.O. / Whitewater. *(lp-iss.Nov99 on 'White & Black'; WB 7524)*
Sep 94. (7"blue) *(EKR 192)* **DEMON CLEANER. / FREEDOM RUN (live)**
(cd-s) *(EKR 192CD1)* – ('A'side) / Day one (to Dave & Chris) / El rodeo / Hurricane.

(cd-s) *(EKR 192CD2)* – ('A'side) / Gardenia (live) / Thumb (live) / Conan trout man (live).

Feb 95. (cd-s) *(EKR 197CD)* **GARDENIA / U.N. SANDPIPER / CONAN TROUT MAN (live)** ☐ ☐

Jun 95. (cd/c) *<(7559 61811-2/-4)>* **. . .AND THE CIRCUS LEAVES TOWN** ☐ ☐
– Hurricane / One inch man / Thee of boozeroony / Gloria Lewis / Phototropic / El rodeo / Jumbo blimp jumbo / Tango zizzle / Size queen / Catamarran / Spaceship landing.

— split in 1995 leaving some recordings below. HOMME formed QUEENS OF THE STONE AGE, which was released by below label as KYUSS' epitaph album. He was joined by **VAN CONNER** – bass (SCREAMING TREES) / **CHRIS GOSS** (MASTER OF REALITY) / **VIC THE STICK** – drums

Man's Ruin Man's Ruin

Jul 97. (10") *(MR 015)* **INTO THE VOID. / FATSO FORGETSO** ☐ ☐

Dec 97. (cd) *<(MR 063)>* **QUEENS OF THE STONE AGE** ☐ ☐
– Into the void / Fatso forgotso / Fatso Forgotso phase II / If only everything / Born to hula / Spiders and vinegaroons. *(re-iss. Aug00; same)*

QUEENS OF THE STONE AGE

— **JOSH HOMME** – vocals, guitar / **NICK OLIVERI** – bass / **ALFREDO HERNANDEZ** – drums

Man's Ruin Man's Ruin

Sep 98. (10"ep/cd-ep) *(MR 141/+CD)* **QUEENS OF THE STONE AGE / BEAVER EP** ☐ ☐
– The bronze / These aren't the droids you're looking for / BEAVER: Absence without leave / Morocco.

Roadrunner Roadrunner

Oct 98. (cd) *<(RR 8674-2)>* **QUEENS OF THE STONE AGE** ☐ ☐
– Regular John / Avon / If only / Walkin' on the sidewalks / You would know / How to handle a rope / Mexicola / Hispanic impressions / You can't quit me baby / Give the mule what he wants / I was a teenage hand model.

— added **DAVE CATCHING** – guitar, steel guitar, piano / **NICKY LUCERO** – drums

— HOMME was the mainman behind The DESERT SESSIONS, a group of musicians (from KYUSS, SOUNDGARDEN and EARTHLINGS) who released late in 1998, a 10"/cd, 'VOL III/IV' for 'Man's Ruin'.

Interscope Interscope

Jun 00. (cd) *<(490683-2)>* **RATED R** 54 ☐
– Feel good hit of the summer / The lost art of keeping a secret / Leg of lamb / Auto pilot / Better living through chemistry / Monsters in the parasol / Quick and to the pointless / In the fade / Tension head / Lightning song / I think I lost my headache. *(lp-iss.Nov00+=; 490864-1)* – Ode to Clarissa. *(cd re-iss. Nov00 w/ free cd+=; same)* – FEEL GOOD HIT OF THE SUMMER EP

Aug 00. (7") *(497387-7)* **THE LOST ART OF KEEPING A SECRET. / ODE TO CLARISSA** 31 -
(cd-s+=) *(497392-2)* – Monsters in the parasol (live).
(cd-s) *(497391-2)* – ('A'side) / Born to hula / ('A'-CD-Rom).

Nov 00. (cd-ep) *(497455-2)* **FEEL GOOD HIT OF THE SUMMER EP** ☐ -
– Feel good hit of the summer / Never say never / You're so vague / Who'll be the next in line / Feel good hit of the summer (CD-ROM video).

– KYUSS compilation –

Oct 00. (cd) *Elektra; <(7559 62571-2)>* **MUCHAS GRACIAS – THE BEST OF KYUSS** ☐ ☐
– U.N. sandpiper / Shine / 50 million year trip (downside up) / Mudfly / Demon cleaner / A day early and a dollar extra / I'm not / Hurricane / Flip the phrase / Fatso forgotso / El rodeo / Gardenia (live) / Thumb (live) / Conan Troutman (live) / Freedom run (live).

LACUNA COIL

Formed: Italy . . . mid-90's by CRISTINA SCABBIA, ANDREA FERRO, RAFFAELE ZAGARIA, CLAUDIO LEO, and LEONARD FORTI. The band recorded a demo under the moniker ETHERAL which they bandied around various European labels. Finally inking a deal with 'Century Media' records', they had to change their name to the more enigmatic LACUNA COIL, as a Greek band were already using their former title. The line-up, as above, recorded their eponymously titled EP during 1997, releasing it a year later to the acclaim of Europe's rock fraternity. This mini-outing placed LC in the goth-metal bracket but they were certainly not stereotypes of the genre. Their unique sound emanates emphatically from the underpinning of SCABBIA's sublime singing voice with FERRO's more melodious vocals. From the time of its recording to the time of its release, LC took on a large European tour supporting label-mates MOONSPELL, and unfortunately the pressures of the road caused rifts in the fledgling band culminating in a break-up on tour, and the recruiting of CRISTIANO MIGLIORE on guitar and CRISTIANO MOZZATI on drums. This new line-up certainly lacked nothing of the former grouping, bringing out their first full set 'IN A REVERIE' (1999), to the appreciation of the rock press. As before, this album showcased LC's hard-edged but tuneful introspective goth meanderings, defiantly securing for themselves the mark of originality. From then on in it was all go for these Italian metallers, taking on a massive amount of touring with, amongst others, THE GATHERING, but still finding time to record and release a further EP 'HALFLIFE' (2000), and most recently another full set, 'UNLEASHED MEMORIES' (2001) to truly establish themselves in the hearts of the metal community.

Album rating: LACUNA COIL mini (*5) / IN A REVERIE (*6) / HALFLIFE mini (*5) / UNLEASHED MEMORIES (*6)

CRISTINA SCABBIA – vocals / **ANDREA FERRO** – vocals / **CRISTANO MIGLIORE** – guitars / **MARCO COTI ZELATI** – bass / **CRISTIANO MOZZATI** – drums

Century Media | Century Media

Jan 98. (m-cd) *(CM 77201CD) <7901>* **LACUNA COIL** [ ] [ ] Apr98
– No need to explain / The secret . . . / This is my dream / Soul into Hades / Falling / Unfantasma tra noi (A ghost between us).

Mar 99. (cd) *(CM 77234CD) <7934>* **IN A REVERIE** [ ] [ ] Jun99
– Circle / Stately lover / Honeymoon suite / My wings / To myself I turned / Cold / Reverie / Veins of glass / Falling again.

— they were now a sextet (unknown addition)

Apr 00. (m-cd) *(77239-2)* **HALFLIFE** [ ] [-]
– Halflife / Trance awake / Senzaline / Hyperfast / Stars.

Feb 01. (cd/pic-lp) *(77360-2/-1) <8060>* **UNLEASHED MEMORIES** [ ] [ ] Mar01
– Heir of a dying day / To live is to die / Purify / Senzafine / When a dead man walks / 1.19 / Cold heritage / Distant sun / A current obsession / Wave of anguish. *(cd+=)* – HALFLIFE

– compilations, etc. –

Nov 00. (d-cd) *Century Media; (77352-2)* **LACUNA COIL / IN A REVERIE** [ ] [-]

L.A. GUNS

Formed: Los Angeles, California, USA . . . 1984, by TRACII GUNS and other brief GUNS N' ROSES and FASTER PUSSYCAT members. After a spell with PAUL BLACK (who would later win substantial royalties in mid-'91 after being uncredited on co-writing duties) on vocals, he was replaced by English-born PHIL LEWIS in 1987, the band signing a worldwide 'Polygram' contract the same year. Recruiting guitarist MICK CRIPPS, bassist KELLY NICKELS and drummer STEPHEN RILEY (ex-W.A.S.P.), the band released their eponymous debut album in early '88, a record showing them at their sleazy best on the likes of 'ONE MORE REASON' and 'HOLLYWOOD TEASE' (originally a minor UK single for LEWIS's old band, GIRL). Yet while the band were fine 'n' dandy within the confines of the insular L.A. glam scene, they didn't quite have the calibre to make the jump to the big league and TRACII could only look on in envy as his old muckers GUNS N' ROSES (who were partly named after the L.A. GUNS frontman) shot to stardom. Despite a further couple of strong albums, 'COCKED AND LOADED' (1989), and 'HOLLYWOOD VAMPIRES' (1991), the band lingered in the metal margins. As the group splintered, TRACII became part of metal supergroup CONTRABAND (who cut a self-titled album) as well as forming a new outfit, KILLING MACHINE. LEWIS, meanwhile, went on to form FILTHY LUCRE. The original line-up (minus LEWIS) subsequently regrouped for 1995's comeback set, 'VICIOUS CIRCLE', an album which attempted a misguided flirtation with grunge to underwhelming effect. If not exactly blazing, the 'GUNS were once again firing on all (well, most) cylinders with 'AMERICAN HARDCORE' (1996), a return to the sleaze-metal of their late 80's heyday. The GILBY CLARKE-produced 'SHRINKING VIOLET' (1999) was an even more authentic trawl through the L.A. of yore with help from that great unsung talent of the glam era JIZZY PEARL, erstwhile frontman with the late, great LOVE/HATE. In 2001, LEWIS was back as the frontman on US-only set 'MAN IN THE MOON'. • **Covered:** I FEEL NICE (Psyclone Rangers) / HIGH ON YOU (Stooges) / STRANGE BOAT (Waterboys) / GUNSLINGER (Bogie Boys) / Rip off (Marc Bolan) / SHOULD I STAY OR SHOULD I GO (Clash) / CUSTARD PIE + HOW MANY MORE TIMES (Led Zeppelin) / ROCK CANDY (Montrose) / COLD GIN (Kiss).

Album rating: L.A. GUNS (*6) / COCKED AND LOADED (*6) / HOLLYWOOD VAMPIRES (*6) / VICIOUS CIRCLE (*3) / AMERICAN HARDCORE (*4) / WASTED mini (*4) / SHRINKING VIOLET (*5) / MAN IN THE MOON (*4) / THE VERY BEST OF L.A. GUNS compilation (*7)

PHILIP LEWIS – vocals (ex-GIRL) / **TRACII GUNS** – lead guitar (ex-GUNS N' ROSES) / **MICK CRIPPS** – guitar / **KELLY NICKELS** – bass / **STEPHEN RILEY** – drums (ex-WASP); repl. BOB

Vertigo | Vertigo

Feb 88. (lp/c)(cd) *(VERH/+C 55)<(814 144-2)>* **L.A. GUNS** [73] [50]
– No mercy / Sex action / One more reason / The bitch is back / Electric gypsy / Nothing to lose / Hollywood tease / One way ticket / Shoot for thrills / Down in the city.

Sep 89. (lp/c/cd) *<(838 592-1/-4/-2)>* **COCKED & LOADED** [45] [38] Jun89
– Letting go / Rip and tear / Never enough / 17 crash / Give a little / The ballad of Jayne / Wheels of fire / Slap in the face / Sleazy come easy go / Malaria / I'm addicted / Magdalaine / Showdown (riot on sunset). *(cd+=)* – I wanna be your man.

Apr 90. (c-s) *<876984>* **THE BALLAD OF JAYNE / I WANNA BE YOUR MAN** [-] [33]

— RILEY left for a time in May'90 although he soon returned

Mercury | Polydor

Jun 91. (cd/c/lp) *<(849 604-2/-4/-1)>* **HOLLYWOOD VAMPIRES** [44] [42]
– Over the edge / Some lie 4 love / Kiss my love goodbye / Here it comes / Crystal eyes / Wild obsession / Dirty luv / My koo ka choo / It's over now / Snake eyes boogie / The ballad of Jayne / Big house.

Nov 91. (7") *(MER 358)* **SOME LIE 4 LOVE. / DIRTY LUV** [61] [ ]
(12"/12"pic-d) *(MERX/+P 358)* – ('A'side) / Slap in the face (live) / Electric gypsy (live).
(cd-s++=) *(MERCD 358)* – Malaria (live).
(10"pic-d) *(MEREP 358)* – ('A'side) / Rip and tear (live) / Sex action (live) / Bitch is back (live).

Dec 91. (7"/7"pic-d) *(MER/+P 361)* **THE BALLAD OF JAYNE. / LIFE** [53] [-]
(12") *(MERX 361)* – ('A'side) / Kiss my love goodbye (live) / Some lie 4 love (live) / Over the edge (live).
(cd-s) *(MERCD 361)* – ('A'side) / Dirty luv (live) / My koo ka choo (live) / Over the edge (live).

Mar 92. (c-s) *<865494>* **IT'S OVER NOW / (3 album excerpts)** [-] [62]

— (Mar'92) **BONES** – drums repl. RILEY

— between 1992 and 1993, L.A. GUNS released a couple of Japanese-only mini-sets, 'LIVE' and 'LACK OF CHARISMA'; now without LEWIS

Polydor | Polydor

Apr 95. (cd/c) *<(523 158-2/-4)>* **VICIOUS CIRCLE** [ ] [ ]
– Face down / No crime / Long time dead / Killing machine / Fade away / Tarantula / Crystal eyes / Nothing better to do / Chasing the dragon / Kill that girl / I'd love to change the world / Who's in control (let 'em roll) / I'm the one / Why ain't I bleeding / Kiss of death.

C.M.C. | C.M.C.

Apr 97. (cd) *<(06076 86205-2)>* **AMERICAN HARDCORE** [ ] [ ] Oct96
– F.N.A. / What I've become / Unnatural act / Give / Don't pray / Pissed / Mine / Kevorkian / Hey world / Next generation / Hugs and needles / I am alive.

— **RALPH SAENZ** – vocals; repl. NICKELS

— the others were **GUNS, RILEY + CRYPT/CRIPPS**

Stand Back | Stand Back

Jul 98. (m-cd) *(MLSB 002) <351>* **WASTED** [ ] [ ] Sep98
– Wasted / Well spent / Heavy head / Forgiving eyes / Ballad of Jayne '98 / Cold gin.

— **JIZZY PEARL** – vocals (ex-LOVE/HATE) repl. RALPH

Perris | Perris

Jun 99. (cd) *(LA 9928-2) <9999>* **SHRINKING VIOLET** [ ] [ ]
– Girl you turn me on / Shrinking violet / Dreamtime / Barbed wire / I'll be there / California / Cherries / Decide / Big lil' thing / It's hard / Bad whiskey / How many more times. *(re-iss. Sep99 on 'Axe Killer'; AXE 305271CD)*

— **LEWIS** was back at the helm with **GUNS + CRIPPS**

not iss. | Spitfire

Apr 01. (cd) *<15179>* **MAN IN THE MOON** [-] [ ]
– Man in the moon / Beautiful / Good thing / Spider's web / Don't call me crazy / Hypnotized / Fast talkin' dream dealer / Out of sight / Turn it around / Scream.

– compilations, etc. –

Jun 98. (cd) *import; <34121>* **HOLLYWOOD REHEARSAL** [-] [ ]
– I feel nice / High on you / Strange boat / Gunslinger / Rip off / Should I stay or should I go / Custard pie / Rock candy / All the way / Guilty / Long time dead (remix) / Dangerous games.

Jun 99. (cd) *Cleopatra; <(CLP 559)>* **GREATEST HITS AND BLACK BEAUTIES** [ ] [ ]

Apr 00. (cd) *Anagram; (CDMZEB 13)* **THE VERY BEST OF L.A. GUNS** [ ] [-]
– Bricks / One more reason / Ritual / Electric gypsy / No mercy / Sex action / Rip 'n' tear / Disbelief / Ballad of Jayne / Time / Heartful of soul / 3 minute atomic egg / One more reason (Julian Beeston remix) / Sex action (intra-Venus remix).

Apr 00. (cd) *Axe Killer; (AXE 305724CD) / Cleopatra; <CLP 772>* **A NITE ON THE STRIP** [ ] [ ]
(re-iss. Jul00 on 'Cleopatra'; same as US)

Aug 00. (cd) *Cleopatra; <(CLP 864)>* **COCKED AND RE-LOADED** [ ] [ ]

LAGWAGON

Formed: Goleta, South California, USA . . . 1990 initially as SECTION 8 by JOEY CAPE and various others. As with many latter day punk acts of their ilk, LAGWAGON underwent almost constant personnel upheaval with a line-up of JOEY, CHRIS, SHAWN, JESSE and DERRICK in place for their 1992 debut album, 'DUH'. The fact it was released on 'Fat Wreck Chords' only served to confirm the band were pitched squarely in the NOFX camp of head-on, harmonised hardcore and more than occasional lyrical buffoonery. Which isn't to say they were incapable of tackling meatier issues, as the likes of 'ISLAND OF SHAME' – from sophomore effort, 'TRASHED' (1994) – attested. 1995's 'HOSS' attempted a more serious approach, leaving out the puerile cover versions and opting for starker song titles. The self deprecating theme behind 'DOUBLE PLADINUM' (1997) at least suggested that as a group, LAGWAGON knew the limits of their potential. By the release of the latter set – which featured erstwhile POSIES guitarist KEN STRINGFELLOW – their revolving door line-up included a couple of renegades from RICH KIDS ON LSD (DAVE RAUN and CHRIS) who both played on 1998's 'LET'S TALK ABOUT FEELINGS'. • **Covered:** BAD MOON RISING (Creedence Clearwater Revival) / BROWN EYED GIRL (Van Morrison) / etc. • **Trivia:** CAPE (on guitar!) and DAVE RAUN also moonlight with punky covers star band, ME FIRST AND THE GIMME GIMMES, who've released two albums in '97 and '99.

Album rating: DUH (*7) / TRASHED (*6) / HOSS (*6) / DOUBLE PLADINUM (*5) / LET'S TALK ABOUT FEELINGS (*6) / LET'S TALK ABOUT LEFTOVERS outtakes (*5)

JOEY CAPE – vocals / **CHRIS** – guitar / **SHAWN** – guitar / **JESSE** – bass / **DERRICK** – drums

Fat Wreck Chords | Fat Wreck Chords

1992. (cd/c/lp) *<FAT 502 CD/MC/LP>* **DUH** [-] [ ]
– Tragic vision / Folied again / Bury the hatchet / Angry days / Noble end / Child inside / Bad moon rising / Beer goggles / Inspector Gadget / Parents guide to living / Mr. Coffee / Of mind and matter / Stop whining / Lag wagon.

Feb 94. (cd) *<(FAT 513-2)>* **TRASHED** [ ] [ ]
– Island of shame / Lazy / Know it all / Stokin' the neighbors / Give it back / Rust / Goin' south / Dis'chords / Coffee and cigarettes / Brown eyed girl / Whipping boy / No one / Bye for now.

Nov 95. (cd/lp) *<(FAT 532 CD/MC/LP)>* **HOSS** [ ] [ ]
– Kids don't like to share / Violins / Name dropping / Bombs away / Move the car / Sleep / Sick / Rifle / Weak / Black eyes / Bro dependent / Razor burn / Shaving your head / Ride the snake.

— **DAVE RAUN** – drums, percussion (ex-RICH KIDS ON LSD, of ME FIRST AND THE GIMME GIMMES) repl. DERRICK / **KEN STRINGFELLOW** – guitar (ex-POSIES) repl. SHAWN

Aug 97. (cd/c/lp) *<FAT 558 CD/MC/LP>* **DOUBLE PLADINUM** [-] [ ]
– Alien 8 / Making friends / Unfurnished / One thing to live / Today / Confession / Bad scene / Smile / Twenty-seven / Choke / Failure / To all my friends.

— **CHRIS** – guitar (ex-RICH KIDS ON LSD) repl. STRINGFELLOW

Nov 98. (10"lp/cd) *<(FAT 578/+CD)>* **LET'S TALK ABOUT FEELINGS** [ ] [ ]
– After you my friend / Gun in your hand / Leave the light on / Change despair / Train / Hurry up and wait / Everything turns grey / Love story / Messengers / Kids are all wrong / May 16 / Owen Meaney.

– compilations, etc. –

Feb 00. (cd) *My Records; <(MR 8056-2)>* **LET'S TALK ABOUT LEFTOVERS** [ ] [ ]
– Feedbag of truckstop poetry / Narrow straits / Burn that fridge when we get to it / Losing everyone / Jimmy Johnson / Eat your words / Want / Bring on the dancing horses / Randal gets drunk / Raise a family / Restrain / No one like you / Brodeo / Wind in your sail / Over the hill / Defeat you / Layman's terms / Jazzy Jeff / The champ / Demented rumours / Truth and justice / No conviction / Jaded ways.

LAIBACH

Formed: Trbovlje, Slovenia, the former Yugoslavia . . . 1980 by TOMAZ HOSTNIK, MILAN FREZ, DEJAN KNEZ and ERVIN MARKOSEK. A musical, nay cultural one-off, LAIBACH took their moniker from the old German name for Slovenia's capital, Ljubljana, a statement of intent that set out their direct opposition to the communist-controlled state of Yugoslavia. One part of a wider art collective, NSK (Neue Slowenische Kunst or New Slovenian Art), LAIBACH worked in tandem with the movement's painting and theatre divisions in a fashion designed to both parody and speak out against the individual subjugation of the communist industrial machine. The early 80's proved tumultuous as the band attempted to develop their crude electro minimalism amid compulsory military service and the suicide of mainman HOSTNIK (his place was taken by IVAN NOVAK). They also experienced open hostility from the Yugoslav authorities, a deal with the state record company severed at the last minute. Following a series of releases through European labels, the band's growing UK profile and numerous art appearances eventually led to a long-term deal with 'Mute'. The result was 'OPUS DEI' (1987), LAIBACH moving away from the avant-garde experimentalism of their earlier releases towards a thunderous, po-faced (and let's face it, often hilarious) industrial-rock sound. Full marks for turning Opus' Euro cheese classic, 'LIFE IS LIFE' into a Balkan funeral march under the title of 'LEBEN HEIST LEBEN', the thrusting broadsword reworking of Queen's 'ONE VISION' aka 'GEBURT EINER NATION', meanwhile, raising disturbing questions about where exactly the band's political sympathies lie; accusations of fascist undercurrents were inevitable, only serving to further shroud the band in myth. Two of rock's holiest cows, The BEATLES and The ROLLING STONES, were next in line for the LAIBACH treatment as the group proceeded to stomp their musical jackboot over the whole 'LET IT BE' (1988) album and 'STONES' classic, 'SYMPATHY FOR THE DEVIL' (1990). While 1990 also saw the release of their acclaimed 'MACBETH' soundtrack (for a production by German theatre company, 'Deutsches Schauspielhaus'), LAIBACH's political context was irrevocably altered with the beginnings of the Balkans confict as Slovenia declared its independence. The new decade has seen the band tackle techno in suitably Wagnerian style with 'KAPITAL' (1992), KRAFTWERK covers set, 'TRANS-SLOVENIA EXPRESS' (1994) and 'NATO' (even more covers), while 1996's 'SARAJEVO – OCCUPIED EUROPE NATO TOUR 1994-1995' documented the band's live excursions against the backdrop of turmoil and war which continues to afflict the region.

Album rating: THROUGH OCCUPIED EUROPE (*4) / LAIBACH (*5) / NOVA AKRPOLA (*5) / OPUS DEI (*6) / LET IT BE (*6) / MACBETH (*6) / KAPITAL (*6) / JESUS CHRIST SUPERSTARS (*6)

IVAN NOVAK – vocals; repl. TOMAZ HOSTNIK who committed suicide in '81 / **MILAN FREZ** + **DEJAN KNEZ** + **ERVIN MARKOSEK**

Staal | not iss.

Dec 83. (c) **THROUGH THE OCCUPIED NETHERLANDS** [-] [-] Dutch
– De Kapal-den Haag (soundboard rec. 30.11.83) / NL Centrum-Amsterdam (live rec. 1.12.83).

Laylah | not iss.

Mar 84. (12") *(LAY 002)* **BOJI. / SILA / BRAT MOJ** [ ] [-]

East-West Trading Co. | not iss.

May 84. (12") *(12EW 3)* **PANORAMA. / DECREE** [ ] [-]

Walter Ulbright | not iss.

1985. (d-lp) **REKAPITULACIJA** (compilation 1980-84) [-] [-] German
– Jaruzelelski / Tod fur Tod / Macht / In mitten von Kampfen / Bruder mein / Du, der du herausforderst / Wir schmieden die Zukunft.

S.K.U.C. | not iss.

May 85. (lp) **LAIBACH** [-] [-] Yugo
– Cari Amici / Sila / Sredi Bojev / Drzava / Dekret / Mi Kujemo bodocnost / Brat moj / Panorama. *(cd-iss. Aug95 on 'Nika'; EFA 13132-2)*

Cherry Red | Wax Trax!

Dec 85. (12") *(12CHERRY 91)* **DIE LIEBE. / DIE LIEBE IST GROSSTE KRAFT, DIE ALLES SCHAFFT** [ ] [-]

Jan 86. (m-lp/m-cd) *(B/CDM RED 67) <WX/+CS/CD 7080>* **NOVA AKROPOLA** [ ] [ ]
– Vier personen / Nova Akropola / Krvav Gruda – Ploona Zemlja / Vojna poena / Ti, zi izzivas / Die liebe / Drzava / Vade retro / Panorama. *(w/ free-lp)* – NEW KONSTERVATIW HAMBURG 1985 (live) – Vier personen / Nova Akropola / Vade retro Satanas / Die liebe / Du der du herausforderst / Der staat. *(re-iss. cd Apr93; same) <US cd re-iss. 1994 on 'Cleopatra'; 9483>*

Side Effects | not iss.

Jul 86. (lp) *(SER 08)* **THE OCCUPIED EUROPE TOUR 1985 (live)** [ ] [-]
– Vade retro / Perspektive / Panorama / Die liebe / Dsava / Vier personen / Slovenska Akropola / Vojna poema / Nova Akropola / Ti, zi izzivas. *<US cd-iss. 1991 on 'Mute'; 61071-2>*

Mute | Wax Trax!

Mar 87. (12") *(12 MUTE 60)* **GEBURT EINER NATION (ONE VISION). / LEBEN HEIBT LEBEN (LIFE IS LIFE)** [ ] [-]

Mar 87. (cd/lp) *(CD+/STUMM 44) <WAXCD 030>* **OPUS DEI**
– Leben heibt leben / Geburt einer nation / Leben-Tod / F.I.A.T. / Opus dei / Transnational / How the west was won / The great seal. *(cd+=)* – Herz-Felde / Jagerspiel / Koza (skin) / Krst (baptism).

Jul 87. (7") *(MUTE 62)* **LIFE IS LIFE. / GERMANIA** [ ] [-]
(12"+=) *(12MUTE 62)* – Life (Opus).

Mute | Mute

Sep 88. (7") *(MUTE 80) <71404>* **SYMPATHY FOR THE DEVIL (WHO KILLED THE KENNEDYS). / SYMPATHY FOR THE DEVIL (SOUL TO WASTE)** [ ] [ ]
(12"ep+=/cd-ep+=) *(MUTE 80 T/CD)* – ('A'numerous versions). *(re-iss. Feb90 cd/c/lp) (CD/MC/LP MUTE 80)*

Oct 88. (cd/c/lp) *(CD/C+/STUMM 58) <75404>* **LET IT BE** [ ] [ ]
– Let it be / Get back / Two of us / Dig a pony / I me mine / Across the universe / Dig it / I've got a feeling / The long and winding road / One after 909 / For you blue / Maggie Mae (auf der Luneburger Heide & was gleicht wohl auf Erden). *(d-c+=)* – OPUS DEI

Dec 88. (7") *(MUTE 91)* **ACROSS THE UNIVERSE. / MAGGIE MAE** [ ] [-]
(12"+=/cd-s+=) *(12/CD MUTE 91)* – Get back. *(re-iss. Dec89)*

Mute | Restless

Jan 90. (cd/c/lp) *(CD/C+/STUMM 70) <71458>* **MACBETH** [ ] [ ]
– Preludium / Agnus dei (Acropolis) / Wutach schlucht / Die zeit / Ohne geld / U.S.A. / 10.05.1941 / Expectans expectavos / Coincidentia oppositorium / Wolf / Agnus dei (Exil und Tod).

Mute Elektra

Apr 92. (12"/cd-s) **WIRTSCHAFT IST TOT (THE ECONOMY IS DEAD). /** [ ] [ ]

Apr 92. (cd/c/lp) *(CD/C+/STUMM 82) <61282>* **KAPITAL (live)** [ ] [ ]
– Decade null / Everlasting in union / Ilumination / Le privilege des morts / Codex Durex / Hymn to the black Sun / Young Europa / The hunter's funeral procession / White law / Wirtschaft ist tot / Torso / Entartete welt / Kinderreich (English version) / Sponsored by Mars / Regime of confidence / State of gravity.

Sep 94. (12"/cd-s) *(12/CD MUTE 117)* **FINAL COUNTDOWN (mixes: Euro / Mark Stent alt / Juno reactor version / Fortran 5 version II)** [ ] [-]

Oct 94. (cd/c/lp) *(CD/C+/STUMM 121) <61714>* **NATO** [ ] [ ]
– NATO / War / Final countdown / In the army now / Dogs of war / Alle gegen alle / Anational reservation / 2 3 2 5 / Mars on River Drina.

Apr 95. (12"/cd-s) *(12/CD MUTE 170)* **IN THE ARMY NOW. / WAR** [ ] [-]

Oct 96. (cd-ep) *(CDMUTE 197)* **JESUS CHRIST SUPERSTAR / GOD IS GOD (optical vocal mix) / GOD IS GOD (coptic rain mix) / GOD IS GOD (diabolical mix) / JESUS CHRIST SUPERSTAR (random logic mix)** [ ] [-]

Oct 96. (cd/lp) *(CD+/STUMM 136) <69027>* **JESUS CHRIST SUPERSTARS** [ ] [ ]
– God is God / Jesus Christ superstar / Kingdom of God / Abuse and confession / Declaration of freedom / Message from the black star / The cross / To the new light / Deus ex machina.

Robot Robot

Jul 97. (cd) *(<efacd 20447-2>)* **ALSO SPRACH JOHANN PAUL II** [ ] [ ]
– Also Sprach Johann Paul II / Transcendental storm / Human redemption / Hell's march epilepsye / Prolaiare proelis domini / Resurrection of the kinderreich / Divine order / Zoroaster 2000 (reces).

– compilations, etc. –

1985. (c) *Staal;* **EIN SCHAUSPIELER** [-] [-] Yugo

Mar 87. (lp) *S.K.U.C.;* **SLOVENSKA AKROPOLA** [-] [-] Yugo
(UK cd-iss. Aug95 on 'Nika'; EFA 20025-2)

Nov 87. (d-lp/cd) *Sub Rosa; (SUB 33006 7/9)* **A BAPTISM** [ ] [-]
(re-iss. cd Nov88 & Oct94; SR 0019CD)

Feb 89. (cd-ep) *Wax;* **PANORAMA / DECREE / DIE LIEBE / DIE LIEBE IST GROSSTE KRAFT, DIE ALLES SCHAFFT** [ ] [-]

Jun 93. (cd) *Grey Area-Mute; (NSK 1CD)* **LJUBLJANA, ZAGREB, BEOGRAD** [ ] [-]

Jul 95. (cd) *Roir USA; (RUSCD 8211)* **LAIBACH** [ ] [ ]

Aug 96. (cd) *Grey Area-Mute; (NSK 2CD)* **OCCUPIED EUROPE NATO TOUR 1994-95 (live)** [ ] [-]

Jun 97. (cd) *Grey Area-Mute; (NSK 3CD)* **M.B. DECEMBER 21st, 1984** [ ] [-]

Steve LAKE (see under ⇒ ZOUNDS)

Mark LANEGAN (see under ⇒ SCREAMING TREES)

LARD (see under ⇒ DEAD KENNEDYS)

LAST CRACK

Formed: Milwaukee, Wisconsin, USA . . . mid 80's by frontman BUDDO BUDDO, who enlisted guitarists DON BAKKEN and PABLO SCHUTER, plus the rhythm section of TODD WINGER and PHIL BUERSTATE. Driven by the seemingly deranged BUDDO, this bunch of genre-splicing metal magpies combined everything from garage-psych and white funk to full-on thrash, as evidenced on their well-received debut set, 'SINISTER FUNKHOUSE #17' (1989). Two years in the making, a second and final album, 'BURNING TIME' was delivered to a similarly enthusiastic critical response, although their fractured sound proved a tad too challenging for mass taste.

Album rating: SINISTER FUNKHOUSE #17 (*6) / BURNING TIME (*6)

BUDDO BUDDO – vocals / **PABLO SCHUTER** – guitar / **DON BAKKEN** – guitar / **TODD WINGER** – bass / **PHIL BUERSTATE** – drums

Roadracer Roadracer

1989. (lp/c/cd) *<(RO 9501-1/-4/-2)>* **SINISTER FUNKHOUSE #17** [ ] [ ]
– Good mourning from the funkhouse / Sudo volcano crush / Blood brothers of the big black bear / Concrete slaughter dogs / Slicing steel / Saraboys cage / The last crack / Shelter / Terse / Thee abyss.

—— **DAVE TRUEHARDT** – bass; repl. WINGER

Roadrunner Roadrunner

May 91. (cd/c/lp) *<(RR 9330-2/-4/-1)>* **BURNING TIME** [ ] [ ]
– Wicked sandbox / Jenny and Todd's mini toboggan / Energy mind / My burning time / Precious human stress / Love, Craig / Kiss the cold / Love or surrender / Mack bolasses / Blue fly, fish sky / Papa mugaya / Down beat dirt messiah / Oooh.
above was, as they say, their last crack

LAW (see under ⇒ RODGERS, Paul)

LAWNMOWER DETH

Formed: Nottingham, England . . . 1987 by the bizarrely pseudonymous QUALCAST MUTILATOR, CONCORDE FACERIPPER, SCHITZO ROTARY SPRINTMASTER, MIGHTYMO DESTRUCTIMO and MR. (COB BREW) FLYMO. Thrash-metal piss-takers inspired by the over-the-top posturing of bands like JUDAS PRIEST, VENOM and SKYCLAD, LAWNMOWER DETH initiated their vaguely horticultural brand of parody in summer '89 via a split album with fellow pranksters METAL DUCK entitled 'QUACK 'EM ALL'. Signing with 'Earache', the group released their much lauded (by less po-faced critics) 'OOH CRIKEY IT'S . . .' (1990), a record featuring such irreverent 'DETH moments as 'SEVENTH CHURCH OF THE APOCALYPTIC LAWNMOWER' and 'CAN I CULTIVATE YOUR GROINAL GARDEN'. An integral part of the Brit-thrash scene alongside the likes of ACID REIGN and XENTRIX, the band became a constant fixture at club venues around the UK with their 'Tiswas'-like live shows. The green-fingered grass-cutters even managed to unearth a comic cover of Kim Wilde's 'KIDS IN AMERICA' in 1991. The joke began wearing a little thin with the release of 'RETURN OF THE FABULOUS BOZO CLOWNS' (1992) and as thrash fell by the wayside as the 90's wore on, so LAWNMOWER DETH finally retired to that great garden shed in the sky following 1993's 'BILLY'.

Album rating: QUACK EM ALL w/ Metal Duck (*5) / OOH CRIKEY IT'S . . . (*6) / THE RETURN OF THE FABULOUS BOZO CLOWNS (*4) / BILLY (*5)

QUALCAST MUTILATOR – vocals / **CONCORDE FACERIPPER** – guitars / **SCHITZO ROTARY SPRINTMASTER** – guitar / **MIGHTYMO DESTRUCTIMO** – bass / **MR. (COB BREW) FLYMO** (b.24 Jul'68) – drums

R.K.T. not iss.

Jun 89. (lp) *(CMO 192)* **QUACK EM ALL** (w/ METAL DUCK) [ ] [-]

Earache Combat

Sep 90. (lp/cd) *(MOSH 025/+CD) <1079>* **OOH CRIKEY IT'S . . .** [ ] [ ] Feb91
– Spook perv happenings in the snooker hall / Betty Ford's clinic / Weebles wobble but they don't fall down / Sheep dip / Lancer with your zancer / Can I cultivate your groinal garden? / Flying killer cobs from the planet Bob / Did you spill my pint? / Seventh church of the apocalyptic lawnmower (skank mix) / Rad dude / Sumo rabbit and his inescapable trap of doom / Maim mower maim / Cobwoman of deth meets Mr. Smellymop / Got no legs? don't come crawling to me / Icky ficky / Judgement day (assume the position) / Ooh crikey / Satan's trampoline / Dodo doe / Duck off / F.A.T. (Fascist And Tubby). *(cd+=)* – Punk as f*** / Sharp fa blades of Hades. *(cd re-iss. Mar99; same)*

—— **KEV** – guitar (ex-ACID REIGN) repl. SCHITZO ROTARY

May 91. (7") *(MOSH 039)* **KIDS IN AMERICA. / BONEYANK BLISTERS** [ ] [-]
(cd-s+=) *(MOSH 039CD)* – Sumo rabbit and his inescapable trap of doom.

Jul 92. (lp/cd) *(MOSH 072/+CD) <1143>* **RETURN OF THE FABULOUS METAL BOZO CLOWNS** [ ] [ ]
– The return of the fabulous metal bozo clowns / Jaggered wedge / Bad toad / Fetcleaner / Drunk in charge of an ugly face / Paranoid polaroid / Frash for cash / Crazy horses / Enter Mr. Formica (icky fricky Pt.II) / Lawnmowers for heroes, comics for zeros / Urban surfer 125 / A is for asswipe / Sorrow (so dark, so scared) / Goldfish podge / R.F. Potts / Wormy eyes / Be scene, not heard / Egg sandwich / Anyone for tinnies / King of the pharoahs / Illinois enema bandi 1: fookin' moovit. *(cd re-iss. Mar99; same)*

Earache Earache

Oct 93. (lp/cd) *(<MOSH 098/+CD>)* **BILLY** [ ] [ ] Jan94
– Somebody, call me a taxi / Billy / I need to be my main / Squeeze / Do you wanna be a chuffed core? / Buddy Holly never wrote a song called we're too punk / Up the junction / If it was grey you'd say its black / Stomach gout / I Narcissus / Kids in America '93 / March of the tweeds / A funny thing about it is / Purple haze. *(cd re-iss. Mar99; same)*

—— finally went to seed at Christmas '94

LEADFOOT

Formed: Raleigh, North Carolina, USA . . . mid-90's by former CORROSION OF CONFORMITY members KARL AGELL and PHIL SWISHER. Signed to 'Roadrunner', the pair convincingly distanced themselves from their former band with the release of 'BRING IT ON' in 1997. The record's supple metallic grooves betrayed a love of classic Southern Rock (LYNYRD SKYNYRD, ALLMAN BROS, BLACKFOOT etc.) without lapsing into parody, ironically foreshadowing COC's own shift towards Southern-influenced material. 1999's 'TAKE A LOOK' followed in a similar vein, featuring a line-up of AGELL, SWISHER, GRAHAM FRY, SCOTT LITTLE and TIM HAISMAN.

Album rating: BRING IT ON (*7) / TAKE A LOOK (*5)

KARL AGELL – vocals (ex-CORROSION OF CONFORMITY) / **PHIL SWISHER** – bass (ex-CORROSION OF CONFORMITY) / GRAHAM FRY – guitar / **SCOTT LITTLE** – guitar / **TIM HAISMAN** – drums

Roadrunner The Music Cartel

Sep 97. (cd) *(RR 8833-2) <TMC 6CD>* **BRING IT ON** [ ] [ ] Jul98
– Bring it on / Soul full of lies / High time / Roll all over you / Right between the eyes / Ripe / Sooner / Young dumb snake / Throwing out the baby / Under the sun / Naked light / Forgotten one.

The Music Cartel The Music Cartel

Nov 99. (cd) *<(TMC 28CD)>* **TAKE A LOOK** [ ] [ ] Oct99
– Redline / Loose cannon / Unkind / Built in a day / War against you / Take a look / Reapin' existence / Drift / Curse the goals / Old West f-over / Certain to be wrong / Blowhole / Panic attack.

LEAD INTO GOLD (see under ⇒ MINISTRY)

LEAF HOUND

Formed: London, England . . . 1969 as BLACK CAT BONES, by PETER FRENCH. He was a veteran of several pub-rock blues outfits, including BRUNNING SUNFLOWER BLUES BAND with BOB BRUNNING. They made one album, 'BULLEN ST. BLUES', with FRENCH and MICK HALLS co-writing most of the material. BLACK CAT BONES (who wanted a replacement for PAUL KOSSOFF) invited FRENCH to join them for the recording of an album, 'BARBED WIRE SANDWICH'. The outfit soon evolved into LEAF HOUND after the introduction of cousin MICK HALLS (with whom he'd been a member of mid-60's band, SWITCH). In 1971, their heavy touring schedule paid off with a deal for 'Decca', who released the album, 'GROWERS OF MUSHROOM', later that year. It failed to sell, although it was regarded by many rock critics as a classic of its genre; heavy progressive-blues in the mould of FREE or LED ZEPPELIN. LEAF HOUND subsequently went to Germany and Scandinavia to promote both the album and the single, 'DROWNED MY LIFE IN FEAR', which never gained a UK release. The album was delayed in Britain, and by the time of its unveiling, FRENCH had already joined ATOMIC ROOSTER. He featured on one album, 'IN HEARING OF', which hit the Top 20, but fed up with the lack of money, he joined Americans CACTUS (formerly VANILLA FUDGE). He then moved to the States in 1972, recording the album, 'OT 'N' SWEATY'. When they split to form BECK, BOGART & APPICE, he was left to recruit new members, although this idea was soon abandoned. Back on British soil and out of work, he answered an ad from the German band RANDY PIE, who in 1977, gave him a new lease of life. They had already released three albums, now gaining an American release with their fourth, 'FAST FORWARD'. Departing after only one album, he was subsequently offered a solo deal with the German 'Polydor' label, bringing back HALLS to augment him on the album, 'DUCKS IN FLIGHT'. He was then involved in the controversial 'DER FUHRER' rock opera, which was masterminded by German group PARZIVAL and was actually an anti-Hitler farce. In 1981, he teamed up with BIDDU, gaining his first UK hit!, 'STATUS ROCK' as The HEADBANGERS. • **Songwriters:** FRENCH + HALLS on most. • **Trivia:** The BLACK CAT BONES lp is worth £75, while 1971 lp is worth nearly 10 times that!.

Album rating: GROWERS OF MUSHROOM (*7) / Black Cat Bones: BARBED WIRE SANDWICH (*5)

BLACK CAT BONES

PETER FRENCH – vocals / **DEREK BROOKS** – guitar / **STU BROOKS** – bass / **BOB WESTON** – guitar / **ROD PRICE** – guitar, vocals / **STEVE MILLINER + ROBIN SYLVESTER** – piano / **PHIL LENOIR** – drums / **BRIAN SHORT** – vocals

Decca Nova | not iss.

Nov 69. (lp) *(SDN 15)* **BARBED WIRE SANDWICH** [ ] [-]
– Chauffeur / Death valley blues / Feelin' good / Please tell my baby / Coming back / Save my love / Four women / Sylvester's blues / Good lookin' woman. *(cd-iss. Aug94 on 'See For Miles'; SEECD 405)*

— **MICK HALLS** – guitar (ex-SWITCH), repl. PRICE who joined FOGHAT

LEAF HOUND

FRENCH / BROOKS / BROOKS / HALLS / + KEITH YOUNG – drums

Decca | not iss.

Oct 71. (lp) *(SKL-R 5094)* **GROWERS OF MUSHROOM** [ ] [-]
– Freelance fiend / Sad road to the sea / Drowned my life in fear / Work my body / Stray / With a minute to go / Growers of mushroom / Stagnant pool / Sawdust Caesar. *(cd-iss. Jul94 on 'See For Miles'+=; SEECD 403)* – It's going to get better / Hip shaker.

— FRENCH had already left to join ATOMIC ROOSTER, but after recording one charting lp 'IN HEARING OF'. In 1972, FRENCH joined American rock band CACTUS, who contained former members of VANILLA FUDGE. They made one lp with him; 'OT 'N' SWEATY'. He returned to the UK in 1974 to do unfruitful auditions for DEEP PURPLE, MANFRED MANN'S EARTH BAND and URIAH HEEP. In 1977, he joined German outfit RANDY PIE to record on their 4th German/US lp 'FAST FORWARD'. He also featured on European double-lp 'ROCK OPERA – DER FUHRER' for 'Harvest' *(1C 188-32508/9)*. He dressed as Josef Goebbels and it also featured MARTI WEBB as Eva Braun. In 1977, he went solo and released 'DUCKS IN FLIGHT', but he made only one more appearance in novelty STATUS QUO pastische poutfit The HEADBANGERS, in which he sang like FRANCIS ROSSI.

PETER FRENCH

— with **BRIAN ROBERTSON** – guitar (of THIN LIZZY) / **DAVE MARKEE** – bass / **KENNY JONES** – drums (ex-FACES)

Polydor | not iss.

1977. (7") *(2042 025)* **GIVE ME YOUR LOVE. / SAME OLD QUESTIONS** [-] [-] German
1978. (lp) *(2417 117)* **DUCKS IN FLIGHT** [-] [-] German

— FRENCH formed The HEADBANGERS in '81 and issued hit 45 'STATUS ROCK'.

Paul LEARY (see under ⇒ BUTTHOLE SURFERS)

LEATHERWOLF

Formed: South California, USA . . . 1983 by MICHAEL OLIVIERI, GEOFF GAYER, CAREY HOWE, MATT HURICH and DEAN ROBERTS. Manly US hair-rock, LEATHERWOLF's debut set, 'ENDANGERED SPECIES' (1985) was enough to attract respected UK label, 'Island', who finally issued the Kevin Beamish-produced 'LEATHERWOLF' in 1988. The album took a more overtly commercial approach and nearly hit the US Top 100, although they struggled to outrun the pop-metal pack and eventually retreated to their collective lair after a final set, 'STREET READY' (1989).

Album rating: ENDANGERED SPECIES (*5) / LEATHERWOLF (*4) / STREET READY (*5)

MICHAEL OLIVIERI – vocals, guitar / **GEOFF GAYER** – guitar / **CAREY HOWE** – guitar / **MATT HURICH** – bass / **DEAN ROBERTS** – drums

Heavy Metal | S.P.V.

Jul 85. (lp/c/cd) *(HMUSA/HMAMC/HMAXD 39)* <47546> **ENDANGERED SPECIES** [ ] [ ]
– Spiter / Endangered species / Tonight's the night / The hook / Season of the witch / Off the track / Kill and kill again / Vagrant / Leatherwolf.

— **PAUL CARMAN** – bass; repl. HURICH

Island | Island

May 88. (lp/c/cd) *(ILPS/ICT/CID 9889)* <90660> **LEATHERWOLF** [ ] [ ]
– Rise or fall / The calling / Share a dream / Cry out / Gypsies & thieves / Bad moon rising / Princess of love / Magical eyes / Rule the night.
Mar 89. (7"/7"pic-d) *(IS/+P 416)* **HIDEAWAY. / TOO MUCH** [ ] [ ]
(12"+=/12"s+=/cd-s+=) *(12IS/ISS/CID 416)* – Rule the night.
Mar 89. (lp/c/cd) *(ILPS/ICT/CID 9927)* <91072> **STREET READY** [ ] [ ]
– Wicked ways / Street ready / Hideaway / Take a chance / Black knight / Thunder / The way I feel / Too much / Lonely road / Spirits in the wind.

— retired from the scene for the 90's

LED ZEPPELIN

Formed: London, England . . . mid '68 out of The NEW YARDBIRDS, by guitar wizard JIMMY PAGE, session bassist JOHN PAUL JONES and frontman ROBERT PLANT. Another session musician, drummer JOHN BONHAM, completed the line-up, arriving in time for their live debut at Surrey University on the 15th October '68. Taking the group name from one of KEITH MOON's catchphrases, "going down like a lead zeppelin", the band came under the wing of PETER GRANT, one of the most notoriously shrewd managers in the history of rock and an integral part of the 'ZEPPELIN legend. Following some early dates in Scandinavia and the UK, GRANT secured a lucrative worldwide deal with 'Atlantic', the group subsequently touring America with fellow proto-metallers, VANILLA FUDGE. Universally saddled with the dubious honour of inventing heavy metal, the group nevertheless started out as a power-blues outfit, as evidenced on their blistering 1969 debut set, the eponymous 'LED ZEPPELIN'. From the beginning it was obvious 'ZEPPELIN had a musical chemistry more electric than any rock'n'roll band that had gone before; in spite of, or perhaps as a result of, the fact that BONHAM and JONES came from a soul background while PLANT and PAGE were coming from the heavy blues/R&B angle, the group had an almost superhuman grasp of dynamics. Whether negotiating the climactic blues of 'BABE I'M GONNA LEAVE YOU' or ripping out the power drill rhythms of 'COMMUNICATION BREAKDOWN', each musician wielded their instrument like a weapon, deadly accurate and timed to perfection. PLANT, meanwhile, had one of the most distinctive, orgasmic blues wails in rock, bringing it down to a rustic canter on the folkier numbers. These would come later, though, the sole folk song on the blues-dominated debut being the trad-based instrumental, 'BLACK MOUNTAIN SIDE'. The album's centrepiece was the tortured 'DAZED AND CONFUSED', PAGE's guitar trawling the depths of black despair, while PLANT put in one of his career best performances over a track which would become a mainstay of the LED ZEPPELIN live extravaganza. These were marathon events, with solos and improvisation aplenty, albeit in a more focussed way than the likes of the GRATEFUL DEAD. The shows were also concentrated, initially at least, in America, where GRANT was intent upon breaking the band. While the debut was a transatlantic Top 10 success, the follow-up, 'LED ZEPPELIN II' (1969), scaled both the UK and US charts later that year. Cited by many as the birthdate of British heavy metal, the sledgehammer, divebombing riff of 'WHOLE LOTTA LOVE' ushered in a new era for rock, blasting the competition out of the water. Recorded on the road, the album was graced with more than a little of the improvisatory tension of the live show; the grungy groove of 'MOBY DICK' panned out to a marathon display of BONHAM's rhythmic alchemy, while the middle part of 'WHOLE LOTTA LOVE' lingered in a kind of suspended animation as PAGE engendered all manner of bizarre effects and PLANT got himself all hot and bothered. 'THANK YOU' and 'RAMBLE ON' indicated the direction 'ZEPPELIN would follow on subsequent releases while 'LIVING LOVING MAID (SHE'S JUST A WOMAN)' and 'BRING IT ON HOME', were itchy, funky blues/metal barnstormers, the latter boasting one of the most effective intros and majestic, f***-off riffs in the 'ZEP pantheon. Prepared at 'Bron-Y-Aur' cottage in rural Wales, 'LED ZEPPELIN III' (1970) was something of a departure, at least in its equal billing for the gentler acoustic folk numbers such as 'THAT'S THE WAY' and 'TANGERINE'. Nevertheless, proceedings opened with the lumbering battlecry of 'IMMIGRANT SONG', while PAGE performed one of his most endearingly rocking solos midway through 'CELEBRATION DAY'. Though the album again topped the British and US charts (without the aid of any UK singles; LED ZEPPELIN famously never released any British singles, all part of GRANT's masterplan), critics were sceptical of the change in emphasis. They soon changed their tune with the arrival of the group's fourth effort, an untitled affair with four mystical runes adorning the cover. This immersion in myth and mysticism (PAGE had even purchased the notoriously haunted 'Boleskine Lodge' on the shores of Loch

Ness, previously home to occult figurehead, Aleister Crowley) was reflected in the material contained within; the epic 'STAIRWAY TO HEAVEN' remains the most (in)famous LED ZEPPELIN song, its pseudo-hippie musings and acoustic strumming leading into one of the most revered guitar solos of all time. Basically, if you want to spank your plank, this is where you're supposed to start. 'MISTY MOUNTAIN HOP' was another hippie fantasy, while 'THE BATTLE OF EVERMORE' was a folk-rock epic blessed by the golden tonsils of SANDY DENNY. 'BLACK DOG' and 'ROCK AND ROLL' were funky, chunky riffathons, the album's heaviest track surprisingly placed at the end of side two, the wailing, harmonica driven, rolling thunder of 'WHEN THE LEVEE BREAKS', arguably 'ZEPPELIN's most hauntingly effective update of the delta blues tradition. BONHAM's drumming didn't get get much better than this, his molten rhythms subsequently sampled by arch-rappers The BEASTIE BOYS on their massive selling debut album. At the other end of the spectrum, the sun-bleached warmth of 'GOING TO CALIFORNIA' was 'ZEPPELIN at their folky, laidback best, PLANT adopting a mellow, down-home drawl. And this was exactly what the group did, spending most of their time on the road and a fair portion of it in America. With British bands not exactly known for their good manners abroad, LED ZEPPELIN had the most infamous reputation by far. Chief suspects were BONHAM and road manager RICHARD COLE, their alleged appetite for groupies and general debauchery the stuff of rock'n'roll legend; any reader with an interest in such matters will no doubt find the gory details in any of the many books written on 'ZEPPELIN's antics. The embodiment of 70's excess, the band even leased their own jet, nicknamed 'The Starship', which reportedly turned into a 'flying brothel'. With LED ZEPPELIN having released their most successful album to date, one of the most successful albums ever, in fact, they were now riding high as probably the biggest group on the planet. They knew they could get away with anything they wanted and with 'HOUSES OF THE HOLY' (1973), they clearly fancied a bit of experimentation. The majority of critics remained unimpressed with their half-baked attempts at funk ('THE CRUNGE') and reggae ('D'YER MAKER'), 'ZEPPELIN sounding more at home on familiar ground, especially the evocative 'OVER THE HILLS AND FAR AWAY' and JONES' scathing 'NO QUARTER'. Regardless of what commentators might've thought, 'ZEPPELIN remained the crown kings of rock, the album predictably topping the charts and the group undertaking their biggest US tour to date. Subsequently activating their own record label, 'Swan Song', the group took artistic control into their own hands, releasing the ambitious double set, 'PHYSICAL GRAFFITI' in Spring '75. While the quality control was spread rather thin in places, there were some unforgettable moments, obviously the exultant 'KASHMIR', but also the affecting 'CUSTARD PIE', the booty-shaking 'TRAMPLED UNDERFOOT' and the obligatory blues odyssey, 'IN MY TIME OF DYING'. Although the group's popularity ensured massive sales, 'PRESENCE' (1976) saw major cracks appearing in the LED ZEPPELIN armoury; in a set which sounded merely slung together, only 'ACHILLES LAST STAND' put up a fight. The double live set, 'THE SONG REMAINS THE SAME' (1976), was also overblown, the album a soundtrack to a rockumentary/movie of the same name featuring live footage from '73 spliced with dodgy 'dream sequences'. Having recovered from a car crash in 1975, PLANT was dealt another blow when his young son, KARAC, died from a viral infection in the summer of '77. Amid much speculation that the group would finally call it a day, LED ZEPPELIN re-emerged in 1979 with 'IN THROUGH THE OUT DOOR', another patchy effort which nevertheless initiated a comeback tour. Following UK dates at Knebworth and a European jaunt, the group went into rehearsals for a full-scale US tour. It never happened. On the 25th of September 1980, BONHAM was found dead after another sizeable drinking session and the group officially split shortly before Christmas. A posthumous collection of outtakes, 'CODA', was issued in late '82, while more recently, the celebrated 'REMASTERS' (1990) set brought together the cream of 'ZEPPELIN's material on shiny, remastered compact disc. While PLANT went on to record solo material in the early 80's, the transatlantic Top 5, 'PICTURES AT ELEVEN' (1982) and the equally fine 'THE PRINCIPLE OF MOMENTS' (1983), PAGE recorded a sole soundtrack effort, 'DEATH WISH II' (1982). PAGE and PLANT finally got back together in 1984 via the mediocre HONEYDRIPPERS R&B/soul project along with JEFF BECK. Then came The FIRM, PLANT and PAGE hooking up with veteran BAD COMPANY frontman, PAUL RODGERS. Despite the expectation, both 'THE FIRM' (1985) and 'MEAN BUSINESS' (1986) were disappointing, suffering from turgid supergroup syndrome. Much more worthy of attention were PLANT's 'SHAKEN 'N' STIRRED' (1985), 'NOW AND ZEN' (1988), and 'MANIC NIRVANA' (1990), the singer maintaining his experimental spirit throughout, dabbling with everything from hip hop rhythms to metallic blues. Even better was 1993's 'FATE OF NATIONS', the likes of '29 PALMS' and a delicate cover of TIM HARDIN's 'IF I WERE A CARPENTER' seeing PLANT in wistfully reflective, folky mood. Save a one-off collaboration with his old mucker, ROY HARPER ('Whatever Happened To Jugula?' 1985), PAGE's only solo outing proper came with 1988's 'OUTRIDER', a competent, if hardly rivetting set of hard rocking blues (vocals courtesy of seasoned hands JOHN MILES and CHRIS FARLOWE). In 1993 however, PAGE teamed up with WHITESNAKE frontman DAVID COVERDALE to record the highly successful but rather derivative album, 'COVERDALE – PAGE'. While PLANT and PAGE teamed up once more in the mid-90's for a startling album of ethnically reworked 'ZEPPELIN classics (including four new tracks), 'NO QUARTER – UNLEDDED' (1994), the prospect of a LED ZEPPELIN reunion looks as improbable as ever and with the death of PETER GRANT (of a heart attack) on the 21st November 1995, another part of the 'ZEPPELIN legend was laid to rest. Still, fans could console themselves with the release of the acclaimed 'BBC SESSIONS' at Christmas '97, featuring a couple of electrifying performances from the earliest part of their career. Early the following year, PAGE & PLANT were back again with a complete set of new recordings, 'WALKING INTO CLARKSDALE' (1998), the material on the album being close to LED ZEPPELIN standard. JOHN PAUL JONES, meanwhile, was working on his solo project, although why the appropriately titled 'ZOOMA' (1999) was ever issued is beyond me; "What is and what should never have been" are words that spring to mind. • **Songwriters:** PAGE + PLANT wrote nearly all with some help from JONES and/or BONHAM. They also covered; I CAN'T QUIT YOU BABY (Otis Rush) / YOU SHOOK ME (Willie Dixon) / BRING IT ON HOME (Sonny Boy Williamson) / GALLOW'S POLE + HATS OFF TO HARPER (trad.) / etc. JIMMY PAGE covered; HUMMINGBIRD (B.B.King). The HONEYDRIPPERS;- SEA OF LOVE (Phil Phillips with the Twilights). ROBERT PLANT: LET'S HAVE A PARTY (Elvis Presley). • **Trivia:** In the early 70's, C.C.S. (aka. ALEXIS KORNER) had a Top 10 hit with 'WHOLE LOTTA LOVE' (later adopted for the Top Of The Pops theme). In 1985, with PHIL COLLINS on drums, LED ZEPPELIN played LIVE AID. JOHN BONHAM's drumming son, JASON, formed his own band, BONHAM in the late 80's. Around the same time, a kitsch mickey-take outfit DREAD ZEPPELIN, hit the music scene, playing reggae adaptations of the group's classics. In 1992, Australian 60's hitmaker and TV personality ROLF HARRIS destroyed 'STAIRWAY TO HEAVEN', hitting the charts in the process. It was even worse than 1985's FAR CORPORATION version, which also hit the UK Top 10. **Early work:** As well as session work with many (THEM, etc.), JIMMY PAGE released a solo single in early '65 ('SHE JUST SATIFIES' / 'KEEP MOVIN'') for 'Fontana' (TF 533) – it's now worth 250 quid! He had earlier played on 45's by NEIL CHRISTIAN & THE CRUSADERS, plus CARTER-LEWIS & THE SOUTHERNERS. JOHN PAUL JONES played in The TONY MEEHAN COMBO, before issuing a solo 45 in April '64 ('A FOGGY DAY IN VIETNAM' / 'BAJA'), for 'Pye' label. ROBERT PLANT had been part of LISTEN, who released one 45 in November '66; ('YOU'D BETTER RUN' / 'EVERYBODY'S GOTTA SAY') (CBS; 202456). He stayed with the label for two solo releases in March '67; ('OUR SONG' / 'LAUGHING, CRYING, LAUGHING' / (202656), and July '67 ('LONG TIME COMING' / 'I'VE GOT A SECRET') (2858). He subsequently teamed up that year with BONHAM, to form Birmingham-based group, BAND OF JOY. All these rare singles now fetch upwards of 100 quid.

Album rating: LED ZEPPELIN (*9) / LED ZEPPELIN II (*10) / LED ZEPPELIN III (*9) / UNTITLED (LED ZEPPELIN IV) (*10) / HOUSES OF THE HOLY (*8) / PHYSICAL GRAFFITI (*10) / PRESENCE (*6) / THE SONG REMAINS THE SAME (*6) / IN THROUGH THE OUT DOOR (*6) / CODA (*5) / REMASTERS compilation (*10) / Robert Plant: PICTURES AT ELEVEN (*6) / PRINCIPLE OF MOMENTS (*7) / MANIC NIRVANA (*7) / FATE OF NATIONS (*7) / Jimmy Page: OUTRIDER (*6) / Page & Plant: UNLEDDED (*7) / WALKING INTO CLARKSDALE (*7) / John Paul Jones: ZOOMA (*3)

ROBERT PLANT (b.20 Aug'48, West Bromwich, England) – vocals (ex-LISTEN) / **JIMMY PAGE** (b. JAMES PATRICK PAGE, 9 Jan'44, Heston, England) – lead guitars (ex-YARDBIRDS) / **JOHN PAUL JONES** (b. JOHN BALDWIN, 3 Jun'46, Sidcup, Kent, England) – bass / **JOHN BONHAM** (b.31 May'48, Redditch, England) – drums

Atlantic Atlantic

Mar 69. (lp) *(588 171) <8216>* **LED ZEPPELIN** 6 10 Feb69
– Good times bad times / Babe I'm gonna leave you / You shook me / Dazed and confused / Your time is gonna come / Black mountain side / Communication breakdown / I can't quit you baby / How many more times. *(re-iss. Mar72 lp/c; K/K4 40031) (cd-iss. Jan87 & 1989 special; 240031) (re-iss. Jul94 & Aug97 cd/c; 7567 82632-2) (lp re-iss. Oct99 on 'Classic'; SD 19126)*

Mar 69. (7") *<2613>* **GOOD TIMES BAD TIMES. / COMMUNICATION BREAKDOWN** - 80

Oct 69. (lp) *(588 198) <8236>* **LED ZEPPELIN II** 1 1
– Whole lotta love / What is and what should never be / The lemon song / Thank you / Heartbreaker / Livin' lovin' maid (she's just a woman) / Ramble on / Moby Dick / Bring it on home. *(re-iss. Mar72 lp/c; K/K4 40037) (cd-iss. Jan87 & 1989 special; 240037) (re-iss. Jul94 & Aug97 cd/c; 7567 82633-2)*

Nov 69. (7") *<2690>* **WHOLE LOTTA LOVE. / LIVING LOVING MAID (SHE'S JUST A WOMAN)** 4 65

Oct 70. (lp) *(2401 002) <7201>* **LED ZEPPELIN III** 1 1
– Immigrant song / Friends / Celebration day / Since I've been loving you / Out on the tiles / Gallows pole / Tangerine / That's the way / Bron-y-aur stomp / Hats off to (Roy) Harper. *(re-iss. Mar72 lp/c; K/K4 50002) (cd-iss. Jan87 & 1989 special; 250002) (cd-iss. Aug97; 7567 82678-2)*

Nov 70. (7") *<2777>* **IMMIGRANT SONG. / HEY HEY WHAT CAN I DO** - 16

Nov 71. (lp) *(2401 012) <7208>* **(UNTITLED – 4 SYMBOLS)** 1 2
– Black dog / Rock and roll / The battle of Evermore / Stairway to Heaven / Misty mountain hop / Four sticks / Going to California / When the levee breaks. *(re-iss. Mar72 lp/c; K/K4 50008) (lilac-lp Nov78; K 50008) (cd-iss. Jul83; 250008) (cd-iss. Jan87 & 1989 special; 250008) (re-iss. Jul94 & Aug97 cd/c; 7567 82638-2/-4)*

Dec 71. (7") *<2849>* **BLACK DOG. / MISTY MOUNTAIN HOP** - 15

Mar 72. (7") *<2865>* **ROCK AND ROLL. / FOUR STICKS** - 47

Apr 73. (lp/c) *(K/K4 50014) <7255>* **HOUSES OF THE HOLY** 1 1
– The song remains the same / The rain song / Over the hills and far away / The crunge / Dancing days / D'yer mak'er / No quarter / The ocean. *(cd-iss. Jan87; 250014) (re-iss. Jul94 & Aug97 cd/c; 7567 82639-2/-4)*

Jun 73. (7") *<2970>* **OVER THE HILLS AND FAR AWAY. / DANCING DAYS** - 51

Oct 73. (7") *<2986>* **D'YER MAK'ER. / THE CRUNGE** - 20

Swan Song Swan Song

Mar 75. (d-lp/d-c) *(SSK/SK4 89400) <200>* **PHYSICAL GRAFFITI** 1 1
– Custard pie / The rover / In my time of dying / Houses of the holy / Trampled underfoot / Kashmir / In the light / Bron-y-aur / Down by the seaside / Ten years

gone / Night flight / The wanton song / Boogie with Stu / Black country woman / Sick again. *(d-cd-iss. Jan87; 294800) (re-iss. Oct94 & Aug97 on 'Atlantic' cd/c; 7567 92442-2)*

Mar 75. (7") *<70102>* **TRAMPLED UNDERFOOT. / BLACK COUNTRY WOMAN** [-] [38]

Apr 76. (lp/c) *(SSK/SK4 59402) <8416>* **PRESENCE** [1] [1]
– Achilles last stand / For your life / Royal Orleans / Nobody's fault but mine / Candy store rock / Hots on for nowhere / Tea for one. *(cd-iss. Jun87; 259402) (re-iss. Oct94 Aug97 on 'Atlantic' cd/c; 7567 92439-2/-4)*

May 76. (7") *<70110>* **CANDY STORE ROCK. / ROYAL ORLEANS** [-] [ ]

Oct 76. (d-lp/d-c) *(SSK/SK4 89402) <201>* **The soundtrack from the film 'THE SONG REMAINS THE SAME' (live)** [1] [2]
– Rock and roll / Celebration day / The song remains the same / Rain song / Dazed and confused / No quarter / Stairway to Heaven / Moby Dick / Whole lotta love. *(d-cd-iss. Feb87; 289402) (cd re-iss. Aug97 on 'Atlantic'; SK2 89402)*

— Above was also a film from concerts at Madison Square Gardens in 1973. It featured some dream sequences / fantasies of each member.

Aug 79. (lp/c) *(SSK/SK4 59410) <16002>* **IN THROUGH THE OUT DOOR** [1] [1]
– In the evening / South bound Saurez / Fool in the rain / Hot dog / Carouselambra / All my love / I'm gonna crawl. *(cd-iss. Jan87; 259410) (re-iss. Oct94 & Aug97 on 'Atlantic' cd/c: 7567 92443-2)*

Dec 79. (7") *<71003>* **FOOL IN THE RAIN. / HOT DOG** [-] [21]

— Disbanded when JOHN BONHAM died after a drinking session 25 Sep'80.

— JOHN PAUL JONES was already a top producer. In 1992, he contributed string arrangements to R.E.M.'s classic album 'Automatic For The People'. ROBERT PLANT went solo and teamed up with JIMMY PAGE in The HONEYDRIPPERS. PAGE also went solo and formed The FIRM.

— In Aug 94; JOHN PAUL JONES turned up on an unusual collaboration (single 'Do You Take This Man') between himself and loud punk-opera diva DIAMANDA GALAS.

– compilations, others, etc. –

on 'Atlantic' unless mentioned otherwise

Nov 82. (lp/c) *Swan Song; (A 0051/+4) <90051>* **CODA** (demos from 68-79) [4] [6] Dec82
– We're gonna groove / Poor Tom / I can't quit you baby / Walter's walk / Ozone baby / Darlene / Bonzo's Montreaux / Walter's walk / Wearing and tearing. *(cd-iss. Jul87; 790051) (cd re-iss. Aug97 on 'Atlantic'; 7567 92444-2)*

Oct 90. (4xcd/4xc/5xlp) *(<7567 82144-2/-4/-1>)* **LED ZEPPELIN: THE REMASTERS BOX** [48] [18]

Nov 90. (d-cd/d-c/t-lp) *(ZEP/+C/CD 1) <82371>* **REMASTERS** [10] [47] Mar92
– Communication breakdown / Babe I'm gonna leave you / Good times bad times / Dazed and confused / Whole lotta love / Heartbreaker / Ramble on / Immigrant song / Celebration day / Since I've been loving you / Black dog / Rock and roll / The battle of Evermore / Misty mountain hop / Stairway to Heaven / The song remains the same / The rain song / D'yer mak'er / No quarter / Houses of the holy / Kashmir / Trampled underfoot / Nobody's fault but mine / Achilles last stand / All my love / In the evening. *(re-iss. cd Sep92; 7567 80415-2) (cd re-iss. Aug97 hit UK No.27; as last)*

Sep 93. (2xcd-box/2xc-box) *(<7567 82477-2/-4>)* **BOXED SET II** [56] [87]

Oct 93. (10xcd-box) *(<7567 82526-2>)* **REMASTERS 2**

Nov 96. (cd) *Tring; (QED 107)* **WHOLE LOTTA LOVE (Bootleg Zep)** [ ] [-]

Sep 97. (cd-s) *(AT 0013CD)* **WHOLE LOTTA LOVE /** [21] [ ]

Nov 97. (d-cd/d-c) *(<7567 83061-2/-4>)* **BBC SESSIONS** [23] [12]
– You shook me / I can't quit you baby / Communication breakdown / Dazed and confused / The girl I love / What is and what should never be / Communication breakdown / Travelling riverside blues / Whole lotta love / Something else / Communication breakdown / I can't quit you baby / You shook me / How many more times / Immigrant song / Heartbreaker / Since I've been loving you / Black dog / Dazed and confused / Stairway to Heaven / Going to California / That's the way / Whole lotta love / Thank you.

Nov 99. (cd/c) *(<7567 83268-2/-4>)* **EARLY DAYS: THE BEST OF LED ZEPPELIN VOLUME ONE** [55] [71]

Mar 00. (cd/c) *(<7567 83278-2/-4>)* **LATTER DAYS: THE BEST OF LED ZEPPELIN VOLUME TWO** [40] [81]

May 00. (cd) *Thunderbolt; (CDTB 210)* **ROCK AND ROLL HIGHWAY** [ ] [-]

ROBERT PLANT

— with **BOBBIE BLUNT** – guitar / **JEZZ WOODRUFFE** – keyboards / **PAUL MARTINEZ** – bass / **COZY POWELL** – drums / guest **PHIL COLLINS** – drums, percussion

Swan Song Swan Song

Jul 82. (lp/c) *(SSK/+4 59418) <8512>* **PICTURES AT ELEVEN** [2] [5]
– Burning down one side / Moonlight in Samosa / Pledge pin / Slow dancer / Worse that Detroit / Fat lip / Like I've never been gone / Mystery title. *(cd-iss. 1984; SSK2 59418)*

Sep 82. (7") *(SSK 19429) <99979>* **BURNING DOWN ONE SIDE. / MOONLIGHT IN SAMOSA** [73] [44]
(12"+=) *(SSK 19429T)* – Far post.

Nov 82. (7") *<99952>* **PLEDGE PIN. / FAT LIP** [-] [74]

— **RITCHIE HAYWARD** – drums (ex-LITTLE FEAT) repl. COZY /

— added **BOB MAYO** – keyboards, guitar

Es Paranza Es Paranza

Jul 83. (lp/c) *(790101-1/-4) <90101>* **THE PRINCIPLE OF MOMENTS** [7] [8]
– Other arms / In the mood / Messin' with the Mekon / Wreckless love / Thru with the two-step / Horizontal departure / Stranger here . . .than over there / Big log. *(cd-iss. 1984; 790101-2)*

Jul 83. (7") *(B 9848)* **BIG LOG. / MESSIN' WITH THE MEKON** [11] [-]
(12"+=) *(B 9848T)* – Stranger here . . . than over there.

Sep 83. (7") *<99844>* **BIG LOG. / FAR POST** [-] [20]

Nov 83. (7") *<99820>* **IN THE MOOD. / HORIZONTAL DEPARTURE** [-] [39]

Jan 84. (7") *(B 6970)* **IN THE MOOD. / PLEDGE PIN (live)** [ ] [-]
(12"+=) *(B 6970T)* – Horizontal departure.

May 85. (7") *(B 9640)* **PINK AND BLACK. / TROUBLE YOUR MONEY** [ ] [-]

May 85. (7") *<99644>* **LITTLE BY LITTLE. / TROUBLE YOUR MONEY** [-] [36]

May 85. (lp/c/cd) *(790265-1/-4/-2) <90265>* **SHAKEN 'N' STIRRED** [19] [20]
– Hip to hoo / Kallalou Kallalou / Too loud / Trouble your money / Pink and black / Little by little / Doo doo a do do / Easily led / Sixes and sevens.

Jul 85. (7") *<99622>* **TOO LOUD. / KALLALOU KALLALOU** [-] [ ]

Aug 85. (7") *(B 9621)* **LITTLE BY LITTLE (remix). / DOO DOO A DO DO** [ ] [-]
(ext.12"+=) *(B 9621T)* – Easily led (live).
(d7"++=) *(B 9621F)* – Rockin' at midnight (live).

— now with **DOUG BOYLE** – guitars / **PHIL SCRAGG** – bass / **PHIL JOHNSTONE** – keyboards, co-writer / **JIMMY PAGE** – guitar / **CHRIS BLACKWELL** – drums, percussion / **MARIE PIERRE, TONI HALLIDAY + KIRSTY MacCOLL** – backing vocals

Jan 88. (7") *(A 9373) <99373>* **HEAVEN KNOWS. / WALKING TOWARDS PARADISE** [33] [ ]
(ext.12"+=/ext.3"cd-s+=) *(A 9373 T/CD)* – Big log.
(ext.12"box+=) *(A 9373TB)* – ('A'-Astral mix).

Feb 88. (lp/c)(cd) *(WX 149/+C)(790863-2) <90863>* **NOW AND ZEN** [10] [6]
– Heaven knows / Dance on my own / Tall cool one / The way I feel / Helen of Troy / Billy's revenge / Ship of fools / Why / White, clean and neat. *(cd+=)* – Walking towards Paradise.

Apr 88. (7") *(A 9348) <99348>* **TALL COOL ONE (remix). / WHITE, CLEAN AND NEAT** [ ] [25]
(12"+=) *(A 9348T)* – ('A'extended).
(3"cd-s++=) *(A 9348CD)* – Little by little.

Aug 88. (7") *(A 9281)* **SHIP OF FOOLS. / HELEN OF TROY** [ ] [-]
(12"+=/12"w-poster+=) *(A 9281 T/TF)* – Heaven Knows (live).
(3"cd-s+=/3"box-cd-s+=) *(A 9281 CD/+B)* – Dimples (live).

Aug 88. (7") *<99333>* **SHIP OF FOOLS. / BILLY'S REVENGE** [-] [84]

— **PAT THORPE** – drums repl. BLACKWELL who became ill

— now with **BLACKWELL, CHARLIE JONES, JOHNSTONE and BOYLE**

Mar 90. (lp/c/cd) *(WX 229/+C/CD) <91336>* **MANIC NIRVANA** [15] [13]
– Hurting kind (I've got my eyes on you) / Big love / S S S & Q / I cried / She said / Nirvana / The dye on the highway / Your ma said you cried in your sleep last night / Anniversary / Liars dance / Watching you.

Mar 90. (7") *<98985>* **HURTING KIND (I'VE GOT MY EYES ON YOU). / I CRIED** [-] [46]

Apr 90. (7") *(A 8985)* **HURTING KIND (I'VE GOT MY EYES ON YOU). / OOMPAH (WATERY BINT)** [45] [-]
(12"+=) *(A 8985T)* – I cried / One love.
(cd-s+=) *(A 8985CD)* – Don't look back / One love.

Jun 90. (7"/c-s) *(A 8945/+C)* **YOUR MA SAID YOU CRIED IN YOUR SLEEP LAST NIGHT. / SHE SAID** [ ] [ ]
(12"/cd-s) *(A 8945 T/CD)* – ('A'side) / ('A'version) / One love.

— with **KEVIN SCOTT MACMICHAEL** – guitar / **PHIL JOHNSTONE** – electric piano / **CHARLIE JONES** – bass / **MICHAEL LEE** – drums / **CHRIS HUGHES** – drums, co-producer / plus guests **FRANCIS DUNNERY, MAIRE BRENNAN, NIGEL KENNEDY + RICHARD THOMPSON**

Fontana Es Paranza

Apr 93. (7") *(FATE 1)* **29 PALMS. / 21 YEARS** [21] [ ]
(c-s+=) *(FATEM 1)* – Dark moon.
(cd-s++=) *(FATEX 1)* – Whole lotta love (you need love).

May 93. (cd/c/lp) *(<514 867-2/-4/-1>)* **FATE OF NATIONS** [6] [34]
– Calling to you / Down to the sea / Come into my life / I believe / 29 palms / Memory song (hello, hello) / If I were a carpenter / Colours of a shade / Promised land / The greatest gift / Great spirit / Network news.

Jun 93. (7"/c-s) *(FATE/+M 2)* **I BELIEVE. / GREAT SPIRIT (acoustic mix)** [64] [ ]
(cd-s+=) *(FATEX 2)* – Hey Jayne.
(12"pic-d++=) *(FATETP 2)* – Whole lotta love (you need love).

Aug 93. (c-s) *(FATEM 3)* **CALLING TO YOU. / NAKED IF I WANT TO** [ ] [ ]
(12"+=/cd-s+=) *(FATE/+X 3)* – 8.05.

Dec 93. (c-s) *(FATEM 2)* **IF I WERE A CARPENTER / I BELIEVE (live)** [63] [ ]
(cd-s+=) *(FATED 4)* – Going to California (live).
(cd-s) *(FATEX 4)* – ('A'side) / Ship of fools (live) / Tall cool one (live).

JIMMY PAGE

— solo with **CHRIS FARLOWE** – vocals / **DAVE LAWSON + DAVID SINCLAIR WHITTAKER + GORDON EDWARDS** – piano / **DAVE PATON** – bass / **DAVE MATTACKS** – drums

Swan Song Swan Song

Feb 82. (lp) *(SSK 59415) <8511>* **DEATH WISH II (Soundtrack)** [40] [50] Mar82
– Who's to blame / The chase / City sirens / Jam sandwich / Of Carole's theme / The release / Hotel rats and photostats / Shadow in the city / Jill's theme / Prelude / Big band, sax and violence / Hypnotizing ways (oh mamma).

— In 1985, PAGE collaborated with friend ROY HARPER on dual album 'WHATEVER HAPPENED TO JUGULA', which hit UK Top 50.

— In 1987, he released soundtrack blue-lp 'LUCIFER RISING' for 'Boleskine House'; *<BHR 666>*

— now guest vocals – **JOHN MILES, ROBERT PLANT, CHRIS FARLOWE JASON BONHAM** – drums / **DURBAN LEVERDE** – bass / **FELIX KRISH, TONY FRANKLIN, BARRYMORE BARLOW** – drums

Geffen Geffen

Jun 88 (lp/c)(cd) *(WX 155/+C)(924188-2) <24188>* **OUTRIDER** [27] [26]
– Wasting my time / Wanna make love / Writes of winter / The only one / Liquid mercury / Hummingbird / Emerald eyes / Prison blues / Blues anthem (if I cannot have your love . . .). *(re-iss. Feb91 & Aug99 cd/c; GEFD/GEFC 24188)*

Jun 88. (7"w-drawn) *(GEF 41)* **WASTING MY TIME. / WRITES OF WINTER** [ ] [-]

T.V.T. T.V.T.

Jul 00. (d-cd; by JIMMY PAGE and BLACK CROWES) *(TVT 61214) <2140>* **LIVE AT THE GREEK (live)** [39] [64]
– Celebration day / Custard pie / Sick again / What is and what should never be / Woke up this morning / Shapes of things / Sloppy drunk / Ten years gone / In my time of dyin' / Your time is gonna come / The lemon song / Nobody's fault but mine / Heartbreaker / Hey hey what can I do / Mellow down easy / Oh well / Shake your

money maker / You shook me / Out on the tiles / Whole lotta love. *(d-cd iss.Jul00 on 'S.P.V.'; SPV 0917202-2)*

– other recordings, etc –

Jan 82. (lp; JIMMY PAGE, SONNY BOY WILLIAMSON & BRIAN AUGER) *Charly; (CR 30193)* **JAM SESSION** (rec.1964) [ ] [-]
– Don't send me no flowers / I see a man downstairs / She was so dumb / The goat / Walking / Little girl, how old are you / It'a a bloody life / Getting out of town.
below featured on session; **JOHN PAUL JONES / ALBERT LEE / NICKY HOPKINS + CLEM CATTINI**

Sep 84. (lp/c/cd; by JIMMY PAGE & FRIENDS) *Thunderbolt; (THBL/THBC/CDTB 007)* **NO INTRODUCTION NECESSARY** [ ] [-]
– Lovin' up a storm / Everything I do is wrong / Think it over / Boll Weevil song / Livin' lovin' wreck / One long kiss / Dixie friend / Down the line / Fabulous / Breathless / Rave on / Lonely weekends / Burn up. *(re-iss. cd May93;)*
below from early 70's featuring; **JOHN BONHAM, JEFF BECK, NOEL REDDING + NICKY HOPKINS** + actually a re-issue of LORD SUTCH AND HEAVY FRIENDS album.

May 85. (lp/c) *Thunderbolt; (THB L/C 2002)* **SMOKE AND FIRE** [ ] [-]
– Wailing sounds / 'Cause I love you / Flashing lights / Gutty guitar / Would you believe / Smoke and fire / Thumping beat / Union Jack car / One for you baby / L-O-N-D-O-N / Brightest lights / Baby come back. *(cd-iss. Aug86; CDTB 2002)*
below featured him in session with:- JET HARRIS & TONY MEEHAN / MICKIE MOST / DAVE BERRY / The FIRST GEAR / MICKEY FINN / solo / etc.

Jan 90. (lp/cd) *Archive Int.; <AIP/+CD 10041>* **JAMES PATRICK PAGE SESSION MAN VOLUME 1** [-] [ ]

Jul 90. (lp/cd) *Archive Int.; <AIP/+CD 10053>* **JAMES PATRICK PAGE SESSION MAN VOLUME 2** [ ] [-]

Aug 92. (cd) *Sony; <AK 52420>* **JIMMY'S BACK PAGES: THE EARLY YEARS** [-] [ ]
In the US, 'EARLY WORKS ' was issued on 'Springboard' <SPB 4038>

HONEYDRIPPERS

ROBERT PLANT – vocals / **JIMMY PAGE** – guitar / **JEFF BECK** – guitar (solo artist) / **NILE RODGERS** – producer, etc.

Es Paranza / Es Paranza

Oct 84. (7") *<99701>* **SEA OF LOVE. / I GET A THRILL** [-] [3]

Nov 84. (10"m-lp/c) *(790220-2/-4) <90220>* **VOLUME 1** [56] [4] Oct84
– I get a thrill / Sea of love / I got a woman / Young boy blues / Rockin' at midnight. *(cd-iss. Feb93; 7567 90220-2)*

Jan 85. (7") *(YZ 33)* **SEA OF LOVE. / ROCKIN' AT MIDNIGHT** [56] [-]

Mar 85. (7") *<99686>* **ROCKIN' AT MIDNIGHT. / YOUNG BOY BLUES** [-] [25]

THE FIRM

JIMMY PAGE – guitar / **PAUL RODGERS** – vocals (ex-FREE, ex-BAD COMPANY) / **TONY FRANKLIN** – bass, keys / **CHRIS SLADE** – drums (ex-MANFRED MANN'S EARTH BAND)

Atlantic / Atlantic

Feb 85. (lp/c/cd) *(781 239-1/-4/-2) <81239>* **THE FIRM** [15] [17]
– Closer / Make or break / Someone to love / Together / Radioactive / You've lost that lovin' feeling / Money can't buy satisfaction / Satisfaction guarenteed / Midnight moonlight.

Feb 85. (7"/7"sha-pic-d) *(A 9586/+P) <89586>* **RADIOACTIVE. / TOGETHER** [ ] [28]
(12") *(A 9586T)* – ('A'-special mix) / City sirens (live) / Live in peace (live).
(12") *(A 9586TE)* – (all 4 above).

Apr 85. (7") *<89561>* **SATISFACTION GUARENTEED. / CLOSER** [-] [73]

Apr 86. (lp/c)(cd) *(WX 43/+C)(781628-2) <81628>* **MEAN BUSINESS** [46] [22] Feb86
– Fortune hunter / Cadillac / All the King's horses / Live in peace / Tear down the walls / Dreaming / Free to live / Spirit of love.

Apr 86. (7") *(A 9458) <89458>* **ALL THE KING'S HORSES. / FORTUNE HUNTER** [ ] [61]

Jun 86. (7") *<89421>* **LIVE IN PEACE. / FREE TO LIVE** [-] [ ]

— In 1993, JIMMY collaborated with DAVID COVERDALE (of WHITESNAKE) to make one hit album 'COVERDALE • PAGE'.

JIMMY PAGE & ROBERT PLANT

— with **CHARLIE JONES** – bass, percussion / **PORL THOMPSON** – guitar, banjo / **MICHAEL LEE** – drums, percussion / **NAJMA AKHTAR** – vocals / **JOE SUTHERLAND** – mandolin, bodhran / **NIGEL EASTON** – hurdy gurdy / **ED SHEARMUR** – hammond organ & orchestral arrangements for (large) English + Egyptian Ensemble + London Metropolitan Orchestra

Fontana / Atlantic

Nov 94. (cd/c/d-lp) *(526362-2/-4/-1) <82706-2/-4/-1>* **NO QUARTER – UNLEDDED** [7] [4]
– Nobody's fault but mine / Thank you / No quarter / Friends / Yallah / City don't cry / Since I've been loving you / The battle of Evermore / Wonderful one / Wah wah / That's the way / Gallows pole / Four sticks / Kashmir.

Dec 94. (7") *(PP 2)* **GALLOWS POLE. / CITY DON'T CRY** [35] [-]
(pic-cd-s+=) *(PPCD 2)* – The rain song.
(pic-cd-s) *(PPDD 2)* – ('A'side) / Four sticks / What is and what should never be.

Mar 95. (cd-ep) *<CD5 85591-2>* **WONDERFUL ONE (2 versions) / WHAT IS AND WHAT SHOULD NEVER BE / WHEN THE LEVEE BREAKS** [-] [ ]

— **PLANT & PAGE** were actually a 4-piece with other rhythm section & co-writers, **CHARLIE JONES** – bass / **MICHAEL LEE** – drums

Mercury / Atlantic

Mar 98. (7") *(PP 3)* **MOST HIGH. / THE WINDOW** [26] [ ]
(cd-s+=) *(PPCD 3)* – Upon a golden horse.
(cd-s) *(PPDD 3)* –

Apr 98. (cd/c/lp) *(558025-2/-4/-1) <83092>* **WALKING INTO CLARKSDALE** [3] [8]
– Shining in the light / When the world was young / Upon a golden horse / Blue train / Please read the letter / Most high / Heart in your hand / Walking into Clarksdale / Burning up / When I was a child / House of love / Sons of freedom.

Jun 98. (7") *(MER 506)* **SHINING IN THE LIGHT. / MOST HIGH (guitar mix)** [ ] [ ]
(cd-s+=) *(MERDD 506)* – How many more times (live).
(cd-s) *(MERCD 506)* – ('A'side) / Walking into Clarksdale (live) / No quarter (live).

JOHN PAUL JONES

Discipline / Discipline

Sep 99. (cd) *<(DGM 9909)>* **ZOOMA** [ ] [ ]
– Zooma / Grind / Smile of your shadow / Bass'n'drums / B fingers / Snake eyes / Nosumi blues / Tidal.

Alvin LEE (see under ⇒ TEN YEARS AFTER)

Geddy LEE (see under ⇒ RUSH)

LEGS DIAMOND

Formed: Los Angeles, California, USA . . . 1976 by bassist MICHAEL DIAMOND and drummer JEFF POOLE, who enlisted vocalist RICK SANFORD and L.A. guitarists MICHAEL PRINCE and ROGER ROMEO. Signed to 'Mercury', the group released their eponymous debut the following year, a popular set of sophisticated hard-rock in the classic British mould which won the band a small but committed UK fanbase. Just as impressive was their 1977 follow-up, 'A DIAMOND IS A HARD ROCK' (surely a candidate for the corniest album title of all time), a set that should've brought them widespread recognition but instead saw them dropped by their label. After a third, rather obvious attempt at capturing the lighter end of the rock spectrum, the group disbanded, although they did reappear as RAG DOLL. In the mid 80's, SANFORD and PRINCE reformed LEGS DIAMOND, signing with metal indie 'Music For Nations' for their comeback set, 'OUT ON BAIL'. A series of competent but largely ignored albums followed over the course of the next decade, the band finally cutting their losses in '93.

Album rating: LEGS DIAMOND (*7) / A DIAMOND IS A ROCK (*6) / FIRE POWER (*6) / OUT ON BAIL (*5) / LAND OF THE GUN (*6) / TOWN BAD GIRL (*6) / CAPTURED LIVE (*4) / THE WISH (*6) / UNCUT DIAMOND collection (*5)

RICK SANFORD – vocals / **MICHAEL PRINCE** – guitar, keyboards / **ROGER ROMEO** – guitar / **MICHAEL DIAMOND** – bass / **JEFF POOLE** – drums

not iss. / Mercury

1977. (lp) *<SRM1-1136>* **LEGS DIAMOND** [-] [ ]
– It's not the music / Stage fright / Satin peacock / Rock and roll man / Deadly dancer / Rat race / Can't find love. *<(UK + cd-iss. Aug00 on 'Zoom Club'; ZCRCD 32)>*

1977. (lp) *<SRM1-1191>* **A DIAMOND IS A HARD ROCK** [-] [ ]
– A diamond is a hard rock / Waiting / Long shot / Woman / Jailbait / Evil / Live a little / Flyin' too high. *<(UK + cd-iss. Aug00 on 'Zoom Club'; ZCRCD 33)>*

not iss. / Cream

1978. (lp) *<1010>* **FIRE POWER** [-] [ ]
– Underworld king / More than meets the eye / You've lost that lovin' feelin' / Remember my name / Chicago / Midnight lady / Help wanted / Come with me / Tragedy / Man at the top.

— split for six years, until **SANFORD, POOLE, PRINCE + CHRISTIE** recruited newcomer, **JIM MAY** – guitar, vocals

Music For Nations / Target

Jun 85. (lp/c) *(MFN/TMFN 52) <TE 1343>* **OUT ON BAIL** [ ] [ ]
– Out on bail / Fugitive / Walkaway / Doomsday flight / Find it out the hard way / Nobody's fool / Seems like a dream / One way ticket.

— **JONATHAN VALEN** – drums (then DUSTY WATSON); repl. POOLE

Mar 86. (lp/c) *(MFN/TMFN 59) <TE 1349>* **LAND OF THE GUN** [ ] [ ]
– My own game / Falling in love / Waitin' for the nite / Steal a heart / Turn to stone / Raggedy man / Rok doktor / Land of the gun. *(cd-iss. Nov90 +=; CDMFN 59)* – OUT ON BAIL

Jun 86. (12") *(12KUT 121)* **TURN TO STONE. / TWISTED LOVE / RIGHT BETWEEN THE EYES** [ ] [-]

Metal Blade / Metal Blade

Nov 90. (cd/c/lp) *(CD/T+/ZORRO 16) <26362>* **TOWN BAD GIRL** [ ] [ ] Jun90
– Town bad girl / City streets / Stage fright / World on fire / Can't get you (out of my mind) / Never enough town / Look in her eyes / Cry no more / I am for you / She did it for love / Nervous.

Music For Nations / not iss.

Jun 92. (cd/c) *(CD/T MFN 137)* **CAPTURED LIVE (live)** [ ] [-]
– Intro: Things to come – Epilogue / Out on bail / Rok doktor / World on fire / Walkaway / I am for you / Guitar solo / Satin eacock / Nervous / Woman / Town bad girl / Wonderworld king / Drum solo / I think I got it / Stage fright / Fan fare.

Oct 93. (cd) *(CDMFN 154)* **THE WISH** [ ] [-]
– Paradise lost / Red light / Be the one / Street justice / Wish song / Every man / In my dreams / What's da matter with U / Hey kid / Nuthin' / Mister destiny / One sin a lifetime / Forever.

— split after above

– compilations, etc. –

Jun 99. (cd) *Zoom Club; (ZCRCD 9)* **UNCUT DIAMOND** [ ] [-]
– Winds of fortune / Between the legs / House on fire / High school queen / Symptoms of passion / Dance hall gigolo / Shell of a man / Fight for it / Hidin' / Gamblin' on you / My own game / Urban desperado / Card shark / Smother me.

LESS THAN JAKE

Formed: Gainesville, Florida, USA . . . 1992 by CHRIS, SHAUN and VINNIE. With the addition of a brass section (consisting of JESSICA, AARON and BUDDY), the group moved away from their initial pop-punk sound toward a ska-revivalist slant. 'PEZCORE' (1994) laid out the musical agenda with good-time ska-punk, unfortunately inspiring a glut of spotty, pasty-faced so-called "ska" bands who, in reality, sound like they wouldn't know a real ska record if it was handed to them by PRINCE BUSTER himself. A further couple of independently-released albums followed – 'LOSERS, KINGS & THINGS WE DON'T UNDERSTAND' (1995) and 'GREASED' (1996) (their 'Grease' tribute) – before LTJ were inevitably caught up in the major label scramble for anything vaguely resembling punk, or at least the tenth-hand version of it being passed off as something new. 'LOSING STREAK' (1996) marked their 'Capitol' debut while 'HELLO ROCKVIEW' followed in 1998. LESS THAN JAKE were subsequently involved with some other interesting releases including a split 7" with MEGADETH and a first UK hit all on their own (in summer 2000) courtesy of 'ALL MY BEST FRIENDS ARE METALHEADS'.

Album rating: "PEZCORE" (*5) / LOSERS, KINGS AND THINGS WE DON'T UNDERSTAND (*5) / LOSING STREAK (*4) / GREASED (*6) / HELLO ROCKVIEW (*5) / LIVE FROM URANUS (*4) / THE PEZ COLLECTION compilation (*6)

CHRIS – vocals, guitar / **SHAUN** – bass / **VINNIE** – drums / **ROGER** repl. SHAUN / added **JESSICA + AARON** – sax

not iss. — Dill

1994. (cd) *<21>* **"PEZCORE"** [-] [ ]
– Liquor store / My very own flag / Johnny Quest (thinks we're sellouts) / Big / Shotgun / Black coffee / Throw the brick / Growing up on a couch / Blindsided / Downbeat / Jen doesn't like me anymore / Out of the crowd / Robo / Where the hell is Mike Sinkovich? / Process / 3 quarts drunk / Boomtown / Short on idea / One last cigarette. *(UK-iss.Feb97 & Aug99 on 'Asian Man'; AM 001CD)*

No Idea — No Idea

1995. (cd) *<NIR 022>* **LOSERS, KINGS AND THINGS WE DON'T UNDERSTAND** [-] [ ]
– Soundman – Soundcheck / 24 hours in Paramus / Whipping boy / Time and a half / Econolodged / Pez king / Where the hell is Mike Sinkovich? / This is going nowhere / Laverne and Shirley / Fucked / 867-5309 (Jenny) / Dukes of Hazzard / Shotgun / Down in the mission / St. James hotel / Glumble / Lucky day / Who holds the power ring? / Wish pig / Awkward age. *(UK-iss.Sep97 & Nov99; same as US)*

1996. (7") *<NIR 035>* **EVIL HAS NO BOUNDARIES. /** [-] [ ]
(UK-iss.Jan97; same as US)

1996. (7") *<NIR 038>* **split w/ KEMURI** [-] [ ]
(UK-iss.Nov99; same as US)

1996. (7") *<NIR 039>* **LOSING STREAK. / MIXOLOGY OF TOM COLLINS** [-] [ ]
(UK-iss.Nov97 & Nov99; same as US)

1996. (m-cd/m-lp) *<NIR 046>* **GREASED** [-] [ ]
– Summer nights / You're the one that I want / Look at me, I'm Sandra Dee / Greased lightnin' / Hopelessly devoted to you / Blue moon / Beauty school dropout / We got together. *(UK lp-iss.Dec97 & Nov99; same as US)*

not iss. — Capitol

Nov 96. (cd/c) *<37235>* **LOSING STREAK** [-] [ ]
– Automatic / Happyman / 9th at the pine / Sugar in your gastank / Shindo / 107 / Johnny Quest (thinks we're sellouts) / Krazy glue / Never going back to New Jersey / How's my driving, Doug Hastings? / Just like Frank / Ask the magic 8 ball / Dopeman / Jen doesn't like me anymore / Rock-n-roll pizzaria / Lockdown.

May 97. (7"ep) *<(LM 019)>* **MUPPETS COVERS EP** [ ] [ ]
(above issued on 'Liquid Meat', below on 'Too Many')

Nov 97. (cd-ep) *<(TM 79)>* **PESTO** [ ] [ ] Mar99
– Good time for change / Black coffee on the table / Process / Green eyed monster.

Oct 98. (cd/c) *<57663>* **HELLO ROCKVIEW** [-] [80]
– Last one out of Liberty city / Help save the youth of America from . . . . / All my best friends are metalheads / Five state drive / Nervous in the alley / Motto / History of a boring town / Great American sharpshooter / Danny says / Big crash / Theme song for H street / Richard Allen George . . . no, it's just . . . . / Scott Farcas takes it on the chin / Al's war. *(UK lp-iss.Feb99 on 'Liberation'; LIB 3781-2) (pic-lp-iss.Mar00 on 'DriveThru'; DRIVETHRU 015)*

not iss. — E.M.I.

Mar 99. (cd) *<50470>* **LIVE FROM URANUS (live)** [-] [ ]
– Liqour store / Time and a half on 2nd Ave. / Econolodged / JUst like Frank / Automatic / Lockdown / Never going back to New Jersey / How's my driving, Doug Hastings / Shindo.

Fueled By Ramon — Fueled By Ramon

Jul 99. (cd) *<(FBR 000)>* **GOODBYE BLUE AND WHITE** [ ] [ ]

Aug 99. (7") *<(LTJ 001)>* **split w/ MEGADETH** [ ] [ ]

Golf — Capitol

Jun 00. (7"m) *(7HOLE 026)* **ALL MY BEST FRIENDS ARE METALHEADS. / HELP SAVE THE YOUTH OF AMERICA FROM EXPLODING (live) / ROCK'N'ROLL PIZZERIA (live)** [51] [ ]
(cd-s+=) *(CDGOLF 026)* – ('A'version).

– compilations, etc. –

Sep 99. (cd) *Moon Ska; (MOONCD 33-045)* **THE PEZ COLLECTION** [ ] [-]
– Al's war / Johnny Quest (thinks we're sellouts) / My very own flag / Liquor store / Jen doesn't like me anymore / Last one out of Liberty city / Son of Dick / Where the hell is Mike Sinkovich? / Robo / Rock'n'roll pizzaria / Whipping boy / 867-5309 (Jenny) / Cheeze / Automatic / Growing up on a couch / Just like Frank / You're the one that I want / We go together / Soundcheck / Fucked / Mixology of Tom Collins / Modern world / Short on ideas / One last cigarette.

May 00. (d-cd) *Golf; (CDHOLE 025)* **HELLO ROCKVIEW / LOSING STREAK** [ ] [ ]

LIBERTY 37

Formed: Swansea, Wales . . . 1996 as TRAVIS by ISHMAEL LEWIS, TIM, TWINK and SIM. Forced to change their name – due to Glasgow's more famous bunch – to APPLECORE, they were then unlucky enough to get grief from The BEATLES' label, 'The Apple Corps'. Despite such inauspicious beginnings, the band eventually secured a deal with 'Beggars Banquet' and released their debut single, 'NO BEAUTY', in 1998. Inspired by the expansive, experimental likes of JANE'S ADDICTION, LEWIS' literary streak (the man is actually an English teacher in his other life) was an integral part of LIBERTY 37's emotive appeal. Dealing in themes of personal transformation, follow-up single, 'REVOLUTION' preceded a Kerrang!-sponsored UK tour with ONE MINUTE SILENCE and PULKAS, while a debut album, 'GREATEST GIFT' hit the shops in summer '99.

Album rating: GREATEST GIFT (*6)

ISHMAEL LEWIS – vocals / **TIM** – guitar / **TWINK** – bass / **SIM** – drums

Org — not iss.

Mar 98. (cd-s) **NO BEAUTY / BADGER SONG / FRANCIE / TAKE IT LIKE A MAN** [ ] [-]

Beggars Banquet — not iss.

May 98. (7"ep/cd-ep) **STUFFED EP** [ ] [-]
– Stuffed / Letter from 10 years ago / IV buddy.

Jan 99. (7") *(BBQ 332)* **REVOLUTION. / TABLETTEN** [ ] [-]
(cd-s+=) *(BBQ 332/+CD)* – Falling out.
(cd-ep) *(BBQ 343CD)* **('A'side) / When we say (acoustic) / Oh river (video) / When we say (video).**

May 99. (7") *(BBQ 336)* **OH RIVER. / LONG SNAKE MOAN** [ ] [-]
(cd-s+=) *(BBQ 336CD)* – Hole in the water.

Jul 99. (cd/lp) *(BBQ CD/LP 210)* **GREATEST GIFT** [ ] [-]
– Liars and murderers / When we say / Stuffed / Oh river / Promise me / ABC / No beauty / Revolution / Falling out / Tabletten / 23rd / Seize the day.

LID (see under ⇒ TROUBLE)

LIFE OF AGONY

Formed: Brooklyn, New York, USA . . . 1989 by KEITH CAPUTO, JOEY Z and ALAN ROBERT. Adding SAL ABRUSCATO, they signed to 'Roadrunner' in 1993, releasing their debut 'RIVER RUNS RED' in the same year. A hybrid of many styles ranging from hardcore/grunge to melodic power-metal, LIFE OF AGONY complemented their uncompromising music with an equally uncompromising, unrelentingly bleak lyrical outlook. Continuing to tour to a fiercely loyal fanbase, the group briefly crossed paths with chart action, when their second set, 'UGLY' hit the US Top 200. 1997's 'SOUL SEARCHING SUN' was arguably their most compelling work to date, the track 'TANGERINE' a vaguely psychedelic/80's/post-grunge fusion and a perfect vehicle for KEITH's refined, melancholy vox. Unfortunately, this was his last outing for the band as he departed a month after the album's release. His replacement was one of the biggest surprises of recent years – and it was no joke! WHITFIELD CRANE of the pukey, pop-metal outfit, UGLY KID JOE, was given the call up, although a long "trip" (no doubt!) around India had certainly changed his ideals and direction. Meanwhile, CAPUTO, having walked out on the band prior to a 1998 European tour and tired of the music industry's unrelenting pressure was back in music city. His much anticipated solo album, 'DIED LAUGHING', emerged in 2000, providing a platform for his wry, twisted worldview. One of the record's most controversial tracks was 'COBAIN (RAINBOW DEADHEAD)', penned by KEITH after he'd read the book 'Who Killed Kurt Cobain?'.

Album rating: RIVER RUNS RED (*6) / UGLY (*7) / SOUL SEARCHING SUN (*7) / LIFE OF AGONY 1989-1999 compilation (*7) / UNPLUGGED AT THE LOWLANDS FESTIVAL '97 posthumous (*6) / Keith Caputo: DIED LAUGHING (*6)

KEITH CAPUTO – vocals / **JOEY Z** – guitars / **ALAN ROBERT** – bass / **SAL ABRUSCATO** – drums

Roadrunner — Roadrunner

Oct 93. (cd) *<(RR 9043-2)>* **RIVER RUNS RED** [ ] [ ]
– This time / Underground / Monday / River runs red / Through and through / Words and music / Thursday / Bad seed / My eyes / Respect / Method of groove / The stain remains / Friday. *(re-iss. May00; same)*

Jun 94. (cd-ep) *(RR 2373-3)* **THIS TIME /** [ ] [ ]

Oct 95. (cd/c/lp) *<(RR 8924-2/-4/-1)>* **UGLY** [ ] [ ]
– Seasons / I regret / Lost at 22 / Other side of the river / Let's pretend / Ugly / Drained / How it would be / Unstable / Damned if I do / Fears / Don't you (forget about me). *(cd re-iss. May00; same)*

— **DAN RICHARDSON** – drums (ex-CRUMBSUCKERS, ex-PRO-PAIN) repl. SAL

Sep 97. (7") *(RR 2266-7)* **WEEDS. / WEEDS (unplugged)** [ ] [ ]
(cd-s) *(RR 2266-3)* – ('A'side) / Tangerine (re-Zep) / River runs red (re-Zamped) / How it would be '97.

Sep 97. (cd/c/lp) *<(RR 8816-2/-4/-1)>* **SOUL SEARCHING SUN** [ ] [ ]
– Hope / Weeds / Gently sentimental / Tangerine / My mind is dangerous / Neg / Led you astray / Heroin dreams / None / Angry tree / Hemophiliac in me / Desire / Whispers. *(cd re-iss. May00; same)*

Dec 97. (cd-ep) *(RR 2253-3)* **DESIRE (remix) / LET'S PRETEND (live) / REGRET (live) / WEEDS (live)** [ ] [ ]
(cd-ep) *(RR 2253-5)* – ('A'side) / Lost at 22 (live) / My mind is dangerous (live) / Seasons (live).

— **WHITFIELD CRANE** – vocals (ex-UGLY KID JOE) repl. CAPUTO who went solo; LOA disbanded in 1999

– compilations, etc. –

Nov 99. (cd) *Roadrunner; <(RR 8580-2)>* **LIFE OF AGONY 1989-1999** ☐ ☐ Oct99
– Here I am, here I stay / Depression / Plexiglass gate / Three companions / Drowning / Dancing with the Devil / Step aside / Colorblind / March of the S.O.D. / Sergeant D and the S.O.D. / Coffee break / Redemption song / How it would be / Tangerine / I regret (live) / Lost at 22 (live).

Aug 00. (cd) *Roadrunner; <(RR 8518-2)>* **UNPLUGGED AT THE LOWLANDS FESTIVAL '97 (live)** ☐ ☐
– Introduction / How it would be / Angry tree / Weeds / Desire / My mind is dangerous / Let's pretend / River runs red / Other side of the river / Seasons / Plexiglass gate / Respect / This time / Method of groove / My eyes.

KEITH CAPUTO

— solo with

Roadrunner Roadrunner

Feb 00. (cd) *<(RR 8654-2)>* **DIED LAUGHING** ☐ ☐ Jan01
– Honeycomb / Razzberry mockery / Selfish / New York City / Home / Cobain (rainbow deadhead) / Neurotic / Dewdrop music / Just be / Lollipop / Upsy daisy / Why / Brandy Duval.

Apr 00. (cd-s) *(RR 2155-3)* **SELFISH / COBAIN (RAINBOW DEADHEAD) / THE GIRL I LOVE (incomplete version)** ☐ [-]

Aug 00. (cd-s; w-drawn) *(RR 2113-3)* **NEW YORK CITY** [-] [-]

LIGOTAGE

Formed: Bristol, England . . . July '83 by petite punkette, BEKI BONDAGE (formerly of VICE SQUAD) and her seasoned punk crew of LINC (ex-CHELSEA), STEVE ROBERTS (ex-UK SUBS) and er, HOMO SEX (ex-MY EYES MY EYES). A surprise signing to 'E.M.I.', LIGOTAGE lasted only one single, 'CRIME AND PASSION', before moving on to 'Picasso' for a live album, 'FORGIVE AND FORGET' (1984). Opening with a ridiculous rendition of Holzt's 'MARS THE BRINGER OF WAR', the band went on to murder Nancy Sinatra's 'THESE BOOTS ARE MADE FOR WALKING' and Jimi Hendrix's 'PURPLE HAZE', many longtime, er BONDAGE fans not forgiving or forgetting in a hurry. The gorgeous BEKI subsequently released three forgettable solo singles before tying up her career for good. Stop press:- Late in 2000, she tried her hand at some ill-advised cover versions on her comeback album, 'COLD TURKEY'. Indeed.

Album rating: FORGIVE AND FORGET (*3) / Beki Bondage: COLD TURKEY (*3)

BEKI BONDAGE (b. REBECCA LOUISE BOND, 3 Jun'63) – vocals / **HOMO SEX** – guitar (ex-MY EYES MY EYES) / **LINC** – bass (ex-CHELSEA) / **STEVE ROBERTS** – drums (ex-UK SUBS, ex-CYANIDE)

E.M.I. not iss.

Jan 84. (7") *(EMI 5446)* **CRIME AND PASSION. / VANITY** ☐ [-]
(12"+=) *(12EMI 5446)* – Execution.

Picasso not iss.

Dec 84. (lp) *(PIKM 005)* **FORGIVE AND FORGET (live)** ☐ [-]
– Mars the bringer of war / The corporation / Crime and passion / The fun goes on / Forgive and forget / End of the century / Misfits / Coming for you / Vanity / Curate / These boots are made for walking / Purple haze.

BEKI BONDAGE

— solo with an unknown backing band

Communique not iss.

Nov 85. (7"m) *(COMM 2)* **DON'T TURN AWAY. / DOLPHINS / HARD TO GET** ☐ [-]
(12"+=) *(COMM12-2)* – The wheel of fortune.

Mar 86. (c-s/7"; as BEKI) *(C+/LITTLE 5)* **OUT OF THE DARKNESS. /** ☐ [-]
(12"+=/12"pic-d+=) *(12LITTLE/+P 5)* –

Ranch Red not iss.

Oct 87. (7"; as BEKI BONDAGE & THE BOMBSHELLS) **ONCE AIN'T ENOUGH. / LOVE OF MONEY** ☐ [-]

— BEKI retired from the music business, until . . .

BEKI with **JON KLEIN, JAMES STEVENSON, PAUL ROONEY, STEVE LAWRENCE, CHRIS BELL + NEAL X** (mainly famous covers)

not iss. Dressed To Kill

Oct 00. (cd) *<DTK 448>* **COLD TURKEY** [-] ☐
– Son of a preacher man / Smells like teen spirit / Be-bop-a-lula / Move over / Foxy lady / Girls got rhythm / Hell raiser / The dock of the bay / Rave on / Telegram Sam / I heard it through the grapevine / The boys are back in town / Cold turkey.

LILLIAN AXE

Formed: Michigan, USA . . . 1987 as STIFF, by RON TAYLOR, STEVIE BLAZE, JON STER, ROB STRATTON and DANNY KING. Inking a deal with 'M.C.A.' and enjoying the production talents of RATT's ROBBIN CROSBY, the band delighted pop-metal fans with the following year's eponymous debut. With healthy export sales, their label deemed to give the follow-up, 'LOVE + WAR' a UK release in 1989. Despite some favourable reviews and an improvement in the songwriting department, the record failed to live up to MCA's commercial expectations and they were summarily dropped. A split in the ranks ensued with DARREN DeLATTA and GENE BARNETT coming in for the departed ROB and DANNY. This line-up returned in 1992, armed with a 'Music For Nations' deal, the group releasing the 'POETIC JUSTICE' album the same year. Though the market for melodic rock had shrunk considerably (especially in the UK), LILLIAN AXE continued releasing rather blunt melodic rock.

Album rating: LILLIAN AXE (*5) / LOVE + WAR (*7) / POETIC JUSTICE (*5) / PSYCHOSCHIZOPHRENIA (*6) / FIELDS OF YESTERDAY collection (*5)

RON TAYLOR – vocals / **STEVIE BLAZE** – guitar / **JON STER** – guitar, keyboards / **ROB STRATTON** – bass / **DANNY KING** – drums

M.C.A. M.C.A.

Oct 88. (lp/c/cd) *<42146>* **LILLIAN AXE** [-] ☐
– Dream of a lifetime / Inside out / Vision in the night / Picture perfect / The more that you get / Misery loves company / Nobody knows / Hard luck / Waiting in the dark / Laughing in your face.

Sep 89. (lp/c/cd) *(MCG/MCGC/DMCG 6060) <6301>* **LOVE + WAR** ☐ ☐
– All's fair in love and war / She likes it on top / Diana / Down on you / The world stopped turning / Ghost of winter / My number / Show a little love / Fool's paradise / Letters in the rain.

— **DARREN DeLATTA** – bass; repl. ROB

— **GENE BARNETT** – drums (ex-DIRTY LOOKS) repl. DANNY

Music For Nations Capitol

Mar 92. (c-s) *<13855>* **TRUE BELIEVERS** [-] ☐

May 92. (c-s) *<13861>* **NO MATTER WHAT** [-] ☐

Jul 92. (cd/c/lp) *(CD/T+/MFN 131) <13129>* **POETIC JUSTICE** ☐ ☐
– Poetic justice / Innocence / True believers / Body double / See you someday / Living in the grey / Digital dreams / Dyin' to live / Mercy / The promised land / No matter what / She's my salvation / A moment of relection.

Sep 93. (cd/c/lp) *(CD/T+/MFN 151) <13198>* **PSYCHOSCHIZOPHRENIA** ☐ ☐
– Crucified / Deep freeze / Moonlight in your blood / Stop the hate / Sign of the times / Needle and your pain / Those who prey / Voices in my walls / Now you know / Deep blue shadows / Day that I met you / Psychoschizophrenia.

— disbanded after above

– compilations, etc. –

Jun 99. (cd) *Z; (ZR 1997013) / Mutiny; <80024>* **FIELDS OF YESTERDAY** (rare material) ☐ ☐
– Death Valley daze / Pulling the rats out / For crying out loud / The last time / Blood on the Moon / Calm before the storm / Daddy long legs / Do it / Twilight in Hell / Become a monster / Thirst / Throw you away / Kill me again.

LIMP BIZKIT

Formed: Jacksonville, Florida, USA . . . 1994 by FRED DURST, WES BORLAND, SAM RIVERS, JOHN OTTO and DJ LETHAL, the latter snatched from the recently defunct, HOUSE OF PAIN. Drawing inevitable comparisons to KORN and RAGE AGAINST THE MACHINE, the band thrust their bass-chunky metal funk/rap into the melting pot of 90's rock with favourable results. Of a generally more sprightly disposition than the aforementioned bands, this goatee-bearded fly-shaded posse released their 'Interscope' debut, 'THREE DOLLAR BILL, Y'ALL$' in the summer of '97. Not content with BIZKIT's minor breakthrough, DURST also guested for COLD, SOULFLY and KORN on their early 1998 sets. With METHOD MAN from WU-TANG CLAN (on the track, 'N 2 GETHER NOW') and a celebrity feast of stars courtesy of KORN, STONE TEMPLE PILOTS and PRIMUS all on show, how could their follow-up album, 'SIGNIFICANT OTHER', fail. In fact, its MTV-friendly hardcore rap was all the rage with trendy young teenagers who helped it get all the way to No.1 on its first week of release. However, the more discerning Brit was not quite convinced (it only reached No.26). The new millennium got off to a flyer via a $2 million deal with Napster which was soon followed by a breakthrough Top 3 single in the UK, 'TAKE A LOOK AROUND' (the theme to 'MI:2'). Better still was when their 3rd set, 'CHOCOLATE STARFISH AND THE HOT DOG FLAVORED WATER' smashed in at No.1 in the US charts that Autumn; it finally reached peak spot in Britain after the 'ROLLIN' single did the same.

Album rating: THREE DOLLAR BILL, Y'ALL$ (*7) / SIGNIFICANT OTHER (*5) / CHOCOLATE STARFISH AND THE HOT DOG FLAVORED WATER (*7)

FRED DURST – vocals / **WES BORLAND** – guitar / **SAM RIVERS** – bass / **JOHN OTTO** – drums / **DJ LETHAL** (b. LEOR DiMANT, 18 Dec'72, Latvia) – turntables (ex-HOUSE OF PAIN)

not iss. Flip

Jun 96. (c-s) *<24894>* **COUNTERFEIT / POLLUTION / STUCK** [-] ☐

Interscope Interscope

Jul 97. (cd) *<(IND 90124)>* **THREE DOLLAR BILL, Y'ALL$** ☐ [22]
– Intro / Pollution / Counterfeit / Stuck / Nobody loves me / Sour / Stalemate / Clunk / Faith / Stinkfinger / Indigo flow / Leech / Everything. *(hit UK No.68 in Aug00)*

Jul 99. (cd/c/d-lp) *(IND/INC/INT2 90335) <490335>* **SIGNIFICANT OTHER** [26] [1]
– Intro / Jusy like this / Nookie / Break stuff / Re-arranged / I'm broke / Nobody like you / Don't go off wondering / 9 teen 90 nine / N 2 gether now / Trust / No sex / Show me what you got / Lesson learned / Outro. *(cd re-iss. Sep00+=; 490788-2)* – Re-arranged (live) / Nookie (live) / N2 gether now / Break stuff (video).

Jul 99. (cd-s) *<promo>* **NOOKIE / COUNTERFEIT / COUNTERFEIT (mix)** [-] [80]

Nov 99. (c-s/cd-s; as LIMP BIZKIT featuring METHOD MAN) *<497183>* **N 2 GETHER NOW** [-] [78]

Nov 99. (-) *<radio cut>* **RE-ARRANGED** [-] [88]

Jul 00. (cd-s) *(497368-2)* **TAKE A LOOK AROUND (THEME FROM MI:2) / FAITH** [3] ☐
(cd-s) *(497369-2)* – ('A'side) / N 2 gether now (live) / Break stuff (CD-Rom video) / ('A'-CD-Rom video).

Oct 00. (cd/d-lp) *(490770-2)* *<490759>* **CHOCOLATE STARFISH AND THE HOT DOG FLAVORED WATER** 1 1
– Intro / Hot dog / My generation / Full nelson / My way / Rollin' (air raid vehicle) / Livin' it up / One / Getcha groove on / Take a look around / It'll be ok / Boiler / Hold on / Rollin' (urban assault vehicle) / Outro. *(special d-cd+=; 490793-2)* – Crushed / Faith / Counterfeit (Lethal Dose mix) / Faith (video) / Nookie (video) / Re-arranged (video) / N2 gether now (video).

Oct 00. (7"pic-d) *(497447-7)* **MY GENERATION. / IT'S LIKE THAT Y'ALL** 15 -
(cd-s+=) *(497447-2)* – Snake in your face.
(cd-s) *(497448-2)* – ('A'side) / Back on da bus / My generation (US mix) / My generation (video).

Jan 01. (c-s) *(INC 97474)* *<radio play>* **ROLLIN' (AIR RAID VEHICLE) / ROLLIN' (URBAN ASSAULT VEHICLE)** 1 65
(cd-s+=) *(IND 97474)* – Take a look around (live) / My generation (live) / ('A'-CD-ROM).

— also in early 2001, FRED DURST teamed up with AARON LEWIS of STAIND to have a US hit single, 'OUTSIDE'

Jun 01. (c-s) *(497574-4)* *<radio play>* **MY WAY / ROLLIN' (Air Raid Vehicle remix)** 6 75
(cd-s) *(497573-2)* – ('A'side) / ('A'-William Orbit mix) / ('A'-DJ Premier remix).
(cd-s) *(497574-2)* – ('A'side) / ('A'-Dub Pistols remix) / ('A'-Dancehall dub remix) / ('A'-Dub Pistols remix instrumental).

LINEA 77

Formed: Turin, Italy . . . 1993 by unknown lads with a penchant for nu-metal. During the mid-90's, they unleashed two demos, 'OGNI COSA AL SUO POSTO' in '94 and 'KUNG FU', the latter for their local independent 'Dracma' records. With a penchant for the sounds of KORN, WILL HAVEN and SYSTEM OF A DOWN, LINEA 77 moved to Milan (and the 'Collapse' imprint) to record their debut album, 'TOO MUCH HAPPINESS MAKES KIDS PARANOID' (1998). With frequent visits to the UK, the 5-piece sparked interest from the mighty Nottingham-based indie-metal imprint, 'Earache', who signed them in October '99. The following Spring, the Italian stallions' aforementioned debut hit the shops and subsequent tours alongside KILL II THIS and EARTHTONE9 ensured their extreme metal was heard. A live favourite was undoubtably their grinding cover of the Bangles' 'WALK LIKE AN EGYPTIAN', the song also a finale to their rush-released sophomore DAVE CHANG-produced album, 'KET.CHUP SUI.CIDE' (2001). Gutteral, disturbing and schizoid, tracks such as 'SMILE', 'CACAO' and 'LO-FI BOY' were post-hardcore fuelled with dynamic sparring rap vocals – these Italian lads had come of age.

Album rating: TOO MUCH HAPPINESS MAKES KIDS PARANOID (*6) / KET.CHUP SUI.CIDE (*7)

unknown

Collapse / not iss.

Oct 98. (cd) **TOO MUCH HAPPINESS MAKES KIDS PARANOID** - - Italy
– Touch / By my Fay / Headtide / Meat / Nosedive / 90° / Big hole man / Tutto quello che ho sempre voluto / Swellfish. *(re-iss. Apr00 on 'Earache'; MOSH 238CD) <US-iss.May00 on 'Caroline'; >*

Earache / Caroline

Jan 01. (cd) *(MOSH 239CD)* **KET.CHUP SUI.CIDE**
– Potato music machine / Ketchup suicide / Tadayuki song / McHuman deluxe / Miss it / Smile / You kimono / Lo-fi boy / Cacao / Moka / Walk like an Egyptian.

LINKIN PARK

Formed: Los Angeles, California, USA . . . 1999 as HYBRID THEORY by high school friends BRAD DELSON, MIKE SHINODA and ROB BOURDON together with JOSEPH HAHN and CHESTER BENNINGTON. Influenced by the likes of NINE INCH NAILS, APHEX TWIN and The ROOTS, LINKIN PARK are yet another act to muscle in on the heavily saturated rap-metal market. Offered a publishing deal after their very first gig at L.A.'s Whisky, the band subsequently signed with 'Warners' for their debut album, 'HYBRID THEORY' (2000). While admittedly pretty fly for white guys, LINKIN PARK, like most bands of their ilk, possess neither the fluid funk of the 'CHILI PEPPERS nor the wiry conviction of RATM. Like most bands of their ilk, however, they seem to have found an audience willing to part with their hard earned cash and are, at the time of writing, racing up the charts.

Album rating: HYBRID THEORY (*6)

CHESTER BENNINGTON – vocals / **MIKE SHINODA** – vocals/MC / **BRAD DELSON** – guitar / **JOSEPH HAHN** – DJ, vocals / **ROB BOURBON** – drums / with **SCOTT KOZIOL** – bass

Warners / Warners

Oct 00. (cd) *<(9362 47755-2)>* **HYBRID THEORY** 9 16 Apr00
– Papercut / One step closer / With you / Points of authority / Crawling / Runaway / By myself / In the end / A place for my head / Forgotten / Cure for the itch / Pushing me away.

— **PHOENIX** – bass; repl. part-timer SCOTT

Jan 01. (10"/c-s) *(W 550 TE/MC)* *<radio play>* **ONE STEP CLOSER. / MY DECEMBER** 24 75
(cd-s+=) *(W 550CD)* – High voltage / ('A'-CD-ROM).

Apr 01. (c-s) *(W 556MC)* **CRAWLING / PAPERCUT (live)** 16 -
(cd-s+=) *(W 556CD)* – (CD-Rom video footage).
(dvds) *(W 556DVD)* – ('A'side) / ('A'live snippets).

Jun 01. (c-s) *(W 562C)* **PAPERCUT / POINTS OF AUTHORITY (live)** 14
(cd-s+=) *(W 562CD)* – Papercut (live).

LINKMEN (see under ⇒ ANTI-PASTI)

LION

Formed: Los Angeles, California, USA . . . 1983 by ex-TYTAN (the English NWOBHM band) vocalist KAL SWAN, plus DOUG ALDRICH, JERRY BEST and MARK EDWARDS. Following a Japanese-only debut, 'POWER LOVE' in 1985, the band signed to 'Scotti Brothers' (home of SURVIVOR), issuing a second set, 'DANGEROUS ATTRACTION' two years later. With SWAN managing an adequate DAVID COVERDALE impersonation, LION's strong melodic rock was given a third and final airing on 'TROUBLE AT ANGEL CITY' (1989). The frontman secured a solo deal in Japan, after EDWARDS' serious car smash forced the group to split.

Album rating: POWER LOVE mini (*4) / DANGEROUS ATTRACTION (*5) / TROUBLE AT ANGEL CITY (*5)

KAL SWAN – vocals (ex-TYTAN) / **DOUG ALDRICH** – guitar / **JERRY BEST** – bass / **MARK EDWARDS** – drums (ex-STEELER)

Fems / not iss.

1985. (m-lp) *(MP 32-5122)* **POWER LOVE** - - Japan
– Power love / Stranger in the city / Victim of circumstance / Hungry for love / Love is a lie / Forgotten sons.

Polydor / Scotti Bros

Jan 88. (lp/cd) *(834 232-1/-2)* *<BFZ 40797>* **DANGEROUS ATTRACTION** Sep87
– Fatal attraction / Armed and dangerous / Hard and heavy / Never surrender / Death on legs / Powerlove / In the name of love / After the fire / Shout it out.

Grand Slam / Grand Slam

1989. (lp) *<(SLAM 5)>* **TROUBLE AT ANGEL CITY**
– Come on / Lock up your daughters / Can't stop the rain / Love is a lie / Victims of circumstance / Stranger in the city / Hungry for love / Hold on / Lonely girl / Forgotten sons. *(UK re-iss. Jul92 on 'Music For Nations' cd/c/lp; CD/T+/MFN 132)*

— folded when EDWARDS was involved in a serious accident and ALDRICH went off to join HURRICANE

LIONHEART

Formed: London, England . . . 1980 by a number of established musicians in the NWOBHM scene, namely DENNIS STRATTON (ex-IRON MAIDEN), STEVE MANN (ex-LIAR), JESS COX (ex-TYGERS OF PAN TANG), ROCKY NEWTON (ex-WILDFIRE) and FRANK NOON (ex-DEF LEPPARD). COX was first to leave in an ongoing cycle of personnel changes which effectively nipped this promising band's potential in the bud. Over the course of the next two years, singers such as JOHN FARNHAM (future solo artist) and REUBEN ARCHER (ex-STAMPEDE) would pass through the ranks, before CHAD BROWN became the band's permanent frontman. The drumstool was also subject to musical chairs, DAVE DUFORT (ex-ANGEL WITCH) making way finally for BOB JENKINS. In the midst of this flux, LIONHEART did manage to lay down a sole eponymous track for the 'Heavy Metal Heroes, Vol.2' compilation, although by the time they'd signed to 'Columbia' the band had adopted a smoother approach. When it eventually appeared, the Kevin Beamish-produced 1984/85 album, 'HOT TONIGHT' disappointed the band's original fans while failing to attract any new ones. After its release, even more line-up changes ensued, PHIL LANZON and ANDY BIERNE being taken from SWEET, while a new vocalist KEITH MURRELL was the last to fill the position having quickly jumped ship to MAMA'S BOYS. NEWTON and MANN subsequently joined MSG, while STRATTON headed for NWOBHM nostalgia in Japan.

Album rating: HOT TONIGHT (*4)

CHAD BROWN – vocals; replaced a series of vocalists (see above) / **STEVE MANN** – guitar, keyboards (ex-LIAR) / **DENNIS STRATTON** – guitar, vocals (ex-IRON MAIDEN) / **ROCKY NEWTON** – bass, vocals (ex-WILDFIRE) / **BOB JENKINS** – drums; replaced a series of drummers

Epic / Epic

Jan 85. (7") *(A 5001)* **DIE FOR LOVE. / DANGEROUS GAMES**

Jan 85. (lp) *(EPC 26214)* *<BFN 39544>* **HOT TONIGHT**
– Wait for the night / Hot tonight / Die for love / Towers of silver / Don't look back in anger / Nightmare / Living in a dream / Another crazy dream / Dangerous game.

— split up after another series of line-up changes (see above)

LIONSHEART

Formed: London, England . . . early 90's by STEVE GRIMMETT, who enlisted twin brothers, MARK and STEVE OWERS, plus GRAHAM COLLETT and ANTHONY CHRISTMAS. A veteran of the UK metal scene, GRIMMETT had previously cut his teeth in GRIM REAPER and ONSLAUGHT, forming LIONSHEART as a more melodic proposition for his full bore vocals. Signed to 'Music For Nations', the band roared into the Japanese arena with their eponymous debut, although British fans didn't exactly see them as a mane (sic!) attraction. Nevertheless, with 'PRIDE IN TACT' and a new line-up (the OWERS replaced by NICK BURR and ZAK BAJJON) LIONSHEART continued to stalk the fringes of the Brit-rock scene.

Album rating: LIONSHEART (*6) / PRIDE IN TACT (*5)

STEVE GRIMMETT – vocals (ex-ONSLAUGHT, ex-GRIM REAPER) / **MARK OWERS** – guitar / **GRAHAM COLLETT** – keyboards / **STEVE OWERS** – bass / **ANTHONY CHRISTMAS** – drums

Music For Nations — not iss.

Jul 92. (cd/c/lp) *(CD/T+/MFN 139)* **LIONSHEART** — -
– Hard enough / World of pain / So cold / Can't believe / All I need / Portrait / Living in a fantasy / Stealer / Going down / Had enough. *(cd+=)* – Ready or not / Have mercy.

Oct 92. (7") *(KUT 148)* **CAN'T BELIEVE. /** — -
(12"+=/cd-s+=) *(12/CD KUT 148)* –

—— the OWERS twins had already departed and were repl. by **NICK BURR** – guitar + / **ZAK BAJJON** – bass

Nov 94. (cd/c/lp) *(CD/T+/MFN 167)* **PRIDE IN TACT** — -
– Deja vu / I'll stand up / I believe in love / Love remains / Something for nothing / Pain in my heart / Gods of war / Stronger than steel / (Take a little) Piece of my heart / Who's the wise man (Jackie's song) / I'll be there / Relentless.

—— disbanded soon after above

LIQUID JESUS

Formed: Los Angeles, California, USA ... 1990 by SCOTT TRACEY and JOHNNY LONELY, who subsequently added BUCK MURPHY, TODD RIGIONE and JOHN MOLO. Briefly touted as the next JANE'S ADDICTION, the band certainly followed in their mentors' footsteps, signing with the local 'Triple X' label and debuting with a self-titled live set. While their influences were obvious, the group's unhinged delivery and incendiary style marked them out as metal mavericks. 'Geffen' were quick to see their potential, releasing their debut studio album, 'POUR IN THE SKY' in 1991. A fractured hybrid of psych, R&B and hard-rock, the record proved to be too eclectic for its own good and the band evaporated into the smog-filled L.A. ether.

Album rating: LIQUID JESUS LIVE (*5) / POUR IN THE SKY (*6)

BUCK MURPHY – vocals / **SCOTT TRACEY** – guitar / **TODD RIGIONE** – guitar / **JOHNNY LONELY** – bass / **JOHN MOLO** – drums

Triple X — Triple X

1990. (cd) *<(TX 51046CD)>* **LIQUID JESUS LIVE (live)**
– Intro / Kool milds brother / W.H.Y.B. / The light / Take my advice / Slight flight / Yesterday / Bleeding hearts / Goodtime baby / Susan's call / Top of the wheel / Dream awhile / Message.

M.C.A. — M.C.A.

Aug 91. (lp/c/cd) *<(MCA/+C/D 10191)>* **POUR IN THE SKY**
– Intro / Finding my way / W.H.Y.B. / No secret / On my way / Better or worse / The light / Sacrifice / The colorful ones / Faith to believe / Feelings flower / Bleed.

Jan 94. (c-s) *<MCAC 10684>* **MIRRORS FOR THE BLIND** -

—— dissolved after above

LIT

Formed: Orange County, California, USA . . . 1990 by songwriting brothers, JEREMY and A. JAY POPOFF; the line-up being completed by KEVIN BALDES and ALLAN SHELLENBERGER. The band, who looked, but didn't sound like the "SINATRA" rat pack, took their influences primarily from COSTELLO and PRESLEY. An EP, 'FIVE SMOKIN' TRACKS FROM LIT' was released in 1996 and didn't really do much for the rap-metal/pop punk quartet, neither did the debut, 'TRIPPING THE LIGHT FANTASTIC', which bagged some excellent reviews. It wasn't until 1999 that LIT unleashed ~'MY OWN WORST ENEMY', the single that predictably sent melodramatic US teens into hyper mode, proving to be just as successful on British shores too. The song was a darkly comic cartoon punk (can you feel the ghosts of early GREEN DAY) track about a white trash alcoholic's misadventures with his argument-happy girlfriend. The album that followed, 'A PLACE IN THE SUN' didn't even graze the US billboard charts and hardly reached boiling-point selling figures in Europe. This could possibly be blamed on the band's rivals, SUGAR RAY, who sounded familiarly similar.

Album rating: FIVE SMOKIN' TRACKS FROM LIT mini (*5) / TRIPPING THE LIGHT FANTASTIC (*6) / A PLACE IN THE SUN (*6)

A. JAY POPOFF – vocals / **JEREMY POPOFF** – guitar / **KEVIN BALDES** – bass / **ALLAN SHELLENBERGER** – drums

not iss. — Malicious Vinyl

Dec 96. (m-cd) *<MV 5001>* **FIVE SMOKIN' TRACKS FROM LIT** -
– Bitter / Fireman / No big thing / Beginning / Stain.

Apr 97. (cd) *<MV 5016>* **TRIPPING THE LIGHT FANTASTIC** -
– Beginning / My world / Fuel / No big thing / Habib / Explode / Bitter / Amount to nothing / Dozer / Fireman / Cadillac / I don't get it.

R.C.A. — R.C.A.

Jun 99. (7"/c-s) *(74321 61265-7/66999-4)* *<radio cut>* **MY OWN WORST ENEMY. / BITTER** 16 — 51 Apr99
(cd-s) *(74321 66999-2)* – ('A'side) / Money / Lovely day.

Jun 99. (cd/c/lp) *(74321 67859-2/-4/-1)* *<07863 67775-2/-4>* **A PLACE IN THE SUN** 55 — 31 Feb99
– Four / My own worst enemy / Down / Miserable / No big thing / Zip-lock / Lovely day / Perfect one / Quicksand / Happy / The best is yet to come undone / A place in the sun.

Sep 99. (c-s) *(74321 70185-4)* **ZIP-LOCK / QUICKSAND** 60
(cd-s+=) *(74321 70185-2)* – ('A'album version).

Aug 00. (c-s) *(888953-4)* **OVER MY HEAD / (other tracks by BLISS and KARMA SLAVE** 37
(above from the movie, 'Titan A.E.', issued on 'E.M.I.')

LITTLE ANGELS

Formed: Scarborough, England . . . May '87 by TOBY JEPSON and MARK PLUNKETT, who had cut their teeth in school band, ZEUS, in 1984. Just over a year later, they formed an embryonic MR. THRUD along with BRUCE JOHN DICKINSON, recruiting his brother JIMMY DICKINSON by the end of the year. Having been spotted by manager Kevin Nixon, they completed the line-up with DAVE HOPPER, appearing on Channel 4's 'Famous For 15 Minutes' on the 20th November '87 as The LITTLE ANGELS. They had already issued an EP on 'Powerstation', a label co-run by their manager, repackaging the material along with some new tracks later in the year as the mini-lp 'TOO POSH TO MOSH'. Securing a deal with 'Polydor', the group supported YNGWIE MALMSTEEN and CINDERELLA on British and US dates, before issuing a single, '90° IN THE SHADE'. A year later (late '89), with drummer MICHAEL LEE replacing HOPPER, they finally delivered a full-length album, 'DON'T PREY FOR ME', a promising if inconsistent set which won the band a solid core of UK fans. Following in the footsteps of classic 80's Brit-rock, the group's effervescent, musclebound sound took occasional sidesteps into American acoustic balladry. Their first taste of major chart action was provided early in 1990, when a track from the aforementioned album, 'KICKIN' UP DUST', hit the UK Top 50. Following a clutch of infectious hit singles, the group utilised songwriter JIM VALLANCE to arrive at a smoother, more overtly Americanised sound with the 'YOUNG GODS' album of early '91. This approach worked commercial wonders, spawning hit after hit with 'BONEYARD', 'PRODUCT OF THE WORKING CLASS', 'YOUNG GODS' and 'I AIN'T GONNA CRY'. Early in '93, with new drummer MARK RICHARDSON (who actually joined a year previously), they issued another set of equally charismatic hard bluesy-rock, which surprisingly entered the UK chart at pole position, although they still failed to break into the US market despite a support slot to VAN HALEN. They subsequently split, leaving behind a 1994 compilation, while the DICKINSONs moved on to become b.l.o.w., releasing a handful of albums in the mid 90's. • **Covers:** TIE YOUR MOTHER DOWN (Queen) / BROKEN WINGS OF AN ANGEL (Hugh Cornwall) / FORTUNATE SON (Creedence Clearwater Revival) / RADICAL YOUR LOVER (co-with; Dan Reed) / BABYLON'S BURNING (Ruts) / OH WELL (Fleetwood Mac) / FUNK 49 (James Gang) / TIRED OF WAITING FOR YOU (Kinks) / WON'T GET FOOLED AGAIN (Who) / JAILHOUSE ROCK (Elvis Presley) / THE MIGHTY QUINN (Bob Dylan) / – Feb '92 – German single cover; FIRST CUT IS THE DEEPEST (Cat Stevens).

Album rating: TOO POSH TO MOSH mini (*5) / DON'T PREY FOR ME (*5) / YOUNG GODS (*6) / JAM (*6) / LITTLE OF THE PAST compilation (*7)

TOBY JEPSON – vocals, acoustic guitar / **BRUCE JOHN DICKINSON** – guitars, banjo / **JIMMY DICKINSON** – keyboards, vocals / **MARK PLUNKETT** – bass, vocals / **DAVE HOPPER** – drums

Song Management — not iss.

Jul 87. (12"ep) *(LAN 001)* **THE '87 EP** — -
– Bad or just no good / Better than the rest / Burning me / Reach for me.

Powerstation — not iss.

Nov 87. (m-lp) *(AMP 14)* **TOO POSH TO MOSH** — -
– (1st EP tracks) / Too posh to mosh / No more whiskey / Down in the night.

—— **MICHAEL LEE** – drums, percussion (ex-HOLOSAIDE) repl. HOPPER

Polydor — Polydor

Nov 88. (7"/7"w-poster/7"pic-d) *(LTL/+D/XP)* **90 DEGREES IN THE SHADE. / ENGLAND ROCKS (live)** — -
(12"+=) *(LTLX 1)* – Big bad world.

Feb 89. (7") *(LTL 2)* **SHE'S A LITTLE ANGEL. / BETTER THAN THE REST** 74 — -
(c-ep+=/12"+=/cd-ep+=) **THE BIG BAD EP** *(LTL EC/EP/CD 2)* – Don't waste my time / Sex in cars.

Sep 89. (7") *(LTL 3)* **DO YOU WANNA RIOT. / MOVE IN SLOW** — -
(12"+=/cd-s+=) *(LTL X/CD 3)* – Some kind of alien (live).
(10"++=) *(LTLXV 3)* – Snatch (edited highlights of below lp).

Nov 89. (lp/c/cd) *(841 254-1/-4/-2)* **DON'T PREY FOR ME**
– Do you wanna riot / Kick hard / Big bad world / Kickin' up dust / Don't prey for me / Broken wings of an angel / Bitter and twisted / Promises / When I get out of here / No solution / She's a little angel. *(c+=)* – Pleasure pyre. *(cd+=)* – Radical your lover (version) / Broken wings of an angel (version). *(re-dist.Jun90)*

Nov 89. (7"/c-s) *(LTL/+CS 4)* **DON'T PREY FOR ME. / RADICAL YOUR LOVER** — -
(ext.12"+=) *(LTLX 4)* – What do you want.
(cd-s++=) *(LTLCD 4)* – ('A'extended Bob Clearmountain mix).
(12") *(LTLXP 4)* – ('A'live) / She's a little angel (live) / Pleasure pyre (live) / Tie your mother down (live).

Feb 90. (7"/7"box) *(LTL/+B 5)* **KICKIN' UP DUST. / ('A'live)** 46 — -
(12"+=) *(LTLX 5)* – Big bad world (Nashville version).
(cd-s+=) *(LTLLCD 5)* – Pleasure pyre (live) / Kick hard (live).
(12"pic-d) *(LTLXP 5)* – ('A'live) / Sex in cars (live) / When I get out of here (live) / Kick hard (live).

Apr 90. (7"/7"box/c-s) *(LTL/+B/CS 6)* **RADICAL YOUR LOVER. / DON'T LOVE YOU NO MORE** 34 — -
(12"+=/12"pic-d-ep+=/cd-ep+=) **GET RADICAL EP** *(LTL X/XP/CD 6)* – ('A'-adult remix) / Promises (live).

Jul 90. (7"/c-s)(7"w-poster) *(LTL/+CS 7)(APLTL 7)* **SHE'S A LITTLE ANGEL. / DOWN ON MY KNEES** 21 — -
(12"+=) *(LTLX 7)* – ('A'-Voodoo mix).
(club.12"+=) *(LTLXP 7)* – When I get out of here (live).
(7") *(LTLT 7)* – ('A'side) / Sex in cars (live).

Jan 91. (7"/c-s) *(LTL/+CS 8)* **BONEYARD. / FORTUNATE SON** [33] [-]
(12"+=) *(LTLX 8)* – Sweet love sedation.
(ext.12"box++=) *(LTLBX 8)* – ('A'-Bonecrusher mix).
(12"pic-d+=) *(LTLXP 8)* – Jump the gun / ('A'album mix).

Feb 91. (cd/c/lp) *(<847 486-2/-4/-1>)* **YOUNG GODS** [17] [ ]
– Back door man / Boneyard / Young gods (stand up, stand up) / I ain't gonna cry / The wildside of life / Product of the working class / That's my kinda life / Juvenile offender / Love is a gun / Sweet love sedation / Smoke in my eyes / Natural born fighter / Feels like the world has come undone (featuring the angel's anthem). *(re-iss. cd Apr95; same)*

Mar 91. (7"/c-s) *(LTL/+CS 9)* **PRODUCT OF THE WORKING CLASS. / REVIVAL** [40] [-]
(12"+=) *(LTLX 9)* – Take it off.
(12"++=) *(LTLXG 9)* – ('A'-Hot sweat'n'groove mix).
(cd-s+=) *(LTLCD 9)* – ('A'-Hot sweat'n'groove mix) / Might like you better.

May 91. (7"/c-s) *(LTL/+CS 10)* **YOUNG GODS. / GO AS YOU PLEASE** [34] [-]
(12"+=) *(LTLX 10)* – Frantic.
(12"box+=/cd-s+=) *(LTL XB/CD 10)* – Bad imitation.

Jul 91. (7"/c-s) *(LTL/+CS 11)* **I AIN'T GONNA CRY. / BABYLON'S BURNING** [26] [-]
(12"+=) *(LTLX 11)* – Funk 49.
(12"++=/cd-s++=) *(LTL BX/CD 11)* – Oh well.

— **MARK 'Rich' RICHARDSON** – drums; repl. LEE

Nov 92. (7"/c-s) *(LTL/+CS 12)* **TOO MUCH TOO YOUNG. / THE FIRST CUT IS THE DEEPEST** [22] [-]
(12"+=/cd-s+=) *(LTL X/CD 12)* – 90 degrees in the shade / Young gods.

Jan 93. (7"/c-s) *(LTL/+CS 13)* **WOMANKIND. / SCHIZOPHRENIA BLUES** [12] [ ]
(12"+=/cd-s+=) *(LTL X/CD 13)* – This is not America.

Jan 93. (cd/c/lp) *(<517 642-2/-4/-1>)* **JAM** [1] [ ]
– The way that I live / Too much too young / Splendid isolation / Soapbox / S.T.W. / Don't confuse sex with love / Womankind / Eyes wide open / The colour of love / I was not wrong / Sail away / Tired of waiting for you (so tired) / S.T.W. (reprise). *(w/ ltd.live cd+lp + extra tracks 1-side of c) (517 676-2/-1)* **LIVE JAM** – She's a little angel / Product of the working class (grooved & jammed) / I ain't gonna cry / Boneyard 1993 (featuring Big Dave Kemp) / Don't prey for me (extended version) / Won't get fooled again. *(re-iss. cd Apr95; same)*

Apr 93. (7"/c-s) *(LTL/+CS 14)* **SOAPBOX (remix). / I GOT THE SHAKES** [33] [-]
(cd-s+=) *(LTLCD 14)* – Womankind (live) / Too much too young (live).
(cd-s) *(LTLCDX 14)* – ('A'side) / Young gods (live) / Jailhouse rock (live) / I ain't gonna cry (live).

Sep 93. (12"/c-s) *(LTL X/CS 15)* **SAIL AWAY. / I AIN'T GONNA CRY (live) / SOAPBOX (live)** [45] [-]
(cd-s) *(LTLCD 15)* – ('A'side) / The mighty Quinn / This ain't the way it's supposed to be.

Mar 94. (c-s) *(LTLCS 16)* **TEN MILES HIGH. / HARD TIMES** [18] [-]
(12"+=/cd-s+=) *(LTL X/CD 16)* – Overrated.
(cd-s) *(LTLDD 16)* – ('A'side) / Just one night (acoustic) / Too much too young (acoustic).

Apr 94. (cd/c/lp) *(<521 936-2/-4/-1>)* **LITTLE OF THE PAST** (compilation) [20] [ ]
– She's a little angel / Too much too young / Radical your lover / Womankind / Boneyard / Kickin' up dust / I ain't gonna cry / Sail away / Young gods / 90 degrees in the shade / Product of the working class / Soapbox / The first cut is the deepest / Ten miles high / I wanna be loved by you / Don't pray for me. *(cd re-iss. Jun99 on 'Spectrum'; 544051-2)*

— now w/out JIMMY + BRUCE DICKINSON who formed b.l.o.w. (released a handful of albums on their own 'Cottage Industry' imprint).

– compilations, etc –

Jun 94. (cd/c/lp) *Essential; (ESM CD/MC/LP 398)* **TOO POSH TO MOSH, TOO GOOD TO LAST!** [18] [-]
– All roads lead to you / Forbidden fruit / I want love (with Doris) / Reach for me / Bad or just no good / Burning me / No more whiskey / Down in the night / Better than the rest / Too posh to mosh / Some kind of alien.

b.l.o.w.

DICKINSON brothers + **BRUCE GOODING** (b. Scotland) – vocals

— note:- the group on 'Paragoric' was in fact a dance outfit

Cottage Industry / not iss.

Mar 95. (cd) *(COTINDCD 1)* **MAN AND GOAT ALIKE** [ ] [-]
– Hand full of nails (featuring – The man who wasn't there) / Jesus loves me / Humble pie / If / Bump it (mono) / Who composed that song? / Dred Indian blue.

Jun 95. (c-ep/cd-ep) *(COTIND MC/CD 4)* **SHROOMIN' AT MOLES** [ ] [-]

May 96. (cd-s) *(COTINDCD 8)* **KISS LIKE CONCRETE** [ ] [-]

Jul 96. (cd-s) *(COTINDCD 9)* **MUSHROOM TEA** [ ] [-]

Aug 96. (cd) *(COTINDCD 10)* **PIGS** [ ] [-]
– Kiss like concrete / Dreams of the dead / Beautiful day / Mushroom tea / Kill yourself (and learn by your mistakes) / King pig / Dead man face / Brief encounter / Don't ride the white house / Sleep tonight.

— disbanded some time later

LITTLE CAESAR

Formed: Los Angeles, California, USA . . . late 80's by RON YOUNG, APACHE, LOUREN MOLINAIRE, FIDEL ANGEL PANIAGUA and TIM MORRIS. Signed to 'Geffen' on the strength of an independently released EP, 'NAME YOUR POISON' (1989), the group subsequently hit the metal scene with an eponymous full-length debut in summer 1990. Earthy R&B-influenced hard-rock, the set included two Motown covers, 'CHAIN OF FOOLS' (a US Top 100 hit) and 'I WISH IT WOULD RAIN', hardly in keeping with their gritty outlaw image. Perhaps an attempt to distance themselves from the L.A. sleaze-rock pack, they acquired the services of the more experienced EARL SLICK (in place of the departed APACHE) for the 1992 follow-up, 'INFLUENCE'. Although the album was met with a more favourable reception, 'Geffen' decided to "plunge the proverbial knife in" and drop them from their burgeoning empire.

Album rating: LITTLE CAESAR (*5) / INFLUENCE (*6)

RON YOUNG – vocals / **APACHE** – guitar, steel guitar / **LOUREN MOLINAIRE** – guitar / **FIDEL ANGEL PANIAGUA** – bass / **TIM MORRIS** – drums

not iss. / Metal Blade

1989. (cd-ep) *<772418-2>* **NAME YOUR POISON** [-] [ ]
– Name your poison / Tastes good to me / God's creation / Tears don't lie.

Geffen / D.G.C.

Aug 90. (7"/c-s) *(GEF 80/+C) <19693>* **CHAIN OF FOOLS. / ROCK-N-ROLL STATE OF MIND** [ ] [88] Jun90
(12"+=/12"pic-d+=/cd-s+=) *(GEF 80 T/TP/CD)* –

Aug 90. (cd)(lp/c) *<(7599 24288-2)> (WX 352/+C)* **LITTLE CAESAR** [ ] [ ] Jun90
– Down-n-dirty / Hard times / Chain of fools / In your arms / From the start / Rock-n-roll state of mind / Drive it home / Midtown / Cajun panther / Wrong side of the tracks / I wish it would rain / Little Queenie. *(re-iss. May92 on 'D.G.C.' cd/c; DGC D/C 19128)*

Feb 91. (c-s) *<19003>* **IN YOUR ARMS / WRONG SIDE OF THE TRACKS** [-] [79]

— **EARL SLICK** – guitar, slide (ex-DIRTY WHITE BOY, ex-DAVID BOWIE, etc.) repl. APACHE

D.G.C. / D.G.C.

May 92. (lp/c/cd) *<(DGC/+C/D 24472)>* **INFLUENCE** [ ] [ ]
– Stand up / You're mine / Turn my world around / Rum and coke / Ballad of Johnny / Ain't got it / Slow ride / Pray for me / Ridin' on / Piece of the action.

— virtually stabbed in the back when Geffen dropped them. YOUNG went on to form MANIC EDEN prior to instigating the band, DIRT

LIVE

Formed: York, Pennsylvania, USA . . . early 90's by EDWARD KOWALCZYK, CHAD TAYLOR, PATRICK DAHLHEIMER and CHAD GRACEY. Coming up with a moniker that both displayed a complete lack of imagination and confused prospective fans, they nevertheless released a competent neo-grunge debut, 'MENTAL JEWELRY' (1991). Produced by JERRY HARRISON (ex-TALKING HEADS), the record (on MCA subsidiary, 'Radioactive') found a large US audience with its rather derivative hybrid of PEARL JAM and R.E.M. Three years in the making, 'THROWING COPPER' eventually scaled the US charts, largely due to a clutch of harder-edged tracks/singles such as, 'SELLING THE DRAMA' and the MTV fave, 'I ALONE'. These semi-classics also cracked the British charts, setting the scene for a show-stealing (LIVE!) slot at the 1995 Glastonbury Fest. A third album, 'SECRET SAMADHI' (1997), repeated the winning formula, although the more discerning fans considered the album overproduced. In October '99, LIVE were back to their near best, the fourth set 'THE DISTANCE TO HERE' winning back most of the fans. • **Covered:** LOVE MY WAY (Psychedelic Furs) / SUPERNATURAL (Vic Chesnutt).

Album rating: MENTAL JEWELRY (*6) / THROWING COPPER (*7) / SECRET SAMADHI (*5) / THE DISTANCE TO HERE (*6)

EDWARD KOWALCZYK – vocals, guitar / **CHAD TAYLOR** – guitar, vocals / **PATRICK DAHLHEIMER** – bass / **CHAD GRACEY** – drums, vocals

Radioactive / Radioactive

Jan 92. (7") *<54387>* **PAIN LIES ON THE RIVERSIDE. / HEAVEN WORE A SHIRT** [-] [ ]

Apr 92. (lp/c/cd) *<(RAR/+C/D 10346)>* **MENTAL JEWELRY** [ ] [73] Jan92
– Pain lies on the riverside / Operation spirit (the tyranny of tradition) / The beauty of Gray / Brothers unaware / Tired of me / Mirror song / Waterboy / Take my anthem / You are the world / Good pain / Mother Earth is a vicious crowd / 10,000 years (peace is now).

Apr 92. (cd-ep) *<54442>* **OPERATION SPIRIT (THE TYRANNY OF TRADITION) (live) / THE BEAUTY OF GRAY (live) / GOOD PAIN / LIES ON THE RIVERSIDE (live)** [-] [ ]

Jun 92. (7") *(RAX 1)* **OPERATION SPIRIT. / HEAVEN WORE A SKIRT** [ ] [-]
(12"+=/cd-s+=) *(RAX T/TD 1)* – Negation / Good pain.

May 94. (c-s) *<54816>* **SELLING THE DRAMA / LIGHTNING CRASHES** [-] [43]

Sep 94. (c-s/cd-s) *(RAX C/TD 11)* **SELLING THE DRAMA. / ('A'acoustic) / WHITE DISCUSSION** [ ] [-]

Oct 94. (cd/c) *<(RAD/RAC 10997)>* **THROWING COPPER** [37] [1] May94
– The dam at Otter Creek / Selling the drama / I alone / Iris / Lightning crashes / Top / All over you / Shit towne / T.B.D. / Stage / Waitress / Pillar of Davidson / White discussion. *(cd hidden track +=)* – Horse.

Feb 95. (7"clear/c-s) *(RAX/+C 13)* **I ALONE. / PAIN LIES ON THE RIVERSIDE** [48] [-]
(cd-s+=) *(RAXTD 13)* – ('A'mix).

Jun 95. (c-s/cd-s) *(RAX C/TD 17)* **SELLING THE DRAMA / THE DAN AT OTTER CREEK** [30] [-]
(cd-s+=) *(RAXXD 17)* – ('A'acoustic).

Sep 95. (c-s) *(RAXC 20)* **ALL OVER YOU / SHIT TOWNE** [48] [-]
(cd-s+=) *(RAXTD 20)* – ('A'live at Glastonbury).
(cd-s) *(RAXXD 20)* – ('A'side) / Waitress (live) / Iris (live at Glastonbury).

Jan 96. (c-s/cd-s) *(RAX C/TD 23)* **LIGHTNING CRASHES / THE BEAUTY OF GRAY (bootleg) / TBD (acoustic)** [33] [-]
(cd-s) *(RAXXD 23)* – ('A'side) / ('A'-live at Glastonbury) / White discussion (live at Glastonbury).

Mar 97. (7"silver) *(RAX 28)* **LAKINI'S JUICE. / SUPERNATURAL (remix)** [29] [-]
(cd-s+=) *(RAXXD 28)* – White discussion (remix).
(cd-s) *(RAD 49023)* – ('A'side) / Pain lies on the riverside (remix) / Selling the drama (acoustic).

Mar 97. (cd/c/d-lp) *<(RAD/RAC/RAR2 11590)>* **SECRET SAMADHI** [31] [1]
– Rattlesnake / Lakini's juice / Graze / Century / Ghost / Unsheathed / Insomnia and the hole in the universe / Turn my head / Heropsychodreamer / Freaks / Merica / Gas Hed goes west.

Jun 97. (7") *(RAX 29)* **FREAKS. / LOVE MY WAY (live)** [60] [ ]
(cd-s+=) *(RAXTD 29)* – Freaks (Labor, Labor, Labor remix).
(cd-s) *(RAXD 29)* – ('A'side) / Lakini's juice (live) / Freaks (live).

Oct 99. (cd) *(RAD 11966) <111966>* **THE DISTANCE TO HERE** [56] [4]
– The dolphin's cry / The distance / Sparkle / Run to the water / Sun / Voodoo lady / Where fishes go / Face and ghost (The children's song) / Feel the quiet river rage / Meltdown / They stood up for love / We walk in the dream / Dance with you.

Jan 00. (cd-s) *(RAXTD 39) <radio cut>* **THE DOLPHIN'S CRY / VINE STREET / LAKINI'S JUICE** [62] [78] Nov99
(cd-s) *(RAXXD 39)* – ('A'side) / Sun (remix) / Turn my head (live) / The dolphin's cry (video).

Kerry LIVGREN (see under ⇒ KANSAS)

LIVING COLOUR

Formed: New York, USA . . . 1984 by English-born guitarist VERNON REID, who had studied performing arts at Manhattan community college. 1986 saw the arrival of COREY GLOVER (vocals) and WILL CALHOUN (drums), with MUZZ SKILLINGS (bass) completing the line-up the following year. After MICK JAGGER clocked the band at a CBGB's gig, he invited the outfit to play on his 'Primitive Cool' album. The 'STONES frontman also produced two demos for the group, helping to secure them a deal with 'Epic'. LIVING COLOUR's debut album, 'VIVID' (1988) attracted a lot of attention if only because the band were an all-black outfit playing hard rock, not so surprising, and in reality a very interesting prospect. Leaving most of their junk-headed contemporaries at the starting post, LIVING COLOUR played rock with the invention of jazz and the spontaneity of funk. 'CULT OF PERSONALITY' was the album's highlight, a masterful blend of cutting political commentary and driving, spiralling riffs while 'GLAMOUR BOYS' was a playful piece of funk-pop vaguely reminiscent of PRINCE. But it was socially and politically aware material that formed the main thrust of the band's output, 'OPEN LETTER (TO A LANDLORD)' and 'WHICH WAY TO AMERICA' pointedly addressing the oppression of African-Americans to an eclectic, always soulful hard rock backing. The band became critical darlings, figureheads for the loose funk-rock movement that included The RED HOT CHILI PEPPERS and latterly FAITH NO MORE. They also won respect from many fellow musicians, REID contributing to KEITH RICHARDS' 'Talk Is Cheap' album, while the likes of LITTLE RICHARD, CARLOS SANTANA and MACEO PARKER all offered their services for LIVING COLOUR's follow-up effort, 'TIME'S UP' (1990). A wildly eclectic range of styles encompassed everything from hardcore thrash ('TYPE') to the PAUL SIMON ('GRACELAND'-era)-like 'SOLACE OF YOU', even spawning a UK Top 20 single with the meandering blues of 'LOVE REARS ITS UGLY HEAD'. Again the critics frothed although the album failed to match the commercial success of its predecessor. The 'BISCUITS' EP (1991) was a stop gap affair, hardly essential but worth hearing for inspired takes on JAMES BROWN's 'TALKIN' LOUD AND SAYING NOTHING' and HENDRIX's 'BURNING OF THE MIDNIGHT LAMP'. Shortly after the record's release, SKILLINGS departed, his replacement being ex-'Sugarhill' session man and TACKHEAD bassist DOUG WIMBISH. A third album, 'STAIN' (1993), a decidedly harder affair, failed to break any new ground or spark any increase in sales, the band eventually splitting two years later when founder REID decided to pursue solo projects (i.e. the 1996 album, 'MISTAKEN IDENTITY'). • **Covers:** SHOULD I STAY OR SHOULD I GO (Clash) / FINAL SOLUTION (Pere Ubu) / MEMORIES CAN'T WAIT (Talking Heads) / BURNING OF THE MIDNIGHT LAMP (Jimi Hendrix) / TALKING LOUD AND SAYING NOTHING (James Brown) / LOVE AND HAPPINESS (Al Green) / SUNSHINE OF YOUR LOVE (Cream). • **Trivia:** COREY played a smart-assed soldier in the Vietnam film, 'Platoon'.

Album rating: VIVID (*7) / TIME'S UP (*7) / STAIN (*6) / PRIDE: THE GREATEST HITS compilation (*7) / Vernon Reid: MISTAKEN IDENTITY (*4)

COREY GLOVER (b. 6 Nov'64) – vocals / **VERNON REID** (b.22 Aug'58, London, England) – guitar / **MANUEL 'MUZZ' SKILLINGS** (b. 6 Jan'60, Queens, N.Y.) – bass / **WILLIAM CALHOUN** (b.22 Jul'64) – drums

Epic Epic

May 88. (7"/7"sha-pic-d) *(LCL/+P 1)* **MIDDLE MAN. / DESPERATE PEOPLE** [ ] [ ]
(12"+=/pic-cd-s+=) *(LCLT/CPLCL 1)* – Funny vibe.

May 88. (lp/c/cd) *(460 758-1/-4/-2) <44099>* **VIVID** [ ] [6]
– Cult of personality / I want to know / Middle man / Desperate people / Open letter (to a landlord) / Funny vibe / Memories can't wait / Broken hearts / Glamour boys / What's your favourite colour? / Which way to America?

Jul 88. (7"/7"g-f)(7"pic-d) *(LCL/+G 2)(CTLCL 2)* **GLAMOUR BOYS. / WHICH WAY TO AMERICA?** [ ] [ ]
(12"+=/cd-s+=) *(LCLCT/CDLCD 2)* – Middle man / Rap track (conversation with LIVING COLOUR).

Sep 88. (7"/7"s) *(LCL/+B 3)* **CULT OF PERSONALITY. / OPEN LETTER (TO A LANDLORD)** [ ] [ ]
(12"+=/cd-s+=) *(LCLT/CDLCL 3)* – Middle Man (live).

Dec 88. (7"/7"s) *(LCL/+Q 4)* **OPEN LETTER (TO A LANDLORD). / CULT OF PERSONALITY (live)** [ ] [-]
(12"+=/cd-s+=) *(LCLT/CDLCL 4)* – Talkin' 'bout a revolution (live).

Feb 89. (7") *<68611>* **CULT OF PERSONALITY. / FUNNY VIBE** [-] [13]

Apr 89. (7") *(LCL 5)* **CULT OF PERSONALITY. / SHOULD I STAY OR SHOULD I GO** [ ] [-]
(12"+=/cd-s+=) *(LCLT/CDLCL 5)* – What's your favourite colour.

Jun 89. (7") *<68934>* **OPEN LETTER (TO A LANDLORD). / TALKIN' 'BOUT A REVOLUTION** [-] [82]

Oct 89. (7"/7"g-f) *(LCL/+G 6) <68548>* **GLAMOUR BOYS (remix). / CULT OF PERSONALITY (live)** [ ] [31] Aug89
(12"+=) *(LCLT 6)* – Memories can't wait.
(pic-cd-s++=) *(CDLCL 6)* – I don't want to know.
(cd-s+=) *(LCLC 6)* – Middle man (live) / Open letter (to a landlord).

Oct 89. (7") *<73010>* **FUNNY VIBE. / ('A'instrumental)** [-] [ ]

Aug 90. (7") *<73575>* **TYPE. / SHOULD I STAY OR SHOULD I GO** [-] [ ]

Aug 90. (7"/c-s) *(LCL/+M 7)* **TYPE. / FINAL SOLUTION** [75] [-]
(12"+=/cd-s+=) *(LCLGT/CDLCL 7)* – Should I stay or should I go? / Middleman (live).

Sep 90. (cd/c/lp) *(466 920-2/-4/-1) <46202>* **TIME'S UP** [20] [13]
– Time's up / History lesson / Pride / Love rears its ugly head / New Jack theme / Someone like you / Elvis is dead / Type / Information overload / Undercover of darkness / Olozy I / Fight the fight / Tag team partners / Solace of you / This is the life. *(cd+=)* – Final solution (live) / Middle man (live) / Love rears its ugly head (soul power mix).

Jan 91. (7"/7"sha-pic-d/c-s) *(656 593-7/-0/-4) <73677>* **LOVE REARS IT'S UGLY HEAD. / ('A'-Soul power mix)** [12] [ ]
(12"+=) *(656 593-6)* – Type (remix).
(cd-s+=/pic-cd+=) *(656 593-2/-5)* – ('A'version) / Love and happiness.

May 91. (c-s,cd-s) *<73800>* **SOLACE OF YOU / SOMEONE LIKE YOU** [-] [ ]

May 91. (7"/c-s) *(656 908-7/-4)* **SOLACE OF YOU. / NEW JACK THEME** [33] [-]
(12"+=) *(656 908-8)* – Elvis is dead (mix).
(cd-s+=) *(656 908-9)* – ('A'live) / Type (live) / Information overload (live) / Desperate people (live).

Jul 91. (7"/12"/cd-ep) **BURNING OF THE MIDNIGHT LAMP / MEMORIES CAN'T WAIT / TALKING LOUD AND SAYING NOTHING** [-] [ ]

Aug 91. (m-cd) *<47988>* **BISCUITS (live)** [-] [ ]
– Burning of the midnight lamp / Memories can't wait (live) / Talking loud and saying nothing / Desperate people (live) / Money talks / Love and happiness.

Oct 91. (7"/c-s) *(657 535-7/-4)* **THE CULT OF PERSONALITY. / LOVE REARS IT'S UGLY HEAD (live)** [67] [-]
(12"+=) *(657 535-6)* – ('A'live) / Pride (live).
(cd-s+=) *(657 535-2)* – Talkin' loud and saying nothing / Burning of the midnight lamp.

—— MUZZ SKILLINGS departed Nov'91, and was replaced (Jun'92) by **DOUG WIMBUSH** (b.22 Sep'56, Hartford, Connecticut) – bass (ex-GEORGE CLINTON, ex-TACKHEAD)

Feb 93. (7") *(658 976-7)* **LEAVE IT ALONE. / 17 DAYS** [34] [ ]
(12"pic-d+=/cd-s+=) *(658 976-6/-2)* – T.V. news / Hemp (extended).

Feb 93. (cd/c/lp) *(472856-2/-4/-1) <52780>* **STAIN** [19] [26]
– Go away / Ignorance is bliss / Leave it alone / B1 / Mind your own business / Auslander / Never satisfied / Nothingness / Postman / W.T.F.F. / This little pig / Hemp / Wall / T.V. news / Love rears its ugly head (live).

Apr 93. (7"pic-d) *(659 173-7)* **AUSLANDER (remix). / AUSLANDER (Dublander mix)** [53] [ ]
(12"colrd+=/pic-cd-s+=) *(659 173-6/-2)* – Auslander (Radio Days mix) / New Jack theme.

May 93. (7"colrd) *(659 300-7)* **NOTHINGLESS. / 17 DAYS** [ ] [ ]
(cd-s+=) *(659 300-2)* – ('A'remix) / ('A'acoustic mix).

Jan 94. (c-ep) *(660 780-4)* **SUNSHINE OF YOUR LOVE / AUSLANDER (overload mix) / ('A'-Adrian Sherwood & S. McDonald mix)** [ ] [ ]
(cd-ep) *(660 780-2) – (first 2 tracks) / ('A'remix) / Love rears its ugly head (extended).*

—— they disbanded early '95 after poor sales

Nov 95. (cd/c) *(481 021-2/-4) <57698>* **PRIDE – THE GREATEST HITS** (compilation) [ ] [ ]
– Pride / Release the pressure / Sacred ground / Visions / Love rears it's ugly head (soul power remix) / These are happy times / Memories can't wait / Cult of personality / Funny vibe / WTFF / Glamour boys / Open letter (to a landlord) / Solace of you / Nothingless / Type / Time's up / What's your favourite colour? (theme song).

– compilations, etc. –

Jul 00. (cd) *Epic; (498784-2) <65276>* **SUPER HITS** [ ] [ ] Jan98

VERNON REID

—— with various personnel

Jul 96. (cd/c) *<(483921-2/-4)>* **MISTAKEN IDENTITY** [ ] [ ]
– C.P. time / Mistaken identity / You say he's just a psychic friend / Who are you (mutation 1) / Lightnin' / Projects / Uptown drifter / Saint Cobain / Important safety instructions (mutation 2) / What's my name / Signed ficticious / Call waiting to exhale (mutation 3) / My last nerve / Freshwater coconut / Mysterious power / Unborne embrace / Who invited you (mutation 4).

LIVING END

Formed: Melbourne, Australia . . . 1991 as The RUNAWAY BOYS by schoolfriends CHRIS CHENEY and SCOTT OWEN. A STRAY CATS obsessive (presumably the 80's revival started a bit earlier down under), CHENEY turned on his mate to the delights of rockabilly and coerced him into learning acoustic double bass. Together with original drummer JOE PIRIPITSI, the pair graduated to playing sweaty renditions of 'BLUE SUEDE SHOES' at weddings, parties and any other venue that'd have them. A domestic debut EP, 'HELLBOUND' revealed a punk-orientated sound not entirely in keeping with their 50's image yet the group's fortunes began to pick up with the release of follow-up EP, 'IT'S FOR YOUR OWN GOOD'. The record (which featured a cover of The Cure's '10:15 SATURDAY NIGHT' topped the Aussie alternative chart and enjoyed heavy rotation on the native Triple J radio station. With the recruitment of new sticksman from the sticks, TRAVIS DEMPSEY, the band went from strength to strength, touring with BLINK 182 and OFFSPRING. A subsequent double A-side single, 'SECOND SOLUTION' / 'PRISONER OF SOCIETY' went ballistic upon its release in late '97, dominating the airwaves, spending nine months in the Top 40 and eventually notching up sales of a cool quarter million. This homegrown success resulted in a surge of interest from major labels keen to sign the band for Europe and America, the hard-gigging trio throwing in their lot with 'Warners' for their long anticipated, eponymous debut album. Released in 1998, the record went platinum in Australia and if not exactly taking the UK/US charts by storm, saw its good-time late 70's Brit-punk throwback sound garnering decent reviews. Their hearty appetite for live work saw them undertake an extensive world tour after which they returned with sophomore set, 'ROLL ON' (2001). • **Note:** not to be confused with the outfit who released 'Stiff Middle Finger' for 'Last Resort' label in 1996 or the band who issued 'Pow' in '99.

Album rating: HELLBOUND w/ IT'S FOR YOUR OWN GOOD (*5) / THE LIVING END (*6) / ROLL ON (*7)

CHRIS CHENEY – vocals, guitar / **SCOTT OWEN** – double bass / **JOE PIRIPITSI** – drums

Shock / not iss.

Dec 95. (cd-ep) **HELLBOUND** – – Austra
– Traces of doubt / Hellbound / Table top show / The living end / Strange / Headlines / Mispent youth / So lonely. *<US cd-iss. Jun98 on 'Reprise'+=; 47032>* – IT'S FOR YOUR OWN GOOD EP

Rapido / not iss.

Dec 96. (cd-ep) **IT'S FOR YOUR OWN GOOD** – – Austra
– From here on in / English army / One more cell / Stay away from me / Problem / 10:15 Saturday night.

Triple J / not iss.

Sep 97. (7") **PRISONER OF SOCIETY. / SECOND SOLUTION** – – Austra
(above was taken from the 'Liive at The Wireless' radio sessions)

— **TRAVIS DEMPSEY** – drums; repl. JOE

not iss. / E.M.I.

Nov 98. (cd-s) *<86164>* **SAVE THE DAY / LONE RANGER / MR. BUSINESSMAN** –

Reprise / Reprise

May 99. (cd) *<(9362 47280-2)>* **THE LIVING END** Nov98
– Prisoner of society / Growing up (falling down) / Second solution / West end riot / Bloody Mary / Monday / All torn down / Save the day / Trapped / Have they forgotten / Fly away / I want a day / Sleep on it / Closing in.

Sep 99. (c-s) *(W 485C) <44724>* **PRISONER OF SOCIETY / SECOND SOLUTION** Jul99
(cd-s+=) *(W 485CDX)* – Prisoner on the inside / Misspent youth (live) / Strange (live).

Sep 99. (cd-s) *<44752>* **TRAPPED / ALL TORN DOWN / LIVING IN SIN / WITCH DOCTOR** –

Apr 01. (c-s) *(W 552C)* **ROLL ON / PICTURES IN THE MIRROR (live)** –
(cd-s+=) *(W 552CD)* – The man with no name (demo).

Apr 01. (cd) *<(9362 48063-2)>* **ROLL ON** Mar01
– Roll on / Pictures in the mirror / Riot on Broadway / Staring at the light / Carry me home / Don't shut the gate / Dirty man / Blood on your hands / Revolution regained / Silent victory / Read about it / Killing the night / Astoria paranoia / Uncle Harry / Prisoner of society (live).

LIZZY BORDEN

Formed: Los Angeles, California, USA . . . 1983. Taking his/their name from the infamous axe murderess, LIZZY BORDEN was backed by his brother JOEY SCOTT HARGES, TONY MATUZAK and MIKE KENNY. Signed to 'Metal Blade' after contributing a track to the 'Metal Massacre IV' compilation, they debuted with the 1984 mini-set, 'GIVE 'EM THE AXE'. Low-rent metal of the schlock-horror cheap thrills variety, LIZZY BORDEN progressed little from their debut proper, 'LOVE YOU TO PIECES' (another corny play-on-words), to late 80's (Billboard denting) efforts like 'MENACE TO SOCIETY' and 'MASTER OF DISGUISE' (a solo outing). Nevertheless, the band were a popular live draw, at least in their native L.A., the double concert set, 'THE MURDERESS METAL ROADSHOW', slightly sharper than their rather rusty studio efforts.

Album rating: GIVE 'EM THE AXE mini (*4) / LOVE YOU TO PIECES (*5) / THE MURDERESS METAL ROADSHOW (*4) / MENACE TO SOCIETY (*5) / TERROR RISING mini (*4) / VISUAL LIES (*5) / MASTER OF DISGUISE (*5) / THE BEST OF LIZZY BORDEN compilation (*6) / DEAL WITH THE DEVIL (*4)

LIZZY BORDEN – vocals / **TONY MATUZAK** – guitar / **MIKE KENNY** – bass / **JOEY SCOTT HARGES** – drums

Roadrunner / Metal Blade

Nov 84. (m-lp) *<1078>* **GIVE 'EM THE AXE** –
– Give 'em the axe / Kiss of death / No time to lose / Long live rock'n'roll.

Jun 85. (lp) *(RR 9771) <72057>* **LOVE YOU TO PIECES**
– Council for the cauldron / Psychopath / Save me / Red rum / Love you to pieces / American metal / Flesh eater / Warfare / Godiva / Rod of iron. *<(cd-iss. Sep96 on 'Metal Blade'; 3984 14089CD)>*

Mar 86. (d-lp) *(RR 9702)* **THE MURDERESS METAL ROADSHOW (live)**
– Council for the caldron / Flesheater / Warfare / No time to lose / Rod of iron / Save me / Godiva / Psychopath / Love you to pieces / Live and let die / Kiss of death / Red rum / American metal / Give em the axe / Finale / Dead serious / Time to die. *<(cd-iss. Sep96 on 'Metal Blade'; 3984 14092CD)>*

Oct 86. (lp) *(RR 9664) <ST-73224>* **MENACE TO SOCIETY**
– Generation aliens / Notorious / Terror on the town / Bloody Mary / Stiletto (voice of command) / Ultra violence / Love kills / Brass tactics / Ursa minor / Menace to society. *<(cd-iss. Sep96 on 'Metal Blade'; 14090-2)>*

Feb 87. (m-lp) *(RR 9621) <73254>* **TERROR RISING**
– White rabbit / Don't touch me there / Catch your death / Terror rising. *<(cd-iss. Sep96 on 'Metal Blade'+=; 14091-2)>* – GIVE 'EM THE AXE

Sep 87. (lp/cd) *(RR/+34 9592) <73288>* **VISUAL LIES**
– Me against the world / Shock / Outcast / Den of thieves / Visual lies / Eyes of a stranger / Lord of the flies / Voyeur (I'm watching you) / Visions. *<(cd-iss. Sep96 on 'Metal Blade'; 3984 14095CD)>*

Oct 87. (7") *(RR 5472)* **ME AGAINST THE WORLD. /**

Aug 89. (lp/cd; solo) *(RR 9454-1/-2) <73413>* **MASTER OF DISGUISE**
– Master of disguise / One false move / Love is a crime / Sins of the flesh / Phantoms never too young / Be one of us / Psychodrama / Waiting in the wings / Roll over and play dead / Under the rose / We got the power.

— their/his (her?) last offering, until they re-formed with line-up **DAN FITZGERALD** – guitar / **JOEY VERA** – bass / **ALEX NELSON** – guitar + **JOEY SCOTT HARGES** – drums

Metal Blade / Metal Blade

Oct 00. (cd) *<(14343-2)>* **DEAL WITH THE DEVIL**
– There will be blood tonight / Hell is for heroes / Deal with the Devil / Zanzibar / Lovin' you is murder / We only come out at night / Generation landslide / The world is mine / State of pain / Believe.

– compilations, etc. –

May 94. (cd) *Metal Blade; (CDMZORRO 72) <14052>* **THE BEST OF LIZZY BORDEN** Jun94
– Me against the world / Notorious / American metal / Master of disguise / Psychopath / Eyes of a stranger / Red rum (live) / Ultra violence / Live and let die / Give 'em the axe / Love kills / Love is a crim / Lord of the flies / Rod of iron.

LLAMA FARMERS

Formed: Greenwich, London, England . . . 1996 by BERNIE SIMPSON, his 14 year-old sister, JENNI and two other school friends BROOKE ROGERS and WILLIAM BRIGGS who all, apparently in their own words, played in the "shitiest band in the school". Rumour had it that this cheeky punk-pop outfit started their fully-fledged odyssey when ROGERS lied to BERNIE, claiming he could play the drums. After a few gigs in their native town, the band somehow managed to blag themselves a support slot with DAVE GROHL's vehicle The FOO FIGHTERS. The LLAMA's supposedly signed on the dotted line after a record label drinking bash ended in sheer madness. Apparently, they topped the main stage bill in Glastonbury because of their name alone, and managed to convince punters that they were "rockin'" due to the infectiousness of 1998's debut single, 'PAPER EYES'. The LLAMA FARMERS' first album appeared in June 1999 under the R.E.M. parody title, 'DEAD LETTER CHORUS', having already breached the UK Top 75 with singles, 'BIG WHEEL' (their classiest piece so far!) and 'GET THE KEYS AND GO'. However, the aforementioned set didn't possess any range or scope, only wallowing in GREEN DAY-esque silliness. From a band who claimed that they didn't like the SEX PISTOLS, they owed much to the 70's filthy idols. Their use of raw angst punk had turned slightly sour by cliched elderly ethics. 'JESSICA' remained the only true song on the set worth pricking your ears up for, the rest, however, was as tame as Roger Rabbit strumming a noisy guitar.

Album rating: DEAD LETTER CHORUS (*5) / EL TOPPO (*6)

BERNIE SIMPSON – vocals, guitar / **JENNI SIMPSON** – bass, vocals / **WILLIAM BRIGGS** – guitar / **BROOKE ROGERS** – drums

Fierce Panda / not iss.

May 98. (7") *(NING 49)* **PAPER EYES. / PVC** –

Jul 98. (7"/cd-s) *(NING 58/+CD)* **ALWAYS ECHOES. / JESSICA / YELLOW** –

Beggars Banquet / Beggars Banquet

Jan 99. (7") *(BBQ 333)* **BIG WHEELS. / MULTI-COLOURED CURTAINS** 67 –
(cd-s+=) *(BBQ 333CD)* – We've gone wrong.

May 99. (7") *(BBQ 335)* **GET THE KEYS AND GO. / ICE LUNGS** 74 –
(cd-s+=) *(BBQ 335CD)* – Weightless.

Jun 99. (cd/lp) *(BBQ CD/LP 212) <80212>* **DEAD LETTER CHORUS** Nov99
– Get the keys and go / Lull / Pomoco / Zorillo / When we were friends / Big wheels / Jessica / Yellow / P.V.C. / Always echoes / Forgot to breathe / Kill will / Picture.

Aug 99. (7") *(BBQ 338)* **YELLOW. / I DON'T WANT TO TALK ABOUT IT** –
(cd-s+=) *(BBQ 338CD)* – Dead letter chorus.

Apr 00. (7") *(BBQ 345)* **SAME SONG. / MOVIE** –
(cd-s+=) *(BBQ 345CD)* – Reflector.

Sep 00. (7") *(BBQ 346)* **SNOW WHITE. / CERTAIN SQUARE** –
(cd-s+=) *(BBQ 346CD)* – Waz.

Oct 00. (cd/lp) *(BBQ CD/LP 217) <80217>* **EL TOPPO** Jan01
– El Toppo / Snow white / More salt / Dodgy fudge / Postcards and moonrock / Feathers / Note on the door / Same song / Ear the C / You bore me / Movie. *(hidden track+=)* – Do you remember the time, we got drunk and . . .

Feb 01. (7") *(BBQ 351)* **NOTE ON THE DOOR. / LITTLE BUGS** [ ] [-]
(cd-s+=) *(BBQ 351CD)* – 7even twists clockwise / Postcards and moonrocks (XfM session) / Note on the door (XfM session).

LODESTAR

Formed: London, England . . . 1995 by SENSER defectors, HEITHAM AL-SAYED (on vocals), JOHN MORGAN (drums) and HAGGIS (bass). Completing the line-up with new to the fold JULES HODGSON (on guitar), the quartet released what was to become their one and only album, the eponymous 'LODESTAR' in late '96. On this, AL-SAYAD kept his distinctive rap/singing technique that had been a trademark with the mighty SENSER, while their musical sound was both rock and blues orientated.

Album rating: LODESTAR (*6)

HEITHAM AL-SAYED – vocals, percussion / **JOHN MORGAN** – drums / **HAGGIS** – bass / **JULES HODGSON** – guitar

Ultimate not iss.

Sep 96. (7") *(TOPP 046)* **ANOTHER DAY. / FORCE OF HABIT** [ ] [-]
(cd-s) *(TOPP 046CD)* – ('A'side) / All you need / 11-8 Koroviev.

Oct 96. (cd/c/lp) *(TOPP CD/MC/LP 049)* **LODESTAR** [ ] [ ]
– Another day / Salter's ducks / Wait a minute / The representative / By halves / Better late than never / Aftertaste / Worthwhile / Soiled blood / Down in the mud / Lilac crest.

Feb 97. (7") *(FEZ 001)* **DOWN IN THE MUD. / SOMNOPOLIS** [ ] [ ]
(cd-s) *(FEZ 001CD)* – ('A'side) / Neat neat neat / ('A'-Primitive mix) / Horse.

— have since split up

LONDON

Formed: er, London, England . . . early 1977 by RIFF REGAN, DAVE WIGHT, STEVE VOICE and JON MOSS. Signed straight out of obscurity to major label, 'M.C.A.', LONDON made their vinyl debut during the summer of '77 with the hopefully titled 'EVERYONE'S A WINNER', a chart duffer that didn't bode well for future releases. The lightweight punks persevered with a further two forgettable singles, both tracks available on their one and only full-length set, 'ANIMAL GAMES', released early the following year. Although frontman, RIFF REGAN went solo, the band's only claim to fame lies in the fact that JON MOSS subsequently drummed for CULTURE CLUB (after a brief spell with The DAMNED and the more obscure EDGE).

Album rating: ANIMAL GAMES (*3)

RIFF REGAN – vocals / **DAVE WIGHT** – guitar / **STEVE VOICE** – bass / **JON MOSS** – drums

M.C.A. not iss.

Jun 77. (7") *(MCA 305)* **EVERYONE'S A WINNER. / HANDCUFFED** [ ] [-]

Sep 77. (7"ep/12"ep) *(MCA 319/+T)* **SUMMER OF LOVE EP** [ ] [-]
– Summer of love / Friday on my mind / No time / Siouxsie Sue.

Nov 77. (7") *(MCA 336)* **ANIMAL GAMES. / US KIDS COLD** [ ] [-]

Jan 78. (lp) *(MCF 2823)* **ANIMAL GAMES** [ ] [-]
– No time / Reaction / Everyone's a winner / Summer of love / Us kids cold / Young / Good looking girls / Animal games / Out on the skids / Speed speed / Swinging London. *(<cd-iss. Nov97 as 'PUNK ROCK COLLECTION' on 'Captain Oi' +=; AHOYCD 077>)* – Everyone's a winner / Handcuffed / Friday on my mind / Siouxsie Sue.

— they split in 1978, MOSS going off to join The DAMNED before helping to form the EDGE (he subsequently became part of CULTURE CLUB).

RIFF REGAN

Apr 78. (7") *(MCA 363)* **ALL THE NICE BOYS & GIRLS. / STRANGERS** [ ] [-]

Feb 79. (7") *(MCA 406)* **JAPANESE GIRLS. / TERROR BABY** [ ] [-]

Jan 80. (7") *(MCA 548)* **YOU CALL ME LUCKY. / JACOBY ISLAND** [ ] [-]

Mar 80. (7") *(MCA 573)* **THE ONLY ONE. / THE LUCKY DUB** [ ] [-]

Epic not iss.

Apr 81. (7") *(EPCA 1124)* **HARD HEARTS DON'T CRY. / MISS MIDWEST FARMER'S DAUGHTER** [ ] [-]

LONDON

Formed: Hollywood, California, USA . . . 1980 by NADIR D'PRIEST, NIKKI SIXX, LIZZY GREY and BOBBY MARKS (PETER SZUCS also augmented on keyboards). This early incarnation featured in the hard-rock docufilm, 'The Decline Of The Western Civilization Part II – The Metal Years', although it would be five years and a plethora of personnel changes before the band came up with their vinyl debut, 'NON-STOP ROCK' (1985). SIXX had already departed to claim his fame with MOTLEY CRUE (BRIAN WEST was his replacement after BLACKIE LAWLESS – future W.A.S.P – had a brief stint), MARKS also flew the nest, the band finding FRED COURY after STEVEN ADLER became part of GUNS N' ROSES (IZZY STRADLIN and SLASH also played live gigs!). A second album, 'DON'T CRY WOLF' (1987) – co-produced with KIM FOWLEY – was without COURY who had taken up his post in CINDERELLA, although it would be a few years later that LONDON would create their own stir. D'PRIEST, WEST and new recruits SEAN LEWIS and TIM YASUI met Noise International executives while they were at an L.A. party/seminar and the quartet were duly signed up. YASUI soon made way for ex-GIUFFRA drummer, ALAN KRIGGER and LONDON were ready to rock again, this time with one-time STEPPENWOLF producer, Richie Podolor at the controls. 'PLAYA DEL ROCK' (1990), saw LONDON receive rave reviews for their "bad attitude" rock'n'roll style, especially with the epic ballad, 'MISS YOU'. Having paid their dues in the last decade and with the music world beginning to take note, the band surprisingly quit the scene.

Album rating: NON-STOP ROCK (*5) / DON'T CRY WOLF (*5) / PLAYA DEL ROCK (*6)

NADIR D'PRIEST – vocals / **LIZZY GREY** – guitar / **BRIAN WEST** – bass; repl. BLACKIE LAWLESS (to W.A.S.P.) who had repl. NIKKI SIXX who formed MOTLEY CRUE (early 80's) / **FRED COURY** – drums; repl. STEVEN ADLER who repl. BOBBY MARKS

Roadrunner not iss.

Nov 85. (lp) *(RR 9733)* **NON-STOP ROCK** [ ] [-]
– Dirty city / Non-stop rock / Werewolves in London / It's rock and roll / Stand back / No tell motel / Party in Hollywood / Masters of the airwaves / Radio stars.

— **WAILIN' J. MORGAN** – drums; repl. COURY who joined CINDERELLA

Axis Metalhead

May 87. (lp) *(AXISLP 1)* *<MHLP 102>* **DON'T CRY WOLF** [ ] [ ]
– Drop the bomb / Set me free / Hit and run lover / Under the gun / Oh darling / Fast as light / Put out the fire / Killing time / We want everything / For whom the bell tolls.

— **SEAN LEWIS** – guitar; repl. GREY

— **ALAN KRIGGER** – drums (ex-GIUFFRA) repl. TIM YASUI who repl. MORGAN

— added **VINCE GILBERT** – keyboards

Noise Int. Noise Int.

Jun 90. (lp) *(NUK 143)* **PLAYA DEL ROCK** [ ] [ ]
– Ride you through the night / Russian winter / It's so easy / Miss you / Money honey / Love games / Heart beat (it's all right) / Hot child in the city / The wall (13-61) / Been around before.

— disbanded some time in the early 90's

LONE STAR

Formed: Cardiff, Wales . . . mid 1975 by ex-UFO guitarist PAUL CHAPMAN, who recruited other Brit-pack musicians KENNY DRISCOLL, TONY SMITH, RICK WORSNOP, PETER HURLEY and DIXIE LEE. Signed to 'C.B.S.', they subsequently secured a support slot with TED NUGENT, gaining enough exposure to ensure healthy sales for their UK charting eponymous debut (produced by ROY THOMAS BAKER) in 1976. With a heavy pomp-rock sound not too far removed from 'ZEPPELIN, early QUEEN or DEEP PURPLE, the group digressed from their trademark fantasy-based lyrics for a cover of The Beatles' 'SHE SAID, SHE SAID'. With frontman JOHN SLOMAN having stepped in for DRISCOLL, the group completed a second set, 'FIRING ON ALL SIX' (1977) and although this scored a higher chart position, the album failed to live up to its title. Unfortunately, LONE STAR were just a few years out of time; punk was at its zenith, while NWOBHM was just around the corner, thus the group's inevitable demise. Most members went on to bigger and better things.

Album rating: LONE STAR (*6) / FIRING ON ALL SIX (*5)

KENNY DRISCOLL – vocals / **PAUL CHAPMAN** – guitar (ex-UFO) / **TONY SMITH** – guitar / **RICK WORSNOP** – keyboards / **PETER HURLEY** – bass / **DIXIE LEE** – drums

C.B.S. C.B.S.

Aug 76. (lp) *(CBS 81545)* *<34475>* **LONE STAR** [47] [ ]
– She said, she said / Lonely soldier / Flying in the reel / Spaceships / A new day / A million stars / Illusions. *(cd-iss. Jul96 on 'Columbia'; 484422-2)*

Nov 76. (7") *(CBS 4751)* **SHE SAID, SHE SAID. / ILLUSIONS** [ ] [ ]

— **JOHN SLOMAN** – vocals (ex-TRAPPER) repl. DRISCOLL (he later re-formed the band)

Aug 77. (7") *(CBS 5520)* **HYPNOTIC MOVER. / ALL OF US TO ALL OF YOU** [ ] [ ]

Aug 77. (lp) *(CBS 82213)* *<34937>* **FIRING ON ALL SIX** [36] [ ]
– The bells of Berlin / The ballad of crafty Jack / Time lays down / Hypnotic mover / Lovely Lubina / Seasons in your eyes / Rivers overflowing / All of us to all of you.

Oct 77. (7") *(CBS 5707)* **SEASONS IN YOUR EYES. / LOVELY LUBINA** [ ] [ ]

— Broke up late 1978 when CHAPMAN re-joined UFO. SLOMAN later joined URIAH HEEP and DIXIE LEE replaced KENNY JONES in WILD HORSES.

– compilations, etc. –

Apr 93. (cd) *Beat Goes On; (BGOCD 183)* **LONE STAR / FIRING ON ALL SIX** [ ] [-]

May 94. (cd) *Windsong; (WINCD 059)* **BBC 1 LIVE IN CONCERT (live)** [ ] [-]

Jon LORD (see under ⇒ DEEP PURPLE)

LORDS OF THE NEW CHURCH (see under ⇒ DEAD BOYS)

Inger LORRE (see under ⇒ NYMPHS)

LOUDNESS

Formed: Tokyo, Japan . . . late 70's by MINORU NIIHARA, AKIRA TAKASAKI, MASAYOSHI YAMASHITA and MUNETAKA HIGUCHI. Throughout the 80's, this English-speaking, girlie looking 4-piece (pre-ladyboys, of course!) released many a hard rockin' set, the most successful of which was 1986's 'LIGHTNING STRIKES', a Top 75 entry in America of all places.

Album rating: THE BIRTHDAY EVE (*5) / DEVIL SOLDIER (*5) / THE LAW OF THE DEVIL'S LAND (*5) / LIVE – LOUD – ALIVE (*5) / DISSOLUTION (*5) / THUNDER IN THE EAST (*6) / LIGHTNING STRIKES (*6) / 8186 LIVE (*5) / HURRICANE EYES (*4) / JEALOUSY (*4) / SOLDIER OF FORTUNE (*3) / ON THE PROWL (*3)

MINORU NIIHARA – vocals / **AKIRA TAKASAKI** – guitar / **MASAYOSHI YAMASHITA** – bass / **MUNETAKA HIGUCHI** – drums

Blow Up / not iss.

1981. (lp) *(AF 7085)* **THE BIRTHDAY EVE** [-] [-] Japan
– Loudness / Sexy woman / Open your eyes / Street woman / To be demon / I'm on fire / High try / Rock shock (more and more). *(Dutch-iss.1984 on 'Roadrunner'; RR 9897)*

Denon / not iss.

1982. (lp) **DEVIL SOLDIER** [-] [-] Japan
– Lonely player / Angel dust / After illusion / Girl / Hard workin' / Loving maid / Rock the nation / Devil soldier. *(Dutch-iss.1984 on 'Roadrunner'; RR 9896)*

1983. (lp) *(7559)* **THE LAW OF THE DEVIL'S LAND** [-] [-] Japan
– Theme of Loudness (part 2) / In the mirror / Show me the way / I wish you were here / Mr. Yes man / The law of the Devil's hand / Black wall / Sleepless night / Speed. *(Dutch-iss.1984 on 'Roadrunner'; RR 9895)*

1984. (d-lp) *(7943/4)* **LIVE – LOUD – ALIVE (live)** [-] [-] Japan
– Opening theme / In the mirror / Roadracer / I was the sun / Fly away / Black wall / Tusk of jaguar – drum solo / Mr. Yes man / Exploder – Heavenward / Loudness / Sleepless night / Speed / Shinkiro / Burning love / Ending theme.

Music For Nations / Atco

Jun 84. (12") *(12KUT 110)* **ROADRACER. / SHINKIRO** [ ] [-]

Jun 84. (lp/c) *(MFN/CMFN 22)* **DISSOLUTION** [ ] [-]
– Crazy doctor / Esper / Butterfly / Revelation / Exploder / Dream fantasy / Milky Way / Satisfaction guaranteed / Aries' lament. *(cd-iss. 1988 on 'Denon'; C38 7134)*

Mar 85. (lp) *(MFN 38)* <90246> **THUNDER IN THE EAST** [ ] [74] Feb85
– Crazy nights / Like Hell / Heavy chains / Get away / We could be together / Run for your life / Clockwork toy / No way out / The lines are down / Never change your mind.

Atco / Atco

Jul 86. (lp) *(790512-1)* <90512> **LIGHTNING STRIKES** [ ] [64] May86
– Let it go / Dark desire / 1000 eyes / Face to face / Who knows / Ashes in the sky / Black star oblivion / Street life dream / Complication. *(cd-iss. Dec86; 790512-2)*

Oct 86. (7") *(B 9498)* **LET IT GO. / 1000 NIGHTS** [ ] [ ]
(12"+=) *(B 9498T)* – Ashes in the sky.

1986. (d-cd) *<55XD 518-9>* **8186 LIVE (live)** [-] [ ]
– Loudness / Rock shock / Dark desire / Streetlife dreams / Crazy doctor / Geraldine / Bass – solo / Drums – solo / Shadows of war (ashes in the sky) / Let it go / 1000 eyes / Face to face / Aries' lament / In the mirror / Guitar – solo / Crazy night / Speed / Farewell.

Aug 87. (lp/c) *(790619-1/-4)* <90619> **HURRICANE EYES** [ ] [ ]
– S.D.I. / This lonely heart / Rock'n'roll gypsy / In my dreams / Take me home / Strike of the sword / Rock this way / In this world beyond / Hungry hunter / So lonely.

1988. (m-cd) *<25XD 995>* **JEALOUSY** [-] [ ]
– Jealousy / Long distance love / Good things going / Die of hunger / Heavier than Hell / Dreamer and schemer.

— **MIKE VESCERA** – vocals; repl. MINORU

Sep 89. (lp/c/cd) *(791283-1/-4/-2)* <91283> **SOLDIER OF FORTUNE** [ ] [ ]
– Danger of love / You shook me / Demon disease / Soldier of fortune / 25 days from home / Faces in the fire / Red light shooter / Run for cover / Long after midnight / Lost without your love.

not iss. / WEA

1991. (cd) *<9031 73694-2>* **ON THE PROWL** [-] [ ]
– Down 'n' dirty / Playin' games / Love toys / Never again / Deadly player / Take it or leave it / Girl / Long distance / In the mirror / Sleepless night / Find a way.

LOUDSPEAKER

Formed: New York, USA . . . 1986 out of 'Alternative Tentacles' combo, The CRUCIFUCKS (singer – DOC CORBIN DART), a controversially named hardcore/punk act with subsequent LOUDSPEAKER hailers, MATT BORRUSO and CHRISTOPHER DOUGLAS. Enlisting former PUSSY GALORE member, KURT WOLF and ex-RHYTHM & NOISE merchant, CHARLES HANSON, the band delivered a one-off 1987 debut single for UK's 'One Little Indian', 'PSYCHOTIC MACHINE'. Resurfacing in the early 90's with singles on 'Sympathy For The Record Industry' and 'Lung', LOUDSPEAKER also delivered their long-awaited debut album, entitled 'SUPERNATURAL' (1992). However, the group went AWOL yet again, only to return with the 1996 follow-up, 'RE-VERTEBRATE'.

Album rating: SUPERNATURAL (*4) / RE-VERTEBRATE (*4) / Crucifucks: THE CRUCIFUCKS (*4) / WISCONSIN (*6)

CRUCIFUCKS

DOC CORBIN DART – vocals / **JAKE** – guitar / **MATT BORRUSO** – bass / **CHRIS DOUGLAS** – drums

Alternative Tentacles / Alternative Tentacles

Dec 84. (lp) *<(VIRUS 38)>* **THE CRUCIFUCKS** [ ] [ ]
– Democracy spawns bad taste / Go bankrupt and die / You give me the creeps / Marching for trash / Legal genocide / I am the establishment / Cops for fertilizer / Hinkley had a vision / By the door / Oh where, oh where? / I was / Similar items / Official terrorism / No one can make me play along with this / Down on my kness.

— **CHRIS DOUGLAS** – drums; repl. SHELLEY who joined SONIC YOUTH

Dec 85. (lp) *<(VIRUS 53)>* **WISCONSIN** [ ] [ ]
– Annual report – Intro / Mountain song / Washington / Resurrection / Earth by invitation only / Laws against laughing / Pig in a blanket / When the top comes off / Concession stand / Wisconsin / Artificial competition / Holiday parade / Savior.

Feb 92. (cd) *<(VIRUS 111)>* **OUR WILL BE DONE** (compilation of above albums) [ ] [ ]

— DART released a solo set, 'PATRICIA', in 1990

LOUDSPEAKER

— **MATT + CHRISTOPHER** plus **KURT WOLF** – guitar (ex-PUSSY GALORE) / **CHARLES HANSON** – bass (ex-RHYTHM & NOISE)

One Little Indian / unknown

Apr 87. (12") *(12TP 5)* **PSYCHOTIC MACHINE. / LIVING WITH THE DEAD** [ ] [ ]

EFA / Patois

Feb 92. (cd) *(EFA 16821CD)* <004> **SUPERNATURAL** [ ] [ ]

— had US singles issued on 'Lung' & 'Sympathy For The Record Industry'

1990's. (7") *<SFTRI 105>* **PRAY. /** [-] [ ]

1990's. (7") *<SFTRI 218>* **KNOCKOUT. /** [-] [ ]
(UK-iss.Jul98; same)

not iss. / Sympathy F

Apr 95. (12"ep) *<SFTRI 285>* **RUBBERNECKERS VS. TAI** [-] [ ]

Another Planet / Another Planet

Jul 96. (cd) *<(AP 6020-2)>* **RE-VERTEBRATE** [ ] [ ]
– California son / Vaporize / Scientific / (Don't) Kill the messenger / Rerun / Supermantra / Lit / April fool / X-ray / Twin / Bassman 10.

CRUCIFUCKS

— re-formed with DART + BREHER

Alternative Tentacles / Alternative Tentacles

Sep 96. (m-cd/m-lp) *<VIRUS 186>* **L.D. EYE** [-] [ ]
– The L.D. eye theme / Lights over Baghdad / The story of Thomas McElwee / Suicide / Officer Powell / Artificial girl / Jeanetta Jones.

LOVE/HATE

Formed: Los Angeles, California, USA . . . mid-80's by JIZZY PEARL, JON E. LOVE, main writer SKID ROSE and JOEY GOLD. Signed by 'C.B.S.', LOVE/HATE (self-proclaimed as the "Stoopidest band in the world"), exploded onto the metal scene in Spring 1990, with the acclaimed 'BLACKOUT IN THE RED ROOM' (1990). A kaleidoscopic starburst of colour and sleazy, funky, doped-up Cali-metal, LOVE/HATE took the best bits of GUNS N' ROSES / FAITH NO MORE and injected them with a manic energy and low-rent strut. While LOVE/HATE's pet obsessions with sex, drugs and alcohol, didn't exactly make for original songwriting themes, there was an undercurrent of narcotic strangeness and irrepressible abandon to much of their material, making the likes of 'TUMBLEWEED', 'FUEL TO RUN' and 'STRAIGHTJACKET' compelling listening. Despite rave reviews, the album inexplicably failed to take off and LOVE/HATE had to content themselves with playing small sweaty dives, while working on material for a follow-up, 'WASTED IN AMERICA' (1992). Not as consistently thrilling as the debut, the record nevertheless consolidated the group's standing as the sultans off scuzz-glam. Unfortunately, the record buying public thought differently, LOVE/HATE promptly dropped when the record yet again failed to launch the group into the major league. A pity, as subsequent albums, 'LET'S RUMBLE' (1993; released on 'R.C.A.') and 'I'M NOT HAPPY' (1995; released on S.P.V.), indicated that LOVE/HATE were losing their inimitable spark. • **Covered:** I AM THE WALRUS (Beatles).

Album rating: BLACKOUT IN THE RED ROOM (*8) / WASTED IN AMERICA (*7) / LET'S RUMBLE (*4) / I'M NOT HAPPY (*4) / LIVIN' OFF LAYLA (*4) / LET'S EAT (*4) / GREATEST AND LATEST collection (*5)

JIZZY PEARL – vocals / **JON E. LOVE** – guitar / **SKID ROSE** – bass / **JOEY GOLD** – drums

C.B.S. / Columbia

Apr 90. (cd/c/lp) *(466 350-2/-4/-1)* <45263> **BLACK OUT IN THE RED ROOM** [ ] [ ]
– Black out in the red room / Rock queen / Tumbleweed / Why do you think they call it dope? / Fuel to run / One more round / She's an angel / Mary Jane / Straightjacket / Slutsy tipsy / Slave girl / Hell, CA. pop 4.

Apr 90. (7"/c-s) *(655 917-7/-4)* **BLACK OUT IN THE RED ROOM. / HELL, CA. POP 4** [ ] [-]
(12"+=/12"pic-d+=/cd-s+=) *(655 917-6/-5-2)* – Tinseltown / Slutsy tipsy.

Aug 90. (7") *(656 112-7)* **SHE'S AN ANGEL. / ONE MORE ROUND** [ ] [-]
(12"+=/cd-s+=) *(656 112-6/-2)* – One more round (live) / Slave girl (live).

Columbia / Columbia

Nov 91. (7") *(657 596-7)* **EVIL TWIN. / YUCCA MAN** [59] [-]
(12"+=/cd-s+=) *(657 596-6/-2)* – I am the snake / Why do you think they call it dope (live).

Feb 92. (cd/c/lp) *(469 453-2/-4/-1)* <46226> **WASTED IN AMERICA** [20] [ ]
– Wasted in America / Spit / Miss America / Cream / Yucca man / Happy hour / Tranquilizer / Time's up / Don't fuck with me / Don't be afraid / Social sidewinder / Evil twin.

Mar 92. (7") *(657 889-7)* **WASTED IN AMERICA. / CASTLES FROM SAND** [38] [-]
(12"+=/cd-s+=) *(657 889-6/-2)* – Soul house tales.

— **DARREN HOUSHOLDER** – guitar; repl. LOVE

R.C.A. / Calibre

Jul 93. (cd/c) *(74321 15311-2/-4/-1)* <1005> **LET'S RUMBLE** [24] [ ] Apr94
– Let's rumble / Spinning wheel / Boozer / Wrong side of the grape / Devil's squaw / Beer money / Here's to you / Sexical / Miracles / Flower.

— **LOVE** returned to repl. HOUSHOLDER

S.P.V. Mayhem

Dec 95. (cd) *(SPV 0851822-2)* <11078> **I'M NOT HAPPY** [ ] [ ] Sep95
– Superfragilistic / Hey man / I'm not happy / The end / Ola mola / Die / Cutting chain / Searchers / We do what we do / Night crawler / Love me down / Lady Jane / I am the walrus.

SK-9 not iss.

Jul 97. (cd) *(6934225)* **LIVIN' OFF LAYLA** [ ] [-]
– Driver / Walk on / Wire / Low branches / Hit the wall / Rubberina / Explode / Downer / Boom boom boom / Thousand faces / Wish I had more time / It shines.

— **JEFF SIMON** – bass; repl. SKID

Perris Perris

Jun 99. (cd) <*(LH3 1001-2)*> **LET'S EAT** [ ] [ ]
– It could happen to me / Don't play your guitar when you're talkin' / Ratboy / Walk on the Moon / No regrets / Heartbreaker / Wrestle the world / Food for the fire.

— it looked all over when JIZZY joined L.A. GUNS

– compilations, etc. –

Jun 00. (cd) *Anagram; (CDMZEB 14) / Cleopatra; (CLP 827>* **GREATEST AND LATEST: THE VERY BEST OF LOVE/HATE** [ ] [ ] Apr00
– Boozer / Yucca man / Tumbleweed / Fuel / Spinning wheel / Superfragilistic / Angel / Dope / Wasted in America / Black out / Driver / Walk on / Wish I had more time.

LOVERBOY

Formed: Vancouver, Canada . . . 1978 by MIKE RENO and PAUL DEAN, veterans of the Canadian rock scene. With a 'C.B.S.' deal in the offing, the group subsequently recruited DOUG JOHNSON, SCOTT SMITH and MATT FRENETTE to complete the line-up, releasing their Bruce Fairbairn-produced debut in Summer '81. The eponymous album narrowly missed the US Top 10, its glossy, insidiously infectious arena-rock and teen dream lyrics striking a chord in the American market and spawning such definitive LOVERBOY singles as 'THE KID IS HOT TONITE' and 'TURN ME LOOSE'. While they didn't exactly push the parameters of rock music, the group were nothing if not reliable, a follow-up set, 'GET LUCKY' (1982), and a third effort, 'KEEP IT UP' (1983), providing another double-punch, multi-platinum fix of FM/MTV-friendly pop/rock. Massive in their native Canada and the States, the group's fluffy sound nevertheless failed to catch on in the UK, perhaps the reason why they took a harder-edged approach on 1985's 'LOVIN' EVERY MINUTE OF IT'. The record failed to sell as well as its immediate predecessors and the group reunited with Fairbairn for 'WILDSIDE' (1987), an album which saw writing contributions from the likes of fellow pop-metaller, JON BON JOVI and BRYAN ADAMS. Despite a huge hit with the 'NOTORIOUS' single, the album failed to reach the Top 40 and after fulfilling touring commitments, LOVERBOY split voluntarily in Spring '88. DEAN went on to release a solo set, 'HARD CORE' (1989), while 'C.B.S.' issued a compilation ('BIG ONES') the same year containing a handful of new tracks. The group eventually reformed in the early 90's, resuming their dedicated touring schedule although new material has yet to surface. LOVERBOY rekindled their careers in 1997 by delivering one more album, 'VI'.

Album rating: LOVERBOY (*6) / GET LUCKY (*6) / KEEP IT UP (*6) / LOVIN' EVERY MINUTE OF IT (*6) / WILDSIDE (*4) / BIG ONES compilation (*7) / LOVERBOY CLASSICS compilation (*7) / VI (*4)

MIKE RENO (b. RYNOSKI) – vocals (ex-MOXY) / **PAUL DEAN** (b.19 Feb'46) – lead guitar (ex-STREETHEART) / **DOUG JOHNSON** – keyboards / **SCOTT SMITH** – bass / **MATT FRENETTE** – drums

C.B.S. Columbia

Feb 81. (7") *(CBS 9577)* <11421> **TURN ME LOOSE. / PRISSY PRISSY** [ ] [35] Jan81
(re-iss. Jul81; A 1371)

Jun 81. (7") <02068> **THE KID IS HOT TONITE. / TEENAGE OVERDOSE** [-] [55]

Jul 81. (lp/c) *(CBS/40 84798)* <36762> **LOVERBOY** [ ] [13] Jan81
– The kid is hot tonight / Turn me loose / Always on my mind / Lady of the 80's / Little girl / Prissy Prissy / D.O.A. / It don't matter / Teenage overdose. *(cd-iss. 1988; CD 84798)*

Jan 82. (7") *(A 1778)* <02589> **WORKING FOR THE WEEKEND. / EMOTIONAL** [ ] [29] Nov81

Feb 82. (lp/c) *(CBS/40 85402)* <37638> **GET LUCKY** [ ] [7] Nov81
– Working for the weekend / When it's over / Jump / Gangs in the street / Emotional / Lucky ones / It's your life / Take me to the top / Watch out. *(cd-iss. Jul89; CD 85402)*

Mar 82. (12") *(A 2212)* **WORKING FOR THE WEEKEND. / TURN ME LOOSE** [ ] [-]

Apr 82. (7") <02815> **WHEN IT'S OVER. / IT'S YOUR LIFE** [-] [26]

— (above featured backing vocals by NANCY WILSON of HEART)

Jun 82. (7") <03054> **LUCKY ONES. / GANGS IN THE STREET** [-] [ ]

Feb 83. (7") <03108> **THE KID IS HOT TONIGHT. / TURN ME LOOSE** [-] [ ]

Apr 83. (7") <03846> **JUMP. / TAKE ME TO THE TOP** [-] [ ]

Jun 83. (7"/12") *(A/TA 3365)* <03941> **HOT GIRLS IN LOVE. / MELTDOWN** [ ] [11]

Aug 83. (lp/c) *(CBS/40 25436)* <38703> **KEEP IT UP** [ ] [7] Jun83
– Hot girls in love / Strike zone / It's never easy / Chance of a lifetime / Queen of the broken hearts / Prime of your life / Passion pit / One-sided love affair / Meltdown. *(cd-iss. 1988)*

Sep 83. (7") <04096> **QUEEN OF THE BROKEN HEARTS. / CHANCE OF A LIFETIME** [-] [34]

Oct 83. (7") *(A 3705)* **QUEEN OF THE BROKEN HEARTS. / LUCKY ONES** [ ] [-]
(d7"+=) *(DA 3705)* – Chance of a lifetime.

Sep 85. (7") *(A 6514)* <05569> **LOVIN' EVERY MINUTE OF IT. / BULLET IN THE CHAMBER** [ ] [9] Aug85

Oct 85. (lp/c) *(CBS/40 26573)* <39953> **LOVIN' EVERY MINUTE OF IT** [ ] [13] Sep85
– Lovin' every minute of it / Steal the thunder / This could be the night / Friday night / Too much too soon / Dangerous / Lead a double life / Destination heartbreak / Bullet in the chamber.

Nov 85. (7") <05711> **DANGEROUS. / TOO MUCH TOO SOON** [-] [65]

Feb 86. (7") *(A 6950)* <05765> **THIS COULD BE THE NIGHT. / IT'S YOUR LIFE** [ ] [10] Jan86

Apr 86. (7") <05867> **LEAD A DOUBLE LIFE. / STEAL THE THUNDER** [-] [68]

Jan 87. (7") *(650 144-7)* <06178> **HEAVEN IN YOUR EYES. / FRIDAY NIGHT** [ ] [12] Jul86
(12"+=) *(650 144-6)* – Lovin' every minute of it.

Sep 87. (7"/7"pic-d) *(651 060-7/-0)* <07324> **NOTORIOUS. / WILD SIDE** [ ] [38] Aug87
(12"+=) *(651 060-6)* – Turn me loose / Emotional.

Sep 87. (lp/c/cd) *(460 045-1/-4/-2)* <40893> **WILDSIDE** [ ] [42]
– Notorious / Walkin' on fire / Break it to me gently / Can't get much better / Love will rise again / Hometown hero / Read my lips / Don't let go / That's where my money goes.

Dec 87. (7") <07652> **READ MY LIPS. / LOVE WILL RISE AGAIN** [-] [ ]

Mar 88. (7") *(651 459-7)* **BREAK IT TO ME GENTLY. / READ MY LIPS** [ ] [-]
(12"+=/cd-s+=) *(651 459-6/-2)* – Working for the weekend.

— disbanded when JOHNSON departed; PAUL DEAN also went solo releasing the album, 'HARD CORE'.

— LOVERBOY re-formed for a one-one in 1996/7

not iss. C.M.C.

Sep 97. (cd) <86220> **VI** [-] [ ]
– Big picture / Love of money / Secrets / Waiting for the night / Nobody cares / Goodbye angel / Create a monster / Hair of the dog / Maybe someday / Spinnin' my wheels / So much for love / Tortured.

– compilations, etc. –

Dec 89. (c-s,cd-s) *Columbia;* <73066> **TOO HOT. / WHEN IT'S OVER** [-] [84]

Jan 90. (lp/c/cd) *Columbia; (466 006-1/-4/-2)* <45411> **BIG ONES** [ ] [ ] Dec89
– Working for the weekend / For you / The kid is hot tonite / Lovin' every minute of it / Lucky ones / This could be the night / Hot girls in love / Turn me loose / Too hot / Ain't looking for love / Notorious / Take me to the top.

Oct 94. (cd) *Columbia;* <66648> **LOVERBOY CLASSICS: THEIR GREATEST HITS** [-] [ ]
– Turn me loose / Working for the weekend / Take me to the top / Kid is hot tonite / This could be the night / Jump / Lovin' every minute of it / Notorious / Almost paradise / Lucky ones / Destination heartbreak / Hot girls in love / When it's over / It's your life / Gangs in the street / Heaven in your eyes.

Apr 95. (cd) *Sony;* <24191> **TEMPERATURE'S RISING** [-] [ ]

Aug 97. (cd) *Sony;* <65272> **SUPER HITS** [-] [ ]

Jun 01. (cd) *Sony;* <62083> **LIVE, LOUD & LOOSE: 1982-1986** [-] [ ]

L7

Formed: Los Angeles, California, USA . . . 1986 by DONITA SPARKS (guitar/vocals) and SUZI GARDNER (guitar/vocals). Recruiting seasoned L.A. punk veteran JENNIFER FINCH on bass and drummer ANNE ANDERSON, the band signed for the small 'Epitaph' label. The feisty punk-metal noise of their 1988 eponymous debut attracted the attention of the now-famous 'Sub Pop' label the following year, DEE PLAKAS replacing ANDERSON and 'SMELL THE MAGIC' (1990) fuelling the band's growing cult reputation. 1990 also saw the girls touring with a relatively unknown NIRVANA, L7's infamous onstage antics almost causing as much of a stir as the headliners. The band were soon snapped up by 'Slash', hitting the UK Top 20 in 1992 with the pop-grunge of the 'PRETEND WE'RE DEAD' single. This was closely followed by the 'BRICKS ARE HEAVY' album, a hard hitting collision of girl power grunge and ultra hard line, often humorous, post-feminist lyrics. The band caused further uproar later that year when DONITA exposed her womanly charms on 'The Word', having already blessed that year's Reading Festival audience with a used tampon. Irreverant yet committed, L7 also formed 'Rock For Choice', a pro-abortion pressure group which won unprecedented support in the male-dominated environs of the music business. 'HUNGRY FOR STINK' (1994) was equally blistering, the frenetic 'FUEL MY FIRE' later covered by The PRODIGY on their landmark 'THE FAT OF THE LAND' album. 'THE BEAUTY PROCESS: TRIPLE PLATINUM' (1997) marked FINCH's final fling with the band before she left to form LYME, the record's move into harder rocking territory signalling a new era for L7 as they attempted to chart the uncertain waters of the post-grunge era. With first GRETA BRINKMAN and then GAIL GREENWOOD at the helm, they went on to record 'SLAP-HAPPY' (1999), an album which came in for some critical flak for sounding too one dimensional. More satisfying for longtime fans was the live set, 'OMAHA TO OSAKA', a visceral aural document culled from various Japanese club dates. • **Songwriters:** Group or SPARKS penned except THREE DAYS (Willie Nelson).

Album rating: L7 (*6) / SMELL THE MAGIC mini (*6) / BRICKS ARE HEAVY (*8) / HUNGRY FOR STINK (*6) / THE BEAUTY PROCESS: TRIPLE PLATINUM (*6) / FROM OSAKA TO OMAHA (*6) / SLAP-HAPPY (*6) / THE BEST OF L7 compilation (*7)

DONITA SPARKS (b. 8 Apr'63, Chicago, Illinois) – vocals, guitar / **SUZI GARDNER** (b. 1 Aug'60, Altus, Oklahoma) – guitar, vocals / **JENNIFER FINCH** (b. 5 Aug'66) – bass, vocals / **ANNE ANDERSON** (b.Chicago) – drums repl.by **ROY KOUTSKY**

not iss. Epitaph

Dec 88. (lp/c/cd) *<E 86401-1/-4/-2>* **L7** [-] [ ]
– Bite the wax tadpole / Cat-o'-nine-tails / Metal stampede / Let's rock tonight / Uncle Bob / Snake handler / Runnin' from the law / Cool out / It's not you / I drink / Ms. 45. *(UK-iss.Jun92; same)*

— **(DEMETRA) DEE PLAKAS** (b. 9 Nov'60, Chicago) – drums repl. ROY

Glitterhouse Sub Pop

Jan 90. (7",7"green) *<SP 58>* **SHOVE. / PACKIN' A ROD** [-] [ ]
(UK-iss.Jan91 on 'Sub Pop'; EFA 08105)

Nov 90. (12"ep,12"purple-ep) *<(SP 79)>* **SMELL THE MAGIC** [ ] [ ] Aug90
– Shove / Til the wheels fall off / Fast'n'frightening / (Right on) Thru / Deathwish / Broomstick. *(cd-ep Oct95+= ; SPCD 79)* – Packin' a rod / Just like me / American society.

Slash Slash

Mar 92. (7"red/c-s) *(LASH/LACS 34)* **PRETEND WE'RE DEAD. / SHIT LIST** [21] [ ]
(12"+=/cd-s+=) *(LASHX/LASCD 34)* – Lopsided head / Mr. Integrity.

Apr 92. (cd/c/lp) *(828 307-2/-4/-1) <26784>* **BRICKS ARE HEAVY** [24] [ ]
– Wargasm / Scrap / Pretend we're dead / Diet pill / Everglade / Slide / One more thing / Mr. Integrity / Monster / Shit list / This ain't pleasure.

May 92. (7"green) *(LASH 36)* **EVERGLADE. / FREAK MAGNET** [27] [ ]
(12"+=/cd-s+=) *(LASHXP/LASHCD 36)* – Scrap.

Sep 92. (7"/c-s) *(LASH/LACS 38)* **MONSTER. / USED TO LOVE HIM** [33] [ ]
(12"+=/cd-s+=) *(LASHX/LASCD 38)* – Diet pill.

Nov 92. (7"/c-s) *(LASH/LACS 42)* **PRETEND WE'RE DEAD. / FAST 'N' FRIGHTENING (live)** [50] [-]
(cd-s+=) *(LASCD 42)* – (Right on) Thru / Shove / Shit list / Diet pill.

— L7 appeared as CAMEL LIPS group in the film 'Serial Mom'.

Jun 94. (7"colrd/12"colrd) *(LASH/LASCS 48)* **ANDRES. / BOMB** [34] [ ]
(cd-s+=) *(LASCD 48)* – (KRXT radio interview).

Jul 94. (cd/c/lp) *<(828 531-2/-4/-1)>* **HUNGRY FOR STINK** [26] [ ]
– Andres / Baggage / Can I run / The bomb / Questioning my sanity / Riding with a movie star / Stuck here again / Fuel my fire / Freak magnet / She has eyes / Shirley / Talk box.

— After recording 1996 album, FINCH left to form LYME. She was repl. by **GRETA BRINKMAN** who appeared on next album, before **GAIL GREENWOOD** (ex-BELLY) took over

Feb 97. (cd/c) *<(828 868-2/-4)>* **THE BEAUTY PROCESS: TRIPLE PLATINUM** [ ] [ ]
– Beauty process / Drama / Off the wagon / I need / Moonshine / Bitter wine / Masses are asses / Bad things / Must have more / Non existant Patricia / Me, myself and I / Lorenza, Giada, Alessandra / Guera.

Feb 97. (c-s/cd-s) *<17403/43834>* **OFF THE WAGON / GUERA / PUNK BROKE (MY HEART)** [-] [ ]

Man's Ruin Man's Ruin

Jan 99. (cd) *<(MR 146CD)>* **FROM OSAKA OR OMAHA** [ ] [ ] Dec98
– L7 medley – Overture: Fast and frightening / Bad things / Must have more / Deathwish / Slide / Bitter wine / Drama / Non-existant Patricia / Pattylean / El Whatusi / Shitlist / Andres / Fast and frightening / Off the wagon / Little one / Lorenza, Giada, Allesandra.

Bongload Bongload

Aug 99. (cd/lp) *<(BL 43 CD/V)>* **SLAP-HAPPY**
– Crackpot baby / On my rockin' machine / Lackey / Human / Livin' large / Freeway / Stick to the plan / War with you / Long green / Little one / Freezer burn / Mantra down.

– compilations, etc. –

Mar 00. (cd) *Slash; <(8573 82064-2)>* **THE BEST OF L7: THE SLASH YEARS** [ ] [ ] May00
– Pretend we're dead / Mr Integrity / Monster / Everglade / Andres / Fuel my fire / Freak magnet / Can I run / Bad things / Off the wagon / Moonshine / Bitter wine.

LUCIFER'S FRIEND

Formed: Hamburg, Germany . . . 1970 out of European beat outfit GERMAN BONDS, by PETER HECHT, DIETER HORNS, PETER HESSLEIN and JOACHIM RIETENBACH. Initially only employed to perform vocal duties on their eponymous 1971 debut, Englishman JOHN LAWTON was installed as frontman proper when the band became a full-time concern following the album's relative success. Unlike other German outfits of that era (i.e. experimentalists TANGERINE DREAM, CAN and AMON DUUL II), LUCIFER'S FRIEND traded in Anglicised heavy-rock in the mould of DEEP PURPLE and URIAH HEEP. Signed to the German arm of 'Vertigo', they delivered a similar follow-up, 'WHERE THE GROUPIES KILLED THE BLUES', although this incorporated more elaborate string arrangements. A third set, 'I'M JUST A ROCK'N'ROLL SINGER', sold in vast quantities on American import, although LAWTON's countrymen seemed disinterested. Now licensed to the 'Passport' label in the States, the group moved into symphonic pomp-jazz stylings, the 1975 album, 'BANQUET' (without JOACHIM) another German success despite a critical backlash. A few personnel changes occured, most notably LAWTON's big career move to URIAH HEEP, his replacement being MIKE STARRS just prior to a worldwide contract with 'Elektra'. In 1978, the revised line-up completed their sixth album, 'GOOD TIME WARRIOR', although by '81's 'MEAN MACHINE', LAWTON was reinstated as frontman. The album failed to rescue the band's flagging career, LAWTON taking off once more to join the short-lived REBEL.

Album rating: LUCIFER'S FRIEND (*6) / WHERE GROUPIES KILLED THE BLUES (*5) / BANQUET (*5) / MIND EXPLODING (*5) / GOOD TIME WARRIOR (*5) / SNEAK ME IN (*5) / MEAN MACHINE (*4) / SUMOGRIP compilation (*6)

JOHN LAWTON – vocals / **PETER HESSLEIN** – guitar, vocals / **PETER HECHT** – keyboards / **DIETER HORNS** – bass, vocals / **JOACHIM RIETENBACH** – drums

Philips Billingsgate

May 71. (7") *(6003 092)* **RIDE THE SKY. / HORLA** [ ] [-]

Aug 71. (lp) *(6305 068) <1002>* **LUCIFER'S FRIEND** [ ] [ ] 1973
– Ride the sky / Everybody's clown / Keep goin' / Toxic shadows / Free baby / Baby you're a liar / In the time of Job when Mammon was a yippie / Lucifer's friend. *(cd-iss. Aug91 on 'Repertoire'+=; (REP 4059)* – Rock'n'roll singer / Satyr's dance / Horla / Our world is a rock'n'roll band / Alpenrosen.

Vertigo Passport

1972. (lp) *(6360 602) <98008>* **WHERE GROUPIES KILLED THE BLUES** [-] [ ] German
– Hobo / Rose on the vine / Mother / Where the groupies killed the blues / Prince of darkness / Summerdream / Delirium / No reason or rhyme / Burning ships. *(cd-iss. Aug91 on 'Repertoire'; REP 4143)*

— added **HERBERT BORNHOLDT** – percussion / **HERB GELLER** – sax / **BOB LANESE** – trumpet

Vertigo Billingsgate

1974. (lp) *(6360 611) <1008>* **I'M JUST A ROCK'N'ROLL SINGER** [-] [ ] German
– Groovin stone / Closed curtain / Born on the run / Blind freedom / I'm just a rock'n'roll singer / Lonely city days / Mary's breakdown / Song for Louie.

— now without JOACHIM

Vertigo Passport

1975. (lp) *(6360 618) <98012>* **BANQUET** [-] [ ] German
– Spanish galleon / Thus spoke Oberon / High flying lady / Goodbye / Sorrow / Dirty old town. *(UK cd-iss. Apr94 on 'Repertoire'; IMS 7017)*

— **KARL HERMANN LUER** – wind, repl. GELLER + LANESE

Vertigo Janus

1976. (lp) *(6360 633) <7030>* **MIND EXPLODING** [-] [ ] German
– Moonshine rider / Blind boy / Broken toys / Fugitive / Natural born mover / Free hooker / Yesterday's ideals. *(cd-iss. Jul98 on 'Repertoire'; RR 7085)*

— **MIKE STARRS** – vocals, repl. LAWTON (to URIAH HEEP) + LUER

Elektra Elektra

1978. (lp) *(K 52081) <63159>* **GOOD TIME WARRIOR** [ ] [ ]
– Old man roller / I'll meet you in L.A. / My love / Good times / Little dancer / Sweet little lady / Gamblin' man / Warriors.

Jan 79. (7") *(K 12329)* **OLD MAN ROLLER. / MY LOVE** [ ] [ ]

— added **ADRIAN ASKEW** – keyboards, vocals

Jun 80. (7") *(K 12428)* **STARDANCER. / 1999** [ ] [ ]

Jul 80. (lp) *(K 52203) <265>* **SNEAK ME IN** [ ] [ ]
– Goodbye girls / Sneak me in / Foxy lady / Love hymn / Stardancer / Indian summer / Don't you know what I like / Cosmic crusader.

— **JOHN LAWTON** – vocals, returned to repl. STARRS + ASKEW

1981. (lp) *(K 52298) <5E 559>* **MEAN MACHINE** [ ] [ ]
– One way street to heartbreak / Hey driver / Fire and rain / Mean machine / Cool hand killer / Action / Born to the city / One night sensation / Let me down slow / Bye bye Sadie.

— disbanded 1983; LAWTON formed REBEL

– compilations, etc. –

Jan 95. (cd) *Essential; (ESSCD 227)* **SUMOGRIP (featuring JOHN LAWTON from URIAH HEEP)** [ ] [-]
– Get in / One way ticket to Hell / You touched me . . . / Step by step / Sgeree / Intruder / Ride the sky / Get out / Heartbreaker / Don't look back / Cadillac / Rebound / Back in the track / Any day now / Free me / You touched me with your heart. *(re-iss. Apr97; same)*

LUDICHRIST (see under ⇒ SCATTERBRAIN)

LUNACHICKS

Formed: Brooklyn, New York, USA . . . 1988 by BECKY, SQUID SID, GINA and SINDI. Reportedly recommended to the influential indie label, 'Blast First' by NY noisemongers, SONIC YOUTH, LUNACHICKS were a garish explosion of colour and scuzzy punk/grunge, North Eastern cousins to the likes of BABES IN TOYLAND and L7. The sassy grunge girls weren't afraid of controversy, taking the name of their debut album, 'BABYSITTERS ON ACID' (1990) from a real-life incident (when a drug-crazed babysitter phoned her employers to tell them their child would be ready and cooked for them arriving back. She was obviously arrested! Sick), the crazed fem-rockers bashing out a racket that would probably scare most black-hearted Norwegian metallers. Their live show was equally raucous, the intergalactic noise terrorists subsequently releasing a slightly improved follow-up set in 1993, 'BINGE PURGE'. Switching labels to 'Go Kart' and replacing BECKY with CHIP, the band staggered on with a further two releases, 'JERK OF ALL TRADES' (1995) and 'PRETTY UGLY' (1997). Following the obligatory live 'DROP DEAD . . .' in '98, The LUNACHICKS were back creating musical havoc in the studio, the results being their fifth set 'LUXURY PROBLEM' (1999).

Album rating: BABYSITTERS ON ACID (*5) / BINGE AND PURGE (*6) / JERK OF ALL TRADES (*6) / PRETTY UGLY (*6) / DROP DEAD LIVE (*5) / LUXURY PROBLEM (*5)

THEO – vocals / **SINDI** – guitar / **GINA** – guitar / **SQUID SID** – bass / **BECKY** – drums

Blast First Plan 9 – Caroline

Apr 89. (d7"ep/cd-ep) *(BFFP 44/+CD)* **SUGAR LUV. / GET OFF THE ROAD // MAKIN' IT (WITH OTHER SPECIES). / JAN BRADY** [ ] [-]

Nov 89. (lp/c/cd) *(BFFP 52/+C/CD) <2105>* **BABYSITTERS ON ACID**
<US-title 'LUNACHICKS'> [ ] [ ]
– Jan Brady / Glad I'm not yew / Babysitters on acid / Makin' it (with other species) / Mabel rock / Theme song / Born 2B mild / Pin eye woman 665 / Cookie core / Octopussy / Sugar luv / Complication. *(re-iss. Oct90; same)*

Apr 90. (7"ep) *(BFFP 55)* **COMPLICATION EP** [ ] [-]
– Cookie monster / etc.

Zuma Safe House

Aug 92. (12"ep/cd-ep) *<2105>* **APATHETIC EP** [-] [ ]
Mar 93. (lp/cd) *(ELUNA 1/+CD) <SH 2107-1/-2>* **BINGE AND PURGE** [ ] [ ] Sep92
– Apathetic / Plugg / P.S. Hell / Binge and purge / Mom / Superstrong / This is serious / Whole lotta B.S. / 2 bad 4 U / 11 / Rip U / C.I.L.L. *(re-iss. Mar96 on 'SPV'; SPV 0844543-2)*

Go Kart Go Kart

Oct 95. (cd/lp) *<(GK 013/+CD)>* **JERK OF ALL TRADES** [ ] [ ] May95
– Drop dead / Fingerful / F.D.S. / Light as a feather / Edgar / Dogyard / Butt plugg / Bitterness Barbie / Deal with it / Brickface and Stucco / Jerk off all trades / Spoilt / Ring and run / Fallopian rhapsody / Insomnia / Why me. *(UK-iss.May97; same)*
Feb 97. (cd) *<(GK 024CD)>* **PRETTY UGLY** [ ] [ ]
– Yeah / Thrown it away / The day Squibs gerbil died / Dear Dotti / Mr. Lady / Spork / What's left / Gone kissin' / Don't want you / Baby / #%@!* / Wing Chun / MMM donuts / Missed it.
Nov 98. (cd/d-lp) *<(GK 042 CDLP)>* **DROP DEAD LIVE (live)** [ ] [ ] Aug98
– Yeah / FDS / The day Squid's gerbil died / Gong kissin / Fingerful / Thrown it away / Don't want you / Jerk of all trades / Wing Chun / Bitterness Barbie / Drop dead / Donuts / Passenger / Buttplug / Crash / Dear Dotti / #%@!* / Spoilt.
Aug 99. (lp/cd) *<(GOKART 051/+CD)>* **LUXURY PROBLEM** [ ] [ ]
– Less teeth more tits / Luxury problem / I'll be the one / Crash / Terror firmer / Say what you mean / Nowhere fast / Bad ass bitch / Shut you out / Cumming into my own / Hope to die / Knuckle sandwich / The return of Brickface & Stucco / Subway / Down at the pub.

Lydia LUNCH

Born: LYDIA KOCH, 2 Jun'59, Rochester, New York, USA. She became part of New York's 'No Wave' scene in 1976-78 when her punk band, TEENAGE JESUS & THE JERKS exploded onto the scene with their discordant, tortured classic, 'ORPHANS'. Towards the end of the decade, the stunning (in more ways than one!) punk banshee disbanded the 'JERKS, forming the short-lived BEIRUT SLUMP. After a solitary US-only single, 'TRY ME', LYDIA embarked on a solo career with the more vocally subdued debut album, 'QUEEN OF SIAM' (1980), a schizoid record that found LUNCH entertaining a gamut of styles including avant-swing-jazz in the shape of the TOM WAITS-esque 'LADY SCARFACE' (!). Ever the experimentalist, LYDIA tried out R&B and funk in her next project, 8-EYED SPY, although this too was just as brief as only a single and a mini eponymous set appeared in '81. The following year, LYDIA unleashed her second solo album, '13:13', an intense, heavy-duty precursor to the girl-grunge likes of HOLE and BABES IN TOYLAND, it featured three of her most effective numbers, 'AFRAID OF YOUR COMPANY', 'THIS SIDE OF NOWHERE' and 'STARES TO . . .'. Subsequent collaborations with The BIRTHDAY PARTY, ROWLAND S. HOWARD, EINSTURZENDE NEUBAUTEN, DIE HAUT and Danish band, SORT SOL, took her overseas to Berlin, although she returned in her own right in 1984 with 'IN LIMBO' (released on CABARET VOLTAIRE's indie imprint, 'DoubleVision'). The following year, LYDIA founded her own 'Widowspeak' label, issuing her 'UNCENSORED' cassette which unearthed her girlhood traumas in the shape of 'DADDY DEAREST'. This mid-80's period also found the provocative punk queen featuring in a series of NY~ "artistic" films, including 'Fingered', in which she gets to grips, so to speak, with long-time beau, JIM THIRLWELL (of FOETUS). Musically, LUNCH kept up her profile via a collaborative effort with mates SONIC YOUTH, 'DEATH VALLEY '69', a spiralling maelstrom of disturbing guitar-noise (inspired by the MANSON killings) over which she stamped her uncompromising authority. In between further solo work, LYDIA spent time in the studio with MICHAEL GIRA (Swans) and JIM FOETUS (as STINKFIST), while also lending her talents to the all-female project, HARRY CREWS, alongside KIM GORDON (of SONIC YOUTH) in late 80's splinter group HARRY CREWS. In the 90's, LUNCH continued to swim against the musical mainstream, her solo albums interspersed with further collaborative work featuring the likes of former X singer, EXENE CERVENKA. • **Songwriters:** LYDIA, except SPOOKY (Association) / DON'T FEAR THE REAPER (Blue Oyster Cult) / WHY DON'T WE DO IT IN THE ROAD (Beatles) / IN MY TIME OF DYING (trad/ Led Zeppelin).

Album rating: QUEEN OF SIAM (*6) / 8-EYED SPY mini (*5) / 13:13 (*7) / IN LIMBO (*5) / THE UNCENSORED (*5) / THE DROWNING OF LUCY HAMILTON mini (*5) / HYSTERIE compilation (*7) / HONEYMOON IN RED (*6) / ORAL FIXATION (*5) / NAKED IN GARDEN HILLS with Harry Crews (*6) / CONSPIRACY OF WOMEN (*6) / SHOTGUN WEDDING with Rowland S. Howard (*5) / RUDE HIEROGLYPHICS with Exene Cervenka (*5) / CRIMES AGAINST NATURE compilation (*7) / WIDOWSPEAK – THE BEST OF LYDIA LUNCH compilation (*8)

TEENAGE JESUS & THE JERKS

LYDIA LUNCH – vocals, guitar / **GORDON STEVENSON** – bass; repl. JIM SCLAVUNOS who repl. JAMES CHANCE / **BRADLY FIELD** – drums; repl. RECK who joined FRICTION

not iss. Migraine

Apr 78. (7") *<CC-333>* **ORPHANS. / LESS OF ME** [-] [ ]
Mar 79. (7") *<CC-334>* **BABY DOLL. / FREUD IN FLOP / RACE MIXING** [-] [ ]
Aug 79. (12"ep,12"pink-ep) *<CC-336>* **PINK** [-] [ ]
– Freud in flop / Race mixing / Baby doll / Burning rubber / Red alert / Orphans / Less of me.

not iss. Ze

Nov 79. (12"ep) *<12011>* **PRE-TEENAGE JESUS** [-] [ ]
– The closet / Less of me / My eyes.
disbanded when she formed . . .

BEIRUT SLUMP

— **LYDIA LUNCH** – vocals, guitar / **ROBERT QUINE** – guitar / **PAT IRWIN** – sax / **GEORGE SCOTT** – bass

not iss. Migraine

Apr 79. (7") *<CC-335>* **TRY ME. / STAIRCASE** [-] [ ]

LYDIA LUNCH

— went solo added piano & was backed by **ROBERT QUINE** – guitar / **PAT IRWIN** – guitar, keyboards / **JACK RUBY** – bass / **DOUGLAS BROWNE** – drums

Celluloid Ze

Nov 80. (lp) *(CEL 2-6561) <33006>* **QUEEN OF SIAM** [ ] [ ]
– Mechanical flattery / Gloomy Sunday / Tied and twisted / Spooky / Los banditos / Atomic bongos / Lady Scarface / A cruise to the Moon / Carnival fat man / Knives in the drain / Blood of tin. *(cd-iss. Jul91 on 'UFO'; WSP 001) (re-iss. cd Aug95 on 'Triple X')*

8 EYED SPY

— were formed by **LUNCH / IRWIN + SCOTT** plus **JIM SCLAVUNOS** – sax / **MICHAEL PAUMGARDEN** – drums

Fetish not iss.

Oct 81. (m-lp) *(FR 2003)* **8 EYED SPY** [ ] [-]
– Diddy wah diddy / Lazy in love / Love split / Dead you me B side / Swamp / Run through the jungle / Motor oil shanty / You twist I shout / Looking for someone / Lightning's girl / Innocence / Boy meets girl / 2 square / I want candy / Ran away dark. *<(cd-iss. Sep97 on 'Atavistic'; ALP 75CD)>*
Feb 82. (7") *(FE 19)* **DIDDY WAH DIDDY. / DEAD YOU ME B SIDE** [ ] [-]

— Had already disbanded, after SCOTT died late in 1981.

LYDIA LUNCH

— went solo, but she first half shared an album with The BIRTHDAY PARTY, then a single with their guitarist ROWLAND S. HOWARD

4 a.d. not iss.

Feb 82. (lp) *(JAD 202)* **THE AGONY & THE ECSTASY** (other side 'Drunk On The Pope's Blood' by BIRTHDAY PARTY) [ ] [ ]
– Afraid of your company / (2).
Sep 82. (12") *(BAD 210)* **SOME VELVET MORNING. ("ROWLAND S.HOWARD & LYDIA LUNCH") / I FELL IN LOVE WITH A GHOST** [ ] [ ]

— now w / **DIX DENNEY** – guitar / **GREG WILLIAMS** – bass / **CLIFF MARTINEZ** – drums

Situation2 Ruby

Jun 82. (lp) *(SITU 6) <JRR 806>* **13:13** [ ] [ ]
– Stares to . . . / 3*3 / This side of nowhere / Snakepit breakdown / Dance of the dead children / Suicide ocean / Lock your door / Afraid of your company. *(cd-iss. Oct89 + Oct94 on 'Line'; LICD 9.00096)*

— Between 1982 + Aug83, she guested on 2 German 12"ep's on labels 'Ripoff' & 'Zensor' respectively. These were; **EINSTÜRZENDE NEUBAUTEN** – 'DURSTIGES TIER' the B-side of 'THIRSTY ANIMAL' + **DIE HAUT** – 'DER KARIBISCHE WESTERN'.

— Next with musicians **PAT PLACE** – guitar / **THURSTON MOORE** – bass + RICHARD EDSON – drums (of SONIC YOUTH) / **KRISTIAN HOFFMAN** – piano / **JIM SCLAVUNOS** – sax

DoubleVision not iss.

Sep 84. (m-lp; some red) *(DVR 5)* **IN LIMBO** [ ] [ ]
– I wish . . . I wish / Friday afternoon / 1000 lies / Some boys / Still burning / What did you do. *(re-iss. 1986 on 'Widowspeak'; WSP 6)*

— Early in 1985, she was again credited on a 12", this time **SONIC YOUTH's** 'DEATH VALLEY '69, which was released on 'Blast First' UK 'Irredescence' US.

Widowspeak Widowspeak

Mar 85. (c) *(WSP 1)* **THE UNCENSORED** [-] [ ]
– Dear whores / Shotgun / Black Romeo / Daddy dearest. *(cd-see ORAL . . .)*
Jun 85. (lp) *(WSP 2)* **THE DROWNING OF LUCY HAMILTON** [ ] [-]
– Emerald pale has disappeared / The drowning / How men die in their sleep / Lucy's lost her head again / 3:20 Thursday morning / A quiet night of murder in . . .
Oct 85. (10"ep) *(WSP 3)* **HEART OF DARKNESS (with NO TREND)** [ ] [-]
Mar 87. (d-lp) *(WSP 8)* **HYSTERIE** (compilation of all material 1976-1986) [ ] [-]
– Red alert / Orphans / The closet / Burning rubber / I woke up dreaming / Reud in flop / Baby doll / Race mixing / Crown of thorns / Red alert / Try me / Staircase / I am the Lord Jesus / Case #14 / See pretty / C-I blue / Tornado warnings / Sidewalk / Swamp / Run through the jungle / Motor oil shanty / Love split with blood / Ran away dark / Diddy wah diddy / Lazy in love / Dead me you B side / I fell in love with a ghost / As she weeps / Caribbean western. *(cd-iss. 1989; WSP 008CD)*
Mar 88. (12"m) *(WSP 013T)* **THE CRUMB. (with THURSTON MOORE) / DONE DUN / DEAD RIVER** [ ] [-]

— next featured backing from **BIRTHDAY PARTY** + recorded 1983-84

Apr 88. (lp) *(WSP 12)* **HONEYMOON IN RED** [ ] [-]
– Done dun / Still burning / Fields of fire / Dead in the head / Some velvet morning / Come fall / So your heart / Dead river / Three kings. *(cd-iss. May90; WSP 12CD)*
Nov 88. (m-lp) *(WSP 14)* **STINKFIST (with CLINT RUIN)** [ ] [-]
– Stinkfist / Meltdown oratorio (part 1,2,3) / Son of Stink.
Sep 89. (lp) *(WSP 16)* **ORAL FIXATION** (spoken word live in Detroit) [ ] [-]
– Dear whores / Shotgun / Black Romeo / Daddy dearest / Oral fixation.

HARRY CREWS

LYDIA LUNCH – vocals, guitar / **KIM GORDON** – bass (of SONIC YOUTH) / **SADIE MAE** – drums

Big Cat Widowspeak

Apr 90. (lp/cd) *(ABB 21/+CD) <24>* **NAKED IN GARDEN HILLS (live in Vienna; late 1988)** [ ] [ ] Nov89

– About the author / Distopia / Gospel singer / (She's in a) Bad mood / Bring me down / S.O.S. / Man hates a man / You're it / Knockout artist / Way out / Car / Orphans.

LYDIA LUNCH

Big Cat | not iss.

Oct 91. (12"ep)(cd-ep) *(ABB 26T)(ABBSCD 26)* **(with CLINT RUIN): DON'T FEAR THE REAPER / CLINCH. / SERPENTINE / WHY DON'T WE DO IT IN THE ROAD** [ ] [-]

Pathological | not iss.

May 91. (cd) *(PATH 6CD)* **C.O.W. (CONSPIRACY OF WOMEN)** [ ] [-]
– The right to revolt / The conspiracy of women.

UFO | not iss.

Oct 91. (cd)(lp) *(UFO-WSP 2CD)(WSP 002)* **SHOTGUN WEDDING** (with ROWLAND S. HOWARD) [ ] [-]
– Burning skulls / In my time of dying / Solar hex / Endless fall / What is memory / Pigeon town / Cisco sunset / Incubator / Black juju. *<re-iss. cd Aug95 on 'Triple X'+=; 51111)>* – Gospel singer. *(d-cd Sep94 w /'TRANCE MUTATION' cd on 'Trident') (d-cd re-iss. Feb01 on 'Burning Airlines'; PILOT 047)*

Clawfist | not iss.

Feb 93. (7") *(X-PIG 19)* **UNEARTHLY DELIGHTS. / BUSTED** [ ] [ ]

Rykodisc | Rykodisc

Nov 95. (cd; LYDIA LUNCH & EXENE CERVENKA) *<(RCD 10326)>* **RUDE HIEROGLYPHICS** [ ] [ ]
– Rude hieroglyphics.

– compilations, etc. –

on 'Widowspeak' unless mentioned otherwise

May 81. (c) *R.O.I.R.; <A 101>* **LIVE (8 EYED SPY)** [-] [ ]
(UK-iss.1992 on 'Danceteria' cd/lp; DAN CD/LP 087)

Feb 90. (cd) *(WSP 19CD)* **DROWNING IN LIMBO** [ ] [ ]
– (THE DROWNING OF LUCY HAMILTON / IN LIMBO) *<US cd-iss. 1995 on 'Atavistic'; 52>*

May 90. (cd) *(WSP 20CD)* **STINKFIST / THE CRUMB** [ ] [-]

Jul 90. (cd) *(WSP 23CD)* **THE UNCENSORED / ORAL FIXATION** [ ] [-]

Jul 93. (3xcd-box) *Triple X; <51157-2>* **CRIMES AGAINST NATURE** [-] [ ]
– Crimes against nature / The beast / Unearthly delights / Cruel story of youth / Daddy dearest / Terminal distraction / Shock corridor / Oral fixation / The right to revolt / Conspiracy of women. *(re-iss. Aug95; same) (re-iss. Nov99 on 'Atavistic'; APL 114CD)*

Apr 98. (d-cd) *CDH Wax; (efa 043992)* **MATRIKAMANTRA** [ ] [-]

Jun 99. (d-cd) *Burning Airlines; (6501131045-2) <PILOT 009>* **WIDOWSPEAK – THE BEST OF LYDIA LUNCH** [ ] [ ]
– Death valley '69 / Endless fall / Why don't we do it in the road? / Some velvet morning / Four cornered room / Suicide ocean / No excuse / A short history of decay (parts 1 & 2) / Escape / A quiet night of murder in Greenwich Connecticut / The need to feed / Der karibische western / Twisted / Past glas / Done dun / Lock your door / Diddy wah diddy / Run through the jungle / Orphans / Son of stink / Still burning / Tornado warnings / Lady scarface. *(re-iss. Feb01; same as US)*

Nov 00. (cd) *Almafame; (ALMACD 18)* **THE DEVIL'S RACETRACK** [ ] [-]

LURKERS

Formed: Uxbridge, London, England . . . late 1976 by HOWARD WALL, ARTURO BASSICK, PETE STRIDE and MANIC ESSO. The first act to be signed to fledgling DIY independent, 'Beggars Banquet', The LURKERS' debut single, 'SHADOW' / 'LOVE STORY', was initially handed out free at gigs in the summer of '77. The flipside, rather than the lead track, stood out for its relentless, uncompromising barrage of 100 mph raw punk rock, taking its lead from the RAMONES but replacing the bubblegum factor with an aggressive edge more akin to MOTORHEAD. ARTURO was soon to be replaced by KYM BRADSHAW in time for their next single, 'FREAK SHOW', another brutally simplistic two and a half minutes which came packaged in artwork courtesy of SAVAGE PENCIL (an illustrator for Sounds and the frontman of fellow punk conspirators, The ART ATTACKS). Another personnel change ensued when brief member, KYM, was substituted for the more experienced NIGEL MOORE, the revised line-up hitting the Top 50 with the more chorus-friendly 'AIN'T GOT A CLUE'. A taster from their Top 60 debut set, 'FULHAM FALLOUT' (1978), its moderate success consolidated by their second Top 50 entry, 'I DON'T NEED TO TELL HER'. 1979 started off promisingly enough when the single, 'JUST THIRTEEN', dented the charts, although the accompanying album, 'GOD'S LONELY MEN', failed to generate much interest either critically or commercially. After two further 45's only just managed to scrape into the charts, The LURKERS began a long slide into oblivion after losing their frontman. Although replacement, MARK FINCHAM took up the reins from 1982's 'THIS DIRTY TOWN', the band joined the bulging ranks of the redundant punk has-beens and continued to churn out albums of limited appeal throughout the 80's and even the 90's. • **Songwriters:** WALL lyrics / STRIDE music. In 1982 STRIDE and EAGLE were the main writers with BASSICK returning in '88 replacing EAGLE. Covered; LITTLE OL' WINE DRINKER ME (Dean Martin) / etc? • **Trivia:** Their early sleeve artwork was created by Sounds journalist and ART ATTACKS frontman SAVAGE PENCIL.

Album rating: FULHAM FALLOUT (*6) / GOD'S LONELY MEN (*5) / LAST WILL AND TESTAMENT – GREATEST HITS compilation (*7) / THIS DIRTY TOWN (*4)

HOWARD WALL – vocals / **PETE STRIDE** – guitar / **ARTURO BASSICK** (b. ARTHUR BILLINGSLEY) – bass / **MANIC ESSO** (b. PETE HAYNES) – drums

Beggars Banquet | not iss.

Jul 77. (7") *(BEG 1)* **SHADOW. / LOVE STORY** [ ] [-]
(re-iss. Aug78 red, blue or white; same)

—— **KYM BRADSHAW** – bass; repl. ARTURO

Oct 77. (7") *(BEG 2)* **FREAK SHOW. / MASS MEDIA BELIEVER** [ ] [-]

—— **NIGEL MOORE** – bass repl. KYM

May 78. (7") *(BEG 6)* **AIN'T GOT A CLUE. / OOH OOH I LOVE YOU** [45] [-]
(with free gold 7"flexi) *(BEG 6 1/2)* **CHAOS BROTHERS FULHAM FALLOUT FIRTY FREE!')**

Jun 78. (lp) *(BEGA 2)* **FULHAM FALLOUT** [57] [-]
– Ain't got a clue / I don't need to tell her / Total war / Hey you / Shadow / Then I kicked her / Go go go / Jenny / Time of year / Self destruct / It's quiet here / Gerald / I'm on heat / Be my prisoner. *(<cd-iss. Nov97 on 'Captain Oi'+=; AHOYCD 073>)* – Shadow / Love story / Freak show / Mass media believer / Ohh ohh I love you / Pills / We are the Chaos brothers / Be my prisoner / Total war / Then I kissed her / I love the dark / Freak show.

Jul 78. (7") *(BEG 9)* **I DON'T NEED TO TELL HER. / PILLS** [49] [-]

Jan 79. (7") *(BEG 14)* **JUST THIRTEEN. / COUNTDOWN** [66] [-]

Apr 79. (lp/c) *(BEGA/BEGC 8)* **GOD'S LONELY MEN** [ ] [-]
– She knows / God's lonely men / Out in the dark / Cyandide / Whatever happened to Mary / Take me back to Babylon / Room 309 / I'll be with you / Non contender / Seven o'clock someday / Sleep on diamonds / Bad times. *(<cd-iss. Nov97 on 'Captain Oi'+=; AHOYCD 074>)* – Just thirteen / Countdown / Suzie is a floozie / Cyanide / New guitar in town / Little old wine drinker / Cold old night / Pick me up / Mary's coming home / New guitar in town / Little old wine drinker.

May 79. (7") *(BEG 19)* **OUT IN THE DARK. / CYANIDE** [72] [-]
(d7"+=) *(BEG 19)* – Suzie is a floozie / Cyanide (pub version).

Nov 79. (7") *(BEG 28)* **NEW GUITAR IN TOWN. / PICK ME UP / LITTLE OL' WINE DRINKER ME** [72] [-]

—— STRIDE teamed up with BOYS member JOHN PLAIN (see below) .

—— Split for a while. STRIDE, HAYNES and MOORE brought in new members **MARK FINCHAM** – vocals repl. WALL

Clay | not iss.

Jun 82. (7") *(CLAY 12)* **THIS DIRTY TOWN (I CAN'T FIND WAY OUT). / WOLF AT THE DOOR** [ ] [-]

Jul 82. (lp) *(CLAY 104)* **THIS DIRTY TOWN** [ ] [-]
– This dirty town / Drag you out / Frankenstein again / Heroin it's all over / One man's meat / Wolf at the door / Shut out the light / Let's dance now / Midnight hour / By the hat. *(re-iss. Dec89; same) <(cd-iss. Apr93; CLAYCD 104)>*

Nov 82. (7"/7"pic-d) *(CLAY 17/+P)* **DRAG YOU OUT. / HEROIN (IT'S ALL OVER)** [ ] [-]

Feb 83. (7") *(CLAY 21)* **FRANKENSTEIN AGAIN. / ONE MAN'S MEAT . . .** [ ] [-]

Mar 84. (12"ep) *(PLATE 7)* **FINAL VINYL** [ ] [-]
– Let's dance now (no time to be strangers) / Midnight hour / By the heart / Frankenstein again.

May 84. (7") *(CLAY 32)* **LET'S DANCE NOW. / MIDNIGHT HOUR** [ ] [-]

—— split '84. Re-formed late '88, **STRIDE & BASSICK** plus **ESSO + MOORE**

Weser | not iss.

Feb 89. (lp) *(efa 2433)* **WILD TIMES AGAIN** [ ] [-]
– Sidewinder / In Soho / Wolverine / Don't fall down / Miss World / Love commando / Rubber room / I can be good / Don't ask me / She go solo / Wild games / Someone out there / In my own world / Fanatical heart / Uptown or downtown. *(cd-iss. Nov94; WL 024332CD)*

Link | not iss.

Jun 89. (m-lp) *(LINKLP 087)* **KING OF THE MOUNTAIN** [ ] [-]
– Brou blue / Never had a beech head / Unfinished business / Going monkee again / King of the mountain (part 1) / Lucky John / King of the mountain (pt.2).

Nov 89. (lp) **LIVE AND LOUD (live early '89)** [ ] [-]
– Ain't got a clue / I don't need to tell her / Unfinished business / Pills / Barbara blue / Rubber room / Just thirteen / Uptown or downtown / Going Monkee again (hey hey hey) / Shadow / New guitar in town / Miss World / I'm on heat / Freak show / Take me back to Babylon / Then I kissed her / Drag you out / Cyanide / Jenny.

Released Emotions | not iss.

Oct 90. (cd)(lp) **POWERJIVE** [ ] [-]
– Powerjive / Lipstick and shampoo / Solitaire / Waiting for you / Things will never be the same / The world of Jenny Brown / Walk like a superstar (talk like a zombie) / Go go girl / Strange desire (burn, burn, burn) / Raven's wings / I close my eyes / Lullaby.

—— **DAN TOZER** – drums joined STRIDE, PLAIN + BASSICK

Weser | Weser

Nov 94. (cd) *(<WL 02460CD>)* **NON-STOP NITROPOP** [ ] [Jul96]
– Don't need a reason / Melt away / Can't stand my room / Hand in the fire / She's another man / Unknown / The show goes on / Frozen out / Jungle creature / Storm in my mind / Rags to riches / Feel it coming / In a dark room.

—— they've since split

– compilations, etc. –

on 'Beggars Banquet' unless mentioned otherwise

1979. (d7"ep) *(BACK 1)* **SHADOW / LOVE STORY. / FREAK SHOW / MASS MEDIA BELIEVER** [ ] [-]

1979. (d7"ep) *(BACK 3)* **I DON'T NEED YO TELL HER. / PILLS / JUST THIRTEEN / COUNTDOWN** [ ] [-]

Nov 80. (lp) *(BOPA 2)* **LAST WILL AND TESTAMENT – GREATEST HITS** [ ] [-]
– I'm on heat / Cyanide / Shadow / Little ol' wine drinker me / Out in the dark / Freak show / Jenny / Self destruct / Ain't got a clue / Take me back to Babylon / Total war / Love story / Then I kicked her / Just thirteen / New guitar in town / She knows. *(re-iss. Jul88 on 'Beggars Banquet-Lowdown' lp/c)(cd; BBL/+C 2)(BBL 2CD)*

Dec 92. (cd) *Dojo; (DOJOCD 74)* **TOTALLY LURKERED** [ ] [-]

Nov 95. (cd) *Anagram; (CDPUNK 69)* **POWERJIVE / KING OF THE MOUNTAIN** [ ] [-]

May 97. (cd) *Anagram; (<CDPUNK 94>)* **THE BEGGARS BANQUET PUNK SINGLES** [ ] [ ]

Dec 97. (cd) *Receiver; (<RRCD 243>)* **TAKE ME BACK TO BABYLON**
Jun 99. (cd) *Harry May; (<MAYOCD 114>)* **AIN'T GOT A CLUE** Apr00
May 00. (cd) *Captain Oi; (<AHOYCD 137>)* **THE BBC PUNK SESSIONS**

PETE STRIDE and JOHN PLAIN

(PLAIN was from The BOYS) + **TONY BATEMAN** – bass / **JACK BLACK** – drums

Beggars Banquet / not iss.

Jan 80. (lp) *(BEGA 17)* **NEW GUITAR IN TOWN** -
– Laugh at me / School girls / Cold cold night / He'll have to go / Just like a clown / Half the time / New guitar in town / Cure for love / Restless kind / You better move on / Pick me up.
May 80. (7") *(BEG 41)* **LAUGH AT ME. / JIMMY BROWN** -

Phil LYNOTT (see under ⇒ THIN LIZZY)

LYNCH MOB

Formed: Los Angeles, California, USA . . . late 80's by DOKKEN outcasts, GEORGE LYNCH and MICK BROWN, who got together with COLD SWEAT singer ONI LOGAN and ex-BEGGARS & THIEVES bassist ANTHONY ESPOSITO. Remaining with 'Elektra', LYNCH and co. debuted with 'WICKED SENSATION' (1990), a basic hard-rockin' album not too far removed from earlier DOKKEN material (thus its healthy US Top 50 sales). It featured a cover of The Rolling Stones' 'STREET FIGHTIN' MAN', their 1992 eponymous second set (with new frontman ROBERT MASON) displaying another key influence with a reworking of Queen's 'TIE YOUR MOTHER DOWN'. Although this was another to feature highly in the US charts, LYNCH MOB folded with GEORGE LYNCH pursuing a solo career (one album 'SACRED GROOVE' appeared the following year). A second spell with DOKKEN in the mid-90's saw GEORGE's time being taken up somewhat, although LYNCH MOB were back in action after his departure. Their comeback set, 'SMOKE THIS' (1999), was predictable hard rock strictly for the LYNCH worthies.

Album rating: WICKED SENSATION (*6) / LYNCH MOB (*7) / SMOKE THIS (*5) / George Lynch: SACRED GROOVE (*5)

ONI LOGAN – vocals (ex-COLD SWEAT) / **GEORGE LYNCH** – guitar (ex-DOKKEN) / **ANTHONY ESPOSITO** – bass (ex-COLD SWEAT) / **MICK BROWN** – drums (ex-DOKKEN)

Elektra / Elektra

Oct 90. (cd)(lp/c) *<(7559 60954-2)>(WX 81/+C)* **WICKED SENSATION** 46
– Wicked sensation / River of love / Sweet sister mercy / All I want / Hell child / She's evil but she's mine / Dance of the dogs / Rain / No bed of roses / Through these eyes / For a million years / Street fightin' man.

—— **ROBERT MASON** – vocals; repl. LOGAN

May 92. (cd)(lp/c) *<(7559 61322-2)>(WX 106/+C)* **LYNCH MOB** 56
– Jungle of love / Tangled in the web / No good / Dream until tomorrow / Cold is the heart / Tie your mother down / Heaven is waiting / I want it / When darkness calls / The secret.
May 92. (c-s) *<64749>* **TANGLED IN THE WEB** -

—— split the following year + GEORGE went solo

Aug 93. (cd/c; by GEORGE LYNCH) *<(7559 61422-2/-4)>* **SACRED GROOVE**
– Memory Jack / Love power from the mama head / Flesh and blood / We don't own this world / I will remember / The beast (part 1) / The beast (part 2) (addiction to the friction) / Not necessary evil / City of the brave / Tierra del fuego. *<cd re-iss. Mar00 on 'Orchard'; 1389>*

—— GEORGE left DOKKEN again + re-formed LYNCH MOB with **RICHARD HARPER** – vocals / plus **DAVID ROZENMEYER + GERRY McCARTHY**

Dream Catcher / Koch Int.

Feb 00. (cd) *(CRIDE 24) <8072>* **SMOKE THIS** Oct99
– World spinning away / Hype-o / Chromeplated / Hollow / Playpalistics / Beg / Relaxin' in the land of Az / Get it together / Indra's net / When I rise / What do you want / Smoke this.

not iss. / Orchard

Mar 00. (cd-s) *<1388>* **SYZYGY** -
– Into the light / All things must pass / Waterfall.

LYNYRD SKYNYRD

Formed: Jacksonville, Florida, USA . . . 1966 initially as MY BACKYARD, by RONNIE VAN ZANT (vocals) who carefully hand picked a line-up of GARY ROSSINGTON (guitar), ALLEN COLLINS (guitar), BOB BURNS (drums) and LARRY JUNSTROM (bass) to realise his boyhood dream of creating an American equivalent to The ROLLING STONES. The band were blown away after witnessing an early incarnation of The ALLMAN BROTHERS, vowing to conquer the world with their own unique take on the roots music of the South. Continually brought to task for having long hair by gym teacher, Leonard Skinner, VAN ZANT and co. packed in school at the earliest opportunity, spending up to sixteen hours a day honing the sound of the band they'd eventually dub LYNYRD SKYNYRD after their schoolhouse nemesis (name slightly changed to protect themselves from enforced circuit training). At the time, the band's home town of Jacksonville boasted a thriving and eclectic music scene that saw the likes of future ALLMAN's DICKY BETTS and BERRY OAKLEY paying their dues, as well as a young TOM PETTY amongst a slew of others. SKYNYRD's first victory in their campaign to resurrect the glory of the South was winning a support slot to psychedelic one-hit wonders, STRAWBERRY ALARM CLOCK. By 1970, the band had almost notched up a mind boggling 1,000 gigs and the real touring hadn't even started. Record wise, they had a limited issue single, 'NEED ALL MY FRIENDS', (released in 1968 by the local 'Shadetree' label) under their belts and in 1971, they issued a second single, 'I'VE BEEN YOUR FOOL', the cut taken from sessions the band had recorded at the famed Muscle Shoals studio in Sheffield, Alabama. Over the course of the sessions, the septet laid down early versions of the tracks that would later become their acclaimed debut, 'PRONOUNCED LEH-NERD SKIN-NERD' (1974), bassist LEON WILKINSON joining the band midway through the sessions, while future BLACKFOOT man, RICKY MEDLOCKE, contributed some drum and vocal parts. Manager ALAN WALDEN touted the demos around various companies to no avail, opportunity eventually knocking in the form of industry mover and shaker extraordinaire, AL KOOPER (ex-BLUES PROJECT), who was in the process of setting up the Atlanta-based 'Sounds Of The South' label with the backing of 'M.C.A.'. The purpose of this venture was to capitalise on the booming Southern music scene and in SKYNYRD, KOOPER knew he'd found a band to take Southern Rock to a new plateau. As Intense and driven as the band themselves, KOOPER constantly clashed with them during the recording of the debut which he had taken upon himself to produce. Nevertheless, KOOPER functioned like an extra member of the group, playing and singing on many of the tracks, his input pivotal in creating one of rock's great debut albums. A simmering gumbo stew that drew influences from the likes of The 'STONES, FREE and CREAM yet was also haunted by the spectre of raw country blues, the album's flagbearer and breathtaking finale was 'FREE BIRD', the song most people think of at the mention of SKYNYRD's name. From BILLY POWELL's piano-led intro (which, after writing, resulted in the former roadie being taken up as a full time member of the band), the song led into a gorgeously melancholy DUANE ALLMAN-style (whom the band would dedicate the song to after he was killed in a motorcycle crash) slide guitar part, eventually building up to a blistering triple guitar climax. The band achieved the latter by overdubbing an extra guitar part by COLLINS, authentically replicating the song live as LEON WILKINSON (who'd left prior to recording the album) later returned, allowing ED KING (who'd filled in as a bass player on the debut) to become a permanent member, switching to guitar and cementing the three-pronged attack of the classic 'SKYNYRD line-up. Alongside 'FREE BIRD', the album contained some of the finest songs of the band's career in the mournful 'TUESDAY'S GONE', VAN ZANT's normally commanding voice sounding as forlorn as hero's MERLE HAGGARD and WAYLON JENNINGS. 'SIMPLE MAN' was another earthy ballad, RONNIE's lyrics as succinct and unpretentious as ever. 'THINGS GOIN' ON', meanwhile, was a biting criticism of underhand political dealings set to a rollicking honky tonk backing. KOOPER secured the band a support slot on The WHO's 1973 American tour, and immediately the band were thrown in at the deep end, playing to stadium sized audiences. Incredibly, at almost every show, the band had won the normally fiercely partisan WHO crowd over by the end of their set and when 'SWEET HOME ALABAMA' (a rousing, tongue-in-cheek rebuke to NEIL YOUNG's 'Southern Man') made the US Top 10 the following year, the band were well on the way to becoming major league stars. 'SECOND HELPING' (1974) almost matched the power of the debut, the vicious sting of 'WORKIN' FOR M.C.A.' contrasting with the strum and slide of 'THE BALLAD OF CURTIS LOWE', a tribute to a black bluesman. And thus lay the contradiction with LYNYRD SKYNYRD; denounced as reactionary rednecks, their music was haunted by the music of black immigrants. As many commentators have noted, SKYNYRD didn't have any defined politics; VAN ZANT was fiercely proud of his upbringing, attempting in his own blunt way to speak out for a part of America that had been discredited after the civil war; charges of racism, however, were way off the mark. Similarly, an anti-firearms song, 'SATURDAY NIGHT SPECIAL', didn't exactly fit with the archetype of the rifle-toting redneck. The song formed the centrepiece of the band's third effort, 'NUTHIN' FANCY' (1975), a harder rockin' affair that nevertheless failed to break any new ground or capture the excitement of the band's live show. The album also marked the first of LYNYRD SKYNYRD's many casualties as BOB BURNS was replaced with ARTIMUS PYLE after freaking out on tour. The band had been on the road almost constantly from their inception and things began coming to a head, the trek that followed the release of 'NUTHIN' FANCY' coming to be dubbed the 'Torture Tour'. The tales of sex, drugs, violence and madness are legendary, VAN ZANT's infamous violent outbreaks particularly nauseating. While ED KING departed, the rest of the band soldiered on under the auspices of the notoriously unpredictable VAN ZANT, his dedication winning unfaltering loyalty despite his temper. KING's replacement was STEVE GAINES, brother of backing singer CASSIE. Though he was only featured on a handful of the tracks on the live 'ONE MORE FROM THE ROAD' (1976), his visceral playing re-energised a flagging 'SKYNYRD, helping to make 'STREET SURVIVORS' (1977) their best release since 'SECOND HELPING'. Inspired by the 'Outlaw' movement that saw country stars like WILLIE NELSON and TOMPALL GLASER moving away from the polished Nashville sound, 'STREET SURVIVORS' was more countrified than any previous release, right down to a cover of MERLE HAGGARD's 'HONKY TONK NIGHT TIME MAN'. It also included VAN ZANT's heartfelt anti-heroin track, 'THAT SMELL'. The song's lyrics and the album's cover art (featuring the band surrounded by flames) were to take on a chilling new resonance when, on October 20, en route to Baton Rouge, the aircraft carrying band and crew plummeted from the sky after both its engines failed. VAN ZANT was killed on impact, as were STEVE and CASSIE GAINES, and assistant road manager DEAN KILPATRICK. The remaining passengers were all seriously injured and the details of the crash were horrific, the effects of the tragedy still resonating to this day. The remaining members decided to disband LYNYRD SKYNYRD, even although 'STREET SURVIVORS' had become their biggest selling album ever, the remnants of 'SKYNYRD forming the ROSSINGTON-COLLINS BAND, who released two forgettable albums at the turn of the decade, COLLINS later forming his own band after the death of his wife KATHY. This wasn't the end to his strife; COLLINS was involved in a serious car accident in 1986 which killed his girlfriend and left him paralysed from the waist down (he died of pneumonia four years later). COLLINS wasn't the only one to suffer in the aftermath of the band's tragedy; suicide, drug addiction and even alleged child abuse dogged the survivors of the plane crash for years to come. In the late 80's, the remaining members regrouped for a memorial tour and subsequent live album, 'SOUTHERN BY THE GRACE OF GOD' (1988), RONNIE's brother, JOHNNY, fronting the band. Another reformation in 1991 resulted in the eponymous 'LYNYRD SKYNYRD 1991', a credible comeback that saw the return of ED KING. The band released a further three albums during the 90's, 'THE LAST REBEL' (1993), the unplugged 'ENDANGERED SPECIES' (1994) and 1997's 'TWENTY', the latter featuring BLACKFOOT man RICKY MEDLOCKE, who'd played on sessions for the debut over a quarter of a century previously. Of late, LYNYRD SKYNYRD have delivered three more sets, 'LYVE FROM STEEL TOWN' (1998), 'EDGE OF FOREVER' (1999) and the ill-advised 'CHRISTMAS TIME AGAIN' (2000). None of these albums captured the intensity of the original line-up, however, and those looking for a comprehensive musical history lesson are pointed in the direction of the 1991 MCA boxed set. Alongside all the essential album cuts, the collection includes a spectral demo version of 'FREEBIRD' as well as unreleased gems like the impassioned 'HE'S ALIVE' and the spine-tingling 'ALL I CAN DO IS WRITE ABOUT IT', as revealing a song as to what drove the late VAN ZANT as the man ever penned. • **Songwriters:** Bulk by VAN ZANT + COLLINS or VAN ZANT + GAINES after '75. When they re-formed in '87, ROSSINGTON, KING and the new VAN ZANDT contributed all. Covered; SAME OLD BLUES + CALL ME THE BREEZE (J.J. Cale) / CROSSROADS (Robert Johnson) / NONE OF US ARE FREE (Mann-Weil-Russell) / etc.

Album rating: PRONOUNCED LEH-NERD SKIN-NERD (*8) / SECOND HELPING (*8) / NUTHIN' FANCY (*6) / GIMME BACK MY BULLETS (*6) / ONE MORE FROM THE ROAD (*8) / STREET SURVIVORS (*7) / SKYNYRD'S FIRST AND.. LAST posthumous (*6) / GOLD AND PLATINUM compilation (*9) / LEGEND rare live (*6) / SOUTHERN BY THE GRACE OF GOD: LYNYRD SKYNYRD TRIBUTE TOUR – 1987 (*5) / LYNYRD SKYNYRD 1991 (*5) / THE LAST REBEL (*5) / LYNYRD SKYNYRD boxed set (*9) / FREEBIRD – THE VERY BEST OF . . . compilation (*8) / ENDANGERED SPECIES (*4) / TWENTY (*4) / LYVE FROM STEEL TOWN (*5) / EDGE OF FOREVER (*5) / CHRISTMAS TIME AGAIN (*2)

RONNIE VAN ZANT (b.15 Jan'48) – vocals / **GARY ROSSINGTON** (b. 4 Dec'51) – guitar / **ALLEN COLLINS** (b.19 Jul'52) – guitar / **GREG WALKER** (or) **LEON WILKESON** (b. 2 Apr'52) – bass / **RICKY MEDLOCKE** (or) **BOB BURNS** – drums

not iss. / Shade Tree

1971. (7") **I'VE BEEN YOUR FOOL. / GOTTA GO** [-] [ ]
(UK-iss.Oct82 on 'M.C.A.'; 799)

— **ED KING** – bass (ex-STRAWBERRY ALARM CLOCK) repl. LEON & GREG / added **BILLY POWELL** (b. 3 Jun'52) – piano (RICKY MEDLOCKE had now formed BLACKFOOT, after contributing vox + drums on 2 tracks 'White Dove' & 'The Seasons')

M.C.A. / M.C.A.

Nov 73. (7") *<40158>* **GIMME THREE STEPS. / MR. BANKER** [-] [ ]
Jan 74. (lp/c) *(MCG/+C 3502) <363>* **PRONOUNCED LEH-NERD SKIN-NERD** [ ] [27] Sep73
– I ain't the one / Tuesday's gone / Gimme three steps / Simple man / Things goin' on / Mississippi kid / Poison whiskey / Free bird. *(re-iss. Jun84 lp/c; MCL/+C 1798) (cd-iss. Jul88; DMCL 1798) (cd re-iss. Nov91; MCLD 19072) (lp re-iss. Nov98 on 'Simply Vinyl'; SVLP 52)*

— added returning **LEON WILKESON** – bass (ED KING now 3rd guitarist)

May 74. (7") *(MCA 136) <40231>* **DON'T ASK ME NO QUESTIONS. / TAKE YOUR TIME** [ ] [ ] Jan74
Oct 74. (lp/c) *(MCF/+C 2547) <413>* **SECOND HELPING** [ ] [12] Apr74
– Sweet home Alabama / I need you / Don't ask me no questions / Workin' for MCA / The ballad of Curtis Loew / Swamp music / The needle and the spoon / Call me the breeze. *(re-iss. 1983 lp/c; MCL/+C 1746) (re-iss. Oct87 on 'Fame' lp/c; FA/TC-FA 3194) (cd-iss. Aug89; DMCL 1746) (cd re-iss. Oct92; MCLD 19073)*
Oct 74. (7") *(MCA 160) <40258>* **SWEET HOME ALABAMA. / TAKE YOUR TIME** [ ] [8] Jul74
Nov 74. (7") *<40328>* **FREE BIRD (edit). / DOWN SOUTH JUKIN'** [-] [19]

— (Dec74) **ARTIMUS PYLE** (b. 15 Jul'48, Spartanburg, South Carolina) – drums repl. BURNS

May 75. (lp/c) *(MCF/+C 2700) <2137>* **NUTHIN' FANCY** [43] [9] Apr75
– Saturday night special / Cheatin' woman / Railroad song / I'm a country boy / On the hunt / Am I losin' / Made in the shade / Whiskey rock-a-roller. *(re-iss. 1983 lp/c; MCL/+C 1760) (cd-iss. Aug87; CMCAD 31003) (cd re-iss. Nov94; MCLD 19074) (cd re-iss. Nov99; MCD 12024)*
Jul 75. (7") *(MCA 199) <40416>* **SATURDAY NIGHT SPECIAL. / MADE IN THE SHADE** [ ] [27] May75

— Reverted to six-piece, when ED KING departed / added backing vocalists **CASSIE GAINES, LESLIE HAWKINS + JO JO BILLINGSLEY**

Feb 76. (7") *(MCA 229) <40532>* **DOUBLE TROUBLE. / ROLL GYPSY ROLL** [ ] [80]
Mar 76. (lp/c) *(MCF/+C 2744) <2170>* **GIMME BACK MY BULLETS** [34] [20] Feb76
– Gimme back my bullets / Every mother's son / Trust / (I got the) Same old blues / Double trouble / Roll gypsy roll / Searching / Cry for the bad man / All I can do is write about it. *(re-iss. Feb82 lp/c; MCL/+C 1653) (cd-iss. Nov99; MCD 12023)*
Jun 76. (7") *<40565>* **GIMME BACK MY BULLETS. / ALL I CAN DO IS WRITE ABOUT IT** [-] [ ]
Aug 76. (7"ep) *(MCA 251)* **FREE BIRD. / SWEET HOME ALABAMA / DOUBLE TROUBLE** [31] [-]
(re-iss. Nov79, hit No.43) (re-iss. May82 hit No.21) (re-iss. Dec83 12"/12"pic-d; MCAT/+P 251)

— added **STEVE GAINES** (b.14 Sep'49, Seneca, Missouri) – 3rd guitar (ex-SMOKEHOUSE)

Oct 76. (7") *<40647>* **TRAVELIN' MAN (live). / GIMME THREE STEPS (live)** [-] [ ]
Oct 76. (d-lp/d-c) *(MCSP/+C 279) <6001>* **ONE MORE FROM THE ROAD (live)** [17] [9] Sep76
– Workin' for MCA / I ain't the one / Searching / Tuesday's gone / Saturday night special / Travelin' man / Whiskey rock-a-roller / Sweet home Alabama / Gimme three steps / Call me the breeze / T for Texas / The needle and spoon / Crossroads / Free bird. *<US cd-iss. 1991 with edited applause> (d-cd-ss.Dec92; MCLDD 19139)*
Nov 76. (7") *<40665>* **FREE BIRD (live). / SEARCHING (live)** [-] [38]
Jan 77. (7") *(MCA 275)* **FREE BIRD (live edit). / GIMME THREE STEPS (live)** [ ] [-]
Oct 77. (lp/c) *(MCG/+C 3525) <3029>* **STREET SURVIVORS** [13] [5]
– What's your name / That smell / One more time / I know a little / You got that right / I never dreamed / Honky tonk night time man / Ain't no good life. *(re-iss. Jul82 lp/c; MCL/+C 1694) (cd-iss. Oct94; MCLD 19248)*

— On 20th Oct'77, a few days after release of above album, the band's tour plane crashed. RONNIE VAN ZANT, STEVE & CASSIE GAINES plus roadie DEAN KILPATRICK were all killed. The remainder all suffered other injuries, but would recover. ARTIMUS went solo, the rest became ROSSINGTON-COLLINS BAND

Jan 78. (7") *(MCA 342) <40819>* **WHAT'S YOUR NAME. / I KNOW A LITTLE** [ ] [13] Nov77
Mar 78. (7") *<40888>* **YOU GOT THAT RIGHT. / AIN'T NO GOOD LIFE** [-] [69]

ROSSINGTON-COLLINS BAND

— formed 1979 by **GARY & ALLEN** with **BILLY POWELL** – keyboards / **LEON WILKESON** – bass / **DALE KRANTZ** – vocals / **BARRY HAREWOOD** – guitars, slide / **DEREK HASS** – drums, percussion

M.C.A. / M.C.A.

Jul 80. (lp/c) *(MCG/+C 4011) <5130>* **ANYTIME, ANYPLACE, ANYWHERE** [ ] [13]
– Prime time / Three times as bad / Don't misunderstand me / Misery loves company / One good man / Opportunity / Getaway / Winners and losers / Sometimes you can put it out. *(re-iss. Jun87 lp/c; MCL/+C 1748) <US cd-iss. Jun88; 31220>*
Aug 80. (7") *(MCA 636) <41284>* **DON'T MISUNDERSTAND ME. / WINNERS AND LOSERS** [ ] [55]
Oct 80. (7") *<51023>* **GETAWAY. / SOMETIMES YOU CAN PUT IT OUT** [-] [ ]
Oct 80. (7") *(MCA 648)* **ONE GOOD MAN. / MISERY LOVES COMPANY** [ ] [-]
Jun 81. (7") *<51218>* **GOTTA GET IT STRAIGHT. / DON'T STOP ME NOW** [-] [ ]
Oct 81. (lp/c) *(MCF/+C 4018) <5207>* **THIS IS THE WAY** [ ] [24]
– Gotta get it straight / Teshauna / Gonna miss it when it's gone / Pine box / Fancy ideas / Don't stop me now / Seems like every day / I'm free today / Next phone call / Means nothing to you.
Oct 81. (7") *(MCA 752)* **TESHAUNA. / GONNA MISS IT WHEN IT'S GONE** [ ] [-]
(12"+=) *(MCAT 572)* – Don't stop me now.

ROSSINGTON

— with **GARY** & his wife **DALE** with **HASS** – drums / **JAY JOHNSON** – guitar / **TIM LINDSAY** – bass

not iss. / Atlantic

Nov 86. (lp) *<81672>* **RETURNED TO THE SCENE OF THE CRIME** [-] [ ]
– Turn it up / Honest hearts / God luck to you / Wounded again / Waiting in the shadows / Dangerous love / Can you forget about my love / Returned to the scene of the crime / Are you leaving me / Path less chosen.
Nov 86. (7") *<89364>* **TURN IT UP. / PATH LESS CHOSEN** [-] [ ]

— now with **TIM LINDSEY** – bass / **TIM SHARPTON** – keyboards / **RONNIE EADES** – sax / **MITCH RIGER** – drums

M.C.A. / M.C.A.

Jul 88. (lp/c/cd; as The ROSSINGTON BAND) *<(MCA/+C/D 42166)>* **LOVE YOUR MAN** [ ] [ ]
– Losin' control / Welcome me home / Call it love / Holdin' my own / Rock on / Love your man / Stay with me / Nowhere to run / Say it from the heart / I don't want to leave you.

ALLEN COLLINS BAND

— with **COLLINS, HAREWOOD, POWELL, WILKESON, HESS,** plus **JIMMY DOUGHERTY** – vocals / **RANDALL HALL** – guitar

not iss. / M.C.A.

1983. (lp) *<39000>* **HERE THERE AND BACK** [-] [ ]
– Just trouble / One known soldier / Hangin' judge / Time after time / This ride's on me / Ready to move / Chapter one / Commitments / Everything you need. *<US cd-iss. 1990's; MCAD 31324>*

— After a spell in prison, POWELL joined Christian band VISION. Also in 1986, ALLEN COLLINS was involved in a car crash which killed his girlfriend, and paralized himself from the waist down. On the 23rd Jan'90 he died of pneumonia.

LYNYRD SKYNYRD

— re-formed Autumn 1987 with **ROSSINGTON, POWELL, PYLE, WILKESON, KING** plus **DALE KRANTZ ROSSINGTON, RANDALL HALL + JOHNNY VAN ZANT** – vocals (ex-• 38 SPECIAL)

M.C.A. M.C.A.

Apr 88. (d-lp/d-c/cd) *(DCMDMCMDC/DMCMD 7004) <8027>* **SOUTHERN BY THE GRACE OF GOD (live)** 68
– Workin' for MCA / That smell / I know a little / Comin' home / You got that right / What's your name / Gimme back my bullets / Swamp music / Call me the breeze / Dixie – Sweet home Alabama / Free bird.

— **LYNYRD SKYNYRD** re-formed again in 1991 with **ROSSINGTON, KING** and **HALL** – guitars / **JOHNNY VAN ZANT** – vocals / **POWELL** – keyboards / **WILKESON** – bass / **PYLE** – percussion, drums / **CUSTER** – drums, percussion

Atlantic Atlantic

Jun 91. (cd/c/lp) *<(7567 82258-2/-4/-1)>* **LYNYRD SKYNYRD 1991** 64
– Smokestack lightning / Keeping the faith / Southern women / Pure & simple / I've seen enough / Good thing / Money man / Backstreet crawler / It's a killer / Mama (afraid to say goodbye) / End of the road.

— extended members **JERRY JONES** – bass, guitar / **DALE KRANTZ-ROSSINGTON** – backing vocals repl. ARTIMUS PYLE

Mar 93. (cd/c) *<(7567 82447-2/-4)>* **THE LAST REBEL** 64
– Good lovin's hard to find / One thing / Can't take that away / Best things in life / The last rebel / Outta Hell in my Dodge / Kiss your freedom goodbye / South of Heaven / Love don't always come easy / Born to run. *(re-iss. cd Feb95; same)*

not iss. Capricorn

Aug 94. (cd/c) *<42028-2>* **ENDANGERED SPECIES** -
– Down south jukin' / Heartbreak hotel / Devil in the bottle / Things goin' on / Saturday night special / Sweet home Alabama / I ain't the one / Am I losin' / All I have is a song / Poison whiskey / Good luck, bad luck / The last rebel / Hillbilly blues.

S.P.V. S.P.V.

Jul 96. (d-cd) *(SPV 0874419-2)* **SOUTHERN KNIGHTS (live)**
– Working for MCA / Ain't the one / Saturday night special / Down south jukin' / Double trouble / T for Texas / Devil in the bottle / That smell / Simple man / Whiskey rock and roller / What's your name / Gimme three steps / Sweet home Alabama / Free bird.

— line-up now **ROSSINGTON, VAN ZANT, WILKESON, POWELL** plus **RICKEY MEDLOCKE** – guitars, vocals (ex-BLACKFOOT) / **HUGHIE THOMASSON** – guitars, vocals / **OWEN HALE** – drums, percussion

May 97. (cd) *(SPV 0854439-2)* **TWENTY** 97
– We ain't much different / Bring it on / Voodoo lake / Home is where the heart is / Travelin' man / Talked myself right into it / Never too late / O.R.R. / Blame it on a sad song / Berneice / None of us are free / How soon we forget.

S.P.V. CMC Int.

Jun 98. (d-cd) *(SPV 0852916-2) <607686147>* **LYVE FROM STEEL TOWN (live)** Apr98
– We ain't much different / Saturday night special / What's your name? / On the hunt / You got that right / Voodoo lake / That smell / Bring it on / Simple man / I know a little / Berneice / Gimme three steps / Sweet home Alabama / Travelin' man / Free bird / (interview pt.1 & 2).

Aug 99. (cd) *(SPV 0852964-2) <86272>* **EDGE OF FOREVER** 96
– Workin' / Full moon night / Preacher man / Mean streets / Tomorrow's goodbye / Edge of forever / Gone fishin' / Through it all / Money back guarentee / G.W.T.G.G. / Rough around the edges / Fla.

Oct 00. (cd) *(SPV 0857102-2) <86298>* **CHRISTMAS TIME AGAIN** Sep00
– Santa's messin' with the kid / Rudolph the red-nosed reindeer / Christmas time again / Greensleeves / Santa Claus is coming to town (with the CHARLIE DANIELS BAND) / Run run Rudolph / Mama's song / Santa Claus wants some lovin' / Classical Christmas / Hallelujah, it's Christmas (with .38 SPECIAL) / Skynyrd family.

– compilations, others, etc. –

All 'M.C.A.' unless otherwise stated.

Oct 78. (lp/c) *(MCG/+C 3529) <3047>* **SKYNYRD'S FIRST AND . . .LAST** (rec.1970-72) 50 15 Sep78
– Down south jukin' / Preacher's daughter / White dove / Was I right or wrong / Lend a helpin' hand / Wino / Comin' home / The seasons / Things goin' on. *(re-iss. Aug81 lp/c; MCL/+C 1627)*

Oct 78. (7") *<40957>* **DOWN SOUTH JUKIN'. / WINO** -

Oct 78. (7"ep) *(MCEP 101)* **DOWN SOUTH JUKIN' / THAT SMELL. / LEND A HELPIN' HAND / CALL ME THE BREEZE** -

Jan 80. (d-lp/d-c) *(MCSP/+C 308) <11008>* **GOLD & PLATINUM** 49 12 Dec79
– Down south jukin' / Saturday night special / Gimme three steps / What's your name / You got that right / Gimme back my bullets / Sweet home Alabama / Free bird / That smell / On the hunt / I ain't the one / Whiskey rock-a-roller / Simple man / I know a little / Tuesday's gone / Comin' home. *(re-iss. Jul82 lp/c; MCDW/+C 456)*

Apr 82. (d-c) *(MCA2 107)* **PRONOUNCED LEH-NERD SKIN-NERD / SECOND HELPING** -

Nov 82. (lp) *<5370>* **THE BEST OF THE REST** -

Jul 84. (7") *Old Gold; (OG 9421)* **FREE BIRD (edit). / SWEET HOME ALABAMA** -
(re-iss. Aug95 on cd-s;)

Sep 86. (d-c) *(MCA2 111)* **NUTHIN' FANCY / GIVE ME BACK MY BULLETS** -

Mar 87. (d-lp/c) *Raw Power; (RAW LP/TC 031)* **ANTHOLOGY** -

Nov 87. (7") *<53206>* **WHEN YOU GOT GOOD FRIENDS. / TRUCK DRIVIN' MAN** -

Nov 87. (lp/c) *(MCF/+C* **LEGEND** (rare live) 41 Oct87
– Georgia peaches / When you got good friends / Sweet little Missy / Four walls of Raiford / Simple man / Truck drivin' man / One in the sun / Mr. Banker / Take your time.

Jan 89. (7"/12") *(MCA/+T 1315)* **FREE BIRD. / SWEET HOME ALABAMA** -

Apr 89. (lp/c/cd) *(MCG/MCGC/DMCG 6046) <42293>* **SKYNYRD'S INNYRDS**

1990. (c-s) *<54306>* **FREE BIRD. / SWEET HOME ALABAMA** -

Feb 92. (3xcd-box) *(MCA3 10390)* **THE DEFINITIVE LYNYRD SKYNYRD COLLECTION**

Mar 94. (cd/c) *Nectar; (NTR CD/C 015)* **FREEBIRD – THE VERY BEST** -
– Saturday night special / Whiskey rock & roller / Workin' for MCA / I ain't the one / Sweet home Alabama / Ballad of Curtis Loew / Tuesday's gone / Gimme 3 steps / The needle & the spoon / Free bird / Call me the breeze / What's your name / Swamp music / Gimme back my bullets / That smell / You got that right.

Sep 94. (cd) *(MCLD 19248)* **STREET SURVIVORS / SKYNYRD'S FIRST AND . . . LAST** -

Sep 96. (cd) *(MCD 1147-2)* **FREEBIRD – THE MOVIE** (live at Knebworth 1976)

Jun 97. (d-cd) *Repertoire; (RR 4637)* **OLD TIME GREATS** -

Nov 98. (cd) *B.M.G.; <44845>* **EXTENDED VERSIONS** -

Nov 98. (cd) *<MCD 11888>* **SKYNYRD'S FIRST** -

Jan 99. (d-cd) *<(MCD 11807)>* **THE ESSENTIAL LYNYRD SKYNYRD** Aug98

Mar 99. (cd) *<MCD 11941>* **THE MILLENNIUM COLLECTION: THE BEST OF LYNYRD SKYNYRD** -

Oct 99. (cd) *<MCD 12041>* **SOLO FLYTES** -

Jan 00. (cd) *Universal; (E 112173-2)* **UNIVERSAL MASTERS COLLECTION** -

Mar 00. (cd) *<112229>* **ALL TIME GREATEST HITS** -

Mar 00. (cd) *Calamari; <12606>* **THE COMPLETE LYNYRD SKYNYRD LIVE** -

Jul 00. (cd) *S.P.V.; (SPV 0762994-2) / C.M.C.; <86293>* **THEN AND NOW** Apr00

Aug 00. (cd) *Universal; <112341>* **DOUBLE TROUBLE** -

Oct 00. (3xcd-box) *Universal; (E 132182-2)* **NUTHIN' FANCY / SECOND HELPING / STREET SURVIVORS** -

Dec 00. (cd) *Universal; (AA 88112429-2) / M.C.A.; <429>* **COLLECTYBLES** Nov00

Apr 00. (cd) *B.M.G.; <45721>* **YESTERDAY AND TODAY** -

Apr 01. (cd) *Spectrum; (544451-2)* **THE ESSENTIAL COLLECTION** -

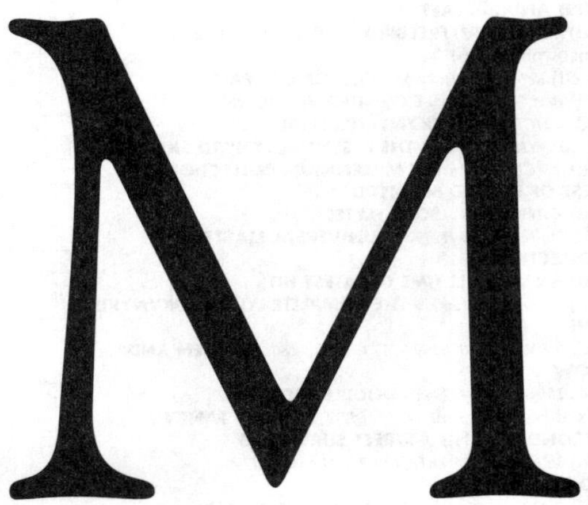

MACABRE

Formed: Chicago, Illinois, USA ... 1987 by CORPORATE DEATH, NEFARIOUS and DENNIS THE MENACE. Reliably sick metal-punksters, MACABRE specialised in tasteless tales of real-life serial killer excess, much in evidence on their 'GRIM REALITY' vinyl debut in '89. Taking black humour to its ultimate conclusion, the group further tested the patience of upstanding citizens with 1990's 'GLOOM', featuring such heartwarming ditties as, 'PATRICK PURDY KILLED FIVE AND WOUNDED THIRTY', 'DAVID BROM TOOK AN AXE' and 'FRITZ HAARMANN THE BUTCHER'. Offensive, yes, listenable, perhaps. After three years carving out their next aural assault, they came up with 'SINISTER SLAUGHTER' (1993), another addition to Nuclear Blast's gory catalogue. Featuring yet another cover art take-off of The BEATLES' 'Sgt. Pepper' – albeit a slightly more interesting one depicting a motley crew of psychopaths and serial killers – the album dedicated each song to a different killer. Among MACABRE's perverse roll call were such infamous anti-icons as Richard Ramirez, John Wayne Gacy, Ted Bundy and of course Jeffrey Dahmer. The latter was to be the sole subject matter of MACABRE's millennial "concept" set, 'DAHMER' (2000), a death-metal rock opera based on the man's horrific life. Humour, if you can call it that, doesn't come much blacker than this but at least the MACABRE trio have their tongue planted at least partly in cheek which is more than can be said for the hordes of po-faced gore obsessed death metallers who clogged up the shelves during the 90's.

Album rating: GLOOM (*4) / SINISTER SLAUGHTER (*6) / DAHMER (*4)

CORPORATE DEATH – vocals, lead guitar / **NEFARIOUS** – bass / **DENNIS THE MENACE** – drums

Vinyl Solution | E.F.A.

Oct 89. (m-lp) *(SOL 18)* **GRIM REALITY** [ ] [ ] 1987
– Serial killer / Mr. Albert Fish / Disease / Mass murder / Son of Sam / Hot rods to Hell / Ed Gein / Natural disaster.

1990. (7"white) **SHIT LIST** [-] [-] German

1990. (cd) *<EFA 17138>* **GLOOM** [-] [ ]
– Embalmer / Trampled to death / Holidays of horror / Fritz Haarmann the butcher / Evil ole soul / Harvey Glatmann / David Brom took an axe / Cremator / I need to kill / Ultra violent / Rat man / Hey Laurie Dann / Patrick Purdy killed five and wounded thirty / Exhumer / Dr. Holmes (he stripped their bones) / The green river murderer (he's still out there) / Funeral home. *(UK-iss.Apr93 lp/cd+=; SOL 20/+CD)* – GRIM REALITY

not iss. | Relapse

1992. (7"ep) **NIGHT STALKER** [-] [ ]

Nuclear Blast | Nuclear Blast

Jun 93. (lp/c/cd) *(NB 070/+MC/CD) <6060>* **SINISTER SLAUGHTER** [ ] [ ] Aug93
– Night stalker: Richard Ramirez / Ted Bundy song / Sniper in the sky: Charles Whitman / Montreal massacre: Mark Lupine / Zodiac: Identity unknown / What the hell did you do?: James Edward / Boston strangler: Albert De Salvo / Mary Bell – Mary Bell (reprise) / Killing spree: Patrick Sherrill / Is it soup yet?: Daniel Rakowitz / White hen decapitator: Michael Bethke / Howard Unrah (what have you done now?) / Gacy's lot: John Wayne Gacy / There was a young man who blew up a plane / Vampire of Dusseldorf: Peter Kurtin / Shotgun Peterson: Christopher Peterson / What's that smell?: Jeffrey Dahmer / Edmond Kemper had a horrible temper / What the heck, Richard Speck (8 nurses you) / Albert was worse than any fish in the sea. *(cd re-iss. Jun96 – US May00-; 6445>* – Fishtails / Behind the wall of sleep / Slaughter thy poser / Freeze dried man.

Jan 95. (cd-ep) *<6891>* **BEHIND THE WALL OF SLEEP** [-] [ ]
– Fishtails / Behind the wall of sleep / Slaughter thy poser / Freeze dried man.

—— folded after above, until . . .

Hammerheart | Decomposed

Jan 00. (10"ep/cd-ep) *(HHR 030/+CD)* **UNABOMBER EP** [ ] [-]
– The unabomber / Ambassador hotel / The brain / David Brom took an axe / Dr. Holmes he stripped their bones / Ed Gein / Serial killer.

Hammerheart | Olympic

Aug 00. (cd) *(HHR 071) <213>* **DAHMER** [ ] [ ] Oct00
– Dog guts / Hitchhiker / In the army now / Grandmother's house / Bloodbank / Exposure / Ambassador hotel / How 'bout some coffee / Bath house / Jeffrey Dahmer and the chocolate factory / Apartment #213 / Drill bit lobotomy / Jeffrey Dahmer blues / McDahmer's / Into the toilet with you / Coming to Chicago / Scrub a dub dub / Konerak / Media circus / Temple of bones / Trial / Do the Dahmer / Baptized / Christopher Scarver / Dahmer's dead / The brain.

MACC LADS

Formed: Macclesfield, England ... 1984 by THE BEATER, MUTTLEY McLAD and CHORLEY THE HORD (named after their hometown, duh!). On a diet of 'BEER + SEX + CHIPS 'N' GRAVY' (the name of their debut vinyl outing), these "hilarious" Northerners came on like the bastard offspring of Bernard Manning, with such P.C. (Politically Calamitous) gems as 'NOW HE'S A POOF', 'SWEATY BETTY' and 'NAGASAKI SAUCE'. Obviously their music was secondary to the lyrics, an all-purpose punkoid assault which, minus the vocal japery, couldn't get arrested. The 'LADS continued in their inimitably ignorant fashion with subsequent albums, 'BITTER, FIT CRACK' (1987), 'LIVE AT LEEDS – THE WHO?' (1988) and 'FROM BEER TO ETERNITY' a surprise UK Top 75 hit in 1989. By the release of 1994's 'ALEHOUSE ROCK', the joke had been long since flogged to death, the group no doubt retreating to a life of carry-outs and take-aways (carried-out the pub and taken-away in a taxi, that is!?).

Album rating: BEER + SEX + CHIPS 'N' GRAVY (*5) / BITTER, FIT CRACK (*4) / LIVE AT LEEDS – THE WHO? (*4) / FROM BEER TO ETERNITY (*4) / THE BEER NECESSITIES (*4) / TURTLE'S HEAD (*4) / TWENTY GOLDEN CRATES compilation (*5) / AN ORIFICE AND A GENITAL collection (*4) / ALEHOUSE ROCK (*3)

THE BEATER – vocals, guitar / **MUTTLEY McLAD** – vocals, bass / **CHORLEY THE HORD** – drums

FM Revolver | not iss.

May 85. (lp) *(WKFMLP 56)* **BEER + SEX + CHIPS 'N' GRAVY** [ ] [-]
– The lads from Macc / Beer + sex + chips 'n' gravy / Boddies / Sweaty Betty / England's glory / Blackpool / Miss Macclesfield / God's gift to women / Get weavin' / Now he's a poof / Nagasaki sauce / Saturday night / Buenos Aires / Charlotte / Failure with girls / Do you love me? / Dan's underpant / Twenty pints / The Macc Lads party. *(re-iss. Aug89 on 'Hectic House' c/cd; HH/+CD 1) (cd-iss. Feb91; WKFMCD 110) (<re-iss. Nov93 on 'Dojo' cd/c; DOJO CD/MC 154>) (cd re-iss. Feb01 on 'Harry May'; MAYDP 015)*

Oct 86. (7"/12") *(HH 1S/+T)* **EH UP! LET'S SUP. /** [ ] [-]
(above single issued on 'Hectic House')

Aug 87. (lp) *(WKFMLP 100)* **BITTER, FIT CRACK** [ ] [-]
– Barrel's round / Guess me weight / Uncle Knobby / Maid of ale / Dan's big log / Got to be Gordon's / Bitter, fit crack / Julie the schooly / Doctor doctor / Torremolinos / Al O'Peesha. *(c-iss.Aug89 on 'Hectic House'; HH 7) (cd-iss. Feb91; WKFMCD 100) (<re-iss. Nov93 on 'Dojo' cd/c+=; DOJO CD/MC 155>)* – Feed your face / Jingle bells.

Nov 87. (7") *(VHF 42)* **JINGLE BELLS. / BARREL'S ROUND** [ ] [-]

Mar 88. (7") *(VHF 44)* **PIE TASTER. / NO SHEEP TIL BUXTON** [ ] [-]
(12"+=) *(12VHF 44)* – Dan's underpant (live).
(re-iss. Aug89 on 'Hectic House'; HH 9)

Aug 88. (lp/c/cd) *(WKFM LP/MC/XD 115)* **LIVE AT LEEDS – THE WHO? (live)** [ ] [-]
– Sweaty Betty / Ben Nevis / Bloink / Do you love me / God's gift to women / Charlotte / Blackpool / Lads from Macc / Now he's a poof / Doctor doctor / Julie the schooly / Guess me weight / Miss Macclesfield / Fat bastard / Get weavin' / Barrel's round / Dan's underpant. *(c re-iss. Aug89 on 'Hectic House'; HH 10) (<re-iss. Mar94 on 'Dojo' cd/c; DOJO CD/MC 161>)*

Hectic House | not iss.

Sep 89. (c/cd/lp) *(HH/+CD/LP 12)* **FROM BEER TO ETERNITY** [72] [-]
– Alton Towers / Geordie girl / Bloik! / No sheep 'til Buxton / All day drinking / Tab after tab / Lucy Lastic / My pub / Dead cat / Lady Muck / Gordon's revenge / Pie taster / Dans round un 'andbag / Ben Nevis / Fluffy pup / Stoppyback / Ugly women / That's gay. *(<re-iss. May94 on 'Dojo' cd/c; DOJO CD/MC 157>)*

Nov 90. (cd/lp) *(HH CD/LP 14)* **THE BEER NECESSITIES** [ ] [-]
– Alcohol / Germans / Fellatio Neil, son / Desperate Dan / Grease stop / Apprentice dentist / Man in the boat / Newcy Brown / McCavity / Chester zoo / Naughty boy / Mr. Methane / More tea vicar? / Two stroke Eddie / Animal testing / Don't fear the sweeper / Poodles. *(<re-iss. May94 on 'Dojo' cd/c; DOJO CD/MC 158>) (cd re-iss. Feb01 on 'Harry May'; MAYOCD 517)*

Sep 91. (m-cd/m-c; shared with VELVET UNDERPANTS) *(HH 17 CD/CS)* **TURTLES HEADS** [ ] [-]
– Piles / Turtles heads / Prestbury girls / VELVET UNDERPANTS: Pissed off mate / Aunty drugs / Vulvahampton.

Up Not Down | not iss.

May 94. (cd/c) *(UPNO CD/MC 1)* **ALEHOUSE ROCK** [ ] [-]
– Piles / Alehouse rock / Back on the pies again / Tart with the heart / Vigilante shanty / Presburt girls / Village idiot / Frogbashing / Gone fishin' / Rockweillers / Father's day / Turtles heads / Dirty glass / Thinking in the dark / Helen of Fowey / Hen night. *(cd re-iss. Mar96 on 'Dojo'; DOJOCD 250) (<cd re-iss. Sep98 on 'Snapper'; SMMCD 536>)*

– compilations, etc. –

Oct 92. (cd/c/lp) *Streetlink; (STR CD/MC/LP 015)* **TWENTY GOLDEN CRATES** [ ] [-]
– No sheep 'til Buxton / Sweaty Betty / Buenos Aires '91 / Beer + sex + chips 'n' gravy / Guess me weight / Maid of ale / Ben Nevis / Blackpool / Dan's underpants / Knock knock / Gordon's revenge / My pub / Charlotte / Dead cat / Boddies / Fluffy pup / Julie the schooly / Lady Muck / Miss Macclesfield / Nagasaki sauce / Barrels round. *(cd+=)* – Twenty pints / Saturday night. *(re-iss. May94 on 'Dojo' cd/c; DOJO CD/MC 115) (<cd re-iss. Sep97 on 'Snapper'; SMMCD 525>)*

Feb 94. (cd/c) *Dojo; (<DOJO CD/MC 141>)* **AN ORIFICE AND A GENITAL** (out-takes 1986-1991) [ ] [ ] Oct94
– Monkees / Eh up! let's sup / Fat bastard / Baggy Anne / Head kicked in / Knutsford / No sleep 'til Buxton / Pie taster / I love Macc / Made of ale / Knock knock / Brevil brevil / Manfred Macc / Buenos Aires '90 / Fellatio Neil, son / Two stroke Eddie /

Even uglier woman. *(<cd re-iss. Apr98 on 'Snapper'; SMMCD 533>) (cd re-iss. Feb01 on 'Harry May'; MAYDP 014)*

Jun 99. (d-cd) *Snapper; (SMMCD 135)* **THE LADS FROM MACC** -

Jun 99. (cd) *Harry May; (<MAYOCD 115>)* **GOD'S GIFT TO WOMEN** Apr00

Nov 99. (d-cd) *Eagle; (EDGCD 109)* **ANTHOLOGY**

May 00. (cd) *Snapper; (SMXCD 102)* **THE BOX** -
– (20 GOLDEN CRATES / FROM BEER TO ETERNITY / AN ORIFICE & A GENTLEMAN)

MACHINE HEAD

Formed: Oakland, California, USA . . . mid '92 by ex-VIOLENCE frontman ROBB FLYNN, LOGAN MADER, ADAM DUCE and CHRIS KONTOS. Dragging the flagging spirit of heavy metal kicking and screaming into the 90's, MACHINE HEAD roared into life with the universally acclaimed, COLIN RICHARDSON-produced debut album, 'BURN MY EYES' (1994). Rupturing eardrums with a bass-heavy bludgeon of mogadon guitars and a vocal style that alternated between CHRIS CORNELL (Soundgarden) and JAMES HETFIELD (Metallica), MACHINE HEAD became the ace in 'Roadrunner's (their label) pack, hitting the UK Top 30. Although they were signed to 'Interscope' in their native land, the group concentrated more on the British metal scene, especially after Kerrang! proclaimed them to be the best machine since ZAK DE LA ROCHA and Co (RATM). In 1995, one of the tracks from the album, 'OLD', was a surprise gatecrasher into the UK Top 50, the single backed by covers of POISON IDEA and CRO-MAGS material. With newcomer DAVE McCLAIN on the drumstool, their much-anticipated second set, 'THE MORE THINGS CHANGE . . .', was finally delivered early in 1997, the UK Top 20 album again proving that no frills, heavy-duty metal was still viable. Another round of ear-bashing was just what the doctor ordered, although not my doctor. Now without guitarist MADER (replaced by AHRUE LUSTER), MACHINE HEAD spurted out their third album, 'THE BURNING RED' (1999). The record entered the US Top 100 (their first to do so!) and the UK Top 20, although what the metal pundits from Kerrang! thought of their version of the Police's 'MESSAGE IN A BOTTLE', I dread to think. – take them away Sgt. STING.

Album rating: BURN MY EYES (*8) / THE MORE THINGS CHANGE . . . (*6) / THE BURNING RED (*4)

ROBB FLYNN – vocals, guitar (ex-VIOLENCE) / **LOGAN MADER** – guitar / **ADAM DUCE** – bass, vocals / **CHRIS KONTOS** – drums

Roadrunner Interscope

Aug 94. (cd) *(RR 90169)* **BURN MY EYES** 25
– Davidian / Old / A thousand lies / None but my own / The rage to overcome / Death church / A nation on fire / Blood for blood / I'm your god now / Real eyes, realize, real lies / Block. *(re-iss. May95 cd/c/lp; RR 9016-2/-4/-1)*

Oct 94. (12") **INFECTED. / PROTOPLAN** -

May 95. (10"pic-d-ep) *(RR 23408)* **OLD / A NATION ON FIRE (demo) / REAL LIES – FUCK IT ALL (demo) / OLD (demo)** 43
(cd-ep) *(RR 23403)* – ('A'side) / Davidian (live) / Hard times (live) / Death church (demo).
(cd-s) *(RR 23405)* – ('A'side) / Death church (convent mix) / Old (eve of apocalypse mix) / The rage to overcome.

Aug 95. (10"pic-d) **DEATH CHURCH. / A NATION ON FIRE (demo)**
(cd-s+=) – Fuck it all (demo) / Old (demo).
(cd-s) – ('A'side) / Old (mix) / The rage to overcome (demo).

—— **DAVE McCLAIN** – drums (ex-SACRED REICH) repl. KONTOS

Mar 97. (cd/c/lp) *(RR 8860-2/-4/-1) <INT 846.371>* **THE MORE THINGS CHANGE . . .** 16
– Ten ton hammer / Take my scars / Struck a nerve / Down to none / The frontlines / Spine / Bay of pigs / Violate / Blistering / Blood of the zodiac.

Nov 97. (cd-ep) *(RR 2257-3)* **TAKE MY SCARS / NEGATIVE CREEP / TAKE MY SCARS (live) / BLOOD FOR BLOOD (live)** 73
(cd-ep) *(RR 2257-5)* – (first 2 tracks) / Ten ton hammer (demo) / Struck a nerve (demo).

—— now without LOGAN MADER who was repl. by **AHRUE LUSTER**

Aug 99. (cd) *<(RR 8651-2)>* **THE BURNING RED** 13 88
– Enter the phoenix / Desire to fire / Nothing left / The blood, the sweat, the tears / Silver / From this day / Exhale the vile / Message in a bottle / Devil with the king's card / I defy / Five / The burning red.

Dec 99. (cd-s) *(RR 2138-3)* **FROM THIS DAY / ALCOHOLOCAUST / HOUSE OF SUFFERING** 74

Jul 00. (cd-ep) *(RR 2093-3)* **YEAR OF THE DRAGON EP**
– The blood, the sweat, the tears / Desire to fire (live) / The blood, the sweat, the tears (live) / From this day (live) / New resistance (demo).

MADAM X

Formed: New York, USA . . . 1983 by sisters MAXINE and ROXY PETRUCCI, along with BRET KAISER and CHRISTOPHER 'GODZILLA' DOLIBER. They soon relocated to L.A., where their tacky sleaze-pop/metal found a natural audience. Signed to 'Jet' records, they released the hackneyed 'HIGH IN HIGH SCHOOL' as a debut single in early '85. Produced by veteran rocker RICK DERRINGER, a long player, 'WE RESERVE THE RIGHT', followed soon after. It's safe to say that MADAM X were regarded as something of a joke in critical circles, reviewers giving the album short thrift while the band's would-be raunchy image failed to attract many record buyers. PETRUCCI wisely bailed out soon after, joining the up and coming all-girl hard-rock group, VIXEN. KAISER also gave up the ghost, his replacement being one SEBASTIAN BACH (future SKID ROW). The modified line-up struggled on for a short period, trying in vain to breathe new life into the group's sagging career prospects. • **Note:** not to be confused with MADAME X who recorded for 'Atlantic'.

Album rating: WE RESERVE THE RIGHT (*4)

BRET KAISER – vocals / **MAXINE PETRUCCI** – guitar / **CHRISTOPHER 'GODZILLA' DOLIBER** – bass / **ROXY PETRUCCI** – drums

Jet Jet

Feb 85. (7"/7"pic-d) *(JET/+P 7044)* **HIGH IN HIGH SCHOOL. / METAL IN MY VEINS**

Mar 85. (lp/c) *(JET LP/CA 242) <39885>* **WE RESERVE THE RIGHT** Nov84
– High in high school / Come one, come all / She's hot tonight / Dirty girls / Max volume / Metal in my veins / Reserve the right to rock / Good with figures / Cat's got your tongue / We want rock / Stand up and fight.

—— **SEBASTIAN BACH** – vocals; repl. KAISER

—— **MARK McCONNELL** – drums; repl. ROXY who joined VIXEN

—— split when DOLIBER formed GODZILLA. BACH found fame in SKID ROW.

MADBALL

Formed: New York, USA . . . 1989 by Florida born vocalist FREDDY CRICIEN, younger brother of AGNOSTIC FRONT's ROGER MIRET. In fact, the young FREDDY had performed alongside them on stage, while the band's VINNIE STIGMA had provided him with the "MADBALL" nickname. AGNOSTIC FRONT were MADBALL's backing band on the debut 1989 single, 'BALL OF DESTRUCTION'. An older and wiser MADBALL (without his brother) retained guitarist STIGMA and drummer WILL SHEPLER, while adding second guitarist MATT HENDERSON and bassist HOYA for a long-awaited follow-up, the EP 'DROPPIN' MANY SUCKERS' (1991). They finally delivered their debut album, 'SET IT OFF', in 1994, a hardcore power-metal affair that barely left the starting gate. Every alternate year from then on, CRICIEN and his po-faced crew blasted out with an odd set of hardcore headbanging, although when the band were not having a ball, the frontman worked as a plumber!

Album rating: SET IT OFF (*6) / DEMONSTRATING MY STYLE (*6) / LOOK MY WAY (*5) / HOLD IT DOWN (*5)

FREDDY CRICIEN – vocals / **VINNIE STIGMA** – guitar (of AGNOSTIC FRONT) / **ROGER MIRET** – bass (of AGNOSTIC FRONT) / **WILL SHEPLER** – drums

not iss. In-Effect

1989. (7") **BALL OF DESTRUCTION. /** -

—— **MATT HENDERSON** – guitar + **HOYA** – bass; repl. ROGER MIRET

not iss. Wreck-age

Dec 91. (cd-ep) *<10>* **DROPPIN' MANY SUCKERS EP** -
– Spit on your grave / Never had it / Across your face / Step on you / No return / The blame / We should care / Get out / It's my life / Ready to fight / Friend or foe.

Roadrunner Roadrunner

Aug 94. (cd) *<(RR 8991-2)>* **SET IT OFF**
– Set it off / Lockdown / New York City / Never had it / It's time / C.T.Y.C. / Across your face / Down by law / Spit on your grave / Face to face / Smell the bacon / Get out / The world is mine / Friend or foe. *(*

Jun 96. (cd/lp) *<(RR 8875-2/-1)>* **DEMONSTRATING MY STYLE**
– Demonstrating my style / Unity / Live or die / Pride (times are changing) / Streets of hate / Back of the bus / Hardcore still lives! / Nuestra familia / 5-0 / Addict / True to the game / Godfather / In memory of . . . / Ball of destruction. *(cd re-iss. May99; same)*

—— now without STIGMA who returned to AGNOSTIC FRONT

—— **JOHN LAFATAA** – drums (ex-MIND OVER MATTER) repl. SHEPLER

Mar 98. (7") *(VR 076)* **BEEN THERE DONE THAT. / TALKIN' TO MYSELF / FOOLS DIE** -
(above issued on 'Victory')

Jun 98. (cd) *<(RR 8807-2)>* **LOOK MY WAY**
– Look my way / Moment of truth / Cut off / Temptation or restraint / Waste of time / False threats / Pushin' me / Walk away / Our family / Lesson of life / All I can take / Been there, done that. *(cd re-iss. May99; same)*

Epitaph Epitaph

Jun 00. (cd/lp) *<(6578-2/-1)>* **HOLD IT DOWN**
– Intro / Can't stop, won't stop / Hold it down / Fall this time / Everyday hate / Done / Say what / D.I.F.M.M. (fuck you) / Show no fear / Never look back / Still searching / Confessions / Thinking to myself / Semper fi.

– compilations, etc. –

May 96. (cd/c/lp) *Century Media; <(CM 77130 CD/MC/LP)>* **BALL OF DESTRUCTION** (early material)
– Smell the bacon (what's with you?) / Discriminate me / We should care / Colossal man / Get out / Last warning / Fight / It's my life / Smell the bacon (what's with you?) / Spit on your grave / Discriminate me / Never had it / Ready to fight / Get out / Across your face / We should care / No return / Step to you / Friend or foe / It's my life / WFMU interview / Over the edge / United blood.

MAD SEASON (see under ⇒ ALICE IN CHAINS)

MAGNUM

Formed: Birmingham, England . . . 1973 by BOB CATLEY and TONY CLARKIN. After initially backing US stars like DEL SHANNON, playing mostly covers (their 1975 debut single was a version of The Searchers' pop hit, 'SWEETS FOR MY SWEET', featuring original vocalist DAVE MORGAN), MAGNUM only really hit their stride after signing to 'Jet' records and fashioning a more characterstic pomp-rock approach, showcased on their debut long player, 'KINGDOM OF MADNESS' (1978). With RICHARD BAILEY, KEX GORIN and COLIN 'Wally' LOWE (MORGAN's replacement) completing the line-up, the group created a distinctive fusion of heavy pomp-metal, orchestration and classical flute flourishes (courtesy of BAILEY), breaking into the UK Top 60 and embarking on a heavy touring schedule, supporting JUDAS PRIEST in the UK and BLUE OYSTER CULT in the States. Though the Leo Lyons-produced 'MAGNUM II' (1979) failed to chart, the band finally broke into the UK Top 40 with the live 'MARAUDER' (1980). This minor success was convincingly consolidated with 'CHASE THE DRAGON' (1982), the group's most impressive and commercially viable (Top 20) set to date. The following year's 'THE ELEVENTH HOUR' (1983) continued in their grandiose, vaguely mystical tradition, although a subsequent disagreement with 'Jet' almost saw the group prematurely disintegrate. In the event, they decided to carry on, 'FM-Revolver' stepping in for the release of the well-received 'ON A STORYTELLER'S NIGHT' (1985). The record proved MAGNUM were far from being a spent force and its Top 30 success led to a major label deal with 'Polydor'. Their ROGER TAYLOR-produced major label debut, 'VIGILANTE' (1986), saw MICKEY BARKER replace SIMPSON on the drum stool, their growing UK popularity gaining substantial support from the metal press. Given their increasingly high profile, it was no surprise when the 'WINGS OF HEAVEN' set made the UK Top 5 in 1988, the album spawning their biggest hit single to date in 'START TALKING LOVE'. With the help of such songwriting pros as RUSS BALLARD and JIM VALLANCE, the KEITH OLSEN-produced 'GOODNIGHT L.A.' (1990) was MAGNUM's most overtly commercial release to date, again making the UK Top 10. The subsequent tour was partly documented in double live set, 'THE SPIRIT' (1991), while more recently the group signed to 'E.M.I.' for 1994's 'ROCK ART' after releasing 'SLEEPWALKING' (1992) on 'Music For Nations'. Against all the odds and flying in the face of fashion, MAGNUM remain perenially popular with aging British rock fans, one of the few such bands to maintain any commercial potential.

Album rating: KINGDOM OF MADNESS (*7) / MAGNUM II (*5) / MARAUDER (*4) / CHASE THE DRAGON (*6) / THE ELEVENTH HOUR (*6) / ON A STORYTELLER'S NIGHT (*6) / VIGILANTE (*5) / WINGS OF HEAVEN (*6) / GOODNIGHT L.A. (*5) / THE SPIRIT (*5) / SLEEPWALKING (*4) / CHAPTER AND VERSE – THE BEST OF MAGNUM compilation (*6) / ROCK ART (*4)

BOB CATLEY – vocals / **TONY CLARKIN** – guitar / **RICHARD BAILEY** – keyboards, flute / **DAVE MORGAN** – bass, vox / **KEX GORIN** – drums

C.B.S. | not iss.

Feb 75. (7") *(CBS 2959)* **SWEETS FOR MY SWEET. / MOVIN' ON** [ ] [-]

— **COLIN 'Wally' LOWE** – bass, vocals repl. MORGAN

Jet | Jet

Jul 78. (7") *(SJET 116)* **KINGDOM OF MADNESS. / IN THE BEGINNING** [ ] [-]

Aug 78. (lp/c) *(JET LP/CA 210)* **KINGDOM OF MADNESS** [58] [ ]
– In the beginning / Baby rock me / Universe / Kingdom of madness / All that is real / The bringer / Invasion / Lords of chaos / All come together. *(re-iss. Mar87 on 'Castle' lp/c/cd; CLA LP/MC/CD 126) (re-iss. Feb89 on 'FM-Revolver' lp/c/cd/pic-lp; WKFM LP/MC/XD/PD 118) (<cd re-iss. Aug99 on 'Essential'; ESMCD 747>)*

Sep 78. (7") *(SJET 128)* **INVASION. / UNIVERSE** [ ] [-]

May 79. (7") *<5059>* **UNIVERSE. / BABY ROCK ME** [-] [ ]

Sep 79. (7") *(JET 155)* **CHANGES. / LONESOME STAR** [ ] [-]

Oct 79. (lp/c) *(JET LP/CA 222)* **MAGNUM II** [ ] [ ]
– Great adventure / Changes / The battle / If I could live forever / Reborn / So cold the night / Foolish heart / Stayin' alive / Firebird / All of my life. *(re-iss. Mar87 on 'Castle' lp/c/cd; CAL LP/MC/CD 125) (re-iss. Feb89 on 'FM-Revolver' lp/c/cd/pic-lp; WKFM LP/MC/CD/PD 119) (<cd re-iss. Aug99 on 'Essential'; ESMCD 748>)*

Nov 79. (7") *(JET 163)* **FOOLISH HEART. / BABY ROCK ME** [ ] [-]

Mar 80. (7") *(JET 175)* **ALL OF MY LIFE (live). / GREAT ADVENTURE (live)** [47] [-]
(d7"+=) *(JET 175)* – Invasion (live) / Kingdom of madness (live).

Apr 80. (lp/c) *(JET LP/CA 230)* **MARAUDER (live)** [34] [ ]
– If I could live forever / The battle / Foolish heart / In the beginning / Reborn / Changes / So cold the night / Lords of chaos. *(re-iss. Mar87 on 'Castle' lp/c/cd; CAL LP/MC/CD 124) (<cd re-iss. Aug99 on 'Essential'; ESMCD 749>)*

— **MARK STANWAY** (b.27 Jul'54) – keyboards repl. BAILEY

Nov 80. (7") *(JET 188)* **CHANGES (live remix). / EVERYBODY NEEDS** [ ] [-]

Feb 82. (7") *(JET 7020)* **LIGHTS BURNED OUT. / LONG DAYS BLACK NIGHTS** [ ] [-]

Mar 82. (lp/pic-lp/c) *(JET LP/PD/CA 235)* **CHASE THE DRAGON** [17] [ ]
– Soldier of the line / On the edge of the world / The spirit / Sacred hour / Walking the straight line / We all play the game / The teacher / The lights burned out. *(cd-iss. Jan87; JETCD 004) (re-iss. Jun88 on 'FM-Revolver' lp/c/cd/pic-lp; WKFM LP/MC/XD/PD 112) (<cd re-iss. Aug99 on 'Essential'; ESMCD 750>)*

Sep 82. (7") *(JET 7027)* **BACK TO EARTH (live). / HOLD BACK YOUR LOVE (live)** [ ] [-]
(d7"+=) *(JET 7027)* – Soldier of the line (live) / Sacred Hour (live).

May 83. (lp/pic-lp/c) *(JET LP/PD/CA 240)* **THE ELEVENTH HOUR** [38] [ ]
– The prize / Breakdown / The great disaster / Vicious companions / So far away / Hit and run / One night of passion / The word / Young and precious souls / The road to Paradise. *(cd-iss. Jan87; JETCD 005) (re-iss. Jun88 on 'FM-Revolver' lp/c/cd/pic-lp; WKFM LP/MC/XD/PD 111) (<cd re-iss. Aug99 on 'Essential'; ESMCD 751>)*

— **JIM SIMPSON** – drums (ex-BLOOMSBURY SET) repl. GORIN / **EDDIE GEORGE** – keyboards repl. STANWAY who also joined ROBIN GEORGE

— **MARK STANWAY** – keyboards returned GRAND SLAM, to repl. EDDIE

FM-Revolver | not iss.

Mar 85. (7") *(VHF 4)* **JUST LIKE AN ARROW. / TWO HEARTS** [ ] [-]
(12"+=) *(12VHF 4)* – The word.

May 85. (lp/s-lp/pic-lp/c/cd) *(WKFM LP/GP/PD/MC/CD 34)* **ON A STORYTELLER'S NIGHT** [24] [-]
– How far Jerusalem / Just like an arrow / Storyteller's night / Before first light / Les morts dansant / Endless love / Two hearts / Steal your heart / All England's eyes / The last dance. *(cd re-iss. Jul93 & Feb98; JETCD 1007)*

May 85. (7"/12") *(VHF/12VHF 10)* **STORYTELLER'S NIGHT. / BEFORE FIRST LIGHT** [ ] [-]

— **CATLEY, CLARKIN, STANWAY + LOWE** recruited new member **MICKEY BARKER** – drums to repl. SIMPSON

Polydor | Polydor

Jul 86. (7") *(POSP 798)* **LONELY NIGHT. / LES MORT DANSANT (live)** [70] [-]
(ext.12") *(POSPX 798)* – Hold back your love (live).
(d7"+=) *(POSPG 798)* – All England's eyes (live) / Hit and run (live).

Oct 86. (7") *(POSP 833)* **MIDNIGHT (YOU WON'T BE SLEEPING). / BACK STREET KID** [ ] [-]
(12"+=) *(POSPX 833)* – ('A'version).
(12"pic-d) *(POSPP 833)* – ('A'version) / Kingdom of madness (live).

Oct 86. (lp/c)(cd)(pic-lp) *(POLD/+C 5198)(POLD 829-986-2)(831708-1Y)* **VIGILANTE** [24] [-]
– Lonely night / Need a lot of love / Sometime love / Midnight (you won't be sleeping) / Red on the highway / Holy rider / When the world comes down / Vigilante / Back street kid.

Feb 87. (7"/ext.12"/cd-s) *(POSP/POSPC/POC 850)* **WHEN THE WORLD COMES DOWN. / VIGILANTE** [ ] [-]

Mar 88. (7"/7"g-f/7"s) *(POSP/+G/P 910)* **DAYS OF NO TRUST. / MAYBE TONIGHT** [32] [-]
(ext.12"+=/ext.12"s+=) *(POSPX/+P 910)* – The spirit (live) / Two hearts (live) / How far Jerusalem (live).
(cd-s+=) *(POC 910)* – ('A'extended) / How far Jerusalem (live).
(12"white-ltd.) *(POSPW 910)* – ('A'side) / The spirit (live) / Two hearts (live).

Apr 88. (lp/c)(cd) *(POLD/+C 5221)(POLD 835 277-2) <835856>* **WINGS OF HEAVEN** [5] [ ] Jul88
– Days of no trust / Wild swan / Start talking love / One step away / It must have been love / Different worlds / Pray for the day / Don't wake the lion (too old to die young). *(pic-lp-iss.Dec88+=; POLDP 5221)* – C'est La Vie. *(re-iss. cd Apr95; same)*

Apr 88. (7"/7"g-f) *(POSP/+G 920)* **START TALKING LOVE. / C'EST LA VIE** [22] [-]
(12"+=/12"red+=) *(POSPX/POSXR 920) – Back to Earth (live) / Storyteller's night (live).*
(cd-s+=) *(POC 920)* – Back to Earth (live) / Sacred hour (live).
(7"sha-pic-d) *(POSPP 920)* – ('A'side) / Days of no trust.

Jun 88. (7") *(POSP 930)* **IT MUST HAVE BEEN LOVE. / CRYING TIME (live)** [33] [-]
(12"+=/12"blue+=) *(POSPX/POSXB 930)* – Lonely night (live) / Just like an arrow (live).
(cd-s+=) *(POCD 930)* – Lights burned out (live) / Lonely night (live) / Cry for you (live).

Jun 90. (7"/c-s) *(PO/+CS 88)* **ROCKIN' CHAIR. / MAMA** [27] [-]
(12"+=/cd-s+=) *(PZ/+CD 8)* – Where do you run to.

Jul 90. (cd/c/lp) *(843568-2/-4/-1)* **GOODNIGHT L.A.** [9] [-]
– Rockin' chair / Mama / Only a memory / Reckless man / Matter of survival / What kind of love is this / Heartbroke & busted / Shoot / No way out / Cry for you / Born to be king.

Aug 90. (7"/c-s) *(PO/+CS 94)* **HEARTBROKE AND BUSTED. / HANGING TREE** [49] [-]
(12"+=/cd-s+=) *(PZ/+CDT 94)* – Cry for you.

Aug 91. (cd/c/d-lp) *(511169-2/-4/-1)* **THE SPIRIT (live)** [50] [ ]
– Introduction / Vigilante / Days of no trust / Mama / Need a lot of love / Pray for the day / Les morts dansants / Reckless man / How far Jerusalem / The spirit / On a storyteller's night / Rocking chair / Kingdom of madness / Sacred hour / When the world comes down. *(cd re-iss. Mar94 on 'Disky' d-cd; DCD 5315) (re-iss. Oct98 on 'Snapper'; SMDCD 188)*

Music For Nations | not iss.

Sep 92. (7"ep/12"ep) *(KUT 148)* **ONLY IN AMERICA. / SLEEPWALKING** [ ] [-]
(12"+=/cd-s+=) *(12/CD KUT 148)* – Just a little bit / Caught in love.

Oct 92. (cd/c/lp) *(CD/T+/MFN 143)* **SLEEPWALKING** [27] [-]
– Stormy weather / Too much to ask / You're the one / The flood / Broken wheel / Just one more heartbreak / Every woman, every man / Only in America / Sleepwalking / Prayer for a stranger / The long ride.

E.M.I. | E.M.I.

Jun 94. (cd/c) *(CD/TC EMD 1066) <829365-2>* **ROCK ART** [57] [ ] Feb95
– We all need to be loved / Hard hearted woman / Back in your arms again / Rock heavy / The tall ships / Tell tale eyes / Love's a stranger / Hush a bye baby / Just this side of Heaven / I will decide myself / On Christmas day.

– compilations, etc. –

Apr 86. (d-lp/c/cd) *Raw Power; (RAW LP/TC/CD 007)* **ANTHOLOGY** [ ] [-]
– In the beginning / Lord of chaos / Kingdom of madness / The bringer / Great adventures / Firebird / Foolish heart / Stayin' alive / If I could live forever / Reborn (live) / Changes (live) / Walking the straight line / We all play the game / The spirit / The prise / Vicious companions / The word / Hit and run / So far away.

Oct 86. (lp/c) *Jet; (JET LP/CA 244)* **VINTAGE MAGNUM** [ ] [-]

Nov 87. (lp/c/cd/pic-lp) *FM Revolver; (WKFM LP/MC/XD/PD 106)* **MIRADOR** [ ] [-]

Feb 88. (d-lp/c/d-cd) *That's Original; (TFO LP/MC/CD 1)* **VINTAGE MAGNUM / THE ELEVENTH HOUR** [ ] [-]

1988. (3"cd-ep) *Special Edition; (CD 3-7)* **THE LIGHTS BURNED OUT / IF I COULD LIVE FOREVER / SACRED HOUR** [ ] [-]

Jul 88. (c/cd) *Knight; (KN MC/CD 10009)* **NIGHTRIDING** [ ] [-]

May 89. (lp/c/cd) *Receiver; (<RR LP/LC/CD 113>)* **MAGNUM LIVE – INVASION (live)** [ ] [ ] May99
(w/ free+=) – (interview disc).

Jun 90. (6xlp-box/6xc-box/6xcd-box) *FM Revolver; (WKFMBX/+C/XD 145)* **FOUNDATION** –
Nov 90. (cd/lp) *Castle; (CCS CD/LP 272)* **THE COLLECTION** –
Apr 93. (cd/c/lp) *Jet; (JET CD/CA/LP 1005)* **ARCHIVE** –
(cd re-iss. Nov97 on 'Rialto'; RMCD 217)
May 93. (cd/c) *Polydor; (519 301-2/-4)* **CHAPTER & VERSE (THE VERY BEST OF MAGNUM)** –
– Rockin' chair / Vigilante / C'est la vie / Heartbroke & busted / On a storyteller's night (live) / Start talking love / Mama / Lonely nights / Crying time / Midnight (remix) / It must have been love / Days of no trust / Don't wake the lion / Just like an arrow / No way out / When the world comes down. *(re-iss. cd Apr95; same)*
Jun 93. (cd/c) *Optima;* **CAPTURED LIVE (live)** –
Nov 93. (cd/c/lp) *Jet; (JET CD/CA/LP 1006)* **KEEPING THE NITE LITE BURNING**
Jun 94. (cd) *Jet; (<JETCD 1008>)* **UNCORKED (THE BEST OF MAGNUM)**
May 95. (cd) *Spectrum; (550 737-2)* **FIREBIRD** –
Sep 95. (cd/c) *Emporio; (EMPR CD/MC 596)* **VINTAGE MAGNUM – ELECTRIC AND ACOUSTIC** –
Feb 99. (d-cd) *;* **THE LAST DANCE** –
Jul 99. (cd) *Cleopatra; <563>* **PROGRESSIVE CLASSICS** –
May 00. (cd) *Zoom Club; (ZCRCD 26)* **DAY OF WONDER – LIVE** –
May 00. (d-cd) *Essential; (ESACD 886)* **ROAD TO PARADISE – THE MAGNUM ANTHOLOGY 1978-1983**

MAHOGANY RUSH

Formed: Montreal, Quebec, Canada . . . Autumn 1970 by FRANK MARINO, who, after recovering in hospital from a bad acid trip, claimed he was visited by an apparition of the recently deceased JIMI HENDRIX!. When he awoke from unconsciousness (or did he?), FRANK was convinced he could play like his idol, although this legendary tale has been questioned repeatedly. MARINO duly recruited PAUL HARWOOD and JIM AYOUB, to form his own "Experience" trio, the MAHOGANY RUSH debut, 'MAXOOM' (1973) extremely derivative of classic HENDRIX. He/they followed in the same path with each successive album, the second set, 'CHILD OF THE NOVELTY' (1974) hitting the US Top 100. By his fourth album, the enigmatically titled, 'MAHOGANY RUSH IV', FRANK was showing worrying signs of guitar originality and innovation. Better experienced live, FRANK MARINO & MAHOGANY RUSH (their recently adapted moniker) released a double concert set in 1978, entitled, er . . . 'LIVE'. In the early 80's, with brother VINCE also contributing guitar (although the identity of his particular spectral visitation remains unclear?), the group released 'WHAT'S NEXT' (1980), the last album for some time to appear under the MAHOGANY RUSH banner, AYOUB subsequently leaving. MARINO then struck out on a solo sojourn, getting off to a good start in 1981 with an acclaimed performance on the 'Heavy Metal Holocaust' bill at Port Vale's football ground. For the next decade, MARINO (occasionally with a re-grouped MAHOGANY RUSH) released a handful of albums, the final set being, 'FROM THE HIP' (1993). • **Covers:** PURPLE HAZE (Jimi Hendrix) / ALL ALONG THE WATCHTOWER (Bob Dylan) / JOHNNY B. GOODE (Chuck Berry) / I'M A KING BEE (Slim Harpo) / NORWEGIAN WOOD (Beatles) / MONA (Bo Diddley) / etc.

Album rating: MAXOOM (*3) / CHILD OF THE NOVELTY (*4) / STRANGE UNIVERSE (*5) / MAHOGANY RUSH IV (*6) / Frank Marino & Mahogany Rush: WORLD ANTHEM (*6) / FRANK MARINO & MAHOGANY RUSH LIVE (*5) / TALES OF THE UNEXPECTED (*5) / WHAT'S NEXT (*4) / Frank Marino: THE POWER OF ROCK AND ROLL (*5) / JUGGERNAUT (*7) / FULL CIRCLE (*7) / DOUBLE LIVE (*5) / DRAGONFLY (THE BEST OF FRANK MARINO & MAHOGANY RUSH) compilation (*6)

FRANK MARINO (b.22 Aug'54, Del Rio, Texas) – vocals, lead guitar / **PAUL HARWOOD** (b.28 Feb'39, Quebec, Canada) – bass / **JIMMY AYOUB** (b. 7 Dec'41, Honolulu, Hawaii) – drums

not iss. Kot'ai

1973. (lp) *<N-936>* **MAXOOM** –
– Maxoom / Buddy / Magic man / Funky woman / Madness / All in your mind / Blues / Boardwalk lady / Back on home / The new beginning. *<re-iss. Feb75 on '20th Century'; T 463>*

not iss. 20th Century

Aug 74. (lp) *<T 451>* **CHILD OF THE NOVELTY** – / 74
– Look outside / Thru the Milky Way / Talking 'bout a feelin' / Child of the novelty / Makin' my wave / A new rock and roll / Changing / Plastic man / Guilt / Chains of (s)pace. *(UK cd-iss. Aug91 on 'Repertoire'; REP 4029)*
Sep 74. (7") *<2111>* **CHILD OF THE NOVELTY. / A NEW ROCK AND ROLL** –
Jun 75. (lp) *<T 482>* **STRANGE UNIVERSE** – / 84
– Tales of the Spanish warrior / The king who stole (. . .the universe) / Satisfy your soul / Land of 1000 nights / Moonlight lady / Dancing lady / Once again / Tryin' anyway / Dear music / Strange universe. *(cd-iss. Aug91 on 'Repertoire'; RR 4028-WZ)*
Jul 75. (7") *<2166>* **SATISFY YOUR SOUL. / BUDDY** –

C.B.S. Columbia

Dec 76. (lp) *(CBS 81417) <34190>* **MAHOGANY RUSH IV** May76
– I'm going away / Man at the back door / The answer / Jive baby / It's begun to rain / Dragonfly / Little sexy Annie / Moonwalk / IV. . . (the emperor).

FRANK MARINO & MAHOGANY RUSH

Jul 77. (lp) *(CBS 81978) <34677>* **WORLD ANTHEM** May77
– Requiem for a sinner / Hey, little lover / Broken heart blues / In my ways / World anthem / Look at me / Lady / Try for freedom. *(cd-iss. Jan98 on 'Columbia'; 489445-2)*
Mar 78. (lp) *(CBS 82621) <35257>* **FRANK MARINO & MAHOGANY RUSH LIVE (live)**
– (introduction) / The answer / Dragonfly / I'm a king bee / (excerpt from "Back door man") / A new rock & roll / Johnny B. Goode / Talkin' 'bout a feelin' / (excerpt from "Who do ya love") / Electric reflections of war / The world anthem / Purple haze.
May 79. (lp) *(CBS 83494) <35753>* **TALES OF THE UNEXPECTED (half studio/ half live)**
– Sister change / All along the watchtower / Norwegian wood (this bird has flown) / Tales of the unexpected / Down, down, down / Door of illusion / Woman / Bottom of the barrel.
Jun 79. (7") *<11077>* **ALL ALONG THE WATCHTOWER. / DOWN, DOWN** –

— brother **VINCE MARINO** contributed guitar to below.

Apr 80. (lp) *(CBS 83897) <36204>* **WHAT'S NEXT** 88 Mar80
– You got livin' / Finish line / Rock me baby / Something's comin' our way / Roadhouse blues / Loved by you / Rock'n'roll hall of fame / Mona.
May 80. (7") *(CBS 8637)* **YOU GOT LIVIN'. / WORLD ANTHEM**
(12"+=) *(CBS12 8637)* – Purple haze (live) / Tales of the unexpected.

FRANK MARINO

solo but with same 2 man backing **HARWOOD + AYOUB** (on same label)

Aug 81. (lp) *(CBS 84969) <37099>* **THE POWER OF ROCK AND ROLL**
– The power of rock and roll / Play my music / Stay with me / Runnin' wild / Crazy Miss Daisy / Go strange / Young man / Ain't dead yet.
Sep 82. (lp) *(CBS 85793) <38023>* **JUGGERNAUT** Aug82
– Strange dreams / Midnight highway / Stories of a hero / Free / Maybe it's time / Ditch queen / For your love / Juggernaut.

MAHOGANY RUSH

— now without AYOUB replaced by **TIMM BIERY**

S.P.V. Grudge

Aug 87. (lp/cd) *(767589) <GR/+D 0951>* **FULL CIRCLE**
– Breakin' away / Imagine / When love is lost / Razor's edge / Hang on / Full circle / Long ago / Had enough / Genesis.

FRANK MARINO & MAHOGANY RUSH

with **VINCE MARINO** – guitar, vocals / **PAUL HARWOOD** – bass / **TIM BIERY** – drums / **CLAUDIO PESAVENTO** – keyboards

Maze Maze

May 89. (d-lp)(cd) *(784 612)(874 614) <85-4614>* **DOUBLE LIVE (live)**
– You got livin' / Midnite highway / Free / Poppy / Roadhouse blues / Who do ya love / Guitar prelude / Electric reflections revisited / Sky symphony to a little town / Rock'n'roll hall of fame / Juggernaut / Strange dreams.

— FRANK now with **VINCE MARINO + ROB HOWELL** – rhythm guitar / **PETER DOWSE** – bass / **TIMM BIERY** – drums / **CLAUDIO PASAVENTO** – keyboards / **ALAN JORDAN** – backing vocals

not iss. Par

Jan 93. (cd) *<13729>* **FROM THE HIP** –
– Babylon revisited / I'm ready / How long / Rise above / Mine all mine / Ride my own wave / Stand / The wall came down.

– compilations, etc. –

Jul 95. (3xcd-box) *Big Beat; (CDWKM2 149)* **THE LEGENDARY MAHOGANY RUSH** –
– (MAXOOM / CHILD OF THE NOVELTY / STRANGE UNIVERSE)
Jul 96. (cd) *Razor & Tie; (RE 2105-2)* **DRAGONFLY (THE BEST OF FRANK MARINO & MAHOGANY RUSH)**

MALEVOLENT CREATION

Formed: Buffalo, New York, USA . . . 1987 by BRET HOFFMANN, PHIL FASCIANA, JEFF JUSKIEWICZ, JASON BLACOWICZ and MARK SIMPSON. The group – who now resided in Florida – eventually secured a deal with 'R.C.' records, the ubiquitous Scott Burns handling production duties on their debut set, 'THE TEN COMMANDMENTS' (1991). This was closely followed by 'RETRIBUTION' (1992), a blistering death-metal hurricane with an ear-shredding momentum that duly attracted the attention of 'Roadrunner' records. By the release of the latter set, SOLSTICE men, ROB BARRETT and ALEX MARQUEZ had replaced JUSKIEWICZ and SIMPSON respectively although BARRETT himself made way for JON RUBIN on 'STILLBORN' (1993). The latter set marked the end of the band's tenure with 'Roadrunner' and after a period of turmoil, a new line-up of FASCIANA, BLACOWICZ, JOHN PAUL SOARES and DERIK RODDY returned with the independently released 'ETERNAL' (1996). Wielding a new improved, more subtly complex sound, the MALEVOLENT CREATION crew were back in 1997 with the 'IN COLD BLOOD' album. This marked the debut of erstwhile SUFFOCATION sticksman DAVE CULROSS, who formed part of another all-new line-up – alongside FASCIANA, veterans HOFFMANN, BARRETT and new man GORDON SIMMS – on 'THE FINE ART OF MURDER' (1998). 'ENVENOMED' (2000), meanwhile, marked almost ten years at the sharp end of extreme metal.

Album rating: THE TEN COMMANDMENTS (*7) / RETRIBUTION (*6) / STILLBORN (*5) / ETERNAL (*5) / JOE BLACK collection (*4) / IN COLD BLOOD (*4) / THE FINE ART OF MURDER (*5) / ENVENOMED (*5)

BRET HOFFMANN – vocals / **PHIL FASCIANA** – guitar / **JEFF JUSKIEWICZ** – guitar / **JASON BLACOWICZ** – bass / **MARK SIMPSON** – drums

R.C. R.C.

Apr 91. (lp/c) *<(RC 9361-1/-4)>* **THE TEN COMMANDMENTS**
– Memorial arrangements / Premature burial / Remnants of withered decay / Multiple stab wounds / Impaled existence / Thou shall kill! / Sacrificial annihilation / Decadence within / Injected sufferage / Malevolent creation. *<(cd-iss. Jan94; RC 9361-2>)*

— **ROB BARRETT** – guitar (ex-SOLSTICE) repl. JUSKIEWICZ

— **ALEX MARQUEZ** – drums (ex-SOLSTICE) repl. SIMPSON

Jun 92. (lp) *<(RC 9181)>* **RETRIBUTION**
– Eve of the apocalypse / Systematic execution / Slaughter of the innocence / Coronation of our domain / No flesh shall be spared / The coldest survive / Monster / Mindlock / Iced. *<(cd-iss. Jan94; RC 9181-2)>*

— **JON RUBIN** – guitar; repl. BARRETT

Roadrunner Roadrunner

Oct 93. (cd/lp) *<(RR 9042-2/-1)>* **STILLBORN**
– Dominated resurgency / The way of all flesh / Dominion of terror / Geared for gain / Stillborn / Ordain the hierarchy / Carnivorous misgivings / Genetic affliction / Ethnic cleansing / Disciple of abhorence.

— **JOHN PAUL SOARES** – guitar; repl. HOFFMANN (JASON now on vox)

— **DEREK RODDY** – drums; repl. MARQUEZ

Bulletproof Pavement

Mar 96. (cd) *(CDVEST 52) <PM 32220CD>* **ETERNAL** Aug96
– No salvation / Blood brothers / Internal desire / Living in fear / Unearthly / Enslaved / Alliance of war / They breed / To kill / Hideous reprisal / Eternal / Tasteful agony.

— **DAVE CULROSS** – drums (ex-SUFFOCATION) repl. RODDY

Pavement Pavement

Jun 97. (cd) *(PM 32258CD)* **IN COLD BLOOD** May97
– Nocturnal overload / Prophecy / Compulsive / Narcotic genocide / Violated / Leech / In cold blood / Vision of malice / IIII II / Preyed upon / Millions / Condemned / Seizure. *(re-iss. Sep98 on 'S.P.V.'; 085-45318-2)*

— **FASCIANA** (+ keyboards) + **CULROSS** brought back **HOFFMANN** – vocals + **ROB BARRETT** – guitar / + **GORDAN SIMMS** – bass

Jun 99. (cd) *<(32293CD)>* **THE FINE ART OF MURDER** Oct98
– To die is at hand / Manic demise / Instinct evolved / Dissect the eradicated / Mass graves / The fine art of murder / Bone exposed / Purge / Fracture / Rictus surreal / Scorn / Day of lamentation / Scattered flesh.

Oct 00. (cd) *<(32361CD)>* **ENVENOMED**
– Homicidal rant / Night of the long knives / Kill zone / Halved / Serial dementia / Bloodline severed / Pursuit revised / Conflict / Viral release / The deviant's march / Envenomed.

– compilations, etc. –

Jan 99. (cd) *Impact; (IRC 1312) / Volcano; <35013>* **JOE BLACK** Apr96
– Joe Black / Self-important freak / Sadistic perversity / No salvation (remix) / To kill (remix) / Tasteful agony (remix) / Genetic affliction ('93 demo) / Raining blood / Remnants of withered decay ('90 demo) / Impaled existence ('90 demo).

Feb 00. (d-cd) *Pavement; <(32341CD)>* **MANIFESTATION – THE BEST OF MALEVOLENT CREATION**
– In cold blood / Condemned / Nocturnal overload / The fine art of murder / Scorn / Blood brothers / Impaled existence / Living in fear / Manic demise / To die is at hand / Infernal desire / Bone exposed / Alliance of war / Mass graves / Joe Black / Self-important freak / Multiple stab wounds / Eve of the apocalypse / Slaughter of innocence / Monster.

MALICE

Formed: Los Angeles, California, USA . . . early 80s by JAMES NEAL and JAY REYNOLDS, who enlisted MICK KANE, MARK BEHN and CLIFF CAROTHERS. In contrast to the majority of their sun-bleached L.A. brethren, MALICE looked to European metal for their musical cues, most obviously JUDAS PRIEST. Snapped up by 'Atlantic' on the strength of their demo recordings (included on the debut), the band debuted in 1985 with 'IN THE BEGINNING', a promising set of serrated twin-guitar power-metal which nonetheless paled in comparison to the emerging thrash sound of the day. A similarly competent follow-up, 'LICENSE TO KILL', was issued in Spring '87, the record making the US Top 200 although the group were already in the process of splintering. Constant in-fighting eventually led to a break-up later that year, only REYNOLDS going on to work with anyone of note, briefly taking up guitar duties with MEGADETH. In 1989, with the unlikely figure of PAUL SABU at the helm, MALICE reformed for a one-off mini-set, 'CRAZY IN THE NIGHT'.

Album rating: IN THE BEGINNING (*7) / LICENSE TO KILL (*6)

JAMES NEAL – vocals / **JAY REYNOLDS** – guitar / **MICK ZANE** – guitar / **MARK BEHN** – bass / **CLIFF CAROTHERS** – drums

Atlantic Atlantic

Oct 85. (lp/c) *(K 781250-1/-4) <81250>* **IN THE BEGINNING**
– Rockin' with you / Into the ground / Air attack / Stellar masters / Tarot dealer / Squeeze it dry / Hellrider / No haven for the raven / The unwanted / Godz of thunder.

Mar 87. (lp/c) *(K 781714-1/-4) <81714>* **LICENSE TO KILL**
– Sinister double / License to kill / Against the empire / Vigilante / Chain gang woman / Christine / Murder / Breathin' down your neck / Circle of fire.

— split early 1988 (REYNOLDS briefly joined MEGADETH)

— **PAUL SABU** – vocals; repl. NEAL

Roadracer Enigma

Aug 89. (m-lp/m-cd) *(RO 9445-1/-2) <73414>* **CRAZY IN THE NIGHT**
– Captive of light / Vice versa / Crazy in the night / Death of glory.

— finally disbanded in '89

Yngwie MALMSTEEN

Born: 30 Jun'63, Stockholm, Sweden. One of the most revered, high profile guitar sorcerors of the 80's, MALMSTEEN was something of a HENDRIX-inspired child prodigy, mastering his instrument by the time he came to play in local bands, POWERHOUSE and RISING. Some demos from this period subseqently came to the attention of L.A. guitar freak and 'Shrapnel' boss, Mike Varney, who enticed MALMSTEEN over to the States. Under Varney's guidance, the young Swede briefly joined STEELER, before striking out on his own and teaming up with GRAHAM BONNET to form ALCATRAZZ (after reportedly turning down offers to join such big guns as KISS and OZZY OSBOURNE). This was also a relatively brief exercise, the group releasing a solo studio set and a live effort. The latter was recorded in Japan where MALMSTEEN was fast gaining a sizeable fanbase, his talent and potential not missed by 'Polydor' who subsequently signed him up to a solo contract. Initiating RISING FORCE, MALMSTEEN recruited JEFF SCOTT SOTO, JENS JOHANSSON and BARRIEMORE BARLOW, releasing an eponymous debut in 1985. Borrowing heavily from RITCHIE BLACKMORE's 70s pseudo-classical guitar innovations, MALMSTEEN updated the style in lightning fingered, clinically proficient fashion, engendering hordes of wet-permed imitators in his wake. With the addition of MARCEL JACOB, 'MARCHING OUT' (1985) continued in much the same fashion, while 'TRILOGY' (1986) employed the vocal services of MARK BOALS, MALMSTEEN concentrating solely on combining his six string histrionics with accessible hooks. Following an accident which put the guitarist out of action for over a year, he eventually returned with a new-look RISING FORCE, another ex-RAINBOW man, JOE LYNN TURNER, at the helm. The resulting album, 'ODYSSEY' (1988), was MALMSTEEN's most overtly commercial release to date, the solos reeled in to a bearable length and the material more song orientated. Where previous releases lingered tantalisingly outside the US Top 40, this album actually made it, just nudging in at No.40. Instead of capitalising on this success, MALMSTEEN opted to release a well under par concert set, 'TRIAL BY FIRE: LIVE IN LENINGRAD' (1989), before dismissing TURNER and going back to the drawing board. He re-emerged the following year with a completely new, all-Swedish line-up (namely MATS OLAUSSON, SVANTE HENRYSSON, MICHAEL VON KNORRING and frontman GORAN EDMAN) for the disappointing 'ECLIPSE' set. This marked the end of MALMSTEEN's association with 'Polydor', the guitarist subsequently inking a deal with 'Elektra' for the equally dull 'FIRE AND ICE' (1992). Yet another new vocalist, MIKE VESCERA, was in place for the 'SEVENTH SIGN' (1994), MALMSTEEN now signed to 'Music For Nations' in the UK. The same year saw the release of a bombastic classical effort, 'NO MERCY' on 'C.M.C.', although fans of MALMSTEEN's limited appeal noodling could content themselves with subsequent albums, 'MAGNUM OPUS' (1995) and poor covers set 'INSPIRATION' (1996). A further series of albums followed through the late 90's including 'FACING THE ANIMAL' (1998), 'LIVE!!' (1998), 'CONCERTO FOR ELECTRIC GUITAR AND ORCHESTRA' (1998) and 'ALCHEMY' (1999). The Scandinavian six-string wizard was back with his RISING FORCE – namely MARK BOALS, MATS OLAUSSON and JOHN MACALUSO – for the millennial 'WAR TO END ALL WARS' (2000), cranking out more than the odd guitar run to end all guitar runs. Although BOALS contributed overwrought vocals to most tracks, the inclusion of three instrumentals catered to the MALMSTEEN diehards.

Album rating: RISING FORCE (*6) / MARCHING OUT (*5) / TRILOGY (*6) / ODYSSEY (*5) / TRIAL BY FIRE: LIVE IN LENINGRAD (*4) / ECLIPSE (*5) / FIRE & ICE (*5) / THE YNGWIE MALMSTEEN COLLECTION compilation (*7) / SEVENTH SIGN (*5) / MAGNUM OPUS (*4) / INSPIRATION (*3) / FACING THE ANIMAL (*5) / LIVE!! (*4) / CONCERTO FOR ELECTRIC GUITAR AND ORCHESTRA . . . (*4) / ALCHEMY (*4) / WAR TO END ALL WARS (*4)

YNGWIE MALMSTEEN'S RISING FORCE

YNGWIE MALMSTEEN – guitars, bass, vocals (ex-STEELER, ex-ALCATRAZZ) / **JEFF SCOTT SOTO** – vocals / **JENS JOHANSSON** – keyboards / **BARRIEMORE BARLOW** – drums (ex-JETHRO TULL)

Polydor Polydor

May 85. (lp) *(<825324-1>)* **RISING FORCE** 60 Apr85
– Black star / Far beyond the sun / Now your ships are burned / Evil eye / Icarus' dream suite op.4 / As above, so below / Little savage / Farewell. *(cd-iss. May85; 825 324-2)*

— added **MARCEL JACOB** – bass

Jun 85. (7"m) *(883073-7)* **I SEE THE LIGHT TONIGHT. / FAR BEYOND THE SUN / I AM A VIKING**

Aug 85. (lp/c)(cd) *(POLD/+C 5183)(<825733>)* **MARCHING OUT** 52
– Prelude / I'll see the light, tonight / Don't let it end / Disciples of Hell / I am a viking / Overture 1383 / Anguish and fear / On the run again / Soldier without faith / Caught in the middle / Marching out.

— **MARK BOALS** – vocals (exTED NUGENT) repl. SOTO + JACOB

— **ANDERS JOHANSSON** – drums; repl. BARLOW

Nov 86. (lp/c)(cd) *(POLD/+C 5204)(<831073-2>)* **TRILOGY** (solo) 44 Oct86
– You don't remember, I'll never forget / Liar / Queen in love / Crying / Fury / Fire / Magic mirror / Dark ages / Trilogy suite op:5.

— **JOE LYNN TURNER** – vocals (ex-RAINBOW) repl. BOALS

— added **BOB DAISLEY** – bass (ex-RAINBOW)

May 88. (lp/c)(cd) *(POLD/+C 5224)(<835451-2>)* **ODYSSEY** 27 40 Apr88
– Rising force / Hold on / Heaven tonight / Dreaming (tell me) / Bite the bullet / Riot in the dungeons / Deja vu / Crystal ball / Now is the time / Faster than the speed of light / Krakatau / Memories. *(cd re-iss. Mar96; same)*

— **BARRY DUNAWAY** – bass, vocals; repl. DAISLEY

Oct 89. (lp/c/cd) *(<839726-1/-4/-2>)* **TRIAL BY FIRE: LIVE IN LENINGRAD (live)** 65
– Liar / Queen in love / Deja vu / Far beyond the sun / Heaven tonight / Dreaming (tell me) / You don't remember, I'll never forget / Guitar solo (trilogy suite opus 5 – Spasebo blues) / Black star / Spanish castle magic.

YNGWIE MALMSTEEN

— now with a complete new line-up:- **GORAN EDMAN** – vocals / **MATS OLAUSSON** – keyboards, vocals / **SVANTE HENRYSSON** – bass, vocals / **MICHAEL VON KNORRING** – drums

Apr 90. (cd/c/lp) *(<843361-2/-4/-1>)* **ECLIPSE** 43 Mar90
– Making love / Bedroom eyes / Save our love / Motherless child / Devil in disguise / Judas / What do you want / Demon driver / Faultline / Eclipse / See you in hell (don't be late) / Eclipse.

Apr 90. (7") *(PO 79)* **MAKING LOVE. /**
(12"+=/cd-s+=) *(PZ/+CD 79)* –

— **BO WERNER** – drums; repl. KNORRING (on most)

Elektra Elektra

Feb 92. (cd/c/lp) *(<7559 61137-2/-4/-1>)* **FIRE AND ICE** 57
– Perpetual / Dragonfly / Teaser / How many miles to Babylon / Cry no more / No mercy / C'est la vie / Leviathan / Fire and ice / Forever is a long time / I'm my own enemy / All I want is everything / Golden dawn / Final curtain.

— **MIKE VESCERA** – vocals; repl. EDMAN

Music For Nations C.M.C.

Mar 94. (cd/c) *(CD/T MFN 158) <6703>* **SEVENTH SIGN** May94
– Never die / I don't know / Meant to be / Forever one / Hairtrigger / Brothers / Seventh sign / Bad blood / Prisoner of your love / Pyramid of cheops / Crash and burn / Sorrow.

— In 1994, MALMSTEEN recorded a classical solo album, 'NO MERCY' for 'CMC'.

Music For Nations Viceroy

Aug 95. (cd/c) *(CD/T MFN 188) <8026>* **MAGNUM OPUS**
– Vengeance / No love lost / Tomorrow's gone / The only one / Die without you / Overture 1622 / Voodoo / Cross the line / Time will tell / Fire in the sky / Amber dawn / Cantabile.

Music For Nations Foundation

Oct 96. (d-cd) *(CDMFN 200) <1401>* **INSPIRATION** Nov96
– Carry on my wayward son / Pictures of home / Gates of Babylon / Manic depression / In the dead of night / The sails of Charon / Demon's eye / Anthem / Child in time / Spanish castle magic / (interview/rarities).

Dream Catcher Mercury

May 98. (cd) *(CRIDE 2) <536737>* **FACING THE ANIMAL** Feb98
– Braveheart / Facing the animal / Enemy / Sacrifice / Like an angel – For April / My resurrection / Another time / Heathens from the north / Alone in Paradise / End of my rope / Only the strong / Poison in your veins / Air on a theme.

Oct 98. (d-cd) *(CRIDE 8) <112722>* **LIVE!!** Aug98
– Resurrection / Facing the animal / Rising force / Bedroom eyes / Far beyond the sun / Like an angel / Braveheart / Seventh sign / Guitar solo / Gates of Babylon / Alone in Paradise / Pictures of home / Never die / Black star / I'll see the light, tonight.

May 99. (cd) *(CRIDE 16) <35764>* **CONCERTO FOR ELECTRIC GUITAR AND ORCHESTRA IN E FLAT MINOR OP.1**
– Icarus dream fanfare / Cavalino rampante / Fugue / Prelude to April / Toccata / Andante / Sarabande / Allegro / Adagio / Vivance / Presto virace / Finale.

Dream Catcher Pony Canyon

Oct 99. (cd) *(CRIDE 20) <1409>* **ALCHEMY** Nov99
– Blitzkrieg / Leonardo / Playing with fire / The stand / Wield my sword / Blue / Legion of the damned / Daemon dance (7,405,926) / Hangar 18, area 51 / Voodoo nights / Asylum: I – Asylum, II – Sky euphoria, III – Quantum leap.

Nov 00. (cd) *(CRIDE 32) <1483>* **WAR TO END ALL WARS**
– Prophet of doom / Crucify / Bad reputation / Catch 22 / Masquerade / Molto arpeggiosa / Miracle of life / The wizard / Preludium / Wild one / Tarot / Instru-mental institution / War to end all wars / Treasure from the east / Requiem.

– compilations, etc. –

Feb 92. (cd/lp) *Polydor; (849271-2/-1)* **THE YNGWIE MALMSTEEN COLLECTION** -
– Black star / Far beyond the sun / I'll see the light tonight / You don't remember, I'll never forget / Liar / Queen in love / Hold on / Heaven tonight / Deja vu / Spasebo blues / Spanish castle magic / Judas / Making love / Eclipse. *(cd re-iss. Mar96; same)*

Apr 00. (cd) *Dream Catcher; (CRIDE 25)* **THE BEST OF YNGWIE MALMSTEEN 1990-1999**

MAMA'S BOYS

Formed: Northern Ireland . . . late 70's by brothers JOHN, PAT and TOMMY McMANUS, who diversified from their traditional folk approach after witnessing Irish act, HORSLIPS, live in 1978. Adopting a hard-rock power trio approach, the main thrust of the group's sound on 'OFFICIAL BOOTLEG' (1980) was searing blues boogie undercut with their ever present folk influences. Comparisons with THIN LIZZY were inevitable, the group's services later requested by none other than PHIL LYNOTT himself on the latter band's 1983 farewell tour. Musically, 'PLUG IT IN' (1982) followed in much the same fashion, while the slightly more refined 'TURN IT UP' attracted the interest of 'Jive' records. The group were subsequently signed up and released the eponymous 'MAMA'S BOYS' in 1984, the record featuring a cover of SLADE's raucous glam chestnut 'MAMA WEER ALL CRAZEE NOW'. As the decade wore on, MAMA'S BOYS' albums increasingly veered towards AOR, the band almost making the UK Top 40 with the impressive 'POWER AND PASSION' (1985), while the decidedly smoother 'GROWING UP THE HARD WAY' (1987) saw the debut of KEITH MURRELL on vocals. Prior to this, TOMMY was diagnosed with leukemia, casting a shadow over their growing success, the drummer eventually dying from an infection in 1994 following a bone marrow transplant (his death precipitating the band's break-up). Nevertheless, MAMA'S BOYS did manage to release a further two albums before their untimely demise, the '91 concert set, 'LIVE TONITE', giving a nod to the band's folk roots with a cover of Joni Mitchell's 'THIS FLIGHT TONIGHT', while 'RELATIVITY' (1992) served as a worthy epitaph.

Album rating: OFFICIAL BOOTLEG (*6) / PLUG IT IN (*6) / TURN IT UP (*6) / POWER AND THE PASSION (*5) / GROWING UP THE HARD WAY (*6) LIVE TONITE (*4) / RELATIVITY (*4)

JOHN McMANUS – vocals, bass / **PAT McMANUS** – lead guitar, fiddle / **TOMMY McMANUS** – drums

Pussy not iss.

1981. (lp) *(PU 001)* **OFFICIAL BOOTLEG** -
– I'm leaving home / Belfast city blues / Hyland rock / Record machine / Rock 'n roll craze / Summertime / Without you / Demon.

Scoff not iss.

Apr 82. (7") *(DT 015)* **BELFAST CITY BLUES. / REACH FOR THE TOP** - - Ireland

Albion not iss.

Oct 82. (7") *(ION 1038)* **IN THE HEAT OF THE NIGHT. / REACH FOR THE TOP** -

Oct 82. (lp/c) *(ULTRA/CULTRA 1)* **PLUG IT IN** -
– In the heat of the night / Burnin' up / Needle in the groove / Reach for the top / Silence is out of fashion / Straight forward / Runaway dreams / Getting out / Belfast city blues. *(re-iss. Jul86 on 'Castle' lp/c; CLA LP/MC 111)*

Jan 83. (7"/12") *(ION/12ION 1041)* **NEEDLE IN THE GROOVE. / HARD HEADED WAYS** -

Spartan not iss.

Sep 83. (7"/12") *(SP/12SP 6)* **TOO LITTLE OF YOU TO LOVE. / FREEDOM FIGHTERS** -

Oct 83. (lp) *(SPLP 001)* **TURN IT UP** -
– Midnight promises / Loose living / Too little of you to love / Late night rendezvous / Crazy Daisy's house of dreams / Face to face / Gentleman rogues / Lonely soul / Shake my bones / Freedom fighters.

Jan 84. (7") *(SP 11)* **MIDNIGHT PROMISES. / LONELY SOUL** -
(12"+=) *(12SP 11)* – High energy weekend.

Jive Jive

Jul 84. (lp/c) *(HIP/+C 15) <8214>* **MAMA'S BOYS**
– Crazy Daisy's house of dreams / Runaway dreams / Mama we're all crazee now / Gentleman rogues / Lonely soul / In the heat of the night / The professor / Midnight promises / Straight forward (no looking back).

Aug 84. (12"m) *(JIVET 71)* **MAMA WEER ALL CRAZEE NOW. / CRAZY DAISY'S HOUSE OF DREAMS / RUNAWAY ROGUES**
(d7"+=) *(JIVEG 71)* – Gentlemen rogues.

Mar 85. (lp/c) *(HIP/+C 24) <8285>* **POWER AND PASSION** 55
– Hard 'n' loud / Straight forward, no looking back / Lettin' go / Needle in the groove / Run / Power & passion / Don't tell mama / The professor II / Let's get high. *(with free 12"pic-d)*

May 85. (7"/7"sha-pic-d/12") *(JIVE/+P 96)* **NEEDLE IN THE GROOVE. / DON'T TELL MAMA**

Nov 85. (7") *(JIVE 110)* **HARD 'N' LOUD. / LETTING GO (remix)**
(12"+=) *(JIVET 110)* – Without you (live).

— added **KEITH MURRELL** – vocals (ex-AIRRACE)

Jul 87. (7") *(MBOY/+T 1)* **HIGHER GROUND. / LAST THING AT NIGHT**
(d7"+=/12"+=/'A'-Captain Love mix.cd-s+=) *(MBOY D/T/CD 1)* – Needle in the groove.

Sep 87. (7"red/12") *(JIVE X/T 152)* **WAITING FOR A MIRACLE. / LIGHTNING STRIKES**

Nov 87. (lp/c/cd) *(HIP/HIPC/CHIP 49) <1059>* **GROWING UP THE HARD WAY**
– Waiting for a miracle / Bedroom eyes / In over my head / Higher ground / Hot blood / Running away / I've had enough / Blacklisted / Last thing at night.

— **MIKE WILSON** – vocals; repl. MURRELL

Music For Nations I.R.S.

Apr 91. (cd/c/lp) *(CD/T+/MFN 114)* **LIVE TONITE (live)** -
– Hot blood / Bedroom eyes / Walk all over me / Rescue me / Needle in the groove / My way home / Last thing at night / Lonely soul / Runaway dreams / Fallin' / Straight forward / The beast / This flight tonight.

C.T.M. I.R.S.

Jun 92. (cd-ep) *(CDS 131103)* **LAUGH ABOUT IT** -

Jul 92. (cd/c) *(CD/MC 131003) <986.958>* **RELATIVITY**
– Judgement day / What you see is what you get / Laugh about it / Don't look back in anger / Cry salvation / Rescue me / My way home / Don't back down / Left and right / Cardboard city / Walk all over me / Fallin' / Moorlough shore. *(<cd-iss. Apr01 on 'Angel Air'; SJPCD 081)>*

— split after TOMMY died of a lung infection on 16th November, 1994

MAMMOTH

Formed: South London, England . . . mid 80's by hard-rock heavyweights, JOHN McCOY and NICKY MOORE, who eventually acquired two more larger than life musicians, BIG MAC BAKER and 'TUBBY' VINNIE REID. Formed on the rather lame premise of presenting an alternative to the pretty boys who ruled 80's metal, MAMMOTH never really made it off the starting blocks. Embroiled in a dispute with their label, 'Jive', almost since their inception, when the eponymous debut was eventually released in 1989, their novelty factor had long since worn off. This was despite a promising start with enjoyably hummable singles like the self-deprecating 'FAT MAN' and 'ALL

THE DAYS'. The album itself was listenable enough, if never really throwing its weight around, MAMMOTH becoming extinct not long after the record's release.

Album rating: MAMMOTH (*5)

NICKY MOORE – vocals, keyboards (ex-SAMSON) / **BIG MAC BAKER** – guitar / **JOHN McCOY** – bass (ex-GILLAN) / **'TUBBY' VINNY REED** – drums, percussion

		Jive	Jive
Jul 87.	(7"/12") *(MOTH/+T 1)* **FAT MAN. / POLITICAL ANIMAL** (cd-s+=) *(MOTHCD 1)* – ('A'-Admiral amour mix) / Bad times.		-
Jan 88.	(7"/12") *(MOTH/+T 2)* **ALL THE DAYS. /**		-
Feb 89.	(7") *(MOTH 3)* **CAN'T TAKE THE HURT. / NONE BUT THE BRAVE** (12"+=/cd-s+=) *(MOTH T/CD 3)* – Political animal.		-
Apr 89.	(lp/c/cd) *(HIP/HIPC/CHIP 56)* <1094> **MAMMOTH** – All the days / Fatman / Can't take the hurt / 30 pieces of silver / Dark star / Bet you wish / Long time coming / Bad times / Home from the storm.		Nov88

—— became extinct in 1989

ManBREAK

Formed: Liverpool, England . . . mid 90's out of the ashes of 25th OF MAY, by chief agitator SWINDELLI, plus MR. BLOND, SNAYKEE, ROY VAN DER KERKOFF and STU BOY STU. They were named after sadistic British Army experiments of the 1950's. In 1996, they became labelmates of fellow angry young people, SKUNK ANANSIE, when they signed on the dotted line for 'One Little Indian'. The band's radical manifesto was informed by a raging sense of social injustice, it's just a pity their lyrical anger didn't translate into their rather tame pop/rock approach, as evidenced on their resulting debut 45, 'NEWS OF THE WORLD'. A further three chart-orientated efforts subsequently flopped, the album 'COME AND SEE' meeting a similar fate, despite the surprising glut of coverage in that bastion of "hard-rock", Kerrang!

Album rating: COME AND SEE (*6)

SWINDELLI – vocals (ex-25th OF MAY) / **MR. BLOND** (aka GARETH) – rhythm guitar, vocals / **SNAYKEE** (aka JOHN) – lead guitar / **ROY VAN DER KERKOFF** – bass / **STU BOY STU** (aka STUART) – drums

		One Little Indian	Almo Sounds
Dec 96.	(7") *(125 TP7)* **NEWS OF THE WORLD. /**		-
Apr 97.	(cd-ep) *(TP7CD)* **WASTED / LET THE GOOD TIMES ROLL / BACK TO BASICS / BELIEVER**		-
Jun 97.	(7"/c-s) *(146 TP7/+C)* **READY OR NOT. / BIG BUDDHA** (cd-s+=) *(146 TP7CD)* – Wasted again / Hangin' around.		-
Aug 97.	(7") *(147 TP7)* **ROUND AND ROUND. / LEARNING TO FLY (ADIN & DUVA)** (cd-s+=) *(147 TP7CD)* – What's the time / Ready or not (live).		-
Nov 97.	(lp/cd) *(TPLP 84/+CD)* <80013> **COME AND SEE** – Ready or not / Kop karma / Morning / News of the world / Wasted / It's on / God's never heard of you / City life / Round and round / Cuts up / Future days / Is everyone still asleep.		Jun97
May 98.	(d12"ep) *(208 TP12)* **ROUND & ROUND (mixes)** – (Dust Junkys club mix) / (Dust Junkys instrumental) / (Manchild epic beat mix) / (Harmonic System long distance mix). (cd-ep) *(208 TP7CD)* – (Brown & nasty radio mix) / (Salt City Orchestra radio mix) / (Tom Lord-Alge radio mix) / (Dust Junkys radio mix) / (Brown & Nasty Bassadelik mix) / (Salt City Orchestra mix).		-
Nov 98.	(cd-s) *(209 TP7CD)* **READY OR NOT /**		-

MANHOLE (see under ⇒ TURA SATANA)

MANIC STREET PREACHERS

Formed: Blackwood, Gwent, South Wales . . . 1988 by JAMES DEAN BRADFIELD (vocals, guitar) and cousin SEAN MOORE (drums). With the addition of former school friends NICKY WIRE (bass) and RICHEY EDWARDS (rhythm guitar), the line-up was complete and the band set about recording their self-financed debut single, 'SUICIDE ALLEY'. The group began to attract attention with the release of the 'NEW ART RIOT' EP (1990), derivative but impassioned neo-punk which drew interest more for the band's defiant slurs on a range of targets (fellow musicians were shown no mercy) than its musical content. While the band looked the part (low rent glamour chic) and namechecked all the right people (RIMBAUD, The CLASH, etc.), their philosophy of kill your idols and then burn out, smacked of contrivance to say the least. When journalist STEVE LAMACQ said as much in an interview with EDWARDS in 1991, the guitarist proceeded to carve '4 REAL' into his arm with a razor, upping the ante in the band's already precarious relationship with the music press and causing furious debate between doubters and obsessive fans. The group proceeded to release a couple of raging singles on 'Heavenly', 'MOTOWN JUNK' and the stinging 'YOU LOVE US' (aimed at the press), before signing to 'Columbia' in 1991. After a couple of minor hits, 'STAY BEAUTIFUL' and 'LOVE'S SWEET EXILE', the MANICS cracked the Top 20 with a re-released 'YOU LOVE US', their much anticipated debut album, 'GENERATION TERRORISTS' following in February 1992. A sprawling double set, it kicked convincingly against the pricks, lashing out at such deserving targets as high street banks ('NAT WEST-BARCLAYS-MIDLAND-LLOYDS') and our beloved monarch ('REPEAT'). The band also proved they had a way with melody and songwriting in the soaring melancholy of 'MOTORCYCLE EMPTINESS'. Despite their original well intentioned claims to break up after the debut, the band rather predictably toured the album and began work on a new collection, 'GOLD AGAINST THE SOUL' (1993). Lacking the vicious kick of the debut, the record nevertheless contained some fine moments in the likes of 'LA TRISTESSE DURERA (SCREAM TO A SIGH)' and 'LIFE BECOMING A LANDSLIDE', reaching No.8 in the album charts. The MANIC STREET PREACHERS continued to court controversy with NICKY WIRE making his infamous comments about MICHAEL STIPE at the 1993 Reading Festival. The following year RICHEY EDWARDS' depression, self-mutilation and anorexia reached a head, the guitarist eventually admitted to a clinic for several weeks. His trauma was detailed in the harrowing '4st 7lb' from their third album, 'The HOLY BIBLE' (1994), a dark night of the soul which centred on such grim topics as Nazi genocide. Then, on 1st February '95, with EDWARDS apparently recovered, he went AWOL from his London hotel. A fortnight later, his abandoned car was found at the Severn Bridge, and rumours of suicide abounded. Even after a protracted police search, there was no trace of the guitarist and at the time of writing , he is still missing. Numerous sightings have since been reported, most notably in Goa, India although the Police have continued to draw a blank. The remaining members eventually decided to carry on, contributing a poignant 'RAIN DROPS KEEP FALLING ON MY HEAD' to the 1995 Warchild charity album, 'HELP', and releasing their fourth album, 'EVERYTHING MUST GO' (1996). The group's most accomplished work to date, the record was preceded by their biggest hit single (No.2), the bitter 'A DESIGN FOR LIFE'. Embellished with soaring strings and lavish arrangements, the band scored with a succession of brilliant songs including 'AUSTRALIA' and the title track, compositions that were almost transcendant in their emotive power, the memory of EDWARDS never far away. It seemed that at last the MANIC STREET PREACHERS had lived up to their early boasts and in early 1997 their talent was recognised when 'EVERYTHING MUST GO' won the coveted Mercury Music Award. The top of the singles chart was the only place the MANICS hadn't been. This was remedied late summer '98 when 'IF YOU TOLERATE THIS YOUR CHILDREN WILL BE NEXT' made No.1, a taster from their massive selling parent album, 'THIS IS THE TRUTH TELL ME YOURS' (1998). Classic anthems such as 'THE EVERLASTING', 'YOU STOLE THE SUN FROM MY HEART', and 'TSUNAMI', also became top selling in the UK charts, although what was happening to their records in America? Not that the staunchly socialist MANICS gave a fig for their Stateside oblivion, content to become the first Western rock band to play in Communist Cuba, that longtime thorn in Uncle Sam's bloated side. No need to ask then, what 'BABY ELIAN' was all about given the Cuba vs USA tussle of summer 2000. The latter track was served up for 'KNOW YOUR ENEMY' (2001), the band's sixth album and one of their most accomplished to date. The almost STOOGES-style savagery of 'FOUND THAT SOUL' (a dual Top 10 single released simultaneously with 'SO WHY SO SAD') set the tone, a blistering punk/garage track that put many of the so called American nu-metal/punk groups to shame and served as a timely reminder of how good angry rock music can be when it comes from the gut and not the marketing strategy. 'OCEAN SPRAY', in contrast, was a poignant homage to JAMES' mum's battle with cancer, Ocean Spray being a brand of cranberry juice used to combat the disease. Yet this album was primarily a politicised affair, again railing against the evils of the USA in the likes of 'FREE SPEECH WON'T FEED MY CHILDREN' and 'LET ROBESON SING', a tribute to the forgotten entertainer/political activist. They may be guilty of naivety, bombast and even double standards but few bands of the modern era write, play and perform with the emotional and political intensity, the dignity and the humbleness of The MANIC STREET PREACHERS; Britain's anaemic music scene (never mind the USA) needs this band now more than ever. • **Covered:** IT'S SO EASY (Guns N' Roses) / UNDER MY WHEELS (Alice Cooper) / SUICIDE IS PAINLESS (Theme from 'Mash') / CHARLES WINDSOR (McCarthy) / THE DROWNERS (Suede) / STAY WITH ME (Faces) / WROTE FOR LUCK (Happy Mondays) / RAINDROPS KEEP FALLING ON MY HEAD (Bacharach-David) / VELOCITY GIRL (Primal Scream) / TAKE THE SKINHEADS BOWLING (Camper Van Beethoven) / I CAN'T TAKE MY EYES OFF YOU (hit; Andy Williams) / TRAIN IN VAIN (Clash).

Album rating: GENERATION TERRORISTS (*8) / GOLD AGAINST THE SOUL (*9) / THE HOLY BIBLE (*9) / EVERYTHING MUST GO (*9) / THIS IS MY TRUTH TELL ME YOURS (*8) / KNOW YOUR ENEMY (*7)

JAMES DEAN BRADFIELD (b.21 Feb'69, Newport) – vocals, guitar / **RICHEY JAMES EDWARDS** (b.27 Dec'69) – rhythm guitar / **NICKY WIRE** (b. NICHOLAS JONES, 20 Jan'69, Tredegar) – bass / **SEAN MOORE** (b.30 Jul'70, Pontypool) – drums

		S.B.S.	not iss.
Aug 89.	(7") *(SBS 002)* **SUICIDE ALLEY. / TENNESSEE (I FEEL SO LOW)**		-
		Damaged Goods	not iss.
Jun 90.	(12"ep) *(YUBB 4)* **NEW ART RIOT** – New art riot / Stip it down / Last exit on yesterday / Teenage 20-20. *(re-iss. Dec91, Jul93 + Sep96, 12"pink-ep/cd-ep; YUBB 4 P/CD)*		-
		Heavenly	not iss.
Jan 91.	(12"ep/cd-ep) *(HVN8 12/CD)* **MOTOWN JUNK. / SORROW 16 / WE HER MAJESTY'S PRISONERS**	92	-
May 91.	(7") *(HVN 10)* **YOU LOVE US. / SPECTATORS OF SUICIDE** (12"+=/cd-s+=) *(HVN 10 12/CD)* – Starlover / Strip it down (live).	62	-
		Caff	not iss.
Jul 91.	(7") *(CAFF 15)* **FEMININE IS BEAUTIFUL: NEW ART RIOT. / REPEAT AFTER ME**		-

Columbia Columbia

Jul 91. (7") *(657337-7)* **STAY BEAUTIFUL. / R.P. McMURPHY** [40] [ ]
(12"+=/12"w-poster/cd-s+=) *(657337-6/-8/-2)* – Soul contamination.
(US-cd-ep+=) – Motown junk / Sorrow 16 / Star lover.
(cd-ep re-iss. Sep97 on 'Epic' hit No.52; MANIC 1CD)

Nov 91. (7") *(657582-7)* **LOVE'S SWEET EXILE. / REPEAT** [26] [-]
(12"+=/cd-s+=) *(657582-6/-2)* – Democracy coma.
(12"ltd.++=) *(657582-8)* – Stay beautiful (live).
(cd-ep re-iss. Sep97 on 'Epic' hit No.55; MANIC 2CD)

Jan 92. (7"/c-s) *(657724-7/-4)* **YOU LOVE US. / A VISION OF DEAD DESIRE** [16] [-]
(12"+=) *(657724-6)* – It's so easy (live).
(cd-s++=) *(657724-2)* – We her majesty's prisoners.
(cd-ep re-iss. Sep97 on 'Epic' hit No.49; MANIC 3CD)

Feb 92. (pic-cd/cd/d-c/d-lp/pic-d-lp) *(471060-0/-2/-4/-1/-9) <52474>* **GENERATION TERRORISTS** [13] [ ]
– Slash 'n' burn / Nat West-Barclays-Midland-Lloyds / Born to end / Motorcycle emptiness / You love us / Love's sweet exile / Little baby nothing / Repeat (stars and stripes) / Tennessee / Another invented disease / Stay beautiful / So dead / Repeat (UK) / Spectators of suicide / Damn dog / Crucifix kiss / Methadone pretty / Condemned to rock'n'roll. *(cd re-iss. Jan99; same)*

Mar 92. (7"/c-s) *(657873-7/-4)* **SLASH 'N' BURN. / AIN'T GOING DOWN** [20] [-]
(12"+=) *(657873-6)* – Motown junk.
(cd-s++=/gold-cd-s++=) *(657873-2/-0)* – ('A'version).
(cd-ep re-iss. Sep97 on 'Epic' hit No.54; MANIC 4CD)

Jun 92. (7"/c-s) *(658083-7/-4)* **MOTORCYCLE EMPTINESS. / BORED OUT OF MY MIND** [17] [-]
(12"pic-d+=) *(658083-8)* – Under my wheels.
(cd-s++=/s-cd-s++=) *(658083-2/-9)* – Crucifix kiss (live).
(cd-ep re-iss. Sep97 on 'Epic' hit No.41; MANIC 5CD)

Sep 92. (7"/cd-s) *(658382-7/-2)* **THEME FROM M.A.S.H. (SUICIDE IS PAINLESS). / ('b'side by 'Fatima Mansions' – Everything I Do (I Do It For You)** [7] [-]

Nov 92. (7") *(658796-7)* **LITTLE BABY NOTHING. / SUICIDE ALLEY** [29] [-]
(12"+=/cd-s+=) *(658796-6/-2)* – Yankee drawl / Never want again.
(cd-ep re-iss. Sep97 on 'Epic' hit No.50; MANIC 6CD)

Jun 93. (c-s) *(659337-4)* **FROM DESPAIR TO WHERE. / HIBERNATION** [25] [-]
(12"+=) *(659337-6)* – Spectators of suicide (Heavenly version).
(cd-s+=) *(659337-2)* – Star lover (Heavenly version).

Jun 93. (cd/c/lp/pic-lp) *(474064-2/-4/-1/-9) <57386>* **GOLD AGAINST THE SOUL** [8] [ ]
– Sleepflower / From despair to where / La tristesse durera (scream to a sigh) / Yourself / Life becoming a landslide / Drug drug druggy / Roses in the hospital / Nostalgic pushead / Symphony of tourette / Gold against the soul.

Jul 93. (7"/c-s) *(659477-7/-4)* **LA TRISTESSE DURERA (SCREAM TO A SIGH). / PATRICK BATEMAN** [22] [-]
(12"+=) *(659477-6)* – Repeat (live) / Tennessee.
(cd-s+=) *(659477-2)* – What's my name (live) / Slash'n'burn (live).

Sep 93. (7"/c-s) *(659727-7/-4)* **ROSES IN THE HOSPITAL. / US AGAINST YOU / DONKEY** [15] [-]
(cd-s+=) *(659727-2)* – Wrote for luck.
(12") *(659727-6)* – ('A'side) / (5-'A' mixes).

Epic Epic

Feb 94. (c-s) *(660070-4)* **LIFE BECOMING A LANDSLIDE / COMFORT COMES** [36] [-]
(12"+=) *(660070-6)* – Are mothers saints.
(cd-s++=) *(660070-2)* – Charles Windsor.

Jun 94. (7"/c-s) *(660447-7/-4)* **FASTER. / P.C.P.** [16] [-]
(10"+=) *(660447-0)* – Sculpture of man.
(cd-s++=) *(660447-2)* – New art riot (in E-minor).

Aug 94. (10"/c-s) *(660686-0/-4)* **REVOL. / TOO COLD HERE** [22] [-]
(cd-s+=) *(660686-2)* – You love us (original Heavenly version) / Love's sweet exile (live).
(cd-s) *(660686-5)* – ('A'side) / (3 live at Glastonbury tracks).

— RICHEY booked himself into a health clinic, after wasting himself down to 5 stone.

Aug 94. (cd/c/pic-lp) *(477421-2/-4/-0) <66967>* **THE HOLY BIBLE** [6] [ ]
– Yes / Ifwhiteamericatoldthetruthforonedayit'sworldwouldfallapart / Of walking abortion / She is suffering / Archives of pain / Revol / 4st 7lb / Mausoleum / Faster / This is yesterday / Die in the summertime / The intense humming of evil / P.C.P.

Oct 94. (10"/c-s) *(660895-0/-4)* **SHE IS SUFFERING. / LOVE TORN US UNDER (acoustic)** [25] [-]
(cd-s+=) *(660895-2)* – The drowners / Stay with me (both live w/ BERNARD BUTLER).
(cd-s) *(660895-5)* – ('A'side) / La tristesse durera (scream to a sigh) / Faster (Dust Brothers remixes).

— RICHEY was now fully recuperated . . . but on 1st Feb '95, he went AWOL again after walking out of London's Embassy Hotel at 7 that morning. Two weeks later, his car was found abandoned and after police frog search the Severn, it was believed he might be dead. By the end of 1995, with RICHEY still missing, the group carried on as a trio.

— Meanwhile, BRADFIELD produced the debut of NORTHERN UPROAR.

Apr 96. (c-s) *(663070-4)* **A DESIGN FOR LIFE / BRIGHT EYES (live)** [2] [-]
(cd-s) *(663070-2)* – ('A'side) / Mr Carbohydrate / Dead passive / Dead trees and traffic islands.
(cd-s) *(663070-5)* – ('A'side) / ('A'-Howard Grey remix) / ('A'-Apollo 440 remix) / Faster (Chemical Brothers remix).

May 96. (cd/c/lp) *(483930-2/-4/-1) <67709>* **EVERYTHING MUST GO** [2] [ ]
– Elvis impersonator: Blackpoool pier / A design for life / Kevin Carter / Enola – alone / Everything must go / Small black flowers that grow in the sky / The girl who wanted to be God / Removables / Australia / Interiors (song for Willem De Kooning) / Further away / No surface at all.

Jul 96. (c-s) *(663468-4)* **EVERYTHING MUST GO / RAINDROPS KEEP FALLING ON MY HEAD (live)** [5] [-]
(cd-s) *(663468-2)* – ('A'side) / Hanging on / Black garden / No-one knows what it's like to be me.
(cd-s) *(663468-5)* – ('A'side) / ('A'-Stealth Sonic Orchestra remix) / ('A'-Chemical Brothers remix).

Sep 96. (c-s) *(663775-4)* **KEVIN CARTER / EVERYTHING MUST GO (acoustic)** [9] [-]
(cd-s) *(663775-2)* – ('A'side) / Horses under starlight / Sepia / First republic.
(cd-s) *(663775-5)* – Kevin Carter busts loose (Jon Carter remix) / ('A'-Stealth Sonic Orchestra mixes).

Dec 96. (c-s) *(664044-4)* **AUSTRALIA / A DESIGN FOR LIFE (live)** [7] [-]
(cd-s) *(664044-2)* – ('A'side) / Velocity girl / Take the skinheads bowling / I can't take my eyes off you (acoustic).
(cd-s) *(664044-5)* – ('A'side) / ('A'-Lionrock remix) / Motorcycle emptiness (Stealth Sonic Orchestra version).

Epic Virgin

Aug 98. (c-s) *(666345-4)* **IF YOU TOLERATE THIS YOUR CHILDREN WILL BE NEXT / KEVIN CARTER (live)** [1] [-]
(cd-s) *(666345-2)* – ('A'side) / Prologue to history / Montana Autumn '78.
(cd-s) *(666345-5)* – ('A'side) / ('A'-Massive Attack remix) / ('A'-The Class Reunion Of The Sunset Marquis mix; aka David Holmes).

Sep 98. (cd/c/lp) *(491703-2/-4/-1) <47579>* **THIS IS MY TRUTH TELL ME YOURS** [1] [ ]
– The everlasting / If you tolerate this your children will be next / You stole the sun from my heart / Ready for drowning / Tsunami / My little empire / I'm not working / You're tender and you're tired / Born a girl / Be natural / Black dog on my shoulder / Nobody loved you / S.Y.M.M.

Nov 98. (c-s) *(666686-4)* **THE EVERLASTING / SMALL BLACK FLOWERS THAT GROW IN THE SUN (live at Nunex)** [11] [-]
(cd-s) *(666686-2)* – ('A'side) / Blackholes for the young / Valley boy.
(cd-s) *(666686-5)* – ('A'extended) / ('A'-Deadly Avenger's Psalm 315) / ('A'-Stealth Sonic Orchestra mix).

Mar 99. (c-s) *(666953-4)* **YOU STOLE THE SUN FROM MY HEART / IF YOU TOLERATE THIS YOUR CHILDREN WILL BE NEXT (live)** [5] [-]
(cd-s) *(666953-2)* – ('A'side) / Socialist serenade / Train in vain (live).
(cd-s) *(666953-5)* – ('A'side) / ('A'mixes by David Holmes & Mogwai).

Jul 99. (c-s) *(667411-4)* **TSUNAMI / MOTOWN JUNK (live)** [11] [-]
(cd-s) *(667411-2)* – ('A'side) / Buildings for dead people / A design for life (video).
(cd-s) *(667411-5)* – ('A'mixes by Cornelius & Stereolab).

Jan 00. (c-s) *(668530-4)* **THE MASSES AGAINST THE CLASSES / CLOSE MY EYES** [1] [-]
(10"+=/cd-s+=) *(668530-6/-2)* – Rock and roll music.

Feb 01. (c-s) *(670832-4)* **SO WHY SO SAD / YOU STOLE THE SUN FROM MY HEART (live from Cardiff Millennium Stadium 31st December 1999)** [8] [-]
(cd-s) *(670832-2)* – ('A'side) / ('A'-Avalanche remix) / Pedestal.

Feb 01. (7") *(670833-7)* **FOUND THAT SOUL. / THE MASSES AGAINST THE CLASSES (live)** [9] [-]
(cd-s) *(670833-2)* – ('A'side) / Locust valley / Ballad of the Bangkok Novotel.

Mar 01. (cd/c/lp) *(501880-2/-4/-1) <10113>* **KNOW YOUR ENEMY** [2] [ ]
– Found that soul / Ocean spray / Intravenus agnostic / So why so sad / Let Robeson sing / The year of purification / Wattsville blues / Miss Europa disco dancer / Dead martyrs / His last painting / My Guernica / The convalescent / Royal correspondent / Epicentre / Baby Elian / Freedom of speech won't feed my children. *(hidden track+=)*

Jun 01. (c-s) *(671253-4)* **OCEAN SPRAY / OCEAN SPRAY (Ellis Island mix)** [15] [-]
(cd-s) *(671253-2)* – ('A'side) / The groundhog days / Just a kid.
(cd-s) *(671253-5)* – ('A'side) / ('A'-Medicine mix) / ('A'-Kinobe mix).

MANOWAR

Formed: New York, USA . . . 1981 by former BLACK SABBATH roadie JOEY DeMAIO and ex-DICTATORS guitarist ROSS THE BOSS. Enlisting the services of ERIC ADAMS and DONNIE HAMZIK, the group set out to become the hoariest, most blatantly bare-chested heavy metal 'he-men' since LED ZEPPELIN's debauched heyday. Taking neolithic man as their role model, MANOWAR signed for 'Liberty' in 1982, the group subsequently being dropped the same year after the label finally realised what they'd let themselves in for. The debut album, 'BATTLE HYMNS' (1982), nevertheless found favour among metal diehards, its tales of war and destruction set to a wall of no-frills bass-heavy bombast. Image wise, MANOWAR certainly looked the part, dressed in open-chested, studded leather jump-suits, etc. Basically, the group took every metal cliche in the book and exaggerated it SPINAL TAP-style, in fact MANOWAR probably inspired the film! Of course, there was a tongue-in-cheek element to all of this, though whether the group's army of headbanging fans realised it is another matter. 'Liberty' certainly weren't impressed and so the group subsequently found a new home at 'Megaforce/Music For Nations' (apparently signing the contract in blood; see what happens when your biro runs out!), releasing 'INTO GLORY RIDE' in 1983. To be fair, the group were consummate musicians and in their field they had few peers, although the MANOWAR musical formula varied little from album to album. The SPINAL TAP connection raised its head again with 'ALL MEN PLAY ON TEN' from 1985's 'SIGN OF THE HAMMER', MANOWAR subsequently gatecrashing the 'The Guinness Book Of World Records' as the loudest band in the world, woarrrgh!! Granted, they may have been capable of fearless decibel terrorism but they were still struggling to sell records and subsequently realising this, they adopted a more mainstream sound for 'FIGHTING THE WORLD'. Despite such gloriously dumb tracks as 'BLOW YOUR SPEAKERS', the record once again failed to change their commercial fortunes and following another flop record, 'KINGS OF METAL' (1988), ROSS THE BOSS departed for pastures (battlefields?) new. Recruiting DEATH DEALER (DAVE SHANKEL to his mum) as a replacement, MANOWAR proudly announced that they were 'KINGS OF METAL' (of course) in 1988 with DeMAIO displaying his bass wizardry on the semi-legendary solo piece, 'STING OF THE BUMBLE BEE'. COLUMBUS was the next to leave, apparently due to family commitments (surely not!), RHINO(?!) recruited as a replacement in time for the 'TRIUMPH OF STEEL' (1992) set. This album marked the end of the group's tenure with 'Atlantic', MANOWAR subsequently engaging 'Geffen' in their eternal battle against "false metal". Though they have yet to achieve that elusive commercial breakthrough, they've become something of an institution, letting their loyal band of metal defenders in on the 'SECRETS OF STEEL' (1993) and assuring the likes of BON JOVI that MANOWAR are actually 'LOUDER THAN HELL' (1996). Lock up your daughters . . .

Album rating: BATTLE HYMNS (*6) / INTO GLORY RIDES (*5) / HAIL TO ENGLAND (*8) / SIGN OF THE HAMMER (*5) / FIGHTING THE WORLD (*6) / KINGS OF METAL (*6) / THE HELL OF STEEL – THE BEST OF MANOWAR compilation (*7) / THE TRIUMPH OF STEEL (*7) / SECRETS OF STEEL (*5) / LOUDER THAN HELL (*2)

ERIC ADAMS – vocals / **ROSS THE BOSS FRIEDMAN** – lead guitar, keyboards (ex-SHAKIN' STREET, ex-DICTATORS) / **JOEY DeMAIO** – bass / **DONNIE HAMZIK** – drums

Liberty | not iss.

Aug 82. (lp/c) *(LBG/TC-LBG 30349)* **BATTLE HYMNS** [ ] [-]
– Death tone / Metal daze / Fast taker / Shell shock / Manowar / Dark avenger / William's tale / Battle hymn. *(cd-iss. Feb00; 524617-2)*

—— **SCOTT COLOMBUS** – drums, percussion; repl. HAMZIK

Music For Nations | Megaforce

Jul 83. (lp/c) *(MFN/TMFN 6)* <*MR 1169*> **INTO GLORY RIDE** [ ] [ ]
– Warlord / Secret of steel / Gloves of metal / Gates of Valhalla / Hatred / Revelation (death's angel) / March for revenge (by the soldiers of death). *(cd-iss. Nov93 on 'Geffen'; GED 24538)*

Oct 83. (12") *(12KUT 102)* **DEFENDER. / GLOVES OF METAL** [ ] [-]
(above features the voice of actor ORSON WELLES)

Feb 84. (lp/c) *(MFN/CMFN 19)* **HAIL TO ENGLAND** [83] [-]
– Blood of my enemies / Each dawn I die / Kill with power / Hail to England / Army of the immortals / Black arrows / Bridge of death. *(cd-iss. Dec88; CDMFN 19) ,(cd re-iss. Nov93 on 'Geffen'; GED 24539)*>

10-Virgin | Grand Slam

Aug 84. (12") *(TEN 30-12)* **ALL MEN PLAY ON TEN. / MOUNTAINS** [ ] [-]

Sep 84. (lp/c) *(DIX/CDIX 10)* <*14*> **SIGN OF THE HAMMER** [73] [ ]
– All men play on ten / Animals / Thor (the power head) / Mountains / Sign of the hammer / The oath / Thunder pick / Guyana (cult of the damned). *(re-iss. Nov90 cd/c; XIDCD/CXID 21)*

Atlantic | Atlantic

Jan 87. (lp/c) <*(790563-1/-4)*> **FIGHTING THE WORLD** [ ] [ ]
– Fighting the world / Blow your speakers / Carry on / Violence and bloodshed / Defender / Drums of doom / Holy war / Master of revenge / Black wind, fire and steel. *(cd-iss. Jul88; 790563-2)*

May 87. (7"/12") *(B/+T 9463)* **BLOW YOUR SPEAKERS. / VIOLENCE AND BLOODSHED** [ ] [-]

Nov 88. (lp/c/cd) <*(K 781930-1/-4/-2)*> **KINGS OF METAL** [ ] [ ]
– Wheels of fire / Kings of metal / Sting of the bumblebee / The crown and the ring (lament of the kings) / Kingdom come / Pleasure slave * / Hail and kill / The warriors prayer / Blood of the kings. *(cd+= *)*

—— The DEATH DEALER (b. DAVE SHANKEL) – guitar; repl. ROSS

—— **RHINO** – drums; repl. COLOMBUS

Oct 92. (cd/c/lp) <*(7567 82423-2/-4/-1)*> **THE TRIUMPH OF STEEL** [ ] [ ]
– Hector storms the wall / The death of Patroclus / Funeral march / Armour of the gods / Hector's final hour / Death Hector's reward / The desecration of Hector's body parts 1 & 2 / The glory of Achilles / Metal warriors / Ride the dragon / Spirit horse of the Cherokee / Burning / The power of thy sword / The demon's whip / Master of the wind.

Geffen | Geffen

Nov 93. (d-cd) <*(GED 24540)*> **SECRETS OF STEEL** [ ] [ ]
– Warlord / Secret of steel / Gloves of metal / Gates of Valhalla / Hatred / Revelation (death's angel) / March for revenge (by the soldiers of death) / Blood of my enemies / Each dawn I die / Kill with power / Hail to England / Army of the immortals / Black arrows / Bridge of death. *<US cd re-iss. Jun98 on 'M.C.A.'; 70558>*

Nov 96. (cd) <*(GED 24925)*> **LOUDER THAN HELL** [ ] [ ]
– Return of the warlord / Brothers of metal pt.1 / The gods made heavy metal / Courage / Number 1 / Outlaw / King / Today is a good day to die / My spirit lives on / The power.

Nuclear Blast | Metal Blade

Mar 99. (cd) *(NB 379-2)* <*14254*> **HELL ON STAGE (live)** [ ] [ ] Apr99
– Metal daze / Dark avenger / March for revenge (by the soldiers of death) / Hatred / Gates of Valhalla / Bridge of death / William's tale / Guyana (cult of the damned) / The warrior's prayer / Blood of the kings / Sting of the bumblebee / Heart of steel / Master of the wind / Outlaw / The power / The crown and the ring. *(t-lp iss.Aug00; NB 379-1)*

– compilations, etc. –

Feb 92. (cd) *Atlantic;* <*(7567 80579-2)*> **THE HELL OF STEEL – THE BEST OF MANOWAR** [ ] [ ]
– Fighting the world / Kings of metal / Demon's whip / The warrior's prayer / Defender / Crown and the ring () / Blow your speakers / Metal warriors / Black wind, fire and steel / Hail and kill / Power of thy sword / Herz aus stahl / Kingdom come / Master of the wind.

Apr 97. (cd) *Connoisseur; (VSOPCD 235)* **ANTHOLOGY** [ ] [-]

Oct 98. (cd) *Mayhem; (11131-2)* **THE VERY BEST OF MANOWAR** [ ] [-]

Feb 99. (cd) *M.C.A.;* <*70101*> **KINGDOM OF STEEL: THE BEST OF MANOWAR** [-] [ ]

Marilyn MANSON

Formed: Fort Lauderdale, South Florida, USA . . . early 90's by the once pneumonia-crippled MANSON (real name BRIAN WARNER), an ordained minister in the Church Of Satan (run by Anton LeVey), provoking the wrath of conservative America. MANSON had begun his infamous career as a music journalist, simultaneously forming MARILYN MANSON & THE SPOOKY KIDS and taking inspiration from schlock-meisters like ALICE COOPER, KISS and surprisingly, veteran UK goth throwbacks, ALIEN SEX FIEND. After interviewing TRENT REZNOR, he/they secured a support slot with Reznor's NINE INCH NAILS, ultimately resulting in a record deal with TRENT's 'Nothing' records. Although the ghoulish Edward Scissorhands lookalike MANSON dated porn-star TRACII LORDS, he caused uproar at a hometown show when he allegedly mouthed ROBIN FINCK's (NIN) "pink oboe". The piercingly contact-lensed MANSON, whose onstage regalia usually included surgical corset and stockings, completed his OTT persona by routinely mutilating himself with knives, light-bulbs and indeed anything that came to hand. Like ALICE COOPER before him, he overshadowed the rest of his band (who comprised DAISY BERKOWITZ, MADONNA WAYNE GACY, SARA LEE LUCAS and smackhead GIDGET GEIN – the latter was deposed by TWIGGY RAMIREZ). Typically subtle as the proverbial sledgehammer, the band members' names were stitched together from glamorous icons and serial killers! As for the music, MANSON's vinyl/cd freakshow began with 1994's sub-goth posturing of 'PORTRAIT OF AN AMERICAN FAMILY'. GINGER took over drum duties for their second set, a collection of remixes entitled 'SMELLS LIKE CHILDREN', which included gruesome versions of SWEET DREAMS (Eurythmics), I PUT A SPELL ON YOU (Screamin' Jay Hawkins) and ROCK'N'ROLL NIGGER (Patti Smith) – he had previously covered Gary Numan's 'DOWN IN THE PARK'. Later that year, MANSON and Co. finally launched a full-scale assault on the moral majority/minority (delete as appropriate) with the inflammatory 'ANTICHRIST SUPERSTAR', which crucified the Billboard chart at No.3. They finally drove a stake through England's conservative heart in 1997, when MANSON (at that time the beau of MTV babe Julia Valet) wowed audiences at secret gigs around the country. By this point, they had also introduced new guitarist ZIM ZUM, who replaced DAISY for the UK Top 20 single, 'BEAUTIFUL PEOPLE', the unholy climax of MANSON's bizarre career to date. Whatever else he is, MANSON is a consummate showman, enticing ghoulish audiences with threats of onstage suicide, the ultimate in 90's entertainment, presumably ? (that's if the Christian extremists don't get 'im first). MANSON (BRIAN) re-invented himself and became a BOWIE-clone/freak "undressed" eunuchoid-fashion on the cover of the bands 1998 US chart-topping set, 'MECHANICAL ANIMALS', "Aladdin INsane" you could say! The Manson who fell to Earth indeed, it looked like we'd have to wait even longer before his "Rock'n'roll Suicide". Earlier in the year, his first book, the autobiographical, 'The Long Hard Road Out Of Hell', was published and contained insights into how WARNER/MANSON's deranged brain evolved. With controversy never a light year away, the man's "evil-metal" music was even brought into question when two MARILYN MANSON-obsessed kamikaze teenagers gunned down thirteen people (12 students and a teacher – another 28 were injured) inside Columbine High School, near Denver. MANSON immediately cancelled the rest of the band's tour and sent his sympathies to the bereaved while answering Right-wing politicians who were intent on blaming MANSON and the world of Heavy Metal – they should ask themselves how easy it was for "easily-led" youngsters (and anyone with that constitution) to obtain firearms and does any other music genre such as Country or Pop get the same media furore when one of its klan goes haywire. Down but not out, the beleaguered scapegoat attempted a resurrection of sorts with 'HOLY WOOD' (2000), summoning up the darker forces which informed 'ANTICHRIST . . .' while retaining the more accessible textures of 'MECHANICAL . . .'. The question is whether MANSON's carefully manicured goth-horror schtick actually has the power to shock anymore. With a career so reliant on image, can the music exist independently once that image has become a cliche? Answers on the back of an inverted cross to the usual address.

Album rating: PORTRAIT OF AN AMERICAN FAMILY (*6) / SMELLS LIKE CHILDREN (*6) / ANTICHRIST SUPERSTAR (*8) / MECHANICAL ANIMALS (*7) / THE LAST TOUR ON EARTH (*5) / HOLY WOOD (*7)

REVEREND MARILYN MANSON (b. BRIAN WARNER, 1969, Canton, Ohio) – vocals / **MADONNA WAYNE GACY** (b. STEPHEN) – keyboards, organ, theremin, saxophone, samples / **DAISY BERKOWITZ** (b. SCOTT MITCHELL PUTESKY) – guitars / **TWIGGY RAMIREZ** – bass; repl. GIDGET GEIN (b.BRAD STEWART) / **SARA LEE LUCAS** (b. FREDDY STREITHORST) – drums

Nothing-Interscope | Nothing-Interscope

Jun 94. (cd-ep) <*INTDM 95902*> **GET YOUR GUNN / MISERY MACHINE / MOTHER INFERIOR GOT HER GUNN / REVELATION No.9** [-] [ ]

Dec 94. (cd/c/d-lp) <*IND 92344*> **PORTRAIT OF AN AMERICAN FAMILY** [ ] [ ]
– Prelude (the family trip) / Cake and sodomy / Lunchbox / Organ grinder / Cyclops / Dope hat / Get your gunn / Wrapped in plastic / Dogma / Sweet tooth / Snake eyes and sissies / My monkey / Misery machine. *(re-iss. cd Jul96 on 'Nothing-Interscope'; same) (lp re-iss. Sep99 on 'Simply Vinyl'; SVLP 121)*

Feb 95. (cd-ep) <*INTDM 95806*> **LUNCHBOX / NEXT MOTHERFUCKER (remix) / DOWN IN THE PARK / BROWN BAG (remix) / METAL (remix)** [-] [ ]

—— **GINGER FISH** – drums; repl. SARA LEE

Aug 96. (cd-ep) *(IND 95504)* **SWEET DREAMS (ARE MADE OF THIS) / DANCE OF THE DOPE HATS (remix) / DOWN IN THE PARK / LUNCHBOX (NEXT MOTHERF****R)** [ ] [ ]

Aug 96. (cd) *<(IND 92641)>* **SMELLS LIKE CHILDREN** [ ] [31] Oct95
– The hands of small children / Diary of a dope fiend / S****y chicken gang bang / Kiddie grinder (remix) / Sympathy for the parents / Sweet dreams (are made of this) / Everlasting c***sucker (remix) / F*** Frankie / I put a spell on you / May cause discoloration of the urine or feces / Scatos, guns and peanut butter / Dance of the dope hats (remix) / White trash (remixed by Tony F. Wiggins) / Dancing with the one-legged . . . / Rock'n'roll nigger. *(cd re-iss. Aug98; same) (lp-iss.May00 on 'Simply Vinyl'; SVLP 208)*

— **ZIM ZUM** – guitar; repl. DAISY after below recording (he subsequently turned up with JACK OFF JILL in '98)

Oct 96. (cd/c) *<(IND 90006-2/-4)>* **ANTICHRIST SUPERSTAR** [73] [3]
– Irresponsible hate anthem / The beautiful people / Dried up, tied up and dead to the world / Tourniquet / Little horn / Cryptorchid / Deformography / Wormboy / Mister Superstar / Angel with the scabbed wings / Kinderfeld / Antichrist superstar / 1996 / Minute of decay / The reflecting God / Man that you fear. *(lp-iss.Nov98 on 'Simply Vinyl'; SVLP 55)*

Jun 97. (cd-ep) *(IND 95541)* **THE BEAUTIFUL PEOPLE / THE HORRIBLE PEOPLE (Danny Sabre remix) / SWEET DREAMS (lp version) / CRYPTORCHID** [18] [ ]
(cd-ep) *(INDX 95541)* – ('A'side) / The not so beautiful people (Jim Thirlwell remix) / Snake eyes and sissies / Deformography.
(10"pic-d) *(INVP 95541)* – The horrible people (Danny Sabre remix) / The not so beautiful people (Jim Thirlwell remix).

Sep 97. (10"pic-d) *(INVP 95552)* **TOURNIQUET. / TOURNIQUET (Prosthetic dance mix)** [28] [ ]
(cd-s+=) *(IND 95552)* – ('A'-Prosthetic dance mix edit).
(cd-s) *(INDX 95552)* – ('A'side) / Lunchbox / Next MF (remix).

Apr 98. (m-cd) *<(IND 95017)>* **REMIX & REPENT** [ ] [ ] Dec97
– The horrible people (remixed by Danny Saber) / Tourniquet (prosthetic dance mix) / Dried up, tied and dead to the world (live in Utica, NY) / Antichrist superstar (live in Hartford, CT) / Man that you fear (acoustic requiem for Antichrist Superstar).

— **JOHNNIE 5** – guitar; repl. ZIM ZUM

Sep 98. (cd/c) *<(IND/INC 98273)>* **MECHANICAL ANIMALS** [8] [1]
– Great big white world / The dope show / Mechanical animals / Rock is dead / Disassociative / The speed of pain / Posthuman / I want to disappear / I don't like the drugs (but the drugs like me) / New model No.15 / User friendly / Fundamentally loathsome / The last day on earth / Coma white. *(ltd-cd-iss. Jun99; IND 90394) (lp-iss.Apr00 on 'Simply Vinyl'; SVLP 195)*

Nov 98. (one-sided-10"pic-d) *(INVP 95610)* **THE DOPE SHOW** [12] [ ]
(cd-s+=) *(IND 95610)* – Sweet dreams (live) / Apple of Sodom (live).
(cd-s+=) *(INDX 95610)* – The beautiful people (live) / ('A'-CD-rom video).

— now without the sacked ZIM ZUM; **JOHN LOWERY** was his replacement

Jun 99. (10"pic-d) *(W 486TE)* **ROCK IS DEAD. / I DON'T LIKE DRUGS (BUT THE DRUGS LIKE ME) (every day mix)** [23] [ ]
(cd-s) *(W 486CD)* – ('A'side) / Man that you fear (acoustic requiem for Antichrist Superstar) / Baxter (television radio edit).
(cd-s) *(W 486CDX)* – ('A'side) / I don't like the drugs (but the drugs like me) (absinthe makes the heart grow fonder mix) / Baxter (I can't see why album version) / ('A'-CD-ROM video).

Nov 99. (d-cd) *<(490524-2)>* **THE LAST TOUR ON EARTH (live)** [61] [ ]
– Inauguration of the mechanical Christ / The reflecting God / Great big white world / Get your gunn / Sweet dreams (are made of this) / Hell outro / Rock is dead / The dope show / Lunchbox / I don't like the drugs (but the drugs like me) / Antichrist superstar / The beautiful people / The irresponsible hate anthem / The last day on Earth. *(UK d-cd+=)* – Coma white / Get off my rocks / Coma white / A rose and a baby Ruth.

Nov 00. (12"pic-d) *(497458-1)* **DISPOSABLE TEENS. / WORKING CLASS HERO / FIVE TO ONE** [12] [–]
(cd-s) *(497437-2)* – (first two tracks) / Diamonds and pollen.
(cd-s) *(497438-2)* – (first & third tracks) / Astonishing panorama of the endtimes.

Nov 00. (cd/d-lp) *(490829-2/-1)* *<490790>* **HOLY WOOD** [23] [13]
– Godeatgod / The love song / The fight song / Disposable teens / Target audience (Narcissus narcosis) / President dead / In the valley of the shadow of Earth / Crucifiction in space / A place in the dirt / The nobodies / The death song / Lamb of God / Born again / Burning flag / Coma black: Eden eye – The apple of discord / Valentine's day / The fall of Adam / King kill 33 / Count to six and die.

Feb 01. (12"pic-d) *(497491-1)* **THE FIGHT SONG. / THE FIGHT SONG (Slipknot remix) / LOVE SONG (remix)** [24] [–]
(cd-s) *(497490-2)* – (first two tracks) / Disposable teens (CD-Rom video).
(cd-s) *(497491-2)* – (first & third tracks) / Disposable teens (remix).

– others, etc. –

Dec 96. (cd-ep) *Interscope; (INTDM 95806)* **LUNCHBOX** [ ] [ ]
Dec 96. (cd-ep) *Interscope; (INTDM 95902)* **GET YOUR GUN** [ ] [ ]
Nov 97. (cd+book) *UFO; (UFOCD 15BX)* **SMELLS LIKE WHITE TRASH** [ ] [–]
Jun 99. (cd-book) *Hallmark; (8086)* **STAR PROFILE** [ ] [–]
Mar 01. (cd; as MARILYN MANSON & THE SPOOKY KIDS) *Nightingale; (ILLUSIONCD 2001)* **BIRTH OF THE ANTI-CHRIST** [ ] [ ]
Mar 01. (cd; as MARILYN MANSON & THE SPOOKY KIDS) *Illusion; (ILLUSIONCD 2002)* **LIVE** [ ] [ ]
Mar 01. (d-cd/CD-Rom; as MARILYN MANSON & THE SPOOKY KIDS) *Illusion; (ILLUSIONCD 2003)* **THE WORD ACCORDING TO MANSON** [ ] [ ]

MANTAS (see under ⇒ VENOM)

MARDUK

Formed: Sweden . . . 1990 as the brainchild of axegrinder MORGAN STEINMEYER HAKANSSON, who rounded off the line-up with ANDREAS AXELSSON, JOAKIM GRAVE and RICHARD KALM; the latter was soon superseded by BOGGE SVENSSON and a second guitarist DEVO ANDERSSON after their controversial 'FUCK ME JESUS' demo hit the scene. Several changes came about during the band's embryonic years, noteably GRAVE taking over vocal duties and the subsequent departure of the man for new drummer FREDRIK ANDERSSON (for more details see below). The album 'DARK ENDLESS' materialised in '92, its black metal overtones delighting their new loyal support. More were to follow:- 'THOSE OF THE UNLIGHT' (1993), 'OPUS NOCTURNE' (1994), 'HEAVEN SHALL BURN . . . WHEN WE ARE GATHERED' (1996). Of their later CD releases, the most interesting was 'PANZER DIVISION MARDUK' (1999) which was a concept obsessed by the Third Reich.

Album rating: DARK ENDLESS (*5) / THOSE OF THE UNLIGHT (*5) / OPUS NOCTURNE (*5) / HEAVEN SHALL BURN WHEN WE ARE GATHERED (*5) / GLORIFICATION mini (*5) / LIVE IN GERMANIA (*5) / NIGHTWING (*5) / PANZER DIVISION (*6) / OBEDIENCE (*5) / INFERNAL ETERNAL (*5) / LE GRANDE DANSE MACABRE (*5)

ANDREAS AXELSSON – vocals / **MORGAN STEINMEYER HAKANSSON** – guitar / **DEVO ANDERSSON** – guitar / **BOGGE SVENSSON** – bass; repl. RICHARD KALM / **JOAKIM GRAVE** – drums

No Fashion / not iss.

1992. (cd) *(NFR 003)* **DARK ENDLESS** [–] [–] Swedish
(UK-iss.Oct94; same)

— GRAVE took over vox from the departing ANDREAS

— **B.WAR** – bass; repl. BOGGE

Osmose / Osmose

1993. (cd) *(OPCD 15)* **THOSE OF THE UNLIGHT** [–] [–] French
– Darkness breeds immortality / Those of the unlight / Wolves / On darkened wings / Burn my coffin / A sculpture of the night / Echoes from the past / Stone stands it's silent vigil.

— added **FREDRIK ANDERSSON** – drums; DEVO departed

Jan 95. (cd/c/lp) *(<OPCD/OPMC/OPLP 28>)* **OPUS NOCTURNE** [ ] [ ] Apr99
– Intro – The appearance of spirits of darkness / Sulphur souls / From subterranean throne profound / Autumnal reaper / Materialized in stone / Untrodden paths (wolves part II) / Opus nocturne / Deme quaden thyrane / The sun has failed.

Feb 96. (7"ep) *(OPEP 06)* **FUCK ME JESUS** [ ] [–]

— **LEGION** – drums (ex-OPTHALAMIA) repl. GRAVE

Jul 96. (cd/lp) *(<OPCD/OPLP 40>)* **HEAVEN SHALL BURN . . . WHEN WE ARE GATHERED** [ ] [ ] Apr99
– Summon the darkness / Beyond the grace of God / Infernal eternal / Glorification of the black God / Darkness it shall be / The black tormentor of Satan / Dracul va domni din nou in Transilvania / Legion.

Oct 96. (m-cd/m-lp) *(OPCD/OPLP 43) <2066>* **GLORIFICATION** [ ] [ ]
– Glorification of the black god / Total desaster / Sex with Satan / Sodomize the dead / The return of darkness & evil.

— now added **PETER TAGTREN** – guitar (of HYPOCRISY)

Jun 97. (cd) *(<OPCD 54>)* **LIVE IN GERMANIA (live)** [ ] [ ]
– Beyond the grace of God / Suphur souls / The black / Darkness it shall be / Materialized in stone / Infernal eternal / On darkened wings / Wolves / Untrodden paths (wolves, pt.33) / Dracula va domni / Legion / Total desaster.

Mar 98. (cd/lp) *(<OPCD/OPLP 64>)* **NIGHTWING** [ ] [ ] Aug98
– Preludium / Bloodtide (XXX) / Of Hell's fire / Slay the Nazarene / Nightwing / Dream of blood and iron / Dracole Wayda / Kaziklu (The Lord Impaler) / Deme quaden thyrane / Anno Domini 1476.

May 99. (cd/lp) *(<OPCD/OPLP 80>)* **PANZER DIVISION MARDUK** [ ] [ ]
– Panzer division Marduk / Baptism by fire / Christraping black metal / Scorched Earth / Beast of prey / Blooddawn / 502 / Fistfucking God's planet.

Regain / Century Media

May 00. (cd-ep) *(BLOOD 003CD) <8034>* **OBEDIENCE EP** [ ] [ ] May01
– Obedience / Funeral bitch / Into the crypts of rays. *<US+=>* – Baptism by fire / Funeral bitch / Dracole wavda.

Dec 00. (d-cd/pic-d-lp) *(BLOOD 007 CD/PLP) <8035>* **INFERNAL ETERNAL** [ ] [ ] May01
– Panzer Division Marduk / Burn my coffin / Baptism by fire / The sun turns black as night / Of Hell's fire / 502 / Materized in stone / Beast of prey / Those of the unlight / Sulphur souls / Dreams of blood and iron / Fistfucking God's planet / On darkened wings / Into the crypts of rays / Still fucking dead / Slay the Nazarene / Departure from the mortals / Legion.

Mar 01. (cd/pic-lp) *(BLOOD 008 CD/LP) <8036>* **LE GRANDE DANSE MACABRE** [ ] [ ] Apr01
– Ars moriendi / Azrael / Pompa funebris 1660 / Obedience unto death / Bonds of unholy matrimony / La grande danse macabre / Death sex ejaculation / Funeral bitch / Summer end / Jesus Christ . . . sodomized.

– compilations, etc. –

Jun 98. (pic-lp) *Osmose; (OPPIC 30)* **FUCK ME JESUS / HERE NO PEACE** [ ] [–]

MARILLION

Formed: Aylesbury, Buckinghamshire, England . . . late '78 initially as SILMARILLION, by MICK POINTER and DOUG IRVINE. Taking their name from a J.R.R. Tolkien novel, they soon shortened it to MARILLION the following year. By this point, the all-instrumental outfit had added STEVE ROTHERY and BRIAN JELLIMAN, subsequently recruiting Scots vocalist, FISH (and DIZ MINNITT), after IRVINE departed late in 1980. By March '82, FISH (aka DEREK WILLIAM DICK), POINTER and ROTHERY, finally completed the line-up with Irishman MARK KELLY and PETE TREWAVAS. The band had now been gigging for almost four years and had built up a sizeable following, something that 'E.M.I.' had noticed before securing them a major deal. Soon after, the company issued 'MARKET SQUARE HEROES', the single denting the UK Top 60. Surprisingly, given their prog-rock pretensions, they were voted the best newcomer in the rock-centric (now defunct) Sounds magazine early in 1983. A second single, 'HE KNOWS, YOU KNOW', hit the Top 40, preceding the release of a debut album, 'SCRIPT FOR A JESTER'S TEAR'. Featuring one of their best-loved tracks, 'GARDEN PARTY' (also a UK Top 20 hit), the record reached the Top 10. With GENESIS pursuing a more commercial direction, MARILLION were perfectly poised to fill the gap in the market; a giant of a man, the enigmatic FISH updated PETER GABRIEL's early 70's vocal mannerisms over a keyboard-dominated backing. Like punk never happened, FISH and the lads took us back a decade, sporting ornate lyrical concepts masterminded by the hulking frontman. A harder-edged affair, the follow-up album, 'FUGAZI' strengthened the band's reputation among British rock fans looking for a genuine alternative to AOR-brushed material churning out of America. In the summer of '85, after a rather unnecessary live mini-set, 'REAL TO REEL', they wooed the mainstream with the wistful love song, 'KAYLEIGH', a near chart topper and an integral part of the conceptual yet accessible 'MISPLACED CHILDHOOD' opus. A UK No.1, the album also featured another top selling ballad, 'LAVENDER' and transformed MARILLION into a stadium-filling live proposition (although America proved impenetrable, 'KAYLEIGH' only scraping into their Hot 100). By 1987's top selling 'CLUTCHING AT STRAWS', FISH was uncomfortable with his newfound pop star status, his drink/drug problems fuelling speculation of an imminent split. The rumours proved all too true, when, just prior to the release of a double live set, 'THE THIEVING MAGPIE', the big man bailed out. While he contemplated a solo career, MARILLION decided to carry on, having found a worthy replacement in STEVE HOGARTH. An unknown quantity to many (although he had fronted minor chart group The EUROPEANS), HOGARTH's fluid, unassuming style nevertheless won over the majority of MARILLION fans, taking the band into unknown territory with the album, 'SEASON'S END' (1989). A competent set, the album's sole weak point was the Top 30 single, 'HOOKS IN YOU'. In 1992, they tried in vain to carry off a cover of Rare Bird's 'SYMPATHY', although this still managed a Top 20 placing, as did a singles collection. MARILLION found it hard to recapture the momentum of their halycon days, that is, until 1994's brilliant return to their conceptual roots with the album, 'BRAVE'. This fusion of folky melodic-rock and quasi-ambient atmospherics was their first to hit the Top 10 for some time, although two albums ('AFRAID OF SUNLIGHT' and the live 'MADE AGAIN') down the line, they finally parted company with 'E.M.I.'. Now on 'Raw Power' (rock's retirement stable), MARILLION subsequently released their 1997 set, 'THIS STRANGE ENGINE', a more accessible outing than previously. Its acoustic musings stood in contrast to 'RADIATION' (1998), a return to meatier, more conceptual waters which nevertheless retained an oblique pop edge. To their credit, MARILLION seemed unwilling to sit on their laurels and churn out music specifically created for their cult fanbase, instead making a concerted effort to update their influences for the new millennium as witnessed on 'MARILLION.COM' (1999). The wittily titled 'ANORAKNOPHOBIA' followed in 2001.

Album rating: SCRIPT FOR A JESTER'S TEAR (*8) / FUGAZI (*6) / REAL TO REEL (*5) / MISPLACED CHILDHOOD (*7) / CLUTCHING AT STRAWS (*6) / THE THIEVING MAGPIE (*5) / SEASON'S END (*5) / A SINGLES COLLECTION 1982-1992 compilation (*8) / HOLIDAYS IN EDEN (*6) / BRAVE (*7) / AFRAID OF SUNLIGHT (*5) / THIS STRANGE ENGINE (*6) / RADIATION (*5) / MARILLION.COM (*4) / ANORAKNOPHOBIA (*5)

FISH (b. DEREK WILLIAM DICK, 25 Apr'58, Dalkeith, Scotland) – vocals / **MARK KELLY** (b. 9 Apr'61, Dublin, Eire) – keyboards repl. BRIAN JELLIMAN / **MICK POINTER** (b.22 Jul'56) – drums / **STEVE ROTHERY** (b.25 Nov'59) – guitar / **PETER TREWAVAS** (b.15 Jan'59) – bass repl. DOUG IRVINE

E.M.I. Capitol

Oct 82. (7") *(EMI 5351)* **MARKET SQUARE HEROES. / THREE BOATS DOWN FROM THE CANDY** [60] [-]
(12"+=/12"pic-d+=) *(12EMI 5351/+P)* – Grendel. *(re-entered.Apr83; hit No.53)*

Jan 83. (7") *(EMI 5362)* **HE KNOWS, YOU KNOW. / CHARTING THE SINGLE** [35] [-]
(12"+=) *(12EMI 5362)* – ('A'extended).

Mar 83. (lp/c) *(EMC/TC-EMC 3429) <12269>* **SCRIPT FOR A JESTER'S TEAR** [7] [ ]
– Script for a jester's tear / He knows, you know / The web / Garden party / Chelsea Monday / Forgotten sons. *(pic-lp.Jun84; EMCP 3429) (cd-iss. Feb87; CDP 746237-2) (re-iss. May90 on 'Fame' cd/c/lp; CD/TC+/FA 3235) (re-iss. Mar96 on 'EMI Gold' cd/c; CD/TC GOLD 1012) (cd re-iss. Aug00; 527115-2)*

Jun 83. (7"/7"sha-pic-d) *(EMI/+P 5393)* **GARDEN PARTY. / MARGARET (live)** [16] [-]
(ext.12"+=/ext.12"w-poster+=) *(12EMI/+P 5393)* – Charting the single (live).

— **ANDY WARD** – drums (ex-CAMEL) replaced POINTER / **IAN MOSLEY** (b.16 Jun'53) – drums (ex-STEVE HACKETT, ex-CURVED AIR) repl. WARD

Jan 84. (7") *(MARIL 1)* **PUNCH AND JUDY. / MARKET SQUARE HEROES (new version)** [29] [-]
(12"+=/12"pic-d+=) *(12MARIL/+P 1)* – Three boats down from the candy (new version).

Mar 84. (lp/pic-lp)(c) *(MRL/+P 1)(TC-MRL 1) <46027>* **FUGAZI** [5] [ ]
– Assassing / Punch and Judy / Jigsaw / Emerald lies / She chameleon / Incubus / Fugazi. *(re-iss. May88 on 'Fame' cd/c/lp; CD/TC+FA 3196) (cd re-iss. May94; CDEMS 1516)*

Apr 84. (7")(ext;12"+=/12"pic-d+=) *(MARIL 2)(12MARIL/+P 2)*
ASSASSING. / CINDERELLA SEARCH [22] [-]

Nov 84. (m-lp/c) *(JEST/TC-JEST 1)* **REAL TO REEL (live)** [8] [ ]
– Assassing / Incubus / Cinderella search / Forgotten sons / Garden party / Market square heroes. *(pic-lp.Jan85; EG 2603036) (re-iss. Nov85 on 'Fame' lp/c/cd+=; FA/TC-FA/CD-FA 3142)* – Emerald lies. *(cd re-iss. Oct87; CDM 752 021-2)*

May 85. (7"/7"pic-d) *(MARIL/+P 3)* **KAYLEIGH. / LADY NINJA** [2] [-]
(ext.12"+=/ext.12"pic-d+=) *(12MARIL/+P 3)* – ('A'-alternative).

Jun 85. (lp/pic-lp)(c)(cd) *(MRL/+P 2)(TC-MRL 2)(CDP 746160-2) <12431>* **MISPLACED CHILDHOOD** [1] [47]
– The pseudo silk kimono / Kayleigh / Lavender / Bitter suite – Heart of Lothian / Waterhole (expresso bongo) / Lords of the backstage / Blind curve / Childhood's end? / White feather. *(cd re-iss. May94; CDEMS 1518) (cd re-iss. Aug00; 527116-20*

Aug 85. (7") *(MARIL 4) <5539>* **LAVENDER. / FREAKS** [5] [ ]
(12"+=/12"pic-d+=) *(12MARIL/+P 4)* – ('A'remix).

Sep 85. (7") *<5493>* **KAYLEIGH. / HEART OF LOTHIAN** [-] [74]

Nov 85. (7") *(MARIL 5)* **HEART OF LOTHIAN. / CHELSEA MONDAY (live)** [29] [-]
(12"+=/12"pic-d+=) *(12MARIL/+P 5)* – ('A'extended).

— Early 1986, FISH teamed up with TONY BANKS (GENESIS) on a single.

Dec 85. (7") *<5561>* **HEART OF LOTHIAN. / LADY NINJA** [-] [ ]

Mar 86. (m-lp) *<15023>* **BRIEF ENCOUNTER** (3 live early '86) [-] [67]
– Freaks / Fugazi / Kayleigh / Lady Ninja / Script for a jester's tear.

May 87. (7") *(MARIL 6) <44043>* **INCOMMUNICADO. / GOING UNDER** [6] [ ]
(12"pic-d+=)(cd-s+=) *(12MARILP 6)(CDMARIL 6)* – ('A'alternate).

Jun 87. (lp/pic-lp)(c/cd) *(EMD/+P 1002)(TC/CD EMD 1002) <12539>*
CLUTCHING AT STRAWS [2] [ ]
– Hotel hobbies / Warm wet circles / That time of the night (the short straw) / Going under * / Just for the record / White Russian / Incommunicado / Torch song / Slainte Mhath / Sugar mice / The last straw. *(cd+= *) (re-iss. 1989 cd)(c/lp; CZ 214)(TC+/ATAK 135) (cd re-mast.Mar99; 498611-2) (cd re-iss. Aug00; 527117-2) (cd re-iss. Feb01; 527117-2)*

Jul 87. (7"/7"pic-d) *(MARIL/+P 7) <44060>* **SUGAR MICE. / TUX ON** [22] [ ]
(12"+=/12"pic-d+=) *(12MARIL/+P 7)* – ('A'extended).

Oct 87. (7") *(MARIL 8)* **WARM WET CIRCLES. / WHITE RUSSIAN (live)** [22] [-]
(12"+=/12"pic-d+=) *(12MARIL/+P 8)* – Incommunicado (live).
(cd-s++=) *(CDMARIL 8)* – Up on top of a rainbow.

Nov 88. (d-cd/c/d-lp) *(CD/TC+/MARL 1) <C 191463>* **THE THIEVING MAGPIE (live)** [25] [ ]
– (intro) / La gazza ladra / Slainte mhath / He knows, you know / Chelsea Monday / Freaks / Jigsaw / Punch and Judy / Sugar mice / Fugazi / Script for a jester's tear / Incommunicado / White Russian / Misplaced childhood part 1:- Pseudo silk kimono – Kayleigh – Lavender – Bitter suite – Heart of Lothian. *(d-cd+=)* – Misplaced childhood part 2:- Waterhole (expresso bongo) – Lords of the backstage – Blind curve – Childhood's end? – White feather.

Nov 88. (7"/7"sha-pic-d) *(MARIL/+P 9)* **FREAKS (live). / KAYLEIGH (live)** [24] [-]
(12"+=/cd-s+=) *(12/CD MARIL 9)* – Childhood's end (live) / White feather (live).

— **STEVE HOGARTH** – vocals (ex-HOW WE LIVE, ex-EUROPEANS, ex-LAST CALL) finally repl. FISH. (He had left to go solo Sep'88).

Aug 89. (c-s/7") *(TC+/MARIL 10)* **HOOKS IN YOU. / AFTER ME** [30] [-]
(12"+=/12"pic-d+=) *(12MARIL 10/+P)* – ('A'-meaty mix).
(cd-s+=) *(CDMARIL 10)* – ('A'-seven mix).

Sep 89. (cd/c/lp) *(CD/TC+/EMD 1011) <C 192877>* **SEASON'S END** [7] [ ]
– King of sunset town / Easter / The uninvited guest / Season's end / Holloway girl / Berlin / After me / Hooks in you / The space. *(c+=/cd+=)* – After me. *(pic-lp.Dec89; EMDPD 1011) (cd re-iss. Aug00; 527118-2)*

Nov 89. (7"/7"sha-pic-d)(c-s) *(MARIL/+PD 11)(TC-MARIL 11)* **THE UNINVITED GUEST. / THE BELL IN THE SEA** [53] [-]
(12"+=/12"pic-d+=)(cd-s+=) *(12MARIL/+P 11)(CDMARIL 11)* – ('A'extended).

Mar 90. (7"/7"pic-d)(c-s) *(MARIL/+P 12)(TC-MARIL 12)* **EASTER. / THE RELEASE** [34] [-]
(12"+=/12"g-f+=)(cd-s+=) *(12MARIL/+G 12)(CDMARIL 12)* – ('A'extended) / The uninvited guest (live).

Jun 91. (c-s/7") *(TC+/MARIL 13)* **COVER MY EYES (PAIN AND HEAVEN). / HOW CAN IT HURT** [34] [-]
(12"+=/cd-s+=) *(12/CD MARIL 13)* – The party.

Jul 91. (cd/c/lp) *(CD/TC+/EMD 1022) <13138>* **HOLIDAYS IN EDEN** [7] [ ]
– Splintered heart / Cover my eyes (pain and Heaven) / The party / No one can / Holidays in Eden / Dry land / Waiting to happen / This town / The rakes progress / 100 nights.

Jul 91. (7"/7"box)(c-s) *(MARIL/+S 14)(TC-MARIL 14)* **NO ONE CAN. / A COLLECTION** [33] [-]
(cd-s+=) *(CDMARIL 14)* – Splintered heart (live).

Sep 91. (c-s/7") *(TC+/MARIL 15)* **DRY LAND. / HOLLOWAY GIRL / AFTER ME** [34] [-]
(12"+=) *(12MARIL 15)* – Substitute.
(10"clear+=) *(10MARIL 15)* – Waiting to happen.
(cd-s+=) *(CDMARIL 15)* – Easter / Sugar mice.
(12"pic-d+=) *(12MARILP 15)* – King of Sunset town.

May 92. (c-s/7") *(TC+/MARIL 16)* **SYMPATHY. / KAYLEIGH (live)** [17] [-]
(cd-s+=) *(MARILS 16)* – I will walk on water.
(12"pic-d+=)(cd-s+=) *(12MARILPD 16)(CDMARIL 16)* – Dry land (live).

Jun 92. (cd/c/d-lp) *(CD/TC+/EMD 1033)* **A SINGLES COLLECTION 1982-1992** (compilation) [27] [-]
– Cover my eyes (pain & Heaven) / Kayleigh / Easter / Warm wet circles / Uninvited guest / Assassing / Hooks in you / Garden party / No one can / Incommunicado / Dry land / Lavender / I will walk on water / Sympathy.

Jul 92. (c-s/7") *(TC+/MARIL 17)* **NO ONE CAN. / A COLLECTION** [26] [-]
(cd-s+=) *(CDMARIL 17)* – Splintered heart.

Feb 94. (cd/c/d-lp) *(CD/TC+/EMD 1054) <28032>* **BRAVE** [10] [ ]
– Bridge / Living with the big lie / Runaway / Goodbye to all that (i) Wave (ii) Mad (iii) The opium den (iv) The slide (v) Standing in the swing / Hard as love / The hollow man / Alone again in the lap of luxury (i) Now wash your hands / Paper lies / Brave / The great escape (i) The last of you (ii) Fallin' from the Moon / Made again. *(cd re-mast.Oct98; 497038-2)*

Mar 94. (c-s/7") *(TC+/EM 307)* **THE HOLLOW MAN. / BRAVE** [30] [-]
(cd-s+=) *(CDEMS 307)* – Marouatte jam.
(cd-s) *(CDEM 307)* – ('A'side) / The last of you – Falling from the Moon (the great escape) / Winter trees.

Apr 94. (c-s) *(TCEM 318)* **ALONE AGAIN IN THE LAP OF LUXURY / LIVING WITH THE BIG LIE (live)** [53] [-]
(12"pic-d+=) *(12EMPD 318)* – The space (live).
(cd-s+=) *(CDEMS 318)* – River (live) / Bridge (live).

(cd-s) *(CDEM 318)* – ('A'side) / Cover my eyes / Slainte Mhath / Uninvited guest (all live).
Jun 95. (c-s/cd-s) *(TC/CD MARIL 18)* **BEAUTIFUL / AFRAID OF SUNRISE / ICON** 29 -
(cd-s) *(CDMARILS 18)* – ('A'side) / Live forever / Great escape (demo) / Hard as love (demo).
Jun 95. (cd/c/lp) *(CD/TC+/EMD 1079)* <33874> **AFRAID OF SUNLIGHT** 16
– Gazpacho / Cannibal surf babe / Beautiful / Afraid of sunrise / Out of this world / Afraid of sunlight / Beyond you / King. *(cd re-mast.Mar99; 498614-2)*

E.M.I. Castle

Mar 96. (d-cd/d-c) *(CD/TC EMD 1094)* <117> **MADE AGAIN (live)** 37
– Splintered heart / Easter / No one can / Waiting to happen / Cover my eyes / The space / Hooks in you / Beautiful / Kayleigh / Lavender / Afraid of sunlight / King // Brave (live in Paris):- Bridge / Living with the big life / Runaway / Goodbye to all that / Wave / Mad / The opium den / Slide / Standing in the swing / Hard as love / Hollow man / Alone again in the lap of luxury / Now wash your hands / Paper lies / Brave / The great escape / The last of you / Falling from the Moon / Made again. *(d-cd re-iss. Feb01 on 'Castle'; CMDDD 123)*

Raw Power Velvel

May 97. (cd/c/pic-lp) *(RAW CD/MC/DP 121)* <79791> **THIS STRANGE ENGINE** 27 Jul97
– Man of 100 faces / One fine day / Eighty days / Estonia / Memory of water / An accidental man / Hope for the future / This strange engine. *(cd re-iss. Feb01 on 'Castle'; CMRCD 071)*
May 97. (cd-s) *(RAWX 1044)* **MAN OF 1000 FACES / BEAUTIFUL / MADE AGAIN / ('A'mix)** -
Oct 97. (cd-s) *(RAWX 1049)* **EIGHTY DAYS / THIS STRANGE ENGINE (extended – live) / BELL IN THE SEA (live)** -
Sep 98. (cd-s) *(RAWX 1051)* **THESE CHAINS / FAKE PLASTIC TREES (live) / MEMORY OF WATER (Big Beat mix)** -
Sep 98. (cd) *(RAWCD 126)* <79760> **RADIATION** 35 Oct98
– Costa del Slough / Under the sun / The answering machine / Three minute boy / Now she'll never know / These chains / Born to run / Cathedral wall / Few words for the dead. <US+=> – Estonia / Memory of water. *(re-iss. Feb01 on 'Castle'; CMRCD 113)*

Raw Power Never

Oct 99. (cd) *(RAWCD 144)* <4505> **MARILLION.COM** 53 Nov99
– A legacy / Deserve / Go / Rich / Enlightened / Built-in bastard radar / Tumble down the years / Interior Lulu / House.

Liberty Sanctuary

May 01. (cd) *(532321-2)* <84506> **ANORAKNOPHOBIA**
– Between you and me / Quartz / Map of the world / When I grow old / Fruit of the wild rose / Separated out / This is the 21st century / If my heart were a ball it would roll uphill.

– compilations etc. –

on 'E.M.I.' unless mentioned otherwise
Jan 88. (cd)(lp) *(CZ 39)(EMS 1295)* **B SIDES THEMSELVES (rare flips)** 64 -
Nov 95. (3xcd-box) *(CDOMB 015)* **THE ORIGINALS** -
– (SCRIPT FOR A JESTER'S TEAR / FUGAZI / MISPLACED CHILDHOOD). *(re-iss. Apr97; same)*
Oct 96. (cd) *EMI Gold; (CDGOLD 1058)* **THE COLLECTION** -
Feb 97. (d-cd) *(CDEMC 3761)* **THE BEST OF BOTH WORLDS** -
Apr 97. (d-pic-lp) *(EMCF 3761)* **THE BEST OF BOTH WORLDS 1982-88** -
Apr 97. (d-pic-lp) *(EMCH 3761)* **THE BEST OF BOTH WORLDS 1989-PRESENT** -
Jun 97. (d-cd) *(CDEM 1603)* **REAL TO REEL / BRIEF ENCOUNTER** -
Jan 00. (cd/c) *Eagle; (EAG CD/MC 033)* **TALES FROM THE ENGINE ROOM** -
– (THIS STRANGE ENGINE remixed + MARILLION & THE POSITIVE LIGHT)

Frank MARINO (see under ⇒ MAHOGANY RUSH)

Bernie MARSDEN

Born: London, England. A former guitarist with BABE RUTH and UFO, the man took up the prestigious lead guitar slot with WHITESNAKE. During this late 70's/early 80's period, he managed to squeeze out two solo albums, 'AND ABOUT TIME TOO' and 'LOOK AT ME NOW'. These featured seasoned hard rock musicians including COZY POWELL, DON AIREY, NEIL MURRAY, JACK BRUCE, JON LORD and IAN PAICE, although this did not ensure any commercial success. MARSDEN enlisted the help of some new musicians and formed BERNIE MARSDEN'S S.O.S., which subsequently became ALASKA. Signing to 'Music For Nations', this symphonic pomp-rock outfit (which numbered vocalist ROBERT HAWTHORN) released two albums, 'HEART OF THE STORM' (1984) and 'THE PACK' (1985). The song 'HEADLINES' was later used on a 1988 TV ad for The Sunday Sport!, thus its re-issue that year, however, MARSDEN had already joined the short-lived MGM.

Album rating: AND ABOUT TIME TOO (*5) / LOOK AT ME NOW (*4) / GREEN AND BLUES (*4) / Alaska: HEART OF THE STORM (*5) / THE PACK (*5) / THE BRONZE YEARS: THE BEST OF ALASKA compilation (*6)

BERNIE MARSDEN – guitar, vocals / **DON AIREY** – keyboards, synthesizers / **JACK BRUCE** – bass / **IAN PAICE** – drums / **JON LORD** – keyboards, synthesizers / **SIMON PHILLIPS** – drums / **NEIL MURRAY** – bass / **COZY POWELL** – drums / **DOREEN CHANTER + IRENE CHANTER** – backing vocals / etc

Parlophone not iss.

May 81. (7") *(R 6047)* **SAD CLOWN. / YOU AND ME** -
May 81. (lp/c) *(PCS/TC-PCS 7215)* **AND ABOUT TIME TOO** -
– You're the one / Song for Fran / Love made a fool of me / Here we go again / Still the same / Sad clown / Brief encounter / Are you ready / Head the ball. *(cd-iss. Oct95 on 'R.P.M.'; RPM 152) (cd re-iss. Mar99 & Nov00 on 'Purple'+=; PUR 313)* – You and me / Who's foolin' who (live) / Shakey ground (live).
Jul 81. (7") *(R 6050)* **LOOK AT ME NOW. / ALWAYS LOVE YOU SO** -
Sep 81. (lp/c) *(PCS/TC-PCS 7217)* **LOOK AT ME NOW** -
– Look at me now / So far away / Who's foolin' who / Shakey ground / Behind your dark eyes / Byblos shack (parts 1 & 2) / Thunder and lightning / Can you do it? (rock city blues) / After all the madness. *(cd-iss. Oct95 on 'R.P.M.'; RPM 153) (cd re-iss. Mar99 & Nov00 on 'Purple'+=; PUR 314)* – Always love you so / Look at me now (live) / Byblos shack (live).
Jan 82. (7") *(R 6053)* **THUNDER AND LIGHTNING. / BYBLOS SHACK** -

ALASKA

BERNIE MARSDEN – guitar / **ROBERT HAWTHORN** – vocals / **BRIAN BADHAMS** – bass / **JOHN MARTER** – drums (ex- MR. BIG, ex-MARILLION)

Music For Nations not iss.

Apr 84. (7"/12") *(KUT 108)* **I NEED YOUR LOVE. / SUSIE BLUE** -
May 84. (lp) *(MFN 23)* **HEART OF THE STORM** -
– Whiteout / Don't say it's over / Voice on the radio / Susie blue / Heart of the storm / I need your love / Can't let go / Other side of midnight / The sorcerer.
Mar 85. (lp) *(MFN 41)* **THE PACK** -
– Run with the pack / Woman like you / Where did they go (Bonneville blues) / Schoolgirl / I help yourself / Miss you tonight / The thing / I really want to know.
May 85. (7"/12") *(KUT/12KUT 116)* **MISS YOU TONIGHT. / VOI** -

Bronze not iss.

Oct 85. (7"/12") *(BRO/+X 196)* **SHOW SOME EMOTION. / YOU DON'T HAVE TO WORRY** -

— Disbanded early 1986, MARSDEN subsequently joined short-lived MGM. In the first half of the 90's, he released two joint efforts with MICK MOODY under the banner of The MOODY MARSDEN BAND. These were 'Essential' cd's 'NEVER TURN YOUR BACK ON THE BLUES' (1993) and 'THE TIME IS RIGHT FOR LIVE' (1994; a double); (ESMCD 182) and (ESDCD 225) respectively.

BERNIE MARSDEN

Essential not iss.

Nov 95. (cd) *(ESSCD 324)* **GREEN AND BLUES** -
– Hideaway / Don't want no woman / If you be my baby / Little girl / Rollin' man / Merry go round / Watchout / Snowy wood / My heart beats like a hammer / Shake your money maker / Love that burns / The welfare (turns its back on you) / Steppin in / The supernatural / Man of the world. *(<re+ US-iss.Apr01 on 'Castle'; CMRCD 181>)*

– compilations, others, etc. –

Sep 88. (7"; by ALASKA) *Music For Nations; (KUT 130)* **HEADLINES. / THE SORCERER** -
May 92. (cd) *Raw Fruit; (FRSCD 007)* **THE FRIDAY ROCK SHOW (live)** -
May 00. (cd; by ALASKA) *Essential; (<ESMCD 889>)* **THE BRONZE YEARS (THE BEST OF ALASKA)** Feb01

MARSEILLE

Formed: London, England . . . 1976 by NEIL BUCHANAN, PAUL DALE, ANDY CHARTERS, STEVE DINWOODIE and KEITH KNOWLES. Signing to the 'Mountain' label, the band debuted in Spring '78 with the 'RED, WHITE AND SLIGHTLY BLUE' set and accompanying single, 'THE FRENCH WAY' (recorded earlier as the soundtrack to the soft-porn film of the same name). With the NWOBHM scene fermenting nicely, the band opted for a more metallic approach on the eponymous 'MARSEILLE' (1979). With the group's label subsequently running into problems, however, MARSEILLE soon found themselves minus a record contract. This marked the end of band activities for more than four years, the group eventually resurfacing with new members SAV PEARSE and MARK HAYS for a third and final set, 'TOUCH THE NIGHT' (1984).

Album rating: RED, WHITE AND SLIGHTLY BLUE (*5) / MARSEILLE (*5) / TOUCH THE NIGHT (*4)

PAUL DALE – vocals / **NEIL BUCHANAN** – guitar / **ANDY CHARTERS** – guitar / **STEVE DINWOODIE** – bass / **KEITH KNOWLES** – drums

Mountain R.C.A.

Mar 78. (7") *(BON 1)* **THE FRENCH WAY. / COLD STEEL** -
Apr 78. (lp) *(TOPC 5012)* **RED, WHITE AND SLIGHTLY BLUE** -
– No time to lose / Can can / She gives me hell / I felt no pain / Dear doctor / The French way / Not tonight Josephine / Men's lib / Motherly love / Percival / Lolita.
Jun 78. (7") *(TOP 39)* **KISS LIKE ROCK'N'ROLL. / CAN-CAN** -
May 79. (7"m) *(BON 2)* **OVER AND OVER. / YOU'RE A WOMAN / CAN-CAN** -
Jun 79. (lp) *(TOPS 125)* <3631> **MARSEILLE**
– Rock you tonight / Armed and ready / Over and over / Lady of the night / Walking thro' the night / Bring on the dancing girls / You're a woman / Don't wanna hurt you / Some like it hot.
Sep 79. (7") *(TOP 49)* **BRING ON THE DANCING GIRLS. / ROCK YOU TONIGHT** -
Feb 80. (7") *(TOP 51)* **KITES. / SOME LIKE IT HOT** -

— took time to find another recording contract

— **SAV PEARSE** – vocals (ex-SAVAGE LUCY) repl. DALE who went solo

— **MARK HAYS** – guitar; repl. CHARTERS

Ultra Noise not iss.

Sep 84. (7") *(WALK 1)* **WALKING ON A HIGHWIRE. / TOO LATE**

Oct 84. (lp) *(ULTRA 3)* **TOUCH THE NIGHT**
– Crazy / Walking on a high wire / After the fall / Touch the night / Reach for the night / Too late / Gatecrashin' / Live now pay later / Open fire.

— split soon after above

MARSHALL LAW

Formed: Birmingham, England . . . 1988 by ANDY PIKE, DAVE MARTIN, ANDY SOUTHWELL, ROG DAVIS and MICK DONOVAN. Heralded as initiating a brave new era for well 'ard Brit-metal, this Brummie bunch displayed all the obvious influences (JUDAS PRIEST, IRON MAIDEN etc, ad(d) nauseam) without any strategy for carrying the music forward. Signed to 'Heavy Metal' records, the band released their eponymous debut in late '89, a hit with certain critics but a stiff with record buying rockers. If MARSHALL LAW had actually made some arresting music, maybe they'd still be around today.

Album rating: MARSHALL LAW (*4) / LAW IN THE RAW (*5) / METAL DETECTOR (*4) / WARNING FROM HISTORY (*4)

ANDY PIKE – vocals / **DAVE MARTIN** – guitar / **ANDY SOUTHWELL** – guitar / **ROG DAVIS** – bass / **MICK DONOVAN** – drums

Heavy Metal not iss.

Dec 89. (lp/c/cd) *(HMR LP/MC/XD 138)* **MARSHALL LAW**
– Armageddon / Under the hammer / Rock the nation / Marshall law / Hearts and thunder / Screaming / We're hot / Feel it / System X / Future shock / When will it end?

Jul 91. (12"ep/cd-ep) *(12HM/HEAVYXD 172)* **POWER CRAZY. /**

— inevitably they split but re-formed later in the 90's

— **LEE MORRIS** – drums; repl. MICK

Neat Metal Feel The Power

Oct 97. (cd) *(NM 008CD)* <106> **LAW IN THE RAW** Mar96
– Chain of youth / Another generation / Screaming / Psychodrama / Searching for paradise / Naked aggression / Under the hammer / System X / Powergame / Hearts and thunder / Marshall law / Leviathan.

Neat Metal Pulse

Nov 97. (cd) <0004> **METAL DETECTOR**
– Osmium / Twisted this / War / Seek and you shall find / Swarm / Feed the need / Devices / Addicted to the pain / Empowerment / The sands of time / Meganoid / The seeds of change / Iridium.

Jun 99. (cd) *(NM 035)* **WARNING FROM HISTORY**
– Foregathering / Victory at last / Locked and loaded / Remembered forever / Harbinger / Blood on blood / Crucified / March of history / Pray for deliverance / God king / Retreat / Searching for Paradise / Powergame.

MARY BEATS JANE

Formed: Ornskoldsvik, Sweden . . . 1991 by MAGNUS NYBERG, URBAN OLSSON, TOMMY APELQUIST and PETER ASP, taking the name from their squabbling girlfriends. With PETER DOLVING subsequently coming in as frontman and BJARNE OLSSON replacing APELQUIST, the group eventually recorded an eponymous debut album of raging alternative grunge-esque rock. Netting them a Swedish Grammy for their troubles, the album was also picked up by 'M.C.A.' for European and American release. Signed to the 'Universal' label, MARY BEATS JANE eventually released a follow-up, 'LOCUST', in 1997. Once again taking the ever-reliable grunge blueprint as their guiding force, MARY BEATS JANE proved that the Swedes could get cathartic with the best of them, their visceral sound recalling the blacker moments of SOUNDGARDEN or ALICE IN CHAINS.

Album rating: MARY BEATS JANE (*5) / LOCUST (*6)

PETER DOLVING – vocals / **MAGNUS NYBERG** – guitar / **URBAN OLSSON** – guitar / **BJARNE OLSSON** – bass / **PETER ASP** – drums

M.C.A. Geffen

1994. (cd-s) **THIS LIFE / BLIND / PARASITE** Sweden

1994. (cd-s) **DAY IN DAY OUT / FIDGET / MEDICINE** Sweden

Sep 94. (7"/c-s) *(MCS/+C 2002)* **OLD /**
(cd-s+=) *(MCSTD 2002)* –

Oct 94. (cd/c/lp) *(MCD/MCC/MCA 11135)* <24724> **MARY BEATS JANE** Nov94
– Neighbourhood psycho / This life / Old / Grind / Blood and oil / War on society / Wasted / Blind / I don't care / Hollowhead / Porno / Corn / Gunshot / Cxxx Cxxx report.

May 95. (12"/cd-s) *(MCST/+D 2046)* **GRIND. /**

Universal not iss.

Apr 97. (cd) *(UND 80371)* **LOCUST**
– Homecoming / Blackeye / Pure / Day in day out / Dogrelish / Fall / Flowered / Corrosion / Cradlewake / Cut / Nail me.

— disbanded after above

J. MASCIS (see under ⇒ DINOSAUR JR.)

MASSACRE

Formed: Florida, USA . . . 1986 by KAM LEE and RICK ROZZ, both original members of DEATH. They found TERRY BUTLER and BILL ANDREWS, working on demo material before putting the band on ice and briefly taking up DEATH duties (all save LEE) once again for 1988's 'Leprosy'. With such high calibre experience behind them, it was only a matter of time before they were snapped up, UK noise merchants 'Earache' securing their signatures at the turn of the decade and releasing a debut album, 'FROM BEYOND' (1991). No-mercy death-metal, the bulk of the material originated from their demo days. The following year saw the release of an EP, 'INHUMAN CONDITIONS', which included a cover of Venom's 'WARHEAD' featuring mainman, CRONOS on guest vocals. With PETE SISON and SYRUS PETERS replacing BUTLER and ANDREWS respectively, they finally issued a belated follow-up, 'PROMISE', in summer '96. • **Note:** Another group called MASSACRE (featuring BILL LASWELL) had an album for 'Celluloid'.

Album rating: FROM BEYOND (*7) / PROMISE (*6)

KAM LEE – vocals (ex-DEATH) / **RICK ROZZ** – guitar (ex-DEATH) / **TERRY BUTLER** – bass (ex-DEATH) / **BILL ANDREWS** – drums (ex-DEATH)

Earache Combat

May 91. (lp/cd) *(MOSH 027/+CD)* <2038> **FROM BEYOND**
– Dawn of eternity / Cryptic realms / Biohazard / Chamber of ages / From beyond / Defeat remains / Succubus / Symbolic immortality / Corpsegrinder. *(w/ free 7")* – PROVOKED. / ACCURSER *(cd+=)* – (below EP tracks). *(cd re-iss. Mar00; same)*

Apr 92. (12"ep/cd-ep) *(MOSH 060 T/CD)* <1110> **INHUMAN CONDITIONS / PLAINS OF INSANITY. / PROVOKED ACCURSER / WARHEAD** Jul92

— **PETE SISON** – bass + **SYRUS PETERS** – drums; repl. TERRY + BILL

Earache Earache

Jul 96. (cd) <(MOSH 096CD)> **PROMISE**
– Nothing / Forever torn / Black soil nest / Promise / Bitter end / Bloodletting / Unnameanable / Where dwells sadness / Suffering / Inner demon. *(re-iss. Apr99; same)*

— disbanded after above

MASTERS OF REALITY

Formed: Syracuse, New York, USA . . . 1981 by CHRIS GOSS and GOODGE. After plugging away on the club scene for most of the decade, the group were spotted by eagle-eyed RICK RUBIN and promptly added to the enviable, eclectic roster of 'Def American'. With TIM HARRINGTON and VINNIE LUDOVICO completing the line-up, the group cut the monumental 'MASTERS OF REALITY' (1989; US title, 'THE BLUE GARDEN'). The fact that they named themselves after a classic 'SABBATH album gives some indication as to where this bunch of maverick retro magpies are coming from, although that's only telling half the story. Complete with cover art not witnessed since the early 70's, and snaking its way through a brooding landscape of queasy psychedelia, malevolent blues, mutant boogie and crunching metal, the album towered over virtually every other comparable release that year despite its failure to notch up many sales. Beginning as it ended, with a wailing desolation worthy of CREEDENCE CLEARWATER REVIVAL's 'Effigy', the record conjured up the ghosts of rock's forsaken past in spellbindingly sinister fashion. With GOSS as voodoo man, his rich, dark-as-treacle tones lulling the listener deep into their weird world, MASTERS OF REALITY were utterly mesmerising. Ditto the lyrics which were no doubt connected somehow to the mystical ephemera adorning the inside sleeve; suffice to say these boys weren't singing about fast cars and groupies. Basically, you need this album. You also need to witness them live, which, for any non-USA resident has been pretty difficult up till now; a tour was initiated after the debut's release but subsequently fell apart amid interpersonal strife before it even reached British shores. GOSS departed, taking the MASTERS OF REALITY name with him; the debut set was subsequently reissued on hip hop label, 'Malicious Vinyl' in 1990 (complete with two extra tracks) while GOSS recruited DANIEL RAY (ex-IGGY POP) and JON LEAMY for touring purposes. HARRINGTON and LUDIVICO, meanwhile, hooked up as The BOGEYMEN, releasing an album, 'THERE'S NO SUCH THING AS . . .' on the same label in summer '91. The MASTERS OF REALITY saga then took its most bizarre turn yet, when GOSS and GOODGE teamed up with veteran drummer GINGER BAKER, recording the 'SUNRISE ON THE SUFFERBUS' (1993) set together. While the album lacked the dark majesty of the GOSS/HARRINGTON-penned debut, it was a compelling listen nonetheless, the heavier material interspersed with surprisingly carefree strumming ('JODY SINGS'), bizarre song fragments ('MADONNA' and 'BICYCLE') and a snatch of very English humour courtesy of BAKER ('T.U.S.A.'). With UK fans' appetites whetted once more via the prospect of an imminent Reading Festival appearance, there was only more disappointment as BAKER departed and yet another tour was abandoned. GOSS subsequently spent most of his time on production work, acting as mentor for apprentice metal mystics, KYUSS, although, to his credit, he kept the MASTERS OF REALITY spirit alive along with GOODGE. Accompanied by new members, BRENDAN McNICHOL, CHRIS JOHNSON and VICTOR INDRIZZO, the pair eventually released a US-only live album in summer '97, 'HOW HIGH THE MOON – LIVE AT THE VIPER ROOM'. Despite accumulating yet more kudos with production for QUEENS OF THE STONE AGE, GOSS disappointed many fans with 'WELCOME TO THE WESTERN LODGE' (1999), an uncharacteristically turgid set recorded in a largely solo capacity with help from aforementioned touring partner LEAMY. Ever the maverick, GOSS will no doubt confound his critics at some point although a return to the genius of his earlier work seems increasingly unlikely.

Album rating: MASTERS OF REALITY (*9) / SUNRISE ON THE SUFFERBUS (*6) / HOW HIGH THE MOON – LIVE AT THE VIPER ROOM (*6) / WELCOME TO THE WESTERN LODGE (*4)

CHRIS GOSS – vocals, guitar, keyboards / **TIM HARRINGTON** – lead guitar / **GOOGE** – bass / **VINNIE LUDOVICO** – drums

Def American / Delicious

May 89. (lp/c/cd) *(838 474-1/-4/-2)* <842904> **MASTERS OF REALITY** Feb89
<US title 'THE BLUE GARDEN'>
– Theme for the scientist of the invisible / Domino / The blue garden / Gettin' high / The candy song / Magical spell / The eyes of tears / Sleepwalkin' / Looking to get rite / Kill the king / John Brown.

Oct 89. (7") *(DEFA 1)* **THE CANDY SONG. / THE BLUE GARDEN** -
(12"+=)(cd-s+=) *(DEFA 1-12)(DEFAC 1)* – Kill the king.

— GOSS departed Oct 89, but he soon retained group name Mar'90. Released above album again on 'Malicious' w /2 extra tracks. He added on tour **DANIEL REY** – guitar (ex-IGGY POP) / **JON LEAMY** – drums. (**GINGER BAKER** – drums; joined Sep 90)

— TIM and VINNIE were to for The BOGEYMEN in 1991. They released an album 'THERE'S NO SUCH THING AS . . .' in Jul'91 on 'Malicious Vinyl'.

— MASTERS OF REALITY re-formed

Vertigo / Chrysalis

Jun 93. (cd/c) *(514 947-2/-4)* <21976> **SUNRISE ON THE SUFFERBUS**
– She got me (when she got her dress on) / J.B. witchdance / Jody sings / Rolling green / Ants in the kitchen / V.H.V. / Bicycle / 100 years (of tears on the wind) / T.U.S.A. / Tilt-a-whirl / Rabbit one / Madonna / Gimme water / The Moon in your pocket.

— BAKER departed and they had to call off a Reading festival spot

— **GOSS** now with **GOOGE** – bass / **BRENDAN McNICHOL** – guitar / **CHRIS JOHNSON** – keyboards / **VIC 'the stick' INDRIZZO** – drums, vocals / guest SCOTT WEILAND (on 1 track)

not iss. / Malicious Vinyl

Jun 97. (cd) <MV 5017-2> **HOW HIGH THE MOON – LIVE AT THE VIPER ROOM (live)** -
– How high the moon / The blue garden / Alder smoke blues / Doralinda's prophecies / She got me (when she got her dress on) / Jindalee Jindalie / John Brown / Tilt-a-whirl swingeroo Joe / Ants in the kitchen goin' down / 100 years (of tears on the wind).

— **GOSS, GOOGE + JOHN LEAMY** – bass, drums, etc + **VICTOR INDRIZZO** – drums

Brownhouse / Spitfire

Jun 99. (cd) *(BRH 9901-2)* <15050> **WELCOME TO THE WESTERN LODGE**
– It's shit / Moriah / The great Spelunker / Time to burn / Take a shot at the clown / Baby Mae / Why the fly? / Ember day / Annihilation of the spirit / Call Dr. Carrion / Boymilk waltz / Lover's sky / Also ran song.

MAXIM (see under ⇒ PRODIGY)

MAX WEBSTER

Formed: Toronto, Canada ... 1973/4 by KIM MITCHELL, TERRY WATKINSON, MIKE TIKA and PAUL KERSLEY. A veteran of the hard-rock scene, the outrageous MITCHELL had played with ZOOM & THE GLADIATORS, cutting his teeth alongside such legendary rock'n'roll names as ALICE COOPER and MC5. His unique vocal style, inimitable stage antics and shearing guitar technique helped the group secure a North American deal with 'Mercury', a debut set, 'HANGOVER', appearing in 1976. With GERRY McCRACKEN replacing KERSEY, a follow-up, 'HIGH CLASS IN BORROWED SHOES' (1977), was well received by their cult audience although they found it difficult to break into either the US or the UK markets. A subsequent deal with 'Capitol' resulted in a further two studio sets, 'MUTINY UP MY SLEEVE' (1978) and 'A MILLION VACATIONS' (1979), while a concert compilation, 'LIVE MAGNETIC AIR' (1979), offered a taste of MAX WEBSTER's infamous live appeal. Commercial success nevertheless proved consistently elusive and by the turn of the decade the group had begun to falter. A final album, 'UNIVERSAL JUVENILES' (1980), appeared on 'Mercury' and by 1982 the group had folded, MITCHELL opting for a solo career. Throughout the 80's, MITCHELL struggled to acquire any major credibility outside Canada, although the 1989 album, 'ROCKLAND', stunned his critics with its blend of distinctive AOR-tinged hard rock. In the 90's, MITCHELL continued to work solo, releasing three fresh but patchy long-players, 'I AM A WILD PARTY' (1990), 'AURAL FIXATIONS' (1992) and 'ITCH' (1994).

Album rating: HANGOVER (*6) / HIGH CLASS IN BORROWED SHOES (*6) / MUTINY UP MY SLEEVE (*5) / A MILLION VACATIONS (*6) / LIVE MAGNETIC AIR (*6) / UNIVERSAL JUVENILES (*5) / DIAMONDS, DIAMONDS compilation (*6) / THE BEST OF MAX WEBSTER featuring KIM MITCHELL compilation (*7) / Kim Mitchell: KIM MITCHELL mini (*4) / AKIMBO ALOGO (*6) / SHAKIN' LIKE A HUMAN BEING (*5) / ROCKLAND (*7) / I AM A WILD PARTY (*4) / AURAL FIXATIONS (*5) / ITCH (*4) / GREATEST HITS compilation (*6)

KIM MITCHELL (b. 1952, Sarnia, Ontario, Canada) – vocals, guitar / **TERRY WATKINSON** – keyboards, vocals / **MIKE TIKA** – bass, vocals / **PAUL KERSEY** – drums, percussion

not iss. / Mercury

Jan 77. (lp) <SRM 1-1131> **HANGOVER** -
– Hangover / Here among the cats / Blowing the blues away / Summer turning blue / Toronto Tontos / Coming off the moon / Only your nose knows / Summer's up / Lily. *<originally Canadian on 'Anthem'; ANR 1-006>*

— **GERRY McCRACKEN** – drums, percussion, repl. KERSEY

Oct 77. (lp) <1160> **HIGH CLASS IN BORROWED SHOES** -
– High class in borrowed shoes / Diamonds diamonds / Gravity / Words to words / America's veins / Oh war! / On the road / Rain child / In context of the Moon. *<also Canadian on 'Anthem'; ANR 1-007>*

— **DAVE MYLES** – bass, vocals, repl. TIKA who still co-produced

Capitol / Capitol

Aug 78. (lp) <(EST 11776)> **MUTINY UP MY SLEEVE**
– Lip service / Astonish me / Let your man fly / Water me down / Distressed / The party / Waterline / Hawaii / Beyond the moon.

Apr 79. (7"/7"pic-d) *(CL/+P 16079)* **PARADISE SKIES. / THE PARTY** 43 -
(12"+=) *(CL12 16079)* – Let your man fly.

May 79. (lp) <(EST 11937)> **A MILLION VACATIONS**
– Paradise skies / Charmonium / Night flights / Sun voices / Moon voices / A million vacations / Look out / Let go the line / Rascal Houdi / Research (at beach resorts).

Jun 79. (7") *(CL 16088)* <4735> **LET GO THE LINE. / MOON VOICES**

Jan 80. (lp/c) *(EST/TCEST 23592)* <12042> **MAGNETIC AIR (live 1976-79)**
– Paradise skies / Night flights / Lip service / Charmonium / Waterline / High class in borrowed shoes / Diamonds diamonds / Gravity / Coming off the moon / Hangover.

Feb 80. (7"m) *(CL 16104)* **NIGHT FLIGHTS (live). / HANGOVER (live) / HIGH CLASS IN BORROWED SHOES (live)** -

— now without WATKINSON who was repl. by guest **DOUG RILEY + DAVE STONE**

Mercury / Mercury

Nov 80. (lp/c) *(6337/7141 144)* <SRMI 3855> **UNIVERSAL JUVENILES**
– In the world of giants / Check / April in Toledo / Juveniles don't stop / Battle scar / Chalkers / Drive and desire / Blue river liquor shine / What do you do with the urge / Cry out your life.

Jan 81. (7") *(MER 59)* **BATTLE SCAR. / APRIL IN TOLEDO**

— split in 1982

– compilations, etc. –

1981. (lp) *Anthem;* <ANR1-1033> **DIAMONDS, DIAMONDS** - - Canada
– Gravity / High class in borrowed shoes / Diamonds, diamonds / Summer's up / Blowing the blues away / Let go the line / A million vacations / The party / Hot spots / Paradise skies / Overnight sensation / Lip service / Hangover.

Nov 91. (cd) *Anthem;* <ANR1-1058> **THE BEST OF MAX WEBSTER featuring KIM MITCHELL** - - Canada
– Check / High class in borrowed shoes / A million vacations / Diamonds, diamonds / Let go the line / Night flights / The party / Hangover / Kids in action / Gravity / Paradise skies / Words to words / Oh war! / Here among the cats / Waterline / Battle scar.

KIM MITCHELL

with **ROBERT SINCLAIR WILSON** – bass, vocals / **PAUL DE LONG** – drums

not iss. / Anthem

1982. (m-lp) <ANM 1-5001> **KIM MITCHELL** - - Canada
– Kids in action / Miss Demeanor / Big best summer / Tennessee water / Chain of events.

— added **PETER FREDETTE** – guitar, keyboards, vocals

Bronze / Anthem

1985. (lp) *(BRON 556)* <1001> **AKIMBO ALOGO** 1984
– Go for soda / That's a man / All we are / Diary for rock'n'roll men / Love ties / Feel it burn / Lager and ale / Rumour has it / Caroline / Called off.

May 85. (7") *(BRO 192)* **GO FOR SODA. / LOVE TIES** -
(12"+=) *(BROX 192)* –

not iss. / Atlantic

Jul 86. (7") <89391> **PATIO LANTERNS. / THAT'S THE HOLD** -

Jul 86. (lp) <781664-1> **SHAKIN' LIKE A HUMAN BEING** -
– Get lucky (boys and girls) / In my shoes / Alana loves me / Patio lanterns / That's the hold / In your arms / City girl / Easy to tame / Cameo spirit / Hitting the ground. *<US cd-iss. 1990's on 'Alert'; ZL 81004>*

— now with **FREDETTE / + MATTHEW GERRARD** – bass / **LOU MOLINO** – drums / **GREG WELLS** – keyboards, vocals / **KIM BULLARD** – keyboards / **RIK EMMETT** – guitar (guest)

1989. (7") <88837> **ROCK N ROLL DUTY. / HARD STREAK** -

1989. (lp/cd) <81963-1/-2> **ROCKLAND** -
– Rockland wonderland / Lost lovers found / Rock n roll duty / Tangle of love / Moodstreet / The crossroads / Expedition sailor / O mercy Louise / This dream / The great embrace. *<US cd-iss. 1990's on 'Alert'; ZL 81010>*

— **GREG CRITCHLEY + MATTHEW FRENETTE** – drums; repl. GERRARD, BULLARD + EMMETT

not iss. / Alert

1990. (cd) <ZL 81017> **I AM A WILD PARTY (live)** -
– I am a wild party / That's the hold / Battle scar / Lager and ale / Deep dive / All we are / Rock n roll duty / Go for soda.

1992. (cd) <81019> **AURAL FIXATIONS** -
– World's such a wonder / Pure as gold / Big smoke / America / Some folks / Find the will / There's a story / Dreamer / Dog and a bone / Flames / Hullabaloo / Honey forget those blues.

Aug 94. (cd,c) <81024> **ITCH** -
– Wonder where and why / Acrimony / Lick yer finger / The U.S. of ache / Lemon wedge / Heartbreakbustop / Your face or mine / Human condition / Stand / Karaoke queen / Cheer us on.

Aug 95. (cd) <82005> **GREATEST HITS** (compilation) -
– Transcendental soda / Rock and roll duty / That's the hold / Go for soda / No more walking away (new song) / Lager and ale / Rocklandwonderland / Easy to tame / Rainbow (new song) / All we are / Patio lanterns / Acrimony / World's such a wonder / Expedition sailor (the other version) / Battle scar / I am a wild party (live) / Hare soda.

Brian MAY (see under ⇒ QUEEN)

MAY BLITZ

Formed: London, England . . .1969 as a 4-piece by drummer TONY NEWMAN, veteran of SOUNDS INCORPORATED and The JEFF BECK GROUP. The group quickly trimmed down to a trio, with JAMES BLACK and REID HUDSON replacing the rhythm section of TERRY POOLE and KEITH BAKER. Signed to cult progressive label, 'Vertigo', they issued their eponymous debut album in late 1970. Beefed-up heavy rock with a distinct progressive edge, the group attracted little interest and split after a follow-up set, 'THE 2nd OF MAY' (1971). • **Trivia:** Both LP's released are worth upwards of £40.

Album rating: MAY BLITZ (*6) / SECOND OF MAY (*5)

TONY NEWMAN – drums, bongos, congas, vibes / **JAMES BLACK** – guitar, vocals / **REID HUDSON** – bass, vocals

Vertigo Paramount

1970. (lp) *(6360 007) <5020>* **MAY BLITZ** [ ] [ ]
– Smoking the day away / I don't know? / Dreaming / Squeet / Tomorrow may come / Fire queen / Virgin waters. *(re-iss. 1989 on 'Beat Goes On'; BGOLP 16)*

Jun 71. (lp) *(6360 037)* **THE 2nd OF MAY** [ ] [–]
– For madmen only / Snakes and ladders / The 25th of December, 1969 / "In part" / 8 mad grim nits / High beech / Honey coloured time / Just thinking.

— Folded in 1972 and TONY mainly went into session work.

– compilations, etc –

Nov 92. (cd) *Beat Goes On; (BGOCD 153)* **MAY BLITZ / THE 2nd OF MAY** [ ] [–]

MAYHEM

Formed: Oslo, Norway ... 1985 by NECROBUTCHER and guitarist EURONYMOUS (born OYSTEIN AARSETH), founder of the Helvete record shop and influential 'Deathlike Silence' label. The epicentre of the weird and wonderful world of Norwegian black metal, MAYHEM debuted in 1987 with the mini-album, 'DEATHCRUSH'. Before the sect managed to unearth a follow-up, frontman DEAD rather unfortunately lived up to his moniker and well er . . . shot himself, eh . . . dead on the 8th of April 1990. He was discovered by EURONYMOUS, who gruesomely rushed out to buy a camera to take some photos. He allegedly snatched fragments of the singer's skull (later arranging them into a necklace!), before calling the authorities. Three years later, his evil ways were cut short and bettered when his sparring partner and fellow black-metallist, COUNT GRISHNACKH (aka VARG VIKERNES of group, BURZUM) frenziedly stabbed him to death after an argument at EURONYMOUS's doorstep on the 10th of August 1993. GRISHNACKH, who had played bass for MAYHEM around this time, was sentenced to 21 years in prison, and while there boasted of prising the knife out of the guitarist's head. The material which EURONYMOUS and his motley crew had been working on prior to his death, was released the following year as 'DE MYSTERIIS DOM SATHANAS' (whath everth thath meanth, but don't recith it too loudly!). True to Satanic style, both MAYHEM and BURZUM refused to die. While the COUNT incredibly worked from his new prison home, the remnants of MAYHEM soldiered on, releasing a third set, 'WOLF'S LAIR ABYSS' at the end of 1997. A live album, 'MEDIOLANUM CAPTA EST' in '99 and a US-only studio return ('GRAND DELARATION OF WAR') have kept the home fires burning – but not literally. • **Note:** Not the same group as the UK outfit that released for 'Riot City' and 'Vigilante'.

Album rating: DEATHCRUSH mini (*6) / DE MYSTERIIS DOM SATHANAS (*7) / LIVE IN LEIPZIG (*6) / WOLF'S LAIR ABYSS (*6) / MEDIOLANUM CAPTA EST (*6) / GRAND DECLARATION OF WAR (*6)

EURONYMOUS (b. OYSTEIN ARSETH) – guitar / **DEAD** – vocals / etc, etc. / **NECROBUTCHER** – bass / **HELLHAMMER** (b. JON) – drums

Deathlike Silence Century Media

1987. (m-lp) *(ANTI-MOSH 003)* **DEATHCRUSH** [–] [–] Norway
– Silvester Anfang / Deathcrush / Chainsaw gutsfuck / Witching hour / Necrolust / (Weird) Manheim. *(UK-iss.May93 & Oct96 lp/cd; ANTI-MOSH 003/+CD)*

— In 1991, DEAD shot himself (see above for more gory details).
below was what they were working on before EURONYMOUS' death

— next with session vocalist **ATTILA CSIHAR** (MANIAC)

Mar 94. (lp/cd) *(ANTI-MOSH 006/+CD) <CM 7767CD>* **DE MYSTERIIS DOM SATHANAS** [ ] [ ]
– Funeral fog / Freezing moon / Cursed in eternity / Pagan fears / Life eternal / From the dark past / Buried by time and dust / De mysteriis Dom Sathanas. *(re-iss. Aug99; same)*

— **HELLHAMMER** and various (**MANIAC + BLASPHEMER**) continued

Misanthropy Misanthropy

Oct 97. (lp/cd) *(<AMAZON 012/+CD>)* **WOLF'S AIR ABYSS** [ ] [ ] Jan98
– Vortex void of humanity (intro) / I am the labyrinth / Fall of Seraphs / Ancient skin / Symbols of bloodswords.

Avante Garde Dwell

May 99. (cd/d-lp) *(AV 039 CD/LP) <DWELL 1062CD>* **MEDIOLANUM CAPTA EST (live)** [ ] [ ] Dec99
– Silvester anfang / Deathcrush / Fall of Seraphs / Carnage / Necrolust / Ancient skin / Freezing moon / Symbols of bloodswords / From the dark past / Chainsaw gutstuck / I am the labyrinth / Pure fucking armageddon. *(cd re-iss. Oct00; same as US)*

not iss. Necropolis

Jun 00. (cd) *<54>* **GRAND DECLARATION OF WAR** [–] [ ]
– Part II / A grand declaration of war / In the lies where upon you lay / A time to die / View from Nihil / (untitled) / II principle / A broadsword and a colder sun / Crystalized pain in deconstruction / Completion in science of agony / To Daimomion / (untitled x2).

– compilations, etc. –

Apr 94. (cd/lp) *Avant Garde; (LPAV/CDAV 004) / Century Media; <7893>* **LIVE IN LEIPZIG (live)** [ ] [ ] Sep97
– Deathcrush / Necrolust / Funeral fog / The freezing moon / Carnage / Buried by time and dust / Pagan fears / Chainsaw gutstuck / Pure fucking armageddon.

— A various artists cd 'TRIBUTE TO EURONYMOUS' was released by 'Necropolis' (NR 009CD).

McAULEY-SCHENKER GROUP (see under ⇒ SCHENKER, Michael)

MC5

Formed: Detroit, Michigan, USA . . . 1965 by ROB TYNER, FED 'SONIC' SMITH and WAYNE KRAMER. After two limited single releases, MC5 (MOTOR CITY FIVE) signed a contract with 'Elektra' in mid '68, helped by counter-cultural activist and DJ, John Sinclair. In addition to becoming the band's manager, he heavily influenced both their political extremism and warped takes on free jazz improvisation. Reflecting the harsher geographical and economic climate of Detroit, the band espoused revolution and struggle as opposed to the love and peace ethos of the sun-kissed Californian flower children. The riotous proto-punk of their legendary, acid-fuelled live show was captured on the controversial debut, 'KICK OUT THE JAMS'. Recorded in late October '68, it eventually hit the shops in May '69 and while the original uncensored pressings contained the line "Kick Out The Jams, Motherfuckers!", the offending word was later supplanted with the milder "Brothers And Sisters". Unfortunately, this wasn't enough to prevent some record stores from refusing to stock the lp, and after the band explicitly aired their views on one of the aforementioned dealers in a local newspaper, they were duly given the boot by Elektra. Nevertheless, the album reached No.30 in America and although it sounds a bit dated to modern ears, it was way radical for the time, remaining an inspiration to each new generation of noiseniks. After a split with Sinclair, the band signed with Atlantic and began to move away from the overtly subversive nature of their earlier material to a more straightahead rock approach, evidenced on their Jon Landau-produced follow-up album, 'BACK IN THE U.S.A.'. Wired rock'n'roll of an impeccable degree, the record didn't fare well in the laid-back, doped-up climate of the early 70's. An ambitious third album in 1971, 'HIGH TIME', featuring horns and even Salvation Army musicians, still failed to cut any commercial ice and the band split in 1972. KRAMER subsequently spent five years in jail for cocaine dealing before embarking on a low key solo career while former manager, Sinclair, was sentenced to ten years in the early 70's for a minor dope charge, serving only two after appeal. Tragically, ROB TYNER died from a heart attack in 1991 aged only 46. Pioneers in the true sense of the word, the MC5 together with the STOOGES were the first real punk bands, the originators who were never bettered. Although KRAMER released the odd obscure 7" throughout the late 70's/80's – during which time he teamed up with JOHNNY THUNDERS as GANG WAR and even worked with the mad, bad and dangerous to know G.G. ALLIN – his solo career only really got back on track via a mid-90's deal with hardcore/punk label 'Epitaph'. The first fruits of this partnership were unleashed in the shape of 'THE HARD STUFF' (1995), an abrasively unsentimental trawl through life's piss-stinking back alleys with guest support from the likes of HENRY ROLLINS and BAD RELIGION. The 'DANGEROUS MADNESS' album followed in 1996, KRAMER once again taking bitter lyrical inspiration from his school-of-hard-knocks background while kicking out the jams 90's style with more ferocity and bile than many of the young pretenders. The same year saw a collaborative effort with fellow Detroit veterans SCOTT MORGAN and DENIZ TEK entitled 'DODGE MAIN', while his rejuvenated solo career continued apace in 1997 with 'CITIZEN WAYNE'. 'LLMF (LIVE LIKE A MOTHERFUCKER' (1998) found KRAMER in his element while a further studio set, 'BEYOND CYBERPUNK', was due to appear some time in 2001. • **Songwriters:** Group compositions, except; I CAN ONLY GIVE YOU EVERYTHING (Them) / TUTTI FRUTTI (Little Richard).

Album rating: KICK OUT THE JAMS (*9) / BACK IN THE USA (*7) / HIGH TIME (*5) / BABES IN ARMS collection (*5) / LOOKING AT YOU collection (*4) / POWER TRIP collection (*5) / Wayne Kramer: DEATHTONGUE (*4) / THE HARD STUFF (*7) / DANGEROUS MADNESS (*5) / CITIZEN WAYNE (*5) / LLMF (*5)

ROB TYNER (b. ROBERT DERMINER, 12 Dec'44) – vocals, harmonica / **WAYNE KRAMER** (b.30 Apr'48) – guitar, vocals, keyboards / **FRED 'SONIC' SMITH** (b. West Virginia) – guitar / **MICHAEL DAVIS** – bass / **DENNIS THOMPSON** – drums

not iss. A.M.G.

1966. (7") *<AMG 1001>* **I CAN ONLY GIVE YOU EVERYTHING. / I JUST DON'T KNOW** [–] [ ]
(above credited to MOTOR CITY FIVE)

not iss. A2.

Mar 68. (7") *<A2 333>* **LOOKING AT YOU. / BORDERLINE** [–] [ ]

— added 6th member **Brother J.C.CRAWFORD** – rapper / narrative

Elektra Elektra

May 69. (7") *(EKSN 45056) <EK 45648>* **KICK OUT THE JAMS. / MOTOR CITY IS BURNING** [ ] [82] Mar 69

May 69. (lp) *(mono/stereo; EKL/EKS 74042)* **KICK OUT THE JAMS** [ ] [30] Mar 69
– Ramblin' rose / Kick out the jams / Come together / Rocket reducer No.62 (rama lama fa fa) / Borderline / Motor city is burning / I want you right now / Starship. *(re-iss. May77.) (re-iss. +cd.Nov91) (re-iss. cd+c Mar93 on 'Pickwick') (re-iss. cd/c Sep95 on 'Warners')*

Aug 69. (7") *(EKSN 45067)* **RAMBLIN' ROSE. / BORDERLINE** [ ] [-]

Atlantic Atlantic

Oct 70. (7") *<2678>* **TONIGHT. / LOOKING AT YOU** [-] [ ]

Nov 70. (lp) *(2400 016) <SD 8247>* **BACK IN THE U.S.A.** [ ] [ ] Feb 70
– Tutti frutti / Tonight / Teenage list / Looking at you / Let me try / High school / Call me animal / The American ruse / Shakin' Street / The human being lawnmower / Back in the U.S.A. *(re-iss. Feb77.) (cd-iss. May93 on 'Rhino-Atlantic')*

1970. (7") *<2724>* **SHAKIN' STREET. / THE AMERICAN RUSE** [-] [ ]

Oct 71. (lp) *(2400 123) <SD 8285>* **HIGH TIME** [ ] [ ]
– Sister Anne / Baby won't ya / Miss X / Gotta keep movin' / Future – Now / Poison / Over nnd over / Skunk (sonically speaking). *(cd-iss. May93 on 'Rhino-Atlantic')*

— (split early '72 when DAVIS departed) THOMPSON, SMITH and DAVIS formed short-lived ASCENSION. FRED SMITH married PATTI SMITH and later formed SONIC'S RENDEZVOUS BAND. TYNER was credited on HOT RODS single, late'77. (see ⇒ EDDIE & THE HOT RODS.

– compilations, etc. –

1969. (7") *A.M.G.; <AMG 1001>* **I CAN ONLY GIVE YOU EVERYTHING. / ONE OF THE GUYS** [-] [ ]

Jul 83. (c) *R.O.I.R.; <A 122>* **BABES IN ARMS** [-] [ ]
(re-iss. Apr90 & Dec92 on 'Danceteria' lp/cd; DAN LP/CD 031)

May 94. (cd) *Receiver; (RRCD 185)* **BLACK TO COMM** [ ] [-]

Oct 94. (10"lp/cd) *Alive; (ALIVE 005/+CD)* **POWER TRIP** [ ] [-]

Nov 94. (cd) *Receiver; (RRCD 193)* **LOOKING AT YOU** [ ] [-]

Feb 95. (10"lp/cd) *Alive; (NER/+CD 2001)* **THE AMERICAN RUSE** [ ] [-]

Mar 95. (10"lp) *Alive; (ALIVE 008)* **ICE PICK SLIM** [ ] [-]
(cd-iss. Feb97; ALIVECD 8)

Sep 95. (10"ep/cd) *Alive; (ALIVE 0010/+CD)* **FRIDAY, THE 13TH** [ ] [-]

Dec 96. (cd) *Dressed To Kill; (DTKLP 002)* **THUNDER EXPRESS – ONE DAY IN THE STUDIO** [ ] [-]

Mar 97. (lp) *Alive; (NER 3008)* **TEENAGE LUST** [ ] [-]

WAYNE KRAMER

— went solo after spending 5 years in prison for cocaine dealing.

Stiff-Chiswick not iss.

Oct 77. (7") *(DEA-SUK 1)* **RAMBLIN' ROSE. / GET SOME** [ ] [-]

Radar not iss.

Jul 79. (7") *(ADA 41)* **THE HARDER THEY COME. / EAST SIDE GIRL** [ ] [-]

not iss. Pure&Easy

1983. (7") *<PE 017>* **NEGATIVE GIRLS. / STREET WARFARE** [-] [ ]

— GANG WAR formed in 1980 with **JOHNNY THUNDERS** – vocals

Zodiac not iss.

1987. (7"ep; WAYNE KRAMER'S GANG WAR) *(800)* **GANG WAR (live at Max's May 1980)** [ ] [-]

May 90. (lp) *(LP 1001)* **GANG WAR** (live/studio) [ ] [-]

— WAYNE had joined the DEVIANTS in 1984 for their album HUMAN GARBAGE.

Curio Progressive

1987. (7"; as WAYNE KRAMER'S DEATH TONGUE) **SPIKE HEELS EP** [-] [ ]

— (WAYNE played late 80's with DAS DAMEN and G.G. ALLIN)

Nov 91. (d-cd/d-lp) *(ITEM 2 CD/LP) <PRO 023>* **DEATH TONGUE** [ ] [ ]
– Take your clothes off / Sike heels / Spend the rent / Negative girls / Death tongue / Leather skull / The scars never show / McArthur Park / Fun in the final days / Who shot you Dutch.

— In Sep'91, ROB TYNER was found dead after suffering heart attack. He was 46.

— with on first **KEITH MORRIS, BRETT REED, MATT FREEMAN, DALE CROVER, JOSH FREESE, BRETT GUREWITZ, CHRIS BAGAROZZI**, etc

Epitaph Epitaph

Jan 95. (cd/c/lp) *<(E 86447-2/-4/-1)>* **THE HARD STUFF** [ ] [ ]
– Crack in the universe / Junkie romance / Bad seed / Poison / Realm of the pirate kings / Incident on Stock Island / Pillar of fire / Hope for sale / Edge of the switchblade / Sharkskin suit.

Feb 96. (cd/lp) *<(86458-2/-1)>* **DANGEROUS MADNESS** [ ] [ ]
– Dangerous madness / Back to DEtroit / Wild America / Something broken in the promised land / Take exit '97 / God's worst nightmare / The boy's got that look in their eyes / Dead man's vest / It's never enough / Rats of illusion / Dead movie stars.

May 97. (cd) *<(6488-2)>* **CITIZEN WAYNE** [ ] [ ]
– Stranger in the house / Back when dogs could talk / Revolution in apt.29 / Down on the ground / Shining Mr. Lincoln's shoes / Dope for democracy / No easy way out / You don't know my name / Count time / Snatched defeat / Doing the work / Farewell to whiskey.

— MC5 were about to reform with KRAMER, DAVIS + THOMSON

— next with rhythm **DOUGLAS LUNN + RIC PARNELL**

Nov 98. (cd/lp) *<(86539)>* **LLMF** (Live Like A Motherfucker) [ ] [ ]
– Bad seed / Stranger in the house / It's never enough / Something broken in the promised land / Take your clothes off / Down on the ground / Junkie romance / Poison / Count time / No easy way out / Crack in the universe / So long, Hank / Kick out the jams / Bomb day in Paris.

– others, etc. –

Nov 96. (cd; by WAYNE KRAMER – DENIZ TEK – SCOTT MORGAN) *Alive; <(ALIVE 25)>* **DODGE MAIN** [ ] [ ]
– City slang / 1.94 / Citizen of time / Future – Now / Fire comin' / 100 fools / The harder they come / Over and over / Better than that / I got a right.

Oct 00. (cd; by WAYNE KRAMER & PINK FAIRIES) *Table Of Elements; <(TOE 3028)>* **COCAINE BLUES 1974-1978** [ ] [ ]
(re-iss. Nov00 on 'Alive'; NER 3028 CD/LP)

Duff McKAGAN

Born: MICHAEL McKAGAN, 5 Feb'64, Seattle, Washington, USA. Famous for having played bass for GUNS N' ROSES, DUFF was also previously a member of punk band TEN MINUTE WARNING, etc. Now picking up the guitar (and other instruments) once again, DUFF set to work on his own solo set. 'BELIEVE IN ME' was relatively successful (UK Top 30) when released in 1993 and even featured old GN'R muckers SLASH, GILBY CLARKE and MATT SORUM; SEBASTIAN BACH, JEFF BECK and LENNY KRAVITZ also turned up on these hard rockin' sessions.

Album rating: BELIEVE IN ME (*5)

DUFF McKAGAN – vocals, guitar (ex-GUNS N' ROSES, ex-TEN MINUTE WARNING) / with **TED ANDREADIS + DIZZY REED** – keyboards / **WEST ARKEEN** – lead guitar (co-wrote 'Man In The Meadow') / plus other guests **SLASH** – lead guitar / **MATT SORUM** – drums (co-wrote 'F@*ked Up Beyond Belief'), **GILBY CLARKE** – guitars (co-wrote '10 Years'), **JOIE MASTROKALOS** – b.vocals (co-wrote 'Just Not There'), **DOC NEWMAN** – vocals (+ co-wrote 'F@*k You'), **SNAKE, SEBASTIAN BACH, LENNY KRAVITZ + JEFF BECK**

Geffen Geffen

Oct 93. (cd/c/lp) *<(GED/GEC/GEF 24605)>* **BELIEVE IN ME** [27] [ ]
– Believe in me / I love you / Man in the meadow / (F@*ked up) Beyond belief / Could it be U / Just not there / Punk rock song / The majority / 10 years / Swamp song / Trouble / F@*k you / Lonely tonite.

Nov 93. (cd-s) *(GED 21865)* **BELIEVE IN ME / BAMBI / CRACKED ACTOR** [ ] [ ]

— In 1997, DUFF couldn't wait for GN'R to regroup and reformed 10 MINUTE WARNING.

Tony McPHEE (see under ⇒ GROUNDHOGS)

MDC

Formed: Austin, Texas, USA . . . 1980 as The STAINS (not the 'S.S.T.' hardcore outfit from L.A.) by drummer AL SCHVITZ. Relocating to the more politically fertile climes of San Francisco, these agit-prop punks announced their enrolment in the DEAD KENNEDYS school of subversion with their unambiguously titled 1981 debut single, 'JOHN WAYNE WAS A NAZI'. Equally uncompromising and inflammatory was the title of their debut long player, 'MILLIONS OF DEAD COPS' (1982). After a further EP 'MULTI-DEATH CORPORATION' the following year, the group went to ground for an extended period before re-emerging with a belated sophomore album, 'SMOKE SIGNALS' (1986). Credited to MILLIONS OF DAMN CHRISTIANS, 1987's set was an attempt at making their hardcore racket more consumer friendly. There were still acoustic guitars to be heard on 'METAL DEVIL COKES' (1989) if only in an ironic context, their blistering sonic assault back with a vengeance on an album which ripped into America's favourite beverage along with other deserving targets. With BILL COLLINS (replacing FRAZER) and MATT FREEMAN (replacing MARES) now on board, MDC delivered two further albums in the first half of the 90's, namely 'HEY COP, IF A HAD A FACE LIKE YOURS' (1992) and 'SHADES OF BROWN' (1994). • **Covered:** BORN UNDER A BAD SIGN + POLITICIAN (Cream) / SPANISH CASTLE MAGIC (Jimi Hendrix) / LOVE POTION No.9 (Clovers) / etc.

Album rating: MILLIONS OF DEAD COPS (*4) / SMOKE SIGNALS (*3) / MILLIONS OF DAMN CHRISTIANS (*4) / MORE DEAD COPS 1981-87 compilation (*4) / METAL DEVIL COKES (*4) / HEY COP, IF I HAD A FACE LIKE YOURS (*3)

"BOXCAR" DAVID DICTOR – vocals / **RON POSNER** – guitar / **FRANCO MARES** – bass; repl. MIKEY "OFFENDER" DONALDSON / **AL SCHVITZ** – drums

Alternative Tentacles Alternative Tentacles

1981. (7") **JOHN WAYNE WAS A NAZI. / BORN TO DIE** [-] [ ]

1982. (lp) *<(VIRUS 26)>* **MILLIONS OF DEAD COPS** [ ] [ ]
– Business on parade / Dead cops – America's so straight / Born to die / Corporate deathburger / Violent rednecks / I remember / John Wayne was a Nazi / Dick for brains / I hate work / My family is a little weird / Greedy and pathetic / Church and state / Kill the light / American achievements. *(re-iss. Apr94 on 'We Bite' lp/cd+=; WB 3109/+CD)* – MORE DEAD COPS 1981-87

— **GORDON FRAZER** – guitar; repl. POSNER

Crass not iss.

Jan 84. (12"ep) *(CRASS12 1984-5)* **MULTI-DEATH CORPORATION EP** [ ] [-]
– Multi-Death Corporation / Selfish shit / Radioactive chocolate / No place to piss / Kleptomaniac.

Radical Radical

Dec 85. (12"ep; as MILLIONS OF DEAD COPS) *<(MDC 3)>* **CHICKEN SQWAWK EP** [ ] [ ]
– Chicken sqwawk / Pecking order / Pay to come along / Evolution in rock / Spanish castle magic / Born under a bad sign.

Dec 86. (lp) *<(MDC 4)>* **SMOKE SIGNALS** [ ] [ ]

We Bite Radical

Nov 87. (lp) *(WB 022) <MDC 5>* **MILLIONS OF DAMN CHRISTIANS** [ ] [ ]
– Millions of damn Christians (Dante's River Styx) / This blood's for you / Who's the terrorist now? / Bye bye Ronnie / Chock full of shit / Mao Tse Tung / Heney Kissmyassinger / Guns for Nicaragua / Politician / S.K.I.N.H.E.A.D. / Sexy and Christian / Your death wish is sick / Massacred and dismembered culture / Police related death. *(cd-iss. Sep93; WB 3022CD)*

Jun 88. (lp) *(WB 033)* <MDC 6> **MORE DEAD COPS 1981-1987** (singles compilation) [ ] [ ]
– John Wayne was a Nazi / Born to die / Multi-Death Corporation / Selfish shit / Radioactive chocolate / No place to piss / Kleptomaniac / Chicken sqwawk / Pecking order / Pay to come along / Evolution in rock / Spanish castle magic / Born under a bad sign. *(cd-iss. Sep93; WB 3033CD)*

Destiny | not iss.

May 89. (lp) *(efa 5147)* **ELVIS: IN THE EHEINLAND (live)** [ ] [-]

Radical | Boner

Sep 89. (lp) *<(efa 1756708)>* **METAL DEVIL COKES** [ ] [ ]
– Huddled masses / Dirty Harry for president / White men in suits / Three blind mice / Tofu spaghetti / Snuffed out / Deep in the heart (of racist Amerikkka) / Acid reindeer / I was a dupe for the RCP / Metal devil cokes / Hole in my soul / Knucklehead / Ain't it funny (how it all works out) / Mongoloid / Love potion No.9 / Something for everyone. *(cd-iss. Apr94 on 'We Bite'; WB 3110CD)*

— **BILL COLLINS** – guitar; repl. FRAZER

— **MATT FREEMAN** – bass; repl. MARES

Mar 92. (lp/c/cd) *(MDC 81/+2/4)* *<MDC 7>* **HEY COP, IF I HAD A FACE LIKE YOURS** [ ] [ ]
– Millions of dead cops / Mark of the farmer / U.S. war #54 / Gig and die in L.A. / Beat somebody up / Nowhere to go / I do not wish / If I had a face / It's later than you think / Lambada me / Jew that got away / Moneypile / Cockrocker / Crime of rape / Black Christmas.

We Bite | New Red Archives

Apr 94. (cd) *(WB 3112CD)* **SHADES OF BROWN** [ ] [ ]
– Shades of brown / Winter of '92 / Someone's behind you again / This land / Thanks for giving me what I didn't want / Greenwash / Slow, stupid and hungry / Hail Satan / Borrowed time / Squat dogs / Welfare line / Spare change / Real food, real people, real bullets / Long time gone / Last train to Castro.

— finally broke up in the mid-90's

MD.45 (see under ⇒ MEGADETH)

MEANSTREAK

Formed: New York, USA . . . 1985 by MARLENE APUZZO and RENA SANDS, who enlisted the services of BETTINA FRANCE, MARTENS PACE and DIANE KEYSER. Taking their cue from metal laydeez such as GIRLSCHOOL, MEANSTREAK proved conclusively (along with The GREAT KAT) that women weren't actually very good at muscle-flexing thrash. Signed to 'Music For Nations', the group released one Alex Perialas (TESTAMENT, ANTHRAX)-produced album, 'ROADKILL' (1988), splitting soon after following the record's rather underwhelming reception.

Album rating: ROADKILL (*3)

BETTINA FRANCE – vocals / **MARLENE APUZZO** – guitar / **RENA SANDS** – guitar / **MARTENS PACE** – bass / **DIANE KEYSER** – drums, percussion

Music For Nations | Mercenary

Oct 88. (cd/c/lp) *(CD/T+/MFN 89)* *<2106>* **ROADKILL** [ ] [ ]
– Roadkill / Searching forever / Snake pit / Nostradamus / It seems to me / Lost stranger / The warning / The congregation.

— split soon after above

MEATHOOK SEED (see under ⇒ NAPALM DEATH)

MEAT LOAF

Born: MARVIN LEE ADAY, 27 Sep'48, Dallas, Texas, USA, his nickname given to him after he trod on the toes of his school master. In 1966 he moved to Los Angeles and formed psychedelic-rock outfit POPCORN BLIZZARD, who opened for The WHO, AMBOY DUKES and The STOOGES, before disbanding in early 1969. That year, MEAT LOAF successfully auditioned for the 'Hair' musical, where he met female soul singer STONEY. In 1970, they made a self-titled lp together for 'Rare Earth', although he soon rejoined the 'Hair' tour in Cleveland, the behemoth subsequently taking the role of Buddha in the musical 'Rainbow'. A year and a half later, he starred in JIM STEINMAN's Broadway musical 'More Than You Deserve', a partnership that was to flower, both creatively and commercially, as the decade wore on. The following year, MEAT LOAF acted/sang in Richard O'Brien's Broadway musical 'The ROCKY HORROR PICTURE SHOW', which was soon made into a film with MEAT LOAF taking the part of EDDIE. He and STEINMAN went on to tour with the comedy show 'National Lampoon', MEAT LOAF playing the part of a priest in the 'Rockabye Hamlet' sketch. Keeping his finger in the rock'n'roll pie, he contributed vocals to TED NUGENT's 1976 set, 'Free For All'. Early the following year, the big man got together again in New York with STEINMAN, starting work on the 'NEVERLAND' project. They signed to 'R.C.A.', although the partnership changed stables (to 'Epic' affiliated label 'Cleveland International') after it was clear the label didn't want to work with producer TODD RUNDGREN. Late in 1977, they finally unleashed the finished article as 'BAT OUT OF HELL', and with heavy tours, the record eventually made the US Top 20 (also hitting the UK Top 10). A bombastic rock opera, the album shook up the punk/new wave dominated music scene, its heavyweight, anthemic choruses and vein-bursting vocal histrionics reclaiming the territory that "rock" had lost in the past few years. It crossed over to such an extent that it became part of nearly everyone's record collection, selling millions in the process and residing in the charts for over eight years. Songs such as 'YOU TOOK THE WORDS RIGHT OUT OF MY MOUTH', 'TWO OUT OF THREE AIN'T BAD', 'PARADISE BY THE DASHBOARD LIGHT' and the epic title track, took rock'n'roll to melodramatic new heights, its crescendos gripping and lulling the listener into submission. Sweating like a builder's arse crack, MEAT LOAF strained and contorted his way through each song with a theatrical passion as yet unwitnessed in rock. However, it wasn't without a price, the hairy one subsequently suffering throat and alcohol problems over the course of the next few years as the pressures of fame took their toll. Nevertheless, he starred in the film 'Roadie' (1980), alongside DEBBIE HARRY and her group BLONDIE. Impatient with MEAT LOAF's problems, STEINMAN released the 'BAD FOR GOOD' (May '81) album under his own name, although this was intended for MEAT. The long-awaited MEAT LOAF follow-up, 'DEAD RINGER FOR LOVE' was finally issued four months later, and although it hit the top of the charts, it only managed to scrape into US Top 50. Having used ELLEN FOLEY as a vocal foil on his last meisterwork, MEAT LOAF employed the powerful tonsils of CHER on the title track (also a hit single). With STEINMAN out of the picture, MEAT LOAF concentrated his activities in Britain, where he soon became a widely known celebrity, losing a few stone in the process. While mid 80's albums like 'MIDNIGHT AT THE LOST AND FOUND' (1983), 'BAD ATTITUDE' (1984) and 'BLIND BEFORE I STOP' (1986) did little to improve his critical standing, fans still came out in their droves for live appearances. Inevitably perhaps, MEAT LOAF and STEINMAN eventually got back together, 'Virgin' (having just lost MIKE OLDFIELD's massive selling 'Tubular Bells II' to 'Warners') being the lucky backer of a million-selling 1993 sequel, funnily enough called 'BAT OUT OF HELL II – BACK INTO HELL'. This provided the once 20-stone rocker with a return to transatlantic chart domination, the accompanying single 'I'D DO ANYTHING FOR YOU (BUT I WON'T DO THAT)'. This rejuvenated the singer's flagging career, a British beef ban unable to prevent MEAT LOAF (and new writer DIANE WARREN) once again making the UK Top 3 with the 'WELCOME TO THE NEIGHBORHOOD' album in 1995; a best of package hit the UK Top 20 late in 1998. • **Songwriters:** MEATLOAF co-wrote w/ PAUL CHRISTIE + others in 1983. P. JACOBS + S. DURKEE took the bulk of the load in 1984. Covered; MARTHA (Tom Waits) / OH WHAT A BEAUTIFUL MORNING (Rogers-Hammerstein) / WHERE ANGELS SING (Davis) / WHATEVER HAPPENED TO SATURDAY NIGHT (Richard O'Brien) / COME TOGETHER + LET IT BE (Beatles).

Album rating: BAT OUT OF HELL (*10) / DEAD RINGER (*6) / MIDNIGHT AT THE LOST AND FOUND (*5) / HITS OUT OF HELL compilation (*7) / BAD ATTITUDE (*6) / MEAT LOAF LIVE AT WEMBLEY (*5) / BLIND BEFORE I STOP (*5) / BAT OUT OF HELL II: BACK INTO HELL (*6) / WELCOME TO THE NEIGHBOURHOOD (*4) / THE VERY BEST OF MEAT LOAF compilation (*7)

STONEY AND MEATLOAF

STONEY – vocals,(who later joined BOB SEGER).

Rare Earth | Rare Earth

Apr 71. (7") *<5027-F>* **WHAT YOU SEE IS WHAT YOU GET. / LADY OF MINE** [-] [71]

Jun 71. (7") *<5033-F>* **IT TAKES ALL KINDS OF PEOPLE. / THE WAY YOU DO THE THINGS YOU DO** [-] [ ]

Oct 71. (7") *(RES 103)* **WHAT YOU SEE IS WHAT YOU GET. / THE WAY YOU DO THE THINGS YOU DO** [ ] [-]
(re-iss. Mar79 on 'Prodigal'; PROD 10)

Oct 72. (lp) *(SRE 3005)* *<R 528-1>* **STONEY AND MEATLOAF** [ ] [ ] Oct71
– Jimmy Bell / She waits by the window / It takes all kind of people / Stone heart / Who is the leader of the people / What you see is what you get / Kiss me again / Sunshine (where's Heaven) / Jessica White / Lady be mine / Everything under the sun. *<(re-iss. Oct78/Mar79 as 'MEATLOAF (FEATURING STONEY AND MEATLOAF)' on 'Prodigal'; P7 10029> (PDL 2010) (re-iss. Oct81 c; CPDL 2010) (re-iss. 1986 as 'MEAT LOAF' on 'Motown'; ZL 72217)*

— Returned to feature in the musical 'Hair' (plus see above biography).

MEAT LOAF

not iss. | R.S.O.

1974. (7") *<RS 407>* **MORE THAN YOU DESERVE. / PRESENCE OF THE LORD** [-] [ ]

Ode | Ode

Oct 75. (7"w-drawn) *(ODS 66304)* **CLAP YOUR HANDS AND STAMP YOUR FEET. / STAND BY ME** [ ] [ ]
(above was recorded in 1973)

— **MEAT LOAF** – vocals / **JIM STEINMAN** – composer, keyboards, percussion / **TODD RUNDGREN** – multi- / **ROY BITTAN** – piano, keyboards / **MAX WEINBERG** – drums / **KASIM SULTAN** – bass / **ROGER POWELL** – synth. / **ELLEN FOLEY + RORY DODD** – back.vox

Epic | Epic

Jan 78. (lp/c)(pic-lp) *(EPC/40 82419)(EPC11 82419)* *<34974>* **BAT OUT OF HELL** [9] [14] Oct77
– You took the words right out of my mouth (hot summer night) / Heaven can wait / All revved up with no place to go / Two out of three ain't bad / Bat out of hell / For crying out loud / Paradise by the dashboard light: (I)- Paradise, (II)- Let me sleep on it, (III)- Praying for the end of time. *(cd-iss. 1983; EPCCDEPC 82419) (re-iss. pic-cd Dec90; 467732-2) (re-iss. Jul91 lp/c+=; EPC/40 82419)* – Dread ringer for love. *(hit UK No.14, re-entered Jan92, peaked again at No.24-Jul92, returned to hit UK No.19 Autumn 1993) (cd re-iss. Jul95; 480411-2) (lp re-iss. Jun99 on 'Simply Vinyl'; SVLP 86)*

Mar 78. (7") *(SEPC 5980)* *<50467>* **YOU TOOK THE WORDS RIGHT OUT OF MY MOUTH. / FOR CRYING OUT LOUD** [33] [ ] Jan78

Jul 78. (7") *(SEPC 6281)* *<50513>* **TWO OUT OF THREE AIN'T BAD. / FOR CRYING OUT LOUD** [32] [11] Mar78

Aug 78. (7") *<50588>* **PARADISE BY THE DASHBOARD LIGHT. / "BAT" OVERTURE** - 39

Sep 78. (7") *(SEPC 6797)* **PARADISE BY THE DASHBOARD LIGHT. / ALL REVVED UP WITH NO PLACE TO GO** [ ] -

Nov 78. (7") *<50634>* **YOU TOOK THE WORDS RIGHT OUT OF MY MOUTH. / PARADISE BY THE DASHBOARD LIGHT** - 39

Jan 79. (7"/ext.12"red) *(SEPC/+12 7018)* **BAT OUT OF HELL. / HEAVEN CAN WAIT** 15 -
(re-iss. Apr81)

—— MEAT LOAF now brought in many session people, including **CHER** on title track.

Sep 81. (lp/c)(pic-lp) *(EPC/40 83645)(EPC11 83645) <36007>* **DEAD RINGER** 1 45
– Peel out / I'm gonna love her for both of us / More than you deserve / I'll kill you if you don't come back / Read 'em and weep / Nocturnal pleasure / Dead ringer for love / Everything is permitted. *(re-iss. Nov85 lp/c; EPC 32692) (cd-iss. Nov87; EPCCD 83645)*

Sep 81. (7") *(EPCA 1580) <02490>* **I'M GONNA LOVE HER FOR BOTH OF US. / EVERYTHING IS PERMITTED** 62 84

Nov 81. (7"/7"pic-d) *(EPCA/+11 1697)* **DEAD RINGER FOR LOVE. / MORE THAN YOU DESERVE** 5 -
(re-iss. Aug88)

Mar 82. (7") *(EPCA 2012)* **READ 'EM AND WEEP. / EVERYTHING IS PERMITTED** [ ] -
(12"+=) *(EPCA 12-2012)* – (interview with MEAT LOAF).

Apr 82. (7") *<02607>* **READ 'EM AND WEEP. / PEEL OUT** - [ ]

1982. (12"ep-clear) *(EPCA 12-2251)* **MEAT LOAF IN EUROPE '82 (live)** [ ] -
– Two out of three ain't bad / You took the words right out of my mouth / I'm gonna love her for both of us / Dead ringer for love.

May 83. (lp)(c) *(EPC 25243)(450360-4)* **MIDNIGHT AT THE LOST AND FOUND** 7 [ ]
– Razor's edge / Midnight at the lost and found / Wolf at your door / Keep driving / The promised land / You never can be too sure about the girl / Priscilla / Don't you look at me like that / If you really want to / Fallen angel. *(re-iss. Jan87 lp/c/cd; EPC 450360-1/-4/-2)*

May 83. (7") *(A 3357)* **IF YOU REALLY WANT TO. / KEEP DRIVING** 59 -
(12"+=/12"pic-d+=) *(TA/WA 3357)* – Lost love.

Jul 83. (7"/7"pic-d) *(A/WA 3511)* **RAZOR'S EDGE. / YOU NEVER CAN BE TOO SURE ABOUT THE GIRL** [ ] -
(12"+=) *(TA 3511)* – Don't look at me like that.

Sep 83. (7"/7"pic-d) *(A/WA 3748)* **MIDNIGHT AT THE LOST AND FOUND. / FALLEN ANGEL** 17 -
(d7"+=/12"+=) *(DA/TA 3748)* – Bat out of Hell (live) / Dead ringer for love (live).

Jan 84. (7") *(A 4080) <04028>* **RAZOR'S EDGE (remix). / PARADISE BY THE DASHBOARD LIGHT** 41 [ ]
(12"+=) *(TA 4080)* – Read 'em and weep.

Arista R.C.A.

Sep 84. (7"/7"sha-pic-d) *(ARIS T/DP 585)* **MODERN GIRL. / TAKE A NUMBER** 17 -
(d7"/12")(12"pic-d) *(ARIST12 585/+D)(ARIPD12 585)* – ('A'-Freeway mix) / ('B'extended).

Nov 84. (lp)(c)(cd) *(206619)(406610)(610187) <5451>* **BAD ATTITUDE** 8 74 May85
– Bad attitude / Modern girl / Nowhere fast / Surf's up / Piece of the action / Jumpin' the gun / Cheatin' in your dreams / Don't leave your mark on me / Sailor to a siren. *(re-iss. May86 on 'Fame' lp/c; FA41/TCFA 3150) (cd re-iss. Jun88 & Feb94; 259049)*

Nov 84. (7"/7"s/7"g-f/7"sha-pic-d) *(ARI ST/PU/SG/SD 600)* **NOWHERE FAST. / CLAP YOUR HANDS** 67 -
(ext.12"+=) *(ARIST12 600)* – Stand by me.

Mar 85. (12") *<14050>* **MODERN GIRL. / ('A'long version)** - [ ]

Mar 85. (7"/7"sha-pic-d) *(ARIS T/D 603)* **PIECE OF THE ACTION. / SAILOR TO A SIREN** 47 [ ]
(d7"+=) *(ARIST 603 + FS603)* – Bat out of Hell (live) / Modern Girl (US remix).
(ext.12"+=) *(ARIST12 603)* – Bad attitude.
(ext.d12"++=) *(ARIST12 603 + FS12 603)* – (see d7"above FS603).

May 85. (7") *<14101>* **(GIVE ME THE FUTURE WITH A) MODERN GIRL. / SAILOR TO A SIREN** - [ ]

Aug 85. (7") *<14149>* **SURF'S UP. / JUMPIN' THE GUN** - [ ]
(12") *<14141>* – ('A'extended) / ('A'side) / Bad attitude.

Aug 86. (7"/7"sha-pic-d/7"white-sha-pic-d/12"/12"pic-d; by MEAT LOAF and JOHN PARR) *(ARIST 666/+P/XP)* **ROCK'N'ROLL MERCENARIES. / REVOLUTIONS PER MINUTE** 31 -

Sep 86. (lp/c/cd) *(207/407/257 741)* **BLIND BEFORE I STOP** 28 [ ]
– Execution day / Rock'n'roll mercenaries / Getting away with murder / One more kiss / Night of the soft parade / Blind before I stop / Burning down / Standing on the outside / Masculine / Man and a woman / Special girl / Rock'n'roll hero. *(re-iss. cd Feb94; 259741)*

Nov 86. (7"/7"sha-pic-d)(10") *(ARIST 683/+P)(ARIST10 683) <89340>* **GETTING AWAY WITH MURDER. / ROCK'N'ROLL HERO** [ ] [ ]
(12") *(ARIST12 683)* – ('A'-Scot free mix)/ ('B'extended).

Feb 87. (7"/12") *(RIS/+T 3)* **BLIND BEFORE I STOP. / EXECUTION DAY** [ ] -
(12"+=) *(RIST 3R)* – Dead ringer for love (live) / Paradise by the dashboard light (live).

Mar 87. (7") *<89303>* **ROCK'N'ROLL MERCENARY. / EXECUTION DAY** - [ ]

Apr 87. (7") *(RIS 14)* **SPECIAL GIRL. / ONE MORE KISS** [ ] -
(12"+=/cd-s+=) *(RIS T/CD 14)* – Dead ringer for love (live) / Paradise by the dashboard light (live).

Oct 87. (7"/ext.12") *(RIS/+T 41)* **BAT OUT OF HELL (live). / MAN AND A WOMAN** [ ] -

Nov 87. (lp/c/cd) *(208/408/258 599)* **LIVE AT WEMBLEY (live)** 60 -
– Blind before I stop / Rock & roll mercenaries / Took the words / Midnight at the lost and found / Modern girl / Paradise by the dashboard light / Two out of three ain't bad / Bat out of Hell. *(free 12"ep/cd+=)* – Masculine / Rock'n'roll medley: Johnny B. Goode – Slow down – Jailhouse rock – Blue suede shoes.

—— now with **MRS LOUD** – female vocal / **ROY BITTAN & BILL PAYNE** – piano / **TIM PIERCE & EDDIE MARTINEZ** – guitar / **KENNY ARONOFF & RICK MAROTTA & BRIAN MEAGHER & JIMMY BRALOWER** – drums / **STEVE BUSLOWE** – bass / **PAT THRALL** – guitar solo / **LENNY PICKETT** – sax / **JEFF BOVA** – synth. & prog. / etc.

Virgin M.C.A.

Sep 93. (cd/c/lp) *(CDV/TCV/V 2710) <10699>* **BAT OUT OF HELL II: BACK INTO HELL** 1 1
– I'd do anything for love (but I won't do that) / Life is a lemon and I want my money back / Rock and roll dreams come through / It just won't quit / Out of the frying pan (and into the fire) / Objects in the rear view mirror may appear closer than they are / Wasted youth / Everything louder than everything else / Good girls go to heaven (bad girls go everywhere) / Back into Hell / Lost boys and golden girls. *(ltd.pic-lp Dec93; VP 2710) (re-iss. Nov95; same)*

Sep 93. (c-s) *<54626>* **I'D DO ANYTHING FOR LOVE (BUT I WON'T DO THAT) / ('A'edit)** - 1

Oct 93. (7"/c-s) *(VS/+C 1443) <54626>* **I'D DO ANYTHING FOR LOVE (BUT I WON'T DO THAT). / BACK INTO HELL** 1 -
(cd-s+=) *(VSCDT 1443)* – Everything louder than everything else (live NYC).
(cd-s) *(VSCDG 1443)* – ('A'side) / You took the words right out of my mouth (live NYC) / Bat out of hell (live NYC).

Jan 94. (c-s) *<54757>* **ROCK AND ROLL DREAMS COME THROUGH / I'D DO ANYTHING FOR LOVE (BUT I WON'T DO THAT) (live)** - 13

Feb 94. (7"pic-d/c-s) *(VSP/VSC 1479)* **ROCK AND ROLL DREAMS COME THROUGH. / WASTED YOUTH** 11 -
(cd-s+=) *(VSCDT 1479)* – I'd do anything for love (but I won't do that) (live NYC).
(cd-s+=) *(VSCDG 1479)* – Heaven can wait (live) / Paradise by the dashboard light (live).

Apr 94. (7"/c-s) *(VS/+C 1492) <54848>* **OBJECTS IN THE REAR VIEW MIRROR MAY APPEAR CLOSER THAN THEY ARE. / TWO OUT OF THREE AIN'T BAD (live)** 26 38
(cd-s) *(VSCDT 1492)* – ('A'side) / Rock and roll dreams come through (live) / All revved up (live).

Oct 95. (c-s) *(VSC 1563) <55134>* **I'D LIE FOR YOU (AND THAT'S THE TRUTH). / I'D DO ANYTHING FOR LOVE (BUT I WON'T DO THAT)** 2 13
(cd-s+=) *(VSCDG 1563)* – Whatever happened to Saturday night.
(cd-s) *(VSCDT 1563)* – ('A'-Fountain Head mix) / Oh, what a beautiful mornin' / Runnin' for the red light (I gotta life).

Oct 95. (cd/c/d-lp) *(CD/TC+/V 2799) <11341>* **WELCOME TO THE NEIGHBOURHOOD** 3 17 Nov95
– When the rubber meets the road / I'd lie for you (and that's the truth) / Original sin / 45 seconds of ecstacy / Runnin' for the red light (I gotta life) / Fiesta de las Almas Perdidas / Left in the dark / Not a dry eye in the house / Amnesty is granted / If this is the last kiss (let's make it last all night) / Martha / Where angels sing.

Jan 96. (c-s) *(VSC 1567) <55174>* **NOT A DRY EYE IN THE HOUSE / I'D LIE TO YOU (AND THAT'S THE TRUTH) (live)** 7 82
(cd-s+=) *(VSCDT 1567)* – Where the rubber meets the road (live).
(cd-s) *(VSCDX 1567)* – ('A'side) / Come together / Let it be.

Apr 96. (c-s) *(VSC 1582)* **RUNNIN' FOR THE RED LIGHT (I GOTTA LIFE) / LIFE IS A LEMON AND I WANT MY MONEY BACK (live) / AMNESTY IS GRANTED** 21 [ ]
(cd-s+=) *(VSCDX 1582)* – Dead ringer for love.
(12"pic-d) *(VSTP 1582)* – ('A'side) / Dead ringer for love (live) / All revved up (live) / Midnight at the lost and found (live).

Nov 98. (cd/c) *(CDV/TCV 2868)* **THE VERY BEST OF MEAT LOAF** (compilation) 14 [ ]
– Home by now / No matter what / Life is a lemon and I want my money back / You took the words right out of my mouth (hot summer night) / Two out of three ain't bad / Modern girl / Rock'n'roll dreams come through / Is nothing sacred / Paradise by the dashboard lights / Heaven can wait / I'd do anything for love (but I won't do that) / A kiss is a terrible thing to waste / I'd lie for you (and that's the truth) / Not a dry eye in the house / Nocturnal pleasure / Dead ringer for love / Midnight at the lost and found / Objects in the rear view mirror may appear closer than they are / Bat out of Hell.

Apr 99. (c-s/cd-s; by MEAT LOAF featuring PATTI RUSSO) *(VSC/+DT 1734)* **IS NOTHING SACRED / NO MATTER WHAT / DEAD RINGER FOR LOVE (live)** 15 [ ]
(cd-s) *(VSCDX 1734)* – ('A'side) / What you see is what you get (live) / Out of the frying pan (and into the fire) (live).

– compilations, others, etc. –

on 'Epic' records (unless stated)

Aug 82. (c-ep) *(EPCA40 2621)* **GREATEST ORIGINAL HITS EP** [ ] -
– Bat out of Hell / Read 'em and weep / Dead ringer for love / I'm gonna love her for both of us. *(7"ep-iss.Mar83; EPCA 2621)*

Jan 85. (lp/c/cd) *(EPC/40/EPCCD 26156)* **HITS OUT OF HELL** 2 [ ]
– Bat out of Hell / Read 'em and weep / Midnight at the lost and found / Two out of three ain't bad / Dead ringer for love / Modern girl / I'm gonna love her for both of us / You took the words right out of my mouth (hot summer night) / Razor's edge / Paradise by the dashboard light. *(re-iss. Mar88 lp/c; 450447-1/-4) (re-iss. cd Mar91 & Jul99; EPC 450447-2)*

Sep 86. (c-ep) *(450131-4)* **MEAT LOAF** [ ] -
– Bat out of Hell / Dead ringer for love / Read 'em and weep / If you really want to / Razor's edge.

Aug 87. (d-lp) *(EPCML 241)* **BAT OUT OF HELL / HITS OUT OF HELL** [ ] -

Jan 88. (7") *Old Gold; (OG 9751)* **BAT OUT OF HELL. / DEAD RINGER FOR LOVE** [ ] -

Feb 89. (7") *Old Gold; (OG 9865)* **YOU TOOK THE WORDS RIGHT OUT OF MY MOUTH. / MIDNIGHT AT THE LOST AND FOUND** [ ] -

Nov 89. (lp/c/cd) *Arista; (210/410/260 363)* **PRIME CUTS** [ ] [ ]

Nov 89. (lp/c/cd; with tracks by BONNIE TYLER) *Telstar; (STAR/STAC/TCD 2361)* **HEAVEN AND HELL** [ ] -
(re-iss. cd-c.May93 & Dec95 on 'Columbia')

Jun 91. (7"/c-s) *(656982-7/-4)* **DEAD RINGER FOR LOVE. / HEAVEN CAN WAIT** 53 [ ]
(12"+=/cd-s+=) *(656982-6/-2)* – Bat out of Hell.

Jun 92. (7"/c-s) *(657491-7/-4)* **TWO OUT OF THREE AIN'T BAD. / MIDNIGHT AT THE LOST AND FOUND** 69 [ ]

(12"+=/cd-s+=) *(657491-6/-2)* – I'm gonna love her for both of us.

Jul 92. (c-s) *M.C.A.; <54557>* **PARADISE BY THE DASHBOARD LIGHT. /** [-] [ ]
(above from the 'Leap Of Faith' soundtrack starring Steve Martin)

Oct 92. (cd/c) *Pickwick; (PWK CD/S 4121)* **ROCK'N'ROLL HERO** [ ] [-]
(re-iss. May94; same)

Feb 93. (cd) *(CDX 82419)* **BAT OUT OF HELL – REVAMPED** [ ] [-]

Feb 93. (d-cd) *(CDX 82419D)* **DEAD RINGER / BAT OUT OF HELL** [ ] [-]

Apr 93. (d-cd) *(474032-2)* **DEAD RINGER / MIDNIGHT AT THE LOST AND FOUND** [ ] [-]
(re-iss. Feb95; 478486-2)

Sep 93. (cd/c) *Ariola; (74321 1528-2/-4)* **THE COLLECTION** [ ] [-]

Dec 93. (12"pic-d-ep/c-ep/pic-cd-ep) *(660006-6/-4/-2)* **BAT OUT OF HELL / READ 'EM AND WEEP. / OUT OF THE FRYING PAN (AND INTO THE FIRE) / ROCK AND ROLL DREAMS COME THROUGH (Jim Steinman)** [8] [ ]

Oct 94. (cd; with BONNIE TYLER) **THE BEST** [ ] [ ]

Oct 94. (cd/c/lp) *Pure Music; (PM CD/MC/LP 7002)* **ALIVE IN HELL (live)** [33] [-]
– (tracks on 'LIVE AT WEMBLEY' album) + (studio tracks;-) Piece of the action / Bad attitude / Surf's up.

Apr 95. (cd) *Arista; (74321 25957-2)* **BLIND BEFORE I STOP / BAD ATTITUDE** [ ] [-]

Jun 96. (cd/c) *Camden; (74321 39336-2/-4)* **ROCK'N'ROLL HERO** [ ] [-]

Jul 98. (cd) *(488674-2)* **THE DEFINITIVE COLLECTION** [ ] [-]

MEAT PUPPETS

Formed: Tempe, Phoenix, Arizona, USA . . . 1980 by brothers CURT and CRIS KIRKWOOD. They were soon snapped up by rising US indie label 'SST' in 1981, after a debut on their own label. Their first recording for the company, 'MEAT PUPPETS 1' (1982), was a demanding blast of howling noise and twisted country that barely hinted at the compelling sound they'd invent with the follow-up 'MEAT PUPPETS II' (1983). A hybrid of mystical GRATEFUL DEAD-like psychedelia that short-fused hardcore punk rock and the country-boy slur of CRIS, the record was the blueprint for most of their subsequent output. 'UP ON THE SUN' (1985) was slightly more polished and saw the band garner snowballing critical acclaim. By the release of 'MIRAGE' (1987), the band had fully realised their desert-rock vision with a collection of weather beaten, psychedelic country classics; tracks like 'BEAUTY' and 'CONFUSION FOG' rank among the MEAT PUPPET's best. Yet the record failed to sell and the band returned to a rawer, ZZ TOP-influenced sound on 'HUEVOS'. This album, together with the more mainstream 'MONSTERS' (1989) and continuing critical praise led to a deal with 'London'. Their major label debut, 'FORBIDDEN PLACES' (1991) was accomplished but lacked the high-noon intensity of their earlier work. After a step-up from KURT COBAIN (see below), the raw 'NO JOKE' (1995) album at last saw The MEAT PUPPETS reaping some financial rewards, sales of the album going on to break the half million mark. Having relocated to Austin, Texas, KIRKWOOD finally re-emerged with a new-look MEAT PUPPETS – featuring ex-PARIAH members KYLE ELLISON and SHANDON SAHM along with ANDREW DUPLANTIS – and a belated album in the shape of 'GOLDEN LIES' (2000). MEAT-ier than most of the band's back catalogue, the album cranked up the amps for a set missing much of the sun-baked strangeness of old but at least partly making up for it with strong, memorable songwriting. • **Songwriters:** Most by CURT, some with CRIS or DERRICK. Covered TUMBLIN' TUMBLEWEEDS (Bob Nolan) / EL PASO CITY (Marty Robbins) / GOODNIGHT IRENE (Leadbelly) / PARANOID + SWEET LEAF (Black Sabbath). • **Trivia:** On 18 Nov'93, CURT & CRIS guested with NIRVANA's on an unplugged MTV spot. The tracks they performed were 'PLATEAU', 'OH ME' and 'LAKE OF FIRE'.

Album rating: MEAT PUPPETS mini (*5) / MEAT PUPPETS II (*7) / UP ON THE SUN (*8) / OUT MY WAY mini (*6) / MIRAGE (*8) / HEUVOS (*6) / MONSTERS (*7) / NO STRINGS ATTACHED compilation (*6) / FORBIDDEN PLACES (*6) / TOO HIGH TO DIE (*7) / NO JOKE! (*6) / LIVE IN MONTANA (*5) / GOLDEN LIES (*5)

CURT KIRKWOOD (b.10 Jan'59, Amarillo, Texas) – guitar, vocals / **CRIS KIRKWOOD** (b.22 Oct'60, Amarillo) – vocals, bass, rhythm guitar / **DERRICK BOSTROM** (b.23 Jun'60, Phoenix) – drums

not iss. World Inv.

Sep 81. (7"ep) **IN A CAR / BIG HOUSE. / DOLFIN FIELD / OUT IN THE GARDINER / FOREIGN LAWNS** [-] [ ]
(cd-ep iss.Nov88 on 'S.S.T.'; SST 044CD)

S.S.T. S.S.T.

Jan 82. (m-lp) *<SST 009>* **MEAT PUPPETS** [-] [ ]
– Reward / Love offering / Blue green god / Walking boss / Melons rising / Saturday morning / Our friends / Tumblin' tumbleweeds / Milo, Sorghum and maize / Meat puppets / Playing dead / Litterbox / Electromud / The goldmine. *(re-iss. May93 lp/c/cd; SST 009/+C/CD) <cd re-iss. Feb99 on 'Rykodisc'; RCD 10466)>*

Apr 84. (lp) *<(SST 019)>* **MEAT PUPPETS II** [ ] [ ] 1983
– Split myself in two / Magic toy missing / Lost plateau / Aurora Borealis / We are here / Climbing / New gods / Oh, me / Lake on fire / I'm a mindless idiot / The whistling song. *(re-iss. May93 lp/c/cd; SST 019/+C/CD) <cd re-iss. Feb99 on 'Rykodisc'; RCD 10467)>*

Apr 85. (lp) *<(SST 039)>* **UP ON THE SUN** [ ] [ ]
– Up on the Sun / Maiden's milk / Away / Animal kingdom / Hot pink / Swimming ground / Bucket head / Too real / Enchanted pork fist / Seal whales / Two rivers / Creator. *(cd-iss. Sep87; SST 039CD) (re-iss. May93 cd/c; SST 039 CD/C) <(cd re-iss. Mar99 on 'Rykodisc'; RCD 10469)>*

Aug 86. (m-lp) *<(SST 049)>* **OUT MY WAY** [ ] [ ]
– She's hot / Out my way / Other kinds of love / Not swimming ground / Mountain line / Good golly Miss Molly. *(cd-iss. Sep87; SST 049CD) (re-iss. May93 cd/c; SST 049 CD/C) <(cd re-iss. Apr99 on 'Rykodisc'; RCD 10468)>*

Apr 87. (lp/cd) *<(SST 100/+CD)>* **MIRAGE** [ ] [ ]
– Mirage / Quit it / Confusion fog / The wind and the rain / Mighty zero / Get on down / Leaves / I am a machine / Beauty / A hundred miles / Love your children forever / Liquified: Mighty zero – I am a machine – Liquified – Rubberneckin'. *(re-iss. May93 cd/c; SST 100 CD/C) <(cd re-iss. May99 on 'Rykodisc'; RCD 10473)>*

Oct 87. (lp/cd) *<(SST 150/+CD)>* **HEUVOS** [ ] [ ]
– Paradise / Look at the rain / Bad love / Sexy music / Crazy / Fruit / Automatic mojo / Dry rain / I can't be counted on at all. *(re-iss. May93 cd/c; SST 150 CD/C) <(cd re-iss. Apr99 on 'Rykodisc'; RCD 10470)>*

Oct 87. (12") *<(PSST 150)>* **I CAN'T BE COUNTED ON AT ALL. / PARADISE** [ ] [ ]

Oct 89. (lp/cd) *<(SST 253/+CD)>* **MONSTERS** [ ] [ ]
– Attacked by monsters / Light / Meltdown / In love / The void / Touchdown king / Party till the world obeys / Flight of the fire weasel / Strings on your heart / Like being alive. *<(cd re-iss. May99 on 'Rykodisc'; (RCD 10471)>*

Nov 90. (d-lp/cd) *<(SST 265/+CD)>* **NO STRINGS ATTACHED** (compilation) [ ] [ ]
– Big house / In a car / Tumblin' tumbleweeds / Reward / The whistling song / New gods / Lost / Lake of fire / Split myself in two / Up on the Sun / Swimming ground / Maiden's milk / Bucket head / Out my way / Confusion fog / I am a machine / Quit it / Beauty / Look at the rain / I can't be counted on at all / Automatic mojo / Meltdown / Like being alive / Attacked by monsters.

London London

Nov 91. (cd/c/lp) *<(828254-2/-4/-1)>* **FORBIDDEN PLACES** [ ] [ ]
– Sam / Nail it down / This day / Open wide / Another Moon / That's how it goes / Whirlpool / Popskull / No longer gone / Forbidden places / Six gallon pie.

Mar 94. (cd/c/lp) *<(828484-2/-4/-1)>* **TOO HIGH TO DIE** [ ] [62]
– Violet eyes / Never to be found / We don't exist / Severed goddess head / Flaming heart / Shine / Backwater / Roof with a hole / Station / Things / Why / Evil love / Comin' down / Lake of fire.

Jul 94. (cd-ep) *<857553>* **BACKWATER / OPEN WIDE / ANIMAL / UP ON THE SUN / WHITE SPORT COAT** [-] [47]

Dec 94. (10"ep) *<1109>* **RAW MEAT EP** [-]
– We don't exist / Up on the sun / El Paso city / White sport coat / Goodnight Irene.

Oct 95. (cd/c) *<(828665-2/-4)>* **NO JOKE!** [ ] [ ]
– Scum / Nothing / Head / Taste of the sun / Vampires / Predator / Poison arrow / Eyeball / For free / Cobbler / Inflamable / Sweet ammonia / Chemical garden.

—— **CURT** recruited entire new band **KYLE ELLISON** – guitar, vocals (ex-PARIAH) / **ANDREW DuPLANTIS** – bass / **SHANDON SAHM** – drums (ex-PARIAH)

Atlantic Atlantic

Sep 00. (cd/c) *<(7567 83402-2/-4)>* **GOLDEN LIES** [ ] [ ]
– Intro / Armed and stupid / I quit / Lamp / Hercules / Batwing / Take off your clothes / You love me / Pieces of me / Push the button / Tarantula / Endless wave / Wipeout / Fat boy (Fat – Requiem).

– compilations, etc. –

Feb 99. (cd) *Rykodisc; <(RCD 1047-2)>* **LIVE IN MONTANA (live December '88)** [ ] [ ]
– Touchdown king / Cotton candy land / Automatic mojo / Plateau / Maiden's milk / Lake of fire / I can't be counted on / Liquified / Dough-rey-mi / S.W.A.T. (get down) – Attacked by monsters / Party till the world obeys / The small hours – Paranoid – Sweet leaf.

MEDULLA NOCTE

Formed: Hereford, Wales . . . 1995 by PAUL CATTEN, NEIL JENKINS, BONES and JAMMER. The band gigged furiously for the next three years before scoring a surprise Kerrang! SOTW with 'ALL OUR FRIENDS ARE DEAD'. More songs about despair and self-loathing could be found on their debut album, 'A CONVERSATION ALONE'; PAUL, in fact, reportedly spent time in a psychiatric ward and is known to be something of an insomniac. An outsider's outsider, CATTEN possibly ranks as one of the most bleak lyricists in the current crop of metal depressives. The product of yet another unhappy childhood, the singer even once famously said to Kerrang! magazine that he'd kill himself if his band split up. He's also been compared to JOY DIVISION's IAN CURTIS, especially with regard to his unhinged live performances. No surprise then that their aforementioned debut album, 'A CONVERSATION ALONE' (1999), was hailed as one of the scariest releases of that year while follow-up, 'DYING ON THE INSIDE' (2000), pushed new boundaries in painfully uneasy listening. The CURE this ain't . . .

Album rating: A CONVERSATION ALONE (*6) / DYING FROM THE INSIDE (*8)

PAUL CATTEN – vocals / **NEIL JENKINS** – guitar / **BONES** – bass / **JAMMER** – drums

Household Name Household Name

Jun 98. (cd) *(<HAUS 017CD>)* **A CONVERSATION ALONE** [ ] [ ] Dec99
– Spat on / A conversation alone / Problem to the solution / Bleed this illness / Choking on dirt / Hooked on masturbation / Don't be a victim / All over friends are dead / All that I ask.

Copro Reds Copro Reds

Jun 00. (cd) *(<COP 016CD>)* **DYING FROM THE INSIDE** [ ] [ ] Oct00
– Deafened by the sound of silence / Twice the trauma / The nervous reaction / Scared of strangers / Has the penny dropped? / Nothing for second / Outcast / Broken state of mind / Inside I'm dying.

ME FIRST AND THE GIMME GIMMES

Formed: Hollywood, California, USA ... 1996 by frontman SPIKE SLAWSON with the help of – on their debut full-set at least! – top hardcore punk friends FAT MIKE (of NOFX) on bass, JOEY CAPE (of LAGWAGON) on guitar, DAVE RAUN (also of LAGWAGON) on drums and CHRIS SHIFLETT (of NO USE FOR A NAME) on guitar. SPIKE was employed at MIKE's label, 'Fat Wreck Chords', and it was there the supergroup (of sorts!?) delivered a series of cover singles under the name of their associated songwriter ('DENVER', 'DIAMOND', 'BILLY', 'BARRY', 'ELTON', etc). Some of these were included on their funpacked debut album, 'HAVE A BALL' (1997), alongside work once(!) classic by JAMES TAYLOR, CARLY SIMON, JACQUES BREL – enough said. Not content with giving us one ball, they decided to give us two, by releasing a follow-up album, 'ARE A DRAG' (1999), in which this time they chose to destroy Broadway/Hollywood musicals (or just simply music!) • **Note:** The ME FIRST on 'Broken' records – who issued a single 'Pinkie' and album 'Awful Friendly' (in '97) – were not the same outfit.

Album rating: HAVE A BALL (*5) / ARE A DRAG (*4) / BLOW IN THE WIND (*6)

SPIKE SLAWSON – vocals / **JOEY CAPE** – guitar (of LAGWAGON) / **CHRIS SHIFLETT** – guitar (of NO USE FOR A NAME) / **FAT MIKE** – bass (of NOFX) / **DAVE RAUN** – drums (of LAGWAGON)

Fat Wreck Chords | Fat Wreck Chords

May 96. (7") *<FAT 531-7>* **DENVER**
– Country road / Leaving on a jet plane.

— also issued similarly titled 45's 'BILLY' – 'Only The Good Die Young', 'PAUL' and 'BARRY' (these were issued on 'Epitaph')

May 97. (cd/c/lp) *<FAT 554 CD/MC/LP>* **HAVE A BALL**
– Danny's song / Leaving on a jet plane / Me and Julio down by the schoolyard / One tin soldier / Uptown girl / I am a rock / Sweet Caroline / Seasons in the sun / Fire and rain / Nobody does it better / Mandy / Rocket man.

Jun 97. (7") *<HR 624-7>* **DIAMOND**
– Sweet Caroline / America.
(above issued on 'Hopeless' records, below on 'Kung Fu')

Jun 97. (7") *<KFS 700-2>* **PAUL**
– Me and Julio down by the schoolyard / I am a rock.

Feb 99. (7") *<DON 20>* **ELTON**
– Rocket man / +1
(above issued on 'Honest Don's)

— **JAKE JACKSON** – guitar (of SWINGIN' UTTERS) repl. CHRIS who later joined The FOO FIGHTERS

Apr 99. (cd/lp) *<FAT 586 CD/LP>* **ARE A DRAG**
– Over the rainbow / Don't cry for me Argentina / Science fiction double feature / Summertime / Favorite things / Rainbow connection / Phantom of the opera song / I sing the body electric / It's raining on prom night / Tomorrow / What I did for love / Stepping out.

May 99. (7"ep) *<LK 219>* **GARF EP**
(above issued on 'Lookout!', below on 'Alternative Tentacles')

May 99. (7"ep) *<VIRUS 226>* **IN YOUR BARCALOUNGER**

Mar 01. (7") *<BYO 071>* **RUNAWAY**
(above issued on 'B.Y.O.')

Mar 01. (lp/cd) *<FAT 820/+CD>* **BLOW IN THE WIND**
– Blowin' in the wind / Sloop John B / Wild world / Who put the bomp / Elenor / My boyfriend's back / All my loving / Stand by your man / San Francisco / I only want to be with you / Runaway / Will you still love me tomorrow / Different drum.

Apr 01. (7") *<15841-7>* **STEVENS**
(above issued on 'Nitro')

MEGADETH

Formed: San Francisco, California, USA ... 1983 by ex-METALLICA guitarist/vocalist, DAVE MUSTAINE, alongside DAVE ELLEFSON (bass), CHRIS POLAND (guitar) and GAR SAMUELSON (drums). MUSTAINE soon secured the band a deal with the small 'Combat' label, who released MEGADETH's breakneck debut album, 'KILLING IS MY BUSINESS ... AND BUSINESS IS GOOD' (1985). Taking the aural assault of METALLICA as a template, MUSTAINE and Co. had carved out an even more intense, speed-driven variation on heavy metal, but unlike many of their similarly speed-obsessed peers, MEGADETH had the instrumental prowess to pull it off. Signing to 'Capitol', the band followed up with 'PEACE SELLS ... BUT WHO'S BUYING?' (1986), after which MUSTAINE sacked both POLAND and SAMUELSON. Replacing them with JEFF YOUNG and CHUCK BEHLER respectively, the band returned in February '88 with a fierce cover of the SEX PISTOLS' 'ANARCHY IN THE U.K.', complete with original 'PISTOLS' guitarist, STEVE JONES. 'SO FAR ... SO GOOD ... SO WHAT!' followed in March, the pinnacle of their career thus far and one of the finest metal albums of that year. Lyrically, MUSTAINE was as reliably pessimistic as ever, 'IN MY DARKEST HOUR' seeing the frontman wracked with bitterness and frustrated rage. Which possibly accounts for his headlong descent into substance abuse following the album's success, MUSTAINE again firing his musicians and not surfacing again until the cover of ALICE COOPER's 'NO MORE MR. NICE GUY' in late '89, his first Top 20 hit. Going on MUSTAINE's track record, there had never been a MR. NICE GUY, although new recruits MARTY FRIEDMAN (guitar) and NICK MENZA (drums) have been with the band now for an unprecedented eight years and MUSTAINE obviously had it together enough to record the critically acclaimed 'RUST IN PEACE' (1990). 'HOLY WARS ... THE PUNISHMENT DUE' was the first single from the album, an uncannily prescient piece of writing in light of the Gulf War, the record made even more eerie by dint of its wailing Arab-esque embellishments. The whole set was more mature, both musically and lyrically, FRIEDMAN ripping out solo's at furious speed, note for perfect note while MUSTAINE tackled subjects from alien cover-ups ('HANGER 18', another Top 30 hit) to the threat of nuclear weapons ('RUST IN PEACE ...POLARIS'). COUNTDOWN TO EXTINCTION (1992) featured equally topical lyrical themes, mainly dealing with the danger to the earth's environment. Musically, the band had inevitably slowed the pace down somewhat; allowing more consideration for melody and structure, MEGADETH scored their biggest success to date, the album reaching No.2 in America, No.5 in Britain. 'SKIN O' MY TEETH' recounted MUSTAINE's brushes with death; rather than banging on about saving the planet, perhaps MUSTAINE should have dealt with his own affairs first as rumours began to surface about drug problems marring sessions for the 'YOUTHANASIA' (1994) album. Nevertheless, by the time of the album's release, MUSTAINE had apparently finally cleaned up and on the strength of the record, no one could really argue. It was another masterful effort, a transatlantic Top 10 that signalled MUSTAINE was hot on the heels of his old muckers METALLICA. After an odds'n'sods collection in '95, the band returned a few years later with 'CRYPTIC WRITINGS', a disappointing affair that should've served as MEGADETH's epitaph. However, they stood their ground for another cocktail of pitbull metal in the shape of 9th set, 'RISK' (1999); another transatlantic Top 30 entry. Having signed off (late in 2000) from 'Capitol' via an obligatory 'best of' package, 'CAPITOL PUNISHMENT: THE MEGADETH YEARS', the group signed a deal with 'Sanctuary' ('Metal-Is' in the UK), releasing the disappointing 'THE WORLD NEEDS A HERO' (2001).

Album rating: KILLING IS MY BUSINESS ... AND BUSINESS IS GOOD (*6) / PEACE SELLS ... BUT WHO'S BUYING? (*8) / SO FAR ... SO GOOD ... SO WHAT? (*7) / RUST IN PEACE (*7) / COUNTDOWN TO EXTINCTION (*7) / YOUTHANASIA (*6) / HIDDEN TREASURES (*5) / CRYPTIC WRITINGS (*4) / RISK (*3) / CAPITOL PUNISHMENT compilation (*6) / THE WORLD NEEDS A HERO (*4)

DAVE MUSTAINE (b.13 Sep'61, La Mesa, Calif.) – vocals, lead guitar (ex-METALLICA) / **CHRIS POLAND** – guitar / **DAVE ELLEFSON** (b.12 Nov'64, Minnesota) – bass / **GAR SAMUELSON** – drums

Music For Nations | Combat

Jun 85. (lp) *(MFN 46) <970546>* **KILLING IS MY BUSINESS ... AND BUSINESS IS GOOD**
– Last rites – Loved to death / Killing in my business . . .and business is good / The skull beneath the skin / These boots / Rattlehead / Chosen ones / Looking down the cross / Mechanix. *(cd-iss. Aug87; CDMFN 46) (pic-lp May88; MFN 46P) (cd re-iss. Nov99 on 'Century Media'; 66034-2)*

— POLAND was replaced by MIKE ALBERT (ex-KING CRIMSON) briefly until his return

Capitol | Capitol

Nov 86. (lp/pic-lp)(c) *(EST/+P 2022)(TCEST 2022) <12526>* **PEACE SELLS ... BUT WHO'S BUYING?** — [76]
– Wake up dead / The conjuring / Peace sells / Devils island / Good mourning – Black Friday / Bad omen / I ain't superstitious / My last words. *(cd-iss. Sep88; CDP 746148-2) (re-iss. Jul94 cd/c; CDEST 2022)*

Nov 87. (7"/7"pic-d) *(CL/+P 476)* **WAKE UP DEAD. / BLACK FRIDAY (live)** [65]
(12"+=,12"w/7"pic-d) *(12CL 476)* – Devil's island (live).

— **CHUCK BEHLER** – drums replaced SAMUELSON / **JEFF YOUNG**– guitar repl. JAY REYNOLDS who had briefly repl. POLAND

Feb 88. (7"/7"pic-d) *(CL/+P 480)* **ANARCHY IN THE U.K. / LIAR** [45]
(12"+=) *(12CL 480)* – 502.

Mar 88. (lp/pic-lp)(c/cd) *(EST/+P 2053)(CD/TC EST 2053) <48148>* **SO FAR ... SO GOOD ... SO WHAT!** [18] [28] Jan88
– Into the lungs of Hell / Set the world afire / Anarchy in the U.K. / Mary Jane / 502 / In my darkest hour / Liar / Hook in mouth.

May 88. (7"/7"pic-d) *(CL/+P 489)* **MARY JANE. / HOOK IN MOUTH** [46]
(12"+=) *(12CL 489)* – My last words.

— Late '88, YOUNG joined BROKEN SILENCE and BEHLER joined BLACK & WHITE

Nov 89. (7"/7"pic-d)(c-s) *(SBK/+PD 4)(TCSBK 4)* **NO MORE MR. NICE GUY. / DEAD ON: Different Breed** [13]
(12"+=/cd-s+=) *(12/CD SBK 4)* – DANGEROUS TOYS: Demon bell (the ballad of Horace Pinker).
(above single released on 'S.B.K.')

— (Mar90) **MUSTAINE + ELLEFSON** bring in new members **MARTY FRIEDMAN** (b. 8 Dec'62, Washington, D.C.) – guitar (ex-CACOPHONY) / **NICK MENZA** (b.23 Jul'64, Germany) – drums

Sep 90. (c-s/7") *(TC+/CLP 588)* **HOLY WARS ... THE PUNISHMENT DUE. / LUCRETIA** [24]
(12"+=/cd-s+=) *(12/CD CLP 588)* – Information.
(12"pic-d) *(12CLP 588)* – ('A'side) / (13-minute interview).

Oct 90. (cd/c)(lp/pic-lp) *(CD/TC EST 2132)(EST/+P 2132) <91935>* **RUST IN PEACE** [8] [23]
– Holy wars . . . the punishment due / Hangar 18 / Take no prisoners / Five magics / Poison was the cure / Lucretia / Tornado of souls / Dawn patrol / Rust in peace . . . Polaris. *(re-iss. Sep94 cd/c; same)*

Mar 91. (7"/7"sha-pic-d) *(CL/+PD 604)* **HANGAR 18. / THE CONJURING (live)** [26]
(cd-s+=) *(12/CD CLG 604)* – ('A'live) / Hook in mouth (live).

Jun 92. (7") *(CLS 662)* **SYMPHONY OF DESTRUCTION. / PEACE SELLS (live)** [15] [-]
(12"clear+=/cd-s+=) *(12CLS/CDCL 662)* – Go to Hell / Breakpoint.
(7"pic-d) *(CLPD 662)* – ('A'side) / In my darkest hour (live).

Jul 92. (cd/c/lp) *(CD/TC+/ESTU 2175)* <98531> **COUNTDOWN TO EXTINCTION** 5 2
– Skin o' my teeth / Symphony of destruction / Architecture of aggression / Foreclosure of a dream / Sweating bullets / This was my life / Countdown to extinction / High speed dirt / Psychotron / Captive honour / Ashes in your mouth.
Oct 92. (c-s) *<44886>* **SYMPHONY OF DESTRUCTION / SKIN O' MY TEETH** - 71
Oct 92. (7"/7"pic-d)(c-s) *(CL/+P 669)(TCCL 669)* **SKIN O' MY TEETH. / HOLY WARS . . . THE PUNISHMENT DUE (General Norman Schwarzkopf)** 13
(cd-s+=) *(CDCL 669)* – ('A'version) / Lucretia.
(10"+=) *(10CL 669)* – High speed drill / (Dave Mustaine interview).
May 93. (c-s/7") *(TC+/CL 692)* **SWEATING BULLETS. / ASHES IN YOUR MOUTH (live)** 26
(12"/cd-s) *(12/CD CL 692)* – ('A'side) / Countdown to extinction (live '92) / Symphony of destruction (gristle mix) / Symphony of destruction (live).
Oct 94. (cd/c/blue-lp) *(CD/TC+/EST 2244)* *<29004>* **YOUTHANASIA** 6 4
– Reckoning day / Train of consequences / Addicted to chaos / A tout le monde / Elysian fields / The killing road / Blood of heroes / Family tree / Youthanasia / I thought I knew it all / Black curtains / Victory.
Dec 94. (7"clear) *(CL 730)* **TRAIN OF CONSEQUENCES. / CROWN OF WORMS** 22
(cd-s+=) *(CDCL 730)* – Peace sells . . . but who's buying? (live) / Anarchy in the UK (live).
(laser-etched 12") *(12CL 730)* – ('A'side) / Holy wars . . . the punishment due (live) / Peace sells . . . but who's buying? (live) / Anarchy in the U.K. (live).
Aug 95. (d-cd) *(CDESTS 2244)* *<33670>* **HIDDEN TREASURES** 28 90
– No more Mr. Nice guy / Breakpoint / Go to Hell / Angry again / 99 ways to die / Paranoid / Diadems / Problems.
Jul 97. (cd/c/lp) *(CD/TC+/EST 2297)* *<38262>* **CRYPTIC WRITINGS** 38 10
– Trust / Almost honest / Use the man / Mastermind / The disintegrators / I'll get even / Sin / A secret place / Have cool, will travel / She-wolf / Vortex / FFF.
Sep 99. (cd) *(499130-2)* *<99134>* **RISK** 29 16
– Insomnia / Prince of darkness / Enter the arena / Crush 'em / Breadline / The doctor is calling / I'll be there / Wanderlust / Ecstasy / Seven / Time: the beginning / Time: the end.
Nov 00. (cd) *(525916-2)* *<25916>* **CAPITOL PUNISHMENT: THE MEGADETH YEARS** (compilation) 66 Oct00
– Kill the king / Dread and the fugitive mind / Crush 'em / Use the man / Almost honest / Trust / A tout le monde / Train of consequences / Sweating bullets / Symphony of destruction / Hangar 18 / Holy wars . . . the punishment due / In my darkest hour / Peace sells. *(hidden tracks+=)*
Metal-Is Sanctuary
May 01. (cd/lp) *(MIS CD/LP 006)* *<84503>* **THE WORLD NEEDS A HERO** 45 16
– Disconnect / The world needs a hero / Moto psycho / 1000 times goodbye / Burning bridges / Promises / Recipe for hate . . . warhorse / Losing my senses / Dread and the fugitive mind / Silent scorn / Return to Hangar / When.

– compilations, etc. –

Mar 97. (3xcd-box) *E.M.I.; (CDOMB 019)* **THE ORIGINALS** -
– (PEACE SELLS . . . BUT WHO'S BUYING / SO FAR . . . SO GOOD . . . SO WHAT / RUST IN PEACE). *(re-iss. Sep00; 528368-2)*

MD.45

DAVE MUSTAINE – guitar / **LEE VING** – vocals (ex-FEAR) / **KELLY LEMIEUX** – bass / **JAMES DE GRASSO** – drums

Capitol Capitol
Jul 96. (cd/c) *(CD/TC EST 2286)* *<36616>* **THE CRAVING**
– Hell's motel / Day the music died / Fight hate / Designer behavior / Cartoon (segue) / The creed / My town / Voices / Nothing is something / Circus (segue) / Hearts will bleed / No pain / Roadman / Alley cat (segue).

MELIAH RAGE

Formed: Boston, Massachusetts, USA ... 1984 by MIKE MUNRO, ANTHONY NICHOLS, JIM KOURY, JESSE JOHNSON and STUART DOWIE. Signed to 'Epic' in late '86, this thrash/heavy duty power-metal outfit released a promising debut, 'KILL TO SURVIVE', in early '89. This was consolidated with a live mini-set in early '89, 'LIVE KILL', while a second studio outing, 'SOLITARY SOLITUDE' (1990), appeared in summer 1990. Again receiving its fair share of critical praise, the record nevertheless failed to take off, MELIAH RAGE's potential subsequently remaining unfulfilled while contemporaries like PANTERA went on to massive success.

Album rating: KILL TO SURVIVE (*5) / SOLITARY SOLITUDE (*6)

MIKE MUNRO – vocals / **ANTHONY NICHOLS** – guitar / **JIM KOURY** – guitar / **JESSE JOHNSON** – bass / **STUART DOWIE** – drums

Epic Epic
Feb 89. (lp/c/cd) *(463257-1/-4/-2)* *<E 44447>* **KILL TO SURVIVE** Nov88
– Beginning of the end / Bates motel / Meliah rage / Deadly existence / Enter the darkness / Impaling doom / The pack.
Nov 89. (m-lp/m-c/m-cd) *(465959-1/-4/-2)* *<6E 45370>* **LIVE KILL (live)**
– Beginning of the end / Kill to survive / Bates motel / Deadly existence / The pack.
Jul 90. (cd/c/lp) *(466675-2/-4/-1)* *<E 46024>* **SOLITARY SOLITUDE**
– Solitary solitude / No mind / Decline of rule / Retaliation / Deliver me / The witching / Lost life / Swallow your soul / Razor ribbon.
— split after a European tour

MELVINS

Formed: Aberdeen, Washington, USA . . . early '85 by BUZZ OSBOURNE, who found LORI BECK and other floating members. Debuting early in 1987 with the patchy 'GLUEY PORCH TREATMENTS', they improved enough in the early 90's to sign for major label 'Atlantic'. In the interim period, this endearingly amateurish outfit (revered by KURT COBAIN, he had been their roadie!) graced a handful of largely ignored albums with their noisy BLACK SABBATH/SWANS fusions. Future MUDHONEY man, MATT LUKIN, appeared on their 1989 set, 'OZMA', before he was replaced by JOE PRESTON. In 1992, the three members simultaneously issued three solo EP's, much in the same way as KISS did in the late 70's. Still a long-time fan, KURT COBAIN worked with them on 1993's 'HOUDINI' set, although his continued patronage didn't do much for their record sales. A couple of uninspiring albums have surfaced during the past few years, the last of which, 'HONKY' was released on the 'Amphetamine Reptile' label. Perhaps the most influential Seattle band of them all, The MELVINS were still kicking out the sludgy jams come the end of the century. 'THE MAGGOT' (1999) marked the first release in a trilogy of albums recorded for MIKE PATTON's 'Ipecac' imprint, featuring an unmissable rendezvous with Peter Green's spine chilling 'GREEN MANALISHI'. 'THE BOOTLICKER' was marginally easier on the ear while 'THE CRYBABY' (2000) – the final part of the series – featured an array of carefully chosen guests including FOETUS' JIM THIRLWELL, HELMET's HENRY BOGNER and even HANK WILLIAMS III (you read that correctly); so, alongside a LEIF GARRET (no, seriously) reading of Nirvana's 'SMELLS LIKE TEEN SPIRIT' were trashings of HANK WILLIAMS' (the original) 'RAMBLIN' MAN' and Merle Haggard's much misunderstood 'OKIE FROM MUSKOGEE'. Continuing in uncharacteristically experimental mode, 'ELECTRORETARD' (2001) was a surprisingly listenable remix album wherein The MELVINS treated the cream of their back catalogue to an electronic going over as well as meting out cover treatment to Pink Floyd's 'INTERSTELLAR OVERRIVE', The Wiper's 'YOUTH OF AMERICA' and The Cows' 'MISSING'. • **Songwriters:** OSBOURNE except; WAY OF THE WORLD + SACRIFICE (Flipper) / BALLAD OF DWIGHT FRY (Alice Cooper) / THE GREEN MANALISHI (Fleetwood Mac) / TEEN SPIRIT (Nirvana) / BLOCKBUSTER (Jesus Lizard) / RAMBLIN' MAN (Hank Williams) / OKEE FROM MUSKOGEE (Merle Haggard) / G.I. JOE (Mike Patton) / YOUTH OF AMERICA (Wipers) / MISSING (Cows) / INTERSTELLAR OVERDRIVE (Pink Floyd).

Album rating: GLUEY PORCH TREATMENTS (*5) / OZMA (*5) / BULLHEAD (*6) / LYSOL compilation (*7) / HOUDINI (*5) / PRICK (*5) / STONER WITCH (*5) / STAG (*5) / HONKY (*4) / THE MAGGOT (*4) / THE BOOTLICKER (*5) / THE CRYBABY (*5) / ELECTRORETARD (*5) / THE COLOSSUS OF DESTINY (*5)

BUZZ OSBOURNE (aka KING BUZZO) – vocals, guitar / **LORI BECK** – bass / **DALE CROVER** – drums

— note that The MELVINS had bootleg singles issued in the mid-late 80's

Volume Alchemy
Feb 87. (lp) *(VM 103)* *<24>* **GLUEY PORCH TREATMENTS**
– Eye flys / Echo head – Don't piece me / Heater moves and eyes / Steve Instant Newman / Influence of atmosphere / Exact paperbacks / Happy grey or black / Leeech / Glow god / Big as a mountain / Heaviness of the load / Flex with you / Bitten into sympathy / Gluey porch treatments / Clipping roses / As was it / Over from under the excrement. *<(cd-iss. Mar01 on 'Ipecac'; IPC 12)>*

Tupelo Boner
Feb 90. (lp/cd) *(TUPLP 7)* *<BR 16/+CD>* **OZMA** 1989
– Vile / Oven / At a glance / Let God be your gardener / Creepy smell / Kool legged / Green honey / Agonizer / Raise a paw / Love thing / Ever since my accident / Revulsion – We reach / Dead dressed / Cranky Messiah / Claude / My small percent shows most / Candy-O. *<cd+=>* – GLUEY PORCH TREATMENTS

— **MATT LUKIN** – bass; repl. LORI

— **JOE PRESTON** – bass repl. LUKIN who joined MUDHONEY

Tupelo Boner
Feb 91. (cd/lp) *(TUP CD/LP 26)* *<BR 25CD>* **BULLHEAD**
– Boris / Anaconda / Ligature / It's shoved / Zodiac / If I had an exorcism / Your blessened / Cow. *<(cd re-iss. Jun99 on 'Boner'; same)>*
Sep 91. (10"ep/cd-ep) *(TUP EP/CD 31)* *<BR 28CD>* **EGGNOG**
– Wispy / Antitoxidote / Hog leg / Charmicarmicat.
Aug 92. (12"ep/cd-ep) *(TUP 39 1/-2)* *<BR 32/+CD>* **KING BUZZO**
– Isabella / Porg / Annum / Skeeter.

— BUZZO augmented by **DALE NIXON** – guitars, etc (on above)
Aug 92. (12"ep/cd-ep) *(TUP 40 1/-2)* *<BR 33/+CD>* **DALE CROVER**
– Hex me / Dead wipe / Respite / Hurter.
Aug 92. (12"ep/cd-ep) *(TUP 41 1/-2)* *<BR 34/+CD>* **JOE PRESTON**
– The eagle has landed / Bricklebrit / Hands first flower.
Nov 92. (cd/c/lp) *(TUP 42 2/4/1)* *<BR 35CD>* **LYSOL** (compilation of above 3)

Amphetam. Reptile Amphetam. Reptile
Jun 92. (7") *<(Scale 44)>* **NIGHT GOAT. / ADOLESCENT WET DREAM**

not iss. Rise
1993. (7") *<RR 76>* **HOOCH. / SKY PUP** -

East West Atlantic
Sep 93. (cd/c) *<(7567 82532-2/-4)>* **HOUDINI**
– Hooch / Set me straight / Sky pup / Joan of Arc / Pearl bomb / Spread eagle Beagle / Night goat / Lizzy / Going blind / Honey bucket / Hag me / Teet / Copache.

— **MARK DEUTROM** – bass; repl. JOE PRESTON
Nov 94. (cd/c/lp) *<(7567 82704-2/-4/-1)>* **STONER WITCH** Oct94
– Skweetis / Queen / Sweet Willy Rollbar / Revolve / Goose freight train / Roadbull / At the stake / Magic pig detective / Shevil / June bug / Lividity.

Mammoth Mammoth

Jul 96. (cd/c/lp) <*(7567-82878-2/-4/-1)*> **STAG**
– The bit / Hide / Bar-X-the rocking M / Yacob's lab / The bloat / Tipping the lion / Black bock / Goggles / Soup / Buck Owens / Sterilized / Lacrimosa / Skin horse / Captain Pungent / Berthas / Cottonmouth.

Amphetam. Amphetam. Reptile Reptile

May 97. (cd) <*(AR 64)*> **HONKY**
– They all must be slaughtered / Mombius Hibachi / Lovely butterfly / Pitfalls in serving warrants / Air breather in the arms of Morphius / Laughing with Lucifer ar Satans's sideshow / How / Harry Lauders walking stick tree / Grin / In the freaktose the bugs are dying.

Aug 98. (cd-ep) <*(AMREP 072CD)*> **MELVINS ALIVE AT F*CKER CLUB** [-] Jun98
– Boris / It's shoved / Bar-X the rocking M / Antioxidote / The bloat / Lizzy / Mombius Hibachi.

Ipecac Ipecac

May 99. (cd) <*(IPC 002CD)*> **THE MAGGOT**
– Amazon / We all love Judy / Manky / The green manalishi / The horn bearer / Judy / See how pretty, see how smart.

Aug 99. (cd) <*(IPC 003CD)*> **THE BOOTLICKER**
– Toy / Let it be me / Black Santa / We we / Up the dumper / Mary lady Bobby kins / Jew boy flower head / Lone rose holding now / Prig.

Feb 00. (cd) <*(IPC 006CD)*> **THE CRYBABY**
– Teen spirit / Blockbuster / Ramblin' man / G.I. Joe / Mine is no disgrace / Spineless / Divorced / Dry drunk / Okee from Muskogee / The man with the laughing hand is dead / Moon pie.

Nov 00. (t-lp) <*(IPC 11)*> **TRILOGY** (3 above)

Man's Ruin Man's Ruin

Feb 01. (cd) <*(MR 2002)*> **ELECTRORETARD**
– Shit storm / Youth of America / Gluey porch treatment / Revolve / Missing / Lonely butterflies / Tipping the lion B / Interstellar overdrive.

Ipecac Ipecac

Apr 01. (cd) *(IPC 14)*> **THE COLOSSUS OF DESTINY**
– The colossus of destiny.

– compilations, others, etc. –

1990's. (7") *Sympathy For The Record Industry;* <*(SFTRI 81)*> **WITH YO HEART NOT YO HANDS. / FOUR LETTER WOMAN / ANAL SATAN**

Jan 92. (cd/c) *C/Z;* <*(CZ 002/+A)*> **MELVINS (live in 1986)**
– Easy as it was / Now a Limo / Grinding process / #2 pencil / At a crawl / Disinvite / Snake appeal / Show off your red hands / Over the underground / Crayfish.

Jan 92. (cd) *Your Choice;* <*(YCR 012/+CD)*> **MELVINS** (early material) Mar94

Nov 92. (5"clear-ep) *Scooby Doo; (SAH 13)* **LOVE CANAL. / CANAL** [-]

Aug 94. (lp/cd) *Amphetamine Reptile;* <*(ARR/+CD 58-333)*> **PRICK**
– How about / Rickets / Pick it n' flick it / Montreal / Chief ten beers / Underground / Chalk people / Punch the lion / Pure digital silence / Larry / Roll another one.

Aug 97. (cd) *Amphetamine Reptile;* <*AR 63CD*> **1996, VOL.1-12** [-]
– Lexicon devil / Pigtro / In the rain / Spread eagle / Leech / Queen / Way of the world / Theme / It's shoved / Forgotten principles / GGIIBBYY / Theresa screams / Poison / Double troubled / Specimen / All at once / Jacksonville / Dallas / Bloat / Fast forward / Nasty dogs and funky kings / HDYF / How – Walking stick tree / Brutal truth – Zodiac.

MERCYFUL FATE

Formed: Copenhagen, Denmark . . . early 80's out of The BRATS, by guitarists MICHAEL DENNER and HANK SHERMANN. This outfit released one album, '1980' for the European arm of 'C.B.S.', before the pair enlisted KING DIAMOND, TIMI GRABBER HANSEN and KIM RUZZ. The influential act were one of the prime movers in the 80's black metal scene, a Euro counterpart to the likes of VENOM, etc. Making their debut on the mini-set, 'A CORPSE WITHOUT A SOUL' (1982), the group's complex style was characterised by frontman KING DIAMOND's bizarre yet effective vocals; his ability to swerve from a demonic growl to a choirboy squeal (often in the space of one line!) was unsettling to say the least. Subsequently signing to 'Roadrunner', the group released 'MELISSA' in 1983, consolidating their underground credentials and touring extensively; another of KING DIAMOND's little foibles was his grotesque face paint, MERCYFUL FATE fashioning a more extreme, satanic version of 70's ALICE COOPER/KISS theatricality. 'DON'T BREAK THE OATH' (1984) brought further acclaim although the time honoured musical differences subsequently sunk the group, SHERMANN going off to form the more melodic FATE while KING DIAMOND embarked on a solo career. Taking DENNER and HANSEN with him, 'DIAMOND initiated a series of concept albums with 'FATAL PORTRAIT' in 1986. Featuring increasingly intricate storylines, albums such as 'THEM' (1988) and 'CONSPIRACY' (1989) lost some of the impact of the early MERCYFUL FATE material, while the group sounded rather tame in comparison to the emerging Scandinavian black metal scene. Through popular demand, the latter group eventually reformed in 1993, releasing 'IN THE SHADOWS' and undertaking a heavy touring schedule. More recently, the group released 'TIME' in 1994. Through the mid-late 90's, both KING DIAMOND and MERCYFUL FATE maintained a surprisingly prolific release schedule although one of the few constant factors in the ever changing 'FATE line-up was the KING himself. His own brand of faux-classical conceit and thespian horror-metal was further pursued on 'THE SPIDER'S LULLABYE' (1995) and 'THE GRAVEYARD' (1996) although the mark of KING DIAMOND's labyrinthine lyrical intrigue was also much in evidence on subsequent MERCYFUL FATE albums such as 'INTO THE UNKNOWN' (1996), 'DEAD AGAIN' (1998) and most recently, the back to basics '9' (1999). The latter two efforts saw the introduction of new guitarist MIKE WEAD in place of the departed MICHAEL DENNER, resulting in a partial loss of the chemistry which had sustained both MERCYFUL FATE and KING DIAMOND's solo albums up to that point. Nevertheless, fans were treated to a few glimpses of the old MF black magic.

Album rating: MERCYFUL FATE mini (*4) / MELISSA (*6) / DON'T BREAK THE OATH (*7) / IN THE SHADOWS (*6) / TIME (*5) / INTO THE UNKNOWN (*5) / DEAD AGAIN (*4) / 9 (*4) / King Diamond: FATAL PORTRAIT (*5) / ABIGAIL (*7) / THEM (*6) / THE DARK SIDES mini (*4) / CONSPIRACY (*5) / THE EYE (*4) / SPIDER'S LULLABYE (*6) / THE GRAVEYARD (*4) / VOODOO (*5) / HOUSE OF GOD (*4)

KING DIAMOND (b. KIM BENDIX PETERSEN, 14 Jun'56) – vocals / **HANK SHERMANN** – guitar / **MICHAEL DENNER** – guitar / **TIMI GRABBER HANSEN** – bass / **KIM RUZZ** – drums

Rave-On not iss.

1982. (m-lp) *(EMLP 002)* **MERCYFUL FATE** [-] [-] Denmark
– A corpse without a soul / Nuns have no fun / Doomed by the living dead / Devil eyes.

Music For Nations Caroline

Oct 83. (lp) *(MFN 10)* <*CAROL 1385*> **MELISSA**
– Evil / Curse of the pharaohs / Into the coven / At the sound of the demon bell / Black funeral / Satan's fall / Melissa. *(re-iss. 1989 on 'Roadrunner' lp/cd; RR/+34 9898) (cd re-mast.Aug00 on 'Roadrunner'; RR 8770-2)*

Nov 83. (12") *(12KUT 106)* **BLACK FUNERAL. / BLACK MASSES** [-]

Music For Nations S.P.V.

Jul 84. (lp) *(MFN 28)* <*85-2089*> **DON'T BREAK THE OATH**
– A dangerous meeting / Nightmare / Desecration of souls / Night of the unborn / The oath / Gypsy / Welcome princess of Hell / To one far away / Come to the sabbath. *(re-iss. 1989 on 'Roadrunner' lp/cd; RR/+34 9835) (re-.mast.Aug00 on 'Roadrunner'; RR 8769-2)*>

—— split into two factions, SHERMANN formed FATE, while DENNER and HANSEN joined the solo KING DIAMOND

KING DIAMOND

KING DIAMOND – vocals / **MICHAEL DENNER** – guitar / **TIMI HANSEN** – bass / **MICKEY DEE** – drums

Roadrunner G.W.D.

Feb 86. (lp/c) *(RR 9721-1/-4)* <*90529*> **FATAL PORTRAIT**
– The candle / The Jonah / The portrait / Dressed in white / Charon / Lurking in the dark / Halloween / Voices from the past / Haunted. *(cd-iss. Nov87; RR34 9721) (cd re-mast.Aug00; RR 8789-2)*

Roadrunner Roadrunner

Jun 87. (lp/pic-lp/c/cd) <*(RR/+6/4/34 9622)*> **ABIGAIL**
– Funeral / Arrival / A mansion in darkness / The family ghost / The 7th day of July 1777 / Omens / The possession / Abigail / Black horseman. *(cd re-mast.Aug00; RR 8788-2)*

Aug 87. (12") *(RR12 5476)* **THE FAMILY GHOST. / SHRINE** [-]

Nov 87. (12") *(RR12 5485)* **NO PRESENTS FOR CHRISTMAS. / CHARON** [-]

Jul 88. (lp/c/cd) <*(RR 9550-1/-4/-2)*> **THEM** 89
– Out from the asylum / Welcome home / The invisible guests / Tea / Mother's getting weaker / Bye, bye, missy / A broken spell / The accusation chair / Them / Twilight symphony / Coming home / Phone call. *(cd re-mast.Aug00; RR 8785-2)*

Oct 88. (m-lp/m-cd) <*(RR 2455-1/-2)*> **THE DARK SIDES**
– Halloween / Them / No presents for Christmas / Shrine / The lake / Phone call.

Aug 89. (lp/pic-lp/c/cd) <*(RR 9461-1/-6/-4/-2)*> **CONSPIRACY**
– At the graves / Sleepless nights / Lies / A visit from the dead / The wedding dream / AMON belongs to THEM / Something weird / Victimized / Let it be done / Cremation. *(re-mast.Aug00; RR 8788-2)*

Nov 90. (cd/c/lp) <*(RR 9346-2/-4/-1)*> **"THE EYE"**
– Eye of the witch / The trial (chambre ardente) / Burn / Two little girls / Into the convent / Father Picard / Behind these walls / The meetings / Insanity / 1642 / The curse. *(re-mast.Aug00; RR 8786-2)*

Dec 91. (cd/c/lp) <*(RR 9287-2/-4/-1)*> **IN CONCERT 1987 (live)**
– Funeral / Arrival / Come to the sabbath / The family ghost / The 7th day of July 1777 / The portrait / (guitar solo; Andy) / The possession / Abigail / (drum solo) / The candle / No presents for Christmas. *(cd re-iss. Feb93; same) (cd re-mast.Aug00; RR 8784-2)*

MERCYFUL FATE

—— reformed with **KING DIAMOND, SHERMANN, DENNER, HANSEN / + MORTEN NIELSEN** – drums

Metal Blade Warners

Jun 93. (cd/c) *(CD/T ZORRO 61)* <*45318*> **IN THE SHADOWS**
– Egypt / The bell witch / The old oak / Shadows / A gruesome time / Thirteen invitations / Room of golden air / Legend of the headless rider / Is that you, Melissa / Return of the vampire . . . 1993. *(cd re-iss. Sep96; 3984 17020CD)*

—— **SNOWY SHAW** – drums (ex-KING DIAMOND) repl. NIELSEN

Metal Blade Priority

Jun 94. (cd-ep) *(CDMZORRO 78)* <*53911*> **THE BELL WITCH E.P.**
– The bell witch / Is that you, Melissa / Curse of the pharaohs / Egypt / Come to the sabbath / Black funeral. *(re-iss. Feb97; 3984 17027CD)*

—— **SHARLEE D'ANGELO** – bass; repl. HANSEN

Oct 94. (cd) *(CDZORRO 80)* <*3984 17028*> **TIME**
– Nightmare be thy name / Angel of light / Witches' dance / The mad Arab / My demon / Time / The preacher / Lady in black / Mirror / The afterlife / Castillo del mortes. *(cd re-iss. Feb97; same as US)*

Aug 96. (cd) <*(3984 18026CD)*> **INTO THE UNKNOWN**
– Lucifer / The uninvited guest / The ghost of change / Listen to the bell / Fifteen men (and a bottle of rum) / Into the unknown / Under the spell / Deadtime / Holy water / Kutulu (the mad Arab part two).

—— **DIAMOND** line-up with **MIKE WEAD + HANK SHERMANN** – guitar / **SHARLEE D'ANGELO** – bass / **BJARNE T. HOLME** – drums

Jun 98. (cd) <(3984 14159CD)> **DEAD AGAIN**
– Torture (1629) / The night / Since forever / The lady who cries / Banshee / Mandrake / Sucking your blood / Dead again / Fear / Crossroads.

Jun 99. (cd/lp) <(14242-2/-1)> **9**
– Last rites / Church of Saint Anne / Sold my soul / House on the hill / Burn in Hell / The grave / Insane / Kiss the demon / Buried alive / 9.

– compilations, etc. –

Nov 87. (lp/cd) *Roadrunner; (RR/+34 9603)* **THE BEGINNING** (early material)

Dec 89. (d-c) *Roadrunner; (RR 49648)* **MELISSA / DON'T BREAK THE OATH** [-]

May 92. (cd/c/lp) *Roadrunner; (RR 9184-2/-4/-1)* **RETURN OF THE VAMPIRE** (THE RARE AND UNRELEASED) [-]

Nov 92. (cd; KING DIAMOND / MERCYFUL FATE) *Roadrunner;* <*(RR 9117-2)*> **A DANGEROUS MEETING**
(re-iss. Mar99; same)

KING DIAMOND

continued a solo career; with **ANDY LaROCQUE** – guitar / **CHRIS ESTES** – bass, keyboards / **DARRIN ATHONY** – drums

Massacre / Metal Blade

Jun 95. (cd) *(MASSCD 062)* <14229> **THE SPIDERS LULLABYE**
– From the other side / Killer / The pltergeist / Dreams / Moonlight / Six feet under / The spider's lullabye / Eastmann's cure / Room 17 / To the morgue.

Sep 96. (cd/pic-lp) *(MASS DP/LP 103)* <17032> **THE GRAVEYARD**
– The graveyard / Black hill sanitarium / Waiting / Heads on the wall / Whispers / I'm not a stranger / Digging graves / Meet me at midnight / Sleep tight little baby / Daddy / Trick or treat / Up from the grave / I am / Lucy forever.

Mar 98. (cd) *(MASSCD 0155)* <14149> **VOODOO**
– Louisiana darkness / "Loa" house / Life after death / Voodoo / A secret / Salem / One down two to go / Sending of dead / Sarah's night / The exorcist / Unclean spirits / Cross of Baron Samedi / If they only knew / Aftermath.

Jun 00. (cd) *(MASCD 0233)* <14308> **HOUSE OF GOD**
– Upon the cross / The trees have eyes / Follow the wolf / House of God / Black devil / The pact / Goodbye / Just a shadow / Help!!! / Passage to Hell / Catacomb / The place is terrible / Peace of mind.

METAL CHURCH

Formed: Seattle, Washington, USA ... 1982 with a line-up of DAVID WAYNE, CRAIG WELLS, KURT VANDERHOOF, DUKE ERICKSON and KIRK ARRINGTON. Building up a grassroots following through constant gigging, the group eventually made it onto vinyl with the independently released 'METAL CHURCH' in 1984. Quasi-thrash of an impressive pedigree, the record's success saw the group tipped as major contenders alongside METALLICA etc, subsequently securing a major label deal with 'Elektra'. A follow-up set, 'THE DARK', eventually surfaced in 1987, a competent set which nevertheless failed to live up to the promise of the debut. A third effort, 'BLESSING IN DISGUISE' (1989), saw founding member WAYNE replaced by MIKE HOWE, the record being the group's last for 'Elektra'. More personnel changes followed prior to the recording of 'THE HUMAN FACTOR', with VANDERHOOF bowing out and being replaced with JOHN MARSHALL. The album marked the end of the band's dalliance with major label muscle, 1994's 'HANGING IN THE BALANCE' being released by the small 'Blackheart' label. Though the group struggled to rise to the heights of their 80's contemporaries and seem rather outdated in today's eclectic metal scene, they retain a hardcore following.

Album rating: METAL CHURCH (*6) / THE DARK (*4) / BLESSING IN DISGUISE (*50 / THE HUMAN FACTOR (*4) / HANGING IN THE BALANCE (*4)

DAVID WAYNE – vocals / **KURDT VANDERHOOF** – guitar / **CRAIG WELLS** – guitar / **DUKE ERICKSON** – bass / **KIRK ARRINGTON** – drums

Elektra / Elektra

Nov 85. (lp/cd) <960 471-1/-2> **METAL CHURCH** [-]
– Beyond the black / Metal church / Merciless onslaught / God of wrath / Hitman / In the blood / (My favourite) Nightmare / Battalions / Highway star. <*originally issued.1984 on 'Banzai'; BRC 1933*>

Nov 86. (lp/c/cd) <(960 493-1/-4/-2)> **THE DARK** [92]
– Ton of bricks / Start the fire / Method to your madness / Watch the children pray / Over my dead body / The dark / Psycho / Line of death / Burial at sea / Western alliance.

— **MIKE HOWE** – vocals; repl. WAYNE

— **JOHN MARSHALL** – guitar; repl. VANDERHOOF

Feb 89. (lp/c/cd) <(K 96087-1/-4/-2)> **BLESSING IN DISGUISE** [75]
– Fake healer / Rest in pieces (April 15, 1912) / Of unsound mind / Anthem to the estranged / Badlands / The spell can't be broken / It's a secret / Cannot tell a lie / The powers that be.

Epic / Epic

Apr 91. (cd/c/lp) *(467816-2/-4/-1)* <EK 47000> **THE HUMAN FACTOR**
– The human factor / Date with poverty / The final word / In mourning / In harm's way / In due time / Agent green / Flee from reality / Betrayed / The fight song.

S.P.V. / Blackheart

May 94. (cd) *(SPV 085-62170)* <BH 1001> **HANGING IN THE BALANCE**
– Gods of second chance / Losers in the game / Hypnotized / No friend of mine / Waiting for a savior / Conductor / Little boy / Down by the river / End of the age / Lovers and madmen / A subtle war.

— seemed to have split from the music biz

METALLICA

Formed: Norvale, California, USA ... 1981 by LARS ULRICH (this Danish-born drummer had previously filled the stool on a UK tour by DIAMOND HEAD, whose songs METALLICA would later cover) and JAMES HETFIELD (guitar vocals; ex-OBSESSION). Recruiting LLOYD GRAND on guitar, the band recorded their first demo, 'NO LIFE TILL LEATHER' and a one-off 7" single, 'LET IT LOOSE'. In early '82, LLOYD was replaced by future MEGADETH mainman DAVE MUSTAINE, while RON McGOVNEY was brought in on bass. After a brief period of relative stability, MUSTAINE was fired for drunkenness early the following year, being replaced by former EXODUS guitarist KIRK HAMMETT. By this point CLIFF BURTON (ex-TRAUMA) had already joined on bass following the departure of McGOVNEY. This was the classic early METALLICA line-up that played on the first three albums, redefining the boundaries of metal and touring constantly until the tragic death of BURTON in 1986. Moving to New Jersey in early '83, the band signed to John Zazula's 'Megaforce' label and unleashed their high octane debut, 'KILL 'EM ALL' (licensed to 'Music For Nations' for UK release). While it certainly wasn't without cliche, both lyrically and musically, there was a vibrancy in the speed and loudness of their sonic attack that drew on hardcore and punk, particularly in 'SEEK AND DESTROY', a track that would come to be a staple of the band's live set. The record also featured, horror of horrors, a track that consisted entirely of a bass solo! But METALLICA weren't trying to resurrect the indulgence of the 70's, their follow-up opus, 'RIDE THE LIGHTNING' (1984), confirming METALLICA's status as one of the most inventive, promising bands in the metal canon. The group had welded a keening sense of melody to their visceral thrash, alternating between grinding, bass heavy, mid-tempo uber-riffing (the title track and 'FOR WHOM THE BELL TOLLS') and all out pummelling ('FIGHT FIRE WITH FIRE' and 'TRAPPED UNDER ICE'). They even came close to ballad territory with the bleakly beautiful 'FADE TO BLACK', arguably one of the best tracks the band have ever penned. Then came 'MASTER OF PUPPETS' (1986), a masterful collection that rightfully saw METALLICA hailed as one of, if not the, foremost metal act in the world, at the heavier end of the spectrum at least. Opening with the relentless fury of 'BATTERY', followed by the epic, breathtaking dynamics of the title track, the album was almost flawless from start to finish, again using the combination of all-out thrashers alternated with bowel-quaking grinders ('THE THING THAT SHOULD NOT BE', 'WELCOME HOME (SANITARIUM)') to maximum effect. The album went Top 30 in the States without the help of a hit single or even radio play, eventually achieving platinum status. The band subsequently toured with metal godfather, OZZY OSBOURNE, playing to rapturous crowds wherever they went. Disaster struck, however, when the band's tour bus crashed on 27th September '86, BURTON losing his life in the accident. METALLICA decided to carry on, replacing BURTON with JASON NEWSTED (ex-FLOTSAM & JETSAM) and fulfilling their touring commitments. The following summer, the band released an EP of covers, '$5.98 EP – GARAGE DAYS REVISITED', a hotch potch of inspired reworkings from the likes of DIAMOND HEAD, BUDGIE and The MISFITS. The record made both the UK and US Top 30, the US edition containing an extra former KILLING JOKE track (see below). Their next album proper, ' ...AND JUSTICE FOR ALL' (1988), was marred by overly ambitious structures and complex arrangements as well as a poor production, subduing the trademark gut intensity. Nevertheless, there were moments of brilliance, most notably with 'ONE', a distressing first person narrative of a soldier kept alive on a life support machine. The song almost made the UK Top 10, winning the band a Grammy the following year for Best Metal Performance. With the eponymous transatlantic No.1, 'METALLICA' (1991), the band entered the major league alongside the likes of U2 and R.E.M. as one of the biggest rock bands in the world. The aptly named Bob Rock had given the record a cleaner, 'big rock' sound that complemented the more melodic and accessible material contained within. Not that METALLICA had gone limp on the Beavis & Butthead element of their fanbase, 'ENTER SANDMAN' was as crunchingly heavy as ever, yet the single possessed a sufficiently strong melodic hook to see it go Top 5 in the UK. With 'NOTHING ELSE MATTERS', METALLICA really had penned a WISHBONE ASH-esque ballad, replete with strings (!) which saw the band notch up another Top 10 UK hit. After undertaking the biggest tour heavy rock has ever seen (obliterating co-headliners GUNS N' ROSES in the process), the band came back with another work of mature rock majesty, 'LOAD' (1996). From morbid metal to LYNYRD SKYNYRD-style rootsy acoustics, METALLICA once more developed and expanded their sonic palate, gaining widespread acclaim. The album went on to sell almost ten million copies, the band headlining the American Lollapolooza tour to promote it, again blowing most of the other acts away. Not exactly the most prolific of bands, METALLICA surpassed themselves by releasing a successor to 'LOAD' the following year, entitled, appropriately enough, 'RE-LOAD'. While other heavy rock acts flounder under the weight of 90's expectations, METALLICA continue to innovate and energise a tired genre, even, God forbid, cutting their hair(!) in line with their new standing as the post-modern kings of metal. In the Spring of '99, HETFIELD, ULRICH and Co were planning an orchestrated performance with composer MICHAEL KAMEN at the helm of the San Francisco Symphony Orchestra, a 'best of' live album, 'S&M' hitting the bemused public later in the year. • **Songwriters:** ULRICH-HETFIELD, bar other covers on record; BLITZKRIEG (Blitzkrieg) / CRASH COURSE IN BRAIN SURGERY + BREADFAN (Budgie) / AM I EVIL? + THE PRINCE + HELPLESS + IT'S ELECTRIC (Diamond Head) /

LAST CARESS – GREEN HELL + DIE DIE MY DARLING (Misfits) / KILLING TIME (Sweet Savage) / THE SMALL HOURS (Holocaust) / THE WAIT (Killing Joke) / STONE COLD CRAZY (Queen) / SO WHAT (Anti-Nowhere League) / SABBRA CADABRA (Black Sabbath) / Medley: EVIL – CURSE OF THE PHARAOHS – SATAN'S FALL – A CORPSE WITHOUT SOUL – INTO THE COVEN (Mercyful Fate) / LOVERMAN (Nick Cave) / WHISKEY IN THE JAR (Thin Lizzy) / TURN THE PAGE (Bob Seger & The Silver Bullet Band) / TUESDAY'S GONE (Lynyrd Skynyrd) / OVERKILL + STONE DEAD FOREVER + DAMAGE CASE + TOO LATE, TOO LATE (Motorhead) / FREE SPEECH FOR THE DUMB + THE MORE I SEE (Discharge) / ASTRONOMY (Blue Oster Cult).

Album rating: KILL 'EM ALL (*7) / RIDE THE LIGHTNING (*8) / MASTER OF PUPPETS (*9) / . . . AND JUSTICE FOR ALL (*7) / METALLICA (*10) / LOAD (*8) / RE-LOAD (*6) / GARAGE INC. (*5) / S&M (*5)

JAMES HETFIELD (b. 3 Aug'63, Los Angeles) – vocals, rhythm guitar (ex-OBSESSION, etc) / **LARS ULRICH** (b.16 Dec'63, Gentoss, Copenhagen, Denmark) – drums / with **LLOYD GRAND** – guitar

not iss. — Bootleg

Dec 81. (7") **LET IT LOOSE. / KILLING TIME** [-] [ ]

— (Jan'82) **DAVE MUSTAINE** (b.13 Sep'63, La Mesa, Calif.) – lead guitar, co-writer / **RON McGOVNEY** – bass repl. GRAND (JEF WARNER also played guitar in 1982)

— (early '83) **KIRK HAMMETT** (b.18 Nov'62, San Francisco) – lead guitar (ex-EXODUS) repl. MUSTAINE who was fired due to drunkeness. He was soon to form rivals MEGADETH.

— **CLIFF BURTON** (b.10 Feb'62) – bass (ex-TRAUMA) replaced McGOVNEY

Music For Nations — Megaforce

Jul 83. (lp) *(MFN 7) <MRI-069>* **KILL 'EM ALL** [ ] [ ]
– Hit the lights / The four horsemen / Motorbreath / Jump in the fire / (Anesthesia) Pulling teeth / Whiplash / Phantom Lord / No remorse / Seek and destroy / Metal militia. *<US re-iss. Mar86; same> (pic-lp.Aug86; MFN 7P) (cd-iss. Apr87; CDMFN 7) <US re-iss. Feb88 on 'Elektra'+=; 60766>* – Am I evil? / Blitzkrieg. *(re-iss. Nov89 on 'Vertigo' lp/c/cd; 838 142-1/-4/-2)*

Jan 84. (12",12"red) *(12KUT 105) <MRS 04>* **JUMP IN THE FIRE /** *[us-only]* WHIPLASH (special neckbrace mix). / SEEK AND DESTROY (live) / PHANTOM LORD [ ] [ ]
(re-iss. Mar86, 7"sha-pic-d; PKUT 105)

Jul 84. (lp/c) *(MFN/TMFN 27) <769>* **RIDE THE LIGHTNING** [87] [100]
– Fight fire with fire / Ride the lightning / For whom the bell tolls / Fade to black / Trapped under ice / Escape / Creeping death / The call of Ktulu. *(re-iss. Sep86 cd/pic-lp; CDMFN 27/CDMFN 27P) <US re-iss. Oct84 on 'Elektra'; 60396> (re-iss. Nov89 on 'Vertigo' lp/c/cd; 838410-1/-4/-2) (cd re-iss. Apr00 on 'DCC'; GZS 1136)*

Music For Nations — Elektra

Nov 84. (12"pic-d/12") *(P+/12KUT 112)* **CREEPING DEATH. / AM I EVIL. / BLITZKRIEG** [ ] [ ]
(re-iss. Jan87 12"gold/12"blue; GV/CV 12KUT 112)

Mar 86. (lp/pic-d-lp)(c/cd) *(MFN 60/+P)(T/CD MFN 60) <9-60439-1>* **MASTER OF PUPPETS** [41] [29]
– Battery / Master of puppets / The thing that should not be / Welcome home (sanitarium) / Disposable heroes / Leper messiah / Orion / Damage, Inc. *(re-iss. Dec87 d-lp; MFN 60DM) (re-iss. May89 on 'Vertigo' lp/c/cd; 838 141-1/-4/-2)*

— **JASON NEWSTEAD** (b. 4 Mar'63, Battle Creek, Missouri) – bass (ex-FLOTSAM AND JETSAM) repl. CLIFF who was killed in tour bus crash 27 Sep'86 Sweden.

Vertigo — Elektra

Aug 87. (12"ep) *(METAL 1-12) <60757>* **$5.98 EP – GARAGE DAYS RE-REVISITED** [27] [28]
– Helpless / Crash course in brain surgery / The small hours / Last caress – Green hell. *<US+=>* – The Wait. *(re-iss. May90 lp/c/cd; 888 788-1/-4/-2)*

Sep 88. (7") *<69357>* **EYE OF THE BEHOLDER. / BREADFAN** [-] [ ]

Sep 88. (12"ep/cd-ep) *(METAL 2-12/CD2)* **HARVESTER OF SORROW. / BREADFAN. / THE PRINCE** [20] [ ]

Oct 88. (d-lp)(c)(cd) *(VERH/+C 61)(836 062-2) <60812>* **. . .AND JUSTICE FOR ALL** [4] [6] Sep88
– Blackened / . . .And justice for all / Eye of the beholder / One / The shortest straw / Harvester of sorrow / The frayed ends of sanity / To live is to die / Dyers eve.

Feb 89. (7") *<69329>* **ONE. / THE PRINCE** [-] [35]
(3"cd-s+=) – Eye of the beholder.

Mar 89. (7")(10"pic-d) *(MET 5)(METPD 5-10)* **ONE. / SEEK AND DESTROY (live)** [13] [-]
(12")(cd-s) *(MET 5-12)(METCD 5)* – ('A'demo) / For whom the bell tolls (live) / Welcome home (sanitarium) (live).
(12"g-f+=) *(METG 5-12)* – Creeping death (live).

Jul 91. (7"pic-d) *(METAL 7) <64857>* **ENTER SANDMAN. / STONE COLD CRAZY** [5] [16]
(12"+=/12"box+=)(cd-s+=) *(METAL/BX 7-12)(METCD 7)* – Holier than thou.

Aug 91. (cd/c/d-lp) *(510022-2/-4/-1) <61113>* **METALLICA** [1] [1]
– Enter sandman / Sad but true / Holier than thou / The unforgiven / Wherever I may roam / Don't tread on me / Through the never / Nothing else matters / Of wolf and man / The god that failed / My friend of misery / The struggle within.

Nov 91. (7"/7"pic-d) *(METAL/METAP 8) <64814>* **THE UNFORGIVEN. / KILLING TIME** [15] [35]
(12"+=)(cd-s+=) *(METAL 8-12)(METCD 8)* – ('A'demo) / So what.

Apr 92. (7"/7"pic-d) *(META L/P 10) <64770>* **NOTHING ELSE MATTERS. / ENTER SANDMAN (live)** [6] [34] Mar92
(12"+=)(cd-s+=) *(METAL 10-12)(METCD 10)* – Harvester of sorrow (live) / ('A'demo).
(live-cd-s+=) *(METCL 10)* – Stone cold crazy (live) / Sad but true (live).

— On tour only **JOHN MARSHALL (of METAL CHURCH)** repl. injured (burnt) HETFIELD

Oct 92. (7"/7"pic-d) *(METAL/METAP 9) <64741>* **WHEREVER I MAY ROAM. / FADE TO BLACK (live)** [25] [82] Jul92
(pic-cd-s+=) *(METCD 9)* – ('A'demo).
(cd-s) *(METCB 9)* – ('A'side) / Last caress – Am I evil? – Battery (live medley).
(12"+=) *(METAL 9-12)* – ('A'demo).

Oct 92. (c-s) *<64696>* **SAD BUT TRUE / SO WHAT?** [-] [98]

Feb 93. (7") *(METAL 11) <64696>* **SAD BUT TRUE. / NOTHING ELSE MATTERS** [20] [-]
(12"+=,12"pic-d+=)(cd-s+=) *(METAL 11-12)(METCD 11)* – Creeping death (live) / ('A'demo).
(pic-cd-s) *(METCH 11)* – ('A'side) / ('B'live) / ('A'live).

Dec 93. (d-cd/d-c) *(518 726-2/-4) <61594>* **LIVE SHIT: BINGE & PURGE (live)** [54] [26]
– Enter sandman / Creeping death / Harvester of sorrow / Welcome home (sanitarium) / Sad but true / Of wolf and man / Guitar doodle / The unforgiven / And justice for all / Solos (bass/guitar) / Through the never / From whom the bell tolls / Fade to black / Master of puppets / Seek & destroy / Whiplash / Nothing else matters / Wherever I may roam / Am I evil? / Last caress / One / Battery. *(d-c+=)* – The four horsemen / Motorbreath / Stone cold crazy. *(also issued 3 videos + book, etc 'METALLICAN')*

May 96. (10"red-ep) *(METAL 12)* **UNTIL IT SLEEPS. / 2x4 (live) / UNTIL IT SLEPS (Moby remix)** [18] [-]
(cd-s) *(METCD 12)* – ('A'-Herman Melville mix) / 2x4 (live) / F.O.B.D. (aka; Until It Sleeps – demo).
(cd-s) *(METCX 12)* – (first & third tracks) / Kill – Ride (medley; Ride the lightning – No remorse – Hit the lights – The four horsemen – Phantom Lord – Fight fire with fire).

May 96. (c-s) *<64276>* **UNTIL IT SLEEPS / OVERKILL** [-] [10]

Jun 96. (cd/c/d-lp) *(532 618-2/-4/-1) <61923>* **LOAD** [1] [1]
– Ain't my bitch / 2 x 4 / The house Jack built / Until it sleeps / King Nothing / Hero of the day / Bleeding me / Cure / Poor twisted me / Wasting my hate / Mama said / Thorn within / Ronnie / The outlaw torn.

Sep 96. (12"ep) *(METAL 13)* **HERO OF THE DAY / MOULDY (aka HERO OF THE DAY – early demo version). / HERO OF THE DAY (outta b sides mix) / OVERKILL** [17] [-]
(cd-ep) *(METCD 13)* – ('A'side) / Overkill / Damage case / Hero of the day (outta b sides mix).
(cd-ep) *(METCX 13)* – ('A'side) / Stone dead forever / Too late too late / Mouldy (aka 'Hero Of The Day' – early demo version).
(cd-ep) *(METCY 13)* – ('A'side) / Overkill / Damage case / Stone dead forever / Too late too late.
(because of length of above, it also hit 47 in UK album charts)

Oct 96. (c-s) *<64248>* **HERO OF THE DAY / KILL – RIDE (medley)** [-] [60]

Nov 96. (7"pic-d) *(METAL 14)* **MAMA SAID. / AIN'T MY BITCH (live)** [19] [ ]
(cd-s) *(METCD 14)* – ('A'side) / King Nothing (live) / Whiplash (live) / ('A'edit).
(cd-s) *(METCX 14)* – ('A'side) / So what (live) / Creeping death (live) / ('A'-early demo).

Feb 97. (cd-s) **KING NOTHING /** [-] [90]

Nov 97. (7") *(METAL 15) <64126>* **THE MEMORY REMAINS. / FOR WHOM THE BELL TOLLS (Haven't Heard It Yet mix)** [13] [28]
(cd-s) *(METCD 15)* – ('A'side) / Fuel for fire / Memory (demo).
(cd-s) *(METDD 15)* – ('A'side) / The outlaw torn (Unencumbered By Manufacturing Restrictions version) / King Nothing (Tepid mix).

— MARIANNE FAITHFULL supplied backing vocals on above single

Nov 97. (cd/c/d-lp) *(536409-2/-4/-1) <62126>* **RELOAD** [4] [1]
– Fuel / The memory remains / The Devil's dance / Unforgiven II / Better than you / Carpe diem baby / Prince Charming / Bad seed / Where the wild things are / Slither / Low man's lyric / Attitude / Fixxer.

Feb 98. (cd-ep) *(METCD 17) <64114>* **THE UNFORGIVEN II / HELPLESS (live) / The four horsemen (live) / Of wolf and man (live)** [15] [59] Mar98
(cd-ep) *(METDD 17)* – ('A'side) / The thing that should not be (live) / The memory remains (live) / King nothing (live).
(cd-ep) *(METCX 17)* – ('A'side) / No remorse (live) / Am I evil? (live) / The unforgiven II (demo).

Jun 98. (cd-ep) *(METCD 16)* **FUEL / SAD BUT TRUE (live) / NOTHING ELSE MATTERS (live)** [31] [ ]
(cd-ep) *(METDD 16)* – ('A'side) / Wherever I roam (live) / One (live).
(cd-ep) *(METED 16)* – ('A'side) / Until it sleeps (live) / ('A'live) / ('A'demo).

Nov 98. (d-cd/d-c/d-lp) *(538351-2/-4/-1) <62323>* **GARAGE INC.** (the covers) [29] [2]
– Free speech for the dumb / It's electric / Sabba cadabra / Turn the page / Die die my darling / Loverman / Mercyful Fate medley:- Evil – Curse of the pharaohs – Satan's fall – A corpse without soul – Into the coven / Astronomy / Whiskey in the jar / Tuesday's gone / The more I see / Helpless / The small hours / The wait / Crash course in brain surgery / Last caress – Green hell / Am I evil? / Blitzkrieg / Breadfan / The prince / Stone cold crazy / So what? / Killing time / Overkill / Damage case / Stone dead forever / Too late, too late.

Nov 98. (cd-ep) *(566591-2)* **TURN THE PAGE / STONE COLD CRAZY (live) / THE WAIT (live) / BLEEDING ME (live)** [ ] [ ]

Feb 99. (cd-s) *(566855-2)* **WHISKEY IN THE JAR / BLITZKREIG (live) / THE PRINCE (live)** [29] [ ]
(cd-s) *(566857-2)* – ('A'side) / The small hours (live) / Killing time (live).
(cd-s) *(566859-2)* – ('A'side) / Last caress – Green hell (live) / Whiskey in the jar (live).

Jun 99. (cd-ep) *(METCD 20)* **DIE DIE MY DARLING / SABBRA CADABRA (live) / MERCYFUL FATE MEDLEY (live)** [ ] [ ]

Nov 99. (d-cd/d-c) *(546797-2/-4) <62463>* **S&M** (with the San Francisco Symphony Orchestra) [33] [2]
– Ecstasy of gold / Call of the Ktulu / Master of puppets / Of wolf and man / The thing that should not be / Fuel / Memory remains / No leaf clover / Hero of the day / Devil's dance / Bleeding me / Nothing else matters / Until it sleeps / For whom the bell tolls / Human / Wherever I may roam / Outlaw torn / Sad but true / One / Enter sandman / Battery. *(re-iss. Apr00; same)*

Mar 00. (cd-s) *(562696-2) <album cut>* **NO LEAF CLOVER / ('A'-enhanced CD-Rom) / "S&M" Documentary (enhanced first 15 minutes)** [ ] [74] Feb00
(cd-s) *(562697-2)* – ('A'side) / (photo gallery and album lyrics CD-Rom) / "S&M" Documentary (enhanced second 15 minutes).
(cd-s) *(562698-2)* – ('A'side) / (Metallica screensaver) / "S&M" Documentary (enhanced third 15 minutes).

Jul 00. (cd-s) *(0113875HWR) <album cut>* **I DISAPPEAR / I DISAPPEAR (instrumental)** [35] [76] Feb00
(above iss.on 'Edel-Hollywood')

– compilations, others, etc. –

Aug 87. (7"ep/7"pic-ep) *Megaforce; <MRS 04/+P>* **WHIPLASH EP** | - | |
Feb 90. (cd/c) *Vertigo; (642 219-2/-4)* **METALLICA**
– (JUMP IN THE FIRE + CREEPING DEATH singles).
May 90. (6x12"box) *Vertigo; (875 487-1)* **THE GOOD, THE BAD & THE LIVE – THE 6 1/2 YEARS ANNIVERSARY COLLECTION** | 56 | - |
Apr 98. (cd) *Ranch Life; (CRANCH 1)* **BAY AREA THRASHERS**
(also pic-lp on 'Collectors Picture Disc Series'; CPD 014)

METAL URBAIN

Formed: Paris, France . . . 1977 as possibly the first Gallic punk-rock act. The band also took the honour of being the first act to release a record on British independent, 'Rough Trade', the track in question being early '78's 'PARIS MAQUIS'. However, CLAUDE PANIK, ERIC DEBRIS, HERMAN SCHWARTZ and NANCY LUGER (a male!) had already issued a French-only debut 7", 'PANIK', two months previously. Pitting growling, politically motivated lyrics against a background/foreground blast of cheap fuzz noise-guitar and a bizarre syncopated drumbeat, METAL URBAIN were musically distinct from most of their UK cousins. Over the course of the next year or so, the Frenchmen released two more singles, 'HYSTERIE CONNECTIVE' and 'SWEET MARILYN', the latter the first to appear under the moniker of the METAL BOYS. DEBRIS also fronted another 'Rough Trade' act, DR. MIX & THE REMIX, releasing a cover of The Stooges' 'NO FUN'. Towards the end of the decade, DEBRIS and Co tackled another cover, 'I CAN'T CONTROL MYSELF', once a hit for the Troggs. The two acts continued to release material simultaneously although both had disappeared in the space of a year.

Album rating: L'AGE D'OR compilation (*6)

CLAUDE PANIK – vocals / **ERIC DEBRIS** – synthesizer, electric drums / **HERMAN SCHWARTZ** – guitar / male **NANCY LUGER** – guitar

Cobra | not iss.
Oct 77. (7") *(COB 7004)* **PANIK. / LADY COCA COLA** | - | - French |
Rough Trade | not iss.
Jan 78. (7") *(RT 001)* **PARIS MAQUIS. / CLE DE CONTACT** | | - |
Radar | not iss.
Sep 78. (7") *(ADA 20)* **HYSTERIE CONNECTIVE. / PAS POUBELLE** | | - |

— now without DEBRIS who joined METAL BOYS and DR. MIX & THE REMIX

— METAL URBAIN issued two further albums, 'LES HOMMES MORT SONT DANGEREUX' (1980 – Byzz; BLPS 8101) and 'DEAD MEN' (1981 – Byzz; BLPS 8107). The former had a free 7" below on 'Celluloid'

Sep 80. (7") *(CEL 16216)* **HYSTERIE CONNECTIVE (mix 2). / ATLANTIS** | - | - French |

DR. MIX & THE REMIX

— **ERIC DEBRIS** – vocals / **PAT VINCENT** – guitar / **MARK TURNER** – bass, synthesizers / **JEAN-PIERRE** – bass, synthesizers / **NICK TURNER** – drums / **LUCY** – saxophone

Rough Trade | not iss.
Jun 79. (7"; as METAL BOYS) *(RT 016)* **SWEET MARILYN. / FUGUE FOR A DARKENED ISLAND** | | - |
Jun 79. (7") *(RT 017)* **NO FUN. / NO FUN (Dr.Mix alone version)** | | - |
Dec 79. (7") *(RT 032)* **I CAN'T CONTROL MYSELF. / ('A'version)** | | - |
Dec 79. (m-lp) *(ROUGH 6)* **WALL OF NOISE** | | - |
– Out of the question / Grey lagoons / No fun / Six dreams / I can't control myself / Supermen / Sister Ray. *(cd-iss. Aug92 on 'Creation – Rev-Ola';)*

Celluloid | not iss.
Oct 80. (12"ep) *(CEL 6585)* **PSYCHEDELIC DESERT EP** | | - |
Dec 80. (lp; as METAL BOYS) *(CEL 2.6560)* **TOKIO AIRPORT** (John Peel session) | | - |
Oct 81. (lp) *(CEL 6589)* **DR. MIX & THE REMIX** | | - |

— disappeared after above

– (METAL URBAIN) compilations –

1989. (lp/cd) *Fan Club; (FC 011/+CD)* **L'AGE D'OR** | | - |
– Hysterie connective / Ghetto / Cle de contact / Lady Coca Cola / Panik / Futurama / Paris maquis / Pop poubelle / 50-50 / Anarchie au palace / E 202 / Numero / Colt 45 / Lady Coke / No fun / Metal urbain / Atlantis / Creve salope / Snuff movie / Ultra violence / Tango sudiste.
Aug 90. (cd/lp; by DR. MIX & THE REMIX) *A.B.C.; (ABCD/BR 041)* **1979-1982** | | - |

METH O.D.

Formed: Glasgow, Scotland . . . 1993/4 as a punk/garage-meets sleaze outfit fronted by the bearded JIMI D'RANGE (also on lead guitar), TRIPPING ELEFANT on guitar, JOHNNY PANTHER on bass and BOB 'Kinetic' KINARDO on drums. Wired-up and with references to everyone under the sun, this combo of swamptrashers were like Tarantino, Russ Meyer and IGGY POP rolled into one huge joint (or concert hall, take your pick!). New drummer, STEFF LE BATTEUR, was in place for their first stab at a long-player, 'TEXAS GOD STARVATION', a record that was er, full of spirit – or something. The METH O.D. were back the following January on a mail-order 7" EP for North Yorkshire-based 'Induce' imprint – licensed to US fanzine Here Be Monsters entitled 'AVOID FREUD'.

Album rating: TEXAS GOD STARVATION (*6)

JIMI D-RANGE – vocals, lead guitar / **TRIPPING ELEFANT** – guitar, vocals / **JOHNNY PANTHER** – bass, vocals / **BOB 'Kenetic' KINARDO** (b. ROBERT KINNAIRD) – drums, vocals

Human Condition | not iss.
Sep 95. (cd-ep) *(HCCD 0010)* **CYBERBILLY E.P.** | | - |
– Elemental / Suftnazi / Storm in abcup / Yum yum girl.

— **STEFF LE BATTEUR** – drums, vocals; repl.

Dec 96. (cd) *(HCCD 002)* **TEXAS GOD STARVATION** | | - |
– Long distance voyeurism / Produktiv konduktor / First zen temple of New York / Dbug now / High school high / August 22 / Goldigger / Big dipper / Kaptain Clearview / Bastard Tarantino.
(below licensed to 'Here Be Monsters')

Induce | not iss.
Jan 97. (7"ep) *(IND/HBM 02)* **AVOID FREUD** | | - |
– dBug / Mindmaster / Bastard Tarantino / Return of the dreaded spaceship.

— METH O.D. are now defunct

METHODS OF MAYHEM

Formed: Los Angeles, California, USA . . . early 1999 by erstwhile MOTLEY CRUE drummer and all round notorious cock-rocker TOMMY LEE, alongside DANNY LOHNER, KEN ANDREWS, SCOT KIRKLAND and CHRIS CHANEY. For METHODS OF MAYHEM's eponymous debut set later that year, LEE gathered together a motley crew of a more fashionably hip-hop bent including TiLo, SNOOP DOGG, KID ROCK, CRYSTAL METHOD, FRED DURST (of LIMP BIZKIT fame) LIL' KIM, MIXMASTER MIKE and even GEORGE CLINTON himself. Tracing the same lineage that runs way back in the day to AEROSMITH's born-again head to head with RUN DMC, MOM set out prove that metal and rap were natural bed fellows through their similar penchant for girls, partying and general obnoxiousness. If it was a relative success then that was at least partly because it was interchangeable with a large portion of the rap-metal currently saturating the market and partly because such a stellar cast were bound to come up with something of interest. And if it didn't generate quite as much headlines as his adventures with PAMMY ANDERSON, at least the record proved LEE was attempting to move with the times.

Album rating: METHODS OF MAYHEM (*5)

TILO – rapper / **TOMMY LEE** (b. THOMAS LEE BASS, 3 Oct'62, Athens, Greece) – drums (ex-MOTLEY CRUE) / **DANNY LOHNER + KEN ANDREWS** – guitars / **SCOTT KIRKLAND** – keyboards / **CHRIS CHANEY** – bass / plus guests **CRYSTAL METHOD, FRED DURST, LIL' KIM, KID ROCK, SNOOP DOGG, GEORGE CLINTON + MIXMASTER MIKE**

Universal | Universal
Jan 00. (12") *<155698>* **GET NAKED** | - | |
Feb 00. (cd) *<(112020-2)>* **METHODS OF MAYHEM** | | 71 |
– Who the hell cares (featuring SNOOP DOGG) / Hypocritical / Anger management / Get naked / New skin (featuring (KID ROCK) / Proposition fuck you (featuring FILTHEE IMMIGRANTS) / Crash / Metamorphosis / Narcotic / Mr. Nosomothers***s (featuring GEORGE CLINTON) / Spun.
Aug 00. (cd-s) *<155733>* **NEW SKIN** | - | |

MIGHTY MIGHTY BOSSTONES

Formed: Boston, Massachusetts, USA . . . 1985 as an 8-piece SPECIALS/MADNESS type ska-rock led by "cool" singer, DICKY BARRETT, an ex user of that nose-numbing powder, cocaine. The line-up was completed by NATE ALBERT, JOE GITTLEMAN, JOE SIROIS, TIM BURTON, DENNIS BROCKENBOROUGH, KEVIN LENEAR and dancer BEN CARR. The forefathers of the currently popular so-called US ska scene, they debuted in 1990 with the 'DEVILS NIGHT OUT' album. However, it would take three years before some kind of commercial breakthrough as 'DON'T KNOW HOW TO PARTY' cracked the US Top 200. The 1994 follow-up, 'QUESTION THE ANSWERS', sold a little better as the group set up their own 'Big Rig' label soon after. Following in the wake of NO DOUBT and RANCID's Stateside success, The MIGHTY MIGHTY BOSSTONES powered their way into the US Top 30 with 1997's 'LET'S FACE IT'. Released a year later in the UK (where Kerrang~! had surprisingly given them column inches) and with the help of a Top 20 hit, 'THE IMPRESSION THAT I GET', it even made the British Top 40. Following the release of stop-gap concert set, 'LIVE FROM THE MIDDLE EAST' (that's Boston, USA, folks), the 'BOSSTONES commanded the faithful to 'PAY ATTENTION' (2000) as they gave another hard-earned lesson in brassy, knees-up Nth generation ska-punk. While wielding a little more gravitas than its predecessor, the record ducked and dived in all the right places with a fair smattering of hooks and a more experimental bent. • **Covers:** SWEET EMOTION (Aerosmith) / AIN'T TALKIN' 'BOUT LOVE (Van Halen) / ENTER SANDMAN (Metallica) / SIMMER DOWN (Bob Marley) / THINK AGAIN (Minor Threat) / etc.

Album rating: DEVILS NIGHT OUT (*6) / MORE NOISE AND OTHER DISTURBANCES (*5) / DON'T KNOW HOW TO PARTY (*4) / QUESTION THE ANSWERS (*6) / SKA-CORE, THE DEVIL AND MORE mini (*5) / LET'S FACE IT (*6) / LIVE FROM THE MIDDLE EAST (*3) / PAY ATTENTION (*6)

DICKY BARRETT – vocals / **NATE ALBERT** (b.1971) – guitar / **JOE GITTLEMAN** (b.1968) – bass / **JOE SIROIS** (b.1971) – drums / **KEVIN LENEAR** (b.1970) – saxophone / **TIM BURTON** (b.1964) – saxophone / **DENNIS BROCKENBOROUGH** (b.1970) – trombone / **BEN CARR** (b.1968) – dancer

Emergo Emergo

Nov 90. (cd) *(EM 9358-1)* **DEVILS NIGHT OUT**
– Devils night out / Howwhywuz, howwhyyam / Drunks and children / Hope I never lose my wallet / Haji / The bartender's song / Patricia / The cave / Do something crazy / A little bit ugly. *(lp-iss.Mar93 on 'Roadrunner'; RR 9358-1) (lp re-iss. Dec96 on 'Taang'; TAANG 044LP) (re-iss. May98 10"d-lp+=/cd; TAANG 044 D/CD)* – WHERE'D YOU GO EP. *(cd re-iss. May98 on 'Roadrunner'; RR 9358-2)*

Taang Taang

Jan 92. (7"ep/cd-ep) *<(TAANG 048/+CD)>* **WHERE'D YOU GO? EP**
– Where'd you go? / Sweet emotion / Enter sandman / Do something crazy / Ain't talkin' 'bout love. *(re-iss. May98; same)*

Jun 92. (lp/cd) *<(TAANG 060/+CD)>* **MORE NOISE AND OTHER DISTURBANCES**
– Awfully quiet / Where'd you go? / Dr. D / It can't hurt / What's at stake / Cowboy coffee / I'll drink to that / Guns and the young / He's back / Bad in plaid / They came to Boston. *(re-iss. May98; same)*

Jan 93. (7") **HARDWARE & LUMBER. / SWIRL**

not iss. Dink-Mercury

Mar 93. (m-cd) *<514 551-2>* **SKA CORE THE DEVIL** -
– Someday I suppose / Think again / Lights out / Police beat / Simmer down / Drugs and kittens / I'll drink to that. *(UK-iss.Jan96 & Jun98 on 'Mercury'; same)*

May 93. (cd) *<514 836-2>* **DON'T KNOW HOW TO PARTY** -
– Almost anything goes / Last dead mouse / Someday I suppose / Don't know how to party / Illegal left / Holy smoke / Issachar / Our only weapon / Man without / Seven thirty seven – Shoe glue / Tin soldiers / What was was over. *(UK-iss.Jun98; same)*

Oct 94. (cd) *<522 845-2>* **QUESTION THE ANSWERS** -
– Bronzing the garbage / Hell of a hat / Pictures to prove it / Dollar and a dream / We should talk / Toxic toast / 365 days / Dogs and chaplains / Jump through the hoops / Kinder words / Sad silence / Stand off. *(UK-iss.Jun98 on 'Mercury'; same)*

May 97. (lp) *(RIG 00050-1) <534 472-2>* **LET'S FACE IT** 27
– Noise brigade / The rascal king / Royal oil / The impression that I get / Let's face it / That bug bit me / Another drinkin' song / Numbered days / Break so easily / Nevermind me / Desensitized / 1-2-8. *(cd-iss. May98 on 'Mercury'; 534 472-2)* – hit UK No.40

Mar 97. (7") *(RIG 00050-2)* **THE IMPRESSION THAT I GET. / IS IT**

Big Rig-Mercury Big Rig-Mercury

Apr 98. (c-ep/cd-ep) *(574 843-4/-2)* **THE IMPRESSION THAT I GET / DESENSITIZED / IS IT / STORM HIT** 12
(cd-ep) *(568 815-2)* –

Jun 98. (c-s) *(566 108-4)* **THE RASCAL KING / A SAD SILENCE** 63
(cd-s+=) *(566 111-2)* – Stand-off.
(cd-s) *(566 109-2)* – ('A'side) / At it again / Hell of a hat.

Nov 98. (cd) *<(558 900-2)>* **LIVE FROM THE MIDDLE EAST (live in Cambridge, Boston)** Sep98
– 1-2-8 / Do somethin' crazy / He's back / Devil's night out / Kinder words / Noise brigade / The rascal king / Hell of a hat / Holy smoke / Hope I never lose my wallet / I'll drink to that / Royal oil / Cowboy coffee / Doves and civilians / Let's face it / Howwhywuz, howwhyam / Dr. D / Where'd you go? / Seven thirty seven – Shoe clue / The impression that I get / Someday I suppose / Lights out.

May 00. (cd/lp) *(542451-2/-1)* **PAY ATTENTION** 74
– Let me be / The skelton song / All things considered / So sad to say / Allow them / High school dance / Over the eggshells / She just happened / Finally / I know more / Riot on Broad Street / One million reasons / Bad news and bad breaks / Temporary trip / Where you come from / The day he didn't die.

MILLENCOLIN

Formed: Orebro, Sweden . . . late 80's by NIKOLA, ERIK and MATHIAS. Named after a skateboarding move and inspired by West Coast hardcore legends like NOFX and BAD RELIGION, the Swedes initially began writing in their own language before switching to English. Subsequently joined by LARZON, the band soon signed to domestic label 'Burning Heart', through whom they issued debut set, 'LIFE ON A PLATE' (1995). The lads soon came to the attention of BRETT GUREWITZ (of BAD RELIGION) who signed them to his US-based 'Epitaph' imprint. The first non-American band to be bestowed with such an honour, MILLENCOLIN released the transitional 'FOR MONKEYS' album in 1997. After completion of the accompanying tour, the band took a year off to do their own thing. NIKOLA guested on FIRESIDE mainman KRISTOFER ASTROM's inaugural solo set, an experience which he maintains has improved his songwriting ability. It was a much matured MILLENCOLIN that regrouped for the GUREWITZ-produced 'PENNYBRIDGE PIONEERS' (2000) – not yet released in the UK – thankfully jettisoning the white-boy ska pretensions of old for a more focused punk sound. • **Covered:** KNOWLEDGE (Operation Ivy) / WHOLE LOT LESS (Sub Society) / COOLIDGE (Descendents) / THAT'S UP TO ME (Scumback) / EVERY BREATH YOU TAKE (Police) / 9 TO 5 (Dolly Parton) / ISRAELITES (Desmond Dekker).

Album rating: LIFE ON A PLATE (*6) / SOME OLD TUNES (*6) / FOR MONKEYS (*5) / THE MELANCHOLY COLLECTION compilation (*6)

NIKOLA – vocals, bass / **ERIK** – guitar / **MATHIAS** – guitar / **LARZON** – drums

Burning Heart Epitaph

Nov 94. (cd-ep) *(BHR 006-2)* **USE YOUR NOSE EP** -
(7"ep-iss.Nov96; BHRMOCLIFF 001)

Oct 94. (cd-ep) *(BHR 016-2)* **SKAUCH EP** -
(7"ep-iss.Nov96; BHRMOCLIFF 002)

Feb 95. (m-cd) *(BHR 019)* **TINY TUNES** -

Mar 95. (cd-ep) *(BHR 021-2)* **DA STRIKE EP** -
(7"ep-iss.Nov96; BHRMOCLIFF 003)

Oct 95. (cd-s) *(BHR 032CDS)* **STORY OF MY LIFE /** -
(7"ep-iss.Aug96 on 'Rugger Bugger'; DUMP 033) (7"ep re-iss. Nov96; BHRMOCLIFF 004)

Oct 95. (cd) *(BHR 033CD) <86467-2>* **LIFE ON A PLATE** Dec95
– Bullion / Olympic / Move your car / Killercrush / Friends 'til the end / Story of my life / Jellygoose / Replay / Vulcan ears / Dr. Jackal & Mr. Hide / Softworld / Buzzer / Ace Frehley / Airhead. *(lp-iss.Jun97; BHRMOCLIFF 008)*

Apr 96. (cd-s) *(BHR 039CD)* **MOVE YOUR CAR** -

Jun 96. (cd) *(BHR 019CD)* **SOME OLD TUNES** -
– Mr. Clean / Chiquita chaser / Diznee time / Domestic subway / Fazil's friend / House of blend / Da strike / Mystic reptile / Dance craze / Einstein crew / Take it or leave it. *(lp-iss.Jun97; BHRMOCLIFF 007) <US-iss.Sep98; 86545-2>*
(above might be 'TINY TUNES' re-issued)

Apr 97. (cd-s) *(BHR 054CD) <86507-2>* **LOZIN' MUST EP** May97
– Lozin' must / Vixen / Story of my life / Israelites.

Apr 97. (cd/lp) *(BHR 056 CD/LP) <86503-2/-1>* **FOR MONKEYS** May97
– Puzzle / Lozin' must / Random I am / Boring planet / Monkey boogie / Twenty-two / Black gold / Trendy winds / Otis / Lights out / Entrance at Rudebrook / Lowlife.

Mar 99. (cd)(lp) *(BHR 087CD)(BHRMOCLIFF 022)* **THE MELANCHOLY COLLECTION** (compilation) -
– In a room / Pain / Shake me / Melack / Nosepicker / Use your nose / Flippin' beans / Yellow dog / Knowledge / Whole lot less / Coolidge / That's up to me / Bit of Muslim / Melancholy protection / Shake me (live) / Niap / Every breath you take / 9 to 5 / Dragster / Elf and his zippo / Israelites / Vixen.

Jun 00. (cd-ep) **FOX / KEMP / PENGUINS & POLARBEARS (live) / NO CIGAR (live)** -

Tralla

Jul 00. (7") *(TREP 090)* **FOX. / KEMP**

Jul 00. (7") *(TREP 185)* **PENGUINS & POLARBEARS (live). / NO CIGAR (live)**

Golf not iss.

May 01. (m-cd) *(CDHOLE 037)* **MILLENCOLIN / MIDTOWN** -
– No cigar / Blackeye / Buzzer / Penguins and polar bears (video) / Fox (video) / (others by Midtown).

MINDFUNK

Formed: New York, USA . . . late 1989 by JASON COPPOLA and PATRICK R. DUBAR, recruiting REED ST. MARK, LOUIS J. SVITEK and JOHN MONTE, the latter two having played together in the mid-80's as M.O.D. (METHOD OF DESTRUCTION). This outfit were a spin-off of BILLY MILANO's S.O.D. (STORMTROOPERS OF DEATH) who also comprised members of ANTHRAX and NUCLEAR ASSAULT. M.O.D. issued three hardcore albums for 'Noise Int.', before calling it a day. MINDFUNK, meanwhile, were signed to 'Epic US' amid a wave of hype at the height of the thrash/metal/funk crossover. Touted as the ultimate in cross genre innovation, when the self-titled debut finally arrived it somehow failed to live up to its tantalising pre-publicity. While the likes of 'SUGAR AIN'T SO SWEET' and 'RIDE AND DRIVE' were heady, visceral stuff, the group were found lacking in the songwriting department. With the album failing to sell as much as expected, the group were promptly given their collective P45, a disheartening experience which no doubt informed the title of their follow-up effort, 'DROPPED' (1993), released on 'Megaforce'. Despite failing to gain the recognition afforded to peers like FAITH NO MORE etc, the group persevered, issuing 'PEOPLE WHO FELL FROM THE SKY' in 1995.

Album rating: MINDFUNK (*7) / DROPPED (*7) / PEOPLE WHO FELL FROM THE SKY (*5) / M.O.D.: U.S.A. FOR M.O.D. (*7) / SURFIN' M.O.D. (*4) / GROSS MISCONDUCT (*5) / RHYTHM OF FEAR (*5) / DEVOLUTION (*4) / LOVED BY THOUSANDS, HATED BY MILLIONS (*5) / DICTATED AGGRESSION (*5)

M.O.D.

BILLY MILANO – vocals (also of STORMTROOPERS OF DEATH; see ANTHRAX) / **LOUIS J. SUITEK** – lead guitar / **JOHN MONTE** – bass / **TIM MALLARBE** – drums

Noise Int. Caroline

Sep 87. (lp/c) *(N 0089/0090) <CAROL/+C 1344>* **U.S.A. FOR M.O.D.**
– Aren't you hungry / Get a real job / I executioner / Don't feed the bears / Ballad of Dio / Trash or be trashed / Let me out / Bubble butt / You're beat / Bushwackteas / Man of your dreams / That noise / Dead man – Most – Captain Crunch / Jim Gordon / Imported society / Spandex enormity / Short but sweet / Parents / Confusion / You're X'ed * / A.I.D.S. / Ruptured nuptuals / Ode to Harry / Hate tank. *(re-iss. Oct89 lp/c; NUK/ZCNUK 089) (re-iss. Feb92 on 'Music For Nations' cd+=*/c/lp; CD/T+/MFN 126) (cd-iss. Aug95 on 'Bulletproof'; CDVEST 61)*

Aug 88. (lp) *<CAROL 1359>* **SURFIN' M.O.D.** -
– Goldfish from Hell / Totally Narley talking by Katrina & Bill / Surfin' U.S.A. / More Narley talking by Katrina & Bill / Surf's up / Sargeant Drexell theme / Billy, Katrina & Alex spot Oofus / Party animal / Still more Narley talk and the party / Crash scene / Bill's big love scene / Color my world / Bill and Katrina split up and the big party scene / Scout / The big final. *(UK cd-iss. Aug95 on 'Bulletproof'; CDVEST 60)* – Surfin' U.S.A. / Surf's up / Sargeant Drexell theme / Mr. Oofus / Party animal / Color my world / Shout / New song.

Roadrunner not iss.

Dec 88. (7"ep/cd-ep) *(RR 2452-1/-2)* **SURFIN' M.O.D.** -
– Surfin' U.S.A. / Surf's up / Sgt. Drexall / Mr. Oofus.

Noise Int. Caroline

Apr 89. (cd/c/lp) *(CD/ZC+/NUK 133) <CAROL 1360>* **GROSS MISCONDUCT**
– No hope / No glove no love / True colors / Accident scene / Godzula / E factor / Gross misconduct / Satan's cronies / In the city / Come as you are / Vents / Theme / P.B.M. / The ride. *(cd re-iss. Aug95 on 'Bulletproof'; CDVEST 58)*

—— disbanded soon after above

MINDFUNK

LOUIS + JOHN recruited **PAT DUBAR** – vocals / **JASON COPPOLA** – rhythm guitar / **REED ST. MARK** – drums (ex-CELTIC FROST)

Epic Epic

Mar 91. (cd/c/lp) *(467790-2/-4/-1)* <46902> **MINDFUNK**
– Sugar ain't so sweet / Ride and drive / Bring it on / Big house / Burning / Fire / Blood runs red / Sister blue / Woke up this morning / Innocence / Touch you.

Nov 91. (12"ep/cd-ep) *(657618-6/-2)* **TOUCH YOU / BANG TIME. / VELVET JANE / SURPRISE TOUCH**

— **JASON EVERMAN** – guitar (ex-NIRVANA), repl. COPPOLA + ST. MARK

Megaforce Megaforce

May 93. (cd/c/lp) *<(CD/T+/ZAZ 3)>* <6914> **DROPPED**
– Goddess / Closer / Drowning / In the way eye / Zootiehead / Wisteria / Mama, Moses and me / 11 ton butterfly / Hogwallow / Billygoat / Hollow.

Music For Nations Megaforce

Mar 95. (cd) *(CDMFN 182)* **PEOPLE WHO FELL FROM THE SKY**

M.O.D.

MILANO with **TIM McMURTIE** – rhythm guitar, vocals / **DAVE CHAVARRE** –

Music For Nations Megaforce

Nov 92. (cd/c/lp) *(CD/T+/MFN 145)* <6909> **RHYTHM OF FEAR**
– Objection – Dead end / Get up and dance / Step by step / Rhymestein / Minute of courage / Irresponsible / Override negative / I, the earth / Spy vs. spy / Intruder / Time Jimmy's revenge / Rally (NYC). *(cd re-iss. Aug95 on 'Bulletproof'; CDMVEST 59)*

Music For Nations Energy

Jun 94. (cd/c/lp) *(CD/T+/MFN 163)* <81109> **DEVOLUTION**
– Land of the free / Devolution / Repent / The angry man / Resist / Crash 'n' burn / Supertouch / Rock tonite / Behind / Running / Time bomb / Unhuman race.

— added **AMASA JUNIS** – vocals / **JOE YOUNG** – guitar, vocals

Jun 96. (cd) *(CDMFN 201)* <1975> **DICTATED AGGRESSION**
– Dictated aggression / Silence your sin / Damaged / Shot glass / Stand or fall / One was Johnny / Nation / Empty vision / In my shoes / U.S. dreams / Just got fired / Whiteout / Brutal beats.

– compilations, etc. –

Nov 95. (cd) *Bulletproof; (CDVEST 66) / Megaforce; <1967>* **LOVED BY THOUSANDS, HATED BY MILLIONS**
– Noize / Aren't you hungry / Spandex enormity / A.I.D.S. / Hate tank '94 / Goldfish from Hell / Surfin' U.S.A. / Mr. Oofus / No glove no love / True colours / In the city / Get up and dance / Rhymestein / Irresponsible / Rally (N.Y.C.) / Ballad of Dio / Bubble butt / Short but sweet / Ode to Harry / Vents / Theme / Bonanza / Buckshot blues / Clubbin' seals / U.S. dreams / He's dead Jim / Get the boot. *(re-iss. Feb99 on 'S.P.V.'; 0761863-2)*

Mar 99. (cd) *S.P.V.; (SPV 07618402)* **U.S.A. FOR M.O.D. / GROSS MISCONDUCT**

Aug 99. (cd) *S.P.V.; (SPV 07618142)* **SURFIN' M.O.D. / RHYTHM OF FEAR**

MINDSTORM

Formed: Canada . . . 1986 by TRAVIS MITCHELL, who recruited AL RODGERS, RUSS BOSWELL, GARY MOFFAT and BRUCE MOFFAT. This quintet released two albums of quality yet highly derivative ZEPPELIN-esque hard-rock, the eponymous 'MINDSTORM' (1987) and 'BACK TO REALITY' (1991) failing to make much of an impact outside their domestic rock scene. They continued to release records in their homeland including two albums 'MINDSTORM III' and 'ZEN'.

Album rating: MINDSTORM (*5) / BACK TO REALITY (*5)

TRAVIS MITCHELL – vocals / **AL RODGERS** – guitar / **RUSS BOSWELL** – bass / **GARY MOFFAT** – keyboards / **BRUCE MOFFAT** – drums

not iss. Aquarius

1987. (lp) <AQCD 545> **MINDSTORM** [-]
– See the future / Go my way / Find the way / Witch doctor / Live hard / End of the line / Whispers / Live to die / One of those days. *(UK-iss.Feb91 on 'Provogue' cd/c/lp; PRD/PRC/PRL 7023-2/-4/-1)*

— added **IAN AUGER** – guitar, keyboards + **MARK CHICHKIN** – guitar

Provogue Provogue

May 91. (cd/c/lp) *<(PRD/PRC/PRL 7012-2/-4/-1)>* **BACK TO REALITY**
– Back to reality / Babylon / Neptune / Love goes blind / Make ends meet / F.T. world / Depths of time / Feelin' satisfied / Burnin' star / Chemical reaction.

Sep 91. (cd-s) *(PRS 1029-2)* **LOVE GOES BLIND /**

1990's. (cd) **MINDSTORM III** [-] [-] Canada
– Sweet lovin' / Weeping widow / Days gone bye / Time it takes / Secret dreams / Oh hell hallelujah / Never get away / Glass windows / Eyes of the times / In the shadows.

1990's. (cd) **ZEN** [-] [-] Canada
– Intro (in your face) / Power pills and effects / Ele mental / Sunny / Break the system / Nitro / Hit me (Tylor's theme) / Fat ass house bitch / Underground flowers / Reverse – Rebel / Mega / Dark thoughts / Ko vs. Ju / Behind the will.

1990's. (cd-s) **BREAK THE SYSTEM / BREAK THE SYSTEM (terpo d'n'b remix) / BREAK THE SYSTEM (stereoman cycleplanet mix) / URBAN FLOAT** [-] [-] Canada

1990's. (cd-s) **ROCK THE HOUSE / HELP ME TO BELIEVE / MOVE THE COLORS** [-] [-] Canada

Zodiac MINDWARP & The LOVE REACTION

Formed: Canada . . . 1985 by former graphic designer MARK MANNING (aka ZODIAC MINDWARP) and his backing group The LOVE REACTION. A 'Mad Max' style mystical hippy/biker-rock pastiche, this tongue-in-cheek troupe were completed by COBALT STARGAZER, HAGGIS (aka KID CHAOS), FLASH EVIL BASTARD and BOOM BOOM KABOOMSKI, their influences taking in everything from STEPPENWOLF to MC5 and of course, MOTORHEAD. Relocating to Britain shortly after their inception, the group soon signed to Dave Balfe's 'Food' label. A lone single, 'WILD CHILD' appeared in summer '85, while a debut mini-lp, 'HIGH PRIEST OF LOVE' was released a year later. By this juncture, SLAM THUNDERHIDE (!) and PAUL BAILEY had replaced KABOOMSKI and HAGGIS respectively, the latter going off to join The CULT. MINDWARP and Co. only really set to work on world domination following a move to 'Mercury' and the Top 20 success of the infectiously dumb 'PRIME MOVER', with its greasy riffs and chest-beating chorus. The low-rent innuendo of 'BACKSEAT EDUCATION' was next up, the single backed with the legendary 'LAGER WOMAN FROM HELL~'! The accompanying album, 'TATTOOED BEAT MESSIAH' (1988) was an enjoyable enough romp if hardly announcing rock's second coming, the record hitting the Top 20 but ultimately failing to live up to the considerable hype which marked its release. Inevitably perhaps, the group soon fell apart after their brief period of late 80's fame, although MINDWARP later reformed the band with STARGAZER, THUNDERHIDE and new recruit SUZY X (aka RICHARD). The revamped outfit signed to the independent 'Musidisc' label, although the subsequent album, 'HOODLUM THUNDER' (1992) and mini-set 'MY LIFE STORY' (1992), failed to generate much interest.
• **Songwriters:** All written by MANNING, except BORN TO BE WILD (Steppenwolf).

Album rating: HIGH PRIEST OF LOVE (*6) / TATTOOED BEAT MESSIAH (*6) / HOODLUM THUNDER (*5) / MY LIFE STORY mini (*4)

ZODIAC MINDWARP (b.MARK MANNING) – vocals / **COBALT STARGAZER** – guitar / **HAGGIS** (aka KID CHAOS) – bass / **FLASH EVIL BASTARD** (b.JAN CYRKA) – guitar / **BOOM BOOM KABOOMSKI** – drums

Food not iss.

Aug 85. (12") *(SNAK 4)* **WILD CHILD. /** [-]
(re-iss. Jun86; same)

— **SLAM THUNDERHIDE** – drums repl. KABOOMSKI

Jul 86. (m-lp) *(WARP 001)* **HIGH PRIEST OF LOVE** [-]
– High priest of love / Hymn of the speed kings / High heel Heaven / Dangerous / Kick start me for love / Wild child (second attempt). *(cd-iss. Jan89; WARP 001CD)*

— guest **PAUL BAILEY** – bass repl. KID CHAOS who joined The CULT

Mercury Mercury

Apr 87. (7") *(ZOD 1)* **PRIME MOVER. / LAUGHING IN THE FACE OF DEATH** [19]
(12"+=) *(ZOD 1-12)* – Hangover from Hell.

Nov 87. (7"/c-s) *(ZOD 2/+22)* **BACKSEAT EDUCATION. / WHORE OF BABYLON** [49]
(12"+=)(cd-s+=) *(ZOD 2-12)(ZODCD 2)* – Lager woman from Hell / Messin' wit.

Feb 88. (lp/c)(cd) *(ZOD LP/MC 1)(832729-2)* **TATTOOED BEAT MESSIAH** [20]
– Prime mover / Skull spark joker / Backseat education / Let's break the law / Driving on holy gasoline / Bad girl city / Untamed stare / Tattooed beat messiah / Spasm gang / Planet girl / Kid's stuff / Messianic reprise. *(c+=/cd+=)* – Born to be wild. *(cd re-iss. Jan00 on 'Spectrum'; 554179-2)*

Mar 88. (7") *(ZOD 3)* **PLANET GIRL. / DOG FACE DRIVER** [63] [-]
(12"+=) *(ZOD 3-12)* – Go-go baby dreams how / Born to be wild.
(pic-cd-s+=) *(ZODCD 3)* – Go-go baby dreams how / Prime mover.

not iss.

Oct 91. (12"/cd-s; as ZODIAC YOUTH) **FAST FORWARD THE FUTURE. / ('A'mix)** [-]
(above as "ZODIAC-YOUTH":- YOUTH = ex-Killing Joke)

— **MINDWARP, STARGAZER + THUNDERHIDE** recruited new member **SUZY X** (aka RICHARD) – bass replaced BAILEY + JAN (later went solo)

Musidisc not iss.

Dec 91. (cd-ep) *(10973-2)* **ELVIS DIED FOR YOU** [-]

Feb 92. (cd/c/lp) *(10864-2/-4/-1)* **HOODLUM THUNDER** [-]
– Elvis / T.B.L.R. / Feed my Frankenstein / Trash adonna / Airline highway / Chainsaw / President / Doctor Jekyll / Hoodlum thunder / Meanstreak.

Jun 92. (12"ep) *(10922-6)* **MEANSTREAK. / TRASH MADONNA / FORCE OF NATURE** [-]
(cd-ep+=) *(10922-2)* – ('A'version).

Nov 92. (m-cd/m-lp) *(10983-2/-1)* **MY LIFE STORY** [-]
– Porno movies I love you / Raw & bleeding / Holy gasoline / Slut freak / My life story.

Stress not iss.

Jun 94. (12") *(12STR 32)* **TOO. /** [-]

– compilations, etc. –

Aug 93. (cd) *Raw Fruit; (FRSCD 011)* **THE FRIDAY ROCK SHOW SESSIONS LIVE AT READING '87 (live)** [-]

MINISTRY

Formed: Chicago, Illinois, USA . . . 1981 by ex-SPECIAL EFFECT member AL JOURGENSEN. The latter bunch included FRANKIE NARDIELLO (who'd replaced TOM HOFFMAN), MARTY SORENSON and HARRY RUSHAKOFF, this synth-pop aggregation releasing a couple of 7" singles and a soundtrack album at the turn of the decade. Continuing in this vein, JOURGENSEN co-formed the 'Wax Trax' label and issued a debut MINISTRY 12" in 1982, 'COLD LIFE'. A further string of limp electro singles and a debut album, 'WITH SYMPATHY' (1983; European title 'WORK FOR LOVE') followed, before JOURGENSEN adopted a decidedly harder electronic sound on 'TWITCH' (1986). Around the same time, the MINISTRY mainman initiated a number of offshoot projects, the most high profile being The REVOLTING COCKS, who included in the ranks RICHARD 23, LUC VAN ACKER (the former later replaced by CHRIS CONELLY of FINI TRIBE). JOURGENSEN was said to have described this bunch as "Disco For Psychopaths", the 12", 'NO DEVOTION' and the long-player, 'BIG SEXY LAND' were aural proof. Another single, 'YOU OFTEN FORGET' (1987) was equally controversial, having already annoyed the PMRC (Parental Music Resource Center) with their overtly blasphemous debut. A live album, 'GODDAMNED SON OF A BITCH' was The REVOLTING COCKS next release in 1988, drummer BILL RIEFLIN now a steady part of both JOURGENSEN's groups. Meanwhile, MINISTRY had recruited bassist PAUL BARKER (and brother ROLAND BARKER), the outfit consolidated their harsher industrial approach with the vicious 1989 set, 'LAND OF RAPE AND HONEY'. To end the decade, MINISTRY unleashed yet another uncompromisingly bleak set of industrial grinding, 'THE MIND IS A TERRIBLE THING TO TASTE', while four months later, The REVOLTING COCKS offered some light relief with a decidedly unsympathetic version of Olivia Newton John's '(LET'S GET) PHYSICAL'. This was lifted from parent album, 'BEERS, STEERS AND QUEERS', the title track a brilliant must-hear send-up of backwoods American perversion. The REVOLTING COCKS gained even more notoriety when a proposed tour (which was to include onstage strippers and livestock) was the subject of an outraged House Of Commons discussion. Having briefly collaborated with JELLO BIAFRA (ex-DEAD KENNEDYS) on a project entitled LARD, JOURGENSEN released a one-off single under the 1000 HOMO DJ's banner, the main track being a cover of Black Sabbath's 'SUPERNAUT'. With the addition of guitarist MIKE SCACCIA and the unhinged guest vocals of GIBBY HAYNES (Butthole Surfers), MINISTRY recorded arguably their finest moment to date, 'JESUS BUILT MY HOTROD'. This was closely followed by MINISTRY's breakthrough Top 40 (on both sides of the Atlantic!) album, 'PSALM 69: THE WAY TO SUCCEED AND THE WAY TO SUCK EGGS', a highly regarded set which saw the group veering towards searing sonic metal. A Top 50 single, 'N.W.O.' followed a successful near headlining slot on the Lollapalooza' 1992 tour, PAUL BARKER also moonlighting in yet another MINISTRY offshoot, LEAD INTO GOLD (releasing the 'AGE OF REASON' a follow-up to 1990's mini-cd 'CHICKS & SPEED'). A year later, The REVOLTING COCKS returned with their inimitably twisted brand of black humour, a version of Rod Stewart's 'DO YA THINK I'M SEXY' one of the highlights of their 1993 album, 'LINGER FICKEN' GOOD'. The two main MINISTRY men, AL JOURGENSEN and PAUL BARKER, replaced the departing RIEFLIN with RAY WASHAM and moved the operation to Texas (JOURGENSEN set up a country label). Late in 1995, after AL escaped a drugs bust, MINISTRY ventured even further into metal territory with the 'FILTH PIG' opus, a collection that contained a murderous version of Bob Dylan's 'LAY LADY LAY'. In 1999, AL, PAUL and the MINISTRY were growling once again at the music industry, 'DARK SIDE OF THE SPOON' (redneck punk, et AL), however the album failed to make its commercial impact – sadly, the release was around the same time as guitarist WILLIAM TUCKER committed suicide by slashing his throat.

Album rating: WORK FOR LOVE (aka WITH SYMPATHY) (*5) / TWITCH (*5) / LAND OF RAPE AND HONEY (*7) / THE MIND IS A TERRIBLE THING TO TASTE (*6) / IN CASE YOU DIDN'T FEEL LIKE SHOWING UP (*4) / PSALM 69: HOW TO SUCCEED AND HOW TO SUCK EGGS (*8) / FILTH PIG (*6) / DARK SIDE OF THE SPOON (*8) / Revolting Cocks: BIG SEXY LAND (*6) / YOU GODAMNED SON OF A BITCH (*5) / BEERS, STEERS & QUEERS (*7) / LINGER FICKEN' GOOD . . . AND OTHER BARNYARD ODDITIES (*6)

SPECIAL EFFECT

AL JOURGENSEN (b. 9 Oct'58, Havana, Cuba) – guitar / **FRANKIE NARDIELLO** – vocals; repl. TOM HOFFMAN / **MARTY SORENSON** – bass / **HARRY RUSHAKOFF** – drums

not iss. | Special Effect

1979. (7"ep) <2955> **MOOD MUSIC EP** [-] [ ]
– I know a girl / Vertigo feeling / Innocense / Dress me dolls.

1980. (lp; soundtrack) <008028> **TOO MUCH SOFT LIVING** [-] [ ]

— also flexidisc from 'Praxis' magazine; HEADACHE. / NUCLEAR GLOOM

not iss. | Thermidor

Oct 81. (7") <T 5> **EMPTY HANDED. / THE HEAT** [-] [ ]

MINISTRY

AL JOURGENSEN – guitar, keyboards, synthesizers, vocals / **LAMONT WELTON** – bass / **STEVO** – drums

Situation 2 | Wax Trax

Mar 82. (12"m) *(SIT 17T)* <110072X> **COLD LIFE. / I'M FALLING / COLD LIFE (dub) / PRIMENTAL** [ ] [ ]

— AL used musicians on next lp; **SHAY JONES** – vocals / **WALTER TURBETT** – guitar / **JOHN DAVIS** – keyboards / **ROBERT ROBERTS** – keyboards / **STEPHEN GEORGE** – drums / **MARTIN SORENSEN** – bass

Arista | Arista

Feb 83. (7"/12") *(ARIST/+12 510)* **WORK FOR LOVE. / FOR LOVE (instrumental)** [ ] [-]

Apr 83. (7"/12") *<9021>* **REVENGE (YOU DID IT AGAIN). / SHE'S GOT A CAUSE** [-] [ ]

Jun 83. (7") *(ARIST 533)* *<9068>* **I WANTED TO TELL HER. / A WALK IN THE PARK** [ ] [ ]
(12"+=) *(ARIST12 533)* *<9102>* – ('A'-Tongue Tied mix).

Sep 83. (lp/c) *(205/405 306)* *<6608>* **WORK FOR LOVE** <US title 'WITH SYMPATHY'> [ ] [96] Jun83
– Work for love / Do the Etawa / I wanted to tell her / Say you're sorry / Here we go / Effigy / Revenge / She's got a cause / Should have known better. *(cd-iss. 1989 as 'WITH SYMPATHY'+=; ARCD 8016) (cd-iss. Mar93 +=; 255 306)* – What He Say.

Nov 83. (7") *(ARIST 549)* **REVENGE (YOU DID IT AGAIN). / EFFIGY** [ ] [-]
(12"+=) *(ARIST12 549)* – Work for love.

— now basically AL solo

Wax Trax | Wax Trax

Oct 85. (12") *(WAXUK 009)* **NATURE OF LOVE. / ('A'-Cruelty mix)** [ ] [-]

Sire | Sire

Apr 86. (lp/c) *(925309-1/-4)* *<25309>* **TWITCH** [ ] [ ]
– Just like you / We believe / All day remix / The angel / Over the shoulder / My possession / Where you at now? / Crash and burn / Twitch (version II). *(cd+=)* – Over the shoulder (mix) / Isle Of Man.

— added partner **PAUL BARKER** (b. 8 Feb'50, Palo Alto, Calif.) – bass, programming (ex-FRONT 242) + **WILLIAM RIEFLIN** (b.30 Sep'60, Seattle, Washington) – drums / **ROLAND BARKER** (b.30 Jun'57, Mountainview, Calif.) – keyboards

Jan 89. (lp/c/cd) *(925799-1/-4/-2)* *<25799>* **THE LAND OF RAPE AND HONEY** [ ] [ ] Nov88
– Stigmata / The missing / Deity / Golden dawn / Destruction / The land of rape and honey / You know what you are / Flashback / Abortive. *(cd+=)* – Hizbollah / I prefer. *(cd re-iss. Dec92; 7599 25799-2)*

Feb 90. (cd/c/lp) *<(7599 26004-2/-4/-1)>* **THE MIND IS A TERRIBLE THING TO TASTE** [ ] [ ] Dec89
– Thieves / Burning inside / Never believe / Cannibal song / Breathe / So what / Test / Faith collapsing / Dream song. *(cd re-iss. Dec92)*

Sep 90. (cd/lp) *<7599 26266-2/-1>* **IN CASE YOU DIDN'T FEEL LIKE SHOWING UP (live)** [-] [ ]
– The missing / deity / So what / Burning inside / Seed / Stigmata. *(UK cd-iss. Dec92 on 'WEA'; same)*

— next with guest **GIBBY HAYNES** (of BUTTHOLE SURFERS)

— added **MIKE SCACCIA** (b.14 Jun'65, Babylon, N.Y.) – guitar

Apr 92. (7") *(W 0096)* **JESUS BUILT MY HOTROD. / TV SONG** [ ] [ ]
(12"+=/cd-s+=) *(W 0096 T/C)* – ('A'-Red line-white line version).

Jul 92. (cd/c/10"lp) *<(7599 26727-2/-4/-1)>* **PSALM 69: HOW TO SUCCEED AND HOW TO SUCK EGGS** [33] [27]
– N.W.O. / Just one fix / TV II / hero / Jesus built my hot rod / Scarecrow / Psalm 69 / Corrosion / Grace.

Jul 92. (10") *(W 0125)* **N.W.O. / F***ED (non lp version)** [49] [ ]
(cd-s+=) *(W 0125CD)* – ('A'extended dance mix).

— **JOURGENSEN + PAUL BARKER + SCACCIA** recruited **RAY WASHAM** – drums (of JESUS LIZARD) / **DUANE BUFORD** – keyboards / **LOUIS SVITEK** – guitar (ex-MINDFUNK)

W.E.A. | Warners

Dec 95. (c-s) *(W 0328C)* **THE FALL / RELOAD** [53] [ ]
(cd-s+=) *(W 0328CD)* – TV III.

Jan 96. (cd/c/lp) *<(9362 45838-2/-4/-1)>* **FILTHPIG** [43] [19]
– Reload / Filth pig / Crumbs / Useless / Lava / Dead guy / The face / Brick windows / Gane show / Lay lady lay / Reload (edit).

Feb 96. (c-s) *(W 0338C)* **LAY LADY LAY / LAY LADY LAY (album version)** [ ] [ ]
(cd-s+=) *(W 0338CD)* – Paisley / Scarecrow (live).

— line-up **JOURGENSEN, BARKER, RAY WASHUM + LOUIS SVITEK**

Jun 99. (cd/c) *<(9362 47311-2/-4)>* **DARK SIDE OF THE SPOON** [ ] [92]
– Supermanbiac soul / Whip or the chain / Bad blood / Eureka pie / Step / Nursing home / Kaif / Vex ans sfolence / 10-10.

— now without guitarist E. WILLIAM TUCKER who committed suicide by slashing his throat (after taking pills) on the 14th May, 1999 (aged 38)

– compilation, others, etc. –

1985. (lp) *Hot Trax; (WAXC 35)* **12" INCH SINGLES 1981-1984** [-] [ ]

REVOLTING COCKS

AL's studio outfit, with FRONT 242 members; LUC and RICHARD 23. The latter was soon replaced CHRIS CONNELLY of FINI TRIBE.

Wax Trax | Wax Trax

Feb 86. (12"m) *(WAXUK 011)* **NO DEVOTION. / ATTACK SHIPS / ON FIRE** [ ] [ ]

Nov 86. (lp)(cd) *(WAXUK 017)(WAX 017CD)* **BIG SEXY LAND** [ ] [ ]
– 38 / We shall cleanse the world / Attack ships on fire / Big sexy land / Union carbide (West Virginia version) / T.V. mind / No devotion / Union carbide (Bhopal version). *(re-iss. Mar92 on 'Devotion' cd/c/lp; CD/T+/DVN 6)*

Feb 87. (12") *(WAXUK 022)* **YOU OFTEN FORGET. / ('A'version)** [ ] [ ]

AL now with **BARKER, VAN ACKER, RIEFLIN + CONNELLY** – vocals

Jun 88. (d-lp/cd) *(WAX UK/CD 037)* **LIVE! - YOU GODDAMNED SON OF A BITCH** (live + 2 studio) [ ] [ ]
– You Goddamned son of a bitch / Cattle grind / We shall cleanse the world / 38 / In the neck / You often forget / TV mind / Union carbide / Attack ships on fire / No devotion. *(re-iss. May92 on 'Devotion' cd/c/lp; CD/T+/DVN 8)*

Mar 89. (12") *<(WAX 042)>* **STAINLESS STEEL PROVIDERS. / AT THE TOP** [ ] [ ]

— **AL + PHIL** were also part of JELLO BIAFRA's (Dead Kennedys) group LARD.

May 90. (cd/c/lp) *(WAX 063 CD/MC/LP)* **BEERS, STEERS + QUEERS** [ ] [ ]
– Beers, steers + queers / (Let's get) Physical / In the neck / Get down / Stainless steel providers / Can't sit still / Something wonderful / Razor's edge. *(cd+=)* – (Let's talk) Physical. *(re-iss. Feb92 on 'Devotion' cd/c/lp; CD/T+/DVN 4)*

May 90. (cd-s) *(WAX 086CD)* **(LET'S GET) PHYSICAL. / (LET'S TALK) PHYSICAL** [ ] [ ]

— now without RIEFLIN (on below only TRENT REZNOR of NINE INCH NAILS)

Apr 91. (12"ep/cd-ep; 1000 HOMO DJ'S) *<WAX 032>* **SUPERNAUT / HEY ASSHOLE / APATHY / BETTER WAYS** [ ] [ ] 1987

Devotion Devotion

Sep 93. (12"ep/cd-ep) *(12/CD DVN 111)* **DA YA THINK I'M SEXY? / SERGIO GUITAR / WRONG (sexy mix)** [61] [ ]

Sep 93. (cd/c/d-lp) *(CD/T+/DVN 22)* **LINGER FICKEN' GOOD . . . AND OTHER BARNYARD ODDITIES** [39] [ ]
– Gila copter / Creep / Mr.Lucky / Crackin' up / Sergio / Da ya think I'm sexy? / The rockabye / Butcher flower's woman / Dirt / Linger ficken' good.

Jun 94. (12"/cd-s) *(12/CD DVN 112)* **CRACKIN' UP. / ('A'-Amylnitrate mix) / GUACOPTER (version 2)** [ ] [-]

PTP

AL, PAUL + WILL (SCORPIO + ALIEN DOG STAR + FRENCHIE L'AMOUR)

Wax Trax Wax Trax

1989. (12) *(WAX 9073)* **RUBBER GLOVE SEDUCTION. / MY FAVOURITE THINGS** [ ] [ ]

ACID HORSE

GALLOPIN' SCORPIO SADDLEBUTT + TENNESSEE KING BIFF + HAROLD SANDOZ + ALIEN DOG STAR

1989. (12") *(WAX 9081)* **NO NAME NO SLOGAN. / ('A'-produced by CABARET VOLTAIRE)** [ ] [ ]

LEAD INTO GOLD

PAUL BARKER with **AL JOURGENSEN + WILD BILL RIEFLIN**

not iss. SPV

1990. (m-cd) *<SPV 91942>* **CHICKS & SPEED** [-] [ ]
– Faster than light / The stripper / Beauty / Idiot / Blackened heart / Hatred.

— added **STUART BANG ZECHMAN** – guitar

Wax Trax Wax Trax

Aug 90. (lp/cd) *<(WAX 116/+CD)>* **AGE OF REASON** [ ] [ ]
– Age of reason / Unreason / Snake oil / A giant on Earth / Faster than light / Lunatic – Genius / Sweet thirteen / Fell from Heaven. *(re-iss. Mar92 on 'Devotion' cd/c/lp; CD/T+/DVN 7)*

MINOR THREAT (see under ⇒ FUGAZI)

MINUTEMEN

Formed: San Pedro, California, USA . . . 1979 originally as The REACTIONARIES, by D. BOON and MIKE WATT (third member GEORGE HURLEY replaced FRANK TONCHE). The band featured on Various Artists US lp's on indie labels 'Radio Tokyo', 'New Alliance' and 'Posh Boy', before signing for 'S.S.T.' (home base of BLACK FLAG and MEAT PUPPETS). For five years they committed many songs (mostly hardcore/jazz! around a minute long!) to EP and LP before having to disband late in 1985 after the untimely death of BOON. From 'PARANOID TIME' to '3-WAY TIE (FOR LAST)', MINUTEMEN showcased their politically leftfield attacks on the establishment including RONNIE REAGAN and JOE McCARTHY. In 1986 the remaining two, MIKE WATT and GEORGE HURLEY re-formed as fIREHOSE alongside guitarist ED CRAWFORD. This trio debuted with an album, 'RAGIN' FULL ON' (1987), their sound slightly mellowing. After an acclaimed 1989 third album 'fROMOHIO', they shifted to 'Columbia', where they scored minor hit albums in the early 90's. • **Covered:** HEY LAWDY MAMA (Steppenwolf) / HAVE YOU EVER SEEN THE RAIN + GREEN RIVER (Creedence Clearwater Revival) / DOCTOR WU (Steely Dan) / THE RED AND THE BLACK (Blue Oyster Cult). fIREHOSE covered WALKING THE COW (Daniel Johnston) / SLACK MOTHERFUCKER (Superchunk). DOS covered PACIFIC COAST HIGHWAY (Sonic Youth) + DON'T EXPLAIN (Billie Holiday).

Album rating: PARANOID TIME (*5) / THE PUNCH LINE mini (*4) / WHAT MAKES A MAN START FIRES? (*7) / DOUBLE NICKELS ON THE DIME (*8) / 3-WAY TIE (FOR LAST) (*6) / PROJECT: MERSH mini n(*6) / BALLOT RESULTS (*7) / firehose: RAGIN', fULL-ON (*6) / fROMOHIO (*8) / FLYING THE FLANNEL (*6) / Mike Watt: BALL-HOG OR TUGBOAT? (*7) / CONTEMPLATING THE ENGINE ROOM (*6) / Dos: DOS (*6)

D. BOON (b. DENNES DALE BOON, 1 Apr'58) – vocals, guitar / **MIKE WATT** (b.20 Dec'57, Portsmouth, Virginia) – bass (also of DOS) / **GEORGE HURLEY** (b. 4 Sep'58, Brockton, Massachusetts) – drums; repl. FRANK TONCHE

S.S.T. S.S.T.

Dec 80. (7"ep) *<SST 002>* **PARANOID TIME** [-] [ ]
– Untitled song for Latin America / Political song for Michael Jackson to sing / Validation / The maze / Definitions / Fascist / Joe McCarthy's ghost. *(UK-iss.Mar83, cd-ep iss.Nov88; same)*

Sep 81. (7"ep) *<NAR 004>* **JOY / BLACK SHEEP. / MORE JOY** [-] [ ]

— <above issued on 'New Alliance'>

Nov 81. (m-lp) *<SST 004>* **THE PUNCH LINE** [-] [ ]
– Search / Tension / Games / Boiling / Disguises / Struggle / Monuments / Ruins / Issued / The punch line / Song for El Salvador / History lesson / Fanatics / No parade / Straight jacket / Gravity / Warfare / Static. *<(cd/c-iss.May93; SST CD/C 004)>*

Feb 83. (lp) *<SST 014>* **WHAT MAKES A MAN START FIRES?** [-] [ ]
– Bob Dylan wrote propaganda songs / One chapter in the book / Fake contest / Beacon sighted through fog / Mutiny in Jonestown / East wind – Faith / Pure joy / '99 / The anchor / Sell or be sold / Only minority / Split red / Colors / Plight / Tin roof / Life as rehearsal / This road / Polarity. *(UK-iss.Aug91 & May93 cd/c; SST 014 CD/C)*

Nov 83. (m-lp) *<SST 016>* **BUZZ OR HOWL UNDER THE INFLUENCE OF HEAT** [-] [ ]
– Self-referenced / Cut / Dream told by Moto / Dreams are free, motherfucker! / Tow jam / I felt like a gringo / Product / Little man with a gun in his hand. *(UK-iss.May93 cd/c; SST 016 CD/C)*

Oct 84. (d-lp) *<(SST 028)>* **DOUBLE NICKELS ON THE DIME** [ ] [ ]
– D.'s car jam – Anxious Mo-Fo / Theatre is the life of you / Vietnam / Cohesion / It's expected I'm gone / Number 1 hit song / Two heads at the end / Do you want new wave or do you want . . . / Don't look now / Shit from an old notebook / Nature without man / One reporter's opinion / Political song for Michael Jackson to sing / Maybe partying will help / Toadies / Retreat / Big foist / God bows to math / Corona / Glory of man / Take 5, D. / My heart and the real world / History lesson, pt.2 / You need the glory / Roar of the masses could be farts / West Germany. *<(cd-iss. Oct87 +=; SST 028CD)>* – THE POLITICS OF TIME lp

Jun 85. (12"ep) *<(SST 034)>* **PROJECT: MERSH** [ ] [ ]
– Cheerleaders / King of the hill / Hey lawdy mama / Take our test / Tour-spiel / More spiel.

— tragedy struck on the 23rd December '85 when D.BOON was killed in a car crash

Jan 86. (lp) *<(SST 058)>* **3 WAY TIE (FOR LAST)** [ ] [ ]
– The price of Paradise / Lost / The big stick / Political nightmare / Courage / Have you ever seen the rain? / The red and the black / Spoken word piece / No one / Stories / What is it? / Ack ack ack / Just another soldier / Situations at hand / Hittin' the bong / Bermuda. *(cd-iss. Aug87; SST 058CD)*

— Broke-up early 1986. WATT guested for CICCONE YOUTH (aka SONIC YOUTH).

– compilations, etc. –

1984. (lp/cd) *New Alliance;* **THE POLITICS OF TIME** (early REACTIONARIES material) [-] [ ]
– The politics of time / Themselves / Please don't be gentle with me / Nothing indeed / No exchange / There ain't shit on TV tonight / This ain't no picnic / Spillage / Untitled song for Latin America / Jesus and tequila / June 16th / Storm in my house / Martin's story / Dr. Wu / World according to nouns / Love dance / Three car jam. *<cd-iss. May93 on 'S.S.T.'; >*

Apr 85. (7"ep) *Reflex; (REFLEX L)* **TOUR SPIEL (live)** [ ] [ ]

Dec 86. (d-lp/cd) *S.S.T.; <(SST 068)>* **BALLOT RESULTS** [ ] [ ]
– Little man with a black gun in his hand / Political song for Michael Jackson to sing / I felt like a gringo / Jesus and tequila / Courage / King of the hill / Bermuda / No one / Mr.Robot's holy orders / Ack ack ack / History lesson (part two) / This ain't no picnic / The cheerleaders / Time / Cut / Split red / Shit you hear at parties / Hell (second take) / Tour-spiel / Take our test / The punch line / Search / Bob Dylan wrote propaganda songs / Badges / Tension / If Reagan played disco / No! no! no! to draft and war – Joe McCarthy ghost. *(re-iss. May93)*

1987. (lp/cd) *S.S.T.; <SST 138/+CD>* **POST-MERSH, VOL.I** [-] [ ]
– THE PUNCH LINE ep / WHAT MAKES A MAN START FIRES lp *(re-iss. May93)*

1987. (lp/cd) *S.S.T.; <SST 139/+CD>* **POST-MERSH, VOL.II** [-] [ ]
– BUZZ OR HOWL UNDER THE INFLUENCE OF HEAT lp / PROJECT: MERSH ep *(re-iss. May93)*

Sep 87. (7"ep) *New Alliance;* **JOY / BLACK SHEEP. / MORE JOY** [ ] [ ]
(re-iss. Feb90 on 'S.S.T.' 10"colrd; SST 214)

May 89. (cd) *S.S.T.; <(SST 165)>* **POST-MERSH, VOL.III** [ ] [ ]

Aug 98. (cd) *S.S.T.; <(SST 363CD)>* **INTRODUCING THE MINUTEMEN** [ ] [ ]

fIREHOSE

MIKE WATT – bass (also of **CRIMONY**, with **PAUL ROESSLER** – keyboards) / **GEORGE HURLEY** – drums / **ED CRAWFORD** (b.26 Jan'62, Steubenville, Ohio) – vocals, guitar (of COLUMBUS)

S.S.T. S.S.T.

Apr 87. (lp/c/cd) *<(SST 079/+C/CD)>* **RAGIN' fULL-ON** [ ] [ ]
– Caroma / Mutiny / Perfect pairs / Chemical wires / Choose and memory / Relating dudes to jazz? / Another theory shot to shit on your . . . / Under the influence of the Meat Puppets / Locked in / Brave captain. *(re-iss. Mar93; same)*

Mar 88. (lp/c/cd) *<(SST 115/+C/CD)>* **If'N** [ ] [ ]
– Sometimes / Hear me / Honey, please / Backroads / From one cums one / Making the freeway / Anger / For the singer of R.E.M. / Operation solitaire / Windmilling / Me & you, remembering / In memory of Elizabeth Cotton / Soon / Thunder child. *(re-iss. Mar93; same)*

Jun 88. (12"ep) *<(SST 131)>* **SOMETIMES. / RHYMIN' SPILIN' / SHE PAINTS PICTURES** [ ] [ ]
(re-iss. Aug93 cd-ep+=; SST 131CD) – For the singer of R.E.M.

Mar 89. (lp/c/cd) *<(SST 235/+C/CD)>* **fROMOHIO** [ ] [ ]
– In my mind / Whisperin' while hollerin' / Mas cojones / What gets heard / Fiddle of the eighties / Time with you / If'n / Understanding / The softest hammer / Vastapol / Let the drummer have some / Liberty for our friend / Some things / Not that shit George.

not iss. New Alliance

1989. (lp,c,cd; as BOOTSTRAPPERS) *<46>* **BOOTSTRAPPERS** [-] [ ]
– Memory is a muscle / Spider baby / New boots / Taxita / Flicker / Third rail / Media dub / D-I-A-L-C-A-S-H / X – Delta / Their faces are green and their hands / Presidential apology / Mud / Indeed / Empty-vee / Long beach dub – Feen / Maneuvres.
(above:- WATT + HURLEY with ELLIOTT SHARP)

Columbia Columbia

Oct 91. (cd/c/lp) *(468422-2/-4/-1)* **fLYIN' THE fLANNEL** [ ] [ ]
– Down with the bass / Up Finnegan's ladder / Can't believe / Walking the cow / Flyin' the flannel / Epoxy for example / O'er the town of Pedro / Too long / The first class / Anti-misogyny manoever / Toolin' song for Dave Alvin / Tienan man dream again / Lost colors / Towin' the line / Losers, boozers and heroes.

Feb 92. (m-cd) *<74152>* **THE LIVE TOTEM POLE EP** [-] [ ]

– The red and the black / Sophisticated bitch / Revolution part 2 / Slack motherfucker / What gets heard / Mannequin / Making the freeway safe for the freeway.
<re-iss. Feb95 as 'THE RED AND THE BLACK'; same>

Mar 93. (cd/c/lp) *(472967-2/-4/-1)* **MR. MACHINERY OPERATOR**
– Formal introduction / Blaze / Herded into pools / Witness / Number seven / Powerful hankerin' / Rocket sled-fuel tank / Quicksand / Disciples of the 3-way / More famous quotes / Sincerely / Hell-hole / 4.29.92 / The cliffs thrown down.

1994. (cd-ep) <*5122*> **BIG BOTTOM POW-WOW**

— disbanded on the 12th of February 1994 after playing a small unadvertised gig. MIKE WATT joined PORNO FOR PYROS after a solo album.

MIKE WATT

Columbia Columbia

Mar 95. (cd/c) *(478375-2/-4)* <*67086*> **MIKE WATT: BALL-HOG OR TUGBOAT?**
– Big train / Against the 70's / Drove up from Pedro / Piss-bottle man / Chinese firedrill / Song for Madonna to sing / Tuff gnarl / Sexual military dynamics / Max and Wells / E-ticket ride / Forever – one reporter's opinion / Song for Igor / Tell 'em boy! / Sidemouse advice / Heartbeat / Maggot brain / Coincidence is either hit or miss.

— now with **NELS CLINE** – guitar / **STEPHEN HODGES** – drums

Jan 98. (cd,c) <*CK 68161*> **CONTEMPLATING THE ENGINE ROOM**
– In the engine room / Red bluff / The bluejackets' manual / Pedro bound! / The boilerman / Black gang coffee / Topsiders / No one says old man (to the old man) / Fireman Hurley / Liberty calls! / In the bunk room / Navy wife / Crossing the equator / Breaking the choke hold / Wrapping around the screw / Shore duty.

DOS

MIKE WATT + his wife **KIRA ROESSLER** – bass (ex-BLACK FLAG)

not iss. New Alliance

1986. (lp) <*NAR 032*> **DOS**
– The fisherman & his wife / Forever / Funk one / Number four / Number one / Number three / Number two / The rabbit and the porcupine / Slow little turtle / Snapshot / Taking away the fire. *(UK cd-iss. May93; NAR 032CD)*

1989. (12"ep) <*NAR 044*> **NUMERO DOS**
– Don't explain / Heartbeat / PCH / I worry, my son / Silence / Number six.

Aug 91. (cd) <*NAR 061*> **UNO CON DOS** (compilation of above 2)
(UK-iss.May93; NAR 061CD)

not iss. Kill Rock Stars

Jun 96. (cd) <*KRS 256*> **JUSTAMENTE TRES**
– Down in the dumps / Dream of San Pedro / Image that / Intense song for Madonna / 'Til the blood ran / Sidemouse advice / Excerpts from a captain's log / To each his dulcinea / Powerful hankerin' / Little doll / Willow weep for me / Even the pain has changed / Formal introduction / Angel face is the Devil's daughter / Number seven / Do you want new wave or do you want the truth? / Number five.

MISERY LOVES CO.

Formed: Uppsala, Sweden . . . early '93 by PATRIK WIREN and ORJAN ORNKLOO, who augmented the band's live appearances with additional musicians JIM EDWARDS, MARRE and BOSSE LUNDSTROM. These three soon made way for permanent members MICHAEL HAHNE, RICHARD STORRONGER and OLLE DAHLSTEDT, the group providing a European alternative to the metallic industrial angst of FEAR FACTORY, NINE INCH NAILS, ALICE IN CHAINS, etc. Following a series of domestic releases on the 'MNW Zone' label, the band secured a deal with UK's 'Earache', delivering an acclaimed eponymous debut set in 1995. Doing little to dispell the stereotype of the depressive, suicide-prone Swede, the album combined a variety of extreme metal styles with a common thread of unrelenting misery. Feted by the likes of Kerrang!, the group built up a steady following in the UK, releasing a follow-up 'NOT LIKE THEM' in 1997. Utilising MINISTRY-esque distorto vocals over bass-quaking grunge/thrash, the record once again proved that these boys were definitely not choosing life, so to speak. It also included a surprising choice of cover version, a barely recognisable reading of XTC's 'A COMPLICATED GAME'. The new millennium saw more MISERY . . . courtesy of the long-awaited but slightly disappointing album, 'YOUR VISION WAS NEVER MINE TO SHARE' (2000).

Album rating: MISERY LOVES CO. (*7) / NOT LIKE THEM (*6) / YOUR VISION WAS NEVER MINE TO SHARE (*5)

PATRIK WIREN – vocals (ex-MIDAS TOUCH, ex-HIGH TECH JUNKIES) / **ORJAN ORNKLOO** – guitar / **MICHAEL HAHNE** – guitar / **RICHARD STORRONGER** – bass / **OLLE DAHLSTEDT** – drums

MNW Zone not iss.

1994. (cd-ep) *(MNWCD 182)* **PRIVATE HELL / THIS IS NO DREAM / HONOUR CODE LOYALTY** Sweden

Earache Earache

1995. (cd-ep) *(MOSH 1995)* **MY MIND STILL SPEAKS / NEED ANOTHER ONE / HAPPY?**

Apr 95. (lp/cd) *(<MOSH 133/+CD>)* **MISERY LOVES CO.**
– My mind still speaks / Kiss your boots / Need another one / Sonic attack / This is no dream / Happy? / Scared / I swallow / Private hell / Only way / Two seconds. *(other cd w/ bonus cd; MOSH 133CDB)* – Need another one / Honour code loyalty / Kiss your boots (kiss my Black Sabbath-y ass version) / Kiss your boots (Open Your Mind mix) / Kiss your boots (NancySinatrekatine mix).

1995. (cd-ep) *(MOSH 135CD)* **KISS YOUR BOOTS (Open Your Mind mix) / (Nancy Sinatraketamine mix) / (Industrial Hazard mix) / (The Urban Jungle mix)**

Mar 96. (cd-ep) *(MOSH 151CD)* **HAPPY? / STRAIN OF FRUSTRATION / THIS IS NO DREAM / PRIVATE HELL / KISS YOUR BOOTS / SONIC ATTACK**

Oct 97. (lp/cd) *(MOSH 184/+CD)* **NOT LIKE THEM**
– It's all yours / A million lies / Prove me wrong / Owe you nothing / A complicated game / Taste it / Deny everything / Them nails / Infected / Feed the creep / Not the only one / Nothing remains. *(d-cd-iss. Sep98; MOSH 184CDT)*

Dec 97. (7") **BLINDED. / KISS YOUR BOOTS (Urban Jungle mix)**

Mar 00. (cd) *(MOSH 231CD)* **YOUR VISION WAS NEVER MINE TO SHARE**
– Your vision was never mine to share / No exit / On the top of the world / Like a suicide / Rise and fall / Damage driven / Never gonna grow up / Into the grey / The drowning man / When everything dies.

MISFITS

Formed: Lodi, New Jersey, USA . . . 1977 by GLENN DANZIG and JERRY ONLY. B-movie punks dominated by the brooding presence and sneering croon of DANZIG, the group (BOBBY STEELE and JOEY IMAGE completing the line-up) gigged at the usual NY haunts such as CBGB's before releasing their debut single, 'COUGH COOL', on the self-financed 'Plan 9' label. This was closely followed by such endearingly amateurish slices of low-rent melodic splatter-punk as 'HORROR BUSINESS' and 'NIGHT OF THE LIVING DEAD EP', as well as a special 'HALLOWEEN' single released in, you guessed it, October (1980). Around the same time, GLENN and Co. supported The DAMNED on a European tour, during which DANZIG wound up in jail after fisticuffs with their roadies. By this point, STEELE had been replaced with JERRY's brother DOYLE, this line-up playing on the belated debut album, 'WALK AMONG US' (1982; one of their only releases issued in the UK). Taking DANZIG's horror/sci-fi obsession to its comic-book conclusion, tracks like 'ASTRO ZOMBIES' and 'I TURNED INTO A MARTIAN' would've done ROKY ERICKSON proud. The painful 'LIVE/EVIL' (1983) featured a guest spot from HENRY ROLLINS on 'We Are 138', while the final album, 'EARTH A.D. / WOLFSBLOOD' (1984) saw the group opting for a decidedly more brutal sonic assault. Although their career spanned only six short years during which time they struggled to achieve even the most passing interest, The MISFITS have since come to be regarded as eminent cult heroes, GUNS N' ROSES, METALLICA and more recently MARILYN MANSON admitting their fondness for the band. A Various Artists tribute compilation, 'VIOLENT WORLD', was released early in 1997 featuring PRONG, NOFX, THERAPY?, while the original band, well at least JERRY and DOYLE, along with new members DR. CHUD and MICHAEL GRAVES, reformed for an album on 'Geffen', 'AMERICAN PSYCHO' (1997) thankfully without heavy-metal frontman DANZIG; another set, 'FAMOUS MONSTERS' was issued in '99.

Album rating: WALK AMONG US (*7) / EVIL – LIVE (*5) / EARTH A.D. (*5) / THE MISFITS compilation (*7) / AMERICAN PSYCHO (*6) / STATIC AGE (*6) / THE MISFITS boxed-set (*7) / FAMOUS MONSTERS (*6)

GLENN DANZIG (b.23 Jun'55, Lodi, New Jersey) – vocals / **BOBBY STEELE** – guitar / **JERRY ONLY** – bass / **JOEY IMAGE** – drums

not iss. Plan 9

1977. (7") <*PL 1001*> **COUGH – COOL. / SHE**

1977. (7") <*PL 1009*> **BULLET EP**
– Horror business / Teenagers from Mars / Children in heat.

1979. (7"ep) <*PL 1011*> **NIGHT OF THE LIVING DEAD EP**
– Night of the living dead / Where eagles dare / Rat fink.

— **DOYLE ONLY** – guitar; repl. STEELE who joined The UNDEAD

— **(ARTHUR) GOOGY** (aka EERIE VON) repl. JOEY

Apr 81. (7"ep) <*PL 1013*> **THREE HITS FROM HELL EP**
– London dungeon / Horror hotel / Ghoul's night out.
(below release licensed to 'Cherry Red' in the UK)

Jul 81. (m-lp) *(PLP 9)* **BEWARE EP**
– Cough – Cool / She / Bullet / We are 138 / Attitude / Hollywood Babylon / Horror business / Teenagers from Mars / Children in heat / Night of the living dead / Where eagles dare / Rat fink / London dungeon / Horror hotel / Ghouls night out. *(cd-iss. 1990's;)* – Halloween / Halloween 2 / 20 eyes (live) / Night of the living dead (live) / Astrozombies (live) / Horror business (live) / London dungeon (live) / All hell breaks loose (live) / We are 138 (live w/ HENRY ROLLINS) / Return of the fly / Last caress.

Oct 81. (7") <*PL 1017*> **HALLOWEEN. / HALLOWEEN II**

not iss. Ruby-WEA

1982. (lp) <*925756-1*> **WALK AMONG US**
– 20 eyes / I turned into a Martian / All Hell breaks loose / Vampira / Nike a go-go / Hate breeders / Mommy, can I go out & kill tonight / Night of the living dead / Skulls / Violent world / Devils whorehouse / Astro zombies / Brain eaters. *(re-iss. +cd Sep88 on 'Ruby-WEA')*

not iss. Aggressive Rock

1983. (lp) <*AG 023*> **EVIL – LIVE (live)**
– 20 eyes / Night of the living dead / Astro zombies / Horror business / London dungeon / All Hell breaks loose / We are 138. *(re-iss. Sep87 on 'Plan 9'; PL 908) (UK-iss.Mar97 on 'Plan 9' lp/cd; PL9/+CD 08)*

— **ROBO** – drums; repl. GOOGY

Feb 84. (lp) <*AG 024*> **EARTH A.D. / WOLF'S BLOOD**
– Earth a.d. / Queen wasp / Devilrock / Death comes ripping / Green Hell / Wolf's blood / Demonomania / Bloodfeast / Hellhound / Die die my darling / We bite. *(cd-iss. Jul91; AGO 572) (cd re-iss. Jan97 on 'Plan 9' lp/cd+=; PL9 02)* – DIE DIE MY DARLING ep

— had already split the previous year. DANZIG released a solo single and formed SAMHAIN with EERIE VON. JERRY and DOYLE formed KRYST THE

CONQUEROR, releasing five track EP augmented by future SKID ROW frontman DAVID SABO.

— The MISFITS re-formed in 1996 with **JERRY ONLY** – bass / **DOYLE** – guitar / **MICHAEL GRAVES** – vocals / **DR. CHUD** – drums

Geffen Geffen

May 97. (cd) *<(GED 24939)>* **AMERICAN PSYCHO**
– Abominable Dr. Phibes / American psycho / Speak of the Devil / Walk among us / The hunger / From Hell they came / Dig up your bones / Blacklight / Resurrection / This island Earth / Crimson ghost / The day of the dead / The haunting / Mars attacks / Hate the living, love the dead / The shining / Don't open til doomsday.

— **MYKE HIDEOUS** – vocals; repl. GRAVES

Roadrunner Roadrunner

Oct 99. (cd/lp) *<(RR 8658-2/-1)>* **FAMOUS MONSTERS**
– King at the gates / Forbidden zone / Lost in space / Dust to dust / Crawling eye / Scream / Witch hunt / Saturday night / Pumpkinhead / Scarecrow man / Di monster die / Living hell / Descending angel / Them / Fiend club / Hunting humans / Helena / Kong unleashed. *(ltd-cd; RR 8658-5)* – Devil doll / 1000 b.c. / Helena.

– compilations, etc. –

1986. (lp/cd) *Plan 9; <PL9/+CD 06>* **LEGACY OF BRUTALITY** -
– Angelfuck / Who killed Marilyn? / Where eagles dare / She / Halloween / American nightmare / Static age / T.V. casualty / Hybrid moments / Spinal remains / Come back / Some kinda hate / Theme for a jackal. *(UK-iss.Jul97; same)*

Jul 86. (lp) *Revolver; (REVLP 74)* **BEST OF THE MISFITS** -

Nov 87. (12"ep) *Plan 9; <PL9-03>* **DIE DIE MY DARLING** -

May 88. (cd) *Plan 9; <PL9CD 1>* **THE MISFITS COLLECTION** -
(UK-iss.Jul97 cd/lp; same)

Oct 95. (cd/lp) *Caroline; <(CAROL 7515-2/-1)>* **THE MISFITS COLLECTION VOL.2**

Feb 97. (4xcd-box) *Caroline; <(CDCAR 7529-2)>* **THE MISFITS BOX SET**

Jul 97. (cd/lp) *Caroline; (CAROL 7520-2/-1)* **STATIC AGE**
– (debut album GLENN DANZIG, JERRY ONLY, FRANCHE COME, MR. JIM) – 14 tracks +; 'She', 'Spinal Remains' and 'In The Doorway')

Mar 00. (cd) *<(PL9CD 02-3)>* **EARTH A.D. / WOLFSBLOOD**

MISSION

Formed: Leeds, England ... late 1985 by ex-SISTERS OF MERCY members WAYNE HUSSEY and CRAIG ADAMS. After falling out with the aforementioned band's singer ANDREW ELDRITCH, the pair recruited SIMON HINKLER (ex-ARTERY) and MICK BROWN (ex-RED LORRY YELLOW LORRY), forming a new band originally under The SISTERHOOD moniker. Calculated to annoy their former colleague, ELDRITCH retaliated by releasing a single under a similar name, HUSSEY and Co. subsequently switching to The MISSION. In Spring '86, the band signed to indie label, 'Chapter 22', releasing the enjoyably amateurish goth theatrics of the 'SERPENT'S KISS' single a couple of months later. Another single, 'GARDEN OF DELIGHT', appeared that summer before the band were snapped up by 'Mercury'. The debut album, 'GOD'S OWN MEDICINE', appeared towards the end of the year, almost making the UK Top 10. Given a bit of a rough ride by critics for its often overbearing goth pompousness, the record was nevertheless a fairly accomplished set of adult rock, a bit like what U2 might have sounded like had they been born in Leeds and developed a penchant for wearing pointy shoes and smearing their faces with flour. The grandiose 'WASTELAND' made No.11 when it was released as a single early the following year, staking The MISSION's claim as the new Goth messiahs and no doubt making ELDRITCH sick to his stomach. But much as they liked to be serious fellows on record, they liked to party hard behind the scenes, CRAIG ADAMS coming a cropper on a particularly gruelling US tour and briefly leaving the band. His temporary replacement was PETE TURNER who filled in for the remainder of the tour and also played at The MISSION's triumphant Reading Festival headlining appearance later that summer. With ADAMS back in the fold, the band began work on a new album with LED ZEPPELIN bassist JOHN PAUL JONES on production chores. The less than impressive result was 'CHILDREN' (1988), a No.2 hit despite its critical lashing. Preceded by the delicate 'BUTTERFLY ON A WHEEL', the 'CARVED IN SAND' album was eventually released to expectant fans in early 1990. More elegantly refined than their normal heavy handed approach, the set remains their most listenable effort, if not their most successful. The band resumed heavy touring following the album's release, HINKLER subsequently storming out on the American jaunt. His replacement for the remainder of the tour was another ex-RED LORRY YELLOW LORRY man, DAVID WOLFENDEN, the band eventually recruiting guitarist ETCH (PAUL ETCHELLS, ex-GHOST DANCE) as a semi-permanent fixture later that year. Following the ambitious 'MASQUE' (1992) set (which featured the violin playing of FAIRPORT CONVENTION's RIC SAUNDERS), MARK THWAITE (ex-SPEAR OF DESTINY) and RIK CARTER (ex-PENDRAGON) were brought in after the departure of ADAMS. Two further albums appeared on the band's own label, 'Equator', following the end of their tenure with 'Mercury', none making any substantial commercial headway. In 1996, The MISSION scraped into the charts with their new 'BLUE' set, although this was a sad swansong for a once enterprising outfit. HUSSEY and crew resurfaced in the late 90's to re-work many of their past faves via the album, 'RESURRECTION' (1999). • **Songwriters:** HUSSEY penned, except LIKE A HURRICANE (Neil Young) / DANCING BAREFOOT (Patti Smith) / SHELTER FROM THE STORM (Bob Dylan) / OVER THE HILLS AND FAR AWAY (Led Zeppelin) / LOVE (John Lennon) / ATOMIC (Blondie). • **Trivia:** In 1991, HUSSEY was ushered off James Whale's late night TV show for being drunk and abusive to its ever-polite presenter!!

Album rating: GOD'S OWN MEDICINE (*7) / CHILDREN (*6) / CARVED IN SAND (*5) / GRAINS OF SAND out-takes (*5) / MASQUE (*5) / SUM AND SUBSTANCE compilation (*7) / NEVERLAND (*4) / BLUE (*4) / RESURRECTION – THE GREATEST HITS (*6)

WAYNE HUSSEY (b.26 May'59, Bristol, England) – vocals, guitar (ex-SISTERS OF MERCY, ex-DEAD OR ALIVE, ex-HAMBI & THE DANCE, ex-WALKIE TALKIES) / **CRAIG ADAMS** – bass (ex-SISTERS OF MERCY, ex-EXPELAIRES) / **SIMON HINKLER** – guitar (ex-ARTERY) / **MICK BROWN** – drums (ex-RED LORRY YELLOW LORRY)

Chapter 22 not iss.

May 86. (7") *(CHAP 6-7)* **SERPENT'S KISS. / WAKE (R.S.V.)** 70 -
(12"+=) *(CHAP 6)* – Naked and savage.

Jul 86. (7") *(CHAP 7)* **GARDEN OF DELIGHT. / LIKE A HURICANE** 50 -
(12"+=) *(12CHAP 7)* – Over the hills and far away / The crystal ocean.
(12"+=) *(L12CHAP 7)* – Dancing barefoot / The crystal ocean.

Mercury Mercury

Oct 86. (7") *(MYSG 1)* **STAY WITH ME. / BLOOD BROTHER** 30
(12"+=) *(MYSGX 1)* – Islands in a stream.

Nov 86. (lp/c)(cd) *(MERH/+C 102)(<830603-2>)* **GODS OWN MEDICINE** 14
– Wasteland / Bridges burning / Garden of delight (hereafter) / Stay with me / Blood brother * / Let sleeping dogs lie / Sacrilege / Dance on glass / And the dance goes on / Severina / Love me to death / Island in a stream *. *(c+=/cd+= *)*

Jan 87. (7") *(MYTH 2)* **WASTELAND. / SHELTER FROM THE STORM** 11
(12"+=) *(MYTHX 2-1)* – Dancing barefoot (live).
('A'-Anniversary mix.12"+=) *(MYTHX 2-2)* – 1969 (live) / Wake (live).
(d7") *(MYTHB 2)* – 1969 (live) / Serpent's kiss (live).

Mar 87. (7"/7"s) *(MYTH/+P 3)* **SEVERINA. / TOMORROW NEVER KNOWS** 25
(12"+=) *(MYTHL 3)* – Wishing well.

— **PETE TURNER** – bass; took over on tour while ADAMS recovered from illness

— **CRAIG ADAMS** was soon back after a 4 month lay-off.

Jan 88. (7") *(MYTH 4)* **TOWER OF STRENGTH. / FABIENNE** 12
(ext.12"+=) *(MYTHX 4)* – Dream on / Breathe (instrumental).
(ext.cd-s+=) *(MTHCD 4)* – Dream on / Breathe (vocal).

Mar 88. (lp/c)(cd) *(MISH/+C 2)(<834263-2>)* **CHILDREN** 2
– Beyond the pale / A wing and a prayer / Fabienne * / Heaven on Earth / Tower of strength / Kingdom come / Breathe / Child's play / Shamera kye / Black mountain mist / Dream on * / Heat / Hymn (for America). *(c+=/cd+= *)*

Jul 88. (7") *(MYTH 6)* **BEYOND THE PALE. / TADEUSZ (1912-1988)** 32
('A'-Armageddon mix.12"+=) *(MYTHX 6)* – Love me to death / For ever more.
('A'-Armageddon mix.cd-s+=) *(MTHCD 6-2)* – Tower of strength (Bombay edit).

Nov 88. (7") *(MYTH 7)* **KINGDOM COME. / CHILD'S PLAY (live)**
(12"+=) *(MYTHX 7)* – The crystal ocean.
(cd-s++=) *(MTHCD 7)* – Garden of delight (live).

— (all formats on above single withdrawn)

Jan 90. (7"/c-s) *(MYTH/MTHMC 8)* **BUTTERFLY ON A WHEEL. / THE GRIP OF DISEASE** 12
(12"+=/cd-s+=/box-cd-s+=)(10"+=) *(MYTHX/MTHCD/MYCDB 8)(MYTH 8-10)* – ('A'-Magni-octopus) / Kingdom come (forever and again).

Feb 90. (cd/c/lp) *(<842251-2/-4/-1>)* **CARVED IN SAND** 7
– Amelia / Into the blue / Butterfly on a wheel / Sea of love / Deliverance / Grapes of wrath / Belief / Paradise (will shine like the Moon) / Hungry as the hunter / Lovely.

Mar 90. (7"/c-s) *(MYTH/MTHMC 9)* **DELIVERANCE. / MR. PLEASANT** 27
(12"+=/cd-s+=/pic-cd-s+=)(10"+=) *(MYTHX/MTHCD/MYCDB 9)(MYTH 9-10)* – Heaven sends us.

May 90. (7"/c-s) *(MYTH/MTHMC 10)* **INTO THE BLUE. / BIRD OF PARADISE** 32
(12"+=/cd-s+=) *(MYTHX/MTHCD 10)* – Divided we fall.

— **DAVID WOLFENDEN** – guitar (ex-RED LORRY YELLOW LORRY) repl. HINKLER.

— (Oct'90) added **ETCH** – guitar (ex-GHOST DANCE)

Oct 90. (cd/c/lp) *(846937-2/-4/-1)* **GRAINS OF SAND** (out-takes) 28
– Hands across the ocean / The grip of disease / Divided we fall / Mercenary / Mr.Pleasant / Kingdom come (forever and again) / Heaven sends you / Sweet smile of a mystery / Love / Bird of passage. *(c+=/cd+=)* – Tower of strength (Casbah mix) / Butterfly on a wheel (Troubadour mix).

Nov 90. (7"/c-s) *(MYTH/MTHMC 11)* **HANDS ACROSS THE OCEAN. / AMELIA / LOVE** 28 -
(12"+=) *(MYTHX 11)* – Amelia (live) / Tower of strength (mix) / Mercenary.
(cd-s+=) *(MTHCD 11)* – Amelia (live) / Stay with me / Mercenary.

Vertigo Mercury

Apr 92. (7"/c-s) *(MYTH/MTHMC 12)* **NEVER AGAIN. / BEAUTIFUL CHAOS** 34 -
(12"+=/cd-s+=) *(MYTHX/MTHCD 12)* – ('A'-F1 mix) / ('A'-Zero G mix.

Jun 92. (cd/c/lp) *<(512121-2/-4/-1)>* **MASQUE** 23
– Never again / Shades of green (part II) / Even you may shine / Trail of scarlet / Spider and the fly / She conjures me wings / Sticks and stones / Like a child again / Who will love me tomorrow? / You make me breathe / From one Jesus to another / Until there's another sunrise. *(re-is.cd/c Aug94; same)*

Jun 92. (7"/c-s) *(MYTH/MTHMC 13)* **LIKE A CHILD AGAIN (remix). / ALL TANGLED UP IN YOU** 30 -
(12"+=/cd-s+=) *(MYTHX/MTHCD 13)* – ('A'-Mark Saunders remix) / Hush a bye baby (child again) (Joe Gibbs remix).

Oct 92. (7"/c-s) *(MYTH/MTHMC 14)* **SHADES OF GREEN. / YOU MAKE ME BREATHE** 49 -
(cd-s) *(MTHCD 14)* – ('A'side) / Sticks and stones / Trail of scarlet / Spider and the fly.
(etched-12"+=) *(MYTHX 14)* – ('A'mix).

— (Nov'92) **MARK THWAITE** – guitar (ex-SPEAR OF DESTINY) repl. HINKLER + ADAMS. Note:- **RIC SAUNDERS** – violin (of FAIRPORT CONVENTION) on last lp

Jan 94. (7") *(MYTH 15)* **TOWER OF STRENGTH (Youth remix). / WASTELAND** [33] [-]
(12"+=) *(MYTHX 15)* – Serpent's kiss.
(cd-s) *(MYTCD 15)* – ('A'mixes) / ('A'-East India Cairo mix) / Deliverance.

Feb 94. (cd/c/d-lp) *<(518447-2/-4/-1)>* **SUM AND SUBSTANCE** (compilation) [49] [ ]
– Never again / Hands across the ocean / Shades of green / Like a child again / Into the blue / Deliverance / Tower of strength / Butterfly on a wheel / Kingdom come / Beyond the pale / Severina / Stay with me / Wasteland / Garden of delight / Like a hurricane / Serpent's kiss / Sour puss / Afterglow.

Mar 94. (7") *(MYTH 16)* **AFTERGLOW. / SOUR-PUSS** [53] [-]
(cd-s+=) *(MYTCD 16)* – Cold as ice / Valentine.

Equator — not iss.

Oct 94. (7"ep/cd-ep) *(HOOK S/CD 001)* **MISSION 1 EP** [ ] [-]
– Raising Cain / Sway / Neverland.

Jan 95. (7"ep/cd-ep) *(HOOK S/CD 002)* **MISSION 2 EP** [73] [-]
– Swoon / Where / Wasting away.
(cd-ep+=) *(HOOKCDR 002)* – ('A'-Resurrection mix).

Feb 95. (cd/c/lp) *(SMEE CD/MC/LP 001)* **NEVERLAND** [58] [-]
– Raising Cain / Sway / Lose myself / Swoon / Afterglow (reprise) / Stars don't shine without you / Celebration / Cry like a baby / Heaven knows / Swim with the dolphins / Neverland / Daddy's going to Heaven now.

Jun 96. (cd/c/lp) *(SMEE CD/MC/LP 002)* **BLUE** [73] [-]
– Coming home / Get back to you / Drown in blue / Damaged / More than this / That tears shall drown the wind / Black & blue / Bang bang / Alpha man / Cannibal / Dying room / Evermore & again.

— HUSSEY and Co called it a day after above; he revived the band with **GEOFF READING** – drums, etc.

Eagle — Cleopatra

Nov 99. (cd) *(EAGCD 055) <CLP 756>* **RESURRECTION – GREATEST HITS** (re-workings) [ ] [ ]
– Prelude: Anniversary / Wasteland / Severina / Love me to death / Interlude: Never forever / Beyond the pale / Deliverance / Without you / Like a child again / Sacrilege / You make me breathe / Crystal ocean / Interlude: Infection / Hands across the ocean / 1969 / Resurrection.

– compilations, others, etc. –

Jun 87. (lp/c) *Mercury; (MISH/+C 1) <832527-1/-4>* **THE FIRST CHAPTER** [35] [ ] May88
(cd-iss. May88; 832527-2)

Jul 94. (cd/lp) *Nighttracks; (CDNT/LPNT 005)* **SALAD DAZE** [ ] [-]

Aug 95. (d-cd) *Mercury; (528805-2)* **CHILDREN / CARVED IN SAND** [ ] [-]

Jan 00. (cd) *Receiver; (RRCD 294)* **EVER AFTER LIVE** [ ] [-]

Feb 00. (cd) *Spectrum; (544228-2)* **TOWER OF STRENGTH** [ ] [-]

MISUNDERSTOOD

Formed: Riverside, California, USA . . . 1965. After one US independent 45, they moved to London and signed to 'Fontana' in 1966. John Ravenscroft (aka JOHN PEEL) became their manager, the band recording a number of tracks before they were all deported back to the States. Two of these tracks were released as singles, 'I CAN TAKE YOU TO THE SUN' (1966) and 'CHILDREN OF THE SUN' (1969). The latter (released after the band had left Britain), was a psychedelic classic, skull-shakingly heavy and featuring a blistering slide guitar. Back in America, a revamped line-up recorded a couple of lighter R&B singles before evolving into the heavier JUICY LUCY. This bunch scored a 1970 UK chart hit with an astounding version of BO DIDDLEY's 'WHO DO YOU LOVE'. The psychedelic material The MISUNDERSTOOD recorded in England was given a full posthumous release on 'Cherry Red' in 1982. • **Songwriters:** Group compositions except; I'M NOT TALKING (Yardbirds) / LITTLE RED ROOSTER (Willie Dixon) / etc. JUICY LUCY covered; WHO DO YOU LOVE (Bo Diddley) / etc.

Album rating: BEFORE THE DREAM FADED (*8) / GOLDEN GLASS (*6)

RICK BROWN – vocals / **GREG TREADWAY** – guitar / **GLENN ROSS CAMPBELL** – steel guitar / **STEVE WHITING** – bass / **RICK MOE** – drums

not iss. — Blues Sound

1966. (7") **YOU DON'T HAVE TO GO. /** [-] [ ]

— **GUY EVANS** – drums repl. MOE **TONY HILL** – guitar (ex-ANSWER) repl. TREADWAY

Fontana — Fontana

Dec 66. (7") *(TF 777)* **I CAN TAKE YOU TO THE SUN. / WHO DO YOU LOVE** [ ] [ ]

— Disbanded when BROWN was drafted into US army. In 1969, **GLENN ROSS** reformed a new line-up (on same label), completed by **STEVE HOARD** – vocals / **NEIL HUBBARD** – guitar (ex-GRAHAM BOND ORGANISATION, ex-GREASY BAND) / **CHRIS MERCER** – saxophone, keyboards (ex-JOHN MAYALL'S BLUESBREAKERS) / **NIC POTTER** – bass / **GUY EVANS** – drums (EVANS joined VAN DER GRAAF . . .) **TONY HILL** later joined HIGH TIDE.

Feb 69. (7") *(TF 998)* **CHILDREN OF THE SUN. / I UNSEEN** [ ] [ ]

May 69. (7") *(TF 1028)* **(YOU'RE) TUFF ENOUGH. / LITTLE RED ROOSTER** [ ] [ ]

Jul 69. (7"; as MISUNDERSTOOD featuring GLENN "FERNANDO" CAMPBELL) *(TF 1041)* **NEVER HAD A GIRL (LIKE YOU BEFORE). / GOLDEN GLASS** [ ] [ ]

— Group evolved into JUICY LUCY, except POTTER who joined VAN DER GRAAF . . .

– compilations, others, etc. –

May 81. (7"m) *Cherry Red; (CHERRY 22)* **CHILDREN OF THE SUN. / WHO DO YOU LOVE / I'LL TAKE YOU TO THE SUN** [ ] [-]

Apr 82. (lp) *Cherry Red; (BRED 32)* **BEFORE THE DREAM FADED** [ ] [-]
– COLOR OF THEIR SOUND:- Children of the sun / My mind / Who do you love? / I unseen / Find a hidden door / I can take you to the sun / BLUE DAY IN RIVERSIDE:- I'm not talkin' / I need your love / You don't have to go / I cried my eyes out / Like I do. *(cd-iss. May92; CDBRED 32)*

Jun 84. (7"m/12"m) *Cherry Red; (THYME 1/+12)* **GOLDEN GLASS. / SHAKE YOUR MONEY MAKER / I'M NOT TALKING** [ ] [-]

Aug 84. (lp) *Time Stood Still; (TSSLP 1)* **GOLDEN GLASS** [ ] [-]
– Never had a girl (like you before) / Golden glass / I don't want to discuss it (you're my girl) / Little red rooster / (You're) Tuff enough / Flamingo music / Freedom / Keep on running / I'm cruisin'.

Mar 97. (cd) *Cherry Red; (CDBRED 142)* **THE LEGENDARY GOLD STAR / GOLDEN GLASS** [ ] [-]

Kim MITCHELL (see under ⇒ MAX WEBSTER)

M.O.D. (see under ⇒ MINDFUNK)

MOIST

Formed: Vancouver, Canada . . . late '92 by DAVID USHER, MARK MAKOWY, KEVIN YOUNG, JEFF PEARCE and PAUL WILCOX. Early in 1994, they exploded onto the music scene with the 'SILVER' album, an independently released set that went on to sell over a quarter of a million copies worldwide after signing with 'Chrysalis'. A winning combination of LED ZEPPELIN-esque rock, R.E.M. harmonies and a U2-like stadium sound, the record spawned three UK hit singles, 'SILVER', 'FREAKY BE BEAUTIFUL' and their best-known track, 'PUSH'. Unfortunately, this has been their only album to date, the band since going to ground. They eventually re-emerged in 1996 with the Canadian/US-only release, 'CREATURE', a set of genuinely angst-ridden but ultimately forgettable alternative rock which struggled to match the immediacy of its predecessor. 'MERCEDES FIVE AND DIME' (2000), meanwhile, featured a distinct retro Brit-rock influence.

Album rating: SILVER (*6) / CREATURE (*4) / MERCEDES FIVE AND DIME (*6)

DAVID USHER – vocals / **MARK MAKOWY** – guitar / **KEVIN YOUNG** – keyboards / **JEFF PEARCE** – bass, vocals / **PAUL WILCOX** – drums

Chrysalis — Capitol

Nov 94. (c-s) *(TCCHS 5016)* **PUSH / MACHINE PUNCH THROUGH** [ ] [-]
(12"+=/cd-s+=) *(12/CD CHS 5016)* – Morphine.

Nov 94. (cd/c) *(CD/TC CHR 6080) <31656>* **SILVER** [35] [ ] May94
– Push / Believe me / Kill for you / Silver / Freaky be beautiful / Break her down / Into everything / Picture Elvis / Machine punch through / This shrieking love / Low low low.

Feb 95. (c-s) *(TCCHS 5019)* **SILVER / BREAK HER DOWN** [50] [-]
(12"clear+=) *(12CHS 5019)* – Kid conductor.
(cd-s+=) *(CDCHS 5019)* – See touch feel.

Apr 95. (12") *(12CHS 5022)* **FREAKY BE BEAUTIFUL. / KILL FOR YOU** [47] [-]
(c-s+=) *(TCCHS 5022)* – Push (acoustic).
(cd-s++=) *(CDCHS 5022)* – Picture Elvis (acoustic).

Aug 95. (c-s/7"purple) *(TCCHS/CHSS 5024)* **PUSH. / MISS YOU** [20] [-]
(cd-s) *(CDCHS 5024)* – ('A'side) / Machine punch through / This shrieking love / Low low low.
(cd-s) *(CDCHSS 5024)* – ('A'side) / ('A'-Youth mix) / ('A'-other mix).

not iss. — Arista

Jan 97. (cd/c) *<18971>* **CREATURE** [-] [ ]
– Hate / Theme from cola / Resurrection / Leave it alone / Creature / Shotgun / Disco days / Tangerine / Better than you / Baby skin tattoo / Ophelia / Gasoline.

not iss. — Capitol

Jun 00. (cd) *<25890>* **MERCEDES FIVE AND DIME** [-] [ ]
– Underground / Push / Breathe / Fish / Comes and goes / Dogs / Alive / Tonight / Pleasing falsetto / Mandolin / Place / Unknown.

MOLLY HATCHET

Formed: Jacksonville, Florida, USA . . . 1971 by DAVE HLUBECK and STEVE HOLLAND. By the time this hard gigging outfit had secured a major label deal with 'Epic' in 1976, DANNY JOE BROWN, DUANE ROLAND, BONNER THOMAS and BRUCE CRUMP had been recruited to complete the line-up. Following in the hard-bitten Southern-Rock traditions of their hometown and wearing their influences on their sleeve from the outset, the group's debut single was a cover of The Allman Brothers' classic 'DREAMS I'LL NEVER SEE', while the eponymous '79 debut set showcased their LYNYRD SKYNYRD/ALLMAN'S multi-guitar duelling boogie in fine style; RONNIE VAN ZANT had even offered to produce the band prior to his tragic death in the 1977 plane crash. With a Top 75 chart placing for the debut, it looked as if MOLLY HATCHET were primed to carry on the mantle of their heroes, a follow-up set, 'FLIRTIN' WITH DISASTER', making the US Top 20 later that year. The group even made it to Europe, playing to receptive crowds and carrying off a highly praised performance at the 1979 Reading Festival. Frontman BROWN was unhappy, however, leaving prior to the recording of 'BEATIN' THE ODDS' (1980), and being replaced with JIMMY FARRAR. The latter's vocals lacked the rough-hewn mellow charm of BROWN and the group lost some of their momentum, the 1981 horn-embellished set, 'TAKE NO PRISONERS' barely making the Top 40. Although BROWN returned in 1983 (with B.B. QUEEN and RIFF WEST replacing CRUMP and THOMAS respectively) for the back-to-basics 'NO GUTS . . . NO GLORY', the record failed to make up lost commercial ground. Another change in direction was effected for the limp 'THE DEED IS DONE' (1985), the album still failing to make the charts despite its radio-pandering content. Finally, after a blistering live set, 'DOUBLE TROUBLE' (1986), the group disbanded with BROWN suffering problems with diabetes. MOLLY HATCHET resurfaced a few years later on 'Capitol' minus founding member, HLUBECK, who was replaced by BOBBY INGRAM. The resulting album, 'LIGHTNING STRIKES TWICE' (1989), was a far cry from their Southern roots, its poor reception sinking the group for another five years; a further set, 'THE DEVIL'S CANYON', was released in summer '96. A second set for 'C.M.C.', 'SILENT REIGN OF HEROES' was duly despatched a few years later. Why? • **Songwriters:** Group compositions except LONG TALL SALLY (Little Richard) / I AIN'T GOT YOU (Yardbirds; b-side) / LET THE GOOD TIMES ROLL (Shirley & Lee) / HIDE YOUR HEART (Kiss) / FREE BIRD (Lynyrd Skynyrd). • **Trivia:** The group name was taken from a 17th century Salem woman who chopped off her husband's head.

Album rating: MOLLY HATCHET (*6) / FLIRTIN' WITH DISASTER (*6) / BEATIN' THE ODDS (*5) / TAKE NO PRISONERS (*5) / NO GUTS . . . NO GLORY (*5) / DOUBLE TROUBLE (*5) / LIGHTNING STRIKES TWICE (*4) / GREATEST HITS compilation (*6) / DEVIL'S CANYON (*4) / SILENT REIGN OF HEROES (*3)

DANNY JOE BROWN (b.1951) – vocals (ex-RUM CREEK) / **STEVE HOLLAND** (b.1954, Dothan, Alabama) – lead guitar (ex-ICE) / **DAVE HLUBECK** (b.1952) – guitar / **DUANE ROLAND** (b. 3 Dec'52, Jefferson, Indiana) – guitar / **BANNER THOMAS** – bass / **BRUCE CRUMP** – drums

Epic Epic

Nov 78. (7") *<50669>* **DREAMS I'LL NEVER SEE. / THE CREEPER** [-] [ ]

May 79. (lp/c) *(EPC/40 83250) <35347>* **MOLLY HATCHET** [ ] [64] Oct78
– Bounty hunter / Gator country / Big apple / The creeper / The price you pay / Dreams I'll never see / I'll be running / Cheatin' woman / Trust your old friend. *(cd-iss. Jul93 on 'Sony Europe')*

Aug 79. (7") *<50773>* **JUKIN' CITY. / GUNSMOKE** [-] [ ]

Oct 79. (lp/c) *(EPC/40 83791) <36110>* **FLIRTIN' WITH DISASTER** [ ] [19] Sep79
– Whiskey man / It's all over now / One man's pleasure / Jukin' City / Boogie no more / Flirtin' with disaster / Good rockin' / Gunsmoke / Long time / Let the good times roll. *(cd-iss. Jul89 on 'Columbia'; CD 462940)*

Oct 79. (7") *<50809>* **IT'S ALL OVER NOW. / GOOD ROCKIN'** [-] [ ]

Feb 80. (7") *(EPC 8221) <50822>* **FLIRTIN' WITH DISASTER. / GUNSMOKE** [ ] [42] Dec79

May 80. (7") *(EPC 8636)* **BOUNTY HUNTER. / BOOGIE NO MORE** [ ] [-]
(12"+=) *(EPC/+13 8636)* – Flirtin' with disaster.

— **JIMMY FARRAR** (b. La Grange, Georgia) – vocals repl. DANNY JOE who released eponymous band solo album summer '81 for 'Epic'.

Sep 80. (7") *<50943>* **BEATIN' THE ODDS. / FEW AND FAR BETWEEN** [-] [ ]

Oct 80. (lp/c) *(EPC/40 84471) <36572>* **BEATIN' THE ODDS** [ ] [25] Sep 80
– Beatin' the odds / Penthouse pauper / Far and few between / Dead and gone / The rambler / Double talker / Poison pen / Sailor / Get her back.

Mar 81. (7") *<50965>* **THE RAMBLER. / GET HER BACK** [-] [91]

Dec 81. (lp/c) *(EPC/40 85296) <37480>* **TAKE NO PRISONERS** [ ] [36]
– Bloody reunion / Respect me in the morning / Long tall Sally / Loss of control / All mine / Lady luck / Power play / Don't mess around / Don't leave me lonely / Dead giveaway.

Jan 82. (7") *<02680>* **POWER PLAY. / BLOODY REUNION** [-] [96]

Apr 82. (7") *<02820>* **LOSS OF CONTROL. / LADY LUCK** [-] [ ]

Jul 82. (7") *<03097>* **DREAMS I'LL NEVER SEE. / FLIRTIN' WITH DISASTER** [-] [ ]

— **DANNY JOE BROWN** – vocals returned to repl. FARRAR / **B.B. QUEEN** (b. BARRY BORDEN, 12 May'54, Atlanta, Georgia) – drums (ex-MOTHER'S FINEST) repl. CRUMP / added **JIMMY GALVIN** – keyboards / **RIFF WEST** (b. 3 Apr'50, Orlando, Florida) – bass repl. THOMAS

Mar 83. (lp/c) *(EPC/40 25244) <38429>* **NO GUTS . . . NO GLORY** [ ] [59]
– Fall of the peacemakers / Under the gun / On the prowl / Both sides / Ain't even close / What's it gonna take / What does it matter? / Kinda like love / Sweet Dixie. *(re-iss. Feb86 lp/c;* **EPC/40 32718**) *(cd-iss. Feb97; 473693-2)*

Apr 83. (7") *<03852>* **SWEET DIXIE. / KINDA LIKE LOVE** [-] [ ]

— **BRUCE CRUMP** – drums returned to repl. QUEEN who joined ILLUSION

Jan 85. (lp/c) *(EPC/40 26213) <39621>* **THE DEED IS DONE** [ ] [ ] Nov84
– Satisfied man / Backstabber / She does she does / Intro piece / Stone in your heart / Man on the run / Good smoke and whiskey / Heartbreak radio / I ain't got you / Straight shooter / Song for the children.

Jan 85. (7"/12") *(EPCA/TA 4848) <04648>* **SATISFIED MAN. / STRAIGHT SHOOTER** [ ] [81] Oct84

Mar 85. (7") *<04714>* **MAN ON THE RUN. / STONE IN YOUR HEART** [-] [ ]

Jan 86. (d-lp/d-c) *(EPC/40 88670) <40137>* **DOUBLE TROUBLE LIVE (live)** [94] [ ] Dec85
– Whiskey man / Bounty hunter / Gator country / Flirtin' with disaster / Stone in your heart / Satisfied man / Bloody reunion / Boogie no more / Walk on the side of angels / Walk with you / Dreams I'll never see / Edge of sundown / Fall of the peacemakers / Beatin' the odds.

— split when BROWN suffered diabetic problems. Re-formed again in '88.

— **BOBBY INGRAM** – guitar, vocals repl. HLUBEK

not iss. Capitol

1989. (lp/c/cd) *<792114-1/-4/-2>* **LIGHTNING STRIKES TWICE** [-] [ ]
– Take Miss Lucy home / There goes the neighborhood / No room on the crew / Find somebody new / The big payback / I can't be watching you / Goodbye to love / Hide your heart / What's the story, old glory / Heart of my soul. *(cd-iss. Dec96 on 'S.P.V.'; 085-4434-2)*

— split but re-formed in the mid 90's.

S.P.V. Mayhem

Aug 96. (cd) *(085-4435-2) <11105>* **DEVIL'S CANYON** [ ] [ ] Nov96
– Down from the mountain / Rolling thunder / Devil's canyon / Heartless land / Never say never / Tatanka / Come hell or high water / Look in your eyes / Eat your heart out / Journey / Dreams I'll never see.

S.P.V. C.M.C.

Jun 98. (cd) *(085-2922-2) <86252>* **SILENT REIGN OF HEROES** [ ] [ ]
– Mississippi moon dog / World of trouble / Silent reign of heroes / Miss Saturday night / Blue thunder / Just remember (you're the only one) / Junk yard dawg / Dead and gone / Saddle tramp / Fall of the peacemakers.

– compilations, others, etc. –

Dec 90. (cd/c) *Epic; <46949>* **GREATEST HITS** [-] [ ]

Michael MONROE (see under ⇒ HANOI ROCKS)

MONSTER MAGNET

Formed: New Jersey, USA . . . 1989 by porn-fixated DAVE WYNDORF (vocalist/guitarist) along with JOHN McBAIN (guitar), JOE CALANDRA (bass) and JOHN KLEINMAN (drums). Signing to European indie label 'Glitterhouse' ('Primo Scree' in the States), MONSTER MAGNET released their eponymous debut in 1991, drawing favourable reviews from the inkies and metal press alike. Akin to a heavier THEE HYPNOTICS, the band were evidently classic psych-rock fetishists with HAWKWIND as an obvious reference point as well as the mogadon riffing of IRON BUTTERFLY etc. Arguably 'grunge' in the true sense of the word; sludgy, filthy, mind-numbingly heavy and bloody scary, 'SPINE OF GOD' (1992) was a tour de force of 'like, heavy, man' drug-rock featuring the legendary album sleeve boast, 'It's a satanic drug thing . . . you wouldn't understand', erm.. right. God knows exactly what kind of drugs these guys were on (DAVE had been apparently selling and taking the stuff since he was 14!) but it sure as hell wasn't 'E'. After a tour supporting SOUNDGARDEN, the band replaced the departing McBAIN with ED MUNDELL, signing with 'A&M' and releasing their major label debut, 'SUPERJUDGE' (1993). Even more of a headbang than 'SPINE..', this was perhaps the heaviest psychedelia ever laid down on vinyl, the likes of 'CYCLOPS REVOLUTION' and 'ELEPHANT BELL' practically redefining the term, while a cover of HAWKWIND's 'BRAINSTORM' was reliably bowel-quaking. 'DOPES TO INFINITY' (1995) carried on in much the same bludgeoning fashion, advising mere mortals who're happy with a pint down the pub (as opposed to munching handfuls of nasty hallucinogens) to 'LOOK TO YOUR ORB FOR THE WARNING', eh? With guitarist PHIL CAIVANO now on board, MONSTER MAGNET's musical spaceship took off once more. Fourth album, 'POWERTRIP' (1998), was exactly that with numbers such as the title track and 'SPACE LORD' greasing up the UK Top 50 early the following year. Following that album's frenzied yet focused sonic onslaught, WYNDORF wound down slightly for 'GOD SAYS NO' (2001), a more diverse and experimental offering featuring a couple of tracks – title effort included – that could, at a pinch, be described as easy going. For fans of the primal MONSTER MAGNET riffola, there's a re-recorded version of 'MEDICINE' from 1992's classic 'SPINE . . .' set although the overwhelming aural suffocation of old is strangely absent. • **Covered:** KICK OUT THE JAMS (MC5).

Album rating: SPINE OF GOD (*8) / SUPERJUDGE (*8) / DOPES TO INFINITY (*7) / POWERTRIP (*6) / GOD SAYS NO (*6)

DAVE WYNDORF – vocals, guitar / **JOHN McBAIN** – guitar / **JOE CALANDRA** – bass / **JOHN KLEINMAN** – drums

Glitterhouse PrimoScree

Nov 90. (12"ep/cd-ep) *(EFA 08123-90)* **MONSTER MAGNET** [-] [-] German
– Snake dance / Tractor / Nod scene / Freak shop USA / Lizard Johnny. *(UK cd-iss. May99 on 'Global Warming'; GRCD 123)*

Oct 91. (m-cd) *(GRCD 158) <CAROL 1471>* **TAB** [ ] [ ]
– Tab / 25 / Longhair / Lord 13. *(re-iss. May99; as US) (re-is.May99; as UK)*

Jun 92. (cd/c/lp) *(GR 017-2/-4/-1) <EFA 08172-08>* **SPINE OF GOD** [ ] [ ] Dec91
– Pill shovel / Medicine / Nod scene / Black mastermind / Zodiac lung / Spine of God / Snake dance / Sin's a good man's brother / Ozium. *(cd re-iss. Mar99 on 'Caroline'; CAROL 1718) (cd re-iss. May99; as original)*

May 93. (12"/cd-s) *(GR/+CD 204)* **EVIL. / ELEPHANT BELL / SPINE OF GOD (live)** [ ] [ ]

— **ED MUNDEL** – lead guitar; repl. McBAIN

A&M A&M

Apr 93. (cd/c/red-lp) *(540 079-2/-4/-1) <31454-0079-2/-4/-1>* **SUPERJUDGE** [ ] [ ]
– Cyclops revolution / Twin earth / Superjudge / Cage around the sun / Elephant bell / Dinosaur vacume / Evil (is going on) / Stadium / Face down / Brainstorm / Black balloon.

May 93. (7") *(580 280-7)* **TWIN EARTH. / NOD SCENE (live)** [67] [ ]
(12"+=/cd-s+=) *(580 281-1/-2)* – Medicine (live).

Mar 95. (7"sha-pic-d) **NEGASONIC TEENAGE WARHEAD. / BLOW 'EM OFF** [49] [ ]
(cd-s+=) – Murder (live) / Superjudge live).
(cd-s) – ('A'side) / Eclipse this / Third alternative / Look into your orb for a warning.

Mar 95. (cd/d-lp) *<(540 315-2/-1)>* **DOPES TO INFINITY** [51] [ ]
– Dopes to infinity / Megasonic teenage warhead / Look to your orb for the warning / All friends and kingdom come / Ego, the living planet / Blow 'em off / Third alternative / I control, I fly / King of Mars / Dead Christmas / Theme from "Masterburner" / Vertigo. *(d-lp+=)* – Forbidden planet.

Apr 95. (7"pic-d) *(581 032-7)* **DOPES TO INFINITY. / I'M FIVE YEARS AHEAD OF MY TIME** [58] [-]
(cd-s+=) *(581 033-2)* – Looking to the orb for a warning.
(cd-s+=) *(581 032-2)* – Dinosaur vacume / Theme from "Masterburner".

— added 5th member, **PHIL CAIVANO** – guitar

Jun 98. (cd) <(540 908-2)> **POWERTRIP** [65] [97]
– Crop circle / Powertrip / Space Lord / Temple of your dreams / Bummer / Baby Gotterdamerung / 19 witches / 3rd eye landslide / See you in Hell / Tractor / Atomic clock / Goliath and the vampires / Your lies become you. *(re-iss. Feb99; same)* *(special d-cd May99; 490377-2)*

Jan 99. (one-sided-7") *(582822-7)* **POWERTRIP** [39] [-]
(cd-s+=) *(582823-2)* – Dead Christmas / ('A'-CD-Rom enhanced).
(cd-s) *(582825-2)* – ('A'side) / Twin Earth / Negasonic teenage warhead (enhanced).

Feb 99. (7"pic-d) *(563274-7)* **SPACE LORD. / THE GAME** [45] [-]
(cd-s) *(563275-2)* – ('A'side) / Big God / ('A'-CD-Rom).
(cd-s) *(563277-2)* – ('A'side) / Kick out the jams / Powertrip.

Interscope Interscope

Oct 00. (cd) <(490749-2)> **GOD SAYS NO** [ ] [ ] Apr01
– Melt / Heads explode / Doomsday / Medicine / God says no / Kiss of the scorpion / All shook out / Gravity well / My little friend / Queen of you / Cry / Take it / Silver future.

MONTROSE

Formed: California, USA ... Autumn '73 by RONNIE MONTROSE, who enlisted the services of guitarist BILL CHURCH, drummer DENNY CARMASSI and frontman SAMMY HAGAR. While both RONNIE and CHURCH had previously earned their crust through session work, including VAN MORRISON's country-esque 'Tupelo Honey' set and the classic 'Listen To The Lion', the groundbreaking hard-rock/heavy-metal they cooked up on the eponymous 'MONTROSE' (1974) was a different kettle of fish completely. Widely cited as one of the best metal debuts (indeed, albums) ever released, the super-charged likes of 'BAD MOTOR SCOOTER' and 'SPACE STATION No.5' achieved new levels of axe-wielding abrasiveness, the tension between HAGAR and MONTROSE almost tangible. Although it failed to break the US Top 100, the record subsequently went platinum and with ALAN FITZGERALD replacing CHURCH, the group worked on a follow-up. The fact that 'PAPER MONEY' was issued a matter of months after the debut only served to highlight its shortcomings, more problems besetting the band when HAGAR was sacked early the following year. BOB JAMES stepped into the frontman's shoes and with the addition of keyboard player, JIM ALCIVER, the band cut 'WARNER BROS PRESENTS MONTROSE!' (1975). The record failed to rekindle the livewire spark of the debut, and after a final effort in 1976, 'JUMP ON IT', MONTROSE called it a day. CHURCH and CARMASSI both subsequently played on HAGAR's solo material, while FITZGERALD and ALCIVER backed RONNIE on his solo debut, 'OPEN FIRE' (1978), a jazzy instrumental affair with EDGAR WINTER guesting on keyboards. The record's radically different approach was given the cold shoulder both critically and commercially, MONTROSE forming the harder rocking GAMMA as a result. This outfit released three albums ('1, 2 and 3!') between '79 and '82, RONNIE eventually resuming his solo career with the 'TERRITORY' set in 1986. Recruiting a band of sorts (numbering future FOREIGNER vocalist, JOHNNY EDWARDS, GLEN LETSCH and JAMES KOTTAK) for 'MEAN' (1987), RONNIE came up with his toughest work in years, although with the addition of synths, the subsequent 'THE SPEED OF SOUND' (1988) saw the guitarist once more taking a more laidback approach. Issued on 'Roadrunner', 1990's 'THE DIVA STATION' was another experimental affair, illustrating MONTROSE's restless creative energy. • **Songwriters:** MONTROSE-HAGAR, until the latter's departure. Covered; CONNECTION (Rolling Stones). RONNIE later covered STAY WITH ME BABY (Walker Brothers). • **Trivia:** RONNIE first sessioned on BEAVER & KRAUSE's 'Gandharva' lp.

Album rating: MONTROSE (*9) / PAPER MONEY (*8) / WARNER BROS PRESENTS (*5) / JUMP ON IT (*6) / Gamma: GAMMA 1 (*3) / GAMMA 2 (*4) / GAMMA 3 (*4) / Ronnie Montrose: OPEN FIRE (*5) / TERRITORY (*4) / MEAN (*5) / THE SPEED OF SOUND (*4) / THE DIVA STATION (*4)

RONNIE MONTROSE (b. Colorado, USA) – guitar (ex-VAN MORRISON, ex-EDGAR WINTER) / **SAMMY HAGAR** (b.13 Oct'47, Monterey, Calif.) – vocals / **BILL CHURCH** – bass (ex-VAN MORRISON sessions) / **DENNY CARMASSI** – drums

Warners Warners

Mar 74. (lp) *(K 46276)* <2740> **MONTROSE** [43] [ ]
– Rock the nation / Bad motor scooter / Space station No.5 / I don't want it / Good rockin' tonight / Rock candy / One thing on my mind / Make it last. *(cd-iss. Nov93; K2 46276)*

Mar 74. (7") <7814> **SPACE STATION NO.5. / MAKE IT EASY** [-] [ ]

Apr 74. (7") *(K 16382)* **BAD MOTOR SCOOTER. / ONE THING ON MY MIND** [ ] [-]

Jul 74. (7") *(K 16428)* <7776> **ROCK THE NATION. / ONE THING ON MY MIND** [ ] [ ] Jan74

—— **ALAN FITZGERALD** – bass repl. BILL (later to SAMMY HAGAR)

Sep 74. (7") <8063> **PAPER MONEY. / THE DREAMER** [-] [ ]

Nov 74. (lp) *(K 56069)* <2823> **PAPER MONEY** [ ] [65]
– Underground / Connection / The dreamer / Starliner / I got the fire / Spaceage sacrifice / We're going home / Paper money. *(cd-iss. Nov93;)*

Nov 74. (7") <8080> **WE'RE GOING HOME. / CONNECTION** [-] [ ]

—— **BOB JAMES** – vocals repl. HAGAR who went solo / added **JIM ALCIVER** – keyboards

Sep 75. (7") <8172> **CLOWN WOMAN. / MATRIARCH** [-] [ ]

Oct 75. (lp) *(K 56170)* <2892> **WARNER BROS. PRESENTS MONTROSE!** [ ] [79]
– Matriarch / All I need / Twenty fight rock / Whaler / Dancin' feet / O lucky man / One and a half / Clown woman / Black train. *(cd-iss. Apr96; 7599 27298-2)*

—— **RANDY JO HOBBS** – bass repl. FITZGERALD (later to SAMMY HAGAR)

Sep 76. (7") <8281> **MUSIC MAN. / TUFT-SIEGE** [-] [ ]

Nov 76. (lp) *(K 56291)* <2963> **JUMP ON IT** [ ] [ ] Sep76
– Let's go / What are you waitin' for / Tuft-sedge / Music man / Jump on it / Rich man / Crazy for you / Merry-go-round.

Nov 76. (7") <8351> **LET'S GO. /** [-] [ ]

—— Disbanded in 1977, CARMASSI joined SAMMY HAGAR

– compilations, others, etc. –

Both below on 'Heavy Metal' UK.

Jun 80. (7") *(HM 8)* **BAD MOTOR SCOOTER. / I DON'T WANT IT** [ ] [-]

Jun 80. (7") *(HM 9)* **SPACE STATION No.5. / GOOD ROCKIN' TONIGHT** [ ] [-]

RONNIE MONTROSE

went solo, augmented by **ALCIVAR, FITZGERALD** plus **RICK SCHLOSSER** – drums / and guest **EDGAR WINTER** – keyboards

Warners Warners

Jan 78. (lp) *(K 56451)* <3134> **OPEN FIRE** [ ] [98]
– Openers / Open fire / Mandolinia / Town without pity / Leo rising / Heads up / Rocky road / My little mystery / No beginning – no end. *(cd-iss. Jan96; 7599 26373-2)*

Jan 78. (7") <8544> **TOWN WITHOUT PITY. / NO BEGINNING NO END** [-] [ ]

GAMMA

was formed by **RONNIE MONTROSE**, retaining **ALCIVAR + FITZGERALD** plus **DAVEY PATTISON** – vocals / **SKIP GALLETTE** – drums

Elektra Elektra

Dec 79. (lp) *(K 52163)* <6E 219> **GAMMA I** [ ] [ ]
– Thunder and lightning / I'm alive / Razor king / No tears / Solar heat / Ready for action / Wish I was / Fight to the finish.

Jan 80. (7") <46555> **I'M ALIVE. / SOLAR HEAT** [-] [60]

Jun 80. (7") *(K 12459)* **THUNDER AND LIGHTNING. / RAZOR KING** [ ] [ ]

—— **GLENN LETSCH** – bass repl. FITZGERALD / **DENNY CARMASSI** – drums (ex-MONTROSE, ex-SAMMY HAGAR) repl. GALLETTE

Sep 80. (lp/c) *(K 52245)* <6E 228> **GAMMA 2** [ ] [65]
– Mean streak / Four horsemen / Dirty city / Voyager / Something in the air / Cat on a leash / Skin and bone / Mayday.

Oct 80. (7") *(K 12480)* <47034> **SOMETHING IN THE AIR. / MAYDAY** [ ] [ ]

Jan 81. (7") <47088> **VOYAGER. /** [-] [ ]

Mar 81. (7") *(K 12517)* **DIRTY CITY. / READY FOR ACTION** [ ] [ ]

—— **MITCHELL FROOM** – keyboards, synth. repl. ALCIVAR

Feb 82. (7") <47423> **RIGHT THE FIRST TIME. / NO WAY OUT** [-] [77]

Mar 82. (lp) *(K 52355)* <60034> **GAMMA 3** [ ] [72]
– What's gone is gone / Right the first time / Moving violation / Mobile devotion / Stranger / Condition yellow / Modern girl / No way out / Third degree.

Apr 82. (7") *(K 13165)* **RIGHT THE FIRST TIME. / CONDITION YELLOW** [ ] [-]

May 82. (7") <47476> **STRANGERS. /** [-] [ ]

—— broke-up again, PATTISON later joined ROBIN TROWER Band in 1987

– compilation –

1980's. (cd) *Warners;* **BEST OF** [-] [ ]
– Meanstreak / Four horsemen / Dirty city / Voyager / Stranger / Condition yellow / No way out / Third degree / Thunder and lightning / I'm alive / Razor king / Modern girl / Right the first time / Wish I was / What's gone is gone / Fight to the finish.

RONNIE MONTROSE

went solo again with band; **HILARY HANES** – bass / **STEVE BELLINO + JOHN HANES + ANDRE B. CHAPMAN** – drums / **PAT FEEHAN + MITCHEL FROOM + KEVIN MONAHAN + DOUG MORTON** – keyboards / **EDGAR WINTER** – saxophone / **BARBARA IMHOFF** – harp / **MICHAEL BEESE** – electric violin

not iss. Passport

Dec 86. (lp/c/cd) <PJ/+C/CD 88009> **TERRITORY** [-] [ ]
– Catscan / I'm gonna be strong / Love you to / Odd man out / I spy / Territory / Synesthesia / Pentagon / Women of Ireland.

—— now with **JOHNNY EDWARDS** – vocals / **GLEN LETSCH** – bass / **JAMES KOTTAK** – drums (later KINGDOM COME)

Enigma Enigma

May 87. (lp/cd) <(ENIG/CDE7 3264)> **MEAN** [ ] [ ]
– Don't damage the rock / Game of love / Pass it on / Hard headed woman / M for machine / Ready, willing and able / Man of the hour / Flesh and blood / Stand.

—— **JOHNNY BEE BEDANJEK** – vocals repl. EDWARDS who joined FOREIGNER / added **PAT FEEHAN** – synthesizer

G.W.R. Enigma

Aug 89. (lp/cd) *(GW LP/CD 53)* <3323-1/-2> **SPEED OF SOUND** [ ] [ ] Apr88
– March / Black box / Hyper-thrust / Monolith / Zero G / Telstar / Sindwinder / Windshear / VTOL / Outer marker inbound.

Roadrunner S.P.V.

Apr 90. (cd/lp) *(RR 9400-2/-1)* <2348-2/-1> **THE DIVA STATION** [ ] [ ]
– Sorcerer / The diva station / Weirding way / New kid in town / Choke canyon / Little demons / Stay with me baby / Quid pro quo / High and dry / Solitaire.

—— with **DAVE MORENO** – bass / **GARY HALL** – synthesizer / **STEVE BELLINO + DON FRANK** – percussion

not iss. I.R.S.

1991. (cd) <13112> **MUTATIS MUTANDIS** [-] [ ]
– Mutatis mutandis / Right saddle – Wrong horse / Heavy agenda / Greed kills / Mercury / Zero tolerance / Velox / Company policy / The nomad / Tonga.

—— now with **CRAIG McFARLAND** – bass / **MICHELE GRAYBEAL** – drums, percussion not iss. Fearless Urge

1994. (cd) <201> **MUSIC FROM HERE** [-] [ ]
– Mr Walker / Primary function / Largemouth / Road to reason / Life after life / Fear not / Indigo spheres / Braindance / The specialist / Walk softly / Wish in one hand.

— with **MYRON DOVE** – bass / **BILLY JOHNSON** – drums / **JOE HEINEMANN** – keyboards / **MICHELE GRAYBEAL** – percussion / **SPENCER NILSEN** – organ / **FITZ HUSTON** – vocals

not iss. SegaMusic

1996. (cd) <124145> **MR BONES** (original soundtrack to Sega Saturn game) [-] [ ]
– Manifesto / Bones is bones / Who's out there? / Don't think, play / The village / In this world / The first thing / Dry moat / The valley / By the way / Red to blue / Shadow monster / Mausoleum / Icy lake / The last word.

– compilations, etc. –

Jul 98. (cd; by GAMMA & RONNIE MONTROSE) *Ranch Life; (CRANCH 5)* **CONCERT CLASSICS** [ ] [ ]
– Ready for action / Thunder and lightning / Razor king / Wish I was / I got the fire / Open fire / Fight to the finish / I'm alive / So you wanna be a rock and roll star / No tears.

MOONSPELL

Formed: Lisbon, Portugal . . . 1989 initially as MORBID GOD by FERNANDO RIBEIRO, RICARDO AMORIM, SERGIO CRESTANA and MIKE GASPAR. Four years on, the Satanists opted for the moniker, MOONSPELL, the band adding PEDRO PAIXAO for their debut release, the demo 'ANNO SATANAE'. English speaking doom/goth-metal in the mould of TYPE O NEGATIVE or SISTERS OF MERCY, MOONSPELL quickly became one of the biggest bands of their ilk in Europe and South America. In 1998, the goths released a fourth set proper, 'SIN/PECADO', while later in the year, RIBEIRO took on extracurricular work, the first an album, 'HERMETICUM' (under the name, DAEMONARCH), the second a novel about a 21st century Jesus Christ.

Album rating: ANNO – SATANAE (*4) / UNDER THE MOONSPELL mini (*4) / WOLFHEART (*6) / IRRELIGIOUS (*4) / SIN/PECADO (*6) / THE BUTTERFLY EFFECT (*5) / Deamonarch: HERMETICUM (*5)

FERNANDO RIBEIRO – vocals / **RICARDO AMORIM** – guitar / **SERGIO CRESTANA** – bass / **MIKE GASPAR** – drums / plus **PEDRO PAIXAO** – synths, samplers

Lion not iss.

1993. (m-cd) **ANNO SATANAE** [-] [-] Polish

Adipocere not iss.

Jul 94. (m-cd) *(CDAR 021)* **UNDER THE MOONSPELL** [ ] [-]
– Allah Akbar~! la Allah ella Allah! / Tenebrarum oratorium (parts 1 & 2) / Opus diabolicum / Chotal Lusitania!

Century Media Century Media

May 95. (cd) *(<CM 7797CD>)* **WOLFHEART** [ ] [ ] Aug95
– Wolfshade (a werewolf masquerade) / Love crimes / . . .Of dream and drama (midnight ride) / Lua d'inverno / Trebaruna / Vampiria / An erotic alchemy / Alma meter. *(d-cd-iss. Dec95; CM 77112CDD)*

Aug 96. (cd/c/lp) *(CM 77123-2/-4/-1)* <7823> **IRRELIGIOUS** [ ] [ ]
– Perverse . . . almost religious / Opium / Awake / For a taste of eternity / Ruin & misery / A poisoned gift / Subversion / Raven claws / Memphisto / Herr Spieglmann / Full moon madness.

Oct 97. (cd-ep) *(CM 77189CD)* **2ECOND SKIN EP** [ ] [-]
– 2econd skin / An erotic alchemy (remix) / Scared / 2econd skin (video). *(with free live cd-ep)* – Opium / Awake / Herr Spiegelmann / Of dreams & drama / Ruin and misery / Mephisto / Alma matter.

Jan 98. (cd) *(CM 77190-2)* <7890> **SIN / PECADO** [ ] [ ] Feb98
– Slow down! / Handmade god / 2econd skin / Abysmo / Flesh / Magdalene / V.C. / Eurotic / Mute / Dekadance / Let the children cum to me / The hanged man / 13!

Oct 99. (cd/lp) *(CM 77290-2/-1)* <7990> **THE BUTTERFLY EFFECT** [ ] [ ] Nov99
– Soulsick / Butterfly FX / Can't bee / Lustmord / Selfabuse / I am the eternal spectator / Soulitary vice / Disappear here / Adaptables / Angelizer / Tired / K.

DAEMONARCH

aka **FERNANDO RIBEIRO**

Century Media Century Media

Aug 98. (cd) *(CM 77240CD)* <7940> **HERMETICUM** [ ] [ ] Oct98
– Lex talionis / Of a thousand young / Corpus hermeticum / Call from the grave / Saniyaca / Nxie angles / Lacuhus / The seventh daemonarch / Hymn to Lucifer.

Gary MOORE

Born: 4 Apr'52, Belfast, N.Ireland. In the late 60's, he joined psychedelic outfit, GRANNY'S INTENTIONS, a band that included NOEL BRIDGEMAN on drums. While they later went on to record the 'HONEST INJUN' album for 'Deram', GARY and NOEL formed SKID ROW with bassist BRENDAN SHIELDS. Relocating to London in 1970, the band signed to 'C.B.S.', releasing two albums of progressive blues rock, 'SKID' (1970) and '34 HOURS' (1971) before MOORE left to form his own outfit (during this time he'd also undertaken some live work with DR. STRANGELY STRANGE, as well as guesting on their 1970 album, 'HEAVY PETTIN''). With a line-up of JAN SCHELHAAS (keyboards, ex-NATIONAL HEAD BAND), JOHN CURTIS (bass), PEARCE KELLY (drums) and session man PHILIP DONNELLY on guitar, The GARY MOORE BAND cut one album in 1973, 'GRINDING STONE'. The group never actually got round to making a follow-up as MOORE joined THIN LIZZY (PHIL LYNOTT had been a brief member of SKID ROW in its earliest incarnation) for three months as a replacement for the departed ERIC BELL. MOORE was eventually succeeded by SCOTT GORHAM and BRIAN ROBERTSON, the guitarist joining COLOSSEUM II and recording three albums with the group, 'STRANGE NEW FLESH' (1976), 'ELECTRIC SAVAGE' (1977) and 'WARDANCE' (1977). In addition to his rapidly improving guitar playing, MOORE sang lead vocals on some tracks, the material significantly heavier than the band's earlier incarnation as a progressive jazz rock outfit. Leaving COLOSSEUM in 1977, MOORE filled in for an injured BRIAN ROBERTSON on THIN LIZZY's American tour, eventually going full time with the band in the summer of 1978. At the same time MOORE resumed his solo career with the help of friends DON AIREY (keyboards; of COLOSSEUM II), JOHN MOLE (bass), SIMON PHILIPS (drums), plus PHIL LYNOTT and BRIAN DOWNEY of THIN LIZZY. Together they recorded an album, 'BACK ON THE STREETS' (1979) and two singles, one of which was the classic 'PARISIENNE WALKWAYS'. Featuring LYNOTT on vocals, the track was an epic piece of emotive axe work, MOORE's undulating soloing among the best work of his career. A Top 10 hit upon its original release in 1979, the track remains the guitarist's most played and most purchased record. Although MOORE remained a member of THIN LIZZY long enough to feature on their seminal UK Top 3 album, 'BLACK ROSE (A ROCK LEGEND)' in 1979, he left the band midway through an American tour, eventually setting up his own outfit, G-FORCE, in 1980. After a solitary eponymous album the same year, the group came to nothing, MOORE joining the GREG LAKE BAND for a couple of years. At the same time he also worked on a solo career, recruiting CHARLIE HUHN (vocals, ex-JACK LANCASTER), TOMMY EYRE (keyboards, ex-GREG LAKE BAND), NEIL MURRAY (bass, ex-WHITESNAKE) and IAN PAICE (drums, ex-WHITESNAKE, ex-DEEP PURPLE, ex-PAICE, ex-ASHTON & LORD, phew!!). The first album, 'CORRIDORS OF POWER' (1982) made the UK Top 30, although it failed to spawn any hit singles. For 1984's 'VICTIMS OF THE FUTURE', MOORE recruited a whole new band again, numbering NEIL CARTER (keyboards, guitar, ex-UFO, ex-WILD HORSES), BOBBY CHOUINARD (drums, although PAICE contributed to the next two albums) and CRAIG GRUBER (bass, ex-BILLY SQIER, although MURRAY appeared on the album). The set almost made the Top 10, while the melancholy ballad-ish 'EMPTY ROOMS' was a minor hit single. Replacing GRUBER first with BOB DAISLEY and then GLENN HUGHES (ex-DEEP PURPLE) while PAUL THOMPSON (ex-ROXY MUSIC) and TED McKENNA (ex-SAHB) took over on drums, MOORE once again hooked up with PHIL LYNOTT for the blistering 'OUT IN THE FIELDS', a No. 5 hit in 1985. Later that summer, a re-issued 'EMPTY ROOMS' went to No.23, while the album, 'RUN FOR COVER' almost made the Top 10. At last MOORE seemed to be on a bit of a roll, hooking up with Irish folk legends, The CHIEFTAINS for 'OVER THE HILLS AND FAR AWAY', another Top 20 hit. 'WILD FRONTIER' (1987) was released early the following Spring and saw MOORE looking back to his Irish roots for inspiration, the cover art depicting a bleak Celtic landscape. On the title track, MOORE tackled the equally bleak Irish political landscape, his wailing riffs echoing his feelings of frustration. With COZY POWELL on drums, 'AFTER THE WAR' (1989) continued in a similar vein, again exploring the Irish question in songs like 'BLOOD OF EMERALDS'. Throughout the 90's, harder-edged rock took a back seat for more blues-orientated material, MOORE releasing the acclaimed 'STILL GOT THE BLUES' in 1990. Subsequent albums 'AFTER HOURS', 'BLUES ALIVE', 'BLUES FOR GREENY' (a tribute to PETER GREEN) and his swansong studio Virgin release 'DARK DAYS IN PARADISE' followed a similar direction. In 1999, MOORE was back in circulation for 'Raw Power' via new album, 'A DIFFERENT BEAT', while 2001's 'BACK TO THE BLUES' (for 'Sanctuary' records) even returned him to the UK Top 60. • **Covered:** DON'T LET ME BE MISUNDERSTOOD (hit; Animals) / SHAPES OF THINGS (Yardbirds) / FRIDAY ON MY MIND (Easybeats) / DON'T YOU TO ME (Hudson Whittaker) / THE BLUES IS ALRIGHT (Milton Campbell) / KEY TO LOVE (John Mayall) / JUMPIN' AT SHADOWS (Duster Bennett) / etc. • **Trivia:** MOORE also sessioned on 1975's 'Peter & The Wolf', and ANDREW LLOYD WEBBER's 1978 lp 'Variations'. In 1980, he was heard on ROD ARGENT's 'Moving Home' & COZY POWELL's 'Over The Top'.

Album rating: GRINDING STONE (*4) / BACK ON THE STREETS (*6) / G-FORCE with G-Force (*5) / CORRIDORS OF POWER (*6) / VICTIMS OF THE FUTURE (*6) / WE WANT MOORE (*6) / RUN FOR COVER (*6) / WILD FRONTIER (*6) / AFTER THE WAR (*6) / STILL GOT THE BLUES (*8) / AFTER HOURS (*7) / BLUES ALIVE (*7) / BLUES FOR GREENY (*7) / BALLADS AND BLUES 1982-1994 compilation (*8) / DARK DAYS IN PARADISE (*4) / OUT IN THE FIELDS – THE VERY BEST OF GARY MOORE compilation (*8) / A DIFFERENT BEAT (*5) / BACK TO THE BLUES (*6)

GARY MOORE BAND

GARY MOORE – guitar, vocals (ex-SKID ROW) with **JAN SCHELHAAS** – keyboards (ex-NATIONAL HEAD BAND) / **JOHN CURTIS** – bass / **PEARCE KELLY** – drums / plus session man **PHILIP DONNELLY** – guitar

C.B.S. Peters

1973. (lp) *(CBS 65527)* <9004> **GRINDING STONE** [ ] [ ]
– Grinding stone / Time to heal / Sail across the mountain / The energy dance / Spirit / Boogie my way back home. *(re-iss. Nov85 lp/c; CBS/40 32699) (re-iss. Oct90 cd/c/lp; 467449-2/-4/-1) (cd re-iss. Jul00 on 'Essential'; ESMCD 914)*

— In 1974 GARY joined THIN LIZZY ⇒ for 3 mths. May75 he joined COLOSSEUM II before returning to THIN LIZZY p/t for 5 mths early'77 and f/t Aug'78.

GARY MOORE

also started a new solo career at this time with friends **DON AIREY** – keyboards (of COLOSSEUM) / **JOHN MOLE** – bass / **SIMON PHILLIPS** – drums / plus THIN LIZZY'S – **PHIL LYNOTT** and **BRIAN DOWNEY**.

M.C.A. Jet

Dec 78. (7") *(MCA 386)* **BACK ON THE STREETS. / TRACK NINE**

Jan 79. (lp) *(MCF 2853)* *<JZ 36187>* **BACK ON THE STREETS** 70
– Back on the streets / Don't believe a word / Fanatical fascists / Flight of the snow moose / Hurricane / Song for Donna / What would you rather bee or wasp / Parisienne walkways. *(re-iss. Aug81 lp/c; MCL/MCLC 1622) (re-iss. Apr92 cd/c; MCL D/C 19011)*

Apr 79. (7") *(MCA 419)* *<5061>* **PARISIENNE WALKWAYS. / FANATICAL FASCISTS** 8
(above single featured PHIL LYNOTT – vocals (of THIN LIZZY)

Oct 79. (7") *MCA 534)* **SPANISH GUITAR. / SPANISH GUITAR (instrumental)** -

Oct 79. (7") *<5066>* **BACK ON THE STREETS. / SONG FOR DONNA** -

G-FORCE

GARY MOORE – guitar, vocals / **TONY NEWTON** – vocals / **WILLIE DEE** – keyboards, bass, vocals / **MARK NAUSEEF** – drums, percussion (ex-THIN LIZZY, ex-ELF, ex-IAN GILLAN BAND)

Jet Jet

Jun 80. (7") *(JET 183)* **HOT GOSSIP. / BECAUSE OF YOUR LOVE**

Jun 80. (lp/pic-lp) *(JET/+PD 229)* **G-FORCE**
– You / White knuckles – Rockin' & rollin' / She's got you / I look at you / Because of your love / You kissed me sweetly / Hot gossip / The woman's in love / Dancin'. *(re-iss. Feb91 on 'Castle' cd/c/lp; CLA CD/MC/LP 212) (cd re-iss. Oct00 on 'Castle'; CMRCD 034)*

Aug 80. (7") *(JET 194)* **YOU. / TRUST YOUR LOVIN'**

Nov 80. (7") *(JET 7005)* **WHITE KNUCKLES – ROCKIN' & ROLLIN'. / I LOOK AT YOU**

— In '81 and '83 he was part of the GREG LAKE BAND. Although he did continue his solo career

GARY MOORE

with **CHARLIE HUHN** – vocals (ex-JACK LANCASTER) / **TOMMY EYRE** – keyboards (ex-GREG LAKE BAND) / **NEIL MURRAY** – bass (ex-WHITESNAKE) / **IAN PAICE** – drums (ex-WHITESNAKE, ex-DEEP PURPLE, ex-PAICE, ex-ASHTON & LORD)

Jet not iss.

Oct 81. (12"ep; as GARY MOORE & FRIENDS) *(JET12 016)* **NUCLEAR ATTACK. / DON'T LET ME BE MISUNDERSTOOD / RUN TO YOUR MAMA** -

Virgin Mirage

Sep 82. (7"/7"pic-d) *(VS/+Y 528)* *<99896>* **ALWAYS GONNA LOVE YOU. / COLD HEARTED** Feb83

Oct 82. (lp/c) *(V/TCV 2245)* *<90077>* **CORRIDORS OF POWER** 30 Apr83
– Don't take me for a loser / Always gonna love you / Wishing well / Gonna' break my heart again / Falling in love with you / End of the world / Rockin' every night / Cold hearted / I can't wait until tomorrow. *(free live 7"ep) (VDJ 34)* – PARISIENNE WALKWAYS. / ROCKIN' EVERY NIGHT / BACK ON THE STREETS *(re-iss. Jun85 lp/c; OVED/+C 210) (cd-iss. Jul85; CDV 2245)*

— **JOHN SLOMAN** – vocals, keyboards repl. HUHN / **DON AIREY** – keyboards (see above) (ex-OZZY OSBOURNE) repl. EYRE

Feb 83. (7"/7"pic-d) *(VS/+Y 564)* *<99856>* **FALLING IN LOVE WITH YOU. / ('A'instrumental)** May83
(12"+=) *(VST 564)* – Wishing well.

— GARY MOORE recruited new personnel after SLOMAN departed / **NEIL CARTER** – keyboards, guitar (ex-UFO, ex-WILD HORSES) repl. AIREY / **BOBBY CHOUINARD** – drums 1/2 repl. PAICE (he appeared on most of next 2 lp's) / on tour Mar 84 **CRAIG GRUBER** – bass (ex-BILLY SQUIER) 1/2 replaced MURRAY (he appeared on lp) (note that all: MURRAY, AIREY and PAICE rejoined past bands WHITESNAKE, OZZY OSBOURNE and DEEP PURPLE respectively)

10-Virgin Mirage

Jan 84. (7"/7"sha-pic-d) *(TEN/+S 13)* **HOLD ON TO LOVE. / DEVIL IN HER HEART** 65 -
(12"+=) *(TEN 13-12)* – Law of the jungle.

Feb 84. (lp/c/cd) *(DIX/+C/CD 2)* *<90154>* **VICTIMS OF THE FUTURE** 12 May84
– Victims of the future / Teenage idol / Shapes of things / Empty rooms / Murder in the skies / All I want / Hold on to love / Law of the jungle. *(re-iss. Jun88 on 'Virgin' lp/c; OVED/+C 206)*

Mar 84. (7"/7"sha-pic-d) *(TEN/+S 19)* **SHAPES OF THINGS. / BLINDER** -
(12"+=) *(TEN 19-12)* – (an interview with Alan Freeman).

Aug 84. (7") *(TEN 25)* **EMPTY ROOMS. / NUCLEAR ATTACK (live)** 51 -
(12"+=) *(TEN 25-12)* – ('A'extended).

Aug 84. (7") **EMPTY ROOMS. / MURDER IN THE SKIES** -

Oct 84. (d-lp/d-c/d-cd) *(GMDL/CGMDL/GMDLD 1)* **WE WANT MOORE (live)** 32 -
– Murder in the skies / Shapes of things / Victims of the future / Cold hearted / End of the world / Back on the streets / So far away / Empty rooms / Don't take me for a loser / Rockin' and rollin'.

— **GLENN HUGHES** – bass (ex-DEEP PURPLE) repl. BOB DAISLEY who repl. GRUBER / **PAUL THOMPSON** (ex-ROXY MUSIC) and **TED McKENNA** (ex-SAHB) took over drums

May 85. (7"/7"sha-pic-d; GARY MOORE & PHIL LYNOTT) *(TEN/+S 49)* **OUT IN THE FIELDS. / MILITARY MAN** 5 -
(12"+=) *(TEN 49-12)* – Still in love with you.
(d7"+=) *(TEND 49)* – Stop messin' around (live).

Jul 85. (7") *(TEN 58)* **EMPTY ROOMS. / OUT OF MY SYSTEM** 23 -
(12"+=) *(TEN 58-12)* – Parisienne walkways (live) / Empty rooms (summer '85).
(d7"+=) *(TEND 58)* – Parisienne walkways (live) / Murder in the skies (live).

Sep 85. (lp/c) *(DIX/CDIX 16)* *<90482>* **RUN FOR COVER** 12 Feb86
– Run for cover / Reach for the sky / Military man / Empty rooms / Out in the fields / Nothing to lose / Once in a lifetime / All messed up / Listen to your heartbeat. *(cd-iss. Feb86 +=; DIXCD 16)* – Out of my system. *(pic-lp-iss.1986; DIXP 16) (re-iss. 1989 on 'Virgin' lp/c; OVED/+C 274)*

— **GARY** now used members of The CHIEFTAINS. Retained **CARTER + DAISLEY**

Dec 86. (7"/7"sha-pic-d) *(TEN/+S 134)* **OVER THE HILLS AND FAR AWAY. / CRYING IN THE SHADOWS** 20 -
(d7"+=) *(TEND 134)* – All messed up (live) / Out in the fields (live).
(12"+=) *(TENT 134)* – All messed up (live) / ('A'version).

Feb 87. (7") *(TEN 159)* **WILD FRONTIER. / RUN FOR COVER (live)** 35 -
(12"+=) *(TENT 159)* – ('A'live) / ('A'extended).
(d7"+=) *(TEND 159)* – Murder in the skies (live) / Wild frontier (live).
(cd-s+=) *(KERRY 159)* – Over the hills and far away / Empty rooms / Out in the fields / Shapes of things.

Mar 87. (lp/c/cd) *(DIX/CDIX/DIXCD 56)* *<90588>* **WILD FRONTIER** 8 May87
– Over the hills and far away / Wild frontier / Take a little time / The loner / Friday on my mind / Strangers in the darkness / Thunder rising / Johnny boy. *(cd+=)* – Crying in the shadows / Over the hills and far away (12"version) / Wild frontier (12"version) *(re-iss. Sep87. WILD FRONTIER (SPECIAL EDITION); DIXG 56) (incl.extra 12"ep) (pic-cd-iss. Jan89; DIXPCD 56) (re-iss. Apr90 on 'Virgin' lp/c; OVED/+C 285)*

Apr 87. (7"/7"pic-d) *(TEN/+P 164)* **FRIDAY ON MY MIND. / REACH FOR THE SKY (live)** 26 -
(12"+=) *(TENT 164)* – ('A'version).
(cd-s+=) *(KERRY 164)* – Parisienne walkways (live) / ('A'-Kool rap version).

Aug 87. (7"/ext.7"s) *(TEN/+C 178)* **THE LONER. / JOHNNY BOY** 53 -
(12"+=) *(TENT 178)* – ('A'live).

Nov 87. (7") *(TEN 190)* **TAKE A LITTLE TIME. / OUT IN THE FIELDS** 75 -
(d7"+=) *(TEND 190)* – All messed up (live) / Thunder rising (live).

— brought back **COZY POWELL** – drums

Virgin Virgin

Jan 89. (7"/7"g-f/7"pic-d) *(GMS/+G/Y 1)* **AFTER THE WAR. / THIS THING CALLED LOVE** 37
(12"+=) *(GMST 1)* – Over the hills and far away.
(3"cd-s+=) *(GMSCD 1)* – Emerald / Thunder rising.

Jan 89. (cd/c/lp) *(CD/TC+/V 2575)* *<91066>* **AFTER THE WAR** 23 Mar89
– After the war / Speak for yourself / Livin' on dreams / Led clones / Running from the storm / This thing called love / Ready for love / Blood of emeralds. *(c+=/cd+=)* – Dunlace (pt.1 & 2) / The messiah will come. *(re-iss. Sep90 lp/c; OVED/+C 335) (cd re-iss. Aug98 on 'VIP-Virgin'; CDVIP 212)*

Mar 89. (7") *(GMS 2)* **READY FOR LOVE. / WILD FRONTIER** 56 -
(12"+=/12"g-f+=/cd-s+=) *(GMS T/TG/CD 2)* – The loner (live).
(3"cd-s+=) *(GMSCDX 2)* – Military man (live).

Apr 89. (7") *<99211>* **SPEAK FOR YOURSELF. / LED CLONES** -

— **CHRIS SLADE** – drums (ex-MANFRED MANN'S EARTH BAND, ex-FIRM) repl. COZY POWELL

Oct 89. (7") *(VS 1219)* **LIVIN' ON DREAMS. / THE MESSIAH WILL COME AGAIN** -
(12"+=) *(VST 1219)* – ('A'extended).

— His band were now **DON AIREY** – keyboards / **BOB DAISLEY + ANDY PYLE** – bass / **GRAHAM WALKER + BRIAN DOWNEY** – drums / **FRANK MEAD** – tenor sax / **NICK PAYN** – sax

Mar 90. (7"/c-s) *(VS/+C 1233)* **OH PRETTY WOMAN. / KING OF BLUES** 48
(12"+=/12"s+=/cd-s+=) *(VS T/TP/CDT 1233)* – The stumble.

Mar 90. (cd/c/lp) *(CD/TC+/V 2612)* *<91369>* **STILL GOT THE BLUES** 13 83 Jun90
– Moving on / Oh pretty woman / Walking by myself / Still got the blues / Texas strut / Too tired / King of the blues / As the years go passing by / Midnight blues / That kind of woman / All your love / Stop messin' around.

May 90. (7"/c-s) *(VS/+C 1267)* *<98854>* **STILL GOT THE BLUES (FOR YOU). / LET ME WITH THE BLUES** 31 97 Jan91
(12"+=) *(VST 1267)* – ('A'extended) / The sky is crying.
(cd-s+=) *(VSCDT 1267)* – Further on up the road / The sky is crying.
(cd-s+=) *(VSCDX 1267)* – Mean cruel woman.

Aug 90. (7") *(VS 1281)* **WALKING BY MYSELF. / ALL YOUR LOVE** 48
(12"+=) *(VST 1281)* – ('A'live).
(cd-s++=) *(VSCDT 1281)* – Still got the blues (live).

Dec 90. (7"; GARY MOORE featuring ALBERT COLLINS) *(VS/+C 1306)* **TOO TIRED. / TEXAS STRUT** 71
(12"+=/cd-s+=) *(VS T/CDT 1306)* – ('A'live).
(cd-s) *(VSCDX 1306)* – ('A'side) / All your love (live) / The stumble.

— He featured on TRAVELING WILBURYS single 'She's My Baby'.

— **WILL LEE + JOHNNY B.GAYDON** – bass repl. PYLE / **ANTON FIG** – drums repl. DOWNEY / **TOMMY EYRE** – keyboards repl. AIREY / added on horns **MARTIN DROVER, NICK PENTELOW, ANDREW LOVE + WAYNE JACKSON RICHARD MORGAN** – oboe / backing vocals – **CAROLE KENYON + LINDA TAYLOR**

Feb 92. (7"/c-s; GARY MOORE & THE MIDNIGHT BLUES BAND) *(VS/+C 1393)* **COLD DAY IN HELL. / ALL TIME LOW** 24
(cd-s+=) *(VSCDT 1393)* – Stormy Monday (live) / Woke up this morning.

Mar 92. (cd/c/lp) *(CD/TC+/V 2684)* *<91825>* **AFTER HOURS** 4
– Cold day in Hell / Don't lie to me (I get evil) / Story of the blues / Since I met you baby / Separate ways / Only fool in town / Key to love / Jumpin' at shadows / The blues is alright / The hurt inside / Nothing's the same.

May 92. (7"/c-s) *(VS/+C 1412)* **STORY OF THE BLUES. / MOVIN' ON DOWN THE ROAD** 40
(cd-s+=) *(VSCDT 1412)* – King of the blues.
(cd-s+=) *(VSCDG 1412)* – Midnight blues (live).

Jul 92. (7"/c-s; GARY MOORE & B.B. KING) *(VS/+C 1423)* **SINCE I MET YOU BABY. / THE HURT INSIDE** 59
(cd-s+=) *(VSCDT 1423)* – Moving on (live) / Texas strut (live).
(cd-s+=) *(VSCDX 1423)* – Don't start me talking / Once in a blue mood (instrumental).

Oct 92. (7"/c-s) *(VS/+C 1437)* **SEPARATE WAYS. / ONLY FOOL IN TOWN** 59
(cd-s+=) *(VSCDT 1437)* – You don't love me (live) / The stumble (live).
(cd-s+=) *(VSCDX 1437)* – Further on up the road (live with ALBERT COLLINS) / Caledonia (live with ALBERT COLLINS).

Apr 93. (7"/c-s) *(VS/+C 1456)* **PARISIENNE WALKWAYS (live '93). / STILL GOT THE BLUES** 32
(cd-s+=) *(VSCDT 1456)* – Since I met you baby (live with B.B. KING) / Key to love.
(cd-s+=) *(VSCDX 1456)* – Stop messin' around / You don't love me.

Pointblank Virgin

May 93. (cd/c/d-lp; as GARY MOORE & THE MIDNIGHT BLUES BAND) *(CD/TC+/V 2716)* **BLUES ALIVE** 8
– Cold day in Hell / Walking by myself / Story of the blues / Oh pretty woman / Separate ways / Too tired / Still got the blues / Since I met you baby / The sky is crying / Further on up the road / King of the blues / Parisienne walkways / Jumpin' at shadows.

— In Jun '94, MOORE teamed up with JACK BRUCE + GINGER BAKER (ex-CREAM, and both solo artists) to form BBM. They had UK Top10 album 'AROUND THE NEXT DREAM' for 'Virgin' records.

Virgin Virgin

Nov 94. (cd/c/lp) *(CD/TC+/V 2768)* **BALLADS AND BLUES 1982-1994** (compilation) 33
– Always gonna love you / Still got the blues / Empty rooms / Parisienne walkways / One day / Separate ways / Story of the blues / Crying in the shadows / With love (remember) / Midnight blues / Falling in love with you / Jumpin' at shadows / Blues for Narada / Johnny boy.
below a tribute to PETER GREEN (ex-Fleetwood Mac) guitarist

— musicians:- **TOMMY EYRE** – keyboards / **ANDY PYLE** – bass / **GRAHAM WALKER** – drums / **NICK PENTELOW + NICK PAYN** – brass

May 95. (cd/c/lp) *(CD/TC+/V 2784)* **BLUES FOR GREENY** 14
– If you be my baby / Long grey mare / Merry go round / I loved another woman / Need your love so bad / The same way / The supernatural / Driftin' / Showbiz blues / Love that burns. *(cd+=)* – Looking for somebody.

Jun 95. (7"ep/c-ep/cd-ep) *(VS/+C/CD 1546)* **NEED YOUR LOVE SO BAD / THE SAME WAY (acoustic). / THE WORLD KEEPS ON TURNIN' (acoustic) / STOP MESSIN' AROUND (acoustic)** 48

— with **GUY PRATT** – bass / **GARY HUSBAND** – drums / **MAGNUS FIENNES + PAUL NICHOLAS** – keyboards

May 97. (c-s) *(VSC 1632)* **ONE GOOD REASON / BEAST OF BURDEN** -
(cd-s+=) *(VSCDT 1632)* – Burning in our hearts / There must be a way.

May 97. (cd/c) *(CDV/TCV 2826)* **DARK DAYS IN PARADISE** 43
– One good reason / Cold wind blows / I have found my love in you / One fine day / Like angels / What are we here for? / Always there for you / Afraid of tomorrow / Where did we go wrong? / Business as usual.

Jun 97. (c-s) *(VSC 1640)* **I HAVE FOUND MY LOVE IN YOU / MY FOOLISH PRIDE** -
(cd-s+=) *(VSCDT 1640)* – All the way from Africa.

Nov 97. (c-s) *(VSC 1674)* **ALWAYS THERE FOR YOU / RHYTHM OF OUR LIVES** -
(cd-s+=) *(VSCDT 1674)* – ('A'mixes).

Oct 98. (cd/c) *(CDV/TCV 2871)* **OUT IN THE FIELDS – THE VERY BEST OF GARY MOORE** (compilation) 54
– After the war / Run for cover / Still in love with you / Parisienne walkways / Out in the fields / Empty rooms / The loner / Shapes of things / Still got the blues / Ready for love / Military man / Wild frontier / Wishing well / Friday on my mind / Cold day in Hell / Over the hills and far away. *(d-cd+=; CDVX 2871)* – Emerald / All messed up (live) / Livin' on dreams (remix) / Military man (live) / Thunder rising (live) / Devil in her heart / Blinder / Reach for the sky (live) / Over the hills and far away (live) / Stop messin' atound (live).

Raw Power Raw Power

Sep 99. (cd) *(RAWCD 142) <550>* **A DIFFERENT BEAT**
– Go on home / Lost in your love / Worry no more / Fire / Surrender / House full of blues / Bring my baby back / Can't help myself / Fat boy / We want love / Can't help myself (E-Z Rollers mix).

Sanctuary Sanctuary

Mar 01. (cd) *(<SANCD 072>)* **BACK TO THE BLUES** 53
– Enough of the blues / You upset me baby / Cold black night / Stormy Monday / Ain't got you / Picture of the Moon / Looking back / The prophet / How many lies / Drowning in tears.

– compilations, etc. –

Jun 84. (lp/c) *Jet; (JET LP/CA 241)* **DIRTY FINGERS** -
(cd-iss. Nov86; JETCD 007) (re-iss. Apr87 on 'Castle' lp/c/cd; CLA LP/MC/CD 131) (cd re-iss. Oct00 on 'Castle'; CMRCD 035)

Jun 84. (7") *Jet; (7043)* **DON'T LET ME BE MISUNDERSTOOD. / SHE'S GOT YOU (live)** -

Oct 85. (lp) *Raw Power; (RAWLP 006)* **WHITE KNUCKLES** -
(re-iss. Apr86 c/cd; RAW TC/CD 006)

Jun 86. (lp/c/cd) *10-Virgin; (XID/CXID/XIDCD 1)* **ROCKIN' EVERY NIGHT** (live in Japan) 99
(re-iss. cd.Jun88; ZIDCD 1) (cd re-iss. Aug97 on 'Disky'; VI 88238-2)

Sep 86. (d-lp/d-c) *Raw Power; (RAW LP/TC 033)* **ANTHOLOGY** -

Jun 87. (lp/c/cd) *Raw Power; (RAW LP/TC/CD 034)* **LIVE AT THE MARQUEE (live)**
(re-iss. Feb91 on 'Castle' cd/c/lp; CLA CD/MC/LP 211) (cd re-iss. Oct00 on 'Castle'; CMRCD 033)

Nov 87. (lp/c) *M.C.A.; (MCL/+C 1864)* **PARISIENNE WALKWAYS** -
(cd-iss. May90; DMCL 1864) (re-iss. Oct92 cd/c; MCL D/C 19076)

Mar 88. (d-lp/c/d-cd) *That's Original; (TFO LP/MC/CD 2)* **G-FORCE / LIVE AT THE MARQUEE** -

1988. (cd-ep) *Special Edition; (CD3-4)* **GARY MOORE E.P.** -
– Don't let me be misunderstood / Parisienne walkways (live) / White knuckles – Rockin' & rollin'.

Jun 90. (cd/c) *Nightriding; (KN CD/MC 10014)* **GOLDEN DECADE OF GARY MOORE** -

Sep 90. (cd/c/lp; by SKID ROW) *Essential; (ESS CD/MC/LP 025)* **GARY MOORE, BRUSH SHIELDS, NOEL BRIDGEMAN** -

Oct 90. (cd/c/d-lp) *Castle; (CCS CD/MC/LP 273)* **THE COLLECTION** -
– Nuclear attack / White knuckles – Rockin' & rollin' / Grinding stone / Spirit / Run to your mama / Don't let me be misunderstood / Bad news / I look at you / She's got you / Back on the streets (live) / Hiroshima / Parisienne walkways (live) / Dancin' / Really gonna rock tonight / Dirty fingers.

Nov 91. (cd-box) *Virgin; (TPAK 18)* **CD BOX SET** -
– (AFTER THE WAR / RUN FOR COVER / WILD FRONTIER)

Feb 92. (cd-box) *Castle; (CLABX 904)* **CD BOX SET** -

Sep 94. (cd/c) *Spectrum; (550 738-2/-4)* **WALKWAYS** -

May 97. (d-cd) *Snapper; (SMDCD 123)* **LOOKING AT YOU** -

Sep 98. (cd) *Essential; (ESMCD 655)* **THE GARY MOORE COLLECTION** -

Oct 00. (d-cd) *Axe Killer; (AXE 306331CD)* **CORRIDORS OF POWER / RUN FOR COVER** -

Thurston MOORE (see under ⇒ SONIC YOUTH)

Vinnie MOORE

Born: 1964, Newcastle, Delaware, USA. A jazz-guitar trained child prodigy, MOORE was taken under the wing of 'Shrapnel' boss, MIKE VARNEY and introduced to Bay Area thrash act, VICIOUS RUMOURS. After only one album, 'SOLDIERS OF THE NIGHT', the six-string virtuoso left the band to pursue a solo career. He debuted with the warmly received instrumental set, 'MIND'S EYE' in 1987, the metal press heralding MOORE as another STEVE VAI or JOE SATRIANI. Its follow-up, 'TIME ODYSSEY' followed the same eclectic blueprint, the minor charting US album combining flying-fingered jazz, blues and metal influences, even extending its reach to an apt Beatles cover, 'WHILE MY GUITAR GENTLY WEEPS' (Beatles). In the early 90's, MOORE released his third album, 'MELTDOWN', working with ALICE COOPER the same year. His sporadic solo career belatedly continued in 1996, an album 'OUT OF NOWHERE' being issued by 'Music For Nations'. Back on 'Shrapnel', VINNIE completed two further long-players 'THE MAZE' (1999) and 'LIVE' (2000).

Album rating: MIND'S EYE (*7) / TIME ODYSSEY (*5) / MELTDOWN (*5) / OUT OF NOWHERE (*4) / THE MAZE (*4) / LIVE! (*5)

VINNIE MOORE – guitars / with **TONY McALPINE** – keyboards / **ANDY WEST** – bass / **TOMMY ALDRIDGE** – drums

Roadrunner Shrapnel

Feb 87. (lp/c/cd) *(RR/+4/34 9635) <SH 1027/+C/CD>* **MIND'S EYE**
– In control / Daydream / Saved by the miracle / Hero without honor / Lifeforce / N.N.Y. / Mind's eye / Shadows of yesterday / The journey.

— added **JORDAN RUDES** – keyboards / **MICHAEL BEAN** – bass / **JOE FRANCO** – drums

Vertigo Mercury

Aug 88. (lp/c)(cd) *(VERH/+C 60)(<834634-2>)* **TIME ODYSSEY** Jun88
– Morning star / Prelude – Into the future / Beyond the door / Message in a dream / As time slips by / Race with destiny / While my guitar gently weeps / The tempest / Pieces of a picture / April sky.

— next w/ **GREG SMITH** – bass / **JOE FRANCO** – drums

not iss. Relativity

1991. (cd-s) **MELTDOWN / COMING HOME / LET'S GO** -

1991. (cd) *<1067>* **MELTDOWN** -
– Meltdown / Let's go / Ridin' high / Earthshaker / Deep sea / Cinema / Midnight rain / Where angels sing / Check it out! / Last chance / Coming home.

— VINNIE joined ALICE COOPER in 1991 for 'Hey Stoopid'

— next with **BRIAN TICHY** – drums

Music For Nations Mayhem

Feb 96. (cd) *(CDMFN 194) <11084>* **OUT OF NOWHERE** Apr96
– With the flow / Losing faith / Echoes / Thunderball / From now on / Time traveller / Vinman's brew / She's only sleeping / Am I only dreaming / 770 days / Move that thang! / Winter sun.

Shrapnel Shrapnel

Jun 99. (cd) *<(SH 1123CD)>* **THE MAZE** Mar99
– The maze / King of kings / Cryptic dreams / Never been to Barcelona / Watching from the light / The thinking machine / Eye of the beholder / Rain / In the healing garden / Fear and trepidation.

Mar 00. (cd) *<(SH 1136CD)>* **LIVE! (live at Palo Alto, California)**
– The thinking machine / The maze / Cryptic dreams / Meltdown / Never been to Barcelona / She's only dreaming / Vinman's brew / Check it out / Rain / Daydream / Watching from the lights / With the flow.

MORBID ANGEL

Formed: Florida, USA ... 1984 by STERLING VON SCARBOROUGH, TREY AZAGTHOTH, RICHARD BRUNELLE and PETE SANDOVAL. In 1986, they laid down tracks for a proposed album 'ABOMINATIONS OF DESOLATION', but unhappy with the results, they shelved this and their label 'Gorque'. The producer of the masters, DAVID VINCENT, actually became the replacement for the departing SCARBOROUGH. Following the issue of an eponymous EP, their debut album, 'ALTARS OF MADNESS', was finally released in 1989, its brutally uncompromising, complex death-metal marking them out as one of the most respected bands in the emerging genre. SANDOVAL and VINCENT also cropped up on a moonlighting project, TERRORIZER. The group featured Californians OSCAR GARCIA (grunting) and JESSE PINTADO (guitar) on their one and only album, 'WORLD DOWNFALL' (1989). MORBID ANGEL toured Europe in the early 90's, also finding time to release a second set, 'BLESSED ARE THE SICK', the band's growing reputation attracting the interest of US label 'Giant' (an affiliated part of Warner Brothers), although they remained on the roster of 'Earache' records in the UK. Two albums, 'COVENANT' (1993) and 'DOMINATION' (1995) have since surfaced, MORBID ANGEL flying the flag for death-metal in the 90's amidst severe competition from more innovative outfits. The seminal extreme metallers – with as much a claim to the Godfathers crown as any band – returned in 1998 with 'FORMULAS FATAL TO THE FLESH', an album which more than a few critics deemed their most realised to date, both in terms of songwriting and complex yet brutally effective musical technique. Fans of AZAGOTH's searing guitar can get a full fix on 'LOVE OF LAVA', a bonus disc of solos free with a limited edition version of the album released in 1999. 'GATEWAYS TO ANNIHILATION' followed in 2000.

Album rating: ALTERS OF MADNESS (*7) / BLESSED ARE THE SICK (*6) / ABOMINATIONS OF DESOLATION (*6) / COVENANT (*6) / ENTANGLED IN CHAOS compilation (*7) / FORMULAS FATAL TO THE FLESH (*5) / GATEWAYS TO ANNIHILATION (*5) / Terrorizer: WORLD DOWNFALL (*6)

STERLING VON SCARBOROUGH – vocals, bass / **TREY AZAGTHOTH** – guitar / **RICHARD BRUNELLE** – guitar / **PETE SANDOVAL** (b. El Salvador) – drums / **MIKE BROWNING** – bass

not iss. Gorque

1986. (lp) *<withdrawn>* **ABOMINATIONS OF DESOLATION** [-] [-]
– The invocation – Chapel of ghouls / Unholy blasphemies / Angel of disease / Azagthoth / The gate – Lord of all fevers / Hell spawn / Abominations / Demon seed / Welcome to Hell. *(finally iss.UK Sep91 on 'Earache' lp/cd; MOSH 048/+CD)*

— **DAVID VINCENT** – vocals, bass (ex-TERRORIZER) repl. SCARBOROUGH and BROWNING (latter formed NOCTURNUS)

Earache Combat

Feb 89. (12"ep) *(MOSH 10)* **MORBID ANGEL** [ ] [-]
Sep 89. (lp/c/cd) *(MOSH 11/+MC/CD)* **ALTERS OF MADNESS** [ ] [-]
– Immortal rites / Suffocation / Visions from the darkside / Maze of torment / Lord of all fevers and plague / Chapel of ghouls / Bleed for the Devil / Damnation / Blasphemy / Evil spells. *(pic-lp Jul90; MOSH 11P) (re-iss. Aug91; same) (cd+=)* – (remixes). *(cd re-iss. Sep97; same)*
Apr 91. (lp/cd)(7"box) *(MOSH 031/+CD)(7MOSH 031) <2032>* **BLESSED ARE THE SICK** [ ] [ ]
– Fall from grace / Brainstorm / Rebel lands / Doomsday celebration / Day of suffering / Blessed are the sick / Thy kingdom come / Unholy blasphemies / Abominations / Desolate ways / The ancient ones / In remembrance. *(cd re-iss. Sep97; same)*
Jan 92. (lp/cd) *(MOSH 048/+CD)* **ABOMINATIONS OF DESOLATION** [ ] [-]
– The invocation – Chapel of ghouls / Unholy blashemies / Angel of disease / Azagthoth / The gate – Lord of all fevers and plagues / Hell spawn / Abominations / Demon seed / Welcome to Hell. *(cd re-iss. Sep97; same)*

Earache Giant

Jun 93. (lp/c/cd) *(MOSH 081/+MC/CD) <24504>* **COVENANT** [ ] [ ]
– Rapture / Pain divine / World of shit (the promised land) / Vengeance is mine / Lion's den / Blood on my hands / Angel of disease / Sworn to black / Nar Mattaru / God of emptiness. *(cd re-iss. Sep97; same)*

— **ERIC RUTAN** – guitar (ex-RIPPING CORPSE) repl. BRUNELLE

May 95. (lp/c/cd) *(MOSH 134/+MC/CD) <24612>* **DOMINATION** [ ] [ ]
– Dominate / Where the slime live / Eyes to see, eyes to hear / Melting / Nothing but fear / Dawn of the angry / This means war / Casar's Palace / Dreaming / Inquisition (burn with me) / Hatework. *(cd re-iss. Sep97; MOSH 123CDSL)*

Earache Earache

Nov 96. (cd/c) *<(MOSH 167 CD/MC)>* **ENTANGLED IN CHAOS (live)** [ ] [ ] Mar97
– Immortal rites / Blasphemy of the holy ghost / Sworn to the black / Lord of all fevers and plagues / Blessed are the sick / Days of suffering / Chapel of ghouls / Maze of torment / Rapture / Blood on my hands / Dominate.

— now without VINCENT + RUTAN. They were subsequently repl. by **STEVE TUCKER** (b.1971, Cincinnati) – vocals, bass (ex-CEREMONY)

Feb 98. (cd/c) *<(MOSH 180CD)>* **FORMULAS FATAL TO THE FLESH** [ ] [ ] Jul99
– Heaving earth / Prayer of hatred / Bil ur-sag / Nothing is not / Chambers of dis / Disturbance in the great slumber / Umulamahri / Hellspawn (the rebirth) / Covenant of death / Hymn to a gas giant / Invocation of the continual one / Ascent through the spheres / Hymnos ritales de guerra / The trooper. *(d-cd-iss. Mar99 +=; MOSH 180CDL)***LOVE OF LAVA** – Heaving earth lava / Prayer of hatred / Bil ur sag / Bil ur sag lava / Nothing is not lava / Chambers of Dis / Umalamaahari / Umalamhri lava / Hellspawn / Covenant of death / Invocation / Dominate lava / Alternative dominate / Dawn of the angry / Burn with me / Eyes to see / Where the slime live.
Sep 00. (lp/cd) *<(MOSH 235/+CD)>* **GATEWAYS TO ANNIHILATION** [ ] [ ]
– Kawazu / Summoning redemption / Ageless, still I am / He who sleeps / To the victor the spoils / At one with nothing / Opening of the gates / Secured limitations / Awakening / I / God of the forsaken.

TERRORIZER

DAVID VINCENT – bass, vocals / **PETE SANDOVAL** – drums / **OSCAR GARCIA** – vocals / **JESSE PINTADO** – drums

Earache Combat

Nov 89. (lp/c/cd) *(MOSH 16/+MC/CD) <2035>* **WORLD DOWNFALL** [ ] [ ]
– After world obliteration / Tear of napalm / Corporation pull in / Resurrection / Need to live / The dead shall rise / Injustice / Storm of stress / Human prey / Condemned system / Enslaved by propaganda / Whirlwind struggle / World downfall / Ripped to shreds. *(cd re-iss. Sep97; same)*

MORDRED

Formed: San Francisco, California, USA . . . 1985 by SCOTT HOLDERBY, DANNY WHITE, JAMES SANGUINETTI, ART LIBOON and GANNON HALL. In at the start of the funk-metal revolution, MORDRED signed to 'Noise' in the late 80's, issuing 'FOOL'S GAME' in Spring '89. Influenced by the likes of RUSH, PIL and P-funk, MORDRED's sound was decidedly more complex than standard-issue Bay Area thrash, though they sometimes tended to over-experiment at the expense of the actual songwriting. They even added a scratch DJ, AARON 'Pause' VAUGHN, for their follow-up album, 'IN THIS LIFE' (1991). Even more energetic and dynamic than the debut, the record was hailed as one of the major potential crossover records of the year and it even nudged its way into the UK Top 75. As intriguing and innovative as it was, the album didn't contain an 'EPIC' or a 'GIVE IT AWAY', MORDRED subsequently languishing in the thrash-funk ghetto. A further album, 'THE NEXT ROOM', appeared in 1994 although by this point the scene was flagging.

Album rating: FOOL'S GAME (*5) / IN THIS LIFE (*6) / VISION mini (*4) / THE NEXT ROOM (*6)

SCOTT HOLDERBY – vocals / **DANNY WHITE** – guitar / **JAMES SANGUINETTI** – guitar / **ART LIBOON** – bass / **GANNON HALL** – drums

Noise Noise

May 89. (lp/c/cd) *(N 135-1/-4/-2) <4812>* **FOOL'S GAME** [ ] [ ]
– State of mind / Spectacle of fear / Every day's a holiday / Spellbound / Sever and splice / The artist / Shatter / Reckless abandon / Super freak / Numb.
Jun 89. (7") *(7MORD 5)* **EVERY DAY'S A HOLIDAY. / SUPERFREAK** [ ] [-]

— added **AARON 'Pause' VAUGHN** – DJ

Feb 91. (cd/c/lp) *(N 159-2/-4/-1) <4829>* **IN THIS LIFE** [70] [ ]
– In this life / The strain / High potency / Window / Esse quam videri / A beginning / Falling away / Killing time / Downtown / Progress / Larger than life.
Sep 91. (12"ep/cd-ep) *(N 0179-6/-3)* **ESSE QUAM VIDERI (radio remix). / INTRO – KILLING TIME (live) / EVERY DAY'S A HOLIDAY (live)** [ ] [-]
(re-iss. Mar92 7")
Jul 92. (12"ep/cd-ep) *(N 170-6/-3)* **FALLING AWAY** [ ] [-]

Noise Futurist

Aug 92. (m-cd) *<1019>* **VISION** [ ] [ ]
– In time / West country hospital / The vagrant / Reach / Closed mind / Vision.

Noise Noise

Aug 94. (cd) *<(N 0211-2)>* **THE NEXT ROOM** [ ] [ ] May95
– Lo-cal, hi-fibre / Skid / Crash / Splinter down / Shut / Pauper's wine / Acrophobia / Murray the mover / In a turn / The trellis / The next room over / Rubber crutch.

— disbanded after above

MORE

Formed: London, England . . . 1980 by KENNY COX, PAUL MARIO DAY, BRIAN DAY, LAURIE MANSWORTH and FRANK DARCH. A solid NWOBHM outfit, the band did better than most of their peers by netting a deal with 'Atlantic'. Early in 1981, they released their debut album, 'WARHEAD', an aptly named affair that pretty well described their incendiary stage shows. However, by the recording of their second album, 'BLOOD AND THUNDER', only COX remained from the original line-up, the guitarist taking on newcomers NICK STRATTON, BARRY NICHOLLS and ANDY JOHN BURTON. Although the album received good press upon its American release, their label declined to issue it in Britain, effectively splitting the band in 1983. However, COX and NICHOLLS later resurfaced in 1985 with a new bunch of musicians, MEL JONES (guitar), PAUL GEORGE (drums) and singer RON JACKSON.

Album rating: WARHEAD (*5) / BLOOD AND THUNDER (*6)

PAUL MARIO DAY – vocals / **KENNY COX** – guitar / LAURIE MANSWORTH – guitar / **BRIAN DAY** – bass / **FRANK DARCH** – drums

Atlantic Atlantic

Feb 81. (lp/c) *(<K/K4 50775>)* **WARHEAD** [ ] [ ]
– Warhead / Fire / Soldier / Depression / Road rocket / Lord of twilight / Way of the world / We are the band / I have no answers.
Mar 81. (7") *(K 11561)* **WE ARE THE BAND. / ATOMIC ROCK** [ ] [ ]

— **COX** changed line-up; **NICK STRATTON** – vocals / **BARRY NICHOLLS** – bass / **ANDY JOHN BURTON** – drums (the DAY brothers subsequently joined WILDFIRE and MANSWORTH joined AIRRACE

Jul 82. (7") *(K 11744)* **TRICKSTER. / HEY JOE** [ ] [ ]
Aug 82. (lp) *<K 50875>* **BLOOD AND THUNDER** [-] [ ]
– Killer on the prowl / Blood and thunder / I just can't believe it / I've been waiting / Traitor's gate / Rock & roll / I wanna take you / Go home / The eye / Nightmare.

— split after the above album didn't get a UK release

Steve MORSE

Formed: 28 Jul'54, Hamilton, Ohio, USA, although from the age of 13 he stayed with his parents in Georgia. Inspired by idols JIMI HENDRIX and LED ZEPPELIN, he took up a post at the University Of Miami, studying under the great classical guitarist Juan Mercadal. It would be at this time, STEVE set up his own band, DIXIE GRIT, who were soon to become The DIXIE DREGS. Along with electric violinist ALLEN SLOAN, bassist ANDY WEST, drummer ROD MORGENSTEIN and last recruit STEVE DAVIDOWSKI on keyboards, this jazz fusion-rock outfit, delivered eight MAHAVISHNU-type sets. Having had even more experience with KANSAS (two albums and a Best Guitarist award in 1982 from Guitar Player), STEVE formed his own hard-rock band to complete his instrumental solo debut, 'THE INTRODUCTION' (1984). Unfairly described as the Mike Oldfield of rodeo rock, MORSE went on to achieve a great deal of critical success via further albums including 'SOUTHERN STEEL' (1991). In 1996, STEVE joined DEEP PURPLE for their 'Purpledicular' set and he has since reformed The DIXIE DREGS while also working in cinema/soundtracks.

Album rating: THE INTRODUCTION (*6) / STAND UP (*6) / HIGH TENSION WIRES (*6) / SOUTHERN STEEL (*7) / COAST TO COAST (*6) / STRUCTURAL DAMAGE (*6)

— solo / with **JERRY PEEK** – bass / **ROD MORGENSTEIN** – drums

Asylum / Elektra Musician

Sep 84. (lp; as STEVE MORSE BAND) *(960 369-1)* *<60369>* **THE INTRODUCTION** ☐ ☐ Aug84
– Cruise missile / General Lee / The introduction / V.H.F. (Vertical Hair Factor) / On the pipe / The whistle / Mountain waltz / Huron River blues medley. *<cd-iss. 1988; 960 369-2> (UK cd-iss. Jan96 on 'WEA'; 7559 60369-2)*

Elektra Elektra

Nov 84. (lp/c) *(EKT 24/+C)* **STAND UP** ☐ ☐
– Books of dreams / English rancher / Rockin' guitars / Distant stars / Pick your poison / Stand up / Travels of Marco Polo / Golden quest / Unity gain.

— in the mid to late 80's, MORSE played with KANSAS

— added **SLOAN, LAVITZ + WEST** (all ex-DIXIE DREGS)

not iss. / M.C.A.

Jun 89. (lp/c/cd) *<MCA/+C/D 6275>* **HIGH TENSION WIRES** ☐ ☐
– Ghostwind / The road home / Country colors / Highland wedding / Third power / Looking back / Leprechaun promenade / Tumeni notes / Endless waves / Modoc.

STEVE MORSE BAND

— with **DAVE LaRUE** – bass / **VAN ROMAINE** – drums

Mar 91. (cd/c) *<(MCA D/C 10112)>* **SOUTHERN STEEL** ☐ ☐
– Cut to the chase / Simple Simon / Vista grande / Sleaze factor / Battle lines / Southern steel / Wolf song / Weekend overdrive / Arena rock / Point counterpoint.

1992. (cd) *<MCD 10565>* **COAST TO COAST** ☐ ☐
– User friendly / Collateral damage / Get it in writing / Morning rush hour / Runaway train / Long lost / The Z / Over easy / Cabin fever / Flat baroque.

— with **DAVE LaRUE** – bass + **VAN ROMAINE** – drums

High Street / High Street

Feb 96. (cd) *<(72902 10332-2)>* **STRUCTURAL DAMAGE** ☐ ☐ Mar95
– Sacred ground / Good to go / Dreamland / Barbary Coast / Smokey mountain drive / Slice of time / Native dance / Just out of reach / Rally cry / Foreign exchange / Structural damage.

Jun 96. (cd) *<(72902 10348-2)>* **STRESSFEST** ☐ ☐ Apr96
– Stressfest / Rising power / Eyes of a child / Nightwalk / Brave new world / Four minutes to live / Easy way / Glad to be / Delicate business / Live to ride.

— STEVE joined DEEP PURPLE in 1996 and later again the DIXIE DREGS

MORTA SKULD

Formed: Milwaukee, USA ... early 90's by DAVE GREGOR, JASON HELLMAN, JASON O'CONNELL and KENT TRUCKEBROD. Signed, appropriately enough to the 'Deaf' label, the group introduced their cranium-splitting brand of death-metal on a debut album, 'DYING REMAINS' (1993). After a few personnel changes when HELLMAN and TRUCKEBROD departed, MORTA SKULD delivered a second set, 'AS HUMANITY FADES' the following year. The record's more focused approach saw them picked up in the UK by 'Peaceville'; a third album, 'FOR ALL ETERNITY' appearing in late '95, while 'Pavement' released 1998's 'SURFACE'.

Album rating: DYING REMAINS (*4) / AS HUMANITY FADES (*5) / FOR ALL ETERNITY (*5) / SURFACE (*4)

DAVE GREGOR – vocals, guitar / **JASON O'CONNELL** – guitar / **JASON HELLMAN** – bass / **KENT TRUCKEBROD** – drums

Deaf / not iss.

Feb 93. (lp/cd) *(DEAF 011/+CD)* **DYING REMAINS** ☐ ☐
– Lifeless / Without sin / Devoured fears / Dying remains / Useless to mankind / Rotting ways / Withering seclusion / Hatred creation / Scarred / Consuming existence. *(cd+=)* – Presumed dead.

— suffered some personnel changes (HELLMAN + TRUCKEBROD left)

Feb 94. (lp/cd) *(DEAF 015/+CD)* **AS HUMANITY FADES** ☐ ☐
– Unknown emotions / Century of ruins / Humanity's lost / Awakening destiny / Paradise of the masses / No world escapes / Different breeds / Sanctuary denied / Relics / Sorrow fields. *(cd+=)* – Through obscurity / In the shadows.

Peaceville / not iss.

Oct 95. (cd) *(CDVILE 57)* **FOR ALL ETERNITY** ☐ ☐
– Bitter / For all eternity / Vicious circle / Justify / Tears / Germ farm / Second thought / Bleeding heart / Crawl inside / Burning daylight.

Pavement / Pavement

Jan 98. (cd) *<(32272CD)>* **SURFACE** ☐ ☐ Feb98
– The killing machines / Save yourself / The anger in disguise / Time will never forget / Surface / Lords of discipline / If I survive / In nothing we trust. *(re-iss. Oct98 on 'S.P.V.'; 084-53203)*

– compilations, etc. –

May 95. (cd) *Peaceville; (CDVILE 60)* **DYING REMAINS / AS HUMANITY FADES** ☐ ☐

MORTIIS

Born: 1975, Notodden, Norway. An original and influential member of Norwegian black metal bad boys EMPEROR, MORTIIS contributed both his bass playing and his penchant for spine-chilling synth textures to a clutch of the band's early recordings. In 1993, he struck out on his own, relocating to Sweden and releasing a solo debut, 'FODT TIL A HERSKE', on his own 'Dark Dungeon' imprint. The saturnine keyboard atmospherics on offer were to become a trademark of the young dark lord's career although perhaps his Lord Of The Rings getup was taking things a bit far; did Spinal Tap ever make it to Scandinavian cinemas? (answers on the back of a bloodstained parchment to the usual address). Sophomore set, 'ANDEN SOM GJORDE' (1994) was followed by the 'SELVMORD' album later that year, released under the auspices of side project VOND. 1995 followed the same pattern with a MORTIIS album, 'KEISER AV EN DIMENSJON UKJENT' and another side project effort, 'FATA MORGANA'. A series of limited edition EP's released in 1996 were later collected together as 'CRYPT OF THE WIZARD' and given a full worldwide release as part of the man's new deal with 'Earache' in 1999. As for new material, MORTIIS released 'THE STARGATE' (1999), a concept album of sorts featuring vocal contributions courtesy of CRADLE OF FILTH's SARAH JEZEBEL DEVA.

Album rating: FODT TIL A HERSKE (*5) / ANDEN SOM GJORDE OPPROR (*5) / SELUMORD as Vond (*4) / THE STARGATE (*5)

MORTIIS – keyboards, synthesizer (ex-EMPEROR)

Malicious / not iss.

1992. (7") **AS THE SHADOWS RISE. /** ☐ ☐ Norway

1993. (cd) **FODT TIL A HERSKE** ☐ ☐ Sweden
– Fodt til a herske (pt.1) / Fodt til a herske (pt.2). *(UK-iss.Oct95 on 'Malicious'; MA 003CD) <US-iss.1997 on 'Projekt'; 1001> (re-iss. Nov99 on 'Earache'; MOSH 229CD)*

1994. (cd) **ANDEN SOM GJORDE OPPROR** ☐ ☐ Sweden
– En mork horisont / Visioner av en eldegammel fremtid. *(UK cd-iss. Feb00 on 'Cold Meat Industry'; CMI 38)*

1994. (cd; as VOND) **SELUMORD** ☐ ☐ Sweden
– Selumord / Nar livet tar farvel / Reisen til en NY verden / Slipp sorgen los. *(re-iss. Oct95 on 'Malicious; MR 004CD) <US-iss.1999 as 'SLIPP SORGEN LOS'>*

1995. (cd) **KEISER AV EN DIMENSJON UKJENT** ☐ ☐ Sweden
– Reisene til grotter og odemarker (Journies to deserts and dungeons) / Keiser av en dimensjon ukjent (Emperor of a dimension unknown). *(UK-iss.Nov99 on 'Cold Meat Industry'; CMI 37CD)*

1995. (cd; as FATA MORGANA) **FATA MORGANA** ☐ ☐ Sweden
– Stargazer / S k din nd / A forest path / Fata Morgana / Distant thunder / The last rainbow king / Purple sky.

1996. (12") **FERDEN OG KALLET. / DA VI BYGDE TARNET** ☐ ☐ Sweden

1996. (12") **UNDER TARNETS SKYGGE. / EN SIRKEL AV KOSMISK KAOS** ☐ ☐ Sweden

1996. (12") **VANDEREN'S SANG. / DEN BORTDREUNE REGNBUEN** ☐ ☐ Sweden

1996. (12") **TROLLMANNENS KRYPT. / STJERNEFODT** ☐ ☐ Sweden

1996. (12") **I MORKET DROMMENDE. / FANGET I KRYSTAL** ☐ ☐ Sweden

CINTECELE DIAVOLUI

— **MORTIIS** and another offshoot

Cold Meat Industry / not iss.

Oct 98. (cd) *(CMI 058CD)* **THE DEVIL'S SONGS** ☐ ☐
– Dance of the dead / Midnight hunt / Soulless / Wedding of the dead / Vampir / Dungeon of horror / The vampire / One soul less for the Devil. *(re-iss. Feb00; same)*

MORTIIS

— was finally back as a solo act; added **SARAH JEZEBEL DEVA** – vocals (of CRADLE OF FILTH)

Earache / Earache

Sep 99. (cd) *(<MOSH 223CD>)* **THE STARGATE** ☐ ☐ Oct99
– Child of curiosity and the old man of knowledge / I am the world / World essence / Across the world of wonders / (Passing by) An old raped village / Towards the gate of stars / Spirit of conquest – The warfare / Army of conquest – The wargare (ever onwards).

– compilations, etc. –

Nov 99. (cd) *Earache; (<MOSH 225CD>)* **CRYPT OF THE WIZARD** (the 12" singles) ☐ ☐

MOTHER LOVE BONE (see under ⇒ PEARL JAM)

MOTHER'S FINEST

Formed: Atlanta, Georgia, USA ... 1974 by husband and wife team, GLENN MURDOCH and JOYCE KENNEDY (aka BABY JEAN), the line-up completed by MOSES MO, MIKE KECK, WIZZARD and B.B. QUEEN. Surely a band out of time, this genre-splicing, multi-racial R&B/funk-metal outfit were treading the boards when LIVING COLOUR were pre-pubescent schoolboys. Signing with 'Epic', the group finally released their eponymous debut in early '77, a promising set which explicitly challenged discrimination on the likes of 'NIGGIZZ CAN'T SING ROCK AND ROLL'. Though they failed to make a major impression on the charts with subsequent funked-up R&B efforts like 'ANOTHER MOTHER FURTHER' (1978) and 'MOTHER FACTOR' (1979), MOTHER'S FINEST built up a loyal following, both in America and in Europe, especially the more open-minded Netherlands. With keyboardist KECK departing in 1980, the group's soulful sound was toughened up on 'IRON AGE' (1981), the original line-up subsequently disintegrating. With new members GREG WILLIS, DOUG BARE, HAROLD SEAY and MATT GREELY, the band cut one more album, 'ONE MOTHER TO ANOTHER' (1983), before finally disbanding in 1984. MOSES subsequently teamed up with B.B. QUEEN (who had been playing with MOLLY HATCHET) again in ILLUSION while BABY JEAN could be heard on GEORGE DUKE's eponymous album. Towards the end of the decade, MURDOCH, WIZZARD and BABY JEAN reformed the band along with JOHN HAYES and DION DEREK for a more laidback effort on 'Capitol', 'LOOKS COULD KILL' (1989). With the funk-rock boom now in full effect, the group seemed to take on a new lease of life, releasing an impressive live set, 'SUBLUXATION' (1990) and the confrontational 'BLACK RADIO WON'T PLAY THIS RECORD' (1992). • **Songwriters:** MURDOCH or some by group except MICKEY'S MONKEY (Miracles) / STRAWBERRY FIELDS FOREVER (Beatles) / etc. **Note:** Not to be confused with other band of the same name, who released an eponymous US lp in 1972 on 'RCA'.

Album rating: MOTHER'S FINEST (*6) / ANOTHER MOTHER FURTHER (*5) / MOTHER FACTOR (*4) / LIVE MUTHA (*5) / IRON AGE (*6) / ONE MOTHER TO ANOTHER (*5) / SUBLUXATION (*7) / BLACK RADIO WON'T PLAY THIS RECORD (*7) / NOT YER MOTHER'S FUNK – THE BEST OF MOTHER'S FINEST compilation (*6)

BABY JEAN (b. JOYCE KENNEDY) – vocals, percussion / **GLENN MURDOCK** – vocals, percussion / **MOSES MO** (b.GARY MOORE) – guitar, vocals / **MIKE KECK** – keyboards / **WIZZARD** (b.JERRY SEAY) – bass, vocals / **B.B. QUEEN** (b.BARRY BORDEN) – drums, percussion

Epic Epic

Sep 76. (7") *(EPC 4613) <50269>* **FIRE. / DONCHA WANNA LOVE ME** [ ] [93] Aug76
Jan 77. (7") *(EPC 4923) <50310>* **RAIN. / MY BABY** [ ] [ ]
Feb 77. (lp) *(EPC 81595) <34179>* **MOTHER'S FINEST** [ ] [ ] Sep76
– Fire / Give you all the love / Niggizz can't sing rock and roll / My baby / Fly with me / Doncha wanna love me / Rain.
Sep 77. (7") *<50407>* **BABY LOVE. / HARD ROCK LOVERS** [-] [58]
Nov 77. (7") *<50438>* **THANK YOU FOR THE LOVE. / DIS GO DIS WAY DIS GO DAT WAY** [-] [ ]
Apr 78. (lp) *(EPC 82037) <34699>* **ANOTHER MOTHER FURTHER** [ ] [ ] Sep77
– Mickey's monkey / Baby love / Thank you for the love / Piece of the rock / Truth'll set you free / Burning love / Dis go dis way, dis go that way / Hard rock lovers.
Jul 78. (7") *(EPC 5987) <50483>* **PIECE OF THE ROCK. / THANK YOU FOR THE LOVE** [ ] [ ] Apr78
Nov 78. (7") *<50596>* **TRUTH'LL SET YOU FREE. / DON'T WANNA COME BACK** [-] [ ]
Jan 79. (lp) *(EPC 83011) <35546>* **MOTHER FACTOR** [ ] [ ] Sep78
– Can't fight the feeling / Tell me / Watch my stylin' / Love changes / Don't wanna come back / Give it up / Mr. Goodbar / I can't believe / More and more.
Feb 79. (7") *<50641>* **LOVE CHANGES. / TRUTH'LL SET YOU FREE** [-] [ ]
Jun 79. (7") *<50679>* **CAN'T FIGHT THE FEELING. / MORE AND MORE** [-] [ ]
Sep 79. (7") *<50784>* **WATCH MY STYLIN'. / SOMEBODY TO LOVE** [-] [ ]
Nov 79. (lp) *<35976>* **LIVE MUTHA (live)** [-] [ ]
– Baby love / Can't fight this feeling / Mickey's monkey / Love changes / Watch my stylin' / Don't wanna come back / Fire / Give you all the love.
Dec 79. (7") *<50848>* **BABY LOVE (live). / HARD ROCK LOVERS (live)** [-] [ ]

—— In 1980, MIKE departed. (MURDOCK now added guitar)

Epic Atlantic

Jul 81. (lp) *(EPC 84924) <19302>* **IRON AGE** [ ] [ ] May81
– Movin' on / All the way / Earthling / Luv drug / Evolution / Gone with th' rain / Illusion / Rock'n'roll nite / Time / U turn me on.

—— **GREG WILLIS** – guitar / **DOUG BARE** – keyboards / **HAROLD SEAY** – drums + **MATT GREELY** – percussion repl. B.B. QUEEN who joined MOLLY HATCHET

Aug 83. (lp/c) *(EPC/40 25363)* **ONE MOTHER TO ANOTHER** [ ] [-]
– Everybody needs somebody / Secret service / Victory / What kind of fool / Take me to the middle (of your luv) / Love me too / Big shot Romeo / In my baby's arms / What you do to me / Some kind of madness.

—— Disbanded in 1984, and MOSES (GARY MOORE) teamed up with B.B.QUEEN to form ILLUSION. JOYCE was heard on GEORGE DUKE's eponymous album. In 1989, they (**KENNEDY** – vocals, **MURDOCK** – vocals + **WIZZARD** – bass, vocals) re-formed, recruiting **JOHN HAYES** – guitar / **DION DEREK** – drums

Capitol Capitol

Oct 89. (cd/c/lp) *<(CD/TC+/EST 2114)>* **LOOKS COULD KILL** [ ] [ ]
– For your love / I'm 'n danger / Legs and lipstick / Dream come true / Stilloveach other / I'll never be the same / Brave and strong / Your wish is my command / Cherish your lover / Heartbreaker. *(c+cd+=)* – Call me mister / Too serious.
Oct 89. (7") *<44416>* **I'M 'N DANGER. /** [-] [ ]

R.C.A. not iss.

Nov 90. (cd/c/lp) *(PD/PK/PL 74836)* **SUBLUXATION (live)** [-] [-] German
– Chain / Truth'll set you free / Call me mister / Mandela song / Mickey's monkey / Give you all the love / Think about me / Cheap spot / Piece of the rock / Strawberry fields forever / Baby love / Somebody to love.
1992. (cd/c) **BLACK RADIO WON'T PLAY THIS RECORD** [-] [ ]

—— split after above

– compilations, etc. –

Jul 97. (cd) *Razor & Tie; (RE 2137)* **NOT YER MOTHER'S FUNK – THE BEST OF MOTHER'S FINEST** [ ] [-]

MOTLEY CRUE

Formed: Los Angeles, California, USA . . . early 1981 by NIKKI SIXX (bass, ex-LONDON) who recruited VINCE NEIL (vocals, ex-ROCK CANDY), TOMMY LEE (drums) and finally MICK MARS (guitar). In 1981, they issued their debut album, 'TOO FAST FOR LOVE', on their own US label, 'Leathur'. From its 'STICKY FINGERS'-esque, crotch-shot cover to the low-rent sleaze-rock contained within, the album announced MOTLEY CRUE's status as wannabe metal successors to the likes of AEROSMITH and The NEW YORK DOLLS. There were certainly worse reference points to have, and the record was an amateurish, minor classic, the title track and 'PIECE OF YOUR ACTION' pouting highlights. After being signed to 'Elektra', the record was re-issued the following year while the band began work on a follow-up with producer Tom Werman. 'SHOUT AT THE DEVIL' (1983) added cod-satanic imagery to their glam fixation while beefing up the guitars. But VENOM this band were not and songs like 'GOD BLESS THE CHILDREN OF THE BEAST' were downright ridiculous. If catchy pop-metal like 'TOO YOUNG TO FALL IN LOVE' was the work of the devil, then God certainly had nothing to fear. Nevertheless, after a nationwide tour supporting KISS, the album hit the US Top 20 and things were looking up for the band. However on the 8th of December '84, VINCE NEIL was involved in a serious car accident; NICK 'RAZZLE' DINGLEY (drummer with HANOI ROCKS) was killed in the crash while two others were injured. NEIL was subsequently ordered to pay $2.5 million compensation and sentenced to 20 days in jail, after being convicted of vehicle manslaughter. The tragedy overshadowed much of the 'THEATRE OF PAIN' (1985) album, a record that went on to sell more than two million copies after its cover of Brownsville Station's 'SMOKIN' IN THE BOYS ROOM' was a Top 20 hit. The album also boasted the surprisingly poignant power ballad, 'HOME SWEET HOME', an MTV favourite later that year. 'GIRLS, GIRLS, GIRLS' (1987) was a marked improvement; the lyrics cementing The 'CRUE's reputation as the 'bad' boys of metal, the music confident and cocksure. Tracks like 'WILD SIDE', showed a newfound adventurousness, the first signs that the band were capable of promotion from the metal second division. Early in 1988, MATTHEW TRIPPE sued the CRUE for royalties, alleging he masqueraded and wrote songs as NIKKI SIXX, while he recovered from a 1983 car crash. This was later proved to be false, although there is still much speculation on how SIXX's face was bloated on some mug pics. Having survived a near-death experience after a heroin o.d., SIXX and the newly cleaned up 'CRUE delivered another album, 'DR. FEELGOOD', which duly topped the US charts (while hitting Top 5 in the UK). It was to be NEIL's parting shot, the singer ousted in the early 90's following media overkill on his war of words with AXL ROSE. While he released a solo album in '93, the group recruited a new frontman, JOHN CORABI, although the subsequent album, 'MOTLEY CRUE' found few takers. NEIL and the group had patched up their differences by 1997, the album, 'GENERATION SWINE' giving them a return to the US Top 5. With VINCE back in the fold it must've seemed a good time to capture some of their rekindled stage fire; 'LIVE: ENTERTAINMENT OR DEATH' (1999) featured a clutch of latter day tracks and a far larger whack from the halcyon days of yore, we're talking early 80's here. If that wasn't enough to please the band's diehard fans then 'NEW TATTOO' (2000) saw MOTLEY CRUE returning to their bad old days in fine style. Out went the half-arsed attempts at alternative metal and serious subject matter; in came scuzz-rock and such time honoured lyrical themes as, well, sex, drugs and rock'n'roll basically, the nastier and filthier the better. They even signed off with a rendition of The Tubes' 'WHITE PUNKS ON DOPE', a somehow more appropriate choice of cover than 'HELTER SKELTER' . . . • **Covered:** HELTER SKELTER (Beatles) / JAILHOUSE ROCK (Leiber-Stoller). • **Trivia:** Late 1985, TOMMY LEE married actress Heather Lockear, although did not last. He is now the spouse of Baywatch actress PAMELA ANDERSON, although in the mid-90's press speculation was rife about an impending split. Around the same time, she gave birth to their first child, although the domestic bliss was short-lived; at the time of writing the couple are heading for a divorce while TOMMY faces a lengthy jail sentence for wife-beating. In Dec '87, MICK married one-time PRINCE girlfriend VANITY (star of 'Purple Rain'). In May '90, NIKKI was hitched to former Playboy centre-fold Brandi Brandt.

Album rating: TOO FAST FOR LOVE (*5) / SHOUT AT THE DEVIL (*6) / THEATRE OF PAIN (*5) / GIRLS, GIRLS, GIRLS (*7) / DR. FEELGOOD (*5) / DECADE OF DECADENCE compilation (*7) / MOTLEY CRUE (*5) / GENERATION SWINE (*5) / THE BEST OF MOTLEY CRUE compilation (*6) / LIVE: ENTERTAINMENT OR DEATH (*4) / NEW TATTOO (*5) / Vince Neil: EXPOSED (*4) / CARVED IN STONE (*3)

VINCE NEIL (b. VINCENT NEIL WHARTON, 8 Feb'61, Hollywood, Calif.) – vocals (ex-ROCK CANDY) / **NIKKI SIXX** (b. FRANK FERRANNO, 11 Dec'58, San Jose, Calif.) – bass (ex-LONDON) / **MICK MARS** (b. BOB DEAL, 3 Apr'56, Huntington, Indiana) – guitar / **TOMMY LEE** (b. THOMAS LE BASS, 3 Oct'62, Athens, Greece) – drums (ex-SUITE 19)

not iss. Leathur

1981. (lp) **TOO FAST FOR LOVE** [-] [ ]
– Live wire / Public enemy No.1 / Take me to the top / Merry-go-round / Piece of your action / Starry eyes / Come on and dance / Too fast for love / On with the show. *(UK-iss.Oct82 as 'MOTLEY CRUE' on 'Elektra' lp/c; K/K4 52425) <US re-iss. Nov83 on 'Elektra'; 60174> (cd-iss. Feb93 on 'Elektra'; 7559 60174-2)*
1982. (7"gig freebie) **TOAST OF THE TOWN. / STICK TO YOUR GUNS** [-] [ ]

Elektra Elektra

Sep 83. (lp/c) *(960 289-1/-4) <60289>* **SHOUT AT THE DEVIL** [ ] [17]
– In the beginning / Shout at the Devil / Looks that kill / Bastard / Knock 'em dead, kid / Danger / Too young to fall in love / Helter skelter / Red hot / Ten seconds 'til love / God bless the children of the beast. *(cd-iss. Jan89; 960 289-2)*
Jul 84. (7") *(E 9756) <69756>* **LOOKS THAT KILL. / PIECE OF YOUR ACTION** [ ] [54] Jan84
(12"+=) *(E 9756T)* – Live wire.
Oct 84. (7"/12") *(E 9732/+T) <69732>* **TOO YOUNG TO FALL IN LOVE. / TAKE ME TO THE TOP** [ ] [90] Jun84
Jul 85. (lp/c) *(EKT 8/+C) <60418>* **THEATRE OF PAIN** [36] [6]
– City boy blues / Smokin' in the boys' room / Louder than Hell / Keep your eye on

the money / Home sweet home / Tonight (we need a lover) / Use it or lose it / Save our souls / Raise your hands to rock / Fight for your rights. *(cd-iss. Jul86; 960 418-2)*

Aug 85. (7"/7"sha-pic-d/12") *(EKR 16/+P/T)* <69625> **SMOKIN' IN THE BOYS' ROOM. / USE IT OR LOSE IT** [71] [16] Jul85
<US-12"> – ('A'side) / Helter skelter / Piece of your action / Live wire.

Oct 85. (7") *<69591>* **HOME SWEET HOME. / RED HOT** [-] [89]

Jan 86. (7"/7"sha-pic-d) *(EKR 33/+P)* **SMOKIN' IN THE BOYS' ROOM. / HOME SWEET HOME** [51] [-]
(12"+=) *(EKR 33T)* – Shout at the Devil.

Jun 87. (lp/c)(cd) *(EKT 39/+C)(960 725-2)* *<60725>* **GIRLS, GIRLS, GIRLS** [14] [2]
– The wild side / Girls, girls, girls / Dancing on glass / Bad bad boogie / Nona / Five years dead / All in the name of . . . / Sumthin' for nuthin' / You're all I need / Jailhouse rock (live).

Jul 87. (7"/7"w-poster) *(EKR 59/+P)* *<69465>* **GIRLS, GIRLS, GIRLS. / SUMTHIN' FOR NUTHIN'** [26] [12] May87
(12"+=/12"pic-d+=) *(EKR 59T)* – Smokin' in the boys' room.

Sep 87. (7") *<69449>* **THE WILD SIDE. / FIVE YEARS DEAD** [-] [ ]

Nov 87. (7") *<69429>* **YOU'RE ALL I NEED. / ALL IN THE NAME OF ROCK** [-] [83]

Jan 88. (7") *(EKR 65)* **YOU'RE ALL I NEED. / WILD SIDE** [23] [-]
(12"+=/12"pic-d+=/12"boxed+=) *(EKR 65 T/+P/B)* – Home sweet home / Looks that kill.

Jul 88. (m-lp/m-cd) *<25XD 1052>* **HOME SWEET HOME** (RAW TRACKS) [-] [ ]
– Live wire / Piece of your action / Too young to fall in love / Knock 'em dead, kid / Home sweet home.

Sep 89. (lp/c)(cd) *(EKT 59/+C)(960 829-2)* *<60829>* **DR. FEELGOOD** [4] [1]
– Same ol' situation (S.O.S.) / Slice of your pie / Rattlesnake shake / Kickstart my heart / Without you / Don't go away mad (just go away) / She goes down / Sticky sweet / Time for a change / T.N.T. (Terror 'n' Tinseltown) / Dr. Feelgood.

Oct 89. (7"/7"sha-pic-d/c-s) *(EKR 97/+P/C)* *<69271>* **DR. FEELGOOD. / STICKY SWEET** [50] [6] Aug89
(ext.12"+=/ext.3"cd-s+=) *(EKR 97 T/CD)* – All in the name of rock.

Nov 89. (c-s) *<69248>* **KICKSTART MY HEART. / SHE GOES DOWN** [-] [27]

Feb 90. (c-s) *<64985>* **WITHOUT YOU. / SLICE OF YOUR LIFE** [-] [8]

Apr 90. (7"/7"pic-d/c-s) *(EKR 109/+P/C)* **WITHOUT YOU. / LIVE WIRE** [39] [-]
(12"+=/cd-s+=) *(EKR 109 T/CD)* – Girls, girls, girls / All in the name of rock.

May 90. (c-s) *<64962>* **DON'T GO AWAY MAD (JUST GO AWAY). / RATTLESNAKE SHAKE** [-] [19]

Aug 90. (c-s) *<64942>* **SAME OL' SITUATION (S.O.S.). / WILD SIDE** [-] [78]

Nov 90. (m-cd) *<WPCP 3462>* **RAW TRACKS II** [-] [ ]

Aug 91. (7"/c-s) *(EKR 133/+C)* *<64848>* **PRIMAL SCREAM. / DANCING ON GLASS** [32] [63]
(12"+=/cd-s+=) *(EKR 133 T/CD)* – Red hot (live) / Dr. Feelgood (live).

Oct 91. (cd)(lp/c) *<(7559 61204-2)>(EKT 95/+C)>* **DECADE OF DECADENCE** (compilation) [20] [2]
– Live wire / Piece of your action / Shout at the Devil / Looks that kill / Home sweet home / Smokin' in the boys' room / Girls, girls, girls / Wild side / Dr. Feelgood / Kickstart my heart / Teaser / Rock'n'roll junkie / Primal scream / Angela / Anarchy in the UK.

Dec 91. (7") *(EKR 136)* *<64818>* **HOME SWEET HOME '91. / YOU'RE ALL I NEED** [37] [37] Nov91
(12"+=/12"pic-d+=/cd-s+=) *(EKR 136 T/TP/CD)* – Without you / ('A'original mix).

— Had already split temporarily Apr'91 to do own projects. The group parted company with VINCE NEIL, who went solo early 1992.

— brought in **JOHN CORABI** (b.26 Apr'59, Philadelphia, Pennsylvania) – vocals (ex-SCREAM)

Feb 94. (7"yellow) *(EKR 180)* **HOOLIGAN'S HOLIDAY. / HYPNOTIZED (demo)** [36] [ ]
(12"+=/cd-s+=/cd-s+=) *(EKR 180 T/CD/CDX)* – ('A'-Brown nose edit) / ('A'-album version a.k.a. The Dregs of Society – featuring – The Slime City Sinners & The Canadian Connection) / Hypnotized (demo).

Mar 94. (cd/c/d-lp) *<(7559 61534-2/-4/-1)>* **MOTLEY CRUE** [17] [7]
– Power to the music / Uncle Jack / Hooligan's holiday / Misunderstood / Loveshine / Poison apples / Hammered / 'Til death us do part / Welcome to the numb / Smoke the sky / Droppin' like flies / Drift away.

May 94. (7"w-drawn) *(EKR 183)* **MISUNDERSTOOD. /** [-] [-]

— **VINCE NEIL** returned to repl. CORABI

Jun 97. (cd/c) *<(7559 61901-2/-4)>* **GENERATION SWINE** [ ] [4]
– Find myself / Afraid / Flush / Generation swine / Confessions / Beauty / Glitter / Anybody out there / Let us prey / Rocketship / Rat like me / Shout at the Devil '97 / Brandon.

Jul 97. (cd-s) *(E 3936CD1)* **AFRAID / AFRAID (Swine mix) / LUST FOR LIFE / WELCOME TO THE PLANET BOOM** [58] [ ]
(cd-s) *(E 3936CD2)* – ('A'side) / Generation swine / Father / Bittersweet.
(cd-s) *(E 3936CD3)* – ('A'-alternative rave mix) / Shout at the Devil '97 / All in the name of . . . (live) / Girls, girls, girls (live).

Virgin Beyond

Nov 98. (cd) *(CDVIR 77)* *<78002>* **THE BEST OF MOTLEY CRUE**
<US-title 'GREATEST HITS'> (compilation & 2 new) [ ] [20]
– Bitter pill / Enslaved / Girls, girls, girls / Kickstart my heart / Wild side / Glitter (remix) / Dr. Feelgood / Same ol' situation / Home sweet home / Afraid / Don't go away mad (just go away) / Without you / Smokin' in the boys room / Primal scream / Too fast for love / Looks that kill / Shout at the Devil '97.

— **RANDY CASTILLO** – drums (ex-OZZY OSBOURNE) repl. TOMMY LEE who formed METHODS OF MAYHEM

Jul 00. (cd) *(CDVIR 117)* *<78120>* **NEW TATTOO** [ ] [41] Jun00
– Hell on high heels / Treat me like the dog I am / New tattoo / Dragstrip superstar / 1st band on the Moon / She needs rock & roll / Punched in the teeth by love / Hollywood ending / Fake / Porno star / White punks on dope.

– compilations, etc. –

Jan 00. (d-cd) *Spitfire; (SPITCD 058) / Beyond; <63985 78034>* **LIVE: ENTERTAINMENT OR DEATH** [ ] [ ] Nov99
– Looks that kill / Knock 'em dead, kid / Too young to fall in love / Live wire / Public enemy #1 / Shout at the Devil / Merry-go-round / Ten seconds to love / Piece of your action / Starry eyes / Helter skelter / Smokin' in the boys' room / Don't go away mad (just go away) / The wild side / Girls, girls, girls / Dr. Feelgood / Without you / Primal scream / Same ol' situation / Home sweet home / Kickstart my heart.

VINCE NEIL

— self-penned collaborations with either STEVE STEVENS + PHIL SOUSSAN or JACK BLADES + TOMMY SHAW except BLONDES HAVE MORE FUN (Rod Stewart) / I WANNA BE SEDATED (Ramones).

VINCE NEIL – vocals, guitar with friends **STEVE STEVENS** – lead guitar, bass / **VIK FOXX** – drums, percussion / **ROBBIE BUCHANAN** keyboards / **ROBBIE CRANE** – bass / **DAVE MARSHALL** – rhythm guitar / **TOMMY FUNDERBURKE, TIMOTHY B. SCHMIDT, DONNA McDANIEL & CHRISTINA NICHOLS** – backing vocals

Hollywood Hollywood

Sep 92. (7"/c-s) *(HWD 123/+C)* **YOU'RE INVITED (BUT YOU'RE FRIEND CAN'T COME). / Luxury Cruiser (by T-RIDE)** [63] [ ]
(12"+=/cd-s+=) *(HWD 123 T/CD)* – Get the hell out of here (by STEVE VAI).

Warners Warners

May 93. (cd/c) *<(9362 45260-2/-4)>* **EXPOSED** [44] [13]
– Look in her eyes / Sister of pain / Can't have your cake / Fine, fine wine / The edge / Can't change me / Set me free / Living is a luxury / You're invited (but your friend can't come) / Gettin' hard / Forever (featuring BOBBY WOMACK).

May 93. (7") **SISTER OF PAIN. / BLONDES (HAVE MORE FUN)** [ ] [ ]
(cd-s+=) – I wanna be sedated.

Sep 95. (cd/c) *<(9362 45877-2/-4)>* **CARVED IN STONE** [ ] [ ]
– Breakin' in the gun / Black promises / The crawl / One way / Skylar's song / Writing on the wall / Make U feel / The rift / One less mouth to feed / Find a dream.

MOTORHEAD

Formed: London, England . . . June '75 by LEMMY (aka IAN KILMISTER; vocals, bass) who decided to form his own band when, after a five year stint with hyperspace hippies HAWKWIND, he was finally given the boot. His sharp exit came after he was briefly detained in Canada on drugs charges; a notorious speed freak, his penchant for amphetamines was directly translated into MOTORHEAD's music, a synapse-crunching racket that somehow lent itself to a tune or two (the title of the band's first single, 'WHITE LINE FEVER', said it all really). Following his departure from HAWKWIND, LEMMY toyed with the name BASTARD, before opting for the MOTORHEAD moniker, the title of the last song he'd penned for his previous band. He subsequently hooked up with LARRY WALLIS (guitar, vocals) of the PINK FAIRIES and LUCAS FOX (drums), although by early '76 these two had been replaced with 'FAST' EDDIE CLARKE and PHIL 'PHILTHY ANIMAL' TAYLOR respectively. The initial line-up had recorded a relatively laid back outing, 'ON PAROLE' for 'United Artists' in 1975, although this was shelved until 1979 when the label cashed in on the band's success. The aforementioned 'WHITE LINE FEVER' single was also held back, 'Stiff' only releasing it once MOTORHEAD's commercial credentials had been established. It was the 'Chiswick' label who finally had the balls to release something, the eponymous 'MOTORHEAD' album in 1977. It was the first opus from the definitive MOTORHEAD line-up, a combination that would become one of the most infamous in the history of heavy metal and create some of the most enduring material in the band's career. Yet while MOTORHEAD were the epitome of headbanging metal, their maniacal energy also attracted hardcore punks in the same way IRON MAIDEN's early performances had a foot in both camps. Over a series of shit kicking albums, 'OVERKILL' (1979), 'BOMBER' (1979) and 'ACE OF SPADES' (1980), MOTORHEAD became a legend, laying the foundations of thrash with testosterone saturated anthems. The latter album was the landmark MOTORHEAD release, its title track the ultimate outlaw anthem and a Top 20 hit to boot. The record went to No.4, illustrating how quickly the band had risen through the metal ranks. While CLARKE and TAYLOR provided the musical fuel, LEMMY was undoubtedly the beast's engine, his dirty, propulsive bass driving MOTORHEAD ever onwards like the aural equivalent of road rage. And crucially, like all genuine badass outlaws, LEMMY was 'orrible!, yet he still got the chicks, and he had style. In bucketloads. Decked out in his white cowboy boots, bullet belt and mutton chop sideburns, he stood centre stage, rooted to the spot, head stretched up to the mike (maybe LIAM GALLAGHER clocked a few shows) like he was summoning up the God of Thunder (possibly). LEMMY didn't sing in the conventional sense, or even in the heavy metal sense, rather he rasped like a piece of industrial strength sandpaper scraped across a blackboard. He also had more charisma than most of the preening queens that passed as frontmen, his sharp wit and biting sense of humour making him quite a celebrity in his own right and ensuring that his band never fell into parody. MOTORHEAD gained further press attention when they hooked up with rock chicks, GIRLSCHOOL, for the 'ST. VALENTINE'S DAY MASSACRE' EP, released, appropriately enough, in February '81. Credited to HEADGIRL (guffaw, guffaw), the assembled n'er do wells ran through a suitably leering version of Johnny Kidd's 'PLEASE DON'T TOUCH'. Their blistering live set was finally laid down on vinyl in the form of 'NO SLEEP 'TIL HAMMERSMITH' (1981), the band's first (and only) No.1 album and deservedly so. Surely the tightest rock band on the planet at that point, MOTORHEAD ran through a hair whipping frenzy of favourites, from 'STAY CLEAN' and '(WE ARE) THE ROAD CREW' to 'IRON HORSE', LEMMY's tribute to Hell's Angel leader, Tramp. This line-up recorded a further album, the slightly disappointing 'IRON FIST' (1982), before CLARKE left to from his own outfit, FASTWAY. His replacement was BRIAN ROBERTSON (ex-THIN LIZZY, ex-WILD HORSES) who played on only one album, 1983's 'ANOTHER PERFECT DAY'. His more subtle style didn't sit well with the trademark MOTORHEAD cacophony and he soon departed for the more appropriate FRANKIE MILLER BAND, PHIL CAMPBELL and MICHAEL BURSTON (aka WURZEL) replacing him. TAYLOR also departed, PETE GILL (ex-Saxon) being recruited to fill the drum stool and complete the new look four piece MOTORHEAD. The new band made their debut on 'NO REMORSE' (1984), a compilation that collected MOTORHEAD's meanest tracks and showcased four new ones, among them the uber-grind of 'KILLED BY DEATH', possibly LEMMY and Co.'s finest hour. The band almost made the Top 20 once again with the BILL LASWELL-produced 'ORGASMATRON' (1986), LEMMY sounding almost inhuman on the brilliant title track; part android, part wild beast. TAYLOR returned to the fold the following year for the 'ROCK 'N' ROLL' album, its 'EAT THE RICH' track used on the 'Comic Strip' film of the same name, in which LEMMY made his acting debut. Another live album followed, 'NO SLEEP AT ALL' (1988), although it failed to make the same commercial impact as its predecessor. Following a move to L.A. (it had to come sooner or later), the band were back in the charts and back on form with '1916' (1991), its title track an unprecedented show of emotion from LEMMY as he narrated the tale of a young soldier lost in battle. The wart-ridden one also indulged his war fixation on the title track to 'MARCH OR DIE' (1992), while the three most recent releases, 'BASTARDS' (1993) and 'SACRIFICE' (1995) have seen MOTORHEAD content to cruise rather than let rip. Still, as long as LEMMY dons his bass and rides into onstage battle, there'll be a willing bunch of masochists ready to have their ears bled dry by the some of the loudest, filthiest rock'n'roll on the face of the earth. After the relatively disappointing 'SNAKE BITE LOVE' (1998), the remorseless sonic abusers returned to restate their claim with 'WE ARE MOTORHEAD' (2000), as loud and obnoxious as anything they'd come up with in the preceding decade. Sadly, the fine classical violin playing with which LEMMY is currently gracing a high profile TV ad (would we kid you on?) is notably absent; maybe next time . . . • **Covers:** LOUIE LOUIE (hit; Kingsmen) / TRAIN KEPT A-ROLLIN' (Johnny Burnette Trio) / PLEASE DON'T TOUCH (Johnny Kidd) / (I'M YOUR) HOOCHIE COOCHIE MAN (Willie Dixon) / CAT SCRATCH FEVER (Ted Nugent).

Album rating: MOTORHEAD (*5) / OVERKILL (*8) / BOMBER (*6) / ACE OF SPADES (*8) / NO SLEEP 'TIL HAMMERSMITH (*9) / IRON FIST (*5) / ANOTHER PERFECT DAY (*5) / NO REMORSE (*7) / ORGASMATRON (*6) / ROCK'N'ROLL (*5) / NO SLEEP AT ALL (*6) / 1916 (*7) / MARCH OR DIE (*5) / SACRIFICE (*5) / PROTECT THE INNOCENT (*6) / EVERYTHING LOUDER THAN EVERYONE ELSE (*6) / WE ARE MOTORHEAD (*5)

LEMMY (b. IAN KILMISTER, 24 Dec'45, Stoke-On-Trent, England) – vocals, bass (ex-HAWKWIND, ex-OPAL BUTTERFLY, ex-SAM GOPAL'S DREAM, ROCKIN' VICKERS) / **PHIL 'ANIMAL' TAYLOR** (b.21 Sep'54, Chesterfield, England) – drums / **FAST EDDIE CLARKE** – guitar, vocals (ex-BLUE GOOSE, ex-CURTIS KNIGHT & ZEUS) (below withdrawn)

Stiff / not iss.

Dec 76. (7") *(BUY 9)* **LEAVING HERE. / WHITE LINE FEVER** [-] [-]
(withdrawn but iss.Dec78 in 'Stiff' box set Nos.1-10)

Chiswick / not iss.

Jun 77. (7",12") *(S 13)* **MOTORHEAD. / CITY KIDS** [ ] [-]
(re-iss. Sep79 on 'Big Beat' 7"colrd/7"pic-d; NS/+P 13)

Aug 77. (lp) *(WLK 2)* **MOTORHEAD** [43] [-]
– Motorhead / Vibrator / Lost Johnny / Iron horse – Born to lose / White line fever / Keepers on the road / The watcher / Born to lose / Train kept a-rollin'. *(re-iss. white-lp 1978; CWK 3008) (re-iss. Sep81 red-lp,clear-lp; WIK 2) (cd-iss. Jun88 & Feb 91 on 'Big Beat'; CDWIK 2)*

Bronze / not iss.

Sep 78. (7") *BRO 60)* **LOUIE LOUIE. / TEAR YA DOWN** [68] [-]

Feb 79. (7"/12") *(BRO/12BRO 67)* **OVERKILL. / TOO LATE, TOO LATE** [39] [-]

Mar 79. (lp,green-lp) *(BRON 515)* **OVERKILL** [24] [-]
– Overkill / Stay clean / Pay your price / I'll be your sister / Capricorn / No class / Damage case / Tear ya down / Metropolis / Limb for limb. *(cd-iss. Jul87 on 'Legacy'; LLMCD 3011) (re-iss. Jul90 on 'Fame' cd/c/lp; CD/TC+/FA 3236) (re-iss. Feb91 on 'Castle' cd/c/lp; CLA CD/MC/LP 178) (re-iss. cd Aug96 on 'Essential'; ESMCD 310)*

Jun 79. (7") *(BRO 78)* **NO CLASS. / LIKE A NIGHTMARE** [61] [-]

Oct 79. (lp,blue-lp) *(BRON 523)* **BOMBER** [12] [-]
– Dead men tell no tales / Lawman / Sweet revenge / Sharpshooter / Poison / Stone dead forever / All the aces / Step down / Talking head / Bomber. *(cd-iss. Jul87 on 'Legacy'; LLMCD 3012) (re-iss. Apr91 on 'Castle' cd/c/lp; CLA CD/MC/LP 227) (re-iss. Aug96 on 'Essential'; ESMCD 311)*

Nov 79. (7",7"blue) *(BRO 85)* **BOMBER. / OVER THE TOP** [34] [-]

Apr 80. (7"ep/12"ep) *(BRO/12BRO 92)* **THE GOLDEN YEARS (live)** [8] [-]
– Leaving here / Stone dead forever / Dead men don't tell tales / Too late, too late.

Bronze / Mercury

Oct 80. (7"/12") *(BRO/+X 106)* **ACE OF SPADES. / DIRTY LOVE** [15] [ ]

Oct 80. (lp/gold-lp) *(BRON/+G 531) <4011>* **ACE OF SPADES** [4] [ ]
– Ace of spades / Love me like a reptile / Shoot you in the back / Live to win / Fast and loose / (We are) The road crew / Fire, fire / Jailbait / Dance / Bite the bullet / The chase is better than the catch / The hammer. *(cd-iss. Aug87 on 'Legacy'; LLMCD 3013) (re-iss. cd Aug96 on 'Essential'; ESMCD 312)*

Feb 81. (7"ep/10"ep; as HEADGIRL) *(BRO/+X 116)*
ST.VALENTINE'S DAY MASSACRE [5] [-]
– Please don't touch (by MOTORHEAD & GIRLSCHOOL) / Emergency (by MOTORHEAD) / Bomber (GIRLSCHOOL).

Jun 81. (lp/gold-lp/c) *(BRON/+G/C 535)* **NO SLEEP 'TIL HAMMERSMITH (live)** [1] [-]
– Ace of spades / Stay clean / Metropolis / The hammer / Iron horse / No class / Overkill / (We are) The road crew / Capricorn / Bomber / Motorhead. *(cd-iss. Aug87 on 'Legacy'; LLMCD 3014) (re-iss. Feb90 on 'Castle' cd/c/lp; CLA CD/MC/LP 179) (re-iss. cd Aug96 on 'Essential'; ESMCD 313)*

Jul 81. (7"/7"pic-d) *(BRO/+P 124)* **MOTORHEAD (live). / OVER THE TOP (live)** [6] [ ]
below, one-off (MOTORHEAD and The NOLANS)

Oct 81. (7"; as YOUNG AND MOODY BAND) *(BRO 130)* **DON'T DO THAT. / HOW CAN I HELP YOU TONIGHT** [63] [-]

Mar 82. (7",7"red,7"blue) *(BRO 146)* **IRON FIST. / REMEMBER ME, I'M GONE** [29] [-]

Apr 82. (lp/c) *(BRNA/+C 539) <4042>* **IRON FIST** [6] [ ]
– Iron fist / Heart of stone / I'm the doctor / Go to Hell / Loser / Sex and outrage / America / Shut it down / Speedfreak / (Don't let 'em) Grind ya down / (Don't need) Religion / Bang to rights. *(re-iss. Mar87 on 'Castle' lp/c/cd; CLA LP/MC/CD 123) (cd re-iss. Aug96 on 'Essential'; ESMCD 372)*

Sep 82. (7"m; by LEMMY & WENDY) *(BRO 151)* **STAND BY YOUR MAN. / NO CLASS (Plasmatics) / MASTERPLAN (Motorhead)** [ ] [-]

— **BRIAN ROBERTSON** (b. 2 Feb'56, Clarkston, Scotland) – guitar, vocals (ex-THIN LIZZY, ex-WILD HORSES) repl. CLARKE who formed FASTWAY

May 83. (7") *(BRO 165)* **I GOT MINE. / TURN YOU AROUND AGAIN** [46] [ ]
(12"+=) *(BROX 165)* – Tales of glory.

May 83. (lp/c) *(BRON/+C 546) <811365>* **ANOTHER PERFECT DAY** [20] [ ]
– Back at the funny farm / Shine / Dancing on your grave / Rock it / One track mind / Another perfect day / Marching off to war / I got mine / Tales of glory / Die you bastard. *(re-iss. Feb91 on 'Castle' cd/c/lp; CLA CD/MC/LP 225) (re-iss. cd Sep96 on 'Essential'; ESMCD 438)*

Jul 83. (7") *(BRO 167)* **SHINE. / HOOCHIE COOCHIE MAN (live)** [59] [-]
(12"+=) *(BROX 167)* – (Don't need) Religion.

— LEMMY with **PHIL CAMPBELL** (b. 7 May'61, Pontypridd, Wales) – guitar / **WURZEL** (b. MICHAEL BURSTON, 23 Oct'49, Cheltenham, England) – guitar both replace ROBERTSON who joined FRANKIE MILLER BAND / **PETE GILL** (b.9 Jun'51, Sheffield, England) – drums (ex-SAXON) repl. TAYLOR

Aug 84. (7"/7"sha-pic-d) *(BRO/+P 185)* **KILLED BY DEATH. / UNDER THE KNIFE** [51] [-]
(12"+=) *(BROX 185)* – Under the knife (version).

Sep 84. (d-lp) *(PRO MOTOR 1)* **NO REMORSE** (compilation) [14] [ ]
– Ace of spades / Motorhead / Jailbait / Stay clean / Killed by death / Bomber / Iron fist / Shine / Dancing on your grave / Metropolis / Snaggletooth / Overkill / Please don't touch / Stone dead forever / Like a nightmare / Emergency / Steal your face / Louie Louie / No class / Iron horse / (We are) The road crew / Leaving here / Locomotive. *(re-iss. 1988 on 'Castle' d-lp/c/cd+=; CLA LP/MC/CD 121)* – Too late, too late. *(re-iss. cd Aug96 on 'Essential'; ESDCD 371) (cd re-iss. Jul97; ESMCD 557)*

G.W.R. / GWR-Profile

Jun 86. (7") *(GWR 2)* **DEAF FOREVER. / ON THE ROAD (live)** [67] [-]
(12"+=) *(GWT 2)* – Steal your face (live).

Aug 86. (lp/c/cd) *(GW LP/TC/CD 1) <1223>* **ORGASMATRON** [21] [ ] Nov86
– Deaf forever / Nothing up my sleeve / Ain't my crime / Claw / Mean machine / Built for speed / Riding with the driver / Doctor Rock / Orgasmatron. *(pic-lp.Aug89; GWPD 1) (re-iss. cd Mar92; CLACD 283)*

— **PHIL CAMPBELL** – drums returned to repl. GILL

Aug 87. (lp/c/cd) *(GW LP/MC/CD 14) <1240>* **ROCK'N'ROLL** [43] [ ] Oct87
– Rock'n'roll / Eat the rich / Blackheart / Stone deaf in the USA / The wolf / Traitor / Dogs / All for you / Boogeyman.

Nov 87. (7") *(GWR 6)* **EAT THE RICH. / CRADLE TO GRAVE** [ ] [ ]
(12"+=) *(GWR 6)* – Power.
(above from the soundtrack of the film 'Eat The Rich')

Oct 88. (lp/c/cd) *(GW LP/MC/CD 31)* **NO SLEEP AT ALL (live)** [79] [ ]
– Dr. Rock / Stay clean / Traitor / Metropolis / Dogs / Ace of spades / Eat the rich / Built for speed / Deaf forever / Just cos you got the power / Killed by death / Overkill. *(cd+=)* – (3 extra). *(re-iss. cd Mar92 on 'Castle' cd/c; CLA CD/MC 285)*

Epic / W.T.G.

Jan 91. (7"/7"sha-pic-d/c-s) *(656578-7/-0/-4)* **THE ONE TO SING THE BLUES. / DEAD MAN'S HAND** [45] [ ]
(12"+=/cd-s+=) *(656578-6/-2)* – Eagle rock / Shut you down.

Jan 91. (cd/c/lp/pic-lp) *(467481-2/-4/-1) <46858>* **1916** [24] [ ] Mar91
– The one to sing the blues / I'm so bad (baby I don't care) / No voices in the sky / Going to Brazil / Nightmare – The dreamtime / Love me forever / Angel city / Make my day / Ramones / Shut you down / 1916.

— **TAYLOR** returned but was soon repl. by **MIKEY DEE** (b.31 Oct'63, Olundby, Sweden) – drums

Aug 92. (cd/c/lp) *(471723-2/-4/-1)* **MARCH OR DIE** [60] [ ]
– Stand / Cat scratch fever / Bad religion / Jack the ripper / I ain't no nice guy / Hellraiser / Asylum choir / Too good to be true / You better run / Name in vain / March or die.

Nov 92. (12"ep/cd-ep) *(658809-6/-2)* **'92 TOUR (live)** [63] [ ]
– Hellraiser / You better run / Going to Brazil / Ramones.

— Above 1st track co-written w / OZZY OSBOURNE

ZYX / not iss.

Nov 93. (cd/lp) *(20263-2/-1)* **BASTARDS** [-] [-] German
– On your feet or on your knees / Burner / Death or glory / I am the sword / Born to raise hell / Don't let daddy kiss me / Bad woman / Liar / Lost in the ozone / I'm your man / We bring the shake / Devils.

Arista / Arista

Nov 94. (7"/c-s; by MOTORHEAD with ICE-T & WHITFIELD CRANE) *(74321 23915-7/-4)* **BORN TO RAISE HELL. / ('A'mix)** [49] [ ]
(12"+=/cd-s+=) *(74321 23915-1/-2)* – ('A'mix).

S.P.V. / C.M.C.

Apr 95. (cd/c/lp) *(SPV 085-7694-2/-4/-1) <86231>* **SACRIFICE** [ ] [ ]
– Sacrifice / Sex & death / Over your shoulder / War for war / Order – Fade to black / Dog-face boy / All gone to hell / Make 'em blind / Don't waste your time / In another time / Out of the sun.

Oct 96. (cd/c) *(SPV 085-1830-2/-4) <86207>* **OVERNIGHT SENSATION** [ ] [ ]
– Civil war / Crazy like a fox / I don't believe a word / Eat the gun / Overnight sensation / Love can't buy you money / Broken / Them not me / Murder show / Shake the world / Listen to your heart.

Mar 99. (d-cd) *(SPV 087-2114-2) <86268>* **EVERYTHING LOUDER THAN EVERYONE ELSE (live)** [ ] [ ]
– Iron fist / Stay clean / On your feet or on your knees / Over your shoulder / Civil war / Burner / Metropolis / Nothing up my sleeves / I'm so bad, baby I don't care / Chase I better than the catch / Take the blame / No class / Overnight sensation / Sacrifice / Born to raise hell / Lost in the ozone / One to sing the blues / Capricorn / Love for sale / Orgasmatron / Going to Brazil / Killed by death / Bomber / Ace of spades / Overkill.

May 00. (cd/lp) *(SPV 0852182-2/-1) <86292>* **WE ARE MOTORHEAD** [ ] [ ]
– See me burning / Slow dance / Stay out of jail / God save the Queen / Out to lunch / Wake the dead / One more fucking time / Stagefright – Crash & burn / (Wearing your) Heart on your sleeve / We are Motorhead.

Jul 00. (cd-s) *(SPV 0602184-3)* **GOD SAVE THE QUEEN / ONE MORE F**KING TIME / GOD SAVE THE QUEEN (enhanced video)** [ ] [-]

– compilations, etc. –

Oct 79. (lp) *Liberty; (LBR 1004)* **ON PAROLE** [65] [-]
– Motorhead / On parole / Vibrator / Iron horse – Born to lose / City kids / Fools / The watcher / Leaving here / Lost Johnny. *(was to be have been released Dec75) (re-iss. May82 on 'Fame' lp/c; FA/TC-FA 3009) (cd-iss. Oct90; CD-FA 3251) (cd remastered Feb97 on 'EMI Gold'; CDGO 2070)*

Nov 80. (7"ep,7"blue-ep,7"pink-ep,7"orange-ep/12"ep,12"blue-ep,12"pink-ep,12"orange-ep) *Big Beat (NS/SWT 61)* **BEER DRINKERS EP** [43] [-]
– Beer drinkers & hell raisers / On parole / Instro / I'm your witch doctor.

Mar 83. (lp/c) *Big Beat; (NED/+C 2)* **WHAT'S WORDS WORTH (live at the Roundhouse 18/2/78)** [71] [-]
– The watcher / Iron horse – Born to lose / On parole (in A) / White line fever / Keep us on the road / Leaving here / I'm your witchdoctor / The train kept a-rollin' / City kids. *(re-iss. Jan90; WIKM 49)*

Aug 82. (d-c) *Bronze; (3574 138)* **OVERKILL / BOMBER** [ ] [-]
Nov 84. (lp/c) *Astan; <2/4 0041>* **RECORDED LIVE (live)** [-] [ ]
Apr 86. (lp/c) *Raw Power; (RAW LP/MC 011)* **ANTHOLOGY** [ ] [-]
(cd-iss. Dec86; RAWCD 011)
Apr 86. (lp/c) *Dojo; (DOJO LP/TC 18)* **BORN TO LOSE** [ ] [-]
1986. (cd) *Legacy; (LLMCD 3004)* **ANTHOLOGY VOL.1** [ ] [-]
Apr 88. (lp/cd) *That's Original; (TFO LP/CD 8)* **OVERKILL / ANOTHER PERFECT DAY** [ ] [-]
1988. (3"cd-ep) *Special Edition; (CD3-10)* **ACE OF SPADES / BOMBER / MOTORHEAD / OVERKILL** [ ] [-]
Nov 89. (lp/cd) *Receiver; (RR LP/CD 120)* **BLITZKREIG ON BIRMINGHAM LIVE '77 (live)** [ ] [-]
Jan 90. (cd/lp) *Receiver; (RR CD/LP 123)* **DIRTY LOVE** [ ] [-]
Apr 90. (cd/d-lp) *Castle; (CCS CD/LP 237)* **WELCOME TO THE BEAR TRAP** [ ] [-]
Apr 90. (cd/c/d-lp) *That's Original; (TFO CD/MC/LP 024)* **BOMBER / ACE OF SPADES** [ ] [-]
Apr 90. (cd/c/lp) *G.W.R.; (GW CD/MC/LP 101)* **THE BIRTHDAY PARTY (live '85)** [ ] [-]
(cd+=) – (3 extra tracks). *(also on 'Roadrunner'; RR 9376-1)*
Jun 90. (cd/c/lp) *Receiver; (RR CD/MC/LP 130)* **LOCK UP YOUR DAUGHTERS (live 1977)** [ ] [-]
Jul 90. (cd) *Marble Arch; (cd)* **GRIND YA DOWN** [ ] [-]
(re-iss. Jul94 on 'Success';)
Jul 90. (cd/c) *Action Replay; (ARLC/CDAR 1014)* **THE BEST OF THE REST OF MOTORHEAD** [ ] [-]
(re-iss. Jul93 cd/c; CDAR/ARLC 1032)
Nov 90. (cd/c/lp) *Knight; (NEX CD/MC/LP 136)* **FROM THE VAULTS** [ ] [-]
Jul 91. (3xcd-box/3xlp-box) *Essential; (ESB CD/LP 146)* **MELTDOWN** [ ] [-]
Feb 92. (3xcd-box) *Castle; (CLABX 901)* **3 ORIGINALS** [ ] [-]
– (NO REMORSE / ACE OF SPADES / NO SLEEP 'TIL HAMMERSMITH)
Feb 92. (cd/lp) *Receiver; (RR CD/LP 005)* **LIVE JAILBAIT (live)** [ ] [-]
Sep 92. (cd/c/lp) *Roadrunner; (RR 9125-2/-4/-1)* **THE BEST OF MOTORHEAD** [ ] [-]
Apr 93. (c/cd) *Tring; (MC+/JHD 081)* **LIVE (live)** [ ] [-]
Jun 93. (4xcd-box) *Receiver; (RRZCD 501)* **MOTORHEAD BOX SET** [ ] [-]
Aug 93. (c-s/12"/cd-s) *W.G.A.F.; (MC/12/CD WGAF 101)* **ACE OF SPADES (THE C.C.N.remix). / ('A'mixes)** [23] [-]
Nov 93. (cd/c/lp) *Castle TV; (CTV CD/MC/LP 125)* **ALL THE ACES** [ ] [-]
Mar 94. (cd/c/lp) *Roadrunner; (RR 9009-2/-4/-1)* **LIVE AT BRIXTON ACADEMY (live)** [ ] [-]
Aug 94. (cd) *Spectrum; (550 724-2)* **ACES HIGH** [ ] [-]
Sep 94. (cd) *Cleopatra; (CLEO 94132)* **IRON FIST AND THE HORDES FROM HELL** [ ] [-]
May 95. (cd) *Spectrum; ()* **ULTIMATE METAL** [ ] [-]
Jul 95. (2xcd-box) *Griffin; (GCD 2192)* **FISTFUL OF ACES / THE BEST OF MOTORHEAD** [ ] [-]
Oct 95. (cd) *Elite; (ELITE 019CD)* **HEADBANGERS** [ ] [-]
Apr 96. (cd/c) *Hallmark; (30369-2/-4)* **MOTORHEAD – LIVE** [ ] [-]
Nov 96. (cd) *Emperio; (EMPRCD 692)* **LIVE** [ ] [-]
Nov 96. (cd) *Steamhammer; (CD 0857694-2)* **WE'RE MOTORHEAD AND WE'RE GONNA KICK YOUR ASS** [ ] [-]
Feb 97. (cd) *Receiver; (RRCD 238)* **STONE DEAD FOREVER** [ ] [-]
May 97. (d-cd) *Snapper; (SMDCD 127)* **TAKE NO PRISONERS** [ ] [-]
Jul 97. (cd) *Going For A Song; (GFS 073)* **MOTORHEAD** [ ] [-]
Aug 97. (4xcd-box) *Essential; (ESBCD 562)* **PROTECT THE INNOCENT** [ ] [-]
Nov 97. (cd) *Rialto; (RMCD 221)* **ARCHIVES** [ ] [-]
Mar 98. (cd/c) *Select-Castle; (SEL CD/MC 502)* **DEAF FOREVER – THE BEST OF MOTORHEAD** [ ] [-]
Apr 98. (cd) *Cleopatra; (<CLP 203>)* **THE SINGLES COLLECTION** [ ] [ ]
Apr 98. (cd) *King Biscuit; <(KBFHCD 002)>* **KING BISCUIT PRESENTS . . .** [ ] [ ]
Oct 98. (3xcd-box) *Essential; (ESMBX 304)* **OVERKILL / BOMBER / ACE OF SPADES** [ ] [ ]
Oct 98. (d-cd) *Essential; (ESSCD 668)* **ALL THE ACES – THE BEST OF MOTORHEAD / THE MUGGER'S TAPES** [ ] [ ]
Jun 99. (cd) *Cleopatra; <(CLP 0497-2)>* **GOLDEN YEARS: THE ALTERNATIVE VERSIONS** [ ] [-]
Jul 00. (cd) *S.P.V.; (06021843)* **GOD SAVE THE QUEEN** [ ] [-]
Aug 00. (d-cd/t-lp) *Metal-Is; (MIS DD/LP 002)* **THE BEST OF MOTORHEAD** [52] [-]
Oct 00. (cd; by LEMMY, SLIM JIM & DANNY B) *S.P.V.; (085-2198-2)* **LEMMY & SLIM JIM / DANNY B** [ ] [-]
Oct 00. (10xcd-box) *Raw Power; (RAWBX 140)* **BORN TO LOSE / LIVE TO WIN** [ ] [ ]

MOTT THE HOOPLE

Formed: Hereford, England . . . Jun '69 by OVEREND WATTS, DALE GRIFFIN, VERDEN ALLEN and MICK RALPHS, who were part of The SHAKEDOWN SOUND with singer STAN TIPPINS. With new manager and producer Guy Stevens placing an ad in a music paper, the group found a replacement frontman in IAN HUNTER (he had once guested on a 45 by CHARLIE WOLFE). Naming themselves MOTT THE HOOPLE (after a novel by Willard Manus), they signed to Chris Blackwell's burgeoning 'Island' label. Their eponymous debut gained a minor chart placing, the record introducing HUNTER's bluesy DYLAN-esque delivery over a tentative set of earthy rock'n'roll. Although three more lacklustre albums were completed in quick succession, the group split in 1972 after the last of them, 'BRAIN CAPERS' failed to match its predecessors' Top 50 status. Fortunately for them, a young DAVID BOWIE was re-establishing himself in the songwriting stakes, the ascending glamster offering the band a lifeline in the form of 'ALL THE YOUNG DUDES'. Securing a new contract with 'C.B.S.', MOTT THE HOOPLE roared into the UK Top 3 with a new lease of life, although VERDEN had departed soon after the recording of the similarily-titled hit parent album. Using the glam-rock craze as their launch pad, the band straddled the widening gap between the teen-pop market and the college circuit. A trio of Top 20 hits in 1973, 'HONALOOCHIE BOOGIE', 'ALL THE WAY FROM MEMPHIS' and 'ROLL AWAY THE STONE' proved that the group were no overnight sensations, although the last of these had been recorded without RALPHS who joined BAD COMPANY. Together with VERDEN's deputy MICK BOLTON, he was replaced by ARIEL BENDER and MORGAN FISHER, two veterans of the British music scene. Releasing 'THE HOOPLE' album as a follow-up to 1973's 'MOTT', the band once again hit the UK and US charts, although the critical tide was turning against glam and everyone connected with it (i.e. SWEET, SLADE, GLITTER, QUATRO, etc). With BENDER (aka LUTHER GROSVENOR) opting to join heavyweights WIDOWMAKER, the band (with ex-BOWIE sidekick, MICK RONSON, now taking on guitar duties) also opted for a harder-edged direction after a single, 'SATURDAY GIGS', failed to scrape into the Top 40. Suffering from exhaustion, HUNTER was eager to follow a less high-profile solo career, RONSON also taking the same route, the pair, in addition touring together as The HUNTER-RONSON BAND. The remainder (OVEREND, DALE and MORGAN) re-grouped in 1975 as MOTT, enlisting the services of new frontman NIGEL BENJAMIN and guitarist RAY MAJORS for a new album, 'DRIVE ON'. Another uninspiring set, 'SHOUTING AND POINTING' was to appear in 1976, the band soon giving up amid general disinterest, although they did resurface as the more overtly hard-rockin' BRITISH LIONS. • **Songwriters:** HUNTER or others wrote most except; YOU REALLY GOT ME (Kinks) / LAUGH AT ME (Sonny Bono) / CROSSROADS (Sir Douglas Quintet) / KEEP A KNOCKIN' (Little Richard) / WHOLE LOTTA SHAKIN' GOIN' ON (Jerry Lee Lewis) / LAY DOWN (Melanie) / COME ON BABY, LET'S GO DOWNTOWN (Crazy Horse) / YOUR OWN BACKYARD (Dion) / etc.

Album rating: MOTT THE HOOPLE (*6) / MAD SHADOWS (*5) / WILD LIFE (*4) / BRAIN CAPERS (*6) / ALL THE YOUNG DUDES (*7) / MOTT (*8) / THE HOOPLE (*7) / LIVE (*4) / DRIVE ON (*3) / SHOUTING AND POINTING (*2) THE BALLAD OF MOTT THE HOOPLE – A RETROSPECTIVE compilation (*8)

IAN HUNTER (b. 3 Jun'46, Shrewsbury, England) – vocals, guitar, piano / **MICK RALPHS** (b.31 May'44) – guitar, vocals / **VERDEN ALLEN** (b.26 May'44) – organ / **OVEREND WATTS** (b.13 May'49, Birmingham, England) – bass, vocals / **DALE 'BUFFIN' GRIFFIN** (b.24 Oct'48, Hereford) – drums, vocals

Island Atlantic

Oct 69. (7") *(WIP 6072)* **ROCK AND ROLL QUEEN. / ROAD TO BIRMINGHAM** [ ] [-]
Nov 69. (lp) *(ILPS 9108) <8258>* **MOTT THE HOOPLE** [66] [ ]
– You really got me / At the crossroads / Laugh at me / Backsliding fearlessly / Rock and roll queen / Rabbit foot and Toby time / Half Moon Bay / Wrath and wroll. *(cd-iss. Jul97 on 'Going For A Song'; GFS 065)*
Jan 70. (7") **ROCK AND ROLL QUEEN. / BACKSLIDING FEARLESSLY** [-] [ ]
Sep 70. (lp) *(ILPS 9119) <8272>* **MAD SHADOWS** [48] [ ]
– Thunderbuck ram / No wheels to ride / You are one of us / Walkin' with a mountain / I can feel / Threads of iron / When my mind's gone.
Feb 71. (lp) *(ILPS 9144) <8284>* **WILDLIFE** [44] [ ]
– Whisky woman / Angel of 8th avenue / Wrong side of the river / Waterloo / Lay down / It must be love / Original mixed-up lad / Home is where I want to be / Keep a knockin'.
Sep 71. (lp) *(ILPS 9178) <8304>* **BRAIN CAPERS** [ ] [ ]
– Death maybe your Santa Claus / Darkness darkness / Your own backyard / Journey / Sweet Angeline / Wheel of the quivering meat conception / Second love / Moon upstairs.
Oct 71. (7") *(WIP 6105)* **MIDNIGHT LADY. / THE DEBT** [ ] [ ]
Dec 71. (7") *(WIP 6112)* **DOWNTOWN. / HOME IS WHERE I WANT TO BE** [ ] [ ]

C.B.S. Columbia

Jul 72. (7") *(8271) <45673>* **ALL THE YOUNG DUDES. / ONE OF THE BOYS** [3] [37]

Sep 72. (lp/c) *(CBS/40 65184) <31750>* **ALL THE YOUNG DUDES** 21 89 Nov72
– Sweet Jane / Momma's little jewel / All the young dudes / Sucker / Jerkin' crocus / One of the boys / Soft ground / Ready for love – After lights / Sea diver. *(cd-iss. Aug98 on 'Columbia'; 491691-2)*

Jan 73. (7") *<45754>* **ONE OF THE BOYS. / SUCKER** - 96

Mar 73. (7") *<45784>* **SWEET JANE. / JERKIN' CROCUS** -

— **MICK BOLTON** – keyboards filled in for departing VERDEN who went solo

May 73. (7") *(1530) <45882>* **HONALOOCHIE BOOGIE. / ROSE** 12

Jul 73. (lp/c) *(CBS/40 69038) <32425>* **MOTT** 7 35 Aug73
– All the way from Memphis / Whizz kid / Hymn for the dudes / Honaloochie boogie / Violence / Drivin' sister / Ballad of Mott The Hoople (March 26, 1972 – Zurich) / I'm a Cadillac – El Camino Dolo Roso / I wish I was your mother. *(cd-iss. 1988 on 'Castle'; CLACD 138X) (cd-iss. Mar95 on 'Rewind'; 467402-2)*

Aug 73. (7") *(1764)* **ALL THE WAY FROM MEMPHIS. / BALLAD OF MOTT THE HOOPLE (MARCH 26, 1972 – ZURICH)** 10 -

Sep 73. (7") *<45920>* **ALL THE WAY FROM MEMPHIS. / I WISH I WAS YOUR MOTHER** -

— **ARIEL BENDER** (b. LUTHER GROSVENOR, 23 Dec'49, Evesham, England) – guitar (ex-SPOOKY TOOTH) replaced RALPHS who joined BAD COMPANY / **MORGAN FISHER** – keyboards (ex-LOVE AFFAIR) repl. BOLTON (above 2 with HUNTER, WATTS and GRIFFIN.)

Nov 73. (7") *(1895)* **ROLL AWAY THE STONE. / WHERE DO YOU ALL COME FROM** 8 -

Mar 74. (7") *(2177) <46035>* **THE GOLDEN AGE OF ROCK'N'ROLL. / REST IN PEACE** 16 96 May74

Mar 74. (lp/c) *(CBS/40 69062) <32871>* **THE HOOPLE** 11 28 Apr74
– The golden age of rock'n'roll / Marionette / Alice / Crash Street kidds / Born late '58 / Trudi's song / Pearl 'n' Roy (England) / Through the looking glass / Roll away the stone.

Apr 74. (7") *<46076>* **ROLL AWAY THE STONE. / THROUGH THE LOOKING GLASS** -

Jun 74. (7") *(2439)* **FOXY FOXY. / TRUDI'S SONG** 33 -

— **BLUE WEAVER** – organ on tour (ex-AMEN CORNER)

Nov 74. (lp/c) *(CBS/40 69093) <33282>* **LIVE** (live; Broadway – Nov73 / Hammersmith – May74) 32 23
– All the way from Memphis / Sucker / Rest in peace / All the young dudes / Walkin' with a mountain / Sweet Angeline / Rose / Medley:- (a) Jerkin' crocus – (b) One of the boys – (c) Rock'n'roll queen – (d) Get back – (e) Whole lotta shakin' – (f) Violence.

— **MICK RONSON** – guitar, vocals (Solo artist, ex-DAVID BOWIE; SPIDERS FROM MARS) repl. ARIEL who formed WIDOWMAKER

Oct 74. (7") *(2754)* **SATURDAY GIGS. / MEDLEY; JERKIN' CROCUS – SUCKER (live)** 41 -

Dec 74. (7") *<10091>* **ALL THE YOUNG DUDES (live). / ROSE** -

— Split Dec'74. HUNTER and RONSON formed duo and went solo.

MOTT

(OVEREND, DALE and **MORGAN)** were joined by **NIGEL BENJAMIN** – vocals (ex-ROYCE) / **RAY MAJORS** – guitar (ex-HACKENSHACK)

C.B.S. Columbia

Aug 75. (7") *(3528)* **MONTE CARLO. / SHOUT IT ALL OUT**

Sep 75. (lp/c) *(CBS/40 69154) <33705>* **DRIVE ON** 45
– By tonight / Monte Carlo / She does it / I'll tell you something / Stiff upper lip / Love now / Apologies / The great white wall / Here we are / It takes one to know one / I can show you how it is.

Oct 75. (7") *(3741)* **BY TONIGHT. / I CAN SHOW YOU HOW IT IS**

Feb 76. (7") *(4055)* **IT TAKES ONE TO KNOW ONE. / I'LL TELL YOU SOMETHING**

Jun 76. (lp/c) *(CBS/40 81289) <34236>* **SHOUTING AND POINTING**
– Shouting and pointing / Collision course / Storm / Career (no such thing as rock'n'roll) / Hold on, you're crazy / See you again / Too short arms (I don't care) / Broadside outcasts / Good times. *(cd-iss. Jan98 on 'Columbia'; SMDCD 312)*

– compilations, etc. –

Oct 72. (lp) *Island; (ILPS 9215) / Atlantic; <7297>* **ROCK'N'ROLL QUEEN** Jul74

Feb 76. (7") *C.B.S.; (3963)* **ALL THE YOUNG DUDES. / ROLL AWAY THE STONE** -
(re-iss. Apr83 on 'Old Gold'; OG 9312)

Mar 76. (lp/c) *C.B.S.; (CBS/40 81225) <34368>* **GREATEST HITS**
– All the way from Memphis / Honaloochie boogie / Hymn for the dudes / Born late '58 / All the young dudes / Roll away the stone / Ballad of Mott The Hoople / Golden age of rock'n'roll / Foxy lady / Saturday gigs. *(re-iss. Jun81 lp/c; CBS/40 32007) (cd-iss. Apr89; CD 32007)*

Mar 81. (lp) *Island; (IRSP 8)* **TWO MILES FROM HEAVEN** -

Mar 81. (lp/c) *Hallmark; (SHM 3055)* **ALL THE WAY FROM MEMPHIS** -

Jul 84. (7") *C.B.S.; (A 4581)* **ALL THE YOUNG DUDES. / HONALOOCHIE BOOGIE** -

1988. (cd) *Castle; (CCSCD 174)* **THE COLLECTION** -

Jun 90. (cd) *Island; (IMCD 87)* **WALKING WITH A MOUNTAIN (BEST OF 1969-1972)**
– Rock and roll queen / At the crossroads / Thunderbuck ram / Whiskey woman / Waterflow / The Moon upstairs / Second love / The road to Birmingham / Black scorpio (mama's little jewel) / You really got me / Walking with a mountain / No wheels to ride / Keep a knockin' / Midnight lady / Death may be your Santa Claus / Darkness darkness / Growing man blues / Black hills.

Jun 92. (7"/c-s) *Columbia; (658177-7/-4)* **ALL THE YOUNG DUDES. / ONCE BITTEN TWICE SHY (by Ian Hunter)**
(cd-s+=) *(658177-2)* – Roll Away The Stone.

Dec 92. (cd) *Edsel; (EDCD 361)* **MOOT THE HOOPLE / MAD SHADOWS** -

Jun 93. (cd) *See For Miles; (SEECD 7)* **MOTT THE HOOPLE FEATURING STEVE HYAMS** -

Nov 93. (d-cd) *Legacy; (CD 46973)* **THE BALLAD OF MOTT THE HOOPLE – A RETROSPECTIVE** -
(re-iss. Jun96 on 'Coulmbia'; 474420-2)

Jun 96. (cd-s) *Old Gold; (126236380-2)* **ALL THE YOUNG DUDES / ONE OF THE BOYS** -

Jul 96. (cd) *Windsong; (WINCD 064)* **THE ORIGINAL MIXED UP KIDS – THE BBC SESSIONS 1970-71** -

Apr 97. (cd) *BR Music; (RM 1547)* **ALL THE YOUNG DUDES** -

Sep 98. (cd) *Spectrum; (554600-2)* **THE BEST OF MOTT THE HOOPLE – THE ISLAND YEARS 1969-1972** -

Nov 98. (cd) *Angel Air; (<SJPCD 029>)* **ALL THE WAY FROM STOCKHOLM TO PHILADELPHIA (live 1971-1972)**

Jun 99. (d-cd; by MOTT) *Angel Air; <(SJPCD 025)>* **LIVE OVER HERE AND OVER THERE 1975-1976**

Oct 99. (d-cd; with Various Artists) *Eagle; (EDGCD 104)* **FRIENDS AND RELATIVES** -

Apr 00. (cd; with Various Artists) *Connoisseur; (VSOPCD 283)* **MOTT THE HOOPLE FAMILY ALBUM** -

Jul 00. (cd) *Angel Air; <(SJPCD 061)>* **ROCK'N'ROLL CIRCUS (live in Wolverhampton 6/4/72)**

Jul 00. (cd; by MOTT) *Angel Air; <(SJPCD 054)>* **THE GOOSEBERRY SESSIONS AND RARITIES**

Sep 00. (d-cd) *Recall; (SMDCD 312)* **A TALE OF TWO CITIES** -

— In Feb'80, MOTT THE HOOPLE tracks were included on double album 'SHADES OF IAN HUNTER – THE BALLAD OF IAN HUNTER & MOTT THE HOOPLE' on 'CBS'; *(88476)*

BRITISH LIONS

MOTT + **JOHN FIDDLER** – vocals (ex-MEDICINE HEAD) repl. NIGEL who joined ENGLISH ASSASSINS

Vertigo R.S.O.

Feb 78. (7") *(6059 192)* **ONE MORE CHANCE TO RUN. / BOOSTER** -

Feb 78. (lp) *(9120 019) <3032>* **BRITISH LIONS** 83 Apr78
– One more chance to run / Wild in the streets / Break this fool / International heroes / Fork talking man / My life in your hands / Big drift away / Booster / Eat the rich.

Apr 78. (7") *(6059 201)* **INTERNATIONAL HEROES. / EAT THE RICH** -

Jul 78. (7") *<898>* **WILD IN THE STREETS. / BOOSTER** - 87

Cherry Red not iss.

May 80. (lp) *(ARED 7)* **TROUBLE WITH WOMEN** -
– Trouble with women / Any port in a storm / Lady don't fall backwards / High noon / Lay down your love / Waves of love / Electric chair / Won't you give him up.

— When they split MORGAN FISHER went solo releasing single 'GENEVE'. GRIFFIN and WATTS went into production incl. HANOI ROCKS.

Bob MOULD (see under ⇒ HUSKER DU)

MOUNTAIN

Formed: The Bronx, New York, USA . . . 1969 by FELIX PAPPALARDI and guitarist LESLIE WEST. A veteran producer, PAPPALARDI had worked with the likes of LOVIN' SPOONFUL, JOAN BAEZ, The YOUNGBLOODS etc., as well as helping CREAM to achieve their groundbreaking power trio crunch. He first came into contact with the girthsome WEST after being landed with the job of producing some salesworthy product by Long Island popsters The VAGRANTS. In the event he failed and the band split; impressed by WEST's guitar skills, however, the natural next move was for the pair to hook up, PAPPALARDI producing WEST's first solo set, 'MOUNTAIN' (1969). The record's encouraging reception duly persuaded the duo to make MOUNTAIN a full-time concern, PAPPALARDI playing bass alongside drummer NORMAN D. SMART and new recruit, keyboard player STEVE KNIGHT. This was the line-up which no doubt caused more than a few bad trips at 'Woodstock' in August '69, the group blasting the hippies with their warp-factor blues/sludge-metal on only their fourth ever gig. The 'MOUNTAIN CLIMBING!' (1970) set was unleashed the following Spring, the rousing 'MISSISSIPPI QUEEN' single pushing the album into the US Top 20. 'NANTUCKET SLEIGHRIDE' (1971) was another sizable Stateside success, its dense title track later used as the theme tune for ITV's long running 'World In Action' series. A third set, 'FLOWERS OF EVIL' (1972) didn't fare so well, the rather predictable organ-dominated riff overkill beginning to grate. A concert set, then, 'MOUNTAIN LIVE – THE ROAD GOES ON FOREVER' (1972), was just what the doctor didn't order, especially one where 'NANTUCKET SLEIGHRIDE' was spun out over a sanity-defying two sides-plus of vinyl; the solo goes on forever, anyone?. Wisely perhaps, PAPPALARDI opted to resume production work and the first incarnation of MOUNTAIN was no more. Along with CORKY LAING, who had replaced SMART in the drum stool, WEST engaged the services of ex-CREAM bassist, JACK BRUCE to form WEST, BRUCE & LAING. The trio secured a deal with 'Columbia', achieving moderate success with the album 'WHY DON'CHA' (1972) and releasing a second set through MOUNTAIN's label, 'Windfall'. By the time a posthumous live album was issued in 1974, WEST had already rejoined PAPPALARDI in a revamped MOUNTAIN, the pair bringing in ALLEN SCHWARZBERG and ROBERT MANN. Worryingly, their first release was a live album, 'TWIN PEAKS' (1974), and a subsequent studio set, 'AVALANCHE' (1974) was met with a muted response. MOUNTAIN faded from view once more, PAPPALARDI recording two solo albums for 'A&M', 'FELIX PAPPALARDI AND CREATION' (1976) and 'DON'T WORRY MUM?' (1979), before retiring to Japan. WEST, meanwhile, released two solo sets for 'R.C.A.', the self-deprecatingly titled 'THE GREAT FATSBY' (1975) and 'THE LESLIE WEST BAND' (1976). Another MOUNTAIN reformation was probably inevitable, however, and it came in 1981, the project later overshadowed by the death of PAPPALARDI, shot dead on 17th April '83 by his wife,

Gail Collins. Ex-RAINBOW and URIAH HEEP man, MARK CLARKE was eventually hired as a replacement and the group cut a disappointing album for 'Scotti Brothers', 'GO FOR YOUR LIFE' (1985). MOUNTAIN were finally buried and WEST once again hooked up with JACK BRUCE for 'THEME' (1988) and 'ALLIGATOR' (1989), the legend given something of a dusting down via the release of 1995's 'Sony' retrospective, 'OVER THE TOP'. • **Songwriters:** WEST-PAPPALARDI penned except; THIS WHEEL'S ON FIRE (Bob Dylan) / ROLL OVER BEETHOVEN (Chuck Berry) / WHOLE LOTTA SHAKIN' GOIN' ON (Jerry Lee Lewis). LESLIE WEST solo covered; RED HOUSE (Jimi Hendrix) / SPOONFUL (Cream) / THE STEALER (Free) / I PUT A SPELL ON YOU (Screaming Jay Hawkins) / HALL OF THE MOUNTAIN KING (Grieg) / DREAM LOVER (Bobby Darin) / THEME FROM EXODUS (Gold) / SEA OF FIRE (Cintron). • **Trivia:** On their live double album 'TWIN PEAKS', they used 1 album and a bit for track 'NANTUCKET SLEIGHRIDE'.

Album rating: LESLIE WEST – MOUNTAIN (*6) / MOUNTAIN CLIMBING! (*7) / NANTUCKET SLEIGHRIDE (*6) / FLOWERS OF EVIL (*6) / THE ROAD GOES ON FOREVER – MOUNTAIN LIVE (*4) / THE BEST OF MOUNTAIN (FEATURING LESLIE WEST & FELIX PAPPALARDI) compilation (*8) / AVALANCHE (*5) / TWIN PEAKS (*4) / GO FOR YOUR LIFE (*4) / OVER THE TOP part compilation (*7) / MAN'S WORLD (*5) / West, Bruce & Laing: WHY DONTCHA (*5) / WHATEVER TURNS YOU ON (*4) / LIVE 'N' KICKIN' (*4) / Leslie West: THE GREAT FATSBY (*4) / THE LESLIE WEST BAND (*3) / THEME (*3) / ALLIGATOR (*4) / DODGIN' THE DIRT (*4)

LESLIE WEST

(b. LESLIE WEINSTEIN, 22 Oct'45, Queens, N.Y.) – vocals, lead guitar (ex-VAGRANTS) / with **FELIX PAPPALARDI** (b.1939) – bass, keyboards / **NORMAN LANDSBERG** – keyboards / **NORMAN D.SMART** (b. Boston) – drums

Bell / Windfall

Sep 69. (lp) <4500> **MOUNTAIN** [-] [72]
– Blood of the sun / Long red / Better watch out / Blind man / Baby I'm down / Dreams of milk & honey / Storyteller man / This wheel's on fire / Look to the wind / Southbound train / Because you are my friend.

Oct 69. (7") *(BLL 1078)* <530> **DREAMS OF MILK AND HONEY. / THIS WHEEL'S ON FIRE** [ ] [ ]

Jan 70. (7") <531> **BLOOD OF THE SUN. / LONG RED** [-] [ ]

MOUNTAIN

named after last album. **STEVE KNIGHT** – keyboards (ex-DEVIL'S ANVIL) repl. LANDSBERG (This line-up appeared at 'Woodstock' festival)

— **CORKY LAING** (b.26 Jan'48, Montreal, Canada) – drums repl. SMART

Mar 70. (lp) *(SBLL 133)* <4501> **MOUNTAIN CLIMBING!** [ ] [17]
– Mississippi queen / Theme for an imaginary western / Never in my life / Silver paper / For Yasgur's farm / To my friend / The laird / Sittin' on a rainbow / Boys in the band. *(re-iss. Aug91 on 'Beat Goes On' cd/c; BGO CD/MC 112) (cd re-iss. Mar95 on 'Columbia'; 472180-2)*

May 70. (7") *(BLL 1112)* <532> **MISSISSIPPI QUEEN. / THE LAIRD** [ ] [21] Mar70

Jun 70. (7") <533> **FOR YASGUR'S FARM. / TO MY FRIEND** [-] [ ]

Oct 70. (7") *(BLL 1125)* **SITTIN' ON A RAINBOW. / TO MY FRIEND** [ ] [-]

Island / Windfall

May 71. (lp) *(ILPS 9148)* <5500> **NANTUCKET SLEIGHRIDE** [43] [16] Jan71
– Don't look around / Taunta (Sammy's tune) / Nantucket sleighride / You can't get away / Tired angels / The animal trainer and the toad / My lady / Travellin' in the dark / The great train robbery. *(cd-iss. Jun89 on 'Beat Goes On'; BGOCD 32)*

Mar 71. (7") <534> **THE ANIMAL TRAINER AND THE TOAD. / TIRED ANGELS** [-] [76]

Jul 71. (7") <535> **TRAVELIN' IN THE DARK. / SILVER PAPER** [-] [ ]

Jan 72. (lp) *(ILPS 9179)* <5501> **FLOWERS OF EVIL** [ ] [35] Dec71
– Flowers of evil / King's chorale / One last cold kiss / Crossroader / Pride and passion / (Dream sequence: Guitar solo) / Roll over Beethoven / Dreams of milk and honey – Variations – Swan theme / Mississippi queen. *(re-iss. Dec91 on 'Beat Goes On' cd/c; BGO CD/MC 113)*

Feb 72. (7") *(WIP 6119)* <536> **ROLL OVER BEETHOVEN. / CROSSROADER** [ ] [ ]

Jun 72. (lp) *(ILPS 9199)* <5502> **MOUNTAIN LIVE – THE ROAD GOES EVER ON (live)** [21] [63] May71
– Long red / Waiting to take you away / Crossroader / Nantucket sleighride. *(re-iss. Dec91 on 'Beat Goes On' cd/c/lp; BGO CD/MC/LP 111)*

Jul 72. (7") <537> **WAITING TO TAKE YOU AWAY. / NANTUCKET SLEIGHRIDE (live excerpt)** [-] [ ]

Island / C.B.S.

Feb 73. (lp) *(ILPS 9236)* <32079> **THE BEST OF MOUNTAIN (FEATURING LESLIE WEST & FELIX PAPPALARDI)** (compilation) [ ] [72]
– Never in my life / Taunta (Sammy's tune) / Nantucket sleighride / Roll over Beethoven / For Yasgur's farm / The animal trainer and the toad / Mississippi queen / King's chorale / Boys in the band / Don't look around / Theme for an imaginary western / Crossroader. *(cd-iss. Apr89 on 'Beat Goes On'; BGOCD 33) (cd re-iss. Dec92 on 'Columbia'; 466335-2)*

— Disbanded mid 1972

WEST, BRUCE & LAING

were formed by ex-MOUNTAIN men and **JACK BRUCE** – vocals, bass (ex-CREAM, etc)

C.B.S. / Columbia

Nov 72. (lp) *(CBS 65314)* <31929> **WHY DONTCHA** [ ] [26] Oct72
– Why dontcha / Out in the fields / The doctor / Turn me over / Third degree / Shake ma thing (Rollin' Jack) / While you sleep / Pleasure / Love is worth the blues / Pollution woman. *(re-iss. Aug85 on 'R.S.O.';) (cd-iss. Apr93 on 'Sony Europe')*

Dec 72. (7") <45751> **SHAKE MA THING (ROLLIN' JACK). / THE DOCTOR** [-] [ ]

Mar 73. (7") <45829> **WHY DONTCHA. / MISSISSIPPI QUEEN** [-] [ ]

R.S.O. / Windfall

Jul 73. (7") *(2090 113)* **DIRTY SHOES. / BACKFIRE** [ ] [ ]

Jul 73. (lp) *(2394 107)* <32216> **WHATEVER TURNS YOU ON** [ ] [ ]
– Backfire / Token / Sifting sand / November song / Rock and roll machine / Scotch krotch / Slow blues / Dirty shoes / Like a plate. *(cd-iss. Apr93 on 'Sony Europe')*

May 74. (lp) *(2394 128)* <32899> **LIVE 'N' KICKIN' (live)** [ ] [ ]
– Play with fire / The doctor / Politician / Powerhouse sod. *(cd-iss. Apr93 on 'Sony Europe')*

MOUNTAIN

had already re-formed late in 1973 with **WEST + PAPPALARDI** bringing in **ALLEN SCHWARZBERG** – drums / **ROBERT MANN** – keyboards

C.B.S. / Columbia

Feb 74. (d-lp) <32818> **TWIN PEAKS** (live in Japan '73) [-] [ ]
– Never in my life / Theme for an imaginary western / Blood of the sun / Guitar solo / Nantucket sleigh ride / Nantucket sleigh ride (conclusion) / Crossroader / Mississippi queen / Silver paper / Roll over Beethoven. *(UK-iss.Nov77; CBS 88095) (cd-iss. Jan98 on 'Columbia'; 472183-2)*

— **DAVID PERRY** – rhythm guitar repl. ALLEN + ROBERT (FELIX now + keyboards)

Epic / Epic

Nov 74. (lp) *(CBS 80492)* <33088> **AVALANCHE** [ ] [ ]
– Whole lotta shakin' goin' on / Sister justice / Alisan / Swamp boy / Satisfaction / Thumbsucker / You better believe it / I love to see you fly / Back where I belong / Last of the sunshine days. *(re-iss. Feb88 on 'Castle' lp/cd; CLA LP/CD 136X)*

— Split again late in '74. FELIX PAPPALARDI signed to 'A&M' and released 2 albums **FELIX PAPPALARDI AND CREATION** (1976) and **DON'T WORRY MUM?** (1979). He retired to Japan, and later (17 Apr'83) was dead, shot by his wife GAIL COLLINS.

LESLIE WEST

went solo with band **CORKY LAING** – drums / **DON KRETMMAR** – bass / **FRANK VICARI** – horns / **etc.**

R.C.A. / Phantom

Feb 75. (7") <10301> **DON'T BURN UP. / E.S.P.** [-] [ ]

Mar 75. (lp) *(RS 1009)* <0954> **THE GREAT FATSBY** [ ] [ ]
– Don't burn me / House of the rising sun / High roller / I'm gonna love you thru the night / E.S.P. / Honky tonk women / If I still had you / Doctor Love / If I were a carpenter / Little bit of love.

Feb 76. (7") <10424> **MONEY – DEAR PRUDENCE. / GET IT UP – SETTING SUN** [-] [ ]

Mar 76. (lp) *(1258)* <701> **THE LESLIE WEST BAND** [ ] [ ]
– Money (watcha gonna do) / Dear Prudence / Get it up (no bass – whatsoever) / Singapore sling / By the river / The twister / Setting sun / Sea of heartache / We'll find a way / We gotta get out of this place.

May 76. (7") <10522> **WE GOTTA GET OUT OF THIS PLACE. / BY THE RIVER** [-] [ ]

— LESLIE WEST retired for a while, until . . .

MOUNTAIN

re-formed in 1981. (**WEST, PAPPALARDI, LAING** and 2 others). In 1984, after death of PAPPALARDI. added **MARK CLARKE** – bass, keyboards (ex-URIAH HEEP, ex-RAINBOW, etc)

not iss. / Scotti Brothers

Apr 85. (lp) *(40006)* **GO FOR YOUR LIFE** [-] [ ]
– Hard times / Spark / She loves her rock (and she loves it hard) / Bardot damage / Shimmy on the footlights / I love young girls / Makin' it in your car / Babe in the woods / Little bit of insanity.

LESLIE WEST

brought in **JACK BRUCE** – vocals, bass / **JOE FRANCO** – drums (ex-TWISTED SISTER)

not iss. / Passport

Apr 88. (lp/cd) <PB 606-1/-2> **THEME** [-] [ ]
– Talk dirty / Motherlode / Theme for an imaginary western / I'm crying / Red house / Love is forever / I ate it / Spoonful / Love me tender.

— In Apr '89, he appeared on Various Artists live cd,c,d-lp,video 'NIGHT OF THE GUITAR' on his next label.

I.R.S. / I.R.S.

Oct 89. (cd) <*(EIRSACD 1017)*> **ALLIGATOR** [ ] [ ]
– Sea of fire / Waiting for the F change / Whiskey / Alligator / I put a spell on you / All of me / The stealer / Medley: Hall of the mountain king – Theme from Exodus / Dream lover.

not iss. / BluesBureau

1994. (cd) <BB 2015> **DODGIN' THE DIRT** [-] [ ]
– Whiskey train / Daddy are you angry / New York state of mind / Sambuca / Juke joint jumping / Easy street / One last lick / Crosscut saw / Hang me out to dry / Wasted years / My friend Sam / Thunderbird / Red house.

MOUNTAIN

— re-formed with **WEST, LAING + CLARKE**

Viceroy / not iss.

1996. (cd) *(34 766-423)* **MAN'S WORLD** [-] [-] German
– In your face / Thunder / Man's world / So fine / Hotel happiness / I'm sorry / I look (power mix) / Is that okay? / Crest of a slump / You'll never be alone / I look (hit mix). *(UK-iss.Jan99 on 'Dream Catcher'; CRIDE 12)*

– compilations, etc. –

Jun 95. (d-cd) *Columbia; (483898-2)* **OVER THE TOP** [ ] [ ]

Mar 96. (cd; LESLIE WEST & MOUNTAIN) *Raven; (RVCD 49)* **BLOOD OF THE SUN** [ ] [-]

Jul 00. (cd) *Columbia; (498783-2)* **SUPER HITS** [ ] [ ] Nov98

MOURNBLADE

Formed: London, England . . . early 80's by DUNKEN MULLET, RICHARD JONES, DEREK JASNOCK, CLIVE BAXTER and JEFF WARD, taking the name from a MICHAEL MOORCOCK novel. The HAWKWIND connection extended to their hard-driving music, which was heavily influenced by the space-rockers' mid 70's period. MOURNBLADE even signed to their heroes' label, 'Flicknife', a debut album, 'TIME'S RUNNING OUT' finally surfacing in 1985. Prior to a couple years of sabbatical, the group supported MOTORHEAD, famously botching the spelling of the word "Hammersmith" on their tour T-shirts. A follow-up, 'LIVE FAST DIE YOUNG', eventually appeared in 1989, the album again steering too close to HAWKWIND for comfort.

Album rating: TIME'S RUNNING OUT (*6) / LIVE FAST DIE YOUNG (*5)

DUNKEN MULLET – vocals / **RICHARD JONES** – guitar / **DEREK JASNOCK** – keyboards / **CLIVE BAXTER** – bass / **JEFF WARD** – drums

Flicknife | not iss.

Jun 85. (lp) *(SHARP 030)* **TIME'S RUNNING OUT** [ ] [-]
– Battlezone / Sidewinder / In the arms of Morpheus / Hunter killer / Titanium hero / Laughter from the mask.

Vanishing Tower | not iss.

Dec 85. (12"ep) *(TVC 03)* **EIN HELDENTRAUM (A HERO'S DREAM) EP** [ ] [-]

G.I. | not iss.

Jan 89. (lp) *(GILP 333)* **LIVE FAST DIE YOUNG** [ ] [-]
– If you can't be good / Red hot reputation / Paradise / Desdemona / Burning ambition / The nearer the bone (the sweeter the meat) / American dream / Crash 'n' burn / Off the rails. *(cd-iss. Nov89; GICD 333)*

— split after above

MOVING SIDEWALKS (see under ⇒ ZZ TOP)

MOVING TARGETS

Formed: Ipswich, Massachusetts, USA . . . early 80's as the brainchild of KEN CHAMBERS. MOVING TARGETS first made it onto vinyl by contributing a handful of tracks to local V/A album sampler, 'Bands That Would Be God', although it would be some time before the band would record in their own right. Eventually securing a deal with fledgling US indie, 'Taang!', CHAMBERS and Co showcased their blistering punk wares on 1986's 'BURNING IN WATER, DROWNING IN FLAMES'. Despite a positive reception, KEN would pursue a number of side projects, BULLET LAVOLTA being the most high profile. CHAMBERS later reassembled MOVING TARGETS with a new line-up that included guitarist, PAT LEONARD, the band slightly off the mark with a belated follow-up set, 'BRAVE NOISE' (1989). The 'TARGETS mainman began a new decade with yet another line-up that boasted the former rhythm section of JONES VERY, JEFF GODDARD and JAMIE VAN BRAMER, along with guitarist BEN SEGAL (prior to the next recording, 'FALL', another backing team were used). Although CHAMBERS continued to record into the 90's, he gradually phased out the MOVING TARGETS name, releasing 'NO REACTION' (1994) in a solo capacity.

Album rating: BURNING IN WATER, DROWNING IN FLAMES (*7) / BRAVE NOISE (*6) / FALL (*5) / Ken Chambers: TAKE THIS RIDE (*5) / NO REACTION (*4)

KEN CHAMBERS – vocals, lead guitar / **unknown**

What Goes On | Taang!

May 88. (lp) *(GOES ON 14)* <TAANG 11> **BURNING IN WATER, DROWNING IN FLAMES** [ ] [ ] 1986
– The other side / Faith / Let me know why / Shape of somethings / Less than gravity / Almost certain – Drone / Urban dub / Always calling / Underground / MTV / Funtime / This world / Squares and circles. *(re-iss. Nov92 on 'Taang!'; TAANG 11LP)*

— CHAMBERS also went into other projects, DRED FOOLE & THE DIN, The GROINOIDS and BULLET LAVOLTA (latters' albums 'THE GIFT' 1989 and 'THE GUN DIDN'T KNOW I WAS LOADED' (1992)

— **PAT LEONARD** – bass; returned to repl. CHUCK FREEMAN

1989. (lp/cd) <TAANG 30/+CD> **BRAVE NOISE** [-] [ ]
– Falling / Brave noise / Nothing changes / Things are going by / Car crash / Separate hearts / Instrumental No.3 / In the way / 2500 club / Into the forest / June 7th / Through the door / Lights. *(UK-iss.Mar93; same as US)*

— **CHAMBERS** recruited **JEFF GODDARD** – bass / **JAMIE VAN BRAMER** – drums (both ex-JONES VERY) **BEN SEGAL** – guitar

— now **CHAMBERS, LEONARD + PAT BRADY** – drums / **CHUCK FREEMAN** – bass

Taang! | Taang!

1990. (7") <(TAANG 43)> **AWAY FROM ME. /** [ ] [ ]

Roadrunner | Taang!

May 91. (cd/lp) *(TG 9304-2/-1)* <TAANG 54> **FALL** [ ] [ ]
– Taang intro / Only fun in life / Fumble / Answer / Can you blame me / Travel music / Away from me / No soul / Blind / Once upon a time / Overrated / Awesome sky / Fake it.

Jun 93. (cd-ep) <TAANG 72> **LAST OF THE ANGELS EP** [-] [ ]
– Last of the angels / Babble / No quarter / Answer II.

KEN CHAMBERS

— now with **PAT** + new drummer **J. ARCARI**

City Slang | City Slang

Dec 92. (7") <(efa 0490645)> **BLOOD & FLOWERS. /** [ ] [ ]

Plastic Head | Plastic Head

Apr 93. (7") <(PHD 001)> **TAKE THIS RIDE. /** [ ] [ ]

Taang! | Taang!

Jun 93. (lp/cd/cd) <(TAANG 73/+MC/CD)> **TAKE THIS RIDE** [ ] [ ]
– Last of the angels / Story / A thousand times / Unwind / The right way / Take this ride / Alright / Reason to believe / Take that away / Answer II / Erase / Drown it out.

Aug 94. (7") <(TAANG 83)> **ABOVE YOU. / TEMPTATION** [ ] [ ]
(cd-s+=) <(TAANG 83CD)> – Jesus Christ superstar / Wiped out / Above you (demo).

— with **JEFF GODDARD** – bass / **GLENN FOSTER BROWN** – keyboards

Nov 94. (cd) <(T 84CD)> **NO REACTION** [ ] [ ]
– Smile / No reaction / In between / Above you / Temptation / Too hard to wait / Here and gone / Operation / No sin / Play the blues / Wintergreen.

— KEN continued with BULLET LAVOLTA

MR. BIG

Formed: San Francisco, Los Angeles, California, USA . . . September '88 by ERIC MARTIN (vocals, ex-solo artist), BILLY SHEEHAN (bass, ex-TALAS, ex-DAVID LEE ROTH), PAT TORPEY (drums) and PAUL GILBERT (guitar, ex-RACER X). This heavy supergroup of sorts named themselves after a track by seminal British blues rockers FREE, securing a deal with 'Atlantic' and releasing their eponymous debut album in 1989. Frenetic hard rock that bordered on metal, SHEEHAN and GILBERT's party trick was playing their instruments with customised power drills (JIMI HENDRIX eat your heart out!). The likes of 'ADDICTED TO THAT RUSH' were impressive slices of breakneck fretboard mastery, yet the band lacked a real songwriting voice to complement MARTIN's earthy vocals. 'LEAN INTO IT' (1991) marked a step forward, taking its cue from a more varied musical palate as evidenced by the neo-psychedelic flavour of 'GREEN TINTED SIXTIES MIND'. The album made the US Top 20 and almost breached the UK Top 40, the band eventually placing themselves squarely on the musical map early the following year with the success of the 'TO BE WITH YOU' single. An acoustic-based, EXTREME-esque ballad, the song was hardly typical of their high octane sound yet it made No.1 in America, No.3 in Britain, no doubt becoming something of a millstone round the band's neck as they tried to capitalise on its success. Despite a further minor hit with 'JUST TAKE MY HEART', the band's third album, 'BUMP AHEAD' (1993) failed to make any commercial impact as they found themselves in the metal margins once more. Following on from a final MR BIG album, 'HEY MAN' (1996), guitarist GILBERT drew on the classic power-pop sounds of his youth for a debut solo set, 'KING OF CLUBS' (1998). 'BEEHIVE LIVE' (1999), meanwhile, was a concert set recorded in Japan – where a large fanbase enjoyed the exclusive release of the 'FLYING DOG' album – and featuring solo material alongside a couple of strangely chosen covers (ELP's 'KARN EVIL 9' and The Osmonds' 'HOLD HER TIGHT'). The aforementioned 'FLYING DOG' finally saw a UK release in early 2000 while 'ALLIGATOR FARM' followed later the same year in the US.

Album rating: MR. BIG (*6) / LEAN INTO IT (*6) / LIVE – MR. BIG (*4) / BUMP AHEAD (*5) / HEY MAN (*4) / BIG, BETTER, BEST compilation (*6) / Paul Gilbert: HENDRIX TRIBUTE (*4) / KING OF CLUBS (*6) / BEEHIVE LIVE (*5) / FLYING DOG (*4) / ALLIGATOR FARM (*4)

ERIC MARTIN (b.10 Oct'60, Long Island, N.Y.) – vocals (ex-solo artist) / **PAUL GILBERT** (b. 6 Nov'66, Pittsburgh, Pennsylvania) – guitar (ex-RACER X) / **PAT TORPEY** (b.13 Dec'59) – drums / **BILLY SHEEHAN** (b.19 Mar'53, Buffalo, N.Y.) – bass (ex-TALAS, ex-DAVID LEE ROTH)

Atlantic | Atlantic

Jul 89. (lp/c/cd) *(781 990-1/-4/-2)* <81990> **MR. BIG** [60] [46]
– Addicted to that rush / Wind me up / Merciless / Had enough / Blame it on my youth / Take a walk / Big love / How can you do what you do / Anything for you / Rock & roll over. *(cd+=)* – 30 days in a hole.

Aug 89. (7") <88860> **ADDICTED TO THAT RUSH. / BLAME IT ON MY YOUTH** [-] [ ]

Jan 90. (c-s) <88805> **WIND ME UP. / MERCILESS** [-] [ ]

Mar 91. (7"/c-s) *(A 7712/+C)* **THE DRILL SONG (DADDY, BROTHER, LOVER, LITTLE BOY). / ROAD TO RUIN** [ ] [-]
(12"+=/cd-s+=) *(A 7712 T/CD)* – Addicted to that rush (live) / Strike like lightning.

Apr 91. (cd/c/lp) <(7567 82209-2/-4/-1)> **LEAN INTO IT** [52] [15]
– Daddy, brother, lover, little boy (the electric drill song) / Alive and kickin' / Green-tinted sixties mind / CDFF lucky this time / Voodoo kiss / Never say never / Just take my heart / My kinda woman / A little too loose / Road to ruin / To be with you. *(re-entered UK chart Feb 92; hit 28)*

May 91. (7") *(A 7702)* **GREEN TINTED SIXTIES MIND. / SHADOWS** [ ] [-]
(12"+=/12"pic-d+=) *(A 7702T/+P)* – Take a walk (live).
(cd-s++=) *(A 7702CD)* – Drilled and confused.

Dec 91. (c-s) <87580> **TO BE WITH YOU. / GREEN TINTED SIXTIES MIND** [-] [1]

Feb 92. (7"/c-s) *(A 7514/+C)* **TO BE WITH YOU. / THE DRILL SONG (DADDY, BROTHER, LOVER, LITTLE BOY) (live)** [3] [-]
(cd-s+=) *(A 7514CD)* – Shy boy (live) / Woman from Tokyo (live).
(12"+=) *(A 7514T)* – Lean into it (live) / A little too loose (live) / Alive and kickin' (live).

Apr 92. (c-s) <87509> **JUST TAKE MY HEART / ROAD TO RUIN** [-] [16]

May 92. (7"/c-s) *(A 7490/+C)* **JUST TAKE MY HEART. / GREEN TINTED SIXTIES MIND** 26 -
(cd-s+=) *(A 7490CD)* – To be with you (live) / Lucky this time (live).
(cd-s+=) *(A 7490CDX)* – Shadow / Strike like lightning.

Jul 92. (7"/c-s) *(A 7468/+C)* **GREEN TINTED SIXTIES MIND. / LOVE MAKES YOU STRONG** 72 -
(12"/pic-cd-s) *(A 7468 T/CD)* – ('A'side) / Just take my heart (acoustic) / Big love / Dirty days in the hole.

Nov 92. (cd/c) *<7567 80523-2/-4>* **LIVE – MR. BIG (live)**
– The drill song (Daddy, brother, lover, little boy) / Alive and kickin' / Green tinted sixties mind / Just take my heart / Road to ruin / Lucky this time / Addicted to that rush / To be with you / 30 days in the hole / Shy baby / Baba O'Riley.

Sep 93. (cd/c/lp) *<7567 82495-2/-4/-1>* **BUMP AHEAD** 61
– Colorado bulldog / The price you gotta pay / Promise her the Moon / What's it gonna be / Wild world / Mr. Gone / The whole world is gonna know / Nothing but love / Temperamental / Ain't seen love like that / Mr.Big.

Oct 93. (7"/c-s) *(A 7310/+C) <87308>* **WILD WORLD. / TEMPERAMENTAL** 59 27
(12"+=/12"pic-d+=) *(A 7310T/+P)* – Long way down.
(cd-s) *(A 7430CD)* – ('A'side) / Rock and roll over / Let yourself go / Voodoo kiss (live).

Feb 94. (c-s) *<87278>* **AIN'T SEEN LOVE LIKE THAT / WHAT'S IT GONNA BE** - 83

Feb 96. (cd/c) *<(7567 80648-2)>* **HEY MAN**
– Trapped in toyland / John Doe / Take cover / The chain / Out of the underground / Into the flame / Mama D / Dancin' right into the flame /

Dec 96. (cd) *(7567 80662-2)* **(V) AT THE HARD ROCK LIVE (live)** - - German
– Alive and kickin' / Green-tinted sixties mind / Where do I fit in? / Jane Doe / Goin' where the wind blows / Take a walk / Voodoo kiss / The chain / Wild world / Take cover / To be with you / Daddy, brother, lover, little boy.

– compilations, etc. –

Apr 97. (cd) *East West; <(7567 80685-2)>* **BIG, BETTER, BEST**
– Addicted to that rush / Rock'n'roll over / Green tinted sixties mind / To be with you / Just take my heart / Daddy, brother, lover, little boy / Wild world / Colorado bulldog / Nothing but love / Promise her the moon / Take cover / Goin' where the wind blows / Seven impossible days / Not one night / Unnatural / Stay together.

PAUL GILBERT

—— solo with a few session players

In-Akustik / not iss.

1994. (cd) *<INAK 1018>* **HENDRIX TRIBUTE** - - Europe
– Red house / Hey Joe / Highway chile / Midnight / Purple haze.

Mayhem / Mayhem

Jun 98. (cd) *<(11119-2)>* **KING OF CLUBS**
– Champagne / Vinyl / Girls who can't read your mind / I'm just in love / The jig / Girlfriend's birthday / Bumblebee / Streetlights / My Naomi / Double trouble / Million dollar smile / The jam.

Mascot / Mascot

Nov 99. (cd) *<(SH 1133CD)>* **BEEHIVE LIVE (live)**
– Heavy disco trip / Be my wife / Get it / Mr. Skin / Down to Mexico / Girls who can read your mind / Tell the truth / Bumblebee / Million dollar smile / Hold her tight / I'm just in love / Red rooster / To be with you / Karn evil 9.

Feb 00. (cd) *<(SH 1138CD)>* **FLYING DOG**
– Get it / Girl crazy / Be my wife / Mr. Skin / Beautiful girls are insane / Midnight Maryanne / Heavy disco trip / Kate is a star / Down to Mexico / Tell the truth / Wrong man / Gilberto concerto.

Mascot / Shrapnel

Feb 01. (cd) *(M 7053CD) <SH 1146CD>* **ALLIGATOR FARM** Sep00
– Better chords / Individually twisted / Cut, cut, cut / Alligator farm / Attitude boy will overcome / Two become one / Lancelot link / Rosalinda told me / Let the computer decide / Koto girl / Dreamed of Victoria / Six billion people / The ballad of the last lions / Whole lotta sonata.

MR. BUNGLE (see under ⇒ FAITH NO MORE)

MR. T EXPERIENCE

Formed: Berkeley/East Bay Gilman Street, California, USA . . . mid-80's by DR. FRANK and an ever revolving sequence of rhythm players. Evolving from the same terrain as megabucks superstars, GREEN DAY and RANCID, the original punk popsters have influenced a generation of gob-slobbering thrashy misfits. RAMONES-esque (in every sense of the description), the quirky ensemble debuted in 1986 with the "so-underground-it's-six-foot-deep", 'EVERYBODY'S ENTITLED TO THEIR OWN OPINION'; later re-issued by 'Lookout!', who else. After a second (and equally as poor as the first) set, MTX made their semi-cult debut for 'Lookout!' with the 'MAKING THINGS WITH LIGHT' (1990) long-player, which helped them gain acknowledgment in the San Francisco neighbourhood. GREEN DAY, who were taken aback by the combo, described themselves as "the little brothers of MTX" when they started to promote their punky antics in the area. Very much like their musical siblings, MTX defined the cartoon punk ethics with their shouty, power chord rock'n'roll that has been very much the same throughout all their releases including such albums as 'MILK, MILK, LEMONADE' (1992), 'OUR BODIES, OUR SELVES' (1994), 'LOVE IS DEAD' (1995) and arguably their best, 'REVENGE IS SWEET AND SO ARE YOU' (1997). The band's latest set (with 'God knows who' in the line up, as it changed so many times that FRANK wittily suggested re-forming as MTX STARSHIP) 'THE ALCATRAZ', finally gained the post-punk credit it deserved when released on these shores in 1999. One only wonders, however, why GREEN DAY are selling out stadiums when it should be the work of their big brother. • **Covered:** PLEASANT VALLEY SUNDAY (hit; Monkees) / NO MILK TODAY (Herman's Hermits) / I FEEL LOVE (Donna Summer) / UP AND DOWN (. . . Moss) / FLYING JELLY ATTACK (. . . Yomano) / SEX OFFENDER (Blondie) / SOMEBODY WANTS TO LOVE YOU (Appel-Cretecos-Farrell) / SPIDERMAN (Harris-Webster) / CAN'T GET THERE FROM HERE (R.E.M.) / SPEED RACER (Shonen Knife) / DON'T GO AWAY GO GO GIRL (Radcliffe-Scott) / etc

Album rating: EVERYBODY'S ENTITLED TO THEIR OWN OPINION mini (*4) / NIGHT SHIFT AT THE THRILL FACTORY (*5) / MAKING THINGS WITH LIGHT (*6) / MILK, MILK, LEMONADE (*7) / OUR BODIES, OUR SELVES (*6) / LOVE IS DEAD (*6) / REVENGE IS SWEET AND SO ARE YOU (*5) / THE ALCATRAZ (*)

DR. FRANK – vocals, guitar / **JON VON** – rhythm guitar, vocals / **AARON** – bass / **ALEX** – drums, vocals

not iss. / Disorder

1986. (m-lp) **EVERYBODY'S ENTITLED TO THEIR OWN OPINION** -
– One big lie / Just your way of saying no / Marine recruiter / Sheep / Surfin' Mozart / Danny Partridge / Scientific / Disconnection / Surfin' cows / I'm in love with Paula Pierce / Big mistake / Pleasany valley Sunday / Mary Mary / Empty experience. *<cd-iss. 1990 on 'Lookout' cd+=; LOOKOUT 39CD> (UK-iss.Jul95 on 'Lookout' cd/lp; same as US)*

not iss. / Rough Trade

1987. (lp) **NIGHT SHIFT AT THE THRILL FACTORY** -
– Now we are twenty-one / Don't know what I'll do if you don't / Predictable / Mind is a terrible thing / Skatin' cows / Go away / What is punk? / The history of the concept of the soul / Say goodnight / Velveeta / She did me in / Wearing out / No milk today / Slagbag / A zillion years / Itching powder in sleeping bags / Dick with ears / I ain't gonna be history / Kenny smokes cloves / Time for your medicine / Boredom zone / At Gilman Street. *<(UK+re-iss. Aug96 on 'Lookout' cd+=/lp; LOOKOUT 144 CD/LP)>*

1989. (m-lp/m-c) *<ROUGH-US 68/+C>* **BIG BLACK BUGS BLEED BLUE BLOOD** -
– Super sonic / Up and down / On the team / At Gilman Street / Dictionary girl / End of the Ramones / Song about a girl who went shopping.

Lookout / Lookout

1990. (cd/lp) *<LOOKOUT 37 CD/LP>* **MAKING THINGS WITH LIGHT** -
– What went wrong / She's no rocket scientist / What's in the cuckoo clock / I don't get it / Zero / Pig Latin / Parasite / I'm breaking out / So long, sucker / Weekend in Hogboro / Psycho girl / The girl who still lives at home / Send me a postcard / Untitled spoken word piece / Now we are twenty-one / Danny Partridge got busted / Marine recruiter / Slagbag / Velveeta / A zillion years / The history of the concept of the soul / Flying jelly attack. *(UK-iss.Jul95; same as US)*

1992. (cd/lp) *<LOOKOUT 49 CD/LP>* **MILK, MILK, LEMONADE** -

Jan 94. (cd/lp) *<LOOKOUT 80 CD/LP>* **OUR BODIES, OUR SELVES** -
– Somebody who cares / Love manifesto / Dustbin of history / Personality seminar / Are you there God? it's me Margaret / Martyr / Even Hitler had a girlfriend / Bridge to Taribithia / I feel love / More than toast / Swallow everything / Not guilty / Game over / Will you still love me when I don't . . .. / Together tonight / God bless America. *(UK cd-iss. Jul95; same as US)*

1993. (7"ep) **GUN CRAZY EP** -

Mar 95. (cd-ep) *<LOOKOUT 106CD>* **. . . AND THE WOMEN WHO LOVE THEM** -
– Tapin' up my heart / My stuped life / I believe in you / All my promises / Checkers speech / We hate all the same things / Now that you are gone.

Jun 95. (7"ep/cd-ep; shared w/ GOOBER PATROL) *<(PAD 001/+CD)>* **FROM OUT OF SPACE E.P.** -
(above issued on 'Punk As Dunk')

Sep 95. (cd-ep) *<(LOOKOUT 126CD)>* **ALTERNATIVE IS HERE TO STAY** Aug95

Jan 96. (lp/cd) *<(LK 134/+CD)>* **LOVE IS DEAD**
– Sackcloth and ashes / Ba ba ba ba ba / I just wanna do it with you / Somebody's song / Thank you (for not being one of them) / Dumb little band / Hangin' on to you / The future ain't what it used to be / I fell for you / Deep deep down / Can I do the thing? / I'd do anything for you / Semi-ok / I'm like yeah, but she's all no / That prozac moment / You're the only one.

—— **JOEL** – bass / **JYM** – drums (joined **DR. FRANK**)

Aug 97. (7") *<(LK 164)>* **AND I WILL BE WITH YOU. /**

Sep 97. (cd/lp) *<(LK 180 CD/LP)>* **REVENGE IS SWEET AND SO ARE YOU** Aug97
– Here she comes / She's coming (over tonight) / Love is dead / Hell of dumb / Lawnmower of love / With my looks an your brains / Weather is here, wish you were . . .. / Another yesterday / Swiss army girlfriend / . . . And I will be with you / Who needs happiness (I'd rather have . . ..) / When I lost you / I don't need you now / Our love will last forever and ever / Some foggy mountain top / You you you.

Sep 99. (cd/lp) *<(LK 232 CD/LP)>* **THE ALCATRAZ**
– I wrote a book about rock and roll / Naomi / elf-pity / Hey Emily / Tomorrow is a harsh mistress / Two of us / Our days are numbered / We're not no one / Re-activate your heart / Perhaps / She's my Alcatraz / I feel for you / We'll get by.

– compilations, etc. –

May 97. (lp/cd) *Lookout; <(LOOKOUT 145/+CD)>* **BIG BLACK BUGS BLEED BLUE BLOOD**
– (the EP tracks) / Flying jelly attack / So long, sucker / Zero / Psycho girl / Fill in the blank / How I made a million in a punk rock . . .. / Look back and crack / Sex offender / Last time I listened to you / Love American style / Somebody wants to love you / Spiderman / Can't get there from here / God bless America / Let's be together tonight / Merry fucking Christmas / Speed racer / T-shirt commercial / Vive le France / More than toast / Swallow everything / God bless Lawrence Livermore / Don't go away go go girl / Hello Kitty Menendez.

M.S.G. (see under ⇒ SCHENKER GROUP, Michael)

MUDHONEY

Formed: Seattle, Washington, USA ... 1988 by MARK ARM (vocals, guitar), STEVE TURNER (guitar), MATT LUKIN (bass) and DAN PETERS (drums). A band boasting impeccable credentials, ARM and TURNER had both graduated from the seminal GREEN RIVER (and The THROWN UPS), while LUKIN had previously been a member of Seattle noisemongers, The MELVINS. With as much a claim to the 'Godfathers of Grunge' crown as labelmates NIRVANA, MUDHONEY released the definitive 'Sub Pop' single in 1988 with 'TOUCH ME I'M SICK'. Arguably one of the few tracks to ever match the primal howl of The STOOGES, the single was a revelation, a cathartically dumb three chord bludgeon with ARM shrieking over the top like a man who was, erm, very sick indeed. A mini-album followed shortly after, the wonderfully titled 'SUPERFUZZ BIGMUFF' (rather disappointingly named after STEVE TURNER's favourite effects pedals, apparently). Visceral, dirty, fuzz-drenched rock'n'roll, this was one of the seminal records of the 80's and the blueprint for "grunge", a term that would later become bastardised to represent a glut of snooze-worthy, sub-metal toss. There was also a deep, underlying sense of unease and melancholy to these songs (especially 'NO ONE HAS' and 'NEED') that gave MUDHONEY an edge over most of their contemporaries, a subsequent cover of SONIC YOUTH'S 'HALLOWEEN' (released as a split single with SONIC YOUTH covering 'TOUCH ME..') sounding positively evil. Given all this, then, the debut album proper, 'MUDHONEY', was regarded as something of a disappointment when it was finally released in late '89. Nevertheless, 'THIS GIFT' and 'HERE COMES SICKNESS' were worth the price of admission alone. By summer '91, MUDHONEY had modified their sound somewhat, releasing the 'LET IT SLIDE' EP as a taster for the forthcoming 'EVERY GOOD BOY DESERVES FUDGE' album (a UK Top 40 hit). The intensity of the EP harked back to 'SUPERFUZZ..', this time with more of a retro garage-punk feel on the blistering 'PAPERBACK LIFE' and 'OUNCE OF DECEPTION'. The album continued in this direction, adding funky (in the loosest sense of the term) hammond organ and harmonica to the mutant guitar buzz. Hell, they even came close to a pop song with 'GOOD ENOUGH'. Following a financial dispute with 'Sub Pop', MUDHONEY followed NIRVANA into the big league, signing with 'Reprise' and releasing the lacklustre 'PIECE OF CAKE' (1992). Having sold their souls to the corporate 'devil', it seemed MUDHONEY had had the life sucked out of them, the rough edges smoothed into a major production gloss. The mini-album, 'FIVE DOLLAR BOB'S MOCK COOTER STEW' (1993) was an improvement but it took Seattle legend, Jack Endino to summon forth the raw spontaneity of old on 'MY BROTHER THE COW' (1995), a return to form of sorts, notably on 'INTO YOUR SCHTIK' and 'GENERATION SPOKESMODEL'. MUDHONEY subsequently took a few years hiatus in which ARM went on tour with his side-project, BLOODLOSS, while TURNER continued with his label, 'Super-Electro' (MUDHONEY were allowed dual output for the imprint) and PETERS guested for solo MIKE JOHNSON (DINOSAUR JR). In the Autumn of '98, the quartet were back once again, although the album, TOMORROW HIT TODAY', disappointed most of their hardcore fanbase. • **Covers:** HATE THE POLICE (Dicks) / EVOLUTION (Spacemen 3) / OVER THE TOP (Motorhead) / PUMP IT UP (Elvis Costello) / TONIGHT I THINK I'M GONNA GO DOWNTOWN (Jimmie Dale Gilmore) / BUCKSKIN STALLION BLUES (Townes Van Zandt). MARK ARM solo:- MASTERS OF WAR (Bob Dylan).

Album rating: SUPERFUZZ BIGMUFF mini (*7) / MUDHONEY (*6) / BOILED BEEF & ROTTING TEETH (*6) / EVERY GOOD BOY DESERVES FUDGE (*7) / PIECE OF CAKE (*5) / MY BROTHER THE COW (*5) / TOMORROW TODAY (*5) / MARCH TO FUZZ compilation (*7)

MARK ARM (b.21 Feb'62, California) – vocals, guitar (ex-GREEN RIVER, ex-THROWN UPS) / **STEVE TURNER** (b.28 Mar'65, Houston, Texas) – guitar (ex-GREEN RIVER, ex-THROWN UPS) / **MATT LUKIN** (b.16 Aug'64, Aberdeen, Washington) – bass (ex-MELVINS) / **DAN PETERS** (b.18 Aug'67) – drums

Glitterhouse Sub Pop

Aug 88. (7",7"brown) <SP 18> **TOUCH ME I'M SICK. / SWEET YOUNG THING AIN'T SWEET NO MORE** [-] [ ]

Oct 88. (12"ep) *(GR 0034)* <SP 21> **SUPERFUZZ BIGMUFF** [ ] [ ]
– No one has / If I think / In 'n' out of grace / Need / Chain that door / Mudride. *(cd-iss. Mar00; same as US)*

Jan 89. (7",7"clear) <SP 26> **('A'side by 'Sonic Youth'). / TOUCH ME I'M SICK** [-] [ ]

Jun 89. (7",7"white) *(GR 060)* <SP 33> **YOU GOT IT (KEEP IT OUTTA MY FACE). / BURN IT CLEAN / NEED (demo)** [ ] [ ]
(re-iss. May93; same)

Oct 89. (7",7"purple,12") *(GR 0070)* <SP 44AA> **THIS GIFT. / BABY HELP ME FORGET / REVOLUTION** [ ] [ ]
(re-iss. May93; same)

Oct 89 (lp/c/cd) *(GR 0069)* <SP 44/+A/B> **MUDHONEY** [ ] [ ]
– This gift / Flat out f***ed / Get into yours / You got it / Magnolia caboose babyshit / Come to mind / Here comes sickness / Running loaded / The further I go / By her own hand / When tomorrow hits / Dead love. *(cd re-iss. Mar00; same as US)*

Jun 90. (7",7"pink) *(GR 0102)* <SP 63> **YOU'RE GONE. / THORN / YOU MAKE ME DIE** [60] [ ]
(re-iss. May93; same)

Sub Pop Sub Pop

Jul 91. (7",12"grey) *(SP 15154)* <SP 95> **LET IT SLIDE. / OUNCE OF DECEPTION / CHECKOUT TIME** [60] [ ]
(cd-s+=) *(SP 95B)* – Paperback life / The money will roll right in.

Aug 91. (lp/c/cd) <*(SP 160/+A/B)*> **EVERY GOOD BOY DESERVES FUDGE** [34] [ ]
– Generation genocide / Let it slide / Good enough / Something so clear / Thorn / Into the drink / Broken hands / Who you drivin' now / Move out / Shoot the Moon / Fuzzgun '91 / Poking around / Don't fade IV / Check out time.

— MARK + STEVE took up time in MONKEYWRENCH, and DAN joined SCREAMING TREES, after below album.

Warners Reprise

Oct 92. (7"/c-s) *(W 0137/+C)* **SUCK YOU DRY. / DECEPTION PASS** [65] [-]
(12"+=/cd-s+=) *(W 0137 T/CD)* – Underride / Over the top.

Oct 92. (cd/c) <*(4509 90073-2/-4)*> **PIECE OF CAKE** [39] [ ]
– No end in sight / Make it now / Suck you dry / Blinding sun / Thirteenth floor opening / Youth body expression explosion / I'm spun / Take me there / Living wreck / Let me let you down / Ritzville / Acetone.

Jan 93. (cd-s) <40741> **BLIDING SUN /** [-] [ ]

Oct 93. (m-cd/m-c/m-lp) <*(9362 45439-2/-4)*> **FIVE DOLLAR BOB'S MOCK COOTER STEW** [ ] [ ]
– In the blood / No song III / Between you & me kid / Six two one / Make it now again / Deception pass / Underide.

— In Mar'94, MUDHONEY released a collab with JIMMIE DALE GILMOUR; 7"yellow/cd-ep 'BUCKSKIN STALLION BLUES' for 'Sub Pop' *(SP 124/305/+CD)* Also a single, 'PUMP IT UP, was released by 'Fox' in April '94

Reprise Reprise

Mar 95. (cd/c/lp) <*(9362 45840-2/-4/-1)*> **MY BROTHER THE COW** [70] [ ]
– Judgement, rage, retribution and thyme / Generation spokesmodel / What moves the heart? / Today, is a good day / Into yer schtik / In my finest suit / F.D.K. (Fearless Doctor Killers) / Orange ball-pen hammer / Crankcase blues / Execution style / Dissolve / 1995.

Apr 95. (7") **INTO YOUR SCHTIK. / YOU GIVE ME THE CREEPS** [ ] [ ]
(above single on 'Super Electro')

May 95. (7"colrd/c-s) *(W 0292/+C)* **GENERATION SPOKESMODEL. / NOT GOING DOWN THAT ROAD AGAIN** [ ] [ ]
(cd-s+=) *(W 0292CD)* – What moves the heart live) / Judgement, rage, retribution and thyme (live).

Amphetam. Reptile Amphetam. Reptile

Aug 95. (7") **GOAT CHEESE. /** [ ] [ ]
(above on 'Amphetamine Reptile' and below on 'Super Electro')

May 98. (ltd-7") *(SE 716)* **NIGHT OF THE HUNTED. / BRAND NEW FACE** [ ] [ ]

Sep 98. (cd) <*(9362 47054-2)*> **TOMORROW HIT TODAY** [ ] [ ]
– A thousand forms of mind / I have to laugh / Oblivion / Try to be kind / Poisoned water / Real low vibe / This is the life / Night of the hunted / Move with the wind / Ghost / I will fight no more forever / Beneath the valley of the underdog.

– compilations, etc. –

Nov 89. (cd-ep) *Tupelo; (TUPCD 009) / Sub Pop;* <SP 62> **BOILED BEEF AND ROTTING TEETH** [ ] [ ]

Jan 00. (cd) *Strange Fruit; (SFRSCD 090)* **THE RADIO SESSIONS** [ ] [-]

Mar 00. (t-lp/d-cd) *Sub Pop;* <*(SP/+CD 500)*> **MARCH TO FUZZ** [ ] [ ]
– In 'n' out of grace / Suck you dry / I have to laugh / Sweet young thing ain't sweet no more / Who you drivin' now / You got it / Judgement, rage, retribution and thyme / Into the drink / A thousand forms of mind / Generation genocide / If I think / Here comes sickness / Let it slide / Touch me I'm sick / This gift / Good enough / Blinding sun / Into your shtik / Beneath the valley of the underdog / When tomorrow hits / Make it now again / Hate the police / Hey sailor / Twenty four / Baby help me forget / Revolution / You stupid asshole / Who is who / Stab yor back / Pump it up / The money will roll right in / Fix me / Dehumanized / She's just 15 / Baby o baby / Over the top / You goive me the creeps / March to fuzz / Ounce of deception / Paperback life / Bushpusher man / Fuzzbeater / Overblown / Run shithead run / King sandbox / Tonight I think I'm gonna go downtown / Holden / Not going down that road again / Brand new face / Drinking for two / Butterfly stroke / Editions of you.

THE FREEWHEELIN' MARK ARM

Sub Pop Sub Pop

Feb 91. (7",7"red,7"green) <*(SP 87)*> **MASTERS OF WAR. / MY LIFE WITH RICKETS** [ ] [ ] Dec90

THROWN UPS

STEVE TURNER + MARK ARM + two others

not iss. Amphetam. Reptile

1987. (7") <*Scale 5*> **FLECH. /** [-] [ ]

1987. (7") <*Scale 7*> **SMILING PANTIES. /** [-] [ ]

1987. (7") <*Scale 9*> **EAT MY DUMP. /** [-] [ ]

1990. (3x7"box) <*Scale 26*> **MELANCHOLY GIRLHOLE** (3 singles boxed) [-] [ ]

Jan 97. (cd) <*AR 55*> **SEVEN YEARS GOLDEN** (compilation) [-] [ ]
– Your band sucks / She's fat / Eat my dump / Flubber mate / Bucking retards / Dude pump / The person in my bowel (is sad) / Fleshy web pit / Elephant crack / My cock is the coin / Hairy crater man / Sparse tits / Smiling panties / Be correct / Melancholy girlhole / Stock boy, superhero / Flech / Lard Butt / Sloppy pud love / Hot lunch / Ladies love me / Scabby like my love / My love is simple / R ladies R bitches / Patty has a problem / Slick lip / Thorp, Thorp.

MONKEYWRENCH

— **MARK + STEVE** plus **TOM PRICE, TIM KERR + MARTIN BLAND**

Sub Pop Sub Pop

1992. (cd) <*(SP 129CD)*> **CLEAN AS A BROKE-DICK DOG** [ ] [ ]
– I call my body home / Angelhead / Cold cold world / Codine / From you / Doubled over again / Great down here / Look back / Bottle up & go / The story as I was told / Notes & chords mean nothing to me / Stop this world / I'm blown.

MUDVAYNE

Formed: Peoria, Illinois, USA . . . 1996 by KUD aka CHAD GRAY, GURRG aka GREG TRIBBETT and sPaG aka MATT McDONOUGH. Following a self-financed debut set, 'KILL I OUGHTA' (1999), the band were signed to 'Epic' for the recording of L.D. 50 (2000), by which time the line-up had been completed by RYKNOW aka RYAN MARTINIE. Sporting a disturbing line in face paint (although they maintain their image comes second to the music) and favouring a fairly pedestrian thrash sound tempered by the odd funky nu-metal flourish, MUDVAYNE have been compared to the likes of FEAR FACTORY, KORN and especially SLIPKNOT with whom they maintain a close working relationship. At their most palatable when KUD substitutes his death growl for a curiously KURT COBAIN-like vocal fragility, MUDVAYNE might be better off leaving the rock theatre stuff to their contemporaries.

Album rating: L.D. 50 (*6)

KUD (b. CHAD GRAY) – vocals / **GURRG** (b. GREG TRIBBETT) – guitar / **RYKNOW** (b. RYAN MARTINIE) – bass; repl. original / **sPaG** (b. MATT McDONOUGH) – drums

not iss. — own label

1999. (cd) **KILL I OUGHTA** [-] [ ]

Epic — Epic

Oct 00. (cd) *(500588-2) <63821>* **L.D. 50** [ ] [85] Aug00
– Monolith / Dig / Internal primates forever / – 1 / Death blooms / Golden ratio / Cradle / Nothing to Gein / Mutatis mutandis / Everything and nothing / Severed / Recombinant resurgence / Prod / Pharmaecopia / Under my skin / (K)now (F)orever / Lethal dosage.

MURDER CITY DEVILS

Formed: Seattle, Washington, USA . . . 1997 by SPENCER MOODY, NATE MANNY, DANN GALLUCI, DEREK FUDESCO, COADY WILLIS and GABE. Veterans of Seattle's ever thriving rock scene (various members had previously played in local acts The UNABOMBERS, AREA 51 and The DEATHWISH KIDS), the 'DEVILS set out to prove that garage'n'roll was still alive and puking in the city even as grunge was taking its last breath. A couple of early singles, 'THREE NATURAL SIXES' and 'DANCE HALL MUSIC' preceded a deal with 'Sub Pop' imprint, 'Die Young Stay Pretty', through whom the band issued their 1997 eponymous debut album. A formative effort which introduced their patented brand of bleak, organ-fuelled retro punk, the record was haunted by the ghosts of The STOOGES, MC5 and NEW YORK DOLLS. The JACK ENDINO-produced 'EMPTY BOTTLES, BROKEN HEARTS' (1999) further enhanced their reputation with many commentators citing them as the Seattle area's most promising newcomers. The biggest thrill of their short career came when PEARL JAM took them out as support on their 'Yield' tour, making the progression from sweaty clubs to stadiums literally overnight. By this point former HOLE keyboard woman, LESLIE HARDY had joined up, making her recording debut via the millennial 'IN NAME AND BLOOD' (2000).

Album rating: MURDER CITY DEVILS (*5) / EMPTY BOTTLES, BROKEN HEARTS (*6) / IN NAME AND BLOOD (*7)

SPENCER MOODY – vocals / **NATE MANNY** – guitar / **DANN GALLUCCI** – guitar / **DEREK FUDESCO** – bass / **COADY WILLIS** – drums / + 7th member/roadie **GABE**

Die Young — Die Young

Sep 97. (lp/cd) *<(DIE/+CD 001)>* **MURDER CITY DEVILS** [ ] [ ] Aug97
– Dance hall music / It's in my heart / Boom swagger room / Get off the floor / Flashbulb / Broken glass / Murder city roit / Sick of dreaming / Make it on my own / Tell you brother.

Sub Pop — Sub Pop

May 99. (lp/cd) *<(SP/+CD 429)>* **EMPTY BOTTLES, BROKEN HEARTS** [ ] [ ] Nov98
– I want a lot now (so come on) / Dancin' shoes / 18 wheels / Left hand right hand / Ready for more / Cradle to the grave / Dear hearts / Hey sailor / Johnny Thunders / Stars in her eyes / Another round on you / Every shitty thing.

—— added **LESLIE HARDY** – keyboards (ex-HOLE)

Oct 99. (7") *<(SP 482)>* **IN THIS TOWN. /** [ ] [ ]

Jun 00. (lp/cd) *<(SP/+CD 497)>* **IN NAME AND BLOOD** [ ] [ ]
– Press gang / I drank the wine / Bunkhouse / Idle hands / Rum and whiskey / I'll come running / Demon brother / Lemuria rising / Somebody else's baby / In this town / No grave but the sea / Fields of fire.

MURDER INC. (see under ⇒ CONNELLY, Chris)

MURPHY'S LAW

Formed: New York, USA . . . mid 80's by JIMMY 'GESTAPO' DRESCHER, ALEX MORRIS, PETE MARTINEZ and PETE HINES. By the release of 1986's eponymous debut album, DRESCHER was already on the hunt for a new hardcore posse, rounding them up in time for a follow-up set, 'BACK WITH A BONG!' (1989). Released on 'Profile' (home to RUN DMC amongst others), the record was another blast of puerile post-adolescent guitar fury that saw MURPHY'S LAW moving in an increasingly metallic direction; the transformation was even more pronounced as the band signed to Kerrang!-friendly European label, 'Roadracer' for third album, 'THE BEST OF TIMES' (1991). It would be some time before DRESCHER and Co returned, the band rocked by the 1994 death (by stabbing) of recent bass player, CHUCK VALLE. The latter's replacement, DEAN RISPER, joined a line-up of DRESCHER, TODD YOUTH and the unfortunately named ERIC ARCE for 1996's comeback set, 'DEDICATED'.

Album rating: MURPHY'S LAW (*6) / BACK WITH A BONG! (*4) / BEST OF TIMES (*5) / DEDICATION (*5)

JIMMY 'GESTAPO' DRESCHER – vocals / **ALEX MORRIS** – guitar / **PETE MARTINEZ** – bass / **PETE HINES** – drums

not iss. — Rock Hotel-Profile

1986. (lp/c/cd) *<1225>* **MURPHY'S LAW** [-] [ ]
– Murphy's law / California pipeline / Sit home and rot / Fun / Beer / Wahoo day / Crucial bar-b-q / A day in the life / Care bear / Isla / Skinhead rebel / I've got a right.

—— **DRESCHER** recruited new musicians

Profile — Profile

Aug 89. (lp/c/cd) *<(FILE R/CT/CD 275)>* **BACK WITH A BONG!** [ ] [ ]
– Intro / Panty raid / Yahoo / Attack of the killer bears / Cavity creeps / Ska song / Quest for Herb / America rules / Rage / Wall of death / Secret agent S.K.I.N. / Push comes to shove / Bong. *(cd re-iss. Sep94 on 'Another Planet' +=; AP 6002-2)* – MURPHY'S LAW

Roadracer — Relativity

Nov 91. (cd/c/lp) *(RO 9240-2/-4/-1) <88561-1070-2/-4/-1>* **THE BEST OF TIMES** [ ] [ ]

—— **DRESCHER** now with **TODD YOUTH** – guitar / **ERIC ARCE** – drums / + **DEAN RISPER** – bass; repl. CHUCK VALLE who was fatally stabbed in an incident in 1994

Another Planet — Another Planet

Apr 96. (cd) **DEDICATED** [-] [ ]

May 96. (7") *<(AP 6504)>* **WHAT WILL THE NEIGHBOURS THINK. /** [ ] [ ]

Second Movement — Second Movement

Apr 96. (12") *(SMR 16)* **20 SECONDS (remix). /** [ ] [ ]

MUSE

Formed: Teignmouth, Devon, England . . . 1997 by MATTHEW BELLAMY, CHRIS WOLSTENHOLME and drummer DOMINIC HOWARD. After playing dingey pubs and damp basements, the 3-piece from the south-west arose when they debuted at the 'In The City' A&R field day in 1998. HOWARD's THOM YORKE-esque vox impressed record pedallers so much that they took the group to America to showcase them for MADONNA's record label 'Maverik' – home to The DEFTONES, ALANIS MORISSETTE and, erm, WANK. The 20-something indie kids released a John Leckie (knob-twiddler for RADIOHEAD, STONE ROSES and somebody called JOHN LENNON) produced EP entitled 'MUSE' at the beginning of 1999, which was only pressed on 999 copies (it can nowadays fetch up to £30). The EP sounded like many earlier RADIOHEAD efforts, with a little MY BLOODY VALENTINE twist thrown in for good measure. MUSE proceeded with the 'MUSCLE MUSEUM' EP and two singles 'UNO' and 'CAVE' before unveiling their debut set 'SHOWBIZ' in late '99. The album boasted nothing special (bar say, the track 'SUNBURN'), except that it may have contained some of the most melodramatic tracks since OASIS's 'WHAT'S THE STORY. . .'. It unleashed a new brand of genre that had the same ideology as Brit Pop: MOR – where have I heard this before? – rock. 2001 saw MUSE go from strength to strength via two major UK hit singles, 'PLUG IN BABY' and 'NEW BORN', both taken from their celebrated Top 3 sophomore set, 'ORIGIN OF SYMMETRY'. • **Note:** The MUSE who released the CD in '97 entitled 'Innocent Voices' were not the same band.

Album rating: SHOWBIZ (*7) / ORIGIN OF SYMMETRY (*7)

MATTHEW BELLAMY – vocals, guitar / **CHRIS WOLSTENHOLME** – bass / **DOMINIC HOWARD** – drums

Dangerous — not iss.

May 98. (cd-ep) *(DREXCDEP 103)* **MUSE EP** [ ] [-]
– Overdue / Cave / Coma / Escape.

Jan 99. (cd-ep) *(DREXCDEP 104)* **MUSCLE MUSEUM EP** [ ] [-]
– Muscle museum / Sober / Uno / Unintented / Instant messenger / Muscle museum #2.

Mushroom — Warners

Jun 99. (7"clear) *(MUSH 50S)* **UNO. / AGITATED** [73] [-]
(cd-s) *(MUSH 50CDS)* – ('A'side) / Jimmy Kane / Forced in.

Sep 99. (7"clear) *(MUSH 58S)* **CAVE / CAVE (instrumental remix)** [52] [ ]
(cd-s+=) *(MUSH 58CDS)* – Twin.
(cd-s) *(MUSH 58CDX)* – ('A'side) / Host / Coma.

Oct 99. (cd/md/c/lp) *(MUSH 59 CD/MC/LP) <47382>* **SHOWBIZ** [69] [ ]
– Sunburn / Muscle museum / Fillip / Falling down / Cave / Showbiz / Unintended / Uno / Sober / Escape / Overdue / Hate this & I'll love you. *(re-iss. Feb00; same)*

Nov 99. (7") *(MUSH 66S)* **MUSCLE MUSEUM. / ('A'live acoustic)** [43] [ ]
(cd-s+=) *(MUSH 66CDS)* – Do we need this?
(cd-s) *(MUSH 66CDSX)* – ('A'extended) / Pink ego box / Con-science.

Feb 00. (7") *(MUSH 68S)* **SUNBURN. / ('A'live)** [22] [ ]
(cd-s+=) *(MUSH 68CDS)* – Ashamed.
(cd-s) *(MUSH 68CDSX)* – ('A'side) / Yes please / Uno (live).

Jun 00. (7"/c-s) *(MUSH 72 S/MCS)* **UNINTENDED. / RECESS** [20] [ ]
(cd-s+=) *(MUSH 72CDS)* – Falling down (live acoustic) / ('A'-CD-ROM).
(cd-s) *(MUSH 72CDSX)* – ('A'side) / Nishe / Hate this & I'll love you (live).

Oct 00. (7") *(MUSH 84S) MUSCLE MUSEUM. / SOBER (The Saint remix)* [25] [-]
(cd-s+=) *(MUSH 84CDS)* – Sunburn (Timo Maas sunstroke remix).

Mar 01. (c-s) *(MUSH 89MCS)* **PLUG IN BABY / NATURE 1** [11] [-]
(cd-s+=) *(MUSH 89CDS)* – Execution commentary.
(cd-s) *(MUSH 89CDSX)* – ('A'side) / Spiral static / Bedroom acoustics.

Jun 01. (7") *(MUSH 92)* **NEW BORN. / SHRINKING UNIVERSE** [12] [-]
(cd-s+=) *(MUSH 92CDS)* – Piano thing / ('A'-video).
(cd-s) *(MUSH 92CDSX)* – ('A'side) / Map of your head / Plug in baby (live).
(12") *(MUSH 92T)* – ('A'-Perfecto remix) / Sunburn (Timo Maas sunstroke remix).
Jun 01. (cd/c/lp) *(MUSH 93 CD/MC/LP)* **ORIGIN OF SYMMETRY** [3] [-]

MY DYING BRIDE

Formed: Bradford, England . . . 1990 by AARON STAINTHORPE, ANDY CRAIGHAN, CALVIN ROBERTSHAW, ADE JACKSON and RICK MIAH. After a one-off single for French label 'Listenable', they secured a deal with 'Peaceville' in 1991. An EP the following year was duly pursued by a debut album, 'AS THE FLOWER WITHERS', a set which featured artwork by cult artist Dave McKean. This doom-laden piece of experimental metal fashioned a more sophisticated variation of the standard death-metal template. With classically-trained violinist MARTIN POWELL now a full-time member, the subsequent album, 'LET LOOSE THE SWANS' was even heavier on the atmospheric orchestration. Three more were to follow in the 90's, 'TRINITY' (1994), 'THE ANGEL AND THE DARK RIVER' (1995) and 'LIKE GODS OF THE SUN' (1996). In the late 90's, MDB soared again with a couple of well above par goth/doom sets, '34.788% COMPLETE' (1998) and 'THE LIGHT AT THE END OF THE WORLD' (1999).

Album rating: AS THE FLOWER WITHERS (*6) / LET LOOSE THE SWANS (*7) / THE ANGEL AND THE DARK RIVER (*6) / TRINITY (*5) / LIKE GODS OF THE SUN (*7) / 34.788% COMPLETE (*5) / THE LIGHT AT THE END OF THE WORLD (*6)

AARON STAINTHORPE – vocals / **ANDY CRAIGHAN** – guitar / **CALVIN ROBERTSHAW** – guitar / **ADE JACKSON** – bass / **RICK MIAH** – drums / part-time until '92 full-time; **MARTIN POWELL** – violin, keyboards

Listenable / not iss.

1990. (12") **GOD IS ALONE. /** [-] [-] France

Peaceville / not iss.

Mar 92. (12"/cd-s) *(VILE 027 T/CD)* **SYMPHONAIRE INFERNUS ET SPERA EMPYRIUM (act 1). / SYMPHONAIRE INFERNUS ET SPERA EMPYRIUM (act II)** [ ] [-]
May 92. (cd/lp) *(CD+/VILE 032)* **AS THE FLOWER WITHERS** [ ] [-]
– Silent dance / Sear me / The forever people / The bitterness and the bereavement / Vast choirs / The return of the beautiful. *(re-iss. cd Apr95; same)* *<US-iss.1996 on 'Futurist'; 11081>*
Feb 93. (12"ep/cd-ep) *(VILE 037 T/CD)* **THE THRASH OF NAKED LIMBS. / LE CERF MALADE / GATHER ME UP FOREVER** [ ] [-]

Peaceville / Futurist

Oct 93. (cd/lp) *(CD+/VILE 039)* *<11046>* **TURN LOOSE THE SWANS** [ ] [ ] Jan94
– Sear me MCMXCIII / Your river / The songless bird / The snow in my hand / The crown of sympathy / Turn loose the swans / Black god. *(re-iss. cd Mar95; same)*
Jan 94. (12") *(VILE 044T)* **I AM THE BLOODY EARTH. / TRANSCENDING (INTO THE EXQUISITE)** [ ] [-]
(cd-s+=) *(VILE 044CD)* – Crown of sympathy (remix).
above featured guest vox of GHOST (of G.G.F.H.)
Oct 94. (cd) *(CDVILE 046)* *<11067>* **TRINITY** [ ] [ ] Oct95
– Symphonaire infernus et spera empyrium / God is alone / De Sade soliloquy / The thrash of naked limbs / Le cerf malade / Gather me up forever / I am the bloody earth / The crown of sympathy (remix) / The sexuality of bereavement. *(<re-iss. Sep95; same>)*
May 95. (cd/c/lp) *(CD/T+/VILE 50)* *<11086>* **THE ANGEL AND THE DARK RIVER** [ ] [ ] May96
– The cry of mankind / From darkest skies / Black voyage / A sea to suffer in / Two winters only / Your shameful heaven. *(d-cd; CDDVILE 50)*

Peaceville / Fierce

Oct 96. (cd/c/lp) *(CD/T+/VILE 65)* *<11103>* **LIKE GODS OF THE SUN** [ ] [ ] Jan97
– Like gods of the sun / The dark caress / Grace unhearing / A kiss to remember / All swept away / For you / It will come / Here in the throat / For my fallen angel. *(also ltd.cd; CDXVILE 65)*

Peaceville / Mayhem

Oct 98. (cd/lp) *(CD+/VILE 74)* *<11127>* **34.788% COMPLETE** [ ] [ ]
– The whore, the cook and the mother / The stance of Evander sinoue / Der uberlebende / Heroin chic / Apocalypse woman / Base level erotica / Under your wings and into your arms.
Nov 99. (cd) *(CDVILE 79)* *<62079>* **THE LIGHT AT THE END OF THE WORLD** [ ] [ ] Mar01
– She is in the dark / Edenbeast / The night he died / The light at the end of the world / The fever sea / Into the lake of ghosts / The Isis script / Christliar / Sear me III.

– compilations, etc. –

Nov 94. (12"box-set) **all singles** [-] [-]

MY OWN VICTIM

Formed: Kentucky, USA . . . 1993 out of HUMAN REMAINS by VIC HILLERICH, BRIAN OMER, JEFF TOY, TODD CONN and IVAN ARNOLD. Eventually picked up by extreme metal label, 'Century Media', the band made their debut with the 'BURNING INSIDE' album in 1995. Their ferocious brand of nu-metallic hardcore reached an artistic pinnacle of sorts on sophomore effort, 'NO VOICE, NO RIGHTS, NO FREEDOM' (1997), an album which received rave write-ups from connoisseurs of the genre. The fact that BIOHAZARD personally requested them as tour support undoubtedly helped raise their profile while the band themselves seemed to have learned a few tricks from the Brooklyn boys. This much was in evidence from even a cursory listen to 'THE WEAPON' (1998), an uncompromising blast of US hardcore aimed point blank at hypocrisy, injustice and greed.

Album rating: BURNING INSIDE (*6) / NO VOICE, NO RIGHTS, NO FREEDOM (*7) / THE WEAPON (*6)

VICTOR HILLERICH – vocals / **BRIAN OMER** – guitar / **JEFF TOY** – guitar / **TODD CONN** – bass / **IVAN ARNOLD** – drums

Century Media / Kingfisher

Mar 95. (cd-ep) *(CM 7708-2)* *<KF 001-2>* **MY OWN VICTIM** [ ] [ ]
Jan 96. (cd/c/lp) *(CM 7805-2/-4/-1)* *<KF 002-2>* **BURNING INSIDE** [ ] [ ] Nov95
– My standpoint / Under the gun / Becoming the enemy / Nothing left to gain / Burning inside / Tied down / On an on / Identity / Push back / Stained / Open scars / Break the system down / Face the facts / To become one.
Feb 97. (cd) *(CM 7852)* *<KF 003-2>* **NO VOICE, NO RIGHTS, NO FREEDOM** [ ] [ ]
– Unjustified / What do you live for? / Ready to explode / One step above / Make a change / Walls apart / Slave / Cornered / Colorblind / From the bottom / No regret.
Mar 98. (cd/lp) *(CM 7905-2/-1)* *<KF 004-2>* **THE WEAPON** [ ] [ ]
– What have we become / Defy the norm / Embrace / Self sacrifice / The weapon / New life / Waste it away / Throw the next stone / Born free / Face up / Something called pride.

MY VITRIOL

Formed: London, England . . . 1998 by Sri Lankan-born singer/songwriter SOM WIJAY-WARDNER and his college mate RAVI KESAVARAM. Taking the name from Graham Greene's classic novel, 'Brighton Rock', the pair cut a 6-track demo EP entitled 'DELUSIONS OF GRANDEUR'. Although more than 200 CDR's were pressed up, less than a quarter were actually playable due to a technical hitch. Luckily, one of these found its way into the hands of Radio 1 DJ Steve Lamacq who duly aired a track on his Evening Session show. Further tracks appeared on compilation albums courtesy of the 'Org' and 'Abuse' labels while the former was to release a debut single proper, 'ALWAYS YOUR WAY' / 'PIECES' in late '99. By this point, the line-up had been completed by SETH TAYLOR and CAROLYN BANNISTER, the four-piece finally landing a deal with 'Infectious' amid much column inches and radio play. The new millennium began with a session for Radio One followed by a couple of live acoustic sessions for X-FM. A much anticipated debut album, 'FINELINES' (2000), hit the shelves in March to widespread acclaim with critics namechecking a host of US noise luminaries including SONIC YOUTH, DINOSAUR JR and SMASHING PUMPKINS. SOM, for his part, cited NIRVANA's 'Smells Like Teen Spirit' as the spark that ignited his much raved over musical bile. A subsequent series of single releases culminated in a Top 40 entry for a re-released 'ALWAYS . . .' while the album nearly breached the Top 20. With a string of festival appearances lined up for summer 2001, MV look set to win over yet more punters with their self-confessed 'C.O.R.'; that's critic-orientated-rock to you . . . • **Covers:** BREAKFAST (irish trad) / WAIT A MINUTE (Wipers) / etc.

Album rating: FINELINES (*7)

SOM WIJAY-WARDNER (b.26 Dec'79) – vocals, guitar (ex-SHOCK SYNDROME) / **SETH TAYLOR** – guitar (ex-MINT 400) / **CAROLYN BANNISTER** – bass, vocals (ex-PRODUCT) / **RAVI KESAVARAM** – drums

Org / not iss.

Jan 00. (cd-ep) **ALWAYS YOUR WAY / PIECES / GROUNDED (demo)** [ ] [-]

Infectious / not iss.

Apr 00. (7") *(INFECT 88S)* **LOSING TOUCH. / TONGUE TIED** [ ] [-]
(cd-s+=) *(INFECT 88CDS)* – Breakfast (live/BBC). *(re-iss. Jan01)*
Jul 00. (7") *(INFECT 89S)* **CEMENTED SHOES. / WAIT A MINUTE** [65] [-]
(cd-s+=) *(INFECT 89CDS)* – All of me. *(re-iss. Jan01)*
Oct 00. (cd-s) *(INFECT 94CDS)* **PIECES / SAFETY ZONES AND CRUMPLE ZONES** [56] [-]
(cd-s) *(INFECT 94CDSX)* – ('A'side) / Another lie / Cemented shoes (live).
Feb 01. (7") *(INFECT 95S)* **ALWAYS: YOUR WAY. / SPOTLIGHTS** [31] [-]
(cd-s+=) *(INFECT 095CDS)* – Game of pricks.
(cd-s) *(INFECT 095CDSX)* – ('A'side) / Losing touch (acoustic) / It came crashing.
Mar 01. (cd/lp) *(INFECT 96 CDX/LP)* **FINELINES** [24] [-]
– Alpha waves / Always: your way / Gentle art of choking / Kohlstream / Cemented shoes / Grounded / C.O.R. / Infantile / Ode to the red queen / Tongue tied / Windows & walls / Taprobane / Losing touch / Pieces / Falling off the floor / Under the wheels.
May 01. (cd-s) *(INFECT 97CDS)* **GROUNDED / OH FATHER / ALWAYS: YOUR WAY** [29] [-]
(cd-s) *(INFECT 97CDSX)* – ('A'side) / Deadlines / Windows and walls (piano).

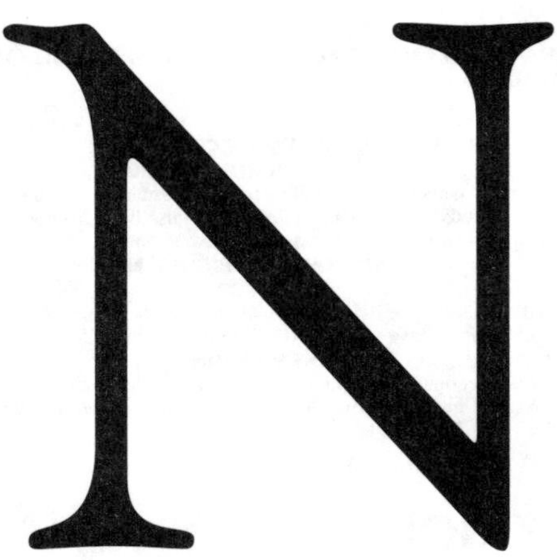

NAILBOMB (see under ⇒ SEPULTURA)

NAKED RAYGUN

Formed: (based) Chicago, Illinois, USA ... 1981 by JEFF PEZZATI, his brother MARCO PEZZATI (who was almost immediately replaced by CAMILO GONZALEZ) and future BIG BLACK member, SANTIAGO DURANGO (who in turn was substituted by JOHN HAGGERTY) with subsequent addition of drummer JIM COLAO. Having garnered an early live reputation for raw (the lads played with their boots on – and nothing else!) hardcore, their first vinyl outing came in the shape of four tracks, 'BOMB SHELTER', 'LIBIDO', 'PARANOIA' and 'WHEN THE SCREAMING STOPS', featured on an Autumn 1981 V/A compilation, 'Busted At Oz' (alongside the EFFIGIES and STRIKE UNDER). With ERIC SPICER newly installed on the drumstool, NAKED RAYGUN fired out a debut EP, 'BASEMENT SCREAMS' before signing to 'Homestead' (stamping ground of DINOSAUR JR and SONIC YOUTH) for whom they released debut album, 'THROB THROB' (1984). Following the replacement of GONZALEZ with PIERRE KEZDY, the band established themselves as one of the Windy City's premier guitar assault units (alongside STEVE ALBINI's noisemongers, BIG BLACK) with 1985's sophomore album, 'ALL RISE'. After parting company with 'Homestead', NAKED RAYGUN initiated their own short-lived imprint, 'Sandpounder' – only a one-off 45, 'VANILLA BLUE', would materialise – before signing to 'Caroline' for 1988's 'JETTISON', which featured a rousing cover of Stiff Little Finger's 'SUSPECT DEVICE'. In '89, they released the follow-up, 'UNDERSTAND?', an album that disappointed many for its occasional ordinariness. One further personnel change (BILL STEPHENS for HAGGERTY) was effected prior to the band's below par swansong set, 'RAYGUN ... NAKED RAYGUN', in 1990.

Album rating: THROB THROB (*5) / ALL RISE (*7) / JETTISON (*7) / UNDERSTAND? (*4) / RAYGUN ... NAKED RAYGUN (*4)

JEFF PEZZATI – vocals, guitar / **JOHN HAGGERTY** – guitar; repl. SANTIAGO DURANGO / **CAMILO GONZALEZ** – bass; repl. MARCO PEZZATI / **ERIC SPICER** – drums; repl. JIM COLAO

not iss. / Ruthless

1983. (7"ep) *<RRNR 03>* **BASEMENT SCREAMS** [-] [ ]

Homestead / Homestead

Mar 85. (lp) *<(HMS 008)>* **THROB THROB** [ ] [ ] Nov84
– Rat patrol / Surf combat / Gear / Metastasis / Leeches / Roller queen / On / I don't know / Libido / Only in America / No sex / Stupid / Managua. *(cd-iss. Jul88 & Mar98; HMS 008CD) <(cd re-iss. Aug99 on 'Quarter Stick'; QS 84CD)>*

—— **PIERRE KEZDY** – bass; repl. GONZALEZ

May 86. (lp) *<(HMS 045)>* **ALL RISE** [ ] [ ] Nov85
– Home of the brave / Dog at large / Knock me down / Mr. Gridlock / The strip / I remember / Those who move / The envelope / Backlash Jack / Peacemaker / New dreams. *(cd-iss. Jul88; HMS 045CD) <(cd re-iss. Aug99 on 'Quarter Stick'; QS 85CD)>*

not iss. / Sandpounder

1987. (7") *<SR 001>* **VANILLA BLUE. /** [-] [ ]
(UK-iss.Oct97; same)

Caroline / Caroline

May 88. (lp/c/cd) *<CAROL 1348-1/-4/-2>* **JETTISON** [-] [ ]
– Soldiers requiem / When the walls come down / Walk in cold / Jettison / Live wire / The mule / Coldbringer / Blight / Free nation / Hammer head / Ghetto mechanic / Suspect device / Vanilla blue. *<(re-iss. Aug99 on 'Quarter Stick'+=; QS 86CD)>* – Roller queen (live) / The strip (live) / Backlash Jack (live).

Feb 89. (lp/c) *(CAR LP/C/CD 6) <CAROL 1371/+C/CD>* **UNDERSTAND?** [ ] [ ]
– Treason / Hips swingin' / Understand? / Entrapment / Bughouse / Wonder beer / Never follow / Too much of you / Vagabond dog / O.K. wait / The sniper song / Which side you're on. *<(cd-iss. Aug99 on 'Quarter Stick'+=; QS 87CD)>* – Mr. Gridlock (live) / I don't know (live).

—— **BILL STEPHENS** – guitar; repl. HAGGERTY who joined PIGBOY

1990. (cd/c/lp) *<CAROL 1642-2/-4/-1>* **RAYGUN ... NAKED RAYGUN** [-] [ ]
– Home / Fever island / The grind / Jazz gone bad / Prepare to die / The promise / Holding you / Strange days / In my head / Camarilla / Terminal. *<(cd re-iss. Aug99 on 'Quarter Stick'; QS 88CD)>*

—— disbanded after above

– compilations, etc. –

Jan 98. (cd) *Dyslexic; <(DYS 21)>* **LAST OF THE DEMOHICANS** [ ] [ ]

NAKED SEE (see under ⇒ FOIL)

NAKED TRUTH

Formed: Atlanta, Georgia, USA ... 1988 by Detroit-born DOUG WATTS, who enlisted JIMMIE WESTLEY, JEFF and BERNARD DAWSON. Hardly the kind of band you'd expect to find in the redneck heart of the US South, this widly eclectic Afro-American outfit relocated to London under the wing of former CLASH manager, BERNIE RHODES. Signed to 'Sony', the group laid down their manic stew of hardcore, jazz and extreme metal with the debut mini-album, 'GREEN WITH RAGE' (1991). With JEFF returning to his native America, the band found a replacement in KWAME BOATEN, who played on an EP, 'READ BETWEEN THE LINES' a year later. Early in 1993 after heavy gigging in the capital and beyond, their first full-length album was completed. 'FIGHT' drew deserved critical praise, its heady musical brew complemented by social conscious lyrics reflecting their unique worldview. However, this was to be their last recording under this moniker, the band taking the name of WATTS as their new nom de plume.

Album rating: GREEN WITH RAGE mini (*6) / FIGHT (*6)

DOUG WATTS – vocals / **JIMMIE WESTLEY** – guitar / **JEFF** – bass / **BERNARD DAWSON** – drums

Sony Soho 2 / Sony

Nov 91. (m-cd/m-c/m-lp) *(469124-2/-4/-1)* **GREEN WITH RAGE** [ ] [ ]
– Pan American alive / King in my home (lovejoy) / Here lies America / Downtown / Brood flows / Harem scares.

—— **KWAME BOATEN** – bass; repl. JEFF

Nov 92. (10"12"/cd-s) *(658429-0/-6/-2)* **READ BETWEEN THE LINES. / FIGHT** [ ] [ ]

Feb 93. (12"ep) *(658949-6)* **BLACK. / HERE LIES AMERICA / I AM HE** [ ] [ ]
(cd-ep+=) *(658949-2)* – Fight.

Mar 93. (cd/c/lp) *(472981-2/-4/-1) <53929>* **FIGHT** [ ] [ ]
– Door / Tormented world / Downtown / Lovejoy / Black / Read between the lines / I am he / Telepathy / Third eye spy / Red river.

not iss. / Midwest

Apr 95. (cd) *<1028>* **BLANKEE** [-] [ ]

—— the band changed their name to WATTS (not the one on 'Estrus')

NAPALM DEATH

Formed: Ipswich, England ... 1982 by "vocalist" LEE DORRIAN and guitarist BILL STEER. Building up a small but fiercely loyal grassroots following by constant gigging, 'DEATH finally made in onto vinyl with 'SCUM' in 1987. Released on the band's own 'Earache' label, the record was a proverbial tale of two halves with NICK BULLEN (bass, vocals), JUSTIN BROADRICK (guitar) and MICK HARRIS (drums) producing side one, while side two was the work of STEER, DORRIAN and JIM WHILTELY. Needless to say, both sides were cranium-shreddingly extreme, pioneering white-hot blasts of a thrash/death-metal/punk hybrid which was duly christened "grindcore". Taking punk's short, sharp shock technique to its ultimate conclusion, many of the tracks were under a minute in length. John Peel's favourite, meanwhile, 'YOU SUFFER', lasted less than a second! The influential and ever eclectic PEEL would subsequently invite the band to record a session that year, acknowledging the group's sonic innovation while large sections of the metal press mocked them. The vocals, particularly, came in for a lot of stick; almost wholly unintelligible sub-human growling is how they might be best described although it's a style that has since been ripped off wholesale by legions of death-metal bands. And while the "singing" may have been incomprehensible to anyone missing a lyric sheet, the growling actually belied a radical political and social agenda, not exactly a priority of your average metal band. By the release of the 54 track (a single lp!) 'ENSLAVEMENT TO OBLITERATION' (1988), if anything more extreme than the debut, SHANE EMBURY had replaced WHITELY on bass. Further line-up changes ensued the following year when DORRIAN and STEER both quit to form their own outfits, CATHEDRAL and CARCASS respectively. Replacements were found in vocalist MARK 'Barney' GREENWAY and Mexican guitarist JESSE PINTADO, the group subsequently heading out on the infamous 'Grindcrusher' European tour. With another American guitarist, MITCH HARRIS, recruited to bolster the group's sound, NAPALM DEATH recorded 'HARMONY CORRUPTION'. Released in late 1990, the opus betrayed a more conventional death/thrash metal sound with longer songs. Prior to the release of the 'UTOPIA BANISHED' (1992) album, MICK HARRIS departed for scary ambient outfit, SCORN, his seat on the drum stool filled by DANNY HERARRA. More heavy touring followed, playing to NAPALM DEATH fans in the most unlikely, furthest flung corners of

the globe. A 1993 cover of the Dead Kennedys' 'NAZI PUNKS FUCK OFF' proved the band hadn't left their roots behind completely and with the acclaimed 'FEAR, EMPTINESS, DESPAIR' (1994), the band finally managed to incorporate their uncompromising vision into a consistent, coherent set of songs. The album was their most successful to date, winning them a support from the music press which was consolidated with subsequent releases 'GREED KILLING' (a mini album; 1995) and 'DIATRIBES' (1996). 'INSIDE THE TORN APART' in '97 and '98's 'BOOTLEGGED IN JAPAN' and 'WORDS FROM THE EXIT WOUND' rounded off their time with the 'Earache' imprint, the latter another brutal barrage of sound with industrial skirmishes thrown in. Signing to 'Dream Catcher', NAPALM DEATH returned to form with two Kerrang!-friendly sets, the mini of cover versions 'LEADERS NOT FOLLOWERS' (1999) and the mind-blowing 'ENEMY OF THE MUSIC BUSINESS' (2000). In addition to their boundary-busting music, NAPALM DEATH have also helped cultivate the more extreme end of the music spectrum via their groundbreaking 'Earache' label, home to such uneasy listening experiences as GODFLESH, MISERY LOVES CO. etc. As well as being involved in EXTREME NOISE TERROR, HARRIS initiated side project MEATHOOK SEED alongside EMBURY and OBITUARY moonlighters DONALD TARDY and TREVOR PERES. Following on from the grindcore dynamics of their 1993 debut album, 'EMBEDDED', the pair were back with new members CHRISTOPHE LAMOURET (of OUT fame), RUSS RUSSELL and IAN TRACEY. The resulting 'BASIC INSTRUCTIONS BEFORE LEAVING EARTH' (1999) was an apocalyptic clash of techno and metal, lyrically inspired by Michael Drosnin's book, 'The Bible Code'.
• **Trivia:** NAPALM DEATH recorded the shortest track ever released (the 1 second) 'YOU SUFFER', for a free 7", given away with an 'Earache' sampler, 'Grindcrusher'. SHANE EMBURY exchanged death threats with another teeth-grinding outfit SORE THROAT (mainly band member RICH MILITIA).
• **Covered:** POLITICIANS (Raw Power) / DEMONIC POSSESSION (Pentagram) / MAGGOTS IN YOUR COFFIN (Repulsion) / NAZI PUNKS FUCK OFF (Dead Kennedys) / etc.

Album rating: SCUM (*5) / FROM ENSLAVEMENT TO OBLITERATION (*6) / HARMONY CORRUPTION (*5) / UTOPIA BANISHED (*6) / DEATH BY MANIPULATION compilation (*7) / FEAR, EMPTINESS, DESPAIR (*4) / GREED KILLING mini (*4) / DIATRIBES (*4) / INSIDE THE TORN APART (*5) / BOOTLEGGED IN JAPAN (*3) / WORDS FROM THE EXIT WOUND (*4) / LEADERS NOT FOLLOWERS mini (*6) / LEADERS NOT FOLLOWERS mini (*6) / ENEMY OF THE MUSIC BUSINESS (*8)/ Meathook Seed: EMBEDDED (*5) / BASIC INSTRUCTIONS BEFORE LEAVING EARTH (*6)

LEE DORRIAN – vocals (also runs own label 'Rise Above') / **BILL STEER** – guitar (also of CARCASS) / **SHANE EMBURY** – bass (also drummer of UNSEEN TERROR) / **MICK HARRIS** – drums (also vocals of EXTREME NOISE TERROR) repl. FRANK HEALEY (other early drummer JUS of HEAD OF DAVID)

Earache Relativity

Jul 87. (lp) *(MOSH 003)* **SCUM** [ ] [-]
– Multinational corporations / Instinct of survival / The kill / Scum / Caught . . .in a dream / Polluted minds / Sacrificed / Siege of power / Control / Born on your knees / Human garbage / You suffer / Life? / Prison without walls / Point of no return / Negative approach / Success? / Deceiver / C.S. / Parasites / Pseudo youth / Divine death / As the machine rolls on / Common enemy / Moral crusade / Stigmatized / M.A.D. / Dragnet. *(c-iss.May89; MOSH 003MC) <US-iss.1991 on 'Relativitity'; 1065> (re-iss. cd Sep94; MOSH 003CD)*

Nov 88. (lp/c/cd) *(MOSH 008/+MC/CD)* **FROM ENSLAVEMENT TO OBLITERATION** [ ] [-]
– Evolved as one / It's a man's world / Lueid fairytale / Private death / Impressions / Unchallenged hate / Uncertainty blurs the vision / Cock rock alienation / Retreat to nowhere / Think for a minute / Display to me . . . / From enslavement to obliteration / Blind to the truth / Social sterility / Emotional suffocation / Practise what you preach / Inconceivable / Worlds apart / Obstinate direction / Mentally murdered / Sometimes / Make way. *(pic-lp iss.Jul90; MOSH 008P) <US-iss.1991 on 'Relativity'; 1066> (re-iss. cd Sep94; same)*

Aug 89. (7") *(7MOSH 014)* **MENTALLY MURDERED. / CAUSE AND EFFECT** [ ] [-]
(12"+=) *(MOSH 014T)* – Rise above / Missing link – Mentally murdered / Walls of confinement / Cause and effect – No manual effort.

—— (Aug'89) **MARK 'Barney' GREENWAY** – vocals (ex-BENEDICTION) repl. LEE (LEE was to join CATHEDRAL, another 'Earache' band) **MITCH HARRIS** (b.Las Vegas, USA) + **JESSE PINTADO** (b.Mexico) – guitars repl. BILL who went full-time with CARCASS)

Aug 90. (7") *(7MOSH 024)* **SUFFER THE CHILDREN. / SIEGE OF POWER** [ ] [-]
(12"+=) *(MOSHT 24)* – Harmony corruption.

Sep 90. (lp/c/cd) *(MOSH 019/+MC/CD) <2020>* **HARMONY CORRUPTION** [67] [ ]
– Vision conquest / If the truth be known / Inner incineration / Malicious intent / Unfit Earth / Circle of hypocrisy / Suffer the children / The chains that bind us / Mind snare / Extremity retained. *(some w/free 12") (re-iss. cd Sep94; same)*

May 91. (7") *(7MOSH 046)* **MASS APPEAL MADNESS. / PRIDE ASSASSIN** [ ] [-]
(12"+=/cd-s+=) *(MOSH 046 T/CD)* – Unchallenged hate / Social sterility.

—— MICK HARRIS was arrested for jewel shop robbery & he left to join SCORN. He was soon replaced by **DANNY HERARRA** – drums

May 92. (lp/c/cd) *(MOSH 053/+MC/CD) <1127>* **UTOPIA BANISHED** [58] [ ] Jun92
– Discordance / I abstain / Dementia access / Christening of the world / The world keeps turning / Idiosyncratic / Aryanisms / Cause and effect (pt.II) / Juidicial slime / Distorting the medium / Got time to kill / Upward and uninterested / Exile / Awake (to a life of misery) / Contemptious. *(free 4 track 7"ep) (re-iss. cd Sep94; same)*

Jun 92. (12"ep/cd-ep) *(MOSH 065 T/CD)* **THE WORLD KEEPS TURNING EP** [ ] [-]
– The world keeps turning / A means to an end / Insanity excursion.

Jul 93. (7"ep/cd-ep) *(MOSH 092/+CD)* **NAZI PUNKS FUCK OFF. / ARYANISMS / ('A'version) / CONTEMPTUOUS (xtreem mix)** [ ] [-]

Earache Sony

May 94. (lp/c/cd) *(MOSH 109/+MC/CD) <64361>* **FEAR, EMPTINESS, DESPAIR** [ ] [ ]
– Twist the knife (slowly) / Hung / Remain nameless / Plague rages / More than meets the eye / Primed time / State of mind / Armageddon X7 / Retching on the dirt / Fasting on deception / Throwaway.

Earache Earache

Nov 95. (10"m-lp/m-c/m-cd) *(<MOSH 146/+MC/CD>)* **GREED KILLING** [ ] [ ]
– Greed killing / My own worst enemy / Self betrayal / Finer truths, white lies / Antibody / All links severed / Plague rages (live).

Jan 96. (10"d-lp/c/cd) *(<MOSH 141/+MC/CD>)* **DIATRIBES** [73] [ ]
– Greed killing / Glimpse into genocide / Ripe for the breaking / Cursed to crawl / Cold forgiveness / My own worst enemy / Just rewards / Dogma / Take the strain / Corrosive elements / Placate, sedate, eradicate / Diatribes / Take the strain.

—— In Nov'96, BARNEY was dismissed and was replaced by vocalist **PHIL VANE** (ex-EXTREME NOISE TERROR). This was brief when **BARNEY** returned

Jan 97. (cd-ep) *(MOSH 168CD)* **IN TONGUES WE SPEAK EP** [ ] [-]
– Food chains / Upward and uninterested / (2 others by COALESCE).

Jun 97. (d-lp/c/cd) *(<MOSH 171/+MC/CD>)* **INSIDE THE TORN APART** [ ] [ ]
– Breed to breathe / Birth in regress / Section / Reflect on conflict / Down in the zero / Inside the torn apart / If systems persist / Prelude / Indispose / Purist realist / Low point / Lifeless alarm / Time will come / Bled dry / Ripe for the breaking.

Nov 97. (cd-rom;ep) *(MOSH 185CD)* **BREED TO BREATHE / ALL INTENSIVE PURPOSES / STRANGER NOW / BLED DRY / TIME WILL COME / SUFFER THE CHILDREN (by; Fatality)** [ ] [-]

Jun 98. (cd) *(<MOSH 209CD>)* **BOOTLEGGED IN JAPAN (live 5th August, 1997)** [ ] [ ] Jul98
– Antibody / My own worst enemy / More than meets the eye / Hung / Greed killing / Suffer the children / Mass appeal madness / Cursed to crawl / Glimpse into genocide / I abstain / Lucid fairytale / Plague rages / Cold forgiveness / Control / Diatribes / Life? / Siege of power / If the truth be known / Unchallenged hate / Nazi punks fuck off / From enslavement to obliteration / The kill / Scum / Ripe for the breaking.

Oct 98. (cd) *(<MOSH 212CD>)* **WORDS FROM THE EXIT WOUND** [ ] [ ]
– The infiltraitor / Repression out of uniform / Next of kin to chaos / Trio-degradable – Affixed by disconcern / Cleanse impure / Devouring depraved / Ulterior exterior / None the wiser? / Clutching at barbs / Incendiary incoming / Throw down a rope / Sceptic in perspective.

Dream Catcher Relapse

Nov 99. (m-cd) *(CRIDE 19M) <6452>* **LEADERS NOT FOLLOWERS** [ ] [ ]
– Politicians / Incinerator / Demonic possession / Maggots in your coffin / Back from the dead / Nazi punks fuck off.

Dream Catcher Spitfire

Sep 00. (cd) *(CRIDE 33) <15164>* **ENEMY OF THE MUSIC BUSINESS** [ ] [ ] Mar01
– Take the poison / Next on the list / Constitutional hell / Vermin / Volume of neglect / Thanks for nothing / Can't play, won't pay / Blunt against the cutting edge / Cure for the common people / Necessarily evil / C.S. (Conservative Shithead) pt.2 / Mechanics of deceit / (The public gets) What the public doesn't want / Fracture in the equation.

– compilations, others, etc. –

May 88. (12"ep) *Strange Fruit; (SFPS 049)* **THE PEEL SESSIONS** (13.9.87) [ ] [-]
– The kill / Prison without walls / Dead part one / Deceiver / Lucid fairytale / In extremis / Blind to the trash / Negative approach / Common enemy / Obstinate direction / Life? / You suffer (Part 2). *(re-iss. May89 c-ep/cd-ep; SFPDS MC/CD 049)*

Dec 89. (cd/c) *Strange Fruit; (SFP MCD/MC 201)* **THE PEEL SESSIONS** (13.9.87 & 8.3.88) [ ] [-]
– (above tracks) / Multi-national corporations / Instinct of survival / Stigatised / Parasites / Moral crusade / Worlds apart / M.A.D. / Divine death / C 9 / Control / Walls / Raging in Hell / Conform or die / S.O.B. *<US-iss.1991 on 'Dutch East India'; 8409>*

Feb 92. (lp/cd) *Earache; (MOSH 051/+CD) / Relativity; <1072>* **DEATH BY MANIPULATION** [ ] [ ]
– Mass appeal madness / Pride assassin / Unchallenged hate / Social sterilty / Suffer the children / Siege of power / Harmony corruption / Rise above / The missing link / Mentally murdered / Walls of confinement / Cause and effect / No mental effort / Multinational corporations / Re address the problem / Changing colours / From the ashes / Understanding / Stalemate / Unchallenged hate (live) / Mentally murdered (live) / Walls of confinement (live).
(with free cd-ep) (re-iss. Oct92 & Sep94; same)

Apr 00. (cd) *Strange Fruit; (SFRSCD 91)* **THE BBC RADIO 1 SESSIONS** [ ] [-]

MEATHOOK SEED

MITCH HARRIS – guitars, etc / **SHANE EMBURY** – bass (of NAPALM DEATH) / with members of OBITUARY on hand:- **TREVOR PERES** – vocals / **DONALD TARDY** – drums

Earache Earache

Mar 93. (lp/cd) *(<MOSH 088/+CD>)* **EMBEDDED** [ ] [ ] Nov93
– Famine sector / A furred grave / My infinity / Day of conceiving / Cling to an image / A wilted remnant / Forgive / Focal point blur / Embedded / Visible shallow self / Sea of tranquility.

—— **HARRIS + EMBURY** continued with **CHRISTOPHE LAMOURET** – vocals (of OUT) / **IAN TRACEY** – drums / plus **RUSS RUSSELL** – electronics

Dream Catcher

Nov 99. (cd) *(CRIDE 21)* **BASIC INSTRUCTIONS BEFORE LEAVING EARTH** [ ] [ ]
– Civilise the world / Elemental / Push away / I think you lie / Beautiful / Dumbshow / Ladder / Black skies / Greed / Build / Questionmark / Lost in the box.

NASHVILLE PUSSY

Formed: Atlanta, Georgia, USA ... 1994 by frontman BLAINE CARTWRIGHT, his guitarist wife, RUYTER SUYS, drummer JEREMY THOMPSON and another female, Amazonian bassist COREY PARKS. NASHVILLE PUSSY caused controversy right from the start, if you thought their moniker was a tad risky, the name of their excellent 1998 debut set, 'LET THEM EAT PUSSY', stirred up even more trouble, but what was riling the moral minority was the album's cover photo shot, portraying both the pantless COREY and RUYTER getting the cunnilingus treatment from a couple of unknown bald geezers. In fact, their original label, 'Amphetamine Reptile', couldn't handle the band (so to speak!), although Mercury offshoot, 'Enclave', came in for them (er, so to speak again!) and unleashed the expletive-ridden TED NUGENT or MOTORHEAD-influenced classic. The crew were subsequently signed to 'Mercury' although their tenure was brief, the Grammy-nominated band dropped along with a host of other artists as a result of the Universal/Polygram merger. A new deal with 'TVT' resulted in 'HIGH AS HELL' (2000), another raucous blast of gratuitously obscene psychobilly sleaze produced by FASTBACKS' KURT BLOCH. Given the record label headaches, British fans eager for a piece of 'PUSSY were forced to shell out on import copies.

Album rating: LET THEM EAT PUSSY (*8) / HIGH AS HELL (*7)

BLAINE CARTWRIGHT – vocals, guitar / **RUYTER SUYS** – guitar / **COREY PARKS** – bass / **JEREMY THOMPSON** – drums

Enclave – Mercury | Amphetam. Reptile

Nov 98. (d-cd) *(558 889-2) <AMREP 069CD>* **LET THEM EAT PUSSY** [ ] [ ] Mar98
– Snake eyes / You're goin' down / Go motherfucker go / I'm the man / All fucked up / Johnny hotrod / 5 minutes to go / Somebody shoot me / Blowin' smoke / First I look at the purse / Eat my dust / Fried chicken and coffee / Kicked in the teeth / Nice boys / Milk cow blues / Headin' for the TEcas border / Sock it to me baby / (I'm) Misunderstood.

TVT | TVT

Sep 00. (cd/lp) *<(TVT 3340-2/-1)>* **HIGH AS HELL** [ ] [ ] May00
– Struttin' cock / Shoot first and run like hell / She's got the drugs / Wrong side of a gun / Piece of ass / High as hell / You ain't right / Go to hell / Rock & roll outlaw / Let's ride / Blowjob from a rattlesnake / Drive.

NASTY SAVAGE

Formed: Brandigan, Florida, USA ... 1983 by former professional wrestler NASTY RONNIE and BEN MEYER. They enlisted the help of DAVID AUSTIN, FRED DREGISCHAN and CURTIS BEESON, who played on their first recordings for the various artists compilation, 'Metal Massacre IV' (1984). This resulted in a deal with 'Metal Blade' ('Roadrunner' UK), an eponymous album appearing in '85. Although this dealt in muscular heavy rock, the band drifted progressively towards hi-tech power metal with touches of thrash on subsequent releases, 'INDULGENCE' (1987), 'ABSTRACT REALITY' and their final effort, the widely-acclaimed 'PENETRATION POINT'. Throughout their career, the band were always more of an exciting live proposition than their studio output might suggest, the ever unpredictable NASTY RONNIE always entertaining with his masochistic antics.

Album rating: NASTY SAVAGE (*6) / INDULGENCE (*7) / ABSTRACT REALITY (*5) / PENETRATION POINT (*5)

NASTY RONNIE – vocals / **DAVID AUSTIN** – guitar / **FRED DREGISCHAN** – bass / **CURTIS BEESON** – drums

Roadrunner | Metal Blade

Sep 85. (lp) *(RR 9752) <14063>* **NASTY SAVAGE** [ ] [ ]
– No sympathy / Gladiator / Fear beyond the vision / Metal knights / Garden of temptation / Asmodeus / Dungeon of pleasure / The morgue / Instigator / Psychopath / End of time. *<(cd-iss. Nov96 on 'Metal Blade'; 3984 14063CD)>*

Roadrunner | Restless

Mar 87. (lp) *(RR 9630) <72186-1>* **INDULGENCE** [ ] [ ]
– Indulgence / Inferno / Hypnotic trance / Incursion dementia / Distorted fanatic.

Feb 88. (lp) *(RR 9566) <72244-1>* **ABSTRACT REALITY** [ ] [ ]
– Abstract reality / Unchained angel / Eromantic vertigo / You snooze, you lose. *(UK-iss.+=)* – Stabbed in the back / Divination / XXX. *(cd-iss. 1989 +=; RR 9566-2)* – INDULGENCE *(cd re-iss. Nov96 on 'Metal Blade'; 3984 14064CD)*

Roadracer | Rotten

Jan 90. (cd/lp) *(RO 9418-2/-1) <2>* **PENETRATION POINT** [ ] [ ]
– Welcome wagon / Irrational / Ritual submission / Powerslam / Sin eater / Penetration point / Puzzled / Horizertical / Family circus.

—— split after above

NAZARETH

Formed: Dunfermline, Scotland ... 1969 out of the ashes of The SHADETTES by DAN McCAFFERTY, PETE AGNEW and DARREL SWEET. With the addition of MANNY CHARLTON, the group turned pro and relocated to London, gaining a record contract with 'Pegasus' in the process. Already armed with a loyal homegrown support, the band released two earthy hard-rock albums for the label between late '71 and mid '72 before moving to 'Mooncrest'. This was the band's turning point, NAZARETH hitting immediately with a Top 10 smash, 'BROKEN DOWN ANGEL'. An obvious focal point for the Caledonian rockers was the mean-looking McCAFFERTY, his whisky-throated wail coming to define the band's sound. Their acclaimed third album, 'RAZAMANAZ' followed soon after, narrowly missing the UK Top 10 but nevertheless spawning another top selling rock classic, 'BAD, BAD BOY'. With ROGER GLOVER (ex-DEEP PURPLE) at the production desk, NAZARETH re-invented Joni Mitchell's classic, 'THIS FLIGHT TONIGHT', the band virtually claiming it as their own with a re-working startling in its stratospheric melodic power. The accompanying, appropriately-named 'LOUD 'N' PROUD' album (also released in '73!), followed the established formula by combining excellent cover versions with original material, thus its Top 10 placing. However, by the following year, only their fifth album, 'RAMPANT' had achieved any degree of success. America finally took NAZARETH to their hearts with the release of the much covered Boudleaux Bryant ballad, 'LOVE HURTS', the single making the US Top 10 in 1975 (JIM CAPALDI of Traffic had pipped them to the post in Britain). McCAFFERTY returned to the UK charts that year in fine fettle with yet another classy cover, Tomorrow's 'MY WHITE BICYCLE'. The frontman even found time to complete and release a full albums worth of covers, the big man and the band suffering a backlash from some of their more hardcore fans. Switching labels to 'Mountain' (home of The SENSATIONAL ALEX HARVEY BAND) late in 1975, the band suffered a dip in profile, although having signed to 'A&M' in America (in the heyday) they consolidated their earlier Stateside success. The ALEX HARVEY connection took another twist with the addition of the latter's clown-faced sidekick ZAL CLEMINSON on guitar. This helped to pull back some of NAZARETH's flagging support, the following JEFF 'Skunk' BAXTER (ex-DOOBIES)-produced set, 'MALICE IN WONDERLAND' hitting Top 30 in America. ZAL departed soon after, his surprising replacement being the American JOHN LOCKE, who in turn (after an album, 'THE FOOL CIRCLE' 1981) was superseded by Glaswegian BILLY RANKIN. For the remainder of the 80's, NAZARETH churned out a plethora of reasonable albums, the band still retaining a North American fanbase while gaining a foothold in many parts of Europe. Founder member MANNY CHARLTON subsequently departed at the turn of the decade, RANKIN returning for their best album for ten years, 'NO JIVE' (1991). Surprisingly, after nearly 30 years in the business, NAZARETH are still plugging away, their most recent effort being 1995's 'MOVE ME'. A host of modern day hard-rockers such as AXL ROSE, MICHAEL MONROE, etc, claim to have been influenced by both McCAFFERTY and his three wise rockers, GUNS N' ROSES even covering 'HAIR OF THE DOG'. With McCAFFERTY, AGNEW and SWEET (plus newcomers JIMMY MURRISON and RONNIE LEAHY) carrying NAZARETH towards the 21st Century, their final album of the millennium was 'BOOGALOO' (1998). Sadly, DARRELL was to die in New Albany, Indiana, USA on the 30th of April, 1999. • **Songwriters:** Group penned, except SHAPES OF THINGS (Yardbirds) / DOWN HOME GIRL (Leiber-Stoller) / I WANT TO DO EVERYTHING FOR YOU (Joe Tex) / TEENAGE NERVOUS BREAKDOWN (Little Feat) / THE BALLAD OF HOLLIS BROWN (Bob Dylan) / YOU'RE THE VIOLIN (Golden Earring) / WILD HONEY (Beach Boys) / SO YOU WANT TO BE A ROCK'N'ROLL STAR (Byrds) / I DON'T WANT TO GO ON WITHOUT YOU (Berns/Wexler). DAN McCAFFERTY solo covered OUT OF TIME (Rolling Stones) / WHATCHA GONNA DO ABOUT IT (Small Faces) / etc.

Album rating: NAZARETH (*6) / EXERCISES (*6) / RAZAMANAZ (*7) / LOUD 'N' PROUD (*6) / RAMPANT (*6) / HAIR OF THE DOG (*7) / CLOSE ENOUGH FOR ROCK'N'ROLL (*5) / PLAY 'N' THE GAME (*4) / GREATEST HITS compilation (*8) / EXPECT NO MERCY (*5) / NO MEAN CITY (*5) / MALCE IN WONDERLAND (*5) / THE FOOL CIRCLE (*4) / 'SNAZ (*4) / 2XS (*4) / SOUND ELIXIR (*4) / THE CATCH (*4) / CINEMA (*4) / SNAKES AND LADDERS (*4) / THE SINGLES COLLECTION compilation (*8) / NO JIVE (*5) / MOVE ME (*4)

DAN McCAFFERTY – vocals / **MANNY CHARLTON** – guitar, vocals / **PETE AGNEW** (b.14 Sep'48) – bass / **DARRELL SWEET** (b.16 May'47, Bournemouth, England) – drums, percussion

Pegasus | Warners

Nov 71. (lp) *(PEG 10) <BS 2615>* **NAZARETH** [ ] [ ] Feb73
– Witchdoctor woman / Dear John / Empty arms, empty heart / If I had a dream / Red light lady / Fat man / Country girl / Morning dew / King is dead. *(re-iss. Apr74 on 'Mooncrest'; CREST 10) (re-iss. Nov 75 & Apr80 on 'Mountain' lp/c; TOPC/TTOPC 5001) (cd-iss. May92 on 'Castle'; CLACD 286) (cd re-iss. Oct99 on 'Essential'; ESMCD 796)*

Jan 72. (7") *(PGS 2)* **DEAR JOHN. / FRIENDS** [ ] [-]

Jun 72. (7") *(PGS 4)* **MORNING DEW. / SPINNING TOP** [ ] [-]

Jun 72. (lp) *(PEG 14) <BS 2639>* **EXERCISES** [ ] [ ] Nov72
– I will not be led / Cat's eye, apple pie / In my time / Woke up this morning / Called her name / Fool about you / Love now you're gone / Madelaine / Sad song / 1692 (Glen Coe massacre). *(re-iss. Apr74 on 'Mooncrest'; CREST 14) (re-iss. Nov75 & Apr80 on 'Mountain' lp/c; TOPS/TTOPS 103) (re-iss. May85 on 'Sahara'; SAH 121) (cd-iss. Feb91 on 'Castle'; CLACD 220)*

Jul 72. (7") *<7599>* **MORNING DEW. / DEAR JOHN** [-] [ ]

Sep 72. (7") *(PGS 5)* **IF YOU SEE MY BABY. / HARD LIVING** [ ] [-]

Mooncrest | A&M

Apr 73. (7") *(MOON 1)* **BROKEN DOWN ANGEL. / WITCHDOCTOR WOMAN** [9] [-]

May 73. (lp/c) *(CREST 1) <SP 4396>* **RAZAMANAZ** [11] [ ]
– Razamanaz / Alcatraz / Vigilante man / Woke up this morning / Night woman / Bad, bad boy / Sold my soul / Too bad, too sad / Broken down angel. *(re-iss. Nov75 & Apr80 on 'Mountain' lp/c; TOPS/TTOPS 104) (re-iss. Oct82 on 'NEMS' lp/c; NEL/NEC 6023) (re-iss. Dec89 on 'Castle' lp/cd; CLA LP/CD 173) (cd re-iss. Sep96 on 'Essential'; ESMCD 370)*

Jul 73. (7"m) *(MOON 9)* **BAD, BAD BOY. / HARD LIVING / SPINNING TOP** [10] [-]

Sep 73. (7") *<1453>* **BROKEN DOWN ANGEL. / HARD LIVING** [-] [ ]

Oct 73. (7") *(MOON 14)* **THIS FLIGHT TONIGHT. / CALLED HER NAME** [11] [-]

Nov 73. (lp/c) *(CREST 4)* *<3609>* **LOUD 'N' PROUD** [10] [ ]
– Go down fighting / Not faking it / Turn on your receiver / Teenage nervous breakdown / Freewheeler / This flight tonight / Child in the sun / The ballad of Hollis Brown. *(re-iss. Nov75 & Apr80 on 'Mountain' lp/c; TOPS/TTOPS 105) (re-iss. Dec89 on 'Castle' lp/cd; CLA LP/CD 174) (cd re-iss. Oct96 on 'Essential'; ESMCD 379)*

Nov 73. (7") *<1469>* **BAD, BAD BOY. / RAZAMANAZ** [-] [ ]

Feb 74. (7") *<1511>* **THIS FLIGHT TONIGHT. / GO DOWN FIGHTING** [-] [ ]

Mar 74. (7") *(MOON 22)* **SHANGHAI'D IN SHANGHAI. / LOVE, NOW YOU'RE GONE** [41] [ ]

May 74. (lp/c) *(CREST 15)* *<3641>* **RAMPANT** [13] [ ]
– Silver dollar forger (parts 1 & 2) / Glad when you're gone / Loved and lost / Shanghai'd in Shanghai / Jet lag / Light my way / Sunshine / a) Shapes of things – b) Space safari. *(re-iss. Nov75 & Apr80 on 'Mountain' lp/c; TOPS/TTOPS 106) (cd-iss. Sep92 on 'Castle'; CLACD 242) (cd re-iss. May97 on 'Essential'; ESMCD 551)*

Jul 74. (7") *<1548>* **SUNSHINE. / THIS FLIGHT TONIGHT** [-] [ ]

Nov 74. (7") *(MOON 37)* *<1671>* **LOVE HURTS. / DOWN** [ ] [8] Nov75

Mar 75. (7") *(MOON 44)* **HAIR OF THE DOG. / TOO BAD, TOO SAD** [ ] [-]

Apr 75. (lp/c) *(CREST 27)* *<4511>* **HAIR OF THE DOG** [ ] [17]
– Hair of the dog / Miss Misery / Guilty * / Changin' times / Beggars day / Rose in the heather / Whisky drinkin' woman / Please don't Judas me. *(In the US, track* repl. by 'Love hurts') (re-iss. Nov75 & Apr80 on 'Mountain' lp/c; TOPS/TTOPS 107) (re-iss. Oct82 on 'NEMS' lp/c; NEL/NEC 6024) (re-iss. May85 on 'Sahara'; SAH 124) (cd-iss. Feb92 on 'Castle'; CLACD 241) (cd re-iss. May97 on 'Essential'; ESMCD 550)*

May 75. (7") *<1671>* **HAIR OF THE DOG. / LOVE HURTS** [-] [ ]

May 75. (7") *(MOON 47)* **MY WHITE BICYCLE. / MISS MISERY** [14] [ ]
(re-iss. 1979 on 'Mountain'; NAZ 10)

Mountain A&M

Oct 75. (7") *(TOP 3)* **HOLY ROLLER. / RAILROAD BOY** [36] [-]

Nov 75. (lp/c) *(TOPS/TTOPS 108)* *<9020>* **GREATEST HITS** (compilation) [54] [ ]
– Razamanaz / Holy roller / Shanghai'd in Shanghai / Love hurts / Turn on your receiver / Bad bad boy / This flight tonight / Broken down angel / Hair of the dog / Sunshine / My white bicycle / Woke up this morning *(re-iss. Oct82 on 'NEMS' lp/c; NEL/NEC 6022) (re-iss. Apr89 on 'Castle' lp/c/cd; CLA LP/MC/CD 149)*

Feb 76. (7") *(TOP 8)* *<1819>* **CARRY OUT FEELINGS. / LIFT THE LID** [ ] [ ]

Mar 76. (lp/c) *(TOPS/TTOPS 109)* *<4562>* **CLOSE ENOUGH FOR ROCK'N'ROLL** [ ] [24]
– Telegram (part 1:- On your way / part 2:- So you want to be a rock'n'roll star / part 3:- Sound check / part 4:- Here we are again) / Vicki / Homesick again / Vancouver shakedown / Born under the wrong sign / Loretta / Carry out feelings / Lift the lid / You're the violin. *(re-iss. May85 on 'Sahara'; SAH 126) (re-iss. Jun90 on 'Castle' lp/c/cd; CLA LP/MC/CD 182)*

Jun 76. (7") *(TOP 14)* **YOU'RE THE VIOLIN. / LORETTA** [ ] [-]

Sep 76. (7") *<1854>* **LIFT THE LID. / LORETTA** [-] [ ]

Nov 76. (7") *(TOP 21)* **I DON'T WANT TO GO ON WITHOUT YOU. / GOOD LOVE** [ ] [-]

Nov 76. (lp/c) *(TOPS/TTOPS 113)* *<4610>* **PLAY 'N' THE GAME** [ ] [75]
– Somebody to roll / Down home girl / Flying / Waiting for the man / Born to love / I want to (do everything for you) / I don't want to go on without you / Wild honey / L.A. girls. *(re-iss. May85 on 'Sahara; SAH 131) (cd-iss. Feb91 on 'Castle'; CLACD 219)*

Dec 76. (7") *<18??>* **I WANT TO (DO EVERYTHING FOR YOU). / BLACK CATS** [-] [ ]

Jan 77. (7") *(TOP 22)* **SOMEBODY TO ROLL. / VANCOUVER SHAKEDOWN** [ ] [ ]

Feb 77. (7") *<1895>* **I DON'T WANT TO GO ON WITHOUT YOU. / I WANT TO DO (EVERYTHING FOR YOU)** [-] [ ]

Apr 77. (7") *<1936>* **SOMEBODY TO ROLL. / THIS FLIGHT TONIGHT** [-] [ ]

Jun 77. (lp) *<4643>* **HOT TRACKS** (compilation) [-] [ ]

Sep 77. (7"ep) *(NAZ 1)* **HOT TRACKS** (compilation) [15] [-]
– Love hurts / This flight tonight / Broken down angel / Hair of the dog. *(re-iss. Jul80; HOT 1) (re-iss. Jan83 on 7"pic-ep on 'NEMS'; NEP 2)*

Nov 77. (lp/c) *(TOPS/TTOPS 115)* *<4666>* **EXPECT NO MERCY** [ ] [82]
– Expect no mercy / Gone dead train / Shot me down / Revenge is sweet / Gimme what's mine / Kentucky fried blues / New York broken toy / Busted / A place in your heart / All the king's horses. *(re-iss. May85 on 'Sahara'; SAH 123) (re-iss. Jun90 on 'Castle' cd/lp; CLA CD/LP 187) (re-iss. cd Sep93 on 'Elite'; ELITE 022CD)*

Jan 78. (7"m) *(NAZ 2)* **GONE DEAD TRAIN. / GREENS / DESOLATION ROAD** [49] [-]

Apr 78. (7") *(TOP 37)* **A PLACE IN YOUR HEART. / KENTUCKY FRIED BLUES** [70] [-]

Apr 78. (7") *<2009>* **SHOT ME DOWN. / KENTUCKY FRIED BLUES** [-] [ ]

Jul 78. (7") *<2029>* **GONE DEAD TRAIN. / KENTUCKY FRIED BLUES** [-] [ ]

—— added **ZAL CLEMINSON** (b. 4 May'49, Glasgow, Scotland) – guitar, synth. (ex-SENSATIONAL ALEX HARVEY BAND)

Jan 79. (7") *(NAZ 3)* *<2116>* **MAY THE SUNSHINE. / EXPECT NO MERCY** [22] [ ]

Jan 79. (lp/c) *(TOPS/TTOPS 123)* *<4741>* **NO MEAN CITY** [34] [88]
– Just to get into it / May the sun shine / Simple solution (parts 1 & 2) / Star / Claim to fame / Whatever you want babe / What's in it for me / No mean city (parts 1 & 2). *(re-iss. May85 on 'Sahara'; SAH 120) (re-iss. May91 on 'Castle' lp/c/cd; CLA LP/MC/CD 213)*

Apr 79. (7",7"purple) *(NAZ 4)* *<2130>* **WHATEVER YOU WANT BABE. / TELEGRAM (PARTS 1, 2 & 3)** [ ] [ ]

Jul 79. (7") *<2158>* **STAR. / EXPECT NO MERCY** [-] [ ]

Jul 79. (7") *(TOP 45)* **STAR. / BORN TO LOVE** [54] [-]

Jan 80. (7") *(TOP 50)* *<2219>* **HOLIDAY. / SHIP OF DREAMS** [ ] [87]

Jan 80. (lp/c) *(TOPS/TTOPS 126)* *<4799>* **MALICE IN WONDERLAND** [ ] [41]
– Holiday / Showdown at the border / Talkin' to one of the boys / Heart's grown cold / Fast cars / Big boy / Talkin' 'bout love / Fallen angel / Ship of dreams / Turning a new leaf. *(re-iss. Sep90 on 'Castle' cd/lp; CLA CD/LP 181)*

Apr 80. (7") *<2231>* **SHIP OF DREAMS. / HEARTS GROWN COLD** [-] [ ]

NEMS A&M

Dec 80. (d7") *(BSD 1)* **NAZARETH LIVE (live)** [ ] [-]
– Hearts grown cold / Talkin' to one of the boys / Razamanaz / Hair of the dog.

—— added **JOHN LOCKE** (b.25 Sep'43, Los Angeles, Calif.) – keyboards (ex-SPIRIT)

Feb 81. (lp/c) *(NEL/NEC 6019)* *<4844>* **THE FOOL CIRCLE** [60] [70]
– Dressed to kill / Another year / Moonlight eyes / Pop the Silo / Let me be your leader / We are the people / Every young man's dream / Little part of you / Cocaine (live) / Victoria. *(re-iss. Feb91 on 'Castle' cd/lp; CLA CD/LP 214)*

Mar 81. (7") *(NES 301)* *<2324>* **DRESSED TO KILL. / POP THE SILO** [ ] [ ]

—— **BILLY RANKIN** – guitar; repl. ZAL who joined TANDOORI CASSETTE

Sep 81. (d-lp/c) *(NELD/NELC 102)* *<6703>* **'SNAZ (live)** [78] [83]
– Telegram (part 1:- On your way – part 2:- So you want to be a rock'n'roll star – part 3:- Sound check) / Razamanaz / I want to do everything for you / This flight tonight / Beggars day / Every young man's dream / Heart's grown cold / Java blues / Cocaine / Big boy / Holiday / Dressed to kill / Hair of the dog / Expect no mercy / Shape of things / Let me be your leader / Love hurts / Tush / Juicy Lucy / Morning dew. *(re-iss. Jan87 on 'Castle' lp/c/cd; CLA LP/MC/CD 130) (cd re-iss. May97 on 'Essential'; ESMCD 531)*

Sep 81. (7") *(NES 302)* *<2378>* **MORNING DEW (live). / JUICY LUCY (live)** [ ] [ ]

Dec 81. (7") *<2389>* **HAIR OF THE DOG (live). / HOLIDAY (live)** [-] [ ]

Jul 82. (7") *(NIS 101)* *<2421>* **LOVE LEADS TO MADNESS. / TAKE THE RAP** [ ] [ ]

Aug 82. (7") *<2444>* **DREAM ON. / TAKE THE RAP** [-] [ ]

Jan 83. (7") *(NIS 102)* **GAMES. / YOU LOVE ANOTHER** [ ] [-]

Feb 83. (lp/c) *(NIN 001)* *<4901>* **2XS** [ ] [ ] Jun82
– Love leads to madness / Boys in the band / You love another / Gatecrash / Games / Back to the trenches / Dream on / Lonely in the night / Preservation / Take the rap / Mexico. *(cd-iss. Feb91 on 'Castle'; CLACD 217)*

Jun 83. (7") *(NIS 103)* **DREAM ON. / JUICY LUCY** [ ] [-]

Vertigo Capitol

Jun 83. (lp) *(812396-1)* **SOUND ELIXIR** [-] [ ] German
– All nite radio / Milk and honey / Whippin' boy / Rain on the window / Backroom boys / Why don't you read the book / I ran / Rags to riches / Local still / Where are you now. *(re-iss. Jul85 on 'Sahara'; SAH 130) (cd-iss. Feb91 on 'Castle'; CLACD 218)*

Jul 83. (7") *(812 544-7)* **WHERE ARE YOU NOW. / ON THE RUN** [-] [-] German

Sep 84. (lp/c) *(VERL/+C 20)* **THE CATCH** [ ] [ ]
– Party down / Ruby Tuesday / Last exit Brooklyn / Moondance / Love of freedom / This month's Messiah / You don't believe in us / Sweetheart tree / Road to nowhere.

Sep 84. (7") *(VER 13)* **RUBY TUESDAY. / SWEETHEART TREE** [ ] [ ]
(12"+=) *(VERX 13)* – This month's messiah / Do you think about it.

Oct 84. (7"/12") *(880 085-1/+Q)* **PARTY DOWN. / DO YOU THINK ABOUT IT** [-] [-] German

1986. (lp/cd) *(830 300-1/-2)* **CINEMA** [-] [-] Europe
– Cinema / Juliet / Just another heartache / Other side of you / Hit the fan / One from the heart / Salty salty / White boy / A veterans song / Telegram / This flight tonight. *(cd-iss. Sep97 on 'Essential'; ESMCD 500)*

1986. (7") *(884 982-7)* **CINEMA. / THIS FLIGHT TONIGHT (live)** [-] [-] Europe
(12"+=) *(884 981-1)* – Telegram (live).

1989. (lp/cd) *(838 426-1/-2)* **SNAKES 'N' LADDERS** [-] [-] Europe
– We are animals / Lady luck / Hang on to a dream / Piece of my heart / Trouble / The key / Back to school / Girls / Donna – Get off that crack / See you, see you / Helpless. *(UK cd-iss. May97 on 'Essential'; ESMCD 501)*

1989. (cd-s) *(874 733-2)* **PIECE OF MY HEART / LADY LUCK / SEE YOU SEE ME** [-] [-] German

1989. (7") *(876 448-7)* **WINNER ON THE NIGHT. / TROUBLE** [-] [-] German
(12"+=/cd-s+=) *(876 448-1/-2)* – Woke up this morning (live) / Bad, bad boy (live).

—— **BILLY RANKIN** – guitar; now totally repl. CHARLTON

Mausoleum Griffin

Nov 91. (cd/c/lp) *(3670010.2/.4/.1)* *<3932>* **NO JIVE** [ ] [ ] 1993
– Hire and fire / Do you wanna play house / Right between the eyes / Every time it rains / Keeping our love alive / Thinkin' man's nightmare / Cover your heart / Lap of luxury / a.The Rowan tree (traditional) – b.Tell me that you love me / Cry wolf. *(cd+=)* – This flight tonight. *(cd re-iss. Sep97 on 'Essential'; ESMCD 502)*

Jan 92. (7") *(3670010.7)* **EVERY TIME IT RAINS / THIS FLIGHT TONIGHT 1991** [ ] [-]
(12"+=/cd-s+=) *(3670010.0/.3)* – Lap of Luxury.

Mar 92. (cd-ep) *(903005.3)* **TELL ME THAT YOU LOVE ME / RIGHT BETWEEN THE EYES / ROWAN TREE – TELL ME THAT YOU LOVE ME (extended)** [ ] [-]

Essential Mayhem

May 97. (cd) *(ESMCD 503)* *<11076>* **MOVE ME** [ ] [ ] Oct95
– Let me be your dog / Can't shake these shakes / Crack me up / Move me / Steamroller / Stand by your beds / Rip it up / Demon alcohol / You had it comin' / Bring it on home to mama / Burning down.

—— **McCAFFERTY, AGNEW + SWEET** added **JIMMY MURRISON** – guitar + **RONNIE LEAHY** – keyboards

S.P.V. C.M.C.

Sep 98. (cd) *(SPV 0851850-2)* *<86263>* **BOOGALOO** [ ] [ ] Jan99
– Lights come down / Cheerleader / Loverman / Open up woman / Talk talk / Nothing so good / Party in the Kremlin / God save the South / Robber and the roadie / Waiting / May Heaven keep you.

—— on the 30th of April, 1999, DARRELL died

– compilations, others, etc. –

Jun 85. (d-lp) *Sahara; (SAH 137)* **20 GREATEST HITS** [ ] [-]

Jun 88. (d-lp/c/cd) *That's Original; (TFO LP/TC/CD 13)* **RAMPANT / HAIR OF THE DOG** [ ] [-]

Jul 88. (7") *Old Gold; (OG 9801)* **LOVE HURTS. / BAD BAD BOY** [ ] [-]

Jul 88. (7") *Old Gold; (OG 9803)* **THIS FLIGHT TONIGHT. / BROKEN DOWN ANGEL** [ ] [-]

Dec 88. (lp/c/cd) *Raw Power; (RAW LP/TC/CD 039)* **ANTHOLOGY** [ ] [-]

Jan 89. (cd-ep) *Special Edition; (CD3-17)* **THIS FLIGHT TONIGHT / BROKEN DOWN ANGEL / LOVE HURTS / BAD, BAD BOY** [ ] [-]

Jun 89. (cd) *Milestones; (MSSCD 102)* **MILESTONES** [ ] [-]
1990. (cd) *Ariola Express; (295969)* **BROKEN DOWN ANGEL** [ ] [-]
Jan 91. (cd/c/d-lp) *Castle; (CLA CD/MC/LP 280)* **THE SINGLES COLLECTION** [ ] [-]
– Broken down angel / Bad, bad boy / This flight tonight / Shanghai'd in Shanghai / Love hurts / Hair of the dog / My white bicycle / Holy roller / Carry out feelings / You're the violin / Somebody to roll / I don't want to go on without you / Gone dead train / A place in your heart / May the Sun shine / Star / Dressed to kill / Morning dew / Games / Love will lead to madness.
Oct 91. (3xcd-box) *Essential; (ESBCD 967)* **ANTHOLOGY** [ ] [-]
Nov 91. (cd) *Windsong; (WINDCD 005)* **BBC RADIO 1 LIVE IN CONCERT** [ ] [-]
Dec 91. (cd) *Dojo; (EARLCD 2)* **THE EARLY YEARS** [ ] [-]
Mar 92. (3xcd-box) *Castle; (CLABX 908)* **SNAZ / RAZAMANAZ / EXPECT NO MERCY** [ ] [-]
Apr 93. (cd) *Sequel; (NEMCD 639)* **FROM THE VAULTS** [ ] [-]
Jun 93. (cd/c) *Optima; (OPTM CD/C 009)* **ALIVE AND KICKING** [ ] [-]
Jun 94. (cd) *BR Music; (BRCD 1392)* **GREATEST HITS** [ ] [-]
Mar 96. (cd) *Disky; (CR 86711-2)* **CHAMPIONS OF ROCK** [ ] [-]
Oct 96. (cd) *Essential; (ESMCD 369)* **GREATEST HITS** [ ] [-]
Jul 98. (d-cd) *Reef; (SRDCD 707)* **LIVE AT THE BEEB** [ ] [-]
(d-cd re-iss. Feb00 on 'Snapper'; SMDCD 272)
Oct 98. (3xcd-box) *Essential; (ESMBX 308)* **RAZAMANAZ / LOUD 'N' PROUD / HAIR OF THE DOG** [ ] [-]
Apr 01. (d-cd)(t-lp) *Receiver; (RDPCD 016)(RRLT 009)* **BACK TO THE TRENCHES (live 1972-1984)** [ ] [-]

DAN McCAFFERTY

with some members of NAZARETH and SAHB

Mountain / A&M

Aug 75. (7") *(TOP 1) <1753>* **OUT OF TIME. / CINNAMON GIRL** [41] [ ]
Oct 75. (lp/c) *(TOPS/TTOPS 102)* **DAN McCAFFERTY** [ ] [ ]
– The honky tonk downstairs / Cinnamon girl / The great pretender / Boots of Spanish leather / Watcha gonna do about it / Out of time / You can't lie to a liar / Trouble / You got me hummin' / Stay with me baby. *(cd-iss. Jul94 on 'Sequel'; NEMCD 640)*
Nov 75. (7") *(TOP 5)* **WHATCHA GONNA DO ABOUT IT. / NIGHTINGALE** [ ] [-]
Mar 78. (7"m) *(DAN 1)* **STAY WITH ME, BABY. / OUT OF TIME / WATCHA GONNA DO ABOUT IT** [ ] [-]
Aug 78. (7") *(TOP 18)* **THE HONKY TONK DOWNSTAIRS. / TROUBLE** [ ] [-]
Aug 79. (7") *(TOP 47)* **BOOTS OF SPANISH LEATHER. / WATCHA GONNA DO ABOUT IT** [ ] [-]

—— with German musicians + **PETE AGNEW** – bass

Mercury / not iss.

1987 (lp/cd) *(830 934-1/-2)* **INTO THE RING** [-] [-] German
– Into the ring / Backstage pass / Starry eyes / My sunny island / For a car / Caledonia / Headin' for South America / The departure (instrumental) / Southern Cross / Where the ocean ends we'll find a new born land / Sally Mary / Island in the Sun / Albatross / The last ones will be the first after all / Reprise.
1987. (7") *(888 397-7)* **STARRY EYES. / SUNNY ISLAND** [-] [-] German
(12"+=/cd-s+=) *(888 397-1/-2)* – Where the ocean ends, we'll find a new born land.

NEBULA

Formed: Los Angeles, California, USA . . . 1997 by former high school mates and FU MANCHU rhythm men MARK ABSHIRE and RUBEN ROMANO, the trio completed by another FU man, guitarist/vocalist EDDIE GLASS. Yet NEBULA certainly stood their ground against their former band, producing some memorable heavy rock in the BLACK SABBATH vein. With the members' musical abilities already proved through frenetic live shows, NEBULA were quickly signed up to the 'Tee Pee' label, who released their first spirited bout of rock, the EP, 'LET IT BURN' (re-issued in 1998 by 'Relapse' with two extra tunes). This mini-set let fans know that they hadn't passed their prime with FU MANCHU, and mixed exciting chunky riffing with hard rock – a must for all air-guitarists. NEBULA followed this up with 'SUN CREATURE' (1999). This EP showed again their influences matching up to some of LED ZEPPELIN's earlier heavier material, with stoner-rock titles like 'ROLLIN' MY WAY TO FREEDOM' and 'SMOKIN' WOMAN' probably their finest yet. The trio's first full-length, 'TO THE CENTER' (1999) was released the same year. Again, as with their former outings, NEBULA's zeal and excitement shone through; standout tracks were 'WHAT YOU'RE LOOKING FOR', and 'COME DOWN'. There was also a good bit of fretboard fingering and extended jams to keep their more chemically relaxed following happy. The album also featured a cover of the Stooges' 'I NEED SOMEBODY', with MARK ARM from MUDHONEY on vocals. 2001 saw NEBULA working with experienced British knob-twiddler, JOHN AGNELLO (who had worked with DINOSAUR JR. and CHAINSAW KITTENS), and he helped create their second full-length piece, 'CHARGED'.

Album rating: TO THE CENTER (*7) / CHARGED (*6)

EDDIE GLASS – vocals, guitar (ex-OLIVELAWN, ex-FU MANCHU) / **MARK ABSHIRE** – bass / **RUBEN ROMANO** – drums

Last Scream / not iss.

Nov 97. (7"ep; split) *(SCREAM 010)* **NEBULA / THAT'S ALL FOLKS** [-] [-] Italy
– Vulcan bomber / Skydiver / THAT'S ALL FOLKS: Aquasphere.

Tee Pee / Tee Pee

Feb 98. (cd-ep) *(TP 001)* **NEBULA** [ ] [ ]
– Anything from you / Full throttle / Back to the dawn / Fall of Icarus. *(re-iss. Sep98 as 12"ep; TP 006LP)*
Oct 98. (cd-ep/12"ep) *<(TP 010/+LP)>* **LET IT BURN** [ ] [ ]
– Elevation / Down the highway / Let it burn / Vulcan bomber / Dragon eye / Raga in the bloodshot pyramid. *<(re-iss. FEb99 on 'Relapse'+=; RR 6991)>* – Sonic titan / Devil's liquid.

Meteor City / Meteor City

Feb 99. (12"ep/cd-ep; split) *<(MCY 002/004)>* **NEBULA / LOWRIDER** [ ] [ ] Nov98
(re-iss. Sep00 as 'SOARING PSYCHEDELIC MASTERPIECES' on 'Century Media' cd/lp; 88995-2/-1)

Man's Ruin / Man's Ruin

Mar 99. (10"ep) *<(MR 133)>* **SUN CREATURE EP** [ ] [ ]
– Rollin' my way to freedom / Sun creature / Smokin' woman.
(cd-ep+=) *<(MR 133CD)>* – Fly on.

Sweet Nothing / Sub Pop

Oct 99. (cd/lp) *(SNCD/SNLP 002) <SP 493>* **TO THE CENTER** [ ] [ ] Aug99
– To the center / Come down / Whatcha looking for / Clearlight / Freedom / Antigone / I need somebody / So low / Synthetic dream / Fields of psilocybin / Between time / You mean nothin'.
May 00. (7"clear) *(7SN 001)* **CLEARLIGHT. / HUMBUCKER** [ ] [-]
(cd-s+=) *(CDSSN 001)* – Full throttle (live).
Apr 01. (7") *(7SN 004)* **DO IT NOW. / COSMIC EGG** [ ] [-]
(cd-s+=) *(CDSSN 004)* – Untitled.
Apr 01. (cd/lp) *(SNCD/SNLP 008) <SP 535>* **CHARGED** [ ] [ ]
– Do it now / Beyond / Giant / Travelin' man's blues / Instant gravitation / This one / Ignition / Shaker / Goodbye yesterday / All the way.

NECROPHAGIA

Formed: Ohio, USA . . . 1983 by the pseudonymous KILLJOY. An appropriate name for a death-metal/thrash-gore outfit, NECROPHAGIA meaning the eating of dead flesh – mmm yummy. However, after a 1987 debut LP, 'SEASON OF THE DEAD' (1987), they disbanded when others (apart from KILLJOY) wanted to become the new QUEENSRYCHE. KILLJOY re-formed ten years later, recruiting the assistance of ANTON CROWLEY, WAYNE FABRA, and DUSTIN HAVNEN. KILLJOY had kept the hope alive and in the meantime he went through several incarnations himself, but all in the death/gore metal spirit of things; his self-titled band, KILLJOY, and CABAL. In 1997 he found his chosen dark crew and NECROPHAGIA rose again. As with the original band their chosen subject matter was horror and gore, a more original idea back in 1987, but in the late 90's it was a fairly staple ingredient of many death metal artists. KILLJOY and his new players though were not just doing it for the shock of it; they were obsessed with horror movies, dedicating NECROPHAGIA's long in coming second album, 'HOLOCAUSTO DE LA MORTE' (1998), to their favourite gore/horror movie director, Lucio Fulgi. This set is a fairly good death metal piece dripping with sick and twisted lyrics; comparable to CHRIS BARNES' work with CANNIBAL CORPSE, and his later band, SIX FEET UNDER, although perhaps with less horror movie references. It is worth noting the side-projects of KILLJOY, who kept himself on his toes, with his own label, 'Baphomet', who signed VIKING CROWN, ANTAEUS, and THORNSPAWN among others. Also worth mentioning is the role KILLJOY played in the metal supergroup, EIBON, which included a roster of PHIL ANSELMO from PANTERA, MANIAC from MAYHEM, and SATYR from SATYRICON. His other musical side-project, the elemental RAVENOUS, also kept KILLJOY in work, with bandmates DAN CORRUES and CHRIS REIFERT.

Album rating: SEASON OF THE DEAD (*5) / HOLOCAUSTO DE LA MORTE (*6) / BLACK BLOOD VOMITORIUM mini (*5) / A LEGACY OF HORROR, GORE AND SICKNESS (*4) / DEATH IS FUN (*4) / Viking Crown: UNORTHODOX STEPS OF RITUAL mini (*4) / INNOCENCE FROM HELL (*5) / Antaeus: CUT YOUR FLESH AND WORSHIP SATAN mini (*4)

KILLJOY – vocals / + unknown

New Renaissance / not iss.

Sep 87. (lp/c/cd) *(NR R/C/CD 15)* **SEASON OF THE DEAD** [ ] [-]
– Season of the dead / Forbidden pleasure / Bleeding torment / Insane for blood / Reincarnation / Ancient slumber / Mental decay / Abomination / Terminal vision / Painful discharge / Beyond and back.

—— split after above when they had a differing musical opinion

—— KILLJOY made a solo/band album (and a demo), 'COMPELLED BY FEAR' (1989). Afterwards he formed CABAL but an album was shelved; NECROPHAGIA were back again in '97 with **KILLJOY** plus **ANTON CROWLEY** – guitar / **WAYNE FABRA** – drums / **DUSTIN HAVNEN** – bass

Plague / Orchard

May 99. (cd) *(PLAGUE 001CD) <132>* **HOLOCAUSTO DE LA MORTE** [ ] [ ] Mar00
– Blood freak / Embalmed yet I breathe / The cross burns black / Deep inside, I plant the Devil's seed / Burning moon sickness / Cadaverous screams of my deceased lover / Children of the vortex / Hymns of divine genocide. *(re-iss. May00; same)*

Red Stream / not iss.

Mar 00. (m-cd) *(RSR 0131)* **BLACK BLOOD VOMITORIUM** [ ] [-]
– And you will live in terror / They dwell beneath / It lives in the woods / Black blood vomitorium.

Baphomet / Baphomet

Oct 00. (cd) *(<BAPH 2114CD>)* **A LEGACY OF HORROR, GORE AND SICKNESS** [ ] [ ]
– Bold funeral / Lust of the naked dead / Semorage / Ready for death / Ancient clumber / Black apparition / Blood thirst / Rental decan / Communion of death / Return to life / Bitchcraft / Autopsy on the living dead / Death is pain / Communion of death / Insane for blood / Rise from the crypt / Hill / Chainsaw lust / Demonic possession. *(d-lp iss.Mar01 on 'Vinyl Collectors'; VC 006)*

—— **JARED FAULK** – bass; repl. HAVNEN

– compilations, others, etc. –

May 01. (cd) *Red Stream; (RSR 0142)* **DEATH IS FUN** ☐ ☐-
– Abomination / Young burial / Black apparition / Chainsaw lust / Death is fun / Intense mutilation / Autopsy on the living dead / Bitchcraft / Power through darkness / Young burial / Chainsaw lust / Autopsy on the living dead.

VIKING CROWN

KILLJOY + others

Hammerheart not iss.

Nov 99. (m-lp/m-cd) *(HHR 054/+CD)* **UNORTHODOX STEPS OF RITUAL** ☐ ☐-
– Intro / Asmodeus rising / Satan ruler of Earth / Lust and destruction / The Judas goat / Unorthodox steps of ritual / Blaspheme / Invocation toward the conjuration of black souls.

Baphomet Baphomet

May 00. (cd) *(<BAPH 2109CD>)* **INNOCENCE FROM HELL** ☐ ☐
– Intro: Song of Faduf / Innocence from Hell / The burning emherf of mockery / Birth of the Devil fetus / The red flame of tin / Overloard of infinite depression / The long and mighty reign of Satan / Raped by an angel / The seventh form of the blood demon / The gathering / Outro: The blood of Sadus.

ANTAEUS

KILLJOY + others

Nov 00. (m-cd) *(<BAPH 2113CD>)* **CUT YOUR FLESH AND WORSHIP SATAN** ☐ ☐
– Inner war / Seventh ceremony / Devotee / Those with no eyes / Specimen 23 / Bleeding blasphemy / Nihil chaos / Daemon.

NECROPHOBIC

Formed: Sweden . . . 1989 by DAVID PARLAND, TOBIAS SIDEGARD, ANDERS STROKIRK and JOAKIM STERNER. The band set out to deliver to the world of death metal their uncompromising version of events, as they later became miffed with other bands of the genre selling-out the style for greater commercial success. Their first three track demo in 1990, 'SLOW ASPHYXIATION', gained these Swedes attention in both the American and European underground metal scene; several of the tunes ending up on a compilation for the Austrian label 'Witchhunt'. Stateside interest in the band culminated in two small outings with 'Wild Rags' records, the second of which, the 7" EP 'THE CALL', got limited pressings but sold out so fast that it has now become a bit of a rarity. After this, NECROPHOBIC looked for a more long-term contract and found this with 'Black Mark Productions', who released the band's first full-length album, 'THE NOCTURNAL SILENCE' (1993). The set was a sinister slice of black metal which was certainly palatable to the rock critics, gaining the band several merits with this fraternity. Shortly after though STROKIRK departed, leaving SIDEGARD to pick up the vocal reins, while MARTIN HALFDAN joined to bolster the guitar sound. Along with this re-shuffle came a long period away from the recording studio, during which time PARLAND bailed out and was replaced by SEBASTIAN RAMSTEDT. 'PHOBIC's next full-length album was 'DARKSIDE' (1997), and, by their own admission, was a response to the watering down of death metal that had been going on in their absence. Thus the group made their album faster, harder and heavier. Two years on though, it seemed NECROPHOBIC were also keen to try out other possibilities with the album, 'THE THIRD ANTICHRIST' (1999) – sticking in a few slow numbers among their normal rabid arrangements. • **Covered:** ENTER THE ETERNAL FIRE (Bathory) / DIE BY THE SWORD (Slayer) / NIGHTMARE (Venom).

Album rating: NOCTURNAL SILENCE (*4) / SPAWNED BY EVIL mini (*3) / DARKSIDE (*6) / THE THIRD ANTICHRIST (*4)

STEFAN HARRVIK – vocals / **DAVID PARLAND** – guitar / **TOBIAS SIDEGARD** – bass / **JOAKIM STERNER** – drums

not iss. Wild Rags

Jan 92. (c-ep) **UNHOLY PROPHECIES EP** ☐- ☐
Jan 93. (7"ep) **THE CALL EP** ☐- ☐
– Shadows of the Moon / The ancients gate / Father of creation.

—— **ANDERS STROKIRK** – vocalsl repl. HARRVIK

Black Mark Black Mark

Aug 93. (cd) *(<BMCD 40>)* **THE NOCTURNAL SILENCE** ☐ ☐ Feb94
– Awakening . . . / Before the dawn / Unholy prophecies / The nocturnal silence / Shadows of the moon / The ancients gate / Sacrificial rites / Father of creation / Where sinners burn.

—— **MARTIN HALFDAN** – guitar; repl. STROKIRK (SIDEGARD + vocals)

May 96. (m-cd) *(BMCD 60)* **SPAWNED BY EVIL** ☐- ☐- Sweden
– Spawned by evil / Die by the sword / Nightmare / Enter the eternal fire.

—— now without PARLAND

Mar 97. (cd) *(<BMCD 96>)* **DARKSIDE** ☐ ☐
– Black moon rising / Spawned by evil / Bloodthirst / Vaneaesectio / Call / Descension.

—— added **SEBASTIAN RAMSTEDT** – guitar

S.P.V. Black Mark

Nov 99. (cd) *(SPV 085-13369-2)* *<BMCD 146>* **THE THIRD ANTICHRIST** ☐ ☐ Nov00
– Rise of the infernal / The third of arrivals / Frozen empire / Into armageddon / Eye of the storm / The unhallowed / Isaz / The throne of souls possessed / He who rideth in rage / Demonic / One last step into the great mist.

—— **JOHAN BERGEBACK** – guitar; repl. HALFDAN

NECROS

Formed: Maumee, Ohio, USA . . . summer '79 by BARRY HENSSLER, BRIAN POLLACK, COREY RUSK and TODD SWALLA. One of the first acts to sign for 'Touch & Go', the NECROS unleashed their debut EP, 'SEX DRIVE', in early '81, experimenting with hardcore punk. Youthful, brash and 'orrible, this outfit was not to be confused with Washington DC's similarly named hardcore troopers who released an eponymous set for 'Dischord' the same year. The Ohio NECROS returned in '83 with a new guitarist, ANDY WENDLER (to replace POLLACK), the man taking up his post for their debut long-player, 'CONQUEST FOR DEATH'. Another sabbatical ensued before the NECROS came back to life with an album on 'Restless', 'TANGLED UP' (1987), a more straight-down-the-line metallic affair that featured the track, 'BIG CHIEF', a title that departing frontman HENSSLER would later use as the moniker for his new band.

Album rating: CONQUEST FOR DEATH (*6) / TANGLED UP (*6) / LIVE OR ELSE (*4)

BARRY HENSSLER – vocals / **BRIAN POLLACK** – guitar / **COREY RUSK** – bass / **TODD SWALLA** – drums

not iss. Touch & Go

Feb 81. (7"ep) **SEX DRIVE / POLICE BRUTALITY. / BETTER NEVER THAN LATE / CASTE SYSTEM** ☐- ☐
Oct 81. (7"ep) *<No.4 1/2>* **THE NECROS EP** ☐- ☐
– I.Q. 32 / Youth camp / Peer pressure / Race riot / Wargame / I hate my school / Past comes back to haunt me / Reject / Public high school.
(above was probably the NECROS from Washington DC on 'Dischord')

—— **ANDY WENDLER** – guitar; repl. POLLACK

1983. (lp) **CONQUEST FOR DEATH** ☐- ☐
– Search for fame / Tarnished words / No one / Satisfy / Bad dream / Police brutality / Andy's shit for brunch / Conquest for death / Count me out / Change / Crying form / Face forward / Friend to all.

Enigma Restless

Jun 87. (lp) *(2203-1)* *<971295>* **TANGLED UP** ☐ ☐
– Gun / Blizzard of glass / Big chief / Open wound / Tangled up / Power of fear / Black water / Noise / 500 years a pack of kools / Nile song / A house full of drunks.

—— HENSSLER bailed out and subsequently formed BIG CHIEF

not iss. Enigma

1989. (lp) *<72220>* **LIVE OR ELSE** ☐- ☐

—— disbanded after above

Vince NEIL (see under ⇒ MOTLEY CRUE)

NEPHILIM (see under ⇒ FIELDS OF THE NEPHILIM)

Mike NESS (see under ⇒ SOCIAL DISTORTION)

NEUROSIS

Formed: Oakland, California, USA . . . 1987 by STEVE VON TILL, DAVE EDWARDSON, SCOTT KELLY, NOAH LANDIS and JASON ROEDER. Hardcore extremists combining a barrage of tribal metal/industrial grind with apocalyptic psychedelia, NEUROSIS debuted in 1988 with the self-explanatory 'PAIN OF MIND' set. The early 90's saw the band's material more readily available to UK audiences following a deal with JELLO BIAFRA's 'Alternative Tentacles' label. Recently re-issued on 'Music For Nations', the 'SOULS AT ZERO' (1992) and 'ENEMY OF THE SUN' (1993) carried on in reliably brutalising style, NEUROSIS' despairing worldview of violence, destruction etc, set to a soul-shredding soundtrack of rhythmically punishing noise. Originally issued as a US-only affair, 'THROUGH SILVER IN BLOOD' (1996), its sanity-threatening assault putting the group at the vanguard of the genre alongside the likes of GODFLESH. With the legendary STEVE ALBINI now at the mixing desk, NEUROSIS completed their 5th set proper, 'TIMES OF GRACE' (1999), another rifftastic, heavy ear-bashing that deserved all the plaudits. While working in the studio, the group – who were now a sextet featuring visual guy PETE INC – found they had some talent in the ambient/avant-garde department. Their alter-ego TRIBES OF NEUROT have since surfaced on numerous occasions since their late 1997 debut, 'SILVER BLOOD TRANSMISSION'.

Album rating: PAIN OF MIND (*7) / SOULS AT ZERO (*6) / ENEMY OF THE SUN (*4) / THROUGH SILVER IN BLOOD (*6) / TIMES OF GRACE (*7) / SOVEREIGN mini (*4)

STEVE VON TILL – vocals, guitar / **DAVE EDWARDSON** – bass, vocals / **SCOTT KELLY** – guitar, vocals / **NOAH LANDIS** – keyboards / **JASON ROEDER** – drums

Alchemy Alchemy

Apr 88. (lp/c) *(VM 105/+C)* **PAIN OF MIND** ☐ ☐
– Pain of mind / Self-taught infection / Reasons to hide / Black / Training / Progress / Stalemate / Bury what's dead / Geneticide / Ingrown / United sheep / Dominoes fall / Life on your knees / Grey. *<(re-iss. May94 on 'Alternative Tentacles' lp/cd; VIRUS 146/+CD)> (d-cd-iss. Nov00 on 'Neurot'; NEUROT 010DCD)*

not iss. Lookout

1991. (lp/cd) *<LOOKOUT/+CD 21>* **THE WORD IS LAW** ☐- ☐
– Double edged sword / The choice / Obsequious obsolescence / To what end? / Tomorrow's reality / Common inconsistencies / Insensitity / Blisters / Life on your knees / Pain of mind / Grey / United sheep / Pollution / Day of the lords. *(cd-iss. May99; LK 21CD)*

Your Choice / Your Choice

Jun 92. (7"ep) *(YCR 014)* **NEUROSIS LIVE (live)**

Alternative Tentacles / Alternative Tentacles

Jun 92. (lp/c/cd) *<(VIRUS 109/+C/CD)>* **SOULS AT ZERO**
– To crawl under one's skin / Souls at zero / Zero / Flight / The web / Sterile vision / A chronological for survival / Stripped. *(c+=/cd+=)* – Takehnase / Empty. *(cd re-iss. Jul99 on 'Neurot'; NER 3)*

Oct 93. (lp/c/cd) *<(VIRUS 134/+C/CD)>* **ENEMY OF THE SUN**
– Lost / Raze the stray / Burning flesh in the year of the pig / Cold ascending / Lexicon / Enemy of the sun. *(c+=/cd+=)* – The time of the beasts / Cleanse.

Iron City / Relapse

Jun 96. (cd/lp) *(ICR 002 CD/LP) <6938>* **THROUGH SILVER IN BLOOD** Apr96
– Through silver in blood / Rehumanize / Eye / Purify / Locust star / Strength of fates / Become the ocean / Aeon / Enclosure in flame. *(cd re-iss. Oct97 on 'Music For Nations'; CDMFN 235)*

—— added **PETE INC** – visuals

Music For Nations / Relapse

Aug 99. (cd/lp) *(CD+/MFN 249) <RR 3419-2/-1>* **TIMES OF GRACE**
– Suspended in light / The doorway / Under the surface / The last you'll know / Belief / Exist / End of the harvest / Descent / Away / Times of grace / The road to sovereignty. *(cd re-iss. Nov99; same as US)*

Music For Nations / Neurot

Oct 00. (m-cd) *(CDMFNM 258) <8>* **SOVEREIGN**
– Prayer / Offering / Flood / Sovereign.

– compilations, etc. –

Oct 97. (d-cd) *Music For Nations; (CDMFN 234)* **SOULS AT ZERO / ENEMY OF THE SUN**

Feb 00. (cd) *Short Wave Warfare; <(SWW 1CD)>* **SHORT WAVE WARFARE**

Dec 00. (cd) *Short Wave Warfare; <(SWW 2CD)>* **ENEMY LIVE – NEW YORK CITY 1994**

TRIBES OF NEUROT

the alter-ego of NEUROSIS

Relapse / Relapse

Jan 98. (cd) *<(RR 6929-2)>* **SILVER BLOOD TRANSMISSION** Jul97
– Primordial uncarved block / Wolf lava / Fires of purification / The accidental process / Fall back to stone / A manifestation by modern means / Achtwan / Continuous regression / Closing in.

Mar 98. (cd; shared w/ WALKING TIMEBOMBS) *<(RR 6972-2)>* **STATIC MIGRATION** Jan98
– Unspoken path / Rust / Recurring birth / March to the sun / Origin unknown / Blood and water / Edgewood / Head of the scorpion.

Feb 98. (m-cd) *<9012>* **REBEGIN** [-]
– intro / Water / Air / Earth / Fire.

Man's Ruin / Man's Ruin

May 98. (10"lp/m-cd) *<(MR 086/+CD)>* **ADAPTATION AND SURVIVAL**

Neurot / Neurot

Sep 99. (cd) *<(NER 005CD)>* **GRACE**
– Suspended in light / The doorway / Under the silence / The last you'll know / Belief / Exist / End of the harvest / Descent / Away / Times of grace / The road to sovereignty.

Nov 00. (cd) *<(NEUROT 009CD)>* **60 DEGREES**
– Trial / Left to wander / Chance encounter / All things must pass / Markandaya / Origin and destiny / Broken ring / Desire and delusion / Cathartides / From Charon to Seoul.

NEVERMORE (see under ⇒ SANCTUARY)

NEW BOMB TURKS

Formed: Columbus, Ohio, USA . . . 1990 by Ohio University students ERIC DAVIDSON, JIM WEBER, MATT REBER and BILL RANDT. Akin to a fusion of IGGY POP, DEAD BOYS and The DWARVES, their brand of melody-fuelled punk was initially heard on US-only singles before they signed to 'Crypt' and issued a highly praised (in underground circles at least) debut album, '!!DESTROY-OH-BOY!!' (1993). A follow-up, 'INFORMATION HIGHWAY REVISITED' (1994), appeared a couple of years later to equally effusive praise and despite a resurgence in interest for nu-punk in the wake of grunge, the band's profile and sales remained low. 1995 saw the release of a collaboration with The ENTOMBED, misanthropically titled 'I HATE PEOPLE', as well as a double set, 'PISSIN' OUT THE POISON', which collected the group's early singles; including a plethora of covers: SUMMER ROMANCE (Rolling Stones) / I WANNA SLEEP (Modern Lovers) / BAD GIRL (New York Dolls) / CHRISTMAS (Phil Spector, etc) / YOUNGBLOOD (Wild Billy Childish) / etc. Subsequently signing with the seminal 'Epitaph' label, the group released 'SCARED STRAIGHT' in 1996 and needless to say turned a tad heavier.

Album rating: !!DESTROY-OH-BOY!! (*5) / INFORMATION HIGHWAY REVISITED (*7) / PISSIN' OUT THE POISON compilation (*6) / SCARED STRAIGHT (*7) / AT ROPE'S END (*6) / THE BIG COMBO (*5) / NIGHTMARE SCENARIO (*6)

ERIC DAVIDSON – vocals / **JIM WEBER** – guitar / **MATT REBER** – bass / **BILL RANDT** – drums

not iss. / Munster

1990's. (7") **DRAGSTRIP RIOT. / CRYIN' INTO THE BEER OF A DRUNK MAN** [-]

not iss. / Bag Of Hammers

1990's. (7") **SHARPEN-UP TIME. / LAISSEZ FAIR STATE** [-]

not iss. / Sympathy F

Jan 93. (cd-s) *<SFTRI 228>* **TRYING TO GET BY. / LAST LOST FIGHT** [-]

Crypt / Crypt

Apr 93. (lp/cd) *(EFA 11560/+D) <32>* **!!DESTROY-OH-BOY!!**
– Born Toulouse-Lautrec / Tail crush / Up for a downside / Tattooed apathethic boys / Dragstrip riot / We give a rat's ass / Runnin' on go / Lone gone sister / Mr. Suit / Let's dress up the naked truth / Hapless attempt / I want my baby . . . dead? / Sucker punch / I'm weak / Tryin' to get by / Cryin' into the beer of a drunk man. *<(re-iss. Feb00; same)>*

Oct 93. (7") *(DAM 26)* **BOTTLE ISLAND. /**
(above issued on 'Damaged Goods') (below on 'Helter Skelter')

Feb 94. (7") *(EFA 402977)* **DOGS ON 45. / (other track by DEVIL DOGS)**
(below on 'Sympathy For The . . .')

Oct 94. (7") *<(SFTRI 319)>* **(GOTTA, GOTTA) SINKING FEELING. /**

Oct 94. (lp/cd) *(EFA 11585-1/-2) <49>* **INFORMATION HIGHWAY REVISITED**
– It slips in / Bullish on / If I only could / Brother Orson Welles / T.A.S. / Fingernail chomp / Dented 'n' spent / Girl can't help it / (Gotta gotta) Sinking feeling / Grandpa atomic / Never will / Apocalyptic dipstick / Lyin' on our backs / I got you bitter end / Straight-on chaser. *<(re-iss. Feb00; same)>*

—— (In Jun'95, they shared a single with The ENTOMBED, 'I HATE PEOPLE')

Oct 95. (d-lp/cd) *(EFA 11598-1/-2) <58>* **PISSIN' OUT THE POISON**
(compilation of all early 45's)
– Tail crush / Out of my mind / Cryin' in the beer of a drunk man / Just head / Let's dress up to the naked truth / Do the pop / Sucker punch / Spinnin' clock / Summer romance / The girl can't help it / Got no proof / Polyester thinking cap / Last lost fight / We need more / Sharpen-up time / Laissez faire state / Croonin' into the beer of a drunk man / Pist / Deathbedside manner / I wanna sleep / Youngblood / Taller order / Bad girl / Ejection / Christmas (baby please come home) / Anal swipe. *<(re-iss. Feb00; same)>*

Fat Wreck Chords / Fat Wreck Chords

Jul 96. (7") *<(FAT 542-7)>* **STICK IT OUT. / STILL NEVER WILL / JOB**

Epitaph / Epitaph

Aug 96. (cd/c/lp) *<(86479-2/-4/-1)>* **SCARED STRAIGHT**
– Hammerless nail / Bachelor's high / Professional gangster / Cultural elite sign-up sheet / Jukebox lean / Jeers of a clown / Look alive jive / Staring down the gift horse / Shoot the offshoot / Drop what you're doin' / Telephone numbrrr / Wrest your hands.

Jun 97. (7") *(WAL 015)* **PROFESSIONAL AGAINSTER. /**
(above single on 'Wallabies' & below on 'Munster')

Jul 97. (7") *(DLM 179)* **DRAGSTRIP RIOT. /** [-]

Mar 98. (7") *(SFTRI 553)* **SNAP DECISION. / JAGUAR RIDE**
(above on 'Sympathy For The Record Industry')

Mar 98. (cd/c/lp) *<(6515-2/-4/-1)>* **AT ROPE'S END**
– Scapegoat soup / Snap decisions / Ally smile / So long silver lining / Veronica Lake / Defiled / Bolan's crash / Raw law / Minimum wages of sin / At rope's end / Common cold shoulder / Aspirin aspirations / Streamline yr skull.

Mar 98. (7"ep/cd-ep) *(1001-7/-2)* **VERONICA LAKE EP**
– Veronica Lake / Snap decision / Double Marlon (rough mix) / Don't Kimosabe me (demo).

Nov 98. (7"ep/cd-ep) *(1011-7/-2)* **RAW LAW / SO LONG SILVER LINING / HAMMERLESS NAIL / TAIL CRUSH**

Apr 99. (cd/lp) *<(BEHIND 001/+LP)>* **THE BIG COMBO**
– Stick it out / Feel it / (Still) Never will / Slung jury / Bachelor's high / Professional againster / Jivin' sister Fanny / Streamline yr skull / Job / Veronica Lake / Don't kimosabe me / Fuck it / So long silver lining (live) / Hammerless nail (live) / Tail crush (live) / Eyes of Satan. (above issued on 'Drop Kick')

Jun 00. (cd/lp) *<(6561-2/-1)>* **NIGHTMARE SCENARIO** Apr00
– Point A to point blank / Automatic teller / End of the great credibility race / Too much / Killer's kiss / Continental cats / Spanish fly by night / The roof / Your beaten heart / Turning tricks / Wine and depression / Quarter to four / Untitled.

NEW ENGLAND

Formed: East Coast, USA . . . 1979 by JOHN FANNON, JIMMY WALDO, GARY SHEA and HIRSH GARDENER. Appearing on the 'Infinity' label, the band's debut album was co-produced by PAUL STANLEY (Kiss), the record subsequently hitting the US Top 50 in summer of the same year. A hard-edged AOR outfit in the airbrushed American tradition, the group's attitude to the (then) current punk explosion was explicitly encapsulated on 'P.U.N.K. (Puny Under Nourished Kid)'. A further two US-only albums, 'EXPLORER SUITE' (1980) and the TODD RUNDGREN-produced 'WALKING WILD' (1981), appeared on 'Elektra' although the band struggled to build on their early chart success and subsequently split. SHEA and WALDO later formed ALCATRAZZ along with GRAHAM BONNET and YNGWIE MALMSTEEN.

Album rating: NEW ENGLAND (*5) / EXPLORER SUITE (*4) / WALKING WILD (*4)

JOHN FANNON – vocals, guitar / **JIMMY WALDO** – keyboards / **GARY SHEA** – bass / **HIRSH GARDENER** – drums

Infinity / Infinity

Apr 79. (7") *<50,013>* **DON'T EVER WANNA LOSE YA. / SHOOT** [-] [40]

Aug 79. (7") *(INF 113)* **DON'T EVER WANNA LOSE YA. / ENCORE** [-]

Aug 79. (lp) *(INS 2005) <9007>* **NEW ENGLAND** [50] May79
– Hello, hello, hello / Don't ever wanna lose ya / P.U.N.K. (Puny Under Nourished Kid) / Shall I run away / Alone tonight / Nothing to fear / Shoot / Turn out the light / The last show / Encore.

Aug 79. (7") *<50,021>* **HELLO, HELLO, HELLO. / ENCORE** [-] [69]

not iss. Elektra

Jul 80. (lp) *<6E-307>* **EXPLORER SUITE** [-] [ ]
– Honey money / Livin' in the eighties / Conversation / It's never too late / Explorer suite / Seal it with a kiss / Hey you're on the run / No place to go / Searchin' / Hope / You'll be born again.

Jun 81. (7") *<47155>* **DDT. / ELEVATOR** [-] [ ]

Jul 81. (lp) *<6E-346>* **WALKING WILD** [-] [ ]
– Walking wild / Holdin' out on me / Don't ever let me go / Love's up in the air / DDT / Get it up / L-5 / She's gonna tear you apart / Elevator / You're there.

Sep 81. (7") *<47205>* **DON'T EVER LET ME GO. /** [-] [ ]

— split soon after above

NEW ENGLAND

Formed: Deptford, London, England ... 1990 by former ATOM SEED bassist CHRIS HUXTER, who recruited PAUL McKENNA, DAVE COOK and IAN WINTERS. An aggressively eclectic outfit who attempted to fuse 70's rock, metal and punk, NEW ENGLAND seemed to burn themselves out prematurely with their uncompromising musical integrity. The sum total of the group's output was a sole album, 'YOU CAN'T KEEP LIVING THIS WAY' (1992), on the independent 'Street Link' label, a highly acclaimed effort which nevertheless failed to make any lasting impression on the UK rock scene.

Album rating: YOU CAN'T KEEP LIVING THIS WAY (*7)

PAUL McKENNA – vocals / **DAVE COOK** – guitar / **CHRIS HUXTER** – bass (ex-ATOM SEED) / **IAN WINTERS** – drums

Street Link not iss.

Oct 92. (cd/lp) *(STR CD/LP 014)* **YOU CAN'T KEEP LIVING THIS WAY** [ ] [-]
– Suicide / Real live mind / Money / Nine / Communication breakdown / We R 4 U2 / No zone / War / Love.

— folded a few months after above

NEW YORK DOLLS

Formed: New York City, New York, USA ... late '71 by JOHNNY THUNDERS, DAVID JOHANSEN, BILLY MURCIA, ARTHUR KANE and RICK RIVETS. In March the following year, RIVETS left to form The BRATS, being swiftly replaced by SYLVAIN SYLVAIN. After a promising start as support act on a FACES British tour, the 'DOLLS' first casualty was MURCIA who died on the 6th of November '72 after drowning in his own bath (not, as widely believed, from a drug overdose). With JERRY NOLAN as a replacement, they signed to 'Mercury' in March '73 and promptly began work on an eponymous debut album with TODD RUNDGREN producing. Released in the summer of that year, 'THE NEW YORK DOLLS' was a proto-punk revelation, a way cool schlock of visceral rock'n'roll which combined the more essential moments of MC5, The PRETTY THINGS, PINK FAIRIES and The SHANGRI-LAS. The ROLLING STONES were another obvious reference point, JOHANSEN a dead-ringer for MICK JAGGER in terms of both vocal style and mascara'd looks. Inevitably, then, THUNDERS was the glam-punk KEITH RICHARDS, Glitter Twins to the JAGGERS/RICHARDS Glimmer coupling. The 'DOLLS' trashy transvestite attire also borrowed heavily from the 'STONES (circa '66 'Have You Seen Your Mother . . .'), although being American they'd obviously taken it to almost cartoon-esque proportions. The likes of 'PERSONALITY CRISIS', 'TRASH' and 'JET BOY' were seminal squalls of guitar abuse, making up in attitude what they lacked in musical ability. Although the record had the critics salivating, commercial success wasn't forthcoming and, unhappy with the record's production, the band opted for SHANGRI-LA's producer, GEORGE MORTON to work on 'TOO MUCH TOO SOON' (1974). Though the album had its moments, again the band had been paired with the wrong producer and the music press were emphatically unimpressed. The lukewarm reviews heightened inter-band tension and the 'DOLLS demise was swift and inevitable. Early the following year, Londoner MALCOLM McLAREN made a last-ditch attempt to save the band, revamping their image to no avail. THUNDERS was the first to leave, departing in 1975 to form The HEARTBREAKERS, while JOHANSEN and SYLVAIN subsequently sacked KANE before finally calling it a day the following Christmas. While THUNDERS went on to most acclaim with his HEARTBREAKERS (dying from an overdose on 23rd April '91), JOHANSEN recorded a number of solo albums, 'DAVID JOHANSEN' (1978), 'IN STYLE' (1979) and 'HERE COMES THE NIGHT' (1981) as well as releasing a 1988 set under the pseudonym of BUSTER POINDEXTER. NOLAN also met an untimely death, almost a year on from THUNDERS (14th January, 1992), suffering a fatal stroke while undergoing treatment for meningitis and pneumonia. A pivotal reference point for not only punk, but the US sleaze/glam metal movement of the mid-80's (FASTER PUSSYCAT, L.A. GUNS, GUNS N' ROSES, et al), The NEW YORK DOLLS influence remains hugely disproportionate to their relatively slim legacy. • **Songwriters:** JOHANSEN with THUNDERS or SYLVAIN. Covered PILLS (Bo Diddley) / DON'T START ME TALKIN' (Sonny Boy Williamson) / SHOWDOWN (Archie Bell) / SOMETHIN' ELSE (Eddie Cochran) / etc. • **Trivia:** Two songs 'PERSONALITY CRISIS' & 'WHO ARE THE MYSTERY GIRLS', appeared on the 1977 Various Artists compilation 'NEW WAVE'. **JOHANSEN's filmography:** 'Married To The Mob', 'Scrooged' and 'The Fisher King'.

Album rating: NEW YORK DOLLS (*8) / TOO MUCH TOO SOON (*7) / LIPSTICK KILLERS exploitation (*5) / ROCK & ROLL compilation (*7) / David Johansen: DAVID JOHANSEN (*6) / IN STYLE (*5) / HERE COMES THE NIGHT (*4) / LIVE IT UP (*5) / SWEET REVENGE (*5) / CRUCIAL MUSIC: THE DAVID JOHANSEN COLLECTION (*6)

DAVID JOHANSEN (b. 9 Jan'50, Staten Island, N.Y.) – vocals / **JOHNNY THUNDERS** (b. JOHN GENZALE, 15 Jul'54) – guitar, vocals / **SYLVAIN SYLVAIN** (b. SIL MIZRAHI) – guitar, vocals repl. RICK RIVETS / **ARTHUR KANE** (b. 3 Feb'51) – bass / **JERRY NOLAN** (b. 7 May'51) – drums repl. BILLY MURCIA who died.

Mercury Mercury

Jul 73. (7") *<73414>* **TRASH. / PERSONALITY CRISIS** [-] [ ]

Aug 73. (lp) *(6338 270) <SRM 675>* **NEW YORK DOLLS** [ ] [ ] Jul73
– Personality crisis / Looking for a kiss / Vietnamese baby / Lonely planet boy / Frankenstein / Trash / Bad girl / Subway train / Pills / Private world / Jet boy. *<US re-iss. 1984; same>*

Nov 73. (7") *(6052 402)* **JET BOY. / VIETNAMESE BABY** [ ] [-]

Jul 74. (lp) *(6338 498) <SRM 1001>* **TOO MUCH TOO SOON** [ ] [ ] May74
– Babylon / Stranded in the jungle / Who are the mystery girls? / (There's gonna be a) Showdown / It's too late / Puss 'n' boots / Chatterbox / Bad detective / Don't start me talkin' / Human being. *<US re-iss. 1984; same>*

Jul 74. (7") *(6052 615) <73478>* **STRANDED IN THE JUNGLE. / WHO ARE THE MYSTERY GIRLS?** [ ] [ ]

Sep 74. (7") *<73615>* **(THERE'S GONNA BE A) SHOWDOWN. / PUSS 'N' BOOTS** [-] [ ]

not iss. Trash

1974. (fan club-7"ep) *<TR 001>* **LOOKING FOR A KISS (live). / WHO ARE THE MYSTERY GIRLS? (live) / SOMETHIN' ELSE (live)** [-] [ ]

— **PETER JORDAN** – bass (the roadie filled in on stage when KANE was drunk)

— Disbanded mid-1975, after **BOBBY BLAIN** – keyboards repl. CHRIS ROBINSON who had repl. THUNDERS (he formed The HEARTBREAKERS with NOLAN). **TOMMY MACHINE** (was last drummer). The NEW YORK DOLLS reformed again with JOHANSEN and SYLVIAN but only toured until late '76. SYLVIAN later formed The CRIMINALS. DAVID JOHANSEN went solo in 1978.

– compilations, others, etc. –

Jun 77. (7"m) *Mercury; (6160 008)* **JET BOY. / BABYLON / WHO ARE THE MYSTERY GIRLS?** [ ] [-]

Jul 77. (d-lp) *Mercury; (6641 631)* **NEW YORK DOLLS / TOO MUCH TOO SOON** [ ] [-]
(re-iss. Apr86; PRID 12)

Nov 81. (c) *R.O.I.R.; <A 104>* **LIPSTICK KILLERS – MERCER ST. SESSIONS** [-] [ ]
(re-iss. May90 on 'Danceteria' cd/lp; DAN CD/LP 038) (re-iss. cd Feb95 & Jun97 on 'ROIR Europe'; 885615027-2) (cd re-iss. Aug00 on 'R.O.I.R.'; RUSCD 8266)

Sep 82. (12"ep) *Kamera; (ERA 13-12)* **PERSONALITY CRISIS / LOOKING FOR A KISS. / SUBWAY TRAIN / BAD GIRL** [ ] [-]
(re-iss. Jul90 on 'See For Miles' cd-ep; SEACD 3)

Sep 84. (red-m-lp) *Fan Club; (FC 007)* **RED PATENT LEATHER (rec. 75)** [-] [-] France
– Girls / Downtown / Private love / Personality crisis / Pills / Something else / Daddy rollin' stone / Dizzy Miss Lizzy. *(cd-iss. Oct88; FC 007CD) (UK cd-iss. Feb93 on 'Receiver'+=; RRCD 173) (cd re-iss. Apr97 on 'Last Call'; 42241-2)*

Oct 84. (7"white) *Fan Club; (NYD 1)* **PILLS (live). / DOWN, DOWN, DOWN TOWN (live)** [-] [-] France

1985. (lp) *Mercury; <8260 941>* **NIGHT OF THE LIVING DOLLS** [-] [ ]

Feb 86. (7",12"pic-d,12"red) *Antler; (DOLLS 1)* **PERSONALITY CRISIS. / SUBWAY TRAIN** [ ] [-]

Feb 86. (7",12"pic-d,12"blue) *Antler; (DOLLS 2)* **LOOKING FOR A KISS. / BAD GIRL** [ ] [-]

1986. (lp; one-side by SEX PISTOLS) *Receiver; (RRLP 102)* **AFTER THE STORM** [ ] [-]
(cd-iss. Jul93; RRCD 102)

Jul 93. (cd) *Receiver; <(RRCD 163)>* **SEVEN DAY WEEKEND** [ ] [ ]

Jul 93. (cd) *Receiver; <(RRCD 173)>* **IN NYC 1975** [ ] [ ]

Oct 94. (cd) *Mercury; (522 129-2)* **ROCK'N'ROLL** [ ] [ ]

Mar 96. (cd) *Skydog; <62256-2>* **PARIS BURNING** [ ] [ ]

Mar 96. (cd) *Skydog; <62257-2>* **NEW YORK TAPES 1972-1973** [ ] [ ]
<(re-iss. Feb00 on 'Munster'; MR 167/+CD)>

Oct 97. (cd) *Red Star; <(RS 7006)>* **TEENAGE NEWS** [ ] [ ]

Nov 98. (cd; shared w/ JOHNNY THUNDERS) *Recall; <(SMDCD 207)>* **STREET TRASH** [ ] [ ]

Nov 98. (cd) *Receiver; <(RRCD 260)>* **I'M A HUMAN BEING (live)** [ ] [ ]

Sep 98. (cd) *Red Star; <(RSR 7006)>* **LIVE IN CONCERT PARIS 1974** [ ] [ ]
<(re-iss. Jun99 on 'Essential'; ESMCD 734)>

Jul 99. (cd) *Big Ear; (109634022-2)* **GLAMOROUS LIFE – LIVE** [ ] [ ]

Apr 00. (lp/cd) *Get Back; (GET 60/+CD)* **THE BIRTH OF THE NEW YORK DOLLS** [ ] [ ]

DAVID JOHANSEN

– vocals, keyboards with his group **STATEN ISLAND BOYS: THOMAS TRASK** – guitar / **JOHNNY RAO** – guitar / **BUZZ VERNO** – bass (ex-CHERRY VANILLA) / **FRANKI LA ROCKA** – drums (ex-CHERRY VANILLA)

Blue Sky Blue Sky

Jul 78. (lp) *(SKY 82335) <34926>* **DAVID JOHANSEN** [ ] [ ] May78
– Funky but chic / Girls / Pain in my heart / Not that much / Donna / Cool metro / I'm a lover / Lonely tenement / Frenchette.

Sep 78. (7") *(BS 6663)* **FUNKY BUT CHIC. / THE ROPE (THE LET GO SONG)** [ ] [ ]

Sep 79. (lp) *(SKY 83745) <JZ 36082>* **IN STYLE** [ ] [ ]
– Melody / She / Big city / She knew she was falling in love / Swaheto woman / Justine / In style / You touched me too / Wreckless crazy / Flamingo road.

Sep 79. (7") *<ZS 92781>* **MELODY. / RECKLESS CRAZY** [-] [ ]

Mar 80. (7"/12") *(SKY/12SKY 8125)* *<BS 2789>* **SWAHETO WOMAN. / SHE KNEW SHE WAS FALLING IN LOVE** Nov79

— with new band **BLONDIE CHAPLIN** – guitar, vocals / **ERNIE BROOKS** – bass / **TOM MANDEL** – organ / **BOBBY BLAIN** – piano / **TONY MACHINE** – drums

Aug 81. (lp) *(SKY 84504)* *<FZ 36589>* **HERE COMES THE NIGHT**
– She loves strangers / Bohemian love pad / You fool me / My obsession / Marquesa de Sade / Here comes the night / Suspicion / Party tonight / Havin' so much fun / Rollin' job / Heart of gold. *(cd-iss. Oct94 on 'Rewind';)*

Sep 81. (7") **HERE COMES THE NIGHT. / SHE LOVES STRANGERS** -

Jun 82. (7") *<ZS 550 3003>* **BOHEMIAN LOVE PAD. / MEDLEY: WE GOTA GET OUT OF THIS PLACE – DON'T BRING ME DOWN (live)** -

1982. (lp) *(ARZ 38004>* **LIVE IT UP** -
(cd-iss. Jan94 on 'Legacy';)

— now with **JOE DELIA** – keyboards / **DAVID NELSON** – guitar / **BRETT CARTWRIGHT** – bass / **DENNIS McDERMOTT** – drums

10-Virgin Passport

Feb 85. (lp) *(DIX 8)* *<PB 6043>* **SWEET REVENGE** Nov84

Mar 85. (7"/12") *(TEN 46/+12)* **HEAR THE NEWS. / KING OF BABYLON**

BUSTER POINDEXTER & HIS BANSHEES OF BLUE

(aka DAVID JOHANSEN)

R.C.A. R.C.A.

Jun 88. (7"/12") *(PB/PT 49581)* *<53577R>* **HOT HOT HOT. / CANNIBAL** 45 Nov87

Jul 88. (lp)(c)(cd) *<6633>* **BUSTER POINDEXTER** 90 Dec87
– Smack dab in the middle / Bad boy / Hot hot hot / Are you lonely for me baby / Screwy music / Good morning judge / Oh me oh my (I'm a fool for you baby) / Whadaya want? / House of the rising sun / Cannibal / Heart of gold.

Jul 88. (7") *<7638>* **OH ME, OH MY (I'M A FOOL FOR YOU BABY). / CANNIBAL** -

1989. (7") *<8914>* **HEART OF GOLD. / HIT THE ROAD JACK** -

1989. (7") **ALL NIGHT PARTY. / ('A'-hot mix)** -

1989. (7") *<9195 – 2572>* **UNDER THE SEA. / DEBOURGE YOURSELF** -

– compilations, etc. –

1990. (cd) *Columbia; <1033>* **CRUCIAL MUSIC: THE DAVID JOHANSEN COLLECTION**
– Girls / Donna / Is this what I get / Animals medley (live) / Frenchette / Melody / Funky but chic / I'm a lover / Cool metro / Flamingo road.

Oct 94. (cd) *Sequel-Rhino; (RSFCD 818)* **BUSTER'S HAPPY HOUR** -

— note:- the album 'DAVID JOHANSEN & THE HARRY SMITHS' was issued in April 2000 for 'Chesky'; *(JD 196)*

NIGHT RANGER

Formed: San Francisco, California, USA . . . 1981 as RANGER by OZZY OSBOURNE guitarist BRAD GILLIS alongside JACK BLADES, JEFF WATSON, ALAN FITZGERALD and KELLY KEAGY. With the group subsequently securing a deal via Neil Bogart's 'Boardwalk' label and adopting the NIGHT RANGER moniker, GILLIS quit The 'OZ and went full-time with his Bay Area baby. 'DAWN PATROL' (1983) was their sole 'Boardwalk' release, the band finding themselves on the 'M.C.A.' roster following the untimely death of Bogart. Despite subsequent conflicts with the label over musical/artistic control etc., the group released a pivotal record in the AOR/pop-metal genre with 1984's 'MIDNIGHT MADNESS'. Keyboard-heavy power ballads like the US Top 5, 'SISTER CHRISTIAN', paved the way for the poodle-maned hordes which would dominate the MTV-friendly American rock scene for the bulk of the 80's, while with '(YOU CAN STILL) ROCK IN AMERICA', the group voiced their right to "rawk" in the face of pop domination. The following year's '7 WISHES' continued in the same vein, making the US Top 10 and spawning another three US Top 20 hits. As the decade wore on, however, the group deliberately pursued a harder-edged direction, 1988's 'MAN IN MOTION' being their poorest selling record to date. Disillusioned, and with record company hassles, the group called it a day, songwriter BLADES forming DAMN YANKEES with TED NUGENT. Although GILLIS and KEAGY reformed the group in 1991, they remained unsigned until the mid 90's, when, with new singer GARY MOON, they released 'FEEDING OFF THE MOJO' (1995). After a live set in '97, NIGHT RANGER returned with yet another patchy album, 'SEVEN' (1998), power ballads we could do without.

Album rating: DAWN PATROL (*7) / MIDNIGHT MADNESS (*7) / 7 WISHES (*7) / BIG LIFE (*5) / MAN IN MOTION (*5) / GREATEST HITS compilation (*6) / LIVE IN JAPAN (*4) / FEEDING OFF THE MOJO (*4) / ROCK IN JAPAN '97 (*4) / THE MILLENNIUM COLLECTION (*6) / SEVEN (*4) / Jeff Watson: LONE RANGER (*4) / AROUND THE SUN (*5)

JACK BLADES (b.24 Apr'54) – vocals, bass (ex-RUBICON) / **BRAD GILLIS** – guitar (ex-RUBICON, ex-OZZY OSBOURNE) / **JEFF WATSON** (b. 4 Nov'56) – guitar / **ALAN 'FITZ'GERALD** (b.16 Jun'54) – keyboards (ex-SAMMY HAGAR, ex-MONTROSE) / **KELLY KEAGY** (b.15 Sep'52) – drums, vocals

Epic Boardwalk

Feb 83. (7") *(EPCA 3210)* *<171>* **DON'T TELL ME THAT YOU LOVE ME. / NIGHT RANGER** 40 Jan83

Feb 83. (lp/c) *(EPC/40 25301)* *<33259>* **DAWN PATROL** 38 Dec82
– Don't tell me that you love me / Sing me away / At night she sleeps / Call my name / Eddie's comin' out tonight / Can't find me a thrill / Young girl in love / Play rough / Penny / Night ranger. *<US cd-iss. Jun88; >*

Apr 83. (7") *<175>* **SING ME AWAY. / PLAY ROUGH** - 54

Jul 83. (7") *<181>* **CALL MY NAME. / YOUNG GIRL IN LOVE** -

Epic Camel-MCA

Nov 83. (7") *<52305>* **(YOU CAN STILL) ROCK IN AMERICA. / LET HIM RUN** - 51

Jan 84. (lp/c) *(EPC/40 25845)* *<5456>* **MIDNIGHT MADNESS** 15 Nov83
– (You can still) Rock in America / Rumours in the air / Why does love have to change / Sister CHristian / Touch of madness / Passion play / When you close your eyes / Chippin' away / Let him run. *(re-iss. Jul84 on 'M.C.A.' lp/c)(cd; MCF/+C 3209)(DIDX 54)* *<US cd-iss. Jun88; >*

M.C.A. Camel-MCA

Apr 84. (7") *(MCA 881)* *<52350>* **SISTER CHRISTIAN. / CHIPPIN' AWAY** 5 Mar84

Jul 84. (7") *<52420>* **WHEN YOU CLOSE YOUR EYES. / WHY DOES LOVE HAVE TO CHANGE** - 14

May 85. (7"/12") *(MCA/+T 973)* *<52591>* **SENTIMENTAL STREET. / NIGHT MACHINE** 8

Jun 85. (lp/c) *(MCF/+C 3278)* *<5593>* **7 WISHES** 10
– Seven wishes / Faces / Four in the morning (I can't take any more) / I need a woman / Sentimental street / This boy needs to rock / I will follow you / Interstate love affair / Night machine / Goodbye. *<US cd-iss. Jun88; >*

Sep 85. (7") *<52661>* **FOUR IN THE MORNING (I CAN'T TAKE ANY MORE). / THE BOY NEEDS TO ROCK** - 19

Nov 85. (7") *<52729>* **GOODBYE. / SEVEN WISHES** - 17

Apr 87. (7") *(MCA 1125)* **THE COLOUR OF YOUR SMILE. / GIRLS ALL LIKE IT** -
(12"+=) *(MCAT 1125)* – When you close your eyes / Don't tell me that you love me.

Apr 87. (lp/c/cd) *(MCF/MCFC/DMCF 3362)* *<5839>* **BIG LIFE** 28
– Big life / The color of your smile / Love is standing near / Rain comes crashing down / The secret of my success / Carry on / Better let it go / I know tonight / Hearts away.

Jun 87. (7") *(MCA 1163)* *<53013>* **THE SECRET OF MY SUCCESS. / CARRY ON** 64 Mar87
(12"+=) *(MCAT 1163)* – Sister Christian (live).

Jul 87. (7") *<53131>* **HEARTS AWAY. / BETTER LET IT GO** - 90

— **JESS BRADMAN** – keyboards; repl. FITZGERALD

Sep 88. (7") *<53364>* **I DID IT FOR LOVE. / WOMAN IN LOVE** - 75

Oct 88. (lp/c/cd) *<6238>* **MAN IN MOTION** - 81
– Man in motion / Reason to be / Don't start thinking (I'm alone tonight) / Love shot me down / Restless kind / Halfway to the sun / Here she comes again / Right on you / Kiss me where it hurts / I dit it for love / Woman in love.

Nov 88. (7") *<53495>* **KISS ME WHERE IT HURTS. / DON'T START THINKING (I'M ALONE TONIGHT)** -

— Disbanded Apr'89, BLADES joined DAMN YANKEES with TED NUGENT. The man subsequently teamed up with TOMMY SHAW (ex-STYX) to form SHAW BLADES and issued a one-off 'Warners' album, 'HALLUCINATION' (9362 45835-2/-4). BRADMAN joined the band of JIMMY BAIN. BRAD, JEFF & KELLY re-formed NIGHT RANGER in Mar'91.

– compilations, others, etc. –

Jul 89. (lp/c/cd) *M.C.A.; (MCG/MCGC/DMCG 6055)* **GREATEST HITS** -
– You can still rock in America / Goodbye / Sister Christian / The secret of my success / Rumours in the air / Sing me away / When you close your eyes / Sentimental street / Restless kind / Eddie's comin' out tonight.

Nov 90. (cd/c) *M.C.A.; (MCA 1002-2/-4)* **LIVE IN JAPAN (live '88)**
– Touch of madness / When you close your eyes / Man in motion / Don't start thinking (I'm alone tonight) / Let him run / Goodbye / Reason to be / Four in the morning (I can't take any more) / Sister Christian / Don't tell me you love me / Halfway to the sun / (You can still) Rock in America.

JEFF WATSON

(solo) with **BRAD GILLIS / SAMMY HAGAR / BOB DAISLEY / CARMINE APPICE / STEVE SMITH + ALLAN HOLDSWORTH**

Roadrunner Shrapnel

Feb 93. (cd) *(RR 9223-2)* *<SH 1055>* **LONE RANGER** Apr92
– Late one night / Cement shoes / Forest of feelings / Night lifer / Picnic island / Morse minor / Osaka rot / Echo chalet / Talking hands / Pipedream / Song for Rebecca.

NIGHT RANGER

GARY MOON – bass (ex-JEFF PARIS) repl. BLADES

not iss. Drive Ent.

Oct 95. (cd) *<46001>* **FEEDING OFF THE MOJO** -
– Mojo / Last chance / Try (for good reason) / Precious time / The night has a way / Do you feel like I do – Tomorrow never knows / Music box / Longest days / Tell me I'm wrong / So far gone.

Zero Zero

Jun 98. (cd) *(XRCN 2004)* *<29345>* **ROCK IN JAPAN '97 (live)**

S.P.V. C.M.C.

Sep 98. (cd) *(SPV 085-1817-2)* *<86257>* **SEVEN** Jul98
– Sign of the times / Jane's interlude / Panic in Jane / Don't ask me why / Kong / Mother mayhem / Soul survivor / Sea of love / Peace sign / When I call on you / Revelation.

– compilations, etc. –

Jul 00. (cd) *Universal; <(AA 88112307-2)>* **THE MILLENNIUM COLLECTION**

JEFF WATSON

— with guest vocalists **AARON HAGAR + STEVE WALSH**

Cleopatra Cleopatra

Jun 99. (cd) <*(CLP 553)*> **AROUND THE SUN** [ ] [ ] May99
– Glass revenge / Life goes on / Around the sun / Follow / Anna waits / Tightrope / Leslie Ann / Man's best friend / Moment of truth / Shadows of winter / Serenity / Ghost town.
(re-iss. Apr00 on 'Frontier'; FRCD 052)

NIGHTSHADE (see under ⇒ Q5)

NIGHTSTICK

Formed: USA . . . mid-90's by frontman/bassist ALEX SMITH, guitarist COTIE COWGILL and songwriting drummer ROBERT WILLIAMS. Exponents of the power/grunge/psyche-metal scene (aka Stoner-rock), NIGHTSTICK poked fun at the establishment (and themselves) during a three-LP period during the late 90's. Their 1997 debut, 'BLOTTER', contained stabs (quite literally) at Pink Floyd's 'SET THE CONTROLS FOR THE HEART OF THE SUN', Lydia Lunch's 'SOME BOYS' and a wild interpretation of George Clinton's 'MOMMY, WHAT'S A FUNKADELIC?'; a 1998 follow-up, 'ULTIMATUM', featured a segue of BERLIOZ's 'DREAM OF THE WITCH'S SABBATH' and Discharge's 'MASSACRE OF INNOCENCE'. With a heavy cocktail of HAWKWIND, MONSTER MAGNET and KYUSS, NIGHTSTICK exposed their uncommerciality and musical cynicism for a third time, via their 1999 set, 'DEATH TO MUSIC', appropriate title, if ever there was one.

Album rating: BLOTTER (*5) / ULTIMATUM (*7) / DEATH TO MUSIC (*5)

ALEX SMITH – vocals, bass / **COTIE COWGILL** – guitar / **ROBERT WILLIAMS** – drums

Relapse Relapse

Mar 97. (cd) <*(RR 6951-2)*> **BLOTTER** [ ] [ ] Jan97
– Workers of the world unite!! / Some boys / Set the controls for the heart of the sun / Mommy, what's a Funkadelic? / Blotter: This is a pig – Only the leaves / Fellating the dying Christ.

Mar 98. (cd) <*(RR 6977-2)*> **ULTIMATUM** [ ] [ ] Jan98
– Ultimatum: "Cut it off, then kill it" / United snakes / The pentagon / Pig in shit / 4 more years / August 6, 1945: a) Flight, b) Fright / Dream of the witch's sabbath – Massacre of innocence (air attack) / Ultimatum: "He . . . is . . . dead . . . wrong (4-track version) / Ultimatum: (live @ Mama Kin's).

Aug 99. (cd) <*(RR 6422-2)*> **DEATH TO MUSIC** [ ] [ ] Jun99
– Babykiller / Jarhead / Young man, old man / (Won't you take me to) Junkytown / The American way / Free man / In Dahmer's room / Boot party theme / Egghead.

NIGHTWING

Formed: London, England . . . 1978 by ex-STRIFE bassist GORDON ROWLEY, who soon got together with ALEX JOHNSON, ERIC PERCIVAL, KENNY NEWTON and STEVE BARTLEY. Influenced by the booming US AOR scene, the band's debut album, 'SOMETHING IN THE AIR' (1980), attempted an English pomp-rock equivalent with promising results. Although PERCIVAL subsequently departed, the band went on to record the harder-edged 'BLACK SUMMER' (1982), endearing them to the fans of the burgeoning NWOBHM. By 1983's 'STAND UP AND BE COUNTED', the band had decided to recruit a full-time vocalist, MAX BACON, although his tenure was brief (he later went on to BRONZ, then GTR – with STEVE HOWE and STEVE HACKETT). DAVE EVANS was brought in as a replacement, while more line-up changes ensued as GLYNN PORRINO took over from the departing JOHNSON. There was little doubt the constant flux was having a detrimental effect on the group's creativity with the disappointing 'KINGDOM COME' (1984) proving their final studio release for over half a decade. Now on the roster of 'Neat Metal', NIGHTWING delivered their comeback set, 'NATURAL SURVIVORS', in 1996.

Album rating: SOMETHING IN THE AIR (*6) / BLACK SUMMER (*7) / STAND UP AND BE COUNTED (*5) / MY KINGDOM COME (*4) / NIGHT OF MYSTERY, ALIVE! ALIVE! (*4) / NATURAL SURVIVORS (*5)

GORDON ROWLEY – vocals, bass (ex-STRIFE) / **ALEC JOHNSON** – guitar / **ERIC PERCIVAL** – guitar / **KENNY NEWTON** – keyboards / **STEVE BARTLEY** – drums

Ovation not iss.

Jul 80. (7") *(OVS 1209)* **BARREL OF PAIN. /** [ ] [-]

Aug 80. (lp) *(OVLP 1757)* **SOMETHING IN THE AIR** [ ] [-]
– Fantasia / Nightwing / Cold love / Edge of a knife / Something in the air / Barrel of pain / Boogie woman / You keep me hanging on / Fantasia (reprise). *(cd-iss. Sep99 on 'Zoom Club'; ZCRCD 15)*

— now without PERCIVAL

Gull not iss.

1982. (lp) *(GULP 1036)* **BLACK SUMMER** [ ] [-]
– Overnight sensation / Bird has flown / Carry on / Long hard road / Searching / Evil woman / Black summer / Don't want to lose you. *(cd-iss. Sep99 on 'Zoom Club'; ZCRCD 16)*

— added **MAX BACON** – vocals

1983. (7") *(GULS 75)* **TREADING WATER. / CALL YOUR NAME** [ ] [-]
(12"+=) *(GULS 75-12)* – Barrel of pain.

1983. (lp) *(GULP 1038)* **STAND UP AND BE COUNTED** [ ] [-]
– Let me be your lover / Treading water / The machine / Dressed to kill / Stand up and be counted / Next Saturday / Still in love with you / Games to play / Call your name / The last song. *(cd-iss. May00 on 'Zoom Club'; ZCRCD 29)*

— **DAVE EVANS** – vocals; repl. BACON who joined BRONZ (later to GTR)

— **GLYNN PORRINO** – guitar; repl. JOHNSON

Feb 84. (7") *(GULS 77)* **NIGHT OF MYSTERY. / DRESSED TO KILL** [ ] [-]

Mar 84. (lp) *(GULP 1040)* **MY KINGDOM COME** [ ] [-]
– Back on the streets / Fingers in the fire / Night of mystery / Give me the love that I want / Cell 151 / The Devil walks behind you / Living behind the 8 ball / Men of war / My kingdom come. *(cd-iss. May97 on 'Long Island'; LIR 00123) (cd re-iss. May00 on 'Zoom Club'; ZCRCD 30)*

Sep 84. (d7") *(GULS 80)* **STRANGERS ARE WELCOME. / GAMES TO PLAY // THE DEVIL WALKS BEHIND YOU. / CELL 151** [ ] [-]

Jun 85. (lp) *(GULP 1043)* **NIGHT OF MYSTERY, ALIVE! ALIVE! (live)** [ ] [-]
– Fantasia / Dressed to kill / Something in the air / Cell 151 / Night of mystery / You keep me hanging on / The Devil walks behind you / Treading water. *(cd-iss. May00 on 'Zoom Club'; ZCRCD 31)*

— split around the same time of above's release, re-formed for below

— **EVANS, PORRINO, ROWLEY, BARTLEY + NEWTON** plus **KERY BESWICK** – keyboards / **BARRY ROBERTS** – drums

Neat Metal not iss.

May 96. (cd) *(NM 009)* **NATURAL SURVIVORS** [ ] [-]
– Islands / Unrequited love / I must be dreaming / Natural survivor / 21st century / Sahara / Here comes the night / All of my life / Take the money and run / She's the woman / Nights in white satin / You've got me falling / Mercenary man / Islands reprise. *(re-iss. Oct97; same)*

NIGHTWISH

Formed: Kitee, Finland . . . late 1996 by TUOMAS HOLOPAINEN, TARJA TURUNEN and EMPPU VUORINEN. In the beginning it was HOLOPAINEN's wish to create acoustic music in a gothic style, but after recording a few tracks, the trio decided to electrify the sound; VUORINEN switching from acoustic to electric guitar, with the band recruiting JUKKA NEVALAINEN on drums. NIGHTWISH then recorded a handful of tracks as a demo which attracted the label, 'Spinefarm', who gave the Finns a two-album deal and released their debut album in late 1997, 'ANGELS FALL FIRST' (1997), a record that incorporated some of the songs from the demo. After this the band had to take a brief sojourn as the members had academic and military duties to attend to. After wrapping up these extra-curricular activities the band came back together with the addition of bassist SAMI VANSKA to record and release their second album, 'OCEANBORN' (1998). The album sold well in their home country and brought them many more admirers from the rest of Europe. In sound they were compared frequently with Italy's goth-metallers, LACUNA COIL, although this was probably due to both bands having female vocalists – they also share the goth obsession with fantasy literature and likewise subject-matter. After a European tour at the turn of the century, the band returned to the studio to work on their third album, 'WISHMASTER' (2000), releasing it within the year. A stand-out track on this set in terms of subject-matter was 'THE KINSLAYER'. The track dealt with HOLOPAINEN's despair with the tragic events of April '99 that befell Colorado's Columbine High School.

Album rating: ANGELS FALL FIRST (*3) / OCEAN BORN (*5) / WISHMASTER (*6)

TARJA TURUNEN (b.17 Aug'77, Helsinki) – vocals / **TUOMAS HOLOPAINEN** (b.25 Dec'76) – keyboards / **EMPPU VUORINEN** (b.24 Jun'78) – guitar / **JUKKA NEVALAINEN** (b.21 Apr'78) – drums, percussion

Spinefarm Century Media

Nov 97. (cd-s) **THE CARPENTER / RED LIGHT IN MY EYES (part II) / ONLY DUST MOVES . . .** [-] [-] Finnish

Mar 98. (cd) *(SPI 47CD)* <*8021*> **ANGELS FALL FIRST** [ ] [ ]
– Beauty and the beast / Elvenpath / The carpenter / Astral romance / Angels fall first / Tutankhamen / Nymphomaniac fantasia / Know why the nightingale sings / Lappi (Lapland): I. Eramaajarvi – II. Witchdrums – III. This moment is . . . – IV. Etiainen.

— added **SAMI VANSKA** (b.26 Sep'76) – bass

Nov 98. (cd-s) **SACRAMENT OF WILDERNESS / THE CROW AND THE WARRIOR / BURNING FLAMES' EMBRACE** [-] [-] Finnish

Dec 98. (cd) <*8027*> **OCEAN BORN** [-] [ ]
– Stargazers / Gethsemane / Devil and the deep dark ocean / Sacrament of wilderness / Passion and the opera / Swanheart / Moondance / The riddler / The pharaoh / sails to Orion / Sleeping sun. *(hidden track+=)* – (untitled).

Feb 99. (cd-s) **WALKING IN THE AIR / NIGHTQUEST / TUTANKHAMEN** [-] [-] Finnish

Aug 99. (cd-ep) *(DRAKKAR 005)* **FOUR BALLADS OF THE ECLIPSE** [-] [-] Finnish
– Sleeping sun / Walking in the air / Swanheart / Angels fall first.

May 00. (cd) *(SPI 87CD)* <*8001*> **WISHMASTER** [ ] [ ] Jul00
– She is my sin / The kinslayer / Come cover me / Wanderlust / Two for tragedy / Wishmaster / Bare grace misery / Crownless / Deep silent complete / Dead boy's poem / Fantasmic.

Jun 00. (cd-s) *(??)* **DEEP SILENT COMPLETE / SLEEPWALKER (unreleased version)** [-] [-] Finnish

NILE

Formed: Greensberg, South Carolina, USA . . . 1993 by KARL SANDERS, CHIEF SPIRES and PETE HAMMOURA. Founded just as death metal was finally dying itself, the strikingly different NILE put a much needed spin on the genre. Inspired by the mysticism and ritual of ancient Egypt, the band not only developed their lyrics and imagery around the subject but spiced up their metal with flutes, gongs and religious-style chanting. 'FESTIVALS OF ATONEMENT' (1995) set the scene and despite their new label going bust prior to the release of acclaimed sophomore effort, 'AMONGST THE CATACOMBS OF NEPHREN-KA' (1998), the band forged ahead with their dark vision. Revelling in the more hellish legends of the ancient kingdom, NILE invoked more tales of woe for 'BLACK SEEDS OF VENGEANCE' (2000). The record even featured real live chanting from a Tibetan monk troupe which the band – now featuring a line-up of SANDERS, SPIRES, TONY LAURENO and DALLAS TOLER-WADE – coaxed into their studio with the promise of a case of beer!

Album rating: AMONGST THE CATACOMBS OF NEPHREN-KA (*6) / BLACK SEEDS OF VENGEANCE (*8) / IN THE BEGINNING collection (*4)

KARL SANDERS – vocals / **CHIEF SPIRES** – vocals, bass / **DALLAS TOLER-WADE** – guitar / **TONY LAURENO** – drums

Relapse Relapse

Sep 98. (cd) *<(RR 6983-5)>* **AMONGST THE CATACOMBS OF NEPHREN-KA** [ ] [ ] Apr98
– Smashing the antiu / Barra edinazzu / Kudurru maqiu / Serpent headed mask / Ramses bringer of war / Stones of sorrow / Die rache krieg lied der assyriche / Howling of the Jinn / Pestilence and iniquity / Opening of the mouth / Beneath the eternal oceans of sand.

Sep 00. (cd) *<(RR 6448-2)>* **BLACK SEEDS OF VENGEANCE** [ ] [ ]
– Invocation of the gate of Aat Ankh en Amenti / Black seeds of vengeance / Defiling the gates of Ishtar / The black flame / Libation unto the shapes who lurk in the shadows / Of the temple of Anhur / Masturbating the war god / Multitude of foes / Chapter for transforming into a snake / Nas akhu she an asbiu / To dream of Ur / The nameless city of the accursed / Khetti satha semsu.

– compilations, etc. –

Feb 00. (cd/lp) *Hammerheart; (<HHR 068 CD/LP>)* **IN THE BEGINNING** [ ] [ ] Nov00
– Divine intent / The black hand of set / Wrought / Immortality through art / Godless / Extinct / The howling of the Jinn / Ramses bronger of war / Der rache kreig leid der Assyriche.

NINE INCH NAILS

Formed: San Francisco, California, USA . . . 1989 by classically trained pianist, TRENT REZNOR. He turned his attention to the darker textures of 'PRETTY HATE MACHINE' in the late 80's following a stint working in a recording studio. A solo effort – the album was written and played wholly by REZNOR – its despair and bitter self-pity were set against walls of churning synths and industrial rhythms, the compelling 'HEAD LIKE A HOLE' subsequently becoming a minor hit thanks to heavy MTV rotation. Around the same time, REZNOR recruited a band and struck out on that year's Lollapolooza trek, previewing a harder hitting, guitar influenced sound. Although the debut album was equal parts DEPECHE MODE/MINISTRY, REZNOR's follow-up, the mini-album, 'BROKEN' (1992), followed the metal/industrial fusion of the live shows. REZNOR seemed more tormented than ever on the likes of 'HELP ME I AM IN HELL', an explicitly masochistic video for the 'HAPPINESS IN SLAVERY' single courting not inconsiderable controversy. A punishing album of remixes, 'FIXED' followed a couple of months later, featuring such good-time party favourites as 'FIST FUCK' and 'SCREAMING SLAVE'. Clearly, REZNOR was rather discontented with his lot, his scary reputation heightened when it was revealed that he'd rented the L.A. pad where Charles Manson and Family had murdered Sharon Tate and her friends back in 1969. While REZNOR was allegedly unaware of this spook factor when he rented the property, it nevertheless gave 'THE DOWNWARD SPIRAL' (1994) a grim new resonance (the album was recorded in said abode). The consummation of everything REZNOR had been working towards, the record was a masterful alternative metal/industrial landmark, exploring the depths of human despair and depravity in its multifarious forms. REZNOR's tormented musings obviously struck a chord with the American populace, the album making No.2 in the US charts while NIN were given a rapturous reception at that year's Woodstock anniversary festival. Another album of remixes, 'FURTHER DOWN THE SPIRAL', appeared the following year, while REZNOR set up his own 'Nothing' label, nurturing such famous talent as the equally scary MARILYN MANSON. It had been five long years since the emergence of any new NINE INCH NAILS material (apart from TRENT producing the soundtrack to Oliver Stone's movie, 'Natural Born Killers', however REZNOR and his nihilistic NIN completed their comeback set, 'THE FRAGILE' (1999). Packed with over twenty apocalyptic tracks it hit the top of the US charts (scraped Top 10 in the UK), doom, gloom and then boom, it was all here for America's forgotten youth of today. • **Songwriters:** 'The Terminator' REZNOR penned except PHYSICAL YOU'RE SO (Adam Ant). • **Trivia:** REZNOR appeared in the 1987 film 'LIGHT OF DAY'.

Album rating: PRETTY HATE MACHINE (*7) / BROKEN (*7) / THE DOWNWARD SPIRAL (*8) / THE FRAGILE (*6)

TRENT REZNOR (b.17 May'65, Mercer, Pennsylvania, USA) – vocals, guitar, keyboards, bass, drums, programming / **JAMES WOOLEY** – keyboards / **RICHARD** – guitar / **CHRIS VRENNA** – drums

Island Nothing-TVT

Nov 90. (12"ep/cd-ep) *(12IS/CID 482)* **DOWN IN IT (skin). / TERRIBLE LIE (mix) / DOWN IN IT (shred – demo)** [ ] [ ]

Sep 91. (7"/10") *(IS/10ISP 484)* **HEAD LIKE A HOLE. / ('A'-Copper mix)** [45] [ ]
(12"+=/cd-s+=) *(12IS/CID 484)* – ('A'-Opal mix).

Sep 91. (cd/c/lp) *(CID/ICT/ILPS 9973) <2610>* **PRETTY HATE MACHINE** [67] [75] Nov90
– Head like a hole / Terrible lie / Down in it / Sanctified / Something I can never have / Kinda I want to / Sin / That's what I get / The only time / Ringfinger.

Nov 91. (c-s/7") *(C+/IS 508)* **SIN. / GET DOWN MAKE LOVE** [35] [ ]
(10"+=/cd-s+=) *(10IS/CID 508)* – Sin (dub).

Sep 92. (m-cd/m-c/m-lp) *(IMCD/ICM/ILPM 8004) <92246>* **BROKEN** [18] [7]
– Pinion / Wish / Last / Help me I am in Hell / Happiness is slavery / Gave up. *(free 7"+/cd+=)* – Physical (you're so) / Suck.

Nov 92. (m-cd/m-c/m-lp) *(IMCD/ICM/ILPM 8005)* **FIXED** (remixes) [ ] [-]
– Gave up / Wish / Happiness is slavery / Throw this away / Fist fuck / Screaming slave.

—— Below was controversally recorded at the house of the Charles Manson murders (some produced by /with FLOOD). Guests on 1 track each were **ADRIAN BELEW + DANNY LOHNER** – guitar / **CHRIS VRENNA + STEPHEN PERKINS + ANDY KUBISZEWSKI +** – drums (live:- **VRENNA, LOHNER, WOOLLEY + ROBIN FINCK)**

Mar 94. (cd/c/d-lp) *(CID/ICT/ILPSD 8012) <92346>* **THE DOWNWARD SPIRAL** [9] [2]
– Mr. Self destruct / Piggy / Heresy / March of the pigs / Closer / Ruiner / The becoming / I do not want this / Big man with a gun / A warm place / Eraser / Reptile / The downward spiral / Hurt.

Mar 94. (cd-ep) *<95938>* **MARCH OF THE PIGS / REPTILLIAN / ALL THE PIGS, ALL LINED UP / A VIOLET FLUID / UNDERNEATH THE SKIN** [-] [59]

Mar 94. (etched-7") *(IS 592)* **MARCH OF THE PIGS. / A VIOLENT FLUID** [45] [-]
(9"+=) *(9IS 592)* – All the pigs, all lined up / Underneath the skin.
(cd-s) *(CID 592)* – ('A'side) / Underneath the skin / Reptillian.
(cd-s+=) *(CIDX 592)* – All the pigs, all lined up / Big man with a gun.

Jun 94. (12"ep/cd-ep) *(12IS/CID 596)* **CLOSER / CLOSER TO GOD / MARCH OF THE FUCKHEADS / HERESY (BLIND) / MEMORABILIA** [25] [-]
(12"ep/cd-ep) *(12ISX/CIDX 596)* – ('A'side) – (deviation) – (further away) / ('A'original) / ('A'-Precursor) / ('A'-Internal).

Jun 94. (c-s) *<98263>* **CLOSER / MARCH OF THE PIGS (live)** [-] [41]

Jun 95. (cd/c) *(IMCD/IMA 8041) <95811>* **FURTHER DOWN THE SPIRAL** (remixes) [ ] [23]
– Piggy (nothing can stop me) / The art of destruction (part one) / Self destruction (part three) / Heresy (version) / The downward spiral (the bottom) / Hurt / At the heart of it all / Ruiner (version) / Eraser (denial: realization) / Self destruction: final.

Sep 97. (cd-ep) *(IND 95542) <9554>* **THE PERFECT DRUG (mixes; original / Meat Beat Manifesto / Plug / Nine Inch Nails / Spacetime Continuum / The Orb)** [43] [46]
(above from the movie 'Lost Highway' on the 'Interscope' imprint)

Aug 99. (c-s/cd-s) *<97026>* **THE DAY THE WORLD WENT AWAY** [-] [17]

Sep 99. (d-cd/d-c/t-lp) *(CIDD/ICT/ILPST 8091) <490473>* **THE FRAGILE** [10] [1]
– Somewhat damaged / The day the world went away / Frail / Wretched / We're in this together / The fragile / Just like you imagined / Even deeper / Pilgrimage / No you don't / La mer / Great below / Way out i through / Into the void / Where is everybody / Mark has been made / Please / Starfuckers Inc. / Complication / I'm looking forward to joining you finally / Pilgrimage / Big come down / Underneath it all.

Nov 99. (cd-s) *(497140-2)* **WE'RE IN THIS TOGETHER / THE DAY THE WORLD WENT AWAY (quiet version) / THE DAY THE WORLD WENT AWAY (Porter Ricks mix)** [39] [ ]
(cd-s) *(497141-2)* – ('A'side) / 10 miles high / The new flesh.
(cd-s) *(497183-2)* – ('A'side) / Complication / The perfect drug.

Nov 00. (cd) *(CID 8102) <490744>* **THINGS FALLING APART** (mixes, etc.) [ ] [67]

NIRVANA

Formed: Aberdeen, Washington, USA . . . 1987 by singer/songwriter/guitarist KURT COBAIN and bassist KRIST NOVOSELIC. Recruiting drummer CHAD CHANNING, they soon became a talking point and pivotal band in nearby Seattle where the likes of SOUNDARDEN and MUDHONEY were major players in the emerging grunge scene. Whereas those bands dealt in raw garage punk/metal, NIRVANA immediately stood out from the pack by dint of the subtle pop melodies which COBAIN craftily incorporated into his songs. They also fast gained a reputation for their ferocious live shows which drew comparisons with early WHO, if only for their sheer nihilistic energy, invariably ending in trashed equipment. Signing, of course, with the hub of the Seattle scene, 'Sub Pop', NIRVANA released their debut single, 'LOVE BUZZ' in October 1988, the album, 'BLEACH', following a year later. One of the seminal 'Sub Pop' releases alongside, MUDHONEY's 'SUPERFUZZ BIGMUFF' and TAD's 'GOD'S BALLS', this was a darkly brooding, often savagely angry collection, driven by bass and fuzz and interspersed with pockets of melody. The likes of 'SCHOOL' and the throbbing 'NEGATIVE CREEP' saw COBAIN lapse into his trademark howl, an enraged, blood curdling shriek, almost primal in its intensity. Conversely, 'ABOUT A GIRL' was an achingly melodic semi-acoustic shuffle, as steeped in hurt as the rest of the album but more resigned than angry. New guitarist JASON EVERMAN had contributed to the record's sonic bludgeon as well as paying for recording costs, although he soon parted ways (he went on to play with the much hyped MINDFUNK) with COBAIN and NOVOSELIC over the ever reliable, 'musical differences'. 'BLEACH' was heartily received by the indie/metal press, NIRVANA embarking on a heavy round of touring, first in the States, then Europe. Following the departure of CHANNING, MUDHONEY's DAN PETERS joined briefly and was involved with the 'SLIVER' single, a brilliant chunk of pop-noise which further enhanced NIRVANA's underground kudos and raised expectations for a follow-up album to fever pitch. 'NEVERMIND'

(1991) let down no-one, except possibly the anally-retentive sad-kids who accused the band of selling out to a major label ('Geffen'). Released immediately after a blinding set at England's Reading festival (where NIRVANA, who probably drew the most frenetic crowd reaction of the day, had to make do with a paltry afternoon slot; the following year they'd be headlining), and with appetites whetted via import copies of 'SMELLS LIKE TEEN SPIRIT', the record was met with an ecstatic press reaction. While the album brought the grunge phenomenon into the mainstream, NIRVANA had already moved on to a blistering power pop/punk sound, best evidenced in the sardonic fury of the aforementioned 'SMELLS . . .'. Here was an anthem for the blank generation, for all the people who'd given up before even starting; COBAIN had condensed the collective frustration/despair/apathy into an incendiary slice of pop genius not witnessed since The SEX PISTOLS' heyday. 'COME AS YOU ARE' was another piece of semi-acoustic bruised beauty while 'TERRITORIAL PISSINGS' was as extreme as the record went, a rabid blast of hardcore punk introduced with a sarcastic send-up pilfered from The YOUNGBLOOD's 60's love 'n' peace classic, 'GET TOGETHER'. Most of the other tracks lay somewhere in between, COBAIN never letting up the intensity level for a minute, whether on the deceptively breezy 'IN BLOOM' or the stinging 'BREED'. For a three piece (the drum seat had now been filled by DAVE GROHL, ex-SCREAM), the group made one hell of a racket, but it was a racket which was never less than 100% focused, the GROHL/NOVOSELIC rhythmic powerhouse underpinning every track with diamond-edged precision. It's fair to say that 'NEVERMIND' literally changed the face of music, American indie bands coming to dominate the scene until the arrival of OASIS in the mid-90's. COBAIN was heralded as the spokesman of a generation, although it was a role he was both unwilling and unable to cope with. As the inevitable, punishing round of touring ensued, the singer's health began to suffer once more; never the healthiest of people, COBAIN suffered from a chronic stomach complaint as well as narcolepsy, a condition which causes the sufferer to sleep for excessive periods of time. What's more, he was concerned that the irony of his lyrics was missed on his growing legions of fans (which now included the macho 'jocks' whom COBAIN so despised) who now doted on his every word. Amid all this confusion, COBAIN was married to HOLE's COURTNEY LOVE on the 24th February '92, the couple almost losing custody of their newborn child, Frances, later that summer following revelations of drug abuse. The end of the year saw the release of a compilation of rare material, 'INCESTICIDE', including two storming VASELINES' (obscure but brilliant Scottish punk-popsters) covers, 'MOLLY'S LIPS' and 'SON OF A GUN'. Rumours of COBAIN's heroin abuse were rife, however, and the singer overdosed twice the following year. 'IN UTERO' (1993) reflected the turmoil, an uncompromising wall of noise (courtesy of STEVE ALBINI) characterising most of the album. The melodies were still there, you just had to dig deeper in the sludge to find them. Despite 'Geffen's misgivings, the record was a transatlantic No.1, its success engendering another round of live work. After a final American show in January, the group set off for Europe, taking a break at the beginning of March. COBAIN remained in Rome, where, on the 4th March, LOVE found him unconscious in their hotel room, the result of an attempted tranquilizer overdose. Although COBAIN eventually recovered, the tour was abandoned and the couple returned to their Seattle home. Though it didn't come as a complete surprise, the music world was stunned nonetheless when, on the 8th April, news broke that COBAIN had finally killed himself, blowing his own head off with a shotgun. The most widely mourned rock'n'roll death since JOHN LENNON, COBAIN's suicide even sparked off a series of 'copycat' incidents in America by obsessive fans. Posthumously released later that year, the acoustic 'UNPLUGGED IN NEW YORK' (1994) live set was heavy going, a tragic poignancy underpinning the spare beauty of tracks like 'DUMB' and 'PENNYROYAL TEA' (from 'IN UTERO') while the heart-rendingly resigned 'ALL APOLOGIES' sounds like COBAIN's final goodbye to a world that he could no longer bear to be a part of. Eventually picking up the pieces, GROHL formed The FOO FIGHTERS, turning his hand to guitar playing/songwriting and recruiting ex-GERM, PAT SMEAR. After time spent campaigning for his native, war torn Yugoslavia, NOVOSELIC returned with his own band, SWEET 75, a collaboration with diminutive Venezuelan lesbian folk-singer, YVA LAS VEGAS. They finally released one unstartling eponymous set in 1997, which just might be their only outing. • **Songwriters:** COBAIN wrote late 80's work. In the 90's, the group were credited with COBAIN lyrics. Covers; LOVE BUZZ (Shocking Blue) / HERE SHE COMES NOW (Velvet Underground) / DO YOU LOVE ME? (Kiss) / TURNAROUND (Devo) / JESUS WANTS ME FOR A SUNBEAM (Vaselines) / D7 (Wipers) / THE MAN WHO SOLD THE WORLD (David Bowie) / WHERE DID YOU SLEEP LAST NIGHT (Leadbelly).

Album rating: BLEACH (*8) / NEVERMIND (*10) / INCESTICIDE collection (*7) / IN UTERO (*10) / UNPLUGGED IN NEW YORK (*9) / FROM THE MUDDY BANKS OF THE WISHKAH (*8) / Sweet 75: SWEET 75 (*4)

KURT COBAIN (b.20 Feb'67, Hoquaim, Washington) – vocals, guitar / **CHRIS NOVOSELIC** (b.16 May'65) – bass / **CHAD CHANNING** (b.31 Jan'67, Santa Rosa, Calif.) – drums

Tupelo Sub Pop

Oct 88. (7") *<SP 23>* **LOVE BUZZ. / BIG CHEESE** [-] [ ]

— Early '89, added **JASON EVERMAN** – guitar Also guest drummer on 2 tracks **DALE CROVER**

Aug 89. (lp,white or green-lp/cd) *(TUP LP/CD 6) <SP 34>* **BLEACH** [ ] [ ] Jun89
– Blew / Floyd the barber / About a girl / School / Paper cuts / Negative creep / Scoff / Swap meet / Mr.Moustache / Sifting / Big cheese. *(cd+=)* – Love buzz / Downer. *<US re-iss. Dec91 hit 89> (re-iss. Feb92 on 'Geffen'; GEFD 24433) (hit UK No.33) (c+=)* – Big cheese. *(re-iss. Oct95 on 'Geffen' cd/c; GFLD/GFLC 19291)*

Dec 89. (12"ep/cd-ep) *(TUP EP8/CD8)* **BLEW / LOVE BUZZ. / BEEN A SON / STAIN** [ ] [-]

— **DAN PETERS** – drums (of MUDHONEY) repl. CHANNING (Apr90)

Jan 91. (7",7"green) *(TUP 25)* **SLIVER. / DIVE** [ ] [ ] Sep 90
(12"+=) *(TUP EP25)* – About a girl (live). *(US-iss.7"blue; SP 72)*
(cd-s++=) *(TUP CD25)* – Spank thru (live).

Feb 91. (7",7"green) *<SP 97>* **MOLLY'S LIPS. / ('Candy' by FLUID)** [-] [ ]

not iss. Communion

Mar 91. (7"colrd) *<Communion 25>* **HERE SHE COMES NOW. / ('Venus In Furs' by MELVINS)** [-] [ ]

— (Apr'91 trio) **DAVE GROHL** (b.14 Jan'69, Warren, Ohio) – drums, vocals (ex-SCREAM) repl. PETERS and EVERMAN, who joined MIND FUNK

Geffen Geffen

Sep 91. (lp/c/cd) *<(DGC/+C/D 24425)>* **NEVERMIND** [7] [1]
– Smells like teen spirit / In bloom / Come as you are / Breed / Lithium / Polly / Territorial pissings / Drain you / Lounge act / Stay away / On a plain / Something in the way. *(cd+=)* – Endless nameless. *(lp re-iss. Nov98 on 'Simply Vinyl'; SVLP 38)*

Oct 91. (c-s/cd-s) *<19050>* **SMELLS LIKE TEEN SPIRIT / EVEN IN HIS YOUTH** [-] [6]

Nov 91. (7"/c-s) *(DGC/+C 5)* **SMELLS LIKE TEEN SPIRIT. / DRAIN YOU** [7] [-]
(12"pic-d+=) *(DGCTP 5)* – Aneurysm.
(cd-s++=) *(DGCCD 5)* – Even in his youth.
(12") *(DGCT 5)* – ('A'side) / Even in his youth / Aneurysm.

Mar 92. (c-s/cd-s) *<19120>* **COME AS YOU ARE. / DRAIN YOU (live)** [-] [32]

Mar 92. (7"/c-s) *(DGC/+C 7)* **COME AS YOU ARE. / ENDLESS NAMELESS** [9] [-]
(12"+=/12"pic-d+=) *(DGCT/+P 7)* – School (live).
(cd-s++=) *(DGCTD 7)* – Drain you (live).

Jul 92. (7"/c-s) *(DGCS/+C 9)* **LITHIUM. / CURMUDGEON** [11] [-]
(12"pic-d+=) *(DGCTP 9)* – Been a son (live).
(cd-s++=) *(DGCSD 9)* – D7 (Peel session).

Jul 92. (c-s,cd-s) *<19134>* **LITHIUM / BEEN A SON (live)** [-] [64]

Nov 92. (7"/c-s) *(GFS/+C 34)* **IN BLOOM. / POLLY** [28] [-]
(12"pic-d+=/cd-s+=) *(GFST P/D 34)* – Sliver (live).

Dec 92. (cd/c/lp) *<(GED/GEC/GEF 24504)>* **INCESTICIDE** (rare material) [14] [39]
– Dive / Sliver / Stain / Been a son / Turnaround / Molly's lips / Son of a gun / (New wave) Polly / Beeswax / Downer / Mexican seafood / Hairspray queen / Aero zeppelin / Big long now / Aneurysm.

— In Feb'93, NIRVANA's 'OH, THE GUILT' appeared on double'A'side with JESUS LIZARD's 'Puss'. Issued on 'Touch & Go' 7"blue/cd-s; *(TG 83/+CD)*. It had UK No.12, and crashed out of the Top 60 the following week!.

— GOODBYE MR MACKENZIE's BIG JOHN played guitar for them in mid'93.

— In Aug'93, KURT COBAIN and WILLIAM S.BURROUGHS narrated 'The Priest, They Call Him By' on 10"lp/cd 'Tim Kerr'; *(92 10/CD 044)*

Aug 93. (7"/c-s) *(GFS/+C 54)* **HEART-SHAPED BOX. / MARIGOLD** [5] [-]
(12"+=/cd-s+=) *(GFST/+D 54)* – Milk it.

Sep 93. (cd/c/lp)<clear-lp> *<(GED/GEC/GEF 24536)><DGC 24607>* **IN UTERO** [1] [1]
– Serve the servants / Scentless apprentice / Heart-shaped box / Rape me / Frances Farmer will have her revenge on Seattle / Dumb / Very ape / Milk it / Penny royal tea / Radio friendly unit shifter / Tourette's / All apologies. *(cd+=)* – Gallons of rubbing alcohol flow through the strip. *(lp re-iss. Nov98 on 'Simply Vinyl'; SVLP 48)*

Dec 93. (7"/c-s) *(GFS/+C 66)* **ALL APOLOGIES. / RAPE ME** [32] [-]
(12"+=/cd-s+=) *(GFST/+D 66)* – MV.

— On the 4th March '94, KURT overdosed while on holiday in Italy and went into a coma. A month later, on the 8th April he committed suicide, by shooting himself through the mouth. He was only 27, and this was certainly the biggest rock star death since JOHN LENNON. For more details see HOLE and the COURTNEY LOVE story.
below album featured **LORI GOLDSTON** – cello + **MEAT PUPPETS' Curt & Cris Kirkwood** on 3rd, 4th & 5th last songs.

Nov 94. (cd/c/white-lp) *<(GED/GEC/GEF 24727)>* **UNPLUGGED IN NEW YORK** (live acoustic) [1] [1]
– About a girl / Come as you are / Jesus doesn't want me for a sunbeam / Dumb / The man who sold the world / Pennyroyal tea / Polly / On a plain / Something in the way / Plateau / Oh me / Lake of fire / All apologies / Where did you sleep last night. *(lp re-iss. Nov98 on 'Simply Vinyl'; SVLP 53)*

— GROHL (now vox, guitar) formed The FOO FIGHTERS with ex-GERMS guitarist PAT SMEAR; meanwhile NOVOSELIC formed the trio SWEET 75

– compilations, etc. –

on 'Geffen' unless mentioned otherwise

Jul 95. (d-cd) *<(GES 00001)>* **BLEACH / INCESTICIDE** [ ] [ ]

Nov 95. (6xcd-s-box) *<(GED 24901)>* **6 CD SINGLE BOXED SET** [ ] [ ]

Oct 96. (cd/c/lp) *<(GED/GEC/GEF 25105)>* **FROM THE MUDDY BANKS OF THE WISHKAH (live)** [4] [1]
– Intro / School / Drain you / Aneurysm / Smells like teen spirit / Been a son / Lithium / Sliver / Spank thru / Scentless apprentice / Heart-shaped box / Milk it / Negative creep / Polly / Breed / Tourette's / Blew.

SWEET 75

KRIST NOVOSELIC – guitar (ex-NIRVANA) / **YVA LAS VEGAS** – vocals, bass / **ADAM WADE** – drums

Geffen Geffen

Aug 97. (cd/c) *<(GED/GEC 25140)>* **SWEET 75** [ ] [ ]
– Fetch / Lay me down / Bite my hand / Red dress / La vida / Six years / Take another stab / Poor Kitty / Ode to Dolly / Dogs / Cantos de Pilon / Nothing / Japan trees / Oral health.

NITZINGER

Formed: Texas, USA . . . early 70's by namesake JOHN NITZINGER, plus rhythm section, CURLY BENTON and LINDA WARING. With NITZINGER's gonzo-boogie guitar style often drawing comparisons to TED NUGENT, the eponymous 1972 album set the raucous blueprint for his subsequent work as well as breaking into the US Top 200. Though rooted in blues-based rock, NITZINGER's albums are notable for their musical diversity, the Texan bringing his inimitable touch to more exotic fare. NITZINGER also wrote material for sludge-metallers BLOODROCK. Following the 'ONE FOOT IN HISTORY' (1973) set, NITZINGER eventually resurfaced with a group of session musicians for 1976's 'LIVE BETTER . . . ELECTRICALLY' before opting for session work himself and going on to work with both ALICE COOPER and (CARL PALMER's) P.M.

Album rating: NITZINGER (*6) / ONE FOOT IN HISTORY (*5) / LIVE BETTER . . . ELECTRICALLY (*4)

JOHN NITZINGER – vocals, guitar / **CURLY BENTON** – bass / **LINDA WARING** – drums, vocals

not iss. Capitol

Aug 72. (lp) *<SMAS 11091>* **NITZINGER** [-] [ ]
– L.A. Texas boy / Boogie queen / Nature of your taste / No sun / My last goodbye / Hero of the war / Tickclick / Witness to the truth / Enigma / Louisiana cock fight / My last goodbye.

—— added **BUGS HENDERSON** – guitar

1973. (lp) *<SMAS 11122>* **ONE FOOT IN HISTORY** [-] [ ]
– Take a picture / Motherlode / God bless the pervert / Earth eater / Driftwood / Let the living grow / Cripple gnat Boune / One foot in history / Uncle John.

—— NITZINGER now used session players including **KENNETH WHITFIELD** – keyboards / **JERRY HARRIS** – bass / **PAUL LEIM + DARREL NORRIS + RANDY REEDER** – drums

20th Century 20th Century

1976. (lp) *(6370 251) <518>* **LIVE BETTER . . . ELECTRICALLY** [ ] [ ]
– Control / Are you with me / Live better electrically / Around / Gimme a wink / Yellow dog / Tell Texas / Vagabond / No way around you / The writing on the wall.

—— went into session work for ALICE COOPER and (CARL PALMER's) P.M.

NOCTURNAL RITES

Formed: Umea, Sweden . . . 1990 by FREDRIK MANNBERG originally as a death-metal band named NECROMONIC, although he experienced a multitude of problems with the line-up culminating in a break-up which left only himself and drummer TOMMY ERIKSSON. The two became three; recruiting bassist NILS ERIKSSON and renaming themselves NOCTURNAL RITES. These guys released a demo in '91, 'THE OBSCURE', however, this did not come to much. While writing material the band realised that their passions lay in metal's past – namely heavy metal supergroups like IRON MAIDEN, JUDAS PRIEST and even ALICE COOPER. Thus they turned away from the burgeoning Scandinavian death metal scene and began writing material worthy of their influences. At this point TOMMY ERIKSSON departed and was succeeded by ULF ANDERSON, with MIKAEL SODERSTROM joining on guitar. After producing a demo in their new-found retro style, the band decided that they needed a singer with the delivery to match the genre. So MANNBERG concentrated on lead and they hired vocalist ANDERS ZACKRISSON. Managing to get a deal with 'Megarocks', the Swedish combo released their debut album, 'IN A TIME OF BLOOD AND FIRE' (1996). Unfortunately the dismal marketing and distribution of the record didn't do the boys any favours and they subsequently signed with metallic/punk bastion 'Century Media'. SODERSTROM left after this initial set and was subsequently replaced by NILS NORBERG who admirably complemented MANNBERG in their dual lead guitar style. This was shown to great effect in their live shows, and on their second full issue, 'TALES OF MYSTERY AND IMAGINATION' (1998). This set was technically very good, and was popular among the metallers who still harked back to the glory days of the 80's stadium rock legends. Shortly after this release, sticksman ANDERSON, left and was replaced by OVE LINGVALL. NOCTURNAL RITES continued in the same power-rock vein with their third full-length release, 'THE SACRED TALISMAN' (1999), keeping their goth-metal fans happy as well with their Tolkein-style subject matter. The turn of the century saw the departure of ZACKRISSON and the recruitment of singer JOHNNY LINDKVIST for their fourth long-player, 'AFTERLIFE' (2000), another tribute to the rock gods of bygone days.

Album rating: IN A TIME OF BLOOD AND FIRE (*4) / TALES OF MYSTERY AND IMAGINATION (*5) / THE SACRED TALISMAN (*5) / AFTERLIFE (*5)

ANDERS ZACKRISSON – vocals / **FREDRIK MANNBERG** – lead guitar / **MIKAEL SODERSTROM** – rhythm guitar / **NILS ERIKSSON** – bass / **ULF ANDERSSON** – drums; repl. TOMMY ERIKSSON

Megarocks not iss.

Nov 96. (cd) *(MRRCD 032)* **IN A TIME OF BLOOD AND FIRE** [ ] [-]
– Sword of steel / Skyline flame / Black death / In a time of blood and fire / Dawnspell / Lady of Ennui / Winds of death / Rest in peace / Dragonisle.

—— **NILS NORBERG** – lead guitar; repl. SODERSTROM

—— **OVE LINGVALL** – vocals; repl. MANNBERG

Century Media Century Media

Apr 98. (cd) *(CM 77208CD) <7908>* **TALES OF MYSTERY AND IMAGINATION** [ ] [ ]
– Ring of steel / Dark secret / Test of time / Lost in time / The vision / Warrior's return / Change the world / Pentagram / Eye of the world / The curse / Burn in Hell.

—— added on below only **MATTHIAS BERNHARDSSON** – keyboards

Mar 99. (cd) *(CM 77232CD) <7932>* **THE SACRED TALISMAN** [ ] [ ]
– Destiny calls / The iron force / Ride on / Free at last / Hold on to the flame / Eternity holds / When fire comes to ice / The legend lives on / The ring's command / Unholy powers / Glorious.

—— **JONNY LINDKVIST** – vocals; repl. OVE

Sep 00. (cd) *(77292-2) <7992>* **AFTERLIFE** [ ] [ ]
– Afterlife / Wake up dead / The sinner's cross / Hell and back / The sign / The Devil's child / Genetic distortion sequence / Sacrifice / Temple of the dead / Hellenium.

NOCTURNUS

Formed: Tampa, Florida, USA . . . late 80's by MIKE BROWNING, following his departure from MORBID ANGEL. He duly recruited SEAN McNENNEY, MIKE DAVIS and LOUIS PANZER, releasing 'THE KEY' on 'Earache' in late summer 1990. A decidedly different take on the death-metal genre, the record drew praise for its inventive and atmospheric use of keyboards, an instrument seldom heard in such a context. A vocalist proper, DAN IZZO, was brought in for the 1992 album, 'THRESHOLDS', another intelligent effort which failed to make any commercial impact. Prior to the release of the 'POSSESS THE PRIEST EP', the group brought in EMO MOWERY as a more permanent replacement for the departed ANDERSON. In the event the record was shelved and the band split, only to rise from Florida's death metal swamps once more at the turn of the decade with 'ETHEREAL TOMB' (2000). Recorded with a rejuvenated line-up of McNENNEY, DAVIS, MOWERY and new drummer RICK BIZZARO, the album wasn't too far removed from the sound of their highly regarded debut if never quite maintaining the quality of sonic innovation.

Album rating: THE KEY (*6) / THRESHOLDS (*5) / ETHEREAL TOMB (*5)

MIKE BROWNING – vocals, drums (ex-MORBID ANGEL) / **SEAN McNENNEY** – guitar / **MIKE DAVIS** – guitar / **LOUIS PANZER** – keyboards

Earache Combat

Sep 90. (lp/cd) *(MOSH 023/+CD) <2029>* **THE KEY** [ ] [ ]
– Lake of fire / Standing in blood / Visions from beyond the grave / Neolithic / BC/AD / Andromeda strain / Droid sector / Destroying the manager / Empire of the sands. *(cd+=)* – Undead journey.

—— **DAN IZZO** took over vocals / added **CHRIS ANDERSON** – bass

May 92. (lp/cd) *(MOSH 055/+CD)* **THRESHOLDS** [ ] [-]
– Climate controller / Tribal vodoun / Nocturne in B M / Arctic crypt / Aquatic / Subterranean infiltrator / After reality / Gridzone. *(cd re-iss. Mar99; same)*

—— **EMO MOWERY** repl. touring bassist JIM O'SULLIVAN who repl. CHRIS

Morbid Sounds not iss.

Jul 94. (cd-s) *(DEAD 02EP)* **POSSESS THE PRIEST / MUMMIFIED** [ ] [-]

—— the band had already split; they re-formed in 1999

not iss. Necropolis

Feb 00. (cd) *<50>* **ETHEREAL TOMB** [-] [ ]
– Orbital decay / Apostle of evil / Edge of darkness / The killing / Search for the trident / Paranormal state / The science of horror / Outland.

NOFX

Formed: Hollywood, California, USA . . . 1984 by 'FAT' MIKE RAKHABIT, ERIC MELVIN, IZZY DREW LYNN and GROGGY NODBEGGAR. Punk-metal/hardcore stalwarts, NOFX's albums are noted primarily for their black humour and cutting wit, their music akin to a more adventurous fusion of BLACK FLAG and BAD RELIGION. The latter band's label, 'Epitaph', recognised NOFX's distinctive talents and the label's mainman GUREWITZ signed them for debut album, 'LIBERATION ANIMATION' (1988) – there had of course been loads of singles, mainly for 'Mystic' records. A further couple of albums followed over the ensuing two years, 'S & M AIRLINES' (1989) and 'RIBBED' (1990), the latter set, in particular, seeing the group gaining more widespread recognition for their wicked way with a humorous lyric and a skull-crushing sonic assault. NOFX (AL HEFE and ERIK SANDON replaced IZZY and GROGGY respectively) continued a fairly prolific recording schedule throughout the 90's (MIKE formed his own 'Fat Wreck Chords' label), and following the success of bands like GREEN DAY, finally made the US and UK charts (Top 75) with 1996's 'HEAVY PETTING ZOO'. True to the band's confrontational style, the artwork depicted a sheep shearer, eh . . . shearing very close to the bone . . . so to speak. In the same year at a New York gig, they dressed up in bizarre female clothing copying the style of tourmates, The LUNACHICKS. Clever-clever as ever, the Californian japesters came up with the wonderful title of 'PUMP UP THE VALUUM' for their millennial album release. In amongst the likes of 'MY VAGINA' and 'CLAMS HAVE FEELINGS TOO', FAT MIKE had actually penned a semi-serious prophecy on the fate of rich rock bands come the full extent of the internet revolution, 'DINOSAURS WILL DIE'. • **Trivia:** FAT MIKE also plays bass for his mates' covers outfit, ME FIRST AND THE GIMME GIMMES, releasing two albums (on his own 'Fat Wreck Chords') and a handful of singles during the late 90's.

Album rating: LIBERATION ANIMATION (*3) / S & M AIRLINES (*4) / RIBBED (*5) / WHITE TRASH, TWO HEEBS AND A BEAN (*5) / PUNK IN DRUBLIC (*7) / I HEARD THEY SUCK LIVE!!! (*5) / HEAVY PETTING ZOO (*5) / SO LONG – AND THANKS FOR ALL THE SHOES (*4) / PUMP UP THE VALUUM (*6)

'FAT' MIKE BURKETT – vocals, bass / **ERIC MELVIN** – guitar / **IZZY DREW LYNN** – guitar / **GROGGY NODBEGGAR** – drums

not iss. Mystic

1984. (7"ep) **FOR A GLORY OF KATE EP** [-] [ ]
– Kasia is the best / Warsaw – The capital city of Poland / Polish lakes rules / Atlanta is shit.

1985. (7"ep) **LIVE YOUR LIFE EP** [-] [ ]
– Live your life / My friends / Six pack girls / Bang gang / Hit it / Hold it back / I.D.

1986. (12"ep) <33-159> **THE ALBUM** [-] [ ]
– No problems / Memories / Beast within / Instrumental Ant attack / Cops and donuts / Iron man / Live your life / My friends / Six pack girls / Bang gang / Hit it / Hold it back / I.D.

1986. (7"ep) **SO WHAT IF WE'RE ON MYSTIC!** [-] [ ]
– Shitting bricks / Mom's rules / On my mind / White bread / Larger in the dark / Too mixed up / Drain bamaged / Bob Turkee.

not iss. Wassail

1987. (7"ep) <1> **THE P.M.R.C CAN SUCK ON THIS** [-] [ ]
– Duelling retards / On the rag / A 200 club / Shut up already / The punk song / Johnny B. good.

1988. (12"ep) **NO F-X** [-] [ ]
– Shut up aleady / Freedumb / Here come the neighborhood /A200 club / Sloppy English / You put your chocolate in my peanut butter / Mr. Jones / Vegetarian mumbo jumbo / Beer bong / Piece / I live in a cake / No problems / On the rag / Truck stop blues.

1987. (7"ep) **DRINKIN', STINKIN', NEVER THINKIN'** [-] [ ]

1988. (lp) **LIBERATION ANIMATION** [-] [ ]
– Shut up already / Freedumb / Here comes the neighbourhood / A 200 club / Sloppy English / You put your chocolate in my peanut butter / Mr. Jones / Vegetarian mumbo jumbo / Beer bong song / Piece / I live in a cake / No problems / On the rag / Truck stop blues. *(UK-iss.Nov92 on 'Epitaph' cd/lp; E 86417-2/-1)*

Epitaph Epitaph

1989. (lp/cd) <E 86405-1/-2> **S & M AIRLINES** [-] [ ]
– Day to daze / Five feet under / Professional crastination / Mean people suck / Vailla sex / S&M airlines / Drug free America / Life O'Riley / You drink you drive you spill / Screamin for change / Jaundiced eye / Go your own way. *(UK-iss.Nov92 cd/c/lp; same)*

Mar 91. (cd/lp) <86410-1/-2> **RIBBED** [-] [ ]
– Green corn / Moron brothers / Showerdays / Food, sex and ewe / Just the flu / El lay / Cheese – Where's my slice? / Together on the sand / Nowhere / Brain constipation / Gonoherpasyphilaids / I don't want you around / Malachi crunch. *(UK-iss.Nov92 cd/c/lp; 6410-2/-4/-1)*

—— **EL HEFE** – guitar, trumpet, vocals / **ERIK GHINT** (b. SANDON) – drums; repl. IZZY DREW + GROGGY NODBEGGAR

Jun 92. (m-cd/m-lp) <(FAT 503-2/-1)> **THE LONGEST LINE** [ ] [ ]
– The death of John Smith / The longest line / Stranded / Remnants / Kill all the white man. *(m-cd re-iss. Dec96; same)*

Nov 92. (7") **LIZA AND LOUISE. / THE FASTEST LONGEST LINE** [-] [ ]
(above 2 issued on 'Fat Wreck Chords')

Jun 93. (cd/lp) <(E 86418-2/-1)> **WHITE TRASH, TWO HEEBS AND A BEAN** [ ] [ ] Nov92
– Soul doubt / Stickin' in my eye / Bob / You're bleeding / Straight edge / Liza and Louise / Bag / Please play this song on the radio / Warm / I wanna be your baby / Johnny Appleseed / She's gone / Buggley eyes.

Jun 94. (7") <(FAT 514-7)> **DON'T CALL ME WHITE. / PUNK GUY** [ ] [ ]
(above issued on 'Fat Wreck Chords')

Jul 94. (cd/c/lp) <(E 86435-2/-4/-1)> **PUNK IN DRUBLIK** [ ] [ ]
– Linoleum / Leave it alone / Dig / Cause / Don't call me white / My heart is yearning / A perfect government / The brews / The quass / Dying degree / Fleas / Lori Meyers / Jeff wears birkenstocks? / Punk guy (cause he does punk things) / The happy guy / Reeko / Scavenger type.

Jul 95. (7") <(FAT 526-1)> **WE AIN'T SHIT. / DRUGS ARE GOOD** [ ] [ ]
(above was actually billed as 'HOFX')

Sep 95. (cd/c/lp) <(FAT 528-2/-4/-1)> **I HEARD THEY SUCK LIVE!! (live)** [ ] [ ]
– Linoleum / You're bleeding / Moron brothers / Punk guy / Bob / Life O'Riley / You drink, you drive, you spill nothing . . . / East Bay / Soul doubt / Kill all the white man / Beer bong / Six pack girls / Together on the sand / Nowhere / The bres / Buggley eyes.
(above 2 releases on 'Fat Wreck Chords') (below on 'Out Of Step')

Sep 95. (10"/cd-s) *(WOOS 6 TOT/CDS)* **LEAVE IT ALONE / DON'T CALL ME WHITE. / SOUL DOUBT (live) / DRUGS ARE GOOD** [ ] [-]

Jan 96. (cd/c) <(E 86457-2/-4)> **HEAVY PETTING ZOO** [60] [63]
– Hobophobic (scared of bums) / Philthy Phil Philanthropist / Freedom lika shopping cart / Bleeding heart disease / Hot dog in a hallway / Release the hostages / Liza / What's the matter with kids today? / Love story / Black and white / Whatever Didi wants / August 8th / Drop the world.

Nov 96. (7"ep) **FUCK THE KIDS** [-] [ ]
– Fuck the kids I / Fuck the kids II / I'm telling Tim / Reagan sucks / My name's Bud / Two on glue / Please stop fucking my mom / Murder the government / Stranger than fishin' / Stupid Canadiens / Eric Melvin Vs. PCP / Always hate hippies.

Nov 97. (cd/c/lp) <(6518-2/-4/-1)> **SO LONG – AND THANKS FOR ALL THE SHOES (live)** [ ] [79]
– 180 degrees / I'm telling him / Dad's bad news / Falling in love / Kill rock stars / Punk rock elite / Murder the government / Stuck in the k-hole again / Desperation's gone / All outta angst / Champs Elysees / Quart in session / Mono syllabic girl / Eat the meek.

Nov 97. (7") <(FAT 561-7)> **ALL OF ME. / THE DESPERATION'S GONE** [ ] [ ]

1999. (7") **TIMMY THE TURTLE. / THE PLAN** [-] [ ]

Nov 99. (cd-s/12") <(FAT 605-2/-1)> **THE DECLINE** (one 18 minute song) [ ] [ ]
(above singles were issued on 'Fat Wreck Chords')

May 00. (cd/c) <(6584-2/-4/-1)> **PUMP UP THE VALUUM** [50] [61]
– And now for something completely similar / Take two placebos and call me lame / What's the matter with parents today? / Dinosaurs will die / Thank God it's Monday / Clams have feelings too / Louise / Stranger than fishin' / Pharmacist's daughter / Bottles to the ground / Total bummer / My vagina / Herojuana / Theme from a NOFX album / Lower.

Jun 00. (7") <(FAT 614-7)> **PODS AND GODS. / WHAT'S THE MATTER WITH PARENTS TODAY** [ ] [ ]
(above issued for 'Fat Wreck Chords')

Oct 00. (cd-s) *(6594-2)* **BOTTLES TO THE GROUND / LOWER / MY NAME IS BUD / DINOSAURS WILL DIE** [ ] [-]

Apr 01. (7"ep) <FAT 624> **SURFER EP** [-] [ ]
– Fun things to fuck (if you're a winner) / Juice head / Three on speed / New happy birthday song? / Talking 'bout to momma / Party enema / Can't get the stink out / Go to work wasted / Fuck da kids / Whoa on the whoas / Three shits to the wind / Puke on cops / I gotta pee / Totally fucked.
(above issued on 'Fat Wreck Chords')

– compilations, etc. –

Oct 94. (cd) *Mystic;* <(MYSTICCD 180)> **MAXIMUM ROCK'N'ROLL (E IS EVERYTHING)** (all the early 'Mystic' material) [ ] [ ] 1991
– Live your life / My friends / Six pack girls / Bang gang / Hit it / Hold it back / I.D. / Cops and donuts / Iron man / Shitting bricks / Mom's rules / On my mind / White bread / Larger in the dark / Too mixed up / Drain bamaged / Bob Turkee / No problems / Memories / Beast within / Instrumental / Ant attack. *(lp-iss.Mar99; MYSTIC 180)*

NOMEANSNO

Formed: Victoria, British Columbia, Canada . . . 1983 by the WRIGHT brothers ROB and JOHN (their name a reference to a woman's right to refuse sexual advances). Deliberately anti-image and fiercely independent from the beginning, NOMEANSNO delivered their debut set, 'MAMA', in 1983 on their own label, 'Wrong'. With darkly caustic social commentary and fragmented, avant-garde fuzzcore their forte, this trio (having recently added ANDREW KERR) certainly weren't in the game of rock stardom. They found a soul mate in JELLO BIAFRA, who subsequently signed/licensed them to the ever bulging roster of 'Alternative Tentacles' in 1984. Several albums followed through the 80's, namely 'SEX MAD' (1987), 'SMALL PARTS ISOLATED AND DESTROYED' (1988), 'WRONG' (1989) and '0+2=1' (1991). A year previously, they were one of the many acts to collaborate with BIAFRA, recording an album, 'THE SKY IS FALLING AND I WANT MY MOMMY' together. More recently, the trio have issued two further, equally barbed sets, 'WHY DO THEY CALL ME MR. HAPPY?' (1993) (Mr. HAPPY being ROB's solo alter-ego) and 'THE WORLDHOOD OF THE WORLD (AS SUCH)' (1995). The snappily titled 'DANCE OF THE HEADLESS BOURGEOISIE' arrived in 1998, confirming the veteran Canadian subversives as leaders in the – admittedly fairly undersubscribed – field of abrasive but curiously rhythmic avant-hardcore. Fittingly then, perhaps, the band even turned their hand to a cover (and there aren't that many around) of Miles Davis' fusion classic, 'BITCHES BREW', carried off in NOMEANSNO style along with The Ramones' 'BEAT ON THE BRAT'; both could be found nestled away in the closing section of 'NO ONE' (2000).

Album rating: SEX MAD (*5) / SMALL PARTS ISOLATED AND DESTROYED (*6) / WHY DO THEY CALL ME MR. HAPPY? (*6) / WRONG (*5) / 0+2=1 (*6) / THE WORLDHOOD OF THE WORLD (AS SUCH) (*6) / DANCE OF THE HEADLESS BOURGEOISE (*6)

ANDREW KERR – guitar (joined after debut) / **ROB WRIGHT** – bass / **JOHN WRIGHT** – drums

not iss. Wrong

1983. (lp) <WRONG 001> **MAMA** [-] [ ]
– Living is free / My roommate is turning into a monster / Red devil / Mama's little boy / We are the chopped / No sex / Rich guns / No rest for the wicked / Living in Detente. *(UK-iss.Nov92 on 'Wrong' cd/c; WRONG 001 CD/C)*

1985. (12"ep) <WRONG > **YOU KILL ME** [-] [ ]
– Body bag / Stop it / Some bodies / Manic depression / Paradise (with BILLY & SARAH GAINES). *<(re-iss. 1990 & Apr00 on 'Alternative Tentacles'+=; VIRUS 86)>* – SEX MAD

Alternative Tentacles Alternative Tentacles

Jan 87. (lp) <(VIRUS 56)> **SEX MAD** [ ] [ ]
– Sex mad / Dad / Obsessed / No fkucign / Hunt the she beast / Dead Bob / Long days / Metrognome / Revenge / Self pity. *<cd-iss. Jun91 +=; VIRUS 56CD>* – YOU KILL ME

Feb 88. (7") <VIRUS 60> **DAD. / REVENGE** [-] [ ]

May 88. (12"ep) <(VIRUS 62)> **THE DAY EVERYTHING BECAME NOTHING** [ ] [ ]
– The day everything became nothing / Dead souls / Forget your life / Beauty and the beast.

May 88. (lp/c/cd) <(VIRUS 63/+MC/CD)> **SMALL PARTS ISOLATED AND DESTROYED** [ ] [ ]
– Brother rat / What Slayde says / Dark ages / Junk / And that's sad / Small parts isolated and destroyed / Victory / Teresa give me that knife / Real love / Lonely. *(cd-iss. as 'THE DAY EVERYTHING BECAME ISOLATED AND DESTROYED', which included last ep)*

Nov 89. (lp/c/cd) <(VIRUS 77/+MC/CD)> **WRONG** [ ] [ ]
– It's catching up / The tower / Brainless wonder / Tired of waiting / Stocktaking / The end of all things / Big Dick / Two lips, two lungs, and one tongue / Rags and bones / Oh no! Bruno! / All lies. *(cd+=)* – Life in Hell / I am wrong.

Apr 90. (12"/cd-s) <(VIRUS 81/+CD)> **THE POWER OF POSITIVE THINKING. / MANIC DEPRESSION** [ ] [ ]

—— early 1991, collaborated with JELLO BIAFRA (Dead Kennedys) on album 'THE SKY IS FALLING AND I WANT MY MOMMY'

Oct 91. (lp/c/cd) <(VIRUS 98/+MC/CD)> **0 + 2 = 1** [ ] [ ]
– Now will you be good? / The fall / 0 + 2 = 1 / The valley of the blind / Mary / Everyday I start to ooze / When putting it all in order ain't enough / The night nothing became everything / I think you know / Ghosts / Joyful reunion.

—— now without KERR who formed HISSANOL with their engineer, SCOTT HENDERSON

Jun 93. (lp/c/cd) <(VIRUS 123/+MC/CD)> **WHY DO THEY CALL ME MR. HAPPY?**
– The land of the living / The river / Machine / Madness and death / Happy bridge / Kill everyone now / I need you (with TONYA WYNNE). *(c+=/cd+=)* – Slowly melting / Lullaby / Cats, sex and Nazis.

— added guitarist/keyboardist (**TOMMY**) and uncredited drummer

Nov 95. (cd/lp) <(VIRUS 171 CD/LP)> **THE WORLDHOOD OF THE WORLD (AS SUCH)** Oct95
– Joy / Humans / Angel or devil / He learned how to bleed / I've got a gun / My politics / Lost / Predators / Wiggley worm / Tuck it away / Victim's choice / State of grace / The jungle.

Dec 97. (12"ep/cd-ep) <(VIRUS 207/+CD)> **WOULD WE BE ALIVE? / YOU ARE NOT THE ONE. / RISE / BIG DICK (alternate version)**

Jun 98. (lp/cd) <(VIRUS 215/+CD)> **DANCE OF THE HEADLESS BOURGEOISE**
– This story must be told / Going nowhere / I'm an asshole / Disappear / Dance of the headless bourgeoisie / The world wasn't built in a day / I can't stop talking / The rape / Give me the push / One fine day.

Sep 00. (d-lp) <(VIRUS 248)> **NO ONE**
– The graveyard shift / Under the sea / Our town / A little too high / Hello, goodbye / The phone call / Bitch's brew / Beat on the brat.

– compilations, others, etc. –

1990's. (7") *Wrong; (WRONG 2)* **BETRAYAL. /**

1990's. (7") *Plastic Head; (ALLIEDN 010)* **OH CANADUH. /**

Jun 91. (d-lp/c/cd) *Konkurrel; (K 031-130) / Alternative Tentacles;* <VIRUS 97/+MC/CD> **LIVE + CUDDLY (live in Europe)**

Oct 94. (cd) *Wrong; (WRONG 13)* **ONE DOWN, TWO TO GO (NO MEANS NO PRESENTS: MR WRIGHT & MR WRONG)**

May 97. (cd/lp) *Konkurrel; (FIRSTFISH 1 CD/LP)* **IN THE FISHTANK** -

John NORUM

Born: Upplands-Vasby, Stockholm, Sweden. After helping to form EUROPE in the early 80's, the guitarist departed just as they were hitting the big time with 'THE FINAL COUNTDOWN' (1986). Not content with their newfound pop-metal crossover, NORUM recorded his debut solo album, 'TOTAL CONTROL'. However, this showed no major change of direction and although he was to surface again in the early 90's (with DON DOKKEN), NORUM virtually quit the business after a second solo set, 'FACE THE TRUTH' (1992). From '95 onwards, NORUM completed work on a handful of other long-players, including fan's fave, 'ANOTHER DESTINATION'. • **Covers:** MASSACRE + KILLER WITHOUT A CAUSE (Thin Lizzy) / SUNSHINE OF YOUR LOVE (Cream). • **Trivia:** His younger sister, TONE, also recorded her blend of AOR, releasing three albums for 'Epic'.

Album rating: TOTAL CONTROL (*5) / LIVE IN STOCKHOLM mini (*4) / FACE THE TRUTH (*5) / ANOTHER DESTINATION (*6) / WORLDS AWAY (*4) / FACE IT LIVE (*5) / SLIPPED INTO TOMORROW (*4)

JOHN NORUM – guitar, vocals (ex-EUROPE) / with **GORAN EDMAN** – vocals (ex-MADISON) / **MARCEL JACOB** – bass (ex-YNGWIE MALMSTEEN) / **PETER HERMANSSON** – drums (ex-220 VOLTS)

Epic Columbia

Mar 88. (7") *(651 493-7)* **LOVE IS MEANT. / IN CHASE OF THE WIND**
(12"+=) *(651 493-6)* – Don't believe a word / ('A'extended).

Mar 88. (lp/c/cd) *(460 203-1/-4/-2)* <44220> **TOTAL CONTROL**
– Let me love you / Love is meant / Too many hearts / Someone else here / Eternal flame / Back on the streets / Blind / Law of life / We'll do what it takes together / In chase of the wind.

May 88. (7"/12") *(651 187-7/-1)* **LET ME LOVE YOU. / WILD ONE** - - Sweden

Jul 88. (7") *(651 614-7)* **BACK ON THE STREETS. / BAD REPUTATION (live)** - - Sweden

1990. (m-lp) *(656 401-6)* **LIVE IN STOCKHOLM (live)** - - German
– Eternal flame / Don't believe a word / Blind / Free birds in flight (studio).

— now with **GLENN HUGHES** – vocals (ex-DEEP PURPLE) / **PETER BALTES** – bass / **HEMPO HILDEN** – drums / + session people

Epic Shrapnel

1992. (cd/lp) *(46944-2/-1)* <SH 1073> **FACE THE TRUTH** - Sweden
– Face the truth / Night buzz / In your eyes / Opium trail / We will be strong / Good man shining / Time will find the answer / Counting on your love / Endica / Still the night / Distant voices.

1992. (7"/12"/cd-s) *657 670-7/-1/-2)* **WE WILL BE STRONG. / FREE BIRDS IN FLIGHT** - - Sweden

1992. (7") *(658 111-7)* **IN YOUR EYES. / STILL THE NIGHT** - - Sweden
(cd-s+=) *(658 111-2)* – Counting on your love.

1992. (7") *(658 132-7)* **FACE THE TRUTH. / DISTANT VOICES** - - Sweden
(cd-s) *(658 132-2)* – Endica.

May 95. (cd) *<SH 1079>* **ANOTHER DESTINATION** -
– Inside / Resurrection time / Strange days / Spirit world / Shimmering highs / Whose side are you on? / Sunshine of your love / Catalina sunset / Half way home / Healing rays / Jillanna.

Shrapnel Shrapnel

Jul 97. (cd) *<SH 1106>* **WORLDS AWAY** -
– Manic distortion / Make a move / C.Y.R. / Where the grass is green / Center of balance / Dogs are barking / Homeland / Wasted labor / Worlds away / Endica (revisted) / From outside in.

Mar 98. (cd) <(SHR 1117)> **FACE IT LIVE '97 (live)**
– Face the truth / Make a move / Good man shining / Wishing well / Resurrection time / Opium trail / Blind / C.Y.R. / Guitar solo / From outside in / Let me love you / Scream of anger.

Mascot Shrapnel

Mar 00. (cd) *(M 7049CD)* <SH 1145> **SLIPPED INTO TOMORROW** Oct00
– Still in the game / Waiting on you / Blackscape / Tico's life / Nobody answers / Losing my mind / Freedom is my truth / Veda / Songs of yesterday / Killer without a cause / Center of balance.

NOSEBLEEDS

Formed: Manchester, England . . . 1977 by ED BANGER, VINI REILLY, PETE CROOKS and TOBY. Although this raw punk outfit only managed to bring out one single, the brilliant 'AIN'T BIN TO NO MUSIC SCHOOL' (complete with orchestra intro, chunky guitars and griping chorus line!), each member went on to better things: ED to fellow 'Rabid' combo, SLAUGHTER & THE DOGS and VINI (with later PETE and TOBY) to the more subdued DURUTTI COLUMN. Billed at times as ED BANGER & THE NOSEBLEEDS, it was no surprise when the loud frontman went solo leaving the rest to audition the likes of STEPHEN MORRISSEY (yes, that one!); future CULT guitarist, BILLY DUFFY, also made an appearance before their final demise.

Album rating: never released any

ED BANGER – vocals / **VINI REILLY** – guitar / **PETE CROOKS** – bass / **TOBY** – drums

Rabid not iss.

Sep 77. (7") *(TOSH 102)* **AIN'T BIN TO NO MUSIC SCHOOL. / FASCIST PIGS** -

— ED joined SLAUGHTER & THE DOGS after a solo single, VINI joined V2 (prior to any releases) and later recalled PETE and TOBY to his DURUTTI COLUMN, the latter also becoming part of The BLUE ORCHIDS.

ED BANGER

Jul 78. (7") *(TOSH 106)* **KINNEL TOMMY. / BABY WAS A BABY** -
(re-iss. Aug78 on 'EMI International'; INT 570)

Spiv not iss.

Nov 81. (7") *(DIV 1)* **I'VE JUST HAD ME CAR NICKED. / P.C. PLOD / SPONGE** -

Cloud Nine not iss.

Jan 83. (7") *(CNS 01)* **POOR PEOPLE. / VICARS IN THE PARK** -

— ED retired from solo work

NOTHINGFACE

Formed: Washington DC, USA . . . 1995 by songwriter MATT HOLT, TOM MAXWELL, BILL GAAL and CHRIS HOUCK. Following 1997's 'PACIFIER' and 1998's 'AN AUDIO GUIDE TO EVERYDAY ATROCITY' albums – released on the 'Dcide' and 'Mayhem' imprints respectively – NOTHINGFACE signed to 'TVT' for their major label debut, 'VIOLENCE' (2000). As the unequivocal title might suggest, these guys are no-nonsense purveyors of heavy, heavy music eschewing the hip-hop posturing of much nu-metal for a more earthy sound rooted in grunge. Recalling the likes of ALICE IN CHAINS and STONE TEMPLE PILOTS with a strong undercurrent of bleak melody carried on slab-like riffing and propelled by a jackhammer rhythm section, the ominous NOTHINGFACE sound was refreshingly out of step with the rock elite of the new millennium.

Album rating: PACIFIER (*5) / AN AUDIO GUIDE TO EVERYDAY ATROCITY (*6) / VIOLENCE (*6)

MATT HOLT – vocals / **TOM MAXWELL** – guitar / **BILL GAAL** – bass / **CHRIS HOUCK** – drums

not iss. DCide

Feb 97. (cd) <1> **PACIFIER** -
– One thing / Pacifier / Lipsdick / Undercut / Defaced / Self punishment / Hitch / Useless / Perfect person / Communion. *(UK-iss.Sep98 on 'Mayhem'; 11147-2)*

not iss. Eat Raw

May 98. (12"ep) <012> **NOTHINGFACE EP** -

Mayhem Mayhem

Sep 98. (cd) <(11148-2)> **AN AUDIO GUIDE TO EVERYDAY ATROCITY**
– Goldtooth / Grinning / So few / Villains / Sleeper / Breathe out / Error in excellence / I, Diablo / The sick.

TVT TVT

Sep 00. (cd) <(TVT 5880)> **VIOLENCE**
– Make your own bones / Bleeder / Same solution / For all the sin / Can't wait for violence / Dead like me / Blue skin / Filthy / Hidden hands / American love / Everlasting godstopper / Piss & vinegar.

— **TOMMY SICKLES** – drums; repl. HOUCK

— part-time **JERRY MONTANO** – bass (ex-DEADLIGHTS) repl. GAAL who went into production/engineering

NOTSENSIBLES

Formed: Burnley, Lancashire, England . . . 1978 by frontman HAGGIS, and his motley crew of SAGE, KEV, ROG and GARY. "Celebrating" the election of a new Conservative government, these northern lads made their memorable debut with a frantic, fun-packed JILTED JOHN-esque ode to the Iron Lady, '(I'M IN LOVE WITH) MARGARET THATCHER'. Tongue-in-cheek shoutalong punk at its vintage best, the track was a turn of the decade favourite and even laid into Sun pundit, Gary Bushell on the B-side. A possible precursor to the TOY DOLLS, they never quite managed to send-up any target as entertainingly as their debut, although they made a fair attempt with their one and only LP, 'INSTANT CLASSIC' (1980).

Album rating: INSTANT CLASSIC (*4)

HAGGIS – vocals / **SAGE** – guitar / **ROG SENSIBLE** – keyboards, bass / **GARY BROWN** – bass / **KEV HEMMINGWAY** – drums

Redball | not iss.

Nov 79. (7"m) *(RR 02)* **(I'M IN LOVE WITH) MARGARET THATCHER. / LITTLE BOXES / GARY BUSHELL'S BAND OF THE WEEK** [ ] [-]
(re-iss. Jan80 on 'Snotty Snail'; NELCOL 1)

Bent | not iss.

Feb 80. (7"m) *(SMALL BENT 5)* **DEATH TO DISCO. / CORONATION STREET HUSTLE / LYING ON THE SOFA** [ ] [-]

Snotty Snail | not iss.

Mar 80. (lp) *(SSLP 1)* **INSTANT CLASSIC** [ ] [-]
– Instant classic / Girl with scruffy hair / Freedom / King Arthur / Death to disco / Ploppy / I am a clone / Little boxes / Sick of being normal / (Love is like) Banging my head against a brick wall / Because I'm mine / Wrong love / Blackpool rock / Daddy won't let me love you song / Don't wanna work anymore.

1980. (7"m) *(NELCOL 3)* **I THOUGHT YOU WERE DEAD. / I MAKE A BALLS OF EVERYTHING I DO / TEENAGE REVOLUTION** [ ] [-]

Sep 81. (7") *(NELCOL 6)* **I AM THE BISHOP. / THE TELEPHONE RINGS AGAIN** [ ] [-]

— sensibly split up after above

– compilations, etc. –

Sep 94. (cd) *Anagram; (CDPUNK 38)* **INSTANT PUNK CLASSICS** (all material) [ ] [-]

NO USE FOR A NAME

Formed: Sunnydale, California, USA . . . 1987 by leader/songwriter, TONY SLY, along with CHRIS DODGE, STEVE PAPOUTSIS and RORY KOFF. Like many acts of their ilk, NUFAN received early coverage through US hardcore fanzine 'Maximum Rock'n'Roll', releasing their first recorded track, 'TURN IT AROUND' via a special maxi-7" produced by the publication. After a further single, 'LET THEM OUT', their long awaited debut album, 'INCOGNITO', was finally issued at the turn of the decade. Sophomore effort 'DON'T MISS THE TRAIN' (1991) preceded a deal with 'Fat Wreck Chords' and a third album, 'THE DAILY GRIND' (1993). By the release of 'LECHE CON CARNE' (1994), the group had undergone numerous personnel changes with only a couple of survivors form the original line-up. Thus SLY and KOFF welcomed MATT RIDDLE and CHRIS SHIFLETT into the fold for 'MAKING FRIENDS' (1997), the latter jumping ship to the FOO FIGHTERS after the recording of 'MORE BETTERNESS' (1999). Erstwhile SUICIDAL TENDENCIES man, DAVE NASSIE, was subsequently recruited for the millennium.

Album rating: INCOGNITO (*6) / DON'T MISS THE TRAIN (*6) / THE DAILY GRIND (*6) / LECHE CON CARNE (*5) / MAKING FRIENDS (*4) / MORE BETTERNESS! (*3)

TONY SLY – vocals, guitar / **CHRIS DODGE** – guitar / **STEVE PAPOUTSIS** – bass / **RORY KOFF** – drums

not iss. | New Red Archives

1989. (7") **LET 'EM OUT. /** [-] [ ]

1990. (cd/c/lp) *<NSA 20>* **INCOGNITO** [-] [ ]
– DMV / Sign the bill / It won't happen again / Hail to the king / Weirdo / Truth hits everybody / Felix / Noitall / I detest / Puppet show / Record thieves / Power bitch. *(UK cd-iss. Oct98 on 'Playing Golf . . .'; CDHOLE 017)*

1991. (cd/c/lp) *<NSA 32>* **DON'T MISS THE TRAIN** [-] [ ]
– Born addicted / Thorn in my side / Looney toon / Tollbridge / Hole / Another step / Don't miss the train / Watching / Punk points / Tan in a can / Death doesn't care / Get out of this town. *(UK cd-iss. Oct98 on 'Playing Golf . . .'; CDHOLE 018)*

1991. (cd-ep) *<NSA 33>* **DEATH DOESN'T CARE EP** [-] [ ]
– Death doesn't care / DMV / Born addicted / Hail to the king.

— **ROBIN PFEFER** – guitar; repl. DODGE

Fat Wreck Chords | Fat Wreck Chords

Sep 93. (lp/cd) *<(FAT/+CD 507)>* **THE DAILY GRIND** [ ] [ ] Jun93
– Until it's gone / Old what's his name / Permanent rust / Bio mag / Count down / Hazardous to yourself / The daily grind / Feeding the fire.

Mar 95. (cd/c/lp) *<(FAT 522 CD/MC/LP)>* **LECHE CON CARNE** [ ] [ ]
– Justified black eye / Couch boy / Soul mate / 51 days / Leave it behind / Redemption song / Straight from the jacket / Fields of agony / Fatal flu / Wood / Alone / Exit.

— **CHRIS SHIFLETT** (also of ME FIRST AND THE GIMME GIMMES) – guitar, vocals; repl. PFEFER

— **MATT RIDDLE** – bass, vocals (ex-PULLEY) repl. PAPOUTSIS

Jun 97. (7") *(7SMS 10)* **split w/ SODA** [ ] [-]
(above issued on 'Sessions')

Aug 97. (cd/c/lp) *<FAT 557 CD/MC/LP>* **MAKING FRIENDS** [-] [ ]
– The answer is still no / Invincible / Growing down / On the outside / A postcard would be nice / Secret / Best regards / Revenge / Sidewalk / 3 month weekend / Sitting duck / Fields of Athenry.

Oct 99. (lp/cd) *<(FAT 593/+CD)>* **MORE BETTERNESS!** [ ] [ ]
– Not your savior / Life size mirror / Chasing rainbows / Lies can't pretend / Why doesn't anybody like me? / Sleeping in / Fairytale of New York / Pride / Always Carrie / Let it slide / Six degrees from misty / Coming too close / Saddest song / Room 19.

— **DAVE NASSIE** – guitar (ex-SUICIDAL TENDENCIES) repl. SHIFLETT who joined FOO FIGHTERS

– compilations, etc. –

Oct 97. (cd) *Playing Golf . . .; (CDHOLE 013)* **THE N.R.A. YEARS** [ ] [-]

Aldo NOVA

Born: ALDO SCARPORUSCIO, Montreal, Canada (of Italian/French descent). Recruiting sidemen MICHAEL PELO, MICHEL LACHAPELLE and DENIS CHARTLAND, songwriter/multi-instrumentalist NOVA recorded a highly praised album of streamlined AOR/pomp-metal under the guiding hand of SANDY PEARLMAN (Blue Oyster Cult). Preceded by the US Top 30 hit, 'FANTASY', the album made the Top 10, NOVA looking to have a promising future in America's rock mainstream. Things went pear-shaped, however, as NOVA subsequently hired a new crew of musicians and proceeded to record a poorly received concept album, 'SUBJECT: ALDO NOVA' (1983). Although a third set, 'TWITCH' (1985), was more in keeping with the style of the debut, NOVA failed to regain lost momentum and subsequently went to ground. At the insistence of friend JON BON JOVI, NOVA finally re-emerged in 1991 with a fine comeback album, 'BLOOD ON THE BRICKS', the axe wizard having recently provided his services on JBJ's 'Blaze Of Glory' set. ALDO retired from solo work for around five years until he finally surfaced with another album, 'NOVA'S DREAM' (1997).

Album rating: ALDO NOVA (*7) / SUBJECT: ALDO NOVA (*6) / TWITCH (*6) / BLOOD ON THE BRICKS (*6) / A PORTRAIT OF . . . compilation (*7) / NOVA'S DREAM (*4)

ALDO NOVA – guitar, vocals, keyboards, bass / with **MICHAEL PELO** – bass / **MICHEL LACHAPELLE** – drums / **DENIS CHARTLAND** – piano

Portrait | Portrait

May 82. (7")<12"> *(A 2081) <02799><02802>* **FANTASY. / UNDER THE GUN** [ ] [23] Mar82

Jun 82. (lp) *(PRT 85287) <37498>* **ALDO NOVA** [ ] [8] Feb82
– Fantasy / Hot love / It's too late / Ball and chain / Heart to heart / Foolin' yourself / Under the gun / You're my love / Can't stop lovin' you / See the light.

Jul 82. (7") *<03001>* **FOOLIN' YOURSELF. / SEE THE LIGHT** [-] [65]

Nov 82. (7") *<03208>* **BALL AND CHAIN. / HEART TO HEART** [-] [ ]

— now with **KEVIN CARLSON** – guitar / **DAVID SIKES + NEAL JASON + STEVE BUSLOWE** – bass / **BILLY CARMASSI + CHUCK BURGI** – drums

Nov 83. (lp/c) *(PRT/40 25482) <38721>* **SUBJECT: ALDO NOVA** [ ] [56] Oct83
– Subject's theme / Armageddon (race cars) / Monkey on your back / Hey operator / Cry baby cry / Victim of a broken heart / Africa (primal love) / Hold back the night / Always be mine / All night long / War suite / Prelude to paradise / Paradise.

Nov 83. (7") *(A 3926)* **MONKEY ON MY BACK. / ARMAGEDDON (RACE CARS)** [ ] [-]

Nov 83. (7") *<05762>* **ALWAYS BE MINE. / ARMAGEDDON (RACE CARS)** [-] [ ]

Jan 84. (7") *(A 4189)* **HOLD BACK THE NIGHT. / HEART TO HEART** [ ] [-]
(d7"+=/12"+=) *(DA/TA 4189)* – Monkey on my back / Hot love.

— **LENNIE PETZE + PAUL KAYAN** – guitar; repl. CARLSON

— **ALLAN SCHWARTZBERG + ANTON FIG** – drums; repl. BURGI

Nov 85. (lp/c) *(PRT/40 26440) <40001>* **TWITCH** [ ] [ ]
– Tonite (lift me up) / Rumours of you / Surrender your heart / If looks could kill / Heartless / Long hot summer / Fallen angel / Stay / Lay your love on me / Twitch.

Nov 85. (7") *<05762>* **RUMOURS OF YOU. / LAY YOUR LOVE ON ME** [-] [ ]

— now with **RANDY JACKSON** – bass / **KENNY ARONOFF** – drums / **GREG MATHIESON** – keyboards / **STEVE SEGAL** – slide guitar

Mercury | Jambco

Jun 91. (cd/c/lp) *<(848 513-2/-4/-1)>* **BLOOD ON THE BRICKS** [ ] [ ]
– Blood on the bricks / Medicine man / Bang bang / Someday / Young love / Modern world / This ain't love / Hey Ronnie (Veronica's song) / Touch of madness / Bright lights.

Jan 92. (c-s) *<866040>* **SOMEDAY** [-] [ ]

— ALDO went into retirement for a while until . . .

not iss. | B.M.G.

Nov 97. (cd) *<41410>* **NOVA'S DREAM** [-] [ ]
– My soul to keep / Is there anybody there? / Dreamwalk / Are you inexperienced? / Excuse me while I scream~~!!! / The pressure's killing me / Pressure cooker / Falling back – An angel whispered / Freedom / Where am I now? / Elaye / Dada / Coming home / Lighting up / Mary Jane / Carlito's way / Wake up!!! / The end. *<US-iss.1999 on 'Demuzik'; 2002>*

– compilations, etc. –

Feb 92. (cd/c) *Epic; <EK/ET 48522>* **A PORTRAIT OF . . .** [-] [ ]
– Fantasy / Hot love / It's too late / Ball and chain / Heart to heart / Foolin' yourself / Under the gun / See the light / Armageddon (race cars) – Armageddon / Monkey on your back / Hey operator / Africa (primal love) – Hold back the night / All night long / Always be mine / Victim of a broken heart / Rumours of you / Tonight (lift me up) / Lay your love on me.

NOVOCAINE

Formed: Newport, Wales . . . 1994 by STEVE EVANS, RUSSELL EDWARDS, RICHARD JACKSON and BERT LEWIS. They made their vinyl debut that year with 'MODERN MAN', raw, gut-wrenching punk-grunge with turps-gargling vocals provided by EVANS. A follow-up, 'TENSION', appeared on the 'Townhill' label a year later, leading to a contract with the more experienced indie imprint, 'Fire'. NOVOCAINE injected even more energy into 1997 albums, the mini 'FRUSTRATION No.10' and 'NERVOUS DISPOSITION'; although the band were saddled with the usual NIRVANA or RADIOHEAD comparisons, they were hotly tipped for greater things in '98/'99 although they split soon after.

Album rating: FRUSTRATION No.10 mini (*6) / NERVOUS DISPOSITION (*7)

STEVE EVANS – vocals / **RICHARD JACKSON** – guitar / **RUSSELL EDWARDS** – bass / **BERT LEWIS** – drums

Liberty Place — not iss.

Jun 94. (7") *(LP 004)* **MODERN MAN. / BRAIN** — -

Townhill — not iss.

Jul 95. (7") *(TIDY 002)* **TENSION. / DADDY'S MONEY** — -

Fire — Velvel

Nov 96. (7") *(BLAZE 107)* **CELLOPHANE WRAPPED NEW HEAD. / 'E'** — -

Jan 97. (m-cd) *(FIREMCD 61) <79742>* **FRUSTRATION NO.10** — Oct97
– Brain / Cellophane wrapped new head / Modern man / Culture me / Sneaky servo? / Tension / Bedroom addict / Daddy's money.

May 97. (7") *(BLAZE 114)* **MOTHER – FATHER. / IN MY HEAD** — -
(cd-s+=) *(BLAZE 114CD)* – My big business.

Jul 97. (7") *(BLAZE 117)* **STONEFACE. / FLAMES** — -
(cd-s+=) *(BLAZE 117CD)* – Bury the hate.

Aug 97. (cd) *(FIRECD 67)* **NERVOUS DISPOSITION** — -
– Walls / Mother – Father / Awake / Bittersoul / Stoneface / Frustration No.10 / Pondlife / Million miles / Sorry (scum like me) / Boring git / Waiting / Analyse / Horses / She knows nothing.

Dec 97. (7") *(BLAZE 118)* **POND LIFE. / BEDROOM ADDICT (alternative version)** — -
(cd-s+=) *(BLAZE 118CD)* – Astronaut / Modern man (radio version).

Feb 98. (7") *(BLAZE 120)* **MILLION MILES. / YOU KNOW ME BETTER THAN THAT** — -
(cd-s+=) *(BLAZE 120CD)* – Control / Asylum.

— looked to have disbanded

NUCLEAR ASSAULT

Formed: New York, USA . . . 1985 by ANTHRAX member DAN LILKER alongside JOHN CONNELLY, ANTHONY BRAMANTE and GLENN EVANS. One of the better outfits among the initial wave of thrash bands in the mid-80's, NUCLEAR ASSAULT stayed more musically in touch with their hardcore roots and attitude while ANTHRAX followed a more metallic path. Signing with 'Music For Nations' thrash offshoot, 'Under One Flag', the band made an immediate impact with their late '86 debut album, 'GAME OVER'. In stark contrast to many thrash acts, NUCLEAR ASSAULT favoured politically aware lyrics, often as uncompromising (see 'HANG THE POPE') as their brutal music. As the movement peaked towards the end of the decade, so NUCLEAR ASSAULT delivered their best work and enjoyed their highest record sales with 'SURVIVE' (1988) and 'HANDLE WITH CARE' (1989), the likes of 'CRITICAL MASS' demonstrating a precision and aggression which saw the band tipped as major contenders for the thash premier league. It wasn't to be though, and following the departure of LILKER in the early 90's (to his more contemporary side project, BRUTAL TRUTH), the band recorded one more album, 'SOMETHING WICKED' (1993) with new members SCOTT METAXAS an DAVE DiPIETRO, before finally splitting.

Album rating: GAME OVER (*6) / THE PLAGUE mini (*5) / SURVIVE (*6) / HANDLE WITH CARE (*6) / OUT OF ORDER (*4) / LIVE AT HAMMERSMITH (*4) / SOMETHING WICKED (*4) / ASSAULT & BATTERY compilation (*6)

DAN LILKER – vocals, bass (ex-ANTHRAX) / **JOHN CONNELLY** – guitar, vocals / **ANTHONY BRAMANTE** – guitar / **GLENN EVANS** – drums

Under One Flag — Combat

Nov 86. (lp) *(FLAG 5) <88561-8118>* **GAME OVER** — Jan87
– L.S.D. / Cold steel / Betrayal / Radiation sickness / Hang the Pope / After the holocaust / Mr. Softee theme / Stranded in Hell / Nuclear war / My America / Vengeance / Brain death. *(re-iss. Aug87 c/cd; T/CD FLAG 5) <US cd+=>* – THE PLAGUE *<cd re-iss. Nov99 on 'Century Media'; 66037-2)>*

Jan 87. (12"m) *(12FLAG 102) <88561-8119>* **BRAIN DEATH. / FINAL FLIGHT / DEMOLITION**

Jul 87. (m-lp/m-c) *(MFLAG/TMFLAG 13) <88561-8155>* **THE PLAGUE**
– Game over / Nightmares / Butt f**k / Justice / The plague / Cross of iron.

Under One Flag — I.R.S.

Jul 88. (cd/c/lp) *(CD/T+/FLAG 21) <42195>* **SURVIVE**
– Brainwashed / Great depression / Equal rights / Good times bad times / Survive / Wired / Technology / F sharp / Fight to be free / Got another quarter / P.S.A. / Rise from the ashes. *(pic-lp Oct88; FLAG 21P)*

Aug 88. (12"m) *(12FLAG 105)* **FIGHT TO BE FREE. / EQUAL RIGHTS / STAND UP** — -

Sep 88. (m-lp) *<977105>* **FIGHT TO BE FREE** -
– Fight to be free / Equal rights / Stand up / Brain death / Final flight / Demolition.

Jul 89. (12"ep) *(12FLAG 107)* **GOOD TIMES BAD TIMES / HANG THE POPE (live). / LESBIANS / MY AMERICA / HAPPY DAYS**

Under One Flag — I.R.S.

Sep 89. (cd/c/lp) *(CD/T+/FLAG 35) <88561-3010>* **HANDLE WITH CARE**
– New song / Critical mass / Inherited hell / Surgery / Emergency / Funky noise / F# (wake up) / When freedom dies / Search & seizure / Torture tactics / Mother's day / Trail of tears. *<(cd re-iss. Nov99 on 'Century Media'; 66041-2)>*

Under One Flag — I.R.S.

Sep 91. (cd/c/lp) *(CD/T+/FLAG 64) <13107>* **OUT OF ORDER**
– Sign in blood / Fashion junkie / Too young to die / Preaching to the deaf / Resurrection / Stop wait think / Doctor butcher / Quocustudiat / Hypocrisy / Save the planet / Ballroom blitz.

Roadracer — Combat

May 92. (cd/lp) *(RO 9167-2/-1) <1100>* **LIVE AT HAMMERSMITH ODEON (live)**
– Intro – The new song / Critical mass / Game over / Nightmares / B.F. / Survive / Torture tactics / Trail of tears / Mother's day / My America / Hang the Pope / Lesbians / Funky noise / Good times bad times. *<(cd re-iss. Aug99 on 'Century Media'; 66016-2)>*

— LILKER departed after concentrating more on his other project, BRUTAL TRUTH. He and BRAMANTE were replaced by **SCOTT METAXAS + DAVE DiPIETRO** (both ex-PROPHET)

Alter Ego — I.R.S.

Apr 93. (cd) *(ALTGOCD 003) <13172>* **SOMETHING WICKED**
– Something wicked / Another violent end / Behind glass walls / Chaos / Forge / No time / To serve man / Madness descends / Poetic justice / Art / The other end.

— disbanded after above

– compilations, etc. –

Sep 97. (cd) *Receiver; <(RRCD 244)>* **ASSAULT AND BATTERY**
– Happy days / Enter darkness / Leaders / Hang the Pope / Radiation sickness / Hypocrisy / Behind the glass walls / No time / Hour shower / Sadam / Preaching to the deaf / Hang the Pope / Ping / Torture tactics / Fight to be free (live) / Trail of tears (live) / Ping again (live) / Butt fuck (live).

NUDESWIRL

Formed: New Jersey, USA . . . 1990 by vocalist/guitarist SHANE GREEN, guitarist DIZ CORTRIGHT, bass player CHRIS WARGO and sticksman, WOODY NEWLAND. Despite hitting the ground running in the alternative metal stakes, NUDESWIRL somehow failed to generate significant interest in their eponymous debut album at the zenith of the grunge explosion in 1993. A New Jersey alternative to BON JOVI's hair-rock, the often evocative strains of GREEN and co's metallic experimentation, together with de rigueur controversial cover art and a support slot to MINDFUNK should've at least ensured a cult audience. It wasn't to be though, the band calling it a day following the departure of their frontman in the mid-90's.

Album rating: NUDESWIRL (*6)

SHANE M GREENE – vocals, guitar / **DIZ CORTRIGHT** – guitar / **CHRISTOPHER VORGA** – bass / **WOODY NEWLAND** – drums

Megaforce — Megaforce

Feb 93. (cd/lp) *(CD+/ZAZ 1) <6911>* **NUDESWIRL**
– Gordon's corner / F sharp / Sooner or later / Disappear / Buffalo / Potato trip / Dog food / When I'm dead / Now nothing / Three / Damned / Ringworm.

— disbanded in June '94 when GREENE departed

Ted NUGENT

Born: 13 Dec'48, Detroit, Michigan, USA. After earlier moving to Chicago, he formed garage/psych-rock band, The AMBOY DUKES in 1966. They soon signed to 'Mainstream' US, releasing a debut single, 'BABY PLEASE DON'T GO' (a Big Joe Williams number, more famously covered by THEM), in 1967. Their eponymous 1968 debut album broke into the US Top 200, and by the summer, the classic psychedelic single, 'JOURNEY TO THE CENTER OF THE MIND', was in the US Top 20. Ironically enough, NUGENT was a vehement non-drug taker, sacking anyone in the band who dabbled with even the softest narcotics (TED preferred hunting animals instead, his love of blood sports was well-publicised). Although The AMBOY DUKES toured constantly in the States for the next couple of years, the band only managed minor chart placings. In 1971, they evolved into TED NUGENT & THE AMBOY DUKES, snapped up by FRANK ZAPPA's 'Discreet' label and subsequently unleashing two albums in the mid-70's before dissolving. In 1975, NUGENT secured a solo deal with 'Epic', shooting up the US Top 30 with an eponymous Tom Werman-produced debut in early '76. By this point, NUGENT had come a long way from his 60's roots, adopting a bare-chested stone-age axe-grinding image (a good few years before MANOWAR). His next album in 1976, 'FREE FOR ALL' (which featured MEAT LOAF) ventured further and was the first to earn him a Top 40 placing in the UK. Abrasive as ever, TED "The Deer Hunter" NUGENT took a break from boasting about his conquests (musical, animal or otherwise . . .) to record his third heavy-metal onslaught, 'CAT SCRATCH FEVER', another acclaimed album which featured such pussy-tickling gems as 'WANG DANG SWEET POONTANG' and the glorious title track. NUGE (who had recently demonstrated his affection for a fan by enscribing his name with a bowie knife on their arm!), reached his 70's climax with the ripping 1978 concert set, 'DOUBLE LIVE GONZO', and although he released two more sturdy studio albums that decade, 'WEEKEND WARRIORS' and 'STATE OF SHOCK', he would never quite attain such testosterone-fuelled heights again. After two middling early 80's albums (one of them being the live 'INTENSITIES IN 10 CITIES'), TED signed to 'Atlantic', delivering a rather poor, directionless affair thoughtfully titled, 'NUGENT' (1982). Taking a few years to recover, the loinclothed one returned in good old feminist-baiting style with 'PENETRATOR' (1984) and 'LITTLE

MISS DANGEROUS' (1986), NUGENT rather unconvincingly claiming that the title track of the latter could cure the emerging AIDS virus. Even more unbelievable was the news that NUGE was forming a new AOR-orientated supergroup, The DAMN YANKEES alongside TOMMY SHAW (Styx), JACK BLADES (Night Ranger) and MICHAEL CARTELLONE (er, drums). This was all too horribly confirmed in 1990 with the release of their eponymous debut, the Top 20 album boasting a US Top 3 smash, 'HIGH ENOUGH'. This quartet released another set in 1992, 'DON'T TREAD', although the only thing The DAMN YANKESS were treading was water. Thankfully NUGE abandoned this project and returned to his familiar bloodthirsty neck of the woods with the 1995 solo album, 'SPIRIT OF THE WILD'. • **Trivia:** In 1973, while working on a new record deal, he featured alongside other stars MIKE PINERA (Iron Butterfly), WAYNE KRAMER (MC5) and FRANK MARINO (Mahogany Rush), on the 'battle of the guitarists' stage shows. • **Note:** There was another group of the same name in the UK called The AMBOY DUKES, who released several singles on 'Polydor', around the mid-60's to '68.

Album rating: JOURNEYS & MIGRATIONS (*7) / TED NUGENT (*7) / FREE FOR ALL (*6) / CAT SCRATCH FEVER (*6) / DOUBLE LIVE GONZO! (*7) / WEEKEND WARRIORS (*5) / STATE OF SHOCK (*5) / SCREAM DREAM (*5) / INTENSITIES IN 10 CITIES (*6) / GREAT GONZOS! THE BEST OF TED NUGENT compilation (*6) / NUGENT (*2) / PENETRATOR (*5) / LITTLE MISS DANGEROUS (*4) / IF YOU CAN'T LICK 'EM, LICK 'EM (*4) / SPIRIT OF THE WILD (*4)

AMBOY DUKES

TED NUGENT – guitar, vox / plus **JOHN DRAKE** – vocals / **STEVE FARMER** – rhythm guitar / **BILL WHITE** – bass / **RICK LOBER** – keyboards / **DAVID PALMER** – drums

Fontana Mainstream

1967. (7") *<676>* **BABY PLEASE DON'T GO. / PSALMS OF AFTERMATH** [-] [ ]

1967. (7") *(TF 971)* **LET'S GO GET STONED. / IT'S NOT TRUE** [ ] [-]

1968. (lp; stereo/mono) *(S+/TL 5468) <6104>* **THE AMBOY DUKES** [ ] [ ] Jan68
– Baby please don't go / I feel free / Young love / Psalms of aftermath / Colors / Let's go get stoned / Down on Philips escalator / The lovely lady / Night time / It's not true / Gimme love. *(cd-iss. Dec92 on 'Repertoire'+=;)* – J.B. special.

— **RUSTY DAY** – vocals repl. DRAKE + FARMER / **ANDY SOLOMAN** – keyboards repl. LOBER / **GREG ARAMA** – bass repl. WHITE
In the UK, they were now called The AMERICAN AMBOY DUKES

London Mainstream

Jul 68. (7") *<684>* **JOURNEY TO THE CENTER OF THE MIND. / MISSISSIPPI MURDERER** [-] [16]

Oct 68. (7") *<693>* **SCOTTISH TEA. / YOU TALK SUNSHINE, I BREATHE FIRE** [-] [ ]

Feb 69. (lp; stereo/mono) *(SH-T/HA-T 8378) <6112>* **JOURNEY TO THE CENTER OF THE MIND** [ ] [74] Aug68
– Mississippi murderer / Surrender to your kings / Flight of the Byrd / Scottish tea / Dr. Slingshot / Journey to the center of the mind / Ivory castles / Why is a carrot more orange than an orange? / Missionary Mary / Death is life / Saint Philips friend / I'll prove I'm right / (Conclusion). *(cd-iss. Dec92 on 'Repertoire'+=; MDCD 0911)* – You talk sunshine, I breathe fire.

1969. (7") *<700>* **PRODIGAL MAN. / GOOD NATURED EMMA** [-] [ ]

1969. (lp; stereo/mono) *(SH-T/HA-T 8392) <6118>* **MIGRATION** [ ] [ ]
– Migration / Prodigal man / For his namesake / I'm not a juvenile delinquent / Good natured Emma / Inside the outside / Shades of green and grey / Curb your elephant / Loaded for bear. *(cd-iss. Dec92 on 'Repertoire'+=;)* – Sobbin' in my mug of bear.

1969. (7") *<704>* **FOR HIS NAMESAKE. / LOADED FOR BEAR** [-] [ ]

1969. (7") *<711>* **MIGRATION. / FLIGHT OF THE BIRDS** [-] [ ]

1969. (lp) *<6125>* **THE BEST OF THE ORIGINAL AMBOY DUKES** (compilation) [-] [ ]

Polydor Polydor

Mar 70. (lp) *<4012>* **MARRIAGE ON THE ROCKS – ROCK BOTTOM** [-] [ ]
– Marriage:- (a) Part 1 – Man / (b) Part 2 – Woman / (c) Part 3 – Music / Breast-fed 'gator (bait) / Get yer guns / Non-conformist wilderbeast man / Today's lesson / Children of the woods / Brain games of the yesteryear / The inexhaustable quest for the cosmic garbage (part 1 & 2) / (excerpt from Bartok).

— **NUGENT** brought in new members **BOB GRANGE** – bass / **KJ KNIGHT** – drums retaining also **ANDY SOLOMAN** (RUSTY DAY joined CACTUS)

TED NUGENT & THE AMBOY DUKES

Mar 71. (lp) *<4035>* **SURVIVAL OF THE FITTEST** (live) [-] [ ]
– Survival of the fittest / Rattle my snake / Mr. Jones' hanging party / Papa's will / Slidin' on / Prodigal man. *(UK-iss.1974 on 'Polydor'; 2675 141)*

— Disbanded in the early 70's, but re-formed with others **BOB GRANGE** – bass / **ANDY JEZOWSKI** – vocals / **GABRIEL MAGNO** – keyboards / **VIC MASTRIANNI** – drums

Discreet Discreet

Jun 74. (lp) *(K 59203) <2181>* **CALL OF THE WILD** [ ] [ ]
– Call of the wild / Sweet revenge / Pony express / Ain't it the truth / Renegade / Rot gut / Below the belt / Cannon balls. *(re-iss. Oct89 on 'Edsel' lp/cd; ED/+CD 278)*

Jun 74. (7") *(K 19200)* **SWEET REVENGE. / AIN'T IT THE TRUTH** [ ] [ ]

— **Rev.ATROCIOUS THEODOLIUS** – guitar, vocals repl. MAGNO

1975. (lp) *(K 59203) <2203>* **TOOTH FANG & CLAW** [ ] [ ]
– Lady luck / Living in the woods / Hibernation / Free flight / Maybelline / The great wjite buffalo / Sasha / No holds barred. *(re-iss. Oct89 on 'Edsel'; lp/cd; ED/+CD 295)*

— TED finally gave up AMBOY DUKES in 1975.

– compilations, etc. –

Apr 73. (d-lp) *Mainstream; <MRL 801>* **JOURNEYS & MIGRATIONS** [-] [ ]
<re-iss. Apr75 on 'Polydor'; 2801> (UK-iss.Feb83 on 'Audio Fidelity'; MRD 5008)

Jun 77. (d-lp) *Polydor; <2664 344)* **MARRIAGE ON THE ROCKS – ROCK BOTTOM / SURVIVAL OF THE FITTEST (AMBOY DUKES)** [ ] [-]

1977. (d-lp) *Warners; (K 69202)* **TWO ORIGINALS OF . . . (AMBOY DUKES)** [ ] [-]
– (CALL OF THE WILD & TOOTH, FANG & CLAW) albums

Jan 91. (cd/c) *Thunderbolt; (CDTB/THBC 097)* **ON THE EDGE** (early AMBOY DUKES material) [ ] [-]
(cd re-iss. Nov98; same)

May 91. (cd/c) *Thunderbolt; (CDTB/THBC 120)* **OVER THE TOP** (early AMBOY DUKES material) [ ] [-]
(cd re-iss. Nov98; same)

Aug 99. (cd; TED NUGENT & THE AMBOY DUKES) *Legacy; (494606-2)* **LOADED FOR BEAR** [ ] [ ]

Jun 00. (d-cd) *Thunderbolt; (CDTBD 010)* **ON THE EDGE / OVER THE TOP** [ ] [-]

TED NUGENT

(solo) with **ROB GRANGE** – bass / **DEREK ST.HOLMES** – vocals, guitar (ex-SCOTT) / **CLIFF DAVIS** – drums / plus guests

Epic Epic

Nov 75. (7") *<50172>* **MOTORCITY MADNESS. / WHERE HAVE YOU BEEN ALL MY LIFE** [-] [ ]

Mar 76. (lp/c) *(EPC/40 33692) <81196>* **TED NUGENT** [56] [28] Nov75
– Stranglehold / Stormtroopin' / Hey baby / Just what the doctor ordered / Snakeskin cowboys / Motor city madhouse / Where have you been all my life / You make me feel right at home / Queen of the forest. *(cd-iss. Aug99 on 'Legacy'; 494605-2)*

Jun 76. (7") *(EPC 3900) <50197>* **HEY BABY. / STORMTROOPIN'** [ ] [72] Mar76

Oct 76. (lp/c) *(EPC/40 81397) <34121>* **FREE-FOR-ALL** [33] [24] Sep76
– Free for all / Dog eat dog / Writing on the wall / Turn it up / Together / Street rats / Hammer down / Light my way / Love you so much I told a lie. *(re-iss. Jan84; EPC 34121) (cd re-mast.Aug99 on 'Legacy'; 494604-2)*

Nov 76. (7") *<50301>* **DOG EAT DOG. / LIGHT MY WAY** [-] [91]

Nov 76. (7") *(EPC 4796)* **DOG EAT DOG. / LOVE YOU SO MUCH I TOLD A LIE** [ ] [-]

Jan 77. (7") *<50363>* **FREE-FOR-ALL. / STREET RAGS** [-] [ ]

Jun 77. (lp/c) *(EPC/40 82010) <34700>* **CAT SCRATCH FEVER** [28] [17]
– Cat scratch fever / Wang dang sweet poontang / Death by misadventure / Live it up / Home bound / Workin' hard, playin' hard / Sweet Sally / A thousand knives / Fist fightin' son of a gun / Out of control. *(cd-iss. Jun89; CD 32252) (cd re-iss. Aug93 on 'Columbia'; 468024-2) (cd re-mast.Aug99 on 'Legacy'; 494603-2)*

Jul 77. (7") *<50425>* **CAT SCRATCH FEVER. / WANG DANG SWEET POONTANG** [-] [ ]

Jul 77. (7") *(EPC 5482)* **CAT SCRATCH FEVER. / A THOUSAND NIGHTS** [ ] [-]

Feb 78. (7") *(EPC 5945) <50493>* **HOME BOUND. / DEATH BY MISADVENTURE** [ ] [70]

Feb 78. (d-lp) *(EPC 88282) <35069>* **DOUBLE LIVE GONZO! (live)** [47] [13]
– Just what the doctor ordered / Yank me, crank me / Gonzo / Baby please don't go / Great white buffalo / Hibernation / Stormtroopin' / Stranglehold / Wang dang sweet poontang / Cat scratch fever / Motor city madhouse.

Mar 78. (7") *<50533>* **YANK ME, CRANK ME (live). / CAT SCRATCH FEVER (live)** [-] [58]

— **CHARLIE HUHN** – vocals, vocals repl. ST. HOLMES (to ST. PARADISE, etc)
DAVID HULL – bass repl. BOB GRANGE (also to ST. PARADISE, who released one eponymous album for 'Warners' in '79)

Nov 78. (lp/c) *(EPC/40 83036) <35551>* **WEEKEND WARRIORS** [ ] [24]
– Need you bad / One woman / I got the feelin' / Tight spots / Venom soup / Smokescreen / Weekend warriors / Cruisin' / Good friends and a bottle of wine / Name your poison.

Dec 78. (7") *<50648>* **NEED YOU BAD. / I GOT THE FEELIN'** [-] [84]

— **WALTER MONAHAN** – bass repl. HULL

Jun 79. (lp/c)<US-pic-lp> *(EPC/40 86092) <36000>* **STATE OF SHOCK** [ ] [18] May79
– Paralyzed / Take it or leave it / Alone / It doesn't matter / State of shock / I want to tell you / It doesn't matter / Satisfied / Bite down hard / Snake charmer / Saddle sore. *(cd-iss. Aug93 on 'Columbia'; 471456-2)*

Jun 79. (7") *<50713>* **I WANT TO TELL YOU. / BITE DOWN HARD** [-] [ ]

Jul 79. (7"m) *(EPC 7723)* **I WANT TO TELL YOU. / PARALYSED / CAT SCRATCH FEVER** [ ] [-]

May 80. (7"/12") *(EPC/12 8640)* **FLESH AND BLOOD. / MOTOR CITY MADHOUSE** [ ] [-]

Jun 80. (lp/c) *(EPC/40 86111) <36404>* **SCREAM DREAM** [37] [13] May80
– Wango tango / Scream dream / Hard as nails / I gotta move / Violent love / Flesh and blood / Spit it out / Come and get it / Terminus El Dorada / Don't cry, I'll be back before you know it baby. *(cd-iss. Aug93 on 'Columbia'; 471458-2)*

Jul 80. (7") *<50907>* **WANGO TANGO. / SCREAM DREAM** [-] [86]

Feb 81. (7") *<01046>* **LAND OF A THOUSAND DANCES. / THE TNT OVERTURE** [-] [ ]

Apr 81. (lp/c) *(EPC/40 84917) <37084>* **(INTENSITIES) IN 10 CITIES** [75] [51]
– Put up or shut up / Spontaneous combustion / My love is like a tire iron / Jailbait / I am a predator / Heads will roll / The flying lip lock / Land of a thousand dances / The TNT overture / I take no prisoners.

Dec 81. (lp/c) *(EPC/40 85408) <37667>* **GREAT GONZOS! THE BEST OF TED NUGENT** (compilation) [ ] [ ]
– Cat scratch fever / Just what the doctor ordered / Free-for-all / Dog eat dog / Motor city madness / Paralysed / Stranglehold / Baby please don't go / Wango tango / Wang dang sweet poontang. *(cd-iss. Feb97 on 'Columbia'; 471216-2)*

— **DEREK ST. HOLMES** – vocals returned from WHITFORD / ST. HOLMES to repl. HUHN / **DAVE KISWINEY** – bass repl. MONAGHAN / **CARMINE APPICE** – drums (ex-VANILLA FUDGE, ex-CACTUS, etc.) repl. DAVIS

Atlantic Atlantic

Aug 82. (lp/c) *(K/K4 50898) <19365>* **NUGENT** [ ] [51] Jul82
– No, no, no / Bound and gagged / Habitual offender / Fightin' words / Good and ready / Ebony / Don't push me / Can't stop me now / We're gonna rock tonight / Tailgunner.

Sep 82. (7") *<89998>* **BOUND AND GAGGED. / HABITUAL OFFENDER** [-] [ ]

Nov 82. (7") *<89978>* **NO, NO, NO. / HABITUAL OFFENDER** [-] [ ]

— **NUGENT** recruited entire new band again! **BRIAN HOWE** – vocals / **ALAN ST. JOHN** – keyboards / **DOUG LABAHN** – bass / **BOBBY CHOUINARD** – drums

Feb 84. (lp/c) *(780 125-1/-4) <80125>* **PENETRATOR** [ ] [56]
– Tied up in love / (Where do you) Draw the line / Knockin' at your door / Don't you want my love / Go down fighting / Thunder thighs / No man's land / Blame it on the night / Lean mean R&R machine / Take me home.

Feb 84. (7") *(A 9705) <89705>* **TIED UP IN LOVE. / LEAN MEAN R&R MACHINE** [ ] [ ]

Apr 84. (7") *<89681>* **(WHERE DO YOU) DRAW THE LINE. / LEAN MEAN R&R MACHINE** [-] [ ]

— Took time out to appear in 'Miami Vice' US TV programme. He also played on charity single 'Stars' by aggregation 'HEAR'N AID' circa Spring 1986.

— **DAVE AMATO** – guitar, vocals repl. HOWE who joined BAD COMPANY / **RICKY PHILIPS** – bass (ex-BABYS) repl. LABAHN

Nov 86. (lp/c/cd) *(K 252388-1/-4/-2) <81632>* **LITTLE MISS DANGEROUS** [ ] [76] Mar86
– High heels in motion / Strangers / Little Miss Dangerous / Savage dancer / Crazy ladies / When your body talks / My little red book / Take me away / Angry young man / Painkiller.

Apr 86. (7") *<89442>* **HIGH HEELS IN MOTION. / ANGRY YOUNG MAN** [-] [ ]

Jul 86. (7") *<89436>* **LITTLE MISS DANGEROUS. / ANGRY YOUNG MAN** [-] [ ]

— **NUGENT** re-recruited **DEREK ST.HOLMES** – vocals, guitar / **DAVE KISWINEY** – bass / plus new drummer – **PAT MARCHINO**

Feb 88. (lp/c/cd) *(K 255385-1/-4/-2) <81812>* **IF YOU CAN'T LICK 'EM . . . LICK 'EM** [ ] [ ]
– Can't live with 'em / She drives me crazy / If you can't lick 'em . . . lick 'em / Skintight / Funlover / Spread your wings / The harder they come (the harder I get) / Separate the men from the boys, please / Bite the hand / That's the story of love.

DAMN YANKEES

TED NUGENT – guitar, vocals / **TOMMY SHAW** (b.11 Sep'53, Montgomery, Alabama) – vocals (ex-STYX) / **JACK BLADES** (b.24 Apr'54, Palm Beach, Calif.) – bass (ex-NIGHT RANGER) / **MICHAEL CARTELLONE** (b. 7 Jun'62, Cleveland, Ohio) – drums, non-s/writer

Warners Warners

Apr 90. (cd/c/lp) *<(7599 26159-2/-4/-1)>* **DAMN YANKEES** [26] [13] Mar90
– Coming of age / Bad reputation / Runaway / High enough / Damn Yankees / Come again / Mystified / Rock city / Tell me how you want it / Piledriver.

Apr 90. (c-s,cd-s) *<19838>* **COMING OF AGE. / TELL ME HOW YOU WANT IT** [-] [60]

Jan 91. (7"/c-s) *(W 0006/+C) <19595>* **HIGH ENOUGH. / PILEDRIVER** [ ] [3] Oct90
(12"+=/cd-s+=) *(W 0006 T/CD)* – Bonestripper.

Apr 91. (c-s,cd-s) *<19408>* **COME AGAIN. / ('A'radio version)** [-] [50]

Aug 92. (cd/c) *<(9362 45025-2/-4)>* **DON'T TREAD** [ ] [22]
– Don't tread on me / Fifteen minutes of fame / Where you goin' now / Dirty dog / Mister please / Silence is broken / Firefly / Someone to believe / This side of Hell / Double coyote / Uprising. *(re-iss. cd Feb95; same)*

Jan 93. (7"/c-s) *<18728>* **WHERE YOU GOIN' NOW. / THIS SIDE OF HELL** [ ] [20] Sep92
(12"+=/cd-s+=) – ('A'version).

Apr 93. (c-s) *<18612>* **SILENCE IS BROKEN / DOUBLE COYOTE** [-] [62]
(12"+=/cd-s+=) – High enough (live) / ('A'live version).

— **STEVE SMITH** – drums (ex-JOURNEY) repl. NUGENT, although the band became SHAW BLADES, releasing one 'Warners' album, 'HALLICINATION' (9362 45835-2/-4).

Ted NUGENT

— returned w/ **DAVE AMATO** – guitar / **CHUCK WRIGHT** – bass / **PAT TORPEY** – drums / + co-writers ST. HOLMES + LUTZ

Atlantic Atlantic

Dec 95. (cd/c) *<(7567 82611)>* **SPIRIT OF THE WILD** [ ] [86] May95
– Thighraceous / Wrong side of town / I shoot back / Toot, fang & claw / Lovejacker / Fred bear / Primitive man / Hot or cold / Kiss my ass / Heart & soul / Spirit of the wild / Just do it like this.

– compilations, others, etc. –

Feb 83. (d-c) *Epic;* **TED NUGENT / FREE FOR ALL** [ ] [-]

Sep 86. (d-lp/d-c) *Raw Power; (RAW LP/TC 026)* **ANTHOLOGY** [ ] [-]
(re-iss. Feb91 on 'Castle' cd/c; CCS CD/MC 282)

Jun 93. (cd) *Sony;* **THE VERY BEST OF TED NUGENT** [ ] [ ]

May 94. (d-cd/d-c) *Epic-Legacy; (CD/40 47039)* **OUT OF CONTROL** [ ] [ ]

May 97. (cd) *Columbia; (471216-2)* **LIVE AT HAMMERSMITH ODEON** [ ] [ ]

NUTZ

Formed: Liverpool, England . . . 1973 by DAVE LLOYD and MICK DEVONPORT along with KEITH MULHOLLAND and JOHN MYLETT. Signed to 'A&M', the band debuted with the eponymous 'NUTZ' in summer '74, their basic hard boogie sound not translating well to vinyl, although they were considered a reliably raucous live proposition. The unimaginative titles of subsequent releases, 'NUTZ TOO' (1975), 'HARD NUTZ' (1977) etc. were indicative of the uninspired material within, and the group soon opted for a change of name (to RAGE) and image in line with the NWOBHM. Beefing up their sound with an additional guitarist, TERRY STEERS, the group signed to French label, 'Carrere', releasing a debut set, 'OUT OF CONTROL' in 1981. RAGE were afforded more interest in Europe, subsequent albums, 'NICE 'N' DIRTY' (1982) and 'RUN FOR THE NIGHT' (1983) failing to capture the interest of UK metal fans despite some encouraging reviews. The band eventually called it a day in '84, after more than a decade of second division status.

Album rating: NUTZ (*5) / NUTZ TOO (*4) / HARD NUTZ (*5) / LIVE CUTZ (*3)

DAVE LLOYD – vocals, guitar / **MICK DEVONPORT** – guitar, vocals / **KEITH MULHOLLAND** – bass, vocals / **JOHN MYLETT** – drums, percussion

A&M A&M

Jun 74. (7") *(AMS 7115)* **AS FAR AS THE EYE CAN SEE. / JUST FOR THE CRACK** [ ] [ ]

Jul 74. (lp) *(AMLS 68256) <3648>* **NUTZ** [ ] [ ]
– Poor man / Ain't no thanks to you / Spoke in a wheel / I can't unwind / Can't tell her why / As far as the eye can see / Love will last forever / Light of day / Round and round / Joke.

Aug 74. (7") *(AMS 7128)* **ROUND AND ROUND. / LIGHT OF DAY** [ ] [ ]

1975. (lp) *(AMLS 68306)* **NUTZ TOO** [ ] [-]
– Nature intended / I want never gets / Take it from me / Change's coming / Dear diary / Is it all for real / Cool me down / R.S.D. / The love you lost / Sinner / Knife edge.

May 75. (7") *(AMS 7160)* **CHANGE'S COMING. / LONG SHIPS** [ ] [ ]

Jan 77. (7") *(AMS 7272)* **SICK AND TIRED. / WALLBANGER** [ ] [ ]

Feb 77. (lp) *(AMLH 64623) <4623>* **HARD NUTZ** [ ] [ ]
– Seeing is believing / I know the feeling / Loser / From here to anywhere / Wallbanger / Pushed around / Beast of the field / Sick and tired / Down on my knees / One more cup of coffee.

Apr 77. (7") *(AMS 7281)* **ONE MORE CUP OF COFFEE. / DOWN ON MY KNEES** [ ] [ ]

— added **KENNY NEWTON** – keyboards

Oct 77. (lp) *(AMLH 68453)* **NUTZ LIVE CUTZ (live)** [ ] [-]
– Seeing is believing / Loser / Pushed around / You better watch out / R.S.D. / Joke / Can be loved / Wallbanger / Knife edge.

— KENNY NEWTON joined NIGHTWING after their split

— changed their name to RAGE

RAGE

LLOYD, DEVONPORT, MULHOLLAND + MYLETT recruited **TERRY STEERS** – guitar

Carrere not iss.

Sep 80. (7") *(CAR 159)* **MONEY. / THANK THAT WOMAN** [ ] [-]

Mar 81. (7") *(CAR 182)* **OUT OF CONTROL. / DOUBLE DEALER** [ ] [-]

Mar 81. (lp/c) *(CAL/CAC 124)* **OUT OF CONTROL** [ ] [-]
– Out of control / What have I done wrong? / She's on fire / Roll the dice / Fallen idol / Money / I didn't wanna to leave / Rage / Thank that woman.

Jul 81. (7") *(CAR 199)* **BOOTLIGGERS. / ROLL THE DICE** [ ] [-]

Jun 82. (lp/c) *(CAL/CAC 138)* **NICE 'N' DIRTY** [ ] [-]
– American radio stations / Wasted years / Woman / Heartbreaker / Silver and gold / Long way from home / Only child / Blame it on the night / Wild cat woman / Ready to go.

Jul 82. (7") *(CAR 240)* **WOMAN. / READY TO GO** [ ] [-]

Oct 83. (7") *(CAR 291)* **NEVER BEFORE. / ROCK FEVER** [ ] [-]

Oct 83. (lp/c) *(CAL/CAC 149)* **RUN FOR THE NIGHT** [ ] [-]
– Cry from a hill / Fantasy / Can't say no / Light years / Ladykiller / No prisoners / Run for the night / Badlands / Never before / Rock fever.

Mar 84. (7") *(CAR 304)* **CRY FROM A HILL. / LADYKILLER** [ ] [-]

— split in 1984, MYLETT was subsequently killed in a car accident. LLOYD was back in form with the group 2 A.M.

N.Y. LOOSE

Formed: Manhattan, New York, USA . . . 1993 as LOOSE by vocalist/guitarist, BRIJETTE WEST and drummer JOHN MELVILLE. With another band already operating under that name, the pair were forced to prefix their moniker with NY prior to the release of a self-financed debut single, 'BITCH'. A potted history of streetwise punk/New Wave from the Big Apple's skool of kool, the track kicked the stagnant Grunge-fixated US indie squarely in the bollocks. BRIJETTE's tough-talking patter and feminist invective also had the critics chattering, some even daring to compare her with COURTNEY LOVE. Bolstering the line-up with two battle-scarred veterans of the NY scene, GARY SUNSHINE (formerly of the blistering but criminally overlooked CIRCUS OF POWER) and DANNY NORDAHL (ex-STIV BATORS), BRIJETTE and Co delivered two further 45's, 'GREEN LITTLE SEMAPHORE' and 'SPIT', the latter a one-off for Chris Parry's offshoot label, 'Non-Fiction'. After a period of label-less instability, the hard-bitten quartet found a home at 'Hollywood' (well, the company, that is) and finally got round to freeing up a debut long-player, 'YEAR OF THE RAT', in '96. Containing a brilliant cover of the Velvet Underground's 'SUNDAY MORNING', although the set turned out to be their swansong.

Album rating: YEAR OF THE RAT (*6)

BRIJETTE WEST – vocals, guitar / **JOHN MELVILLE** – drums

not iss. Loose

1994. (7") **BITCH. /** [-] [ ]

— added **GARY SUNSHINE** – guitar (ex-CIRCUS OF POWER) / **DANNY NORDAHL** – bass (ex-STIV BATORS)

not iss. Holy Plastic

1994. (7") **GREEN LITTLE SEMAPHORE. /** [-] [ ]

Non-Fiction unknown

Apr 95. (7") *(YES 12)* **SPIT. / PRETTY SUICIDE** [ ] [-]

Flipside Flipside

Sep 95. (m-cd) *<(FLIP 70)>* **LOOSEN UP** [ ] [-]

Polydor Hollywood

Sep 96. (cd) <(162049-2)> **YEAR OF THE RAT**
– Pretty suicide / Rip me up / Broken / Apathy is golden / Dragonfly / Sunday morning / Detonator / Song for Margo / Kiss my wheels / Hide / Trash the given chance / Spit.

NYMPHS

Formed: Los Angeles, California, USA . . . 1989 by former model (and one-time girlfriend of deceased SEA HAGS man, CHRIS SCHLOSSHARDT) INGER LORRE along with JET FREEDOM, SAM MERRICK and ALEX KIRST (original bassist ROB GRAVES overdosed with drugs and was replaced by CLIFF D). An emotional volcano waiting to erupt, the group's haphazard momentum rode on the unpredictable LORRE and her well documented antics. Hardly the most stable of frontwomen, her wild-style behaviour together with the constant group in-fighting translated to a visceral live show (a rare event due to contractual hassles etc.) and a cathartic debut set which drew comparisons with the primal howl of PATTI SMITH and IGGY POP. The eponymous album was released by 'Geffen' in 1992, the label having snapped them up pronto amid the considerable hype that surrounded their inception. The company certainly got their money's worth, LORRE infamously urinating over five symbolic poppies on the chief A&R man's desk in protest at their producer decamping to work on GUNS N' ROSES 'Use Your Illusion' set. In another legendary incident, INGER allegedly invited her boyfriend to come on stage so that she could give him a blow job. An unusual remedy for her vox problems, to say the least. Unsurprisingly, following a further mini-set later that summer, 'A PRACTICAL GUIDE TO ASTRAL PROJECTION', the group disintegrated. However, after a few years in the musical wilderness (her boyfriend CHRIS SCHLOSSHARDT of the SEA HAGS od'd in 1991), LORRE returned in Spring '99 with her long-awaited solo effort, 'TRANSCENDENTAL MEDICATION'. The blues-based noise record featured a writing collaboration on the track 'THIEF WITHOUT THE TAKE' with the now deceased JEFF BUCKLEY.

Album rating: THE NYMPHS (*7) / A PRACTICAL GUIDE TO ASTRAL PROJECTION mini (*5) / Inger Lorre: TRANSCENDENTAL MEDICATION (*6)

INGER LORRE (b. LAURIE WENNING, 1966, New Jersey, USA) – vocals / **SAM MERRICK** – guitar / **jet freedom** – guitar / **CLIFF D** – bass / **ALEX KIRST** – drums

D.G.C. D.G.C.

Jun 91. (12"ep/cd-ep) **IMMITATING ANGELS** [-]
Jan 92. (12"ep/cd-ep) **SAD AND DAMNED / DEATH OF A SCENESTER. / JUST ONE HAPPY DAY / THE HIGHWAY (demo)**
Feb 92. (lp/c/cd) <(DGC/+C/D 24366)> **THE NYMPHS** Sep91
– Just one happy day / Cold / 2 cats / Immitating angels / Wasting my days / Heaven / Supersonic / Sad and damned / Death of a scenester / The river / Revolt / The highway.
Jun 92. (m-lp/m-c/m-cd) <(DGCT/+C/D 8)> **A PRACTICAL GUIDE TO ASTRAL PROJECTION**
– Imitating angels / Alright / Cum 'n' get it / Wasting my fays / Highway.

—— split mid '92 after INGER had earlier broken her wrist and two fingers in a car crash

INGER LORRE

LORRE with her own band **DAVE GREEN** – bass / **DAN SMITH** – drums / **KEITH HARTEL** – guitar / **BILL DONAHUE** – keyboards / etc.

Sweet Nothing Triple X

Sep 99. (cd) (SNCD 001) <TX 51248CD> **TRANSCENDENTAL MEDICATION**
– She's not your friend / Beautiful dead / It could happen to you / Gibby Haynes is next / Haunted hill / Devil's priest / Yard of blonde girls / Thief without the take / Dusted / Sweet release / 7b.

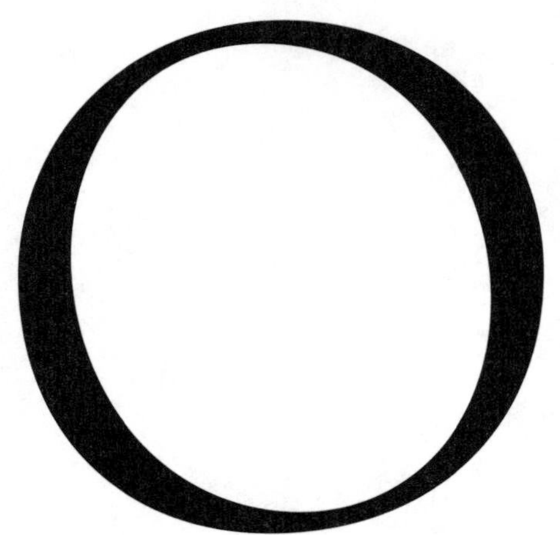

OBITUARY

Formed: Brandon, Florida, USA . . . 1985 as XECUTIONER by JOHN TARDY. Under this moniker, the group cut a couple of tracks for the 'Metal Massacre' compilation series. Adopting the OBITUARY tag, the band (whose line-up was completed by brother DONALD TARDY, ALLEN WEST, TREVOR PERES, DAVID TUCKER) subsequently signed to 'Roadracer' for their heralded (in death-metal circles anyhow) 'SLOWLY WE ROT' (1989) set. Setting TARDY's 'Exorcist'-style growling over a barrage of seismic six-string terrorism and blurred rhythm, OBITUARY won themselves pride of place in the premier league of the death-metal genre. Their readily identifiable logo and suitably grim cover art also helped stamp their identity on the consciousness of metal fans (whether they liked it or not). Following the replacement of WEST and TUCKER with ex-DEATH man, JAMES MURPHY and FRANK WATKINS respectively, the band's profile increased even further with the acclaimed 'CAUSE OF DEATH' (1990). Again produced by the ubiquitous Scott Burns and something of a genre landmark, the record witnessed OBITUARY honing their vicious sonic attack and attempting to come to terms with the outer extremities of the rock format in an uncompromising display of musical viciousness. The aural equivalent of a video nasty, the group continued in their inimitably gory fashion for 'THE END COMPLETE' (1992), ALLEN WEST returning to the fold as MURPHY left for CANCER. The album even gave OBITUARY an unprecedented chart entry(!), the band almost nudging into the UK Top 50. Inevitably, however, TARDY and Co. had to let up at some point and 'WORLD DEMISE' (1994) signalled that, if not exactly mellowing out, the group was willing to temper their hard-headed approach. While metal has moved on to more expansive and eclectic terrain, OBITUARY are still stalking the death-metal graveyard, releasing 'BACK FROM THE DEAD' in 1997. 'DEAD', a year later, was in fact a "live" set comprising songs to sign off with their own sort of obituary.

Album rating: SLOWLY WE ROT (*6) / CAUSE OF DEATH (*7) / THE END COMPLETE (*6) / WORLD DEMISE (*6) / BACK FROM THE DEAD (*6) / DEAD (*5) / ANTHOLOGY compilation (*7)

JOHN TARDY – vocals / **ALLEN WEST** – guitar / **TREVOR PERES** – guitar / **DAVID TUCKER** – bass / **DONALD TARDY** – drums

Roadracer Roadracer

Jun 89. (lp/c/cd) *<(RO 9489-1/-4/-2)>* **SLOWLY WE ROT** ☐ ☐
– Internal bleeding / Godly beings / Till death / Slowly we rot / Immortal visions / Gates to Hell / Words of evil / Suffocation / Intoxicated / Deadly intentions / Bloodsoaked / Stinkupuss. *(cd re-iss. Nov97 & Jun00 on 'Roadrunner'; RR 8768-2)*

— **JAMES MURPHY** – guitar (ex-DEATH) repl. WEST

— **FRANK WATKINS** – bass repl. TUCKER

Sep 90. (cd/c/lp) *<(RO 9370-2/-4/-1)>* **CAUSE OF DEATH** ☐ ☐
– Infected / Body bag / Chopped in half / Circle of the tyrants / Dying / Find the arise / Cause of death / Memories remain / Turned inside out. *(pic-lp Jun91; RO 9370-8) (cd re-iss. Nov97 & JUn00 on 'Roadrunner'; RR 8767-2)*

— JAMES MURPHY left to join CANCER and was repl. by the returning **ALLEN WEST** (WEST subsequently became part of SIX FEET UNDER)

R.C. R.C.

Apr 92. (cd/c/lp) *<(RC 9201-2/-4/-1)>* **THE END COMPLETE** 52 ☐
– I'm in pain / Back to one / Dead silence / In the end of life / Sickness / Corrosive / Killing time / The end complete / Rotting ways. *(cd re-mast.Jun00; RR 8741-2)*

Roadrunner Roadrunner

Sep 94. (cd/c/lp) *<(RR 8995-2/-4/-1)>* **WORLD DEMISE** 65 ☐
– Don't care / World demise / Burned in / Redefine / Paralyzing / Lost / Solid state / Splattered / Final thoughts / Boiling point / Set in stone / Kill for me / Infected (live) / Godly beings (live) / Body bag (live). *(cd re-mast.Jun00; RR 8740-2)*

Apr 97. (cd) *<(RR 8831-2)>* **BACK FROM THE DEAD** ☐ ☐
– Threatening skies / By the light / Inverted / Platonic disease / Download / Rewind / Feed on the weak / Lockdown / Pressure point / Back from the dead / Bullituary. *(re-mast.Jun00; same)*

Apr 98. (cd) *<(RR 8755-2)>* **DEAD (live)** ☐ ☐
– Download / Threatening skies / By the light / Chopped in half / Body bag / Turned inside out / Dying / Cause of death / I'm in pain / Rewind / Till death / Kill for me / I don't care / Back from the dead / Final thoughts / Slowly we rot. *(re-mast.Jun00; same)*

– compilations, etc. –

Jan 01. (cd) *Roadrunner; <(RR 8562-2)>* **ANTHOLOGY** ☐ ☐
– Find the arise (demo) / Til death / Internal bleeding / Intoxicated / Slowly we rot / Cause of death / Dying / Chopped in half / Turned inside out / Back to one / The end complete / I'm in pain / Kill for me / Final thoughts / Don't care / Threatening skies / By the light / Back from the dead / Buried alive / Boiling point (212 degree sporadic mix).

OBSESSED

Formed: Washington, DC, USA . . . early 80's by SCOTT 'WINO' WEINRICH, MARK LAUE and ED GULLI. Emerging from the fertile hardcore scene of their native city, this influential riff-heavy outfit's only official 80's release was a lone EP, 'SODDEN JACKYL', issued on the self-financed 'Invictus' label. With WIENRICH decamping to SAINT VITUS as a replacement for SCOTT REAGERS, OBSESSED was temporarily put on hold. The legacy lived on, however, and in 1990, SAINT VITUS' label, 'Hellbound', proceeded to release an eponymous OBSESSED album comprising early demo material. The reaction was such that WEINRICH was subsequently persuaded to reform the group with new members SCOTT REEDER and GREG ROGERS, releasing 'LUNAR WOMB' the following year. The uncompromising power of the new recordings and the industry respect afforded WEINRICH led to a major label deal with 'Columbia'. With REEDER going off to join another top flight outfit, KYUSS, GUY PINHAS was brought in to complete work an a full-length album, 'THE CHURCH WITHIN' (1993). Unfortunately, the album was lost amid the major label machinations and 'Columbia' declined to take up the option for a follow-up. The band split shortly after and WEINRICH decamped to Hollywood where he became seriously involved in drugs. The singer even ended up sleeping rough while an acute foot infection put him in hospital. This period of strife finally ended after he travelled back to his parents' home in Maryland and gave up hard drugs for good. Rejuvenated, he formed SPIRIT CARAVAN in 1996 alongside GARY ISOM and DAVE SHERMAN. The group initially went under the SHINE moniker, releasing the 'LOST SUN DANCE' EP as their vinyl debut in 1997. The threat of legal action from a similarly named outfit saw them switching to their current tag as they developed their explorative, psychedelic stoner rock. The acclaimed 'JUG FULLA SUN' (1999) – released on 'Tolotta', the label run by FUGAZI man JOE LALLY – was hailed as WEINRICH's most realised effort to date, his 70's biker rock influences subsumed into a denser, trippier style. The follow-up 'DREAMWHEEL' EP was pared down and laid-back in comparison, a taster for the even more cerebral space-rock of 'ELUSIVE TRUTH' (2001).

Album rating: THE OBSESSED (*7) / LUNAR WOMB (*6) / THE CHURCH WITHIN (*6) / INCARNATE compilation (*6) / Spirit Caravan: JUG FULLA SUN (*7) / DREAMWHEEL mini (*5) / ELUSIVE TRUTH (*6)

SCOTT 'WINO' WEINRICH – vocals, guitar / **MARK LAUE** – bass / **ED GULLI** – drums

not iss. Invictus

1980's. (7"ep) **SODDEN JACKYL EP** – ☐

— (1985) WEINRICH replaced SCOTT REAGERS in SAINT VITUS and moved to L.A. He stayed for a few albums, 'BORN TOO LATE' (1987), 'MOURNFUL CRIES' (1988) and 'V' (1989). **WEINRICH** resurrected The OBSESSED, when SAINT VITUS's label 'Hellbound' wanted to release their early demos.

Hellbound Tolotta

1990. (cd/lp) *(H 0008-2/-1) <5>* **THE OBSESSED** ☐ ☐
– Tombstone highway / The way she fly / Forever midnight / Ground out / Fear child / Freedom / Red disaster / Inner turmoil / River of soul.

— **WEINRICH** with newcomers, **SCOTT REEDER** – bass / **GREG ROGERS** – drums (ex-POISON 13)

Jan 92. (cd) *(H 0015-2)* **LUNAR WOMB** ☐ ☐
– Brother blue steel / Bardo / Hiding mask / Spew / Kachina / Jaded / Back to zero / No blame / No mas / Endless circles / Lunar womb / Embryo.

— **GUY PINHAS** – bass (of B.A.L.L., ex-SCREAM) repl. REEDER who joined KYUSS

Columbia Columbia

Apr 94. (cd/c/lp) *(476 504-2/-4/-1) <57342>* **THE CHURCH WITHIN** ☐ ☐ Nov93
– To protect and to serve / Field of hours / Streamlined / Blind lightning / Neatz brigade / A world apart / Skybone / Streetside / Climate of despair / Mourning / Touch of everything / Decimation / Living rain.

— after their split, GUY and GREG would later turn up in GOATSNAKE

– compilations, etc. –

Sep 99. (cd) *Southern Lord; (SUNN 3) / Mia; <10202>* **INCARNATE** ☐ ☐ Jun99
– Yen sleep / Concrete cancer / Peckerwood stomp / Inside looking out / Mental kingdom / Sodden jackal / Iron and stone / Indestroy / Streetside / Mourning / Spirit caravan / Skybone / On the hunt.

SPIRIT CARAVAN

SCOTT WINO – vocals, guitar / **DAVE SHERMAN** – bass / **GARY ISOM** – drums

Tolotta Tolotta

Jun 99. (cd) *<(TOL 04)>* **JUG FULLA SUN** ☐ ☐
– Healing tongue / Courage / Cosmic artifact / Fear's machine / Powertime / Dead love – Jug fulla sun / Fang / Shaw / Melancholy grey / Sea legs / Kill ugly naked / Lost sun dance / No hope goat farm.

Sep 99. (m-cd) *<(MCY 007CD)>* **DREAMWHEEL** ☐ ☐ Nov99
– Dreamwheel / Burnin' in / Re-alignment – High power / Sun stoned / C. yourself. *(re-iss. Jul00 on 'Prison' cd/lp; PRISON 994-2/-1)*
(above on 'Meteor City', below on 'Teepee')

Nov 99. (7") <(MIA 1018)> **split w/ 60 Watt** [ ] [ ]
May 01. (cd/lp) <(TOL 07 CD/LP)> **ELUSIVE TRUTH** [ ] [ ]
– Spirit caravan / Black flower / Retroman / Find it / Futility's reasons / Cloudy mirror / Elusive truth / Darkness and longing / Lifer city / Outlaw wizard / The departure (of Quetzalcoatl).

OBSESSION

Formed: Connecticut, USA . . . 1983 by MIKE VESCARA and BRUCE VITALE, who subsequently added ART MACO, MATT KARUGAS and JAY MEZIAS. Signed to 'Metal Blade' after contributing a track to the label's 'Metal Massacre' compilation, OBSESSION debuted with the 'MARSHALL LAW' album in 1986. Screaming trad metal in typical 80's style, the group moulded their British influences into a hard-hitting, if hardly original, sonic assault. With the group switching labels to 'Enigma', subsequent releases, 'SCARRED FOR LIFE' (1986) and 'METHODS OF MADNESS' (1987) eased off the accelerator slightly. Following MEZIAS' departure for LOUDNESS, however, OBSESSION split.

Album rating: MARSHALL LAW mini (*6) / SCARRED FOR LIFE (*5) / METHODS OF MADNESS (*6)

MIKE VESCARA – vocals / **BRUCE VITALE** – guitar / **ART MACO** – guitar / **MATT KARUGAS** – bass / **JAY MEZIAS** – drums

Enigma / Metal Blade

1986. (m-lp) *(47554)* <MBR 1010> **MARSHALL LAW** [ ] [ ]
– Only the strong will survive / Hatred unto death / The execution / Marshall law.

Enigma / Enigma

Oct 86. (lp) <73212-1> **SCARRED FOR LIFE** [-] [ ]
– Intro – Scarred for life / Winner takes all / Losing my mind / In the end / Bang 'em till they bleed / My Lai 31568 – Take no prisoners / Taking your chance / Run into the night / Tomorrow hides no lies / Shadows of steel / Evil in her eyes.
Oct 87. (lp) <(73262-1)> **METHODS OF MADNESS** [ ] [ ]
– Four play – Hard to the core / High treason / For the love of money / Killer elite / Desperate to survive / Methods of madness / Too wild to tame / Always on the run / Panic in the streets / Missing you / Waiting for your call.

—— MEZIAS quit when VESCARA joined Japanese hard-rockers, LOUDNESS

OCEAN MACHINE (see under ⇒ TOWNSEND, Devin)

Gene OCTOBER (see under ⇒ CHELSEA)

OFFSPRING

Formed: Orange County, California, USA . . . 1984 out of MANIC SUBSIDAL and CLOWNS OF DEATH, by main songwriter DEXTER HOLLAND and GREG KRIESEL. With the addition of JAMES LILJA and KEVIN 'NOODLES' WASSERMAN they adopted THE OFFSPRING moniker, releasing a debut 45, 'I'LL BE WAITING' on the self-financed 'Black' label. With RON WELTY subsequently replacing LILJA, the band began working on demo material, eventually going into the studio with Thom Wilson. The results eventually surfaced in the form of the eponymous 'OFFSPRING' (1989), issued on the 'Nitro' label. An ambitious and experimental fusion of exotic hardcore, its schizoid ramblings not endearing the band to many outside the scene. The next few years were tough for the band as they struggled to find a steady record deal, even tougher for NOODLES who was stabbed at a benefit concert. They eventually found a sympathetic ear in the form of BRAD GUREWITZ (ex-BAD RELIGION) and his burgeoning 'Epitaph' operation, releasing a much improved follow-up album, 'IGNITION' in 1992. However, it wasn't until 1994 and their follow-up, 'SMASH', that OFFSPRING pogo'd into the US charts. Hard on the heels of GREEN DAY's phenomenal worldwide success, the 4-piece found a very successful niche in the larger than life, lads-together ska-core punk rock complete with dayglo choruses and brutally addictive hooklines. The album went on to sell over a million copies in the States and finally gained deserved recognition in Britain, especially after the 'SELF ESTEEM' track became a Top 40 smash early '95! Over the course of the ensuing two years, OFFSPRING almost became part of 'Columbia's roster, although in the end a follow-up, 'INXAY ON THE HOMBRE' appeared on 'Epitaph' in 1997. Building on the winning formula of its predecessor, the album scored another transatlantic Top 20. The dreadlocked DEXTER subsequently teamed up with JELLO BIAFRA (ex-DEAD KENNEDYS) to play some charity gigs under the banner of F.S.U. in aid of the homeless, human rights, etc. Album No.5 'AMERICANA' was delivered late in '98, nobody in their right minds prophecising it would unearth a UK chart-topper in the shape of fun novelty 45, 'PRETTY FLY (FOR A WHITE GUY)'. More of the same was to follow, British hits, 'THE KIDS AREN'T ALRIGHT' and 'SHE'S GOT ISSUES', boosting sales of an otherwise flagging album – a pretty fly move, indeed! Now in the major league of nu-punk heroes, OFFSPRING served up more metallic mania for the masses with 'CONSPIRACY OF ONE', a record which contained precious little in the way of sonic innovation but plenty of shoutalong riffage for longtime fans and the newly converted alike. • **Covered:** HEY JOE (hit; Jimi Hendrix) / SMASH IT UP (Damned) / KILLBOY POWERHEAD (Didjits).

Album rating: THE OFFSPRING (*4) / IGNITION (*6) / SMASH (*7) / IXNAY ON THE HOMBRE (*5) / AMERICANA (*5) / CONSPIRACY OF ONE (*5)

DEXTER HOLLAND (b. BRYAN HOLLAND, 1966) – vocals, guitar / **NOODLES** (b. KEVIN WASSERMAN, 4 Feb'63, L.A.) – guitar / **GREG KRIESEL** (b.20 Jan'65, Glendale, Calif.) – bass / **JAMES LILJA** – drums

not iss. / Black

1987. (7") <none> **I'LL BE WAITING. / BLACKBALL** [-] [ ]

—— **RON WELTY** (b. 1 Feb'71) – drums (ex-FQX) repl. LILJA

not iss. / Nemesis

Aug 88. (7"ep) <NEX 21> **BAGHDAD EP** [-] [ ]
– Get it right / Hey Joe / Baghdad / The blurb.
1989. (cd) <NECDX 44> **THE OFFSPRING** [-] [ ]
– Jennifer lost the war / Elders / Out on patrol / Crossroads / Demons / Beheaded / Tehran / A thousand days / Black ball / I'll be waiting / Kill the president. *(UK-iss.Nov95 on 'Epitaph' cd/c; E 86460-2/-4) (cd re-iss. Jun00 on 'Nitro'; 15803-2)*

Epitaph / Epitaph

Oct 92. (cd/c/lp) <(E 86424-2/-4/-1)> **IGNITION** [ ] [ ]
– Session / We are one / Kick him when he's down / Take it like a man / Get it right / Dirty magic / Hypodermic / Burn it up / No hero / L.A.P.D. / Nothing from something / Forever and a day.
Sep 94. (cd/c/lp) <(E 86432-2/-4/-1)> **SMASH** [21] [4] Apr94
– Time to relax / Nitro (youth energy) / Bad habit / Gotta get away / Genocide / Something to believe in / Come out and play / Self esteem / It'll be a long time / Killboy powerhead / What happened to you / So alone / Not the one / Smash.
Sep 94. (12"/c-s/cd-s) *(EPUK/+MC/CD 001)* **COME OUT AND PLAY. / SESSION / ('A'acoustic)** [ ] [-]
Oct 94. (7") <IGN 3H> <65572> **COME OUT AND PLAY. / COME OUT AND PLAY** [ ] [ ]
(above on 'Ignition'/<'Phantom'> (below ltd. on 'Flying')
Dec 94. (10"ep) *(GOD 008)* **COME OUT AND PLAY EP** [ ] [-]
Feb 95. (7"/c-s/12"/cd-s) *(7/MC/12/CD HOLE 001)* **SELF ESTEEM. / JENNIFER LOST THE WAR / BURN IT UP** [37] [-]
Aug 95. (7"/c-s/cd-s) *(WOOS 2/+CS/CDS)* **GOTTA GET AWAY. / SMASH** [43] [-]
(above single on 'Out Of Step' UK)

—— In the Spring of '96, they were fighting Epitaph and boss BRETT GUREWITZ for the right to sign with another label 'Columbia' in the US-only.

Jan 97. (7"m/cd-s) *(6495-7/-2)* **ALL I WANT. / WAY DOWN THE LINE** [31] [-]
(cd-s+=) *(6491-2)* – Smash it up.
Feb 97. (cd/lp) *(6487-2/-1)* <67810> **IXNAY ON THE HOMBRE** [17] [9]
– Disclaimer / Meaning of life / Mota / Me and my old lady / Cool to hate / Leave it behind / Gone away / I choose / Intermission / All I want / Way down the line / Don't pick it up / Amazed / Change the world.
Apr 97. (7"/cd-s) *(6504-7/-2)* **GONE AWAY. / D.U.I.** [42] [-]
(cd-s+=) *(6498-2)* – Cool to hate / Hey Joe.

Columbia / Columbia

Nov 98. (cd/c) *(491656-2/-4)* <69661> **AMERICANA** [10] [2]
– Welcome / Have you ever / Staring at the sun / Pretty fly (for a white guy) / The kids aren't alright / Feelings / She's got issues / Walla walla / End of the line / No brakes / Why don't you get a job? / Americana / Pay the man. *(pic-lp-iss.May99; 491656-0) (cd re-iss. Feb01; same)*
Jan 99. (7"/c-s) *(666880-7/-4)* <41579> **PRETTY FLY (FOR A WHITE GUY). / ('A'-The Geek mix)** [1] [53] Nov98
(cd-s+=) *(666880-2)* – All I want (live).
Apr 99. (c-s) *(667354-4)* <radio cut> **WHY DON'T YOU GET A JOB? / BEHEADED 1999** [2] [74] Mar99
(cd-s+=) *(667354-2)* – ('A'remix by Baka Boyz) / Pretty fly (for a white guy) (CD-ROM).
(cd-s) *(667354-5)* – ('A'remixes).
Aug 99. (c-s) *(667763-4)* **THE KIDS AREN'T ALRIGHT / PRETTY FLY (FOR A WHITE GUY) (live)** [11] [-]
(cd-s+=) *(667763-2)* – Why don't you get a job? (live).
(cd-s) *(667763-5)* – ('A'side) / Walla walla (live) / Pretty fly (for a white guy) (video).
Nov 99. (c-s) *(668377-4)* <4274> **SHE'S GOT ISSUES / PRETTY FLY (Baka Boyz Low Rider mix)** [41] [ ]
(cd-s+=) *(668377-2)* – ('A'side) / Kids aren't alright (Wise Guys mix) / Kids aren't alright (Wise Guys instrumental).
(cd-s) *(667377-5)* – ('A'side) / All I want (live in Vegas) / Kids aren't alright (CD-Rom video).
Nov 00. (c-s) *(669997-4)* **ORIGINAL PRANKSTER / DAMMIT, I CHANGED AGAIN** [6] [-]
(cd-s+=) *(669997-2)* – Gone away (live).
(cd-s) *(669997-5)* – ('A'side) / Come out swinging / Staring at the sun (live).
Nov 00. (cd/c/lp) *(498481-2/-4/-1)* <61419> **CONSPIRACY OF ONE** [12] [9]
– Intro / Come out swinging / Original prankster / Want you bad / Million miles away / Dammit, I change again / Living in chaos / Special delivery / One fine day / All along / Denial, revisited / Vultures / Conspiracy of one.
Mar 01. (c-s) *(670929-4)* **WANT YOU BAD / THE KIDS AREN'T ALRIGHT (live)** [15] [-]
(cd-s+=) *(670929-2)* – 80 times.
(cd-s) *(670929-5)* – ('A'side) / The kids aren't alright (live) / Autonomy.
Jun 01. (c-s) *(671408-4)* **MILLION MILES AWAY / STARING AT THE SUN (live)** [••] [-]
(cd-s+=) *(671408-2)* – Sin city / ('A'video).
(cd-s) *(671408-5)* – ('A'side) / Dammit, I changed again (live) / Bad habit (live).

OI POLLOI

Formed: Edinburgh, Scotland . . . 1984 by DEGSY ALLAN and Co. Although their moniker might have suggested an association with the "oi" movement, OI POLLOI (which was taken from the ancient Greek meaning of "the common people") had more in common with the likes of CRASS and CONFLICT. After building up a loyal fanbase in the capital, these politically correct anarcho-punks finally made it onto vinyl in early '86, sharing the 'UNLIMITED GENOCIDE' lp with AOA. In fact, OI POLLOI also shared their following two sets, 'MAD AS FUCK (DON'T YOU THINK?)' and 'SKINS 'N' PUNKS II', with TOXIK EPHEX and BETRAYED respectively. Lending their weight to the anti-censorship movement, OI POLLOI contributed one track, 'NO FILTHY NUCLEAR POWER', to the JELLO (BIAFRA) AID compilation album, 'Censorship Sucks', the proceeds from which went towards the cost of the DEAD KENNEDYS frontman's impending court case (cover art by the illustrious Harry Horse!). In 1987, moving in an increasingly punk-metal hybrid direction, the band delivered their first exclusive set, 'UNITE AND WIN', a subsequent two year hiatus broken with the impassioned protest of 'IN DEFENCE OF OUR EARTH' (1990). Having earlier signed to 'Words Of Warning' (home of fellow anti-Nazis, BLAGGERS ITA), they went on to issue the EP 'OMNICIDE' in '92. Despite being largely ignored by the indie press, OI POLLOI battled on. In 1998, the quartet signed to Devon-based 'Ruptured Emotions', delivering their umpteenth 7" EP, 'GUILTY' the same year; their comeback album 'FUAIM CATHAI' was issued in '99.

Album rating: UNLIMITED GENOCIDE shared (*4) / MAD AS FUCK (DON'T YOU THINK?) shared (*4) / SKINS 'N' PUNKS II shared (*4) / UNITE AND WIN (*5) / IN DEFENCE OF OUR EARTH (*5) / TOTAL ANARCHOI compilation (*5) / FIGHT BACK compilation (*5) / FUAIM CATHA! (*5)

DEGSY ALLAN – vocals / **BOB** – guitar / **BOBBY** – bass / **MURRAY** – drums

Children Of The Revolution — not iss.

Jan 86. (lp; shared with AOA) *(GURT 12)* **UNLIMITED GENOCIDE** [ ] [-]
– Go green / You cough they profit / Punx or mice / Nuclear waste / The only release / Apartheid stinx / (others by AOA).

Endangered Musik — not iss.

May 86. (7"ep) *(EDR 5)* **RESIST THE ATOMIC MENACE EP** [ ] [-]
– Hands off Nicaragua / Scum / They shoot children don't they / Resist the atomic menace / Reach for the light. *(re-iss. 1994; same)*

Green Vomit — not iss.

Oct 86. (lp; shared with TOXIK EPHEX) *(PUKE 15)* **MAD AS FUCK (DON'T YOU THINK?)** [ ] [-]
– Go green / Scum / Minority authority / They shoot children, don't they? / The only release? / Foundations for a future / No filthy nuclear power / (others by TOXIC EPHEX).

Oi! — not iss.

Jan 87. (lp; shared with BETRAYED) *(OIR 008)* **SKINS 'N' PUNKS II** [ ] [-]
– Boot down the door / Americans out / Thugs in uniform / Pigs for slaughter / Rich scumbag / Never give in / Minority authority / Skinhead / (others by the BETRAYED).

Oct 87. (lp) *(OIR 011)* **UNITE AND WIN** [ ] [-]
– Punx 'n' skins / We don't need them / Kill the bill / Lowest of the low / Nuclear waste / Commies and Nazis / Pigs for slaughter / Scum / Thrown on the scrapheap / Punx picnic in Princess Street gardens / Mindless few / Unite and win! *(cd-iss. Apr01 on 'Step 1'+=; STEPCD 132)* – SKINS'N'PUNKS lp tracks.

Words Of Warning — not iss.

Jul 90. (lp) *(WOWLP 10)* **IN DEFENCE OF OUR EARTH** [ ] [-]
– Thin green line / 23 hours / When two men kiss / Whale song / What have we done / Victims of a chemical spillage / Anarcho pie / Clachan chalanais / Free the Henge / Nazi scum / World park Antartica. *(cd-iss. May00+=; WOWCD 10)* – Dealer in death / Omnicide / Victims of a gas attack / Die for BP (time to stop the war).

Jan 92. (7"ep) *(WOW 17)* **OMNICIDE EP** [ ] [-]
– Dealer in death / Omnicide / Victims of a gas attack / Die for BP (time to stop the war).

1994. (7"ep; shared with BLOWNAPART) **BASTARDS** [ ] [-]
– Right to choose / Victims of a gas attack / (2 by other group).

Campary — not iss.

1998. (7"ep) **THC EP** [ ] [-]
– THC / Sex with strangers / Simon Weston / Meine augen.

Ruptured Ambitions — not iss.

Sep 98. (7"ep) *(RUP 1)* **GUILTY EP** [ ] [-]
– Guilty / Break the mould / John Major – fuck you / Bash the fash.

Jul 99. (7"ep) *(GRAND 1)* **LET THE BOOTS DO THE TALKING EP** [ ] [-]
– It doesn't have to be like this / Let the boots do the talking / Stay alert / Fuck the national lottery / Threshers – fuck off!

Skuld — not iss.

1999. (lp) **FUAIM CATHA!** [ ] [-]
– The Earth is our mother / Terra-Ist / Take back the land / Religious con / Don't burn the witch / The right to choose / Fuck everybody who voted Tory / Sios leis a' ghniomhachas mhoir / G.L.F. / Willie McRae / Deathcafe / Your beer is shit and your money stinks / Sell-out / No more roads / Hunt the rich / Mindrot / Anti-police aggro.

– compilations, etc. –

Jan 91. (m-lp) *Words Of Warning; (WOWLP 13)* **OUTRAGED BY THE ATOMIC MENACE** [ ] [-]
– Outrage / Thugs in uniform / Resist the atomic menace / Death by night.

Apr 92. (cd) *Released Emotions; (REM 017)* **TOTAL ANARCHOI (some live)** [ ] [-]
– Nuclear waste / Boot down the door / Pigs for slaughter / Scum / Thrown on the scrapheap / Punx picnic / Mindless few / Unite and win / Omnicide (live) / Americans out (live) / Pigs for slaughter (live) / Thugs in uniform (live) / Nazi scum (live) / Nuclear waste (live) / Free the Henge (live) / Punx picnic (live) / State violence, state control (live) * / If the kids are united *. *(re-iss. Nov97 on 'Step 1' cd/lp*-; STEP CD/LP 073)* – (LP w/out *).

Mar 97. (lp) *Campary; (CAMPARY 024)* **FIGHT BACK** [ ] [-]
– (split sides with the BETRAYED and AOA).

OMEGA TRIBE

Formed: North London, England . . . 1982 by ex-FATAL MICROBES guitarist, PETE FENDER, who had previously issued a solo EP, 'FOUR FORMULAS', for 'Xntrix'. Alongside him were a young team of oi/punks, namely HUGH, RADLY and PETER (aka PETEROLEUM YORKIE) and this line-up toured supporting The NIGHTINGALES and TOXIC SHOCK. The 'TRIBE debuted a year later on the 'Crass' label with the EP, 'ANGRY SONGS', following it up with a mini-set, 'NO LOVE LOST' (1983). YORKIE was subsequently replaced by SUNNY and saxophonist, JANE, although only a solitary single and a cassette were forthcoming before they became extinct.

Album rating: NO LOVE LOST mini (*3)

HUGH TWITM'N – vocals, guitar / **PETE LOUDM'N** (b. PETE FENDER) – guitar, vocals (ex-FATAL MICROBES) / **RADLY HARDM'N** (b. DARYL) – bass, vocals / **PETEROLEUM YORKIE BIGM'N** – drums, vocals

Crass — not iss.

May 83. (7"ep) *(221984-10)* **ANGRY SONGS** [ ] [-]

Corpus Christi — not iss.

Dec 83. (m-lp) *(ITS 5)* **NO LOVE LOST** [ ] [-]
– Duty calls / Profit / Aftermath / Freedom, peace and unity / What the hell / Mother of cultivation / My tears / Nature wonder / Pictures / Man made / My tears – reprise (no more wars).

—— **SUNNY** – drums; repl. YORKIE / added **JANE** – sax, flute

Sep 84. (7"/12") *(ITS/+T 12)* **IT'S A HARD LIFE. / YOUNG JOHN** [ ] [-]

96 Tapes — not iss.

Mar 85. (c) *(96-11)* **LIVE AT THE CLARENDON** [ ] [-]

—— disbanded in 1985

OMEN

Formed: Los Angeles, California, USA . . . 1984 by J.D. KIMBALL, KENNY POWELL, JODY HENRY and STEVE WITTIG. After contributing a track to one of the 'Metal Massacre' compilations, OMEN were signed to 'Metal Blade' ('Roadrunner' UK) in 1984. Their debut album, 'BATTLE CRY', surfaced later that year, its unimaginative power-metal failing to mark them out as anything more than second division contenders. A series of similar albums followed in quick succession before KIMBALL eventually departed, his replacement being future ANNIHILATOR frontman COBURN PHARR. The resulting opus, 'ESCAPE TO NOWHERE' (1988) was their final effort for some time, the record's more ambitious approach still failing to bring them any luck; comeback set 'RE-OPENING THE GATES' was issued in 1997.

Album rating: BATTLE CRY (*4) / WARNING OF DANGER (*5) / THE CURSE (*6) / NIGHTMARES (*7) / ESCAPE TO NOWHERE (*5) / TEETH compilation (*6) / REOPENING THE GATES (*5)

J.D. KIMBALL – vocals / **KENNY POWELL** – guitar (ex-SACRED BLADE) / **JODY HENRY** – bass / **STEVE WITTIG** – drums

Roadrunner — Restless

Sep 84. (lp) *(RR 9818)* <71103> **BATTLE CRY** [ ] [ ]
– Death rider / The axeman / Last rites / Dragon's breath / By my wench / Battle cry / Die by the blade / Prince of darkness / Bring out the beast / In the arena. *(cd-iss. Nov96 on 'Metal Blade'; 3984 14215CD)*

Nov 85. (lp) *(RR 9738)* **WARNING OF DANGER** [ ] [ ]
– Termination / Make me your king / Don't fear the night / Ruby eyes (of the serpent) / Warning of danger / Red horizon / Hell's gates / March on / V.B.P. *<US cd-iss. Nov96 on 'Metal Blade'; 14217>*

Mar 86. (m-lp) *(RR 9661)* <73230> **THE CURSE** [ ] [ ]
– The curse / Kill on sight / Holy martyr / Eye of the storm / S.R.B. / Teeth of the hydra / At all cost / Destiny / Bounty hunter / The larch. *(cd-iss. Nov96 on 'Metal Blade'; 3984 14216CD)*

Jun 86. (m-lp) *(RR 9617)* <73266> **NIGHTMARES** [ ] [ ]
– Nightmares / Shock treatment / Dragon's breath / Termination / Bounty hunter / Whole lotta Rosie.

—— **COBURN PARR** – vocals; repl. KIMBALL

Nov 88. (lp/cd) *(RR 9544-1/-2)* <73310> **ESCAPE TO NOWHERE** [ ] [ ]
– It's not easy / Radar love / Escape to nowhere / Cry for the morning / Thorn in your flesh / Poisoned / Nomads / King of the hill / No way out.

—— folded in 1990 when PHARR left to join ANNIHILATOR; POWELL joined STEP CHILD. OMEN re-formed some time later

Massacre — Massacre

Jun 97. (cd) *<(MASSCD 124)>* **REOPENING THE GATES** [ ] [ ]
– Dead march / Uneven plow / Chained / Rain down / Reopening the gates / Everything / Well fed / Crushing day / Saturday / Into the ground.

– compilations, etc. –

Nov 96. (cd) *Metal Blade; <(3984 14206CD)>* **TEETH** [ ] [ ]

ONEIDA

Formed: Brooklyn, New York, USA . . . mid-90's by PAPA CRAZY aka PCRZ, BOBBY MATADOR aka FAT BOBBY, HANOI JANE aka BABY JANE and KID MILLIONS. Committed garage revivalists with a typically experimental NY edge, ONEIDA combine hard-driving retro punk and R&B with frazzled free jazz and even elements of Krautrock. Having built up a healthy reputation amongst the city's music cognoscenti, the band made their vinyl debut in 1997 with 'A PLACE CALLED EL SHADDAI'S'. A second independently released album, 'ENEMY HOGS', followed in 1999 while a prolific start to the new millennium saw the release of both the 'COME ON EVERYBODY LET'S ROCK' set and 'STEEL ROD' EP, the latter featuring a cover of Creedence Clearwater Revival's 'SINISTER PURPOSE'.

Album rating: A PLACE CALLED EL SHADDAI'S (*6) / ENEMY HOGS (*5) / STEEL ROD mini (*5) / COME ON EVERYBODY LET'S ROCK (*5)

(PCRZ) PAPA CRAZY – vocals, guitar / **(FAT) BOBBY MATADOR** – keyboards / **HANOI (BABY) JANE** – bass / **KID MILLIONS** – drums

Turnbuckle Turnbuckle

Dec 97. (cd) <*(TB 009)*> **A PLACE CALLED EL SHADDAI'S**
– Hieronymous / Go there / Salad days / Medium cool / Gandhi for now / Dog days / Ballad of Vaurice / El Shaddai's.

Nov 98. (7") **BEST FRIENDS. / THE LAND OF BUGS**

Turnbuckle Jagjaguwar

Oct 99. (cd) *(TB 018)* <*JAG 29*> **ENEMY HOGS**
– Whitney fortress / Primanti Bros. / Bombay fraud / Give up . . . and move on / Little red dolls / Ginger (bein' free) / Turn it: up (loud) / Gettin' it on / Hard workin' man / Quest for two / Fourth eye / Wicked servant. *(hidden track+=)* – O.L.B. *(re-iss. Apr01 on 'Jagjaguwar'; same as US)*

Jagjajuwar Jagjaguwar

Nov 99. (7") <*(JAG 14)*> **split w/ Songs: Ohia**

Aug 00. (m-cd) <*(JAG 25)*> **STEEL ROD** Nov00
– XXY / Steel rod / Tennessee / Helltrain / Sinister purpose.

Nov 00. (cd) <*(JAG 27)*> **COME ON EVERYBODY LET'S ROCK**
– I love rock / Major havoc / Pure light invasion / Legion of scags / Doin' business in Japan / Snow machine / Slip inside this house / Power animals / Fat Goggy's black thumb.

ONE MINUTE SILENCE

Formed: London, England . . . 1995 initially as touring band, NEAR DEATH EXPERIENCE by Irish-born frontman BRIAN 'Yap' BARRY, guitarist CHRIS IGNATIOU (of German/Greek parentage), Gibraltar-born bassman GLEN DIANI and drummer EDDIE STRATTON. A Brit rap anti-racist answer to RAGE AGAINST THE MACHINE and CLAWFINGER, they signed to 'Big Cat' and released two singles, 'SOUTH CENTRAL' and 'A WASTE OF THINGS TO COME', plus the equally sardonic 'AVAILABLE IN ALL COLOURS' album in '98. Subsequently becoming the latest in a long line of pop/punk/metal signings for Virgin cola/balloon/railway tycoon, Richard Branson's 'V2' imprint, ONE MINUTE SILENCE released three minutes of agit-noise with a re-worked version of 'STUCK BETWEEN A ROCK AND A WHITE FACE'. • **Trivia:** Apparently, GLEN's favourite chat-up line is "How much?".

Album rating: AVAILABLE IN ALL COLOURS (*7) / BUY NOW . . . SAVED LATER (*6)

BRIAN 'Yap' BARRY – vocals / **CHRIS IGNATIOU** – guitar / **GLEN DIANI** – bass / **EDDIE STRATTON** – drums

Big Cat Big Cat

Nov 97. (12"pic-d/cd-s) *(ABB 146 TP/SCD)* **SOUTH CENTRAL. / STUCK BETWEEN A ROCK AND A WHITE FACE / HALF EMPTY** –

Mar 98. (7") *(ABB 156S)* **A WASTE OF THINGS TO COME. / YANK MY DOODLE DANDY** –
(12"+=/cd-s+=) *(ABB 156 T/CD)* – Brain spiller.

Apr 98. (cd) *(ABB 147CD)* <*81847*> **AVAILABLE IN ALL COLOURS**
– New dogs new tricks / South Central / Stuck between a rock and a white face / A more violent approach / Norfuckinmality / For want of a better world / I think therefore I'm damned / Remain calm / Available in all colours / Brainspiller / A waste of things to come / And some ya lose / Pig until proven cop.

V2 V2

Oct 98. (7") *(VVR 500330-7)* **STUCK BETWEEN A ROCK AND A WHITE FACE. / AND COUNTING (demo)** –
(cd-s+=) *(VVR 500330-3)* – Going going gone (demo).

Mar 00. (cd-s) *(VVR 501234-3)* **HOLY MAN / 14 YEARS / I FEEL NOTHING** –

Apr 00. (cd/lp) *(VVR 101236-2/-1)* <*27069*> **BUY NOW . . . SAVED LATER**
– Rise and shine / 1845 / Holy man / It's just a ride / Food for the brain / Fish out of water / Roof of the world / 16 stone pig / 210 dog years / If I can dance / A spoonful of sugar / On deaf ears / A day in the light of / Words. <*US cd+=*> – 14 years / I feel nothing.

Jan 01. (cd-s) *(VVR 501321-3)* **FISH OUT OF WATER / 1845 (demo) / 210 DOG YEARS (demo)** 56 –
(cd-s) *(VVR 501321-6)* – ('A'side) / Holy man (demo) / A day in the light of (demo).

ONSLAUGHT

Formed: Bristol, England . . . 1983 by guitarist NIGE ROCKETT and drummer STEVE GRICE, who enlisted the services of vocalist PAUL MAHONEY and bassist JASON STALLORD. Beginning life as a punk-metal fusion, the group issued an independently released debut album, 'POWER FROM HELL' in 1985. They were soon joined by a new frontman in the shape of SY KEELER, downgrading MAHONEY to bass duties while STALLORD now played rhythm guitar. The resulting album, 'THE FORCE' (1986) was unleashed by 'Under One Flag', its somewhat derivative thrash style demonstrating that the UK scene was yet to carve out its own identity. Bassman JAMES HINDER came in for the departing MAHONEY just prior to a cover of AC/DC's 'LET THERE BE ROCK' being issued as a single. Signed to 'London' records in 1988, ONSLAUGHT subsequently took on a more traditional metal belter in the form of STEVE GRIMMETT (ex-GRIM REAPER), the 'IN SEARCH OF SANITY' set re-recorded with the new singer's vocals. To preview the album's release, 'London' issued two singles, 'SHELLSHOCK' and a re-vamped but toned down 'LET THERE BE ROCK' (ROB TROTMAN replaced STALLORD). The album eventually hit the shops in May '89, its more commercial approach achieving a UK Top 50 placing but alienating the band's thrash fanbase. GRIMMETT departed soon after, his replacement TONY O'HARA never getting a chance to prove himself on vinyl as ONSLAUGHT finally split in 1991.

Album rating: POWER FROM HELL (*6) / THE FORCE (*6) / IN SEARCH OF SANITY (*5)

PAUL MAHONEY – vocals / **NIGE ROCKETT** – guitar / **JASON STALLORD** – bass / **STEVE GRICE** – drums

Children Of the Revolution not iss.

Jun 85. (lp) *(CART 2)* **POWER FROM HELL** –
– Damnation / Onslaught (power from Hell) / Thermonuclear devastation / Skullcrusher 1 / Lord of evil / Death metal / Angels of death / The Devils legion / Street meets steel / Skullcrusher 2 / Witch hunt / Mighty empress. *(re-iss. Mar87 on 'Under One Flag'; FLAG 7) (cd-iss. Oct96 on 'Powerage'; PRAGE 001CD)*

— added **SY KEELER** – vocals (MAHONEY + STALLORD now on bass + rhythm guitar respectively)

Under One Flag Combat

Apr 86. (lp/c) *(FLAG/TFLAG 1)* <*8104*> **THE FORCE**
– Let there be death / Metal forces / Fight with the beast / Demoniac / Flame of the antichrist / Contract in blood / Thrash till the death. *(cd-iss. Dec88; CDFLAG 1)*

— **JAMES HINDER** – bass; repl. MAHONEY

Oct 87. (12"ep) *(12FLAG 103)* **LET THERE BE ROCK. /** –

— **STEVE GRIMMETT** – vocals (ex-GRIM REAPER) + **ROB TROTMAN** – lead guitar; repl. KEELER + STALLORD respectively

London London

Dec 88. (12"ep) *(LONX 215)* **SHELLSHOCK. / CONFUSED / H-EYES** –

Apr 89. (7") *(LON 224)* **LET THERE BE ROCK. / SHELLSHOCK (live)** 50 –
(12"+=/12"s+=/cd-s+=) *(LON X/XP/CD 224)* – Metal forces (live).

May 89. (lp/c/cd) <*(828 142-1/-4/-2)*> **IN SEARCH OF SANITY** 46
– Asylum / In search of sanity / Shellshock / Lightning war / Let there be rock / Blood upon the ice / Welcome to dying / Power play.

Jul 89. (7") *(LON 198)* **WELCOME TO DYING. / NICE 'N' SLEAZY** –
(12"+=) *(LONX 198)* – Atomic punk.

— **TONY O'HARA** – vocals; repl. GRIMMETT (they folded in '91). ROCKETT formed FRANKENSTEIN later that year.

OPERATION IVY (see under ⇒ RANCID)

OPETH

Formed: Stockholm, Sweden . . . 1990 by PETER LINDGRAN and MIKAEL AKERFELDT. Favouring lengthy progressive metal with meandering acoustic guitar interludes, epic themes and gutteral vocals, these Scandinavian gloom merchants released their debut album, 'Orchid', on the 'Candlelight' label in 1995. With a line-up completed by the rhythm section of JOHAN DeFARFALLA and ANDERS NORDIN, they went on to issue a follow-up set, 'MORNINGRISE' (1996) and tour with death metal veterans MORBID ANGEL. A subsequent deal with the 'Century Media' company resulted in a US licensing deal for their first two albums and a transatlantic release for 1998's acclaimed 'MY ARMS, YOUR HEARSE', its title – if not the music – reminiscent of NICK CAVE's classic 'Your Funeral . . . My Trial'. By this point, both DeFARFALLA and NORDIN had been replaced by MARTIN MENDEZ and MARTIN LOPEZ respectively, a line-up which would remain stable over subsequent albums 'STILL LIFE' (1999) and 'BLACKWATER PARK' (2001).

Album rating: ORCHID (*5) / MORNINGRISE (*6) / MY ARMS, YOUR HEARSE (*7) / STILL LIFE (*6) / BLACKWATER PARK (*6)

MIKAEL AKERFELDT – guitar / **PETER LINDGREN** – guitar / **JOHAN DeFARFALLA** – bass, guitars, vocals / **ANDERS NORDIN** – drums, percussion, piano

Candlelight Century Media

Sep 95. (cd) *(CANDLE 010CD)* <*CM 7845*> **ORCHID**
– In mist she was standing / Under the weeping moon / Silhouette / Forest of October / The twilight is my robe / Requiem / The apostle in triumph. *(re-iss. Oct00; CANDLE 053CD)*

Jul 96. (cd) *(CANDLE 015CD)* <*CM 7849*> **MORNINGRISE**
– Advent / The night and the silent water / Nectar / Black rose immortal / To bid you farewell. *(re-iss. Oct00; CANDLE 054CD)*

Jun 98. (cd) *(CANDLE 025CD)* <*CM 7894*> **MY ARMS, YOUR HEARSE** Aug98
– Prologue / April ethereal / When / Madrigal / The amen corner / Demon of the fall / Credence / Karma / Epilogue. *(re-iss. Oct00; CANDLE 055CD)*

— **MARTIN MENDEZ** – bass; repl. JOHAN

— **MARTIN LOPEZ** – drums; repl. ANDERS

Peaceville Peaceville

Oct 99. (cd) *(CDVILE 78)* <*62078*> **STILL LIFE**
– The moor / Godheads lament / Benighted / Moonlapse vertige / Face of Melinda / Serenity painted death / White cluster. *(re-iss. Nov00; same)*

Music For Nations Koch Int.

Mar 01. (cd/lp) *(CD+/MFN 264)* <*8237*> **BLACKWATER PARK** Feb01
– The leper affinity / Bleak / Harvest / The drapery falls / Dirge for November / The funeral portrait / Patterns in the ivy / Blackwater park.

ORANGE GOBLIN

Formed: England ... 1994 initially as OUR HAUNTED KINGDOM by stoner-crew, BEN WARD, JOE HOARI, PETE O'MALLY, MARTYN MILLARD and CHRIS TURNER. Following a 10" release and a split cd with ELECTRIC WIZARD, they signed a deal with LEE DORRIAN's (ex-CATHEDRAL, etc) label, 'Rise Above', who issued a debut album proper, 'FREQUENCIES FROM PLANET TEN'. 'TIME TRAVELLING BLUES' (1998) and 'THE BIG BLACK' (2000) offered up much of the same psychedelic-tinged stoner rock, although they had some way to go before they would become the next KYUSS/QOTSA. • **Covered:** HAND OF DOOM (Black Sabbath) / BLACK SHAPE OF DOOM (Trouble).

Album rating: FREQUENCIES FROM PLANET TEN (*5) / TIME TRAVELLING BLUES (*4) / THE BIG BLACK (*5)

BEN WARD – vocals / **JOE HOARI** – guitar / **PETE O'MALLEY** – guitar / **MARTYN MILLARD** – bass / **CHRIS TURNER** – drums

Rise Above — not iss.

Apr 95. (7"; as OUR HAUNTED KINGDON / + split) *(RISE 011)* **AQUATIC FANATIC. / (other track by Electric Wizard)** □ -

Man's Ruin — Man's Ruin

Feb 97. (cd-ep; split with ELECTRIC WIZARD) *<MR 071>* **NUCLEAR GURU / HAND OF DOOM / (others by ELECTRIC WIZARD)** - □

Nov 97. (10") *(<MR 084>)* **NUCLEAR GURU. / HAND OF DOOM** □ □

Rise Above — The Music Cartel

Dec 97. (cd) *(CDRISE 15)* **FREQUENCIES FROM PLANET TEN** □ -
– The astral project / Magic carpet / Saruman's wish / Song of the purple mushroom fish / Aquatic fanatic / Lothlorian / Land of secret dreams / Orange goblin / Star shaped cloud. *<US-iss.Aug99 on 'The Music Cartel'; TMC 26>*

Oct 98. (cd) *(CDRISE 18) <TMC 16>* **TIME TRAVELLING BLUES** □ □ Feb99
– Blue snow / Solarisphere / Shine / The man who invented time / Diesel (phunt) / Snail hook / Nuclear guru / Lunarville / Airlock 3 / Time travelling blues.

May 00. (cd) *(CDRISE 25) <TMC 36>* **THE BIG BLACK** □ □
– Scorpionca / Quincy the pig boy / Hot magic, red planet / Cozmo bozo / 298 kg / Turbo effalunt (elephant) / King of the hornets / You'll never get to the Moon in that / Alco fuel / The big black. *(lp-iss.Aug00 on 'The Music Cartel'; TMC 36LP)*

ORGANIZATION (see under ⇒ DEATH ANGEL)

ORGY

Formed: Los Angeles, California, USA . . . 1997 by JAY GORDON, RYAN SHUCK, AMIR DERAKH, PAIGE HALEY and BOBBY HEWITT. ORGY became the first group to sign for KORN's 'Elementree' imprint, the latter's mainman, JONATHAN DAVIS, guesting on the track, 'REVIVAL' from their debut album, 'CANDYASS' (1998). In fact, guitarist RYAN had played alongside the aforementioned singer in the band, SEX ART, co-writing 'BLIND', a track which made it onto KORN's debut album. Although their initial inception was KORN-inspired, ORGY were in fact tarty, alternative pop-metal, like DURAN DURAN sharing a bed with MINISTRY. In 1999, ORGY lifted their version of New Order's 'BLUE MONDAY' from the set and nearly had a minor hit. • **Trivia:** Singer, JAY, produced COAL CHAMBER's dark debut in '98.

Album rating: CANDYASS (*6) / VAPOR TRANSMISSION (*4)

JAY GORDON – vocals / **RYAN SHUCK** – guitar / **AMIR DERAKH** – guitar, synthesizer / **PAIGE HALEY** – bass / **BOBBY HEWITT** – drums

Elementree – Reprise — Elementree – Reprise

Apr 99. (cd) *<(9362 46923-2)>* **CANDYASS** □ 32 Sep98
– Social enemies / Stitches / Dissention / Platinum / Fetisha / Fiend / Blue Monday / Gender / All the same / Pantomime / Revival / Dizzy.

Jun 99. (c-s/12"/cd-s) *(W 484 C/T/CD) <F-111 44555>* **BLUE MONDAY. ('A'-Club 69 mix) / ('A'-Top40-single mix)** □ 56 Dec98

Oct 00. (cd) *<47832>* **VAPOR TRANSMISSION** - 16

Ozzy OSBOURNE

Born: JOHN MICHAEL OSBOURNE, 3 Dec'48, Aston, Birmingham, England. After eleven years as frontman for BLACK SABBATH, OSBOURNE was given his marching orders, forming his own BLIZZARD OF OZZ in 1980 alongside LEE KERSLAKE (drums, ex-URIAH HEEP), BOB DAISLEY (bass, ex-RAINBOW, ex-CHICKEN SHACK), DON AVERY (keyboards) and guitar wizard, RANDY RHOADS (ex-QUIET RIOT). Signing to Don Arden's 'Jet' label, OZZY and the band released their self-titled debut in 1980, hitting the UK Top 10 and narrowly missing the US Top 20. Hailed as OZZY's best work since 'SABBATH's heyday, the unholy alliance of RHOADS's music and OSBOURNE's lyrics (which, if anything, looked even more to the 'dark side' than the 'SABBATH material) produced such wonderfully grim fare as 'CRAZY TRAIN', 'SUICIDE SOLUTION' (later the subject of much JUDAS PRIEST-style courtroom controversy) and the epic 'MR. CROWLEY', inspiring multitudes of schoolkids to raise their pinkie and forefinger in cod-satanic salutation. The record went double platinum in the States, as did the follow-up, 'DIARY OF A MADMAN' (1981) (credited to OZZY solo), a cross-Atlantic Top 20 hit. Proving once and for all that the music industry is peopled by hard-bitten control freaks, OZZY proceeded to chomp on a live dove at a record company meeting later that year. Another infamous incident occurred only a few months later when the singer gnashed the head off a bat thrown onstage by a fan at a concert in Des Moines, cementing his reputation as heavy metal monster extraordinaire and public enemy No.1. 1982 proved to be an eventful year for 'the Oz', tragedy striking when his close friend and right hand man, RHODES, died in a plane crash in March. Consolation and a modicum of much needed stability came with his subsequent marriage to Don Arden's daughter, Sharon, on the 4th of July '82, the brave lass subsequently becoming his manager. BRAD GILLIS replaced RHODES for the live album of BLACK SABBATH covers, 'TALK OF THE DEVIL' (1982), before JAKE E. LEE was brought in as a more permanent fixture prior to 'BARK AT THE MOON' (1983). The rhythm section had also undergone numerous personnel changes with a final line-up of TOMMY ALDRIDGE (drums, ex-BLACK OAK ARKANSAS,etc.) and BOB DAISLEY. Another double platinum smash, the release of the record saw OZZY undertaking a mammoth US tour during which he unwittingly relieved himself on a wall of the Alamo monument in San Antonio, consequently being charged and banned from playing there. OZZY had always been a hard drinker and drug user, Sharon finally forcing him to attend the first of many unsuccessful sessions at the Betty Ford Clinic in 1984. His albums continued to sell consistently, particularly in America, despite constant line-up changes. 1988 saw the arrival of guitarist ZAKK WYLDE, heralded as a true successor to the revered RHODES. The late 80's also saw OSBOURNE retiring to his Buckinghamshire mansion with Sharon and his three kids, eventually kicking the booze and re-emerging in 1991 after being cleared of causing the death of three fans. In three separate, well documented cases, parents claimed OZZY's 'SUICIDE SOLUTION' had driven their siblings to kill themselves. 'NO MORE TEARS' (1991) was a triumphant comeback, OSBOURNE claiming the album would be his last and subsequently embarking on a farewell tour. The last two shows of the jaunt were opened by a ROB HALFORD (of JUDAS PRIEST)-fronted BLACK SABBATH, RONNIE JAMES DIO refusing to perform. Talks of a 'SABBATH reunion came to nothing although OZZY couldn't resist another tour and eventually an album, OZZMOSIS (1995). The record made the Top 5 in America where he's still regarded as something of a Metal Godfather; maybe it's the Brummie accent. OZZY has since stunned the metal world by rejoining BLACK SABBATH for concerts and a reunion album in 1998. • **Songwriters:** OZZY lyrics, RHOADS music. OZZY later collaborated with BOB DAISLEY. • **Trivia:** In 1987, he played a bible-punching preacher in the film 'Trick Or Treat'.

Album rating: OZZY OSBOURNE'S BLIZZARD OF OZZ (*7) / DIARY OF A MADMAN (*6) / TALK OF THE DEVIL (*6) / BARK AT THE MOON (*5) / THE ULTIMATE SIN (*5) / TRIBUTE (*8) / NO REST FOR THE WICKED (*5) / JUST SAY OZZY (*5) / NO MORE TEARS (*7) / LIVE & LOUD (*6) / OZZMOSIS (*6) / THE OZZMAN COMETH – THE BEST OF . . . compilation (*8)

OZZY OSBOURNE'S BLIZZARD OF OZZ

OZZY OSBOURNE – vocals (ex-BLACK SABBATH) / **RANDY RHOADS** – guitar (ex-QUIET RIOT) / **LEE KERSLAKE** – drums (ex-URIAH HEEP) / **BOB DAISLEY** – bass (ex-RAINBOW, ex-CHICKEN SHACK) / **DON AVERY** – keyboards

Jet — Jet-CBS

Sep 80. (7") *(JET 197)* **CRAZY TRAIN. / YOU LOOKING AT ME LOOKING AT YOU** 49 -

Sep 80. (lp/c) *(JET LP/CA 234) <36812>* **OZZY OSBOURNE'S BLIZZARD OF OZZ** 7 21 Mar81
– I don't know / Crazy train / Goodbye to romance / Dee / Suicide solution / Mr. Crowley / No bone movies / Revelation (Mother Earth) / Steal away (the night). *(re-iss. Nov87 on 'Epic' lp/c; 450453-1/-4) (cd-iss. Nov87 on 'Jet'; CDJET 234) (re-iss. cd Nov95 on 'Epic'; 481674-2)*

Nov 80. (7") *(JET 7-003) <37640>* **MR. CROWLEY (live). / YOU SAID IT ALL (live)** 46 □ Apr82
(12"+=/12"pic-d+=) *(JET/+P 12-003)* – Suicide solution (live).

Apr 81. (7") *<02079>* **CRAZY TRAIN. / STEAL AWAY (THE NIGHT)** - □

OZZY OSBOURNE

(same line-up, except AVERY)

Oct 81. (lp/c) *(JET LP/CA 237) <37492>* **DIARY OF A MADMAN** 14 16
– Over the mountain / Flying high again / You can't kill rock and roll / Believer / Little dolls / Tonight / S.A.T.O. / Diary of a madman. *(cd-iss. May87; CDJET 237) (re-iss. Apr91 on 'Epic' cd/c; 463086-2/-4) (re-iss. cd Nov95 on 'Epic'; 481677-2)*

Nov 81. (7"/12") *(JET 7/12 017)* **OVER THE MOUNTAIN. / I DON'T KNOW** □ -

Nov 81. (7") *<02582>* **FLYING HIGH AGAIN. / I DON'T KNOW** - □

Feb 82. (7") *<02707>* **LITTLE DOLLS. / TONIGHT** - □

— (Nov'81) **RUDY SARZO** – bass (ex-QUIET RIOT) repl. DAISLEY (to URIAH HEEP) **TOMMY ALDRIDGE** – drums (ex-BLACK OAK ARKANSAS, etc) repl. KERSLAKE

— (Apr'82) **BRAD GILLIS** – guitar (of NIGHT RANGER) repl. RANDY RHOADS who was killed in a light aeroplane crash on 19th Mar'82.

Nov 82. (d-lp/d-c) *(JET DP/CD 401) <38350>* **TALK OF THE DEVIL** (live at Ritz Club, NY) <US-title 'SPEAK OF THE DEVIL'> 21 14
– Symptom of the universe / Snowblind / Black sabbath / Fairies wear boots / War pigs / The wizard / N.I.B. / Sweet leaf / Never say die / Sabbath bloody sabbath / Iron man – Children of the grave / Paranoid. *(re-iss. Sep87 on 'Epic' d-lp/d-c; 451124-1/-4) (cd-iss. Jun89; 451124-2)* – (omits dialogue). *(re-iss. cd/d-lp complete.Jul91 on 'Castle'; CCS CD/LP 296) (re-iss. cd Nov95 as 'SPEAK OF THE DEVIL' on 'Epic'; 481679-2)*

Dec 82. (7"/7"pic-d) *(JET/+P 7-030)* **SYMPTOM OF THE UNIVERSE (live). / N.I.B. (live)** □ -
(12"+=) *(JET 12-030)* – Children of the grave (live).

Feb 83. (7") *<03302>* **IRON MAN (live). / PARANOID (live)** - □

— (Dec'82) **JAKE E. LEE** (b.JAKEY LOU WILLIAMS, San Diego, California, USA) – guitar (ex-RATT) repl. GILLIS who returned to NIGHT RANGER / **DON COSTA** – bass repl. PETE WAY (ex-UFO) who had deputised for the departing RUDY SARZO who had returned to QUIET RIOT. (He later joined WHITESNAKE)

— **OZZY, JAKE E + TOMMY** re-recruited **BOB DAISLEY** to repl. COSTA

Epic CBS Assoc.

Nov 83. (7"/12",12"silver/12"pic-d) *(A/TA/WA 3915)* **BARK AT THE MOON. / ONE UP ON THE B-SIDE** [21] [ ]

Dec 83. (7") *<04318>* **BARK AT THE MOON. / SPIDERS** [-] [ ]

Dec 83. (lp/c) *(EPC/40 25739) <38987>* **BARK AT THE MOON** [24] [19]
– Rock'n'roll rebel / Bark at the Moon / You're no different / Now you see it (now you don't) / Forever / So tired / Waiting for darkness / Spiders. *(re-iss. Apr86 lp/c; EPC/40 32780) (cd-iss. Oct88; CD 32780) (re-iss. cd Nov95; 481678-2)*

Mar 84. (7") *(A 4260) <04383>* **SO TIRED. / FOREVER (live)** [ ] [ ]
(12"+=/d7"+=) *(TA/DA 4260)* – Waiting for darkness / Paranoid (live).

— ALDRIDGE was briefly replaced (Mar-May84) on tour by CARMINE APPICE.

May 84. (7") *(A 4452)* **SO TIRED. / BARK AT THE MOON (live)** [20] [ ]
(12"+=,12"gold+=) *(WA 4452)* – Waiting for darkness / Suicide solution (live) / Paranoid (live).

— **PHIL SOUSSAN** – bass repl. DAISLEY / **RANDY CASTILLO** – drums (ex-LITA FORD BAND) repl. ALDRIDGE

Jan 86. (7"/7"w-poster/12") *(A/QA/TA 6859)* **SHOT IN THE DARK. / ROCK'N'ROLL REBEL** [20] [-]

Feb 86. (lp/c) *(EPC/40 26404) <40026>* **THE ULTIMATE SIN** [8] [6]
– Lightning strikes / Killer of giants / Thank God for the bomb / Never / Shot in the dark / The ultimate sin / Secret loser / Never know why / Fool like you. *(cd-iss. Jul86; CD 26404) (pic-lp Aug86; EPC 11-26404) (re-iss. Feb89 on 'C.B.S.' lp/c/cd; 462496-1/-4/-2) (re-iss. Nov95; 481680-2)*

Mar 86. (7") *<05810>* **SHOT IN THE DARK. / YOU SAID IT ALL** [-] [68]

Jul 86. (7"/12") *(A/TA 7311)* **THE ULTIMATE SIN. / LIGHTNING STRIKES** [72] [-]

1988. (7") *<08463>* **SHOT IN THE DARK. / CRAZY TRAIN** [-] [ ]

— (Aug'88) **ZAKK WYLDE** (b.ZACH ADAMS, 14 Jan'66) – guitar repl. JAKE who formed BADLANDS. / **DAISLEY** returned to repl. SOUSSAN (to BILLY IDOL) / added **JOHN SINCLAIR** – keyboards

Oct 88. (lp/c/cd) *(46258-1/-4/-2) <44245>* **NO REST FOR THE WICKED** [23] [13]
– Miracle man / Devil's daughter / Crazy babies / Breaking all the rules / Bloodbath in Paradise / Fire in the sky / Tattooed dancer / The demon alcohol. *(cd+=)* – Hero. *(re-iss. Jun94 & Nov95; cd/c; 481681-2)*

Oct 88. (7"/7"sha-pic-d) *(653063-0/-9)* **MIRACLE MAN. / CRAZY BABIES** [ ] [-]
(12"+=/12"w-poster/cd-s+=) *(653063-6/-8/-2)* – The liar.

Dec 88. (7") *<08516>* **MIRACLE MAN. / MAN YOU SAID IT ALL** [-] [ ]

Feb 89. (7") *<68534>* **CRAZY BABIES. / THE DEMON ALCOHOL** [-] [ ]

— Earlier in the year OZZY had accompanied LITA FORD on 45 'CLOSE MY EYES FOREVER'. In Apr'89, it was to reach UK/US Top50.

— **TERRY 'GEEZER' BUTLER** – bass was used for tour work late 1988.

Feb 90. (cd/c/lp) *(465940-1/-4/-2) <45451>* **JUST SAY OZZY (live)** [69] [58]
– Miracle man / Bloodbath in Paradise / Shot in the dark / Tattooed dancer / Sweet leaf / War pigs. *(re-iss. cd Nov95; 481517-2)*

— In the late 80's, OZZY retired to his Buckinghamshire mansion with his manager/wife Sharon Arden and 3 kids. He had also kicked his alcohol addiction. Returned 1991 after being cleared of causing death of fan. See last studio line-up. Augmented also by **MICHAEL INEZ** – bass, inspiration repl. BUTLER

Epic Epic Assoc

Sep 91. (7") *(657440-7) <73973>* **NO MORE TEARS. / S.I.N.** [32] [71]
(c-s+=/12"+=/12"pic-d+=/cd-s+=) *(657440-8/-6/-?/-2)* – Party with the animals.

Oct 91. (cd/c/lp) *(467859-2/-4/-1) <46795>* **NO MORE TEARS** [17] [7]
– Mr. Tinkertrain / I don't want to change the world / Mama I'm coming home / Desire / No more tears / S.I.N. / Hellraiser / Time after time / Zombie stomp / A.V.H. / Road to nowhere. *(re-iss. cd Nov95; 481675-2)*

Nov 91. (7") *(657617-7) <74093>* **MAMA I'M COMING HOME. / DON'T BLAME ME** [46] [28] Feb92
(12"+=) *(657617-8)* – I don't know / Crazy train.
(cd-s+=) *(657617-9)* – (Ozzy on the Steve Wright show)
(12"+=) *(657617-6)* – Time after time / Goodbye to romance.
<US-cd-ep+=> *<74265>* – Party with the animals.

Jun 93. (d-cd) *(473798-2) <46795>* **LIVE & LOUD (live)** [ ] [22]
– Intro / Paranoid / I don't want to change the world / Desire / Mr. Crowley / I don't know / Road to nowhere / Flying high again / Guitar solo / Suicide solution / Goodbye to romance / Shot in the dark / No more tears / Miracle man / Drum solo / War pigs / Bark at the Moon / Mama, I'm coming home / Crazy train / Black sabbath / Changes. *(re-iss. Nov95; 481676-2)*

Jun 93. (12"/cd-s) *(659340-6/-2)* **CHANGES (live). / CHANGES / NO MORE TEARS / DESIRE** [ ] [ ]

— next featured **MIKE INEZ** – bass (of ALICE IN CHAINS)

Oct 95. (cd/c/lp) *(481022-2/-4/-1) <67091>* **OZZMOSIS** [22] [4]
– Perry Mason / I just want you / Ghost behind my eyes / Thunder underground / See you on the other side / Tomorrow / Denial / My little man / My Jekyll doesn't hide / Old LA tonight. *(re-iss. Apr99; same)*

Nov 95. (7"pic-d) *(662639-7)* **PERRY MASON. / LIVING WITH THE ENEMY** [23] [ ]
(cd-s+=) *(662639-2)* – The whole world's falling down.
(cd-s) *(662639-5)* – ('A'side) / No more tears / I don't want to change the world / Flying high again.

— **ROBERT TRUJILLO** – bass (ex-SUICIDAL TENDENCIES) – bass repl. INEZ

Aug 96. (12") *(663570-6)* **I JUST WANT YOU. / AIMEE / VOODOO DANCER** [43] [ ]
(cd-s) *(663570-2)* – ('A'side) / Aimee / Mama, I'm coming home.
(cd-s) *(663570-5)* – ('A'side) / Voodoo dancer / Iron man (with THERAPY?).

– compilations, others, etc. –

on 'Epic' UK / 'CBS Assoc.' unless otherwise stated

May 87. (d-lp/c/cd) *(450475-1/-4/-2) <40714>* **TRIBUTE (live 1981 with RANDY RHOADS)** [13] [6]
– I don't know / Crazy train / Revelation (Mother Earth) / Believer / Mr. Crowley / Flying high again / No bone movies / Steal away (the night) / Suicide solution / Iron man – Children of the grave / Goodbye to romance / Paranoid / Dee *[not on cd]*. *(re-iss. Apr93 cd/c;) (re-iss. cd Nov95; 481516-2)*

Jun 87. (7"/12") *(650943-7/-6) <07168>* **CRAZY TRAIN (live 1981). / CRAZY TRAIN (live 1981)** [ ] [ ]

Jul 88. (12"ep/cd-ep) *(652 875-6/-2)* **BACK TO OZZ** [76] [-]
– The ultimate sin / Bark at the Moon / Mr. Crowley / Diary of a madman.

Aug 90. (cd) *Priority; <57129>* **TEN COMMANDMENTS** (rare) [-] [ ]

Mar 93. (d-cd) *(465211-2)* **BARK AT THE MOON / BLIZZARD OF OZZ** [ ] [ ]

Nov 97. (cd/c) *(487260-2/-4)* **THE OZZMAN COMETH – THE BEST OF** [68] [13]
– Black sabbath / War pigs / Goodbye to romance (live) / Crazy train (live) / Mr. Crowley (live) / Over the mountain (live) / Paranoid (live) / Bark at the moon / Shot in the dark / Crazy babies / No more tears / Mama, I'm coming home (live) / I just want you / I don't want to change the world / Back on earth. *(cd+=)* – Fairies wear boots / Beyond the wall of sleep.

Nov 98. (3xcd-box) *Epic; (492655-2)* **DIARY OF A MADMAN / BARK AT THE MOON / THE ULTIMATE SIN** [ ] [-]

OSTROGOTH

Formed: Gent, Belgium . . . 1983 by RUDY VERCRUYSSE and MARIO PAUWELS, who eventually found MARC DEBRAUWER, MARNIX VANDEKAUTER and HANS VANDEKERCKHOVE. Signing to the European 'Mausoleum' label, the group released a debut EP, 'FULL MOON'S EYES' in summer '83. Standard issue hair-whipping power-metal, the group followed a similar formula on their debut album proper, 'ECSTASY AND DANGER' (1985). This was rapidly followed up with 'TOO HOT' later the same year, although the original line-up fell apart soon after. PAUWELS and VERCRUYSSE subsequently re-shaped OSTROGOTH around PETER DE WINT, KRIS TAERWE, JUNO MARTINS and SYLVAIN CHEROTTI. The revamped group released 'FEELINGS OF FURY' in 1987, the record still failing to bring the group any widespread recognition.

Album rating: FULL MOON'S EYES mini (*5) / ECSTASY AND DANGER (*4) / TOO HOT (*6) / FEELINGS OF FURY (*6)

RED STAR (b. MARC DEBRAUWER) – vocals / **SPHINX** (b. RUDY VERCRUYSSE) – guitar / **WHITE SHARK** (b. HANS VANDEKERCKHOVE) – guitar / **BRONCO** (b. MARNIX VANDEKAUTER) – bass / **GRIZZLY** (b. MARIO PAUWELS) – drums, percussion

Mausoleum not iss.

Aug 83. (12"ep) *(BONE12 8310)* **FULL MOON'S EYES** [ ] [-]
– Full moon's eyes / Heroes' museum / Paris by night / Rock fever.

Mar 84. (lp/c) *(SKULL/TAPE7 8319)* **ECSTASY AND DANGER** [ ] [-]
– Queen of desire / Ecstasy and danger / A bitch again / Stormbringer / Scream out / Lords of thunder / The new generation / Do it right.

Dec 85. (lp) *(SKULL 8374)* **TOO HOT** [-] [-] Belgian
– Too hot / Shoot back / Sign of life / The gardens of Marrakesh / Love in the streets / Night women (don't like me) / Endless winterdays / Catch the sound of peace / Halloween.

— **VERCRUYSSE + PAUWELS** recruited **PETER DE WINT** – vocals / **KRIS TAERWE** – keyboards / **JUNO MARTINS** – guitar / **SYLVAIN CHEROTTI** – bass

Ultraprime not iss.

Dec 87. (lp) *(ULT33 1804)* **FEELINGS OF FURY** [ ] [-]
– Conquest / The introduction / Samurai / Love can wait / We are the ace / The hunter / Get out of my life / What the hell is going on / Vlad strigoi.

— disbanded when PAUWELS joined SHELLSHOCK who subsequently became HERMETIC BROTHERHOOD

OUR LADY PEACE

Formed: Toronto, Canada . . . 1994 by RAINE MAIDA (a former criminology student), Bradford-born MIKE TURNER, DUNCAN COUTTS and jazz-trained JEREMY TAGGART. Almost immediately signing to 'Epic' records, they released their debut album 'NAVEED' in '95, a disc that went on to achieve record-breaking triple platinum sales in their native Canada. Unfortunately, DUNCAN didn't appear on the album as he spent a year at university, his temporary substitute being, CHRIS EACRETT. Issued early '96 in the UK, the record's dreamy emotional guitar-rock was akin to a more cerebral LIVE, ALICE IN CHAINS or even U2. 'CLUMSY' (1997) placed the angst-ridden breathlessness and cathartic emotions in a more grown-up context to surprisingly listenable results while the convoluted titled of 1999's 'HAPPINESS IS NOT A FISH THAT YOU CAN CATCH' belied a semi-successful attempt at imbuing both their music and lyrics with a greater sense of purpose. Going even further down that route, 'SPIRITUAL MACHINES' (2001) took Ray Kurzweil's book, 'The Age Of Spiritual Machines: When Computers Exceed Human Intelligence', as the inspiration for a series of meditations upon man's innate frailty and potential for redemption. With TAGGART out of action for part of the recording process due to a mugging, the ubiquitous MATT CAMERON (ex-SOUNDGARDEN) filled in on a couple of tracks. • **Songwriters:** TURNER, MAIDA (+ lyrics), EACRETT and producer ARNOLD LANNI.

Album rating: NAVEED (*8) / CLUMSY (*6) / HAPPINESS . . . IS NOT A FISH YOU CAN CATCH (*5) / SPIRITUAL MACHINES (*6)

RAINE MAIDA (b.1972) – vocals / **MIKE TURNER** (b.1965) – guitars / **CHRIS EACRETT** (b.1971) – bass; repl. DUNCAN COUTTS / **JEREMY TAGGART** (b.1977) – drums

Epic Sony

Feb 96. (cd/c) *(478383-2/-4)* <68170> **NAVEED** [ ] [ ] Mar95
– The birdman / Supersatellite / Starseed / Hope / Naveed / Dirty walls / Denied / Is it safe? / Julia / Under Zenith / Neon crossing.

—— **DUNCAN COUTTS** – bass; returned in '96 to repl. CHRIS

Epic Epic

Sep 97. (cd/c) *(487408-2/-4)* <67940> **CLUMSY** [ ] [76]
– Superman's dead / Automatic flowers / Carnival / Big dumb rocket / 4 a.m. / Shaking / Clumsy / Hello Oskar / Let you down / Story of 100 aisles / Car crash.

Oct 97. (cd-s) <2935> **CLUMSY / CLUMSY (version)** [-] [ ]

Jun 98. (7") *(664331-7)* **SUPERMAN'S DEAD. / STARSEED** [ ] [ ]
(cd-s+=) *(664331-2)* – Let you down.

Nov 99. (cd/c) *(496098-2/-4)* <63707> **HAPPINESS . . . IS NOT A FISH YOU CAN CATCH** [ ] [69] Sep99
– One man army / Happiness and the fish / Potato girl / Blister / Is anybody home / Waited / Thief / Lying awake / Annie / Consequence of laughing / Stealing babies (with ELVIN JONES).

Jan 00. (7"blue) *(668866-7)* **ONE MAN ARMY. / SUPERMAN'S DEAD** [70] [ ]
(cd-s) *(668866-2)* – ('A'side) / Starseed / Clumsy / ('A'-CD-Rom).

Apr 01. (cd) *(502340-2)* <85368> **SPIRITUAL MACHINES** [ ] [81] Mar01
– R.K. intro / Right behind you (Mafia) / R.K. 2029 / In repair / Life / Middle of yesterday / Are you sad? / R.K. 2029 (pt.2) / Made to heal / R.K. 1949 to 97 / Everyone's a junkie / R.K. on death / All my friends / If you believe / The wonderful future.

OUT

Formed: Lille, France . . . 1993 by CHRISTOPHE LAMOURET, CHRISTOPHE TRISTAN, THIBAULT GHEYSENS, JEAN-LOUP DEMEULEMEESTER and an anonymous guitarist. Although a rough (unknown) debut album surfaced in 1995, a subsequent demo tape – featuring the talents of new guitarist ETIENNE FAUQUET – caught the attention of noted producer COLIN RICHARDSON (most famous for his work with FEAR FACTORY). Around the same time, a London gig landed them a deal with 'Roadrunner' and set them up for the recording of a more professional sophomore set. The result was 'X-POSITION' (1999), a state of the art nu-metal affair which enjoyed consistent comparison with the likes of STABBING WESTWARD and KORN. In an all too rare example of positive Anglo-French relations, LAMOURET subsequently teamed up with NAPALM DEATH's MITCH HARRIS and SHANE EMBURY in MEATHOOK SEED.

Album rating: X-POSITION (*5)

CHRISTOPHE LAMOURET – vocals / **ETTIENNE FAUQUET** – guitar / **CHRISTOPHE TRISTRAM** – bass / **JEAN-LOUP DEMEULEMEESTER** – drums / **THIBAULT GHEYSENS** – samples

Roadrunner Roadrunner

Feb 99. (cd) *(<RR 8669-2>)* **X-POSITION** [ ] [ ]
– Lie no limits / Who's alive / Left in limbo / Like a fish / Watch me in / Will / X-position / Nine hates / Girl x man / Bio burger / Les voix du silence. *(re-iss. Jun00; same)*

OVERDOSE

Formed: Brazil . . . 1985 by graphic artist B.Z., CLAUDIO DAVID, SERGIO CICHOVICZ, EDDIE WEBER and ANDRE MARCIA. The group kickstarted their career by sharing one side of an album ('SECULO XX') with fellow Brazilian thrashers SEPULTURA ('Bestial Devastation'). However, while their compadres took off into major league status, OVERDOSE were left holding the baby, so to speak. With contractual problems out of the way, the group toured South America, signing to UK's 'Under One Flag' in 1993. Having released some unknown and rare releases in Brazil, the group were welcomed in Europe via their 6th album, 'PROGRESS OF DECADENCE' (1994). A second UK release, 'SCARS' hit the shops late 1996.

Album rating: PROGRESS OF DECADENCE (*6) / SCARS (*6) / CIRCUS OF DEATH (*5)

B.Z. – vocals / **SERGIO CICHOVICZ** – guitar / **CLAUDIO DAVID** – guitar / **EDDIE WEBER** – bass / **ANDRE MARCIO** – drums

Cogumelo not iss.

1985. (lp; shared with SEPULTURA) **SECULO XX** [-] [-] Brazil

—— Other albums only released in Brazil

Under One Flag Futurist

Nov 94. (cd) *(CDFLAG 83)* <11063> **PROGRESS OF DECADENCE** [ ] [ ]
– Rio, samba e porrado no morro / Street law / Straight to the point / Progress of decadence / Capitalist way / Deep in your mind / Noise from Brazil / Aluquisarrera / Favela / No truce / Faithful death / Stupid generation / Zombie factory.

Music For Nations Futurist

Nov 96. (cd) *(CDMFN 213)* <11097> **SCARS** [ ] [ ] Oct96
– The front / My rage / Manipulated reality / How to pray / Scars / Still primitive / Just another day / School / Last words / Postcards from Hell / Who's guilty? / Out of control – A fairy tale / Nu dos otro and refresco.

—— **FERNANDO PAZZINI** – bass; repl. EDDIE

Pavement Pavement

May 99. (cd) <*(32310CD)*> **CIRCUS OF DEATH** [ ] [ ]
– The zombie factory / Children of war / Dead clouds / Profit / The healer / Violence / A good day to die / Powerwish / Beyond my bad dreams.

OVERKILL

Formed: New York, USA . . . 1984 by BOBBY ELLSWORTH, BOBBY GUSTAFSON, D.D. VERNI and SID FALCK. After self-financing a debut mini-album the same year, the group caught the interest of Johnny Z and his 'Megaforce' label, issuing a full-length set, 'FEEL THE FIRE', in early '86. Utilising GUSTAFSON's distinctive, shearing guitar attack and ELLSWORTH's demonic vocals, the album was a competent if hardly innovative set of power-thrash bludgeon. Enough to place OVERKILL firmly on the metal map, the record was followed-up in 1987 by another slab of howling speed-metal, 'TAKING OVER', the record occasionally veering too close to contemporaries like ANTHRAX and TESTAMENT for critics' comfort. Nevertheless, OVERKILL commanded a loyal fanbase, silencing at least some of their detractors with their most confident set to date, 'UNDER THE INFLUENCE' (1988). Following the release of 'YEARS OF DECAY' (1989), founding member GUSTAFSON quit, OVERKILL subsequently employing a twin guitar attack courtesy of MERRIT GRANT and ROB CANNAVINO. This alteration allowed the group more room to manouvre and the resulting album, 'HORRORSCOPE' (1991), was markedly more dynamic, using tension and release to create a more consistent set of songs which included a cover of Edgar Winter's 'FRANKENSTEIN'. A move to 'East West' for 'I HEAR BLACK' (1993) failed to significantly increase sales, however, and OVERKILL signed to the smaller 'Edel' for the aptly named '10 YEARS OF WRECKING YOUR NECK' (1995). Throughout the 90's, OVERKILL had obviously taken heed of the changing musical climate, increasingly moving towards a more retro approach while still maintaining their trademark punch. During the latter half of the 90's, a handful of albums were also issued for 'C.M.C.', these were 'KILLING KIND' (1996), 'FROM THE UNDERGROUND AND BELOW' (1997), 'NECROSHINE' (1999) and 'COVERKILL' (1999). The latter was indeed a covers set that included versions of the Sex Pistols 'NO FEELINGS', Jethro Tull's 'HYMN 43', Black Sabbath's 'CHANGES', 'NEVER SAY DIE' and 'CORNUCOPIA', Deep Purple's 'SPACE TRUCKIN', Kiss' 'DEUCE', Manowar's 'DEATH TONE', Judas Priest's 'TYRANT', Dead Boys' 'AIN'T NOTHIN' TO DO' and the Ramones 'I'M AGAINST IT'.

Album rating: FEEL THE FIRE (*6) / TAKING OVER (*4) / UNDER THE INFLUENCE (*7) / THE YEARS OF DECAY compilation (*8) / HORRORSCOPE (*7) / I HEAR BLACK (*8) / WRECKING YOUR NECK (*4) / THE KILLING KIND (*5) / FROM THE UNDERGROUND AND BELOW (*5) / NECROSHINE (*5) / COVERKILL (*3)

BOBBY ELLSWORTH – vocals / **BOBBY GUSTAFSON** – guitar / **D.D. VERNI** – bass / **SID FALCK** (aka RAT SKATES) – drums

Noise Megaforce

Feb 86. (lp/cd) *(N 0035)* <MRI 1469> **FEEL THE FIRE** [-] [ ] German
– Raise the dead / Rotten to the core / There's no tomorrow / Second son / Sonic reducer / Hammerhead / Feel the fire / Blood and iron / Kill at command / Overkill. *(UK-iss.Oct89 on 'Noise' lp/cd; NUK/CDNUK 035) (re-iss. Feb92 on 'Music For Nations' cd/c; CD/T MFN 127) (cd re-iss. Feb99 on 'S.P.V.'; SPV 0761844-2)*

Apr 87. (lp/c) *(N 0069)* <781 735-1/-4> **TAKING OVER** [-] [ ] German
– Deny the cross / Wrecking crew / Fear his name / Use your head / Fatal if swallowed / Powersurge / In union we stand / Electro-violence / Overkill II (the nightmare continues). *(UK-iss.Oct89 on 'Noise' lp/c/cd; NUK/ZCNUK/CDNUK 069)*

Under One Flag Megaforce

Oct 87. (12"ep) *(12FLAG 104)* <1974> **F@CK YOU (live)** [ ] [ ]
– F@ck you / Rotten to the core / Hammerhead / Use your head / Electro-violence. *<US cd-iss. 1990 on 'Caroline'; CAROL 1345-2> (UK cd-iss. May97 as 'F@CK YOU AND THEN SOME' on 'S.P.V.'+=; SPV 0851872-2)* – Fuck you / Hole in the sky / Evil never dies / Rotten to the core / Fatal if swallowed / The answer / Overkill.

Megaforce Megaforce

Jun 88. (lp/c/cd) *(781 865-1/-4/-2)* <81865> **UNDER THE INFLUENCE** [ ] [ ]
– Shred / Never say never / Hello from the gutter / Mad gone world / Brainfade / Drunken wisdom / End of the line / Head first / Overkill III (under the influence).

Oct 89. (lp/c/cd) <*(7567 82045-1/-4/-2)*> **THE YEARS OF DECAY** (compilation) [ ] [ ]
– Time to kill / Elimination / I hate / Nothing to die for / Playing with spiders – Skullkrusher / Birth of tension / Who tends the fire / The years of decay / E.vil n.ever d.ies.

—— **MERRIT GANT** – guitar (ex-FAITH OR FEAR) + **ROB CANNAVINO** – guitar repl. GUSTAFSON

Sep 91. (cd/c/lp) <*(7567 82283-2/-4/-1)*> **HORRORSCOPE** [ ] [ ]
– Coma / Infectious / Blood money / Thanx for nothin' / Bare bones / Horrorscope / New machine / Frankenstein / Live young, die free / Nice day . . . for a funeral / Solitude. *(with free 12"; SAM 862)* – COMA / THANX FOR NOTHIN'. / NEW MACHINE / FRANKENSTEIN

—— **TIM MALLARE** – drums; repl. FALCK

East West Atlantic

May 93. (cd/c) <*(7567 82476-2/-4)*> **I HEAR BLACK** [ ] [ ]
– Dreaming in Colombian / I hear black / World of hurt / Feed my head / Shades of grey / Spiritual void / Ghost dance / Weight of the world / Ignorance & innocence / Undying / Just like you.

C.M.C. C.M.C.

Jul 95. (d-cd) <*(CMC 7603)*> **WRECKING YOUR NECK – OVERKILL 1985-1995 LIVE (live)** [ ] [ ]
– Where it hurts / Infectious / Coma / Supersonic hate / Wrecking crew / Powersurge / The wait – New high in lows / Skullkrusher / Spiritual void / Hello from the gutter / Anxiety / Elimination / Fast junkie / World of hurt / Gasoline dream / Rotten to the core / Horrorscope / Under one / New machine / Thanx for nothin' / Bastard nation / Fuck you. *(re-iss. Mar00 on 'S.P.V.'; 0762148-2)*

—— **ELLSWORTH, VERNI + MALLARE** recruited **JOE COMEAU + SEBASTIAN MARINO** – guitars

Concrete C.M.C.

Mar 96. (cd) *(EDEL 008650-2CTR) <87604>* **THE KILLING KIND** ☐ ☐
– Battle / God-like / Certifiable / Burn you down – To ashes / Let me shut that for you / Bold face pagan stomp / Feeding frenzy / The cleansing / The morning after – Private bleeding / God, hard fact. *(re-iss. Mar00 on 'S.P.V.'; SPV 0762159-2)*

S.P.V. C.M.C.

Oct 97. (cd) *(085-1877-2) <86219>* **FROM THE UNDERGROUND AND BELOW** ☐ ☐
– It lives / Save me / Long time dyin' / Genocya / Half past dead / F.U.C.T. / I'm alright / The rip 'n' tear / Promises / Little bit o' murder.

Mar 99. (cd) *(085-1888-2) <86267>* **NECROSHINE** ☐ ☐
– Necroshine / My December / Let us prey / 80 cycles / Revelation / Stone cold Jesus / Forked tongue kiss / I am fear / Black line / Dead man.

Nov 99. (cd) *(085-2154-2) <86279>* **COVERKILL** ☐ ☐ Oct99
– Overkill / No feelings / Hymn 43 / Changes / Space truckin' / Deuce / Never say die / Death tone / Cornucopia / Tyrant / Ain't nothin' to do / I'm against it.

Wendy O'WILLIAMS (see under ⇒ PLASMATICS)

OZ

Formed: Finland . . . 1977 by singer The OZ (aka EERO HAMALAINEN), who soon recruited KARI ELO, TAUNO VAJAVAARA and PEKKA MARK. The band eventually translated their raw, crunching heavy-metal sound onto vinyl in 1982, debuting with 'THE OZ' album (released only in Sweden). Following the record's release, HAMALAINEN and ELO were ousted in favour of the comically monikered SPEEDY FOX, SPOOKY WOLFF and JAY C. BLADE., the revamped line-up subsequently releasing the 'FIRE IN THE RAIN' album in 1983 (German only) This attracted the attention of 'R.C.A.' who signed the band up for a couple of mid-80's efforts, 'III WARNING' and 'DECIBEL STORM', new recruit APE DE MARTINI performing vocal duties. The more commercial approach did the band no favours and they were subsequently dropped. A split was inevitable, although they did reform towards the end of the decade, MARTINI and RUFFNECK bringing in new members MIKE PAUL, MICHAEL LOREDA and T.B. MUEN.

Album rating: THE OZ (*4) / FIRE IN THE RAIN (*5) / ILL WARNING (*6) / DECIBEL STORM (*5) / ROLL THE DICE (*4)

THE OZ (EERO HAMALAINEN) – vocals / **KARI ELO** – guitar / **TAUNO VAJAVAARA** – bass / **'PEKKA' MARK RUFFNECK** – drums

Kraf not iss.

1982. (lp) **THE OZ** [-] [-] Sweden

—— the two mainmen were sacked, EERO + KARI were subsequently repl. by **SPEEDY FOXX + SPOOKY WOLFF** – guitar / **JAY C. BLADE** – bass

Wave not iss.

1983. (lp) *(LP 8006)* **FIRE IN THE BRAIN** [-] [-] German
– Search lights / Fortune / Meglomaniac / Black candles / Gambler / Stop believin' / Free me, leave me / Fire in the brain. *<US cd-iss. Feb97 on 'Black Mark'; BM 112>*

—— **APE DE MARTINI** – vocals; repl. TAUNO (RUFFNECK only original remaining)

R.C.A. Combat

1984. (lp) *(PL 70564) <MX 8013>* **III WARNING** [-] ☐ German
– Third warning / Crucified / Runner / Rock'n'roll widow / Samurai / Born out of time / Too bad to be true / Total metal.

1986. (lp) *(PL 71024)* **DECIBEL STORM** [-] [-] German
– Eyes of the stranger / Starrider / Teenage rampage / Disaster dreamer / Firestarter / Exterminator / Black tattoo / Sound of speed / The show must go on.

—— **APE DE MARTINI + MARK RUFFNECK** recruited a new line-up of **MIKE PAUL + MICHAEL LOREDA** – guitars / **T.B. MUEN** – bass

Black Mark Black Mark

Jan 92. (cd/c/lp) *<(BM CD/CT/LP 11)>* **ROLL THE DICE** ☐ ☐

—— split after above

P (see under ⇒ BUTTHOLE SURFERS)

PAGANS

Formed: Cleveland, Ohio, USA . . . 1977 by MIKE HUDSON and TOMMY GUNN METOFF along with TIM ALLEE and BRIAN MORGAN. Hailing from the same American city that spawned PERE UBU, DEAD BOYS, etc, The PAGANS certainly kicked up an ungodly racket while their brutally defiant lyrics took no prisoners, thriving on alienation and offence. Despite being overlooked during punk's first wave, the greasoid garage crew were subsequently namechecked by a host of latter day hardcore/punk bands. Only four (independently-released) singles appeared during their short career span, the first three on 'Drome': 'THE STREET WHERE NOBODY LIVES', 'NOT NOW, NO WAY' and 'DEAD END AMERICA'. A final 7", 'SIX AND CHANGE', surfaced on 'Neck' records at the turn of the decade, rounding up their short sharp legacy. They re-formed for the odd gig or two throughout the 80's, sparking interest in a handful of retrospective releases for Mark Trehus' 'Treehouse' imprint. • **Covered:** HEART OF STONE (Rolling Stones) / CAN'T EXPLAIN (Who) / SEVENTH SON WIPED OUT (Willie Dixon) / BOY I CAN DANCE GOOD (. . . Carlton) / LITTLE BLACK EGG (. . . Conlon).

Album rating: BURIED ALIVE compilation (*7) / THE GODLIKE POWER OF THE PAGANS compilation (*7) / EVERYBODY HATES YOU compilation (*7)

MIKE HUDSON – vocals / **TOMMY GUNN METOFF** – guitar (ex-CHRONIC) / **TIM ALLEE** – bass / **BRIAN MORGAN** – drums

not iss. — Drome

1978. (7") *<DR 1>* **THE STREET WHERE NOBODY LIVES. / WHAT'S THIS SHIT CALLED LOVE?** [-] [ ]
1978. (7") *<DR 5>* **NOT NOW, NO WAY. / I JUVENILE** [-] [ ]
1978. (7") *<DR 7>* **DEAD END AMERICA. / LITTLE BLACK EGG** [-] [ ]

not iss. — Neck

1979. (7") *<1143>* **SIX AND CHANGE. / SIX AND CHANGE** [-] [ ]

— disbanded Sep'79, METOFF went on to work with DAVE DELUCA, MORGAN with The FRENCHMEN

– compilations, etc. –

1986. (lp) *Treehouse;* **BURIED ALIVE** [-] [ ]
Sep 87. (lp) *Treehouse; <(TR 004)>* **THE GODLIKE POWER OF THE PAGANS** [ ] [ ]
May 89. (lp)(cd) *Resonance; (R33 8921)(08908-2)* **THE STREET WHERE NOBODY LIVES (live)** [ ] [-]
May 95. (cd) *Crypt; <36>* **EVERYBODY HATES YOU** [-] [ ]
– What's this shit called love / Dead end America / Eyes of Satan / The street where nobody lives / Boy I can dance good / Give up / Real world / Six and change / Haven't got the time / Little black egg / Yeah yeah / Heart of stone / Not now no way / I juvenile / Can't explain / Nowhere to run / Give till it hurts / Slow street / Cry 815 / Angela / Seventh son wiped out / Multiple personalities / When I die / Cleveland confidential (real world) / Dead end America / Wall of shame / She's a cadaver (and I gotta have her) / I stand alone / I don't understand / Her name was Jane.
Apr 98. (cd) *Sonic Swirl; (SWIRL 024)* **LIVE ROAD KILL 1978-1979 (live)** [ ] [-]

Jimmy PAGE (see under ⇒ LED ZEPPELIN)

PAICE, ASHTON & LORD (see under ⇒ DEEP PURPLE)

PAIN TEENS

Formed: Houston, Texas, USA . . . 1988 by SCOTT AYERS, his girlfriend BLISS BLOOD, along with KIRK CARR and FRANK GARYMARTIN. Fixated on twisted sexuality and and the more unsavoury impulses of the human psyche, The PAIN TEENS were a natural choice for KING COFFEY's 'Trance Syndicate' imprint, having previously debuted in '89 with the 'CASE HISTORIES' set. First up for the label was 1990's 'BORN IN BLOOD', a sample-hungry collection of fractured but accessible noise experimentation that set the tone for the bulk of their 90's output. Memorably described as the Marquis de Sade put to music, The PAIN TEENS uneasy listening experience continued with 'STIMULATION FESTIVAL' (1992), 'DESTROY ME LOVER' (1993) and 'BEAST OF DREAMS' (1995), the latter recorded after the band had been reduced to a duo of BLISS and SCOTT; by this point their partnership was purely musical. Having already given up live work, the pair retired for an extended sabbatical.

Album rating: CASE HISTORIES (*6) / BORN IN BLOOD (*6) / STIMULATION FESTIVAL (*6) / DESTROY ME, LOVER (*7) / BEAST OF DREAMS (*6)

BLISS BLOOD – vocals, percussion / **SCOTT AYERS** – guitar, samples, drums / **KIRK CARR** – bass / **FRANK GARYMARTIN** – drums

not iss. — Anomie

1988. (12"ep) **PAIN TEENS** [-] [ ]
– Inside me / Unameable / Brown Jenkin / Knife / Shoemaker / Amidst the rubble / World of destruction / Valley of the sun / Symptoms / Where madness dwells / Continuing nightmare / Count Magnus / Tapes / Innsmouth / Freezing wind / The somnambulist. *<cd-iss. Apr98 on 'Charnel'; 32>*
1989. (lp) *<3>* **CASE HISTORIES** [-] [ ]
– Hands in time / Bannoy / Veil of light / Puzzling diagnoses / Wot's de matter / Preppy killer / Unthinkable / Path of destruction / New woman / Bug in a can.

Trance Syndicate — Trance Syndicate

Nov 90. (lp/c/cd) *<(TR 03/+CS/CD)>* **BORN IN BLOOD** [ ] [ ]
– The basement / Pleasures of the flesh / Shotguns / Bad in my head / The way love used to be / Secret is sickness / Lady of flame / Desu evol yaw / She shook me / Christo / My desire / Noh jam.
Jun 92. (lp/cd) *<(TR 10/+CD)>* **STIMULATION FESTIVAL** [ ] [ ]
– Shallow hole / The dead cannot / God told me / Poured out blood / Drowning / Living hell / Indiscreet jewels / Wild world / Daughter of chaos / Evil dirt / Bruised / Dog spirits / Hangman's rope / Apartment #213.
Jul 93. (lp/cd) *<(TR 17/+CD)>* **DESTROY ME, LOVER** [ ] [ ]
– Cool your power / Prowling / Tar pit / Ru 486 / Dominant man / Sexual anorexia / Lisa knew / Body memory / Story of Isaac / Shock treatment.

— now pared down to the couple **BLISS + SCOTT**

Nov 95. (lp/cd) *<(TR 41/+CD)>* **BEAST OF DREAMS** [ ] [ ] Oct95
– Swimming / Manouche / Coral kiss / Accusing eyes / Swamp / Embers and ashes / Voluptus / Moonray / Frigid idol / Skids / Sweet sickness / Invitation.

— split up the following year

PALLAS

Formed: Aberdeen, Scotland . . . 1975 by CRAIG ANDERSON, DEREK HOLT, RONNIE BROWN, GRAEME MURRAY and DEREK FORMAN. Unable to secure a major deal, this neo-Prog rock outfit issued a self-financed EP, 'PALLAS' in 1978. Touring constantly over the next four years, they finally delivered a follow-up single, 'ARRIVE ALIVE', EUAN LAWSON and NIALL MATHEWSON had been called in to replace CRAIG and DEREK respectively. A debut set of 1981 'Granite Wax' demos was finally released by 'Cool King' in 1983 and showed that MARILLION were not the only rock group to adopt keyboards as an overriding influence. EMI's 'Harvest' saw sufficient promise in the band to sign them, the label bringing in EDDIE OFFORD (early producer of YES) to refine their sound on the concept set, 'THE SENTINEL' (1984). The over-complex record was met with mixed reviews, although it still managed to reach No.41 in the UK charts. Shortly after, vocalist ALAN REED replaced LAWSON, a follow-up, 'THE WEDGE' (1986) disappointing all but their mothers and leading to the band being dropped by EMI. Some band members subsequently joined ABEL GANZ, CASINO and COMEDY OF ERRORS, while also relocating to the Netherlands. With former PROMISE drummer COLIN FRASER and keyboard genius MIKE STOBBIE in tow, REED and his PALLAS returned to the fore in the mid-90's, releasing comeback set 'BEAT THE DRUM' (1999), to please their ever faithful following. At the time of writing, the band have recorded a new set, 'THE CROSS AND THE CRUCIBLE' (2001).

Album rating: ARRIVE ALIVE (*5) / THE SENTINEL (*5) / THE WEDGE (*4) / BEAT THE DRUM (*4) / LIVE OUR LIVES (*4)

CRAIG ANDERSON – vocals / **DAVID HOLT** – guitar / **RONNIE BROWN** – keyboards / **GRAEME MURRAY** – bass / **DEREK FORMAN** – drums

Sue-i-cide — not iss.

Feb 78. (7"ep) *(PAL 101)* **PALLAS** [ ] [-]
– Reds under the bed / Thought police / C.U.U.K. / Willmot Dovehouse MP.

— **EUAN LAWSON** – vocals; repl. ANDERSON

— **NIALL MATHEWSON** – guitar; repl. HOLT

Granite Wax — not iss.

Jun 81. (lp) *(GWLP 001)* **ARRIVE ALIVE** [ ] [-]
– Arrive alive / Heart attack *[not on cd]* / Queen of the deep (live) / Crown of thorns / The ripper (live). *(c-iss.Nov82; GWC 002) (re-iss. Feb83 on 'Cool King' lp/c; CKLP/CKC 002) (cd-iss. Feb99 on Germany's 'Inside Out'+=; IOMCD 38)* – 5 to 4 (live) / Flashpoint (live) / Paris is burning / The hammer falls / Stranger (on the edge of time).
May 82. (7") *(GWS 001)* **ARRIVE ALIVE. / STRANGER (ON THE EDGE OF TIME)** [ ] [-]

Cool King — not iss.

Apr 83. (7") *(CK 010)* **PARIS IS BURNING. / THE HAMMER FALLS** [ ] [-]
(12"+=) *(12CK 010)* – Stranger on the edge of time.

Harvest Capitol

Jan 84. (7"/7"pic-d) *(PLS/+P 1)* **EYES IN THE NIGHT (ARRIVE ALIVE). / EAST WEST** [ ] [-]
(12"+=) *(12PLS 1)* – Crown of thorns.

Feb 84. (lp/c) *(SHSP/TC-SHSP 2400124)* *<ST 12350>* **THE SENTINEL** [41] [ ] Aug84
– Eyes in the night (arrive alive) / Cut and run / Rise and fall / Shock treatment / Ark of infinity / Atlantis. *(cd-iss. Oct93 on 'Centaur'; CENCD 001) (cd re-iss. Jun00 on 'S.P.V.'+=; SPV 0853199-2)* – (diff.track order & extras).

Mar 84. (7") *(PLS 2)* **SHOCK TREATMENT. / MARCH ON ATLANTIS** [ ] [-]
(12"+=) *(12PLS 2)* – Heart attack.

— **ALAN REED** – vocals; repl. LAWSON

Apr 85. (7") *(PLS 3)* **STRANGERS. / NIGHTMARE** [ ] [-]
(12"+=/12"pic-d+=) **THE KNIGHTMOVES EP** *(12PLS/+P 3)* – Sanctuary.
(12"+=) **THE KNIGHTMOVES EP** *(12PLSD 3)* – Sanctuary. *(with free 7")* – MAD MACHINE. / STITCH IN TIME

Jan 86. (7") *(PLS 4)* **THROWING STONES AT THE WIND. / CUT AND RUN (live)** [ ] [-]
(12"+=) *(12PLS 4)* – Crown of thorns (live).

Feb 86. (lp/c) *(SHVL/TC-SHVL 850)* **THE WEDGE** [70] [-]
– Dance through the fire / Throwing stones at the wind / Win or lose / Executioner (Bernie Goetz a gun) / A million miles away (imagination) / Ratracing / Just a memory. *(cd-iss. Oct93 as 'KNIGHTMOVES TO THE WEDGE' on 'Centaur'; CDNCD 002) (cd re-iss. Jun00 on 'S.P.V.'+=; SPV 0854115-2)* – (diff.track order & extras)

Apr 86. (7") *(PLS 5)* **WIN OR LOSE. / JUST A MEMORY** [ ] [-]
(12"+=) *(12PLS 5)* – ('A'version).

— folded when EMI-Harvest let them go

— re-formed in the mid-late 90's with EUAN LAWSON making a guest appearance / **MIKE STOBBIE** – on keyboards

— **COLIN FRASER** – drums (ex-PROMISE) repl. FORMAN

Pallas not iss.

Mar 99. (cd) *(PALCD 004)* **BEAT THE DRUM** [ ] [-]
– Call to arms / Beat the drum / Hide and seek / Insomniac / All or nothing / Spirits / Man of principle / Ghosts / Blood and roses / Wilderness years / Fragments of the sun.

Jan 01. (cd) **LIVE OUR LIVES (live)** [ ] [-]
– Intro / Call to arms / Cut & run / Executioner / Hide & seek / Rat racing / Beat the drum / Insomniac / Blood & roses / Fragments. *(w/free cd+=)* – THE ATLANTIS SUITE

PANDEMONIUM

Formed: Alaska, USA . . . 1981 by the RESCH brothers; CHRIS, DAVID and ERIC, who subsequently moved to L.A., recruiting drummer GLENN HOLLAND in the process. Like many bands of their ilk, PANDEMONIUM secured a contract with 'Metal Blade' records after contributing a track to the 'Metal Massacre' compilation, an album proper appearing in 1984 entitled 'HEAVY METAL SOLDIERS'. Formulaic US fare, the album attracted scant interest, HOLLAND later being replaced with DAVE GRAYBILL while CHRIS LATHAM was added to augment the guitar attack. A further couple of albums, 'HOLE IN THE SKY' (1985) and 'THE KILL' (1988) were released to little avail.

Album rating: HEAVY METAL SOLDIERS (*5) / HOLE IN THE SKY (*4) / THE KILL (*4)

CHRIS RESCH – vocals / **DAVID RESCH** – guitar / **ERIC RESCH** – bass / **GLENN HOLLAND** – drums

Roadrunner Metal Blade

1984. (lp) *<1014-1036>* **HEAVY METAL SOLDIERS** [-] [ ]
– Road I'm traveling / Heavy metal soldiers / Little lady liar / The prey / Girls in love / Kitten mittens / This world / Radiation day.

— **DAVE GRAYBILL** – drums + **CHRIS LATHAM** – guitar; repl. HOLLAND

Roadrunner Enigma

Nov 85. (lp) *(RR 9727)* *<72089>* **HOLE IN THE SKY** [ ] [ ]
– Eye of the storm / Look of death / Imagination / Don't touch that dial / Evil face / Nothing left to say / Boys in the bright white sports car / Imprisoned by the snow / After the freeze.

Aug 88. (lp; w-drawn) *(RR 9537)* **THE KILL** [ ] [ ]

— folded after above

PANDORA'S BOX (see under ⇒ STEINMAN, Jim)

PANSY DIVISION

Formed: San Francisco, California, USA . . . 1991, when openly gay frontman, JON GINOLI, placed an ad in a newspaper looking for queer musicians into The Beatles, Buzzcocks and Ramones. He picked three like minded homosexuals, CHRIS FREEMAN, SALLY SCHLOSSTEIN and finally PATRICK GOODWIN, the self-professed "faggot quartet" getting around to releasing their debut album, 'UNDRESSED', in 1993. A couple more basic (s)punk rock sets appeared in the mid '90's before they slapped it on the table with a tongue-in-bum-cheek variation of an AC/DC number, 'FOR THOSE ABOUT TO SUCK COCK . . . WE SALUTE YOU'. The EP poked fun at two other covers of Judas Priest's 'BREAKING THE LAW' and Kiss's 'SWEET PAIN', while KIRK HAMMETT (don't tell anyone!) made a guest spot on 'HEADBANGER'.

Album rating: UNDRESSED (*4) / DEFLOWERED (*4) / PILE UP (*4) / WISH I'D TAKEN PICTURES (*4) / ABSURD POP SONG ROMANCE (*4)

JON GINOLI – vocals / **PATRICK GOODWIN** – guitar / **CHRIS FREEMAN** – bass / **SALLY SCHLOSSTEIN** – drums

Outpunk Outpunk

Jul 93. (7") *<OUT 006>* **BILL AND TED'S HOMO ADVENTURE. / BIG BOTTOM** [ ] [ ]

K not iss.

Oct 94. (7") *(IPU 52)* **JACKSON. / I REALLY WANTED YOU** [ ] [-]

Lookout Lookout

Oct 94. (cd) *<(LOOKOUT 70CD)>* **UNDRESSED** [ ] [ ] 1993
– Versatile / Fem in a black leather jacket / Bunnies / Boyfriend wanted / Story so far / Hippy dude / Curvature / Cocksucker club / Crabby day / Luck of the draw / Rock and roll queer bar / Surrender your clothing / Anthem.

Oct 94. (cd) *<(LOOKOUT 87CD)>* **DEFLOWERED** [ ] [ ]
– Reciprocate / Groovy underwear / Anonymous / Fluffy city / James bondage / Negative queen / Denny / Rachbottomoff / Beercan boy / Kissed / Song of remembrance for old queers / Deep water / Not enough of you to go around / New pleasures / Homosapien.

— rhythm section now **CHRIS BOWE + DAVID AYER**

Mar 95. (cd) *(DAMGOOD 60CD)* *<LOOKOUT 110CD>* **PILE UP** [ ] [ ] Feb95
– I can't sleep / Ring of joy / Fuck Buddy / Cowboys are frequently secretly fond . . . / Flower / Cry for shadow / Real men / Bill & Ted's homosexual adventure / Jack U off / Strip U down / Jackson / Big bottom / Touch my Joe camel / Biggest lie / Denny (naked) / Femme fatale / Trash / Homo Christmas / C.S.F. / Smells like queer spirit. (above issued on 'Damaged Goods' UK)

— now with drummer **DUSTIN DONALDSON**

Feb 96. (lp/cd) *<(LOOKOUT 133/+CD)>* **WISH I'D TAKEN PICTURES** [ ] [ ]
– Horny in the morning / Vanilla / I really wanted you / Dick of death / Expiration date / The summer you let your hair grow out / Wish I'd taken pictures / Pillow talk / This is your life / Don't be so sure / Kevin / Ache / Pee shy / Side walk sale.

Aug 96. (7"ep) *(LOOKOUT 147)* **FOR THOSE ABOUT TO SUCK COCK, WE SALUTE YOU EP** [ ] [-]
– For those about to suck cock, we salute you / Headbanger / Breaking the law / Sweet pain.

Apr 97. (7"ep) *(LOOKOUT 174)* **QUEER TO THE CORE EP** [ ] [ ]

Sep 98. (cd) *<(LK 198CD)>* **ABSURD POP SONG ROMANCE** [ ] [ ]
– – / February 17 / Sweet insecurity / It'll never be the same / Better off just friends / Too beautiful / – / Luv luv luv / – / Best revenge / Bad boyfriend / – / You're gonna need your friends / Tinted windows / – / Glenview / Used to turn me on / Obstacle course / Vicious beauty.

PANTERA

Formed: Texas, USA . . . 1981 by TERRY GLAZE, 'DIAMOND' DARRELL, VINCE ABBOTT and REX ROCKER, taking their name from the Spanish word for panther. Initially a vaguely glam-influenced hard-rock band in the packet-bulging tradition of KISS and AEROSMITH, PANTERA began their career with 'METAL MAGIC' (1983), issued on their own homegrown 'Metal Magic' label. The album was fairly well-received Stateside and saw the band gain a firm foothold on the lower rungs of the hair-rock ladder. With subsequent releases like 'PROJECTS IN THE JUNGLE' (1984) and 'I AM THE NIGHT' (1985), however, the group began to adopt a more muscular approach, consolidated with the arrival of PHIL ANSELMO (as a replacement for GLAZE) on 1988's 'POWER METAL'. With a growing reputation and the help of a recommendation from JUDAS PRIEST's ROB HALFORD, the band secured a major label deal with 'Atco'. The resulting album, 'COWBOYS FROM HELL' (1990) was a dramatic turnaround, gone was the 80's metal garb and cheesy choruses; check shirts, tattoos and a brutally uncompromising thrash-based groove had forcibly taken their place. Clearly, something had made these boys angry and 'A VULGAR DISPLAY OF POWER' (1992) was arguably the most articulate and succinct fix of metallic aggression to be had that year; the likes of 'F**KING HOSTILE' said it all. The record also gave PANTERA their first taste of chart success, the 'WALK' single making the UK Top 40. So it was, then, that the stage was set for PANTERA to both consolidate their position as one of the most unrelentingly intense groups in the nu-metal hierarchy and smash into the UK album chart at pole position with 'FAR BEYOND DRIVEN' (1994). Incredibly their seventh album, the group were now virtually unrecognisable from their rather tame origins, the record's grim vignettes (select 'I'M BROKEN' and 'THROES OF REJECTION' for that ultimate feel-bad factor) were accompanied by a suitably severe Black Sabbath cover, 'PLANET CARAVAN'. The set also saw PANTERA climb to the uppermost regions of the American charts, their services sought out for a contribution to 'The Crow' soundtrack (a cover of Poison Idea's 'THE BADGE'). Silent for most of 1995 (bar ANSELMO who moonlighted with DOWN; sole album, 'NOLA'), PANTERA returned with a vengeance the following year, releasing 'THE GREAT SOUTHERN TRENDKILLERS' (1996). Easing back a little on the speed pedal, the group achieved an even more savagely focused intensity, ANSELMO raging from the depths of his tortured soul. It may have lent his lyrics and delivery a stark harshness, but surviving on the very precipice of existence eventually caught up with ANSELMO when, later that summer (13th July), the singer narrowly escaped death from a heroin overdose, later admitting to being dead for five minutes. Shaken but hardly beaten, PANTERA returned the following year with a well-overdue concert set, 'OFFICIAL LIVE – 101 PROOF', proving that there are still few to match the sheer, unadulterated heaviness of their impact. 'RE-INVENTING THE STEEL' in 2000 kept them high in profile as it returned ANSELMO and Co to the US Top 5.

Album rating: METAL MAGIC (*5) / PROJECTS IN THE JUNGLE (*5) / I AM THE NIGHT (*5) / POWER METAL (*4) / COWBOYS FROM HELL (*6) / A VULGAR DISPLAY OF POWER (*8) / FAR BEYOND DRIVEN (*7) / THE GREAT SOUTHERN

TRENDKILLERS (*6) / OFFICIAL LIVE 101 PROOF (*6) / REINVENTING THE STEEL (*6) / Down: NOLA (*5)

TERRY GLAZE – vocals, guitar / **DARRELL ABBOTT** (b.20 Aug'66, Dallas, Texas) – guitar / **REX ROCKER** (b.REX BROWN, 27 Jul'64, Graham, Texas) – bass / **VINCENT PAUL ABBOTT** (b.11 Mar'64, Dallas) – drums

not iss. | Metal Magic

1983. (lp) *<MMR 1983>* **METAL MAGIC** [-] [ ]
– Ride my rocket / I'll be alright / Tell me if you want it / Latest lover / Biggest part of me / Metal magic / Widowmaker / Nothin' on (but the radio) / Sad lover / Rock out!.

— GLAZE became TERRENCE LEE, DARRELL prefixed the word DIMEBAG and VINCE was now VINNIE PAUL

1984. (lp) *<MMR 1984>* **PROJECTS IN THE JUNGLE** [-] [ ]
– All over tonite / Out for blood / Blue lite turnin' red / Like fire / In over my head / Projects in the jungle / Heavy metal rules! / Only a heartbeat away / Killers / Takin' my life.

1985. (lp) *<MMR 1985>* **I AM THE NIGHT** [-] [ ]
– Hot and heavy / I am the night / Onward we rock! / D.S.G.S.T.S.T.S.M. / Daughters of the queen / Down below / Come-on eyes / Right on the edge / Valhalla / Forever tonight.

— **PHILIP ANSELMO** (b.30 Jun'68, New Orleans, Louisiana) – vocals repl. TERRY

May 88. (lp) *<MMR 1988>* **POWER METAL** [-] [ ]
– Rock the world / Power metal / We'll meet again / Over and out / Proud to be loud / Down below / Death trap / Hard ride / Burnnn! / P*S*T*88.

Atco | Atco

Jul 90. (cd/c/lp) *<7567 91372-2/-4/-1>* **COWBOYS FROM HELL** [ ] [ ]
– Cowboys from Hell / Primal concrete sledge / Psycho holiday / Heresy / Cemetery gates / Domination / Shattered / Clash with reality / Medicine man / Message in blood / The sleep / The art of shredding.

Feb 92. (cd/c/lp) *<7567 91758-2/-4/-1>* **A VULGAR DISPLAY OF POWER** [64] [44]
– Mouth for war / A new level / Walk / F**king hostile / This love / Rise / No good (attack the radical) / Live in a hole / Regular people (conceit) / By demons be driven / Hollow.

Sep 92. (7"/c-s) *(A 5845/+C)* **MOUTH FOR WAR. / RISE** [73] [ ]
(cd-s+=) *(A 5845CD)* – Cowboys from Hell / Heresy.
(12") *(A 5845T)* – ('A'side) / ('A'-superloud mix) / Domination / Primal concrete sledge.

Feb 93. (12"m) *(B 6076T)* **WALK. / COWBOYS FROM HELL / PSYCHO HOLIDAY (live)** [34] [ ]
(cd-ep) *(B 6076CD)* – ('A'side) / Fucking hostile / By demons be driven.
(cd-ep) *(B 6076CDX)* – ('A'side) / No good (attack the radical)/ A new level / Walk (extended remixes by Jim 'Foetus' Thirlwell).

East West | Atco

Mar 94. (12"/cd-s) *(B 5932 T/CD1)* **I'M BROKEN. / SLAUGHTERED** [19] [ ]
(cd-s+=) *(B 5932CD2)* – Domination (live) / Primal concrete sledge.
(cd-s) *(B 5932CD3)* – ('A'side) / Cowboys from Hell (live) / Psycho holiday (live).
(12") *(B 5932X)* – ('A'side) / Walk (cervical edit) / Fuckin' hostile.

Mar 94. (cd/c/lp) *<7567 92302-2/-4/-1>* **FAR BEYOND DRIVEN** [3] [1]
– Strength beyond strength / Becoming / 5 minutes alone / I'm broken / Good friends and a bottle of pills / Hard lines, sunken cheeks / Slaughtered / 25 years / Shedding skin / Use my third arm / Throes of rejection / Planet Caravan.

May 94. (7"white) *(A 8293)* **5 MINUTES ALONE. / THE BADGE** [ ] [ ]

Oct 94. (7") *(A 5836)* **PLANET CARAVAN. / 5 MINUTES ALONE** [26] [ ]
(12") *(A 5836T)* – ('A'side) / Cowboys from Hell / Heresay.
(cd-s) *(A 5836Cd1)* – ('A'side) / The badge / New level / Becoming.
(cd-s) *(A 5836CD2)* – ('A'side) / Domination / Hollow.

May 96. (cd/c/lp) *<7559 61908-2/-4/-1>* **THE GREAT SOUTHERN TRENDKILLERS** [17] [4]
– Drag the waters / War nerve / It can't destroy my body / 13 steps to nowhere / Sandblasted skin / Underground in America / Suicide note (part 1) / Suicide note (part 2).

— On 13th Jul'96, ANSELMO luckily survived a heroin overdose in which he was reported to be dead for five minutes.

Aug 97. (cd/c/lp) *<7559 62068-2/-4/-1>* **OFFICIAL LIVE – 101 PROOF (live)** [54] [15]
– New level / Walk / Becoming / 5 minutes alone / Sandblasted skin / Suicide note (part 2) / War nerve / This love / Dom – Hollow / Strength beyond strength / I'm broken / Cowboys from Hell / Cemetery gates / Fuckin' hostile / Where you come from / I can't hide.

Mar 00. (cd/c) *<7559 62451-2/-4>* **REINVENTING THE STEEL** [33] [4]
– Hellbound / Goddamn electric / Yesterday don't mean shit / You've got to belong to it / Revolution is my name / Death rattle / We'll grind that axe for a long time.. / Uplift / It makes them disappear / It'll cast a shadow.

DOWN

PHIL ANSELMO – vocals / **PEPPER KEENAN** – guitar / **KIRK WINDSTEIN** – guitar / **TODD STRANGE** – bass / **JIMMY BOWER** – drums

East West | East West

Sep 95. (cd/c/lp) *<7559 61830-2/-4/-1>* **NOLA** [68] [57]
– Pray for the locust / Stone the crow / Bury me in smoke / Eyes of the south / Pillars of eternity / Underneath everything / Swan song / Temptation's wings / Jail / Lifer / Rehab / Losing all / Hail the leaf.

PAPA ROACH

Formed: Vacaville, North California, USA . . . 1993 by schoolmates JACOBY SHADDIX aka COBY DICK, DAVE BUCKNER, JERRY HORTON and WILL JAMES, taking the inspiration for their moniker from the PONCHO SANCHEZ album, 'Papa Gato'. Influenced by Bay Area mavericks such as FAITH NO MORE and PRIMUS, the band set out playing a funk/hip-hop hybrid and rapidly built up a loyal local following while making a tentative start to their recording career with 'CACA BONITA' (1995). In 1996, WILL JAMES was replaced by the band's teenage roadie TOBIN ESPERANCE and the lads cut a sophomore album, 'OLD FRIENDS FROM YOUNG YEARS' (1997) on a miniscule budget. Playlisted by many local radio stations, the record – again released on their own 'Onion Hardcore Recordings' imprint – was instrumental in raising PAPA ROACH's profile and before long the Californian upstarts were playing on the same bill as SUICIDAL TENDENCIES, HUMAN WASTE PROJECT, WILL HAVEN etc. 1998's '5 TRACKS DEEP' EP sharpened their rap-metal chops and paved the way for a major label deal with 'Dreamworks'. The Hollywood-based label released the 'INFEST' album in 2000, a record that crept unannounced into the US Top 20 and finally established PAPA ROACH as major league contenders alongside KORN, LIMP BIZKIT, DEFTONES etc. Reliable if not exactly innovative exponents of the increasingly over subscribed nu-metal agenda, P-ROACH (as their fans know and love them) can safely regard themselves as fully paid up members of America's new rock establishment.

Album rating: OLD FRIENDS FROM YOUNG YEARS (*5) / INFEST (*6)

COBY DICK – vocals / **JERRY HORTON** – guitar / **WILL JAMES** – bass / **DAVE BUCKNER** – drums

not iss. | own label

Dec 94. (cd-ep) **POTATOES FOR CHRISTMAS** [-] [ ]
– Coffee thoughts / Mama's dress / Lenny's / Lulu Espidachi / Cheez-z-fux / I love babies / Dendrilopis.

1995. (cd-s) **CACA BONITA** [-] [ ]

— **TOBIN ESPERANCE** – bass; repl. WILL

1997. (cd) **OLD FRIENDS FROM YOUNG YEARS** [-] [ ]
– Intro / Orange drive palms / Liquid diet / GrrBrr / iSEDuF**nDie / Dirty cut freak / Living room / 829 / Peewagon / Hedake / Shut up n die (reprise). *(hidden track+=)* – thanx.

1998. (cd-ep) **5 TRACKS DEEP** [-] [ ]
– Revenge in Japanese / My bad side / July / Tambienemy / Thrown away.

1999. (cd-ep) **LET 'EM KNOW** [-] [ ]
– Walking thru barbed wire / Legacy / Binge / Snakes / Tightrope.

Dreamworks | Dreamworks

Aug 00. (cd) *<(450223-2)>* **INFEST** [9] [5] Apr00
– Infest / Last resort / Broken home / Dead cell / Between angels and insects / Blood brothers *[on explicit version]* / Legacy *[on clean version]* / Revenge / Snakes / Never enough / Binge / Thrown away. *(hidden track+=)* – Tight rope. *(UK re-iss. Feb01 cd/cd+=; 45031 6-2/7-2)* – Dead cell (live) / Last resort (video).

Feb 01. (c-s) *(450920-4) <album cut>* **LAST RESORT / BROKEN HOME (session)** [3] [57] May00
(cd-s+=) *(450920-2)* – Dead cell (session) / ('A'-CD-ROM).
(cd-s) *(450921-2)* – ('A'side) / ('A'session) / Between angels and insects (session).

Apr 01. (c-s) *(450908-4)* **BETWEEN ANGELS AND INSECTS / LAST RESORT (radio)** [17] [-]
(cd-s) *(450908-2)* – ('A'side) / Last resort (live) / Binge (live) / ('A'-CD-ROM).
(cd-s) *(450909-2)* – ('A'side) / Tight rope (live) / Barbed wire (live).

PARADISE LOST

Formed: Halifax, England . . . April '88 by NICK HOLMES, GREGOR McINTOSH, AARON AEDY, STEPHEN EDMONDSON and MATT ARCHER, taking their name from the famous Milton poem. Initially playing death metal combining the grindcore element of the UK scene and the more extreme US sound with a vaguely gothic element, PARADISE LOST made their debut on 'Peaceville' in 1990 with the 'IN DUB' single and 'LOST PARADISE' album. Eschewing the gore-obsessed lyrics of their contemporaries, PARADISE LOST instead opted for a more existential take on the misery of life in keeping with their literary influences. A follow-up, 'GOTHIC' (1991), saw the band moving away from the death-metal genre, slowing things down and abandoning the requisite death grunt as well as adding keyboards (unheard of for a death-metal band!) and female vocals. Subsequently signing with 'Music For Nations', the group further embraced this direction with 'SHADES OF GOD' (1992) and 'ICON' (1993), the latter set especially, seeing them amass long overdue critical acclaim and a swelling crossover fanbase. By the release of the UK Top 20 set, 'DRACONIAN TIMES' (1995), PARADISE LOST had fashioned a compelling sound lying somewhere between METALLICA and The SISTERS OF MERCY with hints of latter-day DEPECHE MODE. Drawing praise form such esteemed admirers as the aforementioned METALLICA and Brazilian maestros SEPULTURA, the group went from strength to strength, the excellent, string-enhanced 'ONE SECOND' (1997) set further underlining their credentials as the foremost purveyors of atmospheric, misery-wallowing, gothic metal. 'HOST' in 1999 and 'BELIEVE IN NOTHING' (2001), disappointed many metal fans – they were accused of sounding more DEPECHE MODE than their true selves. • **Songwriters:** McINTOSH / HOLMES except DEATH WALKS BEHIND YOU (Atomic Rooster) / WALK AWAY (Sisters Of Mercy). • **Trivia:** In Mar'96, NICK HOLMES finished his 1,500 mile leukaemia charity motorcycle ride in Australia, travelling from Ayers Rock to Alice Springs and on to Darwin, raising 4,000 quid in the process.

Album rating: LOST PARADISE (*6) / GOTHIC (*7) / SHADES OF GOD (*6) / ICON (*7) / DRACONIAN TIMES (*8) / ONE SECOND (*8) / REFLECTION compilation (*6) / HOST (*5) / BELIEVE IN NOTHING (*4)

NICK HOLMES – vocals / **GREGOR MacINTOSH** – lead guitar / **AARON AEDY** – rhythm guitar / **STEPHEN EDMONDSON** – bass / **MATT ARCHER** – drums, percussion

Peaceville Rough Trade

Apr 90. (lp/cd) *(VILE 17/+CD)* **LOST PARADISE** [ ] [-]
– Intro / Deadly inner sense / Paradise lost / Our saviour / Rotting misery / Frozen illusion / Breeding fear / Lost Paradise. *(cd+=)* – Internal torment II. *(re-iss. cd Apr95 & Nov00; CDVILEM 17)*

Apr 90. (12") *(VILE 19T)* **IN DUB** [ ] [-]
– Rotting misery (doom dub) / Breeding fear (demolition dub).

Apr 91. (cd/lp) *(CD+/VILE 26)* **GOTHIC** [ ] [ ]
– Gothic / Dead emotion / Shattered / Rapture / Eternal / Falling forever / Angel tears / Silent / The painless / Desolate. *(cd re-iss. Nov00; CDVILEM 26)*

Jan 92. (cd-ep) *(CDVILE 41)* **GOTHIC EP** [ ] [-]
– Gothic / IN DUB (tracks) / The painless (mix). *(re-iss. Jul94; same)*

Music For Nations Metal Blade

Jun 92. (cd/c/lp) *(CD/T+/MFN 135) <14001>* **SHADES OF GOD** [ ] [ ]
– Mortals watch the day / Crying for eternity / Embraced / Daylight torn / Pity the sadness / No forgiveness / Your hand in mine / The word made flesh. *(cd+=)* – As I die.

Oct 92. (12"ep/cd-ep) *(12/CD KUT 150)* **AS I DIE / RAPE OF VIRTUE. / DEATH WALKS BEHIND YOU / ETERNAL (live)** [ ] [-]

Sep 93. (cd/c/d-lp) *(CD/T+/MFN 152) <14021>* **ICON** [ ] [ ]
– Embers fire / Remembrance / Forging sympathy / Joys of the emptiness / Dying freedom / Widow / Colossal rains / Weeping words / Poison / True belief / Shallow seasons / Christendom / Deus misereatur.

Feb 94. (12"ep/cd-ep) *(12/CD KUT 157)* **SEALS THE SENSE** [ ] [-]
– Embers fire / Sweetness / True belief / Your hand in mine (live).

— **LEE MORRIS** – drums (ex-MARSHALL LAW) repl. ARCHER

Music For Nations Relativity

May 95. (c-ep/12"ep/cd-ep) *(T/12/CD KUT 165)* **LAST TIME / I WALK AWAY. / LAID TO WASTE / MASTER OF MISRULE** [60] [-]

Jun 95. (cd/c/lp)(pic-lp) *(CD/T+/MFN 184)(MFNP 184) <1537>* **DRACONIAN TIMES** [16] [ ]
– Enchantment / Hallowed land / The last time / Forever failure / Once solemn / Shadowkings / Elusive cure / Yearn for change / Shades of God / Hands of reason / I see your face / Jaded. *(cd w/ltd cd+=)* – Embers fire (live) / Daylight torn (live) / True belief (live) / Pity the sadness (live) / As I die (live) / Weeping words (demo) / The last time (demo) / I walk away / Laid to waste / Master of misrule / Forever failure (video edit).

Oct 95. (c-ep/12"ep/cd-ep) *(T/12/CD KUT 169)* **FOREVER FAILURE. / ANOTHER DESIRE / FEAR** [66] [-]

Music For Nations Jive

Jun 97. (12"ep) *(12KUT 174)* **SAY JUST WORDS / HOW SOON IS NOW? / SAY JUST WORDS (album mix) / CRUEL ONE** [53] [-]
(cd-ep) *(CDKUT 174)* – Soul courageous. *[repl.2nd track]*
(cd-ep) *(CDXKUT 174)* – Albino flogged black. [repl.4th track]

Jul 97. (cd/c/lp) *(CD/T+/MFN 222) <41616>* **ONE SECOND** [31] [ ]
– One second / Say just words / Lydia / Mercy / Soul courageous / Another day / The sufferer / This cold life / Blood of another / Disappear / Sane / Take me down.

Jul 98. (c-s) *(TKUT 177)* **ONE SECOND / ONE SECOND (remix)** [ ] [-]
(cd-s+=) *(CDKUT 177)* – The hour / Slave.
(cd-s) *(CDXKUT 177)* – ('A'side) / Mercy (live) / This cold life (live).

Music For Nations Mayhem

Sep 98. (cd) *(CDMFN 243) <11160>* **REFLECTION** (compilation) [ ] [ ]
– Say just words / Hallowed land / True belief / Pity the sadness / The eternal / Forever failure (exclusive remix version) / Gothic / One second / Rotting misery (in dub) / The last time / Mercy mercy mercy / Widow / Embers fire / As I die / Soul courageous (live) / Blood of another (live) / As I die (live).

Chrysalis not iss.

Jun 99. (cd) *(520567-2)* **HOST** [61] [-]
– So much is lost / Nothing sacred / In all honesty / Harbour / Ordinary days / It's too late / Permanent solution / Behind the grey / Wreck / Made the same / Deep / Year of summer / Host.

Liberty Liberty

Feb 01. (cd) *(530707-2) <65693>* **BELIEVE IN NOTHING** [ ] [ ] May01
– I am nothing / Mouth / Fader / Look at me now / Illumination / Something real / Divided / Sell it to the world / Never again / Control / No reason / World pretending / Sway / Gone / Waiting for good.

– compilations, etc. –

on 'Music For Nations' unless mentioned otherwise

Apr 96. (d-cd) *(CDMFN 202)* **SHADES OF GOD / ICON** [ ] [-]

Oct 97. (5xcd-ep-box) *(CDMFNB 236)* **THE SINGLES COLLECTION** [ ] [-]

PARADOX

Formed: Germany . . . 1986 by former WARHEAD cohorts CHARLY STEINHAUER and AXEL BLAHA, who soon added MARKUS SPYTH and ROLAND STAHL. Signing to 'Roadrunner' in Europe, this forgettable thrash band debuted with the uninspiring 'PRODUCT OF IMAGINATION' (chance would be a fine thing!). The band went through a number of personnel changes prior to their second and final album, DIETER ROTH, MANFRED SPRINGER and ARMIN DONDERER replacing SPYTH and STAHL on 'HERESY' (1989), a slightly more inventive set.

Album rating: PRODUCT OF IMAGINATION (*4) / HERESY (*7)

CHARLY STEINHAUER – vocals, guitar / **MARKUS SPYTH** – guitar / **ROLAND STAHL** – bass / **AXEL BLAHA** – drums

Roadrunner S.P.V.

Nov 87. (lp) *(RR 9593) <787876>* **PRODUCT OF IMAGINATION** [ ] [ ]
– Opening theme / Paradox / Death, screaming and pain / Product of imagination / Continuation of invasion / Mystery / Kill that beast / Pray to the godz of wrath / Beyond space / Wotan II. *(cd-iss. Apr89 on 'Roadracer'; RO 9593-2)*

— **DIETER ROTH + MANFRED SPRINGER** – guitars; repl. SPYTH

— **ARMIN DONDERER** – bass; repl. STAHL

Roadracer Relix

Dec 89. (lp/cd) *(RO 9506-1/-2) <847871>* **HERESY** [ ] [ ]
– Heresy / Search for perfection / Killtime / Crusaders revenge / The burning / Massacre of the Cathars / Serenity / 700 years on / Castle in the wind.

— folded some time in the early 90's

PARIAH

Formed: Florida, USA . . . 1987 by the EGGER brothers; GARTH, SHAUN and CHRIS, who enlisted the help of guitarist WAYNE DERRICK. The reason for the inclusion of this thrash outfit is purely to differentiate between the slightly superior UK group of the same name. The 1989 album, 'TAKE A WALK' was released on 'Moshroom', the moshers were not amused. Enough said.

Album rating: TAKE A WALK (*3)

GARTH EGGER – vocals / **SHAUN EGGER** – guitar / **WAYNE DERRICK** – guitar / **CHRIS EGGER** – drums

Moshroom not iss.

Feb 89. (lp) *(20002)* **TAKE A WALK** [-] [-] Dutch

— took a long walk after above

PARIAH (see under ⇒ SATAN)

PAW

Formed: Lawrence, Kansas, USA . . . 1990 by the FITCH brothers; GRANT and PETER, plus CHARLES BRYAN and frontman MARK HENNESSY. Signed to 'A&M' on the strength of a Butch Vig-produced demo, PAW released the acclaimed 'DRAGLINE' in summer '93. Tracing their way back through the great American lineage of seminal hardcore/indie rock, PAW sculpted a visceral collection of contemporary yet classic, melody-conscious guitar abuse. Set to everyday tales of smalltown love and life, the record's powerful, empathetic approach brought praise from the indie and metal press alike, PAW going on to tour with the likes of THERAPY and MONSTER MAGNET. A second set, 'DEATH TO TRAITORS', followed in 1995, although the group have yet to turn critical favour into major record sales.

Album rating: DRAGLINE (*8) / DEATH TO TRAITORS (*6)

MARK HENNESSY – vocals / **GRANT FITCH** – guitar / **CHARLES BRYAN** – bass / **PETER FITCH** – drums

A&M A&M

May 93. (12"/cd-s) *(580 293-1/-2)* **JESSIE. / SLOW BURN / BRIDGE** [ ] [ ]

Jul 93. (7"/c-s) *(580 344-7/-4)* **COULDN'T KNOW. / BRIDGE** [ ] [ ]
(cd-s+=) *(580 345-2)* – Dragline.

Aug 93. (cd/c) *<(540 065-2/-4)>* **DRAGLINE** [ ] [ ]
– Gasoline / Sleeping bag / Jessie / The bridge / Couldn't know / Pansy / Lolita / Dragline / Veronica / One more bottle / Sugarcane / Hard pig.

Oct 93. (7"/c-s) *(580 374-7/-4)* **SLEEPING BAG. / IMAGINARY LOVER** [ ] [ ]
(10"+=/cd-s+=) *(580 375-0/-2)* – Suicide shift / Slow burn.

Mar 94. (7"/c-s) *(580 560-7/-4)* **JESSIE. / GASOLINE** [ ] [ ]
(cd-s+=) *(580 561-2)* – Slow burn / The bridge.
(12"red) *(580 561-1)* – ('A'side) / Pansy / Sleeping bag.

Aug 95. (cd/c) *<(540 391-2/-4)>* **DEATH TO TRAITORS** [ ] [ ]
– No such luck / Seasoned glove / Hope I die tonight / Swollen / Last one / Death to traitors / Built low / Glue mouth kid / Texas / Max the silent / Sweet Sally Brown / Badger / Peach / Sunflower.

— not heard much from them since

PEARL JAM

Formed: Seattle, Washington, USA . . . 1991 by JEFF AMENT and STONE GOSSARD, who, together with MARK ARM, STEVE TURNER and ALEX VINCENT had previously played in pivotal Seattle band, GREEN RIVER (ARM and TURNER went on to form the noisier, and some still argue, superior MUDHONEY). Widely held to be the first ever "Grunge" act, GREEN RIVER's distortion-heavy mash-up of punk and metal is best sampled on the 'DRY AS A BONE' EP (1987), one of the first releases on the seminal 'Sub Pop' label. Following the band's demise, GOSSARD, AMENT and BRUCE FAIRWEATHER (who had replaced TURNER in GREEN RIVER) recruited vocalist ANDREW WOOD (ex-MALFUNKSHUN) and drummer GARY GILMOUR to form the short lived MOTHER LOVE BONE. After an EP and a cult debut album, 'APPLE' (1990), WOOD overdosed on heroin (March '90), effectively bringing the band to an untimely end. However, it was within these 70's influenced grooves that AMENT and GOSSARD laid the musical foundations for what would later become PEARL JAM. The group evolved from a tribute project for the dead WOOD put together by SOUNDGARDEN frontman, CHRIS CORNELL. Also featuring GOSSARD, AMENT, guitarist MIKE McCREADY, and SOUNDGARDEN sticksman MATT CAMERON, this loose aggregation released 'TEMPLE OF THE DOG' in 1991, a critically acclaimed opus that laid further groundwork for PEARL JAM's sound. With vocalist EDDIE VEDDER and drummer DAVE KRUSEN (subsequently superceded by DAVE ABBRUZZESE) replacing the SOUNDGARDEN boys, the outfit gradually evolved into PEARL JAM, the band still something of a cult act when their 'Epic' debut was released in America at the tail end of '91. 'TEN' eventually reached No.2 in the US chart and a hefty media buzz ensured a steady flow of UK imports, the record making the British Top 20 upon its February '92 release. With VEDDER penning the lyrics and GOSSARD and AMENT writing the music, 'TEN' was a powerfully assured debut, transforming the grunge monster into a sleekly melodic rock beast. VEDDER's soulful bellow was a key factor, the singer wringing emotion from every note of the anthemic 'ALIVE' and the affecting 'JEREMY'. Granted, comparisons to LED ZEPPELIN were a little unfair, but the band's lumbering sound seemed the antithesis of the cathartic rush with which NIRVANA had revolutionised a stale music scene and KURT COBAIN was spot on with his infamous criticisms, despite cries of sour grapes. While their intentions may have been honourable, PEARL JAM ushered in a tidal wave of dull as dishwater, sub-metal masquerading as grunge, most of it, funnily enough, released on major labels. Nevertheless, the kids loved it, especially the American ones, and the band embarked on a punishing touring schedule, finding time to make a cameo appearance as Matt Dillon's band in 'Singles', the Cameron Crowe film based on the Seattle music scene. As well as standing in for JIM MORRISON when The DOORS were eventually inducted into the Rock 'n' Roll Hall Of Fame, VEDDER performed a heart stopping version of BOB DYLAN's 'Masters Of War' (playing mandolin) at the veteran's annniversary concert in 1993. The same year also saw the release of a PEARL JAM follow-up, 'VS', the band's fiercely loyal fanbase propelling the album straight in at No.1 in the US charts. A more ragingly visceral affair, 'GO' gave VEDDER something to get his teeth into while the more reflective 'DAUGHTER' proved how affecting the band (and particularly VEDDER) could be when they dropped the derivative hard rock assault. Along with their mate NEIL YOUNG, PEARL JAM seemingly have an abiding love of vinyl, releasing 'VITALOGY' (1994) initially on record only, something which didn't prevent the band scaling the US chart once again. While not exactly vital, as the title might suggest, the record saw PEARL JAM going back to basics and injecting their behemoth-rock with a bit of stripped down energy. The following year saw PEARL JAM backing NEIL YOUNG on the so-so 'MIRROR BALL' (1995) album, the fruition of their musical partnership that had begun some years previous. In 1995, each member (except ABBRUZZESE), took time to carry out other projects, although the following year they returned to full force with 'NO CODE', an album that showed a lighter, acoustic side. Unfortunately if not predictably, the fans were not best impressed by the album's more experimental turn and it quickly faded from view after a relatively brief stay at the US No.1 spot and the UK Top 3. More newsworthy was the band's feud with the Ticketmaster agency, a spat which precluded a full-scale tour. While the 'YIELD' (1998) album heralded a return to meatier fare, PEARL JAM records were beginning to follow the time-honoured heavy metal pattern of an initial high chart placing followed by a rapid descent into obscurity. All the signs of a cult, diehard fanbase and one which lapped up both the mammoth US arena tour of summer '98 and its spin-off album, 'LIVE ON TWO LEGS' (1998). Bizarrely enough, the band then proceeded to score their biggest hit in years with a cover of the J.FRANK WILSON chestnut, 'LAST KISS'. Originally part of a fan-club only covers series, the single was given a full release due to popular demand and ended up narrowly missing the US No.1 slot in summer '99. The Tched Blake-produced 'BINAURAL' resumed normal service as PEARL JAM entered the new millennium seemingly oblivious to changing fads and fashions. A GRATEFUL DEAD for the post-grunge generation may be a comparison not too far off the mark although PEARL JAM adopted a slightly different attitude to bootlegging. While the late JERRY GARCIA and crew seemingly encouraged their fans to tape away to their hearts content, VEDDER's mob made a stubborn attempt to out-bootleg the bootleggers by recording every single date of their European and British tours and subsequently releasing them as a series of 72 double-CD sets. JERRY'll be turning in his grave and I was pulling the rest of my hair out updating this discography. • **Songwriters:** VEDDER wrote lyrics / GOSSARD and AMENT the songs except F***IN' UP (Neil Young). GREEN RIVER covered AIN'T NOTHIN' TO DO (Dead Boys) / QUEEN BITCH (David Bowie). • **Trivia:** Backed actor MATT DILLON's band CITIZEN DICK in the 1992 film 'Singles'. VEDDER co-wrote and sang on 2 tracks; 'THE LONG ROAD' + 'THE FACE OF LOVE' on the 1996 movie 'Dead Man Walking'.

Album rating: Green River: REHAB DOLL – DRY AS A BONE (*7) / Mother Love Bone: STARDOG CHAMPION collection (*8) / Pearl Jam: TEN (*10) / VS (*8) / VITALOGY (*7) / NO CODE (*8) / YIELD (*7) / LIVE ON TWO LEGS (*6) / BINAURAL (*7) / Three Fish: THREE FISH (*5) / QUIET TABLE (*5)

GREEN RIVER

MARK ARM (b.21 Feb'62, California) – vocals / **STEVE TURNER** (b.28 Mar'65, Houston, Texas) – guitar / **STONE GOSSARD** (b.20 Jul'66) – guitar / **JEFF AMENT** (b.10 Mar'63, Big Sandy, Montana) – bass / **ALEX VINCENT** – drums

not iss. Homestead

Sep 85. (12"ep) *<HMS 031>* **COME ON DOWN** [-] [ ]
– New god / Swallow my pride / Ride of your life / Corner of my eye / Tunnel of love. *(cd-ep-iss.May94; same)*

—— **BRUCE FAIRWEATHER** – guitar repl. TURNER who later joined MUDHONEY

not iss. I.P.C.

Nov 86. (7"green) *<ICP 01>* **TOGETHER WE'LL NEVER. / AIN'T NOTHIN' TO DO** [-] [ ]

Glitterhouse Sup Pop

Jun 87. (12"ep) *<SP 11>* **DRY AS A BONE** [-] [ ]
– Unwind / Baby takes / This town / PCC / Ozzie. *(UK-iss.Mar91 on 'Tupelo'; TUPLP 17) (cd-iss. May94; same)*

Feb 89. (12"ep) *(GR 0031) <SP 15>* **REHAB DOLL** [ ] [ ] May88
– Searchin' / Ain't nothin' to do / Forever means / Rehab girl / Swallow my pride / Together we'll never / Smilin' and dyin' / Porkfist / Take a dive / One more stitch. (c-ep+=) *<SP 15A>* – Queen bitch. *(US re-iss. c+cd-lp Jul88 as 'DRY AS A BONE' / 'REHAB DOLL')*

—— MARK ARM formed MUDHONEY

MOTHER LOVE BONE

formed by **AMENT, GOSSARD + FAIRWEATHER** plus **ANDREW WOOD** (b.1966) – vocals (ex-MALFUNKSHUN) / **GARY GILMOUR** – drums

Polydor Stardog

Mar 89. (m-lp) *<839011-2>* **SHINE** [-] [ ]
– Thru fade away / Midshaker meltdown / Halfass monkey boy / Medley:- Chloe dancer / Lady Godiva blues.

Jul 90. (cd/c/lp) *<(843191-2/-4/-1)>* **APPLE** [ ] [ ] Mar90
– This is Shangri-la / Stardog champion / Holy roller / Bone China / Come bite the apple / Stargazer / Heartshine / Captain hi-top / Man of golden words / Mr.Danny boy / Capricorn sister / Crown of thorns. *(above 2 re-iss. cd as 'STAR DOG CHAMPION' Sep92 on 'Polydor'; 514177-2 / <314512 884-2>) (hit US No.77)*

—— ANDREW WOOD died on the 19th March '90 after a heroin overdose. AMENT and GOSSARD paid tribute to him by joining with SOUNDGARDEN ⇒ members in off-shoot outfit TEMPLE OF THE DOG. After this project was finished . . . PEARL JAM were formed

PEARL JAM

AMENT + GOSSARD with **EDDIE VEDDER** (b.23 Dec'66, Evanson, Illinois) – vocals / **MIKE McCREADY** (b. 5 Apr'65) – lead guitar / **DAVE ABBRUZZESE** (b.17 May'??) – drums repl. DAVE KRUZON

Epic Epic

Feb 92. (cd/c/lp/pic-lp) *(468884-2/-4/-1/-0) <47857>* **TEN** [18] [2] Dec91
– Once / Even flow / Alive / Why go / Black / Jeremy / Oceans / Porch / Garden / Deep / Release. *(re-dist.Dec92 yellow-cd+=/m-d; 468884-5/-3)* – Alive (live) / Wash / Dirty Frank. *(lp re-iss. Feb99 on 'Simply Vinyl'; SVLP 68)*

Feb 92. (7"white/c-s) *(657572-7/-4)* **ALIVE. / WASH** [16] [ ]
(12"+=/pic-cd-s+=) *(657572-6/-5)* – Once.

Apr 92. (7"/c-s) *(657857-7/-4)* **EVEN FLOW (remix). / OCEANS** [27] [ ]
(12"white+=/cd-pic-s+=) *(657857-8/-2)* – Dirty Frank.

Sep 92. (7"white/c-s) *(658258-7/-4)* **JEREMY. / ALIVE (live)** [15] [ ]
(12"pic-d+=) *(658258-6)* – Footsteps (live).
(pic-cd-s+=) *(658258-4)* – Yellow Ledbetter.

Oct 93. (cd/c/lp) *(474549-2/-4/-1) <53136>* **VS** [2] [1]
– Go / Animal / Daughter / Glorified G / Dissident / W.M.A. / Blood / Rearviewmirror / Rats / Elderly woman behind the counter in a small town / Leash / Indifference.

Oct 93. (12"ep/cd-ep) *(659795-6/-2)* **GO. / ALONE / ELDERLY WOMAN BEHIND THE COUNTER IN A SMALL TOWN (acoustic)** [ ] [ ]
(free c-s+=) *(659795-4)* – Animal (live).

Dec 93. (7"red/c-s) *(660020-7/-4)* **DAUGHTER. / BLOOD (live)** [18] [ ]
(12"+=/cd-s+=) *(660020-6/-2)* – Yellow ledbetter (live).

May 94. (7"/c-s) *(660441-7/-4)* **DISSIDENT. / REARVIEWMIRROR (live)** [14] [ ]
(cd-s+=) *(660441-2)* – Release / Even flow (versions).
(cd-s) *(660441-5)* – ('A'side) / Deep / Even flow / Why go (versions).

—— ABBRUZZESE departed and was repl. after below album by **JACK IRONS** (ex-RED HOT CHILI PEPPERS)

Nov 94. (7"/c-s/cd-s) *(661036-7/-4/-2) <77771>* **SPIN THE BLACK CIRCLE. / TREMOR CHRIST** [10] [58] [18]

Dec 94. (cd/c/d-lp) *(477861-2/-4/-1) <66900>* **VITALOGY** [6] [1]
– Last exit / Spin the black circle / Not for you / Tremor Christ / Nothingman / Whipping / Pry, to / Corduroy / Bugs / Satan's bed / Better man / Aye davanita / Immortality / Stupid mop.

—— McCREADY now also moonlighted for MAD SEASON (see under ALICE IN CHAINS) – lead singer being LAYNE STALEY. Meanwhile, STONE GOSSARD set up own record label 'Loosegroove' and signed MALFUNKSHUN, DEVILHEAD, WEAPON OF CHOICE, BRAD and PROSE AND CONCEPTS.

Feb 95. (7"colrd/c-s/cd-s) *(661203-7/-4/-2)* **NOT FOR YOU. / OUT OF MY MIND (live)** [34] [-]

Dec 95. (7"/cd-s) *(662716-7/-2) <78199>* **MERKINBALL** [25] [7]
– I got I.D. / Long road.
(above both recorded w/ NEIL YOUNG)

—— Group had already featured on NEIL YOUNG's album 'MIRRORBALL'. GOSSARD featured on THERMIDOR's 1996 album 'Monkey On Rico'.

—— mid-96; JEFF AMENT featured for minor supergroup THREE FISH

Aug 96. (7"/c-s/cd-s) *(663539-7/-4/-2) <78389>* **WHO YOU ARE. / HABIT** [18] [31]

Sep 96. (cd/c/d-lp) *(484448-2/-4/-1) <67500>* **NO CODE** [3] [1]
– Sometimes / Habit / Who you are / In my tree / Smile / Hail hail / I'm open / Red mosquito / Lukin / Mankind / Black & red & yellow / Allnight. *(cd re-iss. Aug00; same)*

Jan 98. (7"/c-s) *(665394-7/-4) <78797>* **GIVEN TO FLY. / PILATE** [12] [21]
(cd-s+=) *(665394-2)* – Leatherman.

Feb 98. (cd/c/lp) *(489365-2/-4/-1) <68164>* **YIELD** [7] [2]
– Brain of J. / Faithfull / No way / Given to fly / Wishlist / Pilate / Do the evolution / • / MFC / Low light / In hiding / Push me, pull me / All those yesterdays.

May 98. (7"/c-s) *(665790-7/-4) <78896>* **WISHLIST. / U** [30] [47]
(cd-s+=) *(665790-2)* – Brain of J. (live).

—— **MATT CAMERON** – drums (ex-SOUNDGARDEN) repl. IRONS

Nov 98. (cd/c/d-lp) *(429859-2/-4/-1) <69752>* **LIVE ON TWO LEGS (live)** [68] [15]
– Corduroy / Given to fly / Hail hail / Daughter / Elderly woman behind the

counter in a small town / Untitled / MFC / Go / Off he goes / Even flow / Red mosquito / Nothingman / Do the evolution / Better man / Black / F*ckin' up.

Aug 99. (7"red/cd-s) *(667479-7/-2)* *<79197>* **LAST KISS. / SOLDIER OF LOVE** 42 2 May99

May 00. (7"blue) *(669374-7)* *<79416>* **NOTHING AS IT SEEMS. / INSIGNIFICANCE** 22 49 Apr00
(cd-s+=) *(669374-2)* – ('A'side) / Better man (live) / Footsteps (live).

May 00. (cd/c/lp) *(494590-2/-4/-1)* *<63665>* **BINAURAL** 5 2
– Breakerfall / God's dice / Evacuation / Light years / Nothing as it seems / Thin air / Insignificance / Of the girl / Grievance / Rival / Sleight of hand / Soon forget / Parting ways.

Jul 00. (7"yellow) *(669628-7)* *<79452>* **LIGHT YEARS. / SOON FORGET (live)** 52
(cd-s+=) *(669628-2)* – Grievance (live).

– others, etc. –

on 'Epic' records unless mentioned otherwise

Jul 95. (cd-ep) *Epic; <77935>* **JEREMY / YELLOW LEDBETTER / FOOTSTEPS** - 79

Jan 96. (cd-ep) *Epic; <77938>* **DAUGHTER / YELLOW LEDBETTER (live) / BLOOD (live)** - 97

Sep 00. (d-cd) *(499623-2)* **LIVE: Palau Sant Jordi, Barcelona, Spain – May 25th, 2000** -

Sep 00. (d-cd) *(499624-2)* **LIVE: Parkbuhne, Wuhlheide, Berlin – June 25th, 2000** -

Sep 00. (d-cd) *(499626-2)* **LIVE: Spodek Arena, Katowice, Poland – June 16th, 2000** -

Sep 00. (d-cd) *(499628-2)* **LIVE: The Point Theater, Dublin, Ireland – June 1st, 2000** -

Sep 00. (d-cd) *(499629-2)* **LIVE: SECC Arena, Glasgow, Scotland – June 3rd, 2000** -

Sep 00. (d-cd) *(499630-2)* **LIVE: Sporthalle, Hamburg, Germany – June 26th, 2000** -

Sep 00. (d-cd) *(499631-2)* **LIVE: Spodek Arena, Katowice, Poland – June 15th, 2000** -

Sep 00. (d-cd) *(499632-2)* **LIVE: International Arena, Cardiff, Wales – June 6th, 2000** -

Sep 00. (d-cd) *(499633-2)* **LIVE: Rock Am Ring Eifel, Nurberg, Germany – June 9th, 2000** -

Sep 00. (d-cd) *(499634-2)* **LIVE: Estadio Do Restelo, Lisbon, Portugal – May 23rd, 2000** -

Sep 00. (d-cd) *(499635-2)* **LIVE: Hala Tivoli, Llubljana, Slovenia – June 19th, 2000** -

Sep 00. (d-cd) *(499636-2)* **LIVE: Wembley Arena, London, England – May 29th, 2000** -

Sep 00. (d-cd) *(499637-2)* **LIVE: Wembley Arena, London, England – May 30th, 2000** -

Sep 00. (d-cd) *(499638-2)* **LIVE: Pinkpop, Heerden, Holland – June 12th, 2000** -

Sep 00. (d-cd) *(499639-2)* **LIVE: Evening News Arena, Manchester, England – June 4th, 2000** -

Sep 00. (d-cd) *(499640-2)* **LIVE: FILA Forum, Milan, Italy – June 22nd, 2000** -

Sep 00. (d-cd) *(499641-2)* **LIVE: Rock In Park, Nurnberg, Germany – June 11th, 2000** -

Sep 00. (d-cd) *(499642-2)* **LIVE: Spectrum, Oslo, Norway – June 29th, 2000** -

Sep 00. (d-cd) *(499643-2)* **LIVE: Paegas Arena, Prague, Czechoslavakia – June 14th, 2000** -

Sep 00. (d-cd) *(499644-2)* **LIVE: Bercy, Paris, France – June 8th, 2000** -

Sep 00. (d-cd) *(499646-2)* **LIVE: City Square, Salzburg, Austria – June 18th, 2000** -

Sep 00. (d-cd) *(499647-2)* **LIVE: Velodromo Anaeta, San Sebastian, Spain – May 26th, 2000** -

Sep 00. (d-cd) *(499648-2)* **LIVE: Naval Museum, Stockholm, Sweden – June 28th, 2000** -

Sep 00. (d-cd) *(499649-2)* **LIVE: Arena, Verona, Italy – June 20th, 2000** -

Sep 00. (d-cd) *(499650-2)* **LIVE: Hallenstadion, Zurich, Switzerland – June 23rd, 2000** -

Feb 01. (d-cd) *(501989-2)* *<E2K 85551>* *LIVE: Boston, Massachusetts Vol.1 – August 29th, 2000*

Feb 01. (d-cd) *(501990-2)* *<E2K 85545>* **LIVE: Jones Beach, New York, Vol.3 – August 25th, 2000**

Feb 01. (d-cd) *(501991-2)* *<E2K 85542>* **LIVE: Jones Beach, New York, Vol.2 – August 24th, 2000**

Feb 01. (d-cd) *(501992-2)* *<E2K 85536>* **LIVE: Columbus, Ohio – August 21st, 2000**

Feb 01. (d-cd) *(501993-2)* *<E2K 85518>* **LIVE: Tampa, Florida – August 12th, 2000**

Feb 01. (d-cd) *(501994-2)* *<E2K 85509>* **LIVE: Atlanta, Georgia – August 7th, 2000**

Mar 01. (d-cd) *<(E2K 85208)>* **LIVE: Virginia Beach, Virginia – August 3rd, 2000**

Mar 01. (d-cd) *<(E2K 85503)>* **LIVE: Charlotte, North Carolina – August 4th, 2000**

Mar 01. (d-cd) *<(E2K 85506)>* **LIVE: Greensboro, North Carolina – August 6th, 2000**

Mar 01. (d-cd) *<(E2K 85512)>* **LIVE: West Palm Beach, Florida. Vol.1 – August 9th, 2000**

Mar 01. (d-cd) *<(E2K 85515)>* **LIVE: West Palm Beach, Florida, Vol.2 – August 10th, 2000**

Mar 01. (d-cd) *<(E2K 85521)>* **LIVE: New Orleans, Louisiana – August 14th, 2000**

Mar 01. (d-cd) *<(E2K 85524)>* **LIVE: Memphis, Tennessee – August 15th, 2000**

Mar 01. (d-cd) *<(E2K 85527)>* **LIVE: Nashville, Tennessee – August 17th, 2000**

Mar 01. (d-cd) *<(E2K 85530)>* **LIVE: Indianapolis, Indiana – August 18th, 2000**

Mar 01. (d-cd) *<(E2K 85533)>* **LIVE: Cincinatti, Ohio – August 20th, 2000**

Mar 01. (d-cd) *<(E2K 85539)>* **LIVE: Jones Beach, New York, Vol.1 – August 23rd, 2000**

Mar 01. (d-cd) *<(E2K 85548)>* **LIVE: Saratoga, New York – August 27th, 2000**

Mar 01. (d-cd) *<(E2K 85554)>* **LIVE: Boston, Massachusetts Vol.2 – August 30th, 2000**

Mar 01. (d-cd) *<(E2K 85557)>* **LIVE: Philadelphia, Pennsylvania, Vol.1 – September 1st, 2000**

Mar 01. (d-cd) *<(E2K 85560)>* **LIVE: Philadelphia, Pennsylvania, Vol.2 – September 2nd, 2000**

Mar 01. (d-cd) *<(E2K 85563)>* **LIVE: Washington DC – September 4th, 2000**

Mar 01. (d-cd) *<(E2K 85566)>* **LIVE: Pittsburgh, Pennsylvania – September 5th, 2000**

Mar 01. (d-cd) *<(E2K 85572)>* **LIVE: Toronto, Canada – October 5th, 2000**

Mar 01. (d-cd) *<(E2K 85599)>* **LIVE: Dallas, Texas – October 17th, 2000**

Mar 01. (cd) *(502165-2)* *<E2K 85575>* **LIVE: Detroit, Michigan – October 7th, 2000**

Mar 01. (cd) *(502166-2)* *<E2K 85581>* **LIVE: Chicago, Illinois – October 9th, 2000**

Mar 01. (cd) *(502167-2)* *<E2K 85611>* **LIVE: Las Vegas, Nevada (10th Anniversary Show) – October 22nd, 2000**

Mar 01. (cd) *(502168-2)* *<E2K 85617>* **LIVE: San Diego, California – October 25th, 2000**

Mar 01. (cd) *(502169-2)* *<E2K 85635>* **LIVE: Boise, Idaho – November 3rd, 2000**

Mar 01. (t-cd) *(502170-2)* *<E2K 85641>* **Seattle, Washington – 6th November, 2000**

Apr 01. (cd) *<(E2K 85569)>* **LIVE: Montreal, Canada – October 4th, 2000**

Apr 01. (cd) *<(E2K 85578)>* **LIVE: East Troy, Wisconsin – October 8th, 2000**

Apr 01. (cd) *<(E2K 85584)>* **LIVE: St. Louis, Missouri – October 11th, 2000**

Apr 01. (cd) *<(E2K 85587)>* **LIVE: Kansas City, Missouri – October 12th, 2000**

Apr 01. (cd) *<(E2K 85590)>* **LIVE: Houston, Texas, Vol.1 – October 14th, 2000**

Apr 01. (cd) *<(E2K 85593)>* **LIVE: Houston, Texas, Vol.2 – October 15th, 2000**

Apr 01. (cd) *<(E2K 85602)>* **Lubbock, Texas – October 18th, 2000**

Apr 01. (cd) *<(E2K 85608)>* **LIVE: Phoenix, Arizona – October 21st, 2000**

Apr 01. (cd) *<(E2K 85614)>* **LIVE: Los Angeles, California – October 24th, 2000**

Apr 01. (cd) *<(E2K 85620)>* **LIVE: Fresno, California – October 27th, 2000**

Apr 01. (cd) *<(E2K 85623)>* **LIVE: San Bernadino, California – October 28th, 2000**

Apr 01. (cd) *<(E2K 85623)>* **LIVE: Sacramento, California – October 30th, 2000**

Apr 01. (cd) *<(E2K 85629)>* **LIVE: San Francisco, California – October 31st, 2000**

Apr 01. (cd) *<(E2K 85632)>* **LIVE: Portland, Oregon – November 2nd, 2000**

Apr 01. (cd) *<(E2K 85638)>* **LIVE: Seattle, Washington – November 5th, 2000**

Apr 01. (d-cd) *<(E2K 85805)>* **LIVE: Albuquerque, New Mexico – October 20th, 2000**

THREE FISH

JEFF AMENT – vocals, bass / **ROBBI ROBB** – vocals, guitar (of TRIBE AFTER TRIBE) / **RICHARD STUVERUD** – drums (of FASTBACKS)

Epic Epic

Jun 96. (cd/c/d-lp) *(484118-2/-4/-1)* *<67652>* **THREE FISH**
– Solitude / Song for a dead girl / Silence at the bottom / Intellgent fish / Zagreb / All messed up / Here in the darkness / Hall of intelligent fish / Strangers in my head / Lovely meander / Elusive ones / Build / Stupid fish / A secret place / Laced. *(d-lp+=)* – If miles were alive / Can I come along / Easy way.

Sep 96. (cd-s) **LACED / CAN I COME ALONG? / IF MILES WERE ALIVE . . .**

Jun 99. (cd/c) *<69964>* **QUIET TABLE** -
– Shiva and the astronaut / Tremor void / Myth of Abdou / Once in a day / All these things / Timeless / Hummingbird / My only foe / Transporting / Found a widow / Resonate / Chantreuse.

PEECHEES

Formed: San Francisco, California, USA . . . mid-90's by the cosmopolitan line-up of CHRISTOPHER APPELGREN, CARLOS CANEDO, ROP VASQUEZ and ex-BRATMOBILE stickperson MOLLY NEUMAN. The general critical concensus on these shambolic art-punks was that their shortfall in musicality and originality redeemed itself with attitude aplenty and a healthy irreverence. Over a brace of 7" singles, mainly for the 'Kill Rock Stars' label, The PEECHEES proved that their ebullient racket was ripe for the picking while 'DO THE MATH' (1996), 'GAMES PEOPLE PLAY' (1997) and 'LIFE' (1999) all sneered with abandon.

Album rating: DO THE MATH (*5) / GAMES PEOPLE PLAY (*4) / LIFE compilation (*5)

CHRISTOPHER APPELGREN (b. Kansas City, Missouri) – vocals / **CARLOS CANEDO** (b. Culiacan, Sinaloa) – guitar / **ROP VASQUEZ** (b. Metro Manila, Philippines) – bass / **MOLLY NEUMAN** (b. Washington, D.C.) – drums

Kill Rock Stars / Kill Rock Stars

Jan 96. (lp/cd) *<KRS 255/+CD>* **DO THE MATH** [-] [ ]
– Pepper / Do the math / I could have loved you / Mad doctor / On with Guayabera / Cloud fantasy / Cloud frenzy / Beer city / I don't know too / Tired imagery / Fascist lawn / Slick's living it up (on the bottom . . ..) / Animal.

Mar 97. (7"ep) *(DUMP 041)* **LOVE MOODS** [ ] [-]
(above issued on 'Rugger Bugger')

Sep 97. (lp/cd) *<(KRS 285/+CD)>* **GAMES PEOPLE PLAY** [ ] [ ] Aug97
– Invitation / Antarticists / Lose the motorcade (and live it up) / Right reasons / One for the treble / To be counted / Everybody / Quadruple bypass / New Moscow woman / Can we check in? / Two for the bass / Restart / Return of the rock'n'roll nurse / Feel free / Brass tinsel.

Dec 97. (7") *(ROX 002)* **ANTARTICISTS. / LOVE IS THE LAW** [ ] [-]
(above issued on 'Roxy', below on 'Damaged Goods')

Jul 98. (7") *(DAMGOOD 152)* **SING LIKE ME. / (other track by ELLIOT SMITH)** [ ] [-]

Jan 99. (cd) *<(KRS 315)>* **LIFE** (singles compilation) [ ] [ ]
– Cheap fun / Fine watch / Grease / Patty Coahuila / Genuine article / Tea biscuit to show / Olive oil / Tomfoolery / Maintenance free / Modern soul / New Moscow woman / Quadruple bypass / Well worth talkin' about / You are not / Other ice age / Love is the law / Sing like me / No heart. *(lp-iss.Feb99 on 'Damaged Goods'; DAMGOOD 160LP)*

— disbanded some time in '99

Axel Rudi PELL (see under ⇒ STEELER)

PENNYWISE

Formed: Hermosa Beach, California, USA . . . 1988 by JIM LINDBERG, FLETCHER DRAGGE, JASON THIRSK and BYRON McMACKIN. Yet another band in the mould of OFFSPRING and GREEN DAY to sign to Brett Gurewitz's 'Epitaph' imprint, JIM and Co had obviously grown up listening to both the sounds of Bay Area thrash and classic US hardcore, as evidenced on their eponymous 1991 debut for the label; in 1989 the band had issued the very rare 'A WORD FROM THE WISE'. PENNYWISE finally came to prominence after the Americans finally discovered punk in the mid 90's, cracking the US Top 100 with 'ABOUT TIME' (1995). Tragically, a year after its completion, bass player THIRSK was to meet an untimely death (it is believing he accidently shot himself after a drinking binge), leaving the band very much down but not out. With new man RANDY BRADBURY on board, PENNYWISE scored an even bigger success with their fourth set, 'FULL CIRCLE' (1997); full circle right enough, as we in Britain had been listening to this stuff for the past two decades! 'STRAIGHT AHEAD' in 1999, was basically just that, although the fans would've been impressed as ever.

Album rating: PENNYWISE (*5) / UNKNOWN ROAD (*5) / ABOUT TIME (*5) / FULL CIRCLE (*5) / STRAIGHT AHEAD (*6) / LIVE AT THE KEY CLUB (*4)

JIM LINDBERG – vocals / **FLETCHER DRAGGE** – guitar / **JASON THIRSK** (b.1967) – bass / **BYRON McMACKIN** – drums

not iss. / Thelogian

1989. (lp) *<3>* **A WORD FROM THE WISE** [-] [ ]
– Final chapter / Covers / Depression / No way out / Gone / Wildcard / Maybes / Stand by me.

Epitaph / Epitaph

Oct 91. (cd/c/lp) *<(E 86412-2X/-4X/-1X)>* **PENNYWISE** [ ] [ ]
– Wouldn't it be nice / Rules / Secret / Living for today / Come out fighting / Homeless / Open door / Pennywise / Who's to blame / Fun and games / Kodiak / Side one / No reason why / Bro hymn.

Aug 93. (cd/c/lp) *<(E 86429-2/-4/-1)>* **UNKNOWN ROAD** [ ] [ ]
– Unknown road / Homesick / Time to burn / It's up to me / You can demand / Nothing / Vices / The city is burning / Dying to know / Tester / Try to conform / Give and get / Clear your mind.

May 95. (7"ep) *(T 002)* **WILD CARD EP** [ ] [-]
(above on 'Semaphore')

Jun 95. (cd/c/lp) *<(E 86437-2/-4/-1)>* **ABOUT TIME** [ ] [96]
– Peaceful day / Waste of time / Perfect people / Every single day / Searching / Not far away / Freebase / It's what you do with it / Try / Same old story / I won't have it / Killing time.
(below on 'Out Of Step')

Sep 95. (7") *(WOOS 7S)* **SAME OLD STORY. /** [ ] [ ]
(cd-s+=) *(WOOS 7CDS)* –

— **RANDY BRADBURY** – bass; repl. JASON who died in 1996

Apr 97. (cd/c/lp) *<(86489-2/-4/-1)>* **FULL CIRCLE** [ ] [79]
– Fight till you die / Date with destiny / Get a life / Society / Final day / Broken / Running out of time / You'll never make it / Every time / Nowhere fast / What if I / Go away / Did you really / Bro hymn tribute.

May 99. (cd/c/lp) *<(86553-2/-4/-1)>* **STRAIGHT AHEAD** [ ] [62]
– I need more / Straight ahead / Victim of reality / Can't believe it / Might be a dream / Greed / My way / One voice / American dream / Just for you / Alien / Still can be great / Watch me as I fall / Can't take anymore / Never know / Badge of pride.

Mar 00. (cd-s) **VICTIM OF REALITY** [ ] [-]

Oct 00. (cd/lp) *<(6598-2/-1)>* **LIVE AT THE KEY CLUB (live)** [ ] [ ]
– Unknown road (intro) / Wouldn't it be nice / Living for today / Final chapters / Can't believe it / Unknown road / Homesick / No reason why / Fight till you die / Peaceful day / Society / Straight ahead / Pennywise / Perfect people / Minor threat / Same old story / Alien / Bro hymn.

Jun 01. (cd) *<86600>* **LAND OF THE FREE** [-] [67]

– others, etc. –

all issued on 'Thelogian'

Jun 95. (cd) *<(TF 003CD)>* **WILDCARD / A WORD FROM THE WISE** [ ] [ ] 1992

Jul 95. (7") *(RE 001)* **TOMORROW. / DON'T FEEL NOTHING** [ ] [ ]
(re-iss. Apr97; TPW 02)

Apr 97. (7") *(TPW 01)* **A WORD FROM THE WISE. /** [ ] [ ]

PENTAGRAM

Formed: Virginia, USA . . . 1978 by BOBBY LEIBLING and JOE HASSELVANDER. Struggling for years to find a record deal, prototype black metallers PENTAGRAM eventually decided to self-finance their eponymous 1985 debut album. By this point HASSELVANDER had departed the group, although he did appear on the album alongside VICTOR GRIFFIN and MARTIN SWANEY. Replacing him with STUART ROSE, the band recorded a follow-up set for the 'Firebird' label entitled 'DAY OF RECKONING' (1987). Never managing to attract more than a cult following, PENTAGRAM finally called it a day towards the end of the decade. The 90's brought a new twist to the story, however, as gothic/death-metal label, 'Peaceville', acquired the slim PENTAGRAM catalogue and proceeded to release both albums. This renewed interest inspired LIEBLING to reform the band with the same line-up, subsequently releasing an album's worth of new material in 1995, 'BE FOREWARNED'.

Album rating: PENTAGRAM (*6) / DAY OF RECKONING (*7) / BE FOREWARNED (*6) / REVIEW YOUR CHOICES compilation (*6)

BOBBY LIEBLING – vocals / **VICTOR GRIFFIN** – guitar, keyboards / **MARTIN SWANEY** – bass / **JOE HASSELVANDER** – drums

Pentagram / Pentagram

Jul 85. (lp) *<(DEVIL 4)>* **PENTAGRAM** [ ] [ ]
– Death row / All your sins / Sign of the wolf / The ghoul / Relentless / Run my course / Sinister / The deist / You're lost I'm free / Dying world / 20 buck skin. *(re-iss. Apr93 as 'RELENTLESS' on 'Peaceville' lp/cd; VILE 038/+CD)*

— **STUART ROSE** – drums (on most); repl. HASSELVANDER (to RAVEN)

Firebird / Firebird

Jun 87. (lp) *<(FLAME 6)>* **DAY OF RECKONING** [ ] [ ]
– Day of reckoning / Evil seed / Broken vows / When the screams come / Burning saviour / Madman / Wartime. *(re-iss. Aug93 on 'Peaceville' lp/cd; VILE 040/+CD) (cd re-iss. May95 +=; CDVILE 40)* – RELENTLESS (tracks)

— split in 1990, although the originals reformed in '93

Peaceville / Fierce

Mar 95. (cd/lp) *(CD+/VILE 42) <11069>* **BE FOREWARNED** [ ] [ ]
– Live free and burn / Too late / Ask no more / The world will love again / Vampyre love / Life blood / Wolf's blood / Frustration / Bride of evil / Nightmare gown / Petrified / A timeless heart / Be forewarned.

— a different group released 'Trail Blazer' for 'Nuclear Blast'

Century Media / Century Media

May 98. (cd) *<(CM 77218CD)>* **ANATOLIA** [ ] [ ]

– compilations, etc. –

Jul 99. (cd) *Black Widow; (BWRCD 31)* **REVIEW YOUR CHOICES** [ ] [ ]
– Burning rays / Change of heart / Living in a ram's head / Gorgon's slave / Review your choices / Diver / Bees / I am vengeance / Forever my queen / Mow you down / Downhill slope / Megalania / Gilla.

PENTHOUSE

Formed: Camden, London, England . . . mid 90's by CHARLIE FINKE, JON FREE, GRAEME FLYNN and TIM CEDAR. What the 'STONES might've sounded like had they been born twenty, thirty, or even forty (!) years later, PENTHOUSE traded in a similar scabby vein of dirty, distorted blues as JON SPENCER, if a bit more lascivious. After the release of two independent 45's, 'RIPPED 'N' HAPPY' and 'GAS PORTER BLUES', they signed to 'World Domination', releasing their debut album, 'GUTTER EROTICA', in 1997. From the devilish sleaze of the cover art to the explicit nature of the lyrics, especially opening track/single, 'VOYEUR'S BLUES', the record was the aural equivalent of Soho at its seediest.

Album rating: GUTTER EROTICA (*6)

CHARLIE FINKE – vocals, mouth harp / **JON FREE** – guitar / **GRAEME FLYNN** – bass / **TIM CEDAR** – drums

Kitty Kitty Corporation / not iss.

Nov 95. (7") *(CHOOSY 002)* **RIPPED 'N' HAPPY. / BABY PEELER** [ ] [-]

Apr 96. (7") *(CHOOSY 003)* **GAS PORTER BLUES. / STUNG TRUNKS** [ ] [-]

Syrup / not iss.

Jul 96. (ltd.7") *(SYRUP 001)* **LE STUNT. / Country Teasers: GETAWAY** [ ] [-]

World Domination / Beggars Banquet

Apr 97. (7") *(WDOM 33S)* **VOYEUR'S BLUES. / PLATE OF SLAGS** [ ] [-]
(cd-s+=) *(WDOM 33SCD)* – Le stunt / Tongue Kung Fu.

May 97. (lp/cd) *(WDOM 34/+CD) <80206>* **GUTTER EROTICA** [ ] [ ] Nov98
– Voyeur's blues / Gus' neck / La grotte d'amour / Road rash / The beauty in the beast / A deviant soiree / Harmonic surf spastic / Widow's chagrin / Mare Ingram's

lament / The gin waltz / White coal / Lap dog shuffle / Face down. *(re-iss. Apr98; same) (cd re-iss. Oct98 on 'Beggars Banquet'; BBQMCD 206)*

Nov 97. (cd-ep) *(CRH 00009)* **RECKS EP**
– Baby pealer / Ript'n'happy / Gas porter blues / Strung trunks / Queen of sex / Behemoth.
(above single on 'Carcrashh') *(re-iss. Jan99; CCRASH 004)*

Apr 98. (12"ep/cd-ep) *(PENT 001 T/CD)* **REMIX EP**
– White coal / Voyeur's blues / Road rash / Lap dog shuffle.

Beggars Banquet not iss.

Nov 98. (7") *(BBQ 331)* **VALLEY OF THE SOWS. / INSIDE SLICK**
(cd-s+=) *(BBQ 331CD)* – What meanders.

Jun 99. (cd/lp) *(BBQ CD/LP 211)* **MY IDLE HANDS**
– Creeper's reef / Valley of the sows / Man o' fire / Detunabilly / Petit song / The fool at blood gulley / Head of the wake / Giant haystacks / Nudie Ron / Lil' brown kisses / Beautiful be the indolent / Wot meanders / The 49th ton.

Butcher's Wig not iss.

Nov 00. (7") *(SYRUP 009)* **WHITE SLAVE SPEAKS. / NIGHT JAR**

Joe PERRY PROJECT (see under ⇒ AEROSMITH)

Steve PERRY (see under ⇒ JOURNEY)

PESTILENCE

Formed: Holland . . . 1986 by guitarists RANDY MEINHARD and PATRICK MAMELI, who recruited MARTIN VAN DRUNEN and MARCO FODDIS. Signed to 'Roadrunner', the group attempted to establish themselves in the fertile German thrash scene with a tentative debut album, 'MALLEVS MALEFICARUM' (1988). With MEINHARD subsequently departing to form SACROSANCT, PATRICK UTERWIJK was recruited in time to record the 'CONSUMING IMPULSE' (1989) set, a markedly improved effort which saw the group gaining increasing recognition in death-metal circles. PESTILENCE were dealt another blow, however, when VAN DRUNEN initiated his own outift, ASPHYX. MAMELI extended his talents to the vacant lead vocal spot for two further albums, 'TESTIMONY OF THE ANCIENTS' (1991) and 'SPHERES' (1993), the band finally calling it a day towards the middle of the decade.

Album rating: MALLEVS MALEFICARUM (*4) / CONSUMING IMPULSE (*6) / TESTIMONY OF THE ANCIENTS (*4) / SPHERES (*5)

MARTIN VAN DRUNEN – vocals, bass / **RANDY MEINHARD** – guitar / **PATRICK MAMELI** – guitar / **MARCO FODDIS** – drums

Roadunner not iss.

Oct 88. (lp/cd) *(RR 9519-1/-2)* **MALLEVS MALEFICARUM**
– Mallevs maleficarum / Subordinate to the domination / Commandments / Bacterial surgery / Osculum inflame / Parricade / Extreme junction / Chemo therapy / Cycle of existence / Systematic instruction. *(cd re-iss. Nov98 on 'Displeased'+=; D 00061CD)* – DEMOS

— **PATRICK UTERWIJK** – guitar (ex-THERIAC) repl. MEINHARD

Roadracer S.P.V.

Dec 89. (lp/c/cd) *(RO 9421-1/-4/-2)* <842319> **CONSUMING IMPULSE**
– Dehydrated / The process of suffocation / Suspended animation / The trauma / Chronic infection / Out of the body / Echoes of death / Defy thy master / Proliferous souls / Reduced to ashes.

— VAN DRUNEN left to form his own outfit, ASPHYX

— MAMELI now on lead vocals & guitar

R.C. R.C.

Sep 91. (cd/c/lp) <*(RC 9285-2/-4/-1)*> **TESTIMONY OF THE ANCIENTS**
– Secrecies of horror / Bitterness / Twisted truth / Darkening / Lost souls / Blood / Land of tears / Free us from temptation / Prophetic revelations / Impure / Testimony / Soulless / Presence of the dead / Mindwarp / Stigmatized / In sorrow.

Roadrunner Roadrunner

Aug 93. (cd/c/lp) <*(RR 9081-2/-4/-1)*> **SPHERES**
– Mind reflections / Multiple beings / Level of perception / Aurian eyes / Soul search / Personal energy / Voices from within / Spheres / Changing perspective / Phileas / Demise of time.

— split early in 1994 after being dropped by their label

PETER & THE TEST-TUBE BABIES

Formed: Brighton, England . . . 1978 by PETER BYWATERS, DEREK GREENING, CHRIS MARCHANT and NICHOLAS LOIZIDES. Initially making an appearance with the track 'ELVIS IS DEAD' on 1978's 'Vaultage' compilation – released on local label, Attrix' – PETER and his cronies later surfaced as in-house jesters for the court of Oi!, releasing the self explanatory 'BANNED FROM THE PUBS' on the 'No Future' label in 1982. This was quickly followed by another synapse-shattering commentary, 'RUN LIKE HELL', detailing the trials of trying to chat up the "skirt" down the local disco. Subsequently setting up their own 'Trapper' label, the band released a further two slabs of yobbish three-chord aggro in 'ZOMBIE CREEPING FLESH' and 'THE JINX' prior to a full length debut album, 'THE MATING SOUNDS OF SOUTH AMERICAN FROGS' (1983). Just to make sure people got the message, 'PISSED AND PROUD' emerged as the second full length release of the year, while 'Hairy Pie' served as a vehicle for the cassette-only 'JOURNEY TO THE CENTRE OF JOHNNY CLARKE'S HEAD' (1984) and live set, 'ANOTHER NOISY, LOUD, BLARING PUNK ROCK LP' (1985). The mid-80's also saw the release of the 'ROTTING IN THE FARTSACK' EP, presumably how the boys occupied their time until 1990's assassination of STOCK, AITKEN & WATERMAN songs (artists; Kylie, Jason, Rick, Sinita, et all; yuk!) on the album, 'THE SHIT FACTORY – PLAY . . .'. An erm, pivotal influence on the feminist baiting likes of The MACC LADS, PETER & THE TEST TUBE BABIES could only have been a product of the 80's.
• **Songwriters:** BYWATERS / GREENING except a few covers; LEADER OF THE GANG (Gary Glitter).

Album rating: THE MATING SOUNDS OF SOUTH AMERICAN FROGS (*5) / PISSED AND PROUD compilation (*5) / JOURNEY TO THE CENTRE OF JOHNNY CLARKE'S HEAD (*4) / ANOTHER NOISY, LOUD, BLARING PUNK ROCK LP (*5) / 3x45 (*4) / SOBERPHOBIA (*5) / THE BEST OF . . . compilation (*6) / CRINGE (*4) / ALIEN PUBDUCTION (*4)

PETER BYWATERS – vocals / **DEREK 'Greenback' GREENING** – guitar / **CHRIS 'Trapper' MARCHANT** – bass / **NICHOLAS 'Ogs' LOIZIDES** – drums

No Future not iss.

Jan 82. (7"m) *(OI 14)* **BANNED FROM THE PUB. / MOPED LADS / PEACEHAVEN WILD LADS**

Jul 82. (7") *(OI 15)* **RUN LIKE HELL. / UP YER BUM**

Trapper not iss.

Mar 83. (7"m/12"m) *(EARS/12EARS 1)* **ZOMBIE CREEPING FLESH. / NO INVITATION / SMASH AND GRAB**

Sep 83. (7"/12") *(EARS/12EARS 2)* **THE JINX. / TRAPPER AIN'T GOT A BIRD**

Nov 83. (lp) *(THIN 1)* **THE MATING SOUNDS OF SOUTH AMERICAN FROGS**
– September (part 1) / Guest list / One night stand / Let's burn / The jinx / Blown out again / Easter Bank Holiday / No invitation / Pissed punks (go for it) / Never made it / September (part 2). *<US cd-iss. 1997 on 'Dr.Strange'; 56>*

Mar 84. (12"ep) *(EARFIT 1)* **PRESSED FOR CASH / BLOWN OUT AGAIN (blender version). / (FITS: Peace and quiet but never dreamed it was going to be like this)**

Og & Dells not iss.

Sep 84. (c) *(OD 1)* **JOURNEY TO THE CENTRE OF JOHNNY CLARKE'S HEAD**
– The journey begins / Who the hell is jolly / What's up with Trapper records / Go for it (live) / Banned from the pubs (live) / From the heart / T.Q.G.G.B.J.'s (demo) / Go to the garage mate / The golden voice beckons you / Elvis is dead (live) / Wimpy's are shit (studio) / Reggae meets le punk movement / Tupperware party (demo) / Skin one up Ralph / Keep Britain untidy (demo) / Who the hell is jolly (part 2) / I lust for the disgusting things in life (demo) / All about love (rare demo) / Time to go home. *(cd-iss. Oct94 on 'Dojo'; DOJO 80CD) (cd re-iss. May95 on 'We Bite'; WB 3124-2) <US cd-iss. 1997 on 'Dr.Strange'; 57>*

Jungle not iss.

May 85. (12"white-ep) *(JUNG 21T)* **ROTTING IN THE FART-SACK**
(cd-ep-iss.May95 on 'We Bite'; WB 3127)

Hairy Pie not iss.

May 85. (lp) *(HP 1)* **ANOTHER NOISY, LOUD, BLARING PUNK ROCK LP**
(cd-iss. Oct94 on 'Dojo'; DOJO 67)

May 86. (7") *(TTB 1)* **KEYS TO THE CITY. / KEITH MOON**
(12"+=) *(TTB 12-1)* – Work hard.

Trapper not iss.

Oct 85. (lp) *(NO FEARS 1)* **3 X 45**

Dec 85. (7") *(EARS 3)* **WHIMPEEZ. / NEVER MADE IT**

Hairy Pie not iss.

Oct 86. (lp) *(HP 2)* **SOBERPHOBIA**
– Key to the city / Louise Wouldn't like it / Spirit of Keith Coleman / Allergic to life / All about love / He's on the whiskey (watch out) / Boozanza / Everytime I see her / Ghost in the bedsit / Every second counts. *(re-iss. Feb87 on 'Dojo'; DOJOLP 49) (cd-iss. May95 on 'We Bite'; 3128-2)*

A.B.T. not iss.

Nov 90. (cd/c/lp) **THE SHIT FACTORY (. . .PLAY STOCK, AITKEN AND WATERMAN)**
– I just can't wait / Toy boy / Nothings gonna stop us now / F.L.M. / I'd rather jack / When I fall in love / Love in the first degree / The harder I try / Hand on your heart / Venus / Especially for you / Never gonna give you up / Too many broken hearts / Who's leaving who.

Rebel not iss.

1991. (cd/c/lp) *(SPV 0843001-2/-4/-1)* **CRINGE**
– Cringe / Shit British tour / The gardener / Launch 'em now / Reality calling / The man who did nothing / Weekend warrior / V.D.U. head / Shit it all / There's a penis in my shoulder / Tuinal shuffle / Goodbye forever / Latent psychosis. *(re-iss. cd Mar96; same)*

We Bite Dr.Strange

Jan 96. (cd/lp) *(WB 1139-2/-1)* <55> **SUPERMODELS** Mar97
– Supermodels / Giving up drinking / Shake my world / Mr. Mortgage / U bore me / Temptation / Jetsetter / Love is dead / Crying in the snow / Dog society / Chasing shadows / Bad loser / Let's do lunch / Spacecake / Busy doing nothing.

We Bite Pub City Royal

Jan 98. (cd/lp) *(WB 1176 CD/LP)* <6> **ALIEN PUBDUCTION** Nov98
– Sour grapes / Early grave / 1.4.7.1 / I'm getting pissed for Christmas / Troublemakers / Talk show / Why bother? / Bloody Mary / Big disappointment / Long way from home / Meet you at the all night offy / Nutter / All in her head / Legless / Twenty years / Alien pubduction.

– compilations, etc. –

Dec 83. (lp/c) *No Future; (PUNK/CPUNK 3)* **PISSED AND PROUD**
– Moped lads / Banned from the pubs / Elvis is dead / Up yer bum / Smash and grab raid / Run like hell / Shit stirrer / Intensive care / Keep Britain untidy / Transvestite / Maniac / Disco / Leader of the gang (I am). *(cd-iss. Jul89 & Jun93; CDPUNK 3) <US cd-iss. Jun94 on 'Century Media'; 7768>*

Aug 88. (lp/cd) *Dojo; (DOJO LP/CD 57)* **THE BEST OF PETER & THE TEST-TUBE BABIES**

Jan 92. (cd) *; (AMO 7(?)* **TOTALLY TEST TUBED** – –
(re-iss. May95 on 'We Bite'; WB 3126-2)
May 95. (cd) *We Bite; (WB 3127-2)* **TEN DEADLY SINS** –
Oct 95. (cd) *Anagram; (CDPUNK 64)* **THE PUNK SINGLES COLLECTION** –
Mar 97. (cd) *Dr.Strange; <58>* **TEST TUBE TRASH** –

PETRA

Formed: Fort Wayne, Indiana, USA . . . 1972 by Christian rockers GREG VOLZ and BOB HARTMAN, who enlisted the help of rhythm section JOHN DeGROFF and BILL GLOVER. Signing to 'A&M', this veteran Christian rock band began their vinyl crusade in 1974 with the eponymous 'PETRA' album. Playing earthy, melodic hard rock, the band's fanbase increased as the decade wore on, despite the fact they parted with their label and downgraded to the smaller religious imprint 'Star Song'. There were also major personnel changes around this time with JOHN SLICK, MARK KELLY and KEITH EDWARDS replacing McELYEA, DeGROFF and GLOVER respectively prior to the 1979 release of the 'WASHES WHITER THAN SNOW' album. More line-up changes followed as LOUIE WEAVER replaced EDWARDS on the 'NEVER SAY DIE' album, PETRA entering the most successful period of their career with the likes of 'MORE POWER TO YA' and 'NOT OF THIS WORLD' (1983). In 1984, the group's popularity was confirmed when they were listed in the US publication, 'Performance', as one of the country's most profitable live draws. Throughout the latter half of the 80's, the band's style grew progressively harder in keeping with the general mood of the times, although they could never quite cross over into the charts. Their religious message was as strong as ever, though, the defiant 'THIS MEANS WAR!' (1987) showing PETRA pitting their wits against the ever present dark forces. Perhaps it was these self same forces behind the band's consistent instability, JOHN SCHLITT replacing VOLZ prior to the the latter set, while JOHN LAWRY and RONNIE CATES were recruited in place of SLICK and KELLY respectively with the 'ON FIRE' (1988) set. PETRA kept up fighting the good fight throughout the 90's although not as prolific as they once were, 'NO DOUBT' (1995) – with newcomers DAVID LICHENS on guitar and JIM COOPER on keys – being their penultimate release; their finale set came via 1998's 'GOD FIXATION'. An obvious influence on many Christian metal bands, especially the likes of STRYPER etc., PETRA have nevertheless unfortunately failed to make the same impact as some of their more Satanically-inclined brethren.

Album rating: PETRA (*3) / COME AND JOIN US (*4) / WASHES WHITER THAN SNOW (*4) / NEVER SAY DIE (*5) / MORE POWER TO YA (*5) / NOT OF THIS WORLD (*6) / BEAT THE SYSTEM (*6) / CAPTURED IN TIME AND PLACE (*5) / BACK TO THE STREET (*5) / THIS MEANS WAR! (*5) / ON FIRE (*5) / PETRA MEANS ROCK compilation (*6) / PETRA PRAISE – THE ROCK CRIES (*5) / BEYOND BELIEF (*5) / UNSEEN POWER (*6) / NO DOUBT (*6) / WE NEED JESUS (*5) / GOD FIXATION (*4)

GREG X VOLZ – vocals, guitar / **BOB HARTMAN** – guitar, vocals / **JOHN DeGROFF** – bass / **BILL GLOVER** – drums

not iss. A&M

1974. (lp) *<SP 5061>* **PETRA** –
– Walkin' in the light / Mountains and valleys / Lucas McGraw / Wake up / Back sliding blues / Get back to the bible / Gonna fly away / I'm not ashamed / Storm comin' / Parting thought.

— added **STEVE McELYEA** – keyboards

1977. (lp) *<SP 5062>* **COME AND JOIN US** –
– God gave rock and roll to you / Holy ghost power / Woman don't you know / Sally / Come and join us / Where can I go / Without you / Ask him in / God gave rock and roll to you (reprise).

— **JOHN SLICK** – keyboards, vocals; repl. McELYEA

— **MARK KELLY** – bass, vocals; repl. DeGROFF

— **KEITH EDWARDS** – drums; repl. GLOVER

Star Song Star Song

1979. (lp/c) *<(SRR/SRC 327)>* **WASHES WHITER THAN SNOW**

— **LOUIE WEAVER** – drums, percussion; repl. EDWARDS

1982. (lp/c) *<(SRR/SRC 357)>* **NEVER SAY DIE** 1981
– The colouring song / Chameleon / Angel of light / Killing my old man / Without him we can do nothing / Never say die / I can be friends with you / For Annie / Father of lights / Praise ye the Lord. *(cd-iss. 1989; SSD 8016)*

1983. (lp/c) *<(SRR/SRC 397)>* **MORE POWER TO YA**
– Stand up / Second wind / More power to ya / Judas' kiss / Rose colored stained glass windows / Run for the prize / All over me / Let everything that hath breath / Road to Zion / Disciple.

1983. (lp/c) *<(SRR/SRC 418)>* **NOT OF THIS WORLD**
– Visions / Not of this world / Bema seat / Grave robber / Blinded eyes / Not by sight / Lift him up / Pied piper / Occupy / Godpleaser / Visions (reprise). *(cd-iss. 1989; SSD 8050)*

1985. (7") *<2714>* **BEAT THE SYSTEM. / HOLLOW EYES** –
1985. (lp/c) *<(SSR/SRC 2057)>* **BEAT THE SYSTEM** 1984
– Beat the system / Computer brains / Clean / It is finished / Voice in the wind / God gave rock and roll to you / Witch hunt / Hollow eyes / Speak to the sky / Adonai.

Aug 86. (lp/c) *<(SRR/SRC 2065)>* **CAPTURED IN TIME AND SPACE (live)**
– Beat the system / Computer brains / Clean / Grave robber / Speak to the sky / Hollow eyes / The rock medley: Stand up – Not by sight – Judas' kiss / The mellow medley: Soloring song – Road to Zion – More power to ya / John's solo / Jesus loves you – The race / Bob's solo / Louie's solo / God gave rock and roll to you.

Jan 87. (lp/c/cd) *<(SRR/SRC/SSD 8073)>* **BACK TO THE STREET**
– Back to the street / You are I am / Shakin' the house / King's ransom / Whole world / Another crossroad / Run for cover / Fool's gold / Altar ego / Thankful heart.

— **JOHN SCHLITT** – vocals (ex-HEAD EAST) repl. VOLZ

Sep 87. (lp/c/cd) *(SRR/SRC/SSD 8084) <CDP 74102>* **THIS MEANS WAR!**
– This means war / He came, he saw, he conquered / Get on your knees and fight like a man / I am available / Kenaniah / You are my rock / The water is alive / Don't let your heart be hardened / Dead reckoning / All the king's horses.

— **JOHN LAWRY** – keyboards, vocals; repl. SLICK

— **RONNIE CATES** – bass; repl. KELLY

1988. (lp/c/cd) *(SSR/SSC/SSD 8106)* **ON FIRE**
– All fired up / Hit you where you live / Mine field / First love / Defector / Counsel of the holy / Somebody's gonna praise his name / Open book / Stand in the gap.

1989. (cd) *<SSD 8138>* **PETRA MEANS ROCK** (compilation) –
– Stand up / Get on your knees and fight like a man / Hit you where you live / Killing my old man / Shakin' the house / Second wind / Clean / Not by sight / All fired up / Praise ye the Lord / He came, he saw, he conquered / Without him we can do nothing / Angel of light / Judas' kiss / Let everything that hath breath / Counsel of the holy / God gave rock and roll to you.

Dayspring Elektra

Dec 89. (lp/c/cd) *(DAY R/C/CD 4184) <306700>* **PETRA PRAISE – THE ROCK CRIES OUT**
– I love the Lord / King of kings / Jesus, Jesus, glorious one / The battle belongs to the Lord / Take me in / Salvation belongs to our God / The king of glory shall come in / No weapon weapon formed against us / I will celebrate with the spirit of the Lord / I will sing.

1990. (lp) *(108500) <48546>* **BEYOND BELIEF** – German
– Armed and dangerous / I am on the rock / Creed / Beyond belief / Love / Underground / Seen and not heard / Last daze / What's in a name / Prayer.

Dayspring Elektra

Nov 91. (cd/c) *(DAY CD/C 4218) <EK 48859>* **UNSEEN POWER** Jan92
– Destiny / Who's on the Lord's side / Ready, willing and able / Hand on my heart / I need to hear from you / Dance / Secret weapon / Sight unseen / Hey world / In the likeness of you.

Apr 93. (cd/c) *<EK/ET 57606>* **WAKE-UP CALL** –
– Midnight oil / Good news / Strong convictions / He's been in my shoes / Praying man / Underneath the blood / Sleeping giant / Believer in deed / Marks of the cross / Just reach out.

— added **JIM COOPER** – keyboards + **DAVID LICHENS** – guitar

Word Sony

Oct 95. (cd/c) *(701-962460 X/C) <67302>* **NO DOUBT**
– Enter in / Think twice / Heart of a hero / More than a thousands words / No doubt / Right place / Two are better than one / Sincerely yours / Think on these things / For all you're worth / We hold our hearts out to you.

Apr 98. (cd/c) *(7019967 604/507) <69150>* **GOD FIXATION**
– If I had to die for someone / Hello again / A matter of time / Falling up / Over the horizon / God fixation / Set for life / Magnet of the world / Shadow of a doubt / St. Augustine's pears / The invitation.

– compilations, others, etc. –

Feb 95. (cd) *Capitol; <20014>* **PETRAPHONICS** –
– Radio daze / Why should the father bother? / The coloring song / More power to ya / Road to Zion / Not of this world / Grave robber / Hollow eyes / Thankful heart / Fool's gold / I am available / Don't let your heart be hardened / First love.

Feb 95. (cd) *Capitol; <20022>* **POWER PRAISE** –
– Power praise / Yahweh love / Praise ye the Lord / Without him we can do nothing / Let everything that hath breath / Lift him up / Adonai / You are I am / You are my rock / Somebody's gonna praise his name.

PHANTOM BLUE

Formed: Los Angeles, California, USA . . . 1988 as an all-girl rock act by guitarists NICOLE COUCH and MICHELLE MELDRUM, who enlisted vocalist GIGI HANGACH, bassist KIM NIELSEN and drummer LINDA McDONALD. Nurtured by MIKE VARNEY and signed to his 'Shrapnel' label, the group fared better than most of their all-female peers, MARTY FRIEDMAN (future MEGADETH) co-producing the acclaimed debut album, 'PHANTOM BLUE' (1989). Touring their professional blend of hard-edged metal melodica around the world, it was some time before the girls got round to recording a follow-up. This eventually arrived in the shape of 1993's 'BUILT TO PERFORM', a somewhat disappointing set which nevertheless included a raucous cover of Thin Lizzy's 'BAD REPUTATION'.

Album rating: PHANTOM BLUE (*6) / BUILT TO PERFORM (*4)

GIGI HANGACH – vocals / **NICOLE COUCH** – guitar / **MICHELLE MELDRUM** – guitar / **KIM NIELSEN** – bass / **LINDA McDONALD** – drums

Roadrunner Shrapnel

Jun 89. (lp/c/cd) *(RR 9469-1/-4/-2) <SH 1043/+C/CD>* **PHANTOM BLUE**
– Going mad / Last show / Why call it love / Frantic zone / Slow it down / Walking away / Fought it out / Never too late / Out of control.

Roadrunner Geffen

Oct 93. (cd/c/lp) *(RR 9027-2/-4/-1) <24603>* **BUILT TO PERFORM**
– Nothing good / Time to run / Bad reputation / My misery / Little man / Better off dead / Anti love crunch / Loved ya to pieces / So easy / Lied to me / A little evil / You're free.

— **RANA ROSS** – bass; repl. NIELSEN

— released a third set, as yet unknown (US-only)

PICTURE

Formed: Netherlands . . . 1979 by RONALD VAN PROOYEN and JAN BECHTUM, who enlisted the rhythm section of RINUS VREUGDENHIL and LAURENS 'BAKKIE' BAKKER. Inspired by classic British heavy-rock and metal, the group signed a domestic deal with 'Philips', who released their first two early 80's albums, 'PICTURE' (1980) and 'HEAVY METAL EARS' (the same pair sported by Star Trek's Mr. Spock, perhaps!?). With SHMOULIK AVIGAIL replacing PROOYEN as frontman, the band secured a deal with French label, 'Carrere', the subsequent 'NIGHT HUNTER' (1983) album being PICTURE's first UK release. More personnel changes ensued prior to the 'ETERNAL DARK' (1984) album, PETE LOVELL replacing AVIGAIL in turn. Internal strife led to VREUGDENHIL recruiting a new line-up to play on 'TRAITOR' (1986), the same situation occuring on 'MARATHON' (1987). With such instability, it came as no surprise when PICTURE finally faded soon after.

Album rating: PICTURE (*5) / HEAVY METAL EARS (*5) / DIAMOND DREAMER (*7) / NIGHT HUNTER (*6) / ETERNAL DARK (*5) / TRAITOR (*5) / MARATHON (*6)

RONALD VAN PROOYEN – vocals / **JAN BECHTUM** – guitar, vocals / **RINUS VREUGDENHIL** – bass / **LAURENS BAKKER** – drums

Philips not iss.

Nov 80. (lp) *(6350 054)* **PICTURE** - Dutch
– Dirty street fighter / You can go / Bombers / No more / One way street / You're a fool / Get back or you fall / Rockin' in your brains / He's a player / Fear.

Feb 82. (lp) *(6350 058)* **HEAVY METAL EARS** - - Dutch
– Heavy metal ears / Spend the night with you / Unemployed / I'm just a simple man / Funky town / Out of time / Nighttiger / No no no / Rock & roll – Under your spell.

— **SHMOULIK AVIGAIL** – vocals; repl. PROOYEN

Carrere not iss.

Jul 83. (lp/c) *(CAL/CAC 146)* **NIGHT HUNTER** -
– Lady lightnin' / Night hunter / Hot lovin' / Diamond dreamer / Message from Hell / You're all alone / Lousy lady / The hangman / Get me rock and roll / You're touching me. *(Dutch-iss.Dec83 as 'DIAMOND DREAMER'; 6350 065)*

— **PETE LOVELL** – vocals; repl. AVIGAIL

Jul 85. (lp/c) *(CAL/CAC 217)* **ETERNAL DARK** -
– Eternal dark / Griffons guard the gold / Make your burn / Battle for the universe / The blade / Flying in time / Into the underworld / Tell no lies / Power of evil / Down and out.

— **VREUGDENHIL + LOVELL** recruited new line-up; **CHRIS VAN JAARSUELD + HENRY VAN MANNEN** – guitars / **SHAKE** (b. JACQUES VAN OEVELEN) – drums

1986. (lp) *(824 806-1)* **TRAITOR** - - Dutch
– Traitor / Right now / Fantasies / Dyin' to live / Lost in the night / State of shock / Loud'n proud / Out of control / We don't need to hide.
(above issued on 'Back Door')

— **BERT HEERINK** – vocals (ex-VANDENBERG) repl. LOVELL

— **ROB VAN ENHUIZEN** – guitar; repl. JAARSSUELD

— **RONALD DE GROUW** – keyboards; repl. VAN MANNEN

Mar 88. (lp/c) *(CAL/CAC 228)* **MARATHON** -
– Breakaway / Vampire of the new age / Money / Desperate call / I'm on my way / S.O.S. / Get out of my sight / We just can't lose / Don't keep me waiting.

— disbanded later in 1988

PIGEONHED (see under ⇒ BRAD)

PIGFACE (see under ⇒ BRAIN, Brian)

PINK FAIRIES

Formed: London, England ... 1966 as The SOCIAL DEVIANTS, by RUSSELL HUNTER, MICK FARREN – vocals, SID BISHOP – guitar, CORD REES – bass and two others. In 1967, they shortened their name to The DEVIANTS, luckily finding a millionaire who put up the cash for an album, 'PTOOF', which sold reasonably well on mail order. With DUNCAN SANDERSON replacing CORD, and the recruitment of a new manager (Canadian, Jamie Mandelkau), they issued a second lp, 'DISPOSABLE', another effort showcasing their heavily percussive prog-rock set. Early in '69, PAUL RUDOLPH replaced BISHOP, their third lp, 'DEVIANTS', being issued by 'Transatlantic'. When FARREN left to go solo in October '69, the new line-up (HUNTER, SANDERSON and RUDOLPH) augmented SHAGRAT member TWINK on his debut 'Polydor' album, 'THINK PINK'. The latter had already initiated the idea of The PINK FAIRIES in Colchester, subsequently teaming up with the aforesaid trio under that name. TWINK had also drummed at various stages with The IN-CROWD (who evolved into TOMORROW), and The PRETTY THINGS. Early in 1971, The PINK FAIRIES unleashed their first official 'Polydor' single, 'THE SNAKE', preceding the hippie celebration of the 'NEVER NEVER LAND' album. Their 1972 follow-up, 'WHAT A BUNCH OF SWEETIES', (recorded without TWINK, who had briefly formed The STARS together with another acid casualty, SYD BARRETT) scraped into the UK Top 50. With numerous personnel changes, they decided to disband in March '74, although many re-incarnations lay ahead (for touring purposes only, mainly with friends HAWKWIND).

Album rating: Deviants: Ptoof! (*5) / DISPOSABLE (*5) / DEVIANTS (*5) / Pink Fairies: NEVER NEVER LAND (*6) / WHAT A BUNCH OF SWEETIES (*6) / KINGS OF OBLIVION (*7) / FLASHBACK: PINK FAIRIES compilation (*7) / KILL 'EM & EAT 'EM (*5) / Deviants: HUMAN GARBAGE (*5)

DEVIANTS

DUNCAN SANDERSON – bass / **SID BISHOP** – guitar, sitar / **MICK FARREN** – vocals, piano / **CORD REES** – bass, guitar / **RUSS HUNTER** – drums

Underground not iss.

1967. (lp) *(IMP 1)* **PTOOFF!** -
– Opening / I'm coming home / Child of the sky / Charlie / Nothing man / Garbage / Bun / Deviation street. *(re-iss. May69 on 'Decca' mono/stereo; LK-R/SKL-R 4993) (re-iss. Dec83 on 'Psycho'; PSYCHO 16) (cd-iss. Nov92 on 'Drop Out'; DOCD 1988) (cd re-iss. Sep95 on 'Alive';)*

— **PAUL RUDOLPH** – guitar repl. CORD

Stable not iss.

Oct 68. (lp) *(SLE 7001)* **DISPOSABLE** -
– Somewhere to go / Sparrows and wires / Jamie's song / You've got to hold on / Fire in the city / Let's loot the supermarket / Papa-oo-Mao-Mao / Slum lord / Blind Joe McTurk's last session / Normality jam / Guaranteed too dead / Sidney B. Goode / Last man.

Nov 68. 7") *(STA 5601)* **YOU'VE GOT TO HOLD ON. / LET'S LOOT THE SUPERMARKET** -

— now a trio of SANDERSON, RUDOLPH + HUNTER when BISHOP left, FARREN went solo and released lp in 1970 'MONA (THE CARNIVEROUS CIRCUS).'

Transatla. not iss.

Jan 70. (lp) *(TRA 204)* **THE DEVIANTS** -
– Billy the monster / Broken biscuits / First line / The people suite / Rambling 'B'ask transit blues / Death of dream machine / Play time / Black George does it weith his mouth / Junior narco raiders / People of the city / Metamorphosis exploration. *(re-iss. 1978 on 'Logo'; MOGO 4001) (re-iss. Oct88 on 'Demon'; DEMON 8)*

TWINK

TWINK (b. JOHN ADLER) – drums, vocals (ex-SHAGRAT) (solo, with DEVIANTS)

Polydor not iss.

Jan 71. (lp) *(2343 032)* **THINK PINK** -
– Coming of the other side / Ten thousand words in a cardboard box / Dawn of magic / Tiptoe on the highest hill / Fluid / Mexican grass war / Rock an' roll the joint / Suicide / Three little piggies / Sparrow is a sign. *(re-prom.Apr71; same) (re-iss. Nov97 on 'Twink' cd/lp; TWK CD/LP 7) (re-iss. Jul99 on 'Akarma' cd/lp; AK 64 CD/LP)*

PINK FAIRIES

PAUL RUDOLPH – guitar, vocals / **DUNCAN SANDERSON** – bass, vocals / **RUSSELL HUNTER** – drums now with **TWINK**

Polydor Polydor

Jan 71. (7") *(2058 059)* **THE SNAKE. / DO IT** -

May 71. (lp,pink-lp) *(2383 045)* **NEVER NEVER LAND**
– Do it / Heavenly man / Say you love me / Wargirl / Never never land / Track one side two / Thor / Teenage rebel / Uncle Harry's last freak-out / The dream is just beginning.

— Trimmed to a trio when TWINK joined STARS, before flitting to Morocco. His spot filled by guest **TREVOR BURTON** – guitar (ex-MOVE)

Jul 72. (lp) *(2383 132)* **WHAT A BUNCH OF SWEETIES** 48
– Right on, fight on / Portobello shuffle / Marilyn / The pigs of Uranus / a) Walk, don't run, b) Middle run / I went up, I went down / X-ray / I saw her standing there.

— **MICK WAYNE** – guitar, vox (ex-JUNIOR'S EYES) repl. RUDOLPH (to UNCLE DOG)

Nov 72. (7") *(2059 302)* **WELL WELL WELL. / HOLD ON** -

— **LARRY WALLIS** – guitar, vocals (ex-UFO, ex-SHAGRAT, ex-BLODWYN PIG) repl. MICK. (trio now consisted of LARRY, DUNCAN + RUSSELL)

Jun 73. (lp) *(2383 212)* *<5537>* **KINGS OF OBLIVION**
– City kids / I wish I was a girl / When's the fun begin? / Chromium plating / Raceway / Chambermaid / Street urchin. *(cd-iss. Apr98 on 'Raceway'; RWY 001CD)*

— broke-up Mar74, although **DUNCAN, RUSSELL, PAUL, TWINK & LARRY** re-formed for one-off reunion gig at The Roundhouse 13th Jul'75. Autumn 1975, they officially re-united w / **DUNCAN, RUSSELL & LARRY.** When they added (mid'76) **MARTIN STONE** – guitar (ex-CHILI WILLI, ex-MIGHTY BABY, ex-ACTION, etc.) they returned to studio.

Stiff not iss.

Sep 76. (7") *(BUY 2)* **BETWEEN THE LINES. / SPOILING FOR A FIGHT** -

— Break-up again, and LARRY went solo in 1977.

TWINK & THE FAIRIES

— solo with ex-PINK FAIRIES (**PAUL RUDOLPH**; who had been recently seen in HAWKWIND, etc. / **DUNCAN + RUSSELL**)

Chiswick not iss.

Feb 78. (12"ep) *(SWT 26)* **DO IT '77. / PSYCHEDELIC PUNKAROO / ENTER THE DIAMONDS** -

— Disbanded once again when TWINK moved to Belgium. DUNCAN joined The LIGHTNING RAIDERS.

MICK FARREN

with **TWINK** – drums, percussion, vocals / **SHAGRAT THE VAGRANT** – vocals, percussion / **STEVE HAMMOND** – guitar / **JOHNNY GUSTAFSON** – bass / **PETE ROBINSON** – keyboards

Transatla. not iss.

Apr 70. (lp) *(TRA 212)* **MONA (THE CARNIVEROUS CIRCUS)** -
– Mona (a fragrant) / Carniverous circus part 1: The whole thing starts – But Charlie it's still moving – Observe the ravens – Society 4 the horsemen – Summertime blues / Carniverous circus part 2: Don't talk to Mary – You can't move me – In my window box – An epitaph can point the way – Mona (the whole trip). *(re-iss. Mar84 on 'Psycho'; PSYCHO 20)*

Stiff not iss.

Nov 77. (7"ep; MICK FARREN & DEVIANTS) *(LAST 4)* **SCREWED UP** -
– Outragious contagious / Let's loot the supermarket / Screwed up / Shock horror

— now with **WILKO JOHNSON** – guitar / **ALAN POWER** – drums / **ANDY COLQUHOUN** – bass / **WILL STALL** – brass / **CHRISSIE JANE + SONJA KRISTINA** – backing vox.

Logo not iss.

1978. (lp) *(LOGO 2010)* **VAMPIRES STOLE MY LUNCH MONEY** – Trouble coming every day / Half price drinks / I don't want to go this way / I want a drink / Son of a millionaire / Zombie (live) / Bela Lugosi / People call you crazy / Fast Eddie / Let me in damn you / Self destruction / Drunk in the morning.
1978. (7") *(GO 321)* **HALF PRICE DRINKS. / I DON'T WANT TO GO THIS WAY**
May 79. (7") *(GO 345)* **BROKEN STATUE. / IT'S ALL IN THE PICTURE**

DEVIANTS

— re-formed with **MICK FARREN** – vocals / **LARRY WALLIS + WAYNE KRAMER** – guitar / **DUNCAN SANDERSON** – bass / **GEORGE BUTLER** – drums

Psycho not iss.

May 84. (lp) *(PSYCHO 25)* **HUMAN GARBAGE** (live at Dingwalls '84) – Outragious contagious / Broken statue / Ramblin' Rose / Hey thanks / Screwed up / I wanna drink / Takin' LSD / Police car / Trouble coming every day.

– compilations, etc. –

Sep 92. (cd) *Drop Out; (DOCD 1989)* **PARTIAL RECALL** – (from DEVIANTS 3 / VAMPIRES / all 'MONA; THE CARNIVOROUS CIRCUS')
Jun 97. (cd; MICK FARREN & THE DEVIANTS) *Captain Trip; (CTCD 046)* **FRAGMENTS OF BROKEN DREAMS**

MICK FARREN'S TIJUANA BIBLE

Big Beat not iss.

Feb 93. (cd) *(CDWIK 117)* **GRINGO MADNESS** – Leader hotel / Mark of Zorro / Lone sungularity / Solitaire devil / Spider kissed / Jezebel / Long walk with the devil / Jumping Jack Flash / Movement of the whores on Revolution Plaza / Hippie death cult / Last night the Alhambra burned down / Eternity is a very long time / Memphis psychosis / Riot in Cell Block #9.

PINK FAIRIES

— re-formed 1987 with **TWINK, LARRY, RUSSELL, ANDY + SANDY** (aka DUNCAN)

Demon not iss.

Oct 87. (lp/cd) *(FIEND/+CD 105)* **KILL 'EM AND EAT 'EM** – Broken statue / Fear of love / Undercover of confusion / Waiting for the ice cream to melt / Taking LSD / White girls on amphetamine / Seeing double / Fool about you / Bad attitude / I might be lying. *(cd re-iss. May97; VEXCD 16)*

— Once again, they bit the dust, and TWINK joined MAGIC MUSCLE who made live lp in 1989 'ONE HUNDRED MILES BELOW'. TWINK released another solo lp 'MR. RAINBOW' and then 'MAGIC EYE' both in 1990 for 'Woronzow' label. Reformed in the mid-90's, **TWINK** – drums / **PAUL RUDOLPH** – guitar / **MATTHEW BAILEY** – bass / **CHRIS PINKERTON** – drums

H.T.D. not iss.

Jan 96. (cd) *(HTDCD 46)* **OUT OF THE BLUE AND INTO THE PINK** – Out of the pink / Red house / Going home / Find yourself another fool / Talk to me babe / Oye come va / Youngblood / Steppin' out / Tulsa time / Kansas city / Rambling / Out go the lights: (a) A midnight rambler (excerpt from Stone The Dragon solo), (b) Midnight rambler return.

– compilations, others, etc. –

Jul 75. (lp) *Flashback-Polydor; (2384 071)* **PINK FAIRIES** – The snake / City kids / Wargirl / Portobello shuffle / Heavenly man / Do it / pigs of Uranus / Well well well / Chromium plating / I went up, I went down / Say you love me / Street urchin.
Jun 82. (m-lp) *Big Beat; (WIK 14)* **AT THE ROUNDHOUSE (live July '75)** – City kids / Waiting for the man / Lucille / Uncle Harry's last freakout / Going down.
Oct 84. (m-lp) *Big Beat; (NED 9)* **PREVIOUSLY UNRELEASED** – As long as the price is right / Waiting for the lightning to strike / Can't find a lady / No second chance / Talk of the Devil / I think it's coming back again.
Oct 90. (cd/c) *Polydor; (843894-2/-4)* **THE BEST OF THE PINK FAIRIES**
Jul 91. (cd) *Big Beat; (CDWIK 965)* **LIVE AT THE ROUNDHOUSE / PREVIOUSLY UNRELEASED / TWINK & THE FAIRIES (ep)**
Jan 98. (cd) *Twink; (TWKCD 8)* **NO PICTURE**
Mar 98. (cd) *Cleopatra; (<CLP 01882>)* **THE GOLDEN YEARS 1969-1971**
Jul 98. (d-lp) *Get Back; (GET 514)* **UNCLE HARRY**
Nov 98. (lp/cd) *Total Energy; (NER 3017/+CD)* **DO IT (live)**
May 99. (lp) *Get Back; (GET 527)* **LIVE AT THE WEELY FESTIVAL**

TWINK

Twink not iss.

Mar 86. (7") *(TWK 1)* **APOCALIPSTIC. / HE'S CRYING**
Jul 86. (12"ep) *(TWK 2)* **SPACE LOVER (Rock'n'roll mix 1 & 2). / ('A'-percussion mix) / ('A'-psychedelic mix) / ('A'instrumental)**
Jun 87. (7") *(TWK 3)* **DRIVING MY CAR. / WAR GIRL**
Mar 90. (lp/cd) *(TWK LP/CD 1)* **MR. RAINBOW** – Psychedelic punkaroo / Baron Saturday / Teenage rebel / Mr. Rainbow / Seize the time / The snake / Three jolly little dwarfs / Waygirl / Balloon burning / Do it.
Jun 90. (7") *(7TWK 5)* **PSYCHEDELIC PUNKAROO. /** (12"+=) *(12TWK 5)* –

— in 1991, TWINK collaborated with BEVIS FROND on the album 'Magic Eye'

– compilations, etc. –

Jan 98. (cd/lp) *Twink; (TWK CD/LP 3)* **ODDS AND BEGINNINGS**
Dec 99. (lp) *Get Back; (GET 526)* **FROM THE VAULTS**
Mar 00. (d-lp/cd) *Get Back; (GET 0572 CD/LP)* **THE LOST EXPERIMENTAL RECORDINGS 1970**

PISSING RAZORS

Formed: El Paso, Texas, USA . . . 1994 by MATT LYNCH, EDDY GARCIA, his brother DANNY and original vocalist, "LOCO" PELON; the latter derived the moniker after he described the pain of his recently acquired VD (Venerial Disease). A year later, when LOCO was obviously going that way, MATT decided to call upon high school mate (and fellow former SADIST member), JOE RODRIGUEZ, who had come home to help his then wife rehabilitate herself from drugs (crystal methadone). The frontman, MATT and EDDIE were subsequently joined by RICK VALLES as the tattooed goateed ones blended their own inimitably exuberant metal style, although obviously inspired by the likes of MACHINE HEAD, PANTERA and FEAR FACTORY. In 1996/7, after they distributed their own 'PSYCHO PUNKO METAL GROOVE', they were finally spotted when a 'Noise' A&R man gave them the call-up to the German/European label. Early the following year, the first fruits of their labour were born, the much-heralded eponymous set. JOE's personal life also bore some fruit a few months later – a baby to his 2nd wife. CESAR SOTO replaced LYNCH for their follow-up set, 'CAST DOWN THE PLAGUE' (1999); 'FIELDS OF DISBELIEF' was released the following year.

Album rating: PSYCHO PUNKO METAL GROOVE (*5) / PISSING RAZORS (*7) / CAST DOWN THE PLAGUE (*4) / FIELDS OF DISBELIEF (*6)

JOE RODRIGUEZ (b.1970) – vocals (ex-SADIST) repl. 'LOCO' PELON / **MATT LYNCH** (b.1971) – guitar (ex-SADIST) / **RICK VALLES** (b.1971) – bass; repl. DANNY GARCIA / **EDDIE GARCIA** (b.1966) – drums

not iss. own label

1996. (cd) **PSYCHO PUNKO METAL GROOVE** – World of deceit / Haze of deception / Wasteland / Wall Street man / Fuck you up / Box life / Head strong / Friends / Season to die / Why / I hate you / Down with the cause / (Hillbilly) Control is / Division lines / Nine lives / Voice of reason.

Noise Noise

Jan 98. (cd) *<N 0290-2>* **PISSING RAZORS** Feb98 – Dodging bullets / Tortured / Where we come from / Permanent / Life of a lunatic / World of deceit / Disaster / Desperado / Sounds of doom / Season to die / Silent hatred / For what it's worth / Broken trust.

— **CESAR SOTO** – guitars; repl. LYNCH

Jun 99. (cd) *<N 311-2>* **CAST DOWN THE PLAGUE** Apr99 – Mass corruption / Truth in disguise / Survival of time / Cast down the plague / Box life / Understand / Sympathy / Forever / Vexed / Away / Mistake No.1 / Reality of war / Train of thought.
Aug 00. (cd) *<N 336-2>* **FIELDS OF DISBELIEF** – Between Heaven and Hell / Fork tongue / Ruin / You'll never know / Selfish / Fields of disbelief / Three / Out of control / The other side / Regret / Sever the ties / Choices / Voice of reason / Wasteland.

PIST°ON

Formed: Brooklyn, New York, USA . . . 1995 by HENRY FONT, VAL LUM and two others. Depending on how you read it, their moniker might suggest either car engines or golden showers, although their debut album cover indicated the latter. Released at the end of 1996, 'NUMBER ONE' (also a play on words!), was as sleazy as might be expected, JOSH SILVER's (Type-O Negative) production cleaning up the worst excesses of their dirty, gritty sound. FONT and his female counterpart VAL, were subsequently left to find other members when the original musicians pist°off. The band were now a trio after they found drummer JEFF McMANUS, although he in turn was replaced temporarily after being admitted to hospital with respiratory problems in late '97. Singer FONT and crew were back early in '99 with the long-awaited 'SELL OUT', an even heavier collection of climatic rock.

Album rating: NUMBER ONE (*7) / SELL OUT (*6)

HENRY FONT – vocals, guitar / **VAL LUM** – bass / **PAUL POULOS** – lead guitar / **DANNY JAM KAVADIO** – drums

Music For Nations Music For Nations

Nov 96. (cd/c) *(CD/T MFN 211) <11102>* **NUMBER ONE** Oct96 – Parole / Turbulent / Grey flap / Shoplifters of the world unite / I am no one / Eight sides / Afraid of life / Electra complex / Down and out / Mix me with blood / My feet / Exit wound.

— **JEFF McMANUS** – drums; repl. DANNY

— temp. **JOHNNY KELLY** – drums (of TYPE-O NEGATIVE); repl. McMANUS who suffered illness

Music For Nations Evil Eye

1998. (7"ep) *<3>* **DYKE FIGHT TONIGHT EP**

Music For Nations Mayhem

Mar 99. (cd) *(CDMFN 248) <11145>* **SELL OUT** – Suddenly sober / Rest / 31 degrees / C / Need to know / New car / When I go / Low / Someone / Square / Waiting to die.

PITCHSHIFTER

Formed: Nottingham, England . . . early 1991 by brothers JOHN and MARK CLAYDEN, who were raised on listening to acts like CRASS and FLUX OF PINK INDIANS. A doom-grinding industrial outfit in the mould of MINISTRY and GODFLESH, the initial drummerless line-up also boasted JONATHAN CARTER and STUART TOOLIN. Although they released their debut set, the aptly named 'INDUSTRIAL' (1991) on 'Peaceville', the group subsequently inked a deal with local ambassadors of extremity, 'Earache'. PITCHSHIFTER's first release for the label was the mini-set, 'SUBMIT' (1992), also the first material to feature a conventional drummer, the mysteriously named D CRUSHING. Electronics still featured highly in the group's sonic terrorism manifesto, however, the following year's full-length 'DESENSITIZED' set carrying on in much the same vein. For such an unrelentingly subversive outfit, a remix set was the logical next step and late '94 saw the release of 'PITCHSHIFTER VS . . . THE REMIX WARS', an album featuring deconstructions by the likes of THERAPY, GUNSHOT and BIOHAZARD. Though they've yet to make the same impact as some of their more infamous contemporaries, PITCHSHIFTER continued to fashion ear-shredding soundscapes for a loyal core of fans, the album 'INFOTAINMENT?' (1996) another success. The Nottingham noise crew were subsequently furnished with the chance to bring their racket to a wider audience courtesy of a major label deal with 'Geffen'. The band (now featuring JIM DAVIES in place of the departed TOOLIN) also got up to speed with the internet revolution, cheekily naming their 1998 set, 'www.pitchshifter.com'. A futuristic collision of industrial punk and new fangled drum'n'bass underlined that the lads weren't merely paying lip service to the computer era. Live drum sampling, meanwhile ensured that their sound retained an organic edge. A combination of live instruments and sonic technology again proved an effective recipe on the millennial 'DEVIANT' set, wherein their radical lyrical manifesto proved as uncompromising as ever on the likes of 'HIDDEN AGENDA' and 'EVERYTHING'S FUCKED'. • **Covered:** MAKING PLANS FOR NIGEL (Xtc) / TOUCH ME I'M SICK (Mudhoney).

Album rating: INDUSTRIAL (*7) / SUBMIT mini (*6) / DESENSITIXED (*6) / PITCHSHIFTER VS . . . (*4) / INFOTAINMENT? (*7) / www.pitchshifter.com (*7) / DEVIANT (*6)

(JONATHAN) JS CLAYDEN – vocals / **(MARK) MD CLAYDEN** – bass / **(JONATHAN) JA CARTER** – guitar, programming / **STUART TOOLIN** – guitar

Peaceville | not iss.

1991. (cd/lp) *(CD+/VILE 56)* **INDUSTRIAL** | | –
– Landfill / Brutal cancroid / Gravid rage / New flesh / Catharsis / Skin grip / Inflamator / Eye. *(re-iss. cd Apr95; same)*

—— **D** – drums repl. TOOLIN

Earache | Earache

Mar 92. (m-lp/c/cd) *(MOSH 066/+MC/CD)* **SUBMIT**
– Gritter / Deconstruction / New flesh P.S.I. (remix) / Bastardiser (remix) / Dry riser inlet / Tendrill. *(cd re-iss. Sep97+=; same)* – Deconstruction (live) / Landfill (live).

Oct 93. (lp/c/cd) *(<MOSH 075/+MC/CD>)* **DESENSITIZED** | | Dec93
– Lesson one / Diable / Ephemerol / Triad / To die is to gain / (A higher form of) Killing / Lesson two / Cathode / N/A / Gatherer of data / N.C.M. / Routine. *(cd re-iss. Sep97; same)*

Dec 94. (m-lp/cd) *(<MOSH 095/+CD>)* **PITCHSHIFTER – VS – BIOHAZARD – THERAPY? – GUNSHOT (THE REMIX WARS)** | | Jan95
– Triad (Pitch Shifter remix) / Diable (Therapy? remix) / 'NCM' (Pitch Shifter remix) / Triad (Gunshot remix) / Diable Pitch Shifter remix) / Triad (Biohazard remix) / To die is to gain (Pitch Shifter remix).

May 96. (lp/c/cd) *(<MOSH 137/+MC/CD>)* **INFOTAINMENT?**
– Self relicating PSI / Introductory disclaimer / Underachiever / (We're behaving like) Insects / Virus / Product placement / (Harmless) Interlude / Bloodsweataliva / Hangar 84 / Whiteout / Phoenixology.

—— added **JIM DAVIS** – guitar

Geffen | Geffen

Feb 98. (7"green) *(GFS 22324)* **GENIUS. / MAKING PLANS FOR NIGEL** | 71 | –
(cd-s) *(GFSTD 22324)* – ('A'side) / Floppy disk / Genius (Luke Vibert mix) / You are free (to do as we tell you).

Mar 98. (cd) *(<GED 25163>)* **WWW.PITCHSHIFTER.COM**
– Microwaved / 2nd hand / Genius / Civilised / Subject to status / W.Y.S.I.W.Y.G. / Please sir / Disposable / A better lie / Innit / What's in it for me? / I don't like it / ZXB1. *(cd+=)* – (free samples).

Sep 98. (7"red) *(GFS 22348)* **MICROWAVED. / GENIUS (DJ WAlly)** | 54 |
(cd-s) *(GFSTD 22348)* – ('A'side) / Genius (Deejay Punk-Roc vocal mix) / Genius (CD-Rom).
(cd-s) *(GFSXD 22348)* – ('A'side) / Genius (Deejay Pubk-Roc dub) / Genius (lunatic calm).

M.C.A. | M.C.A.

May 00. (cd) *(<112254-2>)* **DEVIANT** | 35 |
– Condenscension / Wafer thin / Keep it clean / Forget the facts / Hidden agenda / Scene this / Dead battery / As seen on TV / Everything's fucked / Chump change / Stronger / PSIcological.

Oct 00. (cd-s) *(MCSTD 40241)* **DEAD BATTERY / VOTED LEAST LIKELY TO SUCCEED / CHUMP CHANGE (fat controller mix)** | 71 | –
(cd-s) *(MCSXD 40241)* – ('A'side) / Touch me I'm sick / Hidden agenda (Koy-jin mix).

PIXIES

Formed: Boston, Massachusetts, USA . . . 1986 by L.A. born frontman and self-confessed UFO freak, BLACK FRANCIS (real name, deep breath . . . CHARLES MICHAEL KITRIDGE THOMPSON IV) along with guitarist JOEY SANTIAGO. Famously placing a newspaper ad requesting musicians with a penchant for PETER, PAUL AND MARY and HUSKER DU, the only taker was KIM DEAL who subsequently brought in drummer DAVID LOVERING. Originally trading under the moniker PIXIES IN PANOPLY, the band soon trimmed this down to the punchier PIXIES and began kicking up a storm on the Boston music scene with their spiky, angular noise-pop (that's two thirds noise, one third pop) and wilfully cryptic lyrics. Along with fellow Bostonians THROWING MUSES, the band were signed to '4 a.d.' by a suitably impressed Ivo Watts-Russell, the label releasing The PIXIES' debut 'COME ON PILGRIM' in late '87. Stunningly different, the record galvanised the early PIXIES sound, a bizarre hybrid of manic, strangulated vocals (often sung in Spanish), searing melodic noise and schizophrenic, neo-latin rhythms. The album drew an early core of believers but it wasn't until the release of 'SURFER ROSA' (1988) that the band were hailed as the saviours of indie rock. Taking the formula of the debut to its brain splintering conclusion, the likes of 'BONE MACHINE', the incendiary 'SOMETHING AGAINST YOU' and careering 'BROKEN FACE' were utterly compelling in their blistering intensity. The sheer unhinged abandon with which BLACK FRANCIS threw himself into these songs has to be heard to be believed. You begin to fear that the man really has lost it when he asks 'WHERE IS MY MIND' in his inimitable melancholy howl. DEAL was equally affecting on the gorgeous 'GIGANTIC', the track building from a metaphorical whisper to a scream. Truly essential, 'SURFER ROSA' remains one of the most pivotal alternative rock records of the last fifteen years. Following their first headline UK tour, the band hooked up with producer Gil Norton for the 'DOOLITTLE' (1989) album. Previewed by the haunting 'MONKEY GONE TO HEAVEN', the record showcased a cleaner, more pop-friendly sound, most notably on (then) upcoming single, 'HERE COMES YOUR MAN'. Swoonfully poptastic, this song was guaranteed to have even the most miserable SMITHS fan grinning ear to ear, putting the toss that passes for modern 'indie-pop' to eternal shame. The demented 'DEBASER' was another highlight, becoming a dependable fixture at indie discos for oh, aeons. As well as a mammoth world tour, DEAL found time for her side project, The BREEDERS. A collaboration with the delectable TANYA DONELLY (ex-THROWING MUSES), the pair released the acclaimed 'POD' album in 1990. Later that year came 'BOSSANOVA', another breathtaking collection that had the music press in rapture. Lyrically, BLACK was in his element, losing himself in science fiction fantasy while the band raged and charmed in equal measure. The album reached No.3 in the UK charts and The PIXIES could apparently do no wrong, consolidating their position as one of the biggest American acts in Europe. Yet the critics turned on them with the release of 'TROMPE LE MONDE' (1991), in keeping with the times a decidedly grungier affair. Accusations of "Heavy Metal" were way off the mark. In reality, the record was still chokka with stellar tunes, you just had to dig deeper to find them. 'PLANET OF SOUND', 'SPACE (I BELIEVE IN)' and 'MOTORWAY TO ROSWELL' were all quintessential PIXIES, FRANCIS as endearingly fascinated as ever with the mysteries of the universe. Sadly, the singer was soon to turn his obsession into a solo venture, The PIXIES gone almost as quickly as they had arrived, leaving behind a brief but rich sonic legacy. With FRANCIS changing his name to the rather dull FRANK BLACK, he went on to release a moderately successful eponymous solo debut in 1993 and a wryly titled follow-up, 'TEENAGER OF THE YEAR' (1994), DEAL going on to make a further album with The BREEDERS. Inevitably, none of these projects approached the deranged genius of The PIXIES (Rock will never see their like again). The frontman continued to surface periodically and three albums, 'THE CULT OF RAY' (1996), 'FRANK BLACK AND THE CATHOLICS' (1998) and 'PISTOLLERO' (1999), have all met with diminishing fanbase response. 'DOG IN THE SAND' followed in 2001, a more down home effort which featured some of his best songwriting for years. The fact that SANTIAGO was back on board was hardly a hindrance while occasional glimpses of FRANK's legendary lyrical genius suggested there was life in the old (black) dog yet. • **Songwriters:** BLACK FRANCIS penned except; WINTERLONG + I'VE BEEN WAITING FOR YOU (Neil Young) / EVIL HEARTED YOU (Yardbirds) / HEAD ON (Jesus & Mary Chain) / CECILIA ANN (Surftones) / BORN IN CHICAGO (Paul Butterfield's Blues Band) / I CAN'T FORGET (Leonard Cohen). FRANK BLACK solo:- JUST A LITTLE (Beau Brummels) / RE-MAKE, RE-MODEL (Roxy Music) / HANG ON TO YOUR EGO (Beach Boys).

Album rating: COME ON PILGRIM mini (*7) / SURFER ROSA (*10) / DOOLITTLE (*9) / BOSSANOVA (*8) / TROMPE LE MONDE (*7) / DEATH TO THE PIXIES compilation (*8) / Frank Black: FRANK BLACK (*8) / TEENAGER OF THE YEAR (*8) / THE CULT OF RAY (*5) / FRANK BLACK & THE CATHOLICS (*5) / PISTOLLERO (*5) / DOG IN THE SAND (*6)

BLACK FRANCIS (b. CHARLES MICHAEL KITRIDGE THOMPSON IV, 1965, Long Beach, Calif.) – vocals, guitar / **JOEY SANTIAGO** (b.10 Jun'65, Manila, Philippines) – lead guitar / **KIM DEAL** (Mrs.JOHN MURPHY) (b.10 Jun'61, Dayton, Ohio) – bass, vocals / **DAVE LOVERING** (b. 6 Dec'61) – drums

4.a.d. | Elektra

Oct 87. (m-lp) *(MAD 709)* <61296> **COME ON PILGRIM**
– Caribou / Vamos / Islade encounter / Ed is dead / The holiday song / Nimrod's son / I've been tried / Levitate me.

Mar 88. (lp/c)(cd) *(CAD/+C 803)(CAD 803CD)* <61295> **SURFER ROSA**
– Bone machine / Break my body / Something against you / Broken face / Gigantic /

River Euphrates / Where is my mind? / Cactus / Tony's theme / Oh my golly! / Vamos / I'm amazed / Brick is red. *(cd+=)* – COME ON PILGRIM (m-lp)

Aug 88. (12"ep/cd-ep) *(BAD 805/+CD)* **GIGANTIC. / RIVER EUPHRATES. / VAMOS. / IN HEAVEN (LADY IN THE RADIATOR SONG)** [ ] [-]

Mar 89. (7") *(AD 904)* **MONKEY GONE TO HEAVEN. / MANTA RAY** [60] [ ]
(12"+=/cd-s+=) *(BAD 904/+CD)* – Weird at my school / Dancing the manta ray.

Apr 89. (lp/c)(cd) *(CAD/+C 905)(CAD 905CD) <60856>* **DOOLITTLE** [8] [98]
– Debaser / Tame / Wave of mutilation / I bleed / There goes my gun / Here comes your man / Dead / Monkey gone to Heaven / La la love you / Mr. Grieves / Crackity Jones / #13 baby / Silver / Hey / Gouge away.

Jun 89. (7") *(AD 909) <66694>* **HERE COMES YOUR MAN. / INTO THE WHITE** [54] [ ]
(12"+=/cd-s+=) *(BAD 909/+CD)* – Wave of mutilation (UK surf) / Bailey's walk.

— KIM DEAL was also part of amalgamation The BREEDERS

Jul 90. (7"/c-s) *(AD/+C 0009) <66616>* **VELOURIA. / I'VE BEEN WAITING FOR YOU** [28] [ ]
(12"+=/cd-s+=) *(BAD 0009/+CD)* – Make believe / The thing.

Aug 90. (cd)(lp/c) *(CAD 0010CD)(CAD/+C 0010) <60963>* **BOSSANOVA** [3] [70]
– Cecilia Ann / Rock music / Velouria / Allison / Is she weird / Ana / All over the world / Dig for fire / Down to the wall / The happening / Blown away / Hang wire / Stormy weather / Havalina.

Oct 90. (7"/c-s) *(AD/+C 0014) <66596>* **DIG FOR FIRE. / VELVETY (instrumental)** [62] [ ]
(12"+=/cd-s+=) *(BAD 0014/+CD)* – Winterlong / Santo.

May 91. (7") *(AD 1008)* **PLANET OF SOUND. / BUILD HIGH** [27] [ ]
(c-s+=)(12"+=/cd-s+=) *(BADC 1008)(BAD 1008/+CD)* – Evil hearted you / Theme from Narc.

Sep 91. (cd)(lp/c) *(CAD 1014CD)(CAD/+C 1014) <61118>* **TROMPE LE MONDE** [7] [92]
– Trompe de Monde / Planet of sound / Alec Eiffel / The sad punk / Head on / U-mass / Palace of the brine / Letter to Memphis / Bird dream Of the Olympus mons / Space (I believe in) / Subbacultcha / Distance equals rate times time / Lovely day / Motorway to Roswell / The Navajo know.

Nov 91. (12"ep) **ALEC EIFFEL / MOTORWAY TO ROSWELL. / PLANET OF SOUND (live) / TAME (live)** [ ] [-]

Feb 92. (12"ep) *<66444>* **ALEC EIFFEL / LETTER TO MEMPHIS (instrumental). / BUILD LIFE / EVIL HEARTED YOU** [-] [ ]

— Disbanded late in '92, with BLACK FRANCIS going solo as FRANK BLACK.

– compilations, etc. –

on '4 a.d.' / 'Elektra' unless otherwise mentioned

Sep 97. (7") *(AD 7010)* **DEBASER (demo). / #13 BABY** [23] [ ]
(cd-s) *(BAD 7010CD)* – ('A'studio) / Bone machine / Gigantic / Isla de Encanta.
(cd-s) *(BADD 7010CD)* – ('A'live) / Holiday song (live) / Cactus (live) / Nimrod's son (live).

Oct 97. (d-cd/d-c) *(DAD/+C 7011) / <62118>* **DEATH TO THE PIXIES** [28] [ ]
– Cecilia Ann / Planet of sound / Tame / Here comes your man / Debaser / Wave of mutilation / Dig for fire / Caribou / Holiday song / Nimrod's son / U mass / Bone machine / Gigantic / Where is my mind / Velouria / Gouge away / Monkey gone to Heaven / Debaser / Rock music / Broken face / Isla De Encanta / Hangfire / Dead / Into the white / Monkey gone to Heaven / Gouge away / Gouge away / Here comes your man / Alidon / Hey / Gigantic / Crackity Jones / Something against you / Tame / Wave of mutilation / Where is my mind / Ed is dead / Vamos / Tony's theme. *(de-luxe version hit No.20 q-lp/d-cd; DADD 7011/+CD)*

Jul 98. (cd) *(GAD 8013) <62185>* **PIXIES AT THE BBC (live)** [45] [ ]
– Wild honey pie / There goes my gun / Dead / Subbacultcha / Manta Ray / Is she weird? / Ana / Down to the well / Wave of mutilation / Letter to Memphis / Levitate me / Caribou / Monkey gone to Heaven / Hey / In Heaven (lady in the radiator song).

FRANK BLACK

— with **ERIC DREW FELDMAN** – bass, keyboards, synthetics (ex-CAPTAIN BEEFHEART) / **NICK VINCENT** – drums, percussion / + extra guitars **SANTIAGO, MORRIS TEPPER + DAVID SARDY**

4 a.d. — Elektra

Mar 93. (lp/cd)(c) *(CAD 3004/+CD)(CADC 3004) <61467>* **FRANK BLACK** [9] [ ]
– Los Angeles / I heard Ramona sing / Hang on to your ego / Fu Manchu / Places named after numbers / Czar / Old black dawning / Ten percenter / Brackish boy / Two spaces / Tossed (instrumental version) / Parry the wind high, low / Adda Lee / Every time I go around here / Don't ya rile 'em. *(cd re-iss. Jul98; GAD 3004CD)*

Apr 93. (7") *(AD 3005) <8782-2>* **HANG ON TO YOUR EGO. / THE BALLAD OF JOHNNY HORTON** [ ] [ ]
(cd-s+=) *(BAD 3005CD)* – Surf epic.

— same trio augmented by **SANTIAGO, TEPPER + LYLE WORKMAN** – guitar

May 94. (7") *(AD 4007)* **HEADACHE. / ('A'mix)** [53] [-]
(10"/cd-s) *(BADD 4007/+CD)* – ('A'side) / Men in black / At the end of the world / Oddball.
(cd-s) *(BAD 4007CD)* – ('A'side) / Hate me / This is where I belong / Amnesia.

May 94. (d-lp/cd)(c) *(DAD 4009/+CD)(DADC 4009) <61618>* **TEENAGER OF THE YEAR** [21] [ ]
– Whatever happened to Pong? / Thalassocracy / (I want to live on an) Abstract plain / Calistan / The vanishing spies / Speedy Marie / Headache / Sir Rockaby / Freedom rock / Two reelers / Fiddle riddle / Ole Mulholland / Fazer eyes / I could stay here forever / The hostess with the mostest / Superabound / Big red / Space is gonna do me good / White noise maker / Pure denizen of the citizens band / Bad, wicked world / Pie in the sky. *(re-iss. Jul98; GAD 4009CD)*

— FRANK BLACK had earlier in the year teamed up with ex-SEX PISTOL; GLEN MATLOCK to form tribute band FRANK BLACK & THE STAX PISTOLS

Noise Annoys — not iss.

Dec 95. (cd/d-lp) *(ANAN CD/V 7)* **THE BLACK SESSIONS (live in Paris)** [ ] [-]
– Two spaces / (I want to live on an) Abstact plain / Headache / Old black dawning / Superabound / Calistan / The vanishing spies / Sir Rockaby / Big red / The Jacques Tati / Oddball / Men in black / Czar / Freedom rock / (Whatever happened to) Pong / Thalasocracy / White noise maker / Los Angeles / Handyman / Modern age / Jumping beans / (I want to live on an) Abstact plain (acoustic). *(re-iss. Oct97; same)*

— now w/ **LYLE WORKMAN** – lead guitar / **DAVID McCAFFREY** – bass / **SCOTT BOUTIER** – drums

Epic — Warners

Dec 95. (ltd-7") *(662 671-7)* **THE MARXIST. / BETTER THINGS** [ ] [-]

Jan 96. (7") *(662 786-7)* **MEN IN BLACK. / JUST A LITTLE** [37] [-]
(cd-s+=) *(662 786-2)* – Re-make, re-model.
(cd-s) *(662 786-5)* – ('A'side) / You never heard of me / Pray a little faster / Announcement.

Jan 96. (cd/c/lp) *(481 647-2/-4/-1) <43070>* **THE CULT OF RAY** [39] [ ]
– The Marxist / Men in black / Punk rock city / You ain't me / Jesus was right / I don't want to hurt you (every single time) / Mosh, don't pass the guy / Kicked in the taco / Creature crawling / Adventure and the resolution / Dance war / The cult of Ray / Last stand of Shazeb Andleeb.

Jul 96. (7") *(663 463-7)* **I DON'T WANT TO HURT YOU (EVERY SINGLE TIME). / YOU AIN'T ME (live)** [63] [-]
(cd-s+=) *(663 463-2)* – The Marxist / Better things.
(cd-s) *(663 463-5)* – ('A'live) / Men in black (live) / Village of the sun (live) / The last stand of Shazeb Andleeb (live).

FRANK BLACK AND THE CATHOLICS

Play It Again Sam — SpinArt

Apr 98. (7"ep/cd-ep) *(BIAS 347 7/CD)* **ALL MY GHOSTS / LIVING ON SOUL / HUMBOULDT COUNTY MASSACRE / CHANGING OF THE GUARDS** [ ] [-]

May 98. (cd/c/lp) *(BIAS 370 CD/MC/LP) <SPART 67>* **FRANK BLACK AND THE CATHOLICS** [61] [ ]
– All my ghosts / Back to Rome / Do you feel bad about it / Dog gone / I gotta move / I need peace / King and Queen of Siam / Six sixty six / Solid gold / Steak 'n' sabre / Suffering / Man who was too loud. *(ltd-cd+=; BIAS 370CDX)* – All my ghosts / Living on soul / Humboldt county massacre / Changing of the guards.

Mar 99. (cd) *(CDBIAS 390CD) <SPART 70>* **PISTOLLERO** [ ] [ ]
– Bad harmony / I switched you / Western star / Tiny heart / You're such a wire / I loved your brain / Smoke up / Billy Radcliffe / So hard to make things out / Eighty five weeks / I think I'm starting to lose it / I want to rock and roll / Skeleton man / So bay. *(lp-iss.Nov99 on 'SpinArt'; SPART 70)*

Cooking Vinyl — What Are?

Jan 01. (cd) *(FRYCD 098)* **ROBERT ONION** [ ] [-]

Jan 01. (cd) *(COOKCD 200) <4833>* **DOG IN THE SAND** [ ] [ ]
– Blast off / I've seen your picture / St. Francis dam disaster / Robert Onion / Stupid me / Bullet / The swimmer / Hermaphroditos / I'll be blue / Llano del Rio / If it takes all night / Dog in the sand.

Feb 01. (cd-s) *(FRYCD 099)* **ST. FRANCIS DAM DISASTER** [ ] [-]

– compilations, etc. –

Jul 95. (12"ep/cd-ep) *Strange Fruit; (SFPS/+CD 091)* **PEEL SESSION** [ ] [-]
– Handyman / The man who was too loud / The Jacques Tati / Sister Isabel.

Nov 97. (cd-ep; with TEENAGE FANCLUB) *Strange Fruit; (SFRSCD 042)* **THE JOHN PEEL SESSION** [ ] [-]

Mar 01. (cd) *4 a.d.; (GAD 2103CD)* **THE COMPLETE B-SIDES** [53] [-]

PLACEBO

Formed: South London, England . . . October '94 by the cosmopolitan pair of BRIAN MOLKO and STEFAN OLSDAL, who had attended the same school in Luxembourg. They met up again in a London tube having spent time in the States and Sweden respectively. Early the following year, they recruited Swedish drummer, ROBERT SCHULTZBERG, the trio subsequently becoming joint winners of the 'In The City' Battle Of The Bands competition. Late in '95, PLACEBO shared a one-off single, 'BRUISE PRISTINE', with the band, SOUP, on 'Fierce Panda' records. After only a handful of gigs, they signed for 'Deceptive' (home of ELASTICA), leading to tours with ASH, BUSH and WHALE. A solitary single later ('COME HOME'), MOLKO and Co., hit the proverbial jackpot via a deal with Virgin/Hut subsidiary, 'Elevator'. The openly bisexual, cross-dressing MOLKO, drew comparisons with 70's glam idols like BOLAN and BOWIE, the music, however, traded in the glitter for a darker listening experience. Taking the fast lane out of the post-grunge pile-up, they fused elements of avant-garde rock and cerebral metal, MOLKO's paint-stripping shrill drawing comparisons with Rush's GEDDY LEE and DAVID SURKAMP of the more obscure Pavlov's Dog. Their eponymous debut album was released in mid-'96 to a fawning music press, metal-mag Kerrang's strong support helping the record dent the UK Top 40. Hit singles 'TEENAGE ANGST' and the Top 5 'NANCY BOY', helped regenerate sales of a collection which many hailed as one of the years' best. In addition to the more incendiary tracks, the album also contained such hauntingly reflective songs as 'LADY OF THE FLOWERS' and 'HANG ON TO YOUR IQ'. PLACEBO – with STEVE HEWITT replacing SCHULTZBERG – were back with a bang (so to speak!) in the Autumn of '98, two blistering UK Top 5 singles in quick succession, 'PURE MORNING' and 'YOU DON'T CARE ABOUT US', premiering their equally superb sophomore set, 'WITHOUT YOU I'M NOTHING' – 'EVERY YOU EVERY ME' and collaborative title track with MOLKO's idol BOWIE, kept the band in high profile the following year. With 'BLACK MARKET MUSIC' (2000), MOLKO took his brooding sexual vision to its twisted climax on an album which ranks as one of PLACEBO's most darkly satisfying to date. Longtime fans will be glad to know that the ever androgynous frontman is still wrestling with his soiled demons, content to provide a mascara-smeared foil to the bloke-rock clogging up the music biz. • **Songwriters:** Group, except BIGMOUTH STRIKES AGAIN (Smiths) / 20TH CENTURY BOY (T.Rex) / JOHNNY & MARY (Robert Palmer).

Album rating: PLACEBO (*9) / WITHOUT YOU I'M NOTHING (*8) / BLACK MARKET MUSIC (*6)

BRIAN MOLKO (b. 1972) – vocals, guitars, bass / **STEFAN OLSDAL** (b. Sweden) – bass, guitars, keyboards / **ROBERT SCHULTZBERG** – drums, percussion, didgeridoo

Fierce Panda / not iss.

Nov 95. (7") *(NING 13)* **BRUISE PRISTINE. / (Soup: 'Meltdown')** [ ] [-]

Deceptive / not iss.

Feb 96. (7") *(BLUFF 024)* **COME HOME. / DROWNING BY NUMBERS** [ ] [-]
(cd-s+=) *(BLUFF 024CD)* – Oxygen thief.

Elevator / Caroline

Jun 96. (7") *(FLOOR 001)* **36 DEGREES. / DARK GLOBE** [ ] [-]
(cd-s+=) *(FLOORCD 001)* – Hare Krishna.

Jun 96. (cd/c/lp) *(CD/MC/LP FLOOR 002)* <7575> **PLACEBO** [40] [ ] Jul96
– Come home / Teenage angst / Bionic / 36 degrees / Hang on to you IQ / Nancy boy / I know / Bruise pristine / Lady of the flowers / Swallow. *(re-dist.Jan97 hit UK No.5; same)*

Sep 96. (7"/cd-s) *(FLOOR/+CD 003)* **TEENAGE ANGST. / BEEN SMOKING TOO LONG / HUG BUBBLE** [30] [-]
(7"m) *(FLOORX 003)* – ('A'-V.P.R.O. radio session) / Flesh mechanic (demo) / HK farewell.

Jan 97. (7") *(FLOOR 004)* **NANCY BOY. / SLACKERBITCH** [4] [ ]
(cd-s+=) *(FLOORCD 004)* – Bigmouth strikes again / Hug bubble.
(cd-s) *(FLOORCDX 004)* – ('A'side) / Eyesight to the blind / Swallow (Brad Wood mix) / Miss Moneypenny.

May 97. (c-s/cd-s) *(FLOOR MC/CD 005)* **BRUISE PRISTINE / THEN THE CLOUDS WILL OPEN FOR ME / BRUISE PRISTINE (One Inch Punch remix)** [14] [-]
(cd-s) *(FLOORCDX 005)* – ('A'side) / Waiting for the sun of man / Serenity (Lionrock remix).

— **STEVE HEWITT** (b. Northwich, England) – drums; repl. SCHULTZBERG

Elevator / Hut

Aug 98. (cd-ep) *(FLOORCD 6)* **PURE MORNING / MARS LANDING PARTY / LEELOO** [4] [-]
(cd-ep) *(FLOORCDX 6)* – ('A'-lp version) / Needledick / The innocence of sleep.

Sep 98. (c-s/cd-s) *(FLOOR C/CD 7)* <95363> **YOU DON'T CARE ABOUT US / 20TH CENTURY BOY / ION** [5] [ ]
(cd-s) *(FLOORDX 7)* – ('A'side) / ('A'-Les Rhythmes Digitales remix) / ('A'-Howie B remix).

Oct 98. (cd/c/lp) *(CDFLOOR/FLOORMC/FLOORLP 8)* <46531> **WITHOUT YOU I'M NOTHING** [7] [ ] Nov98
– Pure morning / Brick shithouse / You don't care about us / Ask for answers / Without you I'm nothing / Allergic (to thoughts of Mother Earth) / The crawl / Every you every me / My sweet prince / Summer's gone / Scared of girls / Burger queen.

Jan 99. (7") *(FLOORLH 9)* **EVERY YOU EVERY ME. / NANCY BOY (Blue Amazon remix)** [11] [-]
(c-s+=/cd-s+=) *(FLOORCD 9)* – ('A'-Jimmy Cauty remix).
(cd-s) *(FLOORDX 9)* – ('A'side) / ('A'-Sneaker Pimps version) / ('A'-Brothers In Rhythm remix).

Aug 99. (cd-ep; featuring DAVID BOWIE) *(FLOORCD 10)* **WITHOUT YOU I'M NOTHING / ('A'-Unkle remix) / ('A'-Americruiser remix) / ('A'-Brothers In Rhythm remix)** [-] [-] nochart

Jul 00. (c-s/cd-s) *(FLOOR C/CD 11)* **TASTE IN MEN / THEME FROM FUNKY REVEREND / TASTE IN MEN (Alpinestars Kamikaze skimix)** [16] [-]
(cd-s) *(FLOORDX 11)* – ('A'side) / Johnny & Mary / Taste in men (Adrian Sherwood Go Go dub mix).
(12"++=) *(FLOORT 11)* – (all above).

Sep 00. (c-s/cd-s) *(FLOOR C/CD 12)* **SLAVE TO THE WAGE / LENI / BUBBLEGUM** [19] [-]
(cd-s/12"+=) *(FLOOR DX/X 12)* – ('A'-album version) / Holocaust / ('A'-Les Rythmes Digitales new wave mix).

Oct 00. (cd/c/lp) *(CDFLOOR/FLOORMCX/FLOORLP 13)* <10316> **BLACK MARKET MUSIC** [6] [ ]
– Taste in men / Days before you came / Special K / Spite & malice / Passive aggressive / Black-eyed / Blue American / Slave to the wage / Commercial for Levi / Haemoglobin / Narcoleptic / Peeping Tom.

Mar 01. (cd-s) *(CDFLOOR 14)* **SPECIAL K / DUB PSYCHOSIS / PASSIVE AGGRESSIVE (Brothers In Rhythm remix)** [ ] [-]
(12"+=) *(TFLOOR 14)* – Little Mo / Slave to the wage (I can't believe it's a remix).
(cd-s) *(CDFLOORX 14)* – ('A'-Timo Maas remix) / (above 2).

PLANKEYE

Formed: Orange County, California, USA . . . 1993 by SCOTT SILIETTA, LUIS GARCIA, ADAM FERRY and ERIC BALMER, the former and his musical buddies of the Christian persuasion. Never going to be the greatest punk-pop band of all time, PLANKEYE managed to squeeze out a handful of average albums in a prolific mid-90's period that included 'SPILL' (1994), 'SPARK' (1995), 'COMMONWEALTH' (1996) and 'THE ONE AND ONLY' (1997); the latter their debut UK release in February '98. FRANZ LENZ replaced drummer FERRY prior to their fifth set (in as many years), entitled 'RELOCATION' (1999) and they were at least gaining some ground on their punk contemporaries; a sixth long-player, 'STRANGE EXCHANGE', was their latest offering.

Album rating: SPILL (*5) / SPARK (*5) / COMMONWEALTH (*5) / THE ONE AND ONLY (*6) / RELOCATION (*5) / STRANGE EXCHANGE (*5)

SCOTT SILIETTA – vocals, guitar / **ERIC BALMER** – guitar / **LUIS GARCIA** – bass / **ADAM FERRY** – drums

not iss. / Tooth & Nail

1994. (cd) <TNR 1005CD> **SPILL** [-] [ ]
– Good news / Revolution / Power / Open eyes / Scared / Bold / Step away / Free me / Know way / Forever.

1995. (cd) <TNR 1023CD> **SPARK** [-] [ ]
– It's a perfect day Jerome / Open house / Three fold chord / Drive / Boy / Tonight / Wings to fly / Let me go / Questions / Dichotomy / So far from home.

Jun 96. (cd) <TNR 1054CD> **COMMONWEALTH** [-] [ ]
– Whisper to me / B.C. / Push me down (veiled) / Struck by the chord / Placement / He / Bicycle / Beautiful / Who loves you more?

B.E.C. / B.E.C.

Nov 97. (cd) <(BED 7405)> **THE ONE AND ONLY** [ ] [ ] Nov97
– Someday / How much I don't know / Fall down / Playground / It's been so very long / One or the other / Landmarks / Let's try again tomorrow / Compromise / Sterling.

— **FRANK LENZ** – drums; repl. FERRY

Sep 99. (cd) <(BEC 7418CD)> **RELOCATION** [ ] [ ] May99
– Say now that you're sorry / I can't complain / Goodbye / When it comes / Call me liar / Break my fall / Break of dawn / Honey and oil / You got it / Indivisible.

Apr 01. (cd) <BEC 17444> **STRANGE EXCHANGE** [-] [ ]
– This is / The meaning of it all / Chemicals and sleep / Let me be near you / My wife / By design / Remind / Bring it down / The way of the earth.

Robert PLANT (see under ⇒ LED ZEPPELIN)

PLASMATICS

Formed: New York, USA . . . 1978 by porn magnate ROD SWENSON, the brains behind this outrageous, shock-hungry post-punk outfit. To front the band he recruited ex-stripper and porn-star WENDY O'WILLIAMS, backing her up with the colourful RITCHIE STOTTS, WES BEECH, STU DEUTSCH and CHOSEI FUNAHARA, the latter subsequently being replaced by JEAN BEAUVOIR. With a string of US-only indie 45's behind them, The PLASMATICS arrived in Britain under a storm of protest, especially from London's GLC who vehemently objected to their much publicised high-octane stage show (blowing up cars and chainsawing the odd instrument a speciality, while WENDY's topless, sometimes bottomless attire further provoked police heavy-handedness!). Appropriately signing to 'Stiff' records, the spiky-nippled O'WILLIAMS and her crew finally unleashed their debut set, 'NEW HOPE FOR THE WRETCHED' amid a sea of hype in 1980. Although lambasted by the critics it nevertheless hit the UK charts, as did the controversial 'BUTCHER BABY' single. WENDY and the band released two further forgettable albums the following year and it was quite surprising 'Capitol' records took up the option to sign them. Now without BEAUVOIR and DEUTSCH (who were replaced by JUNIOR ROMANELLI and T.C. TOLLIVER), they released the heavier 'COUP D'ETAT' (1982), a change in music and image which left them with few fans. This proved to be The PLASMATICS' epitaph, the bondage-loving WENDY going solo, taking her cue from wildman sidekick, LEMMY and releasing three albums in as many years. The last of these, 'MAGGOTS: THE RECORD', came in 1987, both its concept and cover art reaching a nadir in bad taste. She made her final stand for rock'n'roll excess with the aforementioned LEMMY on a version of Tammy Wynette's country standard, 'STAND BY YOUR MAN'. Spookily enough, both WENDY and TAMMY were to die on the same day (6th April '98), O'WILLIAMS taking her own life by shooting herself. • **Songwriters:** BEECH-BEAUVOIR penned most, until the latter's departure; also covered DREAM LOVER (Bobby Darin) / JAILBAIT (Motorhead).

Album rating: NEW HOPE FOR THE WRETCHED (*6) / BEYOND THE VALLEY OF 1984 (*4) / COUP D'ETAT (*5) / Wendy O'Williams: W.O.W. (*5) / KOMMANDER OF CHAOS (*4) / MAGGOTS: THE RECORD (*3) / DEFFEST! AND BADDEST! (*1)

WENDY O'WILLIAMS – vocals, saxophone, electric chain saw / **RITCHIE STOTTS** – lead guitar / **WES BEECH** – rhythm guitar / **JEAN BEAUVOIR** – bass; repl. CHOSEI FUNAHARA / **STU DEUTSCH** – drums

Vice Squad / P.V.C.

Nov 78. (7";7"red) <VS 101/102> **BUTCHER BABY. / FAST FOOD SERVICE / CONCRETE SHOES** [-] [ ]

Oct 79. (7"/7"lavender) <VS 103/104> **DREAM LOVER. / CORRUPTION / WANT YOU BABY** [-] [ ]

Dec 79. (12"ep/12"ep;yellow) <VS 105/106> **MEET THE PLASMATICS** [-] [ ]
– Sometimes I / Won't you? / Want you baby.

Stiff / Stiff

Jun 80. (7",7"multi-colrd) *(BUY 76)* **BUTCHER BABY. / TIGHT BLACK PANTS** [55] [-]

Jul 80. (12"ep) *(BUYIT 76)* **BUTCHER BABY (re-recorded). / LIVING DEAD (live) / SOMETIMES I (FEEL IT WHEN YOU'RE DOWN ON YOUR KNEES)** [ ] [-]

Sep 80. (7"multi-colrd) *(BUY 91)* **MONKEY SUIT. / SQUIRM (live)** [ ] [-]

Sep 80. (lp,multi-colrd-lp) *(SEEZ 24)* <USE 9> **NEW HOPE FOR THE WRETCHED** [55] [ ]
– Concrete shoes / Butcher baby / Squirm (live) / Corruption / Want you baby / Dream lover / Won't you / Sometimes I / Tight black pants / Monkey suit / Living dead / Test-tube babies. *(cd-iss. Dec92 on 'Dojo'; DOJOCD 79) (re-iss. cd Feb94 on 'Disky'; STIFFCD 16)*

— **JOEY REESE** – drums; repl. DEUTSCH

Nov 81. (m-lp) <WOW 666> **METAL PRIESTESS** (The 2nd Album) [-] [ ]
– Lunacy / Doom song / Sex junkie / Black leather monster / 12 noon / Masterplan.

—— **'JUNIOR' CHRIS ROMANELLI** – bass repl. BEAUVOIR who went solo, after joining LITTLE STEVEN & THE DISCIPLES OF SOUL

Jun 81. (lp) *(WOW 2)* **BEYOND THE VALLEY OF 1984**
– Incantation / Masterplan / Headbanger / Sumer nite / Nothing / Fast food service / Hit man / Living dead / Sex junkie / Plasma jam / Pig is a pig.

—— **T.C. TOLLIVER** – drums, percussion repl. REESE

Capitol Capitol

Nov 82. (lp/c) *<(EST/TC-EST 12237)>* **COUP D'ETAT**
– Put your love in me / Stop / Rock and roll / Counting fairs / No class / Just like on TV / Lightning breaks / Mistress of taboo / Path of glory. *(re-iss. 1986 on 'Revolver' lp/c; REV LP/MC 78) (cd-iss. Mar96 on 'Dojo'; DOJOCD 239) (cd re-iss. Oct00 on 'Razor & Tie'; RE 82215-2)*

—— split 1983

WENDY O'WILLIAMS

went solo, augmented by **ROMANELLI, BEECH + GENE SIMMONS** (of KISS, + their producer)

Music For Nations not iss.

May 84. (7"/12") *(KUT/12KUT 111)* **IT'S MY LIFE. / PRIESTUS**
Jul 84. (lp) *(MFN 24)* **W.O.W.** 100
– I love sex and rock and roll / It's my life / Priestess / Thief in the night / Opus in Cm7 / Ready to rock / Bump and grind / Legends never die / Ain't none of your business. *<US-iss.1987 on 'Passport' lp/c/cd; PB/+C/CD 6034>*

Zebra not iss.

Feb 86. (lp) *(ZEB 7)* **KOMMANDER OF CHAOS**
– Hoy hey (love to rock) / Pedal to the metal / Goin' wild / Ain't none of your business / Party / Jailbait / Bad girl / Fight for the right / F*** that booty.

—— **O'WILLIAMS** re-formed The PLASMATICS with **RAY**

G.W.R. not iss.

Mar 87. (lp; as The PLASMATICS and WENDY O'WILLIAMS) *(GWLP 8)* **MAGGOTS: THE RECORD**
– Overture / Introduction / You're a zombie / Full meal diner / The whites apartment / The day of the humans is gone / The central research laboratory / Valerie and Bruce on the phone / Destroyers / The whites apartment / Bruces bedroom / Brain dead / The whites apartment / Bruces bedroom / Propagators / The whites apartment / Fire escape / Finale.

—— added **WES BEECH** – guitar / **KATRINA ASHTON** – guitar

Mar 88. (lp; as ULTRAFLY & THE HOMETOWN GIRLS) *<PAL 1258>* **DEFFEST! AND BADDEST!**
– Rulers of rock / 10 million $ question / Super Jock / Early days / Know w'am sayin' / I.R.T. (out in space) / Lies intro & 41 / La la land / Laffin' & scratchin'.

– compilations, etc. –

1987. (lp/c/cd) *P.V.C.; <PVC/+C/CD 8929>* **BEYOND THE VALLEY OF 1984 / METAL PRIESTESS**

PLAY DEAD

Formed: Oxford, England . . . Autumn 1980 by ROB, PETE DEAN and WIFF, who were soon supporting the likes of UK DECAY the following summer. Their debut single, 'POISON TAKES A HOLD', was issued around the same time while its follow-up, 'TV EYE', saw the addition of guitarist, STEVE. In 1982, they recorded their first of many John Peel sessions and signed to goth/punk orientated label, 'Jungle', releasing 'PROPAGANDA' in the process. Subsequent tours supporting SEX GANG CHILDREN and KILLING JOKE – with whom they shared a spiritual similarity – paved the way for another string of anthemic singles including the pummelling 'PROPAGANDA'. They finally unleashed their debut album, 'FROM THE PROMISED LAND', in 1984, featuring live favourite 'WALK AWAY', which believe it or not, suggested a gothic BIG COUNTRY, if that's possible! Becoming one of the many acts on the books of the 'Clay' label, PLAY DEAD featured on a December '84 edition of 'The Tube', while going on to tour Scandinavia and other parts of Europe where they were more popular. However, by March '86 (and after another album, 'COMPANY OF JUSTICE'), PLAY DEAD had finally keeled over, metamorphosising into the short-lived BEASTMASTER GENERAL.

Album rating: FROM THE PROMISED LAND (*5) / INTO THE FIRE – LIVE mini (*4) / COMPANY OF JUSTICE (*4) / THE SINGLES 82-85 compilation (*5)

ROB – vocals / **PETE DEAN** – bass / **WIFF** – drums

Fresh not iss.

Jun 81. (7") *(FRESH 29)* **POISON TAKES A HOLD. / INTRODUCTION**

—— added **STEVE** – guitar

Oct 81. (7") *(FRESH 38)* **T.V. EYE. / THE FINAL EPITAPH**

Jungle not iss.

Nov 82. (7") *(JUNG 002)* **PROPAGANDA. / PROPAGANDA (mix)**

Situation 2 not iss.

Sep 83. (7") *(SIT 28)* **SHINE. / PROMISE**
(12"+=) *(SIT 28T)* – Gaze.

Clay not iss.

Apr 84. (7") *(CLAY 31)* **BREAK. / BLOODSTAINS**
(12"+=) *(12CLAY 31)* – The pleasure.
May 84. (lp) *(CLAYLP 11)* **FROM THE PROMISED LAND**
– Isabel / Torn on desire / Walk away / Pleasureland / Return to the east / Holy holy / No motive / Weeping blood.
Jul 84. (7"/12") *(CLAY/12CLAY 35)* **ISABEL. / SOLACE**
Oct 84. (7"/12") *(CLAY/12CLAY 40)* **CONSPIRACY. / SILENT CONSPIRACY**
Feb 85. (7") *(CLAY 42)* **SACROSANCT. / PALE FIRE**
(12"+=) *(12CLAY 42)* – Holy holy / Sacrosanct.
May 85. (m-lp) *(CLAYLP 16M)* **INTO THE FIRE (live)**
– Walk away / Shine / Return to the east / Break / Turn on desire / Sin of sins / The tenant / No motive.

Tanz not iss.

Sep 85. (12"'w-drawn) *(TANZ 1)* **THIS SIDE OF HEAVEN. / LAST DEGREE / THIS SIDE OF HEAVEN (serious mix)**
Nov 85. (lp) *(TANZLP 1)* **COMPANY OF JUSTICE**
(cd-iss. Sep93 on 'Jungle'; FREUDCD 41)
May 86. (12") *(TANZ 2)* **BURNING DOWN. / STILL IN CHAINS**

—— had already split in March when two members (not PETE) formed the BEASTMASTER GENERAL

– compilations, etc. –

Jul 84. (lp/c) *Jungle; (FREUD/+C 003)* **THE FIRST FLOWER**
– Shine / Sin of sins / In silence / Gaze / Propaganda / The tenant / Time / Promise / Propaganda ('84 mix) / Don't leave without me. *(cd-iss. Sep92 +=; FREUDCD 003)* – Sin of sins ('84 mix) / Poison takes a hold / Introduction / T.V. eye / The final epitaph. *(cd re-iss. Jan94 on 'Cleopatra'; CLEO 7519CD)*
Sep 84. (12") *Jungle; (JUNG 17)* **PROPAGANDA (1984 mix). / SIN OF SINS (remix)**
Feb 86. (12"ep) *Jungle; (JUNG 26T)* **IN THE BEGINNING – THE 1981 SINGLES**
Jul 86. (m-lp) *Clay; (CLAYLP 20M)* **THE SINGLES '82-'85**
Aug 86. (lp) *Dojo; (DOJOLP 34)* **CAUGHT FROM BEHIND – LIVE IN ENGLAND, FRANCE, GERMANY AND SWITZERLAND)**
– Break / Last degree / Solace / Shine / Isabel / Sin of sins / Torn on desire / This side of Heaven / Sacrosanct / The tenant.
Mar 87. (lp) *Jungle; (FREUD 015)* **THE FINAL EPITAPH – LIVE (live)**
Jun 92. (cd) *Clay; (CLAYCD 111)* **RESURRECTION** (w/ some remixes)
– Break / Isabel / Walk away / Bloodstains / Solace / No motive / Pleasureland / Pale fire / Sacrosanct / Torn on desire / Holy holy / Return to the east / Conspiracy / Sin of sins (live) / Bloodstains pleasure / Solace / Holy holy.

POINT BLANK

Formed: Texas, USA . . . mid-70's, a line-up of JOHN O'DANIELS, RUSTY BURNS, KIM DAVIS, PHILIP PETTY and PETER 'BUZZY' GRUEN appearing on the eponymous debut album in 1976. Signed to 'Arista' and produced by ZZ TOP guru, Bill Ham, the comparisons with the latter band's gritty desert-boogie were unavoidable. 'SECOND SEASON' (1977) continued in a similar sun-parched mould, although a subsequent move to 'M.C.A.' and a change of personnel (BILL RANDOLPH and STEVE HARDIN recruited in place of PETTY) resulted in a more straightahead, keyboard-enhanced hard-rock approach on 1980's 'AIRPLAY'. Still, fans of the group's more organic style could console themselves with the live tracks on 'THE HARD WAY' (1980), POINT BLANK wigging out over some paint-strippingly intense blues-boogie. The early 80's saw BUBBA KEITH taking over on vocals and a more concerted effort to break into the US AOR market with 'AMERICAN EXCESS' (1981), the 'NICOLE' single nudging into the US Top 40 and giving them their sole sniff at notable chart action. The follow-up, 'ON A ROLL' (1982), failed to hit the commercial target, however, and the band eventually set their sights on other avenues.

Album rating: POINT BLANK (*6) / SECOND SEASON (*5) / AIRPLAY (*4) / THE HARD WAY (*7) / AMERICAN EXCESS (*6) / ON A ROLL (*5)

JOHN O'DANIEL – vocals / **RUSTY BURNS + KIM DAVIS** – guitar, vocals / **PHILIP PETTY** – bass / **PETER 'BUZZY' GRUEN** – drums

Arista Arista

Sep 76. (7") *<0217>* **MOVING. / BAD BEES**
Nov 76. (lp) *(ARTY 135) <AL 4087>* **POINT BLANK** Sep76
– Free man / Wandering / Bad bees / That's the law / Lone star fool / Distance / In this world.
1977. (7") *<0298>* **BACK IN THE ALLEY. / BEAUTIFUL LOSER**
1977. (lp) *(SPARTY 1019) <AL 4137>* **SECOND SEASON**
– Part time lover / Back in the alley / Rock and roll hideaways / Stars and scars / Beautiful loser / Uncle Ned / Tattooed lady / Nasty notions / Waiting for a change.

—— **BILL RANDOLPH** – bass, vocals + **STEVE HARDIN** – keyboards repl. PETTY

M.C.A. M.C.A.

Feb 80. (lp) *(MCF 3049) <3160>* **AIRPLAY** Aug79
– Mean to your Queenie / Two-time loser / Shine on / Penthouse pauper / Danger zone / Louisiana leg / Takin' it easy / Thunder and lightning / Changed my mind.

—— **KARL BERKE** – keyboards, vocals, repl. HARDIN

May 80. (lp) *<5114>* **THE HARD WAY**
– Turning back / The hard way / On the run / Highway star / Rock and roll soldier / Guessing game / Wrong to cry / Thank you mama.
Oct 80. (7") *<41268>* **ROCK AND ROLL SOLDIER. / ON THE RUN**

—— **BUBBA KEITH** – vocals + **MIKE HAMILTON** – keyboards, vocals, repl. O'DANIEL + BERKE

Mar 81. (7") *<51083>* **LET ME STAY WITH YOU TONIGHT. / WALK ACROSS THE FIRE**
Apr 81. (lp) *<5189>* **AMERICAN EXCE$$** 80
– Let me stay with you tonight / Walk across the fire / Nicole / Go on home / The getaway / The way you broke my heart / Restless / Cadillac dragon / Do it all night.
Jun 81. (7") *<51132>* **NICOLE. / RESTLESS** 39
Apr 82. (7") *<52029>* **LET HER GO. / LOVE ON FIRE**
Jun 82. (lp/c) *(MCF/+C 3141) <5312>* **ON A ROLL** Apr82
– On a roll / I just want to know / Love on fire / Don't look down / Great white line / Let her go / Gone Hollywood / Take me up.
Aug 82. (7") *<52071>* **DON'T LOOK DOWN. / TAKE ME UP**

—— Split after above.

POISON

Formed: Harrisburg, Pennsylvania, USA ... March '84 by former SPECTRES members BRET MICHAELS and RIKKI ROCKETT, the line-up completed by BOBBY DALL and C.C. DEVILLE. Like a cartoon bubblegum version of FASTER PUSSYCAT or HANOI ROCKS, this super-glam metal outfit exploded onto the US rock scene in a sea of peroxide bleach circa late '86, their aptly titled debut album, 'LOOK WHAT THE CAT DRAGGED IN' (1986) reaching No.3 in the US charts, aided and abetted by the singalong sleaze anthem, 'TALK DIRTY TO ME'. Needless to say, the rest of the album was painfully amateurish at best, hilarious at worst. Still, the Americans lapped it up and made sure the follow-up, 'OPEN UP AND SAY . . . AAH!' (1988) climbed to No.2. The obligatory "sensitive" ballad, in this case 'EVERY ROSE HAS ITS THORN' was a massive hit on both sides of the Atlantic (US No.1), a lonesome strumathon that EXTREME would've been proud to call their own. The album spawned a further three Stateside singles, including a cover of the old LOGGINS & MESSINA chestnut, 'YOUR MAMA DON'T DANCE'. 'FLESH AND BLOOD' (1990) was the band's most successful album to date, going Top 5 in both the British and American charts, POISON making a conscious effort to distance themselves from their mascara'd days of old. Nevertheless, they retained the ability to release annoyingly pointless pop-metal nonsense like 'UNSKINNY BOP'. By the release of 1993's 'NATIVE TONGUE' opus, the MICHAELS and Co. were trying so painfully hard to create a credible image, they employed the TOWER OF POWER horn section! If they were under the illusion that this would give them instant soul power then POISON were clearly even more clueless than their music gave them credit for. The ploy didn't work and the album failed to sell as much as its predecessor, MICHAELS more newsworthy for his shortlived affair with PAMELA ANDERSON than his music. The POISON posse finally emerged into a radically altered rock landscape in the new millennium with a couple of half-baked albums which will undoubtedly be of interest to hardcore fans only. The bulk of 'CRACK A SMILE . . . AND MORE' (2000) was composed of material from aborted 1994 sessions cobbled together with a few outtakes and MTV Unplugged material. The godawful cover probably tells you all you need to know, although the ageing Glam rockers at least have the grace to poke fun at their increasingly archaic image on the likes of 'TRAGICALLY UNHIP' while a rendition of the Dr. Hook nugget, 'COVER OF THE ROLLING STONE' is worth a laugh. 'POWER TO THE PEOPLE' (2000), meanwhile, featured a mixture of new studio tracks and live cuts from their 1999 comeback tour. The big news for fans is that lead guitar hearthrob C.C. DEVILLE is back in action and even has a shot at lead vocals. • **Trivia:** Late in 1990, BRET co-wrote and produced girlfriend SUSIE HATTON's debut album. He landed the lead role in the 1996 movie 'A Letter From Death Row'.

Album rating: LOOK WHAT THE CAT DRAGGED IN (*6) / OPEN UP AND SAY . . . AAH! (*7) / FLESH & BLOOD (*7) / SWALLOW THIS LIVE (*5) / NATIVE TONGUE (*5) / GREATEST HITS 1986-1996 compilation (*7) / CRACK A SMILE . . . AND MORE collection (*5) / POWER TO THE PEOPLE (*4)

BRET MICHAELS (b. BRET MICHAEL SYCHAK, 15 Mar'63) – vocals / **C.C. DEVILLE** (b. BRUCE ANTHONY JOHANNESSON, 14 May'62, Brooklyn, N.Y.) – lead guitar (ex-SCREAMING MIMI) repl. MATT SMITH / **BOBBY DALL** (b. ROBERT KUY KENDALL, 2 Nov'63, Miami, Florida) – bass / **RIKKI ROCKETT** (b. RICHARD REAM, 8 Aug'61, Mechanicsburg, Pennsylvania) – drums

Music For Nations / Capitol

Oct 86. (lp/pic-lp/c) *(MFN 69/+P/C)* <12523> **LOOK WHAT THE CAT DRAGGED IN** [ ] [3] Jul86
– Cry tough / I want action / I won't forget you / Play dirty / Look what the cat dragged in / Talk dirty to me / Want some, need some / Blame it on you / #1 bad boy / Let me go to the show. *(re-iss. Apr89 lp,pic-lp,c/cd.Apr89; same/MFN 69CD) (re-iss. Jul94 cd/c; same) (re-iss. May96 on 'EMI Gold' cd/c; CD/TC GOLD 1027)*

May 87. (7") *(KUT 125)* <5686> **TALK DIRTY TO ME. / WANT SOME, NEED SOME** [67] [9] Mar87
(12"pic-d+=/12"+=) *(P+/12KUT 125)* – (interview).

Jun 87. (7") <44004> **I WANT ACTION. / PLAY DIRTY** [-] [50]

Aug 87. (7") *(KUT 127)* **CRY TOUGH. / LOOK WHAT THE CAT DRAGGED IN** [ ] [-]
(12"pic-d+=/12"+=) *(P+/12KUT 127)* – ('A'-U.S. remix).
(re-iss. Apr89; same)

Capitol / Capitol

Sep 87. (7") <44038> **I WON'T FORGET YOU. / BLAME IT ON YOU** [-] [13]

Apr 88. (7"/7"w-poster/7"s) *(CL/+P/Z 486)* <44145> **NOTHIN' BUT A GOOD TIME. / LOOK BUT YOU CAN'T TOUCH** [35] [6]
(12"+=/12"g-f+=) *(12CL/+G 486)* – Livin' for a minute.

May 88. (lp/pic-lp)(c/cd)(pic-cd) *(EST/+P 2059)(TC/CD+/EST 2059) (CDP 748493L)* <48493> **OPEN UP AND SAY . . .AAH!** [23] [2]
– Love on the rocks / Nothin' but a good time / Back to the rocking horse / Good love / Tearin' down the walls / Look but you can't touch / Fallen angel / Every rose has its thorn / Your mama can't dance / Bad to be good. *(re-iss. Mar94 cd/c; same) (cd re-iss. Nov99 on 'Axe Killer'; AXE 305333-2)*

Oct 88. (7"/7"s) *(CL/+S 500)* <44191> **FALLEN ANGEL. / BAD TO BE GOOD** [59] [12] Jul88
(12"+=/12"pic-d+=) *(12CL/+P 500)* – (interview).

Oct 88. (7") <44203> **EVERY ROSE HAS ITS THORN. / LIVING FOR THE MINUTE** [-] [1]

Jan 89. (7"/7"s/7"sha-pic-d) *(CL/+S/P 520)* **EVERY ROSE HAS ITS THORN. / BACK TO THE ROCKING HORSE** [13] [-]
(12"+=/12"g-f+=)(cd-s+=) *(12CL/+G 520)(CDCL 520)* – Gotta face the hangman.

Apr 89. (7"/7"green) *(CL/+S 523)* <44203> **YOUR MAMA DON'T DANCE. / TEARIN' DOWN THE WALLS** [13] [10] Feb89
(12"+=/12"green+=)(cd-s+=) *(12CL/+B 523)(CDCL 523)* – Love on the rocks.

Jul 89. (7"/7"s)(c-s) *(CL/+X 539)(TCCL 539)* **NOTHIN' BUT A GOOD TIME. / LIVIN' FOR THE MINUTE** [48] [-]
(12"+=/12"pic-d+=)(cd-s+=) *(12CL/+P 539)(CDCL 539)* – Look what the cat dragged in (live).

Jun 90. (c-s/7") *(TC+/CL 582)* <44584> **UNSKINNY BOP. / SWAMP JUICE (SOUL-O)** [15] [3]
(12"+=/12"pic-d+=)(cd-s+=) *(12CL/+P 582)(CDCL 582)* – Valley of lost souls / Poor boy blues.

Jul 90. (cd/c/lp) *(CD/TC+/EST 2126)* <918132> **FLESH & BLOOD** [3] [2]
– Strange days of Uncle Jack / Valley of lost souls / Unskinny bop / (Flesh and blood) Sacrifice / Swamp juice (soul-o) / Let it play / Life goes on / Come Hell or high water / Ride the wind / Don't give up an inch / Something to believe in / Ball and chain / Life loves a tragedy / Poor boy blues. *(re-iss. cd Sep94;)*

Oct 90. (c-s/7") *(TC+/CL 594)* <44617> **SOMETHING TO BELIEVE IN. / BALL AND CHAIN** [35] [4]
(12"+=) *(12CL 594)* – Look what the cat dragged in / Your mama don't dance / Every rose has its thorn.
(10"yellow+=/cd-s+=) *(10/CD CL 594)* – (Bret Michaels interview).

Jan 91. (c-s,12") <44616> **RIDE THE WIND. / COME HELL OR HIGH WATER** [-] [38]

Apr 91. (c-s,12") <44705> **LIFE GOES ON. / SOMETHING TO BELIEVE IN (acoustic)** [-] [35]

Nov 91. (7"/7"clear) *(CL/+P 640)* **SO TELL ME WHY. / GUITAR SOLO** [25] [ ]
(12"+=/cd-s+=) *(12/CD CL 640)* – Unskinny bop (live) / Ride the wind (live).
(12"pic-d+=/pic-cd-s+=) *(12/CD CLP)* – Only time will tell / No more Lookin' back (poison jazz).

Dec 91. (cd/c/d-lp) *(CD/TC+/ESTU 2159)* <98046> **SWALLOW THIS LIVE** (live / studio tracks *) [52] [51]
– Intro / Look what the dragged in / Look but you can't touch / Good love / I want action / Something to believe in / Poor boy blues / Unskinny bop / Every rose has its thorn / Fallen angel / Your mama don't dance / Nothin' but a good time / Talk dirty to me / So tell me why* / Souls on fire* / Only time will tell* / No more lookin' back (poison jazz).

—— (Nov'91) DeVILLE left, and was replaced (Jun'92) by **RICKIE KOTZEN** (b. 3 Feb'70, Reading, Pennsylvania) – guitar

Feb 93. (c-s/7") *(TC+/CL 679)* <44905> **STAND. / STAND (CHR edit)** [25] [50] Jan93
(cd-s) *(CDCL 679)* – ('A'side) / Native tongue / The scream / Whip comes down / ('A'-lp version).

Feb 93. (cd/c/lp) *(CD/TC+/ESTU 2190)* <98961> **NATIVE TONGUE** [20] [16]
– Native tongue / The scream / Stand / Stay alive / Until you suffer some (Fire and ice) / Body talk / Bring it home / 7 days over you / Richie's acoustic thang / Ain't that the truth / Theatre of the soul / Strike up the band / Ride child ride / Blind faith / Bastard son of a thousand blues.

Apr 93. (7"pic-d/c-s) *(CLP/TCCL 685)* **UNTIL YOU SUFFER SOME (FIRE AND ICE). / STAND (acoustic)** [32] [ ]
(cd-s+=) *(CDCL 685)* – Bastard son of a thousand blues / ('A'mix).
(12"colrd+=) *(12CL 685)* – Strike up the band / ('A'mix).

—— **BLUES SARACENO** (b.17 Oct'71) – guitar; repl. KOTZEN

Feb 97. (cd) *(<CTMCD 312>)* **GREATEST HITS 1986-1996** (compilation + two new) [ ] [ ]
– Nothin' but a good time / Talk dirty to me / Unskinny bop / Every rose has its thorn / Fallen angel / I won't forget you / Stand / Ride the wind / Look what the cat dragged in / I want action / Life goes on / (Flesh and blood) Sacrifice / Cry tough / Your mama don't dance / So tell me why / Something to believe in / Sexual thing / Lay your body down.

Liberty / Capitol

May 00. (cd) *<(524781-2)>* **CRACK A SMILE . . . AND MORE** (rec. 1994 . . .) [ ] [ ] Mar00
– Best thing you ever had / Stand up, make love / Baby gets around a bit / Cover of the Rolling Stone / Be the one / Mr. Smiley / Sexual thang / Lay your body down / No ring, no gets / That's the way (I like it) / Tragically unhip / Doin' as I seen on my TV / One more for the bone / Face the hangman / Your mama don't dance (live unplugged).

not iss. / Cyanide

Jun 00. (cd) <6969> **POWER TO THE PEOPLE** [-] [ ]
– Power to the people / Can't bring me down / The last song / Strange / I hate every bone in your body but mine / live:- Intro / Look what the cat dragged in / I want action / Something to believe in / Love on the rocks / C.C. solo / Fallen angel / Let it play / Riki solo / Every rose has its thorn / Unskinny bop / Nothin' but a good time / Talk dirty to me.

POISON GIRLS

Formed: Brighton, England . . . 1977 by VI SUBVERSA, LANCE D'BOYLE and RICHARD FAMOUS. In her mid-40's by the time of the group's shared debut EP, 'FATAL MICROBES MEET THE POISON GIRLS' – the FATAL MICROBES being a punk band featuring VI's kids! – SUBVERSA was an unlikely but highly articulate and committed hippy-turned-punk frontwoman, guiding the band through more than a decade of anti-establishment, pro-feminist musical activity. The subsequent 'HEX' EP was released on CRASS' own label, while the 'GIRLS collaborated with the staunchly anarchist punks themselves on 1980's bludgeoning 'PERSONS UNKNOWN'. The POISON GIRLS also shared their beliefs and lifestyle, choosing to live in a London commune and spending their spare time campaigning against racism and fascism. A full length debut set, 'CHAPPAQUIDDICK BRIDGE' (1980) followed on the band's own 'Xentrix' label and by the release of 'WHERE'S THE PLEASURE' (1982), the group had begun to widen their musical scope and had moved on from their affiliation with CRASS. Following a brief dalliance with the 'Illuminated' label for 1983's 'SEVEN YEAR SCRATCH', the group reactivated 'Xentrix' with their swansong album, 'SONGS OF PRAISE' (1985), the material, at least lyrically, as uncompromising as ever. Although they kept on keeping on until the end of the 80's, The POISON

GIRLS last vinyl release was 1986's EP, 'THE PRICE OF GRAIN AND THE PRICE OF BLOOD', railing against injustice to the last. While VI's occasionally cackling vocal style may be something of an acquired taste and the slightly GONG-hippy feel to some tracks may be off-putting, 1995's 4CD box set, 'STATEMENT', provides an interesting overview of the band's career.

Album rating: CHAPPAQUIDICK BRIDGE (*5) / TOTAL EXPOSURE (*4) / WHERE'S THE PLEASURE (*6) / 7 YEAR SCRATCH compilation (*6) / SONGS OF PRAISE (*4) / STATEMENT – THE COMPLETE RECORDINGS boxed set (*6)

VI SUBVERSA – vocals, guitar / **RICHARD FAMOUS** – guitar, vocals / **LANCE D'BOYLE** – drums / **PETE FENDER** – bass

Small Wonder — not iss.

Mar 79. (12"ep) *(WEENY 3)* **FATAL MICROBES MEET THE POISON GIRLS**
– Piano lessons / Closed shop / (2 by FATAL MICROBES).

— **BERNHARDT REBOURS** – bass repl. FENDER (of FATAL MICROBES)

Jul 79. (12"ep) *(WEENY 4)* **HEX**
– Old tarts song / Crisis / Ideologically / Bremen song / Political love / Jump mama jump / Under the doctor / Reality attack. *(re-iss. Apr81 on 'Crass'; 421984-1)*

Crass — not iss.

May 80. (7") *(421984-1)* **PERSONS UNKNOWN. / (other track by CRASS)**

— added guests **GEM STONE** – vocals (ex-KILLJOYS) / **NIL** – violin

Oct 80. (lp) *(421984-2)* **CHAPPAQUIDICK BRIDGE**
– Another hero / Hole in the wall / Underbitch / Alienation / Pretty Polly / Good time / Other / Daughter & sons.

Apr 81. (7"m) *(421984-8)* **ALL SYSTEMS GO. / PROMENADE IMMORTELLE / DIRTY WORK**

Jun 81. (7"flexi-free) *(421984-10)* **PRETTY POLLY. / BULLY BOYS (live)**

Xntrix — not iss.

Oct 81. (lp) *(XN 2003)* **TOTAL EXPOSURE (live)**
– Persons unknown / Old tart's song / State control / Tension / Bully boys / Another hero bites / Don't go home tonight / S.S. snoopers / Other / Daughters and sons / Alienation / Fucking mother / Dirty work.

— **CHRIS GRACE** + guest **PETE FENDER** – bass repl. REBOURS

Nov 82. (lp) *(XN 2006)* **WHERE'S THE PLEASURE**
– Where's the pleasure / Lovers are they worth it / I've done it all before / Whisky voice / Menage abattoir / Take the toys / Soft touch / Take the toys – reprise / Velvet launderette / Rio disco stink / Cry no more / Mandy is having a baby / Fear of freedom.

— added **CYNTH ETHICS** – keyboards

Illuminated — not iss.

Jul 83. (7") *(ILL 23)* **ONE GOOD REASON. / CINNAMON GARDEN**

Oct 83. (7") *(ILL 25)* **ARE YOU HAPPY NOW?. / CREAM DREAM**

— **MARTIN HEATH** – bass repl. CHRIS

Xntrix — not iss.

Nov 84. (7") *(XN 2009)* **(I'M NOT A) REAL WOMAN. / TAKE THE TOYS FROM THE BOYS**
(12"+=) *(12XN 2009)* – Perfect crime / Tension.

Jun 85. (lp) *(XN 2008)* **SONGS OF PRAISE**

— **AGENT ORANGE** – drums repl. D'BOYLE

Upright — not iss.

Nov 85. (12"ep) *(UPT 12)* **THE PRICE OF GRAIN AND THE PRICE OF BLOOD**

— **MAX VOLUME** – bass repl. HEATH + ETHICS

— still until split in 1989 after Zagreb concert, but nothing new was released after '86. However, they did a one-off gig in June '95.

– compilations, etc. –

Mar 84. (d-lp) *Xntrix; (RM 101)* **7 YEAR SCRATCH**

Mar 85. (12"ep) *Illuminated; (ILL 33-12)* **ARE YOU HAPPY NOW? (remix) / CREAM DREAM. / MENAGE ABATTOIR / WHISKY VOICE**

May 95. (cd) *Cooking Vinyl; (<COOKCD 086>)* **REAL WOMAN** — Feb97

May 95. (4xcd-box) *Cooking Vinyl; (<COOKCD 087>)* **STATEMENT – THE COMPLETE RECORDINGS 1977-1989**
(re-iss. Jun00; same)

Sep 98. (cd) *Recall; <137>* **POISONOUS**

POISON IDEA

Formed: Portland, Oregon, USA ... late 1980 by JERRY A., PIG CHAMPION, CHRIS TENSE and DEAN JOHNSON. The latter pair were subsequently replaced by numerous rhythm men throughout a torrid decade which saw the remainder/bulk of the band (50 stone between them!) consistently fixated on alcohol and general debauchery. Their first release was an EP of 13 short songs entitled 'PICK YOUR KING', virtually a mini-set featuring an iconic sleeve depicting ELVIS on one side and JESUS on the other. The 1986 debut album, 'KINGS OF PUNK', showed little compromise as they threw their weight behind a vicious set of foul-mouthed hardcore punk. The following year's 'WAR ALL THE TIME' was equally heavy going, while the hilariously titled 'RECORD COLLECTORS ARE PRETENTIOUS ASSHOLES' (1989) suggested that POISON IDEA had little time for trainspotting. Still, they did drag out a surprisingly eclectic bag of covers on 1992's 'PAJAMA PARTY', including suitably harsh renditions of such soul classics as Jimmy Cliff's 'THE HARDER THEY COME' and Booker T & The MGs 'GREEN ONIONS'. By this point, the band had already signed to 'Vinyl Solution', disbanding after 'WE MUST BURN' (1993). After a brief (one album) stint with The GIFT in '94, POISON IDEA lumbered back into view in 1996, the resulting album, 'PIG'S LAST STAND' released for 'Sub Pop'.

• **Songwriters:** JERRY A. + PIG except covers album 'PAJAMA PARTY', which included; WE GOT THE BEAT (Go-Go's) / KICK OUT THE JAMS (MC5) / MOTORHEAD (Motorhead) / ENDLESS SLEEP (Joey Reynolds) / JAILHOUSE ROCK (Elvis Presley) / NEW ROSE (Damned) / etc. The GIFT covered SO THIS IS THE POPS (Tones On Tails).

Album rating: KINGS OF PUNK (*6) / WAR ALL THE TIME (*6) / RECORD COLLECTORS ARE PRETENTIOUS ASSHOLES (*7) / IN YOUR FACE (*6) / FEEL THE DARKNESS (*7) / PAJAMA PARTY (*6) / BLANK, BLACKOUT, VACANT (*6) / WE MUST BURN (*5) / MULTUM IN PARVA by The Gift (*5) / PIG'S LAST STAND (*6)

JERRY A. – vocals / **PIG CHAMPION** (b. TOM ROBERTS) – guitar / **CHRIS TENSE** – bass / **DEAN JOHNSON** – drums

not iss. — unknown

1985. (12"ep) **PICK YOUR KING E.P.**
– Think twice / It's an action / This thing called progress / In my head ache / Underage / Self abuse / Cult band / Last one / Pure hate / Castration / Reggae (I hate) / Give it up / Think fast. *<US cd-iss. Oct91 on 'Taang!'; >*

not iss. — Pusmort

1986. (m-lp) *<6012-10>* **KINGS OF PUNK**
– Lifestyles / Short fuse / God not God / Ugly American / Subtract / Cop an attitude / Death wish kids / Made to be broken / Tormented imp / One by one / Out of the picture. *<(re-iss. Sep91 on 'Taang!' cd/lp; TG 9284-2/-1)>*

— **STEVE 'Three Slayer Hippy' SANFORD** – drums repl. JOHNSON

— added **VEGETABLE** – guitar (ex-MAYHEM)

— **MONDO** – bass (ex-MAYHEM) repl. TENSE (he had been replaced very briefly by TIM PAUL for only one song and one aborted gig; now in GUNTRUCK)

not iss. — Alchemy

Nov 87. (lp/c) *<VM 106/+C>* **WAR ALL THE TIME**
– Temple / Romantic self destruction / Push the button / Ritual chicken / Nothing is final / Motorhead / Hot time / Steel rule / Typical / Murderer / Marked for life. *(UK-iss.Oct93 on 'Vinyl Solution' cd/c/lp; SOL 40 CD/MC/LP)*

not iss. — Bitzcore

1989. (m-lp) *<BC 1658>* **RECORD COLLECTORS ARE PRETENTIOUS ASSHOLES**
– A.A. / Legalize freedom / Cold comfort / Typical / Thorn in my side / Laughing boy / Rubber hisband / Right? / Rich get richer / Don't like it here / Die on your knees / Time to go. *(UK-iss.Sep91 on 'Taang!'; TG 9299-1) (cd-iss. Aug94 on 'Bitzcore'; 1568)*

not iss. — InYourFace

Jul 89. (lp) *<FACE 6>* **POISON IDEA (aka 'GETTING THE FEAR')**

— **MYRTLE TICKNER** – bass (ex-OILY BLOODMEN) repl. VEGETABLE

Sub Pop — Sub Pop

Oct 90. (7",7"green) *(SP 86)* **WE GOT THE BEAT. / TAKEN BY SURPRISE**

Vinyl Solution — Taang!

Oct 90. (lp/cd) *(SOL 025/+CD)* **FEEL THE DARKNESS**
– Plastic bomb / Deep slep / The badge / Just to get away / Gone for good / Death of an idiot blues / Taken by surprise / Alan's on fire / Welcome to Krell / Nation of finks / Backstab gospel / Painkiller / Feel the darkness. *(cd+=)* – Discontent. *(re-iss. Jan97 on 'Epitaph' cd/c/lp; 6463-2/-4/-1)*

Nov 90. (7") **FEEL THE DARKNESS. / ALAN'S ON FIRE**

— **KID COCKSMAN** – guitar (ex-GARGOYLE) repl. VEGETABLE

— **ALDINE STRYCHNINE** – guitar (ex-MAIMED FOR LIFE) repl. KID

Apr 91. (cd-ep) *(VS 32CD)* **OFFICIAL BOOTLEG EP**
– Plastic bomb / Punish me / etc.

— **MONDO** returned to add to the mayhem

Feb 92. (lp/cd) *(SOL 033/+CD) <T 63-2/-4/-1>* **BLANK, BLACKOUT, VACANT**
– Say good bye / Star of Baghdad / Icepicks at dawn / Smack attack / Forever and always / Punish me / Crippled angel / What happened to Sunday? / You're next / Drain / Brigandage / Amy's theme / Vietnamese baby. *(lp w/free 7"live)*

Sep 92. (lp,pink-lp/c/cd) *(SOL 034/+MC/CD)* **PAJAMA PARTY**
– Kick out the jams / Vietnamese baby / We got the beat / Motorhead / Endless sleep / Laudy Miss Clawdy / Jailhouse rock / Flamethrower love / New rose / Doctor doctor / Up front / The harder they come / Green onions.

Apr 93. (cd-ep) *(VS 32CD)* **PUNISH ME EP**

Apr 93. (lp/c/cd) *(SOL 037/+MC/CD)* **WE MUST BURN**
– In order to live / Hung like a saviour / Hard and cheap / Endless blockades for the pussyfooter / It's not the last / When I say stop / Foiled again / Jessie's arms / Slum lord / Stare at the sun / Religion and politics.

— disbanded when TENSE and JOHNSON formed APARTMENT 3G

GIFT

— **JERRY A.** with his wife **MAY MAY DEL CASTRO** – bass, vocals (ex-DESTROY ALL BLONDS) / **SAM HENRY** – drums (ex-WIPERS)

Tim/Kerr — Tim/Kerr

Oct 94. (cd) *<(TK93CD 068)>* **MULTUM IN PARVA**
– Little deranged puppet (part 1) / Sinking ship / OK this is the pops / Don't need a reason / Restless spirit / Little deranged puppet (part 2) / Never too young / Social cleansing / A date with failure / Beyond the tears / Kelly K. / Jezebel / Little deranged puppet (part 3).

POISON IDEA

— re-formed with **JERRY A. + CHAMPION**

Sub Pop Sub Pop

Apr 96. (cd) <(SP 343)> **PIG'S LAST STAND**
– Plastic bomb / Taken by surpise / Truth hurts / Death, agony and screams / Don't ask me why / A.A. / Crippled angle / Stare at the sun / Bela Lugosi is dead / Feel the darkness / Give it up / Blitzkreig bop / Hangover heart attack / Alan's on fire / Up front.

— In Feb'97, PIG CHAMPION was credited on an MDC single, 'I Don't Want To Hurt You Dude', issued on 'Honest Dons'; (DON 004).

– compilations, etc. –

Jan 92. (lp/cd) *Bitzcore; (BC 1667/+CD)* **DUTCH COURAGE**
(re-iss. Aug94; same)

1992. (cd; with JEFF DAHL) *Triple X; <51137>* **JEFF DAHL AND POISON IDEA** -

Aug 94. (cd) *Bitzcore; (BC 1684CD)* **THE EARLY YEARS**

May 00. (cd) *Taang!; <(TAANG 147)>* **BEST OF POISON IDEA**

Chris POLAND

Born: California, USA. Former member of MEGADETH in the 80's, POLAND released his debut 'Roadrunner' album, 'RETURN TO METALOPOLIS' in 1990, while the aforementioned group's 'Rust In Peace' was high in the charts. The guitarist took some comfort from the album's reviews, relocating to Los Angeles the following year after forming DAMN THE MACHINE. Signing to 'A&M' the line-up was completed by DAVE CLEMMONS (guitar, vocals), DAVE RANDI (bass) and his brother MARK (drums), their recordings issued eponymously two years later. The album married together metal, power-rock and even touched on jazz, although the band quickly disintegrated after supporting DREAM THEATER on tour.

Album rating: RETURN TO METALOPOLIS (*5) / DAMN THE MACHINE (*6)

CHRIS POLAND – guitar (ex-MEGADETH) / with **MARK POLAND** – drums

Roadrunner Enigma

Sep 90. (cd/c/lp) *(RR 9348-2/-4/-1) <73590>* **RETURN TO METALOPOLIS**
– Club Ded / Alexandria / Return to Metalopolis / Heinous interruptus / The fall of Babylon / Row of crows / Theatre of the damned / Beelzebub bop / Apparation station / Khazad dum.

DAMN THE MACHINE

CHRIS POLAND – guitar / **DAVE CLEMMONS** – guitar, vocals / **DAVE RANDI** – bass / **MARK POLAND** – drums

not iss. A&M

Jun 93. (cd/c) *<540103-2/-4>* **DAMN THE MACHINE** -
– The mission / Fall of order / Corporate reign / Honor / Lonesome god / On with the dream / Patriot / I will / Silence / Russians / Countryside / Humans.

Jul 93. (cd-ep) **SILENCE / I WILL / I'D LOVE TO CHANGE THE WORLD / CAT FOOD** -

— folded after above

Iggy POP

Born: JAMES JEWEL OSTERBERG, 21 Apr'47, Ypsilanti, Michigan, USA. The son of an English father and American mother, he joined The IGUANAS as a drummer in 1964. They issued a cover of Bo Diddley's 'MONA', which was limited to 1,000 copies sold at gigs. The following year, he became IGGY POP and joined The PRIME MOVERS with bassist RON ASHETON, although they folded, IGGY subsequently moving to Chicago. In 1967, he returned to Michigan and formed The (PSYCHEDELIC) STOOGES with RON and his drummer brother SCOTT. They were soon joined by DAVE ALEXANDER, IGGY making his celluloid debut in the avant-garde film, 'Francois De Moniere' with girlfriend NICO. In 1968, the band gigged constantly, on one occasion IGGY being charged with indecent exposure. The following year, A&R man Danny Fields, while looking to sign MC5, instead signed The STOOGES to 'Elektra', furnishing them with a $25,000 advance. Their eponymous debut (produced by JOHN CALE – another VELVET UNDERGROUND connection), later proved to be way ahead of its time. Tracks such as 'NO FUN', '1969' and 'I WANNA BE YOUR DOG', were howling proto-punk, garage classics, later covered by The SEX PISTOLS, SISTERS OF MERCY and SID VICIOUS! respectively. The album just failed to secure a Top 100 placing, the second album faring even worse commercially, although it was hailed by the more discerning critics of the day as a seminal work. From the primal nihilism of 'DIRT', to the psychedelic kiss-off, 'I FEEL ALRIGHT (1970)', it seemed, to The STOOGES at least, as if flower-power had never happened. They were subsequently dropped by their label, following drug-related problems and dissension in the ranks. IGGY moved to Florida, becoming a greenkeeper while taking up golf more seriously, a healthier pastime than his penchant for self-mutilation. In 1972, he had a chance meeting with DAVID BOWIE and manager TONY DeFRIES, who persuaded IGGY to reform his STOOGES and sign a MainMan management deal, this in turn leading to a 'C.B.S.' contract. After his/their flawed classic, 'RAW POWER' (not one of BOWIE's best productions), they folded again, citing drugs as the cause. It was, however, even more of an embryonic punk record, the amphetamine rush of 'SEARCH AND DESTROY' highly influential on the "blank generation" that would trade-in their STEELY DAN albums for anything with two chords and a sneering vocal. In 1975, IGGY checked in to a psychiatric institute, weaning himself off heroin. His only true friend, BOWIE, who regularly visited him in hospital, invited him to appear on his 'LOW' album. He signed to 'R.C.A.' (home of BOWIE) in 1977, issuing the BOWIE-produced debut solo album, 'THE IDIOT', which, due to the recent "new wave" explosion, broke him into the UK Top 30 and US Top 75. It contained the first BOWIE/POP collaboration, 'CHINA GIRL', later a smash hit for BOWIE. His second solo release, 'LUST FOR LIFE' (also produced by BOWIE in '77), was another gem, again deservedly reaching the UK Top 30 (the title track was later resurrected in 1996 after appearing on the soundtrack to the cult Scottish movie, 'Trainspotting'). In 1979, IGGY moved to 'Arista' records, shifting through various infamous personnel, although his commercial appeal was on the wane. The first half of the 80's saw IGGY desperately trying to carve out a successful solo career while combating his continuing drug problems. Albums such as, 'SOLDIER' (1980), 'PARTY' (1981) and 'ZOMBIE BIRDHOUSE' (1982) marking the nadir of POP's chequered career. Finally teaming up again with BOWIE for 1986's 'BLAH BLAH BLAH', the proclaimed "Godfather Of Punk" at last gained some belated recognition, his revival of a 1957 Johnny O'Keefe hit, 'REAL WILD CHILD', giving IGGY his first Top 10 hit (UK). Still with 'A&M' records and adding ex-SEX PISTOLS guitarist STEVE JONES, he consolidated his recovery with 'INSTINCT' (1988). His new lease of life prompted 'Virgin America' to give IGGY (who had recently taking up acting) a new contract, the 1990 set, 'BRICK BY BRICK' featuring the GN'R talents of SLASH and DUFF McKAGAN. To end the year, IGGY showed his caring side by duetting with former punkette, DEBORAH HARRY, on AIDS benefit single, 'WELL DID YOU EVAH!' (a bigger hit for NANCY Sinatra & LEE Hazlewood in 1971). He resurfaced once again in 1993 with 'AMERICAN CAESAR', a full-length set which contained some of his raunchiest tracks for some time, including 'WILD AMERICA', 'F*****' ALONE' and Richard Berry's 'LOUIE LOUIE'. Busying himself with more film work, he eventually broke his recording silence with an umpteenth album, 'NAUGHTY LITTLE DOGGIE' (1996). Mr. POP was back on song in the Autumn of '99, the album 'AVENUE B' delivering his usual raw power with all the finesse of a man taking a motorcycle ride to Hell. 'NAZI GIRLFRIEND', 'LONG DISTANCE' and even a cover of Johnny Kidd's 'SHAKIN' ALL OVER', all testament to a guy not yet ready to get out his pipe and slippers. • **IGGY covered;** SOMETHING WILD (John Hiatt) / LIVIN' ON THE EDGE OF THE NIGHT (Rifkin / Rackin) / SEX MACHINE (James Brown). • **Trivia:** In 1987, IGGY made a cameo appearance in the film, 'The Color Of Money'. In 1990, his film & TV work included, 'Cry Baby', 'Shannon's Deal', Tales From The Crypt' & 'Miami Vice'. In 1991, he starred in the opera! 'The Manson Family' and five years later, 'The Crow'.

Album rating: Stooges: THE STOOGES (*8) / FUN HOUSE (*10) / RAW POWER as Iggy & the Stooges (*7) / METALLIC K.O. (*5) / Iggy Pop: THE IDIOT (*9) / LUST FOR LIFE (*9) / TV EYE (*3) / NEW VALUES (*5) / SOLDIER (*5) / PARTY (*4) / ZOMBIE BIRDHOUSE (*4) / BLAH-BLAH-BLAH (*6) / INSTINCT (*5) / BRICK BY BRICK (*7) / AMERICAN CAESAR (*6) / NAUGHTY LITTLE DOGGIE (*5) / NUDE & RUDE: THE BEST OF IGGY POP compilation (*8) / AVENUE B (*7)

STOOGES

IGGY POP – vocals / **RON ASHETON** (b. RONALD RANKLIN ASHETON JR., 17 Jul'48, Washington, D.C.) – guitar / **DAVE ALEXANDER** (b. DAVID MICHAEL ALEXANDER, 3 Jun'47, Ann Arbor) – bass / **SCOTT ASHETON** (b. SCOTT RANDOLPH ASHETON, 16 Aug'49, Washington) – drums

Elektra Elektra

Sep 69. (lp) *<(EKS 74051)>* **THE STOOGES** Aug69
– 1969 / I wanna be your dog / We will fall / No fun / Real cool time / Ann / Not right / Little doll. *(re-iss. Mar77; K 42032) <US cd-iss. 1988; 74051-2> (cd-iss. Nov93; 7559 60667-2)*

Oct 69. (7") *<EK 45664>* **I WANNA BE YOUR DOG. / 1969** -

— added guests **STEVE MACKAY** – saxophone / **BILL CHEATHAM** – 2nd guitar

Dec 70. (lp) *<(EKS 74071)>* **FUN HOUSE**
– Down on the street / Loose / T.V. eye / Dirt / I feel alright (1970) / Fun house / L.A. blues. *(re-iss. Mar77; K 42051) <US cd-iss. 1988; 74071-2> (cd-iss. Nov93; 7559 60669-2)*

Dec 70. (7") *<EKM 45695>* **I FEEL ALRIGHT (1970). / DOWN ON THE STREET** -

— broke-up in 1972. **IGGY** re-formed the group with **SCOTT** and **RON** (now bass)

IGGY AND THE STOOGES

JAMES WILLIAMSON – guitar repl. DAVE (died 10 Feb'75)

C.B.S. Columbia

Jun 73. (lp) *(CBS 65586) <KC 32111>* **RAW POWER** May73
– Search and destroy / Gimme danger / Hard to beat * / Penetration / Raw power / I need somebody / Shake appeal / Death trip. *(re-iss. May77 on 'CBS-Embassy'; 31464)*, hit UK No.44, *track repl. by – Your pretty face is going to Hell. *(re-iss. Nov81; CBS 32081) <US cd-iss. 1988 on 'Columbia'; > (UK re-iss. May89 on 'Essential' cd/c/lp; ESS CD/MC/LP 005) (cd-iss. all tracks) (re-iss. May94 & Apr97 on 'Columbia' cd/c; 485176-2/-4) (lp re-iss. Jul98 on 'Simply Vinyl'; SVLP 33)*

Jun 73. (7") *<45877>* **SEARCH AND DESTROY. / PENETRATION** -

— added **SCOTT THURSTON** – keyboards (on last 1974 tour, before disbanding) The ASHETONS formed The NEW ORDER (US version), with RON moving on to DESTROY ALL MONSTERS who had three 45's for UK label 'Cherry Red' in the late 70's.

– compilations, others, etc. –

1977. (white-d-lp) *Visa; <IMP 1015>* **METALLIC K.O.** -
– Raw power / Head on / Gimme danger / Rich bitch / Cock in my pocket / Louie

Louie. *(originally issued 1976 on French 'Skydog'; SGIS 008) (re-iss. May88 as 'METALLIC KO x 2' on 'Skydog' lp/cd; 62232-1/2) (cd-iss. Sep94; same) (re-iss. Sep96 & May98 on 'Dressed To Kill'; DTKLP 001)*

1977. (7"ep) *Bomp; <EP 113>* **I'M SICK OF YOU** [-] [ ]
– I'm sick of you / Tight pants / Scene of the crime.

1977. (7"ep; by IGGY POP & JAMES WILLIAMSON) *Bomp; <EP 114>* **JESUS LOVES THE STOOGES** [-] [ ]
– Jesus loves the Stooges / Consolation prizes / Johanna. *(re-iss. 10"ep.Nov94;)*

1977. (7") *Siamese; <PM 001>* **I GOT A RIGHT. / GIMME SOME SKIN** [-] [ ]
(UK-iss.Dec95 on 'Bomp'; REVENGE 2)

Feb 78. (lp,green-lp; as IGGY POP with JAMES WILLIAMSON) *Radar; (RAD 2) / Bomp; <BLP 4001>* **KILL CITY** [ ] [ ] Nov77
– Sell your love / Kill city / I got nothin' / Beyond the law / Johanna / Night theme / Night theme reprise / Master charge / No sense of crime / Lucky monkeys / Consolation prizes. *(re-iss. ! on 'Elektra';) (cd-iss. Feb89 on 'Line'; LICD 9.00131) (cd-iss. Jan93;) (re-iss. 10"lp Feb95 on 'Bomp'; BLP 4042-10) (cd-iss. ; BCD 4042)*

Apr 78. (7") *Radar; (ADA 4)* **KILL CITY. / I GOT NOTHIN'** [ ] [-]

1978. (7"ep) *Skydog; (SGIS 12)* **(I GOT) NOTHING** [-] [-] France
– I got nothing / Gimme danger / Heavy liquid.

Aug 80. (lp/c) *Elektra; (K/K4 52234) <EF 7095>* **NO FUN** (1969-70 best of THE STOOGES) [ ] [ ]

1983. (lp) *Invasion; <E 1019>* **I GOT A RIGHT** [-] [ ]

1987. (lp) *Revenge; (MIG 2)* **I GOT A RIGHT** [-] [-] France

1987. (7") *Revenge; (SS 1)* **I GOT A RIGHT. / NO SENSE OF CRIME** [-] [-] France

1987. (7") *Revenge; (BF 50) KILL CITY. / I'M SICK OF YOU* [-] [-] France

Dec 87. (lp) *Fan Club; (FC 037)* **RUBBER LEGS** [-] [-] France
– Rubber legs / Open up and bleed / Johanna / Cock in my pocket / Head on the curb / Cry for me. *(free 7")* – GIMME DANGER (live). / I NEED SOMEBODY (live) *(cd-iss. Apr97 on 'Last Call'; 422248)*

1988. (cd-ep) *Revenge; (CAX 1)* **PURE LUST** [-] [-] France
– I got a right / Johanna / Gimme some skin / I got nothing.

1988. (cd-ep) *Revenge; (CAX 2)* **RAW POWER** [-] [-] France
– Raw power / Head on the curb / Purple haze / Waiting for the man.

1988. (12"pink-ep,cd-ep) *Revenge; (CAX 3)* **GIMME DANGER** [-] [-] France
– Gimme danger / Open up and bleed / Heavy liquid / I got nothing / Dynamite boogie.

1988. (7") *Revenge; (SS 6)* **JOHANNA. / PURPLE HAZE** [-] [-] France

Sep 88. (pic-lp; as IGGY & THE STOOGES) *Revenge; (LPMIG 6)* **DEATH TRIP** [-] [-] France

May 88. (cd; as IGGY & THE STOOGES) *Revenge; (HTM 16)* **OPEN UP AND BLEED** [-] [-] France
(re-iss. Feb96 on 'Bomp' cd/lp; BCD/BLP 4051) (cd re-iss. Jul96; 890016)

Dec 88. (lp; as IGGY & THE STOOGES) *Revenge; (MIG 7)* **LIVE AT THE WHISKEY A GO-GO** [ ] [-]
(cd-iss. Nov94 & Feb97; 895104F)

Dec 88. (lp; as IGGY & THE STOOGES) *Electric; (190069)* **RAW STOOGES VOL.1** [-] [-] German

Dec 88. (lp; as IGGY & THE STOOGES) *Electric; (190070)* **RAW STOOGES VOL.2** [-] [-] German

May 92. (cd) *Line; (LICD 921175)* **I'M SICK OF YOU / KILL CITY** [ ] [-]

Jun 94. (cd; IGGY & THE STOOGES) *New Rose; (890028)* **MY GIRL HATES MY HEROIN** [ ] [-]
(re-iss. Feb97 on 'Wrote Music'; 7890028) (re-iss. Sep97 on 'Revenge'; MIG 28)

Jul 94. (cd; IGGY & THE STOOGES) *New Rose; (642100)* **NIGHT OF DESTRUCTION** [ ] [-]
(re-iss. as 6xcd-s-box on 'Wind'; WM 375)

Jul 94. (cd; IGGY & THE STOOGES) *New Rose; (642042)* **TILL THE END OF THE NIGHT** [ ] [-]
(re-iss. Apr97; same) (re-iss. Sep97 on 'Revenge'; MIG 42)

Sep 94. (cd; IGGY & THE STOOGES) *New Rose; (642011)* **LIVE 1971 & EARLY LIVE RARITIES (live)** [ ] [-]
(re-iss. Apr97; same)

Sep 94. (cd; IGGY & THE STOOGES) *New Rose; (895002)* **RAW MIXES VOL.1** [ ] [-]

Sep 94. (cd; IGGY & THE STOOGES) *New Rose; (895003)* **RAW MIXES VOL.2** [ ] [-]

Sep 94. (cd; IGGY & THE STOOGES) *New Rose; (895004)* **RAW MIXES VOL.3** [ ] [-]

Feb 95. (10"lp/cd) *Bomp; (BLP/BCD 4049)* **ROUGH POWER** [ ] [-]

— Also in France;
THE STOOGES(12"ep) / **SHE CREATURES OF HOLLYWOOD HILLS**

Jul 96. (cd) *Revenge; (642050)* **WILD ANIMAL (live 1977)** [ ] [-]

Jul 96. (cd) *Revenge; (893334)* **PARIS HIPPODROME 1977 (live)** [ ] [-]

Jul 96. (cd; as IGGY & THE STOOGES) *Trident; (PILOT 008)* **YOUR PRETTY FACE IS GOING TO HELL** [ ] [-]

Mar 97. (cd; IGGY & THE STOOGES) *Bomp; (BCD 4063)* **YEAR OF THE IGUANA** [ ] [-]

Apr 97. (cd; STOOGES) *Arcade; (301563-2)* **THE COMPLETE RAW MIXES** [ ] [-]

Sep 97. (cd/lp; IGGY & THE STOOGES) *Bomp; (BCD/BLP 4069)* **CALIFORNIA BLEEDING** [ ] [-]

Nov 97. (cd) *King Biscuit; (88003)* **KING BISCUIT FLOWER HOUR** [ ] [-]

Mar 98. (cd) *Snapper; (SMMCD 528)* **LIVE IN L.A. 1973 (live)** [ ] [-]

Apr 98. (cd) *King Biscuit; (KBFHCD 001)* **KING BISCUIT PRESENTS . . .** [ ] [-]

May 88. (12"ep; IGGY & THE STOOGES) *Revenge; (CAX 8MAXI)* **I GOT NOTHING. / SEARCH AND DESTROY / COCK IN MY POCKET** [ ] [-]

Jun 98. (lp; IGGY & THE STOOGES) *Get Back; (GET 33LP)* **RUBBER** [ ] [-]

Nov 99. (7"pic-d; as IGGY & THE STOOGES) *Munster; (MR 7125)* **I GOT NOTHING. /** [ ] [ ]

IGGY POP

— had already went solo, augmented by **DAVID BOWIE** – producer, keyboards / **RICKY GARDINER** – guitar / **TONY SALES** – bass / **HUNT SALES** – drums (latter 2; ex-TODD RUNDGREN) / guest **CARLOS ALOMAR** – guitar

R.C.A. R.C.A.

Feb 77. (7") *<10989>* **SISTER MIDNIGHT. / BABY** [-] [ ]

Mar 77. (lp/c) *(PL/PK 12275) <2275>* **THE IDIOT** [30] [72]
– Sister midnight / Nightclubbing / Fun time / Baby / China girl / Dum dum boys / Tiny girls / Mass production. *(re-iss. Apr90 on 'Virgin' lp/c/cd; OVED/OVEDC/CDOVD 277)*

May 77. (7") *(PB 9093)* **CHINA GIRL. / BABY** [ ] [ ]

— **STACEY HEYDON** – guitar / **SCOTT THURSTON** – keyboards repl. BOWIE + ALOMAR

Sep 77. (lp/c) *(PL/PK 12488) <2488>* **LUST FOR LIFE** [28] [ ]
– Lust for life / Sixteen / Some weird sin / The passenger / Tonight / Success / Turn blue / Neighbourhood threat / Fall in love with me. *(re-iss. 1984 lp/c; NL/NK 82488) (re-iss. Apr90 on 'Virgin' lp/c/cd; OVED/OVEDC/CDOVD 278) (lp re-iss. Nov97 on 'Virgin'; LPCENT 40)*

Oct 77. (7") *(PB 9160)* **SUCCESS. / THE PASSENGER** [ ] [ ]

— **IGGY** retained **THURSTON**, and recruited **SCOTT ASHETON** – drums / **FRED 'SONIC' SMITH** – guitar (ex-MC5) / **GARY RAMUSSEN** – bass (The SALES brothers later to BOWIE's TIN MACHINE)

Apr 78. (7") *(PB 9213)* **I GOT A RIGHT (live). / SIXTEEN (live)** [ ] [ ]

May 78. (lp/c) *(PL/PK 12796)* **TV EYE (live 1977)** [ ] [ ]
– T.V. eye / Funtime / Sixteen / I got a right / Lust for life / Dirt / Nightclubbing / I wanna be your dog. *(cd-iss. Jul94 on 'Virgin'; CDOVD 448)*

— **IGGY / THURSTON** now with **JAMES WILLIAMSON** – guitar, producer / **JACKIE CLARKE** – bass (ex-IKE & TINA TURNER) / **KLAUS KREUGER** – drums (ex-TANGERINE DREAM) / **JOHN HORDEN** – saxophone

Arista Arista

Apr 79. (lp/c) *(SPART/TC-SPART 1092) <4237>* **NEW VALUES** [60] [ ]
– Tell me a story / New values / Girls / I'm bored / Don't look down / The endless sea / Five foot one / How do ya fix a broken part / Angel / Curiosity / African man / Billy is a runaway. *(re-iss. Mar87; 1201144) (re-iss. Oct90 cd/lp; 260/210 997)*

May 79. (7") *(ARIST 255) <0438>* **I'M BORED. / AFRICAN MAN** [ ] [ ]

Jul 79. (7"/7"pic-d) *(ARIP/+D 274)* **FIVE FOOT ONE. / PRETTY FLAMINGO** [ ] [-]

— **IGGY / KREUGER** recruited **IVAN KRAL** – guitar (ex-PATTI SMITH) / **PAT MORAN** – guitar / **GLEN MATLOCK** – bass (ex-SEX PISTOLS, ex-RICH KIDS) / **BARRY ANDREWS** – keyboards (ex-XTC, ex-LEAGUE OF GENTLEMEN) (THURSTON formed The MOTELS)

Jan 80. (lp/c) *(SPART/TC-SPART 1117) <4259>* **SOLDIER** [62] [ ]
– Knockin' 'em down (in the city) / I'm a conservative / I snub you / Get up and get out / Ambition / Take care of me / I need more / Loco mosquito / Mr. Dynamite / Play it safe / Dog food. *<US re-iss. Oct87; 201160> (cd-iss. Apr91; 251 160)*

Jan 80. (7") *(ARIST 327)* **LOCO MOSQUITO. / TAKE CARE OF ME** [ ] [-]

— **IGGY / KRAL** now with **ROB DuPREY** – guitar / **MICHAEL PAGE** – bass / **DOUGLAS BROWNE** – drums (BARRY ANDREWS formed SHRIEKBACK)

May 81. (7") *(ARIST 407)* **BANG BANG. / SEA OF LOVE** [ ] [-]

Jun 81. (lp/c) *(SPART/TC-SPART 1158) <9572>* **PARTY** [ ] [ ]
– Pleasure / Rock and roll party / Eggs on plate / Sincerity / Houston is hot tonight / Pumpin' for Jill / Happy man / Bang bang / Sea of love / Time won't let me. *(re-iss. Jan87 lp/c; 203/403 806) (cd-iss. Sep89 on 'R.C.A.'; 253 806)*

— **IGGY / DuPREY** found new people **CHRIS STEIN** – guitar, producer (ex-BLONDIE) / **CLEM BURKE** – drums (ex-BLONDIE)

Animal-Chrysalis Animal

Aug 82. (7") *(CHFLY 2634)* **RUN LIKE A VILLAIN. / PLATONIC** [ ] [ ]

Sep 82. (lp/c) *(CHR/ZCHR 1399) <APE 6000>* **ZOMBIE BIRDHOUSE** [ ] [ ]
– Run like a villain / The villagers / Angry hills / Life of work / The ballad of Cookie McBride / Ordinary bummer / Eat to be eaten / Bulldozer / Platonic / The horse song / Watching the news / Street crazies.

— In 1984, he sang the title song on Alex Cox's movie 'REPO MAN'. For the same director, he appeared in the 1985 film 'SID & NANCY' about SID VICIOUS.

— **IGGY** now with **ERDAL KIZILCAY** – drums, bass, synthesizers / **KEVIN ARMSTRONG** – guitar / **BOWIE + STEVE JONES** (guest writers)

A&M A&M

Sep 86. (7"/12") *(AM/+Y 358) <2874>* **CRY FOR LOVE. / WINNERS & LOSERS** [ ] [ ]

Oct 86. (lp/c/cd) *<(AMA/AMC/CDA 5145)>* **BLAH-BLAH-BLAH** [43] [75]
– Real wild child (wild one) / Baby, it can't fail / Shades / Fire girl / Isolation / Cry for love / Blah-blah-blah / Hideaway / Winners and losers. *(cd+=)* – Little Miss Emperor. *(cd re-iss. 1989; 395 145-2) (re-iss. Jun91 cd/c; CD/C+/MID 159)*

Nov 86. (7"/12") *(AM/+Y 368) <2909>* **REAL WILD CHILD (WILD ONE). / LITTLE MISS EMPEROR** [10] [ ]

Feb 87. (7") *(AM 374)* **SHADES. / BABY IT CAN'T FAIL** [ ] [ ]
(12"+=) *(AMY 374)* – Cry for love.

Apr 87. (7"/12") *(AM/+Y 392)* **FIRE GIRL. / BLAH-BLAH-BLAH (live)** [ ] [ ]

Jun 87. (7") *(AM 397)* **ISOLATION. / HIDEAWAY** [ ] [ ]
(12"+=) *(AMY 397)* – Fire girl (remix).

— IGGY now with **STEVE JONES** – guitar / **PAUL GARRISTO** – drums (ex-PSYCHEDELIC FURS) / **SEAMUS BEAGHEN** – keyboards / **LEIGH FOXX** – bass

Jul 88. (lp/c/cd) *<(AMA/AMC/ADA 5198)>* **INSTINCT** [61] [ ]
– Cold metal / High on you / Strong girl / Tom tom / Easy rider / Power & freedom / Lowdown / Tuff baby / Squarehead.

Aug 88. (7") *(AM 452)* **COLD METAL. / INSTINCT** [ ] [ ]
(12"+=/12"pic-d+=) *(AM Y/P 452)* – Tuff baby.

Nov 88. (7") *(AM 475)* **HIGH ON YOU. / SQUAREHEAD** [ ] [ ]
(12"+=) *(AMY 475)* – Tuff baby (remix).

— **ALVIN GIBBS** – guitar (ex-UK SUBS) repl. STEVE JONES (continued solo) / **ANDY McCOY** – bass (ex-HANOI ROCKS) repl. FOXX (to DEBORAH HARRY)

Nov 88. (lp/c/cd) **LIVE AT THE CHANNEL (live 17.9.88)** [-] [ ]
(UK-iss.May94 on 'New Rose'; 642005) (re-iss. cd Sep97 on 'Revenge'; MIG 40-41)

— now with **SLASH** – guitar / **DUFF McKAGAN** – bass (both of GUNS N' ROSES) / **KENNY ARONOFF** – drums

Virgin America / Virgin America

Jan 90. (7"/c-s) *(VUS/+C 18) <VSC 1228>* **LIVIN' ON THE EDGE OF THE NIGHT. / THE PASSENGER** [51] [ ]
(12"+=/12"pic-d+=/cd-s+=) *(VUS T/TE/CD 18)* – Nightclubbing / China girl.

Jun 90. (7"/c-s) *(VUS/+C 22)* **HOME. / LUST FOR LIFE** [ ] [ ]
(12"+=/cd-s+=) *(VUS T/CD 22)* – Pussy power / Funtime.

Jul 90. (cd/c/lp) *(CDVUS/VUSMC/VUSLP 19) <91381>* **BRICK BY BRICK** [50] [90]
– Home / Main street eyes / I won't crap out / Candy / Butt town / The undefeated / Moonlight lady / Something wild / Neon forest / Stormy night / Pussy power / My baby wants to rock & roll / Brick by brick / Livin' on the edge of the night. *(c re-iss. Apr92; OVEDC 426)*
(below 'A'side featured **KATE PIERSON** – vox (of B-52's)

Oct 90. (7"/c-s) *(VUS/+C 29) <98900>* **CANDY. / PUSSY POWER (acoustic demo)** [67] [28]
(10"+=/cd-s+=) *(VUS 29)* – My baby wants to rock'n'roll (acoustic demos).
(12"/cd-s) *(VUS T/CD 29)* – ('A'side) / The undefeated / Butt town (acoustic demo).

— Oct 90, IGGY dueted with DEBORAH HARRY on UK Top 50 single 'DID YOU EVAH'; *Chrysalis; CHS 3646)*

— with **LARRY MULLEN** (U2) – drums, percussion / **HAL CRAGIN** – bass / **ERIC SCHERMERHORN** – guitar plus guests **MALCOLM BURN** – guitars, etc

Aug 93. (7"ep/c-ep/12"ep/cd-ep) *(VUS/+C/T/CD 74)* **THE WILD AMERICA EP** [63] [ ]
– Wild America / Credit card / Come back tomorrow / My angel.

Sep 93. (cd/c/d-lp) *(CDVUS/VUSMC/VUSLP 64)* **AMERICAN CAESAR** [43] [ ]
– Character / Wild America / Mixin' the colors / Jealousy / Hate / It's our love / Plastic & concrete / F***in' alone / Highway song / Beside you / Sickness / Boogie boy / Perforation / Problems / Social life / Louie Louie / Caesar / Girls of N.Y

May 94. (10"ep) *(VUS A/C 77)* **BESIDE YOU / EVIL CALIFORNIA. / HOME (live) / FUCKIN' ALONE** [47] [-]
(cd-ep) *(VUSCD 77)* – ('A'side) / Les amants / Louie Louie (live) / ('A'acoustic).

Feb 96. (cd/c/lp) *(CDVUS/VUSMC/VUSLP 102) <41327>* **NAUGHTY LITTLE DOGGIE** [ ] [ ]
– I wanna live / Pussy walk / Innocent world / Knucklehead / To belong / Keep on believing / Outta my head / Shoeshine girl / Heart is saved / Look away.

Sep 99. (cd) *(CDVUS 163) <48216>* **AVENUE B** [ ] [ ]
– No shit / Nazi girlfriend / Avenue B / Miss Argentina / Afraid to get close / Shakin' all over / Long distance / Corruption / She called me daddy / I felt the luxury / Espanol / Motorcycle / Facade.

Oct 99. (7") *(VUS 155)* **CORRUPTION. / ROCK STAR GRAVE** [ ] [-]
(cd-s+=) *(VUSCD 155)* – Hollywood affair.

– compilations, etc. –

May 82. (7") *RCA Gold; (GOLD 549)* **THE PASSENGER. / NIGHTCLUBBING** [ ] [-]
Sep 84. (lp/c) *R.C.A.; (PL/PK 84597)* **CHOICE CUTS** [ ] [-]
Apr 88. (cd-ep) *A&M; (AMCD 909)* **COMPACT HITS** [ ] [-]
– Real wild child (the wild one) / Isolation / Cry for love / Shades.
Jan 92. (cd) *Arista; (262 178)* **POP SONGS** [ ] [-]
Jan 93. (3xcd-box) *Virgin; (TPAK 21)* **LUST FOR LIFE / THE IDIOT / BRICK BY BRICK** [ ] [-]
Jun 93. (cd) *Revenge; (642044)* **LIVE NYC RITZ '86 (live)** [ ] [-]
Aug 93. (cd/c) *Revenge; (642/644 050)* **SUCK ON THIS!** [ ] [-]
Aug 95. (cd) *Skydog;* **WE ARE NOT TALKING ABOUT COMMERCIAL SHIT** [ ] [-]
Aug 95. (cd) *Skydog;* **WAKE UP SUCKERS** [ ] [-]
Aug 96. (cd) *M.C.A.; (MCD 84021)* **THE BEST OF IGGY POP LIVE (live)** [ ] [-]
Sep 96. (cd) *Camden RCA; (74321 41503-2)* **POP MUSIC** [ ] [-]
Oct 96. (cd/c/d-lp) *Virgin; (CDVUS/VUSMC/VUSLP 115)* **NUDE & RUDE: THE BEST OF IGGY POP** [ ] [ ]
– I wanna be your dog / No fun / Search & destroy / Gimme danger / I'm sick of you / Funtime / Nightclubbing / China girl / Lust for life / The passenger / Kill city / Real wild child / Cry for love / Cold metal / Candy / Home / Wild America.
Nov 96. (7"colrd/c-s) *Virgin; (VUS/+C 116)* **LUST FOR LIFE / (GET UP I FEEL LIKE BEING A) SEX MACHINE** [26] [ ]
(cd-s+=) *(VUSCD 116)* – ('A'live) / I wanna be your dog (live).
Dec 96. (cd) *The Network; (3D 013)* **IGGY POP** [ ] [-]
Apr 97. (cd) *Wotre; (642007)* **LIVE IN BERLIN '91** [ ] [-]
Sep 97. (d-cd) *Snapper; (SMDCD 142)* **HEAD ON** [ ] [-]
Nov 97. (cd) *Other People's Music; (OPM 2116CD)* **HEROIN HATES YOU** [ ] [-]
Nov 97. (cd) *Eagle; (EABCD 011)* **THE MASTERS** [ ] [-]
Feb 98. (c-s) *Virgin; (VSC 1689)* **THE PASSENGER /** [22] [-]
(12"+=/cd-s+=) *(VS T/CDT 1689)* –
Aug 98. (cd) *A&M; (540943-2)* **BLAH BLAH BLAH / INSTINCT** [ ] [-]

PORNO FOR PYROS (see under ⇒ JANE'S ADDICTION)

POSSESSED

Formed: San Francisco, California, USA . . . 1983 by JEFF BECCARA, MIKE TARRAO, LARRY LALONDE and MIKE SUS. One of the earlier Bay Area thrash outfits, POSSESSED attracted the interest of 'Combat' records after contributing a track to a 'Metal Blade' compilation. Released by 'Roadrunner' in Europe, the album's ultra fast proto-death metal approach and Satanically preoccupied lyrics engendered POSSESSED to a loyal, if not particularly large cult following. Subsequently signing with 'Under One Flag', the group released an equally infernal follow-up, 'BEYOND THE GATES' (1986), European live shows helping to swell their fanbase. Finally, after the JOE SATRIANI-produced follow-up, 'THE EYES OF HORROR' (1987), the group split amid personal and musical differences, LALONDE going on to great acclaim with PRIMUS.

Album rating: SEVEN CHURCHES (*6) / BEYOND THE GATES (*6) / THE EYES OF HORROR mini (*5)

JEFF BECCARA – vocals, bass / **MIKE TARRAO** – guitar / **LARRY LALONDE** – guitar / **MIKE SUS** – drums

Roadrunner / Combat

Dec 85. (lp) *(RR 9757) <8024>* **SEVEN CHURCHES** [ ] [ ]
– Exorcist / Burning in Hell / Seven churches / Holy hell / Fallen angel / Pentagram / Evil warriors / Satan's curse / Twisted minds / Death metal. *(cd-iss. Apr89 on 'Roadracer'; RO 9757-2) <(cd re-iss. Feb99 on 'Century Media'; CM 66049CD)>*

Under One Flag / Combat

Nov 86. (lp) *(FLAG 3) <8097>* **BEYOND THE GATES** [ ] [ ]
– Intro / The heretic / Tribulation / March to die / Phantasm / No will to live / Beyond the gates / The beasts of the apocalypse / Seance / Restless dead / Dog fight. *(cd-iss. Aug87; CDFLAG 3) <(cd re-iss. Jun99 on 'Century Media'; CM 66015-2)>*

Jun 87. (m-lp) *(MFLAG 16) <8168>* **THE EYES OF HORROR** [ ] [ ]
– Confessions / My belief / The eyes of horror / Swing of the axe / Storm in my mind.

— split after above's release

POWDERFINGER

Formed: Brisbane, Australia . . . 1992 by JON COGHILL, JOHN COLLINS and IAN HAUG; this trio subsequently adding frontman BERNARD FANNING and keyboard player DARREN MIDDLETON. Named after one of NEIL YOUNG's best songs, the group began their career playing classic rock covers by the likes of The DOORS, The ROLLING STONES, LED ZEPPELIN and of course, YOUNG himself. Both a self-financed eponymous debut EP and a follow-up, 'TRANSFUSION' sold well, attracting the attentions of 'Polydor'. 1994 saw the release of a major label debut album, 'PARABLES FOR WOODEN EARS', produced by Tony Cohen (who'd previously worked with The BIRTHDAY PARTY and NICK CAVE). After a further two EP's (see below), the group finally broke through with sophomore album, 'DOUBLE ALLERGIC' (1996). A more melodic and accessible effort which spawned the singles 'PICK YOU UP' and 'DAF', the record resided in the Australian Top 30 for nigh on six months. A more stylistically diverse third album, 'INTERNATIONALIST' (1998) went straight in at No.1 down under and spent more than a year on the chart, earning the group a clutch of industry awards. 'ODYSSEY NUMBER FIVE' (2001) repeated the feat, selling even more copies and turning POWDERFINGER into homeboy superstars. Europe and America were less sure of the band's infectious CROWDED HOUSE-do-grunge sound (especially 'LIKE A DOG') despite a tour with COLDPLAY and an inclusion on the 'Mission Impossible 2' soundtrack.

Album rating: PARABLES FOR WOODEN EARS (*6) / DOUBLE ALLERGIC (*6) / INTERNATIONALIST (*5) / ODYSSEY NUMBER FIVE (*5)

BERNARD FANNING – vocals / **IAN HAUG** – guitar, vocals / **DARREN MIDDLETON** – guitar, keyboards, vocals / **JOHN COLLINS** – bass / **JON COGHILL** – drums, percussion

not iss. / own label

1993. (cd-ep) **POWDERFINGER – BLUE EP** [-] [-] Austra
– Take a light / Sacrifice (black Jack) / Freedom / If I tried / Save your skin / Lighten my load / It's no crime.
1993. (cd-ep) **TRANSFORMER EP** [-] [-] Austra
– Reap what you sow / Change the tide / Blind to reason / Mama Harry / Rise up.
1993. (cd-ep) **MR KNEEBONE EP** [-] [-] Austra
– Swollen tongue / Stitches / Drongo / My urn / I'm splittin' Terry.

Polydor / Polydor

Jul 94. (cd-s) **TAIL / MAY MORNING / SLIP** [-] [-] Austra
Aug 94. (cd) **PARABLES FOR WOODEN EARS** [-] [-] Austra
– Walking stick / Tail / Hurried bloom / Father's pyramid / Bridle you / Citadel / Sink low / Grave concern / Solution / This syrup to exchange / Namaste (instrumental) / Blanket / Save your skin.
Oct 94. (cd-ep) **GRAVE CONCERN / BLIND TO REASON (live) / WHILE MY GUITAR GENTLY WEEPS (live)** [-] [-] Austra
Jan 95. (cd-ep) **SAVE YOUR SKIN / SWEET LIP (live) / SINK LOW (live) / SAVE YOUR SKIN (live)** [-] [-] Austra
Aug 96. (cd-ep) **PICK YOU UP / TOFFEE APPLE / WOBBLY KNEES / COME AWAY** [-] [-] Austra
Sep 96. (cd) **DOUBLE ALLERGIC** [-] [-] Austra
– Skinny Jean / Turtle's head / Pick you up / D.A.F. / Boing boing / Give / Oipic / Living type / JC / Glimpse / Take me in / (Return of) The electric horseman.
Dec 96. (cd-ep) **D.A.F. / BLACKFELLA – WHITEFELLA / IBIS / POGO STYLE** [-] [-] Austra
Mar 97. (cd-ep) **LIVING TYPE / ENTREES / MAINS / DESERTS** [-] [-] Austra
May 97. (cd-ep) **TAKE ME IN / SKINNY JEAN (live) / TAIL (live)** [-] [-] Austra
Jul 98. (cd-ep) **THE DAY YOU COME / POLLY / IRONICAL / JOHN CALLAHAN (demo)** [-] [-] Austra
Aug 98. (cd) *(559201-2)* **INTERNATIONALIST** [-] [-] Austra
– Hindley Street / Belter / The day you come / Already gone / Passenger / Don't wanna be left out / Good-day Ray / Trading places / Private man / Celebrity head / Over my head.
Mar 99. (cd-ep) *(563521)* **ALREADY GONE / CONTROL FREAK / THE DAY YOU COME (Ascension remix) / TOM (demo)** [-] [-] Austra
May 99. (cd-ep) **DON'T WANNA BE LEFT OUT / GOOD-DAY RAY / CORNER BOY / PAULS THEME** [-] [-] Austra
Jul 99. (cd-ep) **PASSENGER / THESE DAYS / PASSENGER (live) / PICK YOU UP (live) / MAXWELL'S GREAT MISTAKE / THAT OL' TRACK** [-] [-] Austra
Mar 01. (cd-ep) *(587945)* **LIKE A DOG / LOVE MY WAY / ODYSSEY #2 (THE MISEDUCATION OF POWDERFINGER)** [-] [-] Austra

Apr 01. (cd) *(<549640-2>)* **ODYSSEY NUMBER FIVE** [ ] [ ]
– Waiting for the sun / My happiness / The metre / Like a dog / Odyssey #5 / Up & down and back again / My kind of scene / These days / We should be together now / Thrilloilogy / Whatever makes you happy. *(cd+=)* – Nature boy / Waiting for the sun (live) / My kind of scene (live) / My happiness (live).

May 01. (cd-ep) **MY HAPPINESS / MY KIND OF SCENE / NATURE BOY / ODYSSEY #1 (demo)** [-] [-] Austra

Cozy POWELL

Born: COLIN POWELL, 29 Dec'47, London, England. Learning drums as a young teenager, he ventured into his first of many bands in 1965. They were The SORCERERS, who stuck around until spring '68 when COZY joined The ACE KEFFORD STAND. ACE was an ex-member of The MOVE and numbered in his ranks brothers DAVE and DENNIS BALL. COZY played on their debut 'Atlantic' 45 in March '69; 'FOR YOUR LOVE. / GRAVY BOOBY JAMM'; (584 260). Meanwhile The SORCERERS had become YOUNGBLOOD and invited COZY to return, although this became a brief stay as the drummer re-joined ACE, DAVE and DENNIS for a short time in BIG BERTHA, before being replaced by MAC POOLE. In the spring of '71, COZY's talents and hard work paid off when JEFF BECK recruited him for his own band/GROUP. During the following sixteen months, COZY enjoyed great success as JEFF's albums, 'Rough And Ready' & 'The Jeff Beck Group' soared high in the charts. In Sep/Oct '72, COZY gigged with American outfit SPIRIT, but was back in Britain a month later to join DAVE and DENNIS BALL in the group BEAST. With vocalist FRANK AIELLO installed, they became BEDLAM in May 1973. This mini-supergroup released an eponymous lp for 'Chrysalis'; (CHR 1048) which didn't chart, COZY subsequently looking to the singles market with 'RAK' manager/producer MICKIE MOST (six years previous, JEFF BECK had secured the services of the same guy). Over the course of the next nine months, COZY enjoyed an unpricedented three UK Top 20 hits, namely 'DANCE WITH THE DEVIL', 'THE MAN IN BLACK' & 'NA NA NA'. He departed from BEDLAM in April '74 to form COZY POWELL'S HAMMER, this band including AIELLO, plus BERNIE MARSDEN (guitar), CLIVE CHAMAN (bass) and DON AIREY (keyboards). BEDLAM toured for a year, although the project was shelved when COZY joined the motor racing circuit for three months, prior to fermenting yet another outfit, STRANGE BREW (alongside DAVE CLEMPSON – guitar and GREG RIDLEY – bass). Like a bad pint, the group went stale and only lasted a month, COZY taking up the chance of joining (RITCHIE) BLACKMORE'S RAINBOW in the Autumn of '75. This was his most fruitful period as this top rock act enjoyed four major selling albums, 'RAINBOW RISING' (1976), 'ON STAGE' (1977), 'LONG LIVE ROCK'N'ROLL' (1978) and 'DOWN TO EARTH' (1979). He said farewell to RAINBOW fans at 1980's Donington Rock Festival, having released his debut (!) solo album, 'OVER THE TOP', a year earlier. In 1981, COZY kept busy as a solo artist and a member of MICHAEL SCHENKER GROUP, appearing on their 'MSG' set the same year. The following year he joined (DAVID COVERDALE's) WHITESNAKE and remained for two albums, 'SAINTS 'N' SINNERS' and 'SLIDE IT IN'. His third album, 'OCTOPUSS' (1983) managed only a minor UK Top 100 placing, the drummer tiring of the solo life. He subsequently worked with GARY MOORE in the mid-80's, before replacing CARL PALMER in the dinosaur supergroup, EMERSON, LAKE & POWELL (still trading under the ELP moniker). This brought them renewed interest, although by 1987 COZY had united with Dutch guitarist JAN AKKERMAN (ex-FOCUS) to form FORCEFIELD. This outfit made I, II & III albums in the late 80's, before COZY was inducted into another heavyweight rock act, BLACK SABBATH, for their 1989 album 'HEADLESS CROSS'. The 90's have been seen COZY decreasing his workload, although he still found time to complete another solo album, 'THE DRUMS ARE BACK' (1992) as well as coaxing the legendary PETER GREEN back into the studio and onto the stage. Tragically, COZY lost his life on the 5th April, 1998, when he died in a car crash. He was only 50 years of age.

Album rating: OVER THE TOP (*5) / TILT (*5) / OCTOPUSS (*4) / THE DRUMS ARE BACK (*4) / THE VERY BEST OF COZY POWELL compilation (*6)

COZY POWELL – drums, percussion with various personnel

R.A.K. Chrysalis

Oct 73. (7") *(RAK 164) <2029>* **DANCE WITH THE DEVIL. / AND THEN THERE WAS SKIN** [3] [49] Feb74

May 74. (7") *(RAK 173)* **THE MAN IN BLACK. / AFTER DARK** [18] [-]

Jul 74. (7") *(RAK 180)* **NA NA NA. / MISTRAL** [10] [-]

— Formed COZY POWELL'S HAMMER, STRANGE BREW before moving to RAINBOW (1975-80)

— solo again, now with **DON AIREY** – keyboards, synthesizers / **BERNIE MARSDEN + GARY MOORE + DAVE CLEMPSON** – guitar / **JACK BRUCE** – bass / **MAX MIDDLETON** – piano

Ariola Polydor

Oct 79. (7") *(ARO 189)* **THEME 1. / OVER THE TOP** [62] [ ]

Oct 79. (lp) *(ARL 5038) <6312>* **OVER THE TOP** [34] [ ]
– Theme 1 / Killer / Heidi goes to town / El Sid / Sweet poison / The loner / Over the top. *(re-iss. Jan83 on 'Fame' lp/c; FA/TCFA 3056)*

Dec 79. (7") *(ARO 205)* **THE LONER. / EL SID** [ ] [ ]

Feb 80. (7") *(ARO 222)* **HEIDI GOES TO TOWN. / OVER THE TOP (part 2)** [ ] [ ]

— next with **FRANK AIELLO + ELMER GANTRY** – vocals / **BERNIE MARSDEN + GARY MOORE + JEFF BECK + KIRBY** – guitar / **NEIL MURRAY + CHRIS GLEN + JACK BRUCE** – bass / **DON AIREY + JOHN COOK** – keyboards / **MEL COLLINS** – sax / **DAVID SANCIOUS** – synthesizers

Polydor Polydor

Aug 81. (7") *(POSP 328)* **SOONER OR LATER. / THE BLISTER** [ ] [ ]

Sep 81. (lp/c) *(POLD/+C 5047) <16342>* **TILT** [58] [ ]
– The right side / Jekyll and Hyde / Sooner or later / Living a lie / Cat moves / Sunset / The blister / Hot rock.

— now with **GARY MOORE / DON AIREY / + JON LORD** – keyboards / **COLIN HODGKINSON** – bass / **MEL GALLEY** – guitar

Apr 83. (lp/c) *(POLD/+C 5093)* **OCTOPUSS** [86] [ ]
– Up on the downs / 633 squadron / Octopuss / The big country / Formula one / Princetown / Dartmoore / The rattler.

— See above details for the many bands COZY joined. Returned solo in '92, aided by BRIAN MAY + JOHN DEACON, JON LORD + STEVE LUKATHER, etc

Odeon not iss.

Aug 92. (cd/c) *(CD/TC ODN 1008)* **THE DRUMS ARE BACK** [ ] [-]
– The drums are back / Ride to win / I wanna hear tou shout / Light in the sky / Return of the 7 / Battle hymn / Legend of the glass mountain / Cryin' / Classical gas / Somewhere in time / Rocket.

– compilations, etc. –

Jul 84. (7") *EMI Golden Grooves; (G 4530)* **DANCE WITH THE DEVIL. / THE MAN IN BLACK** [ ] [-]

Sep 91. (cd) *Elite; (018 CDP)* **SOONER OR LATER** [ ] [-]
– ('TILT' & 'OCTOPUSS')

Sep 92. (cd-s) *Old Gold; (OG 6177)* **DANCE WITH THE DEVIL / NA NA NA / THE MAN IN BLACK** [ ] [-]

Oct 95. (cd-s) *Old Gold; (1262363332)* **THE MAN IN BLACK / DANCE WITH THE DEVIL** [ ] [-]

Jul 99. (d-cd; by COZY POWELL & BIG BERTHA) *Zoom Club; (ZCRCD 17)* **LIVE IN HAMBURG 1970** [ ] [-]

Sep 99. (cd) *Polydor; (<537724-2>)* **THE VERY BEST OF COZY POWELL** [ ] [ ] Jul97
– Theme one / Killer / Sweet poison / The loner / Over the top / Cat moves / Sunset / Hot rock / The blister / Up on the downs / Formula one / Dartmoore / 633 Squadron / Octopuss / The big country / The rattler.

POWERMAN 5000

Formed: Boston, Massachusetts, USA ... 1990 by frontman SPIDER (incidently the younger brother of ROB ZOMBIE!) along with his spikey-topped mystery men ADAM, M.33, DORIAN 27 and AL 3. Firing up a large home-based following after their well-received debut album, 'THE BLOOD SPLAT RATING SYSTEM' (1995), POWERMAN 5000 found themselves being asked to sign for 'DreamWorks'. Re-issuing the record as 'MEGA!! KUNG FU RADIO' in February '97, the metal-rap band were subsequently invited to support the man OSBOURNE on his US 'Ozzfest' tour. With the comic book obsessed quintet augmented by DJ LETHAL (of LIMP BIZKIT) and GINGER FISH (of MARILYN MANSON) on their 1999 follow-up, 'TONIGHT THE STARS REVOLT!', it was no surprise when the band smashed into the US Top 30.

Album rating: THE BLOOD SPLAT RATING SYSTEM – MEGA!! KUNG FU RADIO (*4) / TONIGHT THE STARS WILL REVOLT! (*5)

SPIDER – vocals / **ADAM** – guitar / **M.33** – guitar / **DORIAN 27** – bass / **AL 3** – drums

not iss. Conscience

1995. (cd) **THE BLOOD SPLAT RATING SYSTEM** [-] [ ]

DreamWorks DreamWorks

Feb 97. (cd/c) *<DRD 50005>* **MEGA!! KUNG FU RADIO** (re-working of debut) [-] [ ]
– Public menace, freak, human fly / Organized / Neckbone / Car crash / Earth vs. me / Swim with the sharks / 20 miles to Texas, 25 to Hell / Mega!! kung fu radio / Tokyo vigilante #1 / Boredwitcha / Standing 8 / Even Superman shot himself.

Aug 99. (cd) *<(DRD 50107)>* **TONIGHT THE STARS REVOLT!** [ ] [29] Jul99
– The eye is upon you / Super nova goes pop / When worlds collide / Nobody's real / System 11:11 / Tonight the stars revolt! / AUTOmatic / Son of X-51 / Operate, annihilate / Blast off to nowhere / They know who you are / Good times roll / Watch the sky for me.

– others, etc. –

Mar 97. (cd) *Curve Earth; <16>* **TRUE FORCE** [-] [ ]

PRAYING MANTIS

Formed: London, England ... 1977 by brothers TINO and CHRIS NEOPHYTOU (who were both nicknamed TROY), ROBERT ANGELO and MICK RANSOME. Like IRON MAIDEN, the band released an EP of demo tracks through the help of DJ, Neal Kay, subsequently appearing with the band on the 'EMI' compilation, 'Metal For Muthas'. An eponymous one-off independent single followed on 'Gem' in 1980, prior to line-up changes (STEVE CARROLL for ANGELO and POTTS for RANSOME) and a major label deal with 'Arista'. After a few 45's, the band released their debut album, 'TIME TELLS NO LIES', a disappointing set given their NWOBHM promise, although it did secure a minor UK chart placing. The subsequent lack of interest engendered a line-up change with vocalist BERNIE SHAW replacing CARROLL. A few more personnel shuffles ensued, the band re-naming themselves STRATUS in the process and adopting a more complex, pomp-rock approach. After an album, 'THROWING SHAPES' (1985) failed to take off the group packed it in, SHAW joining URIAH HEEP. In the 90's, the TROY's, with former IRON MAIDEN members PAUL DiANNO and DENNIS STRATTON (completed by drummer BRUCE BISLAND) toured Japan under the banner of The BRITISH ALL STARS. This led to a second PRAYING MANTIS album, 'PREDATOR IN DISGUISE' (1993) – DI'ANNO has since reformed his KILLERS. In 1995, they released the Japanese-only 'TO THE POWER OF TEN', while their first UK album for some time, 'NOWHERE TO HIDE', was issued in 2000.

Album rating: TIME TELLS NO LIES (*5) / PREDATOR IN DISGUISE (*4) / A CRY FOR THE NEW WORLD (*5) / TO THE POWER OF TEN (*5) / NOWHERE TO HIDE (*4) / Stratus: THROWING SHAPE (*4)

TINO 'Troy' NEOPHYTOU – vocals, guitar / **ROBERT ANGELO** – guitar / **CHRIS 'Troy' NEOPHYTOU** – bass, vocals / **MICK RANSOME** – drums

Harvest not iss.

Feb 80. (7") *(HAR 5201)* **THE SOUNDHOUSE TAPES PART 2** [ ] [-]
– Captured city / Johnny Cool.
(12"+=) *(12HAR 5201)* – Ripper.

Gem not iss.

Jul 80. (7") *(GEMS 36)* **PRAYING MANTIS. / HIGH ROLLER** [ ] [-]

— **STEVE CARROLL** – guitars, vocals; repl. ANGELO

— **DAVE POTTS** – drums (ex-TEN YEARS AFTER) repl. RANSOME

Arista Arista

Nov 80. (7") *(ARIST 378)* **CHEATED. / THIRTY PIECES OF SILVER** [69] [-]
(some with free live 7") **FLIRTING WITH SUICIDE. / PANIC IN THE STREETS**

Mar 81. (7") *(ARIST 397)* **ALL DAY AND ALL OF THE NIGHT. / BEADS OF EBONY** [ ] [-]

May 81. (lp) *(SPART 1153)* **TIME TELLS NO LIES** [60] [-]
– Cheated / All day and all of the night / Running for tomorrow / Rich city kids / Lovers to the grave / Panic in the streets / Beads of ebony / Flirting with suicide / Children of the earth.

— **BERNIE SHAW** – vocals (ex-GRAND PRIX) repl. CARROLL

— added **JON BAVIN** – keyboards

Jet not iss.

Sep 82. (7") *(JET 7026)* **TURN THE TABLES. TELL ME THE NIGHTMARE'S WRONG** [ ] [-]

— **CLIVE BURR** – drums (ex-IRON MAIDEN) repl. RANSOME

— the band became . . .

STRATUS

— **ALAN NELSON** – keyboards; repl. BAVIN

Steeltrax not iss.

Sep 85. (lp/c) *(STEEL/+C 31001)* **THROWING SHAPE** [ ] [-]
– Back street lovers / Gimme something / Even if it takes / Give me one more chance / Never say no / Run for your life / Romancer / Enough is enough / So tired.

— split after the failure of above, SHAW joined URIAH HEEP

PRAYING MANTIS

— reformed for the 90's; the **TROY's** with **PAUL DiANNO** – vocals (ex-DiANNO, ex-IRON MAIDEN) / **DENNIS STRATTON** – guitar (ex-IRON MAIDEN) / **BRUCE BISLAND** – drums (ex-WEAPON)

Under One Flag not iss.

Feb 93. (cd) *(CDFLAG 77)* **PREDATOR IN DISGUISE** [ ] [-]
– Can't see the angels / She's hot / This time girl / Time slipping away / Listen to what your heart says / Still want you / The horn / Battle royal / Only you / Borderline / Can't wait forever.

Sep 93. (cd) *(CDFLAG 80)* **A CRY FOR THE NEW WORLD** [ ] [-]
– Rise up again / A cry for the new world / A moment in life / Letting go / One chance / Dangerous / Fight to be free / Open your heart / Dream on / Journeyman / The final eclipse.

not iss. unknown

Nov 95. (cd) **TO THE POWER OF TEN** [-] [-] Japan
– Don't be afraid of the dark / Bring on the night / Ball of confusion / Welcome to my Hollywood / Another time, another place / To the power of ten / Little angel / Victory / Only the children cry / Night and day / Angry man.

Sep 00. (cd) *(FRCD 073)* **NOWHERE TO HIDE** [ ] [-]
– Nowhere to hide / Cruel winter / The clocktower / Can't stop the fire / Future of the world / Whenever I'm lost / You'll never know / River of hope / S.O.S.

- compilations, etc.

Aug 00. (cd) *Zoom Club; (ZCRCD 35)* **LIVE AT LAST (live)** [ ] [-]

Sep 00. (cd) *Zoom Club; (ZCRCD 36)* **CAPTURED ALIVE IN TOKYO CITY (live)** [ ] [-]

PRECIOUS METAL

Formed: Los Angeles, California, USA . . . 1984 as an all-female hard-rock act, by LESLIE KNAUER-WASSER, MARA FOX, JANET ROBIN, ALEX RYLANCE and CAROL M. CONTROL. Inhabiting the male-dominated, shark infested waters of the metal world, the group predictably found it difficult for their work to be judged on its own merits, despite a production job by the respected PAUL SABU on their debut album, 'RIGHT HERE, RIGHT NOW' (1985). A US-only release on 'Mercury', PRECIOUS METAL had moved to an independent by the release of follow-up, 'THAT KIND OF GIRL' (1988). With success proving consistently elusive, the girls finally decided to call it a day after a third and final set, the eponymous 'PRECIOUS METAL' (1990).

Album rating: RIGHT HERE, RIGHT NOW (*4) / THAT KIND OF GIRL (*5) / PRECIOUS METAL (*5) / WHAT YOU SEE IS WHAT YOU GET compilation (*6)

LESLIE KNAUER-WASSER – vocals / **JANET ROBIN** – guitar, vocals / **MARA FOX** – guitar, vocals / **ALEX RYLANCE** – bass, vocals / **CAROL M. CONTROL** – drums

not iss. Mercury

1985. (lp) *<826146-1>* **RIGHT HERE, RIGHT NOW** [-] [ ]
– This girl / Right here, right now / Bad guys / Pretty boy / Emily / Shakin' / Girls nite out / You do something special / Cheesecake / Remembering old times.

Savage Chameleon

Aug 88. (lp/c/cd) *(LP/CASS/CD VAG 001) <D1/D4/D2-74753>* **THAT KIND OF GIRL** [ ] [ ]
– Anybody's lover / All fall down / What you see is what you get / Moving mountains / Seven minutes to midnight / Stand up and shout / That kind of girl / Sweet sweet / Push / Passion's pain.

Sep 88. (7") *(7VAG 001)* **MOVIN' MOUNTAINS. /** [ ] [ ]

Jan 89. (7") *(7VAG 002)* **STAND UP AND SHOUT. / SWEET SWEET** [ ] [ ]

— **JULIA FAREY** – bass, vocals; repl. RYLANCE

1990. (cd/c/lp) *<D2/D4/D1-74834>* **PRECIOUS METAL** [ ] [ ]
– Mr. Big stuff / Trouble / Two hearts / Thrilling life / Forever tonight / Reckless / Eaxier than you think / Nasty habits / Downhill dreamer / In the mood / Howl at the moon / Chasing rainbows.

— broke-up after above

- compilations, etc. -

Sep 98. (cd) *Renaissance; <(RMED 0197CD)>* **WHAT YOU SEE IS WHAT YOU GET** [ ] [ ]
– This girl / Sweet sweet / Cheese cake / Moving mountains / Mr. Big stuff / Emily / What you see is what you get / In the mood / Easier than you think / Right here, right now / All fall down / You do something special / Push / Downhill dreamer / Stand up and shout / Trouble / Pretty boy / That kind of firl / Howl at the Moon / Shakin' / Chasing rainbows.

PRESIDENTS OF THE UNITED STATES OF AMERICA

Formed: Seattle, Washington, USA . . . late 1993 by long-time friends CHRIS BALLEW, JASON FINN and DAVE DEDERER. All veterans of the alternative rock scene in one way or another (BALLEW had even worked as part of BECK's backing band), this "wacky" outfit were akin to a head-on collision between The CARS and DEVO. Combining surreal animal-inspired lyrics and a youthfully enthusiastic, funky pop/punk approach, the band recorded their celebrated debut set. Initially released on the independent 'Pop Llama' label in 1994, the eponymous album was subsequently remixed and reissued the following year after 'Columbia' came out tops in the ensuing bidding war for their presidential signatures. Powered by the success of the 'LUMP' single, the album went on to sell well over a million copies in the States, eventually making the Top 10. The band also made a dent in the UK market, helped by the success of the bizarre 'PEACHES' single. A follow-up set, 'II', eventually appeared in 1996, although this time around they failed to capture the public's attention in quite the same fashion. Early in 1998, the band split up, leaving behind a couple of albums and a miserable leftovers collection, 'PURE FROSTING'. • **Songwriters:** BALLEW and group except KICK OUT THE JAMS (MC5) / WE ARE NOT GOING TO MAKE IT (Ben Reiser) / VIDEO KILLED THE RADIO STAR (Buggles) / CA PLANE POUR MOI (Plastic Bertrand) / DEVIL IN A SLEEPING BAG (Willie Nelson) / CLEVELAND ROCKS (Ian Hunter). • **Trivia:** PEACHES video was directed by ROMAN COPPOLA, son of FRANCIS FORD COPPOLA.

Album rating: PRESIDENTS OF THE UNITED STATES OF AMERICA (*5) / II (*7) / PURE FROSTING part compilation (*3)

CHRIS BALLEW – vocals, two-string basitar (ex-SUPERGROUP) / **DAVE DEDERER** – three-string guitbass, vocals (ex- LOVE BATTERY) / **JASON FINN** – drums, vocals (ex-SKIN YARD, ex-HELIOS CREED)

— released a single on 'Pop Llama' US Mar 95.

Columbia Columbia

Oct 95. (cd/c) *(481039-2/-4) <67291>* **PRESIDENTS OF THE UNITED STATES OF AMERICA** [14] [6] Sep95
– Kitty / Feather pluckn / Lump / Stranger / Boll Weevil / Peaches / Dune buggy / We are not going to make it / Kick out the jams / Body / Back porch / Candy / Naked and famous. *(yellow-lp Apr96; 481039-0)* – (2 extra). *(re-iss. cd Jul96; 484334-2) (w/ free cd+=)* – Dune buggy / Kick / Peaches / Lump / Back porch (versions). *(lp re-iss. Jun98 on 'Munster'; MR 093) (cd re-iss. Jan99; same as original)*

— <above album was originally issued on 'Pop Llama' in the US>

Dec 95. (7"pic-d/c-s) *(662496-7/-4)* **LUMP. / WAKE UP** [15] [-]
(cd-s+=) *(662496-2)* – Carolyn's bootie / Candy's cigarette.

Feb 96. (c-s,cd-s) *<78254>* **PEACHES / CANDY CIGARETTE** [-] [29]

Mar 96. (7") **FUCK CALIFORNIA. / CAROLYN'S BOOTIE** [-] [ ]
above on US label 'C/Z'

Apr 96. (7"pic-d/c-s) *(663107-7/-4)* **PEACHES. / CONFUSION** [8] [-]
(cd-s) *(663107-2)* – ('A'side) / Feather pluckin (live) / Boll Weevil (live) / Dune buggy (live).

Jul 96. (7"pic-d/c-s) *(663489-7/-4)* **DUNE BUGGY. / PEACHES (live)** [15] [-]
(cd-s) *(663489-3)* – ('A'side) / Back porch (live) / Kick out the jams (live) / Video killed the radio star (live).

Oct 96. (7"pic-d) *(663881-7)* **MACH 5. / BODY (live)** [29] [-]
(c-s) *(663817-4)* – ('A'side) / Carolyn's bootie.
(cd-s) *(663817-2)* – ('A'side) / Tremelo blooz / Tiki lounge god.

Nov 96. (cd/c/lp) *(485092-2/-4/-1) <67577>* **II** 36 31
– Ladies and gentlemen part 1 / Lunatic to love / Volcano / Mach 5 / Twig / Bug city / Bath of fire / Tiki god / L.I.P. / Froggie / Toob amplifier / Supermodel / Puffy little shoes / Ladies and gentlemen part 2 / Basketball dream.

—— split leaving behind a few remnants below

Mar 98. (cd/c) *(489702-2/-4) <69201>* **PURE FROSTING** (part compilation)
– Love delicatessen / Video killed the radio star / Mobile home / Japan / Black porch / Man (deposable thumb) / Tiki lounge god / Teenage girl / Slip away / Tremolo blooz / Cleveland rocks / Lump.

Jul 98. (c-s/cd-s) *(W 0450 C/CD)* **VIDEO KILLED THE RADIO STAR / (other tracks by Ellen Dow & Sugarhill Gang / Culture Club** 52 -
(above issued on the 'Maverick/Warners' label)

—— BALLEW was now in a band called, The GIRAFFES

PRETTY MAIDS

Formed: Denmark . . . 1981 by RONNIE ATKINS and KEN HAMMER, who collected together musicians PETE COLLINS, JOHN DARROW and PHIL MOORHEAD. Unlike many European acts of their ilk, PRETTY MAIDS succeeded in securing a brief tenure with a UK label, in the case 'Bullet', who issued an eponymous mini-debut in '83. Not surprisingly, their sound closely resembled classic DEEP PURPLE, an approach that helped them win a deal with 'Epic'. Their derivative formula changed little over major label releases like 'RED, HOT AND HEAVY' (1985) and 'FUTURE WORLD' (1987), although the latter hit the US Top 200. After a lengthy delay, their 4th and final album (produced by ROGER GLOVER, ex-er . . . DEEP PURPLE), 'JUMP THE GUN' eventually appeared in 1990.

Album rating: PRETTY MAIDS mini (*5) / RED, HOT AND HEAVY (*5) / FUTURE WORLD (*7) / JUMP THE GUN (*4) / SIN-DECADE (*4) / STRIPPED (*4) / SCREAM (*5) / SCREAMIN' LIVE (*4) / SPOOKED (*4) / BACK TO BACK – THE BEST OF . . . (*6) / ANYTHING WORTH DOING IS WORTH OVERDOING (*3) / FIRST CUTS . . . AND THEN SOME collection (*4) / CARPE DIEM (*4)

RONNIE ATKINS – vocals / **KEN HAMMER** – guitar / **PETE COLLINS** – guitar / **JOHN DARROW** – bass / **PHIL MOORHEAD** – drums / 6th member **ALAN OWEN** – keyboards

Bullet not iss.

Oct 83. (m-lp) *(CULP 1)* **PRETTY MAIDS** -
– City light / Fantasy / Shelly the maid / Bad boys / Children of tomorrow / Nowhere to run. *(re-iss. 1984 on 'C.B.S.'; CBS 25885) (cd-iss. May99 on 'Massacre'; MASSSH 197)*

—— **RICK HANSON** – guitar; repl. COLLINS

—— **ALLAN DELONG** – bass; repl. DARROW

Epic Epic

Jun 85. (lp) *(EPC/40 26207)* **RED, HOT AND HEAVY**
– Fortuna / Back to back / Red, hot and heavy / Waitin' for the time / Cold killer / Battle of pride / Night danger / A place in the night / Queen of dreams / Little darling.

May 87. (7") *(650 437-7)* **LOVE GAMES. / NEEDLES IN THE DARK**
(12"+=) *(650 437-8)* – Yellow rain.

May 87. (lp/c) *(450 281-1/-4) <40713>* **FUTURE WORLD**
– Future world / We came to rock / Love games / Yellow rain / Loud 'n' proud / Rodeo / Needles in the dark / Eye of the storm / Long way to go.

—— **RICKY MARX** – guitar; repl. HANSON

Columbia not iss.

1990. (cd/c/lp) *(466365-2/-4/-1) <46130>* **JUMP THE GUN** - Danish
– Lethal heroes / Don't settle for less / Rock the house / Savage heart / Young blood / Headlines / Jump the gun / Partners in crime / Attention / Hang tough / Over and out / Dream on.

—— **ATKINS + HAMMER** recruited **KEN JACKSON** – bass + **MICHAEL FAST** – drums, percussion

1992. (cd/c) *(471275-2/-4)* **SIN-DECADE** - - Danish
– Running out / Who said money / Nightmare in the neighbourhood / Sin-decade / Come on tough, come on nasty / Raise your flag / Credit card lover / Know it ain't easy / Healing touch / In the flesh / Please don't leave.

1993. (cd) *(473964-2)* **STRIPPED** - - Danish
– If it ain't gonna change / Please don't leave me / In the minds of the young / Too late, too loud / Say the word / 39 / Heartbeat from Heaven / How does it feel / I'll be there / Savage heart.

Massacre not iss.

Mar 95. (cd/lp) *(MASS CD/LP 047)* **SCREAM** -
– Rise / Scream / Psycho-time-bomb-Planet-Earth / This love / Walk away / No messiah / In a world of your own / Don't turn your sex on me / Adrenaline junkie / Anytime anywhere / When it all comes down.

Nov 95. (cd/lp) *(MASS CD/LP 081)* **SCREAMIN' LIVE (live)** -
– Psycho-time-bomb-Planet-Earth / Rock the house / Rise / Walk away / Scream / Yellow rain / Sin – Decade / Savage heart / No messiah / Please don't leave me / Lovegames / Future world / Back to back / Red hot and heavy.

May 97. (cd) *(MASSCD 119)* **SPOOKED** -
– Resurrection (intro) / Freakshow / Dead or alive / Die with your dreams / Fly me out / Live until it hurts / Spooked / Twisted / If it can't be love / Never too late / Your mind is where the money is / Hard luck woman / The one that should not be.

Mar 99. (cd) *(MASSCD 170)* **ANYTHING WORTH DOING IS WORTH OVERDOING** -
– Snakes in Eden / Destination paradise / Hell on high heels / When the angels cry / Back off / Only in America / With these eyes / Anything worth doing is worth overdoing / Scent of my prey / Face me / Loveshine.
(below was actually released in Scandinavia Nov'00)

Mar 01. (cd) *(MASSCD 251)* **CARPE DIEM** -
– Violent tribe / Carpe diem / Tortured spirit / Wouldn't miss you / Clay / Poisoned pleasures / Until it dies / The unwritten pages / For once in your life / They're all alike / Time awaits for no one / Invisible chains.

– compilations, etc. –

Nov 98. (cd) *Massacre; (MASSCD 169)* **BACK TO BACK . . . THE BEST OF PRETTY MAIDS** -
– Fortuna / Back to back / Attention / Dead or alive / When it all comes down / Forever and eternal / Savage heart / Love games / Walk away / Sin – Decade / Waitin' for the time to come / Yellow rain / Twisted / Future world / Please don't leave me / Red hot and heavy / De bedste til og mine venner.

Jan 00. (cd) *Massacre; (MASSCD 227)* **FIRST CUTS . . . AND THEN SOME** -

PRIDE & GLORY (see under ⇒ WYLDE, Zakk)

(see under ⇒ WYLDE, Zakk)

PRIMAL FEAR

Formed: Germany . . . mid-90's by former GAMMA RAY vocalist RALF SCHEEPERS. With the aid of their long-standing guitar king KAI HANSEN, RALF and his new heavy-metal crew (including guitarist MAT SINNER – also at the controls – and KLAUS SPERLING), PRIMAL FEAR were ready to rock. An eponymous set for 'Nuclear Blast' in 1998, set the ball rolling and concerts went down a storm. With STEFAN LEIBING stepping in on guitar, a sophomore set, 'JAWS OF DEATH' (1999) was delivered and it looked like SCHEEPERS had regained the metal respect he once had with GAMMA RAY. Early in 2001 (and with 5th member/guitarist HENRY WOLTER), PF took off on a world 'Nuclear Blast' tour which coincided with their third and best set so far, 'NUCLEAR FIRE'.

Album rating: PRIMAL FEAR (*7) / JAWS OF DEATH (*6) / NUCLEAR FIRE (*7)

RALF SCHEEPERS – vocals (ex-GAMMA RAY) / **KAI HANSEN** – guitar (of GAMMA RAY) / **MAT SINNER** – guitar (of SINNER) / **KLAUS SPERLING** – drums (ex-PROLOPOWER singer)

Nuclear Blast Nuclear Blast

Mar 98. (lp/cd) *(NB 302/+CD) <6302>* **PRIMAL FEAR** Feb98
– Primal fear / Chainbreaker / Silver and gold / Promised land / Formula one / Dollars / Nine lives / Tears of rage / Speedking / Battalions of hate / Running in the dust / Thunderdome.

—— **STEFAN LEIBING** – guitar (ex-INSANITY) repl. HANSEN

Aug 99. (cd) *(NB 391-2) <6391>* **JAWS OF DEATH** Jul99
– Jaws of death / Final embrace / Save a prayer / Church of blood / Into the future / Under your spell / Play to kill / Nation in fear / When the night comes / Fight to survive / Hatred in my soul / Kill the king.

—— added **HENRY WOLTER** – guitar (ex-THUNDERHEAD)

Jan 01. (cd) *(NB 557-2) <6557>* **NUCLEAR FIRE**
– Angel in black / Kiss of death / Back from Hell / Now or never / Fight the fire / Eye of an eagle / Bleed for me / Nuclear fire / Red rain / Fire on the horizon / Living for metal.

PRIMUS

Formed: Bay Area, San Francisco, California, USA . . . mid-80's by bassist/vocalist LES CLAYPOOL and guitarist TODD HUTH, initially as PRIMATE. Something of a cult phenomenon in their native city, the act's first release was a live affair, 'SUCK ON THIS' (1989), recorded at a local club and released on the band's own 'Prawnsong' label. By this point, JOE SATRIANI protege, LARRY LALONDE, had replaced HUTH who joined fellow Bay Area act, BLIND ILLUSION (CLAYPOOL had once been a member). PRIMUS were hardly purveyors of breakneck rifferama, however, CLAYPOOL's wayward muse fashioning instead a notoriously bizarre, bass-heavy fish stew of thrash, aquatic funk, avant-rock and surreal humour, CLAYPOOL's staccato-snorkle vocals colouring his marine-obsessed tales of fishermen and sturgeon. PRIMUS' first studio effort, 'FRIZZLE FRY' (1990), was released on the American independent label, 'Caroline' ('Virgin' in the UK), many of the songs from the debut reworked, including the brilliant 'JOHN THE FISHERMAN'. The band had also recruited a permanent drummer in TIM 'HERB' ALEXANDER, complementing CLAYPOOL's slippery, knottily intricate bass work. PRIMUS fitted in loosely with the burgeoning funk-metal scene of the day (supporting the likes of FAITH NO MORE, 24-7 SPYZ and LIVING COLOUR) and soon found themselves with a major label contract via 'Interscope', subsequently making their major label debut with the wonderfully titled 'SAILING THE SEAS OF CHEESE' (1991). The record's highlight was a reworked 'TOMMY THE CAT' (from the debut), complete with vocals courtesy of highly respected fellow weirdster, TOM WAITS. Touring with RUSH obviously hadn't damaged the band's street cred too much and the '93 follow-up, 'PORK SODA' made the US Top 10, proving that weird, in PRIMUS' case, was indeed wonderful. The same year, CLAYPOOL teamed up with old colleagues HUTH and JAY LANE to form a side project, SAUSAGE, releasing the album 'RIDDLES ARE ABOUND TONIGHT' (1993). A further (US) Top 10 PRIMUS album appeared in 1995, 'TALES FROM THE PUNCHBOWL', CLAYPOOL proving that he hadn't lost his technicolour, often flippant sense of humour with such lyrical vignettes as 'WYNONA'S BIG BROWN BEAVER'. Prior to the release of 'THE BROWN ALBUM' in '97, a rare line-up change occured with BRIAN MANTIA replacing ALEXANDER. The following year saw the release of a largely disappointing covers mini-album, 'RHINOPLASTY', it looked like PRIMUS were sailing on cheese right enough. The album 'ANTIPOP' in 1999 gave them a welcome return to US Top 50. • **Covers:** MAKING PLANS FOR NIGEL + SCISSOR MAN (Xtc) / INTRUDER + THE FAMILY AND THE FISHING NET (Peter Gabriel) / HAVE A CIGAR (Pink Floyd) / TIPPY TOES

(Meters) / SILLY PUTTY (Stanley Clarke) / AMOS MOSES (Jerry Reed) / BEHIND MY CAMEL (Police) / THE THING THAT SHOULD NOT BE (Metallica) / etc.

Album rating: SUCK ON THIS (*4) / FRIZZLE FRY (*7) / SAILING THE SEAS OF CHEESE (*7) / PORK SODA (*8) / TALES FROM THE PUNCH BOWL (*8) / THE BROWN ALBUM (*6) / RHINOPLASTY mini (*5) / ANTIPOP (*5) / Sausage: RIDDLES ARE ABOUND TONIGHT (*4) / Les Claypool and the Holy Mackerel: HIGHBALL WITH THE DEVIL (*3)

LES CLAYPOOL (b.29 Sep'63, Richmond, Calif.) – vocals, bass (ex-BLIND ILLUSION) / **LARRY LaLONDE** (b.12 Sep'68, Richmond) – guitar (ex-POSSESSED) repl. TODD HUTH (b.13 Mar'63, San Leandro, Calif.) who joined BLIND ILLUSION / **JAY LANE** (b.15 Dec'64, San Francisco) – drums; repl. drum machine

not iss. / Prawn Song

Jan 90. (lp) *<CAROL 160-2>* **SUCK ON THIS (live)** [-] [ ]
– John the fisherman / Groundhog's day / The heckler / Pressman / Jelikit / Tommy the cat / Pudding time / Harold of the rocks / Frizzle fry. *(UK cd-iss. Mar92 on 'Atlantic'; 7567 91833-2) (re-iss. Jun97 on 'Caroline' lp/cd; CAR/+OLCD 1620)*

— **TIM 'HERB' ALEXANDER** (b.10 Apr'65, Cherry Point, New Connecticut) – drums repl. JAY who joined SAUSAGE

Virgin / Caroline

Jul 90. (cd/c/lp) *(CAR CD/C/LP 10) <CAROL 1619-2>* **FRIZZLE FRY** [ ] [ ] Feb90
– To defy the laws of tradition / Ground hog's day / Too many puppies / Mr.Know-it-all / Frizzle fry / John the fisherman / You can't kill Michael Malloy / The toys go winding down / Pudding time / Sathington Willoby / Spaghetti western / Harold of the rocks / To defy. *(cd re-iss. Jun97; CAROLCD 1619)*

Atlantic / Interscope

May 91. (cd/c/lp) *<(7567 91659-2/-4/-1)>* **SAILING THE SEAS OF CHEESE** [ ] [ ]
– Seas of cheese / Here come the bastards / Sgt. Baker / American life / Jerry was a race car driver / Eleven / Is it luck? / Grandad's lil ditty / Tommy the cat / Sathington waltz / Those damned blue collar tweekers / Fish on / Los bastardos. *(re-iss. Feb95; same)*

Jun 92. (cd-ep) *(A 6167CD)* **CHEESY EP 1** <US title 'MISCELLANEOUS DEBRIS'> [ ] [ ]
– Making plans for Nigel / Tommy the cat / Tippy toes / Have a cigar.
(cd-ep) **CHEESY 2** *(A 6167CDX)* – (1st 2 tracks) / Sinister exaggerator / Intruder.

May 93. (cd/c/lp) *<(7567 92257-2/-4/-1)>* **PORK SODA** [56] [7]
– Pork chop's little ditty / My name is mud / Welcome to this world / Bob / D.M.V. / The ol' Diamondback sturgeon (Fisherman's chronicles, part 3) / Nature boy / Wounded Knee / Pork soda / The pressman / Mr.Krinkle / The air is getting slippery / Hamburger train / Pork chop's little ditty / Hail Santa. *(cd re-iss. Jul96 on 'Interscope'; IND 92257)*

Jun 95. (cd/c) *<(IND/INC 92553)>* **TALES FROM THE PUNCHBOWL** [ ] [8]
– Professor Nutbutter's house of treats / Mrs. Blaileen / Wynona's big brown beaver / Southbound pachydern / Space farm / Year of the parrot / Hellbound 17 1/2 (theme from) / Glass sandwich / Del Davis tree farm / De Anza jig / On the tweak again / Over the electric grapevine / Captain Shiner. *(enhanced-cd re-iss. Jul96; IND 92665)*

Dec 95. (c-s) *(A 8129C)* **WYNONA'S BIG BROWN BEAVER / HELLO SKINNY – CONSTANTINOPLE** [ ] [-]
(cd-s+=) *(A 8129CD)* – Have a cigar.
(above issued on 'Atlantic' in the UK)

— early '96, CLAYPOOL featured on ALEX LIFESON'S (Rush) VICTOR project

— (Sep'96) **BRIAN 'Brain' MANTIA** – drums (ex-GODFLESH) repl. TIM

Jul 97. (cd/d-lp) *<(IND/ISC 90126)>* **BROWN ALBUM** [ ] [21]
– The return of Sathington Willoughby / Fisticuffs / Golden boy / Over the falls / Shake hands with beef / Camelback cinema / Hats off / Puddin' Taine / Bob's party time lounge / Duchess and the proverbial mind spread / Restin' bones / Coddington / Kalamazoo / Chastasing of renegade / Arnie.

Aug 98. (m-cd) *<(IND 90214)>* **RHINOPLASTY** [ ] [ ]
– Scissor man / The family and the fishing net / Silly putty / Amos Moses / Behind my camel / Too many puppies / The thing that should not be / Tommy the cat / Bob's party time lounge.

Oct 99. (cd/c) *<(490414-2/-4)>* **ANTIPOP** [ ] [44]
– Intro / Electric Uncle Sam / Natural Joe / Laquerhead / Electric electric / Greet the sacred cow / Mama didn't raise no fool / Dirty drowning man / Ballad of bodacious / Power mad / Final voyage of the liquid sky / Coat tails of a dead man / Heckler.

SAUSAGE

LES CLAYPOOL – vocals, bass / **TODD HUTH** – guitar / **JAY LANE** – drums

East West / East West

Apr 94. (cd/c) *<(6544 92361-2/-4)>* **RIDDLES ARE ABOUND TONIGHT** [ ] [ ]
– Temporary phase / Girls for single men / Caution should be used while driving a motor vehicle or operating machinery / Shattering song / Prelude to fear / Riddles are abound tonight / Here's to the man / Toyz 1988 / Recreating.

LES CLAYPOOL and the HOLY MACKEREL

LES CLAYPOOL with **JAY LANE** – drums / **JOE GORE + CHARLIE HUNTER** – guitar / with **ADAM GATES** – vocals / plus **HENRY ROLLINS** – narrator

not iss. / Interscope

Sep 96. (cd) *<IND 90085>* **HIGHBALL WITH THE DEVIL** [-] [ ]
– Running the gauntlet / Holy mackerel / Highball with the Devil / Hendershot / Calling Kyle / Rancor / Cohibas esplenditos / Delicate tendrils / The awakening / Precipitation / George E. Porge / El sobrante fortnight / Granny's little yard gnome / Me and Chuck / Carolina rig.

PRINCESS PANG

Formed: New York, USA . . . 1986 by JENI FOSTER, RONNIE ROZE and BRIAN KEATS, who recruited guitarists JAY LEWIS and ANDY TYERNON. This female fronted scuzz-rock act elbowed their way onto the scene in 1989 with an eponymous album on 'Metal Blade'. Despite favourable reviews and a British tour in 1990, the group fell apart when JENI decided to bail out.

Album rating: PRINCESS PANG (*4)

JENI FOSTER – vocals / **JAY LEWIS** – guitar / **ANDY TYERNON** – guitar / **RONNIE ROZE** – bass / **BRIAN KEATS** – drums

Roadracer / Metal Blade

Aug 89. (lp/c/cd) *(RO 9471-1/-4/-2) <847934>* **PRINCESS PANG** [ ] [ ]
– Trouble in Paradise / Find my heart a home / South St. kids / No reason to cry / Sympathy / Scream and shout / China doll / Baby blue / Too much too soon / Any way you want it / I'm not playin'.

— folded after JENI departed in 1990

PRISM

Formed: Vancouver, Canada . . . mid 70's by RON TABAK and LINDSAY MITCHELL, who enlisted the services of TOM LAVIN, JOHN HALL, ABE BRYANT and RODNEY HIGGS. Initially an easy-on-the-ear soft rock/pomp outfit, PRISM released two largely forgettable albums for 'Ariola' between 1977 and '78. They changed labels in 1979, 'Capitol' issuing a harder-edged set, 'ARMAGEDDON', which like their second album featured a line-up of TABAK, HALL, MITCHELL, AL HARLOW and ROCKET NORTON. Returning to a more FM-friendly pop-rock sound, they issued a fourth set, 'YOUNG AND RESTLESS' (1980). HENRY SMALL subsequently deposed TABAK, co-writing the track 'DON'T LET HIM KNOW' with fellow Canadian, BRYAN ADAMS on the 'SMALL CHANGE' album. The aforesaid new frontman virtually took over the reins for the sixth and final set, 'BEAT STREET' (1983), the band now in complete disarray, especially when their founder member TABAK was killed in a car crash the following year.

Album rating: PRISM (*5) / SEE FOREVER EYES (*4) / ARMAGEDDON (*6) / YOUNG AND RESTLESS (*5) / SMALL CHANGE (*4) / BEAT STREET (*5) / THE BEST OF PRISM compilation (*6)

RON TABAK – vocals / **LINDSAY MITCHELL** – guitar / **TOM LAVIN** – guitar / **JOHN HALL** – keyboards, vocals / **ABE BRYANT** – bass / **RODNEY HIGGS** – drums

EMI Internat. / Ariola

Sep 77. (lp) *(INS 3014) <50020>* **PRISM** [ ] [ ]
– Spaceship superstar / Open soul surgery / It's over / Take me to the Kaptin / Vladivostock / Freewill / Amelia / Julie / I ain't lookin' anymore.

Jan 78. (7") *(INT 543) <7672>* **SPACESHIP SUPERSTAR. / JULIE** [ ] [82] Oct77

Jan 78. (7") *<7678>* **TAKE ME TO THE KAPTIN. / I AIN'T LOOKIN' ANYMORE** [-] [59]

Jun 78. (7") *(INT 559)* **TAKE ME TO THE KAPTIN. / IT'S OVER** [ ] [-]

— **ALLEN HARLOW** – guitar, bass; repl. LAVIN + BRYANT

— **ROCKET NORTON** – drums; repl. HIGGS

Ariola / Ariola

Jul 78. (lp) *(ARL 5014) <50034>* **SEE FOREVER EYES** [ ] [ ]
– Hello / Flyin' / Nickels and dimes / Crime wave / You're like the wind / N-N-N-No! / Take me away / You're my reason / Just like me / See forever eyes.

Jul 78. (7") *<7714>* **FLYIN'. / CRIME WAVE** [-] [53]

Capitol / Capitol

Mar 80. (7") *(CL 16132) <4832>* **YOU WALKED AWAY AGAIN. / N-N-N-NO!** [ ] [ ]

Mar 80. (lp) *<(EST 12051)>* **ARMAGEDDON** [ ] [ ] Nov79
– Coming home / Jealousy / Virginia / You walked away again / Take it or leave it / Armageddon / Night to remember / Mirror man.

Jul 80. (7") *<4889>* **YOUNG AND RESTLESS. / DECEPTION** [-] [ ]

Jul 80. (lp) *<(EST 12072)>* **YOUNG AND RESTLESS** [ ] [ ]
– American music / Young and restless / Satellite / Party line / Acid rain / Here comes another world / The visitor / Deception / Hideaway / Runnin' for cover.

— **HENRY SMALL** – vocals; repl. TABAK

Mar 82. (7") *(CL 238) <5082>* **DON'T LET HIM KNOW. / WINGS OF YOUR LOVE** [ ] [39] Jan82

May 82. (lp) *<(EST 12184)>* **SMALL CHANGE** [ ] [53] Jan82
– Don't let him know / Turn on your radar / Hole in paradise / Rain / When will I see you again / Heart and soul / When love goes wrong (you're not alone) / In the jailhouse now / Wings of your love.

May 82. (7") *(CL 246) <5106>* **TURN ON YOUR RADAR. / WHEN LOVE GOES WRONG (YOU'RE NOT ALONE)** [ ] [64] Apr82

Aug 82. (7") *<5137>* **HOLE IN PARADISE. / RAIN** [-] [ ]

— **SMALL** recruited session people for final album!

1983. (7") *<5244>* **BEAT STREET. / BLUE COLLAR** [-] [ ]

1983. (lp) *<EST 12266>* **BEAT STREET** [-] [ ]
– Nightmare / Beat street / Dirty mind / Modern times / Is he better than me / Blue collar / Wired / State of the heart / I don't want to want you anymore.

1983. (7") *<5266>* **IS HE BETTER THAN ME. / STATE OF THE HEART** [-] [ ]

— In 1984, TABAK was killed in a car crash.

– compilations, etc. –

1988. (lp) *Phonogram;* **THE BEST OF PRISM** [-] [ ]
– Good to be back / Don't let him know / American music / Party line / Cover girl / Armageddon / See forever eyes / Spaceship superstar / You walked away again / Virginia / Mirror man / Satellite / Turn on your radar / Night to remember / Flyin' / Young and restless / Take me to the kaptin. *(UK cd-iss. Jan98 on 'Renaissance'; RME 0113CD)*

Aug 97. (cd) *Shroom;* *<(SP 9700-2)>* **LIVE 1975-1977** [ ] [ ]

Oct 97. (cd) *Renaissance;* *<(RME 0145CD)>* **FROM THE VAULTS** [ ] [ ]

PRODIGY

Formed: Braintree, Essex, England . . . early 90's by LIAM HOWLETT together with MC MAXIM REALITY, LEEROY THORNHILL and KEITH FLINT. With their roots in hip hop, this irrepressible quartet of techno terrorists spread their first waves of discontent through the harder end of the rave scene, releasing the 'WHAT EVIL LURKS' EP in March '91 on the (then) fledgling 'XL' label. One track, the rave call to arms of 'EVERYBODY IN THE PLACE' would rocket to No.2 the following Christmas, hot on the heels of the PRODIGY's seminal debut hit (No.3), 'CHARLY'. A masterstroke of genius, HOWLETT sampled a veteran Government TV ad warning children off playing with fire (a recurring lyrical obsession) and welded it to fuck-off, hoover synths and a juggernaut breakbeat. The mixed result: proof that ravers had a sense of humour/irony and a string of low-rent imitations sampling everything from 'Sesame Street' to 'Rhubarb and Custard'. Borrowing from ARTHUR BROWN's hoary old chestnut of the same name, 'FIRE' gave the PRODIGY their third Top 20 hit in a row, closely followed by 'THE PRODIGY EXPERIENCE' (1992). More assured and inventive than most of the weak cash-in albums to come out of the 12" dominated rave scene, the record proffered alternate versions of the hits and killer new tracks like the brilliant breakbeat-skank, 'OUT OF SPACE'. By this point the group were also making waves with their formidable live show, still largely gracing raves yet a far cry from your average P.A. featuring a scantily clad diva miming to a 15-minute set. By 1993, HOWLETT was extending his horizons; a much in demand remixer, he worked on material for such diverse acts as DREAM FREQUENCY and FRONT 242 as well as poring over new PRODIGY tracks. The first of these, the wailing 'ONE LOVE' was initially realeased as a white label, apparently to keep in touch with their underground roots. The record still charted of course, going Top 10 in late '93 after a full release. 'NO GOOD START THE DANCE' was the sound of a group in transition, a speeded-up female vocal alternating with a thundering techno assault. The single made the Top 5 in Spring '94, but it was hardly representative of what lay in store on 'MUSIC FOR THE JILTED GENERATION' later that summer. Opening with a sinister tap-tapping typewriter and spoken word intro, then slamming into a dark, twisting techno groove, it was clear HOWLETT was no longer "luvved up". The album was breathtaking in its sweep, mapping out the future of techno, PRODIGY style, incorporating heavy riffing (on the two fingered salute to the Criminal Justice Bill, 'THEIR LAW', a collaboration with POP WILL EAT ITSELF), 70's style funky flute (the evocative '3 KILOS') and even a trio of tracks, 'THE NARCOTIC SUITE', climaxing the album in blistering form. Obvious highlights were the utterly compelling 'VOODOO PEOPLE' (riffs AND funky flute!; arguably The PRODIGY's finest moment to boot) and the military stomp of 'POISON' (complete with techno-gothic video; a must-see). The album was a UK No.1, establishing the band as major contenders who had far outstripped the narrow confines of 'dance', as was evidenced at their shows over the ensuing two years. White-gloved ravers blew their whistles hopefully, waiting in vain for 'CHARLY' or 'NO GOOD START THE DANCE', while more recent converts contorted and thrashed wildly to the new material (when, that is, they weren't threatening to shove the raver's eardrum-rupturing whistles where the sun doesn't shine!). By late '95/early '96, The PRODIGY were also showcasing new material at live gigs, including an incendiary little ditty entitled 'FIRESTARTER'. Primarily KEITH's baby, the 'song' was released as a single in Spring '96, giving The PRODIGY their first No.1. FLINT had, by now, fashioned his once flowing locks into a formidable luminous green mohican and had also developed a stage act that made IGGY POP (circa The STOOGES) look like a librarian. The fine, upstanding British public were subsequently treated to the new improved KEITH via the brilliant video (claustrophobically shot in the London Underground) on Top Of The Pops, resulting in an avalanche of complaints. Of course, the kids loved it, even toddlers were heard to garble 'I'm a twisted firestarter' while dragging their hapless mums into Woolies to bag a copy. As for the song itself, FLINT took a starring role, spitting out his demented cockney threats over depth charge beats. The next single, 'BREATHE', was even better, an ominous JOY DIVISION-esque guitar riff segueing into the hardest funkiest breakbeats this side of The CHEMICAL BROTHERS. Arguably the single of the year, the track raised expectations for the forthcoming PRODIGY opus to fever pitch. Almost inevitably, then, 'THE FAT OF THE LAND' (1997) was something of a letdown. There was nothing to match the dark majesty of 'BREATHE' (included on the album along with 'FIRESTARTER'), but there were plenty of other tracks to 'melt some brains' as HOWLETT put it. The insistent techno-hop of 'DIESEL POWER' (with KOOL KEITH guesting) attested to the group's love of hardcore rap, while the BEASTIE BOYS-sampling 'FUNKY SHIT' and MC MAXIM-led 'MINDFIELDS' were high-octane PRODIGY crowd pleasers. Minus points, however, for the dull collaboration with CRISPIAN MILLS (KULA SHAKER), 'NARAYAN' and the pointless cover of L7's 'FUEL MY FIRE'. Far more compelling was the insidiously funky 'CLIMBATIZE'. But it was the album's opener which had the nation's moral guardians and pro-women groups in a tizzy; whatever the inspiration for 'SMACK MY BITCH UP', The PRODIGY were as defiant and unapologetic as ever. Politics aside, the album may not have fully met expectations but it still trampled on the competition. Live, The PRODIGY remain a revelation, an electric maelstrom of colour and sound (and grimacing!), with an ability to mobilise a crowd unmatched in the musical spectrum. In saying that, if they rely on punk cliches without pushing the boundaries of dance music – which is what they do best – they risk becoming a caricature of themselves.

• **Songwriters:** HOWLETT except samples of BABY D ('Casanova') on 'BREAK & ENTER', and KELLY CHARLES on 'YOU'RE NO GOOD FOR ME'. 'FULL THROTTLE' is also reminiscent of JOAN ARMATRADING's 'Me Myself I'.

Album rating: EXPERIENCE (*8) / MUSIC FOR THE JILTED GENERATION (*10) / THE FAT OF THE LAND (*7)

KEITH FLINT (b.17 Sep'69) – vocals, dancer / **LIAM HOWLETT** (b.21 Aug'71) – keyboards / **MC MAXIM REALITY** (b.KEITH PALMER, 21 Mar'67) – rapper-vox, dancer / **LEEROY THORNHILL** (b.7 Oct'69) – dancer, vocals

X.L. | Elektra

Mar 91. (12"ep) *(XLT 17)* **WHAT EVIL LURKS / WE GONNA ROCK. / ANDROID / EVERYBODY IN THE PLACE** [ ] [-]

Aug 91. (7"/c-s) *(XLS/XLC 21) <66411>* **CHARLY. / CHARLY (original mix)** [3] [ ]
(12"+=/cd-s+=) *(XLT/CDXLS 21)* – Pandemonium / Your love.

Dec 91. (7"/c-s) *(XLS/XLC 26)* **EVERYBODY IN THE PLACE. / G-FORCE (ENERGY FLOW)** [2] [-]
(12"+=) *(XLT 26)* – Crazy man / Rip up the sound system.
(cd-s++=) *(XLS 26CD)* – ('A'remix).

Sep 92. (7"/c-s) *(XLS/XLC 30) <66370>* **FIRE. / JERICHO (original mix)** [11] [ ]
(12"+=/cd-s+=) *(XLT/XLS 30CD)* – Fire (sunrise version) / Jericho (genaside II remix).

Oct 92. (cd/c/lp) *(XLCD/XLMC/XLLP 110) <61365>* **EXPERIENCE** [12] [ ]
– Jericho / Music reach (1/2/3/4) / Wind it up / Your love (remix) / Hyperspeed (G-Force part 2) / Charly (trip into drum and bass version) / Out of space / Everybody in the place (155 and rising) / Weather experience / Fire (sunrise version) / Ruff in the jungle bizness / Death of the Prodigy dancers (live).

Nov 92. (7"/c-s) *(XLS/XLC 35) <66346>* **OUT OF SPACE (remix). / RUFF IN THE JUNGLE BIZNESS (uplifting vibes remix)** [5] [ ] Dec92
(12"+=)(cd-s+=) *(XLT/XLS 35CD)* – ('A'techno underworld remix) / Music reach (1,2,3,4) (live).

Apr 93. (7"/c-s) *(XLS/XLC 39) <66319>* **WIND IT UP (REWOUND). / WE ARE THE RUFFEST** [7] [ ]
(12"+=) *(XLT 39)* – Weather experience (remix).
(cd-s++=) *(XLS 39CD)* – ('A'edit).

Oct 93. (c-ep/12"ep/cd-ep) *(XLC/XLT/XLS 47CD)* **ONE LOVE / RHYTHM OF LIFE (original mix). / FULL THROTTLE (original mix) / ONE LOVE (Jonny L remix)** [8] [-]

May 94. (12"/c-s) *(XLT/XLC 51)* **NO GOOD (START THE DANCE) / NO GOOD (bad for you mix) / NO GOOD (CJ Bolland's museum mix)** [4] [-]
(cd-s+=) *(XLS 51CD)* – No Good (original mix).
below album with **PHIL BENT** – flute / **LANCE RIDDLER** – guitar

X.L. | Mute

Jul 94. (cd/c/d-lp) *(XLCD/XLMC/XLLP 114) <55642>* **MUSIC FOR THE JILTED GENERATION** [1] [ ] Mar95
– Intro / Break & enter / Their law (featuring POP WILL EAT ITSELF) / Full throttle / Voodoo people / Speedway (theme from 'Fastlane') / The heat (the energy) / Poison / No good (start the dance) / One love (edit) – The narcotic suite / 3 kilos / Skylined / Claustrophobic sting.

Sep 94. (12"ep) *(XLT 54) <67007>* **VOODOO PEOPLE (original mix) / VOODOO PEOPLE (Dust Brothers remix). / VOODOO PEOPLE (Haiti Island mix) / GOA (THE HEAT, THE ENERGY PART 2)** [13] [ ]
(cd-ep) *(XLS 54CD)* – (3rd track repl.by) ('A'edit).

Mar 95. (c-s) *(XLC 58)* **POISON ('95) / ('A'-Rat Poison mix) / SCIENIDE** [15] [ ]
(12"+=/cd-s+=) *(XLT/XLS 58CD)* – ('A'-Environmental science dub mix).

X.L. | Geffen

Mar 96. (c-s) *(XLC 70) <17387>* **FIRESTARTER / MOLOTIV BITCH** [1] [30] Jan97
(12"+=/cd-s+=) *(XLT/XLS 70CD)* – ('A'-Empiron mix) / ('A'instrumental).

—— All singles re-issued Apr96 hitting UK Top 75.

Nov 96. (c-ep/12"ep) *(XLC/XLT 80)* **BREATHE / THEIR LAW featuring PWEI (live at Phoenix fesival '96). / POISON (live at the Tourhout & Werchter festival '96)** [1] [ ]
(cd-ep+=) *(XLS 80CD)* – The trick.

Jul 97. (cd/c/lp) *(XL CD/MC/LP 121) <46606>* **THE FAT OF THE LAND** [1] [1]
– Smack my bitch up / Breathe / Diesel power / Funky shit / Serial thrilla / Mindfields / Narayan / Firestarter / Climbatize / Fuel my fire.

Nov 97. (12"/c-s) *(XLT/XLC 90) <43946>* **SMACK MY BITCH UP. / NO MAN ARMY** [8] [89]
(cd-s+=) *(XLS 90CD)* – Minefields (heavy rock dub) / ('A'-DJ Hype remix).

MAXIM

—— solo with various personnel

X.L. | X.L.

May 00. (c-s; by MAXIM featuring SKIN) *(XLC 119)* **CARMEN QUESAY / CARMEN QUEASY (digital dubz digi dub)** [53] [ ]
(12"+=)(cd-s+=) *(XLT 119)(XLS 119CD)* – ('A'instrumental).

Sep 00. (cd-s) *(XLS 121CD)* **SCHEMING / SCHEMING (Blood of Abraham mix) / PRISM** [ ] [-]
(12") *(XLS 121)* – ('A'-original) / (2nd track above) / ('A'-Zed bias mix).
(cd-s) *(XLS 121CD2)* – ('A'-Zed Bias) / ('A'-instrumental) / ('A'-King cheetah more saliva mix).

Oct 00. (cd/c/lp) *(XL CD/MC/LP 134) <342>* **HELL'S KITCHEN** [ ] [ ]
– Hatriao's wall / Killing evhture / Carmen queasy / Spectral wars / Hell's kitchen / Scheming / Worldwind syndicates / Soul yeller / Voiversal scientist / My web / Dominant genes / Backward bullet.

PROMISE

Formed: Aberdeen, Scotland . . . 1985 as FREEBIRD then TOUR DE FORCE by GARETH DAVIES, NODS GRAHAM, COLIN CHAPMAN and DEANNE (IAN BENZIE joined in 1987). Melodic rock/AOR devotees influenced by the likes of JOURNEY, TOTO, AUTOGRAPH, THIN LIZZY and VAN HALEN, the group cut a series of demo tapes which they sold at gigs and used for promotional purposes. As well as magazine coverage and radio airplay throughout Europe and beyond, the band secured a number of high profile support slots to the likes of BIG COUNTRY and RUNRIG. In 1991 rock mag, 'Raw' even nominated them as one of the best unsigned bands in Britain yet they struggled to gain a record deal. This eventually led to the band's demise in 1992 although a subsequent offer of a deal from newly formed independent rock label, 'Now & Then', persuaded them to re-form as The PROMISE (another band were by now using the TOUR DE FORCE moniker) in 1994. A belated eponymous debut album appeared the following year to widespread acclaim and the group performed at the London Astoria's 'Gods Of Hard Rock' festival. Personnel reshuffles and recording hitches delayed the release of a sophomore set although 'HUMAN FIRE' eventually emerged in Spring '95 featuring new members COLIN FRASER and STEVE CRAIG (although the latter has since departed). • **Note:** not to be confused with the mid-90's outfit on 'Station 2 Station' who issued the 'Strange Bird' set in '95.

Album rating: THE PROMISE (*3) / HUMAN FIRE (*4)

IAN BENZIE – vocals, guitar / **GARETH DAVIES** – guitar, vocals / **COLIN CHAPMAN** – drums / **NODS GRAHAM** – guitar, vocals / **DEANNE** – bass

Now & Then — not iss.

Mar 95. (cd) *(NTHEN 014CD)* **THE PROMISE** [ ] [-]
– End of the game / You are the one / Playing dirty / Holdin' out for a miracle / Sleepin' alone / Don't keep me waiting / Holdin' on / Restless / When it rains / Silver lights. *(re-prom.Sep95) <Jap-iss.Aug95 on 'Brunette-Alfa'+=; ALCB 3080>* – Falling / All the way / The thin man.

— **COLIN FRASER** – drums, vocals; repl. CHAPMAN

— **STEVE CRAIG** – keyboards, vocals; repl. DEANNE

Frontiers — not iss.

May 99. (cd) *(FRCD 024)* **HUMAN FIRE** [ ] [-]
– Let's talk about love / Kiss me and kill me / Hold on to love / There goes my heart / When love takes a hand / Hole in my heart / Let the night go on forever / Only a woman / Looking glass / Arms of a stranger. *<Jap-iss.Aug99 on 'Nippon Crown'; CRCL 4506> (UK re-iss. Jul00; same)*

— (late '99) now without STEVE who sessioned for PALLAS

PRONG

Formed: Manhattan, New York, USA . . . mid-80's by TOMMY VICTOR, MIKE KIRKLAND and TED PARSONS. Residing in the grimy Lower East Side of Manhattan (home to the hard-bitten likes of CIRCUS OF POWER), PRONG's first two albums were issued on the small 'Spigot' label, 'PRIMITIVE ORIGINS' (1987) and the acclaimed 'FORCE FED' (1988). Emotive, dada avant-garde thrash-hardcore, featuring uncompromising lyrics sung in the style of KILLING JOKE, PRONG were a critical favourite as well as a fearsome live act. The hypnotic, bass-quaking brilliance of live favourite 'THIRD FROM THE SUN' (a cover of the CHROME track) was almost enough to upstage headliners FAITH NO MORE when they toured with PATTEN and Co. at the turn of the decade. Predictably, then, PRONG soon became the subject of major label attention, the band finally signing with 'Epic' for 1990's 'BEG TO DIFFER'. Another leap forward both musically and stylistically, PRONG's unique take on rock's left-field extreme nevertheless reached a creative peak of sorts with the following year's 'PROVE YOU WRONG'. Veteran noisemongers JIM THIRLWELL (of FOETUS) and (PAUL) RAVEN (of KILLING JOKE) worked on the 1992 remix EP, 'WHOSE FIST IS IT ANYWAY' (upon which ex-FLOTSAM AND JETSAM man, TROY GREGORY, replaced the departing KIRKLAND), its lead track appearing on the 'CLEANSED' (1994) album. The latter set scraped into the lower regions of the UK chart but the group failed to rise above cult status and eventually called it a day following the release of 'RUDE AWAKENING' (1996). The high esteem with which PRONG were regarded within music circles was illustrated by the fact that both VICTOR and PARSONS were snapped up by respected acts, the latter going on to play with GODFLESH, the former with DANZIG. • **Covered:** (GET A) GRIP (ON YOURSELF) (Stranglers).

Album rating: PRIMITIVE ORIGINS (*4) / FORCE FED (*7) / BEG TO DIFFER (*7) / PROVE YOU WRONG (*8) / CLEANSED (*6) / RUDE AWAKENING (*6)

TOMMY VICTOR – vocals, guitar / **MIKE KIRKLAND** – vocals, bass / **TED PARSONS** – drums

Spigot — Spigot

Oct 87. (lp) *<(SPT 1)>* **PRIMITIVE ORIGINS** [ ] [ ] 1986
– Disbelief / Watching / Cling to life / Denial / Dreams like that / In my view / Climate control / Persecution. *(cd-iss. Apr97 on 'Southern'; 18541-2)*

Apr 88. (lp/c) *<(SPT 2/+C)>* **FORCE FED** [ ] [ ]
– Freezer burn / Forgery / Senseless abuse / Primitive origins / Aggravated condition / The coliseum / Decay / It's been decided / Force fed / The taming / Bought and sold / Look up at the Sun / Drainpipe. *<US cd-iss. 1988 on 'Relativity'; 3004> <(cd-iss. Apr97 on 'Southern'; 18542-2)*

Mar 89. (12"ep) *<(SPT 3)>* **THIRD FROM THE SUN (extended). / ('A'version) / MIND THE GAP** [ ] [ ] 1987

Epic — Epic

Apr 90. (cd/c/lp) *(466375-2/-4/-1) <EK 46011>* **BEG TO DIFFER** [ ] [ ]
– For dear life / Steady decline / Lost and found / Your fear take it in hand / Intermenstrual D.S.B. / Right to nothing / Prime cut / Just the same. *(cd+=)* – Third from the sun (live).

Sep 91. (cd/c/lp) *(468945-2/-4/-1) <EK 47460>* **PROVE YOU WRONG** [ ] [ ]
– Irrelevant thoughts / Unconditional / Positively blind / Pointless / Contradictions / Torn between / Brainwave / Territorial rights / (Get a) Grip (on yourself) / Shouldn't have bothered / No way to deny it.

— **TROY GREGORY** – bass, vocals (ex-FLOTSAM AND JETSAM) repl. KIRKLAND

Apr 92. (12"ep/cd-ep) *(658000-6/-2) <74284><74309>* **WHOSE FIST IS IT ANYWAY** [58] [ ]
– Prove you wrong (fuzzbuster mix) / Hell if I could / Get a grip on yourself / Irrelevent thoughts (safety mix) / Talk talk (xanax mix).

Feb 94. (cd/c/lp) *(474796-2/-4/-1) <53019>* **CLEANSING** [71] [ ]
– Another worldly device / Whose fist is it anyway / Snap your fingers, snap your neck / Cut-rate / Broken peace / One outnumbered / Out of this misery / No question / Not of this Earth / Home rule / Sublime / Test. *(cd re-iss. Jan99 on 'Columbia'; 474996-2)*

Jun 94. (cd-ep) *(660069-2)* **SNAP YOUR FINGERS, SNAP YOUR NECK / ANOTHER WORLDLY DEVICE / PROVE YOU WRONG / BEG TO DIFFER** [ ] [ ]
(12"pic-d-ep/cd-ep) *(660069-8/-5)* – ('A'-5 mixes).

Jun 96. (c-s) *(663028-4)* **RUDE AWAKENING. / I ACCEPT NOTHING** [ ] [ ]
(12"orange/cd-s) *(663028-6/-2)* – ('A'side) / ('A'-Subtle as a velvet Doc Marten left version) / ('A'-Subtle as a velvet Doc Marten right version) / ('A'-Detrimental version).

Jul 96. (cd/c/red-lp) *(483651-2/4/1) <66945>* **RUDE AWAKENING** [ ] [ ]
– Controller / Caprice / Unfortunately / Face value / Avenue of the finest / Slicing / Without hope / Mansruin / Innocence gone / Dark signs / Close the door. *(cd+=)* – Proud division.

— disbanded when VICTOR joined DANZIG; PARSONS joined GODFLESH

– compilations, etc. –

Sep 90. (12"ep/c-ep/cd-ep) *Strange Fruit; (SFPS/+C/CD 078)* **THE PEEL SESSION** (22.1.89) [ ] [-]
– Defiant / Decay / Senseless abuse / In my view.

PROPAGANDHI

Formed: Canada . . . early 90's by CHRIS and JORD. The band's original bass player was subsequently replaced by TODD (these guys are obviously going for the minimalist aesthetic), although by that point they already had two albums of agit-prop punk under their belts: 'HOW TO CLEAN EVERYTHING' (1993) and 'LESS TALK, MORE ROCK' (1996). Although still militantly political, the band now admit that their harangues on the latter album went slightly overboard. A more subtle but no less outspoken approach was employed on 'TODAY'S EMPIRES, TOMORROW'S ASHES' (1999), released on 'Fat Wreck Chords' and generally deemed by fans of the genre as the trio's finest moment to date.

Album rating: HOW TO CLEAN EVERYTHING (*5) / LESS TALK, MORE ROCK (*6) / WHERE QUANTITY IS No.1 (*6) / TODAY'S EMPIRES TOMORROW'S ASHES (*7)

CHRIS – vocals, guitar / – bass / **JORD** – drums

Fat Wreck Chords — Fat Wreck Chords

Aug 93. (lp/cd) *<(FAT 506/+CD)>* **HOW TO CLEAN EVERYTHING** [ ] [ ]

Jul 95. (cd; shared with I-SPY) *<(FAT 666)>* **PROPAGANDHI / I-SPY** [ ] [ ]

May 96. (cd/lp) *<(FAT 666 CD/MC/LP)>* **LESS TALK, MORE ROCK** [ ] [ ]

Mar 99. (cd) *<(G7 007)>* **WHERE QUANTITY IS No.1** [ ] [ ]
(above issued on 'G7 Welcoming Committee')

— **TODD** – bass; repl.

Feb 01. (lp/cd) *<(FAT 617/+CD)>* **TODAY'S EMPIRES TOMORROW'S ASHES** [ ] [ ]

PRO-PAIN

Formed: Long Island, New York, USA . . . 1991 out of CRUMBSUCKERS by GARY MESKILL and DAN RICHARDSON. Soon adding TOM KLIMCHUCK and securing the services of producer ALEX PERIALAS, they worked on their pulverising hardcore debut, 'FOUL TASTE OF FREEDOM' (1993). Signed to 'Roadrunner' the following year, PRO-PAIN fell foul of censors with their second set, 'THE TRUTH HURTS' (1994), the authorities banning the record for its alleged obscene sleeve artwork depicting an autopsy scene, accompanied by explicit inner sleeve police photographs. The group had now expanded to a quartet with the addition of NICK ST. DENNIS and MIKE HOLLMAN, who replaced KLIMCHUCK, although the guitarist (with newcomer ROB MOSCHETTI) resumed his PRO-PAIN position on a 1996 set, 'CONTENTS UNDER PRESSURE'. Following on from a 1998 greatest hits set, a new line-up of MESKILL, KLIMCHUCK, ERIC KLINGER and ERIC MATTHEWS delivered another set of uncompromising metallic intensity via 'ACT OF GOD' (1999). Proving there was still room for musical pain in the new millennium, the band released the live 'ROAD RAGE' in mid 2001; the studio set, 'ROUND 6', was delivered at the tail end of 2000.

Album rating: FOUL TASTE OF FREEDOM (*8) / THE TRUTH HURTS (*6) / CONTENTS UNDER PRESSURE (*4) / PRO-PAIN (*5) / THE BEST OF PRO-PAIN compilation (*6) / ACT OF GOD (*6) / ROUND 6 (*5) / ROAD RAGE (*5)

GARY MESKILL – vocals, bass / **TOM KLIMCHUCK** – lead guitar / **DAN RICHARDSON** – drums

Roadrunner Energy

May 93. (cd/c/lp) *(RR 9068-2/-4/-1) <81101>* **FOUL TASTE OF FREEDOM** 1992
– Foul taste of freedom / Death on the dancefloor / Murder 101 / Pound for pound / Every good boy does fine / Death goes on / The stench of piss / Picture this / Iraqnophobia / Johnny Black / Lesson learned / God only knows. *(cd re-iss. Sep99 on 'Digital Dimensions'; DDE 6003CD)*

— **NICK ST. DENNIS** – guitar / **MIKE HOLLMAN** – guitar (ex-POSSESSED) repl. KLIMCHUCK

Aug 94. (cd/c/lp) *(RR 8985-2/-4/-1) <81107>* **THE TRUTH HURTS**
– Make war (not love) / Bad blood / The truth hurts / Put the lights out / Denial / Let sleeping dogs lie / One man army / Down in the dumps / The beast is back / Switchblade knife. *(c+=)* – Death on the dancefloor / Pound for pound / Foul taste of freedom. *(cd re-iss. Sep99 on 'Digital Dimensions'; DDE 6005CD)*

— **KLIMCHUCK** returned and **ROB MOSCHETTI** – rhythm guitar repl. ST. DENNIS + HOLLMAN

Edel Energy

May 96. (cd) *(86622 CIR) <81119>* **CONTENTS UNDER PRESSURE**
– Crush / Shine / State of mind / Gunya down / The mercy killings / Contents under pressure / Against the grain / Box city / Odd man out / Political suicide.

High-Gain Rawhead

Mar 98. (cd) *(HGCD 001) <11113>* **PRO-PAIN** Nov97
– Get real / Time / No love lost / Don't kill yourself to live / Loveihb / Life's hard / Mark my words / My time will come / Smokin' gun / Goosize / Blood red. *(re-iss. Sep99 on 'Digital Dimensions'; DDE 6004CD)*

— **ERIC MATTHEWS** – drums; repl. RICHARDSON

— added **ERIC KLINGER** – guitar

High-Gain Nuclear Blast

Feb 99. (cd) *(HGCD 5531)* **ACT OF GOD**
– Stand tall / In for the kill / Act of God / On parade / I remain / Time will tell / Pride / Love and war / Hopeless? / Burn / All fall down / F.S.U. *(re-iss. Aug99 on 'Digital Dimensions'; DDE 6000CD)*

Nuclear Blast Spitfire

Nov 00. (cd) *(NB 531-2) <15070>* **ROUND 6** Oct00
– Fed up / Desensitize / Substance / All or none / Status quo / F**k it / Psywar / Take it personal / Make some noise / Let live / Thou shall not / Draw blood / Down in flames.

Apr 01. (cd) *(NB 592-2) <15222>* **ROAD RAGE (live)** Jun01
– Stand tall / I remain / Life's hard / Get real / Act of God / Smoking gun / In for the kill / Don't kill yourself to live / Foul taste of freedom / Crush / Shine / Make war not love / State of mind / The stench of piss / Bad blood / Iraqnophobia / Pound for pound.

– compilations, etc. –

Mar 98. (cd) *High-Gain; (HGCD 002) / Mayhem; <11130>* **THE BEST OF PRO-PAIN** Apr98
– Take it back / Make war (not love) / Foul taste of freedom / The truth hurts / Death on the dance floor / Switchblade knife / Murder 101 / Johnny Black / Denial / Pound for pound / State of mind (live) / Shine (live) / Crush (live). *(re-iss. Sep99 on 'Digital Dimensions'; DDE 6001CD) <US re-iss. 2000 on 'Nuclear Blast'; 6752>*

Dec 98. (d-cd) *High-Gain; (HG2CD 5542-2)* **POWER PACK** -

PRUNELLA SCALES (see under ⇒ SKID ROW)

PSYCORE

Formed: Gothenburg, Sweden . . . late '96 by bald man with the weird beard, songwriter MARKUS JAAN, plus CARLOS SEPULVEDA, HANSI BAUMGARTTNER and HANS WILHOLM. The band took time to find a decent recording contract and to save up their own money to finally come up with 1998's 'YOUR PROBLEM' (produced and mixed by themselves at home!). A promotional debut single (on Branson's metal-friendly 'V2'), 'MEDICATION', came out five months earlier while the uncompromising turbo-charged, metal-noisters supported fellow subversives, TURA SATANA and WILL HAVEN. The Swedes returned at the turn of the millennium with a slightly disappointing sophomore set, 'I'M NOT ONE OF US' (2000).

Album rating: YOUR PROBLEM (*6) / I'M NOT ONE OF US (*5)

MARKUS JAAN – vocals / **CARLOS SEPULVEDA** – guitar / **HANSI BAUMGARTTNER** – bass / **HANS WILHOLM** – drums

V2 V2

May 98. (7"white/cd-s) *(VVR 500193-7/-3)* **MEDICATION. / CHOCOLATE MILKSHAKE / POP FOR THE NEW MILLENIUM** -

Jun 98. (7"/cd-s) *(VVR 500222-7/-3)* **FULLBLOOD FREAK / 2002 / THE FULLBLOOD SEQUEL** -

Sep 98. (cd-s) *(VVR 500124-3)* **I GO SOLO / NOTHING / END YOU** -
(cd-s) *(VVR 500303-3)* – ('A'side) / The future is here to stay / Skool / ('A'-CD-Rom).

Oct 98. (cd) *(VVR 100092-2) <27032>* **YOUR PROBLEM**
– I go solo / Dedicated enemy / Fullblood freak / Circus / Chocolate milkshake / Againandagain / Medication / Enemy aftermath / Tune in – turn on – drop dead / The fullblood sequel / Driven / No money, no manners, no mercy.

Jan 00. (internet) *(none)* **THE ZOO (Utah Saints remix) / THE ZOO (An Apathy Allstar Percutation) / I GO SOLO (The Grand P-core Bonanza Of Grang Nip) / BE A BABY (Apathy Allstar's Elektrodelica)** -

Feb 00. (cd) *(VVR 100919-2)* **I'M NOT ONE OF US** -
– Set the record straight / Narrow mind / The zoo / The zoo (part 2) / Smell the cancer / Enemy to myself / Week / You made a monster / Be a baby / My life / Part me part machinery / Pandemonium / Future gone fishing.

Mar 00. (cd-ep) *(VVR 501052-3)* **THE ZOO / THE ZOO (Utah Saints remix) / THE ZOO (Apathy Allstar Mutation) / FRIENDS AND FAMILY / INSIDE MY UNIVERSE** -

PULKAS

Formed: London, England . . . 1996 by LUKE LLOYD, who apparently met the others – MARTIN BOURNE, JULES McBRIDE and ROB LEWIS – on a tube train and decided to form a band. After delivering a demo in '97, they finally inked with 'Earache', who, after issuing a limited edition 7", 'CONTROL', released their debut COLIN RICHARDSON-produced album, 'GREED', in '98. Aggro-metal is the best way to describe this PANTERA or FEAR FACTORY like band.

Album rating: GREED (*7)

LUKE LLOYD – vocals / **MARTIN BOURNE** – guitar / **JULES McBRIDE** – bass / **ROB LEWIS** – drums

Earache not known

Dec 97. (7") **CONTROL. / THIS IS IT** -

Apr 98. (cd) *(MOSH 190CD)* **GREED** -
– Loaded / Rubber room / Drown / Hippy fascist / Betrayal / Control / This is it / Rebirth / Flesh / Eh / Close to the enemy.

PULLEY

Formed: Los Angeles, California, USA . . . 1995 by former TEN FOOT POLE/SCARED STRAIGHT members SCOTT RADINSKY and JORDAN BURNS, JIM CHERRY, MIKE HARDER, and MATT RIDDLE completed the quintet. PULLEY's line-up was made up of seasoned rockers culled from the punk revival and hardcore scene. RADINSKY and BURNS came out of TEN FOOT POLE; unfortunately the singer's former band wanted a more full-time commitment which RADINSKY could not provide having to balance his musical career with his sporting one as a second-string pitcher in major league baseball. HARDER had also formerly sidelined with RADINSKY and BURNS in their other band SCARED STRAIGHT. RIDDLE was originally with FACE TO FACE and CHERRY came from STRUNG OUT, whom BURNS had also done various stints with. Thus PULLEY had no real problems getting a deal with the label 'Epitaph', who released the band's debut full-set 'ESTEEM DRIVEN ENGINE' (1996). Following this outing RIDDLE left the band to become involved with NO USE FOR A NAME, his position being filled by TYLER REBBE. Within a year the boys had penned, recorded and released another full-slice of hardcore/punk revival with '60 CYCLE HUM' (1997). Yet the band only reached full maturity as an outfit two years later when their self-titled third album 'PULLEY' (1999) was delivered. This set showed a much greater degree of integrity in its subject-matter and a more fully formed, hardcore-influenced, punk sound.

Album rating: ESTEEM DRIVEN ENGINE (*4) / 60 CYCLE HUM (*5) / PULLEY (*8)

SCOTT RADINSKY – vocals (ex-TEN FOOT POLE, ex-SCARED STRAIGHT) / **JIM CHERRY** – guitar (ex-STRUNG OUT) / **MIKE HARDER** – guitar (ex-SCARED STRAIGHT) / **MATT RIDDLE** – bass (ex-FACE TO FACE) / **JORDAN BURNS** – drums (ex-TEN FOOT POLE, ex-SCARED STRAIGHT, ex-STRUNG OUT)

Epitaph Epitaph

Oct 96. (cd/c/lp) *<(6470-2/-4/-1)>* **ESTEEM DRIVEN ENGINE**
– Cashed in / Crawl / Eyes open wide / Wok Inn / Four walls / One shot / Barf / She / Lifer / No defense / Silver tongue devil / S.F.B.I.H.Y.D. / Seain' different / All we have.

— **TYLER REBBE** – bass; repl. RIDDLE who joined NO USE FOR A NAME

Nov 97. (cd/c/lp) *<(6521-2/-4/-1)>* **60 CYCLE HUM** Oct97
– If / Locked away / Havasu / Reality / Mandingo / Scab / Where are you now / Hold on / Padded cell 4 walls / Noddin' off / Separated / What / Endless journey / Outside opinion.

Mar 99. (cd/lp) *<(6554-2/-1)>* **PULLEY**
– Working class whore / Soberbeah / Pie / Gone / Over it / Darkside / Nothing to lose / Second best / Just for me / Dog's life / Sick / Intro – Outro.

PUNGENT STENCH

Formed: Vienna, Austria . . . early '88, by frontman MARTIN SCHIRENC, bassman JACEK PERKOWSKI and er, ALEX WANK on drums. This eminently sick bunch of musical undertakers initially emerged into the harsh light of day with the release of a split album alongside The DISHARMONIC ORCHESTRA in 1989. A debut proper appeared the following year, 'FOR GOD YOUR SOUL . . .', a rank crawl through the sewers of death-metal, the record attracting the attention of the ever-extreme 'Nuclear Blast'. The resulting three albums revelled in the blackest of humour, while refining their brutal sound with more eclectic influences.

Album rating: FOR GOD YOUR SOUL . . . FOR ME YOUR FLESH (*7) / BEEN CAUGHT BUTTERING (*5) / DIRTY RHYMES AND PSYCHOTRONIC mini (*4) / CLUB MONDO BIZARRE FOR MEMBERS ONLY (*5)

MARTIN SCHIRENC – vocals, guitar / **JACEK PERKOWSKI** – bass / **ALEX WANK** – drums

S.P.V. not iss.

Aug 89. (lp; shared with DISHARMONIC ORCHESTRA) *(082 932)* **SPLIT**
– Pulsating protoplasma / Dead body love / Miscarriage / In the vault / Rip you without care / (other tracks by DISHARMONIC ORCHESTRA). *(re-iss. Dec90 on 'Nuclear Blast'; NB 019)*

1989. (7"ep) **EXTREME DEFORMITY**
– Extreme deformity / Mucous secretion / Molecular disembowelment.

Aug 90. (cd)(lp) *(842973)(082973)* **FOR GOD YOUR SOUL . . . FOR ME YOUR FLESH**
– Intro – Extreme deformity / Hypnos / For God your soul . . . for me your flesh / Just let me rot / Pungent stench / Bonesawer / Embalmed in sulphuric acid / Blood, pus and gastic juice / Suspended animation / A small lunch. *(re-iss. Apr93; same)*

Nuclear Blast Nuclear Blast

Jan 92. (lp/c/cd) *(NB 052/+C/CD) <6023>* **BEEN CAUGHT BUTTERING**
– Shrunken and mumified bitch / Happy re-birthday / Games of humiliation / S.M.A.S.H. / Brainpan blues / And only hunger remains / Sputter supper / Sick bizarre defaced creation / Splatterday night fever.

Jul 93. (m-lp/m-c/m-cd) *(NB 078/+C/CD)* **DIRTY RHYMES AND PSYCHOTRONIC**
– Praise the names of the musical assassins / Viva la muerte / Why can the bodies fly / Blood, pus and gastric juice (rare groove mix) / Horny little piggy bank / Four 'F' club / Blood, pus and gastric juice (tekkno-house mix).

Mar 94. (lp/c/cd) *(NB 079/+C/CD) <6097>* **CLUB MONDO BIZARRE FOR MEMBERS ONLY** Apr94
– True life / Klyster boogie / Choked just for a joke / Hydrocephalus / I'm a family man / Treatments of pain / In search of the perfect torture / Practice suicide / Fuck bizarre / Rape-pagar con la misma moneda.

— the group have since split

Jimmy PURSEY (see under ⇒ SHAM 69)

PUSSY GALORE

Formed: Washington DC, USA . . . 1985 by JON SPENCER and JULIE CAFRITZ, who first met at college in Providence, Rhode Island, the pair subsequently recruiting drummer JOHN HAMILL. The trio then invited photographer, CRISTINA MARTINEZ, to join up after she'd snapped them for the cover shot of their debut 7"ep, 'FEEL GOOD ABOUT YOUR BODY' (released on their own 'Shove' records). Featuring four tracks of primal hardcore, holocaustic industrial slime and scuzzy garage-punk, the band's nearest musical cousins were SONIC YOUTH, BIG BLACK and HUSKER DU, although PUSSY GALORE were in a noise terrorist league of their own. Adding NEIL HAGGERTY and replacing HAMILL with former SONIC YOUTH man, BOB BERT, they took off to the more sympathetic New York, having slagged off local 'Dischord' label owner IAN McKAYE of MINOR THREAT (later FUGAZI). JON and CRISTINA set up home together, meeting up with the others to record their seriously deranged debut mini-set, 'GROOVY HATE FUCK' (1986), titles such as 'CUNT TEASE', 'TEENY PUSSY POWER' and 'YOU COOK LIKE A JEW', seeing the band court a sense of outrage that would characterise their whole career. In response to SONIC YOUTH's rumoured wholesale makeover of The BEATLES' 'White Album', SPENCER played up to the supposed rivalry by covering The ROLLING STONES' 'EXILE ON MAIN STREET' in its entirety, although only 550 cassettes were pressed. Release No.4 for the label (a joint effort with US label, 'Buy Our Records') came in the shape of 'PUSSY GALORE 5000' (1987), although by this point, CRISTINA, had opted to leave the band rather than further jeopardise her relationship with SPENCER, whom she later married. For their first full-length long-player, 'RIGHT NOW!' (1987), the band – who had now signed to 'Caroline' – were graced with the uncompromising production skills of former BIG BLACK leader, STEVE ALBINI, resulting in a marginally less shambolic, more focused slab of noise which saw the band begin to win over their critics. Later that year, NEIL was temporarily substituted with KURT WOLF, the latter's sole appearance being on the mini-set, 'SUGARSHIT SHARP' (1988). HAGGERTY returned to pick up the pieces on follow-up proper, 'DIAL M FOR MOTHERFUCKER' (1989), although shortly prior to its release, JULIE added another nail to the band's coffin by finally taking her leave. SPENCER recalled HAGGERTY and BERT into the PUSSY GALORE fold for one last ditch attempt, coming in the shape of 'LA HISTORIA DE LA MUSICA ROCK' (1990), upon which the first twisted seeds of SPENCER's subsequent BLUES EXPLOSION were sown with swaggering covers of Elvis's 'CRAWFISH' and Willie Dixon's 'RED ROOSTER' (the latter disguised as 'ERIC CLAPTON MUST DIE'). The 90's saw HAGGERTY form ROYAL TRUX, while JULIE teamed up with SONIC YOUTH's KIM GORDON in FREE KITTEN; a musically re-united JON and CRISTINA also recorded a few albums under the BOSS HOG moniker.
• **Songwriters:** JON and some with JULIE, except DAMAGED (Black Flag) / CRAWFISH (Elvis Presley) / YU GUNG (Einsturzende Neubauten) / LITTLE RED ROOSTER (Willie Dixon) / NO COUNT (Ty Wagner & The Scotchmen).

Album rating: EXILE ON MAIN STREET (*4) / RIGHT NOW! (*6) / DIAL M FOR MOTHERFUCKER (*6) / LA HISTORIA DE LA MUSICA ROCK (*5) / GROOVY HATE FUCK compilation UK (*6) / CORPSE LOVE: THE FIRST YEAR compilation (*6) / Boss Hog: DRINKIN', LECHIN' AND LYIN' (*3) / COLD HANDS (*3) / BOSS HOG (*5)

JON SPENCER – vocals, guitar / **JULIE 'Juicy' CAFRITZ** – guitar / **JOHN HAMILL** – drums

not iss. Shove

Oct 85. (7"ep) *<SHOV 1>* **FEEL GOOD ABOUT YOUR BODY**
– Die bitch / Car fantasy / Constant pain / HC rebellion.

— added **CRISTINA MARTINEZ** – guitar / **NEIL HAGGERTY** – guitar / **BOB BERT** – drums (ex-SONIC YOUTH); repl. HAMMILL who later joined ELEVATOR (he later appeared on supergroups' VELVET MONKEYS Oct90 album 'Rake'.

Jun 86. (m-lp) *<SHOV 2>* **GROOVY HATE FUCK (FEEL GOOD ABOUT YOUR BODY)**
– Asshole / Cunt tease / Just wanna die / Kill yourself / Dead meat / Teeny pussy power / Spit'n'shit / You cook like a Jew / Get out / No count / Spin out. *(UK-iss.compilation Feb89 on 'Vinyl Drip'; SUK 001)*

Dec 86. (c;ltd) *<SHOV 3>* **EXILE ON MAIN STREET**
(same tracks as ROLLING STONES d-lp from 1972)

— CRISTINA had departed in Autumn '86 and she later formed BOSS HOG

Jan 87. (m-lp) *<SHOV 4>* **PUSSY GALORE 5000**
<also issued on US 'Buy Our Records'; BOR 12-010>

Product Inc. Caroline

Sep 87. (lp) *(33PROD 19) <CAROL 1337>* **RIGHT NOW!**
– Pig sweat / White noise / Uptight / Biker rock loser / Wretch / Rope legend / Fuck you, man / White people / New breed / Alright / Knock up / NYC 1999 / Punch out / Pussy stomp / Trash can oil drum / Fix it / Really suck / Rancid / Hell spawn. *(cd-iss. Feb88; PRODCD 19) (re-iss. Feb98 on 'Pussy Galore' cd/lp; PGCD/PGLP 1)*

— **KURT WOLF** – guitar; repl. NEIL

Oct 88. (m-lp/m-c) *(MPROD/+C 15)* **SUGAR SHIT SHARP**
– Yu gung / Adolescent wet dream / Brick / Handshake / Sweet little hi-fi / Renegade. *(re-iss. Mar98 on 'Pussy Galore' lp/cd; PGEP/+CD 001)*

— **NEIL** returned to replace KURT who later joined LOUDSPEAKER

Apr 89. (lp/c/cd) *(INC LP/MC/CD 001) <CAROL 1369-1/-4/-2>* **DIAL M FOR MOTHERFUCKER**
– Understand my love / Kicked out / Undertaker / Dick Johnson / Eat me / Evil eye / Hang on / SM 57 / Solo = sex / D.W.D.A. / 1 hour later / Waxhead / A.D.W.D. 2. *(cd+=)* – Penetration of the centerfold / Handshake / Adolescent wet dream / Sweet little hi-fi / Brick / Renegade!. *(re-iss. Jun94; same) (re-iss. Mar98 on 'Pussy Galore' cd/lp; PGCD/PGLP 002) (lp re-iss. Aug00 on 'Matador'; OLE 213-1)*

Sub Pop Sub Pop

Jun 89. (7") *<SP 37>* **DAMAGED. / (version by TAD)**

not iss. Supernatural

1989. (7") **PENETRATION OF A CENTREFOLD /**

— now a trio of **JON, NEIL + BOB,** when JULIE left later joining FREE KITTEN with KIM GORDON (SONIC YOUTH). She was also became part of VELVET MONKEYS.

Rough Trade Caroline

May 90. (lp/c/cd) *(ROUGH/+C/CD 149) <CAROL 1618-1/-4/-2>* **LA HISTORIA DE LA MUSICA ROCK**
– Dedication / Revolution summer / Will you still have me / Don't Jones me / (Do) The snake / Ship comin' in / Mono! man / Crawfish / Drop dead.

— disbanded finally just after above. JON formed JON SPENCER BLUES EXPLOSION while NEIL formed ROYAL TRUX (BOB joined ACTION SWINGERS with at first, JULIE in tow). In 1990, an alter-ego of PUSSY GALORE going by the name of BOSS HOG, featured CRISTINA and JON.

– compilations, etc. –

Apr 92. (cd/lp) *Hut; (HUT CD/LP 003) / Caroline; <CAROL 1706>*
CORPSE LOVE: THE FIRST YEAR Feb92
– Die bitch / HC rebellion / Contact pain / Car fantasy / Fuck you, man / No count solo / Why would I say it to you / Groovy phone / Shit rain / Don't give a fuck about you / Soundcheck / D.M.P. / Teen pussy power / You look like a Jew / Cunt tease / Just wanna die / Dead meat / Kill yourself / Asshole / Spit 'n shit / Turd on the run / Ventilator blues / Just wanna see his face / Let it loose / Pretty fuck look / Spin out / Walk / Get out.

Feb 98. (lp/cd) *In The Red; (ITR 050/+CD)* **LIVE**

BOSS HOG

CRISTINA + JON plus **JERRY TEEL** – guitar / **KURT WOLF** – guitar / **PETE SHORE** – bass / **CHARLIE ONDRAS** – drums

Amphetam. Reptile Amphetam. Reptile

1989. (c) *<89176>* **DRINKIN', LECHIN' AND LYIN'**

Jan 91. (lp) *<(ARR 41-278)>* **COLD HANDS**

— SPENCER formed The BLUES EXPLOSION but returned to moonlight here as duo with his wife CRISTINA

Jun 93. (m-lp) *(ARR 41-278) <17>* **GIRL POSITIVE**

— the pair added **JENS JURGENSEN** – bass (ex-SAWNS) / **HOLLIS QUEENS** – drums / **MARK BOYCE** – keyboards (ex-GOATS)

Geffen Geffen

Oct 95. (cd) *<(GED 24811)>* **BOSS HOG**
– Winn coma / Sick / Beehive / Ski bunny / Green shirt / I dig you / Try one / What the fuck / White sand / I idolize you / Punkture / Strawberry / Walk in / Texas / Sam.

Mar 96. (12"/cd-s) *(GFST/+D 22098)* **I DIG YOU. /**

— SPENCER concentrated on his BLUES EXPLOSION until . . .

City Slang In The Red

Jan 00. (7") *(20149-7)* **WHITEOUT. / COUNT ME OUT**
(cd-s+=) *(20149-2)* – Structure.

Feb 00. (cd/lp) *(20152-2/-1) <ITR 68>* **WHITEOUT**
– Whiteout / Chocolate / Nursery rhyme / Stereolight / Fear for you / Get it while you wait / Jaguar / Itchy & Scratchy / Trouble / Monkey.

Feb 00. (7") *<(ITR 067)>* **OLD SCHOOL. /**
(above issued on 'In The Red')

Apr 00. (7") *(20156-7)* **GET IT WHILE YOU WAIT. / DRIVE ME CRAZY**
(cd-s+=) *(20156-2)* – Dedicated.

Q5

Formed: Seattle, Washington, USA . . . 1983 by guitarist FLOYD ROSE (more noted for the invention of his Tremelo bar), who enlisted TKO members wholesale, namely singer JONATHAN K, guitarist RICK PIERCE, bassist/keyboardist EVAN SHEELEY and drummer GARY THOMPSON. Appearing on the 'Albatross' label ('Music For Nations' UK), their debut album, 'STEEL THE LIGHT' was initially released in 1984. A concotion of high-octane melodic metal, the album took its cue from the likes of SCORPIONS, etc, although the derivative material attracted little attention. A second set, 'WHEN THE MIRROR CRACKS' (1986), trod the same well-beaten path and the group subsequently split. JONATHAN and RICK reunited in a new group, NIGHTSHADE, in the early 90's.

Album rating: STEEL THE LIGHT (*5) / WHEN THE MIRROR CRACKS (*6) / Nightshade: DEAD OF NIGHT (*4)

JONATHAN K – vocals / **FLOYD ROSE** – guitar / **RICK PIERCE** – guitar / **EVAN SHEELEY** – bass, keyboards / **GARY THOMPSON** – drums

Music For Nations | Albatross

Mar 85. (lp/c) *(MFN/TMFN 39) <826359-1>* **STEEL THE LIGHT** – 1984
– Missing in action / Lonely day / Steel the light / Pull the trigger / Ain't no way to treat a lady / In the night / Come and gone / Rock on / Teenage runaway.

May 85. (12") *(12KUT 115)* **STEEL THE LIGHT. / THAT'S ALRIGHT WITH YOU**

Music For Nations | Squawk

Sep 86. (cd/c/lp) *(CD/T+/MFN 64) <832728-2/-4/-1>* **WHEN THE MIRROR CRACKS**
– Livin' on the borderline / Your tears (will follow me) / Never gonna love again / Stand by me / When the mirror cracks / Runaway / In the rain / I can't wait / Cold heart / Let go.

—— split in 1987, FLOYD went on to work in guitar manufacturing

NIGHTSHADE

JONATHAN SCOTT K – vocals / **RICK PIERCE** – guitar / **ANTHONY MAGNELLI** – bass / **JEFFREY McCORMACK** – drums

Music For Nations | Delinquent

Sep 90. (cd/c/lp) *(CD/TC+/MFN 122) <12>* **DEAD OF NIGHT**
– Surrender / Dead of night / Situation critical / Into knightshade / Rock you sinners / Somebody's watching you / Violent times / Last train home / Still in love with you / Prophesy 1616.

QUARTZ

Formed: Birmingham, England . . . 1974 by singer MIKE TAYLOR and former IDLE RACE guitarist MIKE HOPKINS. They evolved out of BANDYLEGS, recruiting GEOFF NICHOLLS, DEK ARNOLD and MAL COPE after a few years. Taken under the wing of TONY IOMMI (Black Sabbath), the band secured a deal with 'United Artists', the label releasing their eponymous debut in 1977. More melodic than 'SABBATH, it was nevertheless derided by the music press. The record was to be re-issued on 'Jet' in 1979 when the company went bust, leaving the group high and dry, although they did surface with a live album for independent label, 'Reddington's Rare Records'. After releasing a version of Mountain's 'NANTUCKET SLEIGHRIDE' (subsequently used as the theme to ITV's 'Weekend World'), both the album and QUARTZ themselves were taken on by 'Logo', who released a single, 'SATAN'S REVENGE'. Later in 1980, the group found what they thought to be a more secure home with 'M.C.A.', although their tenure only lasted one album, 'STAND UP AND FIGHT'. QUARTZ rocked on to yet another label, 'Heavy Metal' delivering their final album of the decade with the appropriately titled 'AGAINST ALL ODDS' in 1983. NICHOLLS, not surprisingly, was snapped up by BLACK SABBATH, playing keyboards on their 1986 set, 'Seventh Star'. In 1996, QUARTZ were back in circulation via a new set, 'RESURRECTION', a record that saw them covering the Easybeat's 'GOOD TIMES', Rare Bird's 'BIRD MAN', Chuck Berry's 'ROLL OVER BEETHOVEN', Wishbone Ash's 'JAILBAIT' and of course 'NANTUCKET . . .' • **Note:** There were other groups of the same name.

Album rating: QUARTZ)(5) / LIVE QUARTZ (*4) / STAND UP AND FIGHT (*5) / AGAINST ALL ODDS (*5) / RESURRECTION (*5)

MIKE TAYLOR – vocals / **MIKE HOPKINS** – guitar (ex-IDLE RACE) / **GEOFF NICHOLLS** – guitar, keyboards / **DEK ARNOLD** – bass, vocals / **MAL COPE** – drums

U.A. | not iss.

Aug 77. (7") *(UP 36290)* **SUGAR RAIN. / STREET FIGHTING LADY / MAINLINE RIDERS** – -

Sep 77. (lp) *(UAG 30081)* **QUARTZ** – -
– Mainline riders / Sugar rain / Street fighting lady / Hustler / Devil's brew / Smokie / Around and around / Pleasure seekers / Little old lady. *(re-iss. 1979 as 'DELETED' on 'Jet'; JETLP 233)*

Oct 77. (7") *(UP 36317)* **STREET FIGHTING LADY. / MAINLINE RIDERS** – -
(re-iss. 1980 on 'Jet'; SJET 189)

Pye Int. | not iss.

Oct 78. (7") *(7NL 25797)* **BEYOND THE CLOUDS. / FOR GEROMINE** – -

Reddingtons Rare | not issued

1980. (lp) *(REDD 001)* **LIVE QUARTZ (live)** – -
– Street fighting lady / Good times / Mainline rider / Belinda / Count Dracula / Around & around / Roll over Beethoven. *(re-iss. Jul80 on 'Logo'; MOGO 4007)*

1980. (7",7"white,7"blue) *(DAN 1)* **NANTUCKET SLEIGHRIDE. / WILDFIRE** – -

Logo | not iss.

Jun 80. (7") *(GO 387)* **SATAN'S SERENADE. / BLOODY FOOL** – -
(12"blue+=,12"red+=) *(GOT 387)* – Roll over Beethoven (live).

M.C.A. | not iss.

Aug 80/ (7") *(MCA 642)* **STOKING UP THE FIRES OF HELL. / CIRCLES** – -

Aug 80. (lp) *(MCF 3080)* **STAND UP AND FIGHT** – -
– Stand up and fight / Charlie Snow / Can't say no to you / Revenge / Stoking up the fires of Hell / Rock'n'roll child / Questions / Wildfire.

Jan 81. (7") *(MCA 661)* **STAND UP AND FIGHT. / CHARLIE SNOW** – -

Heavy Metal | not iss.

Jun 83. (lp/pic-lp) *(HMR LP/PD 9)* **AGAINST ALL ODDS** – -
– Just another man / Madman / Too hot to handle / Hard road / Tell me why / The wake / Buried alive / Silver wheels / Love 'em and run / Avalon / (It's) Hell, livin' without you.

Dec 83. (7") *(HEAVY 17)* **TELL ME WHY. / STREETWALKER** – -

—— split when NICHOLLS joined BLACK SABBATH

—— re-formed in the mid-90's

Neat Metal | Metal Blade

Oct 96. (cd) *(NM 012CD) <14319>* **RESURRECTION**
– Good times / Around and around / Street fighting lady / Bird man / Dracula / Main line rider / Born to rock the nation / Roll over Beethoven / Jailbait / Belinda / Nantucket sleighride / Pleasure seekers.

QUEEN

Formed: London, England . . . early 1971 by guitarist BRIAN MAY, drummer ROGER TAYLOR and vocalist par excellence FREDDIE MERCURY, bassist JOHN DEACON completing the line-up. MAY had left school in 1963 (with a whopping ten O-levels), joining teen group The OTHERS who issued one single for 'Fontana' in 1965, 'OH YEAH'. Together with TAYLOR, he then went on to form SMILE in 1969, a project that met with little success although they did release one 45 for 'Mercury US', 'EARTH' / 'STEP ON ME'. The pair then hooked up with the Zanzibar-born MERCURY and formed QUEEN in 1971, JOHN DEACON subsequently recruited on bass. After spending most of 1972 in the studio, QUEEN were picked up by 'E.M.I.' when engineer John Anthony sent the company a demo tape. The group made their live debut in April '73 at London's famed Marquee club, but prior to any QUEEN release, FREDDIE MERCURY (as LARRY LUREX!) issued a one-off 'EMI' solo single that summer, 'I CAN HEAR MUSIC' / 'GOIN' BACK' (the former an old BEACH BOYS number). A month later, QUEEN simultaneously unleashed their eponymous Roy Thomas-Baker produced debut album, and single, 'KEEP YOURSELF ALIVE'. Influenced by LED ZEPPELIN and the more garish elements of glam-rock, the group had fashioned a unique, densely layered sound around MERCURY's impressive vocal acrobatics and MAY's fluid, coin-pick guitar style. Though the album didn't exactly set the charts alight, the band subsequently set out on a heavy touring schedule, supporting friends to be, MOTT THE HOOPLE, in late '73. Success eventually came with the piano-led bombast of the 'SEVEN SEAS OF RHYE' single, the track making the Top 10 in February '74 and paving the way for 'QUEEN II' the following month. The album reached No.5, consolidating QUEEN's new position as a headline act; while MERCURY was allegedly known to be fairly shy in real life, onstage he embodied everything that the word QUEEN implied with a passionate theatricality unmatched in rock music. The group really came into their own with the 'KILLER QUEEN' single, an infectious slice of jaunty high camp that reached No.2 in late '74. The following month, QUEEN released their strongest album to date, 'SHEER HEART ATTACK', an eminently listenable collage of killer hooks, neo-metal riffs,

O.T.T. choruses and satin-clad dynamics that contained the likes of 'STONE COLD CRAZY' and the next single, 'NOW I'M HERE'. But QUEEN, to use a particularly crap pun, were finally crowned, commercially at least with the 'BOHEMIAN RHAPSODY' single in late 1975. Surely one of the most annoyingly overplayed singles of all time next to 'Stairway To Heaven', the song was nevertheless something of an innovation at the time, a grandiose epic that gave new meaning to the term 'rock opera'; forget concept albums, QUEEN could condense such lofty conceits into a meagre 6 minutes! The song was accompanied by what is widely regarded as the first promotional video, a quintessentially 70's affair that, in retrospect, resembles the title sequence of 'Doctor Who'. Nevertheless, the single gave QUEEN an astonishing nine week run at the top of the charts over the Christmas period, ensuring similar success for the highly ambitious 'NIGHT AT THE OPERA' (1975) album. Apparently the most expensive project recorded up to that point, the record took QUEEN's bombastic pretensions to new limits, MERCURY's multi tracked vocals setting new standards in studio mastery. While most of QUEEN's work was penned by MERCURY and MAY, TAYLOR and DEACON were also talented songsmiths, the latter contributing one of the group's loveliest songs, 'YOU'RE MY BEST FRIEND', its heartfelt simplicity counterbalancing some of the album's more excessive moments. 'NIGHT AT THE OPERA' also went Top 5 in the States, QUEEN having broken America with their irrepressible stage show earlier that year. Their ascent into world beater status continued with 'A DAY AT THE RACES' (1976), another No.1 album which spawned a further massive hit in 'SOMEBODY TO LOVE' and contained the classic camp of 'GOOD OLD FASHIONED LOVER BOY'. The anthemic double header of the 'WE ARE THE CHAMPIONS' / 'WE WILL ROCK YOU' single reached No.2 the following year, presaging QUEEN's move away from operatic artifice to more straightahead stadium rock. 'NEWS OF THE WORLD' (1977) and 'JAZZ' (1978) confirmed this, both albums selling well despite their lack of inventiveness. The riff-heavy 'FAT BOTTOMED GIRLS' could only have been recorded in the 70's, a gloriously unreconstructed paeon to shapely women that just wouldn't do in todays PC-controlled climate. While other rock monsters of the 70's were washed away on the tide of dour aggression that was punk, QUEEN looked to other musical forms to keep their sound fresh, namely 50's style rockabilly on the classic 'CRAZY LITTLE THING CALLED LOVE', MERCURY coming on like a camp ELVIS in the video, decked out in biker gear with a leather cap, of course, de rigueur. The group also flirted with disco on the bass-heavy 'ANOTHER ONE BITES THE DUST', a US No.1 that was later sampled by GRANDMASTER FLASH. Both tracks were featured on 'THE GAME' (1980), QUEEN'S most consistent album since the mid-70's and a transatlantic chart topper. After a partially successful sidestep into soundtrack work with 'FLASH GORDON' (1980), QUEEN rounded up the highlights of the preceding decade with a multi platinum greatest hits set. While the band had been selling more records of late in the States than the UK, this trend was reversed with 'UNDER PRESSURE', a collaboration with DAVID BOWIE which topped the British charts. 'HOT SPACE' (1982) ranks as one of QUEEN's dodgiest albums but with 'THE WORKS' (1984), QUEEN once again enjoyed a run of Top 10 singles with the likes of 'RADIO GA-GA' and 'I WANT TO BREAK FREE'. While these were listenable enough they lacked the pop brilliance of QUEEN's best 70's work. Live, QUEEN were still a massive draw, MERCURY's peerless ability to work a crowd evidenced on his famous Live Aid appearance in 1985. While the group's back catalogue subsequently clogged up the album charts, QUEEN returned with new material in the shape of 'A KIND OF MAGIC' (1986). Maybe Live Aid went to QUEEN's collective head, the album suffering from a kind of plodding stadium-friendly malaise that saw the group descending into self-parody. Nevertheless, the record made No.1, as QUEEN continued to tour the world and play to record breaking audiences. The band returned to the fray with 'THE MIRACLE' in 1989, another No.1 album that contained few surprises. Nor did 'INNUENDO' (1991), although bearing in mind MERCURY's rumoured failing health, it'd be churlish to criticise what must have been a very difficult album for the singer to finish. On the 23rd of November, 1991, a matter of months after the album's release, MERCURY succumbed to AIDS. The following month, 'BOHEMIAN RHAPSODY' was re-released and once again topped the UK charts, raising money for research into the killer disease. A tribute concert was held the following Spring at Wembley Stadium, the cream of the music world's top drawer stars paying their respects including ELTON JOHN, GUNS N' ROSES, GEORGE MICHAEL and DEF LEPPARD. Inevitably, QUEEN split although a posthumous album was released in 1995, featuring material that MERCURY had been working on prior to his death. While it didn't exactly add anything significant to QUEEN's stunning legacy, it tied up the loose ends, bringing the saga of one of music's most flamboyantly colourful bands to a dignified close. • **MERCURY covered:** THE GREAT PRETENDER (Platters). The CROSS covered FOXY LADY (Jimi Hendrix), BRIAN MAY covered ROLLIN' OVER (Small Faces).

Album rating: QUEEN (*7) / QUEEN II (*6) / SHEER HEART ATTACK (*8) / A NIGHT AT THE OPERA (*7) / A DAY AT THE RACES (*5) / NEWS OF THE WORLD (*6) / JAZZ (*5) / LIVE KILLERS (*7) / THE GAME (*6) / HOT SPACE (*4) / FLASH (*3) / THE WORKS (*4) / A KIND OF MAGIC (*5) / LIVE MAGIC (*6) / THE MIRACLE (*6) / INNUENDO (*6) / QUEEN'S GREATEST HITS compilation (*9) / GREATEST HITS II compilation (*8)

FREDDIE MERCURY (b. FREDERICK BULSARA, 5 Sep'46, Zanzibar, Africa. In 1959, he moved with family to Feltham, Middlesex, England) – vocals, piano / **BRIAN MAY** (b.19 Jul'47, London, England) – guitar, vocals, keyboards / **ROGER MEDDOWS-TAYLOR** (b.26 Jul'49, King's Lynn, Norfolk, England) – drums, vocals / **JOHN DEACON** (b.19 Aug'51, Leicester, England) – bass, vocals

E.M.I. Elektra

Jul 73. (7") *(EMI 2036) <45863>* **KEEP YOURSELF ALIVE. / SON AND DAUGHTER**

Jul 73. (lp/c) *(EMC/TCEMC 3006) <75064>* **QUEEN** 83 Oct73
– Keep yourself alive / Doing all right / Great King Rat / My fairy king / Liar / The night comes down / Modern times rock'n'roll / Son and daughter / Jesus / Seven seas of rhye *[US only] (hit UK No.24 Mar74) (re-iss. Aug82 on 'Fame' lp/c; FA/TCFA 3040) (cd-iss. Nov86; CDP 746204-2) (cd-iss. May88; CDFA 3040) <US cd-iss. Jun91 on 'Hollywood'+=; 61064-2>* – Mad the swine, keep yourself alive (long lost retake) / Liar (1991 remix) *(re-iss. Apr94 on 'Parlophone' cd/c; CD/TC PCSD 139)*

Nov 73. (7") *<45884>* **LIAR. / DOING ALL RIGHT** -

Feb 74. (7") *(EMI 2121) <45891>* **SEVEN SEAS OF RHYE. / SEE WHAT A FOOL I'VE BEEN** 10

Mar 74. (lp/c) *(EMA/TCEMA 767) <75082>* **QUEEN II** 5 49 May74
– Procession / Father to son / White queen (as it began) / Some day one day / The loser in the end / Ogre battle / The fairy feller's master-stroke / Nevermore / The march of the black queen / Funny how love is / Seven seas of rhye. *(re-iss. Apr84 on 'Fame' lp/c; FA/TCFA 3099) (cd-iss. Nov86; CDP 746205-2) (re-iss. May88; CDFA 3099) <US cd-iss. Oct91 on 'Hollywood'+=; 61232-2>* – See what a fool I've been / Ogre battle – 1991 remix / Seven seas of rhye – 1991 remix. *(re-iss. Apr94 on 'Parlophone' cd/c; CD/TC PCSD 140)*

Oct 74. (7") *(EMI 2229) <45226>* **KILLER QUEEN. / FLICK OF THE WRIST** 2 12 Jan75

Nov 74. (lp,red-lp/c-s) *(EMC/TCEMC 3061) <1026>* **SHEER HEART ATTACK** 2 12 Dec74
– Brighton rock / Killer Queen / Tenement funster / Flick of the wrist / Lily of the valley / Now I'm here / In the lap of the gods / Stone cold crazy / Dear friends / Misfire / Bring back that Leroy Brown / She makes me (stormtrooper in stilettoes) / In the lap of the gods . . . revisited. *(re-iss. 1984 lp/c; ATAK/TCATAK 22) (cd-iss. 1984; CDP 746052-2) (cd-iss. Jun88; CDP 746206-2) <US cd-iss. Nov88 on 'Hollywood'+=; 61036-2>* – Stone cold sober – 1991 remix) *(re-iss. Aug93 on 'Parlophone' cd/c; CD/TC PCSD 129)*

Jan 75. (7") *(EMI 2256)* **NOW I'M HERE. / LILY OF THE VALLEY** 11 -

Apr 75. (7") *<45268>* **LILY OF THE VALLEY. / KEEP YOURSELF ALIVE** -

Nov 75. (7") *(EMI 2375) <45297>* **BOHEMIAN RHAPSODY. / I'M IN LOVE WITH MY CAR** 1 9 Dec75

Dec 75. (lp/c) *(EMTC/TCEMTC 103) <1053>* **A NIGHT AT THE OPERA** 1 4
– Death on two legs (dedicated to . . .) / Lazing on a Sunday afternoon / I'm in love with my car / You're my best friend / '39 / Sweet lady / Seaside rendezvous / The prophet's song / Love of my life / Good company / Bohemian rhapsody / God save the Queen. *(re-iss. 1984 lp/c; ATAK/TCATAK 27) (cd-iss. 1984; CDP 746050-2) (cd-iss. Jun88; CDP 746207-2) <US cd-iss. Aug91 on 'Hollywood'+=; 61065-2>* – I'm in love with my car – 1991 remix / You're my best friend – 1991 remix. *(re-iss. Aug93 on 'Parlophone' cd/c; CD/TC PCSD 130)*

Jun 76. (7") *(EMI 2494) <45318>* **YOU'RE MY BEST FRIEND. / '39** 7 16 May76

Nov 76. (7") *(EMI 2565) <45362>* **SOMEBODY TO LOVE. / WHITE MAN** 2 13

Dec 76. (lp/c) *(EMTC/TCEMTC 104) <101>* **A DAY AT THE RACES** 1 5 Jan77
– Tie your mother down / You take my breath away / Long away / The millionaire waltz / You and I / Somebody to love / White man / Good old fashioned lover boy / Drowse / Teo Torriate (let us cling together). *(re-iss. 1984 lp/c; ATAK/TCATAK 28) (cd-iss. 1984; CDP 746051-2) (cd-iss. Jun88; CDP 746208-2) <US cd-iss. Mar91 on 'Hollywood'+=; 61035-2>* – Tie your mother down – remix / Somebody to love – remix. *(re-iss. Aug93 on 'Parlophone' cd/c; CD/TC PCSD 131) (lp re-iss. Nov97; LPCENT 29)*

Mar 77. (7") *(EMI 2593)* **TIE YOUR MOTHER DOWN. / YOU AND I** 31 -

Mar 77. (7") *<45385>* **TIE YOUR MOTHER DOWN. / DROWSE** - 49

May 77. (7"ep) *(EMI 2623)* **QUEEN'S FIRST EP** 17 -
– Good old fashioned lover boy / Death on two legs (dedicated to . . .) / Tenement funster / White Queen (as it began).

Jun 77. (7") *<45412>* **LONG AWAY. / YOU AND I** -

Oct 77. (7") *(EMI 2708) <45441>* **WE ARE THE CHAMPIONS. / WE WILL ROCK YOU** 2 4

Nov 77. (lp/c) *(EMA/TCEMA 784) <112>* **NEWS OF THE WORLD** 4 3
– We will rock you / We are the champions / Sheer heart attack / All dead, all dead / Spread your wings / Fight from the inside / Get down make love / Sleeping on the sidewalk / Who needs you / It's late / My melancholy blues. *(re-iss. 1984 lp/c; ATAK/TCATAK 20) (cd-iss. Jun88; CDP 746209-2) <US cd-iss. Mar91 on 'Hollywood'+=; 61037-2>* – We will rock you – 1991 remix. *(re-iss. Aug93 on 'Parlophone' cd/c; CD/TC PCSD 132)*

Feb 78. (7") *(EMI 2575)* **SPREAD YOUR WINGS. / SHEER HEART ATTACK** 34 -

Apr 78. (7") *<45478>* **IT'S LATE. / SHEER HEART ATTACK** - 74

Oct 78. (7") *(EMI 2870) <45541>* **BICYCLE RACE. / FAT BOTTOMED GIRLS** 11 24 Nov78

Nov 78. (lp/c) *(EMA/TCEAM 788) <166>* **JAZZ** 2 6
– Mustapha / Fat bottomed girls / Jealousy / Bicycle race / If you can't beat them / Let me entertain you / Dead on time / In only seven days / Dreamer's ball / Fun it / Leaving home ain't easy / Don't stop me now / More of that jazz. *(re-iss. 1984 lp/c; ATAK/TCATAK 24) (cd-iss. Jun88; CDP 746210-2) <US cd-iss. Jun91 on 'Hollywood'+=; 61062-2>* – Fat bottomed girls – 1991 remix / Bicycle race – 1991 remix. *(re-iss. Feb94 on 'Parlophone' cd/c; CD/TC PCSD 133)*

Feb 79. (7") *(EMI 2910)* **DON'T STOP ME NOW. / IN ONLY SEVEN DAYS** 9 -

Feb 79. (7") *<46008>* **DON'T STOP ME NOW. / MORE OF THAT JAZZ** - 86

Apr 79. (7") *<46039>* **JEALOUSY. / FUN IT** -

Jun 79. (d-lp/d-c) *(EMSP/TC2EMSP 330) <702>* **LIVE KILLERS (live)** 3 16
– We will rock you / Let me entertain you / Death on two legs / Killer Queen / Bicycle race / I'm in love with my car / Get down, make love / You're my best friend / Now I'm here / Dreamer's ball / '39 / Keep yourself alive / Don't stop me now / Spread your wings / Brighton rock / Bohemian rhapsody / Tie your mother down / Sheer heart attack / We will rock you / We are the champions / God save the Queen. *(re-iss. 1984 lp/c; ATAK/TCATAK 23) (cd-iss. Jun88; CDP 746211-2) <US cd-iss. Nov88 on 'Hollywood'; 61066-2> (re-iss. Apr94 on 'Parlophone' cd/c; CD/TC PCSD 138)*

Jul 79. (7") *(EMI 2959)* **LOVE OF MY LIFE (live). / NOW I'M HERE (live)** 63 -

Aug 79. (7") *<46532>* **WE WILL ROCK YOU (live). / LET ME ENTERTAIN YOU (live)** -

Oct 79. (7") *(EMI 5001)* **CRAZY LITTLE THING CALLED LOVE. / WE WILL ROCK YOU (live)** [2] [-]

Dec 79. (7") *<46579>* **CRAZY LTTLE THING CALLED LOVE. / SPREAD YOUR WINGS** [-] [1]

Feb 80. (7") *(EMI 5022)* **SAVE ME. / LET ME ENTERTAIN YOU (live)** [11] [-]

Jun 80. (7") *(EMI 5076) <46652>* **PLAY THE GAME. / HUMAN BODY** [14] [42]

Jul 80. (lp/c) *(EMA/TCEMA 795) <513>* **THE GAME** [1] [1]
– Play the game / Dragon attack / Another one bites the dust / Need your loving tonight / Crazy little thing called love / Rock it (prime jive) / Don't try suicide / Sail away sweet sister / Coming soon / Save me. *(re-iss. 1984 lp/c; ATAK/TCATAK 21) (cd-iss. Jun88; CDP 746213-2) <US cd-iss. Jun91 on 'Hollywood'+=; 61063-2>* – Dragon attack – 1991 remix. *(re-iss. Feb94 on 'Parlophone' cd/c; CD/TC PCSD 134)*

Aug 80. (7") *(EMI 5102)* **ANOTHER ONE BITES THE DUST. / DRAGON ATTACK** [7] [-]

Aug 80. (7") *<47031>* **ANOTHER ONE BITES THE DUST. / DON'T TRY SUICIDE** [-] [1]

Oct 80. (7") *<47086>* **NEED YOUR LOVING TONIGHT. / ROCK IT (PRIME JIVE)** [-] [44]

Nov 80. (7") *(EMI 5126) <47092>* **FLASH. / FOOTBALL FIGHT** [10] [42] Jan81

Dec 80. (lp/c) *(EMC/TCEMC 795) <518>* **FLASH GORDON (Soundtrack)** [10] [23]
– Flash's theme / In the space capsule (the love theme) / Ming's theme (in the court of Ming the merciless) / The ring (hypnotic seduction of Dale) / Football fight / In the death cell (love theme reprise) / Execution of Flash / The kiss (Aura resurrects Flash) / Arboria (planet of the tree men) / Escape from the swamp / Flash to the rescue / Vultan's theme (attack of the hawk men) / Battle theme / The wedding march / The marriage of Dale and Ming (and Flash approaching) / Flash's theme reprise (victory celebrations) / The hero. *(re-iss. 1984 lp/c; ATAK/TCATAK 26) (cd-iss. Jun88; CDP 746214-2) <US cd-iss. Aug91 on 'Hollywood'+=; 61203-2>* – Flash – 1991 remix. *(re-iss. Apr94 on 'Parlophone' cd/c; CD/TC PCSD 137)*

Nov 81. (lp/c) *(EMTV/TCEMTC 30) <564>* **QUEEN'S GREATEST HITS** (compilation) [1] [14]
– Bohemian rhapsody / Another one bites the dust / Killer queen / Fat bottomed girls / Bicycle race / You're my best friend / Don't stop me now / Save me *[or US= Keep yourself alive / Under pressure]* / Crazy little thing called love / Somebody to love / Now I'm here / Good old-fashioned lover boy / Play the game / Flash / Seven seas of Rhye / We will rock you / We are the champions. *(cd-iss. Aug84; CDP 746033-2) (re-hit at No.7 – Dec91) (re-iss. Jun94 on 'Parlophone' cd/c; CD/TC PCSD 141)*

Nov 81. (7"; by QUEEN and DAVID BOWIE) *(EMI 5250) <47235>* **UNDER PRESSURE. / SOUL BROTHER** [1] [29]

Apr 82. (7") *(EMI 5293) <47452>* **BODY LANGUAGE. / LIFE IS REAL (SONG FOR LENNON)** [25] [11]

May 82. (lp/c) *(EMA/TCEMA 797) <60128>* **HOT SPACE** [4] [22]
– Staying power / Dancer / Back chat / Body language / Action this day / Put out the fire / Life is real (song for Lennon) / Calling all girls / Las Palabras de amor / Cool cat / Under pressure. *(cd-iss. Jun88; CDP 746215-2) (re-iss. Aug89 on 'Fame' cd/c/lp; CD/TC+/FA 3228) <US cd-iss. Mar91 on 'Hollywood'+=; 61038-2>* – Body language – 1991 remix. *(re-iss. Feb94 on 'Parlophone' cd/c; CD/TC PCSD 135)*

Jun 82. (7") *(EMI 5316)* **LAS PALABRAS DE AMOR. / COOL CAT** [17] [-]

Jul 82. (7") *<69981>* **CALLING ALL GIRLS. / PUT OUT THE FIRE** [-] [60]

Aug 82. (7"/ext.12") *(EMI/12EMI 5325) <69941>* **BACKCHAT. / STAYING POWER** [40] [ ]

E.M.I. Capitol

Jan 84. (7") *(QUEEN 1) <5317>* **RADIO GA GA. / I GO CRAZY** [2] [16]
(ext.12") *(12QUEEN 1)* – ('A'dub version).

Mar 84. (lp/c)(cd) *(WORK/TCWORK 1)(CDP 7460160-2) <12322>* **THE WORKS** [2] [23]
– Radio ga ga / Tear it up / It's a hard life / Man on the prowl / Machines (or back to humans) / I want to break free / Keep passing the open windows / Hammer to fall / Is his he world we created?. *<US cd-iss. Dec91 on 'Hollywood'+=; 61233-2>* – Radio Ga Ga (12"mix) / I want to break free (12"mix) / I go crazy. *(re-iss. Feb94 on 'Parlophone' cd/c; CD/TC PCSD 136)*

Apr 84. (7"/ext.12") *(QUEEN/12QUEEN 2) <5350>* **I WANT TO BREAK FREE (remix). / MACHINES (OR BACK TO HUMANS)** [3] [45]

Jul 84. (7"/12"pic-d) *(QUEEN/12QUEENP 3) <5372>* **IT'S A HARD LIFE. / IS THIS THE WORLD WE CREATED?** [6] [72]
(12"+=) *(12QUEEN 3)* – ('A'extended remix).

Sep 84. (7"/'A'-Headbangers-12") *(QUEEN/12QUEEN 4) <5424>* **HAMMER TO FALL. / TEAR IT UP** [13] [ ]

Dec 84. (7"/ext.12") *(QUEEN/12QUEEN 5)* **THANK GOD IT'S CHRISTMAS. / MAN ON THE PROWL / KEEP PASSING OPEN WINDOWS** [21] [-]

— In the mid 80's & before, each individual had also launched solo

Nov 85. (7"/ext-12") *(QUEEN/12QUEEN 6) <5530>* **ONE VISION. / BLURRED VISION** [7] [61]

Feb 86. (7") *<5568>* **PRINCES OF THE UNIVERSE. / A DOZEN RED ROSES FOR MY DARLING** [-] [ ]

Mar 86. (7"/ext.12"/ext.12"pic-d) *(QUEEN/12QUEEN/12QUEENP 7) <5590>* **A KIND OF MAGIC. / A DOZEN RED ROSES FOR MY DARLING** [3] [42] Jun86

May 86. (lp/c)(cd) *(EU/TCEU 3509)(CDP 746267-2) <12476>* **A KIND OF MAGIC** [1] [46]
– One vision / A kind of magic / One year of love / Pain is so close to pleasure / Friends will be friends / Who wants to live forever / Gimme the prize / Don't lose your head / Princes of the universe. *(cd+=)* – A kind of 'A kind of magic – Friends will be friends – Who wants to live forever. *<US cd-iss. Jun91 on 'Hollywood'+=; 61152>* – Forever, One vision.

Jun 86. (7"/7"pic-d) *(QUEEN/+P 8)* **FRIENDS WILL BE FRIENDS. / SEVEN SEAS OF RHYE** [14] [-]
(12"+=) *(12QUEEN 8)* – ('A'extended mix).

Jul 86. (7") *<5633>* **DON'T LOSE YOUR HEAD. / PAIN IS SO CLOSE TO PLEASURE** [-] [ ]

Sep 86. (7") *(QUEEN 9)* **WHO WANTS TO LIVE FOREVER. / KILLER QUEEN** [24] [-]
(12"+=) *(12QUEEN 9)* – ('A'-lp version) / Forever.

Dec 86. (d-lp/c)(cd) *(EMC/TCEMC 3519)(CDP 746413-2)* **LIVE MAGIC (live)** [3] [-]
– One vision / Tie your mother down / I want to break free / Hammer to fall / Seven seas of rhye / We are the champions / Another one bites the dust / Is this the world we created? / Bohemian rhasody / Radio Ga Ga / Friends will be friends / We will rock you / Under pressure / A kind of music / God save the Queen. *(re-iss. Dec91 on 'Parlophone')*

— During this lull in QUEEN activity, FREDDIE MERCURY had released some solo singles and collaborated with MONTSERRAT CABALLE. TAYLOR had formed The CROSS

Parlophone Capitol

Apr 89. (c-s/7") *(TC+/QUEEN 10) <44372>* **I WANT IT ALL. / HANG ON IN THERE** [3] [50]
(12"+=/cd-s+=) *(12/CD QUEEN 10)* – ('A'album version).

May 89. (lp/c/cd) *(PCSD/TCPCSD/CDPCSD 107) <92357>* **THE MIRACLE** [1] [24]
– Party / Khashoggis ship / The miracle / I want it all / The invisible man / Breakthru / Rain must fall / Scandal / Was it all worth it / My baby does me. *(cd+=)* – Hang on in there / Chinese torture / The invisible man (ext). *<US cd-iss. Oct91 on 'Hollywood' ++=; 61134-2>* – Scandal (12"mix).

Jun 89. (c-s/7"/7"sha-pic-d) *(TC+/QUEEN/+PD 11)* **BREAKTHRU. / STEALIN'** [7] [-]
(12"+=/cd-s+=) *(12/CD QUEEN 11)* – ('A'extended).

Aug 89. (c-s/7"/7"clear) *(TC+/QUEEN/+X 12)* **INVISIBLE MAN. / HIJACK MY HEART** [12] [-]
(cd-s+=/12"+=/12"clear+=) *(CD/12 QUEEN/+X 12)* – ('A'extended).

Oct 89. (c-s/7") *(TC+/QUEEN 14) <44457>* **SCANDAL. / MY LIFE HAS BEEN SAVED** [25] [ ]
(12"+=/cd-s+=) *(12/CD QUEEN 14)* – ('A'extended).

Dec 89. (c-s/7") *(TC+/QUEEN 15)* **THE MIRACLE. / STONE COLD CRAZY (live)** [21] [ ]
(12"+=/cd-s+=) *(12/CD QUEEN 15)* – My melancholy blues (live).

Parlophone Hollywood

Jan 91. (c-s/7") *(TC+/QUEEN 16)* **INNUENDO. / BIJOU** [1] [ ]
('A'-Explosion mix; cd-s+=12"+=/12"pic-d+=) *(CD/12 QUEEN/+P 16)* – Under pressure (extended).

Feb 91. (cd/c/lp) *(CD/TC+/PCSD 115) <61020>* **INNUENDO** [1] [30]
– Innuendo / I'm going slightly mad / Headlong / I can't live with you / Don't try so hard / Ride the wild wind / All God's people / These are the days of our lives / Delilah / Hit man / Bijou / The show must go on.

Mar 91. (c-s/7"/7"sha-pic-d) *(TC+/QUEEN/+P 17)* **I'M GOING SLIGHTLY MAD. / HIT MAN** [22] [ ]
(12"+=/cd-s+=) *(12/CD QUEEN 17)* – Lost opportunity.

May 91. (c-s/7") *(TC+/QUEEN 18)* **HEADLONG. / ALL GOD'S PEOPLE** [14] [ ]
(cd-s+=/12"+=/12"pic-d+=) *(CD/12 QUEEN/+P 18)* – Mad the swine.

Oct 91. (c-s/7") *(TC+/QUEEN 19)* **THE SHOW MUST GO ON. / KEEP YOURSELF ALIVE** [16] [ ]
(12"+=) *(12QUEEN 19)* – (Queen talks – interview).
(cd-s++=) *(CDQUEEN 19)* – Body language.
(cd-s) – ('A'side) / Now I'm here / Fat bottomed girls / Los Palabras de amor.

Oct 91. (cd/c/d-lp) *(CD/TC+/PMTV 2) <61311>* **GREATEST HITS II** (compilation) (US title 'CLASSIC QUEEN') [1] [4]
– A kind of magic / Under pressure / Radio Ga Ga / I want it all / I want to break free / Innuendo / It's a hard life / Breakthru / Who wants to live forever / Headlong / The miracle / I'm going slightly mad / The invisible man / Hammer to fall / Friends will be friends / The show must go on / One vision. *(hit UK No.29 in May93)* (US-version +=)– Bohemian rhapsody / Stone cold crazy / One year of love / Tie your mother down / These are the days of our lives / Keep yourself alive.

— On the 23 Nov'91, FREDDIE lost his 2 year silent battle against AIDS. The previous day, it was announced in the news. The rumours had now ended.

Dec 91. (c-s/12"/cd-s/7") *(TC/12/CD+/QUEEN 20) <64794>* **BOHEMIAN RHAPSODY. / THESE ARE THE DAYS OF OUR LIVES** [1] [2]

Jun 92. (12")(c-s) *<64725>* **WE WILL ROCK YOU. / WE ARE THE CHAMPIONS** [-] [52]

Sep 92. (cd) *<61265>* **GREATEST HITS** [-] [11]

Apr 93. (c-ep/cd-ep/7"ep; by GEORGE MICHAEL & QUEEN) *(TC/CD+/R 6340) <61479>* **FIVE LIVE EP** [1] [46] album
– Somebody to love / Medley: Killer – Papa was a rollin' stone / These are the days of our lives (with LISA STANSFIELD) / Calling you.
(cd-ep) *(CDRS 6340)* – ('A'side) / Medley: Killer / Papa was a rollin' stone (with PM DAWN).
(12"+=) *(12RS 6340)* – Medley: Killer / Papa was a rollin' stone – instrumental.

— In the US, the EP's main track 'SOMEBODY TO LOVE', hit No.30; *<64647>*

— In Feb'95, FREDDIE and BRIAN featured on EDDIE HOWELL's re-issued 1977 single 'THE MAN FROM MANHATTAN'.

Oct 95. (c-s) *(TCQUEEN 21)* **HEAVEN FOR EVERYONE / IT'S A BEAUTIFUL DAY** [2] [ ]
(cd-s+=) *(CDQUEEN 21)* – ('A'-lp version).
(cd-s) *(CDQUEENS 21)* – ('A'side) / Keep yourself alive / Seven seas of rhye / Killer queen.

Nov 95. (cd/c/lp) *(CD/TC+/PCSD 167) <62017>* **MADE IN HEAVEN** [1] [58]
– It's a beautiful day / Made in Heaven / Let me live / Mother love / My life has been saved / I was born to love you / Heaven for everyone / Too much love will kill you / You don't fool me / A winter's tale / It's a beautiful day (reprise) / Yeh / Track 13.

Dec 95. (c-s/7") *(TC+/QUEEN 22)* **A WINTER'S TALE. / THANK GOD IT'S CHRISTMAS** [6] [ ]
(cd-s+=) *(CDQUEEN 22)* – Rock in Rio blues.
(cd-s) *(CDQUEENS 22)* – ('A'side) / Now I'm here / You're my best friend / Somebody to love.

Feb 96. (c-s/7") *(TC+/QUEEN 23)* **TOO MUCH LOVE WILL KILL YOU. / WE WILL ROCK YOU / WE ARE THE CHAMPIONS** [15] [ ]
(cd-s+=) *(CDQUEEN 23)* – Spread your wings.

Jun 96. (c-s/7"pic-d) *(TCQUEEN/QUEENP 24)* **LET ME LIVE. / MY FAIRY KING / DOIN' ALRIGHT / LIAR** [9] [ ]
(cd-s) *(CDQUEEN 24)* – ('A'side) / Fat bottomed girls / Bicycle race / Don't stop me now.
Nov 96. (c-s) *(TCQUEEN 25)* **YOU DON'T FOOL ME / ('A'remix)** [17] [-]
(12") *(12QUEEN 25)* – ('A'-Freddie's club + revenge mixes).
(cd-s+=) *(CDQUEEN 25)* – ('A'-Dancing Divas mix) / ('A'-sexy club mix).
Nov 97. (cd/c/d-lp) *(823091-2/-4/-1)* **QUEEN ROCKS** [7] [ ]
– No-one but you / We will rock you / Tie your mother down / Seven seas of rhye / I can't live with you / Hammer to fall / Stone cold crazy / Fat bottomed girls / Keep yourself alive / Tear it up / One vision / Killer queen / Sheer heart attack / I'm in love with my car / Put out the fire / Headlong / It's late / I want it all.
Jan 98. (c-s) *(TCQUEEN 27)* **NO-ONE BUT YOU / TIE YOUR MOTHER DOWN** [13] [ ]
(12"+=/cd-s+=) *(QUEENPD/CDQUEEN 27)* – We will rock you (mix) / Gimme the prize (mix).
Nov 98. (c-s; by QUEEN / WYCLEF JEAN featuring PRAS MICHEL & FREE) *(DRMC 22364)* **ANOTHER ONE BITES THE DUST / (mix)** [5] [ ]
(12"+=/cd-s+=) *(DRM T/CD 22364)* – (Wyclef Jean remix) / (Black Rock Star remix).
(above from the movie, 'Small Soldiers', released on 'Dreamworks')
Dec 99. (7"pic-d; QUEEN & DAVID BOWIE) *(QUEENPD 28)* **UNDER PRESSURE. / BOHEMIAN RHAPSODY** [14] [ ]
(c-s+=/cd-s+=) *(TC/CD QUEEN 28)* – Thank God it's Christmas.
(cd-s) *(CDQUEENS 28)* – ('A'mixes).

— In Jul'00, QUEEN were back at No.1 collaborating with pop group FIVE on a rendition of 'WE WILL ROCK YOU'

– compilations, etc. –

on 'EMI'UK / 'Capitol'US, unless otherwise mentioned.
Dec 85. (14xlp-box) *(QB 1)* **THE COMPLETE WORKS** [ ] [ ]
Nov 88. (3"cd-ep) *(QUECD 1)* **SEVEN SEAS OF RHYE / SEE WHAT A FOOL I'VE BEEN / FUNNY HOW LOVE IS** [ ] [-]
Nov 88. (3"cd-ep) *(QUECD 2)* **KILLER QUEEN / FLICK OF THE WRIST / BRIGHTON ROCK** [ ] [-]
Nov 88. (3"cd-ep) *(QUECD 3)* **BOHEMIAN RHAPSODY / I'M IN LOVE WITH MY CAR / YOU'RE MY BEST FRIEND** [ ] [-]
Nov 88. (3"cd-ep) *(QUECD 4)* **SOMEBODY TO LOVE / WHITE MAN / TIE YOUR MOTHER DOWN** [ ] [-]
Nov 88. (3"cd-ep) *(QUECD 5)* **GOOD OLD FASHIONED LOVER BOY / DEATH ON TWO LEGS (DEDICATED TO . . .) / TENEMENT FUNSTER / WHITE QUEEN (AS IT BEGAN)** [ ] [-]
Nov 88. (3"cd-ep) *(QUECD 6)* **WE ARE THE CHAMPIONS / WE WILL ROCK YOU / FAT BOTTOMED GIRLS** [ ] [-]
Nov 88. (3"cd-ep) *(QUECD 7)* **CRAZY LITTLE THING CALLED LOVE / SPREAD YOUR WINGS / FLASH** [ ] [-]
Nov 88. (3"cd-ep) *(QUECD 8)* **ANOTHER ONE BITES THE DUST / DRAGON ATTACK / LAS PALABRAS DE AMOR** [ ] [-]
Nov 88. (3"cd-ep) *(QUECD 9)* **UNDER PRESSURE / SOUL BROTHER / BODY LANGUAGE** [ ] [-]
Nov 88. (3"cd-ep) *(QUECD 10)* **RADIO GA GA / I GO CRAZY / HAMMER TO FALL** [ ] [-]
Nov 88. (3"cd-ep) *(QUECD 11)* **I WANT TO BREAK FREE / MACHINES (OR BACK TO HUMANS) / IT'S A HARD LIFE** [ ] [-]
Nov 88. (3"cd-ep) *(QUECD 12)* **A KIND OF MAGIC / A DOZEN RED ROSES FOR MY DARLING / ONE VISION** [ ] [-]
Dec 89. (lp/c/cd) *Band Of Joy; (BOJ LP/MC/CD 001)* **QUEEN AT THE BEEB (live)** [67] [-]
Jun 92. (cd) *Parlophone; <CDPCSD 725> / Hollywood; <61104>* **QUEEN: LIVE AT WEMBLEY (live)** [2] [53]
– (above was originally issued UK on video)
Oct 94. (d-cd/d-c) *Parlophone; (CD/TC PCSD 161)* **GREATEST HITS 1 & 2** [37] [ ]
Dec 95. (20xcd-box) *E.M.I.; (QUEENBOX 20)* **ULTIMATE QUEEN** [ ] [ ]
Nov 99. (cd/c/d-lp) *Parlophone; (523452-2/-4/-1)* **GREATEST HITS III** (hits/collaborations & solo material) [5] [ ]
– The show must go on / Under pressure / Barcelona / Too much love / Somebody to love / You don't fool me / Heaven for everyone / Las palabras / Driven by you / Living on my own / Let me live / The great pretender / Princess of the universe / Another one bites the dust / No one but you / These are the days of our lives / Thank God it's Christmas.
Nov 00. (3xcd-box) *Parlophone; (529883-2)* **GREATEST HITS VOL.I, II & III** [63] [ ]

BRIAN MAY

— with **EDDIE VAN HALEN** – guitar / **PHIL CHEN** – bass / **FRED MANDEL** – keyboards / **ALAN GRATZER** – drums etc.

E.M.I. Capitol

Oct 83. (7"; as BRIAN MAY & FRIENDS) *(EMI 5436)* **STARFLEET. / SON OF STARFLEET** [65] [-]
Oct 83. (7"; as BRIAN MAY & FRIENDS) *<B-5278>* **STARFLEET. / STARFLEET (extended)** [-] [ ]
Oct 83. (m-lp/c; as BRIAN MAY & FRIENDS) *(SFLT 107806-1/-4) <15014>* **STARFLEET PROJECT** [35] [ ]
– Starfleet / Let me out / Bluesbreakers.

— In the Autumn of '89, BRIAN MAY wrote the song 'WHO WANTS TO LIVE FOREVER' and gave it to charity for single by youngsters IAN MEESON & BELINDA GHILETT; 'EMI' 7"/12"*(ODO/12ODO 112)*

Parlophone Hollywood

Nov 91. (7"/c-s) *(R/TCR 6304)* **DRIVEN BY YOU. / JUST ONE LIFE (dedicated to the memory of Philip Sayer)** [6] [ ]
(b-guitar version; 12"+=/cd-s+=) *(12R/CDR 6034)* – Driven by you (Ford Ad version).
Sep 92. (7"/c-s) *(R/TCR 6320)* **TOO MUCH LOVE WILL KILL YOU. / I'M SCARED** [5] [ ]
(cd-s+=/s-cd-s+=) *(CDR/+S 6320)* – Driven by you (feat. COZY POWELL + NEIL MURRAY).
Oct 92. (cd/c/lp) *(CD/C+/PCSD 123)* **BACK TO THE LIGHT** [6] [ ]
– The dark / Back to the light / Love token / Resurrection / Too much love will kill you / Driven by you / Nothin' but blue / I'm scared / Last horizon / Let your heart rule your head / Just one life / Rollin' over. *(re-iss. Jun93 in gold-cd; CDPCSDX 123)*

— In Oct'92, BRIAN featured on HANK MARVIN's (Shadows) version of QUEEN's song 'WE ARE THE CHAMPIONS'.

Nov 92. (7"/c-s) *(R/TCR 6329)* **BACK TO THE LIGHT. / NOTHING BUT BLUE (guitar version)** [19] [ ]
(B-guitar cd-s+=) *(CDR 6329)* – Blues breaker.
(cd-s) *(CDRX 6329)* – ('A'side) / Star fleet / Let me out.
Jun 93. (c-s; by BRIAN MAY with COZY POWELL) *(TCR 6351)* **RESURRECTION / LOVE TOKEN** [23] [ ]
(12"pic-d+=/cd-s+=) *(12RPF/CDRS 6351)* – Too much love will kill you (live).
(cd-s) *(CDR 6351)* – ('A'side) / Driven by you (two) / Back to the light (live) / Tie your mother down (live).
Dec 93. (7"/c-s) *(R/TCR 6371)* **LAST HORIZON. / LET YOUR HEART RULE YOUR HEAD** [51] [ ]
(cd-s/s-cd-s) *(CDR/+S 6371)* – ('A'side) / ('A'live) / We will rock you (live) / ('A'album mix).

— **MAY** – vox, guitar with **COZY POWELL** – drums / **NEIL MURRAY** – bass / **SPIKE EDNEY** – keyboards / **JAMIE MOSES** – guitar, vocals / **CATHY PORTER + SHELLEY PRESTON** – vox

Feb 94. (cd/c/d-lp; by BRIAN MAY BAND) *(CD/C+/PCSD 150)* **LIVE AT THE BRIXTON ACADEMY (live London, 15th June 1993)** [20] [ ]
– Back to the light / Driven by you / Tie your mother down / Love token / Headlong / Love of my life / '39 – Let your heart rule your head / Too much love will kill you / Since you've been gone / Now I'm here / Guitar extravagance / Resurrection / Last horizon / We will rock you / Hammer to fall.
May 98. (7") *(R 6498)* **THE BUSINESS (Rock On Cozy mix). / MAYBE BABY** [51] [ ]
(cd-s+=) *(CDR 6498)* – (Brian talks) / ('A'-CD-Rom video).
Jun 98. (cd/c/lp) *(494973-2/-4/-1) <162103>* **ANOTHER WORLD** [23] [ ]
– Space / The business / China belle / Why don't we try again / On my way up / Cyborg / Guv'nor / Wilderness / Slow down / One rainy wish / All the way from Memphis / Another world.
Aug 98. (c-s/cd-s) *(TCR/CDR 6504)* **WHY DON'T WE TRY AGAIN / ONLY MAKE BELIEVE / F.B.I.** [44] [-]

– (MAY) compilations, etc. –

Nov 95. (cd) *Javelin; (HADCD 190)* **THEMES AND DREAMS** [ ] [-]
Dec 95. (cd-s) *Koch; (34337-2)* **BLACK WHITE HOUSE** [ ] [-]

— with APPICE (veteran drummer) + SLASH (of Guns N' Roses)

Feb 96. (cd-s; by BRIAN MAY with CARMINE APPICE'S GUITAR ZEUS) **NOBODY KNEW (BLACK WHITE HOUSE) / NOBODY KNEW (BLACK WHITE HOUSE) (long version)** [ ] [-]

ROGER TAYLOR

E.M.I. Elektra

Aug 77. (7") *(EMI 2679)* **I WANNA TESTIFY. / TURN ON THE T.V.** [ ] [-]
Apr 81. (7") *(EMI 5157)* **FUTURE MANAGEMENT. / LAUGH OR CRY** [49] [-]
Apr 81. (lp/c) *(EMC/TCEMC 3369) <5E-522>* **FUN IN SPACE** [18] [ ]
– No violins / Laugh or cry / Future management / Let's get crazy / My country I & II / Good times are now / Magic is loose / Interlude in Constantinople / Airheads / Fun in space. *(cd-iss. May96 on 'Parlophone'; CDPCS 7380)*
Apr 81. (7") *<E-47151>* **LET'S GET CRAZY. / LAUGH OR CRY** [-] [ ]
Jun 81. (7") *(EMI 5200)* **MY COUNTRY. / FUN IN SPACE** [ ] [-]

E.M.I. Capitol

Jun 84. (7"/ext.12") *(EMI/+12 5478)* **MAN ON FIRE. / KILLING TIME** [66] [-]
Jul 84. (lp/c) *(RTA/TCRTA 1) <EJ-240137-1>* **STRANGE FRONTIER** [30] [ ]
– Strange frontier / Beautiful dreams / Man on fire / Racing in the street / Masters of war / Killing time / Abandon fire / Young love / It's an illusion / I cry for you (love, hope & confusion). *(cd-iss. May96 on 'Parlophone'; CDPCS 7381)*
Aug 84. (7") *(EMI 5490)* **STRANGE FRONTIER. / I CRY FOR YOU (remix)** [ ] [-]
(ext.12"+=) *(EMI12 5490)* – Two sharp pencils.

The CROSS

ROGER with **PETER NOONE** – bass / **CLAYTON MOSS** – guitar / **SPIKE EDNEY** – keyboards / **JOSH MacRAE** – drums

Virgin Virgin

Sep 87. (7"/ext.12")(cd-s) *(VS/+T 1007)(CDEP 10)* **COWBOYS AND INDIANS. / LOVE LIES BLEEDING** [74] [ ]
(c-s+=) *(VSTC 1007)* – ('A'extended).
Jan 88. (7") *(VS 1026)* **SHOVE IT. / ROUGH JUSTICE** [ ] [ ]
(ext.12"+=) *(VS 1026-12)* – ('A'-Metropolix mix).
(cd-s+=) *(CDEP 20)* – Cowboys and Indians / ('A'extended).
Jan 88. (lp/c/cd) *(V/TCV/CDV 2477) <90857>* **SHOVE IT** [58] [ ] Apr88
– Shove it / Heaven for everyone / Love on a tightrope (like an animal) / Cowboys and Indians / Stand up for love / Love lies bleeding (she was a wicked, wily waitress) / Contact. *(cd+=)* – Rough justice – 2nd shelf mix.
Mar 88. (7") *(VS 1062)* **HEAVEN FOR EVERYONE. / LOVE ON A TIGHTROPE (LIKE AN ANIMAL)** [ ] [ ]
(12"+=) *(VST 1062)* – Contact.
Jul 88. (7") *(VS 1100)* **MANIPULATOR. / STAND UP FOR LOVE** [ ] [ ]
(12"+=) *(VS 1100-12)* – ('A'extended).

Parlophone not iss.

Apr 90. (7") *(R 6251)* **POWER TO LOVE. / PASSION FOR TRASH** [ ] [-]
(12"+=/cd-s+=) *(12R/CDR 6251)* – ('A'extended).

May 90. (cd/c/lp) *(CD/TC+/PCS 7342)* **MAD, BAD AND DANGEROUS TO KNOW** [ ] [-]
– On top of the world ma / Liar / Closer to you / Breakdown / Penetration guru / Power to love / Sister blue / Better things / Old men (lay down) / Final destination. *(cd+=)* – Foxy lady.

ROGER TAYLOR

— with **JASON FALLOON** – guitars / **PHIL SPALDING** – bass / **MIKE CROSSLEY** – piano, keyboards / **CATHERINE PORTER** – backing vocals / **JOSHUA J. MacRAE** – programming

Parlophone not iss.

Apr 94. (c-s/7") *(TC+/R 6379)* **NAZIS 1994. / ('A'radio mix)** [22] [-]
(12"red+=) *(12R 6379)* – ('A'extended) / ('A'-Big science mix).
(cd-s++=) *(CDR 6379)* – ('A'kick mix) / ('A'-Schindler's extended mix).
Sep 94. (cd/c) *(CD/TC PCSD 157)* **HAPPINESS?** [22] [-]
– Nazis 1994 / Happiness / Revelations / Touch the sky / Foreign sand / Freedom train / You had to be there / The key / Everybody hurts sometime / Loneliness . . . / Dear Mr. Murdoch / Old friends.

— Below featured a Japanese classically trained drummer, pianist & co-composer **YOSHIKI** plus **JIM CREGAN** – guitars / **PHIL CHEN** – bass / **DICK MARX** – strings arrangement

Sep 94. (c-s/7"colrd; by ROGER TAYLOR & YOSHIKI) *(TC+/R 6389)* **FOREIGN SAND. / ('A'mix)** [26] [-]
(12"pic-d+=/cd-s+=) *(12R/CDR 6389)* – You had to be there / Final destination.
Nov 94. (7") *(R 6399)* **HAPPINESS. / RIDE THE WILD WIND (live)** [32] [-]
(12") *(12R 6399)* – ('A'side) / Dear Mr.Murdoch / Everybody hurts sometime (live) / Old friends (live).
(cd-s) *(CDR 6399)* – ('A'side) / Loneliness / Dear Mr. Murdoch / I want to break free (live).
Sep 98. (7"/cd-s) *(R/CDR 6507)* **PRESSURE ON. / PEOPLE ON STREETS (mashed) / TONIGHT (dub sangria)** [45] [-]
Sep 98. (cd/c/lp) *(496724-2/-4/-1)* **ELECTRIC FIRE** [53] [-]
– Pressure on / Nation of haircuts / Believe in yourself / Surrender / People on the streets / Whispers / No more fun / Tonight / Where are you now / Working class hero / London town c'mon down.
Mar 99. (7") *(R 6517)* **SURRENDER. / LONDON TOWN, C'MON DOWN** [38] [-]
(cd-s+=) *(CDR 6517)* – A nation of haircuts (club cut).
(cd-s) *(CDRS 6517)* – ('A'live) / No more fun (live) / Tonight (live) / ('A'-CD-Rom video).

QUEEN ADREENA

Formed: London, England . . . late 90's by former DAISY CHAINSAW frontwoman KATIE JANE GARSIDE along with fellow DC veteran CRISPIN GLOVER. Following the latter act's flash-in-the-pan success with the 'Love Your Money' single and subsequent doomed reunions, GARSIDE – surprisingly namechecked by COURTNEY LOVE as one of the founders of the Riot Grrrl movement – turned her back on the music business and went off to find herself in the Lake District. Upon her return to London, she hooked up with GLOVER once more and the pair completed their new band with a rhythm section of ORSON WAJIH and BILLY FREEDOM. Debut single, 'COLD FISH, arrived in the summer of '99, featuring GARSIDE's eerie vocals over a barrage of distortion. A true child of nature given to premonitions – of which the band's name was apparently one – and mystical visions, KATIE convincingly stamped her wayward persona over QUEEN ADREENA's debut album, 'TAXIDERMY' (2000).

Album rating: TAXIDERMY (*7)

KATIE JANE GARSIDE – vocals (ex-DAISY CHAINSAW) / **CRISPIN GRAY** – guitar (ex-DAISY CHAINSAW) / **ORSON WAJIH** – bass / **BILLY FREEDOM** – drums

Blanco Y Negro not iss.

Aug 99. (cd-s) *(NEG 118CDX)* **COLD FISH / YESTERDAY'S HYMN** [ ] [-]
Nov 99. (cd-s) *(NEG 121CDX)* **X-ING OFF THE DAYS / A HEAVENLY SURRENDER** [ ] [-]
Feb 00. (10"/cd-s) *(NEG 124 TE/CDX)* **I ADORE YOU. / WEEDS** [ ] [-]
Apr 00. (cd/lp) *(8573 80662-2/-1)* **TAXIDERMY** [ ] [-]
– Cold fish / Soda dreamer / I adore you / Yesterday's hymn / Pretty Polly / Yamaya / Madraykin / X-ing off the days / Hide from time / Friday's child / Sleepwalking / Are the songs my disease / Weeds.
Oct 00. (12"/cd-s) *(NEG 128 TE/CDX)* **PRETTY POLLY. / JOLENE** [ ] [-]

QUEENS OF THE STONE AGE (see under ⇒ KYUSS)

QUEENSRYCHE

Formed: Bellevue, Seattle, Washington, USA . . . 1980 initially as The MOB by high school friends, CHRIS DE GARMO, MICHAEL WILTON, EDDIE JACKSON and SCOTT ROCKENFIELD. With the addition of classically trained vocalist GEOFF TATE, the act assumed the QUEENSRYCHE moniker after an enduring track on their eponymous debut EP. The 12" was released by record shop owners Kim and Diana Harris who had set up the independent '206' label expressly for this purpose. Following the record's underground success, 'EMI America' snapped the band up for a seven album deal and promptly re-issued the record before setting them to work on a debut album with producer James Guthrie. The result was 'THE WARNING' (1984), a rather underwhelming affair handicapped by an unsympathetic final mix. 'RAGE FOR ORDER' (1986) was the first QUEENSRYCHE release to hint at the band's future cerebro-metal direction, TATE's impressive vocal muscle flexing a taster of what was in store with 'OPERATION MINDCRIME' (1988). One of the landmark metal releases of that year, the record was a 1984-style concept affair dealing with media brainwashing and social turmoil, conjuring up a convincingly chilling vision of a future gone wrong. Interspersed with snippets of dialogue, broadcasts etc., the songs effortlessly created an atmosphere of tension and portent, TATE veering between prophetic threat and despairing menace while the band's twin guitar attack raged and insinuated in equal measure. ' . . .MINDCRIME' subsequently went gold in America while selling over a million copies worldwide with nary a hit single to support it. Firmly established as the foremost thinking man's metal band, they could afford to be a bit more instinctive with their next release, the acclaimed 'EMPIRE' (1990). More a collection of set pieces, the record's highlight was the hypnotic 'SILENT LUCIDITY', a US Top 10 hit with heavy MTV rotation, the album itself reaching No.7. Other highlights included the brawny 'JET CITY WOMAN', the final single (save a re-release of 'SILENT LUCIDITY' which made the UK Top 20) before a period of relative inactivity. QUEENSRYCHE finally re-emerged in 1994 with 'PROMISED LAND', a more introspective and meditative effort which nevertheless made the US Top 3, cementing the band's position as prime purveyors of intelligent hard rock/metal. Taking a little too much experimentation on board with their next long-playing effort in '97 ('HEAR IN THE NEW FRONTIER'), QUEENSRYCHE for once failed to get the right response from the buying public. Shifting to 'Atlantic' for 'Q2K' (1999), the band were treading water when the set only managed to squeeze into the US Top 50 for one week.
• **Trivia:** PAMELA MOORE was guest singer on 'SUITE SISTER MARY'.
• **Songwriters:** DeGARMO or TATE / WILSON except; SCARBOROUGH FAIR – CANTICLE (Simon & Garfunkel) / GONNA GET CLOSE TO YOU (Lisa Diabello).

Album rating: THE WARNING (*5) / RAGE FOR ORDER (*7) / OPERATION: MINDCRIME (*8) / EMPIRE (*7) / PROMISED LAND (*6) / HEAR IN THE NEW FRONTIER (*6) / Q2K (*5) / GREATEST HITS compilation (*7)

GEOFF TATE (b.14 Jan'59, Stuttgart, Germany) – vocals / **CHRIS DeGARMO** (b.14 Jun'63, Wenatchee, Washington) – guitar / **MICHAEL WILTON** (b.23 Feb'62, San Francisco, Calif.) – guitar / **EDDIE JACKSON** (b.29 Jan'61, Robstown, Texas) – bass / **SCOTT ROCKENFIELD** (b.15 Jun'63, Seattle, Washington) – drums

EMI America EMI America

Sep 83. (12"ep) *(12EA 162)* *<19006>* **QUEENSRYCHE** [ ] [81] m-lp
– Queen of the Reich / Nightrider / Blinded / The lady wore black. *<first issued 1982 on '206' records; R 101>*
Sep 84. (7") *(EA 183)* **TAKE HOLD OF THE FLAME. / NIGHTRIDER** [ ] [ ]
Sep 84. (lp/c) *(EJ 240220-1/-4)* *<E2 46557>* **THE WARNING** [ ] [61]
– The warning / En force / Deliverance / No sanctuary / NM 156 / Take hold of the flame / Before the storm / Child of fire / Roads to madness. *(cd-iss. Mar87; CDP 746 557-2) (re-iss. Aug91 cd/c; QY 1) (re-iss. cd Oct94 & Apr00; CDP 746557-2)*
Jul 86. (lp/c) *(AML/TCAML 3105)* *<E2 46330>* **RAGE FOR ORDER** [66] [47]
– Walk in the shadows / I dream in infrared / The whisper / Gonna get close to you / The killing words / Surgical strike / Neue regel / Chemical youth (we are rebellion) / London / Screaming in digital / I will remember. *(cd-iss. Feb87; CDP 746330-2) (re-iss. Aug91 cd/c; CD/TC AML 3105) (re-iss. cd Oct94; same)*
Aug 86. (7") *(EA 22)* **GONNA GET CLOSE TO YOU. / PROPHECY** [ ] [ ]
(d7"+=) *(EAD 22)* – Queen of the Reich / Deliverance.

Manhattan Manhattan

May 88. (lp/c/cd) *(MTL/TCMTL/CDMTL 1023)* *<48640>* **OPERATION: MINDCRIME** [58] [50]
– I remember now / Anarchy-X / Revolution calling / Operation: Mindcrime / Speak / Spreading the disease / The mission / Suite Sister Mary / The needle lies / Electric requiem / Breaking the silence / I don't believe in love / Waiting for 22 / My empty room / Eyes of a stranger. *(re-iss. cd Oct94; CDP 748640-2)*
Oct 88. (10"ep) *(10QP 1)* **OVERSEEING THE OPERATION. / EXCERPTS FROM OPERATION MINDCRIME** [ ] [ ]
– Suite sister Mary / I Remember Now / Revolution Calling / Operation: Mindcrime / Breaking The Silence / Eyes Of A Stranger.
Apr 89. (7") *(MT 65)* **EYES OF A STRANGER. / QUEEN OF THE REICH** [59] [ ]
(12"+=/12"g-f+=) *(12MT/+G 65)* – Walk in the shadows / Take hold of the flame.
(cd-s+=) *(CDMT 65)* – Take hold of the flame / Prophecy.

E.M.I. USA E.M.I.

Sep 90. (7"/7"sha-pic-d) *(MT/+PD 90)* **EMPIRE. / SCARBOROUGH FAIR – CANTICLE** [61] [ ]
(12"+=/cd-s+=) *(12/CD MT 90)* – Prophecy.
Sep 90. (cd/c/d-lp) *(CD/TC+/1058)* *<E2 92806>* **EMPIRE** [13] [7]
– Best I can do / The thin line / Jet city woman / Della Brown / Another rainy night (without you) / Empire / Resistance / Silent lucidity / Hand on heart / One and only / Anybody listening?
Apr 91. (7"/7"box/c-s) *(MT/MTS/TCMTP 94)* *<50345>* **SILENT LUCIDITY. / THE MISSION (live)** [34] [9] Mar91
(12"+=) *(12MTP 94)* – Eyes of a stranger.
(cd-s+=) *(CDMT 94)* – Della Brown.
Jun 91. (7"/c-s) *(MT/CTMT 97)* **BEST I CAN. / I DREAM IN INFRARED (acoustic remix)** [36] [ ]
(10"+=) *(10MT 97)* – Prophecy.
(cd-s++=) *(CDMT 97)* – ('A'radio edit).
Aug 91. (7"/7"sha-pic-d) *(MT/+PD 98)* **JET CITY WOMAN. / EMPIRE (live)** [39] [ ]
(12"+=) *(12MTS 98)* – Walk in the shadows (live).
(cd-s) *(CDMT 98)* – ('A'side) / Walk in the shadows (live) / Queen of The Reich.
Nov 91. (cd+video) *<97048>* **OPERATION: LIVECRIME (live)** [-] [38]
Aug 92. (7"/c-s) *(MT/CTMT 104)* **SILENT LUCIDITY. / I DON'T BELIEVE IN LOVE** (live) [18] [-]
(12"pic-d) *(12MTPD 104)* – ('A'side) / Last time in Paris / Take hold of the fame.
(cd-s) *(CDMT 104)* – ('A'side) / Suite Sister Mary (live) / Last time in Paris.
(cd-s) *(CDMTS 104)* – ('A'side) / Eyes of a stranger (live) / Operation: Mindcrime.

Oct 94. (cd/c/clear-lp) *(CD/TC+/MTL 1081)* <30711> **PROMISED LAND** [13] [3]
– 9:28 a.m. / I am I / Damaged / Out of mind / Bridge / Promised land / Disconnected / Lady Jane / My global mind / One more time / Someone else?.

Jan 95. (12"gold) *(12MT 109)* **I AM I. / REAL WORLD / SOMEONE ELSE?** [40] [ ]
(cd-s+=/s-cd-s+=) *(CDMT/+S 109)* – Dirty li'l secret.

Mar 95. (7"pic-d/c-s) *(MTPD/TCMT 111)* **BRIDGE. / THE KILLING WORDS (live)** [40] [ ]
(cd-s+=) *(CDMTS 111)* – The lady wore black (live) / Damaged (live).
(cd-s) *(CDMTSX 111)* – ('A'side) / Silent lucidity (live) / My empty room (live) / Real world (live).

Mar 97. (cd/c) *(CD/TC EMC 3764)* <56141> **HEAR IN THE NEW FRONTIER** [46] [19]
– Sign of the times / Cuckoo's nest / Get a life / Voice inside / Some people fly / Saved / You / Miles away / Reach / All I want / Hit the black / Anytime – anywhere / Spool.

Atlantic Atlantic

Nov 99. (cd) <(7567 83225-2)> **Q2K** [ ] [46] Sep99
– Falling down / Sacred ground / One life / When the rain comes / How could I know / Beside you / Liquid sky / Breakdown / Burning man / Wot kinda man / Right side of my mind.

– compilations, etc. –

1988. (cd) *E.M.I. USA;* <CDP7 90615-2> **QUEENSRYCHE** [-] [ ]

Oct 99. (d-cd) *Axe Killer; (AXE 3052182CD)* **OPERATION: MINDCRIME / QUEEN OF THE RYCHE** [ ] [-]

Jul 00. (cd) *E.M.I.;* <(8 49422-2)> **GREATEST HITS** [ ] [ ]
– Queen of the Reich / The lady wore black / The warning / Take hold of the flame / Walk in the shadows / I dream in infrared / I don't believe in love / Eyes of a stranger / Jet city woman / Empire / Silent lucidity / I am I / The bridge / Sign of the times. *(cd-extra+=)* – Chasing blue skies / Someone else.

QUEERS

Formed: North Hampton, USA ... 1982 by the RAMONES obsessed teenagers, JOE QUEER, VAPID, B-FACE and DANNY PANIC. After the release of a 6-song EP that year they seemed to go into a 5-year hibernation, that is, until their debut album, 'LOVE SONGS' was issued in '88. They resurfaced again with a series of 'Lookout!' (once home of GREEN DAY) sets, including 'BEAT OFF' (1990), 'GROW UP' (1992), 'MOVE BACK HOME' (1995) and 'DON'T BACK DOWN' (1996). In 1998, still with a penchant for sounding like clones of the RAMONES, they moved to another label, 'Hopeless', which best describes their sixth album, 'PUNK ROCK CONFIDENTIAL'. Their blend of cartoon three-chord punk'n'roll will no doubt go down well with the new wave of poppy-punk that American acts were churning out, twenty-odd years too late! • **Covered:** THAT GIRL (Livermore) / GET OVER YOU (Undertones) / HAWAII + DON'T BACK DOWN + LITTLE HONDA (Brian Wilson/Beach Boys) / END IT ALL (Muffs) / SIDEWALK SURFIN' GIRL (Curb-Hatcher) / ANOTHER GIRL (Hernandez) / PRETTY FLAMINGO (Manfred Mann) / I ENJOY BEING A BOY (Banana Splits) + a complete tribute to the Ramones:- ROCKET TO RUSSIA.

Album rating: LOVE SONGS FOR THE RETARDED (*5) / BEAT OFF (*4) / GROW UP (*4) / MOVE BACK HOME (*6) / DON'T BACK DOWN (*4) / PUNK ROCK CONFIDENTIAL (*3) / LATER DAYS AND BETTER DAYS demos (*4) / BEYOND THE VALLEY . . . (*5)

JOE QUEER (b. KING) – vocals, guitar / **VAPID** – guitar, vocals / **B-FACE** (b. BARNARD) – bass, vocals / **DANNY PANIC** – drums

not iss. unknown

1982. (7"ep) **6-SONG EP** [-] [ ]

Lookout Lookout

1988. (lp) <*LOOKOUT 66*> **LOVE SONGS FOR THE RETARDED** [-] [ ]
– You're tripping / Ursula finally has tits / I hate everything / Teenage bonehead / Fuck this world / I can't stop farting / Feeling groovy / Debra Jean / Hi mom, it's me! / Noodlebrain / I can't stand you / Night of the livid queers / Granola head / I won't be / Monster zero / Daydreaming. *(UK-iss.Jul95 cd/c; LOOKOUT 66 CD/MC)*

1990. (lp) <*LOOKOUT 81*> **BEAT OFF** [-] [ ]
– Steak bomb / Drop the attitude fucker / You make me wanna puke / Teenage gluesniffer / Ben Weasel / Voodoo doll / Mirage / Grounded / Live this life / Half shitfaced / Too many twinkies / All screwed up. *(UK-iss.Jul95 cd/c; LOOKOUT 81 CD/MC)*

1990. (lp) <*LOOKOUT 90*> **GROW UP** [-] [ ]
– Squid omelet / Love love love / Boobarella / I met her at the rat / I'll be true to you / Burger king queen / Junk freak / Gay boy / Rambo rat / I don't wanna get involved / Goodbye California / Strip search. *(UK-iss.Jul95 cd/c/lp; LOOKOUT 90 CD/MC/LP)*

—— **HUGH O'NEILL** – drums, bass; repl. VAPID + DANNY PANIC

Feb 95. (cd-ep) <*LOOKOUT 108*> **SURF GODDESS EP** [-] [ ]
– Mirage / Surf goddess / Get over you / +1

May 95. (cd/lp) <*(LOOKOUT 114 CD/LP)*> **MOVE BACK HOME** [ ] [ ]
– She's a cretin / Next stop rehab / High school psychopath II / If you only had a brain / I gotta girlfriend / Hawaii / From your body / Definitely / Everything's going my way / Cut it dude / I can't get invite to the prom / That girl / Peppermint girl.

Jan 96. (cd) <*LOOKOUT 130*> **A DAY LATE AND A DOLLAR SHORT** (compilation) [-] [ ]
– We'd have a riot doing heroin / Terminal rut / Fagtown / I want cunt / Trash this place / Love me / Kicked out the Webelos / Tuly is a wimp / At the mall / I spent the rent / I don't wanna work / I'm useless / This place sucks / Wimpy drives through Harlem / I like young girls / Nuni in New York / Nobody likes me / Nothing to do / Nowhere at all / Mac Arthurs park / Flesh for Tulu / Fuck you / Didn't want some / Meat wagon / Don't puke / Bonehead / Wimpy drives through Harlem / Nothing to do / Gay boy / Nobody likes me / Too many twinkies / Half shitfaced / I live this life / Live broadcast WFMJ 4/11/9?

Oct 96. (cd/lp) <*(LOOKOUT 140 CD/LP)*> **DON'T BACK DOWN** [ ] [ ] Aug96
– No tit / Punk rock girls / I'm ok, you're fucked / Number one / Don't back down / I only drink Bud / I always new / Born to do dishes / Janelle, Janelle / Brush your teeth / Sidewalk surfin' girl / Another girl / Love, love, love / I can't get over you.

Feb 97. (7"ep) <*(LOOKOUT 158)*> **BUBBLEGUM DREAMS EP** [ ] [ ]
– Punk rock girls / Never ever ever / Little Honda / End it all.

Hopeless Hopeless

Jun 98. (cd-ep) *(HR 631CD)* **EVERYTHING'S OK / QUEERBAIT / GET A LIFE AND LIVE IT LOSER / I ENJOY BEING A BOY** [ ] [ ]

Oct 98. (cd/lp) <*(HR 636-2/-1)*> **PUNK ROCK CONFIDENTIAL** [ ] [ ]
– Tamara is a punk / Everything's OK / I didn't puke / Mrs. Brown, you've got an ugly daughter / The sun always shines around you / Rancid motherfuckers / Punk rock confidential / Today I fell in love / Pretty flamingo / Motherfucker / Like a parasite / Idiot savant / I enjoy being a boy / Don't mess it up / Sayonara sucker.

May 00. (lp/cd) <*(HR 643/+CD)*> **BEYOND THE VALLEY . . .** [ ] [ ]
– Uncouth / Little rich working class oi-boy / Strangle the girl / I'm not a mongo anymore / Stupid fucking vegan / In with the out crowd / I wanna know / Journey to the center of your empty mind / I hate your fucking guts / Babyface (boo-hoo-hoo) / My cunt's a cunt / I just called to say fuck you / Just say cunt / Theme from beyond the valley . . .

– compilations, etc. –

1994. (lp; shared with PINK LINCONS) *Just Add Water;* <*001*> **LIVE AT SOME PRICK'S HOUSE** [-] [ ]

Jan 98. (cd) *Clear View;* <*37*> **SUCK THIS LIVE (live)** [-] [ ]
– Squid omelet / We'd have a riot doing heroin / This place sucks / Tulu is a wimp / I want it now / Monster zero / Fuck up / Noodle brain / Granola gead / Hi mom . . . it's me!! / Teenage bonehead / Beer break / I spent the rent / Nothing to do / My old man's a fatso / Fuck you / Fuck the world / I hate everything / Ursula finally has tits / You're tripping.

Nov 98. (cd) *Clear View;* <*28*> **ROCKET TO RUSSIA** [-] [ ]

Apr 99. (cd) *Lookout;* <*(LK 216CD)*> **LATER DAYS AND BETTER DAYS** [ ] [ ]

QUICKSAND

Formed: New York, USA . . . mid 80's by WALTER SCHRIEFELS, SERGIO VEGA, TOM CAPONE and ALAN CAGE. Learning their trade in the cut and thrust NYC scene, the group were finally pulled from the hardcore mire after releasing an eponymous indie debut EP in 1992. Moving away from their roots, QUICKSAND's malignant, subliminal approach was fully realised on the major label debut, 'SLIP', issued on 'Polygram' the following year. The newly instigated 'Island Red' label signed them in 1994, unleashing their first UK release, 'MANIC COMPRESSION' a year later. QUICKSAND resurfaced nearing the end of '97, releasing comeback album, 'HOME IS WHERE I BELONG', early the following year.

Album rating: SLIP (*6) / MANIC COMPRESSION (*6) / HOME IS WHERE I BELONG (*5)

WALTER SCHRIEFELS – vocals, guitar / **TOM CAPONE** – guitar / **SERGIO VEGA** – bass / **ALAN CAGE** – drums

Revelation Revelation

Apr 92. (7"ep/c-ep/cd-ep) *(REVEL 018/+MC/CD)* **QUICKSAND E.P.** [ ] [ ]
– Omission / Clean slate / Unfulfilled / Hypno jam with Dan.

Island Red Island

1993. (cd/lp) <*314 517 685-2/-1*> **SLIP** [-] [ ]
– Fazer / Head to the wall / Dine alone / Slip / Freezing process / Lie and wait / Unfulfilled / Can opener / Omission / Baphomet / Too official / Transparent / How soon is now?

Apr 95. (cd/c/lp) *(CIRD/IRCT/IRLP 1005)* <*526564*> **MANIC COMPRESSION** [ ] [ ]
– Backward / Delusional / Divorce / Simpleton / Skinny (it's overflowing) / Thorn in my side / Landmine spring / Blister / Brown gargantuan / East 3rd St. / Supergenius / It would be cooler if you did. *(lp-iss.Mar95 on 'Revelation'; REV 43LP)*

Jul 95. (7"red) *(IR 107)* **THORN IN MY SIDE. / (other track by "Stanford Prison Experiment")** [ ] [ ]

—— they re-formed in 1997

Siwan Siwan

Jan 98. (cd) <*(SRMC 1030)*> **HOME IS WHERE I BELONG** [ ] [ ]
– Hideaway my song / Sunlight brings shadows / Empty street empty heart / Overcome the pattern – Flying / Time to live / Home is where I belong / Seasongs – Alpha Omega / Hiding it all.

QUIET RIOT

Formed: Los Angeles, California, USA . . . 1975 by KEVIN DuBROW, RANDY RHOADS, KELLY GARNI and DREW FORSYTH. A popular local act, QUIET RIOT were nevertheless far more successful in Japan, where they had two early self-titled albums released on 'Columbia'. Following the departure of RHOADS to OZZY OSBOURNE's band (where his guitar playing would make him a minor legend prior to his untimely death in a plane crash in March '82), QUIET RIOT subsequently disbanded. DuBROW formed erm . . . DuBROW, along with RUDY SARZO and FRANKIE BANALI, before reforming QUIET RIOT in 1982 with the addition of CARLOS CAVAZO. Signing to the new 'Pasha' label, the group stomped to the top of the US charts with the 'METAL HEALTH' (1983), its unexpected success down to their highly infectious cover of Slade's 'CUM ON FEEL THE NOIZE'. An enjoyable if hardly rivetting set of shiny hard-rock, the album went on to sell an amazing five million copies, an incredible feat for a metal band of their ilk. They failed to build on this break, however, the aptly named 'CONDITION

CRITICAL' (1984) proving a weak facsimile of its predecessor as tensions within the group reached breaking point. With SARZO wisely opting to jump ship for WHITESNAKE, CHUCK WRIGHT was recruited as a replacement and the group cut an even more lacklustre third set, 'QR III' (1986). QUIET RIOT subsequently rebelled against DuBROW, ousting him from the band amid claims that he was an 'egomaniac'. PAUL SHORTINO was installed as frontman although the resulting album, 'POWER AND GROOVE' (1988; US title, 'QUIET RIOT') was largely ignored. So it was, then, that the 'RIOT ended as more of a minor disturbance, SHORTINO going on to work with MITCH PERRY while BANALI later enjoyed some recognition as a member of both W.A.S.P. and FASTER PUSSYCAT. DuBROW eventually resurfaced in 1991 as HEAT, along with CAVAZO and new members, KENNY HILARY and PAT ASHBY.

Album rating: QUIET RIOT (*4) / QUIET RIOT II (*4) / METAL HEALTH (*6) / CONDITION CRITICAL (*4) / QR III (*2) / WILD, YOUNG AND CRAZEE compilation (*6) / QUIET RIOT (*3) / TERRIFIED (*4) / DOWN TO THE BONE (*4) / THE RANDY RHOADS YEARS compilation (*5) / THE BEST OF QUIET RIOT compilation (*6) / ALIVE AND WELL (*3)

KEVIN DuBROW (b.29 Oct'55) – vocals / **RANDY RHOADS** (b. 6 Dec'56, Burbank, Calif.) – guitar / **KELLY GARNI** (b.29 Oct'57, Hollywood, Calif.) – bass / **DREW FORSYTH** (b.14 May'56, Hollywood) – drums

Columbia | not iss.

1978. (lp) **QUIET RIOT** [-] [-] Japan
– It's not so funny / Mama's little angels / Tin soldier / Ravers / Back to the coast / Glad all over / Get your kicks / Look in any window / Just how you want it / Riot reunion / Fit to be tied / Demolition derby.

1979. (lp) *<25AP 1192>* **QUIET RIOT II** [-] [-] Japan
– Slick black Cadillac / You drive me crazy / Afterglow (of your love) / Eye for an eye / Trouble / Killer girls / Face to face / Inside you / We've got the magic.

— **RUDY SARZO** (b. 9 Nov'52, Havana, Cuba) – bass repl. GARNI. Disbanded in 1979 when RHOADS joined OZZY OSBOURNE. He was killed in a plane crash in Mar'82. **KEVIN** formed own self-named outfit **DuBROW**, with **SARZO** + drummer **FRANKIE BANALI** (b.14 Nov'53, Queens, N.Y.) QUIET RIOT reformed with **DUBROW, SARZO, BANALI + CARLOS CAVAZO** (b. 8 Jul'59) – guitar

Epic | Pasha

May 83. (lp/c/pic-lp) *(EPC/40 25322) <38443>* **METAL HEALTH** [ ] [1] Apr83
– Metal health / Cum on feel the noize / Don't wanna let you go / Slick black Cadillac / Love's a bitch / Breathless / Run for cover / Battle axe / Let's get crazy / Thunderbird. *(re-iss. Jan87 lp/c; 459984-1/-4) (cd-iss. 1988; CD 25322) (cd re-iss. Jul93 on 'Sony Europe'; EPC 25322)*

Jul 83. (7") *(A 3616) <04005>* **CUM ON FEEL THE NOIZE. / RUN FOR COVER** [ ] [5] Sep83

Nov 83. (7") *(A 3968) <04267>* **METAL HEALTH. / CUM ON FEEL THE NOIZE** [45] [-]
(12"+=/d7"+=) *(TA/DA 3968)* – Love's a bitch / Let's get crazy.

Jan 84. (7") *<04267>* **METAL HEALTH (BANG YOUR HEAD). / ('A'live version)** [-] [31]

Mar 84. (7") *(A 4250)* **BAD BOY. / METAL HEALTH (BANG YOUR HEAD)** [ ] [-]
(12"+=) *(TA 4250)* – Slick black Cadillac.

Jul 84. (lp/c) *(EPC/40 26075) <39516>* **CONDITION CRITICAL** [71] [15]
– Sign of the times / Mama weer all crazee now / Party all night / Stomp your hands, clap your feet / Winners take all / Condition critical / Scream and shout / Red alert / Bad boy / (We were) Born to rock. *(cd-iss. 1988; CD 26075) (re-iss. Oct94 cd/c; 467834-2/-4)*

Aug 84. (7") *(A 4572) <04505>* **MAMA WEER ALL CRAZEE NOW. / BAD BOY** [ ] [51] Jul84
(12"+=) *(TA 4572)* – Love's a bitch.

Oct 84. (7") *(A 4806)* **WINNERS TAKE ALL. / RED ALERT** [ ] [ ]

— (1985) **CHUCK WRIGHT** – bass (ex-GUIFFRIA) repl. SARZO to WHITESNAKE

Aug 86. (lp/c/cd) *(EPC/40/CD 26945) <40321>* **QR III** [ ] [31] Jul86
– Main attraction / The wild and the young / Twilight hotel / Down and dirty / Rise or fall / Put up or shut up / Still of the night / Bass case / The pump / Slave to love / Helping hands.

Sep 86. (7"/12") *(A/TA 7280) <06174>* **WILD AND THE YOUNG. / RISE OR FALL** [ ] [ ]

— **PAUL SHORTINO** (b.14 May'58) – vocals (ex-ROUGH CUTT) repl. DuBROW to LITTLE WOMEN / **SEAN McNABB** – bass repl. WRIGHT

Oct 88. (7") *<08096>* **STAY WITH ME TONIGHT. / CALLING THE SHOTS** [-] [ ]

Nov 88. (lp/c/cd) *(462896-2/-4/-1) <40981>* **QUIET RIOT** [ ] [ ]
– Stay with me tonight / Callin' the shots / Run to you / I'm fallin' / King of the hill / The joker / Lunar obsession / Don't wanna be your fool / Coppin' a feel / In a rush / Empty promises.

— Disbanded finally when SHORTINO joined MITCH PERRY. BANALI went on to WASP and later FASTER PUSSYCAT. In 1991, CAVAZO re-united with DuBROW in HEAT. They were now joined by KENNY HILARY – bass + **PAT ASHBY** – drums

not iss. | Moonstone

1993. (cd) *<28096-3102-2>* **TERRIFIED** [-] [ ]
– Cold day in Hell / Loaded gun / Itchycoo park / Terrified / Rude boy / Dirty lover / Psycho city / Rude, crude mood / Little angel / Resurrection.

not iss. | Kamikaze

Mar 95. (cd) *<1029>* **DOWN TO THE BONE** [-] [ ]
– Dig / Pretty pack o' lies / All day and all of the night / Whatever it takes / Wings of a cloud / Trouble again / Down to the bone / Voodoo brew / Monday morning breakdown / Live til it hurts / Twisted / All wound up / Hell or high water / Wings of a cloud (revisited).

— **DuBROW** and the mid-80's line-up were back

Axe Killer | Cleopatra

Apr 99. (cd) *(AXE 304932CD) <CLP 04892>* **ALIVE AND WELL** [ ] [ ] Aug99
– Don't know what I want / Angry / Alive and well / Ritual / Overworked and underpaid / Slam dunk (way to go) / Too much info / Against the wall / Highway to Hell / Sign of the times / Don't want to let you go / The wild and the young / Mama weer all crazee now / Cum on feel the noize / Metal health.

– compilations, others, etc. –

May 87. (lp/c) *Raw Power; (RAW LP/TC 033)* **WILD, YOUNG AND CRAZEE** [ ] [-]
– Metal health / Cum on feel the noize / Love's a bitch / Mama weer all crazee now / Winner takes all / Condition critical / Bad boy / Main attraction / Wild and the young / Put up or shut up / Slave to love / Let's get crazy.

Feb 94. (cd) *Atlantic; (812271445-2)* **THE RANDY RHOADS YEARS** [ ] [ ]

1996. (cd) *Sony;* **THE BEST OF QUIET RIOT** [-] [ ]

QUIREBOYS

Formed: Newcastle, England . . . 1987 initially as The QUEERBOYS by bassist/vocalist NIGEL MOGG (younger cousin of UFO's PHIL MOGG), the line-up also comprising frontman SPIKE GRAY, guitarists GUY BAILEY and GINGER, keyboard player CHRIS JOHNSTONE and drummer NICK 'COZY' CONNEL. The following year, the band substituted 'QUEER' with 'QUIRE' to remedy the homophobic violence that had marred their early shows. The QUIREBOYS were basically purveyors of unreconstructed bar-room blooze-rock and comparisons with The FACES were inevitible, SPIKE resembling ROD STEWART in both sound and image, if not quite managing to match his premier songwriting skills. Following two independently released singles on the indie label, 'Survival', the band signed to the 'Parlophone' label and dented the UK Top 40 in late '89 with the '7 O'CLOCK' track. Early the following year, the group hit the Top 20 with the 'HEY YOU' single, their debut album, 'A BIT OF WHAT YOU FANCY', reaching No.2 soon after. A swaggering collection of rootsy raunch-rock (other reference points were NAZARETH and The ROLLING STONES), for a time it looked as if the 'BOYS could mount a credible challenge to America's BLACK CROWES. It wasn't to be though, and after a further couple of minor hit singles, it was a further three years before any original material surfaced. When 'BITTER SWEET & TWISTED' (1993) was finally released, the momentum had been lost and the album met with minimal success. The QUIREBOYS split soon after, SPIKE forming GOD'S HOTEL while NIGEL MOGG formed the NANCY BOYS. It was erstwhile guitarist GINGER, however, who went on to notably bigger and better things with metal funsters The WILDHEARTS.
• **Songwriters:** GRAY / BAILEY penned except HEARTBREAKER (Rolling Stones) / HOLD ON, I'M COMING (Hayes-Porter) / BROTHER LOUIE (Hot Chocolate).

Album rating: A BIT OF WHAT YOU FANCY (*6) / LIVE AROUND THE WORLD (*5) / BITTER SWEET & TWISTED (*4) / FROM TOOTING TO BARKING compilation (*5)

SPIKE GRAY – vocals, acoustic guitar, mouth harp / **GUY BAILEY** – guitars, vocals / **NIGEL MOGG** – bass, vocals / **GINGER** – guitar / **CHRIS JOHNSTONE** – keyboards / **NICK 'COZY' CONNEL** – drums

Survival | not iss.

May 88. (7") *(SUR 043)* **MAYFAIR. / MISLED** [ ] [-]
(12"+=) *(SUR12 043)* – Man on the loose.

Oct 88. (7"pic-d/7") *(PD+/SUR 046)* **THERE SHE GOES AGAIN. / HOW DO YA FEEL** [ ] [-]
(12"+=) *(SURT 046)* – Sex party.

— guest **IAN WALLACE** – drums; repl. CONNEL

— **GUY GRIFFIN** – guitar; repl. GINGER

Parlophone | Capitol

Sep 89. (7"/7"pic-d/c-s) *(R/RPD/TCR 6230) <44513>* **7 O'CLOCK. / PRETTY GIRLS** [36] [ ] Jul90
(12"+=/cd-s+=) *(12R/CDR 6230)* – How do ya feel.

— **RUDY RICHMOND** – drums, percussion; repl. WALLACE

Jan 90. (c-s/7") *(TC+/R 6241)* **HEY YOU. / SEX PARTY** [14] [-]
(12"+=/cd-s+=) *(12R/CDR 6241)* – Hoochie coochie man.

Feb 90. (cd/c/lp) *(CD/TC+/R 7335)* **A BIT OF WHAT YOU FANCY** [2] [ ]
– 7 o'clock / Man on the loose / Whippin' boy / Sex party / Sweet Mary Ann / I don't love you anymore / Hey you / Misled / Long time comin' / Roses and rings / There she goes again / Take me home. *(re-iss. Mar94 cd/c; CD/TC+/PCSX 7335)*

Mar 90. (7"/7"g-f/7"sha-pic-d/c-s) *(R/RG/RPDE/TCR 6248)* **I DON'T LOVE YOU ANYMORE. / MAYFAIR (original)** [24] [-]
(12"+=/cd-s+=) *(12R/CDR 6248)* – Hey you (live).

Aug 90. (7"/7"sha-pic-d/c-s) *(R/RPD/TCR 6267)* **THERE SHE GOES AGAIN. / MISLED** [37] [-]
(12"+=) *(12R 6267)* – Heartbreaker (live).
(cd-s++=) *(CDR 6267)* – I don't love you anymore (live).

Dec 90. (cd/c/lp) *(CD/TC+/PRG 1002)* **LIVE AROUND THE WORLD (live)** [ ] [ ]
– Hey you / Sex party / Whippin' boy / Sweet Mary Ann / I don't love you anymore / Heartbreaker / Hold on I'm coming / There she goes again.

Oct 92. (7") *(RS 6323)* **TRAMPS AND THIEVES. / AIN'T LOVE BLIND** [41] [ ]
(12"+=) *(12RS 6323)* – Wild, wild, wild / Can't park here.
(cd-s+=) *(CDRS 6323)* – Wild, wild, wild / Pleasure and pain / Best jobs.
(cd-s+=) *(CDR 6323)* – Can't park here / Hold on, I'm comin' / Heartbreaker.

Feb 93. (c-s) *(TCR 6335)* **BROTHER LOUIE. / CAN'T GET THROUGH** [31] [ ]
(12"+=) *(12RP 6335)* – I don't love you anymore (live).
(cd-s++=) *(CDRS 6335)* – 7 o'clock (live).
(cd-s) *(CDR 6335)* – ('A'side) / Tramps and thieves (live) / Hey you (live) / Sweet Mary Ann (live).

Mar 93. (cd/c/lp) *(CD/TC+/PCSD 120)* **BITTER SWEET & TWISTED** [31] [ ]
– Tramps and thieves / White trash blues / Can't park here / King of New York / Don't bite the hand / Last time / Debbie / Brother Louie / Ode to you (baby just walk) / Hates to please / My Saint Jude / Takes no revenge / Wild, wild, wild / Ain't love blind. *(re-iss. Dec94 on 'Fame' cd/c; CDFA/TCFA 3307)*

— split in 1993

– compilations, etc. –

Sep 91. (m-cd) *Survival; (SURCD 014)* **MINI CD** (early material) ☐ -
Oct 94. (cd/c) *Essential; (ESS CD/MC 222)* **(UNDONE) FROM TOOTING TO BARKING** (early demos) ☐ -
(cd re-iss. Jul96; ESMCD 400)
Feb 97. (d-cd) *E.M.I.; (CTMCD 200)* **A BIT OF WHAT YOU FANCY / BITTER SWEET & TWISTED** ☐ -
Jun 00. (cd) *Snapper; (<SMACD 831>)* **LOST IN SPACE** ☐ ☐
– Don't bite the hand / White trash blues / Can't park here / Tramps and thieves / Misled / Sweet Maryanne / Take no revenge / Roses and rings / Buick McKane / Ode to you / King of New York / Hey you / My Saint Jude / Man on the loose / Whippin' boy / Sex party / Mayfair / Hates to please / Last times / 7 o'clock.

QUOTHORN (see under ⇒ BATHORY)

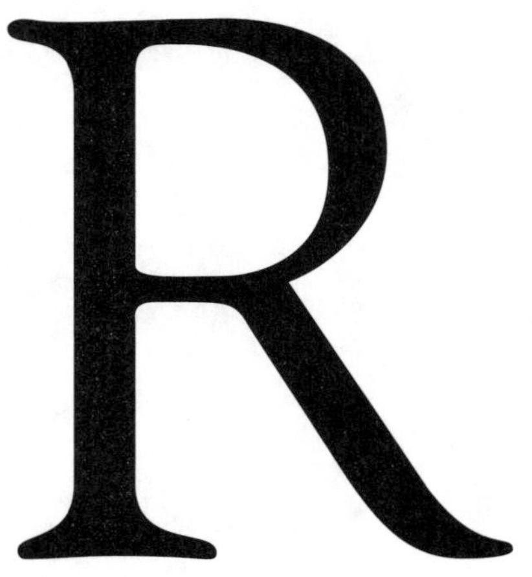

RACER X

Formed: Los Angeles, California, USA . . . mid 80's by JEFF MARTIN, PAUL GILBERT, JOHN ALDERETE and HARRY GSCHOESSER. A fertile seed-bed of future talent, RACER X roared on to the rock scene in 1986 with the gleaming precision metal of 'STREET LETHAL'. They subsequently boosted the line-up with second guitarist BRUCE BOUILLET, around the same time as replacing GSCHOESSER with drummer SCOTT TRAVIS, the newcomers playing on the 1987 follow-up, 'SECOND HEAT' (again on 'Roadrunner'). Once more, PAUL GILBERT was in the driving seat, showcasing his speed-freak axe runs throughout, even attempting a turbo-charged cover of Bowie's 'MOONAGE DAYDREAM'. The guitarist made his last stand on a disappointing live set, before teaming up with BILLY SHEEHAN in MR. BIG. TRAVIS also found some degree of fame, when he became part of JUDAS PRIEST and later FIGHT (with J.P. frontman, ROB HALFORD). Taking on JOHN CORABI and WALT WOODWARD III, the band evolved into SCREAM and after delivering only one album, 'LET IT SCREAM' (1991) they too hit the skids, largely due to CORABI being poached by MOTLEY CRUE. • **Covered:** HEART OF A LION (Judas Priest) / DETROIT ROCK CITY (Kiss).

Album rating: STREET LETHAL (*6) / SECOND HEAT (*7) / EXTREME VOLUME . . . LIVE (*3) / EXTREME VOLUME II – LIVE (*3) / TECHNICAL DIFFICULTIES (*5) / Scream: LET IT SCREAM (*5)

JEFF MARTIN – vocals (ex-SURGICAL STEEL) / **PAUL GILBERT** – guitar / **JOHN ALDERETE** – bass / **HARRY GSCHOESSER** – drums (ex-NOBROS)

Roadrunner Shrapnel

Sep 86. (lp) *(RR 9705) <SH 1023>* **STREET LETHAL**
– Frenzy / Street lethal / Into the night / Blowin' up the radio / Hotter than fire / On the loose / Loud and clear / Y.R.O. / Dangerous love / Getaway / Rock it. *(cd-iss. Mar90 on 'Roadracer'; RO 9705-2)*

— **SCOTT TRAVIS** – drums; repl. GSCHOESSER

— added **BRUCE BOUILLET** – guitar

Dec 87. (lp/cd) *(RR/+34 9601) <SH 1032>* **SECOND HEAT**
– Sacrifice / Gone too far / Scarified / Sunlit nights / Hammer away / Heart of a lion / Motor man / Moonage daydream / Living the hard way / Lady killer.

Nov 88. (lp/cd) *(RR 9530-1/-2) <SH 1038>* **EXTREME VOLUME . . . LIVE (live)**
– Loud and clear / Dangerous love / Bruce's solo / Gone too far / John's solo / She wants control / Scit scat wah / Into the night / Paul's solo / Motor man / Scott's solo / Set the world on fire.

— **CHRIS ARVAN** – guitar; repl. GILBERT who joined MR. BIG

— In 1990, they evolved with JOHN CORABI into SCREAM, when TRAVIS joined JUDAS PRIEST.

– compilations, etc. –

Jan 94. (cd) *Roadrunner; (RR 9142-2) / Shrapnel; <SH 1059>* **EXTREME VOLUME II – LIVE (live)** Dec92
– Hammer away / Poison eyes / Heart of a lion / Moonage daydream / Sunlight nights / Give it to me / On the loose / Rock it / Detroit rock city.

Apr 00. (cd) *Mascot; <M 7046CD>* **TECHNICAL DIFFICULTIES**
– Phallic tractor / Fire of rock / Snakebite / Technical difficulties / Miss mistreater / Bolt in my heart / 17th moon / Waiting / Poison eyes / B.R.O. / God of the sun / Give it to me / The executioner's song / Children of the grave.

SCREAM

CORABI, BOUILLET + ALDERETE plus **WALT WOODWARD III** – drums, percussion

Hollywood Hollywood

Oct 91. (7") *(HWD 112)* **MAN IN THE MOON. /**
(12"+=/cd-s+=) *(HWD 112 TX/CD)* –

Oct 91. (cd/c/lp) *(HWD CD/MC/LP 16) <60994>* **LET IT SCREAM**
– Outlaw / I believe in me / Man in the moon / Father, mother, son / Give it up / Never loved her anyway / Tell me why / Love's got a hold on me / I don't care / Every inch a woman / You are all I need / Catch me if you can.

— folded when CORABI was poached by MOTLEY CRUE to repl. VINCE NEIL. Found a new frontman, BILLY SCOTT, but a change of name to STASH and a different funkier outlook didn't help matters any

RACHEL STAMP

Formed: London, England . . . 1994 by DAVID RYDER-PRANGLEY and WILL CREWDSON after the pair met at a VANESSA PARADIS show . . . Swiftly snatche~~d up by 'Warners', RACHEL STAMP (also featuring SHAHEENA DAX and ROBIN GUY) recorded an experimental debut album which proved a little too adventurous for major label taste; they were unceremoniously relieved of their deal and the record was shelved. Down but not out, the 'STAMP erm, stuck to their guns and wowed the nation's smaller venues with their firtatious nu-glam stylings. A clutch of 7" singles, 'POP SINGER', 'HEY HEY MICHAEL YOU'RE REALLY FANTASTIC' and 'MADONNA . . . CHER . . .' appeared on 'Warners' although their scuzzy-rock task of ridding the world of dad-rock seems an unenviably impossible one. After a further series of unsuccessful singles, the album, 'HYMNS FOR STRANGE CHILDREN', finally surfaced in 2000.

Album rating: HYMNS FOR STRANGE CHILDREN (*6)

DAVID RYDER-PRANGLEY – vocals, bass / **WILL CREWDSON** – guitar / **SHAHEENA DAX** – keyboards / **ROBIN GUY** – drums

WEA WEA

Feb 96. (7") *(WEA 036)* **POP SINGER. /**
(cd-s+=) *(WEA 036CD)* –

Aug 96. (c-s) *(WEA 049C)* **HEY HEY MICHAEL YOU'RE REALLY FANTASTIC / SCIENCE FICTION**
(12"+=/cd-s+=) *(WEA 049 T/CD)* – N.A.U.S.E.A.

Nov 96. (c-s) *(WEA 086C)* **MADONNA . . . CHER . . . / TAMMY MACHINE**
(12"ep+=/cd-ep+=) **BRING ME THE HEAD OF RACHEL STAMP EP** *(WEA 086 T/CD)* – Every night I pray for the bomb / Christmas cardboard.

Bitch Vinyl not iss.

Dec 97. (7") **MY SWEET ROSE. / JE SUIS MAISEE** -
(cd-s+=) – I like girlz / True love.

Jun 98. (cd-ep) *(STAMP 005CD)* **I GOT THE WORM / QUEEN BEE / HEROINE**

Cruisin' Cruisin'

Sep 99. (cd-s) *(CRRS 001)* **SPANK / PINK SKAB / STEALING CLOTHES FROM SHELLEY**

Feb 00. (7") *(CRRS7 002)* **DIDN'T I BREAK MY HEART OVER YOU. / BLACK TAMBOURINE**
(cd-s+=) *(CRRS 002)* – Carmelita.

Feb 00. (cd) *(CRRS 003)* **HYMNS FOR STRANGE CHILDREN**
– Monsters of the new wave / Brand new toy / I got the worm / I wanna be your doll / Ladies and gents / Spank / Didn't I break my heart over you / Take a hold of yourself / Pink scab / Dirty bone / My sweet rose. *(cd re-iss. Oct00 +=; CRRS 003L)* – live:- Brand new toy / Dead girl / Tammy machine / True love / Madonna . . . Cher / Queen bee / Black tambourine / Feel like makin' love / I like girlz / Girl you're just a slave to your man / Hey hey Michael you're really fantastic / Je suis maisee / N.A.U.S.E.A.

May 00. (cd-s) *(CRRS 004)* **HEY HEY MICHAEL YOU'RE REALLY FANTASTIC / I GOT THE WORM / SPANK** -

Oct 00. (cd-s) *(CRRS 005)* **MONSTERS OF THE NEW WAVE / BLACK CHERRY (live) / PLEASE DON'T TOUCH (live)** -

RADIATOR

Formed: Bethnal Green, London, England . . . 1996 by the all-macho trio of JACK COOKE, JANNE JARVIS and CHRIS ROSE. Described as hard-thrusting rock (SABBATH-ish or PRODIGY, come to mind), the trio first came to light when they featured on the 'Gran Turisimo' film soundtrack. After a few singles on 'Chrysalis', hot property RADIATOR delivered their eponymous debut in April '99. Average reviews – depending on what paper you read – led to these retro-rockers cooling down somewhat.

Album rating: RADIATOR (*6)

JACK COOKE – vocals, guitar / **JANNE JARVIS** – bass, vocals / **CHRIS ROSE** – drums, vocals

Chrysalis not iss.

Mar 98. (7") **RESISTOR. / DARK SHOW** -
(cd-s+=) – Feel.

Jul 98. (7") *(CHS 5995)* **BLACK SHINE. / KEEP MY HEAD** -
(cd-s+=) *(CDCHS 5995)* – ('A'version).

Mar 99. (7") *(CHS 5106)* **MAKE IT REAL. / RESONATE** -
(cd-s+=) *(CDCHS 5106)* – A place for myself.
(cd-s) *(CDCHSS 5106)* – ('A'side) / Submission / There's a kind of hush.

Apr 99. (cd/c) *(4 99246-2/-4)* **RADIATOR** -
– I am / Black shine / Generator / Amnesia / Resistor / Untitled love song / Whole inside / Give / Make it real / Feel / Who is your God.

RAGE (see under ⇒ NUTZ)

RAGE

Formed: Germany . . . 1984 as AVENGER, by PETER 'PEAVEY' WAGNER, JOCHEN SCHROEDER, THOMAS GRUNING and JORG MICHAEL, although this group name was abandoned due to a UK band having claimed that moniker. Choosing RAGE (although another rock act from Britain had only recently ditched the name!), they signed to 'Noise' and initiated their speed-metal attack with 1986's 'REIGN OF FEAR'. Neither this set nor the following year's 'EXECUTION GUARANTEED', displayed much imagination, although 'PERFECT MAN' (1988) witnessed RAGE (PEAVEY being the sole remaining member from the original line-up) enjoying a degree of critical praise for their much-improved songwriting. Further releases such as 'SECRETS IN A WEIRD WORLD' (1989), 'REFLECTIONS OF A SHADOW' (1990), etc, refined the band's intricate thrash although they failed to excite audiences beyond their more tolerant homeland.

Album rating: PRAYERS OF STEEL by Avenger (*5) / REIGN OF FEAR (*6) / EXECUTION GUARANTEED (*5) / PERFECT MAN (*7) / SECRETS IN A WEIRD WORLD (*6) / REFLECTIONS OF A SHADOW (*6) / TRAPPED! (*5) / BEYOND THE WALL mini (*5) / THE MISSING LINK (*5) / TEN YEARS IN RAGE compilation (*6) / BLACK IN MIND (*4) / END OF ALL DAYS (*5) / XIII (*4) / GHOSTS (*4)

PETER 'PEAVEY' WAGNER – vocals, bass / **JOCHEN SCHROEDER** – guitar / **THE REAPER** – guitar / **JORG MICHAEL** – drums

Wishbone / not iss.

1984. (lp; as AVENGER) *(WBLP 4)* **PRAYERS OF STEEL** [-] [-] German
– Battlefield / Southcross union / Prayers of steel / Halloween / Faster than hell / Aboration / Rise of the creature / Sword made of steel / Blood lust / Assorted by Satan. *(cd-iss. 1995 on 'Gun'+=; 74321 18259-2)* – Depraved to black / Down to the bone / Prayers of steel / Faster than hell.

—— **THOMAS GRUNING** – guitar; repl. THE REAPER

Noise / not iss.

1986. (lp) *(N 0038)* **REIGN OF FEAR** [ ] [-]
– Scared to death / Deceiver / Reign of fear / Hand of glory / Raw energy / Echoes of evil / Chaste flesh / Suicide / Machinery. *(re-iss. Oct89 cd/lp; CD+/NUK 038)*

—— **RUDY GRAF** – guitar; repl. GRUNING

1987. (lp) *(N 0073)* **EXECUTION GUARANTEED** [ ] [-]
– Down by law / Execution guaranteed / Before the storm (the secret affair) / Streetwolf / Deadly error / Hatred / Grapes of wrath / Mental decay / When you're dead. *(re-iss. Oct89 cd/c/lp; CD/ZC+/NUK 073)*

—— **MANNI SCHMIDT** – guitar; repl. SCHROEDER

—— **CHRIS EFTHIMIADIS** – drums; repl. MICHAEL

May 88. (lp/c/cd) *(N 0112-1/-2/-3)* **PERFECT MAN** [ ] [-]
– Wasteland / In the darkest hour / Animal instinct / Perfect man / Sinister thinking / Supersonic hydromatic / Don't fear the winter / Death in the afternoon / A pilgrim's path / Time and place / Round trip / Between the lines. *(cd+=)* – Symbols of our fear / Neurotic.

Sep 89. (12"ep) *(N 0136)* **INVISIBLE HORIZONS. / LOST SIDE OF THE WORLD / LAW AND ORDER** [ ] [-]

Sep 89. (cd/c/lp) *(CD/ZC+/NUK 137)* **SECRETS IN A WEIRD WORLD** [ ] [-]
– Intro (opus 32 No.3) / Time waits for no one / Make my day / The inner search / Invisible horizons / She / Light into the darkness / Talk to grandpa / Distant voices / Without a trace / Lost side of the world.

Dec 90. (cd/c/lp) *(CD/ZC+/NUK 160)* **REFLECTIONS OF A SHADOW** [ ] [-]
– Introduction (A bit more green) / That's human bondage / True face in everyone / Flowers that fade in my hand / Reflections of a shadow / Can't get out / Waiting for the moon / Saddle the wind / Dust / Nobody knows. *(cd+=)* – Lost side of the world.

May 91. (m-cd/m-lp) *(N 0169-3/-5)* **EXTENDED POWER** [ ] [-]
– Woman / Ashes / Bottlefield / Waiting for the moon / What's up?

Apr 92. (cd/c/lp) *(N 0189-2/-4/-1)* **TRAPPED!** [ ] [-]
– Shame on you / Solitary man / Enough is enough / Medicine / Questions / Take me to the water / Power and greed / The body talks / Not forever / Beyond the wall of sleep / Baby, I'm your nightmare / Fast as a shark / Difference.

Nov 92. (m-cd) *(N 0202-3)* **BEYOND THE WALL** [ ] [-]
– Bury all life / On the edge / I want you / (Those who got) Nothing to lose / Last goodbye / Light into darkness (acoustic version).

Aug 93. (cd/lp) *(N 0217-2/-4/-1)* **THE MISSING LINK** [ ] [-]
– Firestorm / Nevermore / Refuge / The pit & the pendulum / From the underworld / Her diary's black pages / Certain days / Who dares? / Wake me when I'm dead / The missing link.

Sep 94. (cd) *(N 0291-2)* **TEN YEARS IN RAGE – THE ANNIVERSARY** (compilation) [ ] [ ]
– Vertigo / She killed and smiled / Destination day / Take my blood / No sign of life / Submission / The unknown / Dangerous heritage / Prayers of steel / The blow in a row.

Gun / Gun

May 95. (cd) *<(74321 27499-2)>* **BLACK IN MIND** [-] [ ] German
– Black in mind / The crawling chaos / Alive but dead / Sent by the Devil / Shadow out of time / A spider's web / In a nameless time / The icecold hand of destiny / Forever / Until I die / My rage / The price of war / Start! / Tie the rope / Forgive but don't forget / All this time.

May 96. (m-cd) *<6667-2>* **LINGUA MORTIS** [-] [ ]
– In a nameless time / Alive but dead / Medley / All this time / Alive but dead (instrumental orchestra version).

Oct 96. (cd) *(GUN 101CD) <99142>* **END OF ALL DAYS** [ ] [ ] Sep96
– Under control / Higher than the sky / Deep in the blackest hole / End of all days / Visions / Desperation / Voice from the vault / Let the night begin / Fortress / Frozen fire / Talking to the dead / Face behind the mask / Silent victory / Fading hours.

—— (next credited to RAGE & LINGUA MORTIS ORCHESTRA)

Apr 98. (cd) *(GUN 156CD)* **XIII** [ ] [-]
<US-iss.Dec99 on 'B.M.G.'; 52612>

Aug 98. (cd-ep) *(GUN 166CD1)* **IN VAIN (I WON'T GO DOWN) / TURN THE PAGE / INCOMPLETE / IMMORTAL SIN / YESTERDAY** [ ] [-]
(cd-ep) *(GUN 166CD2) (GUN 166CD3)* –

Oct 99. (cd) *(GUN 185CD)* **GHOSTS** [ ] [ ]
– Beginning of the end / Back in time / Ghosts / Wash my sins away / Fear / Love and fear unite / Vanished in haze / Spititual awakening / Love after death / More than a lifetime / Tomorrow's yesterday.

RAGE AGAINST THE MACHINE

Formed: Los Angeles, California, USA . . . 1992 by rapper/vocalist ZACK DE LA ROCHA and guitarist TOM MORELLO along with bassist TIMMY C and drummer BRAD WILK. Signed to 'Epic' partly on the strength of their infamous live reputation, the band divebombed their way into the UK charts after performing the incendiary 'KILLING IN THE NAME OF' on cult 'yoof' TV show (now sadly missed), 'The Word'. One of the most visceral, angry and overtly political records of the 90's, the song formed the centrepiece of their pivotal 1993 eponymous debut album. A revelatory hybrid of monster riffing and knotty hip hop rhythms, the album was venom-spewing and utterly defiant. While detractors argued that the band's position on the roster of a major corporation was untenable, RATM countered that they had to get their message across to as wide an audience as possible. The vital point was that this was one SERIOUSLY angry young man, raging against all kinds of injustice, mainly the ruling white American capitalist system. Most of the tracks (highlights being 'BOMBTRACK', BULLET IN THE HEAD' and 'KNOW YOUR ENEMY') were positively seething with anger but crucially, they were also funky as hell and this is where RATM scored over their square-jawed copyists. Music aside, how many bands in the 90's have had the balls to be openly political?, or rather, how many bands even know the meaning of protest? In a music world of drug-inspired vacancy, RATM provided a vital injection of reality. Putting their money where their mouth was, or rather putting their modesty thereabouts, the band walked on stage naked at a show in Philadelphia, the initials PMRC (Parent Music Resource Centre) scrawled across their respective chests in defiance of the risible censorship organisation. Political dissent was nothing new to either TOM or ZACK, MORELLO's father being a member of the Mau Mau's (Kenyan Guerrillas) who fought for an end to British colonialism while his uncle JOMO KENYATTA was imprisoned, later becoming the Kenyan president. LA ROCHA's father, meanwhile, was a noted L.A. muralist and political activist. While the band continued to stir up controversy with their live work (including a sold out 1993 UK tour and blinding set at the 1994 Glastonbury Festival), a follow-up album wasn't released until 1996. When it eventually surfaced, 'EVIL EMPIRE' was something of a disappointment, lacking the focus and some of the funkiness of the debut, although it did hit US No.1. The cover art too, lacked the impact of the first album (a powerful photo of a buddhist monk setting himself on fire in protest at the Vietnam war). Nevertheless, the group put in a brilliant performance at that year's Reading Festival, whipping the crowd into a frenzy and almost upstaging headliners, The PRODIGY. The impressively talented and ever inventive MORELLO subsequently hooked up with the Essex electro-punks on the acclaimed 'NO MAN ARMY' track. Three years in the making (as per usual), the third album, 'THE BATTLE OF LOS ANGELES' (1999), once again pulled no punches and deservedly topped the US chart (only Top 30 in Britain!). Tracks such as the single, 'GUERRILLA RADIO', 'MIC CHECK' and 'NEW MILLENNIUM HOMES', were certainly the highlights as the band undertook an extensive world tour.

Album rating: RAGE AGAINST THE MACHINE (*9) / EVIL EMPIRE (*7) / THE BATTLE OF LOS ANGELES (*7) / RENEGADES (*8)

ZACK DE LA ROCHA (b.1970, Long Beach, Calif.) – vocals / **TOM MORELLO** (b.1964, New York City, NY) – guitars / **TIMMY C.** (b. TIM COMMERFORD) – bass / **BRAD WILK** (b.1968, Portland, Oregon) – drums

Epic / Epic

Feb 93. (7"/12"white/cd-s) *(658492-7/-6/-2)* **KILLING IN THE NAME. / CLEAR THE LANE / DARKNESS OF GREED** [25] [-]

Feb 93. (cd/c/lp) *(472224-2/-4/-1) <52959>* **RAGE AGAINST THE MACHINE** [17] [45] Nov92
– Bombtrack / Killing in the name / Take the power back / Settle for nothing / Bullet in the head / Know your enemy / Wake up / Fistful of steel / Township rebellion / Freedom. *(lp re-iss. Feb99 on 'Simply Vinyl'; SVLP 69)*

Apr 93. (7") *(659258-7)* **BULLET IN THE HEAD. / BULLET IN THE HEAD (remix)** [16] [-]
(12"/cd-s) *(659258-6/-2)* – Bullet in the head / Settle for nothing.

Sep 93. (7") *(659471-7)* **BOMBTRACK. / ('A'mix)** [37] [-]
(12"+=/cd-s+=) *(659471-6/-2)* – ('A'version).

Feb 94. (cd-s; w-drawn) *(659821-2)* **FREEDOM** [-] [-]

Apr 96. (7"colrd/cd-s) *(663152-7/-2)* **BULLS ON PARADE. / HADDA BE PLAYING ON THE JUKEBOX** [8] [-]

Apr 96. (cd/c/lp) *(481026-2/-4/-1) <57523>* **EVIL EMPIRE** [4] [1]
– People of the sun / Bulls on parade / Vietnow / Revolver / Snakecharmer / Tire me / Down rodeo / Without a face / Wind below / Roll right / Year of tha boomerang.

Aug 96. (7"orange) *(663628-7)* **PEOPLE OF THE SUN. / ZAPATA'S BLOOD (live)** [26] [-]
(cd-s+=) *(663628-2)* – Without a face (live).
(cd-s) *(663628-5)* – ('A'side) / Killing in the name (live) / Bullet in the head (live).

—— TIMMY C. now as **Y.tim.K**

Oct 99. (7") *(668314-7) <79720>* **GUERRILLA RADIO. / THE GHOST OF TOM JOAD** [32] [69]
(cd-s+=) *(668314-2)* – No shelter.
(cd-s) *(668314-5)* – ('A'side) / F*** tha police (live) / Freedom (live).

Nov 99. (cd/c) *(491993-2/-4) <69630>* **THE BATTLE OF LOS ANGELES** [23] [1]
– Testify / Guerrilla radio / Calm like a bomb / Mic check / Sleep now in the fire / Born of a broken man / Born as ghosts / Maria / Voice of the voiceless / New millennium homes / Ashes in the fall / War within a breath.

Apr 00. (7"colrd) *(669136-7)* **SLEEP NOW IN THE FIRE. / ('A'live)** [43] [ ]
(cd-s) *(669136-2)* – ('A'side) / Bulls on parade (live) / ('A'-CD-Rom).
(cd-s) *(669136-5)* – ('A'side) / Guerilla radio (live) / Freedom (live).

Nov 00. (cd/c/lp) *(499921-2/-4/-1) <85289>* **RENEGADES** (covers) [71] [14]
– Microphone fiend / Pistol grip pump / Kick out the jams / Renegades of funk / Beautiful world / I'm housin' / In my eyes / How could I just kill a man / The ghost of

Tom Joad / Down on the street / Street fighting man / Maggie's farm. *(other cd+=; 499921-0/-9/-8/-7)* – Kick out the jams (live) / How could I just kill a man.

- compilations, etc. -

Apr 97. (10"ep) *Revelation; (REV 056)* **PEOPLE OF THE SUN (live) / WITHOUT A FACE (live) / INTRO BLACK STEEL IN THE HOUR OF CHAOS (live). / ZAPATA'S BLOOD (live) / BULLS ON PARADE / HADDA BE PLAYING ON THE JUKEBOX (live)** [ ] [-]

RAGING SLAB

Formed: New York, USA . . . 1983 by GREG STRZEMPKA and ELYSE STEINMAN, who, after some initial personnel changes, settled with the rhythm section of ALEC MORTON and TIM FINEFROCK (the latter drummer came in for KORY CLARKE – future WARRIOR SOUL and T.J. SCAGLIONE – ex-SLAYER). After two independently released sets, the wonderfully titled 'ASSMASTER' (1987) and 'TRUE DEATH' (1988), RAGING SLAB secured a deal with 'R.C.A.' and released the eponymous 'RAGING SLAB' in 1990. Torch bearers of the Southern Rock flag, the group brought the genre bang up to date with more than a little style and tongue-in-cheek humour. LYNYRD SKYNYRD meets METALLICA was a favoured critical description and wasn't too far off the mark, although RAGING SLAB had a raggey-assed funkiness not attributable to either of those bands. Despite favourable reviews, the record failed to sell and the group subsequently moved to what was surely their natural home, the retro-orientated 'Def American'. After finally settling on sticksman PAUL SHEENAN, they created their finest effort to date in 'DYNAMITE MONSTER BOOGIE CONCERT' (1993). A critical fave which further developed their metallic rootsiness, RAGING SLAB finally gained some belated recognition, a renewed interest in flare-rock (i.e. KYUSS, MONSTER MAGNET, etc.) certainly not doing the band any harm. However, STRZEMPKA and Co signed off after a dismal 4th full-set, 'SING MONKEY SING' (1996), their first and last for 'Warners'. Back from the grave, the 'SLAB rose once again to enjoy a little critical success with their country/Southern-fried piece of rock that was 'THE DEALER' album – eat your heart out SKYNYRD.

Album rating: ASSMASTER (*6) / TRUE DEATH mini (*5) / RAGING SLAB (*7) / DYNAMITE MONSTER BOOGIE CONCERT (*8) / SING MONKEY SING (*3) / THE DEALER (*7)

GREG STRZEMPKA – vocals, guitar / **ELYSE STEINMAN** – guitar / **ALEC MORTON** – bass / **TIM FINEFROCK** – drums

not iss. Buy Our..

Sep 88. (lp) <BOR 12-011> **ASSMASTER** [-] [ ]
– Feel too much / Bitch to kill / Mr. Lucky / Miracles / Rocks off is rocks off / Alpha jerk / King Pompadour / Shiny mama / The shield / Assmaster.

1989. (m-lp) <BOR 12-> **TRUE DEATH** [-] [ ]
– In contempt / Get off my jollies / Shrivel / Thunder chucker / I heard the owl.

—— **BOB PANTELLA** – drums; repl. TIM / added **MARK MIDDLETON** – guitar

R.C.A. R.C.A.

Feb 90. (cd/c/lp) *(PD/PK/PL 90396)* <9680> **RAGING SLAB** [ ] [ ] Nov89
– Don't dog me / Jaynde / Sorry's all I got / Waiting for the potion / Get off the jollies / Shiny mama / Geronimo / Bent for silver / When love comes loose / Dig a hole / San Loco. *(cd re-iss. Nov00 on 'Axe Killer'; AXE 306238CD)*

—— **PAUL SHEENAN** – drums; repl. PANTELLA

American Def American

May 94. (cd-s) *(858 437-2)* **TAKE A HOLD / MOVE THAT THANG / WEATHERMAN** [ ] [ ]

Jun 95. (cd) *<(74321 28759-2)>* **DYNAMITE MONSTER BOOGIE CONCERT** [ ] [ ] Apr93
– Anywhere but her / Weatherman / Pearly / So help me / What have you done? / Take a hold / Laughin' and cryin' / Don't worry about the bomb / Lynne / Lord have mercy / National dust / Ain't ugly none.

not iss. Warners

Sep 96. (cd) *<43079>* **SING MONKEY SING** [-] [ ]
– Should'a known / Econoliner / Never comin' down / Nobodies / Lay down / Gracious / C'mon 'n' on / She like ta / Better / Wrong / Gravity / Checkyrd demon / Skull's ending: The beginning – Slab song.

—— the group split after above . . . re-formed below

Tee-Pee Tee-Pee

Feb 01. (cd/lp) *<(TP 029 CD/LP)>* **THE DEALER** [ ] [ ] Jan01
– Here lies / Sir Lord Ford – When electricity came to town / Double wind / Real good time / Too bad / Chasin' the dragon / Flap your boogie flap / That's alright / The ballad of Truly Mae / Bite the lightning / I don't know you / Roadless rider / (What I) See through you / I saw the light / That ain't what I meant / Good mornin' lil' schoolboy.

RAGING SPEEDHORN

Formed: Corby, Northamptonshire, England . . . late 1998 by brothers TONY and JOHN LOUGHLIN alongside FRANK REGAN, GARETH SMITH, DARREN SMITH and GORDON MORISON. While the definition of a RAGING SPEEDHORN – you won't find it in the dictionary, kids – is open to dubious question, the (actually quite hilarious) moniker describes their BLACK SABBATH meets NAPALM DEATH headf**ck fairly well. Bearing titles such as 'RANDOM ACTS OF VIOLENCE', 'NECROPHILIAC GLUE SNIFFER' and 'HIGH WHORE', their 2000 eponymous debut album suggested that these lads weren't exactly contented with their lot. Which is just as well given that the SPEEDHORN crew have been touted as Brit-metal's trump card in breaking the current vice-like grip of US noisemongers on the devil's most fearsome tunes. Having toured with the likes of BIOHAZARD and MINISTRY, Corby's sonic shock troops were subsequently snapped up by 'Epic' Japan where they played a series of gigs alongside AMEN. With high profile support slots coming thick and fast and a new single, 'THE GUSH', released in June 2001, RAGING SPEEDHORN don't look like calming it down anytime soon.

Album rating: RAGING SPEEDHORN (*6)

FRANK REGAN – vocals / **JOHN LOUGHLIN** – vocals / **TONY LOUGHLIN** – guitar / **GARETH SMITH** – guitar / **DARREN SMITH** – bass / **GORDON MORISON** – drums

Green Island not iss.

Aug 00. (cd) *(GIR 003)* **RAGING SPEEDHORN** [ ] [-]
– Superscud / Redweed / Knives and faces / Mandan / Random acts of violence / Thumper / Necrophiliac glue sniffer / Dungeon whippet / Death row dogs / High whore. *(lp-iss.Apr01; GIR 003LP) (re-iss. Jun01; GIR 003X)*

Jun 01. (cd-s) *(GIR 004)* **THE GUSH / THUMPER (video) / HIGH WHORE (live) / THE GUSH (video)** [47] [-]
(cd-s) *(GIRX 004)* – ('A'extended) / Mandan (live) / Dungeon whippet (live).

RAINBOW

Formed: 1975 . . . by former DEEP PURPLE guitar guru, RITCHIE BLACKMORE. Recruiting New York band ELF wholesale, including the esteemed metal warbler RONNIE JAMES DIO, BLACKMORE recorded the eponymous debut album ('RITCHIE BLACKMORE'S RAINBOW') in the summer of '75. While 'PURPLE lumbered towards imminent implosion, BLACKMORE took the Brontosaurus-rock blueprint to mystical new heights, the classic 'MAN ON THE SILVER MOUNTAIN' being the prime example. By the release of the seminal 'RAINBOW RISING' (1976), the ubiquitous COZY POWELL was on the drum stool. The record (released under the slightly clipped moniker of BLACKMORE'S RAINBOW) featured such enduring BLACKMORE stage favourites as 'TAROT WOMAN', 'STARGAZER' and 'A LIGHT IN THE BLACK', arguably the most cohesive set of the guitarist's career. After a live album, more line-up changes ensued, BOB DAISLEY finally stepping in for MARK CLARKE, who had temporarily replaced BAIN (DAVID STONE was now the new keyboard man in place of TONY CAREY). Although 'LONG LIVE ROCK'N'ROLL' (1978) was another hard-rock classic, it wasn't until DIO had departed for BLACK SABBATH that the band enjoyed their greatest success. Recruiting ex-MARBLES vocalist, GRAHAM BONNET, as a replacement, and surprisingly enlisting old 'PURPLE mucker ROGER GLOVER on bass, the band hit the UK Top 10 twice in a row at the turn of the decade with 'SINCE YOU BEEN GONE' and 'ALL NIGHT LONG'. Watertight, marvellously crafted melodic rock, both songs featured on the 'DOWN TO EARTH' (1979) album. POWELL left the following year, as did BONNET, BLACKMORE recruiting JOE LYNN TURNER as frontman. Their next single, 'I SURRENDER', was their biggest hit to date, an epic slice of American-influenced rock that stands among metal's greatest moments. The album, 'DIFFICULT TO CURE' (1981) made the UK Top 5 although it was clear RAINBOW had adopted a more commercial approach in an attempt to break America, subsequent efforts failing to make much impact, however. With no pot of gold at the end of this particular rainbow, BLACKMORE eventually folded the band in 1984, with plans to resurrect the classic Mk.II DEEP PURPLE line-up. Ten years on, BLACKMORE (again leaving 'PURPLE) resurrected another version of RAINBOW, a 1995 album, 'STRANGER IN US ALL', purely for BLACKMORE diehards. The veteran guitarist took a radically different tack on 'SHADOW OF THE MOON' (1998), the first recorded fruits of his collaboration with musical partner/fiancee, CANDICE NIGHT. Released under the moniker of BLACKMORE'S NIGHT (apparently not an awful pun on the old DP chestnut but a reference to the happy couple . . .), the album found RITCHIE and his young vocalist exploring Renaissance-era music via elements of new age, world, rock and folk. Such distinctly un-rock'n'roll instrumentation as pennywhistle, hurdy gurdy and mandolin contributed to the ambience while IAN ANDERSON even made an appearance with a blast of his trademark flute. Written with the anticipation of a full stage tour, 'UNDER A VIOLET MOON' (1999) was similar if less restrained, BLACKMORE again demonstrating his mastery of the acoustic guitar.

Album rating: RITCHIE BLACKMORE'S RAINBOW (*6) / RAINBOW RISING (*8) / LIVE ON STAGE (*4) / LONG LIVE ROCK'N'ROLL (*6) / DOWN TO EARTH (*6) / DIFFICULT TO CURE (*5) / THE BEST OF RAINBOW compilation (*7) / STRAIGHT BETWEEN THE EYES (*5) / BENT OUT OF SHAPE (*4) / FINAL VINYL (*4) / STRANGER IN US ALL (*4) / THE VERY BEST OF RAINBOW compilation (*6) / Blackmore's Night: SHADOW OF THE MOON (*4) / UNDER A VIOLET MOON (*4)

RITCHIE BLACKMORE'S RAINBOW

RITCHIE BLACKMORE (b.14 Apr'45, Weston-Super-Mare, England) – guitar with (ex-ELF) men **RONNIE JAMES DIO** – vocals / **MICKEY LEE SOULE** – keyboards / **CRAIG GRUBER** – bass / **GARY DRISCOLL** – drums

Oyster Oyster

Aug 75. (lp/c) *(OYA 2001)* <6049> **RITCHIE BLACKMORE'S RAINBOW** [11] [30]
– Man on the silver mountain / Self portrait / Black sheep of the family / Catch the rainbow / Snake charmer / Temple of the king / If you don't like rock'n'roll /

Sixteenth century Greensleeves / Still I'm sad. *(re-iss. Aug81 on 'Polydor; 2490 141) (re-iss. Aug83 on 'Polydor' lp/c; SPE LP/MC 7) (cd-iss. 1988 & Jan93 on 'Polydor'; 825089-2) (cd re-iss. Jun99; 547360-2)*

Oct 75. (7") *(OYR 103) <14290>* **MAN ON THE SILVER MOUNTAIN. / SNAKE CHARMER**

— RITCHIE only retained **DIO,** recruiting new members **TONY CAREY** – keyboards / **JIMMY BAIN** – bass / **COZY POWELL** – drums

Polydor Oyster

May 76. (lp/c; as BLACKMORE'S RAINBOW) *(2490 137) <1601>* **RAINBOW RISING** 11 48
– Tarot woman / Run with the wolf / Starstruck / Do you close your eyes / Stargazer / A light in the black. *(re-iss. Aug83 lp/c; SPE LP/MC 35) (cd-iss. Nov86; 823089-2) (cd re-iss. Jun99; 547361-2)*

RAINBOW

Jul 77. (d-lp) *(2657 016) <1801>* **RAINBOW ON STAGE (live)** 7 65
– Kill the king: (a) Man on a silver mountain, (b) Blues, (c) Starstruck / Catch the rainbow / Mistreated / Sixteenth century Greensleeves / Still I'm sad. *(re-iss. Jan84; SPDLP 6) (cd-iss. Nov86; 823656-2)*

Aug 77. (7") *(2066 845)* **KILL THE KING: MAN ON THE SILVER MOUNTAIN. / MISTREATED** 44 -
(re-iss. Jul81; same) ; reached UK No.41

— **MARK CLARKE** – bass (ex-COLOSSEUM, ex-URIAH HEEP) repl. BAIN who joined WILD HORSES / **BOB DAISLEY** – bass (ex-WIDOWMAKER, ex-CHICKEN SHACK) repl. CLARKE / **DAVID STONE** – keyboards (ex-SYMPHONIC SLAM) repl. CAREY

Polydor Polydor

Mar 78. (7") *(2066 913) <14481>* **LONG LIVE ROCK'N'ROLL. / SENSITIVE TO LIGHT** 33
(re-iss. Jul81; same)

Apr 78. (lp/c) *(POLD/+C 5002) <6143>* **LONG LIVE ROCK'N'ROLL** 7 89
– Long live rock'n'roll / Lady of the lake / L.A. connection / Gates of Babylon / Kill the king / The shed (subtle) / Sensitive to light / Rainbow eyes. *(re-iss. Aug83 lp/c; SPE LP/MC 34) (cd-iss. Jan93; 825090-2) (cd re-iss. Jun99; 547363-2)*

Sep 78. (7"red) *(2066 968)* **L.A. CONNECTION. / LADY OF THE LAKE** 40 -
(re-iss. 7"black Jul81; same)

— **BLACKMORE** retained only **COZY POWELL / GRAHAM BONNET** – vocals (ex-Solo artist, ex-MARBLES) repl. DIO who went solo / **ROGER GLOVER** – bass, vocals (ex-DEEP PURPLE) repl. DAISLEY / **DON AIREY** – keyboards repl. STONE

Aug 79. (clear-lp/c) *(POLD/+C 5023) <6221>* **DOWN TO EARTH** 6 66
– All night long / Eyes of the world / No time to lose / Makin' love / Since you been gone / Love's no friend / Danger zone / Lost in Hollywood. *(re-iss. Apr84 lp/c; SPE LP/MC 69) (cd-iss. Dec86; 823705-2) (cd re-iss. Jun99; 547364-2)*

Aug 79. (7") *(POSP 70) <2014>* **SINCE YOU BEEN GONE. / BAD GIRLS** 6 57 Oct79
(re-iss. Jul81; same)

Feb 80. (7") *(POSP 104) <2060>* **ALL NIGHT LONG. / WEISS HEIM** 5
(re-iss. Jul81; same)

— **JOE LYNN TURNER** – vocals, repl. BONNET who continued solo career. / **BOBBY RONDINELLI** – drums repl. POWELL who later joined E.L.P.

Jan 81. (7") *(POSP 221)* **I SURRENDER. / MAYBE NEXT TIME** 3 -
(re-iss. Jul81; same)

Feb 81. (lp/c) *(POLD/+C 5036) <6316>* **DIFFICULT TO CURE** 3 50
– I surrender / Spotlight kid / No release / Vielleicht das nachster zeit (Maybe next time) / Can't happen here / Freedom fighter / Midtown tunnel vision / Difficult to cure. *(re-iss. Aug84 lp/c)(cd; SPE LP/MC 76)(800-018-2) (cd re-iss. Jun99; 547365-2)*

Jun 81. (7") *(POSP 251)* **CAN'T HAPPEN HERE. / JEALOUS LOVER** 20 -

Nov 81. (m-lp) *<502>* **JEALOUS LOVER** -
– Jealous lover / Can't happen here / I surrender / Weiss Helm.

— **DAVE ROSENTHAL** – keyboards; repl. AIREY who joined OZZY OSBOURNE

Polydor Mercury

Mar 82. (7"blue/ext-12"blue) *(POSP/+X 421) <76146>* **STONE COLD. / ROCK FEVER** 34 40

Apr 82. (lp/c) *(POLD/+C 5056) <4041>* **STRAIGHT BETWEEN THE EYES** 5 30
– Death alley driver / Stone cold / Bring on the night (dream chaser) / Tite squeeze / Tearin' out my heart / Power / Miss Mistreated / Rock fever / Eyes of fire. *(cd-iss. Nov83; 800-028-2) (cd re-iss. Apr94; 521709-2) (cd re-iss. Jun99; 547366-2)*

— **BLACKMORE** still had in his ranks **GLOVER, TURNER, ROSENTHAL, /** and **CHUCK BURGI** – drums (ex-BRAND X) repl. RONDINELLI

Aug 83. (7"/7"pic-d) *(POSP/+P 631) <815660>* **STREET OF DREAMS. / IS ANYBODY THERE** 52 60
(12"+=) *(POSPX 631)* – Power (live).

Sep 83. (lp/c)(cd) *(POLD/+C 5116)(<815-305-2>)* **BENT OUT OF SHAPE** 11 34
– Stranded / Can't let you go / Fool for the night / Fire dance / Anybody there / Desperate heart / Street of dreams / Drinking with the devil / Snowman / Make your move. *(cd re-iss. Jun99; 547367-2)*

Oct 83. (7"/7"sha-pic-d) *(POSP/+P 654)* **CAN'T LET YOU GO. / ALL NIGHT LONG (live)** 43
(12"+=) *(POSPX 654)* – Stranded (live).

— Split late '83 . . . BLACKMORE and GLOVER reformed DEEP PURPLE

RITCHIE BLACKMORE'S RAINBOW

— re-formed for comeback concerts & an album. His new band:- **DOOGIE WHITE** – vocals / **PAUL MORRIS** – keyboards / **GREG SMITH** – bass / **JOHN O'REILLY** – drums

Arista Arista

Sep 95. (cd/c) *(74321 30337-2/-4)* **STRANGER IN US ALL**
– Wolf to the Moon / Cold hearted woman / Hunting humans (insatiable) / Stand and fight / Ariel / Too late for tears / Black masquerade / Silence / Hall of the mountain king / Still I'm sad.

– compilations, etc. –

Sep 78. (d-lp) *Polydor; (268 3078)* **RITCHIE BLACKMORE'S RAINBOW / RAINBOW RISING** -

Nov 81. (d-lp/d-c) *Polydor; (POLDV/PODVC 2)* **THE BEST OF RAINBOW** 14
– All night long / Man on the silver mountain / Can't happen here / Lost in Hollywood / Since you been gone / Stargazer / Catch the rainbow / Kill the king / 16th century Greensleeves / I surrender / Long live rock'n'roll / Eyes of the world / Starstruck / A light in the black / Mistreated. *(cd-iss. 1983; 800-074-2)*

Feb 83. (d-c) *Polydor; (3574 141)* **DOWN TO EARTH / DIFFICULT TO CURE** -

Feb 86. (d-lp/d-c)(d-cd) *Polydor; (PODV/+C 8)(<827-987-2>)* **FINYL VINYL** (live 80's material) 87
– Spotlight kid / I surrender / Miss mistreated / Jealous lover / Can't happen here / Tearin' out my heart / Since you been gone / Bad girl / Difficult to cure / Stone cold / Power / Man on the silver mountain / Long live rock'n'roll / Weiss heim. *(d-cd re-iss. Jun99; 547368-2)*

Feb 88. (7") *Old Gold; (OG 9772)* **SINCE YOU BEEN GONE. / ALL NIGHT LONG** -

Oct 89. (d-lp/c/cd) *Connoisseur; (RPVSOP LP/MC/CD 143)* **ROCK PROFILE VOL.1** -
(above credited to RITCHIE BLACKMORE contains early sessions and PURPLE work) (cd.omits interview tracks + 1 song)

Dec 90. (d-cd/c/d-lp) *Connoisseur; (DPVSOP CD/MC/LP 155)* **LIVE IN GERMANY 1976 (live)** -

Jul 91. (cd/d-lp) *Connoisseur; (RPVSOP CD/LP 157)* **ROCK PROFILE VOLUME 2** -
(above also credited to RITCHIE BLACKMORE cont. RAINBOW material, etc.)

Jun 93. (cd-s) *Old Gold; (OG)* **I SURRENDER / SINCE YOU BEEN GONE / ALL NIGHT LONG** -

Jan 94. (cd) *R.P.M.; (RPM 120)* **SESSION MAN** -

Jun 94. (cd) *R.P.M.; (PRM)* **TAKE IT! – SESSIONS 63-68** -

Aug 97. (cd) *Polydor; (537687-2)* **THE VERY BEST OF RAINBOW**

BLACKMORE'S NIGHT

RITCHIE with **CANDICE NIGHT** (b. 8 May'71, Hauppauge, Long Island, New York) – vocals / **LADY GREEN** – violin / etc

Edel Edeltone

Oct 97. (cd) *(0099022WHE) <3755>* **SHADOW OF THE MOON** Feb98
– Shadow of the Moon / The clock ticks on / Be mine tonight / Play minstrel play / Ocean gypsy / Minstrel hall / Magical world / Writing on the wall / Renaissance faire / Memmingen / No second chance / Mond tanz / Spirit of the sea / Greensleeves / Wish you were here. *(re-iss. May98 on 'H.T.D.'; HTDCD 84) (cd re-iss. May00 on 'Candlelight'; LIGHTCD 1)*

— added **JOHN FORD** – bass / **KEVIN DUNNE** – drums / **JENS JOHANSSON** – keyboards / etc.

Pony Canyon Intersound

Jun 99. (cd) *(PCCY 01377) <3741>* **UNDER A VIOLET MOON** Jul99
– Under a violet moon / Castles and dreams / Past time with good company / Morning star / Avalon / Possum goes to Prague / Wind in the willows / Gone with the wind / Beyond the sunset / March the heroes home / Spanish nights (I remember it well) / Catherine Howard's fate / Durch den wald zum balch haus / Fool's gold / Now and then / Self portrait.

RAISM (see under ⇒ IMPALED NAZARENE)

RAM JAM

Formed: East Coast, USA . . . 1976 by BILL BARTLETT, former member of late 60's pop/psychedelia group The LEMON PIPERS. He had come out of early 70's retirement to put down a demo of LEADBELLY's 'BLACK BETTY'. In the summer of '77, the single smashed into the US Top 20, subsequently hitting the UK Top 10 and becoming a classic rock anthem in the process, despite having to compete with the emergence of punk rock. However, further output fell on deaf ears commercially and by the following year, RAM JAM were certified one-hit wonders. The story didn't quite end there though, as the track underwent the inevitable 90's remix treatment, zooming back into UK Top 20 at the turn of the decade.

Album rating: RAM JAM (*5) / PORTRAIT OF THE ARTIST AS A YOUNG RAM (*4)

MIKE SCAVONE – vocals, percussion / **BILL BARTLETT** (b.1949) – guitar, vocals (ex-LEMON PIPERS) / **HOWIE ARTHUR BLAUVELT** – bass, vocals (ex-HASSLES; Billy Joel's late 60's group) / **PETER CHARLES** – drums

Epic Epic

Jul 77. (7") *(EPC 5492) <50357>* **BLACK BETTY. / I SHOULD HAVE KNOWN** 7 18 May77

Oct 77. (lp) *(82215) <34885>* **RAM JAM** 34
– Black Betty / Let it all out / Keep your hands on the wheel / Right on the money / All for the love of rock'n'roll / 404 / High steppin' / Overloaded / Hey boogie woman / Too bad on your birthday.

Nov 77. (7") *(EPC 5806) <50451>* **KEEP YOUR HANDS ON THE WHEEL. / RIGHT ON THE MONEY**

— added **JIMMY SANTORO** – guitar

1978. (lp) *<35287>* **PORTRAIT OF THE ARTIST AS A YOUNG RAM** -
– Gone wild / Pretty poison / The kid next door / Turnpike / Wanna find love / Just like me / Hurricane ride / Saturday night / Runaway runaway / Please, please, please. *<US cd-iss. 1990; 463299-2>*

1978. (7") *<50587>* **PRETTY POISON. / RUNAWAY RUNAWAY** -

— Disbanded after above and once more disappeared. HOWIE died of a heart attack on the 25th October '93.

– compilations, etc. –

Date	Release	UK	US
Jul 82.	(7") *Old Gold; (OG 9193)* **BLACK BETTY. / (other artist)**		-
Jul 84.	(7") *C.B.S.; (A 4585)* **BLACK BETTY. / KEEP YOUR HANDS ON THE WHEEL**		-
Jan 90.	(7"/c-s) *Epic; (655430-7/-4)* **BLACK BETTY (rough'n'ready remix). / ('A'-original mix)** (12"+=/cd-s+=) *(655430-6/-2)* – ('A'-Rough'n'ready edit).	13	

RAMMSTEIN

Formed: Germany . . . 1994 by former East German Olympic swimmer, TILL LINDEMANN, plus his 30-something long-time companions, OLIVER RIEDEL, RICHARD KRUSPE, FLAKE, PAUL LANDERS and CHRISTOPH SCHEIDER. Naming themselves after the German airbase at Rammstein (originally went by the name of ORGASM DEATH GIMMICK), the industrial shock metallers, like a fusion of LAIBACH, MINISTRY and fellow countrymen, EINSTURZENDE NEUBAUTEN, RAMMSTEIN had five hit singles in their home country. This was due to their OTT stage extravaganzas which featured TILL singing (in his native tongue) covered in a metallic coat of fire before he unveiled to show off his muscular, naked body complete with very large dildo strapped upside his leather belt!. Meanwhile, the naked OLIVER (bar his white socks), RICHARD (wearing a white wedding dress) and the rest of the bare-cheeked crew played their aggro-rock to a backdrop of Leni Riefenstahl's (Hitler's fave!) controversial film, 'Olympiad'. A German-only released debut album was finally upstaged by a second, 'SEHNSUCHT' (1997), which went on to surprisingly sell over half a million copies in the States. In the Autumn of '98, RAMMSTEIN were at the centre of some accusations of neo Nazi-ism when English tabloids branded them with that unfortunate tag. Around the same time, the single 'DU HAST' (actually a cover of Depeche Mode's 'STRIPPED') was given a British release and it looked as if these brassnecked technoid show-offs were going to eventually invade our shores. RAMMSTEIN's long-awaited sophomore album, 'MUTTER', was unleashed to the public in Spring 2001, the broody ensemble were now on their way to becoming Germany's best export since SCHENKER and The SCORPIONS.

Album rating: SEHNSUCHT (*7) / MUTTER (*7)

TILL LINDEMANN – vocas / **RICHARD KRUSPE** – guitar / **PAUL LANDERS** – guitar / **OLIVER RIEDEL** – bass / **FLAKE** – keyboards / **CHRISTOPH SCHNEIDER** – drums

		London	Motor – Slash
Nov 97.	(cd) *(537304-2) <539901>* **SEHNSUCHT** – Sehnsucht / Engel / Tier / Bestrafe mich / Du hast / Buck dich / Spiel mit mir / Klavier / Alter Mann / Eifersucht / Kuss mich (fellfrosch) / Engel / Du hast. *(re-iss. Mar99 on 'XIII Bis'; 18795-2)*		45 Jan98
Nov 98.	(cd-s) *(LONCD 422)* **DU HAST / (Jacob Hellner remix) / (Clawfinger remix)**		
		Universal	Universal
Apr 01.	(cd) *<(549639-2)>* **MUTTER** – Mein herz brennt / Links 2 3 4 / Sonne / Ich will / Feuer frei! / Mutter / Spielurhr / Zwitter / Rein raus / Adios / Nebel.		77

RAMONES

Formed: Forest Hills, New York, USA . . . August'74 as a trio by JOHNNY, JOEY and DEE DEE, who all took the working surname RAMONE (although they were brothers only in the loosest sense of the term). One of the prime movers (many would subsequently cite them as the first) in the emergent US punk scene, the band began a residency at the legendary NY club, CBGB's, TOMMY coming in on the drum stool in order to free JOEY up for suitably deranged vocal duties. In June '75, the band were dealt a slight setback when they failed an audition for RICK DERRINGER's 'Blue Sky' label in front of 20,000 fans at a JOHNNY WINTER concert, although later that year manager, Danny Fields, found up and coming new wave label, 'Sire' (run by Seymour Stein) considerably more receptive. Released around the same time as their pivotal (and highly influential) London Roundhouse gig, the band's eponymous summer '76 debut album presented a sound every bit as exhilaratingly juvenile and humorously warped as their leering, mop-topped scruffiness might suggest. Ripping out gloriusly dumb, two-minute buzz-saw classics on such perennial punk subjects as solvent abuse ('I WANNA SNIFF SOME GLUE'), girls (most of the album) and erm, chainsaws ('CHAIN SAW'), The RAMONES had invented themselves as larger than life, cartoon yob no-wavers well ahead of their time, their attitude alone copied by countless two-bit punk bands (and a few great ones) the length and breadth of the British Isles. Barely pausing for breath (or whatever it was these guys inhaled), the new yoik brudders followed up with 'LEAVE HOME' (1977), another strychnine-fuelled session of primitive but tuneful terrace chant anthems, RAMONES style; from this point onwards, the words 'Gabba Gabba Hey' would be forever carved in the stone of the punk lexicon. The album even managed a minor dent in the UK charts, a full scale assault led later that year with the brilliantly throwaway 'SHEENA IS A PUNK ROCKER'. The climax of the early RAMONES blitzkrieg came with 'ROCKET TO RUSSIA' (1977), the lads easing ever so slightly off the gas pedal and taking the credo of mangled, two minute surf-pop to its dayglo conclusion; the hilarious 'CRETIN HOP', 'ROCKAWAY BEACH' and 'TEENAGE LOBOTOMY' remain among the most definitive moments in the RAMONES' dog-eared catalogue. A rather disappointing Top 60 placing failed to do the record justice, although by this stage the band were beginning to make some inroads into the home market. Further evidence, if any was needed, that The RAMONES' chief writer was at the peak of his powers came with the blistering 'Chinese Rocks', a HEARTBREAKERS track co-penned by DEE DEE. With the departure of TOMMY (into production work) the following year, ex-VOID-OID MARC BELL was recruited in his place, rechristened, of course, MARKY RAMONE. Incredibly, the tried and tested formula (with a few notable exceptions, a guitar solo (!) on 'GO MENTAL' and a ballad, 'QUESTIONINGLY') continued to excite with 'ROAD TO RUIN' (1978), their first album to break into the UK Top 40 and the resting place of the legendary 'I WANNA BE SEDATED'. The riotous 'IT'S ALIVE' (1979) captured the RAMONES concert experience head-on, neatly wrapping up the first stage of the boys' career and providing a handy overview of their career to date. Every punk band coped with the scene's fragmentation in their own way, The RAMONES not so wisely choosing to indulge their love of classic 60's pop via the genre's guru, Phil Spector. The results were predictably confused, many longtime RAMONES headbangers balking at their UK Top 10 cover of The Ronettes' 'BABY I LOVE YOU'. Subsequent 80's efforts such as 'PLEASANT DREAMS' (1981) and 'SUBTERRANEAN JUNGLE' (1983) lacked the ragged glory of their earlier work although with the replacement of MARKY with RICHIE (aka RICHARD REINHARDT) in 1984, 'TOO TOUGH TO DIE' (1985) found the band sharpening their attack and presenting a united front against the hardcore pretenders of the day. They couldn't keep it up though, and the limitations of their art really began to bite deep on the bedraggled 'ANIMAL BOY' (1986) and 'HALFWAY TO SANITY' (1987). DEE DEE bailed out after 'BRAIN DRAIN' (1989), replacement C.J. effecting something of a rejuvenation on 'MONDO BIZARRO' (1992). The following year's 'ACID EATERS' saw the band pay tribute to the 60's sounds which had inspired them, while in turn, many of the younger bands who had actually been inspired by The RAMONES would soon be calling the shots at America's major labels. Yet despite this punk revival and the success of such acts as GREEN DAY and OFFSPRING, The RAMONES finally decided to call it a day in early 1996 following the release of the 'ADIOS AMIGOS' set and the accompanying tour. Fans of all ages were shocked to hear the news of JOEY's death in NY on the 15th of April, 2001. • **Songwriters:** DEE DEE and group, except; DO YOU WANNA DANCE (Bobby Freeman) / SURFIN' BIRD (Trashmen) / BABY I LOVE YOU (Ronettes; Phil Spector) / NEEDLES AND PINS (Searchers) / STREET FIGHTIN' MAN (Rolling Stones) / TAKE IT AS IT COMES (Doors) / R.A.M.O.N.E.S. (Motorhead) / ANY WAY YOU WANT IT (Dave Clark) / SPIDER-MAN (Harris-Webster) / etc. In '77, DEE DEE co-wrote 'CHINESE ROCKS' for the HEARTBREAKERS. • **Trivia:** The RAMONES featured in the films 'Blank Generation' (1976) & 'Rock'n'roll High School' (Roger Corman 1979).

Album rating: RAMONES (*9) / LEAVE HOME (*8) / ROCKET TO RUSSIA (*8) / ROAD TO RUIN (*7) / IT'S ALIVE (*6) / END OF THE CENTURY (*7) / PLEASANT DREAMS (*6) / SUBTERRANEAN JUNGLE (*6) / TOO TOUGH TO DIE (*7) / ANIMAL BOY (*6) / HALFWAY TO SANITY (*4) / RAMONES MANIA compilation (*9) / BRAIN DRAIN (*4) / LOCO LIVE (*3) / MONDO BIZARRO (*3) / ACID EATERS (*3) / ADIOS AMIGOS (*5) / WE'RE OUTTA HERE (*5)

JOEY RAMONE (b. JEFFREY HYMAN, 19 May'51) – vocals (was drummer) / **JOHNNY RAMONE** (b. JOHN CUMMINGS, 8 Oct'51, Long Island, N.Y.) – guitar, vocals / **DEE DEE RAMONE** (b. DOUGLAS COLVIN, 18 Sep'52, Fort Lee, Virginia) – bass, vocals / **TOMMY RAMONE** (b. TOM ERDELYI, 29 Jan'49, Budapest, Hungary) – drums

		Sire	Sire
Jul 76.	(lp) *(9103 253) <7520>* **RAMONES** – Blitzkrieg bop / Beat on the brat / Judy is a punk / I wanna be your boyfriend / Chain saw / Now I wanna sniff some glue / I don't wanna go down to the basement / Loudmouth / Havana affair / Listen to my heart / 53rd & 3rd / Let's dance / I don't wanna walk around with you / Today your love, tomorrow the world. *(re-iss. Sep78; SRK 6020) <(cd-iss. Oct99 on 'Rhino'; 7559 27421-2)> <(cd re-mast.Jun01 on 'Rhino'+=; 8122 74306-2)>* – (extra tracks).		May76
Jul 76.	(7") *(6078 601) <725>* **BLITZKRIEG BOP. / HAVANA AFFAIR**		May76
Oct 76.	(7"m) *<734>* **I WANNA BE YOUR BOYFRIEND. / CALIFORNIA SUN (live) / I DON'T WANNA WALK AROUND WITH YOU (live)**	-	
Feb 77.	(7"m) *(6078 603)* **I REMEMBER YOU. / CALIFORNIA SUN (live) / I DON'T WANNA WALK AROUND WITH YOU (live)**		-
Mar 77.	(lp) *(9103 254) <7528>* **LEAVE HOME** – Glad to see you go / Gimme gimme shock treatment / I remember you / Oh oh I love her so / Babysitter * / Suzy is a headbanger / Pinhead / Now I wanna be a good boy / Swallow my pride / What's your game / California sun / Commando / You're gonna kill that girl / You should never have opened that door / California sun. *(re-iss. Jun77 'Carbona Not Glue' replaced *; other re-iss's same) (re-iss. Sep78; SRK 6031) (re-iss. Nov87 on 'Mau Mau'; MAU 602) <(cd re-iss. Oct99 on 'Rhino'; 7599 27422-2)> <(cd re-mast.Jun01 on 'Rhino'+=; 8122 74307-2)>* – (extra tracks).	45	Feb77
May 77.	(7"m,12"m) *(6078 606) <746>* **SHEENA IS A PUNK ROCKER. / COMMANDO / I DON'T CARE**	22	81
Jul 77.	(7"m) *(6078 607) <738>* **SWALLOW MY PRIDE. / PINHEAD / LET'S DANCE (live)**	36	Mar77
Nov 77.	(7"m,12"m) *(6078 611)* **ROCKAWAY BEACH. / TEENAGE LOBOTOMY / BEAT ON THE BRAT**		-
Nov 77.	(7") *<1008>* **ROCKAWAY BEACH. / LOCKET LOVE**	-	66
Dec 77.	(lp) *(9103 255) <6042>* **ROCKET TO RUSSIA** – Cretin hop / Rockaway beach / Here today, gone tomorrow / Locket love / I don't care / Sheena is a punk rocker / We're a happy family / Teenage lobotomy / Do you wanna dance? / I wanna be well / I can't give you anything / Ramona / Surfin' bird / Why is it always this way. *(re-iss. Sep78; SRK 6042) <(cd-iss. Oct99 on 'Rhino'; 7559 27424-2)> <(cd re-mast.Jun01 on 'Rhino'+=; 8122 74309-2)>* – (extra tracks).	60	49 Nov77
Feb 78.	(7") *<1017>* **DO YOU WANNA DANCE?. / BABYSITTER**	-	86

Mar 78. (7"m) *(6078 615)* **DO YOU WANNA DANCE? / IT'S A LONG WAY BACK TO GERMANY / CRETIN HOP** [ ] [-]

— **MARKY RAMONE** (b. MARC BELL, 15 Jul'56) – drums (ex-RICHARD HELL & THE VOID-OIDS, ex-DUST) repl. TOMMY who continued producing others.

Sep 78. (7",7"yellow,12"yellow,12"red) *(SRE 1031) <1025>* **DON'T COME CLOSE. / I DON'T WANT YOU** [38] [ ]

Oct 78. (yellow-lp) *<(SRK 6063)>* **ROAD TO RUIN** [32] [ ]
– I just want to have something to do / I wanted everything / Don't come close / I don't want you / Needles and pins / I'm against it / I wanna be sedated / Go mental / Questioningly / She's the one / Bad brain / It's a long way back. *(cd-iss. Oct99; 7559 27426-2) <(cd re-mast.Jun01 on 'Rhino'+=; 8122 74308-2)>* – (extra tracks).

Nov 78. (7") *<1045>* **NEEDLES AND PINS. / I WANTED EVERYTHING** [-] [ ]

Jan 79. (7") *(SIR 4009)* **SHE'S THE ONE. / I WANNA BE SEDATED** [-] [-]

May 79. (d-lp/c) *(SRK/SRC 26074)* **IT'S ALIVE (live)** [27] [-]
– Rockaway beach / Teenage lobotomy / Blitzkrieg bop / I wanna be well / Glad to see you go / Gimme gimme shock treatment / You're gonna kill that girl / I don't care / Sheena is a punk rocker / Havana affair / Commando / Here today, gone tomorrow / Surfin' bird / Cretin hop / Listen to my heart / California sun / I don't wanna walk around with you / Pinhead / Do you wanna dance? / Chain saw / Today your love, tomorrow the world / Now I wanna be a good boy / Judy is a punk / Suzy is a headbanger / Let's dance / Oh oh I love her so / Now I wanna sniff some glue / We're a happy family. *(cd-iss. Nov93 on 'Warners'; 7599 26069-2) (cd re-iss. Jan96; 9362 46045-2)*
(above album features TOMMY on drums)

Sep 79. (7") *<1051>* **DO YOU WANNA DANCE? / ROCK'N'ROLL HIGH SCHOOL** [-] [ ]

Sep 79. (7") *(SIR 4021)* **ROCK'N'ROLL HIGH SCHOOL. / SHEENA IS A PUNK ROCKER (live) / ROCKAWAY BEACH (live)** [67] [-]

Jan 80. (lp/c) *<(SRK/SRC 6077)>* **END OF THE CENTURY** [14] [44]
– Do you remember rock'n'roll radio? / I'm affected / Danny says / Chinese rock / The return of Jackie and Judy / Let's go / Baby I love you / I can't make it on time / This ain't Havana / Rock'n'roll high school / All the way / High risk insurance. *(re-iss. cd Mar94; 7599 27429-2)*

Jan 80. (7") *(SIR 4031) <49182>* **BABY, I LOVE YOU. / HIGH RISK INSURANCE** [8] [ ]

Apr 80. (7") *<49261>* **DO YOU REMEMBER ROCK'N'ROLL RADIO?. / LET'S GO** [-] [ ]

Apr 80. (7") *(SIR 4037)* **DO YOU REMEMBER ROCK'N'ROLL RADIO?. / I WANT YOU AROUND** [54] [-]

Jul 81. (7") *(SIR 4051) <49812>* **WE WANT THE AIRWAVES. / ALL'S QUIET ON THE EASTERN FRONT** [ ] [ ]

Jul 81. (lp/c) *<(SRK/SRC 3571)>* **PLEASANT DREAMS** [ ] [58]
– We want the airwaves / All's quiet on the Eastern front / The KKK took my baby away / Don't go / You sound like you're sick / It's not my place / She's a sensation / 7-11 / You didn't mean anything to me / Come on now / This business is killing me / Sitting in my room. *(re-iss. cd Mar94 & Jun00; 7599 23571-2)*

Oct 81. (7") *(SIR 4052)* **SHE'S A SENSATION. / ALL'S QUIET ON THE EASTERN FRONT** [ ] [-]

May 83. (lp/c) *(WX/+C 3800) <23800>* **SUBTERRANEAN JUNGLE** [ ] [83]
– Little bit o' soul / I need your love / Outsider / What'd ya do / Highest trails above / Somebody like me / Psycho therapy / Time has come today / My-my kind of girl / In the park / Time bomb / Everytime I eat vegetables It makes me think of you. *(re-iss. cd Mar94 & Jun00; 7599 23800-2)*

Jun 83. (7") *(W 9606)* **TIME HAS COME TODAY. / PSYCHO THERAPY** [ ] [-]
(12"+=) *(W 9606T)* – Baby I love you / Don't come close.

— **RICHIE RAMONE** (b. RICHARD REINHARDT, aka BEAU) – drums (ex-VELVETEENS) repl. MARC

Beggars Banquet | Sire

Nov 84. (7") *<29107>* **HOWLING AT THE MOON (SHA LA LA). / WART HOG** [-] [ ]

Jan 85. (lp/c) *(BEGA/BEGC 59) <25187>* **TOO TOUGH TO DIE** [63] [ ] Oct84
– Mama's boy / I'm not afraid of life / Too young to die / Durango 95 / Wart hog / Danger zone / Chasing the night / Howling at the Moon (sha-la-la) / Daytime dilemma (dangers of love) / Planet Earth 1988 / Human kind / Endless vacation / No go.

Jan 85. (7") *(BEG 128)* **HOWLING AT THE MOON (SHA-LA-LA). / CHASING THE NIGHT** [ ] [-]
(d7"+=)(12"pic-d+=) *(BEG 128D)(BEGTP 128)* – Smash you / Street fighting man.

Jun 85. (7") *(BEG 140)* **BONZO GOES TO BITBURG. / DAYTIME DILEMMA (DANGERS OF LOVE)** [ ] [-]
(12"+=) *(BEG 140T)* – Go home Annie.

Apr 86. (7") *(BEG 157)* **SOMETHING TO BELIEVE IN. / SOMEBODY PUT SOMETHING IN MY DRINK** [69] [-]
(12"+=) *(BEG 157T)* – (You) Can't say anything nice.

May 86. (lp/c) *(BEGA/BEGC 70) <25433>* **ANIMAL BOY** [38] [ ]
– Somebody put something in my drink / Animal boy / Love kills / Apeman hop / She belongs to me / Crummy stuff / My brain is hanging upside down (Bonzo goes to Bitburg) / She belongs to me / Mental hell / Eat that rat / Freak of nature / Hair of the dog / Something to believe in.

Jun 86. (7") *<28599>* **SOMETHING TO BELIEVE IN. / ANIMAL BOY** [-] [ ]

Jul 86. (7") *(BEG 167)* **CRUMMY STUFF. / SHE BELONGS TO ME** [ ] [-]
(12"+=,12"red+=) *(BEG 167 T)* – I don't want to live this life.

— **MARKY RAMONE** – drums returned to repl. CLEM BURKE (ex-BLONDIE) who had repl. RICKY (above now with originals JOEY, DEE DEE and JOHNNY)

Sep 87. (7") *(BEG 198)* **A REAL COOL TIME. / INDIAN GIVER** [ ] [-]
(12"+=) *(BEG 198T)* – Life goes on.

Sep 87. (lp/c) *(BEGA/BEGC 89) <25641>* **HALFWAY TO SANITY** [78] [ ]
– I wanna live / Bop 'til you drop / Garden of serenity / Weasel face / Go lil' Camaro go / I know better now / Death of me / I lost my mind / A real cool time / I'm not Jesus / Bye bye baby / Worm man. *(cd-iss. Dec87 +=; BEGA 89CD)* – Indian giver / Life goes on.

Nov 87. (7"/12") *(BEG 201/+T)* **I WANNA LIVE. / MERRY CHRISTMAS (I DON'T WANT TO FIGHT TONIGHT)** [ ] [ ]

Chrysalis | Sire

Aug 89. (lp/c/cd) *(CHR/ZCHR/CCD 1725) <25905>* **BRAIN DRAIN** [75] [ ] Jun89
– I believe in miracles / Zero zero UFO / Don't bust my chops / Punishment fits the crime / All screwed up / Palisades Park / Pet sematary / Learn to listen / Can't get you outta my mind / Ignorance is bliss / Come back, baby / Merry Christmas (I don't want to fight tonight).

Sep 89. (7") *(CHS 3423)* **PET SEMATARY. / ALL SCREWED UP** [ ] [-]
(12"+=) *(CHS12 3423)* – Zero zero UFO.

Sep 89. (7") *<22911>* **PET SEMATARY. / SHEENA IS A PUNK ROCKER** [-] [ ]

— **C.J. RAMONE** (b. CHRISTOPHER JOSEPH WARD, 8 Oct'65, Long Island, N.Y.) – bass repl. DEE DEE who became rap artist DEE DEE KING

Oct 91. (cd/c/d-lp) *(CCD/ZCHR/CHR 1901)* **LIVE LOCO (live)** [ ] [ ]
– The good, the bad and the ugly / Django 95 / Teenage lobotomy / Psycho therapy / Blitzkrieg bop / Rock'n'roll radio / I believe in miracles / Gimme gimme shock treatment / Rock'n'roll high school / I wanna be sedated / The KKK took my baby away / I wanna live / Bonzo goes to Bitzburg / Too tough to die / Sheena is a punk rocker / Rockaway beach / Pet semetary / Don't bust my shape / Palisades park / Mama's boy / Animal boy / Wart hog / Surfin' bird / Cretin hop / I don't wanna walk around with you / Today your love, tomorrow the world / Pinhead / Somebody put something in my drink / Beat on the brat / Judy is a punk / Chinese rocks / Love kills / Ignorance is bliss.

Radioactive | Radioactive

Sep 92. (cd/c/lp) *<(RAR D/C 10615)>* **MONDO BIZARRO** [ ] [ ]
– Censorshit / The job that ate my brain / Poison heart / Anxiety / Strength to endure / It's gonna be alright / Take it as it comes / Main man / Tomorrow she goes away / I won't let it happen again / Cabbies on crack / Heidi is a heartache / Touring.

Chrysalis | Radioactive

Nov 92. (c-s/7"yellow) *(TC+/CHS 3917)* **POISON HEART. / CENSORSHIT (live)** [69] [-]
(12"+=) *(12CHS 3917)* – Chinese rocks (live) / Sheena is a punk rocker (live).
(cd-s+=) *(CDCHS 3917)* – Rock and roll radio (live).

Dec 93. (cd/c/lp) *(CD/TC+/CHR 6052) <10913>* **ACID EATERS** [ ] [ ]
– Journey to the center of the mind / Substitute / Out of time / The shape of things to come / Somebody to love / When I was young / 7 and 7 is / My back pages / Can't seem to make you mine / Have you ever seen the rain / I can't control myself / Surf city.

— Album of covers; SUBSTITUTE (Who) / I CAN'T CONTROL MYSELF (Troggs) / SURF CITY (Jan & Dean) / OUT OF TIME (Rolling Stones) / THE SHAPE OF THINGS TO COME (Headboys) / etc.

Jun 95. (cd/c/lp) *(CD/TC+/CHR 6104) <11273>* **ADIOS AMIGOS** [62] [ ]
– I don't want to grow up / I'm makin' monsters for my friends / It's not for me to know / The crusher / Life's a gas / Take the pain away / I love you / Cretin family / Have a nice day / Scattergun / Got a lot to say / She talks to rainbows / Born to die in Berlin.

— split after tour early the following year, although they had a brief reunion on the 6th August, 1996 at The Palace, Los Angeles

Eagle | Radioactive

Nov 97. (cd) *(EAGCD 010) <11555>* **WE'RE OUTTA HERE!** [ ] [ ]
– Durango 95 / Teenage lobotomy / Psycho therapy / Blitzkrieg bop / Do you remember rock and roll radio / I believe in miracles / Gimme gimme shock treatment / Rock'n'roll high school / I wanna be sedated / Spider-man / The K.K.K. took my baby away / I just want to have something to do / Commando / Sheena is a punk rocker / Rockaway beach / Pet sematary / The crusher / Love kills / Do you wanna dance / Someone put something in my drink / I don't want you / Wart hog / Cretin hop / R.A.M.O.N.E.S. / Today your love, tomorrow the world / Pinhead / 53rd & 3rd / Listen to your heart / We're a happy family / Chinese rock / Beat on the brat / Any way you want it.

— after what we think is their final release, MARKY RAMONE went solo

– compilations, etc. –

Aug 80. (7") *R.S.O.; (RSO 70) / Sire; <2090 512>* **I WANNA BE SEDATED. / THE RETURN OF JACKIE AND JUDY** [ ] [ ]

— (above from Various Artists Film Soundtrack 'Rock'n'roll High School' also incl. 'Medley: Blitzkrieg bop – Teenage lobotomy – California sun – Pinhead – She's the one')

Nov 80. (7"ep) *Sire; (SREP 1)* **MELTDOWN WITH THE RAMONES** [ ] [ ]
– I just wanna have something to do / Questioningly / I wanna be your boyfriend / Here today, gone tomorrow.

Jun 88. (7") *Sire; <27663>* **I WANNA BE SEDATED. / (part 2)** [-] [ ]

Jun 88. (d-lp/c/cd) *Sire; (925709-1/-4/-2) <25709>* **RAMONES MANIA** [ ] [-]
– I wanna be sedated / Teenage lobotomy / Do you remember rock'n'roll radio? / Gimme gimme shock treatment / Beat on the brat / Sheena is a punk rocker / I wanna live / Pinhead / Blitzkrieg bop / Cretin hop / Rockaway beach / Commando / I wanna be your boyfriend / Mama's boy / Bop 'til you drop / We're a happy family / Bonzo goes to Bitburg / The outsider / Psycho therapy / Wart hog / Animal boy / Needles and pins / Howlin' at the Moon / Somebody put something in my drink / We want the airwaves / Chinese rocks / I just want to have something to do / The KKK took my baby away / Indian giver / Rock'n'roll high school.

Sep 90. (cd/c/d-lp) *Sire; (7599 2620-2/-4/-1)* **ALL THE STUFF (AND MORE)** (demos 1976-77, etc) [ ] [-]

May 99. (d-cd+book) *Megaworld; (MEGBK 02)* **BLITZKREIG BOP** [ ] [-]

Aug 99. (d-cd) *Sire; <(8122 7581-2)>* **HEY HO LET'S GO – THE RAMONES ANTHOLOGY** [ ] [ ]

Aug 00. (cd) *Burning Airlines; <(PILOT 79)>* **YOU DON'T COME CLOSE** [ ] [ ]

May 01. (d-cd) *Sire; <(8122 73557-2)>* **HEY HO LET'S GO (THE RAMONES ANTHOLOGY)** [74] [ ]

— JOEY also on "HOLLY & JOEY" 7" – 1982 'I Got You Babe' on 'Virgin'.

— In August '88, JOHNNY teamed up with DEBBIE HARRY for 7" – 'Go Lil Camara Go'.

DEE DEE RAMONE

writes with **REY**

World Dom. / World Dom.

Jun 94. (cd/lp) *<(1571757-2/-1)>* **I HATE FREAKS LIKE YOU**
– I'm making monsters for my friends / Don't look in my window / Chinese bitch / It's not for me to know / Runaway / All's quiet on the Eastern Front / I hate it / Life is like a little smart Alleck / I hate creeps like you / Trust me / Curse on me / I'm seeing strawberry's again / Lass mich in Fuhe / I'm making monsters for my friends.

Other People's Music / Other People's Music

Sep 97. (cd) *<(OPM 2118CD)>* **ZONKED**
– I'm zonked, los hombres / Fix yourself up / I am seeing UFO's / Get off of the scene / Never never again / Bad horoscope / It's so bizarre / Get out of my room / Someone who don't fit in / Victim of society / My Chico / Disguises / Why is everybody always against Germany.

Blackout / Blackout

Oct 97. (7") *(BLK 5008E7)* **I AM SEEING UFO'S. / BAD HOROSCOPE** [-]

Nov 97. (cd) *(BLK 5008ECD)* **AIN'T IT FUN**
– I'm zonked los hombres / Fix yourself up / I am seeing UFO's / Get off the scene / Never never again / Bad horoscope / It's so bizarre / Get out of the room / Someone who doesn't fit in / Victim of society / My Chico / Disguises / Why is everyone always against Germany / Please kill me.

Corazong

Mar 00. (cd) *(2000 006)* **HOP AROUND** [-]

Eagle

Sep 00. (cd) *(EAGCD 156)* **GREATEST AND LATEST**
– Blitzkrieg bop / Timebomb / Sheena is a punk rocker / Shaking all over / I wanna be sedated / Cretin hop / Teenage lobotomy / Gimme gimme shock treatment / Motorbikin' / Come on now / Cathy's clown / Pinhead / Rockaway beach / Fix yourself up / Sidewalk surfin' / Beat on the brat.

Lee RANALDO (see under ⇒ SONIC YOUTH)

RANCID

Formed: Albany, California, USA . . . 1987 as tattooed ska-punk act, OPERATION IVY, by TIM 'LINT' ARMSTRONG and MATT FREEMAN (alias MATT McCALL), who also numbered JESSE MICHAELS and DAVE MELLO in their ranks. This quartet would become a cult act of the late 80's, although they only managed to squeeze out one album, 'ENERGY', in 1989. ARMSTRONG and FREEMAN continued to work with various outfits, including MDC, a band that they often supported at the infamous Gilman Street Club in Berkeley. In 1990, the pair were joined by BRETT REED and thus RANCID were spawned. After the release of a self-financed EP, 'I'M NOT THE ONLY ONE' in '92, the trio inked a deal with BRETT GUREWITZ's 'Epitaph' records. They subsequently added second guitarist LARS FREDERIKSON, who was to swell the ranks following the release of their well-received eponymous debut in 1993. With the early 90's resurgence of punk and youthful peers such as OFFSPRING and GREEN DAY making commercial headway, RANCID were well placed to capitalise on their particular brand of gut-level hardcore. Following the release of a 1994 EP, 'RADIO RADIO RADIO' on FAT MIKE's (NOFX) independent 'Fat Wreck Chords' label, the band cracked the elusive US Top 100 with their second album, 'LET'S GO' (1994). The following year, RANCID scored with an even higher placed album, ' . . . AND OUT COME THE WOLVES', a Top 60 success. In 1998, like The CLASH over 20 years before them, RANCID adopted some roots reggae and ska into their umpteenth set, 'LIFE WON'T WAIT' (Jamaican, BUJU BANTON and MIGHTY MIGHTY BOSSTONES' mainman DICKY BARRETT guested). The results surprisingly worked as the album went Top 40 in America and Britain. In summer 2000, the mighty RANCID delivered another eponymous album which hit the UK Top 75. • **Trivia:** ARMSTRONG also set up his own label, 'Hellcat', his best signings being DROPKICK MURPHYS, The PIETASTERS, GADJITS, HEPCAT and US BOMBS.

Album rating: Operation Ivy: OPERATION IVY (*6) / Rancid: RANCID (*7) / LET'S GO (*6) / . . .AND OUT COME THE WOLVES (*8) / LIFE WON'T WAIT (*7) / RANCID (*6)

OPERATION IVY

TIM ARMSTRONG – vocals, guitar / **MATT FREEMAN** (as MATT McCALL) – bass / **JESSE MICHAELS** – vocals / **DAVE MELLO** – drums

not iss. / Lookout

Jan 88. (7"ep) **HECTIC EP** [-]

Apr 91. (lp) *<LOOKOUT 10>* **OPERATION IVY** [-]
– Knowledge / Sound system / Jaded / Take warning / The crowd / Bombshell / Unity / Vulnerability / Bankshot / One of these days / Gonna find you / Bad town / Smiling / Caution / Freeze up / Artificial life / Room without a window / Big city / Missionary / Junkie's running dry / Here we go again / Hoboken / Yellin' in my ear / Sleep long / Healthy body / Officer / I got no. *(UK-iss.Oct94 lp/c/cd+=; LOOKOUT 10/+MC/CD)* – HECTIC EP

— they had already split in May '89, DAVE hoined SCHLONG while JESSE became a Buddhist monk! but ten years later formed COMMON RIDER with members from SQUIRTGUN. ARMSTRONG and FREEMAN worked with the DANCE HALL CRASHERS and DOWNFALL, while both joined MDC, FREEMAN more so; he featured on the group's 1990 set, 'Hey Cop, If I Had A face Like Yours'.

RANCID

— **ARMSTRONG + FREEMAN** added **BRETT REED** – drums (ex-SMOG)

not iss. / Lookout

1992. (7"ep) *<LOOK 059>* **RANCID** [-]
– I'm not the only one / etc
(UK-iss.Dec94 & Dec95; same as US)

not iss. / Fat Wreck Chords

1992. (7"ep) *<FAT 509>* **RADIO, RADIO, RADIO EP** [-]
(UK-iss.Apr94; same as US)

Epitaph / Epitaph

May 93. (cd/c/lp) *<(E 86428-2/-4/-1)>* **RANCID**
– Adina / hyena / Detroit / Rats in the hallway / Another night / Animosity / Otta my mind / Whirlwind / Rejected / Injury / The bottle / Trenches / Holiday sunrise / Unwritten rules / Get out of my way / (untitled).

— added **LARS FREDERIKSON** – guitar (ex-UK SUBS)

Jan 95. (cd/c/d-10"lp) *<(E 86434-2/-4/-1)>* **LET'S GO** [97] Jun94
– Nihilism / Radio / Sidekick / Salvation / Tenderloin / Let's go / As one / Burn / Ballad of Jimmy & Johnny / Gunshot / I am the one / Gave it away / Ghetto box / Harry Bridges / Black and blue / St. Mary / Dope sick girl / International cover-up / Solidarity / Midnight / Motorcycle ride / Name / 7 years down.

Jun 95. (7") **ROOTS RADICALS. / I WANNA RIOT** [-]

Aug 95. (cd/c/lp) *<(E 86444-2/-4/-1)>* **. . .AND OUT COME THE WOLVES** [55] [45]
– Maxwell murder / 11th hour / Roots radicals / Time bomb / Olympia Wa. / Lock, step and gone / Junkie man / Listed M.I.A. / Ruby Soho / Daly city train / The way I feel / Avenues and alleyways / As wicked / You don't care nothin' / Wars end / Disorder and disarray / Old friend / She's automatic / Journey to the end of the East Bay.

Oct 95. (7"ep/cd-ep) *(WOOS 8 S/CDS)* **TIME BOMB / THE WAR'S END / BLAST 'EM** [56] [-]
(above issued on 'Out Of Step')

May 96. (7"ep/cd-ep) *(86464-7/-2)* **RUBY SOHO. / THAT'S ENTERTAINMENT / DISORDER AND DISARRAY** [-]

Jun 98. (d-cd/d-c/d-lp) *(6497-2/-4/-1)* *<86497>* **LIFE WON'T WAIT** [32] [35]
– Intro / Bloodclot / Black lung / Life won't wait / New dress / Warsaw / Hooligan / Crane fist / Leicester Square / Backslide / Who would've thought / Cas culture and violence / Wolf / 1998 / Lady Liberty / Wrongful suspicion / Turntable / Something in the world today / Corazon de oro / Coppers.

Aug 98. (7"ep/cd-ep) *(1005-7/-2)* **BLOODCLOT. / ENDRINE / STOP**

Dec 98. (7"ep/cd-ep) *(1009-7/-2)* **HOOLIGANS / CASH, CULTURE AND VIOLENCE (bass drop mix) / THINGS TO COME (dance hall mix)**

Jul 00. (cd/c/lp) *<(0427-2/-4/-1)>* **RANCID** [68]
– Don Giovanni / Disgruntled / It's quite alright / Let me go / I am forever / Poison / Loki / Blackhawk down / Rwanda / Corruption / Antennas / Rattlesnake / Not to regret / Radio Havana / Axiom / Black derby jacket / Meteor of war / Dead bodies / Fuck you / Young Al Capone / Golden gate fields / Churchill Downs.

RAPEMAN (see under ⇒ BIG BLACK)

RATT

Formed: Los Angeles, California, USA . . . 1981 by frontman STEPHEN PEARCY and guitarist ROBBIN CROSBY. By '83, they had augmented the line-up with guitarist WARREN DeMARTINI, bassist JUAN CROUCIER and drummer BOBBY BLOTZER. Following an eponymous mini album the same year on indie label, 'Time Coast', RATT secured a deal with 'Atlantic' records in 1984 with the help of friends/fellow metallers, MOTLEY CRUE. Their major label debut, 'OUT OF THE CELLAR' (1984) was standard issue L.A. pseudo-glam metal fare, although it possessed enough of a pop sensibility to score a fairly respectable stay in the US charts, peaking at No.7. Likewise the infectious single, 'ROUND AND ROUND', which narrowly missed the (US) Top 10. Subsequent releases like 'INVASION OF YOUR PRIVACY' (1985) and 'DANCING UNDERCOVER' (1986) were slight improvements on the debut if not exactly breaking from the pretty-boy formula. Though successive albums failed to create the chart interest of the early releases, the band were a reliable Stateside live draw. Starting the new decade on a high note, the group procured the songwriting midas touch of the ubiquitous DESMOND CHILD for 1990's well received 'DETONATOR', RATT finally beginning to make inroads into the UK market. Just when it seemed they had the pop-metal market by the tail, however, RATT were finally trapped following the departure of both CROSBY and PEARCY in the early 90's. PEARCY went on to form ARCADE, releasing two albums in 1993/94, before RATT reformed three years later. An album, 'COLLAGE', was hugely disappointing especially the sad dance version of 'LOVIN' YOU . . .'. • **Covered:** WALKING THE DOG (Rufus Thomas).

Album rating: RATT (*4) / OUT OF THE CELLAR (*5) / INVASION OF YOUR PRIVACY (*4) / DANCING UNDERCOVER (*4) / REACH FOR THE SKY (*6) / DETONATOR (*5) / RATT & ROLL compilation (*6) / COLLAGE (*3)

STEPHEN PEARCY (b. 3 Jul'56) – vocals / **JAKE E.LEE** – guitar / **WARREN DeMARTINI** (b.10 Apr'63) – guitar / **JUAN CROUCIER** (b.22 Aug'59) – bass (ex-DOKKEN) / **BOBBY BLOTZER** (b.22 Oct'58) – drums

Music For Nations / Time Coast

Jun 83. (m-lp) *(MFN 2)* *<2203>* **RATT**
– Sweet cheater / You think you're tough / U got it / Tell the world / Back for more / Walkin' the dog. *<re-iss. Jun84; same>* *(re-iss. Sep86 on 'Time Coast' lp/c; 790245-1/-4)* *(cd-iss. Jan00 on 'Axe Killer'; 495075-2)*

— **ROBBIN CROSBY** – guitar; repl. LEE (to ROUGH CUTT then OZZY OSBOURNE)

Atlantic / Atlantic

Apr 84. (lp/c) *(780 143-1/-4)* *<80143>* **OUT OF THE CELLAR** [7] Mar84
– Wanted man / You're in trouble / Round and round / In your direction / She wants money / Lack of communication / Back for more / The morning after / I'm insane / Scene of the crime. *(cd-iss. 1988; 780 143-2)*

Sep 84. (7") *(A 9693)* <89693> **ROUND AND ROUND. / THE MORNING AFTER** [ ] [12] Jun84
Sep 84. (7") <89618> **WANTED MAN. / SHE WANTS MONEY** [-] [87]
Nov 84. (7") <89602> **SCENE OF THE CRIME. / LACK OF COMMUNICATION** [-] [ ]
Mar 85. (7") *(A 9573)* **ROUND AND ROUND. / YOU THINK YOU'RE TOUGH** [ ] [-]
(12"+=) *(A 9573T)* – Sweet cheater.
Jun 85. (7"/12") *(A 9546/+T)* <89546> **LAY IT DOWN. / GOT ME ON THE LINE** [ ] [40] May85
Jul 85. (lp/c/cd) *(781 257-1/-4/-2)* <81257> **INVASION OF YOUR PRIVACY** [50] [7] Jun85
– You're in love / Never use love / Lay it down / Give it all / Closer to my heart / Between the eyes / What you give is what you get / Got me on the line / You should know by now / Dangerous but worth the risk.
Jan 86. (7") *(A 9502)* <89502> **YOU'RE IN LOVE. / BETWEEN THE EYES** [ ] [89] Oct85
Oct 86. (lp/c/cd) *(781 683-1/-4/-2)* <81683> **DANCIN' UNDERCOVER** [51] [26]
– Dance / One good lover / Drive me crazy / Slip of the lip / Body talk / Looking for love / 7th Avenue / It doesn't matter / Take a chance / Enough is enough.
Feb 87. (7") <89354> **DANCE. / TAKE A CHANCE** [-] [59]
Oct 88. (lp/c/cd) *(781 929-1/-4/-2)* <81929> **REACH FOR THE SKY** [82] [17]
– City to city / I want a woman / Way cool Jr. / Don't bite the hand that feeds / I want to love you tonight / Chain reaction / No surprise / Bottom line / What's it gonna be / What I'm after.
Dec 88. (c-s,cd-s) <88985> **WAY COOL JR. / CHAIN REACTION** [-] [75]
Apr 89. (c-s,cd-s) <88928> **WHAT I'M AFTER. / I WANT A WOMAN** [-] [ ]
Aug 90. (cd/c/lp) <(7567 82127-2/-4/-1)> **DETONATOR** [55] [23]
– Intro to shame / Shame shame shame / Lovin' you's a dirty job / Scratch that itch / One step away / Hard time / Heads I win, tails you lose / All or nothing / Can't wait on love / Givin' yourself away / Top secret.
Oct 90. (7"/c-s) *(A 7844/+MC)* **LOVIN' YOU'S A DIRTY JOB. / WHAT'S IT GONNA BE** [ ] [ ]
(12"+=/cd-s+=) *(A 7844 T/CD)* – ('A'version).

—— now a quartet when ROBBIN left. In 1992 PEARCY quit also forming TABBO who became ARCADE

Sep 91. (cd/c/lp) <(7567 82260-2/-4/-1)> **RATT & ROLL 81-91** (compilation) [ ] [57]
– Tell the world / Round and round / Wanted man / Back for more / Lack of communication / Lay it down / You're in love / Slip of the lip / Body talk / Way cool Jr. / Lovin' you's a dirty job / Shame shame shame / Givin' yourself away / Nobody rides for free. *(cd+c+=)* – You think you're tough / Dance (part 1) / I want a woman / One step away / Heads I win, tails you lose.

ARCADE

STEPHEN PEARCY – vocals / **FRED COURY** – drums (ex-CINDERELLA) / **FRANKIE WILSEY** – guitar (ex-SEA HAGS) / **JOHNNY ANGEL** – guitar (ex-MICHAEL MONROE) / **MICHAEL ANDREWS** – bass

Epic Epic

Aug 93. (cd) *(472897-2)* <53012> **ARCADE** [ ] [ ] Apr93
– Dancin' with the angels / Nothin' to lose / Calm before the storm / Cry no more / Screamin' S.O.S. / Never goin' home / Messed up world / All shook up / So good . . . so bad / Livin' dangerously / Sons and daughters / Mothers blues.
Aug 93. (cd-s) <77178> **CRY NO MORE** [-] [ ]

—— **DONNIE SYRACUSE** – guitar; repl. ANGEL

Oct 94. (cd/c) <57586> **A/2** [-] [ ]
– Angry / Move / So what / Get off my back / When I'm gone / Welcome / Kidnapped / Chain to me / Room with a view / Your only age / Hot racin'.

—— split after above

RATT

—— re-formed in 1997 with **DeMARTINI, CRUCIER, PEARCY, BLOTZER + ROBBIN CROSBY**

DeRock DeRock

Aug 97. (cd) <(DERCD 097)> **COLLAGE** [ ] [ ] Jul97
– Steel river / Dr. Rock / Diamond time again / Ratt madness / Hold tight / I want it all / Mother blues / Top secret (original) / Take it anyway / Lovin' you (Fonic mix LP version).

– compilations, etc. –

Oct 99. (cd) *Axe Killer;* <(AXE 305325CD)> **NEVER FORGET YOUR PAST (IT'LL COME BACK TO HAUNT YOU)** [ ] [ ]

RAVEN

Formed: Newcastle, England ... 1975 by brothers JOHN and MARK GALLAGHER, plus ROB 'WACKO' HUNTER who completed the line-up in 1980. A precursor to 80's thrash, RAVEN's frenetic guitar mangling was developed over four albums for 'Neat'. Flying high alongside the rest of the NWOBHM flock, this group were most definitely razor-clawed birds of prey, homing in for the kill on the debut set, 'ROCK UNTIL YOU DROP'. Complete with screeching covers of The Sweet's 'HELLRAISER' and 'ACTION', the album actually made the UK Top 75. With no commercial success forthcoming in Britain, the band flew to America (in a plane!?), their "Mad Geordie" reputation and manic live appearances helping them to gain a deal with 'Atlantic' records. Ironically, the resulting album, 'STAY HARD' (1985), was derided by the UK fans as decidedly limp and as the band pandered to the American mainstream, their reputation suffered a fatal blow. Failing to crack the US market, RAVEN eventually came home to roost, the band replacing HUNTER with a new drummer, JOE HASSELVANDER, as they reverted back to their roots with an album, 'NOTHING EXCEEDS LIKE EXCESS' (1989) on thrash label, 'Under One Flag'. Re-forming in the mid-90's, RAVEN have since delivered three further sets, 'GLOW' (1995), 'DESTROY ALL MONSTERS – LIVE IN JAPAN' (1996) and 'EVERYTHING LOUDER' (1997).

Album rating: ROCK UNTIL YOU DROP (*6) / WIPED OUT (*5) / ALL FOR ONE (*6) / LIVE AT THE INFERNO (*7) / STAY HARD (*5) / THE DEVIL'S CARRION compilation (*6) / THE PACK IS BACK (*5) / LIFE'S A BITCH (*4) / NOTHING EXCEEDS LIKE EXCESS (*4) / GLOW (*4) / DESTROY ALL MONSTERS – LIVE IN JAPAN (*4) / EVERYTHING LOUDER (*4)

JOHN GALLAGHER – vocals, bass / **MARK GALLAGHER** – guitar / **ROB 'WACKO' HUNTER** – drums

Neat Discovery

Aug 80. (7") *(NEAT 06)* **DON'T NEED YOUR MONEY. / WIPED OUT** [ ] [-]
Sep 81. (lp) *(NEAT 1001)* **ROCK UNTIL YOU DROP** [63] [-]
– Hard ride / Hell patrol / Don't need your money / Over the top / 39-40 / For the future / Rock until you drop / Nobody's hero / Hellraiser / Action / Lambs to the slaughter / Tyrant of the airways. *(re-iss. May85 lp/pic-lp/c; NEAT/+P/C 1001) (<re-iss. Jul90 on 'Roadrunner' cd/lp; RC 9387-2/-1>) (cd re-iss. Oct91 on 'Castle'; CLACD 257) (cd re-iss. Jan00; NM 036)*
Nov 81. (7") *(NEAT 11)* **HARD RIDE. / CRAZY WORLD** [ ] [-]
Sep 82. (lp) *(NEAT 1004)* **WIPED OUT** [ ] [-]
– Faster than the speed of light / Bring the hammer down / Fire power / Read all about it / To the limit – To the top / Battle zone / Live at the inferno! / Star war / UXB / 20-21 / Hold back the fire / Chain saw. *<US cd-iss. 1990 on 'Roadrunner'; RR 9386> (cd-iss. Jan00; NM 037)*
Oct 82. (12"mauve-ep) *(NEAT 15-12)* **CRASH BANG WALLOP EP** [ ] [-]
– Crash bang wallop / Firepower / Run them down / Rock hard.
May 83. (7") *(NEAT 28)* **BREAK THE CHAIN. / BALLAD OF MARSHALL JACK** [ ] [-]
Jun 83. (lp) *(NEAT 1011)* **ALL FOR ONE** [ ] [-]
– Take control / Mind over metal / Sledgehammer rock / All for one / Run silent, run deep / Hung drawn and quartered / Break the chain / Take it away / Seek and destroy / Athletic rock. *(re-iss. May85 lp/c/cd; NEAT/+C/CD 1011) (cd re-iss. Jan00; NM 038)*
Aug 83. (7"/7"pic-d) *(NEAT 29/+C)* **BORN TO BE WILD. / INQUISITOR** [ ] [-]
(12"+=) *(NEAT 29-12)* – Break the chain.
1984. (d-lp) *(NEAT 1020)* <36133> **LIVE AT THE INFERNO (live)** [ ] [ ]
– I don't need your money / Break the chain / Hell patrol / Live at the inferno / Crazy world / Let it rip / I.G.A.R.B.O. / Wiped out / Fire power / All for one / Forbidden planet / Star war / Tyrant of the airways / Run silent, run deep / Take control / Mind over metal / Crash bang wallop / Rock until you drop / Faster than the speed of light. *(re-iss. May85; same) (re-iss. 1988 on 'Roadrunner'; RR 9808) (cd-iss. Feb99 on 'S.P.V.'; 076-1843-2)*

Atlantic Atlantic

Mar 85. (12") *(RAVEN 1T)* **PRAY FOR THE SUN. / ON AND ON / BOTTOM LINE** [ ] [-]
May 85. (lp/c) *(781 241-1/-4)* <81241> **STAY HARD** [ ] [ ]
– Stay hard / When the going gets tough / On and on / Get it right / Restless child / Power and the glory / Pray for the sun / Hard ride / Extract the action / Bottom line. *(cd-iss. Sep98 on 'Mayhem'; 11137-2)*
Feb 86. (7") <89453> **GIMME SOME LOVIN'. / ON AND ON** [-] [ ]
Mar 86. (lp/c) *(781 629-1/-4)* <81629> **THE PACK IS BACK** [ ] [ ]
– The pack is back / Gimme some lovin' / Screaming the house down / Young blood / Hyperactive / Rock dogs / Don't let it die / Get into your car / All I want / Nightmare ride. *(cd-iss. Sep98 on 'Mayhem'; 11150-2)*
Apr 87. (lp/c) *(781 734-1/-4)* <81734> **LIFE'S A BITCH** [ ] [ ]
– The savage and the hungry / Pick your window / Life's a bitch / Never forgive / Iron league / On the wings of an eagle / Overload / You're a liar / Fuel to the fire / Only the strong survive / Juggernaut / Playing with the razor. *(c+=)* – Finger on the trigger. *(cd-iss. Sep98 on 'Mayhem'; 11143-2)*

—— **JOE HASSELVANDER** – drums; repl. HUNTER who went into production

Under One Flag Combat

Aug 89. (cd/c/lp) *(CD/T+/FLAG 28)* **NOTHING EXCEEDS LIKE EXCESS** [ ] [ ] 1988
– Behemoth / Die for Allah / Gimme a break / Into the jaws of death / In the name of the Lord / Stick it / Lay down the law / You got a screw loose / Thunderlord / The king / Hard as nails / Kick your ass. *<(cd re-iss. Nov99 on 'Century Media'; CM 66043-2)>*

—— split in the early 90's but re-formed in the mid-90's

S.P.V. not iss.

Jun 95. (cd) *(SPV 084-1209-2)* **GLOW** [ ] [-]
– Watch you drown / Spite / True believer / So close / Altar / The dark side / The rocker / Turn on you / Far and wide / Victim / Gimme a reason / Slip away.
Apr 96. (cd) *(SPV 085-1213-2)* **DESTROY ALL MONSTERS – LIVE IN JAPAN (live)** [ ] [-]
May 97. (cd) *(SPV 085-1216-2)* **EVERYTHING LOUDER** [ ] [-]
– Blind eye / No pain, no gain / Sweet Jane / Holy grail / Hungry / Insane / Everything louder / Between the wheels / Losing my mind / Get your fingers out / Wilderness of broken glass / Fingers do the walking.

– compilations, etc. –

Apr 86. (d-lp/c) *Raw Power; (RAW LP/TC 003)* **THE DEVIL'S CARRION** [ ] [-]
Sep 99. (cd) *Massacre; (MASSCD 194)* **RAW TRACKS** [ ] [ ]
Jan 00. (cd) *Massacre; (MASSCD 206)* **ONE FOR ALL** [ ] [ ]
– Seven shades / Double talk / Roll with the punches / Get your motor running / To be broken / Derailed / The hunger inside / Top of the world / In the line of fire / Kangaroo / New religion / Last ride / Big fat mama.

RAVENOUS (see under ⇒ AUTOPSY)

RAZOR

Formed: Guelph, Ontario, Canada . . . 1983 by STACE "SHEEPDOG" McLAREN, DAVE CARLO, MIKE CAMPAGNOLO and MIKE "M-BRO" EMBRO. One of the earliest Canadian power-thrash acts, RAZOR cut their self-financed debut album, 'ARMED AND DANGEROUS' in 1984. A viciously sharp assault, it no doubt helped them sign a deal with Attic subsidiary, 'Viper' ('Roadrunner' UK), a follow-up set, 'EXECUTIONER'S SONG' appearing in the summer '85. In the space of a year or so, the group delivered two further albums, 'EVIL INVADERS' and 'MALICIOUS INTENT', although these were the last to feature the rhythm section of MIKE and M-BRO who had been deposed by ADAM CARLO and ROB MILLS. Dropped by 'Roadrunner', RAZOR sounded a bit rusty on the 'CUSTOM KILLING' set, although by 'VIOLENT RESTITUTION', they had regained their cut-throat edge. The 1991 follow-up, 'OPEN HOSTILITY' proved something of a disappointment, although 1995's 'SHOTGUN JUSTICE' proved just as sharp as its predecessor, the band proving that even the frozen North could supply ear-melting thrash; 'DECIBELS' in '98 would be their final outing.

Album rating: ARMED AND DANGEROUS (*4) / EXECUTIONER'S SONG (*5) / EVIL INVADERS (*5) / MALICIOUS INTENT (*5) / CUSTOM KILLING (*5) / VIOLENT RESTITUTION (*7) / OPEN HOSTILITY (*4) / SHOTGUN JUSTICE (*7) / DECIBELS (*6)

STACE 'Sheepdog' McLAREN – vocals / **DAVE CARLO** – guitars / **MIKE CAMPAGNOLO** – bass / **MIKE "M-BRO" EMBRO** – drums

not iss. Voice

1984. (lp) **ARMED AND DANGEROUS** [-] [ ]
– The end / Killer instinct / Hot metal / Armed and dangerous / Take this torch / Ball and chain / Fast and loud.

Roadrunner Viper

Jun 85. (lp) *(RR 9778)* **EXECUTIONER'S SONG** [ ] [ ]
– Take this torch / Fast and loud / City of damnation / Escape the fire / March of death / Distant thunder / Hot metal / Gatecrasher / Deathrace / Time bomb / The end.

Dec 85. (lp) *(RR 9732)* **EVIL INVADERS** [ ] [ ]
– Nowhere fast / Cross me fool / Legacy of doom / Evil invaders / Iron hammer / Instant death / Cut throat / Speed merchants / Tortured skull / Thrashdance. *(cd-iss. May89 on 'Roadracer'; RO 9732-2)*

Aug 86. (lp) *(RR 9698)* **MALICIOUS INTENT** [ ] [ ]
– Tear me to pieces / Night attack / Grindstone / Cage the ragers / Malicious intent / Rebel onslaught / A.O.D. / Challenge the eagle / Stand before kings / High speed metal / K.M.A.

— **ADAM CARLO** – bass; repl. MIKE / **ROB MILLS** – drums; repl. M-BRO

Steamhammer Flight

Sep 87. (lp) *<FPL 3042>* **CUSTOM KILLING** [-] [ ]
– Survival of the fittest / Shootout / Forced annihilation / Last rites / Snake eyes / White noise / Going under / Russian ballet.

Steamhammer Roadrunner

Dec 88. (lp)(cd) *(087 569)(857 571) <9486>* **VIOLENT RESTITUTION** [-] [ ] German
– The marshall arts / Hypertension / Taste the floor / Behind bars / Below the belt / I'll only say it once / Enforcer / Violent restitution / Out of the game / Edge of the razor / Eve of the storm / Discipline / Fed up / Soldier of fortune.

1991. (cd) **OPEN HOSTILITY** [-] [-] Canada
– In protest / Sucker for punishment / Bad vibrations / Road gunner / Cheers / Red money / Free lunch / Iron legions / Mental torture / Psychopath / I disagree / End of the war.

Fringe Fringe

Mar 95. (lp/cd) *(<FPL/FPD 3094>)* **SHOTGUN JUSTICE** [ ] [ ]
– Miami / United by hatred / Violence condoned / Electric torture / Meaning of pain / Stabbed in the back / Shotgun justice / Parricide / American luck / Brass knuckles / Burning the bridges / Concussion / Cranial stomp / The pugilist.

Hypnotic Hypnotic

Jan 98. (cd) *<(HYPSD 1058CD)>* **DECIBELS** [ ] [-] Canada
– Decibels / Jimi the fly / Life sentence / Liar / The game / Great white lie / Open hostility / Nine dead / Goof soup / Violence . . . gun control / Instant death 1997.

— split after above

– compilations, etc. –

1994. (d-cd) **EXHUMED** [-] [-] Canada
– Killer instinct / Armed and dangerous / Take this torch / Fast and loud / City of damnation / Gatecrasher / Cross me fool / Evil invaders / Iron hammer / Instant death / Speed merchants / Thrash dance / A.O.D. / K.M.A. / Forced annihilation / Snake eyes // The marshall arts / Behind bars / Below the belt / Enforcer / Violent restitution / Edge of the razor / Soldier of fortune / Miami / Electric torture / Meaning of pain / Shotgun justice / Parricide / Brass knuckles.

REALM

Formed: Milwaukee, USA . . . 1985 by guitarists TAKIS KINIS and PAUL LAGANOWSKI, who, after a few false starts found other members MARK ANTONI, STEVE POST and MIKE OLSON. Signing to 'Roadracer', the group attempted to mark out their territory with the ambitious 1988 debut set, 'ENDLESS WAR', a schizophrenic mish-mash of competing styles which turned out a bizarre cover of The Beatles' 'ELEANOR RIGBY'. A follow-up, the strangely-titled 'SUICIETY' was an even more confusing affair that left the band minus a record contract and facing imminent demise.

Album rating: ENDLESS WAR (*4) / SUICIETY (*3)

MARK ANTONI – vocals / **TAKIS KINIS** – guitar / **PAUL LAGANOWSKI** – guitar / **STEVE POST** – bass / **MIKE OLSON** – drums

Roadracer Roadracer

Dec 88. (lp/cd) *<(RO 9509-1/-2)>* **ENDLESS WAR** [ ] [ ]
– Endless war / Slay the oppressor / Eminence / Fate's wind / Root of evil / Eleanor Rigby / This house is burning / Second coming / All heads will turn to the hunt / Mang / Poisoned minds. *(cd+=)* – Theseus and the minotaur.

Oct 90. (cd/c/lp) *<(RO 9406-2/-4/-1)>* **SUICIETY** [ ] [ ]
– Cain rose up (scream bloody murder) / Fragile earth / Energetic discontent / Gateway / Final solution / The brainchild / La Flamme's theory / Dick / Knee deep in blood / Suiciety.

— split after above

RE-ANIMATOR

Formed: Hull, England . . . 1987 by KEVIN INGLESON, MIKE ABEL, JOHN WILSON and MARK MITCHELL. Initially presenting themselves as a thrash band, RE-ANIMATOR came to vinyl life with a debut mini-set in 1989, 'DENY REALITY'. Later that year, the group delivered their first album proper, 'CONDEMNED TO ETERNITY', a record that was condemned to the bargain bin by the more discerning speed-metal freaks. Changing direction in line with the funk-metal vogue, RE-ANIMATOR did little to improve their critical standing with the 'LAUGHING' album. Despite being generally ignored in their home country, the group struggled on with an aptly-titled final set, 'THAT WAS THEN, THIS IS NOW' in 1992.

Album rating: DENY REALITY mini (*5) / CONDEMNED TO ETERNITY (*6) / LAUGHING (*6) / THAT WAS THEN, THIS IS NOW (*6)

KEVIN INGLESON – vocals, guitar / **MIKE ABEL** – guitar / **JOHN WILSON** – bass / **MARK MITCHELL** – drums

Under One Flag not iss.

Feb 89. (m-lp) *(MFLAG 32)* **DENY REALITY** [ ] [-]
– Deny reality / Fatal descent / Re-animator / Follow the masses / O.P.C. / D.U.A.F.

Oct 89. (cd/c/lp) *(CD/T+/FLAG 37) <970437>* **CONDEMNED TO ETERNITY** [ ] [-]
– Low life / Chain of command / Room / Condemned to eternity / Shock treatment / Buried alive / Techno fear / What the funk / Say your prayers. *<US+=>* – DENY REALITY

Feb 91. (cd/c/lp) *(CD/T+/FLAG 53)* **LAUGHING** [ ] [-]
– Rude awakening / Laughing / Kipper 'n' / Research / Another fine mess / Too drunk to f*** / Monkey see, monkey dance / Don't patronise me / Instrumental / Pass the buck / Time and tide / Big black cloud.

Oct 92. (cd/c/lp) *(CD/T+/FLAG 67)* **THAT WAS THEN, THIS IS NOW** [ ] [-]
– Take me away / 2 CV / Cold sweat / Hope / Last laugh / Kick back / Listen up / Sunshine times / That was then, this is now. *(cd+=)* – D.U.A.F.

— disbanded after above

REDD KROSS

Formed: Hawthorne, California, USA . . . late 1978 by schoolboy brothers JEFF McDONALD (then 15) and STEVE (only 11), initially as The TOURISTS (not UK group with ANNIE and DAVE). Completing the line-up with GREG HETSON and RON REYES, they played their first gig in 1979 as RED CROSS, opening for BLACK FLAG. Spotted by DJ and entrepreneur, Rodney Bingenheimer, they subsequently recorded an EP for 'Posh Boy' which led to the "real" International Red Cross threatening to sue them if they didn't change the group name! REDD KROSS, as they were now known, lost GREG HETSON and RON REYES in the process, both moving on to similar hardcore acts, CIRCLE JERKS and BLACK FLAG respectively. Over the course of the early to mid 80's, personnel changed like the weather and output was sparse. However, a few albums had emerged during this lean period, namely 'BORN INNOCENT' (1982) and covers set, 'TEEN BABES FROM MONSANTO' (1984), REDD KROSS not exactly causing an emergency with their trashy psychedelic punk/glam, although their embryonic grunge sound was definitely ahead of its time. Just when recognition seemed to be forthcoming with 1987's 'NEUROTICA', luck ran out as their label, 'Big Time', came a cropper. The McDONALD brothers re-appeared in 1990 with their one-off covers side project, TATER TOTZ, before the pair resurfaced with a new REDD KROSS line-up and a major deal courtesy of 'Atlantic'. A comeback album, 'THIRD EYE', appeared in 1991, the band's subsequent UK output released through 'This Way Up' (home to TINDERSTICKS and IAN McNABB). Another new line-up (namely, EDDIE KURDZIEL, GERE FENNNELLY and BRIAN REITZEL) was in place for 1993's 'PHASESHIFTER', which spawned three singles, 'SWITCHBLADE SISTER', 'LADY IN THE FRONT ROW' and 'VISIONARY', the latter scraping into the UK Top 75 early the following year. Later that summer, the band indulged their love of classic 70's pop with a kitschy cover of the Carpenters' 'YESTERDAY ONCE MORE', a shock UK Top 50 hit which featured SONIC YOUTH paying tribute to Karen & Richard on the B-side. A long hiatus ensued before REDD KROSS entered the fray once more in early '97 with another set of multi-coloured sonic-pop, 'SHOW WORLD', a collection that featured another minor hit single, 'GET OUT OF MYSELF'. • **Covered:** CITADEL (Rolling Stones) / HEAVEN ONLY KNOWS (Shangri-las) / DANCING QUEEN (Abba) / ANN (Stooges) / CEASE TO EXIST (Charles Manson) / etc. • **Trivia:** In 1990, REDD KROSS recorded a soundtrack for the Super-8 film, 'Desperate Teenage Lovedolls'.

Album rating: BORN INNOCENT (*4) / TEEN BABES FROM MONSANTO (*5) / NEUROTICA (*6) / THIRD EYE (*7) / PHASESHIFTER (*6) / SHOW WORLD (*7)

JEFF McDONALD (b.10 Aug'63, Los Angeles) – vocals / **GREG HETSON** – guitar / **STEVE McDONALD** (b.24 May'67) – bass, vocals / **RON REYES** – drums not iss. Posh Boy

1981. (12"ep; as RED CROSS) <PBS 1010> **RED CROSS** [-] [ ]
– Cover band / Annette's got the hits / I hate my school / Clorox girls / S&M party / Standing in front of a poseur.

—— now without HETSON (to CIRCLE JERKS) and REYES (to BLACK FLAG). They were repl. by a BANGLE!? (briefly) and various L.A. session people including **DEZ CADENA** (of BLACK FLAG)

not iss. Smoke 7

1982. (lp) <smk7 103> **BORN INNOCENT** [-] [ ]
– Linda Blair / White trash / Everyday there's someone new / Solid gold / Burn out / Charlie / Tatum O'Tot and the fried vegetables / St. Lita Ford blues / Self respect / Pseudo-intellectual / Kill someone you hate / Look on up at the bottom / Cellulite city / I'm alright / Cease to exist / Notes and chords mean nothing to me. *(UK-iss.Aug92 on 'Frontier' cd/lp; 4609-2L/1L) (re-iss. Aug00 on 'Munster'; MR 186)*

not iss. Enigma

1984. (lp) <71110-1> **TEEN BABES FROM MONSANTO** (covers) [-] [ ]

Big Time Big Time

Sep 87. (lp/c) <(ZL/ZK 71427K)> **NEUROTICA** [ ] [ ]
– Neurotica / Play my song / Frosted flake / Janus, Jeanie and George Harrison / Love is you / Peach Kelli Pop / McKenzie / Ballad of a love doll / What they say / Ghandii is dead (in the cartoon man) / Beautiful bye byes.

East West Atlantic

Apr 91. (cd/c/lp) <(7567 82148-2/-4/-1)> **THIRD EYE** [ ] [ ] Nov90
– The faith healer / Annie's gone / I don't know how to be your friend / Shonen Knife / Bubblegum factory / Where I am today / Zira (call out my name) / Love is not love / 1976 / Debbie & Kim / Elephant flares.

Apr 91. (7") **ANNIE'S GONE. /** [ ] [ ]
(12")(cd-s) –

Seminal Twang not iss.

Jul 92. (7") **TRANCE. /** [ ] [ ]
(cd-s+=) –

—— **McDONALD's** plus **EDDIE KURDZIEL** (b.25 Sep'60, Philadelphia) – guitar / **GERE FENNELLY** (b. 5 Aug'60, San Mateo, Calif.) – keyboards / **BRIAN REITZEL** (b.24 Dec'65, Ukiah, Calif.) – drums

This Way Up Polygram

Jun 93. (7") *(WAY 10-11)* **SWITCHBLADE SISTER. / WHAT'S WRONG WITH ME** [ ] [ ]
(cd-s+=) *(WAY 10-33)* – I don't know how to be your friend (live).

Sep 93. (cd/c/lp) <(518167-2/-4/-1)> **PHASESHIFTER** [ ] [ ]
– Jimmy's fantasy / Lady in the front row / Monolith / Crazy world / Dumb angel / Huge wonder / Visionary / Pay for love / Ms. Lady Evans / Only a girl / Saragon / After school special.

Oct 93. (7"/10") *(WAY 20-11/88)* **LADY IN THE FRONT ROW. / I'LL MEET YOU HALFWAY** [ ] [ ]
(cd-s) *(WAY 20-33)* – ('A'side) / Standing in front of poseur / Oh my lover / Fancy.

Jan 94. (7") *(WAY 27-11)* **VISIONARY. / IT WON'T BE LONG / VISIONARY (acoustic live)** [75] [-]
(12"+=/cd-s+=) *(WAY 27-12/33)* – ('A'side) / Any hour, every day / Oh my lover / Huge wonder (original) / Visionary (acoustic) / Disco bitch.

—— In Sep'94, they shared a single 'YESTERDAY ONCE MORE' with SONIC YOUTH's 'Superstar' (both CARPENTERS covers) hit UK No.45 for 'A&M'; *580792)*

Jan 97. (7"colrd) *(WAY 54-11)* **GET OUT OF MYSELF. / SOCALV8** [63] [-]
(cd-s+=) *(WAY 54-33)* – Teen competition (demo).
(cd-s) *(WAY 54-66)* – ('A'side) / Misery is mother / Jimmy's fantasy.

Feb 97. (cd/c/lp) <(524 275-2/-4/-1)> **SHOW WORLD** [ ] [ ]
– Pretty please me / Stoned / You lied again / Girl god / Mess around / One chord progression / Teen competition / Follow the leader / Vanity mirror / Secret life / Ugly town / Get out of myself / Kiss the goat.

Mar 97. (7") *(WAY 60-11)* **MESS AROUND. / WHAT CHA DOIN' TO THAT GIRL** [ ] [ ]
(cd-s) *(WAY 60-33)* – ('A'side) / Crazy world / Ugly town.
(cd-s) *(WAY 60-66)* – ('A'side) / Sick love / Popular cult.

Jun 97. (7") *(WAY 64-11)* **SECRET LIFE. / DANCING QUEEN** [ ] [ ]
(cd-s+=) *(WAY 64-33)* – Follow the leader.
(cd-s) *(WAY 64-66)* – ('A'side) / Its in the sky / You lied again.

TATER TOTZ

not iss. Positive

1988. (lp) <6010> **ALIEN SLEESTACKS FROM BRAZIL** [-] [ ]

Jul 90. (cd/c/lp) **SGT. SHONEN'S EXPLODING PLASTIC EASTMAN BAND REQUESTS** [-] [ ]
(above was released on 'Gatanska-Giant')

1990. (cd) <6027> **MONO! STEREO** [-] [ ]
– Instant karma! / Rock on / Rain / Who has seen the wind? – Bohemian rhapsody / Telephone piece / Strawberry fields forever / 1,2,3, red light / Luck of the Irish / Sisters, o sisters / Lovely Linda / Shompton in Babylon / Why? / Two virgins #9 / Tomorrow never knows (live) / Cambridge 1969 (live).

Rockville Rockville

Jul 93. (m-cd) <(ROCK 6054-2)> **TATER COMES ALIVE!** [ ] [ ]
– Tomorrow never knows / Rain / Sisters, o sisters / Don't worry Kyoko / Flowers / Sympathy for the Devil / Don't worry Kyoko.

RED HOT CHILI PEPPERS

Formed: Hollywood, California, USA . . . 1983 after four years as ANTHEM, by schoolfriends ANTHONY KIEDIS (aka ANTWAN THE SWAN), Israeli-born HILLEL SLOVAK, MICHAEL 'FLEA' BALZARY and JACK IRONS. This motley bunch of funky funsters then proceeded to sign with 'E.M.I.' stark naked as part of a now famous publicity stunt. The exhibitionist streak was to be a mainstay of their early career, most famously on the cover for the ABBEY ROAD EP (1988), the lads wearing nought but one sock, strategically placed (no prizes for guessing where!) in a send-up of the classic Beatles' album of the same name. With IRONS and SLOVAK under contractual obligations to their own group, WHAT IS THIS?, drummer JACK SHERMAN (ex-CAPTAIN BEEFHEART) and guitarist CLIFF MARTINEZ (ex-WEIRDOS, ex-TEENAGE JESUS & THE JERKS) filled in on the 1984 eponymous debut album, a promising start which introduced the band's mutant funk-punk hybrid. Taking their cue from the cream of 70's funk (obvious reference points were SLY STONE, JAMES BROWN, The METERS, etc.) and injecting it with a bit of L.A. hardcore mayhem, the CHILI PEPPERS came up with such gonzoid grooves as 'GET UP AND JUMP' and 'POLICE HELICOPTER', although the most interesting track was the haunting 'GRAND PAPPY DU PLENTY', a kind of pre-'Twin Peaks' slice of instrumental noir. The GEORGE CLINTON-produced follow-up, FREAKY STYLEY (1985) sounded more cohesive, most impressively on the galvanising defiance of the hypnotic title track. Alongside fairly faithful covers of Sly Stone's 'IF YOU WANT ME TO STAY' and The Meters' 'HOLLYWOOD (AFRICA)', the group "got down" with their own groove thang on the likes of 'JUNGLE MAN' and 'AMERICAN GHOST DANCE'. 'CATHOLIC SCHOOL GIRLS RULE' and 'SEX RAP', meanwhile, left no doubt as to the CHILI PEPPERS' feminist-baiting agenda. While these records were American-only affairs, the band's manic reputation was beginning to reach across the Atlantic, 'UPLIFT MOFO PARTY PLAN' (1988) intoducing the band to a receptive UK audience. Tougher than their earlier releases, the record consolidated the group's place at the forefront of the burgeoning funk-metal explosion, their brash, kaleidoscopic sound injecting a bit of colour and excitement to Blighty's rather dour rock scene. The party was cut somewhat short, however, with the death of SLOVAK in June, yet another victim of a heroin overdose. With KEIDIS also a heroin addict, IRONS (who subsequently formed the band, ELEVEN) obviously didn't like the way things were going and decided to bail out. Eventual replacements were found in guitarist JOHN FRUSCIANTE and drummer CHAD SMITH, the group throwing themselves into the recording of 'MOTHER'S MILK' (1989). Unfairly criticised in some quarters, the album contained some of the CHILI PEPPERS' finest moments to date. 'KNOCK ME DOWN' was an impassioned plea for sanity in the face of drugs hell, the group enjoying MTV exposure for the first time with the video. A brilliant, celebratory cover of Stevie Wonder's 'HIGHER GROUND' also scored with MTV, easing the band slowly out of cultdom. 'TASTE THE PAIN' was an uncharacteristically introspective (by the CHILI's standards anyhow) song, no doubt also borne of the band's recent troubles and showing a newfound maturity in songwriting. More trouble was to follow in April '90, when that young scamp, KIEDIS, was given a 60-day jail sentence for sexual battery and indecent exposure to a female student (the following year, FLEA and SMITH were both charged with offences of a similar nature). As well as clearly possessing red hot libidos, by the early 90's the band had become red hot property following the release of the RICK RUBIN-produced 'BLOOD SUGAR SEX MAGIK' (1991). Their first release for new label, 'Warners', at last the band had fulfilled their potential over the course of a whole album (a US Top 3). With another series of striking videos, the CHILI PEPPERS almost scored a US No.1 with the aching ballad, 'UNDER THE BRIDGE' while the body-jerk funk-rock of 'GIVE IT AWAY' made the UK Top 10. A multi million seller, the album catapulted The RED HOT CHILI PEPPERS into the big league, the band subsequently securing a prestigious headlining slot on the 1992 Lollapalooza tour. Always an utterly compelling live proposition, the group's hyperactive stage show is the stuff of legend, what with KEIDIS' manic athletics and FLEA's (possibly) JIMI HENDRIX-inspired upside down bass playing, hanging feet-up by a rope!!!. By the release of 'ONE HOT MINUTE' (1995), a transatlantic Top 5, FRUSCIANTE had been replaced with DAVE NAVARRO (ex-JANE'S ADDICTION), adding a new dimension to the band's sound. For many, the album was the 'CHILI PEPPERS' peak achievement, from the dreamy 'WALKABOUT' to the japery of 'AEROPLANE', the latter becoming a UK hit single. While many of the group's funk-rock contemporaries folded or fell by the wayside when that scene went out of fashion, the RED HOT CHILI PEPPERS developed into one of America's most entertaining, and biggest selling 'alternative' acts though a combination of sheer hard work, talent and concrete self belief (and no doubt a hefty dose of shagging!). Never the most stable of bands, rumours of a 'PEPPERS split were rife in 1997, although they still managed to hit the UK Top 10 with their fantastic cover of The Ohio Players' 'LOVE ROLLERCOASTER' (straight from the Beavis & Butt-Head film). With the returning FRUSCANTE out from the bench to replace NAVARRO, the band were back with a bang on 1999's 'CALIFORNICATION'. Meanwhile, another stab at the singles chart paid off with a transatlantic Top 20 hit, 'SCAR TISSUE'. • **Songwriters:** Group compositions except other covers; SUBTERRANEAN HOMESICK BLUES (Bob Dylan) / FIRE + CASTLES MADE OF SAND (Jimi Hendrix) / MOMMY WHERE'S DADDY (Frank Zappa) / THEY'RE RED HOT (Robert Johnson) / SEARCH AND DESTROY (Iggy Pop) / SUFFRAGETTE CITY (David Bowie) / WHY DON'T YOU LOVE ME (Hank Williams) / TINY DANCER (Elton John).

Album rating: RED HOT CHILI PEPPERS (*5) / FREAKY STYLEY (*5) / THE UPLIFT MOFO PARTY PLAN (*6) / MOTHER'S MILK (*7) / BLOOD SUGAR SEX MAGIK (*8) / WHAT HITS!? compilation (*7) / PLASMA SHAFT collection (*4) / OUT IN L.A. collection (*3) / ONE HOT MINUTE (*6) / CALIFORNICATION (*6)

ANTHONY KIEDIS (ANTWAN THE SWAN) (b. 1 Nov'62, Grand Rapids, Michigan) – vocals / **HILLEL SLOVAK** (b.13 Apr'62, Haifa, Israel) – guitar / **MICHAEL 'FLEA' BALZARY** (b.16 Oct'62, Melbourne, Australia) – bass / **JACK IRONS** (b.18 Jul'62, Los Angeles, California) – drums

EMI America / EMI America

1984. (lp/c/cd) *<790616-1/-4/-2>* **THE RED HOT CHILI PEPPERS** [-] [ ]
– True men don't kill coyotes / Baby appeal / Buckle down / Get up and jump / Why don't you love me / Green heaven / Mommy where's daddy? / Out in L.A. / Police helicopter / You always sing / Grand pappy du plenty. *(UK-iss.Aug90 on 'EMI Manhattan' cd/c/lp; CD/TC+/MTL 1056) (re-iss. Jun93 on 'Fame' cd/c; CD/TC FA 3297) (lp re-iss. Dec99 on 'Simply Vinyl'; SVLP 156)*

— (Due to contractual reasons, SLOVAK and IRONS couldn't play on debut. They were deputised by session men **JACK SHERMAN** – guitar (ex-CAPTAIN BEEFHEART) / & **CLIFF MARTINEZ** – drums (ex-WEIRDOS, ex-TEENAGE JESUS & THE JERKS)

— **HILLEL SLOVAK** returned from WHAT IS THIS? to repl. SHERMAN guests included **MACEO PARKER + FRED WESLEY** (of FUNKADELIC / PARLIAMENT)

1985. (lp/c/cd) *<790617-1/-4/-2>* **FREAKY STYLIE** [-] [ ]
– Jungle man / Hollywood (Africa) / American ghost dance / If you want me to stay / Never mind / Freaky stylie / Blackeyed blonde / The brothers cup / Battle ship / Lovin' and touchin' / Catholic school girls rule / Sex rap / Thirty dirty birds / Yertle the turtle. *(UK-iss.Aug90 on 'EMI Manhattan' cd/c/lp; CD/TC+/MTL 1057) (re-iss. Dec94 on 'Fame' cd/c; CD/TC FA 3309)*

Aug 85. (7") *(EA 205)* **HOLLYWOOD (AFRICA). / NEVER MIND** [ ] [ ]
(remixed-12"+=) *(12EA 205)* – ('A'dub version).

— **JACK IRONS** returned from WHAT IS THIS? to repl. MARTINEZ

Jan 88. (7") *(EA 241)* **FIGHT LIKE A BRAVE. / FIRE** [ ] [ ]
(12"+=/12"pic-d+=) *(12EA/+P 241)* – ('A'-Mofo mix) / ('A'-Knucklehead mix).

EMI Manhattan / EMI Manhattan

Mar 88. (cd/c/lp) *(CD/TC+/AML 3125) <48036>* **THE UPLIFT MOFO PARTY PLAN** [ ] [ ] Nov87
– Fight like a brave / Funky crime / Me and my friends / Backwoods / Skinny sweaty man / Behind the sun / Subterranean homesick blues / Special secret song inside / No chump love sucker / Walkin' on down the road / Love trilogy / Organic anti-beat box band. *(lp re-iss. Aug00 on 'Simply Vinyl'; SVLP 242)*

May 88. (7"ep) *(MT 41)* **THE ABBEY ROAD EP** [ ] [-]
– Backwoods / Hollywood (Africa) / True men don't kill coyotes.
(12"ep+=) *(12MT 41)* – Catholic school girls rule.

— **ANTWAN & FLEA** (now adding trumpet) brought in new lads **JOHN FRUSCIANTE** (b. 5 Mar'70, New York City) – guitar repl. HILLEL who died (of heroin OD) 25 Jun'88. **CHAD SMITH** (b.25 Oct'62, St. Paul, Minnesota) – drums repl. IRONS who later formed ELEVEN and joined PEARL JAM

E.M.I. USA / E.M.I.

Aug 89. (7"/7"sha-pic-d/12"pic-d) *(MT/MTPD/12MTPD 70)* **KNOCK ME DOWN. / PUNK ROCK CLASSIC / PRETTY LITTLE DITTY** [ ] [ ]
(12") *(12MT 70)* – (first 2 tracks) / Special secret song inside / Magic Johnson.
(cd-s) *(CDMT 70)* – (first 2 tracks) / Jungle man / Magic Johnson.

Aug 89. (cd/c/lp) *(CD/TC+/MTL 3125) <92152>* **MOTHER'S MILK** [ ] [52]
– Good time boys / Higher ground / Subway to Venus / Magic Johnson / Nobody weird like me / Knock me down / Taste the pain / Stone cold bush / Fire / Pretty little ditty / Punk rock classic / Sexy Mexican maid / Johnny kick a hole in the sky. *(lp-iss.Apr01 on 'Simply Vinyl'; SVLP 328)*

Dec 89. (7") *(MT 75)* **HIGHER GROUND. / MILLIONAIRES AGAINST HUNGER** [55] [ ]
('A'-Munchkin mix-cd-s+=) *(CDMT 75)* – Mommy where's daddy / Politician (mini rap).
(12") *(12MT 75)* – ('A'-Munchkin mix) / ('A'dub mix) / Politician (mini rap) / Mommy where's daddy.
(12") *(12MTX 75)* – ('A'side) / ('A'-Munchkin mix) / ('A'dub mix) / Politician (mini rap).

Jun 90. (c-s/7") *(TC+/MT 85)* **TASTE THE PAIN. / SHOW ME YOUR SOUL** [29] [ ]
(12"+=/9"square-pic-d+=) *(12/10 MT 85)* – Castles made of sand (live).
(cd-s++=) *(CDMT 85)* – Never mind.
(remixed-12"+=) *(12MTX 85)* – If you want me to stay / Never mind.

Aug 90. (c-s/7") *(TC+/MT 88)* **HIGHER GROUND. / FIGHT LIKE A BRAVE** [54] [ ]
(12"+=/12"pic-d+=) *(12MT/+PD 88)* – ('A'-Daddy-O mix).
(cd-s+=) *(CDMT 88)* – Behind the sun / Out in L.A.

Warners / Warners

Sep 91. (cd)(d-lp/c) *(7599 26681-2)(WX 441/+C) <26681>* **BLOOD SUGAR SEX MAGIK** [25] [3]
– The power of equality / If you have to ask / Breaking the girl / Funky monks / Suck my kiss / I could have lied / Mellowship slinky in B major / The righteous & the wicked / Give it away / Blood sugar sex magik / Under the bridge / Naked in the rain / Apache Rose peacock / The greeting song / My lovely man / Sir psycho sexy / They're red hot. *(re-iss. Mar92 cd/c; same)*

Dec 91. (c-s,cd-s) *<19147>* **GIVE IT AWAY / SEARCH AND DESTROY** [-] [73]

Mar 92. (c-s,cd-s) *<18978>* **UNDER THE BRIDGE / THE RIGHTEOUS AND THE WICKED** [-] [2]

Mar 92. (7"/s7"/c-s) *(W 0084/+W/C)* **UNDER THE BRIDGE. / GIVE IT AWAY** [26] [-]
(12"/cd-s) *(W 0084 T/CD)* – ('A'side) / Search and destroy / Soul to squeeze / Sikamikanico.

— (the last track also featured on 'Wayne's World' film/single)

— **ZANDER SCHLOSS** (THELONIUS MONSTER) – guitar, repl. FRUSCANTE who went solo 'TO CLARA' in 1994 on 'American'.

Jun 92. (c-s,cd-s) **IF YOU HAVE TO ASK /** [-] [ ]

Aug 92. (7"/c-s) *(W 0126/+C)* **BREAKING THE GIRL. / FELA'S COOK** [41] [ ]
(12"+=/cd-s+=) *(W 0126 T/CD)* – Suck my kiss (live) / I could have lied (live).

— (Aug'92) **ARIK MARSHALL** (b.13 Feb'67, Los Angeles) – guitar (ex-MARSHALL LAW) repl. SCHLOSS

Jun 93. (c-s) *(W 188C)* **GIVE IT AWAY / IF YOU HAVE TO ASK (Friday night fever blister mix)** [ ] [-]
(12"+=/cd-s+=) *(W 188 TP/CD1)* – ('A'-extended + Rasta mixes).
(cd-s) *(W 188CD2)* – ('A'side) / ('A'-Disco Krisco mix) / ('A'-Scott & Garth mix).

Aug 93. (c-s,cd-s) *<18401>* **SOUL TO SQUEEZE / NOBODY WEIRD LIKE ME** [-] [22]

— **DAVE NAVARRO** (b. 7 Jun'67, Santa Monica, Calif.) – guitar (ex-JANE'S ADDICTION) repl. MARSHALL

Jan 94. (c-s) *(W 0225C)* **GIVE IT AWAY / SOUL TO SQUEEZE** [9] [-]
(cd-s+=) *(W 0225CD1)* – ('A'-extended & Rasta mixes).
(cd-s) *(W 0225CD2)* – ('A'side) / If you have to ask (Friday night fever blister mix) / ('A'-Scott & Garth mix) / Nobody weird like me (live).
(12") *(W 0225T)* – ('A'extended) / ('A'-Rasta mix) / If you have to ask (disco krisco mix).

Apr 94. (7"blue/c-s) *(W 0237/+C)* **UNDER THE BRIDGE. / SUCK MY KISS (live)** [13] [-]
(cd-s+=) *(W 0237CD)* – Sikamikanico / Search and destroy (live).
(cd-s) *(W 0237CDX)* – ('A'side) / I could have lied (live) / Fela's cock / Give it away (in progress; demo).

Aug 95. (c-s) *(W 0316C)* **WARPED / PEA** [31] [-]
(cd-s+=) *(W 0316CD)* – Melancholy mechanics.

Sep 95. (cd/c/lp) *<(9362 45733-2/-4/-1)>* **ONE HOT MINUTE** [2] [4]
– Warped / Aeroplane / Deep kick / My friends / Coffee shop / Pea / One big mob / Walkabout / Tearjerker / One hot minute / Falling into grace / Shallow be thy name / Transcending.

Oct 95. (c-s) *(W 0317C)* **MY FRIENDS / LET'S MAKE EVIL** [29] [-]
(12"+=/cd-s+=) *(W 0317 TX/CD)* – Coffee shop / Stretch.

Feb 96. (c-s) *(W 0331C)* **AEROPLANE / SUFFRAGETTE CITY (live)** [11] [-]
(cd-s+=) *(W 0331CD)* – Suck my kiss (live).
(cd-s) *(W 0331CDX)* – ('A'side) / Backwoods (live) / Transcending (live) / Me and my friends (live).

— FLEA + CHAD splintered with THERMIDOR, which was formed by ROBBIE ALLEN and DAVID KING. An album 'MONKEY ON RICO' was released in the Spring.

Jun 97. (7"/c-s/cd-s) *(GFS/+C/TD 22188)* **LOVE ROLLERCOASTER. / Engelbert Humperdinck: Lesbian Seagull** [7] [-]
(above from the 'Beavis & Butt-Head Do America' film; on 'Geffen')

— (Apr'98) **JOHN FRUSCANTE** returned to repl. NAVARRO (who formed SPREAD)

May 99. (c-s) *(W 490C) <16913>* **SCAR TISSUE / GONG LI** [15] [9]
(cd-s+=) *(W 490CD2)* – Instrumental No.1.

Jun 99. (cd/c) *<(9362 47386-2/-4)>* **CALIFORNICATION** [5] [3]
– Around the world / Parallel universe / Scar tissue / Otherside / Get on top / Californication / Easily / Porcelain / Emit remmus / Velvet glove / Savoir / Purple stain / Right on time / Road trippin'.

Aug 99. (c-s) *(W 500C)* **AROUND THE WORLD / YERTLE TRILOGY** [35] [ ]
(cd-s+=) *(W 500CD2)* – Me and my friends.
(cd-s) *(W 500CD1)* – ('A'side) / Parallel universe / Teatro jam.

Jan 00. (cd-s) *(W 510CD1) <album cut>* **OTHERSIDE / HOW STRONG / ROAD TRIPPIN' (without strings) / OTHERSIDE (CD-Rom)** [33] [14]
(cd-s) *(W 510CD2)* – ('A'side) / My lovely man / Around the world (CD-Rom).

Aug 00. (c-s/cd-s) *(W 534 C/CD) <album cut>* **CALIFORNICATION / END OF THE SHOW (live) / I COULD HAVE LIED (live) / END OF SHOW (live)** [16] [69] May00

Jan 01. (c-s) *(W 546C)* **ROAD TRIPPIN' / CALIFORNICATION (live)** [30] [-]
(cd-s+=) *(W 546CD1)* – BloodSugarSexMagick (live) / ('A'-CD-ROM).
(cd-s) *(W 546CD2)* – ('A'side) / Under the bridge (live) / If you have to ask (live).

– compilations, others, etc. –

Oct 92. (cd/c/d-lp) *EMI USA; (CD/TC+/MTL 1071) <94762>* **WHAT HITS!?** [23] [22]
– Higher ground / Fight like a brave / Behind the Sun / Me & my friends / Backwoods / True men don't kill coyotes / Fire / Get up and jump / Knock me down / Under the bridge / Show me your soul / If you want me to stay / Hollywood / Jungle man / The brothers cup / Taste the pain / Catholic school girls rule / Johnny kick a hole in the sky.

Oct 94. (d-cd) *Warners; (9362 45649-2)* **PLASMA SHAFT** (rare mixes/live) [ ] [ ]

Nov 94. (cd/c/lp) *E.M.I.; (CD/TC+/MTL 1062)* **OUT IN L.A.** (rare remixes, demos & live) [61] [82]

Nov 95. (3xcd-box) *E.M.I.; (CDOMB 004)* **THE RED HOT CHILI PEPPERS / FREAKY STYLIE / THE UPLIFT MOFO PARTY PLAN** [ ] [ ]

Apr 98. (cd/c) *EMI-USA; <72434-94139-2/-4>* **ESSENTIAL RED HOT CHILI PEPPERS: UNDER THE COVERS** [-] [ ]

Jun 00. (cd) *E.M.I.; (527294-2)* **MOTHER'S MILK / THE UPLIFT MOFO PARTY PLAN / FREAKY STYLEY** [ ] [-]

RED LETTER DAY

Formed: Portsmouth, England . . . 1983 by frontman ADE, IAN CAMPBELL, PETE WHITE and BRIAN LEE, the latter three soon posted missing and replaced over the course of the ensuing few years by guitarist DAVIE EGAN, bassist KEITH METCALFE and drummer DARYN PRICE respectively. This line-up debuted in early '86 with the single, 'WHEREVER YOU MAY RUN', the record's post-punk stylings catching the ear of Radio One DJ, John Peel, who invited the quartet on his show for a session. Subsequently signing to 'Quiet' records (former stable of NEW MODEL ARMY), they issued two further EP's, 'RELEASED EMOTIONS' and 'TAKE ME IN YOUR ARMS', the former also the name of the label they'd sign to for a shared LP (with The SECT), 'SOFT LIGHTS AND LOUD GUITARS' (1988). Never a prolific band, RED LETTER DAY were also dogged by further personnel changes (METCALFE and EGAN were despatched around '87/'88) although they did finally emerge with their own album proper, 'MORE SONGS ABOUT LOVE AND WAR' (1991). After taking another interminable sabbatical, RLD were back with a limited-edition one-off 7", 'INSOMNIA', in '97, while the following year saw the release of only their second album in a decade and a half, 'LETHAL'; the CD 'HAPPY NEW YEAR' was appropriately delivered around the turn of the millennium.

Album rating: SOFT LIGHTS AND LOUD GUITARS (*5) / MORE SONGS ABOUT LOVE AND WAR (*5)

ADE – vocals, guitar / **DAVIE EGAN** – guitar; repl. IAN CAMPBELL / **KEITH METCALFE** – bass; repl. PETE WHITE / **DARYN PRICE** – drums; repl. BRIAN LEE

Lost Generation | not iss.

Mar 86. (7") *(LG 003)* **WHEREVER YOU MAY RUN. / SUSIE'S BOMBED OUT TONITE** [ ] [-]

Quiet | not iss.

Sep 86. (12"ep) *(QST 15)* **RELEASED EMOTIONS EP** [ ] [-]

Jul 87. (7"ep) *(QS 018)* **TAKE ME IN YOUR ARMS. / MOVING ON / THE DAY I JOINED THE HUMAN RACE** [ ] [-]

— **STEVE** – bass (ex-ORIGINAL MIRRORS) repl. METCALFE

Released Emotions | not iss.

Jul 88. (lp; shared with The SECT) *(REM 001)* **SOFT LIGHTS AND LOUD GUITARS** [ ] [-]
– It's cold outside / American dream / The war starts at midnight / Fade away / Fall apart / Barely alive / Shades / The less i see the more I think of you / The whole world gets me down / Unclean.

— **RAY** – guitar; repl. EGAN

1991. (cd) **MORE SONGS ABOUT LOVE AND WAR** [ ] [-]

— disbanded but re-formed later

Mouthy | not iss.

Feb 97. (ltd-7") **INSOMNIA. /** [ ] [-]

Holier Than Thou | not iss.

Jul 98. (cd) *(HTT 032-2)* **LETHAL** [ ] [-]
– Choose noise / Alison / Insomnia / Lethal / Parallel suburbia / Diva / Clandestine / Wordstoomuch / Four / Insider / Drama queen / Thousand names for God.

Mouthy | not iss.

Nov 99. (cd) *(MOUTHY 014CD)* **HAPPY NEW YEAR** [ ] [ ]

Dan REED NETWORK

Formed: Portland, Oregon, USA . . . 1982 by frontman DAN REED (b. South Dakota), New York-born guitarist BRIAN JAMES, Japanese-born keyboard player BLAKE SAKAMOTO, Jewish-born drummer DAN PRED and black-American bassist MELVIN BRANNON. This cosmopolitan group eventually signed a world wide deal with 'Mercury' in 1987 on the back of the burgeoning funk-rock scene, L.A.'s The RED HOT CHILI PEPPERS and San Francisco's FAITH NO MORE warranting increasing column inches in the metal press. DAN REED NETWORK's take on the genre was less intense, akin to LIVING COLOUR's more chart friendly moments, REED & Co. breaching the lower end of the US charts with their second single, 'RITUAL', in the Spring of '88. Their eponymous Bruce Fairbairn (AOR rock sculptor) produced debut album was released soon after, again cracking the furthest reaches of the Billboard Hot 100 and kicking up a bit of a fuss within the rock fraternity. The NILE RODGERS (CHIC) produced follow-up, 'SLAM' (1989), saw the band making inroads into the UK market, the British metal press singing the band's praises. Their funk was somewhat more taut this time around, inventive enough to catch the ever vigilant ears of The ROLLING STONES who invited them onto their 'Steel Wheels' tour. With their music reaching a considerably larger audience, the band's third effort, 'THE HEAT', made the UK Top 20. The stage seemed to be set for a big break, but somehow it never came. While the group had a compulsive groove, their albums nevertheless consistently lacked a bonafide hit single and the band remained in the also-ran category, eventually splitting in '92. • **Covers:** YOU CAN LEAVE YOUR YOUR HAT ON (Randy Newman) / MONEY (Pink Floyd).

Album rating: DAN REED NETWORK (*7) / SLAM (*6) / THE HEAT (*5) / MIXIN' IT UP – THE BEST OF . . . compilation (*6) / LIVE AT LAST (*6)

DAN REED – vocals / **BRIAN JAMES** – guitar / **BLAKE SAKAMOTO** – keyboards / **DAN PRED** – drums / **MELVIN BRANNON** – bass

Mercury | Mercury

Nov 87. (7"ep) **BREATHLESS EP** [-] [ ]

Feb 88. (7"/12") *<870183>* **RITUAL. / FORGOT TO MAKE HER MINE** [-] [38]

Oct 88. (7") *(MER 269)* **GET TO YOU. / FORGOT TO MAKE HER MINE** [ ] [ ]
(12"+=) *(MERX 269)* – ('A'version).
(cd-s++=) *(MERCD 269)* – Halfway round the world.

Nov 88. (lp/c/cd) *<834 309-1/-4/-2>* **DAN REED NETWORK** [ ] [95] Mar88
– The world has a heart too / Get to you / Ritual / Forgot to make her mine / Tamin' the wild nights / I'm so sorry / Resurrect / Baby don't fade / Human / Halfway round the world / Rock you all night long. *(cd+=)* – Tatiana.

Sep 89. (7") *(DRN 1)* **TIGER IN A DRESS. / AFFECTION** [ ] [ ]
(12"+=) *(DRN 1-12)* – Seven sisters road.
(c-s+=/cd-s+=) *(DRN MC/CD 1)* – Get to you.

Oct 89. (lp/c/cd) *<838 868-1/-4/-2>* **SLAM** [66] [ ]
– Make it easy / Slam / Tiger in a dress / Rainbow child / Doin' the love thing / Stronger than steel / Cruise together / Under my skin / Lover / I'm lonely, please stay / Come back baby / All my lovin' / Seven Sisters road.

Jan 90. (7"/7"pic-d/c-s) *(DRN/+PB/MC 2)* **COME BACK BABY. / BURNIN' LOVE** [51] [ ]
(12"+=)(12"pic-d) *(DRN 2T)(DRNSP 2-12)* – ('A'side) / Come alive / Make it easy.
(cd-s) *(DRNCD 2)* – (all 4 tracks)

Mar 90. (7"/7"g-f) *(DRN/+G 3)* **RAINBOW CHILD. / YOU CAN LEAVE YOUR HEART ON** [60] [ ]
(12"+=/12"yellow+=) *(DRN/+PC 3-12)* – Ritual.
(cd-s++=) *(DRNCD 3)* – Tamin' the wild nights.

Jun 90. (7"/c-s) *(DRN/+MC 4)* **STARDATE 1990. / RAINBOW CHILD (live)** [39] [ ]
(12"+=/12"g-f+=) *(DRN/+G 4-12)* – Ritual / Under my skin.
(cd-s+=) *(DRNCD 4)* – Without you / Come to me.

Aug 90. (7"/c-s) *(DRN/+MC 5)* **LOVER. / MONEY** [45] [ ]
(12"+=/12"yellow+=)(cd-s+=) *(DRN/+G 5-12)(DRNCD 5)* – Ritual (Dido Slam mix).
(12"blue+=) *(DRNB 5-12)* – Forgot to make her mine / Tiger in a dress.

Jul 91. (7") *(MER 345)* **MIX IT UP. / THE HEAT** [49] [ ]
(10"orange+=) *(MERXP 345)* – Slavery.
(12"+=/cd-s+=) *(MER X/CD 345)* – The lonely sun.

Jul 91. (cd/c/lp) *<848 855-2/-4/-1>* **THE HEAT** [15] [ ]
– Baby now I / Blame it on the Moon / Mix it up / The heat / Let it go / Love don't work that way / Money / Chill out / Life is sex / The salt of joy / Take my hand / The lovely sun / Thy will be done / Wake up / Long way to go.

Sep 91. (7"/c-s) *(MER/+MC 352)* **BABY NOW I. / THY WILL BE DONE** [65] [ ]
(10"pic-d+=) *(MERX 352)* – Living with a stranger.
(cd-s++=) *(MERCD 352)* – Stronger than steel.

— disbanded around 1992

– compilations, etc. –

Jul 93. (cd/c/lp) *Mercury; <514979-2/-4/-1>* **MIXIN' IT UP (THE BEST OF)** [-] [ ]
– World has a heart too / Get to you (remix) / Ritual / Rainbow child / Forgot to make her mine / Stardate 1990 / Baby now I / Tamin' the wild nights / Tiger in a dress / Make it easy / Lover / Stronger than steel (acoustic) / Mix it up / Rock you all night long / Baby don't fade / Long way to go (featuring NUNO BETTENCOURT). *(UK cd-iss. Sep98; same as US)*

Nov 97. (d-cd) *Video Media; <737885308326>* **LIVE AT LAST – HALFWAY AROUND THE WORLD** [ ] [ ]

REEF

Formed: London-based from Bath, England . . . 1994 by GARY STRINGER, KENWYN HOUSE, JACK BESSANT and DOMINIC GREENSMITH. Following a PAUL WELLER support slot, REEF were snapped up by corporate giants, 'Sony', hitting the ears of the nation in 1995, when a Minidisc TV commercial featured one of their tracks, 'NAKED'. This became their second! Top 30 hit, although they shunned STILTSKIN-like now-made-it-through-TV-ad comparisons. Their debut album, 'REPLENISH' followed later that summer, a decidedly un-Brit-poppy hybrid of loudmouthed funky, heavy country/blues fusing the rootsy sounds of BLACK CROWES or LENNY KRAVITZ with LED ZEPPELIN. The record crashed into the UK Top 10, REEF wowing festival audiences as well as playing a riotous gig on Newquay beach. The year ended with further controversy when the band made an in-store appearance at Tower records in Birmingham, STRINGER allegedly inciting the crowd to loot CD's from the racks and the show breaking down in confusion as the electricity cut out. After a relatively quiet start to '96, the group returned with the anthemic 'PLACE YOUR HANDS ON' which stormed into the charts at No.6 in October, the track becoming the band's signature tune as well as one of Chris Evan's themes on his 'TFI Friday' show. A follow-up album, the GEORGE DRAKOULIAS-produced 'GLOW', topped the charts in early '97, another rootsy, Glastonbury via American Deep South melange of raunchy, soulful pop with the odd mellow moment like 'CONSIDERATION'. Consolidating their position as Britain's foremost purveyors of unreconstructed 70's via 90's rock, the band undertook another round of festival appearances, including a homecoming gig at rain-drenched Glastonbury. With growing confidence and a two-year lay-off, REEF coasted back in '99 with their third and most critically acclaimed set to date, 'RIDES' (notable for the guest appearance by BECK (HANSEN)'s dad, DAVID CAMPBELL on string arrangements!). A year and a bit later, REEF only managed to make the UK Top 20 with the slightly less adventurous 'GETAWAY' (2000).

Album rating: REPLENISH (*6) / GLOW (*7) / RIDES (*8) / GETAWAY (*6)

GARY STRINGER – vocals / **KENWYN HOUSE** – guitar / **JACK BESSANT** – bass / **DOMINIC GREENSMITH** – drums

Sony-S2 | Sony

Apr 95. (c-s) *(661360-4)* **GOOD FEELING / WAKE** [24] [-]
(cd-s+=) *(661360-2)* – End.
(12"pic-d++=) *(661360-6)* – Water over stone.

May 95. (7"colrd/c-s) *(662062-7/-4)* **NAKED. / CHOOSE TO LIVE** [11] [-]
(cd-s+=) *(662062-2)* – Fade.

Jun 95. (cd/c/lp) *(480698-2/-4/-1) <67281>* **REPLENISH** [9] [ ]
– Feed me / Naked / Good feeling / Repulsive / Mellow / Together / Replenish / Choose to live / Comfort / Loose / End / Reprise.

Jul 95. (7"colrd/c-s) *(662277-7/-4)* **WEIRD. / ACOUSTIC ONE** [19] [-]
(cd-s) *(662277-2)* – ('A'side) / Sunrise shakers / Together / End (live).

— Sep'96, STRINGER sustained a gash in his hand when attacked by a gang in a pub.

Oct 96. (c-s) *(663571-4)* **PLACE YOUR HANDS / UNCOMFORTABLE** [6] [-]
(cd-s+=) *(663571-2)* – The snob / Weird (Australian edit).
(cd-s) *(663571-5)* – ('A'side) / Repulsive (live) / Speak lark (live) / Naked (live).

Jan 97. (c-s) *(664097-4)* **COME BACK BRIGHTER / RESIGNATION** [8] [-]
(cd-s+=) *(664097-2)* – It's not what I need / Hawaiian tooth.
(cd-s) *(664097-5)* – ('A'side) / Back into line / Dom and Gary / Robot part.

Feb 97. (cd/c/lp) *(486940-2/-4/-1) <67971>* **GLOW** [1] [ ]
– Place your hands / I would have left you / Summer's in bloom / Lately stomping / Consideration / Don't you like it? / Come back brighter / Higher vibration / I'm not scared / Yer old / Yer old riff / Lullaby. *(cd re-iss. Jan01; same)*

Mar 97. (7"red/c-s) *(664312-7/-4)* **CONSIDERATION / ALLOTMENT** [13] [-]
(cd-s+=) *(664312-2)* – New thinking / ('A'radio mix).

(cd-s) *(664312-5)* – ('A'side) / Claypits / Higher vibration (live) / Come back brighter (live).

Jul 97. (c-s) *(664703-4)* **YER OLD / SUMMER'S IN BLOOM (live)** 21 -
(cd-s+=) *(664703-2)* – Place your hands (live) / Yer old (Young version).
(cd-s) *(664703-5)* – ('A'side) / Higher vibration (live) / Lately stomping (live) / ('A'live).

Mar 99. (c-s) *(666954-4)* **I'VE GOT SOMETHING TO SAY / FOOT ONE** 15 -
(cd-s+=) *(666954-2)* – Buried.
(cd-s) *(666954-5)* – ('A'side) / Who are you / Choose to live (live).

Apr 99. (cd/c) *(492882-2/-4)* **RIDES** 3 -
– New bird / I've got something to say / Wandering / Metro / Hiding / Sweety / Locked inside / Back in my place / Undone & sober / Who are you / Love feeder / Moaner snap / Funny feeling / Electric Sunday.

May 99. (c-s) *(667373-4)* **SWEETY / TRIUMPHANT ANTHEM** 46 -
(cd-s+=) *(667373-2)* – Bullitt.
(cd-s) *(667373-5)* – ('A'side) / New bird (version) / This day.

Aug 99. (7") *(667851-7)* **NEW BIRD. / BACK IN MY PLACE** 73 -
(cd-s+=) *(667851-2)* – Sweety (video).

Jul 00. (c-s) *(669595-4)* **SET THE RECORD STRAIGHT / GENTLE MORNING** 19 -
(cd-s+=) *(669595-2)* – Haze.
(cd-s) *(669595-5)* – ('A'side) / Life seems so clean / Nothing town.

Aug 00. (cd/c) *(498891-2/-4)* **GETAWAY** 15 -
– Set the record straight / Superhero / Getaway / Solid / All I want / Hold on / Saturday / Won't you listen / Levels / Pretenders / I do not know what they will do.

Dec 00. (cd-s) *(669938-2)* **SUPERHERO / INSIDE OUT / BLOODY MARY / SUPERHERO (secret gig video)** -
(cd-s) *(669938-5)* – ('A'side) / Nothing can change / Whistledown / ('A'-CD-ROM).

May 01. (c-s) *(670822-4)* **ALL I WANT / NAKED (live)** 51 -
(cd-s+=) *(670822-2)* – Come back brighter (live) / ('A'-CD-ROM).

REEL BIG FISH

Formed: Huntington Beach, California, USA . . . early 90's by AARON BARRETT, MATT WONG and ANDREW GONZALES. The band began as a fairly run of the mill outfit covering rock, metal and pop songs. Their real distinction came with their movement towards the ska style, incorporating the rhythm-based horn punctuation of this genre with their punkier leanings. After several different brass section line-ups RBF found a permanent quartet in the shape of GRANT BARRY, SCOTT KLOPFENSTEIN, DAN REGAN, and TAVIS WERTS. Thus the band went from being a rock-orientated trio to becoming a ska-punk driven septet, issuing their debut album 'EVERYTHING SUCKS' (1995) independently. This release caught the attention of the label 'Mojo' who signed and brought out the band's second long-player 'TURN THE RADIO OFF' (1996). This album included the US Top 100 single 'SELL OUT', which over the course of the succeeding year became a bit of an MTV stalwart, rocketing the band into the mainstream. They followed this album up two years later with their third full-set 'WHY DO THEY ROCK SO HARD' (1998). Their jaunty punk-ska style and good humored approach made them popular on campus – their ouput translating well to the keg-fuelled bashes of American students. • **Covered:** UNITY (Operation Ivy).

Album rating: EVERYTHING SUCKS (*5) / TURN THE RADIO OFF (*6) / WHY DO THEY ROCK SO HARD? (*5)

AARON BARRETT – vocals, guitar / **MATT WONG** – bass / **ANDREW GONZALES** – drums / **SCOTT KLOPFENSTEIN** – trumpet, vocals / **TAVIS WERTS** – trumpet / **GRANT BARRY** – trombone / **DAN REGAN** – trombone / **ADAM POLAKOFF** – saxophone

not iss. — own label

1995. (lp) **EVERYTHING SUCKS** -
– I'm cool / Join the club / Call you / Hate you / I'll never be / Boyfriend / Fo'head / Trendy / Skatanic / Why do all girls think they're fat / Say "ten" / I want your girlfriend to be my girlfriend too / Jig / Go away / Beer / Snoop dog, baby / Big ****in' star / **** yourself / Spin the globe / I'm her man / Super hero #5.

Mojo-Universal — Mojo-Universal

Aug 96. (cd/c) *<UND/UNC 53013>* **TURN THE RADIO OFF** - 57
– Sell out / Trendy / Join the club / She has a girlfriend now / Snoop dog, baby / Beer / 241 / Everything sucks / S.R. / Skatanic / All I want is more / Nothin' / Say "ten" / I'll never be / Alternative baby. *<clean version 1997; UND 53108>*

Jan 97. (cd-s) *<1223>* **SHE HAS A GIRLFRIEND NOW** -

Feb 97. (7") *<(US 756036)>* **split w/ GOLDFINGER** -

Apr 97. (cd-s) **SELL OUT /** - 98

Jul 97. (cd-ep) *<53078>* **KEEP YOUR RECEIPT EP** -
– Alternative baby / Why do all the girls think they're fat? / I'm cool / S.R. / Unity.

1997. (cd-s) *<1255>* **BEER / BEER (instrumental)** -

Oct 98. (cd-s) *<1390>* **THE SET UP (YOU NEED THIS) /** -

Oct 98. (cd/c) *<UND/UNC 53159>* **WHY DO THEY ROCK SO HARD?** - 67
– Somebody hates me / Brand new song / She's famous now / You don't know / The set up (you need this) / Thank you for not moshing / I'm cool / I want your girlfriend to be my girlfriend too / Everything is cool / Song #3 / Scott's a dork / Big star / Kids don't like it / Down in flames / We care / Victory over Peter Bones.

REFUSED

Formed: Umea, Sweden . . . 1991 by DENNIS LYXZEN, JONF BRANNSTROM, KRISTOFER STEEN and DAVID SANDSTROM. More often than not REFUSED are placed in the hardcore punk revival bracket, but they fuse together many styles including jazz movements and breakbeat, and unlike some of the punk revivalists of this period their anarchist sensibilities were fairly unquestionable. In many ways they were the forerunners of punky dance bands like The PRODIGY's later incarnation, although incomparable as far as political integrity goes. REFUSED became available to the record buying public with their EP, 'THIS IS THE NEW DEAL' (1993). Following this up the same year with their first full-length set, 'THIS JUST MIGHT BE . . . THE TRUTH' (1993). A period of three years elapsed, with several EP's released, before the band brought out another album, 'FAN THE FLAMES OF DISCONTENT' (1996). On this set they proved their adept musicianship, while never straying from the point of the songs, and the reason why they were doing it in the first place. Something which they continued on into their third full-piece, 'SHAPE OF PUNK TO COME' (1998). On this album though they really took off as far as punk-innovation was concerned; skilfully mixing the hardcore styles with lighter more dance-inspired passages. Unfortunately this record marked the end of the band as a unit. Although the musical creativity of the members did not finish there. REFUSED's frontman, LYXZEN, joined fellow punk-minded idealists LARS STROMBERG (from punk outfit SEPARATION), INGE JOHANSSON from punk art band THE FEMALE ANCHOR OF SADE, SARA ALMGREN from SAIDWAS and the DOUGHNUTS and LUDWIG ALMGREN (also from SAIDWAS) to form the anarcho-punky (INTERNATIONAL) NOISE CONSPIRACY. (I)NC recorded and put out two full-length albums, 'THE FIRST CONSPIRACY' (1999) and 'SURVIVAL SICKNESS' (2000). The former was a collection of 7" singles the band had put out in 1999 on several different labels. The latter on 'Burning Heart' was conceived as a whole unit, and shows the band's mix of punk and hardcore styles with the British Mod sounds of the sixties. LYXZEN also found time in 1999 to write, record, and release, a single and album, 'SONGS IN THE KEY OF RESISTANCE' (1999), with his other outfit, LOST PATROL.

Album rating: THIS JUST MIGHT BE . . . THE TRUTH (*5) / SONGS TO FAN THE FLAMES OF DISCONTENT (*5) / THE SHAPE OF PUNK TO COME mini (*6) / (International) Noise Conspiracy: THE FIRST CONSPIRACY (*6) / SURVIVAL SICKNESS (*6)

DENNIS LYXZEN – vocals / **JON F BRANNSTROM** – guitar / **KRISTOFER STEEN** – bass, guitar / **DAVID SANDSTROM** – drums

House Of Kicks — not iss.

Oct 94. (cd) *(STARTREC 372-2)* **THIS JUST MIGHT BE . . . THE TRUTH** -
– Intro / Pump the brakes / Trickbag / 5th freedom / Untitled / Strength / Our silence / Dust / Inclination / Mark / Tide / Button. *(re-iss. Jan95 on 'We Bite'; WB 3116CD)* *(re-iss. Sep97 on 'Burning Heart'; BHR 062CD)*

Burning Heart — not iss.

Oct 94. (cd-ep) *(BHR 002CD)* **THIS IS THE NEW DEAL** -
– Hate breeds hate / Break / Where's equality? / Soft / I wish.

1995. (cd-ep) **REFUSED LOVES RANDY** - - Sweden
– TV freak / Pump the brakes / Humanology / Re-fused.

1996. (cd-ep) **PUMP THE BRAKES EP** - - Sweden
– Pump the brakes / Perception / Strength / Who died.

Equal Vision — Equal Vision

Mar 97. (m-cd/m-lp) *(<EVR CD/LP 033>)* **THE EVERLASTING EP**
– Burn it / Symbols / Sunflower princess / Everlasting / I am not me / The real / Pretty face.

Burning Heart — Victory

Sep 97. (cd) *(BHR 061CD) <VR 40>* **SONGS TO FAN THE FLAMES OF DISCONTENT** Jun96
– Rather be dead / Coup d'etat / Hook, line and sinker / Return to the closet / Life support addiction / It's not O.K. / Crusader of hopelessness / Worthless is the freedom bought . . . . / This trust will kill again / Beauty / Last minute pointer / The slayer.

Burning Heart — Epitaph

Mar 98. (m-cd) *(BHR 071CD) <82001>* **THE SHAPE OF PUNK TO COME** Oct98
– Worms of the senses – Liberation frequency / The deadly rhythm / Summerholidays vs. punkroutine / Bruitist pome #5 / New noise / The Refused party program / Protest song '68 / Refused are fuckin' dead / The shape of punk to come / Tannhauser – Derive / The Apollo programme was a hoax.

Burning Heart — Honey Bear

May 98. (cd-ep) *(BHR 079CDS) <21>* **THE NEW NOISE THEOLOGY EP** Nov98
– New noise / Blind date / Poetry written in gasoline / Refused are fucking dead.

— after they split, LYXZEN formed The LOST PATROL who released an eponymous set in 1999; 'SONGS IN THE KEY OF RESISTANCE' was issued on Nov'00 on 'Startracks'; *(STAR 7842-2)*

– compilations, etc. –

Sep 97. (cd) *Burning Heart; (BHR 063CD)* **THIS ALBUM CONTAINS OLD SONGS VOL.1** -

Sep 97. (cd) *Burning Heart; (BHR 064CD)* **THIS ALBUM CONTAINS OLD SONGS VOL.2** -

(INTERNATIONAL) NOISE CONSPIRACY

DENNIS LYXZEN – vocals, tambourine / **SARA ALMGREN** – guitar, tambourine, organ (ex-DOUGHNUTS, ex-SAIDIWAS) / **LARS STROMBERG** – guitar, vocals (ex-SEPARATION) / **INGE JOHANSSON** – bass, vocals (ex-FEMALE ANCHOR OF SADE) / **LUDWIG DAHLBERG** – drums (ex-SAIDIWAS)

G-7 — Epitaph

Jun 99. (cd) *(G7 009) <82008>* **THE FIRST CONSPIRACY** -
– The first conspiracy / Abolish work / A new language / Do U know my name? / T.I.M.E.B.O.M.B. / The sin crusade / The blast-off / Young pretenders army / I swear if U do / Airports / Introduction to the . . . / Black mask. *<US-iss.Apr01; same as UK>*

Burning Heart — not iss.

Apr 00. (lp/cd) *(BHR 106-1/-2)* **SURVIVAL SICKNESS** -
– I wanna know about U / The subversive sound / Smash it up / Survival sickness /

The reproduction of death / Imposter costume / Intermission / Only lovers left alive / Do I have to spell it out / Will I ever be quiet / Enslavement blues / Ready steady go!

Big Wheel Big Wheel

Nov 00. (7"ep/cd-ep) *(<BWR 0238/+CD>)* **SMASH IT UP** [ ] [ ]

Sweet Nothing Sub Pop

Mar 01. (7") *(7SN 003)* *<SP 558>* **THE REPRODUCTION OF DEATH. /** [ ] [ ]
(cd-ep iss.May01 on 'Burning Heart'; BHR 123-2)

Riff REGAN (see under ⇒ LONDON)

Vernon REID (see under ⇒ LIVING COLOUR)

RENTALS (see under ⇒ WEEZER)

REO SPEEDWAGON

Formed: Champaign, Illinois, USA ... 1968 by NEAL DOUGHTY and ALAN GRATZER, who soon recruited GARY RICHRATH, TERRY LUTTRELL and GREG PHILBIN. With help from manager Irving Azoff, they signed to 'Epic' records in 1971, releasing their eponymous debut album soon after. Through constant touring and a highly productive recording schedule, the band built up a hefty national following, although early albums like 'LOST IN A DREAM' (1975) and 'THIS TIME WE MEAN IT' (featuring contributions from SLY STONE, of all people; 1975) only managed minor US chart placings. However, by the release of 'R.E.O.' in 1976, frontman CRONIN had returned following a brief period as a solo artist, his co-writing skills (along with RICHRATH) contributing to the band's subsequent breakthrough. The live 'YOU GET WHAT YOU PLAY FOR' (1977) was the group's first multi million seller while the appallingly titled 'YOU CAN TUNE A PIANO, BUT YOU CAN'T TUNA FISH' (1978) followed suit, their first US Top 30 placing. The group were also moving away from the rather faceless snooze-rock of old to a more poppy, hook-laden style, the shift paying off in 1981 when the 'SPEEDWAGON scored dual US No.1's with the melancholic balladry of single, 'KEEP ON LOVING YOU' and accompanying album, 'HI INFIDELITY'. An AOR classic in the mould of JOURNEY, STYX, BOB SEGER or KANSAS, 'HI . . .' was highly melodic, infectious and endearing despite the rather sappy vocal delivery and the group's chronic unfashionability. Tunes like 'TOUGH GUYS' and 'TAKE IT ON THE RUN' made great driving material, though you'd never admit as much to your mates. The follow-up, 'GOOD TROUBLE' (1982) was by all accounts a disappointment although the band were back on track by the mid-80's with the 'WHEELS ARE TURNIN'' (1984) album and its attendant No.1 single, 'CAN'T FIGHT THIS FEELING'. REO SPEEDWAGON continued to enjoy fair to middling US success throughout the remainder of the decade although since the departure of RICHRATH in 1990, the band have struggled to make an impact on the charts. • **Songwriters:** RICHRATH until 1976 when CRONIN returned to co-write most. • **Trivia:** Took their name from a 1911 fire truck.

Album rating: REO SPEEDWAGON (*6) / R.E.O. T.W.O. (*7) / RIDIN' THE STORM OUT (*6) / LOST IN A DREAM (*5) / THIS TIME WE MEAN IT (*5) / R.E.O. (*4) / REO SPEEDWAGON LIVE – YOU GET WHAT YOU PAY FOR (*5) / YOU CAN TUNE A PIANO, BUT YOU CAN'T TUNA FISH (*6) / NINE LIVES (*5) / A DECADE OF ROCK AND ROLL 1970 TO 1980 compilation (*6) / HI INFIDELITY (*6) / GOOD TROUBLE (*4) / WHEELS ARE TURNIN' (*5) / LIFE AS WE KNOW IT (*4) / THE HITS compilation (*6) / THE EARTH, A SMALL MAN, HIS DOG AND A CHICKEN (*3) / A SECOND DECADE OF ROCK AND ROLL 1981-1991 compilation (*5) / BUILDING THE BRIDGE (*3)

GARY RICHRATH (b.18 Oct'49, Peoria, Illinois) – lead guitar / **NEAL DOUGHTY** (b.29 Jul'46, Evanston, Illinois) – keyboards, organ / **ALAN GRATZER** (b. 9 Nov'48, Syracuse, N.Y.) – drums / **TERRY LUTTRELL** – vocals / **GREG PHILBIN** – bass

Epic Epic

Jan 72. (7") *<10827>* **PRISON WOMEN. / SOPHISTICATED LADY** [-] [ ]
Jun 72. (7") *<10847>* **157 RIVERSIDE AVENUE. / FIVE MEN WERE KILLED TODAY** [ ] [ ]
Jul 72. (lp) *(EPC 64813)* *<31089>* **REO SPEEDWAGON** [ ] [ ] Dec71
– Gypsy woman's passion / 157 Riverside Avenue / Anti-establishment man / Lay me down / Sophisticated lady / Five men were killed today / Prison women / Dead at last. *(re-iss. Nov81 on 'C.B.S.'; CBS 32096) (re-iss. Jun93 on 'Sony Collectors' cd/c; 982967-2/-4)*
Aug 72. (7") *<10892>* **GYPSY WOMAN'S PASSION. / LAY ME DOWN** [-] [ ]

—— **KEVIN CRONIN** (b. 6 Oct'51, Evanston) – vocals, guitar repl. LUTTRELL

Dec 72. (lp) *<31745>* **R.E.O. T.W.O.** [-] [ ]
– Let me ride / How the story goes / Little Queenie / Being kind / Music man / Like you do / Flash tan queen / Golden country.
Apr 73. (7") *<10975>* **GOLDEN COUNTRY. / LITTLE QUEENIE** [-] [ ]

—— **MIKE MURPHY** – vocals repl. CRONIN who became unrecorded solo artist

Jan 74. (lp) *<32378>* **RIDIN' THE STORM OUT** [-] [ ]
– Ridin' the storm out / Whiskey night / Oh woman / Find my fortune / Open up / Movin' / Son of a poor man / Start a new life / It's everywhere / Without expression.
Feb 74. (7") *<11078>* **RIDIN' THE NIGHT STORM. / WHISKEY NIGHT** [-] [ ]
Jun 74. (7") *<11132>* **OPEN UP. / START A NEW LIFE** [-] [ ]
Nov 74. (lp) *<32948>* **LOST IN A DREAM** [-] [98]
– Give me a ride / Throw the chains away / Sky blues / You can fly / Lost in a dream / Down by the dam / Do your best / Wild as the western wind / They're on the road / I'm feeling good.
Apr 75. (7") *<50059>* **THROW THE CHAINS AWAY. / SKY BLUES** [-] [ ]

—— **KEVIN CRONIN** returned to repl. MURPHY

Aug 75. (7") *<50120>* **OUT OF CONTROL. / RUNNING BLIND** [-] [ ]
Jul 75. (lp) *<33338>* **THIS TIME WE MEAN IT** [-] [74]
– Reelin' / Headed for a fall / River of life / Out of control / You better realise / Gambler / Candalera / Lies / Dance / Dream weaver.
Nov 75. (7") *<50180>* **HEADED FOR A FALL. / REELIN'** [-] [ ]
Jun 76. (7") *<50254>* **KEEP PUSHIN' / TONIGHT** [-] [ ]
Jun 76. (lp) *<34143>* **R.E.O.** [-] [ ]
– Keep pushin' / Any kind of love / Summer love / Our time is gonna come / Breakaway / Flying turkey trot / Tonight / Lightning.
Nov 76. (7") *<50288>* **FLYING TURKEY TROT. / KEEP PUSHIN'** [-] [ ]
May 77. (7") *<50367>* **RIDIN' THE STORM OUT (live). / BEING KIND (live)** [-] [94]
Aug 77. (d-lp) *(EPC 88265)* *<34494>* **REO SPEEDWAGON LIVE / YOU GET WHAT YOU PLAY FOR (live)** [ ] [72] Mar77
– Like you do / Lay me down / Any kind of love / Being kind (can hurt someone sometimes) / Keep pushin' / (Only) A summer love / Son of a poor man / (I believe) Our time is gonna come / Flying turkey trot / Gary's guitar solo / 157 Riverside Avenue / Ridin' the storm out / Music man / Little Queenie / Golden country.
Aug 77. (7") *<50459>* **FLYING TURKEY TROT (live). / KEEP PUSHIN' (live)** [-] [ ]

—— **BRUCE HALL** (b. 3 May'53) – bass repl. PHILBIN

Jul 78. (lp) *(EPC 82554)* *<35082>* **YOU CAN TUNE A PIANO, BUT YOU CAN'T TUNA FISH** [ ] [29] Apr78
– Roll with the changes / Time for me to fly / Runnin' blind / Blazin' your own trail again / Sing to me / Lucky for you / Do you know where your woman is tonight / The unidentified flying tuna trot / Say you love me or say goodnight. *(re-iss. Sep82; EPC 32115)*
Jun 78. (7") *(EPC 6415)* *<50545>* **ROLL WITH THE CHANGES. / THE UNIDENTIFIED FLYING TUNA TROT** [ ] [58] May78
Jul 78. (7") *<50582>* **TIME FOR ME TO FLY. / RUNNIN' BLIND** [-] [56]
Jul 79. (7") *<50764>* **EASY MONEY. / I NEED YOU TONIGHT** [-] [ ]
Aug 79. (lp/c) *(EPC/40 83647)* *<35988>* **NINE LIVES** [ ] [33]
– Heavy on your love / Drop it (an old disguise) / Only the strong survive / Easy money / Rock'n 'roll music / Take me / I need you tonight / Meet me on the mountain / Back on the road again.
Oct 79. (7") *(EPC 7918)* *<50790>* **ONLY THE STRONG SURVIVE. / DROP IT (AN OLD DISGUISE)** [ ] [ ]
Aug 80. (7") *(EPC 8903)* **ONLY THE STRONG SURVIVE. / MEET ME ON THE MOUNTAIN** [ ] [-]
Nov 80. (7") *<50953>* **KEEP ON LOVING YOU. / TIME FOR ME TO FLY** [-] [1]
Feb 81. (7") *(EPC 9544)* **KEEP ON LOVING YOU. / FOLLOW MY HEART** [7] [-]
Apr 81. (lp/c) *(EPC/40 84700)* *<36844>* **HI INFIDELITY** [6] [1] Dec80
– Don't let him go / Keep on loving you / Follow my heart / In your letter / Take it on the run / Tough guys / Out of season / Shakin' it loose / Someone tonight / I wish you were there. *(re-iss. Nov84 lp/c; EPC/40 32538) (cd-iss. 1988 on 'C.B.S.'; CD 84700) (lp re-iss. Nov98 on 'Simply Vinyl'; SVLP 42)*
Jun 81. (7") *(EPC 1207)* *<01054>* **TAKE IT ON THE RUN. / SOMEONE TONIGHT** [19] [5] Mar81
Jun 81. (7") *<02127>* **DON'T LET HIM GO. / I WISH YOU WERE THERE** [-] [24]
Sep 81. (7") *(EPC 1562)* *<02457>* **IN YOUR LETTER. / SHAKIN' IT LOOSE** [ ] [20] Aug81
Jul 82. (7") *(EPC 2495)* *<02967>* **KEEP THE FIRE BURNIN'. / I'LL FOLLOW YOU** [ ] [7] Jun82
Jul 82. (lp/c) *(EPC/40 85789)* *<38100>* **GOOD TROUBLE** [29] [7]
– Keep the fire burnin' / Sweet time / Girl with the heart of gold / Every now and then / I'll follow you / The key / Back in my heart again / Let's bebop / Stillness of the night / Good trouble. *(re-iss. 1986; EPC 32789)*
Sep 82. (7") *(EPC 2715)* *<03175>* **SWEET TIME. / STILLNESS OF THE NIGHT** [ ] [26] Aug82
Oct 82. (7") *(EPC 2889)* *<03400>* **THE KEY. / LET'S BEBOP** [ ] [ ]
Oct 84. (7") *<04659>* **I DO'WANNA KNOW. / ROCK AND ROLL STAR** [-] [29]
Nov 84. (lp/c/cd) *(EPC/40/CD 26137)* *<39593>* **WHEELS ARE TURNIN'** [ ] [7]
– I do'wanna know / One lonely night / Thru the window / Rock and roll star / Live every moment / Can't fight this feeling / Gotta feel more / Break his spell / Wheels are turnin'.
Jan 85. (7") *<04713>* **CAN'T FIGHT THIS FEELING. / BREAK HIS SPELL** [-] [1]
Feb 85. (7") *(A 4880)* **CAN'T FIGHT THIS FEELING. / ROCK AND ROLL STAR** [16] [-]
(12"+=) *(TA 4880)* – Keep on loving you.
May 85. (7") *(A 6225)* *<04848>* **ONE LONELY NIGHT. / WHEELS ARE TURNIN'** [ ] [19] Mar85
(12"+=) *(TA 6225)* – Take it on the run.
Jul 85. (7") *(A 6466)* *<05412>* **LIVE EVERY MOMENT. / GOTTA FEEL MORE** [ ] [34]
Nov 85. (7") *(A 6673)* **WHEREVER YOU'RE GOING. / SHAKIN' IT LOOSE** [ ] [-]
Mar 87. (7") *(650390-7)* *<06656>* **THAT AIN'T LOVE. / ACCIDENTS CAN HAPPEN** [ ] [16] Jan87
Apr 87. (lp/c/cd) *(450380-1/-4/-2)* *<40444>* **LIFE AS WE KNOW IT** [ ] [28] Feb87
– New way to love / That ain't love / In my dreams / One too many girlfriends / Variety tonight / Screams and whispers / Can't get you out of my heart / Over the edge / Accidents can happen / Tired of getting nowhere.
May 87. (7") *<07055>* **VARIETY TONIGHT. / TIRED OF GETTING NOWHERE** [-] [60]
Oct 87. (7") *(651040-7)* *<07255>* **IN MY DREAMS. / OVER THE EDGE** [ ] [19] Jul87

—— **GRAHAM LEAR** – drums (ex-SANTANA) repl. GRATZER

Sep 88. (7") *(651646-7)* *<07901>* **HERE WITH ME. / WHEREVER YOU'RE GOIN' (IT'S ALRIGHT)** [ ] [20] Jun88
(12"+=/cd-s+=) *(651646-6/-2)* – Keep on loving you / Take it on the run.
Nov 88. (7") *<08030>* **I DON'T WANT TO LOSE YOU. / ON THE ROAD AGAIN** [-] [ ]

— (Apr'89) **MILES JOSEPH** – guitar (ex-PLAYER) repl. RICHRATH

— (1990) **CRONIN, DOUGHTY & HALL** brought in new members **DAVE AMATO** – lead guitar, vocals (ex-TED NUGENT) repl. MILES JOSEPH / **BRYAN HITT** – drums (ex-WANG CHUNG) repl. LEAR / added **JESSE HARMS** – keyboards, vocals (ex-JOHN HIATT, ex-RY COODER)

Aug 90. (7") *<73499>* **LIVE IT UP. / ALL HEAVEN BROKE LOOSE** [-] [ ]

Sep 90. (cd/c/lp) *(467013-1/-4/-2) <45246>* **THE EARTH, A SMALL MAN, HIS DOG AND A CHICKEN** [ ] [ ] Aug90
– Love is a rock / The heart survives / Live it up / All Heaven broke loose / Love in the future / Half way / Love to hate / You won't see me / Can't lie to my heart / L.I.A.R. / Go for broke.

Oct 90. (c-s,cd-s) *<73540>* **LOVE IS A ROCK. / GO FOR BROKE** [-] [65]

Jan 91. (c-s,cd-s) *<73659>* **L.I.A.R. / HALF WAY** [-] [ ]

— split some time in 1991 before re-forming later

not iss. Essential

Jul 96. (cd) *<119>* **BUILDING A BRIDGE** [-] [ ]
– Can't stop rockin' / I still love you / Building the bridge / When I get home / Then I met you / Look the other way / After tonight / Hey wait a minute / One true man / She's gonna love me / Ballad of the Illinois Opry.

– compilations, etc. –

Below releases on 'Epic' unless mentioned.

May 80. (7") *<50858>* **TIME FOR ME TO FLY. / LIGHTNING** [-] [77]

Jul 80. (d-lp/d-c) *(EPC/40 22131) <36444>* **A DECADE OF ROCK'N'ROLL 1970 TO 1980** [ ] [55] Apr80
– Sophisticated lady / Music man / Golden country / Son of a poor man / Lost in a dream / Reelin' / Keep pushin' / Our time is gonna come / Breakaway / Lightning / Like you do / Flying turkey trot / 157 Riverside Avenue / Ridin' the storm out / Roll with the changes / Time for me to fly / Say you love me or say goodnight / Only the strong survive / Back on the road again. *(re-iss. Jul82; same)*

Apr 83. (7") *<03846>* **KEEP THE FIRE BURNIN'. / TAKE IT ON THE RUN** [-] [ ]

Apr 83. (7") *<03847>* **IN YOUR LETTER. / DON'T LET HIM GO** [-] [-]

Aug 84. (7"ep/c-ep) *Scoop; (7SR/7SC 5049)* **6 TRACK HITS** [ ] [-]
– Only the strong survive / Meet me on the mountain / Shakin' it loose / In your letter / I need you tonight / Roll with the changes.

Nov 85. (lp/c) *(EPC/40 26640)* **BEST FOOT FORWARD – THE BEST OF REO SPEEDWAGON** [ ] [-]
(re-iss. Jan92 cd/c; 468603-2/-4) (cd re-iss. Oct94; 477510-2)

Feb 86. (7"ep) *Old Gold; (OG 4010)* **KEEP ON LOVIN' YOU. / (2 other tracks by 'Journey' & 'Meat Loaf')** [ ] [-]

Jun 88. (lp/c/cd) *(460856-1/-4/-2) <44202>* **THE HITS** [ ] [56]
(cd/c re-iss. Jul98; 465595-2/-4)

Aug 88. (3"cd-s) <> **KEEP ON LOVIN' YOU. / TIME FOR ME TO FLY** [-] [ ]

Oct 91. (cd/c/lp) *(468958-2/-4/-1)* **A SECOND DECADE OF ROCK'N'ROLL 1981-1991** [ ] [ ]
– Don't let him go / Tough guys / Take it on the run / Shakin' it loose / Keep the fire burnin' / Roll with the changes / I do wanna know / Can't fight this feeling / Live every moment / That ain't love / One too many girlfriends / Variety tonight / Back on the road again / Keep on loving you '89 / Love is a rock / All Heavens broke loose / L.I.A.R. / Live it up.

Jan 00. (cd) *(495324-2)* **THE BALLADS** [ ] [ ]

REPLACEMENTS

Formed: Minneapolis, Minnesota, USA ... 1980 originally as The IMPEDIMENTS by the STINSON brothers – TOMMY and BOB – along with CHRIS MARS and chief songwriter/frontman, PAUL WESTERBERG. Legendary purveyors of ramshackle three-chord punk rock, The REPLACEMENTS' early efforts were so lo-fi they were off the end of the scale. Signed to Minneapolis indie stalwart, 'Twin Tone', the band debuted with 'SORRY MA, FORGOT TO TAKE OUT THE TRASH' (1981), the record's raw-nerve attitude, cathartic melodies and twisted humour shining through the garden shed (and a particularly dilapidated one at that) production. The following year's 'STINK' stepped on the gas and upped the nihilism ('GIMME NOISE', 'FUCK SCHOOL') although 'HOOTENANNY' (1983) and 'LET IT BE' (1984) used the hormonal energy to more satisfying and constructive ends. The latter set, especially, saw WESTERBERG's breathtakingly intuitive way with a melody reach fruition; granted, the likes of 'GARY'S GOT A BONER' didn't suggest another ELVIS COSTELLO in the ascendant but the bruised beauty of 'SIXTEEN BLUE' put WESTERBERG head and shoulders above most of his contemporaries (with the honourable exception of, perhaps, HUSKER DU). The record's charms were powerful enough to attract the major label attentions of 'Sire' and in late '85, The REPLACEMENTS released the Tommy Erdelyi (formerly TOMMY RAMONE)-produced 'TIM'. Furnished with a bigger budget, the group tempered their ragged sound while retaining much of the threadbare authenticity, the hooks as razor sharp as ever. It was to be the last album to feature the departing BOB, the band's notoriously shambolic live appearances robbed of the man's more erm, eccentric tendencies (playing in a dress – radical for the time! – or indeed in the nude, was not uncommon). With ROBERT 'SLIM' DUNLAP brought in as a replacement (ha!), the band recorded what many fans and critics alike regard as their finest hour, 'PLEASED TO MEET ME' (1987). More musically adventurous in line with their growing eclecticism, the album also found WESTERBERG's songwriting prowess at its unprecedented best, 'SKYWAY' soaring heavenward while 'CAN'T HARDLY WAIT' was the killer pop song he'd been threatening to pen since the band's inception. Criminally, the rave reviews and positive momentum surrounding the album's release failed to translate into sales, The REPLACEMENTS sounding strangely muted on 1989's 'DON'T TELL A SOUL', despite the return of BOB STINSON. While the minor concessions to commerciality resulted in a Top 60 US chart entry, the band were on their last legs and 1990's 'ALL SHOOK DOWN' was a WESTERBERG solo effort in all but name. The split eventually came in 1992, TOMMY forming BASH & POP (who released an album, 'FRIDAY NIGHT IS KILLING ME' the following year), while WESTERBERG worked on his solo debut proper, '14 SONGS' (1993). Although the writing was faultless, the record lacked the unkempt charm of old, any chance of a full REPLACEMENTS reunion suffering a serious setback as BOB succumbed to a drugs overdose the following year. In the latter half of the 90's (while MARS was also delivering the odd album), WESTERBERG found acceptance – in the way of US chart fame – via two further sets, 'EVENTUALLY' (1996) and 'SUICAINE GRATIFACTION' (1999). • **Songwriters:** Penned by WESTERBERG, except; I WILL DARE (Kiss) / ROUTE 66 (Nelson Riddle Orchestra) / 20TH CENTURY BOY (T-Rex) / HEY GOOD LOOKING (Bo Diddley) / CRUELLA DE VILLE (from '1001 Dalmations'). • **Trivia:** Were quoted after a tour as saying 'Better hours, 9 to 5; 9 at night to 5 in the morning, that is'. Their '87 single 'ALEX CHILTON', was dedicated to legendary BOX TOPS leader.

Album rating: SORRY MA, FORGOT TO TAKE OUT THE TRASH (*4) / STINK mini (*4) / HOOTENANNY (*6) / BOINK!! compilation (*7) / LET IT BE (*8) / TIM (*7) / PLEASED TO MEET ME (*8) / DON'T TELL A SOUL (*6) / ALL SHOOK DOWN (*6) / ALL FOR NOTHING – NOTHING FOR ALL compilation (*7) / Paul Westerberg: 14 SONGS (*5) / EVENTUALLY (*6) / SUICAINE GRATIFACTION (*7) / Chris Mars: HORSESHOES AND HAND GRENADES (*5) / 75% LESS FAT (*5) / TENTERHOOKS (*6) / ANONYMOUS BOTCH (*5)

PAUL WESTERBERG (b.31 Dec'60) – vocals, rhythm guitar / **BOB STINSON** (b.17 Dec'59) – lead guitar / **TOMMY STINSON** (b. 6 Oct'66, San Diego, Calif.) – bass / **CHRIS MARS** (b.26 Apr'61) – drums

not iss. Twin Tone

1981. (lp) *<TTR 8123>* **SORRY MA, FORGOT TO TAKE OUT THE TRASH** [-] [ ]
– Takin' a ride / Careless / Customer / Hanging downtown / Kick your door down / Otto / I bought a headache / Rattlesnake / I hate music / Johnny's gonna die / Shiftless when idle / More cigarettes / Don't ask why / Something to do / I'm in trouble / Love you till Friday / Shut up / Raised in the city. *(UK-iss.Mar88 on 'What Goes On'; GOES ON 017) (cd-iss. Apr93 on 'Roadrunner'; RR 9089-2) (cd re-iss. Mar95; TTR 8123-2)*

1981. (7") *<TTR 8120>* **I'M IN TROUBLE. / IF ONLY YOU WERE LONELY** [-] [ ]

1982. m-(lp) *<TTR 8228>* **STINK** [-] [ ]
– Kids don't follow / Fuck school / Stuck in the middle / God damn job / White and lazy / Dope smokin' moron / Go / Gimme noise. *(UK-iss.Mar88 on 'What Goes On'; GOES ON 020) (cd-iss. Apr93 on 'Roadrunner'; RR 9090-2) (cd re-iss. Mar95; 8228-2)*

1983. (lp) *<TTR 8332>* **HOOTENANNY** [-] [ ]
– Hootenanny / Run it / Color me impressed / Will power / Take me down to the hospital / Mr. Whirly / Within your reach / Buck hill / Lovelines / You lose / Hayday / Treatment bound. *(UK-iss.Mar88 on 'What Goes On'; GOES ON 021) (cd-iss. Apr93 on 'Roadrunner'; RR 9091-2) (cd re-iss. Feb95; TTR 8332-2)*

1984. (12") *<TTR 8440>* **I WILL DARE. / 20TH CENTURY BOY / HEY GOOD LOOKING (live)** [-] [ ]

Zippo Twin Tone

Oct 84. (lp) *(ZONG 002) <TTR 8441>* **LET IT BE**
– I will dare / We're comin' out / Tommy gets his tonsels out / Black diamond / Androgynous / Unsatisfied / Seen your video / Gary's got a boner / Sixteen blue / Answering machine. *(cd-iss. Apr93 on 'Roadrunner'; RR 9092-2) (cd-iss. Mar95)*

1985. (c) **THE SHIT HITS THE FAN (live bootleg)** [-] [ ]

Sire Sire

Nov 85. (lp/c) *(K 925330-1/-4) <25330>* **TIM** [ ] [ ]
– Hold my life / I'll buy / Kiss me on the bus / Dose of thunder / Waitress in the sky / Swingin' party / Bastards of young / Lay it down clown / Left of the dial / Litle mascara / Here comes a regular. *(cd-iss. Jul93; 7599 25330-2)*

Mar 86. (7") *(W 8727)* **SWINGIN' PARTY. / LEFT OF THE DIAL** [ ] [-]

May 86. (7") *(W 8679)* **KISS ME ON THE BUS. / LITTLE MASCARA** [ ] [-]

— **ROBERT 'SLIM' DUNLAP** (b.14 Aug'51, Plainview, Minnesota) – keyboards repl. BOB (he was to die on the 18th of February 1995 o.d.)

Apr 87. (lp/c/cd) *(K 925557-1/-4/-2) <25557>* **PLEASED TO MEET ME** [ ] [ ]
– I.O.U. / Alex Chilton / I don't know / Nightclub jitters / The ledge / Never mind / Valentine / Shooting dirty pool / Red red wine / Skyway / Can't hardly wait. *(cd re-iss. Jul93; 7599 25557-2)*

Jun 87. (7") *(W 8297)* **ALEX CHILTON. / ELECTION DAY** [ ] [-]
(12"+=) *(W 8297T)* – Nightclub jitters / Route 66.

Jul 87. (7") *<28151>* **CAN'T HARDLY WAIT. / COOL WATER** [-] [ ]

— **BOB STINSON** – guitar returned to repl. SLIM who went solo

Jan 89. (lp/c/cd) *(K 925721-1/-4/-2) <25721>* **DON'T TELL A SOUL** [ ] [57]
– Talent show / Back to back / We'll inherit the Earth / Achin' to be / They're blind / Anywhere's better than here / Asking me lies / I won't / Rock'n'roll ghost / Darlin' one. *(cd re-iss. Jul93; 7559 25831-2)*

Apr 89. (7") *<22992>* **I'LL BE YOU. / DATE TO CHURCH (with TOM WAITS)** [-] [51]
(below w/ guests **STEVE BERLIN / MICHAEL BLAIR / BELMONT TENCH / JOHN CALE /** etc.

Sep 90. (cd/c/lp) *<(7599 26298-2/-4/-1)>* **ALL SHOOK DOWN** [ ] [69]
– Merry go round / One wink at a time / Nobody / Bent out of shape / Sadly beautiful / Someone takes the wheel / When it began / All shook down / Attitude / Happy town / Torture / My little problem / The lost. *(cd re-iss. Jul93 & Feb95; same)*

— (Mar'91) **STEVE FOLEY** – drums; repl. MARS who went solo

— disbanded late in 1991, TOMMY formed BASH & POP, while WESTERBERG and MARS went solo

– compilations, others, etc. –

Apr 86. (m-lp/m-c) *Glass; (MGA LP/MC 016)* **BOINK!!** [ ] [-]
– Color me impressed / White and lazy / Within your reach / If only you were lonely / Kids don't follow / Nowhere is my home / Take me down to the hospital / Go.

Nov 97. (d-cd) *Reprise; <(9362 46807-2)>* **ALL FOR NOTHING / NOTHING FOR ALL**
– Left of the dial / Kiss me on the bus / Bastards of young / Here comes a regular / Skyway / Alex Chilton / The ledge / Can't hardly wait / I'll be you / Achin' to be / Talent show / Anywhere's better than here / Merry-go-round / Sadly beautiful / Nobody / Someone take the wheel / Can't hardly wait (the TIM version) / Birthday gal / Beer for breakfast / Till we're nude / Election day / Jungle rock / All he wants to do is fish / Date to church / Cruella De Ville / We know the night / Portland / Wake up / Satellite / Like a rolling pin / Another girl, another planet / Who knows / All shook down.

REVOLTING COCKS (see under ⇒ MINISTRY)

RHINOCEROS

Formed: (based) Los Angeles, California, USA . . . 1968 by the "supergroup" of MICHAEL FORFARA, BILLY MUNDI, DOUG HASTINGS, DANNY WEIS and newcomer JOHN FINLAY as lead singer. Although the super part was always questioned by critics, they had Top 50 hit early in 1969 with instrumental 'APRICOT BRANDY', which was used as the Radio 1 theme in the 70's. Just prior to this, their eponymous debut album started to hover around the outside of the US Top 100, as did their awful follow-up 'SATIN CHICKENS' in autumn of '69. 'Elektra' released their third set 'BETTER TIMES ARE COMING', but this was certainly not a good prediction, as the band split up soon after.

Album rating: RHINOCEROS (*5)

JOHN FINLEY – vocals / **ALAN GERBER** – keyboards, vocals, harps, flute / **MICHAEL FORFARA** – organ / **DANNY WEIS** – guitar / **DOUG HASTINGS** – guitar (ex-BUFFALO SPRINGFIELD, ex-DAVID ACKLES) / **JERRY PENROD** – bass (ex-IRON BUTTERFLY) / **BILLY MUNDI** – drums (ex-MOTHERS OF INVENTION, ex-EARTH OPERA, ex-TIM BUCKLEY)

Elektra Elektra

Oct 68. (7") *<45640>* **I WILL SERENADE YOU. / YOU'RE MY GIRL** [-]

Dec 68. (7") *<45647>* **APRICOT BRANDY. / WHEN YOU SAY YOU'RE SORRY** [-] [46]

Jan 69. (7") *(EKSN 45051)* **APRICOT BRANDY. / YOU'RE MY GIRL (I DON'T WANT TO DISCUSS IT)** [-]

Feb 69. (lp) *<(EKS 74030)>* **RHINOCEROS** Dec68
– When you say you're sorry / It's the same old way / I've been there / Apricot brandy / That time of the year / I need love / You're my girl (I don't want to discuss it) / Belbuekus / Along comes tomorrow / I will serenade you.

Mar 69. (7") *<45659>* **I NEED LOVE. / BELBUEKUS** [-]

Apr 69. (7") *(EKSN 45058)* **I WILL SERENADE YOU. / BELBUEKUS** [-]

— **PETER HODGSON** – bass (ex-BAMBOO), repl. PENROD

Dec 69. (lp) *<(EKS 74056)>* **SATIN CHICKENS** Sep69
– Satin doll / Monkee man / Find my hand / Top of the ladder / Sugar foot rag / Don't come crying / Chicken / It's the same thing / In a little room / Funk butt / Back door.

Feb 70. (7") *(EKSN 45080) <45677>* **BACK DOOR. / IN A LITTLE ROOM** Oct69

— **LARRY LEISHMAN** – guitar, repl. HASTINGS (to DANNY O'KEEFE) + GERBER

— **DUKE EDWARDS** – drums, repl. MUNDI who went into many sessions

Jun 70. (7") *(2101 009) <45691>* **OLD AGE. / LET'S PARTY** May70

Sep 70. (lp) *(2469 006) <74075>* **BETTER TIMES ARE COMING** Jul70
– Old age / Sweet, nice'n'high / Insanity / Let's party / It's a groovy world / Better times / Just me / Happiness / Somewhere / Lady of fortune / Rain child.

Jan 71. (7") *<45694>* **IT'S A GROOVY WORLD. / BETTER TIMES** [-]

— Disbanded when WEIS + HODGSON formed BACKSTAGE.

RICO

Born: ENRICO CAPUANO, 23 Jun'71, Glasgow, the son of an Italian taxi driver and a Scottish-Irish shop assistant. Having scoured his older brother's record collection on more than several occasions, the young RICO decided he'd take up drumming and played in local punk bands during the mid to late 80's. His most treasured memory was unearthing a portastudio at school. He borrowed the equipment for a while but was moved to finding his own second-hand bits and bobs when his music teacher reclaimed it. Back at his parents' house in Paisley, RICO set up his own garage studio, although some of the neighbours haven't spoken to him since. Influenced by everyone from PiL, THE THE and NINE INCH NAILS, RICO set about creating his own homegrown one man band. From working by day at a £70 a week fast-food outlet, to working with other bands in his soundproofed studio, the greasy-haired RICO developed the self-obsessed skills needed to achieve his breakthrough. For three years between 1995 and 1998, the man pulled out all the stops to get the right mixes for his debut album. A limited-edition promo of the track, 'THIS AND THAT' (a f**ked up song, if ever there was one!), circulated around by late '98, while 'E.M.I.' produced his debut single proper, 'ATTACK ME'. The aforementioned debut set for 'Chrysalis', 'SANCTUARY MEDICINES', was finally unleashed to the public in August '99, its stark, paranoid undercurrents did indeed have all the hallmarks of NIN's TRENT REZNOR. Like mixing his favourite whiskey liquor (Jack Daniels, Jim Beam or Southern Comfort), anger and tension were always at the core of most of the album's contents.

Album rating: SANCTUARY MEDICINES (*5)

RICO – vocals, drums, guitar, effects

E.M.I. not iss.

May 99. (cd-ep) *(CDEM 538)* **ATTACK ME EP** [-]
– Attack me / Burst / Millennium mutants.

Chrysalis not iss.

Jul 99. (c-s) *(CHS 5111)* **SMOKESCREEN / THIS AND MATT** [-]
(cd-s+=) *(CDCHS 5111)* – Worst dream.

Aug 99. (cd) *(499063-2)* **SANCTUARY MEDICINES** [-]
– Shave your head / Aeroplane / Smokescreen / Black limo / Float / Overload / Sanctuary medicines / This and that / State / Attack me / Dear God.

Nov 99. (7") *(CHS 5113)* **SHAVE YOUR HEAD. / THE DOSE** [-]
(cd-s) *(CDCHSS 5113)* – ('A'side) / Next caller please / Digging the hole.
(cd-s) *(CDCHS 5113)* – ('A'side) / ('A'-Bury The Dead mix) / ('A'-Out Of Your Head mix).

Jul 00. (cd-s) *(CDCHSS 5117)* **FLOAT / AEROPLANE / SANCTUARY MEDICINES / FLOAT (video)** [-]
(cd-s) *(CDCHS 5117)* – ('A'-live in the studio) / Black limo (live in the studio) / Dear God (live in the studio).

RIOT

Formed: New York, USA . . . 1976 by MARK REALE, GUY SPERANZA, L.A. KOUVARIS, PETER BITELLI and JIMMY IOMMI. Signed to 'Ariola', the band made more of an impression in Europe than their native America, both with their debut album, 'ROCK CITY' (1978) and its follow-up, 'NARITA' (1980). The latter set was released on 'Capitol', RIOT undergoing the first of their countless personnel and label changes (RICK VENTURA replaced KOUVARIS). By the turn of the decade, KIP LEMING and SANDY SLAVIN were in place for the recording of their third set, 'FIRE DOWN UNDER', although this was knocked back by Capitol as being unlikely to sell. However, 'Elektra' took both the album and the group on board, eventually releasing the record in 1981. Despite continuing critical acclaim for their classy hard rock/metal, RIOT foundered with the exit of SPENENZA. The frontman's replacement, RHETT FORRESTER, graced a fourth set, 'RESTLESS BREED', although he only stuck around for one more independently issued album, 'BORN IN AMERICA' (1984). RIOT were dispersed in the mid 80's, REALE instigating a renewed disturbance in 1988 with a fresh line-up. Armed with a new major label contract via 'Epic/CBS', the band delivered two further albums, 'THUNDERSTEEL' (1988) and 'THE PRIVILEGE OF POWER' (1990), before order was restored. Sadly, around the time of a one-off comeback album, 'NIGHTBREAKER' (1994), former frontman, FORRESTER was killed during an attempted robbery; the 1996 cut 'THE BRETHREN OF THE LONG HOUSE' was subsequently issued in '98. With newcomer DiMEO on vocals, RIOT delivered two further below par sets, 'SHINE ON' (1998) and 'SONS OF SOCIETY' (1999).

Album rating: ROCK CITY (*6) / NARITA (*5) / FIRE DOWN UNDER (*6) / RESTLESS BREED (*5) / BORN IN AMERICA (*4) / THUNDERSTEEL (*6) / RIOT LIVE 1980 (*6) / PRIVILEGE OF POWER (*5) / NIGHTBREAKER (*5) / THE BRETHREN OF THE LONG HOUSE (*5) / SHINE ON (*4) / SONS OF SOCIETY (*4)

GUY SPERANZA – vocals, guitar / **MARK REALE** – guitar / **L.A. KOUVARIS** – guitar / **JIMMY IOMMI** – bass / **PETER BITELLI** – drums

Ariola Ariola

1978. (lp) *(ARL 5007)* **ROCK CITY**
– Desperation / Warrior / Rock city / Overdrive / Angel / Tokyo rose / Heart of fire / Gypsy queen / This is what I get. *(cd-iss. Feb93 on 'Metal Blade'; CDMZORRO 54) (cd re-iss. Jun96 on 'Metal Blade'; 3984 14009CD)*

— **RICK VENTURA** – guitar; repl. KOUVARIS

Capitol Capitol

May 80. (lp) *<(EST 12081)>* **NARITA**
– Waiting for the taking / 49er / Kick down the wall / Born to be wild / Narita / Here we come again / Do it up / Hot for love / White rock / Road racin'.

— **KIP LEMING** – bass; repl. IOMMI

— **SANDY SLAVIN** – drums; repl. BITELLI

Elektra Elektra

Aug 81. (7") *<47218>* **OUTLAW. / ROCK CITY** [-]

Sep 81. (lp) *(K 52315) <546>* **FIRE DOWN UNDER** [99] Aug81
– Swords and tequila / Fire down under / Feel the same / Outlaw / Don't bring me down / Don't hold back / Altar of the king / No lies / Run for your life / Flashbacks. *(cd-iss. Jan96 on 'Warners'; 7559 60576-2) (cd re-iss. Sep97 on 'High Vaultage'; HV 1021)*

Oct 81. (7") *(K 12565)* **OUTLAW. / ROCK CITY**

— **RHETT FORRESTER** – vocals, harmonica; repl. SPERANZA

Jun 82. (lp) *<(K 52398)>* **RESTLESS BREED**
– Hard lovin' man / C.I.A. / Restless breed / When I was young / Loanshark / Loved by you / Over to you / Showdown / Dream away / Violent crimes. *(cd-iss. Jan96 on 'Warners'; 7559 60134-2)*

not iss. Quality

Jan 84. (lp) *<1008>* **BORN IN AMERICA** [-]
– Born in America / You burn in me / Wings of fire / Running from the law / Devil woman / Vigilante killer / Heavy metal machine / Where soldiers rule / Gunfighter / Promised land. *<re-iss. 1989 on 'Grand Slam'; SLAM 6> <(cd-iss. May99 on 'Metal Blade'; 14234-2)>*

— **MARK REALE** recruited an entire new line-up; **TONY MOORE** – vocals / **DON VAN STAVERN** – bass / **BOBBY JARZOMBEK** – drums

Epic CBS Assoc.

Sep 88. (lp/c/cd) *(460 976-1/-4/-2) <44232>* **THUNDERSTEEL** May88
– Thundersteel / Fight or fall / Sign of the crimson storm / Flight of the warrior / On wings of eagles / Johnny's back / Bloodstreets / Run for your life / Buried alive (tell tale heart).

May 90. (cd/c/lp) *(466486-2/-4/-1) <45132>* **THE PRIVILEGE OF POWER**

– On your shoes / Metal soldiers / Runaway / Killer / Dance of death / Storming the gates of Hell / Maryanne / Little Miss Death / Black leather and glittering steel / Race with the Devil on a Spanish highway (revisited).

S.P.V. — Metal Blade

Jun 94. (cd) *(SPV 084-6222-2)* <14239> **NIGHTBREAKER**
– Soldier / Destiny / Burn / In your eyes / Nightbreaker / Medicine man / Silent scream / Magic maker / I'm on the run / Babylon / Outlaw.

Rising Sun — Metal Blade

Jul 98. (cd) *(RS 0072962CD)* <14240> **THE BRETHREN OF THE LONG HOUSE** (German 1996) — - — German
– The last of the Mohicans / Wounded heart / Rolling thunder / Rain / Holy land / The brethren of the long house / Blood of the English / Out in the fields / Ghost dance / Shenandoah / Glory calling / Mohicans reprise / Santa Maria. *(with free live-cd+=)* – Minutes to showtime / On your knees . . . in Tokyo! / Metal soldiers / Runaway / Tokyo rose . . . in Osaka! / Rock city / Outlaw / Killer / Skins & bones (parts 1 & 2) / Johnny's back . . . in Tokyo! / Ladies & gentlemen / Japan cakes / Narita / Warrior / The dressing room – The encore begins . . . in Tokyo.

— **DiMEO** – vocals; repl. MOORE

Metal Blade — Metal Blade

Oct 98. (cd) <*(14182-2)*> **SHINE ON**
– Black water / Angel's eyes / Soldier / The man / Kings are falling / Bloodstreets / Swords and tequila / Cry for the dying / Irish trilogy: Inishmore (forsaken heart) – Inishmore – Danny boy / Liberty / Gypsy / The last of the Mohicans / Thundersteel / Outlaw / Warrior.

Sep 99. (cd) <*(14249-2)*> **SONS OF SOCIETY**
– Snake charmer / On the wings of life / Sons of society / Twist of fate / Bad machine / Cover me / Dragon fire / The law / Time to bleed / Somewhere / Promises.

– compilations, etc. –

1989. (cd) *CBS-Sony;* <*CSCS 5024*> **RIOT LIVE (live)** — -
– Hard lovin' man / Showdown / Loved by you / Loanshark / Restless breed / Swords and tequila. *(UK-iss.Jul92 on 'Metal Blade'; CDZORRO 55) (cd re-iss. Jun96 on 'Metal Blade'; 3984 14011CD)*

RIOT SQUAD

Formed: Mansfield, England . . . 1982, comprising WAYNE BUTLER, PAUL PALMER and two unknown members (not to be confused with another outfit around the same time who released 'Total Onslaught' – in fact, the RIOT SQUAD moniker was used by a reasonably successful mod combo in the mid-60's). Anyway, these hardcore skins with protest oi/punk leanings were a different kettle of fish altogether. Defiant and anarchic from the outset, RIOT SQUAD unleashed two anti-establishment 45's in 1982, namely 'FUCK THE TORIES' and 'RIOT IN THE CITY', before WAYNE and PAUL enlisted two new recruits, LEE BUTLER and CHEDD. This line-up completed three further similarly provocative singles for their own 'Rot' label, the musical blind alley of subsequent album, 'NO POTENTIAL THREAT' (1984), arresting their progress as the band split.

Album rating: THE COMPLETE PUNK COLLECTION compilation (*4)

– vocals / – guitar / **WAYNE BUTLER** – bass / **PAUL PALMER** – drums

Rondelet — not iss.

Aug 82. (7"m) *(ROUND 23)* **FUCK THE TORIES. / WE ARE THE RIOT SQUAD / CIVIL DESTRUCTION** — -

Sep 82. (7"m) *(ROUND 25)* **RIOT IN THE CITY. / WHY SHOULD WE / RELIGION DOESN'T MEAN A THING** — -

— **LEE BUTLER** – vocals; repl.

— **CHEDD** (b. PAUL) – bass; repl. (WAYNE now lead guitar)

Rot — not iss.

Jun 83. (7"ep) *(ASS 1)* **DON'T BE DENIED** — -
– Lost cause / Suspicion / Unite and fight / Police power.

Sep 83. (7"ep) *(ASS 2)* **I'M OK FUCK YOU** — -
– Society's fodder / In the future / Friday night hero.

Jan 84. (7") *(ASS 3)* **THERE AIN'T NO SOLUTION. / GOVERNMENT SCHEME** — -

Mar 84. (lp) *(ASS 13)* **NO POTENTIAL THREAT** — -
– No potential threat / Ten years time / Hate the law / Hidden in fear / Lost cause (demo) / Unite and fight (demo).

— disbanded later in '84

– compilations, etc. –

Jan 95. (cd) *Anagram; (CDPUNK 41)* **THE COMPLETE PUNK COLLECTION** — -

ROCK BITCH

Formed: In communes between England & France . . . 1997 as a 7-piece pagan, sex-metal extravaganza; description:- BABE (blonde bimbette half naked with hand prints on breasts – oh, and she sings!), JULIE (body-painted, ginger-haired, basque-popping she-devil – oh and she sings too!), LUCI (sultry dancer/slut!, long black-haired and naked but from stockings and black tape-wrapping around her intimate parts!), BEAST (the normally-attired, lucky male guitarist), JO (girl next door/hippy and er, drummer!), AMANDA THE BITCH (the bass-playing Morticia of the band!) and keyboardist NIKKI (the naked Lady Godiva of the outfit, what outfit!). ROCK BITCH soon found themselves the centre of distraction after several European shows (Scotland, Wales and even Norway, being the most infamous) were interrupted by riot police. The shock tactics paraded for all and sundry (bare flesh and simulated sex) became the subject of discussion by churches who attended a few gigs singing hymns; the group stopped to join in! What really riled up the Jesus Brigade and American fundamentalists was when during every show, LUCI threw a golden condom into the audience inviting the lucky person to er, come on stage and "give her one". As for records (vinyl,cd), well I suppose they'll probably have a criminal one first!

Album rating: MOTOR DRIVEN BIMBO (*5)

BABE + JULIE – vocals / **BEAST** – guitar / **NIKKE** – keyboards / **AMANDA THE BITCH** – bass / **JO** – drums / **LUCI** – slut

S.P.V. — S.P.V.

Jun 99. (cd) <*(085-21062)*> **MOTOR DRIVEN BIMBO**
– Snafu / The church / Eveline / Baby / Sex and the Devil / Open letter / Nympho / Innocence / Lucifer / Essex girl / Tell me / Bride of Christ / Diva.

ROCKET FROM THE CRYPT

Formed: San Diego, California, USA . . . 1989 by half-Portuguese singer, SPEEDO (JOHN REIS), alongside PETEY X, ATOM, JC 2000 and ND. REIS left school and joined PITCHFORK, a hardcore band who rapidly evolved into DRIVE LIKE JEHU (other members of this outfit being RICK FROBERG, MIKE KENNEDY and MARK TROMBINO), the frontman continuing to moonlight for the latter outfit through his early career with the 'CRYPT. Kick-ass speedball R&R punks/greasers drawing on the earthiest of 50's tradition, ROCKET FROM THE CRYPT were as suave as Vegas-era ELVIS with the attitude and sound of their heroes, The MISFITS (who they initially supported). In a further bid to boost their street cred, RFTC also claimed to have opened for two of the most legendary figures in black music, JAMES BROWN and SUN RA. On the recording front, the lads issued a plethora of singles for various hip US underground labels (the tracks were later collected together for UK consumption as 'ALL SYSTEMS GO!'), along the way releasing a debut album, 'PAINT AS A FRAGRANCE' (1991) and picking up sax player, APOLLO NINE. They unearthed a second album, 'CIRCA: NOW!', a year later and although the ROCKET-fuelled formula varied little, there was an audible improvement in the musicianship. While their mid-90's release schedule was as prolific as ever, they finally settled on a long-term deal with 'Interscope' ('El-e-mental' in the UK) in 1995. Towards the end of that year, they finally made their critical breakthrough on the UK alt-rock scene with the 'SCREAM, DRACULA, SCREAM!' album. It also lent them a modicum of commercial success scraping into the UK Top 40 and spawning no less than three hit singles, the last of which, 'ON A ROPE', found them threatening the Top 10. In the best tradtion of the DEAD BOYS or the SAINTS, however, ROCKET FROM THE CRYPT were in their element on stage blasting out their visceral, three-chord mainline rock'n'roll, NME recognising their talent by bestowing upon them a Brat Award for Best Newcomer. In the summer of '98, the slicked-back six-piece resurfaced with their second major label album, 'RFTC', a slightly subdued, more pop/rock-orientated affair that only just scraped into the UK Top 75. • **Songwriters:** Group, except GOLD (MC5). • **Trivia:** SPEEDO recently married ND's sister.

Album rating: PAINT AS A FRAGRANCE (*5) / CIRCA: NOW! (*5) / ALL SYSTEMS GO compilation (*7) / THE STATE OF ART IS ON FIRE mini (*5) / HOT CHARITY mini (*4) / SCREAM, DRACULA, SCREAM! (*8) / RFTC (*6) / ALL SYSTEMS GO 2 compilation (*7)

SPEEDO (b. JOHN REIS) – vocals, guitar / **ND** (aka ANDY) – guitar / **PETEY X** – bass, bass vocals / **ATOM** (aka ADAM) – drums / **JC 2000** (aka JAY) – trumpet, percussion, organ, vocals

not iss. — Pushead

1990. exist? (7"red) <*200772*> **CUT IT LOOSE. / GLAZED** — -

Helter Skelter — not iss.

1991. (7"ep) <*HS 92712*> **YUM KIPPERED EP** — - — - Italian
– Bad Ninja / Goodbye / Kill the funk (there will be no funk in Outer Space). *(UK-iss.Apr95 c-s/cd-s; same)*

not iss. — Headhunter

Feb 91. (lp/c/cd) <*HED 003/+MC/CD*> **PAINT AS A FRAGRANCE** — -
– French guy / Maybellene / Shy boy / Basturds / Velvet touch / Evil party / Stinker / Jiggy jig / Weak superhero / Thumbmaster. *(cd-iss. Mar93; same +UK)*

— added **APOLLO NINE** (aka PAUL) – saxophone, vocals

not iss. — Sympathy F

Jun 92. (7"m) <*SFTRI 179*> **BOY CHUCKER. / JUMPER K. BALLS / LEFTY** — -

not iss. — Sub Pop

Jun 92. (7"blue-ep) <*SP 154*> **NORMAL CARPET RIDE / WHERE ARE THE FUCKERS. / SLUMBER QUEEN / FLIP THE BIRD** — -

not iss. — Drunken Fish

Jul 92. (one-sided-7"gold) <*DF 02*> **GOLD** — -

not iss. — Standard

Oct 92. (7") <*SR 72*> **CHA CHA CHA. / (other track by DEADBOLT)** — -

not iss. — Merge

Nov 92. (7") <*MRG 035*> **PIGEON EATER. / (THE) PASTE THAT YOU LOVE** — -

not iss. — Pussheads

Dec 92. (d7") **PUSS MORT. / (other by SEPTIC DEATH)** — -

Headhunter — Headhunter

Jan 93. (lp/c/cd) <*(HED 015/+MC/CD)*> **CIRCA: NOW!** — — Nov92
– Short lip fuser / Hippy dippy do / Ditch digger / Don't Darlene / Killy kill / Hairball alley / Sturdy wrists / March of dimes / Little arm / Dollar / Glazed.

not iss. | Drunken Fish

Apr 93. (7",7"clear) <DF 05> **PURE GENIUS. / LIFT AND LOVE** [-] [ ]

not iss. | Merge

Feb 94. (12") <1994> **BURNT MOUTH OFF LIAR. / UFO UFO UFO** [-] [ ]

Bacteria Sour | not iss.

May 94. (7") *(SOUR 2V/3V)* **BLOODY THIRSTY BUTCHERS. /** [ ] [ ]

not iss. | Sympathy F

1995. (10"ep) <SFTRI 320> **THE STATE OF THE ART IS ON FIRE** [-] [ ]
– Light me / A+ in arson class / Rid or ride / Human torch / Ratsize / Human spine / Trouble / Masculine intuition.

El-e-mental | Interscope

Oct 95. (m-lp) *(ELM 27LP)* <92595> **HOT CHARITY** [ ] [ ] Aug95
– Pushed / Guilt free / Poison eye / My arrow's aim / Feathered friends / Cloud over Branson / Lorna Doom / Shucks / Pity yr paws.

Dec 95. (cd/c)<lp> *(ELM 34 CD/MC)* <92596-2/-4><Hed 54> **SCREAM, DRACULA, SCREAM!** [40] [ ] Oct95
– Middle / Born in '69 / On a rope / Young livers / Drop out / Used / Ball lightning / Fat lip / Suit city / Heater hands / Misbeaten / Come see, come saw / Salt future / Burnt alive.

El-e-mental | Interscope

Jan 96. (7"/cd-s) *(ELM 32 S/CD)* **BORN IN '69. / CIAO PATSY** [68] [-]

Apr 96. (7"/c-s) *(ELM 33 S/MC)* **YOUNG LIVERS. / BURNING ARMY MEN** [67] [-]
(cd-s+=) *(ELM 33CD)* – Lumps.

Sep 96. (cd-ep) *(ELM 38CD1)* **ON A ROPE / ALONE / WHO NEEDS YOU / YOUNG LIVERS (Mark Radcliffe session)** [12] [-]
(cd-ep) *(ELM 38CD2)* – ('A'-White Room version) / Allergic reaction / Transcendent crankiness / Suit city (Mark Radcliffe session).
(cd-ep) *(ELM 38CD3)* – ('A'-Ghetto box mix) / You and I / Intro – Don't Darlene (Mark Radcliffe session) / Lorna Doom (Mark Radcliffe session).

Nov 96. (7"ep) *(SFTRI 373)* **PLAYS THE MUSIC MACHINE EP** [ ] [ ] Oct96
(above on 'Sympathy For The Record Industry' / 'Kill Rock Stars' US)

Jun 98. (10"pic-d-ep) *(ELM 47TPIC)* **WHEN IN ROME (DO THE JERK). / TARZAN / TIGER FEET TONITE** [ ] [-]

Jul 98. (cd/c/lp) *(ELM 50 CD/MC/LP)* <90167> **RFTC** [63] [ ] Jun98
– Eye on you (with HOLLY GOLIGHTLY) / Break it up / I know / Panic scam / Made for you / Lipstick / You gotta move / Your touch / Let's get busy / Dick on a dog / Back in the state / When in Rome / Run kid run. *(also ltd-cd; ELM 50CDQ)*

Aug 98. (10") *(ELM 48TEN)* **LIPSTICK. / HOT HEART** [64] [-]
(cd-s) *(ELM 48CDS1)* – ('A'side) / Heads are gonna roll / Cheetah.
(cd-s) *(ELM 48CD2)* – ('A'side) / When in Rome (do the jerk) / Stranglehold.

— In Oct'98, the group were on a split 7" with JULIAN Y SUS HERMANOIS for 'Vinyl Communication' (VC 76)

Nov 98. (7") *(ELM 49S)* **BREAK IT UP. / TURKISH REVENGE** [ ] [-]
(cd-s+=) *(ELM 49CDS1)* – Crack attack.
(cd-s) *(ELM 49CDS2)* – ('A'side) / U.S. Army / Raped by ape.

Flapping Jet | Flapping Jet

Oct 99. (m-lp) <(FJ 010)> **5 SONG EP** [ ] [ ]
<(re-iss. Aug00; FLAP 010)>

Glazed | Glazed

Jan 00. (7") <(GLZ 001)> **DANCING BIRDS. /** [ ] [ ]

– compilations, etc. –

Dec 93. (lp/cd) *Sympathy For The Record Industry; (SFTRI 558/+CD) / Hedhunter; <Hed 023>* **ALL SYSTEMS GO** [ ] [ ]
– Live the funk / Bad song Ninja / Goodbye / Boy chucker / Jumper K. balls / Lefty / Normal carpet ride / Where are the fuckers / Slumber queen / Flip the bird / Cha cha cha / Pressure's on / Pigeon eater / (The) Paste that you love / Pure genius / Lift and love / Press darlings / Filly fill again / Chantilly face. *(cd re-iss. Dec98; same)*

Oct 99. (lp/cd) *Swami; <(SWA 2001/+CD)>* **ALL SYSTEMS GO 2** [ ] [ ]
– Tarzan / UFO x3 / Birdman / Ciao Patsy / Heads are gonna roll / Cheetah / Turkish revenge / US aim / Raged by an age / Crack party / Stranglehold / 10 forward / Call it a clue / Cut it loose / Hot heart / I drink blood / Slow / Who needs you / Allergic reaction / You and I / Transcendent crankiness / Lose your clown / Burning army man / Ballot fire / Nobobby / Ushering in a new age of quarrel.

DRIVE LIKE JEHU

JOHN REIS – guitar / **RICK FROBERG** – vocals, guitar / **MIKE KENNEDY** – bass / **MARK TROMBINO** – drums

not iss. | Merge

1992. (7") <MRG 023> **HAND OVER FIST. / BULLET TRAIN TO VEGAS** [-] [ ]

Headhunter | Headhunter

Jan 93. (lp/cd) <(HED/+CD 008)> **DRIVE LIKE JEHU** [ ] [ ] Dec91
– Caress / Spikes to you / Step on chameleon / O pencil sharp / Atom Jack / If it kills you / Good luck in jail / Turn it off / Future home of Stucco monstrosity.

El-e-mental | Cargo

May 94. (cd) *(ELM 22CD)* <EFA 17690-2> **YANK CRIME** [ ] [ ]
– Here come the Rome plows / Do you compute / Golden brown / Luau / Super unison / New intro / New math / Human interest / Sinews. *(lp-iss.Aug94 on 'Cargo'; HED 037)*

ROCK GODDESS

Formed: Wandsworth, London, England . . . early 80's (when they started recording a demo), by schoolgirl sisters JODY and JULIE TURNER, who invited playground chum, TRACEY LAMB to join up on bass duties. The girls made their first tentative steps into the music business with gigs around London and a contribution to the 'Making Waves' compilation. A family affair, ROCK GODDESS were managed by the TURNERs' father, the band soon securing a deal with 'A&M'. An eponymous debut album appeared in 1983, its Brit-metal approach endearing the group to fans of the rapidly splintering NWOBHM and securing a UK Top 75 chart placing. Prior to the release of follow-up, 'HELL HATH NO FURY', later that year, DEE O'MALLEY replaced the departing LAMB. Although the album again breached the lower end of the chart and received encouraging reviews, ROCK GODDESS failed to gain the exposure enjoyed by their older forebears GIRLSCHOOL. The final nail in the coffin came when O'MALLEY herself left prior to the independently issued, French-only 'YOUNG AND FREE' (1987) set, ROCK GODDESS splitting soon after with JODY initiating her own band.

Album rating: ROCK GODDESS (*6) / HELL HATH NO FURY (*5) / YOUNG AND FREE (*4)

JODY TURNER – vocals, guitar / **TRACEY LAMB** – bass / **JULIE TURNER** – drums / guest **DONNICA CAMON** – guitar, keyboards

A&M | not iss.

Nov 82. (7"pic-d/12") *(AMS/+X 8263)* **HEAVY METAL ROCK'N'ROLL REVIVAL. / SATISFIED THEN CRUCIFIED** [ ] [-]

Feb 83. (7") *(AMS 8311)* **MY ANGEL. / IN THE HEAT OF THE NIGHT** [64] [-]
(12"+=) *(AMSX 8311)* – Over love's gone.

Feb 83. (lp/c) *(AMLH/CAM 68554)* **ROCK GODDESS** [65] [-]
– Heartache / Back to you / The love lingers still / To be betrayed / Take your love away / My angel / Satisfied with crucified / Start running / Make my night / One way love / Heavy metal rock'n'roll.

— **DEE O'MALLEY** – bass; repl. LAMB, who later joined GIRLSCHOOL

Oct 83. (lp/c) *(AMLX/CXM 68560)* **HELL HATH NO FURY** [84] [-]
– Hold me down / No more / Gotta let your hair down / Don't want your love / In the night / Visitors are here / I've seen it all before / You've got fire / It will never change / God be with you.

Mar 84. (7"/7"pic-d) *(AM/+P 185)* **I DIDN'T KNOW I LOVED YOU (TILL I SAW YOU ROCK AND ROLL). / HELL HATH NO FURY** [57] [-]
(12"+=) *(AMX 185)* – In the night.

— In 1986, O'MALLEY departed just prior to the release of below

Just In | not iss.

1987. (lp) **YOUNG AND FREE** [-] [-] France
– Young and free / Hello / So much love / Jerry / Streets of the city / The party never ends / Love has passed me by / Raiders / Love is a bitch / Boys will be boys / Sexy eyes / Rumour / Turn me loose / Hey lover. *(UK cd-iss. Jul94 on 'Thunderbolt'; CDTB 155)*

— when they split, JODY took off on a solo career

– compilations, etc. –

Jun 98. (cd) *Renaissance; (RMED 0218CD)* **ROCK GODDESS / HELL HATH NO FURY** [ ] [-]

ROCKHEAD

Formed: 1992, by guitarist BOB ROCK (b. ROBERT JENS ROCK, Winnipeg, Canada), who was better known as a producer for hard/heavy acts, BON JOVI, METALLICA, AEROSMITH and MOTLEY CRUE. He enlisted the services of vocalist STEVE JACK, bassist JAMEY KOSH and drummer CHRIS TAYLOR, signing to 'E.M.I.' in the process. An eponymous album featuring BILLY DUFFY (The Cult) and RICHIE SAMBORA (Bon Jovi), hit the shops in 1993, a derivative hard-rock set which never proved itself to critics.

Album rating: ROCKHEAD (*6)

BOB ROCK – guitar / **STEVE JACK** – vocals / **JAMEY KOSH** – bass / **CHRIS TAYLOR** – drums

E.M.I. | Capitol

Mar 93. (cd/c/lp) *(CD/TC+/EMC 3649)* <98369> **ROCKHEAD** [ ] [ ]
– Bed of roses / Chelsea rose / Heartland / Lovehunter / Death do us part / Warchild / Sleepwalk / Hell's back door / Hard rain / Angelfire / Webhead / Baby wild / House of cards.

Jun 93. (12") *(12CHELS 1)* **CHELSEA ROSE. / SLEEPWALK** [ ] [ ]
(cd-s+=) *(CDCHELS 1)* – Angelfire.

— returned to production work

Paul RODGERS

Born: 17 Dec'49, Middlesborough, England. The grits n' honey voice behind both FREE and BAD COMPANY, RODGERS struck out on a solo career following the demise of the latter band in the early 80's. Recorded at RODGERS' home studio with the singer laying down all the instrumental parts himself, 'CUT LOOSE' (1983) was largely unremarkable fare from a man eminently capable of R&B/hard-rock genius. His next project, The FIRM (a collaboration with JIMMY PAGE and ROBERT PLANT), also failed to do the business over the course of two average albums in the mid-80's. Declining to join a reformed BAD COMPANY in 1986, RODGERS eventually resurfaced in the early 90's as one half of The LAW with ex-WHO drummer KENNY JONES. Releasing a sole lacklustre album, 'THE LAW' (1991), the duo certainly didn't rewrite any rules and a general lack of interest saw the group locked away for good. RODGERS' emerged again a couple of years later with the star-studded 'MUDDY WATERS BLUES: A TRIBUTE TO MUDDY WATERS' (1993). As the title suggested, the record was an interpretation of RODGERS' fave blues numbers featuring the likes of JEFF BECK, STEVE MILLER, NEAL SCHON and BUDDY GUY to name but a few. His most consistent effort since the BAD COMPANY days, the album surprisingly made the UK Top 10. The following year saw the release of a live EP featuring a trio of Hendrix covers, namely 'PURPLE HAZE', 'STONE FREE' and 'LITTLE WING'. A set of original material, 'NOW', eventually appeared in 1997 on the 'S.P.V.' label, released around the same time as a live set running through old FREE and BAD COMPANY classics. At the close of the millennium, RODGERS returned with another album, 'ELECTRIC' (1999), a record that was a slight throwback to his FREE and BAD COMPANY days.

Album rating: CUT LOOSE (*4) / MUDDY WATERS BLUES (*7) / NOW (*5) / LIVE (*4) / ELECTRIC (*5) / the Law: THE LAW (*4)

PAUL RODGERS – vocals, instruments

Atlantic Atlantic

Nov 83. (lp/c) *(780 121-1/-4) <80121>* **CUT LOOSE**
– Fragile / Cut loose / Live in peace / Sweet sensation / Rising sun / Boogie mama / Morning after the night before / Northwinds / Superstar woman / Talking guitar blues.

Nov 83. (7") *(A 9749) <89749>* **CUT LOOSE. / TALKING GUITAR BLUES**

Jan 84. (7") *<89709>* **MORNING AFTER THE NIGHT BEFORE. / NORTHWINDS** –

— Early in 1985, he joined The FIRM (see under ⇒ LED ZEPPELIN). In the 90's he returned to the studio.

The LAW

RODGERS wrote some material w/ **BRYAN ADAMS / DAVID GILMORE / CHRIS REA.** Covered: MISS YOU IN A HEARTBEAT (Def Leppard).

RODGERS – vocals / **KENNY JONES** – drums (ex-WHO, ex-SMALL FACES)

Atlantic Atco

Mar 91. (7") **LAYING DOWN THE LAW. / TOUGH LOVE**
(12"+=/cd-s+=) – That's when you fall.

Apr 91. (cd/c/lp) *<(7567 82195-2/-4/-1)>* **THE LAW** 61
– For a little ride / Miss you in a heartbeat / Stone cold / Come save me (Julianne) / Laying down the law / Nature of the beast / Stone / Anything for you / Best of my love / Tough love / Missing you bad girl.

Paul RODGERS

(solo) with **JASON BONHAM** – drums / **PINO PALLADINO** – bass / **IAN HATTON** – rhythm guitar / plus **JIMMIE WOOD** – harmonica / **RONNIE FOSTER** – organ / **MARK T.WILLIAMS** – bass drum and guest lead guitarists on each of the 15 tracks; **BUDDY GUY / TREVOR RABIN / BRIAN SETZER / JEFF BECK / JEFF BECK / STEVE MILLER / TREVOR RABIN / DAVID GILMOUR / SLASH / GARY MOORE / BRIAN MAY / JEFF BECK / NEAL SCHON / RICHIE SAMBORA / NEAL SCHON**

Victory Victory

Jun 93. (cd/c) *(828424-2/-4) <480013>* **MUDDY WATERS BLUES: A TRIBUTE TO MUDDY WATERS** 9 91
– Muddy Water blues (acoustic version) / Louisiana blues / I can't be satisfied / Rollin' stone / Good morning little school girl (part 1) / I'm your hoochie coochie man / She's alright / Standing around crying / The hunter / She moves me / I'm ready / I just want to make love to you / Born under a bad sign / Good morning little school girl (part 2) / Muddy Water blues (electric version). *(free-cd 'THE HISTORY'; re-recordings of FREE and BAD COMPANY hits)* – All right now / Wishing well / Fire & water / Bad company / Feel like making love / Can't get enough.

— Album 'MUDDY WATER BLUES' songs stemming from MUDDY WATERS, RODGERS, SONNY BOY WILLIAMSON, WILLIE DIXON or BOOKER T. JONES.

Jan 94. (7"ep/c-ep/cd-ep) *(ROG ER/MC/CD 1)* **MUDDY WATER BLUES / PURPLE HAZE (live) / STONE FREE (live) / LITTLE WING (live)** 45 –
(cd-ep) *(ROCDP 1)* – ('A'side) / The hunter (live) / Stone free (live) / Nature of the beast (live) .

— More covers; PURPLE HAZE + STONE FREE + LITTLE WING (Jimi Hendrix).

S.P.V. S.P.V.

Jan 97. (cd-s) *(<SPV 0554462-3>)* **SOUL OF LOVE / ALL RIGHT NOW (live) / FEEL LIKE MAKIN' LOVE / SOUL OF LOVE (version)**

Feb 97. (cd) *(SPV 085-4466-2)* **NOW** 30
– Soul of love / Overloaded / Heart of fire / Saving grace / All I want is you / Chasing shadows / Nights like this / Shadow of the sun / Holding back the storm.

Mar 97. (cd) *(SPV 085-4467-2)* **LIVE (The Loreley Tapes)**
– Little bit of love / Be my friend / Feel like making love / Louisiana blues / Muddy Waters blues / Rolling stone / I'm ready / Wishing well / Mister Big / Fire and water / The hunter / Cant get enough / Alright now.

Nov 99. (cd) *(SPV 085-9702) <86294>* **ELECTRIC** Jun00
– Deep blue / Walking tall / Find a way / China blue / Love rains / Over you / Drifters / Freedom / Jasmine flower / Conquistadora.

RODS

Formed: New York, USA . . . 1980 by DAVID FEINSTEIN (ex-ELF), who recruited STEPHEN FARMER and CARL CANEDY. A workmanlike, if persistent metal power trio, The RODS were nevertheless a source of some excitement when they revved their way onto the metal scene in 1980 with the independently issued 'ROCK HARD' album. The interest surrounding the record's release led to a deal with 'Arista', GARY BORDONARO replacing FARMER prior to their eponymous major label debut. A touched up version of the debut with a handful of extra tracks, the record brought The RODS' high-octane sound to a wider audience. A follow-up set, 'WILD DOGS' (1982), failed to build on this promise and the band soon found themselves minus a record label. A further clutch of albums followed, varying in quality from fair to middling, a completely revamped line-up in place for a final effort in 1987, 'HEAVIER THAN THOU'.

Album rating: ROCK HARD (*6) / THE RODS (*6) / WILD DOGS (*5) / IN THE RAW (*3) / THE RODS LIVE (*5) / LET THEM EAT METAL (*6) / HEAVIER THAN THOU (*5)

DAVID FEINSTEIN – vocals, guitar (ex-ELF) / **STEPHEN FARMER** – bass, vocals / **CARL CANEDY** – drums

not iss. Primal

1980. (lp) *<1001>* **ROCK HARD** –
– Sit down honey / Music man / In your panties / Power lover / Roll with the night / Hungry for some love / Get ready to rock & roll / Crank it up / Rock hard / Gettin' higher / You better run / Woman.

— **GARY BORDONARO** – bass; repl. FARMER

Arista Arista

Sep 81. (lp/c) *(SPART/TCART 1182) <9558>* **THE RODS**
– Power lover / Crank it up / Hungry for some love / Music man / Woman / Nothing going on in the city / Get ready to rock'n'roll / Ace in the hole / Rock hard / Roll with the night. *(cd-iss. Sep97 on 'High Vaultage'; HV 1015)*

Feb 82. (7") *(ARIST 457)* **POWER LOVER. / NOTHING GOING ON IN THE CITY**
(12"+=) *(ARIST12 457)* – Crank it up / Getting higher.

May 82. (7") *(ARIST 467)* **YOU KEEP ME HANGIN' ON. / WINGS OF FIRE**

Jul 82. (lp/c) *<(SPART/TCART 1196)>* **WILD DOGS**
– Too hot to stop / Waiting for tomorrow / Violation / Burned by love / Wild dogs / You keep me hangin' on / Rockin'n'rollin' again / End of the line / No sweet talk, honey / The night lives to rock. *(cd-iss. Sep97 on 'High Vaultage'; HV 1016)*

Aug 82. (7"/12") *(ARIST/+12 484)* **TOO HOT TO STOP. / POWER LOVER**

not iss. Shrapnel

1983. (lp) *<SH 1005>* **IN THE RAW** –
– Hurricane / Can't get enough of the fun / Witches' brew / Go for broke / Hot love / Hot city / Streetfighter / Evil woman / Hold on for your life / Another night on the town.

Music For Nations not iss.

Jan 84. (lp/c) *(MFN/TMFN 16)* **THE RODS LIVE (live)** –
– I live for rock n' roll / Hellbound / Born to rock / The viper / Speed demon / Hurricane / Devil's child / Rabid thunder / Cold sweat and blood.

Jul 84. (lp) *(MFN 29)* **LET THEM EAT METAL** –
– Let them eat metal / White lightning / Nuclear skies / Rock warriors / Bad blood / She's so tight / Got the fire burnin' / I'm a rocker / She's such a bitch.

— added **RICK CAUDLE** – vocals / **ANDY McDONALD** – guitar / **EMMA ZALE** – keyboards

— (1986) **FEINSTEIN + CANEDY** recruited **CRAIG GRUBER** – bass (ex-ELF) / **SHMOULIC AVIGAL** – vocals (ex-PICTURE)

Zebra not iss.

Jan 87. (lp) *(ZEB 9)* **HEAVIER THAN THOU**
– Heavier than thou / Make me a believer / Angels never run / Crossfire / I'm gonna rock / She's trouble / Born to rock / Chains of love / Communication breakdown / Fool for your love / Cold sweat and love / The music man.

— disbanded some time in 1987

ROGUE MALE

Formed: London, England . . . 1984 by JIM LYTTLE, JOHN FRASER BINNIE, KEVIN COLLIER and STEVE KINGSLEY. Signing to 'Music For Nations', the group debuted in 1985 with the 'FIRST VISIT' album. With lyrics (penned by the Irish-born LYTTLE) taking at least some of their inspiration from the frontman's troubled home country, ROGUE MALE's sound was confrontational and uncompromising, a combination of punk energy and rock grime. Though signed to a major label in America ('Elektra'), the group were unable to make any headway in the US market and duly concentrated on Britain with a follow-up album, 'ANIMAL MAN'. It was another set scarred by gritty social realism, even including a raging cover of The Who's 'REAL ME'. The record failed to sell, however, ROGUE MALE sinking without trace.

Album rating: FIRST VISIT (*6) / ANIMAL MAN (*6)

JIM LYTTLE – vocals, guitar / **JOHN FRASER BINNIE** – guitar / **KEVIN COLLIER** – bass (ex-LE GRIFFE) / **STEVE KINGSLEY** – drums

Music For Nations Elektra

May 85. (12") *(12KUT 114)* **ALL OVER YOU. / REAL ME**

May 85. (lp) *(MFN 40) <60423>* **FIRST VISIT**
– Crazy motorcycle / All over you / First visit / Get off my back / Dressed incognito / Unemployment / On the line / Devastation / Look out.

— session man **CHARLIE MORGAN** – drums; repl. KINGSLEY

Jul 86. (12") *(12KUT 122)* **BELFAST. / ROUGH TOUGH (PRETTY TOO) / TAKE NO SHIT** –

Jul 86. (lp) *(MFN 68)* **ANIMAL MAN** –
– Progress / L.U.S.T. / Take no shit / You're on fire / Real me / Animal man / Belfast / Job centre / Low rider / The passing.

— **DANNY FURY** – drums; repl. MORGAN

— split after above

Henry ROLLINS

Born: HENRY GARFIELD, 13 Feb'61, Washington DC, USA. After cutting his teeth in the 'straight edge' (militantly clean living) hardcore punk scene of the late 70's, ROLLINS made his name with the seminal BLACK FLAG. Recruited in time for their 'DAMAGED' (1981) opus, ROLLINS added a manic intensity to the brilliant 'SIX PACK' as well as new numbers like 'LIFE

OF PAIN' and the title track. So extreme was the record that MCA's top man, Al Bergamo, tried to block the record's release even though thousands of copies had already been pressed. ROLLINS honed his writing and performing talents over a further series of albums, eventually going solo after the release of 'LOOSE NUT' (1985). 'HOT ANIMAL MACHINE' (1987) was a crudely visceral debut, ROLLINS indicating that, if anything, his solo career was going to be even more uncompromising than his work with BLACK FLAG. Later the same year, the singer released the mini album, 'DRIVE BY SHOOTING' under the pseudonym, HENRIETTA COLLINS AND THE WIFE-BEATING CHILD HATERS, a taste of ROLLINS' particularly tart brand of black humour. By 1988, The ROLLINS BAND line-up had solidified around guitarist CHRIS HASKETT (who'd played on the earlier releases), bassist ANDREW WEISS and drummer SIMON CAIN, releasing the IAN MACKAYE (of hardcore gurus, FUGAZI)-produced 'LIFE TIME' (1988) album later that year. An incendiary opus, the record was The ROLLINS BAND blueprint, setting the agenda for future releases with a lyrical incisiveness and musical ferocity that would be hard to equal. Following a slot on the hugely successful 1991 Lollapalooza tour, The ROLLINS BAND moved from cult status to a major label deal with 'Imago/RCA', releasing 'THE END OF SILENCE' in early '92. Fiercely self-analytic, ROLLINS had always used the stage and the rock medium, to a certain extent, as a kind of therapy, dredging up his childhood demons and tackling them head on. With '. . ..SILENCE', ROLLINS had penned his most introspective work to date, leaving no stone unturned. The fact that he'd had seen his best friend, Joe Cole, gunned down in cold blood had obviously deeply affected the singer and subsequently the material on the album. This intensely personal exorcism is what made ROLLINS' shows so damn compelling; for ROLLINS, this was far and beyond mere entertainment, for the most part at least, and this was no doubt a major contributing factor in the band's constant live work. As well as a punishing regime of physical exercise, ROLLINS found time to run his own publishing company, 2.13.61 (showcasing work of underground authors as well as ROLLINS' own material, including his acclaimed collection of short stories, 'Black Coffee Blues') and tour his darkly observant, often hilarious and ultimately inspiring spoken word sets. A choice selection of the latter were included on the double-set, 'BOXED LIFE' (1993). The ROLLINS BAND, meanwhile, returned in 1994 with 'WEIGHT', their most commercially successful set to date, and a record which finally made inroads into the UK market, almost making the Top 20. Musically, the album was more accessible than its predecessor, firmly establishing ROLLIN's & Co. as 'alternative rock' heavyweights. More recently, ROLLINS has expanded his jack-of-all-trades CV with another burst of acting (he'd made his onscreen debut alongside LYDIA LUNCH in 1991's 'Kiss Napoleon Goodbye'), appearing in 'The Chase' and 'Johnny Mnemonic' as well as scoring a cameo in the much heralded De Niro/Pacino face-off, 'Heat'. In mid '96, ROLLINS was the subject of a lawsuit (an 8-figure sum) by Imago for allegedly signing with 'Dreamworks' while under contract, the singer claiming he was let go by the major distributors of the label, 'B.M.G.'. Despite all this, the singer returned to the fray in 1997 with a new album, 'COME IN AND BURN', the record actually appearing on 'Dreamworks'. Come the new millennium, ROLLINS had parted company with his longtime backing musicians and teamed up with MOTHER SUPERIOR, a three-piece unit who had already been making waves in their own right. The resulting 'GET SOME GO AGAIN' (2000) was an impressively back to basics effort from a man who just seems to get angrier with age. With ROLLINS becoming something of an all-round celebrity, it remains to be seen whether he can retain the outsider intensity of old (though it wouldn't be an idea to argue with the man!). • **Covers:** GHOST RIDER (Suicide) / EX-LION TAMER (Wire) / DO IT (Pink Fairies) / LET THERE BE ROCK (Ac-Dc) / FRANKLIN'S TOWER (Grateful Dead).

Album rating (music only): HOT ANIMAL MACHINE (*6) / LIFE TIME (*5) / DO IT! (*6) / HARD VOLUME (*6) / TURNED ON (*6) / THE END OF SILENCE (*8) / WEIGHT (*7) / BLACK COFFEE BLUES mini (*5) / COME IN AND BURN (*5) / GET SOME GO AGAIN (*6)

HENRY ROLLINS – vocals (ex-BLACK FLAG, ex-SOA) / with **CHRIS HASKETT** (b. Leeds, England) – guitar (ex-SURFIN' DAVE) / **BERNIE WANDEL** – bass / **MICK GREEN** – drums

Fundam. — Texas Hotel

Jul 87. (lp) *(SAVE 024) <TXH 001>* **HOT ANIMAL MACHINE** ☐ ☐
– Black and white / Followed around / Lost and found / There's a man outside / Crazy lover / A man and a woman / Hot animal machine I / Ghost rider / Move right in / Hot animal machine 2 / No one. *(cd-iss. Oct88 +=; SAVE 024CD) – . (cd re-iss. Mar94 on 'Intercord'; 986976)*

— In Oct'87, he shared 'LIVE' lp with GORE, released on Dutch 'Eksakt' label; *EKSAKT 034*

Dec 87. (lp; solo) *<TXH 005>* **BIG UGLY MOUTH** (spoken word live early '87) [-] ☐
(UK cd-iss. Mar93 on '1/4 Stick'; QS 9CD)
(below saw him do a reverse MICHAEL JACKSON and black-up)

Jan 88. (12"ep; as HENRIETTA COLLINS and THE WIFEBEATING CHILDHATERS featuring HENRY ROLLINS) *(HOLY 5) <TXH 03>* **DRIVE BY SHOOTING** ☐ ☐ Aug87
– Drive by shooting (watch out for that pig) / Ex-lion tamer / Hey Henriezza / Can you speak this? / I have come to kill you / Men are pigs.

ROLLINS BAND

retained **HASKETT** and recruited **ANDREW WEISS** – bass / **SIMEON CAIN** – drums

Sep 88. (lp/cd) *(SAVE 065/+CD) <TXH >* **LIFE TIME** ☐ ☐
– Burned beyond recognition / What am I doing here / 1000 times blind / Lonely / Wreck-age / Gun in mouth blues / You look at you / If you're alive / Turned out. *(cd+=)* – What am I doing here? / Burned beyond recognition / Move right in / Hot animal machine 2. *(cd re-iss. Mar94 on 'Intercord'; 986977)*

World Service — Texas Hotel

Jan 89. (lp) *(SERVM 004) <TXH 013CD>* **DO IT! (live/studio)** ☐ ☐ Apr89
– Do it / Move light in / Next time / Joe is everything, everything is Joe / Black and white / Lost and found / Followed around / Wreck age / Lonely / Hot animal machine #1 / You look at you / Gun in mouth blues / Turned out / Thousand times blind / No one. *(re-iss. cd Mar94 on 'Intercord'; 986978)*

Apr 89. (d-lp; solo) *<TXH 015>* **SWEATBOX** (spoken word live) [-] ☐
(UK d-cd-iss. Mar93 on '1/4 Stick'; QS 10CD)

Nov 89. (m-lp/cd) *(SERV 010 LP/CD) <TXH >* **HARD VOLUME** ☐ ☐
– Hard / What have I got / I feel like this / Planet Joe / Love song / Turned inside out / Down and away. *(cd+=)* – Joyriding with Frank. *(cd-iss. Mar94 on 'Intercord'; 986979)*

— In 1989, a Swiss cassette found its way into UK; 'READINGS: SWITZERLAND' on 'Action' *ACTIONK 001*

— In 1990, WARTIME was an extra-curricular activity headed by ROLLINS and ANDREW WEISS. An cd-ep surfaced 'FAST FOOD FOR THOUGHT' on 'Chrysalis'; *MPCD 1753*

1990. (lp; solo) *<TXH >* **LIVE AT McCABE'S (spoken word live)** [-] ☐
(UK cd-iss. Mar93 on '1/4 Stick'; QS 11CD)

not iss. — Sub Pop

1990. (7",7"red,7"pink) *<SP 72>* **I KNOW YOU. / EARACHE MY EYE** [-] ☐

1/4 Stick — 1/4 Stick

Nov 90. (lp/cd) *<(QS 02/+CD)>* **TURNED ON (live '89)** ☐ ☐
– Lonely / Do it / What have I got / Tearing / Out there / You didn't need / Hard / Followed around / Mask / Down & away / Turned inside out / The Dietmar song / Black & white / What do you do / Crazy lover.

— in July '91, HENRY ROLLINS & The HARD-ONS released their collaboration 'LET THERE BE ROCK' issued on 'Vinyl Solution' (VS 30/+CD)

Imago-RCA — Imago-RCA

Feb 92. (12") *(PT 49113)* **LOW SELF OPINION. / LIE, LIE, LIE** ☐ ☐

Feb 92. (cd/c/d-lp) *(PD/PK/PL 90641) <21006>* **THE END OF SILENCE** ☐ ☐
– Low self opinion / The end of silence / Grip / Tearing / You didn't need / Almost real / Obscene / What do you do? / Blues jam / Another life / Just like you.

Aug 92. (7") *(72787 87250-18-7)* **TEARING. / EARACHE IN MY EYE (live)** [54] ☐
(12"+=/cd-s+=) *(72787 87250-18-1/-2)* – (There'll be no) Next time / Ghost rider.

Jan 93. (2xcd-box/2xc-box) *(72787 21009-2/-4)* **THE BOXED LIFE** (compilation of alter-ego workings) ☐ ☐

— In early '94, he acted in the film 'The Chase', and was about to be seen in 'Johnny Mnemonic'.

— **MELVIN GIBBS** – bass repl. HASKINS who left in 1993.

Apr 94. (cd/c/clear d-lp) *<(72787 21034-2/-4/-1)>* **WEIGHT** [22] [33]
– Disconnect / Fool / Icon / Civilized / Divine object of hatred / Liar / Step back / Wrong man / Volume 4 / Tired / Alien blueprint / Shine.

Aug 94. (7"/c-s) *(74321 213057-7/-4)* **LIAR. / DISCONNECT** [27] ☐
(cd-s+=) *(74321 213057-2)* – Right here too much / Nightsweat.

not iss. — Thirsty Ear

Apr 97. (m-cd) *<21321>* **BLACK COFFEE BLUES** [-] ☐
– Black coffee blues / Invisible woman blues / Monster / Exhaustion blues / I know you.

Dreamworks — Dreamworks

Apr 97. (cd/c) *<(DRD/DRC 50011)>* **COME IN AND BURN** ☐ [89] Mar97
– Shame / Starve / All I want / The end of something / On my way to the cage / Thursday afternoon / During a city / Neon / Spilling over the side / Inhale exhale / Saying goodbye again / Rejection / Disappearing act.

Jul 97. (7") *(DRMS 22271)* **THE END OF SOMETHING. / ALSO RAN** ☐ [-]
(cd-s) *(DRMCD 22271)* – ('A'side) / ('A'-We Change remix) / Threshold.
(cd-s) *(DRMXD 22271)* – ('A'side) / ('A'-Grooverider remix) / Stray.

Feb 00. (cd) *<(450216-2)>* **GET SOME GO AGAIN** ☐ ☐
– Illumination / Get some go again / Monster / Love's so heavy / Thinking cap / Action / I go day glo / Are you ready / On the day you let yourself down / Brother interior / Hotter and hotter / Illuminator. *(d-cd+=; 450971-2)* – Side by side / 100 miles / Fuck yo mama / What have I got / Get some go again (video) / Action (live) / E.P.K.

– compilations, etc. –

Mar 93. (d-cd) *1/4 Stick; (QS 12CD)* **HUMAN BUTT** (book readings) ☐ ☐ 1991

Mar 93. (cd-box) *1/4 Stick; (QS 13CD)* **DEEP THROAT** ☐ ☐
– (all 4 spoken word releases).

Nov 94. (d-cd) *Imago; <(74321 24238-2)>* **GET IN THE VAN** (book readings; life on the road with BLACK FLAG) ☐ ☐

Nov 94. (book) *Imago;* **HENRY: PORTRAIT OF A SINGER SINGER** (spoken word) ☐ ☐

Jul 96. (cd) *Thirsty Ear; <2.13.61>* **EVERYTHING** (spoken word) [-] ☐

Oct 98. (cd) *Dreamworks; <(DRD 50054)>* **THINK TANK** (spoken word) ☐ ☐

ROSE TATTOO

Formed: Sydney, Australia . . . 1977 initially as BUSTER BROWN, by ANGRY ANDERSON, MICHAEL COCKS, MICK 'GEORDIE' LEECH, PETER WELLS and DALLAS 'DIGGER' ROYALL. Trading in balls-to-the-wall, bruising blues/boogie rock, ROSE TATTOO unleashed their testosterone-saturated debut in 1978 on the Australian 'Albert' label. Entitled 'ROSE TATTOO' for domestic release and 'ROCK'N'ROLL OUTLAWS' in Europe, the record saw the Aussies gaining a cult fanbase both at home and abroad; presumably a young AXL ROSE was listening somewhere in Indiana, GUNS N' ROSES later covering the blistering 'NICE BOYS' on their debut 'Live ?!*@ Like A Suicide' set. On stage, ROSE TATTOO also became something of a legend, the group reaching UK shores in summer '81 when they performed at the Reading Festival. 'ASSAULT & BATTERY' (1981) compounded ROSE TATTOO's hard-men image, the aptly named ANDERSON sounding well angry as he bellowed out his hard-bitten tales of life on the wrong side of the tracks. Following a third set, 'SCARRED FOR LIFE' (1982), the group splintered on the accompanying US tour. ANDERSON and LEECH subsequently created a new line-up along with GREG JORDAN, ROBERT BOWRON and JOHN MEYER, the 'SOUTHERN STARS' (1984) set surfacing in 1984. This was a short-lived arrangement, however, the group finally splitting soon after. Essentially a solo album by ANDERSON, 'BEATS FROM A SINGLE DRUM' (1987) was nevertheless issued under the ROSE TATTOO moniker. More influential than their relatively slim back catalogue might suggest, the original line-up eventually reformed in 1993 to support G N' R on their Australian tour.

Album rating: ROCK'N'ROLL OUTLAWS (*7) / ASSAULT AND BATTERY (*7) / SCARRED FOR LIFE (*6) / SOUTHERN STARS (*6) / BEATS FROM A SINGLE DRUM (*5) / NICE BOYS DON'T PLAY ROCK'N'ROLL compilation (*6) / 25 TO LIFE (*5)

ANGRY ANDERSON – vocals / **MICHAEL COCKS** – lead guitar / **PETER WELLS** – slide guitar, vocals / **MICK 'GEORDIE' LEECH** – bass / **DALLAS 'DIGGER' ROYALL** – drums

—— released on 'Albert' in Australia

WEA Mirage

Apr 81. (lp/c) *(CAL/CAC 125) <19280>* **ROCK'N'ROLL OUTLAWS** (Australian rel.1978 as 'ROSE TATTOO') [ ] [ ] Nov80
– Rock'n'roll outlaw / Nice boys / The butcher and fast Eddy / One of the boys / Remedy / Bad boy for love / T.V. / Stuck on you / Tramp / Astra Wally. *(re-iss. Aug90 on 'Streetlink' cd/c/lp; STR CD/MC/LP 002) (cd re-iss. Aug91 & Mar00 on 'Repertoire'; REP 2049-WZ)*

May 81. (7") *(CAR 191)* **BAD BOY FOR LOVE. / TRAMP** [ ] [-]

Jul 81. (7"/7"pic-d) *(CAR 200/+P) <3782>* **ROCK'N'ROLL OUTLAW. / REMEDY** [60] [ ]

Sep 81. (lp/c) *(CAR/CAC 127) <18342>* **ASSAULT & BATTERY** [40] [ ]
– Out of this place / All the lessons / Let it go / Assault & battery / Magnum maid / Rock'n'roll is king / Manzil madness / Chinese Dunkirk / Sidewalk Sally / Suicide city. *(re-iss. Aug90 on 'Streetlink' cd/lp; STR CD/LP 003) (cd re-iss. Aug91 & Mar00 on 'Repertoire'; REP 4011-WZ)*

Oct 81. (7") *(CAR 210)* **ROCK'N'ROLL IS KING. / I HAD YOU FIRST** [ ] [-]

Dec 81. (d7") *(CAR 220)* **ASSAULT AND BATTERY. / ASTRA WALLY // ONE OF THE BOYS. / MANZIL MADNESS** [ ] [-]

—— **ROBIN RILEY** – guitar; repl. COX who joined HEAVEN

1982. (7") *(AP 854)* **WE CAN'T BE BEATEN. / FIGHTIN' SONS** [-] [-] Austra

1982. (7") *(AP 898)* **BRANDED. / DEAD SET** [-] [-] Austra

WEA not iss.

Nov 82. (lp/c) *(CAL/CAC 144)* **SCARRED FOR LIFE** [ ] [-]
– Scarred for life / We can't be beaten / Juice on the loose / Who's got the cash / Branded / Texas / It's gonna work itself out / Sydney girls / Dead set / Revenge. *(cd-iss. Mar00 on 'Repertoire'; REP 4049)*

Dec 82. (7") *<99923>* **SCARRED FOR LIFE. /** [-] [ ]

1983. (7") *(AP 1007)* **IT'S GONNA WORK ITSELF OUT. / SYDNEY GIRLS** [-] [-] Austra

Mar 83. (7") *(CAR/+P 263)* **IT'S GONNA WORK ITSELF OUT. / FIGHTIN' SONS** [ ] [-]

—— **ANDERSON + LEECH** recruited new members **JOHN MEYER** – guitar / **GREG JORDAN** – slide guitar / **ROBERT BOWRON** – drums

Albert not iss.

1984. (7") *(AP 1299)* **I WISH. / WILD ONE** [-] [-] Austra

1985. (7") *(AP 1384)* **FREEDOM'S FLAME. / NEVER TOO LOUD** [-] [-] Austra

1985. (lp) *(240569-1)* **SOUTHERN STARS** [ ] [-]
– Southern stars / Let us live / Freedom's flame / I wish / Saturday's rage / Death or glory / The pirate song / You've been told / No secrets / The radio said rock'n'roll is dead. *(re-iss. Aug90 on 'Streetlink' cd/lp; STR CD/LP 005) (cd re-iss. Aug91 & Mar00 on 'Repertoire'; REP 4050-WZ)*

1985. (7") *(AP 1444)* **NO SECRETS. / LET US LIVE** [-] [-] Austra

below releases were in fact ANGRY ANDERSON solo, although ROSE TATTOO were credited due to contractual roblems

Mushroom Pacific

1986. (7") *(K 9837)* **BORN TO BE WILD. / SUNS GONNA SHINE** [-] [-] Austra

1986. (7") *(K 66)* **CALLING. / WIN AT ANY COST** [-] [-] Austra

1986. (7") *(K 187)* **GET IT RIGHT. / MICHAEL O'RILEY** [-] [-] Austra

1987. (lp/cd) *(LP/CD 53217)* **BEATS FROM A SINGLE DRUM** [-] [-] Austra
– Calling / Frightened kid / Suddenly / Runaway / Winnie Mandela / Get it right / Say goodbye / Falling / Clear and simple / Michael O'Riley. *(UK-iss.Apr89 by ANGRY ANDERSON on 'Food For Thought' cd/c/lp; CD/T+/GRUB 11)*

1987. (7") *(K 248)* **FALLING. / WINNIE MANDELA** [-] [-] Austra

—— ANGRY ANDERSON went solo in name, releasing mainly mainstream singles/albums (i.e. the UK Top 3 hit 'SUDDENLY' Nov'88). In September '91, ANDERSON released the album, 'BLOOD FROM STONE' for 'Music For Nations'.

– compilations, etc. –

Aug 91. (cd) *Repertoire; (REP 2010-WZ)* **ANGRY METAL** [ ] [-]
(re-iss. Mar00; same)

1992. (cd) *; <470053-2>* **NICE BOYS DON'T PLAY ROCK'N'ROLL** [-] [-] Austra

Oct 92. (cd) *Streetlink; (STRCD 024)* **THE BEST OF ROSE TATTOO** [ ] [-]
(re-iss. Jun95 on 'Dojo'; DOJOCD 126)

Mar 00. (d-cd) *Repertoire; (REP 4601)* **NEVER TOO LOUD** [ ] [-]

Nov 00. (cd/d-lp) *S.P.V.; (<085/089-7209-2>)* **25 TO LIFE (live)** [ ] [ ]
– Out of this place / Bad boy for love / Assault and battery / Tramp / Butcher and fast Eddy / Rock & roll is king / Rock and roll outlaw / We can't be beaten / Astra walley / Scarred for life / Remedy / Juice on the loose / Who's got the cash / One of the boys / Nice boys / Manzil madness / Suicide city.

ROSSINGTON-COLLINS BAND
(see under ⇒ LYNYRD SKYNYRD)

David Lee ROTH

Born: 10 Oct'55, Bloomington, Indiana, USA. Suffering from hyperactivity from an early age, he attended a child clinic at the age of eight. His family subsequently moved to Pasadena, where he later joined the group, MAMMOTH, in 1973. Two years later, this outfit had evolved into VAN HALEN, ROTH taking centre stage as their inimitably OTT frontman over a period of ten years. During this time, the group became one of the biggest hard rock/metal acts in the world as well as regularly hitting the pop charts. By the mid-80's, however, ROTH was getting restless, recording a mini solo album, 'CRAZY FROM THE HEAT', as a side project in early '85. Scoring a US Top 3 hit with one of its singles, a memorable cover of The Beach Boys' 'CALIFORNIA GIRLS', 'Diamond' DAVE finally decided to take the plunge and leave VAN HALEN later that summer. Enlisting a cast of crack rock troopers including guitarist STEVE VAI (ex-FRANK ZAPPA) and much touted bassist, BILLY SHEEHAN (ex-TALAS, future MR. BIG), ROTH cut a fully fledged solo album, 'EAT 'EM AND SMILE'. Released in the summer of '86, the album was roundly praised in the rock press, making the US Top 5. Alive with the singer's infectious enthusiasm and natural talent for showmanship, the record was a consistently entertaining listen, the brilliant 'YANKEE ROSE' making the US Top 20. Its follow-up, 'SKYSCRAPER', duly appeared a couple of years later, the sleeve depicting DAVE in the throes of his latest obsession, rock climbing. Fittingly then, there was a lofty, widescreen sound to much of the album, the soaring 'JUST LIKE PARADISE' giving ROTH his first solo UK Top 10 hit. By the release of 'A LITTLE AIN'T ENOUGH' (1991), both VAI and SHEEHAN had departed, the album missing their instrumental spark and underlining ROTH's increasingly formulaic approach. Though the album made the US Top 5, it failed to spawn any hit singles, ROTH subsequently sacking his band and heading for New York. Not that he fared much better in the Big Apple, the singer running into personal problems and failing to kickstart his ailing career with the poor 'YOUR FILTHY LITTLE MOUTH' (1994). Not a man to be held down for long, motormouth DAVE subsequently re-united with VAN HALEN. • **Songwriters:** ROTH written (most with STEVE VAI '86-88), except JUST A GIGOLO (Ted Lewis) / I AIN'T GOT NOBODY (Marian Harris) / THAT'S LIFE (hit; Frank Sinatra) / TOBACCO ROAD (Nashville Teens).

Album rating: CRAZY FROM THE HEAT mini (*5) / EAT 'EM AND SMILE (*7) / SKYSCRAPER (*5) / A LITTLE AIN'T ENOUGH (*4) / YOUR FILTHY LITTLE MOUTH (*3)

DAVID LEE ROTH – vocals (ex-VAN HALEN) with **DEAN PARKS + EDDIE MARTINEZ + SID McGINNIS** – guitar / **EDGAR WINTER** – keyboards, sax, synthesizers, vocals / **JAMES NEWTON HOWARD** – synthesizers / **WILLIE WEEKS** – bass / **JOHN ROBINSOB** – drums / **SAMMY FIGUEROA** – percussion / **BRIAN MANN** – synthesizers

Warners Warners

Feb 85. (7") *(W 9102) <29102>* **CALIFORNIA GIRLS. / ('A'remix)** [68] [3] Jan85
(above featured CARL WILSON of THE BEACH BOYS on backing vocals)

Feb 85. (m-lp/m-c) *(925222-1/-4) <25222>* **CRAZY FROM THE HEAT** [91] [15]
– Easy street / Just a gigolo – I ain't got nobody / Coconut Grove / California girls.

Apr 85. (7") *(W 9040) <29040>* **JUST A GIGOLO – I AIN'T GOT NOBODY. / ('A'remix)** [ ] [12] Mar85

—— **STEVE VAI** – guitar (ex-FRANK ZAPPA) / **BILLY SHEEHAN** – bass (ex-TALAS) / **BRETT TUGGLE** – keyboards / **GREGG BISSONETTE** (b. 9 Jun'59) – drums

Jul 86. (7"/7"sha-pic-d) *(W 8656/+P) <28656>* **YANKEE ROSE. / SHYBOY** [ ] [16]
(12"+=) *(W 8656T)* – Easy street.

Jul 86. (lp/c)(cd) *(WX 56/+C)(925470-2) <25470>* **EAT 'EM AND SMILE** [28] [4]
– Yankee Rose / Shyboy / I'm easy / Ladies' nite in Buffalo? / Goin' crazy! / Tobacco Road / Elephant gun / Big trouble / Bump and grind / That's life.

Sep 86. (7") *<28584>* **GOIN' CRAZY! / OOCO DEO CALOR (Spanish version)** [-] [66]

Nov 86. (7") *<28511>* **THAT'S LIFE. / BUMP AND GRIND** [-] [85]

—— **MATT BISSONETTE** – bass repl. SHEEHAN who joined OZZY OSBOURNE

Jan 88. (lp/c)(cd) *(WX 140/+C)(925671-2) <25671>* **SKYSCRAPER** [11] [6]
– Knucklebones / Just like paradise / The bottom line / Skyscraper / Damn good / Hot dog and a shake / Stand up / Hina / Perfect timing / Two fools a minute. *(cd+=)* – California girls / Just a gigolo – I ain't got nobody. *(re-iss. Jan89 lp/c)(cd; WX 236/+C)(925824-2)*

Feb 88. (7") *(W 8119) <28119>* **JUST LIKE PARADISE. / THE BOTTOM LINE** [27] [6] Jan88
(12"pic-d+=/3"cd-s+=) *(W 8119 TP/CD)* – Yankee Rose.

Apr 88. (7") *<28108>* **STAND UP. / KNUCKLEBONES** [-] [64]

Jul 88. (7") *<27825>* **DAMN GOOD. / SKYSCRAPER** [-] [ ]

Jul 88. (7"/12") *(W 7753/+T)* **DAMN GOOD. / STAND UP** [72] [-]

Nov 88. (7") *(W 7650)* **CALIFORNIA GIRLS. / JUST A GIGOLO** [ ] [-]
(12"+=) *(W 7650T)* – I ain't got nobody.
(cd-s++=) *(W 7650CD)* – Yankee Rose.

—— (Apr'89-Jan'90) **ROCKY RICHETTE** – guitar (ex-STEPPENWOLF, ex-BLACK ROSE) repl. STEVE VAI who went solo and joined WHITESNAKE

—— (Oct'90) **TODD JENSEN** – bass (ex-HARLOW) repl. MATT / **DEZZI REXX + JOE HOLMES** – guitar repl. JASON BECKER + ROCKY RICHETTE

W.E.A. Warners

Dec 90. (7"/c-s) *(W 0002/+C)* **A LITTLE AIN'T ENOUGH. / BABY'S ON FIRE** [32] [ ]
(12"+=/cd-s+=) *(W 0002 T/CD)* – Tell the truth.

Jan 91. (cd)(lp/c) *<(7599 26477-2)>(WX 403/+C)* **A LITTLE AIN'T ENOUGH** 4 18
– A little ain't enough / Shoot it / Lady Luck / Hammerhead shark / Tell the truth / Baby's on fire / 40 below / Sensible shoes / Last call / The dogtown shuffle / It's showtime! / Drop in the bucket.

Mar 91. (7"/5"sha-pic-d) *(W 0016/+P/C)* **SENSIBLE SHOES. / A LIL AIN'T ENOUGH**
(12"/cd-s) *(W 0016 T/CD)* – ('A'side) / California girls / Just a gigolo / I ain't got nobody.

Feb 94. (7"/c-s) *(W 0229/+C)* **SHE'S MY MACHINE. / MISSISSIPPI POWER** 64
(cd-s+=) *(W 0229CD1)* – Land's edge / Yo breathin' it.
(cd-s+=) *(W 0229CD2)* – ('A'mixes).

Mar 94. (cd/c/lp) *<(9362 45391-2/-4/-1)>* **YOUR FILTHY LITTLE MOUTH** 28 78
– She's my machine / Everybody's got the monkey / Big train / Experience / A little luck / Cheatin' heart cafe / Hey, you never know / No big 'ting / Yo breathin' it / Your filthy little mouth / Land's edge / Night life / Sunburn / You're breathin' it (urban NYC mix).

May 94. (7"/c-s) *(W 0249/+C)* **NIGHT LIFE. / JUMP (live)** 72
(cd-s+=) *(W 0249CD1)* – She's my machine (live).
(cd-s) *(W 0249CD2)* – ('A'side) / Panama (live) / Big train (live) / Experience (live).

— returned to VAN HALEN in 1996.

– compilations, etc. –

Nov 97. (cd/c) *Warners; <(8122 72941-2/-4)>* **THE BEST OF DAVID LEE ROTH**
– Don't piss me off / Yankee rose / A lil' ain't enough / Just like Paradise / Big train / Big trouble / It's showtime / Hot dog and a shake / Skyscraper / Shyboy / She's my machine / Stand up / Tobacco road / Easy street / California girls / Just a gigolo / I ain't got nobody / Sensible shoes / Goin' crazy / Ladies nite in Buffalo / Land's edge.

Uli John ROTH (see under ⇒ ELECTRIC SUN)

ROTTING CHRIST

Formed: Athens, Greece . . . 1987 under the joint helm of brothers SAKIS and THEMIS TOLIS, and backed by KOSTAS and ANDREAS. Inspired by the emergence of the Black Metal scene in Northern Europe, the rather impiously named ROTTING CHRIST thrashed their first dark chords onto tape with their mini-set 'PASSAGE TO ARCTURO'(1989). Later, recruiting the unpretentiously named GEORGE on keyboard, the line-up was complete. Signing to French label 'Osmose' the boys from Athens really put the classical world on the metal map with their first full set 'THY MIGHTY CONTRACT' (1993), following this up a year later with the equally brutal metal of 'NON SERVIAM' (1994). These first two full-length studio outings brought them to the attention of 'Century Media' and through this, greater distribution in the US as well as Europe. Recording for their new masters what is perhaps RC's most highly regarded album 'TRIARCHY OF THE LOST LOVERS' (1996), the boys slowed the pace of their earlier style, edging towards a slightly more melodious sound, but still sustaining the phenomenal power of their earlier outings on such standout numbers as 'KING OF A STELLAR WAR'. RC continued on this more tuneful and accessible vein with their next set 'A DEAD POEM' (1997). Although this album is perhaps more approachable for the wider metal market than their earlier outings, it's most certainly not their acoustic set (although they did lean towards an acoustic sound for the final track 'IRA INCENSUS'). RC followed this up with the more gothic metal strains of 'SLEEP OF ANGELS' (1999), but certainly not to the rapturous praise of their former set. The turn of the century saw the release of 'KHRONOS 666' (2000), acclaimed by the more extreme death metallers for RC's return to a harder sound, although still catering for their newer goth-metal following.

Album rating: PASSAGE TO ARCTURO mini (*4) / THY MIGHTY CONTRACT (*4) / NON SERVIAM (*4) / SATANAS TEDEUM mini (*4) / TRIARCHY OF THE LOST LOVERS (*6) / DEAD POEM (*6) / DER PERFEKTE TRAAM mini (*4) / SLEEP OF THE ANGELS (*6) / KHRONOS 666 (*6)

SAKIS TOLIS – vocals, guitar / **KOSTAS** – guitar / **ANDREAS** – bass / **THEMIS TOLIS** – drums

unknown / not iss.

1989. (m-lp; split) **ROTTING CHRIST / SOUND POLLUTION** - - Greece

— added **GEORGE** – keyboards

Decapitated / not iss.

Nov 89. (m-cd) *(DEC 003)* **PASSAGE TO ARCTURO** -
– Intro – Ach Golgotha / Old coffin spirit / The forest of N'Gai / The mystical meeting / Gloria de domino inferni – Inside the eye of Algond. *(re-iss. Nov93 & Nov95 & Dec98 on 'Unisound'; USRDEC 003CD)* – Feast of the grand whore / The forest of N'Gai (reprise).

Obscure Plasma / not iss.

1991. (7"ep; split w/ MOMENTUM) **FEAST OF THE GRAND WHORE** - - Greece
– The hills of the crucifixion / Feast of the grand whore / The nereid of Esgalduin / Restoration of the infernal kingdom / The sixth communion.

1992. (7") **DAWN OF THE ICONOCLAST. /** - - Greece

Osmose / not iss.

1993. (7"ep) **APOKATHELOSIS** - - French
– Visions of the dead lovers / The mystical meeting.

1993. (cd) **THY MIGHTY CONTRACT** - - French
– The sign of evil existence / Transform all suffering into plagues / Agmenth, thy gift / His sleeping majesty / Exiled archangels / Dive the deepest abyss / The coronation of the serpent / The 4th knight of revelation (part I, II). *(<UK+US-iss.Nov97 on 'Century Media'+=; CM 77196CD>)* – Visions of the dead lover / The mystical meeting.

Unisound / not iss.

Nov 94. (cd) *(USR 012CD)* **NON SERVIAM** -
– The fifth illusion / Wolfera the chacal / Non serviam / Morality of a dark age / Where mortals have no pride / Fethroesforia (instrumental) / Mephesis of black crystal / Ice shaped god / Saturn unlock Avey's son.

Nov 95. (m-cd) *(USR 015CD)* **SATANAS TEDEUM** -
– The hills of crucifixion /Feast of the grand whore / The nereid of Esqualdium / Restoration of the infernal kingdom / The sixth commission.

Century Media / Century Media

May 96. (cd/c/lp) *(CM 77128 CD/MC/LP)* *<7828>* **TRIARCHY OF THE LOST LOVERS**
– King of a stellar war / A dynasty from the ice / Snowing still / Shadows follow / One with the forest / Diastric alchemy / The opposite bank / The first field of the battle.

Oct 97. (cd) *<7866>* **A DEAD POEM** -
– Sorrowful farewell / Among two storms / A dead poem / Out of spirits / As if by magic / Full colour is the night / Semigod / Ten miles high / Between times / Ira incensus.

Nov 98. (m-cd) *(CM 77247CD)* **DER PERFEKTE TRAAM (THE PERFECT DREAM)** -
– Der perfekte traam (the perfect dream) / Moonlight / Shadows follow / Diastric alchemy / A dynasty from the ice / The first field of the battle / King of a stellar war.

Jan 99. (cd) *(CM 77248CD)* *<7948>* **SLEEP OF THE ANGELS** Mar99
– Cold colours / After dark I feel / Victoriatus / Der perfeckte craum (The perfect dream) / You my flesh / The world made end / Sleep the sleep of angels / Delusions / Imaginary zone / Thine is the kingdom. *(hidden track+=)* – Moonlight.

Sep 00. (cd/lp) *(77294-2/-1)* *<7994>* **KHRONOS 666**
– Thou art blind / If it ends tomorrow / My sacred path / Aeternatus / Art of sin / Lucifer over London / Law of the serpent / You are I / Khronos / Fateless / Time stands still / Glory of sadness.

ROUGH CUTT

Formed: Los Angeles, California, USA . . . mid-80's by PAUL SHORTINO and cohorts AMIR DERAKH, MATT THOR and DAVID ALFORD. Signing to 'Warners', this identikit spandex-metal outfit released an eponymous debut in summer '85 to universal indifference. Despite scoring some second division support slots, their label let them go after a further stultifyingly average set, 'WANTS YOU!' (1986), SHORTINO going on to (marginally) greater things with an ailing QUIET RIOT while the remaining members formed JAILHOUSE.

Album rating: ROUGH CUTT (*5) / WANTS YOU! (*4) / Paul Shortino: BACK ON TRACK (*5) / IT'S ABOUT TIME (*4) / BOOKED TOURED RELEASED (*4) / STAND OR FALL (*4)

PAUL SHORTINO – vocals / **AMIR DERAKH** – guitar / **MATT THOR** – bass / **DAVID ALFORD** – drums

Warners / Warners

Jul 85. (lp) *(925 268-1)* *<25268>* **ROUGH CUTT**
– Take her / Piece of my heart / Never gonna die / Dreamin' again / Cutt your heart out / Black widow / You keep breaking my heart / Kids will rock / Dressed to kill / She's too hot.

Nov 86. (lp/c) *(925 484-1/-4)* *<25484>* **WANTS YOU!**
– Rock the USA / Bad reputation / Don't settle for less / Hot 'n' heavy / Take a chance / We like it loud / Double trouble / You wanna be a star / Let 'em talk / The night cries out (for you).

— abandoned by the label which led to SHORTINO joining QUIET RIOT. The remainder formed JAILHOUSE, while SHORTINO subsequently went solo in the 90's.

PAUL SHORTINO

— with **JEFF NORTHRUP** – guitar / + other session people

Bulletproof / Bulletproof

Mar 94. (cd) *(CDVEST 3)* **BACK ON TRACK**
– The kid is back in town / Body and soul / Girls like you / Pieces / Bye-bye to love / Everybody can fly / Give me love / Remember me / Rough life / Forgotten child / Where there's a life.

Hi-Gain / Hi-Gain

Jun 98. (cd) *<(HGCD 0890)>* **IT'S ABOUT TIME**

U.S.G. / U.S.G.

Jun 99. (cd) *<(USG 1030CD)>* **BOOKED TOURED RELEASED**

not iss. / Orchard

2000. (cd) *<2353>* **STAND OR FALL** -
– Stand or fall / Take me into the fire / Devil in my heart / There goes another love / I know you want me / All of my life / Honesty / Same thing / You can't lose / Broke n' busted.

ROYAL TRUX

Formed: Chicago, Illinois, USA . . . 1987 by Calvin Klein model and self-confessed junkie, JENNIFER HERRERA and PUSSY GALORE's NEIL HAGERTY, who had originally met in a New York sewer two years previously. Lo-fi avant-garde terrorists from the stable of BEEFHEART or ZAPPA that shifted more into The 'STONES (early 70's era), the difference being the sultry JANE BIRKEN style-vox of HERRERA. Following the junkie freeform chaos of earlier albums (by this point she had kicked her habit), the couple signed to 'Virgin'-offshoot, 'Hut' in 1994 and finally got it together for the most focused album of their career to date, the David Briggs-produced 'THANK YOU' (1995). Reportedly cleaned up and newly relocated to Virginia,

HAGGERTY and HERRERA had created a work of hip swivelling, ground-in-the-dirt rock'n'roll drawing inevitable comparisons with the early 70's glory of The ROLLING STONES while recreating the spirit of such less readily remembered boogie merchants as BLACK OAK ARKANSAS and GRAND FUNK RAILROAD, the legendary 'TRUX musical bloody mindedness bubbling under the surface. An unlikely UK tour with TEENAGE FANCLUB helped raise their profile, yet perhaps not surprisingly, it seemed ROYAL TRUX weren't destined for mainstream indie success and following the release of 'SWEET SIXTEEN' (1997), the pair relocated to the more familiar surroundings of US indie label, 'Domino', issuing the 'ACCELERATOR' album in 1998. The aptly titled 'VETERANS OF DISORDER' (1999), meanwhile, provided a right ROYAL TRUX racket, or at least half of it did. Split fairly evenly between two and a half minute minor classics and a trio of longer noisefests, the album provided a bridge between old and new without losing any of the shambolic, subversive edge. In contrast, 'POUND FOR POUND' (2000) found HERRERA and HAGERTY once again kicking back in the musical equivalent of a battered old leather armchair, content to crank out bruised rock'n'roll free from the pressures of experimentation.

Album rating: UNTITLED – ROYAL TRUX (*4) / TWIN INFINITIVES (*4) / CATS AND DOGS (*6) / THANK YOU (*6) / SWEET SIXTEEN (*5) / ACCELERATOR (*6) / VETERANS OF DISORDER (*8) / POUND FOR POUND (*6)

JENNIFER HERRERA – vocals / **NEIL HAGERTY** – guitar, vocals (ex-PUSSY GALORE) / with guests

not iss. Royal

Jan 89. (lp) **UNTITLED** [-] [ ]
– Air / Move / Hallucination / Sometimes / Lightning boxer / Blood flowers / Sun on the run. *<cd-iss. Jan92 & Dec96 as 'ROYAL TRUX' on 'Drag City'; DC 5> (UK-iss.Jun93 on 'Domino' cd/lp' WIG CD/LP 5)*

not iss. Drag City

1990. (d-lp) **TWIN INFINITIVES** [-] [ ]
– Solid gold tooth / Ice cream / Jet pet / RTX – USA / Kool down wheels / Chances are the comets in our future / Yin Jum verses the vomit creature / Osiris / (Edge of the) Ape oven / Florida Avenue theme / Lick my boots / Glitterbust / Funky son / Ratcreeps / New York Avenue bridge. *(UK-iss.Jan94 on 'Domino'; WIGCD 8)*

—— **KEN NASTA** – drums; repl. unknown

Domino Drag City

Jul 93. (cd/lp) *(WIG CD/LP 6) <DC 32CD>* **CATS AND DOGS** [ ] [ ] Jun93
– Teeth / The flag / Friends / The spectre / Skywood greenback mantra / Turn of the century / Up the sleeve / Hot and cold skulls / Tight pants / Let's get lost / Driving in that car (with the eagle on the hood).

Oct 93. (12"ep/cd-ep) *(RUG 8 T/CD)* **DOGS OF LOVE EP** [ ] [-]

Oct 94. (7") *(RUG 27)* **MERCURY. / SHOCKWAVE RIDER** [ ] [-]

—— added **DAN BROWN** – bass / **CHRIS PYLE** – drums / **ROBBIE ARMSTRONG** – percussion / with guests RIAN MURPHY + DAVID BERMAN

Hut Virgin + Drag City

Feb 95. (7") *(HUT 50)* **MAP OF THE CITY. / NATIONAL MOTHER** [ ] [-]

Feb 95. (cd)(c/lp) *(CDHUT 23)(HUT MC/LP 23) <40141><DG 66>* **THANK YOU** [ ] [ ]
– A night to remember / The sewers of Mars / Ray O Vac / Map of the city / Granny grunt / Lights on the levee / Fear strikes out / (Have you met) Horror James / You're gonna lose / Shadow of the wasp.

May 95. (10"/cd-s) *(HUT EN/CD 56)* **YOU'RE GONNA LOSE. / HIBISCUS (live) / HOT AND COLD (live)** [ ] [-]

—— now without 5th member

Apr 97. (cd) *(CDHUT 43) <42752>* **SWEET SIXTEEN** [ ] [ ] Feb97
– Don't try too hard / Morphic resident / Pickup / Cold joint / Golden rules / You'll be staying in romm 323 / Can't have it both ways / 10 days 12 nights / Microwave made / Sweet sixteen / I'm looking through you / Roswell seeds and stems / Pol Pot pie.

Domino Drag City

Apr 98. (7"m) *(RUG 065)* **I'M READY. / P.T. 20 / MR CRUMP DON'T LIKE IT** [ ] [-]

Apr 98. (cd/lp) *(WIG CD/LP 045) <DC 145CD>* **ACCELERATOR** [ ] [ ]
– I'm ready / Yellow kid / Banana question / Another year / Juicy, juicy, juice / Liar / New bones / Follow the winner / Stevie.

Jun 98. (7") *(RUG 069)* **LIAR. / MONEY FOR NOTHING** [ ] [-]
(cd-s+=) *(RUG 069CD)* – P.T. 20 / Mr. Crump don't like it.

Aug 98. (12"ep/cd-ep) *(RUG 076 T/CD) <DC 154>* **3 SONG EP** [ ] [ ]
– Deafer than blind / The United States vs. one 1974 Cadillac El Dorado Sedan / Run, shaker life.

Aug 99. (7") *(RUG 097)* **WATERPARK. / WATERPARK (version)** [ ] [ ]
(cd-s) *(RUG 097CD)* – ('A'side) / Old Yank / The new, new bones.

Sep 99. (cd/lp) *(WIG CD/LP 068)* **VETERANS OF DISORDER** [ ] [ ]
– Waterpark / Stop / The exception / Second skin / Witch's tit / Lunch money / Yo see! / Sickazz dog / Coming-out party / Blue is the frequency.

Jan 00. (12"ep/cd-ep) *(RUG 105 T/CD)* **RADIO VIDEO EP** [ ] [ ]
– The inside game / Victory chimp / Episode 3 / Dirty headlines / Mexican comet on my mind.

May 00. (12") *(JAGZ 001T)* **DIRTY HEADLINES** [ ] [ ]

Jun 00. (cd/lp) *(WIG CD/LP 081)* **POUND FOR POUND** [ ] [ ]
– Call out to the lions / Fire hill / Platinum tips / Accelerator / Deep country sorceror / Sunshine and grease / Blind navigator / Teenage murder mystery / Small thief / Dr.Gone. *<lp-iss.Aug00 on 'Drag City'; DC 188>*

Aug 00. (7") *(RUG 113)* **SUNSHINE AND GREASE. / TEENAGE MURDER MYSTERY** [ ] [-]
(cd-s+=) *(RUG 113CD)* – Zing zang / Dirty headlines (mix).

– compilations, etc. –

May 97. (7") *<(DC 42)>* **MERCURY. /** [ ] [ ]

Nov 97. (d-cd/t-lp) *Domino; (WIG 040 CD/LP) / Drag City; <DC 93>* **SINGLES LIVE UNRELEASED** (rarities, etc) [-] [ ]
– Esso dame / Mercury / No fixed address / Red tiger / Lucy Peaupaux / June night afternoon / Steal your face / Back to school / Faca amolada / Luminous dolphin / Spike cyclone / Vile child / Law man / Shockwave rider / Chairman blow / Womban / Cut you loose / Baghdad buzz / Hero – Zero / Statik Jakl / Gett off / Teeth / Cleveland / Theme from M*A*S*H / Strawberry soda / Sunflavor / Love is . . . / Ratcreeps / Hair beach / Sometimes / Signed, confused / Aviator blues.

RTZ (see under ⇒ BOSTON)

RUBICON (see under ⇒ FIELDS OF THE NEPHILIM)

RUB ULTRA

Formed: London, England . . . summer 1993 by WILL, his sister SARAH, STEVE, CHARLIE and PETE. Signed to indie label, 'Hi-Rise', this group debuted in 1994 with the 'KORPORATE FYNGER TACTIK' EP, following it up with a full length album, 'LIQUID BOOTS AND BOILED SWEETS' in 1995. It would be a further two years before any new material surfaced, the group switching labels before releasing the brilliantly titled 'WEE WEE PADS 4 ALL THE LADS' (1997).

Album rating: LIQUID BOOTS AND BOILED SWEETS (*6)

WILL – vocals / **STEVE** – guitar / **CHARLIE** – bass / **PETE** – drums / **SARAH** – vocals, percussion

Hi-Rise not iss.

Nov 94. (12"ep/cd-ep) *(FLAT T/SCD 11)* **KORPORATE FYNGER TACTIK EP** [ ] [-]
– Cosmyk fruit centre / That's your load / Honey is my thing.

Sep 95. (7") *(FLAT 22)* **BROWN BOX NITRO. / WIND IT** [ ] [-]
(cd-s+=) *(FLATSCD 22)* – Earth adjustment.

Oct 95. (cd) *(FLATCD 21)* **LIQUID BOOTS AND BOILED SWEETS** [ ] [-]
– Brown box nitro (dog's life) / Blasted freak / Health horror and the vitamin urge / Oily man eel / Your nasty hair / Generate / Whale boy / Free toy / Cat's gone underground / Suspend your belief / Castles / Voodoo accident.

S.A.D. not iss.

Mar 97. (12") *(SAD 007)* **WEE WEE PADS 4 ALL THE LADS** [ ] [-]

RUNAWAYS

Formed: Los Angeles, California, USA . . . mid-1974 by the notorious solo star turned record producer KIM FOWLEY (along with teen lyricist, KARI KROME), who set out to create a female RAMONES. After successfully applying to his music paper ad, JOAN JETT became the first to join, followed soon after by SANDY WEST and MICKI STEELE. With a few gigs under their belt, STEELE was replaced by CHERIE CURRIE, while the line-up was finalised with the addition of LITA FORD and JACKIE FOX. This was the formation that played a rooftop session on a Los Angeles apartment block in early 1976, an event that helped secure a record deal with 'Mercury'. While their eponymous debut was hitting the shops, the girls (average age 16) made their New York debut at CBGB's in September '76 supporting TELEVISION and TALKING HEADS. Dragging glam-metal by the pubic hair and injecting it with punk energy, tracks such as 'CHERRY BOMB' and 'HOLLYWOOD' saw The RUNAWAYS lumped in with the fermenting US New Wave scene. Early in '77, they released a second album, 'QUEENS OF NOISE', and like its predecessor it too failed to capitalize on the hype. Internal tensions were coming to a head around the time of the Japanese-only (The RUNAWAYS were huge in the Far East) live set, VICKI BLUE standing in for the worn out JACKIE FOX, while the blonde CURRIE finally split for a solo career (JOAN JETT taking over vocal duties). Adopting a harder-edged approach, the new line-up released yet another album, 'WAITIN' FOR THE NIGHT' (1978), the last to feature LITA FORD (another RUNAWAY to go onto a semi-successful solo career) and VICKI BLUE (who had attempted suicide). Although LAURIE McCALLISTER was brought in as a brief replacement, she didn't play on a posthumous covers set, 'AND NOW . . . THE RUNAWAYS', the band having already finally split. JOAN JETT was the third and most successful member to carve out a solo niche, however, FOWLEY subsequently resurrected the name (minus any original members!) for a less than impressive 1987 set, 'YOUNG AND FAST'. • **Trivia:** The JOAN JETT & THE RUNAWAYS album was entirely made up of covers; Slade's 'MAMA WEER ALL CRAZEE NOW' being one of them.

Album rating: THE RUNAWAYS (*7) / QUEENS OF NOISE (*6) / LIVE IN JAPAN (*5) / WAITIN' FOR THE NIGHT (*4) / AND NOW . . . THE RUNAWAYS (*3) / THE BEST OF THE RUNAWAYS compilation (*6) / YOUNG AND FAST (*3)

CHERIE CURRIE (b.1960) – vocals who repl. MICKI STEELE (was part-time vox, bass) / **LITA FORD** (b.23 Sep'59, London, England) – lead guitar, vocals / **JOAN JETT** (b.22 Sep'60, Philadelphia, Pennsylvania) – rhythm guitar, vocals / **JACKIE FOX** – bass / **SANDY WEST** (b.1960) – drums

Mercury Mercury

Sep 76. (7") *(6167 392) <73819>* **CHERRY BOMB. / BLACKMAIL** [ ] [ ]

Nov 76. (lp) *(9100 029) <SRM1 1090>* **THE RUNAWAYS** [ ] [ ] Jun 76
– Cherry bomb / You drive me wild / Is it day or night? / Thunder / Rock and roll / Lovers / American nights / Blackmail / Secrets / Dead end justice.

Feb 77. (lp) *(9100 032) <SRM1 1126>* **QUEENS OF NOISE** [ ] [ ] Jan 77
– Queens of noise / Take it or leave it / Midnight music / Born to be bad / Neon angels on the road to ruin / Midnight music / I love playin' with fire / California Paradise / Hollywood heartbeat / Johnny Guitar.

Feb 77. (7") *<73890>* **HEARTBEAT. / NEON ANGELS ON THE ROAD TO RUIN** [-] [ ]

Feb 77. (7") *(6167 493)* **QUEENS OF NOISE. / BORN TO BE BAD** [ ] [-]

Oct 77. (lp) *(9100 046)* **LIVE IN JAPAN (live)** [ ] [-]
– Queens of noise / California Paradise / All right you guys / Wild thing / Gettin' hot / Rock and roll / You drive me wild / Neon angels on the road to ruin / I wanna be where the boys are / Cherry bomb / American nights / C'mon.

—— (Jul'77) **VICKI BLUE** – bass repl. FOX who suffers from nervous exhaustion. **JETT** took over lead vocals, when CURRIE left to go solo.

Oct 77. (7") *(6167 587)* **SCHOOL DAYS. / WASTED** [ ] [-]
Dec 77. (lp) *(9100 047)* *<SRM1 3075>* **WAITIN' FOR THE NIGHT** [ ] [ ]
– Little sister / Wasted / Gotta get out tonight / Wait for me / Fantasies / School days / Trash can murders / Don't go away / Waitin' for the night / You're too possessive.

—— **LAURIE McALLISTER** – bass repl. VICKI BLUE when she attempted suicide. Split late 1978, when LITA FORD went solo after the recording of final album below.

Cherry Red / not iss.

Jul 79. (lp,colrd-lp) *(ARED 3)* **AND NOW . . . THE RUNAWAYS** [ ] [-]
– Saturday night special / Eight days a week / Mama weer all crazee now / I'm a million / Right now / Takeover / My buddy and me / Little lost girls / Black leather. *<re-iss. US 1981 as 'LITTLE LOST GIRLS' on 'Rhino' lp><pic-lp; RNLP 70861><RNDF 250> <cd-iss. US 1987; R2 70861> (cd-iss. Jul93 on 'Anagram'; CDGRAM 63)*
Aug 79. (7") *(CHERRY 8)* **RIGHT NOW. / BLACK LEATHER** [ ] [-]

—— JOAN JETT went solo backed by her BLACKHEARTS

—— re-formed for a one-off (with no originals)

not iss. / Allegience

1987. (lp) **YOUNG AND FAST** [-] [ ]

– compilations, others, etc. –

Feb 80. (lp) *Cherry Red; (BRED 9)* **FLAMING SCHOOLGIRLS** (live/studio) [ ] [-]
Sep 82. (lp/c) *Mercury; (MERB/+C 12)* **THE BEST OF THE RUNAWAYS** [ ] [ ]
1981. (12"ep) *Rhino; <RNEP 602>* **MAMA WEER ALL CRAZEE NOW** [-] [ ]
Apr 82. (pic-lp/lp; JOAN JETT & THE RUNAWAYS) *Cherry Red; (P+/LAKER 1)* **I LOVE PLAYING WITH FIRE** [ ] [-]
1992. (cd) *Mercury; <838 583-2>* **NEON ANGELS** [-] [ ]
Jun 94. (10"lp) *Marilyn; (FM 1004)* **BORN TO BE BAD** [-] [-] France

RUNNING WILD

Formed: Hamburg, Germany . . . 1981 by ROCK'N'ROLF, who enlisted STEPHAN, THE PREACHER and HASCHE. Initially purveying cliched black metal, the band signed to 'Noise' and incredibly topped the German charts with their debut long player, 'GATES TO PURGATORY' (1985). A follow-up, 'BRANDED AND EXILED' (1985; and with newcomer MAJK MOTI) followed in a similar vein, although by the release of 'UNDER JOLLY ROGER' (1987), the satanic trappings had been ditched in favour of a well dodgy pirate image and more accessible power-metal approach. A series of line-up changes preceded the 1988 live set, with JENS BECKER replacing THE PREACHER. The sea-faring nonsense continued with 'PORT ROYAL' (1989) and 'DEATH OR GLORY' (1990), the latter marking the first fruits of their deal with 'E.M.I.'. The fact they had signed to a major was an indication of their ever buoyant popularity in Germany despite minimal interest in the UK. After a final set on 'Noise', however, the band were well and truly consigned to Davy Jones' Locker. With more personnel changes abound (see below discog), RUNNING WILD trotted out several other sets, namely 'BLAZON STONE' (1991), 'PILE OF SKULLS' (1995), 'BLACK HAND INN' (1995), 'MASQUERADE' (1995), 'THE RIVALRY' (1998) and 'VICTORY' (2000). File under "those crazy Germans".

Album rating: GATES OF PURGATORY (*6) / BRANDED AND EXILED (*6) / UNDER JOLLY ROGER (*6) / READY FOR BOARDING (*5) / PORT ROYAL (*4) / DEATH OR GLORY (*4) / BLAZON STONE (*5) / THE FIRST YEARS OF PIRACY compilation (*6) / MASQUERADE (*5) / THE RIVALRY (*5) / VICTORY (*4)

ROCK'N'ROLF - vocals, guitar / **THE PREACHER** - guitar / **STEPHAN** - bass, vocals / **(STEFAN) HASCHE** - drums

Noise / S.P.V.

1984. (12") *(N 0010)* **WALPURGIS NIGHT. /** [-] [-] German
1984. (lp)(cd) *(N 0012)(NCD 001)* **GATES TO PURGATORY** [-] [-] German
– Victims of state power / Black demon / Preacher / Soldiers of Hell / Diabolic force / Adrian S.O.S. *(cd+=)* – Genghis Khan / Prisoner of our time. *(re-iss. Oct89 cd/lp; CD+/NUK 012) (cd re-iss. Jun99; NCD 0001)*

—— **MAJIK MOTI** – guitar; repl. THE PREACHER

1985. (lp) *(N 0030) <SPV 084 7735>* **BRANDED AND EXILED** [-] [ ] German
– Branded and exiled / Gods of iron / Realm of shades / Mordor / Fight the oppression / Evil spirit / Marching to die / Chains and leather. *(re-iss. Oct89 cd/lp; CD+/NUK 030) (cd re-iss. Jun99; N 00303)*
1987. (lp) *(N 0062) <SPV 086 4427>* **UNDER JOLLY ROGER** [-] [ ]
– Under Jolly Roger / War in the gutter / Raw hide / Beggar's night / Raise your fist / Land of ice / Diamonds of the black chest / Merciless game. *(re-iss. Oct89 cd/c/lp; CD/ZC+/NUK 062) (cd re-iss. Jun99; N 0064)*

—— **JENS BECKER** – bass; repl. STEPHAN

1988. (lp/c/cd) *(N 0108-1/-2/-3) <SPV 44722>* **READY FOR BOARDING (live)** [-] [ ]
– Hymn of Long John Silver / Under Jolly Roger / Genghis Khan / Raise your fist / Purgatory / Mordor / Diabolic force / Raw hide / Adrian (S.O.S.) / Prisoner of our time. *(re-iss. Oct89 cd/c/lp; CD/ZC+/NUK 108) (cd re-iss. Jun99; same)*

—— **IAIN FINLAY** – drums; repl. HASCHE

Feb 89. (lp/c/cd) *(N 0122-1/-2/-3) <SPV 085-4713>* **PORT ROYAL** [-] [ ]
– Port Royal / Raging fire / Into the arena / Vaschitschun / Final gates / Conquistadores / Blown to kingdom come / Warchild / Mutiny / Calico Jack. *(re-iss. Oct89 cd/c/lp; CD/ZC+/NUK 122) (cd re-iss. Jun99; N same)*

E.M.I. / Circle Blue

Nov 89. (7") *(EM 116)* **BAD TO THE BONE. / BATTLE OF WATERLOO** [ ] [ ]
(12"+=/cd-s+=) *(12/CD EM 116)* – March on.
Feb 90. (cd/c/lp) *(CD/TC+/EMC 3568) <N.CD.004UX>* **DEATH OR GLORY** [ ] [ ] 1995
– Riding the storm / Renegade / Evilution / Running blood / Highland glory (the eternal fight) / Marooned / Bad to the bone / Tortuga Bay / Death or glory / Battle of Waterloo. *(cd+=)* – March on. *<US cd++=>* – Hanged, drawn and quartered / Win or be drowned.

—— **AXEL MORGAN** – guitar; repl. MOTI

—— **U.E.** – drums; repl. IAIN

Noise / Circle Blue

May 91. (cd/c/lp) *(N 0171-2/-4/-1) <N.CD.005UX>* **BLAZON STONE** [ ] [ ] 1995
– Blazon stone / Lonewolf / Slavery / Fire & ice / Little Big Horn / Over the rainbow / White masque / Rolling wheels / Bloody red rose / Straight to hell / Heads or tails. *<US cd+=>* – Billy the kid / Genocide / Dancing on a minefield. *(cd re-iss. Jun99; N 0320-2)*

—— **THOMAS SMUSZYNSKI** – bass; repl. BECKER

—— **STEFAN SCHWARZMANN** – drums; repl. U.E.

1995. (cd) *<N.CD.006UX>* **PILE OF SKULLS** [-] [ ]
– Chamber of lies / Whirlwind / Sinister ice / Black wings of death / Fistful of dynamite / Roaring thunder / Pile of skulls / Lead or gold / White buffalo / Jennings revenge / Treasure island / Beggars night. *(cd re-iss. Jun99; N 0322-2)*

—— **THILO HERMANN** – guitar; repl. AXEL

—— **JORG MICHAEL** – drums; repl. STEFAN

1995. (cd) *<N.CD.007UX>* **BLACK HAND INN** [-] [ ]
– The curse / Black Hand Inn / Mr. Deadhead / Souless / The privateer / Fight the fire of hate / The phantom of Black Hand hill / Freewind rider / Powder & iron / Dragonmen / Genesis (the making and the fall of man) / Poisoned blood. *(UK-iss.Jun99; N 0319-2)*
1995. (cd/lp) *(N 0261-2/-1)* **MASQUERADE** [-] [-] German
– The contract – The crypts of Hades / Masquerade / Demonized / Black soul / Lions of the sea / Rebel at heart / Wheel of doom / Metalhead / Soleil royal / Men in black / Underworld. *(UK-iss.Jun99; N 0318CD)*

Gun / Gun

Feb 98. (cd) *(GUN 155CD)* **THE RIVALRY** [ ] [ ]
Jan 00. (cd) *(GUN 187CD)* **VICTORY** [ ] [ ]

– compilations, etc. –

Jan 92. (cd/c/lp) *Noise; (N 0184-2/-4/-1)* **THE FIRST YEARS OF PIRACY** [ ] [-]
– Under Jolly Roger / Branded and exiled / Soldiers of Hell / Raise your fist / Walpurgis night / Fight the oppression / Marching to die / Raw ride / Diamonds of the black chest / Prisoner of our time. *(cd re-iss. Jun99; same)*

RUSH

Formed: Toronto, Canada . . . 1969 by ALEX LIFESON, GEDDY LEE and JOHN RUTSEY. Initially a hard-rock power outfit in the classic British mould of CREAM and LED ZEPPELIN, they toured local bars and clubs, culminating in a hometown support slot with The NEW YORK DOLLS. Immediately prior to this (1973), RUSH formed their own label, 'Moon', issuing a cover of Buddy Holly's 'NOT FADE AWAY' as their debut 45. An eponymous debut followed in early '74 and was soon picked up by DJ, Donna Halper, who sent a copy to Cliff Burnstein at 'Mercury' records. The company signed RUSH for a 6-figure sum, re-mixing (courtesy of Terry 'Broon' Brown) and re-releasing the record to minor US success (bubbled under the Top 100). Although a tentative start, GEDDY's helium-laced shrill was employed to stunning effect on tracks such as 'WORKING MAN', 'FINDING MY WAY' and 'WHAT YOU'RE DOING'. However, with drummer NEIL PEART replacing RUTSEY, RUSH began to develop the unique style which would characterise their classic 70's work. As well as being a consummate sticksman, PEART masterminded the band's lyrical flights of fantasy, beginning with 'FLY BY NIGHT' (1975). With the conceptually similar YES still world-beating favourites, RUSH found it difficult to progress commercially. Creatively however, the trio attempted to wrestle the symphonic-rock crown from their transatlantic neighbours with such mystical, grandiose fare as 'BY-TOR AND THE SNOW DOG'. Later the same year, they released the under par 'CARESS OF STEEL', which featured the self-indulgently lengthy 'FOUNTAIN OF LAMNETH'. This stage of RUSH's career reached its zenith in 1976 with the concept album, '2112', based on the work of novelist and philosopher Ayn Rand. Boasting a spectacular side-long 20-minute title track/overture, this feted prog-rock/sci-fi classic gave RUSH their long-awaited breakthrough, the record almost achieving a US Top 60 placing. In the course of the previous three years, the band's fanbase had swelled considerably, enabling them to get away with releasing a live double set, 'ALL THE WORLD'S A STAGE'. Featuring electrifying renditions of RUSH's most exquisite material to date, the album was hailed as an instant classic, its Top 40 success in the States leading to massive import sales in Europe. This persuaded the band to bring their live show to Britain/Europe, their wildly enthusiastic reception encouraging them to stay on in Wales and record 'A FAREWELL TO KINGS'. Not surprisingly, the album made the UK (& US) Top 40, its success boosted by a UK Top 40 hit/EP, 'CLOSER TO THE HEART' early the following year. 1978's 'HEMISPHERES' set was the last to feature PEART's trademark epics, the album consolidating the band's growing UK support, while their native Canada lavished upon them the title, 'Ambassadors Of Music'. While many bands of their ilk floundered critically, RUSH began the 80's on a high note, scoring a rare UK Top 20 hit single with 'SPIRIT OF RADIO'. Taken from their million-selling 'PERMANENT WAVES' opus, the track was characteristic of the shorter, leaner sound that RUSH would pursue throughout the coming decade.

Not escaping the increasing technological influence of 80's music, the band adopted a more keyboard-orientated approach on albums such as 'MOVING PICTURES' (1981), 'SIGNALS' (1982), 'GRACE UNDER PRESSURE' (1984) and 'POWER WINDOWS' (1985). Finally parting company with their longstanding producer, TERRY BROWN, they further refined their sound on the 1987 album, 'HOLD YOUR FIRE', which spawned a near UK Top 40 single, 'TIME STAND STILL' (credited AIMEE MANN of 'TIL TUESDAY). After the compulsory live set, 'A SHOW OF HANDS', the band opted for a fresh start with 'Atlantic', 'PRESTO' (1989) being the first fruits of this new alliance. Incredibly, despite regular critical derision from the trendier sections of the music press, RUSH have gone on to even greater success in the 90's, both 'ROLL THE BONES' (1991) and 'COUNTERPARTS' (1993) making the US Top 5 (now only Top 30 in Britain!). Certainly, PRIMUS' well-documented admiration has done the band no harm, LIFESON even bringing in the latter band's LES CLAYPOOL for a guest spot on his ill-advised VICTOR project. The same year (1996), RUSH released their umpteenth set, 'TEST FOR ECHO', the band looking good for their 30th anniversary just prior to the millennium. Of late (November 2000 to be exact), GEDDY LEE has become a solo artist, releasing his debut solo album 'MY FAVOURITE HEADACHE' to lukewarm reviews. • **Trivia:** Early in 1982, GEDDY guested for BOB & DOUG McKENZIE (aka Rick Moranis & Dave Thomas) on their US Top 20 single 'Take Off'.

Album rating: RUSH (*6) / FLY BY NIGHT (*6) / CARESS OF STEEL (*5) / 2112 (*8) / ALL THE WORLD'S A STAGE (*8) / A FAREWELL TO KINGS (*7) / HEMISPHERES (*6) / PERMANENT WAVES (*6) / MOVING PICTURES (*7) / EXIT . . . STAGE LEFT (*5) / SIGNALS (*6) / GRACE UNDER PRESSURE (*5) / POWER WINDOWS (*5) / HOLD YOUR FIRE (*5) / A SHOW OF HANDS (*5) / PRESTO (*5) / CHRONICLES compilation (*7) / ROLL THE BONES (*5) / COUNTERPARTS (*4) / TEST FOR ECHO (*5) / DIFFERENT STAGES live compilation (*5) / Alex Lifeson: VICTOR (*3) / Geddy Lee: MY FAVOURITE HEADACHE (*5)

GEDDY LEE (b. GARY LEE WEINRIB, 29 Jul'53, Willowdale, Toronto, Canada) – vocals, bass, keyboards / **ALEX LIFESON** (b. ALEX ZIVOJINOVICH, 27 Aug'53, Surnie, British Columbia, Canada) – lead guitar / **JOHN RUTSEY** – drums

not iss. Moon

1973. (7") **NOT FADE AWAY. / YOU CAN'T FIGHT IT** [-] []

Mercury Mercury

Aug 74. (7") *<73623>* **FINDING MY WAY. /** [-] []

Feb 75. (lp) *(9100 011) <1011>* **RUSH** [] [] Jul74
– Finding my way / Need some love / Take a friend / Here again / What you're doing / In the mood / Before and after / Working man. *(c-iss.Apr82; 7142 365) (re-iss. Jun83 lp/c; PRICE/PRIMC 18) (cd-iss. Apr87; 822 541-2)*

Feb 75. (7") *<73647>* **WHAT YOU'RE DOING. / IN THE MOOD** [-] []

—— (Autumn '74) **NEIL PEART** (b.12 Sep'52, Hamilton, Ontario, Canada) – drums, vocals, lyrics repl. RUTSEY

Apr 75. (lp) *(9100 013) <1023>* **FLY BY NIGHT** [] [] Feb75
– Anthem / Best I can / Beneath, between and behind / By-Tor & the snowdog: (i) At the tobes of Hades – (ii) Across the Styx – (iii) Of the battle – (iv) Epilogue / Fly by night / Making memories / Rivendell / In the end. *(c-iss.Apr82; 7142 389) (re-iss. Jun83 lp/c; PRICE/PRIMC 19) (cd-iss. Apr87; 822 542-2)*

May 75. (7") *<73681>* **FLY BY NIGHT. / ANTHEM** [-] []
<re-iss. Dec77; 73990>

Nov 75. (7") *<73737>* **BASTILLE DAY. / LAKESIDE PARK** [-] []

Mar 76. (lp) *(9100 018) <1046>* **CARESS OF STEEL** [] [] Oct75
– Bastille day / I think I'm going bald / Lakeside Park / The necromancer: (I) Unto darkness – (II) Under the shadow – (III) REturn of the prince / In the valley / Didacts and narpets / No one at the bridge / Panacea / Bacchus plateau / The fountain. *(c-iss.Apr82; 7142 421) (re-iss. Jun83 lp/c; PRICE/PRIMC 20) (cd-iss. Apr87; 822 543-2)*

Jun 76. (lp) *(9100 039) <1079>* **2112** [] [61] Apr76
– Overture / The temples of Syrinx / Discovery / Presentation / Oracle. The dream / Soliliquy / Grand finale / A passage to Bangkok / The twilight zone / Lessons / Tears / Something for nothing. *(re-iss. Jan85 lp/c; PRICE/PRIMC 79) (cd-iss. Apr87; 822 545-2)*

Jun 76. (7") *<73803>* **LESSONS. / THE TWILIGHT ZONE** [-] []

Mar 77. (d-lp) *(6672 015) <7508>* **ALL THE WORLD'S A STAGE (live)** [] [40] Sep76
– Bastille day / Anthem / Fly by night / In the mood / Something for nothing / Lakeside park / Overture / The temple of Syrinx / Presentation / Soliloquy / Grand finale / By-Tor and the snowdog / In the end / Working man / Finding my way / What you're doing. *(c-iss.Apr78; 7553 047) (re-iss. Sep84 d-lp/d-c; PRID/+C 1) (cd-iss. Apr87 – = a few tracks; 822 552-2)*

Dec 76. (7") *<73873>* **FLY BY NIGHT (live). / IN THE MOOD (live) / SOMETHING FOR NOTHING (live)** [-] [88]

Feb 77. (7") *<73912>* **THE TEMPLES OF SYRINX. / MAKING MEMORIES** [-] []

Sep 77. (lp) *(9100 042) <1184>* **A FAREWELL TO KINGS** [22] [33]
– A farewell to kings / Xanadu / Closer to the heart / Cinderella man / Madrigal / Cygnus X-1. *(re-iss. Apr86 lp/c; PRICE/PRIMC 92) (cd-iss. Apr87; 822 546-2)*

Nov 77. (7") *<73958>* **CLOSER TO THE HEART. / MADRIGAL** [-] [76]

Jan 78. (7"ep) *(RUSH 7)* **CLOSER TO THE HEART. / BASTILLE DAY / THE TEMPLES OF SYRINX** [36] [-]
(12"ep+=) *(RUSH 12)* – Anthem.

Nov 78. (lp)(c)<US-pic-lp> *(9100 059)(7142 647) <3743>* **HEMISPHERES** [14] [47]
– Prelude / Apollo (bringer of wisdom) Hemispheres / Dionysus (bringer of love) / Armageddon (the battle of heart and mind) / Cygnus (bringer of balance) / The sphere (a kind of dream) / Circumstances / The trees / La villa Strangiato. *(cd-iss. Apr87; 822 547-2) (re-iss. Mar88 lp/c; PRICE/PRIMC 118)*

Jan 79. (7") *<74051>* **CIRCUMSTANCES. / THE TREES** [-] []

Jan 80. (lp)(c) *(9100 071)(7142 720) <4001>* **PERMANENT WAVES** [3] [4]
– Spirit of radio / Freewill / Jacob's ladder / Entre nous / Different strings / Natural science. *(cd-iss. Apr87; 822 548-2)*

Feb 80. (7") *<76044>* **SPIRIT OF RADIO. / CIRCUMSTANCES** [-] [51]

Feb 80. (7") *(RADIO 7)* **SPIRIT OF RADIO. / THE TREES** [13] [-]
(12"+=) *(RADIO 12)* – Working man.

Apr 80. (7") *<76060>* **DIFFERENT STRINGS. / ENTRE NOUS** [-] []

Feb 81. (7") *<76095>* **LIMELIGHT. / XYZ** [-] [55]

Feb 81. (lp/c) *(6337/7141 160) <4013>* **MOVING PICTURES** [3] [3]
– Tom Sawyer / Red Barchetta / XYZ / Limelight / The camera eye / Witch hunt (part III of fear) / Vital signs. *(cd-iss. 1983; 800 048-2)*

Mar 81. (7") *(VITAL 7)* **VITAL SIGNS. / IN THE MOOD** [41] [-]
(12"+=) *(VITAL 12)* – A passage to Bangkok / Circumstances.

May 81. (7") *<76109>* **TOM SAWYER. / WITCH HUNT** [-] [44]

Oct 81. (7") *<76124>* **FREEWILL (live). / CLOSER TO THE HEART (live)** [-] []

Oct 81. (d-lp/d-c) *(6619/7558 053) <7001>* **EXIT . . . STAGE LEFT (live)** [6] [10]
– The spirit of radio / Red Barchetta / YYZ / A passage to Bangkok *[not on cd]* / Closer to the heart / Beneath, between and behind / Jacob's ladder / Broon's bane / The trees / Xanadu / Freewill / Tom Sawyer / La villa Strangiato. *(cd-iss. Apr87; 822 551-2)*

Oct 81. (7") *(EXIT 7)* **TOM SAWYER (live). / A PASSAGE TO BANGKOK (live)** [25] [-]
(12"+=) *(EXIT 12)* – Red Barchetta (live).

Dec 81. (7") *(RUSH 1) <76124>* **CLOSER TO THE HEART (live). / THE TREES (live)** [] [69]

Aug 82. (7") *(RUSH 8) <76179>* **NEW WORLD MAN. / VITAL SIGNS (live)** [42] [21]
(12"+=) *(RUSH 8-12)* – Freewill (live).

Sep 82. (lp/c) *(6337/7141 243) <403>* **SIGNALS** [3] [10]
– Subdivisions / The analog kid / Chemistry / Digital man / The weapon / New world man / Losing it / Countdown. *(cd-iss. 1983; 810 002-2)*

Oct 82. (7") *<76196>* **SUBDIVISIONS. / COUNTDOWN** [-] []

Oct 82. (7"/7"pic-d) *(RUSH/+P 9)* **SUBDIVISIONS. / RED BARCHETTA (live)** [53] [-]
(12"+=) *(RUSH 9-12)* – Jacob's ladder (live).

Apr 83. (7"/7"sha-pic-d) *(RUSH 10/+PD)* **COUNTDOWN. / NEW WORLD MAN** [36] []
(12"+=) *(RUSH 10-12)* – Spirit of radio (live) / (interview excerpts).

Apr 84. (lp/c)(cd) *(VERH/+C 12)(818 476-2) <818476>* **GRACE UNDER PRESSURE** [5] [10]
– Distant early warning / After image / Red sector A / The enemy within / The body electric / Kid gloves / Red lenses / Between the wheels.

May 84. (7") *(RUSH 11)* **THE BODY ELECTRIC. / THE ANALOG KID** [56] []
(10"red+=/12"+=) *(RUSH 11 10/12)* – Distant early warning.

Oct 85. (7") *(RUSH 12) <884191>* **THE BIG MONEY. / TERRITORIES** [] [45]
(12"+=) *(RUSH 12-12)* – Red sector A (live).
(d7"+=) *(RUSHD 12)* – Closer to the heart / Spirit of radio.
(7"g-f) *(RUSHG 12)* – ('A'side) / Middletown dreams.

Nov 85. (lp/pic-lp/c)(cd) *(VERH/+P/C 31)(826 098-2) <826098>* **POWER WINDOWS** [9] [10] Oct85
– The big money / Grand designs / Manhattan project / Marathon / Territories / Middletown dreams / Emotion detector / Mystic rhythms.

Oct 87. (7") *(RUSH 13)* **TIME STAND STILL. / FORCE TEN** [41] []
(12"pic-d+=) *(RUSHP 13-12)* – The enemy within (live).
(12"++=) *(RUSH 13-12)* – Witch hunt (live).

Nov 87. (lp/c)(cd) *(VERH/+C 47)(832 464-2) <832464>* **HOLD YOUR FIRE** [10] [13] Sep87
– Force ten / Time stand still / Open secrets / Second nature / Prime mover / Lock and key / Mission / Turn the page / Tai Shan / High water.

Mar 88. (7") *(RUSH 14)* **PRIME MOVER. / TAI SHAN** [] []
(12"+=) *(RUSH 14-12)* – Open secrets.
(12"++=) *(RUSHR 14-12)* – New world man (live).
(cd-s+=) *RUSHCD 14)* – Distant early warning (live) / New world man (live).
(7"white) *(RUSHR 14)* – ('A'side) / Distant early warning (live).

Jan 89. (d-lp/c/cd) *(836 346-1/-4/-2) <836346>* **A SHOW OF HANDS (live)** [12] [21]
– (intro) / The big money / Subdivisions / Marathon / Turn the page / Manhattan project / Mission / Distant early warning / Mystic rhythms / Witch hunt (part III of fear) / The rhythm method / Force ten / Time stand still / Red sector A / Closer to the heart.

Atlantic Atlantic

Dec 89. (lp/c)(cd) *(WX 327/+C)(782 040-2) <82040-1/-4/-2>* **PRESTO** [27] [16] Nov89
– Show don't tell / Chain lightning / The pass / War paint / Scars / Presto / Superconductor / Anagram (for Mongo) / Red tide / Hand over fist / Available light.

Jan 90. (7") **SHOW DON'T TELL. /** [-] []

Sep 91. (cd)(lp/c) *<(7567 82293-2)>(WX 436/+C)* **ROLL THE BONES** [10] [3]
– Dreamline / Bravado / Roll the bones / Face up / Where's my thing? (part IV 'Gangster Of Boats' trilogy) / The big wheel / Heresy / Ghost of a chance / Neurotica / You bet your life.

Feb 92. (7") *(A 7524)* **ROLL THE BONES. / SHOW DON'T TELL** [49] []
(cd-s+=) *(A 7524CD)* – (interviews) / Anagram.
(7"sha-pic-d) *(A 7524TE)* – ('A'side) / The pass / It's a rap part 1.

Apr 92. (7") *(A 7491)* **GHOST OF A CHANCE. / DREAMLINE** [] []
(cd-s+=) *(A 7491CD)* – Chain lightning / Red tide.

Oct 93. (cd/c/lp) *<(7567 82528-2/-4/-1)>* **COUNTERPARTS** [14] [2]
– Animate / Stick it out / Cut to the chase / Nobody's hero / Between sun & moon / Alien shore / The speed of love / Double agent / Leave that thing alone / Cold fire / Everyday glory.

Sep 96. (cd/c) *<(7567 82925-2/-4)>* **TEST FOR ECHO** [25] [5]
– Test for echo / Driven / Half the world / The color of right / Time and motion / Totem / Dog years / Virtuality / Resist / Limbo / Carve away the stone.

Nov 98. (t-cd/d-c) *(7567 80921-2/-4) <83122>* **DIFFERENT STAGES (live history)** [] [35]
– Dreamline / Limelight / Driven / Bravado / Animate / Show don't tell / Trees / Nobody's hero / Closer to the heart / 2112 – Overture / Temples in Syrinx – Discovery – Presentation – Oraci (e the dream – Soliloquy – Grand finale) / Test for echo / Analog kid / Freewill / Roll the bones / Stick it out / Resist / Leave that thing alone / Neil's solo / Natural science / Spirit of radio / Tom Sawyer / XYZ / Bastille day / By Tor and the snow dog / Xanadu / Farewell to kings / Something for nothing / Cygnus X-1 / Anthem / Working man / Fly by night / In the mood / Cinderella man.

– compilations, others, etc. –

on 'Mercury' unless otherwise mentioned

May 78. (t-lp)(d-c) *(6641 779)(7649 103)* <9200> **ARCHIVES** [ ] [ ] Apr78
– (RUSH / FLY BY NIGHT / CARESS OF STEEL)

Sep 81. (lp/c) *<6337/7141 171)* **RUSH THROUGH TIME** [-] [ ]

Feb 88. (7") *Old Gold; (OG 9767)* **SPIRIT OF RADIO. / CLOSER TO THE HEART** [ ] [-]

Oct 90. (d-cd/d-c/t-lp) *Vertigo; (838 936-2/-4/-1) / Mercury; <838936>* **CHRONICLES** [42] [51] Sep90
– Finding my way / Working man / Fly by night / Anthem / Bastille day / Lakeside park / 2112: a) Overture, b) The temples of Syrinx / What you're doing (live) / A farewell to kings / Closer to the heart / The trees / La villa Strangiato / Freewill / Spirit of radio/ / Tom Sawyer / Red barchetta / Limelight / A passage to Bangkok (live) / Subdivisions / New world man / Distant early warning / Red sector A / The big money / Manhattan project / Force ten / Time stand still / Mystic rhythms (live) / Show don't tell.

VICTOR

ALEX LIFESON – guitar, bass, keyboards / **BILL BELL** – wobble & slide guitar, co-writer / **PETER CARDINALI** – bass / **BLAKE MANNING** – drums / + guests EDWIN – vocals (of I MOTHER EARTH) + LES CLAYPOOL – bass (of PRIMUS)

Atlantic Atlantic

Feb 96. (cd/c) *<(7567-82852-2/-4)>* **VICTOR** [ ] [99] Jan96
– Don't care / Promise / Start today / Mr. X / At the end / Sending a warning / Shut up shuttin' up / Strip and go naked / The big dance / Victor / I am the spirit.

GEDDY LEE

with **BEN MONK** – guitar, violin (ex-FM) / **MATT CAMERON** – drums (ex-SOUNDGARDEN)

Atlantic Atlantic

Nov 00. (cd) *<(7567 83384-2)>* **MY FAVOURITE HEADACHE** [ ] [ ]
– My favourite headache / The present tense / Window to the world / Working at perfekt / Runaway train / The angels' share / Moving to Bohemia / Home on the strange / Slipping / Still / Grace to grace.

SABBAT

Formed: England . . . mid 80's by MARTIN WALKYIER, ANDY SNEAP, FRAZER CRASKE and SIMON NEGUS. Famous for bagging a glossy Kerrang! spread before even releasing a record, SABBAT were mystical pagan curios in a thrash scene saturated by pedestrian, axe-abusing bores. Signing to 'Noise', the band more or less lived up to the initial hype with debut set, 'HISTORY OF A TIME TO COME' (1988), their elaborate stage show attempting to visualise the intricate lyrical tapestries in suitably medieval style. A conceptual affair based on the Brian Bates novel, 'The Way Of Wyrd', 'DREAMWEAVER' (1989) witnessed SABBAT accumulating even greater critical acclaim from their growing band of admirers. Just when it seemed as if the band were poised to cross over from cultdom, internal tension led to the departure of frontman WALKYIER (who went on to form SKYCLAD). His replacement was RITCHIE DESMOND, WAYNE BANKS coming in for CRASKE who had also left, while NEIL WATSON was added to augment the guitar attack. The resulting album was a pale reflection of the original SABBAT sound, the group subsequently disbanding amid general disinterest.

Album rating: HISTORY OF A TIME TO COME (*6) / DREAMWEAVER (*7) / MOURNING HAS BROKEN (*4)

MARTIN WALKYIER – vocals / **ANDY SNEAP** – guitar / **FRAZER CRASKE** – bass / **SIMON NEGUS** – drums

Noise / not iss.

Mar 88. (lp/c) *(NUK/ZCNUK 098)* **HISTORY OF A TIME TO COME** [ ] [-]
– A cautionary tale / Hosanna in excelsis / Behind the crooked cross / Horned is the hunter / I for an eye / For those who died / A dead man's robe / The church bizarre. *(cd-iss. Oct89; CDNUK 098) (cd re-iss. Jul00; N 0099-2)*

May 89. (cd/c/lp) *(CD/ZC+/NUK 132)* **DREAMWEAVER** [ ] [-]
– The beginning of the end (intro) / The clerical conspiracy / Advent of insanity / Do dark horses dream of nightmares / The best of enemies / How have the mighty fallen / Wildfire / Mythistory / Happy never after outro).

— **RITCHIE DESMOND** – vocals; repl. WALKYIER who formed SKYCLAD

— **WAYNE BANKS** – bass + **NEIL WATSON** – guitar; repl. CRASKE

Mar 91. (cd/c/lp) *(N 0162-2/-4/-1)* **MOURNING HAS BROKEN** [ ] [-]
– The demise of history / Theological void / Paint the world black / Dumbstruck / The voice of time / Dreamscape / Without a trace / Mourning has broken.

— split in 1992, SNEAP formed GODSEND

SACRED REICH

Formed: Phoenix, Arizona, USA . . . 1985 by JASON RAINEY, PHIL RIND, GREG HALL and JEFF MARTINEK. The latter was replaced by WILEY ARNETT in 1987. Signing to 'Roadrunner', the group released 'IGNORANCE' later the same year, a promising debut which saw SACRED REICH tipped as serious thrash-metal contenders. Like NUCLEAR ASSAULT, the group were more concerned with the harsh realities of day to day life in America than the normal metal subjects of sex, violence and the occult. Harsh critics of the US system, SACRED REICH dealt with the country's Central American foreign policy in the title track of the 'SURF NICARAGUA' (1988) mini-album, a set which also included the group's pulverising cover of Black Sabbath's 'WAR PIGS'. 'THE AMERICAN WAY' (1990) was SACRED REICH's most accomplished work to date, RIND's political commentary more biting than ever on the relentless title track and the environmental crie de coeur, 'CRIMES AGAINST HUMANITY'. Subsequently replacing HALL with DAVE McLAIN and signing to 'Hollywood' records, the group made their major label debut in 1993 with 'INDEPENDENT'. However, this was to be their only effort for the imprint as the band shifted to 'Metal Blade' for a further two sets, 'HEAL' (1996) and the live retrospective 'STILL IGNORANT' (1997).

Album rating: IGNORANCE (*7) / SURF NICARAGUA mini (*5) / THE AMERICAN WAY (*6) / INDEPENDENT (*5) / HEAL (*5) / STILL IGNORANT (*5)

PHIL RIND – vocals, bass / **WILEY ARNETT** – lead guitar; repl. JEFF MARTINEK / **JASON RAINEY** – rhythm guitar / **GREG HALL** – drums

Roadrunner / Metal Blade

Nov 87. (lp) *(RR 9578)* <73306> **IGNORANCE** [ ] [ ]
– Death squad / Victim of demise / Layed to rest / Ignorance / No believers / Violent solutions / Rest in peace / Sacred Reich / Administrative decisions. *(cd-iss. 1989; RR 9578-2) (re-iss. Sep91 on 'Metal Blade' cd/c/lp; CD/T+/ZORRO 30) (cd re-iss. Mar96 on 'Metal Blade'; 3984 17008CD)*

Dec 88. (m-lp/m-cd) *(RR 9512-1/-2)* <73359> **SURF NICARAGUA** [ ] [ ]
– Surf Nicaragua / One nation / War pigs / Draining you of life. *(cd+=)* – Ignorance / Death squad. *(re-iss. Aug92 on 'Music For Nations' cd/c; CD/TM ZORRO 47) (cd reiss.Mar96 on 'Metal Blade'; 3984 17009CD)*

Roadracer / Metal Blade

Oct 89. (12"ep/cd-ep) *(RO 9431-1/-2)* <SPV 083 7975> **ALIVE AT THE DYNAMO (live)** [ ] [ ]
– Surf Nicaragua / Violent solutions / War pigs / Death squad.

May 90. (cd/c/lp) *(RO 9392-2/-4/-1)* <73560> **THE AMERICAN WAY** [ ] [ ]
– Love . . . hate / Crimes against humanity / I don't know / State of emergency / The American way / Who's to blame / The way it is / 31 flavors. *(cd re-iss. Jun91; RO 9392-5)*

— **DAVE McCLAIN** – drums; repl. HALL

Hollywood / Hollywood

Feb 93. (cd/c/lp) <*(HR 61369-2/-4)*> **INDEPENDENT** [ ] [ ]
– Independent / Free / Just like that / Supremacy / If only / Crawling / Pressure / Product / I never said goodbye / Open book / Do it.

Metal Blade / Metal Blade

Feb 96. (cd/lp) <*(3984 14106 CD/LP)*> **HEAL** [ ] [ ]
– Blue suit, brown shirt / Heal / Break through / Low / Don't / Jason's idea / Ask Ed / Who do you want to be / See through my eyes / I don't care / Power of the written word.

Nov 97. (cd) <*(3984 14145CD)*> **STILL IGNORANT (live)** [ ] [ ]
– The American way / Administrative decisions / One nation / Independent / State of emergency / Power of the written word / Heal / Blue suit, brown shirt / Who's to blame / Violent solutions / War pigs / Death squad / Surf Nicaragua.

— they disbanded in 1999

– compilations, etc. –

Oct 89. (c) *Roadrunner; (RR 9578-4)* **IGNORANCE / SURF NICARAGUA** [ ] [-]

S.A.D.O.

Formed: Germany . . . 1983 by ANDRE COOK, WOLFGANG EICHOLZ, MATTHIAS MOSER, STEPHAN NEUMANN and MATTI KAEBS. As the name might suggest, this bunch used kinky sex as their overriding theme, their infamous stage show leaving little to the imagination. Musically, the group dealt in melodic power metal, as evidenced on their 'Noise' debut, 'SHOUT' (1984). It was a further three years before the release of a follow-up, 'CIRCLE OF FRIENDS' (1987) ironically enough preceding the en masse departure of all S.A.D.O. members (to form the band V2) bar COOK. Recruiting a new line-up, COOK soldiered on with the harder-edged 'DIRTY FANTASY' (1988), before changing his mind and deciding that, well, he was a 'SENSITIVE' (1990) guy at heart with a penchant for AOR. Not surprisingly, S.A.D.O. were consigned to the PVC-lined bin of metal history soon after.

Album rating: SHOUT (*5) / CIRCLE OF FRIENDS (*4) / DIRTY FANTASY (*5) / ANOTHER KIND OF . . . mini (*4) / SENSITIVE (*4)

ANDRE COOK – vocals / **WOLFGANG EICHOLZ** – guitar / **MATTHIAS MOSER** – guitar / **STEPHAN NEUMANN** – bass / **MATTI KAEBS** – drums

Noise / S.P.V.

1984. (lp) *(N 0011)* **SHOUT** [-] [-] German
– Shout / American hero / Rubber bondage / Women and whiskey / The rage / Run baby run / Death / Rock'n roll thunder / Alone.

— **C.F. BRANK** – bass; repl. NEUMANN

— **SIMON D'BROUIER** – guitar; repl. repl. EICHOLZ

— **ALEXANADER REICH** – guitar; repl. MOSER

1987. (lp) *(N 0091)* **CIRCLE OF FRIENDS** [-] [-] German
– Intro / My dream / Goodbye Mr.G / 219 uniform / Circle of friends / American gambler / Obscene rock'n'roll / Julie's vacation / Savage girl / Thanks given. *(re-iss. Oct89 cd/c/lp; CD/ZC+/NUK 091)*

— all but COOK left to form V2; newcomers were **JORG POWILEIT + ANDY MALECEK** – guitar / **ALEXANDER REMDE** – bass / **CHRIS KUHLMEY** – drums

Aug 88. (cd/c/lp) *(CD/ZC+/NUK 115)* **DIRTY FANTASY** [ ] [-]
– The door / Dirty charms / Riches make enemies / I'm never ever blue / Strike back / Cities on flame / On the races / Gamblin' fool / Dancing in the dark / Homicide.

DUNCAN O'NEILL – bass; repl. REMDE / **DANNY** – drums; repl. KUHLMEY

1989. (m-lp) **ANOTHER KIND OF . . .** [-] [-] German

— **MOSER** returned to repl. JORG + ANDY

Feb 90. (cd/c/lp) *(CD/ZC+/NUK 147)* <SPV 4032> **SENSITIVE** [ ] [ ]
– Talk about me / Just married! / Women and whiskey / Dear Miss J. / Another kind of . . . / Every time / Bad lovin' / Time out / Love lies / Run baby run.

— split after above

SAGA

Formed: Toronto, Ontario, Canada . . . 1977 by MICHAEL SADLER and STEVE NEGUS, who subsequently recruited the CRICHTON brothers, JIM and IAN, plus a fifth member PETER ROCHAN. A synth-heavy pomp-rock act with an enduring line in sci-fi concepts, SAGA rather enterprisingly self-financed their eponymous debut album in 1978, the record attracting the attention of 'Polydor', who signed them up for a worldwide deal. Synth player ROCHAN was replaced by GREGG CHADD prior to the release of a second set, 'IMAGES AT TWILIGHT' (1980), SAGA's popularity increasing both in the UK and US. Yet another keyboard change was affected prior to the 'SILENT KNIGHT' (1980) album, JIM GILMOUR coming in for CHADD. While the live 'IN TRANSIT' (1982) set appeared on 'Polydor', SAGA were subsequently dropped by the label and ironically, their first single for new label 'Portrait', 'ON THE LOOSE' gave them a Top 30 hit in America later that year. An album, 'WORLDS APART' (1981) also made the US Top 30, SAGA enjoying the most commerically fruitful period of their career despite the label difficulties. 'HEADS OR TAILS' (1983) and 'BEHAVIOUR' (1985) didn't fare quite so well, GILMOUR and NEGUS subsequently departing and putting together their own outfit, GNP. Adding CURT CRESS, SAGA label-hopped onwards, the 1987 set, 'WILDEST DREAMS', receiving a US-only release on 'Atlantic', while the SAGA saga finally came to an end with 'THE BEGINNER'S GUIDE TO THROWING SHAPES' (1980), released on 'BMG' in the UK.

Album rating: SAGA (*4) / IMAGES AT TWILIGHT (*5) / SILENT KNIGHT (*5) / WORLDS APART (*5) / HEADS OR TAILS (*4) / BEHAVIOUR (*4) / WILDEST DREAMS (*4) / BEGINNERS GUIDE TO THROWING SHAPES (*4) / SECURITY OF ILLUSION (*4) / STEEL UMBRELLAS (*4) / GENERATION 13 (*3) / PLEASURE & THE PAIN (*4) / DEFINING MOMEMTS – GREATEST HITS compilation (*6) / DETOURS LIVE (*5) / FULL CIRCLE (*5) / HOUSE OF CARDS (*6)

MICHAEL SADLER – vocals, keyboards, synthesizer / **IAN CRICHTON** – guitar / **JIM CRICHTON** – bass / **PETER ROCHAN** – keyboards, synthesizers, vocals / **STEVE NEGUS** – drums

Polydor Maze

1978. (lp) *(2424 175) <8001>* **SAGA**
– How long / Humble stance / Climbing the ladder / Will it be you (chapter 4) / The perfectionist / Give 'em the money / Ice nice / Tired world (chapter six). *(cd-iss. Mar98 as 'PHASE ONE 1978' on 'Midstream'; SA 98051)*

— **GREG CHADD** – keyboards, synthesizer, vocals; repl. ROCHAN

Aug 80. (lp) *(2391 437) <8002>* **IMAGES AT TWILIGHT**
– It's time / See them smile / Slow motion / You're not alone / Take it or leave it / Images / Hot to cold / Mouse in a maze. *(cd-iss. 1988; 825 254-2)*

Sep 80. (7") *(2095 246)* **IT'S TIME. / MOUSE IN A MAZE**

— **JIM GILMOUR** – keyboards, vocals; repl. CHADD

Dec 80. (lp) *(2374 166) <8004>* **SILENT NIGHT**
– Don't be late / What's it gonna be / Time to go / Compromise / Too much to lose / Help me out / Someone should / Careful where you step. *(cd-iss. 1988; 821 934-2)*

Feb 81. (7") *(POSP 228)* **SYNOPSIS: CAREFUL WHERE YOU STEP. / HOW LONG**
(12"+=) *(POSPX 228)* – Take it or leave it.

1982. (lp) *<8006>* **IN TRANSIT** –
– Careful where you step / Don't be late / Humble stance / Wind him up / How long / No regrets / A brief case / You're not alone / On the loose. *(UK cd-iss. 1988 on 'Polydor'; 800 100-2)*

Portrait Portrait

Jan 83. (7") *(PRTA 2958) <03359>* **ON THE LOOSE. / FRAMED** 26 Nov82

Feb 83. (lp) *(PRT 25054) <38246>* **WORLDS APART** 29 Oct82
– On the loose / Wind him up / Amnesia / Framed / Time's up / Interview / No regrets (chapter V) / Conversations / No stranger (chapter VIII). *(cd-iss. 1988 on 'Polydor'; 821 479-2)*

Mar 83. (7") *(PRTA 3053) <03791>* **WIND HIM UP. / AMNESIA** 64

Oct 83. (7"/12") *(A/TA 3817) <04178>* **THE FLYER. / THE WRITING** 79

Nov 83. (lp) *(PRT 25740) <38999>* **HEADS OR TAILS** 92 Oct83
– The flyer / Cat walk / Sound of strangers / The writing / Intermission / Social orphan / Vendetta (still helpless) / Scratching the surface / The pitchman. *(cd-iss. 1988 on 'Polydor'; 815 410-2)*

Jan 84. (7"/12") *(A/TA 4067) <04361>* **SCRATCHING THE SURFACE. / THE SOUND OF STRANGERS**

Sep 85. (7"/12") *(A/TX 6515) <05463>* **WHAT DO I KNOW? / EASY WAY OUT**

Sep 85. (lp/c) *(PRT/40 26579) <40145>* **BEHAVIOUR** 87
– Listen to your heart / Take a chance / What do I know? / Misbehaviour / Nine lives of Miss Midi / You and the night / Out of the shadows / Easy way out / Promises / Here I am / Goodbye (once upon a time).

Jan 86. (7"/12") *(A/TX 6840)* **TAKE A CHANCE. / YOU AND THE NIGHT**

— **CURT CRESS** – drums, percussion; repl. NEGUS + GILMOUR, who later formed GNP

not iss. Atlantic

Sep 87. (7") *<89195>* **ONLY TIME WILL TELL. / THE WAY OF THE WORLD** –

Oct 87. (lp/cd) *<25860-1/-2>* **WILDEST DREAMS** –
– Don't put out the fire / Only time will tell / Wildest dreams / Chase the wind / We've been here before / The way of the world / Angel / Don't look down.

BMG Bonaire

1989. (lp/cd) *(210/260 367)* **BEGINNERS GUIDE TO THROWING SHAPES**
– How do I look / Starting all over / Shape / Odd man out / Nineties / Scarecrow / As I am / Waiting in the wings / Giant.

Bonaire Bonaire

1993. (cd) *<BNA 0011>* **SECURITY OF ILLUSION** –
– Entrance / Mind over matter / Once is never enough / Alone again tonight / I'll leave it in your hands / The security of illusion / Stand up / Days like these / Voila! / No man's land / Without you.

1994. (cd) *(523054-2) <BNA 0012>* **STEEL UMBRELLAS** – German
– Why not? / (You were) Never alone / Bet on this / Shake that tree / Password pirate – Access code – Password pirate / I walk with you / (Walking on) Thin ice / Steamroller / Say goodbye to Hollywood / Feed the fire.

1995. (cd) *<BNA 0014>* **GENERATION 13** –
– Chances are #1 / Generation 13 / All will change / The cross (home #3) / Danger whistle / Leave her alone / I'll never be like you #1 / My name is Sam (finding a friend) / The 13th generation / The cross / The learning tree / I'll never be like you #2 / Snake oil / We hope you're feeling better (the test) / My name is Sam (your time is up) / Generation 13 (theme #2) / Where are you now / Screw 'em / No strings attached / All will change (it's happening to me!) / The victim / One small step / Sam's new friend / We hope you're feeling better / Chances are #2.

— **NEGUS** returned to the fold

Jun 97. (cd) *<BNA 0016>* **THE PLEASURE & THE PAIN**
– Heaven can wait / How do you feel? / Welcome to the zoo / Where's my money? / You're not alone '97 / Taxman / You were made for me / Gonna give it to ya / Fantastically wrong / Pleasure & the pain.

S.P.V. S.P.V.

May 98. (cd) *<SPV 088-1800-2>* **DETOURS LIVE (live)** Nov99
– In the hall of the mountain King William / How long / The perfectionist / Careful where you sleep / Ice nice / Don't be late / Interview / Wind him up / Welcome to the zoo / Take a chance / William's walkabout / The cross / Scratching the surface / On the loose / The security of illusion / I walk with you / Time's up / Heaven can wait / The flyer / You're not alone / Framed / Humble stance.

Aug 99. (cd) *(SPV 085-2146-2)* **FULL CIRCLE** –

Feb 01. (cd) *<SPV 085-7216-2>* **HOUSE OF CARDS** Apr01
– God knows / The runaway / Always there / Ashes to ashes / Once in a lifetime / So good so far / Only human / That's how we like it! / Watching the clock / We'll meet again / Money talks / House of cards.

Apr 01. (cd-s) *(SPV 055-72344-3)* **MONEY TALKS**

– compilations, etc. –

1994. (cd) *Bonaire; <BNA 0013>* **DEFINING MOMENTS – GREATEST HITS** –
– Without you / Catwalk / Times up / Listen to your heart / Wind him up / You and the night / Don't be late / On the loose / Nine lives of Miss Midi / Ice nice / (Walking on) Thin ice / Odd man out / Once is never enough / I walk with you / (Goodbye) Once upon a time. *(<UK + re-iss. Mar98 on 'Varase Sarabande'; VSD 1007)>*

Oct 95. (cd) *Bonaire; <BNA 0015>* **THE SAGA SOFTWORKS** –
– Generation 13 / What you see is what you get / All things will change (it's happening to me!) / The victim / One small step / Sam's new friend / We hope you're feeling better / Chances are #2.

Greg SAGE (see under ⇒ WIPERS)

SAIGON KICK

Formed: Miami, Florida, USA ... 1990 by MATT KRAMER, JASON BIELER, TOM DeFILE and PHIL VARONE. Subsequently signing to Atlantic subsidiary 'Third Stone', SAIGON KICK tackled the rock/metal scene with a hard-driving eponymous debut in Spring '91. Building on the promise of the debut, the group scored a US Top 100 placing with a follow-up set, 'THE LIZARD' (1992). Further success came in the form of accompanying single, 'LOVE IS ON THE WAY', which touched down into the 20. CHRIS McLERNON subsequently came on for the sidelined DeFILE, although the whistle was finally blown on their career following the lacklustre 1993 third set, 'WATER' (a patchy cover of Bowie's 'SPACE ODDITY' hardly improving matters).

Album rating: SAIGON KICK (*5) / THE LIZARD (*5) / WATER (*4)

MATT KRAMER – vocals / **JASON BIELER** – guitar / **TOM DeFILE** – bass / **PHIL VARONE** – drums

Third Stone Third Stone

Apr 91. (cd/c/lp) *<7567 91634-2/-4/-1>* **SAIGON KICK**
– New world / What you say / What do you do / Suzy / Colours / Coming home / Love of God / Down by the ocean / Acid rain / My life / Month of Sundays / Ugly / Come take me now / I.C.U. *(re-iss. cd Nov93; same)*

Jun 92. (cd/c/lp) *<7567 92158-2/-4/-1>* **THE LIZARD** 80
– Cruelty / Hostile youth / Feel the same way / Freedom / God of 42nd Street / My dog / Peppermint tribe / Love is on the way / The lizard / All alright / Sleep / All I want / Body bags / Miss Jones / World goes round / Chanel.

Aug 92. (c-s,cd-s) *<98530>* **LOVE IS ON THE WAY / SLEEP** – 12

Nov 92. (7"/c-s) *(A 7451/+C)* **LOVE IS ON THE WAY. / HOSTILE YOUTH** –
(12"/cd-s) *(A 7451 T/CD)* – ('A'side) / All I want / Hey hey hey / Colors (acoustic).

— **CHRIS McLERNON** – bass; repl. DeFILE

Oct 93. (cd/c) *<7567 92300-2/-4>* **WATER**
– One step closer / Space oddity / Water / Torture / Fields of rape / I love you / Sgt. Steve / My heart / On and on / The way / Sentimental girl / Close to you / When you were mine / Reprise.

— split after above

SAINTS

Formed: Brisbane, Australia . . . 1976 by ED KUEPPER and CHRIS BAILEY alongside KYM BRADSHAW and IVOR HAY. The quartet had barely begun an apprenticeship on the Sydney music scene when their debut effort, 'I'M STRANDED' (released on 'Fatal' in Australia), won a Single Of The Week award in punk-friendly music paper, 'Sounds'. Hi-octane rock'n'roll ignited by KUEPPER's scathing guitar playing and IGGY POP-style drawl, the domestically released track saw The SAINTS hailed as Australia's most vital contribution to the punk war effort and bagged them a major label deal with 'Harvest' into the bargain. Relocating to the UK, the band enjoyed widespread acclaim for their similarly titled debut album, released in the summer of '77 alongside their only Top 40 hit, 'THIS PERFECT DAY'. A subsequent EP, 'ONE TWO THREE FOUR', found them demolishing standards, 'LIPSTICK

ON YOUR COLLAR' and 'RIVER DEEP MOUNTAIN HIGH', while 1978's 'KNOW YOUR PRODUCT' single and accompanying album, 'ETERNALLY YOURS', flirted with a brassier sound. Never a punk band in the conventional sense, The SAINTS refused to kow-tow to prevailing fashion and suffered the resulting damage to their credibilty. To make matters worse, KUEPPER left after the release of 1978's 'PREHISTORIC SOUNDS' with the remaining line-up having crumbled by the end of the year. While the former frontman went on to follow his own idiosyncratic path and enjoy cult acclaim with The LAUGHING CLOWNS and a subsequent solo career, CHRIS BAILEY later reformed The SAINTS at the turn of the decade with a line-up of CHRIS BARRINGTON, JANINE HALL, MARK BIRMINGHAM and IVOR HAY. Signed to French label, 'New Rose', the remodelled band released 'THE MONKEY PUZZLE' in 1981, the following year's 'CASABLANCA' and 1984's 'WHAT WE DID ON OUR HOLIDAYS' issued as BAILEY solo albums. Featuring former BIRTHDAY PARTY man, TRACY PEW, until his untimely death in 1986, The SAINTS continued to record sporadically throughout the 80's and on into the 90's with varying line-ups. • **Songwriters:** Penned by BAILEY and KUEPPER, until the latter's departure. Covered RIVER DEEP MOUNTAIN HIGH (Phil Spector) / LIPSTICK ON YOUR COLLAR (Connie Francis).

Album rating: I'M STRANDED (*6) / ETERNALLY YOURS (*6) / PREHISTORIC SOUNDS (*6) / THE MONKEY PUZZLE (*4) / A LITTLE MADNESS TO BE FREE (*5) / LIVE IN A MUD HUT (*5) / ALL FOOLS DAY (*6) / SONGS OF SALVATION compilation (*8) / HOWLING (*5)

CHRIS BAILEY – vocals / **ED KUEPPER** (b. EDMUND) – guitar / **KYM BRADSHAW** – bass / **IVOR HAY** – drums

Fatal | Sire

Sep 76. (7") *(MA 7158) <1005>* **(I'M) STRANDED. / NO TIME** [ ] [ ] Jun77

Harvest | Sire

May 77. (7") *(HAR 5123)* **EROTIC NEUROTIC. / ONE WAY STREET** [ ] [-]

May 77. (lp) *(SHSP 4065) <SRK 6039>* **(I'M) STRANDED** [ ] [ ]
– (I'm) Stranded / One way street / Wild about you / Messin' with the kid / Erotic neurotic / No time / Kissin' cousins / Story of love / Demolition girl / Nights in Venice. *(cd-iss. Nov97 on 'Triple X'; TX 51243CD)*

Jul 77. (7") *(HAR 5130)* **THIS PERFECT DAY. / LIES** [34] [ ]
(12") *(12HAR 5130)* – ('A'side) / Do the robot.

—— **ALGY WARD** – bass repl. BRADSHAW who joined The LURKERS

Sep 77. (7"ep) *(SHSM 2028)* **ONE TWO THREE FOUR** [ ] [-]
– Lipstick on your collar / One way street / Demolition girl / River deep mountain high.

Feb 78. (7") *(11673)* **KNOW YOUR PRODUCT. / RUN DOWN** [ ] [-]

Mar 78. (lp) *(SHSP 4078) <SRK 6055>* **ETERNALLY YOURS** [ ] [ ]
– Know your product / Lost and found / Memories are made of this / Private affair / A minor aversion / No, your product / This perfect day / Run down / Ostralia / New center of the universe / Untitled / Misunderstood. *(re-iss. Nov87 on 'Fan Club'; FC 035) (cd-iss. May94 on 'New Rose'; 422309) (cd re-iss. Nov97 on 'Triple X'; TX 51244CD)*

Aug 78. (7") *(11795)* **SECURITY. / ALL TIMES THROUGH PARADISE** [ ] [-]

Sep 78. (lp) *(SHSP 4094)* **PREHISTORIC SOUNDS** [ ] [-]
– Swing for the crime / All times through Paradise / Everyday's a holiday, every night's a party / Brisbane / Church of indifference / Crazy Googenheimer blues / Everything's fine / The prisoner / Security / This time / This heart of mine / The chameleon / Save me. *(re-iss. Nov87 on 'Fan Club'; FC 036) (cd-iss. May94 on 'New Rose'; 422312)*

—— Disbanded late 1978. KUEPPER formed The LAUGHING CLOWNS and WARD joined The DAMNED. In 1980, **CHRIS BAILEY** re-formed The SAINTS recruiting **CHRIS BARRINGTON** – guitar / **JANINE HALL** – bass / **MARK BIRMINGHAM** – drums / guest **IVOR HAY** – keyboards

New Rose | not iss.

Apr 80. (12"ep) *(NEW 1)* **PARALYTIC TONIGHT DUBLIN TOMORROW EP** [ ] [-]
– Simple love / Roses / On the waterfront / Call it mine.

Oct 80. (7") *(NEW 3)* **ALWAYS. / IN THE MIRROR** [ ] [-]

Jan 81. (lp) *(ROSE 1)* **THE MONKEY PUZZLE** [ ] [-]
– Miss wonderful / Always / Paradise / Let's pretend / Someday / Monkeys (let's go) / Mystery dream / Simple love / The ballad / Dizzy Miss Lizzy. *(free live 7"m w.a.)* – **(I'M) STRANDED. / SECURITY / THIS PERFECT DAY** *(cd-iss. 1980's+=; ROSE 1CD)* – (above 12"ep)

Flicknife | not iss.

Feb 83. (7") *(FLS 215)* **FOLLOW THE LEADER. / ANIMAL** [ ] [-]

SAINTS

—— **TRACY PEW** – bass (ex-BIRTHDAY PARTY) repl. JANINE HALL

New Rose | not iss.

Dec 84. (7") *(NEW 43)* **IMAGINATION. / PRISONER (live)** [ ] [-]

Dec 84. (lp) *(ROSE 38)* **A LITTLE MADNESS TO BE FREE** [ ] [-]
(cd-iss. 1985 +=; ROSE 38CD) – (extra live tracks)

Mar 85. (7") *(NEW 37)* **GHOST SHIP. / WRAPPED UP & BLUE** [ ] [-]

May 85. (lp) *(ROSE 55)* **LIVE IN A MUD HUT (live)** [ ] [-]
– Ghost ship / Imagination / Follow the leader / Know your product / etc.

—— TRACY PEW died of cancer in November '86

—— **BAILEY + HAY** with **RICHARD BURGMANN** – bass + **ARCHIE LaRIZZA** – drums

Polydor | TVT

Oct 86. (7") *(POSP 825)* **THE TEMPLE OF THE LORD. / CELTIC BALLAD** [ ] [-]
(12"+=) *(POSPX 825)* – How to avoid disaster.

Oct 86. (lp/c) *(POLD/+C 5203) <TVT 2111-1/-4/-2>* **ALL FOOLS DAY** [ ] [ ] 1987
– Just like fire would / First time / Hymn to Saint Jude / See you in Paradise / Love or imagination / Celtic ballad / Empty page / Big hits (on the underground) / How to avoid disaster / Blues on my mind / Temple of the Lord / All fools day.

Mar 87. (7") *(POSP 848)* **JUST LIKE FIRE WOULD. / EAST IS EAST** [ ] [-]
(12"+=) *(POSPX 848)* – Casablanca.

—— split but BAILEY re-formed 1989 with **LaRIZZA / + IAIN SHEDDEN** – drums / **BARRINGTON 'BAZ' FRANCIS** – guitar / **JOE CHIOFALO** – keyboards

Mushroom | TVT

Jan 90. (7") *(MRI 01)* **GRAIN OF SAND. / MAD RACE** [ ] [-]
(12"+=) *(MRI 01T)* – Minus a ride.

Jan 90. (cd/c/lp) *(MRI CD/MC/LP 001) <TVT 2121-2/-4/-1>* **PRODIGAL SON** [ ] [ ] Nov89
– Grain of sand / Fire and brimstone / Friend of the people / Before Hollywood / Sold out / Ghost ships / Massacre / Tomorrow / Stay / Shipwreck / The music goes round my head.

1992. (cd) **PERMANENT REVOLUTION** [-] [ ]
– Grain of sand (Zydeco version) / One night with you / Wild and wicked world / Pick up the pieces / Running away / Revolution in my life / Friday the 13th / Love or imagination / Cartoon life / Idiot blues.

1992. (12"etched) **GRAIN OF SAND. / CARTOON** [-] [ ]

—— disbanded after above but re-formed in the mid-90's; **BAILEY** with **IAN WALSH** – guitar + **ANDREAS JORNVILL** – drums

Blue Rose | Triple X

Oct 96. (cd) *(BLUCD 029) <TX 51245CD>* **HOWLING** [ ] [ ] Jan98
– Howling / Shadows / Something, somewhere, sometime / Something wicked / Only stone / Good Friday / Blown away / Last and laughing mile / You know I know / Only dreaming / Second coming / All for nothing.

Last Call | Amsterdamned

Apr 98. (cd) *(303777-2) <70019>* **EVERYBODY KNOWS THE MONKEY** [ ] [ ] Oct98
– What do you want / Easy money / Working overtime / Fall of an empire / Mustard / Vaguely Jesus / What are you waiting for / Everything turns sour / Playboy of the western world / Come back and visit / S+M+M's / Glorious wonder.

– compilations, etc. –

Aug 77. (7") *Power Exchange; (PX 242)* **(I'M) STRANDED. / (B-side by Chuck Stanley)** [ ] [-]

Mar 82. (lp) *New Rose; (ROSE 11)* **OUT IN THE JUNGLE** [ ] [-]
(cd-iss. 1988; ROSE 11CD) (re-iss. Oct90 on 'Flicknife'; SHARP 106)

Nov 86. (lp) *Razor; (RAZ 21)* **THE BEST OF THE SAINTS (77-78)** [ ] [-]

Dec 89. (lp) *Raven;* **SCARCE SAINTS** [-] [-] Austra

Jan 90. (lp/c/cd) *Fan Club; (FC 060/+C/CD)* **THE NEW ROSE YEARS (GREATEST HITS)** [ ] [-]
(cd+=) – (5 extra tracks)

Feb 91. (cd) *Raven; (<9>)* **SONGS OF SALVATION 1976-1988** [-] [ ] Austra

Jul 95. (lp/cd) *Hot; (HOT 1053/+CD)* **THE MOST PRIMITIVE BAND IN THE WORLD (live from The Twilight Zone, Brisbane 1974)** [ ] [-]
– Wild about you / Do the robot / One way street / Knock on wood / Erotic neurotic / River deep mountain high / Lies / Stranded / Messin' with the kid / Misunderstood.

Oct 96. (cd) *EMI Gold; (CDGO 2069)* **KNOW YOUR PRODUCT (THE BEST OF THE SAINTS)** [ ] [-]
– (I'm) Stranded / This perfect day / Lipstick on your collar / River deep mountain high / Demolition girl / One way street / Story of love / Kissin' cousins / No time / Wild about you / Messin' with the kid / Nights in Venice / Do the robot / Know your product / Run down / Lost and found / Memories are made of this / Private affaie / Minor aversion / No. your product / Swing for the crime / All times through paradise.

SALTY DOG

Formed: Los Angeles, California, USA . . . mid-80's by MIKE HANNON and KHURT MAIER. With the line-up completed by JIMMI BLEACHER and SCOTT LANE (later replaced by PETE REEVEN). Eventually securing a deal with 'Geffen', the band released a fine debut album, 'EVERY DOG HAS ITS DAY' in 1990. Previewed by the brilliant blues/funk-rock raunch of the 'COME ALONG' single, the album drew countless comparisons with LED ZEPPELIN, BLEACHER's PLANT-esque warbling certainly adding weight to the claims. Like 'ZEPPELIN, SALTY DOG were also unafraid to pay tribute to their blues mentors, running through a cover of Willie Dixon's 'SPOONFUL'. Despite the critical acclaim, SALTY DOG prematurely came to an end following the departure of BLEACHER soon after the debut's release. A shame, as they walked the L.A. cock-rock thing like they talked it, unlike many groups of a similar ilk.

Album rating: EVERY DOG HAS ITS DAY (*7)

JIMMI BLEACHER (b. Youngstown, Ohio) – vocals, guitar, harmonica / **PETE REEVEN** (b. Canada) – guitars; repl. SCOTT LANE / **MIKE HANNON** (b. Colombus, Ohio) – bass, vocals / **KHURT MAIER** (b. Sacramento, Calif.) – drums, percussion

Geffen | Geffen

Feb 90. (cd/c/lp) *<(7559 24270-2/-4/-1)>* **EVERY DOG HAS ITS DAY** [ ] [ ]
– Come along / Cat's got nine / Ring my bell / Where the sun don't shine / Spoonful / Just like a woman / Sim sala bim / Keep me down / Heave hard (she comes easy) / Lonesome fool / Slow daze / Sacrifice / Nothin' but a dream. *(re-iss. Aug91 cd/c; GEF D/C 24270)*

—— **DARREL BEACH** (b. Dallas, Texas) – vocals (ex-DT ROXX) repl. BLEACHER

—— folded early in '92

SAMAEL

Formed: Switzerland . . . 1987 by VORPHALACK, MASMISEIM and XYTRAS. A self-financed debut EP, 'MEDIEVAL PROPHECY', caught the attention of French label, 'Osmose', who issued SAMAEL's first long player, 'WORSHIP HIM' (1991). While this dealt in fairly pedestrian extreme black metal, 1992's 'BLOOD RITUAL' was a more focused effort which substituted the spit and thrash for decelerated power and more inventive instrumentation.

The success of these experiments led to the recruitment of a full-time keyboard man, RODOLPHE H, who made his debut on 'CEREMONY OF OPPOSITES' (1994). The first fruits of their new deal with death metal bastion, 'Century Media', the album was another step forward with more lavish use of synth textures in the pursuit of creepy atmospherics. 'PASSAGE' (1996) went even further, fully revolutionising SAMAEL's sound with lunar-themed post-metal symphonies orbiting around an apocalyptic, neo-industrial backdrop. XYTRAS even went on to create his own unique version of the album in 1998, released as a solo effort. VORPH, meanwhile, manned the production helm for a couple of albums by fellow 'Century Media' band ROTTING CHRIST. SAMAEL regrouped – along with extra guitarist KAOS – in 1999 for 'ETERNAL', a record which continued to flirt with the possibilities of cross-fertilisation without making quite the same impact as its predecessor. • **Covered:** I LOVE THE DEAD (Alice Cooper).

Album rating: WORSHIP HIM (*4) / BLOOD RITUAL (*5) / REBELLION mini (*4) / CEREMONY OF OPPOSITES (*6) / PASSAGE (*7) / EXODUS mini (*4) / ETERNAL (*6) / Xytras: PASSAGE (*4)

VORPHALACK – vocals, guitar / **XYTRAS** – drums, keyboards / **MASMISEIM** – bass

own label — not iss.

1990. (cd-ep) **MEDIEVAL PROPHECY** [-] [-] Swiss

Osmose — not iss.

1991. (cd) **WORSHIP HIM** [-] [-] French
– Sleep of death / Worship him / Knowledge of the ancient kingdom / Morbid metal / Rite of Cthulhu / The black face / Into the pentagram / Messenger of the light / Last benediction / The dark. *(re-iss. Dec94 as 'SAMAEL 1987-92' on 'Century Media'; CM 77085-2) <US-iss.1993 on 'JL America'; 41080>*

Dec 92. (cd/c/lp) *(OS 9737-2/-4/-1) <7737>* **BLOOD RITUAL** [ ] [ ]
– Epilogue / Beyond the nothingness / Poison infiltration / After the sepulture / Macabre operetta / Blood ritual / Since the creation . . . / Eith the gleam of the torches / Total consecration / Bestial devotion / Until the chaos.

Century Media — Century Media

Mar 94. (cd) *(CM 77064CD) <7764>* **CEREMONY OF OPPOSITES** [ ] [ ]
– Black trip / Celebration of the fourth / Son of Earth / Till we meet again / Mask of the red death / Baphomet's throne / Flagellation / Crown / To our martyrs / Ceremony of opposites. *(pic-lp Jan95; CM 77067-1)*

— added **RODOLPHE H** – keyboards

Apr 95. (m-cd) *(CM 77099CD) <7799>* **REBELLION** [ ] [ ]
– Rebellion (new venture) / After the sepulture / I love the dead / Static journey / Into the pentagram.

Sep 96. (cd) *(CM 77127CD) <7827>* **PASSAGE** [ ] [ ]
– Rain / Shining kingdom / Angel's decay / My saviour / Jupiteran vibe / The ones who came before / Liquid soul dimension / Moonskin / Born under Saturn / Chosen race / A man in your head.

May 98. (m-cd) *(CM 77127CD) <7910>* **EXODUS** [ ] [ ]
– Exodus / Tribes of Cain / Son of Earth / Winter solstice / Ceremony of opposites / From Malkuth to Kether.

— the remaining **VORPH** recruited **KAOS** – guitar

Aug 99. (cd/lp) *(77185-2/-1) <7885>* **ETERNAL** [ ] [ ] Sep99
– Year zero / Alilleurs / Together / Ways / The cross / Us / Surpra karma / I / Nautilus & zeppelin / Infra galaxia / Being / Radiant star.

XYTRAS

— solo after he broke away from SAMAEL

Feb 98. (cd) *(CM 77202CD)* **PASSAGE** [ ] [-]
– Regen / Glanzendes konigreich / Des engels untergang / Jupiterianische schwingungen / Die vorher kamen / Der stamn Kains / Mondhaut / Mein retter / Wintersonnenwende / Ein mench im kopf.

Richie SAMBORA (see under ⇒ BON JOVI)

SAMHAIN (see under ⇒ DANZIG)

SAMSON

Formed: London, England . . . 1978 by PAUL SAMPSON alongside BRUCE BRUCE, CHRIS AYLMER and CLIVE BURR. One of the earliest and most pivotal bands to emerge from the NWOBHM, SAMSON nevertheless existed in the shadow of IRON MAIDEN, whom they supported in the early days and to whom they lost two of their most talented members. BURR was the first to go, the entertainingly novelty-masked THUNDERSTICK replacing him prior to the debut album, 'SURVIVORS' (1979). As the metal renaissance stepped up a gear, the group were subsequently signed to 'R.C.A.'-subsidiary, 'Gem', making their major label debut in 1980 with 'HEAD ON'. The record sparked considerable interest in the band, gatecrashing the Top 40 and seeing SAMSON garner a growing following of lank-haired youths. Another well-received set, 'SHOCK TACTICS', followed in '81, the last to feature the vocal jousting of BRUCE BRUCE, or BRUCE DICKINSON as he became known in IRON MAIDEN, going on to massive worldwide fame with the group while SAMSON languished in the second division. His replacement was the girthsome NICKY MOORE, his gritty vocals enhancing the inherent bluesiness of the group's melodic hard-rock on the enduring 'BEFORE THE STORM' (1982) set. The inimitable THUNDERSTICK had also departed prior to the recording of this set, MEL GAYNOR (who rather sensibly went on to greater things with SIMPLE MINDS) recruited temporarily before future FM man, PETE JUPP, was found as a more secure replacement. Still, these were testing times for the band (the NWOBHM having run its course) and despite another consummate set of solid blues-metal, 'DON'T GET MAD – GET EVEN' (1984), SAMSON's popularity diminished with each passing year. PAUL eventually called it a day in '85, a posthumous live set, 'THANK YOU AND GOOD NIGHT', released the same year much to the latter's consternation, the SAMSON frontman fighting its release in court. The singer eventually teamed up with MOORE again in a variation on the SAMSON theme, PAUL SAMSON'S EMPIRE, along with JO JULIAN, JOHN McCOY and EDGAR PATRICK. This purely studio-based project released a sole album in 1986, 'JOINT FORCES', PAUL subsequently taking a completely different group of NWOBHM veterans out on the road to tour the album. He then resurrected the plain old SAMSON name with yet another new crew of musicians, releasing a mini-set, 'AND THERE IT IS', in summer '88. Never giving up the ghost, PAUL continued releasing solid, if rather predictable material into the 90's. • **Note:** The 80's SAMSON are not to be confused with progressive band of the early 70's, who issued an album 'Are You Samson?'.

Album rating: SURVIVORS (*5) / HEAD ON (*6) / SHOCK TACTICS (*6) / BEFORE THE STORM (*7) / DON'T GET MAD – GET EVEN (*7) / THANK YOU AND GOODNIGHT (*6) / JOINT FORCES (*5) / HEAD TACTICS compilation (*6) / AND THERE IT IS mini (*4) / REFUGEE (*6) / SAMSON (*4)

BRUCE BRUCE (b. DICKINSON) – vocals / **PAUL SAMPSON** – guitar, vocals / **THUNDERSTICK** (b. BARRY GRAHAM) – drums repl. BURR who joined IRON MAIDEN / **CHRIS AYLMER** – bass

Lightning — not iss.

Oct 78. (7") *(LIG 547)* **TELEPHONE. / LEAVIN' YOU** [ ] [-]

Mar 79. (7") *(LIG 553)* **MR. ROCK'N'ROLL. / DRIVIN' MUSIC** [ ] [-]

Laser — not iss.

Jun 79. (lp) *(LAP 1)* **SURVIVORS** [ ] [-]
– It's not as easy as it seems / I wish I was the saddle of a schoolgirl's bike / Big brother / Tomorrow or yesterday / Koz / Six foot under / Inside out / Wrong side of time. *(re-iss. Jun84 on 'Thunderbolt' lp/c; THB L/C 001) (cd-iss. Aug91 & Jul93 on 'Repertoire'; REP 4039-WZ) (cd re-iss. Mar00 on 'Air Raid'; AIRCD 7)*

Jun 79. (7") *(LAS 6)* **MR. ROCK'N'ROLL. / PRIMROSE SHUFFLE** [ ] [-]

E.M.I. — not iss.

May 80. (7"w-drawn) *(EMI 5061)* **VICE VERSA. / HAMMERHEAD** [ ] [-]

Gem — not iss.

Jun 80. (7") *(GEMS 34)* **VICE VERSA. / HAMMERHEAD** [ ] [-]

Jun 80. (lp) *(GEMLP 108)* **HEAD ON** [34] [-]
– Hard times / Take it like a man / Vice versa / Manwatcher / Too close to rock / Thunderburst / Hammerhead / Hunted / Take me to your leader / Walking out on you. *(cd-iss. Aug91 & Jul93 on 'Repertoire'; REP 4037-WZ) (cd re-iss. Mar00 on 'Air Raid'; AIRCD 9)*

Aug 80. (7") *(GEMS 38)* **HARD TIMES (remix). / ANGEL WITH A GUN** [ ] [-]

R.C.A. — not iss.

May 81. (7"pic-d) *(RCA 67)* **RIDING WITH THE ANGELS. / LITTLE BIG MAN** [55] [-]

May 81. (lp/c) *(RCA LP/K 5031)* **SHOCK TACTICS** [ ] [-]
– Riding with the angels / Earth mother / Nice girl / Blood lust / Go to Hell / Bright lights / Once bitten / Gimme crime / Communion. *(cd-iss. Aug91 & Jul93 on 'Repertoire'; REP 4038-WZ) (cd re-iss. Mar00 on 'Air Raid'; AIRCD 8)*

— **NICKY MOORE** – vocals (ex-TIGER) repl. BRUCE who joined IRON MAIDEN / **PETE JUPP** – drums repl. MEL GAYNOR (future SIMPLE MINDS) who repl. THUNDERSTICK (had replaced himself with himself – i.e. the unmasked BARRY GRAHAM)

Polydor — not iss.

Jul 82. (7"/7"pic-d) *(POSP/+P 471)* **LOSING MY GRIP. / PYRAMID TO THE STARS** [63] [-]
(12"+=) *(POSPX 471)* – Mr. Rock'n'roll (live) / Tomorrow or yesterday (live).

Oct 82. (7") *(POSP 519)* **LIFE ON THE RUN. / DRIVING WITH ZZ!** [ ] [-]
(d7"+=) *(POSPG 519)* – Walking out on you (live) / Bright lights (live).

Nov 82. (lp) *(POLS 1077)* **BEFORE THE STORM** [ ] [-]
– Danger zone / Stealing away / Red skies / I'll be round / Test of time / Life on the run / Turn out the light / Losing my grip / Young idea.

Feb 83. (7"/7"pic-d) *(POSP/+P 554)* **RED SKIES. / LIVIN', LOVIN', LYIN'** [65] [-]
(12"+=) *(POSPX 554)* – Running out of time.

Feb 84. (7"/7"pic-d) *(POSP/+P 670)* **ARE YOU READY? / FRONT PAGE NEWS** [ ] [-]
(12"+=) *(POSPX 670)* – La grange.

Mar 84. (lp) *(POLD 5132)* **DON'T GET MAD – GET EVEN** [ ] [-]
– Are you ready? / Love hungry / Burning up / The fight goes on / Don't get mad – get even / Into the valley / Bite on the bullet / Doctor Ice / Front page news / Leaving love (behind).

Apr 84. (7") *(POSP 680)* **THE FIGHT GOES ON. / RIDING WITH THE ANGELS (re-recording)** [ ] [-]
(12"+=) *(POSPX 680)* – Vice versa (live).

— disbanded 1985, after **DAVE COLWELL** – rhythm guitar / **MERV GOLDWORTHY** – bass repl. AYLMER

Metal Masters — not iss.

Mar 85. (lp) *(METALP 102)* **THANK YOU AND GOOD NIGHT (live)** [ ] [-]
– Bite on the bullet / Into the valley / Losing my grip / Vice versa / Love hungry / Tomorrow or yesterday / Mr. Rock & roll / Don't get mad – get even / Test of time / Are you ready. *(cd-iss. Feb95 on 'Thunderbolt'; CDTB 160)*

— NICKY MOORE joined ULI ROTH

PAUL SAMSON'S EMPIRE

with **NICKY MOORE** – vocals / **JO JULIAN** – guitar / **JOHN McCOY** – bass / **EDGAR PATRICK** – drums

Raw Power — not iss.

May 86. (lp/c) *(RAW LP/TC 018)* **JOINT FORCES** [ ] [-]
– Burning emotion / No turning back / Russians / Tales of the fury / Reach out

to love / The chosen few / Tramp / Power of love / Tell me. *(cd-iss. Sep94 on 'Thunderbolt'; CDTB 148)*

— to tour, PAUL brought in **DAVE COLWELL** – guitar, keyboards (ex-SAMSON) / **MARK BRABBS** – drums (ex-TANK, ex-DUMPY'S RUSTY NUTS) / **SAM BLUE** – vocals / **KEVIN RIDDLES** – bass, synth. (ex-ANGELWITCH, ex-TITAN)

SAMSON

— re-formed with **PAUL** bringing in **MICK WHITE** – vocals / **TOBY SADLER** – keyboards / **DAVE BOYCE** – bass / **CHARLIE MACK GOLIE** – drums

Metal Masters — not iss.

Jul 88. (m-lp) *(METALPM 126)* **AND THERE IT IS** -
– Tomorrow / Don't turn away / I must be crazy / Good to see you / The silver screen.

— (Jan'89) **PETER SCANLON** – vocals repl. WHITE

Communique — not iss.

Aug 90. (cd/c/lp) *(CMG CD/MC/LP 001)* **REFUGEE** -
– Good to see you / Can't live without your love / Turn on the lights / Love this time / Room 109 / State of emergency / Look to the future / Someone to turn to / Too late / Samurai sunset / The silver screen. *(cd re-iss. Sep95 on 'Thunderbolt'; CDTB 163)*

Aug 93. (cd) *(CMGCD 008)* **1993** -
– Hey you / Dream / Back to you / The word / Room 109 / Slip away / Can you imagine / It ain't fair / Use it before you lose it / The edge / When will I see you again. *(<re-iss. Feb96 on 'Thunderbolt'; CDTB 159>)*

– compilations, etc. –

Apr 84. (12"ep) *Thunderbolt; (THBE 1.003)* **MR. ROCK'N'ROLL / PRIMROSE SHUFFLE. / TELEPHONE / LEAVIN' YOU** -

Sep 84. (lp) *Thunderbolt; (THBL 015)* **LAST RITES** -

Mar 86. (7"/12"pic-d) *Capitol; (CL/12CLP 395)* **VICE VERSA (remix). / LOSING MY GRIP (remix)** -

Mar 86. (lp/c; SAMSON featuring BRUCE DICKINSON) *Capitol; (EST/TC-EST 2006)* **HEAD TACTICS** -

Dec 90. (cd/c/lp) *Raw Fruit; (FRS CD/MC/LP 001)* **THE FRIDAY ROCK SHOW SESSIONS – LIVE AT READING 1981 (live)** -
(cd re-iss. Aug91 & Jul93 on 'Repertoire'; RR 4040-CC) (cd re-iss. Mar00 on 'Air Raid'; AIRCD 10)

Jan 91. (cd/c/lp) *Connoisseur; (VSOP CD/MC/LP 151)* **PILLARS OF ROCK** -
– Danger zone / Stealing away / Red skies / Losing my grip / Running out of time / Driving with ZZ! / Young idea / Test of time / Leaving love (behind) / The fight goes on / Don't get mad, get even / Doctor Ice / Front page news / Bite on the bullet / Into the valley / Tomorrow or yesterday / Mr. Rock'n'roll / Love hungry.

Jul 93. (cd) *Great Expectations; (PIPCD 054)* **1988** -

Nov 94. (cd; by PAUL SAMSON) *Thunderbolt; (CDTB 157)* **LIVE AT THE MARQUEE (live)** -

Apr 95. (cd) *Thunderbolt; (CDTB 169) / Magnum; <59>* **THE BEST OF SAMSON 1985-1990: BURNING EMOTION** -

Sep 97. (cd) *High Vaultage; (HV 1006)* **THE BBC SESSIONS** -

Mar 98. (d-cd) *Eagle; (EDMCD 027)* **THE MASTERS** -

Jul 99. (d-cd) *Zoom Club; (CRCD 18)* **PAST PRESENT AND FUTURE** -

Sep 99. (cd) *Delta; (47009)* **TEST OF TIME** -

SANCTUARY

Formed: Seattle, Washington, USA . . . 1985 by WARREL DANE, LENNY RUTLEDGE, SEAN BLOSL, JIM SHEPPARD and DAVE BUDBILL. Fronted by the impressively blonde-maned WARREL DANE, this group were fortunate enough to secure the patronage of MEGADETH's DAVE MUSTAINE. Instrumental in getting SANCTUARY signed to 'Epic', MUSTAINE also produced their debut album, 'REFUGE DENIED'. A fairly run-of-the-mill affair, the album displayed little promise although the band put in some powerful live shows on their ensuing tour with MEGADETH. A slightly improved follow-up, 'INTO THE MIRROR BLACK' (1990) failed to advance their cause and inevitably they split. Having abandoned SANCTUARY for a few years, DANE and SHEPPARD formed a new metal project (with PAT O'BRIEN, JEFF LOOMIS and VAN WILLIAMS) under the title of NEVERMORE. Four albums have since surfaced, 'NEVERMORE' (1995), 'THE POLITICS OF ECSTASY' (1996), 'DREAMING NEON BLACK' (1999) and 'DEAD HEART IN A DEAD WORLD' (2000).

Album rating: REFUGE DENIED (*5) / INTO THE MIRROR BLACK (*6) / Nevermore: NEVERMORE (*6) / IN MEMORY mini (*5) / THE POLITICS OF ECSTASY (*7) / DREAMING NEON BLACK (*7) / DEAD HEART IN A DEAD WORLD (*5)

WARREL DANE – vocals / **LENNY RUTLEDGE** – guitar, vocals / **SEAN BLOSL** – guitar, vocals / **JIM SHEPPARD** – bass / **DAVE BUDBILL** – drums, vocals

Epic — Epic

Apr 88. (lp/c/cd) *(460 811-1/-4/-2) <40920>* **REFUGE DENIED** Nov87
– Battle angels / Termination force / Die for my sins / Soldiers of steel / Sanctuary / White rabbit / Ascension to destiny / The third war / Veil of disguise.

Apr 90. (cd/c/lp) *(465 876-2/-4/-1) <45085>* **INTO THE MIRROR BLACK**
– Future tense / Taste revenge / Long since dark / Epitaph / Eden lies obscured / The mirror black / Seasons of destruction / One more murder / Communion.

— split after above, DANE and SHEPPARD formed NEVERMORE in the mid-90's

NEVERMORE

WARREL DANE – vocals / **JIM SHEPPARD** – bass / **PAT O'BRIEN** – guitar / **JEFF LOOMIS** – guitar / **VAN WILLIAMS** – drums

Century Media — Ill Labels

Apr 95. (cd) *(CM 77091CD) <ILL 01>* **NEVERMORE**
– What tomorrow knows / C.B.F. / Sanity assassin / Garden of gray / Sea of possibilities / Hurting words / Timothy Leary / Godmoney.

Century Media — Century Media

Jul 96. (m-cd) *(CM 77121CD) <7821>* **IN MEMORY**
– Optimist or pessimist / Matricide / In memory / Silent hedges – Double dare / The sorrowed man.

Nov 96. (cd) *(CM 77132CD) <7832>* **THE POLITICS OF ECSTASY**
– Seven tongues of God / This sacrament / Next in line / Passenger / The politics of ecstasy / Lost / Tiananmen man / Precognition / 42147 / Learning.

— now without SHEPPARD who had already gone solo

— added **TIM CALVERT** – guitar (ex-FORBIDDEN)

Jan 99. (cd) *(CM 77191-2) <7891>* **DREAMING NEON BLACK**
– Ophidian / Beyond within / The death of passion / I am the dog / Dreaming neon black / Deconstruction / The fault of the flesh / The lotus eaters / Poison godmachine / All play dead / Cenotaph / No more will / Forever.

Oct 00. (cd) *(77310-2) <8010>* **DEAD HEART IN A DEAD WORLD**
– Narcosynthesis / We disintigrate / Inside four walls / Evolution 169 / The river dragon has come / The heart collector / Engines of hate / The sound of silence / Insignificant / Believe in nothing / Dead heart in a dead world.

SANTERS

Formed: Canada . . . 1980 by guitarist/vocalist RICK SANTERS, who along with his drum-playing brother MARK, recruited bass man RICK LAZAROFF. A worthy heavy blues-rock outfit, SANTERS achieved a degree of fame in their native Canada, mastermind RICK having earned a reputation as a solid session man. After two domestic releases, the 'SHOT DOWN IN FLAMES' (1981) album, and the 'MAYDAY' EP, the group were licensed to 'Heavy Metal' for the UK, releasing the 'RACING TIME' set in 1982. After a final set, 'GUITAR ALLEY' (1984), RICK returned to session work.

Album rating: SHOT DOWN IN FLAMES (*5) / RACING TIME (*5) / GUITAR ALLEY (*4) / Rick Santers: REVITALIZE (*5)

RICK SANTERS – vocals, guitar, keyboards / **RICK LAZAROFF** – bass, vocals / **MARK SANTERS** – drums

not iss. — Ready

1981. (lp) *<LR 014>* **SHOT DOWN IN FLAMES** - - Canada
– The rapper / Crazy ladies / You turn me on / Time after time / Lost and found / Shot down in flames / Caught in the wind / Paths of heart / Points of resistance.

1982. (12"ep) *<ER 023>* **MAYDAY EP** - - Canada
– Mistreatin' heart / Still I am / Time after time / You turn me on.

Heavy Metal — Passport

Dec 82. (lp) *(HMILP 4)* **RACING TIME** -
– Mistreatin' heart / Mystical eyes / Still I am / A dog without a home / Road to Morocco / Two against the world / Back streets / Winter freeze / Hard time lovin' you / Racing time.

Jun 84. (lp) *(HMUSA 3) <PB 6036>* **GUITAR ALLEY**
– Can't shake you / Hotline / High risk / Hate to love you / Too young to die / Loa / Black magic / All right now / Baby blue / Dreaming.

— folded after failure of above

RICK SANTERS

not iss. — unknown

1990's. (cd) **1st SHOT** - - Canada
– Mistreatin' heart / Caught in the wind / Hotline / Shot down in flames / Still I am / The rapper / Hard time lovin' you / Black magic / Time after time / Hate to love you / Road to Morocco / Paths of the heart / Back streets / Too young to die.

1990's. (cd) **2nd SHOT** - - Canada
– Can't shake you / Mystical eyes / Crazy ladies / High risk / All right now / Racing time / Dog without a home / You turn me on / Baby blue / Lost and found / Winter freeze / Points of resistance / Two against the world / Dreaming.

Dandelion — Dandelion

Jan 98. (cd) *<(DSD 19604)>* **REVITALIZE**
– Ashes / No gonna die / The dream / Do you remember me / Celebration / Angel from Heaven / Break down the walls / Love don't come easy / Do no time / Never wanna let you go.

SARAYA

Formed: New Jersey, USA . . . 1987 intially as ALSACE LORRAINE, by the delectable SANDI SARAYA and her sidekick keyboard-player, GREGG MUNIER. Concocting a flimsy yet occasionally endearing brand of AOR metal-lite, the band enjoyed minor US chart success with their eponymous '89 debut album and its attendant single, 'LOVE HAS TAKEN ITS TOLL'. With REY, TAYLOR and BONFANTE all subsequently leaving, however, the group were forced to hire new members, TONY BRUNO and BARRY DUNAWAY coming in for follow-up set, 'WHEN THE BLACKBIRD SINGS' (1991). A combination of changing musical climate, inertia and loss of momentum saw the record failing to chart, SARAYA subsequently calling it a day.

Album rating: SARAYA (*5) / WHEN THE BLACKBIRD SINGS (*4)

SANDI SARAYA – vocals / **GREGG MUNIER** – keyboards, vocals / **TONY REY** – guitar, vocals / **GARY 'SKID' TAYLOR** – bass, vocals / **CHUCK BONFANTE** – drums

Polydor — Polydor

Jul 89. (lp/c/cd) *<(837 764-1/-4/-2)>* **SARAYA** 79 Apr89
– Love has taken it's toll / Healing touch / Get u ready / Gypsy child / One night away / Alsace Lorraine / Runnin' out of time / Back to the bullet / Fire to burn / St. Christopher's medal / Drop the bomb.

Jul 89. (7") *<(889 292-7)>* **LOVE HAS TAKEN ITS TOLL. / RUNNIN' OUT OF TIME** [ ] [64] Jun89
(12"+=) *(889 293-1)* – ('A'extended).
Oct 89. (7") *<889 976-7>* **BACK TO THE BULLET. / FIRE TO BURN** [-] [63]
Dec 89. (7") *<07316>* **TIMELESS LOVE. / SHOCKER (THE DUDES OF WRATH)** [-] [85]
(above from the movie 'Shocker' on 'S.B.K.' and written and produced by DESMOND CHILD)

— **TONY BRUNO** – guitar, vocals + **BARRY DUNAWAY** – bass, vocals; repl. REY, TAYLOR + BONFANTE

May 91. (cd/c/lp) *<(849 087-2/-4/-1)>* **WHEN THE BLACKBIRD SINGS** [ ] [ ]
– Queen of Sheba / Bring back the light / Hitchin' a ride / When you see me again . . . / Tear down the wall / Seducer / When the blackbird sings . . . / Lion's den / In the shade of the sun / White highway / New world.
Jun 91. (7") *(PO 149)* **SEDUCER. /** [ ] [ ]
(12"+=/cd-s+=) *(PZ/+CD 149)* –

— she disbanded her group after the failure to shift album copies

SARKOMA

Formed: USA . . . early 90's by songwriter/guitarist STUART JOHNSON, BRIAN CARTER, MIKE HILLENBURG, TONY CHRISMAN and AARON INGRAM. A short-lived venture for this alt-metal act, they nevertheless managed to tour midwest America and deliver a couple of releases, the mini 'COMPLETELY DIFFERENT' (1992) and the disappointing 'INTEGRITY'.

Album rating: COMPLETELY DIFFERENT mini (*4) / INTEGRITY (*4)

BRIAN CARTER – vocals / **MIKE HILLENBURG** – guitar / **STUART JOHNSON** – guitar / **TONY CHRISMAN** – bass / **AARON INGRAM** – drums

Grindcore Grindcore

Jul 92. (m-cd) *<(GC 189805)>* **COMPLETELY DIFFERENTLY** [ ] [ ]
– Sometimes / Dog / Trolls opinion (Brian's song) / 2 a friend / Holidays / N.E.S.

Bulletproof Bulletproof

Jun 94. (cd) *(CDVEST 16)* **INTEGRITY** [ ] [ ]
– Tuesdays / Tabula rasa / Hoveldaze / George / Universal footsteps / Blue horizon / Mortamer / Paper / Less by one / Tung.

— they split soon after above

SASSAFRAS

Formed: Wales . . . 1972 by TERRY BENNETT, DAI SHELL, RALPH EVANS, RICKY JOHN HOLT and ROBERT JONES, who played their good-time rockin' boogie mostly in the shadow of STATUS QUO and CANNED HEAT. These three-chord (non-)wonders released three critically lambasted sets, 'EXPECTING COMPANY' (1973), 'WHEELIN' AND DEALIN' (1975) and 'RIDING HIGH' (1976); the band even having time to lay down their version of The Beatles' 'I AM THE WALRUS' on a 'Chrysalis' set, 'Over The Rainbow – The Last Concert Live!'.

Album rating: EXPECTING COMPANY (*4) / WHEELIN' 'N' DEALIN' (*3) / RIDING HIGH (*3) / SASSAFRAS (*3)

TERRY BENNETT – vocals / **DAI SHELL** – guitar / **RALPH EVANS** – guitar, vocals / **RICKY JOHN HOLT** – bass, vocals / **ROBERT JONES** – drums

Polydor not iss.

1973. (lp) *(2383 245)* **EXPECTING COMPANY** [ ] [-]
– Electric chair / Busted country blues / Beans and things / Across the sea of stars / School days / The way of me / The goose that laid the golden egg / (a) Expecting company, (b) Meanwhile back in Merthyr.
Jul 74. (7") *(2058 497)* **OH MY, DON'T IT MAKE YOU WANNA CRY. / KANSAS CITY WINE** [ ] [-]

— **STEVE FINN** – bass, repl. RICKY on tracks before he returned

— **CHRIS SHARLEY** – drums, repl. ROBERT but he returned for 3rd lp

Chrysalis not iss.

Mar 75. (7") *(CHS 2063)* **WHEELIN' 'N' DEALIN'. / MOONSHINE** [ ] [-]
1975. (lp) *(CHR 1076)* **WHEELIN' 'N' DEALIN'** [ ] [-]
– Wheelin' 'n' dealin' / Highway skies / Hamburg song / Moonshine / Peanut man / Box car hobo / Ohio / Soul destroyer.
Jul 76. (7") *(CHS 2098)* **SMALL TOWN TALK. / LONG SHOT LOVER** [ ] [-]
1976. (lp) *(CHR 1100)* **RIDING HIGH** [ ] [-]
– Riding high / Nothin' to lose / Bad blood / See through a mountain / New York collapse / Small town talk / Long shot lover / The band refuse to play / Keep rock & roll (like it used to be).

not iss. H&L

1978. (lp) *<69027>* **SASSAFRAS** [-] [ ]

— **EDDIE WILLIAMS** – guitar + **JEFF JONES** – drums, repl. TERRY + ROBERT

— disbanded after above

SATAN

Formed: Newcastle, England . . . 1981 out of NWOBHM band, BLITZKRIEG by TREVOR ROBINSON, RUSS TIPPINS, STEVE RAMSEY, GRAEME ENGLISH and ANDY REED (who was soon to be replaced by SEAN TAYLOR). A prized artefact among collectors, the band's debut single, 'KISS OF DEATH', was released on the small 'Guardian' label the same year. A succession of personnel changes subsequently held up work on an album, frontman ROBINSON replaced by IAN SWIFT, who in turn was succeeded by BRIAN ROSS. 'COURT IN THE ACT' eventually appeared on 'Neat' records in 1984, its frenetic metal assault anticipating the emerging thrash genre. Although the album received encouraging reviews, the group were unhappy with their black-metal image and changed their name to BLIND FURY, yet again enlisting a new singer, LOU TAYLOR. The resulting album, 'OUT OF REACH' (1985), appeared on 'Roadrunner', its more accessible hard-rock sound still failing to bring the band any commercial success. With TAYLOR departing, the band brought in another new vocalist, MICHAEL JACKSON (no not that one!), reverting to the name SATAN and signing with the 'Steamhammer' label. Two heavy duty albums, 'INTO THE FUTURE' (1986) and 'SUSPENDED SENTENCE' (1987) followed in quick succession, although the group again decided to ditch the name amid concerns that it was being misinterpreted. Adopting the PARIAH moniker, the band released 'THE KINDRED' in 1988, an even tougher affair no doubt born of continuing frustration. The cuttingly titled 'BLAZE OF OBSCURITY' (1989) would become the group's epitaph as SATAN (or PARIAH) finally threw in the towel after almost a decade of largely fruitless struggle.

Album rating: COURT IN THE ACT (*5) / OUT OF REACH as Blind Fury (*5) / INTO THE FUTURE mini (*4) / SUSPENDED SENTENCE (*5) / Pariah: THE KINDRED (*6) / BLAZE OF OBSCURITY (*5)

TREVOR ROBINSON – vocals / **RUSS TIPPINS** – guitar / **STEVE RAMSEY** – guitar / **GRAEME ENGLISH** – bass / **SEAN TAYLOR** – guitar; repl. ANDY REED

Guardian not iss.

Sep 82. (7") *(GRC 145)* **KISS OF DEATH. / HEADS WILL ROLL** [ ] [-]

— **BRIAN ROSS** – vocals; repl. IAN SWIFT who repl. ROBINSON

Neat Metal Blade

Jan 84. (lp) *(NEAT 1012)* *<70666>* **COURT IN THE ACT** [ ] [ ]
– Into the fire / Trial by fire / Blades of steel / No turning back / Broken treaties / Break free / Hunt you down / The ritual / Dark side of innocence / Abone in the dock. *(cd-iss. Apr97 on 'Neat Metal'; NM 019)*

— **LOU TAYLOR** – vocals; repl. BRIAN ROSS

Roadrunner not iss.

Jun 85. (lp; as BLIND FURY) *(RR 9814)* **OUT OF REACH** [ ] [-]
– Do it loud / Out of reach / Evil eyes / Contact rock and roll / Living on the edge / Dynamo (there is a place) / Back inside / Dance of the crimson lady (part 1).

— **MICHAEL JACKSON** (obviously not that one) – vocals; repl. TAYLOR

Steamhammer not iss.

1986. (lp) *(60-1898)* **INTO THE FUTURE** [ ] [-]
– Key to oblivion / Hear evil, see evil, speak evil / Fuck you / The ice man.

S.P.V. Steamhammer

1987. (lp) *(08 1837)* *<7003>* **SUSPENDED SENTENCE** [ ] [ ]
– 92nd symphony / Who dares wins / 11th commandment / Suicidal justice / Vandal (hostile youth) / S.C.U.M. (Socially Condemned Undesirable Misfits) / Avalance of a million hearts / Calculated execution. *(cd-iss. 1989 +=; 85-1819)* – INTO THE FUTURE

— were forced into changing their moniker

PARIAH

— same line-up as SATAN

1988. (lp)(cd) *(08-7526)(085-7528)* **THE KINDRED** [ ] [-]
– Gerrymander / The rope / Scapegoat / Foreign bodies / La guerra / Inhumane / Killing for company / Icons of hypocrisy / Promise of remembrance.
Jun 89. (lp)(cd) *(08-7594)(085-7595)* **BLAZE OF OBSCURITY** [ ] [-]
– Missionary of mercy / Puppet regime / Canary / Blaze of obscurity / Retaliate! / Hypochondriac / Enemy within / The brotherhood.

— folded in 1990

SATCHEL (see under ⇒ BRAD)

Joe SATRIANI

Born: 15 Jul'57, Bay Area, San Francisco, California, USA, although he was raised in Carle Place, Long Island. In addition to working as a guitar teacher (STEVE VAI and METALLICA's KIRK HAMMETT are among his more famous ex-pupils), six-string maestro SATRIANI played in various rock outfits (i.e. The SQUARES), before eventually making his vinyl debut in 1985 with an eponymous EP. A debut album, 'NOT OF THIS EARTH' (1987) followed soon after, introducing SATRIANI as more then yet another fretboard acrobat; conventional song structures and strong melodies were given just as much emphasis as the (admittedly impressive) soloing and flying-fingered technicality. So it was then, that SATRIANI attracted conventional rock fans and guitar freaks alike, a follow-up effort, 'SURFING WITH THE ALIEN' (1987), hitting the US Top 30, a remarkable feat for an instrumental opus. A master of mood, SATRIANI's forte was the ability to segue smoothly from grinding jazz-tinged raunch rock like 'SATCH BOOGIE' into the beautiful lilt of 'ALWAYS WITH YOU, ALWAYS WITH ME'. 'FLYING IN A BLUE DREAM' (1989) developed this approach, a flawless album which took in everything from dirty boogie ('BIG BAD MOON') to PRINCE-esque white funk ('STRANGE') as well as the obligatory ballad (the corny yet heartfelt 'I BELIEVE'), careering guitar juggernauts ('BACK TO SHALLA-BAL') and even a back-porch banjo hoedown (!), 'THE PHONE CALL'. The album also introduced SATRIANI the singer, and as might be expected, his vocal talents didn't quite match his celebrated axe skills. Nevertheless, it was a brave attempt to advance even further down the song-centric route and his voice did have a certain sly charm although the most affecting tracks on the album remained the new-agey efforts where SATRIANI was talking through his instrument (so to speak!); just listen to the likes of 'THE FORGOTTEN', lie back and melt! A third effort followed in 1992, 'THE EXTREMIST' almost making the UK Top 10 and consolidating SATRIANI's reputation as one of the foremost players of his era. A double set, 'TIME MACHINE' (1993) collected rare and previously released material with a smattering of new tracks while a fourth album proper was eventually released in the form of the eponymous 'JOE SATRIANI' (1995), following the guitarist's brief stint in DEEP PURPLE. In 1997, a live set appeared although this was shared alongside fellow guitar troopers STEVE VAI and ERIC JOHNSON. Veteran collaborators HAMM and CAMPITELLI were back in place for 1998's 'CRYSTAL PLANET', a welcome return to the all-instrumental inventiveness of his late 80's work. While this further explored the parameters of his own unique sonic territory, 'ENGINES OF CREATION' (2000) found SATRIANI gamely attempting to translate his six-string alchemy into an electronic framework. As with JEFF BECK's recent plunge into the digital age, the album worked best when the guitar components went with the electronic flow rather than trying to stem it. • **Trivia:** JOE also guested on ALICE COOPER's 'Hey Stoopid' and SPINAL TAP's 'Break Like The Wind'.

Album rating: NOT OF THIS EARTH (*6) / SURFING WITH THE ALIEN (*7) / FLYING IN A BLUE DREAM (*8) / THE EXTREMIST (*5) / TIME MACHINE part compilation (*6) / JOE SATRIANI (*6) / G3 LIVE IN CONCERT with Eric Johnson & Steve Vai (*7) / CRYSTAL PLANET (*6) / ENGINES OF CREATION (*5)

JOE SATRIANI – guitar, bass, keyboards, percussion, etc. / with band **JEFF CAMPITELLI** – drums, percussion, DX / **JOHN CUNIBERTI** – percussion, vocals / **BONGO BOB SMITH** – electronics, drums / **JEFF KREEGER** – synthesizer

not iss. Rubina

1985. (12"ep) <1> **JOE SATRIANI** -
– Banana mango / Dreaming #11 / I am become death / Saying goodbye.

Food For Thought Combat

Feb 87. (lp) *(GRUB 7)* <88561-8110-2> **NOT OF THIS EARTH** Nov86
– Not of this Earth / The snake / Rubina / Memories / Brother John / The enigmatic / Driving at night / Hordes of locusts / New day / The headless horseman. *(re-iss. Sep88 cd/c; CD/T GRUB 7) (re-iss. Feb93 cd/c/lp; CD/T+/GRUB 7X) (re-iss. May93 on 'Relativity' cd/c; 462972-2/-4)*

— he was now joined by **STU HAMM** – bass / **JONATHAN MOVER** – drums

Food For Thought Relativity

Nov 87. (lp) *(GRUB 8)* <8195> **SURFING WITH THE ALIEN** 29
– Surfing with the alien / Ice 9 / Crushing day / Always with you, always with me / Satch boogie / Hill of the skull / Circles / Lords of Karma / Midnight / Echo. *(re-iss. Sep88 cd/c; CD/T GRUB 8) (re-iss. Feb93 cd/c/lp; CD/T+/GRUB 8X) (re-iss. May93 on 'Relativity' cd/c; 462973-2/-4)*

Jun 88. (7") *(YUM 112)* **ALWAYS WITH YOU, ALWAYS WITH ME. / SURFING WITH THE ALIEN**

Dec 88. (12"ep) *(YUMT 114)* <8265> **DREAMING #11** 42 m-lp
– The crush of love / Ice 9 / Memories (live) / Hordes of locusts (live). *(re-iss. May93 on 'Relativity' cd-ep/c-ep; 473604-2/-4)*

— SATRIANI now on vocals for 6 tracks & returned to original line-up

Nov 89. (cd/c/lp) *(CD/T+/GRUB 14)* <1015> **FLYING IN A BLUE DREAM** 23
– Flying in a blue dream / The mystical potato head groove thing / Can't slow down / Headless / Strange / I believe / One big rush / Big bad moon / The feeling / The phone call / Day at the beach (new rays from an ancient Sun) / Back to Shalla-bal / Ride / The forgotten (part one) / The forgotten (part two) / The bells of Lal (part one) ? The bells of Lal (part two) / Into the light. *(re-iss. Feb93 cd/c/lp; CD/T+/GRUB 14X) (re-iss. May93 on 'Relativity' cd/c; 465995-2/-4)*

Mar 90. (7") *(YUM 118)* **BIG BAD MOON. / DAY AT THE BEACH (NEW RAYS FROM AN ANCIENT SUN)** Nov89
(12"+=/cd-s+=) *(YUMT 118)* – ('A'extended).

Mar 91. (7") **I BELIEVE. / FLYING IN A BLUE DREAM**
(12"+=/cd-s+=) – ('A'remix).

— now with **ANDY JOHNS** on production, etc.

Epic Relativity

Aug 92. (cd/c/lp) *(471672-2/-4/-1)* <1053> **THE EXTREMIST** 13 22
– Friends / The extremist / War / Cryin' / Rubina's blue sky happiness / Summer song / Tears in the rain / Why / Motorcycle driver / New blues.

Feb 93. (12"ep/cd-ep) *(658953-2/-4)* **THE SATCH EP** 53
– The extremist / Cryin' / Banana mango / Crazy.

Nov 93. (2xcd/2xc/3xlp) *(474515-2/-4/-1)* <1177> **TIME MACHINE** (out-takes & new) 32 95
– Time machine / The mighty turtle head / All alone (a.k.a. left alone) / Banana mango 11 / Thinking of you / Crazy / Speed of light / Baroque / Dweller of the threshold / Banana mango / Dreaming #11 / I am become death / Saying goodbye / Woodstock jam / Satch boogie / Summer song / Flying in a blue dream / Cryin' / The crush of love / Tears in the rain / Always with me, always with you / Big bad Moon / Surfing with the alien / Rubina / Circles / Drum solo / Lords of Karma / Echo.

Oct 95. (cd/c) *(481102-2/-4)* <1500> **JOE SATRIANI** 21 51
– Cool #9 / If / Down down down / Luminous flesh giants / SMF / Look my way / Home / Moroccan sunset / Killer bee bop / Slow down blues / (You're) My world / Sittin' 'round. *(re-iss. Aug00; same)*

May 97. (cd/c; shared with ERIC JOHNSON & STEVE VAI) *(487539-2/-4)* **G3 LIVE IN CONCERT (live 2nd November, 1996 at Northrop Auditorium, Minneapolis)**
– Cool No.9 / Flying in a blue dream / Summer song / (tracks by ERIC JOHNSON) / (tracks by STEVE VAI) / The jam songs (featuring all 3 G's):- Going down. *(video+=)* – My guitar wants to kill your mama / Red house. *(cd re-iss. Aug00; same)*

Mar 98. (cd/c) *(489473-2/-4)* <68018> **CRYSTAL PLANET** 32 50
– Up in the sky / House full of bullets / Crystal planet / Love thing / Trundrumbalind / Lights of Heaven / Raspberry jam delta-V / Ceremony / With Jupiter in mind / Secret player / A train of angels / A piece of liquid / Psycho monkey / Time / Z.Z.'s song.

Mar 00. (cd) *(497665-2)* <67860> **ENGINES OF CREATION**
– Devil's side / Flavor crystal / Borg sex / Until we say goodbye / Attack / Champagne / Clouds race across the sky / The power cosmic 2000 (part 1) / The power cosmic 2000 (part 2) / Slow and easy / Engines of creation.

– compilations, etc. –

Oct 94. (3xcd-box) *Relativity; (477519-2)* **NOT OF THIS EARTH / SURFING WITH THE ALIEN / FLYING IN A BLUE DREAM**

SATYRICON

Formed: Norway ... 1992 by mainman SATYR alongside guitarist KVELDULV and drummer FROST. Under the auspices of SATYR's own 'Moonfog' label, the band initiated their black metal crusade with 1994's 'DARK MEDIEVAL TIMES' and 'THE SHADOWTHRONE'. A split effort with ENSLAVED, 'THE FOREST', followed in 1996 along with a third album proper, 'NEMESIS DIVINA'. That year also saw the demonic trio touring with GORGOROTH and DISSECTION, although the corpse-painted SATYR would become increasingly tired of the genre's strict confines and increasingly corny trappings. This was the thinking behind the more experimental, folk-inflected 'REBEL EXTRAVAGANZA' (1999), the band's first release for 'Nuclear Blast'. SATYR was also a key member of black metal supergroup EIBON alongside FENIRZ (of DARKTHRONE), MANIAC (MAYHEM) and erm, PHIL ANSELMO (of PANTERA . . .). A highly unlikely combination but one which worked fairly well on 'MIRROR SOUL JESUS', a track featured on the latest 'Moonfog' sampler. There are plans to record a whole album while ANSELMO subsequently took the calculated risk of inviting SATYRICON to open for PANTERA on their UK tour. • **Covered:** ORGASMATRON (Motorhead)

Album rating: DARK MEDIEVAL TIMES (*5) / THE SHADOWTHRONE (*5) / THE FOREST shared w/ Enslaved (*5) / NEMESIS DIVINA (*6) / REBEL EXTRAVAGANZA (*6)

SATYR – vocals / **KVELDULV** – guitar / **FROST**– drums

Moonfog Century Media

Sep 94. (cd) *(FOG 001)* **DARK MEDIEVAL TIMES** -
– Walk the path of sorrow / Dark medieval times / Skyggedans / Min hyllest til vinterland / Into the mighty forest / The dark castle in the deep forest / Taakeslottet.

Nov 94. (cd) *(FOG 003)* **THE SHADOWTHRONE** -
– Hvite krists dod / In the mist by the hills / Woods to eternity / Vikingland / Dominions of Satyricon / The king of the Shadowthrone / I en svart list.

Feb 96. (cd/lp; split with ENSLAVED) *(FOG 009 CD/LP)* **THE FOREST / ENSLAVED** -
– Black winds / The forest is my throne / Min hyllest til vinterland / The night of triumphator / (others by ENSLAVED).

Mar 96. (cd) *(FOG 012CD)* <7820> **NEMESIS DIVINA** Apr97
– The conquering – The dawn of a new age / Forhekset / Mother North / Du son hater gud / Immortality passion / Nemesis divina / Transcendental requiem of slaves.

Jun 97. (12"/cd-s) *(FOG 014/+CD)* **MEGIDDO. / ORGASMATRON** -

— now down to just SATYR + FROST

Nuclear Blast Nuclear Blast

Oct 99. (cd) *(NB 418-2)* <6418> **REBEL EXTRAVAGANZA**
– Tied in bronze chains / Filthgrinder / Rhapsody in filth / Havoc vulture / Prime evil renaissance / Supersonic journey / End of journey / A moment of clarity / Down south, up north / The scorn torrent.

1990's. (m-cd/m-lp; ltd) **INTERMEZZO II** (remixes) - - Norway

SAUSAGE (see under ⇒ PRIMUS)

SAVAGE

Formed: Mansfield, England ... 1978 by CHRIS BRADLEY, WAYNE RENSHAW, ANDY DAWSON and MARK BROWN. A dyed-in-the-wool NWOBHM outfit, SAVAGE debuted with 'LOOSE 'N' LETHAL' on the 'Ebony' label, its razor-sharp riffing garnering encouraging reviews and seeing the group following in the shoes of Brit-metal stalwarts like JUDAS PRIEST. UK success wasn't forthcoming, however, despite a growing European fanbase, the band changing tack and adopting a more considered sound on the EP, 'WE GOT THE EDGE'. Now on the 'Zebra' label, SAVAGE eventually released a second album in 1985, 'HYPERACTIVE'. Despite what its title might suggest, the album carried on in the same fashion, consequently lacking the visceral punch of the debut. With reaction to their new direction muted, at least in Britain, SAVAGE eventually lost heart and called it a day the following year.

Album rating: LOOSE N' LETHAL (*7) / HYPERACTIVE (*5) / HOLY WARS (*4) / BABYLON (*4) / XTREME MACHINE (*3)

CHRIS BRADLEY – vocals, bass / **ANDY DAWSON** – guitar / **WAYNE REDSHAW** – guitar / **MARK BROWN** – drums

Ebony not iss.

Nov 83. (lp) *(EBON 12)* **LOOSE 'N' LETHAL** -
– Let it loose / Cry wolf / Berlin / Dirty money / Ain't no fit place / On the rocks / The China run / White hot. *(cd-iss. Apr97 on 'Neat Metal'+=; NM 017)* – No cause to kill / The Devil take you / Back on the road.

Zebra not iss.

Nov 84. (12"ep) *(12RA 4)* **WE GOT THE EDGE. / RUNNING SCARED / SHE DON'T NEED YOU** -

Jun 85. (lp/c) *(ZEB/CZEB 4)* **HYPERACTIVE** -
– We got the edge / Eye for an eye / Hard on your heels / Blind hunger / Gonna tear

ya heart out / Stevies vengeance / Cardiac / All set to sting / Keep it on ice. *(cd-iss. Apr97 on 'Metal Anagram'+=; CDMETAL 10)* – Running scared / She don't need you / We got the power.

— folded soon after above, although they re-formed in the mid 90's

Neat Metal Neat Metal

Nov 95. (cd) *(<NM 004CD>)* **HOLY WARS**
– Headstrong (cult of one) / Anthem / How? / This means war / Down 'n' dangerous (machine gun) / Suffer the children / Fashion by force / Twist / Streets of fire / Let the world go crazy / Glory boys / Let it loose '95.

Oct 97. (cd) *(<NM 016CD>)* **BABYLON**
– Space cowboy / Temple of deceit / Babylon / Rainmaker / Snake dance / Cyberhead / TV nation / Rat race / Sister sleaze / No ordinary day.

Jul 00. (cd) *(<NM 024X>)* **XTREME MACHINE**
– Control freak / Smiling assassin / Choke / Xtreme machine / Promised land / Drowning man / Creepshow / Living with uncertainty / Thorns / New messiah / The evil we can do / Hyde.

SAVATAGE

Formed: Florida, USA . . . 1983 out of METROPOLIS and AVATAR, by brothers JON and CRISS OLIVA. AVATAR had come together in 1978 (KEITH COLLINS and STEVE 'DOC' WACHOLZ completing the line-up), although this power-metal act released only one rare EP, 'CITY BENEATH THE SURFACE'. Changing their name to SAVATAGE, the band signed to 'Metal Blade' ('Music For Nations' UK) and debuted with mini-set, 'THE DUNGEONS ARE CALLING' (1984). Influenced by IRON MAIDEN, BLACK SABBATH and JUDAS PRIEST, the group's thundering power-chord smash was characterised by the glass-shattering shrill of frontman JON OLIVA. A follow-up set, 'SIRENS' (1984), led to a major label deal with 'Atlantic', although SAVATAGE alienated many of their fans with the overtly commercial 'FIGHT FOR THE ROCK' in 1986. Back on track for the following year's 'HALL OF THE MOUNTAIN KING', SAVATAGE had created their most critically acclaimed work to date (bubbled under the US Top 100). The record's epic reach also signalled the beginning of SAVATAGE's dalliance with the dreaded rock opera. To their credit, they managed to carry it off fairly convincingly on the string-enhanced 'GUTTER BALLET' and 'STREETS' (1991). The latter was the last to feature OLIVA in a full frontal capacity, the singer subsequently concentrating on writing although he did perform backing vocals. ZACHARY STEVENS was brought in as a replacement on the 'EDGE OF THORNS' set in 1993, although tragedy was to strike later that year as JON's brother, CRISS, was involved in a fatal car accident. Eventually carrying on, SAVATAGE recruited ex-TESTAMENT guitarist, ALEX SKOLNICK, who made his debut on the following year's 'HANDFUL OF RAIN', issued on 'Bulletproof'. The mid-90's saw another change of label as the band signed to 'Edel', releasing 'DEAD WINTER DEAD' (1995). Still going strong, the group issued 'WAKE OF MAGELLAN' in 1997. With JON OLIVA back to replace ZACHARY, SAVATAGE issued the 'POETS AND MADMEN' set in 2001.

Album rating: SIRENS (*5) / THE DUNGEONS ARE CALLING mini (*6) / POWER OF THE NIGHT (*4) / FIGHT FOR THE ROCK (*4) / HALL OF THE MOUNTAIN KING (*6) / GUTTER BALLET (*6) / STREETS: A ROCK OPERA (*7) / EDGE OF THORNS (*6) / HANDFUL OF RAIN (*5) / DEAD WINTER DEAD (*6) / GHOST IN THE RUINS tribute (*5) / FROM THE GUTTER TO THE STAGE compilation (*6) / THE WAKE OF MAGELLAN (*5) / JAPAN LIVE '94 (*5) / POETS AND MADMEN (*4)

AVATAR

JON OLIVA – vocals, guitar, keyboards / **CRISS OLIVA** – guitar / **KEITH COLLINS** – bass / **STEVE 'DOC' WACHOLZ** – drums

not iss. Par

1983. (7"ep) *<PAR 1002>* **CITY BENEATH THE SURFACE. / SIRENS / THE WHIP** -

SAVATAGE

— same line-up

1983. (lp) *<PAR 1050>* **SIRENS** -
– Sirens / Holocaust / I believe / Rage / On the run / Twisted little sister / Living for the night / Scream murder / Out on the streets. *(UK-iss.Sep84 on 'Music For Nations'; MFN 48) (cd-iss. 1988; CDMFN 48) (cd re-iss. Mar97 on 'Metal Blade'; 3984 14076CD)*

Music For Nations Metal Blade

Mar 85. (m-lp) *(MFN 42)* **THE DUNGEONS ARE CALLING** 1984
– The dungeons are calling / By the grace of a witch / Visions / Midas knight / City beneath the surface / The whip. *(cd-iss. 1988; CDMFN 42) (cd re-iss. Mar97 on 'Metal Blade'; 3984 14075CD)*

Atlantic Atlantic

Aug 85. (lp) *(781 247-1) <81247>* **POWER OF THE NIGHT**
– Power of the night / Unusual / Warriors / Necrophilia / Washed out / Hard for love / Fountain of youth / Skull session / Stuck on you / In the dream. *(cd re-iss. Dec97 on 'Edel'; 0089482CTR)*

— **JOHNNY LEE MIDDLETON** – bass; repl. COLLINS

May 86. (lp/c) *(781 634-1/-4) <81634>* **FIGHT FOR THE ROCK**
– Fight for the rock / Out on the streets / Crying for love / Day after day / The edge of midnight / Hyde / Lady in disguise / She's only rock'n'roll / Wishing well / Red light paradise. *(cd re-iss. Dec97 on 'Edel'; 0089462CTR)*

Sep 87. (lp/c) *(781 775-1/-4) <81775>* **HALL OF THE MOUNTAIN KING**
– 24 hours ago / Beyond the doors of the dark / Legions / Strange wings / Prelude to madness / Hall of the mountain king / The price you pay / White witch / Last dawn / Devastation. *(cd re-iss. Dec97 on 'Edel'; 008982CTR)*

— added **CHRISTOPHER CAFFERY** – guitar, bass

Jan 90. (cd/c/lp) *(782 008-2/-4/-1) <82008>* **GUTTER BALLET**
– Of rage and war / Gutter ballet / Temptation revelation / When the crowds are gone / Silk and steel / She's in love / Hounds / The unholy / Mentally yours / Summer's rain. *(cd+=)* – Thorazine shuffle. *(cd re-iss. Dec97 on 'Edel'; 0089442CTR)*

— reverted to a quartet when CAFFERY departed

Oct 91. (cd/c/lp) *<(7567 82320-2/-4/-1)>* **STREETS – A ROCK OPERA**
– Streets / Jesus saves / Tonight he grins again / Strange reality / A little too far / You're alive / Sammy and Tex / Can you hear me now / New York City don't mean nothing / Ghost in the ruins / Agony and ecstasy / Heal my soul / Somewhere in time / Believe. *(cd re-iss. Dec97 on 'Edel'+=; 0089452CTR)* – St. Patrick's.

— **ZACHARY STEVENS** – vocals (ex-WHITE WITCH) repl. JON (although he was still on backing vox)

Mar 93. (cd/c) *<(7567 82488-2/-4)>* **EDGE OF THORNS**
– Edge of thorns / He carves his stone / Lights out / Skraggy's tomb / Labyrinths / Follow me / Exit music / Degrees of sanity / Conversation piece / All that I bleed / Damien / Miles away / Sleep. *(cd re-iss. Nov97 on 'Edel'; 0089492CTR)*

— In October 1993, CRISS was killed in a car crash

— **ALEX SKOLNICK** – guitar (ex-TESTAMENT) repl. CRISS

Bulletproof Bulletproof

Aug 94. (cd) *(CDVEST 32)* **HANDFUL OF RAIN**
– Taunting cobras / Handful of rain / Chance / Stare into the sun / Castles burning / Visions / Watching you fall / Nothing's going on / Symmetry / Alone you breathe.

Concrete Atlantic

Oct 95. (d-cd) *(086202RAD) <82850>* **DEAD WINTER DEAD**
– Overture / Sarajevo / This is the time (1990) / I am / Starlight / Doesn't matter anyway / This isn't what we meant / Mozart and madness / Memory (dead winter dead intro) / Dead winter dead / One child / Christmas eve (Sarajevo 12/24) / Not what you see / City beneath the surface (live) / 24 hours (live).

Nov 97. (cd) *(0089832CTR)* **THE WAKE OF MAGELLAN**
– The ocean / Welcome / Turns to me / Morning sun / Another way / Blackjack guillotine / Paragons of innocence / Complaint in the system (Veronica Guerin) / Underture / The wake of Magellan / Anymore / The storm / The hourglass.

— **JON OLIVA** – vocals; repl. ZACHARY

S.P.V. Nuclear Blast

Apr 01. (cd/lp) *(SPV 0857215-2/-1) <NB 6618>* **POETS AND MADMEN**
– Stay with me a while / There is a silence / Commissar / I seek power / Drive / Morphine child / Rumor / Man in the mirror / Surrender / Awaken / Back to reason. *(other cd+=; SPV 0857215-0)* – Shotgun innocence.

Apr 01. (cd-s) *(SPV 055727229-3)* **COMMISSAR / DRIVE / VOYAGE** -

– compilations, etc. –

Jan 96. (cd) *Intercord; (IRSCD 993015)* **JAPAN LIVE '94 (live)** -

Apr 96. (cd) *(SPV 085 1214-2)* **GHOST IN THE RUINS** (a tribute to Criss Oliva) -
– City beneath the surface / 24 hours ago / Legions / Strange wings / Gutter ballet / When the crowds are gone / Of rage and war / The dungeons are calling / Sirens / Hounds / Criss intro / Hall of the mountain king / Post script. *<US-iss.Sep99 as 'THE FINAL BELL' on 'Nuclear Blast'; NB 6477>*

Feb 97. (cd) *Edel; (0089392CTR)* **FROM THE GUTTER TO THE STAGE** -

Apr 97. (cd) *Hengest; (IRSCD 993015)* **LIVE** -

Jul 00. (cd) *S.P.V.; (SPV 31021930)* **GHOST IN THE RUINS / HANDFUL OF RAIN** -

SAWYER

Formed: Edinburgh, Scotland . . . early 1994 by JOHN MACKIE, IAIN H, ANDREW HUNTER and ALAN FINDLAY. One of the many up and coming 'Human Condition' bands (remember IDLEWILD), SAWYER were all of the following: claustrophobic, uneasy and grotesque, something like MARK E SMITH sparring musically with STEVE ALBINI or even NAPALM DEATH having a bender with MARTIN HANNETT at the controls – the truth is, producer JAMIE WATSON was at the proverbial helm. Their debut, a double-pack 7" led by the bludgeoning 'GHETTY CHASUN', definitely stirred the listener into submission. However, for the latter half of the 90's, SAWYER were posted AWOL, although a few personnel changes (DEREK ANDERSON and ALAN WILSON replacing HUNTER), might have set them back slightly – who knows. Back in circulation (after six New Years, burb!), the brutal 5-piece finally delivered some (much delayed) fresh product via the debut album, 'ON THE SEVEN' (2000). The wilderness years had certainly paid off and with US groups (i.e. FUGAZI, etc) biting the dust, it was time was for these Caledonian Grunge-Metallers to make the grade.

Album rating: ON THE SEVEN (*7)

JOHN MACKIE – vocals / **IAIN H.** – guitar, vocals / **ANDREW HUNTER** – bass, guitar / **ALAN FINDLAY** – drums

Human Condition not iss.

Oct 94. (d7"ep) *(HC 007)* **GHETTY CHASUN. / TORN // GUY. / G.M.** -

— **DEREK ANDERSON** – guitar + **ALAN WILSON** – bass; repl. HUNTER

Jun 00. (cd) *(HCCD 0027)* **ON THE SEVEN** -
– In the evening you could be anything in the evening / Johnny the wadd / (It's a) Dry heat / 20 etc / 20 etc version / The world is endless / Osoba / He gave what he could / No rule / In the evening reprise / Ghetty chasun / The counties.

SAXON

Formed: Barnsley, Yorkshire, England . . . 1977 as SON OF A BITCH by BIFF BYFORD, PAUL QUINN, GRAHAM OLIVER, STEVE DAWSON and PETE GILL. Changing their name to the slightly less hoary SAXON, the group managed to secure a deal with French label, 'Carrere', releasing their eponymous debut in Spring '79. With their vaguely biker, road warrior image and Spinal Tap-friendly lyrics (check out 'STALLIONS OF THE HIGHWAY'!), the group came to characterise the NWOBHM, subsequently competing with IRON MAIDEN in a two horse race that saw SAXON beaten hands down. Nevertheless, the group released a string of hard-driving NWOBHM classics, beginning with the UK Top 5 'WHEELS OF STEEL' in 1980. The extent of the group's popularity among the metal hordes was illustrated as they scored two Top 20 singles in succession, with the album's title track and '747 (STRANGERS IN THE NIGHT)'. Road hungry to a man, SAXON embarked on their first major headlining tour in support of the record, keeping their profile high with the release of another set later that year, 'STRONG ARM OF THE LAW'. While this album perhaps lacked their trademark heavy/melodic punch, they came storming back the following year with the infamous 'DENIM AND LEATHER' (wot no spandex?) (1981), surely a cue for the likes of MANOWAR if ever there was one. The record again made the UK Top 10, spawning another two Top 20 hits with 'AND THE BANDS PLAYED ON' and 'NEVER SURRENDER'. These were SAXON's glory days, although inevitably it couldn't last; by the release of 'CRUSADER', the band were caught up in a vain attempt to crack the American market. Produced by AOR knob-twiddler, Kevin Beamish, 'CRUSADER' (1984) was a blatant attempt at securing FM radio play which only served to alienate some of their fans. Although the album made the Top 20, their next effort, 'INNOCENCE IS NO EXCUSE' (1985), struggled to dent the charts while old NWOBHM muckers, IRON MAIDEN were in the process of worldwide metal domination. Undeterred, the group made an attempt to return to a harder style on 'ROCK THE NATIONS' (1986). An inappropriate cover of Christopher Cross's 'RIDE LIKE THE WIND', however, signalled that they wouldn't be chasing METALLICA's throne just yet. In an effort to get back to their roots, SAXON undertook a UK club tour in 1990, playing material from their classic early 80's period to receptive audiences and, for once, decent reviews. In what appeared to be a final attempt to break the US market, the group signed to the American 'Enigma' label ('Virgin Int.' in the UK) for the 'SOLID BALL OF ROCK' (1991) set. Although once again their Stateside efforts amounted to not that much, SAXON's resilience won out with a clutch of 90's albums which, if never standing any chance of winning young converts, at least pleased stalwart fans. The likes of 'FOREVER FREE' (1993), 'DOGS OF WAR' (1995) and 'UNLEASH THE BEAST' (1997) were no-frills efforts making absolutely no concessions to market trends. 'METALHEAD' (1999) continued to fly their true colours, BYFORD and Co content to be the curators of vintage NWOBHM in the new millennium.

Album rating: SAXON (*6) / WHEELS OF STEEL (*7) / STRONG ARM OF THE LAW (*6) / DENIM AND LEATHER (*6) / THE EAGLE HAS LANDED (*6) / POWER AND THE GLORY (*6) / CRUSADER (*5) / INNOCENCE IS NO EXCUSE (*4) / ROCK THE NATIONS (*4) / DESTINY (*5) / ROCK'N'ROLL GYPSIES (*4) / SOLID BALL OF ROCK (*4) / THE BEST OF SAXON compilation (*7) / DOGS OF WAR (*3) / UNLEASH THE BEAST (*4) / METALHEAD (*5)

BIFF BYFORD (b. PETER BYFORD, 5 Jan'51) – vocals / **PAUL QUINN** – lead guitar / **GRAHAM OLIVER** – lead guitar / **STEVE DAWSON** – bass / **PETE GILL** – drums (ex-GLITTER BAND)

Carrere / Capitol

May 79. (lp) *(CAL 110)* **SAXON** [ ] [-]
– Rainbow theme / Frozen rainbow / Big teaser / Judgement day / Stallions of the highway / Backs to the wall / Still fit to boogie / Militia guard. *(re-iss. Jan86 on 'Capitol' lp/c; EMS/TC-EMS 1161) (cd-iss. Aug99; 521295-2)*

Jun 79. (7") *(CAR 118)* **BIG TEASER. / STALLIONS OF THE HIGHWAY** [ ] [-]

Nov 79. (7") *(CAR 129)* **BACKS TO THE WALL. / MILITIA GUARD** [ ] [-]
(re-iss. Jun80 on 'HM'; HM 6) – hit UK No.64

Mar 80. (7") *(CAR 143)* *<7300>* **WHEELS OF STEEL. / STAND UP AND BE COUNTED** [20] [ ]

Mar 80. (lp/c) *(CAR/CAC 115)* *<SQ 12515>* **WHEELS OF STEEL** [5] [ ]
– Motorcycle man / Stand up and be counted / 747 (strangers in the night) / Wheels of steel / Freeway mad / See the light shining / Street fighting gang / Suzie hold on / Machine gun. *(re-iss. Mar85 on 'Fame' lp/c; FA41 3143-1/-4) (re-iss. Jun93 on 'Optima')*

Jun 80. (7") *(CAR 151)* **747 (STRANGERS IN THE NIGHT). / SEE THE LIGHT SHINING** [13] [-]

Sep 80. (7") *(CAR 165)* **SUZIE HOLD ON. / JUDGEMENT DAY (live)** [ ] [-]

Nov 80. (lp/c) *(CAL/CAC 120)* *<17679>* **STRONG ARM OF THE LAW** [11] [ ]
– Heavy metal thunder / To hell and back again / Strong arm of the law / Taking your chances / 20,000 ft. / Hungry years / Sixth form girls / Dallas 1 p.m. *(re-iss. Mar86 on 'E.M.I.'; EMS 1162) (re-iss. May87 on 'Fame' lp/c; FA/TC-FA 3176)*

Nov 80. (7"/12") *(CAR 170/+T)* **STRONG ARM OF THE LAW. / TAKING YOUR CHANCES** [63] [-]

Apr 81. (7"/7"pic-d) *(CAR 180/+P)* **AND THE BANDS PLAYED ON. / HUNGRY YEARS / HEAVY METAL THUNDER** [12] [ ]

Jul 81. (7") *(CAR 204)* **NEVER SURRENDER. / 20,000 FT.** [18] [ ]
(d7"+=) *(SAM 134)* – Bap-shoo-ap! (live) / Street fighting gang.

Sep 81. (lp/c) *(CAL/CAC 128)* **DENIM AND LEATHER** [9] [ ]
– Princess of the night / Never surrender / Out of control / Rough and ready / Play it loud / And the bands played on / Midnight rider / Fire in the sky / Denim and leather. *(re-iss. Mar86 on 'E.M.I.' blue-lp; EMS 1163) (re-iss. May87 on 'Fame' lp/c; FA/TC-FA 3175) (cd-iss. Oct87; CDFA 3175) (re-iss. Oct96 on 'EMI Gold' cd/c; CD/TC GOLD 1011)*

Oct 81. (7") *(CAR 208)* **PRINCESS OF THE NIGHT. / FIRE IN THE SKY** [57] [-]

— **NIGEL GLOCKER** – drums (ex-TOYAH, etc.) repl. GILL who joined MOTORHEAD

May 82. (pic-lp/c) *(CAL/CAC 137)* **THE EAGLE HAS LANDED (live)** [ ] [-]
– Motorcycle man / 747 (strangers in the night) / Princess of the night / Strong arm of the law / Heavy metal thunder / 20,000 ft. / Wheels of steel / Never surrender / Fire in the sky / Machine gun. *(re-iss. May86 on 'E.M.I.' lp/c; ATAK/TC-ATAK 74) (cd-iss. Jul89 on 'E.M.I.'; CZ 210) (cd re-iss. Aug99 on 'E.M.I.'; 521297-2)*

Mar 83. (pic-lp/c) *(CAL/CAC 147)* *<38719>* **POWER AND THE GLORY** [15] [ ]
– Power and the glory / Redline / Warrior / Nightmare / This town rocks / Watching the sky / Midas touch / The eagle has landed. *(re-iss. May86 on 'E.M.I.' lp/c; ATAK/TC-ATAK 75) (cd-iss. Jul89; CZ 209) (cd re-iss. Mar99 on 'Axe Victim'; AXE 304612CD) (cd re-iss. Aug99 on 'E.M.I.'; 521303-2)*

Apr 83. (7"/7"pic-d) *(SAXON/+P 1)* **POWER AND THE GLORY. / SEE THE LIGHT SHINING** [32] [-]
(12"+=) *(SAXONT 1)* – Denim and leather.

Jul 83. (7"/7"pic-d) *(CAR/+P 284)* **NIGHTMARE. / MIDAS TOUCH** [50] [-]
(12"+=) *(CART 284)* – 747 (strangers in the night).

Jan 84. (7"/12") *(CAR/+T 301)* **SAILING TO AMERICA. / A LITTLE BIT OF WHAT YOU FANCY** [ ] [-]

Feb 84. (lp/c/pic-lp) *(CAL/CAC/CALP 200)* *<39284>* **CRUSADER** [18] [ ]
– The Crusader prelude / A little bit of what you fancy / Sailing to America / Set me free / Just let me rock / Bad boys (like to rock'n'roll) / Do it all for you / Rock city / Run for your lives. *(re-iss. May86 on 'E.M.I.' lp/c; EMS/TC-EMS 1168) (cd-iss. 1988; 817849-2)*

Mar 84. (7"/12") *(CAR/+T 323)* **DO IT ALL FOR YOU. / JUST LET ME ROCK** [ ] [-]

Parlophone / Capitol

Aug 85. (7"/7"sha-pic-d) *(R/RP 6103)* **BACK ON THE STREETS. / LIVE FAST DIE YOUNG** [75] [-]
(12"+=) *(12RA 6103)* – ('A'extended).

Sep 85. (lp/c/pic-lp) *(SAXON/TCSAXON/SAXONP 2)* *<12420>* **INNOCENCE IS NO EXCUSE** [36] [ ]
– Rockin' again / Call of the wild / Back on the streets / Devil rides out / Rock'n'roll gipsy / Broken heroes / Gonna shout / Everybody up / Raise some hell / Give it everything you've got. *(cd-iss. Feb00 on 'Axe Killer'; AXE 305552CD)*

Mar 86. (7"/7"pic-d) *(R/RP 6112)* **ROCK'N'ROLL GYPSY. / KRAKATOA** [71] [ ]
(12"+=) *(12RA 6112)* – Medley: Heavy metal thunder – Stand up and be counted – Taking your chances – Warrior.

— **PAUL JOHNSON** – bass; repl. DAWSON (GLOCKER briefly to G.T.R.)

E.M.I. / Capitol

Aug 86. (7") *(EMI 5575)* **WAITING FOR THE NIGHT. / CHASE THE FADE** [66] [-]
(12"+=) *(12EMI 5575)* – ('A'extended).

Aug 86. (lp/c) *(EMC/TC-EMC 3515)* *<12519>* **ROCK THE NATIONS** [34] [ ]
– Rock the nations / Battle cry / Waiting for the night / We came here to rock / You ain't no angel / Running hot / Party 'til you puke / Empty promises / Northern lady. *(cd-iss. Feb88; CZ 38) <US cd-re-iss. Oct96; C2 46371>*

Oct 86. (7"/7"sha-pic-d/12"clear) *(EMI/EMP/12EMI 5587)* **ROCK THE NATIONS. / 747 / AND THE BANDS PLAYED ON** [ ] [-]

Jan 87. (7") *(EMI 5593)* **NORTHERN LADY. / EVERYBODY UP (live)** [ ] [ ]
(12"+=) *(12EMI 5587)* – Dallas 1 p.m. (live).

— **NIGEL DURHAM** – drums repl. GLOCKER

Feb 88. (7"/7"sha-pic-d) *(EM/+P 43)* **RIDE LIKE THE WIND. / RED ALERT** [52] [ ]
(12"+=) *(12/CD EM 43)* – Back on the streets (live).

E.M.I. / Enigma

Mar 88. (cd/c/lp) *(CD/TC+/EMC 3543)* *<73339-2>* **DESTINY** [49] [ ]
– Ride like the wind / Where the lightning strikes / I can't wait anymore / Calm before the storm / S.O.S. / Song for Emma / For whom the bell tolls / We are strong / Jericho siren / Red alert.

Apr 88. (7"/7"s) *(EM/+P 54)* **I CAN'T WAIT ANYMORE. / BROKEN HEROES (live)** [71] [-]
(12"+=) *(12EM 54)* – Gonna shout (live).

— **TIM NIBS CARTER** – bass repl. JOHNSON

Enigma / Enigma

Nov 89. (lp/c/cd) *(ENVLP/TCENV/CDENV 535)* *<73370>* **ROCK'N'ROLL GYPSIES** (live '88 Hungary) [ ] [ ]
– Power and glory / Bands played on / Rock the nations / Dallas 1pm / Broken heroes / Battle cry / Rock'n'roll gypsy / Northern lady / I can't wait anymore / This town rocks. *(cd+=)* – The eagle has landed / Just let me rock. *(re-iss. Dec89 on 'Roadrunner' lp/c/cd; RR 9416-1/-4/-2)*

Virgin Int. / Charisma

Jan 91. (cd/c/lp) *(CD/MC/LP VIR 4)* *<91672>* **SOLID BALL OF ROCK** [ ] [ ]
– Solid ball of rock / Alter of the gods / Requiem (we will remember) / Lights in the sky / I just can't get enough / Baptism of fire / Ain't gonna take it / I'm on fire / Overture in B-minor – Refugee / Bavarian beaver / Crash dive.

Mar 91. (7"/7"sha-pic-d) *(DINS/+Y 105)* **WE WILL REMEMBER. / ALTAR OF THE GODS** [ ] [-]
(12"+=/cd-s+=) *(DINS T/ 105)* – Reeperbahn stomp.

— **NIGEL GLOCKER** – drums; returned to rel. DURHAM

Warhammer / not iss.

Apr 93. (12"/cd-s) **IRON WHEELS. / FOREVER FREE** [ ] [-]

May 93. (cd/c/lp) *(WAR CD/MC/LP 10)* **FOREVER FREE** [ ] [-]
– Forever free / Hole in the sky / Just wanna make love to you / Get down and dirty / Iron wheels / One step away / Can't stop rockin' / Nighthunter / Grind / Cloud nine.

H.T.D. / S.P.V.

Mar 95. (cd) *(HTDCD 35)* **DOGS OF WAR** [ ] [ ]
– Dogs of war / Burning wheels / Don't worry / Bug twin rolling (coming home) / Hold on / The great white buffalo / Demolition alley / Walking through Tokyo / Give it all away / Yesterday's gone. *(re-iss. Nov96 on 'S.P.V.'; 085-7601-2)*

S.P.V. / C.M.C.

Oct 97. (cd) *(SPV 085-1876-2)* *<862221>* **UNLEASH THE BEAST** [ ] [ ]
– Gothic dreams / Unleash the beast / Terminal velocity / Circle of light / The thin

red light / Ministry of fools / The preacher / Bloodletter / Cut out the disease / Absent friends / All hell breaking loose.

— **FRITZ RANDOW** (b. Germany) – drums; repl. GLOCKER

Aug 99. (cd) *(SPV 085-2150-2) <21502>* **METALHEAD**
– Metalhead / Are we travellers in time / Conquistador / What goes around / Song of evil / All guns blazing / Prisoner / Piss off / Watching you / Sea of life / Untitled.

– compilations, others, etc. –

Jun 80. (7") *Heavy Metal; (HM 5)* **BIG TEASER. / RAINBOW THEME / FROZEN RAINBOW** 66 -
Apr 81. (7") *WEA; (SPC 8)* **WHEELS OF STEEL. / 747 (STRANGERS IN THE NIGHT)** -
Jul 83. (c-ep) *Carrere; (RCXK 013)* **FLIPHITS** -
– 747 (strangers in the night) / And the bands played on / Never surrender / Princess of the night.
Dec 84. (lp/c) *Carrere; (CAL/CAC 212)* **GREATEST HITS – STRONG ARM METAL** -
(re-iss. Jan86 on 'Parlophone' lp/c; ATAK/TC-ATAK 58) (cd-iss. 1988; 823 680-2)
Oct 88. (d-lp/c/cd) *Raw Power; (RAW LP/TC/CD 038)* **ANTHOLOGY** -
Jan 90. (cd/c/d-lp) *Connoisseur; (VSOP CD/MC/LP 147)* **BACK ON THE STREETS** -
– Power and the glory / Backs to the wall / Watching the sky / Never surrender / Princess of the night / Motorcycle man / 747 (Strangers in the night) / Wheels of steel / Nightmare / Back on the streets / Rock'n'roll gypsy / Broken heroes / Devil rides out / Party 'til you puke / Rock the nations / Waiting for the night / I can't wait anymore / We are the strong. *(d-lp+=)* – Midnight rider / Ride like the wind.
Sep 90. (cd/c/d-lp) *Essential; (ESS CD/MC/LP 132)* **GREATEST HITS LIVE! (live)** -
Mar 91. (cd/c/lp) *E.M.I.; (CD/TC+/EMS 1390)* **THE BEST OF SAXON** -
(cd re-iss. Aug95 on 'Smashing';)
Oct 92. (cd-ep) *Old Gold; (OG 6181)* **AND THE BAND PLAYED ON / 747 (AND THE BAND PLAYED ON) / NEVER SURRENDER** -
Jan 96. (cd) *Intercord; (IRS 993011CD)* **LIVE AT THE MONSTERS OF ROCK, DONINGTON (live)** -
Oct 96. (cd) *EMI Gold; (CDGOLD 1055)* **A COLLECTION OF METAL** -
Feb 97. (d-cd) *E.M.I.; (CTMCD 201)* **WHEELS OF STEEL / STRONG ARM OF THE LAW** -
Apr 97. (cd) *Interchord; (<IRSCD 993011>)* **DONINGTON 1980 (live)**
(<re-iss. Nov99 on 'Angel Air'; SJPCD 045>)
Jul 98. (cd) *C.M.C.; (<CMC 186258>)* **THE EAGLE HAS LANDED VOL.2**
Oct 98. (cd) *E.M.I.; (497772-2)* **THE BBC SESSIONS / LIVE AT READING**
Jul 00. (d-cd) *Axe Killer; (AXE 305593CD)* **STRONG ARM OF THE LAW / DENIM AND LEATHER** -
Sep 00. (cd) *Angel Air; (<SJPCD 070>)* **DIAMONDS AND NUGGETS**
Sep 00. (cd) *Zoom Club; (<ZCRCD 43>)* **LIVE IN THE RAW**

SCANNER

Formed: Germany ... 1987 out of LION'S BREED, by MICHAEL KNOBLICH (yes, an unfortunate surname), TOM S. SOPHA, AXEL A.J. JULIUS, MARTIN BORK and WOLFGANG KOLORZ. A quasi-thrash power metal outfit preoccupied with science fiction, SCANNER found a sympathetic home at 'Noise' records and a loyal, if cult following for their conceptual debut, 'HYPERTRACE' (1988). With new recruit, S.L. COE replacing KNOBLICH, 'TERMINAL EARTH' (1990) carried on where the first album left off. Nothing has been heard from them since, possibly they've joined NASA.

Album rating: HYPERTRACE (*5) / TERMINAL EARTH (*4) / MENTAL RESERVATION (*4) / DELIVERY (*5)

MICHAEL KNOBLICH – vocals / **TOM S. SOPHA** – guitar / **AXEL A.J. JULIUS** – guitar / **MARTIN BORK** – bass / **WOLFGANG KOLORZ** – drums

Noise / not iss.

Oct 88. (cd/c/lp) *(CD/ZC+/NUK 111)* **HYPERTRACE** -
– Warp 7 / Terrion / Locked out / Across the universe / R.M.U. / Grapes of fear / Retaliation positive / Killing fields. *(cd+=)* – Wizard force. *(cd re-iss. Sep98; N 0111-3)*

— **S.L. COE** – vocals (ex-ANGEL DUST) repl. KNOBLICH

Feb 90. (cd/c/lp) *(CD/ZC+/NUK 141)* **TERMINAL EARTH** -
– The law / Not alone / Wonder / Buy or die / Touch the light / Terminal earth / From the dust of ages / The challenge. *(cd+=)* – Telemania / Lady. *(cd re-iss. Sep98; N 0141-2)*

— split sometime in the early 90's . . . until

Massacre / Massacre

Oct 95. (cd) *(<MASSCD 058>)* **MENTAL RESERVATION**
– Break the seal / Upright liar / After the storm / Your infallible smile / Conception of a cure / Out of nowhere / Into a brave man's mind / Nightmare / Rubberman / Wrong lane society / 2oth century crusade.

Earache / Earache

May 97. (d-lp/cd) *(<MOSH 174/+CD>)* **DELIVERY**
– The spirit of speech / Digital anchor / Treble spin / Fingerbug / Heidi / Barcode / Radio sprite / Throne of hives / Affaire / Vie one / My lost love hunting your lost face.

SCAT OPERA

Formed: USA ... 1988 by ERNIE BRENNAN, STEVE YATES, JOHN O'REILLY and MARK DIMENT. Famous for five minutes at the height of the funk-metal craze (late 80's/early 90's), SCAT OPERA recorded a promising 'Music For Nations' album in 1991, 'ABOUT TIME'. In addition to their bass-sprung musical propulsion, the band could pen an incisive lyric or two. It wasn't enough though, and along with the likes of fellow also rans, HEADS UP etc., SCAT OPERA failed to crossover, splitting after a second set, 'FOUR GONE CONFUSION' (1992).

Album rating: ABOUT TIME (*6) / FOUR GONE CONFUSION (*5)

ERNIE BRENNAN – vocals / **STEVE YATES** – guitar / **JOHN O'REILLY** – bass / **MARK DIMENT** – drums

Music For Nations / Caroline

Mar 91. (cd/c/lp) *(CD/T+/MFN 111) <CAROL 2212>* **ABOUT TIME** Oct91
– Premonition / B.G.V. / About time / Family man / Tarred with the same brush / Filo / Pighead / Be mine / On your own / Flex / Overture.
Oct 92. (cd/c/lp) *(CD/T+/MFN 140)* **FOUR GONE CONFUSION** -
– Reminisce in bitterness / Geee-forced / The points of madness / Think big / Inferiority complex I.C. / (I dig that) Oral mastication / Sit down, shut up and listen / Babble on tongue / Men and their tiny minds / Old fuddy duddy / Calculated.

— folded sometime later in the early 90's

SCATTERBRAIN

Formed: New York, USA ... late 80's by former LUDICHRIST members, TOMMY CHRIST and PAUL NIEDER. An NY hardcore act specialising in stinging humour, LUDICHRIST released two albums for the 'Combat' label, 'IMMACULATE DECEPTION' (1987) and 'POWERTRIP' (1988). Recruiting GUY BROGNA and MIKE BOYKO, the band became SCATTERBRAIN, signing to the 'In-Effect' label and releasing the acclaimed 'HERE COMES TROUBLE' in 1990. Revamping their hardcore in line with the funk-metal vogue, SCATTERBRAIN were akin to a cartoon combination of SUICIDAL TENDENCIES and FAITH NO MORE, the album gaining considerable support from Kerrrang! and figuring fairly high in the end-of-year polls. They were also popular in their native USA, the debut hitting the US Top 200 and lodging there for four months. The following year's 'SCAMBOOGERY' didn't fare so well, however, SCATTERBRAIN tiring of the corporate world of major labels and subsequently moving to UK independent, 'Bulletproof' for 1994's 'MUNDUS INTELLECTUALS'. • **Note:** Not to be confused with the SCATTERBRAIN of Germany, who issued a few releases in the early 80's.

Album rating: Ludichrist: IMMACULATE DECEPTION (*5) / POWERTRIP (*5) / Scatterbrain: HERE COMES TROUBLE (*7) / SCAMBOOGERY (*6) / MUNDUS INTELLECTUALIS (*4)

LUDICHRIST

TOMMY CHRIST – vocals / **PAUL NIEDER** – guitar

We Bite / Combat Core

Oct 88. (lp) *(WEBITE 34)* **IMMACULATE DECEPTION** 1987
– Fire at the firehouse / Most people are dicks / Murder bloody murder / Blown into the arms of Christ / Big business / Only as directed / Games once played / Green eggs and ham / Immaculate deception / You can't have fun / Government kids / Legal murder / Down with the ship / Thinking of you / Tylenol / Mengele / Young white and well behaved / Last train to Clarksville / God is everywhere. *(cd-iss. Sep93; WB 3034-2) <(cd re-iss. May99 on 'Century Media'; CM 66060CD)>*
Oct 88. (lp) *(WEBITE 35) <88561-8246-1>* **POWERTRIP**
– Powertrip / Z.A.D. / Stuff to fill graves / The tip of my mind / Damage done / T.B.O.S. / This party sucks / Johnny Pump / Yesterday for you / And so it goes / The well-dressed man disguise / Iwo Jima / One for the road. *<(cd re-iss. Jun99 on 'Century Media'; 66059-2)>*

— changed their moniker to

SCATTERBRAIN

TOMMY CHRIST – vocals / **PAUL NIEDER** – guitar / **GUY BROGNA** – bass / **MIKE BOYKO** – drums

Elektra / In-Effect

Jun 90. (cd/c/lp) *<3012-2/-4/-1>* **HERE COMES TROUBLE**
– Here comes trouble / Earache my eye / That's that / I'm with stupid / Down with the ship (slight return) / Sonata #3 / Mr. Johnson and the juice crew / Goodbye freedom, hello mom / Outta time / Don't call me dude / Drunken milkman. *(UK-iss.Oct91 cd/c/lp; 7559 61254-2/-4/-1) <(cd re-iss. Oct99 on 'Century Media'; 66085-2)>*
1990. (cd-s) **DOWN WITH THE SHIP / SLIGHT RETURN / EARACHE MY EYE / GOODBYE FREEDOM, HELLO MOM** -
1990. (cd-ep) **RETURN OF THE DUDES TOUR EP** -
– Don't call me dude / Mozart sonata #3 / Down with the ship (live) / Earache my eye (live) / Goodbye freedom, hello mom (live).
Nov 91. (cd/c/lp) *<(7559 61224-2/-4/-1)>* **SCAMBOOGERY**
– Big fun / Fine line / Dark side of the pepsi generation / Grandma's house of babes / Sanata No.11 / Bartender / Scamboogery / Swiss army girl / Logic / Down the road.

Bulletproof / Pavement

Sep 94. (cd) *(CDVEST 33) <15004>* **MUNDUS INTELLECTUALIS**
– Write that hit / Beer muscles / Everybody does it / A funny thing / How could I love you / Dead man blues / Down with the ship.

— disbanded shortly after above

Michael SCHENKER (GROUP)

Born: 10 Jan'55, Savstedt, Germany. Famous for forming teutonic rockers The SCORPIONS with his brother RUDOLF in 1971, he went on to join English band, UFO, with whom he cut four albums (PHENOMENON / FORCE IT / NO HEAVY PETTIN' / LIGHTS OUT). SCHENKER subsequently

returned to Germany in 1978 where he briefly rejoined The SCORPIONS for the 1979 album, 'LOVEDRIVE', augmenting them live before striking out on his own and forming the MICHAEL SCHENKER GROUP. Recruiting GARY BARDEN, MO FOSTER, SIMON PHILIPS and ex-COLOSSEUM II keyboard whizz, DON AIREY, the guitarist released an eponymous debut in 1980. Dominated by SCHENKER's sizzling axework, the album smashed into the UK Top 10, the guitarist's impressive pedigree ensuring healthy sales. For the subsequent tour, however, SCHENKER made the first personnel changes (PAUL RAYMOND, CHRIS GLEN and COZY POWELL replacing AIREY, FOSTER and PHILIPS respectively) in what would become a familiar pattern and no doubt contribute to the group's eventual spiral into mediocrity. This was the line-up which played on 'MSG' (1981), SCHENKER ripping out what could be his theme tune in 'ATTACK OF THE MAD AXEMAN'. Like The SCORPIONS, MSG enjoyed obsessive adulation in Japan, as witnessed on 1982's barnstorming double live set, 'ONE NIGHT AT BUDOKAN'. More line-up changes ensued, chief among them being ex-RAINBOW vocalist, GRAHAM BONNET replacing BARDEN, while former RORY GALLAGHER sticksman, TED McKENNA, was recruited in place of POWELL (who joined WHITESNAKE). With BONNET's earthier tones and significant songwriting input, the resulting album, 'ASSAULT ATTACK' (1982) was a bluesier affair albeit with SCHENKER's stinging guitar still vying for attention. Following BONNET's resumption of his solo career, BARDEN was welcomed back into the fold for 'BUILT TO DESTROY' (1983) and 'ROCK WILL NEVER DIE' (1984), two lacklustre albums which didn't exactly do much for SCHENKER's reputation. Inevitably, the group splintered, with the guitarist going back to Germany to reconsider his battle plan. When he resurfaced in late '87 with 'PERFECT TIMING', the 'M' in MSG now stood for McAULEY, SCHENKER having teamed up with former FAR CORPORATION / GRAND PRIX vocalist ROBIN McCAULEY for a more accessible melodic rock approach. The group enjoyed moderate success although by the release of 1992's 'M.S.G.', they seemed bankrupt of ideas and the record was roundly slated by critics. Marginally more inspired was the 'CONTRABAND' (1991) project, a collaboration with the likes of TRACII GUNS and BOBBY BLOTZER. The days of the guitar hero may well be over, however, and SCHENKER has been conspicuous by his absence from the metal scene for most of the 90's. After an extended absence the ageing teutonic axeman returned to the fray in the late 90's with a flurry of releases beginning with 1997's comeback set, 'WRITTEN IN THE SAND'. 1999 saw the release of both the 'UNFORGIVEN' studio set and a concert double set from the subsequent tour, 'THE UNFORGIVEN WORLD TOUR: LIVE'. Another live set, 'FLYING GOD' was released the same year. Come the new millennium, his guitar playing was as surprisingly virile as it had ever been with 'ADVENTURES OF THE IMAGINATION' (2000), an all-instrumental affair featuring veteran skins pounder AYNSLEY DUNBAR.
• **Trivia:** CONTRABAND covered Mott The Hoople's 'ALL THE WAY FROM MEMPHIS'.

Album rating: MICHAEL SCHENKER GROUP (*5) / MSG (*4) / ONE NIGHT AT BUDOKAN (*6) / ASSAULT ATTACK (*4) / BUILT TO DESTROY (*4) / ROCK WILL NEVER DIE (*4) / PORTFOLIO compilation (*6) / McAuley-Schenker Group: PERFECT TIMING (*5) / SAVE YOURSELF (*4) / MSG (*4) / Michael Schenker (Group): WRITTEN IN THE SAND (*4) / FLYING GOD (*4) / THE UNFORGIVEN (*5) / THE UNFORGIVEN WORLD TOUR (*4) / ADVENTURES OF THE IMAGINATION (*6)

MICHAEL SCHENKER – lead guitar (ex-SCORPIONS, ex-UFO) / **GARY BARDEN** – vocals / **DON AIREY** – keyboards (ex-COLOSSEUM II) / **MO FOSTER** – bass / **SIMON PHILLIPS** – drums

Chrysalis Chrysalis

Aug 80. (lp/c) *(<CHR/ZCHR 1302>)* **MICHAEL SCHENKER GROUP** [8] [100]
– Armed and ready / Cry for the nations / Victim of illusion / Bijou pleasurette / Feels like a good thing / Into the arena / Looking out from nowhere / Tales of mystery / Lost horizons. *(re-iss. Jun84 on 'Fame' lp/c; FA41 3105-1/-4) (<cd-iss. Feb00 on 'Liberty'; 524630-2>)*

Aug 80. (7"colrd) *(CHS 2455)* **ARMED AND READY. / BIJOU PLEASURETTE** [53] [ ]

Oct 80. (7"clear) *(CHS 2471)* **CRY FOR THE NATIONS. / INTO THE ARENA (live)** [56] [ ]
(12"+=) *(CHS12 2471)* – Armed and ready (live).

— **PAUL RAYMOND** – keyboards (ex-UFO, etc.) repl. AIREY / **CHRIS GLEN** – bass (ex-SENSATIONAL ALEX HARVEY BAND) repl. FOSTER / **COZY POWELL** – drums (ex-RAINBOW, ex-Solo artist) repl. PHILLIPS

Aug 81. (7"clear) *(CHS 2541)* **READY TO ROCK. / ATTACK OF THE MAD AXEMAN** [ ] [ ]

Sep 81. (lp/c) *(<CHR/ZCHR 1336>)* **MSG** [14] [81]
– Ready to rock / Attack of the mad axeman / On and on / Let sleeping dogs lie / But I want more / Never trust a stranger / Looking for love / Secondary motion. *(cd-iss. May86; CCD 1336)*

Feb 82. (d-lp/d-c) *(<CTY/ZCTY 1375>)* **ONE NIGHT AT BUDOKAN (live)** [5] [ ]
– Armed and ready / Cry for the nations / Attack of the mad axeman / But I want more / Victim of illusion / Into the arena / On and on / Never trust a stranger / Let sleeping dogs lie / Courvoisier concert / Lost horizons / Doctor doctor / Are you ready to rock. *(d-cd-iss. Sep91; CCD 1375) (cd re-iss. Jun96 on 'Beat Goes On'; BGOCD 312)*

— **GRAHAM BONNET** – vocals (ex-RAINBOW, ex-Solo, ex-MARBLES) repl. BARDEN + RAYMOND / **TED McKENNA** – drums (ex-SENSATIONAL ALEX HARVEY BAND, ex-RORY GALLAGHER) repl. COZY who joined WHITESNAKE

Sep 82. (7"clear,7"pic-d) *(CHS 2636)* **DANCER. / GIRL FROM UPTOWN** [52] [ ]
(12"+=) *(CHS12 2636)* – ('A'extended).

Oct 82. (lp/c/pic-lp) *(<CHR/ZCHR/PCHR 1393>)* **ASSAULT ATTACK** [19] [ ]
– Assault attack / Rock you to the ground / Dancer / Samurai / Desert song / Broken promises / Searching for a reason / Ulcer. *(cd-iss. Aug96 on 'Beat Goes On'; BGOCD 321)*

— **GARY BARDEN** – vocals returned to repl. BONNET who went solo / added **DEREK ST. HOLMES** – keyboards (ex-TED NUGENT) (on tour **ANDY NYE** – keyboards)

Sep 83. (lp/c/pic-lp) *(<CHR/ZCHR/PCHR 1441>)* **BUILT TO DESTROY** [23] [ ]
– Rock my nights away / I'm gonna make you mine / The dogs of war / Systems failing / Captain Nemo / Still love that little devil / Red sky / Time waits (for no one) / Walk the stage. *(cd-iss. Jan97 on 'Beat Goes On'; BGOCD 344)*

Jun 84. (lp/c) *(<CUX/ZCUX 1470>)* **ROCK WILL NEVER DIE (live)** [24] [ ]
– Captain Nemo / Rock my nights away / Are you ready to rock / Attack of the mad axeman / Into the arena / Rock will never die / Desert song / I'm gonna make you mine / Doctor, doctor.

— When CHRIS GLEN departed, most of others also departed

McAULEY-SCHENKER GROUP

— added **ROBIN McAULEY** (b.20 Jan'53, County Meath, Eire) – vox (ex-FAR CORPORATION) / **MITCH PERRY** – guitar / **ROCKY NEWTON** – bass / **BOBO SCHOPF** – drums

E.M.I. Capitol

Oct 87. (7") *(EM 30) <44079>* **GIMME YOUR LOVE. / ROCK TILL YOU'RE CRAZY** [ ] [ ]
(12"+=/12"remix+=) *(12EM/+S 30)* – ('A'extended).

Oct 87. (cd/c/lp) *(CD/TC+/EMC 3539) <46985>* **PERFECT TIMING** [65] [95]
– Gimme your love / Here today, gone tomorrow / Don't stop me now / No time for losers / Follow the night / Get out / Love is not a game / Time / I don't wanna lose / Rock 'til you're crazy.

Jan 88. (7"/12"/12"remix) *(EM/12EM/12EMS 40) <44113>* **LOVE IS NOT A GAME. / GET OUT** [ ] [ ]

Apr 88. (7") *<44156>* **FOLLOW THE NIGHT. / DON'T STOP ME NOW** [-] [ ]

— **McAULEY & SCHENKER** now with **BOBO SCHOPF** – drums / **STEVE MANN** (b.9 Aug'56) – rhythm guitar / **ROCKY NEWMAN** (b.11 Sep'57) – bass (ex-LIONHEART)

Oct 89. (cd/c/lp) *(CD/TC+/EMC 3567) <92752>* **SAVE YOURSELF** [ ] [92]
– Save yourself / Bad boys / Anytime / Get down to bizness / Shadow of the night / What we need / I am your radio / There has to be another way / This is my heart / Destiny. *(cd+=)* – Take me back.

Apr 90. (c-s/7") *(TC+/EM 127) <44471>* **ANYTIME. / WHAT WE NEED** [ ] [ ]
(12"+=/12"pic-d+=/cd-s+=) *(12EM/12EMPD/CDEM 127)* – ('A'version).

— **SCHENKER** with **ROBIN McAULEY** – vocals / **JEFF PILSON** – bass (ex-DOKKEN) / **JAMES KOTTAK** – drums (ex-KINGDOM COME)

E.M.I. Impact

Feb 92. (12"ep/cd-ep) **NEVER ENDING NIGHTMARE** [ ] [ ]
– Nightmare / Bad boys (acoustic) / What happens to me (acoustic) / We believe in love (acoustic) / Nightmare (album version).

Feb 92. (cd)(c/lp; as SCHENKER – McAULEY) *(CDP 798487-2)(EUS MC/LP 3) <10385>* **M.S.G.** [ ] [ ]
– Eve / Paradise / When I'm gone / The broken heart / We believe in love / Crazy / Invincible / What happens to me / Lonely nights / This night is gonna last forever / Never ending nightmare. *(cd re-iss. Jul96 on 'Beat Goes On'; BGOCD 316)*

Zero Michael Schenker

Dec 97. (cd) *(XRCN 1283) <109>* **WRITTEN IN THE SAND** [ ] [ ]
– Brave new world / Cry no more / I believe / Back to life / Written in the sand / Essenz / Love never dies / I will be there / Take me through the night / Down the drain / Into the arena / Cry for nations.

Feb 99. (cd) *(XRCN 10009)* **FLYING GOD** [ ] [-]
– A self made man / Venus / Pushed to the limit / Stopped by a bullet (of love) / Dreaming of summer / Doctor doctor '95 / Lights out '95 / Brave new world / Essenz / Written in the sand / Back to life / I believe / Into the arena / Cry for the nations.

S.P.V. Shrapnel

Feb 99. (cd) *(085-1868-2) <SH 1126>* **THE UNFORGIVEN** [ ] [ ]
– Rude awakening / The mess I've made / In and out of time / Hello angel / Fat city N.O. / Tower / Pilot of your soul / Forever and more / Turning off the emotion / Live for today / Illusion / The storm.

Oct 99. (d-cd) *(085-2153-2) <SH 1131>* **THE UNFORGIVEN WORLD TOUR LIVE (live)** [ ] [ ]
– Armed and ready / Only you can rock me / Natural thing / Pushed to the limit / Written in the sand / Captain Nemo / Into the arena / Essence / Pilot of your soul / The mess I've made / Fat city / On and on / Attack of the mad axeman / Assault attack / Another piece of meat / Love to love / Too hot to handle / Lights out / Bijou pleasurette – Positive forward / Doctor doctor / Rock bottom.

Mar 00. (cd) *(085-2172-2) <SH 1140>* **ADVENTURES OF THE IMAGINATION** [ ] [ ]
– Achtung fertig, los / Open gate / Three fish dancing / Michael Schenker, Junior / Aardvark in a VW smoking a cigar / I want to be with you / Old man with sheep on Mars / At the end of the day / Hand in hand.

– compilations, etc. –

Jun 87. (lp/c)(cd) *Chrysalis; (CNW/ZCNW 1)(MPCD 1598)* **PORTFOLIO** [ ] [-]
– Doctor doctor (UFO) / Rock bottom (UFO) / Rock will never die / Armed and ready / Ready to rock / Assault attack / Ulcer / Attack of the mad axeman / I'm a loser / Reasons to love / Too hot to handle / Only you can rock me (UFO) / Lights out (UFO) / Arbory hill / Love drive (SCORPIONS) / Searching for a reason / Rock my nights away / Captain Nemo.

Jul 91. (cd/c) *Castle; (CCS CD/MC 294)* **THE COLLECTION** [ ] [-]

Oct 92. (cd/c) *Chrysalis; (CD/TC CHR 1949)* **THE ESSENTIAL MICHAEL SCHENKER GROUP** [ ] [-]

Apr 93. (cd) *Connoisseur; (VSOPCD 185)* **ANTHOLOGY** [ ] [-]
– (with UFO tracks) *(re-iss. Aug95 on 'Griffin';)*

Nov 93. (cd) *Windsong; (WINCD 043)* **BBC RADIO 1 LIVE IN CONCERT (live)** [ ] [-]

Apr 94. (cd) *Chrysalis; (CDCHR 6071)* **THE STORY OF MICHAEL SCHENKER GROUP** [ ] [-]

Jun 94. (cd/c) *Music Club; (MC CD/TC 160)* **ARMED AND READY – THE BEST OF MICHAEL SCHENKER GROUP** [ ] [-]
Mar 97. (cd; SCHENKER & McAULEY GROUP) *Disky; (CR 86993-2)* **CHAMPIONS OF ROCK** [ ] [-]

CONTRABAND

MICHAEL SCHENKER – guitar / **RICHARD BLACK** – vocals (of-SHARK ISLAND) / **TRACII GUNS** – guitar (of-L.A.GUNS) / **SHARE PEDERSON** – bass (of-VIXEN) / **BOBBY BLOTZER** – drums (of-RATT)

E.M.I. Impact

Mar 91. (cd/c/lp) *(CD/TC+/EMC 3594) <10247>* **CONTRABAND** [ ] [ ] Jun91
– All the way from Memphis / Kiss by kiss / Ultimate outrage / Bad for each other / Loud guitars, fast cars and wild, wild living / Good rockin' tonight / Stand / Tonight you're mine / Hang on to yourself.
Jul 91. (c-s/7") *(TC+/EM 195) <54089>* **ALL THE WAY FROM MEMPHIS. / LOUD GUITARS, FAST CARS AND WILD, WILD LIVING** [65] [ ]
(12"+=/cd-s+=) *(12/CD EM 195)* – (3-'A'versions).
(12"pic-d+=) *(12EMP 195)* – ('A'-Balls to the wall version).
Oct 91. (c-s) *<54161>* **HANG ON TO YOURSELF. / LOUD GUITARS, FAST CARS AND WILD, WILD LIVING** [-] [ ]

Neal SCHON & Jan HAMMER (see under ⇒ JOURNEY)

SCORN

Formed: Birmingham, England . . . early 90's by ex-NAPALM DEATH drummer MICK HARRIS and NICK BULLEN. Initially augmented by JUSTIN BROADRICK, these seasoned noise manipulators debuted with the 'VAE SOLIS' album in '92, a dense fusion of sonic terrorism and a natural progression from what NAPALM DEATH had originally set out to achieve. Later that year, BROADRICK left to concentrate on his own GODFLESH project, PAT McCAHAN stepping in for the 'DELIVERANCE' EP. SCORN kept up a fairly prolific recording schedule over the forthcoming two years, releasing 'COLOSSUS' (1993) and 'EVANESCENCE' (1994), the latter set drawing increasing attention to the band and resulting in a full-blown remix album, 'ELLIPSIS' (featuring such electronic/industrial pioneers as COIL and MEAT BEAT MANIFESTO). In 1997, they issued two sets, one a Belgian-only affair, 'ZANDER', the other, 'LOGGHI BAROGGHI' appearing via their long-standing relationship with 'Earache' records.

Album rating: VAE SOLIS (*5) / COLOSSUS (*6) / EVANESCENCE (*7) / ELLIPSIS (*6) / GYRAL (*6) / LOGGHI BAROGGHI (*5) / ZANDER (*5) / WHINE (*5) / ANAMNESIS 1994-1998 compilation (*5)

MICK HARRIS – drums (ex-NAPALM DEATH, of PAINKILLER) / **NICK BULLEN** – bass, vocals / + **JUSTIN BROADRICK** – guitar

Earache Combat

Mar 92. (12"ep/cd-ep) *(MOSH 061 T/CD) <1154>* **LICK FOREVER DOG / ON ICE. / HEAVY BLOOD / LICK FOREVER DOG (dub)** [ ] [ ]

Earache Earache

Apr 92. (d-lp/c/cd) *(<MOSH 054/+MC/CD>)* **VAE SOLIS** [ ] [ ]
– Spasm / Suck and eat you / Hit / Walls of my heart / Lick forever dog / Thoughts of escape / Deep in – Eaten over and over / On ice / Heavy blood / Scum after death (dub) / Fleshpile (edit) / Orgy of holiness / Still life. *(cd re-iss. Mar99; same)*
— **PAT McCAHAN** – guitar (ex-CANDIRU) repl. BROADRICK who joined GODFLESH
Oct 92. (12"ep/cd-ep) *(MOSH 078 T/CD)* **DELIVERANCE** [ ] [-]
– Deliverance through dub / Delivered / To high heaven / Black sun rising. *(cd-ep re-iss. Feb97; MOSH 176CD)*
Apr 93. (10"ep/cd-ep) *(MOSH 093 T/CD)* **WHITE IRISES BLIND / (mix). / BLACK ASH DUB / DRAINED / HOST OF SCORPION** [ ] [-]
Jun 93. (lp/c/cd) *(MOSH 091/+MC/CD)* **COLOSSUS** [ ] [-]
– Endless / Crimson seed / Blackout / The sky is loaded / Nothing hunger / Beyond / Little angel / White irises blind / Scorpionic / Night ash black / Sunstroke. *(cd re-iss. Apr99; same)*
Jun 94. (d-lp/cd) *(<MOSH 113/+CD>)* **EVANESCENCE** [ ] [ ] Aug94
– Silver rain fell / Light trap / The falling / Automata / Days passed / Dreamspace / Exodus / Night tide / End / Slumber.
Aug 94. (12") *(MOSH 122T)* **SILVER RAIN FELL. / SILVER RAIN FELL (Meatbeat Manifesto remix)** [ ] [-]
Jun 95. (5x12"box/cd) *(SCORN 001/+CD) <111>* **ELLIPSIS** [ ] [ ]
– Dreamscape (Coil mix) / Silver rain fell (Meat Beat Manifesto mix) / Exodus (Scorn mix) / Dreamscape (Coil – Shadow vs. Executioner mix) / Night ash black (Bill Laswell – slow black underground river mix) / Night tide (Scanner – Flaneur Electronique mix) / Falling (Autechre FR 13 mix) / The end (P.C.M. – nightmare mix) / Automata (Germ mix) / Light trap (Scorn mix) / Dreamscape (Coil mix).
— now without BULLEN
Nov 95. (lp/cd) *(SCORN 002/+CD) <144>* **GYRAL** [ ] [ ]
– Six hours one week / Time went slow / Far in out / Stairway / Forever turning / Black box / Hush / Trondheim – Gaule.
Oct 96. (12") *(DOSS12 003)* **LEAVE IT OUT. /** [ ] [-]
(above single on 'Possible') (below two on Belgian label 'KK')
Feb 97. (cd) *(KK 152) <INV 76>* **ZANDER** [-] [-] Belgian
<above iss. on 'Invisible' US>
— next with **ERALDO BENOCCHI** – guitar
Oct 97. (d-lp/cd) *(KK 174/+CD) <113>* **WHINE (live & studio)** [-] [-] Belgian
– Not answering / Twitcher / Strand / Beat 3 / Well sorted / Check the sonic / 416 / Aurora / Beat 4 / Beat 2 (mix) / Beat 3 (mix) / Who know (mix).
Sep 97. (cd) *(<MOSH 158CD>)* **LOGGHI BAROGGHI** [ ] [ ]
– Look at that / Do the geek / Next days / Sponge / Out of / It's on / Logghi barogghi / Black box 2 / Nut / Mission / Pithering twat / Fumble / Weakener / Go.

– compilations, etc. –

Feb 97. (cd) *Earache; (MOSH 175CD)* **WHITE IRISES BLIND EP / LICK FOREVER DOG** [ ] [-]
Mar 99. (cd) *Invisible; <(INV 8005CD)>* **ANAMNESIS: RARITIES 1994-1998** [ ] [ ]
– Almost human / Maker of angels / Scorpionic / Geeked (original) / Get up / Wallpaper dub / Trap / Tamper / Beat 2 version / State of that / Dreamscape (unstable sidereal oneirscopic mix).

SCORPIONS

Formed: Hanover, Germany . . . 1971 by the SCHENKER brothers (MICHAEL and RUDOLPH) together with KLAUS MEINE, LOTHAR HEINBERG and WOLFGANG ZIONY. After a well-received debut, 'LONESOME CROW' (1973), on the domestic 'Brain' records, the band underwent a turbulent series of personnel changes which resulted in ULRICH ROTH replacing MICHAEL (who went on to join U.F.O.), JURGEN ROSENTHAL replacing ZIONY and FRANCIS BUCHHOLZ coming in for the departing LOTHAR. Signing worldwide to 'R.C.A.', the new-look SCORPIONS released a follow-up, 'FLY TO THE RAINBOW' in 1974. Archetypal German hard-rock, The SCORPIONS' sound consisted of initially jazz-inflected, lumbering riffs punctuated with piercing solos and topped off with MEINE's strangely accessible nasal whine. They developed this approach over a number of 70's albums, 'IN TRANCE' (1976), erm.. 'VIRGIN KILLERS' (1977), etc. The live 'TOKYO TAPES' (1979) brought the first half of the group's career to a neat close, ROTH subsequently departing to form ELECTRIC SUN, disillusioned at the band's increasingly commercial direction. His replacement was MATHIAS JABS although MICHAEL SCHENKER returned briefly, guesting on three tracks for the 'LOVEDRIVE' (1979) set. Now signed to 'Harvest' ('Mercury' in the States), the group had produced their most radio-friendly collection to date, the album taking them into the UK (Top 40) and US (Top 60) charts for the first time. 'ANIMAL MAGNETISM' (1980) fared even better, almost breaking the UK Top 20 with the NWOBHM in full swing, the record also featuring the anthemic live favourite, 'THE ZOO'. 'BLACKOUT' (1982) finally broke the group in America, achieving double platinum status. 1984's 'LOVE AT FIRST STING' fared even better, selling twice as much as its predecessor and spawning a Top 30 hit single with the stop-start riffing of 'ROCK YOU LIKE A HURRICANE'. The SCORPIONS were now seemingly tailoring their music for the US market, concentrating more on melody and hooklines with each successive release. Save for the massive selling concert set,'WORLD WIDE LIVE' (1985), it was to be a further four years before the group released a new album as they became the first Western rock group to play in the Soviet Union, 'SAVAGE AMUSEMENT' finally surfacing in 1988. The SCORPIONS' anthemic rock continued to attract a bigger audience Stateside than in Britain, the group scoring a Top 5 US hit single (and a worldwide No.1) in 1991 with the lighter-waving ballad, 'WIND OF CHANGE'. Sadly not referring to MEINE finally having that awful mullet cut off, the song instead dealt with the sweeping changes in the communist bloc (a version was actually recorded in Russian!). They continued to eschew tales of loose women and 'crazy' nights for more serious political matters on 'FACE THE HEAT' (1993), exploring the social effect of their country's reunification. Four albums have since emerged from the German dinosaurs, 'LIVE BITES' (1995), 'PURE INSTINCT' (1995), 'EYE TO EYE' (1999) and the year 2000's METALLICA-meets-orchestra type effort 'MOMENT OF GLORY', a record that featured The Berlin Philharmonic!

Album rating: ACTION (or) LONESOME CROW (*4) / FLY TO THE RAINBOW (*4) / IN TRANCE (*6) / VIRGIN KILLERS (*6) / TAKEN BY FORCE (*4) / TOKYO TAPES (*5) / LOVEDRIVE (*6) / ANIMAL MAGNETISM (*5) / BLACKOUT (*6) / LOVE AT FIRST STING (*6) / WORLD WIDE LIVE (*6) / SAVAGE AMUSEMENT (*5) / CRAZY WORLD (*4) / FACE THE HEAT (*4) / LIVE BITES (*3) / DEADLY STING compilation (*6) / PURE INSTINCTS (*4) / EYE TO EYE (*3) / MOMENT OF GLORY with the Berliner Philharmonica (*4)

KLAUS MEINE (b.25 May'52) – vocals / **MICHEL SCHENKER** (b.10 Jan'55, Savstedt, Germany) – lead guitar / **RUDOLF SCHENKER** (b.31 Aug'52, Hildesheim, Germany) – guitar (ex-COPERNICUS) / **LOTHAR HEIMBERG** – bass / **WOLFGANG DZIONY** – drums

Brain not iss.

1973. (lp) *<1001>* **LONESOME CROW** [-] [-] German
– It all depends / Action / Lonesome crow / I'm goin' mad / Leave me / In search of the peace of mind / Inheritance. *(re-iss. Aug74 as 'I'M GOIN' MAD & OTHERS' on 'Billingsgate'; 1004) (re-iss. Nov77 as 'GOLD ROCK' on 'Brain'; 004 0016) (re-iss. May80 as 'ACTION' on 'Brain'; 0040 150) (UK-iss.Nov82 on 'Heavy Metal' lp/c/pic-lp; HMI LP/MC/PD 2) (cd-iss. 1988 on 'Brain'; 825 739-2) (re-iss. Jul91 on 'Metal Masters' cd/c/lp; METAL MCD/K/PS 114)*
— (Jun'73) **ULRICH ROTH** – lead guitar repl. MICHAEL who joined UFO / **JURGEN ROSENTHAL** – drums repl. WOLFGANG / **FRANCIS BUCHHOLZ** (b.19 Feb'50) – bass repl. LOTHAR

R.C.A. R.C.A.

Nov 74. (lp) *(RS 1023) <APL-1 4025>* **FLY TO THE RAINBOW** [ ] [ ]
– Speedy's coming / They need a million / Drifting Sun / Fly people fly / This is my song / Fly away / Fly to the rainbow. *(re-iss. Oct85 lp/c; NL/NK 70084) (cd-iss. Apr88; ND 70084)*
Apr 75. (7") *<10574>* **SPEEDY'S COMING. / THEY NEED A MILLION** [-] [ ]
— (1975) **RUDY LENNERS** – drums repl. JURGENS

Mar 76. (lp) *(RS 1039) <PPL-1 4028>* **IN TRANCE** [ ] [ ]
– Dark lady / In trance / Life's like a river / Top of the bill / Living and dying / Robot man / Evening wind / Sun in my hand / Longing for fire / Night lights. *(re-iss. Jun83; INTS 5251) (re-iss. 1984 lp/c; NL/NK 70028) (cd-iss. Feb90; ND 70028)*

Nov 76. (7") *<10691>* **IN TRANCE. / NIGHT LIGHTS** [-] [ ]

Feb 77. (lp) *(PPL1 4225) <APL-1 4225>* **VIRGIN KILLERS** [ ] [ ]
– Pictured life / Catch your train / In your park / Backstage queen / Virgin killer / Hell cat / Crying days / Polar nights / Yellow raven. *(re-iss. Apr88 lp/cd; NL/ND 70031)*

— **HERMAN RAREBELL** (b.18 Nov'53, Lubeck, Germany) – drums (ex-STEPPENWOLF) repl. RUDY

Apr 78. (lp/c) *(PL/PK 28309) <APL-1 2628>* **TAKEN BY FORCE** [ ] [ ]
– Steamrock fever / We'll burn the sky / I've got to be free / The riot of your time / The sails of Charon / Your light / He's a woman she's a man / Born to touch your feelings. *(re-iss. Sep81 lp/c; RCA LP/K 3024) (re-iss. Oct88 lp/c/cd; NL/NK/ND 70081)*

Feb 79. (d-lp) *(NL 28331)* **THE TOKYO TAPES (live)** [ ] [ ]
– All night long / Pictured life / Backstage queen / Polar nights / In trance / We'll burn the sky / Suspender love / In search of the peace of mind / Fly to the rainbow / He's a woman, she's a man / Speedy's coming / Top of the bill / Hound dog / Long tall Sally / Steamrock fever / Dark lady / Kojo no tsuki / Robot man. *(re-iss. 1984 lp/c; NL/NK 70008) (d-cd-iss. Nov88; PD 70008)*

— (Dec'78) **MATHIAS JABS** (b.25 Oct'56) – lead guitar repl. ULRICH who formed ELECTRIC SUN. **MICHAEL SCHENKER** also guested on 3 tracks on next album, joining **KLAUS, RUDOLF, HERMAN, FRANCIS + MATHIAS**

Harvest Mercury

Mar 79. (7") *<76008>* **LOVING YOU SUNDAY MORNING. / COAST TO COAST** [-] [ ]

Apr 79. (lp/c) *(SHSP/TC-SHSP 4097) <3795>* **LOVEDRIVE** [36] [55]
– Loving you Sunday morning / Another piece of meat / Always somewhere / Coast to coast / Can't get enough / Is there anybody there? / Lovedrive / Holiday. *(re-iss. Nov83 on 'Fame' lp/c; FA41 3080-1/-4) (cd-iss. Nov88; CDFA 3080)*

May 79. (7") *(HAR 5185)* **IS THERE ANYBODY THERE? / ANOTHER PIECE OF MEAT** [39] [-]

Aug 79. (7"/12") *(HAR/12HAR 5188)* **LOVEDRIVE. / COAST TO COAST** [69] [-]

Apr 80. (lp/c) *(SHSP/TC-SHSP 4113) <3825>* **ANIMAL MAGNETISM** [23] [52]
– Make it real / Don't make no promises (your body can't keep) / Hold me tight / Twentieth century man / Lady starlight / Fallin' in love / Only a man / The zoo / Animal magnetism. *(re-iss. Aug85 on 'E.M.I.'; ATAK/TC-ATAK 48) (re-iss. May89 on 'Fame' cd/c/lp; CD/TC+/FA 3217)*

May 80. (7") *(HAR 5206) <76070>* **MAKE IT REAL. / DON'T MAKE NO PROMISES (YOUR BODY CAN'T KEEP)** [72] [ ]

Jul 80. (7") *<76084>* **LADY STARLIGHT. /** [-] [ ]

Aug 80. (7") *(HAR 5212)* **THE ZOO. / HOLIDAY** [75] [-]

— In 1981, MICHAEL SCHENKER briefly returned to repl. JABS while MEINE had throat surgery. Everything resumed as 1980 line-up re-appeared in 1982.

Mar 82. (lp/c) *(SHVL/TC-SHVL 823) <4039>* **BLACKOUT** [11] [10]
– Blackout / Can't live without you / No one like you / You give me all I need / Now! / Dynamite / Arizona / China white / When the smoke is going down. *(re-iss. May85 on 'Fame' lp/c; FA/TCFA 3126) (re-iss. Nov88; CDFA 3126)*

Mar 82. (7"/7"pic-d) *(HAR/+P 5219) <76153>* **NO ONE LIKE YOU. / NOW!** [64] [65] Jun82

Jul 82. (7") *(HAR 5221)* **CAN'T LIVE WITHOUT YOU. / ALWAYS SOMEWHERE** [63] [-]

Feb 84. (7") *(HAR 5225) <818440>* **ROCK YOU LIKE A HURRICANE. / COMING HOME** [ ] [25]

Mar 84. (lp/c) *(SHSP 24-0007-1/-4) <814981>* **LOVE AT FIRST STING** [17] [6]
– Bad boys running wild / Rock you like a hurricane / I'm leaving you / Coming home / The same thrill / Big city nights / As soon as the good times roll / Crossfire / Still loving you. *(re-iss. Nov87 on 'E.M.I.' lp/c; ATAK/TC-ATAK 69) (re-iss. Aug89 on 'Fame' cd/c/lp; CD/TC+/FA 3224)*

Aug 84. (7"/12"/12"pic-d) *(HAR/12HAR/12HARP 5231)* **BIG CITY NIGHTS. / BAD BOYS RUNNING WILD** [ ] [-]

Mar 85. (7") *(HAR 5232) <880082>* **STILL LOVING YOU. / HOLIDAY** [ ] [64] Jun84
(12"+=) *(12HAR 5232)* – Big city nights.

Jun 85. (d-lp/d-c) *(SCORP/TC-SCORP 1) <824344>* **WORLD WIDE LIVE (live)** [18] [14]
– Countdown / Coming home / Blackout / Bad boys running wild / Loving you Sunday morning / Make it real / Big city nights / Coast to coast / Holiday / Still loving you / Rock you like a hurricane / Can't live without you / Another piece of meast / Dynamite / The zoo / No one like you / Can't get enough (part 1) / Six string sting / Can't get enough (part 2). *(d-cd-iss. Feb86; CDP 746155-2)*

Jun 85. (7") *(HAR 5237)* **NO ONE LIKE YOU (live). / THE ZOO (live)** [ ] [-]

Apr 88. (cd/c/lp)(pic-lp) *(CD/TC+/SHSP 4125) <832963>* **SAVAGE AMUSEMENT** [18] [5]
– Don't stop at the top / Rhythm of love / Passion rules the game / Media overkill / Walking on the edge / We let it rock . . . you let it rock / Every minute every day / Love on the run / Believe in love. *(pic-lp-iss.May88; SHSPP 4125)*

May 88. (7"/7"box/7"pic-d) *(HAR/+X/P 5240) <870323>* **RHYTHM OF LOVE. / WE LET IT ROCK . . . YOU LET IT ROLL** [59] [75]
(12"+=) *(12HAR 5240)* – Love on the run (mix).

Aug 88. (7"/7"pic-d) *(HAR 5241)* **BELIEVE IN LOVE. / LOVE ON THE RUN** [ ] [-]
(12"+=) *(12HAR 5241)* – ('A'version).

Feb 89. (7") *(HAR 5242)* **PASSION RULES THE GAME. / EVERY MINUTE EVERY DAY** [74] [-]
(12"+=/12"pic-d+=) *(12HAR/+P 5242)* – Is there anybody there?
(cd-s++=) *(CDHAR 5242)* – ('A'extended).

Vertigo Mercury

Nov 90. (cd/c/lp) *(846908-2/-4/-1) <846908>* **CRAZY WORLD** [ ] [21]
– Tease me please me / Don't believe her / To be with you in Heaven / Wind of change / Restless nights / Lust or love / Kicks after six / Hit between the eyes / Money and fame / Crazy world / Send me an angel. *(re-dist.Oct91; hit UK No.27)*

Dec 90. (7"/c-s) *(VER/+MC 52)* **DON'T BELIEVE HER. / KICKS AFTER SIX** [ ] [-]
(12"+=/12"g-f+=/cd-s+=) *(VER X/XG/CD 52)* – Big city nights / Holiday (live).

Mar 91. (7"red/c-s) *(VER/+MC 54)* **WIND OF CHANGE. / RESTLESS NIGHTS** [53] [-]
(12"red+=) *(VERXP 54)* – The zoo (live)
(cd-s+=) *(VERCD 54)* – To be with you in Heaven / Blackout (live).
(12"red+=) *(VERPX 54)* – Zoo (live).

May 91. (c-s,cd-s) *<868180>* **WIND OF CHANGE / MONEY AND FAME** [-] [4]

Sep 91. (7"/c-s) *(VER/+MC 58)* **WIND OF CHANGE. / RESTLESS NIGHTS** [2] [-]
(12"pic-d+=) *VERX 58)* – Hit between the eyes / Blackout (live).
(cd-s+=) *(VERCD 58)* – Blackout (live) / To be with you in Heaven.

Nov 91. (c-s,cd-s) *<868956>* **SEND ME AN ANGEL / RESTLESS NIGHTS** [-] [44]

Nov 91. (7"/c-s) *(VER/+MC 60)* **SEND ME AN ANGEL. / WIND OF CHANGE (Russian)** [27] [-]
(12"+=/cd-s+=) *(VER X/CD 60)* – Tease me, please me (live) / Lust or love (live).

— (May'92) BUCHHOLZ departed repl. by **RALPH RIECKERMANN** (b. Lubeck) – bass

Mercury Mercury

Sep 93. (cd/c/lp) *(<518280-2/-4/-1>)* **FACE THE HEAT** [51] [24]
– Alien nation / No pain, no gain / Someone to touch / Under the same sun / Unholy alliance / Woman / Hate to be nice / Taxman woman / Ship of fools / Nightmare Avenue / Lonely nights / Destin / Daddy's girl

Nov 93. (c-s) *(MERMC 395)* **UNDER THE SAME SUN / SHIP OF FOOLS** [ ] [ ]
(12"+=) *(12MER 395)* – Alien nation / Rubber fucker.
(cd-s++=) *(MERCD 395)* – Partners in crime.

Apr 95. (cd) *(526903-2)* **LIVE BITES (live)** [ ] [ ]
– Tease me, please me / Is anybody / Rhythm of love / In trance / No pain no gain / When the smoke is going down / Ave Maria no morro / Living for tomorrow / Concerto in V / Alien nation / Hit between the eyes / Crazy world / Wind of change / Heroes don't cry / White dove.

— line-up **KLAUS, RUDOLF, MATTHIAS + RALPH** were joined by **CURT CRESS + PITTI HECHT** – drums / **LUKE HERZOG + KOEN VAN BAEL** – keyboards

East West Atlantic

May 96. (cd/c/lp) *(0630 14524-2) <82913>* **PURE INSTINCT** [ ] [99]
– Wild child / But the best for you / Does anyone know / Stone in my shoe / Soul behind the face / Oh girl (I wanna be with you) / When you came into my life / Where the river flows / Time will call your name / You and I / Are you the one?

Jun 96. (c-s/cd-s) *(W 0042 C/CD)* **YOU AND I / SHE'S KNOCKING AT MY DOOR / YOU AND I (extended)** [ ] [-]

Coalition – eastwest Coalition – eastwest

Mar 99. (7"pic-d) *(COLA 074)* **TO BE NO.1. / MIND LIKE A TREE** [ ] [-]
(cd-s+=) *(COLA 074CD)* – ('A'-CD-Rom version).

Mar 99. (cd) *<(3984 26830-2)>* **EYE TO EYE** [ ] [ ]
– Mysterious / To be No.1 / Obsession / 10 light years away / Mind like a tree / Eye to eye / What you give you get back / Skywriter / Yellow butterfly / Freshly squeezed / Priscilla / Du bist so schmutzig / Aleyah / Moment is a million years.

EMI Classics EMI Classics

Jul 00. (cd; with The Berliner Philharmonica) *(<CDC 557019-2>)* **MOMENT OF GLORY** [ ] [ ]
– Hurricane 2000 (rock you like a hurricane) / Moment of glory / Send me an angel (with ZUCCHERO) / Wind of change / Medley: Crossfire – Dynamite – He's a woman she's a man / Deadly sting suite / Here in my heart (with LYNN LIECHTY) / Still loving you / Big city nights / Lady Starlight (with LYNN LIECHTY).

Sep 00. (cd-ep; with The Berliner Philharmonica) *(8891410)* **HERE IN MY HEART / WIND OF CHANGE / MOMENT OF GLORY (video)** [ ] [ ]

– compilations, etc. –

on 'R.C.A.' unless mentioned otherwise

Nov 79. (12"ep) *(PC 9402)* **ALL NIGHT LONG / FLYING TO THE RAINBOW. / SPEEDY'S COMING / IN TRANCE** [ ] [-]

Sep 81. (lp/c) *(RCA LP/K 3035) <3516>* **THE BEST OF THE SCORPIONS** [ ] [ ] Nov79
– Steamrock fever / Pictured life / Robot man / Backstage queen / Speedy's coming / Hell-cat / He's a woman, she's a man / In trance / Dark lady / The sails of Charon / Virgin killer. *(re-iss. Feb89 lp/c/cd; NL/NK/ND 74006)*

Nov 89. (cd/c/lp) *E.M.I.; (CD/TC+/EMD 1014) / Mercury; <842002>* **BEST OF ROCKERS 'N' BALLADS** [ ] [43]
(re-iss. Sep91 on 'Fame'; CD/TC FA 3262)

Feb 90. (lp/c/cd) *(NL/NK/ND 74517) <5085>* **THE BEST OF THE SCORPIONS, VOL.2** [ ] [ ] Jul84

Feb 90. (cd) *(ND 70672)* **HOT AND HEAVY** [ ] [ ]

Nov 90. (cd/c/lp) *E.M.I.; (CD/TC+/EMC 3586)* **STILL LOVING YOU** [ ] [ ]
(re-iss. Feb92 cd/c/lp; CD/TC+/EMD 1031)

Dec 90. (cd/c/lp) *Connoisseur; (VSOP CD/MC/LP 156)* **HURRICANE ROCK** [ ] [-]

Oct 91. (3xcd-box) *E.M.I.; (CDS 797963-2)* **SCORPIONS 3 CD SET** [ ] [-]
– (WORLDWIDE LIVE / SAVAGE AMUSEMENT / ROCKERS 'N' BALLADS)

Dec 91. (cd/c) *(ND/NK 75029)* **HOT AND SLOW (THE BEST OF THE BALLADS)** [ ] [-]

Sep 93. (cd) *(74321 15119-2)* **HOT AND HARD** [ ] [ ]

Feb 95. (cd) *E.M.I.; (CDEMC 3698)* **DEADLY STING** [ ] [ ]

Sep 99. (cd) *E.M.I.; (497013-2)* **THE BEST OF THE SCORPIONS** [ ] [-]

Mar 00. (d-cd) *Axe Killer; (<AXE 305646CD>)* **IN TRANCE / VIRGIN KILLER** [ ] [ ]

SCRATCH ACID (see under ⇒ JESUS LIZARD)

SCREAM

Formed: Washington, DC, USA . . . 1982 by PETER STAHL, his brother FRANZ STAHL, SKEETER THOMPSON and KENT STAX. Signed to IAN McKAYE's (Minor Threat) label 'Dischord', they recorded three hardcore/punk albums, 'STILL SCREAMING' (1983), 'THIS SIDE UP' (1985) and 'BANGING THE DRUM' (1987). DAVE GROHL (later a member of NIRVANA and The FOO FIGHTERS) subsequently became their drummer in '88, sticking around for a couple of late 80's live albums and the studio set, 'NO MORE CENSORSHIP'. However, the group floundered at the turn of the decade, GROHL becoming a grunge figurehead alongside KURT COBAIN and the STAHL brothers forming the West Coast rock outfit, WOOL. The siblings recruited AL BLOCH (on bass) and CHRIS BRATTON (on drums), before embarking on a journey to the centre of raw edged rock with the mini-debut, 'BUDSPAWN' (1993). The set contained much of the same material produced by SCREAM, in fact, it may have been confusing due to the fact that the two sounded so alike. WOOL managed to enforce the RAMONES punk trait while adding the same filth as they once did in SCREAM. Of course, DAVE GROHL became a huge fan by the time of the band's second set, the un-boxed(!) 'BOX SET' (1995), a slightly more diverse affair than the previous one. Grungy guitars dabbling with muted dynamics and improvised jazz rock like they were some kind of fearsome narcotic, backed STAHL's messy, almost legendary vocals, crediting the set's garage rock theme. Later, after the subsequent death of grunge, the band split, joining various other outfits, including baseball capped rockers and bearded weirdos GOATSNAKE.

Album rating: STILL SCREAMING (*5) / THIS SIDE UP (*5) / BANGING THE DRUM (*6) / NO MORE CENSORSHIP (*5) / SCREAM – LIVE (*4) / FUMBLE (*4) / Wool: BUDSPAWN mini (*4) / BOX SET (*5)

PETER STAHL – vocals / **FRANZ STAHL** – guitar / **SKEETER THOMPSON** – bass / **KENT STAX** – drums

Dischord Dischord

1983. (lp) <DISCHORD 9> **STILL SCREAMING** [-] [ ]
(UK-iss.1988; same)

—— Also in 1984 they issued 'BOUNCING BABIES' compilation on 'Fountain Of Youth'.

1985. (lp) <DISCHORD 15> **THIS SIDE UP** [-] [ ]
(UK-iss.1988; same)

Nov 87. (lp/c) *(DISCHORD 25/+C)* **BANGING THE DRUM** [ ] [ ]
– Banging the drum / People, people / I.C.Y.U.O.D. / Nod to the east / Mineshaft burning / Rhythm beating / Feel like that / Walking by myself / When I rise / Sing it up kidz.

—— **DAVE GROHL** – drums; repl. KENT around this time

Konkurrel not iss.

Sep 88. (lp) *(K 001-113)* **LIVE IN EUROPE (AT VAN HALL, AMSTERDAM)** [ ] [-]

R.A.S. Torso

Dec 88. (lp/cd) *(RAS/RASCD 4001)* <2614248> **NO MORE CENSORSHIP** [ ] [ ]
– Hit me / No more censorship / Fucked without a kiss / No escape / Building dreams / Take it from the top / Something in my head / It's the time / Binge / Run to the sun / In the beginning.

YourChoice not iss.

1990. (lp) *(010)* **SCREAM – LIVE (live)** [ ] [-]
– C.W.W. Pt.II / I.C.Y.O.U.D. / The zoo closes / Hot smoke and sasafrass / Fight / American justice / Show and tell / Sunmaker / No escape / Take it from the top / Dancing madly backwards / Hit me.

—— disbanded in 1990 after GROHL joined NIRVANA and later FOO FIGHTERS. Another SCREAM were formed in the early 90's, but they were from L.A.

Jul 93. (lp/c) <(DIS 82 V/C)> **FUMBLE** [ ] [ ]
– Caffine dream / Sunmaker / Mardi Gras / Land torn down / Gods look down / Gas / Dying days / Poppa says / Rain. *(cd-iss. w/ 'BANGING THE DRUM'; DIS 82D)*

– compilations, etc. –

Jul 93. (cd) *Dischord;* <(DIS 81CD)> **STILL SCREAMING / THIS SIDE UP** [ ] [ ]
– Came without warning / Bedlam / Solidarity / Your wars – Killer / Piece of her time / Human behavoir / Stand / Fight – American justice / New song / Laissez faire / Influenced / Hygiene / Cry wolf / Total mash / Who knows? who cares? / Amerarockers / U. suck A. – We're fed up / Ultra violence – Screamin' / Violent youth / Bet you never thought / Things to do today / This side up / Gluesniff / Still screaming / No money down / Show and tell me baby / Zoo closes at dark / I look when you talk / Iron curtain / Walking song dub.

WOOL

—— were formed by the **STAHL's** who recruited **AL BLOCH** – bass / **PETE MOFFETT** – drums (ex-GOVERNMENT ISSUE)

Parallel External

May 93. (m-cd/m-c/m-lp) *(ALL CD/C/P 1)* <162111> **BUDSPAWN** [ ] [ ] Nov92
– S.O.S. / Slightly under / Clear my head / Wait / Medication / Eff.

—— **CHRIS BRATTON** – drums; repl. MOFFETT who later joined BURNING AIRLINES

London Polygram

Feb 95. (cd/c) <(828498-2/-4)> **BOX SET** [ ] [ ] Nov94
– Eden / Kill the crow / Eat some ziti / Superman is dead / B-350 / Chances are / Coalinga / Speak / God rest his soul / Blackeye / Take a look. *<lp-iss.on 'Bongload'; BL 15>*

SCREAM (see under ⇒ RACER X)

SCREAMING JETS

Formed: Newcastle, Australia . . . early 1989 by high school friends DAVE GLEESON and GRANT WALMSLEY together with RICHARD LARA, PAUL WOSEEN and BRAD HEANEY. All veterans of the local rock scene despite their tender age, the band gigged relentlessly around the Hunter Valley area, building a reputation as an uncompromising, blistering live act. Having scooped the JJJ national battle of the bands contest, the 'JETS secured a deal with 'Roo Art', the label run by INXS manager Chris Murphy. An EP and a debut album, 'ALL FOR ONE' (1991), set out the band's agenda with a raw rock sound in the time honoured mould of greasy, Antipodean rockers like AC/DC and ROSE TATTOO. A domestic Top 10 hit single with 'BETTER' set them on the road to Australian fame while high profile UK and US support slots put their name on the international map. Sophomore effort, 'TEAR OF THOUGHT' (1992) preceded extensive touring and an appearance at the Rock Am Ring Festival in Germany. Although 1994 saw LARA and HEANEY replaced by JIMI HOCKING and CRAIG ROSEVEAR respectively, a surprise domestic hit with the ballad, 'HELPING HAND', propelled sales of their first two albums to platinum status in their homeland. A belated third set, 'WORLD GONE CRAZY', eventually appeared in 1997 by which time the band were bigger than ever in their homeland, despite (or perhaps partly because of!) GLEESON's infamous onstage rants. Having weathered everything the music industry could throw at them, The SCREAMING JETS were worldly wise verterans by the release of 'SCAM' (2000), its title dedicated to one of the world's most notoriously dirty businesses.

Album rating: ALL FOR ONE (*6) / TEAR OF THOUGHT (*5) / SCREAMING JETS (*6) / WORLD GONE CRAZY (*5) / HITS & PIECES compilation (*6) / SCAM (*4)

DAVE GLEESON – vocals / **GRANT WALMSLEY** – guitar / **RICHARD LARA** – guitar / **PAUL WOSEEN** – bass / **BRAD HEANEY** – drums

Roo Art Roo Art

Nov 90. (cd-s) **C'MON** [-] [-] Austra

Mar 91. (cd-s) **BETTER** [-] [-] Austra

Jul 91. (cd/c/lp) *(<848441-2/-4/-1>)* **ALL FOR ONE** [ ] [ ]
– C'mon / Better / Needle / No point / Shine on / Starting out / Stop the world / Blue sashes / Sister tease / Got it / The only one.

Aug 91. (cd-s) **SHINE ON** [-] [-] Austra

Jun 92. (cd-ep) **LIVING IN ENGLAND EP** [-] [-] Austra

WEA WEA

Aug 92. (cd-s) **THINK / TUNNEL** [-] [-] Austra

Jan 93. (cd-s) **SHIVERS** [-] [-] Austra

Feb 93. (cd/c) *(450990678-2/-4)* <92270-2/-4> **TEAR OF THOUGHT** [ ] [ ] Oct92
– Dream on / Here I go / Meet anybody / Alright / Night child / Helping hand / Everytime / Living in England / Think / Best of you / Rich bitch / Tunnel / Hard drugs / Sick and tired / Shivers / Feeble.

Jul 93. (cd-s) **HERE I GO** [-] [-] Austra

Nov 93. (cd-s) **HELPING HAND** [-] [-] Austra

Oct 95. (cd-s) **FRIEND OF MINE** [-] [-] Austra

Oct 95. (cd) **SCREAMING JETS** [-] [-] Austra
– Figure it out / Sacrifice / Sad song / High as a kite / Otherside / Disappear / Bloodshed / Impossible / Friend of mine / Life and death / Refer madness / In a jam.

Apr 96. (cd-s) **SACRIFICE** [-] [-] Austra

Oct 97. (cd) **WORLD GONE CRAZY** [-] [-] Austra
– Elvis (I remember . . .) / When I go / Strength / Jurisdiction / Eve of destruction / Drowning / Drowning / Dying to see you / Holding on / Stay awhile / October grey / Black and white / In and out / Silence lost / World gone crazy.

not iss. Universal

Jun 00. (cd-s) **SHINE OVER ME** [-] [-] Austra

Oct 00. (cd) **SCAM** [-] [-] Austra
– Individuality / Realise / Shine over me / Watching the grass grow / No way out / The protest song / Higher with you / Thinkin' about you / Overexcited / Maggots / Hitting myself in the head / Close to you / I need your love / Don't be sorry.

– compilations, etc. –

Oct 99. (cd) *B.M.G.; (61655)* **HITS & PIECES** [-] [-] Austra
– C'mon / Better / I need your love / Sad song / Helping hand / Blue sashes / Needle / Living in England / Individuality / Sacrifice / Shivers / October grey / Elvis (I remember. . .) / Eve of destruction / Tunnel / Silence lost / Shine on / Impossible.

SCREAMING TREES

Formed: Ellensburg, Washington, USA . . . 1985 by girthsome brothers VAN and GARY LEE CONNER along with frontman MARK LANEGAN and drummer MARK PICKEREL. Following early effort, 'CLAIRVOYANCE' (1986) for the tiny 'Velvetone' label, the group signed to respected US indie, 'S.S.T.', making their debut with the convincing 'EVEN IF AND ESPECIALLY WHEN' (1987). Fuelled by raging punk, The SCREAMING TREES were nevertheless characterised by the spectral hue of 60's psychedelia running through much of their music, LANEGAN's exotic, JIM MORRISON-esque vocals adding an air of brooding mystery on the likes of fans' favourite, 'TRANSFIGURATION'. Another couple of stirring sets, 'INVISIBLE LANTERN' (1988) and 'BUZZ FACTORY' (1989), followed before the group released a one-off EP for 'Sub Pop'. With the emerging grunge phenomenon in nearby Seattle on the cusp of world domination, The SCREAMING TREES were obviously a promising prospect for major label A&R and it came as little surprise when they signed for 'Epic'. That same year, prior to their debut for the label, the various 'TREES occupied themselves with solo projects, GARY LEE forming PURPLE OUTSIDE and releasing 'MYSTERY LANE', while brother VAN issued the eponymous 'SOLOMON GRUNDY' set the same year, both appearing on 'New Alliance'. Best of the lot, however, was LANEGAN's windswept 'WINDING SHEET', an intense, largely acoustic collection featuring a cover of Leadbelly's 'WHERE DID YOU SLEEP LAST NIGHT' (as later covered in frightening style by KURT COBAIN). Co-produced by CHRIS CORNELL, the subsequent SCREAMING TREES effort, 'UNCLE ANAESTHESIA' (1991), saw the group moving towards a more overt 70's rock sound, while 'SWEET OBLIVION' (1992) saw PICKEREL replaced with BARRETT MARTIN on a more low-key set which stood at odds with the grunge tag unwillingly forced on the band. Augmented by such Seattle "luminaries" as TAD and DAN PETERS (MUDHONEY) along with DINOSAUR JR.'s J. MASCIS, LANEGAN cut an acclaimed solo follow-up, 'WHISKEY FOR THE HOLY GHOST' (1993), before beginning the long and arduous work on the material which would eventually come to make up 'DUST' (1996). Widely held up as the group's most affecting work to date, the George Drakoulias-produced album perfectly captured their threadbare grit and world-weary mysticism, the disparate elements of their sound finally fusing in harmony and exorcising the lingering spirit of grunge. During the latter part of the 90's, LANEGAN was again a solo artist, two albums for 'Sub Pop' ('Beggars Banquet' in Britain), 'SCRAPS AT MIDNIGHT' (1998) and 'I'LL TAKE CARE OF YOU' (1999), being released to mixed response and sliding out of the hard/grunge-rock circle. Meanwhile, VAN CONNOR was back in action via GARDENER, a collaborative duo that also featured Seaweed's AARON STAUFFER. In mid '99, this supergroup of sorts delivered their Lo-Fi psychedelic album for 'Sub Pop', 'NEW DAWNING TIME'. • **Covered:** SLIDE MACHINE (13th Floor Elevators). • **Note:** Not to be confused with the English band on 'Native' records.

Album rating: OTHER WORLDS mini (*4) / EVEN IF AND ESPECIALLY WHEN (*7) / INVISIBLE LANTERN (*5) / BUZZ FACTORY mini (*5) / UNCLE ANAESTHESIA (*6) / ANTHOLOGY – THE S.S.T. YEARS 1985-1989 compilation (*7) / SWEET OBLIVION (*7) / DUST (*9) / Mark Lanegan: THE WINDING SHEET (*6) / WHISKEY FOR THE HOLY GHOST (*7) / SCRAPS AT MIDNIGHT (*6) / I'LL TAKE CARE OF YOU (*8)

MARK LANEGAN (b.25 Nov'64) – vocals / **GARY LEE CONNER** (b.22 Aug'62, Fort Irwin, Calif.) – guitar, vocals / **VAN CONNER** (b.17 Mar'67, Apple Valley, Calif.) – bass, vocals / **MARK PICKEREL** – drums, percussion

not iss. Velvetone

1986. (m-lp) **CLAIRVOYANCE** [-] [ ]

S.S.T. S.S.T.

Feb 87. (m-lp/m-cd) *<SST/+C/CD 105>* **OTHER WORLDS** [-] [ ]
– Like I said / Pictures in my mind / Turning / Other worlds / Barriers / Now your mind is next to mine. *(UK-iss.May93; same as US)*

Sep 87. (lp/cd) *<(SST 132/+CD)>* **EVEN IF AND ESPECIALLY WHEN** [ ] [ ]
– Transfiguration / Straight out to any place / World painted / Don't look down / Girl behind the mask / Flying / Cold rain / Other days and different planets / The pathway / You know where it's at / Back together / In the forest. *(cd re-iss. May93; same)*

Jul 88. (12"ep; shared w/ BEAT HAPPENING) *(AGARR 020) <110>*
POLLY PEREGUIN E.P. [ ] [-]
(above issued on UK '53rd & 3rd') <US-iss.on 'Positive'>

Sep 88. (lp/c/cd) *<(SST 188/+C/CD)>* **INVISIBLE LANTERN** [ ] [ ]
– Ivy / Walk through to the other side / Line & circles / Shadow song / Grey diamond desert / Smokerings / The second I awake / Invisible lantern / Even if / Direction of the sun / Night comes creeping / She knows.

Mar 89. (m-lp/m-cd) *<(SST 248/+CD)>* **BUZZ FACTORY** [ ] [ ]
– Where the twain shall meet / Windows / Black sun morning / Too far away / Subtle poison / Yard trip / Flower web / Wish bringer / Revelation revolution / The looking glass cracked / End of the universe.

Glitterhouse Sub Pop

Dec 89. (d7"w /1-white) *(GR 80) <SP 48B>* **CHANGE HAS COME. / DAYS / / FLASHES. / TIME SPEAKS HER GOLDEN TONGUE** [ ] [ ]
(re-iss. Dec90 cd-ep+=; GRCD 80) – I've seen you before. *(re-iss. May93; same)*

— LEE CONNER also formed PURPLE OUTSIDE in 1990, releasing 'MYSTERY LANE'. Brother VAN with SOLOMON GRUNDY issued eponymous same year also for 'New Alliance'.

Epic Epic

Oct 90. (12"ep) *<73539>* **UNCLE ANAESTHESIA / WHO LIES IN DARKNESS. / OCEAN OF CONFUSION / SOMETHING ABOUT TODAY (numb inversion version)** [-] [ ]

Jun 91. (cd/c/lp) *(467 307-2/-4/-1) <EK 46800>* **UNCLE ANAESTHESIA** [ ] [ ] Mar91
– Beyond this horizon / Bed of roses / Uncle anaesthesia / Story of her fate / Caught between / Lay your head down / Before we arise / Something about today / Alice said / Time for light / Disappearing / Ocean of confusion / Closer.

— **BARRETT MARTIN** (b.14 Apr'67, Olympia, Washington) – drums repl. PICKEREL who later joined TRULY

Oct 92. (cd/c/lp) *(471 724-2/-4/-1) <48996>* **SWEET OBLIVION** [ ] [ ]
– Shadow of the season / Nearly lost you / Dollar bill / More or less / Butterfly / For celebrations past / The secret kind / Winter song / Troubled times / No one knows / Julie Paradise.

Feb 93. (12"ep/pic-cd-ep) *(658 237-6/-2)* **NEARLY LOST YOU. / E.S.K. / SONG OF A BAKER / WINTER SONG (acoustic)** [50] [-]

Apr 93. (7"pic-d) *(659 179-7)* **DOLLAR BILL. / (THERE'LL BE) PEACE IN THE VALLEY FOR ME (acoustic)** [52] [-]
(12"colrd+=/cd-s+=) *(659 179-6/-2)* – Tomorrow's dream.

Jul 96. (cd/c/lp) *(483 980-2/-4/-1) <64178>* **DUST** [32] [ ]
– Halo of ashes / All I know / Look at you / Dying days / Make my mind / Sworn and broken / Witness / Traveler / Dime western / Gospel plow.

Sep 96. (7") *(663 351-7)* **ALL I KNOW. / WASTED TIME** [ ] [ ]
(cd-s+=) *(663 351-2)* – Silver tongue.
(cd-s) *(663 351-5)* – ('A'side) / Dollar bill / Nearly lost you / Winter song (acoustic).

Nov 96. (7"white) *(663 870-7)* **SWORN AND BROKEN. / BUTTERFLY** [ ] [-]
(cd-s+=) *(663 870-2)* – Dollar bill (U.S. radio session) / Caught between – The secret kind (U.S. radio session).

— on a long holiday from each other, maybe for ever, VAN CONNER now moonlighting in VALIS with DAN PETERS of MUDHONEY, while BARRETT plays on tour with R.E.M., while joining PETER BUCK's supergroup, TUATARA. LANEGAN continued solo (see below)

– compilations, others, etc. –

Nov 91. (d-lp/d-cd) *<(SST 260/+CD)>* **ANTHOLOGY . . . THE S.S.T. YEARS 1985-1989** [ ] [ ]

MARK LANEGAN

— with on first **MICHAEL JOHNSON** – guitar / **JACK ENDINO** – bass, guitar / **KURT COBAIN** – guitar, vocals / **CHRIS NOVOSELIC** – bass / **MARK PICKEREL** – drums / **STEVE FISK** – keyboards

Glitterhouse Sub Pop

May 90. (red-lp/cd) *(GR 085/+CD) <SP 61>* **THE WINDING SHEET** [ ] [ ]
– Mockingbirds / Museum / Undertow / Ugly Sunday / Down in the dark / Wild flowers / Eyes of a child / The winding sheet / Woe / Ten feet tall / Where did you sleep last night? / Juarez / I love you little girl. *(c+cd+=)* – I love you little girl. *(re-iss. Apr94 & Oct99; same)*

Sep 90. (7") **DOWN IN THE DARK. /** [ ] [ ]

— next w / **J.MASCIS + MARK JOHNSON** (Dinosaur Jr.) / **TAD DOYLE** (Tad) / **DAN PETERS** (Mudhoney) / **KURT FEDORA** (Gobblehoof)

Sub Pop Sub Pop

Jan 94. (lp/cd) *<(SP/+CD 78249)>* **WHISKEY FOR THE HOLY GHOST** [ ] [ ]
– The river rise / Borracho / House a home / Kingdoms of rain / Carnival / Riding the nightingale / El Sol / Dead on you / Shooting gallery / Sunrise / Pendulum / Jesus touch / Beggar's blues. *(cd re-iss. Oct99; SPCD 132)*

May 94. (cd-ep) *<(SPCD 131-327)>* **HOUSE A HOME / SHOOTING GALLERY / UGLY SUNDAY / SUNRISE** [ ] [ ]

Beggars Banquet Sub Pop

Jul 98. (cd) *(BBQCD 204) <SP 419>* **SCRAPS AT MIDNIGHT** [ ] [ ]
– Hospital roll call / Hotel / Stay / Black bell ocean / Last one in the world / Wheels / Waiting on a train / Day and night / Praying ground / Because of this.

Sep 98. (7"colrd) *(BBQ 328)* **STAY. / SLIDE MACHINE** [ ] [ ]
(cd-s+=) *(BBQ 328CD)* – Death don't have no mercy.

Sep 99. (cd/lp) *(BBQ CD/LP 215)* **I'LL TAKE CARE OF YOU** [ ] [ ]
– Carry home / I'll take care of you / Shiloh town / Creeping coastline of lights / Ba dee da / Consider me / On Jesus program / Little Sadie / Together again / Shanty man's life / Boogie boogie.

SCREECHING WEASEL

Formed: Chicago, Illinois, USA ... mid-80's by 'Maximumrocknroll' columnist and RAMONES obsessed punk rocker BEN FOSTER (who soon adopted his WEASEL moniker). Although the line-up was to fluctuate wildly over the course of their career, the early 'WEASEL crew consisted – in addition to BEN himself – of JOHN JUGHEAD, STEVE CHEESE and VINNI BOVINE. An eponymous debut album arrived the following year on the 'Underdog' label, albeit in a limited pressing. More widely available was 'BOOGADABOOGADABOOGADA' (1989), by which point WARREN OZZFISH had joined up with BRIAN VERMIN following not long after (as replacements for BOVINE and CHEESE respectively). The pseudonymous japery continued unabated as OZZFISH was replaced by DANNY VAPID for a further string of EP's. With VAPID and VERMIN subsequently leaving to from SLUDGEWORTH, WEASEL temporarily split up the band only to later reform his shock punk-revival troops for a renewed assault on good taste: a line-up of WEASEL, JUGHEAD and VAPID were joined by new members DAVE NAKED and DAN PANIC for 'MY BRAIN HURTS' (1991). Further personnel changes ensued although a surprising surge in creativity saw the release of 'WIGGLE' (1992), 'RAMONES' (a cover of the entire classic debut by the infamous NY brudders) (1993), 'ANTHEM FOR A NEW TOMORROW' (1993) and 'HOW TO MAKE ENEMIES AND IRRITATE PEOPLE' (1994), the latter a farewell set recorded with the help of GREEN DAY's MIKE DIRNT. WEASEL then formed The RIVERDALES with VAPID and PANIC, a group which again took their influence from The RAMONES and were basically SCREECHING WEASEL in all but name. With JUGHEAD soon returning to the fold, the band reverted to the SCREECHING WEASEL moniker once more although this was to cause legal difficulties and eventually lead to yet another split. In the meantime, the 'BARK LIKE A DOG' album eventually found a sponsor in the shape of the 'Fat Wreck Chords' label. An umpteenth version of the 'WEASEL returned towards the turn of the decade with a further three albums, 'TELEVISION CITY DREAMS' (1998), 'EMO' (1999) and 'TEEN PUNKS IN HEAT' (2000). • **Covered:** RAMONES numbers by the score plus I CAN SEE CLEARLY (Johnny Nash) / AIN'T GOT NO SENSE (Kerr-Lewis-Mahon-Stipanitz) / I THINK WE'RE ALONE NOW (Tommy James & The Shondells) / I FALL TO PIECES (Cochran-Howard) / etc.

Album rating: SCREECHING WEASEL (*5) / BOOGADABOOGADABOOGADA! (*5) / MY BRAIN HURTS (*7) / WIGGLE (*6) / RAMONES (*5) / ANTHEMS FOR A NEW TOMORROW (*6) / HOW TO MAKE ENEMIES AND IRRITATE PEOPLE (*5) / KILL THE MUSICIANS compilation (*6) / BARK LIKE A DOG (*4) / TELEVISION CITY DREAMS (*4) / EMO (*5) / Riverdales: RIVERDALES (*3) / STORM THE STREETS (*5)

BEN WEASEL – vocals / **(JOHN) JUGHEAD** – guitar / **VINNIE BOVINE** – bass / **STEVE CHEESE** – drums

not iss. Underdog

1987. (lp) **SCREECHING WEASEL** [-] [ ]
– Say no! to authority / Wanna die / Society / California sucks / Murder in the Brady house / I can't stand myself / My song / High ambitions / March of the lawnmowers / Leave me alone / Don't touch my car / 7-11 / Cows / Work. *(UK cd-iss. Jan98 on 'Vermiform'; VML 072) <cd-iss. 1999 on 'Liberation'+=; 37813>* – Wavin' gerbs / Liar / O.M.W. / Clean-cut ass-hole / Raining needles / B.P.D. / Experience the

Ozzfish / Jockpunk / K-mart blues / Bates motel / Hardcore hippie / What is right / Yeah right / In the hospital / I feel like shit / I hate Led Zeppelin / American suicide / A political song for Screeching Weasel / Twinkie winkie / Stoned and stupid / Life sucks / I wanna be naked! / My right / Hey suburbia / Ashtray.

— **WARREN OZZFISH** – bass (ex-OZZFISH EXPERIENCE) repl. BOVINE

Wet Spots / Roadkill

Oct 88. (lp) *(WETLP 5) <001>* **BOOGADABOOGADABOOGADA!**
– Dingbat / Love / Zombie / This ain't Hawaii / We skate / Police insanity / Stupid over you / Runaway / I hate Led Zeppelin / My right / Nicaragua / Sunshine / I wanna be naked / Ashtray / American suicide / Psychiatrist / Mad at the paper boy / I love to hate / More problems / Supermarket fantasy / Holy hardcore / Professional distribution / Used cars / Hunter / I believe in UFO's / Hey suburbia. *<(re-iss. /UK-iss.1993/Jan97 on 'Lookout!' lp/c/cd; LOOKOUT 62/+C/CD)>*

— **BRIAN VERMIN** – drums; repl. CHEESE

— **DANNY VAPID** (b. SCHAFER) – bass (ex-IGOR SKULLS, ex-GENERATION WASTE vocalist) repl. WARREN

not iss. / Limited Potential

1989. (7"ep) **PUNKHOUSE EP** -

not iss. / Shred Of Dignity

1991. (7"ep) **PERVO-DEVO. /** -

— split when VERMIN + VAPID joined SLUDGEWORTH

— **BEN + JUGHEAD** re-formed with **DAVE NAKED** (b. ROBINSON) who was subsequently repl. by **VAPID (now on guitar, vocals) + JOHN PERSONALITY** (b. SULLIVAN) – bass, vocals (who repl. GUB) / **DAN PANIC** (b. LUMLEY) – drums

Lookout! / Lookout!

Nov 91. (lp/c/cd) *<LOOKOUT 50/+C/CD>* **MY BRAIN HURTS** -
– Making you cry / Slogans / Guest list / Veronica hates me / I can see clearly / Cindy's on methadone / Science of myth / What we hate / Teenage freakshow / Kamala's too nice / Don't turn out the lights / Fathead / I wanna be with you tonight / My brain hurts. *(UK-iss.Jan97; same as US)*

Nov 92. (lp/c/cd) *<LOOKOUT 63/+C/CD>* **WIGGLE** -
– Hanging around / I'm not in love / One step beyond / I was a high school psychopath / Crying in my beer / Slomotion / Like a parasite / Joanie loves Johnny / Second floor east / Automatic rejector / Jeannie's got a problem with her uterus / Sad little girl / Ain't got no sense / It's all in my head / Teenage slumber party / Danny is a wimp / Going home. *(UK-iss.Jan97; same as US)*

— **JOE KING** – guitar, vocals; repl. JOHN P
(below issued on 'Selfless')

Mar 93. (lp) *<(SLFS 17)>* **RAMONES** (covers) Nov92
– Blitzkreig bop / Beat on the brat / Judy is a punk / I wanna be your boyfriend / Chainsaw / Now I wanna sniff some glue / I don't wanna go down to the basement / Loudmouth / Havana affair / Listen to my heart / 53rd & 3rd / Let's dance / I don't wanna walk around with you / Today your love, tomorrow the world. *<(cd-iss. Nov98 as 'BEAT ON THE BRAT' on 'Lookout'+=; LK 213CD)>* – (Nothing's gonna) Turn me off (of . . ..) / Pretty girls don't talk to me / I don't care anymore / Why'd you have to leave.

— now without **JOE KING** (VAPID back to bass + BEN added guitar)

Oct 93. (lp/c/cd) *<LOOKOUT 76/+C/CD>* **ANTHEM FOR A NEW TOMORROW** -
– I'm gonna strangle you / Falling apart / Leather jacket / Rubber room / Inside out / Peter Brady / I, robot / Every night / Totally / Three sides / I don't wanna be friends / Cancer in my body / Thrift store girl / Panic / Trance / Claire Monet / A new tomorrow. *(UK cd-iss. Oct94 & Jan97; same as US)*

— **MIKE DIRNT** – bass, vocals (of GREEN DAY) repl. VAPID

Sep 94. (lp/c/cd) *<LOOKOUT 97/+C/CD>* **HOW TO MAKE ENEMIES AND IRRITATE PEOPLE** -
– Planet of the dupes / 86 / I love yer nuts on Monday / Johnny is that beer? / Slime pond / Burnt out squirrel / If I was Hugh / Nobody bites you / Da genitals / Smurf goddess / Kathy's not too light / Kathy's on the moon / I wrote ignatius J. Reilly. *(UK cd-iss. Jun95 & Jan97; same as US)*

— split early the following year

RIVERDALES

— were formed by **WEASEL (FOSTER), VAPID (SCHAFER) + PANIC (LUMLEY)**; latter also now a member of SQUIRTGUN and later COMMON RIDER

Sep 95. (cd/lp) *<(LOOKOUT/+LP 120)>* **THE RIVERDALES** Jul95
– Fun tonight / Judy go home / Wanna be alright / Back to you / Not over me / She's gonna break your heart / I think about you during the . . . . Rehabilitated / Plan 13 / Outta sight / In your dreams / Hampton beach.

Honest Don / Honest Don

Sep 97. (lp) *<(HDN 00010)>* **STORM THE STREETS**
– Make way / Mental retard / Don't let them beat my baby / Cementhead / Riverdale stomp / Dyna-mole / I will make it up to you / Blood on the ice / I don't wanna go to the party / Kick your head in / I accuse my parents / Boy in the plastic bubble / Give it up / I am not a freak.

SCREECHING WEASEL

— had re-formed inbetween above albums (trio + **JUGHEAD**)

Fat Wreck Chords / Fat Wreck Chords

Dec 96. (cd/c/lp) *<FAT 547 CD/MC/LP)>* **BARK LIKE A DOG**
– Get off my back / Cool kids / First day of summer / You'll be in my dreams today / You blister my paint / Stupid girl / Phasers on kill / Handcuffed to you / (She got) Electroshocked / It's not enough / I will always be there / You name is tattooed on my heart.

Lookout! / Lookout!

Jan 97. (7") *<(LOOKOUT 75)>* **YOU BROKE MY FUVKING HEART. /**

Jan 97. (7") *<(LOOKOUT 86)>* **SUZANNE'S GETTING MARRIED. /**

Jun 97. (7") *(VMFM 31)* **FORMULA 27. /** -
(above issued on 'Vermiform')

Feb 98. (12"ep/cd-ep) *<(LK 190/+CD)>* **MAJOR LABEL DEBUT EP** Jan98
– Last Janelle / D.I.Y. / Compact disc / Hey asshole / Racist society / Nightbreed.

Fat Wreck Chords / Fat Wreck Chords

Aug 98. (lp/cd) *<(FAT 572/+CD)>* **TELEVISION CITY DREAM**
– Count to three / Speed of mutation / Dummy up / Your morality / Dirty needles / Breaking point / Outside of you / We are the Generation X / Identity crisis / First day of winter / Plastic bag / I don't give a fuck / Only a test / Pervert at large / Burn it down.

Lookout! / Lookout!

May 99. (cd/lp) *<(LK 227 CD/LP)>* **EMO**
– Acknowledge / Sidewalk warrior / Static / Scene / Let go / Regroup / Passion / Linger / Last night / 2-7 split / On my own / Bark like a dog.

– compilations, etc. –

Jun 95. (cd) *Lookout!; <(LOOKOUT 95CD)>* **KILL THE MUSICIANS** Apr95
– Kamala's too nice / Punkhouse / Fathead / Good morning / I need therapy / I think we're alone now / Something wrong / This bud's for me / I wanna be homosexual / She's giving me the creeps / I fall to pieces / Celena / Radio blast / Girl next door / Achtung / Judy is a punk / Chainsaw / Now I wanna sniff some glue / Havana affair / Soap opera / Stab stab stab / Six a.m. / Hey suburbia / American dream / Mary was an anarchist / Around on you / Goodbye to you / Veronica hates me / I can see clearly / Supermarket fantasy / Science of myth. *<(re-iss. Jan97; same)>*

Feb 00. (d-cd) *Lookout; <(LK 239CD)>* **THANK YOU VERY LITTLE**

SEA HAGS

Formed: San Francisco, California, USA . . . 1985 by RON YOCOM, FRANKIE WILSEY, CHRIS SCHLOSSHARDT and ADAM MAPLES. An L.A. band in spirit if not geographical location, this notoriously debauched bunch of rock'n'roll retro-bates staggered onto the sleaze-rock scene in 1989 with their one and only album, 'THE SEA HAGS'. With a demo produced by KIRK HAMMETT (METALLICA) and an album produced by MIKE CLINK (of 'Appetite For Destruction' fame), the band were on track to follow in the footsteps of their heroes AEROSMITH with a low-slung set of crotch-level metal. Of course, it came as little surprise (given the band's reputation) when SCHLOSSARDT – the boyfriend at the time of The NYMPHS' INGER LORRE – was found dead from an alleged drug overdose, effectively leaving The SEA HAGS all washed up.

Album rating: SEA HAGS (*7)

RON YOCOM – vocals, guitar / **FRANKIE WILSEY** – guitar / **CHRIS SCHLOSSHARDT** – bass / **ADAM MAPLES** – drums

Chrysalis / Chrysalis

May 89. (lp/c/cd) *(CHR/ZCHR/CCD 1665) <41665>* **THE SEA HAGS**
– Half the way valley / Doghouse / Too much T-bone / Someday / Back to the grind / Bunkbed creek / In the mood for love / Miss fortune / All the time / Three's a charm / Under the night stars.

Jul 89. (7") *(CHS 3396)* **HALF THE WAY VALLEY. /**
(12"+=) *(CHS12 3396)* –

— split after SCHLOSSHARDT died of a drug overdose. WILSEY became WILSEX and joined ARCADE, a RATT off-shoot.

SEND NO FLOWERS

Formed: Bristol, England . . . 1993 as AGENT ORANGE by MATT BRADBURY and STEVE RENDELL. With SCOTT LEACH, DOMINIC GEARON and TOM BROMAN completing the line-up, the band subsequently earned themselves a deal with 'East West' following strong support from Kerrang! and a growing live reputation. Having created a uniquely English and consistently inventive take on the US grunge-metal sound, they debuted with the 'MONOTONY' EP in late '95, following it up with the 'DOWNFALL' single and a debut album, 'JUICE' (1996). This was promoted with the 'BITTER TASTE' EP, boasting an acerbic cover of The Beatles' classic 'EVERYBODY'S GOT SOMETHING TO HIDE EXCEPT ME AND MY MONKEY'. Unfortunately the album sales failed to meet major label expectations and SEND NO FLOWERS were ultimately sent packing. The band split in frustration although some members later released a one-off single, 'STRUNG OUT' under the SHINEOLA moniker in early '97.

Album rating: JUICE (*6)

MATT BRADBURY – vocals / **STEVE RENDELL** – guitar / **SCOTT LEACH** – guitar / **DOMINIC GEARON** – bass / **TOM BROMAN** – drums

East West / Atlantic

Oct 95. (cd-ep) *(EW 004CDX)* **MONOTONY E.P.**
– Monotony / Fireman / Scars / Yellowback.

Feb 96. (7"clear) *(EW 016X)* **DOWNFALL. / PROFIT MARGIN**
(cd-s+=) *(EW 016CDX)* –

Mar 96. (cd/c) *(0630 12954-2/-4)* **JUICE**
– Effervescent smile / Bitter taste / Porcelain / Fireman / Monotony / Candidate / Sepia / Wrong / Cold / Downfall / Animal feeder. *(c+=)* – Yellowback.

Jul 96. (7"orange-ep/cd-ep) *(EW 056/+CD)* **BITTER TASTE / EVERYBODY'S GOT SOMETHING TO HIDE EXCEPT ME AND MY MONKEY. / CANDIDATE (demo) / BITTER TASTE (demo)**

— parted company with the label and changed their name to . . .

SHINEOLA

Shine / not iss.

Jan 97. (7") *(SHINE 001)* **STRUNG OUT. / LESS** -

SENSER

Formed: Wimbledon, London, England . . . late 1990 initially as a trio by NICK MICHAELSON, KERSTIN HAIGH and JAMES BARRETT. With the line-up subsequently augmented by Saudi Arabian vocalist/rapper, HEITHAM AL-SAYED, DJ ANDY CLINTON, bassist/engineer HAGGIS and drummer JOHN MORGAN, SENSER developed into a formidably eclectic soundclash attracting such labelling attempts as "the British RAGE AGAINST THE MACHINE". They were certainly as fiercely indignant about political inertia and injustice, although they soundtracked their anger with a slightly more schizophrenic musical assault. Aligning themselves with the free festival/crusty scene, the group's first tour was supporting uber-hippies OZRIC TENTACLES in 1992, although the first SENSER single, 'EJECT' was more molten metal-hip hop than mushroom meandering. Released on 'Ultimate' in summer '93, the single enjoyed wildly enthusiastic reviews across the board, from the inkies to the metal and dance press. Likewise their two follow-up efforts, 'THE KEY' and 'SWITCH', the former scraping into the Top 50 while the latter featured a rivetting mash-up of Public Enemy's SLAYER-sampling classic, 'SHE WATCH CHANNEL ZERO'. It served as a brutal taster for the group's genre splicing debut album, 'STACKED UP' (1994), a groundbreaking collision of dub, rap, riffing, scratching and two-fingered defiance best evidenced in the frantic 'AGE OF PANIC', a subsequent single release later that summer. Despite continuing acclaim and riotous live appearances, however, the group splintered the following year with HEITHAM, MORGAN and HAGGIS forming LODESTAR alongside guitarist JULES HODGSON. Recruiting DJ AWE, SENSER carried on with its original core members, releasing a one-off single in summer '96, 'CHARMING DEMONS'. • **Songwriters:** Group except; SHE WATCH CHANNEL ZERO (Public Enemy). 'PEACE' was co-written w / TIM MORTON.

Album rating: STACKED UP (*8) / ASYLUM (*5)

HEITHAM AL-SAYED (b.1970, Riyadh, Saudi Arabia) – vocals, piano, bongos / **KERSTIN HAIGH** (b.1969, Balham, London) – vocals, flute / **NICK MICHAELSON** (b.1969, London) – guitar / **JAMES BARRETT** (b. 1970, London) – bass / **ANDY CLINTON** (b. 1969, Buckinghamshire) – DJ / **HAGGIS** (b. 1966, Edinburgh, Scotland) – bass, soundman, engineer / **JOHN MORGAN** (b. London, 1970) – drums

Ultimate | A&M

Jun 93. (12"/cd-s) *(Topp 016 t/cd)* **EJECT / DON'T LOSE YOUR SOUL. / (other mixes)** [ ] [-]

Sep 93. (7") *(Topp 019)* **THE KEY. / NO COMPLY** [47] [-]
(12"+=/cd-s+=) *(Topp 019 t/cd)* – ('A'-radio mix) / ('A'-Liquid lunch mix).

Mar 94. (7") *(Topp 022)* **SWITCH. / CHANNEL ZERO** [39] [-]
(12"+=/cd-s+=) *(Topp 022 t/cd)* – ('A'-Depth Charge mix) / Age of panic (Eat Static mix).

Apr 94. (cd/c/d-lp) *(Topp cd/mc/lp 008) <540347>* **STACKED UP** [4] [ ] Jan95
– States of mind / The key / Switch / Age of panic / What's going on / One touch one bounch / Stubborn / Door game / Peanut game / Peace / Eject / No comply / Worth.

Jul 94. (c-s) *(Topp 027mc)* **AGE OF PANIC. / LOOKING DOWN THE BARREL OF A GUN (live)** [52] [-]
(12"+=/c-s+=/cd-s+=) *(Topp 027 t/mcs/cd)* – ('A'-Sick man mix).

— now without HEITHAM, JOHN MORGAN + HAGGIS who formed LODESTAR with guitarist JULES HODGSON. An eponymous album in September '96, also for 'Ultimate' was another metallic-rap affair. The aforementioned were replaced by **DJ AWE** – scratching

Jul 96. (7"/c-s) *(Topp 045mc)* **CHARMING DEMONS. / HEADCASE** [42] [-]
(cd-s) *(Topp 045cd)* – ('A'-Keep on dreaming vocal mix) / ('A'-DJ Awe mix) / ('A'-Keep on dreaming dub mix).

— **PAUL SODEN** – drums; repl. MORGAN

Feb 98. (7") *(Topp 061)* **ADRENALIN. / ROWS OF PEOPLE** [ ] [-]
(cd-s) *(Topp 061cd)* – ('A'side) / ('A'-Ladyboy remix) / Spunk.

Mar 98. (7") *(Topp 066)* **BREED. / TRIED AND UNTESTED** [ ] [-]
(cd-s) *(Topp 066cd)* – ('A'side) / Breed (featuring DJ Awe & Kerstin) / 6's & 7's.
(12"/cd-s) *(Topp 066 t/cdx)* – ('A'side) / ('A'-Anorak mix) / ('A'-De Senser mix).

Apr 98. (cd/c/lp) *(Topp cd/mc/lp 064)* **ASYLUM** [73] [-]
– Book of flies / Charming demons / Adrenalin / Strange asylum / Burn out / Desensitised / Breed / Lizard / Oyster / Weatherman. *(d-cd-iss. Feb99 +=; Toppcdx 064)* – Charming demons (DJ Awe mix) / Eye laleid / Tried and untested / Om (Harry Hogg mix) / Rows of people / Gabba man.

SENTENCED

Formed: Finland . . . early 90's by MIIKA TENKULA and SAMI LOPAKKA. Staying true to the peculiar Scandinavian passion for all things (musically) fiendish, the Finns managed to release their debut album 'SHADOWS OF THE PAST', through an obscure French label. TANELI JARVA was added to the line-up for 1992's more fully realised follow-up set, 'NORTH FROM HERE', itself preceding a 1993 EP entitled 'THE TROOPER'. The fact that the lead track was a cover of the IRON MAIDEN classic only served to confirm the impression that the band were moving inexorably away from their black metal roots to a more accessible NWOBHM style. 'AMOK' (1995) was the last album to feature JARVA who was subsequently replaced by VILLE LAIHIALA for 1997's 'DOWN'. Following on from the 1998 retrospective, 'STORY: A RECOLLECTION', the veteran metal troupe entered the new millennium with 'CRIMSON' (2000).

Album rating: SHADOWS OF THE PAST (*4) / NORTH FROM HOME (*5) / AMOK (*6) / LOVE AND DEATH mini (*4) / DOWN (*6) / FROZEN (*5) / CRIMSON (*5)

MIIKA TENKULA – guitar / **SAMI LOPAKKA** – guitar

unknown | not iss.

1991. (cd) **SHADOWS OF THE PAST** [-] [-] French
– When the moment of death arrives / Rot to death / Disengagement / Rotting ways to misery / The truth / Suffocated beginning of life / Beyond the distant valleys / Under the suffer / Descending curtain of death. *(UK re-iss. Jan96 on 'Century Media'+=; CM 7716CD)* – Wings / In memoriam / Mythic silence (as they wander in the mist).

— added **TANELI JARVA** – vocals, bass

1992. (cd) **NORTH FROM HOME** [-] [-] Finland
– My sky is darker than thine / Wings / Fields of blood, harvester of hate / Capture of fire / Awaiting the winter frost / Beyond the wall of sleep / Northern lights / Epic / The trooper / Desert by night / In memoriam / Awaiting the winter frost. *<US-iss.1995 on 'Century Media'; 7746>*

Spinefarm | not iss.

Feb 94. (cd-ep) *(SPI 15CDS)* **THE TROOPER / DESERT BY NIGHT / IN MEMORIAM / AWAITING THE WINTER FROST** [ ] [-]

Century Media | Century Media

Apr 95. (cd/c/lp) *(CM 77076 CD/MC/LP) <7776>* **AMOK** [ ] [ ]
– The war ain't over! / Phenix / New age messiah / Forever lost / Funeral spring / Nepenthe / Dance on the graves / Moon magick / The golden stream of Lapland.

Oct 95. (m-cd) *(CM 77101) <7801>* **LOVE AND DEATH** [ ] [ ]
– The way I wanna go / Obsessed / Dreamlands / White wedding / Love and death.

— **VILLE LAIHIALA** – vocals; repl. JARVA

Nov 96. (cd) *(CM 77146CD) <7846>* **DOWN** [ ] [ ] Feb97
– Intro – The gate / Noose / Shadegrown / Bleed / Keep my grave open / Crumbling down (give up hope) / Sun won't shine / Ode to the end / 0132 / Warrior of life (reaper redeemer) / I'll throw the first rock.

Nov 97. (cd) *(CM 77199CD) <7899>* **STORY: A RECOLLECTION** (compilation) [ ] [ ] Jan98
– Noose / Nepenthe / Sun won't shine / Dance on the graves / The way I wanna go / White wedding / My sky is darker than thine / The trooper / New age messiah / Desert by night / No tomorrow / The truth / Awaiting the winter frost / Crumbling down (give up hope) / In memoriam.

Aug 98. (cd) *(CM 77246CD) <7946>* **FROZEN** [ ] [ ]
– Kaamos / Farewell / Dead leaves / For the love I bear / One with misery / The suicider / The rain comes falling down / Grave sweet grave / Burn / Drown together / Let go (the last supper) / Mourn.

Feb 00. (cd) *(77346-2) <8046>* **CRIMSON** [ ] [ ]
– Bleed in my arms / Home in despair / Fragile / No more beating as one / Broken / Killing me killing you / Dead moon rising / The river / One more day / With bitterness and joy / My slowing heart.

SEPTIC DEATH

Formed: San Francisco, California, USA . . . 1986 by PUSHEAD, an illustrator turned singer who worked for the likes of METALLICA and The MISFITS. The fact that there was plenty of support from the likes of JELLO BIAFRA, JAMES HETFIELD and Co, should have made the inspiringly-monikered SEPTIC DEATH a force to be reckoned with. From the early days at The Farm in San Francisco, this hardcore/punk combo (like FLIPPER and MILLIONS OF DEAD CHILDREN) were all the rage for just over half a decade. During this period, they released a couple of singles and two LP's, 'NOW THAT I HAVE THE ATTENTION' (1988) and 'GORE STORY' (1992). Recent interest has surrounded this cult band and a few more CD collections have been unearthed.

Album rating: NOW THAT I HAVE THE ATTENTION (*4) / GORE STORY (*4) / SOMEWHERE IN TIME live (*6) / ATTENTION compilation (*6)

PUSHEAD – vocals / + musicians

Pusmort | Pusmort

Dec 88. (7") *<(PUS007 03)>* **KICHIGAI. /** [ ] [ ]

Dec 88. (lp) *<(0012-01D)>* **NOW THAT I HAVE THE ATTENTION** [ ] [ ]
<re-iss. Apr95; same>

Lemon Flower | Lemon Flower

Jun 92. (lp) *<(LF 021)>* **GORE STORY** [ ] [ ]

— split after above

– compilations, etc. –

Oct 97. (cd) *Lost & Found; (LF 283CD)* **SOMEWHERE IN TIME (live at the Farm June 86)** [ ] [-]
– Negative threat / Child / Hardware / Fear / Poison mask / Control / Demon inside me / Quit / Insanity.

1990's. (cd) *Southern; <2301>* **ATTENTION** [-] [ ]
– Burial / Disinfect / Forest of the megalomaniac / Quit / Dream silent / Child / Terrorain / Thaw (cold world) / Poison mask / Hardware / Silence / Evolution garden / Unprotected games / Change / Demon / Control / Sweat of a nightmare / Core of reality / Negative threat / Never trust / Mental cancer / Fear / Advantage / Gore story / Kharma khamatic.

Feb 01. (cd) *Prank; <40>* **CHUMOKU** [-] [ ]

SEPULTURA

Formed: Belo Horizonte, Brazil . . . 1983 by brothers MAX and schoolboy IGOR CAVALERA alongside JAIRO T. and PAOLO JR., taking the name SEPULTURA from the MOTORHEAD song, 'Dancing On Your Grave' (Sepultura meaning 'grave' in Portuguese). Influenced largely by black metal bands such as VENOM, as well as British punk, SEPULTURA's earliest release was a split album with fellow Brazilian death metallers, OVERDOSE, entitled 'BESTIAL DEVASTATION' (1984). Another rudimentary thrash effort followed in 'MORBID VISIONS' (1985), again released on the small 'Cogumelo' label. It was nevertheless enough to see the band snapped up by 'Roadrunner', who released the 'SCHIZOPHRENIA' set in early '87. With ANDREAS KISSER replacing JAIRO T, SEPULTURA at last began to focus some of their unbridled sonic savagery, MAX's trademark growl assuming the bowel quaking chill it had always threatened as the ubiquitous Scott Burns worked his magic at the mixing desk. With BURNS in a production capacity, the masterful 'BENEATH THE REMAINS' (1989) finally signalled the arrival of a major force on the international metal scene. Breathtakingly dynamic, the album twisted and turned like a joyrider on speed, switching from breakneck thrash to pummeling sludge-riffing with untrammelled ferocity. Though you still couldn't actually make out what CAVALERA was saying, the unearthly roar of his voice was a revelation, almost an instrument in itself with its own rhythmic thrust. And while many thrash acts gave the impression of playing aggressively purely because that's what was expected of them, the likes of 'INNER SELF' and 'STRONGER THAN HATE' reeked of the genuine frustration, despair and disillusionment of growing up in an impoverished third world country. One of the last great thrash albums of the 80's, the record marked the end of the first stage in SEPULTURA's development; the next album, 'ARISE' (1991), was released as the scene was in its death throes and on this showing it was clear they weren't going to be left behind. On many tracks, the pace was slowed to a seismic turbo-Sabbath grind, gut-wrenchingly heavy and immensely powerful; SEPULTURA were redefining the boundaries of metal with each successive release. Already massive in Brazil (SEPULTURA had played the huge 'Rock In Rio' festival in 1990), the group narrowly missed the UK Top 10 with 'CHAOS A.D.' (1993). Taking the more basic approach of its predecessor even further, the record adopted a markedly more political lyrical stance than anything they'd released to date, the anger ferociously focused into bitter diatribes like 'SLAVE NEW WORLD'. Having previously injected a malignant power into MOTORHEAD's 'Orgasmatron' (which even LEMMY couldn't muster) a couple of years back, here SEPULTURA steamrollered NEW MODEL ARMY's 'The Hunt', proving that punk was as close as metal, if not more so, to the group's charred heart. But SEPULTURA really guaranteed their place in the rock hall of fame with 'ROOTS' (1996), voted by Kerrang! magazine as one of the best metal albums ever released. Stunning in both its stylistic breadth and unrelenting intensity, this was the masterpiece SEPULTURA had been working towards from the beginning of their career. Leaving most of their peers banging their heads on the starting post, the record embraced the cultural heritage of their native Brazil (with the help of rainforest tribe, the Xavantes) to concoct a haunting fusion of ethno-metal and hypnotic tribal spiritualism. The rock world was stunned when SEPULTURA disbanded early in 1997, one of the few metal acts to quit while they were on top (MAX has since formed SOULFLY, taking up where 'ROOTS' more rhythmic sound left off). However, that was certainly not the end, as SEPULTURA regrouped the following year complete with new frontman, DERRICK GREEN. An excellent comeback set, 'AGAINST', astonished most hardcore fans, GREEN's earthy vocal chords giving the group another dimension. • **Songwriters:** Group penned, except DRUG ME (Dead Kennedys) / SYMPTOM OF THE UNIVERSE (Black Sabbath) / CLENCHED FIST (Ratos De Porao) / INTO THE CRYPT OF RAYS + PROCREATION (OF THE WICKED) (Celtic Frost) / GENE MACHINE – DON'T BOTHER ME (Bad Brains).

Album rating: MORBID VISIONS (*4) / SCHIZOPHRENIA (*7) / BENEATH THE REMAINS (*9) / ARISE (*6) / CHAOS A.D. (*7) / ROOTS (*9) / BLOOD-ROOTED compilation (*7) / AGAINST (*8)

MAX CAVALERA (b.MASSIMILANO A. CAVALERA, 4 Aug'69) – vocals, guitar / **JAIRO T** – guitar/ **PAULO JR.** (b.PAULO XISTO PINTO JR., 30 Apr'69) – bass / **IGOR CAVALERA** (b.4 Sep'70) – drums

Cogumelo | not iss.

Nov 84. (m-lp; shared with OVERDOSE) *(803248)* **BESTIAL DEVASTATION** [-] [-] Brazil
– Bestial devastation / Antichrist / Necromancer / Warriors of death. *(cd-iss. Mar97 on 'Bestial'; SBD 001)*

Nov 85. (lp) **MORBID VISIONS** [-] [-]
– Morbid visions / Mayhem / Troops of doom / War / Crucifixion / Show me the wrath / Funeral rites / Empire of the damned / The curse. *(UK-iss.Apr89 on 'Shark' German; SHARK 004) (UK-iss.Nov91 on 'Roadracer' w/ 'BESTIAL DEVASTATION' cd/c/lp; RO 9276-2/-4/-1) (re-iss. Apr94 + Aug95 on 'Roadrunner'; same)*

— **ANDREAS KISSER** (b.24 Aug'68, Sao Bernado Do Campo, Brazil) – lead guitar; repl. JAIRO T

Shark | New Renaissance

Feb 88. (lp/cd) *(SHARK/+CD 006)* **SCHIZOPHRENIA** [-] [ ] German
– Intro / From the past comes the storms / To the wall / Escape to the void / Inquisition symphony / Screams behind the shadows / Septic schizo / The abyss / R.I.P. (Rest In Pain). *(c+=/cd+=)* – Troops of doom. *(re-iss. cd/c/lp Apr94 & Aug95 & May00 on 'Roadrunner'; RR 8764-2)*

Roadracer | Roadracer

Apr 89. (lp/c/cd) *<(RO 9511-1/-4/-2)>* **BENEATH THE REMAINS** [ ] [ ]
– Beneath the remains / Inner self / Stronger than hate / Mass hypnosis / Sarcastic existence / Slaves of pain / Lobotomy / Hungry / Primitive future. *(re-iss. Apr94 & Aug95 on 'Roadrunner'; same)*

Mar 91. (cd/c/lp/pic-lp) *<(RO 9328-2/-4/-1/-8)>* **ARISE** [40] [ ]
– Arise / Dead embryonic cells / Desperate cry / Murder / Subtraction / Altered state / Under siege (regnum Irae) / Meaningless movements / Infected voice. (pic-lp+=) – Orgasmatron. *(re-iss. Apr94 & Aug95 on 'Roadrunner'; same)*

Mar 91. (c-ep/12"ep/cd-ep) *(RO 2424-4/-6/-3)* **UNDER SIEGE (REGNUM IRAE). / TROOPS OF DOOM (re-recorded) / ORGASMATRON** [ ] [ ]

Feb 92. (c-ep/12"ep/cd-ep) *(RO 2406-4/-6/-3)* **ARISE. / INNER SELF (live) / TROOPS OF DOOM (live)** [ ] [ ]

Roadrunner | Epic

Sep 93. (7"pic-d-ep/c-ep/12"ep/cd-ep) *(RR 2382-7/-4/-6/-3)* **TERRITORY. / POLICIA / BIOTECH IS GODZILLA** [66] [ ]

Oct 93. (cd/c/lp) *(RR 9000-2/-4/-1) <57458>* **CHAOS A.D.** [11] [32]
– Refuse-Resist / Territory / Slave new world / Amen / Kaiowas / Propaganda / Biotech is Godzilla / Nomad / We who are not as others / Manifest / The Hunt / Clenched fist *(cd-tin-box.Mar94; 9000-0) (+=)* – Policia / Inhuman nature. *(re-iss. Aug95+=; same)* – Chaos B.C. / Kaiowas (tribal jam) / Territory (live) / Amen – Inner self (live). *(re-iss. Oct96; same)*

— Early in '94, MAX was arrested and fined for stamping on the Brazilian flag. He is said to have done it accidentally.

Feb 94. (7"ep/c-ep/12"ep/12"purple-ep/cd-ep/s-cd-ep) *(RR 2377-7/-4/-6/-8/-3/-5)* **REFUSE – RESIST. / INHUMAN NATURE / PROPAGANDA** [51] [ ]

May 94. (cd-s) *(RR 2374-3)* **SLAVE NEW WORLD / DESPERATE CRY** [46] [ ]
(c-ep/etched-12"ep/cd-ep) *(RR 2374-4/-8/-5)* – ('A'side) / Crucificados Pelo systema / Drug me / Orgasmatron (live).

Feb 96. (7"colrd) *(RR 2320-7)* **ROOTS BLOODY ROOTS. / SYMPTOM OF THE UNIVERSE** [19] [ ]
(cd-s) *(RR 2320-2)* – ('A'side) / Procreation (of the wicked) / Refuse – resist (live) / Territory (live).
(cd-s) *(RR 2320-5)* – ('A'side) / Propaganda (live) / Beneath the remains (live) / Escape to the void (live).

Feb 96. (cd/c/lp) *<(RR 8900-2/-4/-1)>* **ROOTS** [4] [27]
– Roots bloody roots / Attitude / Cut-throat / Ratamahatta / Breed apart / Straighthate / Spit / Lookaway / Dusted / Born stubborn / Jasco / Itsari / Ambush / Endangered species / Dictatorshit. *(cd+=)* – Chaos B.C. / Symptom of the universe / Kaiowas (live). *(re-iss. Oct96 as 'THE ROOTS OF SEPULTURA' cd w/ bonus cd of 20 unreleased + rare tracks; RR 8900-8)*

Aug 96. (7") *(RR 2314-7)* **RATAMAHATTA. / MASS HYPNOSIS (live)** [23] [ ]
(cd-s) *(RR 2314-2)* – ('A'side) / War / Slave new world (live) / Amen – Inner self (live).
(cd-s) *(RR 2314-5)* – ('A'side) / War / Roots bloody roots (demo) / Dusted (demo).

Dec 96. (7") *(RR 2299-7)* **ATTITUDE. / DEAD EMBRYONIC CELLS (live)** [46] [ ]
(cd-s) *(RR 2299-2)* – ('A'side) / Lookaway (master vibe mix) / Mine.
(cd-s) *(RR 2299-5)* – ('A'side) / Kaiowas (tribal jam) / Clenched fist (live) / Biotech is Godzilla (live).

— split late '96, when MAX was told he was no longer wanted. He subsequently formed SOULFLY, while SEPULTURA went to ground for a year. They returned with a new singer **DERRICK GREEN** (ex-ALPHA JERK)

Oct 98. (cd/c/lp) *(<RR 8700-2/-4/-1>)* **AGAINST** [40] [82]
– Against / Choke / Rumors / Old earth / Floaters in mud / Boycott / Tribus / Common bonds / F.O.E. / Reza / Unconscious / Kamaitachi / Drowned out / Hatred aside / T3rcermillennium.

Nov 98. (cd-s) *(RR 2219-3)* **CHOKE / GENE MACHINE (demo) / DON'T BOTHER ME (demo) / AGAINST (demo)** [ ] [ ]

Jul 99. (cd-s) *(RR 2169-3)* **AGAINST / THE WASTE / TRIBUS / COMMON BONDS (Alternate mix)** [ ] [ ]

– compilations, etc. –

Nov 89. (cd) *Shark; (CDSHARK 012)* **MORBID VISIONS / CEASE TO EXIST** [-] [-] German

May 90. (c) *Shark; (SHARKMC 017)* **SCHIZOPHRENIA / MORBID VISIONS** [-] [-] German

Aug 97. (cd) *Roadrunner; (<RR 8821-2>)* **BLOOD ROOTED** [ ] [ ]
– Procreation (of the wicked) / Inhuman nature / Policia / War / Criucificados pelo sistema / Symptom of the universe / Mine / Lobotomy / Dusted / Roots bloody roots / Drug me / Refuse – resist / Slave new world / Propaganda / Beneath the remains / Escape to the void / Kaiowas / Clenched fist / Biotech is Godzilla. *(re-iss. May00; same)*

May 00. (cd) *Roadrunner; <(RR 8765-2)>* **MORBID VISIONS / BESTIAL DEVASTATION** [ ] [ ]

NAILBOMB

MAX CAVALERA + ALEX NEWPORT (of FUDGE TUNNEL)

Roadrunner | Epic

Mar 94. (cd/c/lp) *(RR 9055-2/-4/-1)* **POINT BLANK** [62] [ ]
– Wasting away / Vai toma no cu / 24 hour bullshit / Guerillas / Blind and lost / Sum of your achievements / Cockroaches / For f***'s sake / World of shit / Exploitation / Religious cancer / Shit panata / Sick life. *(re-iss. Aug95; same)*

Oct 95. (cd/c/lp) *(RR 8910-2/-4/-1)* **PROUD TO COMMIT COMMERCIAL SUICIDE** [ ] [ ]
– Wasting away / Guerrillas / Cockroaches / Vai toma no co / Sum of your achievements / Religious cancer / Police truck / Exploitation / World of shit / Blind and lost / Sick life / While you sleep, I destroy your world / Zero tolerance.

SEVENDUST

Formed: Atlanta, Georgia, USA ... 1994 initially as CRAWLSPACE by MORGAN ROSE, VINCE HORNSBY, CLINT LOWERY, JOHN CONNOLLY and LAJON WITHERSPOON, the latter a black funk singer poached from his brother COREY's band (now a STUCK MOJO member). One single, 'MY RUIN' was independently issued under this moniker (also appeared on V/A set 'Mortal Kombat: More Kombat') and was to subsequently surface on the SEVENDUST debut album. Under the wing of manager, JAY JAY FRENCH (ex-TWISTED SISTER), the band signed to 'TVT', although it was by sheer chance as the label's A&R men were detoured by a hard-of-hearing cab driver who took them to one of their gigs, not a strip club as requested. Their bruising, aggro-rock sound (with similarities between LIVING COLOUR and/or MINISTRY) was soon being given radio airplay in the States via an excellent eponymous set in '97. A second set, 'HOME' (1999) repeated the riff-laden formula, only this time it payed off with a US

Top 20 placing. MORGAN, meanwhile (who'd married COAL CHAMBERS' RAYNA FOSS), was possibly up for a bit of paternity leave following the subsequent birth of their new baby.

Album rating: SEVENDUST (*6) / HOME (*6)

LAJON WITHERSPOON – vocals / **CLINT LOWERY** – guitar / **JOHN CONNOLLY** – guitar / **VINCE HORNSBY** – bass / **MORGAN ROSE** – drums

TVT TVT

Sep 98. (cd/c) *<(TVT 5730-2/-4)>* **SEVENDUST** ☐ ☐ Apr97
– Black / Bitch / Terminator / Too close to hate / Wired / Prayer / Face / Speak / Will it bleed / My ruin / Born to die.

Loud-Epic TVT

Oct 99. (cd/c) *(4961579) <5820>* **HOME** ☐ 19
– Home / Denial / Headtrip / Insecure / Reconnect / Waffle / Rumble fish / Licking cream / Grasp / Crumble / Feel so / Grasshopper / Bender.

SEVEN MARY THREE

Formed: Orlando, Florida, USA . . . 1992 by the 4-piece of JASON ROSS, JASON POLLOCK, CASEY DANIEL and GITI KHALSA. Signed to 'Atlantic' records on the strength of an independently released debut 'CHURN' (1995), the band cruised into the US Top 40 with the 'CUMBERSOME' single. Taken from the Top 30 album, 'AMERICAN STANDARD', the track's title accurately described the band's post-grunge sound, akin to a heavy COUNTING CROWS or even COLLECTIVE SOUL. The aforesaid album caused considerable controversy with artwork depicting a farmer about to behead a chicken with an axe. In the summer of '97, SMT returned with a third effort, 'ROCKCROWN', although this only managed to dent the US Top 75.

Album rating: CHURN (*6) / AMERICAN STANDARD (*7) / ROCKCROWN (*6) / ORANGE AVE. (*5)

JASON ROSS – vocals, guitar / **JASON POLLOCK** – guitar / **CASEY DANIEL** – bass / **GITI KHALSA** – drums

not iss. Independent

1995. (cd) **CHURN** - ☐

Mammoth–Atlantic Mammoth–Atlantic

Apr 96. (7"/c-s) *(A 5688/+C) <98111>* **CUMBERSOME. / SHELF LIFE** ☐ 39 Jan96
(cd-s+=) *(A 5688CD)* – ('A'acoustic).

Apr 96. (cd/c) *<(7567 92633-2/-4)>* **AMERICAN STANDARD** ☐ 24 Jan96
– Cumbersome / Favorite dog / Punch in punch out / Margaret / Devil boy / My my / Lame / Anything / Headstrong / Roderigo / Water's edge.

Jun 97. (cd/c) *<(7567 83018-2/-4)>* **ROCKCROWN** ☐ 75
– Lucky / Rockcrown / Needle can't burn / Honey of generation / Home stretch / People like new / Make up your mind / Gone away / Times like these / I could be wrong / Angry blue / Houdini's angels / This evening's great excuse / Player piano / Oven.

Jul 98. (cd,c) *<83114>* **ORANGE AVE.** - ☐
– Peel / Over your shoulder / Chasing you / Each little mystery / In-between / Joliet / Super-related / Flagship Eleanor / Southwestern state / Hang on / Blessing in disguise / Devil's holy joke.

Nov 98. (cd-s) **OVER YOUR SHOULDER** - ☐

707

Formed: Detroit, Michigan, USA . . . 1979 by KEVIN RUSSELL, PHIL BRYANT and JIM McCLARTY. Signed to a domestic deal with 'Casablanca' records, 707's eponymous debut introduced the band's sophisticated, distinctively Amercian blend of heavy pomp-rock. Despite employing a harder-edged approach, 'THE SECOND ALBUM' (1981) hit the US Top 200, even spawning a Top 60 hit in 'I COULD BE GOOD FOR YOU'. Adding KEVIN CHALFANT and TOD HOWARTH, the band switched labels to 'Boardwalk' for the Keith Olsen-produced 'MEGA FORCE' (1982) set, its title track (also the theme tune for the 'Megaforce' film) providing 707 with another minor chart hit. This marked the end of the road for the band, however, as internal tensions finally resulted in a split. While HOWARTH went on to play with FREHLEY'S COMET, CHALFONT subsequently backed up KIM CARNES before augmenting NIGHT RANGER. In the early 90's he was instrumental in forming hard rock act, The STORM.

Album rating: 707 (*4) / THE SECOND ALBUM (*4) / MEGA FORCE (*4)

KEVIN RUSSELL – vocals, guitar / **PHIL BRYANT** – bass, vocals / **JIM McCLARTY** – drums, percussion / **DUKE McFADDEN** – keyboards, guitar, vocals

not iss. Casablanca

Feb 80. (lp) *<7213>* **707** - ☐
– I could be good for you / Let me live my life / One way highway / Save me / You who needs to know / Slow down / Feel this way / Waste of time / Whole lot better.

Sep 80. (7") *<2280>* **I COULD BE GOOD FOR YOU. / LET ME LIVE MY LIFE** - 52

— now without McFADDEN

Jan 81. (lp) *<7248>* **THE SECOND ALBUM** - ☐
– Tonite's your nite / Millionaire / Live with the girl / Strings around my heart / Pressure rise / Rockin' is easy / City life / Life without her / Love on the run / The party's over.

— added **KEVIN CHALFANT** – vocals / **TOD HOWARTH** – keyboards, guitar, vocals

not iss. Boardwalk

Jun 82. (lp) *<NB1 33253>* **MEGA FORCE** - ☐
– Mega force / Can't hold back / Get to you / Out of the dark / Hell or high water / We will last / Hello girl / Write again / No better feeling / Heartbeat.

Jun 82. (7") *<146>* **MEGA FORCE. / HELL OR HIGH WATER** - 62

Sep 82. (7") *<153>* **WE WILL LAST. / NO BETTER FEELING** - ☐

Nov 82. (7") *<163>* **OUT OF THE DARK. / NO BETTER FEELING** - ☐

— folded in 1983, HOWARTH went on to play with FREHLEY'S COMET. CHALFANT went onto back singer KIM CARNES and augment the group NIGHT RANGER. He subsequently helped form The STORM in the early 90's.

7 SECONDS

Formed: Reno, Nevada, USA . . . 1981 by KEVIN SECONDS, STEVE YOUTH and drummer TROY MOWAT, the latter being deposed first by TOM BORHINO and then BIX BIGLER. After completing a couple of self-financed demo cassettes for 'Vicious Scam', the group signed to JELLO BIAFRA's 'Alternative Tentacles' label – then still in its infancy – for a solitary EP, 'SKIN, BRAINS AND GUTS'. Released in summer '82, the record's lyrical concerns were reflected in such archetypal hardcore titles as 'REDNECK SOCIETY', 'ANTI-KLAN' and 'RACISM SUCKS'. Moving on to the 'Better Youth Organisation' (also home to YOUTH BRIGADE), 7 SECONDS continued their crusade through the mid-80's with a trio of albums, 'THE CREW' (1984), 'WALK TOGETHER ROCK TOGETHER' (1985) and 'NEW WIND' (1986), the last of which saw the return of TROY. Like many US hardcore bands, they gravitated towards a more accessible punk-metal crossover as the 80's wore on, signing to 'Restless' ('G.W.R.' in the UK) for a further two sets. More independent releases followed in the early 90's, although 7 SECONDS finally hit paydirt with a major label deal courtesy of 'Epic'. Despite criticism that their music had been progressively diluted, the veteran punksters kept the faith with 'THE MUSIC, THE MESSAGE' (1995).

Album rating: THE CREW (*5) / WALK TOGETHER ROCK TOGETHER mini (*4) / NEW WIND (*4) / OLD SCHOOL compilation (*5) / THE MUSIC, THE MESSAGE (*4)

KEVIN SECONDS – vocals, guitar / **STEVE YOUTH** – bass / **BIX BIGLER** – drums; repl. TROY (other early drummer, TOM BORHINO)

— issued 2 cassettes on 'Vicious Scam' US

not iss. Alternative Tentacles

Jul 82. (7"ep) *<VIRUS 15>* **SKIN, BRAINS AND GUTS** - ☐
– Skin, brains and guts / No authority / Redneck society / Baby games / Racism sucks / This is my life / Anti-klan / I hate sports / We're gonna fight.

Better Youth Org'n Better Youth Org'n

Sep 84. (lp/c) *<(BYO 5/+C)>* **THE CREW** ☐ ☐
– The crew / Clenched fists / Black eyes / Colourblind / Aim to please / Boss / Young 'til I die / Red and black / Die hard / I have a dream / Bully / Trust / Here's your warning / Spread / Not just boys fun / Rock together. *<US cd-iss. 1989 inc. live tracks; BYO 5CD>* – Here's your warning / Definite choice / Not just boys fun / This is the angry (part 2) / Straight on / You lose / What if there's a war in America.

Jun 85. (m-lp/m-c) *<(BYO 10/+C)>* **WALK TOGETHER ROCK TOGETHER** ☐ ☐
– Regress no way / We're gonna fight it / In your face, spread / 99 red balloons / Remains to be seen / Walk together, rock together / How do you think you'd feel / Strength.

— **TROY MOWAT** – drums; returned to repl. BIX

Sep 86. (lp/c) *<(BYO 14/+C)>* **NEW WIND** ☐ ☐

G.W.R. Restless

1988. (lp) *(GWLP 49) <72276-1>* **OURSELVES** ☐ ☐
– Escape and run / Far away friends / Save ourselves / If I abide / Wish I could help / Sleep / Sister / Middleground / When one falls / Some sort of balance / Seven years. *(cd-iss. Jul95 on 'Restless'; same as US)*

1989. (lp) *<72344-1>* **SOULFORCE REVOLUTION** - ☐
– Satyagraha / Busy like people / I can sympathise / It makes a lot sense now / Mother's day / Tribute freedom landscape / Copper ledge / Tickets to a better place / 4 a.m. in Texas / Soul to keep. *(UK cd-iss. Jul95 on 'Restless; same as US)*

not iss. Headhunter

Jul 93. (cd/c/lp) *<HED 028-2/-4/-1>* **OUT THE SHIZZY** - ☐
– Shizzy / His way, go away / Happy rain / Free to space / Weak link / Reuben said / Yet again / G / Widespread / Motionary / Naked / Nate / Some kind of sign.

Epic Epic

Dec 95. (cd/c) *<(481454-2/-4)>* **THE MUSIC, THE MESSAGE** ☐ ☐
– Ghost / Such and such / The music, the message / Kinda future / My gravity / See you tomorrow / Get a different life / Talkbox / My list / First ya told us / Born without a mind / Punk rock teeth / Girl song / I can remember / Even better plan / The kids are united.

– compilations, etc. –

1988. (lp) *Head Hunter;* **OLD SCHOOL** (early material) - ☐

Nov 95. (cd) *Headhunter; <053>* **ALT.MUSIC.HARDCORE** - ☐
– ('SKINS, BRAINS & GUTS') + 5 years of lies / Drug control / Bottomless pit / Fight your own fight / Committed for life / This is the angry / Aggro / War in the head / The kids are united.

7 YEAR BITCH

Formed: Seattle, Washington, USA . . . 1991 by SELENE VIGIL, STEFANIE SARGENT, ELIZABETH DAVIS and VALERIE AGNEW. Not short of selling points, this all-female Seattle act generated an immediate buzz with their debut single, 'LORNA', the girls' righteously browned off, distortion-drenched racket earning them fawning column inches and a PEARL JAM support slot. Even the shock death of SARGENT wasn't enough to halt the band's momentum and after a period of uncertainty they decided to carry on with new guitarist ROICI DUNNE. In the meantime the ladies released a compilation – dedicated to SARGENT – of their work to date, 'SICK 'EM', on the local 'C/Z' label; despite shying away from any real connection with the militant Riot Grrrl movement, titles like 'DEAD MEN DON'T RAPE' spelled out in black and white exactly where this band was coming from. A debut album proper, 'VIVA ZAPATA!' finally arrived in 1994, its title and subject matter no doubt influenced by sterling politico-rap tourmates RAGE AGAINST THE MACHINE. With encouraging reviews and a further round of high profile touring it was only a matter of time before the girls moved on up to a major, 'Atlantic' clinching their signatures and releasing follow-up set, 'GATO NEGRO' in 1996. • **Covered:** IT'S TOO LATE (Jim Carroll) / GO! (Tones On Tails).

Album rating: SICK 'EM (*6) / VIVA ZAPATA! (*6) / GATO NEGRO (*6)

SELENE VIGIL – guitar / **STEFANIE SARGENT** – guitar / **ELIZABETH DAVIS** – bass / **VALERIE AGNEW** – drums

not iss. unknown

1991. (7") **LORNA. /** [-] [ ]

10 Past 12 10 Past 12

Jul 92. (10"pic-ep) *<(DUMP 009)>* **ANTIDISESTABLISHMENTARIANISM EP** [ ] [ ]
– 8 ball / No fuckin' war / You smell / Lonely / Dead men don't rape.

C/Z C/Z

Oct 92. (lp/cd) *<(CZ 048/+CD)>* **SICK 'EM** [ ] [ ]
– Chow down / Tired of nothing / Knot / In lust you trust / Sink / Gun / Lorna / You smell lonely / No fucking war / Dead men don't rape / 8-ball deluxe / Can we laugh now?

—— tragically, STEFANIE died a month before above release date

—— she was repl. by **ROICI DUNNE** – guitar

May 95. (cd) *<CZ 078>* **VIVA ZAPATA!** [-] [ ]
– The scratch / Hip like junk / M.I.A. / Derailed / Cats meow / Rock a bye / It's too late / Damn good and well / Kiss my ass goodbye / Icy blue / Get lit.

—— (mid '96) **LISA FAYE** – guitar (ex-MUDWIMMIN) repl. DUNNE

not iss. Atlantic

Mar 96. (cd/c/lp) *<82873-2/-4/-1>* **GATO NEGRO** [-] [~]
– The history of my future / Crying shame / Disillusion / Deep in the heart / The midst / 24,900 miles per hour / Whoopie cat / Miss understood / Sore subject / Rest my head / 2nd hand / Jack.

not iss. Man's Ruin

1996. (7") *<MR 026>* **MISS UNDERSTOOD. / GO!** [-] [ ]

—— disbanded after above

SEX GANG CHILDREN

Formed: London, England . . . 1982 out of PANIC BUTTON by ANDI SEX GANG and DAVE ROBERTS, who in turn recruited TERRY McLEAY and ROB STROUD. Rapidly building up a cult following, this bunch of ghoulish goth-fetish merchants (who took their offensive moniker from a line in a William Burroughs novel) released a self-financed, cassette-only live album, 'NAKED', later the same year. An appearance at Leeds' Futurama festival helped push their debut vinyl release, 'BEASTS!', an EP consisting mainly of reworked material from 'NAKED' and their first release for 'Illuminated'. A follow-up single, 'INTO THE ABYSS' rounded the year off as the band became indie chart favourites with their patented brand of scratchy guitar, shrieking, often unintelligible vocals and general musical chaos. 'SEBASTIANE', the first single from debut album, 'SONG AND LEGEND' (1983) threw grating violin into the already crowded mix courtesy of MARC & THE MAMBAS member, GINI HEWES. 1983 also saw the release of a compilation album put together by ROBERTS; entitled 'THE WHIP', it featured a duet between ANDI and MARC ALMOND, 'THE HUNGRY YEARS'. The subsequent departure of STROUD was temporarily solved by the recruitment of ex-THEATRE OF HATE man, NIGEL PRESTON; he stayed for one single, 'MAURITIA MAYER', released on 'Clay' records after The 'GANG were dropped by 'Illuminated'. Matters became even more confused as another temp sticksman, DEATH CULT's RAY MONDO, was deported as the band returned from an American tour. To add insult to injury, ROBERTS jumped ship for his new band, the catchily monikered CARCRASH INTERNATIONAL, before 1983 was out. ANDI and McLEAY soldiered on briefly with new recruits CAM CAMPBELL and KEVIN MATTHEWS before Mr SEX GANG struck out for a solo career and effectively brought the band to an end. Renewed interest following the release of a retrospective album in 1991 led to a short-lived Stateside reformation, an independently released set of new material, 'MEDEA', surfacing in 1993. • **Trivia:** Produced by NICKY GARRETT (ex-UK SUBS) early on, before TONY JAMES (ex-GENERATION X) took over.

Album rating: SONG AND LEGEND (*4) / BEASTS (*3) / ECSTASY AND VENDETTA OVER NEW YORK (*3) / THE HUNGRY YEARS: BEST OF THE SEX GANG CHILDREN compilation (*6) / Andi SexGang: BLIND! (*5) / ARCO VALLEY (*3)

ANDI SEX GANG (b. ANDREW HAYWARD) – vocals, guitar / **TERRY MacLEAY** (b. Scotland) – guitar / **DAVE ROBERTS** – bass, acoustic guitar / **ROB STROUD** – drums

Illuminated not iss.

Jun 82. (12"ep) *(ILL 11-12)* **BEASTS** [ ] [-]
– Cannibal queen / Times of our lives / Sense of elation. *(re-iss. Feb85)*

Oct 82. (7") *(ILL 15)* **INTO THE ABYSS. / DEICHE** [ ] [-]

Mar 83. (7") *(ILL 20)* **SONG AND LEGEND. / SEBASTIANE** [ ] [-]

Mar 83. (lp) *(JAMS 666)* **SONG AND LEGEND** [ ] [-]
– The crack-up / German nun / State of mind / Sebastiane / Draconian dream / Shout and scream / Killer K / Cannibal queen / Kill machine / Song and legend. *(re-iss. Apr86 on 'Dojo' lp/cd; DOJO LP/CD 16)*

Jun 83. (12"m) *(ILL 22-12)* **SEBASTIANE / MONGOLIA. / WHO ON EARTH CAN THAT BE** [ ] [-]

—— **NIGEL PRESTON** – drummer (ex-THEATRE OF HATE) repl. STROUD who formed Huddersfield outfit AEMOTU CRII, then PINK AND BLACK

Clay not iss.

Sep 83. (7"/ext.12") *(CLAY/12CLAY 27)* **MAURITIA MAYER. / CHILDREN'S PRAYER** [ ] [-]

—— **RAY MONDO** – drums (ex-DEATH CULT) repl. PRESTON who was swopped into same band

—— DAVE ROBERTS left late '83 to form CAR CRASH INTERNATIONAL. Trimmed to just ANDI and TERRY with new bassist **CAM CAMPBELL** and drummer **KEVIN MATTHEWS** when RAY was deported back to home country Sierra Leone. They split in 1984, but got the 7-year itch and reformed due to support in the US. **ANDI / DAVE** (now on guitar) / **GERALD SANTANA** (b. USA) – bass / + drummer

– compilations, etc. –

Dec 83. (lp) *Illuminated; (JAMS 34)* **BEASTS** [ ] [-]
– Beasts / Cannibal queen / Who on Earth can that be / Sense of elation / Into the abyss / Deiche / Salvation / Mongolia / Times of our lives. *(re-iss. Aug86 on 'Dojo'; DOJOLP 30)*

Jul 84. (12") *Illuminated; (ILL 39-12)* **DEICHE. / DRACONIAN DREAM** [ ] [-]

Aug 84. (c) *R.O.I.R.; (A 127)* **ECSTASY AND VENDETTA OVER NEW YORK (live)** [ ] [-]
(cd-iss. Aug94 on 'Cleopatra'; CLEO 3833)

Sep 85. (12") *Saderal; (SLS 12-001)* **DEICHE. / BEASTS** [ ] [-]

Apr 86. (lp/c) *Dojo; (DOJO LP/TC 13)* **RE-ENTER THE ABYSS** [ ] [-]

May 88. (lp) *Arkham House; (AHLP 1001)* **NIGHTLAND USA, 1983 (live)** [ ] [-]

May 88. (lp) *Sex; (SEX 2)* **LIVE IN LONDON AND GLASGOW (live)** [ ] [-]

Dec 91. (cd/lp) *Receiver; (RR CD/LP 149)* **THE HUNGRY YEARS: THE BEST OF THE SEX GANG CHILDREN** [ ] [-]

May 94. (cd) *Cleopatra; <(CLEO 6957)>* **PLAY WITH CHILDREN** [ ] [ ]

Aug 99. (cd) *Dressed To Kill; <(DRESSCD 156)>* **DEICHE** [ ] [ ]
– Deiche / Salvation / Mongolia / Times of our lives / Beasts / Cannibal queen / Who on earth can that be? / Sense of elation / Into the abyss / People with dirty faces.

Aug 99. (cd) *Dressed To Kill; <(DRESSCD 157)>* **POP UP** [ ] [ ]

Sep 99. (cd) *Dressed To Kill; <(DRESSCD 187)>* **MEDEA** [ ] [ ]
– Barbarossa / Guy wonder / Alien baby / Medea / Giaconda smile / Smile / Arms of Cicero / Boss and beauty / Shattered room / Sugar pill.

Sep 99. (cd) *Dressed To Kill; <(DRESSCD 189)>* **VEIL** [ ] [ ]

Sep 00. (cd) *Metrodome; (MCCD 0010)* **DEMONSTRATION** [ ] [-]

Apr 01. (cd) *Triple X; (<TX 60026CD>)* **EMPYRE AND FALL** [ ] [ ]
– State of mind / Killer K / Shout and scream / Sebastiane / Beats / Into the abyss (extended) / Deiche / Times of our lives / Draconian dream.

ANDI SEX GANG

Illuminated not iss.

Sep 84. (7") *(ILL 52)* **LES AMANTS D'UN JOUR. / OH HENRY** [ ] [-]

Jan 85. (lp) *(JAMS 48)* **BLIND** [ ] [-]
– Welcome to my world / Boss and beauty / Dead metal / Ecstasy and vendetta / Ida-ho / Last chants for the slow dance / The quick gas gang / Dying fall / Immigrant / Oh Henry / I've done it all before / Strike blind / Gas reprise. *(cd-iss. Jun93 on 'Trident'; TMI 1) (<re-iss. cd Mar94 on 'Cleopatra'; CLEO 5122-2>) (cd re-iss. Aug99 on 'Dressed To Kill'; DRESS 186)*

Mar 85. (7") *(ILL 53)* **IDA-HO. / QUICK GAS GANG** [ ] [-]
(12"+=) *(ILL 53-12)* – You don't know me.

Revolver not iss.

Sep 86. (12"m) *(12REV 27)* **THE NAKED AND THE DEAD. / YOU DON'T KNOW ME / THE QUICK AND THE DEAD** [ ] [-]
below featured MICK RONSON – guitar

Jungle Jungle

Nov 88. (7") *(JUNG 42)* **SEVEN WAYS TO KILL A MAN. /** [ ] [-]
(12"+=) *(JUNG 42T)* –

Nov 88. (lp) *(FREUD 24) <51185>* **ARCO VALLEY** [ ] [ ] Feb89
– 7 ways to kill a man / Queen of broken dreams / Power waits / Jesus phoned / Les amants d'un jour / Rock revo / Station 5 / Christian circus Joe / Assassin years / Belgique blue. *(re-iss. Jul89 c/cd; FREUD/+C/CD 24) (cd re-iss. Aug95 on 'Triple X'; TX 511852CD) (cd re-iss. Oct99 on 'Metrodome'; METRO 241)*

Mar 89. (7") *(JUNG 48)* **ASSASSIN YEARS. /** [ ] [-]
(12"+=) *(JUNG 48T)* –

not iss. Cleopatra

1993. (cd,c) *<5861>* **GOD ON A ROPE** [-] [ ]
– Bormann chain – Victor Jara / Psyche Sara / Pig of a god: Heartless Harvey – Comedy / Captain Careful – Tin house, glass . . . / Almagordo – Miriam pain / Cold hard stone / Atom dance / Patient performers / Violin valley / Egypt's ancient lovers – The last great / God dies.

—— next with **ADRIAN PORTAS** – multi / **KEVIN MATTHEWS** – drums

Triple X Triple X

Aug 95. (m-cd) *(<TX 51186CD>)* **WESTERN SONGS FOR CHILDREN** [ ] [ ] May95
– Diamond girls / Heaven shines for you / Welcome to my world / Waiting for the assassin / Beauty of lovers.

Oct 95. (cd; by ANDI SEX GANG & MICK ROSSI) *(TX 51195CD)* **GABRIEL AND THE GOLDEN HORN** [ ] [ ]

SEX PISTOLS

Formed: London, England . . . summer 1975 out of The SWANKERS by PAUL COOK, STEVE JONES and GLEN MATLOCK, the latter two regular faces at MALCOLM McLAREN'S 'Sex' boutique on the capital's King's Road. With the NEW YORK DOLLS already on his CV, McLAREN was well qualified to mastermind the rise and fall of The SEX PISTOLS as he dubbed his new plaything, the entrepeneur/svengali installing another 'Sex' customer, the green-haired JOHN LYDON, as a suitably sneering frontman. JONES soon renamed the latter JOHNNY ROTTEN, informing his farting rear-end, "You're rotten, you are"; the tone of the SEX PISTOLS was set. After a few local gigs, the group supported JOE STRUMMER's 101'ers in April '76, their bedraggled, low-rent bondage chic troupe of followers including the likes of SIOUXSIE SIOUX (later of BANSHEES fame) and one SID VICIOUS, allegedly the perpetrator behind the infamous glass-throwing incident at the 100 Club punk all-dayer in which a girl was partially blinded. Controversy, intentional or otherwise, hung around the group like a bad smell and made The SEX PISTOLS into minor legends with barely one single under their belts. Signed to 'E.M.I.' for £40,000, their debut release, 'ANARCHY IN THE U.K.' (having already shocked those of a sensitive disposition after being aired on the 'So It Goes' TV pop show) was finally released in November '76. An inflammatory slice of primal nihilism which surpassed even The STOOGES' finest efforts, the track initially climbed into the Top 40 before being unceremoniously withdrawn following the band's riotous appearance on a local chat/news programme, 'Today'. With JONES swearing copiously at presenter Bill Grundy, the tabloids had a field day, stirring up the moral majority and prompting more "must we subject our pop kids to this filth" editorials than you could shake a snotty stick at. 'E.M.I.' of course, bailed out (writing off the advance as a particularly bad debt) early the following year, while MATLOCK was fired around the same time for being, well, er . . . too nice. His replacement was the aforementioned VICIOUS, a suitably violent and abusive character who duly became more of a punk anti-hero/caricature than McLAREN could ever have dreamed. After a short period in label limbo, The 'PISTOLS signed to 'A&M' in March '77 for another six figure sum; the honeymoon period was probably the shortest in recording history as the band's infamous antics at the post-signing party, together with protests from other artists on the label saw the UK's foremost punk band once again minus a recording contract. Once again, the band retained the loot from the advance and once again, a single, 'GOD SAVE THE QUEEN', was withdrawn (some copies did find their way into circulation and now fetch considerably more than the original 50p price tag). Arguably The SEX PISTOLS' defining moment, this jaw-clenching two-fingured salute to the monarchy and everything it represented was to truly make the band public enemy No.1, its release coinciding sweetly with her highness' silver jubilee year. Re-released by new label 'Virgin' (virtually the only company willing to take the band on for a meagre £15,000 advance), the single was predictably banned by the BBC, though that didn't prevent it from outselling the official No.1 at the time, Rod Stewart's 'I Don't Want To Talk About It'. That long, hot summer also saw the band hiring a boat and sailing up and down the Thames in a publicity stunt which ended in chaos; cue yet more controversy and howls of derision from the nation's moral guardians. Knuckle-headed English royalists decided to take matters into their own hands, both COOK and ROTTEN attacked in separate incidents as another blankly brilliant single, 'PRETTY VACANT', gatecrashed the Top 10. Previewed by the seething, squalling outrage of 'HOLIDAYS IN THE SUN', the legendary debut album, 'NEVER MIND THE BOLLOCKS, HERE'S THE SEX PISTOLS' was finally released at the end of the year. While the record undeniably contained some filler, it remains the classic punk statement, the blistering 'BODIES' and the gleeful kiss-off to their former employers, 'E.M.I.', almost standing up against the intensity of the singles (included in their entirety). As ever, controversy clouded its release, the album reaching No.1 in spite of the word 'Bollocks' – a near contravention of the 1889 Indecent Advertisements Act(!) – resulting in boycotts from many major outlets. Constantly on the verge of falling apart, the band subsequently flew to America for a string of chaotic dates, the final round of blanks in The SEX PISTOLS' depleted armoury. Amid sporadic showdowns with Deep South cowboys and SID's ever worsening heroin problem, ROTTEN (bowing out on stage in San Francisco with the immortal phrase "Ever get the feeling you've been cheated") effectively ended the whole sorry affair with his departure after the final gig. While LYDON (the name he now reverted back to) went on to form PUBLIC IMAGE LTD., McLAREN had other ideas for the splintered remains of the band, namely jetting off to Rio De Janeiro to record a single with exiled trainrobber, RONNIE BIGGS. The result, 'NO ONE IS INNOCENT (A PUNK PRAYER BY RONNIE BIGGS)', made the Top 10 in summer '78, although VICIOUS was absent from the recording, holed up in New York with his similarly addicted girlfriend, Nancy Spungeon. He did find time to record a peerless rendition of Paul Anka's 'MY WAY', the single taking on an added poignancy following his untimely but hardly surprising death early the following year; out on bail after being charged with the murder of Spungeon in October, VICIOUS succumbed to a fatal heroin overdose on the 2nd of February '79. The following month saw the belated release of McLAREN's pet project, an artistically licensed celluloid account of The SEX PISTOLS' history entitled 'THE GREAT ROCK'N'ROLL SWINDLE'. Widely criticised for its its blatant exclusion of GLEN MATLOCK, the glaring absence of ROTTEN as an active participant and its paper-thin storyline, the movie was nevertheless an occasionally exhilirating, often hilarious trip through the misspent youth of Britain's best-loved punk band. While a perfunctory cover of Eddie Cochran's 'C'MON EVERYBODY' (a posthumous VICIOUS recording) made the Top 10 later that summer and 'Virgin' continued to flog The SEX PISTOLS' dead corpse with a variety of exploitation jobs, COOK and JONES fomed the short-lived PROFESSIONALS. Although they didn't invent punk, The SEX PISTOLS certainly helped popularise it and while they were at least partly responsible for an avalanche of unlistenably amateurish shit, the band's uncompromising approach permanently altered the machinations of the music industry and took three-chord rock'n'roll to its ultimate conclusion. Despite the fact original fans had long since given up on the UK ever descending into anarchy, the original 'PISTOLS line-up of LYDON, MATLOCK, JONES and COOK reformed in summer '96 for a handful of outdoor gigs and an accompanying live album. Opinion was divided as to whether this blatantly commercial venture (billed as "The Filthy Lucre Tour") was in keeping with the original punk spirit; probably not, although few paying punters complained about what was subsequently hailed as one of the events of the summer and it was certainly a safer bet than the new GREEN DAY album . . . **• Songwriters:** Group compositions, until COOK & JONES took over in 1978. They also covered; NO FUN (Stooges) / ROCK AROUND THE CLOCK (Bill Haley) / JOHNNY B. GOODE (Chuck Berry) / STEPPING STONE (Boyce-Hart) / etc. **• Trivia:** In 1979, they took McLAREN to court for unpaid royalties. In 1986, the official receiver, through McLAREN paid a 7-figure out of court settlement to LYDON, JONES, COOK and SID's mother.

Album rating (selective): NEVER MIND THE BOLLOCKS, HERE'S THE SEX PISTOLS (*10) / THE GREAT ROCK'N'ROLL SWINDLE soundtrack (*8) / FLOGGING A DEAD HORSE compilation (*8) / KISS THIS compilation (*8) / FILTHY LUCRE LIVE (*6)

JOHNNY ROTTEN (b. JOHN LYDON, 31 Jan'56) – vocals / **STEVE JONES** (b. 3 Sep'55) – guitar / **GLEN MATLOCK** (b.27 Aug'56) – bass / **PAUL COOK** (b.20 Jul'56) – drums

E.M.I. | not iss.

Nov 76. (7") *(EMI 2566)* **ANARCHY IN THE U.K. / I WANNA BE ME** [38] [-]

— (Feb'77) **SID VICIOUS** (b.JOHN RITCHIE, 10 May'57) – bass, vocals (ex-SIOUXSIE & THE BANSHEES) repl. MATLOCK who soon formed RICH KIDS

A&M | not iss.

Mar 77. (7"w-drawn) *(AMS 7284)* **GOD SAVE THE QUEEN. / NO FEELINGS** [-] [-]

— Were soon paid off yet again. Above copies filtered through and soon became a collectors item).

Virgin | Warners

May 77. (7") *(VS 181)* **GOD SAVE THE QUEEN. / DID YOU NO WRONG** [2] [-]

— (above was banned by the BBC, and outsold the official No.1 at the time; Rod Stewart's 'I Don't Want To Talk About It'.)

Jul 77. (7") *(VS 184)* **PRETTY VACANT. / NO FUN** [6] [-]

Oct 77. (7") *(VS 191)* **HOLIDAYS IN THE SUN. / SATELLITE** [8] [-]

Nov 77. (7") **PRETTY VACANT. / SUBMISSION** [-] [ ]

Nov 77. (lp/c) *(V/TCV 2086)* <3147> **NEVER MIND THE BOLLOCKS, HERE'S THE SEX PISTOLS** [1] [106]
– Holidays in the sun / Bodies / No feelings / Liar / God save the Queen / Problems / Seventeen / Anarchy in the UK / Submission / Pretty vacant / New York / E.M.I. *(7" free w/some copies of 'Submission'; SPOTS 001)* – **SUBMISSION** (one-sided). *(pic-lp Jan78; VP 2086) (re-iss. Oct86 lp/c; OVED/+C 136) (cd-iss. Oct86; CDV 2086) (re-iss. cd May93; CDVX 2086) (re-iss. 1996 on cd w/ free 'SPUNK' bootleg tracks) <cd-iss. Jul96 on 'Alex; 5695>*

— ROTTEN left, reverted to JOHN LYDON and created new band PUBLIC IMAGE LTD. His place was temporarily taken by **RONNIE BIGGS** (the Great Train Robber escapee now exiled in Brazil) 'A'-side vocals / **SID VICIOUS** – 'B'side vocals

Jun 78. (7") *(VS 220)* **NO ONE IS INNOCENT (A PUNK PRAYER BY RONNIE BIGGS). / MY WAY** [7] [-]
(12") *(VS 220-12 A1/2)* – The biggest blow (a punk prayer by Ronnie Biggs) / My way.
(12"+=) *(VS 220-12 A3)* – (above listing) / (interview).

— On 11 Oct'78, SID was charged with the murder of girlfriend NANCY SPUNGEN. MALCOLM McLAREN/'Virgin' bailed him out, but he died 2 Feb'79 of drug overdose. The 1979/80 singles were all taken from THE GREAT ROCK'N'ROLL SWINDLE film.

Feb 79. (7") *(VS 240)* **SOMETHING ELSE. / FRIGGIN' IN THE RIGGIN'** [3] [-]

Mar 79. (d-lp/d-c) *(VD/TCV 2510)* <45083> **THE GREAT ROCK'N'ROLL SWINDLE (Film Soundtrack)** [7] [ ]
– God save the Queen symphony / Rock around the clock / Johnny B. Goode / Roadrunner / Black Arabs / Watcha gonna do about it (* on some) / Who killed Bambi? / Silly thing / Substitute / No lip / (I'm not your) Stepping stone / Lonely boy / Somethin' else / Anarchie pour le UK / Einmal war Belsen vortrefflich / No one is innocent / My way / C'mon everybody / E.M.I. / The great rock'n'roll swindle / You need hands / Friggin' in the riggin'. *(re-iss. 1-lp May80; V 2168) (re-iss. Apr89 lp/c; OVED/+C 234) (d-cd iss.Jul86; CDVD 2510) (re-iss. cd May93; CDVDX 2510)*

Apr 79. (7") *(VS 256)* **SILLY THING. / WHO KILLED BAMBI?** [6] [ ]

— (above 'A'vocals – **STEVE JONES**, 'B'vocals – **EDDIE TENPOLE TUDOR)** (below 'A'vocals – **SID VICIOUS)**

Jun 79. (7") *(VS 272)* **C'MON EVERYBODY. / GOD SAVE THE QUEEN SYMPHONY / WATCHA GONNA DO ABOUT IT** [3] [ ]

Aug 79. (lp/c) *(VR/ 2)* **SOME PRODUCT: CARRI ON SEX PISTOLS** [6] [-]
– The very name (the Sex Pistols) / From beyond the grave / Big tits across America / The complex world of Johnny Rotten / Sex Pistols will play / Is the Queen a moron / The fuckin' rotter. *(cd-iss. May93; CDVR 2)*

Oct 79. (7") *(VS 290)* **THE GREAT ROCK'N'ROLL SWINDLE. / ROCK AROUND THE CLOCK** [21] [ ]

Dec 79. (lp/c; by SID VICIOUS) *(V/TCV 2144)* **SID SINGS** [30] [-]
– Born to lose / I wanna be your dog / Take a chance on me / (I'm not your) Stepping stone / My way / Belsen was a gas / Somethin' else / Chatterbox / Search and destroy / Chinese rocks / My way. *(re-iss. Aug88 lp/c; OVED/+C 85)* (cd-iss. Feb89; *CDV 2144)*

— There were other SID VICIOUS exploitation releases later.

Feb 80. (lp/c) *(V/TCV 2142)* **FLOGGING A DEAD HORSE** [23] [-]
– (singles compilation) *(re-iss. Apr86 lp/c; OVED/+C 165) (cd-iss. Oct86; CDV 2142)*

Jun 80. (7") *(VS 339)* **(I'M NOT YOUR) STEPPING STONE. / PISTOLS PROPAGANDA** [21] [-]

— COOK and JONES were now The PROFESSIONALS

– compilations, exploitation releases –

Note; on 'Virgin' until mentioned otherwise.

Jan 80. (lp) *Flyover; (YX 7247)* **THE BEST OF . . . AND WE DON'T CARE** [ ] [-]
Dec 80. (6x7"box) *(SEX 1)* **PISTOLS PACK** [ ] [-]
– GOD SAVE THE QUEEN. / PRETTY VACANT / / HOLIDAYS IN THE SUN. / MY WAY / / SOMETHING ELSE. / SILLY THING / / C'MON EVERYBODY. / THE GREAT ROCK'N'ROLL SWINDLE / / STEPPING STONE. / ANARCHY IN THE U.K. / / BLACK LEATHER. / HERE WE GO AGAIN
(below 45 credited EDDIE TENPOLE TUDOR)
Sep 81. (7") *(VS 443)* **WHO KILLED BAMBI?. / ROCK AROUND THE CLOCK** [ ] [-]
1983. (7") *(VS 609)* **ANARCHY IN THE UK. / NO FUN** [ ] [-]
(12"+=) *(VS 609-12)* – E.M.I.
Jan 85. (7"/7"pic-d)(12") *Cherry Red; (PISTOL 76P)(12PISTOL 76)* **LAND OF HOPE AND GLORY. ("EX-PISTOLS") / FLOWERS OF ROMANSK** [69] [-]
Jan 85. (m-lp) *Chaos; (MINI 1)* **THE MINI-ALBUM** [ ] [-]
(pic-m-lp.Jan86; AMPL 37) (cd-iss. Mar89; APOCA 3)
Mar 87. (7",7"yellow,7"pink) *Chaos; (DICK 1)* **SUBMISSION. / NO FEELINGS** [ ] [-]
(12",12"colrd) *(EXPORT 1)* – ('A'side) / Anarchy in the U.K.
Feb 85. (lp) *Receiver; (RRLP 101)* **THE ORIGINAL PISTOLS LIVE (live)** [ ] [-]
(pic-lp Jun86 on 'American Phono.'; APKPD 13) (re-iss. Jan89 on 'Dojo'; DOJOLP 45) (re-iss. May86 on 'Fame' lp/c; FA 41-3149-1/-4) (cd-iss. Jul89; CDFA 3149)
1985. (lp) *Receiver; (RRLP 102)* **AFTER THE STORM** [ ] [-]
(above with tracks by NEW YORK DOLLS) (cd-iss. Jul91; RRCD 102)
Aug 85. (lp) *Konnexion;* **LIVE WORLDWIDE (live)** [ ] [-]
Nov 85. (lp) *Receiver;* **WHERE WERE YOU IN '77** [ ] [-]
Nov 85. (lp/pic-lp) *Bondage;* **BEST OF SEX PISTOLS LIVE (live)** [ ] [-]
Nov 85. (lp) *Hippy;* **NEVER TRUST A HIPPY** [ ] [-]
Nov 85. (lp) *'77 Records;* **POWER OF THE PISTOLS** [ ] [-]
Feb 86. (lp) *McDonald-Lydon; (JOCK 1)* **THE LAST SHOW ON EARTH (live)** [ ] [-]
Apr 86. (12") *McDonald-Lydon; (JOCK 1201)* **ANARCHY IN THE U.K. (live). / FLOGGING A DEAD HORSE** [ ] [-]
Aug 86. (lp) *McDonald-Lydon; (JOCKLP 3)* **THE SEX PISTOLS 10th ANNIVERSARY ALBUM** [ ] [-]
Aug 86. (12"ep) *Archive 4; (TOF 104)* **ANARCHY IN THE UK / I'M A LAZY SOD. / PRETTY VACANT / SUBSTITUTE** [ ] [-]
Jan 87. (6xlp-box) *McDonald-Lydon; (JOCK BOX1)* **THE FILTH AND THE FURY** [ ] [-]
– FILTH & THE FURY / LAST SHOW ON EARTH / 10th ANNIVERSARY ALBUM / ITALIAN DEMOS / NO FUTURE USA / THE REAL SID & NANCY
May 88. (lp/cd) *Restless; <72255-1/-2>* **BETTER LIVE THAN DEAD (live)** [-] [ ]
Jun 88. (cd/lp) *M.B.C.; (JOCK/+LP 12)* **IT SEEMED TO BE THE END UNTIL THE NEXT BEGINNING** [ ] [-]
Jun 88. (3"cd-s) *(CDT 3)* **ANARCHY IN THE U.K. / E.M.I. / NO FUN** [ ] [-]
Oct 88. (m-lp) *Specific; (SPAW 101)* **ANARCHY WORLDWIDE** [ ] [-]
Oct 88. (cd-ep) *Specific; (SPCFC 102)* **CASH FOR CHAOS** [ ] [-]
– Submission (live) / God save the Quen / Liar.
Oct 88. (cd-ep) *Classic Tracks; (CDEP 13C)* **THE ORIGINAL PISTOLS (live)** [ ] [-]
– Anarchy in the U.K. / Pretty vacant / No fun / Substitute.
Dec 88. (3"cd-s) *(CDT 37)* **GOD SAVE THE QUEEN / DID YOU NO WRONG / DON'T GIVE ME NO LIP CHILD** [ ] [-]
Jun 89. (lp,pink-lp,green-lp/c) *Link; (LINK LP/MC 063)* **LIVE AND LOUD (live)** [ ] [-]
(cd-iss. Oct92; LINKCD 063)
Dec 89. (lp/c/cd,pic-cd) *Receiver; (RR LP/MC/CD 117)* **NO FUTURE U.K.?** [ ] [-]
Feb 90. (cd/c) *Action Replay; (CDAR/ARLC 1008)* **THE BEST OF AND THE REST OF THE SEX PISTOLS** [ ] [-]
1990. (12"blue-ep) *Receiver; (REPLAY 3012)* **THE EARLY YEARS LIVE** [ ] [-]
– Anarchy in the U.K. / Pretty vacant / Liar / Dolls (aka 'New York').
Jan 91. (d-lp) *Receiver; (RRLD 004)* **PRETTY VACANT** [ ] [-]
(d-cd-iss. Jul93; RRDCD 004)
Sep 92. (7"/c-s) *(VS/+C 1431)* **ANARCHY IN THE U.K. / I WANNA BE ME** [33] [ ]
(cd-s+=/s-cd-s+=) *(VSCD T/X 1431)* – ('A'demo).
Oct 92. (cd) *Streetlink; (STRCD 019)* **EARLY DAZE – THE STUDIO COLLECTION** [ ] [-]
(re-iss. May93 on 'Dojo'; DOJOCD 119)
Oct 92. (cd/c/d-lp) *(V/TC/CDV 2702) / Alex; <2931>* **KISS THIS** [10] [ ]
– Anarchy in the UK / God save the Queen / Pretty vacant / Holidays in ther Sun / I wanna be me / Did you no wrong / No fun / Satellite / Don't give me no lip child / (I'm not your) Stepping stone / Bodies / No feelings / Liar / Problems / Seventeen / Submission / New York / E.M.I. / My way / Silly thing. // *(cd w/bonus cd+=)* **LIVE IN TRONDHEIM 21st JULY 1977** :- Anarchy in the UK / I wanna be me / Seventeen / New York / E.M.I. / No fun / No feelings / Problems / God save the Queen.
Nov 92. (7") *(VS 1448)* **PRETTY VACANT. / NO FEELINGS (demo)** [56] [-]
(12"+=) *(VST 1448)* – Satellite (demo) / Submission (demo).
(cd-s+=) *(VSCDG 1448)* – E.M.I. (demo) / Satellite (demo).
(cd-s) *(VSCDT 1448)* – ('A'side) / Seventeen (demo) / Submission (demo) / Watcha gonna do about it?
Mar 93. (cd) *Dojo; (DOJOCD 66)* **LIVE AT CHELMSFORD PRISON** [ ] [-]
Nov 93. (cd) *Dojo; (DOJOCD 73)* **BETTER LIVE THAN DEAD** [ ] [-]
Jul 95. (cd) *Dojo; (DOJOCD 216)* **WANTED – THE GOODMAN TAPES** [ ] [-]
Oct 95. (d-cd) *Essential; (ESDCD 321)* **ALIVE** [ ] [-]
Jan 96. (cd) *Dojo; (DOJOCD 222)* **PIRATES OF DESTINY** [ ] [-]
Jan 97. (7") *Man's Ruin; (MR 053)* **split with the UGLYS** [ ] [-]
Mar 97. (7") *Man's Ruin; (MR 056)* **split with the SOPHISTICATES** [ ] [-]
Jun 97. (cd) *Emporio; (EMPRCD 716)* **RAW** [ ] [-]

— The original SEX PISTOLS re-formed at the back end of '95. Messrs LYDON, JONES, COOK + MATLOCK finally returned live on 24th June 1996, with packed out Finsbury Park concert. Embarked on their 'Filthy Lucre' tour soon after.

Virgin America / Caroline

Jul 96. (7"silver) *(VUS 113)* **PRETTY VACANT – LIVE. /** [18] [-]
(cd-s+=) *(VUSCD 113)* –
Aug 96. (cd/c/lp) *(41926) <7541>* **FILTHY LUCRE LIVE (live)** [26] [ ]
– Seventeen / New York / Did you no wrong / God save the Queen / Liar / Satellite / (I'm not your) Stepping stone / Holidays in the sun / Submission / No feelings / Pretty vacant / E.M.I. / Problems / Anarchy in the UK / No fun.

— JONES was also part-member of trans-Atlantic supergroup, NEUROTIC OUTSIDERS, alongside DUFF McKAGAN and MATT SORUM (Guns N' Roses) and JOHN TAYLOR (Duran Duran). They released an eponymous album for 'Maverick' in August '96 and from it they lifted the single, 'JERK'.

SHADOW KING (see under ⇒ GRAMM, Lou)

SHAKIN' STREET

Formed: Paris, France . . . 1975 by Tunisian-born FABIENNE SHINE and her co-pensmith ERIC LEWY. They enlisted the help of ARMIK TIGRANE, MIKE WINTER and JEAN-LOU KALINOWSKI, signing to 'C.B.S.' in the process. A no-frills heavy rock'n'roll band in the classic mould of The STOOGES and MC5 (from whom they took their name), SHAKIN' STREET's debut, 'VAMPIRE ROCK' (1978) nevertheless stood in the shadows of its mighty forebears. Things really got shakin' with the arrival of ROSS THE BOSS (formerly of fellow scuzz rockers, The DICTATORS), his uncompromising style together with the SANDY PEARLMAN (Blue Oyster Cult) production rendering 'SHAKIN' STREET' a minor classic. Ultimately the 'STREET proved to be something of a dead end, however, ROSS leaving to set up MANOWAR and the band splitting soon after.

Album rating: VAMPIRE ROCK (*5) / SHAKIN' STREET (*6)

FABIENNE SHINE – vocals, harmonica / **ERIC LEWY** – guitar / **ARMIK TIGRANE** – guitar / **MIKE WINTER** – bass / **JEAN-LOU KALINOWSKI** – drums

C.B.S. / not iss.

1978. (lp) *(CBS 82610)* **VAMPIRE ROCK** [ ] [-]
– Vampire rock / Where are you babe / Love song / Living with a dealer / No time to lose / Yesterday's papers / Celebration 2000 / Blues is the same / Speedy lady.

— **ROSS THE BOSS FUNICELLO** – guitar (ex-DICTATORS) repl. TIGRANE

Apr 78. (7") *(CBS 8512)* **SUSIE WONG. / EVERY MAN, EVERY WOMAN IS A STAR** [ ] [ ]
May 80. (lp) *(CBS 84115)* **SHAKIN' STREET** [ ] [-]
– No compromise / Solid as a rock / No time to lose / Soul dealer / Susie Wong / Every man, every woman is a star / Generation X / So fine / I want to box you.

— **DUCK McDONALD** – guitar (ex-THRASHER) repl. ROSS who formed MANOWAR

— subsequently folded some time in 1981

– compilations, etc. –

1989. (cd) *<SS 80>* **LIVE AND RAW (live 1980)** [-] [ ]

SHAM 69

Formed: London, England . . . 1976 by JIMMY PURSEY, ALBIE SLIDER, MARK CAIN and DAVE PARSONS (the latter two replacing original members BILLY BOSTIK and NEIL HARRIS – who himself had replaced the curiously monikered JOHN GOODFORNOTHING – respectively). Inspired by The SEX PISTOLS, PURSEY set out making pogo-friendly, dumbly anthemic punk with a fiercely working class agenda, issuing a statement of intent with an independently released, JOHN CALE-produced single, 'I DON'T WANNA'. Subsequently signing with 'Polydor', the band made their major label debut with the inimitable 'BORSTAL BREAKOUT' in early '77, following it up with a partly live album, 'TELL US THE TRUTH'. What really took their terrace chant appeal to the masses, however, was the subsequent trio of hit singles led by 'ANGELS WITH DIRTY FACES'; 'HURRY UP HARRY' and 'IF THE KIDS ARE UNITED' followed into the Top 10 shortly after, the latter track (complete with hilarious chirpy cockney intro) a well meant but naive call for youthful brotherhood. Which kind of summed up SHAM 69's fate; PURSEY's idealistic working class warrior philosophy backfired as the air-punching punk-by-numbers began attracting more and more face-punching neo-Nazi skinheads. Despite a considered attempt to brush up on the lads-on-the-loose formula with their third set, 'THE ADVENTURES OF THE HERSHAM BOYS' (1979), Top 10 success only seemed to make the situation worse. PURSEY finally disbanded SHAM 69 in the summer of '79 only to reform a couple of months later for a final album, 'THE GAME' (1980). This failed to chart and PURSEY subsequently pursued a low key solo career, initially with 'Polydor' (who released his 1980 debut set, 'IMAGINATION CAMOUFLAGE') then with 'Epic', before going on to record a series of one-off singles for various indie labels. With this going nowhere fast, PURSEY and PARSONS resurrected SHAM 69 in 1987, releasing a largely ignored album, 'VOLUNTEER' the following year. Retreating from view for a further four years, they were back yet again in the 90's, releasing a string of albums for the diehards and playing regular gigs on the punk nostalgia circuit. • **Songwriters:** Penned by PURSEY-PARSONS except; YOU'RE A BETTER MAN THAN I (Yardbirds) / WITH A LITTLE HELP FROM MY FRIENDS (Beatles). The WANDERERS covered THE TIMES THEY ARE A-CHANGIN' (Bob Dylan). • **Trivia:** PURSEY appeared on Various Artists lp, 'The Whip', in '83.

Album rating: TELL US THE TRUTH (*6) / THAT'S LIFE (*5) / ADVENTURES OF THE HERSHAM BOYS (*5) / THE GAME (*4) / THE FIRST, THE BEST AND THE LAST compilation (*7) / VOLUNTEER (*2) / INFORMATION LIBRE (*2) / KINGS AND QUEENS (*3) / SOAPY WATER & MR MARMALADE (*1)

JIMMY PURSEY (b. Hersham, Surrey, England) – vocals / **DAVE PARSONS** – guitar repl. NEIL HARRIS who had repl. JOHNNY GOODFORNOTHING / **ALBIE SLIDER** (b. ALBERT MASKAIL) – bass, vocals / **MARK CAIN** – drums repl. BILLY BOSTIK

Step Forward — not iss.

Oct 77. (7"m/12"m) *(SF 4/+12)* **I DON'T WANNA. / RED LONDON / ULSTER** — [ ] [-]
(re-iss. 1979; same)

— **DAVE TREGANNA** – bass, vocals repl. ALBIE

Polydor — Sire

Jan 78. (7") *(2058 966)* **BORSTAL BREAKOUT. / HEY LITTLE RICH BOY** — [ ] [-]
Feb 78. (lp) *(2383 491) <6060>* **TELL US THE TRUTH** (some live) — 25 [ ]
– We gotta fight / Rip off / Ulster / George Davis is innocent / They don't understand / Borstal breakout / Family life / Hey little rich boy / I'm a man, I'm a boy / What about the lonely / Tell us the truth / It's never too late / Whose generation. *(re-iss. Mar89 on 'Receiver'; RRD 001) (cd-iss. Mar96 on 'Dojo'; DOJOCD 256)*
Apr 78. (7") *(2059 023)* **ANGELS WITH DIRTY FACES. / COCKNEY KIDS ARE INNOCENT** — 19 [-]
Jul 78. (7") *(2059 050)* **IF THE KIDS ARE UNITED. / SUNDAY MORNING NIGHTMARE** — 9 [-]
Oct 78. (7") *(POSP 7)* **HURRY UP HARRY. / NO ENTRY** — 10 [ ]
Nov 78. (lp) *(2442 158)* **THAT'S LIFE** — 27 [-]
– Leave me alone / Who gives a damn / Everybody's right, everybody's wrong / That's life / Win or lose / Hurry up Harry / Evil way (live) / Reggae pick up (part 1) / Sunday morning nightmare / Reggae pick up (part 2) / Angels with dirty faces / Is this me or is this you. *(re-iss. Jul88 on 'Skunx'; SHAMX 1) (cd-iss. Mar96 on 'Dojo'; DOJOCD 257)*
Mar 79. (7"m) *(POSP 27)* **QUESTIONS AND ANSWERS. / I GOTTA SURVIVE (live) / WITH A LITTLE HELP FROM MY FRIENDS** — 18 [-]
Jul 79. (7"m) *(POSP 64)* **HERSHAM BOYS. / I DON'T WANNA (live) / TELL US THE TRUTH (live)** — 6 [-]
(12"m+=) *(POSPX 64)* – I'm a man, I'm a boy (live).
Sep 79. (lp) *(POLD/+C 5025)* **THE ADVENTURES OF THE HERSHAM BOYS** — 8 [-]
– Money / Fly dark angel / Joey's on the street / Cold blue in the night / You're a better man than I / Hersham boys / Lost on Highway 46 / Voices / Questions and answers / What have we got. *(free 12") (2812 045)* – IF THE KIDS ARE UNITED. / BORSTAL BREAKOUT *(cd-iss. Mar96 on 'Dojo'; DOJOCD 258)*
Oct 79. (7") *(POSP 82)* **YOU'RE A BETTER MAN THAN I. / GIVE A DOG A BONE** — 49 [-]

— Disbanded for two months Jul'79. **MARK GOLDSTEIN** – drums repl. CAIN

Mar 80. (7") *(POSP 136)* **TELL THE CHILDREN. / JACK** — 45 [-]
May 80. (lp) *(2442 173)* **THE GAME** — [ ] [-]
– The game / Human zoo / Lord of the flies / Give a dog a bone / In and out / Tell the children / Spray it on the wall / Dead or alive / Simon / Deja vu / Poor cow / Run wild run free / Unite and win. *(re-iss. Mar89 on 'Receiver'; RRLD 002) (cd-iss. Mar96 on 'Dojo'; DOJOCD 259)*
Jun 80. (7") *(2059 259)* **UNITE AND WIN. / I'M A MAN** — [ ] [-]
Nov 80. (lp) *(2383 596)* **THE FIRST, THE BEST AND THE LAST** (compilation) — [ ] [-]
– Borstal breakout / Hey little rich boy / Angels with dirty faces / Cockney kids are innocent / If the kids are united / Sunday morning nightmare / Hurry up Harry / Questions and answers / Give the dog a bone / Hersham boys / Tell the children / Unite & win. *(free 7"ep live)(RIOT 1 – 2816 028) (cd-iss. Apr94; 513429-2).*

— Had already splintered, with PURSEY going solo

WANDERERS

(TREGANNA, PARSONS + GOLDSTEIN) added **STIV BATORS** – vocals (ex-DEAD BOYS)

Polydor — not iss.

Mar 81. (7") *(POSP 237)* **READY TO SNAP. / BEYOND THE LAW** — [ ] [-]
May 81. (lp) *(POLS 1028)* **THE ONLY LOVERS LEFT ALIVE** — [ ] [-]
– Fanfare for 1984 / No dreams / Dr.Baker / Take them and break them / Little bit frightening / It's all the same / The times they are a-changin' / Ready to snap / Can't take you anymore / Sold your soul for fame / Circles of time / There'll be no end fanfare.
Jun 81. (7") *(POSP 284)* **THE TIMES THEY ARE A-CHANGIN'. / (IT'S A) LITTLE BIT FRIGHTENING** — [ ] [-]

— Split Aug'81, TREGANNA followed BATORS into LORDS OF THE NEW CHURCH. PARSONS formed FRAMED later in 1982.

JIMMY PURSEY

Polydor — not iss.

Sep 80. (7") *(POSP 154)* **LUCKY MAN. / BLACK AND WHITE ROCK REGGAE** — [ ] [-]
Oct 80. (lp) *(2442 180)* **IMAGINATION CAMOUFLAGE** — [ ] [-]
– Moon morning funday / Have a nice day / Lucky man / You never can tell / Situation's vacant / Playground soldier / White trash / Fifty-fifty / Freak show / Your mother should have told you / Just another memory.

Epic — not iss.

Jun 81. (7") *(EPCA 1336)* **ANIMALS HAVE MORE FUN. / SUS** — [ ] [-]
Nov 81. (7") *(EPCA 1830)* **NAUGHTY BOYS LIKE NAUGHTY GIRLS. / WHO'S MAKING YOU HAPPY** — [ ] [-]
Feb 82. (lp) *(EPC 85235)* **ALIEN ORPHAN** — [ ] [-]
– Alien orphan / The first deadly kiss / I'm a human being / One invite only / Why (he shouldn't be here) / Who's making you happy / Spies / Jungle west one / Oh isn't it a weird weird world / One night in Paris / Technical / Naughty boys like naughty girls.
Feb 82. (7") *(EPCA 2118)* **ALIEN ORPHAN. / CONVERSATIONS** — [ ] [-]

Code Black — not iss.

Jan 83. (lp) **REVENGE IS NOT THE PASSWORD** — [ ] [-]
Feb 83. (7") **MAN WORRIES MAN. / ?** — [ ] [-]

An Eskimo — not iss.

May 84. (12"/7"; as JAMES T. PURSEY) *(CODE 02/+7)* **IF ONLY BEFORE. / ABOVE AND BEYOND** — [ ] [-]

Videocat — not iss.

Sep 86. (7"/12") *(JIMMY/+T 1)* **ZAP POW. / ('A'-Bass camp mix)** — [ ] [-]

SHAM 69

re-formed in '87. (**PURSEY, PARSONS,** +2)

Legacy — Legacy

Jul 87. (7") *(LGY 69)* **RIP AND TEAR. / THE GREAT AMERICAN SLOWDOWN** — [ ] [-]
Feb 88. (7") *(LGY 71)* **OUTSIDE THE WAREHOUSE. / ('A'version)** — [ ] [-]
(12"+=) *(LGY/+T 71)* – How the west was won.
Jun 88. (lp/c) *(<LLP/LLK 117>)* **VOLUNTEER** — [ ] [ ]
– Outside the warehouse / Wicked tease / Wallpaper / Mr.Know it all / As black as sheep / How the west was won / That was the day / Rip and tear / Bastard club / Volunteer. *(cd-iss. Dec89; LLCD 117) (cd re-iss. Mar92 on Castle'; CLACD 274)*

Rotate — not iss.

Nov 92. (cd/lp) *(ROT CD/LP 006)* **INFORMATION LIBRE** — [ ] [-]
– Break on through / Uptown / Planet trash / Information libretaire / Caroline's suitcase / Feel it / King Kong drinks Coca-Cola / Saturdays and Strangeways / Breeding dinosaurs / Wild and wonderful. *(cd re-iss. Nov95 on 'Dojo'; DOJOCD 236)*

C.M.P. — not iss.

Nov 92. (12") **M25. /** — [ ] [-]
Mar 93. (7") **UPTOWN. / BORSTAL BREAKOUT** — [ ] [-]
(12"+=) – Flowers / Wild and wonderful.
Nov 93. (cd) **KINGS & QUEENS** — [ ] [-]
– Action time vision / I don't wanna / Ulster boy / They don't understand / Tell us the truth / Borstal breakout / Family life / The kids are united / Hurry up Harry / Hey little rich boy / Bosnia / Reggae giro. *(re-iss. Jul95 on 'Dojo';)*
Oct 93. (cd-ep) *(CMCCD 002)* **ACTION TIME & VISION / BOSNIA / HEY LITTLE RICH BOY / REGGAE GIRO** — [ ] [-]

Red Cat — not iss.

Jul 95. (cd) *(A1CD 001)* **SOAPY WATER & MR. MARMALADE** — [ ] [-]
(re-iss. May98 on 'Rhino'; 301279-2)

– compilations, others, etc. –

Oct 82. (12"ep) *Polydor; (POSPX 602)* **ANGELS WITH DIRTY FACES / BORSTAL BREAKOUT. / HURRY UP HARRY / IF THE KIDS ARE UNITED** — [ ] [-]
Nov 86. (lp/c) *Receiver; (RRLP/RRLC 104)* **ANGELS WITH DIRTY FACES – THE BEST OF SHAM 69** — [ ] [-]
Dec 87. (lp) *Link; (LINKLP 004)* **LIVE AND LOUD (live)** — [ ] [-]
Apr 88. (lp) *Link; (LINKLP 025)* **LIVE AND LOUD VOL.2** — [ ] [-]
May 89. (lp/cd) *Receiver; (RRLP/CD 112)* **THE BEST OF THE REST OF SHAM 69** — [ ] [-]
Oct 89. (cd/c/lp) *Castle; (CLA CD/MC/LP 153)* **COMPLETE LIVE (live)** — [ ] [-]
Apr 90. (cd/c) *Action Replay; (CDAR/ARLC 1011)* **SHAM 69 LIVE (live)** — [ ] [-]
Aug 90. (cd/lp) *Receiver;* **LIVE AT THE ROXY (live tapes '77)** — [ ] [-]
Jul 91. (cd) *Dojo; (DOJOCD 62)* **LIVE AT THE CBGB'S** — [ ] [-]
Apr 93. (cd) *Dojo; (DOJOCD 95)* **SHAM'S LAST STAND** — [ ] [-]
(re-iss. Jun99 on 'Snapper'; SMMCD 540)
Oct 93. (cd) *Dojo; (DOJOCD 105)* **LIVE IN JAPAN (live)** — [ ] [-]
Nov 93. (cd) *Windsong; (WINCD 049)* **BBC RADIO 1 LIVE IN CONCERT (Live)** — [ ] [-]
Mar 95. (cd; shared with 999) *Step-1;* **LIVE AND LOUD** — [ ] [-]
Sep 95. (cd) *Emporio; (EMPRCD 582)* **SHAM 69 LIVE** — [ ] [-]
Dec 95. (cd) *Essential; (ESDCD 350)* **LIVE / THE BEST OF SHAM 69** — [ ] [-]
Jun 96. (cd/c) *Hallmark; (30446-2/-4)* **UNITED** — [ ] [-]
Jun 97. (cd) *Essential; (<ESMCD 512>)* **THE BEST OF SHAM 69** — [ ] [-]
Jul 97. (cd) *Empty; (efaCD 12359)* **THE A FILES** — [ ] [-]
Mar 98. (d-cd) *Eagle; (EDMCD 030)* **THE MASTERS** — [ ] [-]
Mar 98. (cd/c) *Castle Select; (SEL CD/MC 504)* **THE VERY BEST OF THE HERSHAM BOYS** — [ ] [-]
Oct 98. (7"; shared with DIE TOTEN HOSEN) *M Tradegy; (MT 385)* **SAWBLADE SERIES #19** — [ ] [-]
Jun 99. (cd) *Essential; (ESMCD 733)* **LIVE IN ITALY** — [ ] [ ]
Oct 99. (d-cd) *Essential; (<ESDCD 780>)* **ANGELS WITH DIRTY FACES – THE BEST OF SHAM 69** — [ ] [ ]
May 00. (cd) *Captain Oi; (<AHOYCD 139>)* **RARITIES 1977-1980** — [ ] [ ]

SHARK ISLAND

Formed: Los Angeles, California, USA . . . 1986 out of glam-metal outfit, The SHARKS by RICHARD BLACK, SPENCER SERCOMBE, MICHAEL GUY, TOM RUCCI and WALT WOODWARD. Recording an eponymous, self-financed album in 1987, 'S'COOL BUS', the band were the subject of some interest from 'A&M', who signed them to a development deal. Although no album was funded, this did result in two SHARK ISLAND tracks being used in the soundtrack to metal-goof flick, 'Bill And Ted's Excellent Adventure'. The group subsequently underwent a number of line-up changes (CHRIS HEILMAN replacing RUCCI and GUY, GREG ELLIS replacing

WOODWARD) before being picked up by 'Epic' and releasing the 'LAW OF THE ORDER' album in 1990. Enjoying widespread praise in the metal press, particularly for BLACK's much improved vocal prowess, the album marked SHARK ISLAND out as definite contenders. Strangely enough, the band's profile has been almost non existent since, although BLACK was instrumental in the CONTRABAND project alongside MICHAEL SCHENKER and various L.A. metal figures.

Album rating: ALTER EGO as Sharks (*4) / S'COOL BUS (*6) / LAW OF THE ORDER (*6)

SHARKS

RICHARD BLACK (b. CZERNY) – vocals / **SPENCER SERCOMBE** – guitar / **JIM VOLPICELLI** – bass, vocals / **DAVE BISHOP** – drums

not iss. Sharks

1982. (lp) *<SM 1002>* **ALTER EGO** [-] [ ]
– Into the wheel / Whirlpool / Rock kids / Already gone / Hard to get / Under the table / Intermission / L.A. rock / Shoot to kill.

SHARK ISLAND

— **BLACK + SERCOMBE** found new musicians **MICHAEL GUY** – guitar / **TOM RUCCI** – bass / **WALT WOODWARD** – drums (ex-AMERICADE)

not iss. Shark

1987. (lp) **S'COOL BUS** [-] [ ]

— **CHRIS HEILMAN** – bass (ex-BERNIE TORME) repl. RUCCI + GUY

— **GREGG ELLIS** – drums; repl. WOODWARD

Epic Epic

Apr 90. (cd/c/lp) *(465956-2/-4/-1) <EK 45043>* **LAW OF THE ORDER** [ ] [ ]
– Paris calling / Shake for me / Somebody's falling / Bad for each other / Passion to ashes / Spellbound / Get some strange / Why should I believe / Ready or not / Chain.

— BLACK went on to collaborate with MICHAEL SCHENKER in the one-off project, CONTRABAND, which included all-star line-up from RATT, VIXEN and L.A. GUNS

Tommy SHAW (see under ⇒ STYX)

sHEAVY

Formed: St.John's, Newfoundland, Canada . . . 1993 as GREEN MACHINE by DAN MOORE and REN SQUIRES. Also comprising STEVE HENNESSEY, STERLING ROBERTSON and PAUL GROUCHY, the group unsurprisingly attracted little interest in Canada's frozen north and instead looked to the wider markets of the USA and Europe. Following 1994's independently released demo/debut EP, 'REPRODUCTION', the band adopted the sHEAVY moniker so as not to clash with an American indie outfit of the same name. ROBERTSON had also departed by this point, reducing the group to a quartet for the recording of a follow-up demo, 'SLAVES TO FASHION'. A 7" single on the Montreal label, 'Mag Wheel', featured a cover of Black Sabbath's 'TOMORROW'S DREAM' while sHEAVY's self financed debut album, 'BLUE SKY MIND' (1996) offered up a more comprehensive overview of the the band's retro, stoner metal sound. LEE DORIAN (of NAPALM DEATH and CATHEDRAL fame) was sufficiently impressed to offer the Canadians a deal on his 'Rise Above' label, through which 'THE ELECTRIC SLEEP' album was issued to positive reviews in 1998; noted poster artist Frank Kozik released their material on his 'Man's Ruin' label. A third album, 'CELESTIAL HI-FI', arrived in 2000. • **Covered:** THUMB + GREEN MACHINE (Kyuss) / TOMORROW'S DREAM + WAR PIGS (Black Sabbath).

Album rating: BLUE SKY MIND (*7) / THE ELECTRIC SLEEP (*6) / BORN TOO LATE split w/ Church Of Misery (*5) / CELESTIAL HI-FI (*5)

STEVE HENNESSEY – vocals / **DAN MOORE** – guitar / **STERLING MORRISON** – guitar / **PAUL GROUCHY** – bass / **REN SQUIRES** – drums

not iss. Dallas Tarr

1993. (c-ep) *<demo>* **REPRODUCTION** [-] [-] Canada
– Gun it jam / Dalas Tar / Dreamer's mind / Month of Sundays / Psycho universe / Thumb (live) / Green machine (live) / Crock (live).

1994. (c-ep) *<demo>* **SLAVES TO FASHION** [-] [-] Canada
– First / Shining path / Dalas tar / The everlasting / Dreamer's mind / Lonely & me / Crock / Psycho universe / Month of Sundays / Boogie woogie baby.

1995. (7",7"clear) **DALAS TAR. / UNTITLED / TOMORROW'S DREAM** [-] [-] Canada
(above issued on 'Mag Wheel') *<re-iss. Jan99; same>*

1996. (cd) **BLUE SKY MIND** [-] [-] Canada
– Mountains of madness / Blue sky mind / Domelight / Cosmic overdrive / Sea of tomorrow / Supa-hero / The gun it jam / Psycho universe (live). *(cd+=)* – SLAVES TO FASHION demo

1997. (c; split with AFTER FOREVER) **LIVE AT THE LOFT (live)** [-] [-] Canada
– Suitcase blues / Mountains of madness / Blue sky mind / Domelight / Psycho universe / Shinier path jam (live in studio) / (others by AFTER FOREVER).

— (all above recordings were of very limited quantities)

Rise Above The Music Cartel

Mar 98. (cd) *(CDRISE 17) <TMC 15>* **THE ELECTRIC SLEEP** [ ] [ ] Feb99
– Virtual machine / Velvet / Destiny rainbow / Electric sleep / Born in a daze / Automation / Savannah / Saving me from myself / Oracle / Stardust. *<US+=>* – The last parade.

Dec 99. (cd; split with CHURCH OF MISERY) *(G2 09CD)* **BORN TOO LATE** [ ] [ ]
– (CHURCH OF MISERY tracks) / Destiny's rainbow '96 / Suitcase blues (live) / Mountains of madness (live) / Blue sky mind (live) / Domelight (live) / War pigs.
(above issued on 'Game Two')

Mar 00. (cd) *(CDRISE 26) <TMC 37>* **CELESTIAL HI-FI** [ ] [ ] May00
– Hyper faster / What's up Mr. Zero? / Stingray part II / Solarsphere / Strange gods, strange altars / Celestial hi-fi / Mountains of madness / Persona / A Utopian interlude / Gemini (the twins) / Tales from the afterburner.

SHELLAC (see under ⇒ BIG BLACK)

SHELTER

Formed: New York, USA . . . 1990 out of 80's skacore band, YOUTH OF TODAY, by RAY CAPPO (also in side project, BETTER THAN A THOUSAND), PORCELL, FRANKLIN RHI and DAVE DiCENSO. One of the few (no, the only!) Hare Krishna hardcore/metal acts to emerge from a scene that is better known for its venom-spewing bile and righteous anger than positive vibes and good karma; CAPPO had actually spent a few years in India studying all things spiritual. After the release of their debut, 'PERFECTION OF DESIRE' (1990), SHELTER found a new home at 'Roadrunner', releasing their long-awaited follow-up proper, 'MANTRA', in 1995. While these two albums relied largely on a full-bore hardcore assault, 1997's 'BEYOND PLANET EARTH' attempted to transcend the genre, illuminating the material with an infectious vibrancy lacking in many of their peers. • **Covers:** WE CAN WORK IT OUT (Beatles). • **Trivia:** J, guitarist of WHITE ZOMBIE, performed on a few tracks.

Album rating: PERFECTION OR DESIRE (*5) / QUEST FOR CERTAINTY mini (*4) / ATTAINING THE SUPREME collection (*6) / MANTRA (*6) / BEYOND PLANET EARTH (*6) / WHEN 20 SUMMERS PASS (*6)

RAY CAPPO – vocals / **PORCELL** – guitar / **FRANKLIN RHI** – bass / **DAVE DiCENSO** – drums, percussion

Revelation Revelation

Apr 92. (lp/c/cd) *(<REVEL 016/+MC/CD>)* **PERFECTION OF DESIRE** [ ] [ ] 1991
– Turn it around / In the name of comfort / Enough / Society based on bodies / Death and dying / Photographs lie / Shelter.

May 95. (m-cd) *<REV 066>* **QUEST FOR CERTAINTY** [-] [ ]
– In defense of reality / Quest for certainty / The news / After forever / Freewill / Saranagati / A society based on bodies (live) / Death and dying (live) / (untitled tracks). *(UK-iss.Mar98; REV 066CD)*

May 95. (c-s) *<11>* **SHELTER BHAJAN** [-] [ ]

May 95. (c-s) *<12>* **STANDARD TEMPLE** [-] [ ]

Aug 95. (lp/cd) *<7>* **ATTAINING THE SUPREME** [-] [ ]
– Better way / One concern / In praise of others / Consumer / Progressive man / Not just a package / Hands of time / Knowledge of the absolute / Busy doing nothing / Shelter. *(UK-iss.Apr97 on 'Equal Vision'; EVR 007/+CD)*

Roadrunner Roadrunner

Oct 95. (cd/c/lp) *<(RR 8938-2/-4/-1)>* **MANTRA** [ ] [ ]
– Message of the Bhagavat / Civilized man / Here we go / Appreciation / Empathy / Not the flesh / Chance / Mantra / Surrender to your T.V. / Letter to a friend / Metamorphosis. *(cd re-iss. May99; same)*

Nov 95. (12"/cd-s) *(RR 2323-6/-3)* **HERE WE GO. / APPRECIATION** [ ] [-]
(cd-s) *(RR 2323-2)* – ('A'side) / Progressive man.

Sep 97. (cd/c/lp) *<(RR 8828-2/-4/-1)>* **BEYOND PLANET EARTH** [ ] [ ]
– Revealed in reflection / I know so little (so well) / Rejuvenate / Alone on my birthday / Hated to love / Refusal / Whole wide world / Helpless / Beyond planet earth / Time's ticking away / Man or beast / In praise of others / Eleventh day of the Moon / Man or beast.
(cd re-iss. May99; same)

Feb 98. (cd-ep) *(RR 2261-3)* **WHOLE WIDE WORLD / SHELTER / MAN OR BEAST (End Of The Millennium mix) / WE CAN WORK IT OUT** [ ] [ ]

Century Media Century Media

Apr 00. (cd/lp) *<(77303-2/-1)>* **WHEN 20 SUMMERS PASS** [ ] [ ]
– When 20 summers pass / In the van again / Song of Brahma / Don't walk away / Public eye / If there's only today / Loss disguised as gain / Spirits blinded / Crushing someone you love / Look away / Killer of my dreams / I can't change history.

Apr 01. (10") *(VH 052)* **THE POWER OF POSITIVE THINKING** [ ] [-]
(above issued on 'Vacation House')

Jun 01. (cd/lp) *<(77371-2/-1)>* **THE PURPOSE THE PASSION** [ ] [ ]

SHINEOLA (see under ⇒ SEND NO FLOWERS)

SHIVA

Formed: England . . . early 80's by the multi-instrumentalist JOHN HALL, who enlisted the help of ANDY SKUSE and CHRIS LOGAN. An ambitious fusion of various 70's hard-rock influences, SHIVA saw through their short career with 'Heavy Metal' records. Preceded by a couple of 45's, a sole album, 'FIREDANCE', appeared in late '82, although LOGAN departed soon after. PHIL WILLIAMS was brought in as replacement although his tenure was short-lived, SHIVA subsequently splitting.

Album rating: FIREDANCE (*5)

JOHN HALL – vocals, guitar, keyboards / **ANDY SKUSE** – bass, keyboards / **CHRIS LOGAN** – drums

Heavy Metal not iss.

Feb 82. (7") *(HEAVY 13)* **ROCK LIVES ON. / SYMPATHY** [ ] [-]

Nov 82. (7") *(HEAVY 16)* **ANGEL OF MONS. / STRANGER LANDS** [ ] [-]

Nov 82. (lp) *(HMRLP 6)* **FIREDANCE** [ ] [-]
– How can I / En cachent / Wild machine / Borderline / Stranger lands / Angel of

Mons / Rendezvous with death / User / Call me in the morning / Shiva. *(cd-iss. Jan97 on 'Anagram'+=; CDMETAL 8)* – Rock lives on / Sympathy.

— (1983) **PHIL WILLIAMS** – drums; repl. LOGAN

— folded soon afterwards

SHOOTYZ GROOVE

Formed: The Bronx, New York, USA . . . 1992 by the largely Hispanic/latin crew of MC SENSE, MC SEASON, guitarist DONNY and the rhythm section of SPEC and DOSE. While the BEASTIE BOYS pretended to have a rough'n'ready NY background, these guys were the real thing, trading old skool hip hop science with heavy guitar licks and organic beats. Following on from early 1994's promising debut EP, 'RESPECT' (a live affair recorded in NY's Queens district), the group unleashed their equally promising major label ('Mercury') debut album, 'JAMMIN' IN VICIOUS ENVIRONMENTS' later the same year. The record underlined the fact that SHOOTYZ GROOVE were dyed-in-the-wool homeboys embracing rock music rather than metallers clumsily affecting a lumbering groove and a few verses of rap-style shouting. After touring with big name acts from both the metal and hip hop scenes, the band underwent a period of uncertainty as SPEC left and they parted company with 'Mercury'. A replacement was found in PAUL 'FREAK LOVE' while a concert set, 'Live J.I.V.E.' emerged in 1995. The 'GROOVE posse finally found a stable home at 'Roadrunner' where they released the sharper, punk/ska influenced 'HIPNOSIS' (1997). Their hard-hitting positive vibes were given an even more effective studio translation in 1999 with 'HIGH DEFINITION', wherein the New Yorkers even had a successful go at XTC's 'DEAR GOD'.

Album rating: RESPECT mini (*5) / JAMMIN' IN VICIOUS ENVIRONMENTS (*6) / HIPNOSIS (*7) / HIGH DEFINITION (*6)

SENSE – rapper / **SEASON** – rapper / **DONNY** – guitar / **SPEC** – bass / **DOSE** – drums (surnames:- BAEZ, RADELJIC, RAMIREZ, RODRIGUEZ + MACELI)

Abstract Mercury

Aug 93. (c-ep/cd-ep) *<518224-4/-2>* **RESPECT (live)** [-] [ ]
– Buddah blessed / Craze / Buddahful day / Soulfreak / Rockin' in the wilderness.

May 95. (cd/c/lp) *(ABT 101 CD/MC/LP) <522465-2/-4/-1>* **JAMMIN' IN VICIOUS ENVIRONMENTS** [ ] [ ] Nov94
– Respect / In the ocean / Sol / Joint / Soulfreak / Walkin' the frog / Maxin' (clockin' Z's) / Craze / Crooked is the path / Level / Come w/ cha best / Carry on / R.I.T.W.

Roadrunner Roadrunner

Jun 97. (cd) *<(RR 8829-2)>* **HIPNOSIS** [ ] [ ]
– Regardless / Manhole / Lillypad / Once / Interzone / Anchor / Fantasy #5 / Triangle music / Groovyland / Nothing for you / Damond mind / Other side / Reverse side / 8,000,000 times. *(re-iss. May99; same)*

Reprise Reprise

Sep 99. (cd-s) *(W 501CD)* **L TRAIN (radio) / L TRAIN (album) / CALL OUT RESEARCH HOOK #1 & 2** [ ] [-]

Oct 99. (cd) *<(9362 47359-2)>* **HIGH DEFINITION** [ ] [ ] Jun99
– Mad for it / Young city boys and girls / L train / Faithful / So much time / Dear God / Blow your top / NYC minute / Put down the mics / You have all been warned / Easily.

Paul SHORTINO (see under ⇒ ROUGH CUTT)

SHOTGUN MESSIAH

Formed: Skovde, Sweden . . . early 80's as SHYLOCK, then KING PIN by HARRY K. CODY, TIM SKOLD and STIXX GALORE, who were subsequently joined by frontman ZINNY J. SAN. Under the KING PIN moniker, they issued their debut (Swedish-only) album, 'WELCOME TO BOP CITY', the record subsequently re-issued (1990) as/by the renamed SHOTGUN MESSIAH following their move to L.A. in 1988. Something of a minor glam/sleaze classic, the record stood out from the peroxide crowd by dint of CODY's (Satriani/Vai-influenced) nimble fingered axework. When ZINNY departed amicably after a hectic touring schedule, it looked like SHOTGUN MESSIAH's battle plan had backfired. However, SKOLD rather resourcefully switched to a vocal role, BOBBY LYCON drafted in as the new bass player on the appropriately-titled 'SECOND COMING' (1991). This line-up recorded a further EP of covers (including Iggy Pop's 'SEARCH AND DESTROY', New York Dolls' 'BABYLON' and Ramones' '53 & A 3RD'), before STIXX and LYCON left SKOLD and CODY to get on with it. They did this in fine style, performing a musical volte face and cutting an album of electro-industrial metal, 'VIOLENT NEW BREED' (1993). Unfortunately, this proved to be SHOTGUN MESSIAH's final blast, SKOLD now pursuing a solo career.

Album rating: WELCOME TO BOP CITY (or) SHOTGUN MESSIAH (*7) / SECOND COMING (*6) / I WANT MORE mini (*4) / VIOLENT NEW BREED (*6)

ZINNY J. SAN – vocals (ex-EASY ACTION) / **HARRY K. CODY** – guitar / **TIM SKOLD** – bass / **STIXX GALORE** – drums

Music For Nations Combat

Jul 90. (lp/c) *(MFN/TMFN 105) <88561-1012-2>* **SHOTGUN MESSIAH** (debut remixed) [ ] [ ]
– Bop city / Don't care about nothin' / Shout it out / Squeezin' teazin' / The explorer / Nowhere fast / Dirt talk / I'm your love / Nervous.
(above was originally released in 1988 by KING PIN as 'WELCOME TO BOP CITY')

— **BOBBY LYCON** – bass; repl. SAN (SKOLD now on vocals)

Roadrunner Combat

Nov 91. (cd/c/lp) *(RR 9239-2/-4/-1) <88561-1060>* **SECOND COMING** [ ] [ ]
– Sexdrugsrock'n'roll / Red hot / Nobody's home / Living without you / Heartbreak Blvd. / I want more / Trouble / Ride the storm / I wanna know / Babylon / Free / You and me / Can't fool me.

Nov 92. (m-cd) *(RR 9103-2) <88561 1151-2>* **I WANT MORE** [ ] [ ]
– I want more / Search and destroy / 53rd and 3rd / Babylon / Nobody's home.

— **CODY + SKOLD** now employed drum machines, synths, etc, after STIXX + LYCON departed

Sep 93. (cd/c) *(RR 9036-2/-4) <88561-1164-2/-4>* **VIOLENT NEW BREED** [ ] [ ]
– I'm a gun / Come down / Violent breed / Enemy in me / Revolution / Monkey needs / Rain / Jihad / Side F-X / Sex / Overkill / I come in peace.

— folded sometime later, TIM going solo in the process

SHY

Formed: Birmingham, England . . . 1982 by singer TONY MILLS, who introduced into the line-up STEVE HARRIS, PAT McKENNA, MARK BADRICK and ALAN KELLY. Adopting the style and execution of Americanised AOR pomp wholesale, this band certainly weren't shy about their influences. MILLS' vocal athletics, introduced on the 1983 debut set, 'ONCE BITTEN, TWICE SHY', were something of an acquired taste, press reaction decidedly mixed. With ROY STEPHEN DAVIS replacing BADRICK, the group signed to 'R.C.A.', their second album 'BRAVE THE STORM' (1985) refining the band's solid approach. This was further developed on 'EXCESS ALL AREAS' (1987), a record which arguably ranks as their most consistent despite a pointless cover of Cliff Richard's 'DEVIL WOMAN'. Unfortunately SHY suffered equally modest record sales, RCA subsequently letting the band go. After a one-off 45 for 'FM Records', the thick-skinned SHY secured themselves a new deal with 'M.C.A.', releasing the ROY THOMAS BAKER-produced 'MISSPENT YOUTH' in 1989. Roundly slated, the album's overtly commercial material cut no ice with the band's dwindling fanbase, SHY soon finding themselves minus a deal once more. After an early 90's hiatus, the group resurfaced with a new singer, JOHN WARD, who graced their comeback single in 1994, a cover of The Rolling Stones' 'IT'S ONLY ROCK'N'ROLL'. In the late 90's, after a few filler demo/live packages, SHY returned from the wilderness; the album 'LET THE HAMMER FALL' (2000) described it perfectly.

Album rating: ONCE BITTEN TWICE SHY (*5) / BRAVE THE STORM (*5) / EXCESS ALL AREAS (*6) / MISSPENT YOUTH (*4) / WELCOME TO THE MADHOUSE (*4) / REGENERATION collection (*4) / LIVE IN EUROPE collection (*3) / LET THE HAMMER FALL (*3)

TONY MILLS – vocals / **STEVE HARRIS** – guitar / **PAT McKENNA** – keyboards / **MARK BADRICK** – bass / **ALAN KELLY** – drums

Ebony Ebony

Nov 83. (lp) *(<EBON 15>)* **ONCE BITTEN TWICE SHY** [ ] [ ]
– Deep water / Take it all away / Give me a chance / Think of me / Tonight / Chained by desire / Reflections / Once bitten, twice shy. *(cd-iss. Apr00 on 'Neat Metal'; NM 030)*

— **ROY STEPHEN DAVIS** – bass; repl. BADRICK

R.C.A. R.C.A.

Mar 85. (7") *(PB 40053)* **HOLD ON (TO YOUR LOVE). / STRANGERS IN TOWN** [ ] [-]
(12"+=) *(PT 40054)* – ('A'extended).

May 85. (lp/c) *(PL/PK 70605)* **BRAVE THE STORM** [ ] [ ]
– Hold on (to your love) / My Apollo / Reflections / Keep the fires burning / The hunter / Brave the storm / Wild wild woman / Caught in the act / Was I wrong.

May 85. (7") *(PB 40229)* **REFLECTIONS. / THE HUNTER** [ ] [-]
(12"+=) *(PT 40230)* – Deep water.

Apr 87. (7") *(PB 41295)* **YOUNG HEART. / RUN FOR COVER** [ ] [-]
(12"+=) *(PT 41296)* – Don't want to lose your love.

May 87. (lp/c/cd) *(PK/PL/PD 71221)* **EXCESS ALL AREAS** [ ] [-]
– Emergency / Can't fight the nights / Young hearts / Just love me / Break down the walls / Under fire / Devil woman / Talk to me / When the love is over / Telephone.

Jun 87. (7"m) *(SHY 100)* **UNDER FIRE. / YOUNG HEART / BREAK DOWN THE WALLS** [ ] [-]

FM Records not iss.

Feb 88. (12"ep) *(12VHF 43)* **JUST LOVE ME / DEEP WATER. / HOLD ON (TO YOUR LOVE) / BREAK DOWN THE WALLS** [ ] [-]

— (now as SHY ENGLAND in the States)

M.C.A. M.C.A.

Oct 89. (7") *(MCA 1369)* **GIVE IT ALL YOU'VE GOT. / SHE'S GOT WHAT IT TAKES** [ ] [ ]
(12"+=/cd-s+=) *(MCAT/DMCA 1369)* – How does it feel.
(12") *(MCATT 1369)* – ('A'remixes).

Oct 89. (lp/c/cd) *(MCG/MCGC/DMCG 6069) <6371>* **MISSPENT YOUTH** [ ] [ ]
– Burnin' up / Pub / Money / Never trust a stranger / After the love has gone / Give it all you've got / Broken heart / Shake the nation / When you need someone / Love on the line / Make my day / Encore.

Jan 90. (7") *(MCA 1391)* **MONEY. /** [ ] [-]
(12"+=/12"s+=) *(MCAT/+B 1391)* –

Apr 90. (7") *(MCA 1399)* **BROKEN HEART. /** [ ] [ ]
(12"+=/12"s+=) *(MCAT/+B 1399)* –

— MILLS left some time in 1990. He was replaced in 1992 by **JOHN WARD**

Parachute not iss.

Sep 94. (c-s) *(GRMC 4)* **IT'S ONLY ROCK'N'ROLL /** [ ] [-]
(cd-s+=) *(GRCD 2)* –

— folded until . . .

Neat Metal | not iss.

May 99. (cd) *(NM 033)* **REGENERATION** (rare) [ ] [-]
– If it ain't love / When you're bad you're better / When you need someone / Only you / Someday / Blind rage, blind fury / Long time coming / Dangerous ground / Are you ready? / You're gonna get what's coming to ya / Girls like you / Lonely man / Changing / What would your daddy do? / She's too dangerous. *<US-iss.May01; same as UK>*

May 99. (cd) *(NM 034)* **LIVE IN EUROPE (live)** [ ] [-]
– Telephone / Can't fight the nights / Talk to me / When love is over / Young heart / Devil woman / Break down the walls / Emergency / Chained by desire / Money / Shake the nations / When you need someone / If you want it / Make my day. *<US-iss.May01; same as UK>*

Jan 00. (cd) *(NM 039)* **LET THE HAMMER FALL** [ ] [-]
– Let the hammer fall / Steal me / Maybe tonight / Showdown / It's over / Why does our love have to end? / All your love tonight / You're gonna lose her / Time after time / Standing in the line of fire / Love is just another word / Set the night on fire. *<US-iss.May01; same as UK>*

SICK OF IT ALL

Formed: New York City, New York, USA . . . 1986 by brothers LOU and PETE KOLLER, along with EDDIE and E.K. An influential, uncompromising straight-edged band, SOIA were a pivotal part of the late 80's NY hardcore scene, early albums such as 'BLOOD, SWEAT & NO TEARS' (1989) and 'JUST LOOK AROUND' (1991) akin to a more vicious combination of RANCID and The BEASTIE BOYS. Their third (half live) set, 'WE STAND ALONE' (1992), was the last with EDDIE and E.K, the pair being replaced by CRAIG SETARI and ARMIN MAJIDI respectively for their first major label outing, 'SCRATCH THE SURFACE' (1994). Like many bands of their ilk, SOIA were snapped up amid the punk/hardcore revival of the early 90's, the group signing away their particular soul with 'East West'. During this time, a number of exploitation releases flooded the market, the band taking until 1997 to release a follow-up, 'BUILT TO LAST'. Now on the 'Fat Wreck Chords' roster, SOIA delivered their umpteenth full-set, 'CALL TO ARMS' (1999), a record that bridged the hardcore gap between the mid-80's and late 90's. SICK OF IT ALL had also helped their roadie, TOBY MORSE, to get his/their stage party piece act, H2O, get off the ground. • **Covered:** BORSTAL BREAKOUT (Sham 69).

Album rating: BLOOD, SWEAT AND NO TEARS (*6) / WE STAND ALONE (*5) / JUST LOOK AROUND (*6) / SCRATCH THE SURFACE (*6) / BUILT TO LAST (*6) / CALL TO ARMS (*7)

LOU KOLLER – vocals / **PETE KOLLER** – guitar / **EDDIE** – bass / **E.K.** – drums

not iss. | Revelation

1987. (7"ep) *<3>* **SICK OF IT ALL** [-] [ ]
– It's clobberin' time – Just lies / Pete's sake / Friends like you / Bullshit justice / Pay the price / Pushed too far – Give respect / Deal / N.S. – My revenge. *<cd-iss. Sep97; same>*

not iss. | Combat

1989. (lp,c,cd) *<3005>* **BLOOD, SWEAT AND NO TEARS** [-] [ ]
– The blood and the sweat / Clobberin' time – Pay the price / Give respect / Breeders of hate / Pushed too far / Friends like you / B.S. justice / Rat pack / Pete's sake / Stick together / G.I. Joe head stomp / Alone / My life / World full of hate / My revenge / No labels / Disillusion / Deal / Injustice system! *<(UK cd-iss. May99 on 'Century Media'; CM 66007-2)>*

1992. (cd/c) *<88561-3017-2/-4>* **JUST LOOK AROUND** [-] [ ]
– We want the truth / Locomotive / Pain strikes / Shut me out / What's goin' on / Never measure up / Just look around / Violent generation / Shield / Now it's gone / We stand alone / Will we survive / Indust. *(UK cd-iss. May95 on 'Roadrunner'; RR 9191-2) <(re-iss. Aug99 on 'Century Media' cd/lp; 66008-2/-1)>*

not iss. | In-Effect

1992. (cd) *<468100-2>* **WE STAND ALONE** (rec.1990/91) [-] [ ]
– What's goin' on / Betray / We stand alone / Disillusion / My revenge – World full of hate / Pete's sake / Injustice system / The deal / G.I. Joe head stomp / Pushed too far / The blood & the sweat / Politics.

—— **CRAIG SETARI** – bass + **ARMIN MAJIDI** – drums; repl. EDDIE + E.K.

East West | East West

Nov 94. (cd/c/lp) *<(7567 92422-2/-4/-1)>* **SCRATCH THE SURFACE** [ ] [ ]
– No cure / Inserrection / Consume / Goatless / Maladjusted / Free spirit / Desperate fool / Force my hand / Cease fire / Farm team / Return to reality / Scratch the surface / Step down / Who sets the rules. *(lp re-iss. Apr97 on 'Equal Vision'; EVR 023)*

Jan 95. (12"etched) *(A 8202X)* **SCRATCH THE SURFACE. / BORSTAL BREAKOUT** [ ] [ ]
(cd-ep+=) *(A 8202EP)* – Consume / Straight ahead.

Mar 97. (cd/c) *<(7596 62008-2/-4)>* **BUILT TO LAST** [ ] [ ]
– Good lookin' out / Built to last / Closer / One step ahead / Us vs them / Laughingstock / Don't follow / Nice / Busted / Burn 'em down / End the era / Chip away / Too late / Jungle. *(lp-iss.May97 on 'Equal Vision'; EVR 036)*

Fat Wreck Chords | Fat Wreck Chords

Feb 99. (cd/lp) *<(FAT 582 CD/LP)>* **CALL TO ARMS** [ ] [ ]
– Let go / Call to arms / Potential for a fall / Falter / The future is mine / Guilty / Falling apart / Sanctuary / Morally confused / Hindsight / Martin / Pass the buck / Quiet man / Drastic / Patsy.

– compilations, etc. –

on 'Lost & Found' unless mentioned otherwise

Dec 93. (cd) *<(LF 073CD)>* **LIVE IN A WORLD FULL OF HATE** [ ] [ ] Apr95
– Injustice system! / It's clobberin' time / Violent generation / Alone / Pain strikes / Shut me out / Pushed too far / Friends like you / Locomotive / World full of hate / Just look around / What's going on / Give respct / Disillusion / No labels / Pete's sake / G.I. Joe head stomp / We want the truth / Blood and the sweat / Shield / We stand alone / Indist. / My life / Betray.

May 94. (cd) *(LF 083CD)* **THE REVELATION RECORDINGS 1987-89** [ ] [-]

May 94. (m-cd) *(LF 084MCD)* **SPREADING THE HARDCORE REALITY** [ ] [-]

Jan 95. (d-lp) *(LF 121)* **LIVE IN A WORLD FULL OF HATE / BROTHER AGAINST BROTHER (by The Rykers)** [ ] [-]

SIGH

Formed: Japan . . . 1989 by the trio of MIRAI, SHINICHI and SATOSHI – surely a better moniker might have been chosen. Concocting an unlikely fusion of grindcore, black metal, opera, avant-garde and Oriental folk music, these children of the sun were not yer average run of the mill metal outfit; in fact they were the weirdest rock act to hit the scene for some time. Initially signed to the late, great (and mortal) EURONYMOUS' label, 'Deathlike Silence' (see MAYHEM), SIGH delivered one album, 'SCORN DEFEAT' (1994), before settling with 'Cacophonous'. There, they created some of the most unique Black metal, via the LP's 'INFIDEL ART' (1995), the groundbreaking mini-set 'GHASTLY FUNERAL THEATRE' (1997), the equally brilliant 'HAIL HORROR HAIL' (1997) and the most recent 'SCENARIO IV: DREAD DREAMS' (1999); truly schizoid!

Album rating: SCORN DEFEAT (*6) / INFIDEL ART (*6) / GHASTLY FUNERAL THEATRE mini (*6) / HAIL HORROR HAIL (*7) / SCENARIO IV: DREAD DREAMS (*6)

MIRAI – vocals, bass, keyboards / **SHINICHI** – guitar, bass / **SATOSHI** – drums, percussion

Deathlike Silence | not iss.

Apr 94. (cd) *(ANTiMOSH 007CD)* **SCORN DEFEAT** [ ] [-]
– A victory of Dakini / The knell / At my funeral / Gundali / Ready for the final war / Weakness within / Taste defeat. *(re-iss. Aug99; same)*

Cacophonous | Cacophonous

Dec 95. (cd) *(NIHIL 7CD)* **INFIDEL ART** [ ] [-]
– Izuna / The zombie terror / Desolation / The last elegy / Suicidogenic / Beyond centuries.

Feb 97. (m-cd) *(NIHIL 17CD)* **GHASTLY FUNERAL THEATRE** [ ] [-]
– Intro: Soushiki / Shingontachikawa / Doman seman / Imiuta / Shikigami / Outro: Higeki. *<US-iss.Feb00; same as UK>*

Dec 97. (cd) *(NIHIL 24CD)* **HAIL HORROR HAIL** [ ] [-]
– Hail horror hail / 47 49 / 12 souls / Burial / The dead sing / Invitation to die / Pathetic / Curse of Izanagi / Seed of eternity. *<US-iss.Feb00; same as UK>*

Sep 99. (cd) *(<NIHIL 34CD>)* **SCENARIO IV: DREAD DREAMS** [ ] [ ] Feb00
– Diabolic suicide / Internal cries / Black curse / Iconoclasm in the 4th desert / In the mind of a lunatic / Severed ways / Imprisoned / Waltz: dread dreams / Divine graveyard.

SILVERCHAIR

Formed: Newcastle, Australia . . . 1992 by schoolmates DANIEL JOHNS, his songwriting partner BEN GILLIES and CHRIS JOANNOU. After winning a national talent contest, SILVERCHAIR were lucky enough to have one of their tracks, 'TOMORROW', playlisted by Australia's foremost "alternative" radio stations. Released as a single in summer 1994, the song scaled the domestic charts, the pubescent schoolboys becoming overnight sensations. A follow-up, 'PURE MASSACRE' repeated the feat, as did their debut album, 'FROGSTOMP', its enjoyable, if cliched grunge/rock stylings proving a massive (Top 10) hit in the States. Finally given a British release in late summer '95, the album squeezed into the Top 50, although it didn't have quite the same impact. Early the following year, their track 'ISRAEL'S SON' was cited by the lawyer of two teenage Americans who were charged with murdering one of their own relatives. The SILVERCHAIR rollercoaster continued early in 1997 with the 'FREAKSHOW' album, a set that once again took its cue from the cream of American alt-rock (i.e. PEARL JAM, STONE TEMPLE PILOTS, etc.) and predictably performed well in the US charts. The lads even began to progress a little further in Britain, the Top 40 album spawning two similarly successful singles, 'FREAK' and 'ABUSE ME'. Returning with a third album, 'NEON BALLROOM' (1999), SILVERCHAIR sold out to the mainstream and bypassed their metallic roots for a more tuneful, string-laden style. However, the record still coined in enough sales for it to dent the US Top 50 (UK Top 30), although the boyz to men development had certainly not worked critically. • **Trivia:** Concert pianist, DAVID HELFGOTT (the movie 'Shine' was made about him!), guested on the track, 'EMOTION SICKNESS'.

Album rating: FROGSTOMP (*7) / FREAKSHOW (*5) / NEON BALLROOM (*4)

DANIEL JOHNS – vocals, guitar / **CHRIS JOANNOU** – bass / **BEN GILLIES** – drums

Columbia | Columbia

Jul 95. (12") *(662264-6)* **PURE MASSACRE. / STONED** [71] [ ]
(cd-s+=) *(662264-2)* – Acid rain / Blind.

Sep 95. (7"/c-s) *(662395-7/-4)* **TOMORROW. / BLIND (live)** [59] [ ]
(cd-s) *(662395-2)* – ('A'side) / Leave me out (live) / Undecided (live).

Sep 95. (cd/c) *(480340-2/-4)* *<67247>* **FROGSTOMP** [49] [9] Aug95
– Israel's son / Tomorrow / Faultline / Pure massacre / Shade / Blind / Leave me out / Suicidal dream / Madman / Undecided / Cicada / Findaway.

Feb 97. (cd/c/pic-lp) *(487103-2/-4/-1)* *<67905>* **FREAKSHOW** [38] [12]
– Slave / Freak / Abuse me / Lie to me / No association / Cemetry / Pop song for us rejects / Door / Learn to hate / Petrol and chlorine / Roses / Nobody came.

Mar 97. (10"/cd-s) *(664076-0/-5)* **FREAK. / SLAVE / (interview)** [34] [ ]
(cd-s) *(664076-2)* – ('A'side) / New race / Punk song #2 / (interview with Daniel, Ben & Chris).

Jul 97. (c-s/cd-s) *(664790-4/-2)* **ABUSE ME / FREAK (Remix for us rejects) / BLIND** [40] [ ]
(cd-s) *(664790-5)* – ('A'side) / Surfin' bird / Slab (Nick Laurnoise mix).

Feb 99. (7"/cd-s) *(667088-7/-2)* **ANTHEM FOR THE YEAR 2000. / MILLENNIUM BUG** [ ] [-]

Mar 99. (cd/c) *(493309-2/-4)* *<69816>* **NEON BALLROOM** [29] [50]
– Emotion sickness / Anthem for the year 2000 / Ana's song (open fire) / Spawn again / Miss you love / Dearest helpless / Do you feel the same / Black tangled heart / Point of view / Satin sheets / Paint pastel princess / Steam will rise.

May 99. (7") *(667345-7)* **ANA'S SONG (OPEN FIRE). / ('A'-acoustic)** [45] [ ]
(cd-s+=) *(667345-5)* – Trash.
(cd-s) *(667345-2)* – ('A'side) / Anthem for the year 2000 (Paul Mac remix) / London's burning.

Aug 99. (cd-ep) **MISS YOU LOVE / WASTED / FIX ME / MINOR THREAT** [ ] [-]

SILVERHEAD

Formed: London, England . . . early 70's by frontman MICHAEL DES BARRES, future BLONDIE bassist NIGEL HARRISON, STEVIE FOREST, ROD DAVIES and PETE THOMPSON. One of the best kept secrets of the glam-rock era, SILVERHEAD, complete with the magnetic DES BARRES, signed to DEEP PURPLE's 'Purple' label, releasing a debut 45, 'ACE SUPREME' in 1972. This heavyweight glitter-rock effort failed to make any headway, likewise their eponymous debut album which drew comparisons with T.REX and SLADE. The following year, ROBBIE BLUNT came in for the departing FOREST, a second album, '16 AND SAVAGED' doing little to stop an impending split. After a one-off solo 45, DES BARRES resurfaced in DETECTIVE, a heavier proposition which caught the eye of JIMMY PAGE. The 'ZEPPELIN axeman snapped the band up for his new 'Swan Song' label, although after only two albums, 'DETECTIVE' (1977) and 'IT TAKES ONE TO KNOW ONE' (1978) the outfit (also numbering ex-YES man, TONY KAYE) folded. After some session work, DES BARRES went solo, recording his debut album, 'I'M ONLY HUMAN' for 'Dreamland' in 1980. Again, success proved elusive, the singer subsequently forming supergroup, CHEQUERED PAST, who also featured NIGEL HARRISON and CLEM BURKE (from BLONDIE), STEVE JONES (ex-SEX PISTOLS!) and TONY SALES (ex-BOWIE, IGGY POP and TODD RUNDGREN). Another commercial non-starter, this punk/metal influenced troupe disbanded after only one eponymous album in 1984. DES BARRES released a follow-up solo set a year later, abandoning this career path after being asked to replace ROBERT PALMER (on tour only) in the DURAN DURAN offshoot, POWER STATION. This signalled the end of DES BARRES' dalliance with the music industry, the singer subsequently substituting the stage for the small screen and landing himself a job as a TV actor. • **Trivia:** DES BARRES was married to former supergroupie, PAMELA DES BARRES (of GTO's), author of rock expose, 'I'm With The Band'. She later became an actress, appearing in US TV shows 'Roseanne', 'MacGyver' and 'WKRP'.

Album rating: SILVERHEAD (*6) / 16 & SAVAGED (*5) / Detective: DETECTIVE (*5) / IT TAKES ONE TO KNOW ONE (*4) / LIVE (*4) / Michael Des Barres: I'M ONLY HUMAN (*4) / SOMEBODY UP THERE LIKES ME (*4) / Chequered Past: CHEQUERED PAST (*5)

MICHAEL DES BARRES – vocals / **STEVIE FOREST** – guitar, vocals / **ROD "ROOK" DAVIES** – guitar, vocals / **NIGEL HARRISON** – bass / **PETE THOMPSON** – drums, percussion

Purple / M.C.A.

1972. (7") *(PUR 104)* **ACE SUPREME. / NO NO NO** [ ] [ ]

1972. (lp) *(PURL 700)* *<306>* **SILVERHEAD** [ ] [ ]
– Long legged Lisa / Underneath the light / Ace supreme / Johnny / In your eyes / Rolling with my baby / Wounded heart / Sold me down the river / Rock and roll band / Silver boogie. *(re-iss. Jun85; TPSA 7506) (cd-iss. Apr97 on 'Repertoire'; RR 4645)*

1973. (7") *(PUR 110)* **ROLLING WITH MY BABY. / IN YOUR EYES** [ ] [ ]

— **ROBBIE BLUNT** – guitar, slide guitar, repl. FOREST

1973. (lp) *(PURL 701)* *<391>* **16 AND SAVAGED** [ ] [ ]
– Hello New York / More than your mouth can hold / Only you / Bright light / Heavy hammer / Cartoon princess / Rock out Claudette rock out / This ain't a parody / 16 and savaged. *(re-iss. Jun85; TPSA 7511) (cd-iss. Jun97 on 'Repertoire'; REP 4646WY)*

— disbanded, HARRISON joined NITE CITY before being found by US hitmakers BLONDIE

Oct 74. (7"; MICHAEL DES BARRES) *(PUR 123)* **LEON. / NEW MOON TONIGHT** [ ] [-]

DETECTIVE

MICHAEL DES BARRES – vocals / **MICHAEL MONARCH** – guitar / **TONY KAYE** – keyboards (ex-YES, ex-BADGER) / **BOBBY PICKET** – bass / **JOHN HYDE** – drums

Swan Song / Swan Song

Jun 77. (lp) *(59405)* *<SS 8417>* **DETECTIVE** [ ] [ ] May77
– Recognition / Got enough love / Grim reaper / Nightingale / Detective man / Ain't none of your business / Deep down / Wild hot summer nights / One more heartache. *(cd-iss. Jan96 on 'Warners'; 7567 91415-2)*

May 78. (lp) *(59406)* *<SS 8504>* **IT TAKES ONE TO KNOW ONE** [ ] [ ] Jan78
– Help me up / Competition / Are you talkin' to me / Dynamite / Something beautiful / Warm love / Betcha won't dance / Fever / Tear jerker. *(cd-iss. May96 on 'Warners'; 7567 91416-2)*

1978. (lp) *<LAAS 002>* **LIVE (live)** [-] [ ]

— DES BARRES guested on GENE SIMMONS's (of KISS's solo album).

MICHAEL DES BARRES

with **NIGEL HARRISON** – bass / **JOHN GOODSALL** – guitar / **PAUL DELPH** – keyboards, vocals / **RIC PARNELL** – drums

Dreamland / Dreamland

Jan 81. (7") *(DLSP 7)* *<106>* **I'M ONLY HUMAN. / CATCH PHRASE** [ ] [ ]

May 81. (lp) *(2394 279)* *<15001>* **I'M ONLY HUMAN** [ ] [ ]
– Bated breath / I'm only human / Someone somewhere in the night / Nothing's too hard / Right or wrong / Dancin' on the brink of disaster / Boy meets car / Scandal papers / Five hour flight / Catch phrase / Bullfighter / I don't have a thing to wear / Outro.

1981. (7") *(DLSP 9)* **SOMEONE SOMEWHERE IN THE NIGHT. / FIVE HOUR FLIGHT** [ ] [-]

1981. (7") *<108>* **NOTHING'S TOO HARD. / BOY MEETS CAR** [-] [ ]

A&M / A&M

Mar 84. (7"/12"; MICHAEL DES BARRES & HOLLY KNIGHT) *(AM/+X 183)* **OBSESSION. / WOMAN'S WEAPON** [ ] [ ]

CHEQUERED PAST

DES BARRES / NIGEL HARRISON / + STEVE JONES – guitar, vocals (ex-SEX PISTOLS) / **TONY SALES** – keyboards (ex-TODD RUNDGREN) / **CLEM BURKE** – drums (ex-BLONDIE)

Heavy Metal / EMI America

Sep 84. (7") *<8229>* **HOW MUCH IS TOO MUCH? / ONLY THE STRONG (WILL SURVIVE)** [-] [ ]

Nov 84. (lp/c) *(HMUSA/HMAMC 53)* *<ST 17123>* **CHEQUERED PAST** [ ] [ ] Sep84
– A world gone wild / Are you sure Hank done it this way / Let me rock / Never in a million years / How much is too much? / Only the strong (will survive) / Underworld / No knife / Tonight and every night.

MICHAEL DES BARRES

with session people incl. **ANDY TAYLOR + STEVE JONES + LAURENCE JUBER** – guitar / **PHILIP CHEN** – bass / **JIM KELTNER** – drums / **KEVIN SAVIGAR** – keyboards

M.C.A. / M.C.A.

Jul 86. (7") *<52870>* **MONEY DON'T COME EASY. / CAMERA EYES** [-] [ ]

Aug 86. (lp) *<5763>* **SOMEBODY UP THERE LIKES ME** [-] [ ]
– Money don't come easy / Do you belong / Is there somebody else / Everything reminds me of you / I can see clearly now / Somebody up there likes me / Too good to be sad / Locked in the cage of love / Camera eyes / Thinking with your body.

— Early in 1986, he had replaced ROBERT PALMER live in DURAN DURAN off-shoot POWER STATION, before he became actor?

SILVER MOUNTAIN

Formed: Malmo, Sweden . . . 1978 by group mastermind JONAS HANSSON, who recruited MORGAN ALM, INGEMAR STENQVIST and MARTEN HEDENER. Taking their cue from the British metal/hard-rock scene, SILVER MOUNTAIN issued a sole (now very rare) single in '79, 'AXEMAN & THE VIRGIN'. One complete line-up change (JENS JOHANSSON, PER STADIN and ANDERS JOHANSSON), three years and a deal with 'Roadrunner' later, the group released a belated debut album, 'SHAKIN' BRAINS' (1983). The JOHANSSON brothers departed shortly after to team up with YNGWIE MALMSTEEN, CHRISTER MENTZER drafted in as a replacement frontman while MARTEN HEDENER returned to fill the drum stool. This new configuration lasted only one studio album, 'UNIVERSE' (1985), the record again only released in Holland. After a live set recorded in Japan (where SILVER MOUNTAIN were held in some regard), MENTZER was superseded by ERIK BJORN NEILSON, while KJELL GUSTAVSON replaced HEDENER. SILVER MOUNTAIN's final release, 'ROSES AND CHAMPAGNE' (1988), was a more overtly commercial affair issued on HANSON's own 'Hex' label. Following the band's demise, HANSSON relocated to America where he continued a low profile recording career.

Album rating: SHAKIN' BRAINS (*5) / UNIVERSE (*5) / HIBIYA – LIVE IN JAPAN '85 (*4) / ROSES AND CHAMPAGNE (*4)

JONAS HANSSON – guitar, vocals / **MORGAN ALM** – guitar / **INGEMAR STENQVIST** – bass / **MARTEN HEDENER** – drums

Eutone / not iss.

1979. (7") *(EUSM 227)* **AXEMAN & THE VIRGIN. / MAN OF NO PRESENT EXISTENCE** [-] [-] Sweden

— **JONAS** brought in complete new line-up; **JENS JOHANSSON** – keyboards / **PER STADIN** – bass / **ANDERS JOHANSSON** – drums

Roadrunner / not iss.

1983. (lp) *(RR 9884)* **SHAKIN' BRAINS** [-] [-] Dutch
– 1789 / Aftermath / Always / Necrosexual killer / Destruction song / Vikings / Looking for you / Spring maiden / King of the sea / Keep on keepin' on.

— **CHRISTER MENTZER** – vocals; repl. JENS

— **MARTEN HEDENER** – drums; repl. ANDERS

1985. (lp) *(RR 9800)* **UNIVERSE** [-] [-] Dutch
– Shakin' brains / Universe / Call of the lords / Handled roughly / Why / Help me / Walking in the shadow / Too late / Niagara.

S.M.S. / not iss.

1986. (lp) *(SP25-5281)* **HIBIYA – LIVE IN JAPAN '85 (live)** [-] [-] Japan
– Shakin' brains / Universe / Always / Why / Handled roughly / Meaningless / Walking in the shadow.

— **ERIK BJORN NIELSEN** – keyboards; repl. MENTZER

— **KJELL GUSTAVSON** – drums; repl. HEDENER

Hex / not iss.

1988. (lp) *(HRLP 881)* **ROSES AND CHAMPAGNE** [ ] [-]
– Romeo & Juliet / Light the light / Where are you / Forest of cries / Coming home / Paris / Paradise smile / Not you baby / Down town junkie.

— folded late in '89

SILVERWING

Formed: Macclesfield, England . . . 1980 by the ROBERTS brothers, DAVE and STEVE, plus TREVOR KIRKPATRICK and ALISTAIR TERRY. An OTT glitter metal outfit, they flew onto the scene with an infamous debut single in summer 1980, 'ROCK AND ROLL ARE FOUR LETTER WORDS' (never!). However, it was almost two years before they got round to issuing a follow-up, appropriately titled, 'SITTING PRETTY'. A third 45, 'THAT'S ENTERTAINMENT', preceded their belated debut album, 'ALIVE AND KICKING', although ironically the group were dead and buried soon after.

Album rating: ALIVE AND KICKING (*5)

TREVOR KIRKPATRICK – vocals, guitar / **STUART McFARLANE** – guitar / **DAVE ROBERTS** – bass / **STEVE ROBERTS** – drums

Mayhem not iss.

Aug 80. (7") *(SILV 001)* **ROCK AND ROLL ARE FOUR LETTER WORDS. / HIGH CLASS WOMAN** -

Apr 82. (7") *(SILV 002)* **SITTING PRETTY. / TEENAGE LOVE** -
(12"+=) *(SILV 002-12)* – Flashbomb fever / Rock'n'roll mayhem.

— **ALISTAIR TERRY** – guitar; repl. McFARLANE who joined MACAXE

Nov 82. (7") *(SILV 003)* **THAT'S ENTERTAINMENT. / FLASHBOMB FEVER** -

Bullet not iss.

Jul 83. (lp) *(BULP 1)* **ALIVE AND KICKING** -
– That's entertainment / Sittin' pretty / Teenage love affair / Flashbomb fever / Love ya / Everybody's singing / Everything happens at night / Soldier girl / Adolescent sex / Rock and roll mayhem / Rock and roll are four letter words.

— the group evolved into PET HATE, although the ROBERTS' reformed for live appearances in 1988 with **IVOR GRIFFITH** – vocals / **PAUL ROLAND** – guitar

Gene SIMMONS (see under ⇒ KISS)

SIMPLE AGGRESSION

Formed: Independence, Kentucky, USA . . . Autumn '89 by ERIC JOHNS, JAMES CARR, DARRIN McKINNEY, DAVE SWART and KENNY SOWARD, who subsequently moved to Cincinnati. Signed to Music For Nations subsidiary, 'Bulletproof', the group released their one and only album, 'FORMULATIONS IN BLACK' (1994), a hard-edged, bass slapping metallic assault which surprisingly failed to catch the attention of either press or public.

Album rating: FORMULATIONS IN BLACK (*5) / GRAVITY (*6)

ERIC JOHNS – vocals / **JAMES CARR** – guitar / **DARRIN McKINNEY** – guitar / **DAVE SWART** – bass / **KENNY SOWARD** – drums

Bulletproof Leviathan

Apr 94. (cd) *(CDVEST 1) <1993-2>* **FORMULATIONS IN BLACK** Jul94
– Quiddity / Formulation in black / Lost / Psychoradius / Sea of eternity / Of winter / Simple aggression / Frenzy / Madd / Spiritual voices / Jedi mind trick / Share your pain.

May 96. (cd) *<19961>* **GRAVITY** -
– In my nature / Art of discipline / Swimming in quicksand / Eternity suite / Hated / Devotion / Release / Demon smile / Lifeguard / Why?

— they must have split some time after above

SINK (see under ⇒ STUPIDS)

SINNER

Formed: Munich, Germany . . . 1980 by MATTHIAS LASCH (aka MAT SINNER), who lined up likeminded JUDAS PRIEST lovers/musicians WOLFGANG WERNER, CALO RAPALLO, FRANKY MITTELBACH and EDGAR PATRIK. Feeding on a musical diet of imported NWOBHM, SINNER (with whatever unrepentant musicians were seemingly available at the time) released a clutch of amateurish albums in the early to mid 80's, from 'WILD 'N' HEAVY' (their debut) to 'DANGEROUS CHARM' (1987). The re-formed SINNER rose again in '92, releasing a further batch of uninspiring records on the German 'No Bull' label. Still relatively big in their homeland, the 5-piece secured a deal with 'Nuclear Blast', releasing two much-improved metal sets, 'THE NATURE OF EVIL' (1998) and 'THE END OF SANCTUARY' (2000).

Album rating: WILD 'N' EVIL (*4) / FAST DECISION (*4) / DANGER ZONE (*4) / TOUCH OF SIN (*4) / COMIN' OUT FIGHTING (*4) / DANGEROUS CHARM (*3) / BACK TO THE BULLET (*4; Mat Sinner) / NO MORE ALIBIS (*5) / GERMANY ROCKS – THE BEST OF SINNER compilation (*5) / RESPECT (*4) / BOTTOM LINE (*4) / IN THE LINE OF FIRE (*4) / JUDGEMENT DAY (*5) / THE NATURE OF EVIL (*5) / THE SECOND DECADE – THE BEST OF SINNER compilation (*7) / THE END OF SANCTUARY (*5)

MATTHIAS LASCH (aka MAT SINNER) – vocals, bass / **WOLFGANG WERNER** – guitar, vocals / **CALO RAPALLO** – guitar, vocals / **FRANKY MITTELBACH** – keyboards, vocals / **EDGAR PATRIK** – drums

Sri Lanka not iss.

1982. (lp) *(SL 7001)* **WILD 'N' EVIL** - - German
– Loser of love / No speed limit / Murder / Ridin' the white horse / Lost in a dream / Heat of the night / F.T.A. / Freerider / Shakin' the Devil's hand / The sin / Trouble.

— **HELMO STONER** – guitar; repl. WERNER + RAPALLO

Scratch not iss.

1983. (lp) *(95001)* **FAST DECISION** - - German
– Runnin' wild / Crazy / Prelude #7 / Magic / One lost look / Fast decision / Trouble boys / In the city / Chains / Rockin'.

— **MICK SHIRLEY** – guitar; repl. MITTELBACH

— **RALF SCHULZ** – drums; repl. PATRIK

Noise not iss.

1984. (lp) *(N 0013)* **DANGER ZONE** - - German
– Danger zone / No place in Heaven / Scene of a crime / Lupo Manaro / Fast, hard & loud / The shiver / Razor blade / Shadow in the night / Wild winds / Rattlesnake.

— **MATS + STONER** recruited **HERMANN FRANK** – guitar / **BERNIE VAN DER GRAAF** – drums

1985. (lp) *(N 0026)* **TOUCH OF SIN** - - German
– Born to rock / Emerald / Bad girl / Shout / The storm broke loose / Out of control / Too late to run away / Hand of fate / Masquerade / Open arms.

1986. (lp) *(N 0049)* **COMIN' OUT FIGHTING** - - German
– Hypnotized / Faster than light / Comin' out fighting / Age of rock / Rebel yell / Lost in a minute / Don't tell me (that the love is gone) / Germany rocks / Playing with fire / Mad house.

— **ANDY SUSEMIHL + ARMIN MUCKE** – guitars; repl. FRANK

— **MATHIAS ULMER** – keyboards; repl. STONER

Nov 87. (lp/c/cd) *(N 0101-1/-4/-2)* **DANGEROUS CHARM** - - German
– Concrete jungle / Knife in my heart / Dangerous charm / Everybody needs somebody to love / Nobody rocks like you / Tomorrow doesn't matter tonight / Fight the fight / Back in my arms / Gipsy / Desperate heart.

— split after they were dropped by their label; re-formed again in the 90's after MAT SINNER released a solo album, 'BACK TO THE BULLET' for 'BMG Ariola'.

Posh not iss.

Oct 92. (cd) *(904008-2)* **NO MORE ALIBIS** -
– When a heart breaks / Good times / Where were you / Burning heart / Boys in trouble / Save me / I'm not over you yet / Thrill of a lifetime / So excitable / Don't wanna lose you / Chasing my dreams. *(re-iss. Mar96 on 'No Bull'; 34346-2)*

No Bull Saraya

Oct 95. (cd) *(34261-2)* **BOTTOM LINE** -
– The biggest lie / Rose of yesterday / When silence falls / All men are heroes / I can't stop the fire / We'll make it alright / Rage of a hurricane / Mercy killer / Dead end street / In the heart of the young / Hearts of steel / Say goodbye.

Dec 95. (cd) *(34270-2)* **RESPECT** -
– Respect / Things get started / Fire in the dark / Don't let this dream die young / Modern world / Beds are burning / Little victory / Every little step / Believer / Valley of tears / Shattered dreams / Knife in my heart / What's so bad about feeling good.

May 96. (cd) *(34347-2)* **IN THE LINE OF FIRE (LIVE IN EUROPE) (live)** -

Sep 97. (cd) *(332231) <431015>* **JUDGEMENT DAY** Nov98
– Used to the truth / Troublemaker / Jump the gun / Judgement day / Pray for mercy / White lightning / Blue tattoo / School of hard knocks / The fugitive / Death walker / Streets of sin. *(re-iss. Jun98 on 'High Gain'; HGCD 0616)*

— MAT also sidelined for a while with PRIMAL FEAR

Nuclear Blast Nuclear Blast

Jul 98. (cd) *(NB 324-2) <6324>* **THE NATURE OF EVIL**
– Devil's river / A question of honour / Justice from Hell / The nature of evil / Some truth / Dark soul / Faith and conviction / Rising / Walk on the dark side / Trust no one / The sun goes down.

— new line-up with **MAT** was **BENNY WOLTER** – guitars (ex-THUNDERHEART) / **ALEX BEYROTH** – guitars / **FRANK ROSSLER** – keyboards / **ULI KUSCH** – drums (of HELLOWEEN)

May 00. (cd) *(NB 471-2) <6471>* **THE END OF SANCTUARY**
– Signed sealed and delivered / Blood relations / The end of sanctuary / Pain in your neck / Edge of the blade / The prophecy / Destiny / Congress of deceit / Heavy duty / Night of the wolf / Broken world / Hand of the saint.

– compilations, etc. –

1994. (cd) *Noise;* **GERMANY ROCKS – THE BEST OF SINNER** - - German

Nov 99. (d-cd) *Nuclear Blast; (NB 441-2) <6441>* **THE SECOND DECADE – THE BEST OF SINNER** Jan99
– The second decade / Jump the gun / When the silence / Devil's river / Used to the truth / Question of honour / The truth is out there / Balls to the wall / Judgement day / The biggest / Streets of sin / Rage of hurricane / The nature of evil / Born to rock / Respect.

SISTER DOUBLE HAPPINESS

Formed: San Francisco, California, USA . . . 1986 by two former members of The DICKS, namely LYNN PERKO and GARY FLOYD. This semi-legendary Texan politico-punk act debuted on a shared album, 'LIVE AT RAULS' with The BIG BOYS, before finally unleashing two further sets, 'KILL FROM THE HEART' (1983) and 'THESE PEOPLE' (1985). Having subsequently split, they teamed up with BEN COHEN and MIKEY DONALDSON, SISTER DOUBLE HAPPINESS initiating their crusade in 1988 with an eponymous album on L.A. indie label, 'S.S.T.'. Carrying on the blues/punk spirit of the DICKS, the record's rawhide intensity and bludgeoning, blistering hard rock'n'roll was convincingly carried off by the gravel-gargling vocals of GARY FLOYD, the overall effect sufficiently impressive to attract 'Warners' subsidiary, 'Reprise'. Disappointingly, the band's belated major label debut, 'HEART & MIND' (featuring guests JOHN CALE and RODDY BOTTUM), failed to capture their trademark piledriving power and by the time of the record's 1992 UK release, DONALDSON had been replaced by JEFF PALMER. FLOYD and Co were freed from the constraints of a big budget studio with 'UNCUT' (1993) – released on 'Dutch East India' – and went for broke on the blues wailing, harmonica-huffing 'HORSEY WATER' (1994), released on 'Sub Pop'. FLOYD had already issued a 'Glitterhouse' solo set, 'WORLD OF TROUBLE', a month previously and following the subsequent demise of SISTER DOUBLE HAPPINESS, would go on to release 'BROKEN ANGELS' (1995) as The GARY FLOYD BAND.

Album rating: SISTER DOUBLE HAPPINESS (*7) / HEART AND MIND (*6) / UNCUT (*6) / HORSEY WATER (*6) / Dicks: KILL FROM THE HEART (*5) / THESE PEOPLE (*5)

DICKS

GARY FLOYD – vocals / **GLEN** – guitar, bass / **BUXF** – bass, vocals, guitar / **PAT** – drums

not iss. Selfless

1981. (m-lp; shared with the BIG BOYS) **LIVE AT RAUL'S (live)**

S.S.T. S.S.T.

Oct 83. (lp) <*(SST 017)*> **KILL FROM THE HEART**
– Anti-Klan (part 1) / Rich daddy / No Nazi's friend / Marilyn Buck / Kill from the heart / Little boys' feet / Pigs run wild / Bourgeois fascist pig / Anti-Klan (part 2) / Purple haze / Right wing – White wing / Dicks can'd swim: 1. Cock jam – 2. Razor blade dance.

— **LYNN PERKO** – drums; repl. PAT

Alternative Tentacles Alternative Tentacles

Jul 85. (lp) <*(VIRUS 43)*> **THESE PEOPLE**
– The police (force) / Off duty sailor / Executive dive / Sidewalk begging / Lost and divided / Dead in a motel room / Cities are burning / Doctor daddy / Decent and clean / Legacy of man / Little rock'n'roller / George Jackson.

— disbanded the following year and evolved into (see below)

– compilations, etc. –

Jun 93. (7"; shared with the BIG BOYS) *Selfless; (SFLS 10-7)* **LIVE AT RAUL'S**

Apr 97. (cd) *Alternative Tentacles;* <*(VIRUS 200CD)*> **DICKS 1980-1986**

SISTER DOUBLE HAPPINESS

GARY FLOYD – vocals / **BEN COHEN (ex-POLKACIDE)** – guitar / **MIKEY DONALDSON** – bass / **LYNN PERKO** – drums

S.S.T. S.S.T.

Jul 88. (lp) <*(SST 162)*> **SISTER DOUBLE HAPPINESS**
– Sister double happiness / Freight train / Let me in / Cry like a baby / On the beach / Poodle dog / It's our life / I tried / Sweet talker / Get drunk and die / You don't know me. *(re-iss. May93 cd/c; SST 162 CD/C)*

— **JEFF PALMER** – bass; repl. DONALDSON

Reprise Reprise

Feb 92. (cd-s) <*40356*> **HEY KIDS / WHEEL'S A' SPINNING / SWEET-TALKER (acoustic) / LIGHTNING STRUCK**

May 92. (cd/c) <*(7599 26657-2/-4)*> **HEART AND MIND** Apr91
– Bobby Shannon / Ain't it a shame / Exposed to you / Sweet talker / You don't know me / The sailor song / Dark heart / Heart and mind / Hey kids / I'm drowning / Don't worry / You for you.

Sub Pop Dutch East

Dec 92. (7") <*SP 77*> **DON'T WORRY. / WHEELS A' SPINNING**

Jun 93. (7") <*(SP 104-276)*> **DO WHAT YOU GOTTA DO. /**
(cd-s+=) <*(SPCD 104-276)*> –

Jul 93. (lp/cd) *(SP/+CD 105-277)* <*2029*> **UNCUT** Jun93
– San Diego / Will you come / Ashes / Whipping song / Doesn't make sense / Honey don't / Keep the city clean / Do what you gotta do / Where do we run / No good for you / Lightnin' / Louise.

— **MILES MONTALBANO** – bass + **DANNY ROMAN** – guitar; repl. PALMER

Sub Pop Sub Pop

Nov 94. (lp/cd) <*(SP/+CD 137-337)*> **HORSEY WATER** Oct94
– Jack freak / Gurden jail / Bad line / Holly said / Waiting for anyone / A+R man / Heart of ice / Who's been fucking you / Sweet home California / Everything will be alright tomorrow.

— split after above, GARY had already recorded a solo set

– compilations, etc. –

Dec 99. (cd) *Innerstate;* <*(INNER 7006)*> **A STONE'S THROW FROM LOVE: LIVE & ACOUSTIC AT THE GREAT AMERICAN MUSIC HALL 6/17/92**
– No good for you / Here I go again / Maybe / You for you / Lightning struck / Absense / The sailor song / Running back again / Exposed to you / Hey kids / No big thang / Dark heart / Motherless children / Sweet talker / Wheels a spinning.

GARY FLOYD

Glitterhouse Glitterhouse

Sep 94. (cd) <*(GRCD 316)*> **WORLD OF TROUBLE**
– Maybe / A better man / World of trouble / Franklyn & Susie / Absence / Dallas / Tough / Wayfaring stranger / Lazarus / From the darkness (to the light). *(re-iss. Nov97; same)*

Oct 94. (7") <*(THM 002)*> **MORE THAN A LIFETIME. /**
(above issued on 'Tres Hombres')

— next with **DANNY ROMAN** – guitar / **JONATHAN BURNSIDE** – guitars / **KENNEY DALE JOHNSON** – drums / **ED IVEY** – bass, mandolin, etc / **DAVE ZIRBEL** – pedal steel

Jun 95. (cd; as the GARY FLOYD BAND) <*(GRCD 367)*> **BROKEN ANGELS**
– Won't be so sad / Spirit on the wind / More than a lifetime / One backdoor man / King bee / Laredo / Don't send me away / Loving you (is all I ever need) / Wild side of life / Baby spends my money / Angel flying too close to the ground / Can't do that.

Innerstate Innerstate

Nov 99. (cd) <*(INNER 7004)*> **BACKDOOR PREACHER MAN** Mar00
– Spirit on the wind / Don't send me away / Franklyn & Susie / Can't be satisfied / Won't be so sad / Spoonful / Wayfaring stranger / Bodean / A better man / More than a lifetime / The rejected ones / World of trouble / Can't do that / King Bee (kissing cousins version) / Angel flying close to the ground / Honey bee / From the darkness (to the light).

SISTERS OF MERCY

Formed: Leeds, England ... 1980 by frontman/lyricist extraordinaire, ANDREW ELDRITCH along with guitarist, GARY MARX. The original "goth" combo, ELDRITCH and Co. were among the first acts to define the genre in its lasting image of black-clad, po-faced rockers meditating on dark, impenetrable lyrics, decipherable only for those willing to substitute make-up for flour or wear pointy boots (and, more importantly, never to emerge in daylight!). For their early releases, the group employed a drum machine, christened Doktor Avalanche, issuing material on their self-financed label, 'Merciful Release'. Following the debut single, 'DAMAGE DONE', ELDRITCH and MARX recruited guitarist BENN GUNN and bassist CRAIG ADAMS, fleshing out the sound on a further series of 7 and 12 inchers, the 'ALICE' EP drawing widespread interest with its goth/alternative/dance fusion. GUNN was then replaced with ex-DEAD OR ALIVE guitarist, WAYNE HUSSEY, for the piledriving theatrics of 'TEMPLE OF LOVE'. During this time, the group had also built up a live reputation, supporting the likes of The BIRTHDAY PARTY and The PSYCHEDELIC FURS as well as appearing at the Leeds Futurama festival. Word was spreading, and in 1984, The SISTERS OF MERCY and their label were signed to a worldwide deal with 'WEA'. A debut album, 'FIRST AND LAST AND ALWAYS', appeared the following year, a worthwhile effort which saw the group almost break into the UK Top 10. Yet only a month after the record's release, the band announced they were to split, tension between ELDRITCH and MARX resulting in the latter leaving the group first. After a final concert at London's Royal Albert Hall, a bitter legal battle ensued between ELDRITCH and ADAMS/HUSSEY. At stake was the SISTERS OF MERCY moniker, ELDRITCH eventually winning out, though not before he'd hastily released a single and album, 'GIFT' (1986), under The SISTERHOOD, primarily to prevent ADAMS and HUSSEY using the title. The latter two subsequently formed The MISSION while ELDRITCH relocated to Berlin/Hamburg, retaining ex-GUN CLUB bassist, PATRICIA MORRISON (who'd played on 'GIFT') and recording 'FLOODLAND' (1987) with the help of his ever-faithful drum machine. The preceding single, 'THIS CORROSION' was suitably grandiose, all ominous vocals and OTT production courtesy of JIM STEINMAN, the single giving ELDRITCH his first UK Top 10 hit. The album achieved a similar feat, incorporating a more overtly rhythmic feel to create a kind of doom-disco sound (perfect for goths who couldn't dance anyway!). MORRISON subsequently left, ELDRITCH recruiting an array of diverse musicians including TIM BREICHENO, ANDREAS BRUHN and punk veteran, TONY JAMES (ex-SIGUE SIGUE SPUTNIK, ex-GENERATION X) to record 'VISION THING' (1990). Employing a more commercial hard rock sound, 'MORE' was one of The SISTERS' most effective singles to date while again the album was a Top 20 success. Further acclaim came in 1992 with the surprisingly consistent retrospective, 'SOME GIRLS WANDER BY MISTAKE' (1992), and its attendant single, a brilliant re-vamp of 'TEMPLE OF LOVE', Israeli warbler, OFRA HAZA, adding that extra mystical touch. After a 1991 joint tour with PUBLIC ENEMY (nice idea, but probably taking the Lollapollooza ethic a bit too far) was abandoned after poor ticket sales, not much has been heard from The SISTERS OF MERCY. ELDRITCH remains an enigmatic figure, any significant activity normally resulting in intense interest from the music press. The odds are that he'll return, though whether in the guise of The SISTERS OF MERCY remains to be seen. • **Covered:** EMMA (Hot Chocolate) / 1969 (Stooges) / GIMME SHELTER (Rolling Stones) / KNOCKIN' ON HEAVEN'S DOOR (Bob Dylan).

Album rating: FIRST AND LAST AND ALWAYS (*8) / GIFT (*7; as Sisterhood) / FLOODLAND (*8) / VISION THING (*7) / SOME GIRLS WANDER BY MISTAKE compilation (*8) / GREATEST HITS VOLUME 1 – A SLIGHT CASE OF OVERBOMBING compilation (*7)

ANDREW ELDRITCH (b. ANDREW TAYLOR, 15 May'59, East Anglia, England) – vocals / **GARRY MARX** (b. MARK PEARMAN) – guitar / + drum machine DOKTOR AVALANCHE

Merciful Release not iss.

1980. (7"m) *(MR 7)* **THE DAMAGE DONE. / WATCH / HOME OF THE HITMAN**

— added **BEN GUNN** (b. BENJAMIN MATTHEWS) – guitar / **CRAIG ADAMS** (b. 4 Apr'62) – bass (ex-EXPELAIRES)

C.N.T. not iss.

Feb 82. (7") *(CNT 002)* **BODY ELECTRIC. / ADRENOCHROME**

Merciful BrainEater

Nov 82. (7") *(MR 015)* **ALICE. / FLOORSHOW**

Mar 83. (7") *(MR 019)* **ANACONDA. / PHANTOM**

Apr 83. (12"ep) *(MR 021)* **ALICE. / FLOORSHOW / 1969 / PHANTOM**

May 83. (12"ep) *(MR 023)* **THE REPTILE HOUSE**
– Kiss the carpet / Lights / Valentine / Burn / Fix. *(re-iss. Apr94)*

— **WAYNE HUSSEY** (b. JERRY LOVELOCK, 26 May'58, Bristol, England) – guitar (ex-DEAD OR ALIVE, ex-HAMBI & THE DANCE) repl. BEN

Oct 83. (7") *(MR 027)* **TEMPLE OF LOVE. / HEARTLAND**

(ext.12"+=) *(MRX 027)* – Gimme shelter.
Jun 84. (7"; as The SISTERS) *(MR 029)* **BODY AND SOUL. / TRAIN** [46] [-]
(12"+=) *(MR 029T)* – After hours / Body electric.

Merciful Release / Elektra

Oct 84. (7") *(MR 033)* **WALK AWAY. / POISON DOOR** [45] [-]
(above w/free 7"flexi) *(MR 033 – SAM 218)* – Long Train.
(12"+=) *(MR 033T)* – On the wire.
Feb 85. (7") *(MR 035)* **NO TIME TO CRY. / BLOOD MONEY** [63] [-]
(12"+=) *(MR 035T)* – Bury me deep.
Mar 85. (lp/c) *(MR 337 L/C) <60405>* **FIRST AND LAST AND ALWAYS** [14] [ ]
– Black planet / Walk away / No time to cry / A rock and a hard place / Marian / First and last and always / Possession / Nine while nine / Amphetamine logic / Some kind of stranger. *(cd-iss. Jul88; 240616-2) (re-iss. re-mastered.Jul92 on 'East West' lp/c; MR 571 L/C) (cd re-mast.Jun92; 9031 77379-2)*

— disbanded mid-'85 . . . GARRY MARX helped form GHOST DANCE. HUSSEY and ADAMS formed The MISSION after squabbles with ANDREW over use of group name.

— **ELDRITCH** with ever faithful drum machine adopted

The SISTERHOOD

— recruited **PATRICIA MORRISON** (b.14 Jan'62) – bass, vocals (ex-FUR BIBLE, ex-GUN CLUB) / **JAMES RAY** – guitar / **ALAN VEGA** – synthesizers (ex-SUICIDE) / **LUCAS FOX** – drums (ELDRITCH moved to Berlin, Germany)

Merciful / not iss.

Feb 86. (7") *(SIS 001)* **GIVING GROUND (remix). / GIVING GROUND (album version)** [ ] [-]
Jul 86. (lp/c) *(SIS 020/+C)* **GIFT** [90] [-]
– Jihad / Colours / Giving ground / Finland red, Egypt white / Rain from Heaven. *(cd-iss. Sep89; SIS 020CD) (re-iss. Jul94 cd/c; 1131684-2/-4)*

— JAMES RAY went solo (backed with The PERFORMANCE), subsequently issuing a couple of 45's, 'MEXICO SUNDOWN BLUES' and 'TEXAS', for 'Merciful Release'. At the turn of the decade, he and his new outfit, JAMES RAY'S GANGWAR, issued a few more, 'DUSTBOAT' and 'WITHOUT CONSCIENCE', the former from a part compilation set, 'A NEW KIND OF ASSASSIN' (1989). In 1992 and '93, the band delivered two more, 'DIOS ESTA DE NUESTRO LADO' and 'THIRD GENERATION'.

The SISTERS OF MERCY

— were once again **ELDRITCH + MORRISON** obtaining rights to name

Merciful-WEA / Elektra

Sep 87. (7") *(MR 39)* **THIS CORROSION. / TORCH** [7] [ ]
(c-s+=/12"+=/cd-s+=) *(MR 39 C/T/CD)* – Colours.
Nov 87. (lp/c)(cd) *(MR 441 L/C)(242246-2) <60762>* **FLOODLAND** [9] [ ]
– Dominion / Mother Russia / Flood I / Lucretia my reflection / 1959 / This corrosion / Flood II / Driven like the snow / Neverlan. *(c+=)–* Torch. *(cd-s++=) –* Colours.
Feb 88. (7") *(MR 43)* **DOMINION. / SANDSTORM / UNTITLED** [13] [-]
(d12"+=) *(MR 43TB)* – Emma.
(c-s+=/3"cd-s+=) *(MR 43 C/CD)* – Ozy-Mandias.
May 88. (7"/ext.12"/ext.3"cd-s) *(MR 44/+T/CD)* **LUCRETIA MY REFLECTION. / LONG TRAIN** [20] [ ]

— (Feb'90) **ELDRITCH** w/drum machine, recruited complete new line-up / **TONY JAMES** (b.1956) – bass, vocals (ex-SIGUE SIGUE SPUTNIK, ex-GENERATION X) / **ANDREAS BRUHN** (b. 5 Nov'67, Hamburg, Germany) – guitar / **TIM BRICHENO** (b. 6 Jul'63, Huddersfield, England) – guitar (ex-ALL ABOUT EVE) / guests were **MAGGIE REILLY** – b.vocals (ex-MIKE OLDFIELD) / **JOHN PERRY** – guitar (ex-ONLY ONES)

Oct 90. (7"/c-s) *(MR 47/+C) <66595>* **MORE. / YOU COULD BE THE ONE** [21] [ ]
(cd-s+=/cd-s+=) *(MR 47CD/+X)* – ('A'extended).
Oct 90. (cd)(c/lp) *(9031 72663-2)(MR 449 C/L) <61017>* **VISION THING** [11] [ ]
– Vision thing / Ribons / Destination Boulevard / Something fast / When you don't see me / Doctor Jeep / More / I was wrong. *(cd re-iss. Jul00; same)*
Dec 90. (7") *(MR 51)* **DOCTOR JEEP. / KNOCKIN' ON HEAVEN'S DOOR (live)** [37] [ ]
(12"+=/cd-s+=) *(MR 51 T/CD)* – ('A'extended).
(ext.12") *(MR 51TX)* – Burn (live) / Amphetamine logic (live).

— (Oct91) **TONY JAMES** split from ELDRITCH amicably.

— Next featured vocals by **OFRA HAZA**

East West / Elektra

Apr 92. (7") *(MR 53)* **TEMPLE OF LOVE (1992). / I WAS WRONG (American fade)** [3] [ ]
(ext.12"+=) *(MR 53T)* – Vision thing (Canadian club mix).
(cd-s+=) *(MR 53CD)* – When you don't see me (German release).
Apr 92. (cd)(c/d-lp) *(9031 76476-2)(MR 449 C/L) <61306>* **SOME GIRLS WANDER BY MISTAKE** (1980-1983 material) [5] [ ]
– Alice / Floorshow / Phantom / 1969 / Kiss the carpet / Lights / Valentine / Fix / Burn / Kiss the carpet (reprise) / Temple of love / Heartland / Gimme shelter / Damage done / Watch / Home of the hitmen / Body electric / Adrenochrome / Anaconda.

— now just **ANDREW ELDRITCH** on own with guests

Aug 93. (7"/c-s) *(MR 59/+C)* **UNDER THE GUN. / ALICE (1993)** [19] [-]
(12"+=/cd-s+=) *(MR 59 T/CD)* – ('A'-Jutland mix).
Aug 93. (cd/c/d-lp) *(4509 93579-2/-4/-1) <61399-2/-4>* **GREATEST HITS VOLUME 1 – A SLIGHT CASE OF OVERBOMBING** (compilation) [14] [ ]
– Under the gun / Temple of love (1992) / Vision thing / Detonation boulevard / Doctor Jeep / More / Lucretia my reflection / Dominion – Mother / This corrosion / No time to cry / Walk away / Body and soul.

— ELDRITCH and his gang seem to have split from the music scene

– compilations, etc. –

Jan 94. (cd) *Cleopatra; <(CLEO 6642CD)>* **FIRST, LAST FOREVER** [ ] [ ]

SIX FEET UNDER

Formed: 1995, in the beginning as a side project for CHRIS BARNES from CANNIBAL CORPSE and ALLEN WEST from OBITUARY; the two of them recruiting TERRY BUTLER (from DEATH) and GREG GALL. Due to the death-metal star status of BARNES and WEST the debut album, 'HAUNTED' (1995) – released on 'Metal Blade' imprint – was eagerly anticipated by fans and critics alike, but unfortunately did not deliver, being seen by many as a money spinner that neither vocalist BARNES or guitarist WEST put much real effort into. Due to disputes that had been growing within CANNIBAL CORPSE, BARNES exited this band for good, turning his full attention towards SFU. This new concern of the singer certainly manifested itself on 'WARPATH' (1997), SFU's second album. On this set the tunes were much more up to the standard devotees of BARNES' and WEST's former output had come to expect. There was lashings of the to-be-expected, over-the-top, almost comical gore-soaked lyrics and subject matter, although not to the same degree as BARNES' work with his former band. 'MAXIMUM VIOLENCE' (1999), the third LP from the group continued in the same, but simple, death-metal formula as far as the music went. Lyrically BARNES seemed to parody himself unfortunately, death for death's sake; STEVE SWANSON replaced WEST. The turn of the century saw the emission of 'GRAVEYARD CLASSICS' (2000). This compilation of SFU covering classic metal was, to all intents and purposes, fairly embarrassing. They did the originals no justice, and did themselves a disservice by releasing it. • **Covered:** GRINDER (Judas Priest) / WRATHCHILD (Iron Maiden) / JAILBREAK (Thin Lizzy) / HOLOCAUST (Savatage) / T.N.T. (Ac/Dc) / SWEET LEAF (Black Sabbath) / PIRANHA (Exodus) / SON OF A BITCH (Accept) / (I'M NOT YOUR) STEPPIN' STONE (Boyce-Hart) / CONFUSED (AngelWitch) / CALIFORNIA UBER ALLES (Dead Kennedys) / SMOKE ON THE WATER (Deep Purple) / BLACKOUT (Scorpions) / PURPLE HAZE (Jimi Hendrix) / IN LEAGUE WITH SATAN (Venom). • **Note:** not to be confused with hard-rock outfit of the mid-80's.

Album rating: HAUNTED (*3) / ALIVE AND DEAD mini (*6) / WARPATH (*7) / MAXIMUM VIOLENCE (*5) / GRAVEYARD CLASSICS (*3)

CHRIS BARNES – vocals (ex-CANNIBAL CORPSE) / **ALLEN WEST** – guitar (ex-OBITUARY) / **TERRY BUTLER** – bass (ex-DEATH) / **GREG GALL** – drums

Metal Blade / Metal Blade

Oct 95. (cd) *<(14093-2)>* **HAUNTED** [ ] [ ] Sep95
– The enemy inside / Silent violence / Lycanthropy / Atill alive / Beneath a black sky / Human target / Remains of you / Suffering in ecstasy / Tomorrow's victim / Torn to the bone / Haunted.
Oct 96. (m-cd) *<(14118-2)>* **ALIVE AND DEAD** [ ] [ ]
– Insect / Drowning / Grinder / Suffering in ecstasy (live) / Human target (live) / Lycanthropy (live) / Beneath a black sky (live).
Aug 97. (cd) *<(14128-2)>* **WARPATH** [ ] [ ]
– War is coming / Nonexistence / A journey into darkness / Animal instinct / Death or glory / Burning blood / Manipulation / 4:20 / Revenge of the zombie / As I die / Night visions / Caged and disgraced. *(lp-iss.Nov97; 3984-14128LP)*

— **STEVE SWANSON** – guitar; repl. ALLEN WEST

Jul 99. (cd/lp) *<(14243-2/-1)>* **MAXIMUM VIOLENCE** [ ] [ ]
– Feasting on the blood of the insane / Bonesaw / Victim of the paranoid / Short cut to Hell / No warning shot / War machine / Mass murder / Brainwashed / Torture killer / The graveyard Earth / Hacked to pieces. *(cd+=) –* Wrathchild / Jailbreak.
Dec 00. (cd) *<(14341-2)>* **GRAVEYARD CLASSICS** [ ] [ ] Oct00
– Holocaust / T.N.T. / Sweet leaf / Piranha / Son of a bitch / (I'm not your) Steppin' stone / Confused / California uber alles / Smoke on the water / Blackout / Ourple haze / In league with Satan.

SKID ROW

Formed: Dublin, Ireland . . . 1968 by 16 year-old guitarist GARY MOORE with PHIL LYNOTT (vocals, bass), ERIC BELL (guitar) and BRIAN DOWNEY (drums), the line-up being dramatically altered a year later, when all but MOORE departed to form THIN LIZZY. These future "Vagabonds Of The Western World" were replaced by BRENDAN "BRUSH" SHIELS and NOEL BRIDGEMAN, the revamped band releasing a couple of Irish 45's, before signing to 'C.B.S.' in 1970. Their debut album grazed the UK Top 30, its promising fusion of hard-edged power blues and progressive jazz-rock landing US support slots to the likes of CANNED HEAT and SAVOY BROWN. A follow-up set, '34 HOURS' surfaced in 1971, although it soon became clear that MOORE's talents were mushrooming beyond the group's limited parameters. PAUL CHAPMAN was subsequently secured as MOORE's replacement, his tenure short-lived as the group finally crashed the following year.

Album rating: SKID (*6) / 34 HOURS (*5)

BRUSH SHIELS – vocals, bass / **GARY MOORE** – guitar, vocals / **NOEL BRIDGEMAN** – drums, vocals

Song / not iss.

1969. (7") **NEW PLACES, OLD FACES. / MISDEMEANOR DREAM FELICITY** [-] [-] Irish
1969. (7") **SATURDAY MORNING MAN. / MERVYN ALDRIDGE** [-] [-] Irish

C.B.S. Columbia

1970. (7") *(CBS 4893)* **SANDIE'S GONE. / (part 2)** [ ] [ ]

Oct 70. (lp) *(CBS 63965)* **SKID ROW** [30] [-]
– Mad dog woman / Virgo's daughter / Heading home again / An awful lot of woman / Unco-up showband blues / For those who do / After I'm gone / The man who never was / Felicity. *(cd-iss. Aug94 on 'Columbia'; 477360-2)*

Apr 71. (7") *(CBS 7181)* **NIGHT OF THE WARM WITCH. / MR. DELUXE** [ ] [ ]

1971. (lp) *(CBS 64411) <30913>* **34 HOURS** [ ] [ ]
– "Night of the warm witch" including (a. The following morning) / "First thing in the morning" including (a. The last thing at night) / "Mar" / "Go, I'm never gonna let you" (part 1) including ("Go, I'm never gonna let you" part 2) / "Lonesome still" / "The love story" (part 1) including ("The love story" part 2) ("The love story" part 3) ("The love story" part 4). *(cd-iss. 1990's on 'Repertoire'; REP 4073) (cd re-iss. May95 on 'Columbia'; 480525-2)*

— **PAUL CHAPMAN** – guitar, vocals, repl. GARY MOORE who joined folkies DR. STRANGELY STRANGE before going solo, etc in 1973. BRIDGEMAN later sessioned for CLANNAD and joined The WATERBOYS.

– compilations, etc. –

Jun 76. (lp) *Release; (RRL 8001)* **ALIVE & KICKING** [-] [-] Irish

Apr 87. (lp/c; as GARY MOORE / BRUSH SHIELS / NOEL BRIDGEMAN) *C.B.S.; (450 263-1/-4)* **SKID ROW** [ ] [-]
– Benedict's cherry wine / Saturday morning man / Crystal ball / Mr. Deluxe / Girl called winter / Morning star avenue / Silver bird. *(cd-iss. Jun94 on 'Castle'; CLACD 343) (cd re-iss. Aug00 on 'Snapper'; SMMCD 608)*

SKID ROW

Formed: New Jersey, New York, USA . . . late '86 by DAVE 'Snake' SABO and RACHEL BOLAN (male!). Following the addition of SCOTTI HILL, ROB AFFUSO and Canadian born frontman SEBASTIAN BACH, the band line-up was complete, a subsequent management deal (with Doc McGhee) and a support slot on BON JOVI's 1989 US tour a result of SABO's personal connection with JON BON JOVI. Signed worldwide to 'Atlantic' in 1988, the group enjoyed heavy MTV coverage of their summer '89 debut single, 'YOUTH GONE WILD', BACH's blonde-haired good looks and brattish behaviour proving a compelling focal point. Combining the metallic glam of MOTLEY CRUE / L.A. GUNS with the nihilistic energy of the SEX PISTOLS, their eponymous debut album narrowly missed the US Top 5, going on to sell a staggering four million copies. Sales were boosted by the Top 10 success of subsequent singles, the angst-ridden '18 AND LIFE' and token ballad, 'I REMEMBER YOU'. Controversy followed after BACH was charged with assault (following a bottle throwing incident), the singer escaping jail with three years' probation. With their reputation as rock bad boys complete, the group stormed into the US No.1 slot (UK No.5) with a follow-up, 'SLAVE TO THE GRIND' (1991). A more aggressive affair, the punk influence was more pronounced with the group even releasing a fiery cover of the 'Pistols' 'HOLIDAYS IN THE SUN' (originally recorded as part of the 1989 metal compilation, 'Stairway To Heaven, Highway To Hell') as the B-side of the 'WASTED TIME' single. No hits were forthcoming, however, and the record failed to match sales of the debut. A third album eventually appeared in 1995, 'SUBHUMAN RACE', the record faring better in the UK (Top 10) than their native USA where it barely made the Top 40. The man BOLAN (RACHEL, that is), had already released his own album billed under the unlikely tag of PRUNELLA SCALES (Basil Fawlty would not be amused). The band's subsequent demise saw BACH forming an unlikely alternative "supergroup", THE LAST HARD MEN with BREEDERS guitarist KELLEY DEAL, FROGS guitarist JIMMY FLEMION and SMASHING PUMPKINS sticksman JIMMY CHAMBERLAIN. Although the band managed only a one-off cover of Alice Cooper's 'SCHOOL'S OUT' (for the soundtrack to the movie, 'Scream'), before DEAL and CHAMBERLAIN returned to their respective bands, BACH retained FLEMION for a solo project which also involved various minor-league metal faces. The appallingly titled 'BRING 'EM BACH ALIVE' (1999) was culled from the band's Japanese tour, featuring a raft of SKID ROW nuggets alongside a few new studio efforts. • **Songwriters:** BOLAN w/ SNAKE + BACH or BOLAN w / AFFUSO + HILL. Covered PSYCHO THERAPY (Ramones) / C'MON AND LOVE ME (Kiss) / DELIVERING THE GOODS (Judas Priest) / WHAT YOU'RE DOING (Rush) / LITTLE WING (Jimi Hendrix).

Album rating: SKID ROW (*6) / SLAVE TO THE GRIND (*6) / B-SIDE OURSELVES collection (*4) / SUBHUMAN RACE (*5) / 40 SEASONS – THE BEST OF SKID ROW compilation (*6) / Prunella Scales: DRESSING UP THE IDIOT (*5) / Sebastian Bach: BRING 'EM BACK ALIVE (*5)

SEBASTIAN BACH (b. SEBASTIAN BIERK, 3 Apr'68, Bahamas) – vocals; repl. MATT FALLON / **DAVE 'Snake' SABO** (b.16 Sep'62) – guitar / **SCOTTI HILL** (b.31 May'64) – guitar / **RACHEL BOLAN** (b. 9 Feb'64) – bass / **ROB AFFUSO** (b. 1 Mar'63) – drums

Atlantic Atlantic

Nov 89. (7"/7"sha-pic-d) *(A 8935/+P) <88935>* **YOUTH GONE WILD. / SWEET LITTLE SISTER** [42] [99] May89
(12"+=/cd-s+=) *(A 8935T)* – Makin' a mess (live).

Dec 89. (lp/c/cd) *(K 781936-1/-4/-2) <81936>* **SKID ROW** [30] [6] Feb89
– Big guns / Sweet little sister / Can't stand the heartache / Piece of me / 18 and life / Rattlesnake shake / Youth gone wild / Here I am / Makin' a mess / I remember you / Midnight – Tornado. *(cd re-iss. Feb95; same)*

Jan 90. (7"one-sided/7"sha-pic-d) *(A 8883/+P) <88883>* **18 AND LIFE. / MIDNIGHT – TORNADO** [12] [4] Jul89
(12"+=/cd-s+=) *(A 8883 T/CD)* – Here I am (live).

Mar 90. (7"/7"s/c-s) *(A 8886/+X/C) <88886>* **I REMEMBER YOU. / MAKIN' A MESS** [36] [6] Nov89
(12"+=/cd-s+=) *(A 8886 TW/CD)* – Big guns.
(10"+=) *(A 8886T)* – ('A'live).

East West Atlantic

Jun 91. (7"sha-pic-d/c-s) *(A 7673/+C) <87673>* **MONKEY BUSINESS. / SLAVE TO THE GRIND** [19] [ ]
(12"+=/cd-s+=) *(A 7673 TW/CD)* – Riot act.

Jun 91. (cd)(lp/c) *<(7567 82242-2)>(WX 423/+C)* **SLAVE TO THE GRIND** [5] [1]
– Monkey business / Slave to the grind / The threat / Quicksand Jesus / Psycho love / Get the fuck out / Livin' on a chain gang / Creepshow / In a darkened room / Riot act / Mudkicker / Wasted time.

Sep 91. (7"/c-s) *(A 7603/+C)* **SLAVE TO THE GRIND. / C'MON AND LOVE ME** [43] [-]
(12") *(A 7603TX)* – ('A'side) / Creepshow / Beggar's day.
(cd-s++=) *(A 7603CD)* – (above 'B'side).

Nov 91. (7") *(A 7570)* **WASTED TIME. / HOLIDAYS IN THE SUN** [20] [-]
(12"+=) *(A 7570T)* – What you're doing / Get the fuck out (live).
(cd-s+=) *(A 7570CD)* – Psycho love / Get the fuck out (live).
(12"pic-d) *(A 7570TP)* – ('A'side) / Psycho love.

Dec 91. (c-s,cd-s) *<87565>* **WASTED TIME / C'MON AND LOVE ME** [-] [88]

Aug 92. (7"/c-s) *(A 7444/+C)* **YOUTH GONE WILD. / DELIVERIN' THE GOODS** [22] [-]
(12"+=/cd-s+=) *(A 7444 T/CD)* – Get the funk out / Psycho therapy.

Sep 92. (m-cd/m-c) *<(7567 82431-2/-4)>* **B-SIDE OURSELVES** [ ] [58]
– Psychotherapy / C'mon and love me / Deliverin' the goods / What you're doing / Little wing.

Mar 95. (cd/c/lp) *<(7567 82730-2/-4/-1)>* **SUBHUMAN RACE** [8] [35]
– My enemy / Firesign / Bonehead / Beat yourself blind / Eileen / Remains to be seen / Subhuman race / Frozen / Into another / Face against my soul / Medicine jar / Breakin' down / Ironwill.

Nov 95. (7"colrd) *(A 7135)* **BREAKIN' DOWN. / RIOT ACT (live)** [48] [ ]
(cd-s) *(A 7135CD1)* – ('A'side) / Firesign (demo) / Slave to the grind (live) / Monkey business (live).
(cd-s) *(A 7135CD2)* – ('A'side) / Frozen (demo) / Beat yourself blind (live) / Psychotherapy (live).

— split early in 1996, but will reform under a new banner in '98/'99. **SEAN McCABE** – vocals; repl. BACH who went solo

– compilations, etc. –

Jul 98. (cd/c) *Atlantic; <(7567 83103-2/-4)>* **40 SEASONS – THE BEST OF SKID ROW** [ ] [ ]
– Youth gone wild / 18 and life / Piece of me / I remember you / Threat / Psycho love / Monkey business / Quicksand Jesus / Slave to the grind / Into another (mix) / Frozen / My enemy / Breakin' down (mix) / Beat yourself blind (live) / Forever / Fire in the hole.

PRUNELLA SCALES

RACHEL BOLAN – bass, guitar, vocals / **TOMMY SOUTHARD** – guitar / **PHIL VARONE** – drums

Mutiny Mutiny

Aug 97. (cd) *<(80008-2)>* **DRESSING UP THE IDIOT** [ ] [ ] May97
– Crisp / Dead man / Freak machine / When / Fifty tons of life / Don't let the flowers die / TV is king / Tom's river / Had to look / Talk myself down.

SEBASTIAN BACH

BACH with **JIMMY FLEMION** – guitar (ex-FROGS) / **RICHIE SCARLET** – guitar (ex-FREHLEY'S COMET) / **MARK "BAM BAM" McCONNELL** – drums / **LARRY** – bass, rhythm guitar

not iss. Spitfire

Nov 99. (cd) *<15041>* **BRING 'EM BACH ALIVE** [-] [ ]
– Rock & roll / Done bleeding / Superjerk, superstar, supertears / Blasphemer / Counterpunch / Slave to the grind (live) / Frozen (live) / 18 & life (live) / Beat yourself blind (live) / Riot act (live) / Mudkicker (live) / In a darkened room (live) / Monkey business – Godzilla (live) / The most powerful man in the world (live) / I remember you (live) / Youth gone wild (live).

SKIN

Formed: London, England . . . 1991 as TASTE by ex-JAGGED EDGE guitarist, MYKE GRAY along with previous bandmate ANDY ROBBINS, ex-BRUCE DICKINSON man, DICKIE FLISZAR and frontman NEVILLE MacDONALD, formerly of Welsh heavies, KOOGA. Changing their name to SKIN to avoid confusion with the late 60's blues act of the same name, the group attempted to bring some credibilty to melodic Brit-metal, signing to the hip 'Parlophone' label and injecting their sound with a 90's verve and style lacking in their more traditional contemporaries. Building up a grassroots fanbase through consistent touring, the group scored a minor Top 75 hit in late '93 with their debut release, the cheekily titled 'SKIN UP EP'. Further singles, 'HOUSE OF LOVE' and 'MONEY' achieved successively higher chart placings in Spring '94, the latter making the UK Top 20. It came as no surprise, then, when the eponymous debut, 'SKIN' (1994) launched into the Top 10, its polished, bluesy hard-rock taking up the mantle of acts like THUNDER and FM. Although they scored a further string of minor singles chart successes, SKIN couldn't keep up their early momentum and by the release of follow-up set, 'LUCKY' (1996), were struggling to make the Top 40. Like so many similar acts before them, SKIN struggled to live up to high expectations and were inevitably dropped by their major label paymasters. Battling on, the band resurfaced with the independently released 'EXPERIENCE ELECTRIC' in 1997, their diehard fans putting the record into the Top 75. • **Songwriters:**

GRAY, some w/others, except HANGIN' ON THE TELEPHONE (Blondie) / PUMP IT UP (Elvis Costello) / ROCK CANDY (Montrose) / RADAR LOVE (Golden Earring) / SHOULD I STAY OR SHOULD I GO (Clash) / EXPRESS YOURSELF (Madonna) / UNBELIEVABLE (EMF) / SPEED KING (Deep Purple) / ROCK AND ROLL (Led Zeppelin) / MY GENERATION (Who) / SILLY THING (Sex Pistols) / HIT ME WITH YOUR RHYTHM STICK (Ian Dury) / DOG EAT DOG (Adam & The Ants) / COME TOGETHER (Beatles) / ONE WAY (Levellers) / THE MUPPET SONG (hit; Muppets).

Album rating: SKIN (*5) / LUCKY (*5) / EXPERIENCE ELECTRIC (*6) / HASTA LA VISTA BABY compilation (*6)

NEVILLE MacDONALD (b. Ynysybwl, Wales) – vocals (ex-KOOGA) / **MYKE GRAY** (b.12 May'68) – guitar (ex-JAGGED EDGE) / **ANDY ROBBINS** – bass, vocals / **DICKIE FLISZAR** (b. Germany) – drums, vocals (ex-BRUCE DICKINSON)

Parlophone — not iss.

Dec 93. (12"ep/cd-ep) *(12R/CDR 6363)* **SKIN UP EP** [67] [-]
– Look but don't touch / Shine your light / Monkey.

Mar 94. (12"ep/c-ep/cd-ep) *(12R/TCR/CDR 6374)* **HOUSE OF LOVE / GOOD TIME LOVIN'. / THIS PLANET'S ON FIRE / TAKE IT EASY** [45] [-]

Apr 94. (c-s) *(TCR 6381)* **MONEY / ALL I WANT / FUNKTIFIED** [18] [-]
(cd-s) *(CDR 6381)* – (1st 2 tracks) / Unbelievable / Down down down.
(12"pic-d) *(CDR 6381)* – (1st & 3rd tracks) / Express yourself.
(cd-s) *(CDRS 6381)* – (1st & 3rd tracks) / Express yourself / Unbelievable.

May 94. (cd/c/lp) *(CD/TC+/PCSD 151)* **SKIN** [9] [-]
– Money / Shine your light / House of love / Colourblind / Which are the tears / Look but don't touch / Nightsong / Tower of strength / Revolution / Raised on radio / Wings of an angel. *(re-iss. Oct94 d-cd+=; CDPCST 151)* – Unbelievable / Pump it up / Hangin' on the telephone / Express yourself / Funkified / Monkey / Should I stay or should I go / Dog eat dog / Down, down, down / Good good lovin'.

Jul 94. (c-s) *(TCR 6387)* **TOWER OF STRENGTH / LOOK BUT DON'T TOUCH (live) / UNBELIEVABLE (live)** [19] [-]
(12"+=/cd-s+=) *(12R/CDR 6387)* – ('A'live).
(cd-s) *(CDRS 6387)* – ('A'side) / Money (live) / Shine your light (live) / Colourblind (live).

Oct 94. (c-s) *(TCR 6391)* **LOOK BUT DON'T TOUCH. / HANGIN' ON THE TELEPHONE** [33] [-]
(cd-s+=) *(CDR 6391)* – Should I stay or should I go / Dog eat dog.
(12"pic-d/cd-s) *(12R/TCR 6391)* – ('A'side) / Should I stay or should I go / Pump it up / Money.

May 95. (12"ep) *(12R 6409)* **TAKE ME DOWN TO THE RIVER. / SPEED KING (live) / NEED YOUR LOVE SO BAD (live) / HOUSE OF LOVE (live)** [26] [-]
(cd-ep) *(CDR 6409)* – ('A'side) / Rock and roll (live) / Ain't talkin' 'bout love (live) / Rock candy (live).
(cd-ep) *(CDRS 6409)* – ('A'side) / Radar love (live) / Come together (live) / My generation (live).

Mar 96. (cd-s) *(CDR 6426)* **HOW LUCKY YOU ARE / SPIT ON YOU / I BELIEVE** [32] [-]
(12"pic-d+=) *(12R 6426)* – Sweet Mary Jane.
(cd-s) *(CDRS 6426)* – ('A'side) / Back door man / Sweet Mary Jane.

Apr 96. (cd/c/d-lp) *(CD/TC+/PCSD 168)* **LUCKY** [38] [-]
– Spit on you / How lucky are you / Make it happen / Face to face / New religion / Escape from reality / Perfect day / Let love rule your heart / Juliet / No way out / Pray / One nation / I'm alive / Inside me inside you.

May 96. (7"colrd-ep/cd-ep) *(R/CDR 6433)* **PERFECT DAY / THE MUPPET SONG (MAH NA MAH NA). / I GOT YOU / SILLY THING** [33] [-]
(cd-ep) *(CDRS 6433)* – ('A'side) / The Muppet song (mah na mah na) / Hit me with your rhythm stick / One way.

Snapper – Reef — Snapper – Reef

Sep 97. (cd) *(<SRECD 705>)* **EXPERIENCE ELECTRIC** [72] [ ] Dec97
– Experience electric / Only one / Blow my mind / Shine like diamonds / Pleasure / Love like suicide / Tripping / Soul / Falling / Winners and losers / Bittersweet / Aphrodite's child.

– compilations, etc. –

Jun 00. (d-cd) *Recall; (SMDCD 277) / Snapper; <709>* **HASTA LA VISTA BABY** [ ] [ ]
– Krusher intro / Experience electric / The only one / Blow my mind / No way out / Make it happen / Soul / Shine like diamonds / Let love rule your heart / Tripping / Love like suicide / Perfect day / How lucky you are / Unbelievable / Mah na mah na / Money / Shine your light / House of love / Colour blind / Take me down to the river / Look but don't touch / Tower of strength.

SKINLAB

Formed: San Francisco, California, USA . . . 1995 by STEEV ESQUIVEL, MIKE ROBERTS, GARY WENDT, and PAUL HOPKINS. SKINLAB came out of the Bay Area metal scene; their output tending towards skate-park friendly, ultra heavy metal although with alt-rock leanings. With some well-placed demo tapes and a little help from fellow San Franciscans MACHINE HEAD, the band managed to ink a deal with metal/punk label 'Century Media'. They released their debut full-set, 'BOUND, GAGGED AND BLINDFOLDED' in 1997. This album unleashed on the public SKINLAB's version of events, fully of chunky riffage and a heavy rhythm section to complement it. Unfortunately a monumental round of touring led to the departure of ROBERTS and WENDT. SKINLAB managed to find more than ample replacements though, courtesy of SCOTT SARGEANT (from KILLING CULTURE) and SNAKE (formerly with SKREW). The new recruits on rhythm and lead certainly bolstered SKINLAB's sound. This was evident on the band's follow up album, 'DISEMBODY: THE NEW FLESH' (1999). The sophomore album showed a far more mature and heavier approach. Maybe the brand of weed they were smoking was finally getting through.

Album rating: BOUND, GAGGED AND BLINDFOLDED (*6) / DISEMBODY: THE NEW FLESH (*7)

STEEV ESQUIVEL – vocals, bass / **MIKE ROBERTS** – guitar / **GARY WENDT** – guitar / **PAUL HOPKINS** – drums

Century Media — Century Media

Apr 97. (cd/lp) *(CM 77174/+LP)* *<7874>* **BOUND, GAGGED AND BLINDFOLDED** [ ] [ ]
– When pain comes to surface / Dissolve / Race of hate / Paleface / Down / Promised / Stumble / The art of suffering / Ten seconds.

— **SCOTT SARGEANT** – guitar + **SNAKE** – guitar (ex-SKREW) repl. MIKE + GARY

Nov 98. (cd-ep) *<(CMA 7939CD)>* **EYESORE** [ ] [ ]
– So far from the truth / Noah / Raza Odiada (Pito Wilson) / When pain comes to surface (demo) / Paleface (live).

Mar 99. (cd) *(CM 77238CD)* *<7938>* **DISEMBODY: THE NEW FLESH** [ ] [ ]
– So far from the truth / Know your enemies / No sympathy (for the Devil) / Scapegoat / Breathe / I name my pain / Excellerate / Coward / Second skin (new flesh) / Looks can be deceiving.

SKINNY PUPPY

Formed: Vancouver, Canada . . . 1983 by NIVEK OGRE (aka DAVID OGILVIE), cEVIN KEY and BILL LEEB. Basically a distorted industrial electronic dance outfit influenced by THROBBING GRISTLE or CABARET VOLTAIRE, their first release in 1985, 'REMISSION', saw them fuse teutonic electro with an early form of acid-house! Live performances combined footage of vivisection experiments with a splattering of fake stage blood and samples of the voice of killer, Charles Manson. DWAYNE GOETTEL was added during the mid-80's, his debut appearance being on the album, 'CLEANSE, FOLD AND MANIPULATE', a record that brought them critical acclaim. Their credibility was partly lost after signing to 'Capitol', the conglomerate plucking them from the depths of Euro-indie obscurity (i.e. 'Nettwerk'). However, by 1990 their sound had incorporated a new off-kilter beat, highlighted on the album, 'TOO DARK PARK'. In August 1995, tragedy struck when heroin addict, DWAYNE, died of a suspected overdose. A final postscript set, 'THE PROCESS', surfaced in early '96, although members have since splintered into DOWNLOAD and PIGFACE. The former had also released two albums for 'Westcom' prior to DWAYNE's death ('SIDEWINDER', 'FURNACE' and in 1996, 'EYES OF STANLEY PAIN'). KEY had also been part of TEARGARDEN with LEGENDARY PINK DOTS' mainman, EDWARD KA-SPEL.

Album rating: REMISSION mini (*5) / BITES (*6) / MIND: THE PERPETUAL INTERCOURSE (*6) / CLEANSE, FOLD AND MANIPULATE (*7) / VIVIsectVI (*6) / RABIES (*6) / SPASMOLYTIC (*5) / TOO DARK PARK compilation (*7) / LAST RIGHTS (*6) / BACK AND FORTH 2 (*5) / THE PROCESS (*6)

NIVEK OGRE (b. DAVID OGILVIE, 5 Dec'62) – vocals / **cEVIN KEY** (b. KEVIN CROMPTON, 13 Feb'61) – percussion, synthesizer / **BILL LEEB** –

Scarface — Nettwerk

Jun 85. (m-lp) *(MFACE 010)* *<30082>* **REMISSION** [ ] [ ]
– Smothered hope / Glass houses / Far too frail / Solvent / Sleeping beast / Brap.

— now without LEEB who formed FRONTLINE ASSEMBLY

Feb 86. (lp) *(FACE 15)* *<30002>* **BITES** [ ] [ ]
– Assimilate / The choke / Blood on the wall / Church / Deadline / Last call / Basement / Tomorrow. *('REMISSION AND BITES' cd-iss. Jan87 on 'Play It Again Sam'; BIAS 048) <US on 'SPV'; 857100>*

Play It Again Sam — not iss.

1986. (12") *(BIAS 037)* **DIG IT. / THE CHOKE** [ ] [-]

Capitol — Capitol

Feb 87. (cd/c) *<C2/C4 90467>* **MIND: THE PERPETUAL INTERCOURSE** [-] [ ]
– One time one place / God's gift (maggot) / Three blind mice / Love / Stairs and flowers / Antagonism / 200 years / Dig it / Burnt with water. *(cd-iss. 1988 on 'Nettwerk'; NT CD 037)* – Chainsaw / Addiction / Stairs and flowers (dub) / Deep down trauma hounds. *(re-iss. lp Aug89 on 'Play It Again Sam'; BIAS 43)*

— added **DWAYNE GOETTEL** (b. 1 Feb'64) – keyboards, samples

Nettwerk — Nettwerk

May 87. (12"/c-s) *(NTM/+C 6305)* **CHAINSAW. /** [ ] [ ]

Oct 87. (12") *(NT12 3010)* **ADDICTION. /** [ ] [ ]

Capitol — Nettwerk

Jan 88. (lp/c) *(EST/TCEST 2052)* *<46922>* **CLEANSE FOLD AND MANIPULATE** [ ] [ ]
– First aid / Addiction / Shadow cast / Draining faces / The mourn / Second tooth / Tear or beat / Deep down / Trauma hounds / Anger / Epilogue. *(cd-iss. Sep93; NET 019CD)*

1988. (12") *(12CL 517)* **CENSOR (extended). / PUNK IN PARK ZOO'S / CENSOR** [ ] [ ]

Nov 88. (lp/c)(cd) *(EST/TCEST 2079)(CDP 791 040-2)* *<91040>* **VIVIsectVI** [ ] [ ] Jul88
– Dogshit / VX gas attack / Harsh stone white / Human disease (S.K.U.M.M.) / Who's laughing now? / Testure? / State aid / Hospital waste / Fritter (Stella's home). *(cd+=)* – Yes he ran / Punk in park zoos / The second opinion / Funguss. *(re-iss. cd Sep93 on 'Nettwerk'; NET 021CD)*

— added guest producer **AL JOURGENSEN** – guitar, vocals (MINISTRY)

Nettwerk — Capitol

Jul 90. (lp/cd) *(NET 023/+CD)* *<93007>* **RABIES** [ ] [ ] Jan90
– Rodent / Hexonxonx / Two time grime / Fascist Jockitch / Worlock / Rain / Tin omen / Rivers / Choralone / Amputate / Spahn dirge (live).

Nov 90. (cd-ep) *(NET 024CD)* **SPASMOLYTIC** [ ] [-]

Feb 91. (cd) *(NET 026CD) <94683>* **TOO DARK PARK; TWELVE INCH ANTHOLOGY** (compilation) [ ] [ ]
– Convulsion / Tormentor / Sasmolytic / Rash reflection / Natures revenge / Short lived poison / Grave wisdom / T.F.W.O. / Morpheus laughing / Reclamation. *(re-iss. Sep93; same)*

Apr 92. (cd) *(NET 038CD) <98037>* **LAST RIGHTS** [ ] [ ]
– Hinder / Killing game / Cancelled / Xception / Catbowl / Hurtful 2 / Rivers end / Fester / Premonition / Wrek / Epilogue 2. *(re-iss. Sep93; same) (cd re-iss. Nov99; 670030072-2)*

— now without OGRE. Tragically on 23 August '95, GOETTEL died of a heroin overdose. They were both featured on below album.

American Warners

Feb 96. (cd) *(74321 31097-2) <43057>* **THE PROCESS** [ ] [ ]
– Jahya / Death / Candle / Hardset head / Cult / The process / Crucible / Blue Serge / Morter / Amnesia / Cellar heat.

– compilations, etc. –

1990. (cd/lp) *Nettwerk; <30041>* **12" ANTHOLOGY** [-] [ ]
(cd re-iss. Feb99; same)

1991. (cd) *Nettwerk; <30061>* **AIN'T IT DEAD YET (live)** [-] [ ]
– Intro / Anger / Choke / Addiction / Assimilate / First aid / Dig it / One time one place / Deep down trauma hounds / Chainsaw / Brap / Smothered hope. *(re-iss. Feb99; same)*

Jan 93. (cd) *Nettwerk; <30078>* **BACK AND FORTH SERIES VOL.2** [-] [ ]
– Intro (live in Winnipeg) / Sleeping beast / K-9 / Monster radio man / Quiet solitude / Pit / Sore in a masterpiece – Dead of winter / Unovis on a stick / To a baser nature / A.M. – Meat flavour / My voice sounds like shit / Smothered hope / Explode the P.A. / Assimilate / Edge of insanity.

May 96. (d-cd) *Westcom; (0892240-2) / Nettwerk; <30103>* **BRAP** (rare material) [ ] [ ] Apr96

Aug 98. (cd) *Nettwerk; (NET 024CD)* **SPASMOLYTIC** [ ] [ ]

Oct 98. (cd) *Nettwerk; <30128>* **REMIX DAYS TEMPER** [-] [ ]

Jan 00. (cd) *Nettwerk; (30148-2)* **SINGLES COLLECTION** [ ] [ ]

Jan 00. (cd) *Nettwerk; (30149-2)* **B-SIDES COLLECTION** [ ] [ ]

SKREW

Formed: Austin, Texas, USA . . . 1991 out of ANGKOR WAT by ADAM "BUNNE" GROSSMAN and OPOSSUM (aka DANNY LOHNER), who, after their scary debut industrial-metal album, 'BURNING IN WATER' (1992), expanded the line-up for subsequent touring commitments, recruiting JIM VOLLENTINE, BRANDON WORKMAN, DOUG SHAPPUIS and MARK DUFOUR. This worked well enough to convince GROSSMAN that a more live instrumental feel would benefit the next studio album, 'DUSTED' (1994) which proved a more conventionally heavy affair while still retaining an innovative, open ended feel. Signing to 'Metal Blade', GROSSMAN moved progressively further from his industrial beginnings on successive releases, 'SHADOW OF DOUBT' (1996) and 'ANGEL SEED XXIII' (1997), piling on the dense, metallic riffs with a vengeance.

Album rating: BURNING IN WATER, DROWNING IN FLAME (*7) / DUSTED (*6) / SHADOW OF DOUBT (*6) / ANGEL SEED XXIII (*6)

ADAM "BUNNE" GROSSMAN – vocals, guitar / **OPOSSUM** (b. DANNY LOHNER) – guitar / + session people

Devotion Metal Blade

May 92. (cd/c/lp) *(CD/T+/DVN 15) <26948>* **BURNING IN WATER, DROWNING IN FLAME** [ ] [ ] Dec91
– Orifice / Burning in water, drowning in flame / Cold angel press / Charlemagne / Gemini / Indestructible / Feast / Once alive / Sympathy for the Devil / Poisonous / Prey flesh. *(cd re-iss. Jun96 on 'Metal Blade'; 3984 17015CD)*

— added **DOUG SHAPPUIS** – guitar / **BRANDON WORKMAN** – bass / **MARK DUFOUR** – drums / **JIM VOLLENTINE** – keyboards

Devotion Scarface

May 94. (cd) *(CDDVN 28) <53902>* **DUSTED** [ ] [ ]
– In tongues / Picasso trigger / Jesus skrew superstar / Skrew saves / Season for whither / Sour / Mouthful of dust / Godsong.

Metal Blade Metal Blade

Apr 96. (cd) *<(3984 17025CD)>* **SHADOW OF DOUBT** [ ] [ ]
– She said / Black eye / Knotted twig / Head / Swallow / Sam I am / Going down / Generator / Dark ride / Crawl.

Oct 97. (cd) *<(3984 14142CD)>* **ANGEL SEED XXIII** [ ] [ ]
– Open up / Sea man / Seventh eye / King of the hole / Porcelain / Kosmo's seed / Sputnik / Angel suck / Horsey(man) / Slip.

— disbanded after above

SKREWDRIVER

Formed: Blackpool, England . . . late '76 by IAN STEWART, RON HARTLEY, KEVIN McKAY and GRINNY. Unashamed white-power skinheads, SKREWDRIVER were part of punk's lower division vanguard alongside the likes of CHELSEA, COCK SPARRER and EATER. Signed to the capital's 'Chiswick' label (once home of JOE STRUMMER's 101'ERS), SKREWDRIVER began their notorious recording career in Spring 1977 with the boorish 'YOU'RE SO DUMB' (a blueprint for the UK "oi" movement no doubt). Half a year on, with the 'PISTOLS riding high at No.1, the lads released the self-explanatory 'ANTI-SOCIAL' single backed by a painfully raw cover of The Rolling Stones' '19th NERVOUS BREAKDOWN'. In November that year, their debut (mini) album, 'ALL SKREWED UP' hit the shops, its 45rpm playing speed something of a novelty for the time; its only redeeming feature was a punked-up version of The Who's 'WON'T GET FOOLED AGAIN'. SKREWDRIVER found it hard to get their message across, the majority of punks now finding the pop/punk-friendly anthems of SHAM 69 and their ilk more palatable. During the early 80's, SKREWDRIVER became media hate figures, presented by the tabloids as the unacceptable face of the far right neo-Nazis. The music press were just as scathing in their criticism, the music obviously taking a backseat to the so-called message of tracks like 'VOICE OF BRITAIN' and 'RETURN OF ST. GEORGE'. Still beloved of racists and bigots today, SKREWDRIVER continue to ply their ugly trade at one-off gigs and extremist rallies.

Album rating: ALL SKREWED UP (*3)

IAN STEWART – vocals / **RON HARTLEY** – guitar / **KEVIN McKAY** – bass / **GRINNY** – drums

Chiswick not iss.

Apr 77. (7") *(S 11)* **YOU'RE SO DUMB. / BETTER OFF CRAZY** [ ] [-]

Oct 77. (7") *(NS 18)* **ANTI-SOCIAL. / 19TH NERVOUS BREAKDOWN** [ ] [-]

Nov 77. (m-lp; @45rpm) *(CH 3)* **ALL SKREWED UP** [ ] [-]
– Where's it gonna end / Government action / Back street kids / Gotta be young / I don't need your love / I don't like you / Anti-social / Streetfight / (Too much) Confusion / 9 till 5 / Jailbait / Unbeliever / We don't pose / The only one / Won't get fooled again. *(German-iss.lp @33rpm; WIK 3)* – (3 extra included in above).

Mar 78. (7"; shelved) *(NS 28)* **STREETFIGHT. / UNBELIEVER** [-] [-]

T.J.M. not iss.

Jan 80. (7"ep) *(TJM 4)* **SKREWDRIVER EP** [ ] [-]
– Built up, knocked down / A case of pride / Breakout.

Skrewdriver not iss.

Sep 82. (12"ep) *(SKREW 1T)* **BACK WITH A BANG** [ ] [-]

White Noise not iss.

1983. (7"m) *(WN 1)* **WHITE POWER. / SMASH THE I.R.A. / SHOVE THE DOVE** [ ] [-]

1983. (7") *(WN 2)* **VOICE OF BRITAIN. / SICK SOCIETY** [ ] [-]

1984. (7"m) *(WN 3)* **WHEN THE BOAT COMES IN. / WHITE WORKING CLASS MAN / RETURN OF ST. GEORGE** [ ] [-]

— disbanded as a musical recording unit but still played sporadic live gigs and appeared at a few rallies

SKUNK ANANSIE

Formed: London, England . . . early 1994 by striking, shaven-headed black lesbian frontwoman, SKIN and bassist CASS LEWIS. With ACE and ROBBIE FRANCE completing the line-up, SKUNK ANANSIE kicked up enough of a stink to get themselves signed after only a handful of gigs. Their first single, however, was an unofficial limited edition mail order affair lifted from a BBC Radio One Evening Session, 'LITTLE BABY SWASTIKKKA'. A debut single proper, 'SELLING JESUS' hit the shops and the Top 50 in March '95, its controversial content attracting even more interest than the band's burgeoning live reputation. A further couple of furious indie-metallic missives followed in the shape of 'I CAN DREAM' and 'CHARITY', while the band hooked up with labelmate BJORK on her 'Army Of Me' single. Surely one of the most radical acts to ever be associated with the metal scene, the intense interest surrounding scary SKIN and her uncompromising musical vision/political agenda guaranteed a Top 10 placing for the debut album, 'PARANOID & SUNBURNT' (1995). One of the record's most soul-wrenching tracks, 'WEAK', became their biggest hit to date (Top 20) the following January, SKIN's cathartic howl akin to a more soulful PATTI SMITH. Temporary replacement LOUIS was succeeded in turn by MARK RICHARDSON prior to their next Top 20 hit, 'ALL I WANT', one of the many highlights on their second set, 'STOOSH' (1996). Even more scathing than their debut, this angst-ridden collection saw SKUNK ANANSIE championed by Kerrang!, the lead track, 'YES IT'S FUCKING POLITICAL' summing things up perfectly. Riding high in the end of year polls, the Top 10 album contained a further three hit singles, 'TWISTED (EVERYDAY HURTS)', 'HEDONISM (JUST BECAUSE YOU FEEL GOOD)' and 'BRAZEN (WEEP)'. Subsequently signing to 'Virgin' records, SKIN and her band previewed their excellent third album, 'POST ORGANIC CHILL' (1999), with yet another Top 20 single, 'CHARLIE BIG POTATO'; sonic ballads 'SECRETLY' and 'LATELY' followed it into the UK charts shortly afterwards. • **Songwriters:** SKIN – ARRAN, some with other two.

Album rating: PARANOID & SUNBURNT (*7) / STOOSH (*9) / POST ORGANIC CHILL (*8)

SKIN (b. DEBORAH DYER, 3 Aug'67, Brixton, London) – vocals / **ACE** (b. MARTIN KENT, 30 Mar'67, Cheltenham, England) – guitar / **CASS LEWIS** (b. RICHARD LEWIS, 1 Sep'60) – bass / **ROBBIE FRANCE** – drums

One Little Indian Sony

Mar 95. (10"white/c-s) *(101 TP10/TP7C)* **SELLING JESUS. / THROUGH RAGE / YOU WANT IT ALL** [46] [-]
(cd-s+=) *(101 TP7CD)* – Skunk song.
(re-iss. Mar99; same)

Jun 95. (10"lime/c-s) *(121 TP10/TP7C)* **I CAN DREAM. / AESTHETIC ANARCHIST / BLACK SKIN SEXUALITY** [41] [-]
(cd-s+=) *(121 TPCD)* – Little baby Swastikkka.
(re-iss. Mar99; same)

— **LOUIS** – drums; repl. ROBBIE

Aug 95. (c-s) *(131 TP7C)* **CHARITY / I CAN DREAM (version)** [40] [-]
(cd-s+=) *(131 TP7CD)* – Punk by numbers.
(cd-s+=) *(131 TP7CDL)* – Kept my mouth shut.
(10"colrd) *(131 TP10)* – ('A'side) / Used / Killer's war.
(re-iss. Mar99; same)

Sep 95. (lp/c/cd) *(TPLP 55/+C/CD)* <67216> **PARANOID & SUNBURNT** [8] [ ]
– Selling Jesus / Intellectualise my blackness / I can dream / Little baby swastikkka / All in the name of pity / Charity / It takes blood & guts to be this cool but I'm still just a cliche / Weak / And here I stand / 100 ways to be a good girl / Rise up. *(cd re-iss. Mar99; same)*

Jan 96. (c-s) *(141 TP7C)* **WEAK / TOUR HYMN** [20] [-]
(cd-s+=) *(141 TP7CD)* – Selling Jesus ('Strange Days' film version).
(cd-s) *(141 TP7CDL)* – ('A'side) / Charity (clit pop mix) / 100 ways to be a good girl (anti matter mix) / Rise up (Banhamoon mix).
(re-iss. Mar99; same)

Apr 96. (c-s) *(151 TP7C)* **CHARITY / I CAN DREAM (live)** [20] [-]
(cd-s+=) *(151 TP7CD)* – Punk by numbers (live).
(cd-s) *(151 TP7CDL)* – ('A'side) / And here I stand (live) / It takes blood & guts to be this cool but I'm still just a cliche (live) / Intellectualise my blackness (live).
(re-iss. Mar99; same)

—— **MARK RICHARDSON** (b.28 May'70, Leeds, England) – drums; repl. LOUIS

Sep 96. (7") *(161 TP7)* **ALL I WANT. / FRAGILE** [14] [-]
(cd-s+=) *(161 TP7CD)* – Punk by numbers / Your fight.
(cd-s) *(161 TP7CDL)* – ('A'side) / But the sex was good / Every bitch but me / Black skinhead coconut dogfight.
(re-iss. Mar99; same)

Oct 96. (lp/c/cd) *(TPLP 85/+C/CD)* <67555> **STOOSH** [9] [ ]
– Yes it's fucking political / All I want / She's my heroine / Infidelity (only you) / Hedonism (just because you feel good) / Twisted (everyday hurts) / We love your apathy / Brazen (weep) / Pickin on me / Milk is my sugar / Glorious pop song.

Nov 96. (c-s) *(171 TP7C)* **TWISTED (EVERYDAY HURTS) / SHE'S MY HEROINE (polyester & cotton mix)** [26] [-]
(cd-s+=) *(171 TP7CD1)* – Milk in my sugar (cement mix) / Pickin on me (instrumental pick'n'mix).
(cd-s) *(171 TP7CD2)* – ('A'-Cake mix) / Pickin on me (pick'n'mix) / Milk in my sugar (instrumental cement mix) / Yes it's fucking political (comix).
(re-iss. Mar99; same)

Jan 97. (c-ep/cd-ep) *(181 TP7C+D)* **HEDONISM (JUST BECAUSE YOU FEEL GOOD) / SO SUBLIME / LET IT GO / STRONG** [13] [-]
(cd-ep) *(181 TP7CDL)* – ('A'side) / Song recovery / Contraband / I don't believe.
(re-iss. Mar99; same)

Jun 97. (cd-ep) *(191 TP7CD1)* **BRAZEN (WEEP) / TWISTED (EVERYDAY HURTS) (radio 1 session) / ALL I WANT (radio 1 session) / IT TAKES BLOOD & GUTS TO BE THIS COOL BUT I'M STILL JUST A CLICHE (radio 1 session)** [11] [-]
(cd-ep) *(191 TP7CD2)* – ('A'-Dreadzone remix) / ('A'-Hani's Weeping club mix) / ('A'-Ventura's Underworld mix) / ('A'-Stealth Sonic Orchestra remix) / ('A'-Cutfather & Joe electro mix).
(cd-ep) *(191 TP7CD3)* – ('A'-Junior Vasquez's Arena anthem) / ('A'-Paul Oakenfold & Steve Osborne mix) / ('A'-Dreadzone's instrumental mix) / ('A'-Junior Vasquez's riff dub) / ('A'-Hani's Hydro instrumental mix). *(re-iss. Mar99; same)*

Virgin Virgin

Mar 99. (c-s) *(VSC 1725)* **CHARLIE BIG POTATO / FEEL / 80'S MELLOW DRONE** [17] [ ]
(cd-s+=) *(VSCDT 1725)* – ('A'-CD-Rom video).
(cd-s) *(VSCDX 1725)* – ('A'side) / Sane / Jack knife ginal.

Mar 99. (cd/c/lp) *(CD/TC+/V 2881)* **POST ORGANIC CHILL** [16] [ ]
– Charlie big potato / On my hotel T.V. / We don't need who you think you are / Tracey's flaw / The skank heads / Lately / Secretly / Good things don't always come to you / Cheap honesty / You'll follow me down / And this is nothing that I thought I had / I'm not afraid.

May 99. (c-s/cd-s) *(VSC/+DT 1733)* **SECRETLY / KING PSYCHEDELIC SIZE / PAINKILLERS** [16] [ ]
(cd-s) *(VSCDX 1733)* – ('A'side) / Breathing / ('A'-Optical vocal mix).

Jul 99. (c-s/cd-s) *(VSC/+DT 1738)* **LATELY / THE DECADENCE OF YOUR STARVATION / CHARLIE BIG POTATO (Smokin' Jo skin up mix)** [33] [ ]
(cd-s) *(VSCDX 1738)* – ('A'side) / This pill's too painful / Secretly (Armand Van Helden's mix).

Oct 99. (c-s/cd-s) *(VSC/+DT 1754)* **YOU'LL FOLLOW ME DOWN / YOU'LL FOLLOW ME DOWN (The Rollo & Sister Bliss mix) / YOU'LL FOLLOW ME DOWN (Golden Ashes mix)** [ ] [-]
(cd-s) *(VSCDX 1754)* – ('A'side) / Hedonism (just because you make me feel good) (live) / The skank heads (live).

—— In Jun'2000, SKIN was featured on MAXIM (of the PRODIGY's) debut single, 'Carmen Queasy'

SKYCLAD

Formed: England . . . 1991 by ex-SABBAT frontman, MARTIN WALKYIER, who recruited STEVE RAMSEY, GRAEME ENGLISH and KEITH BAXTER. Famous for being quite possibly the only thrash-folk exponents in the metal sphere, SKYCLAD numbered a violinist (FRITHA JENKINS) among their ranks, not exactly a common sight in the world of exploding amps and all-men-play-on-10-bravado. Signed to 'Noise', the group introduced their unashamedly pagan agenda with the 1991 debut set, 'THE WAYWARD SONS OF MOTHER EARTH'. Interest in the band was initially fairly intense, although subsequent albums such as 'JONAH'S ARK' (1993) and 'PRINCE OF THE POVERTY LINE' (1994) moved ever further towards a folk-based sound, alienating many fans who'd originally been enthralled by early pioneering efforts. In the mid-90's, SKYCLAD moved to 'Massacre' records, ironically enough getting even more pastoral on 'OUI AVANT-GARDE A CHANCE' (1996) and more recently 'THE ANSWER MACHINE?' (1997) with new fiddler, GEORGE BIDDLE.

Album rating: THE WAYWARD SONS OF MOTHER EARTH (*6) / A BURNT OFFERING FOR THE BONE IDOL (*5) / TRACKS FROM THE WILDERNESS mini (*4) / JONAH'S ARK (*4) / PRINCE OF THE POVERTY LINE (*4) / THE SILENT WHALES OF LUNAR SEA (*(*6) / IRRATIONAL ANTHEMS (*6) / OUI AVANT-GARDE A CHANCE (*5) / THE ANSWER MACHINE? (*5) / VINTAGE WHINE (*4) / FOLKEMON (*4)

MARTIN WALKYIER – vocals (ex-SABBAT) / **STEVE RAMSEY** – guitar / **GRAEME ENGLISH** – bass / **KEITH BAXTER** – drums / **FRITHA JENKINS** – violin

Noise Noise

May 91. (cd/c/lp) *(N 0163-2/-4/-1)* <4839> **THE WAYWARD SONS OF MOTHER EARTH** [ ] [ ]
– The sky beneath my feet / Trance dance (a dreamtime walkabout) / A minute's piece / The widdershins jig / Our dying island / Intro: Pagan man / The cradle will fall / Skyclad / Moongleam and meadowsweet / Terminus.

Mar 92. (cd/c/lp) *(N 0186-2/-4/-1)* **A BURNT OFFERING FOR THE BONE IDOL** [ ] [-]
– War and disorder / A broken promised land / Spinning Jenny / Salt on the earth (another man's poison) / Karmageddon (the suffering silence) / Ring stone round * / Men of Straul / R'Vannith / The declaration of indifference / Alone in death's shadow. *(cd+= *) (cd re-iss. Nov96; same)*

Nov 92. (m-cd) *(N 0194-2)* **TRACKS FROM THE WILDERNESS** [ ] [-]
– Emerald / A room next door / When all else fails / The declaration of indifference / Spinning Jenny / Skyclad. *(re-is.Nov96; same)*

Apr 93. (cd-ep) *(N 0209-3)* **THINKING ALOUD / THE CRADLE WILL FALL (live) / WIDDERSHINS jig (live)** [ ] [-]

May 93. (cd/c/lp) *(N 0209-2/-4/-1)* **JONAH'S ARK** [ ] [-]
– Thinking aloud / Cry of the land / Schadenfreude / A near life experience / The wickedest man in the world / Earth mother, the sun and the furious host / The ilk of human blindness / Tunnel visionaries / A word to the wise / Bewilderbeast / It wasn't meant to end this way.

Jun 93. (cd-ep) *(N 0209-3)* **THINKING ALLOWED / THE CRADLE WILL FALL (live) / THE WIDDERSHINS JIG (live)** [ ] [-]

Mar 94. (cd/c/lp) *(N 0239-2/-4/-1)* **PRINCE OF THE POVERTY LINE** [ ] [-]
– Civil war dance / Cardboard city / Sins of emission / Land of the rising slum / The one piece puzzle / A bellyful of emptiness / A dog in the manger / Gammadion seed / Womb of the worm / The truth famine. *(cd re-iss. Nov96; same)*

Apr 94. (7"m) *(N 0239-5)* **BROTHER BENEATH THE SKIN. / WIDDERSHINS JIG / CRADLE WILL FALL** [ ] [-]

Apr 95. (cd/lp) *(N 0228-2/-4)* **THE SILENT WHALES OF LUNAR SEA** [ ] [-]
– Still spinning shrapnel / Just what nobody wanted / Art-Nazi / Jeopardy / Brimstone ballet / A stranger in the garden / Another fine mess / Turncoat rebellion / Halo of flies / Desperanto (a song for Europe?) / The present imperfect.

Massacre Century Media

Jan 96. (cd/lp/pic-lp) *(MASS CD/LP/PD 084)* <7853> **IRRATIONAL ANTHEMS** [ ] [ ]
– Inequality street / The wrong song / Snake charming / Penny dreadful / The sinful ensemble / My mother in darkness / The spiral staircase / No deposit, no return / Sabre dance / I dubious / Science never sleeps / History lessens / Quantity time.

Nov 96. (cd) *(MASSCD 104)* <7854> **OUI AVANT-GARDE A CHANCE** [ ] [ ] Aug97
– If I die laughing, it'll be an act of God / Great blow for a day job / Constance eternal / Postcard from Planet Earth / Jumping my shadow / Bombjour! / History lessons (the final examination) / A badtime story / Come on Eileen / Master race / Bombed out (instru-mental) / Penny dreadful (full shilling mix).

—— **GEORGE BIDDLE** – violin; repl. JENKINS

Sep 97. (cd) *(MASSCD 128)* **THE ANSWER MACHINE?** [ ] [-]
– A clown of thorns / Building a ruin / Worn out sole to heel / Single phial / Helium / The thread of evermore / Eirenarch / Troublesometimes / Isle of Jura / Fainting by numbers / My naked I / Catherine at the wheel / Dead angels on ice.

Mar 99. (cd/lp) *(MASS CD/LP 178)* **VINTAGE WHINE** [ ] [ ]
– Kiss my sweet brass / Vintage whine / On with their heads / Silver cloud's dark lining / Well beside the river / No strings attached / Bury me / Cancer of the heart / Little miss take / Something to cling to / By George.

May 99. (cd-ep) *(MASSSH 203)* **SKYCLAD** [ ] [ ]

Nuclear Blast Nuclear Blast

Nov 00. (cd) *(NB 502-2)* <6502> **FOLKEMON** [ ] [ ] Jan01
– The great brain robbery / Think back and lie of England / Polkageist / Crux of the message / The disenchanted forest / The antibody politic / When God locs-off / You lost my memory / De ja-vu ain't what it used to be / Any old irony.

– compilations, etc. –

Nov 96. (cd) *Noise; (N 0275-2)* **OLD ROPE** [ ] [-]
– The Widdershins jig / Skyclad / Spinning Jenny (live) / Alone in death's shadow / Thinking allowed? / The wickedest man in the world / Earth mother, the sun and the furious host / Cardboard city / Land of the rising slum / The one-piece puzzle / Just what nobody wanted / Brother beneath the skin / The present imperfect / The cradle will fall / The declaration of indifference (live) / Ring stone round / Men of straw.

SLADE

Formed: Wolverhampton, Midlands, England . . . 1964 as The VENDORS, by DAVE HILL and DON POWELL, becoming The IN-BE-TWEENS the following year and recording a demo EP for French label, 'Barclay'. Their official debut 45, 'YOU BETTER RUN' (with newcomers NODDY HOLDER and JIMMY LEA), flopped late in '66, the group retiring from studio activity until 1969 when they became AMBROSE SLADE at the suggestion of Fontana's Jack Baverstock. A belated debut album, 'BEGINNINGS', sold poorly although ex-ANIMALS bass player, CHAS CHANDLER, recognised the band's potential after spotting them performing in a London night club (the band now residing in the capital) and subsequently became their manager/producer. Kitted out in bovver boots, jeans, shirt and braces, SLADE topped their newly adopted 'ard look with skinheads all round, CHANDLER moulding the band's image and sound in an attempt to distance them from the fading hippy scene. Although they attracted a sizable grassroots following, SLADE's appropriately titled first album, 'PLAY IT LOUD' (on 'Polydor') failed to translate into sales. However, they finally cracked the UK Top 20 in May 1971 via a rousing cover of Bobby Marchan's 'GET DOWN AND GET WITH IT', the track bringing SLADE into the living rooms of the nation through a Top Of The Pops appearance. By this point, HOLDER and Co. had grown some hair, painted their boots sci-fi silver and initiated the roots of "Slademania" (foot-stomping now all the rage). The noisy, gravel-throated HOLDER (complete with tartan trousers, top hat and mutton-chop sideburns), the bare-chested, glitter-flecked HILL and the not so flamboyant LEA and POWELL, became part of the glam-metal brigade later in the year, 'COZ I LUV YOU' hitting the top of the charts for 4 weeks. Competing with the likes of GARY GLITTER, T. REX and SWEET, the lads amassed a string of anthemic UK chart toppers over the ensuing two years, namely 'TAKE ME BACK 'OME', 'MAMA WEER ALL CRAZEE NOW', 'CUM ON FEEL THE NOIZE', 'SKWEEZE ME PLEEZE ME' and the perennial festive fave 'MERRY XMAS EVERYBODY'. The noize level was markedly lower on the pop-ballad, 'EVERYDAY' (1974), a song that only hit No.3, glam-rock/pop shuddering to a halt around the same time. Their chart-topping albums, 'SLAYED?' (1972), 'SLADEST' (1973) and 'OLD NEW BORROWED AND BLUE' (1974) were now shoved to the back of people's record collections, PINK FLOYD, MIKE OLDFIELD and GENESIS now vying for the attention of the more discerning rock fan. Late '74 saw the release of a film/rockumentary 'SLADE IN FLAME'; issued as an album, it only managed a Top 10 placing. SLADE found it even harder to compete with the burgeoning punk/new wave scene, only re-emerging into the Top 10 in 1981 with 'WE'LL BRING THE HOUSE DOWN', released on their own 'Cheapskate' records. Three years later, the loveable rogues with the 'Bermingim' accent scored yet again, 'MY OH MY' just narrowly missing the No.1 spot, while the follow-up, 'RUN RUNAWAY' made the Top 10. Both records surprised observers by cracking the elusive US charts, the former hitting No.37, the latter No.20; a year previously, metal act, QUIET RIOT had taken Slade's 'CUM ON FEEL THE NOIZE' into the US Top 5 and subsequently charted with another, 'MAMA WEER ALL CRAZEE NOW'. SLADE continued on their merry way, untroubled by the fashion crimes of the 80's. The following decade saw the band chart once more, 'RADIO WALL OF SOUND' blasting out HOLDER's frantic yell to an appreciative Kerrang!- friendly audience. The jovial HOLDER has regained his footing as a celebrity in the 90's, VIC REEVES and BOB MORTIMER giving him and SLADE the highest accolade by inventing a whole series of irreverent sketches based around the band. OASIS, too, have contributed to the cult of NODDY, regularly performing 'CUM ON FEEL THE NOIZE' on stage. • **Songwriters:** HOLDER-LEA or LEA-POWELL penned except IN-BETWEENS:- TAKE A HEART (Sorrows) / CAN YOUR MONKEY DO THE DOG (Rufus Thomas) / YOU BETTER RUN (Rascals). AMBROSE SLADE:- BORN TO BE WILD (Steppenwolf) / AIN'T GOT NO HEAT (Frank Zappa) / IF THIS WORLD WERE MINE (Marvin Gaye) / FLY ME HIGH (Justin Hayward) / MARTHA MY DEAR (Beatles) / JOURNEY TO THE CENTER OF MY MIND (Ted Nugent). SLADE:- THE SHAPE OF THINGS TO COME (Max Frost & The Troopers; Mann-weill) / ANGELINA (Neil Innes) / COULD I (Griffin-Royer) / JUST A LITTLE BIT (?) / DARLING BE HOME SOON (Lovin' Spoonful) / LET THE GOOD TIMES ROLL (Shirley & Lee) / MY BABY LEFT ME – THAT'S ALL RIGHT (Elvis Presley) / PISTOL PACKIN' MAMA (Gene Vincent) / SOMETHIN' ELSE (Eddie Cochran) / OKEY COKEY (seasonal; trad) / HI HO SILVER LINING (Jeff Beck) / STILL THE SAME (Bob Seger) / YOU'LL NEVER WALK ALONE (Rogers-Hammerstein) / AULD LANG SYNE (trad.) / SANTA CLAUS IS COMING TO TOWN (festive) / LET'S DANCE (Chris Montez) / etc.

Album rating: Ambrose Slade: BEGINNINGS (*4) / Slade: PLAY IT LOUD (*4) / SLADE ALIVE! (*5) / SLAYED? (*6) / SLADEST compilation (*7) / OLD, NEW, BORROWED AND BLUE (*5) / SLADE IN FLAME (*6) / NOBODY'S FOOLS (*5) / WHATEVER HAPPENED TO SLADE (*4) / SLADE ALIVE VOL.2 (*5) / RETURN TO BASE (*4) / WE'LL BRING THE HOUSE DOWN (*5) / TILL DEAF US DO PART (*4) / ON STAGE (*5) / THE AMAZING KAMIKAZE SYNDROME (*4) / ROGUES GALLERY (*4) / YOU BOYZ MAKE BIG NOIZE (*4) / WALL OF HITS compilation (*6) / FEEL THE NOIZE: THE VERY BEST OF SLADE compilation (*8)

The IN-BE-TWEENS

JOHNNY HOWELLS – vocals / **MICKEY MARSTON** – guitar / **DAVE HILL** (b. 4 Apr'52, Fleet Castle, Devon, England) – guitar / **DAVE JONES** – bass / **DON POWELL** (10 Sep'50, Bilston, Staffordshire) – drums

Barclay / not iss.

1965. (7"ep) **TAKE A HEART / LITTLE NIGHTINGALE. / (2 tracks by 'The Hills')** – / – France

1965. (7"ep) **TAKE A HEART. / CAN YOUR MONKEY DO THE DOG / OOP OOP I DO** – / – France

—— **NODDY HOLDER** (b. NEVILLE HOLDER, 15 Jun'50, Walsall, England) – vox, guitar repl. HOWELLS / **JIM LEA** (b.14 Jun'52, Wolverhampton) – bass, piano repl. MARSTON + JONES

Columbia / not iss.

Nov 66. (7"; as N' BETWEENS) *(DB 8080)* **YOU BETTER RUN. / EVIL WITCHMAN** □ / –

AMBROSE SLADE

(HOLDER, HILL, LEA + POWELL)

Fontana / Fontana

Apr 69. (lp) *(STL 5492)* <67592> **BEGINNINGS** □ / □
– Genesis / Everybody's next one / Knocking nails into my house / Roach daddy / Ain't got no heat / Pity the mother / Mad dog Cole / Fly me high / If this world were mine / Martha my dear / Born to be wild / Journey to the centre of my mind. *(re-iss. Jun91 & Jun99 on 'Polydor' cd/c; 849 185-2/-4)*

May 69. (7") *(TF 1015)* **GENESIS. / ROACH DADDY** □ / –

SLADE

(same line-up + label)

Oct 69. (7") *(TF 1056)* **WILD WINDS ARE BLOWING. / ONE WAY HOTEL** □ / –

Mar 70. (7") *(TF 1079)* **SHAPE OF THINGS TO COME. / C'MON C'MON** □ / –

Polydor / Cotillion

Sep 70. (7") *(2058 054)* **KNOW WHO YOU ARE. / DAPPLE ROSE** □ / –

Nov 70. (lp) *(2383 026)* <9035> **PLAY IT LOUD** □ / □
– Raven / See us here / Dapple rose / Could I / One way hotel / The shape of things to come / Know who you are / I remember / Pouk Hill / Angelina / Dirty joker / Sweet box. *(re-iss. Jun91 cd/c; 849 178-2/-4)*

May 71. (7"m) *(2058 112)* <44128> **GET DOWN AND GET WITH IT. / DO YOU WANT ME / THE GOSPEL ACCORDING TO RASPUTIN** 16 / □

Polydor / Polydor

Oct 71. (7") *(2058 155)* **COZ I LUV YOU. / LIFE IS NATURAL** 1 / –

Jan 72. (7") *(2058 195)* <15041> **LOOK WOT YOU DUN. / CANDIDATE** 4 / □

Jan 72. (7") <15044> **COZ I LOVE YOU. / GOTTA KEEP A-ROCKIN' (live)** – / □

Mar 72. (lp) *(2383 101)* <5508> **SLADE ALIVE! (live)** 2 / □
– Hear me calling / In like a shot from my gun / Darling be home soon / Know who you are / Gotta keep on rockin' / Get down and get with it / Born to be wild. *(re-iss. Nov84 lp/c; SPE LP/MC 84) (re-iss. Jun91 cd/c; 841 114-2/-4)*

May 72. (7") *(2058 231)* <15046> **TAKE ME BAK 'OME. / WONDERIN'** 1 / 97 Sep72

Aug 72. (7") *(2058 274)* <15053> **MAMA WEER ALL CRAZEE NOW. / MAN WHO SPEAKS EVIL** 1 / 76 Nov72

Nov 72. (7") *(2058 312)* <15060> **GUDBUY T'JANE. / I WON'T LET IT 'APPEN AGAIN** 2 / 68 Mar73

Dec 72. (lp)(c) *(2383 163)* <5524> **SLAYED?** 1 / 69
– How d'you ride / The whole world's goin' craze / Look at last nite / I won't let it 'appen again / Move over / Gudbuy t'Jane / Gudbuy gudbuy / Mama weer all crazee now / I don't mind / Let the good times roll. *(cd-iss. May91; 849 180-2)*

Feb 73. (7") *(2058 339)* <15069> **CUM ON FEEL THE NOIZE. / I'M MEE, I'M NOW AN' THAT'S ORL** 1 / 98 May73

Jun 73. (7") *(2058 377)* **SKWEEZE ME PLEEZE ME. / KILL 'EM AT THE HOT CLUB TONITE** 1 / –

Jul 73. (7") <15080> **LET THE GOOD TIMES ROLL. / FEEL SO FINE – I DON' MINE** – / □

Polydor / Reprise

Sep 73. (7") *(2058 407)* **MY FRIEND STAN. / MY TOWN** 2 / –

Sep 73. (lp) *(2442 119)* <2173> **SLADEST** (compilation) 1 / □
– Wild things are blowing / Shape of things to come / Know who you are / Pounk Hill / One way hotel / Get down and get with it / Coz I luv you / Look wot you dun / Tak me bak ome / Mama weer all crazee now / Gudbuy t'Jane / Look at last night / Cum on feel the noize / Skweeze me pleeze me. *(cd-iss. Mar93; 837 103-2)*

Sep 73. (7") <1182> **SKWEEZE ME PLEEZE ME. / MY TOWN** – / □

Polydor / Warners

Dec 73. (7") *(2058 422)* <7759> **MERRY XMAS EVERYBODY. / DON'T BLAME ME** 1 / □
(re-iss. Dec80, Dec81 (No.32), Dec82 (No.67), Dec83 (No.20), Dec84 (No.47).

Feb 74. (lp) *(2383 261)* <2770> **OLD NEW BORROWED AND BLUE**
<US title 'STOMP YOUR HANDS, CLAP YOUR FEET'> 1 / □
– Just want a little bit / When the lights are out / My town / Find yourself a rainbow / Miles out to sea / We're really gonna raise the roof / Do we still do it / How can it be / Don't blame me / My friend Stan / Everyday / Good time gals. *(cd-iss. May91; 849 181-2)*

Mar 74. (7") *(2058 453)* <7777> **EVERYDAY. / GOOD TIME GALS** 3 / □

Jun 74. (7") *(2058 492)* **THE BANGIN' MAN. / SHE DID IT TO ME** 3 / –

Jul 74. (7") <7808> **WHEN THE LIGHTS ARE OUT. / HOW CAN IT BE** – / □

Oct 74. (7") *(2058 522)* **FAR FAR AWAY. / OK YESTERDAY WAS YESTERDAY** 2 / –

Nov 74. (lp) *(2442 126)* <2865> **SLADE IN FLAME (Film Soundtrack)** 6 / 93
– How does it feel? / Them kinda monkeys can't swing / So far so good / Summer song (wishing you were here) / O.K. yesterday was yesterday / Far far away / This girl / Lay it down / Standin' on the corner. *(re-iss. Nov82 on 'Action Replay'; REPLAY 1000) (cd-iss. May91; 849 182-2)*

Feb 75. (7") *(2058 547)* **HOW DOES IT FEEL. / SO FAR SO GOOD** 15 / –

Apr 75. (7") <8134> **HOW DOES IT FEEL. / O.K. YESTERDAY WAS YESTERDAY** – / □

May 75. (7") *(2058 585)* **THANKS FOR THE MEMORY (WHAM BAM THANK YOU MAM). / RAINING IN MY CHAMPAGNE** 7 / –

Nov 75. (7") *(2058 663)* **IN FOR A PENNY. / CAN YOU JUST IMAGINE** 11 / –

Jan 76. (7") *(2058 690)* **LET'S CALL IT QUITS. / WHEN THE CHIPS ARE DOWN** 11 / –

Mar 76. (lp) *(2383 377)* <2936> **NOBODY'S FOOLS** 14 / □
– Nobody's fools / Do the dirty / Let's call it quits / Pack up your troubles / In for a penny / Get on up / L.A. jinx / Did your mama ever tell ya / Scratch my back / I'm a talker / All the world is a stage. *(cd-iss. May91; 849 183-2)*

Apr 76. (7") *(2058 716)* **NOBODY'S FOOL. / L.A. JINX** □ / –

Apr 76. (7") <8185> **NOBODY'S FOOL. / WHEN THE CHIPS ARE DOWN** – / □

Barn-Polydor / not iss.

Feb 77. (7") *(2014 105)* **GYPSY ROADHOG. / FOREST FULL OF NEEDLES** [48] [-]

Mar 77. (lp) *(2314 103)* **WHATEVER HAPPENED TO SLADE** [ ] [-]
– Be / Lightning never strikes twice / Gypsy roadhog / Dogs of vengeance / When fantasy calls / One eyed Jacks with moustaches / Big apple blues / Dead men tell no tales / She's got the lot / It ain't love but it ain't bad / The soul, the fall and the motion. *(cd-iss. May93; 849 184-2)*

Apr 77. (7") *(2014 106)* **BURNING IN THE HEAT OF LOVE. / READY STEADY KIDS** [ ] [-]

Oct 77. (7") *(2014 114)* **MY BABY LEFT ME – THAT'S ALL RIGHT (Medley). / O.H.M.S.** [32] [-]

Mar 78. (7") *(2014 121)* **GIVE US A GOAL. / DADDIO** [ ] [-]

Oct 78. (7") *(2014 127)* **ROCK'N'ROLL BOLERO. / MY BABY'S GOT IT** [ ] [-]

Nov 78. (lp) *(2314 106)* **SLADE ALIVE VOL.2** [ ] [-]
– Get on up / Take me bak 'ome / Medley: My baby left me – That's all right / Be / Mama weer all crazee now / Burning in the heat of love / Everyday / Gudbuy t' Jane / One-eyed Jacks with moustaches / C'mon feel the noize. *(cd-iss. May93; 849 179-2)*

Barn / not iss.

Mar 79. (7"yellow) *(BARN 002)* **GINNY GINNY. / DIZZY MAMA** [ ] [-]

Oct 79. (7") *(BARN 010)* **SIGN OF THE TIMES. / NOT TONIGHT JOSEPHINE** [ ] [-]

Oct 79. (lp) *(NARB 003)* **RETURN TO BASE** [ ] [-]
– Wheels ain't coming down / Hold on to your hats / Chakeeta / Don't waste your time / Sign of the times / I'm a rocker / Nuts, bolts and screws / My baby's got it / I'm mad / Lemme love into ya / Ginny, Ginny.

Dec 79. (7") *(BARN 011)* **OKEY COKEY. / MY BABY'S GOT IT** [ ] [-]

Cheapskate / not iss.

Sep 80. (7"ep) *(CHEAP 5)* **SLADE ALIVE AT READING '80 (live)** [44] [-]
– When I'm dancing I ain't fightin' / Born to be wild / Somethin' else / Pistol packin' mama / Keep a rollin'.

Nov 80. (7") *(CHEAP 11)* **MERRY XMAS EVERYBODY. / OKEY COKEY / GET DOWN AND GET WITH IT** [70] [-]

Jan 81. (7") *(CHEAP 16)* **WE'LL BRING THE HOUSE DOWN. / HOLD ON TO YOUR HATS** [10] [-]

Mar 81. (lp/c) *(SKATE/KAT 1)* **WE'LL BRING THE HOUSE DOWN** [25] [-]
– Night starvation / Wheels ain't coming down / I'm a rocker / Nuts, bolts and screws / We'll bring the house down / Dizzy mama / Hold on to your hats / Lemme love into ya / My baby's got it / When I'm dancing I ain't fightin'. *(cd-iss. Nov96 on 'Castle'; CLACD 418) (cd re-iss. Sep99; 547412-2)*

Mar 81. (7") *(CHEAP 21)* **WHEELS AIN'T COMING DOWN. / NOT TONIGHT JOSEPHINE** [60] [-]

May 81. (7") *(CHEAP 24)* **KNUCKLE SANDWICH NANCY. / I'M MAD** [ ] [-]

R.C.A. / CBS-Assoc.

Sep 81. (7") *(RCA 124)* **LOCK UP YOUR DAUGHTERS. / SIGN OF THE TIMES** [29] [-]

Nov 81. (lp/c) *(RCA LP/K 6021)* **TILL DEAF US DO PART** [ ] [-]
– Rock and roll preacher (hallelujah I'm on fire) / Ruby red / Lock up your daughters / Till deaf us do part / That was no lady that was my wife / She brings out the devil in me / A night to remember / M'hat m'coat / It's your body not your mind / Let the rock and roll out of control / Knuckle sandwich Nancy / Till deaf resurrected. *(cd-iss. Apr93 & Nov96 on 'Castle'; CLACD 377 & 415) (cd re-iss. Sep99; 547407-2)*

Mar 82. (7") *(RCA 191)* **RUBY RED. / FUNK PUNK AND JUNK** [51] [-]
(d7"+=) *(RCAD 191)* – Rock'n'roll preacher (live) / Take me back 'ome (live).

Nov 82. (7") *(RCA 291)* **(AND NOW – THE WALTZ) C'EST LA VIE. / MERRY XMAS EVERYBODY (ALIVE & KICKIN')** [50] [-]

Dec 82. (lp/c) *(RCA LP/K 3107)* **ON STAGE (live)** [ ] [-]
– Rock and roll preacher / When I'm dancing I ain't fightin' / Tak me bak 'ome / Everyday / Lock up your daughters / We'll bring the house down / A night to remember / Mama weer all crazee now / Gudbuy t'Jane / You'll never walk alone. *(cd-iss. Jul93 & Nov96 on 'Castle'; CLACD 380 & 420) (cd re-iss. Sep99; 547413-2)*

Nov 83. (7"m) *(RCA 373)* **MY OH MY. / MERRY XMAS EVERYBODY (live) / KEEP YOUR HANDS OFF MY POWER SUPPLY** [2] [-]

Dec 83. (lp/c) *(PL/PK 70116)* **THE AMAZING KAMIKAZE SYNDROME** [49] [-]
– Slam the hammer down / In the doghouse / Run runaway / High and dry / My oh my / Cocky rock boys / Ready to explode / (And now – The waltz) C'est la vie / Cheap 'n' nasty love / Razzle dazzle man. *(cd-iss. Apr93 & Nov96 on 'Castle'; CLACD 381 & 419) (cd re-iss. Sep99; 547411-2)*

Jan 84. (7"/12") *(RCA/+T 385)* **RUN RUNAWAY. / TWO TRACK STEREO, ONE TRACK MIND** [7] [-]

Apr 84. (lp) *<39336>* **KEEP YOUR HANDS OFF MY POWER SUPPLY** [-] [33]
<cd-iss. 1988; ZK 3936>

Apr 84. (7") *<04398>* **RUN RUNAWAY. / DON'T TAME A HURRICANE** [-] [20]

Jul 84. (7") *<04528>* **MY OH MY. / HIGH AND DRY** [-] [37]

Nov 84. (7") *(RCA 455)* **ALL JOIN HANDS. / HERE'S TO . . . (THE NEW YEAR)** [15] [-]
(12"+=) *(RCAT 455)* – Merry xmas everybody (live & kickin').

Jan 85. (7") *(RCA 475)* **7 YEAR (B)ITCH. / LEAVE THEM GIRLS ALONE** [60] [-]
(12"+=) *(RCAT 475)* – We'll bring the house down (live).

Mar 85. (lp/c) *(PL/PK 70604) <39976>* **ROGUES GALLERY** [ ] [ ]
– Hey ho wish you well / Little Sheila / Harmony / Myzsterious Mizster Jones / Walking on water, running on alcohol / 7 year (b)itch / I'll be there / I win, you lose / Time to rock / All join hands. *(cd-iss. Sep99; 547406-2)*

Mar 85. (7",7"pic-d) *(PB 40027)* **MYZSTERIOUS MIZSTER JONES. / MAMA NATURE IS A ROCKER** [50] [-]
(ext.12"+=) *(PT 40028)* – My oh my (piano and vocal version).

Apr 85. (7") *<04865>* **LITTLE SHEILA. / LOCK UP YOUR DAUGHTERS** [-] [86]

Nov 85. (7") *(PB 40449)* **DO YOU BELIEVE IN MIRACLES. / MY OH MY (swing version)** [54] [-]
(d7"+=) *(PB 40549)* – (see below d12" for extra tracks)
(12"+=) *(PT 40450)* – Time to rock.
(12"++=) *(PT 40550)* – Santa Claus is coming to town / Auld lang syne / You'll never walk alone.

Feb 87. (7"/12") *(PB 4113 7/8)* **STILL THE SAME. / GOTTA GO HOME** [73] [-]
(d7"+=) *(PB 41147D)* – The roaring silence / Don't talk to me about love.

Apr 87. (7") *(PB 41271)* **THAT'S WHAT FRIENDS ARE FOR. / WILD WILD PARTY** [ ] [-]
(12"+=) *(PT 41272)* – Hi ho silver lining / Lock up your daughters (live).

Apr 87. (lp/c/cd) *(PL/PK/PD 71260)* **YOU BOYZ MAKE BIG NOIZE** [ ] [-]
– Love is like a rock / That's what friends are for / Still the same / Fools go crazy / She's heavy / We won't give in / Won't you rock with me / Ooh la la in L.A. / Me and the boys / Sing shout (knock yourself out) / The roaring silence / It's hard having fun nowadays / You boyz make big noize / Boyz (instrumental). *(cd re-iss. Apr93 & Nov96 on 'Castle'; CLACD 379 & 417) (cd re-iss. Sep99; 547408-2)*

Cheapskate-RCA / not iss.

Jun 87. (7") *(BOYZ 1)* **YOU BOYZ MAKE BIG NOIZE. / ('A'instrumental)** [ ] [-]
(12"+=) *(TBOYZ 1)* – ('A'-USA mix).

Nov 87. (7") *(BOYZ 2)* **WE WON'T GIVE IN. / LA LA IN L.A.** [ ] [-]

Nov 88. (7") *(BOYZ 3)* **LET'S DANCE (1988 remix). / STANDING ON THE CORNER** [ ] [-]
(cd-s+=) *(BOYZCD 3)* – Far far away / How does it feel.

Polydor / not iss.

Oct 91. (7"/c-s) *(PO/+CS 180)* **RADIO WALL OF SOUND. / LAY YOUR LOVE ON THE LINE** [21] [-]
(cd-s+=) *(PZCD 180)* – Cum on feel the noize.

Nov 91. (cd/c/lp) *(511 612-2/-4/-1)* **WALL OF HITS** (compilation & new hits) [34] [ ]
– Get down and get with it / Coz I luv you / Look wot you dun / Take me bak 'ome / Gudbuy t'Jane / Cum on feel the noize / Skweeze me pleeze me / My friend Stan / Everyday / Bangin' man / Far far away / Let's call it quits / My oh my / Run run away / Radio wall of sound / Universe / Merry Xmas everybody. *(cd/c+=)* – How does it feel / Thanks for the memory (wham bam thank you mam).

Nov 91. (7"/c-s) **UNIVERSE. / MERRY CHRISTMAS EVERYBODY** [ ] [-]
(12"+=/cd-s+=) – Gypsy roadhog.

—— no new material as yet

– compilations, etc. –

on 'Polydor' unless stated otherwise

Jun 80. (12"ep) *Six Of The Best; (SUPER45 3)* **SIX OF THE BEST** [ ] [-]
– Night starvation / When I'm dancing I ain't fightin' / I'm a rocker / Don't waste your time / Wheels ain't coming down / Nine to five.

Nov 80. (lp) *(POLTV 13)* **SLADE SMASHES** [21] [-]

Apr 81. (d-lp/d-c) *(2689/3539 101)* **THE STORY OF SLADE** [ ] [-]
(cd-iss. VOL.1 & VOL.2 Nov90 on 'Bear Tracks'; BTCD 97941-1/-2)

Dec 81. (7"ep) *(POSP 399)* **CUM ON FEEL THE NOIZE / COZ I LUV YOU. / TAKE ME BAK 'OME / GUDBUY T'JANE** [ ] [-]
(12"ep+=) *(POSPX 399)* – Coz I luv you.

Dec 82. (7"/7"pic-d) *Speed; (SPEED/+P 201)* **THE HOKEY COKEY. / GET DOWN AND GET WITH IT** [ ] [-]

May 84. (lp/c) *(SLAD/+C 1)* **SLADE'S GREATS** [ ] [-]

Nov 85. (7"/12") *(POSP/+X 780)* **MERRY CHRISTMAS EVERYBODY (remix). / DON'T BLAME ME** [48] [-]
(re-iss. Dec86, hit No.71)

Nov 85. (lp/c) *Telstar; (STAR/STAC 2271)* **CRACKERS – THE SLADE CHRISTMAS PARTY ALBUM** [34] [-]

1988. (cd-ep) *Counterpoint; (CDEP 12C)* **HOW DOES IT FEEL / FAR FAR AWAY / (2 tracks by Wizzard)** [ ] [-]

Mar 89. (3"cd-ep) *R.C.A.; (PD 42637)* **MY OH MY / KEEP YOUR HANDS OFF MY POWER SUPPLY / RUNAWAY / ONE TRACK STEREO, ONE TRACK MIND** [ ] [-]

Apr 91. (cd/c/lp) *R.C.A.; (ND/NK/NL 74926)* **COLLECTION 81-87** [ ] [-]
(re-iss. Apr93 on 'Castle' cd/c; CCS CD/MC 372) (cd re-iss. Sep99 on 'Polydor'; 547410-2)

Dec 95. (c) *Prestige; (CASSGP 0253)* **KEEP ON ROCKIN'** [ ] [-]

Jan 97. (cd/c) *(537 105-2/-4)* **GREATEST HITS – FEEL THE NOIZE** [19] [-]
– Get down and get with it / Coz I luv you / Look wot you dun / Take me bak 'ome / Mama weer all crazee now / Gudbuy t'Jane / Cum on feel the noize / Skweeze me pleeze me / My friend Stan / Everyday / Bangin' man / Far far away / How does it feel to feel / In for a penny / We'll bring the house down / Lock up your daughters / Oh my my / Run run away / All join hands / Radio wall of sound / Merry Xmas everybody. *(re-iss. Dec99 as 'GREATEST HITS – FEEL THE NOIZE'; same)*

Mar 97. (cd) *Music Corp; (TMC 9606)* **THE GENESIS OF SLADE** [ ] [-]

Dec 98. (c-s; SLADE VS FLUSH) *Polydor; (563352-4)* **MERRY XMAS EVERYBODY '98 REMIX / ('A'remix)** [30] [-]
(12"+=) *(563353-1)* – ('A'mix).
(cd-s+=) *(563353-2)* – Cum on feel the noize.

SLAMMER

Formed: Bradford, England . . . 1987 by PAUL TUNNICLIFFE, ENZO ANNECCHINI, MILO ZIVANOVIC, RUSSELL BURTON and GAGIC. Bright young hopes of the Brit-thrash scene, SLAMMER were lucky/unlucky enough to be one of the first bands of their ilk snapped up by a major label. The resulting album, 'THE WORK OF IDLE HANDS' (1989) was released to generally favourable reviews but subsequently failed to create the fuss that 'Warners' had anticipated. Unceremoniously dropped, SLAMMER were picked up by 'Heavy Metal' records, who issued their follow-up set, 'NIGHTMARE SCENARIO' in Spring '91. Again, the record scraped negligible sales and SLAMMER duly called it a day soon after.

Album rating: THE WORK OF IDLE HANDS (*5) / NIGHTMARE SCENARIO (*4)

PAUL TUNNICLIFFE – vocals / **ENZO ANNECCHINI** – guitar / **MILO ZIVANOVIC** – guitar / **RUSSELL BURTON** – bass / **ANDY GAGIC** – drums

WEA not iss.

Jun 89. (lp/c)(cd) *(WX 273/+C)(246000-2)* <46000> **THE WORK OF IDLE HANDS** [ ] [-]
– Tenement zone / If thine eye / Johnny's home / Razor's edge / Hellbound / Hunt you down / Gods' prey / Fight or fall / No excuses. *(cd+=)* – Born for war.

Heavy Metal not iss.

Oct 90. (12"ep/cd-ep) *(12HM/HEAVYXD 66)* **BRING THE HAMMER DOWN. / I.O.U. / MANIAC** [ ] [-]

Apr 91. (cd/c/lp) *(HMR XD/MC/LP 170)* **NIGHTMARE SCENARIO** [ ] [-]
– What's your pleasure? / Greed / In the name of God / Just another massacre / Architect of pain / Every breath / I know who I am / Corruption / Think for yourself / L'ultima.

—— disbanded in June '91 when they were dropped by their record company

SLANT 6

Formed: Washington DC, USA ... mid 1992 by MYRA POWER, CHRISTINA BILLOTTE and MARGE MARSHALL. Taking their unusual moniker from a Dodge engine (c.1960's), this all-female trio began their vinyl career with a sporadic series of 7" singles and V/A compilation appearances. Having signed to local hardcore bastion, 'Dischord', SLANT 6 released their debut long-player, 'SODA POP * RIP OFF', in early '94, more an overview of their progress to date rather than a cohesive body of work in itself. IAN MacKAYE (of FUGAZI) also offered his knob-twiddling skills to the follow-up, 'INZOMBIA' (1995), which developed the group's girly punk guitar assault without offering any real innovation.

Album rating: SODA POP * RIP OFF (*6) / INZOMBIA (*4)

CHRISTINA BILLOTTE – vocals, guitar (ex-AUTOCLAVE) / **MYRA POWER** – bass (ex-LUCKY 13) / **MARGE MARSHALL** – drums, organ

Dischord Dischord

Jul 93. (7") <*DIS 85V*> **WHAT KIND OF MONSTER ARE YOU? /** [ ] [ ]

Mar 94. (cd/lp) <*DIS 91 CD/V*> **SODA POP * RIP OFF** [ ] [ ]
– Don't you ever? / Nights x9 / Love shock / Double edged knife / Time expired / Invisible footsteps / Poison arrows shot at heroes / Don't censor me / Blood song / Soda pop * rip off / Become your ghost / Blue angel / March 6* / What kind of monster are you? / Semi-ble tile / Thirty-thirty vision.

May 95. (cd/lp) <*DIS 94 CD/V*> **INZOMBIA** [ ] [ ]
– G.F.S. / Babydoll / Click-click / Instrumental / Ladybug superfly / Retro duck / Partner in crime / Victim of your own desires / Eight swimming pools / Insider spider / Mascaria / Inzombia.

—— disbanded after above

SLASH'S SNAKEPIT

Formed: Los Angeles, California ... mid 90's by renegade G N'R axe hero SLASH. Frustrated by worsening musical differences with AXL ROSE, SLASH found an outlet for his bluesy hard-rock passions in a side project featuring G N'R drummer MATT SORUM (although he was to leave before the debut album's release), ex-G N'R guitarist GILBY CLARKE, ALICE IN CHAINS man MIKE INNEZ and ex-JELLYFISH frontman ERIC DOVER. Written jointly with DOVER, 'IT'S FIVE O'CLOCK SOMEWHERE' (1995) eventually emerged into the vacuum waiting to be filled by a G N'R album. While the blues-rock on offer didn't fill that vacuum fully, it satisfied many fans craving for a fix of SLASH's distinctive, fluid soloing. Come the accompanying tour, the guitarist was enjoying himself so much, he finally parted company with ROSE amid much controversy. Following the record's success, SLASH eventually assembled a whole new line-up (see below) for a belated, low-key sophomore album, 'AIN'T LIFE GRAND' (2000).

Album rating: IT'S FIVE O'CLOCK SOMEWHERE (*6) / AIN'T LIFE GRAND (*5)

SLASH – guitar with **MATT SORUM + GILBY CLARKE / + ERIC DOVER** – vocals (ex-JELLYFISH)/ **MIKE INEZ** – bass (of ALICE IN CHAINS)

Geffen Geffen

Feb 95. (cd/c/lp) <*(GED/GEC/GEF 24730)*> **IT'S FIVE O'CLOCK SOMEWHERE** [15] [70]
– Neither can I / Dime store rock / Beggars and hangers-on / Good to be alive / What do you want to be / Monkey chow / Soma city ward / Jizz da pit / Lower / Take it away / Doin' fine / Be the ball / I hate everybody (but you) / Back and forth again.

—— now with **MATT LAUG** – drums / **RYAN ROXIE** – guitar, vocals / **JACK DOUGLAS** – sitar, vocals / **ROD JACKSON** – vocals

Koch Koch

Oct 00. (cd/c) <*(KOC CD/MC 8198)*> **AIN'T LIFE GRAND** [ ] [ ]
– Been there lately / Just like anything / Shine / Mean bone / Back to the moment / Life's sweet drug / Serial killer / The truth / Landslide / Ain't life grand / Speed parade / Alien.

SLAUGHTER

Formed: Las Vegas, Nevada, USA ... September '88 by MARK SLAUGHTER and DANA STRUM (both ex-VINNIE VINCENT INVASION). With the line-up completed by TIM KELLY and BLAS ELIAS, the group remained with 'Chrysalis' (home to VVI) for their million selling debut, 'STICK IT TO YA' (1990). Formulaic but professional commercial metal characterised by the tonsil torturing vocals of SLAUGHTER, the album slowly but surely worked its way up the Billboard chart as the group enjoyed widespread exposure supporting big guns KISS. A follow-up, 'WILD LIFE' (1992), surfaced a couple of years later although despite reaching the US Top 10, the record failed to achieve the commercial success enjoyed by its predecessor. With 'grunge' now firmly established as the youthful music of choice, SLAUGHTER's pop-metal preening seemed out of date, more problems besetting the band as TIM KELLY was charged with drug offences. It was 1995 before they resurfaced, issuing the independently released 'FEAR NO EVIL' to general disinterest. One of the first acts signed to metal dinosaur label 'C.M.C.', SLAUGHTER had finally resigned themselves to life on the margins of rock's radically reshaped landscape alongside hordes of other stragglers from the golden era of hair-metal. No longer having to cater to the demands of MTV and commercial radio programmers, the band had also toughened up their sound without altering its basic melodic hard-rock structure. 'REVOLUTION' (1997) followed in much the same vein although 'ETERNAL LIVE' (1998) drew heavily on the band's better known material, its release a testament to their enduring Stateside concert appeal. After the tragic death of guitarist TIM KELLY, SLAUGHTER made a brave return with 'BACK TO REALITY' (1999), replacement JEFF BLANDO grinding out the riffs on an album which deviated little from the latter day formula.

Album rating: STICK IT TO YA (*5) / STICK IT TO YA LIVE (*4) / THE WILD LIFE (*5) / FEAR NO EVIL (*4) / REVOLUTION (*4) / ETERNAL LIVE (*4) / BACK TO REALITY (*5) / MASS SLAUGHTER: THE BEST OF SLAUGHTER compilation (*6)

MARK SLAUGHTER – vocals / **TIM KELLY** – guitar / **DANA STRUM** – bass / **BLAS ELIAS** – drums

Chrysalis Chrysalis

Apr 90. (cd/c/lp) *(CCD/ZCHR/CHR 1702)* <*21702*> **STICK IT TO YA** [ ] [18] Feb90
– Eye to eye / Burnin' bridges / Up all night / Spend my life / Thinking of June / She wants more / Fly to the angels / Mad about you / That's not enough / You are the one / Give me your heart / Desperately / Loaded gun. *(cd+=)* – Fly to the angels (acoustic) / Wingin' it.

Aug 90. (7"/7"pic-d) *(CHS/+P 3556)* <*23486*> **UP ALL NIGHT. / EYE TO EYE** [62] [27] Apr90
(12"pic-d+=/cd-s+=) *(CHS P12/CD 3556)* – Stick it to ya (medley); Mad about you – Burning bridges – Fly to the angels.

Aug 90. (c-s,cd-s) <*23527*> **FLY TO THE ANGELS / DESPERATELY** [-] [19]

Jan 91. (7"/7"pic-d) *(CHS/+P 3634)* **FLY TO THE ANGELS. / UP ALL NIGHT (live)** [55] [-]
(12"pic-d+=) *(CHSP12 3634)* – Loaded gun.
(cd-s++=) *(CHSCD 3634)* – ('A'acoustic version).

Nov 90. (m-cd,m-c) <*21816*> **STICK IT LIVE (live)** [-] [ ]
– Burnin' bridges / Eye to eye / Fly to the angels / Up all night / Loaded gun.

Dec 90. (c-s,cd-s) <*23605*> **SPEND MY LIFE / SHE WANTS MORE** [-] [39]

Mar 92. (cd/c/lp) *(CCD/ZCHR/CHR 1911)* <*21911*> **THE WILD LIFE** [64] [8]
– Reach for the sky / Out for love / The wild life / Days gone by / Dance for me baby / Times they change / Move to the music / Real love / Shake this place / Streets of broken hearts / Hold on / Do ya know. *(cd+=)* – Old man / Days gone by (acoustic version).

Aug 92. (c-s,cd-s) <*50401*> **REAL LOVE / SHE WANTS MORE (live)** [-] [69]

S.P.V. C.M.C.

Jun 95. (cd) *(SPV 085-7600-2)* <*7403*> **FEAR NO EVIL** [ ] [ ] May95
– Like there's no tomorrow / Get used to it / Searchin' / It'll be alright / Let the good times roll / Breakdown n' cry / Hard times / Divine order / Yesterday's gone / Prelude / Outta my head / Unknown destination.

May 97. (cd) <*86214*> **REVOLUTION** [-] [ ]
– American pie / Heaven it cries / Tongue 'n' groove / Can we find a way? / Stuck on you / Hard to say goodbye / Revolution / Guck / Heat of the moment / Rocky mountain way / You're my everything / I'm gone / Ad-majorem-vei-gloriam. *(UK-iss.May98 on 'S.P.V'; 085-1812-2)*

Sep 98. (cd) *(SPV 085-1816-2)* <*86249*> **ETERNAL LIVE** [ ] [ ] May98
– Rock the world / Get used to it / Shout it out / Mad about you / Spend my life / Fly to the angels / Real love / Dance for me / Searchin' / Wild life / Move to the music / Up all night.

—— **JEFF BLANDO** – guitar; repl. KELLY who died

Aug 99. (cd) *(SPV 085-2143-2)* <*607-686276-2*> **BACK TO REALITY** [ ] [ ] Jun99
– Killin' time / All fired up / Take me away / Dangerous / Trailer park boogie / Love is forever / Bad groove / On my own / Silence of Ba / Headin' for a dream / Nothin' left to lose.

Utopian Vision not iss.

Jul 00. (cd) *(UVMCD 010)* **SURRENDER OR DIE** [ ] [-]

– compilations, etc. –

Mar 95. (cd) *Capitol;* <*32696*> **MASS SLAUGHTER: THE BEST OF SLAUGHTER** [-] [ ]
– Up all night / Fly to the angels / Spend my life / Days gone by / Eye to eye / Real love / Loaded gun / Burnin' bridges / Reach for the sky / Streets of broken hearts / You are the one / Shake this place / She wants more / Mad about you / The wild life / Hold on / Fly to the angels (live) / Up all night (live).

SLAUGHTER & THE DOGS

Formed: Manchester, England ... 1976 by WAYNE BARRETT, MIKE ROSSI, HOWARD BATES and MAD MUFFET. Emerging from a fertile Manchester punk scene concentrated around the city's Electric Circus venue, SLAUGHTER AND THE DOGS were initially signed to local independent label, 'Rabid', through which they issued a debut single, 'CRANKED UP REALLY HIGH'. Signed to 'Decca' in the wake of the punk explosion, the band issued their one and only album, the provocatively titled 'DO IT DOG STYLE', in 1978. Featuring such enduring aggro anthems as 'WHERE HAVE ALL THE BOOT BOYS GONE' (their major label debut single), the record was a first-wave mini-classic played out with more than a passing nod to the proto-punk glam of The NEW YORK DOLLS (especially with regards to

BARRETT's THUNDERS-like vocals!). One famous admirer, of course, was a young STEVEN MORRISSEY, auditioned but not taken on for the vacant role of lead singer after BARRETT's subsequent departure. With ROSSI eventually taking over the post and future CULT man BILLY DUFFY added on guitar, the group re-emerged as SLAUGHTER (nothing to do with the American metal-boys!). When that name didn't work, they rather unadvisedly adopted the STUDIO SWEETHEARTS moniker before finally splitting after a brief period with BARRETT back in the fold. More often mentioned for the big name connections rather than their actual music, SLAUGHTER AND THE DOGS nevertheless remain one of the key players in the early punk scene. • **Songwriters:** BARRETT-ROSSI except; QUICK JOEY SMALL (Kasenetz-Katz Singing Orchestral Circus) / I'M WAITING FOR THE MAN (Velvet Underground).

Album rating: WHERE HAVE ALL THE BOOT BOYS GONE compilation (*6)

WAYNE BARRETT – vocals / **MIKE ROSSI** – guitar / **HOWARD BATES** – bass / **MAD MUFFET** (b. BRIAN CRANFORD) – drums

Rabid not iss.

Jun 77. (7") *(TOSH 101)* **CRANKED UP REALLY HIGH. / THE BITCH** [ ] [-]

Decca not iss.

Sep 77. (7") *(FR/LF 13723)* **WHERE HAVE ALL THE BOOT BOYS GONE. / YOU'RE A BORE** [ ] [-]

Nov 77. (7") *(FR 13743)* **DAME TO BLAME. / JOHNNY T** [ ] [-]

Feb 78. (7") *(FR 13758)* **QUICK JOEY SMALL. / COME ON BACK** [ ] [-]

above featured **MICK RONSON** – guitar (ex-DAVID BOWIE)

May 78. (lp) *(SKL 5292)* **DO IT DOG STYLE** [ ] [-]
– Where have all the boot boys gone / Victims of the vampire / Boston babies / I'm waiting for the man / I'm mad / You're a bore / Quick Joey Small / Keep on trying / We don't care / Since you went away / Who are the mystery girls / Dame to blame. *(re-iss. 1989 colrd-lp on 'Damaged Goods'; FNARR 2) (<cd-iss. Mar00 on 'Captain Oi'; AHOYCD 131>)*

Rabid not iss.

Dec 78. (lp) *(HAT 23)* **LIVE SLAUGHTER RABID DOGS (live)** [ ] [-]
(re-iss. Mar 89 on 'Receiver'; RRLP 109)

— **ED BANGER** (EDDIE GARRITY) – guitar (ex-NOSEBLEEDS) repl. WAYNE

T.J.M. not iss.

Mar 79. (12"ep) *(TJM 3)* **IT'S ALRIGHT / EDGAR ALLEN POE. / TWIST & TURN / UFO** [ ] [-]

D.J.M. not iss.

Jun 79. (7") *(DJS 10915)* **I BELIEVE. (as "STUDIO SWEETHEARTS") / IT ISN'T ME** [ ] [-]

Nov 79. (7") *(DJS 10927)* **YOU'RE READY NOW. / RUNAWAY** [ ] [-]

SLAUGHTER

— **PHIL ROWLAND** – drums (ex-EATER) repl. MUFFET

— WAYNE BARRETT also returned to repl. BILLY DUFFY who joined THEATRE OF HATE

Feb 80. (7") *(DJS 10936)* **EAST SIDE OF TOWN. / ONE BY ONE** [ ] [-]

Mar 80. (lp) *(DJF 20566)* **BITE BACK** [ ] [-]
– Now I know / What's wrong boy / Won't let go / All over now / She ain't gonna show / Heel in New York / Crashing out with Lucy / Chasing me / It's in the mind / East side of town / Don't wanna die. *(<cd-iss. Jun00 on 'Captain Oi'+=; AHOYCD 142>)* – I'm the one / One by one / What's wrong boy (live).

Jun 80. (7") *(DJS 10945)* **I'M THE ONE. / WHAT'S WRONG BOY? (live) / HELL IN NEW YORK** [ ] [-]

SLAUGHTER & THE DOGS

— now without ED BANGER

Thrush not iss.

Feb 83. (12"ep) *(THRUSH 1)* **HALF ALIVE** [ ] [-]
– Twist and turn / Cranked up really high (live) / Where have all the boot boys gone (live).

— split after above

– compilations, etc. –

Jun 83. (lp) *Thrush; (THRUSHLP 1)* **THE WAY WE WERE** [ ] [-]

Nov 88. (7",7"red or green) *Damaged Goods; (FNARR 1)* **WHERE HAVE ALL THE BOOT BOYS GONE. / YOU'RE A BORE / JOHNNY T** [ ] [-]

May 89. (lp) *Receiver; (RRLP 14)* **LIVE AT THE FACTORY (live 1981)** [ ] [-]
– Now I know / Hell in New York / Runaway / Mystery girls / What's wrong boy? / You're ready now / Johnny T / Boston babies / All over now.

Jun 89. (lp) *Link; (LINKLP 092)* **SLAUGHTERHOUSE TAPES** [ ] [-]

Feb 92. (cd/lp) *Receiver; (RR CD/LP 151)* **SHOCKING** [ ] [-]

Mar 94. (cd) *Receiver; (RRCD 183)* **WHERE HAVE ALL THE BOOT BOYS GONE** [ ] [-]

Sep 98. (cd) *Captain Oi; (<AHOYCD 050>)* **CRANKED UP REALLY HIGH** [ ] [ ]

SLAVE RAIDER

Formed: USA . . . 1987 by CHAINSAW CAINE, with NICCI WIKKID, LANCE SABIN, LETITIA RAE and er . . . THE ROCK (on drums). Tacky sensation merchants fronted by the eye-patched CAINE, SLAVE RAIDER were signed up by the British label, 'Jive', the group subsequently making a concerted effort to win over the UK rock scene with their debut album, 'TAKE THE WORLD BY STORM'. Of course, SLAVE RAIDER did nothing of the sort, 'Jive' duly pairing them up with respected producer Chris Tsangerides for a second shot at the big time with 'WHAT DO YOU KNOW ABOUT ROCK'N'ROLL' (1989). It was clear SLAVE RAIDER had barely mastered the basics, the band eventually splitting after being dropped by their label.

Album rating: TAKE THE WORLD BY STORM (*5) / WHAT DO YOU KNOW ABOUT ROCK'N'ROLL? (*4)

CHAINSAW (CHARLIE) CAINE – vocals / **NICCI WIKKID** – guitar / **LANCE SABIN** – guitar / **LETITIA RAE** – bass / **THE ROCK** – drums

Jive Jive

Mar 88. (lp/c) *(HIP/+C 60) <1088>* **TAKE THE WORLD BY STORM** [ ] [ ]
– Take the world by storm / Back stabbing / Make some noise / Burning too hot / Long way from home / Survival of the fittest / The Devil comes out in me / Black hole.

Apr 89. (7") *(JIVE 198)* **YOUNG BLOOD. /** [ ] [ ]
(12"+=) *(JIVET 198)* –

Apr 89. (lp/c/cd) *(HIP/HIPC/CHIP 68) <1141>* **WHAT DO YOU KNOW ABOUT ROCK'N'ROLL?** [ ] [ ]
– Is there rock'n'roll in Heaven / Bye bye baby / Sin city social / High priest of good times / What do you know about rock'n'roll? / Iron bar motel / Jailbreak / Youngblood / Keep on pushing / Rollercoaster / Magistrate / Guilty / Wreckin' machine.

— folded when they were dropped by their record company

SLAYER

Formed: Los Angeles, California, USA . . . late 1981 by TOM ARAYA, JEFF HANNEMAN, KERRY KING and former jazz drummer, DAVE LOMBARDO. One of the heaviest, fastest and generally more extreme outfits to emerge from the initial wave of thrash-metal, SLAYER recorded their first couple of releases, 'SHOW NO MERCY' (1984) and the 'HAUNTING THE CHAPEL' EP (1984) for the 'Metal Blade' label. A largely unfocussed blur of manic drumming and powerdrill guitar shredding, these early efforts also showcased a lyrical excess to match the 'music', heralding a new era in which initially thrash outfits, then death-metal merchants, trawled new depths of goriness (the PMRC would probably use the term depravity). 'HELL AWAITS' (1985) followed in much the same fashion and it wasn't until the epochal 'REIGN IN BLOOD' (1987) that SLAYER began to assume the status of metal demi-gods. Cannily signed up by RICK RUBIN to the ultra-hip 'Def Jam' (home to such groundbreaking rap outfits as The BEASTIE BOYS and PUBLIC ENEMY), SLAYER not only benefitted from the added kudos of a 'street' label but were touted by the rock press as having produced the ultimate speed-metal album. From its trademark black-period Goya-esque artwork to the breakneck precision of the playing and the wildly controversial lyrical fare ('NECROPHOBIC', 'RAINING BLOOD' etc.), 'REIGN IN BLOOD' was a landmark metal release, which in many respects has never been bettered in its respective field. The biggest fuss, however, was reserved for 'ANGEL OF DEATH', a track detailing the horrific atrocities of Nazi butcher, Joseph Mengele. 'Def Jam's distributor, 'Columbia' refused to handle the album, with 'Geffen' stepping in to facilitate the group's first Top 100 (US) entry. While SLAYER allegedly hold right-wing political views, the disturbingly soft-spoken ARAYA maintains that his lyrics do not promote war or violence but merely reflect the darker aspects of humanity. Whatever, there was no denying the power of SLAYER's music, especially on the more composed 'SOUTH OF HEAVEN' (1988). No doubt finally realising that only too often they sacrificed effectiveness for speed, SLAYER took their proverbial foot off the accelerator. Sure, there were still outbursts of amphetamine overkill, but with the likes of the apocalyptic title track, the chugging fury of 'MANDATORY SUICIDE' (complete with chilling spoken word outro) and a raging cover of Judas Priest's 'DISSIDENT AGGRESSOR', SLAYER had at last harnessed the malign potential which they had always promised. The record brought the band an unprecedented UK Top 30 chart placing, proof that the group were now being taken seriously as major thrash contenders alongside METALLICA, MEGADETH and ANTHRAX. The acclaimed 'SEASONS IN THE ABYSS' (1990) confirmed that SLAYER were not merely contenders but challengers for the thrash throne. With 'SEASONS..', the group succeeded in combining their instinct for speed with a newfound maturity, resulting in one of the most intense yet accessible metal records ever released. The doom-obsessed, bass-crunching likes of 'EXPENDABLE YOUTH', 'SKELETONS OF SOCIETY' and the brooding title track recalled the intensity of prime 70's BLACK SABBATH while even the harder tracks like 'WAR ENSEMBLE' and 'BLOOD RED' displayed traces of melody. The obligatory lyrical shock tactics came with 'DEAD SKIN MASK' an eery meditation reportedly inspired by serial killer, Ed Gein. Again produced by RUBIN and released on his fledgling 'Def American' label, the album made the UK Top 20 and finally broke the group into the US Top 40. Promoting the record with the legendary 'Clash Of The Titans' tour (also featuring MEGADETH, SUICIDAL TENDENCIES and TESTAMENT), SLAYER had finally made it into the metal big league and summing up the first blood-soaked chapter of their career, the group duly released the live double set, 'DECADE OF AGGRESSION' (1991). Amid much rumour and counter-rumour, LOMBARDO finally left the band for good in Spring '92, ex-FORBIDDEN sticksman, PAUL BOSTOPH, drafted in as a replacement. A long-awaited sixth set, 'DIVINE INTERVENTION', finally arrived in 1994, a consolidation of SLAYER's hallowed position in the metal hierarchy and the group's first assault on the US Top 10. The heaviest band ever (as Kerrang! readers acclaimed them!) spewed back with 'UNDISPUTED ATTITUTE' (1996), although it was 1998's 'DIABOLUS IN MUSICA' (apparently a "devilish" musical scale banned by churches in the

15th century!) which brought their brutal gore back to the fore. • **Songwriters:** ARAYA words / HANNEMAN music, also covered IN-A-GADDA-DA-VIDA (Iron Butterfly) / DISORDER + WAR + UK 82 (as 'US 92'; 3 from 1993 film 'Judgment Night') (Exploited). 'UNDISPUTED ATTITUDE' album all covers; ABOLISH GOVERNMENT (TSOL) / I WANNA BE YOUR DOG (Iggy Pop) / (GBH) / GUILTY OF BEING WHITE (Minor Threat) / other covers from (Verbal Abuse), (D.I.), (Dr Know) and (DRI).

Album rating: SHOW NO MERCY (*5) / HELL AWAITS (*7) / REIGN IN BLOOD (*9) / SOUTH OF HEAVEN (*9) / SEASONS IN THE ABYSS (*8) / DECADE OF AGGRESSION (*8) / DIVINE INTERVENTION (*7) / UNDISPUTED ATTITUDE (*6) / DIABOLUS IN MUSICA (*5)

TOM ARAYA (b. 6 Jun'61, Chile) – vocals, bass / **JEFF HANNEMAN** (b.31 Jan'64) – lead guitar / **KERRY KING** (b. 3 Jun'64, Huntington Park, Calif.) – lead guitar / **DAVE LOMBARDO** (b.16 Feb'65) – drums

Roadrunner Metal Blade

Jun 84. (lp) *(RR 9868)* *<MBR 1013>* **SHOW NO MERCY** [ ] [ ] Feb84
– Evil has no boundaries / The antichrist / Die by the sword / Fight till death / Metalstorm – Face the slayer / Black magic / Tormentor / The final command / Crionics / Show no mercy. *<US re-iss. pic-lp Dec88; 72214-1> (re-iss. Aug90 on 'Metal Blade' cd/c/lp; CD/T+/ZORRO 7) (cd re-iss. Feb96 on 'Metal Blade'; 3984 14032CD)*

Oct 84. (12"ep) *(RR12 55087)* **HAUNTING THE CHAPEL. / CHEMICAL WARFARE / CAPTOR OF SIN** [ ] [ ]
(re-iss. Oct89 as cd-ep; RR 2444-2)

Roadrunner Enigma

May 85. (lp/c) *(RR 9795-1/-4)* *<72297>* **HELL AWAITS** [ ] [ ]
– Hell awaits / Kill again / At dawn they sleep / Praise of death / Necrophiliac / Crypts of eternity / Hardening of the arteries. *(cd-iss. Feb89; RR34 9795) (re-iss. Aug90 on 'Metal Blade' cd/c/lp; CD/T+/ZORRO 8) (cd re-iss. Feb96 on 'Metal Blade'; 3984 14031CD)*

London Def Jam

Apr 87. (lp/c/pic-lp) *(LON LP/C/PP 34)* *<24131>* **REIGN IN BLOOD** [47] [94] Oct86
– Angel of death / Piece by piece / Necrophobic / Alter of sacrifice / Jesus saves / Criminally insane / Reborn / Epidemic / Post mortem / Raining blood. *(cd-iss. Dec94 on 'American'; 74321 24848-2)*

May 87. (7"red) *(LON 133)* **CRIMINALLY INSANE (remix). / AGGRESSIVE PERFECTER** [64] [ ]
(12"+=) *(LONX 133)* – Post mortem.

Jun 88. (lp/c)(cd) *(LON LP/C 63)(828 820-2)* *<24203>* **SOUTH OF HEAVEN** [25] [57]
– South of Heaven / Silent scream / Live undead / Behind the crooked cross / Mandatory suicide / Ghosts of war / Read between the lies / Cleanse the soul / Dissident aggressor / Spill the blood. *(cd re-iss. Dec94 on 'American'; 74321 24849-2)*

Sep 88. (12") *(LONX 201)* **MANDATORY SUICIDE. / IN-A-GADDA-DA-VIDA** [ ] [-]

American Def American

Oct 90. (cd/c/lp) *(849 6871-2/-4/-1)* *<24307>* **SEASONS IN THE ABYSS** [18] [40]
– War ensemble / Blood red / Spirit in black / Expendable youth / Dead skin mask / Hallowed point / Skeletons of society / Temptation / Born of fire / Seasons in the abyss. *(cd re-iss. Dec94 on 'American'; 74321 24850-2)*

Oct 91. (d-cd/d-c/d-lp) *(510 605-2/-4/-1)* *<26748>* **DECADE OF AGGRESSION (live)** [29] [ ]
– Hell awaits / The anti-Christ / War ensemble / South of Heaven / Raining blood / Altar of sacrifice / Jesus saves / Dead skin mask / Seasons in the abyss / Mandatory suicide / Angel of death / Hallowed paint / Blood red / Die by the sword / Black magic / Captor of sin / Born of fire / Post mortem / Spirit in black / Expendable youth / Chemical warfare. *(cd re-iss. Dec94; 74321 24851-2)*

Oct 91. (7") *(DEFA 9)* **SEASONS IN THE ABYSS (live). / AGGRESSIVE PERFECTOR (live)** [51] [ ]
(12"+=) *(DEFA 9-12)* – Chemical warfare.
(12"pic-d+=)(cd-s+=) *(DEFAP 9-12)(DEFAC 9)* – ('A'-experimental).

—— (May'92) **PAUL BOSTAPH** (b. 4 Mar'65, Hayward, Calif.) – drums repl. LOMBARDO

Oct 94. (cd/c/lp) *(74321 23677-2/-4/-1)* *<26748>* **DIVINE INTERVENTION** [15] [8]
– Killing fields / Sex. murder. art / Fictional reality / Dittohead / Divine intervention / Circle of beliefs / SS-3 / Serenity in murder / 213 / Mind control.

Sep 95. (7"ep) *(74321 26234-7)* **SERENITY IN MURDER / RAINING BLOOD. / DITTOHEAD / SOUTH OF HEAVEN** [ ] [-]
(cd-s) *(74321 26234-2)* – ('A'side) / At dawn they sleep (live) / Dead skin mask (live) / Divine intervention (live).
(cd-s) *(74321 31248-2)* – ('A'side) / Angel of death / Mandatory suicide / War ensemble.

—— (after below) **JOHN DETTE** – drums (ex-TESTAMENT) repl. BOSTOPH who joined lightweight TRUTH ABOUT SEAFOOD

May 96. (cd/c/10"d-lp) *(74321 35759-2/-4/-1)* *<43072>* **UNDISPUTED ATTITUDE** [31] [34]
– Disintigration – Free money / Verbal abuse – Leeches / Abolish government – Superficial love / Can't stand you / Ddamm / Guilty of being white / I hate you / Filler – I don't want to hear it / Spiritual law / Sick boy / Mr. Freeze / Violent pacification / Richard hung himself / I wanna be your god / Gemini. *(cd w/ free cd+=)(74321 38325-2)* – Witching hour / Dittohead / Divine intervention.

Sub Pop Sub Pop

Aug 96. (7") *<(SP 368)>* **ABOLISH GOVERNMENT. /** [ ] [ ]

—— there was also a SLAYER tribute album released Nov95; 'SLATANIC SLAUGHTER' on 'Black Sun' cd/lp; *BS 003 CD/LP)*

Columbia Columbia

Jun 98. (cd/c/lp) *(491302-2/-4/-1)* *<69192>* **DIABOLUS IN MUSICA** [27] [31]
– Bitter peace / Death's head / Stain of mind / Overt enemy / Perversions of pain / Love to hate / Desire in the name of God / Screaming from the sky / Wicked / Point / Scrum. *(cd re-iss. Aug00; same)*

– compilations, etc. –

Dec 88. (lp/c) *Roadrunner; (RR/+34 9574) / Enigma; <72015-1>* **LIVE UNDEAD (live 1984)** [ ] [ ] Oct87
– Black magic / Die by the sword / Captor of sin / The antichrist / Evil has no boundaries / Show no mercy / Aggressive perfector / Chemical warfare. *(re-iss. Sep91 on 'Metal Blade' cd/c/lp; CD/T+/ZORRO 29) (cd re-iss. Feb96 on 'Metal Blade'+=; 3984 14011CD)* – HAUNTING THE CHAPEL

SLEDGEHAMMER

Formed: Slough, England . . . 1978 by MIKE COOKE, TERRY PEARCE and KEN REVELL. With a MOTORHEAD support slot as their first gig, SLEDGEHAMMER got off to a promising start, their semi-legendary eponymous debut single proving a favourite among fans of the burgeoning NWOBHM movement. Despite a series of high profile support slots, subsequent singles failed to make any impact and it was almost five years before the band secured a release for their debut set, 'BLOOD ON THEIR HANDS'. By this point, the momentum had long been lost and the record was widely ignored.

Album rating: BLOOD ON THEIR HANDS (*3)

MIKE COOKE – vocals, guitar / **TERRY PEARCE** – bass / **KEN REVELL** – drums, percussion

S.R.T. not iss.

1979. (7") *(SRTS79CUS 395)* **SLEDGEHAMMER. / FEEL GOOD** [ ] [-]
(re-iss. 1980 on 'Valiant'; STRONG 1) (re-iss. 1980 on 'Valiant'; ROUND 2)

Slammer not iss.

Jan 81. (7") *(CELL 2)* **LIVING IN DREAMS. / FANTASIA** [ ] [-]
1982. (7") *(MRSB 2)* **IN THE MIDDLE OF THE NIGHT. /** [ ] [-]

—— **JOHN JAY** – bass, keyboards, vocals

Illuminated not iss.

Feb 85. (lp) *(JAMS 32)* **BLOOD ON THEIR HANDS** [ ] [-]
– Over the top 1914 / Perfumed garden / Feel good / Food and sex mad / 1984 / Sledgehammer / Garabandal.

Mar 85. (7"sha-pic-d) *(ILL 333)* **IN THE QUEUE. / OXFORD CITY** [ ] [-]

—— folded a few years later after the single 'PORNO PEAT' was withdrawn

SLEEP

Formed: San Jose, California, USA . . . early 90's by AL CISNEROS, MAT PIKE and CHRIS HAKIUS. A short-lived stoner-metal outfit, SLEEP issued a 'VOLUME ONE' set, before their thunderingly dense album in 1993, 'SLEEPS HOLY MOUNTAIN'. Dusting down molten slabs of Sabbath-esque riffs and scary psychedelia from the bowels of the late 60's/early 70's, they successfully captured that quasi-mystical vibe essential to any budding flare-rock act. Despite widespread praise and heavy touring, SLEEP's scheduled second set, 'DOPE SMOKER' (with a tentative release date of 1995) failed to materialise, as the band nodded into eternal slumber. • **Note:** Another SLEEP released records for 'Meantime' in 1990.

Album rating: VOLUME ONE (*5) / SLEEPS HOLY MOUNTAIN (*7)

AL CISNEROS – vocals, bass / **MAT PIKE** – guitar / **CHRIS HAKIUS** – drums

Tupelo Tupelo

Feb 92. (cd/c/lp) *(TUP CD/MC/LP 034)* *<RTD 344 4134>* **VOLUME ONE** [ ] [ ]
– Stillborn / The suffering / Numb / Anguish / Catatonic / Nebuchadnezzar's dream / The wall of yawn / Prey. *(cd re-iss. Jul00; same)*

Earache Earache

Mar 93. (lp/c/cd) *<(MOSH 079/+MC/CD)>* **SLEEPS HOLY MOUNTAIN** [ ] [ ] Nov93
– Dragonaut / The druid / Evil gypsy – Solomon's theme / Some grass / Aquarian / Holy mountain / Inside the sun / From beyond / Nain's baptism. *(cd re-iss. Sep97; same)*

—— an album, 'DOPE SMOKER' was penciled in for release in 1995, although this was withdrawn when they disbanded

Sleep Dopesmoker

Oct 98. (cd) *(ZZ 001)* *<DS 1>* **JERUSALEM** [ ] [ ] Jun98
– Jerusalem (6 versions). *(re-iss. Jan99 on 'Rise Above'; CDRISE 19) <US re-iss. Feb99 on 'The Music Cartel'; TMC 12>*

SLIPKNOT

Formed: Des Moines, Iowa, USA . . . 1995 by members 0, 1, 2, 3, 4, 5, 6, 7 and 8 – aka DJ SID WILSON, JOEY JORDISON, PAUL GRAY, CHRIS FEHN, JAMES ROOT, CRAIG JONES, SHAWN CRAHAN, MIC THOMPSON and singer (or screamer) COREY TAYLOR. The menacing 9-piece recorded and released the now rare album 'MATE, FEED, KILL, REPEAT' in 1996, receiving mass attention from record labels in the process. The ensemble signed with 'Roadrunner' in 1997 and released their self-titled debut album in 1999. The album (predictably) gained a huge cult following from the widespread majority of dysfunctional teens all over the globe. In a way, it's not hard to describe SLIPKNOT's music: fast, heavy, vicious, ferocious, venomous and crude – in fact a few journos made them out to be Rock's answer to 'The Texas Chainsaw Massacre'. The mask-clad spooksters have found their niche within the flow of sports metal in the US; bands such as KORN and white chumps LIMP BIZKIT thrive off the money made from these double-bass drum pedallers. But as a band, the angsty punk-metallers are not bad, mixing in a blend of tricky, thumping and downright blastferic lyrics along with the pounding guitars and drums. It's what grandmothers have nightmares about.

Album rating: SLIPKNOT (*8)

COREY TAYLOR – vocals / **MIC THOMPSON** – guitar / **JIM ROOT** – guitar / **PAUL GRAY** – bass / **JOEY JORDISON** – drums / **CHRIS FEHN** – percussion / **SHAWN CRAHAN** – percussion / **CRAIG JONES** – samples, programmes / **SID WILSON** – DJ

not iss. | unknown

1996. (cd) **MATE, FEED, KILL, REPEAT** [-] [ ]

Roadrunner | Roadrunner

Jun 99. (cd) *<(RR 8655-2)>* **SLIPKNOT** [37] [51]
– 74261000027 / Eyel ESS / Wait and bleed / Surfacing / Spit it out / Tattered and torn / Frail limb nursery / Purity / Liberate / Prosthetics / No life / Diluted / The only one. *(other cd+=; RR 8655-5)* – Me inside / Get this / Interloper (demo) / Despise (demo). *(pic-lp iss.Aug00; RR 8655-6)*

Feb 00. (cd-s) *(RR 2112-5)* **WAIT AND BLEED / SPIT IT OUT (overcaffeinated hyper-molt mix) / SIC (Spaceship Console mix) / WAIT AND SEE (live promo video)** [27] [ ]

Sep 00. (7") *(RR 2090-7)* **SPIT IT OUT. / SURFACING (live)** [28] [ ]
(cd-s+=) *(RR 2090-3)* – Wait and bleed (live) / ('A'-video).

S*M*A*S*H

Formed: Welwyn Garden City, Hertfordshire, England . . . 1992 as SMASH AT THE BLUES by ED BORRIE, SALVADOR ALESSI and ROB HAIGH. One of the most fiercely political bands since The CLASH (an obvious influence alongside the PISTOLS and the ANGELIC UPSTARTS), S*M*A*S*H made an immediate impact in summer '93 with the 'REAL SURREAL' single. Issued on their own 'Le Disques De Popcor' label, the track was followed up by early '94's 'SHAME', a double A-sided NME/Melody Maker single of the week and the subject of much controversy due to its flip side, 'LADY LOVE YOUR CUNT' (the title a reference to an essay by Germaine Greer). By this point the band were also being heralded as leaders of the much hyped "New Wave Of New Wave" scene alongside THESE ANIMAL MEN (they had previously shared an album, 1993's 'WHEELERS, DEALERS AND CHRISTINE KEELERS'), the press coverage not exactly harming them as incendiary live performances blazed a trail across the UK. The band subsequently signed to 'Hi-Rise' along with THESE ANIMAL MEN, releasing a mini-set compilation of their work to date, 'S*M*A*S*H SPRING 1994'. It broke the Top 30, as did the controversial '(I WANT TO KILL) SOMEBODY' – which infamously included a hit list of Tory MP's – the subject of censorship from Radio One. The band's political beliefs were further underlined when they played an Anti-Nazi League rally alongside BILLY BRAGG, the fact that they were more effective in a live environment than the studio confirmed with the release of a full length debut album, 'SELF ABUSED' (1994). Criticisms centred around the thin production yet amidst all the buzzsaw bluster were genuinely affecting moments such as 'REFLECTIONS OF YOU (REMEMBER ME)', 'TIME' etc. Whatever, the album failed to sell and the band concentrated on a US tour, supported by a one-off single on 'Sub Pop', 'BARRABAS'. Their return to British shores was marked with the release of mini-set, 'ANOTHER LOVE (SONG)' (1995), although it contained only a handful of genuinely new tracks. With Brit-pop now dominating the music scene, S*M*A*S*H's moment seemed to have passed and following a final single, 'REST OF MY LIFE', they officially split.

Album rating: SELF ABUSED (*6) / ANOTHER LOVE (SONG) mini (*5)

ED BORRIE – vocals, guitar / **SALVADOR ALESSI** – bass / **ROB HAIGH** – drums (ex-NIGHTMARE, ex-ASTRONAUTS)

Les Disques | not iss.

Jul 93. (7") *(POPCOR 001)* **REAL SURREAL. / DRUGS AGAIN / REVISITED NO.3** [ ] [-]

Dec 93. (c-ep) *(POPCOR 002)* **WHEELERS, DEALERS & CHRISTINE KEELERS** [ ] [-]
– Self-abused / Kill somebody / Altruism / Bang bang bang / (5 other tracks by THESE ANIMAL MEN)

Feb 94. (7",7"pink/one-sided7"red) *(POPCOR 003/+V)* **LADY LOVE YOUR CUNT. / SHAME** [ ] [-]

Hi-Rise | Hut

Mar 94. (m-cd/m-c/m-lp) *(FLATM CD/TC/LP 2) <3>* **S*M*A*S*H SPRING 1994** [28] [ ]
– Real surreal / Drugs again / Revisited No.3 / Lady love your c*** / Shame.

Jul 94. (c-ep/12"ep/cd-ep) *(FLATS TC//CD 5)* **(I WANT TO) KILL SOMEBODY (Topper mix). / ('A'-Keith LeBlanc mix) / ('A'Gunshot headhunter mix) / ('A'-Bragg reshuffle mix)** [26] [ ]

Sep 94. (cd/c/lp) *(FLAT CD/MC/LP 6) <HUSCD 6>* **SELF ABUSED** [59] [ ]
– Revisited No.5 / Barrabas / Oh ovary / Altruism / Reflections of you (remember me) / Self abused / Scream silent / Another love / Another shark in the deep end of my swimming pool / Real surreal / Dear Lou / Bang bang bang (granta 25) / Time. *(cd+=)* – A.L.L.Y.C. *(also other lp++=; FLATLPX 6)* – Trainspotter.

Nov 94. (7") *(SP 276)* **BARRABAS (PILOTED). / TURN ON THE WATER** [ ] [ ]
(above single on 'Sub Pop')

Feb 95. (m-cd/m-c/m-lp) *(FLATM CD/TC/LP 10)* **ANOTHER LOVE (SONG) EP** [ ] [-]
– Another love (Bobbit mix) / Petal buzz / You've got a friend who's a friend of mine / Reflections of you (remember me) (live) / Time (live) / Self abused (live) / Another love (uncut).

Popcor | not iss.

Jan 96. (7"/cd-s) *(POPCOR 9/+CD)* **THE REST OF MY LIFE. /** [ ] [-]

—— broke up after above

SMASHING PUMPKINS

Formed: Chicago, Illinois, USA . . .late 80's by BILLY CORGAN, JAMES IHA, D'ARCY WRETZKY. The son of a jazz guitarist and former member of local goth band, The MARKED, CORGAN initiated The SMASHING PUMPKINS as a three piece using a drum machine, before the band recruited sticksman, JIMMY CHAMBERLAIN. After a debut single for a local label, 'I AM ONE', and the inclusion of two tracks on a local compilation album, the group came to the attention of influential Seattle label, 'Sub Pop'. After only one single, 'TRISTESSA', The SMASHING PUMPKINS moved once more, signing to Virgin subsidiary, 'Hut', in the UK, 'Caroline' in America. Produced by BUTCH VIG, a debut album, 'GISH', was released in early '92, its grunge pretensions belying a meandering 70's/psychedelic undercurrent which distanced the band from most of their contemporaries. Nevertheless, the group amassed a sizable student/grassroots following which eventually saw the debut go gold in the States, a re-released 'I AM ONE' sneaking into the UK Top 75 later that year. With the masterful 'SIAMESE DREAM' (1993), the band went from underground hopefuls to alternative rock frontrunners, the album fully realising the complex 'PUMPKINS sound in a delicious wash of noise and gentle melody. Influenced by acoustic LED ZEPPELIN fused with slices of 70's PINK FLOYD, CORGAN's croaky but effective voice was at its best on the pastel, NIRVANA-esque classics, 'TODAY' and 'DISARM', while the 'PUMPKINS went for the jugular on the likes of 'CHERUB ROCK', 'ROCKET' and 'GEEK U.S.A.'. The album made the Top 5 in Britain, Top 10 in the States, selling multi-millions and turning the band into a 'grunge' sensation almost overnight, despite the fact that their mellotron stylings and complex arrangements marked them out as closer in spirit to prog-rock than punk. Amidst frantic touring, the band released the outtakes/B-sides compilation, 'PISCES ISCARIOT' (1994), the next album proper surfacing in late '95 as the sprawling double set, 'MELLON COLLIE AND THE INFINITE SADNESS'. Dense and stylistically breathtaking, the album veered from all-out grunge/thrash to acoustic meandering and avant-rock doodlings, a less cohesive whole than its predecessor but much more to get your teeth into. Inevitably, there were criticisms of self-indulgence, though for a two-hour set, there was a surprising, compelling consistency to proceedings; among the highlights were 'BULLET WITH BUTTERFLY WINGS', 'TONIGHT, TONIGHT' and the visceral rage of '1979'. The record scaled the US charts, where The SMASHING PUMPKINS were almost reaching the commercial and critical heights of NIRVANA, the group also taking Britain by storm, headlining the 1995 Reading Festival. Never the most stable of bands, disaster struck the following year when new boy (keyboard player) JONATHAN MELVOIN died of a drugs overdose and heroin addict CHAMBERLAIN was finally kicked out. More recently (early 1998), IHA released an acclaimed solo album of acoustic strumming ('LET IT COME DOWN') while the others recorded fresh songs with a drum machine, taking things full circle. That summer, the 'PUMPKINS showed a softer side to their character when the mournful but still effective album, 'ADORE', hit the Top 5. 1999 saw two major personnel changes via the return of CHAMBERLAIN and the departure of D'ARCY (who was replaced by ex-HOLE bassist MELISSA); one last set would appear in 2000. • **Songwriters:** CORGAN, except several with IHA. Covered; A GIRL NAMED SANDOZ (Eric Burdon & The Animals) / LANDSLIDE (Fleetwood Mac) / DANCING IN THE MOONLIGHT (Thin Lizzy) / NEVER LET ME DOWN (Depeche Mode) / YOU'RE ALL I'VE GOT TONIGHT (Cars) / CLONES (WE'RE ALL) (Alice Cooper) / DREAMING (Blondie) / A NIGHT LIKE THIS (Cure) / DESTINATION UNKNOWN (Missing Persons) / SAD PETER PAN with Red Red Meat (Vic Chesnutt). • **Miscellaneous:** IHA and D'ARCY set up their own label, 'Scratchie', for whom the outfit, FULFLEJ recorded an album ('Wack-Ass Tuba Riff') in 1996 with the pair making guest appearances.

Album rating: GISH (*6) / SIAMESE DREAM (*9) / MELLON COLLIE AND THE INFINITE SADNESS (*9) / PISCES ISCARIOT compilation (*5) / THE AEROPLANE FLIES HIGH boxed set (*6) / ADORE (*5) / James Iha: LET IT COME DOWN (*5)

BILLY CORGAN (b.17 Mar'67) – vocals, guitar / **JAMES IHA** (b.26 Mar'68, Elk Grove, Illinois) – guitar / **D'ARCY (WRETZKY)** (b. 1 May'68, South Haven, Michigan) – bass, vocals / **JIMMY CHAMBERLIN** (b.10 Jun'64, Joliet, Illinois) – drums

not iss. | Limited Potential

Apr 90. (7") *<Limp 006>* **I AM ONE. / NOT WORTH ASKING** [-] [ ]

Glitterhouse | Sub Pop

Dec 90. (7",7"pink) *<SP 90>* **TRISTESSA. / LA DOLLY VITA** [-] [ ]
(UK-12"+=; May93) *(SP 10-137)* – Honeyspider.

Hut | Caroline

Aug 91. (12") *(HUTT 6)* **SIVA. / WINDOW PAINE** [ ] [-]

Feb 92. (12"ep/cd-ep) *(HUTT/CDHUT 10)* **LULL EP** [ ] [-]
– Rhinoceros / Blue / Slunk / Bye June (demo).

Feb 92. (cd/c/lp) *(HUT CD/MC/LP 002) <1705>* **GISH** [ ] [ ] Aug91
– I am one / Siva / Rhinoceros / Bury me / Crush / Suffer / Snail / Tristessa / Window paine / Daydream. *(re-iss. May94; diff.versions cd/lp; HUT CDX/LPX 002)*

Jun 92. (c-ep/12"ep/cd-ep) *(HUT C/T/CD 17)* **PEEL SESSIONS** [ ] [-]
– Siva / A girl named Sandoz / Smiley.

Aug 92. (12"ep/cd-ep) *(HUTT/CDHUT 18)* **I AM ONE. / PLUME / STARLA** [73] [-]
(10"ep) *(HUTTEN 18)* – ('A'side) / Terrapin (live) / Bullet train to Osaka.

Jun 93. (7"clear) *(HUT 31)* **CHERUB ROCK. / PURR SNICKETY** [31] [-]
(12"/cd-s) *(HUTT/CDHUT 31)* – ('A'side) / Pissant / French movie theme / (Star spangled banner).

Jul 93. (cd/c/d-lp) *(HUT CD/MC/LP 011) <88267>* **SIAMESE DREAM** [4] [10]
– Cherub rock / Quiet / Today / Hummer / Rocket / Disarm / Soma / Geek U.S.A. / Mayonaise / Spaceboy / Silverfuck / Sweet sweet / Luna. *(d-lp re-iss. Dec99 on 'Caroline'; CAROL 17401)*

Sep 93. (7"red) *(HUT 37)* **TODAY. / APATHY'S LAST KISS** [44] [-]
(c-s/12"/cd-s) *(HUTC/HUTT/CDHUT 37)* – ('A'side) / Hello kitty kat / Obscured.

Feb 94. (7"purple) *(HUT 43)* **DISARM. / SIAMESE DREAM** [11] [-]
(12"/cd-s) *(HUT T/CD 43)* – ('A'side) / Soothe (demo) / Blew away.
(cd-s) *(HUTDX 43)* – ('A'side) / Dancing in the moonlight / Landslide.

Oct 94. (cd/c/gold-lp) *<39834>* **PISCES ISCARIOT** (compilation of B-sides & rarities) [-] [4]
– Soothe / Frail and bedazzled / Plume / Whir / Blew away / Pissant / Hello Kitty Kat / Obscured / Landslide / Starla / Blue / A girl named Sandoz / La dolly vita / Spaced. *<w/free gold-7"; CAR 1767-7>* **NOT WORTH ASKING. / HONEY SPIDER II** *(UK-iss.Oct96 cd/c/lp; HUT CD/MC/LP 41)*

Hut Virgin

Dec 94. (7"peach) *(HUTL 48)* **ROCKET. / NEVER LET ME DOWN** [ ] [-]
(4x7"box-set) *(SPBOX 1)* **SIAMESE SINGLES** – (last 3 singles 1993-94 + above)

Oct 95. (c-s/cd-s) *(HUT C/CD 63) <38522>* **BULLET WITH BUTTERFLY WINGS / . . .SAID SADLY** [20] [25]

Oct 95. (d-cd/d-c) *(CD/TC HUTD 30) <40861>* **MELLON COLLIE AND THE INFINITE SADNESS** [4] [1]
– DAWN TO DUSK:- Mellon Collie and the infinite sadness / Tonight, tonight / Jellybelly / Zero / Here is no why / Bullet with butterfly wings / To forgive / An ode to no one / Love / Cupid de Locke / Galapogos / Muzzle / Porcelina of the vast oceans / Take me down. // TWILIGHT TO STARLIGHT:- Where boys fear to tread / Bodies / Thirty-three / In the arms of sleep / 1979 / Tales of a scorched Earth / Thru the eyes of Ruby / Stumbleine / X.Y.U. / We only come out at night / Beautiful / Lily (my one and only) / By starlight / Farewell and goodnight. *(re-iss. Apr96 as t-lp+=; HUTTLP 30)* – Tonight reprise / Infinite sadness.

— added on tour **JONATHAN MELVOIN** – keyboards (ex-DICKIES) (brother of WENDY; ex-WENDY & LISA, ex-PRINCE)

Jan 96. (c-ep/12"ep/cd-ep) *(HUT C/T/CD 67) <38547>* **1979 / UGLY. / BELIEVE / CHERRY** [16] [12]
(12"ep/cd-ep; Mar96) *(HUT TX/CDX 67)* – 1979 REMIXES: Vocal / Instrumental / Moby / Cement.

May 96. (c-ep) *(HUTC 69) <38547>* **TONIGHT, TONIGHT / MELADORI MAGPIE / ROTTEN APPLES** [7] [36] Jun96
(cd-ep+=) *(HUTCD 69)* – Medellia of the gray skies.
(cd-ep) *(HUTDX 69)* – ('A'side) / Jupiter's lament / Blank / Tonite (reprise).

— On 12th Jul'96, MELVOIN died of a heroin overdose. CHAMBERLIN, who found him dead, was charged with drug offences and sacked by the remaining trio who were said to sick of his long-lasting drug addiction. In August, they were replaced for tour by **DENNIS FLEMION** – keyboards (ex-FROGS) + **MATT WALKER** – drums (of FILTER)

Sep 96. (m-cd) *(HUTCD 73) <38545>* **ZERO EP** [ ] [46] May96
– Zero / God / Mouths of babes / Tribute to Johnny / Marquis in spades / Pennies / Pastichio medley: (excerpts).

Nov 96. (cd-ep) *(HUTCD 78) <38574>* **THIRTY THREE / THE LAST SONG / THE AEROPLANE FLIES HIGH (TURNS LEFT, LOOKS RIGHT) / TRANSFORMER** [21] [39]
(cd-ep) *(HUTDX 78)* – ('A'side) / The bells / My blue Heaven.

Nov 96. (5xcd-ep;box) *<SPBOX 2>* **THE AEROPLANE FLIES HIGH** [-] [42]
– (BULLET WITH BUTTERFLY WINGS / 1979 / TONIGHT, TONIGHT / THIRTY THREE / ZERO)

— early in '97, CORGAN provided six songs for 'RANSOM' film soundtrack credited to conductor JAMES HORNER (Hollywood HR 62086-2)

Jun 97. (c-s) *(W 0404C)* **THE END IS THE BEGINNING IS THE END / THE BEGINNING IS THE END IS THE BEGINNING** [10] [ ]
(cd-s+=) *(W 0404CD)* – The ethers tragic / The guns of love disastrous.
(12"/cd-s) *(W 0410 T/CD)* – ('A'mixes; 2 Fluke mixes / 2 Rabbit in The Moons mixes / Hallucination Gotham mix).
(above from the film 'Batman And Robin' on 'Warners')

May 98. (7") *(HUT 101) <38647>* **AVA ADORE. / CZARINA** [11] [42] Jun98
(c-s+=/cd-s+=) *(HUT C/CD 101)* – Once in a while.

Jun 98. (cd/c/d-lp) *(CDHUT/TCHUT/HUTDLP 51) <45879>* **ADORE** [5] [2]
– To Sheila / Ava adore / Perfect / Daphne decends / Once upon a time / Tear / Crestfallen / Appels + oranjes / Pug / The tale of Dusty and Pistol Pete / Annie-dog / Shame / Behold! the night mare / For Martha / Blank page / 17.

Sep 98. (c-s/cd-s) *(HUT C/CD 106) <38650>* **PERFECT / SUMMER / PERFECT (Nellee Hooper mix)** [24] [54]
(cd-s) *(HUTDX 106)* – ('A'side) / Daphne descends (Oakenfold Perfecto mix) / Daphne descends (Kerry B mix).

— **CHAMBERLAIN** was now back in the fold

— **MELISSA AUF DER MAUR** – bass (ex-HOLE) repl. D'ARCY

Feb 00. (c-s/cd-s) *(HUT C/CD 127)* **STAND INSIDE YOUR LOVE / SPEED KILLS** [23] [-]

Feb 00. (cd/c/d-lp) *(CDHUT/HUTMC/HUTDLP 59) <48936>* **MACHINA / THE MACHINES OF GOD** [7] [3]
– The everlasting gaze / Rain drops & sun showers / Stand inside your love / I of the mourning / The sacred and profane / Try, try, try / Heavy metal machine / This time / The imploding voice / Glass and the ghost children / Wound / The crying tree of Mercury / With every light / Blue skies bring tears / Age of innocence.

Sep 00. (cd-s) *(HUTCD 140)* **TRY, TRY, TRY / HERE'S TO THE ATOM BOMB** [73] [-]

— the band split after above single

JAMES IHA

JAMES IHA – vocals, guitar / **NEAL CASAL** – guitar / **ADAM SCHLESINGER** – piano (of FOUNTAINS OF WAYNE) / **GREG LEISZ** – steel guitar / **JOHN GINTY** – hammond organ / **SOLOMON SNYDER** – bass / **MATT WALKER** – drums / **NINA GORDON** (of VERUCA SALT) also a part of initial basement set-up

Feb 98. (cd/c/lp) *(CDHUT/HUTMC/HUTLP 47) <45411>* **LET IT COME DOWN** [ ] [ ]
– Be strong now / Sound of love / Beauty / See the sun / Country girl / Jealousy / Lover, lover / Silver string / Winter / One and two / No one's gonna hurt you.

Feb 98. (12"ep/cd-ep) *(HUT T/CD 99)* **BE STRONG NOW / MY ADVICE. / TAKE CARE / FALLING** [ ] [ ]

Pat SMEAR / RUTHENSMEAR (see under ⇒ GERMS)

SNAKE RIVER CONSPIRACY

Formed: San Jose, California, USA . . . 1999 by JASON SLATER and TOBEY TORRES. Bored by the increasingly bland direction taken by his erstwhile band THIRD EYE BLIND, SLATER subsequently worked as a studio engineer, crafting the songs which would eventually make up 'SONIC JIHAD' (2000). Introduced to the sultry TORRES through mutual friends, SLATER wasted little time in installing the former go-go dancer as frontwoman while he provided the hybrid electro-sleaze/industrial/metal backdrop. Given the studio-boffin basis of the band, comparisons to GARBAGE were inevitable, although SLATER's JOHN BARRY swipes and cover of The Smiths' 'HOW SOON IS NOW?' suggested a more maverick talent. The quaintly titled 'SMELLS LIKE TEEN PUNK MEAT' EP followed later that year while UK fans were treated to a support slot with MY RUIN.

Album rating: SONIC JIHAD (*7)

TOBEY TORRES (b.1972) – vocals / **JASON SLATER** – bass, electronics, etc (ex-THIRD EYE BLIND)

Morpheus Reprise

Oct 99. (cd-ep) *(MORPH 003CD)* **VULCAN MIND HELD EP** [ ] [ ]
– Vulcan / She said, she said / Coke & vaseline.

Jul 00. (cd-ep) *(MORPH 004CD)* **SMELLS LIKE TEEN PUNK MEAT EP** [ ] [ ]
– Somebody hates you / Breed (Loadblower mix) / Homicide / Vulcan (CD-ROM video).

Oct 00. (cd) *(MORPH 008CD) <9362 47701-2>* **SONIC JIHAD** [ ] [ ] Apr00
– Breed / Casualty / You and your friend / Lovesong / Act your age / More than love / Strangled / Oh well / Somebody hates you / Vulcan / How soon is now?

SNAPCASE

Formed: Buffalo, New York, USA . . . 1989 as SOLID STATE by TIM REDMOND (their drummer) and frontman DARYL TABERSKI. Part of the don't drink/don't smoke/don't do drugs/don't do . . . the new SNAPCASE line-up was completed by like-minded, straight-edged guitarists FRANK VICARIO and JOHN SALEMI (bassist DUSTIN PERRY was to join much later). After appearances on a handful of V/A compilations, the band bagged a record contract with 'Victory' who issued their debut set, 'LOOKINGLASSSELF', in 1994. A second full-length, 'PROGRESSION THOUGH UNLEARNING' (1997), took three years to hit the shops, although the 'CASE were definitely making inroads into the earlobes of the young punk/hardcore contingent. By the time of their long-awaited third album, 'DESIGNS FOR AUTOMOTION' (2000), SNAPCASE were certainly taking more chances with the diverse sound and tours with EARTH CRISIS, etc, helped boost their profile.

Album rating: LOOKINGLASSELF (*6) / PROGRESSION THROUGH UNLEARNING (*6) / DESIGNS FOR AUTOMOTION (*5)

DARYL TABERSKI – vocals / **JOHN SALEMI + FRANK VICARIO** – rhythm guitars + bass / **TIM REDMOND** – drums

Victory Victory

Apr 94. (lp/cd) *(VR 13/+CD)* **LOOKINGLASSELF** [ ] [ ]
– Drain me / Filter / Incarnation / Deceived / Lookinglasself / No bridge / Covered / Another's life / Fields of illusion. *(cd re-iss. Sep96; same)*

Nov 95. (7"ep/cd-ep) *(VR 24/+CD)* **STEPS** [ ] [ ]
– Cognition / Steps / Windows / Run and fall.

Apr 97. (lp/cd) *(VR 51/+CD)* **PROGRESSION THROUGH UNLEARNING** [ ] [ ]
– Caboose / Guilty by ignorance / Harrison Bergeron / Priceless / Zombie prescription / Killing yourself to live / She suffocates / Weak tyrant / Vent / Breaking and reaching.

— (late 90's) added **DUSTIN PERRY** – bass (ex-THREADBARE)

Aug 99. (cd-s; split) *<(EVR 051CD)>* **SNAPCASE VS BOY SETS FIRE** [ ] [ ]
– Energy dome / Truth hits everybody / (2 by BOY SETS FIRE).
(above issued on 'Equal Vision')

Feb 00. (cd) *<(VR 100CD)>* **DESIGNS FOR AUTOMOTION** [ ] [ ] Jan00
– Target / Disconnector / Bleeding orange / Typecast modulator / Are you tuned in? / Twentieth nervous breakdown / Energy dome / Ambition now / Break the static / Blemish / Box seat.

SNFU

Formed: Edmonton, Alberta, Canada . . . early 80's by MISTER CHI PIG (aka MARC BEKLE) and his brother BRENT. A persistent if workmanlike hardcore/punk act that always existed in the shadow of their more critically revered countrymen, D.O.A., SNFU began life on the 'Better Youth Organisation' label (also home to YOUTH BRIGADE) with debut album, ' . . .AND NO ONE ELSE WANTED TO PLAY' (1984). Like many hardcore outfits, they were dogged by numerous personnel changes and weren't particularly prolific although three further albums, 'IF YOU SWEAR, YOU'LL CATCH NO FISH' (1986), 'BETTER THAN A STICK IN THE EYE' (1989) and 'THE LAST OF THE BIG TIME SUSPENDERS' (1991), appeared before MARC completely overhauled the band. Bringing in ROB JOHNSON and DAVID REES, the new SNFU signed to modern punk specialist, 'Epitaph', where they continued to churn out brash, unadulterated hardcore to order throughout the 90's.

Album rating: . . . AND NO ONE ELSE WANTED TO PLAY (*4) / IF YOU SWEAR YOU'LL CATCH NO FISH (*5) / BETTER THAN A STICK IN THE EYE (*4) / LAST OF THE BIG TIME SUSPENDERS (*3) / SOMETHING GREEN AND LEAFY THIS WAY COMES (*3) / ONE VOTED MOST LIKELY TO SUCCEED (*3) / FYULABA (*3)

MISTER CHI PIG (alias MARC BEKLE) – vocals / **BRENT BEKLE** – guitar / **JIMMY SCHMITZ** – bass / **JOHN CARD** – drums

Better Youth Org'n — Better Youth Org'n

1984. (lp/c) <(BYO 9/+C)> **. . . AND NO ONE ELSE WANTED TO PLAY** [ ] [ ]
– Broken toy / She's not on the menu / Money matters / I'm real scared / Joy ride / Seeing life through the bottom of a glass / Cannibal cafe / Misfortune / Plastic surgery kept her beautiful / Gravedigger / Bodies in the wall / Get off your ass / Loser at life – Loser at death / This is the end. *(re-iss. Oct96 lp/cd; BYO 9/+CD)*

— CARD joined D.O.A.

1986. (lp/c) <(BYO 17/+C)> **IF YOU SWEAR, YOU'LL CATCH NO FISH** [ ] [ ]
– Devil's voice / Where's my legs? / Better homes and gardens / Scarecrow / Black cloud / I forget / Ceiling / Mind like a door / He's not getting older, he's getting younger / Electric chair / Welcome to my humble life of disarray / Snapping turtle. *(re-iss. Oct96 lp/cd; BYO 17/+CD)*

Cargo — Cargo

1989. (lp/cd) <(CAR 001/+CD)> **BETTER THAN A STICK IN THE EYE** [ ] [ ]
– Time to buy a Futon / G.I. Joe gets angry with humankind / The quest for fun / Tears / In the first place / Postman's pet peeve / What good Hollywood? / The happy switch / Straightening out the shelves / Thee maul that eats peephole / Tour tantram / Wild world. *(re-iss. Jul95 & Oct96 lp/cd; CAR 001/+CD)*

Jan 92. (lp/cd) <CAR 011/+CD> **LAST OF THE BIG TIME SUSPENDERS** [-] [ ]
– The kitchen kreeps / Cannibal cafe / Beautiful, unlike you and I / Gimme some water / I know more than you / I'm real scared / I used to write songs / The electric chair / Visiting the bad again / She's not on the menu (Dunce mix) / Appraise the Lord / Wonder what they're thinking / Grunt, groan, rant and rave. *(UK-iss.Jul95 & Oct96; same as US)*

— **MARC BELKE** (aka MISTER CHI PIG) – guitar, vocals / **ROB JOHNSON** – bass / **DAVID REES** – drums

Epitaph — Epitaph

Dec 93. (cd/c/lp) <(E 86430-2/-4/-1)> **SOMETHING GREEN AND LEAFY THIS WAY COMES** [ ] [ ]
– All those opposed / Reality is a ride on the bus / Joni Mitchell tapes / Bomb / Tin fish / Painful reminder / Costume trunk / Gladky in gloom / This is a goodbye / Strangely strange / X-creep / Trudging / Great mind eraser / Limping away / Seven minutes closer to death / Watering hole.

May 95. (cd/c/lp) <(E 86441-2/-4/-1)> **THE ONE VOTED MOST LIKELY TO SUCCEED** [ ] [ ]
– Rusty rake / A better place / Big thumbs / Drunk on a bike / Manuel / My mold collection / Bumper stickers / Eri's had a bad day / The king of skin / Mutated dog / Bizarre novelties / Lovely little Frankenstein / One last loveshove.

Sep 96. (cd/c/lp) <(86472-2/-4/-1)> **FYULABA** [ ] [ ]
– Step stranger / You make me thick / Bobbitt / Better than Eddie Vedder / Don't have the cow / Fate / Dean Martian / Charlie still smirks / Spaceghost, the twins & blip / My pathetic past.

Alternative Tentacles — Alternative Tentacles

Apr 00. (12"ep/cd-ep) <(VIRUS 238/+CD)> **THE PING PONG EP** [ ] [ ]
– Questions, questions, questions / I'm your carpet / Slavetrader / Zipperhead club / Quentin Tarantino can't act!

– compilations, etc. –

Sep 98. (cd) *Aquarius;* <587> **LET'S GET IT RIGHT THE FIRST TIME** [-] [ ]
– I forget / Eddie Vedder / Loser at life / Don't have the cow / Bobbitt / Fate / Big thumbs / Painful reminder / Rusty rake / Eric's had a bad day / You make me tick / Drunk on a bike / Charlie still smirks / Reality / Gravedigger / Cannibal cafe / Victims of the womanizer / Watering hole.

SNOT

Formed: Santa Barbara, California, USA . . . 1995 by LYNN STRAIT and MIKE DOLING. With JOHN 'TUMOR' FAHNESTOCK, SONNY MAYO and JAMIE MILLER completing the line-up, the band scored their first gig supporting MANHOLE at L.A.'s 'Roxy'. A sufferer of Tourette's syndrome as well as an ex-junkie who'd spent time in jail, STRAIT possessed a hard-bitten magnetism and a generosity of spirit which won him many friends in L.A.'s thriving nu-metal scene. Word spread quickly and soon SNOT had a 'Geffen' debut album in the shops entitled 'GET SOME' (1997). Although the record initially failed to clock up quite as many sales as their label might have liked, STRAIT and Co stole the show at that year's Ozzfest. The exposure – quite literally as a naked STRAIT found himself on a felony charge! – helped boost sales and things were looking sweet for the band. Yet just as sessions were due to begin for a second album, tragedy struck. On the night of 11th December, 1998, STRAIT was killed instantly when his car hit a truck on the freeway near his Santa Barbara home. He was only 30 years old. Although his death brought SNOT to a premature halt, DOLING – who went on to join SOULFLY – was determined to make sure that STRAIT wouldn't be forgotten. He duly initiated the tribute project 'Strait Up' (1999), a record utilising the music which was to become the second SNOT album. Lyrics were handled by close friends of the man and the album's credits featured the cream of the contemporary metal scene.

Album rating: GET SOME (*8)

JAMES LYNN STRAIT (b. 1968, Manhasset, New York) – vocals / **MIKE DOLING** – guitar / **SONNY MAYO** (b. Washington DC) – guitar / **JOHN 'Tumor' FAHNESTOCK** (b. Pennsylvania) – bass / **JAMIE MILLER** (b. Washington DC) – drums

not iss. — Geffen

1997. (cd/c) **GET SOME** [-] [ ]

— **MIKE SMITH** – guitar; repl. MAYO

— **SHANNON LARKIN** – drums (ex-UGLY KID JOE) repl. MILLER

— tragically, on the 11th of December, 1998, LYNN was killed in a crash just minutes from his home

SNUFF

Formed: Hendon, London, England . . . 1986 by DUNCAN REDMONDS, SIMON CRIGHTON and ANDY WELLS. Leavening the "straight edge" seriousness of much hardcore from across the pond, SNUFF set out their agenda with 'NOT LISTENING ANYMORE', a debut single that struck a chord with Radio One DJ John Peel. Released on the 'Workers Playtime' label in the spring of '89, it was to feature in the man's final Festive 50 of the 80's. By that time, it had also appeared on first album, 'SNUFF SAID . . .', the comic book funsters introducing their penchant for mind-bogglingly unpronounceable titles, raucous, good-time melodic hardcore/punk and amphetamine party-piece cover trashings of pop hits such as Tiffany's 'I THINK WE'RE ALONE NOW'. Famed for their manic live shows and diehard following, it came as a bit of a surprise when they split in summer '91 after a final gig at Kilburn National Ballroom. With healthy patronage from American practitioners such as GREEN DAY and NOFX, however, the lads were persuaded to re-group in 1994 along with new members, trombonist DAVE and hammond player LEE. Subsequently signing to 'Deceptive', the trio returned in characteristic style at Xmas '95 with a version of the theme from vintage Brit TV sitcom, 'WHATEVER HAPPENED TO THE LIKELY LADS'. A comeback album, 'DEMMAMUSSABEBONK' (1996), meanwhile, saw LOZ replacing SIMON but demonstrated the trio had lost none of their roughneck charm or sense of humour. On the contrary, the trio entered the most prolific period of their career, releasing a mini-covers set, 'POTATOES AND MELONS AT WHOLESALE PRICES (DIRECT TO YOU THE PUBLIC)' in '97 and a further long player, 'TWEET TWEET MY LOVELY', the following year. In April '99, members of SNUFF and LEATHERFACE united in Honest Dons outfit, DOGPISS, releasing one album 'EINE KLEINE PUNKMUSIK'. 'NUMB NUTS' (2000) took the SNUFF campaign into the new millennium with a whopping 16 tracks, all reliably under the 3 minute mark. 'BLUE GRAVY: PHASE 9', meanwhile, was a mini-set by comparison although its willingness to experiment with everything from 60's R&B, ska and soul to neo-psychedelia was a shot in the eye to anyone who'd written them off as a one-trick novelty act. • **Covers:** CAN'T EXPLAIN (Who) / DO NOTHING + YOU'RE WONDERING NOW (Specials) / REACH OUT I'LL BE THERE (Four Tops) / I CAN SEE CLEARLY NOW (Johnny Nash) / I THINK WE'RE ALONE NOW (Rubinoos) / PURPLE HAZE (Jimi Hendrix) / IN SICKNESS & IN HEALTH (Chas & Dave) / MAGIC MOMENTS (hit. Perry Como) / RIVERS OF BABYLON (hit. Boney M) / SHADOWS OF LOVE (Dozier-Holland-Holland) / SOUL LIMBO (Booker T.) / etc. • **Trivia:** SNUFF also did versions of themes for TV commercials (Bran Flakes + Shake'n'vac + Cadbury's Flake) and more recently 'ANY OLD IRON'.

Album rating: SNUFF SAID . . . (*6) / REACH (*5) / DEMMAMUSSABEBONK (*7) / POTATOES AND MELONS AT WHOLESALE PRICES (*6) / TWEET TWEET MY LOVELY (*5) / NUMB NUTS (*5) / BLUE GRAVY PHASE 9 (*7)

SIMON CRIGHTON (b.11 Dec'66) – guitar, vocals / **DUNCAN REDMONDS** (b.22 Aug'64) – drums, vocals / **ANDY WELLS** (b. 4 Jul'63) – bass

Workers Playtime — Aftertan

Apr 89. (7"ep/cd-ep) *(PLAY 008)* **NOT LISTENING ANYMORE EP** [ ] [-]
– Not listening / Dead and buried / That's enough / For both sides – No one home.*(re-iss. Jul96; same)*

Nov 89. (lp/c/cd) *(PLAY-LP/MC/CD 010)* **SNUFF SAID: GORBLIMEYGUVSTONEMEIFHEDIDN'TTHROWA WOBBLERCHACHACHACHACHACHACHACHA YOU' REGOINGHOMEINACOSMICAMBULANCE** [ ] [ ]
– Words of wisdom / Some how / Now you don't remember / Not listening / I see – H.M. Trout / Too late / Another girl / I think we're alone now / Win some lose some / Pass me by / Keep the best / Night of the Li's / Purple haze / Little git / What kind of love. *(re-iss. Apr95; same)* <US cd-iss. 1996 on 'Fat Wreck Chords'+=; 543> – NOT LISTENING EP

Apr 90. (12"ep/cd-ep) *(PLAY 011-T/CD)* **FLIBBEDDEDYDIBBIRDDYDOB** [ ] [-]
– Rods and mockers / Do nothing / Shake'n'black / Can't explain / Ecstasy / Reach out / Hazy shade of winter / Do it quick / City attacked by rats / Bran flakes / In sickness & in health. *(12"ep re-iss. Mar95; same)* <US cd-iss. Aug96 on 'Fat Wreck Chords'; 544>

— split August '91 after mail-order final gig lp 'KILBURN NATIONAL BALLROOM 17/11/90'. ANDY joined LEATHERFACE for a few years.

10 Past 12 — not iss.

Jul 91. (12"ep) **THAT'S FINE. / I CAN SEE CLEARLY NOW / YOU'RE WONDERING NOW** [ ] [-]

Apr 92. (lp/cd) *(PARKA 003/+CD)* **REACH** [ ] [-]
– I know what you want / Teabag / The damage is done / Spend, spend, spend / If I tried / Hellbound / Smile (that's fine) / It's you / Bingo / Ichola buddha / Porro / Sweet dreams. *(re-iss. Jun97 on 'K'; KLP 012)*

— **DUNCAN, ANDY + SIMON** re-formed in 1994, although the latter was replaced a year later by **LOZ** – guitar, vocals. Other 2 members were **DAVE** – trombone / **LEE M** – hammond organ, vocals (late bass)

Deceptive / Fat Wreck Chords

Dec 95. (7"one-sided) *(BLUFF 019)* **THEME FROM 'WHATEVER HAPPENED TO THE LIKELY LADS'** [ ] [-]
Feb 96. (cd/c/lp) *(BLUFF 023 CD/MC/LP) <533>* **DEMMAMUSSABEBONK** [ ] [ ]
– Vikings / Defeat / Dick trois / Martin / Nick Northern / Batten down the hatches / G to D / Sunny places / Horse and cart / Squirrels / Cricklewood / B / Punchline / Who.
Mar 96. (7"ep/cd-ep) *(BLUFF 026/+CD)* **LONG BALL TO NO-ONE (EP)** [ ] [-]
– Caught in session / Nick Northern / Walk / Dow dow boof boof.
Aug 96. (7"ep/cd-ep) *(BLUFF 033/+CD)* **DO DO DO (EP)** [ ] [-]
– Standing in the shadows of love / I will survive / Soul limbo / It must be boring being in Snuff.
Jun 97. (10"m-lp/m-cd) *(BLUFF 042 TN/CD) <556>* **POTATOES AND MELONS AT WHOLESALE PRICES (DIRECT TO YOU THE PUBLIC)** [ ] [ ]
– Rivers of Babylon / Whatever happened to the Likely Lads / Shadows of love / Soul limbo / Come and gone / It must be boring being Snuff / Ye olde folke twatte / Magic moments / Russian fields / Time dub / Pink purple.
Apr 98. (7"ep/cd-ep) *(BLUFF 061/+CD) <563>* **SCHMINKIE MINKIE PINKIE EP** [ ] [ ] May98
– Nick Motown / Spicy / Medaka no gakoh / Bit cosy.
May 98. (cd/lp) *(BLUFF 056 CD/LP) <562>* **TWEET TWEET MY LOVELY** [ ] [ ]
– No reason / Ticket / Timebomb / Lyehf taidu leikh / Nick Motown / Brickwall / Arsehole / Bob / All you need / Etc. / The thief / Verdidn't / Bit cosy / Take me home (piss off).
Nov 98. (7") *(BLUFF 065)* **YUKI. / ROMEO & JULIET** [ ] [-]
(cd-s+=) *(BLUFF 065CD)* – Rockafeller skank.
Oct 99. (7"ep/cd-ep) *(BLUFF 072/+CD)* **DOWN BY YURR EP** [ ] [ ]
– Pixies / Chalk me down for more / 2 winds / Sweet dreams.
Mar 00. (cd/lp) *(BLUFF 074 CD/LP) <601>* **NUMB NUTS** [ ] [ ]
– Pixies / It's a long way down / SQ11 / Marbles / Numb nuts / Reach / Another wet weekend / EFL vs concrete / Fuck off / Yuki / Hilda Ogden and thick plottens / Soup of the day / Cake / Bottom of the river / Chalk me down for more / Romeo and Juliet / Rockafeller skank.
May 00. (7"ep/cd-ep) *(BLUFF 076/+CD)* **SWEET DAYS EP** [ ] [ ]
– Sweet days / Inmate / Combination mullet / Bacharach.

12:10 / Fat Wreck Chords

May 01. (m-cd/10"m-lp) *(1210 01 CD/V) <FAT 627>* **BLUE GRAVY PHASE 9** [ ] [ ] Jun01
– Split / Prisoner abroad / Blue gravy / Emperor / Damaged / Ichola buddha / Night of the Li's / Caught in session (live) / Ecstacy (live).

– compilations, etc. –

Jan 95. (cd) *Vinyl Japan; (ASKCD 048)* **KILBURN NATIONAL 27.11.90 (live)** [ ] [-]
(re-iss. Jan97; same)
Sep 97. (cd/lp) *Vinyl Japan; (MASKCD/ASKLP 073)* **CAUGHT IN SESSION** [ ] [-]
Oct 98. (cd) *Konkurrel; (FISH 4CD)* **IN THE FISHTANK** [ ] [ ]
Oct 99. (7"ep/cd-ep) *V8; (004/005)* **AUSTRALIAN TOUR EP** [ ] [ ]

SOCIAL DISTORTION

Formed: Fullerton, Orange County, California, USA ... summer 1978 by the AGNEW brothers RIKK (vocals) and FRANK, plus MIKE NESS and CASEY ROYER. With the AGNEWS subsequently departing the following year (to form The ADOLESCENTS), NESS took over vocals while DENNIS DANELL came in on bass and CARROT was recruited as the new sticksman. This wholesale personnel upheaval signalled early on that this band's ride was going to be anything but easy. Things got off to a promising start though, the group signing a one-off deal with Robbie Fields' 'Posh Boy' records, the label releasing the 'MAINLINER' 7". In true DIY fashion, SOCIAL DISTORTION then decided to form their own '13th Floor' records, a further line-up change seeing new boys DEREK O'BRIEN (of DI) and BRENT LILES (DANNELL moving to rhythm guitar, a key element in the development of the band's sound) gracing the belated debut album, 'MOMMY'S LITTLE MONSTER' (1983). A record celebrated in hardcore circles, the album nevertheless distinguished itself from the lemming-like pack by dint of its pop nous and freewheeling R&B undertow (critical references to The ROLLING STONES were rife). Despite the acclaim, SOCIAL DISTORTION almost went belly-up as NESS battled with drug problems. After time in a detox unit, NESS returned in 1988 with a new line-up (CHRIS REECE and JOHN MAURER having replaced O'BRIEN and LILES respectively) and equally belated follow-up set, 'PRISON BOUND'. Like The ROLLING STONES themselves had done in the past, NESS attempted to introduce roughshod country (obviously influenced by 'outlaw' artists such as JOHNNY CASH and MERLE HAGGARD) into his band's equation with impressive results. No doubt buffeted by his difficult experiences, NESS' material was now markedly more considered, the band's 1992 major label follow-up (having been snapped up by 'Epic'), 'BETWEEN HEAVEN AND HELL' trawling the personal depths of NESS' drug hell. Musically, the SOCIAL DISTORTION sound was earthier and grittier than ever, combining trad authenticity with righteous anger. Four years in the making and graced by the ubiquitous CHUCK BISCUITS, the wittily titled 'WHITE LIGHT, WHITE HEAT, WHITE TRASH' (1996) was arguably the group's most affecting album to date, the US Top 30 record even including a paint-stripping makeover of their Rolling Stones cover, 'UNDER MY THUMB'. MIKE NESS took the independent route by releasing a solo set in Spring '99, 'CHEATING AT SOLITAIRE', a rootsy album which featured BRUCE SPRINGSTEEN, BRIAN SETZER and covers including Dylan's 'DON'T THINK TWICE' and Hank Williams' 'YOU WIN AGAIN'.

Album rating: MOMMY'S LITTLE MONSTER (*5) / PRISON BOUND (*6) / SOCIAL DISTORTION (*7) / SOMEWHERE BETWEEN HEAVEN AND HELL (*7) / WHITE LIGHT, WHITE HEAT, WHITE TRASH (*9) / Mike Ness: CHEATING AT SOLITAIRE (*6) / UNDER THE INFLUENCES (*5)

MIKE NESS – vocals, guitar / **DENNIS DANELL** – bass repl. FRANK / **CARROTT** – drums; repl. CASEY who formed The ADOLESCENTS with other early members RIKK and FRANK AGNEW / guitarists **TIM MAG + DANNY FURIOUS** (ex-AVENGERS) were also early members. The former later joined D.I.

not iss. / Posh Boy

Nov 81. (7") *<PBS 11>* **MAINLINER. / PLAYPEN** [-] [ ]

— **DEREK O'BRIEN** – drums, vocals repl. CARROTT

— added **BRENT LILES** – bass (DANELL switched to rhythm guitar)

not iss. / 13th Story

1982. (7"ep) *<SD 4501>* **1945 EP** [-] [ ]
1983. (7") *<SD 4502>* **ANOTHER STATE OF MIND. / MOMMY'S LITTLE MONSTER** [-] [ ]
1984. (lp) **MOMMY'S LITTLE MONSTER** [-] [ ]
– The creeps / Another state of mind / It wasn't a pretty picture / Telling them / Hour of darkness / Mommy's little monster / Anti-fashion / All the answers / Moral threat. *(UK-iss.Dec95 on 'Timebomb' cd/lp; 43500-2/-1) (cd-iss. Sep96 on 'R.C.A.'; 0930 43500-2)*

— (1985) **JOHN MAURER** – bass repl. LILES who joined AGENT ORANGE

— **CHRIS REECE** – drums (ex-LEWD) repl. O'BRIEN (full-time D.I.)

G.W.R. / Enigma

Feb 89. (lp) *(GWLP 43)-<772251>* **PRISON BOUND** [ ] [ ] 1988
– It's the law / Indulgence / Like an outlaw / Backstreet girl / Prison bound / No pain no gain / On my nerves / I want what I want / Lawless / Lost child. *(re-iss. Dec95 on 'Timebomb' cd/lp; 43501-2/-1) (cd-iss. Sep96 on 'R.C.A.'; 0930 43501-2)*

Epic / Epic

May 90. (cd/c/lp) *<(46055-2/-4/-1)>* **SOCIAL DISTORTION** [ ] [ ]
– So far away / Let it be me / Story of my life / Sick boys / Ring of fire / Ball and chain / It coulda been me / She's a knockout / A place in my heart / Drug train.
1990. (cd-ep) *<73571>* **STORY OF MY LIFE / 1945 (live) / MOMMY'S LITTLE MONSTER (live) / PRETTY THING / SHAME ON ME** [-] [ ]
1992. (7") *<74229>* **BAD LUCK. / BYE BYE BABY** [-] [ ]
Sep 92. (cd/lp) *<(471343-2/-1)>* **SOMEWHERE BETWEEN HEAVEN AND HELL** [ ] [76] Feb92
– Cold feelings / Bad luck / Making believe / Born to lose / Bye bye baby / When she begins / 99 to life / King of fools / Sometimes I do / This time darlin'. *(cd+=)* – Ghost town blues.

— **CHUCK BISCUITS** – drums (ex-DANZIG, etc.) repl. REECE

Sep 96. (cd/c) *(484374-2/-4) <64380>* **WHITE LIGHT, WHITE HEAT, WHITE TRASH** [ ] [27]
– Dear lover / Don't drag me down / Intitled / I was wrong / Through these eyes / Down on the world again / When the angels sing / Gotta know the rules / Crown of thorns / Pleasure seeker / Down here / Under my thumb.
Nov 96. (7"red) *(663955-7)* **I WAS WRONG. / RING OF FIRE** [ ] [ ]
(cd-s+=) *(663955-2)* – Born to lose.

Time Bomb / Time Bomb

Jul 98. (lp/cd) *(TB 70930/+CD) <43516>* **LIVE AT THE ROXY (live)** [ ] [ ] Jun98
– Story of my life / Bad luck / Under my thumb / Prisin bound / Mommy's little monster / Mass hysteria / Creeps / Another state of mind / Let it be me / No pain, no gain / Cold feelings / Telling them / I was wrong / 1945 / Don't drag me down / Ball and chain / Ring of fire.

– compilations, etc. –

Dec 95. (cd/lp) *Time Bomb; (43502-2/-1)* **MAINLINER** [ ] [ ]

MIKE NESS

Time Bomb / Time Bomb

Apr 99. (cd/c) *<43524-2/-4>* **CHEATING AT SOLITAIRE** [ ] [80]
– Devil in Miss Jones / Don't think twice / Misery loves company / Crime don't pay / Rest of our lives / You win again / Cheating at solitaire / No man's friend / Charmed life / Dope fiend blues / Ballad of a lonely man / I'm in love with my car / If you leave before me / Long black veil / Send her back.
Nov 99. (cd/c) *<43536-2/-4>* **UNDER THE INFLUENCES** (covers) [ ] [ ]
– I walk the line / Let that jukebox keep on playing / Funnel of love / You're for me / I fought the law / Six more miles (to the graveyard) / All I can do is cry / My brand of the blues / One more time / Thief in the night / Once a day / World's worst loser / Gambling man (roving gambler) / Mansion on a hill / Wildwood flower.

S.O.D. (see under ⇒ ANTHRAX)

SODOM

Formed: Germany ... 1983 by ANGEL RIPPER, AGGRESSOR and WITCHHUNTER. Inspired by British black metal acts such as VENOM, the band debuted in 1985 with the 'IN THE SIGN OF EVIL' EP, a precursor to the band's first full length release, 'OBSESSED BY CRUELTY' (1986). A raging slice of teutonic thrash, the album saw SODOM stake their somewhat cliched claim in the emerging German extreme metal scene alongside KREATOR etc. The first release to feature new guitarist FRANK BLACKFIRE, the album's follow-up, 'PERSECUTION MANIA', represented something of an improvement, another German-only affair which nevertheless saw the band attract some interest in the UK. After a double live effort, the band continued with their preoccupation for war on studio sets, 'AGENT ORANGE' (1989) and 'AUSGEBOMBT' (1990). The same year, BLACKFIRE decamped to KREATOR, MICHAEL HOFFMAN coming in for the passable 1991 set, 'BETTER OFF DEAD'. Dallying with death metal on 'TAPPING THE VEIN' (1993), SODOM continued releasing albums into the 90's, 'MASQUERADE IN BLOOD' (1995) being their first of several sets for the 'S.P.V.' stable.

Album rating: OBSESSED BY CRUELTY (*4) / PERSECUTION MANIA (*5) / MORTAL WAY OF LIFE (*6) / AGENT ORANGE (*6) / BETTER OFF DEAD (*5) / TAPPING THE VEIN (*4) / TEN BLACK YEARS compilation (*6) / 'TIL DEATH US DO PART (*4) / CODE RED (*5)

(TOM) ANGEL RIPPER – vocals, bass / **AGGRESSOR** – guitar / **(CHRIS) WITCHHUNTER** – drums

Steamhammer Roadracer

1985. (12"ep) *(602 120)* **IN THE SIGN OF EVIL** [-] [-] German
– Outbreak of evil / Blasphemer / Burst command 'til war / Sepulchural voice / Witching metal. *(UK cd-iss. Jul89 on 'S.P.V.'; 607 598) (UK cd re-iss. Feb97; SPV 085-7533)*

Jun 86. (lp) *(SH 0040)* **OBSESSED BY CRUELTY** [-] [-] German
– Deathlike equinoxe / After the deluge / Obsessed by cruelty / Fall of majesty town / Nuctemeron / Pretenders to the throne / Witchhammer / Volcanic slut. *(cd-iss. 1988 on 'S.P.V.'; 85-7533) (cd-iss. Apr93 +=; SPV 076-75332CD)*

—— **(FRANK) BLACKFIRE** – guitar; repl. DESTRUCTOR, who repl. GRAVE VIOLATOR, who repl. AGGRESSOR

Jun 88. (lp)(cd) *(08-7507)(85-7509) <RC 9495>* **PERSECUTION MANIA** [-] [ ] German
– Nuclear winter / Electrocution / Iron fist / Persecution mania / Enchanted land / Procession to Golgatha / Christ passion / Conjuration / Bombenhagel / Outbreak of evil / Sodomy and lust / The conqueror / My atonement. *(UK cd-iss. Feb97; SPV 857509)*

Jan 89. (d-lp/cd) *(08-7575)(85-7576) <RC 9480>* **MORTAL WAY OF LIFE (live)** [-] [-] German
– Persecution mania / Outbreak of evil / The conqueror / Iron fist / Obsessed by cruelty / Nuclear winter / Electrocution / Blashemer / Enchanted land / Sodomy & lust / Christ passion / Bombenhagel / My atonement. *(UK cd-iss. Feb97; SPV 857576)*

Jun 89. (lp)(cd) *(08-7596)(85-7597)* **AGENT ORANGE** [-] [-] German
– Agent Orange / Tired and red / Incest / Remember the fallen / Magic dragon / Exhibition bout / Ausgebombt / Baptism of fire. *(UK cd-iss. Feb97; SPV 847597)*

Aug 89. (12") *(502 123)* **EXPOSURE OF DOOM. /** [-] [-] German

Mar 90. (12") *(507 604)* **AUSGEBOMBT / DON'T WALK AWAY / INCEST** [-] [-] German

—— **MICHAEL HOFFMAN** – guitar; repl. BLACKFIRE who joined KREATOR

Nov 90. (cd/lp) *(84/08 – 76261)* **BETTER OFF DEAD** [-] [-] German
– Eye for an eye / Saw is the law / Capture the flag / Never healing wound / Resurrection / Shellfire defence / Turn your head around / Bloodtrials / Better off dead / Stalinorgel.

S.P.V. Century Media

Apr 93. (cd/c/lp) *(084-76542 CD/MC/LP) <7739>* **TAPPING THE VEIN** [ ] [ ]
– Body parts / Skinned alive / One step over the line / Deadline / Bullet in the head / The crippler / Wachturm – Erwachet / Tapping the vein / Back to war / Hunting season / Reincarnation.

S.P.V. not iss.

May 94. (12"/cd-s) *(SPV 055-76723-3/-2)* **BUTT WITH WHIPPED CREAM. /** [ ] [-]

May 94. (cd/lp) *(SPV 084/008 7676-2/-1)* **GET WHAT YOU DESERVE** [ ] [-]
– Get what you deserve / Jabba the hut / Jesus screamer / Delight in slaying / Die stummel ursel / Freaks of nature / Eat me / Unbury the hatchet / Into perdition / Sodomized / Fellows in misery / Tribute to Moby Dick / Silence is consent / Erwachet / Gomorrah / Angel dust.

Nov 94. (cd/c/lp) *(084-7685-2/-4/-1)* **MAROONED (live)** [ ] [-]
– Intro / Outbreak of evil / Jabba the hut / Agent orange / Jesus screamer / Ausgebombt / Tarred and feathered / Abuse / Remember the fallen / An eye for an eye / Tired and red / Eat me! / Die stumme ursel / Sodomized / Gomorrah / One step over the line / Freaks of nature / Aber bitte mi sahne / Silence is consent / Wachturm – Erwachet / Stalinhagel / Fraricide / Gone to glory. *<US cd-iss. Oct00>*

Jul 95. (cd/c/lp) *(085-7696-2/-4/-1)* **MASQUERADE IN BLOOD** [ ] [-]
– Masquerade in blood / Gathering of minds / Field of honour / Braindead / Verrecke / Shadow of damnation / Peasemaker's law / Murder in my eyes / Unwanted youth / Mantelman / Scum / Hydrophobia / Let's break the law. *<US cd-iss. Oct00 on 'Steamhammer'; 1767696>*

Gun Gun

Feb 97. (cd) *(GUN 119CD) <90342>* **'TIL DEATH US DO PART** [ ] [ ]
– Frozen screams / Fuck the police / Gisela / That's what an unknown killer diarized / Hanging judge / No way out / Polytoximaniac / 'Til death do us unite / Hazy shade of winter / Suicidal justice / Wander in the valley / Sow the seeds of discord / Master of disguise / Schwerter zu pflugscharen / Hey, hey, hey rock'n'roll star.

Drakkar Pavement

Jun 99. (cd) *(DRAKKAR 003CD) <32335>* **CODE RED** [ ] [ ] Oct99
– Intro / Code red / What Hell can create / Tombstone / Liquidation / Spiritual demise / Warlike conspiracy / Cowardice / The vice of killing / Visual buggery / Book burning / The wolf and the lamb / Addicted to abstinence.

– compilations, etc. –

Feb 97. (d-cd) *S.P.V.; (SPV 086-1834-2)* **TEN BLACK YEARS (THE BEST OF SODOM)** [ ] [-]
– Tired and red / Saw is the law / Agent Orange / Wachturn – Erwachtet / Sodomy and lust / Remember the fallen / Nuclear winter / Outbreak of evil / Resurrection / Bombenhagel / Masquerade in blood / Bullet in the head / Stalinhagel / Shellshock / Angel dust / Hunting season / Abuse / 100 days of Sodom / Gomorrah / Unwanted youth / Tarred and feathered / Iron fist / Jabba the hut / Silence is consent / Incest / Shellfire defence / Gone to glory / Fraticide / Verrecke / One step over the line / My atonement / Sodomized / Aber bitte mit sahne / Die stumme ursei / Mantlemann.

Jul 00. (cd) *S.P.V.; (31021970)* **PERSECUTION MANIA / OBSESSED BY CRUELTY** [ ] [-]

SOLITUDE AETURNUS

Formed: Texas, USA . . . by guitarist JOHN PEREZ, who recruited vocalist ROBERT LOWE, guitarist EDGAR RIVERA, bassist LYLE and drummer WOLF. A doom-metal outfit in the mould of CATHEDRAL etc., SOLITUDE AETURNUS signed to 'Roadracer' in 1991, releasing a debut set, 'INTO THE DEPTHS OF SORROW', the same year. Taking a more spiritual/mystical approach than many bands of their ilk, the band's sound was characterised by LOWE's impressive feats of vocal flight. A follow-up set, 'BEYOND THE CRIMSON HORIZON', appeared in 1992, the group subsequently switching labels to 'Bulletproof' and developing a harder-edged approach on 'THROUGH THE DARKEST HOUR' (1994). An independently released fourth set, 'DOWNFALL', eventually appeared in 1997.

Album rating: INTO THE DEPTHS OF SORROW (*6) / BEYOND THE CRIMSON HORIZON (*6) / THROUGH THE DARKEST HOUR (*7) / DOWNFALL (*6) / ADAGIO (*7)

ROBERT LOWE – vocals / **JOHN PEREZ** – guitar / **EDGAR RIVERA** – guitar / **LYLE** – bass / **WOLF** – drums

Roadracer Roadracer

Sep 91. (cd/c/lp) *<(RO 9265-2/-4/-1)>* **INTO THE DEPTHS OF SORROW** [ ] [ ]
– Dawn of antiquity (a return to despair) / Opaque divinity / Transcending sentinels / Dream of immortality / Destiny falls to ruin / White ship / Mirror of sorrow / Where angels dare to tread.

May 92. (cd/lp) *<(RO 9168-2/-1)>* **BEYOND THE CRIMSON HORIZON** [ ] [ ]
– Seeds of the desolate / Black castle / The final sin / It came upon one night / The hourglass / Beneath the fading sun / Plague of procession / Beyond . . .

Bulletproof Pavement

Nov 94. (cd) *(CDVEST 35) <32214>* **THROUGH THE DARKEST HOUR** [ ] [ ] Jan95
– Falling / Haunting the obscure / The 8th day: Mourning / The 9th day: Awakening / Pain / Pawns of anger / Eternity (dreams part II) / Perfect insanity / Shattered my spirit.

Hengest Pavement

Jan 97. (cd) *(IRSCD 99302-2) <32252>* **DOWNFALL** [ ] [ ] Jul96
– Phantoms / Only this (and nothing more) / Midnight dreams / Together and wither / Elysium / Deathwish / These are the nameless / Chapel of burning / Concern.

Massacre Slipdisc

Aug 98. (cd) *(MASSCD 161) <638001>* **ADAGIO** [ ] [ ] Feb99
– My endtime / Days of prayer / Believe / Never / Isis / Personal god / Mental pictures / Insanity's circles / The fall / Lament / Empty faith / Spiral descent / Heaven and Hell.

– compilations, etc. –

Nov 98. (d-cd) *S.P.V.; (085-5327-2)* **DOWNFALL / THROUGH THE DARKEST HOUR** [ ] [ ]

SONA FARIQ

Formed: East London, England . . . 1997 by MICHAEL FRANKEL, DOM BOUFFARD, WASIF HUSAIN, and ABRAR HAFIZ. These heavy alternative metallers were on a mission to have as much aggro-fuelled fun as possible. Their sound blends the hardcore side of the inspirational and innovative BAD BRAINS and that of RAGE AGAINST THE MACHINE, with say the metal funkiness of FISHBONE. The band being British, but of Asian origin, many critics lazily described their music as political, which the band themselves strongly denied, prefering to see their output in a more high-emotion inducing context; their live sets being rowdy and frenetic to say the least. Their self-titled debut album came out to huge critical claim in 2000, especially in a stale period in which British metal and hardcore was languishing; the American nu-metallers attracting most of the chart attention. SF's first album was a solid piece of heavy rock helped on by the seasoned knob-twiddler, CHRIS SHELDON (of FOO FIGHTERS and FEEDER fame). Stand-out tracks on this outing include the single 'DROP THE BOMB' and the energetic 'WE BE ON FIRE'.

Album rating: SONA FARIQ (*8)

MICHAEL FRANKEL – vocals / **DOM BOUFFARD** – vocals, guitar / **ABRAR HAFIZ** – bass / **WASIF HUSAIN** – drums

Blue Dog not iss.

Nov 98. (cd-s) **DO NOT RETURN (mixes; original / Big Hair / Alex Jazzupstart / Dave Ball & Ingo Vauk)** [ ] [-]

WEA not iss.

Nov 99. (cd-s) *(promo)* **LOVE YOU CRAZY / HEY CHICA / BURN BABY CRAZY** [-] [-]

Jul 00. (cd-s) *(WEA 278CD)* **DROP THE BOMB. / DON'T LET GO / DROP THE BOMB (Manchild vocal mix)** [ ] [-]
(12") *(WEA 278T)* – ('A'mixes; radio / Manchild vocal / Black Star Liner / Bomb disposal).

Jul 00. (cd/c) *(8573 83042-2/-4)* **SONA FARIQ** [ ] [-]
– Drop the bomb / We be on fire / Do not return / Killer B / Move on / Love you crazy / So perfect / Dr. John / Brown / Zoo / Hey Chica / Me and mescalito.

Nov 00. (cd-s) *(WEA 310CD)* **MOVE ON** [ ] [-]

SONIC YOUTH

Formed: New York City, New York, USA . . . early 1981 by THURSTON MOORE and KIM GORDON. They replaced an early embryonic rhythm section with LEE RANALDO and RICHARD EDSON. After numerous releases on various US indie labels (notably Glenn Branca's 'Neutral' records), they signed to 'Blast First'in the U.K. First up for the label was 'BAD MOON RISING' in 1985, showing them at their most menacing and disturbing, especially on the glorious 'DEATH VALLEY 69' (a macabre reference to killer Charles Manson) with LYDIA LUNCH providing dual vox. They subsequently secured a US deal with 'S.S.T.', heralding yet another socially passionate thrash effort with 'EVOL'. A sideline project, CICCONE YOUTH, saw KIM and the lads plus MIKE WATT (of fIREHOSE), take off MADONNA's 'INTO THE GROOVE(Y)', which became a surprise dancefloor fave. Two more classic pieces, 'SISTER' (1987) & 'DAYDREAM NATION' (1988), finally secured them a major deal with 'D.G.C.' (David Geffen Company). In the early 90's, they smashed into the UK Top 40 with the album 'GOO', featuring a cameo by CHUCK D (of PUBLIC ENEMY) on the track/single 'KOOL THING'. The album, which sweetened their garage-punk/art-noise collages with melodic hooks, also included their deeply haunting tribute to KAREN CARPENTER, 'TUNIC (SONG FOR KAREN)'. They supported PUBLIC ENEMY that year, also stepping out with NEIL YOUNG on his 'Ragged Glory' tour in '91 (much to the distaste of YOUNG's more conservative fans!). In 1992, many thought 'DIRTY' to be a disappointment, the record being overproduced and overtaken by their new rivals and labelmates NIRVANA. By the mid-late 90's, they had returned to ground roots with acoustic psychedelia and the albums, 'EXPERIMENTAL JET SET' (1994), 'WASHING MACHINE' (1995) and 'A THOUSAND LEAVES' (1998) were again lauded by the alternative music press. All members had also taken on side solo projects, KIM featuring in all-star punk-grunge affair, FREE KITTEN. SONIC YOUTH returned towards the end of the decade with an appropriately-titled set, 'GOODBYE 20th CENTURY' (1999), a record in which they took on the works of avant-garde composers CHRISTIAN WOLFF, JOHN CAGE and CORNELIUS CARDEW. 'NYC GHOSTS & FLOWERS' (2000) was also a tribute of sorts, inspired by the beat poets who once upon a time fed their wayward muse on the Big Apple's mean streets. Featuring an Allen Ginsberg-derived title and William Burroughs cover art, the album was only partly successful in capturing the wild-eyed passion of the era. • **Songwriters:** MOORE / RANALDO / GORDON compositions, except I WANNA BE YOUR DOG (Stooges) / TICKET TO RIDE + WITHIN YOU WITHOUT YOU (Beatles) / BEAT ON THE BRAT + others (Ramones) / TOUCH ME, I'M SICK (Mudhoney) / ELECTRICITY (Captain Beefheart) / COMPUTER AGE (Neil Young). Their off-shoot CICCONE YOUTH covered INTO THE GROOVE (Madonna) / ADDICTED TO LOVE (Robert Palmer) / IS IT MY BODY (Alice Cooper) / PERSONALITY CRISIS (New York Dolls) / CA PLANE POUR MOI (Plastic Bertrand) / MOIST VAGINA = (MV) (Nirvana). FREE KITTEN covered: OH BONDAGE UP YOURS (X-Ray Spex). • **Trivia:** Early in 1989, they were featured on hour-long special TV documentary for Melvyn Bragg's 'The South Bank Show'.

Album rating: CONFUSION IS SEX (*6) / KILL YR IDOLS (*4) / BAD MOON RISING (*8) / EVOL (*8) / SISTER (*9) / DAYDREAM NATION (*9) / GOO (*9) / DIRTY (*7) / EXPERIMENTAL JET SET, TRASH AND NO STAR (*6) / WASHING MACHINE (*8) / A THOUSAND LEAVES (*6) / GOODBYE 20th CENTURY (*7) / NYC GHOSTS & FLOWERS (*4) / Lee Ranaldo: FROM HERE TO INFINITY (*4) / EAST JESUS (*7) / Thurston Moore: PSYCHIC HEARTS (*8) / ROOT (*7)

THURSTON MOORE (b.25 Jul'58, Coral Gables, Florida) – vocals, guitar / **KIM GORDON** (b.28 Apr'53, Rochester, N.Y.) – vocals, bass / **LEE RANALDO** (b. 3 Feb'56, Glen Cove, N.Y.) – vocals, guitar repl. ANN DEMARIS / **RICHARD EDSON** – drums repl. DAVE KEAY

Neutral / not iss.

Feb 84. (m-lp) *(ND 01)* **SONIC YOUTH (live)** [-] [-] German
– The burning spear / I dreamt I dreamed / She's not alone / I don't want to push it / The good and the bad. *(re-iss. cd Oct87 on 'S.S.T.'; SSTCD 097)*

— **JIM SCLAVUNOS** – drums repl. EDSON

Feb 84. (lp) *(ND 02)* **CONFUSION IS SEX** [-] [-] German
– Inhuman / The world looks red / Confusion is next / Making the nature scene / Lee is free / (She's in a) Bad mood / Protect me you / Freezer burn / I wanna be your dog / Shaking Hell. *(re-iss. cd Oct87 on 'S.S.T.'; SSTCD 096)*

— **BOB BERT** – drums repl. SCLAVUNOS (still featured on 2 tracks)

Zensor / not iss.

Oct 83. (m-lp) *(ZENSOR 10)* **KILL YR. IDOLS** [-] [-] German
– Protect me you / Shaking Hell / Kill yr. idols / Brother James / Early American.

not iss. / Ecstatic Peace

1984. (c) *<none>* **SONIC DEATH (SONIC YOUTH LIVE)** [-]
– Sonic Death (side 1) / Sonic Death (side 2). *(UK cd-iss. Jul88 on 'Blast First'; BFFP 32CD>*

not iss. / Iridescence

Dec 84. (12"; by SONIC YOUTH & LYDIA LUNCH) *<1-12>*
DEATH VALLEY '69. / BRAVE MEN (RUN IN MY FAMILY) [-]

Blast First / Homestead

Mar 85. (lp) *(BFFP 1) <HMS 016>* **BAD MOON RISING**
– Intro / Brave men rule / Society is a hole / I love her all the time / Ghost bitch / I'm insane / Justice is might / Death valley '69. *(cd-iss. Nov86+=; BFFP 1CD)* – Satan is boring / Flower / Halloween. *<US cd re-iss. 1995 on 'Geffen'; 24512>*

Jun 85. (12"ep; by SONIC YOUTH & LYDIA LUNCH) *(BFFP 2)*
<HMS 012> **DEATH VALLEY '69. / I DREAMT I DREAMED / INHUMAN / BROTHER JAMES / SATAN IS BORING**

Jan 86. (12",12"yellow) *(BFFP 3)* **HALLOWEEN. / FLOWER** [-]

Jan 86. (7") *(BFFP 3)* **FLOWER. / REWOLF (censored)** [-]
(12") – ('A'side) / Satan is boring (live).

Mar 86. (etched-12") *(BFFP 3-B)* **HALLOWEEN II** [-]

— **STEVE SHELLEY** (b.23 Jun'62, Midland, Michigan) – drums repl. BOB BERT who joined PUSSY GALORE

Blast First / S.S.T.

May 86. (lp/c) *(BFFP 4/+C) <SST/+C/CD 059>* **EVOL**
– Green light / Star power / Secret girl / Tom Violence / Death to our friends / Shadow of a doubt / Marilyn Moore / In the kingdom / Madonna, Sean and me. *(cd-iss. Nov86+=; BFFP 4CD)* – Bubblegum. *<US cd re-iss. 1995 on 'Geffen'; 24513>*

Jul 86. (7") *(BFFP 7) <SST 80>* **STAR POWER. / BUBBLEGUM**
(12"+=) *(BFFP 7T) <SST 80-12>* – Expressway.

— added guest **MIKE WATT** – bass (of fIREHOSE)

Nov 86. (12"; as CICCONE YOUTH) *(BFFP 8)* **INTO THE GROOVE(Y). / TUFF TITTY RAP / BURNIN' UP**

Jun 87. (lp/c/cd) *(BFFP 20/+C/CD) <SST/+C/CD 134>* **SISTER**
– White cross / (I got a) Catholic block / Hot wire my heart / Tuff gnarl / Kotton crown / Schizophrenia / Beauty lies in the eye / Stereo sanctity / Pipeline – killtime / PCH. *(cd+=)* – Master-Dik (original). *<US cd re-iss. 1995 on 'Geffen'; 24514>*

Jan 88. (m-lp) *(BFFP 26T)* **MASTER-DIK**
– Master-Dik / Beat on the brat / Under the influence of the Jesus & Mary Chain: Ticket to ride / Ringo – He's on fire – Florida oil / Chines jam / Vibrato – Guitar lick – Funky fresh / Our backyard / Traffik.

Blast First / Capitol

Jan 88. (lp/c/cd; as CICCONE YOUTH) *(BFFP 28/+C/CD)*
<C1/C4/C2 75402> **THE WHITEY ALBUM** [63]
– Needle-gun (silence) / G-force / Platoon II / Macbeth / Me & Jill / Hendrix Cosby / Burnin' up / Hi! everybody / Children of Satan / Third fig / Two cool rock chicks / Listening to Neu! / Addicted to love / Moby-Dik / March of the Ciccone robots / Making the nature scene / Tuff titty rap / Into the groovey. *<US cd re-iss. 1995 on 'Geffen'; 24516>*

Feb 88. (d-one-sided-7"on 'Fierce') *(FRIGHT 015-016)* **STICK ME DONNA MAGICK MOMMA / MAKING THE NATURE SCENE (live)** [-]
(also soon issued as normal-7")

Blast First / Torso

Oct 88. (d-lp/c/cd) *(BFFP 34/+C/CD) <2602339>* **DAYDREAM NATION** [99]
– Teenage riot / Silver rocket / The sprawl / 'Cross the breeze / Eric's trip / Total trash / Hey Joni / Providence / Candle? / Rain king / Kissability / Trilogy: The wonder – Hyperstation – Eliminator Jr.

— Late in '88, KIM teamed up with LYDIA LUNCH and SADIE MAE to form one-off project HARRY CREWS. Their live appearences were issued in Apr 90 as 'NAKED IN GARDEN HILLS' for 'Big Cat' UK + 'Widowspeak' US.

Feb 89. (12") *(BFFP 46)* **TOUCH ME, I'M SICK. / (Halloween; by MUDHONEY)**

W.E.A. / D.G.C.

Jun 90. (cd/c/lp) *<(7599 24297-2/-4/-1)>* **GOO** [32] [96]
– Dirty boots / Tunic (song for Karen) / Mary-Christ / Kool thing / Mote / My friend Goo / Disappearer / Mildred Pierce / Cinderella's big score / Scooter + Jinx / Titanium expose. *(re-iss. cd Oct95 on 'Geffen'; GFLD 19297)*

Sep 90. (7"/c-s) **KOOL THING. / THAT'S ALL I KNOW (RIGHT NOW)** [-]
(12"+=) – ('A'demo version).
(cd-s++=) – Dirty boots (rock & roll Heaven version).

— In Autumn '90, THURSTON was part of 'Rough Trade' supergroup VELVET MONKEYS.

D.G.C. / D.G.C.

Apr 91. (m-lp/m-c/m-cd) *(DGC/+C/D 21634)* **DIRTY BOOTS** (all live, except the title track) [69] [-]
– Dirty boots / The bedroom / Cinderella's big scene / Eric's trip / White kross. *(re-iss. cd Apr92; DGLD 19060)*

— Early in '92, THURSTON and STEVE also teamed up with RICHARD HELL's off-shoot group The DIM STARS.

Jun 92. (7") *(DGCS 11)* **100%. / CREME BRULEE** [28] [-]
(10"orange+=/12"+=) *(DGC V/T 11)* – Hendrix necro.
(cd-s++=) *(DGCTD 11)* – Genetic.

Jul 92. (d-lp/c/cd) *<(DGC/+C/D 24485)>* **DIRTY** [6] [83]
– 100% / Swimsuit issue / Theresa's sound-world / Drunken butterfly / Shoot / Wish fulfillment / Sugar Kane / Orange rolls, angel's spit / Youth against fascism / Nic fit / On the strip / Chapel Hill / JC / Purr / Creme brulee. *(d-lp+=)* – Stalker. *(re-iss. cd Oct95; GFLD 19296)*

Geffen / D.G.C.

Oct 92. (7") *(GFS 26)* **YOUTH AGAINST FASCISM. / PURR** [52] [-]
(10"colrd+=) *(GFSV 26)* – ('A'version).
(12"++=/cd-s++=) *(GFST/+D 26)* – The destroyed room (radio version)

Apr 93. (7"/c-s) *(GFS/+C 37)* **SUGAR KANE. / THE END OF THE END OF THE UGLY** [26] [-]
(10"blue+=/cd-s+=) *(GFS V/TD 37)* – Is it my body / Personality crisis.

Apr 94. (10"silver/c-s/cd-s) *(GFS V/C/TD 72)* **BULL IN THE HEATHER. / RAZORBLADE** [24] [-]

May 94. (cd/c/blue-lp) *<(GED/GEC/GEF 24632)>* **EXPERIMENTAL JET SET, TRASH AND NO STAR** [10] [34]
– Winner's blues / Bull in the heather / Starfield road / Skink / Self-obsessed and sexxee / Bone / Androgynous mind / Quest for the cup / Waist / Doctor's orders / Tokyo eye / In the mind of the bourgeois reader / Sweet shine.

— In Sep 94; 'A&M' released CARPENTERS tribute album, which contained their single 'SUPERSTAR'. It was combined with also another cover from REDD KROSS, and reached UK No.45.

Oct 95. (cd/c/d-lp) *<(GED/GEC/GEF 24925)>* **WASHING MACHINE** [39] [58]
– Becuz / Junkie's promise / Saucer-like / Washing machine / Unwind / Little trouble girl / No queen blues / Panty lies / Becuz coda * / Skip tracer / The diamond sea. *(cd+= *)*

Apr 96. (12"/cd-s) *(GRS T/D 22132)* **LITTLE TROUBLE GIRL. / MY ARENA / THE DIAMOND SEA (edit)** [-]

Feb 98. (12"ep/cd-ep; SONIC YOUTH & JIM O'ROURKE) *(SYR 003/+CD)* **INVITO AL CIELO EP**
– Invito al cielo / Hungara vivo / Radio-Amatoroj.
(above issued on own 'Sonic Youth Records')

May 98. (d-cd/d-lp) *<(GED/GEF 25203)>* **A THOUSAND LEAVES** 38 85
– Contre le sexisme / Sunday / Female mechanic now on duty / Wildflower soul / Hoarfrost / French tickler / Hits of sunshine (for Allen Ginsberg) / Karen Koltrane / The ineffable me / Snare / Girl / Heather angel.

Jun 98. (7") *(GFS 22332)* **SUNDAY. / MOIST VAGINA** 72 -
(cd-s+=) *(GFSTD 22332)* – Silver panties / ('A'edit).

—— THURSTON collaborated with DON FLEMING and JIM DUNBAR on the freeform/experimental project, FOOT, releasing 'S/T' for 'God Bless'

Smells Like / Smells Like

Nov 99. (d-lp/d-cd) *<(SYR 04/+CD)>* **GOODBYE 20th CENTURY**
– Edges / Six / Six for new time for Sonic Youth / + – / Voice piece for soprano / Pendulum music // Having never written a note for percussion / Six / Burdocks / Four / Piano piece #3 / enfantine / Treatise.

Geffen / Geffen

May 00. (cd/lp) *<(490665-2/-1)>* **NYC GHOSTS AND FLOWERS**
– Free city rhymes / Renegade princess / Nevermind (what was it anyway) / Small flowers crack concrete / Side 2 side / Streamsonik subway / NYC ghosts and flowers / Lightnin'.

– compilations, others, etc. –

Feb 92. (cd) *Sonic Death; <(SD 13001)>* **GOO DEMOS LIVE AT THE CONTINENTAL CLUB (live)** Nov89

Mar 95. (cd/c) *Blast First; (BFFP 113 CD/C)* **CONFUSION IS SEX / KILL YR IDOLS** -

Mar 95. (cd) *Warners-Rhino; (8122 71591-2)* **MADE IN THE U.S.A.**
(1986 soundtrack)

Apr 95. (cd) *Blast First; (BFFP 119CD)* **SCREAMING FIELDS OF SONIC LOVE** -

May 97. (pic-lp) *Sonic Death; (SYLB 1)* **LIVE IN BREMEN (live)** -

Jun 97. (12"ep/cd-ep) *Sonic Youth; (SYR 1/+CD)* **SYR VOL.1**
– Anagrama / Improvisation ajout'e / Tremens / Mieux: de corrosion.

Jul 98. (cd) *S.K.R.; (SKR 1)* **SILVER SESSION FOR JASON KNUTH**

Aug 98. (cd) *Goofin' (GOO 2CD)* **HOLD THAT TIGER (live 1987)**

Jul 00. (cd; by SONIC YOUTH & YAMATSUKA EYE) *Ecstatic Peace; <(E 38CD)>* **TV SHIT**

LEE RANALDO

Blast First / S.S.T.

Jul 87. (m-lp/c) *(BFFP 9/+C)* *<SST 113>* **FROM HERE ⇒ ETERNITY**
– Time stands still / Destruction site / Ouroboron / Slodrown / New groove loop / Florida flower / Hard left / Fuzz-locusts / To Mary / Lathe speaks / The resolution / King's egg. *(re-iss. May93 on 'S.S.T.' lp/c/cd; same as US)*

not iss. / Blast First

Oct 95. (cd) *<BFFPCD 103>* **EAST JESUS** -
– Bridge / Time stands still / Destruction site / Oroboron / Slo drone / Some distortion / Live #1 / New groove loop / Some hammering . . . / Walker grooves / Fuxx – Locusts / To Mary (x2) / Lathe speaks / Deva, Spain / Resolution – King's Ogg.

FREE KITTEN

KIM GORDON – vocals, bass, guitar / **JULIE CAFRITZ** – vocals, guitar (ex-PUSSY GALORE)

Wiiija / Ecstatic Peace

1992. (7") **OH BONDAGE UP YOURS. /** -

—— there were other singles collected on their compilation, see below

1992. (m-cd) *<E#22>* **CALL NOW** -
– Falling backwards / + 5

—— added **MARK IBOLD** – bass (of PAVEMENT) + **YOSHIMI** – drums, trumpet

Jun 94. (cd) *(WIJ 036CD)* **UNBOXED** (compilation)
– Skinny butt / Platinumb / Smack / Falling backwards / Oneness / Dick / Yoshimi Vs. Mascis / Oh bondage up yours / 1-2-3 / Party with me punker / John Stark blues / Guilty pleasures / Sex boy / Cleopatra / Loose lips / Oh baby.

Jan 95. (7"one-sided) *(LTD 002)* **HARVEST SPOON** -

Feb 95. (cd/lp) *(WIJ 041 CD/V)* **NICE ASS**
– Harvest sppon / Rock of ages / Proper band / What's fair / Kissing well / Call back / Blindfold test / Greener pastures / Revlon liberation orchestra / The boaster / Scratch the D.J. / Secret sex friend / Royal flush / Feelin' / Alan Licked has ruined music for an entire generation.

Feb 96. (7"ep) *(WIJ 047V)* **PUNKS SUING PUNKS EP** -
– Kitten bossa nova / Punk v. punk / Coco's theme.

Oct 97. (12"ep) *(WIJ 074)* **CHINATOWN EXPRESS. / NEVER GONNA SLEEP / GAA** -

Oct 97. (cd/lp) *(WIJ CD/LP 1076)* **SENTIMENTAL EDUCATION**
– Teenie weenie boppie / Top 40 / Never gonna sleep / Strawberry milk / Played yrself / Dr. Spooky's spatialized Chinatown express / Bouwerie's boys / Records sleep / Picabo who / Sentimental education / One forty five / Eat cake / Gaa / Daddy long legs / Noise doll.

THURSTON MOORE

Geffen / D.G.C.

May 95. (cd/c/d-lp;colrd 3-sides) *<(GEF/GEC/GED 24810)>* **PSYCHIC HEARTS**
– Queen bee and her pals / Ono soul / Psychic hearts / Pretty bad / Patti Smith math scratch / Blues from beyond the grave / See-through play-mate / Hang out / Feathers / Tranquilizor / Staring statues / Cindy (rotten tanx) / Cherry's blues / Female cop / Elergy for all dead rock stars.

Forced Exposure / Forced Exposure

Dec 96. (cd; by JIM SAUTER, DON DIETRICH & THURSTON MOORE) *<(FE 015)>* **BAREFOOT IN THE HEAD** (rec. 1988)
– All doors look alike / Tanned moon / On the phrase "ass-backwards" / The date-reduced loaf / Concerning the sun as a cool solid.

Victo / Victo

Mar 97. (cd) *<(VICTOCD 045)>* **PIECE FOR JETSUN DOLMA**

Corpus Hermeticum / Corpus Herme

Apr 97. (cd) *(HERMES 011)* **KLANGFARBENMELODIE**

Father Yod / Father Yod

May 97. (cd; by THURSTON MOORE & PHIL MILSTEIN) *(HOTYOD 1)* **SONGS WE TAUGHT THE LORD VOL.2** -

Little Brother / Little Brother

Jul 97. (cd; by THURSTON MOORE & NELS CLINE) *<(LB 011CD)>* **PILLOW WAND**
(re-iss. Feb99 on 'Skycap'; RTD 3012002-2)

Xeric / Xeric

Aug 98. (cd/lp; by LOREN MAZZACANE CONNORS, JEAN-MARC MONTERA, THURSTON MOORE & LEE RANALDO) *<(X 99 0/5)>* **mmmr**
– (untitled) / (untitled) / (untitled).

Lo Record. / Lo Record.

Oct 98. (cd/lp) *<(LCD/LLP 011)>* **ROOT** (V/A remixes)

Fourth Dimension / Fourth Dimension

Feb 99. (10"lp) *<(FDCD 57)>* **NOT ME. / LYDIA's MOTH**

Materiali Sonori / Materiali Sonori

Mar 99. (cd; by THURSTON MOORE, EVAN PARKER & WALTER PRATI) *<(MASDO 90106)>* **THE PROMISE**
– The promise / Is / Our future / Our promise / Are / Children / All children. *(lp-iss.Apr99 on 'Get Back'; FT 803)*

SOUL ASYLUM

Formed: Minneapolis, Minnesota, USA . . . 1981 as LOUD FAST RULES, by ex-AT LAST guitarist DAN MURPHY and ex-SHITS frontman DAVE PIRNER, who were subsequently joined by KARL MUELLER then PAT MORLEY. Very much in the mould of HUSKER DU and The REPLACEMENTS, SOUL ASYLUM joined the latter at 'Twin Tone' records, while the former's BOB MOULD produced their 1984 debut album, 'SAY WHAT YOU WILL'. Later that year, MORLEY departed while the rest of the band took a break, SOUL ASYLUM subsequently returning in 1986 with GRANT YOUNG on their follow-up, 'MADE TO BE BROKEN'. A fusion of 60's pop and 70's punk, the album (also produced by MOULD) showed PIRNER blossoming into a cuttingly perceptive lyricist. Later that year, the band delivered another fine set, 'WHILE YOU WERE OUT', the record attracting major label attention in the form of 'A&M'. Fulfilling their contract with 'Twin Tone', SOUL ASYLUM cut a covers set, 'CLAM DIP AND OTHER DELIGHTS', displaying their wide range of tastes from Barry Manilow's 'MANDY' to Foreigner's 'JUKEBOX HERO'. In 1988, A&M issued the LENNY KAYE and ED STASIUM produced album, 'HANG TIME', an endearing collection of gleaming power-pop nuggets that occasionally veered off the beaten track into country. Their second and final release for A&M, 'SOUL ASYLUM AND THE HORSE THEY RODE IN ON' (1990), saw PIRNER spiral into despair despite the album's critical acclaim. Disillusioned with the major label inertia, the frontman took a break from amplified noise while his colleagues resumed their day jobs. Staking their chances on yet another major label, SOUL ASLYLUM subsequently signed to 'Columbia' and achieved almost instanteous success with the album 'GRAVE DANCERS UNION' in 1992. This was mainly due to the massive interest in the TOM PETTY-esque 'RUNAWAY TRAIN', a single that hit the American Top 5 in the summer of '93. The track's radio-friendly success paved the way for more typically abrasive numbers as 'SOMEBODY TO SHOVE' and 'BLACK GOLD', PIRNER landing on his feet as he wooed sultry actress, Winona Ryder (he appeared with her in the film, 'Generation X'). SOUL ASYLUM subsequently became MTV darlings and friends of the stars, such luminaries as BOB DYLAN, PETER BUCK and GUNS N' ROSES professing to fan status. In 1995, they returned with a new drummer, STERLING CAMPBELL, and a new album, 'LET YOUR DIM LIGHT SHINE', another worldwide seller which spawned the melancholy Top 30 gem, 'MISERY'. MURPHY and PIRNER (latter part-time) had also moonlighted in the countrified GOLDEN SMOG with among others the JAYHAWKS' GARY LOURIS and MARC PERLMAN. An EP of covers in '92 was finally followed up by an album in '96, 'DOWN BY THE OLD MAINSTREAM'. A few years later y'all supergroup added BIG STAR's JODY STEPHENS to replace the drumming PIRNER, a second set, WEIRD TALES', gaining many plaudits. • **Covers:** MOVE OVER (Janis Joplin) / RHINESTONE COWBOY (Glen Campbell) / BARSTOOL BLUES (Neil Young) / SEXUAL HEALING (Marvin Gaye) / ARE FRIENDS ELECTRIC (Tubeway Army) / SUMMER OF DRUGS (Victoria Williams) / WHEN I RAN OFF AND LEFT HER (Vic Chesnutt).

Album rating: SAY WHAT YOU WILL (*6) / MADE TO BE BROKEN (*6) / WHILE YOU WERE OUT (*6) / HANG TIME (*6) / CLAM DIP AND OTHER DELIGHTS (*5) / SOUL ASYLUM AND THE HORSE THEY RODE IN ON (*8) / GRAVE DANCERS UNION (*7) / LET YOUR DIM LIGHTS SHINE (*6) / CANDY FROM A STRANGER (*5)

DAVE PIRNER (b.16 Apr'64, Green Bay, Wisconsin) – vocals, guitar / **DAN MURPHY** (b.12 Jul'62, Duluth, Minnesota) – guitar, vocals / **KARL MUELLER** (b.27 Jul'63) – bass / **PAT MORLEY** – drums, percussion

Rough Trade Twin Tone

Aug 84. (m-lp) <TT 8439> **SAY WHAT YOU WILL** [-] [ ]
– Long day / Voodoo doll / Money talks / Stranger / Sick of that song / Walking / Happy / Black and blue / Religiavision. *<US re-iss. May89+=; same>* – Dragging me down / Do you know / Spacehead / Broken glass / Masquerade. *(UK cd-iss. Mar93 as 'SAY WHAT YOU WILL CLARENCE . . . KARL SOLD THE TRUCK' on 'Roadrunner'; RR 9093-2) (cd re-iss. Mar95 on 'Twin Tone'; TTR 8439-2)*

— **GRANT YOUNG** (b. 5 Jan'64, Iowa City, Iowa) – drums, percussion; repl. MORLEY

Sep 86. (lp) *(ROUGH 102)* <TT 8666> **MADE TO BE BROKEN** [ ] [ ]
– Tied to the tracks / Ship of fools / Can't go back / Another world another day / Made to be broken / Never really been / Whoa! / New feelings / Growing pain / Lone rider / Ain't that tough / Don't it (make your troubles seem small). *(cd-iss. Mar93 on 'Roadrunner'+=; RR 9094-2)* – Long way home. *(cd re-iss. Sep98 on 'R.C.A.'; 74321 60573-20)*

Sep 86. (7") **TIED TO THE TRACKS. /** [-] [ ]

What Goes On Twin Tone

Mar 88. (lp) *(GOES ON 16)* <TT 8691> **WHILE YOU WERE OUT** [ ] [ ] 1987
– Freaks / Carry on / No man's land / Crashing down / The judge / Sun don't shine / Closer to the stars / Never too soon / Miracles mile / Lap of luxury / Passing sad daydream. *(cd-iss. Mar93 on 'Roadrunner'; RR 9096-2) (cd re-iss. Feb95 on 'Twin Tone'; TTR 8691-2)*

May 88. (m-lp) *(GOES ON 22)* <TT 8814> **CLAM DIP AND OTHER DELIGHTS** [ ] [ ] 1987
– Just plain evil / Chains / Secret no more / Artificial heart / P-9 / Take it to root / Jukebox hero / Move over / Mandy / Rhinestone cowboy. *(cd-iss. Mar93 on 'Roadrunner'; RR 9097-2) (cd re-iss. Feb95 on 'Twin Tone'; TTR 8814-2)*

— split but re-formed adding guest **CADD** – sax, piano

A&M A&M

Jun 88. (7"/12") *(AM/+Y 447)* **SOMETIME TO RETURN. / PUT THE BOOT IN** [ ] [-]
(12"-iss.Jun91 +=; same) – Marionette.

Jun 88. (lp/c/cd) *(AMA/AMC/CDA 5197)* <395197-1/-4/-2> **HANG TIME** [ ] [ ]
– Down on up to me / Little too clean / Sometime to return / Cartoon / Beggars and choosers / Endless farewell / Standing in the doorway / Marionette / Ode / Jack of all trades / Twiddly dee / Heavy rotation. *(re-iss. Sep93 cd/c; CD/C MID 189)*

Aug 88. (7") *(AM 463)* **CARTOON. / TWIDDLY DEE** [ ] [-]
(12"+=) *(AMY 463)* – Standing in the doorway.

Sep 90. (cd/c/lp) *(395318-2/-4/-1)* **SOUL ASYLUM & THE HORSE THEY RODE IN ON** [ ] [ ] 1989
– Spinnin' / Bitter pill / Veil of tears / Nice guys (don't get paid) / Something out of nothing / Gullible's travels / Brand new shine / Grounded / Don't be on your way / We / All the king's friends. *(re-iss. Sep93 cd/c; CD/C MID 190)*

Jan 91. (7") **EASY STREET. / SPINNING** [ ] [ ]
(12"+=) – All the king's friends / Gullible's travels.

Columbia Columbia

Oct 92. (cd/c/lp) *(472253-2/-4/-1)* <48896> **GRAVE DANCERS UNION** [ ] [11]
– Somebody to shove / Black gold / Runaway train / Keep it up / Homesick / Get on out / New world / April fool / Without a trace / Growing into you / 99% / The Sun maid. *(re-dist.Jul93; hit UK No.52) (UK No.27 early '94)*

Mar 93. (10"ep/cd-ep) *(659 088-0/-2)* **BLACK GOLD. / BLACK GOLD (live) / THE BREAK / 99%** [ ] [ ]

May 93. (c-s,cd-s) *<74966>* **RUNAWAY TRAIN / NEVER REALLY BEEN (live)** [-] [5]

Jun 93. (7"/c-s) *(659 390-7/-4)* **RUNAWAY TRAIN. / BLACK GOLD (live)** [37] [-]
(12"+=) *(659 390-6)* – By the way / Never really been (live).
(cd-s++=) *(659 390-2)* – Everybody loves a winner. (- Black Gold).
(above single returned into UK chart Nov'93 to hit No.7)

Aug 93. (12"ep/cd-ep) *(659 649-6/-2)* **SOMEBODY TO SHOVE / SOMEBODY TO SHOVE (live). / RUNAWAY TRAIN (live) / BY THE WAY (demo)** [34] [-]
(c-ep) *(659 649-4)* – ('A'side) / Black gold (live) / Runaway train (live).

Jan 94. (7"/c-s) *(659 844-7/-4)* **BLACK GOLD. / SOMEBODY TO SHOVE** [26] [-]
(cd-s+=) *(659 844-2)* – Closer to the stairs / Square root.
(cd-s+=) *(659 844-5)* – Runaway train (live).

Mar 94. (7"/c-s) *(660 224-7/-4)* **SOMEBODY TO SHOVE. / BY THE WAY** [32] [-]
(cd-s+=) *(660 224-2)* – Stranger (unplugged) / Without a trace (live).
(cd-s++=) *(660 224-5)* – ('A'mix).

— **STERLING CAMPBELL** – drums; repl. YOUNG

Jun 95. (cd/c) *(480 320-2/-4)* *<57616>* **LET YOUR DIM LIGHT SHINE** [22] [6]
– Misery / Shut down / To my own devices / Hopes up / Promises broken / Bittersweetheart / String of pearls / Crawl / Caged rat / Eyes of a child / Just like anyone / Tell me when / Nothing to write home about / I did my best.

Jun 95. (c-s,cd-s) *<77959>* **MISERY / HOPE** [-] [20]

Jul 95. (7"white/c-s) *(662 109-7/-4)* **MISERY. / STRING OF PEARLS** [30] [-]
(cd-s+=) *(662 109-2)* – Hope (demo) / I did my best.

Nov 95. (c-s) *(662 478-4)* **JUST LIKE ANYONE / DO ANYTHING YOU WANNA DO (live)** [52] [-]
(cd-s+=) *(662 478-2)* – Get on out (live).
(cd-s) *(662 478-5)* – ('A'side) / You'll live forever (demo) / Fearless leader (demo).

Feb 96. (c-s,cd-s) *<78215>* **PROMISES BROKEN / CAN'T EVEN TELL (live)** [-] [63]

— now a trio of **PIRNER, MURPHY + MUELLER**

May 98. (cd/c) *(487265-2/-4)* *<67618>* **CANDY FROM A STRANGER** [ ] [ ]
– Creatures of habit / I will still be laughing / Close / See you later / No time for waiting / Blood into wine / Lies of hate / Draggin' out the lake / Blackout / The game / Cradle chain.

SOULFLY

Formed: based – Phoenix, Arizona, USA . . . 1997 by ex-SEPULTURA mainman, MAX CAVALERA, the Brazilian enlisting the aid of LUCIO (JACKSON BANDIERA), MARCELO D. RAPP and punk rocker, ROY MAYORGA. MAX had recently found faith in God after his step-son, Dana (also son of wife/manager, Gloria) died; his other sons, Zyon and Igor also had serious illnesses. The man never changed his "ungod"-like vocal chords though, and SOULFLY (under the production of Ross Robinson) unleashed their thrillingly diverse eponymous set in the Spring of '98. The contrast between the tribal 'UMBABARAUMA' and the grinding 'NO' somehow worked, the latter's refreshingly metal assault on the ears and the line, "no motherf***in' HOOTIE & THE BLOWFISH", supplying the definitive "ROCK!!!" highlight of the year! The 'PRIMITIVE' set in 2000 kicked off with the excellent 'BACK TO THE PRIMITIVE', certainly one of the highlights of the year.

Album rating: SOULFLY (*8) / PRIMITIVE (*6)

MAX CAVALERA – vocals, 4-string guitar (ex-SEPULTURA) / **JACKSON BANDIERA** (aka LUCIO) – guitars (ex-CHICO SCIENCE) / **MARCELO D. RAPP** – bass (ex-MIST) / **ROY "RATA" MAYORGA** – drums (ex-AGNOSTIC FRONT, ex-SHELTER, ex-NAUSEA, ex-CHAOS USA)

Roadrunner Roadrunner

Mar 98. (ltd;cd-ep) *(RR 2238-3)* **BLEED / NO HOPE = NO FEAR / CANGACEIRO / AIN'T NO FEEBLE BASTARD** [ ] [-]

Apr 98. (cd/c/lp) *(<RR 8748-2/-4/-1>)* **SOULFLY** [16] [79]
– Eye for an eye / No hope = no fear / Bleed / Tribe / Bumba / First commandment / Bumbklaatt / Soulfly / Umbabarauma / Quilombo / Fire / The song remains insane / No / Prejudice / Karmageddon. *(special cd+=; RR 8748-9)* – Cangaceiro / Ain't no feeble bastard / The possibility of life's destruction. *(re-iss. May99 d-cd+=; RR 8748-8)*– Tribe (fuck shit up mix) / Qilombo (extreme ragga dub mix) / Umbabarauma (World Cup remix) / No hope = no fear (live) / Bleed (live) / Quilombo (live) / The song remains the insane (live) / Eye for an eye (live) / Tribe (tribal terrorism mix) / Umbabarauma (Brasilia '70 remix) / Quilombo (Zumbi dub remix) / Soulfly (eternal spirit remix).

Jun 98. (ltd;cd-ep) *(RR 2231-3)* **UMBABARAUMA / UMBABARAUMA (World Cup mix) / TRIBE (extended) / UMBABARAUMA (World Cup instrumental)** [ ] [-]

May 99. (cd-s) *(RR 2203-3)* **TRIBE (fuck shit up mix) / QUILOMBO (Zumbi dub mix) / TRIBE (tribal terrorism mix)** [ ] [-]

— **MIKEY DOLING** – guitar; repl. BANDIERA

— **JOE NUNEZ** – drums, percussion; repl. MAYORGA

Sep 00. (cd/pic-lp) *(<RR 8565-2/-1>)* **PRIMITIVE** [45] [32]
– Back to the primitive / Pain / Bring it / Jumpdafuckup / Mulumbo / Son song / Boom / Terrorist / The prophet / Soulfly II / In memory of . . . / Flyhigh. *(special cd+=; RR 8565-5)* – Eye for an eye (live) / Tribe (live) / Soulfire / Soulfly (universal spirit mix).

Dec 00. (cd-s) *(RR 2067-3)* **BACK TO THE PRIMITIVE / TERRORIST (total deconstruction mix) / BACK TO THE PRIMITIVE (dub shit up mix) / BACK TO THE PRIMITIVE (CD-Rom video)** [ ] [-]

SOULS AT ZERO (see under ⇒ WRATHCHILD AMERICA)

SOULWAX

Formed: Ghent, Belgium . . . 1995 by brothers STEPHEN and DAVID DeWAELE, who enlisted the help of STEFAAN VAN LEUVEN, STEPHANE MISSEGHERS and INGE FLIPS. By their own admission the DeWAELE brothers' major influences came from classic 80's metal; i.e. AC/DC and VAN HALEN. Yet being the sons of a famed Belgian radio DJ (Zaki DeWaele), the boys benefitted from his large musical knowledge, making SOULWAX's output far more rounded and eclectic than just a cloning of their childhood heroes. After the release of a successful EP in 1995, the group travelled Stateside to record their debut full-set 'LEAVE THE STORY UNTOLD' (1996). For this project they enlisted the help of producer CHRIS GOSS of MASTERS OF REALITY fame. Their sound on this LP definitely has elements of metal but the use of organ and other less power rock patterns at times pigeonholed the the band in the Alt-rock camp. They finally followed this release with their second full-length, 'MUCH AGAINST EVERYONE'S ADVICE' (2000). Between the albums the DeWAELE siblings continued on their extra-curricular activites of directing promo videos and hosting TV shows, surprisingly also managing to keep SOULWAX going as a full-time concern.

Album rating: LEAVE THE STOLD UNTOLD (*6) / MUCH AGAINST EVERYONE'S ADVICE (*7)

STEPHEN DeWAELE – vocals / **DAVID DeWAELE** – guitar / **INGE FLIPS** – keyboards / **STEFAAN VAN LEUVEN** – bass / **STEPHANE MISSEGHERS** – drums

Play It Again Sam Play It Again Sam

Dec 96. (cd) **LEAVE THE STORY UNTOLD** [-] [-] Belgian
– Intro / Reruns (Daisy Duke) / Caramel / Kill your darlings / Great continental suicide note / Soul simplicity / Rooster / Tales of a dead scene / Hammer & tongues / Spending the afternoon in a slowly revolvin' door / The about it song / Long distance zoom / Vista grande / Acapulco gold.

Nov 99. (10"ep/cd-ep) *(PIASB 006 T/CD)* **TOO MANY DJ'S / MUCH AGAINST EVERYONE'S ADVICE / OVERWEIGHT KARATE KID / CUT SOME SLACK (live)** [ ] [-]

Feb 00. (7") *(PIASB 018)* **CONVERSATION INTERCOM. / I GO TO SLEEP** [65] [-]
(cd-s) *(PIASB 018CD)* – ('A'side) / ('A'-Vocoder intermix) / The salty knowledge of tears.

Apr 00. (cd/lp) *(PIASB 010 CD/LP)* **MUCH AGAINST EVERYONE'S ADVICE** [ ] [ ]
– Conversation intercom / Saturday / When logic die / Much against everyone's advice / Overweight karate kid / Proverbial pants / The salty knowledge of tears / Flying without wings / More than this / Too many DJ's / Temptingly yours / Scream / Funny. *(cd re-iss. Oct00 +=; PIASB 010CDX)* – Saturday (Morning After Thrill mix) / Conversation intercom (live) / Overweight karate kid (live) / Temptingly yours (live) / Conversation (vocoder mix) / Mike Rule (Joe Cream mix) / Saturday (Roger Manning mix).

Jun 00. (7") *(PIASB 026)* **MUCH AGAINST EVERYONE'S ADVICE. / STARFISH AND COFFEE** [56] [-]
(cd-s) *(PIASB 026CD)* – ('A'side) / Flying without wings / My cruel joke.
(cd-s) *(PIASB 026CDX)* – ('A'side) / Cut some slack.

Sep 00. (cd-s) *(PIASB 036CD)* **TOO MANY DJ'S / TOO MANY DJ'S (Tim Love Lee mix) / WOULDN'T IT BE GOOD** [40] [-]
(12"/cd-s) *(PIASB 036 T/CDX)* – ('A'side) / Popfile / Children of the revolution.

Feb 01. (7") *(PIASB 046)* **CONVERSATION INTERCOM. / SATURDAY (live)** [50] [-]
(cd-s) *(PIASB 046CD)* – ('A'side) / Caramel / Tales of a dead scene.
(cd-s) *(PIASB 046CDX)* – ('A'side) / ('A'-Ladytron mix) / I go to sleep.

SOUND BARRIER

Formed: Los Angeles, California, USA . . . 1980, initially as COLOUR, by the all-black quartet of BERNIE K., SPACEY T., STANLEY E. and DAVE BROWN. No doubt inspired by the likes of MOTHER'S FINEST and BAD BRAINS, SOUND BARRIER proved that the metal scene was not the sole reserve of blonde maned American boys, signing to 'M.C.A.' and releasing a US-only debut set, 'TOTAL CONTROL' (1983). The record's musical melting pot of funk, soul and metal was obviously ahead of its time (it would be a further five years before LIVING COLOUR managed to take a similar hybrid to the masses) and the group were promptly dropped amid poor sales. Soldiering on with an independently released mini-set, 'BORN TO ROCK', the group were subsequently picked up by 'Metal Blade'. The resulting album, 'SPEED OF LIGHT' (1986) was something of a compromise, SOUND BARRIER breaking shortly after as BERNIE joined MASI, SPACEY joined STANLEY in LIBERTY and LECH was recruited by JOSHUA.

Album rating: TOTAL CONTROL (*6) / BORN TO ROCK mini (*4) / SPEED OF LIGHT (*4)

BERNIE K. – vocals / **SPACEY T.** – guitar, vocals / **STANLEY E.** – bass, vocals / **DAVE BROWN** – drums

not iss. / M.C.A.

1983. (lp) *<5396>* **TOTAL CONTROL** [-] [ ]
– Other side / Total control / Rock without the roll / Mayday / Second thoughts / Nobody cares / Don't put me on hold / Hey U / Rock on the wild side.

not iss. / Pit Bull

1984. (m-lp) *<PBR 002>* **BORN TO ROCK** [-] [ ]
– Conquer the world / Born to be wild / Raging heart / Born to rock / Do or die.

—— **EMIL LECH** – bass; repl. STANLEY who later joined LIBERTY

Enigma / Metal Blade

1986. (lp) *<2114-1>* **SPEED OF LIGHT** [ ] [ ]
– Speed of light / Gladiator / On the level (head banger) / What price glory? / Hollywood (down on your luck) / Fight for life~ / Aim for the top / Hard as a rock / On to the next adventure.

—— folded when BERNIE joined MASI, while SPACEY formed LIBERTY and EMIL joined JOSHUA. The outfit who released for the 'Compact Organisation' label in the mid 80's were nothing to do with this SOUND BARRIER.

SOUNDGARDEN

Formed: Seattle, Washington, USA . . . 1984 by lead singer CHRIS CORNELL, guitarist KIM THAYIL and bassist HIRO YAMAMOTO. With the addition of drummer MATT CAMERON in '86, the band became one of the first to record for the fledgling 'Sub Pop' label, releasing the 'HUNTED DOWN' single in summer '87. Two EP's, 'SCREAMING LIFE', and 'FOPP' followed, although the group signed to 'S.S.T.' for their debut album, 'ULTRAMEGA OK' (1988). Despite its lack of focus, the record laid the foundations for what was to follow; a swamp-rich miasma of snail-paced, bass-crunch uber-riffing, wailing vocals and punk attitude shot through with bad-trip psychedelia (i.e. not something to listen to last thing at night). And with the Grammy-nominated 'LOUDER THAN LOVE' (1989), the group's major label debut for 'A&M', SOUNDGARDEN harnessed their devilish wares onto infectious melodies and fuck-off choruses; one listen to the likes of 'HANDS ALL OVER', 'LOUD LOVE' and the tongue-in-cheek brilliance of 'BIG DUMB SEX' was enough to convince you that these hairy post-metallers were destined for big, grunge-type things. Success wasn't immediate however, the album failing to make a dent beyond the Sub-Pop in-crowd and a few adventurous metal fans. YAMAMOTO departed soon after the record's release, his replacement being ex-NIRVANA guitarist JASON EVERMAN, who was succeeded in turn by BEN SHEPHERD. CORNELL and CAMERON subsequently got together with future PEARL JAM mambers, EDDIE VEDDER, STONE GOSSARD and JEFF AMENT to form TEMPLE OF THE DOG, releasing an eponymous album in early '91 to critical acclaim. SOUNDGARDEN, meanwhile, finally got their break later that year when 'BADMOTORFINGER' broke the US/UK Top 40. An even more accessible proposition, the record combined a tighter, more driven sound with pop/grunge hooks and their trademark cerebral lyrics to create such MTV favourites as 'JESUS CHRIST POSE' and 'OUTSHINED'. 'RUSTY CAGE' was another juggernaut riffathon, while 'SEARCHING WITH MY GOOD EYE CLOSED' meted out some of the most brutal psychedelia this side of MONSTER MAGNET. A high profile support slot on GUNS N' ROSES' 'Lose Your Illusion' tour afforded the band valuable exposure in the States, their crossover appeal endearing them to the metal hordes on both sides of the Atlantic. Previewed by the Top 20 'SPOONMAN' single, SOUNDGARDEN's masterful fourth set, 'SUPERUNKNOWN' (1994), finally gave the group long overdue success, scaling the US charts and going Top 5 in Britain. Constructed around a head-spinning foundation of acid-drenched retro-rock and JIM MORRISON-esque doom, this epic album spawned the Grammy-winnning 'BLACK HOLE SUN' while 'FELL ON BLACK DAYS' stands as one of their most realised pieces of warped psychedelia to date. Following a world tour with the likes of The SMASHING PUMPKINS, the group began work on 'DOWN ON THE UPSIDE' (1996). Another marathon set boasting sixteen tracks, the record inevitably failed to garner the plaudits of its predecessor; the claustrophobia of old had given way to a marginally more strightforward melodic grunge sound, evidenced to best effect on the likes of 'BURDEN IN MY HAND'. Subversiveness was still the key word; 'TY COBB's mutant country-punk and gonzoid expletive-filled attitude was reminiscent of MINISTRY's seminal 'Jesus Built My Hotrod'. The album ultimately proved to be their swan song, SOUNDGARDEN subsequently pushing up the daisies as of April '97. CORNELL (now in his mid-30's!) returned as a solo artist a few years later, although a largely timid soft-rock debut, 'EUPHORIA MORNING' (1999) – featuring the JEFF BUCKLEY tribute, 'WAVE GOODBYE' – saw the man lose his "metal" credentials. • **Songwriters:** Most by CORNELL and group permutations. Covered SWALLOW MY PRIDE (Ramones) / FOPP (Ohio Players) / INTO THE VOID tune only (Black Sabbath) / BIG BOTTOM (Spinal Tap) / EARACHE MY EYE (Cheech & Chong) / I CAN'T GIVE YOU ANYTHING (Ramones) / HOMOCIDAL SUICIDE (Budgie) / I DON'T CARE ABOUT YOU (Fear) / CAN YOU SEE ME (Jimi Hendrix) / COME TOGETHER (Beatles).

Album rating: ULTRAMEGA OK (*7) / LOUDER THAN LOVE (*8) / BADMOTORFINGER (*9) / SUPERUNKNOWN (*9) / DOWN ON THE UPSIDE (*6) / A-SIDES compilation (*8) / Chris Cornell: EUPHORIA MORNING (*4) / Temple Of The Dog: TEMPLE OF THE DOG (*7)

CHRIS CORNELL (b.20 Jul'64) – vocals, guitar / **KIM THAYIL** (b. 4 Sep'60) – lead guitar / **HIRO YAMAMOTO** (b.13 Apr'61) – bass / **MATT CAMERON** (b.28 Nov'62, San Diego, Calif.) – drums, percussion

not iss. / Sub Pop

Jun 87. (7"blue) *<SP 12a>* **NOTHING TO SAY. / HUNTED DOWN** [-] [ ]

Oct 87. (12"ep,orange-12"ep) *<SP 12>* **SCREAMING LIFE** [-] [ ]
– Hunted down / Entering / Tears to forget / Nothing to say / Little Joe / Hand of God.

Aug 88. (12"ep) *<SP 17>* **FOPP** [-] [ ]
– Fopp / Fopp (dub) / Kingdom of come / Swallow my pride.

S.S.T. / S.S.T.

Nov 88. (m-lp/c/cd) *<(SST 201/+C/CD)>* **ULTRAMEGA OK** [ ] [ ]
– Flower / All your lies / 665 / Beyond the wheel / 667 / Mood for trouble / Circle of power / He didn't / Smokestack lightning / Nazi driver / Head injury / Incessant mace / One minute of silence. *(re-iss. Oct95;)*

May 89. (12"ep/c-ep/cd-ep) *<(SST 231/+C/CD)>* **FLOWER. / HEAD INJURY / TOY BOX** [ ] [ ]

A&M / A&M

Sep 89. (lp/c/cd) *<(AMA/AMC/CDA 5252)>* **LOUDER THAN LOVE** [ ] [ ]
– Ugly truth / Hands all over / Gun / Power trip / Get on the snake / Full on Kevin's mom / Loud love / I awake / No wrong no right / Uncovered / Big dumb sex / Full on (reprise).

Apr 90. (10"ep/cd-ep) *(AM X/CD 560)* **HANDS ALL OVER** [ ] [-]
– Hands all over / Heretic / Come together / Big dumb sex.

Jul 90. (7"ep/12"ep) *(AM/+Y 574)* **THE LOUD LOVE E.P.** [ ] [-]
– Loud love / Fresh deadly roses / Big dumb sex (dub) / Get on the snake.

—— **JASON EVERMAN** (b.16 Aug'67) – bass (ex-NIRVANA) repl. HIRO who later formed TRULY after working in a bike shop.

Oct 90. (7",7"purple/green) *<SP 83>* **ROOM A THOUSAND YEARS WIDE. / H.I.V. BABY** [-] [ ]
(above issued on 'Sub Pop')

—— **BEN SHEPHERD** (b. HUNTER SHEPHERD, 20 Sep'68, Okinawa, Japan) – bass repl. JASON

Oct 91. (cd/c/lp) *(395374-2/-4/-1)* *<5374>* **BADMOTORFINGER** [39] [39]
– Rusty cage / Outshined / Slaves & bulldozers / Jesus Christ pose / Face pollution / Somewhere / Searching with my good eye closed / Room a thousand years wide / Mind riot / Drawing flies / Holy water / New damage.

Mar 92. (7") *(AM 862)* **JESUS CHRIST POSE. / STRAY CAT BLUES** [30] [-]
(cd-s+=) *(AMCD 862)* – Into the void (stealth).

Jun 92. (7"pic-d) *(AM 874)* **RUSTY CAGE. / TOUCH ME** [41] [-]
(12"+=/cd-s+=) *(AM Y/CD 874)* – Show me.
(cd-s+=) *(AMCDX 874)* – Big bottom / Earache my eye.

Nov 92. (7") *(AM 0102)* **OUTSHINED. / I CAN'T GIVE YOU ANYTHING** [50] [-]
(12"+=/cd-s+=) *(AM 0102 T/CD)* – Homocidal suicide.
(cd-s+=) *(AM 0102CDX)* – I don't care about you / Can't you see me.

Feb 94. (7"pic-d/c-s) *(580 538-7/-4)* **SPOONMAN. / FRESH TENDRILS** [20] [-]
(12"clear+=/cd-s+=) *(580 539-1/-2)* – Cold bitch / Exit Stonehenge.

Mar 94. (cd/c/orange-d-lp) *(540215-2/-4/-1)* *<0198>* **SUPERUNKNOWN** [4] [1]
– Let me drown / My wave / Fell on black days / Mailman / Superunknown / Head down / Black hole Sun / Spoonman / Limo wreck / The day I tried to live / Kickstand / Fresh tendrils / 4th of July / Half / Like suicide / She likes surprises.

Apr 94. (7"pic-d/c-s) *(580594-7/-4)* **THE DAY I TRIED TO LIVE. / LIKE SUICIDE (acoustic)** [42] [-]
(12"etched+=/cd-s+=) *(580595-1/-2)* – Kickstand (live).

Aug 94. (7"pic-d/c-s) *(580736-7/-4)* **BLACK HOLE SUN. / BEYOND THE WHEEL (live) / FELL ON BLACK DAYS (live)** [12] [-]
(pic-cd-s+=) *(580753-2)* – Birth ritual (demo).
(cd-s) *(580737-2)* – ('A'side) / My wave (live) / Jesus Christ pose (live) / Spoonman (remix).

Jan 95. (7"pic-d/c-s) *(580947-7/-4)* **FELL ON BLACK DAYS. / KYLE PETTY, SON OF RICHARD / MOTORCYCLE LOOP** [24] [-]
(cd-s) *(580947-2)* – ('A'side) / Kyle Petty, son of Richard / Fell on black days (video version).
(cd-s) *(580947-5)* – ('A'side) / Girl u want / Fell on black days (early demo).

May 96. (7"red/cd-s) *(581620-7/-4)* **PRETTY NOOSE. / JERRY GARCIA'S FINGER** [14] [-]
(cd-s) *(581620-2)* – ('A'side) / Applebite / An unkind / (interview with Eleven's Alain and Natasha).

May 96. (cd/c/d-lp) *(540526-2/-4/-1) <0526>* **DOWN ON THE UPSIDE** [7] [2]
– Pretty noose / Rhinosaur / Zero chance / Dusty / Ty Cobb / Blow up the outside world / Burden in my hand / Never named / Applebite / Never the machine forever / Tighter & tighter / No attention / Switch opens / Overfloater / An unkind / Boot camp.

Sep 96. (7"/cd-s) *(581854-7/-2)* **BURDEN IN MY HAND. / KARAOKE** [33] [-]
(cd-s) *(581855-2)* – ('A'side) / Bleed together / She's a politician / (Chris Cornell interview).

Dec 96. (7") *(581986-7)* **BLOW UP THE OUTSIDE WORLD. / DUSTY** [38] [-]
(cd-s+=) *(581987-2)* – Gun.
(cd-s) *(581986-2)* – ('A'side) / Get on the snake / Slice of spacejam.

— split on the 9th of April 1997

– compilations, etc –

Oct 93. (cd) *A&M; (CDA 24118)* **LOUDER THAN LOUD / BADMOTORFINGER** [ ] [ ]

Oct 93. (c/cd) *Sub Pop; (SP/+CD 12)* **SCREAMING LIFE / FOPP** [ ] [ ]

Nov 97. (cd) *A&M; (540833-2) <0833>* **A-SIDES** [ ] [63]
– Nothing to say / Flower / Loud love / Hands all over / Get on the snake / Jesus Christ pose / Outshined / Rusty cage / Spoonman / The day I tried to live / Black hole sun / Fell on black days / Pretty noose / Burden in my hand / Blow up the outside world / Ty Cobb / Bleed together.

CHRIS CORNELL

Sep 99. (cd/c) *<(490412-2/-4)>* **EUPHORIA MORNING** [31] [18]
– Can't change me / Flutter girl / Preaching the end of the world / Follow my way / When I'm down / Mission / Wave goodbye / Moonchild / Sweet euphoria / Disappearing one / Pillow of your bones / Steel rain.

Oct 99. (7") *(497173-7)* **CAN'T CHANGE ME. / FLUTTER GIRL** [62] [ ]
(cd-s+=) *(497173-2)* – Nowhere but you.
(cd-s) *(497174-2)* – ('A'side) / When I'm down / ('A'-video).

TEMPLE OF THE DOG

splinter-group feat. **CORNELL + CAMERON** plus **STONE GOSSARD / JEFF AMENT** (both ex-MOTHER LOVE BONE, future PEARL JAM)

A&M A&M

Jun 92. (cd/c/lp) *(395 350-2/-4/-1) <5350>* **TEMPLE OF THE DOG** [ ] [5]
– Say hello to Heaven / Reach down / Hunger strike / Pushing forward back / Call me a dog / Times of trouble / Wooden Jesus / Your saviour / 4-walled world / All night thing.

Oct 92. (7"pic-d/c-s) *(AM 0091/+C)* **HUNGER STRIKE. / ALL NIGHT THING** [51] [ ]
(12"+=/cd-s+=) *(AM 0091 T/CD)* – Your saviour.

HATER

MATT + BEN plus **JOHN McBAIN** – guitar (of MONSTER MAGNET)

Sub Pop Sub Pop

Aug 93. (7") *<(SP 233)>* **CIRCLES. / GENOCIDE** [ ] [ ]

A&M A&M

Sep 93. (cd/c) *(540 137-2/-4) <0137>* **HATER** [ ] [ ]
– Mona bone jakon / Who do I kill? / Tot finder / Lion and lamb / Roadside / Down undershoe / Circles / Putrid / Blistered / Sad McBain. *(re-iss. cd May95; same)*

WELLWATER CONSPIRACY

MATT + JOHN once again

3rd Gear 3rd Gear

Mar 98. (cd) *<(3G 17)>* **DECLARATION OF CONFORMITY** [ ] [ ]
– Sleeveless / Shel Talmy / The ending / Sandy / Far side of your moon / Lucy leave / Green undertow / Enebrio / You do you / Space travel in the blink of an eye / Nati bati yi / Declaration of conformity / Trowerchord / Palomar observatory. *(lp-iss.on 'Super Electro'; SUPER 07LP)*

Time Bomb Time Bomb

Jan 99. (cd) *<(43523-2)>* **BROTHERHOOD OF ELECTRIC: OPERATIONAL DIRECTIVES** [ ] [ ]
– Destination 24 / Compellor / Teen lambchop / Hal McBlaine / Born with a tail / Destination 7 / Red light, green light / B.O.U. / Psycho Scrimm / Van vanishing / Right of left field / Ladder to the moon / Dark passage / Good pushin' / Dr. Browne Dr. Greene / Jefferson experiment. *(lp-iss.Oct99 on '3rd Gear'; 3G 24)*

2000. (cd-ep) *<3G 29>* **WELLWATER CONSPIRACY** [-] [ ]
– Tidepool telegraph / Now invisibly / Farside of the moon (live) / Of dreams. *(above issued on '3rd Gear')*

— there's also a new release in May'01, but so far US-only

SOUTHERN DEATH CULT (see under ⇒ CULT)

SPACE AGE PLAYBOYS (see under ⇒ WARRIOR SOUL)

SPARROW (see under ⇒ STEPPENWOLF)

SPECIAL EFFECT (see under ⇒ MINISTRY)

SPEEDEALER

Formed: Lubbock, Texas . . . 1994 as REO SPEEDEALER (surely THE band name of the decade?!) by JEFF HIRSHBERG, RODNEY SKELTON, HARDEN HARRISON and ERIC SCHMIDT. Sadly, after the threat of legal action from AOR veterans REO SPEEDWAGON, the band were forced to clip their moniker's wings although the song, so to speak, remained the same. Hailing from the same sonic cattle ranch as the late lamented RAGING SLAB, while drawing influences from scuzz-rock godfathers like MOTORHEAD, these no-nonsense garage-punks issued their eponymous debut album on the 'Royalty' imprint in 1998. The same label released follow-up, 'HERE COMES DEATH' the following year although Royalty's subsequent bankruptcy saw the record sink without trace. Determined to keep their profile high, they played a gig almost every single night through 1999. This punishing schedule eventually bore fruit when top A&R man Michael Alago, signed the band to his 'Palm Pictures' label and gave 'HERE COMES . . .' the full re-release it deserved.

Album rating: HERE COMES DEATH (*6)

JEFF HIRSHBERG – vocals, guitar / **ERIC SCHMIDT** – guitar / **RODNEY SKELTON** – bass / **HARDEN HARRISON** – drums

not iss. Royalty

1998. (lp) *<12>* **SPEEDEALER** [-] [ ]

Palm Pictures Palm Pictures

Oct 00. (cd) *(PALMCD 2051)* **HERE COMES DEATH** [ ] [ ]
– Hit it and run / CCCP (Cold War blues) / You lose, I win / Nobody's hell like mine / Cream #1 / Sasparilla / Death / Hate you better / No more / Drink me dead / 1:50 a.m. / Washed up / Ansinthe / We are diseased / Dealer's choice / Tweeked / California tumbles into sea.

Bronx Cheer not iss.

Apr 01. (7"ep) *(200001BC)* **THE TRANSATLANTIC SPEED TRIALS** [ ] [-]
– Hate you better / Pig fucker / (other two by Social Lepers).

SPEEDBALL BABY

Formed: New York, USA . . . early 1994 when Bostonians RON WARD (ex-drummer of BLOOD ORANGES) and MATT VERTA-RAY (ex-MADDER ROSE) met at a friend's wedding. Completing the line-up with the rhythm section of ALI SMITH and DAVE ROY, the band signed to 'Matador' sub-label, 'P.C.P.', releasing their eponymous EP later that year. Mixing up a Molotov Cocktail of JON SPENCER-esque primal blues and raucous punk, the band served it neat on the following year's mini-set, 'GET STRAIGHT FOR THE LAST SUPPER'. The record even included a clutch of mangled covers, including the Ramones' 'BLITZKRIEG BOP' and Van Morrison's 'T.B. SHEETS'. Making a foray into major label land via MCA's 'Fort Apache' subsidiary, SPEEDBALL BABY released their debut album proper, 'CINEM~A!' (1996). Issued a year later in Britain (on 'Konkurrent'), its release coincided with that of a mini-set on 'Sympathy For The Record Industry', 'I'M GONNA STOMP MR. HARRY LEE'.

Album rating: CINEMA! (*6)

RON WARD – vocals (ex-BLOOD ORANGES) / **MATT VERTA-RAY** – guitar (ex-MADDER ROSE) / **ALI SMITH** – bass / **DAVE ROY** – drums

P.C.P. P.C.P.

Dec 94. (7"ep) *<(PCP 018-1)>* **SPEEDBALL BABY EP** [ ] [ ]
– Fucked up town / Black eyed girl / Percoset.
(cd-ep+=) *(PCP 018-2)* – Corn river.

Aug 95. (10"m-lp/m-cd) *<(PCP 023-1/-2)>* **GET STRAIGHT FOR THE LAST SUPPER** [ ] [ ]
– Phoenix hotel / Five dollar priest / Blitzkreig bop / Ballad of the thin / Pillbilly / Milking stool blues / T.B. sheets / The edge / Phoenix hotel pt.1.

Konkurrent Fort Apache-MCA

Mar 98. (cd) *(K 182CD) <11425>* **CINEMA!** [ ] [ ] Sep96
– Stranger's skin / Rubber connection / Black cat moan / Suicide girl / Black eyed girl / Dog on fire / Skull poppin', skin tastin', love . . . / Shakin' it loose / Cinema! / Toss my head / Mr. Heat / Dancin' with a fever / Drug owl.

Sympathy F Sympathy F

Apr 98. (10"m-lp/m-cd) *<(SFTRI 531/+CD)>* **I'M GONNA STOMP MR. HARRY LEE** [ ] [ ]
– Pin-up cowboy / Hate you baby / Pocket fulla fish (spoken word) / Lakeside story / Blackish man / Don't turn blue / Speedball petite.

SPEEDWAY BLVD.

Formed: USA . . . 1979 by ROY HERRING, GREGG HOFFMAN, JORDAN RUDES, DENNIS FELDMAN and GLENN DOVE. Another band spiritually akin to the likes of MOTHER'S FINEST, this multi-racial heavy rock outfit primed their musical engine with a variety of exotic styles, as evidenced on their debut 'Epic' album, 'SPEEDWAY BOULEVARD' (1980).

Unfortunately, SPEEDWAY BOULEVARD skidded to a halt before they'd really had a chance to trailblaze their way through the rock scene.

Album rating: SPEEDWAY BLVD. (*5)

ROY HERRING – vocals, piano / **GREGG HOFFMAN** – guitar, vocals / **JORDAN RUDES** – keyboards / **DENNIS FELDMAN** – bass, vocals / **GLENN DOVE** – drums

not iss. Epic

1980. (7") *<50879>* **SPEEDWAY BLVD. / (THINK I BETTER) HOLD ON** [-] [ ]

1980. (lp) *<NJE 36533>* **SPEEDWAY BOULEVARD** [-] [ ]
– Speedway blvd. / Chinatown / (Think I better) Hold on / Dog in the distance / Out of the fire / Telephoto lens / Prisoner of time / Money, money / (Call my name) Rock magic / A boulevard nite.

1980. (7") *<50936>* **SPEEDWAY BLVD. / OUT OF THE FIRE** [-] [ ]

— after their brief foray as a band, FELDMAN joined BALANCE, subsequently joining the backing band of MICHAEL BOLTON

SPELL

Formed: Denver, Colorado, USA ... 1991 by GARRETT SHAVLIK, CHANIN FLOYD and TIM BECKMAN. All veterans of the American punk/hardcore scene (especially SHAVLIK, a former member of early 'Sub Pop' act The FLUID and friend of the late KURT COBAIN), the trio got together after a drunken, impromptu jam session and set about creating a suitably intense, post-grunge sound. With such an impressive track record, the band were able to bypass the independent sector and secure a deal with 'Island Red', no mean feat. A debut single, 'SUPERSTAR', preceded the 'MISSISSIPPI' album, released in early '95 and drawing comparisons with the likes of The AFGHAN WHIGS, CHANIN's vocal adding a feminine slant reminiscent of The BREEDERS. • **Note:** Not to be confused with the 'Mute' band of the same name who issued the single, 'BIG RED BALLOON'.

Album rating: MISSISSIPPI (*4)

TIM BECKMAN – guitar, vocals (ex-ROPE) / **CHANIN FLOYD** – bass, vocals (ex-57 LESBIANS) / **GARRETT SHAVLIK** – drums, vocals (ex-FLUID)

Island Red Island Red

Mar 95. (7") *(IR 105)* **SUPERSTAR. / HAZEL MOTES** [ ] [ ]
(cd-s+=) *(CIRD 105)* – Best friend (demo). *(7" w/free 7")*

Apr 95. (cd/c/lp) *(CIRD/IRCT/IRLP 1003)* **MISSISSIPPI** [ ] [ ]
– Dixie / Seems to me / Superstar / More / Straight to Hell / 4-B / Hazel motes / Safe / Mom / Bring the old man.

— disbanded after above

SPELLBOUND

Formed: Uppsala, Sweden ... 1984 by brothers ALF and OLA STRANDBERG, who recruited HANS FROBERG, J.J. MARSH and THOMPSON. Signed to the 'Sonet' label after contributing a track to their 'Swedish Metal' compilation, SPELLBOUND issued a debut set, 'BREAKING THE SPELL' in 1984. Hard, melodic Euro-rock, the album was popular in the group's native Sweden, import copies leading to some interest in the UK. After a second set, 'ROCKIN' RECKLESS' (1986), the group parted company with 'Sonet' the following year. Although they cut a further series of tracks for another label, these remained unreleased and the band eventually folded in 1989 when HASSE formed SOLID BLUE.

Album rating: BREAKING THE SPELL (*5) / ROCKIN' RECKLESS (*4)

HANS FROBERG – vocals, guitar / **J.J. MARSH** – guitar, vocals / **ALF STRANDBERG** – guitar, keyboards, vocals / **THOMPSON** – bass, vocals / **OLA STRANDBERG** – drums, percussion

Sonet not iss.

1984. (lp) *(SMLP 2)* **BREAKING THE SPELL** [ ] [-]
– Seducer / Love taker / Burning love / Crack up the sky / Hooked on metal / Raise the roof / Passion kills / Loud and dirty / Piece of my heart / Rock the nation. *(re-iss. Jul87; SNTF 934) (cd-iss. 1995; SMCD 2/527 524-2)*

May 86. (7") *(SON 2294)* **MY KINDA GIRL. / GONE ROCKIN'** [ ] [-]

Jun 86. (lp) *(SNTF 952)* **ROCKIN' RECKLESS** [ ] [-]
– Rockin' reckless / My kinda girl / Love on the run / Drinking alone / Shot of love / Streetprowler / Dying for your touch / Mistreated heart / Hear it up / Sing you goodbye. *(cd-iss. 1995; 952/527 526-2)*

Sep 86. (7") *(SON 2306)* **ROCKIN' RECKLESS. / ON THE PROWL** [ ] [-]

— dropped by the label in '87, they subsequently disbanded when HASSE formed SOLID BLUE

Jon SPENCER BLUES EXPLOSION

Formed: New York City, New York, USA ... 1991 by former PUSSY GALORE namesake, JON SPENCER and ex-HONEYMOON KILLERS, JUDAH BAUER and RUSSELL SIMINS. Hardly blues in the conventional sense, SPENCER rather puts the emphasis on EXPLOSION, grinding out a bass-less groove-noise and howling out lip-curled soundbites. It was a formula that had its roots in the primal sludge of PUSSY GALORE and the first instalment in the JSBX saga carried on where that band left off, kind of. Released by 'Caroline' in the States and Virgin subsidiary, 'Hut', in Britain, the eponymous STEVE ALBINI-produced album surfaced in Spring '92, showcasing SPENCER's newly adopted blues drawl and revelling in defiantly dishevelled guitar abuse. Although some critics argued that SPENCER was all mouth and no trousers, so to speak, the man answered in strutting style on the likes of 'BELLBOTTOMS', one of the highlights from 1994's acclaimed 'ORANGE' album; that record, together with its 1993 predecessor, 'EXTRA WIDTH' (both released on 'Matador') really set out the band's manifesto of fractured 70's groove-funk, semi-detached melodies, hand claps, sweat dripping testimonial and sheer distorted noise. Sure, it might've been a style over substance white trash/noise interpretation of delta blues in the loosest sense but SPENCER's tongue was planted firmly in his cheek and following MTV exposure and a tour with The BEASTIE BOYS, JSBX were suddenly big news. A subsequent remix EP roped in such luminaries as BECK and if a move to 'Mute' seemed a little strange, there was no denying the blistering potential of 'NOW I GOT WORRY' (1996). From the delirious swagger of '2KINDSA LOVE' (surely a companion piece, if there ever was one, to MUDHONEY's 'Touch Me I'm Sick') to the disembodied static of Dub Narcotic's 'FUCK SHIT UP', SPENCER sounded as if he'd finally cut that deal down at the crossroads. Still, the man's recorded work only tells half the story; if you really want a baptism by BLUES EXPLOSION fire then you'll have to catch them live. 1998's STEVE ALBINI-produced set, 'ACME', was another adrenalin-fuelled taste of rock'n'roll blues although experimental sidesteps were always on show. Of late, an 'ACME +' remix LP has surfaced while his collaboration with the DUB NARCOTIC SOUND SYSTEM, 'SIDEWAYS SOUL', has also been issued. • **Songwriters:** SPENCER/ group except; LOVIN' UP A STORM (Willie Dixon)

Album rating: A REVERSE WILLIE HORTON (aka JON SPENCER BLUES EXPLOSION) (*5) / CRYPT-STYLE collection (*5) / EXTRA WIDTH (*6) / ORANGE (*7) / MO' WIDTH collection (*5) / NOW I GOT WORRY (*7) / ACME (*7) / ACME PLUS out-takes (*5) /

JON SPENCER – vocals, guitar / **JUDAH BAUER** – guitar / **RUSSELL SIMINS** – drums

not iss. In The Red

Oct 91. (7") *<ITR 007>* **SHIRT JAC. / LATCH-ON** [-] [ ]

Jan 92. (7") *<ITR 011>* **SON OF SAM. / BENT** [-] [ ]

Mar 92. (7") *<ITR 019>* **TRAIN NO.3. / TRAIN NO.1** [-] [ ]

not iss. Public Popcam

Feb 92. (lp) *<PORK 1>* **A REVERSE WILLIE HORTON** [-] [ ]
– Write a song / IEV / Exploder / Rachel / Chicken walk / White tail / '78 style / Changed / What to do / Eye to eye / Eliza Jane / History of sex / Come back / Support-a-man / Maynard Ave. / Feeling of love / Vacuum of loneliness / Intro A / Biological / Water man. *<cd-iss. Apr92 as 'BLUES EXPLOSION' on 'Caroline'; CAROLCD 1719> (UK-iss.Dec93 on 'Hut' cd/lp; HUT CD/LP 3) (cd re-iss. Jun97 & Sep98 on 'Caroline'; same as US)*

not iss. Clawfist

Jun 92. (7") *<13>* **HISTORY OF SEX. / WRITE A SONG / SMOKE CIGARETTES** [-] [-] mail-o

not iss. Sub Pop

Nov 92. (7"green) *<SP 180>* **BIG YULE LOG BOOGIE. / MY CHRISTMAS WISH** [-] [ ]

Matador Matador

Aug 93. (cd/c/lp; as BLUES EXPLOSION) *<(OLE 052-2/-4/-1)>* **EXTRA WIDTH** [ ] [ ] Nov93
– Afro / History of lies / Black slider / Soul letter / Soul typecast / Pant leg / Hey mom / Big road / Train No.2 / Inside the world of the blues explosion / The world of sex.

Feb 94. (7",7"white; as BLUES EXPLOSION) *<(OLE 077-7)>* **AFRO. / RELAX-HER** [ ] [ ] Jul93

Oct 94. (cd/c/lp) *<(OLE 105-2/-4/-1)>* **ORANGE** [ ] [ ]
– Bellbottoms / Ditch / Dang / Very rare / Sweat / Cowboy / Orange / Brenda / Dissect / Blues x men / Full grown / Flavor / Greyhound.

Feb 95. (7"white) *(OLE 111-7)* **BELLBOTTOMS. / MISS ELAINE** [ ] [-]
(12") *(OLE 111-1)* – ('A'remix) / Flavor 1 / Flavor 2.
(cd-s+=) *(OLE 111-2)* – Soul typecast / Greyhound (part 1 & 2).
(the REMIXES ep of above iss.May95)

Mute Matador – Capitol

Sep 96. (cd/c/lp) *(cd/c+/stumm 132) <OLE 193 – 53553>* **NOW I GOT WORRY** [50] [ ]
– Skunk / Identify / Wail / Fuck shit up / 2Kindsa love / Love all of me / Chicken dog / Rocketship / Dynamite lover / Hot shot / Can't stop / Firefly child / Eyeballin / R.L. got soul / Get over here / Sticky. *(re-iss. May97; same)*

Oct 96. (7") *(MUTE 202)* **2 KINDSA LOVE. / LET'S SMERF** [ ] [ ]
(cd-s) *(CDMUTE 202)* – ('A'side) / Fish sauce / Cool Vee.

Apr 97. (7"m) *(MUTE 204)* **WAIL. / JUDAH LOVE THEME / RADIO SPOT** [66] [ ]
(7"m) *(LMUTE 204)* – ('A'-Mario C remix) / Afro (live) / Flavor (live).
(cd-s) *(CDMUTE 204)* – ('A'video mix) / Yellow eyes / Buscemi / Turn up Greene.

Oct 98. (cd/lp) *(CD+/STUMM 154) <OLE 322 – 95566>* **ACME** [72] [ ]
– Calvin / Magical colours / Do you wanna get heavy? / High gear / Talk about the blues / I wanna make it all right / Lovin' machine / Bernie / Blue green Olga / Give me a chance / Desperate / Torture / Attack.

Nov 98. (7"yellow) *(MUTE 222)* **MAGICAL COLOURS. / CONFUSED** [ ] [-]
(cd-s) *(CDMUTE 222)* – ('A'side) / Bacon / Get down lover.

Mar 99. (7"orange) *(MUTE 226)* **TALK ABOUT THE BLUES. / WAIT A MINUTE (Moby mix)** [ ] [-]
(12") *(12MUTE 226)* – ('A'side) / Lovin' machine (Automator mix) / Calvin (zebra ranch) / ('A'-Saints and sinners remix).
(cd-s+=) *(CDMUTE 226)* – ('A'-video).

Jun 99. (7") *(SMALL 004)* **NEW YEAR (DESTROYER). / other track by Barry Adamson** [ ] [-]
(above issued on 'Slut Smalls')

Aug 99. (7") *(MUTE 239)* **HEAVY. / GIVE YA SOME HELL** [ ] [ ]
(12") *(12MUTE 239)* – ('A'side) / 2 kindsa love (Duck rock remix) / Attack

(Detroit) / Do you wanna get heavy? (Duck rock hip'n'bass remix).
(cd-s) *(CDMUTE 239)* – ('A'side) / 2 kindsa love / Blues power / Attack (Detroit).

Sep 99. (cd/d-lp) *(CD+/STUMM 184)* **ACME PLUS** (out-takes)
– Wait a minute / Get down lover / Confused / Magical colors (31 flavors) / Not yet / Get old / Bacon / Blue green / Olga (remix) / Heavy (remix) / Lap dance / Right place, wrong time / Leave me alone so I can rock again / Soul trance / Electricity / New year / Chowder / TATB (for the saints and sinners mix) / Hell / I wanna make it alright (Zebra ranch).

– compilations, others, etc. –

Mar 94. (cd/lp) *Crypt; (EFA 11502-2/-1) <29>* **CRYPT-STYLE** (rec.1991 NYC) Apr92
– Lovin' up a storm / Support a man / White tail / Maynard Ave. / '78 style / Chicken walk / Mo' chicken – Let's get funky / Watermain / Like a hawk / Big headed baby / Write a song / Eye to eye / Feeling of love / Kill a man / Rachel / History of sex / Comeback / The vacuum of loneliness.

Nov 96. (7") *In The Red; <(ITR 42)>* **GET WITH IT. / DOWN LOW**

Feb 97. (lp/cd) *Au Go Go; <(ANDA 166/+CD)>* **MO' WIDTH** Jan95
– Afro / Out of luck / Cherry lime / Rob K / Ole man trouble / Wet cat blues / Johnson / There stands the glass / Lion cut / Beat of the traps / Memphis soul typecast.

Oct 97. (7") *Au Go Go; <(ANDA 231)>* **ROCKETSHIP. / CHOCOLATE JOE** – – Austra
(cd-s) *<(ANDA 231CD)>* – ('A'side) / Down low / Dynamite lover / Flavor / Full grown.

SPIDER

Formed: Merseyside, England . . . 1976 by the brothers BRIAN and ROB E. BURROWS, who subsequently recruited SNIFFA and COL HARKNESS. After cutting their teeth on the local live scene, SPIDER followed the bright lights to London, subsequently issuing a series of independently released singles which brought widespread comparisons with boogie-meisters STATUS QUO. Having built up a solid reputation, they were subsequently picked up by 'R.C.A.', making their major label debut with the 'ROCK'N'ROLL GYPSIES' (1982) album. Although the record scraped into the Top 75, it failed to cross over into the wider rock arena and SPIDER were promptly dropped from 'R.C.A.'s roster. Rescued by 'A&M', the group were given free rein to write even more songs about "rock'n'roll" on the 'ROUGH JUSTICE' (1984) set. Again, the record failed to sell and SPIDER found themselves minus a contract once more. With STU HARWOOD subsequently replacing the curiously named SNIFFA, SPIDER crawled on, releasing an independently released third set, 'RAISE THE BANNER' (1986) before calling it a day.

Album rating: ROCK'N'ROLL GYPSIES (*5) / ROUGH JUSTICE (*5) / RAISE THE BANNER (FOR ROCK'N'ROLL) (*4)

BRIAN BURROWS – vocals, bass / **SNIFFA** – guitar / **COL HARKNESS** – guitar, vocals / **ROB E. BURROWS** – drums

Alien not iss.

Jul 80. (7") *(ALIEN 14)* **CHILDREN OF THE NIGHT. / DOWN 'N' OUT** –

Oct 80. (7") *(ALIEN 16)* **COLLEGE LUV. / BORN TO BE WILD** –

City not iss.

Aug 81. (7") *(NIK 7)* **ALL THE TIME. / FEEL LIKE A MAN** –

Creole not iss.

Mar 82. (7") *(CR 30)* **TALKIN' 'BOUT ROCK'N'ROLL. / 'TIL I'M CERTAIN** –

R.C.A. not iss.

Aug 82. (d7") *(RCA 268)* **ROCK'N'ROLL WILL FOREVER LAST. / DID YA LIKE IT BABY? // AMAZING GRACE MEDLEY (part 1). / (part 2)** –

Oct 82. (lp/c) *(RCA LP/K 3101)* **ROCK'N'ROLL GYPSIES** 75 –
– A.W.O.L. / Talkin' 'bout rock'n'roll / Part of the legend / Did ya like it baby? / Them that start the fighting (don't fight) / What you're doing to me / Lady (I'm dyin' for you) / 'Til I'm certain / Rock'n'roll forever will last / All the time.

Nov 82. (7") *(RCA 294)* **TALKIN' 'BOUT ROCK'N'ROLL. / DOWN 'N' OUT** –

Feb 83. (7") *(RCA 313)* **WHY D'YA LIE TO ME. / FOOTLOOSE** 65 –
(12"+=) *(RCAT 313)* – 9 to 5.

A&M not iss.

Mar 84. (7"/7"sha-pic-d) *(AM/+P 180)* **HERE WE GO ROCK'N'ROLL. / DEATH ROW** 57 –
(12"+=) *(AMX 180)* – I just wanna make love to you.

Apr 84. (lp) *(AMLX 68563)* **ROUGH JUSTICE** 96 –
– Here we go rock'n'roll / Morning after the night before / Rock'n'roll gypsies / Martyred (for what I love) / Time to go now / Death row / The minstrel / You make me offers (I can't refuse) / Midsummer morning.

Jul 84. (7") *(AM 204)* **BREAKAWAY. / MORNING AFTER THE NIGHT BEFORE** –
(12"+=) *(AMX 204)* – Rock'n'roll gypsy.

— **STU HARWOOD** – guitar; repl. SNIFFA

P.R.T. not iss.

Mar 86. (7") *(7P 344)* **GIMME GIMME IT ALL. / ROCK TONIGHT** –
(ext.12"+=) *(12P 344)* – Did ya like it baby.
(d7"+=) *(7PX 344)* – (live recording from Kerrang corner).

1986. (lp) *(N 6556)* **RAISE THE BANNER (FOR ROCK'N'ROLL)** –
– Raise the banner (for rock'n'roll) / Gimme gimme it all / I'm not the only one / Need to know 'bout you / When you hear that song / 'Bad boys / Mind, heart, body'n'soul / Rock tonite / Games in the park / So sorry.

— folded after above, BRIAN becoming a cartoonist and record sleeve designer

SPIDER

Formed: New York, USA . . . 1978 by South Africans AMANDA BLUE, KEITH LENTIN and ANTON FIG, who had previously been in the group HAMMAK. With HOLLY KNIGHT and JIMMY LOWELL completing the line-up, the group signed to the 'Dreamland' label with the help of ACE FREHLEY (FIG having played on the KISS guitarist's 1978 debut solo set). Weaving a silky pop-rock web, SPIDER crept into the nether regions of the US Top 40 in 1980 with their debut single, 'NEW ROMANCE'. An eponymous album followed later that year, SPIDER scoring a second minor (US) hit with the 'EVERYTHING IS ALRIGHT' single. A follow-up album, 'BETWEEN THE LINES' (1981), spawned a further hit in 'IT DIDN'T TAKE LONG', although the band subsequently changed their name to SHANGHAI.

Album rating: SPIDER (*5) / BETWEEN THE LINES (*5)

AMANDA BLUE – vocals / **KEITH LENTIN** – guitar / **ANTON FIG** – drums / **HOLLY KNIGHT** – keyboards / **JIMMY LOWELL** – bass (ex-RIFF RAFF)

R.S.O. Dreamland

Jun 80. (7") *(2090 441) <100>* **NEW ROMANCE (IT'S A MYSTERY). / CROSSFIRE** 39 Apr80

Aug 80. (lp) *(2394 260) <5000>* **SPIDER** May80
– New romance (it's a mystery) / Burning love / Shady lady / Everything is alright / Crossfire / Little darlin' / Brotherly love / What's going on / Don't waste your time / Zero.

Dreamland Dreamland

Aug 80. (7") *(DSLP 4) <103>* **EVERYTHING IS ALRIGHT. / SHADY LADY** 86 Jul80

Oct 80. (7") *<105>* **LITTLE DARLIN'. /** –

May 81. (7") *<111>* **IT DIDN'T TAKE LONG. / I LOVE** – 43

May 81. (7") *(DSLP 11)* **BETTER BE GOOD TO ME. / I LOVE** –

Jun 81. (lp) *(2394 298) <5007>* **BETWEEN THE LINES**
– Change / I think I like it / Between the lines / It didn't take long / Going by / Better be good to me / Can't live this way anymore / Faces are changing / Go and run / I love.

— changed their name to SHANGHAI, due to UK band of the same name. KNIGHT subsequently joined DEVICE, while FIG became a noted session man.

SPIDERS (see under ⇒ COOPER, Alice)

SPINAL TAP

Formed: USA . . . late 70's as a razor sharp satire on the inherent ridiculousness of the metal scene by comedy writer MICHAEL McKEAN and comedic actors NIGEL TUFNELL and DEREK SMALLS. Initially activated for a TV sketch, the idea was transformed into a celebrated full length feature film documenting the trials and tribulations of life as a struggling British metal band undertaking a ruinous US tour. Stonehenge stage props, cucumbers down trousers, amps that went up to 11 (!), drummers dying in "bizarre gardening accidents" – in fact every metal cliche in the book (and some that weren't) was exploited in such hilariously deadpan style that many moviegoers were convinced they were watching a real-life rockumentary. Entitled 'This Spinal Tap', the 1984 film was accompanied by a soundtrack of the same name boasting such unforgettable 'TAP classics as 'BIG BOTTOM', '(LISTEN TO THE) FLOWER PEOPLE' and 'SEX FARM'. Although the film was a relative failure at the time, SPINAL TAP have since become a rock'n'roll institution and a comeback set was inevitable. Featuring such luminaries as JEFF BECK, SLASH and CHER, 'BREAK LIKE THE WIND' (1992) brought the band belated chart success, scraping into the lower regions of the UK and US charts. Although there wasn't a movie sequel to complement the album, fans could relive those spandex-clad 80's days with such wonderfully unreconstructed fare as 'BITCH SCHOOL', incredibly a UK Top 40 hit. Essential viewing for anyone with delusions of metal grandeur.

Album rating: THIS IS SPINAL TAP film (*8) / BREAK LIKE THE WIND (*5)

DAVID ST. HUBBINS (MICHAEL McKEAN) – vocals / **NIGEL TUFNELL** (CHRISTOPHER GUEST) – lead guitar / **DEREK SMALLS** (HARRY SHEARER) – bass / + er . . . drummers including RIC PARNELL

Polydor Polydor

Sep 84. (lp/c) *<(817 846-1/-4)>* **THIS IS SPINAL TAP** (soundtrack) – Apr84
– Hell hole / Tonight I'm gonna rock you tonight / Heavy duty / Rock and roll creation / America / Cups and cakes / Big bottom / Sex farm / Stonehenge / Gimme some money / (Listen to the) Flower people. *(UK-iss.Mar89 on 'Priority' lp/c; LUS LP/MC 2) (cd-iss. Aug90; 817 846-2)*

— the trio added guests, JEFF BECK, SLASH, DWEEZIL ZAPPA, JOE SATRIANI, STEVE LUKATHER + CHER

M.C.A. M.C.A.

Mar 92. (7"/c-s) *(MCS/+C 1624)* **BITCH SCHOOL. / SPRINGTIME** 35
(12"pic-d+=/cd-s+=) *(MCS TP/D 1624)* –

Mar 92. (lp/c/cd) *<(MCA/+C/D 10514)>* **BREAK LIKE THE WIND** 51 61
– Bitch school / The majesty of rock / Diva fever / Just begin again / Cash on delivery / The sun never sweats / Rainy day sun / Break like the wind / Stinkin' up the great outdoors / Springtime / Clam caravan / Christmas with the Devil / All the way home.

Apr 92. (7"/c-s) *(MCS/+C 1629)* **THE MAJESTY OF ROCK. / STINKIN' UP THE GREAT OUTDOORS** 61
(cd-s+=) *(MCSTD 1629)* – exclusive "talk with Tap" part 3.

— like their drummers, all seemed to have disappeared

SPINESHANK

Formed: Los Angeles, California, USA . . . late 1996 out of the ashes of BASIC ENIGMA, by youthful lads JONNY SANTOS, Armenian-born MIKE SARKISYAN, ROB GARCIA and TOM DECKER. Friends of KORN, ORGY, COAL CHAMBER and SYSTEM OF A DOWN, they signed to stalwart metal label, 'Roadrunner'. Influenced by labelmates, FEAR FACTORY, SPINESHANK bulldozed George Harrison's 'WHILE MY GUITAR GENTLY WEEPS' on their debut album, 'STRICTLY DIESEL' (1998).

Album rating: STRICTLY DIESEL (*6) / THE HEIGHT OF CALLOUSNESS (*5)

JONNY SANTOS – vocals / **MIKE SARKISYAN** – guitar / **ROB GARCIA** – bass / **TOM DECKER** – drums

Roadrunner Roadrunner

Sep 98. (cd) <*(RR 8725-2)*> **STRICTLY DIESEL** □ □
– Intake / Stovebolt / Shinebox / Where we fall / Detatched / Slipper / 40 below / Strictly diesel / Grey / 28 / While my guitar gently weeps / If it breathes / Mend / Stain.

Oct 00. (cd) <*(RR 8563-2)*> **THE HEIGHT OF CALLOUSNESS** □ □
– Asthmatic / The height of callousness / Synthetic / New disease / (Can't be) Fixed / Cyanide 2600 / Play God / Malnutrition / Seamless / Negative space / Transparent.

SPIRIT CARAVAN (see under ⇒ OBSESSED)

SPIRITUAL BEGGARS

Formed: Halmstad, Sweden . . . 1992 by vocalist/bassist SPICE (HAIRY, that is!), ex-CARCASS guitar ace MIKE AMOTT and drummer LUDWIG WITT. Stoner-rock fusing cosmic psych with hard SABBATH/PURPLE rock, their eponymous album appeared in '94, before the band signed to UK metal imprint, 'Music For Nations'. A second and third set, 'ANOTHER WAY TO SHINE' (1996) and 'MANTRA III' (1998) were well-received in Kerrang! circles. Around the same period, AMOTT was also involved with another project, ARCH ENEMY and could be heard on CANDLEMASS's 1998 set.

Album rating: SPIRITUAL BEGGARS mini (*5) / ANOTHER WAY TO SHINE (*5) MANTRA III (*7) / AD ASTRA (*8)

SPICE – vocals, bass / **MIKE AMOTT** – guitar (ex-CARCASS) / **LUDWIG WITT** – drums (ex-FIREBIRD)

Wrong Again not iss.

1994. (m-cd) *(WAR 002CD)* **SPIRITUAL BEGGARS** □ [-]
– Yearly dying / Pelekas / The space inbetween / If this is all / Under silence / Magnificent obsession. *(UK-iss.Apr96; same)*

Music For Nations Music For Nations

Mar 96. (cd) *(CDMFN 198)* **ANOTHER WAY TO SHINE** □ [-]
– Magic spell / Blind mountain / Misty valley / Picking from the box / Nowhere to go / Entering into peace / Sour stains / Another way to shine / Past the sound of whispers.

—— added **PER WILBERG** – keyboards / and on tour **STEFAN ISEBRING** – percussion

Feb 98. (cd) *(CDMFN 231)* **MANTRA III** □ [-]
– Homage to the betrayed / Monster astronauts / Euphoria / Broken morning / Lack of prozac / Superbossanova / Bad karma / Send me a smile / Cosmic romance / Inside charmer / Sad queen boogie / Mushroom tea girl.

Apr 00. (cd/lp) *(CD+/MFN 252)* <*61008*> **AD ASTRA** □ □ Jul00
– Left brain ambassadors / Wonderful world / Sedated / Angel of betrayal / Blessed / Per aspera ad astra / Save your soul / Until the morning / Escaping the fools / Of dark rivers / The goddess / Mantra.

SPLIT BEAVER

Formed: Wolverhampton, England . . . 1981 by DARREL WHITEHOUSE, MIKE HOPPER, ALAN REES and MICK DUNN. As well as possibly offending lovers of small furry rodents everywhere, SPLIT BEAVER subjected metal fans to a whole album's worth of fannying around. Understandably titled 'WHEN HELL WON'T HAVE YOU' (1982), the record fumbled its way through a limp set of trad heavy rock. Clearly, every week was a bad week for SPLIT BEAVER.

Album rating: WHEN HELL WON'T HAVE YOU (*2)

DARREL WHITEHOUSE – vocals / **MIKE HOPPER** – guitar / **ALAN REES** – bass / **MICK DUNN** – drums

Heavy Metal not iss.

Sep 81. (7") *(HEAVY 7)* **SAVAGE. / HOUND OF HELL** □ [-]

Jun 82. (lp) *(HMRLP 3)* **WHEN HELL WON'T HAVE YOU** □ [-]
– Savage / Going straight / Gimme head / Cruisin' / Levington gardens / Hounds of hell / Likewise / Living in and out / Get out, stay out / The baliff.

—— split the beaver for the last time

SPONGE

Formed: Detroit, Michigan, USA . . . 1994 out of the ashes of LOUDHOUSE, by VINNIE DOMBROWSKI, MIKE CROSS, TIM CROSS, JOEY MAZZOLA and CHARLIE GROVER (the latter being replaced by JIMMY PALUZZI). Following the release of one independent single, 'THE CRASH', SPONGE were soaked up by 'Columbia' as the next great white hope of Grunge. A couple of singles, 'MOLLY (SIXTEEN CANDLES)' and 'PLOWED', along with a debut album, 'ROTTING PINATA' (1995), revealed the band to be firmly in the epic melodic-grunge mould of PEARL JAM, vocalist DOMBROWSKI a throaty dead ringer for EDDIE VEDDER. The album (which made the Top 60 in the States) also had its fair share of 80's-esque guitar solos, no doubt endearing them to the more trad elements of the American metal fraternity (although there were moments of light and shade such as 'FIELDS', what The POLICE might've sounded like had they grown up in L.A.). Accompanying single, 'PLOWED', even scraped into the UK Top 75 although no further success in the British market would be forthcoming. It was a different story in America of course, where their sales approached the half million mark, a follow-up album, 'WAX ECSTATIC' also making the Top 60. Yet sales weren't good enough to please 'Columbia' who duly dropped SPONGE into the indie wilderness. Signing to the 'Beyond' label, the band licked their wounds and came up with 'NEW POP SUNDAY' (1999), an unashamed homage to classic hard rock which ironically found them sounding more comfortable with themselves than ever.

Album rating: ROTTING PINATA (*6) / WAX ECSTATIC (*6) / NEW POP SUNDAY (*6)

VINNIE DOMBROWSKI – vocals / **MIKE CROSS** (b. RYGIEL) – guitar / **TIM CROSS** (b. RYGIEL) – bass / **JOE MAZZOLA** – guitar / **JIMMY PALUZZI** – drums, vocals; repl. CHARLIE GROVER

Suburban Suburban

Feb 95. (12") *(SUBBASE 48)* **THE CRASH. / SHABBUTZ** □ □

Columbia Work

Jul 95. (c-s,cd-s) <*77976*> **MOLLY (SIXTEEN CANDLES) / I HATE MYSELF** [-] [55]

Aug 95. (7") *(662316-7)* **PLOWED. / WELCOME HOME** [74] [-]
(cd-s+=) *(662316-2)* – Severed hearty mums.

Sep 95. (cd/c) *(476982-2/-4)* <*57800*> **ROTTING PINATA** □ [58] Feb95
– Pennywheels / Rotting pinata / Giants / Neenah Menasha / Miles / Plowed / Drownin' / Molly / Fields / Rainin. *(cd+=)* – Candy corn.

Oct 95. (7"/c-s) *(662547-7/-4)* **MOLLY (SIXTEEN CANDLES) / COWBOY EYES** □ [-]
(cd-s+=) *(662547-2)* – ('A'live) / Seventeen.

Columbia Columbia

Aug 96. (cd/c/lp) *(484186-2/-4/-1)* <*67578*> **WAX ECSTATIC** □ [60] Jun96
– My putty / Got to be a bore / Wax ecstatic (to sell Angelina) / Drag queen of Memphis / I am Anastasia / Silence is their drug / Have you seen Mary / My baby said / Death of a drag queen / Velveteen.

not iss. Beyond

Apr 99. (cd) <*78038*> **NEW POP SUNDAY** [-] □
– My lacklustre love / Polyanna / Live here without you / 1,000 times / All American world / Radio prayer line / New pop Sunday / Planet girls / When you're on fire baby, roll / Disconnected / Lucky.

SPREAD EAGLE

Formed: New York, USA . . . late 80's by RAY WEST, PAUL DiBARTOLO, ROB DeLUCA and TOMMI GALLO. A cross between, say, JUNKYARD and CIRCUS OF POWER, SPREAD EAGLE traded in crotch-level blooze-metal with an unashamed line in trad sexism which didn't sit well with more enlightened critics. Signed to 'M.C.A.', the group delivered their eponymous debut album in Spring 1990, which, sentiments of 'BACK ON THE BITCH' aside, packed a convincing enough punch to stake its claim among the hordes of gutter-rock wannabes. A follow-up set, 'OPEN TO THE PUBLIC' (1993) mined a less controversial lyrical vein although no one took much notice.

Album rating: SPREAD EAGLE (*7) / OPEN TO THE PUBLIC (*5)

RAY WEST – vocals / **PAUL DiBARTOLO** – guitar / **ROB DeLUCA** – bass / **TOMMI GALLO** – drums

M.C.A. M.C.A.

May 90. (cd/c/lp) *(DMCG/MCGC/MCG 6092)* <*6383*> **SPREAD EAGLE** □ □
– Broken city / Back on the bitch / Switchblade serenade / Hot sex / Suzy suicide / Dead of winter / Scratch like a cat / Thru these eyes / Spread eagle / 42nd Street / Shotgun kiss.

—— session men helped out GALLO, who was the first to leave the band

1993. (cd/c) **OPEN TO THE PUBLIC** [-] □
– Devil's road / Revolution maker / Shine / If I can't have you . . . / Fade away / Preacher man / King of the dogs / Rhythm machine / High horses / This is my world / Faith.

SPY

Formed: USA . . . 1979 by DAVID NELSON, JOHN VISLOCKY, DAVE LE BOLT, DANNY SEIDENBERG, MICHAEL VISCEGLIA and ROB GOLDMAN. Signed to 'C.B.S.' subsidiary, 'Kirshner' (home of KANSAS), SPY released a sole eponymous album in 1980. Revealing themselves to be talented purveyors of grandiose symphonic rock, SPY even employed a violinist in their ranks. Despite critical approval, however, SPY failed to uncover the secret of chart success and promptly faded from view.

Album rating: SPY (*5)

JOHN VISLOCKY – vocals / **DAVID NELSON** – guitar, vocals / **DAVE LE BOLT** – keyboards / **MICHAEL VISCEGLIA** – bass / **DANNY SEIDENBERG** – violin, viola, keyboards / **ROB GOLDMAN** – drums not iss. Kirshner

1980. (lp) <*NJZ 36378*> **SPY** [-] [ ]
– Crimson queen / Easy street / The best we can do / Can't complain / Ruby twilight / Love's there / Feelin' shining through / Anytime, anyplace / When I find love.

—— folded after the failure of above, most went into session work

SPYS

Formed: New York, USA . . . 1981 by former FOREIGNER members AL GREENWOOD and ED GAGLIARDI. They recruited JOHN BLANCO, JOHN DIGAUDIO and BILLY MILNE and subsequently signed to 'E.M.I'. Yet more American musical espionage, SPYS launched their AOR offensive with an eponymous album in summer '82. Their hard-edged, keyboard-dominated approach persuaded sufficient civilians to part with their cash that SPYS earned themselves a chart placing in the lower regions of the US Top 100. A follow-up set, 'BEHIND ENEMY LINES' was released in 1983 amid contractual hassles and SPYS subsequently went to ground.

Album rating: SPYS (*5) / BEHIND ENEMY LINES (*4)

JOHN BLANCO – vocals / **AL GREENWOOD** – keyboards (ex-FOREIGNER) / **JOHN DIGAUDIO** – guitar / **BILLY MILNE** – drums

not iss. EMI America

Aug 82. (7") <*8124*> **DON'T RUN MY LIFE. /** [-] [82]
Aug 82. (lp) <*ST 17073*> **SPYS** [-] [ ]
– Don't run my life / She can't wait / Ice age / Danger / Over her / Desiree / Don't say goodbye / Into the night / Hold on (when you feel you're falling) / No harm done.
Sep 83. (lp) <*ST 17098*> **BETWEEN ENEMY LINES** [-] [ ]
– Rescue me / Midnight fantasy / Behind enemy lines / Sheep don't talk back / Reaction / Heartache / Race against time / Younger days / Can't stop us now.

—— folded soon after above, GREENWOOD joined JOE LYNN TURNER

Billy SQUIER

Born: 12 May'50, Wellesley Hills, Massachusetts, USA. Although he spent some time in New York in the late 60's, SQUIER returned to Boston in the early 70's to join power-pop outfit, The SIDEWINDERS. A shortlived affair, the band split after a sole LENNY KAYE-produced album, SQUIER subsequently forming PIPER, who released two albums for A&M ('PIPER' and 'CAN'T WAIT') before disbanding. Offered a solo deal by 'Capitol' in 1979, SQUIER debuted with the impressive 'TALE OF THE TAPE' (1980), a hard rocking set undercut with supple rhythms ('BIG BEAT' was a favourite among hip hop sample fiends) and overlaid with power-pop melodies. He finally hit the big time the following year with the equally well received 'DON'T SAY NO', the album reaching the US Top 5 and eventually going multi-platinum with the help of the smouldering 'THE STROKE' single. While SQUIER became a household name in the States, he was virtually unknown in Britain, despite a tour with WHITESNAKE and an appearance at the Reading Festival. Whatever, his continuing US success no doubt made up for it, SQUIER scoring another massive hit album with 'EMOTIONS IN MOTION' (1982). By 1984's 'SIGNS OF LIFE', the singer had begun collaborating with MEATLOAF maestro, JIM STEINMAN, his subsequent material veering ever more towards the mainstream with one eye on the lucrative MTV market. Nevertheless, SQUIER's fifth album, 'ENOUGH IS ENOUGH' (1986), failed to break the US Top 50, future releases such as 'HEAR AND NOW' (1989) and 'CREATURES OF HABIT' (1991) not even receiving a UK release, such was the British rock scene's disinterest. With a return to the meatier sound of the debut, however, 1993's 'TELL THE TRUTH' was deemed suitable for the UK market, the record garnering some interest if hardly kickstarting his career. • **Trivia:** In 1983, SQUIER wrote and performed in the film 'Fast Times At Ridgemont High'.

Album rating: TALE OF THE TAPE (*7) / DON'T SAY NO (*6) / EMOTIONS IN MOTION (*5) / SIGNS OF LIFE (*5) / ENOUGH IS ENOUGH (*5) / HEAR AND NOW (*4) / CREATURES OF HABIT (*4) / REACH FOR THE SKY compilation (*6) / HAPPY BLUE (*4)

PIPER

BILLY SQUIER – vocals, guitar (ex-SIDEWINDERS) / **ALAN LAINE NOLAN + TOMMY GUNN** – guitar / **DANNY McGARY** – bass / **RICHIE FONTANA** – drums

not iss. A&M

Mar 77. (lp) <*SP 4615*> **PIPER** [-] [ ]
– Out of control / Whatcha gonna do / The road / Sail away / Who's your boyfriend (I gotta feelin') / Telephone relation / The last time / 42nd Street / Can't live with ya . . .can't live without ya.
May 77. (7") <*1918*> **THE ROAD. / WHO'S YOUR BOYFRIEND (I GOT A FEELIN')** [-] [ ]
Oct 77. (7") <*1969*> **CAN'T WAIT. / BLUES FOR THE COMMON PEOPLE** [-] [ ]
Nov 77. (lp) <*SP 4654*> **CAN'T WAIT** [-] [ ]
– Can't wait / Drop by and stay / See me through / Little Miss Intent / Now ain't the time / Bad boy / Comin' down off your love / Anyday / Blues for the common man.

BILLY SQUIER

went solo with band **DAVID SANCIOUS** – keyboards / **BRUCE KULICK** – guitar / **BUCKY BALLARD** – bass / **BOBBY CHOUNARD** – drums

Capitol Capitol

Mar 80. (7") <*4877*> **YOU SHOULD BE HIGH LOVE. / LIKE I'M LOVIN' YOU** [-] [ ]
May 80. (7") <*4901*> **THE BIG BEAT. / MUSIC'S ALRIGHT** [-] [ ]
Jul 80. (lp/c) <*(EST/TC-EST 12062)*> **THE TALE OF THE TAPE** [ ] [ ] Apr80
– The big beat / Calley oh / Rich kid / Like I'm lovin' you / Who knows what a love can do / You should be high love / Who's your boyfriend / The music's all right / Young girls.
Aug 80. (7") *(CL 16160)* **YOU SHOULD BE HIGH LOVE. / MUSIC'S ALL RIGHT** [ ] [-]

—— **SQUIER** retained only **CHOUNARD** and enlisted **GARY SHARAF** – guitar / **ALAN ST. JOHN** – keyboards / **MARK CLARK** – bass

May 81. (lp/c) <*(EST/TC-EST 12146)*> **DON'T SAY NO** [ ] [5] Apr81
– In the dark / The stroke / My kinda lover / You know what I like / Too daze gone / Lonely is the night / Whadda you want from me / Nobody knows / I need you / Don't say no. *(cd-iss. Apr87 on 'E.M.I.'; CDP 746479-2)*
May 81. (7") <*5005*> **THE STROKE. / TOO DAZE GONE** [-] [17]
Jun 81. (7") *(CL 206)* **IN THE DARK. / LONELY IS THE NIGHT** [ ] [-]
Aug 81. (7") <*5040*> **IN THE DARK. / WHADDA YOU WANT FROM ME** [-] [35]
Aug 81. (7") *(CL 214)* **THE STROKE. / MY KINDA LOVER** [52] [-]
Nov 81. (7") <*5037*> **MY KINDA LOVER. / CHRISTMAS IS THE TIME TO SAY I LOVE YOU** [-] [45]
Feb 82. (7") *(CL 231)* **TOO DAZE GONE. / WHADDA YOU WANT FROM ME** [ ] [-]

—— **JEFF GOLUB** – guitar + **DOUG LABAHN** – bass repl. SHARAF + CLARK

Jul 82. (7") *(CL 261)* <*5135*> **EMOTIONS IN MOTION. / CATCH 22** [ ] [68]
Sep 82. (lp/c) <*(EST/TC-EST 12217)*> **EMOTIONS IN MOTION** [ ] [5] Jul82
– Everybody wants you / Emotions in motion / Learn how to live / In your eyes / Keep me satisfied / It keeps you rockin' / One good woman / She's a runner / Catch 22 / Listen to the heartbeat. *(cd-iss. Apr87; CZ 72)*
Jan 83. (7") *(CL 273)* <*5163*> **EVERYBODY WANTS YOU. / KEEP ME SATISFIED** [ ] [32] Oct82
Jan 83. (7") <*5202*> **SHE'S A RUNNER. / IN YOUR EYES** [-] [75]
Nov 83. (7") <*5303*> **CHRISTMAS IS THE TIME TO SAY I LOVE YOU. / WHITE CHRISTMAS** [-] [ ]

—— **SQUIER** with more session people employed collaborator **JIM STEINMAN**

Jun 84. (7") *(SQ 1)* <*5370*> **ROCK ME TONITE. / CAN'T GET NEXT TO YOU** [ ] [15]
(d7"+=) *(SQD 1)* – She's a runner / Listen to the heartbeat.
Sep 84. (lp/c) *(EJ 240192-1/-4)* <*12361*> **SIGNS OF LIFE** [ ] [11] Jul84
– All night long / Rock me tonite / Eye on you / Take a look behind ya / Reach for the sky / (Another) 1984 / Fall for love / Can't get next to you / Hand-me-downs / Sweet release. *(cd-iss. Apr87; CZ 71)*
Oct 84. (7") <*5422*> **ALL NIGHT LONG. / CALLEY OH** [-] [75]
Dec 84. (7") <*5416*> **EYE ON YOU. / CALLEY OH** [-] [71]

—— **T.M. STEVENS** – bass repl. DOUG

Sep 86. (7") *(CL 433)* <*5619*> **LOVE IS THE HERO. / LEARN HOW TO LIVE** [ ] [80]
(12"+=) *(12CL 433)* – ('A'extended).
Nov 86. (lp/c) *(EST/TC-EST 2024)* <*12483*> **ENOUGH IS ENOUGH** [ ] [61] Oct86
– Shot o' love / Love is the hero / Lady with a tenor sax / All we have to give / Come home / Break the silence / Powerhouse / Lonely one / Til it's over / Wink of an eye. *(cd-iss. Mar88; BU 1)*
Nov 86. (7") <*5657*> **SHOT O' LOVE. / ONE GOOD WOMAN** [-] [ ]
Jun 89. (7") <*44420*> **DON'T SAY YOU LOVE ME. / TOO MUCH** [-] [58]
Jul 89. (lp/c/cd) <*48748-1/-4/-2*> **HEAR AND NOW** [-] [64]
– Rock out – Punch someone / Don't say you love me / Don't let me go / Tied up / (I put a) Spell on you / G.O.D. / Mine tonite / The work song.
Aug 89. (7") <*44456*> **DON'T LET ME GO. /** [-] [ ]
Apr 91. (cd/c/lp) <*94303*> **CREATURES OF HABIT** [-] [ ]
– Facts of life / Strange fire / Alone in your dreams (don't say goodbye) / (L.O.V.E.) Four letter world / Young at heart / Nerves on ice / She goes down / Lover / Hollywood / Hands of seduction / Conscience point.
Apr 93. (cd/c) *(CD/TC EST 2194)* <*98690*> **TELL THE TRUTH** [ ] [ ]
– Angry / Tryin' to walk a straight line / Rhythm (a bridge too far) / Hercules / Lovin' you ain't so hard / Timebomb / Stranger to myself / Girl's all right / Break down / Not a colour / Mind-machine / Shocked straight.

J-Bird J-Bird

Sep 98. (cd) <*(JBD 80256)*> **HAPPY BLUE** [ ] [ ]
– Happy blue / The pursuit of happiness / She will / Grasping for oblivion / If you would hate me less, I'd love you more / Stroke me blues / More than words can say / Inferno (everybody cries sometimes) / Long way to fall / River / Two.

– compilations, etc. –

1995. (cd) *Capitol;* **16 STROKES** [-] [ ]
Feb 96. (d-cd) *Polydor;* <*529296*> **REACH FOR THE SKY** [-] [ ]
– Who's your boyfriend / Little miss intent / You should be high love / The big beat / In the dark / Lonely is the night / My kinda lover / Nobody knows / The stroke / Everybosy wants you / Emotions in motion / Learn how to live / She's a runner / (Another) 1984 / Fall for love / All night long / Rock me tonite / Reach for the sky / Love is the hero / Lady with a tenor sax / Til it's over / Rock out – Punch somebody / Stronger / Don't let me go / G.O.D. / Hands of seduction / She goes down / Lover / (L.O.V.E.) a four letter word / The girl's all right / Lovin' you ain't so hard / Hercules / Time bomb.
Apr 98. (cd) *Cema;* <*19399*> **BEST OF . . .** [-] [ ]
Mar 00. (cd) *EMI-Capitol;* <*24495*> **LIVE** [-] [ ]

SQUIRREL BAIT

Formed: Louisville, Kentucky, USA . . . 1985 by DAVID GRUBBS, PETER SEARCY, BRIAN McMAHAN, BRITT WALFORD and ETHAN BUCKLER (the latter two subsequently made way for BEN DAUGHTREY and CLARK JOHNSON respectively during debut session cuts). A seminal indie hardcore act with a neat line in adolescent humour, SQUIRREL BAIT set their first musical trap in early '86 with an eponymous HUSKER DU-esque album for Steven Joerg's 'Homestead' imprint. Their lifespan was brief however, the band effectively extinct as college captured them following the release of the excellent 'SKAG HEAVEN' (1987). While most of the posse were buried in their books, SEARCY formed The BIG WHEEL and GRUBBS (with JOHNSON) worked on a trio of thrash-metal/noise sets as BASTRO, the latter two surprisingly featuring drummer, JOHN McENTIRE, before he crawled off to form TORTOISE. The most famous by-product of SQUIRREL BAIT, however, was SLINT, an influential indie outfit formed from the ashes of the former band's final line-up (i.e. McMAHAN, WALFORD, DAVID PAJO and ETHAN BUCKLER). In 1991, GRUBBS initiated GASTR DEL SOL, a more intelligent, musically complex proposition which originally saw him working with BUNDY K BROWN and the ubiquitous McENTIRE (in a guest capacity) on the 1993 mini-set, 'THE SERPENTINE SIMILAR'. The latter sticksman also featured on the following single, '20 SONGS LESS', a collaboration with GRUBBS and JIM O'ROURKE (BUNDY had already joined TORTOISE). Having been part of the 'TeenBeat' operation, GASTR DEL SOL signed with 'Drag City' for 1994's acclaimed long-player, 'CROOKT, CRACKT, OR FLY', a subtle, spellbinding record that made genuine innovations in the use of dense acoustic guitar textures and traversed the boundaries of standard indie-rock structures. Never one to shirk a challenge, GRUBBS (and some local friends/musicians) took it upon himself to create a mini-orchestral suite scored to the usual freeform rules, the resulting 17-minute long 'HARP FACTORY ON LAKE STREET' (1995), taking the post-rock ethos into uncharted territory. The following year, GASTR DEL SOL returned to a more song-based approach on 'UPGRADE & AFTERLIFE', a slightly disappointing set which featured a cover of John Fahey's 'DRY BONES IN THE VALLEY'. The partnership of GRUBBS and O'ROURKE was tied up with the 'CAMOUFLEUR' (1998) album, an impressive swansong that found the pair in a more reflective mood, dabbling in a cinematic mix of folk and avant-jazz influences. Around the same time, GRUBBS was carving out his own "new age" solo career, releasing three albums, 'BANANA CABBAGE . . .' (1997), 'THE THICKET' (1998) and with MATS GUSTAFSSON, 'APERTURA' (1999), before the turn of the century.

Album rating: SQUIRREL BAIT (*6) / SKAG HEAVEN (*7) / Bastro: RODE HARD AND PUT UP WET (*4) / DIABLO GUAPO (*4) / SING THE TROUBLED BEAST (*5) / Gastr Del Sol: THE SERPENTINE SIMILAR mini (*6) / CROOKT, CRACKT, OR FLY (*7) / UPGRADE & AFTERLIFE (*5) / CAMOUFLEUR (*7) / David Grubbs: BANANA CABBAGE POTATO LETTUCE ONION ORANGE (*3) / THE THICKET (*5) / THE COXCOMB (*5) / APERTURA with Mats Gustafson (*5)

PETER SEARCY – vocals / **BRIAN McMAHAN** – guitar, vocals / **DAVID GRUBBS** – guitar / **CLARK JOHNSON** – bass; repl. ETHAN BUCKLER / **BEN DAUGHTREY** – drums; repl. BRITT WALFORD (played on two debut tracks)

Homestead Homestead

Jan 86. (lp) *<(HMS 028-1)>* **SQUIRREL BAIT**
– Hammering so hard / Thursday / Sun god / When I fall / The final chapter / Mixed blessing / Disguise. *<(cd/lp-iss.Feb97 on 'Drag City'; DEX 10/DC 102)>*

Nov 86. (7") **KID DYNAMITE. / SLAKE TRAIN COMING**

Mar 87. (lp/cd) *<(HMS 072-1/-2)>* **SKAG HEAVEN**
– Kid Dynamite / Vigil's return / Black light poster child / Choose your poison / Short straw wins / Too close to the fire / Slake train coming / Rose Island road / Tape to California. *<(cd/lp-iss.Feb97 on 'Drag City'; DEX 11/DC 103)>*

— split in 1988, singer SEARCY forming BIG WHEEL with guitarist and co-songwriter, GLENN TAYLOR, along with the rhythm section of MIKE BRADEN and SCOTT LANKFORD. The quartet released hard-rock/metal album, 'EAST END' for 'Giant' records in 1989, while two further albums, 'HOLIDAY MANOR' (1992) and 'SLOWTOWN' (1993) surfaced for 'Mammoth'.

BASTRO

— meanwhile, **GRUBBS + JOHNSON** formed this outfit

Homestead Homestead

Sep 88. (m-lp/m-c) *<(HMS 111/+C)>* **RODE HARD AND PUT UP WET**

— added **JOHN McENTIRE** – drums

Apr 89. (7") *<(HMS 137)>* **SHOOT ME A DEAR. /**

Jul 89. (lp/c/cd) *<(HMS 132-1/-4/-2)>* **DIABLO GUAPO**
– Tallow waters / Filthy five filthy ten / Guapo / Flesh-coloured house / Short-haired robot / Can of whoopass / Decent skin / Engaging the reverend / Wurlitzer / Pretty smart on my part / Hoosier logic / Shoot me a deer.

1990. (cd/c/lp) *<HMS 164-2/-4/-1>* **SING THE TROUBLED BEAST** [-]
– Demons begone / Krakow, Illinois / I come from a long line of ship-builders / Tobacco in the sink / Recidivist / Floating home / Jefferson-in-drag / The sifter / Noise – Star / Recidivist.

— disbanded after above, McENTIRE later formed TORTOISE

STABBING WESTWARD

Formed: Macomb, Illinois, USA . . . 1990 by CHRISTOPHER HALL and WALTER FLAKUS, who after the release of a self-financed EP, recruited the rhythm section of JIM SELLERS and DAVID SUYCOTT (who replaced temp CHRIS VRENNA from NiN); second guitarist STUART ZECKMAN was added when they moved to Chicago. Hard-hitting US alt-rock with base elements of tribal industrial hardcore held together by well-structured melodies, the STABBING WESTWARD sound first hit the shops courtesy of 'Columbia' late in '93. Aired live to British fans via a worthy half hour slot at that year's Reading Festival, the album in question, 'UNGOD', was sufficiently impressive to see the band hired to contribute towards the soundtracks of movies, 'The Cable Guy' and 'Escape From L.A.'. In 1995/96, SW shuffled the pack a little when both SUYCOTT and ZECKMAN were superseded by new drummer ANDY KUBISZEWSKI. The band's growing reputation was consolidated with the release of sophomore set, 'WITHER, BLISTER, BURN & PEEL' (1996), which steadily headed northward up the US Top 100. Later that year, frontman HALL gave a full, er . . . frontal for the August edition of female top-shelf mag, 'Playgirl'. HALL and Co continued their.. er.. rise to fame with a third set, 'DARKEST DAYS' (1998), nearly poking the Top 50. However, towards the end of the millennium STABBING WESTWARD were dropped by their major. Undaunted, they picked themselves back up once again (added new guitarist DERREK HAWKINS) and celebrated their fifteenth year together by releasing a slightly more radio-friendly eponymous fourth set in summer 2001.

Album rating: UNGOD (*7) / WITHER, BLISTER, BURN & PEEL (*7) / DARKEST DAYS (*6) / STABBING WESTWARD (*5)

CHRISTOPHER HALL – vocals, guitar / **WALTER FLAKUS** – keyboards / **STUART ZECKMAN** – guitar / **JIM SELLERS** – bass / **DAVID SUYCOTT** – drums

Columbia Columbia

May 94. (cd/c/lp) *(475735-2/-4/-1) <CK/CT+/53614>* **UNGOD** Dec93
– Lost / Control / Nothing / ACF / Lies / Ungod / Throw / Violent mood swings / Red on white / Can't happen here.

Sep 94. (12"/cd-s) *(660426-6/-2)* **NOTHING. / LIES** [-]

— **ANDY KUBISZEWSKI** – drums, guitar; repl. SUYCOTT + ZECKMAN

May 96. (cd/c) *(481580-2/-4) <66152>* **WITHER, BLISTER, BURN & PEEL** [67] Jan96
– I don't believe / Shame / What do I have to do? / Why? / Inside you / Falls apart / So wrong / Crushing me / Sleep / Slipping away.

Jun 98. (cd-s) *<3277>* **SAVE YOURSELF / SAVE YOURSELF (longer)** [-]

Nov 98. (cd-s) *<41803>* **HAUNTING ME (versions)** [-]
(above from the movie 'Faculty')

Aug 99. (cd/c) *(488533-2) <68006>* **DARKEST DAYS** [52] Apr98
– Darkest days / Everything I touch / How can I hold on? / Drugstore / You complete me / Save yourself / Haunting me / Torn apart / Sometimes it hurts / Drowning / Desperate now / Goodbye / When I'm dead / The thing I hate / On your way down / Waking up beside you. *(hidden track+=)* – Hopeless.

— added on tour **DERREK HAWKINS** – guitar

Koch Koch

Jun 01. (cd) *(KOCD 38924)* **SO FAR AWAY / SO FAR AWAY (album) / LAST TIME** [-]

Jun 01. (cd) *<(KOCCD 8295)>* **STABBING WESTWARD** [47] May01
– So far away / Perfect / I remember / Wasted / Happy / The only thing / Angel / Breathe you in / High / Television.

STAGE DOLLS

Formed: Trondheim, Norway . . . 1983 by TORSTEIN FLAKNE, TERJE STORLI and ERLAND ANTONSON. Signed to 'Mercury' Norway, the group debuted in 1985 with the 'SOLDIER'S GUN' album, a competent set taking its cue from melodic American hard rock/AOR. With STEINAR KROKSTAD replacing ANTONSEN, the band made their UK debut with a follow-up set, 'COMMANDOS' (1987). Although they failed to gain any widespread British recognition, STAGE DOLLS scored a minor US chart hit with the 'LOVE CRIES' single in early 1990. While this small victory led to some high profile support slots, the group failed to consolidate the success and subsequently split following final album, 'STRIPPED' (1992).

Album rating: SOLDIER'S GUN (*6) / COMMANDOES (*7) / STAGE DOLLS (*6) / STRIPPED (*5)

TORSTEIN FLAKNE – vocals, guitar (ex-KIDS) / **TERJE STORLI** – bass / **ERLAND ANTONSEN** – drums (ex-SUBWAY SECT)

Mercury Mercury

1985. (lp/cd) *<824 553-1/-2>* **SOLDIER'S GUN** [-] Norway
– Queen of the hearts / Soldier's gun / Ten tons / While the bombs are falling / Tonight / Left foot boogie / Way of the world / Red rose / Photograph / Shout.

— **STEINAR KROKSTAD** – drums; repl. ANTONSEN

Big Time not iss.

1987. (lp/cd) *(ZL/ZD 71485)* **COMMANDOS** [-]
– Prelude / Heart to heart / Commandos / Yesterday's rain / Young hearts / Rock you / Magic / Who's lonely now / America / Don't look back.

Polydor Chrysalis

Feb 90. (7") *(PO 68) <23366>* **LOVE CRIES. / HANOI WATERS** [46] Jul89
(12"+=/cd-s+=) *(PZ/+CD 68)* – Don't stop believin'.

Feb 90. (cd/c/lp) *(841 259-2/-4/-1) <21716>* **STAGE DOLLS** Aug89
– Still in love / Wings of steel / Lorraine / Waitin' for you / Love cries / Mystery / Don't stop believin' / Hanoi waters / Ammunition.

Apr 90. (7"/7"g-f/c-s) *(PO/+G/CS 78)* **STILL IN LOVE. /**
(12"+=) *(PZ 78)* –

Apr 92. (cd/c/lp) *(513 167-2/-4/-1)* **STRIPPED**
– Stand by you / Life in America / Left foot boogie / Love don't bother me / Money / Sorry (is all I can say) / In the heat / Let's get crazy / Goodbye to Amy / Rock this city / Livin' on borrowed time / Down on me.

— split soon after above album

STAIND

Formed: Springfield, Massachusetts, USA . . . Xmas 1994 by vocalist AARON LEWIS and guitarist MICHAEL MUSHOK, the pair almost immediately hooking up with drummer JON WYSOCKI and an unknown original bassist; JOHNNY APRIL would become their 4-string plucker after their first gig in February '95. In late '96, the quartet self-financed a debut album, 'TORMENTED', its title pretty much giving the game away as to their miserabilist nu-metal approach. Spurred on by healthy sales, the band jumped at the chance to play on the same bill as LIMP BIZKIT in late 1997. While that band's ubiquitous lead singer, FRED DURST, initially took vocal exception to STAIND's quasi-Satanic cover art, an impassioned performance on the night persuaded him they were worthy of his new label. After trying and failing to contact DURST by phone, they travelled to a LIMP BIZKIT gig and left a new demo tape for the man's perusal. He was suitably impressed and soon STAIND were cutting their major label debut for the 'Elektra'-backed 'Flip' imprint with Terry Date (SOUNDGARDEN, DEFTONES, PANTERA etc.) at the production helm. 'DYSFUNCTION' arrived in Spring '99, pulling few punches and even less surprises with a solid if uninspiring set of treacle-thick post-grunge. The record went down a storm nevertheless, spawning three sizeable rock radio hits in 'JUST GO', 'MUDSHOVEL' and 'HOME'. Tours with KID ROCK, KORN and LIMP BIZKIT followed and STAIND were subsequently named as the headline act for MTV's 'Return Of The Rock' jaunt. Amid the media circus and general mayhem, a sophomore album, 'BREAK THE CYCLE', appeared in 2001, the record hitting No.1 in the States but earning short thrift from the likes of Kerrang!

Album rating: TORMENTED (*5) / DYSFUNCTION (*6) / BREAK THE CYCLE (*4)

AARON LEWIS – vocals / **MICHAEL MUSHOK** – guitar / **JOHNNY APRIL** – bass / **JON WYSOCKI** – drums

not iss. | own label

Oct 96. (cd) **TORMENTED** [-] [ ]
– Tolerate / Come again / Break / Painful / Nameless / Mudshuvel / See thru / Question / No one's kind / Self destruct / Walls.

Elektra | Elektra

Mar 00. (cd) *<(7559 62356-2)>* **DYSFUNCTION** [ ] [74] Apr99
– Suffocate / Just go / Me / Raw / Mudshovel / Home / A flat / Crawl / Spleen. *(hidden track+=)* – Excess baggage.

Feb 01. (-; as AARON LEWIS of STAIND with FRED DURST)
<radio play> **OUTSIDE** [-] [56]

Apr 01. (-) *<radio play>* **IT'S BEEN AWHILE** [-] [22]

Jun 01. (cd/c) *<(7559 62626-2/-4)>* **BREAK THE CYCLE** [ ] [1] May01
– Open your eyes / Change / Warm safe place / It's been a while / Can't believe / Fade / Suffer / Waste / For you / Outside (with FRED DURST) / Take it / Pressure / Epiphany.

STAMPEDE

Formed: London, England ... 1981 by ex-LIONHEART trio, REUBEN ARCHER and his brother LAURENCE, plus FRANK NOON. They enlisted the help of COLIN BOND, prior to NOON being replaced with EDDIE PARSONS. Signed to 'Polydor' and favouring archetypal heavy Brit-rock, STAMPEDE thundered onto the scene in 1983 with a live debut album recorded at the Reading Festival, 'THE OFFICIAL BOOTLEG'. A follow-up album, 'HURRICANE TOWN' (1983), was released to general disinterest and it became clear that STAMPEDE had run their course. • **Note:** Not to be confused with a German outfit who issued an album in '81.

Album rating: THE OFFICIAL BOOTLEG (*5) / HURRICANE TOWN (*5)

REUBEN ARCHER – vocals / **LAURENCE ARCHER** – guitar / **COLIN BOND** – bass, synthesizer / **EDDIE PARSONS** – drums, percussion; repl. FRANK NOON who joined BERNIE TORME

Polydor | not iss.

Sep 82. (7"/12") *(POSP/+X 507)* **DAYS OF WINE AND ROSES. / PHOTOGRAPHS** [ ] [-]

Jan 83. (lp) *(ROCK 1)* **THE OFFICIAL BOOTLEG** (live at Reading) [ ] [-]
– Missing you / Moving on / Days of wine and roses / Hurricane town / Shadows of the night / Bavy driver / The runner / There and back.

May 83. (7") *(POSP 592)* **THE OTHER SIDE. / RUNNER** [ ] [-]

Jul 83. (lp) *(POLS 1083)* **HURRICANE TOWN** [ ] [-]
– I've been told / Love letters / Casino junkie / The other side / Turning in circles / Hurricane town / Girl / The runner / Mexico.

— got trampled on by the media which led to LAURENCE joining GRAND SLAM. He subsequently released a solo album, 'L.A.'

STAMPIN' GROUND

Formed: Cheltenham, England ... 1995 by IAN GLASPER and TONY MOWBRAY who recruited ADAM FRAKES-SIME, SCOTT ATKINS and ADRIAN STOKES. Unrelentingly determined self-starters in the time honoured hardcore mould, STAMPIN' GROUND booked their own grinding gig schedule and even played thir initial shows for free. Similarly, GLASPER formed his own 'Blackfish' label for material by other worthy punkmeisters; debuts 'STAMPIN' GROUND' a mini-set and 'DEMONS RUN AMOK' were issued on 'We Bite'. Covering their costs by canny merchandising, the quintet won a loyal cult following who devoured sophomore set, 'AN EXPRESSION OF REPRESSED VIOLENCE' (1998) and 'CARVED FROM EMPTY WORDS' (2000). Although the latter was released via 'Century Media', GLASPER and Co still had the option of self-financing the occasional EP.

Album rating: STAMPIN' GROUND mini (*6) / DEMONS RUN AMOK (*6) / AN EXPRESSION OF REPRESSED VIOLENCE (*6) / CARVED FROM EMPTY WORDS (*6)

ADAM FRAKES-SIME – vocals / **TONY 'MOBS' MOWBRAY** – guitar / **SCOTT ATKINS** – guitar / **IAN GLASPER** – bass / **ADRIAN 'ADE' STOKES** – drums

We Bite | not iss.

Sep 96. (m-cd) *(WB 1148MCD)* **STAMPIN' GROUND** [ ] [-]

Jun 97. (cd) *(WB 1169CD)* **DEMONS RUN AMOK** [ ] [-]

Century Media | Century Media

Oct 98. (lp/cd) *(CM 77237/+CD)* **AN EXPRESSION OF REPRESSED VIOLENCE** [ ] [-]

Jul 00. (cd/lp) *(77337-2/-1) <7837>* **CARVED FROM EMPTY WORDS** [ ] [ ] Apr00
– Officer down / Outside looking in / The symmetry of hatred / Bathe my wounds / Everybody owes a death / Fundamental truth / By whatever means neccessary / Nothing changes nothing / Mid-death crisis / Ultimatum.

STANFORD PRISON EXPERIMENT

Formed: Los Angeles, California, USA . . . early 90's by MARIO JIMINEZ, MIKE STARKEY, MARK FRASER and DAVEY LATTER. Taking their moniker from an infamous 70's experiment-gone-wrong at California's Stanford College (wherein students took on the opposing roles of Warders and Prisoners in a mock-up jail scenario), this uncompromising quartet set out to expose societal indoctrination via a basic but intense hardcore assault. Signed to the 'World Domination' imprint, they unleashed their inaugural single, 'MR. TEACHER DAD', in Spring 1994, preceding an eponymous album the following month. In '95, SPE were back to terrorise the establishment with a second set of fierce, no holds barred (oops! sorry) jailhouse rock, 'THE GATO HUNCH'. Of late, the band seem to have gone AWOL.

Album rating: STANFORD PRISON EXPERIMENT (*5) / THE GATO HUNCH (*6)

MARIO JIMINEZ – vocals / **MIKE STARKEY** – guitar, vocals / **MARK FRASER** – bass / **DAVEY LATTER** – drums

World Domination | World Domination

May 94. (7") *<(WDOM 008S)>* **MR. TEACHER DAD. / OPEY OF THE MASSES** [ ] [ ]

Jun 94. (cd) *<(WDOM 009CD)>* **STANFORD PRISON EXPERIMENT** [ ] [ ]
– Disbelief / Take it / Written apology / Supermonkey / Get on / Course / What's an epidemic / Mr. Teacher dad / It's expected I'm gone / Frozen / Sheepshit / Rob hates.

Oct 94. (7") **SUPERMONKEY. /** [ ] [ ]

— In July '95, their track, 'YOU'RE THE VULGARIAN', featured on the B-side of a QUICKSAND single for 'Island Red' (IR 107)

Sep 95. (cd) *<(WDOM 020CD)>* **THE GATO HUNCH** [ ] [ ]
– You're the vulgarian / Repeat removal / (Very) Put out / Cansado / Flap / So far, so good / El nuevo / Accomplice / Harcord idiot / Swoon / Worst case scenario.

— escaped from the music biz after above

Paul STANLEY (see under ⇒ KISS)

Jack STARR

Born: American STARR went solo in 1984 after playing guitar with heavy metal outfit, VIRGIN STEELE, subsequently enlisting the services of relative rock veterans RHETT FORRESTER, GARY BORDONARO and CARL CANEDY. Securing a deal with UK label, 'Music For Nations', STARR released a debut set, OUT OF DARKNESS', in 1984. Consummately executed melodic metal, the record introduced STARR as a would-be fretboard messiah. For the following year's US-only 'ROCK THE AMERICAN WAY', STARR had dispensed with his original line-up and recruited a cast of musicians that numbered FRANK VESTRY, JOHN RODRIQUEZ and TONY GALTIERI. STARR switched line-ups yet again for the 1986 set, 'NO TURNING BACK', hiring the backing band, BURNING STARR. While his albums have become progressively more accessible, JACK's star seems to have faded completely in the 90's, his last release to date being the 'BURNING STAR' (1990) set.

Album rating: OUT OF DARKNESS (*6) / ROCK THE AMERICAN WAY (*5) / NO TURNING BACK (*5) / BLAZE OF GLORY (*5) / BURNING STARR (*5) / A MINOR DISTURBANCE (*4)

JACK STARR – guitar / with **RHETT FORRESTER** – vocals (ex-RIOT) / **GARY BORDONARO** – bass (ex-RODS) / **CARL CANEDY** – drums (ex-RODS)

Music For Nations | Passport

Aug 84. (lp) *(MFN 34) <PB 6037>* **OUT OF DARKNESS** [ ] [ ]
– Concrete warrior / False messiah / Scorcher / Wild in the streets / Can't let you walk away / Chains of love / Eyes of fire / Odile / Let's get crazy again.

— now with **FRANK VESTRY** – vocals / **JOHN RODRIGUEZ** – bass / **TONY GALTIERI** – drums

Passport | Passport

Nov 85. (lp; by JACK STARR'S BURNING STAR) *<(PBL 101)>* **ROCK THE AMERICAN WAY** [ ] [ ]
– Rock and roll is the American way / In your arms again / Woman / Heat of the night / Born to rock / She's on fire / Live fast, rock hard / Fight the thunder.

— now with **MIKE TERRELLI** – vocals / **THUMPER** – bass / **MARK EDWARDS** – drums

U.S.Metal | U.S.Metal

Nov 86. (lp; by JACK STARR'S BURNING STAR) *<US 4>* **NO TURNING BACK** [-] [ ]
– No turning back / Light in the dark / Fire and rain / Call of the wild / Road warrior /

Prelude in C minor / Evil never sleeps / Path of destruction / M-1 / Avenging angel / Run for your life / Coda.

— **FREE BASS** – bass; repl. THUMPER

— **JIM HARRIS** – drums; repl. EDWARDS

Nov 87. (lp) <(US 8)> **BLAZE OF GLORY** □ □
– Stand up and fight / Overdrive / Blaze of glory / F.F.Z. (Free Fire Zone) / Go down fighting / Burning Starr / Mad at the world / Mercry killer / Metal generation / Excursion.

Jan 90. (lp/cd) <(US 16/+CD)> **BURNING STARR** □ □ 1989
– Send me an angel / Bad times / Fool for love / Hold back the night / Love can't wait / Out of the blue / New York women / Tear down the wall / Break the ice / Remember tomorrow / Good girls gone bad.

not iss. Cariola

1991. (cd) <C7001-2> **A MINOR DISTURBANCE** - □
– Exodus / Post modern funk / A minor disturbance / Interlude in the afternoon / Sundance strut / Love in the rain / Last thing on my mind / New York City blues / Nothing to declare / Last date.

not iss. Jack Starr

1994. (c-s) **OXYGEN 1** - □

— seems to have taken a hiatus for the rest of the 90's

STARZ

Formed: New York, USA . . . 1975 as The FALLEN ANGELS by BRENDAN HARKIN, JOEY X DUBE and PETER SWEVAL who recorded a soundtrack to a 70's porno flick before getting their act together and forming the highly regarded heavy glam act, STARZ. With the line-up completed by guitarist RICHIE RANNO and frontman MICHAEL LEE SMITH, the group signed to 'Capitol', releasing an eponymous debut in 1976. Album sales were given a high-heeled kick as STARZ scored two minor US hits in a row with '(SHE'S JUST A) FALLEN ANGEL' and 'CHERRY BABY'. The latter single was lifted from the band's stompalong follow-up set, 'VIOLATION' (1977), a record which breached the lower echelons of the Top 100. STARZ scored further minor hits with tracks from 'ATTENTION SHOPPERS!' (1977) and 'COLISEUM ROCK' (1979), although they never quite managed to break through and capture the limelight from peers such as KISS. After a final tour, the band split in 1980, although the STARZ legend never really faded as SMITH and RANNO's new band, HELLCAT, carried on the legacy.

Album rating: STARZ (*7) / VIOLATION (*7) / ATTENTION SHOPPERS! (*5) / COLISEUM ROCK (*7) / posthumous: BRIGHTEST STARZ (*6) / LIVE IN CANADA (*5) / PISS PARTY (*5) / DO IT WITH THE LIGHTS ON (*4) / LIVE IN ACTION (*4)

MICHAEL LEE SMITH – vocals, guitar / **BRENDAN HARKIN** – guitar, vocals / **RICHIE RANO** – guitar / **JOEY X DUBE** – bass / **PETER SWEVAL** – drums

Capitol Capitol

Sep 76. (lp) <(EST 11539)> **STARZ** □ □ Aug76
– Boys in action / Detroit girls / Live wire / Monkey business / Night crawler / Now I can / Over and over / Pull the plug / (She's just a) Fallen angel / Tear it down. <cd-iss. 1991 on 'Metal Blade'; 26558>

Dec 76. (7") <4343> **(SHE'S JUST A) FALLEN ANGEL. / MONKEY BUSINESS** - 95

Apr 77. (7") (CL 15916) <4399> **CHERRY BABY. / ROCK SIX TIMES** □ 33 Mar77

May 77. (lp) <(EST 11617)> **VIOLATION** □ 89 Apr77
– Cherry baby / Rock six times / Sing it, shout it / Violation / Subway terror / All night long / Cool one / S.T.E.A.D.Y. / Is that a street light or the moon? <cd-iss. 1991 on 'Metal Blade'; 26559>

Jul 77. (7") (CL 15932) <4434> **SING IT, SHOUT IT. / SUBWAY TERROR** □ 66 Jun77

— **ORVILLE DAVIS** – bass, vocals; repl. SWEVAL

Apr 78. (lp) <(EST 11730)> **ATTENTION SHOPPERS!** □ □ Feb78
– Hold on to the night / She / Third time's the charm / (Any way that you want it) I'll be there / Waitin' on you / X-ray spex / Good ale we seek / Don't think / Johnny all-alone. <cd-iss. 1991 on 'Metal Blade'; 26570>

May 78. (7") (CL 15986) <4546> **(ANY WAY THAT YOU WANT IT) I'LL BE THERE. / TEXAS** □ 79 Mar78

May 78. (7") <4566> **HOLD ON TO THE NIGHT. / TEXAS** - 78

— **BOBBY MESSANO** – guitar, vocals; repl. HARKIN

Oct 78. (7") <4637> **SO YOUNG, SO BAD. / COLISEUM ROCK** - 81

Feb 79. (lp/c) <(EST/TC-EST 11861)> **COLISEUM ROCK** □ □
– So young, so bad / Take me / No regrets / My sweet child / Don't stop now / Outfit / Last night I wrote a letter / Coliseum rock / It's a riot / Where will it end. <cd-iss. 1991 on 'Metal Blade'; 26571>

— split in 1980, RANNO and DUBE forming their own outfit with OETER SCANCE on bass. They evolved into The HELLCATS, although this was without DUBE, who was replaced by DOUG MADICK (ex-PRISM) and the return of MICHAEL LEE SMITH. The HELLCATS released two melodic rock albums, 'HELLCATS' (1982) and 'HELLCATS KIDS' (1987) both for 'King Klassic'. BOBBY MESSANO went into session work for the 'Atlantic' stable, and after working with FIONA, he released his own solo album, 'MESSANO' (1989).

– compilations, etc. –

Jan 85. (lp/c) *Heavy Metal America; (HMUSA/HMAMC 8)* **BRIGHTEST STARZ** □ -
– Rock six times / Cherry baby / Pull the plug / So young, so bad / Violation / Subway terror / Sing it, shout it / She / Coliseum rock / Boys in action.

May 85. (7") *FM Revolver; (VHF 6)* **SO YOUNG, SO BAD. /** □ -

Oct 85. (lp/c) *Heavy Metal America; (HMUSA/HMAMC 46)* **LIVE IN CANADA (live)** □ -
– Rock six times / Subway terror / Where will it end / Nitecrawler / Outfit / Last night I wrote a letter / No regrets / It's a riot / Waitin' on you / Coliseum rock / Take me.

Nov 85. (yellow-lp/c) *Heavy Metal America; (MHUSA/HMAMC 50)* **PISS PARTY** □ -
– Reggae plug / That's alright mamma – Mountain dew / Devil with the blue dress / Good golly Miss Molly / Interview / P*ss party.

1986. (7") *Capitol; (SPSR 405)* **BOYS IN ACTION. / STARZ ADZ** □ -

1987. (lp) *Performance; (PERF 386)* **DO IT WITH THE LIGHTS ON** - □

Dec 89. (d-lp/cd) *Roadracer; (RO 9427-1/-2) / Relix; <847997>* **LIVE IN ACTION (live)** □ □

Jul 99. (cd) *G.B.; (GB 1003)* **GREATEST HITS LIVE** □ -

Jan 00. (cd) *Performance; <(DCC 0001CD)>* **REQUIEM** □ □
– Vidi OD / Love and pain / You called his name / Rough & ready / Backstreet survivor / Texas / Nite crawler / Fallen angel / Hold on to the night / Can't take it no more / Waitress / Fannin' the fire / I ain't no Einstein.

Jan 00. (cd) *Performance; <(DCC 0003CD)>* **BACK IN THE DAY** □ □

Jan 00. (d-cd) *Performance; <(DCC 0005CD)>* **LIVE IN LOUISVILLE** □ □

Jan 00. (cd) *D.C.C.; <(DCC 0006CD)>* **LIVE AT THE FOX THEATRE** □ □

Jan 00. (cd) *D.C.C.; <(DCC 0007CD)>* **LIVE IN TEXAS THEATRE** □ □

Jan 00. (cd) *D.C.C.; <(DCC 0008CD)>* **LIVE AT THE EL MOCAMBO** □ □

Jan 00. (d-cd) *D.C.C.; <(DCC 0009CD)>* **AGORA** □ □

Jan 00. (cd) *D.C.C.; <(DCC 0017CD)>* **LIVE AT THE CALDERONE** □ □

Jan 00. (cd) *D.C.C.; <(DCC 0018CD)>* **JAM** □ □

STATIC-X

Formed: based – Los Angeles, California, USA . . . 1997 by WAYNE STATIC and KEN JAY, who'd met while working in a Chicago record store. They soon recruited Japanese-born KOICHI FUKADA and California native TONY CAMPOS, building up a genuine grass roots fanbase in thrall to their guttural, technologically enhanced metal. A subsequent deal with 'Warners' led to the release of a debut album, 'WISCONSIN DEATH TRIP' (1999), earning a fair whack of airtime on US rock radio via the tracks, 'PUSH IT', 'I'M WITH STUPID' and 'BLED FOR DAYS'. By the time the record had gone platinum, FUKADA had been replaced by TRIPP REX EISEN, the erstwhile DOPE guitarist making his debut on sophomore effort, 'MACHINE' (2001).

Album rating: WISCONSIN DEATH TRIP (*5) / MACHINE (*6)

WAYNE STATIC (b. WAYNE WELLS, Michigan) – vocals, guitar, programming / **KOICKI FUKADA** – guitar / **TONY CAMPOS** – bass / **KEN JAY** – drums

Warners Warners

May 99. (cd/c) <(9362 47271-2/-4)> **WISCONSIN DEATH TRIP** □ □ Mar99
– Push it / I'm stupid / Bled for days / Love dump / I am / Otsegolation / Stem / Sweat of the bud / Fix / Wisconsin death trip / The trance is the motion / December.

Jan 00. (cd-s) <44782> **PUSH IT** □ -

Sep 00. (12") (F 1114490-2) **LOVE DUMP** □ -
(above issued on ~Higher Education')

— **TRIPP REX EISEN** – guitar (ex-DOPE) repl. FUKADA

Jun 01. (cd/c) <(9362 47948-2/-4)> **MACHINE** 56 11
– Bien venidos / Get to the gone / Permanence / Black and white / This is not / Otsego undead / Cold / Structural defect / . . .In a bag / Burn to burn / Machine / A dios alma perida.

STATUS QUO

Formed: London, England ... 1962 as The SPECTRES, by schoolboys ALAN LANCASTER, ALAN KEY, MIKE ROSSI (aka FRANCIS) and JESS JAWORSKI. They subsequently added JOHN COGHLAN to replace BARRY SMITH, and, by the mid-60's were playing a residency at Butlin's holiday camp, where ROY LYNES took over from JESS. In July '66, they signed to 'Piccadilly' records but failed with a debut 45, a Leiber & Stoller cover, 'I (WHO HAVE NOTHING)'. They released two more flops, before they changed name in March '67 to The TRAFFIC JAM. After one 45, they chose an alternative moniker, The STATUS QUO, due to the more high profile TRAFFIC making the charts. In October '67, MIKE ROSSI reverted back to his real Christian name, FRANCIS, the band adding a second guitarist, RICK PARFITT. Now re-signed to 'Pye' records, they unleashed their first single, 'PICTURES OF MATCHSTICK MEN', giving them a breakthrough into the UK Top 10 (it also hit No.12 in the States – their only Top 50 hit). This was an attempt to cash-in on the hugely popular psychedelic scene, an enjoyable pastiche nevertheless, which remains one of their most enduring, timeless songs. The following year, they were again in the Top 10 with 'ICE IN THE SUN', another taken from the same blueprint. Soon after, the band shed their psychedelic trappings, opting instead for a blues/boogie hard rock sound a la CANNED HEAT. After two more Top 30 hits in the early 70's, their biggest and best being, 'DOWN THE DUSTPIPE', they jumped ship in 1972, signing to 'Vertigo' records. With their trademark blue jeans and (sometimes) white T-shirts, they became one of the top selling bands of the 70's. Their 3-chord-wonder barrage of rock'n'roll had few variations, a disappointing 1971 set, 'DOG OF TWO HEAD' nevertheless hiding a minor classic in 'MEAN GIRL' (a hit two years later). Flying high once more in early '73, STATUS QUO hit the Top 10 with 'PAPER PLANE', the single lifted from the accompanying album, 'PILEDRIVER' (which featured a cover of The Doors' 'ROADHOUSE BLUES'!). The 'QUO said 'HELLO' in fine fashion nine months later, the chart-topping album widely regarded as ROSSI and Co.'s 12-bar tour de force, the hit single 'CAROLINE' also making the Top 5. The following year, another Top 10'er, 'BREAK THE RULES' (from the 'QUO' album), saw the band rather ironically sticking steadfastly to their tried and tested formula. This same formula served them well throughout the mid 70's, their commercial peak coming with 'DOWN DOWN', a No.1 single from the similarly successful 'ON THE LEVEL' album. They followed this with 'BLUE FOR YOU', a set that was lapped up by the massed ranks of the 'QUO army and featured two classy, almost credible hit singles, 'RAIN' and 'MYSTERY SONG'. A hairy eight-legged hit machine, the band just kept on rockin' oblivious to the punk upstarts; perhaps the song most readily identifiable with STATUS QUO, the cover of John Fogerty's 'ROCKIN' ALL OVER THE WORLD' "rocked" the nation in 1977, everyone from housewives to headbangers getting down with their air-guitar. Although they kept their notoriously die-hard following, the band became something of a reliable joke in the music journals as they veered more and more into R&B-by-numbers pop-rock territory, 1984's cover of Dion's 'THE WANDERER' being a prime example. Two years previous, COGHLAN departed (possibly after hearing the same three chords just once too many), the group bringing in PETE KIRCHNER until 1986 when JEFF RICH replaced him. That same year, yet another founder member, LANCASTER, bailed out, keyboard player, ANDY BOWN (a part-time member since '74) become a full-time fifth member. Hardly recognisable as a 'QUO single, the dreary 'IN THE ARMY NOW' almost took ROSSI, PARFITT and Co. back to the top of the charts in '86 (having earlier wowed the world at LIVE AID). STATUS QUO's past musical misdemeanours paled dramatically against the unforgivable early 90's medley, entitled 'ANNIVERSARY WALTZ' (25th unfortunately). The song found them vying for the knees-up-Mother Brown position previously held by cockney "entertainers", CHAS & DAVE. Enough said. • **Songwriters:** LANCASTER (until his departure) or ROSSI and PARFITT. In the early 70's, ROSSI and tour manager BOB YOUNG took over duties. Covered; SPICKS AND SPECKS (Bee Gees) / GREEN TAMBOURINE (Lemon Pipers) / SHEILA (Tommy Roe) / ICE IN THE SUN + ELIZABETH DREAMS + PARADISE FLAT + others (Marty Wilde – Ronnie Scott) / JUNIOR'S WAILING (Steamhammer) / DOWN THE DUSTPIPE (Carl Grossman) / THE PRICE OF LOVE (Everly Brothers) / WILD SIDE OF LIFE (Tommy Quickly) / IN THE ARMY NOW (Bolland-Bolland) / RESTLESS (Jennifer Warnes) / WHEN YOU WALK IN THE ROOM (Jackie DeShannon) / FUN, FUN, FUN (Beach Boys) / I CAN HEAR THE GRASS GROW (Move) / YOU NEVER CAN TELL (Chuck Berry) / GET BACK (Beatles) / SAFETY DANCE (Men Without Hats) / RAINING IN MY HEART (Buddy Holly) / DON'T STOP (Fleetwood Mac) / PROUD MARY (Creedence Clearwater Revival) / LUCILLE (Little Richard) / JOHNNY AND MARY (Robert Palmer) / GET OUT OF DENVER (Bob Seger) / THE FUTURE'S SO BRIGHT (Timbuk 3) / ALL AROUND MY HAT (Steeleye Span) / etc.

Album rating: PICTURESQUE MATCHSTICKABLE MESSAGES FROM THE STATUS QUO (*5) / SPARE PARTS (*4) / MA KELLY'S GREASY SPOON (*4) / DOG OF TWO HEAD (*6) / PILEDRIVER (*6) / HELLO! (*7) / QUO (*6) / ON THE LEVEL (*6) / BLUE FOR YOU (*5) / STATUS QUO LIVE! (*6) / ROCKIN' ALL OVER THE WORLD (*6) / IF YOU CAN'T STAND THE HEAT (*6) / WHATEVER YOU WANT (*6) / 12 GOLD BARS compilation (*8) / JUST SUPPOSIN' (*6) / NEVER TOO LATE (*5) / 1+9+8+2 (*5) / FROM THE MAKERS OF . . . compilation/live (*6) / BACK TO BACK (*4) / 12 GOLD BARS, VOL.2 compilation (*6) / IN THE ARMY NOW (*6) / AIN'T COMPLAINING (*5) / PERFECT REMEDY (*3) / ROCKIN' ALL OVER THE YEARS compilation (*7) / ROCK 'TIL YOU DROP (*5) / LIVE ALIVE QUO (*4) / THIRSTY WORK (*4) / DON'T STOP (*3) / UNDER THE INFLUENCE (*3) / FAMOUS IN THE LAST CENTURY (*3) / Francis Rossi: KING OF THE DOGHOUSE (*3)

MIKE ROSSI (b. FRANCIS, 29 Apr'49, Forest Hill, London) – vocals, guitar / **ROY LYNES** (b.25 Oct'43, Surrey, Kent) – organ, vocals repl. JESS JAWORSKI / **ALAN LANCASTER** (b. 7 Feb'49, Peckham, London) – bass, vocals / **JOHN COGHLAN** (b.19 Sep'46, Dulwich, London) – drums repl. BARRY SMITH

Piccadilly — not iss.

Sep 66. (7"; as The SPECTRES) *(7N 35339)* **I (WHO HAVE NOTHING). / NEIGHBOUR, NEIGHBOUR** [ ] [-]
Nov 66. (7"; as The SPECTRES) *(7N 35352)* **HURDY GURDY MAN. / LATICA** [ ] [-]
— (above was not the DONOVAN song)
Feb 67. (7"; as The SPECTRES) *(7N 35368)* **(WE AIN'T GOT) NOTHIN' YET. / I WANT IT** [ ] [-]
Jun 67. (7"; as TRAFFIC JAM) *(7N 35386)* **ALMOST THERE BUT NOT QUITE. / WAIT JUST A MINUTE** [ ] [-]

The STATUS QUO

— added **RICK PARFITT** (b. RICHARD HARRISON, 12 Oct'48, Woking, Surrey) – guitar, vocals / MIKE now **FRANCIS ROSSI**

Pye — Cadet Concept

Nov 67. (7") *(7N 17449)* *<7001>* **PICTURES OF MATCHSTICK MEN. / GENTLEMAN JOE'S SIDEWALK CAFE** [7] [12] May68
Apr 68. (7") *(7N 17497)* *<7015>* **BLACK VEILS OF MELONCHOLY. / TO BE FREE** [ ] [ ] Jul69
Aug 68. (lp) *(NSPL 18220)* *<LSP 315>* **PICTURESQUE MATCHSTICKABLE MESSAGES FROM THE STATUS QUO** (US-title 'MESSAGES FROM THE STATUS QUO') [ ] [ ]
– Black veils of meloncholy / When my mind is not live / Ice in the Sun / Elizabeth dreams / Gentleman Joe's sidewalk cafe / Paradise flat / Technicolour dreams / Spicks and specks / Sheila / Sunny cellophane skies / Green tambourine / Pictures of matchstick men. *(re-iss. Oct87 on 'P.R.T.' lp/c/cd; PYL/PYM/PYC 6020) (cd re-iss. Dec89 on 'Castle'; CLACD 168)*
Aug 68. (7") *(7N 17581)* *<7006>* **ICE IN THE SUN. / WHEN MY MIND IS NOT ALIVE** [8] [70]
Jan 69. (7"w-drawn) *(7N 17650)* **TECHNICOLOR DREAMS. / PARADISE FLAT** [-] [-]
Feb 69. (7") *(7N 17665)* **MAKE ME STAY A BIT LONGER. / AUNTIE NELLIE** [ ] [-]
Mar 69. (7") *<7010>* **TECHNICOLOR DREAMS. / SPICKS AND SPECKS** [-] [ ]
May 69. (7") *(7N 17728)* **ARE YOU GROWING TIRED OF MY LOVE. / SO ENDS ANOTHER LIFE** [46] [-]
Sep 69. (lp) *(NSPL 18301)* **SPARE PARTS** [ ] [-]
– Face without a soul / You're just what I'm looking for / Mr.Mind detector / Antique Angelique / So ends another life / Are you growing tired of my love / Little Miss Nothing / Poor old man / The clown / Velvet curtains / When I awake / Nothing at all. *(re-iss. Oct87 on 'P.R.T.' lp/c/cd; PYL/PYM/PYC 6021) (re-iss. Aug90 on 'Castle' cd/c/lp; CLA CD/MC/LP 205) (re-mast.Aug98 on 'Essential'+=; ESMCD 625)* – (extra tracks).
Oct 69. (7") *(7N 17825)* *<7017>* **THE PRICE OF LOVE. / LITTLE MISS NOTHING** [ ] [ ]

Pye — Janus

Mar 70. (7") *(7N 17907)* *<127>* **DOWN THE DUSTPIPE. / FACE WITHOUT A SOUL** [12] [ ]
Sep 70. (lp) *(NSPL 18344)* *<3018>* **MA KELLY'S GREASY SPOON** [ ] [ ]
– Spinning wheel blues / Daughter / Everything / Shy fly / (April) Spring, Summer and Wednesdays / Junior's wailing / Lakky lady / Need your love / Lazy poker blues / (a) Is it really me – (b) Gotta go home. *(re-iss. Oct87 on 'P.R.T.'; PYL/PYM/PYC 6022) (cd re-iss. Dec89 on 'Castle'; CLACD 169)*

STATUS QUO

— now a quartet of **ROSSI, PARFITT, LANCASTER + COGHLAN** when LYNES departed
Oct 70. (7") *(7N 17998)* *<141>* **IN MY CHAIR. / GERDUNDULA** [21] [ ]
(re-iss. Jun79)

Pye — Pye

Jun 71. (7") *(7N 45077)* *<65000>* **TUNE TO THE MUSIC. / GOOD THINKING** [ ] [ ]
Dec 71. (lp/c) *(NSPL 18371)* *<3301>* **DOG OF TWO HEAD** [ ] [ ]
– Umleitung / Nanana / Something going on in my head / Mean girl / Nanana / Gerdundula / Railroad / Someone's learning / Nanana. *(cd-iss. 1986 on 'P.R.T.'; CDMP 8837) (re-iss. Oct87 on 'P.R.T.' lp/c/cd; PYL/PYM/PYC 6023) (re-iss. Aug90 on 'Castle' cd/c/lp; CLA CD/MC/LP 206) (re-mast.Aug98 on 'Essential'+=; ESMCD 626)* – (extra tracks).

Vertigo — A&M

Jan 73. (7") *(6059 071)* **PAPER PLANE. / SOFTER RIDE** [8] [-]
Jan 73. (lp) *(6360 082)* *<4381>* **PILEDRIVER** [5] [ ]
– Don't waste my time / O baby / A year / Unspoken words / Big fat mama / Paper plane / All the reasons / Roadhouse blues. *(re-iss. May83 lp/c; PRICE/PRIMC 17) (cd-iss. Feb91; 848 176-2)*
May 73. (7") *<1425>* **DON'T WASTE MY TIME. / ALL THE REASONS** [-] [ ]
Jul 73. (7") *<1443>* **PAPER PLANE. / ALL THE REASONS** [-] [ ]
Sep 73. (7") *(6059 085)* **CAROLINE. / JOANNE** [5] [-]
Sep 73. (lp) *(6360 098)* *<3615>* **HELLO!** [1] [ ]
– Roll over lay down / Claudie / A reason for living / Blue eyed lady / Caroline / Softer ride / And it's better now / Forty-five hundred times. *(re-iss. May83 lp/c; PRICE/PRIMC 16) (cd-iss. Feb91; 848 172-2)*
Feb 74. (7") *<1510>* **CAROLINE. / SOFTER RIDE** [-] [ ]
Apr 74. (7") *(6059 101)* **BREAK THE RULES. / LONELY NIGHT** [8] [-]
May 74. (lp/c) *(9102/7231 001)* *<3649>* **QUO** [2] [ ]
– Backwater / Just take me / Break the rules / Drifting away / Don't think it matters / Fine fine fine / Lonely man / Slow train. *(re-iss. Aug83 lp/c; PRICE/PRIMC 38)*

Vertigo — Capitol

Nov 74. (7") *(6059 114)* *<4039>* **DOWN DOWN. / NIGHT RIDE** [1] [ ]
Feb 75. (lp/c) *(9102/7231 002)* *<11381>* **ON THE LEVEL** [1] [ ]
– Little lady / Most of the time / I saw the light / Over and done / Nightride / Down down / Broken man / What to do / Where I am / Bye bye Johnny. *(re-iss. Aug83 lp/c; PRICE/PRIMC 39) (cd-iss. Feb91; 848 175-2)*
Apr 75. (7") *<4125>* **BYE BYE JOHNNY. / DOWN DOWN** [-] [ ]
May 75. (7"ep) *(QUO 13)* **STATUS QUO LIVE! (live)** [9] [-]
– Roll over lay down / Gerdundula / Junior's wailing.
Feb 76. (7") *(6059 133)* **RAIN. / YOU LOST THE LOVE** [7] [ ]
Mar 76. (lp/c) *(9102/7231 006)* *<11509>* **BLUE FOR YOU** <US title 'STATUS QUO'> [1] [ ]
– Is there a better way / Mad about the boy / Ring of a change / Blue for you / Rain / Rolling home / That's a fact / Ease your mind / Mystery song. *(re-iss. Dec83 lp/c; PRICE/PRIMC 55)*
Jul 76. (7") *(6059 146)* **MYSTERY SONG. / DRIFTING AWAY** [11] [ ]
Dec 76. (7") *(6059 153)* **WILD SIDE OF LIFE. / ALL THROUGH THE NIGHT** [9] [ ]
Mar 77. (d-lp)(d-c) *(6641 580)(7599 171)* *<11623>* **LIVE! (live)** [3] [ ]
– Junior's wailing / (a) Backwater, (b) Just take me / Is there a better way / In my chair / Little lady / Most of the time / Forty-five hundred times / Roll over lay down / Big fat mama / Caroline / Bye bye Johnny / Rain / Don't waste my time / Roadhouse blues. *(re-iss. Sep84; d-lp/d-c; PRID/+C 5) (d-cd-iss. Feb92 & Aug98; 510 334-2)*
Oct 77. (7") *(6059 184)* **ROCKIN' ALL OVER THE WORLD. / RING OF A CHANGE** [3] [ ]
Nov 77. (lp)(c) *(9102 014)(7231 012)* *<11749>* **ROCKIN' ALL OVER THE WORLD** [5] [ ]
– Hard time / Can't give you more / Let's ride / Baby boy / You don't own me / Rockers rollin' / Rockin' all over the world / Who am I? / Too far gone / For you / Dirty water / Hold you back. *(re-iss. Aug85 lp/c; PRICE/PRIMC 87) (cd-iss. Feb91; 848 173-2)*
Aug 78. (7") *(QUO 1)* **AGAIN AND AGAIN. / TOO FAR GONE** [13] [-]
Oct 78. (lp)(c) *(9102 027)(7231 017)* **IF YOU CAN'T STAND THE HEAT** [3] [-]
– Again and again / I'm giving up my worryin' / Gonna teach you to love me / Someone show me home / Long legged Linda / Oh! what a night / Accident prone / Stones / Let me fly / Like a good girl. *(cd-iss. see-compilations)*
Nov 78. (7") *(QUO 2)* **ACCIDENT PRONE. / LET ME FLY** [36] [-]
Sep 79. (7") *(6059 242)* **WHATEVER YOU WANT. / HARD RIDE** [4] [-]
Oct 79. (lp)(c) *(9102 037)(7231 025)* **WHATEVER YOU WANT** [3] [-]
– Whatever you want / Shady lady / Who asked you / Your smiling face / Living on an island / Come rock with me / Rockin' on / Runaway / High flyer / Breaking away. *(cd-iss. see-compilations)*
Nov 79. (7") *(6059 248)* **LIVING ON AN ISLAND. / RUNAWAY** [16] [-]
Apr 80. (lp/c) *(QUO TV/MC 1)* **12 GOLD BARS** (compilation) [3] [-]
– Rockin' all over the world / Down down / Caroline / Paper plane / Break the rules / Again and again / Mystery song / Roll over lay down / Rain / The wild side of life / Whatever you want / Living on an island. *(cd-iss. Nov83; 800 062-2)*
Oct 80. (7") *(QUO 3)* **WHAT YOU'RE PROPOSIN'. / AB BLUES** [2] [-]

Oct 80. (lp/c) *(6302/7144 057)* **JUST SUPPOSIN'** 4 -
– What you're proposin' / Run to mummy / Don't drive my car / Lies / Over the edge / The wild ones / Name of the game / Coming and going / Rock'n'roll.

Dec 80. (7") *(QUO 4)* **DON'T DRIVE MY CAR. / LIES** 11 -

Feb 81. (7") *(QUO 5)* **SOMETHING 'BOUT YOU BABY I LIKE. / ENOUGH IS ENOUGH** 7 -

Mar 81. (lp/c) *(6302/7144 104)* **NEVER TOO LATE** 2 -
– Never too late / Something 'bout you baby I like / Take me away / Falling in falling out / Carol / Long ago / Mountain lady / Don't stop me now / Enough is enough / Riverside. *(cd-iss. Oct83; 800 053-2)*

Nov 81. (7"m) *(QUO 6)* **ROCK'N'ROLL. / HOLD YOU BACK / BACKWATER** 8 -

— **PETE KIRCHNER** – drums (ex-ORIGINAL MIRRORS, ex-HONEYBUS, etc.) repl. COUGHLAN who formed PARTNERS IN CRIME

Mar 82. (7") *(QUO 7)* **DEAR JOHN. / I WANT THE WORLD TO KNOW** 10 -

Apr 82. (lp/c) *(6302/7144 189)* **1+9+8+2** 1 -
– She don't fool me / Young pretender / Get out and walk / Jealousy / I love rock and roll / Resurrection / Dear John / Doesn't matter / I want the world to know / I should have known / Big man. *(cd-iss. Oct83; 800 035-2)*

Jun 82. (7") *(QUO 8)* **SHE DON'T FOOL ME. / NEVER TOO LATE** 36 -

Oct 82. (7"/7"pic-d) *(QUO/+P 10)* **CAROLINE (live). / DIRTY WATER (live)** 13 -
(12"+=) *(QUO 10-12)* – Down down (live).

Nov 82. (t-lp/3xlp-box) *(PRO LP/BX 1)* **FROM THE MAKERS OF . . .** (compilation & 2 lp-sides live) 4 -
– Pictures of matchstick men / Ice in the Sun / Down the dustpipe / In my chair / Junior's wailing / Mean girl / Gerdundula / Paper plane / Big fat mama / Roadhouse blues / Break the rules / Down down / Bye bye Johnny / Rain / Mystery song / Blue for you / Is there a better way / Again and again / Accident prone / The wild side of life / Living on an island / What you're proposing / Rock and roll / Something 'bout you baby I like / Dear John / Caroline / Roll over lay down / Backwater / Little lady / Don't drive my car / Whatever you want / Hold you back / Rockin' all over the world / Over the edge / Don't waste my time.

Sep 83. (7"/7"blue) *(QUO/+B 11)* **OL' RAG BLUES. / STAY THE NIGHT** 9 -
(ext.12"+=) *(QUO 11-12)* – Whatever you want (live).

Oct 83. (lp/c)(cd) *(VERH/+C 10)(814 662-2)* **BACK TO BACK** 9 -
– A mess of blues / Ol' rag blues / Can't be done / Too close to the ground / No contrast / Win or lose / Marguerita time / Your kind of love / Stay the night / Going down town tonight. *(cd re-iss. see-compilations)*

Oct 83. (7") *(QUO 12)* **A MESS OF BLUES. / BIG MAN** 15 -
(ext.12"+=) *(QUO 12-12)* – Young pretender.

Dec 83. (7"/7"pic-d) *(QUO/+P 14)* **MARGUERITA TIME. / RESURRECTION** 3 -
(d7"+=) *(QUO 14-14)* – Caroline / Joanne.

May 84. (7") *(QUO 15)* **GOING DOWN TOWN TONIGHT. / TOO CLOSE TO THE GROUND** 20 -

Oct 84. (7"/12"clear) *(QUO/+P 16)* **THE WANDERER. / CAN'T BE DONE** 7 -

Nov 84. (d-lp/c)(cd) *(QUO TV/MC 2)(822 985-2)* **12 GOLD BARS VOL.2** (compilation) 12 -
– What you're proposing / Lies / Something 'bout you baby I like / Don't drive my car / Dear John / Rock and roll / Ol' rag blues / Mess of the blues / Marguerita time / Going down town tonight / The wanderer. / (includes VOL.1).

— **ROSSI + PARFITT** enlisted **ANDY BOWN** – keyboards (ex-HERD) (He was p/t member since 1974) / **JEFF RICH** – drums (ex-CLIMAX BLUES BAND) repl. KIRCHNER / **RHINO EDWARDS** (r.n.JOHN) – bass (ex-CLIMAX BLUES BAND) repl. LANCASTER

May 86. (7"/7"sha-pic-d) *(QUO/+PD 18)* **ROLLIN' HOME. / LONELY** 9 -
(12"+=) *(QUO 18-12)* – Keep me guessing.

Jul 86. (7") *(QUO 19)* **RED SKY. / DON'T GIVE IT UP** 19 -
(12"+=)(12"w-poster+=) *(QUO 19-12)(QUOPB 19-1)* – The Milton Keynes medley (live).
(d7"+=) *(QUOPD 19)* – Marguerita time.

Aug 86. (lp/c)(cd) *(VERH/+C 36)(830 049-2)* **IN THE ARMY NOW** 7 -
– Rollin' home / Calling / In your eyes / Save me / In the army now / Dreamin' / End of the line / Invitation / Red sky / Speechless / Overdose.

Sep 86. (7"/7"pic-d) *(QUO/PD 20)* **IN THE ARMY NOW. / HEARTBURN** 2 -
(d7"+=) *(QUODP 20)* – Marguerita time / What you're proposin'.
('A'-military mix.12"+=) *(QUO 20-12)* – Late last night.

Nov 86. (7") *(QUO 21)* **DREAMIN'. / LONG-LEGGED GIRLS** 15 -
('A'-wet mix.12"+=) *(QUO 21-12)* – The Quo Christmas cake mix.

Mar 88. (7"/7"s) *(QUO/+H 22)* **AIN'T COMPLAINING. / THAT'S ALRIGHT** 19 -
(ext.12"+=) *(QUO 22-12)* – Lean machine.
(cd-s++=) *(QUOCD 22)* – In the army now (remix).

May 88. (7"/7"s) *(QUO/+H 23)* **WHO GETS THE LOVE?. / HALLOWEEN** 34 -
(ext.12"+=) *(QUO 23-12)* – The reason for goodbye.
(cd-s++=) *(QUOCD 23)* – The wanderer (Sharon the nag mix).

Jun 88. (lp/c)(cd) *(VERH/+C 58)(834 604-2)* **AIN'T COMPLAINING** 12 -
– Ain't complaining / Everytime I think of you / One for the money / Another shipwreck / Don't mind if I do / I know you're leaving / Cross that bridge / Cream of the crop / The loving game / Who gets the love? / Burning bridges / Magic.

— (Below single was a re-working of 'ROCKIN' ALL . . . ' for Sport Aid)

Aug 88. (7") *(QUAID 1)* **RUNNING ALL OVER THE WORLD. / MAGIC** 17 -
(12"+=) *(QUAID 1-12)* – ('A'extended).
(cd-s++=) *(QUACD 1)* – Whatever you want.

Nov 88. (7") *(QUO 25)* **BURNING BRIDGES (ON AND OFF AND ON AGAIN). / WHATEVER YOU WANT** 5 -
(ext.12"+=/cd-s+=) *(QUO 25-12/CD25)* – Marguerita time.

Oct 89. (7"/c-s) *(QUO/+MC 26)* **NOT AT ALL. / GONE THRU THE SLIPS** 50 -
(12"+=)(cd-s+=) *(QUO 26-12/CD26)* – Every time I think of you.

Nov 89. (lp/c/cd) *(842 098-1/-4/-2)* **PERFECT REMEDY** 49 -
– Little dreamer / Not at all / Heart on hold / Perfect remedy / Address book / The power of rock / The way I am / Tommy's in love / Man overboard / Going down for the first time / Throw her a line / 1,000 years.

Dec 89. (7"/7"pic-d/c-s) *(QUO/+P/MC 27)* **LITTLE DREAMER. / ROTTEN TO THE BONE** -
(12"+=)(12"g-f+=/cd-s+=) *(QUO 27-12)(QUO X/CD 27)* – Doing it all for you.

Oct 90. (7"/7"silver/c-s) *(QUO/+G/MC 28)* **THE ANNIVERSARY WALTZ – (PART 1). / THE POWER OF ROCK** 2 -
(12"+=/cd-s+=) *(QUO 28-12/CD28)* – Perfect remedy.

Oct 90. (cd/c/d-lp) *(846 797-2/-4/-1)* **ROCKIN' ALL OVER THE YEARS** (compilation) 2 -
– Pictures of matchstick men / Ice in the Sun / Paper plane / Caroline / Break the rules / Down down / Roll over lay down / Rain / Wild side of life / Whatever you want / What you're proposing / Something 'bout you baby I like / Rock'n'roll / Dear John / Ol' rag blues / Marguerita time / The wanderer / Rollin' home / In the army now / Burning bridges / Anniversary waltz (part 1).

Dec 90. (7"/c-s) *(QUO/+MC 29)* **THE ANNIVERSARY WALTZ – (PART 2). / DIRTY WATER (live)** 16 -
(12"+=/cd-s+=) *(QUO 29-12/CD29)* – Pictures of matchstick men – Rock'n'roll music – Lover please – That'll be the day – Singing the blues.

Aug 91. (7"/c-s) *(QUO/+MC 30)* **CAN'T GIVE YOU MORE. / DEAD IN THE WATER** 37 -
(12"+=/cd-s+=) *(QUO 30-12/CD30)* – Mysteries from the ball.

Sep 91. (cd/c/lp) *(510 341-2/-4/-1)* **ROCK 'TIL YOU DROP** 10 -
– Like a zombie / All we really wanna do (Polly) / Fakin' the blues / One man band / Rock 'til you drop / Can't give you more / Warning shot / Let's work together / Bring it on home / No problems. *(cd+=/c+=)* – Good sign / Tommy / Nothing comes easy / Fame or money / Price of love / Forty-five hundred times. *(re-iss. Feb93)*

Jan 92. (7"/c-s) *(QUO/+MC 32)* **ROCK 'TIL YOU DROP. / Awards Medley:- CAROLINE – DOWN DOWN – WHATEVER YOU WANT – ROCKIN' ALL OVER THE WORLD** 38 -
(12"+=/cd-s+=) *(QUO 32-12/CD32)* – Forty-five hundred times.

Polydor not iss.

Oct 92. (7"/c-s) *(QUO/+MC 33)* **ROADHOUSE MEDLEY (ANNIVERSARY WALTZ 25). / ('A'extended)** 21
(cd-s+=) *(QUOCD 33)* – ('A'mix).
(cd-s+=) *(QUODD 33)* – Don't drive my car.

Nov 92. (cd/c/lp) *(517 367-2/-4/-1)* **LIVE ALIVE QUO (live)** 37
– Roadhouse medley:- Roadhouse blues – The wanderer – Marguerita time – Living on an island – Break the rules – Something 'bout you baby I like – The price of love – Roadhouse blues / Whatever you want / In the army now / Burning bridges / Rockin' all over the world / Caroline / Don't drive my car / Hold you back / Little lady.

— In May 94; their 'BURNING BRIDGES' tune, was used for Manchester United Football Squad's UK No.1 'Come On You Reds'.

Jul 94. (7"colrd/c-s) *(QUO/+MC 34)* **I DIDN'T MEAN IT. / WHATEVER YOU WANT** 21 -
(cd-s+=) *(QUODD 34)* – Down down / Rockin' all over the world.
(cd-s) *(QUOCD 34)* – ('A'side) / ('A'-Hooligan version) / Survival / She knew too much.

Aug 94. (cd/c/lp) *(523607-2/-4/-1)* **THIRSTY WORK** 13 -
– Goin' nowhere / I didn't mean it / Confidence / Point of no return / Sail away / Like it or not / Soft in the head / Queenie / Lover of the human race / Sherri don't fail me now! / Rude awakening time / Back on my feet / Restless / Ciao ciao / Tango / Sorry.

Oct 94. (7"colrd/c-s) *(QUO/+MC 35)* **SHERRI DON'T FAIL ME NOW!. / BEAUTIFUL** 38 -
(cd-s+=) *(QUOCD 34)* – In the army now.
(cd-s) *(QUODD 34)* – ('A'side) / Tossin' and turnin' / Down to you.

Nov 94. (7"/c-s/cd-s) *(QUO/+MC/CD 36)* **RESTLESS (re-orchestrated). / AND I DO** 39 -

PolygramTV not iss.

Oct 95. (7"/c-s) *(577 512-7/-4)* **WHEN YOU WALK IN THE ROOM. / TILTING AT THE MILL** 34 -
(cd-s+=) *(577 512-2)* – ('A'version).

Feb 96. (7"/c-s; STATUS QUO with The BEACH BOYS) *(576 262-7/-4)* **FUN FUN FUN. / MORTIFIED** 24 -
(cd-s+=) *(576 262-2)* – ('A'mix).
below album features all covers. They sued Radio One for not playing the above hit on their playlist after it charted. The QUO finally lose out in court and faced costs of over £50,000.

Feb 96. (cd/c) *(531 035-2/-4)* **DON'T STOP** 2 -
– Fun, fun, fun (with The BEACH BOYS) / When you walk in the room / I can hear the grass grow / You never can tell (it was a teenage wedding) / Get back / Safety dance / Raining in my heart (with BRIAN MAY) / Don't stop / Sorrow / Proud Mary / Lucille / Johnny and Mary / Get out of enver / The future's so bright (I gotta wear shades) / All around my hat (with MADDY PRIOR).

Apr 96. (7"/c-s) *(576 634-7/-4)* **DON'T STOP. / TEMPORARY FRIEND** 35 -
(cd-s+=) *(576 635-2)* –

Oct 96. (7"/c-s; STATUS QUO with MADDY PRIOR) *(575 944-7/-4)* **ALL AROUND MY HAT. / I'LL NEVER GET OVER YOU** 47 -
(cd-s+=) *(575 945-2)* – Get out of Denver.

— FRANCIS ROSSI also issued solo releases, the album 'KING OF THE DOGHOUSE' was out in Sept'96

Eagle Spitfire

Mar 99. (c-s) *(EAGCS 075)* **THE WAY IT GOES / UNDER THE INFLUENCE** 39 -
(cd-s) *(EAGXS 075)* – ('A'side) / Sea cruise.

Mar 99. (cd/c) *(EAG CD/MC 076)* <5035> **UNDER THE INFLUENCE** 26 Jul99
– Twenty wild horses / Under the influence / Round and round / Shine on / Little white lies / Keep 'em coming / Little me and you / Making waves / Blessed are the meek / Roll the dice / Not fade away.

May 99. (c-s) *(EAGCS 101)* **LITTLE WHITE LIES / I KNEW THE BRIDE** 47 -
(cd-s+=) *(EAGXS 101)* – Pictures of matchstick men (1999).

Sep 99. (c-s) *(EAGCS 105)* **TWENTY WILD HORSES / ANALYSE TIME** 53 -
(cd-s+=) *(EAGXS 105)* – Destruction day.

Universal Universal

Apr 00. (cd/c) *(157814-2/-4)* **FAMOUS IN THE LAST CENTURY** [19] [ ]
– Famous in the last century / Old time rock'n'roll / Way down / Rave on / Roll over Beethoven / When I'm dead and gone / Memphis Tennessee / Sweet home Chicago / Crawling from the wreckage / Good golly Miss Molly / Claudette / Rock'n'me / Hound dog / Runaround Sue / Once bitten twice shy / Mony mony / Famous in the last century (reprise).

May 00. (c-s) *(158013-4)* **MONY MONY /** [48] [-]
(cd-s+=) *(158013-2)* –

– compilations, etc. –

Dec 69. (lp) *Marble Arch; (MALS 1193)* **STATUS QUOTATIONS** [ ] [-]
Mar 73. (7") *Pye; (7N 45229) / <65017>* **MEAN GIRL. / EVERYTHING** [20] [ ]
May 73. (lp/c) *Pye; (NSPL/ZCP 18402)* **THE BEST OF STATUS QUO** [32] [-]
– Down the dustpipe / Gerdundula / In my chair / Umleitung / Lakky lady / Daughter / Railroad / Tune to the music / April, Spring, Summer and Wednesdays / Mean girl / Spinning wheel blues. *(cd-iss. 1986 on 'P.R.T.'; CDNSP 7773)*
Jun 73. (lp/c) *Golden Hour; (GH/ZCGH 556)* **A GOLDEN HOUR OF . . .** [ ] [-]
(re-iss. Apr90 on 'Knight' cd/c; KGH CD/MC 110)
Jul 73. (7") *Pye; (7N 45253)* **GERDUNDULA. / LAKKY LADY** [ ] [-]
1975. (lp) *Starline;* **ROCKIN' AROUND WITH** [ ] [-]
Oct 75. (lp/c) *Golden Hour; (GH/ZCGH 604)* **DOWN THE DUSTPIPE: THE GOLDEN HOUR OF . . . VOL.2** [20] [-]
Sep 76. (lp/c) *Pye; (PKL/ZCPKB 5546)* **THE REST OF STATUS QUO** [ ] [-]
Jan 77. (lp/c) *Pye; (FILD 005)* **THE STATUS QUO FILE SERIES** [ ] [-]
(re-iss. Sep79 on 'P.R.T.';)
Apr 77. (12"ep) *Pye; (BD 103)* **DOWN THE DUSTPIPE / MEAN GIRL. / IN MY CHAIR / GERDUNDULA** [ ] [-]
Apr 78. (lp) *Hallmark; (HMA 257)* **PICTURES OF MATCHSTICK MEN** [ ] [-]
May 78. (lp)(c) *Marble Arch; (HMA 260)(HSC 322)* **STATUS QUO** [ ] [-]
Aug 78. (d-lp/d-c) *Pickwick; (PDA/PDC 046)* **THE STATUS QUO COLLECTION** [ ] [-]
May 79. (7"yellow) *Flashback-Pye; (FBS 2)* **PICTURES OF MATCHSTICK MEN. / DOWN IN THE DUSTPIPE** [ ] [-]
(re-iss. 7"black Apr83 on 'Old Gold'; OG 9298)
Jun 79. (lp,orange-lp/c) *Pye; (NPSL/ZCP 18607)* **JUST FOR THE RECORD** [ ] [-]
Jun 80. (d-lp/d-c) *P.R.T.; (SPOT/ZCSPT 1028)* **SPOTLIGHT ON . . .** [ ] [-]
Sep 80. (d-lp/d-c) *Pickwick; (SSD/+C 8035)* **STATUS QUO** [ ] [-]
Oct 81. (10"lp/c) *P.R.T.; (DOW/ZCDOW 2)* **FRESH QUOTA** (rare) [74] [-]
Jun 82. (c) *P.R.T.; (ZCTON 101)* **100 MINUTES OF . . .** [ ] [-]
Jul 82. (7") *Old Gold; (OG 9142)* **MEAN GIRL. / IN MY CHAIR** [ ] [-]
Oct 82. (lp/c) *P.R.T.; (SPOT/ZCSPT 1028)* **SPOTLIGHT ON . . . VOL.II** [ ] [-]
Apr 83. (lp/c) *Contour; (CN/+4 2062)* **TO BE OR NOT TO BE** [ ] [-]
(cd-iss. Apr91 on 'Pickwick'; PWKS 4051P)
Jul 83. (10"lp/c) *P.R.T.; (DOW/ZCDOW 10)* **WORKS** [ ] [-]
Jul 84. (lp/c) *Vertigo; (818 947-2/-4)* **LIVE AT THE N.E.C. (live)** [83] [-] Dutch
(UK cd-iss. Jul91; 818 947-2)
Sep 85. (7") *Old Gold; (OG 9566)* **CAROLINE. / DOWN DOWN** [ ] [-]
Oct 85. (lp/c) *Flashback; (FBLP/ZCFBL 8082)* **NA NA NA** [ ] [-]
Nov 85. (7") *Old Gold; (OG 9567)* **ROCKIN' ALL OVER THE WORLD. / PAPER PLANE** [ ] [-]
(re-iss. Aug89 & Sep90)
Nov 85. (d-lp/c) *Castle; (CCS LP/MC 114)* **THE COLLECTION** [ ] [-]
(cd-iss. 1988; CCSCD 114)
Oct 87. (lp/c/cd) *P.R.T.; (PYL/PYM/PYC 6024)* **QUOTATIONS VOL.1 – (THE EARLY YEARS)** [ ] [-]
Oct 87. (lp/c/cd) *P.R.T.; (PYL/PYM/PYC 6025)* **QUOTATIONS VOL.2 – (ALTERNATIVES)** [ ] [-]
Sep 88. (lp/pic-lp/c/cd) *P.R.T.; (PYZ/PYX/PYM/PYC 4007)* **FROM THE BEGINNING (1966-67)** [ ] [-]
Apr 89. (c)(cd) *Legacy; (C 903)(GHCD 3)* **C90 COLLECTOR** [ ] [-]
Sep 90. (cd/c/d-lp) *Castle; (CCS CD/MC/LP 271)* **B SIDES AND RARITIES** [ ] [-]
Dec 90. (3xcd-box/3xlp-box) *Essential; (ESS CD/LP 136)* **THE EARLY WORKS** [ ] [-]
Feb 91. (cd) *Vertigo; (848 087-2)* **WHATEVER YOU WANT / JUST SUPPOSIN'** [ ] [-]
Feb 91. (cd) *Vertigo; (848 088-2)* **NEVER TOO LATE / BACK TO BACK** [ ] [-]
Feb 91. (cd) *Vertigo; (848 089-2)* **QUO / BLUE FOR YOU** [ ] [-]
(re-iss. Sep97; same)
Feb 91. (cd) *Vertigo; (848 090-2)* **IF YOU CAN'T STAND THE HEAT / 1+9+8+2** [ ] [-]
Sep 91. (d-cd) *Decal; (CDLIK 81)* **BACK TO THE BEGINNING** [ ] [-]
Nov 91. (cd) *Pickwick; (PWKS 4087P)* **THE BEST OF STATUS QUO 1972-1986** [ ] [-]
May 93. (cd/c) *Spectrum; (550002-2/-4)* **A FEW BARS MORE** [ ] [-]
Feb 94. (cd) *Dojo; (EARLD 8)* **THE EARLY YEARS** [ ] [-]
Aug 94. (cd/c) *Matchstick; (MAT CD/MC 291)* **STATUS QUO** [ ] [-]
Sep 94. (cd/c) *Spectrum; (550190-2/-4)* **IT'S ONLY ROCK'N'ROLL** [ ] [-]
Mar 95. (cd) *Connoisseur; (VSOPCD 213)* **THE OTHER SIDE OF STATUS QUO** [ ] [-]
May 95. (cd/c) *Spectrum; (550727-2/-4)* **PICTURES OF MATCHSTICK MEN** [ ] [-]
Jun 95. (cd/c) *Savanna; (SSL CD/MC 204)* **ICE IN THE SUN** [ ] [-]
(re-iss. Apr97 on 'Pulse' cd/c; PLS CD/MC 206)
Jul 96. (cd/c) *Truetrax; (TRT CD/MC 198)* **THE BEST OF STATUS QUO** [ ] [-]
Oct 97. (d-cd/d-c) *Polygram TV; (553507-2/-4)* **WHATEVER YOU WANT – THE VERY BEST OF** [13] [-]
Mar 99. (cd) *Castle Select; (SELCD 555)* **MATCHSTICK MEN – THE PSYCHEDELIC YEARS** [ ] [-]
Mar 99. (cd) *Spectrum; (554891-2)* **THE ESSENTIAL STATUS QUO VOL.1** [ ] [-]
Aug 99. (cd) *Spectrum; (554896-2)* **THE ESSENTIAL STATUS QUO VOL.2** [ ] [-]
Aug 99. (cd) *Castle Pie; (PIESD 005)* **ICE IN THE SUN** [ ] [-]
Feb 00. (cd) *Spectrum; (554897-2)* **THE ESSENTIAL STATUS QUO VOL.3** [ ] [-]
Jul 00. (cd) *Delta No.10; (CD 23106)* **ROCKIN' ALL OVER THE WORLD** [ ] [-]
Sep 00. (cd/c) *Pulse; (PLS CD/MC 206)* **ICE IN THE SUN** [ ] [-]
Sep 00. (d-cd) *Castle; (CCSCD 821)* **THE SINGLES COLLECTION 1968-1972** [ ] [-]

STEELER

Formed: Bochum, Germany . . . 1981 originally as SINNER by guitar maestro AXEL RUDI PELL and singer PETER BURTZ. With the addition of VOLKER KRAWCZAK, VOLKER JAKEL and BERTRAM FREWER, they signed to the German indie label, 'Earthshaker'. More line-up changes ensued when THOMAS EDER and JAN YILDIRAL replaced FREWER and JAKEL prior to the recording of their eponymous debut set in 1984. The German-only release established the group's blend of typical teutonic melodic metal as well as functioning as a platform for PELL's six string histrionics. By the release of third set, 'STRIKE BACK' (1987), STEELER had begun moving towards a more commercial approach and following 1988's 'UNDERCOVER ANIMAL', PELL disbanded the project completely in favour of a solo career. Recruiting frontman CHARLIE HUHN along with German metal scene veterans JOERG DEISINGER and JORG MICHAEL, PELL made his solo debut the following year with the 'WILD OBSESSION' set. Much in the trad guitar hero mould, PELL's work failed to attract the plaudits of say, JOE SATRIANI although he did attract a loyal European following. He even secured the services of vocalist BOB ROCK for follow-up set, 'NASTY REPUTATION' (1991). PELL continued recording and releasing albums in incredibly prolific style throughout the 90's, 'MAGIC' didn't live up to its name in 1997. • **AXEL covers:** WHEN A BLIND MAN CRIES (Deep Purple) / WISHING WELL (Free) / JULY MORNING (Uriah Heep).

Album rating: STEELER (*5) / RULIN' THE EARTH (*5) / STRIKE BACK (*4) / UNDERCOVER ANGEL (*4) / Axel Rudi Pell: WILD OBSESSION (*6) / NASTY REPUTATION (*7) / THE BALLADS (*5) / BETWEEN THE WALLS (*5) / MADE IN GERMANY (*4) / BLACK MOOD PYRAMID (*5) / MAGIC (*4) / OCEANS OF TIME (*4) / THE BALLADS VOL.2 (*4) / THE MASQUERADE BALL (*4) / THE WIZARDS CHOSEN FEW compilation (*6)

PETER BURTZ – vocals / **AXEL RUDI PELL** – guitar / **THOMAS EDER** – guitar; repl. BERTRAM FREWER / **VOLKER KRAWCZAK** – bass / **JAN YILDIRAL** – drums; repl. VOLKER JAKEL

Earthshaker not iss.

Aug 84. (lp) *(ES 4001)* **STEELER** [-] [-] German
– Chains are broken / Gonna find some place in Hell / Heavy metal century / Sent from the evil / Long way / Call her Princess / Love for sale / Hydrophobia / Fallen angel.
Jun 85. (lp) *(ES 4009)* **RULIN' THE EARTH** [-] [-] German

— **HERVE ROSS** – bass; repl. KRAWCZAK

Steam-hammer not iss.

Feb 87. (7") *(SH 0067)* **NIGHT AFTER NIGHT. / WAITING FOR A STAR** [-] [-] German
Nov 87. (lp)(cd) *(08-18 90)(85-1861)* **STRIKE BACK** [-] [-] German
– Chain gang / Money doesn't count / Danger comeback / Icecold / Messing around with fire / Rockin' the city / Strike back / Night after night / Waiting for a star.
1988. (lp)(cd) *(08-75 10)(85-7512)* **UNDERCOVER ANIMAL** [-] [-] German
– (I'll be) Hunter or hunted / Undercover animal / Shadow in the redlight / Hard breaks / Criminal / Rely on rock / Stand tall / The deeper the night / Knock me out / Bad to the bone.

— split after above, AXEL went solo

AXEL RUDI PELL

— with **CHARLIE HUHN** – vocals / **JORG DEISINGER** – bass (of BONFIRE) / **JORG MICHAEL** – drums (ex-RAGE) / + sessions from GEORGE HAHN + RUDIGER KONIG – keyboards / VOLKER KRAWCZAK + THOMAS "BODO" S

Steam-hammer not iss.

1989. (lp)(cd) *(SPV 08-7609)(SPV 84-7610)* **WILD OBSESSION** [-] [-] German
– Wild cat / Call of the wild dogs / Slave of love / Cold as ice / Broken heart / Call her Princess / Snake eyes / Hear you calling me / Return of the Calyph from the apocalypse of Babylon / (Don't trust the) Promised dreams.

— **BOB ROCK** – vocals; repl. HUHN

1991. (lp/c/cd) *(SPV 008 7634-1/-4/-2)* **NASTY REPUTATION** [-] [-] German
– I will survive / Nasty reputation / Fighting the law / Wanted man / When a blind man cries / Land of the giants / Firewall / Unchain the thunder / Open doors, pt.I: Experience, pt.II: The journey, pt.III: Sugar big daddy.

— **VOLKER KRAWCZAK** – bass + **KAI RAGLEWSKI** – keyboards; repl. DEISINGER

Jul 93. (cd) *(SPV 084-7664-2)* **THE BALLADS** [ ] [-]
– You want love / Forever young / Dreams of passion / Your life (not close enough to Paradise) / Tearin' out my heart / When a blind man cries / Broken heart (demo) / Open doors, pt.2: The journey / Falling tears / Broken heart.
Jun 94. (cd) *(SPV 084-7682-2)* **BETWEEN THE WALLS** [ ] [-]
– The curse / Talk of the guns / Warrior / Cry of the gypsy / Casbah / Outlaw / Wishing well / Innocent child / Between the walls / Desert fire.
May 95. (cd) *(SPV 085-7697-2)* **MADE IN GERMANY (live)** [ ] [-]
– Talk of the guns / Nasty reputation / Mistreated / Warrior / Snake eyes / Casbah / Call her princess / Fire on the mountain.
May 96. (cd) *(SPV 085-1828-2)* **BLACK MOOD PYRAMID** [ ] [-]
– Return of the pharaoh (intro) / Gettin' dangerous / Fool fool / Hole in the sky / Touch the rainbow / Sphinx' revenge / You and I / Silent angel / Black moon pyramid / Serenade of darkness / Visions in the night / Aqua solution / Aquarius dance / Silent angel (guitar version).

Jun 97. (cd) *(SPV 085-1836-2)* **MAGIC** [ ] [-]
– Swamp castle overture / Nightmare / Playing with fire / Magic / Turned to stone / The clown is dead / Prisoners of the sea / Light in the sky / The eyes of the lost.
Jul 98. (cd) *(SPV 085-1814-2)* **OCEANS OF TIME** [ ] [-]
– Slaves of twilight / Pay the price / Carousel / Ashes from the oath / Ride the rainbow / The gates of the seven seals / Oceans of time / Prelude to the Moon / Living on the wildside / Holy creatures.
Mar 99. (cd) *(SPV 085-1867-2)* **THE BALLADS VOL.2** [ ] [-]
Apr 00. (cd) *(SPV 085-2169-2)* **THE MASQUERADE BALL** [ ] [-]
– The arrival (intro) / Carls of black / Voodoo nights / Night and rain / The masquerade ball / Tear down the walls / The line / Hot wheels / The temple of the holy ghost / July morning.
Nov 00. (cd) *(SPV 089-7207-2)* **THE WIZARDS CHOSEN FEW** (compilation) [ ] [-]
– Broken dreams / Carousel / The masquerade ball / Ghosthunter / Oceans of time / Still I'm sad / Come back to me / Burn – Purple haze – Call her princess / Total eclipse / Eternal prisoner / Fool fool / Casbah / Snake eyes / Mistreated / Magic / The clown is dead / Nasty reputation / Land of the giants / Hear you calling me.

– compilations, etc. –

Jul 00. (cd) *S.P.V.; (SPV 31021940)* **WILD OBSESSION / NASTY REPUTATION** [ ] [-]

STEELER (see under ⇒ KEEL)

STEEL POLE BATH TUB

Formed: Bozeman, Montana, USA . . . late 80's by DALE FLATTUM, MIKE MORASKY and DARREN MOR-X (former MR EPP, an outfit which also featured future MUDHONEY members, MARK ARM and STEVE TURNER). Relocating to San Francisco, they signed to 'Tupelo', where they set about causing maximum aural damage with their particularly twisted brand of industrial grunge-metal, calling up the damned soul of BLACK SABBATH and The STOOGES via the latter day sonic terrorism of MINISTRY. In 1989, SPBT delivered their debut album, 'BUTTERFLY LOVE', although it would be the following year's MELVINS collaboration, 'SWEET YOUNG THING' (borrowed from old muckers, MUDHONEY) that would bring them more exposure in the emerging Seattle grunge scene. Around the same time, the lads issued their follow-up set, 'LURCH', which featured an industrial strength remake of 'HEY BO DIDDLEY'. Their busiest year to date, 1991, saw STEEL POLE BATH TUB release another long-player, 'TULIP', while collaborating with fellow SF resident and former DEAD KENNEDYS frontman, JELLO BIAFRA, on the TUMOUR CIRCUS project. Two further SPBT sets, 'THE MIRACLE OF SOUND IN MOTION' (1993) and 'SOME COCKTAIL SUGGESTIONS' (1994), preceded a major label deal with 'Slash'. Although the band had cleaned up their act somewhat, 'SCARS FROM FALLING DOWN' (1995), their slightly watered down sound disappeared down the proverbial corporate plughole. • **Covered:** CHEMICAL WARFARE (Dead Kennedys) / THE GHOST (Willie Nelson).

Album rating: BUTTERFLY LOVE (*6) / LURCH (*6) / TULIP (*6) / THE MIRACLE OF SOUND IN MOTION (*5) / SOME COCKTAIL SUGGESTIONS (*5) / SCARS FROM FALLING DOWN (*5)

DALE FLATTUM – vocals, bass / **MIKE MORASKY** – guitar, vocals / **DARREN MOR-X** – drums

Tupelo Tupelo

1989. (lp) **BUTTERFLY LOVE** [-] [ ]
Jul 90. (7") **SWEET YOUNG THING (w/ MELVINS) /** [ ] [ ]
Jul 90. (cd/lp) *<(TUP CD/LP 15)>* **LURCH** [ ] [ ]
– Christine / Hey you / Paranoid / I am Sam I am / Bee sting / Swerve / Heaven on dirt / Lime away / The river / Time to die / Welcome aboard it's love / Hey Bo Diddley / Thru the windshields of love / Tear it apart.
Feb 91. (cd/lp) *<(TUP CD/LP 27)>* **TULIP** [ ] [ ]
– Soul cannon / Sister / Quark / One thick second / Pirate 5 / Mercurochrome / Wonders of dust / The scarlet / Misty Mt. Blowtorch / Myrna Loy / Pause.
May 92. (7"/cd-s) **BOZEMAN. / BORSTAL** [ ] [ ]
Apr 93. (cd/lp) *>(TUP 47-2/-1)>* **THE MIRACLE OF SOUND IN MOTION** [ ] [ ]
– Pseudoephedrine hydrochloride / Train to Miami / Exhale / Thumbnail / Down all the days / Cartoon / Bozeman / Borstal / 594 / Waxl.
Jan 94. (m-cd/m-c/m-10"lp) *<(TUP 051-2/-4/-1)>* **SOME COCKTAIL SUGGESTIONS** [ ] [ ]
– Ray / Living end / Slip / Hit it / Speaker phone / Wasp jar.

Slash Slash

Jan 96. (cd/c) *<(828 685-2/-4)>* **SCARS FROM FALLING DOWN** [ ] [ ] Nov95
– 500 club / Population / Home is a rope / Conversation / Twist / Everything / 3 of cups / Four barrels / Decline / Kansas City / Friday.

– compilations, etc. –

1992. (lp) *Your Choice; <(YCR 015)>* **LIVE** [ ] [ ]
Jul 94. (cd) *Your Choice; <(YCLS 019)>* **LIVE (live)** [ ] [ ]

Jim STEINMAN

Born: 1956, New York, USA. Raised in California, STEINMAN formed his first band when still in high school, the catchily titled CLITORIS THAT THOUGHT IT WAS A PUPPY. A talented lad, he also penned the off-Broadway musical, 'More Than You Deserve', the same year (1974), which is where he met girthsome performer, MEAT LOAF. STEINMAN relocated to New York the following year, touring alongside the 'LOAF and eventually collaborating with him on the soon-to-be-massively famous 'Bat Out Of Hell' album. Produced by TODD RUNDGREN and eventually released in 1978, the album went on to become one of the biggest selling recordings of all time. It also established STEINMAN as a much-in-demand man with a midas touch in the songwriting department. Due to MEAT LOAF's subsequent health/vocal problems, STEINMAN eventually released the follow-up, 'BAD FOR GOOD', as a solo project in 1981. Once again utilising the production/multi-instrumental skills of RUNDGREN and the backing muscle of the E-STREET BAND, the record nevertheless lacked the theatrical overload of MEAT's vocals for which the material was obviously written. While the album made the Top 10 in Britain, it didn't fare so well in the States, and STEINMAN concentrated largely on production work for most of the 80's. He wrote and produced BONNIE TYLER's No.1 'Total Eclipse Of The Heart' and subsequently went on to produce many acts including SISTERS OF MERCY (two tracks on their 'Floodland' set) and DEF LEPPARD, although the latter collaboration (1984) was aborted. Though an eventual MEAT LOAF follow-up, 'Dead Ringer' (1981), used STEINMAN material, it would be more than a decade before the pair would work together again. STEINMAN's next high profile project was the 'ORIGINAL SIN' (1989) album, a deranged hard-rock opera focussing on the theme of sex. Though masterminded by STEINMAN, the record was credited to PANDORA'S BOX, a band of session musicians fronted by ELAINE CASWELL and backed up with a posse of scary females. Despite garnering rave reviews from the metal press, the album failed to do much commercially and in the early 90's STEINMAN finally reunited with MEAT LOAF for the long anticipated follow-up to 'Bat..'. Needless to say the album was a humungous success all over again, STEINMAN's services currently as sought after as ever. • **Trivia:** 'LEFT IN THE DARK' was later covered by BARBRA STREISAND!

Album rating: BAD FOR GOOD (*5) / Pandora's Box: ORIGINAL SIN (*7)

JIM STEINMAN – keyboards, vocals (ex-MEAT LOAF) with **RORY DODD** – vox / **TODD RUNDGREN** – multi / **E-STREET BAND** (see; Bruce SPRINGSTEEN)

Epic Cleveland

May 81. (lp/c)(pic-lp) *(EPC/40 84361)(EPC11 84361) <36531>* **BAD FOR GOOD** [7] [63]
– Bad for good / Lost boys and golden girls / Love and death and an American guitar / Stark raving love / Out of the frying pan (and into the fire) / Surf's up / Dance in my pants / Left in the dark. *(free-7") (SXPS 117)* – THE STORM. / ROCK'N'ROLL DREAMS COME THROUGH *(cd-iss. Jan87 & Feb00; 472042-2)*
Jun 81. (7") *(EPCA 1236) <02111>* **ROCK'N'ROLL DREAMS COME THROUGH. / LOVE AND DEATH AND AN AMERICAN GUITAR** [52] [32] May81
(12"blue+=) *(EPCA13 1236)* – The storm.
Aug 81. (7") *(EPCA 1561) <02595>* **LOST BOYS AND GOLDEN GIRLS. / LEFT IN THE DARK** [ ] [ ] Oct81
Oct 81. (7") *(EPCA 1707) <02539>* **DANCE IN MY PANTS. / LEFT IN THE DARK** [ ] [ ] Jul81

JIM STEINMAN'S FIRE INC.

M.C.A. M.C.A.

May 84. (7"/12") *(MCA/+T 889) <52377>* **TONIGHT IS WHAT IT MEANS TO BE YOUNG. / HOLD THAT SNAKE (Ry Cooder)** [67] [ ]
Sep 84. (7") *<52693>* **NOWHERE FAST. / ONE BAD STUD (Blasters)** [-] [ ]
Sep 84. (7") *(MCA 920)* **NOWHERE FAST. / THE SORCEROR (Marilyn Martin)** [ ] [-]
(above from the film 'Streets Of Fire')

— Went back into production until the late 80's, when he formed

PANDORA'S BOX

with **ELAINE CASWELL** – vocals / **EDDIE MARTINEZ** – guitar / **STEVE BUSLOWER** – bass / **ROY BITTAN** – piano / **JEFF BITTAN** – piano / plus **backing singers ELLEN FOLEY, DELIRIA WILDE, GINA TAYLOR, HOLLY SHERWOOD + LAURA THEODORE.**

Vertigo E.M.I.

Oct 89. (7") *(VS 1216)* **IT'S ALL COMING BACK TO ME NOW. / I'VE BEEN DREAMING UP A STORM RECENTLY** [51] [ ]
(c-s+=) *(VSC 1216)* – Pray lewd / Teenager in love.
(12"+=/cd-s+=) *(VS T/CD 1216)* – Pray lewd / Requiem metal.
Nov 89. (cd/c/lp) *(CD/TC+/V 2605) <42985>* **ORIGINAL SIN** [ ] [ ]
– The invocation / Original sin (the natives are restless today) / 20th century fox / Safe sex (when it comes 2 loving U) / Good girls go to Heaven (bad girls go everywhere) / Requiem metal / I've been dreamin' up a storm recently / It's all coming back to me now / The opening of the box / The want ad / My little red book / It just won't quit / Pray lewd / The flute ain't what it used to be. *(cd re-iss. Apr97 on 'Virgin VIP'; CDVIP 171)*
Mar 90. (7") *(VS 1227)* **GOOD GIRLS GO TO HEAVEN (BAD GIRLS GO EVERYWHERE). / REQUIEM METAL** [ ] [ ]
(12"+=/cd-s+=) *(VS T/CD 1227)* – Pray lewd / Pandora's house; room to roam.
Jun 90. (7"m) *(VS 1275)* **SAFE SEX. / I'VE BEEN DREAMIN' UP A STORM / REQUIEM METAL** [ ] [ ]
(12"+=/cd-s+=) *(VST 1275)* – Pray lewd.

— STEINMAN subsequently teamed up once again with MEAT LOAF on his 'BAT OUT OF HELL II – BACK TO HELL'.

STEPPENWOLF

Formed: Toronto, Canada . . . 1966 as blues band SPARROW, by JOHN KAY, plus MICHAEL MONARCH, GOLDY McJOHN, RUSHTON MOREVE and JERRY EDMONTON. After one-off 45 for 'Columbia', they soon relocated to Los Angeles following a brief stay in New York. There, they met producer Gabriel Mekler, who suggested the STEPPENWOLF name (after a Herman Hesse novel). They quickly signed to 'Dunhill' and recorded their eponymous 1968 debut, which included that summer's No.2 classic biker's anthem, 'BORN TO BE WILD'. This success resurrected the album's appeal, which finally climbed to the higher echelons of the charts. The track was subsequently used on the 1969 film, 'Easy Rider', alongside another from the debut, 'THE PUSHER'. While both songs were enjoyable, hot-wired romps through dusty blues-rock terrain, the pseudo-intellectual musings and less than inspired songwriting of JOHN KAY made the multitude of subsequent STEPPENWOLF releases hard going. Nevertheless, the band hit US Top 3 with the colourful psychedelia of the 'MAGIC CARPET RIDE' (1968) single, its parent album, 'STEPPENWOLF THE SECOND' (1969) notching up a similar placing in the album charts. By the early 70's, the band were experiencing diminishing chart returns and split after the 1972 concept album, 'FOR LADIES ONLY'. KAY recorded a couple of solo albums before reforming STEPPENWOLF in 1974. Signed to 'C.B.S.' then 'Epic', the band failed to resurrect their early momentum, although they continued to inflict their tired biker-rock on an oblivious music world right up until the 90's. • **Songwriters:** KAY written, except; THE PUSHER + SNOW BLIND FRIEND (Hoyt Axton) / SOOKIE SOOKIE (Grant Green) / BORN TO BE WILD (Dennis Edmonton; Jerry's brother) / I'M MOVIN' ON (Hank Snow) / HOOCHIE COOCHIE MAN (Muddy Waters). • **Trivia:** BORN TO BE WILD coined a new rock term in the their lyrics "heavy metal thunder". Early in 1969, they contributed some songs to another cult-ish film, 'Candy'.

Album rating: STEPPENWOLF (*6) / THE SECOND (*6) / AT YOUR BIRTHDAY PARTY (*6) / MONSTER (*7) / STEPPENWOLF 'LIVE' (*5) / STEPPENWOLF 7 (*5) / STEPPENWOLF GOLD – THEIR GREAT HITS compilation (*7) / FOR LADIES ONLY (*5) / FORGOTTEN SONGS AND UNSUNG HEROES (*5; by John Kay) / REST IN PEACE collection (*4) / 16 GREATEST HITS compilation (*7) / MY SPORTIN' LIFE (*4; by John Kay) / SLOW FLUX (*4) / HOUR OF THE WOLF (*3) / SKULLDUGGERY (*3) / REBORN TO BE WILD (*3) / ALL IN GOOD TIME (*3; by John Kay) / John Kay & Steppenwolf: LIVE IN LONDON (*4) / WOLF TRACKS (*3) / ROCK & ROLL REBELS (*4) / RISE & SHINE (*4) / BORN TO BE WILD: A RETROSPECTIVE compilation (*7)

JOHN KAY (b. JOACHIM F. KRAULEDAT, 12 Apr'44, Tilsit, Germany) – vox, guitar / **MICHAEL MONARCH** (b. 5 Jul'50, Los Angeles, California, USA) – guitar / **GOLDY McJOHN** (b. JOHN GOADSBY, 2 May'45) – organ / **RUSHTON MOREVE** (b.1948, Los Angeles) – bass / **JERRY EDMONTON** (b. JERRY McCROHAN, 24 Oct'46, Canada) – drums, vocals

C.B.S. / Columbia

1966. (7"; as The SPARROW) *(202342) <43755>* **TOMORROW'S SHIP. / ISN'T IT STRANGE**

1967. (7"; as The SPARROW) *<43960>* **GREEN BOTTLE LOVER. / DOWN GOES YOUR LOVE LIFE** [-]

1967. (7"; as JOHN KAY) *<44769>* **TWISTED. / SQUAREHEAD PEOPLE** [-]

— **JOHN RUSSELL MORGAN** – bass repl. MOREVE. He was killed in car crash on 1st Jul'81.

R.C.A. / Dunhill

Nov 67. (7") *<4109>* **A GIRL I KNOW. / THE OSTRICH** [-]

Apr 68. (7") *(RCA 1679) <4123>* **SOOKIE SOOKIE. / TAKE WHAT YOU NEED** Jan68

May 68. (lp; mono/stereo) *(RD/SF 7974) <50029>* **STEPPENWOLF** [6] Jan68
– Sookie Sookie / Everybody's next one / Berry rides again / Hoochie coochie man / Born to be wild / Your wall's too high / Desperation / The pusher / A girl I know / Take what you need / The ostrich. *(re-iss. Apr70 on 'Stateside'; SSL 5020); hit No.59 (re-iss. Jun87 on 'M.C.A.' lp/c; MCL/+C 1857) (cd-iss. Jul87; CMCAD 31020) (re-iss. Apr92 cd/c; MCL D/C 19019)*

Aug 68. (7") *(RCA 1735) <4138>* **BORN TO BE WILD. / EVERYBODY'S NEXT ONE** [2] Jun68
(re-iss. May69 on 'Stateside'; SS 8017); hit No.30

Stateside / Dunhill

Oct 68. (7") *(SS 8003) <4160>* **MAGIC CARPET RIDE. / SOOKIE SOOKIE** [3] Sep68
(re-iss. Sep69; SS 8027)

Jan 69. (lp; stereo/mono) *(S+/SL 5003) <50053>* **STEPPENWOLF THE SECOND** [3] Nov68
– Faster than the speed of life / Tighten up your wig / None of your doing / Spiritual fantasy / Don't step on the grass, Sam / 28 / Magic carpet ride / Disappointment number (unknown) / Lost and found by trial and error / Hodge, podge strained through a Leslie / Resurrection / Reflections. *(cd-iss. Jun87 on 'M.C.A.'; CMCAD 31021)*

— **LARRY BYROM** (b.27 Dec'48, USA) – guitar repl. MONARCH / **NICK ST.NICHOLAS** (b. KLAUS KARL KASSBAUM, 28 Sep'43, Pion, Germany) – bass repl. RUSSELL

Mar 69. (7") *(SS 8013) <4182>* **ROCK ME. / JUPITER CHILD** [10] Feb69

Jun 69. (lp; stereo/mono) *(S+/SL 5011) <50060>* **AT YOUR BIRTHDAY PARTY** [7] Mar69
– Don't cry / Chicken wolf / Lovely meter / Round and down / It's never too late / Sleeping dreaming / Jupiter child / She'll be better / Cat killer / Rock me / God fearing man / Mango juice / Happy birthday.

May 69. (7") *<4192>* **IT'S NEVER TOO LATE. / HAPPY BIRTHDAY** [-] [51]

Aug 69. (7") *<4205>* **MOVE OVER. / POWER PLAY** [-] [31]

Dec 69. (7") *<4221>* **MONSTER. / BERRY RIDES AGAIN** [-] [39]

Jan 70. (7") *(SS 8035)* **MONSTER. / MOVE OVER** [-]

Jan 70. (lp) *(SSL 5021) <50066>* **MONSTER** [43] [17] Nov69
– Monster / Suicide / America / Draft resister / Power play / Move over / Fag / What would you do (if I did that to you) / From here to there eventually. *(cd-iss. Sep91 on 'Beat Goes On'; BGOCD 126)*

Mar 70. (7") *(SS 8038)* **THE PUSHER. / YOUR WALL'S TOO HIGH** [-]

Jun 70. (7") *(SS 8049) <4234>* **HEY LAWDY MAMA. / TWISTED** [35] Apr70

Jun 70. (d-lp) *(SSL 5029) <50075>* **STEPPENWOLF 'LIVE' (live)** [16] [7] Apr70
– Sooki, Sooki / Don't step on the grass Sam / Tighten up your wig / Hey lawdy mama / Magic carpet ride / The pusher / Corina, Corina / Twisted / From here to there eventually / Born to be wild. *(re-iss. Oct74 on 'A.B.C.'; ABCL 5007) (cd-iss. Aug98 on 'Beat Goes On'; BGOCD 412)*

Sep 70. (7") *(SS 8056) <4248>* **SCREAMING NIGHT HOG. / SPIRITUAL FANTASY** [62] Aug70

Probe / Dunhill

Nov 70. (7") *(PRO 510) <4261>* **WHO NEEDS YA. / EARSCHPLITTENLOUDENBOOMER** [54]

Nov 70. (lp) *(SPBA 6254) <50090>* **STEPPENWOLF 7** [19]
– Ball crusher / Forty days and forty nights / Fat Jack / Renegade / Foggy mental breakdown / Snow blind friend / Who needs ya / Earschplittenloudenboomer / Hippo stomp.

Mar 71. (7") *(PRO 525) <4269>* **SNOW BLIND FRIEND. / HIPPO STOMP** [60] Feb71

— **KENT HENRY** – guitar repl. BYROM

— **GEORGE BIONDO** (b. 3 Sep'45, Brooklyn, N.Y.) – bass repl. NICK

Jul 71. (7") *(PRO 534) <4283>* **RIDE WITH ME. / FOR MADMEN ONLY** [52]

Oct 71. (7") *(PRO 544) <4292>* **FOR LADIES ONLY. / SPARKLE EYES** [64]

Oct 71. (lp) *(SPBA 6260) <50110>* **FOR LADIES ONLY** [54]
– For ladies only / I'm asking / Shackles and chains / Tenderness / The night time's for you / Jadet strumpet / Sparkle eyes / Black pit / Ride with me / In hopes of a garden.

— disbanded Feb'72, EDMUNTON and McJOHN formed MANBEAST

JOHN KAY

went solo, augmented by **KENT HENRY + GEORGE BIONDO** plus **HUGH SULLIVAN** – keyboards / **PENTII WHITNEY GLEN** – drums / etc. (same label)

Apr 72. (lp) *(1054) <50120>* **FORGOTTEN SONGS AND UNSUNG HEROES**
– Many a mile / Walk beside me / You win again / To be alive / Bold marauder / Two of a kind / Walking blues / Somebody / I'm moving on.

Apr 72. (7") *<4309>* **I'M MOVIN' ON. / WALK BESIDE ME** [-] [52]

Jul 72. (7") *<4319>* **YOU WIN AGAIN. / SOMEBODY** [-]

Jul 73. (7") *<4351>* **MOONSHINE. / NOBODY LIVES HERE ANYMORE** [-]

Jul 73. (lp) *(6274) <50147>* **MY SPORTIN' LIFE**
– Moonshine / Nobody lives here anymore / Drift away / Heroes and devils / My sportin' life / Easy evil / Giles of the river / Dance to my song / Sing with the children.

Sep 73. (7") *(PRO 601) <4360>* **EASY EVIL. / DANCE TO MY SONG**

STEPPENWOLF

re-formed (**KAY, McJOHN, EDMUNTON, BIONDO**) plus **BOBBY COCHRAN** – guitar repl. KENT (first and last with horn section)

C.B.S. / Mums

Oct 74. (lp) *(80358) <33093>* **SLOW FLUX** [47] Sep74
– Gang war blues / Children of the night / Justice don't be slow / Get into the wind / Jeraboah / Straight shootin' woman / Smokey factory blues / Morning blue / A fool's factory / Fishin' in the dark.

Oct 74. (7") *(MUM 2679) <6031>* **STRAIGHT SHOOTIN' WOMAN. / JUSTICE DON'T BE SLOW** [29] Sep74

Jan 75. (7") *<6034>* **GET INTO THE WIND. / MORNING BLUE** [-]

Apr 75. (7") *(MUM 3147) <6036>* **SMOKEY FACTORY BLUES. / A FOOL'S FANTASY**

— **ANDY CHAPIN** – keyboards repl. McJOHN who went solo

Aug 75. (7") *(MUM 3470) <6040>* **CAROLINE (ARE YOU READY). / ANGEL DRAWERS**

Sep 75. (lp) *(69151) <33583>* **HOUR OF THE WOLF**
– Caroline (are you ready for the outlaw world) / Annie, Annie over / Two for the love of one / Just for tonight / Hard rock road / Someone told a lie / Another's lifetime / Mr. Penny pincher.

— **WAYNE COOK** – keyboards repl. ANDY

Epic / Epic

May 77. (lp) *(81328) <34120>* **SKULLDUGGERY**
– Skullduggery / Roadrunner / Rock and roll song / Train of thought / Life is a gamble / Pass it on / Sleep / Lip service.

Dec 77. (lp) *<34382>* **REBORN TO BE WILD** (remixes) [-]
– Straight shootin' woman / Hard rock road / Another's lifetime / Mr. Penny pincher / Smokey factory blues / Caroline / Get into the wind / Gang war blues / Children of night / Skullduggery.

— Disbanded yet again.

JOHN KAY

with **LARRY BYROM** – slide guitar / **MAC McANALLY** – guitar / **CLAYTON IVEY** – keyboards / **BOB WRAY** – bass / **ROGER CLARK** – drums

Mercury / Mercury

Jun 78. (lp) *(9110 054) <1-3715>* **ALL IN GOOD TIME**
– Give me some news I can use / The best is barely good enough / That's when I think of you / Ain't nobody home (in California) / Ain't nothin' like it used to be / Business is business / Show me how you'd like it done / Down in New Orleans / Say you will / Hey, I'm alright.

Jun 78. (7") *<74004>* **GIVE ME SOME NEWS I COULD USE. / SAY YOU WILL** [-]

Jun 78. (7") *(6167 683)* **GIVE ME SOME NEWS I CAN USE. / BUSINESS IS BUSINESS** [-]

— In the early 80's, KAY and group toured as

JOHN KAY & STEPPENWOLF

with **MICHAEL PALMER** – guitar / **BRETT TUGGLE** – keyboards / **CHAD PERRY** – bass / **STEVEN PALMER** – drums not iss. Allegiance

Dec 81. (lp) **LIVE IN LONDON (live)** -
– Sookie Sookie / Give me news I can use / You / Hot night in a cold town / Ain't nothin' like it used to be / Magic carpet ride / Five finger discount / Hey lawdy mama / Business is business / Born to be wild / The pusher.

Dec 81. (7") *<3909>* **HOT TOME IN A COLD TOWN. /** -

— **WELTON GITE** – bass repl. CHAD / added **MICHAEL WILK** – keyboards

not iss. CBS-Sony

1983. (lp) *<DIDZ 10010>* **WOLFTRACKS** -
– All I want is all you got / None of the above / You / Every man for himself / Five finger discount / Hold your head up / Hot night in a cold town / Down to earth / For rock'n'roll / The balance. *(UK-iss.May97 as 'FIVE FINGER DISCOUNT' on 'C.M.C.'; 10045-2)*

— now with **ROCKET RITCHOTTE** – guitar, vocals + **MICHAEL WILK** – keyboards, bass / **RON HURST** – drums, vocals. Finally issued new material 1988.

Disky Qwil

May 88. (lp/c/cd) *(979209-1/-4/-2) <1560>* **ROCK & ROLL REBELS** Sep87
– Give me life / Rock and roll rebels / Hold on (never give up, never give in) / Man on a mission / Everybody knows you / Rock steady (I'm rough and ready) / Replace the face / Turn out the lights / Give me news I can use / Rage.

I.R.S. I.R.S.

Aug 90. <(cd/c/lp)> *(EIRSA 1037) <241066-2/-4/-1)* **RISE & SHINE**
– Let's do it all / Time out / Do or die / Rise & shine / The wall / The daily blues / Keep rockin' / Rock'n'roll war / Sign on the line / We like it, we love it (we want more of it). *<(cd re-iss. Jul98 on 'C.M.C.'; CMC 823910-2)>*

A-Play A-Play

May 97. (cd) *(CD 10045-2)* **FIVE FINGERS DISCOUNT** -
– Five fingers discount / You / All I want is what you got / None of the above / Balance / Down to earth / Hot night in a cold town / Hold your head up / For rock'n'roll / Every man for himself.

C.M.C. Winter Harvest

Jul 98. (cd) *(CMC 823908-2)* **PARADOX**
Jul 98. (cd) *(CMC 823909-2) <3310>* **FEED THE FIRE**
– Rock & roll rebels / Rock steady (I'm rough & ready) / Hold on (never give up, never give in) / Everybody knows you / (Give me) News I can use / Replace the face / Bad attitude / Man on a mission / Rage / Feed the fire.

– compilations, others, etc. –

— on 'Probe' UK / 'Dunhill' US unless mentioned otherwise

Jul 69. (lp) *Stateside; (5015) / Dunhill; <50060>* **EARLY STEPPENWOLF** 29
(live from 1967 as The SPARROW)
– Power play / Howlin' for my baby / Goin' upstairs / Corina Corina / Tighten up your wig / The pusher.

Mar 71. (lp) *(SPB 1033) <50099>* **STEPPENWOLF GOLD** 24
– Born to be wild / It's never too late / Rock me / Hey lawdy mama / Move over / Who needs ya / Magic carpet ride / The pusher / Sookie Sookie / Jupiter's child / Screaming night hog. *(re-iss. Oct74 on 'A.B.C.'; ABCL 8613) (re-iss. Aug80 on 'M.C.A.'; 1502) (re-iss. Aug81 lp/c; MCM/+C 1619) (re-iss. Jan83 on 'Fame' lp/c; FA/TCFA 3052)*

Jul 72. (lp) *(SPB 1059) <50124>* **REST IN PEACE** 62 Jun72
Mar 73. (lp) *(SPB 1071) <50135>* **16 GREATEST HITS** Feb73
(re-iss. Oct74 on 'A.B.C.'; ABCL 5028) (cd-iss. Feb91 on 'M.C.A.'; MCAD 37049)

Jun 80. (7") *M.C.A.; (MCA 614)* **BORN TO BE WILD. / THE PUSHER**
(re-iss. Apr83 on 'Old Gold'; OG 9323)

Jul 85. (lp/c) *M.C.A.; (MCM/+C 5002)* **GOLDEN GREATS**
– Born to be wild / It's never too late / Rock me / Hey lawdy mama / Move over / Who needs ya / Monster / Snow blind friend / Magic carpet ride / The pusher / Sookie sookie / Jupiter's child / Screaming dog night / Ride with me / For ladies only / Tenderness.

1991. (cd) *M.C.A.; <MCA 10389>* **BORN TO BE WILD: A RETROSPECTIVE** -
Aug 91. (cd/c) *Knight; (KN CD/MC 10022)* **NIGHTRIDING** -
Apr 93. (cd) *Movieplay Gold; (MPG 74016)* **BORN TO BE WILD** -
Jan 94. (cd) *Legacy;* **TIGHTEN UP YOUR WIG – THE BEST OF JOHN KAY & SPARROW**
Dec 96. (cd) *Beat Goes On; (BGOCD 336)* **AT YOUR BIRTHDAY PARTY / STEPPENWOLF** -
May 97. (cd) *Experience; (EXP 029)* **STEPPENWOLF** -
Feb 99. (c-s/cd-s) *M.C.A.; (MCS C/TD 48104)* **BORN TO BE WILD / MAGIC CARPET RIDE / ROCK ME** 18
Feb 99. (cd) *M.C.A.; (MCLD 19386)* **THE BEST OF STEPPENWOLF**
Mar 99. (cd) *Beat Goes On; (BGOCD 450)* **STEPPENWOLF / STEPPENWOLF II** -

STIFF LITTLE FINGERS

Formed: Belfast, N.Ireland . . . 1977 by teenagers JAKE BURNS, HENRY CLUNEY, ALI McMORDIE and GORDON BLAIR, the latter soon being replaced by BRIAN FALOON. Famously taking their name from a line in a VIBRATORS' b-side, the group began life as a CLASH covers band. Taken under the wing of journalist, GORDON OGILVIE (who subsequently became both band manager and BURNS' writing partner), the group began to rely on original material, releasing their incendiary 1978 debut single, 'SUSPECT DEVICE'. / 'WASTED LIFE' on the self-financed 'Rigid Digits' label. Wound tight, both lyrically and musically, with the frustration and anger of living in war-torn Belfast, the record introduced SLF as one of the most visceral and compelling punk bands since The SEX PISTOLS. Championed by the ever vigilant John Peel, the single led to a deal with 'Rough Trade' who jointly released a follow-up single, 'ALTERNATIVE ULSTER', the track rapidly assuming legendary status, although it was originally penned for release as a magazine flexi-disc. A debut album, 'INFLAMMABLE MATERIAL', followed in early '79, a raging, politically barbed howl of punk protest which lined up all the aforementioned tracks alongside such definitive SLF material as 'STATE OF EMERGENCY' and 'JOHNNY WAS'. Storming into the Top 20, the album expanded their already voracious fanbase, the group undertaking their first major headlining tour to promote it. The insistent, bass-heavy pop-punk dynamics of 'GOTTA GETAWAY' marked the debut of JIM REILLY (replacing the departing FALOON on the drum stool) and no doubt fuelled a thousand teenage runaway fantasies while the vicious 'STRAW DOGS' marked the group's major label debut for 'Chrysalis'. Early the following year, SLF scored their sole Top 20 hit with 'AT THE EDGE', another seething account of BURNS' troubled youth in Northern Ireland and arguably one of the group's finest moments. 'NOBODY'S HEROES' (1980) saw a move towards a more varied musical palette and a distinctly melodic feel, notably on the title track although 'TIN SOLDIERS' was as brutal as ever. The seminal live album, 'HANX!' (1980) gave the band their only Top 10 success later that year, surprising given the band's increasingly commercial approach as witnessed on the infectious 'JUST FADE AWAY' (possibly the only song ever written about a woman harassing a man!). A centerpiece of the 'GO FOR IT' (1981) set, the single stood in stark contrast to the insipid cod-reggae that so many punk bands, SLF unfortunately included, were now falling back on. 'NOW THEN' (1982) was an uncomfortable attempt to branch out even further into uncharted pop/rock territory, BURNS leaving soon after to form JAKE BURNS & THE BIG WHEEL. This effectively spelled the end for the band, and after a farewell tour, they called it a day. The live demand for SLF was so strong, however, that they were able to regroup in 1987, new material eventually surfacing in 1991 following the replacement of the disillusioned McMORDIE with ex-JAM bassist BRUCE FOXTON. The album in question, 'FLAGS AND EMBLEMS', hardly set the rock world alight, gigs predictably characterised by diehard fans shouting for old favourites. 'GET A LIFE' (1994) was similarly formulaic and, without being precious, one can't help but wonder how such a vital, influential band are now reduced to basically retreading past glories for a greying audience. • **Songwriters:** BURNS penned, some with OGILVIE. They also covered JOHNNY WAS (Bob Marley) / RUNNING BEAR (Johnny Preston) / WHITE CHRISTMAS (Bing Crosby) / LOVE OF THE COMMON PEOPLE (Nicky Thomas) / THE MESSAGE (Grandmaster Flash). • **Trivia:** JAKE once applied for a job as a Radio 1 producer.

Album rating: INFLAMMABLE MATERIAL (*8) / NOBODY'S HEROES (*7) / HANX! (*6) / GO FOR IT (*5) / NOW THEN (*5) / ALL THE BEST compilation (*8) / NO SLEEP TILL BELFAST (*5) / SEE YOU UP THERE! (*5) / FLAGS AND EMBLEMS (*5) / GET A LIFE (*4) / TINDERBOX (*4)

JAKE BURNS – vocals, lead guitar / **HENRY CLUNEY** – guitar / **ALI McMORDIE** – bass / **BRIAN FALOON** – drums; repl. GORDON BLAIR who later joined RUDI

Rigid Digits not iss.

Mar 78. (7") *(SRD-1)* **SUSPECT DEVICE. / WASTED LIFE** -
(re-iss. Jun78) (re-iss. Mar79 on 'Rough Trade'; RT 006)

Rough Trade not iss.

Oct 78. (7") *(RT 004)* **ALTERNATIVE ULSTER. / '78 R.P.M.** -
Feb 79. (lp) *(ROUGH 1)* **INFLAMMABLE MATERIAL** 14 -
– Suspect device / State of emergency / Here we are nowhere / Wasted life / No more of that / Barbed wire love / White noise / Breakout / Law and order / Rough trade / Johnny was / Alternative Ulster / Closed groove. *(re-iss. Mar89 on 'E.M.I.' lp/c(cd); EMC/TC-EMC 3554)(CDP 792105-2) <US cd-iss. 1992 on 'Restless'; 72363>*

— **JIM REILLY** – drums repl. FALOON

May 79. (7") *(RT 015)* **GOTTA GETAWAY. / BLOODY SUNDAY** -

Chrysalis Chrysalis

Sep 79. (7") *(CHS 2368)* **STRAW DOGS. / YOU CAN'T SAY CRAP ON THE RADIO** 44 -
Feb 80. (7") *(CHS 2406)* **AT THE EDGE. / SILLY ENCORES: RUNNING BEAR – WHITE CHRISTMAS** 15 -
Mar 80. (lp/c) *(CHR/ZCHR 1270)* **NOBODY'S HEROES** 8
– Gotta getaway / Wait and see / Fly the flag / At the edge / Nobody's hero / Bloody dub / Doesn't make it alright / I don't like you / No change / Suspect device / Tin soldiers. *(re-iss. Mar89 on 'E.M.I.' lp/c(cd); EMC/TC-EMC 3555)(CDP 792106-2) <US cd-iss. 1992 on 'Restless'; 72364>*

May 80. (7") *(CHS 2424)* **TIN SOLDIERS. / NOBODY'S HERO** 36 -
Jul 80. (7") *(CHS 2447)* **BACK TO FRONT. / MR FIRE COAL-MAN** 49 -
Sep 80. (lp/c) *(CHR/ZCHR 1300)* **HANX! (live)** 9 -
– Nobody's hero / Gotta getaway / Wait and see / Barbed wire love / Fly the flag / Alternative Ulster / Johnny was / At the edge / Wasted life / Tin soldiers / Suspect device. *(re-iss. Feb89 on 'Fame-EMI' lp/c/cd; FA/TC-FA/CD-FA 3215) <US cd-iss. 1992 on 'Restless'; 72365>*

Mar 81. (7"m) *(CHS 2510)* **JUST FADE AWAY. / GO FOR IT / DOESN'T MAKE IT ALRIGHT (live)** 47 -
Apr 81. (lp/c) *(CHR/ZCHR 1339)* **GO FOR IT** 14 -
– Roots, radicals, rockers and reggae / Just fade away / Go for it / The only one / Hits and misses / Kicking up a racket / Safe as houses / Gate 49 / Silver lining / Piccadilly Circus. *(re-iss. Feb89 on 'Fame-EMI' lp/c/cd+=; FA/TC-FA/CD-FA 3216)* – Back to front. *<US cd-iss. 1992 on 'Restless'; 72366>*

May 81. (7") *(CHS 2517)* **SILVER LINING. / SAFE AS HOUSES** 68 -

— **BRIAN 'DOLPHIN' TAYLOR** – drums (ex-TOM ROBINSON BAND) repl. REILLY

Jan 82. (7"ep) *(CHS 2580)* **R.E.P. PAY 1.10 OR LESS EP** 33 -
– Listen / Sad-eyed people / That's when your blood bumps / Two guitars clash.

Apr 82. (7") *(CHS 2601)* **TALK BACK. / GOOD FOR NOTHING** -
Aug 82. (7"/12") *(CHS/+12 2637)* **BITS OF KIDS. / STANDS TO REASON** 73 -
Sep 82. (lp/c) *(CHR/ZCHR 1400)* **NOW THEN** 24 -
– Falling down / Won't be told / Love of the common people / The price of admission / Touch and go / Stands to reason / Bits of kids / Welcome to the whole week / Big city night / Talkback / Is that what you fought the war for. *(cd-iss. Dec94 on 'Fame'; CDFA 3306) (cd re-iss. Apr97 on 'EMI Gold'; CDGOLD 1090)*

Jan 83. (d-lp/d-c) *(CTY/ZCTY 1414)* **ALL THE BEST** (compilation) 19
– Suspect device / Wasted life / Alternative Ulster / '78 R.P.M. / Gotta getaway / Bloody Sunday / Straw dogs / You can't say crap on the radio / At the edge / Running bear / White Christmas / Nobody's hero / Tin soldiers / Back to front / Mr. Fire

coal-man / Just fade away / Go for it / Doesn't make it alright / Silver lining / Safe as houses / Sad eyed people / Two guitars clash / Listen / That's when your blood bumps / Good for nothing / Talkback / Stand to reason / Bits of kids / Touch and go / The price of admission / Silly encores *[not on cass]. (d-cd-iss. Jun88; CCD 1414) (re-iss. Sep91 on 'E.M.I.' d-cd/d-c; CD/TC EM 1428) <US d-cd-iss. 1995 on 'One Way'; 18429>*

Feb 83. (7") *(CHS 2671)* **THE PRICE OF ADMISSION. / TOUCH AND GO** [ ] [-]

— Had already disbanded late 1982. McMORDIE joined FICTION GROOVE and DOLPHIN joined SPEAR OF DESTINY after stint with GO WEST.

JAKE BURNS & THE BIG WHEEL

— were formed by **JAKE** plus **NICK MUIR** – keyboards / **SEAN MARTIN** – bass / **STEVE GRANTLEY** – drums

Survival | not iss.

Jul 85. (7"/12") *(SRD/+T 2)* **ON FORTUNE STREET. / HERE COMES THAT SONG AGAIN** [ ] [-]

Mar 86. (7"/12") *(SRD/+T 3)* **SHE GREW UP. / RACE YOU TO THE GRAVE** [ ] [-]

Jive | not iss.

Feb 87. (7"/ext.12") *(JIVE/+T 139)* **BREATHLESS. / VALENTINE'S DAY** [ ] [-]

STIFF LITTLE FINGERS

— re-formed in 1987 by **BURNS, TAYLOR, CLUNEY & McMORDIE**

Link | not iss.

Apr 88. (d-lp,green-d-lp) *(LP 026)* **LIVE AND LOUD (live)** [ ] [-]
– Alternative Ulster / Roots radicals rockers and reggae / Silver lining / Wait and see / Gotta getaway / Just fade away / Wasted life / The only one / Nobody's hero / At the edge / Listen / Barbed wire love / Fly the flag / Tin soldiers / No sleep till Belfast / Suspect device / Johnny was. *(re-iss. May88 as 'NO SLEEP TILL BELFAST' on 'Kaz' c/cd; KAZ MC/CD 6) (cd-iss. Sep89; CD 026)*

Skunx | not iss.

Jun 88. (12"ep) *(SLFX 1)* **NO SLEEP TILL BELFAST (live)** [ ] [-]
– Suspect device / Alternative Ulster / Nobody's hero.

Virgin | Caroline

Mar 89. (12"ep/cd-ep) *(SLF/+CD 1)* **ST.PATRIX** (the covers live) [ ] [-]
– The wild rover / Love of the common people / Johnny Was.

Apr 89. (d-lp/d-c/d-cd) *(VGD/+C/CD 3515) <CAROL 1377-1/-4/-2>* **SEE YOU UP THERE! (live)** [ ] [ ]
– (intro: Go for it) / Alternative Ulster / Silver lining / Love of the common people / Gotta getaway / Just fade away / Piccadilly Circus / Gate 49 / Wasted life / At the edge / Listen / Barbed wire love / Fly the flag / Tin soldiers / The wild rover / Suspect device / Johnny was.

— (Mar'91) **BRUCE FOXTON** – bass (ex-JAM, ex-solo) repl. McMORDIE

Essential | Taang!

Oct 91. (cd/c/lp)(pic-lp) *(ESS CD/MC/LP 171)(EPDLP 171)* **FLAGS & EMBLEMS** [ ] [-]
– (It's a) Long way to Paradise (from here) / Stand up and shout / Each dollar a bullet / The cosh / Beirut Moon / The game of life / Human shield / Johnny 7 / Dread burn / No surrender. *(cd re-iss. Jul95 on 'Dojo'; DOJOCD 243)*

Oct 91. (cd-ep) *(ESSX 2007)* **BEIRUT MOON / STAND UP AND SHOUT / (JAKE interview)** [ ] [-]

Jan 94. (12"ep) *(ESS 2035)* **CAN'T BELIEVE IN YOU. / SILVER LINING (unplugged) / LISTEN (unplugged) / WASTED LIFE (unplugged)** [ ] [-]
(cd-ep) *(ESSX 2035)* – ('A'side) / ('A'extended) / Alternative Ulster (featuring RICKY WARWICK of The ALMIGHTY) / Smithers-Jones (live with BRUCE FOXTON vocals).

Feb 94. (cd/c) *(ESS CD/MC 210) <TAANG 100>* **GET A LIFE** [ ] [ ] Oct94
– Get a life / Can't believe in you / The road to kingdom come / Walk away / No laughing matter / Harp / Forensic evidence / Baby blue ((what have they been telling you?) / I want you / The night that the wall came down / Cold / When the stars fall from the sky / What if I want more? i*(re-iss. Apr97; ESMCD 488)*

Jun 94. (12"/cd-s) **HARP. / SHAKE IT OFF / NOW WHAT WE WERE (PRO PATRIA MORI)** [ ] [-]

— **STEVE GRANTLEY** – drums (ex-JAKE BURNS . . .) repl. TAYLOR

Spitfire | Taang!

Jun 97. (cd/lp) *(SLF 100 CD/LP) <T 137>* **TINDERBOX** [ ] [ ] Jul97
– You never hear the one that hits you / (I could) Be happy yesterday / Tinderbox / Dead of night / The message / My ever changing moral stance / Hurricane / You can move mountains / River flowing / You don't believe in me / In your hand / Dust in my eye / Roaring boys (part 1) / Roaring boys (part 2).

– compilations, etc. –

Sep 86. (12"ep) *Strange Fruit; (SFPS 004)* **THE PEEL SESSIONS (12.9.78)** [ ] [-]
– Johnny was / Law and order / Barbed wire love / Suspect device. *(c-ep-iss.May87; SFPSC 004) (cd-ep-iss.Jul88; SFPCD 004)*

Nov 89. (lp/c/cd) *Strange Fruit; (SFR LP/MC/CD 106) / Dutch East India; <8103>* **THE PEEL SESSIONS** [ ] [ ]

Oct 89. (12"ep) *Link; (LINK 1203)* **THE LAST TIME. / MR.FIRE-COAL MAN / TWO GUITARS CLASH** [ ] [-]

Apr 91. (cd) *Streetlink; (STRCD 010)* **GREATEST HITS LIVE (live)** [ ] [-]
(re-iss. May93 on 'Dojo'; DOJOCD 110) (re-iss. Feb99 on 'Recall'; SMMCD 538)

Oct 91. (cd) *Link; (AOK 103)* **ALTERNATIVE CHARTBUSTERS** [ ] [-]

Oct 89. (cd/green-lp) *Limited Edition; (LTD EDT 2 CD/LP)* **LIVE IN SWEDEN (live)** [ ] [-]

Dec 92. (cd) *Dojo; (<DOJOCD 75>)* **FLY THE FLAGS – LIVE AT BRIXTON ACADEMY (27/9/91)** [ ] [ ] Oct94

Aug 93. (cd) *Windsong; (<WINCD 037>)* **BBC RADIO 1 LIVE IN CONCERT (live)** [ ] [ ]

Mar 95. (cd) *Dojo; (DOJOCD 224)* **PURE FINGERS LIVE – ST.PATRIX 1993** [ ] [-]

Sep 98. (cd) *PinHead; (PINCD 105)* **STAND UP AND SHOUT** [ ] [-]

Mar 99. (cd) *Harry May; (<MAYOCD 105>)* **TIN SOLDIERS** [ ] [ ]

Jun 99. (cd) *Snapper; (SMMCD 516)* **PURE FINGERS LIVE** [ ] [ ]

Mar 00. (d-cd) *Recall; (SMMCD 276)* **INSPIRED – A COLLECTION** [ ] [ ]

STILTSKIN

Formed: West Lothian, Scotland . . . 1989 by songwriter PETER LAWLOR and JAMES FINNEGAN. The latter had played with HUE AND CRY, while LAWLOR had just returned from the States. They soon found ROSS McFARLANE, who had played with SLIDE, while 1993 saw them recruiting singer RAY WILSON. STILTSKIN came to the attention of the nation when their NIRVANA-esque track 'INSIDE' was aired on a Levi jeans TV commercial (the one where the quaker girls go to a lake and see what appears to be a naked man in the water, only to find he is just breaking in his new jeans). The Television company were then inundated with enquiries on who was the group/artist on its soundtrack, and where could they buy it. Unfortunately it hadn't yet been released, although due to public demand it eventually surfaced in April 1994. Now with growling lyrics, the single crashed into the UK No.5 and was soon topping the charts. However, by the end of the year, bad album reviews of their debut, 'THE MIND'S EYE', had already made them yesterday's men. LAWLOR subsequently had a brief stint as a solo artist, while WILSON stunned the rock world in 1996 by replacing PHIL COLLINS in GENESIS.

Album rating: THE MIND'S EYE (*4)

RAY WILSON – vocals / **PETER LAWLOR** – guitars, mandolin, vocals / **JAMES FINNIGAN** – bass, keyboards / **ROSS McFARLANE** – drums, percussion

Whitewater | East West

May 94. (7"/c-s) *(LEV 1/+C)* **INSIDE. / AMERICA** [1] [ ]
(12"+=/cd-s+=) *(LEV 1 T/CD)* – ('A'extended).

Sep 94. (7"/c-s) *(WWR/+C 2)* **FOOTSTEPS. / SUNSHINE & BUTTERFLIES (live)** [34] [-]
(cd-s+=) *(WWRD 2)* – ('A'extended).

Oct 94. (cd/c/lp) *(WW L/M/D 1) <61785>* **THE MIND'S EYE** [17] [ ] Jan95
– Intro / Scared of ghosts / Horse / Rest in peace / Footsteps / Sunshine and butterflies / Inside / An illusion / America / When my ship comes in / Prayer before birth.

Mar 95. (7"ep/c-ep/cd-ep) *(WWR/+C/D 3)* **REST IN PEACE. / THE POLTROON / INSIDE (acoustic)** [ ] [-]

— LAWLOR has now formed his own self-named group. In 1996, WILSON took the place of PHIL COLLINS in GENESIS.

LAWLOR

PETER with his own band

Water | not iss.

May 96. (c-s/cd-s) *(WAT 1 MC/CD)* **MAD ALICE LANE** [ ] [-]

STONE FURY

Formed: Los Angeles, California, USA . . . 1983 by frontman LENNY WOLF (who had just arrived in L.A. from Hamburg, Germany) and guitarist BRUCE GOWDY, completing the line-up with the rhythm section of RICK WILSON and JODY CORTEZ. Signing to 'M.C.A.', WOLF wore his influences glaringly on his sleeve from the off, doing his best ROBERT PLANT impression to a churning 'ZEPPELIN groove on debut set 'BURNS LIKE A STAR' (1985). The album was a minor Stateside success, hanging around the US Top 200 for a few months, a follow-up, 'LET THEM TALK', eventually appearing a couple of years later. The rest, as they say, is history, WOLF returning to Germany to meditate upon his next career move; an even more 'ZEPPELIN-esque outfit going under the name of KINGDOM COME. GOWDY, meanwhile, formed the band WORLD TRADE.

Album rating: BURNS LIKE A STAR (*5) LET THEM TALK (*5)

LENNY WOLF – vocals, guitar / **BRUCE GOWDY** – guitar, vocals / **RICK WILSON** – bass, vocals / **JODY CORTEZ** – drums, percussion

M.C.A. | M.C.A.

Oct 84. (7") *<52464>* **BREAK DOWN THE WALL. / MAMA'S LOVE** [-] [ ]

Mar 85. (lp/c) *(MCF/+C 3249) <5522>* **BURNS LIKE A STAR** [ ] [ ] Nov84
– Break down the wall / I hate to sleep alone / Life is too lonely / Don't tell me why / Mamas love / Burns like a star / Tease / Hold it / Shannon you lose.

Mar 85. (7") *<52523>* **BURNS LIKE A STAR. / LIFE IS TOO LONELY** [-] [ ]

— RICK + JODY were repl. by session men, **DEAN CORTEZ** – bass / **VINNIE COLAITUA** – drums / **ALAN PASQUA + JIM LANG + RICHARD LANDIS** – keyboards / **REED NIELSEN** – electro-drums

Nov 86. (7") *<52942>* **LET THEM TALK. / I SHOULD'VE TOLD YOU** [-] [ ]

Nov 86. (lp) *<5788>* **LET THEM TALK** [-] [ ]
– Too late / Lies on the run / Let them talk / Babe / Eye of the storm / Doin' what I feel / Let the time take care / Stay.

— disbanded when WOLF returned to Germany for a year. He returned to America and formed the highly successful KINGDOM COME, while GOWDY formed WORLD TRADE

STONE TEMPLE PILOTS

Formed: Los Angeles, California, USA . . . 1987 as MIGHTY JOE YOUNG by WEILAND and ROBERT DeLEO. Recruiting DeLEO's brother, DEAN and ERIC KRETZ, they opted for the less frenetic San Diego as a musical base, changing their moniker to STONE TEMPLE PILOTS (thankfully changed from the considerably more controversial SHIRLEY TEMPLE'S PUSSY). After a few years on the hard/alternative rock circuit, they finally signed to 'Atlantic', the fruits of their labour, 'CORE' released in '92. Critical raves saw the album climb up the US chart (eventually reaching Top 3), songs like 'SEX TYPE THING' and 'PLUSH' drawing inevitable comparisons with PEARL JAM; WEILAND's vocals especially, were from the EDDIE VEDDER school of gravel-throated cool. After the aforementioned tracks were issued as UK singles, the album surfaced in the British Top 30 a full year on from its original release date, WEILAND's carrot-topped mop marking him out as a distinctive focal point for the band. LED ZEPPELIN and ALICE IN CHAINS were other obvious reference points, a second album, 'PURPLE' (1994), building on these influences to create a more cerebral post-grunge sound. The fact that the album rocketed into the American charts at No.1 was a measure of the group's lofty standing in the echelons of US alt-rock. WEILAND's love of nose candy and associated pleasures was no secret in the music world, the frontman narrowly avoiding a sizeable prison stretch for possession. Early in 1996, STP delivered a third (Top 5) album, 'TINY MUSIC . . . SONGS FROM THE VATICAN GIFT SHOP', accompanying touring commitments severely disrupted when WEILAND was ordered by the court to attend a rehab centre while awaiting trial (he was later cleared). The following year, WEILAND continued his self-destructive behaviour, STP's future looking bleak as the remaining band members formed TALK SHOW. A WEILAND solo effort, '12 BAR BLUES' (1998), was poorly received by critics and fans alike, while a long 18 months (and after more WEILAND arrests!) saw the group back together on a 'NO.4' set in 1999 – needless to say this type of music had died in Britain ages ago. • **Songwriters:** Lyrics: WEILAND + R. DeLEO / KRETZ most of music except covers DANCING DAYS (Led Zeppelin).

Album rating: CORE (*7) / PURPLE (*7) / TINY MUSIC . . . SONGS FROM THE VATICAN GIFT SHOP (*7) / NO.4 (*4) / Talk Show: TALK SHOW (*5) / Scott Weiland: 12 BAR BLUES (*5)

(SCOTT) WEILAND (b.27 Oct'67, Santa Cruz, Calif.) – vocals / **DEAN DeLEO** (b.23 Aug'61, New Jersey) – guitar / **ROBERT DeLEO** (b. 2 Feb'66, New Jersey) – bass / **ERIC KRETZ** (b. 7 Jun'66, Santa Cruz) – drums

Atlantic Atlantic

Nov 92. (cd/c/lp) *<(7567 82418-2/-4/-1)>* **CORE** [ ] [3]
– Dead and bloated / Sex type thing / Wicked garden / No memory / Sin / Creep / Piece of pie / Naked Sunday / Plush / Wet my bed / Crackerman / Where the river goes. *(re-dist.Sep93, hit UK No.27)*

Mar 93. (12"/cd-s) *(A 5769 T/CD)* **SEX TYPE THING. / PIECE OF ME** [60] [-]

Aug 93. (7"/c-s) *(A 7349/+C)* **PLUSH. / SEX TYPE THING (swing version) / PLUSH (acoustic)** [23] [-]
(12"+=/cd-s+=) *(A 7349 T/CD)* – ('A'side) / ('B'live version) / Sin.

Nov 93. (7"/c-s) *(A 7293/+C)* **SEX TYPE THING. / WICKED GARDEN** [55] [-]
(12"+=/cd-s+=) *(A 7293 TP/CD)* – Plush (acoustic).
(cd-s+=) *(A 7293CDX)* –

Jun 94. (cd/c/purple-lp) *<(7567 82607-2/-4/-1)>* **PURPLE** [10] [1]
– Meatplow / Vasoline / Lounge fly / Interstate love song / Still remains / Pretty penny / Silvergun Superman / Big empty / Unglued / Army ants / Kitchenware & candybar!. *(cd+=/c+=)* – Gracious melodies.

Aug 94. (c-ep/12"ep/cd-ep) *(A 5650 C/T/CD)* **VASOLINE / MEATPLOW. / ANDY WARHOL / CRACKERMAN** [48] [-]

Dec 94. (7"purple/c-s) *(A 7192 K/C)* **INTERSTATE LOVE SONG. / LOUNGE FLY** [53] [-]
(cd-s+=) *(A 7192CD)* – ('A'live).
(cd-s++=) *(A 7192CDX)* – Vasoline (live).

— In summer '95, WEILAND was credited on a MAGNIFICENT BASTARDS single, 'Mockingbird Girl'; other tracks by Devo & Stomp.

Mar 96. (cd/c/lp) *<(7567 82871-2/-4/-1)>* **TINY MUSIC . . . SONGS FROM THE VATICAN GIFT SHOP** [31] [4]
– Press play / Pop's love suicide / Tumble in the rough / Big bang baby / Lady picture show / And so I know / Tripping on a hole in a paper heart / Art school girl / Adhesive / Ride the cliche / Daisy / Seven caged tigers.

Apr 96. (c-s) *(A 5516C)* **BIG BANG BABY / ADHESIVE** [ ] [-]
(cd-s+=) *(A 5516CD)* – Daisy.

— the group had to cancel promotion tours due to WEILAND being ordered by a Pasadena court to attend a live-in drug rehabilitation programme. He discharged himself for a few days in July '96 and gave himself up to the LAPD who had issued a warrant for his arrest; WEILAND was subsequently cleared. The other members (ROBERT DeLEO + KRETZ) started working on a side-project VITAMIN, which became TALK SHOW after recruiting frontman DAVID COUTTS

TALK SHOW

— **ERIC KRETZ + ROBERT DeLEO + DEAN DeLEO / + DAVE COUTTS** – vocals (ex-TEN INCH MEN)

Oct 97. (cd/c) *<(7567 83040-2/-4)>* **TALK SHOW** [ ] [ ]
– Ring twice / Hello hello / Everybody loves my car / Peeling an orange / So long / Wash me down / End of the world / John / Behind / Morning girl / Hide / Fill the fields.

SCOTT WEILAND

plays nearly every instrument, SHERYL CROW guests on accordion!

May 98. (cd/c) *<(7567 83084-2/-4)>* **12 BAR BLUES** [ ] [42] Apr98
– Desperation #5 / Barbarella / About nothing / Where's the man / Divider / Cool kiss / The date / Son / Jimmy was a stimulator / Lady, your roof brings me down / Mockingbird girl / Opposite octave reaction.

Jun 98. (7"pink/c-s) *(AT 0035/+C)* **BARBARELLA. / MOCKINGBIRD GIRL** [ ] [ ]
(cd-s+=) *(AT 0035CD)* – ('A'-album version).

STONE TEMPLE PILOTS

— re-formed again

Oct 99. (cd/c) *<(7567 83255-2/-4)>* **NO.4** [ ] [6]
– Down / Heaven and hot rods / Pruno / Church on Tuesday / Sour girl / No way out / Sex and violence / Glide / I got you / MC5 / Atlanta.

Apr 00. (-) *<album cut>* **SOUR GIRL** [-] [78]

Jun 00. (cd) *<83449>* **SHANGRI-LA DEE DA** [-] [9]

STONY SLEEP

Formed: Islington, London, England . . . 1993 by guitar playing singer, BEN SMITH, his brother CHRISTIAN and their schoolmate, WILL SALMON. The soft grunge outfit began when BEN and CHRISTIAN played awful cover versions of MUDHONEY classics, and after practising in a dingey basement for ten months, the ensemble realised that they would achieve nothing as a small school band (whose only influence was 90's Seattle). Protagonist BEN began reading Truman Capote novels which subsequently sparked his imagination for lyrical folly. After six continuous gigs (and an alleged tiff with 'E.M.I.'), STONY SLEEP signed with 'Big Cat' who issued their debut single, 'THIS KITTEN IS CLEAN', in 1996; 'MUSIC FOR CHAMELEONS', their first set, appeared a year later. Highly influenced by the Capote novel, the lazy fuzz bass and BEN's pop vox recuperating from post-grunge angst, it was plainly clear that the band were trying their hardest to diminish any references to PEARL JAM or NIRVANA, fitting closely beside The PIXIES, only somewhat MOR and with a lot more mascara. However, two years later STONY SLEEP were still rattling out their soft pop/rock thang! 'A SLACK ROMANCE', which was radically different from their debut, managed to please new fans as well as old and it was unclear where their fortunes lay.

Album rating: MUSIC FOR CHAMELEONS (*5) / A SLACK ROMANCE (*5)

BEN SMITH – vocals, guitar / **WILL SALMON** – bass / **CHRISTIAN SMITH** – drums

Big Cat not iss.

Jun 96. (7") *(ABB 111S)* **THIS KITTEN IS CLEAN. /** [ ] [-]
(cd-s+=) *(ABB 111SCD)* –

Mar 97. (7") *(ABB 141S)* **ABSURD. / SPOOKY FRUIT** [ ] [-]
(cd-s+=) *(ABB 141SCD)* – Spirit of an actomorph / Leaf shadow.

Jun 97. (7") *(ABB 136S)* **SHE HAD ME. /** [ ] [-]
(cd-s+=) *(ABB 136SCD)* –

Jul 97. (lp/cd) *(ABB 138/+CD)* **MUSIC FOR CHAMELEONS** [ ] [-]
(above was to have been issued in Sep'96; *ABB 113/+CD)*

Nov 97. (cd-ep) *(ABB 153SCD)* **THIS KITTEN IS CLEAN** [ ] [-]

Jul 98. (7") *(ABB 500273-7)* **MIDMAY. / CHRISTMAS ON MARS** [ ] [-]
(cd-s+=) *(ABB 500273-3)* – Wake up / Goodbye.

Nov 98. (7") *(ABB 500292-7)* **LADY LAZARUS. / THE TRIP** [ ] [-]
(cd-s+=) *(ABB 500292-3)* – Stargazer.

Mar 99. (cd) *(ABB 100293-2)* **A SLACK ROMANCE** [ ] [-]

Apr 99. (7") *(ABB 500475-7)* **KHARTOUM. / WONDERING WHY** [ ] [-]
(cd-s+=) *(ABB 500475-3)* – Cut wide open.

STOOGES (see under ⇒ POP, Iggy)

STORM (see under ⇒ JOURNEY)

STORMWITCH

Formed: Germany . . . 1981 by LEE TAROT, ANDY ALDRIAN, STEVE MERCHANT, RONNY PEARSON and PETE LANCER. No, not a bunch of expatriate Englishmen, but a posse of Germans who changed their names (presumably) in pursuit of a more credible image. Unfortunately, they couldn't quite replicate an English sound and their albums made little impression outside their native land. Nevertheless, they persevered into the 90's, finally calling it a day after 1994's 'SHOGUN'.

Album rating: WALPURGIS NIGHT (*5) / TALES OF TERROR (*4) / STRONGER THAN HEAVEN (*5) / THE BEAUTY AND THE BEAST (*5) / EYE OF THE STORM (*4) / THE BEST OF . . . compilation (*6) / SHOGUN (*4)

ANDY ALDRIAN – vocals / **LEE TAROT** (b. HAROLD SPENGLER) – guitar / **STEVE MERCHANT** – guitar / **RONNY PEARSON** – bass / **PETE LANCER** – drums

Powerstation not iss.

1985. (lp) **WALPURGIS NIGHT** [-] [-] German
– Allies of the dark / Dorian Grey / Cave of Steenfoll / Priest of evil / Flower in the wind / Warlord / Excalibur / Thunderland. *(re-iss. Aug91 on 'Laserlight' cd/c; 15/79 391)*

1985. (lp) **TALES OF TERROR** [-] [-] German

Sep 86. (lp) *(941 312)* **STRONGER THAN HEAVEN** [-] [-] German
– Intro / Rats in the attic / Eternia / Jonathan's diary / Slave to the moonlight / Stronger than Heaven / Ravenlord.

Gama | not iss.

Jan 88. (lp) *(GAMA 880763)* **THE BEAUTY AND THE BEAST** [ ] [-]
– Call of the wicked / The beauty and the beast / Just for one night / Emerald eye / Tears by the firelight / Tigers of the sea / Russia's on fire / Cheyenne (where the eagles retreat) / Welcome to Bedlam. *(re-iss. Aug91 on 'Laserlight' cd/c; 15/79 348)*

Hot Blood | not iss.

1989. (lp)(cd) *(871-91)(HBCD 87)* **EYE OF THE STORM** [-] [-] German
– Paradise / Heart of ice / I want you around / King in the ring / Tarred and feathered / Eye of the storm / Another world apart / Steel in the red light / Rondo a la Turca / Take me home.

S.P.V. | not iss.

Oct 94. (cd) *(SPV 84.7684-2)* **SHOGUN** [ ] [-]
– Stranded / Liar / Garden of pain / Seven faces (and two hearts) / Forbidden / Victory is mine / Let lessons begin / The king of winds / She's the sun / Good times – bad times / I'll never forgive / Somewhere.

— split soon after above

– compilations, etc. –

1992. (cd) *(54064)* **THE BEST OF . . .** [-] [-] German
– The beauty and the beast / Welcome to Bedlam / Emerald eye / Tears by the firelight / Stronger than Heaven / Point of no return / Walpurgis night (live) / Rats in the attic / King in the ring / Paradise / Eye of the storm.

Izzy STRADLIN

Born: 8 Apr'62, JEFFREY ISBELL, 8 Apr'62, Lafayette, Indiana, USA. STRADLIN began his career with hometown friend AXL ROSE in the massive heavy metal outfit GUNS N' ROSES in 1985. After irrevocable differences between himself and ROSE, STRADLIN departed the band to pursue his musical career via his newly formed band the JU JU HOUNDS. In this band, where STRADLIN got to call the shots, the guitarist was freed from playing the pastiched heavy metal style of his former group, and instead opted for a more traditional heavy rock sound. His major influences came from the 70's rock of AEROSMITH and The ROLLING STONES; KEITH RICHARDS and RON WOOD certainly being high on his list of mentors. STRADLIN's best solo work came later in the decade with his solo album '117 DEGREES' (1998). On this piece the former small-town boy managed to show that both his fret-picking and songwriting abilities were well worthy of attention. Perhaps the only criticism that could be laid at the foot of this hard/heavy rock album was its nostalgic feel; linking STRADLIN with the unashamed FREE-style copycats the BLACK CROWES. Yet like them STRADLIN did make it sound modern, albeit nostalgic, to fresh ears not accustomed to the sounds of yesteryears.
• **Covered:** PRESSURE DROP (Toots & The Maytals) / MEMPHIS (Chuck Berry) / UP JUMPED THE DEVIL (Dawson-Koumis).

Album rating: IZZY STRADLIN & THE JU JU HOUNDS (*6) / 117 DEGREES (*5)

IZZY STRADLIN – vocals, guitar / **RICK RICHARDS** – guitar (ex-GEORGIA SATELLITES) / **JIMMY ASHHURST** – bass (ex-BROKEN HOMES) repl. MARK DUTTON (ex-BURNING TREE) / **CHARLIE QUINTANA** – drums; repl. DONI GREY (ex-BURNING TREE)

Geffen | Geffen

Sep 92. (7"/c-s) *(GFS/+C 25)* **PRESSURE DROP. / BEEN A FIX** [45] [ ]
(12"pic-d+=/cd-s+=) *(GFST/+D 25)* – Came unplugged / Can't hear 'em.
Oct 92. (cd/c/lp) *<(GED/GEC/GEF 24490)>* **IZZY STRADLIN AND THE JU JU HOUNDS** [52] [ ]
– Somebody knockin' / Pressure drop / Time gone by / Shuffle it all / Bucket o' trouble / Train tracks / How will it go / Cuttin' the rug / Take a look at the guy / Come on now inside. *(cd-iss. Jun97 & Aug99; same)*
Dec 92. (c-s) *(GFSC 33)* **SHUFFLE IT ALL. /** [ ] [ ]
(12"+=/cd-s+=) *(GFST R/D 33)* –

— IZZY temporarily deputised for the injured (broken wrist) GILBY on mid '93 tours.

Mar 98. (cd) *<(GED 25202)>* **117°** [ ] [ ]
– Ain't it a bitch / Gotta say / Memphis / Old hat / Bleedin / Parasite / Good enough / 117° / Here before you / Up jumped the Devil / Grunt / Freight train / Methanol / Surf roach.

STRANGEWAYS

Formed: Scotland . . . mid-80's by the sibling pairing of IAN (guitar) and DAVID STEWART (bass), the rest of the quartet being made up from vocalist TONY LIDDELL and drummer JIM DRUMMOND. Signed to 'Arista' backed 'Bonaire', this JOURNEY-meets-KANSAS hard-rock outfit released three albums from the mid to late 80's, the eponymous 'STRANGEWAYS' (1986), 'NATIVE SONS' (1987) – with new American-born singer TERRY BROCK – and 'WALK IN THE FIRE' (1989). Having had a little success in the States, the band surprisingly parted company, only to return for a another stab at the AOR market in the late 90's.

Album rating: STRANGEWAYS (*5) / NATIVE SONS (*6) / WALK IN THE FIRE (*4) / AND THE HORSE (*5) / ANY DAY NOW (*4) / GREATEST BITS compilation (*6)

TONY LIDDELL – vocals / **IAN STEWART** – guitar / **DAVID STEWART** – bass / **JIM DRUMMOND** – drums

Bonaire – Arista | Bonaire – Arista

Mar 86. (7") *(108 104)* **CLOSE TO THE EDGE. / HOLD BACK YOUR LOVE** [ ] [-]
(12"+=) *(608 104)* – Heartbeat zone.
Mar 86. (lp/c) *(207/407 648) <207417>* **STRANGEWAYS** [ ] [ ]
– The kids need love / Hold back your love / Close to the edge / Heart break zone / Cry out / Power play / Breakin' down the barriers / Now it's gone / More than promises / Hold tight. *(cd re-iss. Apr98 on 'Hangdog'; HDRCD 01001)*

— **TERRY BROCK** (b. Atlanta, USA) – vocals; repl. LIDDELL

Nov 87. (7") *(BON 6)* **ONLY A FOOL. / EMPTY STREET** [ ] [-]
(12"+=) *(BON12 6)* – Stand up & shout (live) / Breaking down the barriers (live).
Jan 88. (lp/c/cd) *(208/408/258 579) <6569>* **NATIVE SONS** [ ] [ ]
– Dance with somebody / Only a fool / So far away / Where do we go from here / Goodnight L.A. / Empty streets / Stand up and shout / Shake the seven / Never going to lose it / Face to face. *(cd re-iss. Apr98 on 'Hangdog'; HDRCD 02002)*
Dec 89. (lp/c/cd) *<9662-1/-4/-2>* **WALK IN THE FIRE** [-] [ ]
– Where are they now? / Danger in your eyes / Love lies dying / Everytime you cry / Talk to me / Living in the danger zone / Modern world / Into the night / Walk in the fire / After the hurt is gone.
(cd re-iss. Apr98 on 'Hangdog'; HDRCD 03003)

— BROCK left and the band folded for a while

Hangdog | not iss.

Apr 98. (cd) *(HDRCD 04004)* **AND THE HORSE** [ ] [-]
Apr 98. (cd) *(HDRCD 05005)* **ANY DAY NOW** [ ] [-]
Feb 99. (cd) *(HDRCD 06006)* **GREATEST BITS** (compilation) [ ] [-]
– Love lies dying / Only a fool / It's alright / Where are they now / Face to face / Talk to me / Out of the blue / Never gonna lose it / Great awakening / Every time you cry / So far away / Fallen angel / Shake the seven / Hold back your love / Where do we go from here.

STRAPPING YOUNG LAD (see under ⇒ TOWNSEND, Devin)

STRAPPS

Formed: London, England . . . 1975 by ROSS STAGG, NOEL SCOTT, JOE READ and MICK UNDERWOOD. Issued by 'Harvest', STRAPPS' eponymous debut brought comparisons with classic DEEP PURPLE and like their heroes, they amassed a sizable following in Japan. UK success proved far more elusive, however, with subsequent albums 'SECRET DAMAGE' (1977) and 'SHARP CONVERSATION' (1978) failing to elevate the group above second division status. Their final effort, 'BALL OF FIRE' (title ring any bells?), was withdrawn shortly after its release in 1979, with UNDERWOOD subsequently joining GILLAN (who incidentally, had been in DEEP PURPLE).

Album rating: STRAPPS (*5) / SECRET DAMAGE (*5) / SHARP CONVERSION (*4)

ROSS STAGG – vocals, guitar / **NOEL SCOTT** – keyboards / **JOE READ** – bass / **MICK UNDERWOOD** – drums (ex-QUATERMASS)

Harvest | Harvest

Mar 76. (7") *(HAR 5108)* **IN YOUR EAR. / RITA B** [ ] [ ]
Apr 76. (lp) *(SHSP 4055)* **STRAPPS** [ ] [-]
– Schoolgirl funk / Dreaming / Rock critic / Oh the night / Sanctuary / I long to tell you too / In your ear / Suicide.
Feb 77. (7") *(HAR 5119)* **CHILD OF THE CITY. / SOFT TOUCH** [ ] [-]
Mar 77. (lp) *(SHSP 4064) <11621>* **SECRET DAMAGE** [ ] [ ]
– Down to you / The pain of love / Child of the city / Never never wanna go home / I wanna know / Soft touch / Violent love.
Jun 78. (7") *(HAR 5163)* **TURN OUT ALRIGHT. / TAKE IT, BREAK IT** [ ] [-]
Jun 78. (lp) *(SHSP 4088)* **SHARP CONVERSATION** [ ] [-]
– Let the music play / Rock'n'roll sensation / Be strong / Turn out alright / You're only my life / Prisoner of love / It's your dream / Might or maybe / Look to the east / Break my fall.

— in 1979, an album 'BALL OF FIRE' was withdrawn before its release

— disbanded when UNDERWOOD joined GILLAN

STRATUS (see under ⇒ PRAYING MANTIS)

STRETCHHEADS

Formed: Glasgow, Scotland . . . 1987 by ANDY and PHIL ('DR. TECHNOLOGY' and 'FAT BASTARD'), adding MOFUNGO DIGGS and RICHIE DEMPSEY from their Paisley school days. Serving up a platter of fun hardcore (The EX were an early inspiration), The STRETCHHEADS were an unorthodox rock concept (they wore flashy shirts and balaclavas on stage!) in that Scots bands rarely ventured into this comic book grunge-esque genre (CHOU PAHROT eat your cage out!). Poking fun at number one pop act at the time, BROS, was indeed their first musical mission, 'BROS ARE PISH' (Pish is Scots slang for urine or indeed No.1's!), being the debut EP in question. Early the following year, a full-set of weird ideas was unveiled via their debut set, 'FIVE FINGERS, FOUR THINGERS, A THUMB, A FACELIFT AND A NEW IDENTITY' (1989). Moving from Charles Cosh's 'Moshka' (once home of The SHAMEN) to top indie imprint 'Blast First' (and with MR JASON replacing DEMPSEY on drums), the zany quartet had three releases during a prolific early 90's spell. 'EYEBALL ORIGAMI AFTERMATH WIT VEGETARIAN LEG' was a fine ooh-ah! EP, while the danceable 12" '23 SKINNER (HAVE A BANG ON THIS NUMBER)' featured a sample from the American TV sitcom theme 'Rhoda', also present on their second fool-set (sic!), 'PISH IN YOUR SLEAZEBAG' (1991). However, by the time NIRVANA's 'Nevermind' had hit the shops that Autumn, the group were facing indie oblivion. In fact, it took another couple of years and a comeback 10"EP, 'BARBED ANAL EXCITER', before the band went to ground.

Album rating: FIVE FINGERS, FOUR THINGERS, A THUMB, A FACELIFT AND A NEW IDENTITY (*4) / PISH IN YOUR SLEAZEBAG (*6)

PHIL 'FAT BASTARD' – vocals / **ANDY 'DR. TECHNOLOGY'** – guitar / **MOFUNGO DIGGS** – bass / **RICHIE DEMPSEY** – drums

Moshka not iss.

Nov 88. (7"ep) *(SOMA 5)* **BROS ARE PISH EP** -
– Bros are pish / I should be so lucky / Confront / Headache / Everything's going to break in a minute / Worry.

Jan 89. (lp) *(SOMALP 2)* **FIVE FINGERS, FOUR THINGERS, A THUMB, A FACELIFT AND A NEW IDENTITY** -
(cd-iss. 1991; SOMACD 2)

— **MR. JASON** – drums; repl. DEMPSEY who later surfaced with FENN and the PH FAMILY

Blast First not iss.

Nov 90. (7"ep) *(BFFP 56)* **EYEBALL ORIGAMI AFTERMATH WIT VEGETARIAN LEG EP** -
– Afghanistan bananastan / Incontinent of sex / Omnipresent octopus (Russell Grant) / New thing in Egypt (Boney M).

Jan 91. (12") *(BFFP 57T)* **23 SKINNER (HAVE A BANG ON THIS NUMBER). /** -

Feb 91. (lp/c/cd) *(BFFP 58/+C/CD)* **PISH IN YOUR SLEAZEBAG** -
– Spaceape / Trippy dreadzone / A freakout / Incontinent of sex / Crazy desert man / Housefire up yer f***ing arse music / Machine gun in Delhi (Gary Newman's round the world trip) / Ognob / Acid Sweeney / Mao Tse tungs meat challenge / Space jam / HMS average nostril / Three pottery owls (with innuendo) / Hairy mousaka / Fly feast / 23 skinner (the theme from 'Rhoda') / Housewife up yer f***ing arse music. *(cd+=)* – Afghanistan bananastan / Incontinent of sex / Omnipresent octopus (Russell Grant) / New thing in Egypt (Boney M).
below was a posthumous release due to their demise

Jul 93. (10"ep) *(BFFP 68)* **BARBED ANAL EXCITER EP** -

— p6 (aka PHIL) subsequently turned up on a PH FAMILY release, 'Important Information' c.1997

Pete STRIDE & John PLAIN (see under ⇒ LURKERS)

Joe STRUMMER (see under ⇒ CLASH)

STRYPER

Formed: Orange County, California, USA . . . 1981 initially as ROXX REGIME, by the SWEET brothers, MICHAEL and ROBERT, who converted to Christianity after witnessing preacher Jimmy Swaggart. Completing their line-up with TIMOTHY GAINES and OZ FOX, the group subsequently relocated to Los Angeles and secured a deal with 'Enigma'. Armed with a calculated marketing campaign and a retina-challenging outfit of garish yellow and black stripes, the group set out on a crusade to make a significant dent in the hearts of the largely heathen metal scene. Debuting in 1984 with 'THE YELLOW AND BLACK ATTACK', STRYPER honed their melodic rock over the course of the 80's, reaching a commercial and critical peak with 1987's platinum selling 'TO HELL WITH THE DEVIL'. MICHAEL's choirboy vocals and cutesy pin-up status certainly did the band no harm, attracting the attention of secular fans who helped put the accompanying single, 'HONESTLY' into the US Top 30. Still, the faithful weren't quite so impressed with the more commercial 'IN GOD WE TRUST' (1988), STRYPER subsequently deciding that a more mean 'n' moody image would be more helpful in spreading the good word. Not surprisingly, they were badly mistaken, the disastrous 'AGAINST THE LAW' (1990) effectively damning the band's career. With no miraculous recovery in sight, MICHAEL eventually departed in 1992, STRYPER finally laid to rest.

Album rating: THE YELLOW AND THE BLACK ATTACK (*6) / SOLDIERS UNDER COMMAND (*6) / TO HELL WITH THE DEVIL (*7) / IN GOD WE TRUST (*5) / AGAINST THE LAW (*5) / CAN'T STOP THE ROCK compilation (*6)

MICHAEL SWEET – vocals / **OZ FOX** – guitar / **TIMOTHY GAINES** – bass / **ROBERT SWEET** – drums

not iss. Enigma

1984. (m-lp) *<E 1064>* **THE YELLOW AND THE BLACK ATTACK** -
– Loud 'n' clear / My love I'll always show / You know what to do / Co'mon rock / You won't be lonely / Loving you / Reasons for the season. *(UK-iss.Apr87 on 'Music For Nations'; MFN 74) <US remixed.Aug86 +=; 73207>* – From wrong to right. *(cd-iss. Aug89; CDMFN 74)*

Sep 85. (lp) *<72077>* **SOLDIERS UNDER COMMAND** - 84
– Soldiers under command / Makes me wanna sing / Together forever / First love / The rock that makes me roll / Reach out / (Waiting for) A love that's real / Together as one / Surrender / Battle hymn of the Republic (glory, glory hallelujah). *(UK-iss.Feb87 on 'Music For Nations'; MFN 72) (cd-iss. Aug89; CDMFN 72)*

Nov 85. (7") *(STRY 1)* **WINTER WONDERLAND. / REASONS FOR THE SEASON**

Music For Nations Enigma

Feb 87. (lp) *(MFN 70) <73237>* **TO HELL WITH THE DEVIL** 32 Nov86
– Abyss (to hell with the Devil) / To hell with the Devil / Calling on you / Free / Honestly / The way / Sing-along song / Rockin' the world / All of me / More than a man. *(cd-iss. Aug87; CDMFN 70) (re-iss. Aug90 on 'Enigma' cd/c/lp; CDENV/TCENV/ENVLP 1009)*

Apr 87. (7") *(KUT 126)* **CALLING ON YOU. / FREE**
(12"+=) *(12KUT 126)* –

Oct 87. (7") *<75009>* **HONESTLY. / SING-ALONG-SONG** - 23

Enigma Enigma

Aug 88. (7"/7"pic-d/c-s) *(ENV/ENVS/ENCS 1) <75019>* **ALWAYS THERE FOR YOU. / IN GOD WE TRUST** 71 Jul88
(12"+=) *(ENVT 1)* – Soldiers under command.
(cd-s) *(ENVCD 1)* – ('A'side) / Reign / Soldiers under command (live) / (Robert Sweet interview; part 1).

Aug 88. (lp/c/cd) *(ENVLP/TCENV/CDENV 501) <73317>* **IN GOD WE TRUST** 32 Jul88
– In God we trust / Always there for you / Keep the fire burning / I believe in you / Writings on the wall / It's up 2 U / World of you and I / Come to the everlife / Lonely / The reign. *(also pic-lp; PENVLP 501) (re-iss. Aug90 cd/c/lp; CDENV/TCENV/ENVLP 108)*

Oct 88. (7") *<75028>* **I BELIEVE IN YOU. / TOGETHER FOREVER (live)** - 88

Aug 90. (cd/c/lp) *(CDENV/TCENV/ENVLP 1010) <73527>* **AGAINST THE LAW** 39
– Against the law / Two time woman / Rock the people / Two bodies (one mind, one soul) / Not that kind of guy / Shining star / Ordinary man / Lady / Caught in the middle / All for one / Rock the hell out of you.

— disbanded in 1992 when MICHAEL took off

– compilations, etc. –

Oct 91. (cd/c/lp) *Hollywood; (HWD CD/MC/LP 8) / Intercord; <845.167>* **CAN'T STOP THE ROCK**
– I believe in you / Can't stop the rock / Soldiers under command / Free / Always there for you / Lady / To hell with the Devil / In God we trust / Honestly / Two bodies (one mind one soul) / Together as one / You know what to do.

STUCK MOJO

Formed: Atlanta, Georgia, USA . . . 1990 by BONZ, RICH WARD, COREY LOWERY and BUD FONTSERE. BONZ (pronounced 'Bones') is a black Irishman who was born in Japan to a stationed US Air Force father and who followed in his father's footsteps at the age of 17 (he left after four years). The others (RICH and BUD) played major league football while COREY was from an Indian tribe called the Tuscadora. Akin to an aggressive URBAN DANCE SQUAD or CLAWFINGER with a love for WWF wrestling (they made a promo video with DIAMOND DALLAS PAGE!), STUCK MOJO released a trio of lovingly-titled albums for 'Century Media', namely 'SNAPPIN' NECKS' (1995), 'PIGWALK' (1996) and 'RISING' (1998). During the course of the next two years, 'MOJO delivered another two sets, 'HVY, VOL.1' (1999) and 'DECLARATION OF A HEADHUNTER' (2000).

Album rating: SNAPPIN' NECKS (*5) / VIOLATED mini (*4) / PIGWALK (*5) / RISING (*5) / HVY1 (*5) / DECLARATION OF A HEADHUNTER (*5)

BONZ – vocals / **RICH WARD** – guitar / **COREY LOWERY** – bass / **BUD FONTSERE** – drums

Century Media Century Media

Aug 95. (cd/c/lp) *(CM 77088 CD/MC/LP) <7788>* **SNAPPIN' NECKS** Mar95

May 96. (m-cd) *(CM 77122CD) <7822>* **VIOLATED**
– Violated / U.B. Otch / Sweet leaf / Pizzaman / F.O.D. / Monster.

Sep 96. (cd/c/lp) *(CM 77133 CD/MC/LP) <7833>* **PIGWALK**
– Pigwalk / Mental meltdown / (Here comes) The monster / Twisted / The sermon / Despise / Animal / Only the strong survive / Violated / Inside my head / Down breeding.

Apr 98. (lp/cd) *(CM 77188/+CD) <7888>* **RISING**
– Intro / Crooked figurehead / Trick / Assassination of a pop star / Rising / Southern pride / Enemy territory / Back in the saddle / Dry / Throw the switch / Hang 'em high (loser's theme) / Tears / Pipe bomb / Suburban ranger.

Nov 99. (cd) *(CM 77288-2) <7988>* **HVY1 (live)** Sep99
– 2 minutes of death / Mental meltdown / Monster / Twisted / Crooked figurehead / Trick / Rising / Enemy territory / Back in the saddle / Throw the switch / Tears / F.O.D. / Not promised tomorrow / Southern pride / Pipe bomb / Reborn / My will / Untitled.

Jul 00. (cd/lp) *(77291-2/-1) <7991>* **DECLARATION OF A HEADHUNTER**
– A lesson in insensituity / Hate breed / Set the tone / April 29th / Raise the deadman / Drawing blood / An open letter / Give war a chance / Feel it comin' down / The one / Evilution / Declaration / The ward is my shepherd / Walk the line.

STUPIDS

Formed: Ipswich, Suffolk, England . . . December '83 by a loose, pseudonymous crew with a core of TOMMY STUPID, MARTY TUFF, ED WENN and STEVIE SNAX. Inspired by US hardcore icons such as The CIRCLE JERKS and SUICIDAL TENDENCIES, The STUPIDS took their own irreverent approach to slamdiving and skateboarding via a series of albums on their own 'Children Of The Revolution Records'. A precursor to bands like SNUFF and The SENSELESS THINGS, The STUPIDS quickly acquired cult status, a deal with 'Vinyl Solution' ensuring a wider audience for the 'VAN STUPID' (1987) and 'JESUS MEETS THE STUPIDS' (1987) albums (by the release of which MARTY had been substituted with PAULY PIZZA) while the continuing support of John Peel made sure they were heard by a varied cross section of the indie community. Comparisons were often drawn between The STUPIDS and Aussie hardcore pranksters The HARD-ONS, both bands sharing a juvenile sense of humour and a dedication to anarchic live sets. Never the most stable of bands, it came as little surprise when they finally fell apart in 1989. The various band members were also simultaneously involved with their own bands (BAD DRESS SENSE, SCHNOZZER and FRANKFURTER II), ED and PAULY subsequently forming SINK at the turn of the decade.

Album rating: PERUVIAN VACATION (*6) / RETARD PICNIC (*6) / VAN STUPID (*6) / JESUS MEETS THE STUPIDS (*6)

TOMMY STUPID (b. WITHERS) – vocals, guitar, drums / **ED SHRED** (b. WENN) – guitar, bass, vocals / **STEVIE SNAX** – bass / **MARTY TUFF** – guitar

Children Of The Revolution — not iss.

Mar 85. (7"ep) *(COR 3)* **VIOLENT NUN EP**
May 86. (lp) *(GURT 9)* **PERUVIAN VACATION**
(cd-iss. Sep93 on 'Clay'+=; CLAYCD 116) – VIOLENT NUN EP / Leave your ears behind / (11 rare tracks).
Oct 86. (lp) *(GURT 15)* **RETARD PICNIC**
– The memory burns / Sleeping troubles / Terrordome / Heard it all before / Jesus, do what you have to do / Yah dude!! / Something's got to give / Hawaiian vacation / Shaded eyes / Frankfurter / Slumber party massacre / Waltz of the new wavers / Your little world / Killed by a cripple / We suck / Peoiple in your neighbourhood / I'm so lazy / Wipe out. *(cd-iss. Nov93 on 'Clay'+=; CLAYCD 117)* – (Stupids flexi / Feedback sessions / Retard Picnic out-takes).

— **PAULY PIZZA** – bass; repl. MARTY

Vinyl Solution — not iss.

May 87. (m-lp) *(SOL 2)* **VAN STUPID**
Jul 87. (lp; as BAD DRESS SENSE) *(SOL 4)* **GOODBYE . . . IT WAS FUN**
– G.C.B. / Could I ever / Truth / Cynical smile / Life's demand / Never mine / Always away / Need to love.

— no ED or TOMMY on above

Aug 87. (12"ep) *(FART 1)* **meet (FRANKFURTER) ep**
– Eat me / etc.
Dec 87. (lp) *(SOL 7)* **JESUS MEETS THE STUPIDS**
– Skid row / You never win / Do you really have to? / Fridge / Blue blood / Slit your wrists / etc *(w/free 7"ep)*

— disbanded the following year

– compilations, etc. –

Sep 88. (12"ep) *Strange Fruit; (SFPS 054)* **PEEL SESSIONS** (12.5.87)
– Life's a drug / Heard it all before / Shaded eyes / Dog bog / Stupid Monday.

SINK

ED SHRED (aka WENN) – vocals, guitar / **PAULY** – bass

Poontang — not iss.

Jan 89. (7"ep) *(POON 1)* **TAKE THE HOSSES WITH THE LOSSES**
– Diamonds / I hate yourself / Some lilac evening / Mama sink / Birthday song / For what it's worth (acoustic).
Jun 89. (7"ep) *(POON 2)* **ON THE TRACKS, FEELING BLUE**
– Blue noodles / Slippin' thru my hands / Blues man / Fire and brimstone / If only you were lonely.

Decoy — not iss.

Jan 90. (lp) *(DYL 6)* **ANOTHER LOVE TRIANGLE**

— new guitarist (ex-PERFECT DAZE)

Jun 90. (lp) **OLD MAN SNAKE AND THE FAT BLACK PIG**
(above might have been abandoned)
Nov 90. (lp/cd) *Decoy; (DYL 21/+CD)* **MAMA SINK THE FIRST 18 YEARS (1963-1989)** (compilation of first 2 EP's)

City Slang — unknown

Jan 92. (lp/cd) *(EFA 04072/+CD)* **VEGA-TABLES**

X-Mist — not iss.

Oct 92. (7") *(EFA 1548-7)* **100 TONS. /**

— disappeared after above

ST. VITUS

Formed: Los Angeles, California, USA . . . 1979 as TYRANT by SCOTT REAGERS, DAVE CHANDLER, MARK ADAMS and ARMANDO ACOSTA. By the time the fledgling 'S.S.T.' label had released their eponymous 1984 debut album, the BLACK SABBATH protoges had assumed the SAINT VITUS moniker and set out their doom/stoner metal agenda. Although REAGERS exited after sophomore effort, 'HALLOW'S VICTIM' (1985), the vacuum of his absence was filled with erstwhile OBSESSED frontman SCOTT WEINRICH. The latter made his debut on 'BORN TOO LATE' (1986), a record which garnered considerable underground acclaim. Yet subsequent releases such as 1987's 'THIRSTY AND MISERABLE' EP and 1988's 'MOURNFUL CRIES' album failed to consolidate their position and the band parted company with 'SST'. Concentrating on the European market, they signed a new deal with 'Hellbound' records who issued 'V' in 1989 to little fanfare. With WEINRICH subsequently leaving to reform OBSESSED, SAINT VITUS danced on for a last gasp effort, 'C.O.D.' (1992), with replacement singer CHRISTIAN LINDERSSON. Finally, in 1995, the original line-up regrouped for a further album, 'DIE HEALING', their last release to date.

Album rating: ST. VITUS (*5) / HALLOW'S VICTIM mini (*5) / BORN TOO LATE (*6) / MOURNFUL CRIES (*5) / V (*5) / C.O.D. (*5) / DIE HEALING (*5) / HEAVIER THAN THOU compilation (*7)

SAINT VITUS

SCOTT WEINRICH – vocals / **DAVID CHANDLER** – guitar / **MARK ADAMS** – bass / **ARMANDO ACOSTA** – drums

S.S.T. — S.S.T.

Jun 85. (lp) <*(SST 022)*> ⇒*ST. VITUS* — 1984
– Saint Vitus / White magic – Black magic / The psychopath / Burial at sea. *(c-iss.May93; SST 022C)*
Nov 85. (12"ep) <*(SST 042)*> **THE WALKING DEAD**
– Darkness / White stallions / The walking dead. *(c-iss.May93; SST 042C)*
Apr 86. (m-lp) <*(SST 052)*> **HALLOW'S VICTIM**
(c-iss.May93; SST 052C)
Oct 86. (lp/cd) <*(SST 082/+CD)*> **BORN TOO LATE**
– Born to late / Clear windowpane / Dying inside / H.A.A.G. / The lost feeling / The war starter. *(w/free 12"ep)* – THIRSTY AND MISERABLE EP *(c-iss.May93; SST 082C)*
Jul 87. (12"ep) <*(SST 119)*> **THIRSTY AND MISERABLE**
– The end of the end / Thirsty and miserable / Look behind you. *(c-iss.May93; SST 119)*
Sep 88. (lp/cd) <*(SST 161/+CD)*> **MOURNFUL CRIES**
– The creeps / Dragon time / Shooting gallery / Bitter truth / The troll / Looking glass. *(c-iss.May93; SST 161C)*
Feb 91. (d-lp/cd) <*(SST 266/+CD)*> **HEAVIER THAN THOU** (compilation)
– Clear windowpane / Born too late / Look behind you / Thirsty and miserable / Dying inside / Lost feeling / H.A.A.G. / Shooting gallery / Bitter truth / Dragon time / War is our destiny / White stallions / White magic – Black magic / Saint Vitus. *(c-iss.May93; SST 226C)*

— likely to be two separate bands below is SAINT VITUS on German label

Hellhound — S.P.V.

Apr 90. (cd) *(H 0005-2)* <*SPV 68062*> **V**
– Living backwards / I bleed black / When emotion dies / Patra (Petra) / Ice monkey / Jack Frost / Angry man / Mind-food.
Jan 91. (cd) *(H 0010-2)* **LIVE (live)**
– Living backwards / Born too late / The war starter / Mind-food / Looking glass / White stallions / Look behind you / Dying inside / War is our destiny / Mystic lady / Clear windowpane.
May 92. (cd) *(H 0017-2)* **C.O.D.**
– Intro / Children of doom / Planet of judgement / Shadow of a skeleton / (I am) The screaming banshee / Plague of man / Imagination man / Fear / Get away / Bela / A timeless tale / Hallow's victim (exhumed).
1995. (cd) *(H 0035-2)* **DIE HEALING** — German
– Dark world / One mind / Let the end begin / Trail of pestilence / Sloth / Return of the zombie / In the asylum / Just another notch.

— split after above

STYX

Formed: Chicago, Illinois, USA . . . 1964 as The TRADEWINDS by DENNIS DE YOUNG and neighbours, the PANOZZO twins (CHUCK and JOHN). After meeting JOHN CURULEWSKI at university and duly recruiting him as guitarist, the group briefly changed their name to TW4 before eventually settling on STYX (after the mythical Greek river). With the line-up augmented by a second guitarist, JAMES YOUNG, the group came to the attention of Bill Traut, who signed them to his 'Wooden Nickel' label. Initially touting a classical/art-rock fusion with overblown vocal arrangements, the group debuted with the eponymous 'STYX' in 1972. Although the album spawned a US Hot 100 single in 'BEST THING', subsequent sets such as 'THE SERPENT IS RISING' (1974) and 'MAN OF MIRACLES' (1974), failed to yield any chart action. Things changed in the mid-70's as CURULEWSKI was replaced with guitarist/vocalist/co-writer, TOMMY SHAW, who, along with DE YOUNG, would help steer the band in a more commercial direction. Widely credited with inventing pomp-rock, STYX only really started to take their falsetto-warbling excess to the masses following a move to 'R.C.A.'. Almost instantaneous success came in late '74/early '75 when the label re-issued 'LADY' (from 1972's 'STYX II'), a strident slice of bombastic pop which marched into the US Top 10. Follow-up sets, 'EQUINOX' (1976) and 'CRYSTAL BALL' (1976) appeared on 'A&M', STYX slowly but surely swelling their fanbase with widescale touring and an increasingly radio-friendly sound. The big break finally came in 1977 with the multi-million selling 'THE GRAND ILLUSION' album and accompanying Top 10 crossover hit, 'COME SAIL AWAY'. The following year's 'PIECES OF EIGHT' (1978) achieved a fine balance between melody, power and stride-splitting vocal histrionics, although it was 'CORNERSTONE' (1980) which furnished the group with their sole No.1 single, the syrupy 'BABE'. A lavishly packaged pomp concept piece, 'PARADISE THEATER' (1980) became the group's first (and only) No.1, even making the Top 10 in Britain(!) Arguably among the group's most affecting work, the record spawned two US Top 10 singles, 'THE BEST OF TIMES' and 'TIME ON MY HANDS'. Yet another concept piece (centering on the increasingly controversial issue of censorship), 'KILROY WAS HERE' (1983), appeared in 1983, the last STYX studio album of the decade. The following year saw both DE YOUNG and SHAW releasing solo debuts, 'DESERT MOON' and 'GIRLS WITH GUNS' respectively. Both sets performed relatively well, although DE YOUNG's poppier affair spawned a Top 10 hit single with the title track. Subsequent mid to late 80's efforts (DE YOUNG's 'BACK TO THE WORLD' and 'BOOMCHILD', SHAW's 'WHAT IF' and 'AMBITION') failed to capture the public's imagination and the inevitable STYX reformation album was released in 1990. Despite the absence of SHAW (his replacement being GLEN BURTNIK), who had joined DAMN YANKEES, 'EDGE OF THE CENTURY' was a relative success, housing a massive US Top 3 hit in 'SHOW ME THE WAY'. Come the late 90's the band were back again with another reformation – this time with SHAW in the ranks – and a live comeback album, 'RETURN TO PARADISE'. While this had consisted largely of old material, 'BRAVE NEW WORLD' (1999) was a set of brand spanking new stuff at least making an attempt to sound contemporary but simultaneously railing against the march of time and the current musical climate. Fans also longing for the old days could torture themselves at will with the self explanatory 'STYX WORLD: LIVE 2001'.

Album rating: STYX (*4) / STYX II (*6) / THE SERPENT IS RISING (*5) / MAN OF MIRACLES (*6) / EQUINOX (*6) / CRYSTAL BALL (*6) / THE GRAND ILLUSION (*7) / PIECES OF EIGHT (*7) / THE BEST OF STYX compilation (*6) / CORNERSTONE (*7) / PARADISE THEATER (*8) / KILROY WAS HERE (*6) / CAUGHT IN THE ACT – LIVE (*4) / EDGE OF THE CENTURY (*5) / GREATEST HITS compilation (*8) / RETURN TO PARADISE (*3) / BRAVE NEW WORLD (*3) / STYX WORLD: LIVE 2001 (*3)

DENNIS DeYOUNG (b.18 Feb'47) – vocals, keyboards / **JOHN CURULEWSKI** – guitar / **JAMES YOUNG** (b.14 Nov'48) – guitar / **CHUCK PANOZZO** (b.20 Sep'47) – bass / **JOHN PANOZZO** – drums

not iss. — Wooden Nickel

Sep 72. (lp) <BXLI 1008> **STYX** [-] [ ]
– Movement for the common man: Children of the land – Street collage – Fanfare for the common man – Mother Nature's matinee / Right away / What has come between us / Best thing / Quick is the beat of my heart / After you leave me. *(UK-iss.Jul80 as 'STYX I' on 'R.C.A.'; 3593) (cd re-iss. Jan99 on 'One Way'; OW 35130)*

Sep 72. (7") *<0106>* **BEST THING. / WHAT HAS COME BETWEEN US** [-] [82]

Jul 73. (7") *<0111>* **I'M GONNA MAKE YOU FEEL IT. / QUICK IS THE BEAT OF MY HEART** [-] [ ]

Jul 73. (lp) *<BXLI 1012>* **STYX II** [-] [ ]
– You need love / Lady / A day / You better ask / Little fugue in "G" / Father O.S.A. / Earl of Roseland / I'm gonna make you feel it. *<re-dist.Jan75, hit US No.20> (UK-iss.Jul80 as 'LADY' on 'R.C.A.'; 3594)*

Sep 73. (7") *<0116>* **LADY. / YOU BETTER ASK** [-] [ ]

Feb 74. (lp) *<BXLI 0287>* **THE SERPENT IS RISING** [-] [ ]
– Witch wolf / The grove of Eglantine / Young man / As bad as this / Winner take all / 22 years / Jonas Psalter / The serpent is rising / Krakatoa / Hallelujah chorus. *(UK-iss.Jul80 on 'R.C.A.'; 3595)*

Oct 74. (7") *<10027>* **LIES. / 22 YEARS** [-] [ ]

Nov 74. (lp) *<BWLI 0638)* **MAN OF MIRACLES** [-] [ ]
– Rock & roll feeling / Havin' a ball / Golden lark / A song for Suzanne / A man like me / Best thing / Evil eyes / Southern woman / Christopher Mr. Christopher. *(UK-iss.Jul80 on 'R.C.A.'; 3596)*

R.C.A. — R.C.A.

Feb 75. (7") *(RCA 2518) <10102>* **LADY. / CHILDREN OF THE LAND** [ ] [6] Dec74

Jul 75. (7") *<0252>* **YOUNG MAN. / UNFINISHED SONG** [-] [ ]

May 75. (7") *<10272>* **YOU NEED LOVE. / YOU BETTER ASK** [-] [88]

Nov 75. (7") *<10329>* **BEST THING. / HAVIN' A BALL** [-] [ ]

A&M — A&M

Feb 76. (lp) *(AMLH 64559) <4559>* **EQUINOX** [ ] [58] Dec75
– Light up / Lorelei / Mother dear / Lonely child / Midnight ride / Born for adventure / Prelude 12 / Suite Madame Blue.

Mar 76. (7") *(AMS 7220) <1786>* **LORELEI. / MIDNIGHT RIDE** [ ] [27] Feb76

Jul 76. (7") *<1818>* **LIGHT UP. / BORN FOR ADVENTURE** [-] [ ]

— **TOMMY SHAW** (b.11 Sep'53, Montgomery, Alabama) – lead guitar repl. CURULEWSKI

Oct 76. (lp) *(AMLH 64604) <4604>* **CRYSTAL BALL** [ ] [66]
– Put me on / Mademoiselle / Jennifer / Crystal ball / Shooz / This old man / Clair de Lune – Ballerina.

Jan 77. (7") *(AMS 7273) <1877>* **MADEMOISELLE. / LIGHT UP** [ ] [36] Nov76

Feb 77. (7") *<1900>* **JENNIFER. / SHOOZ** [-] [ ]

Jun 77. (7") *(AMS 7299) <1931>* **CRYSTAL BALL. / PUT ME ON** [ ] [ ]

Aug 77. (lp/c) *(AMLH/CAM 64637) <4637>* **THE GRAND ILLUSION** [ ] [6] Jul77
– The grand illusion / Fooling yourself (the angry young man) / Superstars / Come sail away / Miss America / Man in the wilderness / Castle walls / The grand finale. *(cd-iss. Jul87; CDA 3223)*

Oct 77. (7") *(AMS 7321) <1977>* **COME SAIL AWAY. / PUT ME ON** [ ] [8] Sep77

Mar 78. (7") *(AMS 7343) <2007>* **FOOLING YOURSELF (THE ANGRY YOUNG MAN). / THE GRAND FINALE** [ ] [29] Feb78

Sep 78. (lp/c)<US-pic-d> *(AMLH/CAM 64724) <4724>* **PIECES OF EIGHT** [ ] [6]
– Great white hope / I'm O.K. / Sing for the day / The message / Lords of the ring / Blue collar man (long nights) / Queen of spades / Renegade / Pieces of eight / Aku-aku.

Oct 78. (7"/12"colrd) *(AMS/+P 7388) <2087>* **BLUE COLLAR MAN (LONG NIGHTS). / SUPERSTARS** [ ] [21] Sep78

Mar 79. (7",7"red) *(AMS 7446) <2110>* **RENEGADE. / SING FOR THE DAY** [ ] [16] [41]

Sep 79. (7") *(AMS 7489) <2188>* **BABE. / I'M OK** [6] [1] Sep79

Jan 80. (lp/c) *(AMLK/CKM 63711) <3711>* **CORNERSTONE** [36] [2] Oct79
– Lights / Why me / Babe / Never say never / Boat on the river / Borrowed time / First time / Eddie / Love in the moonlight.

Dec 79. (7") *<2206>* **WHY ME. / LIGHTS** [-] [26]

Mar 80. (7") *<2228>* **BORROWED TIME. / EDDIE** [-] [64]

Mar 80. (7") *(AMS 7512)* **BOAT ON THE RIVER. / COME SAIL AWAY** [ ] [-]

May 80. (7") *(AMS 7528)* **LIGHTS. / RENEGADE** [ ] [-]

Jan 81. (lp/c) *(AML H/K 63719) <3719>* **PARADISE THEATER** [8] [1]
– A.D. 1928 / Rockin' the Paradise / State street Sadie / Too much time on my hands / She cares / Snowblind / Nothing ever goes as planned / The best of times / Half-penny, two-penny / A.D. 1958. *(cd-iss. Jun84; CDA 63719) (re-iss. Oct92 cd/c; CD/C MID 154)*

Jan 81. (7") *(AMS 8102) <2300>* **THE BEST OF TIMES. / LIGHT** [42] [3]
(d-lazer-etched-7") – ('A'side) / PARADISE THEATER

Mar 81. (7",7"colrd) *(AMS 8118) <2323>* **TOO MUCH TIME ON MY HANDS. / QUEEN OF SPADES** [ ] [9]

Jul 81. (7") *<2348>* **NOTHING EVER GOES AS PLANNED. / NEVER SAY NEVER** [-] [54]

Nov 81. (7") *(AMS 8175)* **ROCKIN' THE PARADISE. / SNOWBLIND** [ ] [-]

Feb 83. (lp/c) *(AMLX/CAM 63734) <3734>* **KILROY WAS HERE** [67] [3]
– Mr. Roboto / Cold war / Don't let it end / High time / Heavy metal poisoning / Just get through this night / Double life / Haven't we been here before / Don't let it end (reprise). *(cd-iss. Apr84; CDA 63734)*

Mar 83. (7") *(AMS 8308) <2525>* **MR. ROBOTO. / SNOWBLIND** [ ] [3] Feb83

May 83. (7"/7"sha-pic-d) *(AM/+P 120) <2543>* **DON'T LET IT END. / ROCKIN' THE PARADISE** [56] [6] Apr83

Jun 83. (7") *<2560>* **HAVEN'T WE BEEN HERE BEFORE. / DOUBLE LIFE** [-] [ ]

Aug 83. (7") *<2568>* **HIGH TIME. / DOUBLE LIFE** [-] [48]

Apr 84. (d-lp/d-c) *(AMLH/CAM 66704) <6514>* **CAUGHT IN THE ACT – LIVE (live)** [44] [31]
– Music time / Mr. Roboto / Too much time on my hands / Babe / Snowblind / The best of times / Suite Madame Blue / Rockin' the Paradise / Blue collar man (long night) / Miss America / Don't let it end / Fooling yourself (the angry young man) / Crystal ball / Come sail away.

May 84. (7") *(AM 197) <2625>* **MUSIC TIME (live). / HEAVY METAL POISONING (live)** [ ] [40]

— the band rested activities while their main members DeYOUNG and SHAW went solo

DENNIS DeYOUNG

A&M — A&M

Sep 84. (lp/c/cd) *<(AMA/AMC/CDA 5006)>* **DESERT MOON** [ ] [29]
– Don't wait for heroes / Please / Boys will be boys / Fire / Desert Moon / Suspicious / Gravity / Dear darling (I'll be there).

Oct 84. (7"/12") *(AM/+X 218) <2666>* **DESERT MOON. / GRAVITY** [ ] [10] Sep84

Dec 84. (7") *<2692>* **DON'T WAIT FOR HEROES. / GRAVITY** [-] [83]

Feb 85. (7") *<2709>* **SUSPICIOUS. / DEAR DARLING (I'LL BE THERE)** [-] [ ]

Apr 86. (lp,c) *<5109>* **BACK TO THE WORLD** [-] [ ]
– This is the time / Warning shot / Call me / I'll get lucky / Unanswered prayers / Southbound Ryan / Person to person / Black wall.

Mar 86. (7") *<2816>* **CALL ME. / PLEASE** [-] [54]

Jun 86. (7") *<2839>* **THIS IS THE TIME. / SOUTHBOUND TRAIN** [-] [93]
(above from the film, 'The Karate Kid II')

M.C.A. — not iss.

Nov 88. (7") *<53293>* **BENEATH THE MOON. / BOOMCHILD** [-] [ ]

Dec 88. (lp,c,cd) **BOOMCHILD** [-] [ ]
– Beneath the moon / The best is yet to come / What a way to go / Harry's hands / Boomchild / Who shot daddy? / Outside looking in again / Won't go wasted.

Feb 89. (7") *<53376>* **OUTSIDE LOOKING IN AGAIN. / BOOMCHILD** [-] [ ]

TOMMY SHAW

solo, with **STEVE HOLLEY** – drums (ex-WINGS, ex-ELTON JOHN) / **PETER WOOD** – keyboards (ex-AL STEWART) / **BRIAN STANLEY** – bass (ex-GRAHAM PARKER)

A&M — A&M

Sep 84. (7") *<2676>* **GIRLS WITH GUNS. / HEADS UP** [-] [33]

Oct 84. (lp/c) *<(AMA/AMC 5020)>* **GIRLS WITH GUNS** [ ] [50]
– Girls with guns / Come in and explain / Lonely school / Heads up / Kiss me hello / Fading away / Little girl would / Outside in the rain / Free to love you / The race is on.

Dec 84. (7") *<2696>* **LONELY SCHOOL. / COME IN AND EXPLAIN** [-] [60]

Jan 85. (7") *(AM 231)* **LONELY SCHOOL. / HEADS UP** [ ] [-]
(12"+=) *(AMY 231)* – Girls with guns.

Apr 85. (7") *<2715>* **FREE TO LOVE YOU. / COME IN AND EXPLAIN** [-] [ ]

Sep 85. (7") *<2773>* **REMO'S THEME (WHAT IF). / KISS ME HELLO** [-] [81]
(above from the film 'Remo: The Adventure Begins')

Nov 85. (lp,c) *<5097>* **WHAT IF** [-] [87]
– Jealousy / Remo's theme (What if?) / Reach for the bottle / Friendly advice / This is not a test / See me now / True confessions / Count on you / Nature of the beast / Bad times.

Dec 85. (7") *<2800>* **JEALOUSY. / THIS IS NOT A TEST** [-] [ ]

— Enlisted new band: **TERRY THOMAS** – guitar, keyboards / **TONY BEARD** – drums / **WIX** – keyboards / **FELIX KRISH** – bass / **RICHIE CANNATA** – saxophone / **STEVE ALEXANDER** – percussion

Atlantic — Atlantic

Sep 87. (lp/c/cd) *(781 798-2/-4/-1) <81798>* **AMBITION** [ ] [ ]
– No such thing / Dangerous game / The weight of the world / Ambition / Ever since the world began / Are you ready for me / Somewhere in the night / Love you too much / The outsider / Lay them down.

Sep 87. (7") *<89183>* **NO SUCH THING. / THE OUTSIDER** [-] [ ]

May 88. (7") *(A 9138) <89138>* **EVER SINCE THE WORLD BEGAN. / THE OUTSIDER** [ ] [75] Feb88
(12"+=) *(AT 9138)* – No such thing.

STYX

— STYX were back, although without SHAW (who joined DAMN YANKEES, and later SHAW BLADES), who was deposed by **GLEN BURTNIK** – lead guitar

Nov 90. (cd/c/lp) *(395327-2/-4/-1) <5327>* **EDGE OF THE CENTURY** [ ] [63] Oct90
– Love is the ritual / Show me the way / Edge of the century / Love at first sight / All in a day's work / Not dead yet / World tonite / Carrie Ann / Homewrecker / Back to Chicago.

Dec 90. (7"/7"pic-d) *(AM/+X 709) <1525>* **LOVE IS THE RITUAL. / HOMEWRECKER** [ ] [80] Oct90
(12"+=/cd-s+=) *(AM Y/CD 709)* – Babe.

Feb 91. (7"/c-s) *<1536>* **SHOW ME THE WAY. / BACK TO CHICAGO** [ ] [3] Dec90
(12"+=/cd-s+=) – Don't let it end.

Mar 91. (c-s,cd-s) *<1548>* **LOVE AT FIRST SIGHT / WORLD TONITE** [-] [25]

— re-formed again with **DeYOUNG, SHAW, YOUNG + PANOZZO**

S.P.V. — C.M.C.

Aug 98. (d-cd) *(SPV 0852918-2) <86212>* **RETURN TO PARADISE (live)** [ ] [ ] May97
– On my way / Paradise / Rockin' the paradise / Blue collar man / Lady / Too much time on my hands / Snowblind / Suite Madame blue / Crystal ball / The grand illusion / Foolish yourself (the angry young man) / Show me the way / Boat on the river / Lorelei / Babe / Miss America / Come sail away / Renegade / Best of times / Dear John.

C.M.C. C.M.C.

Jun 99. (cd) <(86275-2)> **BRAVE NEW WORLD**
– I will be your witness / Brave new world / While there's still time / Number one / Best new face / What have they done to you / Fallen angel / Everything is cool / Great expectations / Heavy water / High crimes and misdemeanors (hip hop-crazy) / Just fell in / Goodbye Roseland / Brave new world (reprise).

— **LAWRENCE GOWAN** – vocals; repl. DeYOUNG

Jun 01. (cd) <(86311-2)> **STYX WORLD: LIVE 2001 (live)**
– Rockin' the paradise / High enough / Lorelei / A criminal mind / Love is the ritual / Boat on the river / Half-penny, two penny / Sing for the day / Snowblind / Sometimes love just ain't enough / Crystal ball / Miss America / Come sail away.

– compilations, others, etc. –

Oct 79. (lp/c) *R.C.A.; (PL/PK 13116)* <3597> **THE BEST OF STYX**
– You need love / Lady / I'm gonna make you feel it / What has come between us / Southern woman / Rock & roll feeling / Winner take all / Best thing / Witch wolf / The grove of Eglantine / Man of miracles. *(cd-iss. 1992; PD 83597)*

Apr 78. (7"ep) *A&M; (AMS 7355)* **MADEMOISELLE / COME SAIL AWAY. / CRYSTAL BALL / LORELEI** -

1978. (7") *Wooden Nickel-RCA; <11205>* **BEST THING. / WINNER TAKE ALL** -

Sep 85. (7") *Old Gold; (OG 9545)* **BABE. / THE BEST OF TIMES** -

Jan 87. (12"ep) *Old Gold; (OG 4013)* **BABE / THE BEST OF TIMES. / (2 by The Tubes)** -

Apr 88. (cd-ep) *A&M; (AMCD 904)* **COMPACT HITS** -
– Babe / Come sail away / Rockin' the Paradise / The best of times.

May 95. (cd) *A&M; (396959-2)* **BOAT ON THE RIVER**

Jul 97. (cd) *A&M; (540465-2)* **THE BEST OF TIMES – THE BEST OF STYX**

Jul 99. (d-cd) *One Way; <(OW 35144)>* **THE SERPENT IS RISING / MAN OF MIRACLES**

Sep 00. (cd; shared with REO SPEEDWAGON) *Sanctuary; <86299>* **ARCH ALLIES: LIVE AT RIVERPORT (live)** -

SUBHUMANS

Formed: Vancouver, Canada ... late 70's by WIMPY BOY, MIKE GRAHAM, GERRY USELESS and GREG DIMWIT. Pioneering the Canadian hardcore/punk scene, they released a series of singles beginning with 'DEATH TO THE SICKOIDS', in late '78. Two further 45's for 'Quintessence', 'DEATH WAS TOO KIND' and 'FIRING SQUAD', displayed the uncompromisingly politically correct stance which would eventually see GERRY end up in jail. Following their debut album, 'INCORRECT THOUGHTS' later in 1980, the bass player was sentenced to ten years for his part in a bombing campaign which took in such targets as a nuclear components factory, a hydro-power station and several sex shops. He was subsequently replaced by bass player, RON, while the band had already found a new drummer, JIM IWAGAMA to fill in for GREG JAMES. The upheaval undoubtedly put a brake on their career and only one further album ('NO WISHES, NO PRAYERS') appeared before WIMPY BOY (BRIAN GOBLE) and GREG joined D.O.A.

Album rating: INCORRECT THOUGHTS (*7) / NO WISHES, NO PRAYERS (*6)

WIMPY BOY (b. BRIAN GOBLE) – vocals (ex-SKULLS) / **MIKE GRAHAM** – guitar / **GERRY USELESS** (b. GERRY HANNAH) – bass / **GREG DIMWIT** (b. GREG JAMES) – drums

not iss. SI

Dec 78. (7") <A00> **DEATH TO THE SICKOIDS. / OH CANADUH** -

not iss. Quintessence

Feb 80. (12"ep) <QEP12 02> **DEATH WAS TOO KIND / FUCK YOU. / INQUISITION DAY / SLAVE TO MY DICK** -

Jun 80. (7") <QS 105> **FIRING SQUAD. / NO PRODUCTIVITY** -

not iss. Friends

Nov 80. (lp) <FR 008> **INCORRECT THOUGHTS** -
– The scheme / New order / Behind my smile / Out of line / Big picture / Dead at birth / Urban gorillas / War in my head / Firing squad / Slave to my dick / Death to the sickoids / Greaser boy / Model of stupidity / We're alive / Refugee / Let's go down to Hollywood and shoot people. *(UK-iss.Apr88 on 'CD Presents'; CD 036)*

— **JIM IWAGAMA** – drums; repl. GREG JAMES who joined POINTED STICKS, although he returned and was joined by **RON** – bass; who had repl. the jail-bound GERRY (see above)

not iss. S.S.T.

1983. (lp) **NO WISHES, NO PRAYERS** -

— they split when GOBLE and JAMES joined D.O.A. (the latter was the elder brother of their CHUCK BISCUITS)

SUBHUMANS

Formed: Melksham, Wiltshire, England ... 1981 by main writer DICK LUCAS, BRUCE, GRANT and TROTSKY. Inspired by the uncompromising ideology of CRASS, anarcho-punks The SUBHUMANS concerned themselves with human rights, vegetarianism and a hankering for the downfall of the Tories. This much was evident from a series of EP's in the early 80's, namely, 'DEMOLITION WAR', 'REASONS FOR EXISTENCE' and 'RELIGIOUS WARS'. The self-explanatory 'THE DAY THE COUNTRY DIED', was the title of their late 1982 debut album, although this was the last recording to feature GRANT who was replaced by PHIL. The following year, the band set up their own label, 'Bluurg', to release both their own recordings and those of other acts with a similarly militant outlook. Moving towards a more heavyweight punk sound, LUCAS and Co continued to release the odd album or two before they metamorphosed into ska/reggae/punk fusion act, CULTURE SHOCK, in 1987. Towards the end of the decade, by which time they had delivered three albums, DICK broke away to spearhead his own outfit, CITIZEN FISH. Driving home his 90's free spirit message more successfully than ever before, LUCAS continued to command the festival/crusty crowd with a conscientious but ebullient mixture of politico skank-punk beginning with the 'FREE SOULS IN A TRAPPED ENVIRONMENT' set. CITIZEN FISH are still going strong (if that's the right term), their most recent piece of work being the album, 'LIFE SIZE' (2001).

Album rating: THE DAY THE COUNTRY DIED (*6) / TIME FLIES ... BUT AEROPLANES CRASH (*5) / FROM THE CRADLE TO THE GRAVE (*5) / WORLDS APART (*5) / EP-LP (*5) / 29:29 SPLIT VISION (*5) / Culture Shock: GO WILD! (*5) / ONWARDS AND UPWARDS (*5) / ALL THE TIME (*5) / Citizen Fish: FREE SOULS IN A TRAPPED ENVIRONMENT (*6) / WIDER THAN A POSTCARD (*5) / MILLENNIA MADNESS (*5) / THIRST (*4) / ACTIVE INGREDIENTS (*5) / LIFE SIZE (*4)

DICK (b. RICHARD LUCAS) – vocals / **BRUCE** – guitar / **GRANT** – bass / **TROTSKY** – drums

Spiderleg not iss.

Nov 81. (7"ep) *(SOB 1)* **DEMOLITION WAR** -
– Parasites / Drugs of youth / Animal / Who's gonna fight in the third world war / Society / Human error. *(re-iss. 1988 on 'Bluurg'; XEP 1)*

Apr 82. (7"ep) *(SDL 5)* **REASONS FOR EXISTANCE** -
– Big city / Reason for existance / Cancer / Peroxide. *(re-iss. 1988 on 'Bluurg'; XEP 2)*

Aug 82. (7"ep) *(SDL 7)* **RELIGIOUS WARS** -
– Religious wars / Love is . . . / Work experience / It's gonna get worse. *(re-iss. 1988 on 'Bluurg'; XEP 3)*

Dec 82. (lp) *(SDL 9)* **THE DAY THE COUNTRY DIED** -
– All gone dead / Ashtray dirt / Killing / Minority / Nothing I can do / Mickey Mouse is dead / Dying world / Subvert city / Big brother / No / New age / I don't wanna die / Zyklon B-movie / No more gigs / Black and white / 'Til the pigs come round. *(re-iss. 1988 on 'Bluurg' lp/c; XLP 1/+C) (cd-iss. Jun91 lp/c/cd; XLP 1/+C/CD)*

— **PHIL** – bass; repl. GRANT

Bluurg not iss.

Jun 83. (7"ep) *(FISH 2)* **EVOLUTION / SO MUCH MONEY. / GERM / NOT ME**

Nov 83. (12"ep) *(FISH 5)* **TIME FLIES . . . BUT AEROPLANES CRASH** -

Jun 84. (lp/c) *(FISH 8/+C)* **FROM THE CRADLE TO THE GRAVE** -
– Forget / Waste of breath / Where's the freedom? / Adversity / Reality is waiting for a bus / Wake up screaming / Rain / From the cradle to the grave. *(cd-iss. Mar92; FISH 8CD)*

Dec 84. (7"ep) *(FISH 10)* **RATS EP** -

Jan 86. (lp/c) *(FISH 12/+C)* **WORLDS APART** -
– 33322 / British disease / Heads of state / Apathy / Fade away / Businessmen / Someone is lying / Pigman / Can't hear the words / Get to work on time / Carry on laughing / Straightline thinking / Ex teenage rebel / Power games / 33322. *(cd-iss. Nov91; FISH 12CD)*

Oct 86. (lp/c) *(FISH 14/+C)* **EP-LP** -
– Parasites / Drugs of youth / Animal / Society / Who's gonna fight in the third world war? / Human error / Big city / Peroxide / Reason for existence / Cancer / Religious wars / Love is . . . / It's gonna get worse / Work experience / Evolution / So much money / Germ / Not me. *(cd-iss. Nov91; FISH 14CD)*

Oct 87. (lp/c) *(FISH 16/+C)* **29:29 SPLIT VISION** -
– Somebody's mother / Think for yourself / Walls of silence / Heroes / Dehumanisation / Worlds apart / New boy / Time flies. *(cd-iss. Mar92; FISH 16CD)*

— had already split early '87, and above was postumous

– compilations, others –

Jun 91. (lp/c/cd) *Bluurgh; (FISH 12/+C/CD)* **TIME FLIES . . . BUT AEROPLANES EP / RATS EP** -

CULTURE SHOCK

DICK, BRUCE, PHIL + TROTSKY

Bluurg not iss.

May 87. (lp) *(FISH 18)* **GO WILD** -
– Punks on postcards / Go wild (my son) / Messed up / Six foot rooms / Ten per cent off / Circles / Mother's on the phone / All (messed up) together. *(<re-iss. Feb93; same>)*

Apr 88. (lp/c) *(FISH 20/+C)* **ONWARDS & UPWARDS** -
– Pressure / Colour T.V. / Fast forward / You are not alone / Joyless / If you don't like it / Civilization street / United / Catching flies / When the fighting's over / Open mind surgery / Don't worry about it / I.S.D. *(<cd-iss. Feb93; FISH 20CD>)*

Nov 89. (lp/c) *(FISH 23/+C)* **ALL THE TIME!** -
– Countdowns / Twenty questions / Upside down / The time it takes / Four minutes / Northern Ireland / Northern Ireland (dub) / Onwards. *(<re-iss. Feb93; same>)*

– compilations, etc. –

Aug 95. (cd) *Bluurg;* **GO WILD / ALL THE TIME!** -

CITIZEN FISH

DICK, PHIL + TROTSKY with **JASPER** – bass

Bluurg Bluurg

Oct 90. (lp/c/cd) *(<FISH 24/+C/CD>)* **FREE SOULS IN A TRAPPED ENVIRONMENT**
– Supermarket song / Break into a run / Rainbows / Possession / Small scale wars / Home economics / Paint / Talk is cheap / Face off / Youth / Flesh and blood / Get off the phone / Experiment Earth / How to write ultimate protest songs / Charity. *(cd-iss. Apr94; (FISH 24CD)*

Mar 92. (lp/c/cd) *(<FISH 26/+C/CD>)* **WIDER THAN A POSTCARD**
– Sink or swim / Language barrier / Same old starving millions / Conditional silence / Big big house / Mind bomb / Chili pain / Give me Beethoven / Talk it over / Offended / Central nervous system / Traffic lights / Smells like home.

Nov 93. (lp/cd) *(FISH 28/+CD)* **LIVE FISH (live)** [ ] [-]
Jan 94. (lp/c/cd) *(<FISH 31/+C/CD>)* **FLINCH** [ ] [ ]
– TV dinner / Naked / Small talk / Time control / Dividing lines / Media men / Bag lady / First impressions / Wet cement / Circular vision / Social insecurity / Invisible people / Flinch.

Bluurg Lookout

1990's. (7") *<LK 60>* **DISPOSABLE DREAM. / FLESH AND BLOOD II** [-] [ ]
Sep 95. (lp/cd) *(FISH 34/+CD)* *<LK 123>* **MILLENNIA MADNESS** [ ] [ ] Oct95
– P.C. musical chairs / Next big thing / Can't be bothered / 2000 and one / Panic in the supermarket / Can't complain / Faster / Phone in sick / Refugees go west / Backlash / Friends / Skin.

Lookout Lookout

Sep 96. (cd/lp) *(<LK 152>)* **THIRST** [ ] [ ]
– Feeding / Pop songs / City on a river / Used to work / Plasticash / Scene 496: Care in a Melksham / Words on overtime / Talk about the weather / Catholic sex confession / Criminal / What Charlie said / Fill me up.
Nov 98. (7") *(<LK 209>)* **HABIT. /** [ ] [ ]
Jun 99. (cd) *<LK 212>* **ACTIVE INGEDIENTS** [-] [ ]
– Active ingredients / The Bob song / Oslo / Bitter and twisted / Digging a hole / Sacred cows / Pills / Habit / Isolated incidents / Barking / Heard it all before / Deep neurotic / Not for sale.

Honest Don's Honest Don's

Jun 01. (lp/cd) *(<DON 036/+CD>)* **LIFE SIZE** [ ] [ ]
– Over the fence / Revolution / Out of control / Picture this / Internal release / Autographs / Back to zero / Choice of viewing / Lose the instructions / Somewhere to go / Shrink the distance / Will swap.

SUBLIME

Formed: Long Beach, California, USA . . . 1988 by BRAD NOWELL, ERIC WILSON and FLOYD 'BUD' GAUGH. Signing to M.C.A. off-shoot 'Gasoline Alley', two albums passed virtually unoticed until the untimely drugs death of BRADLEY on 25th of May '96; at least they made it on to MTV while also gaining US radio play for the single, 'WHAT I GOT'. This became a minor hit, a ska-punk semi-classic which only served to underline what might've been, the accompanying eponymous third set going on to sell over two million copies Stateside. • **Songwriters:** NOWELL except RIVERS OF BABYLON (Brent Dowe & James McNaughton; hit for Boney M) / TRENCHTOWN ROCK (Bob Marley). • **Trivia:** NO DOUBT's GWEN STEFANI guested on the track, 'SAW RED'. • **Note:** Don't get confused with UK group of the late 80's and another dance-orientated outfit from '93.

Album rating: 40 oz. TO FREEDOM (*5) / ROBBIN' THE HOOD (*6) / SUBLIME (*7) / SECOND-HAND SMOKE posthumous (*5) / SUBLIME LIVE – STAND BY YOUR VAN (*4) / ACOUSTIC: BRADLEY NOWELL (*4) / GREATEST HITS compilation (*6)

BRAD NOWELL (b. 1968) – vocals, guitar / **ERIC WILSON** – bass / **BUD** (b. FLOYD GAUGH) – drums

not iss. Gasoline Alley

1993. (cd) *<GASD 11413>* **40oz TO FREEDOM** [-] [ ]
– What I got / Pawn shop / Same in the end / Caress me down / Doin' time / April 29, 1992 (Miami) / Ballad of Johnny Butt / Burritos / Garden grove / Seed / Paddle out / Under my voodoo / Get ready / Jailhouse / Santeria / What I got (reprise). *<re-iss. mid-96 as 'SUBLIME' hit US No.13> (UK-iss.Jan98; same)*
1994. (cd) *<GASD 11475>* **ROBBIN' THE HOOD** [-] [ ]
– Waiting for Bud / Steady B loop dub / Raleigh sililoquy part I / Pool shark / Steppin' razor / Greatest-hits / Free loop dub – Q-ball / Saw red / The work that we do / Lincoln highway dub / Pool shark / Cisco kid / Raleigh soliloquy part II / S.T.P. / Boss D.J. / I don't care too much for reggae / Falling idols / All you need / Freeway time in la county jail / Mary / Raleigh soliloquy part III. *(UK-iss.Jan98; same)*

— tragically, BRAD died of a heroin overdose on 25th May '96 leaving behind a wife, a child and their final recordings below.

M.C.A. Gasoline Alley

Jun 97. (7"yellow/c-s) *(MCS/+C 48045)* **WHAT I GOT (Super No Mofo edit). / RIVERS OF BABYLON** [71] [-]
(cd-s+=) *(MCSTD 48045)* – All you need / What I got (reprise).
Sep 97. (m-cd) *<GASD 11678>* **WHAT I GOT . . . THE 7 SONG EP** [-] [ ]
– What I got / 40 oz. to freedom / D.J.S. / All you need / Same in the end / The work that we do / Doin' time.
Nov 97. (cd/c) *<GAS D/C 11714>* **SECOND-HAND SMOKE** (collection of out-takes) [-] [28]
– Doin' time / Get out! / Romeo / New realization / Don't push / Slow ride / Chick on my tip / Had a date / Trenchtown rock / Badfish / Drunk drivin' / Saw red / Garbage grove / April 29th, 1992 / Superstar punami / Legal dub / What's really goin' wrong / Doin' time / Thanx dub.
Dec 97. (cd-ep) *<55390>* **DOIN' TIME /** [-] [87]
Jun 98. (cd/c) *<GAS D/C 11798>* **STAND BY YOUR VAN: SUBLIME LIVE . . . (live)** [-] [49]
– Don't push / Right back / New thrash / Let's go get stoned / Greatest hits / Date rape / S.T.P. / Badfish / D.J.S. / The work that we do / Pool shark / Ebin / All you need / Waiting for my Ruca / Caress me down / KRS-One.
Nov 98. (cd) *<11889>* **ACOUSTIC: BRADLEY NOWELL & FRIENDS** [-] [ ]
– Wrong way / Saw red / Foolish fool / Don't push / Mary / Big salty tears / Boss D.J. / Garden grove / Rivers of Babylon / Little district / KRS-One / Marley medley: Guava jelly – This train / What happened / The eye of Fatima / Freeway time in L.A. county jail / Pool shark / It's who you know.
Nov 99. (cd/c) *<12125>* **GREATEST HITS** (compilation) [-] [ ]
– What I got / The wrong way / Santeria / 40 oz. to freedom / Smoke two joints / Date rape / Saw red / Badfish / Doin' time / Poolshark.

SUGAR

Formed: Minneapolis, USA . . . 1992 by former HUSKER DU frontman/co-writer, BOB MOULD. Upon the demise of the latter act in 1987, MOULD signed to 'Virgin America' and subsequently entered PRINCE's 'Paisley Park' studios to lay down his first solo set, 'WORKBOOK' (1989). Augmented by the former PERE UBU rhythm section of ANTON FIER and TONY MAIMONE and employing cellists JANE SCARPANTONI and STEVE HAIGLER, MOULD confounded expectations with a largely acoustic affair trading in melodic distortion for fragments of contemplative melancholy; only the closing 'WHICHEVER WAY THE WIND BLOWS' acknowledged the sonic assault of prime HUSKER DU. Despite the guaranteed critical plaudits and the more accessible nature of the material, 'WORKBOOK's sales were modest. Perhaps as a reaction, the following year's 'BLACK SHEETS OF RAIN' – again recorded with FIER and MAIMONE – was a searing return to bleaker, noisier pastures; 'HANGING TREE' remains among the most tormented work of MOULD's career, while the likes of 'HEAR ME CALLING' and 'IT'S TOO LATE' combined keening melody with blistering soloing/discordant riffing in patented MOULD fashion. When this album also failed to take off, the singer parted comapny from 'Virgin' and undertook a low-key acoustic tour. His wilderness period was brief, however, the emerging grunge vanguard citing HUSKER DU as a massive influence and inspiring MOULD to form another melodic power trio. Comprising of fellow songwriter/bassist, DAVE BARBE and drummer MALCOLM TRAVIS, SUGAR signed to 'Creation' and proceeded to cut one of the most feted albums of the era in 'COPPER BLUE' (1992). Leaner, tighter and cleaner, the record's bittersweet pop-hardcore crunch finally provided MOULD with a springboard for commercial success; a UK Top 10 hit, the album even spawned a Top 30 hit single in the sublime 'IF I CAN'T CHANGE YOUR MIND'. 'BEASTER', 1993's mini-album follow-up, took tracks from the 'COPPER BLUE' sessions and buried them in a multi-tiered blanket of howling distortion. Unsurprisingly it failed to spawn a hit, although its Top 3 success was no doubt sweet for the ever contrary MOULD, his follow-up proper, 'FILE UNDER EASY LISTENING (F.U.E.L.)' (1994), suggesting that he'd become bored with the whole concept. MOULD eventually disbanded the project in Spring '96, releasing a third solo album the same year, simply titled 'BOB MOULD'. • **Songwriters:** MOULD and now same with others. Covered; SHOOT OUT THE LIGHTS (Richard Thompson).

Album rating: Bob Mould: WORKBOOK (*7) / BLACK SHEETS OF RAIN (*6) / Sugar: COPPER BLUE (*9) / BEASTER mini (*7) / FILE UNDER: EASY LISTENING (*7) / BESIDES collection (*6) / Bob Mould: BOB MOULD (*8) / THE LAST DOG AND PONY SHOW (*7)

BOB MOULD

BOB MOULD – vocals, guitar, etc (ex-HUSKER DU) / with **ANTON FIER** – drums / **TONY MAIMONE** – bass, (both ex-PERE UBU) / **JANE SCARPANTONI** – cello (of TINY LIGHTS) / **STEVE HAIGLER** – cello

Virgin Virgin

Jun 89. (7") *(VUS 2)* **SEE A LITTLE LIGHT. / ALL THOSE PEOPLE KNOW** [ ] [-]
(12"+=/cd-s+=) *(VUS 2T/CD2)* – Shoot out the lights / Composition for the young and the old (live).
Jul 89. (lp/cd) *(VUS LP/CD 2)* *<91240>* **WORKBOOK** [ ] [ ] Apr89
– Sunspots / Wishing well / Heartbreak a stranger / See a little light / Poison years / Sinners and their repentances / Lonely afternoon / Brasilia crossed the Tranton / Compositions for the young and old / Dreaming, I amd / Whichever way the wind blows. *(re-iss. Sep90; OVED 340)*
Aug 90. (cd/c/lp) *(VUS CD/MC/LP 21)* *<91395>* **BLACK SHEETS OF RAIN** [ ] [ ] May90
– Black sheets of rain / Stand guard / It's too late / One good reason / Stop your crying / Hanging tree / The last night / Hear me calling / Out of your life / Disappointed / Sacrifice – let there be peace.

Virgin Virgin

May 94. (cd) *(CDVM 9030)* *<39587>* **THE POISON YEARS** (compilation from first two sets) [ ] [ ] Jul94

SUGAR

BOB MOULD – vox, guitar, keyboards, percussion / **DAVE BARBE** – bass (ex-MERCYLAND) / **MALCOLM TRAVIS** – drums, percussion (ex-ZULUS)

Creation Rykodisc

Jul 92. (cd-ep) *<1024>* **HELPLESS / NEEDLE HITS E / IF I CAN'T CHANGE YOUR MIND / TRY AGAIN** [-] [ ]
Aug 92. (12"ep)(cd-ep) *(CRE 126T)(CRESCD 126)* **CHANGES / NEEDLE HITS E. / IF I CAN'T CHANGE YOUR MIND / TRY AGAIN** [ ] [-]
Sep 92. (cd/lp)(c) *(CRE CD/LP 129)(C-CRE 129)* *<RCD/RACS 10239>* **COPPER BLUE** [10] [ ]
– The act we act / A good idea / Changes / Helpless / Hoover dam / The slim / If I can't change your mind / Fortune teller / Slick / Man on the Moon.
Oct 92. (7"ep/c-ep) *(CRE/+CS 143)* *<1030>* **A GOOD IDEA. / WHERE DIAMONDS ARE HALOS / SLICK** [65] [ ]
(12"ep+=)(cd-ep+=) *(CRE 143T)(CRESCD 143)* – Armenia city in the sky.
Jan 93. (7"/c-s) *(CRE/+CS 149)* **IF I CAN'T CHANGE YOUR MIND. / CLOWN MASTER** [30] [ ]
(12"+=) *(CRE 149T)* *<1031>* – Anyone (live) / Hoover dam (live).
(cd-s) *(CRESCD 149)* *<1032>* – ('A'side) / The slim / Where diamonds are halos.
Apr 93. (m-cd/m-lp)(m-c) *(CRE CD/LP 153)(C-CRE 153)* *<50260>* **BEASTER** [3] [ ]
– Come around / Tilted / Judas cradle / JC auto / Feeling better / Walking away.
Aug 93. (7") *(CRE 156)* **TILTED. / JC AUTO (live)** [48] [-]

Aug 94. (7"/c-s) *(CRE/+CS 186)* **YOUR FAVORITE THING. / MIND IS AN ISLAND** [40] [ ]
(12"+=)(cd-s+=) *(CRE 186T)(CRESCD 186)* <1038> – Frustration / And you tell me (T.V. mix).

Sep 94. (cd/lp)(c) *(CRE CD/LP 172)(C-CRE 172)* <10300> **FILE UNDER EASY LISTENING (F.U.E.L.)** [7] [50]
– Gift / Company book / Your favorite thing / What you want it to be / Gee angel / Panama city hotel / Can't help it anymore / Granny cool / Believe what you're saying / Explode and make up.

Oct 94. (7"/c-s) *(CRE/+CS 193)* **BELIEVE WHAT YOU'RE SAYING. / GOING HOME** [73] [ ]
(cd-s+=) *(CRESCD 193)* <1039> – In the eyes of my friends / And you tell me.

Dec 94. (cd-ep) <*RCD5 1040*> **GEE ANGEL / EXPLODE AND MAKE UP / SLIM / AFTER ALL THE ROADS HAVE LED TO . . .** [-] [ ]

Jul 95. (d-cd) <*10321*> **BESIDES** (compilation of b-sides, live, etc) [-] [ ]

— disbanded and BARBE formed BUZZHUNGRY / TRAVIS went to CUSTOMIZED

BOB MOULD

Creation Rykodisc

Apr 96. (cd/lp) *(CRE CD/LP 188)* <10342> **BOB MOULD** [52] [ ]
– Anymore time between / I hate alternative rock / Fort Knox, King Solomon / Next time that you leave / Egoverride / Thumbtack / Hair stew / Hair stew / Deep karma canyon / Art crisis / Roll over and die.

— now with **MATT HAMMON** – drums / **ALISON CHESLEY** – cello

Aug 98. (7") *(CRE 206)* **CLASSIFIEDS. / MOVING TRUCKS** [ ] [-]

Aug 98. (cd/lp) *(CRE CD/LP 215)* <10443> **THE LAST DOG AND PONY SHOW** [58] [ ]
– New #1 / Moving trucks / Taking everything / First drag of the day / Classifieds / Who was around? / Skintrade / Vaporub / Sweet serene / Megamaniac / Reflecting pool / Along the way / (interview).

SUGAR RAY

Formed: Los Angeles, California, USA ... 1989 out of cover outfit The SHRINKY DINX by MARK McGRATH (of Irish parentage), RODNEY SHEPPARD, MURPHY KARGES, STAN FRAZIER and DJ HOMOCIDE (aka CRAIG BULLOCK). Signed to Atlantic offshoot label 'Lava' in 1994, this dayglo bunch of funky pop-metal funsters debuted the following year with the 'LEMONADE & BROWNIES' set. While that record hinted at an endearing BEASTIES-esque charm, the group only really hit their saucy stride on follow-up set, 'FLOORED' (1997). Trading in hood-down, shout-along metal/rap with a winking undercurrent of dancefloor cheesiness, the record didn't come within a whisker of taking itself seriously (on the majority of tracks anyhow), stretching the limits of good natured fun with a cover of 'STAND AND DELIVER' (Adam & The Ants). While the album received encouraging reviews and the 'FLY' single was an MTV favourite, SUGAR RAY have still to capture the hearts (and groins) of the rock scene at large. Kicking off 1999 with a proverbial bang and now complete with sneakers and loud shirts, SUGAR RAY had a couple of massive American hits beginning with 'EVERY MORNING'. Taken from their sunkissed album, '14:59' (which also contained second Top 10'er, 'SOMEDAY'), the band could do no wrong. For now! • **Covered:** ABRACADABRA (Steve Miller Band).

Album rating: LEMONADE & BROWNIES (*6) / FLOORED (*6) / 14:59 (*6)

MARK McGRATH (b.1969) – vocals / **RODNEY SHEPPARD** (b.1966) – guitar / **MURPHY KARGES** (b.1966) – bass (ex-WEIRDOS) / **STAN FRAZIER** (b. CHARLES STANTON FRAZIER, 1968) – drums / **DJ HOMOCIDE** (b. CRAIG BULLOCK, 1971) – turntables (ex-ALCHOLIKS)

Atlantic Atlantic

Aug 95. (7"/c-s) *(A 7143/+C)* **MEAN MACHINE. / WANGO TANGO** [ ] [-]
(cd-s+=) *(A 7143CD)* – White minority / Wasted.
(re-iss. May96; same)

Sep 95. (cd) <*(7567 82743-2)*> **LEMONADE & BROWNIES** [ ] [ ]
– Snug harbor / Iron mic / Rhyme stealer / Hold your eyes / Big black woman / Dance party USA / Danzig needs a hug / 10 seconds down / Streaker / Scuzzboots / Caboose / Drive by / Mean machine / Greatest.

Feb 96. (7"/c-s) *(A 7111/+C)* **IRON MIC. / CABOOSE** [ ] [-]
(cd-s+=) *(A 7111CD)* – Mean machine (live) / Dr J (live).

Aug 97. (cd) <*(7567 83006-2)*> **FLOORED** [ ] [12] Jun97
– R.P.M. / Breathe / Anyone / Fly / Speed home California / High anxiety / Tap, twist, snap / American pig / Stand and deliver / Cash / Invisible / Right direction / Fly (reprise).

Jan 98. (7"/c-s) *(AT 0008/+C)* **FLY. / FLY (rock)** [58] [-]
(cd-s+=) *(AT 008CD)* – Tap, twist, snap.

May 99. (c-s/cd-s) *(AT 0065 C/CD)* <84462> **EVERY MORNING / RIVERS / AIM FOR ME** [10] [3] Jan99

Jun 99. (cd/c) <*(7567 83151-2/-4)*> **14:59** [60] [17] Jan99
– New direction / Every morning / Falls apart / Personal space invader / Live and direct / Someday / Aim for me / Ode to the lonely hearted / Burning dog / Even though / Abracadabra / Glory / New direction.

Oct 99. (c-s) *(AT 0071C)* <84536> **SOMEDAY / EVERY MORNING (acoustic)** [ ] [7] Jun99
(cd-s) *(AT 0071CD)* – ('A'acoustic).

Jan 00. (-) <*radio play*> **FALLS APART** [-] [29]

May 01. (-) <*radio play*> **WHEN IT'S OVER** [-] [26]

Jun 01. (cd) <*83414*> **SUGAR RAY** [-] [ ]

SUICIDAL TENDENCIES

Formed: Venice, California, USA ... 1982 by MIKE MUIR, LOUICHE MAYOREA and AMERY SMITH. Signing to the small 'Frontier' label, the group debuted in 1984 with the eponymous 'SUICIDAL TENDENCIES'. Vaguely political hardcore skate-punk, the record was a promising start, the frantic 'INSTITUTIONALIZED' summing up their two-fingered defiance towards the "American Dream", complete with a brilliantly surreal video. With RALPH HERRERA and ROCKY GEORGE replacing AMERY and ESTES respectively, they signed to 'Virgin' worldwide, eventually releasing a follow-up effort, 'JOIN THE ARMY' (1987). The album significantly broadened the band's musical framework and when SUICIDAL TENDENCIES were really cooking, there were few acts who could match their compelling mash-up of punk, metal and bass-heavy melodic hardcore. MUIR's drawling vocals were one of the main weapons in their bandana'd, check-shirted armoury, the singer coming on like some streetsmart Godfather of skate-punk. Alongside high-octane wipe-outs like the seminal 'POSSESSED TO SKATE' and the blistering 'WAR INSIDE MY HEAD', more reflective numbers like 'A LITTLE EACH DAY' packed twice the emotional punch with half the bravado. SUICIDAL TENDENCIES also slowed things down on the the title track, its grinding groove and insistent quasi-rapping making it one of the most effective cuts on the album. On the strength of MUIR's lyrics, he's one troubled guy and his depictions of depression and anxiety are certainly more affecting and convincing than many. The dour but honestly titled 'HOW WILL I LAUGH TOMORROW . . . WHEN I CAN'T EVEN SMILE TODAY?' (1988) continued the journey through MUIR's bleak mindset, most effectively on the gonzoid 'TRIP AT THE BRAIN'. The album saw a decidedly more metallic influence creeping in which was even more pronounced on 1989's 'CONTROLLED BY HATRED / FEEL LIKE SHIT . . . DEJA VU', the monster riffing often suffocating SUICIDAL's natural exuberance. The acclaimed 'LIGHTS ... CAMERA ... REVOLUTION' (1990) was an entirely different affair, the group paying heed to the funk/rap-metal revolution (which they arguably had at least something of a hand in starting). The single, 'SEND ME YOUR MONEY', was an upbeat jibe against TV evangelism (a perennial metal favourite) built on an elasticated bass groove. The whole album was more commercial overall with an unsettling display of positivity in the lyrics, a Top 60 UK chart placing indicating the group's brief firtation with the mainstream. SUICIDAL TENDENCIES promoted the album with an opening slot on the 'Clash Of The Titans' tour alongside such thrash heavyweights as TESTAMENT, MEGADETH and SLAYER, not exactly complementary company. It was clear MUIR was more into shaking his booty at this stage and together with new SUICIDAL bass player, ROBERT TRUJILLO, the singer took his funk-metal urges to their ultimate and rather unremarkable conclusion with side project INFECTIOUS GROOVES. The group released three albums, 'THE PLAGUE THAT MAKES YOUR BOOTY MOVE, IT'S THE INFECTIOUS GROOVE' (1991), 'SARSIPPIUS' ARK' (1993) and 'GROOVE FAMILY CYCO' (1994), although none threatened the likes of the 'CHILI PEPPERS. SUICIDAL TENDENCIES, meanwhile, returned as angry as ever with 'THE ART OF REBELLION' (1992) and 'SUICIDAL FOR LIFE' (1994), the latter album boasting no less than four tracks with the word 'fuck' in the title. Despite the current vogue for all things snotty, punky and funky, it seems that SUICIDAL TENDENCIES have yet again been shamefully overlooked, many groups aping the style and verve of a band that literally helped to invent the concept of musical cross-fertilisation. One thing's for sure, SUICIDAL TENDENCIES will never be able to claim their rightful crown with albums as disappointing as 'FREEDUMB' (1999), a US-only affair which found the band woefully short of inspiration. In particular, MUIR's lyrical sharpness seemed uncharacteristically blunted with his lack of focus rubbing off on the rest of the band. 'FREE YOUR SOUL AND SAVE MY MIND' (2000) was a marked improvement, released simultaneously with the latest effort from INFECTIOUS GROOVES, 'MAS BORRACHO' (2000). • **Trivia:** MUIR appeared on TV show 'Miami Vice' in 1992.

Album rating: SUICIDAL TENDENCIES (*6) / JOIN THE ARMY (*7) / HOW WILL I LAUGH TOMORROW . . . (*6) / CONTROLLED BY HATRED / FEEL LIKE SHIT . . . DEJA VU (*5) / LIGHTS . . . CAMERA . . . REVOLUTION (*7) / THE ART OF REBELLION (*6) / STILL CYCO AFTER ALL THESE YEARS (*6) / SUICIDAL FOR LIFE (*5) / PRIME CUTS compilation (*6) / FREEDUMB (*4) / FREE YOUR SOUL . . . AND SAVE MY MIND (*5) / Infectious Grooves: THE PLAGUE THAT MAKES YOUR BOOTY (*5) / SARSIPPIUS' ARK (*5) / GROOVE FAMILY CYCO (*4) / MAS BORRACHO (*5)

MIKE MUIR – vocals / **GRANT ESTES** – guitar / **LOUICHE MAYOREA** – bass / **AMERY SMITH** – drums

not iss. Frontier

1984. (lp) <*FLP 1011*> **SUICIDAL TENDENCIES** [-] [ ]
– Suicide's an alternative / You'll be sorry / I shot the Devil / Won't fall in love today / Memories of tomorrow / I want more / I saw your mommy . . . / 2 sided politics / Suicidal failure / Sublimal / Institutionalized / Possessed / Fascist pig. *(UK-iss.Jan88 & Sep91 on 'Virgin' cd+=/c/lp; CD/TC+/V 2495)* – Possessed to skate / Human guinea pig / Two wrongs don't make a right. *(re-iss. Apr97 on 'Epitaph' cd/c/lp; 0104-2/-4/-1)*

— **RALPH HERRERA** – drums repl. AMERY / **ROCKY GEORGE** – guitar repl. ESTES

Virgin Caroline

Apr 87. (7") *(VS 967)* **POSSESSED TO SKATE. / HUMAN GUINEA PIG** [ ] [ ]
(12"+=/12"pic-d+=) *(VS 967-12)* – Two wrongs don't make a right (but they make me feel better).

Apr 87. (cd/c/lp) *(CD/TC+/V 2424)* <1336> **JOIN THE ARMY** 81 100
– Suicidal maniac / Join the army / You got, I want / A little each day / The prisoner / War inside my head / I feel your pain and I survive / Human guinea pig / Possessed to skate / No name, no words / Cyco / Looking in your eyes / Two wrongs don't make a right (but they make me feel better). *(re-iss. Apr90 lp/c; OVED/+C 307)*

Jan 88. (12"m) *(VST 1039)* **INSTITUTIONALIZED. / WAR INSIDE MY HEAD / CYCO**

—— added **MIKE CLARK** – rhythm guitar

—— **BOB HEATHCOTE** – bass; repl. MAYORGA

Virgin Epic

Aug 88. (12") *(VST 1127)* **TRIP AT THE BRAIN. / SUICYCO MANIA**

Sep 88. (cd/c/lp) *(CD/TC+/V 2551)* <44288> **HOW WILL I LAUGH TOMORROW . . . WHEN I CAN'T EVEN SMILE TODAY?**
– Trip at the brain / Hearing voices / Pledge your allience / How will I laugh tomorrow . . . when I can't even smile today? / The miracle / Surf and slam / If I don't wake up / Sorry? / One too many times / The feeling's back. *(cd+=)* – Suicyco mania.

Epic Epic

Jun 89. (cd/c/lp) *(465 399-2/-4/-1)* <45244> **CONTROLLED BY HATRED / FEEL LIKE SHIT . . . DEJA VU**
– Master of no mercy / How will I laugh tomorrow (video edit) / Just another love song / Walking the dead / Choosing my own way of life / Controlled by hatred / Feel like shit . . . deja vu / It's not easy / How will I laugh tomorrow (heavy emotion mix). *(re-iss. Oct94 cd/c; same)*

Jul 90. (cd/c/lp) *(466 569-2/-4/-1)* <45389> **LIGHTS . . . CAMERA . . . REVOLUTION** 59
– You can't bring me down / Lost again / Alone / Lovely / Give it revolution / Get whacked / Send me your money / Emotion No.13 / Disco's out / Murder's in / Go'n breakdown.

Oct 90. (7"ep/7"sha-pic-ep/12"ep/cd-ep) *(656 332-7/-0/-6/-2)* **SEND ME YOUR MONEY / YOU CAN'T BRING ME DOWN. / WAKING THE DEAD / DON'T GIVE ME YOUR NOTHING**

—— **ROBERT TRUJILLO** – bass / **JOSH FREESE** – drums; repl. BOB + RALPH

Jul 92. (cd/c/lp) *(471 885-2/-4/-1)* <48864> **THE ART OF REBELLION** 52
– Can't stop / Accept my sacrifice / Nobody hears / Tap into the power / Monopoly on sorrow / We call this mutha revenge / Medley: I wasn't meant to feel this – Asleep at the wheel / Gotta kill Captain Stupid / I'll hate you better / Which way to free / It's going down / Where's the truth.

Jul 93. (cd/c/lp) *(473749-2/-4/-1)* <46230> **STILL CYCO AFTER ALL THESE YEARS**
– Suicide's an alternative / Two sided politics / Subliminal / I shot the Devil / Won't fall in love today / Institutionalized / War inside my head / Don't give me your nothin' / Memories of tomorrow / Possessed / I saw your mommy . . . / Fascist pig / A little each day / I want more / Suicidal failure.

Jun 94. (cd/c/lp) *(476 885-2/-4/-1)* <57774> **SUICIDAL FOR LIFE** 82
– Invocation / Don't give a f***! / No f***'n problem / Suicyco muthaf***a / F***ed up just right! / No bullshit / What else could I do? / What you need's a friend / I wouldn't mind / Depression and anguish / Evil / Love vs. loneliness / Benediction.

—— line-up: **MIKE MUIR** plus **MIKE CLARK + DEAN PLEASANTS** – guitar / **JOSH PAUL** – bass / **BROOKS WACKERMAN** – drums

Jun 97. (cd/c) *(484123-2/-4)* **PRIME CUTS** (compilation)
– You can't bring me down / Join the new army / Lovely / Institutionalised / Gotta kill Captain Studio / Berserk / I saw your mommy / Pledge your allegiance / Feeding the addiction / I wasn't meant to feel this / Asleep at the wheel / Send me your money / No fuck'n problem / Go skate / Nobody hears / How will I laugh tomorrow.

Suicidal Suicidal

Jan 99. (m-cd) <*(SR 0014CD)*> **SIX THE HARD WAY** Nov98
– Freedumb / Cyco vision / Refuse / What's the word? / Fascist pig (live) / I saw your mommy (live).

Nuclear Blast Suicidal

Aug 99. (cd) *(NB 368-2)* <*SR 0015CD*> **FREEDUMB**
– Freedumb / Ain't gonna take it / Scream out / Half way up my head / Cyco vision / I ain't like you / Naked / Hippie killer / Built to survive / Get sick / I'll buy myself / Gaigan go home / Heaven.

Oct 00. (cd) *(NB 528-2)* <*SR 0018CD*> **FREE YOUR SOUL . . . AND SAVE MY MIND** Aug00
– Self destruct / Su casa es mi casa / No more no less / Free your soul . . . and save my mind / Pop song / Bullenium / Animal / Straight from the heart / Cyco speak / Start your brain / Public dissension / Children of the bored / Got mutation / Charlie Monroe / Home.

– compilations, etc. –

Jun 92. (cd/c) *Virgin; (CD/TC VM 9003)* **F.N.G.**

INFECTIOUS GROOVES

were formed by **MUIR + ROBERT TRUJILLO** – bass + **STEPHEN PERKINS** – drums (ex-JANE'S ADDICTION) / **ADAM SIEGAL + DEAN PLEASANTS** – guitar

Epic Epic

Oct 91. (cd/c/lp) *(468 729-2/-4/-1)* <47402> **THE PLAGUE THAT MAKES YOUR BOOTY MOVE, IT'S THE INFECTIOUS GROOVE**
– Punk it up / Therapy / I look funny? / Stop funk'n with my head / I'm gonna be my king / Closed session / Infectious grooves / Infectious blues / Monster skank / Back to the people / Turn your head / You lie . . . and yo breath stank / Do the sinister / Mandatory love song / Infecto groovalistic / Thanx but no thanx.

—— **JOSH FREESE** – drums repl. PERKINS

Mar 93. (cd/c/lp) *(473 591-2/-4/-1)* <53131> **SARSIPPIUS' ARK**
– Intro / Turtle wax (funkaholics anonymous) / No cover – 2 drink minimum / Immigrant song / Caca de kick / Don't stop, spread the jam! / Three headed mind pollution / Slo-motion slam / A legend in his own mind (ladies love 'sip) / Infectious Grooves / The man behind the man / Fame / Savor da flavor / No budget – Dust off the 8-track! / Infectious Grooves / You pick me up (just to throw me down) / Therapy / Do the sinister / Big big butt, by infectiphibian / Spreck.

May 94. (cd/c/lp) *(475 929-2/-4/-1)* <57279> **GROOVE FAMILY CYCO**
– Violent & funky / Boom boom boom / Frustrated again / Rules go out the window / Groove family cyco / Die like a pig / Do what I tell ya / Cousin Randy / Why / Made it.

XIII Bis Suicidal

Jul 00. (cd) *(15345-2)* <*SR 0017CD*> **MAS BORRACHO** Aug00
– Citizen of the nation / Just a little bit / Lock it in the pocket (and throw away the key) / Good for nothing / Borracho / Good times are out to get you / Wouldn't you like to know / Going, going, gone / 21st Century surf odyssey / Please excuse THS funk / Fill you up / What goes up / Leave me alone / Suicidal tendencies – Su casa es mi casa / My head – The beard / No mercy fool! – Chosen my own way of life / Creeper – Rollin' in the rain / Cyco Miko – Strugglin'.

SUNDOWN (see under ⇒ CEMETARY)

SUNNA

Formed: Bristol, England . . . 1999 by Londoner JON HARRIS, DJ FLATLINE, IAN MacLAREN, SHANE GOODWIN and RICHIE MILLS. Signed to MASSIVE ATTACK's 'Melankolic' label, these downbeat mood merchants filter a variety of retro, industrial, electronic and alternative metal influences through a skewed post-millennial perspective bearing more than a hint of HARRIS' trip-hop background. Take 'GRAPE' for instance, one of the stand-out tracks from their 'ONE MINUTE SCIENCE' (2000) debut set, which floats from the speakers like classic PINK FLOYD before metamorphosing into a seething NINE INCH NAILS-style nightmare. Kind of like an aural bad trip really . . .

Album rating: ONE MINUTE SILENCE (*6)

JON HARRIS – vocals, guitar / with **DJ FLATLINE** (aka NEIL DAVIDGE) – DJ / **IAN MacLAREN** – guitar / **SHANE GOODWIN** – bass / **RICHIE MILLS** – drums

Astralwerks Astralwerks

Jun 00. (7") *(SAD 8)* **O.D. / GRAPE** -
(cd-s+=) *(SADG 8)* – Burning holes / ('A'-Alpha mix).

Oct 00. (cd-s) *(SADG 9)* **POWER STRUGGLE / WEATHER CONTROLLER / POWER STRUGGLE (James Lavelle remix)** -

Nov 00. (cd) *(CDSAD 11)* <49708> **ONE MINUTE SILENCE** Aug00
– I'm not trading / Preoccupation / Power struggle / I miss / Insanity pulse / Too much / O.D. / Forlorn / Grape / One conditioning / 7%.

Mar 01. (cd-s) *(SADG 11)* **I'M NOT TRADING (full-length version) / GRAVE (live) / I'M NOT TRADING (U.N.K.L.E. in utero)** -

SUNNY DAY REAL ESTATE

Formed: Seattle, Washington, USA . . . early 90's by JEREMY ENIGK, WILLIAM GOLDSMITH, NATE MENDEL and DAN HOERNER. On the strength of a self-financed debut 45, 'SONG NUMBER 8 – SONG NUMBER 9', they signed to veteran US indie label, 'Sub Pop', who released their debut album, 'DIARY', the following year. As their name might suggest, SDRE offered up a brighter take on the grunge formula of their hometown, even going so far as to package their album in a day-glo pink sleeve. Despite a further promising eponymous release, the band effectively sold up with the sudden departure of ENIGK who'd converted to Christianity. MENDEL and GOLDSMITH in turn joined ex-NIRVANA drummer DAVE GROHL in his new FOO FIGHTERS project. However, GOLDSMITH broke away from the aforesaid chartbusters to hook up once more with ENIGK and breathe some new life into SDRE in the shape of a comeback album, 'HOW DOES IT FEEL TO BE SOMETHING ON' (1998).

Album rating: DIARY (*7) / SUNNY DAY REAL ESTATE (*6) / HOW IT FEELS TO BE SOMETHING ON (*7)

JEREMY ENIGK (b.16 Jul'74) – vocals, guitar / **DAN HOERNER** (b.13 May'69) – vocals, guitar / **NATE MENDEL** (b. 2 Dec'68) – bass / **WILLIAM GOLDSMITH** (b. 4 Jul'72) – drums

not iss. One Day I Stopped Breathing

1993. (7") **SONG NUMBER 8 – SONG NUMBER 9. /** -

Sub Pop Sub Pop

Jun 94. (lp/cd) *(SP/+CD 121-302)* <*SP 246/+CD*> **DIARY**
– Seven / In circles / Song about an angel / Round / 47 / Blankets were the stairs / Pheurton skeurto / Shadows / 48 / Grendel / Sometimes.

Oct 95. (lp/cd) <*(SP/+CD 316)*> **UNTITLED** ("The Pink Album")
– Friday / Theo B / Red elephant / 5/4 / Waffle / 8 / Iscarabaid / J'nuh / Rodeo Jones.

—— split when JEREMY found God and became a disciple of Jesus. MENDEL and GOLDSMITH were recruited by DAVE GROHL in The FOO FIGHTERS.

—— **ENIGK + GOLDSMITH** reformed SDRE in 1998 with a new bassist **J PALMER**

Sep 98. (cd) <*(SP 409)*> **HOW IT FEELS TO BE SOMETHING ON**
– Pillars / Roses in water / Every shining time you arrive / Two promises / 100 million / How it feels to be something on / The prophet / Guitar and video games / The hark's own private fuck / Days were golden.

JEREMY ENIGK

with a plethora of session people

1996. (cd) <*SP 323*> **RETURN OF THE FROG QUEEN** -
– Abegail Anne / Return of the frog queen / Lewis hollow / Lizard / Carnival / Call me steam / Explain / Shade and black hat / Fallen heart.

1998. (cd-ep) <*SP 58*> **THE END SESSIONS** (U.S. tour 1997) -
– Abegail Anne / Return of the frog queen / Lizard / Carnival / Explain.

SUPERSUCKERS

Formed: Tucson, Arizona, USA . . . late 80's as BLACK SUPERSUCKERS (after a porn mag!) by EDDIE SPAGHETTI, DAN BOLTON, RON HEATHMAN and DAN SIEGAL. Following a series of singles on various US indie labels – collected together on 1992 compilation, 'THE SONGS ALL SOUND THE SAME' – the band relocated to Seattle (long before the media circus arrived) in search of work, shortened their name to SUPERSUCKERS, signed to 'Sub Pop' and embarked on a campaign of good-time grunge creation. Debut album proper, the Jack Endino-produced 'THE SMOKE OF HELL' (1992), drew comparisons with Australia's long lost COSMIC PSYCHOS while a subsequent tour with 'Sub Pop' rockabilly preacher The REVEREND HORTON HEAT brought the SUCKER musical punch to British shores for the first time. While never exactly threatening to claim NIRVANA's crown, the band continued to churn out reliably un-challenging, reinforced three-minute grunge-pop over albums such as 'LA MANO CORNUDA' (1994), 'THE SACRILICIOUS SOUNDS OF . . .' (1995) and the self-explanatory 'MUST'VE BEEN HIGH' (1997). • **Covered:** BURNIN' UP (Madonna) / WHAT LOVE IS . . . (Dead Boys) / RAZZAMANAZZ (Nazareth).

Album rating: THE SMOKE OF HELL (*6) / LA MANO CORNUDA (*6) / THE SACRILICIOUS SOUNDS OF . . . (*5) / MUST'VE BEEN HIGH (*5) / THE SONGS ALL SOUND THE SAME compilation (*5)

EDDIE SPAGHETTI – vocals, bass / **RON HEATHMAN** – guitar / **DAN BOLTON** – guitar / **DAN SEIGAL** – drums

—— released a number of 7" singles for Sympathy For The Record Industry

Musical Tragedies | eMpTy

Jul 92. (cd) *(EFA 11351)* <162> **THE SONGS ALL SOUND THE SAME** (compilation) [ ] [ ] Nov91
– Alright / Saddle tramp / Poor / Burnin' up / Gravity Bill / Sex & outrage / What love is . . . / Junk / 4-stroke / The girl I know / Razzamanazz.

Sub Pop | Sub Pop

Sep 92. (7") **LIKE A BIG FUCKIN' TRAIN. /** [-] [ ]
Oct 92. (cd)(lp) *(SP 212CD)(SP 50-212)* <SP 164> **THE SMOKE OF HELL** [ ] [ ] Sep92
– Coattail rider / Luck / I say fuck / Alone and stinking / Caliente / Tasty greens / Hell city, Hell / Hot rod rally / Drink and complain / Mighty Joe Young / Ron's got the cocaine / Sweet'n'sour Jesus / Retarded Bill / Thinking 'bout revenge.
May 93. (7") <(SP 23-265)> **DEAD HOMIEZ. / HELL CITY HELL** [ ] [ ]
(cd-s+=) <(SPCD 23-265)> –
Apr 94. (cd/lp) <(SP CD/LP 120-301)> **LA MANO CORNUDA** [ ] [ ]
– Creepy jackalope eye / Seventeen poles / High ya! / On the couch / Clueless / Sugie / Mudhead / Gold top / How to maximize your kill count / I was born without a spine / Glad, damn glad / She's my bitch / The schmooze.
May 94. (7") <(SP 125-308)> **400 BUCKS. / (other track by REVEREND HORTON HEAT)** [ ] [ ]
Oct 94. (7") <(SP 141-345)> **ON THE COUCH. / CAN'T RESIST** [ ] [ ]
(cd-s+=) <(SPCD 141-345)> – Nitroglycerine / Hangliders.

—— **RICK SIMS** – guitar (ex-DIDJITS) repl. HEATHMAN

Jul 95. (7") <(SP 314)> **BORN WITH A TAIL. / HITTING THE GRAVEL** [ ] [ ]
(cd-s+=) <(SPCD 314)> – ('A'version) / Run like a motherfucker.
Sep 95. (7") <(SP 315)> **MARIE. /** [ ] [ ]
(cd-s+=) <(SPCD 3145)> –
Sep 95. (lp/c/cd) <(SP 303/+A/CD)> **THE SACRILICIOUS SOUNDS OF THE SUPERSUCKERS** [ ] [ ]
– Bad bad bad / Born with a tail / 19th most powerful woman in rock / Doublewide / Bad dog / Money into sin / Marie / Thing about that / Ozzy / Run like a motherfucker / Hittin' the gravel / Stoned if you want it / My victim / Don't go blue.
Nov 96. (7") <(SP 384)> **LEAVE THIS TOWN. / (B-side by TENDERLOIN)** [ ] [ ]
Sep 97. (lp/cd) <(SP/+CD 380)> **MUST'VE BEEN HIGH** [ ] [ ] Mar97
– Must've been high / Dead in the water / Barricade / Roamin' 'round / Hungover together / Non-addictive marijuana / Captain / Blow you away / Roadworn and weary / Hangin' out with me.

SURVIVOR

Formed: Chicago, Illinois, USA . . . 1978 by JIM PETERIK and FRANK SULLIVAN. They were joined by vocalist DAVE BICKLER and a couple of session players for their 1980 eponymous debut, released on the 'Scotti Brothers' label. With the addition of permanent members, STEPHEN ELLIS and MARC DOUBRAY, however, the group began to find an AOR niche. PETERIK was already a veteran of the rock scene (he'd fronted early 70's hitmakers, IDES OF MARCH and released a solo set, 'DON'T FIGHT THAT FEELING' in 1976 on 'Epic') and his writing partnership with SULLIVAN eventually bore commercial fruit with the massive success of 'EYE OF THE TIGER'. Used as the theme tune for Sylvester Stallone boxing film, 'Rocky III', the single's beefy guitar stabs and chest-beating chorus saw it scale the charts in both Britain and America. The accompanying album, while containing nothing as visceral as the title track, nevertheless managed a reasonable transatlantic chart run, narrowly missing the top spot in the States. A third album, 'CAUGHT IN THE GAME' (1983) wasn't nearly as successful, its harder-edged approach obviously scaring off the pop fans they'd snagged with their previous effort. Reworking their strategy yet again, the group subsequently replaced BICKLER with ex-COBRA singer JIMI JAMISON. The resulting album, 'VITAL SIGNS' (1984), achieved a neat balance between FM-friendliness and their power-AOR approach, the record spawning two US Top 10 singles and enjoying an extended stay in the album charts. Despite scoring with another 'Rocky' theme tune (the US/UK Top 5 'BURNING HEART', which, incidentally, wasn't included on the album), 'WHEN SECONDS COUNT' (1986) was a relative failure, as was their final effort, 'TOO HOT TO SLEEP' (1989). • **Songwriters:** PETERIK-SULLIVAN compositions. The pair also wrote material for • 38 SPECIAL.

Album rating: SURVIVOR (*4) / PREMONITION (*4) / EYE OF THE TIGER (*5) / CAUGHT IN THE GAME (*4) / VITAL SIGNS (*5) / WHEN SECONDS COUNT (*4) / TOO HOT TO SLEEP (*4) / BEST OF . . . compilation (*6)

DAVE BICKLER – vox, synth. / **FRANK SULLIVAN** – lead guitar, vocals (ex-MARIAH) / **JIM PETERIK** – keyboards, guitar, vocals (ex-Solo artist, ex-IDES OF MARCH) / **DENNIS JOHNSON** – bass / **GARY SMITH** – drums

Scotti Bros | Scotti Bros

Mar 80. (7") *(K 11453)* <511> **SOMEWHERE IN AMERICA. / FREELANCE** [ ] [70] Feb80
Nov 80. (lp/c) *(K/K4 50698)* <7107> **SURVIVOR** [ ] [ ] Mar80
– Somewhere in America / Can't getcha offa my mind / Let it be now / As soon as love finds me / Youngblood / Love has got me / The whole town's talkin' / 20-20 / Freelance / Nothing can shake me (from your love) / Whatever it takes.
Nov 80. (7") <517> **REBEL GIRL. / FREELANCE** [-] [ ]

—— **STEPHAN ELLIS** – bass + **MARC DROUBAY** – drums; repl. JOHNSON + SMITH

Aug 81. (7") <02435> **SUMMER NIGHTS. / LOVE IS ON MY SIDE** [-] [ ]
Nov 81. (7") *(SCTA 1903)* <02560> **POOR MAN'S SON. / LOVE IS ON MY SIDE** [ ] [33] Oct81
Feb 82. (lp/c) *(SCT/40 85289)* <37549> **PREMONITION** [ ] [82] Oct81
– Chevy nights / Summer nights / Poor man's son Heart's a lonely hunter / Light of a thousand smiles / Take you on a Saturday / Runway lights / Love is on my side.
Feb 82. (7") <02700> **SUMMER NIGHTS. / TAKE YOU ON A SATURDAY** [-] [62]
Jul 82. (7"/7"pic-d/12") *(A/SCTA11/TA 2411)* <02912> **EYE OF THE TIGER. / TAKE YOU ON A SATURDAY** [1] [1] Jun82
(above from the film 'Rocky III')
Jul 82. (lp/c) *(SCT/40 85845)* <38062> **EYE OF THE TIGER** [12] [2] Jun82
– Eye of the tiger / Feels like love / Hesitation dance / The one that really matters / I'm not that man anymore / Children of the night / Ever since the world began / American heartbeat / Silver girl. *(re-iss. Feb86 on 'Epic' lp/c/cd; EPC/40/CDSCT 32537)*
Sep 82. (7",7"pic-d) *(SCTA 2813)* <03213> **AMERICAN HEARTBEAT. / SILVER GIRL** [ ] [17]
Jan 83. (7") *(SCTA 3038)* <03485> **THE ONE THAT REALLY MATTERS. / HESITATION DANCE** [ ] [74]
Oct 83. (lp/c) *(SCT/40 25575)* <38791> **CAUGHT IN THE GAME** [ ] [82]
– Caught in the game / Jackie don't go / I never stopped loving you / It doesn't have to be this way / Ready for the real thing / Half-life / What do you really think / Slander / Santa Ana winds.
Nov 83. (7") *(A 3789)* <04074> **CAUGHT IN THE ACT. / SLANDER** [ ] [77] Oct83
Feb 84. (7") <04347> **I NEVER STOPPED LOVING YOU. / READY FOR THE REAL THING** [-] [ ]
Jul 84. (7") *(CAN 1021)* <880053> **THE MOMENT OF TRUTH. / IT DOESN'T HAVE TO BE THIS WAY** [ ] [63] Jun84
(above from the film 'The Karate Kid', issued on 'Casablanca')

—— **JIMI JAMISON** – vocals (ex-COBRA) repl. BICKLER

Sep 84. (7") *(A 4737)* <04603> **I CAN'T HOLD BACK. / I SEE YOU IN EVERYONE** [ ] [13]
Nov 84. (7") *(A 4946)* <04685> **HIGH ON YOU. / BROKEN PROMISES** [ ] [8] Jan85
Dec 84. (lp/c) *(SCT/40 26126)* <39578> **VITAL SIGNS** [ ] [16] Sep84
– I can't hold back / High on you / First night / The search is over / Broken promises / Popular girl / Everlasting / It's the singer not the song / I see you in everyone / Moment of truth. *(cd-iss. 1986 on 'Bellaphon'; 290-14-030)*
Jun 85. (7"/12") *(A/TA 6344)* <04871> **THE SEARCH IS OVER. / IT'S THE SINGER NOT THE SONG** [ ] [4] Apr85
Aug 85. (7") <05579> **FIRST NIGHT. / FEELS LIKE LOVE** [-] [53]
(below single from the film 'Rocky IV')
Nov 85. (7"/7"pic-d) *(A/WA 6708)* <05663> **BURNING HEART. / FEELS LIKE LOVE** [5] [2] Oct85
(12"+=) *(TX 6708)* – Eye of the tiger.
(d7"+=) *(DA 6708)* – Take you on a Saturday.
Nov 86. (lp/c) *(450 136-1/-4)* <40457> **WHEN SECONDS COUNT** [ ] [49]
– How much love / Keep it right here / Is this love / Man against the world / Rebel son / Oceans / When seconds count / Backstreet love affair / In good faith / Can't let you go.
Nov 86. (7"/ext.12") *(650 195-7/-6)* <06381> **IS THIS LOVE. / CAN'T LET YOU GO** [ ] [9] Oct86
Feb 87. (7") <06705> **HOW MUCH LOVE. / BACKSTREET LOVE AFFAIR** [-] [51]
Apr 87. (7") <07070> **MAN AGAINST THE WORLD. / OCEANS** [-] [86]

—— live guests **PETER JOHN VETTESE** – keyboards / **BILL SYNIAR** – bass / **MICKEY CURRY** – drums; repl. ELLIS + DROUBAY

Polydor | Scotti Bros

Oct 88. (7") <08067> **DIDN'T KNOW IT WAS LOVE. / RHYTHM OF THE CITY** [-] [61]
Jan 89. (7") <68526> **ACROSS THE MILES. / BURNING BRIDGES** [-] [74]
Apr 89. (lp/c/cd) *(836 589-1/-4/-2)* <44282> **TOO HOT TO SLEEP** [ ] [ ] Oct88
– She's a star / Desperate dreams / To hot to sleep / Didn't know it was blue / Rhythm of the city / Here comes desire / Across the miles / Take me I'm the one / Can't give it up / Burning bridges.
Nov 91. (cd/c; as JIMI JAMISON) <75220-2/-4> **WHEN LOVE COMES DOWN** [-] [ ]
Jan 92. (c-s; as JIMI JAMISON) <75300> **WHEN LOVE COMES DOWN** [-] [ ]

—— disbanded after above album . . . re-formed

Frontiers | Frontiers

Jul 00. (cd; as JIMI JAMISON'S SURVIVOR) *(FRCD 019)* <7200-2> **EMPIRES** [ ] [ ]
– Dream too far / First day of love / November rain / Have mercy / Empires / Calling America / Just beyond the clouds / Love is alive / Cry tough / Run from the thunder / I'm always here.

– compilations, etc. –

on 'Scotti Bros' unless mentioned otherwise

Mar 86. (7"/12") *(A/TA 6989)* **I CAN'T HOLD BACK. / BURNING HEART** [ ] [-]
Nov 86. (lp) *Bellaphon; (288-14-001)* **THE VERY BEST OF SURVIVOR** [ ] [-]
Aug 93. (cd/c) *(518 139-2/-4)* **GREATEST HITS** [ ] [ ]
Oct 98. (cd) *Spectrum; (554624-2)* **PRIME CUTS** [ ] [-]

SVEN GALI

Formed: Toronto, Canada . . . 1988 by DEE CERNILE, ANDY FRANK, DAVE WANLESS and SHAWN MAHER. Recruiting NY born GREGG GERSON, they began their apprenticeship on the local live circuit before finding a contract with 'Ariola' in the early 90's. Their eponymous 1993 debut set brought widespread comparisons with US attitude-metallers SKID ROW, its high-octane punch faring particularly well in their native Canada. A follow-up set, 'IN WIRE', appeared in 1995, although the band have so far failed to translate their early promise into international success.

Album rating: SVEN GALI (*7) / IN WIRE (*5)

DAVE WANLESS (b. London, England) – vocals / **DEE CERNILE** – guitar / **ANDY FRANK** – guitar / **SHAWN MAHER** – bass / **GREGG GERSON** – drums

R.C.A. Ariola

Mar 93. (cd/c) *<(74321 11442-2/-4)>* **SVEN GALI** [ ] [ ]
– Under the influence / Tie dyed skies / Sweet little gypsy / In my garden / Freakz / Love don't live here anymore / Stiff competition / Real thing / Whisper in the rain / 25 hours a day / Here today, gone tomorrow / Disgusteen. *(cd re-iss. Sep99 on 'Axe Killer'; AXE 20527CD)*

May 95. (cd/c) *<(74321 28211-2/-4)>* **IN WIRE** [ ] [ ]
– What you give / Keeps me down / Worms / Make me / Red moon / Tired of listening / Shallow / Truth / Rocking chair / Helen / Who said?

SWA

Formed: Los Angeles, California, USA . . . 1983 by ex-BLACK FLAG man CHUCK DUKOWSKI alongside RICHARD FORD, MERRILL WARD and GREG CAMERON. Not one of the most promising bands on the eclectic 'S.S.T.' roster, SWA combined the adrenaline of West Coast hardcore with elements of BLACK SABBATH/FLAG-style dirge-rock. Debut album, 'YOUR FUTURE (IF YOU HAVE ONE)' (1985) set out their musical stall, followed by 1986's 'SEX DR.' The guitar slot was reshuffled for 1987's 'XCIII', SYLVIA JUNCOSA injecting a dose of six-string electricity into the sludge. With the latter subsequently going off for a solo career, PHIL VAN DUYNE stepped in for 1989's 'WINTER', which, like its follow-up, 'VOLUME', failed to win the band any significant exposure.

Album rating: YOUR FUTURE (IF YOU HAVE ONE) (*5) / SEX DOCTOR (*5) / XCIII (*6) / WINTER (*5) / VOLUME (*4) / EVOLUTION 85-87 compilation (*6)

MERRILL WARD – vocals / **RICHARD FORD** – guitar / **CHUCK DUKOWSKI** – bass, vocals (ex-BLACK FLAG) / **GREG CAMERON** – drums / **PAUL ROESSLER** – keyboards (guest)

S.S.T. S.S.T.

Sep 85. (lp/c) *<(SST 053/+C)>* **YOUR FUTURE (IF YOU HAVE ONE)** [ ] [ ]
– Rip it up / Until you bleed / 10 miles of hate / Creeps / Simon's thing / Caravan / Islands in the freeway / Myth / Sine cosine X / In my heart.

1986. (m-lp/m-c) *<(SST 073/+C)>* **SEX DOCTOR** [ ] [ ]
– Big ride / Round and round / The evil and the good / Catacombs / Sea and sky / Sex doctor / The only one / Oklahoma / Onslaught.

— **SYLVIA JUNCOSA** – lead guitar (of TO DAMASCUS) repl. FORD

1987. (lp/c) *<(SST 093/+C)>* **XCIII** [ ] [ ]
– Faker's blues / Optimist / Succumb / Heartbreaker / Arroyo / Prayer / So long.

Jul 88. (12"ep) *<(SST 153)>* **ARROYO** [ ] [ ]

Aug 88. (cd) *<(SST 157CD)>* **EVOLUTION 85-87** (compilation) [ ] [ ]
– Simon's thing / Sine cosine X / Until you bleed / Creeps / Islands in the freeway / 10 miles of hate / Catacombs / Sea and sky / Sex Doctor / Oklahoma / Big ride / The evil and the good / Faker's blues / Optimist / Evolution / Arroyo / So long / Succumb.

— **PHIL VAN DUYNE** – guitar, vocals; repl. JUNCOSA who went solo

Mar 89. (lp/c/cd) *<(SST 238/+C/CD)>* **WINTER** [ ] [ ]
– Conquest / Chances are / I wanna know / Intro / Headphones / Goddess / Winter / The man upstairs / Talking behind your back / Mass confusion / Desire / King of the pit / Bad acid / Wasting my time.

— WARD departed before below (VAN DUYNE took over most of vocals) while former SACCHARINE TRUST frontman, **JACK BREWER** helped out

Nov 91. (lp/cd) *<(SST 282/+CD)>* **VOLUME** [ ] [ ] Oct91
– Pull the plug / Force the issue / My god / Decline / I like destruction / Jordan '88 / Get over / The emptiness inside / The outsider / The end of the universe / Crak Jack / True love / The chill of uncertainty / You made a killer out of me.

— split after above, DUKOWSKI formed another outfit

SWANS

Formed: New York, USA . . . 1982 as a vehicle for the musical experimentation of MICHAEL GIRA. With an initial line-up of GIRA, ROLI MOSSIMAN, NORMAN WESTBURG, HARRY CROSBY and JONATHAN KANE, SWANS made their less than graceful debut with an EP in 1982, following it up with debut album, 'FILTH' (1983), both releases appearing – in Europe at least – on the German 'Zensor' label. Subsequently signing to British indie imprint, 'K.422', and replacing KANE with IVAN NAHEM, the band unleashed the pulverising 'COP' (1984) album. A harsh lesson in rock deconstruction, the record found GIRA and Co taking a metamorphic pneumatic drill to the form and pounding it till it barely even resembled music. Lyrically, GIRA was also scraping the margins, focusing on the blackest, most violent, paranoid and disturbing elements of life's dark side; 'RAPING A SLAVE' for instance, this controversial track also appearing as the lead track to a subsequent EP. Not music to play to your grandchildren then, but a brutally honest response to what GIRA perceived as the rotten core of human (and certainly American) society. Previewed by the memorably titled 'TIME IS MONEY (BASTARD)', 'GREED' (1986) was the next instalment in SWANS' dismantling of the capitalist rock beast, taking horror-industrial minimalism to new depths via a skeletal soundtrack of stark piano and percussion. Introducing the haunting vocals of JARBOE (MOSSIMAN had decamped to form WISEBLOOD), the 'HOLY MONEY' album continued along the same (production) lines later that year. 1987 proved a turning point as GIRA and JARBOE created SKIN as an outlet for their more fragile, acoustic creations, albums such as 'BLOOD, WOMEN, ROSES' (1987) and 'SHAME, HUMILITY, REVENGE' (1988) representing a more endearing flipside to the brutality of SWANS. Both albums appeared on 'Product Inc.', as did SWANS' 'CHILDREN OF GOD' (1988), a double set which introduced a new rhythm section (TED PARSONS and ALGYS 'AL' KIZYS) and found the band showing definite signs of mellowing. The shift was underlined with a surprise acoustic reading of Joy Division's 'LOVE WILL TEAR US APART', issued as a single in summer '88. Incredibly, perhaps, the band signed to corporate giant, 'M.C.A.', in 1989, releasing 'THE BURNING WORLD' as their major label debut. The partnership didn't last long, however, GIRA and JARBOE subsequently forming their own 'Young God' label for the release of '10 SONGS FOR ANOTHER WORLD', a third SKIN project issued under the revamped moniker WORLD OF SKIN (after Brit cock-rockers SKIN claimed the name). 1991's 'WHITE LIGHT FROM THE MOUTH OF INFINTIY' moved even further away from the rampant nihilism of GIRA's earlier work, the man sounding uncannily like NICK CAVE (ironically another former prophet of doom who now seems to have found at least a measure of spiritual redemption) in places; while the brilliantly morose 'FAILURE' was the GIRA we all know and love, 'SONG FOR THE SUN' was positively joyous, suggesting there was indeed some light filtering through to the man's formerly opaque world view. Subsequent 90's albums, 'LOVE OF LIFE' (1992), 'OMNISCENCE' (1992), 'THE GREAT ANNIHILATOR' (1995) and 'SOUNDTRACKS FOR THE BLIND' (1996) continued in a similarly (relatively) accessible vein although the latter marked their ahem, SWAN(S)-song as GIRA and JARBOE decided the project had reached its natural conclusion. Nevertheless, 1995 had proved a fruitful year for SWANS-related material as GIRA launched a book, 'The Consumer And Other Stories', through HENRY ROLLINS' publishing operation, '21/3/61' as well as his debut solo set, 'DRAINLAND'. JARBOE, meanwhile, also released a debut solo set the same year, 'SACRIFICIAL CAKE'.

Album rating: FILTH (*6) / COP (*7) / GREED (*6) / HOLY MONEY (*6) / CHILDREN OF THE GOD (*7) / FEEL GOOD NOW (*6) / THE BURNING WORLD (*6) / WHITE LIGHT FROM THE MOUTH OF INFINITY (*7) / THE GREAT ANNIHILATOR (*6) /

MICHAEL GIRA – vocals (ex-LITTLE CRIPPLES) / **ROLI MOSSIMAN** – piano, percussion / **NORMAN WESTBURG** – guitar / **HARRY CROSBY** – bass / **JONATHAN KANE** – drums, percussion

Zensor Labour

1982. (7"ep) **EP #1** [-] [ ]
(UK-iss.Sep90 on 'Young God'; YGEP 001)

Zensor Neutral

1983. (lp) *<ND 02>* **FILTH** [-] [ ]
– Stay here / Big strong boss / Blackout / Power for power / Freak / Right wrong / Thank you / Weakling / Gang. *(UK-iss.Sep90 on 'Young God' cd+=/c/lp; TG CD/MC/LP 1)* – Speak / Laugh / Sensitive skin / Take advantage. *(re-iss. Sep90 on 'Young God' lp/cd; YG LP/CD 001) (cd re-iss. Aug94 on 'Sky'; SKY 75061CD)*

K.422 P.V.C.

— **IVAN NAHEM** – drums; repl. JONATHAN who joined The HOOD

Nov 84. (lp) *(KCC 001)* **COP** [ ] [-]
– Half life / Job / Why hide / Clayman / I crawled / Raping a slave / Your property / Cop / Butcher / Thug / Young god / This is mine. *(cd-iss. Jan89 ; KCCCD 001)*

Feb 85. (12"ep) *(KDE 12-1)* **I CRAWLED / RAPING A SLAVE. / YOUNG GOD / THIS IS MINE** [ ] [-]

Jan 86. (12") *(KDE 12-2)* **TIME IS MONEY (BASTARD). / SEALED IN SKIN / TIME IS MONEY (mix)** [ ] [-]

Mar 86. (lp) *(KCC 2)* **GREED** [ ] [ ]
– Time is money (bastard) / Money is flesh / Another you / Greed.

— **JARBOE** – keyboards, vox; repl. MOSSIMAN who formed WISEBLOOD

Sep 86. (lp) *(KCC 3)* **HOLY MONEY** [ ] [ ]
– A hanging / You need me / Fool / A screw (holy money) / Another you / Money is flesh / Coward / A screw (mix) / Black mail / A screw . *(cd-iss. Feb88 +=; KCCCD 3)* – GREED

Sep 86. (12") *(KDE 3-12)* **A SCREW (HOLY MONEY). / BLACKMAIL / A SCREW** [ ] [-]

Nov 86. (d-lp) **PUBLIC CASTRATION IS A GOOD IDEA (live)** [ ] [-]
– Money is flesh / Fool / A screw / Anything for you / Coward / A hanging / Stupid child / Another you.

— **TED PARSONS** – drums + **ALGYS 'AL' KIZYS** – bass; repl. NAHEM + CROSBY who both formed OF CABBAGES AND KINGS (they issued a few releases, mainly an eponymouse set plus the 'FACE' album in '88.

Product Inc Caroline

Aug 87. (7") *(PROD 16)* **NEW MIND. / I'LL SWALLOW YOU** [ ] [-]
(12"+=) *(12PROD 16)* –

Oct 87. (d-lp/c)(cd) *(33/C PROD 17)(PRODCD 17) <CAROL 1346-1/-4/-2>* **CHILDREN OF GOD** [ ] [ ]
– New mind / In my garden / Sex god sex / Blood and honey / Like a drug / You're not real, girl / Beautiful child / Trust me / Blackmail / Real love. *(cd+=)* – Our love lies.

Jun 88. (7"red) *(PROD 23)* **LOVE WILL TEAR US APART. / TRUST ME** [ ] [-]
(12"+=/cd-s+=) *(PROD 23 T/CD)* – ('A'-Black version) / New mind (purple version).
(12"red+=) *(PROD 23B)* – Our love lies.

Love not iss.

Aug 88. (d-lp) *(LOVE ONE)* **FEEL GOOD NOW** [ ] [-]

— guests incl. **STEVEN** – bass + **VINNY** – drums repl. ALGYS + TED

M.C.A. not iss.

Apr 89. (7") *(MCA 1322)* **SAVED. / NO CRUEL ANGEL** [ ] [-]
(12"+=/cd-s+=) *(MCAT/DMCAT 1332)* – See you more.

May 89. (lp/c/cd) *(MCG/MCGC/DMCG 6047)* **THE BURNING WORLD** [ ] [-]
– The river that runs with love won't run dry / Let it come down / Can't find my way home / Mona Lisa, Mother Earth / (She's a) Universal emptiness / Saved / I remember who you are / Jane Mary, cry one tear / See no more / God damn the sun.

Aug 89. (7") *(MCA 1347)* **CAN'T FIND MY WAY HOME. / UNIVERSAL EMPTINESS** [ ] [-]
(12"+=/12"g-f+=)(cd-s+=) *(MCAT/+G 1347)(DMCAT 1347)* –

— w/ guests **ANTON FIER** (GOLDEN PALOMINOES) / **CLINTON STEELE** (MARY MY HOPE) / **HAHN ROWE** (HUGO LARGO)

Young God not iss.

Apr 91. (cd/c/d-lp) *(YG CD/MC/LP 003)* **WHITE LIGHT FROM THE MOUTH OF INFINITY** [ ] [-]
– Better than you / Power and sacrifice / You know nothing / Song for dead time / Will we survive / Love will save you / Failure / Song for the sun / Miracle of love / When she breathes / Why are we alive? / The most unfortunate lie. *(cd re-iss. Aug94 on 'Sky'; SKY 75060CD)*

Nov 91. (cd/c/lp) *(YG CD/MC/LP 004)* **BODY TO BODY, JOB TO JOB** (compilation of live & out takes from 1982-85) [ ] [-]
– I'll cry for you / Red sheet / Loop 33 / Your game / Seal it over / Whore / We'll hang out for that / Half life / Loop 21 / Get out / Job / Loop 1 / Mother, my body disgusts me / Cop / Only I can hear, only I can touch / Thug. *(cd re-iss. Aug94 on 'Sky'; SKY 75063CD)*

Feb 92. (cd/c/lp) *(YG CD/MC/LP 005)* **LOVE OF LIFE** [ ] [-]
– Love of life / The golden boy that was swallowed by the sea / The other side of the world / Her / The sound of freedom / Amnesia / Identity / In the eyes of nature / She crys / God loves America / No cure for the lonely. *(cd re-iss. Aug94 on 'Sky'; SKY 75064CD)*

Apr 92. (12") **LOVE OF LIFE (M. Gira remix). / AMNESIA (Martin Bisi re mix)** [ ] [-]
(cd-s+=) – Picture of Maryanne.

Young God Dog Gone

Oct 92. (cd/c/lp) *(YG CD/MC/LP 007) <5160>* **OMNISCENCE** [ ] [ ] Jan93
– Mother's milk / Pow r sac / Will serve / Her / Black eyed dog / Amnesia / Love of life / (----) / The other side of the world / Rutting / God loves America / Omnipotent. *(cd re-iss. Aug94 on 'Sky'; SKY 75160CD)*

Young God Invisible

Jan 95. (cd/d-lp) *(YG CD/LP 009) <INV 35CD>* **THE GREAT ANNIHILATOR** [ ] [ ]
– In / I am the sun / She lives! / Celebrity lifestyle / Mother, father / Blood promise / Mind / Body / Light / Sound / My buried child / Warm / Alcohol the seed / Killing for company / Mother's milk / Where does a body end / Telepathy / The great annihilator / Out.

Aug 96. (10") *(ART 01)* **ANIMUS. / FAILURE** [ ] [-]
(above issued on 'Arts & Commerce')

Young God Atavistic

Oct 96. (d-cd) *(YGCD 010) <61959>* **SOUNDTRACKS FOR THE BLIND** [ ] [ ]
– Red velvet corridor / I was a prisoner in your skull / Helpless child / Live through me / Yumyab killers / Beautiful days / Volcano / Mellothumb / All lined up / Surrogate 2 / How they suffer / Animus / Red velvet wound / Sound / Her mouth is filled with honey / Bloodsection / Jypogirl / Minus something / Empathy / I love you this much / YRP / Fans lament / Secret friends / Final sac / YRP 2 / Surrogate drone.

– compilations, etc. –

Nov 92. (cd) *K.422; (KCC 001CD)* **COP / YOUNG GOD** [ ] [-]
(re-iss. Aug94 on 'Sky'; SKY 75068CD)

Nov 92. (cd) *K.422;* **GREED / HOLY MONEY** [ ] [-]
(re-iss. Aug94 on 'Sky'; SKY 75069CD)

Mar 96. (cd) *Atavistic; <57>* **KILL THE CHILD (live)** [-] [ ]

May 96. (cd) *Atavistic; <58>* **REAL LOVE** [-] [ ]

Jun 96. (cd) *World Service; (RTD 1573140-2)* **DIE TUR IST ZU** [ ] [-]
– Liget's breath / Hilfios kind / Ich sehe die alle in einer reihe / Y.R.P. / You know everything / M-F / Sound section.

— disbanded in '97

SWEET 75 (see under ⇒ NIRVANA)

SWORD

Formed: Montreal, Canada . . . 1981 by RICK HUGHES and DAN HUGHES, who recruited MIKE PLANT and MIKE LAROCK. Something of a well kept secret, SWORD's debut album, 'METALIZED' (1986), is especially held in high regard by fans of power metal, its intense melodic assault winning the band tour support with such legends as MOTORHEAD and METALLICA. Despite this exposure and continuing critical backing for a second set, 'SWEET DREAMS' (1988), SWORD failed to carve out a sufficently profitable niche and splintered soon after.

Album rating: METALIZED (*7) / SWEET DREAMS (*5)

RICK HUGHES – vocals, keyboards / **MIKE PLANT** – guitar, keyboards, vocals / **MIKE LAROCK** – bass / **DAN HUGHES** – drums

Roadracer Aquarius

1986. (lp) *<AQR 541>* **METALIZED** [-] [ ]
– F.T.W. (Follow The Wheel) / Children of Heaven / Stoned again / Dare to spit / Outta control / The end of the night / Runaway / Where to hide / Stuck in rock / Evil spell. *(UK-iss.Aug89 on 'G.W.R.'; GWLP 10)*

1988. (lp/c) *(RO 9476-1/-4) <84-7885>* **SWEET DREAMS** [ ] [ ]
– Sweet dreams / The trouble is / Land of the brave / Back off / Prepare to die / Caught in the act / Until death do us part / The threat / Life on the sharp edge / State of shock. *(re-iss. Dec89 on 'G.W.R.' cd/c/lp; GW CD/TC/LP 45)*

— split in the early 90's

SWORDMASTER

Formed: Gothenburg, Sweden . . . 1993 by WHIPLASHER (who was also a member of OPTHALAMIA), NIGHTMARE, THUNDERBOLT and NICKY TERROR; where was LIGHTNING then. The former two had initiated the death/black-metal outfit after meeting at a riotous party in which all hell broke loose, apparently. With the help of KING DIAMOND axeman turned producer, ANDY LA ROCQUE, SWORDMASTER cut a few demo tracks and were rewarded when the 'Osmose' metal imprint signed them on. The following year in 1997, WHIPLASHER and his apocalyptic crew surfaced with 'POSTMORTEM BLUES', heralding a new beginning for yet another Scandic black-metal combo. The 100 mph 'DEATHRAIDER' mini-set in '98, fared even better critically, as did second set proper, 'MORIBUND TRANSGORIA' (1999); sticksman INFERNO had now substituted for NICKY.

Album rating: POSTMORTEM TALES (*5) / DEATHRAIDER mini (*6) / MORIBUND TRANSGORIA (*5)

WHIPLASHER – vocals / **NIGHTMARE** – guitar / **THUNDERBOLT** – bass / **NICKY TERROR** – drums

Osmose Osmose

Jun 97. (cd/lp) *(OPCD/OPLP 055)* **POSTMORTEM TALES** [ ] [ ]
– Intro: Indeathstries – The masters' possession / Crush to dust / Postmortem tales / Past redemption / Claws of death / Blood legacy / The serpent season / Metallic devastation / Black ace.

Jun 98. (m-cd/m-lp) *(OPCD/OPLP 058)* **DEATHRAIDER** [ ] [ ]
– Deathraider 2000 / Firefall of the fireball / Necronaut psychout / Iron corpse / Stand for the fire demon.

— **INFERNO** – drums; repl. TERROR

Mar 99. (cd-ep) *(<FMP 004CD>)* **WRATHS OF TIME / UPON BLOOD AND ASHES . . . / CONSPIRACY / OUTRO** [ ] [ ] Jun98
(above issued on 'Full Moon')

Nov 99. (cd/lp) *(OPCD/OPLP 084)* **MORIBUND TRANSGORIA** [ ] [-]
– Deathspawn of the Eibound / Towards erotomech eye / The angels and the masters / Metalmorphosis – The sweat of Cain / Sulphur skelethrones / Moribund trangoria / Doom at motordome / The grotesque xtravaganza.

SYMPOSIUM

Formed: Kensington, London, England . . . early '96 by fresh-faced youths and former Catholic school choirboys, ROSS CUMMINS, HAGOP TCHAPARIAN (part Armenian), WOJTEK GODZISZ (fully Polish), WILL McGONAGLE and JOSEPH BIRCH. Taking their cue from the noisy pop-punk fusion of GREEN DAY and ASH, these religiously fanatic QPR (a West London football club) fans bounded onto the indie scene in 1996 with the 'DRINK THE SUNSHINE' single. Their debut effort for 'Infectious' (home of ASH), the lads proceeded to gatecrash the Top 30 with their follow-up, 'FAREWELL TO TWILIGHT', a taster from their spunky, CLIVE LANGER/ALAN WINSTANLEY-produced Top 30 debut set, 'ONE DAY AT A TIME' (1997). • **Songwriters:** GODZISZ or CUMMINGS except HARD DAY'S NIGHT (Beatles).

Album rating: ONE DAY AT A TIME mini (*7) / ON THE OUTSIDE (*8)

ROSS CUMMINS – vocals / **HAGOP TCHAPARIAN** – guitar / **WILL McGONAGLE** – guitar / **WOJTEK GODZISZ** – bass / **JOSEPH BIRCH** – drums

Infectious not iss.

Oct 96. (7") *(infect 30s)* **DRINK THE SUNSHINE. / DISAPPEAR** [ ] [-]
(cd-s+=) *(infect 30cd)* – Smiling.

Mar 97. (7") *(infect 34s)* **FAREWELL TO TWILIGHT. / XANTHEIN** [25] [-]
(7") *(infect 34sx)* – ('A'side) / Song.
(cd-s++=) *(infect 34cd)* – Easily scared.

May 97. (7") *(infect 37s)* **ANSWER TO WHY I HATE YOU. / JIM** [32] [-]
(cd-s+=) *(infect 37cd)* – Natural.
(cd-s) *(infect 37cdx)* – ('A'side) / Torquoise / Keeping the secret.

Aug 97. (7") *(infect 44s)* **FAIRWEATHER FRIEND. / ('A'live)** [25] [-]
(cd-s+=) *(infect 44cd)* – Greeting song / Just so.
(cd-s+=) *(infect 44cdx)* – The answer to why I love you (live) / Disappear (live).

Oct 97. (m-cd/m-c/m-lp) *(infect 49 cd/mc/lp)* **ONE DAY AT A TIME** [29] [-]
– Drink to the sunshine / Farewell to twilight / Puddles / Fairweather friend / One day at a time / Fizzy / Girl with brains in her feet / Smiling.

Nov 97. (7"purple) *(infect 50s)* **DRINK THE SUNSHINE. / FIZZY** [ ] [-]

Mar 98. (7") *(infect 52s)* **AVERAGE MAN. / TWIST** | 45 | - |
(cd-s) *(infect 52cd)* – ('A'side) / Journey / Little things / Me.
(cd-s) *(infect 52cdx)* – ('A'side) / Hard day's night (live).
May 98. (7"pic-d) *(infect 55s)* **BURY YOU. / SCHOSTAKOWICH** | 41 | - |
(cd-s) *(infect 55cd)* – ('A'side) / Serenade the idiot / Standing honoured / Higher.
(cd-s) *(infect 55cdx)* – ('A'side) / Fluorescent / Mairamout / ('A'-CD-ROM video clip).
May 98. (cd/c/lp) *(infect 56 cd/mc/lp)* **ON THE OUTSIDE** | 32 | - |
– Impossible / The answer to why I hate you / Bury you / Blue / The end / Nothing special / Circles squares and lines / Stay on the outside / Paint the stars / Obsessive compulsive disorder / Natural / Way.
Jul 98. (7") *(infect 57s)* **BLUE. / LIFE OF RILEY** | 48 | - |
(cd-s+=) *(infect 57cd)* – Carnival.
(cd-s) *(infect 57cdx)* – ('A'side) / Cartwheels / Ode to the frogs.

Curveball **not iss.**

May 99. (7") *(SYMP 001S)* **KILLING POSITION. / WALL OF SILENCE / THE END (live)** | | |
(cd-s+=) *(SYMP 001CD)* – Hard day's night (live at Reading).

– compilations, etc. –

Nov 99. (cd) *Strange Fruit; (SFRSCD 088)* **LIVE AND IN SESSION** | | - |

SYSTEM OF A DOWN

Formed: Los Angeles, California, USA . . . late '94 by expatriot Armenians, SERJ TANKIAN (looks like JELLO BIAFRA~ with an afro hairdo), DARON MALAKIAN and SHAVO ODADJIAN, the trio almost immediately adding JOHN DOLMAYAN. Produced by RICK RUBIN, their '98 eponymous debut revealed them to be anthemic and politically emotional noise-merchants in the mould of COAL CHAMBER or FAITH NO MORE, stretching punk-metal into jazzy Armenian folk.

Album rating: SYSTEM OF A DOWN (*8)

SERJ TANKIAN – vocals / **DARON MALAKIAN** – guitar / **SHAVO ODADJIAN** – bass / **JOHN DOLMAYAN** – drums

American – Columbia **American-Columbia**

Oct 98. (cd) *(491209-2)* **SYSTEM OF A DOWN** | | |
– Suite-pee / Know / Sugar / Suggestions / Spiders / Ddevil / Soil / War? / Mind / Peephole / CUBErt / Darts / P.L.U.C.K.

TAD

Formed: Seattle, Washington, USA . . . 1988 by namesake Idaho-born TAD DOYLE and KURT DANIELSON, both graduates of BUNDLES OF PISS (the group, that is). With STEVE WIED on drums, they subsequently signed to cult US indie label 'Sub Pop' and after one single, 'RITUAL DEVICE', TAD unleashed their classic debut (mini) album 'GOD'S BALLS' (1989). A claustrophobic trawl through the fetid back alleys of grunge, the gargantuan DOYLE laid down the foundations of the genre with a monolithic grind which brought to mind early doom merchants, BLACK SABBATH. Subsequently issuing a cover of Black Flag's 'DAMAGED' and touring with stablemates NIRVANA, the group employed the services of the illustrious STEVE ALBINI to produce a noisier follow-up set, 'SALT LICK' (1990). However, in early '91, the artwork on their third album, '8-WAY SANTA' (featuring a photograph of a hairy man – not TAD – resting his hand on a woman's breast), caused the woman in question to proceed with a lawsuit which resulted in its removal from the shelves. The record saw the grunge behemoths lightening up a little and actually indulging in some melodies/choruses to impressive effect. The brilliant 'JINX' adequately described the band's regular brushes with the fickle hand of fate; amongst other incidents, DOYLE and Co. narrowly missed being blown up by the I.R.A. in a Belfast hotel, survived a lightning strike and miraculously escaped being crushed by a stray boulder! It wasn't all bad, for DOYLE anyway, who subsequently scored a small (not big!) part in the Cameron Crowe film, 'Singles'. Meanwhile, TAD recruited a new drummer, REY WASHAM (to replace JOSH) and, along with the rest of the grunge pack, signed to a major label ('Giant'). The ensuing album, 'INHALER' (1993), saw the band once more throwing their weight around and indicating that commercial compromise was some way off. They moved to 'Music For Nations' for a one-off concert set, 'LIVE ALIEN BROADCAST' (1994), before they majored in 1995 with the 'East West' empire, releasing 'INFRARED RIDING HOOD' the same year. Like fellow instigators MUDHONEY, TAD remain a footnote in the major label grunge rewrite, while acts such as STONE TEMPLE PILOTS, BUSH, etc. coin it in. Oh the irony!

Album rating: GOD'S BALLS (*8) / SALT LICK (*7) / 8-WAY SANTA (*8) / INHALER (*6) / LIVE ALIEN BROADCAST (*4) / INFRARED RIDING HOOD (*6)

TAD DOYLE – vocals, guitar / **KURT DANIELSON** – bass, vocals / **STEVE WIED** – drums

Glitterhouse / Sub Pop

Aug 88. (7",7"clear) <SP 19> **RITUAL DEVICE. / DAISY**

May 89. (m-lp) *(GR 0051)*<SP 27> **GOD'S BALL** — Mar89
– Behemoth / Pork chop / Helot / Tuna car / Cyanide bath / Boiler room / Satan's chainsaw / Hollow man / Nipple belt / Ritual device.

Jun 89. (7") <SP 37> **DAMAGED 1. / DAMAGED 2 (by Pussy Galore)**

— **GARY THORSTENSEN** – guitar / **JOSH SINDER** – drums repl. WIED

Jan 90. (7",7"green) <SP 55> **LOSER. / COOKING WITH GAS**

Apr 90. (m-lp) *(GR 0076)*<SP 49> **SALT LICK** — Feb90
– Jinx / Giant killer / Wired god / Delinquent / Hedge hog / Flame tavern / Trash truck / Stumblin' man / Jack Pepsi / Candy / 3-D witchhunt / Crane's cafe / Plague years. *(US-cd/c incl. 'GOD'S BALL'; SP49 B/A)*

Sub Pop / Sub Pop

Dec 90. (7",7"yellow) <SP 80> **JINX. / SANTA**

Jan 91. (fan club-cd-s) <SP 99B> **JACK PEPSI. / PLAGUE YEARS**

Mar 91. (lp/c/cd) <*(SP 89/+A/B)*> **8-WAY SANTA**
– Jinx / Giant killer / Wired god / Delinquent / Hedge hog / Flame tavern / Trash truck / Stumblin' man / Jack Pepsi / Gandi / 3-D witch hunt / Crane's cafe / Plague years.

Feb 93. (12"/cd-s) *(SP/+CD 229)* <SP 182> **SALEM. / WELT / LEPER**

— **TEXAS REY WASHAM** – drums (ex-RAPEMAN, ex-SCRATCH ACID) repl. JOSH

Mechanic / Giant

Oct 93. (cd/c/lp) <*(4321 16570-2/-4/-1)*> **INHALER**
– Grease box / Throat locust / Leafy incline / Lucimo! / Ulcer lycanthorpe / Just bought the farm / Rotor / Paregoric Pansy / Gouge.

Music For Nations / Futurist

Jan 95. (cd) *(CDMFN 181)* <*11065*> **LIVE ALIEN BROADCASTS**
– Throat locust / Just bought the farm / Paregoric / Delinquent / Rotor / Pale corkscrew / Stumblin' man / Demon seed / Sunday drive / Jack.

East West / Atlantic

May 95. (cd/c/lp) <*(7559 61789-2/-4)*> **INFRARED RIDING HOOD**
– Ictus / Emotional cockroach / Red eye angel / Dementia / Halycon nights / Tool marks / Mystery copter / Particle accelerator / Weakling / Thistle suit / Bullhorn bludge.

— **MIKE MONGRAIN** – drums; repl. WASHAM

Amphetam. Reptile / Amphetam. Reptile

May 98. (7") *(SCALE 096)* **OBSCENE HAND. / KEVORKIAN'S HOLIDAY**

Up / Up

Jul 98. (7") *(UP 055)* **TAD. /**

TALAS

Formed: Buffalo, New York, USA . . . 1979 by BILLY SHEEHAN, a bass player of immense talent. He invited into his band, DAVE CONSTANTINO (guitar) and PAUL VARGA (drums), issuing an eponymous self-financed debut set the following year. This led to a deal with 'Food For Thought', the resulting follow-up, 'SINK YOUR TEETH INTO THAT' (1982) being another hard rocking platform for SHEEHAN's dextrous bass plucking. His much envied skills were subsequently sought out by UFO who wanted a quick replacement for the WAYSTED-bound, PETE WAY. He eventually resurrected the TALAS name with a complete new line-up numbering PHIL NARO (vocals), MITCH PERRY (guitar) and MARK MILLER (drums), a concert set, 'LIVE SPEED ON ICE' surfacing in 1984. The record proved to be TALAS's epitaph as SHEEHAN took up an offer from the solo venturing, DAVID LEE ROTH. He gained even greater success as part of semi-supergroup MR.BIG alongside PAUL GILBERT.

Album rating: TALAS (*5) / SINK YOUR TEETH INTO THAT (*6) / LIVE SPEED ON ICE (*4) / THE TALAS YEARS compilation (*6)

BILLY SHEEHAN – vocals, bass / **DAVE CONSTANTINO** – guitar / **PAUL VARGA** – drums, vocals

not iss. / Evenfall

1980. (lp) <EF 401> **TALAS**
– See saw / Stop! in the name of love / Most people / She don't know / Any other day / My little girl / Thick head / You / Expert on me / Baby, it sure looks great. *(UK-iss.Sep91 on 'Metal Blade' cd/lp; CD+/ZORRO 32)*

not iss. / Relativity

1982. (lp) <EMCL 8001> **SINK YOUR TEETH INTO THAT**
– Sink your teeth into that / Hit and run / NV 43345 / High speed on ice / Shy boy / King of the world / Outside lookin' in / Never see me cry / Smart lady / Hick town. *(UK-iss.Aug86 on 'Food For Thought'; GRUB 1) (cd-iss. Sep91; CDGRUB 1)*

— now with **PHIL NARO** – vocals (ex-CHAIN REACTION) / **MITCH PERRY** – guitar / **MARK MILLER** – drums

not iss. / Combat

1984. (lp) <MX 8005> **LIVE SPEED ON ICE (live)**
– Sink your teeth into that / Crystal clear / The Farandole / Do you feel any better / Lone rock / King of the world / Inner mounting flame / 7718 (3 A 17) / High speed on ice / Shyboy.

— SHEEHAN had already been on the wanted list for some time (he had helped out UFO on a 1982 European tour), so it wasn't surprising when he joined DAVE LEE ROTH. He subsequently formed the highly fruitful MR. BIG.

– compilations, etc. –

1990. (cd; as BILLY SHEEHAN) *Combat;* <1020> **THE TALAS YEARS**
– Sink your teeth into that / Hit and run / NV4 3345 / High speed on ice / Shy boy / King of the world / Outside lookin' in / Never see me cry / Smart lady / Hick town / Sink your teeth into that (live) / Crystal clear / The farandole / Do you feel any better / Lone rock / King of the world / Inner mounting flame / 7718 (3A17) / High speed on ice (live) / Shy boy (live).

TALK SHOW (see under ⇒ STONE TEMPLE PILOTS)

TANGIER

Formed: Philadelphia, USA . . . 1984 by whiskey-throated vocalist BILL MATTSON and main songwriter DOUG GORDON, who subsequently completed the line-up with MIKE KOST, ROCCO MAZELLA and MARK HOPKINS. This formation initially toured the group's footstomping hard/blues rock, the latter two eventually being succeeded by CARL SAINT and BOBBY BENDER respectively. Their hard work eventually paid off as the band secured a deal with 'Atco', the debut album, 'FOUR WINDS' (1989), displaying TANGIER's earthy AOR and duly scraping them a place in the US Top 100 (the single, 'ON THE LINE', having already achieved a similar feat). At the turn of the decade, the band chose another frontman, MIKE LeCOMPTE to replace both MATTSON and SAINT for the second and final set, 'STRANDED' (1991). Despite its melodic approach, it lingered in the nether regions of the US charts, TANGIER possibly going back to the drawing board or even exotic holiday brochures for another thought-provoking moniker.

Album rating: FOUR WINDS (*5) / STRANDED (*5)

BILL MATTSON – vocals / **DOUG GORDON** – guitar / **CARL SAINT** – guitar; repl. ROCCO MAZELLA / **GARRY NUTT** – bass; repl. MIKE KOST / **BOBBY BENDER** – drums; repl. MARK HOPKINS

Atco Atco

Jul 89. (lp/c/cd) *(979125-1/-4/-2) <91251>* **FOUR WINDS** [ ] [91]
– Ripcord / Mississippi / On the line / In time / Four winds / Fever for gold / Southbound train / Sweet surrender / Bad girl / Good lovin'.

Jul 89. (7") *<99208>* **ON THE LINE. / SWEET SURRENDER** [-] [67]

— now without MATTSON + SAINT, who were repl. by **MIKE LeCOMPTE** – vocals, keyboards, guitar

Feb 91. (cd/c/lp) *<(7567 91603-2/-4/-1)>* **STRANDED** [ ] [ ]
– Down the line / Caution to the wind / You're not the lovin' kind / Since you been gone / Takes just a little time / Excited / Back in the limelight / Stranded / It's hard if ya can't find love.

— their new AOR approach won no new fanbase, thus their quick demise

TANK

Formed: London, England . . . 1980 by former punk rocker, ALGY WARD (ex-DAMNED, ex-SAINTS), plus the BRABBS brothers PETER and MARK. The following year, TANK signed to 'Kamaflage' records, rolling out their FAST EDDIE CLARKE-produced debut 45, 'DON'T WALK AWAY'. In fact, the MOTORHEAD veteran worked on most of their early work, 'FILTH HOUND OF HADES' (1982), drawing inevitable comparisons to LEMMY and Co., although it still managed to career into the UK Top 40. Later that year, TANK blasted out another barrage of blackened metal shrapnel, 'POWER OF THE HUNTER', although this was their last for the soon-to-be defunct label. Adding guitarist MICK TUCKER, they signed a deal with 'Music For Nations', releasing a concept set, 'THIS MEANS WAR' (1983), based on the current Falklands Conflict. The BRABBS departed prior to another dubiously war-inspired album, 'HONOUR AND BLOOD' (1984), their places having been filled by GRAEME CRALLAN (guitarist CLIFF EVANS augmenting on tour). With GARY TAYLOR now powering TANK's rhythm engine, the band reported for duty in 1988 with the eponymous 'TANK' album before going AWOL once again.

Album rating: FILTH HOUNDS OF HADES (*6) / POWER OF THE HUNTER (*7) / THIS MEANS WAR (*7) / HONOUR AND BLOOD (*4) / ARMOURED PLATED compilation (*6) / TANK (*3) / RETURN OF THE FILTH HOUNDS LIVE (*4)

ALGY WARD – vocals, bass (ex-DAMNED, ex-SAINTS) / **PETER BRABBS** – guitar, vocals / **MARK BRABBS** – drums

Kamaflage Action

Sep 81. (7"m) *(KAM 1)* **DON'T WALK AWAY. / SHELLSHOCK / HAMMER ON** [ ] [-]

Feb 82. (7") *(KAM 3)* **TURN YOUR HEAD AROUND. / STEPPIN' ON A LANDMINE** [ ] [-]

Mar 82. (lp) *(KAMLP 1) <4149>* **FILTH HOUNDS OF HADES** [33] [ ]
– Shellshock / Struck by lightning / Run like hell / Blood, guts & beer / T.W.D.A.M.O. (That's What Dreams Are Made Of) / Turn your head around / Heavy artillery / Who needs love songs / Filth hounds of Hades / (He fell in love with a) Stormtrooper. *(w/free 7") (KAMF 1)* – DON'T WALK AWAY (live). / THE SNAKE *(cd-iss. Aug91 on 'Repertoire'; REP 4149-WP)*

Kamaflage This Record Co.

Sep 82. (7") *(KAM 7)* **CRAZY HORSES. / FILTH BITCH BOOGIE** [ ] [-]

Oct 82. (lp) *(KAMLP 3) <4150>* **POWER OF THE HUNTER** [ ] [ ]
– Walking barefoot over glass / Pure hatred / Biting and scratching / Some came running / T.A.N.K. / Used leather (hanging loose) / Crazy horses / Set your back on fire / Red skull rock / Power of the hunter. *(cd-iss. Aug91 on 'Repertoire'; REP 4150-WP)*

Nov 82. (7"pic-d) *(KAP 1)* **(HE FELL IN LOVE WITH A) STORMTROOPER. / BLOOD GUTS AND BEER** [ ] [-]

— added **MICK TUCKER** – guitar (ex-WHITE SPIRIT)

Music For Nations Attic

May 83. (m-lp/m-c) *(MFN/TMFN 3)* **THIS MEANS WAR** [ ] [-]
– Just like something from Hell / Hot lead cold steel / This means war / Laughing in the face of war / (If we go) We go down fighting / I (won't ever let you down) / Echoes of a distant battle. *(pic-lp Jun83; MFN 3P) (cd-iss. Sep97 on 'High Vaultage'; HV 1008)*

Jul 83. (7") *(KUT 101)* **ECHOES OF A DISTANT BATTLE. / THE MAN THAT NEVER WAS** [ ] [-]
(12"+=) *(12KUT 101)* – Whichcatchewedmycuckoo.

— the BRABBS were repl. by **GRAEME CRALLAN** – drums (CLIFF EVANS also augmented guitar on tour)

Dec 84. (lp) *(MFN 26)* **HONOUR AND BLOOD** [ ] [-]
– The war drags ever on / When all Hell freezes over / Honour and blood / Chain of fools / W.M.L.A. (Wasted My Love Away) / Too tired to wait for love / Kill. *(cd-iss. Sep97 on 'High Vaultage'; HV 1009)*

— **GARY TAYLOR** – drums; repl. TUCKER

G.W.R. Enigma

Mar 88. (lp/c/cd) *(GW LP/TC/CD 23) <71405>* **TANK** [ ] [ ]
– Reign of thunder / March on, sons of Nippon / With your life / None but the brave / The enemy below / Lost / (The hell they must) Suffer / It fell from the sky.

— split in 1989 when on tour in the States; re-formed briefly below

Rising Sun Rising Sun

Aug 98. (cd) *(<RS 0082032CD>)* **RETURN OF THE FILTH HOUNDS (live)** [ ] [ ]
– This means war / Echoes of a distant battle / T.W.D.A.M.O. / And then we heard the thunder / Don't walk away / Honour and blood / Power of the hunter / Shellshock / In the last hour before dawn.

– compilations, etc. –

Apr 86. (d-lp/c) *Raw Power; (RAW LP/TC 009)* **ARMOURED PLATED** [ ] [-]
– Don't walk away / Power of the hunter / Run like hell / Filth hounds of Hades / (He fell in love with a) Stormtrooper / Red skull rock / The snake / Who needs love songs / Steppin' on a landmine / Turn your head around / Crazy horses / Some came running / Hammer on / Shellshock / T.W.D.A.M.O. / Biting and scratching / Used leather (hanging loose) / Blood, guts and beer / Filth bitch boogie / T.A.N.K.

TANKARD

Formed: Germany . . . 1982 by hardened beer-drinkers GERRE, AXEL, ANDY, FRANK and OLIVER. Perhaps the only metal outfit devoted solely to the pleasures of alcohol, TANKARD slurred their way on to the thrash scene with their 'Noise' records debut, 'ZOMBIE ATTACK' (1986). A concept piece of sorts, 'CHEMICAL INVASION' (1987), reflected upon the outrageous practice of polluting good German beer with additives. Their third album, appropriately titled, 'THE MORNING AFTER' (1988), saw them at their beer-soaked best, the track 'SHIT-FACED' describing in no uncertain terms what it meant to be a TANKARD drinker. Unsurprisingly, their quintessentially German brand of humour failed to light UK fans' fire, although 90's albums such as, 'HAIR OF THE DOG' (1990), 'THE MEANING OF LIFE' (1990), 'FAT UGLY AND LIVE' (1991) and 'STONE COLD SOBER' (1992) were a good soundtrack preceding a good night on the piss. TANKARD and its contents went flat in 1994, after a disastrous attempt to go "serious" on their final thrash-metal effort, 'TWO-FACED'.

Album rating: ZOMBIE ATTACK (*5) / CHEMICAL INVASION (*5) / THE MORNING AFTER (*6) / HAIR OF THE DOG (*4) / THE MEANING OF LIFE (*5) / FAT, UGLY AND LIVE (*4) / STONE COLD SOBER (*5) / ALIEN mini (*5) / TWO FACED (*4) / DISCO DESTROYER (*4) / KINGS OF BEER (*4)

GERRE – vocals / **AXEL** – guitar / **ANDY** – guitar / **FRANK** – bass / **OLIVER** – drums

Noise not iss.

Nov 86. (lp) *(N 0046)* **ZOMBIE ATTACK** [-] [-] German
– Zombie attack / Acid death / Mercenary / Maniac forces / Alcohol / (Empty) Tankard / Thrash till death / Chains / Poison / Screamin' victims. *(UK-iss.Oct89 cd/c/lp; CD/ZC+/NUK 046)*

Nov 87. (lp) *(N 0096)* **CHEMICAL INVASION** [-] [-] German
– Total addiction / Tantrum / Don't panic / Puke / For a thousand beers / Chemical invasion / Farewell to a slut / Traitor / Alcohol. *(pic-lp Mar88; NP 0096) (UK-iss.Oct89 cd/c/lp; CD/ZC+/NUK 096) (re-iss. Nov97 c/cd; N 0097/+2)*

1988. (lp/cd) *(N 0123-1/-3)* **THE MORNING AFTER** [-] [-] German
– Commandments / Shit-faced / TV hero / F.U.N. / Try again / The morning after / Desperation / Feed the lohocla / Help yourself / Mon Cheri. *(UK-iss.Oct89 cd/c/lp; CD/ZC+/NUK 123)*

Apr 89. (m-lp/m-cd) *(N 0131-1/-3)* **ALIEN** [ ] [-]
– Alien / 666 packs / Live to dive / Remedy / (Empty) Tankard.

Apr 90. (cd/c/lp) *(CD/ZC+/NUK 150)* **HAIR OF THE DOG** [ ] [-]
– The morning after / Alien / Don't panic / Zombie attack / Chemical invasion / Commandments / Tantrum / Maniac forces / Shit-faced / (Empty) Tankard.

Sep 90. (cd/c/lp) *(CD/ZC+/NUK 156)* **THE MEANING OF LIFE** [ ] [-]
– Open all night / We are us / Dancing on our grave / Mechanical man / Beermuda / Meaning of life / Space beer / Always them / Wheel of rebirth / Barfly.

Jul 91. (cd/c/lp) *(N 0166-2/-4/-1)* **FAT, UGLY AND LIVE (live)** [ ] [-]
– The meaning of life / Mercenary / Beermuda / Total addiction / Poison / We are us * / Maniac forces * / Live to die / Chemical invasion / The morning after / Space beer / Medley:- Alcohol – Puke – Mon Cheri – Wonderful life / (Empty) Tankard. *(cd+= *)*

Jun 92. (cd/c/lp) *(N 0190-2/-4/-1)* **STONE COLD SOBER** [ ] [-]
– Jurisdiction / Broken image / Mindwild / Ugly beauty / Centrefold / Behind the back / Stone cold sober / Blood, guts and rock'n'roll / Lost and found (Tantrum part 2) / Sleeping with the past / Freibier / Of strange people talking under Arabian skies.

Feb 94. (cd/c/lp) *(N 0233-2/-4/-1)* **TWO-FACED** [ ] [-]
– Death penalty / R.T.V. / Betrayed / Nation over nation / Days of the gun / Cities in flames / Up from zero / Two-faced / Ich brauch meinen suff / Cyberworld / Mainhattan / Jimmy B. Bad.

Century Media Century Media

Apr 98. (cd) *(CM 77209-2)* **DISCO DESTROYER** [ ] [ ]
– Serial killer / http://www.Planetwide-Suicide.com / Hard rock dinosaur / Queen of hearts / U-R-B / Mr. Superlover / Tankard roach motel / Another perfect day / Death by whips / Away! / Face of the enemy / Splendid boyz / Disco destroyer.

Jun 00. (cd) *(CM 77274-2)* **KINGS OF BEER** [ ] [ ]
– Flirtin' with disaster / Dark exile / Hot dog inferno / Hell bent for Jesus / Kings of beer / I'm so sorry! / Talk show prostitute / Incredible loudness / Land of the free / Mirror, mirror / Tattoo coward.

TAPROOT

Formed: Ann Arbor, Michigan, USA . . . 1997 by University of Michigan students STEPHEN RICHARDS, MIKE DeWOLF, PHIL LIPSCOMB and JARROD MONTAGUE. Inspired by the likes of NIRVANA and RAGE AGAINST THE MACHINE, TAPROOT began using the internet for publicity and eventually appropriated a fan's web page as their official site. With a bit of DIY improvement, the site soon generated enough interest for the band to distribute a demo to LIMP BIZKIT mainman FRED DURST. A growing friendship ended in tears after DURST allegedly offered a below par deal and TAPROOT looked elsewhere, resulting in a now infamous answering machine message from the pissed off 'BIZKIT mainman. Undeterred, the group released their self-produced debut album, 'SOMETHING MORE THAN NOTHING' (1998) off their own steam, following it up with the 'MENTOBE' EP. Their internet endeavours together with word of mouth publicity soon attracted major label interest, the band signing with 'Atlantic' for their second album, 'GIFT'

(2000). Awarded 5 stars by Kerrang!, the record bore favourable comparison with rap-influenced nu-metal pioneers such as KORN and DEFTONES with a conspicuous lack of any contrived image going in their favour.

Album rating: GIFT (*7)

STEPHEN RICHARDS – vocals / **MIKE DeWOLF** – guitar / **PHIL LIPSCOMB** – bass / **JARROD MONTAGUE** – drums

Atlantic Atlantic

Sep 00. (cd) *<(7567 83341-2)>* **GIFT** Jun00
– Smile / Again and again / Emotional times / Now / 1 nite stand / Believed / Mentobe / I / Mirror's reflection / Dragged down / Comeback / Impact.

Mar 01. (cd-s) *(AT 0099CD)* **AGAIN AND AGAIN (clean version) / DAY BY DAY / SMILE (clean version)** -

TASTE (see under ⇒ GALLAGHER, Rory)

TATER TOTZ (see under ⇒ REDD KROSS)

TATTOOED LOVE BOYS

Formed: London, England ... 1987 by GARY MIELLE and MICK RANSOME, who enlisted CRIS C.J. JAGDHAR and DARAYUS Z. KAYE. Building a live reputation around the English capital, the band issued a one-off single, 'WHY WALTZ WHEN YOU CAN ROCK'N'ROLL' for the 'Thunderbolt' label, known for its re-issues rather than its new signings. Opting for a transfer to 'Episode', the 'BOYS finally made their mark with their debut album, 'BLEEDING HEARTS AND NEEDLE MARKS' (1989). The bleach-blonde sleaze metal on show suggested that this bunch were serious L.A. wannabes, the record tracing an outline from NEW YORK DOLLS to HANOI ROCKS. C.J. subsequently took off for fellow London upstarts, The QUIREBOYS, before finding even greater fame as a member of The WILDHEARTS. Beefing up their sound, they enlisted two guitarists, MARC AHA CHAN and ADAM GODZIKOWSKI to play on their follow-up set, 'NO TIME FOR NURSERY RHYMES' (1990). However, these two didn't feature in the band's future plans as a major reshuffle saw them and DARAYUS being replaced by NICK SINGLETON, CHRIS DANBY and DEAN MARSHALL, a mooted third album never appearing.

Album rating: BLEEDING HEARTS AND NEEDLE MARKS (*6) / NO TIME FOR NURSERY RHYMES (*4)

GARY MIELLE – vocals / **CRIS C.J. JAGDHAR** – guitar / **DARAYUS Z. KAYE** – bass / **MICK RANSOME** – drums (ex-PRAYING MANTIS)

Thunderbolt not iss.

Jul 88. (12") *(TLB 001)* **WHY WALTZ WHEN YOU CAN ROCK'N'ROLL. /** -

Episode Caroline

May 89. (lp/c/cd) *(LUS LP/MC/CD 1) <CAROL/+C/CD 1380>* **BLEEDING HEARTS AND NEEDLE MARKS**
– Why waltz when you rock'n'roll / Read my lips / Stale lipstick / Ride lonesome / Doin' it for the jazz / Sweet little ragamuffin / Stikky stuff / Chase the ace / Saturday nite / Who ya bringing to the party.

— **MARC AHA CHAN** – guitars (ex-GIN $LING) + **ADAM GODZIKOWSKI** – guitar; repl. C.J. who joined QUIREBOYS (and later WILDHEARTS)

Aug 89. (12") *(12LUS 1)* **BREAKDOWN DEAD AHEAD / SNAKEBITE. / (YOU WON'T SEE ME) GROWING OLD WITH GRACE (live) / THE HOP (live)** -

Aug 90. (cd/c/lp) *(LUS CD/MC/LP 7)* **NO TIME FOR NURSERY RHYMES** -
– No time for nursery rhymes / Real long way / Mystery train / Fat cat / Breakdown dead ahead / Doin' damage / White lightning / Snakebite / Shake dog shake / Blood on roses. *(re-iss. Nov91 on 'Music For Nations' cd/c/lp; CD/T+/MFN 120)*

— **NICK SINGLETON** – guitar; repl. MARC

— **CHRIS DANBY** – rhythm guitar; repl. ADAM

— **DEAN MARSHALL** – bass; repl. DARAYUS

— folded soon after above

TEASER (see under ⇒ VANDENBERG)

TEMPLE OF THE DOG (see under ⇒ SOUNDGARDEN)

TEN YEARS AFTER

Formed: Nottingham, England . . . summer '65 (originally as covers act The JAYBIRDS in 1961) by ALVIN LEE (vocals and guitar) and LEO LYONS (bass). The following year, they relocated to London, recruiting RIC LEE (drums) and CHICK CHURCHILL (keyboards) and adopting the name, TEN YEARS AFTER. A key forerunner of the forthcoming British blues revival (i.e. FLEETWOOD MAC, CHICKEN, SAVOY BROWN, etc.), LEE, known for his nimble fingered, lightning strike guitar playing, secured a deal (through manager, Chris Wright) with Decca offshoot label, 'Deram'. An eponymous debut set was released in '67, although the prevailing trend for for everything flower-power ensured the record met with limited interest. Building up a strong grassroots following through electric stage shows, TEN YEARS AFTER took a calculated risk by releasing a live set recorded at Klook's Kleek, 'UNDEAD' (1968), the album rewarding TYA with a Top 30 breakthrough. Early in '69, they released a third set, 'STONEDHENGE', a surprise Top 10 success (the record also saw them crack the American market) that included their best piece to date, 'HEAR ME CALLING'. To coincide with a forthcoming Woodstock appearance, the band delivered their second set of the year, 'SSSSH', not exactly a hush hush affair but a blistering melange of blues, boogie and country that became the first of three consecutive UK Top 5 albums (US Top 20, well nearly!). LEE's celebrated performance of the epic 11 minute track 'GOIN' HOME' at the aforesaid Woodstock Festival went down in rock history, thrusting the band into the premier league of blues rock acts (the song featured on the subsequent film and soundtrack). The band blazed their way through the early 70's on albums, 'CRICKLEWOOD GREEN' and 'WATT', the former spawning a UK Top 10 hit, 'LOVE LIKE A MAN' in 1970. A subsequent change of both label ('Chrysalis') and music style (following the prevailing trend for electronic progressive rock) for late '71's 'A SPACE IN TIME', saw the band losing substantial ground (critically and commercially). However, due to a Top 40 hit, 'I'D LOVE TO CHANGE THE WORLD', the album still maintained Top 20 status in the US. The ensuing few years saw TEN YEARS AFTER treading water, albums such 'ROCK & ROLL MUSIC TO THE WORLD' (1972), 'TEN YEARS AFTER (RECORDED LIVE)' (1973) and 'POSITIVE VIBRATIONS' (1974) poor reflections of his/their former achievements. It was clear by the last of these that LEE was eager to experiment outside the band framework, a 1973 collaborative project with US gospel singer, MYLON LeFEVRE, resulting in 'ON THE ROAD TO FREEDOM'. The guitarist then formed a new outfit, ALVIN LEE & CO. releasing a handful of unconvincing albums in the mid 70's. From that point on, LEE alternated between various solo incarnations and in 1989 (after a trial at a 4-day German festival the previous year), he reformed a revamped TEN YEARS AFTER for a one-off album, appropriately titled, 'ABOUT TIME'. LEE continues to spread the blues gospel to an ever faithful band of ageing worldwide disciples.

• **Songwriters:** Apart from basic covers act The JAYBIRDS, ALVIN LEE penned and co-wrote with STEVE GOULD in the 80's. Covered; HELP ME (Sonny Boy Williamson) / SPOONFUL (Willie Dixon) / AT THE WOODCHOPPER'S BALL (Woody Herman) / SWEET LITTLE SIXTEEN (Chuck Berry) / GOOD MORNING LITTLE SCHOOLGIRL (Don & Bob) / GOING BACK TO BIRMINGHAM (Little Richard) / etc.

Album rating: TEN YEARS AFTER (*6) / UNDEAD (*7) / STONEDHENGE (*6) / SSSSH (*7) / CRICKLEWOOD GREEN (*7) / WATT (*6) / A SPACE IN TIME (*5) / ALVIN LEE & COMPANY compilation (*6) / ROCK'N'ROLL MUSIC TO THE WORLD (*4) / RECORDED LIVE (*4) / ON THE ROAD TO FREEDOM (*4; by Alvin Lee & Mylon LeFevre) / POSITIVE VIBRATIONS (*4) / IN FLIGHT (*4; by Alvin Lee & Co.) / GOIN' HOME! THEIR GREATEST HITS compilation (*7) / PUMP IRON! (*5; by Alvin Lee & Co.) / LET IT ROCK (*4; by Alvin Lee) / ROCKET FUEL (*4; by Alvin Lee – Ten Years Later) / RIDE ON (*4; Alvin Lee – Ten Years Later) / FREE FALL (*4; by Alvin Lee Band) / RX5 (*3; by Alvin Lee Band) / DETROIT DIESEL (*4; by Alvin Lee) / ABOUT TIME (*5) / ZOOM (*4; by Alvin Lee) / THE ESSENTIAL TEN YEARS AFTER compilation (*7) / NINETEEN NINETY FOUR (*4; by Alvin Lee) / I HEAR YOU ROCKIN' (*3; by Alvin Lee) / LIVE IN VIENNA (*3; by Alvin Lee) / PURE BLUES (*4; by Alvin Lee & Ten Years After)

(Aug'65) **ALVIN** (b. GRAHAM BARNES, 19 Dec'44) – vocals, guitar + **LEO** (b.30 Nov'43, Bedfordshire) – bass; recruited **RIC LEE** (b.20 Oct'45, Cannock, England) – drums (ex-MANSFIELDS), repl. JAYBIRDS drummer DAVE QUIGMIRE

— added **CHICK CHURCHILL** (b. 2 Jan'49, Mold, Wales) – keyboards

Deram Deram

Oct 67. (lp; mono/stereo) *(DML/SML 1015) <18009>* **TEN YEARS AFTER**
– I want to know / I can't keep from crying sometimes / Adventures of a young organ / Spoonful / Losing the dogs / Feel it for me / Love until I die / Don't want you woman / Help me. *(cd-iss. May88; 820 532-2)*

Feb 68. (7") *(DM 176) <85027>* **PORTABLE PEOPLE. / THE SOUNDS**

Aug 68. (lp; mono/stereo) *(DML/SML 1023) <18016>* **UNDEAD (live at Klook's Kleek)** 26
– I may be wrong, but I won't be wrong always / Woodchopper's ball / Spider in my web / Summertime – Shantung cabbage / I'm going home. *(cd-iss. Jun88; 820 533-2)*

Nov 68. (7") *(DM 221) <85035>* **HEAR ME CALLING. / I'M GOING HOME**

Feb 69. (lp; mono/stereo) *(DML/SML 1029) <18021>* **STONEDHENGE** 6 61
– Going to try / I can't live without Lydia / Woman trouble / Skoobly-oobly-doobob / Hear me calling / A sad song / Three blind mice / No title / Faro / Speed kills. *(cd-iss. Apr89; 820 534-2) (cd-iss. Jul97 on 'Beat Goes On'; BGOCD 356)*

Aug 69. (lp) *(SML 1052) <18029>* **SSSSH** 4 20
– Bad scene / Two time woman / Stoned woman / Good morning little schoolgirl / If you should love me / I don't know that you don't know my name / The stomp / I woke up this morning. *(re-iss. Jul75 on 'Chrysalis' lp/c; CHR/ZCHR 1083) (cd-iss. Mar94 on 'Chrysalis'; CD25CR 05) (cd re-iss. Feb97 on 'Beat Goes On'; BGOCD 338)*

Apr 70. (lp) *(SML 1065) <18038>* **CRICKLEWOOD GREEN** 4 14
– Sugar the road / Working on the road / 50,000 miles beneath my brain / Year 3,000 blues / Me and my baby / Love like a man / Circles / As the sun still burns away. *(re-iss. Jul75 on 'Chrysalis' lp/c; CHR/ZCHR 1084) (re-iss. Dec92 on 'Fame' cd/c; CD/TC FA 3287) (re-iss. Jul94 cd/c; CD/TC CHR 1084) (cd re-iss. Oct96 on 'EMI Gold'; CDGOLD 1052) (lp-iss.Aug00 on 'Simply Vinyl'; SVLP 235)*

May 70. (7") *(DM 299) <7529>* **LOVE LIKE A MAN. / LOVE LIKE A MAN (live at 33 rpm)** 10 98
(re-iss. while still into UK chart run; DM 310)

Jan 71. (lp) *(SML 1078) <18050>* **WATT** 5 21
– I'm coming on / My baby left me / Think about the times / I say yeah / The band with no name / Gonna run / She lies in the morning / Sweet little sixteen. *(re-iss. Jul75 on 'Chrysalis' lp/c; CHR/ZCHR 1085) (cd-iss. Apr97 on 'Beat Goes On'; BGOCD 345)*

Chrysalis Columbia

Nov 71. (lp/c) *(CHR/ZCHR 1001) <30801>* **A SPACE IN TIME** 36 17 Aug71
– One of these days / Here they come / I'd love to change the world / Over the hill / Baby won't you let me rock'n'roll you / Once there was a time / Let the sky fall /

Hard monkeys / I've been there too / Uncle Jam. *(cd-iss. Jun97 on 'Beat Goes On'; BGOCD 351)*

Sep 71. (7") *<45457>* **I'D LOVE TO CHANGE THE WORLD. / LET THE SKY FALL** - 40

Jan 72. (7") *<45530>* **BABY WON'T YOU LET ME ROCK'N'ROLL YOU. / ONCE THERE WAS A TIME** - 61

Oct 72. (lp/c) *(CHR/ZCHR 1009) <31779>* **ROCK & ROLL MUSIC TO THE WORLD** 27 43
– You give me loving / Convention prevention / Turned off T.V. blues / Standing at the station / You can't win them all / Religion / Choo choo mama / Tomorrow I'll be out of town / Rock & roll music to the world. *(cd-iss. May97 on 'Beat Goes On'; BGOCD 348)*

Nov 72. (7") *<45736>* **CHOO CHOO MAMA. / YOU CAN'T WIN THEM ALL** - 89

Feb 73. (7") *<45787>* **TOMORROW, I'LL BE OUT OF TOWN. / CONVENTION PREVENTION** -

Jul 73. (7") *<45915>* **I'M GOING HOME. / YOU GIVE ME LOVING** -

Jul 73. (d-lp/d-c) *(CTY/ZCTY 1049) <32288>* **TEN YEARS AFTER (RECORDED LIVE)** 36 39 Jun73
– One of these days / You give me loving / Good morning little schoolgirl / Hobbit / Help me / Classical thing / Scat thing / I can't keep from cryin' sometimes (part 1) / Extension on one chord / I can't keep from cryin' sometimes (part 2) / Silly thing / Slow blues in 'C' / I'm going home / Choo choo mama. *(cd-iss. Apr97 on 'Beat Goes On'; BGOCD 341)*

Apr 74. (lp) *(CHR 1060) <32851>* **POSITIVE VIBRATIONS** 81
– Nowhere to run / Positive vibrations / Stone me / Without you / Going back to Birmingham / It's getting harder / You're driving me crazy / Look into my life / Look me straight into the eyes / I wanted to boogie.

Apr 74. (7") *<46061>* **I WANTED TO BOOGIE. / IT'S GETTING HARDER** -

— Disbanded after CHICK CHURCHILL made a solo album 'YOU AND ME' in Feb'74 (CHR 1051).

ALVIN LEE & MYLON LeFEVRE

with the US solo gospel singer plus TRAFFIC members on session plus GEORGE HARRISON and RON WOOD

Nov 73. (7") *<45987>* **SO SAD. / RIFFIN** -

Nov 73. (lp) *(CHR 1054) <32729>* **ON THE ROAD TO FREEDOM**
– On the road to freedom / The world is changing / So sad (no love of his own) / Fallen angel / Funny / We will shine / Carry me load / Lay me back / Let 'em say what they will / I can't take it / Riffin / Rockin' til the sun goes down.

Jan 74. (7") *(CHS 2020)* **THE WORLD IS CHANGING. / RIFFIN**

ALVIN LEE & CO.

with **NEIL HUBBARD** – guitar / **ALAN SPENNER** – bass / **TIM HINKLEY** – keyboards / **IAN WALLACE** – drums / **MEL COLLINS** – saxophone

Nov 74. (d-lp) *(CTY 1069) <33187>* **ALVIN LEE & CO: IN FLIGHT (live gig)** 65
– (intro) / Let's get back / Ride my train / There's a feeling / Running around / Mystery train / Slow down / Keep a knocking / How many times / I've got my eyes for you baby / I'm writing you a letter / Got to keep moving / Going through the door / Don't be cruel / Money honey / I'm writing you a letter / You need love love love / Freedom for the stallion / Every blues you've ever heard / All life's trials. *(cd-iss. Jun00 on 'Repertoire'; REP 4702)*

— touring band **HINKLEY / ANDY PYLE** – bass / **BRYSON GRAHAM** – drums / studio **RONNIE LEAHY** – keyboards / **STEVE THOMPSON** – bass / **IAN WALLACE** – drums

Oct 75. (lp) *(CHR 1094) <33796>* **PUMP IRON!** Sep75
– One more chance / Try to be righteous / You told me / Have mercy / Julian Rice / Time and space / Burnt fungus / The darkest night / It's alright now / Truckin' down the other way / Let the sea burn down. *(cd-iss. Jun00 on 'Repertoire'; REP 4703)*

— an album 'SAGUITAR' was shelved in 1976

Dec 78. (lp/c; ALVIN LEE) *(CHR/ZCHR 1190)* **LET IT ROCK** -
– Chemicals, chemistry, mystery & more / Love the way you rock me / Ain't nobody / Images shifting / Little boy / Downhill lady racer / World is spinning faster / Through with your lovin' / Time to mediate / Let it rock. *(cd-iss. Jun00 on 'Repertoire'; REP 4704)*

ALVIN LEE – TEN YEARS LATER

with **TOM COMPTON** – drums / **MICK HAWKSWORTH** – bass (ex-ANDROMEDA)

Polydor R.S.O.

Apr 78. (lp) *(2344 103) <3033>* **ROCKET FUEL**
– Rocket fuel / Gonna turn you on / Friday the 13th / Somebody's calling me / Ain't nothin' shakin' / Alvin's blue thing / Baby don't you cry / The Devil's screaming. *(cd-iss. Mar00 on 'Repertoire'; REP 4788)*

Sep 79. (lp) *(2310 678) <3049>* **RIDE ON (live studio)** May79
– Ain't nothin' shakin' / Scat encounter / Hey Joe / Going home / Too much / It's a gaz / Ride on cowboy / Sitin' here / Can't sleep at nite. *(cd-iss. Mar00 on 'Repertoire'; REP 4787)*

Sep 79. (7") *(2001 930)* **RIDE ON COWBOY. / SITTIN' HERE** -

Sep 79. (7") **RIDE ON COWBOY. / CAN'T SLEEP AT NITE** -

ALVIN LEE BAND

— retained **COMPTON** and added **STEVE GOULD** – guitar (ex-RARE BIRD) / **MICKEY FEAT** – bass (ex-STREETWALKERS)

Avatar Atlantic

Oct 80. (lp) *(AALP 5002)* **FREE FALL**
– I don't wanna stop / Take the money / One lonely hour / Heartache / Stealin' / Ridin' truckin' / No more lonely nights / City lights / Sooner or later / Dustbin city. *(cd-iss. Jun00 on 'Repertoire'; REP 4705)*

Nov 80. (7") *(AAA 106)* **I DON'T WANNA STOP. / HEARTACHE** -

Mar 81. (7") **RIDIN' TRUCKIN'. /** -

Jul 81. (7") *(AAA 109)* **TAKE THE MONEY. / NO MORE LONELY NIGHTS** -

Oct 81. (7") **CAN'T STOP. /** -

Nov 81. (lp) *(AALP 5006) <19306>* **RX5**
– Hang on / Lady luck / Can't stop / Wrong side of the law / Nutbush city limits / Rock-n roll guitar picker / Double loser / Fool no more / Dangerous world / High times. *(cd-iss. Jun00 on 'Repertoire'; REP 4706)*

Dec 81. (7") *(AAA 117)* **ROCK'N'ROLL GUITAR PICKER. / DANGEROUS WORLD**

Mar 82. (7") *(AAA 122)* **NUTBUSH CITY LIMITS. / HIGH TIMES**

— **MICK TAYLOR** – guitar (ex-ROLLING STONES) / **FUZZY SAMUELS** – bass (ex-CROSBY, STILLS & NASH) repl. GOULD & FEAT

— split early 1982.

ALVIN LEE

recorded another solo with **LYONS + GEORGE HARRISON**

Viceroy 21 records

Aug 86. (cd) *(VIN 8032-2) <210019>* **DETROIT DIESEL** Feb87
– Detroit diesel / Shot in the dark / Too late to run for cover / Talk don't bother me / Ordinary man / Heart of stone / She's so cute / Back in my arms again / Don't want to fight / Let's go. *(cd-iss. Apr97 on 'Viceroy'; same)*

Sep 86. (7") **DETROIT DIESEL. / LET'S GO** -

Jan 87. (7") **HEART OF STONE. / SHE'S SO CUTE** -

— Signed to 'No Speak' records, but had no releases. In Apr'89, ALVIN guested on Various Artists live cd,c,-d-lp 'NIGHT OF THE GUITAR' for 'I.R.S.' label.

TEN YEARS AFTER

originals re-formed with **ALVIN LEE + STEVE GOULD** plus?

Chrysalis Chrysalis

Nov 89. (lp/c/cd) *(CHR/ZCHR/CCD 1722) <21722>* **ABOUT TIME**
– Highway of love / Let's shake it up / I get all shook up / Victim of circumstance / Going to Chicago / Wild is the river / Saturday night / Bad blood / Working in a parking lot / Outside my window / Waiting for the judgement day.

Nov 89. (7") *(CHS 3447)* **HIGHWAY OF LOVE. / ROCK & ROLL MUSIC TO THE WORLD**

ALVIN LEE

Sequel Domino

Oct 92. (cd/c) *(NED CD/MC 225) <8003>* **ZOOM**
– A little bit of love / Jenny Jenny / Remember me / Anything for you / The price of this love / Real life blues / It don't come easy / Lost in love / Wake up moma / Moving the blues / Use that power. *(re-iss. Oct95 on 'Thunderbolt' cd)(c; CDTB 171)(CTC 0201)*

H.T.D. not iss.

Oct 93. (cd/c) *(HTD CD/MC 14)* **NINETEEN NINETY FOUR** -
– Keep on rockin' / Long legs / I hear you knockin' / I want you (she's so heavy) / I don't give a damn / Give me your love / Play it like it used to be / Take it easy / My baby's come back to me / Boogie all day / Bluest blues / Ain't nobody's business if I do. *(cd re-iss. Mar95 & Sep99 on 'Thunderbolt'; CDTB 150) (cd re-iss. Mar00 on 'Last Call'; 422486)*

Viceroy Viceroy

Mar 94. (cd) *(<VIC 8012-2>)* **I HEAR YOU ROCKIN'**
– Keep on rockin' / Long legs / I hear you knockin' / Ain't nobody's business / Bluest blues / Boogie all day / My baby's come back to me / Take it easy / Play it like it used to play / Give me your love / I don't give a damn / I want you (she's so heavy). *(re-iss. Apr97; same)*

Coast To Coast Viceroy

Mar 95. (cd) *(CTC 0201) <8030>* **LIVE IN VIENNA (live)** Feb96
– Keep on rockin' / Long legs / I hear you knockin' / Hear me calling / Love like a man / Johnny B.Goode / I don't give a damn / Good morning little schoolgirl / Skooboly oobly doobob / Help me baby / Classical thing / Going home / Rip it up. *(re-iss. Apr97 on 'Viceroy'; VIC 80302) (re-iss. Oct98 on 'Thunderbolt'; CDTB 171) (re-iss. Mar00 on 'Last Call'; 422507)*

ALVIN LEE & TEN YEARS AFTER

Chrysalis Capitol

Jul 95. (cd/c) *(CD/TC CHR 6102) <33450>* **PURE BLUES**
– Don't want you woman / Bluest blues / I woke up this morning / Real life blues / Stomp / Slow blues in 'C' / Wake up moma / Talk don't bother me / Every blues you've ever heard / I get all shook up / Lost in love / Help me / Outside my window.

— Aug'95, ALVIN was credited on GUITAR CRUSHER cd 'MESSAGE TO MAN' on 'In-Akustik'; *INAK 9034*

– compilations, others, etc. –

Mar 72. (lp/c; by ALVIN LEE) *Deram; (SML/KSCM 1096)* **ALVIN LEE & COMPANY** 55
– The sounds / Rock your mama / Hold me tight / Standing at the crossroads / Portable people / Boogie on. *(cd-iss. Jan89; 820 566-2)*

Aug 75. (lp/c) *Chrysalis; (CHR/ZCHR 1077) / Deram; <18072>* **GOIN' HOME – THEIR GREATEST HITS** Jul75

Sep 76. (lp/c) *Chrysalis; (CHR/ZCHR 1107)* **ANTHOLOGY**

Feb 77. (lp/c) *Chrysalis; (CHR/ZCHR 1134)* **THE CLASSIC PERFORMANCES OF . . .**
(cd-iss. 1987; CCD 1134)

Feb 79. (c) *Teldec; (CP4 22436)* **GREATEST HITS VOL.1** -

Feb 79. (c) *Teldec; (CP4 23252) GREATEST HITS VOL.2* -

May 80. (lp/c) *Hallmark; (SHM/HSC 3038)* **TEN YEARS AFTER** -

Mar 81. (lp) *Decca; (TAB 12)* **HEAR ME CALLING** -

Oct 83. (7") *Old Gold; (OG 9342)* **LOVE LIKE A MAN. / (B-side by THEM)** -

Nov 85. (d-lp/c) *Castle; (CCS LP/MC 115)* **THE COLLECTION** -
– Hear me calling / No title / Spoonful / I can't keep from crying sometimes / Standing at the crossroads / Portable people / Rock your mama / Love like a man / I want to know / Speed kills / Boogie on / I may be wrong but I won't be wrong

always / At the woodchopper's ball / Spider in your web / Summertime / Shantung cabbage / I'm going home. *(re-iss. Jul91 cd/c; CCS CD/MC 293) (cd re-iss. Aug95 on 'Griffin';)*

Feb 87. (lp) *See For Miles; (SEE 80)* **ORIGINAL RECORDINGS: VOL.1** [ ] [-]

Jun 87. (lp) *See For Miles; (SEE 90)* **ORIGINAL RECORDINGS: VOL.2** [ ] [-]
(cd-iss. Nov93; SEECD 387)

May 88. (d-lp/c/cd) *Chrysalis; (CHR/ZCHR/MPCD 1639)* **PORTFOLIO** [ ] [ ]

Dec 90. (cd/c/lp) *Raw Fruit; (FRS CD/MC/LP 003)* **LIVE AT READING 1983 (live)** [ ] [-]

Oct 92. (cd/c) *Chrysalis; (CD/TC CHR 1857)* **THE ESSENTIAL TEN YEARS AFTER** [ ] [-]

Jul 93. (cd) *Code 90; (NINETY 3)* **LIVE (live)** [ ] [-]

Sep 93. (cd) *Traditional Line; (TL 001327)* **LOVE LIKE A MAN** [ ] [-]

Mar 95. (cd; by ALVIN LEE) *Magnum; (MMGV 064)* **RETROSPECTIVE** [ ] [-]

Nov 95. (3xcd-box) *Chrysalis; (CDOMB 011)* **CRICKLEWOOD GREEN / WATT / A SPACE IN TIME** [ ] [-]

Nov 96. (cd) *Disky; <(DC 86678-2)>* **I'M GOING HOME** [ ] [ ]

Nov 97. (cd; by ALVIN LEE & TEN YEARS AFTER) *Chrysalis; (CDCHR 6129)* **SOLID ROCK** [ ] [ ]

Aug 00. (cd) *Chrysalis; (528499-2)* **THE BEST OF TEN YEARS AFTER** [ ] [ ]

TERRAPLANE (see under ⇒ THUNDER)

TERRORIZER (see under ⇒ MORBID ANGEL)

TERRORVISION

Formed: Bradford, England . . . August 1990 as The SPOILT BRATZ, by TONY WRIGHT, MARK YATES, LEIGH MARKLEW and SHUTTY, who, after locating manager Al Rhodes, changed their moniker to TERRORVISION (taking the name from an obscure 60's B-movie). Signed to 'E.M.I.' on the strength of a demo, they persuaded the company to furnish them with their very own imprint, 'Total Vegas', subsequently debuting with the 'THRIVE EP' early in '92. Melding disparate metal influences into a sticky sweet pop assault, TERRORVISION were akin to THERAPY? and CHEAP TRICK fighting it out in a bouncy castle (fans included?!). A series of singles and a debut album, 'FORMALDEHYDE' (1992/93), failed to launch them into superstardom just yet, although one track, 'NEW POLICY ONE' gave them their first taste of the Top 50. Their first single of '94, 'MY HOUSE' (originally a flop in '92), fared a lot better (Top 30) and the accompanying GIL NORTON-produced album, 'HOW TO MAKE FRIENDS AND INFLUENCE PEOPLE' became a regular fixture in the charts over the coming year. In addition, TERRORVISION proved themselves to be a remarkably consistent singles outfit, five Top 30 smashes, 'OBLIVION', 'MIDDLEMAN', 'PRETEND BEST FRIEND', 'ALICE WHAT'S THE MATTER' and 'SOME PEOPLE SAY' all lifted from the album. Festival stalwarts, the "wacky" quartet took every opportunity to frequent the summer circuit, frontman WRIGHT a manic ball of energy and a dependably entertaining live bet. In 1996, the Kerrang! darlings were back, wreaking chart havoc with a Top 5 single, 'PERSEVERANCE' (perhaps a reference to the horror of festival bogs!) and a Top 10 album, 'REGULAR URBAN SURVIVORS'. Two Top 20 tracks, 'CELEBRITY HIT LIST' and 'BAD ACTRESS', ensured TERRORVISION remained in the public eye, WRIGHT becoming a bit of a lad while guesting in a TV quiz show hosted by Mark Lamaar, 'Never Mind The Bollocks'. 'SHAVING PEACHES' was next up for the tongue-n-cheeky Northerners, the 1998 album a tad disappointing although it did contain the original version of No.2 hit, 'TEQUILA' – the band had now invented a pub-dance singalong number! (were SPLODGENESSABOUNDS the last group to do so?). • **Covered:** PSYCHO KILLER (Talking Heads) / THE MODEL (Kraftwerk) / THE PASSENGER (Iggy Pop) / SURRENDER (Cheap Trick) / WISHING WELL (Free) / I'LL BE YOUR SISTER (Chris Bell) / YOU'VE REALLY GOT A HOLD OF ME (Smokey Robinson) / MOONAGE DAYDREAM (David Bowie).

Album rating: FORMALDEHYDE (*7) / HOW TO MAKE FRIENDS AND INFLUENCE PEOPLE (*8) / REGULAR URBAN SURVIVORS (*6) / SHAVING PEACHES (*5) / GOOD TO GO (*4)

TONY WRIGHT (b. 6 May'68) – vocals / **MARK YATES** (b. 4 Apr'68) – guitars / **LEIGH MARKLEW** (b.10 Aug'68) – bass / **SHUTTY** (b.20 Mar'67) – drums

Total Vegas E.M.I.

Feb 92. (12"ep/cd-ep) *(12/CD VEGAS 1)* **THRIVE EP** [ ] [-]
– Urban space crime / Jason / Blackbird / Pain reliever.

Oct 92. (7") *(VEGAS 2)* **MY HOUSE. / COMING UP** [ ] [-]
(12"+=/cd-s+=) *(12/CD VEGAS 2)* – Tea dance.

Dec 92. (cd/c/green-lp) *(ATVR CD/MC/LP 1)* **FORMALDEHYDE** [ ] [-]
– Problem solved / Ships that sink / American T.V. / New policy one / Jason / Killing time / Urban space crime / Hole for a soul / Don't shoot my dog / Desolation town / My house / Human being / Pain reliever / Tea dance. *(re-iss. May93 cd/s-cd/c/lp; VEGAS CD/CDS/MC/LP 1) (w/out last 2 tracks, hit UK No.75)*

Jan 93. (12"ep/cd-ep) *(12/CD ATVR 1)* **PROBLEM SOLVED / CORPSE FLY. / WE ARE THE ROADCREW / SAILING HOME** [ ] [-]

Jun 93. (12"ep/12"ep w-poster) *(12/12P VEGAS 3)* **AMERICAN T.V. / DON'T SHOOT MY DOG AGAIN / KILLING TIME** [63] [-]
(cd-ep) *(CDVEGAS 3)* – ('A'side) / Psycho killer / Hole for a soul.

Oct 93. (7"green) *(VEGAS 4)* **NEW POLICY ONE. / PAIN RELIEVER (live)** [42] [-]
(12"/12"w poster) *(12 VEGAS/+SP 4)* – ('A'side) / Ships that sink (live) / Problem solved (live).
(cd-s) *(CDVEGAS 4)* – ('A'side) / Psycho killer (live) / Tea dance (live) / My house (live).
(cd-s) *(CDVEGASS 4)* – ('A'side) / American TV (live) / New policy one (live) / Still the rhythm (live).

Jan 94. (7"green) *(VEGAS 5)* **MY HOUSE. / TEA DANCE** [29] [-]
(12") *(12VEGAS 5)* – ('A'side) / ('A'machete mix) / Psycho killer (extended mix).
(cd-s) *(CDVEGAS 5)* – ('A'-Attic mix) / Down under / ('A'Machete mix).
(cd-s) *(CDVEGASS 5)* – ('A'side) / Discotheque wreck / ('A'-Machete mix).

Mar 94. (7") *(VEGAS 6)* **OBLIVION (mix). / WHAT DO YOU DO THAT FOR?** [21] [-]
(cd-s+=) *(CDVEGAS 6)* – Problem solved (by DIE CHEERLEADER) / Oblivion (demo).
(cd-s) *(CDVEGASS 6)* – ('A'side) / The model (with DIE CHEERLEADER) / Remember Zelda (written by DIE CHEERLEADER).
(12") *(12VEGAS 6)* – (above 3) / Problem solved (by DIE CHEERLEADER).

Apr 94. (cd/c/lp/s-lp) *(VEGAS CD/MC/LP/LPX 2)* **HOW TO MAKE FRIENDS AND INFLUENCE PEOPLE** [18] [-]
– Alice what's the matter / Oblivion / Stop this bus / Discotheque wreck / Middleman / Still the rhythm / Ten shades of grey / Stab in the back / Pretend best friend / Time o the signs / What the doctor ordered / Some people say / What makes you tick.

Jun 94. (c-s) *(TCVEGAS 7)* **MIDDLEMAN / OBLIVION** [25] [-]
(12"copper/cd-s) *(12/CD VEGAS 7)* – ('A'side) / Surrender / The passenger.
(cd-s) *(CDVEGASS 7)* – ('A'side) / I'll be your sister / Wishing well.

Aug 94. (c-s) *(TCVEGAS 8)* **PRETEND BEST FRIEND / MIDDLEMAN (live)** [25] [-]
(12") *(12VEGAS 8)* – ('A'side) / Alice what's the matter (live) / Stop the bus (live) / Discotheque wreck (live).
(cd-s) *(CDVEGAS 8)* – ('A'side) / Time o' the signs (live) / Oblivion (live) / ('A'-Danny Does Vegas mix).
(cd-s) *(CDVEGAS 8)* – ('A'side) / What makes you tick (live) / Still the rhythm (live) / ('A'-Alice pretends mix).

Oct 94. (c-s) *(TCVEGAS 9)* **ALICE, WHAT'S THE MATTER (oh yeah mix) / SUFFOCATION** [24] [-]
(12") *(12VEGAS 9)* – ('A'-Junkie J mix) / ('B'side) / ('A'-Psycho bitch mix) / ('A'-All Carmen on the Western Front).
(cd-s) *(CDVEGAS 9)* – ('A'side) / Psycho killer (acoustic) / ('A'-Kill your Terrorvision mix) / What shall we do with the drunken sailor?
(cd-s) *(CDVEGASS 9)* – ('A'side) / ('A'-Junkie J mix) / Discotheque wreck (acoustic) / ('A'demo).

Mar 95. (7"/c-s) *(VEGAS/TCVEGAS 10)* **SOME PEOPLE SAY. / MR. BUSKERMAN / OBLIVION** [22] [-]
(cd-s) *(CDVEGAS 10)* – ('A'side) / This drinking will kill me / ('A'-Oblivious mix) / Oblivion.
(cd-s) *(CDVEGASS 10)* – ('A'side) / Blood on my wheels / ('A'extended) / Oblivion.

Feb 96. (7"blue) *(VEGAS 11)* **PERSEVERANCE. / WAKE UP** [5] [-]
(cd-s+=) *(CDVEGAS 11)* – What goes around comes around.
(cd-s) *(CDVEGASS 11)* – ('A'side) / Sick and tired / Hard to feel.

Mar 96. (cd/c/lp) *(VEGAS CD/TC/LP 3)* **REGULAR URBAN SURVIVORS** [8] [-]
– Enteralterego / Superchronic / Perseverance / Easy / Hide the dead girl / Conspiracy / Didn't bleed red / Dog chewed the handle / Junior / Bad actress / If I was you / Celebrity hit list / Mugwump.

Apr 96. (c-s) *(TCVEGAS 12)* **CELEBRITY HIT LIST / YOU REALLY GOT A HOLD ON ME** [20] [-]
(cd-s+=) *(CDVEGAS 12)* – Tom Petty loves Veruca Salt.
(cd-s) *(CDVEGASS 12)* – ('A'side) / Don't come here / Crossed line on the grapevine.

Jul 96. (12"ep) *(12VEGAS 13)* **BAD ACTRESS / TOO STONED TO DANCE (un-do-able handbag mix). / CONSPIRACY (hexadecimal dub) / CONSPIRACY (hexadecimal mix)** [10] [-]
(cd-s) *(CDVEGAS 13)* – ('A'side) / Fobbed off / Too stoned to dance / Bad actress (alternative strings).
(cd-s) *(CDVEGASS 13)* – ('A'side) / Oblivion / Middleman / Funny feels fine.

Jan 97. (10"clear-ep) *(10VEGAS 14)* **EASY / EASY (live). / CELEBRITY HIT LIST (live) / SOME PEOPLE SAY (live)** [12] [-]
(cd-ep) *(CDVEGAS 14)* – ('A'side) / Middleman (live) / My house (live) / Bad actress (live).
(cd-ep) *(CDVEGASS 14)* – ('A'side) / Discotheque wreck (live) / Pretend best friend (live) / Enteralterego (live).

Sep 98. (7") *(VEGAS 15)* **JOSEPHINE. / REASONS TO DECEIVE** [23] [-]
(cd-s+=) *(CDVEGASS 15)* – Go Jerry.
(cd-s) *(CDVEGAS 15)* – ('A'side) / Falling down / 28 hours.

Oct 98. (cd/c) *(496132-2/-4)* **SHAVING PEACHES** [34] [-]
– III wishes / Josephine / Hypnotised / Can't get you out of my mind / In your shoes / Swings and roundabouts / Day after day / Left to the right / Cantankerous / Tequila / Vegas / Babyface / Spanner in the works / When I die / On a mission. *(cd re-iss. Feb99; 499608-2)*

Jan 99. (12"/cd-s) *(12/CD VEGAS 16)* **TEQUILA (the Mint Royale chaser) / TEQUILA (album version) / TEQUILA (Mint Royale slammer)** [2] [-]
(cd-s) *(CDVEGASS 16)* – ('A'-Mint Royale shot) / (album version) / Risk worth taking.

May 99. (c-s) *(TCVEGAS 17)* **III WISHES / MOONAGE DAYDREAM / TEQUILA (Mint Royale shot mix)** [42] [-]
(cd-s) *(CDVEGAS 17)* – (first & third tracks) / If that's what it takes.
(cd-s) *(CDVEGASS 17)* – ('A'side) / ('A'-Scuba Z remix) / 100 things.

Papillion not iss.

Jan 01. (7") *(BTFLY 0007)* **D'YA WANNA GO FASTER? / IT'S THE CD'S OR ME** [28] [-]
(cd-s) *(BTFLYS 0007)* – ('A'side) / Tequila (Mint Royale shot) / Tequila (video).
(cd-s) *(BTFLYX 0007)* – ('A'side) / ('A'-Dylan rhymes mix) / ('A'-Lypid mix).

Feb 01. (cd) *(BTFLYCD 0011)* **GOOD TO GO** [48] [-]
– D'ya wanna go faster? / Come home Beanie / Friends and family / Sometimes I'd like to kill her / Alone / Fists of fury / Unhappy millionaire / Days like these / From out of nothing / Subway / Goldmine jamjar.

Apr 01. (7") *(BTFLY 0010)* **FISTS OF FURY. /** [ ] [-]
(cd-s) *(BTFLYS 0010)* –
(cd-s) *(BTFLYX 0010)* –

– compilations, etc. –

Sep 00. (3xcd-box) *E.M.I.; (528373-2)* **FORMALDEHYDE / HOW TO MAKE FRIENDS AND INFLUENCE PEOPLE / REGULAR URBAN SURVIVORS** [ ] [-]

TESLA

Formed: Sacramento, California, USA . . . 1985 originally as CITY KID by JEFF KEITH, TOMMY SKEOCH, FRANK HANNON, BRIAN WHEAT and TROY LUCCKETTA. Offering up unashamedly unreconstructed hard rock in a ballsy, bluesy stylee, TESLA broke into the US Top 40 almost immediately with their acclaimed 'Geffen' debut, 'MECHANICAL RESONANCE' (1987). Naming themselves after forgotten pioneering scientist, Nikola Tesla, the title of the group's debut was a reference to one of his theories. Strangely, given the band's avowed attempts to bestow the man with some belated recognition, there was precious little lyrical comment on Tesla's fate or indeed anything even resembling an intellectual/scientific theme. Instead, self-explanatory titles like 'EZ COME EZ GO', '2 LATE 4 LOVE' and 'MODERN DAY COWBOY' were a more accurate guide as to where TESLA were coming from. Musically, the group's reputation was at least partly deserved, TESLA packing a tight, gritty punch lying somewhere between MONTROSE, BAD COMPANY and VAN HALEN. One of the group's main strengths lay in vocalist KEITH, the frontman having apparently learned his trade by singing along to the radio in his previous life as a trucker. Equally adept at slow burning moodiness (the brilliant 'BEFORE MY EYES' from the debut) and lighters-aloft ballads as metal belters, KEITH's way with a slowie gave TESLA a US Top 10 in late '89 with 'LOVE SONG', its success boosting sales of TESLA's equally acclaimed follow-up, 'THE GREAT RADIO CONTROVERSY' (1989). A US Top 20, the album also saw the group gaining popularity in the UK where it breached the Top 40. A period of heavy touring followed, with the live 'FIVE MAN ACOUSTICAL JAM' set appearing in early '91. Its title taken from 70's hippies, THE FIVE MAN ACOUSTICAL BAND (whose classic protest chestnut, 'SIGNS', was covered in fine form), the album was a hugely enjoyable stripped down affair which saw the group running through such choice cover material as 'TRUCKIN' (Grateful Dead), 'LODI' (Creedence Clearwater Revival) and a particularly inspired 'WE CAN WORK IT OUT' (Beatles). Later that year, it was followed-up with another Top 20 success, the re-amplified 'PSYCHOTIC SUPPER', again demonstrating why TESLA remain one of America's most consistently successful rock'n'raunch bands. No-frills to the last, TESLA even rode out the grunge trend with 1994's 'BUST A NUT', the record again making the US Top 20 when lesser trad acts buckled. • **Songwriters:** KEITH-HANNON penned, except AIN'T SUPERSTITIOUS (Willie Dixon) / RUN RUN RUN (Jo Jo Gunne) / MOTHER'S LITTLE HELPER (Rolling Stones) / ROCK THE NATION (Montrose).

Album rating: MECHANICAL RESONANCE (*6) / THE GREAT RADIO CONTROVERSY (*6) / FIVE MAN ACOUSTICAL JAM (*6) / PSYCHOTIC SUPPER (*7) / BUST A NUT (*5) / TIME'S MAKIN' CHANGES: THE BEST OF TESLA compilation (*6)

JEFF KEITH (b.12 Oct'58, Texarkana, Arkansas) – vox / **TOMMY SKEOCH** (b. 5 Feb'62, Santa Monica, Calif.) – guitar, vocals / **FRANK HANNON** (b. 3 Oct'66) – guitar, keyboards / **BRIAN WHEAT** (b. 5 Nov'62) – bass, vocals / **TROY LUCCKETTA** (b. 5 Oct'59, Lodi, Calif.) – drums (ex-ERIC MARTIN BAND)

Geffen Geffen

Jan 87. (lp/c/cd) *(924120-1/-4/-2)* <24120> **MECHANICAL RESONANCE** [ ] [32]
– Ez come ez go / Cumin' atcha live / Gettin' better / 2 late 4 love / Rock me to the top / We're no good together / Modern day cowboy / Changes / Little Suzi (on the up) / Love me / Cover queen / Before my eyes. *(re-iss. Jan91 & Sep97 lp/c/cd; GEF/+C/D 24120)*

Apr 87. (7") <28353> **LITTLE SUZI (ON THE UP). / (SEE YOU) COMIN' ATCHA (live)** [-] [91]

Apr 87. (7") *(GEF 19)* **LITTLE SUZI (ON THE UP). / BEFORE MY EYES** [ ] [-]
(12"+=) *(GEF 19T)* – Comin' atcha live (remix).

Aug 87. (7") *(GEF 28)* **MODERN DAY COWBOY. / ('A'version)** [ ] [-]
(12"+=) – Love live / Cover queen (live).

Feb 89. (lp/c)(cd) *(WX 244/+C)(924224-2)* <24224> **THE GREAT RADIO CONTROVERSY** [34] [18]
– Hang tough / Lady luck / Heaven's trail (no way out) / Be a man / Lady days, crazy nights / Did it for the money / Yesterdaze gone / Makin' magic / The way it is / Flight to nowhere / Love song / Paradise / Party's over. *(re-iss. Jan91 & Sep97 lp/c/cd; GEF/+C/D 24224)*

Oct 89. (7") *(GEF 74)* <22856> **LOVE SONG. / AIN'T SUPERSTITIOUS** [ ] [10] Sep89
(12"+=/cd-s+=) *(GEF 74 T/CD)* – Run run run.

Feb 90. (c-s,cd-s) <19948> **THE WAY IT IS / RUN RUN RUN** [-] [55]

Feb 91. (d-lp/c/cd) <(GEF/+C/D 24311)> **FIVE MAN ACOUSTICAL JAM** [59] [12] Nov90
– Comin' atcha live – Truckin' / Heaven's trail (no way out) / The way it is / We can work it out / Signs / Gettin' better / Before my eyes / Paradise / Lodi / Mother's little helper / Modern day cowboy / Love song / Tommy's down home / Down fo' boogie.

Apr 91. (7")<c-s> *(GFS 3)* <19653> **SIGNS. / DOWN FO' BOOGIE** [70] [8] Dec90
(12"+=/12"blue+=/cd-s+=) *(GFS T/XTD 3)* – Little Suzi (acoustic live).

Sep 91. (7") *(GFS 13)* **EDISON'S MEDICINE. / ROCK THE NATION** [ ] [-]
(12"+=) *(GFST 13)* – Had enough.
(12"blue+=/cd-s+=) *(GFS X/CD 13)* – Run run run.

Sep 91. (lp/c/cd) <(GEF/+C/D 24424)> **PSYCHOTIC SUPPER** [44] [13]
– Change in the weather / Edison's medicine / Don't de-rock me / Call it what you want / Song and emotion / Time / Government personnel / Freedom slaves / Had enough / What you give / Stir it up / Can't stop / Talk about it.

Nov 91. (c-s,cd-s) <19113> **CALL IT WHAT YOU WANT / CHILDREN'S HERITAGE** [-] [ ]

Dec 91. (7") *(GFS 15)* **CALL IT WHAT YOU WANT. / FREEDOM SLAVES** [ ] [-]
(12"+=/cd-s+=) *(GFST/+D 15)* – Children's heritage / Cotton fields.

Apr 92. (c-s,cd-s) <19117> **WHAT YOU GIVE / COTTON FIELDS** [-] [86]

Aug 94. (cd/c) <(GED/GEC 24713)> **BUST A NUT** [51] [20]
– The gate – Invited / Solution / Shine away / Try so hard / She want she want / Need your lovin' / Action talks / Mama's fool / Cry / Earthmover / A lot to lose / Rubberband / Wonderful world / Games people play. *(cd-iss. Aug99; same)*

—— had already split before compilation below

Nov 95. (cd) <24833> **TIME'S MAKIN' CHANGES: THE BEST OF TESLA** [-] [ ]
– Modern day cowboy / Gettin' better / Little Suzi / Heaven's trail (no way out) / The way it is / Love song / Signs / Paradise / Edison's medicine / Song & emotion / What you give / Mama's fool / A lot to lose / Steppin' over / Changes.

TESTAMENT

Formed: Bay Area, San Francisco, USA . . . 1983 as LEGACY, by STEVE SOUZA, DEREK RAMIREZ, ERIC PETERSON, GREG CHRISTIAN and LOUIS CLEMENTE. The group subsequently adopted the TESTAMENT moniker with key members, frontman CHUCK BILLY and six-string wizard ALEX SKOLNICK, replacing SOUZA and RAMIREZ respectively. Signing with Johnny Z's 'Atlantic' subsidiary label, 'Megaforce', the group resurrected the title of their former outfit for the debut set, 'THE LEGACY' (1987). One of the classic 80's thrash releases, the album introduced TESTAMENT as one of the genre's classier outfits, if not exactly a threat to METALLICA or ANTHRAX. Stage favourites like 'OVER THE WALL' and 'BURNT OFFERINGS' were included on the mini-album follow-up, 'LIVE IN EINDHOVEN', recorded at the city's annual thrash-bash, The Dynamo Festival. A follow-up proper, 'THE NEW ORDER' (1988) built on the early promise, establishing the band as favourites, particularly in the UK where the album almost made the Top 75. The songwriting was markedly improved, with the pulverisingly infectious 'DISCIPLES OF THE WATCH' displaying a previously absent grasp of dynamics and melody. TESTAMENT only really confessed their metal credentials with the acclaimed 'PRACTICE WHAT YOU PREACH' (1989), however, the album's more accessible approach furnishing the group with their first UK Top 40 entry, while the lyrics showcased a newfound maturity. Released to coincide with their high profile slot on the 'Clash Of The Titans' tour (in such esteemed company as SLAYER, MEGADETH and SUICIDAL TENDENCIES), 'SOULS OF BLACK' (1990) was even more successful, although some critiscised its lack of focus. It was two years before TESTAMENT returned with 'THE RITUAL' (1992), the last recording to feature SKOLNICK (who decamped to SAVATAGE) and CLEMENTE. The next set of new material, 'LOW' (1994), saw SKOLNICK's position finally filled by death-metal veteran, JAMES MURPHY, the music unsurprisingly taking a more extreme turn. While arguably, TESTAMENT have so far failed to realise their full potential, they remain among the Bay Area's favourite sons, 'LIVE AT THE FILLMORE' (1995) documenting a fiery performance at the legendary San Franciscan venue. While 1997's 'DEMONIC' was a fine if unadventurous addition to the TESTAMENT catalogue, 'THE GATHERING' (1999) ranked as the band's most thrilling outing in years. So called because it boasted an all-star guest line-up of JAMES MURPHY, STEVE DiGIORGIO and DAVE LOMBARDO, the album went for the thrash jugular with merciless fury. If nothing else, the record proved that this almost forgotten genre could still pulse with the thickest and reddest of musical blood. • **Songwriters:** Group compositions, except NOBODY'S FAULT (co-with STEVE TYLER of AEROSMITH).

Album rating: THE LEGACY (*7) / THE NEW ORDER (*7) / PRACTICE WHAT YOU PREACH (*6) / SOULS OF BLACK (*5) / THE RITUAL (*5) / RETURN TO THE APOCALYPTIC CITY (*5) / LOW (*4) / LIVE AT THE FILLMORE (*5) / DEMONIC (*4) / SIGNS OF CHAOS – THE BEST OF TESTAMENT compilation (*5) / THE GATHERING (*4)

CHUCK BILLY – vocals / **ALEX SKOLNICK** – guitar / **ERIC PETERSON** – guitar / **GREG CHRISTIAN** – bass / **LOUIE CLEMENTE** – drums

East West Atlantic

Jun 87. (lp/c) *(781 741-1/-4)* <81741> **THE LEGACY** [ ] [ ] Nov86
– Over the wall / The haunting / Burnt offerings / Raging waters / C.O.T.L.O.D. (Curse of the legions of death) / First strike is deadly / Do or die / Alone in the dark / Apocalyptic city.

Dec 87. (lp/c) *(780 226-1/-4)* <80226> **LIVE IN EINDHOVEN (live)** [ ] [ ]
– Over the wall / Burnt offerings / Do or die / Apocalyptic city / Reign of terror.

Apr 88. (7") *(A 9092)* **TRIAL BY FIRE. / NOBODY'S FAULT** [ ] [-]
(12"+=) *(TA 9092)* – Reign of terror.

May 88. (lp/c/cd) *(781 849-1/-4/-2)* <81849> **THE NEW ORDER** [81] [ ]
– Eerie inhabitants / The new order / Trial by fire / Into the pit / Hypnosis / Disciples of the watch / The preacher / Nobody's fault * / A day of reckoning / Musical death (a dirge). *(cd+= *)*

Aug 89. (lp/c)(cd) *(WX 297/+C)(782 009-2)* <82009> **PRACTICE WHAT YOU PREACH** [40] [77]
– Practice what you preach / Perilous nation / Envy life / Time is coming / Blessed in contempt / Greenhouse effect / Sins of omission / The ballad / Nightmare (coming back to you) / Confusion fusion. *(cd re-iss. Feb95; K 782009-2)*

Oct 90. (cd/c/lp) <(7567 82143-2/-4/-1)> **SOULS OF BLACK** [35] [73]
– Beginning of the end / Face in the sky / Falling fast / Souls of black / Absence of light / Love to hate / Malpractise / One man's fate / The legacy / Seven days of May.

May 92. (cd/c/lp) *<(7567 82392-2/-4/-1)>* **THE RITUAL** 48 55
– Signs of chaos / Electric crown / So many lies / Let go of my world / The ritual / Deadline / As the seasons grey / Agony / The sermon / Return to serenity / Troubled dreams.

Apr 93. (cd/c/lp) *<(7567 82487-2/-4/-1)>* **RETURN TO THE APOCALYPTIC CITY**
– Over the wall / So many lies / The haunting / Disciplines of the watch / Reign of terror / Return to serenity.

Oct 94. (cd/c) *<(7567 82645-2/-4)>* **LOW**
– Low / Legions (in hiding) / Hail Mary / Trail of tears / Shades of war / P.C. / Dog faced gods / All I could bleed / Urotsukidoji / Chasing fear / Ride / Last call.

Music For Nations — Burnt Offering

Aug 95. (cd) *(CDMFN 186)* **LIVE AT THE FILLMORE (live)**
– The preacher / Alone in the dark / Burnt offerings / A dirge / Eerie inhabitants / The new order / Low / Urotsukidoji / Into the pit / Souls of black / Practice what you preach / Apocalyptic city / Hail Mary / Dog faced gods / Return to serenity / The legacy / Trail of tears. *(re-iss. May00 on 'Spitfire'; SPITMCD 003)*

— drummer JOHN DETTE joined SLAYER

Music For Nations — Fierce

Jun 97. (cd/c) *(CD/T MFN 221) <11107>* **DEMONIC**
– Demonic refusal / Burning times / Together as one / Jun-jun / John Doe / Murky waters / Hatred's rise / Distorted lives / New eyes of old / Ten thousand thrones / Nostrovia. *(cd re-iss. May00 on 'Spitfire'; SPITCD 002)*

Mayhem — Mayhem

May 98. (cd) *<(9086 11120CD)>* **SIGNS OF CHAOS – THE BEST OF TESTAMENT** (compilation) Nov97
– Signs of chaos / Electric crown / New order / Alone in the dark / Dog faced gods / Demonic refusal / Ballad / Souls of black / Trial by fire / Low / Practice what you preach / Over the wall / Legacy / Return to serenity / Perilous nation / Sails of Charon / Draw the line.

— **CHUCK BILLY + PETERSON** recruited **JAMES MURPHY** – guitar (ex-DEATH, ex-OBITUARY, ex-CANCER + a solo artist – one set, 'Feeding The Machine') / **DAVE LOMBARDO** – drums (ex-SLAYER) + **STEVE DiGIORGIO** – bass (ex-SADUS, ex-DEATH)

U.S.G. — Spitfire

Jul 99. (cd) *(USG 1033CD) <5001>* **THE GATHERING** Jun99
– D.N.R. (Do Not Resuscitate) / Down for life / Eyes of wrath / True believer / 3 days in darkness / Legions of the dead / Careful what you wish for / Riding the snake / Allegiance / Sewn shut eyes / Fall of Sipledome. *(re-iss. May00 on 'Spitfire'; SPITCD 001)*

THEATRE OF TRAGEDY

Formed: Norway . . . 1993 by RAYMOND I. ROHONYI, LIV KRISTINE ESPENAES, FRANK CLAUSSEN, LORENTZ ASPEN, TOMMY OLSSON, EIRIK T. SALTROE and HEIN FRODE HANSEN. A seminal influence in the development of gothic black metal, THEATRE OF TRAGEDY's elaborate, dramatic style pitched the ogre-like vocals of ROHONYI against KRISTINE's ethereal warbling. Chuck in some Olde English lyrics with KING DIAMOND-style character shuffling and you had a recipe for bat-winged success. The considerable impact of their eponymous 'Massacre' debut album – released in 1995 – led to a US licensing deal with 'Century Media', which in turn gave wider exposure to 1997's 'VELVET DARKNESS THEY FEAR'. While the group's approach may have seemed more like farce than tragedy to some metalheads, their European fanbase was considerable, particularly in Germany. The gothic aesthetes continued to expand their sound with 'AEGIS' (1998), incorporating more electronic ambience into proceedings. Changes were afoot come the end of the decade with both OLSSON and SALTROE departing prior to the release of 'MUSIQUE' (2000), a record which was even more indebted to teutonic computer forefathers such as Kraftwerk while acknowledging the influence of modern mechanical manglers like NIN. • **Covered:** DECADES (Joy Division).

Album rating: THEATRE OF TRAGEDY (*5) / VELVET DARKNESS THEY FEAR (*5) / A ROSE FOR THE DEAD mini (*4) / AEGIS (*6) / MUSIQUE (*4) / Liv Kristine: DEUS EX MACHINA (*3)

RAYMOND I. ROHONNIY – vocals / **LIV KRISTINE ESPENAES** – vocals / **FRANK CLAUSSEN** – guitars / **TOMMY OLSSON** – guitars, programming / **EIRIK T. SALTRO** – bass / **HEIN FRODE HANSEN** – drums / **LORENTZ ASPEN** – synthesizer

unknown — not iss.

1995. (cd) **THEATRE OF TRAGEDY** -
– A hamlet for a slothful vassal / Cheerful dirge / To these words I behold no tongue / Hollow-hearted, heart-departed / . . .A distance there is . . . / Sweet thou art / Mire / Dying – I only feel apathy / Monotone. *<US-iss.1998 on 'Century Media'; 7902> (UK-iss.May99 on 'Massacre'; MASSSH 195)*

Massacre — Century Media

Sep 96. (cd-s) **DER TANZ DER SCHATTEN (club mix) / BLACK AS THE DEVIL PAINTETH / A HAMLET FOR A SLOTHFUL VASSAL / DER TANZ DER SCHATTEN** - - Norway

Oct 96. (cd/pic-lp) *(MASS CD/LP 107) <7881>* **VELVET DARKNESS THEY FEAR** Aug97
– Velvet darkness they fear / Fair & 'guilding copesmate death / Bring forth ye shadow / Seraphic deviltry / And when he falleth / Der tanz der schatten / Black as the Devil painteth / On whom the moon doth shine / Masquerader and Phoenix.

Apr 97. (m-cd) *(MASSCD 130)* **A ROSE FOR THE DEAD** -
– A rose for the dead / Der spiegel / As the shadows dance / And when he falleth (remix) / Black as the Devil painteth (remix) / Decades.

May 98. (cd/pic-cd) *(MASS CD/DP 159) <7933>* **AEGIS** Aug98
– Cassandra / Lorelei / Angelique / Aoede / Siren / Venus / Poppaea / Bacchante. *(also w/book; MASSP 159)*

Jul 98. (cd-s) *(MASSCD 166)* **CASSANDRA (cheap wine edit) / AOEDE (edit) / CASSANDRA (album)** -

— now without OLSSON + SALTRO

Nuclear Blast — Nuclear Blast

Sep 00. (cd-s) **IMAGE / MACHINE / FRAGMENT (element remix) / MACHINE (VNH nation mix)** - - Norway

Nov 00. (cd) *(<NB 568-2>)* **MUSIQUE**
– Machine / City of life / Fragment / Musique / Commute / Radio / Image / Crash / Concrete / Retrospect / Reverie / Space age / New man.

Jan 01. (cd-ep) **MACHINE / MACHINE (VNV Nation mix) / MACHINE (Element / Tarsis remix) / RADIO (Kallisti remix) / REVERIE (Current chill mix) / IMAGE (French) / IMAGE (enhanced video)** - - Norway

– compilations, etc. –

Mar 01. (m-cd) *Massacre; (MASSDP 267)* **INTERSPECTIVE** -
– Samantha / Virago / Lorelei (Icon of coil remix) / The masquerader and phoenix (phoenix mix) / On whom the Moon doth shine (unburn mix) / Der tanz der schatten (club mix).

LIV KRISTINE

— vocalist with **GUNTHER ILLS** – producer/technician

Massacre — not iss.

Feb 98. (cd) *(MASCD 0154)* **DEUS EX MACHINA** -
– Requiem / Deus ex machina / In the heart of Juliet / 3 am / Waves of green / Take good care / Huldra / Portrait: el tulle med 0yne Bla / Good vibes bad vibes / Outro.

Mar 98. (cd-ep) *(MASSCD 0151)* **3 AM (club) / 3 AM / HULDRA (part II / GOOD VIBES, BAD VIBES** -

1998. (cd-s) **TAKE GOOD CARE (radio) / TAKE GOOD CARE (album) / IN THE HEART OF JULIET (forever mix)** - - Norway

May 99. (cd) *(MASSSH 200)* **ONE LOVE (mixes)** -

THEE HYPNOTICS

Formed: High Wycombe, Buckinghamshire, England . . . late 80's by JAMES JONES, RAY HANSON, WILL PEPPER and MARK THOMPSON. After a debut single on the 'Hipsville' label, the band were picked up by 'Beggars Banquet' offshoot, 'Situation 2', releasing the epic 'JUSTICE IN FREEDOM' early the following year. A third single, 'SOUL TRADER', brought further cult acclaim while a live mini-set, 'LIVE'R THAN GOD' (1989) appeared on the fledgling American 'Sub Pop' label as the band were briefly associated with the nascent grunge scene. Certainly, THEE HYPNOTIC's retro sound had more in common with the likes of SOUNDGARDEN, GREEN RIVER etc., than any British indie acts, the distorted mogadon riffing and leadweight vocals of 'COME DOWN HEAVY' (1990) confirming their status as harbingers of stoner rock. Produced by CHRIS ROBINSON of fellow archivists The BLACK CROWES, 'SOUL, GLITTER AND SIN' (1991) received further praise from both the rock and indie press without really making much headway in either scene. Hedonism turned to tragedy the following year, however, as new bassist CRAIG PIKE died of a heroin overdose. It would be another two years before the release of 'THE VERY CRYSTAL SPEED MACHINE' (1995), on 'S.P.V.' and subsequently re-issued after gaining a new deal with Rick Rubin's 'American' label. • **Covered:** ROCK ME BABY (B.B. King).

Album rating: LIVE'R THAN GOD! (*6) / COME DOWN HEAVY (*6) / SOUL, GLITTER AND SIN (*5) / THE VERY CRYSTAL SPEED MACHINE (*6)

JIM JONES – vocals / **RAY HANSON** – guitar / **WILL PEPPER** – bass / **MARK THOMPSON** – drums

Hipsville — not iss.

Jul 88. (7"; HYPNOTICS) *(HIP 1)* **LOVE IN A DIFFERENT VEIN. / ALL NIGHT LONG** -

Situation 2 — Sub Pop

Mar 89. (12"ep) *(SIT 056T)* **JUSTICE IN FREEDOM. / PREACHIN' & RAMBLIN' / CHOOSE MY OWN WAY** -

Sep 89. (7") *(SIT 062)* **SOUL TRADER. / EARTH BLUES** -
(12"+=) *(SIT 062T)* – Rock me baby (live).

Oct 89. (m-lp/m-c/m-cd) *(SITUM 026/+CD) <SP 54/+B>* **LIVE 'R THAN GOD (live Powerhouse, London)** Jan90
– All night long / Let's get naked / Revolution stone / Rock me baby / Justice in freedom. *(re-dist.Jul91; same)*

Situation 2 — Beggars Banquet

May 90. (7") *(SIT 067)* **HALF MAN, HALF BOY. /** -
(12"+=/cd-s=) *(SIT 067 T/CD)* –

Jun 90. (lp/cd) *(SITU 28/+CD) <2320>* **COME DOWN HEAVY**
– Half man, half boy / All messed up / Unearthed / Release the feeling / Resurrection Joe / Let it come down heavy / Bleeding heart / What to do / Sonic lament / Revolution stone.

— recruited **RAT SCABIES** – drums (ex-DAMNED) to repl. THOMPSON

Sep 91. (12"ep/cd-ep) *(SIT T/CD)* **SHAKE DOWN** -
– Loco / etc.

Oct 91. (lp/cd) *(SITU 35/+CD) <61079>* **SOUL, GLITTER & SIN: TARGET FROM THE SONIC UNDERWORLD**
– Shakedown / Kissed by the flame / The big fix / Point blank mystery / Soul accelerator / Black river shuffle / Cold blooded heart / Coast to coast. *(cd+=)* – Samedi's cookbook / Don't let it get you down.

Jan 92. (12"ep/cd-ep) *(SIT T/CD)* **COAST TO COAST / SHAKEDOWN / SOUL ACCELERATOR** -

— **CRAIG PIKE** – bass (also ex-IGGY POP) repl. PEPPER

— CRAIG died (o.d.) on 30th June '93.

S.P.V. Warners

Mar 95. (cd) *(SPV 084 8906-2) <45600>* **THE VERY CRYSTAL SPEED MACHINE** [ ] [ ]
– Keep rollin' on / Heavy liquid / Phil's drum acropolis / Goodbye / If the good Lord loves ya / Ray's baudelaire / Caroline inside out / Tie it up / Down in the hole / Peasant song / Fragile / Look what you've done / Broken morning has. *(re-iss. Jul95 on 'American'; 74321 26451-2)*

Rocket not iss.

Nov 98. (7") **EARTH BLUES '99. / THING 4U** [ ] [-]

THERAPY?

Formed: Belfast, N. Ireland . . . summer '89 by ANDY CAIRNS, MICHAEL McKEEGAN and FYFE EWING. After failing to attract major label interest, they took the DIY route and issued a double A-side debut single, 'MEAT ABSTRACT' / 'PUNISHMENT KISS' (1990) on their own bitterly named 'Multifuckingnational' label. With the help of Radio One guru, John Peel and Silverfish's LESLIE RANKINE, the band secured a deal with London indie label, 'Wiiija'. The following year, they released two mini-sets in quick succession, 'BABYTEETH' and 'PLEASURE DEATH', the latter nearly breaking them into the Top 50 (both topping the independent charts). This initial early 90's period was characterised by a vaguely industrial hardcore/proto-grunge sound lying somewhere between American noiseniks, BIG BLACK and HUSKER DU. Their mushrooming street kudos tempted 'A&M' into offering them a deal and in 1992 THERAPY? made their major label debut with the Top 30 single, 'TEETHGRINDER', following it up with their first album proper, 'NURSE'. A Top 40 injection, its blunt combination of metal/punk and ambitious arrangements something of a love-it-or-hate-it affair. The following year, they released a trio of Top 20 singles, starting off with the 'SHORTSHARPSHOCK EP' which opened with the classic 'SCREAMAGER' track. In the first few months of '94, THERAPY? once again crashed into the charts with 'NOWHERE', an adrenaline rush of a single, that preceded their Mercury-nominated Top 5 album, 'TROUBLEGUM'. However, by the release of 1995's 'INFERNAL LOVE', the band affected something of a musical departure from their stock-in-trade indie-metal extremity with aching ballads (including a heart-rending cover of Husker Du's 'DIANE') and string flourishes courtesy of MARTIN McCARRICK. The cellist (who also appeared on their 1994 set) was made full-time member in early 1996, while EWING was replaced by GRAHAM HOPKINS. A long time in the making, the album 'SEMI-DETACHED', was delivered to a muted response from the critics in '98 and was their last for a major label. Although it opened in fine style with Top 30 hit, 'CHURCH OF NOISE', the rest of the tracks were below par. THERAPY? tried hard to re-establish themselves with 1999's 'SUICIDE PACT – YOU FIRST' set, the group's fanbase becoming more rhetorical with each listen. • **Songwriters:** Mostly CAIRNS or group penned, except TEENAGE KICKS (Undertones) / INVISIBLE SUN (Police) / WITH OR WITHOUT YOU (U2) / BREAKING THE LAW (Judas Priest) / C.C. RIDER (hit; Elvis Presley) / ISOLATION (Joy Division) / TATTY SEASIDE TOWN (Membranes) / NICE 'N' SLEAZY (Stranglers) / REUTERS (Wire) / VICAR IN A TUTU (Smiths). • **Trivia:** In 1994, they featured w/ OZZY OSBOURNE on 'IRON MAN' for a BLACK SABBATH tribute album.

Album rating: BABYTEETH mini (*5) / PLEASURE DEATH mini (*6) / NURSE (*7) / TROUBLEGUM (*8) / INFERNAL LOVE (*5) / SEMI-DETACHED (*5) / SUICIDE PACT – YOU FIRST compilation (*5)

ANDY CAIRNS (b.22 Sep'65, Antrim, N.Ireland) – vocals, guitar / **MICHAEL McKEEGAN** (b.25 Mar'71, Antrim) – bass / **FYFE EWING** – drums

Multifuck-ingnational not iss.

Aug 90. (7") *(MFN 1)* **MEAT ABSTRACT. / PUNISHMENT KISS** [ ] [-]

Wiiija not iss.

Jul 91. (m-lp) *(WIJ 9)* **BABYTEETH** [ ] [-]
– Meat abstract / Skyward / Punishment kiss / Animal bones / Loser cop / Innocent X / Dancin' with Manson. *(re-iss. Mar93 + Jun95 on 'Southern' cd/c/red-m-lp; 18507-2/-4/-1)*

Jan 92. (m-lp) *(WIJ 11)* **PLEASURE DEATH** [52] [-]
– Skinning pit / Fantasy bag / Shitkicker / Prison breaker / D.L.C. / Potato junkie. *(re-iss. Sep92 on 'A&M';) (re-iss. Mar93 + Jun95 on 'Southern' cd/c/m-lp; 18508-2/-4/-1)*

A&M A&M

Oct 92. (7"purple) *(AM 0097)* **TEETHGRINDER. / SUMMER OF HATE** [30] [-]
(12") *(AMY 0097)* – ('A'side) / Human mechanism / Sky high McKay(e).
(cd-s+=) *(AMCD 0097)* – (all four songs above).
(12") – *(AMX 0097)* – ('A'-Tee hee dub mix) / ('A'-Unsane mix).

Nov 92. (cd/c/lp) *(540044-2/-4/-1)* **NURSE** [38] [-]
– Nausea / Teethgrinder / Disgracelands / Accelerator / Neck freak / Perversonality / Gone / Zipless / Deep skin / Hypermania.

Mar 93. (7"pink-ep/c-ep/12"ep/cd-ep) *(AM/+MC/Y/CD 208)* **SHORTSHARPSHOCK EP** [9] [-]
– Screamager / Auto surgery / Totally random man / Accelerator.

—— In May93, they appeared on the B-side of PEACE TOGETHER single 'BE STILL', covered The Police's 'INVISIBLE SUN' on 'Island' records.

Jun 93. (7"grey-ep/c-ep/12"ep/cd-ep) *(580304-7/-4/-1/-2)* **FACE THE STRANGE EP** [18] [-]
– Turn / Speedball / Bloody blue / Neck freak (re-recording).

Aug 93. (7"clearorblue-ep/c-ep/cd-ep) *(580360-7/-4/-2)* **OPAL MANTRA / INNOCENT X (live). / POTATO JUNKIE (live) / NAUSEA (live)** [13] [-]

Sep 93. (cd) *<POCM 1033>* **HATS OFF TO THE INSANE** (compilation) [-] [ ]
– Screamager / Auto surgery / Totally random man / Turn / Speedball / Opal mantra.

Jan 94. (7"ep/c-ep/cd-ep) *(580504-7/-4/-2)* **NOWHERE / PANTOPON ROSE. / BREAKING THE LAW / C.C. RIDER** [18] [-]
(cd-s) *(580 504-2)* – ('A'side) / ('A'-Sabres Of Paradise mix) / ('A'-Therapeutic Distortion mix).

Feb 94. (cd/c/lp,green-lp) *(540196-2/-4/-1)* **TROUBLEGUM** [5] [-]
– Knives / Screamager / Hellbelly / Stop it you're killing me / Nowhere / Die laughing / Unbeliever / Trigger inside / Lunacy booth / Isolation / Turn / Femtex / Unrequited / Brainsaw.
above album guests **PAGE HAMILTON** – lead guitar (of HELMET) / **MARTIN McCARRICK** (b.29 Jul'62, Luton, England) – guitar, cello (of THIS MORTAL COIL) / **LESLEY RANKINE + EILEEN ROSE** – vocals

Feb 94. (7"yellow-ep/c-ep/cd-ep) *(580534-7/-4/-2)* **TRIGGER INSIDE / NICE'N'SLEAZY. / REUTERS / TATTY SEASIDE TOWN** [22] [-]
(12"ep) *(580534-1)* – ('A'side) / ('A'-Terry Bertram mix 1 & 2) / Nowhere (Sabres of Paradise mix 1 & 2).

May 94. (7"red-ep/c-ep/cd-ep) *(580588-7/-4/-2)* **DIE LAUGHING / STOP IT YOU'RE KILLING ME (live). / TRIGGER INSIDE (live) / EVIL ELVIS (the lost demo)** [29] [-]
(12") *(580588-1)* – ('A'-David Holmes mix 1 & 2).

—— In May '95, they hit No.53 UK with remix of 'INNOCENT X', with ORBITAL on the B-side, 'Belfast' / 'Wasted (vocal mix)'.

May 95. (7"orange) *(581504-7)* **STORIES. / STORIES (cello version)** [14] [-]
(c-s+=/cd-s+=) *(581105-4/-2)* – Isolation (Consolidated synth mix).

Jun 95. (cd/c/red-lp) *(540379-2/-4/-1)* **INFERNAL LOVE** [9] [-]
– Epilepsy / Stories / A moment of clarity / Jude the obscene / Bowels of love / Misery / Bad mother / Me vs you / Loose / Diane / 30 seconds.

Jul 95. (c-s/cd-s) *(581163-4/-2)* **LOOSE / OUR LOVE MUST DIE / NICE GUYS / LOOSE (Photek remix)** [25] [-]
(cd-s) *(581165-2)* – ('A'side) / Die laughing (live) / Nowhere (live) / Unbeliever (live).
(7"green/one-sided-12") *(581162-7/-1)* – ('A'side) / ('A'-Photek remix).

Nov 95. (7"red-ep/c-ep/cd-ep) *(581293-7/-4/-2)* **DIANE / JUDE THE OBSCENE (acoustic) / LOOSE (acoustic) / 30 SECONDS (acoustic)** [26] [-]
(cd-ep) *(581291-2)* – ('A'side) / Misery (acoustic) / Die laughing (acoustic) / Screamager (acoustic).

—— Jan 96, **GRAHAM HOPKINS** (b.20 Dec'75, Dublin, Ireland) – drums (ex-MY LITTLE FUNHOUSE) repl. FYFE. Also added full-time **MARTIN McCARRICK**

Mar 98. (7"red) *(582538-7)* **CHURCH OF NOISE. / 60 WATT BULB / ('A'-Messenger mix)** [29] [-]
(cd-s) *(582539-2)* – (first & third tracks) / Suing God / ('A'-CD-Rom video).

Mar 98. (cd/c) *(540891-2/-4)* **SEMI-DETACHED** [21] [-]
– Church of noise / Tightrope walker / Black eye, purple sky / Lonely, cryin', only / Born too soon / Stay happy / Safe / Straight life / Heaven's gate / Don't expect roses / Tramline / The boy's asleep. *(also iss.6x7"box; 582548-7)*

May 98. (7"blue) *(582684-7)* **LONELY, CRYIN', ONLY. / SKYWARD** [32] [-]
(cd-s) *(582685-2)* – ('A'side) / High noon / Diane (new version) / Teethgrinder (new version).
(cd-s) *(044121-2)* – ('A'side) / Kids stuff / Disgracelands / ('A'-CD-Rom video).

Ark 21 not iss.

Oct 99. (cd) *(153972-2)* **SUICIDE PACT – YOU FIRST** [61] [-]
– He's not that kind of girl / Wall of mouths / Jam jar jail / Hate kill destroy / Big cave in / Six mile water / Little tongues first / Ten year plan / God kicks / Other people's misery / Sister / While I pursue my way unharmed.

– compilations, etc. –

Mar 92. (cd) *1/4 Stick; <QUARTERSTICK 8>* **CAUCASIAN PSYCHOSIS** [-] [ ]
– (BABYTEETH + PLEASURE DEATH)

THERION

Formed: Sweden . . . late 80's by CHRISTOFER JOHNSSON and a crew of death-metallists, OSKAR FORSS, PETER HANSSON and ERIK GUSTAFSON. This was the line-up which appeared on the 1990 debut set, 'OF DARKNESS', although follow-up, 'BEYOND SANCTORUM' (1991) was recorded as a trio following the departure of GUSTAFSON. By the release of 'SYMPHONY MASSES: HO DRAKON HO MEGAS' (1993), JOHNSSON had taken on a whole new backing group consisting of MAGNUS BARTHELSON, ANDREAS WALLAN WAHL and PIOTR WAWRZENIUK. As the title suggested, the album found JOHNSSON incorporating classically inspired orchestrations into his black metal maelstrom. For the recording of both the 'BEAUTY IN BLACK' EP (1995) and 'LEPACA KLIFFOTH' (1995) album, the band had again been pared back to a trio of JOHNSSON, WAWRZENIUK and newcomer FREDRIK ISAKSSON although the musical chairs were shuffled yet again for 1996's epic 'THELI'; regarded by many afficionados of the genre as THERION's finest moment, the album's symphonic portent was partly fashioned by new faces JONAS MELBERG and LARS ROSENBERG. 'A'ARAB ZARAQ LUCID DREAMING' (1997) saw comparatively little upheaval although incredibly by the release of 'VOVIN' (1998), JOHNSSON was working with another completely new line-up numbering TOMMY ERIKSSON, JAN KAZDA and WOLF SIMONS. With no new studio material appearing in 1999, THERION disciples were instead graced with an odd'n'sods collection rather grandly titled 'CROWNING OF ATLANTIS' and featuring covers of Manowar's 'THOR (THE POWERHEAD)', Accept's 'SEAWINDS' and Loudness' 'CRAZY NIGHTS'. Effectively JOHNSSON's solo vision rather than any kind of group project, THERION released their umpteenth studio album, 'DEGGIAL', in 2000, with, surprise, surprise, another new line-up: KRISTIAN NIEMANN, JOHAN NIEMANN and SAMI KARPINNEN. Come 2001, the veteran metal composer was 'BEYOND SANCTORUM'.

Album rating: OF DARKNESS ... (*4) / BEYOND SANCTORIUM (*5) / SYMPHONY MASSES: HO DRAKON HO MEGAS (*4) / LEPACA KLIFFOTH (*4) / THELI (*4) / VOVIN (*6) / CROWNING OF ATLANTIS (*5) / DEGGIAL (*5)

— **CHRISTOFER JOHNSSON** – guitar / with **OSKAR FORSS** – drums / **PETER HANSSON** – keyboards, guitar, bass / **ERIK GUSTAFSON** – bass

House Of Kicks | not iss.

1990. (12"ep) **TIME SHALL TELL** [ ] [-]

Deaf | not iss.

Mar 91. (lp/cd) *(DEAF 006/+CD)* **OF DARKNESS . . .** [ ] [-]
– The return / Asphyxiate with fear / Morbid reality / Megalomaniac / A suburb to Hell / Genocidal raids / Time shall tell / Dark eternity.

— now without ERIK

Active | not iss.

Mar 92. (cd/lp) *(CD+/ATV 23)* **BEYOND SANCTORIUM** [ ] [-]
– Future consciousness / Pandemonium outbreak / Cthulhu / Symphony of the dead / Beyond sanctorium / Enter the depths of eternal darkness / Illusions of life / The way / Paths / Tyrants of the damned / Cthulhu (demo) / Future consciousness (demo) / Symphony of the dead (demo) / Beyond sanctorium. *<US cd-iss. 2001 on 'Nuclear Blast'; 6578>*

— **PIOTR WAWRZENIUK** – drums; repl. OSKAR

— **ANDREAS WALLAN WAHL** – bass + **MAGNUS BARTHELSON** – guitar; repl. HANSSON

Megarock | Pavement

1993. (cd) *<32205>* **SYMPHONY MASSES – HO DRAKON HO MEGAS** [-] [ ] Sweden
– Baal reginon / Dark princess Naamah / A black rose (covered with tears, blood and sweat) / Symphoni draconis inferni / Dawn of perishness / The eye of eclipse / The ritualdance of the Yezidis / Powerdance / Procreation of eternity / Ho drakon ho megas: The dragon throne – Fire.

— **FREDRIK ISAKSSON** – bass; repl. BARTHELSON + WAHL

Nuclear Blast | Nuclear Blast

Mar 95. (cd-ep) *(NB 125-2)* **THE BEAUTY IN BLACK** [ ] [ ]
Apr 95. (lp/c/cd) *(<NB 127/+MC/CD>)* **LEPACA KLIFFOTH** [ ] [ ] Jul95
– The wings of the hydra / Melez / Arrival of the darkest queen / The beauty in black / Riders of Theli / Black / Darkness eve / Sorrows of the Moon / Let the new day begin / Lepaca kliffoth / Evocation of Vovin. *(cd re-iss. Nov96; NB 216CD)*

— **JONAS MELLBERG** – guitar + **LARS ROSENBERG** – bass; repl. ISAKSSON

Jul 96. (cd-s) *(NB 178CD)* **THE SIREN OF THE WOODS** [ ] [ ]
Sep 96. (cd) *(NB 179CD) <6179>* **THELI** [ ] [ ] Jan97
– Preludium / To mega Therion / Cults of the shadow / In the desert of set / Interludium / Nightside of Eden / Opus eclipse / Invocation of Naamah / The siren of the woods / Grand finale – Postludium.

— now without MELLBERG

May 97. (cd) *<6249>* **A'ARAB ZARAQ LUCID DREAMING** [-] [ ] Sweden
– In remembrance / Black fairy / Fly to the rainbow / Children of the damned / Under Jolly Roger / Symphony of the dead / Here comes the tears / Enter transcendental sleep / The quiet desert / Down the qliphothic tunnel / Up to Netzach – Floating back / The fall into eclipse / Enter transcendental sleep / The gates to A'arab Zaraq are open / The quiet desert / Down the qliphothic tunnel / Up to Netzach / Floating back.

— **JOHNSSON** recruited newcomers **MARTINA HORNBACHER** – vocals / **THOMMY ERIKSSON** – guitar / **JAN KAZDA** – bass / **WOLF SIMON** – drums

May 98. (cd) *(NB 317-2) <6317>* **VOVIN** [ ] [ ]
– The rise of Sodom and Gomorrah / Birth of Venus illegitima / Wine of Aluqah / Clavicula nox / The wild hunt / Eye of Shiva / Blacksun – Draconian trilogy (parts 1-3: The opening – Morning star – Black diamonds) / Raven of dispersion.
Jun 99. (cd) *(NB 398-2) <6398>* **CROWNING OF ATLANTIS** [ ] [ ] Jul99
– Crowning of Atlantis / Mark of Cain / Clavicula nox / Crazy nights / From the Dionysian days / Thor / Seawinds / To mega therion (live) / The wings at the hydra (live) / Black sun (live).

— **JOHNSSON** now with **KRISTIAN NIEMANN** – rhythm guitar / **JOHANN NIEMANN** – bass / **SAMI KARPPINEN** – drums

Jan 00. (cd) *(NB 442-2) <6442>* **DEGGIAL** [ ] [ ] Mar00
– Seven secrets of the Sphinx / Eternal return / Enter Vril-Ya / Ship of Luna / The invincible / Deggial / Emerald crown / Flesh of the gods / Via nocturna (part 1 & 2) / O fortuna.

THESE ANIMAL MEN

Formed: Brighton, England . . . 1991 by JULIAN HOOLIGAN (HEWINGS), BOAG, PATRICK (HUSSEY) and STEVE MURRAY. Hailed as flag bearers for the hopelessly contrived 'New Wave Of New Wave' scene – as well as encouraging a glut of pointless third-rate punk throwbacks, it was also the root cause of Brit-pop – THESE ANIMAL MEN emerged in 1993 with a track on the 6-band 'Fierce Panda' punk compilation EP 'Shaggin' In The Streets'. A debut cassette EP, 'WHEELERS, DEALERS AND CHRISTINE KEELERS' (shared with S*M*A*S*H), featured five tracks, the mini-set later to resurface as 'TOO SUSSED?' in '94. Having reinvented themselves (after rather dodgy beginnings) as a would-be CLASH for the 90's – complete with retro-Adidas-chic image – the band thrived on notoriety rather than any engaging musical talent, the 'SPEEED KING' single predictably baiting the usual suspects (i.e. MP's, local councils etc.) but failing to say anything new, either musically or lyrically. After a further single, 'THIS IS THE SOUND OF YOUTH', a debut album, '(COME ON, JOIN) THE HIGH SOCIETY' surfaced later that year, critics divided over its amateur pop-punk sloganeering but generally agreeing that they'd captured something of the zeitgeist. With the mid-90's onset of the aforementioned Brit-pop, the band found themsleves somewhat sidelined despite a more expansive musical outlook on mini-set, 'TAXI FOR THESE ANIMAL MEN' (1995) and follow-up album for Virgin-offshoot, 'Hut', 'ACCIDENT AND EMERGENCY' (1997).

Album rating: TOO SUSSED? mini (*5) / (COME ON, JOIN) THE HIGH SOCIETY (*6) / TAXI FOR THESE ANIMAL MEN (*5) / ACCIDENT AND EMERGENCY (*5)

BOAG – vocals / **JULIAN HOOLIGAN (HEWINGS)** – guitar / **PATRICK (HUSSEY)** – bass / **STEVE MURRAY** – drums

Les Disques De Popcor | not iss.

Dec 93. (c-ep) **WHEELERS, DEALERS AND CHRISTINE KEELERS** [ ] [-]
– (5 tracks; see TOO SUSSED? m-lp) / (4 tracks by S*M*A*S*H)

Hi-Rise | Vernon Yard

Mar 94. (7") *(FLAT 2)* **SPEEED KING. / JOBS FOR THE BOYS** [ ] [-]
Apr 94. (7") *(FLAT 3)* **YOU'RE NOT MY BABYLON. / WHO'S THE DADDY NOW?** [ ] [-]
Jun 94. (cd/c/m-lp) *(FLAT MCD/MTC/MLP 4) <VUSCD 4>* **TOO SUSSED?** [39] [ ]
– Too sussed? (live) / Speeed king / Jobs for the boys / Who's the daddy now? / You're not my Babylon.
Sep 94. (7"ep;pic-d/c-ep/12"ep/cd-ep) *(FLAT/+C/T/CD 7)* **THIS IS THE SOUND OF YOUTH. / SAIL AROUND THE WORLD / HOOLIGAN'S PROGRESS** [72] [-]
Sep 94. (cd/c/lp) *(FLAT CD/MC/LP 8)* **(COME ON, JOIN) THE HIGH SOCIETY** [62] [-]
– Sharp kid / Empire building / Ambulance / This year's model / You're always right / Flawed is beautiful / This is the sound of youth / Sitting tenant / Too sussed? / (Come on, join) The high society / We are living / High society (return).
Mar 95. (m-cd/m-c/m-lp) *(FLAT CD/MC/LP 14)* **TAXI FOR THESE ANIMAL MEN** [64] [-]
– You're always right / Nowhere faces / My human remains / False identification / Wait for it.

Hut | not iss.

Jan 97. (7"/cd-s) *(HUT/+CD 76)* **LIFE SUPPORT MACHINE. / (MY) MAGAZINE / APRIL 7th** [62] [-]
(cd-s) *(HUTDX 76)* – ('A'side) / Wichita lineman / Hammond heavy (emptyheads).
Mar 97. (7") *(HUT 81)* **LIGHT EMITTING ELECTRICAL WAVE. / SISTE ANNE** [72] [-]
(cd-s+=) *(HUTCD 81)* – Seamen's mission lament / Louis Louis. (cd-s) *(HUTDX 81)* – Every bullet's (got my name on it).
Apr 97. (cd)(c/lp) *(CDHUT 40)(HUT MC/LP 40)* **ACCIDENT AND EMERGENCY** [ ] [-]
– Life support machine / So sophisticated / When your hands are tied / Monumental moneymaker / Riverboat captain / New wave girl / 24 hours to live / Going native / Ambulance man / Light emitting electrical wave / April 7th.

— the group have since split up

THERMADORE

Formed: Los Angeles, California, USA ... 1995 by songwriter ROBBIE ALLEN (a one-time roadie for the RED HOT CHILI PEPPERS) who enlisted ex-MARY'S DANISH members CHRIS WAGNER, DAVID KING and in a guest capacity, JULIE RITTER. Heading straight into major label land via a deal with 'Atlantic', THERMADORE made their debut with the album, 'MONKEY ON RICO' (1996), the freewheeling cast of alt-rock veterans sculpting a brooding post-grunge landscape that concluded with a re-working of 'EVERYTHING'S ALRIGHT' (from 'Jesus Christ Superstar').

Album rating: MONKEY ON RICO (*6)

ROBBIE ALLEN (b. 1964) – vocals, guitar / **CHRIS WAGNER** – bass (ex-MARY'S DANISH) / **DAVID KING** – guitar (ex-MARY'S DANISH) / guest incl. **JULIE RITTER** – vocals (ex-MARY'S DANISH) / **CHAD SMITH + JOSH FREESE + STONE GOSSARD**

Holiday-Atlantic | Holiday-Atlantic

May 96. (cd/c) *<(7567 82874-2/-4)>* **MONKEY ON RICO** [ ] [ ] Mar96
– Three days / Amerasian / Missing / Go / Spinning / Candywrapper / Pushing / Punk rock beating / Santa Rosa / Anton / Everything's alright.
above was their last as the group were a loose unit

THIN LIZZY

Formed: Dublin, Ireland . . . 1969 by PHIL LYNOTT and BRIAN DOWNEY together with ERIC BELL and ERIC WRIXON (the latter leaving after the first 45). After a debut single for 'Parlophone' Ireland, the group relocated to London in late 1970 at the suggestion of managers, Ted Carroll and Brian Tuite, having already signed to 'Decca'. 'THIN LIZZY' (1971) and 'SHADES OF A BLUE ORPHANAGE' (1972) passed without much notice, although the group scored a surprise one-off UK Top 10 with 'WHISKEY IN THE JAR'. A traditional Irish folk song, THIN LIZZY's highly original adaptation married plangent lead guitar and folk-rock arrangements to memorable effect. The accompanying album, 'VAGABONDS OF THE WESTERN WORLD' (1973), failed to capitalise on the song's success, although it gave an indication of where the band were headed with the hard-edged likes of 'THE ROCKER'. BELL departed later that year, his replacement being ex-SKID ROW axeman GARY MOORE, the first of many sojourns the guitarist would enjoy with 'LIZZY over the course of his turbulent career. He was gone by the Spring tour of the following year (subsequently joining COLOSSEUM II), the trademark twin guitar attack introduced on that tour courtesy of JOHN CANN and ANDY GEE. They were soon replaced more permanently by SCOTT GORHAM and BRIAN ROBERTSON, THIN LIZZY signing a new deal with 'Vertigo' and releasing the 'NIGHTLIFE' set in late '74. Neither that album nor 1975's 'FIGHTING' succeeded in realising the group's potential, although the latter gave them their first Top 60 entry on the album chart. Partly due to the group's blistering live shows and partly down to the massive success of 'THE BOYS ARE BACK IN TOWN', 'JAILBREAK' (1976) was a transatlantic Top 20 smash. One of the band's most consistent sets of their career, it veered from the power chord rumble and triumphant male bonding of 'THE BOYS . . .' to the epic Celtic clarion call of 'EMERALD'. The brooding, thuggish rifferama of the title track was another highlight, LYNOTT's rich, liquor-throated drawl sounding by turns threatening and conspiratorial. 'JOHNNY THE FOX' (1976) followed into the UK Top 20 later that year, a record which lacked the continuity of its predecessor but nevertheless spawned another emotive, visceral hard rock single in 'DON'T BELIEVE A WORD'. This is what marked THIN LIZZY out from the heavy-rock pack; LYNOTT's outlaw-with-a-broken-heart voice and the propulsive economy of the arrangements were light-years away from the warbling and posturing of 70's proto-metal. Accordingly, 'LIZZY were one of the few rock bands who gained any respect from punks and indeed, LYNOTT subsequently formed an extra curricular project with The DAMNED's RAT SCABIES as well as working with ex-SEX PISTOLS, PAUL COOK and STEVE JONES (as The GREEDIES on the Christmas 1980 single, 'A MERRY JINGLE'). A 1977 US tour saw MOORE fill in for ROBERTSON who'd injured his hand in a fight, although the Scots guitarist was back in place for a headlining spot at the 'Reading Festival' later that year. 'BAD REPUTATION' was released the following month, preceded by the R&B-flavoured 'DANCING IN THE MOONLIGHT' single and furnishing the group with their highest chart placing to date (UK Top 5). But it was through blistering live work that THIN LIZZY had made their name and they finally got around to releasing a concert set in 1978. 'LIVE AND DANGEROUS' remains deservedly revered as a career landmark, as vital, razor sharp and unrestrained as any live set in the history of rock. Later that summer, THIN LIZZY again took to the road with MOORE (ROBERTSON departed to form WILD HORSES) undertaking his third stint in the band alongside MARK NAUSEEF who was deputising for an absent DOWNEY. Previewed by the keening exhilaration of 'WAITING FOR AN ALIBI', the 'BLACK ROSE (A ROCK LEGEND)' (1979) set was the last great THIN LIZZY album. Placing all-out rockers alongside more traditionally influenced material, the set produced another two major UK hits in the defiant 'DO ANYTHING YOU WANT TO DO' and the poignant 'SARAH', a beautifully realised tribute to LYNOTT's baby daughter. MOORE, meanwhile, had been enjoying solo chart success with 'PARISIENNE WALKWAYS', the THIN LIZZY frontman guesting on vocals. By late '79, MOORE was out, however, and LYNOTT secured the unlikely services of another Scot, MIDGE URE, to fulfill touring commitments. When the latter subsequently departed to front ULTRAVOX, LYNOTT replaced him with ex-PINK FLOYD man, SNOWY WHITE. 1980 saw LYNOTT marrying Caroline Crowther (daughter of LESLIE) and releasing his first solo set, 'SOLO IN SOHO'. Although it hit the UK Top 30, the record sold poorly, a shame as it contained some of his most endearingly experimental work. The classic 'YELLOW PEARL' (co-written with URE) nevertheless scored a Top 20 placing and was later used as the theme tune for 'Top Of The Pops'. Later that year saw the release of 'CHINATOWN', the title track giving THIN LIZZY yet another hit. A further patchy album, 'RENEGADE' followed in late '81, THIN LIZZY's popularity clearly on the wane as it struggled to break the Top 40. With the addition of ex-TYGERS OF PAN TANG guitarist JOHN SYKES and keyboardist DARREN WHARTON, the group released something of a belated comeback album in 'THUNDER AND LIGHTNING' (1983). It was to be THIN LIZZY's swansong, however; by the release of live set, 'LIFE' (1983), the group had already split, LYNOTT and DOWNEY forming the short-lived GRAND SLAM. LYNOTT eventually carried on with his solo career (he'd previously released a second set, 'THE PHIL LYNOTT ALBUM' in 1982) in 1985, after settling his differences with MOORE. The pair recorded the driving 'OUT IN THE FIELDS', a UK Top 5 hit and a lesson in consummate heavy-rock for the hundreds of dismal 80's bands wielding a guitar and a poodle haircut. A follow-up single, '19', proved to be LYNOTT's parting shot, the Irishman dying from a drugs overdose on the 4th of January '86. As family, rock stars and wellwishers crowded into a small chapel in Southern Ireland for LYNOTT's low-key funeral, the rock world mourned the loss of one of its most talented, charismatic and much-loved figureheads. • **Songwriters:** PHIL LYNOTT and Co. and also covers of ROSALIE (Bob Seger) / I'M STILL IN LOVE WITH YOU (Frankie Miller).

Album rating: THIN LIZZY (*4) / SHADES OF A BLUE ORPHANAGE (*4) / VAGABONDS OF THE WESTERN WORLD (*5) / NIGHTLIFE (*5) / FIGHTING (*6) / JAILBREAK (*8) / JOHNNY THE FOX (*8) / BAD REPUTATION (*6) / LIVE AND DANGEROUS (*9) / BLACK ROSE – A ROCK LEGEND (*6) / CHINATOWN (*5) / ADVENTURES OF THIN LIZZY compilation (*8) / RENEGADE (*5) / THUNDER AND LIGHTNING (*7) / LIFE (*7) / DEDICATION – THE VERY BEST OF THIN LIZZY compilation (*8) / Phil Lynott: SOLO IN SOHO (*4) / THE PHIL LYNOTT ALBUM (*6) / THE BEST OF PHIL LYNOTT & THIN LIZZY – SOLDIER OF FORTUNE compilation (*7)

PHIL LYNOTT (b.20 Aug'51, from Brazillian + Irish parents. Raised from 3 by granny in Crumlin, Dublin) – vocals, bass (ex-ORPHANAGE, ex-SKID ROW brief) / **ERIC BELL** (b. 3 Sep'47, Belfast, N.Ireland) – guitar, vocals (ex-DREAMS) / **BRIAN DOWNEY** (b.27 Jan'51) – drums (ex-ORPHANAGE) / **ERIC WRIXON** – keyboards

Parlophone | not iss.

1970. (7"; as THIN LIZZIE) *<DIP 513>* **THE FARMER. / I NEED YOU** [-] [-] Ireland

— now a trio (+ without WRIXON)

Decca | London

Apr 71. (lp) *(SKL 5082) <594>* **THIN LIZZY** [ ] [ ]
– The friendly ranger at Clontarf Castle / Honesty is no excuse / Diddy Levine / Ray-gun / Look what the wind blew in / Eire / Return of the farmer's son / Clifton Grange Hotel / Saga of the ageing orphan / Remembering. *(cd-iss. Jan89 on 'Deram'+=; 820 528-2)* – Dublin / Remembering (part 2) / Old moon madness / Things ain't working out down at the farm.

Aug 71. (7"ep) *(F 13208)* **NEW DAY** [ ] [-]
– Things ain't working out down on the farm / Remembering pt.II / Old moon madness / Dublin.

Mar 72. (lp) *(TXS 108)* **SHADES OF A BLUE ORPHANAGE** [ ] [-]
– The rise and dear demise of the funky nomadic tribes / Buffalo gal / I don't want to forget how to jive / Sarah / Brought down / Baby face / Chatting today / Call the police / Shades of a blue orphanage. *(cd-iss. Nov88 on 'Deram'; 820 527-2)*

Nov 72. (7") *(F 13355) <20076>* **WHISKEY IN THE JAR. / BLACK BOYS IN THE CORNER** [6] [ ]

May 73. (7") *(F 13402) <20078>* **RANDOLPH'S TANGO. / BROKEN DREAMS** [ ] [ ]

Sep 73. (lp) *(SKL 5170) <636>* **VAGABONDS OF THE WESTERN WORLD** [ ] [ ]
– Mama nature said / The hero and the madman / Slow blues / The rocker / Vagabonds (of the western world) / Little girl in bloom / Gonna creep up on you / A song for while I'm away. *(cd-iss. May91 on 'Deram'+=; 820969-2)* – Whiskey in the jar / Black boys on the corner / Randolph's tango / Broken dreams.

Nov 73. (7") *(F 13467)* **THE ROCKER. / HERE I GO AGAIN** [ ] [-]

— **GARY MOORE** (b. 4 Apr'52, Belfast) – guitar, vocals (ex-SKID ROW) repl. BELL (later MAINSQUEEZE)

Apr 74. (7") *(F 13507) <20082>* **LITTLE DARLIN'. / BUFFALO GIRL** [ ] [ ]

— (on tour May'74) **JOHN CANN** – guitar (ex-ATOMIC ROOSTER, ex-BULLITT) / **+ ANDY GEE** – guitar (ex-ELLIS) both repl. GARY MOORE who joined COLOSSEUM II. These temp. guitarists were deposed by **SCOTT GORHAM** (b.17 Mar'51, Santa Monica, Calif.) + **BRIAN ROBERTSON** (b.12 Sep'56, Glasgow, Scotland)

Vertigo | Vertigo

Oct 74. (7") *(6059 111)* **PHILOMENA. / SHA LA LA** [ ] [-]

Nov 74. (lp) *(6360 116) <SRMI 1107>* **NIGHTLIFE** [ ] [ ]
– She knows / Night life / It's only money / Still in love with you / Frankie Carroll / Showdown / Banshee / Philomena / Sha-la-la / Dear heart. *(re-iss. Aug83 lp/c; PRICE/PRIMC 31) (cd-iss. Jun89; 838029-2)*

Jan 75. (7") *<202>* **SHOWDOWN. / NIGHT LIFE** [-] [ ]

Jun 75. (7") *(6059 124)* **ROSALIE. / HALF CASTE** [ ] [-]

Aug 75. (lp)(c) *(6360 121)(7138 070) <SRMI 1108>* **FIGHTING** [60] [ ]
– Rosalie / For those who love to live / Suicide / Wild one / Fighting my way back / King's vengeance / Spirit slips away / Silver dollar / Freedom song / Ballad of a hard man. *(re-iss. Aug83 lp/c; PRICE/PRIMC 32) (cd-iss. Jun89; 842433-2) (cd re-iss. Mar96 on 'Mercury'; 532296-2)*

Oct 75. (7") *(6059 129)* **WILD ONE. / FOR THOSE WHO LOVE TO DIE** [ ] [-]

Nov 75. (7") *<205>* **WILD ONE. / FREEDOM SONG** [-] [ ]

Vertigo | Mercury

Mar 76. (lp)(c) *(9102 008)(7138 075) <SRMI 1081>* **JAILBREAK** [10] [18]
– Jailbreak / Angel from the coast / Running back / Romeo and the lonely girl / Warriors / The boys are back in town / Fight or fall / Cowboy song / Emerald. *(re-iss. Oct83 lp/c; PRICE/PRIMC 50) (cd-iss. Jun89; 822785-2) (cd re-iss. Mar96 on 'Mercury'; 532294-2)*

Apr 76. (7") *(6059 139)* **THE BOYS ARE BACK IN TOWN. / EMERALD** [8] [-]

Apr 76. (7") *<73786>* **THE BOYS ARE BACK IN TOWN. / JAILBREAK** [-] [12]

Jul 76. (7") *(6059 150)* **JAILBREAK. / RUNNING BACK** [31] [-]

Sep 76. (7") *<73841>* **THE COWBOY SONG. / ANGEL FROM THE COAST** [-] [77]

Oct 76. (lp)(c) *(9102 012)(7138 082) <SRMI 1119>* **JOHNNY THE FOX** [11] [52]
– Johnny / Rocky / Borderline / Don't believe a word / Fools gold / Johnny the fox meets Jimmy the weed / Old flame / Massacre / Sweet Marie / Boogie woogie dance. *(re-iss. May83 lp/c; PRICE/PRIMC 11) (cd-iss. May90; 822687-2) (cd re-iss. Mar96 on 'Mercury'; 532295-2)*

Nov 76. (7") *<73867>* **ROCKY. / HALF-CASTE** [-] [ ]

Jan 77. (7") *(LIZZY 1)* **DON'T BELIEVE A WORD. / OLD FLAME** [12] [-]

Jan 77. (7") *<73882>* **JOHNNY THE FOX MEETS JIMMY THE WEED. / OLD FLAME** [-] [ ]

— BRIAN ROBERTSON became injured, GARY MOORE deputised (on 6 mths. tour only)

Aug 77. (7") *(6059 177) <73945>* **DANCING IN THE MOONLIGHT. / BAD REPUTATION** [14] [ ]

Sep 77. (lp)(c) *(9102 016)(7231 011) <SRMI 1186>* **BAD REPUTATION** [4] [39]
– Soldier of fortune / Bad reputation / Opium trail / Southbound / Dancing in the moonlight (it's caught me in its spotlight) / Killer without a cause / Downtown sundown / That woman's gonna break your heart / Dear Lord. *(re-iss. May83 lp/c; PRICE/PRIMC 12) (cd-iss. Apr90; 842434-2) (cd re-iss. Mar96 on 'Mercury'; 532298-2)*

Apr 78. (7") *(LIZZY 2)* **ROSALIE; COWBOY'S SONG (live medley). / ME AND THE BOYS** [20] [-]

Vertigo | Warners

Jun 78. (d-lp) *(9199 645) <3213>* **LIVE AND DANGEROUS (live)** [2] [84]
– Jailbreak / Emerald / South bound / Rosalie – Cowgirls' song / Dancing in the moonlight (it's caught me in its spotlight) / Massacre / Still in love with you / Johnny the fox meets Jimmy the weed / Cowboy song / The boys are back in town / Don't believe a word / Warriors / Are you ready / Suicide / Sha la la / Baby drives me crazy / The rocker. *(re-iss. Nov84; d-lp/d-c; PRID/+C 6) (cd-iss. Jun89; 838030-2) (cd re-iss. Mar96 on 'Mercury'; 532297-2)*

Jul 78. (7") *<8648>* **COWBOY SONG. / JOHNNY THE FOX (MEETS JIMMY THE WEED)** [-] [ ]

— In Autumn'78 tour, DOWNEY was deputised by MARK NAUSEEF. **GARY MOORE** – guitar, vocals returned to repl. ROBERTSON who formed WILD HORSES

Feb 79. (7") *(LIZZY 3)* **WAITING FOR AN ALIBI. / WITH LOVE** 9 -

Apr 79. (lp/c) *(9102/7231 032) <3338>* **BLACK ROSE (A ROCK LEGEND)** 2 81
– Do anything you want to / Toughest street in town / S & M / Waiting for an alibi / Sarah / Got to give it up / Get out of here / With love / A roisin dubh (Black rose) A rock legend part 1. Shenandoah – part 2. Will you go lassy go – part 3. Danny boy – part 4. The mason's apron. *(re-iss. Sep86 lp/c; PRICE/PRIMC 90) (cd-iss. Jun89; 830392-2) (cd re-iss. Mar96 on 'Mercury'; 532299-2)*

— Apr'79, LYNOTT's vox feat. on GARY MOORE's Top 10 hit 'Parisienne Walkways'.

Jun 79. (7") *(LIZZY 4)* **DO ANYTHING YOU WANT TO. / JUST THE TWO OF US** 14 -

Jun 79. (7") *<49019>* **DO ANYTHING YOU WANT TO. / S & M** -

Sep 79. (7") *(LIZZY 5)* **SARAH. / GOT TO GIVE IT UP** 24 -

Sep 79. (7") *<49078>* **WITH LOVE. / GO TO GIVE IT UP** -

— (for 2 months-late'79) **MIDGE URE** (b. JAMES URE, 10 Oct'53, Glasgow) – guitar (ex-SLIK, ex-RICH KIDS) repl. GARY MOORE who went solo. URE joined ULTRAVOX when repl. by **SNOWY WHITE**

May 80. (7") *(LIZZY 6)* **CHINATOWN. / SUGAR BLUES** 21 -

Sep 80. (7") *(LIZZY 7)* **KILLER ON THE LOOSE. / DON'T PLAY AROUND** 10 -
(d7"+=) *(LIZZY 7/+701)* – Got to give it up (live) / Chinatown (live).

Oct 80. (lp/c) *(6359/7150 030) <3496>* **CHINATOWN** 7
– We will be strong / Chinatown / Sweetheart / Sugar blues / Killer on the loose / Having a good time / Genocide (the killing of buffalo) / Didn't I / Hey you. *(re-is.Sep86, cd-iss. Jun89)*

Oct 80. (7") *<49643>* **KILLER ON THE LOOSE. / SUGAR BLUES** -

Nov 80. (7"; as The GREEDIES) *(GREED 1)* **A MERRY JINGLE. / A MERRY JANGLE** 28 -
above also featured STEVE JONES + PAUL COOK (ex-SEX PISTOLS)

Feb 81. (7") *<49679>* **WE WILL BE STRONG. / SWEETHEART** -

Apr 81. (7"ep/12"ep) *(LIZZY 8/+12)* **LIVE KILLERS (live)** 19 -
– Are you ready / Opium trail / Dear Miss lonely heart / Bad reputation.

Jul 81. (7") *(LIZZY 9)* **TROUBLE BOYS. / MEMORY PAIN** 53 -

Nov 81. (lp/c) *(6359/7150 083) <3622>* **RENEGADE** 38
– Angel of death / Renegade / The pressure will blow / Leave this town / Hollywood (down on your luck) / No one told him / Fats / Mexican blood / It's getting dangerous. *(cd-iss. Jun90; 842435-2)*

Feb 82. (7"/7"pic-d) *(LIZZY/+PD 10) <50056>* **HOLLYWOOD (DOWN ON YOUR LUCK). / THE PRESSURE WILL BLOW** 53
(10"one-sided) *(LIZZY 10)* – ('A'side only)

— **LYNOTT + DOWNEY** recruited new members **JOHN SYKES** – guitar (ex-TYGERS OF PAN TANG) repl. GORHAM **DARREN WHARTON** – keyboards repl. SNOWY WHITE went solo + re-joined PINK FLOYD

Feb 83. (d7"/12") *(LIZZY 11 11-12/22)* **COLD SWEAT. / BAD HABITS / DON'T BELIEVE A WORD (live). / ANGEL OF DEATH (live)** 27 -

Mar 83. (lp/c) *(VERL/+C 3) <23831>* **THUNDER AND LIGHTNING** 4
– Thunder and lightning / This is the one / The sun goes down / The holy war / Cold sweat / Someday she is going to hit back / Baby please don't go / Bad habits / Heart attack. *(initial copies with free live 12")* – EMERALD / KILLER ON THE LOOSE. / THE BOYS ARE BACK IN TOWN / HOLLYWOOD *(cd-iss. Jun89; 810490-2)*

Apr 83. (7"/12") *(LIZZY 12/+12)* **THUNDER AND LIGHTNING. / STILL IN LOVE WITH YOU (live)** 39 -

Jul 83. (7") *(LIZZY 13)* **THE SUN GOES DOWN (remix). / BABY PLEASE DON'T GO** 52 -
(12"+=) *(LIZZY 13/+12)* – ('A'remix).

Nov 83. (d-lp/d-c) *(VERD/+C 6) <23986>* **LIFE (live)** 29
– Thunder & lightning / Waiting for an alibi / Jailbreak / Baby please don't go / The holy war / Renegade / Hollywood / Got to give it up / Angel of death / Are you ready / Boys are back in town / Cold sweat / Don't believe a word / Killer on the loose / The sun goes down / Emerald / Roisin dubh (Black rose) A rock legend part 1. Shenandoah – part 2. Will you go lassy go – part 3. Danny boy – part 4. The mason's apron / Still in love with you / The rocker. *(4th side featured past members) (cd-iss. Aug90; 812882-2)*

— Had already concluded proceedings. LYNOTT and DOWNEY formed short-lived GRAND SLAM. Tragically, PHIL LYNOTT died of heart failure on the 4th January '86.

– compilations, others –

Aug 76. (lp/c) *Decca; (SKL/KSKC 5249)* **REMEMBERING – PART ONE** -

Jan 78. (7"m) *Decca; (F 13748)* **WHISKEY IN THE JAR. / SITAMOIA / VAGABOND OF THE WESTERN WORLD** -

Aug 79. (7"m) *Decca; (THIN 1)* **THINGS AIN'T WORKING OUT DOWN ON THE FARM. / THE ROCKER / LITTLE DARLIN'** -

Sep 79. (lp) *Decca; (SKL 5298)* **THE CONTINUING SAGA OF THE AGEING ORPHANS** -

Apr 81. (lp/c) *Vertigo; (LIZ TV/MC 001)* **ADVENTURES OF THIN LIZZY** 6 -
– Whiskey in the jar / Wild one / Jailbreak / The boys are back in town / Don't believe a word / Dancing in the moonlight / Waiting for an alibi / Do anything you want to / Sarah / Chinatown / Killer on the loose.

Dec 81. (lp/c) *Decca; (KTBC/TAB 28)* **ROCKERS** -
(re-iss. Oct93 on 'Deram' cd/c; 820 526-2/-4)

Mar 83. (cd) *Vertigo; (800 060-2)* **LIZZY KILLERS** -

Oct 83. (7") *Old Gold; (OG 9330)* **WHISKEY IN THE JAR. / THE ROCKER** -

Nov 83. (lp/c) *Contour; (CN/+4 2066)* **THE BOYS ARE BACK IN TOWN** -

Jan 85. (7") *Old Gold; (OG 9484)* **DANCING IN THE MOONLIGHT. / DON'T BELIEVE A WORD** -

Nov 85. (d-lp/c) *Castle; (CCS LP/MC 117)* **THE COLLECTION** -
(cd-iss. Jul87; CCSCD 117)

Nov 85. (lp/c) *Karussel Gold; (822694-1/-4)* **WHISKEY IN THE JAR** -

Apr 86. (lp/c) *Contour; (CN/+4 2080)* **WHISKEY IN THE JAR** -

Aug 86. (12"ep) *Archive 4;* **WHISKEY IN THE JAR / THE ROCKER. / SARAH / BLACK BOYS ON THE CORNER** -

Nov 87. (lp/c/cd) *Telstar; (STAR/STAC/TCD 2300)* **THE BEST OF PHIL LYNOTT & THIN LIZZY – SOLDIER OF FORTUNE** 55 -
– Whiskey in the jar / Waiting for an alibi / Sarah / Parisieene walkways / Do anything you want to / Yellow pearl / Chinatown / King's call / The boys are back in town / Rosalie (cowboy's song) / Dancing in the moonlight / Don't believe a word / Jailbreak. *(cd+=)* – Out in the fields / Killer on the loose / Still in love with you.

Feb 88. (7") *Old Gold; (OG 9764)* **THE BOYS ARE BACK IN TOWN. / ('B'by Bachman-Turner Overdrive)** -

Jun 89. (lp) *Grand Slam; <SLAM 4>* **LIZZY LIVES (1976-84)** -

Jan 91. (7"/c-s) *Vertigo; (LIZZY/LIZMC 14)* **DEDICATION. / COLD SWEAT** 35 -
(12"+=/cd-s+=) *(LIZZY1/LIZCD 14)* – Emerald (live) / Still in love with you.
(12"pic-d+=) *(LIZP1 14)* – Bad reputation / China town.

Feb 91. (cd/c/lp) *Vertigo; (848 192-2/-4/-1)* **DEDICATION – THE VERY BEST OF THIN LIZZY** 8 -
– Whiskey in the jar / The boys are back in town / Jailbreak / Don't believe a word / Dancing in the moonlight / Rosalie – Cowgirl song (live) / Waiting for an alibi / Do anything you want to / Parisienne walkways (with GARY MOORE) / The rocker / Killer on the loose / Sarah / Out in the fields (with GARY MOORE) / Dedication. *(cd+=/c+=)* – Still in love with you (live) / Bad reputation / Emerald / Chinatown.

Mar 91. (7"/c-s) *Vertigo; (LIZZY/LIZMC 15)* **THE BOYS ARE BACK IN TOWN. / SARAH** 63 -
(12"/cd-s) *(LIZZY1/LIZCD 15)* – ('A'side) / Johnny the fox / Black boys on the corner / Me and the boys.

Oct 92. (cd) *Windsong; (WINCD 024)* **BBC RADIO 1 LIVE IN CONCERT** -

Nov 94. (cd/c) *Strange Fruit; (SFR CD/MC 130)* **THE PEEL SESSIONS** -

Jan 96. (cd/c) *Polygram; (528113-2/-4)* **WILD ONE – THE VERY BEST OF THIN LIZZY** 18 -

Mar 96. (cd) *Spectrum; (552085-2/-4)* **WHISKEY IN THE JAR** -

Jan 00. (cd) *Universal; (E 844945-2)* **UNIVERSAL MASTERS COLLECTION**

Jun 00. (cd) *S.P.V.; (SPV 085-2199-2)* **ONE NIGHT ONLY** -

PHIL LYNOTT

(solo) but with THIN LIZZY members.

Vertigo Warners

Mar 80. (7"/12") *(SOLO 1/+12)* **DEAR MISS LONELY HEARTS. / SOLO IN SOHO** 32 -

Apr 80. (lp)(pic-lp) *(9102 038)(PHIL 1) <3405>* **SOLO IN SOHO** 28
– Dear Miss lonely hearts / King's call / A child's lullaby / Tattoo / Solo in Soho / Girls / Yellow pearl / Ode to a black man / Jamaican rum / Talk in '79. *(re-iss. Sep85 lp/c; PRICE/PRIMC 88) (cd-iss. Jul90; 842564-2)*

Jun 80. (7") *(SOLO 2) <49272>* **KING'S CALL. / ODE TO A BLACK MAN** 35

Mar 81. (7"yellow) *(SOLO 3)* **YELLOW PEARL. / GIRLS** 56 -
(re-iss. Dec81 – 12"; SOLO 3-12)
(above was later the TV theme for 'Top Of The Pops')

Aug 82. (7") *(SOLO 4)* **TOGETHER. / SOMEBODY ELSE'S DREAM** -
(12"+=) *(SOLO 4-12)* – ('A'dance version).

Sep 82. (7") *(SOLO 5)* **OLD TOWN. / BEAT OF THE DRUM** -

Oct 82. (lp/c) *(6359/7150 117)* **THE PHIL LYNOTT ALBUM** -
– Fatalistic attitude / The man's a fool / Old town / Cathleen / Growing up / Together / Little bit of water / Ode to Liberty (the protest song) / Gino / Don't talk about me baby. *(cd-iss. Jul90; 842564-2)*

— May'85, GARY MOORE & PHIL hit UK Top 5 with 'OUT IN THE FIELDS'.

Polydor not iss.

Nov 85. (7") *(POSP 777)* **19. / 19 (dub)** -
(12"+=) *(POSPX 777)* – A day in the life of a blues singer.
(d7"+=; 1 pic-d) *(POSPD 777)* – THIN LIZZY; Whiskey in the jar – The rocker.

– (PHIL LYNOTT) posthumous –

Jan 87. (7") *Vertigo; (LYN 1)* **KING'S CALL. / YELLOW PEARL** 68 -
(12"+=) *(LYN 1-12)* – Dear Miss lonely hearts (live).

THIRD EYE BLIND

Formed: San Francisco, California, USA ... mid-90's by frontman, STEPHAN JENKINS (JASON SLATER, future SNAKE RIVER CONSPIRACY mainman was also a member during TEB's early inception). After supporting OASIS in their home city, TEB signed a lucrative deal with 'Elektra' for whom they delivered their first US Top 5 hit, 'SEMI-CHARMED LIFE'. That Spring of '97 also saw the band gain massive sales for their eponymous debut set which also climbed into the Top 30. Musically, they were nothing startling or adventurous (lying inbetween STEVE MILLER and the SPIN DOCTORS), although classy acoustic alt-rock/pop tunes did help the band achieve some kind of steady fanbase. Sophomore set, 'BLUE' (1999), was another to hit the US Top 40, it sales helped no doubt by the success of single, 'NEVER LET YOU GO', the following year.

Album rating: THIRD EYE BLIND (*6) / BLUE (*5)

STEPHAN JENKINS – vocals, guitar / **KEVIN CADOGAN** – guitar / **REN KLYCE** – keyboards / **ARION SALAZAR** – bass, keyboards

Elektra Elektra

Jun 97. (c-s) *(E 4181C) <64137>* **SEMI-CHARMED LIFE. / TATTOO OF THE SUN** 4 Mar97
(cd-s+=) *(E 4181CD)* – London.

Jun 97. (cd/c) *<(7559 62012-2/-4)>* **THIRD EYE BLIND** 25 Apr97
– Losing a whole year / Narcolepsy / Semi-charmed life / Jumper / Graduate / How's it going to be / Thanks a lot / Burning man / Good for you / London / I want you / Background / Motorcycle drive-by / God of wine.

Sep 97. (7"/c-s) *(E 3907/+C)* **SEMI-CHARMED LIFE. / TATTOO OF THE SUN** 33 -
(cd-s+=) *(E 3907CD)* – London.
(re-iss. May98; same)

Nov 97. (7") *(E 3883)* **GRADUATE. / HORROR SHOW** [ ] [ ]
(c-s+=/cd-s+=) *(E 3883 C/CD)* – ('A'remix).
Mar 98. (c-s/cd-s) *(E 3863 C/CD) <64130>* **HOW'S IT GOING TO BE / SEMI-CHARMED LIFE / HORROR SHOW** [51] [9] Nov97
Jul 98. (7") *(E 3832)* **LOSING A WHOLE YEAR. / HORROR SHOW** [ ] [ ]
(cd-s+=) *(E 3832CD)* – Graduate (remix).
Nov 98. (-) *<radio play>* **JUMPER / GRADUATE (remix)** [-] [5]
May 00. (cd/c) *<(7559 62415-2/-4)>* **BLUE** [ ] [40] Nov99
– Anything / Wounded / 10 days late / Never let you go / Deep inside of you / 1000 Julys / Ode to maybe / Red summer sun / Camouflage / Farther / Slow motion / Darkness / Darwin.
Jun 00. (c-s/cd-s) *(E 7050 C/CD) <album cut>* **NEVER LET YOU GO / NEVER LET YOU GO (version) / ANYTHING** [ ] [14] Jan00
Jul 00. (-) *<radio play>* **DEEP INSIDE OF YOU** [-] [69]

THIRD WORLD WAR

Formed: London, England . . . early 70's by main songwriter, TERRY STAMP, JIM AVORY and TONY ASHTON. Signing to the 'Fly' label (home of T. REX), they unleashed their powerful politically-motivated eponymous debut set in 1971. Hailed by many as a precursor to 70's punk rock and 80's hardcore, especially with reference to the uncompromising lyrical content, the group battled their way through the dying embers of the capital's counter-culture scene with their working class rallying calls. A second album, 'II', released the following year, took its cue from the burgeoning bovver/stomp-rock scene that SLADE were cultivating, however, it failed to impress to public, the group going their separate ways soon after. In 1975, STAMP released a solo album, 'FAT STICKS', for 'A&M' (AMLH 63329), featuring seasoned musicians JIM AVORY, TONY NEWMAN, MIKE MORAN, OLLIE HALSALL, HERBIE FLOWERS and ALAN SPENNER.

Album rating: THIRD WORLD WAR (*8) / THIRD WORLD WAR II (*7)

TERRY STAMP – vocals, guitar / **JIM AVORY** – bass / **TONY ASHTON** – keyboards / JIM PRICE – horns / **SPEEDY** – percussion / **WINGY** – harmonica / **FRED SMITH** – drums / **BOBBY KEYS** – sax

Fly / not iss.

Apr 71. (7") *(BUG 7)* **ASCENSION DAY. / TEDDY TEETH GOES SAILING** [ ] [-]
May 71. (lp) *(FLY 4)* **THIRD WORLD WAR** [ ] [-]
– Ascension day / M.I.5's alive / Teddy teeth goes sailing / Working class man / Shepherds Bush cowboy / Stardom road – part I / Stardom road – part II / Get out of my bed you dirty red / Preaching violence. *(cd-iss. May95 on 'Repertoire'; REP 4560-WP) (cd re-iss. Jul97 on 'Spalax'; 14504)*

— **JOHN KNIGHTSBRIDGE + RAY FLACKE** – guitars / **JOHN HAWKEN** – piano / **CRAIG COLLINGE** – drums; repl. ASHTON, SPEEDY, WINGY, KEYS + SMITH

Jul 71. (7") *(BUG 11)* **URBAN ROCK. / WORKING CLASS MAN** [ ] [-]

Track / not iss.

1972. (lp) *(2406 108)* **THIRD WORLD WAR II** [ ] [-]
– Yobo / Urban rock / Coshing old lady blues / Rat crawl / I'd rather cut cane for Castro / Factory canteen news / Hammersmith guerrilla. *(cd-iss. May95 on 'Repertoire'; REP 4566-WP) (cd re-iss. Jul97 on 'Spalax'; 14538)*

— disbanded after above. KNIGHTSBRIDGE and HAWKEN were later part of BOX OF FROGS with ex-YARDBIRDS members.

• 38 SPECIAL

Formed: Jacksonville, Florida, USA . . . 1975 by DONNIE VAN ZANT (younger brother of LYNYRD SKYNYRD's deceased singer, RONNIE), who recruited DON BARNES, JEFF CARLISI, KEN LYONS and the double-barrelled drum assault of STEVE BROOKINS and JACK GRONDIN. Named after the infamous hand-gun, they quickly set about issuing an eponymous debut for 'A&M', a set that featured a guest spot by DAN HARTMAN (ex-EDGAR WINTER). Initially trading in Southern-fried boogie via barroom commerciality, the group drifted towards AOR on their subsequent albums. Eventually breaking through in their homeland at the turn of the decade with a single and album of the same name, 'ROCKIN' INTO THE NIGHT', they went on to even greater success in the early 80's. Albums such as the definitive 'WILD-EYED SOUTHERN BOYS' (1980), 'SPECIAL FORCES' (1982) and 'TOUR DE FORCE' (1983) saw the band becoming regular fixtures in the US Billboard charts, while they also scored with a few hit singles, notably 'CAUGHT UP IN YOU'. After a few years in the proverbial wilderness, the band returned to full-bore in 1986, blasting back into the US Top 20 with 'STRENGTH IN NUMBERS'. The following year, °38 SPECIAL took another side step into film work when they provided 'BACK TO PARADISE' for the soundtrack of 'Revenge Of The Nerds II'. A few personnel changes ensued prior to the release of a 1988 album, 'ROCK'N'ROLL STRATEGY', and although they delivered a back-to-basics set in the early 90's, 'BONE AGAINST STEEL', their commercial appeal had unfortunately gone rusty. After a prolonged absence of more than six years, °38 SPECIAL returned to the fray in 1997 with comeback set, 'RESOLUTION', featuring a line-up of VAN ZANT, BARNES, JUNSTROM and DANNY CHAUNCEY. Co-penned with professional songwriter JIM PETERIK, the record displayed a marked improvement in quality and an admirable attempt to bring the band's sound up to date. It was certainly given the seal of approval by fans, many of whom would've been among the crowd at Sturgis, South Dakota's 1999 biker festival where °38 SPECIAL recorded 'LIVE AT STURGIS ROCK' (1999). DONNIE, meanwhile, had collaborated with his sibling JOHNNY on 1998's 'BROTHER TO BROTHER' album. Released as simply VAN ZANT, the record – again featuring the writing talents of PETERIK – was squarely in the balls-to-the-wall Southern Rock tradition, its reception sufficiently encouraging to warrant the recording of a follow-up set. 'VAN ZANT II' arrived in 2001, a second helping of no frills guitar boogie which featured contributions from the likes of country-rocker KENNY WAYNE SHEPHERD. • **Songwriters:** DONNIE VAN ZANT or current group members with some covers. Their later contributor JOHN CASCELO of The JOHN MELLENCAMP band, died in 1992.

Album rating: .38 SPECIAL (*5) / SPECIAL DELIVERY (*5) / ROCKIN' INTO THE NIGHT (*6) / WILD-EYED SOUTHERN BOYS (*6) / SPECIAL FORCES (*6) / TOUR DE FORCE (*6) / STRENGTH IN NUMBERS (*5) / FLASHBACK compilation (*6) / ROCK & ROLL STRATEGY (*4) / BONE AGAINST STEEL (*4) / RESOLUTION (*4) / LIVE AT STURGIS (*4) / Van Zant: BROTHER TO BROTHER (*4) / VAN ZANT II (*4)

DONNIE VAN ZANT (b.11 Jun'52) – vocals, guitar / **DON BARNES** – guitar, vox / **JEFF CARLISI** – guitar / **STEVE BROOKINS** – drums / **JACK GRONDIN** – drums / **KEN LYONS** – bass

A&M / A&M

May 77. (lp) *(AMLH 64638) <4638>* **• 38 SPECIAL** [ ] [ ]
– Long time gone / Fly away / Around and around / Play a simple song / Gypsy belle / Four wheels / Tell everybody / Just hang on / Just wanna rock & roll.
Jul 77. (7") *<1946>* **LONG TIME GONE. / FOUR WHEELS** [-] [ ]
Sep 77. (7") *<1964>* **TELL EVERYBODY. / PLAY A SIMPLE SONG** [-] [ ]

— **LARRY JUNSTROM** – bass repl. LYONS

Jun 78. (lp) *(AMLH 64684) <4684>* **SPECIAL DELIVERY** [ ] [ ]
– I'm a fool for you / Turnin' to you / Travelin' man / I been a mover / What can I do / Who's been messin' / Can't keep a good man down / Take me back.
Jul 78. (7") *<2051>* **I'M A FOOL FOR YOU. / TRAVELIN' MAN** [-] [ ]
Dec 79. (lp) *(AMLH 64782) <4782>* **ROCKIN' INTO THE NIGHT** [ ] [57]
– Rockin' into the night / Stone cold believer / Take me through the night / Money honey / The love that I've lost / You're the captain / Robin Hood / You got the deal / Turn it on.
Mar 80. (7") *<2205>* **ROCKIN' INTO THE NIGHT. / ROBIN HOOD** [ ] [43] Jan80
Jun 80. (7") *<2242>* **STONE COLD BELIEVER. / (part 2)** [-] [ ]
Jun 80. (7") *(AMS 7535)* **STONE COLD BELIEVER. / ROCKIN' INTO THE NIGHT** [ ] [-]
(12"+=) *(AMSP 7535)* – Robin Hood.
Mar 81. (lp/c) *(AMLH/CMX 64835) <4835>* **WILD-EYED SOUTHERN BOYS** [ ] [18] Feb81
– Hold on loosely / First time around / Wild-eyed Southern boys / Back alley Sally / Fantasy girl / Hittin' & runnin' / Honky tonk dancer / Throw out the line / Bring it on.
Mar 81. (7") *(AMS 8120) <2316>* **HOLD ON LOOSELY. / THROW OUT THE LINE** [ ] [27] Feb81
May 81. (7") *<2330>* **FANTASY GIRL. / HONKY TONK DANCER** [-] [52]
Aug 81. (7") *(AMS 8155)* **FIRST TIME AROUND. / FANTASY GIRL / ROCKIN' INTO THE NIGHT** [ ] [-]
Jun 82. (7") *(AMS 8228) <2412>* **CAUGHT UP IN YOU. / FIRESTARTER** [ ] [10] Apr82
Jun 82. (lp/c) *(AMLH/CXM 64888) <4888>* **SPECIAL FORCES** [ ] [10] May82
– Caught up in you / Back door stranger / Back on the track / Chain lightnin' / Rough-housin' / You keep runnin' away / Breakin' loose / Take 'em out / Firestarter.
Aug 82. (7") *(AMS 8246) <2431>* **YOU KEEP RUNNIN' AWAY. / PRISONERS OF ROCK'N'ROLL** [ ] [38]
Oct 82. (7") *<2505>* **CHAIN LIGHTNIN'. / BACK ON THE TRACK** [-] [ ]
Jan 84. (7") *(AM 174) <2594>* **IF I'D BEEN THE ONE. / 20th CENTURY FOX** [ ] [19] Nov83
Feb 84. (lp/c) *(AMLX/CXM 64971) <4971>* **TOUR DE FORCE** [ ] [22] Nov83
– If I'd been the one / Back where you belong / One time for old times / See me in your eyes / Twentieth century fox / Long distance affair / I oughta let go / One of the lonely ones / Undercover lover. *(cd-iss. 1988; 394971-2)*
Feb 84. (7") *<2615>* **BACK WHERE YOU BELONG. / UNDERCOVER LOVER** [-] [20]
Apr 84. (7") *<2633>* **LONG DISTANCE AFFAIR. / ONE TIME FOR OLD TIMES** [-] [ ]
Sep 84. (7") *<5405>* **TEACHER TEACHER. / 20th CENTURY FOX** [-] [25]
(above single from the feature film 'Teachers', issued on 'Capitol')
May 86. (7") *(AM 321) <2831>* **LIKE NO OTHER NIGHT. / HEARTS ON FIRE** [ ] [14] Apr86
(12"+=) *(AMY 321)* –
May 86. (lp/c) *(AMA/AMC 5115) <5115>* **STRENGTH IN NUMBERS** [ ] [17]
– Somebody like you / Like no other night / Last time / Once in a lifetime / Just a little love / Has there ever been a goodbye / One in a million / Hearts on fire / Against the night / Never give an inch.
Jul 86. (7") *<2854>* **SOMEBODY LIKE YOU. / AGAINST THE NIGHT** [-] [48]
Oct 86. (7") **LAST TIME. / ONE IN A MILLION** [-] [ ]
Jul 87. (7") *<2955>* **BACK TO PARADISE. / REVENGE OF THE NERDS – THEME** [-] [41]
Aug 87. (lp,c,cd) *<3910>* **FLASHBACK** (compilation) [ ] [35]
– Back to Paradise / Hold on loosely / If I'd been the one / Caught up in you / Fantasy girl / Same old feeling / Back where you belong / Teacher, teacher / Like no ther night / Rockin' into the night. *(free live 12"ep)* – Rough housin' / Wild eyed Southern boys / Stone cold believer / Twentieth century fox.

— next album as THIRTY EIGHT SPECIAL

— (1988) **MAX CARL** – vocals, keyboards repl. BARNES

DANNY CLANCY – guitar repl. BROOKINS (said new members now alongside **VAN ZANT, CARLISI, GRONDIN + LUNDSTROM**

Oct 88. (7") *<1246>* **ROCK & ROLL STRATEGY. / LOVE STRIKES** [-] [ ]
Oct 88. (lp,c,cd) *<5218>* **ROCK & ROLL STRATEGY** [-] [61]
– Rock & roll strategy / What's it to ya? / Little Sheba / Comin' down tonight / Midnight magic / Second chance / Hot 'Lanta / Never be lonely / Chattahoochee / Innocent eyes / Love strikes.
Apr 89. (7") *(AM 507) <1273>* **SECOND CHANCE. / COMING DOWN TONIGHT** [ ] [6] Feb89

Jun 89. (7") *<1424>* **COMIN' DOWN TONIGHT. / CHATTAHOOCHEE** [-] [ ]

—— **BOBBY CAPPS** – keyboards; repl. CARL

—— **SCOTT HOFFMAN** – drums repl. CLANCY

Charisma Charisma

Jul 91. (c-s,cd-s) *<98773>* **THE SOUND OF YOUR VOICE / LAST THING I EVER DO** [-] [33]

Jan 92. (cd/c/lp) *(CDCUS/CUSMC/CUSLP 6) <91640>* **BONE AGAINST STEEL** [ ] [ ] Aug91
– The sound of your voice / Signs of love / Last thing I ever do / You definately got me / Rebel to rebel / Bone against steel / You be the dam, I'll be the water / Jimmy Gillum / Tear it up / Don't wanna get it dirty / Burning bridges / Can't shake it / Treasure.

—— re-formed in 1997 with **DONNIE, DON, DANNY + LARRY**

S.P.V. Razor & Tie

Aug 97. (cd) *(SPV 0851875-2) <2829>* **RESOLUTION** [ ] [ ] Jun97
– Fade to blue / Just can't leave you alone / Deja voodoo / Find my way back / Changed by love / After the fire is gone / Miracle man / Shelter me / Homeless guitar / Saving grace / She loves to talk / Trouble / Shatter the silence.

S.P.V. C.M.C.

Feb 00. (cd) *(SPV 085-2977-2) <86281>* **LIVE AT STURGIS (live)** [ ] [ ] Nov99
– Rockin' into the night / 20th Century fox / Back where you belong / Wild-eyed southern boys / Fade to blue / If I'd been the one / Rebel to rebel / Take 'em out / Deja voodoo / Fantasy girl / Caught up in you / Hold on loosely / Just one girl.

VAN ZANT

—— DONNIE + JOHNNY (of LYNYRD SKYNYRD + solo artist) with **CHRIS PELCER** – strings / **PAT BUCHANAN** – guitar / **JIM PETERIK** – guitar (ex-IDES OF MARCH) / **ROBERT WHITE JOHNSON** – percussion

S.P.V. C.M.C.

Mar 98. (cd) *(SPV 085-18900-2) <86236>* **BROTHER TO BROTHER** [ ] [ ] Feb98
– Rage / Can't say it loud enough / Show me / I'm a want you kinda man / Right side up / Brother to brother / Livin' a lie / That was yesterday / Downright and dangerous / Black bottom road / Friend.

Mar 01. (cd) *(SPV 085-7218-2) <86301>* **VAN ZANT II** [ ] [ ]
– Oklahoma / Get what you got comin' / Heart of an angel / Is it for real / Imagination / At least I'm free / Baby get blue / What's the world coming to / Wildside / Alive.

31st FEBRUARY (see under ⇒ ALLMAN BROTHERS BAND)

THOR

Born: JON-MIKL THOR. A former Mr. North America and body builder, the man mountain took his name from a character in a Marvel comic. He initiated his own band comprising his wife PANTERA on vocals, guitarist STEVE PRICE, bassist KEITH ZAZZI and drummer MIKE FAVATA. In 1978, mere mortals were promised a musclebound extravaganza in the form of THOR's debut set, 'KEEP THE DOGS AWAY'. In the event, its rather lame metal posturing and poor production probably didn't even keep the odd stray chihuahua at bay! It took four years for THOR to regain his superhero powers, a tame 7" single, 'OVER TO YOU', doing little to establish him as a metal god. Early in '84, he relaunched himself once more on the unsuspecting British public, a set of Marquee gigs and a mini-set, appropriately titled 'UNCHAINED', briefly holding the attention of vaguely amused metal punters. He subsequently returned to his homeland (America, not Valhalla!) and with a stage show that SPINAL TAP would've been proud of, the caged THOR proceeded to display his immortal powers by blowing up hot water bottles (as normal earthlings would do with balloons!). On the vinyl front, the rampant THOR commanded 'LET THE BLOOD RUN RED' and 'THUNDER ON THE TUNDRA', although it was 'ONLY THE STRONG' (1985 LP) who could brave a second listen. The following year saw JON-MIKL THOR (as he was now known) enter the film industry with a role in the movie, 'Recruits', a project that inspired his final album, 'RECRUITS: WILD IN THE STREETS' (1986). He subsequently sought out his mate Zeus and retired to life in the clouds after appearing in the film, 'Zombie Nightmare'.

Album rating: KEEP THE DOGS AWAY (*4) / UNCHAINED mini (*4) / ONLY THE STRONG (*5) / LIVE IN DETROIT (*4) / RECRUITS: WILD IN THE STREETS (*5)

THOR – vocals / **PANTERA** (b. RUSTY HAMILTON) – vocals / **STEVE PRICE** – guitar / **KEITH ZAZZI** – bass / **MIKE FAVATA** – drums

not iss. Three Hats

1978. (lp) *<2337>* **KEEP THE DOGS AWAY** [-] [ ]
– Keep the dogs away / Sleeping giant / Catch a tiger / I'm so proud / Tell me lies / Military matters / Superhero / Wasted / Rosie / Thunder. *(UK-iss.Jun85 on 'Gull'; GULP 1042)*

K.A. not iss.

Nov 82. (7") *(KA 11)* **OVER TO YOU. / ANITA** [ ] [-]

—— **KARL COCHRAN** – guitar; repl. PRICE

Ultranoise Mongol Horde

Feb 84. (m-lp) *(NOISE 102) <MONGOL 3>* **UNCHAINED** [ ] [-] Canada
– Lightning strikes again / Anger / Rock the city / Lazer eyes / When gods collide / Death march.

Albion not iss.

Apr 84. (7"pic-d) *(ION 165)* **LET THE BLOOD RUN RED. / WHEN GODS COLLIDE** [ ] [-]

Jun 84. (7"pic-d/7") *(P+/ION 168)* **THUNDER ON THE TUNDRA. / HOT FLAMES** [ ] [-]
(12"+=) *(12ION 168)* – ('A'extended).

Roadrunner Enigma

Apr 85. (lp) *(RR 9790) <72044-1>* **ONLY THE STRONG** [ ] [ ]
– 2045 / Only the strong / Start raising hell / Knock 'em down / Let the blood run red / When gods collide / Rock the city / Now comes the storm / Thunder on the tundra / Hot flames / Ride of the chariots.

Jul 85. (7") *(RR 5513)* **KNOCK 'M' DOWN. / LIGHTNING STRIKES (live)** [ ] [-]
(12"+=) *(RR12 5513)* – Anger (live) / ('A'live).

Raw Power not iss.

Apr 86. (lp/c) *(RAW LP/TC 008)* **LIVE IN DETROIT (live)** [ ] [-]
– Thunder on the tundra / Let the blood run red / Knock 'em down / Rock the city / Lightning strikes / Anger / Keep the dogs away / Hot flames / Now comes the storm / When gods collide.

G.W.R. not iss.

1986. (7"; as JON-MIKL THOR) *(GWR 3)* **RECRUITS. / WE LIVE TO ROCK** [ ] [-]

1986. (lp; as JON-MIKL THOR) *(GWLP 3)* **RECRUITS: WILD IN THE STREETS** [ ] [-]
– Recruits (ride hard, live free) / Heartbreak choir / Who's to blame / Warhammer / Ragnarok / Rebirth / Long ride from hell / We live to rock / Lady of the night / Energy.

—— disappeared after above

THORNS

Formed: Oslo, Norway . . . 1989 as the brainchild of SNORRE RUCH. In the plethora of Norwegian metal bands THORNS stood out as a massive inspiration to the other bands of their ilk. As death metal gurus THORNS are more than an enigma, producing in their original incarnation only a few demos and half an LP shared with EMPEROR. Yet from this spartan source THORNS managed to show the way out of the mundanity of black metal; opening the genre up to experimentation through electronica and other assorted influences and styles. THORNS laid the groundwork for the innovations of bands like ARCTURUS and IN THE WOODS. The reason behind the huge lapse in material that occured between the circulation of their original demos in the early 90's and the release of their debut album in 2001, was somewhat darker. RUCH was sent to prison in 1994 for the part he played in the murder of OYSTEIN AARSETH, who formerly played in MAYHEM. RUCH drove VARG VIKERNES to AARSETH's flat on the night of the murder, but has claimed several times he had no knowledge of VIKERNES intentions. On being released from prison it was clear that time inside had not dampened RUCH's musical leanings or experimental touch. A split album with EMPEROR was first to appear in early '99, although this was a very low-key affair. Multi-instrumentalist SNORRE subsequently teamed up with black metal luminaries in the shape of SATYR WONGRAVEN (from SATYRICON), HELLHAMMER (from MAYHEM) and BJORN DENCKER. This all-star black metal band worked on and released the THORNS (extremely) long awaited debut album 'THORNS' (2001); and their patient fanbase were not disappointed.

Album rating: split w/ EMPEROR (*6) / THORNS (*7)

SNORRE RUCH – guitar, multi / with **BJORN 'ALDRAHN' DENCKER** – vocals / **SATYR WONGRAVEN** – guitar (of SATYRICON) / **HELLHAMMER** – drums (of MAYHEM)

Moonfog Moonfog

Mar 99. (cd; split w/ EMPEROR) *(FOG 019CD)* **THORNS / EMPEROR** [ ] [ ]
– (EMPEROR tracks) / Thus march the nightspirit / Melas khole / The discipline of Earth / Cosmic keys. *(also cd-box; FOG 019BX)*

Feb 01. (cd) *(FOG 026CD)* **THORNS** [ ] [-]
– Existence / World playground deceit / Shifting channels / Stellar master elite / Underneath the universe I / Underneath the universe II / Interface to God / Vortex.

THORNSPAWN

Formed: San Antonio, Texas, USA . . . 1993 by BLACKTHORN, SWORNGHOUL and LORD NECRON. Unsurprisingly, these lovely young lads took their cue from the Norwegian black metal mob across the Atlantic, recording a couple of rough demo tapes and making a name for themselves on the underground scene. After a string of high (well, relatively speaking) profile support slots to the likes of DEICIDE, the group inked a deal with the 'Baphomet' label (run by KILLJOY of NECROPHAGIA fame). With ex-NECROVORE man, BJORN HAGA, installed as fourth member, the quartet cut their debut album, 'BLOOD OF THE HOLY, TAINT THY STEEL' (2000). An EP, 'EMPRESS FROM THE REALMS OF BLASPHEMY', followed in 2001.

Album rating: BLOOD FOR THE HOLY, TAINT THY STEEL (*5)

BLACKTHORN – drums, vocals / **LORD NECRON** – guitar / **SWORNGHOUL** – guitar / added **BJORN HAGA** – bass (ex-NECROVORE)

Baphomet Baphomet

Apr 00. (cd) *<(BAPH 2103CD)>* **BLOOD OF THE HOLY, TAINT THY STEEL** [ ] [ ]
– Blood of the holy, taint thy steel / Man, thy name is Satan / Storming the heavens / Ancient path / Bringer of malevolent storms / Dominions of darkness / Thrones of Suspira.

Feb 01. (cd-ep) <*(BAPH 2116CD)*> **EMPRESS FROM THE REALMS OF BLASHEMY**
– Empress from the realms of blasphemy / Everlasting siege of the Aeerasoldiers / Empress from the realms of blasphemy (#2).

THOUGHT INDUSTRY

Formed: Michigan, USA . . . early 90's by BRENT OBERLIN, CHRIS LEE, PAUL ENZIO and DUSTIN DONALDSON. Signing to 'Metal Blade', the band released 'SONGS FOR INSECTS' (1992), their critically bewildering diversity of extreme musical styles included metal, hardcore, industrial, etc. the only common thread running through the band's unrelenting intensity and nihilistic lyrical content. A second set appeared the following year, the interestingly titled, 'MODS CARVE THE PIG . . .'. Early in '96, THOUGHT INDUSTRY issued a long-awaited follow-up, 'OUTER SPACE IS JUST A MARTINI AWAY', while their best effort so far, 'BLACK UMBRELLA' was given light eighteen months later.

Album rating: SONGS FOR INSECTS (*6) / MODS CARVE THE PIG: ASSASSINS, TOADS AND GOD'S FLESH (*6) / OUTER SPACE IS JUST A MARTINI AWAY (*5) / BLACK UMBRELLA (*6) / RECRUITED TO DO GOOD DEEDS FOR THE DEVIL (*4)

BRENT OBERLIN – vocals, bass / **PAUL ENZIO** – guitar / **CHRIS LEE** – guitar / **DUSTIN DONALDSON** – drums

Metal Blade | Metal Blade

Jul 92. (cd) *(CDZORRO 45)* **SONGS FOR INSECTS**
– Third eye / Songs for insects / Corner stone / Daughter mobius / Alexander Vs the puzzle / Ballerina / The chalice vermillion / The flesh is weak / Blistered text and bleeding pens / Bearing an hourglass.

Oct 93. (cd) *(CDZORRO 65)* **MODS CARVE THE PIG: ASSASSINS, TOADS AND GOD'S FLESH**

Metal Blade | Metal Blade

Jan 96. (cd) *(3984 14101CD)* **OUTER SPACE IS JUST A MARTINI AWAY**

Jul 97. (cd) *(3984 14131)* **BLACK UMBRELLA**

May 98. (cd) *(14161-2)* **RECRUITED TO DO GOOD DEEDS FOR THE DEVIL**

THRASHER

Formed: New York, USA . . . mid 1984 by the 'Combat' label, who wanted to release a super session album featuring thrash/hard rock musicians. They employed the services of ex-RODS drummer turned producer CARL CANEDY (now with JACK STARR), who in turn worked with guitarist ANDY McDONALD on the songwriting aspect. An array of heavy-metal musicians (young and old) came into the studio, these included vocalists RHETT FORRESTER, DICKIE PETERSON and MARYANN SCANDIFFIO, guitarists DAN SPITZ, JACK STARR and KIM SIMMONDS, bassists KENNY AARONSON, BILLY SHEEHAN, MARS COWLING and GARY BORDONARO. The self-titled album was delivered soon after, although the project remained a one-off as CANEDY became a much sought after producer for the likes of EXCITER, HELLSTAR, POSSESSED and ATTILA.

Album rating: THRASHER (*5)

CARL CANEDY – drums, producer (ex-RODS) / **RHETT FORRESTER** (RIOT) + **DICKIE PETERSON** (BLUE CHEER) + **MARYANNE SCANDIFFIO** (BLACK LACE) – vocals / **DAN SPITZ** (ANTHRAX) + **KIM SIMMONDS** (SAVOY BROWN) + **JACK STARR** (VIRGIN STEELE) – guitars / **BILLY SHEEHAN** (TALAS) + **KENNY AARONSON** (DERRINGER) + **MARS COWLING** (PAT TRAVERS BAND) + **GARY BORDONARO** (RODS) – bass

Music For Nations | Combat

Jun 85. (lp) *(MFN 45)* <*MX 8017*> **THRASHER**
– Hot and heavy / Ride the viper / Widowmaker / Black lace and leather / She likes it rough / Slipping away / Burning at the speed of light / Bad boys / Never say die.

—— as said, just a one-off

3 COLOURS RED

Formed: London, England . . . 1995 by vocalist/bassist PETE VUCKOVIC and Geordie guitarist CHRIS McCORMACK, who recruited drummer KEITH BAXTER and guitarist BEN HARDING (ex-SENSELESS THINGS). Named after the Kieslowski film of the same name, the band issued their debut 45, 'THIS IS MY HOLLYWOOD' early '97, which immediately led to them signing with 'Creation'. Their first release for the label, the 3-chord pop punk/rock thrash 'NUCLEAR HOLIDAY' homed in on the UK Top 20, narrowly missing its target. 'SIXTY MILE SMILE' however, achieved this feat as did their debut album, 'PURE'. The band subsequently gained a groundswell of support, gigging heavily with the likes of KISS, ANTHRAX and SKUNK ANANSIE, becoming crown princes of the metal press in the process. Early in 1999, 3 COLOURS RED were previewing their Dave Eringa-produced Top 20 sophomore set, 'REVOLT', with a near Top 10 hit, 'BEAUTIFUL DAY'. 'THIS IS THE TIME' followed it into the charts soon afterwards, however, this would be their last release as the quartet disbanded after the Reading/Leeds festivals. McCORMACK returned in 2000 with a new act, GRAND THEFT AUDIO, a sort of supergroup that included ex-members of The WILDHEARTS; GTA's minor hit 'WE LUV U' was not indeed a cover of the Stones' hit – no Grand Theft then after all.

Album rating: PURE (*7) / REVOLT (*7) / Grand Theft Audio: BLAME EVERYONE (*6)

PETE VUCKOVIC (b.16 Feb'71, Tiveton, Devon, England) – vocals, bass (ex-DIAMOND HEAD) / **CHRIS McCORMACK** (b.21 Jun'73, South Shields, England) – guitar, vocals (ex-HONEYCRACK) / **BEN HARDING** (b.31 Jan'65, Stoke-On-Trent, England) – guitar, vocals (ex-SENSELESS THINGS) / **KEITH BAXTER** (b.19 Feb'71, Morcambe, England) – drums

Fierce Panda | not iss.

Mar 96. (7"/cd-s) *(NING 17/+CD)* **THIS IS MY HOLLYWOOD. / HATE SLICK** | | -

Creation | Sony

Jan 97. (7"/c-s) *(CRE/+CS 250)* **NUCLEAR HOLIDAY. / HUMAN FACTORY** | 22 | -
(cd-s+=) *(CRESCD 250)* – My own gauge.

Mar 97. (7") *(CRE 254)* **SIXTY MILE SMILE. / ANISEED (live)** | 20 | -
(cd-s) *(CRESCD 254)* – ('A'side) / Zip the morals / Till I'm ready.
(cd-s) *(CRESCD 254X)* – ('A'side) / This is my Hollywood (live) / Nerve gas (live).

Apr 97. (7") *(CRE 265)* **PURE. / HATESLICK (live)** | 28 | -
(cd-s) *(CRESCD 265)* – ('A'side) / Throughbreeze / Fake apology.
(cd-s) *(CRESCD 265X)* – ('A'side) / Mental blocks (live) / Nuclear holiday (live).

May 97. (cd/lp)(c) *(CRE CD/LP 208)(C-CRE 208)* <*67958*> **PURE** | 16 |
– This is my Hollywood / Nerve gas / Nuclear holiday / Copper girl / Sixty mile smile / Sunny in England / Alright ma / Mental blocks / Fit boy & faint girl / Halfway up the downs / Hateslick / Love's cradle / Aniseed. *(cd re-iss. Sep99; same)*

Jun 97. (7") *(CRE 270)* **COPPER GIRL. / SUNNY IN ENGLAND (live)** | 30 | -
(cd-s) *(CRESCD 270)* – ('A'side) / Inside / This opera.
(cd-s) *(CRESCD 270X)* – ('A'side) / Sixty mile smile (live) / Alright ma (live).

Oct 97. (7") *(CRE 277)* **THIS IS MY HOLLYWOOD. / INSIDE (live)** | 48 | -
(cd-s) *(CRESCD 277)* – ('A'side) / On no ones side / Sunny in England (demo).
(cd-s) *(CRESCD 277X)* – ('A'side) / ('A'-Ice-T sober mix) / Yellow hair carriage / Pure (live).

Oct 98. (7"ep/cd-ep) *(CRE/+SCD 304)* **PARALYSE EP** | | -
– Paralyse / Throwing the world away / Say something / Room with a view.

Jan 99. (7"/c-s) *(CRE/+CS 308)* **BEAUTIFUL DAY. / BEAUTIFUL DAY (acoustic)** | 11 | -
(cd-s) *(CRESCD 308)* – ('A'side) / God shape hole / A fine time for it.
(cd-s) *(CRESCD 308X)* – ('A'side) / I want you / Paralyse (Junkie XL mix).

Feb 99. (cd/c/lp) *(CRECD/CCRE/CRELP 227)* <*69884*> **REVOLT** | 17 |
– Paralyse / Pirouette / Beautiful day / Cancel the exhibition / Intermission / Song on the radio / Paranoid people / Back to the city / This is my time / Be myself / Calling to the outside / Age of madness.

May 99. (c-s) *(CRECS 313)* **THIS IS MY TIME / PARANOID PEOPLE (demo)** | 36 | -
(cd-s) *(CRESCD 313)* – ('A'side) / Everything / www.sad.
(cd-s) *(CRESCD 313X)* – ('A'side) / All the fun of the unfair / If.

—— disbanded in August '99; McCORMACK helped form GRAND THEFT AUDIO

GRAND THEFT AUDIO

CHRIS McCORMACK – guitar / **JAY BUTLER** – vocals (ex-realTV) / **RALPH JEZZARD** – bass, programming (ex-WILDHEARTS, ex-SENSELESS THINGS) / **RITCH BATTERSBY** – drums, programming (ex-WILDHEARTS)

Sci-Fi | Sire

Oct 00. (cd) <*31141*> **BLAME EVERYONE** | - |
– Death to the infidels / We luv U / Stoopid ass / Rock the house / Wake up / Grey, black and white / As good as it gets / Drugs and girls / Avarice / Dead man leaving.

Mar 01. (7"ep/cd-ep) *(SCIFI 1/+CD)* **WE LUV U / REFUSING THE LAST LINE / FUK U IZ IT / UNDER THE LANDFILL** | 65 | -

3 DOORS DOWN

Formed: Escatawpa, nr. Biloxi, Mississippi, USA . . . late 90's by vocalist/drummer BRAD ARNOLD, MATT ROBERTS and TODD HARRELL; added CHRIS HENDERSON soon after. Described by some pundits as bland all-American – similar in some respects to drummer/singer PHIL COLLINS – their local radio station WCPR in Biloxi frequently spun their records. Clones to CREED – i.e. big stadium rock and with God on their side; they're all believers – it looked like 3 DOORS DOWN would be another to break in the US but not the UK.

Album rating: THE BETTER LIFE (*5)

BRAD ARNOLD – vocals, drums / **MATT ROBERTS** – guitar / **CHRIS HENDERSON** – guitar / **TODD HARRELL** – bass

Universal | Universal

Jan 00. (-) <*radio play*> **KRYPTONITE** | - | 3

Sep 00. (cd) <*(153920-2)*> **THE BETTER LIFE** | | 7 Feb00
– Kryptonite / Loser / Duck and run / Not enough / Be like that / Life of my own / The better life / Down poison / By my side / Smack / So I need you.

Oct 00. (-) <*radio play*> **LOSER** | - | 55

—— added drummer when BRAD took on vocal duties on stage

M.C.A. | not iss.

Apr 01. (cd-s) *(MCSTD 40251)* **KRYPTONITE / KRYPTONITE (acoustic sic) / KRYPTONITE (video)** | | -

311

Formed: Omaha, Nebraska, USA . . . 1990 by NICK HEXUM, TIMOTHY J. MAHONEY, P-NUT, CHAD SEXTON and S.A. MARTINEZ. Taking their moniker from the American emergency number, the band signed to the newly resurrected 'Capricorn' label, issuing their debut disc, 'MUSIC' in 1993. Fed mainly on a rap/funk-metal diet of RAGE AGAINST THE MACHINE and RED HOT CHILI PEPPERS, the album, along with their 1994 follow-up, 'GRASSROOTS' built up some local support which translated into a chart call-out two years later with the eponymous US Top 20, '311' set. In 1997, it was all systems go, as 311 were mobilized into the Top 5 with 'TRANSISTOR', although Britain still remained oblivious to their street-chase thrills. Following the 1998 release of disappointing concert set, 'LIVE', the 311 posse were back on the case with 'SOUNDSYSTEM' (1999), clocking up the decibels with their dizzying meltdown of various attitude-friendly music styles. With erstwhile POLICE producer HUGH PADGHAM lending his expertise, the band reined in most of the excess aural flab which had fleshed out the album's predecessor. With a millennial UK breakthrough seemingly as far off as ever, 311 returned in 2001 with 'FROM CHAOS'.

Album rating: MUSIC (*5) / GRASSROOTS (*5) / 311 (*6) / TRANSISTOR (*6) / LIVE (*4) / SOUNDSYSTEM (*5) / FROM CHAOS (*4)

NICK HEXUM – vocals, guitar / **TOMOTHY J. MAHONEY** – guitar / **P-NUT** – bass / **CHAD SEXTON** – drums / **S.A. MARTINEZ** – vocals, turntables

Capricorn Capricorn

Nov 93. (cd/c) *<42008>* **MUSIC** [-] [ ]
– Welcome / Freak out / Visit / Paradise / Unity / Hydrophonic / My stoney baby / Nix hex / Plain / Feels so good / Do you right / Fat chance.

Jun 95. (cd/c) *(477894-2/-4) <42026>* **GRASSROOTS** [ ] [ ] Jul94
– Lucky / Homebrew / Nutsympton / 8:16 a.m. / Omaha stylee / Apples science / Taiyed / Silver / Grassroots / Salsa / Lose / Six / Offbeat / 1-2-3.

Oct 96. (cd/c) *(532 530-2/-4) <42041>* **311** [ ] [12] Jul95
– Down / Random / Jack O'Lantern's weather / All mixed up / Hive / Guns / Misdirected hostility / Purpose / Loco / Brodels / Don't stay home / D.L.M.D. / Sweet / T & P combo.

Nov 96. (cd-ep) **ENLARGED TO SHOW DETAIL EP** [-] [95]
– Tribute / Let the cards fall / Gap / Firewater.

Aug 97. (cd) *<(536181-2)>* **TRANSISTOR** [ ] [4]
– Transistor / Prisoner / Galaxy / Beautiful disaster / Inner light spectrum / Electricity / What was I thinking / Jupiter / Use of time / Continuous life / No control / Running / Color / Light years / Creature feature / Tune in / Rub a dub / Starshines / Strangers / Borders / Stealing happy hour.

Nov 98. (cd) *<(538263-2)>* **LIVE (live)** [ ] [77]
– Down / Homebrew / Beautiful disaster / Misdirected hostility / Freak out / Nix hex / Applied science / Omaha stylee / Tribute / Galaxy / Light years / Hydrophonic / Who's got the herb? / Feels so good.

Oct 99. (cd) *<(546645-2)>* **SOUNDSYSTEM** [ ] [9]
– Freeze time / Come original / Large in the margin / Flowing / Can't fade me / Life's not a race / Strong all along / Sever / Eons / Evolution / Leaving Babylon / Mindspin / Livin' and rockin'.

Jun 01. (cd) *<32184>* **FROM CHAOS** [-] [10]
– You get worked / Sick tight / You wouldn't believe / Full ride / From chaos / I told myself / Champagne / Hostile apostle / Wake your mind up / Amber / Uncalm / I'll be here awhile.

THREE FISH (see under ⇒ PEARL JAM)

THROWN UPS (see under ⇒ MUDHONEY)

THUNDER

Formed: South London, England . . . mid '89 by main songwriter LUKE MORLEY, LUKE BOWES and GARY JAMES, who had all been part of Reading festival specialists, TERRAPLANE. This derivative Brit-rock outfit, who formed around 1982, released two melodic, workmanlike albums, 'BLACK AND WHITE' (1986) and 'MOVING TARGET' (1987), before they disintegrated in early '88; a planned career in America coming to an abrupt end. From the ashes of TERRAPLANE's crash came THUNDER, the core of the former act recruiting BEN MATTHEWS and MARK LUCKHURST (aka SNAKE) and signing to 'E.M.I.' through agent Malcolm McKenzie. Hailed as rock's great white hopes, THUNDER rolled around the country relentlessly, building up a grassroots fanbase which subsequently saw their debut ANDY 'Duran Duran' TAYLOR-produced set, 'BACK STREET SYMPHONY' (1990) go gold. Rootsy heavy rock in the mould of BAD COMPANY, AEROSMITH and LED ZEPPELIN, the album spawned a series of hit singles, 'DIRTY LOVE', 'BACKSTREET SYMPHONY', Spencer Davis Group's 'GIMME SOME LOVIN' and a re-issue of 'SHE'S SO FINE'. They subsequently played the Cathouse in New York and were given a deal with EMI's US counterpart 'Capitol', although they tasted only minor success with the 'DIRTY LOVE' single. Sticking to their hard-rock guns, THUNDER went from strength to strength, two further albums, 'LAUGHING ON JUDGEMENT DAY' (1992) and 'BEHIND CLOSED DOORS' (1995), both storming the UK Top 5, although the latter was recorded without SNAKE, who had been superseded by MIKAEL HOGLUND. Although the group maintained healthy singles/albums sales, they surprised many by downshifting to the former compilation label, 'Raw Power' (now home to BRUCE DICKINSON and HELLOWEEN amongst others). The resulting album, 'THE THRILL OF IT ALL' (early '97), still managed to crack the Top 20, having already spawned a hit single, 'DON'T WAIT UP'. • **Covers:** GET IT ON (T.Rex) / WITH A LITTLE HELP FROM MY FRIENDS (Beatles) / GIMME SHELTER (Rolling Stones) / 5.15 (Who) / ALL THE WAY FROM MEMPHIS (Mott The Hoople) / IN A BROKEN DREAM (hit; Python Lee Jackson) / STAY WITH ME (Rod Stewart & The Faces) / PLAY THAT FUNKY MUSIC (Wild Cherry) / MY BROTHER JAKE (Free) / ONCE IN A LIFETIME (Talking Heads) / DANCE TO THE MUSIC (Sly & The Family Stone). • **Trivia:** SNAKE once appeared on Top Of The Pops as bass player on OWEN PAUL's hit, 'You're My Favourite Waste Of Time'.

Album rating: Terraplane: BLACK AND WHITE (*5) / MOVING TARGET (*4) / Thunder: BACK STREET SYMPHONY (*6) / LAUGHING ON JUDGEMENT DAY (*7) / BEHIND CLOSED DOORS (*5) / THEIR FINEST HOUR (AND A BIT) compilation (*6) / THE THRILL OF IT ALL (*5) / LIVE (*4) / GIVING THE GAME AWAY (*4) / THEY THINK IT'S ALL OVER . . . AND IT IS NOW (*5)

TERRAPLANE

DANNY BOWES – vocals / **LUKE MORLEY** – guitar / **RUDY RIVIERE** – guitar / **NICK LINDEN** – bass, piano / **GARY JAMES** – drums

City not iss.

Mar 83. (7") *(NIK 8)* **I SURVIVE. / GIMME THE MONEY** [ ] [-]

Epic not iss.

Dec 84. (7") *(A 4936)* **I CAN'T LIVE WITHOUT YOUR LOVE. / BEGINNING OF THE END** [ ] [-]
(12"+=) *(TX 4936)* – Let the wheels go round.

Mar 85. (7"/12") *(A/TX 6110)* **I SURVIVE. / ALL NIGHT AND DAY (live)** [ ] [-]

Jul 85. (7") *(A 6352)* **WHEN YOU'RE HOT. / TOUGH KIND OF LOVE** [ ] [-]
(12"+=) *(TX 6352)* – If you could see yourself.

Oct 85. (7") *(A 6584)* **TALKING TO MYSELF. / GET YOUR FACE OUT OF MY DREAMS** [ ] [-]
(12"+=) *(TX 6584)* – Gimme the money.

—— RUDY only appeared on 1 track from next album.

Jan 86. (lp/c) *(EPC/40 26439)* **BLACK AND WHITE** [74] [-]
– Don't walk away / When you're hot / I can't live without your love / Talking to myself / You can't hurt me anymore / I survive / Right betweeen the eyes / Black and white / I'm the one / Get your face out of my dream / Couldn't handle the tears. *(c+=)* – Tough kind of love / Beginning of the end / All night and day. *(cd-iss. Jan98; 489451-2)*

Jan 87. (7"/7"sha-pic-d) *(TERRA/+P 1)* **IF THAT'S WHAT IT TAKES. / LIVING AFTER DARK** [ ] [-]
(12"+=) *(TERRAT 1)* – ('A'-19th Nervous Breakdown mix) / Drugs.

Jun 87. (7") *(TERRA 2)* **GOOD THING GOING. / A NIGHT OF MADNESS** [ ] [-]
(12"+=) *(TERRAT 2)* – The good life.
(c-s++=) *(MCTERRAC 2)* ('A'version).

Aug 87. (7") *(TERRA 3)* **MOVING TARGET. / WHEN I SLEEP ALONE** [ ] [-]
(d7"+=/12"+=) *(TERRA G/T 3)* – I survive (live) / I can't live without your love.

Sep 87. (lp/c/cd) *(EPC 460157-1/-4/-2)* **MOVING TARGET** [ ] [ ]
– If that's what it takes / Good thing going / Promised land / Moving target / Hostage to fortune / Heartburn / Hearts on fire / I will come out fighting / Nothing on but the radio. *(cd+=)* – Moving target (extended) / When I sleep alone / I can't live without your love (live) / I survive (live).

Feb 88. (7") *(TERRA 4)* **IF THAT'S WHAT IT TAKES. / LIVING AFTER DARK** [ ] [-]
(12"+=/cd-s+=) *(TERRA T/Q 4)* – ('A'-19th Nervous Breakdown mix) / Drugs.

—— Disbanded early 1988 after a stint in the US

THUNDER

BOWES + MORLEY brought back **GARY 'Harry' JAMES** – drums, with also **BEN MATTHEWS** – guitar, keyboards / **MARK 'Snake' LUCKHURST** – bass

E.M.I. Geffen

Oct 89. (7"/7"s) *(EM/+S 111)* **SHE'S SO FINE. / GIRL'S GOING OUT OF HER HEAD** [ ] [-]
(12"+=)(cd-s+=) *(2EMP 111)(CDEM 1)* – Another shot of love (live).

Jan 90. (7"/7"pic-d/c-s) *(EM/EMPD/TCEM 126)* **DIRTY LOVE. / FIRED UP** [32] [-]
(12"+=/12"pic-d+=) *(12EM/+P 126)* – She's so fine (live).
(cd-s++=) *(CDEM 126)* – Brown sugar (live).

Feb 90. (cd/c/lp) *(CD/TC+/EMC 3570) <24384>* **BACK STREET SYMPHONY** [21] [ ] Apr91
– She's so fine / Dirty love / Don't wait for me / Higher ground / Until my dying day / Back street symphony / Love walked in / An Englishman on holiday / Girl's going out of her head / Gimme some lovin'. *(cd+=/c+=)* – Distant thunder. *(pic-lp Nov90; PDEMC 3570) (re-iss. Sep94 cd/c; same)*

Apr 90. (c-s/7") *(TC+/EM 137)* **BACK STREET SYMPHONY. / NO WAY OUT OF THE WILDERNESS** [25] [-]
(12"+=/12"pic-d+=) *(12EM/+PD 137)* – An Englishman on holiday (live).
(cd-s++=) *(CDEM 137)* – Girl's going out of her head (live).

Jul 90. (c-s/7") *(TC+/EM 148)* **GIMME SOME LOVIN'. / I WANNA BE HER SLAVE** [36] [-]
(c-s+=/12"+=/cd-s+=) *(TC/12/CD EM 148)* – Dirty love (live).
(10"+=) *(10EM 148)* – Until the night is through.

Sep 90. (c-s/7") *(TC+/EM 158)* **SHE'S SO FINE. / I CAN STILL HEAR THE MUSIC** [34] [-]
(12"+=/12"pic-d+=) *(12EM/+P 158)* – Don't wait for me (live . . .).
(ext.10"red+=) *(10EM 158)* – Back street symphony (live . . .).
(cd-s) *(CDEM 158)* – ('A'side) / Back street symphony (live at Donington) / Don't wait for me (live at Donington).

Oct 90. (c-s,cd-s) *<44547>* **SHE'S SO FINE. / GIMME SOME LOVIN'** [-] [ ]

Feb 91. (c-s/7") *(TC+/EM 175)* **LOVE WALKED IN. / FLAWED TO PERFECTION (demo)** [21] [-]
(12"+=/12"pic-d+=/cd-s+=) *(12EM/12EMPD/CDEM 175)* – Until my dying day (live).
(10"white+=) *(10EM 175)* – World problems: a solution.

Apr 91. (cd-s) *<19026>* **DIRTY LOVE. / GIRL'S GOING OUT OF HER HEAD** [-] [55]

Aug 92. (c-s/7") *(TC+/EM 242)* **LOWLIFE IN HIGH PLACES. / BABY I'LL BE GONE** [22] [-]
(cd-s) *(CDEM 242)* – ('A'side) / Back street symphony / She's so fine / Love walked in.
(cd-s) *(CDEMS 242)* – ('A'side) / With a little help from my friends / She's my inspiration / Low life in high places (demo).

Aug 92. (cd/c/d-lp) *(CD/TC+/EMD 1035)* *<24486>* **LAUGHING ON JUDGEMENT DAY** [2] [ ]
– Does it feel like love? / Everybody wants her / Low life in high places / Laughing on judgement day / Empty city / Today the world stopped turning / Long way from home / Fire to ice / Feeding the flame / A better man / The moment of truth / Flawed to perfection / Like a satellite / Baby I'll be gone. *(re-iss. Mar94 cd/c; same)*

Oct 92. (c-s/7") *(TC+/EM 249)* **EVERYBODY WANTS HER. / DANGEROUS RHYTHM** [36] [-]
(12"pic-d+=) *(12EMPD 249)* – Higher ground (acoustic).
(cd-s) *(CDEM 249)* – ('A'side) / Dirty love (acoustic) / Higher ground (acoustic) / Dirty love.

Feb 93. (c-s/7") *(TC+/BETTER 1)* **A BETTER MAN. / LOW LIFE IN HIGH PLACES (live)** [18] [-]
(12"/cd-s) *(12/CD BETTER 1)* – ('A'side) / New York, New York (Harry's theme) / Lazy Sunday (live) / Higher ground (live).

Jun 93. (12"ep/cd-ep) *(12/CD EM 272)* **LIKE A SATELLITE** [28] [-]
– Like a satellite / The damage is done / Like a satellite (live) / Gimme shelter.

Jan 95. (7"pic-d/c-s) *(EMPD/TCEM 365)* **STAND UP. / (interview)** [23] [-]
(cd-s+=) *(CDEM 365)* – The fire is gone (demo) / Life in a day (demo).
(cd-s) *(CDEMS 365)* – ('A'side) / One pretty woman / It happened in this town.

— now without SNAKE, who was repl. by **MIKAEL HOGLUND**

Jan 95. (cd/c/lp) *(CD/TC+/EMD 1076)* **BEHIND CLOSED DOORS** [5] [-]
– Moth to the flame / Fly on the wall / I'll be waiting / River of pain / Future train / 'Til the river runs dry / Stand up / Preaching from a chair / Castles in the sand / Too scared to live / Ball and chain / It happened in this train.

Feb 95. (c-s) *(TCEM 367)* **RIVERS OF PAIN / DOES IT FEEL LIKE LOVE** [31] [-]
(cd-s+=) *(CDEM 367)* – Everybody wants her (live) / All the way from Memphis (live).
(cd-s) *(CDEMS 367)* – ('A'side) / 5.15 (live) / You don't know what love is (demo).
(12"pic-d) *(12EMPD 367)* – ('A'side) / Move on / All the way from Memphis (live).

Apr 95. (c-ep) *(TCEM 372)* **CASTLES IN THE SAND / A BETTER MAN / SHE'S SO FINE / DIRTY LOVE** [30] [-]
(cd-s) *(CDEM 372)* – ('A'side) / Stand up (live acoustic) / Move over (live).
(cd-s) *(CDEMS 372)* – ('A'side) / I hear you knocking (live acoustic) / River of pain (live acoustic).

Sep 95. (c-s) *(TCEM 384)* **IN A BROKEN DREAM / 'TIL THE RIVER RUNS DRY** [26] [-]
(cd-s) *(CDEM 384)* – ('A'side) / Love walked in / Dirty love (demo).
(cd-s) *(CDEMS 384)* – ('A'side) / Stay with me / An Englishman on holiday.

Sep 95. (cd/c/d-lp) *(CD/TC+/EMD 1086)* **THEIR FINEST HOUR (AND A BIT)** (compilation) [22] [-]
– Dirty love / River of pain / Love walked in / Everybody wants her / In a broken dream / Higher ground '95 / Back street symphony / A better man / Gimme shelter / Like a satellite / Low life in high places / Stand up / Once in a lifetime / Gimme some lovin' / Castles in the sand / She's so fine.

Raw Power Raw Power

Jan 97. (c-s/cd-s) *(RAW M/X 1019)* **DON'T WAIT UP / WELCOME TO THE PARTY / HIRSUITE BOOGIE** [27] [-]
(flexi-cd-s) *(RAWX 1020)* – ('A'version); repl. 3rd track.
(12") *(RAWX 1020)* – ('A'extended) / Every word's a lie.

Feb 97. (cd/c/d-lp) *(<RAW CD/MC/LP 115>)* **THE THRILL OF IT ALL** [14] [ ]
– Pilot of my dreams / Living for today / Love worth dying for / Don't wait up / Something about you / Welcome to the party / The thrill of it all / Hotter than the sun / This forgotten town / Cosmetic punk / You can't live your life.

Mar 97. (c-s/cd-s) *(RAW M/X 1043)* **LOVE WORTH DYING FOR / SOMEBODY TO LOVE / LETHAL COMBINATION** [60] [-]
(cd-s+=) *(RAWX 1030)* – ('A'side) / Bed of roses / Bring it on home.

— **CHRIS CHILDS** – bass, vocals; repl. HOGLAND

Eagle not iss.

Jan 98. (c-s) *(EAGCS 016)* **THE ONLY ONE / YOU CAN'T LIVE YOUR LIFE IN A DAY (the Nomis sessions)** [31] [-]
(cd-s) *(EAGXA 016)* – ('A'side) / Too bad / This forgotten town (acoustic) / Something about you (the Nomis session).
(cd-s) *(EAGXB 016)* – ('A'live) / Pilot of my dreams (live) / Stand up (live) / Everybody wants her (live).

Feb 98. (d-cd) *(EDGCD 016)* **LIVE (live)** [35] [-]
– Welcome to the party / Higher ground / Don't wait up / Low life in high places / Gimme some lovin' / Empty city / Until my dying day / A better man / Does it feel like love? / Dance to the music / She's so fine // Backstreet symphony / An Englishman on holiday / I'll be waiting / Laughing on judgement day / Like a satellite / Moth to the flame / Living for today / The only one / Love walked in / River of pain / Dirty love.

Jun 98. (c-s) *(EAGCS 030)* **PLAY THAT FUNKY MUSIC / ONCE IN A LIFETIME** [39] [-]
(cd-s+=) *(EAGXS 030)* – Like a satellite.
(cd-s) *(EAGXA 030)* – ('A'side) / My brother Jake / I'm one.

Mar 99. (c-s) *(EAGCS 037)* **JUST ANOTHER SUICIDE (YOU WANNA KNOW) / MONTANA MOUNTAIN WOMAN** [49] [-]
(cd-s+=) *(EAGXS 037)* – Duelling harmonicas.
(cd-s) *(EAGXA 037)* – ('A'side) / With a little help from my friends (live) / She's so fine (live).

Mar 99. (cd/c) *(EAG CD/MC 046)* **GIVING THE GAME AWAY** [48] [-]
– Just another suicide (you wanna know) / All I ever wanted / Giving the game away / You'll still need a friend / Rolling the dice / Numb / Play that funky music / 'Til it shines / Time to get tough / It's another day / It could be tonight.

Papillion not iss.

Jul 00. (d-cd) *(BTFLYCD 0004)* **THEY THINK IT'S ALL OVER . . . AND IT IS NOW (live farewell)** [ ] [-]
– Stand up / Low life in high places / Forgotten town / Once in a lifetime / Pinball wizard / Close to you / Lola / Better man / Welcome to the party / River of pain / Higher ground / Pilot of my dreams / Backstreet symphony / Until my dying day / Fly on the wall / Love walked in / Just another suicide / Gimme shelter / Play that funky music / Dirty love.

– compilations, etc. –

Jun 99. (cd) *E.M.I.; (521046-2)* **THE RARE, THE RAW AND THE BEST** [ ] [-]

Apr 00. (cd) *EMI Gold; (525520-2)* **GIMME SOME . . .** [ ] [-]

Sep 00. (3xcd-box) *EMI; (528377-2)* **BACKSTREET SYMPHONY / LAUGHING ON JUDGEMENT DAY / BEHIND CLOSED DOORS** [ ] [-]

THUNDERHEAD

Formed: Hanover, Germany . . . 1987 by American TED "BULLET" PULIT, HENRIK WOLTER, OLE HEMPLEMAN, who subsequently added the drummer ALEX SCOTTI. Although based in Germany, THUNDERHEAD bore little resemblance to their fellow Euro-metallers, opting instead for a hard-nosed Anglo-American grit-metal approach. Having delivered their debut album, 'BEHIND THE EIGHT-BALL' on domestic label, 'Intercord', the band signed to 'Enigma' in the States where there was sufficient interest in their basic sound. With strong UK import sales of their debut, 'Music For Nations' took the band on for two further sets, 'BUSTED AT THE BORDER' (1990) and 'CRIME PAYS' (1991). Their musical approach varied little from release to release and THUNDERHEAD soon found themselves resigned to their home market once again, albums such as 'KILLING WITH STYLE' (1993) and 'WERE YOU TOLD THE TRUTH ABOUT HELL' (1995) appealing to diehards only.

Album rating: BEHIND THE EIGHT-BALL (*5) / BUSTED AT THE BORDER (*6) / CRIME PAYS (*5) / KILLING WITH STYLE (*4) / CLASSIC KILLER LIVE (*4) / WERE YOU TOLD THE TRUTH ABOUT HELL (*4)

TED "BULLET" PULIT – vocals, guitar / **HENRIK WOLTER** – guitar, vocals (ex-VIVA) / **OLE HEMPLEMAN** – bass, vocals (ex-TALON) / **ALEX SCOTTI** – drums

Intercord Enigma

Oct 89. (lp/cd) *(145/845 122)* *<73575-2>* **BEHIND THE EIGHT-BALL** [-] [ ] German
– Behind the eight-ball / Ready to roll / Take it to the highway / (You don't keep me) Satisfied / The fire's burning / Let go / Open all night / Life in the city / Just another lover / Straight shooter / Take me to the limit. *(cd+=)* – Beyond the universe.

Music For Nations not iss.

Sep 90. (cd/c/lp) *(CD/T+/MFN 110)* **BUSTED AT THE BORDER** [ ] [-]
– Busted at the border / 42nd Street / Good till the last drop / The darker side of yesterday / No security / Hard kind of woman / Terrified / 25 or 6 to 4 / Face to lace / Wicked love. *(cd+=)* – Caught between the lies.

Nov 91. (cd/c/lp) *(CD/T+/MFN 116)* **CRIME PAYS** [ ] [-]
– City cornered man / Make it hard / N.T. you let me down / Crime pays / Let the dog loose / Forgive and forget you / Torture ride / Live with it / What mama don't know / Life is only a goodbye / Ain't no trust.

Gun C.M.C.

Dec 93. (cd) *(GUN 030)* *<6303>* **KILLING WITH STYLE** [-] [ ] Aug94
– Young and useless / 8-ball / Overload (more than a buck) / Just when I try / Movin' on / Save me / House of swallow / Whips and chains / Down in desperation / Hard times / Redline / Loosen up your grip.

Apr 94. (cd) *(GUN 040)* **CLASSIC KILLERS LIVE (live)** [-] [-] German
– Intro / Young and useless / Satisfied / Overload / The darker side of yesterday / House of sawllow (live) / Whips and chains / Crime pays / Busted at the border / Movin' on / 8-bald / Face to lace / Behind the 8-ball / Take it to the highway / Ace of spades.

Jun 95. (cd) *(GUN 068)* *<4177-2>* **WERE YOU TOLD THE TRUTH ABOUT HELL** [-] [-] German
– Hangin' by a thread / Crash course in life / The absence of angels / Snap / Thanx / Here's to you America / Schizophrenic mind / Inside of the dark side / Premonition / The show has just begun / Zero the hero.

Nov 95. (cd) *<25862>* **THE BALLADS '88-'95** (compilation) [-] [ ]
– Rescue me / That's the way / Darker side of yesterday / Let him run / Movin' on / Good things never last / Life in the city / Loosen up your grip / Down in desperation / Behind blue eyes.

Aug 99. (cd) *(GUN 178CD)* **THE WHOLE DECADE** (compilation) [ ] [-]
– Whips and chains / Hanging by a thread / Young and useless / Busted at the border / Behind the eight ball / Take it to the highway / Payback time / Rescue me / Behind blue eyes / Snap / House of swallow / Crash course in life / Face to lace / Ace of spades / Good things never last / The absence of angels / Overload / What mama don't know / That's the way.

S.P.V. S.P.V.

Nov 99. (cd) *(085-2156-2)* **UGLY SIDE** [ ] [-]

Johnny THUNDERS

Born: JOHN ANTHONY GENZALE, 15 Jul'52, Leesburg, Florida, USA. Having been an integral part of The NEW YORK DOLLS in the first half of the 70's, vocalist/guitarist THUNDERS formed new wave/punk act, The HEARTBREAKERS alongside ex-'DOLLS drummer, JERRY NOLAN and ex-TELEVISION bassist, RICHARD HELL. After an initial gig as a trio, they picked up extra guitarist, WALTER LURE, although this incarnation was short-lived as RICHARD promptly departed to form his own RICHARD HELL & THE VOID-OIDS. Filling the void with BILLY RATH, they were invited to London by ex-'DOLLS manager, MALCOLM McLAREN, who offered

them a support slot with his punk proteges, The SEX PISTOLS (on their 'Anarchy' tour of late '76). The HEARTBREAKERS subsequently signed to UK label, 'Track', issuing their debut 45, 'CHINESE ROCKS' (a tribute to oriental narcotics co-written with DEE DEE RAMONE), in early '77; both the lead track and the B-side, 'BORN TO LOSE', drawled out with inimitably wasted NY cool. In September of that "Jubilee" year, the group released their much-anticipated debut album, 'L.A.M.F.' (New York street slang for 'Like A Mother F***** '), and although it suffered from terrible production provided by SPEEDY KEEN (ex-THUNDERCLAP NEWMAN), the set still managed a Top 60 placing in Britain. So bad was the record's sound that NOLAN left in protest, further calamity befalling the band as they found themselves on the wrong side of the immigration authorities having abandoned their label. Deported back to NY, the band inevitably splintered despite having recruited a replacement drummer, TY STYX. THUNDERS subsequently returned to London where he recorded a solo album, 'SO ALONE' (1978) aided and abetted by the cream of the UK new wave scene including PETER PERRETT (The Only Ones), CHRISSIE HYNDE (Pretenders), PAUL COOK and STEVE JONES (Sex Pistols) and even PHIL LYNOTT (Thin Lizzy)! In the interim, THUNDERS teamed up with SID VICIOUS in the ill-fated, unfortunately named, The LIVING DEAD (SID was to die shortly afterwards). Just prior to the turn of the decade, The HEARTBREAKERS regrouped in New York with THUNDERS masterminding the affair and prefixing the band name with his own; the resulting stage set, 'LIVE AT MAX'S KANSAS CITY' stands as testament to what might have been. In the 80's, THUNDERS released a series of sporadic albums/singles mostly for UK indie label, 'Jungle', although he never managed to shake off the cult legend tag. Sadly, THUNDERS died in New Orleans on the 23rd of April 1991, the circumstances remaining shrouded in mystery until a subsequent autopsy revealed what most people suspected, that he'd overdosed on heroin.
• Covered: CAN'T KEEP MY EYES OFF YOU (Andy Williams) / DO YOU LOVE ME (Brian Poole & The Tremeloes) / DOWNTOWN (Petula Clark) / LIKE A ROLLING STONE (Bob Dylan) / CRAWFISH (Elvis Presley) / QUE SERA SERA (hit; Doris Day). 'COPY CATS' was a complete covers album.

Album rating: Heartbreakers: L.A.M.F. (*7) / Johnny Thunders: SO ALONE (*7) / Johnny Thunders & The Heartbreakers: LIVE AT MAX'S KANSAS CITY (*7) / D.T.K. (*6) / Johnny Thunders: IN COLD BLOOD (*5) / TOO MUCH JUNKIE BUSINESS collection (85) / HURT ME (*6) / QUE SERA SERA (*5) / STATIONS OF THE CROSS collection (*4) / COPY CATS with Patti Palladin (*5) / GANG WAR (*4) / BOOTLEGGING THE BOOTLEGGERS (*4)

HEARTBREAKERS

JOHNNY THUNDERS – vocals, guitar / **JERRY NOLAN** (b. 7 May'46) – drums / **WALTER LURE** (b.22 Apr'49) – guitar, vocals / **BILLY RATH** – bass, vocals repl. RICHARD HELL who formed his own group

Track | not iss.

May 77. (7"/12") *(2094 135/+T)* **CHINESE ROCKS. / BORN TO LOSE** [ ] [-]
Sep 77. (lp) *(2409 218)* **L.A.M.F.** [55] [-]
– Born to lose / Baby talk / All by myself / I wanna be loved / It's not enough / Get off the phone / Chinese rocks / Pirate love / One track mind / I love you / Goin' steady / Let go. *(re-iss. May85 as 'L.A.M.F. – REVISITED' on 'Jungle' lp,pink-lp/pic-lp; FREUD 4/+P) <(re-iss. Sep96 as 'THE LOST '77 MIXES' cd/c/lp; FREUD CD/C/LP 044)>*
Nov 77. (7") *(2094 137)* **ONE TRACK MIND. / CAN'T KEEP MY EYES OFF YOU (live) / DO YOU LOVE ME (live)** [ ] [-]
Mar 78. (7"w-drawn) *(2094 142)* **IT'S NOT ENOUGH. / LET GO** [ ] [-]

— split early '78 after being deported back to New York, NOLAN joined SNATCH, while RATH and LURE disappeared

JOHNNY THUNDERS

— returned to London and went solo using session people

Real-W.E.A. | not iss.

May 78. (7") *(ARE 1)* **DEAD OR ALIVE. / DOWNTOWN** [ ] [-]
Sep 78. (7"/12"pink,12"blue) *(ARE 3/+T)* **YOU CAN'T PUT YOUR ARMS AROUND A MEMORY. / HURTIN'** [ ] [-]
Oct 78. (lp) *(RAL 1)* **SO ALONE** [ ] [-]
– Pipeline / You can't put your arms around a memory / Great big kiss / Ask me no questions / Leave me alone / Daddy rolling stone / London boys / Untouchable / Subway train / Downtown. *<(re-iss. Jul92 & Feb95 on 'Warners' lp/cd; 7599 26982-2)>*

JOHNNY THUNDERS & THE HEARTBREAKERS

— re-formed '79, with **WALTER, BILLY / + STYX** – drums

Beggars Banquet | Max's Kansas

Jul 79. (7") *(BEG 21)* **GET OFF THE PHONE (live). / I WANNA BE LOVED (live)** [ ] [-]
Sep 79. (lp) *(BEGA 9) <DTK 213>* **LIVE AT MAX'S KANSAS CITY (live)** [ ] [ ]
– (intro) / Milk me / Chinese rocks / Get off the phone / London / Take a chance / One track mind / All by myself / Let go / I love you / Can't keep my eyes on you / I wanna be loved / Do you love me?. *(cd-iss. Jul91; BBL 9CD) <(cd-iss. Dec95 on 'ROIR USA'; RUSCD 8219)>*

— Split again '79. In 1980, THUNDERS joined WAYNE KRAMER'S GANG WAR.

JOHNNY THUNDERS

solo again with **WALTER LURE** – guitar / **BILLY ROGERS** – drums

New Rose | not iss.

Dec 82. (7") *(NEW 14)* **IN COLD BLOOD / ('A'live)** [-] [-] France
Jan 83. (d-lp) *(NR 18)* **IN COLD BLOOD** (some live) [-] [-] France
– In cold blood / Just another girl / Green onions / Diary of a lover / Look at my eyes / Live: (intro) / Just another girl / Too much junkie business / Sad vacation / Louie Louie / Gloria / Treat me like a nigger / Do you love me / Green onions / 10 commandments. *(re-iss. Apr94 lp/cd; 422367) (re-iss. cd Jun95 on 'Dojo'; DOJOCD 221) <(cd re-iss. Aug97 on 'Essential'; ESMCD 589)> (lp re-iss. Mar98 on 'Munster'; MR 142)*
Jan 84. (7"m) *(NEW 27)* **HURT ME. / IT'S NOT ENOUGH / LIKE A ROLLING STONE** [ ] [-]
Jan 84. (lp) *(ROSE 26)* **HURT ME** [ ] [-]
– So alone / It ain't me babe / Eve of destruction / You can't put your arms round a memory / You're so strange / I'm a boy in a girl / Lonely planet boy / Sad vacation / Hurt me / Diary of a lover / Ask me no questions. *(cd-iss. May94; 422366) (re-iss. cd Jul95 on 'Dojo'; DOJOCD 217) <(cd re-iss. Aug97 on 'Essential'; ESMCD 588)> (lp re-iss. Mar98 on 'Munster'; MR 142)*

Jungle | not iss.

Oct 85. (7"/7"pic-d; by JOHNNY THUNDERS with PATTI PALLADIN) *(JUNG 23/+P)* **CRAWFISH. / TIE ME UP (LOVE KNOT)** [ ] [-]
(ext.12"+=) *(JUNG 23T)* – ('A'-Bayou mix).

— (w/ PATTI PALLADIN – vocals (ex-SNATCH, FLYING LIZARDS)

Dec 85. (lp) *(FREUD 9)* **QUE SERA, SERA** [ ] [-]
– Que sera, sera / Short lives / M.I.A. / I only wrote this song for you / Little bit of whore / Cool operator / Blame it on mom / Tie me up / Alone in a crowd / Billy boy / Endless party. *(pic-lp iss.Jun87; FREUDP 09) <(cd-iss. Dec94; FREUDCD 49)>*
Jun 87. (7") *(JUNG 33)* **QUE SERA SERA. / SHORT LIVES** [ ] [-]
(12"+=) *(JUNG 33T)* – I only wrote this song.

JOHNNY THUNDERS & PATTI PALLADIN

May 88. (7") *(JUNG 38)* **SHE WANTS TO MAMBO. / UPTOWN** [ ] [ ]
(12"+=) *(JUNG 38T)* – Love is strange.
Jun 88. (lp/c/cd) *(FREUD/+C/CD 20)* **YEAH, YEAH, I'M A COPY CAT** [ ] [-]
– Can't seem to make you mine / Baby it's you / She wants to mambo / Treat her right / Uptown to Harlem / Crawfish / Alligator wine / Two time loser / Love is strange / (I was) Born to cry / He cried (she cried) / Let me entertain you (part 1 & 2). *(re-iss. cd Nov96; same)*
Jan 89. (7") *(JUNG 43)* **(I WAS) BORN TO CRY. / TREAT HER RIGHT** [ ] [-]
(12"+=) *(JUNG 43T)* – Can't seem to make her mine.

— THUNDERS died on the 23rd April '91, aged 38. He left three children from his first marriage plus another 3 year-old daughter, Jamie, conceived while he'd lived in Sweden with his girlfriend, Suzanne. JERRY NOLAN died on the 14th January '92 of a stroke (aged 45) after a bout of pneumonia and meningitis. Original drummer, BILLY MURCIA, also died in the 90's.

– compilations, etc. –

on 'Jungle' unless otherwise mentioned

Nov 82. (lp,pink-lp,white-lp/pic-lp) *(FREUD/+P 1)* **D.T.K. – LIVE AT THE SPEAKEASY (live)** [ ] [-]
<cd-iss. Aug94 on 'Receiver'; R 191>
May 83. (7"ep) *(JUNG 1)* **VINTAGE '77** [ ] [-]
– Let go / Chinese rocks / Born to lose.
1983. (c) *R.O.I.R.; <A 118>* **TOO MUCH JUNKIE BUSINESS** [-] [ ]
(cd-iss. Feb95 on 'ROIR Europe'; same) <US 'Combat'; 5029>
Mar 84. (7"/7"pic-d) *(JUNG 14/+P)* **GET OFF THE PHONE. / ALL BY MYSELF** [ ] [-]
(12"+=) *(JUNG 14X)* – Pirate love.
Jun 84. (lp) *A.B.C.; (ABCLP 2)* **LIVE AT THE LYCEUM BALLROOM 1984 (live)** [ ] [-]
<re-iss. Jun91 on 'Receiver' lp/c/cd; RR LP/LC/CD 134>
Feb 85. (7") *Twins; (T 1702)* **BORN TO LOSE. / IT'S NOT ENOUGH** [ ] [-]
May 85. (7"ep/12"ep) *(JUNG 18/+X)* **CHINESE ROCKS / BORN TO LOSE / ONE TRACK MIND / I WANNA BE LOVED** [ ] [-]
Feb 87. (c) *R.O.I.R.; (A 146) / Combat; <5028>* **STATIONS OF THE CROSS** [-] [ ]
(re-iss. cd Jul94 on 'Receiver'; RRCD 188) (re-iss. cd Feb95 on 'ROIR Europe'; same)
May 88. (box-lp) *(JTBOX 1)* **THE JOHNNY THUNDERS ALBUM COLLECTION** [ ] [-]
Feb 90. (lp/cd) *(FREUD/+CD 30)* **BOOTLEGGIN' THE BOOTLEGGERS** [ ] [-]
Jan 92. (cd) *Fan Club;* **LIVE AT MOTHERS (live)** [ ] [-]
(re-iss. Mar98 on 'Munster'; MR 140)
Feb 92. (cd) *Bomp; (BCD 4039)* **WHAT GOES AROUND (live)** [ ] [-]
Oct 92. (cd) *Fan Club; (422365)* **HAVE FAITH (live solo)** [ ] [-]
<(re-iss. Aug96 on 'Mutiny'; MUT 8005CD)>
Dec 93. (cd) *Anagram; (CDGRAM 70)* **CHINESE ROCKS – THE ULTIMATE LIVE COLLECTION (live)** [ ] [-]
(lp-iss.Sep99 on 'Get Back'; GET 49)
Sep 94. (cd) *Skydog; (62251)* **VIVE LE REVOLUTION – LIVE PARIS, 1977 (live JOHNNY THUNDERS & THE HEARTBREAKERS)** [ ] [-]
Nov 94. (cd) *Essential; (ESDCD 226)* **ADD WATER AND STIR – LIVE IN JAPAN 1991 (live)** [ ] [ ]
Apr 96. (cd) *Dojo; (DOJOCD 231)* **THE STUDIO BOOTLEGS** [ ] [ ]
Oct 97. (cd) *Anagram; (CDMGRAM 117)* **BELFAST ROCKS** [ ] [ ]
(re-iss. Jul00 on 'Triple X'; TX 0031CD)
Feb 99. (cd) *Mogul; (MNR 003)* **LIVE CRISIS** [ ] [ ]
Apr 99. (d-cd) *Receiver; <(RRDCD 009)>* **SAD VACATION** [ ] [ ]
May 99. (cd) *Sonic; (SRCD 0020)* **INTERNAL POSSESSION** [ ] [ ]
Sep 99. (7"pink) *(JUNG 62)* **CHINESE ROCKS. /** [ ] [-]
Sep 99. (7") *(JUNG 63)* **ONE TRACK MIND. /** [ ] [-]

Oct 99. (d-cd) *Jungle; (FREUDCD 60)* **BORN TO LOSE**
May 00. (cd) *Amsterdamned; (TX 70030CD)* **IN THE FLESH**
May 00. (cd) *Receiver; <(RRCD 288)>* **PLAY WITH FIRE – JOHNNY THUNDERS LIVE**

THUNDERSTICK

Formed: London, England . . . 1982 by drummer THUNDERSTICK (born: BARRY GRAHAM), who'd been around in various guises (actually just one: a rapist's balaclava!) with metal bands, IRON MAIDEN and SAMSON. After an appearance with GILLAN on his 'For Gillan Fans Only' album, he set about completing his group with BEN K. REEVE (guitar), COLIN HEART (guitar), NEIL HAY (bass) and VINNIE MONROE (vocals). This line-up was virtually abandoned (all but REEVE) after he met American pin-up, JODEE VALENTINE, who subsequently became his vocalist and wife in 1983/4. The others, guitarists WANGO WIGGINS and CRIS MARTIN were to play on a 1983 single and a 1984 album, 'BEAUTY AND THE BEASTS', a set that didn't quite deliver. A few years later, BARRY was divorced from JODEE and the group as he returned to his second love, SAMSON.

Album rating: BEAUTY AND THE BEASTS (*1)

BARRY GRAHAM (aka THUNDERSTICK) – drums / **JODEE VALENTINE** – vocals / **CRIS MARTIN** – guitar / **WANGO WIGGINS** – guitar / **BEN K. REEVE** – bass

Thunderbolt not iss.

Nov 83. (7"ep/12"ep) *(THBE 1001/1002)* **FEEL LIKE ROCK'N'ROLL / ALECIA. / BURIED ALIVE / RUNAROUND** -
Apr 84. (lp/c) *(THB L/C 008)* **BEAUTY AND THE BEASTS** -
– Contact angel / Afraid of the dark / Another turnaround / Heartbeat (in the night) / Rich girls (don't cry) / In the name of the father / Long way to go.

— split in 1986 when THUNDERSTICK the drummer re-joined SAMSON

TIGERTAILZ

Formed: South Wales, Wales . . . 1986 by STEVIE JAMES (aka STEEVI JAIMZ), JAY PEPPER, PEPSI TATE and American ACE FINCHAM. The following year, they issued a self-financed single 'SHOOT TO KILL', leading to a deal with 'Music For Nations' and a debut album, 'YOUNG AND CRAZY'. Devoured by the homegrown fanbase, the albums' second-hand American style glam-metal met with derision in certain sections of the rock press. However, with replacement singer KIM HOOKER, the band's fortunes changed dramatically. With the late 80's vogue for all things sleazy and tacky, the Welsh rarebits became blonde figureheads of sorts for the burgeoning UK glam scene. The resulting album, 'BESERK' (1990) shocked many by hitting the UK Top 40, although they couldn't maintain their momentum and ended up chasing their own tails with covers of Megadeth's 'PEACE SELLS (BUT WHO'S BUYING)' and Metallica's 'CREEPING DEATH' on the b-side of subsequent single, 'HEAVEN'. When FINCHAM departed, the remainder found it even tougher going in the short-lived, WAZBONES.

Album rating: YOUNG AND CRAZY (*5) / BEZERK (*5) / WAZBONES (*4) / LIVE IN CONCERT (*4)

STEEVI JAIMZ – vocals / **JAY PEPPER** – guitar / **PEPSI TATE** – bass (ex-TREASON, ex-CRASH K.O.) / **ACE FINCHAM** – drums (ex-TREASON, ex-CRASH K.O.)

Tailz not iss.

Mar 87. (12") *(TAILZ 001)* **SHOOT TO KILL. / SHES SO HOT / LIVING WITHOUT YOU** -

Music For Nations S.P.V.

Nov 87. (lp) *(MFN 78) <970578>* **YOUNG AND CRAZY**
– Star attraction / Hollywood killer / Livin' without you / Shameless / City kids / Shoot to kill / Turn me on / She's too hot / Young and crazy / Fall in love again. *(pic-lp Jan88; MFN 78P) (re-iss. Aug89 cd/c; CD/T MFN 78)*
Jun 88. (7") *(KUT 129)* **LIVIN' WITHOUT YOU. / NINE LIVEZ**
(12"+=) *(12KUT 129)* – For a few dollars more.

— **KIM HOOKER** – vocals (ex-RANKELSON) repl. JAIMZ who formed own outfit, ST. JAIMZ

Jun 89. (7") *(KUT 132)* **LOVE BOMB BABY. / ('A'version)** 75
(12"+=) *(12KUT 132)* – She's too hot (live) / Few dollarz more (live).
Jan 90. (cd/c/lp) *(CD/T+/MFN 96) <84-8512>* **BESERK** 36
– Sick sex / Love bomb baby / I can fight dirty too / Heaven / Noise level critical / Love overload / Action city / Twist and shake / Squeeze it dry / Call of the wild.
Jun 90. (c-s/7") *(T+/KUT 134)* **NOISE LEVEL CRITICAL. / MURDERESS**
(12"+=/cd-s+=) *(12/CD KUT 134)* – Million dollar smile.
Feb 91. (7") *(KUT 137)* **HEAVEN. / PEACE SELLS (BUT WHO'S BUYING)** 71
(12"+=) *(12KUT 137)* – Creeping death.
(cd-s+=) *(CDKUT 137)* – ('A'extended).

— FINCHAM left in 1992, the remainder became WAZBONES before TIGERTAILZ were back in '95

Minority One not iss.

Aug 95. (12"/cd-s) *(12/CD MIN 102)* **BELLY OF THE BEAST** -
(cd-s) *(CDMIN 102X)* –
Sep 95. (cd) *(MIN 04CD)* **WAZBONES** -
– Tear your fucking heart out / Dirty needles / Belly of the beast / Pig face / Love junk II / Make me bleed / Perish / Instruct your mind / Love can kill / The name of the game.
Oct 96. (cd) *(MIN 06CD)* **LIVE IN CONCERT (live)** -

— disbanded after above

TILES

Formed: Detroit, Michigan, USA . . . 1993 by PAUL RARICK, CHRIS HERIN, JEFF WHITTLE and MARK EVANS. After unveiling a melodic prog-rock sound with their 1994 eponymous debut album, TILES recruited veteran RUSH producer TERRY BROWN to oversee the recording of 'FENCE THE CLEAR' (1997). Unsurprisingly, commentators continually compared the album to Canada's most famous rock band, not necessarily a bad thing considering that RUSH fans would certainly enjoy the carefully constructed songwriting on offer. With 'PRESENTS OF MIND' (1999), the group made a more concerted attempt to carve out their own niche.

Album rating: TILES (*4) / FENCE THE CLEAR (*5) / PRESENTS OF MIND (*4)

PAUL RARICK – vocals / **CHRIS HERIN** – lead guitar / **JEFF WHITTLE** – bass / **MARK EVANS** – drums

S.P.V. Standing Pavement

Dec 95. (cd) *<SPR 94001>* **TILES** -
– Analysis paralysis / Token pledge / Retrospect / Trading places / Bridges of Grace / Dancing dogs / Scattergram / Dress rehearsal / Supply and demand.
May 98. (cd) *(SPV 085285-2) <SPR 97001>* **FENCE THE CLEAR** Dec97
– Patterns / Beneath the surface / Cactus valley / Another's hand / The wading pool / Gameshow / Fallen pieces / Changing the guard / Gabby's happy song / Checkerboards.

not iss. Magna Carta

Nov 99. (cd) *<9038>* **PRESENTS OF MIND** -
– Static / Modification / Crossing swords / Facing failure / The learning curve / Ballad of the sacred cows / The sandtrap jig / Taking control / Safe procedures / Reasonable doubt / Patterns (live) / Token pledge (live).

TOBRUK

Formed: Birmingham, England . . . early 1982 by SNAKE, NIGEL EVANS, MICK NEWMAN, MIKE BROWN, JEM DAVIS and EDDIE FINCHER. Missing the NWOBHM boat by a few years, the band opted instead for a more high-gloss melodic metal approach. After a one-off 45, 'WILD ON THE RUN', for the pivotal (in the metal circles anyway) 'Neat', they signed to 'Parlophone', unleashing the Lance Quinn-produced album of the same name in 1985. By the following year, TOBRUK were no more, their battle to release a second set as 'IN MOTION' was finally scuppered, although it did resurface two years later as 'PLEASURE AND PAIN'.

Album rating: WILD ON THE RUN (*5) / PLEASURE AND PAIN (*5)

SNAKE – vocals / **NIGEL EVANS** – guitar / **MICK NEWMAN** – guitar / **JEM DAVIS** – keyboards / **MIKE BROWN** – bass / **EDDIE FINCHER** – drums

Neat not iss.

Sep 83. (7") *(NEAT 32)* **WILD ON THE RUN. / THE SHOW MUST GO ON** -

Parlophone E.M.I.

Mar 85. (7") *(R 6093)* **FALLING. / LIKE LIGHTNING** -
(12"+=) *(12R 6093)* – Under the gun.
Mar 85. (lp/c) *(TK/TC-TK 1) <12430>* **WILD ON THE RUN**
– Wild on the run / Falling / Running from the night / Hotline / Rebound / Poor girl / She's nobody's angel / Breakdown / Going down for the third time. *(c+=)* – The show must go on.
Aug 85. (7") *(R 6101)* **ON THE REBOUND. / POOR GIRL** -
(12"+=) *(12R 6101)* – Falling (extended).

FM Revolver not iss.

May 88. (lp/c/cd) *(WKFM LP/MC/XD 105)* **PLEASURE AND PAIN** -
– Rock'n'roll casualty / Love is in motion / Alley boy / No paradise in Heaven / Burning up / Two hearts on the run / Let me out of here / Cry out in the night / Set me on fire / Promises, promises.

— split some time earlier, above was to have been released in 1986 as 'IN MOTION'.

TODAY IS THE DAY

Formed: Nashville, Tennessee, USA . . . 1992 by STEVE AUSTIN, who recruited the talent of MIKE HERRELL and BRAD ELROD. This band's output is extemely hard to categorise, and rightly so, as their recorded material varies from extreme metal to alternative rock with huge amounts of sampling, industrial sounds and eerie keyboard work to name but a few of the elements that are blended into this progressive noise-rock. This music was certainly for the connoisseur listener who might've been looking for innovation in his/her metal. On releasing an EP on TITD's own label, 'Supernova', the band caught the ear of Tom Hazelmeyer at 'Amphetamine Reptile', who rapidly signed the group and released their full-length debut, 'SUPERNOVA' (1993). This set showed the sheer skill and invention of the trio to the metal world at large. It was extreme but in the most provactive sense, questioning the listeners ability to follow its complexity, moving from black metal riffing and tempo, to rapid changes of pace and volume, but definitely within an albeit complex framework. Their second set, 'WILLPOWER' (1994), followed soon after, and it was as progressive as the former album with many critics finding it easier to take. What stands out most about this set was its integrity and lyrical power in dealing with the multitude of emotions of the isloated individual. Following its release the band did an enormous amount of touring, in which time HERRELL decided to take his leave and AUSTIN opted for replacing the bassist with a keyboard player, SCOTT WEXTON, thus keeping the trio format intact. TITD's next album was the self-titled, 'TODAY IS THE DAY' (1996), and with the installation of WEXTON, AUSTIN choose to experiment with a far more electronic sound with the keyboards creating soundscapes on which his skilled guitar playing created an atmosphere of detachment. The band's fourth full-length outing, 'TEMPLE OF THE MORNING STAR' (1997) was released on 'Relapse'; another line-up change was to be MIKE HYDE replacing ELROD on drums and CHRIS REESER supplanting WEXTON on keyboard. This set followed in the footsteps of the third album, though with a more metal style tempo to the proceedings. Following on from this, AUSTIN once again changed TITD's roster, swapping HYDE for BRANN DAILOR and making the addition of BILL KELLIHER on the long-left-absent bass slot. TITD's fifth set, 'IN THE EYES OF GOD' (1999), included all the innovative elements that made the band so distinct, and at the same time was the most all-out metal album they had produced so far. The turn of the century saw the release of the odd compilation, 'LIVE TILL YOU DIE' (2000). This piece comprised live recordings, acoustic songs, demos, weird samples and covers including the Beatles' 'WHY DON'T WE DO IT IN THE ROAD', Bad Company's, 'FEEL LIKE MAKIN' LOVE', and, most bizarrely, Chris Isaak's, 'WICKED GAME'.

Album rating: SUPERNOVA (*7) / WILLPOWER (*7) / TODAY IS THE DAY (*6) / TEMPLE OF THE MORNING STAR (*7) / IN THE EYES OF GOD (*7) / LIVE 'TIL YOU DIE (*5)

STEVE AUSTIN – vocals, guitar / **MIKE HERRELL** – bass / **BRAD ELROD** – drums

Amphetam. Reptile / Amphetam. Reptile

Aug 93. (lp/cd) *(AAR 44-290/+CD)* <22> **SUPERNOVA**
– Black Dahlia / 6 dementia satyr / Silver tongue / Blind man at the mystic lake / Adult world / The begging / The kick inside / Goose is cooked / Timeless / Rise / The guilt barber / Self portrait.

Nov 94. (lp/cd) *(AAR 57-354/+CD)* <33> **WILLPOWER**
– Willpower / My first knife / Nothing to lose / Golden calf / Sidewinder / Many happy returns / Simple touch / Promised land.

— **SCOTT WEXTON** – keyboards; repl. HERRELL

Apr 96. (lp/cd) *(AAR 71-014/+CD)* <46> **TODAY IS THE DAY** Mar96
– Hai piranha / Marked / Bugs death march / A man of science / Realization / Black iron prison / Mountain people / Ripped off / The tragedy / She is in fear of death / I love my woman / Dot matrix.

— **AUSTIN** enlisted newcomers **CHRIS REESER** – keyboards + **MIKE HYDE** – drums

Relapse / Relapse

Oct 97. (cd) *<(RR 6964-2)>* **TEMPLE OF THE MORNING STAR** Sep97
– Temple of the morning star / The man who loves to hurt himself / Blindspot / High as the sky / Miracle / Kill yourself / Mankind / Pinnacle / Crutch / Root of all evil / Satan is alive / Rabid lassie / Friend for life / My life with you / I see you / Hermaphrodite. *(hidden track+=)* – Temple of the morning star – Sabbath bloody sabbath.

— **BILL KELLIHER** – bass; repl. REESER

— **BRANN DAILOR** – drums; repl. HYDE

Aug 99. (cd) *<(RR 6424-2)>* **IN THE EYES OF GOD** Jul99
– In the eyes of God / Going to Hell / Spotting a unicorn / Possession / The color of psychic power / Mayari / Soldier of fortune / Bionic cock / Argali / Afterlife / Humself / Daddy / Who is the black angel? / Martial law / False reality / The Russian child porn ballet / The cold harshness of being wroung throughout your entire life / Honor / Worn out / There is no end.

Sep 00. (cd) *<(RR 6457-2)>* **LIVE 'TIL YOU DIE (live)** Aug00
– The colour of psychic power / Pinnacle / Feel like makin' love / Temple of the morning star / Wicked game / Crutch / Ripped off (acoustic) / High as the sky / In the eyes of God / Users / T.D.A. / Blindspot / Why don't we do it in the road? / Afterlife / The man who loves to hurt himself.

TOILET BOYS

Formed: New York City, New York, USA . . . 1997 by the MISS GUY (a dangerous blonde with stockings, er . . . you could say!) and ELECTRIC EDDIE. Having secured a surprise gig at bisexual club, 'Squeezebox', the pair swiftly gathered together a backing band. Although some original members were subsequently replaced by SEAN, ROCKIT and VOMIT, The TOILET BOYS' lurid stage show (complete with flame-spitting guitar) and gender bending scuzz-rock rapidly attracted a cult audience. Popular in both New York and Los Angeles, the group issued a string of 7" singles and EP's prior to the release of their acclaimed mini-set, 'LIVING LIKE A MILLIONAIRE' (1999). A further EP, 'SAINTS AND SINNERS' followed in 2001 although their stated mission of steering rock music away from the monochrome angst of nu-metal was hardly a safe bet.

Album rating: LIVING LIKE A MILLIONAIRE mini (*5) / COME AND GET IT! (*6) / SINNERS AND SAINTS mini (*5)

GUY – vocals / **SEAN** – guitar / **ROCKET** – guitar / **ADAM VOMIT** – bass / **ELECTRIC EDDIE** – drums

R.A.F.R. / R.A.F.R.

Feb 99. (m-cd) *<(RAFR 02)>* **LIVING LIKE A MILLIONAIRE** Jul99
– Rocket city / Turn it up / Another day in the life / Go go boy / Electric / Living like a millionaire. *(m-lp iss.Mar01 on 'Cold Front'; CF 019)*

Livewire / Livewire

May 99. (cd) *<(LW001-2)>* **COME AND GET IT!**
– Go to hell / Shine on / Another day / You got it / Millionaire / Blue halo / Do or die / Hard / Ride / Broken home / Black fairies.

Cold Front / Cold Front

Jul 99. (m-cd) *<(CF 0022CD)>* **SINNERS AND SAINTS** Jan01
– P.H.L.N. 2000 / Special / Blue halo / Do or die / Influence / Ride / Black fairies. *(pic-lp iss.Jul00; CF1 22)*

TOOL

Formed: Hollywood, California, USA . . . 1990 by ADAM JONES, MAYNARD JAMES KEENAN, PAUL D'AMOUR and DANNY CAREY. Signing to 'Zoo' records, TOOL showcased their claustrophobic, nihilistic nu-metal on the 1992 mini-set, 'OPIATE'. Creating a buzz with high-profile supports to the likes of HENRY ROLLINS, TOOL subsequently hammered out a full album's worth of HELMET-like savage intensity with 'UNDERTOW' (1993), a record with such bluntly titled tracks as 'PRISON SEX' (also a single), 'INTOLERANCE' and 'BOTTOM' (the latter featuring the aforementioned ROLLINS). The album went on to sell over a million copies in the States, having only reached the Top 50. Three years later, after extensive touring, they resurfaced in dramatic fashion with 'AENIMA', the record bolting straight to No.2, surprising many who had yet to acquire a taste for TOOL. An ensuing legal battle with 'Freeworld Entertainment' lasted two years before the band agreed a joint deal for subsequent recordings. While TOOL then underwent a hard earned sabbatical, KEENAN hooked up with BILLY HOWERDEL (TOOL guitar tech), PAZ LENCHANTIN, TOY VAN LEEUWEN and JOSH FREESE to form A PERFECT CIRCLE. After making their debut at L.A.'s Viper Room in summer '99, the group released the 'MER DE NOMS' album in 2000. With songwriting duties shared by KEENAN and HOWERDEL, the record carried on in the dark spirit of TOOL while drawing a string-enhanced gothic cloak (or cape, even) around KEENAN's emotionally ravaged vocals. Following the release of the millennial 'SALIVAL' box set, TOOL themselves re-entered the fray in 2001 with the widely acclaimed 'LATERALUS', an ineffably complex work of shifting textures, oblique mood and inscrutable lyrics carrying the mystical torch of its predecessor into a parallel sonic universe. Kerrang! hailed it as one of the greatest albums ever recorded, grand claims which will no doubt leave those humble TOOL lads unfazed.

Album rating: OPIATE mini (*5) / UNDERTOW (*6) / AENIMA (*7) / SALIVAL live (*6) / LATERALUS (*8) / A Perfect Circle: MER DE NOMS (*6)

MAYNARD JAMES KEENAN – vocals / **ADAM JONES** – guitar / **PAUL D'AMOUR** – bass / **DANNY CAREY** – drums

Zoo-RCA / Zoo

Jul 92. (m-cd/m-c/m-lp) *<(72445 11027-2/-4/-1)>* **OPIATE**
– Sweat / Hush / Part of me / Cold and ugly (live) / Jerk-off (live) / Opiate.

Apr 93. (cd/c) *<(72445 11052-2/-4)>* **UNDERTOW** 50
– Intolerance / Prison sex / Sober / Bottom / Crawl away / Swamp song / Undertow / 4 degrees / Flood / Disgustipated.

Mar 94. (12"grey/cd-s) *(74321 19432-1/-2)* **PRISON SEX. / UNDERTOW (live) / OPIATE (live)**

Jul 94. (12"/cd-s) *(74321 22043-1/21849-2)* **SOBER. / INTOLERANCE**

— **JUSTIN CHANCELLOR** – bass; repl. D'AMOUR

Oct 96. (cd/c/lp) *(61422 31144-2/-4/-1)* *<72445 11087-2/-4/-1>* **AENIMA** 2
– Stinkfist / Eulogy / H. / Useful idiot / Forty six & 2 / Message to Harry Manback / Hooker with a penis / Intermission / Jimmy / Die eier von Satan / Pushit / Cesaro summability / Aenima / (-)Ions / Third eye.

A PERFECT CIRCLE

MAYNARD JAMES KEENAN – vocals / **BILLY HOWERDEL** – guitar, keyboards, programming, vocals / **PAZ LENCHANTIN** – bass / **TROY VAN LEEUWEN** – guitar (ex-FAILURE, ex-ENEMY) / **JOSH FREESE** – drums (ex-GUNS N' ROSES, ex-VANDALS)

Virgin / Virgin

May 00. (cd/lp) *(CDVUS/VUSLP 173)* <49253> **MER DE NOMS** 55 4
– The hollow / Magdalena / Rose / Judith / Orestes / 3 Libras / Sleeping beauty / Thomas / Renholder / Thinking of you / Brena / Over.

Jul 00. (cd-s) *(VUSCD 168)* **JUDITH / MAGDALENA (live) / BRENA (live) / ORESTES (demo)** –
(7"/7") *(VUS/+X 168)* – (same tracks).

Nov 00. (7"/cd-s) *(VUS/+DX 181)* **THE HOLLOW. / THE HOLLOW (Bunk mix)** 72 –
(cd-s) *(VUSCD 181)* – ('A'side) / ('A'-Constantly consuming mix) / Judith (Danny Lohner mix).

Jan 01. (7") *(VUS 184)* **3 LIBRAS. / MAGDALENA (live)** 49
(cd-s) *(VUSCD 184)* – ('A'side) / ('A'-All main courses remix) / Judith (live) / ('A'-CD ROM).
(cd-s) *(VUSDX 184)* – ('A'live) / ('A'-Feel my ice dub) / Sleeping beauty (live).

TOOL

— were back (see last line-up)

Music For Nations / Volcano

Feb 01. (cd-set; w/dvd/vhs) *(DVDMFN/VFN 18)* <31159> **SALIVAL** 38
– Third eye (live) / Part of me (live) / Pushit (live) / Message to Harry Manback II / Merkarba (live) / You lied (live) / No quarter / L.A.M.C. / Sober (video) / Prison sex (video) / Aenima (video) / Stinkfist (video).

Volcano / Volcano

May 01. (cd/c) *(921013-2)* <31160> **LATERALUS** 16 1
– The grudge / Eon blue apocalypse / The patient / Mantra / Schism / Parabol / Parabola / Tricks and leeches / Lateralus / Disposition / Reflection / Triad / Faaip de Oiad.

May 01. (-) *<radio play>* **SCHISM** – 76

TORA TORA

Formed: Memphis, Tennessee, USA ... 1987 by ANTHONY CORDER, KEITH DOUGLAS, PATRICK FRANCIS and JOHN PATTERSON. Taking the name from a VAN HALEN song (on the album, 'Women And Children First', or possibly the evacuation cry at Pearl Harbour!), they signed to 'A&M', unleashing their debut set, 'SURPRISE ATTACK' in 1989. Hard-driving macho hair-rock in the mould of BULLETBOYS, etc., TORA TORA divebombed into the US Top 50. A second set, 'WILD AMERICA' (1992), failed to emulate its predecessor, the band surrendering to hard-rock obscurity.

Album rating: SURPRISE ATTACK (*5) / WILD AMERICA (*4)

ANTHONY CORDER – vocals / **KEITH DOUGLAS** – guitar / **PATRICK FRANCIS** – bass / **JOHN PATTERSON** – drums

A&M | A&M

Apr 90. (cd/c/lp) *(CDA/AMC/AMA 5261)* **SURPRISE ATTACK** [ ] [47] Jul89
– Love's a bitch / 28 days / Hard times / Guilty / Phantom rider / Walkin' shoes / Riverside drive / She's good she's bad / One for the road / Being there.

May 90. (7") *(AM 557)* *<1425>* **WALKIN' SHOES. / DANCING WITH A GYPSY** [ ] [86] Jul89
(12"+=) *(AMY 557)* –

May 90. (7") *<1485>* **PHANTOM RIDER. / ONE FOR THE ROAD** [-] [ ]

Jul 90. (7") *<1456>* **GUILTY. / SHE'S GOOD SHE'S BAD** [-] [ ]

May 92. (cd/c) *<(39-5371-2/-4)>* **WILD AMERICA** [ ] [ ]
– Wild America / Amnesia / Dead man's band / As time goes by / Lay your money down / Shattered / Dirty secrets / Faith healer / Cold fever / Nowhere to go but down / City of kings.

—— folded after virtual failure of their second album

Bernie TORME

Born: Dublin, Ireland. Initially throwing his lot in with the burgeoning punk scene after relocating to London in the mid-70's, TORME played with SCRAPYARD before forming his own band and releasing a couple of singles on 'Jet' records, 'I'M NOT READY' and 'WEEKEND'. Though delivered in a rough-hewn punk style, TORME's talents didn't escape the notice of former DEEP PURPLE shouter, IAN GILLAN, who subsequently poached his services for a trio of albums, 'Mr Universe', 'Glory Road' and 'Future Shock'. During this time he'd kept a finger in the solo pie, releasing a further couple of singles including a cover of The Kinks' 'ALL DAY AND ALL OF THE NIGHT', TORME finally parting company with GILLAN in mid-'81. Recruiting a new band numbering PHIL SPALDING, NIGEL GLOCKER, MARK HARRISON and COLIN TOWNS, the guitarist finally cut a solo debut set, 'TURN OUT THE LIGHTS' (1982). Later the same year, TORME formed The ELECTRIC GYPSIES along with FRANK NOON and EVERTON WILLIAMS, issuing a sole single, Betty Wright's 'SHOORAH SHOORAH', before he took up another challenging high profile guitar slot, hooking up with OZZY OSBOURNE as a replacement for RANDY RHODES (who had recently lost his life in a plane crash). This position proved to be short-lived and TORME returned to Britain soon after, resurrecting The 'GYPSIES with a new line-up and releasing an eponymous album in late '83 and a concert set, 'LIVE', the following year. Along with PHIL LEWIS, CHRIS HEILMANN and IAN WHITEWOOD, the guitarist then initiated the humbly named TORME, releasing a couple of albums, 'BACK TO BABYLON' (1985) and 'DIE PRETTY, DIE YOUNG' (1987) before heading to America along with LEWIS. While the latter formed sleaze act, L.A. GUNS, TORME teamed up with TWISTED SISTER's DEE SNIDER in the DESPERADOS outfit. This was another short-lived collaboration and the Irishman finally returned to the UK, reverted back to the plain old BERNIE TORME moniker and released a covers set, 'ARE WE THERE YET?' (1991). This was followed a couple of years later by another independently released album, 'DEMOLITION BALL' (1993), and while the guitarist remains a cult attraction he issued only one further 90's release, the appropriately titled 'WILD IRISH' (1997).

Album rating: TURN OUT THE LIGHTS (*5) / ELECTRIC GYPSIES (*5) / LIVE (*4) / BACK TO BABYLON (*5) / DIE PRETTY DIE YOUNG (*5) / OFFICIAL LIVE BOOTLEG special (*4) / ARE WE THERE YET? (*5) / DEMOLITION BALL (*5)

BERNIE TORME – vocals, guitar, etc. / with his own band

Jet | not iss.

Oct 78. (7",7"orange; as BERNIE TORME BAND) *(JET 126)* **I'M NOT READY. / FREE** [ ] [-]

Mar 79. (7"ep; as BERNIE TORME BAND) *(JET 137)* **WEEKEND / SECRET SERVICE. / ALL NIGHT / INSTANT IMPACT** [ ] [-]

Island | not iss.

1980. (7"pink) *(WIP 6586)* **THE BEAT. / I WANT / BONY MORONIE** [ ] [-]

Parole | not iss.

Apr 81. (7") *(PURL 5)* **ALL DAY AND ALL OF THE NIGHT. / WHAT'S NEXT** [ ] [-]
(also issued Apr81 on 'Fresh'; FRESH 7)

—— **TORME** with **PHIL SPALDING** – bass / **NIGEL GLOCKER + MARK HARRISON** – drums / **COLIN TOWNS** – keyboards

Kamaflage | not iss.

1982. (7") *(KAM 5)* **AMERICA. / CHELSEA GIRLS** [ ] [-]

Jun 82. (white-lp/c) *(KAM LP/C 2)* **TURN OUT THE LIGHTS** [ ] [-]
– Turn out the lights / Painter man / Lies / America / Getting there / Possession / No reply / Chelsea girls / India / Oh no! *(cd-iss. Jun96 on 'Retrowrek'; RETRK 101)*

—— now with **FRANK NOON** – drums (ex-DEF LEPPARD) / **EVERTON WILLIAMS** – bass (ex-BETHNAL)

Oct 82. (d7"; by BERNIE TORME & ELECTRIC GYPSIES) *(KAM 8)* **SHOORAH SHOORAH. / STAR // SEARCH AND DESTROY (live). / POSSESSION (live)** [ ] [-]

—— with The ELECTRIC GYPSIES: **JAMES C. BOND** – bass (ex-STAMPEDE) / **RON REBEL** – drums (ex-McCOY)

Zebra | Enigma

Oct 83. (7") *(RA 1)* **I CAN'T CONTROL MYSELF. / BLACK SUNDAY** [ ] [-]

Oct 83. (lp/c) *(ZEB/CZEB 1)* **ELECTRIC GYPSIES** [ ] [-]
– Wild west / 20th century / Lightning strikes / Too young / Call of the wild / D.I.S.E. / Presences / I can't control myself / Go on. *(cd-iss. Jun96 on 'Retrowrek'; RETRK 102)*

Jan 84. (7"/12") *(RA/12RA 2)* **MY BABY LOVES A VAMPIRE. / LIGHTNING STRIKES** [ ] [-]

1984. (m-lp) *(MZEB 3)* **LIVE (live)** [ ] [-]
– Intro – Presences / Wild west / Turn on the lights / Lightning strikes / Getting there / Too young / No easy way.

TORME

—— with **PHIL LEWIS** – vocals (ex-GIRL) / **CHRIS HEILMANN** – bass / **IAN WHITEWOOD** – drums

Aug 85. (7") *(RA 5)* **ALL AROUND THE WORLD. /** [ ] [-]

Sep 85. (red-lp) *(ZEB 6)* *<73434>* **BACK TO BABYLON** [ ] [ ]
– All around the world / Star / Eyes of the world / Burning bridges / Hardcore / Here I go / Family at war / Front line / Arabia / Mystery train. *(cd-iss. Jul91; CDZEB 6)*

Mar 86. (7"ep/12"ep) *(RA/12RA 6)* **STAR / KERRAP. / T.V.O.D. / LOVE, GUNS AND MONEY** [ ] [-]

Heavy Metal | not iss.

Jun 87. (lp) *(HMRLP 94)* **DIE PRETTY DIE YOUNG** [ ] [-]
– Let it rock / The real thing / Ready / Sex action / The ways of the east / Killer / Memphis / Louise / Crimes of passion / Ghost train. *(w/free 12"; 12HM 95) (re-iss. Nov89 cd/c; HMR XD/MC 94)*

—— TORME joined DESPERADO with DEE SNIDER of TWISTED SISTER

Jun 91. (cd/c/lp; as BERNIE TORME) *(HMR XD/MC/LP 168)* **ARE WE THERE YET?** [ ] [-]
– Teenage kicks / Come the revolution / Let it rock / All around the world / Mystery train / Search and destroy / Shoo-rah shoo-rah / Wild west / Star / Turn out the lights (live) / Lies / Chelsea girls.

Bleeding Hearts | not iss.

Apr 93. (cd) *(CDBLEED 2)* **DEMOLITION BALL** [ ] [-]
– Fallen angel / Black sheep / Action / Ball and chain / Slip away / Long time coming / Spinnin' your wheels / Don't understand / Industry / Draw the line / U.S. maid / Let it go / Walk it / Man o' means.

BERNIE TORME

RetroWrek | RetroWrek

Oct 97. (cd) *(<RETRK 103>)* **WILD IRISH** [ ] [ ] Feb95
– Rat / Ghost walking / Follow the leader / Bad blood / Howling at the Moon / River / Walk, don't run / Lonesome train / One more heartache / Yesterday and nowhere / Howling at the Moon (live) / Ghost walking (live) / Rat (live) / Graveyard (live).

– compilations, etc. –

Apr 86. (lp/c) *Raw Power (RAW LP/MC 010)* **BACK WITH THE BOYS** [ ] [-]

Jul 87. (lp) *Onsala Int.; (ONS 3)* **OFFICIAL LIVE BOOTLEG (live)** [ ] [-]
(cd-iss. Jul87 on 'The CD Label'; CDTL 006) (cd re-iss. 1991 on 'Thunderbolt'; CDTB 112)

Devin TOWNSEND

Born: Canada. A prolific songwriter, whose madball antics led him to release a "joke" record taking the piss out of GREEN DAY and RANCID (although for Japanese ears only!). His teen years were spent dodging schoolwork and learning guitar, the manic "bi-polar" (a type of depression) lad finally graduating with a musical scholarship in the early 90's. DEVIN sent demos to various companies and it was 'Relativity' who signed him up for a lucrative record deal, initiating his vocal talents on STEVE VAI's 'Passion And Warfare' set. The man subsequently wrote and starred on STRAPPING YOUNG LAD's debut album, 'HEAVY AS A REALLY HEAVY THING' (1995), a masterful onslaught of FEAR FACTORY meeting JUDAS PRIEST-like metal that seemingly went down well in Japan. SYL (whose line-up was completed by JED SIMON, BYRON STROUD, GENE HOGLAN and MATTEO CARATOZZOLLO), delivered a second album, 'CITY' (1997), a cracking set of intense metal/hard-rock, that in fact led to DEVIN spending some time in a mental institution to recuperate. A third long-player, the fake-live 'NO SLEEP 'TIL BEDTIME' (June '98), was issued only a month after another project of his was unleashed, OCEAN MACHINE. Another equally impressive metal/hard rock act, their debut recording, 'BIOMECH', was a little lighter but nonetheless similar to SYL. A grandiose and symphonic solo set, 'INFINITY', rounded off what was definitely a very busy year. • **Trivia:** In 1995/96, DEVIN also moonlighted for the likes of FRONT LINE ASSEMBLY and The WILDHEARTS.

Album rating: INFINITY (*7) / Strapping Young Lad: HEAVY AS A REALLY HEAVY THING (*6) / CITY (*7) / NO SLEEP 'TIL BEDTIME (*6) / Ocean Machine: BIOMECH (*5)

STRAPPING YOUNG LAD

DEVIN TOWNSEND – vocals, guitar / **JED SIMON** – guitar / **MATTEO CARATOZZOLLO** – keyboards / **BYRON STROUD** – bass / **GENE HOGLAN** – drums

Century Media | unknown

Apr 95. (cd/c) *(CM 77092 CD/MC)* **HEAVY AS A REALLY HEAVY THING** □ □
– Strapping young lad / In the rainy season / etc.

1997. (cd) **CITY** □ □
– Home nucleonics /

Jun 98. (cd) *(CM 77227CD)* **NO SLEEP 'TIL BEDTIME** (live in the studio) □ □
– Velvet Kavorkian / All hail the new flesh / Oh my f***ing god / Home nucleonics / etc / Japan / Centipede.

OCEAN MACHINE

DEVIN TOWNSEND with various guests

U.S.G. | U.S.G.

May 98. (cd) *<(USG 1021-2)>* **BIOMECH** □ □

DEVIN TOWNSEND

U.S.G. | U.S.G.

Nov 98. (cd) *(USG 10282)* **INFINITY** □ □

Dec 98. (cd-s) *(USG 10284)* **CHRISTEEN / WILD COLONIAL BOY / NIGHT** □ □

Mike TRAMP (see under ⇒ FREAK OF NATURE)

TRAPEZE

Formed: Wolverhampton, England . . . 1968 by GLENN HUGHES and MEL GALLEY, who had spent the previous two years with pop act, FINDER'S KEEPERS. Three 45's were released during this period, 'LIGHT'. / 'COME ON NOW' (C.B.S.; 202249), 'ON THE BEACH'. / 'FRIDAY KIND OF MONDAY' (Fontana; TF 892) and 'SADIE (THE CLEANING LADY)'. / 'WITHOUT HER' (Fontana; TF 938). TRAPEZE were completed by DAVE HOLLAND, and two from The MONTANAS: JOHN JONES and TERRY ROWLEY, although the latter two returned to the aforesaid outfit after TRAPEZE's eponymous debut for The MOODY BLUES' label 'Threshold'. This 1970 JOHN LODGE-produced set was riddled with hard rock and blues numbers, possibly a little too derivative for a chart appearance. Now a tighter trio, they continued for the next few years, releasing albums, 'MEDUSA' (1971), 'YOU ARE THE MUSIC' (1972), although they had a major setback when HUGHES chose wisely to join rock giants, DEEP PURPLE. He was replaced by ROB KENDRICK and PETE WRIGHT, the band now a quartet for their fourth album (their first for 'Warners'), 'HOT WIRE' (1974). It was followed by another long player called 'TRAPEZE'!, although this was their last for some time, as the group took a hiatus for a couple of years. Between 1978 and 1981, they released two albums, the last containing GALLEY as the sole survivor, drummer HOLLAND having moved on to JUDAS PRIEST.

Album rating: TRAPEZE (*5) / MEDUSA (*6) / YOU ARE THE MUSIC . . . WE'RE JUST THE BAND (*4) / HOT WIRE (*5) / TRAPEZE (*4) / HOLD ON (*5) / DEAD ARMADILLOS – LIVE IN TEXAS (*3) / HIGH FLYERS compilation (*6)

JOHN JONES – vocals, trumpet (ex-MONTANAS) / **GLENN HUGHES** – bass, vocals (ex-FINDER'S KEEPERS), ex-NEWS) / **MEL GALLEY** – guitar (ex-FINDER'S KEEPERS) / **DAVE HOLLAND** – drums / **TERRY ROWLEY** – keyboards, guitar, flute (ex-MONTANAS)

Threshold | Threshold

1969. (7") *(TH 2) <67001>* **SEND ME NO MORE LETTERS. / ANOTHER DAY** □ □

1970. (lp) *(THS 2)* **TRAPEZE** □ -
– It's only a dream / The giant's dead hoorah! / Over / Nancy Gray / Fairytale / Verily verily / Fairytale / It's my life / Am I / Suicide / Wings / Another day / Send me no more letters / It's only a dream. *(cd-iss. Feb94 on 'London'; 820954-2)*

— now a trio and without JONES + ROWLEY (latter guested on 1974/1978 albums)

1971. (lp) *(THS 4)* **MEDUSA** □ -
– Black cloud / Jury / Your love is alright / Touch my life / Seagull / Makes you wanna cry / Medusa. *(cd-iss. Feb94 on 'London'; 820955-2)*

1971. (7") *<67005>* **BLACK CLOUD. /** - □

1972. (7") *(TH 11) <67011>* **COAST TO COAST. / YOUR LOVE IS ALRIGHT** □ □

1972. (lp) *(THS 8)* **YOU ARE THE MUSIC . . . WE'RE JUST THE BAND** □ -
– Keepin' time / Coast to coast / What is a woman's role / Way back to the bone / Feelin' so much better now / Will our love end / Loser / You are the music. *(cd-iss. Feb94 on 'London'; 820956-2)*

1974. (lp) *<THS 11>* **THE FINAL SWING** (compilation) - □
– Send me no more letters / Your love is alright / Black cloud / Medusa / Coast to coast / Will our love end / You are the music / Good love / Dats it.

— **ROB KENRICK** – guitar + **PETE WRIGHT** – bass; repl. HUGHES who joined DEEP PURPLE (GALLEY now added lead vocals)

Warners | Warners

1974. (lp) *(K 56064) <2828>* **HOT WIRE** □ □
– Back street love / Take it on down the road / Midnight flyer / Wake up, shake up / Turn it on / Steal a mile / Goin' home / Feel it inside.

Aug 75. (7") *(K 16606)* **SUNNY SIDE OF THE STREET. / MONKEY** □ -

1975. (lp) *(K 56165) <2887>* **TRAPEZE** □ □
– Star breaker / It's alright / Chances / The raid / On the sunny side of the street / Gimmie good love / Monkey / I need you / Soul stealer / Nothing for nothing.

— line-up:- **GALLEY, HOLLAND + WRIGHT**

— **PAUL GOALBY** – vocals, guitar; repl. KENDRICK

Aura | not iss.

Oct 79. (lp/c) *(AUL/AUC 708)* **HOLD ON** □ -
– Don't ask me how I know / Take good care / When you get to Heaven / Livin' on love / Hold on / Don't break my heart / Running / You are / Time will heal. *(was actually issued in limited form in 1978 as 'RUNNING'; same) (cd-iss. Aug96 on 'See For Miles'; SEECD 450)*

Jan 80. (7") *(AUS 114)* **DON'T ASK ME HOW I KNOW. / TAKE GOOD CARE** □ -

May 80. (7") *(AUS 116)* **RUNNING AWAY. / DON'T BREAK MY HEART** □ -

— **STEVE BRAY** – drums; repl. HOLLAND who joined JUDAS PRIEST

Nov 81. (lp) *(AUL 717)* **DEAD ARMADILLOS – LIVE IN TEXAS (live)** □ -
– Back street love / Hold on / Midnight flyer / You are the music we're just the band / Black cloud / Way back to the bone. *(cd-iss. Oct96 on 'See For Miles'; SEECD 462)*

— split in 1982, GALLEY joined WHITESNAKE, while GOALBY joined URIAH HEEP

– compilations, etc. –

Oct 86. (lp) *Bandit; (BRF 2001)* **WAY BACK TO THE BONE** □ -
– Coast to coast / Loser / Your love is alright / Touch my life / Way back to the bone / Seagull / Black cloud / You are the music / Medusa.

Jan 96. (cd) *London; (820957-2)* **HIGH FLYERS (THE BEST OF TRAPEZE)** □ -

Pat TRAVERS

Born: 1954, Toronto, Canada. Having previously played guitar in his brother's rock outfit, TRAVERS moved to London and formed his own band with the aid of PETER 'MARS' COWLING on bass and the experienced ROY DYKE on drums (ex-ASHTON, GARDNER & DYKE). Debuting big time at that year's Reading Festival, TRAVERS and Co. played numbers from his eponymous 'Polydor' album, a record that was full of high energy B&B (boogie'n'blues). DYKE departed soon after and was replaced by NICKO McBRAIN for a follow-up set, 'MAKIN' MAGIC' (1977); regarded as his greatest achievement, it managed to scrape into the UK Top 40. Adding short-time members SCOTT GORHAM (guitar; ex-THIN LIZZY) and TONY CAREY (keyboards), TRAVERS released another album that year, 'PUTTING IT STRAIGHT', although this was the last to feature McBRAIN who was to claim his fame with IRON MAIDEN. He was substituted by American, TOMMY ALDRIDGE, straight from the backwaters of BLACK OAK ARKANSAS to the shores of England and TRAVERS' fourth album, 'HEAT IN THE STREET' (1979). A fifth set, the live 'GO FOR WHAT YOU KNOW' (1979), saw The PAT TRAVERS BAND (as they were now credited) make the US Top 30, followed by a similarly successful studio album, 'CRASH AND BURN' in 1980. However, these creative attempts to redefine turn-of-the-decade hard/blues rock drew short shrift from the critics and it seemed TRAVERS' band was becoming a bit of a conveyor belt for talent. Another two top names to leave for higher plains were ALDRIDGE (to OZZY OSBOURNE) and THRALL (to HUGHES/THRALL and ASIA), TRAVERS once again credited solo on 1981's 'RADIO-ACTIVE'. This US Top 40 entry retained the ever-faithful COWLING, plus newcomers SANDY GENNARO on drums and former SANTANA percussionist MICHAEL SHRIEVE. TRAVERS released two more efforts in the ensuing few years, 'BLACK PEARL' (1982) and 'HOT SHOTS' (1984) before virtually taking the rest of the 80's off. The guitarist re-surfaced in the early 90's with a clutch of rootsy blues-orientated albums, starting with 'BOOM BOOM'(1991) and 'BLUES TRACKS' (1992; for 'Roadrunner'!).

Album rating: PAT TRAVERS (*6) / MAKIN' MAGIC (*6) / PUTTING IT STRAIGHT (*6) / HEAT IN THE STREET (*6) / GO FOR WHAT YOU KNOW (*6) / CRASH AND BURN (*6) / RADIO ACTIVE (*5) / PAT TRAVERS' BLACK PEARL (*5) / HOT SHOT (*5) / SCHOOL OF HARD KNOCKS (*4) / BOOM BOOM (*5) / BLUES TRACKS (*5) / JUST A TOUCH (*4) / BLUES MAGNET (*4) / HALFWAY TO SOMEWHERE (*4) / LOOKIN' UP (*4) / BLUES TRACKS VOL.2 (*5) / DON'T FEED THE ALLIGATORS (*4)

PAT TRAVERS – vocals, guitar, keyboards / with **PETER 'MARS' COWLING** – bass / **ROY DYKE** – drums (ex-ASHTON, GARDNER & DYKE)

Polydor | Polydor

Jun 76. (lp) *(2383 395) <6079>* **PAT TRAVERS** □ □
– Stop and smile / Fellin' right / Magnolia / Makes no difference / Boom boom (out go the lights) / Mabelline / Hot rod Lincoln / As my life flies / Medley (parts 1 & 2).

— **NICKO McBRAIN** – drums; repl. DYKE

— guests were **CLIVE EDWARDS** – drums / **GLENN HUGHES** – vocals

Mar 77. (lp) *(2383 436) <6103>* **MAKIN' MAGIC** 40 □
– Makin' magic / Rock'n'roll Susie / You don't love me / Stevie / Statesboro blues / Need love / Hooked on music / What you mean to me. *(re-iss. Sep81; 2384 122)*

Apr 77. (7") *(2058 877)* **ROCK'N'ROLL SUSIE. / MAKES NO DIFFERENCE** □ -

May 77. (7") *<14416>* **WHAT YOU MEAN TO ME. / STEVIE** - □

— added **TONY CAREY** – keyboards / **SCOTT GORHAM** – guitar

Oct 77. (lp) *(2383 471) <6121>* **PUTTING IT STRAIGHT** □ 70
– Life in London / It ain't what it seems / Runnin' for the future / Lovin' you / Off beat ride / Gettin' betta / Dedication / Speakeasy.

Jan 78. (7") *<14473>* **LIFE IN LONDON. / DEDICATION (part 2)** - □

— **PAT THRALL** – guitar, vocals (ex-AUTOMATIC MAN) repl. GORHAM + CAREY

— **TOMMY ALDRIDGE** – drums (ex-BLACK OAK ARKANSAS) repl. McBRAIN who joined IRON MAIDEN

Jan 79. (7") *<14529>* **GO ALL NIGHT. / HAMMERHEAD** - □

Apr 79. (lp) *(POLD 5005)* *<6170>* **HEAT IN THE STREET** 99 Oct78
– Heat in the street / Killers instinct / I tried to believe / Hammerhead / Go all night / Evie / Prelude / One for me and one for you.

PAT TRAVERS BAND

Aug 79. (red-lp,lp) *(POLS 1011)* *<6202>* **PAT TRAVERS BAND LIVE! GO FOR WHAT YOU KNOW (live)** 29 Jul79
– Hooked on music / Gettin' betta / Go all night / Boom boom (out go the lights) / Stevie / Makin' magic / Heat in the street / Makes no difference.
Aug 79. (7") *<2003>* **BOOM BOOM (OUT GO THE LIGHTS) (live). / GO ALL NIGHT (live)** - 56
Sep 79. (7") *(PB 77)* **BOOM BOOM (OUT GO THE LIGHTS) (live). / STATESBORO BLUES (live)** -
Apr 80. (7") *(POSP 144)* **IS THIS LOVE. / SNORTIN' WHISKEY** -
Apr 80. (lp) *(POLS 1017)* *<6262>* **CRASH AND BURN** 20 Mar80
– Crash and burn / Can't be right / Snortin' whiskey / Born under a bad sign / Is this love / The big event / Love will make you strong / Material eyes.
Apr 80. (7") *<2080>* **IS THIS LOVE. / LOVE WILL MAKE YOU STRONG** - 50
Aug 80. (7") *(POSP 164)* **YOUR LOVE CAN'T BE RIGHT. / SNORTIN' WHISKEY** -
(12"+=) *(POSPX 164)* – Life in London / Evie / Rock'n'roll Susie.
1980. (7") *<2107>* **SNORTIN' WHISKEY. / STATESBORO BLUES** -

— during recordings **THRALL + ALDRIDGE** moved on to bigger things (i.e. OZZY OSBOURNE) and were repl. by **SANDY GENNARO** – drums + **MICHAEL SHIEVE** – percussion (ex-SANTANA)

PAT TRAVERS

May 81. (lp/c) *(2391 499)* *<6313>* **RADIO ACTIVE** 37 Mar81
– New age music / My life is on the line / (I just wanna) Live it my way / I don't wanna be awake / I can love you / Untitled / Feelin' in love / Play it like you see it / Electric detective.
May 81. (7") *<2167>* **MY LIFE IS ON THE LINE. / ELECTRIC DETECTIVE** -

— **DON HARRIS** – keyboards; repl. SHRIEVE

Oct 82. (lp) *(2391 553)* *<6361>* **PAT TRAVERS' BLACK PEARL** 74
– I la la la love you / I'd rather see you dead / Stand up / Who'll take the fall / The fifth / Misty morning / Can't stop the heartaches / Amgwanna kick booty / Rockin'.
Nov 82. (7") *<2223>* **I'D RATHER SEE YOU DEAD. / ROCKIN'** -

— band now completed by **JERRY RIGGS** – guitar / **BARRY DUNAWAY** – bass / **PAT MARCHINO** – drums

Apr 84. (lp) *<821064-1>* **HOT SHOT** -
– I gotta fight / Killer / Just try talking (to those dudes) / Hot shot / Women on the edge of love / In the heat of the night / Louise / Tonight / Night into day.

— took the rest of the 80's off

Episode / not iss.
Jul 90. (cd/c/lp) *(LUS CD/MC/LP 4)* **SCHOOL OF HARD KNOCKS** -
– The fight goes on / Chevrolet / If you want love / Purple jazz / Whatcha gonna do without me / School of hard knocks / Help me / Misty morning (in New Orleans) / Via veneto / All or nothing / Only man / Don't say you me / Daddy long legs / Guitars from Hell.

— now with **THRALL, ALDRIDGE + COWLING + JERRY RIGGS + SCOTT ZYMOWSKI**

Essential / Essential
Apr 91. (cd/c/lp) *(ESS CD/MC/LP 140)* **BOOM BOOM (live)** -
– Snorting whiskey / Life in London / I la la la love you / Getting better / Watcha gonna do without me / Daddy long legs / Heat in the street / School of hard knocks / Help me / Stevie / Ready or not / Boom boom (out go the lights) / Born under a bad sign / Guitars from Hell. *(cd re-iss. Mar00; ESMCD 866)*

Roadrunner / Blues Bureau
Sep 92. (cd) *(RR 9147-2)* *<BB 2002>* **BLUES TRACKS**
– Memory pain / Calling card blues / I can't quit you / Statesboro blues / I've got news for you / I ain't superstitious / Built for comfort / Mystery train / Just got paid / Sitting on top of the world.
Oct 93. (cd) *(RR 9045-2)* *<BB 2014>* **JUST A TOUCH**
– The riff / Too cool woman blues / You don't love me / The pain / Wasted years / I've fallen / Daydream / Amanda / The more things change / Miss glory.

Provogue / Blues Bureau
Sep 94. (cd) *(PRD 70682)* *<BB 2022>* **BLUES MAGNET**
– Blues magnet / Travelin' blues / Lil' southern belle / Rock yer blues away / This world we live in / She gets the lovin' / Elaine / Fall to pieces / Tore up (from the floor up) / You shouldn't have hurt me.
Sep 95. (cd) *(PRD 70842)* *<BB 2028>* **HALFWAY TO SOMEWHERE**
– Just enough money / Time out / Walk in my shoes / Steppin' out / Look me up / Party tonight / Just like a dream / Hard times / No escape / Freight train.
Oct 96. (cd) *(PRD 70972)* *<BB 2034>* **LOOKIN' UP**
– Ice queen / Lookin' up / Hypnotized / Dusty blues / Too much (is never enough) / Bad little girl / Right to complain / A good fool is hard to find / Bad feelin's again / Suburban blues.

Blues Bureau / Blues Bureau
Sep 99. (cd) *<(BB 2038-2)>* **BLUES TRACKS VOL.2** Apr98
– I guess I'll go away / Pack it up / Outside woman blues / Your cash ain't nothin' but trash / Whipping post / Take it back / Taxman / Purple haze / Bring it on home to me / I don't know / Walkin' by myself / One more heartache.
Apr 00. (cd) *(BB 2042-2)* **DON'T FEED THE ALLIGATORS**

– compilations, etc. –

Mar 90. (cd) *Polydor; (841 208-2)* **AN ANTHOLOGY VOL.1** -
Mar 90. (cd) *Polydor; (841 209-2)* **AN ANTHOLOGY VOL.2** -
Jun 92. (cd) *Windsong; (WINCD 017)* **IN CONCERT (BBC RADIO 1 LIVE IN CONCERT)** -
Sep 97. (cd) *Strange Fruit; (SFRSCD 038)* **THE PAT TRAVERS BAND** -
Sep 99. (cd) *Dressed To Kill; (PATT 33)* **BORN UNDER A BAD SIGN**

TREEPEOPLE

Formed: Boise, Idaho, USA . . . late 80's by DOUG MARTSCH, SCOTT SCHMALJOHN, PAT BROWN and WAYNE RHINO. Debuting on the 'Toxic Shock' label with 1989's 'GUILT, REGRET, EMBARRASSMENT', this pre-grunge alternative outfit were spiritual cousins to the likes of GREEN RIVER and HUSKER DU, employing a twin-guitar attack that never veered too far from punk primitivism while putting an emphasis on melody. Sticksman, RHINO was replaced by TONY DALLAS REED for 1992's 'C/Z'-released follow-up, 'SOMETHING VICIOUS FOR TOMORROW', a record that mauled The Smiths' 'BIGMOUTH STRIKES AGAIN'. In true Spinal Tap style, yet another drummer, ERIC AKRE, was in place for 'JUST KIDDING' (1993), the band summing up the slacker ethos with 'ANYTHING'S IMPOSSIBLE'. MARTSCH was the next one to climb down, leaving the TREEPEOPLE and later joining BUILT TO SPILL; the gap was subsequently filled with JOHN POLLE and ERIC CARNELL, the line-up on the band's fourth and final album, 'ACTUAL RE-ENACTMENT' (1994).

Album rating: GUILT, REGRET, EMBARRASSMENT (*6) / SOMETHING VICIOUS FOR TOMORROW (*4) / JUST KIDDING (*7) / ACTUAL RE-ENACTMENT (*5)

DOUG MARTSCH – vocals, guitar / **SCOTT SCHMALJOHN** – guitar, vocals / **PAT BROWN** – bass / **WAYNE RHINO** – drums

not iss. / Toxic Shock
1989. (cd) *<23>* **GUILT, REGRET, EMBARRASSMENT** -
– No doubt / Andy Warhol / GRE / Lost / Transitional devices / Pity / (I'm gonna) Miss you (when you're gone) / Wasted on you / Stay / Chunks of milk / Everytime when I fall down and my head . . . / Trailer park.

— **TONY DALLAS REED** – drums; repl. the departing RHINO (on some)

C/Z / C/Z
Mar 92. (lp/cd) *<(CZ 040/+CD)>* **SOMETHING VICIOUS FOR TOMORROW**
– Liquid boy / It's alright now ma / Something vicious for tomorrow / Big mouth strikes again / Filter / Ad campaigns / Funnelhead / Party / Tongues on thrones / Lives / Radio man / Size of a quarter / Time whore. *<US cd-iss. w/+=>* – TIME WHORE EP (tracks above)

— **ERIC AKRE** – drums (ex-CHRIST ON A CRUTCH) repl. BROWN (REED took over bass!)

1993. (cd) *<CZ 54>* **JUST KIDDING** -
– Today / In C / Cartoon brew / Ballard bitter / Clouds and faces / Fishbasket / Nod and blink / Anything's impossible / Neil's down / Outside in.

— **SCHMALJOHN + AKRE** recruited newcomers (**JOHN POLLE** – guitar + **ERIC CARNELL** – bass) when MARTSCH left to form BUILT TO SPILL

1994. (cd) *<CZ 80>* **ACTUAL RE-ENACTMENT** -
– What'd I mean to think you said / Feed me / Slept through mine / Heinz von Foerster / Boot straps / Liver vs. heart / Better days / Bag of wood / Low / Will we ever / Too long.

TRIBE AFTER TRIBE

Formed: South Africa . . . mid 80's out of The ASYLUM KIDS by ROBBI ROBB and ROBBY WHITELAW. In 1987, they were forced to leave their country due to their anti-apartheid stance, relocating to the more amiable L.A. in the process. TRIBE AFTER TRIBE retained their Afro acid-rock, recruiting local drummer PK to redefine their socio-political stance on an eponymous debut set in '91. CHRIS FRAZIER subsequently replaced the aforesaid sticksman prior to a second album, 'LOVE UNDER WILL' (1993). After a lengthy spell away from the scene (in which he worked with PEARL JAM's JEFF AMENT in the THREE FISH project/album), TRIBE AFTER TRIBE, now encouraged by PEARL JAM and KINGS X (whose members helped them out in the recording studio), resurfaced with a third long-player, 'PEARLS BEFORE SWINE' (1997).

Album rating: TRIBE AFTER TRIBE (*5) / LOVE UNDER WILL (*5) / PEARLS BEFORE SWINE (*5)

ROBBI ROBB – vocals, guitar / **ROBBY WHITELAW** – bass / **PK** – drums

East West / Megaforce
Sep 91. (cd/c/lp) *<(7567 82235-2/-4/-1)>* **TRIBE AFTER TRIBE**
– Remember / Build a subway / Sally / Just for a while / Come to see you fall / The mode / White boys in the jungle / Rolling stoney / What are we now / Everything and more / Out of control / Poor Afrika.

— **CHRIS FRAZIER** – drums (ex-STEVE VAI) repl. PK

Megaforce / Megaforce
Jun 93. (cd/c/d-lp) *(CD/T+/ZAZ 4)* *<6914>* **LOVE UNDER WILL** Jul93
– Hold on / Ice below / The spell / Dance of the Wu Li masters / I spit / Nikita / Congo sky / World of promises / Proud and beautiful / Let's go outside / Delight / Lovers: (a) The face of the sun, (b) In the dark, (c) Babalon.
Aug 93. (cd-s) *<CDP 961>* **ICE BELOW / CHILDSPEAK / SINNER MAN** -

— **ROBB** (returned from a stint with THREE FISH) recruited new members **BUTCH REYNOLDS** – drums + **JOEY VERA** – bass to repl. CHRIS + ROBBY respectively

Bulletproof / Bulletproof
Apr 97. (cd) *(CDVEST 82)* **PEARLS BEFORE SWINE**
– Boy / Lazurus / The ballad of Winnie Mandela / Oh-oh / Senor / Fire dancers / Bury me / Pat on the back / The heart / Murder on the ice / Hopeless the clown.

TRIBE 8

Formed: San Francisco, California, USA . . . 1991 by LYNN BREEDLOVE, LYNN FLIPPER, SLADE BELLUM, TANTRUM and LESLIE NEWMAN. Having met while working for a lesbian escort service, the girls decided to form a band with the promise of not only riches and loads of female groupies but a platform for their zealous feminism and radical politics. As heard on their 1993 debut set, 'BY THE TIME WE GET TO COLORADO', TRIBE 8's queercore punk caught the attention of JELLO BIAFRA who quickly procured them for his 'Alternative Tentacles' label. While not prancing around on stage with a dildo sticking out of her tartan trousers, BREEDLOVE was hard at work in the studio with her bosom buddies, banging out the likes of 'ALLEN'S MOM' (1994), 'FIST CITY' (1995) and 'SNARKISM' (1996). The dyke warriors reached their artistic zenith with 'ROLE MODELS FOR AMERIKA' (1998), choosing none other than The SPICE GIRLS as support for the subsequent tour. • **Covered:** THINK (Aretha Franklin) / RADAR LOVE (Golden Earring) / RISE ABOVE (Black Flag).

Album rating: BY THE TIME WE GET TO COLORADO mini (*5) / FIST CITY (*5) / SNARKISM (*6) / ROLE MODELS FOR AMERIKA (*5)

LYNN BREEDLOVE – vocals / **LESLIE MAH** (b. NEWMAN) – lead guitar, vocals / **LYNN FLIPPER** – rhythm guitar, vocals / **LYNN PAYNE** – bass, vocals / **SLADE BELLUM** – drums, vocals

not iss. — own label

1992. (7"ep/c-ep/cd-ep) **THERE'S A DYKE IN THE PIT EP** — -

not iss. — Lickout

1993. (7") **BITCHES IN BREW. /** — -

Outpunk — Outpunk

Jun 93. (cd/c) *<(OUT 7 CD/MC)>* **BY THE TIME WE GET TO COLORADO**
– Lezbophobia / 1 party 2 many / Masochist's medley / Easy virtue / Censor this / Crash crush.

Nov 94. (7"ep/cd-ep) *<OUT 13/+CD>* **ALLEN'S MOM** — -

Alternative Tentacles — Alternative Tentacles

Jan 95. (cd) *<VIRUS 156CD>* **FIST CITY** — -
– Manipulate / Seraphim / Butch in the streets / Romeo and Julio / What? / Kick / Neanderthal dyke / Freedom / Allen's mom / Femme bitch top / Think / Flippersnapper / Barnyard poontang / All I can do / Frat pig. *(UK-iss.Apr00; same as US)*

Nov 95. (cd-ep) *<VIRUS 173>* **ROADKILL CAFE EP** — -
– Wrong bathroom / Radar love / Ice cream man (live) / Manipulate (live).

May 96. (cd/lp) *<(VIRUS 181 CD/LP)>* **SNARKISM** — Apr96
– Republican lullaby / Tranny chaser / She said / A sad poem / Ez virtue / Checking out your babe / Jim, darby & Sid / Wrong bathroom / People hate me / Mendo hoo-ha / Oversize ego / Dead clothed boys / Speed fortress.

Mar 98. (cd/lp) *<(VIRUS 212 CD/LP)>* **ROLE MODELS FOR AMERIKA**
– Sunbears / Old skool, new skool / Sleep deprivation / Junkyard dog / Ta ta ta ta's / What the papers didn't say / Queen of the scene / Castration song #22 / Rise above / Daredevil delivery / Het punx (Opie 'n' Alli's song) / Takin' out the trash / Estrofemme / Haldol shuffle / Prison blues / Hapa girl / Sunbears (extended dance mix).

—— split soon after above

TRIBES OF NEUROT (see under ⇒ NEUROSIS)

TRIBUTE TO NOTHING

Formed: London, England . . . early '92 by brothers JIM and BEN TURNER, the pubescent schoolboys subsequently turning it into a family affair and recruiting their younger brother, SAM (two further musicians were used early on). Licensed by their local education authority to prevent charges of truancy while they were gigging, the young scamps were offered a deal with the brand new 'Kinglake' imprint. They debuted with the 'OFFICE JOBS' EP late in '93 (surely a record NOT born of experience!), following it up with '24 HRS', a track reminiscent of early DEAD KENNEDYS, although their overall image was more in line with the prevailing NIRVANA worship. Like HANSON brought up on hardcore, the siblings continued in precocious fashion with a further clutch of singles on the 'Free' label. A long awaited debut set, 'STRAIGHT LINE' (1997), was quickly followed by another album in the same year, 'WRENCH', the trio finally coming of age.

Album rating: STRAIGHT LINE (*6) / WRENCH (*6) / THIS IS FREEDOM (*5)

JIM TURNER (b. 1979) – vocals, bass / **SAM TURNER** (b. 1980) – guitar / **BEN TURNER** (b. 1977) – drums

Kinglake — not iss.

Nov 93. (7"ep) *(KLR 001)* **OFFICE JOBS EP** — -

Apr 94. (7") *(KLR 003)* **24 HRS. / YET AGAIN** — -

Free — not iss.

Nov 94. (7") *(FOC 9)* **CAN'T GET UP. /** — -

Jun 95. (7"blue) *(FOC 10)* **THINK YOU SHOULD. / DO SOMETHING** — -
(cd-s+=) *(FOCCD 10)* – Lost your mind.

Apr 96. (7") *(FOC 11)* **STRAIGHT LINE. /** — -
(cd-s+=) *(FOCCD 11)* –

Lockjaw — not iss.

Jun 97. (cd-ep) *(LJCD 001)* **FINDING MY OWN MIND / R.T.A. / CLAMP / CATCH YOUR GRIP** — -

Jun 97. (cd) *(LJCD 002)* **STRAIGHT LINE** — -
– Straight line / Find it / Cecil / Could I / Think you should / Do something / How could things / Don't care.

Oct 97. (cd) *(LJCD 004)* **WRENCH** — -
– Backdown / Time to see / Finding my own mind / Should the quiet / Two minutes of hate / R.T.A. / Fight for life / Prevention / 212 / Catch your grip / Blue alloy / Timebomb.

Nov 98. (cd-s) *(LJCDS 011)* **ENEMY / SICKNESS / LOSE** — -

Oct 99. (cd) *(LJCD 017)* **THIS IS FREEDOM** — -
– Understand / This is freedom / Easy target / Panic / Strain / Self opinion / You'll see me rising / Transparent skin / Enemy / Cut / Background.

TRIPPING DAISY

Formed: Dallas, Texas, USA . . . 1991 by lyricist TIM DeLAUGHTER, WES BERGGREN, MARK PIRRO and BRYAN WAKELAND. Signed to 'Island', the band debuted with the 'BILL' album in 1994. Sporting a psychedelic punk / hard-rock sound similar to JANE'S ADDICTION (DeLAUGHTER's whining vocals a bizarre cross between PERRY FARRELL and LIAM GALLAGHER!), the group soon attracted a growing following on the American alternative scene. With media coverage also gathering strength, the band released a follow-up set, 'i am an ELASTIC FIRECRACKER' (complete with sleevework by deceased artist, Gugliemo Achille Cavellini) in early '96. The record was their most successful to date, scraping into the lower regions of the US Top 100, while the swaggering 'PIRANHA' single made the Top 75.

Album rating: BILL (*5) / i am an ELASTIC FIRECRACKER (*8)

TIM DeLAUGHTER – vocals, guitar / **WES BERGGREN** – guitar / **MARK PIRRO** – bass / **BRYAN WAKELAND** – drums

Island Red — Dragon St.

Jul 94. (cd/c/lp) *(CIRD/IRCT/IRLP 1001) <70392>* **BILL** — Nov92
– My umbrella / One through four / Lost and found / Change of mind / On the ground / The morning / Blown away / Brown-eyed pickle boy / Miles and miles of pain / Triangle. *<cd re-iss. 1997 on 'Polygram'; 555002>*

Jul 94. (12"ep/cd-ep) *(12IR/CIRD 102)* **MY UMBRELLA / IT'S SAFE, IT'S SOCIAL (live). / GET IT ON (live) / WE'RE ONLY GONNA DIE (live)** — -

Island — Island

Feb 96. (c-s/7") *(C+/IS 636)* **I GOT A GIRL. / MARGARITA TROPENZANDO** — -
(12"+=/cd-s+=) *(12IS/CID 636)* – Cause tomb shop / Noose.

Feb 96. (cd/lp) *(CIRD/IRLP 1004) <524112>* **i am an ELASTIC FIRECRACKER** — 95 Aug95
– Rocket pop / Bang / I got a girl / Piranha / Motivation / Same dress new day / Trip along / Raindrop / Step behind / Noose / Prick / High.

Mar 96. (7") *(IS 638)* **PIRANHA. / CREATURE** — 72 -
(12"+=/cd-s+=) *(12IS/CID 638)* – High.

1997. (m-cd) *<531095>* **TIME CAPSULE** — -
– Rise / Cause tomb shop / Creature / Boobie the clown / I'm a fish / Blue train.

—— added **ERIC DREW FELDMAN** – producer, multi (ex-CAPTAIN BEEFHEART, ex-FRANK BLACK)

Jul 98. (cd) *<(524518-2)>* **JESUS HITS US LIKE AN ATOM BOMB**
– Field day jitters / Waited a light year / Sonic bloom / Bandaids for Mire / Mechanical breakdown / Your socks have no name / Geeareohdoubleyou / New plains medicine / Our drive to the sun – Can a man mark / Human contact / Pillar / 8 ladies / About the movies / Tiny men / Indian poker (pt.2 & 3).

TRIUMPH

Formed: Canuck, Toronto, Canada . . . September 1975 by RIK EMMETT (vocals/guitar), MIKE LEVINE (bass/keyboards) and GIL MOORE (drums). Taking high-tech power-metal to its extremes, TRIUMPH issued two well-sought after albums in their homeland; with import copies streaming over the American border and overseas, they soon found a home at 'R.C.A.' (packaging a compilation of both 'TRIUMPH' and 'ROCK AND ROLL MACHINE' as their debut non-domestic release). Similar but more rockier than fellow countrymen, RUSH (also a trio!), TRIUMPH delivered their first US/UK set proper, 'JUST A GAME' in 1979. With spectacular shows (involving laser-lighting, flame-throwers and dry ice, etc) gathering word-of-mouth momentum all over the States, the album finally hit the Top 50; the single from it, 'HOLD ON', also achieved similar success. The virtuoso showmanship of the band, highlighted by EMMETT's high-pitched larynx, went on to challenge RUSH as Canada's premier act. Although slagged by the critics, TRIUMPH scored with a string of Top 50 albums such as 'PROGRESSIONS OF POWER' (1980), 'ALLIED FORCES' (1981), 'NEVER SURRENDER' (1982), 'THUNDER SEVEN' (1984; now on 'M.C.A.'), the live set 'STAGES' (1985; complemented by 4th member, guitarist RICK SANTERS) and 'THE SPORT OF KINGS' (1986), before finally moving down the rock road with 'SURVEILLANCE' (1987). When EMMETT departed in 1988, it seemed the band would split, but ill-advisedly they carried on with a new guitarist, PHIL XENIDES, MOORE now taking over vocal duties. • **Note:** don't be confused with another TRIUMPH who issued the album 'Cry Freedom' in 1989.

Album rating: TRIUMPH (*4) / ROCK'N'ROLL MACHINE (*4) / ROCK'N'ROLL MACHINE UK compilation (*5) / JUST A GAME (*4) / PROGRESSIONS OF POWER (*6) / ALLIED FORCES (*6) / NEVER SURRENDER (*6) / THUNDER SEVEN (*5) / STAGES (*5) / THE SPORT OF KINGS (*4) / SURVEILLANCE (*5) / CLASSICS compilation (*6) / CRY FREEDOM (*4) / EDGE OF EXCESS (*4)

RIK EMMETT (b.10 Jul'53, Streetsville, Ontario) – vocals, guitar / **MIKE LEVINE** (b. 1 Jun'49) – bass, keyboards, synthesizers / **GIL MOORE** (b.12 Feb'51) – drums, percussion, vocals

not iss. Attic

1976. (lp) <LAT 1012> **TRIUMPH** - - Canada
– 24 hours a day / Be my lover / Don't take my life / Street fighter / Street fighter (reprise) / What's another day of rock'n'roll / Easy life / Let me get next to you / Blinding light show – Moonchild. *(UK-iss.Mar82;)*

1977. (lp/silver-lp) <LAT/+X 1036> **ROCK 'N ROLL MACHINE** - - Canada
– Takes time / Bringing it on home / Little Texas shaker / New York City streets / The city: War march – El Duende agonizante – Minstrels lament / Rocky mountain way / Rock and roll machine. *<US-iss.May79 on 'R.C.A.'; 2982>*

R.C.A. R.C.A.

Oct 78. (lp) *(1-2982)* **ROCK'N'ROLL MACHINE** (compilation of first 2 albums) -
– Takes time / Bringing it on home / Rocky mountain way / Street fighter / Street fighter (reprise) / 24 hours a day / Blinding light show – Moonchild / Rock & roll machine. *(re-iss. Jun87 on 'M.C.A.' lp/c; MCL/+C 1856)*

Nov 78. (7") *<11440>* **BRINGING IT ON HOME. / ROCKY MOUNTAIN WAY** -

May 79. (lp/c) *(PL/PK 13224) <3224>* **JUST A GAME** 48 Apr79
– Movin' on / Lay it on the line / Young enough to cry / American girls / Just a game / Fantasy serenade / Hold on / Suitcase blues. *(re-iss. Sep81 lp/c; INTS/INTK 5154)*

Jun 79. (7") *(PB 1569) <11569>* **HOLD ON. / JUST A GAME** 38
(12") *(PT 1569) <11620>* – ('A'extended).

Oct 79. (7") *<11690>* **LAY IT ON THE LINE. / AMERICAN GIRLS** - 86

Jan 80. (7") *(PB 9451)* **AMERICAN GIRLS. / MOVIN' ON** -

Apr 80. (lp/c) *(PL/PK 13524) <3524>* **PROGRESSIONS OF POWER** 61 32 Mar80
– I live for the weekend / I can survive / In the night / Nature's child / Woman in love / Take my heart / Tear the roof off / Fingertalkin' / Hard road. *(re-iss. Sep81 lp/c; RCA LP/K 3039) (re-iss. Jun87 on 'M.C.A.' lp/c; MCL/+C 1852)*

May 80. (7") *(PB 1945) <11945>* **I CAN SURVIVE. / NATURE'S CHILD** 91

Oct 80. (7"/12") *(RCA/+T 13)* **I LIVE FOR THE WEEKEND. / LAY IT ON THE LINE** 59 -

Sep 81. (lp/c) *(RCA LP/K 6002) <3902>* **ALLIED FORCES** 64 23
– Fool for your love / Magic power / Air raid / Allied forces / Hot time (in this city tonight) / Fight the good fight / Ordinary man / Petite etude / Say goodbye. *(cd-iss. 1987 on 'M.C.A.'; MCAD 5542)*

Oct 81. (7"/12") *(RCA/+T 135)* **ALLIED FORCES. / HOT TIME IN THIS CITY** -

Jan 82. (7") *<13035>* **ALLIED FORCES. / SAY GOODBYE** -

Mar 82. (7") *(RCA 15) <12298>* **MAGIC POWER. / FIGHT THE GOOD FIGHT** 51 Sep81

Feb 83. (lp/c) *(RCA LP/K 6067) <4382>* **NEVER SURRENDER** 26 Jan83
– Too much thinking / A world of fantasy / A minor prelude / All the way / Battle cry / Overture (processional) / Never surrender / When the lights go down / Writing on the wall / Epilogue (resolution).

Mar 83. (7"/7"pic-d) *(RCA/+PD 319) <13443>* **A WORLD OF FANTASY. / TOO MUCH THINKING**

May 83. (7") *<13510>* **WHEN THE LIGHTS GO DOWN. / ('A'long version)** -

Jul 83. (7") *<13539>* **BATTLE CRY. / ALL THE WAY** -

M.C.A. M.C.A.

Jan 85. (7") *<52520>* **SPELLBOUND. / COOL DOWN** -

Mar 85. (lp/c) *(MCF/+C 3246) <5537>* **THUNDER SEVEN** 35 Dec84
– Spellbound / Rock out, roll on / Cool down / Follow your heart / Times goes by / Midsummer's daydream / Time canon / Killing time / Stranger in a strange land / Little boy blues. *(cd-iss. Feb87; MCAD 5537)*

Mar 85. (7") *<52540>* **FOLLOW YOUR HEART. / STRANGER IN A STRANGE LAND** - 88

Oct 85. (7") *<52744>* **HOLD ON (live). / MIND GAMES (live)** -

Nov 85. (d-lp/d-c) *(MCMD/+C 7002) <8020>* **STAGES (live)** 50
– When the lights go down / Never surrender / Allied forces / Hold on / Magic power / Rock and roll machine / Lay it on the line / A world of fantasy / Druh mer selbo / Midsummer's daydream / Spellbound / Follow your heart / Fight the good fight / Mind games / Empty inside. *(cd-iss. Jul87; MCAD 7002)*

Sep 86. (lp/c) *(MCF/+C 3331) <5786>* **THE SPORT OF KINGS** 33 Aug86
– Tears in the rain / Somebody's out there / What rules my heart / If only / Hooked on you / Take a stand / Just one night / Embrujo / Play with the fire / Don't love anybody else but me / In the middle of the night. *(cd-iss. Apr87; MCAD 5786)*

Nov 86. (7") *<53014>* **HOOKED ON YOU. / JUST ONE NIGHT** -

Feb 87. (7") *(MCA 118) <52898>* **SOMEBODY'S OUT THERE. / FOLLOW YOUR HEART** 27 Aug86
(12"+=) *(MCAT 118)* – Magic power / I live for the weekend.

— STEVE MORSE (of KANSAS) made an appearance on 2 tracks below.

Nov 87. (lp/c/cd) *<42083-2/-4/-1>* **SURVEILLANCE** - 82
– Prologue: Into the forever / Never say never / Headed for nowhere / All the king's horses / Carry on the flame / Let the light (shine on me) / Long time gone / Rock you down / Prelude: The waking dream / On and on / All over again / Running in the night.

— (Nov'88) EMMETT departed and was repl. by **PHIL XENIDES** – guitar (MOORE now on vocals)

Jan 93. (cd) *<80012>* **EDGE OF EXCESS** -
– Child in the city / Troublemaker / It's over / Edge of excess / Turn my back on love / Ridin' high again / Black sheep / Boy's nite out / Somewhere tonight / Love in a minute.

— finally called it a day after above

– compilations, etc. –

Nov 89. (lp/cd) *M.C.A.; <MCA/+D 42283>* **CLASSICS** -
– Tears in the rain / Hold on / I live for the weekend / Magic power / Follow your heart / A world of fantasy / Fight the good fight / Spellbound / Somebody's out there / Lay it on the line / Rock & roll machine.

TROUBLE

Formed: Chicago, Illinois, USA . . . 1979 by ERIC WAGNER, BRUCE FRANKLIN and RICK WARTELL, who subsequently added SEAN McALLISTER and JEFF OLSON. Something of a cult act throughout their long career, TROUBLE only really started to gather the plaudits they deserved at the turn of the 90's. Signing with 'Metal Blade' and debuting with the eponymous 'TROUBLE' in 1984, the group proved themselves to be masterful doom metal merchants, drawing on prime BLACK SABBATH and helping to instigate a retro-metal movement which would gather strength as the decade wore on. The only thing which held them back was the spiritual element of their lyrics, hardly a plus point in the evil-fixated world of heavy metal. Personnel problems following the release of 'THE SKULL' (1985) were also a hindrance, OLSON leaving for the ministry (the pulpit, not AL JOURGENSEN's mob!) and McALLISTER being replaced by RON HOLZNER. The group released a further album, 'RUN TO THE LIGHT' (1987), before being handpicked by Rick Rubin for his 'Def American' label. Ensconced at what was surely the band's spiritual home (they were in the esteemed company of fellow retro connoisseurs MASTERS OF REALITY), WAGNER and Co. came up with their best effort to date in the plainly titled 'TROUBLE' (1990). Combining a 'ZEPPELIN/'SABBATH groove with swirling psychedelia on such hipster shaking wigouts as 'AT THE END OF MY DAZE', the group set a precedent for such heralded latter day flare merchants as KYUSS. 'MANIC FRUSTRATION' (1992) saw TROUBLE's hippy-metal formula reach maturation and the critical chorus reach fever pitch, yet despite Rubin's normally midas touch, the group continued to linger in obscurity. Subsequently parting company with Rubin's label, TROUBLE went back to their roots, selling records at shows before eventually securing a deal with 'Music For Nations'. Of late (1997 to be exact), WAGNER has collaborated on the one-off project, LID, with ANATHEMA axegrinder DANNY CAVANAGH; the album in question being 'IN THE MUSHROOM', which featured two covers:- the Beatles' 'DON'T LET ME DOWN' and the Monkees' 'RANDY SCOUSE GIT'. • **Note:** Not the same group as the 1987 TROUBLE on 'Epic'.

Album rating: TROUBLE (PSALM 9) (*7) / THE SKULL (*6) / RUN TO THE LIGHT (*6) / TROUBLE (*6) / MANIC FRUSTRATION (*8) / PLASTIC GREEN HEAD (*5) / Lid: IN THE MUSHROOM (*7)

ERIC WAGNER – vocals / **BRUCE FRANKLIN** – guitar / **RICK WARTELL** – guitar / **SEAN McALLISTER** – bass / **JEFF OLSON** – drums

Steamhammer Metal Blade

1984. (lp) *(SH 0022) <47543>* **TROUBLE** (PSALM 9)
– The tempter / Assassin / Victim of the insence / Revelation / Bastards will pay / The fall of Lucifer / Endtime / Psalm 9. *(UK cd-iss. May96 as 'PSALM 9' on 'Metal Blade'; 3984 14068CD)*

Jul 85. (lp) *(SH 0027) <47544>* **THE SKULL**
– Pray for the dead / Fear no evil / The wish / Truth is, what is / Wickedness of man / Gideon / The skull. *(UK-iss.1988 on 'Roadrunner'; RR 9791) (cd-iss. May96 on 'Metal Blade'; 3984 14069CD)*

— **RON HOLZNER** – bass; repl. McALLISTER

— **DENNIS LESH** – drums; repl. OLSON who became a minister

Roadrunner Enigma

Jul 87. (lp) *(RR 9606)* **RUN TO THE LIGHT**
– Misery show / Thinking of the past / Peace of mind / Born in a prison / Tuesday's child / Beginning. *(cd-iss. May94 on 'Metal Blade'; CDMZORRO 74) (cd re-iss. May96 on 'Metal Blade'; 3984 14051CD)*

— **BARRY STERN** – drums (ex-ZOETROPE) repl. LESH

American Def American

Feb 90. (cd/c/lp) *(842 421-2/-4/-1)* **TROUBLE**
– At the end of my daze / The wolf / Psychotic reaction / A sinner's fame / The misery shows (Act II) / R.I.P. / Black shapes of doom / Heaven on my mind / E.N.D. / All is forgiven.

Sep 92. (cd/c) *(512 556-2/-4)* **MANIC FRUSTRATION**
– Touch the sky / 'Scuse me / The sleeper / Fear / Rain / Tragedy man / Memory's garden / Plastic green card / Hello strawberry skies / Mr. White / Breathe . . .

— **JEFF OLSON** – drums; repl. LESH

Bulletproof Bulletproof

Apr 95. (cd) *(CDVEST 45)* **PLASTIC GREEN HEAD**
– Plastic green head / The eye / Flowers / Porpoise song / Opium-eater / Hear the earth / Another day / Requiem / Below me / Long shadows fall / Tomorrow never knows.

– compilations, etc. –

Apr 91. (d-lp/d-c/d-cd) *Metal Blade; (ZORRO 19/+M/CD)* **PSALM 9 / THE SKULL** -

LID

ERIC WAGNER – vocals / **DANNY CAVANAGH** – guitar (of ANATHEMA) / + 2 more

Peaceville The Music Cartel

Jun 97. (cd) *(CDVILE 67) <TMC 10>* **IN THE MUSHROOM** Sep98
– L.I.D. / Mary Agnes / The dream is over / In the mushroom / Window pain / RX / You are here / Randy Scouse git / Alive / For all my life / Don't let me down.

Walter TROUT

Born: 6 Mar'51, Atlantic City, New Jersey, USA. Influenced by ROBIN TROWER and JIMI HENDRIX, TROUT took up posts with blues giants, JOHN MAYALL and CANNED HEAT. The 90's saw the guitarist move into solo work, setting up his own band which included JIM TRAPP, LEROY

LARSON and DAN ABRAMS. Mainly releasing sets for the 'Provogue' stable ('Silvertone' for 1994's 'TELLIN' STORIES' was the exception), WALTER and Co subsequently became live favourites all around the globe. 1995's 'BREAKING THE RULES' saw TROUT (and the ever faithful TRAPP) being joined by newcomers BERNARD PERSHEY and MARTIN GERSCHWITZ, the new WALTER TROUT BAND still going strong well into the millennium.

Album rating: LIFE IN THE JUNGLE (*7) / PRISONER OF A DREAM (*6) / TRANSITION (*4) / NO MORE FISH JOKES (*4) / TELLIN' STORIES (*5) / BREAKING THE RULES (*6) / POSITIVELY BEALE STREET (*6)

WALTER TROUT – guitar, vocals / **JIM TRAPP** – bass / **LEROY LARSON** – drums / **DAN ABRAMS** – keyboards

Provogue Provogue

Jun 90. (cd/c/lp) *<(PRD/PRC/PRL 7020-2/-4/-1)>* **LIFE IN THE JUNGLE**
– Good enough to eat / Mountain song / Life in the jungle / Spacefish / Red house / She's out there somewhere / Frederica (I don't need you / In my mind / Cold cold feeling / Serve me right to suffer.

Jan 91. (cd-s) **LIFE IN THE JUNGLE. /**

— **KLAS ANDERHILL** – drums; repl. LEROY

Oct 91. (cd/c/lp) *<(PRD/PRC/PRL 7026-2/-4/-1)>* **PRISONER OF A DREAM**
– Prisoner of a dream / The love that we once knew / Sweet as a flower / Love in vain / Victor the cajun / Girl from the North Country / False alarm / Say goodbye to the blues / You're the one / Earrings on the table / Tribute to Muddy Waters.

— **LEROY LARSON** – drums; repl. ANDERHILL

Oct 92. (cd/c/lp) *<(PRD/PRC/PRL 7044-2/-4/-1)>* **TRANSITION**
– Motivation of love / Endless variety / Transition / Running in place / Deeper shade of blue / Got to kill the monkey / Face the night / Playing with gloves on / She's missing / Fast moving traffic.

Jun 93. (cd/c) *<(PRD/PRC 7051-2/-4)>* **NO MORE FISH JOKES**
– Dust my broom / If you just try / False alarm / Life in the jungle / Girl from the North Country / Victor the cajun / Earrings on the table / Motivation of love / Playing with gloves on / The love what we once knew / Prisoner of a dream / Going down.

Silvertone Silvertone

Mar 94. (cd/lp) *<(ORE CD/LP 530)>* **TELLIN' STORIES**
– I can tell / Tremble / Wanna see the morning / I need to belong / Runnin' blues / On the rise / Time for movin' on / Head hung down / Please don't go / Tellin' stories / Somebody's cryin' / Take of yo' business.

Provogue Provogue

May 95. (cd-s) *(PRS 1082-2)* **TO BEGIN AGAIN**

— **MARTIN GERSCHWITZ** – keyboards; repl. ABRAMS

— **BERNARD PERSHAY** – drums; repl. LARSON

Jun 95. (cd/c) *<(PRD/PRC 7076-2/-4)>* **BREAKING THE RULES**
– To begin again / How much do you want / Under my skin / Like a stranger / Surrounded by Eden / Breaking the rules / The reason I'm gone / I don't wanna be lonely / Put it right back / Lady luck / Watch her dance.

Jun 96. (cd-s) *(PRM 2088-2)* **BREAKING THE RULES / DEATH LETTER BLUES / LIFE IN THE JUNGLE / LADY LUCK**

May 97. (cd) *<(PRD 7104-2)>* **POSITIVELY BEALE STREET**
– Got a broken heart / Obstacles in my way / One way street / Tender heart / Come home / Marie's mood / Hardtime blues / In love with you again / Don't worry about it / Song for a wanderer / Temptation / Walkin' in the rain / If you ever change your mind / Jules well / Let me be the one / Boo.

Ruf Ruf

Apr 99. (cd) *<(RUF 1035)>* **LIVIN' EVERY DAY**
– Livin' every day / Let me know / Playin' with a losin' hand / Sweet butterfly / I thought I heard the Devil / Through the eyes of love / Nothin' but the blues / City man / Fool for love / Say what you mean / Apparations / Junkyards in your eyes / Love that we once knew / Prisoner of a dream.

Jun 00. (d-cd) *<(RUF 1051)>* **LIVE TROUT (live)**
– Walkin' in the rain / I can tell / Say what you mean / The reason I'm gone / Come home / Walter speaks / Livin' every day / Let me know / Finally gotten over you / Gotta broken heart / Walter speaks again / I shall be released / Serve me right to suffer / Good enough to eat.

– compilations, etc. –

Feb 00. (cd) *Provogue; (PRD 7121-2)* **FACE THE MUSIC – LIVE ON TOUR**
– Got a broken heart / Hard time blues / The reason I'm gone / Come home / Marie's mood / Too much biz / Obstacles / Tired of sleeping alone / On the rise.

Robin TROWER

Born: 9 Mar'45, London, England. TROWER had an initial period with 60's outfit The PARAMOUNTS, who subsequently metamorphosed into PROCOL HARUM. He had been an integral part of this rock act since the 'HOMBURG' hit single, staying for five albums, 'PROCOL HARUM' (1967), 'SHINE ON BRIGHTLY' (1968), 'A SALTY DOG' (1969), 'HOME' (1970) and 'BROKEN BARRICADES' (1971), before the now HENDRIX-inspired TROWER set up his own band, JUDE. This deeply blues-rooted short-lived supergroup featured FRANKIE MILLER on husky vox, CLIVE BUNKER (ex-JETHRO TULL) on drums and JAMES DEWAR (ex-STONE THE CROWS) on bass. The latter was re-united with TROWER when the guitarist launched his solo career after re-signing to 'Chrysalis' (incidentally, also the home of PROCOL HARUM) in 1972. A debut album, 'TWICE REMOVED FROM YESTERDAY', appeared the following year featuring REG ISADORE on drums plus DEWAR on bass and soulful vocals!, TROWER (face-contortionist extroadinaire) nearly having his first solo breakthrough into the US Top 100. 1974's 'BRIDGE OF SIGHS' made up for it tenfold, this and his 1975 set, 'FOR EARTH BELOW' (1975) both cracking the US Top 10. ISADORE had been replaced on the latter by former SLY & THE FAMILY STONE man, BILL LORDAN and a live set in 1976 repeated the same feat. TROWER and his band continued to gain further album chart experience, sets such as 'LONG MISTY DAYS' (1976), 'IN CITY DREAMS' (1977), 'CARAVAN TO MIDNIGHT' (1978) and 'VICTIMS OF THE FURY' (1980), all making the US Top 40 (also selling moderately well in Britain). In 1981, TROWER and LORDAN teamed up with JACK BRUCE (ex-CREAM), delivering yet another success story, 'B.L.T.', while the following year's 'TRUCE' was strictly a BRUCE / TROWER effort. The rest of the 80's plodded on a bit for the man with the souped-up Fender Stratocaster, a change of labels to 'GNP Crescendo' in '86 giving him his last US Top 100 appearance with his umpteenth set, 'PASSION'. Another shift two years later, this time to 'Atlantic' was not so fruitful, albums 'TAKE WHAT YOU NEED' and 'IN THE LINE OF FIRE' (1990) for the TROWER or blues connoisseur only. More recently, TROWER, who had rejoined PROCOL HARUM for a reunion set, 'THE PRODIGAL STRANGER' in 1991/92, made two albums for UK 'Demon' records, '20th CENTURY BLUES' (1994) and 'SOMEDAY BLUES' (1997). The millennium began in fine style courtesy of return to form set, 'GO MY WAY', a record that opened with a classy 9 minute title track. • **Songwriters:** Mostly TROWER-DEWAR compositions, except; MAN OF THE WORLD (Fleetwood Mac) / ROCK ME BABY (B.B. King) / I CAN'T WAIT MUCH LONGER (Frankie Miller) / FURTHER ON UP THE ROAD (BB King) / SAILING (Sutherland Brothers) / RECONSIDER BABY (Lowell Folsom) / etc.

Album rating: TWICE REMOVED FROM YESTERDAY (*6) / BRIDGE OF SIGHS (*7) / FOR EARTH BELOW (*6) / ROBIN TROWER LIVE! (*7) / LONG MISTY DAYS (*5) / IN CITY DREAMS (*4) / CARAVAN TO MIDNIGHT (*4) / VICTIMS OF THE FURY (*5) / B.L.T. (*5; as B.L.T.) / TRUCE with Jack Bruce (*4) / BACK IT UP (*5) / BEYOND THE MIST (*5) / PASSION (*5) / PORTFOLIO compilation (*7) / TAKE WHAT YOU NEED (*5) / IN THE LINE OF FIRE (*4) / 20th CENTURY BLUES (*5) / SOMEDAY BLUES (*4) / GO MY WAY (*6)

ROBIN TROWER – guitar (ex-JUDE, ex-PROCOL HARUM) / **JAMES DEWAR** (b.12 Oct'46, Glasgow, Scotland) – vocals, bass (ex-JUDE, ex-STONE THE CROWS) / **REG ISADORE** (b. West Indies) – drums (ex-QUIVER)

Chrysalis Chrysalis

Mar 73. (lp/c) *(<CHR/ZCHR 1039>)* **TWICE REMOVED FROM YESTERDAY**
– I can't wait much longer / Daydream / Hannah / Man of the world / I can't stand it / Rock me baby / Twice removed from yesterday / Sinner's song / Ballerina.

Mar 73. (7") *(CHS 2009)* **MAN OF THE WORLD. / TAKE A FAST TRAIN**

Mar 74. (7") **TOO ROLLING STONED. / MAN OF THE WORLD** -

Apr 74. (lp/c) *(<CHR/ZCHR 1057>)* **BRIDGE OF SIGHS** 7
– Day of the eagle / Bridge of sighs / In this place / The fool and me / Too rolling stoned / About to begin / Lady love / Little bit of sympathy. *(re-iss. Jan82; same) (cd-iss. Mar94; CD25CR 15)*

May 74. (7") *(CHS 2046)* **TOO ROLLING STONED. / LADY LOVE** -

— **BILL LORDAN** – drums (ex-SLY & THE FAMILY STONE) repl. REG to HUMMINGBIRD

Feb 75. (lp/c) *(<CHR/ZCHR 1073>)* **FOR EARTH BELOW** 26 5
– Shame the devil / It's only money / Confessin' midnight / Fine day / Alethea / A tale untold / Gonna be more suspicious / For Earth below.

Mar 76. (lp/c) *(<CHR/ZCHR 1089>)* **ROBIN TROWER LIVE! (live)** 15 10
– Too rolling stoned / Daydream / Rock me baby / Lady love / I can't wait much longer / Alethea / Little bit of sympathy.

Oct 76. (lp/c) *(<CHR/ZCHR 1107>)* **LONG MISTY DAYS** 31 24
– Some rain falls / Long misty days / Hold me / Caledonia / Pride / Sailing / S.M.O. / I can't live without you / Messin' the blues.

Nov 76. (7") *(CHS 2124)* **CALEDONIA. / MESSIN' THE BLUES** 82

— added **RUSTEE ALLEN** – bass (ex-SLY & THE FAMILY STONE)

Sep 77. (lp/c) *(<CHR/ZCHR 1148>)* **IN CITY DREAMS** 58 25
– Somebody calling / Sweet wine of love / Bluebird / Falling star / Further up the road / Smile / Little girl / Love's gonna bring you round / In city dreams.

— added **PAULHINO DACOSTA** – percussion

Aug 78. (lp/c) *(<CHR/ZCHR 1189>)* **CARAVAN TO MIDNIGHT** 37
– My love (burning love) / Caravan to midnight / I'm out to get you / Lost in love / Fool / It's for you / Birthday boy / King of the dance / Sail on.

Sep 78. (7",7"red) *(CHS 2247)* **IT'S FOR YOU. / MY LOVE (BURNING LOVE) / IN CITY DREAMS**

Jan 79. (7") *(CHS 2256)* **IT'S FOR YOU. / MY LOVE (BURNING LOVE)**

— reverted to the trio of the mid-70's; (**TROWER, DEWAR + LORDAN**)

Jan 80. (7") *(CHS 2402)* **VICTIMS OF THE FURY. / ONE IN A MILLION**

Jan 80. (lp/c) *(<CHR/ZCHR 1215>)* **VICTIMS OF THE FURY** 61 34
– Jack and Jill / Roads to freedom / Victims of the fury / The ring / Only time / Into the flame / The shout / Madhouse / Ready for the taking / Fly low.

Apr 80. (7") *(CHS 2423)* **JACK AND JILL. / THE SHOUT**

— **JACK BRUCE** (b.14 May'43, Glasgow, Scotland) – vocals, bass (ex-CREAM, ex-JOHN MAYALL'S BLUESBREAKERS, ex-Solo artist) repl. DEWAR

Feb 81. (lp/c; as B.L.T.) *(<CHR 1324>)* **B.L.T.** 37
– Into money / What it is / Won't let you down / No island lost / It's too late / Life on earth / Once the bird has flown / Carmen / Feel the heat / End game.

Feb 81. (7"; as B.L.T.) *(CHS 2497)* **WHAT IT IS. / INTO MONEY**

— trimmed to a duo plus with drummer **REG ISADORE**

Jan 82. (lp/c; by JACK BRUCE & ROBIN TROWER) *(<CHR/ZCHR 1352>)* **TRUCE**
– Gonna shut you down / Gone too far / Thin ice / The last train to the stars / Take good care of yourself / Fall in love / Fat gut / Shadows touching / Little boy lost.

ROBIN TROWER

— went solo again, augmented by **DEWAR / DAVE BRONZE** – bass / **BOBBY CLOUTER + ALAN CLARKE** – drums

Sep 83. (lp/c) *(<CHR/ZCHR 1420>)* **BACK IT UP** [ ] [ ]
– Back it up / River / Black to red / Benny dancer / Time is short / Islands / None but the brave / Captain midnight / Settling the score. *(cd-iss. Jul99 on 'Beat Goes On'; BGOCD 426)*

Music For Nations | Passport

Jun 85. (lp/c) *(MFN/TMFN 51) <PB/+C/CD 6049>* **BEYOND THE MIST** [ ] [ ]
– The last time / Keeping a secret / The voice (live) / Beyond the mist (live) / Time is short (live) / Back it up (live) / Bridge of sighs (live).

— still retained **BRONZE,** and also with **DAVEY PATTISON** – vox (ex-GAMMA) / **PETE THOMPSON** – drums

P.R.T. | GNP Cres..

Feb 87. (lp/c/cd) *(PRTN/ZCN/PRTCD 6563) <GNPD 2187>* **PASSION** [ ] [100] Dec86
– Caroline / Secret doors / If forever / Won't even think about you / Passion / No time / Night / Bad time / One more world. *(cd-iss. GNPD 2187)*

— retained **PATTISON**

Atlantic | Atlantic

Jun 88. (lp/c/cd) *(781 838-1/-4/-2) <81838>* **TAKE WHAT YOU NEED** [ ] [ ] May88
– Tear it up / Take what you need (from me) / Love attack / I want you home / Shattered / Over you / Careless / Second time / Love won't wait forever.

— now with **PATTISON** – vox / **JOHN REGAN** – bass / **AL FRITSCH + PEPPY CASTRO** – backing vocals / **BOBBY MAYO + MATT NOBLE** – keyboards / **TONY BEARD** – drums

Mar 90. (cd/c/lp) *<782 080-2/-4/-1>* **IN THE LINE OF FIRE** [-] [ ]
– Sea of love / Under the gun / Turn the volume up / Natural fact / If you really want to find love / Every body's watching you now / Isn't it time / (I would) Still be here for you / All that I want / (Let's) Turn this fight into a brawl / Climb above the rooftops.

— ROBIN then re-joined the reformed PROCOL HARUM in 1991

— now w/ **LIVINGSTONE BROWNE** – bass / **CLIVE MAYUYU** – drums

Demon | V-12

Nov 94. (cd/c) *(FIEND CD/C 753) <50001>* **20th CENTURY BLUES** [ ] [ ]
– 20th century blues / Prisoner of love / Precious gift / Whisper up a storm / Extermination blues / Step into the dark / Rise up like the Sun / Secret place / Chase the bone / Promise you the stars / Don't lose faith in tomorrow / Reconsider baby.

Jun 97. (cd) *(FIENDCD 931) <50020>* **SOMEDAY BLUES** [ ] [ ]
– Next in line / Feel so bad / Someday blues / Crossroads / I want you to love me / Inside out / Shining through / Looking for a true love / Extermination blues / Sweet little angel.

Orpheus | V2

Jul 00. (cd) *(7576 670600-2) <50040>* **GO MY WAY** [ ] [ ] Jun00
– Go my way / Breathless / Into dust / Run with the wolves / Too much joy / Blue soul / This old world / On your own / Take this river / Long hard game / In my dream.

– compilations, etc. –

Jul 87. (d-lp/c)(cd) *Chrysalis; (CNW/ZCNW 3)(MPCD 1600)* **PORTFOLIO** [ ] [ ]
– Bridge of sighs / Too rolling stoned / For Earth below / Caravan to midnight / Day of the eagle / Shame the Devil / Fine day / Daydream (live) / Lady Love (live) / Alethea (live) / Caledonia (live) / Messin' the blues / Blue bird / Victims of fury / Madhouse / Into money / Gonna shut you down / Thin ice / Benny dancer. *(re-iss. cd Mar93; same)*

Aug 91. (cd/c/d-lp) *Castle; (CCS CD/MC/LP 291)* **THE ROBIN TROWER COLLECTION** [ ] [-]

Apr 92. (cd) *Windsong; (WINCD 013)* **BBC RADIO 1 LIVE IN CONCERT (live)** [ ] [-]

May 94. (cd) *Connoisseur; (VSOPCD 197)* **ANTHOLOGY** [ ] [-]

Feb 97. (cd) *Beat Goes On; (BGOCD 339)* **TWICE REMOVED FROM YESTERDAY / BRIDGE OF SIGHS** [ ] [-]

Mar 97. (cd) *Beat Goes On; (BGOCD 347)* **FOR EARTH BELOW / ROBIN TROWER LIVE!** [ ] [-]

Apr 97. (cd) *Beat Goes On; (BGOCD 349)* **LONG MISTY DAYS / IN CITY DREAMS** [ ] [-]

May 97. (cd) *Beat Goes On; (BGOCD 352)* **CARAVAN TO MIDNIGHT / VICTIMS OF THE FURY** [ ] [-]

Aug 98. (cd) *Beat Goes On; (BGOCD 411)* **BLT / TRUCE** [ ] [-]

Oct 98. (cd) *King Biscuit; (<KBFHCD 020>)* **KING BISCUIT PRESENTS . . .** [ ] [ ]

TRULY

Formed: Seattle, Washington, USA . . . 1995 by former SOUNDGARDEN bassman HIRO YAMAMOTO, who gathered together drummer MARK PICKEREL (from SCREAMING TREES) and ex-STORYBOOK KROOKS singer/guitarist/songwriter ROBERT ROTH. This trio would have been *thee* grunge supergroup but for one thing, they didn't play grunge. TRULY chose to widen their musical horizons with self-indulgent progressive experiments, witnessed at times on the patchy debut set, 'FAST STORIES . . . FROM KID COMA' (1995). A second, more low-key long-player, 'FEELING YOU UP', appeared in '98, although 'Capitol' records were not involved.

Album rating: FAST STORIES . . . FROM KID COMA (*6) / FEELING YOU UP (*5) / TWILIGHT CURTAINS (*5)

ROBERT ROTH – vocals, guitar (ex-STORYBOOK KROOKS) / **HIRO YAMAMOTO** – bass (ex-SOUNDGARDEN) / **MARK PICKEREL** – drums (ex-SCREAMING TREES)

not iss. | Sub Pop

Oct 91. (cd-ep) *<SP 118>* **TRULY EP** [-] [ ]
– Heart and lungs / Color is magic / Truly drowning / Married in the playground.

1993. (7") *<SP 201>* **LESLIE'S COUGHING UP BLOOD. / VIRTUALLY** [-] [ ]

Capitol | Capitol

Feb 96. (cd) *(CDEST 2278) <28414>* **FAST STORIES . . . FROM KID COMA** [ ] [ ] Jun95
– Blue Flame Ford / Four girls / If you don't let it die / Hot summer 1991 / Blue lights / Leslie's coughing up blood / Hurricane dance / Angelhead / Tragic telepathic (soul slasher) / Virtually / So strange / Strangling / Chlorine.

Headhunter | Thick

Mar 98. (lp/cd) *(HUK 003/+CD) <52>* **FEELING YOU UP** [ ] [ ]
– Intro / Public access girls / Twilight curtains / Wait 'til the night / Air raid / It's on your face / EM7 / Come hither / Leatherette tears / The possessions / Repulsion.

Sweet Nothing | Sweet Nothing

Jun 00. (cd) *<(SNCD 004)>* **TWILIGHT CURTAINS** [ ] [ ]

TRUST

Formed: France . . . 1978 by BERNARD BONVOISIN and NORBERT 'NONO' KRIEF, who added RAYMOND MANNA and JEAN-EMILE 'JEANNOT' HANELA. A band who, like their heroes AC/DC, were admired within certain sections of the punk fraternity, TRUST's jagged agit-rock was a constant thorn in the side of the French authorities. Signed to 'C.B.S.' France, the band issued their eponymous debut in 1979, building up a fearsome reputation among the country's rebellious youth. The acclaimed 'REPRESSION' album followed in early '81, another controversial effort with such inflammatory tracks as 'DEATH INSTINCT' and 'PARIS IS STILL BURNING'. These tracks were from the English language version, translated for BONVOISIN by SHAM 69 mainan, JIMMY PURSEY, the Frenchman's attempts meeting with some criticism. After a UK tour with IRON MAIDEN, personnel changes ensued; NICKO McBRAIN replaced JEAN-EMILE, while MOHAMMED 'MOHO' CHEMLEKH was added on guitar prior to the impressive 'SAVAGE' (1982; French title 'MARCHE OU CREVE'). A rare football-style personnel 'transfer' was subsequently arranged in 1983 as McBRAIN played musical drum chairs with IRON MAIDEN's CLIVE BURR on the eponymous 'TRUST' set. TRUST's popularity began to diminish with the synth enhanced 'ROCK'N'ROLL' (1985) set, the record proving to be their last for five years. After the inevitable split, BONVOISIN struck out on a brief solo career, while KRIEF worked with French chanteur, JOHNNY HALLIDAY. The late 80's witnessed renewed interest in the band as ANTHRAX covered two TRUST tracks, 'ANTISOCIAL' and 'SECTS', prompting a brief reformation for a live set, 'PARIS BY NIGHT' (1979).

Album rating: TRUST (*7) / REPRESSION (*6) / MARCHE OU CREVE (*7) / TRUST (*6) / MAN'S TRAP (*5) / ROCK'N'ROLL (*4) / THE BEST OF TRUST compilation (*6) / PARIS BY NIGHT – LIVE (*4)

BERNARD BONVOISIN – vocals / **NORBERT KRIEF** – guitar / **RAYMOND MANNA** – bass / **JEAN EMILE 'JEANNOT' HANELA** – drums

C.B.S. | not iss.

1979. (lp) *(83732)* **TRUST** [-] [-] France
– Prefabriques / Palace / Le matteur / Bosser huit heures / Comme une damne / Dialogue de sourds / L'elite / Police – milice / H & D / Rode on / Toujours pas une tune. *(cd-iss. 1990's on 'Epic'; EPC 473576-2)*

— **YVES 'VIVI' BRUSCO** – bass; repl. MANNA

Feb 81. (lp/c) *(CBS/40 84958)* **REPRESSION** [ ] [-]
– Antisocial / Mr. Comedy / In the name of the race / Death instinct / Walk alone / Paris is still burning / Pick me up, put me down / Get out your claws / Sects / Le mitard.

Mar 81. (7") *(A 1006)* **ANTISOCIAL. / SECTS** [ ] [-]

— added **MOHAMMED 'MOHO' CHEMLEKH** – guitar

— **NICKO McBRAIN** – drums; repl. JEAN-EMILE

May 82. (lp/c) *(CBS/40 85546)* **SAVAGE** (French title 'MARCHE OU CREVE) [ ] [-]
– The big illusion / The savage / Repression / The junta / Mindless / Loneliness / Work or die / The crusades / Your final gig.

— **CLIVE BURR** – drums (ex-IRON MAIDEN) repl. McBRAIN (yes, it's true!)

Epic | not iss.

1983. (lp) *(25666)* **TRUST** [-] [-] French
– Par compromission / Varsovie / Les armes aux yeux / Ideal / Le pouvoir et la gloire / Purgatoire / Le pacte / La luxure / Jugement dernier.

— **THIBEAULT ABRIAL** – guitar; repl. FARID

1984. (lp) *(26026)* **MAN'S TRAP** [-] [-] French
– Hell on the seventh / Uptown martyrs / Have a care for a shadow / Fireball / Power of the knife / Black angel / Against the law / Man's trap / '84.

— basically trio of **BONVOISON, KRIEF + BRUSCO** adding a couple of synth players

1984. (lp) *(26194)* **ROCK'N'ROLL** [-] [-] French
– Chacun sa haine / Mongolo's land / Paris / Les notables / Avenir / Serre les poings / I shall return / Rock'n'roll star / Surveille ton look.

— disbanded when BONVOISON worked on a couple of solo albums and KRIEF joined JOHNNY HALLIDAY. Renewed interest led to both reforming TRUST, recruiting **BRUSCO** + new bassist **FREDERICK**

Celluloid | not iss.

1989. (d-lp/cd) *(63001-1/-2)* **PARIS BY NIGHT – LIVE (live)** [-] [-] French
– Paris by night / Sors tes griffes / Les templiers / Paris / Saumur / Instinct de mort / Anti-social / Par compromission / I shall return / Marche ou creve / Fatalite / Ton dernier acte / Au nom de la race / L'elite.

— re-formed late in 1999

XIII Bis XIII Bis

Jun 00. (cd) *(526290-2)* **NI DIEU NI MAITRE**
– Manque de trop / Fin de siecle / Morice / Marechal / Chaque homme / Chair and honour / Question d'ethique / Edouard / Revolutionaire / Dieu et conservateur le diable est liberal / Droles de gens / Pensees.

– compilations, etc. –

Feb 88. (lp/c) *Premier-Sony; (450594-1/-4)* **THE BEST OF TRUST** [-]
– Antisocial / L'elite / Bosser hult heures / M comedie / Le mitard / Serre les poings / Police milice / Saumur / Ideal / Ton dernier acte.

1990s. (d-cd) *Epic; (EPC 478020-2)* **TRUST / REPRESSION** [-] [-] France

TSATTHOGGUA

Formed: Germany . . . 1995 by the usual pseudonymous suspects NORTH WIND (on vocals), guitarists NAR MARRATUK and PERVERTED PETE, bassist FALSE PROPHET and drummer LIGHTNING BOLT. Influenced by KREATOR and SODOM, the tongue twistingly-monikered TSATTHOGGUA (taken from an HP Lovecraft novel) set out their Black speed-metal stall via a debut album, 'HOSANNA BIZARRE' (1996). Morbid S&M and other shock tactics were used to rope in the doom-laden punters, in fact a second set went even one better in the schlock department. Entitled 'TRANS CUNT WHIP' (1998), this was not one to ask your mother to buy for you at Christmas while talking to the local priest in the queue. No, this was safely for the brown paper bag brigade, its downright nastiness and perversions a treat for purveyors of the darker side of the Satanic metal scene.

Album rating: HOSANNA BIZARRE (*5) / TRANS CUNT WHIP (*6)

NORTH WIND – vocals, keyboards / **NAR MARRATUK** – guitar / **PERVERTED PETE** – guitar / **FALSE PROPHET** – bass / **LIGHTNING BOLT** – drums

Osmose Osmose

Jul 96. (cd) *(OPCD 035)* **HOSANNA BIZARRE** [-]
– Heirs of fire / 2000 V kum / Niemals geboren / Intrude into immortality / Hosanna bizarre / The belief – The life / Seventh solitude / Worm of sin / Dionysis' ecstasy. *<US-iss.Apr99; same as UK>*

May 98. (cd/lp) *(<OPCD/OPLP 061>)* **TRANS CUNT WHIP** Aug98
– Trans cunt whip / La O Tgatthoggua / Status sturmer / To the credo of inversion / Golden shower / Endeavour to pace / In dope we trust / Angel of the universe / Courtesan Mary slut.

T.S.O.L.

Formed: as TRUE SOUNDS OF LIBERTY, Long Beach, California, USA . . . 1980 by JACK GREGGORS, RON EMORY, MIKE ROCHE and TODD BARNES. They made their eponymous debut (an EP) for 'Posh Boy', an album, 'DANCE WITH ME', following shortly after. Their second set of the year, 'BENEATH THE SHADOWS', moved on from hardcore to basic punk rock, showing signs of British influence (i.e. DAMNED or STRANGLERS), with the addition of keyboard player, BOB KUEHN. In 1983, having recruited a second guitarist, FRANK AGNEW (borrowed from The ADOLESCENTS), T.S.O.L. were involved in a riot with fans and police at a gig on Sunset Boulevard. A year later, they veered off into glam-metal when GREGGORS joined CATHEDRAL OF TEARS then TENDER FURY. Both he and BARNES were subsequently replaced by JOE WOOD and MITCH DEAN respectively, the resulting album, 'CHANGE TODAY?' (1984), a poor reflection of their passionate early work (another album 'REVENGE' – '86, was just as bad). By 1990's 'STRANGE LOVE' set, all original members had departed, as did any remaining credibility. As an alternative, the initial line-up reformed for some gigs as THE ORIGINAL TSOL. • **Trivia:** JACK GREGGORS changed his name for each release (aka GRISHAM, LLOYD, etc).

Album rating: DANCE WITH ME (*6) / BENEATH THE SHADOWS (*6) / CHANGE TODAY (*6) / HIT AND RUN (*6) / THOUGHTS OF YESTERDAY compilation (*7) / TSOL LIVE (*4) / STRANGE LOVE (*4)

JACK GREGGORS (b. GRISHAM) – vocals / **RON EMORY** – guitar / **MIKE ROCHE** – bass / **(FRANCIS GERALD) 'TODD' BARNES** – drums

not iss. Posh Boy

1981. (7"ep) *<PBS 1013>* **T.S.O.L.** [-]
– Superficial love / Property is theft / No way out / Abolish government / Silent majority / World War III.

not iss. Frontier

1981. (lp) *<FLP 1002>* **DANCE WITH ME** [-]
– Sounds of laughter / Core blue / Triangle / 80 times / I'm tired of life / Love storm / Silent scream / Funeral march / Die for me / Peace thru power / Dance with me. *(UK-iss.Apr88 on 'Weird Systems'; WS 033)*

— added **BOB KUEHN** – keyboards

Alternative Tentacles Alternative Tentacles

Apr 82. (7"ep) *<(VIRUS 10)>* **WEATHERED STATUES**
– Man and machine / Weathered statues / Thoughts of yesterday / Word is.

Dec 82. (lp; as TRUE SOUNDS OF LIBERTY) *<(VIRUS 29)>* **BENEATH THE SHADOWS**
– Soft focus / Forever old / She'll be saying / Beneath the shadows / Send my thoughts / Glass streets / Other side / Walk alone / Wash away / Waiting for you. *(UK-iss.1989 on 'GWR'; GWLP 52) <re-iss. 1989 on 'Restless'; 72338>*

— **JOE WOOD** – vocals, guitar (ex-HATED) repl. JACK who joined CATHEDRAL OF TEARS, then TENDER FURY

— **MITCH DEAN** – drums (ex-JONESES) repl. BARNES

— BOB KUEHN also departed and turned up backing BOB DYLAN!

Enigma Enigma

1984. (lp) *<ENIG 1076-1>* **CHANGE TODAY?** [-]
– Blackmagic / Just like me / In time / Red shadows / Flowers by the door / American zone / It's gray / John / Nice guys / How do. *(UK-iss.Nov86; same as US)*

Nov 86. (lp) *(ENIG 3211-1) <US-cd 971203>* **REVENCHE**
– No time / Nothin' for you / Memories / Colors / Madhouse / Revenche / Change today / Still the same / Your eyes / Everybody's a cop.

Jun 87. (lp) *(ENIG 3263-1) <US-cd 971263>* **HIT AND RUN**
– It's too late / Road and gold / The name is love / Dreamer / Good mornin' blues / Hit and run / Not alone anymore / Sixteen / Stay with me / Where did I go wrong / You can try.

Restless Restless

1988. (lp) *<72249-2>* **TSOL LIVE (live)** [-]
– Sixteen / Introduction / Red shadows / Hit and run / Nothin' for you / It's gray / It's too late / Colors (take me away) / The name is love / Road house blues / No time / Dreamer / All along the watchtower / Road of gold.

— now without ROCHE and EMORY, who were repl. by 2 unknowns

May 90. (cd/lp) *(LS 939-2/-1) <73541>* **STRANGE LOVE**
– Hell on Earth / Strange love / In the wind / Angel / White lightning / One shot away / Blow by blow / Candy / Let me go / Stop me at the edge / Good goodbye.

— split when the originals also made a comeback

Triple X Triple X

Dec 91. (cd) *<TX 51070CD>* **LIVE '91 (live)** [-]
– Silent screen / World War II / Abolish government / Triangle / Wash away / Funeral march / Superficial love / Thoughts of yesterday / I'm tired / Love story / Man and machine / Property is theft / Dance with me / Code blue. *(UK-iss.Aug95 & Nov98; same as US)*

— GRISHAM subsequently formed JOYKILLER, who signed to 'Epitaph'.

– compilations, etc. –

1987. (lp) *Posh Boy; <88150>* **THOUGHTS OF YESTERDAY 1981-1987** [-]
– Peace thru' power / Poverty is theft / Word is / Abolish government – Silent majority / Weathered statues / Thoughts of yesterday / Superficial love / Man and machine / No way out / World War III / Youths of age / Inside looking out / Blind resistance / etc *(UK-iss.Oct94 on 'Poshboy'; EFA 12214-2)*

Jul 95. (cd) *Restless; (772581-2)* **HELL & BACK TOGETHER 1984-1990**

Nov 97. (cd/c/lp) *Nitro; (15814-2/-4/-1)* **TSOL / WEATHERED STATUES**

TUMOUR CIRCUS (see under ⇒ DEAD KENNEDYS)

TURA SATANA

Formed: Los Angeles, California, USA . . . 1994 as MANHOLE, by TAIRRIE B, SCOTT UEDA, RICO VILLASENOR and MARCELO PALOMINO. TAIRRIE B (pronounced Terry), complete with bleached blonde hair (the rap MADONNA!), had originally released her own solo album, 'THE POWER OF A WOMAN' in 1990. She was groomed as the protege of EAZY E (Niggaz With Attitude), the album being issued on his 'Comptown' label (she subsequently experimented with early 90's 'Geffen' act, SUGARTOOTH). MANHOLE and TAIRRIE B (now jet black on top) released one album, 'ALL IS NOT WELL', in 1996, before being forced to change the group name the following year. Around the same time, they came up with TURA SATANA (taken from the cult movie character/supervixen, 'Faster Pussycat'), releasing a follow-up, 'RELIEF THROUGH RELEASE', later that Autumn. Infamous for her domineering personality and single minded determination, TAIRRIE clashed regularly with the band and eventually walked out. She subsequently recruited Manchester outfit BUSHAQ, to back her on a new solo project entitled MY RUIN. The resulting 'SPEAK AND DESTROY' emerged in Autumn '99, while the accompanying tour saw a different line-up featuring former TURA SATANA colleague MARCELO PALOMINO amongst others. Yet another line-up was in place for the recording of 'A PRAYER UNDER PRESSURE OF VIOLENT ANGUISH' (2000), a severley pissed off collection of emotionally loaded musical outbursts featuring an unlikely but appropriate cover of Nick Cave's classic 'DO YOU LOVE ME' alongside a blistering hidden-track reading of Black Flag's 'MY WAR' (they had earlier covered Gloria Jones' 'TAINTED LOVE'). The 'BEAUTY FIEND' single railed against the rock industry's inherent sexism while 'ROCKSTAR' was a heartfelt tribute to late SNOT vocalist LYNN STRAIT, a close personal friend of TAIRRIE who appeared on the debut MANHOLE album. • **Songwriters:** lyrics TAIRRIE B. / music SCOTT UEDA and group. Covered NEGATIVE CREEP (Nirvana) / PIECE OF MY HEART (Janis Joplin). MY RUIN covered MY WAR (Black Flag).

Album rating: Tairrie B: THE POWER OF A WOMAN (*3) / Manhole: ALL IS NOT WELL (*5) / Tura Satana: RELIEF THROUGH RELEASE (*7) / My Ruin: SPEAK AND DESTROY (*6) / A PRAYER UNDER PRESSURE OF VIOLENT ANGUISH (*6)

TAIRRIE B

M.C.A. Comptown

Sep 90. (c-s/12") *<53989/53900>* **SWINGIN' WIT "T". / ('A'versions)** [-]

Nov 90. (7") *(MCA 1455) <24025>* **MURDER SHE WROTE. /** [71] Apr90
(12"+=/cd-s+=) *(MCA T/CD 1455)* –

Nov 90. (lp/c/cd) *<(MCA/+C/D 6409)>* **THE POWER OF A WOMAN** Apr90
– Swingin' wit "T" / Anything you want / Vinnie tha' moocha / Step 2 this / Murder she wrote / Packin' a punch / Let the beat rock / Player / Schoolly's in / Ruthless bitch.

MANHOLE

TAIRRIE B. (b. THERESA BETH) – vocals / **SCOTT UEDA** (b. 1 Feb'71) – guitars / **RICO VILLASENOR** (b. 1 Sep'67) – bass, vocals / **MARCELO PALOMINO** (b.13 Dec'69) – drums

Noise / not iss.

Mar 96. (12"ep/cd-ep) *(N 0268-6/-3)* **LOS ANGELES** [ ] [-]
– Victim (clean) / Victim (street) / Clean / Kiss or kill.

May 96. (cd) *(N 0268-2)* **ALL IS NOT WELL** [ ] [-]
– Hypocrite / Sickness / Kiss or kill / Break / Empty / Put your head out / Victim / Clean / Roughness / Six feet deep / Cycle of violence / Down / Down (reprise). *<(re-iss. Jan98 & Oct99 now as TURA SATANA; same as above)>*

TURA SATANA

—— was their new moniker

Noise / Noise

Jul 97. (cd-ep) *(N 0282-3)* **SCAVENGER HUNT / SCAVENGER HUNT (Superstar remix) / SCAVENGER HUNT (Sacrilegous Sick66 remix) / PIECE OF MY HEART** [ ] [-]

Sep 97. (cd) *<(N 0282-2)>* **RELIEF THROUGH RELEASE** [ ] [ ]
– Welcome to violence / Luna / Dry / Venus Diablo / Unclean / Flux / Eternalux / Storage / Scavenger hunt / Negative creep / Relapse / Last rites / Omnia vinat amor.

—— **BRIAN HARRAH** – guitar (ex-SPITKISS) repl. SCOTT

Apr 98. (cd-ep) *(N 0300-3)* **VENUS DIABLO / SICKNESS / SCAVENGER HUNT (live) / VENUS DIABLO (live)** [ ] [-]

—— a new guitarist repl. HARRAH who joined PROFESSIONAL MURDER MUSIC

MY RUIN

TAIRRIE B – vocals / **MELANIE MAKAIWI** – guitar / **LANCE WEBBER** – guitar / **MEGAN MATTOX** – bass / **MARCELO PALOMINO** – drums / **TODD OSENBAUGH** – keyboards, samples

Snapper / Spitfire

Jul 99. (7"/cd-s) *(SMAS 7/CD 106)* **TAINTED LOVE. / BLASPHEMOUS GIRL / SCARS** [ ] [-]

Aug 99. (cd) *(SMACD 820) <15056>* **SPEAK AND DESTROY** [ ] [ ]
– Prologue / Terror / Preacher / Tainted love / Blasphemous girl / Close your eyes / Absolution / Horrible pain / Monster / Sick with it / My beautiful flower / Diavolina / June 10th / Bright red scream / Cosmetic / Sychopant / Epilogue / Beware of God.

Oct 99. (7"/cd-s) *(SMAS 7/CD 109)* **TERROR** [ ] [-]

—— **YAEL** – drums; repl. MARCELO, LANCE + TODD

Sep 00. (7"/cd-s) *(SMAS 7/CD 121)* **BEAUTY FIEND. / MASOCHRIST / MY WAR** [ ] [-]

Sep 00. (cd) *(SMACD 833) <15129>* **A PRAYER UNDER PRESSURE OF VIOLENT ANGUISH** [ ] [ ] Jan01
– Morning prayer / Beauty fiend / Stick it to me / Heartsick / Rock star / Sanctuary / Miss Ann Thrope / Hemorrhage / Letter to the editor / Let it rain / Post noise revelation / Do you love me / Evening prayer. *(bonus+=)* – My war.

Joe Lynn TURNER (see under ⇒ FANDANGO)

TWELFTH NIGHT

Formed: Reading, England ... 1980 by ANDY REVELL, RICK BATTERSBY, CLIVE MITTEN and BRIAN DEVOIL. Began their short but productive career as an intrumental techno outfit somewhat similar to YES or RUSH. Their debut self-financed album, 'LIVE AT THE TARGET' showed off their long overdrawn musical epics. A cassette 'SMILING AT GRIEF' was released early in 1982, before the introduction of Christian frontman, GEOFF MANN. He stayed for one studio album 'FACT AND FICTION', before he too departed, having been replaced by ANDY SEARS. Their next album, 'ART & ILLUSION', produced by the esteemed-to-be, GIL NORTON, hit the UK Top 100 and was easily their greatest achievement. In 1986 they signed to 'Charisma', releasing their final eponymous effort the same year.

Album rating: LIVE AT THE TARGET (*6) / SMILING AT GRIEF (*5) / FACT AND FICTION (*6) / LIVE AND LET LIVE (*6) / ART & ILLUSION (*8) / TWELFTH NIGHT (*5) / COLLECTORS ITEM compilation (*6)

ANDY REVELL – guitar / **RICK BATTERSBY** – keyboards, synthesizer / **CLIVE MITTEN** – bass, keyboards / **BRIAN DEVOIL** – drums

Twelfth Night / not iss.

Dec 80. (7") *(TN 001)* **THE CUNNING MAN. / FUR HELENE** [ ] [-]

Feb 81. (lp) *(TN 002)* **LIVE AT THE TARGET** [ ] [-]
– Fur Helene (part 1) / After eclipse / East to west / Sequences.

Jan 82. (c) *(TN 003)* **SMILING AT GRIEF** [ ] [-]
– East of Eden / This city / The honeymoon is over / Creepshow / Puppets (intro) / Puppets / Make no sense / The three dancers / Fur Helene (part 2).

—— added **GEOFF MANN** – vocals (REVELL + MITTEN also backing vox)

Jan 83. (lp) *(TN 006)* **FACT AND FICTION** [ ] [-]
– We are sane / World without end / Creepshow / Poet sniffs a flower / Human being / Love song / Fact and fiction.

Revolution / not iss.

Nov 82. (7") *(REV 009)* **ELEANOR RIGBY. / EAST OF EDEN** [ ] [-]

Music For Nations / not iss.

Feb 84. (lp) *(MFN 18)* **LIVE AND LET LIVE (live at The Marquee, 4th & 5th November, 1983)** [ ] [-]
– The ceiling speaks / The end of the endless majority / We are sane / Fact and fiction / The poet sniffs a flower / Sequences. *(cd-iss. Feb97 on 'Cyclops'; CYCL 050)*

—— **ANDY SEARS** – vocals; repl. GEOFF

Oct 84. (lp) *(MFN 36)* **ART AND ILLUSION** [83] [-]
– Counterpoint / Art and illusion / C.R.A.B. / Kings and queens / First new day.

Charisma / Virgin

May 86. (7"pic-d) *(CB 424)* **SHAME. / BLUE POWDER MONKEY** [ ] [-]
(12"+=) *(CB 424-12)* – ('A'extended).

Jul 86. (lp/c) *(CHC/+MC 72)* **TWELFTH NIGHT** [ ] [ ]
– Last song / Pressure / Jungle / The craft / Blue powder monkey / Theatre / Shame / This is war / Take a look. *(re-iss. Nov86; CASG 1174)*

Aug 86. (7") *(CB 425)* **TAKE A LOOK. / BLONDON FAIR** [ ] [-]

—— split after above

- compilations, etc. -

Mar 91. (cd/c/d-lp) *Food For Thought; (CD/TC+/GRUB 18)* **COLLECTORS ITEM** [ ] [-]
– We are sane / Sequences / Art and illusion / First new day / Take a look / Blondon fair / The collector / Love song.

12 RODS

Formed: Ohio, USA . . . 1992 (moved to Cincinnati & Minnesota in 1994) by RYAN OLCOTT, his brother EV OLCOTT and CHRISTOPHER McGUIRE. All three were classically-trained, geeky-looking lads on a noisy-pop mission to revive punk and electro at the same time. Signing a worldwide deal with Richard Branson's new imprint, 'V2', 12 RODS unleashed the weird, 'GAY?' mini-set late in '97. The following summer saw the trio make a minor breakthrough with the equally zany, 'SPLIT PERSONALITY'.

Album rating: GAY? mini (*5) / SPLIT PERSONALITIES (*6)

RYAN OLCOTT – vocals, guitar / **EV OLCOTT** – synthesizer, guitar / **CHRISTOPHER McGUIRE** – drums

V2 / V2

Nov 97. (m-cd) *(VVR 100098-2) <27509>* **GAY?** [ ] [ ] Oct97
– Red / Make-out music / Gaymo / Mexico / Friend / Revolute.

Jun 98. (7"/cd-s) *(VVR 500230-7/-3)* **SPLIT PERSONALITY. / STELLA / BABIES** [ ] [-]

Apr 99. (cd) *(VVR 100237-2) <27015>* **SPLIT PERSONALITIES** [ ] [ ] Jul98
– Split personality / Red / I am faster / Chromatically declining me / Part of 2 / Stupidest boy / I wish you were a girl / Lovewaves / Make-out music / Girl sun.

28 DAYS

Formed: Melbourne, Australia . . . 1996 by frontman JAY DUNNE, along with SIMON HEPBURN, DAMIAN GARDINER and a drummer named ADAM. Despite denying any kind of contrived image or sound, 28 DAYS fall squarely into the punk/rap/nu-metal category beloved of just about every new American rock band to invade British shores. Clearly influenced by the likes of The BEASTIE BOYS, BAD RELIGION and The OFFSPRING complete with baggy trousers and hooded tops to match, the Aussie brats kicked off their domestic career with a couple of EP's and an eponymous album towards the decade's close. With the hip hop-hating ADAM out of the way (replaced by SCOTT MURRAY) and with the addition of DJ JEDI MASTER JAY, the band were ready to resume activities. Having already surprisingly topped the charts in their homeland with 'UPSTYLEDOWN', the band foisted the album upon the British public in Autumn 2000. The record was subsequently re-promoted the following Spring with two single releases ('RIP IT UP' and 'SUCKER') as support.

Album rating: 28 DAYS (*5) / UPSTYLEDOWN (*7)

JAY DUNNE – vocals / **SIMON HEPBURN** – guitar / **DAMIAN GARDINER** – bass / **ADAM** – drums

Stubble / not iss.

1999. (cd-s) **GOODBYE / DRINK IT UP (live) / DO YOU AGREE?** [-] [-] Austra

1999. (cd) *(STUB 004)* **28 DAYS** [-] [-] Austra
– Sand / Kool / Empty one / 1988 / She's waiting / Rise above / This songs about you / Ball of hate / 28 days / Do our part. *(hidden track+=)*– La tune.

1999. (cd-s) **HERE WE GO EP** [-] [-] Austra
– Sucker / Goodbye / Kool (remix).

—— **SCOTT MURRAY** – drums; repl. ADAM / added **JEDI MASTER JAY** – DJ

Mushroom / not iss.

2000. (cd-ep) *(MUSH 81CDS)* **KID INDESTRUCTIBLE EP** [ ] [-]
– Never give up / La tune / The right place / Kid indestructible / Kool.

Sep 00. (cd) *(MUSH 332805)* **UPSTYLEDOWN** [ ] [-]
– The bird / Know the score / Sucker / Jedi vs. the kause / Goodbye / Time for us to leave / Rip it up / Song for Jasmine / I remember / Spicy fingers / Rollin gang / What you know / Don't touch my turntables / Deadly like / Information overload / Kill the fake (seshoo). *(re-iss. Mar01; same)*

Feb 01. (7") *(MUSH 88S)* **RIP IT UP. / KOOL** [ ] [-]
(cd-s+=) *(MUSH 88CDS)* – The right place.

May 01. (7") *(MUSH 91S)* **SUCKER. / KID INDESTRUCTIBLE (live)** [ ] [-]
(cd-s+=) *(MUSH 91CDS)* – Never give up (the Randywong mix).

24-7 SPYZ

Formed: South Bronx, New York, USA ... 1986 by JIMI HAZEL. With a line-up completed by PETER 'FLUID' FOREST, RICK SKATORE and ANTHONY JOHNSON, the group debuted in 1989 with the album, 'HARDER THAN YOU'. Released on local funk-metal label, 'In-Effect', the record drew comparisons with the likes of FISHBONE and LIVING COLOUR, purveying a head-spinning collage of soul, funk, hardcore, reggae and metal. More adventurous than many acts of a similar ilk, 'GUMBO MILLENNIUM' (1990) further developed 24-7 SPYZ's uncompromising philosophy although sometimes the wilful eclecticism grated. With the rap-metal craze at its height, the album picked up its fair share of critical acclaim and for a while it looked as if the band might build commercially upon their newfound recognition. Although FLUID and JOHNSON left soon after the record's release, they were quickly replaced with JEFF BRODNAX and JOEL MAITOZA respectively, the group netting a major label deal with 'East West'. Wasting no time, the group promptly set about recording a third set, a mini entitled 'THIS IS . . . 24-7 SPYZ' (1991), closely followed by the acclaimed 'STRENGTH IN NUMBERS' (1992). Though the record met with some of the best reviews of their career, 24-7 SPYZ failed to achieve crossover success and make the all-important commmercial breakthrough.

Album rating: HARDER THAN YOU (*6) / GUMBO MILLENNIUM (*6) / THIS IS . . . 24-7 SPYZ mini (*5) / STRENGTH IN NUMBERS (*5) / TEMPORARILY DISCONNECTED (*5) / HEAVY METAL SOUL BY THE POUND (*5) / 6 (*4)

PETER 'Fluid' FOREST – vocals / **JIMI HAZEL** – guitar / **RICK SKATORE** – bass / **ANTHONY JOHNSON** – drums

London In-Effect

Sep 89. (lp/c/cd) *(828167-2/-4/-1)* <3006> **HARDER THAN YOU** [ ] [ ] Aug89
– Grandma dynamite / Jimi'z jam / Spyz dope / Social plague / I must go on / Ballots not bullets / Jungle boogie / Spill my guts / Sponji reggae / Tango skin polka / Pillage / New drug. *(re-iss. Apr91; same)*

Nov 89. (7") *(LON 246)* **GRANDMA DYNAMITE. / JIMI'Z JAM** [ ] [ ]
(12"+=) *(LONX 246)* –

Epic In-Effect

Sep 90. (cd/c/lp) *(467120-2/-4/-1)* <3014> **GUMBO MILLENNIUM** [ ] [ ]
– John Connelly's theory / New super hero worship / Deathstyle / Dude u knew / Culo posse / Don't push me / Spyz on piano / Valdez 27 million? / Don't break my heart / We'll have power / Racism / Heaven and Hell / We got a date / Dome defenders' memories.

— **JEFF BRODINAX** – vocals; repl. FOREST

— **JOEL MAITOZA** – drums; repl. JOHNSON

East West Atlantic

Nov 91. (m-cd/m-lp) *<(7567 91807-2/-1)>* **THIS IS 24-7 SPYZ** [ ] [ ]
– Tick – tick – tick / Stuntman / My desire / Peace and love / Earthquake.

Jul 92. (cd/c/lp) *<(7567 92166-2/-4/-1)>* **STRENGTH IN NUMBERS** [ ] [ ]
– Break the chains / Crime story / Judgement day / Understanding / Got it goin' on / My desire / Purple / Stuntman / Earth and sky / Room No.9 / Sireality / Last call / I'm not going / Traveling day.

Enemy Enemy

Feb 95. (cd) *<EMY 150-2>* **TEMPORARILY DISCONNECTED** [ ] [ ]
– Dogs come out / Outta mind, outta time / Fire and water / Why / Body thief / Choose me / Heart of fire / Stoner / Boots / Agfroovendee! / Choose me (mix). *(UK-iss.Sep97; same as US)*

Sep 96. (cd) *<60020>* **HEAVY METAL SOUL BY THE POUND** [-] [ ]
– Spyz in da house / Love and peace / Yeah x3 / If I could / Burned / Simple minded Simon / Eyes don't lie / Earth and sky / Interlude / El lame / Free to be / Let your fancy flow / Crushonya / No hope for niggaz / Love for sale / Clique / Save the world.

Sep 97. (cd) *<(EMY 1552)>* **6** [ ] [ ]
– Spyz in da house / Love and peace / Yeah x3 / If I could / Burned / Simple-minded Simion / Eyes don't lie / Interlude / El lame / Free to be / Let your fancy flow / Crushonya / No hope for niggaz / Love for sale / Clique / 7 and 7 is / Along comes Mary.

TWINK (see under ⇒ PINK FAIRIES)

TWINKEYZ

Formed: Sacramento, California, USA . . . 1976 by DONNIE JUPITER, KEITH McKEE, TOM DARLING and vocalist HONEY. One of California's first punk-influenced acts, the TWINKEYZ made their debut in 1977 with a single, 'ALIENS IN OUR MIDST', on the tiny 'Grok' label. Bizarrely enough, the band gained a foothold on continental Europe, where Dutch label, 'Plurex', released their one and only album, 'ALPHA JERK'. While the latter was available in the UK, a final single, 'WATCH OUT FOR HER KISS' was released exclusively onto the Dutch market in 1980 prior to the band's final split. • **Covered:** YOU'RE GONNA MISS ME (13th Floor Elevators).

Album rating: ALPHA JERK (*5) / ALIENS IN OUR MIDST compilation (*6)

DONNIE JUPITER – vocals, rhythm guitar / **HONEY** – vocals, bass, guitar / **TOM DARLING** – lead guitar, bass, vocals / **KEITH McKEE** – drums, vocals

not iss. Grok

1977. (7"white) *<1.00>* **ALIENS IN OUR MIDST. / ONE THOUSAND REASONS** [-] [ ]

1978. (7"opalescent) *<2.00>* **E.S.P. / CARTOON LAND** [-] [ ]

Plurex not iss.

Aug 79. (lp) *(1000)* **ALPHA JERK** [-] [-] Dutch
– Aliens in our midst / Tonight again / Sweet nothing / 1000 reasons / Cartton land / E.S.P. / Twinkeyz theme / That's the way it goes / Alpha jerk / Strange feeling / Wild love.

Oct 80. (7") *(0019)* **WATCH OUT FOR HER KISS. /** [-] [-] Dutch

— after they split, DARLING joined The VEIL (and later GAME THEORY)

– compilations, etc. –

Jun 98. (cd) *Anopheles; (ANOPHELES 003)* **ALIENS IN OUR MIST** [ ] [ ]
– Aliens in our midst / Tonight again / Sweet nothing / 1,000 reasons / Cartoon land / E.S.P. / Twinkeyz theme / That's the way it goes / Alpha jerk / Strange feeling / Wild love / My plea / Watch out for her kiss / Moonbabies / Little Joey / Cartoon land (live) / Twinkeyz theme (live) / Aliens in our midst (live) / Space-age rock queen (live) / Radar burning (live) / You're gonna miss me (live).

TWISTED SISTER

Formed: Ho-Ho-Kus, New Jersey, USA . . . early 1973 by main songwriter DEE SNIDER, JAY JAY FRENCH, EDDIE OJEDA, MARK 'The Animal' MENDOZA and TONY PETRI (soon replaced with A.J. PERO). They signed to an unknown German label in the 70's and following a one-off independent single, 'I'LL NEVER GROW UP', this shock-rock troupe of mascara'd metal mavericks decided to try their luck on the other side of the pond. Signing for the small 'Secret' label, they subsequently released the 'RUFF CUTS' EP in summer '82, gigging around London to encouraging reactions. A few months later, they issued a debut album, the Pete Way (UFO) produced 'UNDER THE BLADE'. Although the record was a pale reflection of the band's war-paint rock'n'roll attack, an infamous appearance on ~Channel 4 TV show, 'The Tube', together with a celebrated performance at The Reading Festival was enough to attract major label interest in the form of 'Atlantic'. Like a cross between MANOWAR and The NEW YORK DOLLS, TWISTED SISTER leered into living rooms around the country via a Top Of The Pops romp through The Who's 'I AM (I'M ME)', SNIDER no doubt putting many unsuspecting people off their dinner with his frightwigged, Bette Midler-from-hell image. The single made the UK Top 20 in 1983, as did the accompanying album, 'YOU CAN'T STOP ROCK'N'ROLL', TWISTED SISTER proving the hype was justified with another show-stopping performance at that year's Monsters Of Rock Festival. Up until this point, America had been largely oblivious to their gutter-rock sons although they began to take notice with the 'STAY HUNGRY' (1984) set and its anthemic accompanying single, 'WE'RE NOT GONNA TAKE IT' (another Who cover). The album made the US Top 20, while the single narrowly missed a similar achievement; it looked as if TWISTED SISTER were about to clean up in the US teen-rebel/pop-metal stakes but it all went horribly wrong as subsequent album, 'COME OUT AND PLAY' (1985), languished in the chart margins (despite being graced with such high profile guests as ALICE COOPER, BILLY JOEL (!) and DON DOKKEN) and a headlining tour was woefully undersubscribed. With JOE FRANCO replacing PERO, the band eventually attempted a comeback in 1987 with 'LOVE IS FOR SUCKERS', although its more considered approach fared equally badly. It came as no surprise when they were dropped, splitting soon after with SNIDER going on to a short-lived solo career before forming DESPERADO, then WIDOWMAKER. During the 80's, SNIDER had to defend himself against 'The American Moral Majority' as TWISTED SISTER were one of the bands the PMRC tried to censor, a charge that their material might corrupt teenagers being thrown out of court (it seems you really can't stop rock'n'roll!). • **Covers:** LEADER OF THE PACK (Shangri-la's) / IT'S ONLY ROCK'N'ROLL (Rolling Stones) / LET THE GOOD TIMES ROLL (Shirley & Lee).

Album rating: UNDER THE BLADE (*4) / YOU CAN'T STOP ROCK'N'ROLL (*6) / STAY HUNGRY (*5) / COME OUT AND PLAY (*5) / LOVE IS FOR SUCKERS (*4) / BIG HITS AND NASTY CUTS compilation (*6) / LIVE AT HAMMERSMITH (*5) / Widowmaker: BLOOD AND BULLETS (*6)

DEE SNIDER (b. DANIEL, 15 Mar'55, Massapequa, Long Island, New York) – vocals / **JAY JAY FRENCH** (b. JOHN SEGALL 20 Jul'54, New York City) – guitar / **EDDIE OJEDA** (b. 5 Aug'54, The Bronx, New York) – guitar / **MARK 'The Animal' MENDOZA** (b.13 Jul'56, Long Island, N.Y.) – bass (ex-DICTATORS) / **A.J.PERO** (b.14 Oct'59, Staten Island, New York) – drums repl. TONY PETRI

Secret not iss.

Jul 82. (12"ep) *(SHH 137-12)* **RUFF CUTS** [ ] [-]

Sep 82. (lp/c) *(SECX/TSECX 9)* **UNDER THE BLADE** [70] [-]
– What you don't know (sure can hurt you) / Bad boys (of rock'n'roll) / Run for your life / Sin after sin / Shoot 'em down / Destroyer / Under the blade / Tear it loose / Day of the rocker. *<US-iss.Jun85 on 'Atlantic'+=; 81256>* – I'll never grow up, now! *(cd-iss. Jun88; SECX 1) (re-iss. 1988 on 'Roadrunner' lp/cd; RR/+34 9946) (cd re-iss. Feb00 on 'Spitfire'; SPITCD 024)*

Atlantic Atlantic

Mar 83. (7") *(A 9854)* **I AM (I'M ME). / SIN AFTER SIN** [18] [-]
(12") *(TA 9854)* – ('A'side) / Tear it loose / Destroyer / It's only rock'n'roll.

May 83. (lp/c) *(A 0074/+4)* <80074> **YOU CAN'T STOP ROCK'N'ROLL** [14] [ ]
– The kids are back / Like a knife in the back / Ride to live, live to ride / I am (I'm me) / The power and the glory / We're gonna make it / I've had enough / I'll take you alive / You're not alone (Suzette's song) / You can't stop rock'n'roll.

May 83. (7"/7"sha-pic-d) *(A 9827/+P)* **THE KIDS ARE BACK. / SHOOT 'EM DOWN** [32] [-]
(12") *(A 9827T)* – ('A'side) / What you don't know sure can't hurt you / Bad boys of rock / Run for your love.

Aug 83. (7"m) *(A 9792)* **YOU CAN'T STOP ROCK'N'ROLL. / LET THE GOOD TIMES ROLL (live) / FEEL SO FINE** [43] [-]
(12") *(A 9792T)* – ('A'side) / Feel the power / Heat of love / One man woman.

May 84. (lp/c) *(780 156-1/-4)* <80156> **STAY HUNGRY** [34] [15]
– Stay hungry / We're not gonna take it / Burn in Hell / Horror-teria (the beginning):- a) Captain Howdy – b) Street justice / I wanna rock / The price / Don't let me down / The beast / S.M.F.

May 84. (7") *(A 9657)* **WE'RE NOT GONNA TAKE IT. / THE KIDS ARE BACK** [58] [-]
(12"+=) *(A 9657T)* – ('A'version) / You can't stop rock'n'roll.

Jun 84. (7") *<89641>* **WE'RE NOT GONNA TAKE IT. / YOU CAN'T STOP ROCK'N'ROLL** [-] [21]

Aug 84. (7") *<89617>* **I WANNA ROCK. / THE KIDS ARE BACK** [-] [68]

Sep 84. (7") *(A 9634)* **I WANNA ROCK. / BURN IN HELL (live)** -
(12"+=) *(A 9634T)* – S.M.F. (live).
Feb 85. (7"/12") *(A 9591/+T) <89591>* **THE PRICE. / S.M.F.**
Dec 85. (lp/cd/pic-lp) *(781275-1/-2/1P) <81275>* **COME OUT AND PLAY** 95 53
– Come out and play / Leader of the pack / You want what we got / I believe in rock'n'roll / The fire still burns / Be chrool to you scuel / I believe in you / Out on the streets / Lookin' out for #1 / Kill or be killed.
Jan 86. (7"/7"g-f/7"sha-pic-d) *(A 9478/+F/P) <89478>* **LEADER OF THE PACK. / I WANNA ROCK** 47 53 Nov85
(d7"+=/12"+=) *(A 9478 D/T)* –
Mar 86. (7") *(A 9435)* **YOU WANT WHAT WE GOT. / STAY HUNGRY** -
(12"+=) *(A 9435T)* – We're not gonna take it / King of fools.
Apr 86. (7") *<89445>* **YOU WANT WHAT WE GOT. / SHOOT 'EM DEAD** -

—— **JOE FRANCO** – drums; repl. PERO

Jul 87. (lp/c)(cd) *(WX 120/+C)(781772-2) <81772>* **LOVE IS FOR SUCKERS** 57 74
– Wake up (the sleeping giant) / Hot love / Love is for suckers / I'm so hot for you / Tonight / Me and the boys / One bad habit / I want this night (to last forever) / You are all that I need / Yeah right.
Oct 87. (7") *<89215>* **HOT LOVE. / TONIGHT** -

—— Disbanded after the album. DEE SNIDER went solo, although he was dropped by 'Elektra' records. In 1988, he formed DESPERADO with BERNIE TORME (ex-GILLAN) and CLIVE BURR (ex-IRON MAIDEN). Early 1991, they issued an eponymous debut album for 'Metal Blade-Warners'. They scrapped this project to form new WIDOWMAKER.

– compilations, others, etc. –

Jan 90. (7") *Old Gold; (OG 9940)* **THE KIDS ARE BACK. / I AM (I'M ME)** -
Mar 92. (cd/c/lp) *Atlantic; <(7567 82380-2/-4/-1)>* **BIG HITS AND NASTY CUTS – THE BEST OF TWISTED SISTER**
– We're not gonna take it / I wanna rock / I am (I'm me) / The price / You can't stop rock'n'roll / The kids are back / Shoot 'em down / Under the blade / I'll never grow up, now / Be chrool to your scuel / I believe in you / Out in the streets / Lookin' out for #1 / Kill or be killed. *(c+=)* – It's only rock'n'roll. *(cd++=)* – Tear it loose.
Oct 94. (cd) *Music For Nations; (CDMFN 170) / C.M.C.; <86229>* **LIVE AT HAMMERSMITH (live)**
(re-iss. Sep98 on 'S.P.V.'; SPITCD 024)
Feb 00. (cd) *Spitfire; <(SPITCD 023)>* **CLUB DAZE: THE STUDIO SESSIONS VOL.1**

WIDOWMAKER

DEE SNIDER – vocals / **AL PITRELLI** – guitar (ex-ASIA, ex-DANGER DANGER, ex-GREAT WHITE, ex-ALICE COOPER) / **MARC RUSSELL** (b. London, England) – bass (ex-BEKI BONDAGE) / **JOE FRANCO** – drums (ex-GOOD RATS, ex-DORO, ex-VINNY MOORE, ex-LESLIE WEST)

Music For Nations — Esquire

Apr 94. (cd) *(CDMFN 161) <74301>* **BLOOD AND BULLETS** Jul92
– Emaheevul / The widowmaker / Evil / The lonely ones / Reason to kill / Snot nose kid / Blood and bullets (pissin' against the wind) / Gone bad / Blue for you / You're a heartbreaker / Calling for you / We are the dead.

Music For Nations — C.M.C.

Oct 94. (cd) *(CDMFN 175) <86903>* **STAND BY FOR PAIN**
– Killing time / Long gone / Protect & serve / Ready to fall / Circles / Stand by for pain / Just business / The iron road / Bad rain / Your sorrow / Cry a dying man's tears / All things must change.

—— disbanded after above

TWO (see under ⇒ HALFORD, Rob)

TYGERS OF PAN TANG

Formed: Whitley Bay, Newcastle-Upon-tyne, England . . . 1978 by JESS COX, ROBB WEIR, ROCKY LAWS and BRIAN DICK. Frontrunners of the early NWOBHM scene, the band's debut single, 'DON'T TOUCH ME THERE', was one of the first ever releases on the recently formed 'Neat' label, a name that would become synonymous with Northern heavy metal throughout the early 80's (and beyond?). The single's success in metal circles led to a deal with 'M.C.A.' and a subsequent Top 20 debut album, 'THE WILD CAT', at the turn of the decade. COX departed soon after, however, his replacement being ex-PERSIAN RISK frontman, JON DEVERILL. The guitar attack was also strengthened, axe maestro JOHN SYKES becoming a TYGER around the same time. This line-up scored a minor hit single in early '81 with 'HELLBOUND', while the accompanying album, 'SPELLBOUND', scraped into the UK Top 40. Later the same year, a third set, 'CRAZY NIGHTS', was met with a muted response and the band were dealt a further blow with the departure of SYKES early in '82. Replacing him with ex-PENETRATION man, FRED PURSER, caused something of a fuss, although the band went on to release their most successful album to date in 'THE CAGE' (1982). Instead of building on this success, they became enmeshed in a protracted dispute with their record company, only DEVERILL and DICK remaining after the dust had settled. With new members DAVID DONALDSON, STEVE LAMB and NEIL SHEPHERD, the revamped 'TYGERS finally emerged from the music business jungle in 1985, with an album, 'THE WRECK-AGE', on 'Music For Nations'. It was met with scant interest and it became clear that their musical claws just weren't sharp enough to compete as thrash came to dominate the metal scene. They finally crawled back into their lair for good after a final album, 'BURNING IN THE SHADE' (1987), although the TYGERS OF PAN TANG name still provokes fond memories in older rock fans. • **Songwriters:** Group compositions until THOMPSON and DEVERILL took over in 1985. Covered; TUSH (ZZ Top) / LOVE POTION No.9 (Clovers) / RENDEZVOUS (R.P.M.).

Album rating: WILD CAT (*5) / SPELLBOUND (*4) / CRAZY NIGHYTS (*4) / THE CAGE (*6) / THE WRECK-AGE (*3) / BURNING IN THE SHADE (*3) / ON THE PROWL – THE BEST OF TYGERS OF PAN TANG compilation (*6)

JESS COX – vocals / **ROBB WEIR** – guitar, vocals / **ROCKY LAWS** – bass, vocals / **BRIAN DICK** – drums, percussion

Neat — not iss.

Jan 80. (7") *(NEAT 03)* **DON'T TOUCH ME THERE. / BAD TIMES** -

M.C.A. — M.C.A.

Mar 80. (7"m) *(MCA 582)* **DON'T TOUCH ME THERE. / BURNING UP / BAD TIMES** -
Jun 80. (7"m) *(MCA 612)* **ROCK'N'ROLL MAN. / ALRIGHT ON THE NIGHT / WILD CATS** -
Jul 80. (lp/c) *(MCF/+C 3075) <3270>* **WILD CAT** 18
– Euthanasia / Slave to freedom / Don't touch me there / Money / Killers / Fireclown / Wild catz / Suzie smiled / Badger badger / Insanity. *(re-iss. May83 on 'Fame' lp/c; FA/TC-FA 3063) (re-iss. Sep86 lp/c; MCL/+C 1610) (cd-iss. Jul93 on 'Repertoire'; REP 4014-WZ) (cd re-iss. May97 & Feb00 on 'Neat'; EDGY 101)*
Aug 80. (7") *(MCA 634)* **SUZIE SMILED. / TUSH** -
Oct 80. (7") *(MCA 644)* **EUTHANASIA. / STRAIGHT AS A DIE** -

—— **JON DEVERILL** – vocals (ex-PERSIAN RISK) repl. JESS who joined LIONHEART

—— added **JOHN SYKES** (b.29 Jul'59, Cardiff, Wales) – guitar

Feb 81. (7") *(MCA 672)* **HELLBOUND. / DON'T GIVE A DAMN** 48 -
(w/ free 7"+=) **THE AUDITION TAPES** – Bad times / Don't take nothin'.
Mar 81. (7"m) *(MCA 692)* **THE STORY SO FAR. / SILVER AND GOLD / ALL OR NOTHING** -
Apr 81. (lp/c) *(<MCF/+C 3104>)* **SPELLBOUND** 33
– Gangland / Take it / Minotaur / Hellbound / Mirror / Silver and gold / Tyger Bay / The story so far / Blackjack / Don't stop by. *(re-iss. Jun87 lp/c; MCL/+C 1747) (cd-iss. Jul93 on 'Repertoire'; REP 4015-WZ) (cd re-iss. May97 & Feb00 on 'Neat'; EDGY 102)*
Jun 81. (7") *(MCA 723)* **DON'T STOP BY. / SLAVE TO FREEDOM** -
(12"+=) *(MCAT 723)* – Raised on rock.
Nov 81. (7") *(MCA 755)* **LOVE DON'T STAY. / PARADISE DRIVE** -
Nov 81. (lp/c) *(<MCF/+C 3123>)* **CRAZY NIGHTS** 51
– Do it good / Love don't stay / Never satisfied / Running out of time / Crazy nights / Down and out / Lonely man / Make a stand / Raised on rock. *(w/ free 12")* – The stormlands / Slip away. *(re-iss. Feb84 lp/c+=; MCL/+C 1780)* – (above 2). *(cd-iss. May97 & Feb00 on 'Neat'; EDGY 103)*
Jan 82. (7") *(MCA 759)* **DO IT GOOD. / SLIP AWAY** -
Mar 82. (7"/7"pic-d) *(MCA/+P 769)* **LOVE POTION No.9. / THE STORMLANDS** 45 -
Mar 82. (7") *<52204>* **LOVE POTION No.9 / LONELY AT THE TOP** -

—— **FRED PURSER** – guitar (ex-PENETRATION) repl. SYKES who joined THIN LIZZY

Jun 82. (7",7"white,7"blue,7"red) *(MCA 777)* **RENDEZVOUS. / LIFE OF CRIME** 49 -
Aug 82. (lp/c) *(<MCF/+C 3150>)* **THE CAGE** 13
– Rendezvous / Lonely at the top / Letter from L.A. / Paris by air / Tides / Making tracks / The cage / Love potion No.9 / You always see what you want to see / Danger in Paradise / The actor. *(re-iss. Jun84 lp/c; MCL/+C 1797) (cd-iss. May97 & Feb00 on 'Neat'; EDGY 104)*
Aug 82. (7"/7"pic-d) *(MCA/+P 790)* **PARIS BY AIR. / LOVE'S A LIE** 63 -
Oct 82. (7"/ext.12") *(MCA/+T 798)* **MAKING TRACKS. / WHAT YOU'RE SAYING** -

—— **DEVERILL + DICK** were joined by newcomers **STEVE LAMB** – guitar / **DAVID DONALDSON** – bass / **NEIL SHEPHERD** – guitar

Oct 83. (7") *(MCA 841)* **LONELY AT THE TOP. / YOU ALWAYS SEE WHAT YOU WANT TO SEE** -

Music For Nations — not iss.

Jun 85. (lp/c) *(MFN/TMFN 50)* **THE WRECK-AGE** -
– Waiting / Protection / Innocent eyes / Desert of no love / The wreck-age / Women in cages / Victim / Ready to run / All change faces / Forgive and forget. *<Us cd-iss. 2001 on 'Spitfire'>*

—— (Sep'86) – guest **STEVE THOMPSON** – keyboards, bass repl. NEIL SHEPHERD + DONALDSON

Zebra — not iss.

May 87. (lp) *(ZEB 10)* **BURNING IN THE SHADE** -
– The first (the only one) / Hit it / Dream ticket / Sweet lies / Maria / Hideaway / Open to seduction / The circle of the dance / Are you there? / The memory fades.

– compilations, etc. –

Aug 86. (lp) *Neat; (NEAT 1037)* **FIRST KILL** -
– Slave to freedom / Angel / Straight as a die / Final answer / Euthanasia / Shakespeare road / Don't take nothing / Alright on the night / Bad times / Small town flirt. *(cd-iss. 1991 on 'Castle'; CLACD 258)*
Jun 98. (cd) *Half Moon; (MHNCD 042)* **ON THE PROWL – THE BEST OF TYGERS OF PAN TANG** -
– Don't touch me there / Slave to freedom / Suzie smiled / Insanity / Hellbound / The mirror / Silver and gold / The story so far / Don't stop by / Love don't stay / Running out of time / Crazy nights / Make a stand / Love potion No.9 / Rendezvous / Lonely at the top / Paris by air / Danger in paradise.

TYKETTO

Formed: New York, USA . . . 1987 by former WAYSTED frontman, DANNY VAUGHN, who gathered together the line-up of JIMI KENNEDY, MICHAEL CLAYTON, BROOKE ST. JAMES and initially former bandmate, JIMMY DILELLA. Signed to 'Geffen', the group debuted in 1991 with the 'DON'T COME EASY' album, an earthy set of easy going hard rock in the mould of WHITE LION etc. TYKETTO subsequently toured with the latter act, while WHITE LION bassist, JAMES LOMENZO, was briefly hired as a replacement for the departing KENNEDY. A more permanent member was found in JAIMIE SCOTT, who played on follow-up set, 'STRENGTH IN NUMBERS'. Although the album was completed and in the final stages of preparation for release, 'Geffen' backed out at the last minute and TYKETTO found themselves in limbo. They eventually signed to 'Music For Nations', who belatedly released the album in early '94. By this point, however, the early momentum had been lost and the album was met with minimal interest. While a third effort, 'SHINE', appeared in 1995, and a concert set, 'TAKE OUT AND SERVED UP LIVE' in '96, TYKETTO have never achieved the success which their early promise seemed to suggest was imminent.

Album rating: DON'T COME EASY (*5) / STRENGTH IN NUMBERS (*6) / SHINE (*5) / TAKE OUT & SERVED UP LIVE (*5)

DANNY VAUGHN – vocals, guitar, mouth harp (ex-WAYSTED) / **BROOKE ST. JAMES** – guitars / **JIMI KENNEDY** – bass / **MICHAEL CLAYTON** – drums, percussion

Geffen Geffen

Oct 91. (c-s) *<19109>* **WINGS** [-] [ ]

Nov 91. (lp/cd) *<DGC/+D 24317>* **DON'T COME EASY** [-] [ ]
– Forever young / Wings / Burning down inside / Seasons / Standing alone / Lay your body down / Walk on fire / Nothing but love / Strip me down / Sail away.

— **JAIMIE SCOTT** – bass; repl. JAMES LOMENZO (ex-WHITE LION) who repl. KENNEDY

Music For Nations C.M.C.

Feb 94. (cd) *(CDMFN 157) <7103>* **STRENGTH IN NUMBERS** [ ] [ ]
– Strength in numbers / Rescue me / End of the summer days / Ain't that love / Catch my fall / The last sunset / All over me / Write your name in the sky / Meet me in the night / Why do you cry / Inherit the wind / Standing alone.

Mar 95. (cd-ep) *(CDKUT 163)* **STANDING ALONE / THE LAST SUNSET / LAY YOUR BODY DOWN (live)** [ ] [-]

Nov 95. (cd) *(CDMFN 195)* **SHINE** [ ] [-]
– Jamie / Rawhigh / Radio Mary / Get me there / High / Ballad of Ruby / Let it go / Long cold winter / I won't cry / Shine.

Jul 96. (cd) *(CDMFN 207)* **TAKE OUT & SERVED UP LIVE (live)** [ ] [-]
– Forever young / Tearin up the night / Standing alone / Drag the river / Wait forever / Burnin down inside / Lay your body down / Let it go / Seasons / Nothin but love / Shine / Get me there / The end of the summer days / High / Jamie.

— disbanded after above

TYLA (see under ⇒ DOGS D'AMOUR)

TYPE O NEGATIVE

Formed: Brooklyn, New York, USA . . .1988 by PETER STEELE (ex-CARNIVORE). One of the more compelling original bands skulking around the fringes of the metal scene, TYPE O NEGATIVE caused controversy from the off with the shocking artwork for the unambiguously titled debut album, 'SLOW, DEEP, HARD' (1991). Issued by 'Roadracer', the record's sleeve resembled a phallic symbol (talking of symbols, sex ones that is, the musclebound STEELE apeared naked in the August '95 edition of Playgirl!). A follow-up, meanwhile, 'THE ORIGIN OF THE FECES' (1992), featured a cover which left even less to the imagination, while music contained within its grooves lent the band's goth/industrial NIN-esque metal hybrid a demonic ambience. With something of a cult building around the band, 'BLOODY KISSES' (1993), became their most successful to date, while 1996's 'OCTOBER RUST' made it into the UK Top 30. In the more experimental climate of the mid 90's metal scene, TYPE O NEGATIVE have emerged from the margins to become a significant player. Autumn '97 saw the release of an EP devoted to different mixes of TYPE O's Neil Young cover, 'CINNAMON GIRL'. Select the wittily titled 'DEPRESSED MODE' mix for maximum black humour value. Their fifth set, 'WORLD COMING DOWN' (1999), was another to reach both the US and UK Top 50. • **Covered:** BLACK SABBATH (Black Sabbath).

Album rating: SLOW, DEEP AND HARD (*6) / THE ORIGIN OF THE FECES (*5) / BLOODY KISSES (*7) / OCTOBER RUST (*6) / WORLD COMING DOWN (*5)

PETE STEELE – vocals, bass / **JOSH SILVER** – keyboards / **KENNY HICKEY** – guitar

Roadracer Roadracer

May 91. (cd/lp) *<(RO 9313-2/-1)>* **SLOW, DEEP AND HARD** [ ] [ ]
– Unsuccessfully coping with the natural beauty of infidelity / Der untermensch / Xero tolerance / Prelude to agony / Glass walls of limbo (dance mix) / The misinterpretation of silence and its disastrous consequences / Gravitational constant: G = 6.67 x 10-8 cm 3 gm-1 sec-2.

Roadrunner Roadrunner

Feb 92. (cd/lp) *<(RR 9006-2/-4)>* **THE ORIGIN OF THE FECES (live)** [ ] [ ]
– I know you're fucking someone someone else / Are you afraid / Gravity / Pain / Kill you tonight / Hey Pete / Kill you tonight (reprise) / Paranoid. *(re-iss. Nov94 cd/c; same) (cd re-iss. Nov97; RR 8762-2)*

— added **JOHNNY KELLY** – drums

Aug 93. (cd/c/lp) *<(RR 9100-2/-4/-1)>* **BLOODY KISSES** [ ] [ ]
– Machine screw * / Christian woman / Black No.1 (Little Miss Scare-all) / Fay Wray come out to play * / Kill all the white people * / Summer breeze / Set me on fire / Dark side of the womb * / We hate everything * / Bloody kisses (a death in the family) / 3.0.1.F. * / Too late: Frozen / Blood & fire / Can't lose you. *(cd+=/c+=*) (lp+=)* – Suspended in dusk.

Feb 94. (cd-s) *(RR 2378-3)* **CHRISTIAN WOMAN / ('A'mixes) / SUSPENDED IN DUSK** [ ] [ ]

Aug 96. (cd-ep) **MY GIRLRIEND'S GIRLFRIEND / BLACK SABBATH (from 'The Satanic Perspective') / BLOOD & FIRE (remix)** [ ] [ ]

Sep 96. (cd/c/d-lp) *<(RR 8874-2/-4/-1)>* **OCTOBER RUST** [26] [42]
– Bad ground / Love you to death / Be my druidess / Green man / Red water (Christmas mourning) / My girlfriend's girlfriend / Die with me / Burnt flowers fallen / In praise of Bacchus / Cinnamon girl / The glorious liberation of the people's technocratic republic of Vinnland by the combined forces of the United Territories of Europa / Wolf moon (including zoanthrobe paranoia) / Haunted / ?.

Nov 96. (cd-ep) **LOVE YOU TO DEATH (radio) / SUMMER BREEZE (rejected radio) / LOVE YOU TO DEATH (album)** [-] [-] mail-o

Sep 97. (cd-ep) *(RR 2270-3)* **CINNAMON GIRL (Depressed Mode mix) / CINNAMON GIRL (US radio mix) / CINNAMON GIRL (extended mix)** [ ] [-]

Sep 99. (cd) *<(RR 8660-2)>* **WORLD COMING DOWN** [49] [39]
– Skip it / White slavery / inus / Everyone I love is dead / Save the sane / Liver / World coming down / Creepy green light / Everything dies / Lung / Pyretta blaze / Hallows eve / Day tripper (medley).

Nov 99. (cd-s) *(RR 2130-3)* **EVERYTHING DIES / 12 BLACK RAINBOWS / EVERYTHING DIES (album version)** [ ] [ ]

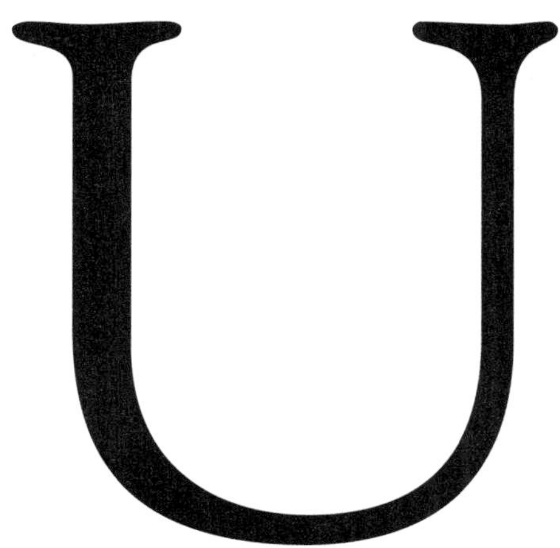

U.D.O.

Formed: Germany ... 1987 by former ACCEPT frontman, UDO DIRKSCHNEIDER, who recruited a line-up of MATTHIAS DEITH, ANDY SUSEMIHL, THOMAS S and STEFAN SCHWARZMANN. Remaining with 'R.C.A.' (for whom ACCEPT recorded in the late 80's), DIRKSCHNEIDER attempted to get back to his lung-lacerated roots on debut set, 'ANIMAL HOUSE' (1988). Released to some positive reviews, it appeared that U.D.O. might reclaim the ground lost by ACCEPT since their screaming heyday. However, successive releases such as 'MEAN MACHINE' (1989) and the appropriately-titled 'FACELESS WORLD' (1990) were shackled by their formulative approach. All those years of vein-straining finally caught up with DIRKSCHEIDER in mid-1990, when the man suffered a heart attack during a German tour. He had sufficiently recovered by the following year, coming blasting back with 'TIMEBOMB', the set as roaringly metallic as ever.

Album rating: ANIMAL HOUSE (*5) / MEAN MACHINE (*4) / FACELESS WORLD (*4) / TIMEBOMB (*6) / SOLID (*4) / NO LIMITS (*4) / THE BEST OF U.D.O. compilation (*5) / HOLY (*4)

UDO DIRKSCHNEIDER – vocals / **MATTHIAS DEITH** – guitar / **ANDY SUSEMIHL** – guitar / **THOMAS S.** – bass / **STEFAN SCHWARZMANN** – drums

R.C.A. R.C.A.

Mar 88. (lp/c) *(PL/PK 71552) <6881>* **ANIMAL HOUSE**
– Animal house / Go back to hell / They want war / Black widow / In the darkness / Lay down the law / We want it loud / Warrior / Coming home / Run for cover.

Apr 89. (lp/c/cd) *(PL/PK/PD 71994) <9716>* **MEAN MACHINE**
– Don't look back / Break the rules / We're history / Painted love / Mean machine / Dirty boys / Streets on fire / Lost passion / Sweet little child / Catch my fall / Still in love with you.

Mar 90. (cd-ep) *(PD 43514)* **HEART OF GOLD / BLITZ OF LIGHTNING / LIVING ON THE FRONTLINE** - - German

Apr 90. (cd/c/lp) *(PD/PK/PL 74510) <2266>* **FACELESS WORLD**
– Heart of gold / Blitz of lightning / System of life / Faceless world / Stranger / Living on a frontline / Trip to nowhere / Can't get enough / Unspoken words / Future land.

— While he was performing in concert mid-1990 in Germany, UDO suffered a heart attack, although he fully recovered by 1991.

Apr 91. (cd/c/lp) *(PD/PK/PL 74953)* **TIMEBOMB** -
– The gutter / Metal eater / Thunderforce / Overloaded / Burning heat / Back in pain / Timebomb / Powersquad / Kick in the face / Soldiers of darkness / Metal maniac master mind.

— split for a while until the latter half of the 90's

Gun Gun

Sep 97. (cd) *(GUN 122CD) <6725>* **SOLID** Mar97
– Independence day / Two faced woman / Desperate halls / The punisher / Devil's dice / Bad luck / Preachers of the night / Hate stinger / Braindead hero / Pray for the hunted / The healer.

May 98. (cd) *(GUN 158CD) <6724>* **NO LIMITS**

Sep 99. (cd) *(GUN 177CD)* **THE BEST OF U.D.O.** (compilation)
– Warrior / The gutter / Metal eater / Black widow / Animal house / Timebomb / Living on a frontline / Break the rules / Coming home / Unspoken words / Go back to hell / Mean machine / Restricted area / They want war / We want it loud / Future land / In the darkness.

Nuclear Blast Nuclear Blast

Nov 99. (cd) *(NB 435-2) <6435>* **HOLY** Feb00
– Holy / Raiders of beyond / Shout it out / Recall the sin / Thunder in the tower / Back off / Friends will be friends / State run operation / Danger / Ride the storm / Cut me out.

U.F.O.

Formed: North London, England ... 1969 initially as HOCUS POCUS, by PHIL MOGG, PETE WAY, MICK BOLTON and ANDY PARKER. Gaining a deal with 'Beacon' records in the early 70's, UFO had a surprising degree of success in Japan and Germany, where their blend of boogified space-rock (embellished with extended jams) sold like hotcakes. Their version of Eddie Cochran's 'C'MON EVERYBODY' (1972) was a massive hit in the far east, although Britain had previously shunned their pretentiously unremarkable first two albums, the thoughtfully titled 'UFO 1' and 'UFO 2 – FLYING' (both 1971). When BOLTON departed in 1972, his place was filled by a succession of guitarists, MICHAEL SCHENKER (ex-SCORPIONS) finally getting the permanent job the following year when BERNIE MARSDEN (who had replaced LARRY WALLIS; ex-PINK FAIRIES) departed for a bit of WILD TURKEY. Signing to 'Chrysalis' in 1974, UFO changed their style dramatically, hard-rock becoming their paymaster with classic songs such as 'DOCTOR, DOCTOR' and 'ROCK BOTTOM' featuring "heavily" on their label debut that year, 'PHENOMENON'. Between mid '74 and early '75, they added a fifth member, PAUL CHAPMAN (ex-SKID ROW), although the group soon reverted to a quartet when the guitarist joined LONE STAR. 'FORCE IT' was pushed out in the same year, the album immediately securing a Top 75 placing in the States where SCHENKER's fingering on his "Flying V" style guitar was as much talked about as the record. For their follow-up set, the mildly disappointing 'NO HEAVY PETTIN' (1976), they added keyboard player, DANNY PEYRONEL, although he was subsequently replaced by PAUL RAYMOND on the 1977 disc, 'LIGHTS OUT'. A definite improvement, UFO landed in America properly this time, hitting their Top 30 with a blistering attack on tracks such as 'TOO HOT TO HANDLE' and a cover of Love's 'ALONE AGAIN OR'. 1978's 'OBSESSION' (featuring the classic hard-rock anthem, 'ONLY YOU CAN ROCK ME'), was again plucked from the stars, although after a live set, 'STRANGERS IN THE NIGHT' (1979), SCHENKER decided to return to The SCORPIONS. PAUL CHAPMAN returned for one GEORGE MARTIN-produced album, 'NO PLACE TO RUN' (1980), although it was clear the only thing taking off in UFO was the group members. PAUL RAYMOND joined SCHENKER in his new group and was replaced by NEIL CARTER prior to the recording of their 1981 set, 'THE WILD, THE WILLING AND THE INNOCENT', an aggressive piece of class that made its mark in Britain. All seemed well after 'MECHANIX' peaked at No.8 in the British charts in '82, however, PETE WAY was another to jump ship, the bassist eventually reappearing in his WAYSTED outfit. Former punk PAUL GRAY (from The DAMNED and EDDIE & THE HOT RODS), filled in on the 1983 set, 'MAKING CONTACT', although this was hardly the standard their fans had come to expect. They split soon after, MOGG and cohorts reforming many times over the next decade but never quite getting off the ground. • **Songwriters:** Mostly WAY / MOGG or CHAPMAN / MOGG, with both variations sometimes adding SCHENKER or CARTER. • **Trivia:** PHIL MOGG's nephew, NIGEL MOGG, became relatively famous in the band, The QUIREBOYS.

Album rating: U.F.O. 1 (*2) / U.F.O. 2 – FLYING (*3) / LIVE IN JAPAN (*5) / PHENOMENON (*6) / FORCE IT (*6) / NO HEAVY PETTIN' (*5) / LIGHTS OUT (*7) / OBSESSION (*8) / STRANGERS IN THE NIGHT (*8) / NO PLACE TO RUN (*6) / THE WILD, THE WILLING + THE INNOCENT (*8) / MECHANIX (*6) / MAKING CONTACT (*5) / HEADSTONE – THE BEST OF U.F.O. compilation (*7) / MISDEMEANOUR (*4) / AIN'T MISBEHAVIN' (*4) / HIGH STAKES AND DANGEROUS MEN (*5) / LIGHTS OUT IN TOKYO (*5) / WALK ON WATER (*3) / COVENANT (*4) / Mogg/Way: EDGE OF THE WORLD (*5) / CHOCOLATE BOX (*4)

PHIL MOGG (b.1951) – vocals / **PETE WAY** – bass / **MICK BOLTON** – guitar / **ANDY PARKER** – drums

Beacon Rare Earth

1970. (7") *(BEA 161)* **SHAKE IT ABOUT. / EVIL** -

Jan 71. (lp) *(BES 12) <524>* **UFO**
– Unidentified flying object / Boogie / C'mon everybody / Shake it about / Melinda / Timothy / Follow you home / Treacle people / Who do you love / Evito. *(cd-iss. Apr91 on 'Line'; GACD 900691) (cd re-iss. Feb99 on 'Repertoire'; RR 4742)*

Jan 71. (7") *(BEA 165)* **COME AWAY MELINDA. / UNIDENTIFIED FLYING OBJECT** -

Jun 71. (7") *(BEA 172)* **BOOGIE FOR GEORGE. / TREACLE PEOPLE** -

Oct 71. (7") *(BEA 181)* **PRINCE KAJUKU. / THE COMING OF PRINCE KAJUKU** -

Oct 71. (lp) *(BEAS 19)* **UFO 2 – FLYING** -
– Silver bird / Star storm / Prince Kajuku / Coming of Prince Kajuku / Flying. *(re-iss. Feb72; same) (cd-iss. Apr91 on 'Line'; GACD 900694) (cd re-iss. Feb99 on 'Repertoire'; RR 4743)*

Nova not iss.

1972. (lp) *(621454)* **UFO: LIVE (live in Japan)** - - German
– C'mon everybody / Who do you love / Loving cup / Prince Kajaku – The coming of Prince Kajuku / Boogie for George / Follow you home. *(UK-iss.1982 on 'AKA'; AKP 2) (cd-iss. Oct98 on 'Repertoire'; RR 4698)*

— In 1972, they issued a few 45's in Japan, incl. 'C'MON EVERYBODY'.

— (Jun'73) **MICHAEL SCHENKER** (b.10 Jan'55, Savstedt, Germany) – guitar repl. BERNIE MARSDEN to WILD TURKEY. BERNIE had repl. LARRY WALLIS (Nov'72) who had repl. BOLTON (Feb'72). WALLIS went on to PINK FAIRIES

Chrysalis Chrysalis

Mar 74. (7") *(CHS 2040)* **DOCTOR DOCTOR. / LIPSTICK TRACES**

May 74. (lp/c) *(<CHR/ZCHR 1059>)* **PHENOMENON**
– Too young to know / Crystal light / Doctor doctor / Space child / Rock bottom / Oh my / Time on my hands / Built for comfort / Lipstick traces / Queen of the deep. *(cd-iss. Oct91 on 'Episode'; LUSCD 10) (cd re-iss. Feb00 on 'Liberty'; 524628-2)*

Jul 75. (lp/c) *(<CHR/ZCHR 1074>)* **FORCE IT** 71
– Let it roll / Shoot shoot / High flyer / Love lost love / Out in the street / Mother Mary / Too much of nothing / Dance your life away / This kid's – Between the walls. *(cd-iss. Feb00 on 'Liberty'; 524599-2)*

— (Sep'75) added **DANNY PEYRONEL** – keyboards (ex-HEAVY METAL KIDS)

May 76. (lp/c) *(<CHR/ZCHR 1103>)* **NO HEAVY PETTING**
– Natural thing / I'm a loser / Can you roll her / Belladonna / Reasons love / Highway lady / On with the action / A fool in love / Martian landscape.

— (Jul'76) **PAUL RAYMOND** – keyboards, guitar (ex-SAVOY BROWN) repl. DANNY

Apr 77. (7") *(CHS 2146)* **ALONE AGAIN OR. / ELECTRIC PHASE**

May 77. (lp/c) *(<CHR/ZCHR 1127>)* **LIGHTS OUT** 54 23
– Too hot to handle / Just another suicide / Try me / Lights out / Gettin' ready / Alone again or / Electric phase / Love to love. *(cd-iss. 1987; ACCD 1127) (cd-re-iss. Jul91 on 'Episode'; LUSCD 9) (cd re-iss. Aug99 on 'EMI'; 521309-2)*

Jun 77. (7") **TOO HOT TO HANDLE. / ELECTRIC PHASE** -

Jun 78. (lp/c) *(<CDL/ZCDL 1182>)* **OBSESSION** 26 41
– Only you can rock me / Pack it up (and go) / Arbory Hill / Ain't no baby / Lookin' out for No.1 / Hot 'n' ready / Cherry / You don't fool me / Lookin' out for No.1 (reprise) / One more for the rodeo / Born to lose. *(cd-iss. Sep91 on 'Episode'; LUSCD 11) (cd re-iss. Aug99 on 'EMI'; 521310-2)*

Jul 78. (7"red) *(CHS 2241)* **ONLY YOU CAN ROCK ME. / CHERRY / ROCK BOTTOM** 50

Dec 78. (d-lp/d-c) *(CJT/ZCJT 1) <1209>* **STRANGERS IN THE NIGHT (live)** 8 42
– Natural thing / Out in the street / Only you can rock me / Doctor doctor / Mother Mary / This kid's / Love to love / Lights out / Rock bottom / Too hot to handle / I'm a loser / Let it roll / Shoot shoot. *(cd-iss. Sep91; CCD 1209) (cd re-iss. Mar94; CD25CR 22)*

Jan 79. (7"clear) *(CHS 2287)* **DOCTOR DOCTOR (live). / ON WITH THE ACTION (live) / TRY ME** 35

Mar 79. (7"clear) *(CHS 2318)* **SHOOT SHOOT (live). / ONLY YOU CAN ROCK ME (live) / I'M A LOSER (live)** 48

— (Nov'78) **PAUL CHAPMAN** – guitar returned to repl. SCHENKER who joined The SCORPIONS and later formed his own self-named group.

Jan 80. (7"red) *(CHS 2399)* **YOUNG BLOOD. / LIGHTS OUT** 36

Jan 80. (lp/c) *(<CDL/ZCDL 1239>)* **NO PLACE TO RUN** 11 51
– Alpha Centauri / Lettin' go / Mystery train / This fire burns tonight / Gone in the night / Young blood / No place to run / Take it or leave it / Money money / Anyday.

— (Aug'80) **WAY, MOGG, CHAPMAN + PARKER** recruited **NEIL CARTER** – keyboards, guitar (ex-WILD HORSES) repl. PAUL RAYMOND who joined MICHAEL SCHENKER GROUP

Oct 80. (7"clear) *(CHS 2454)* **COULDN'T GET IT RIGHT. / HOT 'N' READY (live)**

Jan 81. (lp/c) *(<CHR/ZCHR 1307>)* **THE WILD, THE WILLING AND THE INNOCENT** 19 77
– Chains chains / Long gone / The wild, the willing and the innocent / It's killing me / Makin' moves / Lonely heart / Couldn't get it right / Profession of violence.

Jan 81. (7"clear) *(CHS 2454)* **LONELY HEART. / LONG GONE** 41

Jan 82. (7"clear) *(CHS 2576)* **LET IT RAIN. / HEEL OF A STRANGER / YOU'LL GET LOVE** 62

Feb 82. (lp/c) *(<CHR/ZCHR 1360>)* **MECHANIX** 8 82
– The writer / Something else / Back into my life / You'll get love / Doing it all for you / We belong to the night / Let it rain / Terri / Feel it / Dreaming.

Apr 82. (7"/7"pic-d) *(CHS/+P 2607)* **BACK INTO MY LIFE. / THE WRITER**

— (Jun'82) on tour **BILLY SHEEHAN** – bass (ex-TALAS) repl. PETE WAY who formed FASTWAY and briefly joined OZZY OSBOURNE (later WAYSTED)

Jan 83. (lp/c) *(<CHR/ZCHR 1402>)* **MAKING CONTACT** 32
– Blinded by a lie / Diesel in the dust / A fool for love / You and me / When it's time to rock / The way the wild wind blows / Call my name / All over you / No getaway / Push, it's love.

Mar 83. (7"/7"pic-d) *(CHS/+P 2672)* **WHEN IT'S TIME TO ROCK. / EVERYBODY KNOWS** 70
(12"+=) *(CHS12 2672)* – Push it's love.

— Disbanded when MOGG suffered a nervous breakdown on stage. He resurrected the band in 1984 with **PAUL RAYMOND / PAUL GRAY** – bass (ex-DAMNED) / **JIM SIMPSON** – drums (ex-MAGNUM) / **ATOMIK TOMMY M.** – guitar (b. Japan)

Oct 85. (7"/7"sha-pic-d) *(UFO/+P 1)* **THIS TIME. / THE CHASE** -
(12"+=) *(UFOX 1)* – ('A'extended).

Nov 85. (lp/c) *(<CHR/ZCHR 1518>)* **MISDEMEANOR** 74
– This time / One heart / Night run / The only ones / Meanstreets / Name of love / Blue / Dream the dream / Heaven's gate / Wreckless.

Feb 86. (7"red) *(UFO 2)* **NIGHT RUN. / HEAVEN'S GATE**
(12"+=) *(UFOX 2)* – ('A'extended).

— (late '86) **DAVID 'Jake' JACOBSON** – guitar (ex-ERIC MARTIN) repl. RAYMOND

FM Revolver — not iss.

Mar 88. (lp/c/cd) *(WKFM LP/MC/XD 107)* **AIN'T MISBEHAVIN'** -
– Between a rock and a hard place / Another Saturday night / At war with the world / Hunger in the night / Easy money / Rock boyz, rock.
(cd+=) – Lonely cities (of the heart). *(pic-lp Jan89; WKFMHP 107)*

— Disbanded Spring 1988. PHIL went into production mainly for his nephew NIGEL MOGG's new band QUIREBOYS

— **MOGG + WAY** re-united **UFO** adding **LAURENCE ARCHER** – guitar (ex-GRAND SLAM) / **CLIVE EDWARDS** – drums (ex-WILD HORSES) / **JEM DAVIS** – keyboards

Essential — Victory

Nov 91. (12"ep/cd-ep) **ONE OF THOSE NIGHTS. / AIN'T LIFE SWEET / LONG GONE** -

Feb 92. (cd/c/lp) *(ESM CD/MC 178)* **HIGH STAKES AND DANGEROUS MEN** -
– Borderline / Primed for time / She's the one / Ain't life sweet / Don't want to lose you / Burnin' fire / Running up the highway / Back door man / One of those nights / Revolution / Love deadly love / Let the good times roll. *(cd re-iss. Mar00; ESMCD 864)*

Feb 93. (cd/c) *(ESS CD/MC 191) <VICP 5204>* **LIGHTS OUT IN TOKYO LIVE (live)** Nov92
– Running up the highway / Borderline / Too hot to handle / She's the one / Cherry / Back door man / One of those nights / Love to love / Only you can rock me / Lights out / Doctor, doctor / Rock bottom / Shoot, shoot / C'mon everybody. *(cd re-iss. Apr95; ESSCD 386) (cd re-iss. Mar00; ESMCD 863)*

— The UFO who released '3RD PERSPECTIVE' in 1997 was not the same group

Eagle — C.M.C.

Nov 95. (cd/c) *(EAG CD/MC 009) <86239>* **WALK ON WATER**
– A self made man / Venus / Pushed to the limit / Stopped by a bullet (of love) / Darker days / Running on empty / Knock, knock / Dreaming of summer / Doctor, doctor / Lights out / Fortune town / I will be there / Public enemy #1. *(re-iss. Jan00; same)*

MOGG/WAY

Roadrunner — Roadrunner

Nov 97. (cd) *(<RR 8804-2>)* **EDGE OF THE WORLD**
– Change brings a change / All out of luck / Gravy train / Fortune town / Highwire / Saving me from myself / Mother Mary / House of pain / It's a game / History of flames / Spell on you / Totaled. *(re-iss. May99; same)*

S.P.V. — S.P.V.

Oct 99. (cd) *(<085-2155-2>)* **CHOCOLATE BOX**
– Muddy's gold / Jerusalem / Too close to the sun / This is a life / Lying and dying / King of the city / Death in the family / Whip that groove / Last man in space / Sparkling wine.

UFO

— re-formed yet again

S.P.V. — Shrapnel

Jul 00. (d-cd) *(087-2189-2) <SH 1142-2>* **COVENANT**
– Love is forever / Unreveled / Miss the lights / Midnight train / Fool's gold / In the middle of madness / The smell of money / Rise again / Serenade / Cowboy joe / The world and his dog / Mother Mary / Let it roll / This kids / Love to love / Out in the street / Pushed to the limit / Venus.

– compilations, others, etc. –

1973. (d-lp) *Decca; (SD 30311/2)* **U.F.O. 1 / FLYING** -

Dec 82. (d-c) *Chrysalis; (ZCDP 107)* **MECHANIX / LIGHTS OUT** -

Aug 83. (d-lp/d-c) *Chrysalis; (CTY/ZCTY 1437)* **HEADSTONE – THE BEST OF U.F.O.** 39 -
– Doctor doctor / Rock bottom / Fool for your loving / Shoot shoot / Too hot to handle / Only you can rock me / Love drive (SCORPIONS) / She said she said (LONE STAR) / Lights out / Armed and ready (MICHAEL SCHENKER GROUP) / Young blood / Criminal tendencies / Lonely heart / We belong to the night / Let it rain / Couldn't get it right / Electric phase / Doing it all for you.

Nov 85. (d-lp/d-c) *Castle; (CCS LP/MC 101)* **THE COLLECTION** -

Apr 87. (d-lp/c/cd) *Raw Power; (RAW LP/TC/CD 029)* **ANTHOLOGY** -
– Rock bottom / Built for comfort / Highway lady / Can you roll her / Fool for love / Shoot shoot / Too hot to handle / Gettin' ready / Only you can rock me / Looking for number one / Hot 'n' ready / Mystery train / No place to run / Profession and violence / Chains chains / Something else / Doing it for all of you / When it's time to rock / Diesel in the dust. *(cd re-iss. Jan94; CCSCD 316)*

Sep 89. (cd) *Line; (GACD 900704)* **SPACE METAL** -

Apr 92. (cd) *Windsong; (WINCD 016)* **BBC LIVE IN CONCERT (live)** -

Oct 92. (cd/c) *Chrysalis; (CD/TC CHR 1888)* **ESSENTIAL U.F.O.** -

Nov 92. (cd) *Dojo; (EARLD 9)* **EARLY YEARS** -

Mar 94. (cd/c) *Music Club; (MC CD/TC 153)* **TOO HOT TO HANDLE: THE BEST OF U.F.O.** -

May 94. (cd) *Beat Goes On; (BGOCD 229)* **OBSESSION / NO PLACE TO RUN** -

Jun 94. (cd) *Essential; (ESDCD 218)* **TNT (live in Texas)** -
(re-iss. Mar00; ESMCD 862)

Aug 94. (cd) *Beat Goes On; (BGOCD 228)* **NO HEAVY PETTING / LIGHTS OUT** -

Sep 94. (cd) *Beat Goes On; (BGOCD 230)* **THE WILD, THE WILLING AND THE INNOCENT / MECHANIX** -

Oct 94. (cd) *Beat Goes On; (BGOCD 227)* **PHENOMENOM / FORCE IT** -

May 95. (cd) *Spectrum; (550743-2)* **DOCTOR, DOCTOR** -

Nov 95. (cd) *M&M; (M&MCD 1)* **HEAVEN'S GATE LIVE (live)** -
(re-iss. May98 on 'Indelible'; INDELCD 18)

Jul 96. (cd) *EMI Gold; (CDGOLD 1050)* **THE BEST OF U.F.O.** -

Jul 96. (cd) *Beat Goes On; (BGOCD 319)* **MAKING CONTACT / MISDEMEANOUR** -

May 97. (d-cd) *Snapper; (SMDCD 122)* **THE X-FACTOR – OUT THERE . . . AND BACK** -

Feb 98. (cd) *Disky; <(WB 88595-2)>* **UNIDENTIFIED FLYING OBJECT**

Oct 98. (d-cd) *Repertoire; (RR 4720)* **TIME TO ROCK**

Apr 99. (cd) *EMI; (499403-2)* **BBC SESSIONS / IN CONCERT**

Jun 99. (cd) *Zoom Club; (ZCRCD 1)* **ON WITH THE ACTION (live at the Roundhouse 1976)**

Sep 99. (d-cd) *Zoom Club; (ZCRCD 20)* **WEREWOLVES OF LONDON (live 1988)** -

May 00. (cd) *Brilliant; (BT 33037)* **UFO LIVE IN LONDON (live)** -

Aug 00. (cd) *EMI; (528502-2)* **THE BEST OF U.F.O.**

UGLY KID JOE

Formed: Isla Vista, North California, USA . . . 1989 by students WHITFIELD CRANE and KLAUS EICHSTADT. With the line-up completed by ROGER LAHR, CORDELL CROCKETT and MARK DAVIS, UGLY KID JOE soon earned a reputation as irreverent metal funsters. 'Mercury' subsequently won the race for their signatures and soon had a platinum mini-album on their hands with 'AS UGLY AS THEY WANNA BE'. Its main selling point was the inclusion of the transatlantic Top 10 smash, 'EVERYTHING ABOUT YOU', a sarcastic, tongue-in-cheek tirade aimed at some hapless female. Musically, UGLY KID JOE traded in funky, sleazy pop/metal with attitude, not too far removed from LOVE/HATE for whom CRANE had worked as a guitar technician. A debut album proper, 'AS UGLY AS THEY WANNA BE', followed later that year, almost making the UK Top 10. By turns amusing and annoying, UGLY KID JOE nevertheless had a way with an infectious tune, the album spawning another US/UK Top 10 single with a hard-hitting cover of Harry Chapin's 'CATS IN THE CRADLE'. By 1994, DAVE FORTMAN and SHANNON LARKIN had replaced LAHR and DAVIS respectively while later that year, CRANE was credited on the MOTORHEAD single, 'BORN TO RAISE HELL' alongside ICE-T. A belated follow-up album finally appeared in summer '95, the oh so amusingly titled 'MENACE TO SOBRIETY'. • **Songwriters:** Most by CRANE-EICHSTADT or group, except SIN CITY (Ac/Dc) / N.I.B. (Black Sabbath).

Album rating: AS UGLY AS THEY WANNA BE mini (*5) / AMERICA'S LEAST WANTED (*6) / MENACE TO SOBRIETY (*5) / MOTEL CALIFORNIA (*4) / AS UGLY AS IT GETS: THE VERY BEST OF . . . compilation (*6)

WHITFIELD CRANE (b.19 Jan'68, Palo Alto, Calif.) – vocals / **KLAUS EICHSTADT** (b.19 Dec'67, Redwood City, Calif.) – guitar / **ROGER LAHR** – guitar / **CORDELL CROCKETT** (b.21 Jan'65, Livermore, Calif.) – bass / **MARK DAVIS** (b.22 Apr'64, Phoenix, Arizona) – drums

Mercury | Stardog-Mercury

May 92. (m-cd/m-c/m-lp) *<(868823-2/-4/-1)>* **AS UGLY AS THEY WANNA BE** [9] [4 Jan92]
– Madman / Whiplash liquor / Too bad / Everything about you / Sweet leaf – Funky fresh country club / Heavy metal.

May 92. (7"/c-s) *(MER/+MC 367) <866632>* **EVERYTHING ABOUT YOU. / WHIPLASH LIQUOR** [3] [9 Mar92]
(12"+=/cd-s+=) *(MER X/CD 367)* – Sin city.

Aug 92. (7"/c-s) *(MER/+MC 374)* **NEIGHBOR. / EVERYTHING ABOUT YOU (clean edit)** [28] [ ]
(12") *(MERX 374)* – ('A'side) / Funky fresh country club.
(cd-s) *(MERCD 374)* – ('A'side) / Funky fresh country club / Cats in the cradle.

Sep 92. (cd/c/lp) *<(512571-2/-4/-1)>* **AMERICA'S LEAST WANTED** [11] [27]
– Neighbor / Goddamn devil / Come tomorrow / Panhandlin' prince / Busy bee / Don't go / So damn cool / Same side / Cat's in the cradle / I'll keep tryin' / Everything about you / Madman ('92 remix) / Mr. Recordman. *(re-iss. Apr95 cd/c;)*

Oct 92. (7"/c-s) *(MER/+MC 383)* **SO DAMN COOL. / NEIGHBOR** [44] [ ]
(cd-s+=) *(MERCD 383)* – Panhandlin' Prince.

Mar 93. (7"/c-s) *(MER/+MC 385) <864888>* **CATS IN THE CRADLE. / PANHANDLIN' PRINCE** [7] [6 Feb93]
(12"+=/cd-s+=) *(MER X/CD 385)* – Whiplash liquer (live) / Neighbor (live).

Jun 93. (7"/c-s) *(MER/+MC 389)* **BUSY BEE. / CATS IN THE CRADLE (live)** [39] [ ]
(cd-s) *(MERCD 389)* – ('A'side) / Come together (live) / Don't go (live) / Everything about you (live).

— (Jun'92) **DAVE FORTMAN** (b.11 Jul'67, Orlando, Florida) – guitar (ex-SUGARTOOTH) repl. LAHR

— (1994) **SHANNON LARKIN** – drums (ex-WRATHCHILD AMERICA, ex-SOULS AT ZERO) repl. DAVIS

— Nov'94; WHITFIELD CRANE was credited on MOTORHEAD's single 'Born To Raise Hell' alongside ICE-T.

Mercury | Mercury

Jun 95. (cd/c) *(528282-2/-4) <526997>* **MESSAGE TO SOBRIETY** [25] [ ]
– Intro / God / Tomorrow's world / Clover / C.U.S.T. / Milkman's son / Suckerpath / Cloudy skies / Jesus rode a Harley / 10-10 / V.I.P. / Oompa / Candle song / Slower than nowhere.

Jun 95. (12") *(MERX 435)* **MILKMAN'S SON. / CANDLE SONG (Dave – vocals) / TOMORROW'S WORLD** [39] [ ]
(cd-s) *(MERCDX 435)* – (first 2 tracks) / So damn cool (live) / Neighbour (live).
(cd-s) – ('A'side) / Suckerpath (demo) / God (1994 version) / C.U.S.T. (demo).

Raw Power | Evilution

Oct 96. (d-cd/d-c) *(RAW CD/MC 113) <127>* **MOTEL CALIFORNIA** [ ] [ ]
– It's a lie / Dialogue / Sandwich / Rage against the answering machine / Would you like to be there / Little red man / Bicycle wheels / Father / Undertow / Shine / Strange / 12 cents / Sweeping up.

Nov 96. (cd-s) *(RAWX 1027)* **SANDWICH (clean cut radio) / SANDWICH (original) / SANDWICH (instrumental)** [ ] [ ]
(12") *(RAWX 1029)* – Bicycle wheels.

— after they split, CRANE joined LIFE OF AGONY

– compilations, etc. –

Aug 98. (cd) *Mercury; <(558867-2)>* **AS UGLY AS IT GETS: THE VERY BEST OF . . .** [ ] [ ]
– Madman / Neighbor / Cat's in the cradle / Everything about you / Tomorrow's world / God / Busy bee / C.U.S.T. / Milkman's son / N.I.B. / Goddamn devil / Slower than nowhere / Funky fresh country club.

UK SUBS

Formed: London, England . . . Spring '76 by former R&B singer CHARLIE HARPER and guitarist NICKY GARRETT. This hardy punk outfit – completed by PAUL SLACK and PETE DAVIS – made their vinyl debut in early '78 on the various artists LP, 'Farewell To The Roxy' before issuing a debut single on the small 'City' label. Although the band arrived a bit late for the punk party, their subsequent signing to R.C.A. subsidiary, 'Gem', resulted in a string of minor hit singles beginning with the frantic three-chord stomp of 'STRANGLEHOLD' in summer '79. Along with the excellent 'TOMORROW'S GIRLS', the track was featured on debut album, 'ANOTHER KIND OF BLUES' (1979), an amphetamine-fuelled collection of simple but effective hooklines and RAMONES-style lyrics. The following month saw the release of an EP with an unlikely cover of The Zombies' 'SHE'S NOT THERE' as the lead track, the busy schedule continuing apace with the classic 'WARHEAD' single early in 1980. 'BRAND NEW AGE' hit the Top 20 later that year, although its success was outstripped by seminal live set, 'CRASH COURSE'; while the UK SUBS were perhaps a second division outfit in the shadow of The CLASH etc., there was no doubting their onstage power and formidable aura of HARPER in full flight. The record made the Top 10, an all-time best that the 'SUBS would struggle to emulate as their commercial fortunes began to wane in the early 80's. Personnel upheavals dogged the band, SLACK and DAVIS replaced by ALVIN GIBBS and STEVE ROBERTS prior to the band's last charting album, 'DIMINISHED RESPONSIBILITY' (1981). The subsequent departure of co-songwriter GARRETT dealt a blow that the UK SUBS never really recovered from, HARPER continuing to release workmanlike albums such as 'FLOOD OF LIES' (1983) and 'HUNTINGTON BEACH' (1985) to an ever diminishing core of fans. At the dawn of the 90's HARPER was still fronting the latest incarnation of the UK SUBS, 'MAD COW FEVER's hackneyed collection of pub-rock favourites a far cry from the band's late 70's heyday. • **Covered:** SHE'S NOT THERE (Zombies) / I'M WAITING FOR THE MAN (Velvet Underground) / I WALKED WITH A ZOMBIE (13th Floor Elevators) / ROUTE '66 (hit; Nelson Riddle) / BABY PLEASE DON'T GO (hit; Them). • **Trivia:** HARPER had also been part of garage-influenced URBAN DOGS between 1983-85.

Album rating: ANOTHER KIND OF BLUES (*5) / BRAND NEW AGE (*5) / CRASH COURSE (*6) / DIMINISHED RESPONSIBILTY (*5) / ENDANGERED SPECIES (*4) / FLOOD OF LIES (*3) / GROSS OUT U.S.A. (*2) / HUNTINGTON BEACH (*4) / KILLING TIME (*3) / JAPAN TODAY (*3) / IN ACTION: TENTH ANNIVERSARY (*3) / MAD COW FEVER (*3) / NORMAL SERVICE RESUMED (*3) / SCUM OF THE EARTH – THE BEST OF . . . compilation (*6) / OCCUPIED (*3) / QUINTESSENTIALS (*4) / Charlie Harper: STOLEN PROPERTY (*3)

CHARLIE HARPER (b. DAVID CHARLES PEREZ, 25 Apr'44) – vocals, rhythm guitar / **NICKY GARRETT** – lead guitar / **PAUL SLACK** – bass / **PETE DAVIS** – drums

City | not iss.

Dec 78. (7"clear,7"blue,7"green,7"orange,7"red) *(NIK 5)* **C.I.D. / I LIVE IN A CAR / B.I.C.** [ ] [-]
(re-iss. Oct79 on 'Pinnacle'; PIN 22)

Gem-RCA | R.C.A.

Jun 79. (7"red) *(GEMS 5)* **STRANGLEHOLD. / WORLD WAR / ROCKERS** [26] [-]

Aug 79. (7"blue) *(GEMS 10) <PB 11766>* **TOMORROW'S GIRLS. / SCUM OF THE HEART / TELEPHONE NUMBERS** [28] [ ]

Oct 79. (blue-lp) *(GEMLP 100)* **ANOTHER KIND OF BLUES** [21] [ ]
– C.I.D. / I couldn't be you / I live in a car / Tomorrow's girl / Killer / World war / Rockers / I.O.D. / T.V. blues / Lady Esquire / All I wanna know / Crash course / Young criminals / B.I.C. / Disease / Strangleho1d. *(re-iss. Sep91 on 'Abstract' cd/c; AAB CD/TC 801) (cd-iss. Jul95 on 'Dojo'; DOJOCD 226) (cd re-iss. + Jul98 on 'Diabolo'; DIAB 86-2) (<cd re-iss. Mar00 on 'Captain Oi'; AHOYCD 134>)*

Nov 79. (7"green-ep) *(GEMS 14)* **SHE'S NOT THERE / KICKS. / VICTIM / THE SAME THING** [36] [-]

Feb 80. (7"brown) *(GEMS 23)* **WARHEAD. / I'M WAITING FOR THE MAN / THE HARPER** [30] [-]

Apr 80. (clear-lp) *(GEMLP 106)* **BRAND NEW AGE** [18] [-]
– You can't take it anymore / Brand new age / Public servant / Warhead / Barbie's dead / Organised crime / Rat race / Emotional blackmail / Kicks / Teenage / Dirty girls / 500 c.c. / Bomb factory. *(re-iss. Sep91 on 'Abstract' cd/c; AAB CD/TC 802) (cd-iss. Jul95 on 'Dojo'; DOJOCD 228) (<cd re-iss. May00 on 'Captain Oi'; AHOYCD 143>)*

May 80. (7"pink,7"orange) *(GEMS 30)* **TEENAGE. / LEFT FOR DEAD / NEW YORK STATE POLICE** [32] [-]

Sep 80. (purple-lp) *(GEMLP 111)* **CRASH COURSE (live)** [8] [-]
– C.I.D. / I couldn't be you / I live in a car / Tomorrow's girl / Left for dead / Kicks / Rat race / New York state police / Warhead / Public servant / Telephone numbers / Organised crime / Rockers / Brand new age / Dirty girls / The same thing / Crash course / Teenage / Killer / Emotional blackmail. *(w/ free-12") (re-iss. Sep91 on 'Abstract' cd/c; AAB CD/TC 803) (cd-iss. Jul95 on 'Dojo'; DOJOCD 229) (<cd re-iss. Jun00 on 'Captain Oi'; AHOYCD 140>)*

— **ALVIN GIBBS** – bass (ex-USERS, ex-HELLIONS) repl. SLACK

— **STEVE ROBERTS** – drums; repl. DAVIS

Oct 80. (7"yellow) *(GEMS 42)* **PARTY IN PARIS. / FALL OF THE EMPIRE** [37] [-]

Feb 81. (red-lp) *(GEMLP 112)* **DIMINISHED RESPONSIBILITY** [18] [-]
– You don't belong / So what / Confrontation / Fatal / Time and matter / Violent city / Too tired / Party in Paris / Gangster / Face the machine / New order / Just another jungle / Collision cult. *(re-iss. Sep91 on 'Abstract' cd/c; AAB CD/TC 804) (cd-iss. Jul95 on 'Dojo'; DOJOCD 232) (<cd re-iss. Jul00 on 'Captain Oi'; AHOYCD 143>)*

Apr 81. (7"blue) *(GEMS 45)* **KEEP ON RUNNIN' (TILL YOU BURN). / PERFECT GIRL** [41] [-]
(7"ep+=) **KEEP RUNNIN' EP** *(GEMEP 45)* – Ice age / Party in Paris (French version).

NEMS | not iss.

Nov 81. (7") *(NES 304)* **COUNTDOWN. / PLAN OF ACTION** [ ] [-]

— **KIM WYLIE** – drums; repl. ROBERTS who joined CYANIDE then LIGOTAGE

Abstract | not iss.

Oct 82. (7"red-ep) *(ABS 012)* **SHAKE UP THE CITY** [ ] [-]
– Self destruct / Police state / War of the roses.

Oct 82. (red-lp) **ENDANGERED SPECIES** [ ] [-]
– Endangered species / Living dead / Countdown / Ambition / Fear of girls / Lay down and die / Down on the farm / Sensitive boys / Divide by 8, multiply by 5 / Ice age / I robot / Flesh wound. *(re-iss. Jun90 on 'Link'; CLINK 4) (<cd-iss. Dec98 on 'Captain Oi'; AHOYCD 097>)*

— **CHARLIE HARPER** recruited entire new band **CAPTAIN SCARLET** – guitar repl. GARRETT who formed REBEKKA FRAME / **PAUL SLACK** – bass returned to repl. GIBBS who joined URBAN DOGS / **STEVE JONES** – drums repl. WYLIE

Fall Out | not iss.

Aug 83. (7") *(FALL 017)* **ANOTHER TYPICAL CITY. / STILL LIFE** [ ] [-]
(12"+=) *(FALL12 017)* – Veronique.

Oct 83. (lp/c) *(FALL LP/CLP 018)* **FLOOD OF LIES** [ ] [-]

– Flood of lies / Veronique / Soldiers of fortune / Db's / Tampa Bay / After the war / Vilent revolution / In the red / Dress code / Still life / Revenge of the yellow devils / Another typical city / In the wild / Seas. *(cd-iss. 1995; FALLCD 018)*

Sep 84. (12"ep) *(FALL12 024)* **MAGIC / PRIVATE ARMY. / THE SPELL / MULTIPLE MINDS / PRIMARY STRENGTH** ☐ -

— **HARPER** again + new members **JOHN FALLON** – guitar / **JEZZ MONCUR** – bass / **RAB FAE BEITH** – drums (ex-WALL, ex-PATRIK FITZGERALD)

Jan 85. (lp) *(FALLLP 031)* **GROSS OUT U.S.A. (live)** ☐ -
– Intro / Emotional blackmail / New barbarians / In the wild / Veronique / Flood of lies / Warhead / Limo life / Disease / Violent revolution / Soldiers of fortune / Ice-age / Dress code / Telephone numbers / Stranglehold / You don't belong / Party in Paris. *(cd-iss. 1995; FALLCD 031)*

Jun 85. (7"red,7"blue) *(FALL 036)* **THIS GUN SAYS. / SPEAK FOR MYSELF / WANTED** ☐ -

Red Flame | not iss.

Dec 85. (lp/c) *(RFB LP/CA 1)* **HUNTINGTON BEACH** ☐ -
– Rock'n'roll savage / Between the eyes / Suicide taxi / Party animal / The unknown / Miss Tennage USA / Huntington / All the king's horses / Juke box / Sk8 tough / Death row / Bullshitter / Dirty boy / All change for Hollywood / Blinding stories. *(re-iss. Jun90 on 'FM-Revolver' cd/c/lp; REV XD/MC/LP 150) (<cd re-iss. Jun99 on 'Captain Oi'; AHOYCD 114>)*

Apr 86. (7"ep) *(RFBSIN 1)* **LIVE IN HOLLAND – TENTH ANNIVERSARY (live)** ☐ -
– Stranglehold / New barbarians / Tomorrow's girls / Between the eyes.

Apr 86. (lp/c) *(RFB LP/CA 2)* **IN ACTION: TENTH ANNIVERSARY** (compilation) ☐ -
(re-iss. Mar90 on 'FM-Revolver' cd/c/lp; REV XD/MC/LP 142) (cd re-iss. Jul99 on 'Solid Inc.'; CDRNB 001)

Fall Out | New Red Archives

Dec 87. (12") *(FALL12 044)* **HEY SANTA (LEAVE THESE KIDS ALONE). / THUNDERBIRD** ☐ -

Dec 87. (lp) *(FALLLP 045)* **JAPAN TODAY (live)** ☐ -
– Another Cuba / Funk rap / Streets on fire / Sex object / Warzone / Japan inc. / (interview) / Comin' back / Thunderbird / Hey! Santa / Street legal / Captain Scarlett / Skateboard Billy / Surf bastard / Angel. *(cd-iss. Apr93; FALLCD 045)*

Mar 89. (lp/c/cd) *(FALL LP/C/CD 047)* <06> **KILLING TIME** (reunion album) ☐ ☐
– Yellowman / Motivator / Lower East Side / Drag me down / Never say you won't / Magalopolis / Planet I / Killing time / Holy land / American motors / Big Apple / Killing with kindness / Sabre dance / No heart / Fear to go / Nico. *(cd has extra tracks)*

— latest UK SUBS alongside **HARPER** were **ALAN LEE** – guitar / **FLEA DAVE FARRELLY** – bass / **MATTHEW McCOY** – drums

— **DARRELL BARTH** – guitar; repl. LEE

Released Emotions | not iss.

Feb 89. (12"ep) *(REM 004)* **THE MOTIVATOR / COMBAT ZONE / FASCIST REGIME. / AULD LANG SYNE / CYCLE SLUTS FROM HELL** ☐ -

Fall Out | Amsterdamned

Feb 91. (cd/c/lp) *(FALL CD/C/LP 048)* **MAD COW FEVER** ☐ -
– I walked with a zombie / Mandarins of change / Boneyard / Welfare mother / Saints and sinners / Pearl divers / Roadhouse blues / Talkin' 'bout you / Road runner / Route '66 / Pills / Baby please don't go / Last bus boogie / Ecology blues.

— **DAVIS + CAMPBELL** repl. LEE + FARRELLY

Sep 93. (cd/lp) *(FALL CD/LP 050)* **NORMAL SERVICE RESUMED** ☐ -
– Dumfux / Killer time / Jodie Foster / Here comes Alex / Ozone death / Strangeways / Joyride / Believe in yourself / Down on the farm / Mohawk radio / Brixton / Reaper / All the people / Squat the world / Lydia.

Nov 93. (7"ep/cd-ep) *(FALL 051/+CD)* **THE ROAD IS HARD, THE ROAD IS LONG EP** ☐ -
– Jodie Foster / Here comes Alex / Killer time / Another Cuba / Lydia.

Apr 96. (cd/lp) *(FALL CD/LP 052)* <5> **OCCUPIED** ☐ ☐ Mar97
– Let's get drunk / Shove it / DF 118 / Solutions / Public address / Revolving boys / One of the girls / Darkness / Not so secret wars / Infidel / MPRI.

Fall Out | New Red Archives

Apr 97. (cd/lp) *(FALL CD/LP 054)* <69> **QUINTESSENTIALS** ☐ ☐ May97
– Jump on it / Your ego / War on the Pentagon (parts 1 & 2) / Quintessentials / State of alert / The day of the dead / AK47 / Media man / Mouth on a stick / Outside society / Bitter and twisted / Accident prone / Killer cops / Psychosis.

Apr 98. (7"red) *(FALL 056)* **RIOT '98. /** ☐ -

– compilations, etc. –

Jun 82. (c-ep) *Chaos; (LIVE 009)* **LIVE AT GOSSIPS (live)** ☐ -

Oct 82. (blue-lp) *Abstract; (AABT 300)* **RECORDED '79-'81** ☐ -

Apr 84. (lp/c) *Mausoleum; (AMOK/KOMA 788005)* **DEMONSTRATION TAPES** (rare demos) ☐ -

Apr 86. (lp) *Dojo; (DOJOLP 28)* **SUB STANDARDS** ☐ -

Jun 86. (c) *R.O.I.R.; (A 142)* **LEFT FOR DEAD (ALIVE IN HOLLYWOOD)** ☐ -
(cd-iss. Nov94; RE 412CD) (cd re-iss. Nov99; RUSCD 8256)

Jul 86. (lp) *Killerwatt; (KILP 2001)* **RAW MATERIAL** ☐ -

Apr 90. (lp) *Released Emotions;* **GREATEST HITS (LIVE IN PARIS)** ☐ -
(cd-iss. Jun93 on 'Dojo'; DOJOCD 130)

May 91. (blue-lp) *Abstract; (AABT 800)* **THE SINGLES 1978-1982** ☐ -
(cd-iss. Apr93 on 'Get Back'; GBR 001)

Dec 91. (cd) *Streetlink; (STRCD 017)* **DOWN ON THE FARM (A COLLECTION OF THE LESS OBVIOUS)** ☐ -
(re-iss. Apr93 on 'Dojo'; DOJOCD 117)

Mar 92. (cd) *Released Emotions; (REM 012CD)* **EUROPE CALLING** ☐ -
(re-iss. Jul98 on 'Pinhead'; PINCD 101)

May 93. (cd) *Get Back; (BGR 002)* **ANOTHER KIND OF BLUES / CRASH COURSE** ☐ -

May 93. (cd) *Get Back; (BGR 003)* **BRAND NEW AGE / DIMINISHED RESPONSIBILITY** ☐ -

Jun 93. (cd/c) *Optima; (OPTM CD/C 016)* **PUNK AND DISORDERLY** ☐ -

Jul 93. (cd/lp) *Receiver; (RRCD/RRLP 146)* **LIVE AT THE ROXY (live)** ☐ -
(lp re-iss. Jul00 on 'Get Back'; GET 61)

Aug 93. (cd/c) *Music Club; (MCCD/MCTC 120)* **SCUM OF THE EARTH – THE BEST OF THE UK SUBS** ☐ -

Feb 94. (cd) *Loma; (LOMACD 7)* **ENDANGERED SPECIES / HUNTINGTON BEACH** ☐ -

May 95. (cd) *C.A.S.; (CD 43000-2)* **THE PUNK IS BACK** ☐ -

Sep 95. (cd) *Anagram; (CDPUNK 66)* **THE PUNK SINGLES COLLECTION** ☐ -

Jul 96. (cd) *Cleopatra; (<CLP 9703-2>)* **THE PUNK CAN TAKE IT** ☐ ☐

Oct 96. (cd) *Cleopatra; (<CLP 9826-2>)* **SELF DESTRUCT: PUNK CAN TAKE IT VOL.2** ☐ ☐

Nov 96. (4xcd-box) *Abstract; (SUBBOX 1)* **UK SUBS BOX SET** ☐ -

Mar 97. (cd/lp) *Fallout; (FALL CD/LP 53)* **THE PEEL SESSIONS (1978-1979)** ☐ -

Jun 97. (cd) *Anagram; (CDMGRAM 113) / Cleopatra; <9929>* **RIOT** ☐ ☐ Mar97
(re-iss. Mar00; CDPUNK 115)

Jul 98. (cd) *PinHead; (PINCD 101)* **EUROPE CALLING** ☐ -

Oct 98. (cd) *Captain Oi; (<AHOYCD 093>)* **PUNK ROCK RARITIES** ☐ -

Nov 98. (3xcd-box) *Get Back; (GBRBOX 100CD)* **FASCIST REGIME** ☐ -
– (ANOTHER KIND OF BLUES / CRASH COURSE / BRAND NEW AGE / DIMINISHED RESPONSIBILITY / SINGLES 1978-1982)

Mar 99. (cd) *Harry May; (MAYOCD 107)* **WARHEAD** ☐ ☐

May 99. (d-cd) *Fallout; (FALLCD 055)* **SUBMISSION – THE BEST OF UK SUBS 1982-1998** ☐ -

Nov 99. (cd) *Rejected; (REJ 1000024)* **LIVE AT THE WARZONE** ☐ -

Jan 00. (cd) *Metrodome; (METRO 323)* **STRANGLEHOLD** ☐ -

CHARLIE HARPER

Gem | not iss.

Jul 80. (7") *(GEMS 35)* **BARMY LONDON ARMY. / TALK IS CHEAP** 68 -

Ramkup | not iss.

Jul 81. (7") *(CAC 005)* **FREAKED. / JO** ☐ -

Flicknife | not iss.

Feb 82. (lp) *(SHARP 100)* **STOLEN PROPERTY** ☐ -
– Hoochie coochie man / Femme fatale / Hey Joe / Louie Louie / Pills / Light my fire / I'm waiting for the man / etc.

Fall Out | not iss.

Nov 82. (7"; CHARLIE HARPER'S URBAN DOGS) *(FALL 008)* **NEW BARBARIANS. / SPEED KILLS / COCAINE** ☐ -

Mar 83. (7"; CHARLIE HARPER'S URBAN DOGS) *(FALL 011)* **LIMO LIFE. / WARHEAD** ☐ -

ULTRAVIOLENCE

Formed: England ... 1992 by JOHNNY VIOLENT and probably not named after the simiilarly titled DEATH ANGEL album. Following a session with early fan, Radio One DJ, John Peel, VIOLENT signed to EMI subsidiary, 'Food', releasing the 'VENGEANCE' EP in 1992. A sonically uncompromising mash-up of electronic grinding and uranium scraping metal, the appropriately monikered ULTRAVIOLENCE soon found a more suitable home at 'Earache' records. Debuting with the 'I, DESTRUCTOR' EP, JOHNNY/ULTRAVIOLENCE followed up with a full-length album, 'LIFE OF DESTRUCTOR' (1994). Around the same time, he released the interestingly titled 'JOHNNY IS A BASTARD' single under his own name. A second JOHNNY VIOLENT release followed later that year, 'NORTH KOREA GOES BANG!'. After a number of collaborations with various industrial/left-field artists including DUB WAR, a second ULTRAVIOLENCE album, 'PSYCHODRAMA' (1996), still failed to break through to most metallers. • **Covers:** PARANOID (Black Sabbath).

Album rating: LIFE OF DESTRUCTOR (*7) / PSYCHO DRAMA (*5) / KILLING GOD (*5)

JOHNNY VIOLENT – vocals, etc.

Food | not iss.

1992. (ep) **VENGEANCE EP** ☐ -

Earache | Earache

Oct 93. (12"ep/cd-ep) *(MOSH 102 T/CD)* **I, DESTRUCTOR E.P.** ☐ -
– I, destructor / Zeus / Treason. *(remixed by Lenny Dee – Mar94; MOSH 103TR)*

Jun 94. (lp/cd) *(<MOSH 103/+CD>)* **LIFE OF DESTRUCTOR** ☐ ☐ Oct94
– I am destructor / Electric chair / Joan / Hardcore motherfucker / Digital killing / Only love / We will break / Hiroshima / Destructor's fall / Death of a child. *(cd re-iss. Sep97; same)*

Jun 94. (7"; as JOHNNY VIOLENT) *(7MOSH 117)* **JOHNNY IS A BASTARD. / PULL THE TRIGGER** ☐ -

Dec 94. (12"; as JOHNNY VIOLENT) *(MOSH 128T)* **NORTH KOREA GOES BANG! / U.S. INTERVENTION** ☐ -

— made a recording with DUB WAR

Jan 96. (lp/cd) *(<MOSH 142/+CD>)* **PSYCHODRAMA** ☐ ☐
– Birth – Jessica / The reject / Disco boyfriend / Pimp / Psychodrama / Birth hitman / Stone faced / Murder academy / Hitman's heart / Contract / Lovers / Suicide pact / God's mistake / Searching hell / Heaven is oblivion. *(cd re-iss. Sep97; same)*

Jul 97. (12"/cd-s) *(MOSH 148 T/CD)* **HEAVEN IS OBLIVION. / DISCO BOYFRIEND** ☐ ☐
(cd-s) *(MOSH 148CDD)* – ('A'mixes).

Dec 97. (7") *(7MOSH 205)* **STILL. /** ☐ -

Mar 98. (cd) *(MOSH 191CD)* **KILLING GOD** ☐ -
– Dawn / Adultery / Paranoid / Still / Bombs in my head / Facilitator / Masochist / Killing God / Strangled / Horror / Immolation.

Oct 98. (cd-s; split) *(MOSH 218CD)* **PARANOID / Generation X-ed: Industrial Is Dead** ☐ -

ULVER

Formed: Norway ... 1993 by vocalist GARM, who was a member of another black metal outfit ARCTURUS – ulver means wolf in Norwegian. In fact this black metal act incorporated ambient folk and the works of William Blake ('THE MARRIAGE OF HEAVEN AND HELL'), although ULVER's version was completed in 1999 after three other sets, 'BERGTATT' (1995), 'KVELDSSANGER' (1996) and 'NATTENS MADRIGAL: THE MADRIGAL OF NIGHT' (1997). The first of these, 'BERGTATT', was apparently about a Norse tale involving maidens plucked by mountain people, while 'KVELDSSANGER' (aka 'Twilight Songs') was mainly uneasy acoustic doom. Signed to US-based 'Century Media', GARM and his line-up of musicians (HAAVARD, AISMAL, SKOLL and AIWARIKIAR) recorded 'NATTENS MADRIGAL'. The aforementioned ' . . . HEAVEN AND HELL' was completely different to their previous meanderings and featured the talents of SAMOTH and INSAHN (from EMPEROR), FENRIZ (from DARKTHRONE) and some unknown female on vocals. 'METAMORPHOSIS' and 'PERDITION CITY' followed in 1999 and 2001 respectively.

Album rating: BERGTATT (*5) / KVELDSSANGER (*5) / NATTENS MADRIGAL: THE MADRIGAL OF NIGHT (*6) / THEMES FROM WILLIAM BLAKE'S MARRIAGE OF HEAVEN AND HELL (*5) / METAMORPHOSIS (*6) / PERDITION CITY (*6)

GARM (b. RYGG) – vocals (of ARCTURUS) / **HAAVARD** (b. YLWIZAKER) – lead/acoustic guitar / **AISMAL** – rhythm guitar / **SKOLL** – bass / **AIWARIKIAR** – drums

Head Not Found | not iss.

Aug 95. (cd) *(HNF 005CD)* **BERGTATT** [ ] [-]
– I Troldskog faren vild / Soelen gaaer bag Aase need / Graablick blev hun vaer / Een Stemme locker / Bergtatt – ind i Fjeldkamrene. *(re-iss. Aug99; same)*

Feb 96. (cd) *(HNF 014CD)* **KVELDSSANGER** [ ] [-]
– Ostenfor sol og Vestenfor maane / Ord / Hoyfjeldsbilde / Nattleite / Kveldssang / Naturmystikk / A cappella – Sielens sang / Hiertets vee / Kledt i nattens farger / Halling / Utreise / Sofu-or paa allfers lund / Ulvsblakk. *(re-iss. Sep99; same)*

Century Media | Century Media

Mar 97. (cd) *(CM 77158CD) <7858>* **NATTENS MADRIGAL (THE MADRIGAL OF NIGHT)** [ ] [ ]
– Wolf and fear / Wolf and the Devil / Wolf and hatred / Wolf and man / Wolf and the Moon / Wolf and passion / Wolf and destiny / Wolf and the night.

Jester | Jester

Feb 99. (d-cd) *(TRICK 001)* **THEMES FROM WILLIAM BLAKE'S MARRIAGE OF HEAVEN AND HELL** [ ] [ ]
– The argument, plate 2 / Plate 3 / Plate 3, following / The voice of the Devil, plate 4 / Plates 5-6 / A memorable fancy, plates 6-7 / Proverbs of Hell, plates 7-10 / Plate 11 / Intro / A memorable fancy, plates 12-13 / Plate 14 / A memorable fancy, plate 15 / Plates 16-17 // A memorable fancy, plates 17-20 / Intro / Plates 21-22 / A memorable fancy, plates 22-24 / Intro / A song of liberty, plates 25-27.

Nov 99. (cd) *(TRICK 006)* **METAMORPHOSIS** [ ] [ ]
– Of wolves and vibrancy / Gnosis / Limbo central (theme from Perdition City) / Of wolves and withdrawal.

Apr 01. (cd) *(TRICK 007)* **PERDITION CITY** [ ] [ ]
– Lost in moments / Porn piece or the scars of cold kisses / Hallways of always / Tomorrow never knows / The future sound of music / We are the dead / Dead city centres / Catalept / Nowhere – Catastrophe.

UNCLE KRACKER

Born: MATT SHAFER, Detroit, Michigan, USA. Having met and bonded with KID ROCK back in 1987, SHAFER soon became the Rap-Rock superbrat's right hand man and made his vinyl debut via a contribution to ROCK's 1991 album, 'Grits Sandwiches For Breakfast'. He also had a hand in the writing of his sidekick's massive 'DEVIL WITHOUT A CAUSE' opus and generally paved the way for his own solo career. Signed to KID ROCK's 'Atlantic' subsidiary, 'Top Dog', SHAFER – in the guise of UNCLE KRACKER – finally uneashed his own album in the shape of 'DOUBLE WIDE' (2000). A finger lickin' deep fry-up of twangin hang-dog country, shit-kicking hard rock and hick hip-hop with a dollop of Detroit humour, the album was a mite more accessible than his compadres recent outings although that didn't stop KID ROCK and his TWISTED BROWN TUCKER crew making their mark.

Album rating: DOUBLE WIDE (*5)

UNCLE KRACKER – rapping, DJ / with **JIMMIE BONES** – keyboards, vocals / **JASON KRAUSE + KENNY OLSON** – guitar / **MICHAEL BRADFORD** – bass / **STEFANIE EULINBERG** – drums

not iss. | Atlantic

Apr 00. (cd/c) *<83279>* **DOUBLE WIDE** [-] [7]
– Intro / Better days / What 'chu lookin' at? / Follow me / Heaven / Steaks 'n shrimp / Who's your uncle? / Whiskey & Walter / I can, I can, I can / Aces & 8's / You can't take me.

Feb 01. (-) *<radio play>* **FOLLOW ME** [-] [5]

UNCLE SAM

Formed: New York, USA ... 1987 by LARRY MILLAR, the guitarist completing the line-up with DAVID GENTNER, BILL PUROL and JEFF MANN. With such incendiary spiritual forebears as MC5 and The DICTATORS, UNCLE SAM were something of a back to basics boot-in-the-ass for the more intricately ponderous thorough bands of the day. Signed to the independent 'Razor' records, the group debuted with 'HEAVEN OR HOLLYWOOD' and received a resounding thumbs up from the metal press. Like The STOOGES and the The MC5 before them, however, UNCLE SAM's two-fingered genius nearly burned itself out after a follow-up set, 'LETTERS FROM LONDON' (1990). Two years on, they signed to 'Roadrunner', delivering 'WILL WORK FOR FOOD' (1993), before really coming into their own with 'Communique' set, 'FOURTEEN WOMEN, FIFTEEN DAYS', their best so far.

Album rating: HEAVEN OR HOLLYWOOD (*4) / LETTERS FROM LONDON (*5) / WILL WORK FOR FOOD (*4) / FOURTEEN WOMEN, FIFTEEN DAYS (*6)

LARRY MILLAR – guitar / **DAVID GENTNER** – vocals / **BILL PUROL** – bass / **JEFF MANN** – drums

Razor | Skeller

Oct 88. (lp/cd) *(RAZ/+CD 38) <3MC TA3>* **HEAVEN OR HOLLYWOOD** [ ] [ ]
– Live for the day / Don't be shy / Alice D / No reason why / The candyman / Don't you ever / All alone / Peace of mind, piece of body / Under sedation / Heaven or Hollywood. *(cd+=)* – Steppin' stone / Train kept arollin. *(cd re-iss. Nov90 on 'Skeller'; 3MC CD3)*

Dec 90. (12") *(3MT 12)* **WHISKEY SLICK. /** [ ] [ ]

1991. (cd) *<55>* **LETTERS FROM LONDON** [-] [ ]

Roadrunner | Roadrunner

Mar 93. (cd) *(<RR 9080-2>)* **WILL WORK FOR FOOD** [ ] [ ]

Communique | Communique

Nov 93. (cd) *(CMGCD 010) <39>* **FOURTEEN WOMEN . . . FIFTEEN DAYS** [ ] [ ] Sep93
– Long gun / Stripped of innocence / Caretaker / Carnival knowledge / Dirty & Co / Your hotel or mine / Draggin' the coffin / Ever grey / Fallout shelter / Fourteen women . . . fifteen days.

— split after above

UNIDA

Formed: Palm Springs, California, USA ... 1996 as THIRTEEN by JOHN GARCIA, ARTHUR SEAY and MIGUEL 'MIKE' CANCINO. GARCIA had initially started working with the latter two while still a member of SLO BURN, the ill-fated project (their slim legacy amounted to the 'Amusing The Amazing' EP) he'd worked on after the legendary KYUSS split in 1995. With DAVE DINSMORE completing UNIDA's line-up, the rock'n'stoners set about recording a debut EP, 'THE BEST OF WAYNE-GRO'. While this saw the light of day towards the end of '98, a full length set finally arrived in the shape of 'COPING WITH THE URBAN COYOTE' (1999). DINSMORE was subsequently replaced with SCOTT REEDER.

Album rating: split w/ DOZER (*6) / COPING WITH THE URBAN COYOTE (*7)

JOHN GARCIA – vocals / **ARTHUR SEAY** – guitar / **DAVE DINSMORE** – bass / **MIKE CANCINO** – drums

Meteor City | Meteor City

Feb 99. (lp/cd) *(MCY 003/+CD)* **split w/ DOZER** [ ] [ ] Apr99
– Flower girl / Red / Delta Alba plex / Wet pussycat / (others by DOZER).

Man's Ruin | Man's Ruin

Aug 99. (cd/lp) *<(MR 175CD)>* **COPING WITH THE URBAN COYOTE** [ ] [ ]
– Thorn / Black woman / Plastic / Human tornado / If only two / Nervous / Dwarf it / You wish.

— **SCOTT REEDER** – bass; repl. DINSMORE

UNIFIED THEORY (see under ⇒ BLIND MELON)

UNSANE

Formed: New York City, New York, USA ... 1989 by CHRIS SPENCER, PETE SHORES and CHARLIE ONDRAS. This unhinged trio released a couple of obscure 45's, including a one-off for 'Sub Pop', 'VANDAL-X'. However, in June 1992, ONDRAS was found dead after a fatal drug overdose; the posthumous 'SINGLES 89-92' collection hit the shops not long after. The story didn't finish there however, as a willing replacement, VINNY SIGNORELLI filled the drumstool. Early 1994, UNSANE returned with a long-awaited debut album proper, 'TOTAL DESTRUCTION' on 'City Slang', drawing comparisons to fellow noise merchants, NEUROSIS. Although subsequent sets failed to fulfil their early potential, things looked more promising after MTV played their 'SCRAPE' video. In 1997, DAVE CURRAN stood in for the departing SHORES and made his debut on the unfortunately titled album, 'OCCUPATIONAL HAZARD' (1998); earlier that year, SPENCER had been badly beaten up outside an Austrian night club!

Album rating: UNSANE (*5) / THE SINGLES 1989-1992 compilation (*6) / TOTAL DESTRUCTION (*5) / SCATTERED, SMOTHERED AND COVERED (*6) / ATTACK IN JAPAN (*5) / AMREP CHRISTMAS (*5) / OCCUPATIONAL HAZARD (*7)

CHRIS SPENCER – vocals, guitar / **PETE SHORES** – bass / **CHARLIE ONDRAS** – drums

not iss. | unknown

1989. (7") **BURN / THIS TOWN. / URGE TO KILL** [-] [ ]

Sub Pop | Sub Pop

Sep 90. (7",7"cream) *<(SP 76)>* **VANDAL-X. / STREETSWEEPER** [ ] [ ]

City Slang | Matador

Nov 91. (cd/c/lp) *<OLE 009>* **UNSANE** [-] [ ]
– Organ donor / Bath / Maggot / Cracked up / Slag / Exterminator / Vandal-X / HLL / Aza-2000 / Cut / Action man / White hand.

Nov 92. (cd/c/lp) *(EFA 04913CD)* *<OLE 047>* **THE SINGLES 1989-1992 (compilation)** Feb93
– Burn / This town / Urge to kill / Vandal-X / Streetsweeper / Concrete bed / My right / Jungle music / Blood boy / 4-stix / Boost / El mundo. *(cd+=)* – Blood boy.

—— **VINNY SIGNORELLI** – drums (ex-SWANS); repl. ONDRAS who OD'd Jun'92

Jan 94. (cd/lp) *(EFA 04926-2/-1)* *<OLE 070>* **TOTAL DESTRUCTION**
– Body bomb / Straight / Black book / Trench / Dispatched / Throw it away / Broke / Road trip / Wayne / Get away / S.O.S. / 455. *<re-iss. Dec94 on 'Atlantic'; 92306>*

S.P.V. Amphetam. Reptile

Dec 95. (cd) *(SPV 0844578-2)* *<AR 039CD>* **SCATTERED, SMOTHERED AND COVERED**
– Scrape / Alleged / Blame me / Out / Can't see / Get off my back / Blew / Empty cartridge / No loss / Test my faith / Rion / Swim. *(re-iss. Mar99; same)*

Mar 97. (cd) *(SPV 0854591-2)* **ATTACK IN JAPAN** -
– Scrape / Trench / Out / Straight / Streetsweeper / Body bomb / Empty cartridge / Urge to kill / 4 stix / Swim / Exterminator. *(re-iss. Mar98 on 'Z'; ZIKSBB 022)*

Man's Ruin Man's Ruin

Sep 96. (12") *<MR 024>* **SICK. / NO SOUL** -

Jul 97. (cd) *<(MR 069CD)>* **AMREP CHRISTMAS (live)**
– Sick / Straight / Out / No soul / Can't see / Body bomb / Test of faith / Swim / 4 sticks / Empty cartridge / Get off my back / Special guest appearance. *(re-iss. Aug00; same)*

—— **DAVE CURRAN** – bass; repl. SHORES

Runt Relapse

Mar 98. (cd/lp) *(RUNT 22 CD/LP)* *<RR 6976-2>* **OCCUPATIONAL HAZARD** Feb98
– Committed / This plan / Over me / Take in the stray / Stop / Wait to lose / Sick / Hazmat / Smell likes rain / Lead / Humidifier / Scam / Understand. *(cd re-iss. Dec99 on 'Lockjaw'; LJCD 006)*

Mar 98. (7"ep) *(PAN 019)* **ERASE-YER-HEAD #5**
– Committed / No soul / HINT:- Trafics (parts 1-3).
(above issued on 'Pandemonium' and shared with the group, HINT)

– compilations, etc. –

Oct 93. (m-cd) *Strange Fruit; (SFRCD 123) / Matador; <OLE 74>* **PEEL SESSIONS** Sep94
– Organ donor – Streetsweeper – Jungle music / Bath / Broke / Body bomb / HLL / Black book, Vol.II.

UNWOUND

Formed: Tumwater, Olympia, Washington, USA . . . 1990/91 by JUSTIN TROSPER, VERN RUMSEY and BRANDT SANDENO. The earliest release from this post-punk indie noise-rock group was in 1992 when UNWOUND issued two singles for 'Kill Rock Stars' before recording an album. The self-titled album was delayed as drummer SANDENO left the band (subsequently replaced by SARAH LUND), resurfacing in 1995 for the 'Honey Bear' label. By that time, the band had three albums under their belt, the exhilarating 'FAKE TRAIN' (1993), 'NEW PLASTIC IDEAS' (1994) and 'THE FUTURE OF WHAT' (1995). The band's sound came close to something between FUGAZI, SONIC YOUTH and the BUZZCOCKS, while their melodies and structures were put to great effect and the distortion added a raw element to the post-Washington grunge/punk scene. In 1996, the group added 'REPETITION' to their list of albums, releasing their best long-player to date, ~'CHALLENGE FOR A CIVILIZED SOCIETY'. The stand out track on the album was ~'UNTITLED', a startling wig-out that went from hardcore rock to calm sax-laden jazz to violent punk, and all in eight minutes.

Album rating: UNWOUND (*5) / FAKE TRAIN (*5) / NEW PLASTIC IDEAS (*6) / THE FUTURE OF WHAT (*7) / REPETITION (*5) / CHALLENGE FOR A CIVILIZED SOCIETY (*6) / FURTHER LISTENING compilation (*7) / A SINGLE HISTORY 1991-1997 compilation (*6) / LEAVES TURN INSIDE YOU (*7)

JUSTIN TROSPER – vocals, guitar / **VERN RUMSEY** – bass / **BRANDT SANDENO** – drums

—— released a single for 'Gravity' and in '92 recorded an album (see below)

Kill Rock Stars Kill Rock Stars

—— released a few singles for the label

—— (Jul'92) **SARAH LUND** – drums (ex-WITCHYPOO, ex-BELGIAN WAFFLES) repl. SANDENO

Mar 94. (lp/cd) *<(KRS 210/+CD)>* **FAKE TRAIN** Jul93
– Dragnalus / Lucky acid / Nervous energy / Valentine card / Kantina / Were, are and was or is / Honourosis / Pure pan sugar / Gravity slips / Star spangled hell / Ratbite / Feeling real.

Apr 94. (cd/lp) *<(KRS 223 CD/V)>* **NEW PLASTIC IDEAS**
– Entirely different matters / What was wound / Envelope / Hexenzsene / Abstraktions / All soul's day / Usual dosage / Arboretum / Fiction friction.

Jul 95. (cd) *<(KRS 245CD)>* **THE FUTURE OF WHAT** Apr95
– New energy / Demolished / Natural disasters / Re-enact stupid / Equally stupid / Pardon my French / Descension / Accidents on purpose / Petals like bricks / Vern's answer to the masses / Here come the dogs / Disappoint / Swan / Full explanation of answer / Excuse me but pardon my French.

Apr 96. (cd) *<KRS 261CD>* **REPETITION** -
– Message received / Corpse pose / Unauthorized autobiography / Lowest common denominator / Sensible / Lady elect / Fingernails on a chalkboard / Murder movies / Next exit / Devoid / Go to Dallas an take a left / For your entertainment.

Dec 97. (12"ep) *<(KRS 288)>* **THE LIGHT AT THE END OF THE TUNNEL IS A TRAIN / XLNT / UNTITLED 3 + 2**

Jan 98. (lp/cd) *<(KRS 289/+CD)>* **CHALLENGE FOR A CIVILIZED SOCIETY**
– Data / Laugh track / Meets the plastics / The world is flat / Sonata for loudspeakers / Mile me deaf / No tech / Side effects of being tired / Lifetime achievement award / What went wrong. *<(re-iss. Jan99 on 'Matador' cd=/lp+=; OLE 335-2/-1)>* – THE LIGHT AT THE END OF THE TUNNEL IS A TRAIN EP

Matador Matador

Apr 01. (d-cd/d-lp) *<(OLE 469-2/-1)>* **LEAVES TURN INSIDE YOU**
– We invent you / Look a ghost / December / Treachery / Terminus / Demons sing love songs / Off this century / One lick less / Scarlette / October all over / Summer freeze / Radio Gra / Below the salt / Who cares.

– compilations, others, etc. –

Aug 95. (cd/lp) *Honey Bear; <7>* **UNWOUND** (debut) -

May 99. (cd) *Matador; (OLE 341-2)* **FURTHER LISTENING** -
– All soul's day / Corpse pose / You bite my tongue / Here comes the dogs / Envelope / Rising blood / Dragnalus / Equally stupid / Unauthorised autobiography / Arboretum / Valentine card / Kantina / Were, are and was or is / Petals are like bricks / Murder movies / Miserific condition / The kid is gone / Message received / Swan / Hating in D.

Jul 99. (lp) *Lovitt; (LVT 004LP)* **UNWOUND LIVE IN EUROPE (live)** -

Sep 99. (lp/cd) *Kill Rock Stars; <(KRS 345/+CD)>* **A SINGLE HISTORY 1991-1997**
– Mile me deaf / Broken E strings / Totally / MK ultra / Seen not heard / Caterpillar / Miserific condition / Everything is weird / Negated / Said serial / Census / Plight / Stumbling block / Eternalux / New radio hit / The light at the end of the tunnel is a train / Crab nebula.

Mar 01. (12"ep) *Speakerphone; (SIS 2)* **IN LONDON** -
– Hexenzsene / Side effects of being tired / Kantina / Were are and was or is.

URGE

Formed: St. Louis, Missouri, USA . . . 1987 by STEVE EWING and KARK GRABLE, who recruited JERRY LOST and JOHN PESSONI after three self-financed releases, 'BUST ME DAT FORTY' (1989), 'PUTTIN' THE BACKBONE BACK' (1990) and 'MAGICALLY DELICIOUS' (1992), the latter with added trio, saxophonist BILL REITER plus trombonists MATT KWIAKOWSKI and TODD PAINTER. Hip-hop punk/funk-metal/ska taking off from FISHBONE, URGE were all the rage for further long-players, 'RECEIVING THE GIFT OF FLAVOR' (1995) and 'MASTER OF STYLES' (1998). • **Trivia:** NIK HEXXAM added his vox on 'JUMP RIGHT IN'.

Album rating: RECEIVING THE GIFT OF FLAVOR (*5) / MASTER OF STYLES (*6)

STEVE EWING – vocals / **KARL GRABLE** – bass / unknown 2

not iss. PAG

1989. (c) *<PAG 1>* **BUST ME DAT FORTY** -

1990. (c) *<PAG 2>* **PUTTIN' THE BACKBONE BACK** -

—— added **BILL REITER** – saxophone / **MATT KWIATKOWSKI** – trombone / **TODD PAINTER** – trombone, keyboards

1992. (c) *<PAG 3>* **MAGICALLY DELICIOUS** -

—— **JERRY LOST** – guitar; repl. unknown
JOHN PESSONI – drums, vocals; repl. unknown

1993. (cd-s) *<PAG 4>* **FAT BABIES IN THE MIX** -

1995. (cd/c) *<PAG 7>* **RECEIVING THE GIFT OF FLAVOR** -
– Brainless / All washed up / Where do we go / Drunk asshole / Don't ask why / Open all night / Take away / Frying pan / I remember / Damn that shit is good / It's gettin' hectic / Violent opposition / Dirty rat. *<re-iss. Nov96 on 'Epic'; 67783>* *(UK-iss.Feb97 on 'Epic' cd/c; 486674-2/-4)*

Immortal – Epic Immortal – Epic

Apr 98. (cd/c) *<(EK 69152-2/-4)>* **MASTER OF STYLES**
– If I were you / Straight to Hell / Jump right in / S.L.O.B. / Played out / Closer / Gene machine / My apology / Divide and conquer / Identity crisis / Going down / Prayer for rain.

URGE OVERKILL

Formed: Chicago, Illinois, USA . . . 1986 by NATIONAL 'NASH' KATO, EDDIE 'KING' ROESSER and BLACKIE 'BLACK CAESAR' ONASSIS. Naming themselves after a FUNKADELIC track and setting out on a mission to resurrect the cream of 70's kitsch in a post-modern punk style, URGE OVERKILL made their debut in 1987 with the self-financed 'STRANGE, I . . .' EP. Chicago's hip 'Touch & Go' label were alert to the possibilities, snatching them up for a debut album, 'JESUS URGE SUPERSTAR' (1989). AC/DC and CHEAP TRICK were the most common reference points, though all in the best possible taste of course, the lads even indulging in a cover of Jimmy Webb's 'WICHITA LINEMAN' to make sure people got the message. The main criticism was the ropey production, BUTCH VIG making sure that 'AMERICRUISER' (1990) didn't head the same way. Another alternative figurehead, STEVE ALBINI, oversaw the graft on the acclaimed 'SUPERSONIC STORYBOOK' (1991), their partnership subsequently turning sour when the former BIG BLACK man publicly chastised them for their defiant decadence (well, that's if you can call touring Chicago in a horse-drawn carriage sipping aperatifs decadence) and concrete commitment to all things kitsch. A stop-gap mini-set, 'STULL', preceded their signing to 'Geffen', a record that featured their peerless take on Neil Diamond's 'GIRL YOU'LL BE A WOMAN SOON'. Later featured as a key inclusion on the soundtrack to Quentin Tarantino's masterful 'Pulp Fiction', the song was also a UK Top 40 hit in its own right without actually drawing in many moviegoers to the weird and wonderful universe of URGE OVERKILL itself, no doubt the name putting them off! Their first major label release, 'SATURATION' (1993) further distanced them from the harsh extremism of their hometown punk scene, the band benefitting from residual interest in the insurgent grunge movement and scoring two minor UK hit singles. Amid the wave of mid-

90's publicity following the 'Pulp Fiction' success, URGE OVERKILL were inspired to release their most lovable album to date, 'EXIT THE DRAGON' (1995).

Album rating: JESUS URGE SUPERSTAR (*4) / AMERICRUISER (*4) / THE SUPERSONIC STORYBOOK (*6) / STULL mini (*6) / SATURATION (*7) / EXIT THE DRAGON (*8)

NATIONAL 'Nash' KATO (b.31 Dec'65, Grand Forks, North Dakota) – vocals, guitar / **EDDIE 'King' ROESER** (b.17 Jun'69, Litchfield, Minnesota) – bass / **BLACKIE 'Black Caesar' ONASSIS** (b. JOHNNY ROWAN, 27 Aug'67, Chicago) – vocals, drums

not iss. Ruthless

1987. (12"ep) **STRANGE, I . . .** [-] [ ]

Touch & Go Touch & Go

May 89. (lp) <(TGLP 37)> **JESUS URGE SUPERSTAR**
– God Flintstone / Very sad trousers / Your friend is insane / Dump dump dump / Last train to Heaven / The Polaroid doll / Head on / Crown of laffs / Dubbledead / Easter '88 / Wichita lineman / Eggs.

Jun 90. (cd/c/lp) <(TG CD/MC/LP 52)> **AMERICRUISER**
– Ticket to L.A. / Blow chopper / 76 ball / Empire builder / Faroutski / Viceroyce / Out on the airstrip / Smokehouse. *(cd+=)* – JESUS URGE SUPERSTAR

Mar 91. (cd/c/lp) <(TG CD/MC/LP 70)> **THE SUPERSONIC STORYBOOK**
– The kids are insane / The candidate / (Today is) Blackie's birthday / Emmaline / Bionic revolution / What is artane? / Vacation in Tokyo / Henhough: The greatest story ever told / Theme from Navajo.

Roughneck Touch & Go

Jun 92. (m-cd/m-lp) *(NECKM CD/MC 009)* <TG CD/LP 86> **STULL**
– Girl you'll be a woman soon / Stull (part 1) / Stitches / What's this generation coming to / (Now that's) The barclouds / Goodbye to Guyville. *(cd re-iss. Aug96 on 'Nectar'; NTMCD 522)*

Geffen Geffen

Jun 93. (cd/c/lp) <(GED/GEC/GEF 24529)> **SATURATION**
– Sister Havana / Tequilla sundae / Positive bleeding / Back on me / Woman 2 woman / Bottle of fur / Crackbabies / The stalker / Dropout / Erica Kane / Nite and grey / Heaven 90210. *(cd+=)* – Operation: Kissinger.

Aug 93. (7"/c-s) *(GFS/+C 51)* **SISTER HAVANA. / WOMAN 2 WOMAN** [67] [ ]
(12"+=/cd-s+=) *(GFST/+D 51)* – Operation: Kissinger.

Oct 93. (7"red/c-s) *(GFS/+C 57)* **POSITIVE BLEEDING. / NITE AND GREY** [61] [ ]
(12"+=/cd-s+=) *(GFST/+D 57)* – Quality love (Hong Kong demo).

Nov 94. (c-s) *(MCSC 2024)* <54935> **GIRL YOU'LL BE A WOMAN SOON / (track by The Tornadoes)** [37] [59]
(cd-s+=) *(MCSTD 2024)* – (tracks by other artists).
above from the cult Tarantino film, 'Pulp Fiction', on 'M.C.A.'

Aug 95. (cd/c/lp) <(GED/GEC/GEF 24818)> **EXIT THE DRAGON**
– Jaywalkin' / The break / Need some air / Somebody else's body / Honesty files / This is no place / The mistake / Take me / View of the rain / Last night – Tomorrow / Tin foil / Monopoly / And you'll say / Digital black epilogue. *(cd re-iss. Feb98; same)*

— disbanded soon after above

– compilations, etc. –

Jul 95. (d-cd/t-lp) *Edel; (6613 2/1 RAD)* **10 YEARS OF WRECKING** [ ] [-]

URIAH HEEP

Formed: London, England . . . early 1970 by guitarist MICK BOX and vocalist DAVID BYRON, who had both cut their proverbial teeth in mid 60's outfit, The STALKERS (BYRON had also featured in a cover version hits compilation singing alongside REG DWIGHT, er . . . ELTON JOHN!). In 1968, the pair became SPICE, having found musicians PAUL NEWTON (ex-GODS), ROY SHARLAND and ALEX NAPIER. A solitary 45 was issued on 'United Artists', 'WHAT ABOUT THE MUSIC' failing to sell in any substantial quanties, although it has since become very rare. Taking their new moniker, URIAH HEEP, from a character in Dickens' 'David Copperfield' novel, the band enlisted some seasoned musicians, KEN HENSLEY (ex-GODS, ex-TOE FAT) and NIGEL OLLSON (ex-SPENCER DAVIS GROUP, ex-PLASTIC PENNY) to replace ROY SHARLAND and ALEX NAPIER. Now signed to 'Vertigo' and on a hefty diet of hard rock that critics lambasted for allegedly plagiarising LED ZEPPELIN, URIAH HEEP delivered their debut album, 'VERY 'EAVY, VERY 'UMBLE', in 1970. Although this did little to change music press opinions, the record contained at least two gems, 'GYPSY' and a cover of Tim Rose's 'COME AWAY MELINDA'. Drummer KEITH BAKER filled in for the ELTON JOHN bound OLLSON, prior to their follow-up set, 'SALISBURY' (1971), which, like its predecessor sold better in Germany and other parts of Europe. People were beginning to take BYRON's at times, high-pitched warblings seriously, the classic track 'BIRD OF PREY' (which was criminally left off the US version), being a perfect example. Later that year, 'LOOK AT YOURSELF' (on the new 'Bronze' imprint and featuring new drummer, IAN CLARKE) was released to some decent reviews, the celebrated 10 minute plus epic, 'JULY MORNING' (with an outstanding guest synth/keys spot from MANFRED MANN), helping it to touch the UK Top 40, while breaking the US Top 100. A steadier formation was found while recording their fourth album, 'DEMONS AND WIZARDS' (1972), GARY THAIN (ex-KEEF HARTLEY) took over from short-stop, MARK CLARKE (who had replaced NEWTON in November '71), while HENSLEY's old mate, LEE KERSLAKE superseded CLARKE. The results were outstanding, the disc going Top 30 and gold on both sides of the Atlantic, with tracks such as 'THE WIZARD' and 'EASY LIVIN' (also a US Top 40 hit), URIAH HEEP standards. 'THE MAGICIAN'S BIRTHDAY' (1972) did much of the same, lifted from the record, 'SWEET LORRAINE' and 'BLIND EYE' both became minor US favourites. 1973 saw another two gold albums being released, a live one and their first for 'Warner Bros' in the States, 'SWEET FREEDOM', while HENSLEY even found time to release a solo set, 'PROUD WORDS ON A DUSTY SHELF'. Their live disc contained a live rock'n'roll medley, featuring their interpretations of ROLL OVER BEETHOVEN, BLUE SUEDE SHOES, MEAN WOMAN BLUES, HOUND DOG, AT THE HOP and WHOLE LOTTA SHAKIN' GOIN' ON, some of their more discerning fans awaiting 1974's more sombre studio set, 'WONDERWORLD'. A bad period indeed for URIAH HEEP, THAIN was near-fatally electrocuted on stage in Dallas, Texas, subsequently resulting in major conflicts with the manager, Gerry Bron. His personal problems and drug-taking (while recovering from his injuries) led to URIAH HEEP being kept in a state of limbo for some months and after lengthy group discussions, THAIN was finally asked to leave in February '75 (tragically, on the 19th of March, 1976, he died of a drug overdose). Another bloke with considerable talents, JOHN WETTON (ex-KING CRIMSON, ex-FAMILY, ex-ROXY MUSIC etc.), was quickly drafted in to record 'RETURN TO FANTASY' (1975) and although the record hit the UK Top 10, it barely scratched out a Top 100 US placing. HENSLEY delivered a second solo set that year, 'EAGER TO PLEASE'. Appropriately titled, it failed to get off the starting blocks, a thing that could be said of 'HEEP's next album, 'HIGH AND MIGHTY' (1976), which only checked in at No.55 in the British charts. Disillusioned by their lack of success and the sacking of BYRON (he had formed ROUGH DIAMOND), WETTON too decided to jump ship. Their places were filled by vocalist, JOHN LAWTON and bassist more famous to BOWIE fans, TREVOR BOLDER; the 'HEEP that the band had become soldiered on while punk rock in '77 became yet another stumbling block. Subsequent albums (with various comings and goings) 'FIREFLY' (1977), 'INNOCENT VICTIM' (1977), 'FALLEN ANGEL' (1978) and 'CONQUEST' (1980) all failed both commercially and critically. After a break from music in the early 80's, URIAH HEEP returned with a new line-up, BOX enlisting the services of LEE KERSLAKE, PETE GOALBY (vocals), JOHN SINCLAIR (keyboards) and BOB DAISLEY (bass) to complete a comeback album of sorts, 'ABOMINOG', a record that returned them to the charts on both sides of the Atlantic in 1982. Another, 'HEAD FIRST' (1983), showed the rock world they had not given up just yet, in fact, URIAH HEEP are still going strong a decade and a half later, although their output has led to derision from all circles except that of a loyal fanbase in Kerrang!. They even became the first ever heavy-rock act to play in the U.S.S.R. A few years later, the band plucked up some degree of courage in covering a heavy rock version of Argent's 'HOLD YOUR HEAD UP', which became a track on the 1989 set, 'THE RAGING SILENCE'. URIAH HEEP will be best remembered for their "very 'eavy, very 'ard" 70's sound and style, much mimicked by a plethora of 80's rock acts too numerous and risky to mention (apart from SPINAL TAP, maybe). • **Songwriters:** Majority by HENSLEY or BOX/THAIN. In 1976 all members took share of work.

Album rating: VERY 'EAVY . . . VERY 'UMBLE (*5) / SALISBURY (*5) / LOOK AT YOURSELF (*6) / DEMONS AND WIZARDS (*7) / MAGICIAN'S BIRTHDAY (*6) / URIAH HEEP LIVE! (*5) / SWEET FREEDOM (*5) / WONDERWORLD (*5) / RETURN TO FANTASY (*5) / THE BEST OF URIAH HEEP compilation (*7) / HIGH AND MIGHTY (*5) / FIREFLY (*4) / INNOCENT VICTIM (*3) / FALLEN ANGEL (*3) / CONQUEST (*3) / ABOMINOG (*4) / HEAD FIRST (*4) / EQUATOR (*4) / LIVE IN MOSCOW (*3) / RAGING SILENCE (*4) / STILL HEAVY, STILL PROUD (*4) / DIFFERENT WORLD (*4) / SEA OF LIGHT (*4) / SPELLBINDER (*4) / SONIC ORIGAMI (*5) / THE BEST OF URIAH HEEP, VOL.1 compilation (*6) / Ken Hensley: PROUD WORDS ON A DUSTY SHELF (*5) / EAGER TO PLEASE (*4) / FREE SPIRIT (*4) / ANTHOLOGY compilation (*5) / David Byron: TAKE NO PRISONERS (*4)

DAVID BYRON (b.29 Jan'47, Epping, Essex, England) – vocals / **MICK BOX** (b. 8 Jun'47, London, England) – guitar, vocals / **ROY SHARLAND** – organ / **PAUL NEWTON** – bass, vocals / **ALEX NAPIER** – drums

U.A. not iss.

Dec 68. (7"; as SPICE) *(UP 2246)* **WHAT ABOUT THE MUSIC. / IN LOVE** [ ] [-]

— now without SHARLAND who joined ARTHUR BROWN, etc. / added **KEN HENSLEY** (b.24 Aug'45) – keyboards, guitar, vox (ex-GODS, ex-TOE FAT) / **NIGEL OLLSON** – drums (ex-SPENCER DAVIS GROUP, ex-PLASTIC PENNY) repl. NAPIER (on all lp except 2 tracks)

Vertigo Mercury

Jun 70. (lp) *(6360 006)* <61294> **VERY 'EAVY . . . VERY 'UMBLE**
<US-title 'URIAH HEEP'>
– Gypsy / Walking in your shadow / Come away Melinda / Lucy blues / Dreammare / Real turned on / I'll keep on trying / Wake up (set your sights). *(re-iss. 1971 on 'Bronze'; ILPS 9142) (re-iss. Apr77 on 'Bronze'; BRNA 142) (re-iss. Apr86 on 'Castle' lp/c; CLA LP/MC 105) (cd-iss. Dec90;) (re-iss. cd Jan96 on 'Essential'; ESMCD 316)*

Jul 70. (7") <73103> **GYPSY. / REAL TURNED ON** [-] [ ]

Nov 70. (7") <73145> **COME AWAY MELINDA. / WAKE UP (SET YOUR SIGHTS)** [-] [ ]

— **KEITH BAKER** – drums (ex-BAKERLOO) repl. OLLSON who joined ELTON JOHN

Jan 71. (7") <73174> **HIGH PRIESTESS. /** [-] [ ]

Jan 71. (lp) *(6360 028)* <61319> **SALISBURY**
– Bird of prey * / The park / Time to live / Lady in black / High Priestess / Salisbury. *<US copies repl. *, with =)* – Simon the bullet freak. *(re-iss. 1971 on 'Bronze'; ILPS 9152) (re-iss. Jul77 on 'Bronze'; BRNA 152) (re-iss. Apr86 on 'Castle' lp/c; CLA LP/MC 106) (cd-iss. Apr89; CLACD 106) (re-iss. cd Jan96 on 'Essential'; ESMCD 317)*

Mar 71. (7") *(6059 037)* **LADY IN BLACK. / SIMON THE BULLET FREAK** [ ] [-]

— **IAN CLARKE** – drums (ex-CRESSIDA) repl. BAKER

— guest was **MANFRED MANN** – moog synthesizer / keyboards

Bronze Mercury

Nov 71. (lp) *(ILPS 9169) <614>* **LOOK AT YOURSELF** [39] [93] Sep71
– Look at yourself / I wanna be free / July morning / Tears in my eyes / Shadows of grief / What should be done / Love machine. *(re-iss. Apr77; BRNA 169) (re-iss. Apr86 on 'Castle' lp/c; CLA LP/MC 107) (cd-iss. Apr89; CLACD 107) (re-iss. cd Jan96 on 'Essential'; ESMCD 318)*

Dec 71. (7") *(WIP 6111)* **LOOK AT YOURSELF. / SIMON THE BULLET FREAK** [ ] [-]

Dec 71. (7") *<73243>* **LOVE MACHINE. / LOOK AT YOURSELF** [-] [ ]

Feb 72. (7") *<73254>* **I WANNA BE FREE. / WHAT SHOULD BE DONE** [-] [ ]

— (Nov71) **LEE KERSLAKE** – drums, vocals (ex-GODS, ex-TOE FAT) repl. IAN (Feb'72) / **GARY THAIN** (b. New Zealand) – bass, vocals (ex-KEEF HARTLEY) repl. MARK CLARKE (ex-COLOSSEUM to TEMPEST) who had repl. NEWTON (Nov'71)

May 72. (lp) *(ILPS 9193) <630>* **DEMONS AND WIZARDS** [20] [23]
– The wizard / Traveller in time / Easy livin' / Poet's justice / Circle of hands / Rainbow demon / All my life / (a) Paradise – (b) The spell. *(re-iss. Apr77; BRNA 193) (re-iss. Apr86 on 'Castle' lp/c; CLA LP/MC 108) (cd-iss. Apr89; CLACD 108) (re-iss. cd Jan96 on 'Essential'; ESMCD 319) (lp re-iss. Jan97 on 'Original'; ORRLP 003)*

May 72. (7") *<73271>* **THE WIZARD. / WHY** [-] [ ]

Jun 72. (7") *(WIP 6126)* **THE WIZARD. / GYPSY** [ ] [-]

Jul 72. (7") *<73307>* **EASY LIVIN' / ALL MY LIFE** [-] [39]

Aug 72. (7") *(WIP 6140)* **EASY LIVIN'. / WHY** [ ] [-]

Nov 72. (lp) *(ILPS 9213) <652>* **THE MAGICIAN'S BIRTHDAY** [28] [31]
– Sunrise / Spider woman / Blind eye / Echoes in the dark / Rain / Sweet Lorraine / Tales / The magician's birthday. *(re-iss. Jul77; BRNA 213) (re-iss. Apr86 on 'Castle' lp/c; CLA LP/MC 109) (cd-iss. Apr89; CLACD 109) (re-iss. cd Jan96 on 'Essential'; ESMCD 339)*

Jan 73. (7") *<73349>* **BLIND EYE. / SWEET LORRAINE** [-] [97] [91]

May 73. (d-lp) *(ISLD 1) <7503>* **URIAH HEEP LIVE (live)** [23] [37]
– Sunrise / Sweet Lorraine / Traveller in time / Easy livin' / July morning / Tears in my eyes / Gypsy / Circle of hands / Look at yourself / The magician's birthday / Love machine / Rock'n'roll medley:- Roll over Beethoven – Blue suede shoes – Mean woman blues – Hound dog – At the hop – Whole lotta shakin' goin' on. *(re-iss. Apr77; BRSP 1) (cd-iss. Jun96 on 'Essential'; ESMCD 320)*

May 73. (7") *<73406>* **JULY MORNING (live). / TEARS IN MY EYES (live)** [-] [ ]

Bronze Warners

Sep 73. (lp) *(ILPS 9245) <2724>* **SWEET FREEDOM** [18] [33]
– Dreamer / Stealin' / One day / Sweet freedom / If I had the time / Seven stars / Circus / Pilgrim. *(re-iss. Apr77; BRNA 245) (cd-iss. Jan96 on 'Essential'; ESMCD 338)*

May 74. (7") *(BRO 7) <7738>* **STEALIN'. / SUNSHINE** [ ] [91] Oct73

Jun 74. (lp) *(ILPS 9280) <2800>* **WONDERWORLD** [23] [38]
– Wonderworld / Suicidal man / The shadows and the winds / So tired / The easy road / Something or nothing / I won't mind / We got we / Dreams. *(re-iss. Apr77; BRNA 280) (cd-iss. May96 on 'Essential'; ESMCD 380)*

Aug 74. (7") *(BRO 10) <8013>* **SOMETHING OR NOTHING. / WHAT CAN I DO** [ ] [ ]

— **JOHN WETTON** (b.12 Jul'49, Derby, England) – bass, vocals (ex-KING CRIMSON, ex-ROXY MUSIC, ex-FAMILY) repl. THAIN (He died of a drug overdose 19 May'76) Line-up now **BYRON, BOX, HENSLEY, KERSLAKE & WETTON**

Jun 75. (lp) *(ILPS 9335) <2869>* **RETURN TO FANTASY** [7] [85]
– Return to fantasy / Shady lady / Devil's daughter / Beautiful dream / Prima Donna / Your turn to remember / Showdown / Why did you go / A year or a day. *(re-iss. Jul77; BRNA 385) (cd-iss. May96 on 'Essential'; ESMCD 381)*

Jun 75. (7") *<8132>* **PRIMA DONNA. / STEALIN'** [-] [ ]

Jun 75. (7") *(BRO 17)* **PRIMA DONNA. / SHOUT IT OUT** [ ] [-]

May 76. (lp) *(ILPS 9384) <2949>* **HIGH AND MIGHTY** [55] [ ]
– One way or another / Weep in silence / Misty eyes / Midnight / Can't keep a good band down / Woman of the world / Footprints in the snow / Can't stop singing / Make a little love / Confession. *(re-iss. Apr77; BRNA 384) (re-iss. Mar91 on 'Castle' cd/lp; CLA CD/LP 191) (re-mast.Jul97 on 'Essential'; ESMCD 468)*

Jun 76. (7") *(BRO 27)* **ONE WAY OR ANOTHER. / MISTY EYES** [ ] [ ]

— **JOHN LAWTON** – vocals (ex-LUCIFER'S FRIEND) repl. BYRON to ROUGH DIAMOND / **TREVOR BOLDER** – bass (ex-David Bowie's SPIDERS FROM MARS, ex-WISHBONE ASH) repl. WETTON who joined BRYAN FERRY BAND, and later UK and ASIA

Feb 77. (lp) *(ILPS 9483) <3013>* **FIREFLY** [ ] [ ]
– Been away too long / Sympathy / Who needs me / Wise man / The hanging tree / Rollin' on / Do you know / Firefly. *(re-iss. Apr77; BRNA 483) (re-iss. Mar91 on 'Castle' cd/lp; CLA CD/LP 190) (re-mast.Jul97 on 'Essential'; ESMCD 559)*

Apr 77. (7") *(BRO 37)* **WISE MAN. / CRIME OF PASSION** [ ] [-]

Oct 77. (7") *(BRO 47) <8581>* **FREE ME. / MASQUERADE** [ ] [ ]

Nov 77. (lp) *(BRON 504) <3145>* **INNOCENT VICTIM** [ ] [ ]
– Keep on ridin' / Flyin' high / Roller / Free 'n' easy / Illusion / Free me / Cheat 'n' lie / The dance / Choices. *(re-iss. Dec90 on 'Castle' cd/lp; CLA CD/LP 210)*

Bronze Chrysalis

Sep 78. (lp) *(BRNA 512) <1204>* **FALLEN ANGEL** [ ] [ ]
– Woman of the night / Falling in love / One more night (last farewell) / Put your lovin' on me / Come back to me / Whad'ya say / Save it / Love or nothing / I'm alive / Fallen angel. *(re-iss. Feb90 on 'Castle' cd/c/lp; CLA CD/MC/LP 176) (re-mast.Jul97 on 'Essential'; ESMCD 561)*

Oct 78. (7") *(BRO 62)* **COME BACK TO ME. / CHEATER** [ ] [ ]

— **JOHN SLOMAN** – vocals (ex-LONE STAR) repl. LAWTON / **CHRIS SLADE** (b.30 Oct'46) – drums (ex-MANFRED MANN'S EARTH BAND) repl. LEE to OZZY OSBOURNE

Jan 80. (7") *(BRO 88)* **CARRY ON. / BEING HURT** [ ] [-]

Feb 80. (lp/c) *(BRON/+C 524)* **CONQUEST** [ ] [-]
– No return / Imagination / Feelings / Fools / Carry on / Won't have to wait too long / Out on the street / It ain't easy. *(re-iss. Dec90 on 'Castle' cd/lp; CLA CD/LP 208) (re-mast.Aug97 on 'Essential'; ESMCD 570)*

Jun 80. (7") *(BRO 96)* **LOVE STEALER. / NO RETURN** [ ] [ ]

— **GREGG DETCHETT** – keyboards (ex-PULSAR) repl. HENSLEY to solo & BLACKFOOT

Jan 81. (7") *(BRO 112)* **THINK IT OVER. / MY JOANNA NEEDS TUNING** [ ] [-]

— split 1981 when SLOMAN developed a throat infection (he later formed BADLANDS). CHRIS SLADE joined GARY NUMAN then DAVID GILMOUR and later joined The FIRM. DETCHETT later joined MIKE + THE MECHANICS. BOLDER re-joined WISHBONE ASH. Early 1982, URIAH HEEP re-formed with **BOX** bringing back **LEE KERSLAKE** plus new **PETE GOALBY** – vocals (ex-TRAPEZE) / **JOHN SINCLAIR** – keyboards (ex-HEAVY METAL KIDS) / **BOB DAISLEY** – bass (ex-OZZY OSBOURNE, ex-RAINBOW, ex-WIDOWMAKER, etc)

Bronze Mercury

Feb 82. (7"ep) *(BRO 143)* **THE ABOMINATOR JUNIOR EP** [ ] [-]
– On the rebound / Tin soldier / Song of a bitch.

Mar 82. (lp/c) *(BRON/+C 538) <4057>* **ABOMINOG** [34] [56]
– Too scared to run / Chasing shadows / On the rebound / Hot night in a cold town / Running all night (with the lion) / That's the way that it is / Prisoner / Hot persuasion / Sell your soul / Think it over. *(re-iss. Apr86 on 'Castle' lp/c; CLA LP/MC 110) (cd-iss. Apr89; CLACD 110) (re-mast.Aug97 on 'Essential'; ESMCD 571)*

May 82. (7") *(BRO 148)* **THAT'S THE WAY THAT IT IS. / HOT PERSUASION** [ ] [-]

May 82. (7") *<76177>* **THAT'S THE WAY THAT IT IS. / SON OF A BITCH** [-] [ ]

May 83. (lp/c) *(BRON/+C 545) <812313>* **HEAD FIRST** [46] [ ]
– The other side of midnight / Stay on top / Lonely nights / Sweet talk / Love is blind / Roll-overture / Red lights / Rollin' the rock / Straight through the heart / Weekend warriors. *(re-iss. Dec90 on 'Castle' cd/lp; CLA CD/LP 209) (re-mast.Jul97 on 'Essential'; ESMCD 572)*

Jun 83. (7"/7"pic-d) *(BRO/+P 166)* **LONELY NIGHTS. / WEEKEND WARRIORS** [ ] [-]

Aug 83. (7") *(BRO 168)* **STAY ON TOP. / PLAYING FOR TIME** [ ] [-]
(d7"+=) *(BROG 168)* – Gypsy / Easy livin' / Sweet Lorraine / Stealin'.

— **TREVOR BOLDER** – bass returned to repl. DAISLEY

Portrait CBS Assoc.

Mar 85. (7"/7"sha-pic-d) *(TA/WA 6103)* **ROCKERAMA. / BACK STAGE GIRL** [ ] [ ]

Mar 85. (lp) *(PRT 26414)* **EQUATOR** [79] [ ]
– Rockarama / Bad blood / Lost one love / Angel / Holding on / Party time / Poor little rich girl / Skools burnin' / Heartache city / Night of the wolf. *(cd-iss. Feb99 on 'Columbia'; 493339-2)*

May 85. (7"/7"pic-d) *(A/WA 6309)* **POOR LITTLE RICH GIRL. / BAD BLOOD** [ ] [-]

— **BERNIE SHAW** – vocals (ex-GRAND PRIX, ex-PRAYING MANTIS) repl. GOALBY / **PHIL LANZON** – keyboards (ex-GRAND PRIX, etc) repl. SINCLAIR (above 2 now alongside **BOX, BOLDER, KERSLAKE**)

Legacy Legacy-Sony

Jul 88. (lp/c/cd) *(LLP/LLK/LLCD 118) <848811>* **LIVE IN MOSCOW (live)** [ ] [ ]
– Bird of prey / Stealin' / Too scared to run / Corrina / Mister Majestic / The wizard / July morning / Easy livin' / That's the way that it is / Pacific highway. *(cd+=) – Gypsy. (cd re-iss. 1992 on 'Castle'; CLACD 276) (cd re-iss. Mar98 on 'Essential'; ESMCD 611)*

Sep 88. (7") *(LGY 65)* **EASY LIVIN' (live). / CORRINA (live)** [ ] [-]
(12"red+=) *(LGYT 65)* – Gypsy (live).

Apr 89. (7") *(LGY 67)* **HOLD YOUR HEAD UP. / MIRACLE CHILD** [ ] [-]
(12"+=) *(LGYT 67)* – ('A'extended).

Apr 89. (lp/pic-lp/c/cd) *(LLP/LLPPD/LLK/LLCD 120) <848812>* **RAGING SILENCE** [ ] [ ]
– Hold your head up / Blood red roses / Voice on my TV / Rich kid / Cry freedom / Bad bad man / More fool you / When the war is over / Lifeline / Rough justice. *(cd re-iss. Feb93 on 'Castle'; CLACD 277) (cd re-iss. Mar98 on 'Essential'; ESMCD 612)*

Jul 89. (7") *(LGY 101)* **BLOOD RED ROSES. / ROUGH JUSTICE** [ ] [-]
(12"+=) *(LGYT 101)* – Look at yourself.

1990. (cd) *(LLCD 133)* **STILL 'EAVY, STILL PROUD (live)** [-] [-] Swedish
– Gypsy / Lady in black / July morning / Easy livin' / The easy road / Free me / The other side of midnight / Mr Majestic / Rich kid / Blood red roses.

Feb 91. (cd) *(LLCD 137)* **DIFFERENT WORLD** [ ] [-]
– Blood on stone / Which way will the wind blow / All God's children / All for one / Different world / Step by step / Seven days / First touch / One on one / Cross that line / Stand back. *(UK re-iss. 1990's on 'Castle'; CLACD 279) <US-iss.Nov94 on 'Griifin'; 239> (cd re-iss. Mar98 on 'Essential'; ESMCD 614)*

H.T.D. H.T.D.

Apr 95. (cd/c/lp) *(<HTD CD/MC/LP 33>)* **SEA OF LIGHT** [ ] [ ]
– Against the odds / Sweet sugar / Time of revelation / Mistress of all time / Universal wheels / Fear of falling / Spirit of freedom / Logical progression / Love in silence / Words in the distance / Fires of hell / Dream on. *(cd re-iss. Dec96 on 'S.P.V.'; 085-7695-2)*

Oct 95. (cd-s) *(CDHTD 102)* **DREAM ON /** [ ] [-]

S.P.V. Spitfire

Jul 96. (cd) *(0857699-2) <5034>* **SPELLBINDER (live)** [ ] [ ] Jun99
– Devil's daughter / Stealin' / Bad bad man / Rainbow demon / Words in a distance / The wizard / Circle of hands / Gypsy / Look at yourself / Lady in love / Easy livin'.

Eagle Spitfire

Sep 98. (cd) *(EAGCD 043)* **SONIC ORIGAMI** [ ] [ ]
– Between two worlds / I hear voices / Protect little heart / Heartless land / Only the young / In the moment / Question / Change / Shelter from the rain / Everything in life / Across the miles / Feels like / The golden palace / Sweet pretender.

– compilations, etc. –

Nov 75. (lp) *Bronze; (ILPS 9375) / Mercury; <1070>* **THE BEST OF URIAH HEEP** [ ] [ ]
– Gypsy / Bird of prey / July morning / Look at yourself / Easy livin' / The wizard / Sweet Lorraine / Stealin' / Lady in black / Return to fantasy. *(re-iss. Apr77; BRNA 375) (cd-iss. Apr90 on 'Sequel';)*

1983. (12"ep) *Bronze; (HEEP 1)* **EASY LIVIN' / SWEET LORRAINE. / GYPSY / STEALIN'** -
Apr 86. (d-lp/c/cd) *Raw Power; (RAW LP/TC/CD 012)* **ANTHOLOGY** -
1986. (cd) *Legacy; (LLHCD 3003)* **ANTHOLOGY** -
Mar 87. (lp/c/cd) *Raw Power; (RAW LP/MC/CD 030)* **LIVE IN EUROPE 1979 (live)** -
May 88. (d-lp/c/cd) *That's Original; (TFO LP/MC/CD 7)* **LOOK AT YOURSELF / VERY 'EAVY, VERY 'UMBLE** -
1988. (d-lp/c) *Castle; (CCS LP/MC 177)* **THE URIAH HEEP COLLECTION** -
Dec 88. (cd-ep) *Special Edition; (CD 3-16)* **LADY IN BLACK / JULY MORNING / EASY LIVIN'** -
Dec 88. (lp/c/cd) *Castle; (HEEP LP/TC/CD 1)* **LIVE AT SHEPPERTON '74 (live)** -
(re-iss. Dec90 cd/lp; CLA CD/LP 192) (re-mast.Jul97 on 'Essential'; ESMCD 590)
Aug 89. (d-lp/c/cd) *Castle; (CCS LP/MC/CD 226)* **THE COLLECTION** -
Jun 90. (3xcd/5xlp) *Essential; (ESB CD/LP 022)* **TWO DECADES IN ROCK** -
Jul 90. (cd/c) *Raw Power; (RAW CD/MC 041)* **URIAH HEEP LIVE (live)** -
Oct 91. (cd/c) *Elite; (ELITE 020 CD/MC)* **ECHOES IN THE DARK** -
– Echoes in the dark / The wizard / Come away Melinda / Devil's daughter / Hot persuasion / Showdown / I'm alive / Look at yourself / Spider woman / Woman of the night / I want to be free / Gypsy / Sunrise / Bird of prey / Love machine / Lady in black *(re-iss. Sep93; same)*
Nov 91. (cd) *Sequel; (NEXCD 184)* **EXCAVATIONS FROM THE BRONZE AGE** -
Feb 92. (3xcd-box) *Castle; (CLABX 903)* **3 ORIGINALS** -
– (FIREFLY / HEAD FIRST / DEMONS AND WIZARDS)
Jan 95. (cd) *Spectrum; (550 730-2)* **LADY IN BLACK** -
May 95. (cd) *Spectrum; (550 731-2)* **FREE ME** -
Oct 95. (d-cd) *H.T.D.; (CDHTD 561)*
Mar 96. (4xcd-box) *Essential; (ESFCD 298)* **A TIME OF REVELATION – 25 YEARS ON** -
May 96. (cd) *Red Steel; (RMCCD 0193)* **THE LANSDOWNE TAPES** -
Oct 96. (cd) *Essential; (<ESMCD 418>)* **THE BEST OF URIAH HEEP, VOL.1**
Oct 97. (cd) *Essential; (<ESMCD 594>)* **THE BEST OF URIAH HEEP, VOL.2**
May 98. (cd) *King Biscuit; (KBFHCD 008) <88027-2>* **URIAH HEEP IN CONCERT (live)** Jun97
Oct 98. (3xcd-box) *Essential; (ESMBX 306)* **VERY 'EAVY, VERY 'UMBLE / SALISBURY / LOOK AT YOURSELF** -
Oct 98. (3xcd-box) *Essential; (ESMBX 307)* **FIREFLY / INNOCENT VICTIM / FALLEN ANGEL** -
Jan 00. (d-cd) *Essential; (<ESDCD 818>)* **ANTHOLOGY**
Jan 00. (d-cd) *Essential; (<ESDCD 819>)* **LIVE IN EUROPE 1979**
Jan 00. (cd) *Members Edition; (UAE 3089-2)* **URIAH HEEP** -
Jul 00. (cd) *S.P.V.; (31021920)* **SEA OF LIGHT / SPELLBINDER**

KEN HENSLEY

solo while still a member of URIAH HEEP

Bronze Warners

May 73. (lp) *(ILPS 9223)* **PROUD WORDS ON A DUSTY SHELF**
– When evening comes / From time to time / King without a throne / Rain / Proud words / Fortune / Black-hearted lady / Go down / Cold Autumn Sunday / The last time. *(re-iss. Oct77; BRNA 223)*
Jun 73. (7") *<73410>* **WHEN EVENING COMES. / FORTUNE** -
Mar 75. (7") *(BRO 15)* **IN THE MORNING. / WHO WILL SING TO YOU** -
Apr 75. (lp) *(ILPS 9307)* **EAGER TO PLEASE**
– Eager to please / Stargazer / Secret / Through the eyes of a child / Part three / The house on the hill / Winter or summer / Take and take / Longer shadows / In the morning / How shall I know. *(re-iss. Oct77; BRNA 307) (cd-iss. Jun93 on 'Repertoire';)*

— He left URIAH HEEP in 1980 and quickly made another solo album 'FREE SPIRIT' (BRON/+C 533) (cd also on 'Repertoire'. Two 45's were lifted from it 'THE SYSTEM' & 'NO MORE'. 'THE BEST OF KEN HENSLEY' issued Mar90 on 'Sequel' cd/lp; *NEX CD/LP 104)*. In Jun'94, KEN HENSLEY issued new cd 'FROM TIME TO TIME' on 'Red Steel'; *RMCCD 0195)*

– compilations, etc. –

Jan 00. (cd) *Essential; (ESMCD 824)* **ANTHOLOGY**
– When evening comes / From time to time / Proud words on a dusty shelf / Rain / Fortune / Cold Autumn Sunday / How shall I know / Through the eyes of a child / Winter or summer / House on the hill / Part three / When / Woman / New routine / Inside the mystery / Brown eyed boy.

DAVID BYRON

solo + while a URIAH HEEP member

Bronze Warners

Jan 76. (lp) *(ILPS 9824)* **TAKE NO PRISONERS**
– Man full of yesterday / Sweet rock and roll / Steamin' along / Silver white man / Love song / Midnight flyer / Saturday night / Roller coaster / Stop hit me with a white one.

— Later in '76, he split from HEEP to form ROUGH DIAMOND and continued solo. ROUGH DIAMOND made own self-named lp in 1977 for 'Island'.

U.S. BOMBS

Formed: Orange County, California, USA ... mid 90's by extrovert skateboarding hero of the late 70's/early 80's, DWAYNE PETERS. Completing the line-up with KERRY MARTINEZ, CHUCK BRIGGS, STEVE REYNOLDS and ALEX GOMEZ, this basic punk rock outfit (not another one!) released the appallingly titled 'NEVER MIND THE OPENED MINDS' track as a debut single in early '97. After an album proper on the 'Disaster' imprint, they hooked up with hardcore nerve centre 'Epitaph' for the 'WAR BIRTH' long player. Their association with the label subsequently led to the group signing with TIM ARMSTRONG's (RANCID) operation, 'Hellcat'.
• **Covered:** THAT'S LIFE (hit; Frank Sinatra).

Album rating: GARIBALDI GUARD! (*5) / NEVER MIND THE OPENED MINDS mini (*4) / PUT STRENGTH IN FINAL . . . (*5) / WAR BIRTH (*5) / THE WORLD (*6)

DWAYNE PETERS – vocals / **KERRY MARTINEZ** – guitar / **CHUCK BRIGGS** – guitar / **STEVE REYNOLDS** – bass / **ALEX GOMEZ** – drums

Alive Alive

Jan 96. (cd-ep) *<ALIVE 17>* **U.S. BOMBS EP** -
– Go back home / Retreats / U.S. bombs / Call box.
Apr 96. (lp) *<ALIVE 19>* **GARIBALDI GUARD!** -
– Intro / All the bodies / Deadly kiss / Rumble beach / Spaghetti / Bon voyage / Retreads / Monsters / Don't wanna go / Underdog / No love / Go back home / Not alright / Walkin' blind. *(UK-iss.Aug99; same)*
Mar 97. (m-lp/m-cd) *<(ALIVE/+CD 24)>* **NEVER MIND THE OPENED MINDS**
– Sex machine / Ballad of Sid / Slow down / Neverland / Outside / Ballad of Sid (reprise).

Disaster Alive

Jun 97. (cd) *(DIS 1) <ALIVECD 033>* **PUT STRENGTH IN FINAL . . .**
– The way it is / Holly cost / Dime runner / Mob family / World on / Time is loose / Demolition girl / Bubble gum / Academy awards / Just a mess / All the fun / Track rockets.

— **WADE WALSTON** – bass; repl. REYNOLDS

— **CHIP** – drums; repl. GOMEZ

Epitaph Epitaph

Oct 97. (cd/c/lp) *<(80404-2/-4/-1)>* **WAR BIRTH** Sep97
– That's life / Orange crunch / Jaks / War storyville / 12-25 / Outta touch / U.S. of hate / War birth / The hand me downs / Rocks in Memphis / Beetle boot / Her and me / Don't need you / No company town.

not iss. Epitaph

Jun 99. (cd) *<80417>* **THE WORLD** -
– The world / Goin' out / Yanks & Rebs / Bombs not food / Isolated ones / Skater dater / Hobroken dreams / Don't take it back / New approach / Billy club / Checkpoint / 76ixties / Nothin' on us / Joe's tune / In fuck with you / Salute the dead / Madagascar / Not enough.

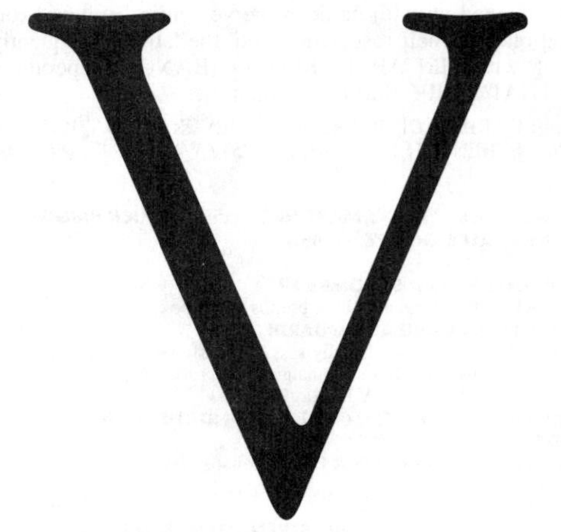

Steve VAI

Born: STEVEN CIRO VAI, 6 Jun'60, Carve Place, Long Island, New Jersey, USA. Taught as a young teenager by the great JOE SATRIANI (his neighbour), he went on to join FRANK ZAPPA's ever-changing band of musicians, playing on albums from 'Tinseltown Rebellion' (1981) to 'Frank Zappa Meets The Mothers Of Prevention' (1986). During a ZAPPA interim (and there's not many of these!), VAI found time to issue a solo album, 'FLEX-ABLE', which, after its initial copies were sold out on the small 'Akashic', went like hotcakes on the larger stable, 'Relativity'. Now much in demand, the superb axeman became part of ALCATRAZZ, briefly replacing YNGWIE MALMSTEEN for one album in '85. During a spell of activity that would even put ZAPPA to shame, the young man played the guitar-grinding Devil in Walter Hill's movie 'Crossroads', while also finding time to lay down all the six-string work for PUBLIC IMAGE LTD.'s 'Album' set. The egocentric DAVID LEE ROTH was the next person to seek out his services, VAI staying and co-writing on two albums, 'Eat 'Em And Smile' (1986) and 'Skyscraper' (1987) before moving on to WHITESNAKE and playing on their 'Slip Of The Tongue' (1989) set. The following year, while still a member of the aforementioned outfit, VAI released his long-awaited follow-up, 'PASSION AND WARFARE', a remarkable and innovative disc which brought delightfully fresh experimentation to the world of guitarslinging hard-rock. Its reviews and his consummate CV ensured it a Top 20 placing on both sides of the Atlantic, marking out VAI, alongside his teacher, SATRIANI as one of the greatest young guitarists in the world. In 1993, he turned his head to more commercially viable roots, his band VAI taking on an old ZAPPA vocalist, TERRY BOZZIO for the album, 'SEX & RELIGION'. Over the course of the next few years, VAI released a few more sets, 'ALIEN LOVE SECRETS' (1995) and 'FIRE GARDEN' (1996), both moderate sellers in Britain. More recently, VAI has turned up on a collaboration live set, '3G' alongside ERIC JOHNSON and who else but JOE SATRIANI.

Album rating: FLEX-ABLE mini (*6) / PASSION AND WARFARE (*7) / SEX & RELIGION (*5) / ALIEN LOVE SECRETS (*5) / FIRE GARDEN (*6) / G3: LIVE IN CONCERT with Joe Satriani & Eric Johnson (*7) / THE ULTRA ZONE (*5)

STEVE VAI – guitar, keyboards, bass, etc.

Music For Nations / Akashic

1984. (lp) *(MFN 31)* **FLEX-ABLE** ☐ ☐
– Little green men / Viva women / Lovers are crazy / The boy / Salamanders in the sun / Girl song / Attitude song / Call it sleep / Junkie / Bill is private parts / Next stop Earth / There's something dead in here. *(re-iss. Sep86 on 'Food For Thought' lp/c; GRUB/TGRUB 3) (cd-iss. 1989; CDGRUB 3) (cd re-iss. Jun97 on 'Relativity-Epic'; 487871-2)*

— now with **DAVE ROSENTHAL** – keyboards / **STU HAMM** – bass / **CHRIS FRAZIER** – drums

Food For Thought / Relativity

May 90. (cd/c/lp) *(CD/C+/GRUB 17) <1037>* **PASSION AND WARFARE** 8 18
– Liberty / Erotic nightmares / The animal / Answers / The riddle / Ballerina 12-24 / For the love of God / The audience is listening / I would love to / Blue powder / Greasy kid's stuff / Alien water kiss / Sisters / Love secrets. *(pic-lp Nov90; GRUB 17P) (re-iss. Oct93 on 'Epic' cd/c; 467109-2/-4)*

— His new band were **TIM STEVENS** – bass / **TERRY BOZZIO** – drums / with **DEVIN TOWNSEND** – vocals / **WILL RILEY** – keyboards / **SCOTT THUNES** – bass / **ABE LABORIEL JR.** – drums

Relativity-Epic / Relativity-Epic

Jul 93. (cd/c/lp; as VAI) *(473947-2/-4/-1) <1132>* **SEX & RELIGION** 17 48
– An earth dweller's return / Here & now / In my dreams with you / Still my bleeding heart / Sex and religion / Dirty black hole / Touching tongues / State of grace / Survive / Pig / The road to Mt.Calvary / Deep down into the pain / Rescue me or bury me.

Aug 93. (12"pic-ep/cd-ep) *(659491-6/-2)* **DEEP DOWN INTO THE PAIN. / JUST CARTILAGE / DEEP DOWN IN THE PAIN (edit)** ☐ ☐

Nov 93. (12"pic-ep/cd-ep) *(659614-6/-2)* **IN MY DREAMS WITH YOU. / EROTIC NIGHTMARES / I WOULD LOVE TO** ☐ ☐

Apr 95. (cd/c) *(478586-2/-4) <1245>* **ALIEN LOVE SECRETS** 39 ☐
– Mad horsie / Juice / Die to live / The boy from Seattle / Ya yo gakk / Kill the guy with the ball – The God eaters / Tender surrender.

Sep 96. (cd/c) *(485062-2/-4)* **FIRE GARDEN** 41 ☐
– There's a fire in my house / Crying machine / Dyin' day / Whookam / Blowfish / Mysterious murder of Christian Tierra's lover / Hand on heart / Bangkok / Fire garden suite / Deepness / Little alligator / All about Eve / Aching burger / Brother / Damn you / When I was a little boy / Genocide / Warm regards.

May 97. (cd/c; shared with JOE SATRIANI & ERIC JOHNSON) *(487539-2/-4)* **G3 LIVE IN CONCERT** (live 2nd November, 1996 at the Northrop Auditorium, Minneapolis) ☐ ☐
– (tracks by JOE SATRIANI) / (tracks by ERIC JOHNSON) / Answers / For the love of God / The attitude song / The jam songs (featuring all 3 G's):- Going down. *(video+=)* – My guitar wants to kill your mama / Red house.

Sep 99. (cd/c) *<69817>* **THE ULTRA ZONE** - ☐
– Blood & tears / The ultra zone / Oooo / Frank / Jiboom / Voodoo acid / Windows to the soul / Silent within / I'll be around / Lucky charms / Fever dream / Here I am / Asian sky.

– compilations, etc. –

Dec 98. (cd) *Relativity; (492858-2)* **FLEX-ABLE LEFTOVERS** ☐ ☐

VAIN

Formed: Bay Area, San Francisco, USA . . . 1987 by DAVY VAIN alongside JAMES SCOTT, DANNY WEST, ASHLEY MITCHELL, TOM RICKARD. The fact that DAVY had produced top Bay Area thrashers, DEATH ANGEL, alone indicated that his group were not yet another bunch of feckless poseurs in the ever expanding glam pack. Snapped up by the ever vigilant 'Island' label, the band launched their career with the compelling 'BEAT THE BULLET' single in the summer of '89. A debut album, 'NO RESPECT' followed soon after, the record kicking into touch most hard rock releases of the day. Despite the ensuing critical acclaim, the group were subsequently dropped by 'Island' after internal changes at the label. After a brief spell in ROAD CREW with GUNS N' ROSES' STEVEN ADLER, DAVY resurrected VAIN for a second release, 'MOVE ON IT' (1993), issued on 'Heavy Metal'.

Album rating: NO RESPECT (*6) / MOVE ON IT (*7) / FADE (*5)

DAVY VAIN – vocals / **JAMES SCOTT** – guitar / **DANNY WEST** – guitar / **ASHLEY MITCHELL** – bass / **TOM RICKARD** – drums

Island / Island

Jul 89. (7"/7"pic-d) *(IS/+P 432)* **BEAT THE BULLET. / SECRETS** ☐ ☐
(12"+=/cd-s+=/3"cd-s+=) *(12IS/CID/CIDX 432)* – Smoke and shadows.

Aug 89. (lp/c/cd) *(ILPS/ICT/CID 9938) <91272>* **NO RESPECT** ☐ ☐
– Secrets / Beat the bullet / Who's watching you / 1000 degrees / Aces / Smoke and shadows / No respect / Laws against love / Down for the 3rd time / Icy / Without you / Ready.

— **DANNY FURY** – drums (ex-KILL CITY DRAGONS) repl. RICKARD

Heavy Metal / Heavy Metal

Sep 94. (cd) *<(HMRXD 194)>* **MOVE ON IT** ☐ ☐
– Breakdown / Whisper / Long time ago / Ivy's dream / Hit & run / Family / Planets turning / Get up / Crumpled glory / Resurrection / Ticket outta here.

Revolver / not iss.

Aug 97. (cd) *(REVXD 216)* **FADE** ☐ ☐
– Holdin' on / Shooting star / Quick step to love / Powder blue / Dee Dee / Languish / Hollow's spin / Voyeurism / Layin' low / Can't get back.

Jackie Rainbow / Jackie Rainbow

Jan 00. (cd; by DAVY VAIN) *<(JR 0001)>* **IN FROM OUT OF NOWHERE** ☐ ☐
– Push me over / Fly again / Yellow / Electric / Come on now / New York / Sugar shack / Trinity / In from out of nowhere / Not your space man / Capsule.

VANDALS

Formed: Los Angeles, California, USA . . . 1982 by STEVO (JENSEN), JAN NILS ACKERMAN, JOE ESCALANTE and STEVE PFAUTER; WARREN FITZGERALD, JOSH FREESE and DAVE QUACKENBRUSH all subsequently passed through their ranks. The VANDALS were stalwarts of the west coast hardcore punk scene, persevering for nearly two decades. Most probably it was the band's good-humored attitude and willingness to make their audience laugh which gave them their endurance. Although their output did veer towards the political, it seldom, if ever, trod the tear-down-the-establishment rantings one thinks of as punk subject matter. It was the boys' willingness to have a good time and put on a good show that kept them in their fans' hearts. Musically the VANDALS have never really turned heads, but they have always done interesting stunts as on the early album 'FEAR OF A PUNK PLANET' (1991) – see further below. It also included one of their more comical masterpieces 'GIRLS TURN 18 EVERYDAY'. The VANDALS moved through successive small labels throughout the 1990's, dropping their parcels of fun on the way. Perhaps their most ludicrous full-length album was their yuletide offering 'CHRISTMAS WITH THE VANDALS: OI TO THE WORLD' (1996), featuring such seasonal numbers as 'CHRISTMAS TIME FOR MY PENIS', turning into hardcore punk's answer to WEIRD AL YANKOVIC. They continued steadily on towards the end of the millennium; setting up their own label 'Kung Fu', two albums being released in quick succession – 'HITLER BAD, VANDALS GOOD' (1998) and ' . . . PLAY

REALLY BAD ORIGINAL COUNTRY TUNES' (1999). The turn of the century saw them touring with among others the slightly more serious PEARL JAM. • **Trivia:** On 1991's comeback set, 'FEAR OF A PUNK PLANET' (a play on words of the PUBLIC ENEMY album!) – a certain KELSEY GRAMMER (aka 'Frazier' in US sitcom 'Cheers'!) narrated some dialogue while DWEEZIL and MOON UNIT (offspring of FRANK ZAPPA) also contributed. • **Covered:** SUMMER LOVIN' (hit from 'Grease') / TEENAGE IDOL (Gary Lewis & The Playboys) / COME OUT FIGHTING (Pennywise; Jason Matthew Thirsk tribute) / etc.

Album rating: PEACE THRU VANDALISM mini (*5) / WHEN IN ROME DO AS THE VANDALS (*6) / SLIPPERY WHEN ILL (*3) / FEAR OF A PUNK PLANET (*4) / SWEATIN' TO THE OLDIES: THE VANDALS LIVE (*3) / LIVE FAST DIARREA (*1) / THE QUICKENING (*4) / CHRISTMAS WITH THE VANDALS: OI TO THE WORLD! er, festive (*2) / HITLER BAD, VANDALS GOOD (*6) / PLAY REALLY BAD ORIGINAL COUNTRY TUNES (*4)

STEVO (JENSEN) – vocals / **JAN NILS ACKERMANN** – guitar / **STEVE PFAUTER** – bass / **JOE ESCALANTE** – drums

not iss. Epitaph

Dec 82. (m-lp) *<VEP 1>* **PEACE THRU VANDALISM** -
– Wanna be manor / Urban struggle / The legend of Pat Brown / Pirate's life / H.B. hotel / Anarchy burger (hold the government).

— **CHALMER LUMARY** – bass, vocals; repl. BRENT TURNER who repl. PFAUTER

Hybrid not iss.

Oct 85. (lp) *(HYBLP 3)* **WHEN IN ROME DO AS THE VANDALS** -
– Ladykiller / Bad birthday bash / Master race (in outer space) / Big brother vs. Johnny Sako / Mohawk town / Viking suit / Hocus pocus / I'm a fly / Slap of luv / Airstream / Rico. *<US-iss.Jan89 on 'Restless' cd/c; 72288-2/-4>* *<re-iss. May92; 72508-2/-4>*

G.W.R. Restless

Feb 89. (lp)<cd/c> *(GWLP 39) <72289-2/-4>* **SLIPPERY WHEN ILL**
– Clowns are experts / Susanville / Desert woman / In America / Elvis decanter / Goop all over the phone / Shi'ite punk / Gator hide / Long hair queer / Lady killa.

— (late 80's) **ESCALANTE** (now on bass) took over control inviting in new members **DAVE QUACKENBUSH** – vocals / **WARREN FITZGERALD** – guitar / **JOSH FREESE** – drums

Roadrunner Restless

Sep 91. (cd/lp) *(RR 9278-2/-1) <72508-2>* **FEAR OF A PUNK PLANET**
– Pizza tran (she delivers) / Rog / Join us for pong / Hey homes! / Girls turn 18 every day / Kill my tenant / Summer lovin' / The day Farrah Fawcett died / Anti / Small wonder / Phone machine. *<(cd re-iss. Jul95 on 'Triple X'; TX 51094CD)>*

Triple X Triple X

Jul 95. (cd) *<(TX 51154CD)>* **SWEATIN' TO THE OLDIES: THE VANDALS LIVE (live)** Nov94
– Anarchy burger (hold the government) / The legend of Pat Brown / Join us for pong / Pizza tran (she delivers) / Master race (in outer space) / Wanna be manor / Mohawk town / Ladykiller / Girls turn 18 every day / Hey homes! / H.B. hotel / Pirate's life / Summer lovin' / Urban struggle / Teenage idol / Goop all over the phone. *(re-iss. Nov99 on 'Kung Fu' cd/c/d-lp; 78771-2/-4/-1)*

Nitro Nitro

Sep 95. (cd/c/lp) *<(15802-2/-4/-1)>* **LIVE FAST DIARREA**
– Let the bad times roll / Take it back / And now we dance / I have a date / Supercalifragilisticexpialidocious / Power moustache / N.I.M.B.Y. / Ape shall never kill ape / Live fast diarrea / Happy birthday to me / Change my pants (I don't wanna) / Get in line / Johnny two bags / Kick me / Soup of the day. *(cd re-iss. Aug99; same)*

Oct 96. (cd/c/lp) *<(15806-2/-4/-1)>* **THE QUICKENING**
– Stop smiling / It's a fact / Marry me / Allah! / Tastes like chicken / (But then) She spoke / How (did this loser get this job) / Hungry for you / Failure is the best revenge / Aging orange / Canine euthanasia / Moving up / (I'll make you) Love me / Choosing your masters / I believe. *(cd re-iss. Aug99; same)*

Oct 96. (cd/c/lp) *<7876-2/-4/-2>* **CHRISTMAS WITH THE VANDALS: OI TO THE WORLD!** (festive!) -
– A gun for Christmas / Grandpa's last Christmas / Thanx for nothing / Oi to the world! / Nothing's going to ruin my holiday / Christmas time for my penis / I don't believe in Santa Claus / My first Xmas as a woman / Dance of the sugarplum fairies / Here I am Lord / C-H-R-I-S-T-M-A-S / Hang myself from the tree. *(UK-iss.Jun98; same as US)*

Dec 96. (7") *<(KFS7 001)>* **split w/ ASSORTED JELLYBEANS**
(above two issued on their own 'Kung Fu' label)

Aug 98. (cd/c/lp) *<(15817-2/-4/-1)>* **HITLER BAD, VANDALS GOOD**
– People that are going to Hell / Cafe 405 / My girlfriend's dead / I know, huh? / Money's not an issue / I've got an ape drape / If the gov't could read my mind / Too much drama / Come out fighting / Euro-barge / F'd up girl / Idea for a movie / OK / So long, farewell. *(cd re-iss. Aug99; same)*

Kung Fu Kung Fu

Oct 99. (cd/c/lp) *<78776-2/-4/-1>* **PLAY REALLY BAD ORIGINAL COUNTRY TUNES** -

– compilations, etc. –

Dec 89. (cd/c) *Restless; <72327-2/-4>* **PEACE THRU VANDALISM / WHEN IN ROME DO AS THE VANDALS** -
<(cd re-iss. Feb99 on 'Time Bomb'; 43503-2)>

VANDENBERG

Formed: Netherlands ... early 80's by ADJE VANDENBERG, who had previously been in the band, TEASER (they released one eponymous BAD COMPANY-esque album in 1978). VANDENBERG resurfaced with his new group, settling for musicians BERT HEERINK, DICK KEMPER and JOS ZOOMER to augment him in the studio, having signed for 'Atco'. Trading in Americanised melodic hard-rock with a distinctly Euro edge, the group also functioned as a platform for ADRIAN's flash-harry guitar mastery. An eponymous debut album was fairly well-received upon its late '82 release, especially in the USA, where the band attracted a core fanbase having scored a Top 40 hit, 'BURNING HEART'. A further two albums followed in the middle of the decade, 'HEADING FOR A STORM' (1984) and 'ALIBI' (1985), although they never quite cut the commercial mustard. The band finally folded 1986 as ADRIAN eventually accepted DAVID COVERDALE's persistent invitations to join WHITESNAKE.

Album rating: Teaser: TEASER (*5) / Vandenberg: VANDENBERG (*5) / HEADING FOR A STORM (*5) / ALIBI (*5) / THE BEST OF VANDENBERG compilation (*6)

TEASER

ADRIAN 'ADJE' VANDENBERG (b. ADJE, 31 Jan'54) – guitar, keyboards / **JOS VELDHUIZEN** – vocals / **PETER VAN EYK** – bass / **NICO DE GOOIJER** – drums

Vertigo not iss.

1978. (lp) *(6413 506)* **TEASER** - - German
– What you need is love / I've sold my soul to rock'n'roll / Ride on train / Don't break my heart / Don't try to change me / I need love / Leave me if you want to / I'm a bad man / It's gonna be alright / Do it to me.

VANDENBERG

ADRIAN VANDENBERG; with **BERT HEERINK** – vocals / **DICK KEMPER** – bass / **JOS ZOOMER** – drums

Atco Atco

Nov 82. (lp) *(K 50904) <90005>* **VANDENBERG** 65
– Your love is in vain / Back on my feet / Wait / Burning heart / Ready for you / Too late / Nothing to lose / Lost in a city / Out in the streets.

Dec 82. (7") *<99947>* **BURNING HEART. / READY FOR YOU** - 39

Jan 84. (lp) *(790 121-1) <90121>* **HEADING FOR A STORM**
– Friday night / Welcome to the club / Time will tell / Different worlds / This is war / I'm on fire / Heading for a storm / Rock on / Waiting for the night.

Feb 84. (7") *<99792>* **FRIDAY NIGHT. /** -

Oct 85. (lp/c) *(790 295-1/-4) <90295>* **ALIBI**
– All the way / Pedal to the metal / Once in a lifetime / Voodoo / Dressed to kill / Fighting against the world / How long / Prelude mortale / Alibi / Kamikaze.

Oct 85. (7") *(B 9610) <99610>* **ONCE IN A LIFETIME. / VOODOO**

— disbanded in 1986 after HEERINK was replaced; ADRIAN VANDENBERG joined WHITESNAKE

– compilations, etc. –

Jun 88. (lp/c/cd) *Atlantic; (790 928-1/-4/-2) / Atco; <90928>* **THE BEST OF VANDENBERG**
– Your love is in vain / Nothing to lose / Rock on / Burning heart / Wait / Welcome to the club / Prelude mortale / Alibi / Different worlds / Pedal to the metal / Fighting against the world.

VANDEN PLAS

Formed: Germany ... 1990 by guitarist STEPHEN LILL, his brother ANDREAS LILL on drums, vocalist ANDY KUNTZ, GUNTER WERNO on keyboards and TORSTEN REICHERT on bass. It is safe to say that VANDEN PLAS are leaders in the world they call progressive metal, comparable to the other dons of this genre DREAM THEATRE, although most defiantly carving out their own style. They showcased this style to huge critical acclaim on their debut album 'COLOUR TEMPLE' (1995). To the uninitiated, this album epitomises the genre in utilising tuneful and complex Prog-rock arrangements with the unmistakable power of metal. With the rock press behind them, VANDEN PLAS were free to manoeuvre a little, and a year on they released their acoustic mini-album 'AcCULT' (1996), a record featuring, among their own material, a cover of Ray Charles' 'GEORGIA ON MY MIND'. VANDEN PLAS took the fans' praise as a green light to experiment and so hit the gas with a return to basics, Prog-rock studio-based album in the shape of 'THE GOD THING' (1997), placing LILL's fretboard mastery against a backdrop of orchestral arrangements. With the rock tabloids firmly behind them, the band came out with the concept album 'FAR FROM GRACE' (1999), each song being a narrative about origins and the quest for the prelapsarian time. Yet to shrug off any sceptics who thought they were studio hermits, the millennium saw them bringing out their first live album 'SPIRIT OF LIVE' (2000), taken from a sold-out concert in Paris' Elysee Montmatre.

Album rating: COLOUR TEMPLE (*5) / AcCULT mini (*3) / THE GOD THING (*6) / FAR OFF GRACE (*5) / SPIRIT OF LIVE (*5)

ANDY KUNTZ – vocals / **STEPHEN LILL** – guitar / **GUNTER WERNO** – keyboards / **TORSTEN REICHERT** – bass / **ANDREAS LILL** – drums

unknown not iss.

Jun 91. (cd-s) **KEEP ON RUNNING** - - German

Mons not iss.

Apr 92. (cd-ep) *(CD 1891)* **FIRE / DAYS OF THUNDER / RIDIN' THE WIND** - - German

Apr 94. (cd) *(10005)* **COLOUR TEMPLE** - - German
– Father / Push / When the wind blows / My crying / Soul survives / Anytime / Judas / Back to me / How many tears.

Aug 94. (cd-s) **AS IST FUR EUCH** - - German
(above was a special single for 1.FC Kaiserslautern)

Dream Circle not iss.

Nov 96. (cd-ep) *(DCD 9629)* **AcCALT** -
– Intro – My crying / Intro – Kayleigh / Father / Georgia on my mind / How many tears / Des hauts, des bas. *(Europe +=)* – Days of thunder / Fire.

S.P.V. Inside Out

Dec 97. (cd) *(SPV 0852857-2)* **THE GOD THING** [ ] [-]
– Fire blossom / Rainmaker / Garden of stones / In you: I believe / The day I die / Crown of thorns / We're not God / Salt in my wounds / You fly / Raing in my heart.

Oct 99. (cd) *(SPV 0853170-2) <2002>* **FAR OFF GRACE** [ ] [ ]
– I can see / Far off grace / Into the sun / Where is the man / Iodic rain / I don't miss you / Inside of your head / Fields of hope / I'm in you / Kiss of death.

Oct 00. (cd) *(SPV 0764135-2) <2018>* **SPIRIT OF LIVE (live)** [ ] [ ]
– I can see / Into the sun / Soul survives / How many tears / Journey to Paris / Spirit of life / Iodic rain / You fly / Far from grace / Rainmaker.

VAN HALEN

Formed: Pasadena, California, USA . . . 1975 by brothers ALEX and EDDIE VAN HALEN. Recruiting blonde-maned high priest of metal cool, DAVE LEE ROTH, and bass player MICHAEL ANTHONY, the quartet initially traded under the MAMMOTH moniker. As VAN HALEN, the group built up a solid reputation as a covers outfit on L.A.'s Sunset Strip, gradually introducing original material into their set. Eventually signed to 'Warners' after being spotted by in-house producer, Ted Templeman, the group released their eponymous debut album in 1977. Coming at a time when hard rock was in seemingly terminal stagnation with punk snapping at its heels, 'VAN HALEN' redefined the boundaries of the genre; from the back cover shot of a shirtless ROTH (chest-wig de rigueur!) sporting leather flares to the opening three chord mash-up of The KINKS' 'YOU REALLY GOT ME', VAN HALEN dripped effortless cool, the golden elixir of sun-bleached Californian coursing through their collective veins. Then there was 'AIN'T TALKIN' 'BOUT LOVE', EDDIE casually reeling off the razor-edged, caterwauling riff (recently resurrected by dance bods, APOLLO FOUR FORTY) while ROTH drawled his most lascivious, sneering drawl. And basically, this was what set VAN HALEN apart from the spandex pack; ROTH actually sang rather than screeching like an asphyxiated budgie, while in EDDIE VAN HALEN, the group boasted one of the most inventive and single-mindedly talented guitarists in the history of metal. O.K., 'ERUPTION' may be responsible for countless fret-wank crimes but it's still impossible not to be impressed by the man's vision, his innovations (flying-fingered hammer-ons, leaving a still smoking cigarette nudged in at the top of the fretboard etc.) becoming base material for any aspiring 80's guitar hero. Essentially, VAN HALEN were glamourous as opposed to glam, and for a few heady years they made heavy metal desirable. Though the debut album barely nudged into the US Top 20, it would go on to sell in excess of five million copies and remains one of THE classic hard-rock releases. A follow-up, 'VAN HALEN II' (1979) didn't pack quite the same punch, although it made the US Top 10 and spawned the group's first hit single, the dreamy 'DANCE THE NIGHT AWAY'. 'WOMEN AND CHILDREN FIRST' (1980) and 'FAIR WARNING' (1981) consolidated the band's standing, both commercially and critically although it wasn't until 'DIVER DOWN' (1982) that VAN HALEN began to cast their net wider. A cover of Roy Orbison's 'PRETTY WOMAN' gave them another US Top 20 hit, the album going Top 5 as a result. The following year, EDDIE famously flashed his fretboard skills on MICHAEL JACKSON's 'Beat It', gaining valuable crossover exposure although by this point, VAN HALEN were already one of the biggest hard rock acts in the world. This was proved with the massive success of the '1984' (released in 1984, funnily enough!) opus and attendant synth-heavy No.1 single, 'JUMP'. For many people, especially in Britain, this was the first time they'd witnessed "Diamond" DAVE in action, the loose-limbed singer, as ever, performing death-defying feats of stage acrobatics in the accompanying video. While the album saw VAN HALEN successfully tackling obligatory 80's experimentation (which did for many of their peers), the likes of 'HOT FOR TEACHER' carried on the grand tradition of tongue-in-cheek lewdness and six-string trickery. Incredibly, at the peak of their success, ROTH buggered off for a solo career, taking his not inconsiderable wit, charisma and sly humour with him. Though VAN HALEN chose to rumble on, it was a rather different beast which reared its head in early '86 with the single, 'WHY CAN'T THIS BE LOVE'. With ex-MONTROSE man, SAMMY HAGAR on vocals, VAN HALEN had created their most consistently accessible and musically ambitious set to date in '5150' (1986), although the absence of ROTH's cheeky innuendo was glaringly obvious. If not gone completely, the group chemistry had been irrevocably altered, in effect, making VAN HALEN just another hard rock band, albeit highly professional and massively successful. '5150' gave the revamped group their first US No.1 album, the record not doing too badly in the UK either. 'OU812' (1988) was another multi-million selling No.1, VAN HALEN now virtually a US institution guaranteed multi-platinum sales with every successive release. 'FOR UNLAWFUL CARNAL KNOWLEDGE' (1991), or 'F.U.C.K.' in its abbreviated form (very clever, lads) saw the group adopt a heavier approach although this didn't prevent it from selling in bucketloads, VAN HALEN holding their own in the age of grunge when many of their contemporaries suddenly seemed embarrassingly outdated. A long overdue live album, 'RIGHT HERE, RIGHT NOW', finally appeared in 1993, while a rare European tour no doubt helped boost UK sales of 'BALANCE' (1995), yet another US No.1 album and their first Top 10 placing in Britain. DAVE LEE ROTH returned during the same year; however after a compilation set in which he appeared on a few new songs, the man departed once more, this time to be replaced by ex-EXTREME frontman, GARY CHERRONE. • **Covered:** FAIR WARNING (Aerosmith) / A POLITICAL BLUES (Little Feat) / WON'T GET FOOLED AGAIN (Who). • **Trivia:** In April '81, EDDIE married actress Valerie Bertinelli.

Album rating: VAN HALEN (*8) / VAN HALEN II (*7) / WOMEN AND CHILDREN FIRST (*7) / FAIR WARNING (*6) / DIVER DOWN (*6) / 1984 (*7) / 5150 (*5) / OU812 (*6) / FOR UNLAWFUL CARNAL KNOWLEDGE (*6) / LIVE: RIGHT HERE, RIGHT NOW (*6) / BALANCE (*5) / THE BEST OF: VOLUME ONE compilation (*8) / VAN HALEN III (*5)

EDDIE VAN HALEN (b.26 Jan'57, Nijmegen, Netherlands) – guitar / **DAVID LEE ROTH** (b.10 Oct'55, Bloomington, Indiana) – vocals / **MICHAEL ANTHONY** (b.20 Jun'55, Chicago, Illinois) – bass / **ALEX VAN HALEN** (b. 8 May'55, Nijmegen) – drums

Warners Warners

Feb 78. (7") *(K 17107) <8515>* **YOU REALLY GOT ME. / ATOMIC ROCK PUNK** [ ] [36] Jan78

Apr 78. (lp/c) *(K/K4 56470) <3075>* **VAN HALEN** [34] [19] Feb78
– Runnin' with the Devil / Eruption / You really got me / Ain't talkin' 'bout love / I'm the one / Jamie's cryin' / Atomic punk / Feel your love tonight / Little dreamer / Ice cream man / On fire. *(cd-iss. Jul86; K2 56470) (cd re-iss. Feb95; K2 56470) (cd re-iss. Jan01; 9362 47737-2)*

Apr 78. (7") *(K 17162) <8556>* **RUNNIN' WITH THE DEVIL. / ERUPTION** [ ] [84]

Jul 78. (7") *<8631>* **JAMIE'S CRYIN'. / I'M THE SAME** [-] [ ]

Sep 78. (7") *<8707>* **AIN'T TALKIN' BOUT LOVE. / FEEL YOUR LOVE TONIGHT** [-] [ ]

Apr 79. (lp/c) *(K/K4 56616) <3312>* **VAN HALEN II** [23] [6]
– You're no good / Dance the night away / Somebody get me a doctor / Bottoms up! / Outta love again / Light up the sky / Spanish fly / D.O.A. / Women in love / Beautiful girls. *(cd-iss. Mar87; K2 56616) (cd re-iss. Jan01; 9362 47738-2)*

May 79. (7"/7"pic-d) *(K 17371/+P) <8823>* **DANCE THE NIGHT AWAY. / OUTTA LOVE AGAIN** [ ] [15] Apr79

Sep 79. (7") *<49035>* **BEAUTIFUL GIRLS. / D. O. A.** [-] [84]

Apr 80. (lp/c) *(K/K4 56793) <3415>* **WOMEN AND CHILDREN FIRST** [15] [6]
– And the cradle will rock . . . / Everybody wants some / Fools / Romeo delight / Tora! Tora! / Loss of control / Take your whiskey home / Could this be magic? / In a simple rhyme. *(cd-iss. Jun89; K 923415-2) (cd re-iss. Jan01; 9362 47739-2)*

Apr 80. (7") *<49501>* **AND THE CRADLE WILL ROCK. / COULD THIS BE MAGIC** [-] [55]

Aug 80. (7") *(K 17645)* **AND THE CRADLE WILL ROCK. / EVERYBODY WANTS SOME!!** [ ] [-]

May 81. (7") *<49751>* **SO THIS IS LOVE. / HEAR ABOUT IT LATER** [-] [ ]

May 81. (lp/c) *(K/K4 56899) <3540>* **FAIR WARNING** [49] [6]
– Mean street / Dirty movies / Sinner's swing / Hear about it later / Unchained / Push comes to shove / So this is love? / Sunday afternoon in the dark / One foot out of the door. *(cd-iss. Jun89; K 923540-2) (cd re-iss. Jan01; 9362 47740-2)*

Feb 82. (7") *(K 17909) <50003>* **(OH) PRETTY WOMAN. / HAPPY TRAILS** [ ] [12] Jan82

May 82. (7") *<29986>* **DANCING IN THE STREET. / THE BULL BUG** [-] [38]

May 82. (lp/c) *(K/K4 57003) <3677>* **DIVER DOWN** [36] [3]
– Where have all the good times gone / Hang 'em high / Cathedral / Secrets / Intruder / (Oh) Pretty woman / Dancing in the street / Little guitars (intro) / Little guitars / Big bad Bill (is sweet William now) / The bull bug / Happy trails. *(cd-iss. Jan84; K2 57003) (cd re-iss. Jan01; 9362 47718-2)*

May 82. (7") *(K 17957)* **DANCING IN THE STREET. / BIG BAD BILL (IS SWEET WILLIAM NOW)** [ ] [-]

Aug 82. (7") *<29929>* **BIG BAD BILL (IS SWEET WILLIAM NOW). / SECRETS** [-] [ ]

Jan 84. (lp/c/cd) *(923985-1/-4/-2) <23985>* **1984 (MCMLXXXIV)** [15] [2]
– 1984 / Jump / Panama / Top Jimmy / Drop dead legs / Hot for teacher / I'll wait / Girl gone bad / House of pain. *(re-iss. cd/c Feb95; same) (cd re-iss. Jan01; 9362 47741-2)*

Jan 84. (7") *<29384>* **JUMP. / HOUSE OF PAIN** [-] [1]

Jan 84. (7") *(W 9384)* **JUMP. / RUNNIN' WITH THE DEVIL** [7] [-]
(12"+=) *(W 9384T)* – House of pain.

Apr 84. (7") *<29307>* **I'LL WAIT. / GIRL GONE BAD** [-] [13]

Apr 84. (7") *(W 9273) <29250>* **PANAMA. / GIRL GONE BAD** [61] [13] Jun84
(12"+=) *(W 9273T)* – Dance the night away.

Jun 84. (7") *(W 9213)* **I'LL WAIT. / DROP DEAD LEGS** [ ] [-]
(12"+=) *(W 9213T)* – And the cradle will rock / (Oh) Pretty woman.

Jun 85. (7") *(W 9199) <29199>* **HOT FOR TEACHER. / LITTLE PREACHER** [ ] [56] Oct84
(12"+=) *(W 9199T)* – Hear about it later.

— (Jun'85) Trimmed to a trio, when DAVID LEE ROTH went solo full-time. Early '86 added **SAMMY HAGAR** (b.13 Oct'47, Monterey, Calif.) – vocals (ex-MONTROSE, ex-Solo Artist)

Mar 86. (7"/7"sha-pic-d/12") *(W 8740/+P/T) <28740>* **WHY CAN'T THIS BE LOVE. / GET UP** [8] [3]

Apr 86. (lp/c)(cd) *(W 5150/+C)(925394-2) <25394>* **5150** [16] [1]
– Good enough / Why can't this be love / Get up / Dreams / Summer nights / Best of both worlds / Love walks in / "5150" / Inside. *(re-iss. cd/c Feb95; same)*

Jun 86. (7"/7"sha-pic-d/12") *(W 8642/+P/T) <28702>* **DREAMS. / INSIDE** [62] [22] May86

Aug 86. (7") *<28626>* **LOVE WALKS IN. / SUMMER NIGHTS** [-] [22]

Oct 86. (7") *<28505>* **BEST OF BOTH WORLDS. / ('A'live)** [-] [ ]

May 88. (7"/12") *(W 7891/+T) <27891>* **BLACK AND BLUE. / APOLITICAL BLUES** [ ] [34]

Jun 88. (lp/c)(cd) *(WX 177/+C)(K 925732-2) <25732>* **OU812** [16] [1]
– Mine all mine / When it's love / A.F.U. (naturally wired) / Cabo wabo / Source of infection / Feels so good / Finish what ya started / Black and blue / Sucker in a 3-piece. *(cd+=)* – Apolitical blues.

Jul 88. (7") *<27827>* **WHEN IT'S LOVE. / CABO WABO** [-] [5]

Jul 88. (7") *(W 7816)* **WHEN IT'S LOVE. / APOLITICAL BLUES** [28] [-]
(12"+=/12"pic-d+=/cd-s+=) *(W 7816 T/TP/CD)* – Why can't this be love.

Sep 88. (7") *<27746>* **FINISH WHAT YA STARTED. / SUCKER IN A 3-PIECE** [-] [13]

Feb 89. (7") *(W 7565) <27565>* **FEELS SO GOOD. / SUCKER IN A 3 PIECE** [63] [35] Jan89
(12"+=/cd-s+=) *(W 7565 T/CD)* – Best of both worlds (live).

Jun 91. (7"/c-s) *(W 0045/+C)* **POUNDCAKE. / PLEASURE DOME** [74] [-]
(12"+=/cd-s+=) *(W 0045 T/CD)* – (interview).

Jul 91. (cd)(lp/c) *(7599 26594-2)(WX 420/+C) <26594>* **FOR UNLAWFUL CARNAL KNOWLEDGE** [12] [1]

– Poundcake / Judgement day / Spanked / Runaround / Pleasure dome / In 'n' out / Man on a mission / The dream is over / Right now / 316 / Top of the world.

Sep 91. (7") *<19151>* **TOP OF THE WORLD. / POUNDCAKE** [-] [27]

Oct 91. (7"/c-s) *(W 0066/+C)* **TOP OF THE WORLD. / IN 'N' OUT** [63] [-]
(cd-s+=) *(W 0066CD)* – Why can't this be love (extended) / When it's love / Dreams.

Feb 92. (c-s,cd-s) *<19059>* **RIGHT NOW / MAN ON A MISSION** [-] [55]

Feb 93. (d-cd/d-c) *<(9362 45198-2/-4)>* **LIVE: RIGHT HERE, RIGHT NOW (live)** [24] [5]
– Poundcake / Judgement day / When it's love / Spanked / Ain't talkin' 'bout love / In'n'out / Dreams / Man on a mission / Ultra bass / Pressure dome – Drum solo / Panama / Love walks in / Runaround/ / Right now / One way to rock / Why can't this be love / Give to love / Finished what ya started / Best of both worlds / 316 / You really got me – Cabo wabo / Won't get fooled again / Jump / Top of the world.

Mar 93. (7"/c-s/cd-s) *(W 0155/+C/CD)* **JUMP (live). / LOVE WALKS IN (live)** [26] [-]
(cd-s+=) *(W 0155CDX)* – Eagles fly (live) / Mine, all mine (live).

Jan 95. (7"purple/c-s) *(W 0280 X/C)* **DON'T TELL ME (WHAT LOVE CAN DO). / BALUCHITHERIUM** [27] [-]
(cd-s+=) *(W 0280CD)* – Why can't this be love (live)/ Poundcake (live)/ Panama (live).
(cd-s) *(W 0280CDX)* – ('A'side)/ Judgement day (live)/ Dreams (live)/ Top of the world (live).

Jan 95. (cd/c/lp) *<(9362 45760-2/-4/-1)>* **BALANCE** [8] [1]
– The seventh seal / Can't stop lovin' you / Don't tell me (what love can do) / Amsterdam / Big fat money / Strung out / Not enough / Aftershock / Doin' time / Baluchitherium / Take me back (deja vu) / Feelin'.

Mar 95. (7"/c-s) *(W 0288/+C)* *<17909>* **CAN'T STOP LOVIN' YOU. / CROSSING OVER** [33] [30]
(cd-s+=) *(W 0288CD)* – Man on a mission / Right now.
(cd-s) *(W 0288CDX)* – ('A'side) / Best of both worlds (live) / One way to rock (live) / When it's love (live).

Jun 95. (c-s) *(W 0302C)* **AMSTERDAM / RUNAROUND (live)** [ ] [-]
(cd-s) *(W 0302CDX)* – ('A'side) / Finish what ya started (live).

Aug 95. (c-s,cd-s) *<17810>* **NOT ENOUGH / AMSTERDAM** [-] [97]

—— **DAVID LEE ROTH** returned on 2 tracks below ('Me Wise Magic' & 'Can't Get This Stuff No More') to repl. HAGAR

Oct 96. (cd/c) *<(9362 46474-2/-4)>* **THE BEST OF: VOLUME ONE** (compilation) [45] [1]

—— ROTH's ego led to the old reunion failing. **GARY CHERONE** (ex-EXTREME) became frontman and co-writer.

Mar 98. (cd/c) *<(9362 46662-2/-4)>* **VAN HALEN III** [43] [4]
– Neworld / Without you / One I want / From afar / Dirty water dog / Once / Fire in the hole / Josephina / Year to the day / Primary / Ballot or the bullet / How many say I.

– others, etc. –

Jun 80. (7") *Atlantic; (HM 10)* **RUNNIN' WITH THE DEVIL. / D.O.A.** [52] [-]

VANILLA FUDGE

Formed: New York City, New York, USA . . . 1965 as The PIGEONS. They became VANILLA FUDGE in late '66, and after their debut at The Village Theater (Fillmore East), they were signed up by 'Atlantic'. Their po-faced, psychedelic-symphonic rock often degenerated into dirty, leaden dirges and VANILLA SLUDGE would've been a more accurate name for this proto-metallic band. Nevertheless, in 1967 they were unique, if nothing else than for their unqualified heaviness and they enjoyed chart success with their first release, a characteristically over the top and drawn out rendition of The SUPREMES' 'YOU KEEP ME HANGIN' ON'. The self-titled debut album followed later that summer and contained similarly overblown and amusing covers, The BEATLES' 'ELEANOR RIGBY' and 'TICKET TO RIDE' among them. Follow-up albums were inconsistent, the band's original material falling woefully short of matching the strength of the covers they'd made their name with and, after the band split in mid '69, TIM BOGERT and CARMINE APPICE formed the short lived CACTUS with RUSTY DAY and JIM McCARTY. Purveying straight-down-the-line hard rock, the band cut three albums, 'CACTUS' (1970), 'ONE WAY. . .OR ANOTHER' (1971) and 'RESTRICTIONS' (1972) before BOGERT and APPICE joined JEFF BECK in the supergroup BECK, BOGERT & APPICE. • **Songwriters:** STEIN or group compositions, with mainly other covers :- BANG BANG (Cher) / SEASON OF THE WITCH (Donovan) / I CAN'T MAKE IT ALONE (Goffin-King) / THE WINDMILLS OF YOUR MIND (Legrand-Bergyan). CACTUS also covered several standards. • **Trivia:** In the summer of '69, they played the Seattle Pop Festival at Woodenville, Washington.

Album rating: VANILLA FUDGE (*7) / THE BEAT GOES ON (*5) / RENAISSANCE (*5) / NEAR THE BEGINNING (*5) / ROCK & ROLL (*4) / Cactus: CACTUS (*5) / ONE WAY . . . OR ANOTHER (*4) / RESTRICTIONS (*3) / 'OT 'N' SWEATY (*3) / Vanilla Fudge: MYSTERY (*3) / THE BEST OF (PSYCHEDELIC SUNDAE) compilation (*7)

MARK STEIN (b.11 Mar'47, Bayonne, New Jersey) – vocals, organ / **VINCE MARTELL** (b.11 Nov'45, Bronx, NY) – guitar, vocals / **TIM BOGERT** (b.27 Aug'44) – bass, vocals / **CARMINE APPICE** (b.15 Dec'46, Staten Island, NY) – drums, vocals

Atlantic Atco

Jun 67. (7") *<6590>* **YOU KEEP ME HANGIN' ON. / COME BY DAY, COME BY NIGHT** [-] [67]
<US re-prom.Jul68, hit No.6>

Jul 67. (7") *(584 123)* *<6590>* **YOU KEEP ME HANGIN' ON. / TAKE ME FOR A LITTLE WHILE** [18] [-]

Sep 67. (lp; mono/stereo) *(587/588 086)* *<33224>* **VANILLA FUDGE** [31] [6]
– Ticket to ride / People get ready / She's not there / Bang bang / Illusions of my childhood – part one / You keep me hanging on / Illusions of my childhood – part two / Take me for a little while / Illusions of my childhood – part three / Eleanor Rigby. *(cd-iss. May93; 7567 90390-2)*

Oct 67. (7") *(584 139)* **ILLUSIONS OF MY CHILDHOOD. / ELEANOR RIGBY** [ ] [-]

Feb 68. (lp; mono/stereo) *(587/588 100)* *<33237>* **THE BEAT GOES ON** [ ] [17]
– Sketch / Variation on a theme from Mozart's Divertimento No.13 in F / Old black Joe / Don't fence me in / 12th Street rag / In the mood / Hound dog / I want to hold your hand – I feel fine – Day tripper – She loves you / The beat goes on / Beethoven's fur Elise and theme from Moonlight Sonata / The beat goes on / Voices in time: – Neville Chamberlain – Winston Churchill – F.D. Roosevelt – Harry S. Truman – John F.Kennedy / Merchant / The game is over / The beat goes on. *(cd-iss. Jun92 & Jul93 on 'Repertoire'+=; RR 4261)* *<(cd re-iss. Nov98 on 'Sundazed'; SC 6142)>*

Apr 68. (7") *(584 179)* *<6554>* **WHERE IS MY MIND?. / THE LOOK OF LOVE** [ ] [73] Jan68

Jun 68. (lp; mono/stereo) *(587/588 110)* *<33244>* **RENAISSANCE** [ ] [20]
– The sky cried – When I was a boy / Thoughts / Paradise / That's what makes a man / The spell that comes after / Faceless people / Season of the witch. *(cd-iss. Jul93 on 'Repertoire'+=; REP 4126)* – You keep me hangin' on (7" version) / Come by day, come by night / People. *<(cd re-iss. Nov98 on 'Sundazed'; SC 6143)>*

Sep 68. (7") *<6616>* **TAKE ME FOR A LITTLE WHILE. / THOUGHTS** [-] [38]

Nov 68. (7") *<6632>* **SEASON OF THE WITCH. / (part 2)** [-] [65]

Atco Atco

Feb 69. (lp) *(228 020)* *<33278>* **NEAR THE BEGINNING** (half studio / half live) [ ] [16]
– Shotgun / Some velvet morning / Where is happiness / Break song. *(cd-iss. Jul93 on 'Repertoire'+=; REP 4127)* – Good good lovin' (unedited) / Shotgun (single version) / People (single version). *<(cd re-iss. Nov98 on 'Sundazed'; SC 6144)>*

Mar 69. (7") *(584 257)* *<6655>* **SHOTGUN. / GOOD GOOD LOVIN'** [ ] [68]

Jun 69. (7") *<6679>* **SOME VELVET MORNING. / PEOPLE** [-] [ ]

Jul 69. (7") *(584 276)* **SOME VELVET MORNING. / THOUGHTS** [ ] [-]

Oct 69. (lp) *(228 029)* *<33303>* **ROCK & ROLL** [ ] [34]
– Need love / Lord in the country / I can't make it alone / Street walking woman / Church bells of St. Martin's / The windmills of your mind / If you gotta make a fool of somebody. *(cd-iss. Jul93 on 'Repertoire'+=; REP 4168)* – Good good lovin' / Shotgun / Where is my mind / Need love (7" version). *<(cd re-iss. Nov98 on 'Sundazed'; SC 6145)>*

Nov 69. (7") *<6703>* **I CAN'T MAKE IT ALONE. / NEED LOVE** [-] [ ]

Jan 70. (7") *<6728>* **LORD IN THE COUNTRY. / THE WINDMILLS OF YOUR MIND** [-] [ ]

—— Had already folded mid '69. STEIN formed BOOMERANG and MARTELL retired.

CACTUS

were formed Feb'70 by **BOGERT & APPICE** with **RUSTY DAY** – vocals, mouth harp (ex-AMBOY DUKES / TED NUGENT) / **JIM McCARTY** – guitar (not of YARDBIRDS)

Atlantic Atco

Jul 70. (lp) *(2400 020)* *<SD 33340>* **CACTUS** [ ] [54]
– Parchman farm / My lady from south of Detroit / Bro. Bill / You can't judge a book by the cover / Let me swim / No need to worry / Oleo / Feel so good. *(cd-iss. Jan96; 7567 80290-2)*

Oct 70. (7") *<6792>* **YOU CAN'T JUDGE A BOOK BY THE COVER. / BRO BILL** [-] [ ]

Mar 71. (7") *<6811>* **LONG TALL SALLY. / ROCK'N'ROLL CHILDREN** [-] [ ]

Jul 71. (lp) *(2400 114)* *<SD 33356>* **ONE WAY . . . OR ANOTHER** [ ] [88] Mar71
– Long tall Sally / Rock out whatever you feel like / Rock'n'roll children / Big mam boogie / Feel so bad / Hometown bust / One way . . .or another.

Sep 71. (7") *<6842>* **TOKEN CHOKIN'. / ALASKA** [-] [ ]

—— (May71) added **DUANE HITCHINGS** – piano

Jan 72. (7") *<6872>* **EVIL. / SWEET SIXTEEN** [-] [ ]

Apr 72. (lp) *(K 40307)* *<SD 33377>* **RESTRICTIONS** [ ] [ ] Nov71
– Restrictions / Token chokin' / Guiltness glider / Evil / Alaska / Sweet sixteen / Bag drag / Mean night in Cleveland. *(cd-iss. Jul93 on 'Repertoire')*

—— **PETE FRENCH** – vocals (ex-ATOMIC ROOSTER) McCARTY and DAY

Oct 72. (lp) *(K 50013)* *<SD 7011>* **'OT & SWEATY** (live/studio) [ ] [ ]
– Swim / Bad mother boogie / Our lil' rock and roll thing / Bad stuff / Bring me down / Bedroom Mazurka / Telling you / Underneath / The arches.

Oct 72. (7") *<6901>* **BAD MOTHER BOOGIE. / BRINGING ME DOWN** [-] [ ]

—— Disbanded and DUANE retained some of name NEW CACTUS BAND issuing an album, 'SON OF CACTUS' and single 'BILLIE GYPSY WOMAN' in 1973. TIM and CARMINE teamed up with JEFF BECK ⇒ in supergroup BECK, BOGERT & APPICE. CARMINE joined MIKE BLOOMFIELD's band KGB in the mid-70's. He later joined ROD STEWART and in the 80's with RICK DERRINGER formed DNA.

VANILLA FUDGE

re-formed originals 1982 and again in 1984.

Atco Atco

Jul 84. (lp/c) *<(90149-1/-4)>* **MYSTERY** [ ] [ ]
– Golden age dreams / Jealousy / Mystery / Under suspicion / It gets stronger / Walk on by / My world is empty / Don't stop now / Hot blood / The stranger.

Jul 84. (7") *<99729>* **MYSTERY. / THE STRANGER** [-] [ ]

—— Folded again, although they briefly got together for Atlantic 40 year bash mid-'88.

– compilations, others, etc. –

1970. (lp; as PIGEONS) *Wand; <687>* **WHILE THE WORLD WAS EATING** [-] [ ]

1974. (lp) *Midi; (MID 0033)* **STAR COLLECTION** [ ] [-]

1982. (lp/c) *Atco; <90006-2>* **GREATEST HITS** [-] [ ]

1991. (cd) *Rhino; <R2 70798>* **VANILLA FUDGE LIVE (live)** [-] [ ]

Mar 93. (cd) *Atlantic; (8122 71154-2)* **THE BEST OF VANILLA FUDGE (PSYCHEDELIC SUNDAE)** [ ] [ ]
– You keep me hangin' on / Where is my mind? / The look of love / Ticket to ride /

Come by day, come by night / Take me for a little while / That's what makes a man / Season of the witch / Shotgun / Thoughts / Faceless people / Good good lovin' / Some velvet morning / I can't make it alone / Lord in the country / Need love / Street walking woman / All in your mind.

Aug 95. (cd) *Atlantic; (7567 90006-2)* **THE BEST OF VANILLA FUDGE** [ ] [-]

Jul 94. (cd/c) *Success;* **YOU KEEP ME HANGIN' ON** [ ] [-]

Jul 96. (cd; CACTUS) *Atlantic; (8122 72411-2)* **CACTOLOGY** [ ] [ ]

VAN ZANT (see under ⇒ • 38 SPECIAL)

VARDIS

Formed: England . . .1979 as QUO VARDIS by guitarist STEVE ZODIAC, alongside ALAN SELWAY and GARY PEARSON. Boogie merchants in the mould of STATUS QUO, albeit harder and heavier, VARDIS were subsequently obliged to drop the QUO part of their name after a one-off single, '100 M.P.H.' on the independent 'Red Ball' imprint. With the adonis-maned ZODIAC as a focal point, the group attracted a sizable fanbase amid the burgeoning NWOBHM scene. Following a second indie single, 'IF I WERE KING', the group were signed to the 'Logo' label. The debut album, also entitled '100 M.P.H.', was a live affair, reflecting the fact that VARDIS were most effective on stage. Live work was clearly the band's bread and butter, VARDIS touring constantly, including gigs with HAWKWIND. A storming heavy bubblegum cover of the latter band's 'SILVER MACHINE' was included on the follow-up album, 'THE WORLD'S INSANE'. As the 80's progressed, however, VARDIS began to lose momentum, founder member SELWAY departing after the eponymous 'QUO VARDIS' (1982). The band battled on with TERRY HORBURY as a replacement, finally calling it a day after the 'VIGILANTE' (1986) album.

Album rating: 100 M.P.H. (*5) / THE WORLD'S INSANE (*6) / QUO VARDIS (*4) / THE LION'S SHARE collection (*4) / VIGILANTE (*4) / THE BEST OF VARDIS compilation (*6) / THE WORLD'S INSANE double comp (*5)

STEVE ZODIAC – vocals, guitar / **ALAN SELWAY** – bass / **GARY PEARSON** – drums

Redball not iss.

Sep 79. (7"ep; as QUO VARDIS) *(RR 017)* **100 MPH** [ ] [-]

Castle not iss.

Apr 80. (7") *(CQUEL 2)* **IF I WERE KING. / OUT OF THE WAY** [ ] [-]

Logo not iss.

Aug 80. (d7") *(VAR 1)* **LET'S GO. / SITUATION NEGATIVE // 100 MPH. / OUT OF THE WAY** [ ] [-]

Oct 80. (lp/c) *(MOGO 4012)* **100 M.P.H.** [ ] [-]
– Out of the way / Move along / The lion's share / Situation negative / Destiny / The loser / Living out of touch / Let's go / 100 m.p.h. / Dirty money / If I were king. *(re-iss. Dec86 on 'Razor'; METALPS 115)*

Nov 80. (7") *(VAR 2)* **TOO MANY PEOPLE. / THE LION'S SHARE** [ ] [-]
(free-7") *(VARFREE 2)* **BLUE ROCK. / I MISS YOU**

Feb 81. (7") *(VAR 3)* **SILVER MACHINE. / COME ON** [ ] [-]

Apr 81. (lp/c) *(LOGO/KLOGO 1026)* **THE WORLD'S INSANE** [ ] [-]
– Power under foot / Money grabber / The world's insane / Blue rock (I miss you) / Silver machine / Police patrol / All you'll ever need / Curse the gods / Love is dead / Steamin' along.

May 81. (7"m) *(VAR 4)* **ALL YOU'LL EVER NEED. / IF I WERE KING / JUMPING JACK FLASH** [ ] [-]

Feb 82. (7") *(GO 408)* **TO BE WITH YOU. / GARY GLITTER (part 1)** [ ] [-]

Mar 82. (lp/c) *(LOGO 1034)* **QUO VARDIS** [ ] [-]
– Do I stand accused? / Where there's mods there's rockers / Please do / Dream with me / Gary Glitter part one / Walking / To be with you / Together tonight / Boogie blitz / The plot to rock the world. *(free-d7"+=) (VARFREE 1)* – SITUATION NEGATIVE. / JEEPSTER // TOO MANY PEOPLE. / STEAMIN'

— **TERRY HORBURY** – bass (ex-DIRTY TRICKS) repl. SELWAY

Big Beat not iss.

Jan 85. (7"/12") *(NS/+T 103)* **STANDING IN THE ROAD. / FREEZING HISTORY** [ ] [-]

Raw Power not iss.

Sep 86. (lp/c) *(RAW LP/TC 022)* **VIGILANTE** [ ] [-]
– Don't mess with the best / Radio rockers / Learn how to shoot straight / All the world's eyes / I wanna be a guitar hero (just for you) / Bad company (the contract) / I must be mad / Wild sound / Radioactive / Running.

— split soon after above. Not to be confused with a dance group who released a 12", 'PAST AND PRESENT'.

– compilations, etc. –

Jul 83. (lp) *Razor; (RAZ 3)* **THE LION'S SHARE** [ ] [-]
– Let's go! / Living out of touch / Move along / Destiny / Too many people / The lion's share / If I were king / Police patrol / Blue rock (I miss you) / Steamin' along / Boogie blitz / Walking.

Sep 97. (cd) *Anagram; (CDMETAL 12)* **THE BEST OF VARDIS** [ ] [-]
– Situation negative / Let's go / 100 mph / Dirty money / If I were king / Destiny / Silver machine / Police patrol / Steamin' along / Blue rock / Jumping Jack Flash / Do I stand accused / Where there's mods there's rockers / Gary Glitter / Together tonight / Boogie blitz / Jeepster / Don't mess with the best / Radio rockers / Bad company.

Aug 00. (d-cd) *Essential; (ESACD 935)* **THE WORLD'S INSANE** (mostly all their work) [ ] [-]

V.A.S.T.

Formed: Humboldt County, California, USA . . . mid-90's, the brainchild of teenage axe-grinder and multi-instrumentalist, JON CROSBY. Initially inspired by classical music, the young CROSBY became engrossed with The BEATLES after meeting a girl called Michelle and subsequently learned to play the famous Lennon/McCartney ditty of the same name. From there it was but a short hop and a jump to METALLICA and JOE SATRIANI, CROSBY duly joining a guitar workshop after moving to San Francisco with his mother. The boss of the local 'Shrapnel' label heard one of his demos and, at the tender age of 13, CROSBY was tipped as a six-string wizard in waiting. He eventually opted for home study over school in order to spend more time on his music, becoming increasingly interested in leftfield electronic/industrial sounds. He first began using the VAST moniker at the age of 16 and earned his initial break a few years later when a local radio station championed his demo. A major label bidding war ensued and CROSBY elected to sign with 'Elektra', releasing his highly acclaimed 'VISUAL AUDIO SENSORY THEATRE' album in 1998 (released in the UK on 'Mushroom' in summer '99). A completely self-realised project, the record's claustrophobic, orchestrated soundscapes were lauded by the likes of METALLICA's LARS ULRICH and won CROSBY fans from across the musical spectrum. With his follow-up, 'MUSIC FOR PEOPLE' (2000), JON took his touring band (THOMAS FROGGATT, STEVE CLARK and JUSTIN COTTA) into the studio although again most of the album was written almost entirely by CROSBY himself. Featuring orchestration from the Bombay Recording Orchestra and utilising flute, trombone, harpsichord etc, alongside the electronics, the album's gothic atmospherics occasionally conjured up TRENT REZNOR's brooding early material while the spectre of The BEATLES circa Sergeant Pepper's hovered obliquely.

Album rating: VISUAL AUDIO SENSORY THEATER (*6) / MUSIC FOR PEOPLE (*6)

JON CROSBY – multi, guitar / with **FRED MAHER** – drums, programming, producer / **JAMES LO** – drums / **ALAN ELLIOTT** – arranger of 18-piece orchestra

Mushroom Elektra

Jul 99. (7") *(MUSH 52S)* **PRETTY WHEN YOU CRY. / PRETTY WHEN YOU CRY (Trailerman electro bump mix)** [ ] [-]
(cd-s+=) *(MUSH 52CDS)* – You (Robert Miles remix).

Jul 99. (cd) *(MUSH 48CD) <62173>* **VISUAL AUDIO SENSORY THEATER** [-] [ ] Apr98
– Here / Touched / Dirty hole / Pretty when you cry / I'm dying / Flames / Temptation / Three doors / Niles edge / Somewhere else to be / (untitled) / You.

Oct 99. (7") *(MUSH 56S)* **TOUCHED. / TOUCHED (Ble Amazon's break the chain vocal mix)** [ ] [-]
(cd-s+=) *(MUSH 56CDS)* – I'm dying (Overdog mix).

— **CROSBY** now with **JUSTIN COTTA** – guitar / **THOMAS FROGGATT** – bass / **STEVE CLARK** – drums

Sep 00. (7") *(MUSH 79S)* **FREE. / TOUCHED** [55] [-]
(cd-s) *(MUSH 79CDS)* – ('A'side) / ('A'-Ben Grosse radio mix) / ('A'-Black Noise remix).
(cd-s) *(MUSH 79CDSX)* – ('A'side / Lady of dreams.

Sep 00. (cd) *(MUSH 03CD) <62511>* **MUSIC FOR PEOPLE** [ ] [ ]
– The last one alive / Free / I don't have anything / The gates of rock'n'roll / What else do I need / Blue / Land of shame / A better place / Song without a name / We will meet again / My TV and you / Lady of dreams.

VELVET VIPER (see under ⇒ ZED YAGO)

VENGEANCE

Formed: Netherlands . . . 1982 by LEON GOEWIE, ARJEN LUCASSEN, OSCAR HOLLERMAN, JAN BIJLSMA and JOHN SNELLS. Snapped up by 'C.B.S.' Holland, the group released an eponymous debut album in late '84, showcasing their stocky brand of US-style hard-rock melodica. The rather amusingly-titled, 'WE HAVE WAYS TO MAKE YOU ROCK' (1986), preceded a full fledged move to 'Epic' worldwide, although such classy albums as 'TAKE IT OR LEAVE IT' and 'ARABIA' (1989) apparently fell through the cracks. Frontman GOEWIE was relaced in mid-1990 with Englishman IAN PARRY, although the group have been conspicuous by their absence from the metal scene for most of the 90's.

Album rating: VENGEANCE (*4) / WE HAVE WAYS TO MAKE YOU ROCK (*3) / TAKE IT OR LEAVE IT (*4) / ARABIA (*5)

LEON GOEWIE – vocals / **ARJEN LUCASSEN** – guitar / **OSCAR HOLLERMAN** – guitar / **JAN BIJLSMA** – bass / **JOHN SNELS** – drums

C.B.S. not iss.

Nov 84. (lp) **VENGEANCE** [-] [-] Dutch
– Down and out / Tonight, tonight / Get out / You took me by surprise / Metal days / Destroyer / Prisoners of the night / On the run / Vengeance.

Sep 86. (lp/c) *(CBS/40 26898)* **WE HAVE WAYS TO MAKE YOU ROCK** [ ] [-]
– She's the woman / Dreamworld / Power of the rock / May Heaven strike me down / I'll come running / Second to none / Only the wind / Love lies bleeding / We shall rock. *(cd-iss. 1988+=; 460651-2)* – Deathride to glory (live) / Down and out (live) / Tonight, tonight (live). *(cd re-iss. Jun98 on 'Pseudonym'; CDP 1054)*

1986. (12"ep) *(127081)* **ONLY THE WIND (live)** [-] [-] German
– Only the wind / Deathride to glory / Down and out / Tonight, tonight.

— **PETER VERSCHUREN** – guitar; repl. HOLLERMAN

Epic not iss.

Feb 88. (7") *(651149-7)* **ROCK'N'ROLL SHOWER. / CODE OF HONOUR** [ ] [-]
(12"+=) *(651149-6)* – Only the wind (special remix) / Deathride to glory (live).

Feb 88. (lp/c) *(460070-1/-4)* **TAKE IT OR LEAVE IT** [ ] [-]
– Take it or leave it / Code of honour / Rock'n'roll shower / Take me to the limit / Engines / Hear me out / Women in the world / Looks of a winner / Ain't gonna take you home.

— **JAN SOMERS** – guitar; repl. PETER

Jun 89. (lp/c) *(463437-1/-4)* **ARABIA** [ ] [-]
– Arabia / Broadway – Hollywood – Beverly Hills / Castles in the air / The best gunfighter in town / Children in the streets / Cry of the sirens / That's the way the story goes / Wallbanger / If lovin' you is wrong / How about tonight. *(d-cd-iss. Jun98 on 'Pseudonym'; CDP 1060)*

— **IAN PARRY** (b.England) – vocals; repl. LEON (before they split)

— VENGEANCE re-formed some time later

Transmission not iss.

Nov 97. (cd) *(TM 011)* **BACK FROM FLIGHT 19** [ ] [-]
– Planet Zilch / Follow a trend / Dreamulator / Darkside of the brain / Loaded gun / She said / Lonely girl / Right to the core / PG 16 / Live or die / Flight 19.

Pseudonym not iss.

May 00. (cd) *(CDP 1071DD)* **WINGS OF AN ARROW** [ ] [-]
– The last of the fallen heroes / Wings of an arrow / Trouble in town / As the last teardrop falls / One 'o' mine / Edge of time / Outta control / Blood money / Outta my head / Funky little lady / Football crazy / Hold on tight / Keepin' up with the Joneses / As the last teardrop falls.

VENOM

Formed: Newcastle, England . . . 1979 by CRONOS (CONRAD LANT), MANTAS (JEFF DUNN) and ABADDON (TONY BRAY). One of the most infamous bands ever to crawl out of the North East, VENOM are widely regarded as being the demonic inspiration for hundreds of scary black metal acts, and may well have instigated the genre. True to their self-proclaimed position as satanic grand masters, VENOM allegedly refused to support anyone, spitting out their debut album, 'WELCOME TO HELL' (1981) without having played one solitary gig. Critics were all the more stunned, then, at its merciless occult assault and proto-thrash fury. Although signed to 'Neat', VENOM made the rest of the NWOBHM acts sound like kindergarten amateurs. When the band did eventually begin playing gigs, they were forced to play halls rather than clubs, their notorious, pyro-happy stage set a mite dangerous for the narrow confines of a small club. VENOM's self-explanatory follow-up set, 'BLACK METAL' (1982) still remains the benchmark against which many Beelzebub-friendly bards compare themselves. By the release of 'AT WAR WITH SATAN' (1983), however, VENOM had begun to take a more considered approach to writing and playing, some fans unhappy that the musical mayhem of old was being compromised (although it did contain the classic 'AAAAARGH!!'). The record even gave the trio some belated chart success, breaking into the UK Top 75. Though the band were still packing in the crowds live, 'POSSESSED' (1985) was another slightly disappointing studio set. MANTAS was upset with the way things were going and finally bailed out after the double concert set, 'EINE KLEINE NACHTMUSIK' (1986). MIKE H and JIM C were recruited in his place, the revamped line-up recording a further two albums, 'CALM BEFORE THE STORM' (1987) and 'PRIME EVIL' (1989). Although MANTAS finally returned at the end of the decade, it was clear VENOM were now a pale shadow of the infernally inclined thrash/death bands they'd helped to spawn. To make things worse, CRONOS then departed to form his own outfit, a lightweight affair miles away from the original VENOM ethos. Recruiting TONY 'THE DEMOLITION MAN' DOLAN as a replacement frontman, the increasingly moribund black metallers stumbled on for a further three albums, finally laying the beast to rest after the 1992 set, 'THE WASTE LANDS'.

Album rating: WELCOME TO HELL (*7) / BLACK METAL (*7) / AT WAR WITH SATAN (*6) / POSSESSED (*5) / EINE KLEINE NACHTMUSIK (*4) / THE SINGLES '80-'86 compilation (*6) / CALM BEFORE THE STORM (*5) / PRIME EVIL (*5) / TEAR YOUR SOUL APART mini (*4) / TEMPLES OF ICE (*4) / THE WASTE LANDS (*4) / CAST IN STONE (*5) / IN MEMORIUM – THE BEST OF VENOM compilation (*5) / Mantas: WINDS OF CHANGE (*5)

CRONOS (b. CONRAD LANT) – vocals, bass / **MANTAS** (b. JEFF DUNN) – guitar / **ABADDON** (b. TONY BRAY) – drums

Neat Combat

Jan 81. (lp) *(NEAT 1002)* **WELCOME TO HELL** [ ] [-]
– Sons of Satan / Welcome to Hell / Schizo / Mayhem with mercy / Poison / Live like an angel (die like a Devil) / Witching hour / One thousand days in Sodom / Angel dust / In league with Satan / Red light fever. *(purple-lp iss.Jan85; NEATP 1002) <US-iss.Jan85 on 'Combat'+=; MX 8032>* – In nomine Satanas / Bursting out. *(re-iss. Apr89 on 'Roadrunner'; RR 9707) (cd re-iss. Oct91 on 'Castle'; CLACD 255)*

Jan 82. (7") *(NEAT 08)* **IN LEAGUE WITH SATAN. / LIVE LIKE AN ANGEL, DIE LIKE A DEVIL** [ ] [-]

Jan 82. (lp) *(NEAT 1005)* **BLACK METAL** [ ] [-]
– Black metal / To Hell and back / Buried alive / Raise the dead / Teacher's pet / Leave me in Hell / Sacrifice / Heaven's on fire / Countess Bathory / Don't burn the witch – At war with Satan (intro). *(cd-iss. Jun85; NEATCD 1005) (re-iss. Apr89 on 'Roadrunner'; RR 9708) <US-iss.Jan85 on 'Combat'+=; MX 8030>* – Acid queen / Blood lust / Die hard. *(cd re-iss. Oct91 on 'Castle'; CLACD 254)*

Aug 82. (7"/7"purple) *(NEAT/+P 13)* **BLOODLUST. / IN NOMINE SATANAS** [ ] [-]

Neat Megaforce

May 83. (7")<7"pic-d> *(NEAT 27) <LOM 1 – NEAT 027>* **DIE HARD. / ACID QUEEN** [ ] [ ]
(12"+=) *(NEAT 27-12)* – Bursting out.

Jun 83. (lp) *(NEAT 1015) <8031>* **AT WAR WITH SATAN** [64] [ ]
– At war with Satan / Rip ride / Genocide / Cry wolf / Stand up (and be counted) / Women, leather and Hell / Aaaaaarrghh!. *(pic-lp iss.Apr84; NEATP 1015) (cd-iss. Jun85; NEATCD 1015) (re-iss. Apr89 on 'Roadrunner'; RR 349869) (cd re-iss. Nov91 on 'Castle'; CLACD 256)*

Feb 84. (7"/7"mauve) *(NEAT/+P 38)* **WARHEAD. / LADY LUST** [ ] [-]
(12"+=/12"blue+=) *(NEAT/+P 38-12)* – Gates of Hell.

Jan 85. (lp,blue-lp/c/pic-lp) *(NEAT/+C/P 1024)* **POSSESSED** [ ] [-]
– Powerdrive / Flytrap / Satanarchist / Burn this place (to the ground) / Harmony dies / Possessed / Hellchild / Moonshine / Wing and a prayer / Suffer not the children / Voyeur / Mystique / Too loud (for the crowd). *(re-iss. Apr89 on 'Roadrunner'; RR 9794) (cd-iss. Jun94 on 'Castle'; CLACD 402)*

Feb 85. (7"/7"pic-d/7"sha-pic-d) *(NEAT/+P/SHAPE 43)* **MANITOU. / WOMAN** [ ] [-]
(12"+=) *(NEAT 43-12)* – Dead of night.
(c-s++=) *(NEATC 43)* – (Dutch radio interview).

Sep 85. (7"/7"sha-pic-d) *(NEAT/+S 47)* **NIGHTMARE. / SATANARCHIST** [ ] [-]
(12"+=) *(NEAT 47-12)* – F.O.A.D.
(w-drawn; 12"++=/12"pic-d++=) *(NEAT/+SP 47-12)* – Warhead (live).
(c-s+++=) *(NEATSC 47)* – (radio intro to) Warhead / Venoms.

Dec 85. (12"ep) *(NEAT 53-12)* **HELL AT HAMMERSMITH (LIVE IN '85) (live)** [ ] [-]
– Witching hour / Teacher's pet / Poison. *(re-iss. Dec95; same)*

— Recorded unreleased 'DEADLINE' album early in 1986.

Dec 86. (d-lp/d-c) *(NEAT/+C 1032)* **EINE KLEINE NACHTMUSIK (live '85-'86)** [ ] [-]
– Too loud (for the crowd) / Seven gates of Hell / Leave me in Hell / Nightmare / Countess Bathory / Die hard / Schizo / (guitar solo by Mantas) / The chanting of the priest / Satanachist / Fly trap / Warhead / Buried alive / Love amongst / (bass solo by Cronos) / Welcome to Hell / Bloodlust. *(cd-iss. Nov87; NEATXS 1032) (re-iss. Apr89 on 'Roadrunner'; RR 9639) (cd re-iss. Feb00; NEATCD 1032)*

— **MIKE H + JIM C** – guitars; repl. MANTAS who went solo

Filmtrax A.J.K.

Jan 87. (lp/c) *(MOMENT/+C 115) <AJK 632-2>* **CALM BEFORE THE STORM** [-] [ ] Italy
– Black Xmas / The chanting of the priest / Metal punk / Under a spell / Calm before the storm / Fire / Beauty and the beast / Deadline / Gypsy / Muscle. *(cd-iss. Nov87; MOMCD 115) (cd re-iss. Feb00 on 'Neat Metal'; NM 029CD)*

Under One Flag Maze

Oct 89. (cd/c/lp)(pic-lp) *(CD/T+FLAG 36)(FLAG 36P) <1064>* **PRIME EVIL** [ ] [ ]
– Prime evil / Parasite / Blackened are the priests / Carnivorous / Skeletal dance / Magalomania / Insane / Harder than ever / Into the fire / Skool daze . *(cd+=)* – Live like an angel (die like a Devil).

— **MANTAS** returned to repl. MIKE H + JIM C

— **TONY (THE DEMOLITION MAN) DOLAN** – vocals, bass; repl. CRONOS who also formed own named band.

Nov 90. (m-lp/m-cd) *(CD+/MFLAG 50)* **TEAR YOUR SOUL APART** [ ] [-]
– Skool daze / Bursting out / The ark / Civilized / Angel dust / Hellbent.

May 91. (cd/c/lp) *(CD/T+/FLAG 56)* **TEMPLES OF ICE** [ ] [-]
– Tribes / Even in Heaven / Trinity MCMXLV 0530 / In memory of (Paul Miller 1964-1990) / Faerie tale / Playtime / Acid / Arachnid / Speed king / Temples of ice.

Nov 92. (cd/c/lp) *(CD/T+/FLAG 72)* **THE WASTE LANDS** [ ] [-]
– Cursed / I'm paralysed / Black legions / Riddle of steel / Need to kill / Kissing the beast / Crucified / Shadow king / Wolverine / Clarisse.

— split after above, although the original line-up did record below

Warhead not iss.

Sep 96. (cd) *(CMCD 101)* **THE SECOND COMING** [ ] [-]
– Seven gates of Hell / Die hard / Welcome to hell / Leave me in hell / Countess Bathory / Buried alive / Don't burn the witch / In nomine satanas / Schitzo / Nightmare / Black metal / Witching hour.

S.P.V. C.B.H.

Dec 97. (cd) *(088-1881-2)* **CAST IN STONE** [ ] [ ]
– The evil one / Raised in Hell / All Devil's eye / Bleeding / Destroyed and damned / Domus mundi / Flight of the Hydra / God's forsaken / Mortals / Infectious / Kings or evil / You're all gonna die / Judgement day / Swarm / Intro / Bloodlust / Die hard / Acid queen / Bustin' out / Warhead / Ladylust / Manitou / Rip ride / Venom.

May 00. (cd) *(085-2175-2)* **RESURRECTION** [ ] [ ]
– Resurrection / Vengeance / War against Christ / All there is fear / Pain / Pandemonium / Loaded / Firelight / Black flame of Satan / Control freak / Disbeliever / Man, myth & magic / Thirteen / Leviathan.

– compilations, etc. –

Feb 86. (lp) *Metalworks; (APK 12)* **LIVE 1984-1985 (live)** [ ] [-]

Apr 86. (d-lp/c) *Raw Power; (RAW LP/TC 001)* **FROM HELL TO THE UNKNOWN** [ ] [-]

Jul 86. (pic-lp) *A.P.K.; (APKPD 12)* **OBSCENE MIRACLE** [ ] [-]

Jul 86. (lp) *Powerstation; (941317)* **SPEED REVOLATION** [ ] [-]

Sep 86. (lp/c) *Raw Power; (RAW LP/TC 024)* **THE SINGLES '80-'86** [ ] [-]
(cd-iss. Aug87; RAWCD 024) (cd-iss. Nov91 on 'Castle'; CLACD 246)

Jul 87. (cd) *The CD Label; (CDTL 004) / American Phonograph; <APK 12>* **LIVE OFFICIAL BOOTLEG (live)** [ ] [ ]
(re-iss. 1991 on 'Thunderbolt'; CDTB 110)

1987. (cd) *O.W.I.L.; (TU 7903)* **IN CONCERT (live)** [-] [ ]

1989. (cd) *Roadrunner; (RR 49653)* **WELCOME TO HELL / BLACK METAL** [ ] [-]

1989. (lp) *Roadrunner; (RR 9659)* **GERMAN ASSAULT (live)** [ ] [-]

Mar 93. (cd/c) *Music Club; (MC CD/TC 097)* **IN MEMORIUM – THE BEST OF VENOM 1981-1991** [ ] [-]
– Angel dust / Raise the dead / Red light fever / Buried alive / Witchin' hour / At war with Satan / Warhead / Manitou / Under a spell / Nothing sacred / Dead love / Welcome to Hell / Black metal / Countess Bathory / 1000 days in Sodom / Prime evil / If you wanna war / Surgery.

Apr 93. (cd/c) *Castle; (CCS 367) / Griffin; <172>* **SKELETONS IN THE CLOSET (live 83-84)** [ ] [ ] 1994

Nov 93. (cd) *Bleeding Hearts; (CDBLEED 7)* **OLD, NEW, BORROWED AND BLUE** [ ] [-]
(re-iss. Jul99 on 'Aspire-Voiceprint'; ASVP 011CD)

Apr 96. (cd) *Receiver; (<RRCD 212>)* **BLACK REIGN** [ ] [ ]

May 97. (d-cd) *Snapper; (<SMDCD 120>)* **FROM HEAVEN TO THE UNKNOWN** [ ] [ ]

Jun 98. (cd) *Cleopatra; (<CLEO 3052>)* **NEW LIVE AND RARE** [ ] [ ]

Jul 99. (m-cd) *Aspire-Voiceprint; (ASVP 010CD)* **LIVE 1996** [ ] [-]

Sep 99. (d-cd) *Receiver; (<RRCD 240>)* **BURIED ALIVE** [ ] [ ]

Oct 99. (cd) *Thunderbolt; (CDTB 110)* **LIVE OFFICIAL BOOTLEG**
May 00. (cd) *Receiver; (<RRCD 266>)* **THE COURT OF DEATH**
Aug 00. (cd) *Connoisseur; (VSOPCD 320)* **THE COLLECTION** -

MANTAS

solo with **PETER HARRISON** – vocals / **ALISTAIR BRAACKEN** – guitar

Neat Roadrunner

Oct 88. (lp/cd) *(NEAT/+CD 1042) <RR 95151>* **WINDS OF CHANGE**
– Let it rock / Deceiver / Hurricane / King of the ring / Western days / Winds of change / Desperado / Nowhere to hide / Sayonara . *(cd re-iss. Jan96; same)*

VICE SQUAD

Formed: Bristol, England . . . early 1978 from the ashes of local bands CONTINGENT and TV BRAKES, the line-up featuring 15 year old peroxide blonde bombshell BEKI BONDAGE, DAVE BATEMAN, MARK HAMBLY and SHANE BALDWIN. Issued on their own 'Riot City' label in 1980, 'LAST ROCKERS' was a promising if overwrought debut single. A doom-laden warning set in the aftermath of a nuclear holocaust, the track bordered on SIOUXSIE & THE BANSHEES conceptualism in its distinct three-part musical structure. Following a further EP, 'RESURRECTION', the band – and their label – were picked up by E.M.I. offshoot, 'Zonophone' for a hastily recorded debut album, 'NO CAUSE FOR CONCERN' (1981). Doubters were given plenty of ammunition with what was clearly a rush job, the band subsequently taking more care over follow-up, 'STAND STRONG STAND PROUD' (1982). Amid increasingly strained band relations, BONDAGE soon opted for a solo career, enjoying a brief hype as BEKI & THE BOMBSHELLS. VICE SQUAD, meanwhile, were still on the case, enlisting a new frontwoman, LIA, and releasing a string of singles and a third album, 'SHOT AWAY' (1985) before finally handing in their badges. • **Trivia:** Rhythm section, HAMBLY and BALDWIN, also moonlighted with oi/punks, CHAOTIC DISCHORD. • **Songwriters:** BOND – BATEMAN penned except THE TIMES THEY ARE A-CHANGIN' (Bob Dylan) / TEENAGE RAMPAGE (Sweet).

Album rating: NO CAUSE FOR CONCERN (*5) / STAND STRONG STAND PROUD (*4) / SHOT AWAY (*4) / LAST ROCKERS – THE SINGLES compilation (*5)

BEKI BONDAGE (b. REBECCA BOND, 3 Jun'63) – vocals (ex-CONTIGENT) / **DAVE BATEMAN** – guitar / **MARK HAMBLY** – bass (ex-TV BRAKES) / **SHANE BALDWIN** – drums

Riot City not iss.

Jan 81. (7"m) *(RIOT 1)* **LAST ROCKERS. / LATEX LOVE / LIVING ON DREAMS** -
May 81. (7"m) *(RIOT 2)* **RESURRECTION. / YOUNG BLOOD / HUMANE** -

Zonophone not iss.

Oct 81. (lp) *(ZEM 103)* **NO CAUSE FOR CONCERN** 32 -
– Young blood / Coward / Nothing / Summer fashion / 1981 / Saturday night special / Offering / The times they are a-changin' / Evil / Angry youth / It's a sell-out / Still dying / Last rockers. *(cd-iss. Oct93 on 'Dojo'+=; DOJOCD 167)* – (So) What for the 80's / Sterile. *(lp-iss.Jan98; DOJOLP 167)*
Feb 82. (7"m) *(Z 26)* **OUT OF REACH. / (SO) WHAT FOR THE 80'S / STERILE** 68 -
Apr 82. (7"m) *(Z 30)* **ROCK'N'ROLL MASSACRE. / STAND STRONG AND PROUD / TOMORROW** -
May 82. (lp) *(ZEM 104)* **STAND STRONG STAND PROUD** 47 -
– Stand strong stand proud / Humane / Cheap / Gutterchild / Rock'n'roll massacre / Fist full of dollars / Freedom begins at home / Out of reach / Saviour machine / No right of reply / Death wish / Propaganda. *(cd-iss. Nov93 on 'Dojo'+=; DOJOCD 170)* – Tomorrow's soldier / Darkest hour / Citizen / Scarred for life / Faceless men.
Sep 82. (7"m) *(Z 34)* **CITIZEN. / SCARRED FOR LIFE / FACELESS MEN** -

— **LIA** – vocals; repl. BEKI who formed LIGOTAGE before going solo

— **SOOTY** – guitar; repl. MARK

Anagram not iss.

Nov 83. (7") *(ANA 16)* **BLACK SHEEP. / NEW BLOOD** -
(12"+=) *(12ANA 16)* – The pledge.
Apr 84. (7") *(ANA 22)* **YOU'LL NEVER KNOW. / WHAT'S GOING ON** -
(12"+=) *(12ANA 22)* – The times they are a-changin'.
Jan 85. (7") *(ANA 26)* **TEENAGE RAMPAGE. / HIGH SPIRITS** -
Feb 85. (lp) **SHOT AWAY** -
– New blood / Take it or leave it / Out in the cold / Nowhere to hide / You'll never know / Rebels and kings / Playground / The rest of your life / What's going on / Killing time / Teenage rampage / Black sheep. *(cd-iss. Feb94 +=; CDPUNK 28)*– The times they are a changin' / High spirits / New blood (version) / The pledge / Nothing.

— they split after above

– compilations, etc. –

1982. (12"ep) *Riot City; (RIOT12 1/2)* **VICE SQUAD SINGLES** -
Feb 92. (cd) *Abstract; (AABT 805CD)* **LAST ROCKERS – THE SINGLES** -
– Last rockers / Living on dreams / Latex love / Young blood / Humane / Resurrection / Out of reach / (So) What for the 80's / Sterile / Stand strong stand proud / Tomorrow's soldier / Rock'n'roll massacre / Darkest hur / Upright citizen / Scarred for life / Faceless men. *(lp-iss.Nov96; DOJOLP 167)*
Apr 95. (cd) *Cleopatra; (<CL 5100>)* **LIVE AND LOUD**
Mar 97. (cd) *Anagram; (<CDPUNK 89>)* **THE COMPLETE PUNK SINGLES COLLECTION**
Aug 97. (cd) *Anagram; (CDPUNK 99)* **THE BBC SESSIONS** -
(lp-iss.Jun98 on 'Get Back'; GET 29LP)
Jul 99. (cd) *Rhythm Vicar; (PREACH 013CD)* **RESURRECTION** -
Sep 99. (cd) *Captain Oi; (AHOYCD 123)* **RARITIES**
Jun 00. (cd) *Anagram; (<CDPUNK 116>)* **THE VERY BEST OF VICE SQUAD**
Jul 00. (12"ep/cd-ep) *Combat Rock; (CR 041 EP/MCD)* **LAVENDER HILL MOB EP** -

VICIOUS RUMOURS

Formed: Bay Area, San Francisco, USA . . . 1983 by GEOFF THORPE, DAVE STARR, LARRY HOWE and GARY ST. PIERRE. Signed to 'Roadrunner', the band drafted in precocious axe wizard, VINNIE MOORE prior to the recording of debut album, 'SOLDIERS OF THE NIGHT' (1985). Stinging power-metal/proto-thrash, the record resoundingly convinced critics that VICIOUS RUMOURS, and especially MOORE, weren't all talk. The latter's association with the band was short-lived, however, and the guitarist subsequently went on to other projects. The hard-hitting 'DIGITAL DICTATOR' saw more line-up changes, with CARL ALBERT replacing ST. PIERRE and MARK McGEE coming in on guitar. Their burgeoning reputation was such that the group were soon picked up by 'Atlantic'. Despite releasing two albums of solid power-metal, 'VICIOUS RUMOURS' (1990) and 'WELCOME TO THE BALL' (1991), the group's lack of musical identity and commercial appeal eventually saw them dropped!! Back in the independent sector, they released 'WORD OF MOUTH' in 1994 on the 'Rising Sun' imprint. Another album, 'SOMETHING BURNING' was duly delivered on the 'Massacre' label in 1996. • **Trivia:** Not to be confused with British punk band of same name, who released records in the mid-80's on 'Dork', 'Oily' & 'Link'.

Album rating: SOLDIERS OF THE NIGHT (*6) / DIGITAL DICTATOR (*5) / VICIOUS RUMOURS (*6) / WELCOME TO THE BALL (*6) / WORD OF MOUTH (*5) / SOMETHING BURNING (*5) / CYBERCHRIST (*4)

GARY ST. PIERRE – vocals / **GEOFF THORPE** – guitar, vocals / **DAVE STARR** – bass / **LARRY HOWE** – drums / + 5th member **VINNIE MOORE** – guitar

Roadrunner Roadrunner

Nov 85. (lp) *(RR 9734)* **SOLDIERS OF THE NIGHT** -
– Premonition / Ride (into the sun) / Medusa / Soldiers of the night / Murder / March or die / Blitz the world / Invader / In fire / Domestic bliss / Blistering winds. *(cd-iss. Apr89 on 'Roadracer'; RO 9734) (cd-iss. Feb93; RO 9734-2)*

— **TERRY MONTANA** – guitar (for live work); repl. MOORE who went solo

— (1986) **CARL ALBERT** – vocals; repl. ST.PIERRE

— **MARK McGEE** – guitar, vocals; repl. MONTANA

Feb 88. (lp/cd) *(RR 9571-1/-2)* **DIGITAL DICTATOR**
– Replicant / Digital dictator / Minute to kill / Towns on fire / Lady took a chance / Worlds and machines / The crest / R.L.H. / Condemned / Out of the shadows.

Atlantic Atlantic

Feb 90. (cd/c/lp) *<(7567 82075-2/-4/-1)>* **VICIOUS RUMOURS**
– Don't wait for me / World church / On the edge / Ship of fools / Can you hear it / Down to the temple / Hellraiser / Electric twilight / Thrill of the hunt / Axe and smash.
Nov 91. (cd/c/lp) *<(7568 22761-2/-4/-1)>* **WELCOME TO THE BALL**
– Abandoned / You only live twice / Raise your hands / Children / Dust to dust / Savior from anger / Strange behaviour / Sex stepsisters / Mastermind / When love comes down / Ends of the Earth.

S.P.V. Rising Sun

Jun 94. (cd) *<(SPV 084-6223-2)>* **WORD OF MOUTH**

Massacre Massacre

Jul 96. (cd/lp) *(MASS CD/LP 091)* **SOMETHING BURNING**
May 98. (cd) *(MASSCD 142)* **CYBERCHRIST**

VICTOR (see under ⇒ RUSH)

VIKING CROWN (see under ⇒ NECROPHAGIA)

Vinnie VINCENT INVASION

Formed: Detroit, Michigan, USA . . . 1985 by ex-KISS guitarist VINNIE VINCENT with bassist DANA STRUM. Signing to 'Chrysalis', the group debuted in the summer of '86 with the eponymous, 'VINNIE VINCENT INVASION'. Receiving a thumbs-up from the music press, the album's safe but thrilling hard-rock pyrotechnics almost saw it scrape into the US Top 60. With original singer ROBERT FLEISHMAN dispensed with soon after the record's release, a then unknown singer by the name of MARK SLAUGHTER was drafted in to fulfill touring commitments and work on a second album, 'ALL SYSTEMS GO'. The record short-circuited both critically and commercially, the 'INVASION subsequently curtailed as SLAUGHTER and STRUM went on to form the eminently more successful SLAUGHTER.

Album rating: VINNIE VINCENT INVASION (*6) / ALL SYSTEMS GO (*5)

VINNIE VINCENT – guitar (ex-KISS) / **ROBERT FLEISHMAN** – vocals (ex-JOURNEY) / **DANA STRUM** – bass / **BOBBY ROCK** – drums

Chrysalis Chrysalis

Aug 86. (lp/c) *<(CHR/ZCHR 1529>* **VINNIE VINCENT INVASION** 64
– Boys are gonna rock / Shoot u full of love / No substitute / Animal / Twisted / Do you wanna make love / Back on the streets / I wanna be your victim / Baby-o / Invasion.

— **MARK SLAUGHTER** – vocals; repl. FLEISHMAN

Apr 88. (lp/c/cd) *<CHR/ZCHR/CCD 1626>* **ALL SYSTEMS GO** [ ] [64]
– Ashes to ashes / Dirty rhythm / Love kills / Naughty naughty / Burn / Let freedom rock / That time of year / Heavy pettin' / Ecstasy / Deeper and deeper / Breakout.

Apr 89. (7") *(INVS 1)* **LOVE KILLS. / ANIMAL** [ ] [-]
(12"+=) *(INVSX 1)* – Shoot you full of love.

— group folded when MARK and DANA formed own band, SLAUGHTER

VIO-LENCE

Formed: Bay Area, San Francisco, USA . . . 1985 as The DEATH PENALTY by guitarists PHIL DEMMEL and TROY FUA, who immediately completed the line-up with vocalist JERRY BURR (who was replaced a year later by SEAN KILLIAN), bassist EDDIE BILLY (replaced by DEEN DELL) and drummer PERRY STRICKLAND. FUA was also to depart in 1986, ROBB FLYNN taking over co-guitar duties for their 'ETERNAL NIGHTMARE' album for 'Mechanic' records in 1988. The album sold reasonably well hitting the US Top 200 for just over a month, the group subsequently gaining a bit of notoriety when they gave away a free bag of sickness with a similarly titled single (fetchingly catalogued, VOMIT 1). Moving on to JOHNNY Z's 'Megaforce' label, VIO-LENCE's follow-up, 'OPPRESSING THE MASSES' (1990) was the subject of some controversy in relation to the lyrics on one particularly gory track, 'TORTURE TACTICS'. A further independently released album, 'NOTHING TO GAIN', followed in Spring '93, although the band's derivative thrash sound had evolved little over the years and they eventually wound the band up. FLYNN, of course, went onto even more violent musical mayhem with the mighty MACHINE HEAD.

Album rating: ETERNAL NIGHTMARE (*5) / OPPRESSING THE MASSES (*6) / NOTHING TO GAIN (*4)

SEAN KILLIAN – vocals; repl. JERRY BURR / **PHIL DEMMEL** – guitar / **ROBB FLYNN** – guitar; repl. TROY FUA / **DEEN DELL** – bass; repl. EDDIE BILLY / **PERRY STRICKLAND** – drums

M.C.A. Mechanic

Aug 88. (lp/c/cd) *(MCF/MCFC/DMCF 3423)* *<42187>* **ETERNAL NIGHTMARE** [ ] [ ]
– Eternal nightmare / Serial killer / Phobophobia / Calling in the coroner / T.D.S. take it as you will / Bodies on bodies / Kill on command.

Oct 88. (7") *(VOMIT 1)* **ETERNAL NIGHTMARE. /** [ ] [ ]

not iss. Megaforce

1990. (cd/lp) *<82105-2/-1>* **OPPRESSING THE MASSES** [-] [ ]
– I profit / Officer nice / Subterfuge / Engulfed by flames / World in a world / Mentally afflicted / Liquid courage / Oppressing the masses.

not iss. Caroline

Jun 91. (cd-ep) *<CAROL 1711-2>* **TORTURE TACTICS** [-] [ ]
– Torture tactics / Officer Nice (live) / Gutterslut / Dicks of death.

Bleeding Hearts not iss.

Mar 93. (cd/lp) *(CD+/BLEED 4)* **NOTHING TO GAIN** [ ] [-]
– Atrocity / 12-gauge justice / Ageless eyes / Pain of pleasure / Virtues of vice / Killing my words / Psychotic memories / No chains / Welcoming party / This is system / Color of life. *(cd re-iss. Nov97; same)*

— after their split only FLYNN went on to greater things, MACHINE HEAD

VIRGINIA WOLF (see under ⇒ BONHAM)

VIRGIN STEELE

Formed: USA . . . early 80's by DAVID DeFEIS, JACK STARR, JOE O'REILLY and JOEY AYVAZIAN. Dealing in metal for the man's man, VIRGIN STEELE showcased their typically 80's sound on an eponymous 1983 debut on 'Megaforce' ('Music For Nations' in Europe). Internal tension led to the departure of axe guru STARR after the 'GUARDIANS OF THE FLAME' (1983) set, EDWARD PURSINO drafted in as a replacement. Although VIRGIN STEELE thundered gallantly on with 'NOBLE SAVAGE' (1986) and 'THE AGE OF CONSENT' (1989), the obvious absence of STARR only went to prove that it was never the same after the first time.

Album rating: VIRGIN STEELE (*6) / GUARDIANS OF THE FLAME (*4) / NOBLE SAVAGE (*4) / THE AGE OF CONSENT (*4) / THE MARRIAGE OF HEAVEN AND HELL PART 1 (*4) / THE MARRIAGE OF HEAVEN AND HELL PART TWO (*4) / INVICTUS (*4) / THE HOUSE OF ATREUS (ACT 1) (*4) / MAGICIAN FIRE MUSIC (*4)

DAVID DeFEIS – vocals, keyboards / **JACK STARR** – guitar / **JOE O'REILLY** – bass / **JOEY AYVAZIAN** – drums

Music For Nations Maze

Jan 83. (lp) *(MFN 1)* **VIRGIN STEELE** [ ] [ ]
– Danger zone / American girl / Dead end kids / Drive on thru / Still in love with you / Children of the storm / Pictures on you / Pulverizer / Living in sin / Virgin Steele.

Jun 83. (lp) *(MFN 5)* **GUARDIANS OF THE FLAME** [ ] [ ]
– Don't say goodbye (tonight) / Burn the sun / Life of crime / The redeemer / Birth through fire / Guardians of the flame / Metal city / Hell or high water / Go all the way / A cry in the night.

Dec 83. (7") *(KUT 104)* **A CRY IN THE NIGHT. / I AM THE ONE** [ ] [ ]
(12"+=) *(12KUT 104)* – Go down fighting / Virgin Steele.

— **EDWARD PURSINO** – guitar; repl. JACK STARR who went solo

Steamhammer Cobra

Jan 86. (lp) *(08-1863)* **NOBLE SAVAGE** [-] [ ] German
– We rule the night / I'm on fire / Thy kingdom come / Image of a faun at twilight / Noble savage / Fight tooth and nail / The evil in her eyes / Rock me / Don't close your eyes / The angel of light. *(cd-iss. Nov96 on 'T&T'; TT 0028-2)*

not iss. Maze

May 89. (cd) *<85-4605>* **THE AGE OF CONSENT** [-] [ ]
– On the wings of the night / Seventeen / Tragedy / Stay on top / Chains of fire / The burning of Rome / Let it roar / Lion in winter / Cry forever / We are eternal. *(cd-iss. Sep97 on 'T&T'; TT 0032-2)*

— split after above, although they reformed in the mid 90's

T&T T&T

1994. (cd) *(TT 0012-2)* **THE MARRIAGE OF HEAVEN AND HELL PART 1** [-] [-] German
– I wiil come for you / Weeping of the spirits / Blood and gasoline / Self crucifixion / Last supper / Warrior's lament / Trail of tears / The raven song / Forever I will roam / I wake up screaming / House of dust / Blood of the saints / Life among the ruins / The marriage of Heaven and Hell.

1995. (cd) *(TT 0019-2)* **THE MARRIAGE OF HEAVEN AND HELL PART 2** [-] [-] German
– A symphony of Steele / Crown of glory / From chaos to creation / Twilight of the gods / Rising unchained / Transfiguration / Prometheus the fallen one / Emalaith / Strawgirl / Devil – Angel / Unholy water / Victory is mine / The marriage of Heaven and Hell revisited.

Apr 98. (cd) *<(TT 0034-2)>* **INVICTUS** [ ] [ ]
– The blood of vengeance / Invictus / Mind, body, spirit / In the arms of the death god / Through blood and fire / Sword of the gods / God of our sorrows / Vow of honour / Defiance / Dust from the burning / Amaranth / A whisper of death / Dominion day / A shadow of fear / Theme: Marriage of Heaven and Hell / Veni, vidi, vici.

Oct 99. (cd) *<(TT 0042-2)>* **THE HOUSE OF ATREUS (ACT 1)** [ ] [ ]
– Kingdom of the fearless (the destruction of Troy) / Blaze of glory (the watchman's song) / Through the ring of fire / Prelude in A minor (the voyage home) / Death darkly closed their eyes / In triumph or tragedy / Return of the king / Flames of the black star (the arms of Herakles) / Narcissus / And Hecate smiled / A song of prophecy (piano solo) / Child of desolations / G minor invention / Day of wrath / Great sword of flame / The gift of Tantalos / Iphigenia in Hades / The fire god / Garden of landation / Agony and shine / Gate of kings / Via sacra.

Jul 00. (cd) *<(TT 0050-2)>* **THE HOUSE OF ATREUS (ACT II): MAGICIAN FIRE MUSIC** [ ] [ ]
– Wings of vengeance / Hymns to the gods of night / Fire of ecstasy / The oracle of Apollo / The voice as weapon / Moira / Nemesis / The wine of violence / A token of my hatred / Summoning the powers / Flames of thy power / Arms of Mercury / By the gods / Areopages / The judgement of the sun / Hammer of the woods / Guilt or innocence / The waters of Acheron / Fantasy and figure in D minor (the death of) / Resurrection day.

VISION OF DISORDER

Formed: Long Island, New York, USA . . . 1992 by MIKE KENNEDY, MATT BAUMBACH, TIM WILLIAMS, BRENDON COHEN and MIKE FLEISCHMANN. These alternative metallers spent several years doing their local rock circuit, gaining many loyal fans through their spirited live sets and inspiring the multitude with their refreshingly angst-ridden lyrics. Admirers included punks, thrashers, and straight-down-the-line metallers. Unfortunately the band had to do without a bass player for a while as FLEISHMANN took a brief sojourn in the early days. VOD really gained wider attention with their release of the 1995 single, 'STILL' on the 'Supersoul' label. Although the sound on this small offering is fairly gritty and undeveloped, it served to show the potential within the band, and its popularity gave the boys their ticket to make their first full-length album, 'VISION OF DISORDER' (1996), the following year. This debut full-set definitely consolidated all the reasons for their staunch following and gained them many more supporters. One of these fans was PHIL ANSELMO, PANTERA's frontman, who indeed guested on their second album, 'IMPRINT' (1998); the track in question being 'BY THE RIVER'. This record shot VOD into the metal limelight and led the band to re-record and re-work tracks from their original demos for their third full-set, 'FOR THE BLEEDERS' (1999). Still going strong in the year of the space odyssey VOD pushed out their fourth set, 'FROM BLISS TO DEVASTATION' (2001). • **Covered:** SOUL CRAFT (Bad Brains).

Album rating: STILL mini (*5) / VISION OF DISORDER (*6) / IMPRINT (*7) / FOR THE BLEEDERS re-recordings (*5) / FROM BLISS TO DEVASTATION (*5)

TIM WILLIAMS – vocals / **MATT BAUMBACH** – guitar / **MIKE KENNEDY** – guitar / **MIKE FLEISCHMAN** – bass / **BRENDON COHEN** – drums

not iss. Strive For Togetherness

1995. (m-cd) *<SFT 10CD>* **STILL** [-] [ ]
– Through my eyes / Choke / Beneath the green / Watch out / D.T.O. / No regrets. *(UK-iss.Aug97 on 'Sonic Rendezvous'; FORCE 002CD) (UK re-iss. Apr98; same as US)*

Roadrunner Roadrunner

Apr 97. (cd) *<(RR 8861-2)>* **VISION OF DISORDER** [ ] [ ] Oct96
– Element / Watering disease / Through my eyes / Viola / Liberation / Divide / Ways to destroy one's ambition / Suffer / Zone zero / D.T.O. / Excess / Gloom. *(re-iss. May99; same)*

Jun 98. (7"ep) *(CRISIS 019)* **RESURRECTING REALITY EP** [ ] [-]
– Clone / Soul craft / Element / Ways to destroy one's ambition.
(above issued on 'Crisis')

Aug 98. (cd) *<(RR 8793-2)>* **IMPRINT** [ ] [ ] Jul98
– What you are / Twelve steps to nothing / Landslide / By the river / Imprint / Colorblind / Rebirth of tragedy / Locust of the dead / Up in you / Clone / Jada bloom. *(re-iss. May00; same)*

Go Kart Go Kart

Aug 99. (lp/cd) <(GOKART 056/+CD)> **FOR THE BLEEDERS** (re-recordings of demos) [ ] [ ]
– Choke / Adelaide / Watch out / 713 / For the bleeders / No regret / Formula for failure (1999 version) / Beneath the green / Take them out (1999 version) / In the room.

not iss. T.V.T.

Jun 01. (cd) <6300> **FROM BLISS TO DEVASTATION** [-] [ ]
– Living to die / Southbound / Itchin' to bleed / Sunshine / On the table / From bliss to devastation / Downtime misery / Pretty hate / Without you / Overrun / Done in / Regurgitate / Walking the line.

VIXEN

Formed: Minnesota, USA . . . 1980 (not to be confused with MARTY FRIEDMAN's outfit of '83). This all-female quartet was initially instigated by guitarist JAN KUEHNEMUND, who invited vocalist/bassist GAYLE ERICKSON (now DeMATOFF), keyboard player CINDY BOETTCHER and drummer LAURIE HEDLUND into the line-up; they'd also uprooted to Los Angeles. The latter three were subsequently replaced by JANET GARDNER (in 1983), former Playboy pin-up ROXY PETRUCCI (in 1985) and SHARE PEDERSEN (in '86); other members to come and go in the early stages were bassist PIA MAIOCCO (STEVE VAI's wife), guitarist TAMMY IVANOV, lead vocalist NOEL BUCCI and LIZA CARBE on bass. In 1984, the 4-piece VIXEN (JAN, TAMMY, PIA and LAURIE) cut half a dozen tracks for the movie, 'Hardbodies', although it would be another few years before they would receive their big break. Signing to EMI subsidiary 'Manhattan' in 1988, these "Barbie Dolls Of Metal" became darlings of the metal press, bringing glamour back to the hard rock world in the process. That year, they debuted with a RICHARD MARX / FEE WAYBILL-penned single, 'EDGE OF A BROKEN HEART', lifted from their eponymous debut album, it too climbing high into the American Billboard charts. Taking their image from a hybrid of ROCK GODDESS and HEART, their sound from BON JOVI, the foxy ladies began the following year with a few more transatlantic hits, 'CRYIN' and 'LOVE MADE ME' (UK-only). A second set, 'REV IT UP' (1990), disappointed many, including their label, who duly dropped them from their roster, although the record and its accompanying singles still managed to chart. VIXEN subsequently split in '91, PEDERSEN enjoying her part in the one-off supergroup, CONTRABAND, while ROXY formed the short-lived, MAXINE. In 1998, VIXEN (PETRUCCI, GARDNER, plus MAXINE PETRUCCI and GINA STILE) – no original members! – re-emerged with a brand new album, 'TANGERINE', a surprisingly decent set of songs that somehow went unnoticed by the buying public. • **Songwriters:** The group penned most although the second album used outside pensmiths (aka JEFF PARIS). The prolific writer of many a hard rock gem, DIANE WARREN, penned their track 'IT WOULDN'T BE LOVE'. • **Note:** A big thankyou to JAN for providing the correct details for this biog – the enclosed photo also showed me what I missed out on.

Album rating: VIXEN (*7) / REV IT UP (*6) / TANGERINE (*5) / FULL THROTTLE: THE BEST OF VIXEN compilation (*7)

JANET GARDNER (b.21 Mar'62, Alaska, USA) – vocals, rhythm guitar; repl. TAMMY IVANOV who repl. keyboard player CINDY BOETTCHER / **JAN KUEHNEMUND** – lead guitar / **SHARE PEDERSON** (b.21 Mar'63, Minnesota, USA) – bass; repl. PIA MAIOCCO / **ROXY PETRUCCI** (b.17 Mar'62, Detroit, USA) – drums; repl. LAURIE HEDLUND

Manhattan Manhattan

Aug 88. (7"/7"sha-pic-d) (MT/+PD 48) <50141> **EDGE OF A BROKEN HEART. / CHARMED LIFE** [51] [26]
(12"+=) (12MT 48) – ('A'extended).
(cd-s) (CDMT 48) – ('A'side) / Love made me (live) / Cryin' (live).
(re-iss. Aug89; same) – hit UK No.59

Sep 88. (cd/c/lp) (CD/TC+/MTL 1028) <46991> **VIXEN** [66] [41]
– Edge of a broken heart / I want you to rock me / Cryin' / American dream / Desperate / One night alone / Hellraisers / Love made me / Waiting / Cruisin'. (cd+=) – Charmed life. (re-iss. Aug91 on 'Fame' cd/c/lp; CD/TC+/FA 3256)

Feb 89. (7"/7"g-f/7"sha-pic-d) (MT/+G/PD 60) <50167> **CRYIN'. / DESPERATE** [27] [22] Jan89
(12"+=/12"pic-d+=) (12MT/+P 60) – ('A'extended).
(cd-s+=) (CDMT 60) – Give it away / Edge of a broken heart.

EMI USA EMI USA

May 89. (7"/7"sha-pic-d) (MT/+PD 66) **LOVE MADE ME (remix). / GIVE IT AWAY** [36] [-]
(12"+=/12"pic-d+=/cd-s+=) (12MT/12MTPD/CDMT 66) – Cruisin' (live) / Edge of a broken heart (live) / Hellraisers (live).

Jul 90. (c-s/7") (TC+/MT 87) <50302> **HOW MUCH LOVE. / WRECKING BALL** [35] [44]
(12"+=/12"pic-d+=/cd-s+=) (12MT/12MTPD/CDMT 87) – Bad reputation.

Aug 90. (cd/c/lp) (CD/TC+/MT 1054) <92923> **REV IT UP** [20] [52]
– Rev it up / How much love / Love is a killer / Not a moment too soon / Streets in Paradise / Hard 16 / Bad reputation / Fallen hero / Only a heartbeat away / It wouldn't be love / Wrecking ball.

Oct 90. (c-s) <50332> **LOVE IS A KILLER / BAD REPUTATION** [-] [71]

Oct 90. (c-s/7") (TC+/MT 91) **LOVE IS A KILLER. / STREETS IN PARADISE** [41] [-]
(10"+=) (10MT 91) – Edge of a broken heart (live acoustic).
(cd-s++=) (CDMT 91) – I want you to rock me (live).
(12"pic-d+=) (12MTPD 91) – The jam (live) / I want you to rock me (live).

Mar 91. (c-s/7") (TC+/MT 93) **NOT A MINUTE TOO SOON. / FALLEN HERO** [37] [-]
(ext;12"pic-d+=/cd-s+=) (12MTPD/CDMT 93) – Desperate (demo).
(10"+=) (10MT 93) – Give it away (demo).

—— (Nov'91) folded when ROXY left to form/join group MAXINE

—— VIXEN re-formed again; **ROXY + JANET** plus **MAXINE PETRUCCI + GINA STILE**

C.M.C. C.M.C.

May 98. (cd) <86246> **TANGERINE** [ ] [ ]
– Page / Tangerine / Never say never / Peace / Barely breathin' / Bleed / Stay / Shut up / Machine / Air balloon / Can't control myself. (re-iss. Jan00 on 'Eagle'; EAG CD/MC 028)

– compilations, etc. –

Mar 99. (cd) Razor & Tie; <(RE 82188)> **FULL THROTTLE: THE BEST OF VIXEN** [ ] [ ]
– How much love / Love made me / Cryin' / Not a minute too soon / Charmed life / Love is a killer / Edge of a broken heart / Streets in Paradise / I want you to rock me (live) / Fallen hero / Bad reputation / Give it away / Cruisin'.

VOIVOD

Formed: Jonquierer, Canada . . . 1983 by DENIS BELANGER (aka SNAKE), DENIS D'AMOUR (aka PIGGY), JEAN-YVES THERIAULT (aka BLACKY) and MICHAEL LANGEVIN (aka AWAY). A defiantly left-field futurist-thrash outfit, VOIVOD immediately caused a stir with their debut album, 'WAR AND PAIN' (1984). Willfully obscure, the group combined techno-industrial and punk elements into their dense mesh of sound. Initially signed to 'Roadrunner', the group moved to 'Noise Int.' for follow-up set, 'RRROOOAAARRR' (1986). Successive albums, 'DIMENSION HATROSS' (1988) and the breakthrough 'NOTHINGFACE' (1989) were if anything, stranger, the latter featuring a weird version of Pink Floyd's 'ASTRONOMY DOMINE'. It was also the band's major label debut for 'M.C.A.', VOIVOD now hot property with their intricate, genre defying sound; by this point they'd left their thrash roots well behind and were truly exploring 'THE OUTER LIMITS OF METAL', on the 1993 album of the same name. Signed to 'Hypnotic' in the mid 90's, they released two further albums, 'NEGATRON' (1995) and 'PHOBOS' (1997).

Album rating: WAR AND PAIN (*7) / RRROOOAAARRR (*6) / KILLING TECHNOLOGY (*7) / DIMENSION HATROSS (*6) / NOTHINGFACE (*6) / ANGEL RAT (*5) / THE BEST OF VOIVOD compilation (*7) / THE OUTER LIMITS (*5) / NEGATRON (*5) / PHOBOS (*6) / KRONIK (*5) / LIVES (*5)

DENIS BELANGER (SNAKE) – vocals / **DENIS D'AMOUR** (PIGGY) – guitar, keyboards / **MICHEL LANGEVIN** (AWAY) – drums / **JEAN-YVES THERIAULT** (BLACKY) – bass

Roadrunner Metal Blade

Sep 84. (lp) (RR 9825) <MBR 1026> **WAR AND PAIN** [ ] [ ]
– Voivod / Warriors of ice / Suck your bone / Iron gang / War and pain / Blower / Live for violence / Black city / Nuclear war. (cd-iss. May89 on 'Roadracer'; RO 9825-2) (cd re-iss. May94 on 'Metal Blade'; CDMZORRO 75) (cd re-iss. Jun97 on 'Metal Blade'; 3984 41449CD)

Noise Int. Combat

May 86. (lp/c) (N 0040) <03612-44846-2> **RRROOOAAARRR** [ ] [ ]
– Korgull the exterminator / Fuck off & die / Slaughter in a grave / Ripping headaches / Horror / Thrashing rage / Helldriver / Build your weapons / To the death! (re-iss. Oct89 cd/lp; CD+/NUK 040)

May 87. (lp/c) (NUK/ZCNUK 058) <03612 44845-2> **KILLING TECHNOLOGY** [ ] [ ]
– Killing technology / Overreaction / Tornado / Forgotten in space / Ravenous medicine / Order of the blackguards / This is not an exercise. (cd-iss. Oct89; CDNUK 058)

Oct 87. (12"pic-d) (NPD 085) **TOO SCARED TO SCREAM. / COCKROACHES** [ ] [-]

Apr 88. (lp/c) (N 0106-1/-4) <4800-2-U> **DIMENSION HATROSS** [ ] [ ]
– . . .Prolog . . .experiment / Tribal convictions / Chaosmongers / Technocratic manipulators / . . .Epilog . . .macrosolutions to megaproblems / Brain scan / Psychic vacuum / Cosmic drama. (cd-iss. Oct89; CDNUK 106)

Noise Mechanic

Nov 89. (lp/c/cd) (N 0142-1/-4/-2) <6326> **NOTHINGFACE** [-] [ ] German
– The unknown knows / Nothingface / Astronomy domine / Missing sequences / X-ray mirror / Inner combustion / Pre-ignition / Into my hypercube / Sub-effect. (re-iss. 1991 on 'Noise Int.' lp/c; N 0142-1/-4)

—— now without JEAN-YVES, who was repl. by **PIERRE ST-JEAN**

M.C.A. M.C.A.

Oct 91. (cd/c/lp) (MCD/MCC/MCA 10293) <MRSD 10293> **ANGEL RAT** [ ] [ ]
– Shortwave intro / Panorama / Clouds in my house / The prow / Best regards / Twin dummy / Angel rat / Golem / The outcast / Nuage fractal / Freedoom / None of the above.

Jul 93. (cd/c/lp) <(MCD/MCC/MCA 10701)> **THE OUTER LIMITS** [ ] [ ]
– Fix my heart / Moonbeam rider / Le pont noir / The Nile song / The lost machine / Time warp / Jack Luminous / Wrong-way street / We are not alone.

Hypnotic Pet Rock

Oct 95. (cd) (HYP 001CD) <60019> **NEGATRON** [ ] [ ] Nov95
– Insect / Project X / Nanoman / Reality / Negatron / PLanet Hell / Meteor / Cosmic conspiracy / Bio TV / Drift / D.N.A. (Don't No Anything).

Aug 97. (cd) (HYPSD 1057) **PHOBOS** [ ] [ ]
– Catalepsy I / Rise / Mercury / Phobos / Bacteria / Temps mort / The tower / Quantum / Neutrino / Forlorn / Catalepsy II / M-body / 21st century schizoid man.

Nov 98. (cd) (HYP 1065CD) **KRONIK** [ ] [ ]
– Forlorn / Nanaman / Mercury / Vortex / Drift / Erosion / Ion / Project X / Cosmic conspiracy / Astronomy domine / Nuclear war.

Century Media Century Media

Apr 00. (cd) (77282-2) **VOIVOD LIVES (live)** [ ] [ ]
– Insect / Tribal convictions / Nanoman / Nuclear war / Planet Hell / Negatron / Project X / Cosmic conspiracy / Ravenous medicine / Voivod / In league with Satan.

– compilations, etc. –

Nov 92. (cd/c) *Noise Int.; (NO 196-2/-4) / Combat; <FUTIRIST 1014>*
THE BEST OF VOIVOD
– Voivod / Ripping headaches / Korgul the extermintor / Tornado / Ravenous machine / Cockroaches / Tribal convictious / Psychic vacuum / Astronomy domine / The unknown knows / Panorama / The prow.

VOODOO GLOW SKULLS

Formed: Riverside, California, USA . . . 1988 by hardcore brothers FRANK and EDDIE CASILLAS, who – with JERRY "SAPO" O'NEILL and other bro JORGE CASILLAS making up the line-up – changed their sound dramatically after a few years of obscurity. The style was now full-blown, in-yer-face Ska-punk, the quartet now expanding to a 7-piece with the addition of horn section JOEY HERNANDEZ, BRODIE JOHNSON and JOE "ROCKHEAD" McNALLY. This line-up released a few 7" singles, before completing their full-length debut, 'WHO IS? THIS IS?', in 1993. Touring alongside the similarly-styled MIGHTY MIGHTY BOSSTONES, VGS signed to 'Epitaph' records. They issued their sophomore set, 'FIRME' (1995), a record that was duly delivered in English and Spanish/Hispanic versions. 'BAILE DE LOS LOCOS' (1997) and 'THE BAND GEEK! MAFIA' (1998) showed the band's fun punk-ska ethos was gaining ground on young audiences who'd missed the genres first time round. A Spanish-language collection, 'EXITOS AL CABRON' (1999), marked time before they finally delivered their fifth set proper, 'SYMBOLIC' (2000). • **Covered:** HERE COMES THE SUN (trad) / CHARLIE BROWN (Coasters) / etc.

Album rating: WHO IS? THIS IS? (*5) / FIRME (*5) / BAILE DE LOS LOCOS (*5) / THE BAND GEEK! MAFIA (*6) / EXITOS AL CABRON collection (*5) / SYMBOLIC (*6)

FRANK CASILLAS – vocals / **EDDIE CASILLAS** – guitar / **JORGE CASILLAS** – bass / **JERRY "SAPO" O'NEILL** – drums / **JOEY HERNANDEZ** – saxophone / **JOE "ROCKHEAD" McNALLY** – trumpet / **BRODIE JOHNSON** – trombone

not iss. Dr. Strange

1993. (cd) *<DSR 018CD>* **WHO IS? THIS IS?** [-]
– Insubordination / Dirty rats / Give in / You're the problem / Sin berguensa (si habla Espanol) / Wife and kid / Country phuck / Dog pile / Here comes the sun / Too many secrets / Cheap guy / Migra (mas Espanol) / Ugly stick / Bossman / Revenge of the nerds. *(UK-iss.Jan96; same as US) (pic-lp Mar97; DSR 018P)*

Epitaph Epitaph

Oct 95. (cd/c/lp) *<(86454-2/-4/-1)>* **FIRME**
– Shoot the moon / Closet monster / Charlie Brown / Drunk tank / Jocks from Hell / Trouble walking / Give me someone I can trust / Empty bottles / Fat Randy / Thift shop junkie / El coo cooi / Method to this madness / Construction / Malas Palabras / Nicotine fit / Land of misfit toys.

Jun 97. (cd/c/lp) *<(6492-2/-4/-1)>* **BAILE DE LOS LOCOS** May97
– Baile de los locos / Here we are again / My soul is sick / Bulletproof / Elephantitis / Los hombres no Lloran / Nazican / Freeballin / Motel six / Kids will have to pay / Nowhere left to go / This ain't no disco.

Jul 98. (cd/c/lp) *<(6535-2/-4/-1)>* **THE BAND GEEK! MAFIA**
– Human pinata / Symptomatic / Love letter / They always come back / Walkin' frustration / Yo no tengo tiempo (para ti) / Left for dead / The band geek! mafia / Brodie Johnson weekend / Delinquent song / Hieroglyphics / Misunderstood / Hit a guy with glasses / Stranded in the jungle.

Sep 00. (cd/lp) *<(6582-2/-1)>* **SYMBOLIC**
– We're back / Say goodnight / Drop in / Musical therapy / The silencer / Orlando's not here / The Devil made me do it / El mas chingon / The last party / Symbolic / San Bernadino / Casa blanca / Cancion de mala suerte.

– compilations, etc. –

Aug 99. (cd) *Grita!; <60023>* **EXITOS AL CABRON** [-]
– Yo no tengo tiempo (para ti) / Sin berguensa / Adicto a tienda sequnda mano / Rancho grande / Botellas vacias / Cielito lindo / Feliz navidad / El coo cooi / Randy Gordo / Celda Borrachera / Migra.

VOW WOW (see under ⇒ BOW WOW)

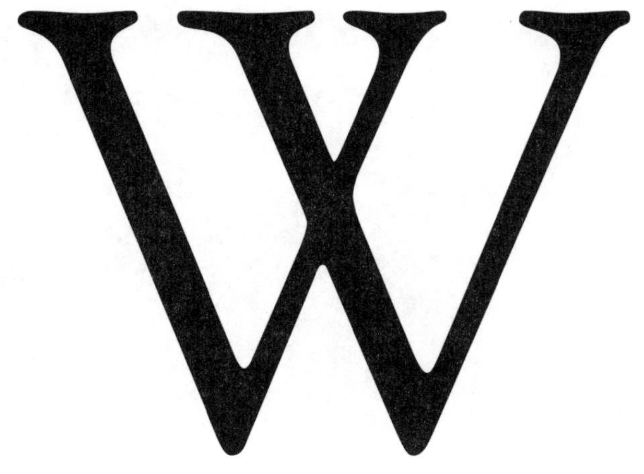

John WAITE (see under ⇒ BABYS)

Joe WALSH

Born: 20th Nov'47, Wichita, Kansas, USA, the classically-trained son of a piano playing mother. In 1969, having spent the previous four years imitating the fret work of guitar idols, JEFF BECK and JIMMY PAGE, while studying at Kent State University (in Cleveland, Ohio), WALSH joined The JAMES GANG. He quit the 'GANG for a solo career late in '71, after contributing his much lauded star quality to three studio albums, 'YER ALBUM', 'RIDES AGAIN' and 'THIRDS'. Keeping his hard-rock roots firmly intact and adding harmonies, WALSH named his new backing band, BARNSTORM (KENNY PASSARELLI on bass and JOE VITALE on drums), also the title of his debut US Top 100 album released in '72. A follow-up, the strangely-titled 'THE SMOKER YOU DRINK, THE PLAYER YOU GET' (with the addition of ROCKE GRACE on keyboards and JOE LALA on percussion), thundered up the American charts into the Top 10. The single from it, 'ROCKY MOUNTAIN WAY' (Top 30), complete with his new 'talkbox', became a classic in its own right, the guitar work and countrified wail of WALSH making him a focal point par excellence. His third set, 'SO WHAT' (1974), featured guest spots from The EAGLES, J.D. SOUTHER and DAN FOGELBERG (JW produced and performed on his 'Souvenirs'), while BARNSTORM took a back seat on around half the tracks. The record just failed to match its predecessor, WALSH subsequently forming a new stage band comprising of drummer RICKY FATAAR (ex-BEACH BOYS), bassist BRYAN GAROFALO and keyboard players DAVID MASON and PAUL HARRIS, a concert set, 'YOU CAN'T ARGUE WITH A SICK MIND', belatedly reaching the Top 20 in the Spring of '76. By this time, WALSH had shocked the rock world, taking the place of BERNIE LEADON in The EAGLES, his contributions to their classic 'Hotel California' (1976), certainly giving the once proud kings of country-rock a harder edge. He remained with the group for the rest of the 70's, reactivating his solo career in 1978 with the celebrated hit single 'LIFE'S BEEN GOOD' taken from another platinum album, 'BUT SERIOUSLY FOLKS . . .'. From 1980 to 1988, he became a semi-serious candidate at the US presidential elections, his recording work understandably a little sporadic and unremarkable during this time (although he did find time to perform a cameo appearance in the 'Blues Brothers' film). Mellowed-down soft-rock albums such as 'THERE GOES THE NEIGHBORHOOD' (1981), 'YOU BOUGHT IT – YOU NAME IT' (1983), 'THE CONFESSOR' (1985) and 'GOT ANY GUM' (1987). all sold moderately well in the states, the former more successful due to the appearance of another major hit, 'LIFE OF ILLUSION'. In 1991, WALSH released his umpteenth set, 'ORDINARY AVERAGE GUY', probably never a truer self-analysis of one of the great guitarists of the 70's. A few years later, the man was back on the "Vote For Me" campaign trail, subsequently rejoining The EAGLES on a reunion set; the album did little to win back the critics, although their concerts sold out everywhere. • **Covered:** WILL YOU STILL LOVE ME TOMORROW? (Goffin-King) / WE GOTTA GET YOU A WOMAN (Todd Rundgren) / IN-A-GADDA-DA-VIDA (Iron Butterfly) / SHAKE YOUR BOOTY (KC & The Sunshine Band) / etc.

Album rating: BARNSTORM (*6) / THE SMOKER YOU DRINK, THE PLAYER YOU GET (*7) / SO WHAT (*5) / YOU CAN'T ARGUE WITH A SICK MIND (*6) / BUT SERIOUSLY FOLKS . . . (*5) / SO FAR SO GOOD – THE BEST OF JOE WALSH compilation (*8) / THERE GOES THE NEIGHBOURHOOD (*5) / YOU BOUGHT IT – YOU NAME IT (*4) / THE CONFESSOR (*4) / GOT ANY GUM? (*4) / ORDINARY AVERAGE GUY (*5) / SONGS FOR A DYING PLANET (*3) / A FUTURE TO THIS LIFE (*3) / LOOK WHAT I DID~: THE JOE WALSH ANTHOLOGY compilation (*8)

JOE WALSH – vocals, guitar (ex-JAMES GANG) with his band BARNSTORM: **KENNY PASSARELLI** – bass / **JOE VITALE** – drums

Probe | Dunhill

Oct 72. (7") *<4327>* **MOTHER SAYS. / I'LL TELL THE WORLD ABOUT YOU** [-] [ ]

Jan 73. (lp) *(6268) <50130>* **BARNSTORM** [ ] [79] Oct72
– Here we go / Midnight visitor / One and one / Giant bohemoth / Mother says / Birdcall morning / Home / I'll tell the world about you / Turn to stone / Comin' down. *(re-iss. Oct74 on 'A.B.C.'; ABCL 5022)*

— added **ROCKE GRACE** – keyboards / **JOE LALA** – percussion

Aug 73. (7") *(PRO 600) <4361>* **ROCKY MOUNTAIN WAY. / (DAYDREAM) PRAYER** [ ] [23]
(UK-iss.Jul75 on 'A.B.C.'; 4061)

Sep 73. (lp) *<50140>* **THE SMOKER YOU DRINK, THE PLAYER YOU GET** [ ] [6] Jun73
– Rocky mountain way / Bookends / Wolf / Midnight moodies / Happy ways / Meadows / Dreams / Days gone by / (Daydream) Prayer. *(re-iss. quad.Oct74 on 'A.B.C.'; ABCL 5033) (cd-iss. Apr92 on 'M.C.A.'; MCLD 19020)*

Jan 74. (7") *(PRO 611) <4373>* **MEADOWS. / BOOKENDS** [ ] [89] Dec73
(re-iss. Mar76 on 'A.B.C.'; 4105)

— In 1974, he sessioned for EAGLES, B.B. KING, etc., and produced DAN FOGELBERG

— Solo; used past BARNSTORM members on a couple of tracks, plus new studio & live line-up **DAVID MASON + PAUL HARRIS** – keyboards / **BRYAN GAROFOLO** – bass / **RICKY FATAAR** – drums (ex-BEACH BOYS) / **TOM STEPHENSON** – keyboards

Anchor | Dunhill

Dec 74. (lp) *(ABCL 5055) <50171>* **SO WHAT** [ ] [11]
– Welcome to the club / Falling down / Pavane / Time out / All night laundromat blues / Turn to stone / Help me thru the night / County fair / Song for Emma.

Feb 75. (7") *(ABC 4035) <15026>* **TURN TO STONE. / ALL NIGHT LAUNDROMAT BLUES** [ ] [93]

— although he was still a solo artist, WALSH joined EAGLES late '75.

A.B.C. | A.B.C.

Apr 76. (lp) *(ABLC 5156) <932>* **YOU CAN'T ARGUE WITH A SICK MIND (live)** [28] [20]
– Walk away / Meadows / Rocky mountain way / Tell me / Help me through the night / Turn to stone. *(re-iss. Jan83 on 'Fame' lp/c; FA/TCFA 3051) <US cd-iss. Jun88; 31120>*

Apr 76. (7") *<12115>* **TIME OUT (live). / HELP ME THRU THE NIGHT (live)** [-] [ ]

Jun 76. (7") *(ABC 4121)* **WALK AWAY (live). / HELP ME THRU THE NIGHT (live)** [ ] [-]

— WALSH used mainly session people + VITALE

Asylum | Asylum

Jun 78. (7") *(K 13129) <45493>* **LIFE'S BEEN GOOD. / THEME FROM BOAT WEIRDOS** [14] [12]

Jun 78. (lp/c) *(K/K4 53081) <141>* **BUT SERIOUSLY, FOLKS . . .** [16] [8]
– Over and over / Second hand store / Indian summer / At the station / Tomorrow / Inner tube / Theme from Boat Weirdos / Life's been good. *(cd-iss. Feb93 on 'WEA'; 7559 60527-2)*

Nov 78. (7") *(K 13141) <45536>* **OVER AND OVER. / AT THE STATION** [ ] [ ]
below from the film 'Urban Cowboy'. B-side by GILLEY'S URBAN COWBOY BAND. On 'Full Moon' in America.

Jun 80. (7") *(K 79146) <46639>* **ALL NIGHT LONG. / ORANGE BLOSSOM SPECIAL / HOEDOWN** [ ] [19] May80

— now an ex-EAGLES man after that group's split

May 81. (7") *<47144>* **A LIFE OF ILLUSION. / ROCKETS** [-] [34]

May 81. (7") *(K 12533)* **A LIFE OF ILLUSION. / DOWN ON THE FARM** [ ] [-]

May 81. (lp/c) *(K/K4 52285) <523>* **THERE GOES THE NEIGHBORHOOD** [ ] [20]
– Things / Made your mind up / Down on the farm / Rivers (of the hidden funk) / A life of illusion / Bones / Rockets / You never know.

Jul 81. (7") *<47197>* **MADE YOUR MIND UP. / THINGS** [-] [ ]

Jan 82. (7") *<69951>* **WAFFLE STOMP. / THINGS** [-] [ ]

Full Moon | Warners

Jun 83. (7") *<29611>* **SPACE AGE WHIZ KIDS. / THEME FROM ISLAND WEIRDOS** [-] [52]

Jul 83. (lp/c) *(923884-1/-4) <23884>* **YOU BOUGHT IT – YOU NAME IT** [ ] [48]
– I can play that rock & roll / Told you so / Here we are now / The worry song / I.L.B.T.'s / Space age whiz kids / Love letters / Class of '65 / Shadows / Theme from Island weirdos. *(cd-iss. Jul84; 923884-2) (cd re-iss. Jul96 on 'WEA'; 7559 23884-2)*

Aug 83. (7") *<29519>* **I CAN PLAY THAT ROCK & ROLL. / HERE WE ARE NOW** [-] [ ]

Sep 83. (7") *(W 9841)* **LOVE LETTERS. / TOLD YOU SO** [ ] [-]

Nov 83. (7") *<29454>* **LOVE LETTERS. / I.L.B.T.'s** [-] [ ]

Jun 85. (7") *<28910>* **I BROKE MY LEG. / GOOD MAN DOWN** [-] [ ]

Jun 85. (lp/c) *(925281-1/-4) <25281>* **THE CONFESSOR** [ ] [65] May85
– Problems / I broke my leg / Bubbles / Slow dancing / 15 years / Confessor / Rosewood bitters / Good man down / Dear John. *(cd-iss. Jul88; 925606-2)*

— now with **CHAD CROMWELL** – drums / **DAVID COCHRAN + RICK THE . . . PLAYER** – bass / **MARK RIVERA** – saxophone / **JOHN DAVID SOUTHER + JIMI JAMISON** – backing vocals

Aug 87. (lp/c/cd) *(925606-1/-4/-2) <25606>* **GOT ANY GUM?** [ ] [ ] Jul87
– The radio song / Fun / In my car / Malibu / Half of the time / Got any gum? / Up to me / No peace in the jungle / Memory lane / Time. *(cd re-iss. Jan96 on 'WEA'; 7599 25606-2)*

Aug 87. (7") *<28304>* **THE RADIO SONG. / HOW YA DOIN'** [-] [ ]

Nov 87. (7") *<28225>* **IN MY CAR. / HOW YA DOIN'** [-] [ ]

Epic | Pyramid-Epic

Jul 91. (cd/c/lp) *(468128-2/-4/-1) <47384>* **ORDINARY AVERAGE GUY** [ ] [ ] May91
– Two sides to every story / Ordinary average guy / The gamma goochee / All of a sudden / Alphabetical order / Look at us now / I'm actin' different / Up all night / You might need somebody / Where I grew up (prelude to schooldays).

Jul 91. (7") *<73843>* **ORDINARY AVERAGE GUY. / ALPHABETICAL ORDER** [-] [ ]

May 92. (cd/c) *<ZK 78916>* **SONGS FOR A DYING PLANET** [-] [ ]
– Shut up / Fairbanks, Alaska / Coyote love / I know / Certain situations / Vote for me / Theme from baroque weirdos / Friend song / It's all right /

Will you still you love me tomorrow? / Decades / Song for a dying planet.

Apr 95. (cd-ep; JOE WALSH & LITA FORD) **A FUTURE TO HIS LIFE /** [-] [ ]

Apr 95. (cd) *<71888>* **A FUTURE TO THIS LIFE** (ROBOCOP: THE SERIES SOUNDTRACK) [-] [ ]
– A future to this life / Guilty of the crime / Fire and brimstone / Chutes and ladders / Flannel / Jacket / We gotta get you a woman / I only have eyes for you / Stuff ya gotta watch / In-a-gadda-da-vida / Shake your booty / Robocop adventure.

– compilations, others, etc. –

Jun 77. (7") *A.B.C.; (12426>* **ROCKY MOUNTAIN WAY. / TURN TO STONE** [-] [ ]

Jun 77. (12"ep) *A.B.C.; (ABE 12-002)* **PLUS FOUR EP** [39] [-]
– Rocky mountain way / Turn to stone / Meadows / Walk away.

Oct 78. (lp/c) *A.B.C.; (ABCL/+C 5240) <1083>* **SO FAR SO GOOD – THE BEST OF JOE WALSH** [ ] [71]
– Rocky mountain way / Welcome to the club / Bookends / Walk away / Mother says / Turn to stone / Here we go / Pavane / Time out / Meadows. *(re-iss. 1983 on 'M.C.A.' lp/c; MCL/+C 1751) (cd-iss. 1987; MCAD 1601) (cd re-iss. Jun97 on 'Half Moon'; HMNCD 007)*

Aug 82. (7") *M.C.A.; (MCA 787)* **ROCKY MOUNTAIN WAY. / TURN TO STONE** [ ] [-]
(12"pic-d+=) *(MCATP 787)* – Funk 49.

Apr 86. (7") *Old Gold; (OG 9599)* **ROCKY MOUNTAIN WAY. / (b-side by Poco)** [ ] [-]

Oct 87. (d-cd) *M.C.A.; (DMCL 1874)* **THE SMOKER YOU DRINK . . . / YOU CAN'T ARGUE WITH A SICK MIND** [ ] [-]
(re-iss. Apr92; MCLD 19020) (re-iss. Jul96; MCD 33728)

Sep 89. (lp/c) *Raw Power; (RAW LP/TC 036)* **WELCOME TO THE CLUB** [ ] [-]

May 94. (cd/c; JOE WALSH & THE JAMES GANG) *Pickwick; (PWK S/MC 4207)* **ALL THE BEST** [ ] [-]

Jul 95. (d-cd) *M.C.A.; (MCD 11233)* **LOOK WHAT I DID: THE JOE WALSH ANTHOLOGY** [ ] [-]
– Tuning, part 1 / Take a look around / Funk #48 / Bomber / Tend my garden / Funk #49 / Ashes, the rain and I / Walk away / It's all the same / Midnight man / Here we go / Midnight visitor / Mother says / Turn to stone / Comin' down / Meadows / Rocky mountain way / Welcome to the club / All night laundry mat blues / Country fair / Help me thru the night / Life's been good / Over and over / A life of illusion / Theme from the Island Weirdos / I can play that rock and roll / I.L.B.T.'s / Space age whiz kids / Rosewood bitters / Shut up / Decades / Song for a dying planet / Ordinary average guy (live with GLENN FREY).

Jun 97. (cd) *Half Moon; (HMNCD 007)* **THE BEST OF JOE WALSH** [ ] [ ]

Steve WALSH (see under ⇒ KANSAS)

WAR (see under ⇒ HYPOCRISY)

WARFARE

Formed: Newcastle, England . . . 1984 by former punk, (PAUL) EVO (ex-ANGELIC UPSTARTS), together with GUNNER and FALKEN. A brutal combination of proto-thrash and punk, the band signed to local metal indie, 'Neat' and commenced battle with the self-explanatory, 'THE NOISE, FILTH AND FURY' EP. The follow-up single, a scathing parody of Frankie Goes To Hollywood's 'TWO TRIBES', was the closest WARFARE came to mainstream fame, the track even enjoying national airplay amid all the FGTH hysteria of the day! Early the following year came the debut album proper, 'WARFARE – PURE FILTH'. There were unmistakable similarities to fellow Northern chaos merchants, VENOM, CRONOS and his devilish crew actually contributing to one track, the tasteless 'ROSE PETALS FALL FROM HER FACE'. MOTORHEAD were another reference point, LEMMY sufficiently impressed enough to undertake production chores on a follow-up set, 'METAL ANARCHY' (1986). A third album, 'MAYHEM FUCKIN' MAYHEM' (1987) continued in similarly blunt fashion, tracks such as 'PROJECTIVE VOMIT' and 'ATOMIC SLUT' making the album an essential purchase for that special person in your life. EVO masterminded yet another thrashing of a popular classic that summer, Robert Palmer's 'ADDICTED TO LOVE', getting the WARFARE treatment this time around. Still, that feat of musical vision was nothing compared to snagging LINDISFARNE (North East folkies, as if you didn't know) sax player MARTI CRAGG for the 'CONFLICT OF HATRED' (1988) album. Two years later, WARFARE launched their most bizarre offensive to date with concept piece, 'HAMMER HORROR', a partially successful tribute to the horror masters of previous 40 years. The album wasn't wholly well received and shortly after, WARFARE announced they were going AWOL from the live and studio front.

Album rating: PURE FILTH (*4) / METAL ANARCHY (*5) / MAYHEM F***IN' MAYHEM – HARDCORE '88 (*5) / CONFLICT OF HATRED (*4) / HAMMER HORROR . . . (*5) / DECADE OF DECIBELS compilations (*6)

(PAUL) EVO – vocals, drums (ex-ANGELIC UPSTARTS) / **GUNNER** – guitar / **FALKEN** – bass

Neat / not iss.

Jul 84. (7"ep) *(NEAT 41)* **THE NOISE, FILTH AND FURY EP** [ ] [-]
– Burn the Kings Road / The new age of total warfare / Noise, filth and fury.

Nov 84. (12"m) *(NEAT 45-12)* **TWO TRIBES (metal noise mix). / HELL / BLOWN TO BITS** [ ] [-]

Jan 85. (lp) *(NEAT 1021)* **PURE FILTH** [ ] [-]
– Warning / Total armageddon (full scale attack) / Noise, filth & fury / Let the show go on / Break out / Collision / Rabid metal / Dance of the dead / Limit crescendo / Rose petals fall from her face. *(free-7")* – THIS MACHINE KILLS. / BURN THE KING'S ROAD

Jun 85. (12"ep) *(NEAT 49-12)* **TOTAL DEATH EP** [ ] [-]
– Metal anarchy / Rape / Burning up / Destroy.

Jan 86. (lp) *(NEAT 1029)* **METAL ANARCHY** [ ] [-]
– Intro / Electric mayhem / Warfare / Death vigilance / Wrecked society / Living for the last days / Disgrace / Military shadow / Metal anarchy / Psycho express.

Dec 86. (10") **MAYHEM F***IN' MAYHEM. /** [ ] [-]

Jul 87. (7") *(NEAT 58)* **ADDICTED TO LOVE (Mayhem mix). / HUNGRY DOGS (live)** [ ] [-]

Nov 87. (lp/c) *(NEAT/+C 1040)* **MAYHEM F***IN' MAYHEM – HARDCORE '88** [ ] [-]
– Abortion sequence / Hungry dogs / Generator / You've really got me / Ebony dreams / Extremely finance / Projectile vomit / Mayhem, fuckin' mayhem / Atomic slut / Machine gun breath / Murder on Melrose.

— next feat. **MANTAS** – guitar (of VENOM) / **MARTI CRAGGS** – sax (of LINDISFARNE) / **IRENE HUME** – vocals (ex-PRELUDE)

Mar 88. (lp/c/cd) *(NEAT/+C/CD 1044)* **CONFLICT OF HATRED** [ ] [-]
– Waxworks / Revolution / Dancing in the flames of insanity / Evolution / Fatal vision / Deathcharge / Order of the dragons / Elite forces / Rejoice the feast of quarantine / Noise, filth and fury.

FM-Revolver / not iss.

Jun 90. (cd/c/lp) *(REV XD/MC/LP 147)* **HAMMER HORROR (40 Years Of Hammer Films 1949-1989)** [ ] [-]
– Hammer horror / Plague of the zombies / Ballad of the dead / Phantom of the opera / Baron Frankenstein / A velvet rhapsody / Solo of shadows / Prince of darkness / Tales of the gothic genre / Scream of the vampire part 1. *(re-iss. cd Apr93 on 'Silva Screen'; FILMCD 130)*

— split some time in the early 90's

– compilations, etc. –

Nov 93. (cd) *Bleeding Hearts; (CDBLEED 8)* **DECADE OF DECIBELS** [ ] [-]

WARLOCK

Formed: Dusseldorf, Germany . . . Autumn 1982 by DORO PESCH, RUDY GRAF, PETER SZIGETI, FRANK RITTEL and MICHAEL EURICH. Fronted by blonde bombshell PESCH, the group made their debut in 1984 with 'BURNING THE WITCHES'. Hardly as demonic as either the band name or album title might suggest, WARLOCK touted teutonic power metal with a distinct melodic edge, not too far removed from what many British bands were doing at the time but obviously with a heavy Germanic influence. Highlights of the debut album were the hard-hitting title track and the lovelorn PESCH torch song, 'WITHOUT YOU'. Her striking blue-eyed Aryan looks did the band no harm at all in picking up a major label deal, WARLOCK subsequently signing with 'Vertigo' and releasing 'HELLBOUND' in 1985. A third set, 'TRUE AS STEEL' (1986), signalled a move towards a more commercial hard rock sound, PESCH and the boys duly relocating to New York. It was almost a completely new line-up which recorded 'TRIUMPH AND AGONY' (1987) the following year, a half-baked pop-metal effort which came in for some scathing reviews. Having alienated most of WARLOCK's original fans, it was only a matter of time before the group folded, the lightweight 'FORCE MAJEURE' (1989) being essentially PESCH's solo debut (it also included a version of PROCOL HARUM's 'A WHITER SHADE OF PALE'). The eponymous 'DORO' (1990) was a similarly misguided set of mainstream chaff, not even a GENE SIMMONS production credit rescuing it from terminal bargain-bin status. By the release of the belated 'ANGELS NEVER DIE' in 1993, the metal scene had changed beyond recognition and the rock vixen approach once again fell on deaf ears. A lesson in musical integrity.

Album rating: BURNING THE WITCHES (*5) / HELLBOUND (*6) / TRUE AS STEEL (*4) / TRIUMPH AND AGONY (*5) / Doro & Warlock: FORCE MAJEURE (*4) / RARE DIAMONDS compilation (*5) / Doro: DORO (*3) / ANGELS NEVER DIE (*3) / DORO LIVE (*3) / MACHINE II MACHINE (*3) / CALLING THE WILD (*3)

DORO PESCH (b. DOROTHEE, 3 Jun'64) – vocals / **RUDY GRAF** – guitar / **PETER SZIGETI** – guitar / **FRANK RITTEL** – bass / **MICHAEL EURICH** – drums

Mausoleum / not iss.

Mar 84. (lp/c) *(SKULL/+7 8325)* **BURNING THE WITCHES** [ ] [-]
– Signs of Satan / After the bomb / Dark fade / Homocide rocker / Without you / Metal racer / Burning the witches / Hateful guy / Holding me. *(re-iss. Mar87 on 'Vertigo' lp/c)(cd; VERH/+C 42)(<830 902-2>)*

Nov 84. (7") *(GUTS 8402)* **WITHOUT YOU. / BURNING THE WITCHES** [ ] [-]

Vertigo / Mercury

Jul 85. (lp/c/cd) *(<824 660-1/-4/-2>)* **HELLBOUND** [ ] [ ]
– Hellbound / All night / Earthshaker rock / Wrathchild / Down and out / Out of control / Time to die / Shout it out / Catch my heart.

Jan 86. (m-lp) *(VERX 27)* **FIGHT FOR ROCK** [-] [-] German
– Fight for rock / Mr. Gold / Midnite in China / You hurt my soul (on'n'on) / Turn it on / Evil.

Aug 86. (lp/c)(cd) *(VERH/+C 41)(<830 237-2>)* **TRUE AS STEEL** [ ] [ ]
– Mr. Gold / Fight for rock / Love in the danger zone / Speed of sound / Midnite in China / Vorwarts, all right! / True as steel / Lady in a rock'n'roll hell / Love song / Igloo on the moon (reckless).

— **TOMMY BOLAN** (b.1966, New York) – guitar; repl. SZIGETI

Oct 87. (12") *(870 398-1)* **FUR IMMER. / KISS OF DEATH / METAL TANGO** [ ] [-]

Nov 87. (lp/c)(cd) *(VERH/+C 50)(830 237-2) <832804>* **TRIUMPH AND AGONY** [ ] [80]
– All we are / Three minute warning / I rule the ruins / Kiss of death / Make time for love / East meets west / Touch of evil / Metal tango / Cold, cold world / Fur immer.

— disbanded when DORO went solo

DORO

— augmented by **TOMMY BOLAN + TOMMY HENRIKSEN** – bass

Vertigo Mercury

Feb 89. (12") *(872 609-1)* **A WHITER SHADE OF PALE / HELLRAISER. / EARTHSHAKER ROCK / OUT OF CONTROL** [ ] [–]

Mar 89. (lp/c/cd; as DORO AND WARLOCK) *<(838 016-1/-4/-2)>* **FORCE MAJEURE** [ ] [ ]
– A whiter shade of pale / Save my soul / World gone wild / Mission of mercy / Angels with dirty faces / Beyond the trees / Hard times / Hellraiser / I am what I am / Cry wolf / Under the gun / River of tears / Bis aufs blut.

Apr 89. (12"ep) *(876 169-1)* **HARD TIMES / FUR IMMER (live). / I RULE THE RUINS / SAVE MY SOUL** [–] [–] German

— with **GENE SIMMONS** (of KISS) – co-writer, executive producer

Jun 90. (cd/c/lp) *<(846 194-2/-4/-1)>* **DORO** [ ] [ ]
– Unholy love / I had too much to dream / Rock on / Only you / I'll be holding on / Something wicked this way comes / Rare diamond / Broken / Alive / Mirage.

Mar 91. (cd/c/lp; DORO & WARLOCK) *<(848 353-2/-4/-1)>* **RARE DIAMONDS** (compilation) [ ] [–]
– All we are / Unholy love / Fur immer / True as steel / East meets west / Rare diamond / You hurt my soul / Hellbound / A whiter shade of pale / Burning the witches / Without you / Love song / Out of control / Beyond the trees.

Mar 93. (cd/c) *(514 309-2/-4)* **ANGELS NEVER DIE** [ ] [–]
– Eyes on you / Bad blood / Last day of my life / Born to bleed / Cryin' / You ain't lived (till you're loved to death) / So alone together / All I want / Enough for you / Heaven with you / Don't go / Alles ist gut.

Dec 93. (cd/c) *(518 680-2/-4)* **DORO LIVE (live)** [–] [–] German
– I rule the ruins / Hellbound / Only you / Bad blood / So alone together / Fall for me again / Fur immer / Metal tango / Let's rock forever / Eye on you / All we are / Enough for you / I am what I am / Whenever I think of you / Children of the night / Burning the witches / Alles ist gut.

1996. (cd/c/lp) *(526 804-2/-4/-1)* **MACHINE II MACHINE** [–] [–] German
– Tie me up / The want / Ceremony / Machine II machine / Are they comin' for me / Can't stop thinking about you / Don't mistake it for love / Desperately / Love is a thrill / Welcome to the tribe / Like whiskey straight / In freiheit stirat mein hers.

— her band now incl. **ANDREAS BRUHN** – bass, guitar, etc / **ERIC SINGER** – drums / **CHRIS LIETZ** – keyboards / **JOE TAYLOR** – guitar / (and guests)

S.P.V. Koch

Oct 00. (cd/d-lp) *(SPV 0857204-2/-1)* *<8151>* **CALLING THE WILD** [ ] [ ] Sep00
– Terrovision / I give my blood (dedication) / White wedding / I wanna live / Kiss me like a cobra / Love me forever / Pain / Give me a reason / Fuel / Scarred / Now or never / Alone again / Constant danger / Burn it up.

Apr 01. (cd-s) **WHITE WEDDING / WHITE WEDDING (album version) / I ADORE YOU / WHITE WEDDING (cd-video)** [ ] [–]

WARRANT

Formed: Los Angeles, California, USA . . . 1986 by JOEY ALLEN, ERIK TURNER, JERRY DIXON and STEVEN SWEET, who subsequently recruited hearthrob singer JANI LANE. After a couple of years slogging it out on Sunset Strip, they were the subject of intense major label interest and signed their talents up to 'Columbia'. With pretty boy glam bands going down a storm, WARRANT were well placed to score with their streamlined pop-metal and slyly cheeky sexual innuendos. It came as no surprise, then, when a debut single, 'DOWN BOYS', cracked the US Top 30. The accompanying BEAU HILL-produced album, 'DIRTY ROTTEN FILTHY STINKING RICH' (1989), eventually made the Top 10 following the massive success of MTV-friendly ballads, 'HEAVEN' and 'SOMETIMES SHE CRIES', the former narrowly missing the No.1 slot. A follow-up set, 'CHERRY PIE' (1990), was even more successful, the coy title track making the Top 10 while WARRANT enjoyed the teen adulation in the calm before the grunge storm. By the following year, WARRANT were already making a concerted effort to distance themselves from their knicker-wetting fanbase and with the 'DOG EAT DOG' (1992) album, they attempted a "serious" approach. This had the effect of alienating them from their former fanbase, while failing to endear them to a more streetwise audience. Disillusioned, LANE departed for a solo career, and although he later rejoined, subsequent 'Music For Nations' albums, 'ULTRAPHOBIC' (1995) and 'BELLY TO BELLY VOL.1' (1997) were released to minimal interest. • **Songwriters:** JANI LANE, except cover of TRAIN, TRAIN (Blackfoot).

Album rating: DIRTY ROTTEN FILTHY STINKING RICH (*5) / CHERRY PIE (*6) / DOG EAT DOG (*5) / ULTRAPHOBIC (*5) / THE BEST OF WARRANT compilation (*6) / BELLY TO BELLY VOL.1 (*4) / GREATEST AND LATEST part compilation (*5)

JANI LANE – vocals / **JOEY ALLEN** – guitar / **ERIK TURNER** – guitar / **JERRY DIXON** – bass / **STEVEN SWEET** – drums

C.B.S. Columbia

Apr 89. (7") *<68606>* **DOWN BOYS. / COLD SWEAT** [–] [27]

Jun 89. (lp/c/cd) *(465052-2/-4/-1)* *<44383>* **DIRTY ROTTEN FILTHY STINKING RICH** [ ] [10] Mar89
– 32 pennies / Down boys / Big talk / Sometimes she cries / So damn pretty (should be against the law) / D.R.F.S.R. / In the sticks / Heaven / Ridin' high / Cold sweat.

Sep 89. (7"/7"s) *(HEAVN/+Q 1)* *<68985>* **HEAVEN. / IN THE STICKS** [ ] [2] Jul89
(12"+=/12"pic-d+=/cd-s+=) *(HEAVN T/P/C 1)* – Cold sweat.

Oct 89. (c-s,cd-s) *<73035>* **BIG TALK. / D.R.F.S.R.** [–] [93]

Dec 89. (c-s,cd-s) *<73095>* **SOMETIMES SHE CRIES / 32 PENNIES / IN A RAG JAR** [–] [20]

Sep 90. (cd/c/lp) *(467190-2/-4/-1)* *<45487>* **CHERRY PIE** [ ] [7]
– Cherry pie / Uncle Tom's cabin / I saw red / Bed of roses / Sure feels good to me / Love in stereo / Blind faith / Song and dance man / You're the only hell your mama ever raised / Mr. Rainmaker / Train, train.

Oct 90. (7"/7"pic-d/c-s) *(656258-7/-0/-4)* *<73510>* **CHERRY PIE. / THIN DISGUISE** [59] [10] Sep90
(12"+=/pic-cd-s+=) *(656258-8/-5)* – Heaven / D.R.F.S.R.

Dec 90. (c-s,cd-s) *<73597>* **I SAW RED / ('A'acoustic)** [–] [10]

Feb 91. (7"/c-s) *(656686-7/-4)* **CHERRY PIE. / THIN DISGUISE** [35] [–]
(d7"+=/12"+=/cd-s+=) *(656686-0/-6/-5)* – Heaven / D.R.F.S.R.

Apr 91. (c-s,cd-s) *<73644>* **UNCLE TOM'S CABIN / SURE FEELS GOOD TO ME** [–] [78]

Jun 91. (c-s,cd-s) *<73598>* **BLIND FAITH / MR. RAINMAKER** [–] [88]

Mar 92. (c-s,cd-s) *<74207>* **WE WILL ROCK YOU / BLIND FAITH (acoustic)** [–] [83]
(above from the film 'Gladiator')

Columbia Columbia

Sep 92. (cd/c/lp) *(472033-2/-4/-1)* *<52584>* **DOG EAT DOG** [74] [25]
– Machine gun / The hole in my wall / April 2031 / Andy Warhol was right / Bonfire / The bitter pill / Hollywood (so far, so good) / All my bridges are burning / Quicksand / Let it rain / Inside out / Sad Theresa.

Sep 92. (c-s,cd-s) *<74445>* **MATCHING GUN / INSIDE OUT** [–] [ ]

Nov 92. (c-s,cd-s) **THE BITTER PILL. / QUICKSAND** [–] [ ]

Music For Nations C.M.C.

Mar 95. (cd) *(CDMFN 183)* *<7203-2>* **ULTRAPHOBIC** [ ] [ ]
– Undertow / Followed / Family picnic / Sun of one / Chameleon / Crawl space / Live inside you / High / Ride #2 / Ultraphobic / Stronger now.

C.M.C. C.M.C.

May 97. (cd) *<(0607 686200-2)>* **BELLY TO BELLY VOL.1** [ ] [ ]
– In the end / Feels good / Letter to a friend / A.Y.M. / Indian giver / Falling down / Interlude / Solid / All 4 U / Coffeee house / Interlude / Vertigo / Room with a view / Nobody else.

Zebra Zebra

Apr 00. (cd) *<(CDMZEB 12)>* **GREATEST AND LATEST** (part compilation) [ ] [ ]
– Cherry pie / The Jones / Downboys / Southern comfort / Hollywood (so far, so far) / Uncle Tom's cabin / Sometimes she cries / 32 pennies / Heaven / Thin disguise / I saw red / Bad tattoo / Cherry pie (Sigue Sigue Sputnik remix) / Downboys (razed in black remix) / 32 pennies (Meeks remix) / Downboys (Julian Beeston remix).

– compilations, etc. –

Jul 96. (cd) *Columbia; (484012-2) / Sony; <64775>* **THE BEST OF WARRANT** [ ] [ ]
– Down boys / 32 pennies / D.R.F.S.R. / Big talk / Sometimes she cries / Cherry pie / Thin disguise / Uncle Tom's cabin / I saw red / Bed of roses / Mr. Rainmaker / Sure feels good to me / Hole in my wall / Machine gun / We will rock you. *(re-iss. May99; same)*

WARRIOR

Formed: Los Angeles, California, USA . . . 1984 by PARRAMORE McCARTY, TOMMY ASAKAWA, JOE FLOYD, BRUCE TURGON and JIMMY VOLPE (the WARRIOR moniker now spare, after the UK group abandoned it after a few releases on their own label). A much heralded metal outfit touting armour-plated bombast and cliched lyrics, WARRIOR were signed to Virgin subsidiary '10' on the strength of a demo tape. When their debut 'FIGHTIN' FOR THE EARTH' (1985) finally saw the harsh light of day, however, the rock media decided fairly and squarely that WARRIOR had not put their money where their chainmail was and dismissed them as chancers. Both frontmen McCARTY and bassist TURGON went on to play with STEVE STEVEN'S ATOMIC PLAYBOYS, the latter rejoining LOU GRAMM (ex-BLACK SHEEP) in the new SHADOW KING outfit.

Album rating: FIGHTING FOR THE EARTH (*3)

PARRAMORE McCARTY – vocals / **TOMMY ASAKAWA** – guitar / **JOE FLOYD** – guitar / **BRUCE TURGON** – bass (ex-BLACK SHEEP) / **JIMMY VOLPE** – drums

10-Virgin not iss.

Feb 85. (7"/12"pic-d) *(TEN/+Y 38)* **FIGHTING FOR THE EARTH. / ONLY THE STRONG SURVIVE** [ ] [–]

Jun 85. (lp/c) *(XID/CDIX 9)* **FIGHTING FOR THE EARTH** [ ] [–]
– Fighting for the earth / Only the strong survive / Ruler / Mind over matter / Defenders of creation / Day of the evil . . . (beware) / Cold fire / PTM 1 / Welcome abroad. *(re-iss. Jun88; same)* *<US cd-iss. 1991 on 'Metal Blade'; 26531>*

— disbanded in 1986, McCARTY joined STEVE STEVEN'S ATOMIC PLAYBOYS, while TURGON rejoined old mucker LOU GRAMM in the group SHADOW KING. The WARRIOR who released 'LET BATTLE COMMENCE' in '94 was not the same band

WARRIOR SOUL

Formed: New York, USA . . . 1989 by one-time video-DJ, KORY CLARKE, alongside JOHN RICCO, PETE McCLANAHAN and PAUL FERGUSON. This celebrated cerebro-metal quartet first came to the attention of rock fans in 1990 with their 'Geffen' debut, 'LAST DECADE, DEAD CENTURY'. One of the earliest "nu-metal" acts, WARRIOR SOUL took the musical bad acid nightmare of the 60's dream gone wrong and set it to socio-political commentary on the terminal condition of modern day America, CLARKE coming on like a latter day JIM MORRISON. Dark, dense and brooding, the creeping decay of WARRIOR SOUL's music was a perfect backdrop for CLARKE, the frontman spitting out more of his apocalyptic poetry on the following set, 'DRUGS, GOD AND THE NEW REPUBLIC' (1991). Having already supported the likes of METALLICA, WARRIOR SOUL further refined their live approach on a US jaunt with QUEENSRYCHE. Critical darlings, WARRIOR SOUL became more revered with subsequent releases, 'SALUTATIONS FROM THE GHETTO NATION' (1992) and 'CHILL PILL'

(1993), although they struggled to achieve the same high profile enjoyed by more successful alternative metal acts. With the latter record representing something of a climax to CLARKE's spiteful diatribes, 1994's 'SPACE AGE PLAYBOYS' took a more inspiring approach. The record was also their first for 'Music For Nations', their swansong in '96 going under the lovely no-messing title of 'FUCKER'! Just when you thought you'd heard the last of KORY, he was back with a new metal-glam line-up (JOHNNY JETSON, RILEY BAXTER and STEVE DELUXE) under the banner of the SPACE AGE PLAYBOYS. Alcohol-infused tracks such as 'I WANT SOME PUSSY' and 'TOKYO GIRLS GO BANG BANG' were typical "shag-nasty" fodder; it was as if KORY had never disappeared. • **Covered:** TWENTY FOUR HOURS (Joy Division).

Album rating: LAST DECADE, DEAD CENTURY (*7) / DRUGS, GOD AND THE NEW REPUBLIC (*5) / SALUTATIONS FROM THE GHETTO NATION (*7) / CHILL PILL (*5) / THE SPACE AGE PLAYBOYS (*6) / FUCKER (*4) / CLASSICS compilation (*7) / Space Age Playboys: NEW ROCK UNDERGROUND (*6) / LIVE IN LONDON (*4)

KORY CLARKE – vocals / **JOHN RICCO** – guitar / **PETE McCLANAHAN** – bass / **PAUL FERGUSON** – drums

Geffen Geffen

Apr 90. (cd)(lp/c) *<(7599 24285-2)>(WX 344/+C)* **LAST DECADE DEAD CENTURY**
– I see the ruins / We cry out / The losers / Downtown / Trippin' on ecstasy / One minute year / Superpower dreamland / Charlie's out of prison / Blown away / Lullaby / In conclusion. *(cd+=)* – Four more years. *(re-iss. Aug91 cd/c; DGC D/C 24285)*

Jun 91. (lp/c/cd) *<(DGC/+C/D 24389)>* **DRUGS, GOD AND THE NEW REPUBLIC**
– Intro / Interzone / Drugs, God and the new republic / The answer / Rocket 88 / Jump for joy / My time / Real thing / Man must live as one / Hero / The wasteland / Children of the winter.

— **MARK EVANS** – drums; repl. FERGUSON

Jul 92. (7") *(DGC 10)* **HERO. / GHETTO NATION**
(12"+=/cd-s+=) *(DGCT/+D 10)* – Twenty-four hours.

Sep 92. (cd/c/lp) *<(GED/GEC/GEF 24488)>* **SALUTATIONS FROM THE GHETTO NATION**
– Love destruction / Blown / Shine like it / Dimension / Punk and belligerent / Ass-kickin / The party / The golden shore / Trip rider / I love you / The fallen / Ghetto nation.

Oct 93. (cd/c) *<(GED/GEC 24608)>* **CHILL PILL**
– Mars / Cargos of doom / Song in your mind / Shock um down / Let me go / Ha ha ha / Concrete frontier / I want some / Soft / High road. *(cd re-iss. Jul97; same)*

— **SCOTT DUBOIS** – drums; repl. EVANS

— **X. FACTOR** – guitar; repl. RICCO who later formed NUMB

Music For Nations Futurists

Oct 94. (cd/c/lp) *(CD/T+/MFN 172) <11072>* **THE SPACE AGE PLAYBOYS**
– Rocket engines / The drug / Let's get wasted / No no no / Television / The pretty faces / The image / Rotten soul / I wanna get some / Look at you / Star ride / Generation graveyard.

Sep 96. (cd) *(CDMFN 204)* **FUCKER** -
– NYC girl / Gimme some of this / Punk rock'n'roll / Turn on / 5 ways to the gutter / Stun fun / My sky / Makin' it / Raised on riots / American / Kiss me / This joy / Can't fix / Come to me / Last decade dead century / If you think you're dead.

— the band had already split in '95

– compilations, etc. –

Sep 00. (cd) *Dream Catcher; (CRIDE 34)* **CLASSICS**
– Love destruction / Downtown / Punk and belligerent / Song in your mind / Super power dreamland / The losers / We are the government Cargoes of doom / Blown away / Trippin' on ecstasy / The wasteland / The drug / Let's get wasted / Rotten soul / I wanna get some / Blown.

SPACE AGE PLAYBOYS

KORY CLARKE – vocals / **JOHNNY JETSON** – guitar / **RILEY BAXTER** – bass (ex-KILLING MACHINE) / **STEVE DELUXE** – drums

Dream Catcher

Feb 99. (cd) *(CRIDE 10)* **NEW ROCK UNDERGROUND**
– Buzz on / The band gets high / Rocket girl / Jets / Phaze out / Cities, scenes and thieves / Ambient guru / Rock'n'roll guru / Tokyo girls go bang bang / I want some pussy.

Oct 99. (cd) *(CRIDE 18)* **LIVE IN LONDON (live)**
– It's time to party / Rocket girl / Jets / I want some pussy / Tokyo girls / Cities scenes and thieves / Band gets high / Phaze out / Rock'n'roll limo / All that glitters.

W.A.S.P.

Formed: Los Angeles, California, USA . . . 1983 as W.A.S.P. (We Are Sexual Perverts/White Anglo Saxon Protestants?, just two of the many possibilities touted by fans and commentators alike over the years, the debate now enshrined in metal myth) by 6'4" New Yorker (ex-NEW YORK DOLLS reincarnation), BLACKIE LAWLESS, together with CHRIS HOLMES, RANDY PIPER and TONY RICHARDS. Coming on like a cartoon ALICE COOPER with about as much subtlety as a sledgehammer, W.A.S.P. held fast by every heavy metal cliche in the book (as well as inventing a few of their own), confirming every parent's worst nightmare about "that awful music". In spite of this, or more likely because of it, they were one of the most entertaining and amusing metal bands of the 80's. Who else would've had the balls to sign to a respected major like 'Capitol' then expect them to release 'ANIMAL (FUCK LIKE A BEAST)'? In the event, 'Music For Nations' did the honors and 'Capitol' consoled themselves with a marginally less offensive debut album, 'W.A.S.P.' (1984). LAWLESS and Co. didn't trade on outrage alone, no, surprisingly they actually had songs, hooks and melodies to back them up, tracks like 'I WANNA BE SOMEBODY' expoiting the same teen rebel formula perfected by KISS / TWISTED SISTER in equally anthemic style. Lyrics aside, W.A.S.P. caused even greater consternation among the pseudo-liberals at the PMRC with their gleefully unreconstructed stage show. A tongue-in-cheek gorefest with plenty of fake blood, topless women being 'tortured', BLACKIE flaunting his famous cod-piece etc., the W.A.S.P. live experience became the stuff of legend, although by the time the group had graduated from seedy L.A. clubs to theatres and stadiums, things had been considerably toned down. With STEPHEN RILEY replacing RICHARDS, the group released a follow-up set in September '85, 'THE LAST COMMAND'. A transatlantic Top 50 chart hit, the album was a slight improvement on the debut featuring such enduring stage favourites as the howling 'WILD CHILD' and 'BLIND IN TEXAS'. Amid continuing battles with their would-be censors and a new bassist, JOHNNY ROD, W.A.S.P. released a third set, 'INSIDE THE ELECTRIC CIRCUS', in late '86, showing their unlikely musical influences with covers of Uriah Heep's 'EASY LIVIN' and Ashford & Simpson's (made famous by Humble Pie) 'I DON'T NEED NO DOCTOR'. 'LIVE . . . IN THE RAW' (1987) marked a kind of last stand of the old W.A.S.P., the closing of the first turbulent period of their career before they turned all 'professional' on us. With the help of keyboard veteran (KEN HENSLEY), W.A.S.P. substituted the blood and guts for a surprisingly mature set of state-of-society ruminations. Still, LAWLESS bellowing along to 'REBEL IN THE F.D.G.' (Fucking Decadent Generation, apparently), sounds just a tad ridiculous if not hypocritical. The set provided the group with their biggest UK success to date (boosted by a furious Top 20 cover of The Who's 'REAL ME') although the change of approach didn't go down too well in the States. HOLMES subsequently departed in less than amicable circumstances, while LAWLESS revamped the band in 1990 as BLACKIE LAWLESS AND WASP, recruiting a line-up of ROD, HENSLEY, FRANKIE BANALI and BOB GULLICK for 1992's 'THE CRIMSON IDOL'. A concept album of all things, the record nevertheless gave LAWLESS a brief tenure in the UK Top 30. After touring the record and releasing the 'FIRST BLOOD, LAST CUTS' (1993) compilation, BLACKIE officially went solo, releasing 'STILL NOT BLACK ENOUGH' (1995) on the 'Raw Power' label. While he still commands a diehard fanbase, LAWLESS' golden days of controversy and outrage seem to be over. W.A.S.P.'s shlock-rock pales into almost non-existent insignificance next to the genuinely stomach churning output of modern death-metal acts, but can these young whippersnappers boast a fire-breathing cod-piece!?, can they heck as like! • **Songwriters:** Most written by LAWLESS and PIPER, except PAINT IT BLACK (Rolling Stones) / LOCOMOTIVE BREATH (Jethro Tull) / LONG WAY TO THE TOP + WHOLE LOTTA ROSIE (Ac-Dc) / SOMEBODY TO LOVE (Jefferson Airplane). • **Trivia:** Late in 1989, the lucky HOLMES married metal-songstress LITA FORD.

Album rating: W.A.S.P. (*5) / THE LAST COMMAND (*6) / INSIDE THE ELECTRIC CIRCUS (*6) / LIVE . . . IN THE RAW (*4) / THE HEADLESS CHILDREN (*5) / THE CRIMSON IDOL (*6) / FIRST BLOOD, LAST CUTS compilation (*6) / STILL NOT BLACK ENOUGH (*4) / KILL, F**, DIE (*3) / DOUBLE LIVE ASSASSINS (*3) / HELLDORADO (*3) / DOUBLE LIVE ASSASSINS (*5)

BLACKIE LAWLESS (b. STEVE DUREN, 4 Sep'54, Florida) – vocals, bass (ex-SISTER, ex-NEW YORK DOLLS) / **CHRIS HOLMES** (b.23 Jun'61) – lead guitar (ex-SISTER) / **RANDY PIPER** – rhythm guitar / **TONY RICHARDS** – drums

Music For Nations not iss.

Apr 84. (12",12"white/7"sha-pic-d/7") *(12/P+KUT 109)* **ANIMAL (F**K LIKE A BEAST). / SHOW NO MERCY** -
(re-iss. 12"pic-d.May85; PIG 109) (re-iss. 12"/12"w-poster, Feb88; 12KUT/+P 109) **LIVE ANIMAL. / DB BLUES / ANIMAL**; *hit UK 61)*

Capitol Capitol

Aug 84. (lp/c) *(EJ 240195-1/-4) <12343>* **W.A.S.P.** 51 74
– I wanna be somebody / L.O.V.E. machine / The flame / B.A.D. / School daze / Hellion / Sleeping (in the fire) / On your knees / Tormentor / The torture never stops. *(re-iss. Jun88 on 'Fame' lp/c; FA/TCFA 3201) (cd-iss. May89; CDFA 3201) (re-iss. Jul94 cd/c; CDP 746661-2/-4) (cd re-iss. Sep97 on 'Snapper'; SMMCD 501)*

Sep 84. (7")(12"/12"pic-d) *(CL 336)(12CL/+P 336)* **I WANNA BE SOMEBODY. / TORMENTOR (RAGEWARS)** -

Jan 85. (7"/12") *(CL/12CL 344)* **SCHOOLDAZE. / PAINT IT BLACK** -

— **STEPHEN RILEY** – drums (ex-KEEL) repl. RICHARDS

Sep 85. (lp/c) *(EJ 240429-1/-4) <12435>* **THE LAST COMMAND** 48 49
– Wild child / Ballcrusher / Fistful of diamonds / Jack action / Widowmaker / Blind in Texas / Cries in the night / The last command / Running wild in the streets / Sex drive. *(re-iss. May89 on 'Fame' cd/c/lp; CD/TC+/FA 3218) (re-iss. Jul94 cd/c; CD/TC EST 2025) (cd re-iss. Sep97 on 'Snapper'; SMMCD 502)*

Oct 85. (7"/7"pic-d) *(CL/+P 374)* **BLIND IN TEXAS. / SAVAGE** -
(12"+=/12"pic-d+=) *(12CL/+P 374)* – I wanna be somebody (live).

Jun 86. (7") *(CL 388)* **WILD CHILD. / MISSISSIPPI QUEEN** 71 -
(d7"+=) *(CLD 388)* – On your knees / Hellion.
(12"+=) *(12CL 388)* – ('A'-wild mix).

— **JOHNNY ROD** (b. 8 Dec'57, Missouri) – bass (ex-KING KOBRA) repl. PIPER

— **BLACKIE** now also rhythm guitar

Sep 86. (7"/7"pic-d) *(CL/+P 432)* **9.5 N.A.S.T.Y. / EASY LIVING** 70 -
(12"+=) *(12CL 432)* – Flesh and fire.

Oct 86. (lp/c; as WASP) *(EST/TCEST 2025) <12531>* **INSIDE THE ELECTRIC CIRCUS** 53 60
– The big welcome / Inside the electric circus / I don't need no doctor / 95 nasty / Restless gypsy / Shoot it from the hip / I'm alive / Easy living / Sweet cheetah / Mantronic / King of Sodom and Gomorrah / The rock rolls on. *(cd-iss. Apr87; CDP 746346-2) (re-iss. May89 lp/c)(cd; ATAK/TCATAK 133)(CZ 212) (re-iss. Jul90 on*

'Fame' cd/c/lp; CD/TC+/FA 3238) (re-iss. Jul94 cd/c; same) (cd re-iss. Feb98 on 'Snapper'; SMMCD 505)

Aug 87. (7") *(CL 458) <44063>* **SCREAM UNTIL YOU LIKE IT. / SHOOT IT FROM THE HIP (live)** 32 —
(12"+=/12"pic-d+=) *(12CL/+P 458)* – Sleeping (in the fire).

Sep 87. (cd/c/lp) *(CD/TC+/EST 2040) <48053>* **LIVE . . . IN THE RAW (live)** 23 77
– Inside the electric circus / I don't need no doctor / L.O.V.E. machine / Wild child / 9.5 N.A.S.T.Y. / Sleeping (in the fire) / The manimal / I wanna be somebody / Harder faster / Blind in Texas. *(cd+=)* – Scream until you like it (theme from 'Ghoulies II'). *(re-iss. Jul94 cd/c; same) (cd re-iss. Feb98 on 'Snapper'; SMDCD 506)*

Oct 87. (7"/7"s/7"w-poster/7"sha-pic-d) *(CL/+B/S/P 469)* **I DON'T NEED NO DOCTOR. / WIDOW MAKER (live)** 31 -
(12"+=/12"w-poster+=) *(12CL/+P 469)* – Sex drive (live).

— now basic trio of **BLACKIE, CHRIS & JOHNNY** when STEPHEN joined L.A. GUNS. **FRANKIE BANALI** – drums (of QUIET RIOT) filled in temp. / added guest **KEN HENSLEY** – keyboards (ex-URIAH HEEP, ex-BLACKFOOT)

Feb 89. (7"/7"pic-d/7"purple) *(CL/+P/M 521)* **MEAN MAN. / LOCOMOTIVE BREATH** 21 -
(12"+=/12"g-f+=/cd-s+=) *(12CL/12CLP/CDCL 521)* – For whom the bells toll.

Apr 89. (cd/c/lp) *(CD/TC+/EST 2087) <48942>* **THE HEADLESS CHILDREN** 8 48
– The heretic (the lost child) / The real me / The headless children / Thunderhead / Mean man / The neutron bomber / Mephisto waltz / Forever free / Maneater / Rebel in the F.D.G. *(pic-lp Oct89; ESTPD 2087) (re-iss. Jul94 cd/c; same) (cd re-iss. Apr98 on 'Snapper'; SMMCD 509)*

May 89. (7"/7"blue/7"pic-d) *(CL/+G/PD 534)* **THE REAL ME. / THE LAKE OF FOOLS** 23 -
(12"+=/12"w-poster+=/cd-s+=) *(12CL/12CLS/CDCL 534)* – War cry.

Aug 89. (7"/7"s/7"sha-pic-d)(etched-12")(c-s) *(CL/+S/P 546)(12CLS 546)(TCCL 546)* **FOREVER FREE. / L.O.V.E. MACHINE (live '89)** — -
(12"+=/cd-s+=) *(12/CD CL 546)* – Blind in Texas (live'89).

— JOHNNY ROD left in 1989 as band split. Reformed in August 1990 as BLACKIE LAWLESS & WASP, but they soon returned to original name. **BLACKIE, JOHNNY, KEN, FRANKIE** + new member **BOB KULICK** – guitar

Parlophone Capitol

Mar 92. (7"/7"pic-d) *(RS/+P 6308)* **CHAINSAW CHARLIE (MURDERS IN THE NEW MORGUE). / PHANTOM IN THE MIRROR** 17 -
(12"+=/cd-s+=) *(12/CD RS 6308)* – The story of Jonathan (prologue to the crimson idol – part I).

— the April tour added **DAN McDADE** – guitar / **STET HOWLAND** – drums

May 92. (7"crimson/7"pic-d) *(RS/RPD 6314)* **THE IDOL. / THE STORY OF JONATHAN (PROLOGUE TO THE CRIMSON IDOL – PART II)** 41 -
(12"+=/pic-cd+=) *(12/CD RS 6314)* – The eulogy.

Jun 92. (cd/c/red-lp) *(CD/TC+/PCS 118) <99443>* **THE CRIMSON IDOL** 21 — May93
– The Titanic overture / The invisible boy / Arena of pleasure / Chainsaw Charlie (murders in the New Morgue) / The gypsy meets the boy / Doctor Rockter / I am one / The idol / Hold on to my heart / The great misconceptions of me. *(cd re-iss. Mar98 on 'Snapper'; SMMCD 507)*

Oct 92. (7"/7"pic-d) *(R/RPD 6324)* **I AM ONE. / WILD CHILD** 56 -
(10"+=) *(10RG 6324)* – Charlie chainsaw / I wanna be somebody.
(cd-s) *(CDRS 6324)* – ('A'side) / The invisible boy / The real me / The great misconception of me.

Capitol Capitol

Oct 93. (7") *(CL 698)* **SUNSET & BABYLON. / ANIMAL (F**K LIKE A BEAST)** 38 -
(cd-s+=) *(CDCL 698)* – Sleeping in the fire / I wanna be somebody.
(12"+=) *(12CL 698)* – School daze / On your knees.
(12"pic-d) *(12CLP 698)* – ('A'side) / Hellion / Show no mercy.

Oct 93. (cd/c/lp) *(CD/TC+/ESTG 2217) <80517>* **FIRST BLOOD . . . LAST CUTS** (compilation) 69 — May94
– Animal (f**k like a beast) / L.O.V.E. machine (remix) / I wanna be somebody (remix) / On your knees / Blind in Texas (remix) / Wild child (remix) / I don't need no doctor (remix) / Sunset and Babylon / The real me / The headless children / Mean man / Forever free / Chainsaw Charlie / The idol / Hold on to my heart / Rock and roll to death.

Raw Power Raw Power

Jun 95. (7"sha-pic-d) *(RAWT 1007)* **BLACK FOREVER. / GOODBYE AMERICA** — -
(cd-s+=) *(RAWX 1005)* – Skin walker / One tribe.
(cd-s) *(RAWX 1006)* – ('A'side) / Long way to the top / Whole lotta Rosie.

Jun 95. (cd/c/lp) *<(RAW CD/MC/LP 103)>* **STILL NOT BLACK ENOUGH** 52 — Jan96
– Still not black enough / Somebody to love / Black forever / Scared to death / Goodbye America / Keep holding on / Rock and roll to death / Breathe / I can't / No way out of here. *(cd re-iss. Feb00 on 'Essential'; ESMCD 790)*

— line-up; **LAWLESS + HOWLAND** plus **MICHAEL DUDA** – bass + the returning **CHRIS HOLMES**

Mar 97. (cd-s) *(RAWX 1041)* **KILL, F**K, DIE /** — -

Apr 97. (cd) *(<RAWCD 114>)* **KILL, F**K, DIE** — — Apr99
– Kill, f**k, die / Take the addiction / My tortured eyes / Killahead / Kill your pretty face / Foetus / Little death / U / Wicked death / Horror. *(re-iss. Feb00 on 'Essential'; ESMCD 791)*

Snapper CMC Int.

Feb 98. (cd) *<86237>* **DOUBLE LIVE ASSASSINS** - —
– The medley / Wild child / Animal (fuck like a beast) / L.O.V.E. machine / Killahead / I wanna be somebody / U / The real me / Kill your pretty face / The horror // Blind in Texas / The headless children / The idol / Crimson idol medley: Little death – Mean man – Rock'n'roll to death.

May 99. (cd) *(SMACD 818) <86269>* **HELLDORADO** — —
– Drive by / Helldorado / Don't cry (just suck) / Damnation alley / Dirty balls / High on the flames / Cocaine cowboys / Don't die tonight / Saturday night cockfight / Hot rods to Hell.

Feb 00. (d-cd) *(SMDCD 275)* **DOUBLE LIVE ASSASSINS (live)** — —
– Medley: On Your knees / I don't need no doctor / Hellicon / Chainsaw Charlie (murders in the Rue Morgue) / Wild child / Animal (fuck like a beast) / L.O.V.E. machine / Killahead / I wanna be somebody / U / The real me / Kill your pretty face / Horror / Blind in Texas / The headless children / Idol / Crimson idol medley / Little death / Mean man / Rock'n'roll death.

– compilations, etc. –

Mar 00. (cd) *Snapper; (SMACD 825)* **BEST OF THE REST 1984-2000** — -

May 00. (3xcd-box) *Snapper; (SMXCD 106)* **THE BOX** — —
– (W.A.S.P. / THE LAST COMMAND / THE HEADLESS CHILDREN)

WATCHTOWER

Formed: Texas, USA . . . mid 80's by JASON McMASTER, DOUG KEYSER, BILLY WHITE and RICK COLALUCA. A densely complex fusion of thrash and avant-garde metal with mind-boggling dynamics, WATCHTOWER debuted with an independently released, US-only debut, 'ENERGETIC DISASSEMBLY', in 1985. McMASTER subsequently went on to play with the highly-touted DANGEROUS TOYS, the frontman replaced with ALAN TECCHIO. By the release of follow-up, 'CONTROL AND RESISTANCE' (1990), WHITE had also been succeeded, the breathtakingly talented JARZOMBEK taking up the slack. Despite cult acclaim, WATCHTOWER's challenging sound proved to be too much for the metal masses and they've since faded from view.

Album rating: ENERGETIC DISASSEMBLY (*5) / CONTROL AND RESISTANCE (*5)

JASON McMASTER – vocals / **BILLY WHITE** – guitar / **DOUG KEYSER** – bass / **RICK COLALUCA** – drums, percussion

not iss. Zombo

1985. (lp) *<44452>* **ENERGETIC DISASSEMBLY** - —
– Violent change / Asylum / Tyrants in distress / Social fears / Energetic disassembly / Argonne Forest / Cimmerian shadows / Meltdown. *(cd-iss. Dec97 on 'Institute Of Art'; RTD 3970002CD)*

— **ALAN TECCHIO** – vocals; repl. McMASTER who joined DANGEROUS TOYS

— **RON JARZOMBEK** – guitar; repl. WHITE

Noise S.P.V.

Feb 90. (cd/c/lp) *(N 0140-2/-4/-1) <85-4784>* **CONTROL AND RESISTANCE** — —
– Instruments of random murder / The eldritch / Mayday in Kiev / The fall of reason / Control and resistance / Hidden instincts / Life cycles / Dangerous toy.

— split after above

Jeff WATSON (see under ⇒ NIGHT RANGER)

Mike WATT (see under ⇒ MINUTEMEN)

WAYSTED

Formed: USA . . . 1982 by legendary ex-UFO bassman, PETE WAY, who recruited RONNIE KAYFIELD, PAUL RAYMOND, FRANK NOON and SCots frontman, FIN. Signed to 'Chrysalis' (home of WAY's previous outfit, UFO), WAYSTED released a fine debut set, 'VICES', in Autumn '83. Earthy hard-rock characterised by FIN's gravel-throated rasp, the second was met with encouraging reviews, even if it did contain a JEFFERSON AIRPLANE cover, 'SOMEBODY TO LOVE'. The first of many line-up changes which would plague WAYSTED's career came when BARRY BENEDETTA replaced PAUL RAYMOND. The ensuing tour saw the band playing with OZZY OSBOURNE and MOTLEY CRUE, perfect company for infamous party animal, WAY. More personnel changes followed as the aforementioned BENEDETTA, KAYFIELD and NOON exited. Various members came and went through the recording of the eponymous 'WAYSTED' (1984), although PAUL CHAPMAN (another ex-UFO man) remained a fairly constant figure. WAYSTED's debut for new label, 'Music For Nations', the record managed to scrape a UK Top 75 placing. A third set, 'THE GOOD THE BAD AND THE WAYSTED' (1985), was the last to feature FIN as DANNY VAUGHN was drafted in to take his place. Subsequently securing a new major label deal, this time with 'Parlophone', the revamped WAYSTED released the more polished 'SAVE YOUR PRAYERS'. Despite its classy approach, the album wasn't enough to sustain WAYSTED's flagging career, matters made worse when CHAPMAN departed and VAUGHN went off to form TYKETTO. The musical chairs finally came to an end in late '87, when WAY patched things up with a still-kicking, UFO.

Album rating: VICES (*6) / WAYSTED (*6) / THE GOOD, THE BAD, THE WAYSTED (*6) / COMPLETELY WAYSTED compilation (*6) / SAVE YOUR PRAYERS (*5)

FIN (b. IAN MUIR, Glasgow, Scotland) – vocals (ex-FLYING SQUAD) / **RONNIE KAYFIELD** (b.Philadelphia, USA) – lead guitar (ex-HEARTBREAKERS, ex-FRAGILE) / **PETE WAY** – bass (ex-UFO, ex-FASTWAY, ex-OZZY OSBOURNE, ex-MICHAEL SCHENKER GROUP) / **PAUL RAYMOND** – rhythm guitar, keyboards (ex-UFO, ex-OZZY OSBOURNE) / **FRANK NOON** – drums (ex-DEF LEPPARD, ex-BERNIE TORME)

Chrysalis Chrysalis

Sep 83. (lp/c) *(<CHR/ZCHR 1438>)* **VICES** 78 —
– Love loaded / Women in chains / Sleazy / Night of the wolf / Toy with the passion / Right from the start / Hot love / All belongs to you / Somebody to love. *(cd-iss. Jun99 on 'Zoom Club'; ZCRCD 5)*

Oct 83. (7") *(CHS 2736)* **CAN'T TAKE THAT LOVE AWAY. / WOMEN IN CHAINS** [ ] [-]

— **BARRY BENEDETTA** (b.Philadelphia) – rhythm guitar (ex-FRAGILE) repl. PAUL RAYMOND

Music For Nations / not iss.

Sep 84. (lp/c) *(MFN/TMFN 31)* **WAYSTED** [73] [-]
– Won't get out alive / The price you pay / Rock steady / Hurt so good / Cinderella boys.

May 85. (7"/12") *(KUT/12KUT 117)* **HEAVEN TONIGHT. / BALL AND CHAIN** [ ] [-]

May 85. (lp/c) *(MFN/TMFN 43)* **THE GOOD THE BAD AND THE WAYSTED** [ ] [-]
– Hang 'em high / Hi ho my baby / Heaven tonight / Manuel / Dead on your legs / Rolling out the dice / Land that lost the love / Crazy 'bout the stuff / Around and around. *(cd-iss. Dec92; CDMFN 43)*

— the remaining **WAY** recruited **PAUL CHAPMAN** – guitar (ex-UFO) + **DANNY VAUGHN** – vocals; to repl. FIN

— **JOHN DITEDDORO** – drums; repl. JERRY SHIRLEY, who repl. NOON

Parlophone / Capitol

Nov 86. (7") *(R 6142)* **BLACK AND BLUE. / OUT OF CONTROL** [ ] [-]
(12"+=) *(12R 6142)* – Wild nights.

Nov 86. (lp/c) *(PCS/TC-PCS 7307)* *<12369>* **SAVE YOUR PRAYERS** [ ] [ ] Mar87
– Walls fall down / Black & blue / Singing to the night / Hell comes home / Hero's die young / Heaven tonight / How the west was won / Wild night / Out of control / So long.

Feb 87. (7") *(R 6150)* *<5685>* **HEAVEN TONIGHT. / FIRE UNDER THE WHEELS** [ ] [ ]
(12"+=) *(12R 6150)* – Hell comes home.

— folded after above, VAUGHN was later frontman for TYKETTO

– compilations, etc. –

Sep 86. (lp/c) *Raw Power; (RAW LP/TC 019)* **COMPLETELY WAYSTED** [ ] [-]
May 00. (cd) *Zoom Club; (ZCRCD 24)* **YOU WON'T GET OUT ALIVE** [ ] [-]
May 00. (cd) *Zoom Club; (ZCRCD 28)* **WILDERNESS OF MIRROR SAVE YOUR . . .** [ ] [-]

WEEZER

Formed: Los Angeles, California, USA . . .1993 by RIVERS CUOMO, MATT SHARP and PATRICK WILSON. Signing to 'Geffen' and recruiting final member, BRIAN BELL, the group released their eponymous RIC OCASEK-produced debut album in September '94. Helped by the transatlantic success of singles such as 'UNDONE – THE SWEATER SONG' and the pogo-pop of 'BUDDY HOLLY', the album became one of the year's biggest sellers. Often described as The PIXIES meeting The BEACH BOYS, their blaring college 'nerd'-rock saw WEEZER riding the crest of an American 'new wave' triggered by the likes of GREEN DAY and OFFSPRING. Meanwhile, MATT SHARP was also busy with a side project, The RENTALS (comprising CHERIELYNN WESTRICH, ROD CERVERA, PETRA HADEN, PAT WILSON and JIM RICHARDS), releasing an album of New Wave-esque songs in 'RETURN OF THE RENTALS' (1995/96). A second WEEZER album, 'PINKERTON' (1996), was much of the same, although it brought the band a bit of grief when the American security firm of the same name brought legal action; the band have been inactive since. Stop press: WEEZER released their third long-awaited set, 'THE GREEN ALBUM', in May 2001, bringing back geek-rock to the masses. • **Songwriters:** CUOMO, a few w/ WILSON.

Album rating: WEEZER (*7) / PINKERTON (*7) / THE GREEN ALBUM (*8) / Rentals: RETURN OF THE RENTALS (*5) / SEVEN MORE MINUTES (*6)

RIVERS CUOMO – vocals / **BRIAN BELL** – guitar, vocals / **MATT SHARP** – bass, vocals / **PATRICK WILSON** – drums

Geffen / D.G.C.

Jan 95. (7"blue) *(GFS 85)* *<19378>* **UNDONE – THE SWEATER SONG. / HOLIDAY** [35] [57] Sep94
(c-s+=/cd-s+=) *(GFS C/TD 85)* – Mykel & Carli / Susanne.

Feb 95. (cd/c/lp) *<(GED/GEC/GEF 24629)>* **WEEZER** [23] [16] Aug94
– My name is Jonas / No one else / The world has turned and left me here / Buddy Holly / Undone – the sweater song / In the garage / Holiday / Only in dreams.

Apr 95. (7"/c-s) *(GFS/+C 88)* **BUDDY HOLLY. / JAMIE** [12] [-]
(cd-s+=) *(GFSTD 88)* – My name is Jonas / Surf wax America.

Jul 95. (10"ep/c-ep/cd-ep) *(GFS V/C/TD 95)* **SAY IT AIN'T SO (remix). / NO ONE ELSE (live acoustic) / JAMIE (live acoustic)** [37] [ ]

Sep 96. (7"/c-s) *(GFS/+C 22167)* **EL SCORCHO. / YOU GAVE YOUR LOVE TO ME SOFTLY** [50] [-]
(cd-s+=) *(GFSTD 22167)* – Devotion.

Oct 96. (cd/c) *<(GED/GEC 25007)>* **PINKERTON** [43] [19]
– Tired of sex / Getchoo / No other one / Why bother / Across the sea / Good life / El Scorcho / Pink triangle / Falling for you / Butterfly.

RENTALS

MATT SHARP – vocals, bass, Moog synthesizer / plus **CHERIELYNN WESTRICH** – vocals / **ROD CERVERA** – guitar / **PETRA HADEN** – violin, vocals / **JIM RICHARDS** – keyboards / **PAT WILSON** – drums

Warners / Maverick

Jan 96. (cd/c) *<(9362 46093-2/-4)>* **RETURN OF THE RENTALS** [ ] [ ] Nov95
– Love I'm searching for / Waiting / Friends of P. / Move on / Please let that be you / My summer girl / Brilliant boy / Naive / These days / Sweetness and tenderness.

Mar 96. (c-s) *(W 0340C)* **FRIENDS OF P. / SO SOON** [ ] [ ]
(cd-s+=) *(W 0340CD)* – Love I'm searching for.

Sire / Sire

Apr 99. (cd/c) *<(9362 46680-2/-4)>* **SEVEN MORE MINUTES** [ ] [ ]
– Getting by / Hello hello / She says it's alright / Cruise / Barcelona / Say goodbye forever / Overlee / Big daddy C / Keep sleeping / The man with two brains / Must be wrong / Insomnia / She says it's alright (reprise) / My head is in the sun / Jumping around.

WEEZER

— re-formed for 2001

May 01. (cd) *(493061-2)* *<493045>* **THE GREEN ALBUM** [31] [4]
– Don't let go / Photograph / Hash pipe / Island in the sun / Crab / Knockdown drag out / Smile / Simple pages / Glorious days / O girlfriend / I do *[UK-only]*.

WEIRDOS

Formed: Los Angeles, California, USA . . . 1976 initially as The BARBIES then The LUXURIOUS ADULTS by brothers JOHN and DIX DENNEY, with others CLIFF ROMAN, DAVID TROUT and NICKEY BEAT. In 1977, they unleashed the first of many cult-punk 45's, 'DESTROY ALL MUSIC', which somehow found its way by import to UK shores. A number of sporadic singles followed, although internal wrangles led to a split in 1981. They did however re-form in the early 90's, and even got round to an album going by the name of 'CONDOR'. Despite their lack of recognition during their short lifespan, this punk/new wave outfit are now regarded by many critics as US pioneers of the movement.

Album rating: WEIRD WORLD 1977-1981 TIME CAPSULE VOLUME ONE compilation (*8)

JOHN DENNEY – vocals / **DIX DENNEY** – guitar / **CLIFF ROMAN** – guitar / **DAVID TROUT** – bass / **NICKEY BEAT** – drums

not iss. / Dangerhouse

1977. (7") **DESTROY ALL MUSIC. /** [-] [ ]
1978. (7") *<SP 1063>* **WE GOT THE NEUTRON BOMB. / SOLITARY CONFINEMENT** [-] [ ]

— **BILLY PERSONS** – bass repl. TROUT

— **DANNY BENAIR** – drums repl. NICKEY

not iss. / Bomp

1979. (12"ep) *<W 3>* **WHO? WHAT? WHEN? WHERE? WHY?** [-] [ ]
– Jungle rock / Happy people / Big shot / Hitman / Idle life / Fort U.S.A.

not iss. / Numbskull

1979. (7") *<none>* **SKATEBOARDS TO HELL. / ADULTHOOD** [-] [ ]

— **WILLY WILLIAMS** – bass; repl. PERSONS

— **ART FOX** – drums; repl. BENAIR

not iss. / Rhino

1980. (12"ep) *<RNEP 508>* **ACTION DESIGN** [-] [ ]
– The hideout / I feel / Break on through / Helium bar.

— split but re-formed nearly a decade later. **DENNEY's + ROMAN**

Frontier / Frontier

1990. (cd/lp) *<(4623-2L/1L)>* **CONDOR** [ ] [ ]
May 91. (cd/lp) *(4630-2L/-4L/-1L)* **WEIRD WORLD 1977-1981 TIME CAPSULE VOLUME ONE** (compilation) [ ] [ ]
– Weird world / Arms race / Pagan / Helium bar / Rhythm syndrome / Fallout / Fort U.S.A. / Happy people / Message from the underworld / Teenage / I'm not like you / We got the neutron bomb / Solitary confinement / Life of crime.

— THE WEIRDOS FEATURING MR. GASSER cd from '95 was from surf band

WELLWATER CONSPIRACY (see under ⇒ SOUNDGARDEN)

Leslie WEST (see under ⇒ MOUNTAIN)

WHALE

Formed: Stockholm, Sweden . . . 1993 by former alternative comedian, HENRIK SCHYFFERT along with hip-hop producer, GORDON CYRUS and part-time actress/former punk, CIA SORO. Anthemic debut single, 'HOBO HUMPIN SLOBO BABE', was only intended as a one-off collaboration for 'East West', although WHALE landed a deal with 'Virgin' after its MTV/European success. A further two suitably salacious singles, 'PAY FOR ME' and 'I'LL DO YA' were also given heavy rotation on MTV and WHALE finally came within breathing distance of the Top 40 with mini-album, 'WE CARE' in mid-'95. On the back of this, they re-issued 'HOBO HUMPIN' and had an even bigger smash, especially in Britain, where it made No.15. Hip-hop thrash-punk with knee-trembling, sexual overtones, the WHALE sound was akin to an x-rated fusion of The BEASTIE BOYS and BJORK. After a gap of almost three years, the group (now minus CYRUS) returned in summer '98 with a single, 'FOUR BIG SPEAKERS', released as WHALE featuring BUS 75. A further two singles and an album, 'ALL DISCO DANCE MUST END IN BROKEN BONES' (1998) were all delivered in WHALE's uncompromising style but failed to generate the same fuss they'd been afforded last time round.

Album rating: WE CARE (*7) / ALL DISCO DANCE MUST END IN BROKEN BONES (*5)

HENRIK SCHYFFERT – instruments, etc / **GORDON CYRUS** – DJ, producer / **CIA SORO** – vocals

East West | Atlantic

Mar 94. (c-s) *(98281)* **HOBO HUMPIN' SLOBO BABE / EYE 242** [ ] [ ]
(12"+=/cd-s+=) *(98281)* – Lips. *(re-iss. Aug94; same)*

Hut | Virgin

May 95. (m-cd/m-c/m-lp) *(DGHUTM/HUTMMC/HUTMLP 24) <1793>* **PAY FOR ME** [ ] [ ]
– Pay for me / I think no / Darling Nikki / Buzzbox babe / Trying. *<US re-iss. Aug95; 38504>*

Hut | Feedback

Jul 95. (c-s) *(HUTC 51) <WH 125>* **I'LL DO YA / THE NOW THING** [53] [ ]
(ext-12"+=/cd-s+=) *(HUT T/DG 51)* – Sexy MM.

Hut | Virgin

Jul 95. (cd/c/lp) *(CDHUT/HUTMC/HUTLP 25) <40560>* **WE CARE** [42] [ ]
– Kickin' / That's where it's at / Pay for me / Eurodog / I'll do ya / Electricity / Hobo humpin' slobo babe / Tryzasnice / Happy in you / I miss me / Young, dumb & full of c*** / I'm cold / Born to raise hell.

Nov 95. (c-s) *(HUTC 64)* **HOBO HUMPIN' SLOBO BABE / YOU AND YOUR SISTER** [15] [-]
(cd-s+=) *(HUTCD 64)* – Singer star.
(cd-s) *(HUTDX 64)* – ('A'side) / ('A'-Doggy Style mix) / ('A'-Sniffin' plankton mix) / ('A'-Skorpio mix).

— CYRUS departed and was repl. by guitarist **JON JEFFERSON KLINGBERG** plus **HEIKKI KIVIAHO** – bass / **JORGEN WALL** – drums

Hut | Imprint

Jun 98. (cd-s; WHALE featuring BUS 75) *(HUTCD 96)* **FOUR BIG SPEAKERS / 14 ROCK STREET / ANYWHERE BUT HERE** [69] [-]
(cd-s) *(HUTDX 96)* – ('A'side) / ('A'-Cut La Roc remix) / ('A'-U-ziq remix).

Aug 98. (cd-s) *(HUTCD 102)* **CRYING AT AIRPORTS / HEAVY STICK / SPITTING INDOORS** [ ] [-]
(12"/cd-s) *(HUT T/DX 102)* – ('A'side) / ('A'mixes; Shawn J Period featuring Mos Def / Friends Wigga-no-no remake).

Aug 98. (cd) *(CDHUT 52) <110718>* **ALL DISCO DANCE MUST END IN BROKEN BONES** [ ] [ ]
– Crying at airports / Deliver the juice / Roadkill / Smoke / CTRL / Four big speakers / Go where you're feeling free / Into the strobe / Puma gym / You're no better than you feel / 2 cord song.

Mar 99. (12"/c-s/cd-s) *(HUT T/C/CD 110)* **DELIVER THE JUICE. / ('A'radio edit) / INTO THE STROBE** [ ] [-]

WHEATUS

Formed: Long Island, New York, USA . . . late 90's by frontman/songwriter BRENDAN BROWN together with his brother PETER, PHIL JIMENEZ and RICH LEIGEY (subsequently replaced by MIKE McCABE). Trailed by the massive US hit single, 'TEENAGE DIRTBAG' (with a video featuring 'American Pie' stars Jason Biggs and Mena Suvari), the band's eponymous major label debut album hit the shops in summer 2000. Bursting with spunky 3 minute volleys of clever clever teenage commentary, the record covered familiar power-pop/punk territory with the requisite big choruses and geeky attitude although a surprise inclusion was an apparently sincere cover of Erasure's 80's hit, 'A LITTLE RESPECT'. The aforementioned 'TEENAGE . . .' was subsequently featured in the film 'Loser' and went on to hit the UK Top 10 in early 2001; probably youth's anthem of the millennium so far – annoyingly catchy to the max and a namecheck for IRON MAIDEN to boot!

Album rating: WHEATUS (*6)

BRENDAN BROWN – vocals, guitar / **PHIL JIMENEZ** – keyboards, percussion / **RICH LEIGEY** – bass / **PETER BROWN** – drums

Columbia | Sony

Jul 00. (12") *<79468>* **TEENAGE DIRTBAG. / (other track by Prozzak)** [-] [ ]

Jan 01. (cd/c) *(499605-2/-4) <62146>* **WHEATUS** [7] [ ] Aug00
– Truffles / Sunshine / Teenage dirtbag / A little respect / Hump 'em n' dump 'em / Leroy / Hey, Mr. Brown / Love is a mutt from Hell / Punk ass bitch / Wannabe gangster. *(cd+=)* – Teenage dirtbag (video).

— (Jul'00) **MIKE McCABE** – bass; repl. LEIGEY

Feb 01. (c-s) *(670796-4)* **TEENAGE DIRTBAG / NEVER WRITE A SONG / MR. BROWN (with club audience)** [2] [-]
(cd-s+=) *(670796-2)* – ('A'-CD-ROM).

WHITE LION

Formed: Brooklyn, New York, USA . . . 1983 by MIKE TRAMP and VITO BRATTA (before heading to America, Danish-born TRAMP had previously enjoyed success in his native country with the group, MABEL). WHITE LION signed a six-figure deal with 'Elektra' that year, and with FELIX ROBINSON and NICKY CAPOZZI completing the line-up, the group recorded a debut set, 'FIGHT TO SURVIVE'. The label were unhappy with it, however, and the collection was shelved along with their contract. Subsequently surfacing in Japan on 'RCA-Victor', the record was finally given a Stateside release in 1986 by indie label, 'Grand Slam'. By this point, TRAMP and BRATTA had found a new rhythm section in JAMES LOMENZO and GREGG D'ANGELO, securing a deal with 'Atlantic'. 'PRIDE' was released to massive US success in 1987, its high quality songwriting raising the band well above the average spandex 'n' hairsray crew and resulting in two ballad-esque Top 10 hits, the affecting 'WAIT' and the tearjerking 'WHEN THE CHILDREN CRY'. Apart from the songs, the group's main asset was pretty-boy TRAMP, his cutesy vocals complementing perfectly the group's hard-edged AOR approach. 'BIG GAME' (1989) was equally impressive if not quite as commercial as its predecessor, the set including a passable cover of Golden Earring's 'RADAR LOVE' alongside the trademark fluff-rock like 'LITTLE FIGHTER'. The record failed to repeat their earlier success and the group subsequently enlisted yet another rhythm section, this time consisting of seasoned players, TOMMY 'T-Bone' CARADONNA and JIMMY DeGRASSO. A third and final effort, 'MANE ATTRACTION' (1991) lacked the sparkle characterising the best of their work and despite some belated UK Top 40 success, the record failed to break the US Top 50. TRAMP finally disbanded WHITE LION towards the end of '91, going on to form FREAK OF NATURE.

Album rating: FIGHT TO SURVIVE (*7) / PRIDE (*5) / MANE ATTRACTION (*4) / THE BEST OF WHITE LION compilation (*6)

MIKE TRAMP (b. Denmark) – vocals (ex-MABEL) / **VITO BRATTA** (b. 1 Jul'63) – guitar (ex-DREAMER) / **FELIX ROBINSON** – bass (ex-ANGEL) / **DAVE CAPOZZI** – drums

RCA Victor | not iss.

1985. (lp) **FIGHT TO SURVIVE** [-] [-] Japan
– Broken heart / Cherokee / Fight to survive / Where do we run / In the city / All the fallen men / All burn in Hell / Kid of 1000 faces / El Salvador / The road to Valhalla. *<US-iss.Apr88 on 'Grand Slam' lp/cd; SLAM/+CD 1) (UK-iss.Jul92 on 'Music For Nations' cd/c/lp; CD/T+/MFN 130)*

— **JAMES LOMENZO** – bass repl. DAVE SPITZ who had repl. ROBINSON / **GREGG D'ANGELO** – drums (ex-ANTHRAX) repl. CAPOZZI

Atlantic | Atlantic

Jul 87. (lp/c/cd) *(781 768-1/-4/-2) <81768>* **PRIDE** [ ] [11] Sep87
– Hungry / Lonely nights / Don't give up / Sweet little loving / Lady of the valley / Wait / All you need is rock n roll / Tell me / All join our hands / When the children cry.

Jan 88. (7") *(A 9178)* **WAIT. / ALL JOIN OUR HANDS** [ ] [-]
(12"+=) *(A 9178T)* – Lady of the valley.

Feb 88. (7") *<89126>* **WAIT. / DON'T GIVE UP** [-] [8]

Jun 88. (7") *<89051>* **TELL ME. / ALL JOIN OUR HANDS** [-] [58]

Jul 88. (7") *(A 9063)* **WAIT. / ALL YOU NEED IS ROCK'N'ROLL** [ ] [-]
(12"+=) *(A 9063 T)* – Lonely nights.

Mar 89. (7") *(A 9015) <89015>* **WHEN THE CHILDREN CRY. / LADY OF THE VALLEY** [ ] [3] Oct88
(12"+=/12"remix+=) *(A 9015T/+W)* – Tell me (live).

Jun 89. (lp/c)(cd) *(WX 277/+C)(781 969-2) <81969>* **BIG GAME** [47] [19]
– Goin' home tonight / Dirty woman / Little fighter / Broken home / Baby be mine / Living on the edge / Let's get crazy / Don't say it's over / If my mind is evil / Radar love / Cry for freedom.

Jun 89. (7") *<88874>* **LITTLE FIGHTER. / LET'S GET CRAZY** [-] [52]

Oct 89. (7") *(A 8836) <88836>* **RADAR LOVE. / IF MY MIND IS EVIL** [ ] [59] Sep89
(12"+=/cd-s+=) *(A 8836 T/CD)* – Wait (live).

Feb 90. (7") *<88767>* **DIRTY WOMAN. / CRY FOR FREEDOM** [-] [ ]

— **TOMMY 'T-Bone' CARADONNA** – bass (ex-ALICE COOPER) repl. LOMENZO / **JIMMY DeGRASSO** – drums (ex-Y&T) repl. D'ANGELO

Apr 91. (7"/c-s) *(A 7727/+C)* **LIGHTS AND THUNDER. / SHE'S GOT EVERYTHING** [ ] [ ]
(cd-s+=) *(A 7727CD)* – Fight to survive (live).

Apr 91. (cd)(lp/c) *<(7567 82193-2)>(WX 415/+C)* **MANE ATTRACTION** [31] [61]
– Lights and thunder / Broken heart / Leave me alone / Love don't come easy / You're all I need / Warsong / It's over / Till death do us apart / Out with the boys / Farewell to you.

Jun 91. (7") **LOVE DON'T COME EASY. / LITTLE FIGHTER (live rehearsal)** [ ] [ ]
(12"+=) – Don't give up.
(cd-s+=) – When the children cry.

— Disbanded late 1991, MIKE TRAMP formed FREAK OF NATURE, with **JERRY BEST** – bass / **OLIVER STEFFENSON + KENNY KORADE** – guitars / **JOHNNY HARO** – drums

– compilations, etc. –

Nov 93. (cd/c) *Atlantic; <(7567 82425-2/-4)>* **THE BEST OF WHITE LION** [ ] [ ]
– Wait / Radar love / Broken heart / Hungry / Little fighter / Lights and thunder / All you need is rock'n'roll / When the children cry / Love don't come easy / Cry for freedom / Lady of the valley / Tell me / Farewell to you.

Oct 99. (cd) *Cleopatra; <(CLP 719)>* **REMEMBERING WHITE LION – THE GREATEST HITS** [ ] [ ]

WHITE SISTER

Formed: USA . . . 1983 by GARRI BRANDON, DENNIS CHURCHILL, RICK CHADOCK and RICHARD WRIGHT. Signed to the American arm of 'Heavy Metal' records, WHITE SISTER released their eponymous debut in early '85. Inspired by the likes of KANSAS and STYX, the group's striking pomp tapestries of lush keyboard washes and streamlined AOR were showcased here to lasting effect. The metal public weren't convinced, however, and after a further set, the criminally titled 'FASHION BY PASSION', WHITE SISTER split in 1988.

Album rating: WHITE SISTER (*5) / FASHION BY PASSION (*4)

GARRI BRANDON – vocals, keyboards / **DENNIS CHURCHILL** – vocals, bass / **RICK CHADOCK** – guitar, vocals / **RICHARD WRIGHT** – drums

Heavy Metal | Heavy Metal

Jan 85. (lp) *<(HMUSA 7)>* **WHITE SISTER** [ ] [ ]
– Don't say that you're mine / Straight from the heart / Love don't make it right / Breakin' all the rules / Whips / Can't say no / Promises / Walk away / One more night / Just for you. *(cd-iss. Sep00 on 'Zoom Club'; ZCRCD 39)*

FM-Revolver | Heavy Metal

Oct 86. (7"/12") *(VHF/12VHF 32)* **TICKET TO RIDE. / FASHION BY PASSION** [ ] [ ]

Oct 86. (lp/c) *(WKFM LP/MC 76)* **FASHION BY PASSION** [ ] [ ]
– A place in the heart / Fashion by passion / Dancin' on midnight / Save me tonight / Ticket to ride / April / Until it hurts / Troubleshooters / Lonely teardrops / A place in the heart (reprise). *(cd-iss. Jun87; WKFMXD 76) (pic-lp.May88; WKFMPD 76)*

— Folded in 1988

WHITESNAKE

Formed: London, England . . . late 70's by ex-DEEP PURPLE vocalist, DAVID COVERDALE (b.22 Sep'49, Slatburn-On-Sea, Yorkshire, England). After leaving 'PURPLE, COVERDALE recorded two fine sets of bluesy hard-rock, 'DAVID COVERDALE'S WHITESNAKE' (1977) and 'NORTHWINDS' (1978), taking the name for his new outfit from the former and retaining a core of musicians which included such seasoned veterans as MICKY MOODY, BERNIE MARSDEN and NEIL MURRAY. Signing to 'EMI International', he/they debuted with the 'SNAKEBITE' EP in summer '78, the record's highlight being a smoky cover of Bobby Bland's 'AIN'T NO LOVE IN THE HEART OF THE CITY'. The group subsequently hit the UK Top 50 with their debut album, 'TROUBLE' (1978), the record adding the keyboard skills of ex-DP man, JON LORD. While they followed it up with the overlooked 'LOVE HUNTER' in 1979, they only really broke through with the 'READY AN' WILLING' (1980) set, the success of its attendant single pushing the album into the UK Top 10. The band were certainly ready, willing and able to fill the gap in the market left by the now defunct DEEP PURPLE, their musical prowess securing them an enviable live reputation if not quite measuring up in the songwriting department. Consequently then, the band's only official concert set, 'LIVE . . . IN THE HEART OF THE CITY' (1980), ranks as one of the most consistent recordings of their career. However their most successful album to date (narrowly missing No.1), 'COME AN' GET IT' (1981) was something of a disappointment, the group moving away from their bluesy roots towards a neutered hard-rock sound. Critics also rounded on COVERDALE's notoriously sexist, cliche-ridden lyrics, complaints which were water off a duck's back to the blonde-maned, mouth-full-of-plums cock-rocker. Despite personnel shuffles which saw new faces such as MEL GALLEY, COLIN 'Bomber' HODGKINSON and COZY POWELL, 'SAINTS AN' SINNERS' (1982) failed to remedy matters although it went Top 10 nevertheless. With the addition of ex-TYGERS OF PAN TANG guitarist, JOHN SYKES, COVERDALE had finally found a sympathetic writing partner as evidenced on the much improved 'SLIDE IT IN' (1984). Blatant innuendo was still high on the agenda, but then again, that's what COVERDALE excelled at, his panting and moaning all over the shop on the epic climax-blues stomp, 'SLOW AN' EASY', actually as effective as it was hilarious. Never the most stable of bands, the tour that followed saw WHITESNAKE eventually reduced to SYKES and COVERDALE, even LORD bogging off to join the reformed DEEP PURPLE. Recruiting TONY FRANKLIN and CARMINE APPICE, the group eventually returned with the eponymous 'WHITESNAKE 1987' (1987, funnily enough), sleeker, (some might say) sexier, and considerably more commercial than ever before. Previewed by the Top 10 LED ZEPELLIN-esque, 'STILL OF THE NIGHT', the album stormed both the British and US charts. The latter track was the hardest fare on offer, however, the bulk of the album made up of limp MTV ballads like 'IS THIS LOVE' and ravamps of old songs, the infectious reworking of 'HERE I GO AGAIN' (the original can be found on 'SAINTS AN' SINNERS') giving the group their first and only No.1. While the album no doubt alienated many of their previously loyal older fans, it sold millions, finally giving COVERDALE the success he'd long been after. It didn't do much for the group's stability, however, as SYKES split for BLUE MURDER and COVERDALE once again recruited a whole new line-up numbering ADRIAN VANDENBURG, RUDY SARZO, TOMMY ALDRIDGE and VIVIAN CAMPBELL. Guitar wizard STEVE VAI subsequently replaced CAMPBELL and this line-up gave a rather lacklustre headlining performance at the 1989 Monsters Of Rock Festival, the highly anticipated 'SLIP OF THE TONGUE' (1989) equally uninspiring. Unsurprisingly, the record failed to match the giddy commercial heights of its predecessor and COVERDALE put the band on ice while he subsequently hooked up with JIMMY PAGE for the successful 'COVERDALE ° PAGE' album in 1993. Last sighted on a tour of Europe in support of a 1994 greatest hits collection, DAVID COVERDALE & WHITESNAKE delivered a UK Top 40 comeback album, 'RESTLESS HEART' in 1997. With the metal/hard-rock scene changing almost beyond recognition, it looks unlikely that WHITESNAKE can repeat the glory days of the late 80's . . . the nostalgia circuit beckons. Well, maybe not quite yet, it seems there's life in the old dog yet. While his new image may shock a few of his older fans, not to mention a few small children, the song, basically remains the same on COVERDALE's 2000 solo set, 'INTO THE LIGHT'. His first since 'NORTHWINDS' back in '78, the record featured a solid if unadventurous selection of the man's trademark bluesy hard rock and histrionic balladry, co-written largely with veteran guitarist EARL SLICK. • **Trivia:** On the 17th of February '89, COVERDALE married actress Tawny Kittaen, who had previously featured on their video of 'IS THIS LOVE'.

Album rating: NORTHWINDS (*7; by David Coverdale) / TROUBLE (*5) / LOVEHUNTER (*6) / READY AN' WILLING (*6) / LIVE . . . IN THE HEART OF THE CITY (*6) / COME AND GET IT (*6) / SAINTS 'N' SINNERS (*4) / SLIDE IN IT (*5) / 1987 (*5) / SLIP OF THE TONGUE (*5) / WHITESNAKE'S GREATEST HITS compilation (*8) / COVERDALE – PAGE (*5) / RESTLESS HEART (*5) / David Coverdale: INTO THE LIGHT (*5)

DAVID COVERDALE

(solo) – vocals (ex-DEEP PURPLE) with **MICK MOODY** – guitar (ex-JUICY LUCY, ex-SNAFU) / **TIM HINKLEY** – keyboards / **SIMON PHILLIPS** – drums / **DELISLE HARPER** – bass / plus **RON ASPERY** – sax / **ROGER GLOVER** – producer, bass, keyboards

Purple | not iss.

May 77. (lp) *(TPS 3509)* **DAVID COVERDALE'S WHITESNAKE** [ ] [-]
– Lady / Blindman / Goldie's place / Whitesnake / Time on my side / Peace lovin' man / Sunny days / Hole in the sky / Celebration. *(cd-iss. Aug00 on 'Connoisseur'+=; VSOPCD 313)* – Peace lovin' man (version) / Sunny days (version).

May 77. (7") *(PUR 133)* **HOLE IN THE SKY. / BLINDMAN** [ ] [-]

— **COVERDALE** retained only **MOODY** and recruited **BERNIE MARSDEN** – guitar (ex-PAICE, ASHTON & LORD, ex-UFO, ex-WILD TURKEY) / **NEIL MURRAY** – bass (ex-COLOSSEUM, ex-NATIONAL HEALTH) / **BRIAN JOHNSON** – keyboards + **DAVID DOWELL** – drums (both ex-STREETWALKERS)

Feb 78. (7") *(PUR 136)* **BREAKDOWN. / ONLY MY SOUL** [ ] [-]

Mar 78. (lp) *(TPS 3513)* **NORTHWINDS** [ ] [-]
– Keep on giving me love / Northwinds / Give me kindness / Time & again / Queen of hearts / Only my soul / Say you love me / Breakdown. *(re-iss. Apr84 on 'Fame' lp/c; FA41 3097-1/-4) (cd-iss. Aug00 on 'Connoisseur'+=; VSOPCD 314)* – Shame the Devil / Sweet mistreater.

Jun 78. (7") **BREAKDOWN. / BLOODY MARY** [-] [ ]

DAVID COVERDALE'S WHITESNAKE

PETE SOLLEY – keyboards repl. JOHNSTON

EMI Int. | Sunburst

Jun 78. (lp) *<5C 062-61290>* **SNAKEBITE** [ ] [-]
– Come on / Bloody Mary / Ain't no love in the heart of the city / Steal away / Keep on giving me love / Queen of hearts / Only my soul / Breakdown.

Jun 78. (7"ep,7"white-ep) *(INEP 751) <915>* **SNAKEBITE EP** [61] [ ]
– Bloody Mary / Steal away / Come on / Ain't no love in the heart of the city.

— **JON LORD** (b. 9 Jun'41, Leicester, England) – keyboards (ex-PAICE, ASHTON & LORD, ex-DEEP PURPLE) repl. SOLLEY

Oct 78. (7") *(INT 568)* **LIE DOWN. / DON'T MESS WITH ME** [ ] [-]

Oct 78. (lp) *(INS 3022) <937>* **TROUBLE** [50] [ ]
– Take me with you / Love to keep you warm / Lie down (a modern love song) / Day tripper / Night hawl (vampire blues) / The time is right for love / Trouble / Belgian Tom's hat trick / Free flight / Don't mess with me. *(re-iss. Sep80 on 'United Artists'; UAG 30305) (re-iss. May82 on 'Fame' lp/c; FA/TCFA 3002) (re-iss. May90 cd/c/lp; CD/TC+/FA 3234) (re-iss. Jun87 on 'E.M.I.' lp/c; EMS/TCEMS 1257) (cd-iss. Apr88 on 'E.M.I.'; CZ 9)*

Mar 79. (7") *(INT 578)* **THE TIME IS RIGHT FOR LOVE. / COME ON (live)** [ ] [-]

Apr 79. (7") **THE TIME IS RIGHT FOR LOVE. / BELGUIN TOM'S HAT TRICK** [-] [ ]

U.A. | U.A.

Oct 79. (lp/c) *(UAG 30264) <981>* **LOVE HUNTER** [29] [ ]
– Long way from home / Walking in the shadow of the blues / Help me thro' the day / Medicine man / You 'n' me / Mean business / Love hunter / Outlaw / Rock'n'roll women / We wish you well. *(re-iss. Apr84 on 'Fame' lp/c; FA/TCFA 3095) (cd-iss. Apr88; CDFA 3095) (cd re-iss. Jul94 on 'E.M.I.'; CDEMS 1529)*

Oct 79. (7"m) *(BP 324)* **LONG WAY FROM HOME. / TROUBLE (live) / AIN'T NO LOVE IN THE HEART OF THE CITY (live)** [55] [-]

Nov 79. (7") **LONG WAY FROM HOME. / WE WISH YOU WELL** [-] [ ]

WHITESNAKE

— with **IAN PAICE** (b.29 Jun'48, Nottingham, England) – drums (ex-PAICE, ASHTON & LORD, ex-DEEP PURPLE) repl. DOWELL

U.A. | Mirage-Atlantic

Apr 80. (7"m) *(BP 352)* **FOOL FOR YOUR LOVING. / MEAN BUSINESS / DON'T MESS WITH ME** [13] [-]

Jun 80. (lp/c) *(UAG 30302) <19276>* **READY AN' WILLING** [6] [90]
– Fool for your loving / Sweet talker / Ready an' willing / Carry your load / Blindman / Ain't gonna cry no more / Love man / Black and blue / She's a woman. *(re-iss. Sep85 on 'Fame' lp/c; FA/TCFA 3134) (cd-iss. Apr88; CDFA 3134) (cd re-iss. Jul94 on 'E.M.I.'; CDEMS 1526) (cd re-iss. Feb00 on 'Axe Killer'; **AXE 305526CD**)*

Jul 80. (7"m) *(BP 363)* **READY AN' WILLING. / NIGHT HAWK (VAMPIRE BLUES) / WE WISH YOU WELL** [43] [-]

Jul 80. (7") *<3672>* **FOOL FOR YOUR LOVING. / BLACK AND BLUE** [-] [53]

Oct 80. (7") *<3766>* **SWEET TALKER. / AIN'T GONNA CRY NO MORE** [-] [ ]

Nov 80. (d-lp/d-c) *(SNAKE/TC2SNAKE 1) <19292>* **LIVE . . . IN THE HEART OF THE CITY (live)** [5] [ ]
– Come on * / Sweet talker / Walking in the shadow of the blues / Love hunter / Fool for your loving / Ain't gonna cry no more / Ready an' willing / Take me with you * / Might just take your life / Lie down * / Ain't no love in the heart of the city / Trouble * / Mistreated. *<cd-iss. Jul88 on 'Underdog'; CDS 790860-2>* – <omits *> *(re-iss. Nov91 on 'Fame' cd/c; CD/TC FA 3265) (re-iss. Jul94 on 'E.M.I.' cd/c; CD/TC EMS 1525)*

Nov 80. (7"/12") *(BP/12BP 381) <3794>* **AIN'T NO LOVE IN THE HEART OF THE CITY (live). / TAKE ME WITH YOU (live)** [51] [ ]

Liberty | Atlantic

Apr 81. (7") *(BP 395)* **DON'T BREAK MY HEART AGAIN. / CHILD OF BABYLON** [17] [-]

Apr 81. (lp/c) *(LBG/TCLBG 30327) <16043>* **COME AN' GET IT** [2] [ ]
– Come an' get it / Hot stuff / Don't break my heart again / Lonely days, lonely nights / Wine, women an' song / Child of Babylon / Would I lie to you / Girl / Hit an' run / Till the day I die. *(re-iss. May89 on 'Fame' cd/c/lp; CD/TC+/FA 3219) (re-iss. Jul94 on 'E.M.I.' cd/c; CD/TC EMS 1528)*

May 81. (7") *(BP 399)* **WOULD I LIE TO YOU. / GIRL** [37] [-]
Jun 81. (7") *<3844>* **DON'T BREAK MY HEART AGAIN. / LONELY DAYS, LONELY NIGHTS** [-] [ ]

— **COVERDALE** retained **MOODY + LORD** and brought in **MEL GALLEY** – guitar (ex-TRAPEZE) repl. MARSDEN who formed ALASKA / **COLIN 'Bomber' HODGKINSON** (b.14 Oct'45) – bass (ex-BACK DOOR) repl. MURRAY to GARY MOORE / **COZY POWELL** (b.29 Dec'47, Cirencester, England) – drums (ex-JEFF BECK, ex-RAINBOW, Solo Artist, ex-BEDLAM) repl. PAICE who joined GARY MOORE

Liberty Geffen

Oct 82. (7"pic-d) *(BP 416)* **HERE I GO AGAIN. / BLOODY LUXURY** [34] [-]
Nov 82. (lp/c/pic-lp) *(LBG/TCLBG/LBGP 30354) <2-24173>* **SAINTS AN' SINNERS** [9] [ ]
– Young blood / Rough an' ready / Blood luxury / Victim of love / Crying in the rain / Here I go again / Love an' afection / Rock'n'roll angels / Dancing girls / Saints an' sinners. *(re-iss. 1985 lp/c; ATAK/TCATAK 10) (re-iss. May87 on 'Fame' lp/c; FA/TCFA 3177) (cd-iss. Apr88; CDFA 3177) (cd re-iss. Jul94 & Jul98 on 'E.M.I.'; CDEMS 1521)*
Aug 83. (7"/7"sha-pic-d) *(BP/+P 420)* **GUILTY OF LOVE. / GAMBLER** [31] [-]

— now a quintet, when MICK MOODY departed

Jan 84. (7"/12") *(BP/12BP 422)* **GIVE ME MORE TIME. / NEED YOUR LOVE SO BAD** [29] [-]

— **NEIL MURRAY** – bass returned to repl. HODGKINSON / added **JOHN SYKES** (b.29 Jul'59) – guitar (ex-TYGERS OF PAN TANG)

Feb 84. (lp/c) *(WHITE/TCWHITE 1) <4018>* **SLIDE IT IN** [9] [40] Aug84
– Gambler / Slide it in / Standing in the shadow / Give me more time / Love ain't no stranger / Slow an' easy / Spit it out / All or nothing / Hungry for love / Guilty of love. *(cd-iss. Apr88 on 'E.M.I.'; CZ 88) (pic-lp 1984 w/extra US mixes; LBGP 240-000-0)*
Apr 84. (7"/7"pic-d) *(BP/+P 423)* **STANDING IN THE SHADOWS. / ALL OR NOTHING (US mix)** [62] [-]
(12"+=) – ('A'-US remix).
Aug 84. (7") *<29171>* **LOVE AIN'T NO STRANGER. / GUILTY OF LOVE** [-] [ ]
Feb 85. (7"/12") *(BP/12BP 424)* **LOVE AIN'T NO STRANGER. / SLOW AN' EASY** [44] [-]
(12"white+=) *(BP12 424)* – Slide it in.

— split for a while in 1984 when JON LORD re-joined DEEP PURPLE. **WHITESNAKE** were re-formed by **COVERDALE + SYKES** and new musicians **TONY FRANKLIN** – bass (ex-The FIRM) repl. MURRAY and GALLEY / **CARMINE APPICE** – drums (ex-BECK, BOGERT & APPICE) repl. POWELL to E.L.P.

EMI Int. Geffen

Mar 87. (7"/7"white) *(EMI/+W 5606)* **STILL OF THE NIGHT. / HERE I GO AGAIN (1987)** [16] [-]
(12"+=/12"pic-d+=) *(12EMI/+P 5606)* – You're gonna break my heart again.
Apr 87. (cd/c/lp) *(CD/TC+/EMC 3528) <24099>* **WHITESNAKE 1987** [8] [2]
– Still of the night / Bad boys / Give me all your love / Looking for love / Crying in the rain / Is this love / Straight for the heart / Don't turn away / Children of the night. *(also on pic-lp; EMCP 3528) (cd+=)* – Here I go again '87 / You're gonna break my heart again. *(re-iss. Jul94 cd/c; CD/TC EMS 1531)*
May 87. (7"/7"sha-pic-d) *(EM/+P 3)* **IS THIS LOVE. / STANDING IN THE SHADOWS** [9] [-]
(12"+=/12"white+=) *(12EM/+P 3)* – Need your love so bad.
(cd-ep++=/7"ep++=) *(EMX/CDEM 3)* – Still of the night.
Jun 87. (7") *<28331>* **STILL OF THE NIGHT. / DON'T TURN AWAY** [-] [79]
Jul 87. (7") *<28339>* **HERE I GO AGAIN. / CHILDREN OF THE NIGHT** [-] [1]
Oct 87. (7") *<28233>* **IS THIS LOVE. / BAD BOYS** [-] [2]
Oct 87. (c-s/12"/7") *(TC/12+/EM 35)* **HERE I GO AGAIN '87 (US mix). / GUILTY OF LOVE** [9] [-]
(7"etched/10"white/cd-s) *(EMP/10EM/CDEM 35)* – ('A'side) / ('A'-US remix).
Jan 88. (7"/7"white) *(EM/+W 23)* **GIVE ME ALL YOUR LOVE. / FOOL FOR YOUR LOVING** [18] [-]
(12"+=/12"white) *(12EMP/+W 23)* – Don't break my heart again.
(3"cd-s+=) *(CDEM 23)* – Here I go again (USA remix).
Jan 88. (7") *<28103>* **GIVE ME ALL YOUR LOVE. / STRAIGHT FROM THE HEART** [-] [48]

— **COVERDALE** completely re-modelled line-up when SYKES formed BLUE MURDER. He was replaced by **ADRIAN VANDENBURG** (b. Netherlands) – guitar (ex-VANDENBERG) / **RUDY SARZO** (b. 9 Nov'52, Havana, Cuba) – bass (ex-OZZY OSBOURNE, ex-QUIET RIOT) repl. FRANKLIN / **TOMMY ALDRIDGE** – drums (ex-OZZY OSBOURNE, ex-BLACK OAK ARKANSAS) repl. APPICE (Dec88) / **STEVE VAI** (b. 6 Jun'60, Carle Place, N.Y.) – guitar (solo Artist, ex-FRANK ZAPPA, DAVID LEE ROTH) repl. VIVIAN CAMPBELL

Nov 89. (cd/c/lp) *(CD/TC+/EMD 1013) <24249>* **SLIP OF THE TONGUE** [10] [10]
– Slip of the tongue / Cheap an' nasty / Fool for your loving / Now you're gone / Kitten's got claws / Wings of the storm / The deeper the love / Judgement day / Slow poke music / Sailing ships. *(re-iss. Jul94 cd/c; CD/TC EMS 1527)*
Nov 89. (7"/7"s)<US-c-s> *(EM/+P 123) <22715>* **FOOL FOR YOUR LOVING ('89). / SLOW POKE MUSIC** [43] [37]
(c-s+=) *(TCEM 123)* – ('A'version).
(12"+=/12"white+=) *(12EM/+P 1243)* – Walking in the shadow of the blues.
Jan 90. (7") *<19951>* **THE DEEPER THE LOVE. / SLIP OF THE TONGUE** [-] [28]
Feb 90. (c-s/7"/7"pic-d) *(TC+/EM/+PD 128)* **THE DEEPER THE LOVE. / JUDGEMENT DAY** [35] [-]
(12"white+=) *(12EMS 128)* – Sweet lady luck.
(12"++=/cd-s++=) *(12/CD EM 128)* – Fool for your lovin' (Vai voltage mix).
Aug 90. (c-s/7"/7"sha-pic-d) *(TC+/EM+/PD 150) <19976>* **NOW YOU'RE GONE (remix). / WINGS OF THE STORM** [31] [96] May90
(12"+=/12"pic-d+=/cd-s+=) *(12EM/12EMPS/CDEM 150)* – Kittens got claws / Cheap an' nasty.

DAVID COVERDALE

Epic Epic

Sep 90. (7"/c-s) *(656 292-7/-4)* **THE LAST NOTE OF FREEDOM. / (track by HANS ZIMMER)** [ ] [ ]
(12"+=) *(656 292-6)* – (track by other artist).
(cd-s++=) *(656 292-2)* – ('A'version).

COVERDALE• PAGE

DAVID COVERDALE – vocals / **JIMMY PAGE** – guitar (ex-LED ZEPPELIN, ex-solo artist) / **JORGE CASAS** – bass / **DENNY CARMASSI** – drums (ex-MONTROSE) / **RICKY PHILIPS** – bass / **LESTER MENDEL** – keyboards / **JOHN HARRIS** – acoustic harmonica / **TOMMY FUNDERBUCK** – backing vocals

E.M.I. Geffen

Mar 93. (cd/c/lp) *(CD/TC+/EMD 1041) <24487>* **COVERDALE• PAGE** [4] [5]
– Shake my tree / Waiting on you / Take me for a little while / Pride and joy / Over now / Feeling hot / Easy does it / Take a look at yourself / Don't leave me this way / Absolution blues / Whisper a prayer for the dying *(re-iss. Jul94 cd/c; same)*
Jun 93. (c-s/12"pic-d) *(12EMPD/TCEM 270)* **TAKE ME FOR A LITTLE WHILE. / EASY DOES IT** [29] [ ]
(cd-s) *(CDEM 270)* – ('A'side) / ('A'acoustic) / Shake my tree (the crunch mix) / ('A'edit).
Sep 93. (7"pic-d/c-s) *(EMPD/TCEM 279)* **TAKE A LOOK AT YOURSELF. / WAITING ON YOU** [ ] [ ]
(cd-s+=) *(CDEM 279)* – ('A'acoustic) / ('A'girls version).

DAVID COVERDALE & WHITESNAKE

E.M.I. Capitol

May 97. (c-s/cd-s) *(TC/CD EM 471)* **TOO MANY TEARS / THE DEEPER THE LOVE / IS THIS LOVE** [46] [ ]
(cd-s) *(CDEMS 471)* – ('A'part 1) / Can't stop now / ('A'part 2).
Jun 97. (cd/c) *(CD/TC EMD 1104)* **RESTLESS HEART** [34] [ ]
– Don't fade away / All in the name of love / Restless heart / Too many tears / Crying / Stay with me / Can't go on / You're so fine / Your precious love / Take me back again / Woman trouble blues.
Oct 97. (c-s) *(TCEM 495)* **DON'T FADE AWAY / OI** [ ] [ ]
(cd-s+=) *(CDEM 495)* – Anything you want / Don't fade away.

DAVID COVERDALE

— with various session people

E.M.I. Dragonfly

Sep 00. (cd-s) *(CDEM 574)* **LOVE IS BLIND / LOVE IS BLIND (radio) / SHE GIVE ME** [ ] [-]
Sep 00. (cd) *(528124-2) <12251>* **INTO THE LIGHT** [75] [ ] Oct00
– Into the light / River song / She give me / Don't you cry / Love is blind / Slave / Cry for love / Living on love / Midnight blue / Too many tears / Don't lie to me / Where you may go.

– compilations, etc. –

Apr 88. (d-lp/c/cd) *Connoisseur; (VSOP LP/MC/CD 118)* **THE CONNOISSEUR COLLECTION** [ ] [-]
– (DAVID COVERDALE's first 2 solo albums)
Jun 88. (cd) *M.C.A.;* **GREATEST HITS** [-] [ ]
Jul 94. (cd/c/lp) *E.M.I.; (CD/TC+/EMD 1065) / Geffen; <24620>* **WHITESNAKE'S GREATEST HITS** [4] [ ]
– Still of the night / Here I go again / Is this love / Love ain't no stranger / Looking for love / Now you're gone / Slide it in / Slow an' easy / Judgement day / You're gonna break my heart again / The deeper the love / Crying in the rain / Fool for your loving / Sweet lady luck.
Jul 94. (7"/7"white/c-s) *E.M.I.; (EM/EMS/TCEM 329)* **IS THIS LOVE. / SWEET LADY LUCK** [25] [ ]
(cd-s+=) *(CDEM 329)* – Now you're gone.
Nov 95. (3xcd-box) *E.M.I.; (CDOMB 016)* **SLIDE IT IN / 1987 / SLIP OF THE TONGUE** [ ] [ ]
Mar 99. (cd) *EMI; (499508-2)* **STARKERS IN TOKYO** [ ] [ ]
Jun 00. (d-cd) *Axe Killer; (AXE 3055482CD)* **1987 / SLIP OF THE TONGUE** [ ] [ ]

WHITE SPIRIT

Formed: London, England ... 1975, by JANICK GERS and GRAEME CRALLAN, the line-up eventually solidifying around BRUCE RUFF, MALCOLM PEARSON and PHIL BRADY. Using the NWOBHM as a touchpaper, WHITE SPIRIT ignited their career with an indie 45 on 'Neat', following it up with a one-off for 'E.M.I.', 'RED SKIES'. Though their sound was a fairly cut'n'dried take on classic 70's hard-rock embellished with pomp keyboards, the group were subsequently procured by 'M.C.A.'. An eponymous debut album was eventually issued later that year, although their occasionally intoxicated blend didn't exactly set the metal scene (or the charts) alight. After a final single, 'HIGH UPON HIGH', the group were extinguished, although they reformed a year later with BRIAN HOWE and MICK TUCKER replacing RUFF and PEARSON respectively. This attempt was another damp squib, however, and WHITE SPIRIT finally evaporated. GERS went on to greater things with GILLAN and later IRON MAIDEN, while HOWE took up with BAD COMPANY.

Album rating: WHITE SPIRIT (*5)

BRUCE RUFF – vocals / **JANICK GERS** – guitar / **MALCOLM PEARSON** – keyboards / **PHIL BRADY** – bass / **GRAEME CRALLEN** – drums

Neat / not iss.

May 80. (7") *(NEAT 05)* **BACK TO THE GRIND. / CHEETAH** [ ] [-]

M.C.A. / not iss.

Aug 80. (7") *(MCA 638)* **MIDNIGHT CHASER. / SUFFRAGETTE** [ ] [-]

Sep 80. (lp) *(MCF 3079)* **WHITE SPIRIT** [ ] [-]
– Midnight chaser / Red skies / High upon high / Way of the kings / No reprieve / Don't be fooled / Fool for the gods.

Nov 80. (7") *(MCA 652)* **HIGH UPON HIGH. / NO REPRIEVE** [ ] [-]

— Disbanded in 1981, but re-formed a year later. **BRIAN HOWE** – vocals; repl. RUFF / **MICK TUCKER** – guitar; repl. PEARSON

— JANICK GERS joined GILLAN, and was last seen in IRON MAIDEN for the 90's. HOWE was to join BAD COMPANY and TUCKER was to appear in TANK

WHITE WOLF

Formed: Toronto, Canada . . . 1975 as SLAMM before opting for the WARRIOR moniker and finally WHITEWOLF, the line-up being crystallised around DON WILK, CAM McLEOD, RICK NELSON (not that one!), LES SCHWARTZ and LORIS BOLZON. After years of scrambling around on the local circuit, this hungry pack of classy pomp-rockers were eventually snapped up by 'R.C.A.', releasing their debut set, 'STANDING ALONE', in late '84. A favourite among AOR buffs, the record nevertheless failed to sink its teeth into the charts. The appropriately named 'ENDANGERED SPECIES' (1986), marked the end of the group's recording career, WHITEWOLF subsequently returning to their collective lair.

Album rating: STANDING ALONE (*4)

DON WILK – vocals, keyboards / **CAM McLEOD** – guitar / **RICK NELSON** – guitar / **LES SCHWARTZ** – bass / **LORIS BOLZON** – drums

R.C.A. / R.C.A.

Nov 84. (lp/c) *(PL/PK 70559)* <*NFL1-8042*> **STANDING ALONE** [ ] [ ]
– Standing alone / Headlines / Shadows in the night / What the war will bring / Night rider / Homeward bound / Metal thunder / Trust me.

Feb 85. (12") <*13946*> **SHADOWS OF THE NIGHT. / NIGHT RIDER / STANDING ALONE** [-] [ ]

Jul 86. (12") <*14360*> **SHE. / ('A'version)** [-] [ ]

Jul 86. (lp) <*AFL-1 9555*> **ENDANGERED SPECIES** [-] [ ]
– Just like an arrow / One more time / Ride the storm / Time waits for no one / She.

— split in 1986

WHITE ZOMBIE

Formed: New York City, New York, USA . . . 1985 by frontman ROB 'ZOMBIE' STRAKER, guitarist TOM GUAY, drummer IVAN DePLUME and female bassist SEAN YSEULT. Fresh from an unhealthy diet of BLACK SABBATH and horror B-movies, this cartoon-esque bunch of schlock-rockers set out on their demonic trail in 1987 with a debut mini-set, 'PSYCHO-HEAD BLOWOUT', for the US indie 'Silent Explosion'. A year later, their first full-length album, 'SOUL CRUSHER', was unleashed to an unsuspecting public, although the British still awaited their landing party by early '89. A third set, 'MAKE THEM DIE SLOWLY' came out around this time, produced by the seasoned BILL LASWELL and released on 'Caroline' records, its funky death-metal slowly unearthing itself and finding underground success from both metal and alternative rock audiences. J (JOHN RICCI) had replaced GUAY at this point, although his stay was short-lived when he was in turn superseded by JAY YUENGER. In the early 90's and now on the bulging, money-spinning roster of 'Geffen', WHITE ZOMBIE went to work on a new album with producer, ANDY WALLACE. The results were mindblowing in every conceivable sense, 'LA SEXORCISTO: DEVIL MUSIC VOLUME 1' (1992), being the musical carcass that The STOOGES and KISS once spewed out. Inevitably, twisted tracks such as 'WELCOME TO PLANET MOTHERFUCKER (PSYCHOHOLIC SLAG)', 'THUNDERKISS '65', etc. (lyrics, care of the warped brain of ROB), saw the band reach the American Top 30, cracking open the skull of any youth into terror-metal (even "real" cartoon pair, Beavis & Butt-head loved them, 'ZOMBIE being a highlight on the duo's various artists album). The band were rewarded with a heavy metal Grammy the following year as the band went on a mighty touring schedule across the globe, only halting to find a replacement for the departing DePLUME. In 1995, having substituted temp PHILO with (ex-TESTAMENT) drummer JOEY TEMPESTA, they rooted out a second long-player for the label, 'ASTROCREEP 2000: SONGS OF LOVE, DESTRUCTION, AND OTHER SYNTHETIC DELUSIONS OF THE ELECTRIC HEAD' (whew!). Conceptual and groundbreaking yet again, it duly scurried up the charts and into the Top 10 (also cracked the UK Top 30), demented titles such as 'EL PHANTASMO AND THE CHICKEN-RUN BLAST-O-RAMA' carrying off where the predecessor left off. During the summer of '96, they surprised many by issuing some danceable remixes of earlier tracks going under the title of 'SUPER SEXY SWINGIN' SOUNDS', a Top 20 hit in their own country. WHITE ZOMBIE split in 1997, although the solo ROB ZOMBIE (retaining TEMPESTA) released an album, 'HELLBILLY DELUXE' (1998) and after failing to come up with the score for 'The Crow 3' movie, launched his own label, 'Zombie A Go-Go'. Meanwhile, YSEULT resurrected her moonlighting project, FAMOUS MONSTERS, releasing a second CRAMPS/B-52's style 45, 'KNOCK KNOCK HALLOWEEN' (the first, 'MONSTER GIRLS – ARE GO!', was issued a few years previously) and a debut album, 'IN THE NIGHT' (1998). • **Covers:** STRAKER/ZOMBIE except CHILDREN OF THE GRAVE (Black Sabbath) / GOD OF THUNDER (Kiss). FM covered CLOCK STRIKES TEN (Cheap Trick).

Album rating: PSYCHO-HEAD BLOWOUT mini (*4) / SOUL CRUSHER (*4) / LA SEXORCISTO: DEVIL MUSIC VOLUME 1 (*7) / ASTROCREEP 2000: SONGS OF LOVE AND DESTRUCTION . . . (*6) / SUPER SEXY SWINGIN' SOUNDS dance remixes (*7) / Rob Zombie: HELLBILLY DELUXE (*6)

ROB 'ZOMBIE' STRAKER (b.1966) – vocals, guitar / **TOM GUAY** – guitar / **SEAN YSEULT** – bass / **IVAN DePLUME** – drums

not iss. / Silent Explosion

Feb 87. (m-lp) <*SILENT 001*> **PSYCHO-HEAD BLOWOUT** [-] [ ]

Jan 88. (lp) <*(SILENT 002)*> **SOUL CRUSHER** [ ] [ ]

— **J** (b. JOHN RICCI) – guitar; repl. TOM

Caroline / Caroline

Feb 89. (lp/c/cd) <*(CAR LP/C/CD 3)*> **MAKE THEM DIE SLOWLY** [ ] [ ]
– Demonspeed / Disaster blaster / Murderworld / Revenge / Acid flesh / Power hungry / Godslayer.

— **JAY YUENGER** (b.1967, Chicago, Illinois) – guitar; repl. RICCI

Jul 89. (12"ep) *(CLNT 1)* **GOD OF THUNDER. / LOVE RAZOR / DISASTER BLASTER 2** [ ] [ ]

Geffen / Geffen

Mar 92. (lp/c/cd) <*(GEF/+C/D 24460)*> **LA SEXORCISTO: DEVIL MUSIC VOL.1** [ ] [26]
– Welcome to Planet Motherfucker (psychoholic slag) / Knuckle duster (Radio 1-A) / Thunderkiss '65 / Black sunshine / Soul-crusher / Cosmic monsters inc. / Spiderbaby (yeah-yeah-yeah) / I am legend / Knuckle duster (Radio 2-B) / Thrust! / One big crunch / Grindhouse (a go-go) / Starface / Warp asylum.

— **JOHN TEMPESTA** – drums (ex-TESTAMENT, ex-EXODUS) repl.PHILO (PHIL BUERSTATTE), who had briefly repl. DePLUME

May 95. (c-s) *(GFSC 92)* **MORE HUMAN THAN HUMAN / BLOOD, MILK AND SKY (KERO KERO KEROPFI AND THE SMOOTH OPERATOR)** [51] [-]
(10"+=/cd-s+=) *(GFST/+D 92)* – ('A'-Jeddak of the Tharks super mix).

May 95. (cd/c/lp) *(GED/GEC/GEF 24806)*> **ASTROCREEP 2000: SONGS OF LOVE AND DESTRUCTION AND OTHER SYNTHETIC DELUSIONS OF THE ELECTRIC HEAD** [25] [6]
– Electric head part I (the agony) / Super charger Heaven / Real solution No.9 / Creature of the wheel / Electric head part II (the ecstasy) / Grease paint and monkey brains / I, zombie / More human than human / El Phantasmo and the chicken-run blast-o-rama / Blur the technicolor / Blood, milk and sky. *(c+=/cd+=)* – The sidewalk ends where the bug parade begins.

May 96. (12"ep) *(GFST 22140)* **ELECTRIC HEAD PART II (THE ECSTASY) / EL PHANTASMO AND THE CHICKEN-RUN BLAST-O-RAMA. / SUPER CHARGER HEAVEN / MORE HUMAN THAN HUMAN (The Warlord Of Mars mega mix)** [31] [-]
(cd-ep) *(GFSTD 22140)* – (first 2 tracks) / More human than human (Princess of Helium ultra) / Blood, milk & sky (Im-Ho-Tep 3,700 year old boogie mix).
(cd-ep) *(GFSXD 22140)* – (tracks except second) / Thunder kiss '65 (Swinging Lovers extended mix).

Oct 96. (cd/c) <*(GED/GEC 24976)*> **SUPERSEXY SWINGIN' SOUNDS** (dance remixes!) [ ] [17] Aug96
– Phantasmo / Blood, milk & sky / Real solution / Electronic head pt.1 / I'm your boogie man / Electronic head pt.2 / More human than human / I, zombie / Grease paint & monkey brains / Blur the technicolour / Super charger Heaven.

— WHITE ZOMBIE looked to have split, J YUENGER went onto produce FU MANCHU while YSEULT moonlighted in the all-girl surf-rock act, FAMOUS MONSTERS

ROB ZOMBIE

— with **TEMPESTA** + **DANNY LOHNER** – guitar (ex-NINE INCH NAILS, ex-SKREW) / **BLASKO** – bass

Aug 98. (cd/c) <*(GED/GEC 25212)*> **HELLBILLY DELUXE** [37] [5]
– Call of the zombie / Superbeast / Dragula / Living dead girl / Perversion / Demonoid phenomenon / Spookshow baby / How to make a monster / Meet the creeper / The ballad of resurrection Joe and Rosa Whore / What lurks on Channel X? / Return of the phantom stranger / Beginning of the end.

Dec 98. (7"pic-d) *(GFS 22367)* <*1213*> **DRAGULA. / DRAGULA (Hot Rod Herman mix)** [44] [ ]
(cd-s+=) *(GFSTD 22367)* – ('A'-video).
(7"pic-d) *(GFX 22367)* – ('A'side) / Halloween (she's so mean).

Interscope / Interscope

Oct 99. (cd) <*(490349-2)*> **AMERICAN MADE MUSIC TO STRIP BY** (HELLBILLY DELUXE remixed) [ ] [38]

FAMOUS MONSTERS

— **DEVIL DOLL** (aka YSEULT) – guitar / **VAMPIRE GIRL** (aka KATIE CAMPBELL) – bass / **FRANKIE STEIN** – drums

Fire / unknown

Aug 95. (cd-ep) *(BLAZE 90CD)* **SUMMERTIME EP** [ ] [ ]
– Monster girls – are go! / etc

— **SHE-ZILLA** (aka CAROL CUTSHALL) – drums; repl. FRANKIE STEIN

Estrus / Estrus

Oct 98. (7") <*(ES 7130)*> **KNOCK KNOCK HALLOWEEN. /** [ ] [ ]

Bongload / Bongload

Oct 98. (cd) <*(BL 37)*> **IN THE NIGHT** [ ] [ ]
– Murder beach U.S.A. / In the night! / Lone wolf massacre / Destroy puny earthlings! / Bloody Mary / The haunting of Planet Earth / Hairy eyeball / Outerspace deathrace #13 / Satan sends a rat! / Vampire cosmonaut / Oui monstre, oui / F is for fiend / Clock strikes 10 / International monster presentation / When I grow up.

Estrus Estrus

Oct 99. (cd) <ES 1261CD>> **AROUND THE WORLD IN 80 BIKINIS!**
– Monster girls are go!!! / Blood of Frankenstein / Monsters over Tokyo! / The werewolf wiggle / Monster stomp, bite, burn! / Skullhunter-uh-oh! / Boo! (hoo hoo) / The reluctant ghoul / Blood of Frankenstein / Bloody Mary / Outerspace deathrace / Destroy puny earthlings / Actual monster party.

WHITFORD / ST. HOLMES (see under ⇒ AEROSMITH)

WIDOWMAKER

Formed: London, England . . . 1975 by the supergroup formation of vocalist STEVE ELLIS (ex-LOVE AFFAIR), guitarist ARIEL BENDER (ex-MOTT THE HOOPLE), bassist BOB DAISLEY (ex-CHICKEN SHACK), drummer PAUL NICHOLLS (ex-LINDISFARNE) and guitarist HUW LLOYD LANGTON (ex-HAWKWIND). Signing to 'Jet' records, these hard-rock troopers should've secured immediate success after supporting The WHO on their football stadium multi-band day outs at Parkhead and Charlton. Their eponymous debut was released early the following year, containing some excellent numbers, 'WHEN I MET YOU, 'AIN'T TELLING YOU NOTHIN' and 'PIN A ROSE ON ME', although it failed to break them through. ELLIS and LANGTON subsequently left the group later that year, the latter rejoining HAWKWIND, while JOHN BUTLER was drafted in as a replacement for the US Top 200 set, 'TOO LATE TO CRY' (1977), released on 'United Artists'. However, while WIDOWMAKER were singing 'HERE COMES THE QUEEN', a large chunk of the nation's youth were spitting out 'God Save The Queen' as the punk revolution kicked in. Supergroup or no supergroup, WIDOWMAKER couldn't compete and split a few months after the album's release, DAISLEY going on to join a plethora of groups including RAINBOW, OZZY OSBOURNE, etc.

Album rating: WIDOWMAKER (*6) / TOO LATE TO CRY (*5)

STEVE ELLIS – vocals (ex-LOVE AFFAIR) / **ARIEL BENDER** (b. LUTHER GROSVENOR) – guitar (ex-SPOOKY TOOTH, ex-MOTT THE HOOPLE) / **HUW LLOYD LANGTON** – guitar (ex-HAWKWIND, ex-LEO SAYER) / **BOB DAISLEY** – bass (ex-CHICKEN SHACK, ex-BROKEN GLASS) / **PAUL NICHOLLS** – drums (ex-LINDISFARNE, ex-SKIP BIFFERTY)

Jet U.A.

Feb 76. (7") (JET 766) **ON THE ROAD. / PIN A ROSE ON ME** -
Mar 76. (lp) (2310 432) <LA 642> **WIDOWMAKER**
– Such a shame / Pin a rose on me / On the road / Straight faced fighter / Ain't telling you nothing / When I met you / Leave the kids alone / Shine a light on me / Running free / Got a dream. *(cd-iss. Aug94 on 'Jet/Line'; JECD 9008580)*
Apr 76. (7") (JET 767) **WHEN I MET YOU. / PIN A ROSE ON ME**
Jun 76. (7") (JET 782) **PIN A ROSE ON ME. / ON THE ROAD**

— **JOHN BUTLER** – vocals; repl. ELLIS (LANGTON also left, rejoining HAWKWIND and releasing solo albums)

U.A. U.A.

Apr 77. (lp) (UAG 30038) <LA 723> **TOO LATE TO CRY**
– Too late to cry / The hustler / What a way to fall / Here comes the queen / Mean what you say / Something I can do without / Sign the papers / Pushin' and pullin' / Sky blues.
Jun 77. (7") (UP 36263) **WHAT A WAY TO FALL. / HERE COMES THE QUEEN**

— split in July that year, DAISLEY joined a plethora of groups including RAINBOW, OZZY OSBOURNE and URIAH HEEP.

WIDOWMAKER (see under ⇒ TWISTED SISTER)

WILD DOGS

Formed: Los Angeles, California, USA . . . 1983 by MATTHEW T McCOURT, JEFF MARK, DANNY KRUTH and DEAN CASTRONOVO. Rabid heavy-metal borrowing heavily from precision Euro practitioners such as JUDAS PRIEST and ACCEPT, WILD DOGS were snapped up by Mike Varney's 'Shrapnel' records. After two sets of barking metal madness, the eponymous 'WILD DOGS' (1983) and 'MAN'S BEST FRIEND' (1984), the Californian canines were signed to a promising deal with 'Enigma' ('Music For Nations' in the UK). By this point, DANNY and MATTHEW had been replaced with RICK BARTEL and MICHAEL FURLONG, the latter lending his tonsil-torturing talents to a third set, 'REIGN OF TERROR' (1987).

Album rating: WILD DOGS (*4) / MAN'S BEST FRIEND (*4) / REIGN OF TERROR (*4)

MATTHEW T. McCOURT – vocals / **JEFF MARK** – guitars / **DANNY KRUTH** – bass / **DEAN CASTRONOVO** – drums

not iss. Shrapnel

1983. (lp) <SH 1003> **WILD DOGS** -
– Life is just a game / The tonight show / The evil in me / Born to rock / Never gonna stop / Two wrongs / Take another prisoner / I need a love / You can't escape your lies.
1984. (lp) <SH 1012> **MAN'S BEST FRIEND** -
– Livin' on the streets / Not stoppin' / Woman in chains / Beauty and the beast / Believe in me / Rock's not dead / Endless nights / Ready or not / Stick to your guns.

— **MICHAEL FURLONG** – vocals; repl. MATTHEW

— **RICK BARTEL** – bass; repl. KRUTH

Music For Nations Enigma

Nov 87. (lp) (MFN 80) <73241> **REIGN OF TERROR**
– Metal fuel (in the blood) / Man against machine / Call of the dark / Siberian vacation / Psychoradio / Streets of Berlin / Spellshock / Reign of terror / We rule the night.

WILDFIRE

Formed: London, England . . . 1983 by seasoned NWOBHM players, PAUL MARIO DAY, MARTIN BUSHELL, JEFF SUMMERS, JEFF BROWN and BRUCE BISLAND. Signed to the 'Mausoleum' label, the group made their debut in summer '84 with 'BRUTE FORCE AND IGNORANCE'. While that description could be applied to more than a few metal acts, WILDFIRE acquitted themselves well with a competent set of upstanding Brit-metal. Though they never actually set the metal scene alight, WILDFIRE were nothing if not prolific, releasing an impressive second set, 'SUMMER LIGHTNING' later that year. A lone single in Spring '85, 'JERUSALEM', proved to be their final spark of life as the flames finally extinguished and the various members went their separate ways. BROWN and BISLAND both went on to join GARY BARDEN's new outfit, STATETROOPER.

Album rating: BRUTE FORCE AND IGNORANCE (*4) / SUMMER LIGHTNING (*4)

PAUL MARIO DAY – vocals / **MARTIN BUSHELL** – guitar / **JEFF SUMMERS** – guitar / **JEFF BROWN** – bass / **BRUCE BISLAND** – drums

Mausoleum not iss.

Jun 84. (lp/c) (SKULL/TAPE7 8307) **BRUTE FORCE AND IGNORANCE** -
– Violator / Victim of love / Another daymare / Lovelight / Search and destroy / Redline / Wildfire / Goldrush / If I tried / Eyes of the future.
Nov 84. (lp) <SKULL 8338> **SUMMER LIGHTNING** -
– Prelude in F flat minor / The key / Summer lightning / Gun runner / Give me back your heart / Nothing lasts forever / Natural selection / Fight fire with fire / Blood money / Passion for the sun / Screaming in the night.
Nov 84. (7") (GUTS 8403) **NOTHING LASTS FOREVER. / BLOOD MONEY** -
Mar 85. (7") (GUTS 8405) **JERUSALEM. /** -

WILDHEARTS

Formed: London, England . . . 1989 by Northern-born guitarist GINGER, guitarist CJ (CHRIS JADGHAR), vocalist SNAKE, bassist JULIAN and drummer STIDI (ANDREW STIDOLPH): all veterans of the late 80's hard-rock/glam-metal scene. STIDI and SNAKE subsequently dropped out the following year, GINGER taking over lead vocal duties, while a guy called PAT filled in on drums prior to BAM (of DOGS D'AMOUR fame) grabbing the sticks. By the summer of '91, a new line-up introduced 19 year-old DANNY McCORMICK to the proceedings and after difficulties with their initial record label, 'Atco', they signed to 'East West' (GINGER would later slate them at most opportunities!). The following year, The WILDHEARTS were finally on their hard-rockin' way with the much-touted, 'MONDO-AKIMBO-A-GO-GO', an EP that was premiered while supporting their mates, The MANIC STREET PREACHERS. Like a punk/metal fusion of The RUTS, The CULT or The MANICS, GINGER and Co. delivered a mini-set, 'DON'T BE HAPPY . . . JUST WORRY' (a play on words from a Bobby McFerrin hit!), featuring the gorefest, 'SPLATTERMANIA'. Slagging everyone from IZZY STRADLIN of GUNS N' ROSES (he chucked them off his tour after only one gig!) to their producer, Simon Efeny, the wild ones toasted the release of their first full-length effort, 'EARTH VS THE WILDHEARTS' (1993), a set that saw the return of STIDI. The record managed to scrape into the UK Top 50, aided by some loveable tracks such as 'GREETINGS FROM SHITSVILLE', 'TV TAN' and a near Top 30 hit, 'CAFFEINE BOMB'. Much of 1994 was spent in personnel turmoil; STIDI was substituted by RITCH BATTERSBY, while CJ was in and out of the band more times than even he could recall. McCORMACK too had his moments, the hardy bassman dislocating his knee during their first number at the Reading Festival, while six months later, he smashed the computer of a Kerrang! journalist, who had said he was about to leave the band. Meanwhile, at the start of '95, a couple of singles had torn into the UK charts, 'IF LIFE IS LIKE A LOVE BANK I WANT AN OVERDRAFT' and 'I WANNA GO WHERE THE PEOPLE GO', the latter one of the many highlights on their glorious Top 10 "comeback" album, 'P.H.U.Q.'. CJ's departure had caused a few problems, none more so when interim (ex-SENSELESS THINGS) guitarist MARK KEDS was posted missing in Japan causing the band to cancel a Phoenix Festival spot; they subsequently found JEFF STREATFIELD. Growing hostility between them and their record company (who issued the 'FISHING FOR LUCKIES' set just one too many times), led to The WILDHEARTS branching out on their own label, 'Round', issuing two hit singles, 'SICK OF DRUGS' and 'RED LIGHT – GREEN LIGHT' in '96. Late the following year, and now on 'Mushroom' records, the group released a couple of Top 30 singles, 'ANTHEM' and 'URGE', which surprisingly didn't push up the sales of third album proper, 'ENDLESS, NAMELESS'. With The WILDHEARTS out of the way by the end of the year, GINGER looked to other pursuits. However, a five week stint in a Bangkok prison put paid to any musical activity; he was arrested for being drunk after missing his flight home. Licking his wounds, he was back early in '99 with a new project, CLAM ABUSE, a duo that featured American ALEX KANE (or CLINT ABUSE, as he was better known at the time). • **Songwriters:** GINGER, except some by others. • **Trivia:** In 1993, the group featured in a Channel 4 play, 'Comics'.

Album rating: DON'T BE HAPPY . . . JUST WORRY (*6) / EARTH VERSUS THE WILDHEARTS (*6) / P.H.U.Q. (*8) / THE BEST OF THE WILDHEARTS compilation (*8) / ENDLESS, NAMELESS (*5) / Clam Abuse: STOP THINKING (*4)

GINGER (b. DAVID WALLS, 17 Dec'64, South Shields, England) – vocals, guitar (ex-QUIREBOYS) / **BAM** – drums (ex-DOGS D'AMOUR) / **CJ** (CHRIS JAGDHAR) – guitar, vocals (ex-TATTOOED LOVE BOYS) / **DANNY McCORMACK** (b.28 Feb'72, South Shields) – bass, vocals (ex-ENERGETIC KRUSHER)

East West East West

Mar 92. (12"ep/12"white-ep/cd-ep) *(YZ 669 T/TX/CD)* **MONDO-AKIMBO-A-GO-GO** [ ] [-]
– (Nothing ever changes but the) Shoes / Turning American / Crying over nothing / Liberty cap.

Nov 92. (2xm-cd/c/2x12"m-lp) *(4509 91202-2/-4/-1)* **DON'T BE HAPPY . . . JUST WORRY** [ ] [-]
– (above 4 tracks; with 4 new ones:-) Splattermania / Weekend (5 days long) / etc. *(cd w/ anti-dance mixes of 'MONDO . . .') (re-iss. Apr 94 cd/c; 4509 96067-2/-4)*

— **ANDREW 'STIDI' STIDOLPH** – drums; returned to repl. BAM who returned to DOGS D'AMOUR

Sep 93. (cd/c/lp) *(4509 93201-2/-4/-1) <92315>* **EARTH VERSUS THE WILDHEARTS** [46] [ ]
– Greetings from Shitsville / TV tan / Everlone / Shame on me / Loveshit / The miles away girl / My baby is a headf*** / Suckerpunch / News of the world / Love u til I don't. *(cd+=/c+=)* – Drinking about life. *(re-iss. Feb94 cd/c; 4509 94859-2/-4)*

Oct 93. (7"brown) *(YZ 773)* **GREETINGS FROM SHITSVILLE. / THE BULLSHIT GOES ON** [ ] [-]

Nov 93. (7"pic-d/c-s) *(YZ 784 P/C)* **TV TAN. / SHOW A LITTLE EMOTION** [53] [ ]
(12"+=/cd-s+=) *(YZ 784 T/CD)* – Dangerlust / Down on London.

— **RITCH BATTERSBY** (b.RICHARD, 29 Jun'68, Birmingham, England) – drums (ex-RADIO MOSCOW) repl. STIDI

Feb 94. (7"green/c-s) *(YZ 794/+C)* **CAFFEINE BOMB / GIRLFRIENDS CLOTHES** [31] [-]
(12"+=/cd-s+=) *(YZ 794 T/CD)* – Shut your fuckin' mouth and use your fuckin' brain / And the bullshit goes on.

— added on tour **WILL DOWNING** – keyboards (ex-GRIP) on tour

Jun 94. (etched10"ep/c-ep/cd-ep) *(YZ 828 TE/C/CD)* **SUCKERPUNCH / BEAUTIFUL THING YOU. / TWO-WAY IDIOT MIRROR / 29 x THE PAIN** [38] [-]

— (Jul'94) temp **DEVON TOWNSEND** – guitar (ex-STEVE VAI) repl. CJ who formed, although only briefly, HONEYCRACK. He returned for the Reading Festival August 1994 before taking WILL to the aforementioned outfit

Dec 94. (mail order m-cd) *(4509 99039-2)* **FISHING FOR LUCKIES** [-] [-]
– Sky babies / Inglorious / Do the channel bop / Shizophronic / Geordie in wonderland / If life is like a love bank I want an overdraft.

Jan 95. (10"ep/c-ep/cd-ep/s-cd-ep) *(YZ 874 TEX/C/CD/CDX)* **IF LIFE IS LIKE A LOVE BANK I WANT AN OVERDRAFT / GEORDIE IN WONDERLAND. / HATE THE WORLD DAY / FIRE UP** [31] [-]

Apr 95. (10"ep/c-ep/cd-ep/s-cd-ep) *(YZ 923 TEX/C/CD/CDX)* **I WANNA GO WHERE THE PEOPLE GO / SHANDY BANG. / CAN'T DO RIGHT FOR DOING WRONG / GIVE THE GIRL A GUN** [16] [-]

May 95. (cd/c/lp)(s-cd) *(0630 10404-2/10653-4/10654-1)(0630 10437-2)* **P.H.U.Q.** [6] [-]
– I wanna go where the people go / V-day / Rust in lust / Baby strange / Nita nitro / Jonesing for Jones / Woah shit, you got through / Cold patootie tango / Caprice / Be my drug / Naivety play / In Lilly's garden / Getting it.

— **MARK KEDS** – guitar (ex-SENSELESS THINGS) finally repl. C.J.

Jul 95. (10"ep/c-ep/cd-ep/cd-ep) *(YZ 967 TEX/C/CD/CDX)* **JUST IN LUST / MINDSLIDE. / FRIEND FOR FIVE MINUTES / S.I.N. (IN SIN)** [28] [-]

— **JEF STREATFIELD** (b. 8 Jun'71, Southampton, England) – guitar repl. KEDS who went AWOL in July

Nov 95. (cd/c)(lp) *(0630 14855-2/-4)(0630 14888-1)* **FISHING FOR MORE LUCKIES** [ ] [-]

— disbanded at the end of '95 although they quickly reformed

Round – East West not iss.

Apr 96. (c-ep/cd-ep) *(WILD 1 C/CD)* **SICK OF DRUGS / UNDERKILL / BAD TIME TO BE HAVING A BAD TIME / SKY CHASER HIGH** [14] [ ]
(cd-ep) *(WILD 1CDX)* –

May 96. (3D-cd/c/d-lp) *(0630 14855-2/-4/-1)* **FISHING FOR LUCKIES** (re-issue from late '94) [16] [-]
– Inglorious / Sick of drugs / Red light – green light / Schitzophonic / Soul searching on Planet Earth / Do the channel bop / Mood swings & roundabouts / In like Flynn / Sky babies / Nite songs.

Jun 96. (7"ep/c-ep/cd-ep) *(WILD 2/+C/CD)* **RED LIGHT – GREEN LIGHT EP** [30] [-]
– Red light – green light / Got it on Tuesday / Do anything / The British all-American homeboy crowd.

Nov 96. (cd/c) *(0630 17212-2/-4)* **THE BEST OF THE WILDHEARTS** (compilation) [ ] [-]
– I wanna go where the people go / T.V. tan / Sick of drugs / 29 x the pain / Caffeine bomb / Geordie in wonderland / Suckerpunch / Just in lust / Greetings from Shitsville / In Lilly's garden / My baby is a headfuck / If life is like a love bank I want an overdraft / Nothing ever changes but the shoes / Red light – green light / Beautiful me, beautiful you / Splattermania.

Mushroom not iss.

Aug 97. (7") *(MUSH 6S)* **ANTHEM. / HE'S A WHORE** [21] [-]
(cd-s) *(MUSH 6CD)* – ('A'side) / So good to be back home / Time to let you go.
(cd-s) *(MUSH 6CDX)* – ('A'side) / The song formerly known as / White lies.

Oct 97. (7") *(MUSH 14S)* **URGE. / FUGAZI (DO THE FAKE)** [26] [-]
(cd-s+=) *(MUSH 14CDS)* – Kill me to death.

Oct 97. (cd/c) *(MUSH 13 CD/MC/LP)* **ENDLESS, NAMELESS** [41] [-]
– Junkenstein / Nurse maximum / Anthem / Urge / Pissjoy / Soundog Babylon / Now is the colour / Heroin / Why you lie / Thunderfuck.

— split after above, DANNY formed The YO-YO'S (with TOM, NEIL and BLADS) in '98, releasing their debut single, 'OUT OF MY MIND', in December. GINGER subsequently joined the band, SUPERSHIT 666, alongside DREGEN (Backyard Babies) and NICKE ANDERSON (Hellacopters). Meanwhile, BATTERSBY helped form GRAND THEFT AUDIO.

– compilations, etc. –

Mar 98. (cd/d-lp) *Kuro Neko; (NKEK/+LP 3)* **ANARCHIC AIRWAVES – THE WILDHEARTS AT THE BBC** [ ] [-]

Sep 98. (cd) *Kuro Neko; (KNEK 4)* **LANDMINES & PANTOMIMES – THE LAST OF THE WILDHEARTS . . .?** [ ] [-]

CLAM ABUSE

GINGER (aka CLAM SAVAGE) + **CLINT ABUSE** (b. ALEX KANE)

Infernal Global Warning not iss.

Jul 99. (cd) *(INFERNAL 001CD)* **STOP THINKING** [ ] [-]
– Sing like a girl / I think I love you / Message to Geri / Unlucky in love / .com together / Falling in bed with you / Sunday driving on a Thursday afternoon / For that girl, everything is groovy / Barney sings the blues / She's so taboo / There's always someone more fucked up than you.

WILD HORSES

Formed: London, England . . . 1978 by two Scots-born hard-rockers BRIAN ROBERTSON (ex-THIN LIZZY) and JIMMY BAIN (ex-RAINBOW), who had met while the latter was with HARLOT; he had earlier been guitarist with THREE'S A CROWD. Taking the name from a well-known ROLLING STONES track, they recruited two more experienced players, NEIL CARTER and CLIVE EDWARDS. Signed to 'E.M.I.' on the quality of their pedigree, WILD HORSES opened the starting gate on their career in late '79 with the single, 'CRIMINAL TENDENCIES'. Criticised for their notably unoriginal hard rock sound, the 'HORSES nevertheless bolted into the UK Top 40 with their eponymous debut album, released in the Spring the following year. CARTER was subsequently relaced by JOHN LOCKTON, and, gee'd up by the enthusiastic reception reserved for their live work, the group released an improved second set, the earthy 'STAND YOUR GROUND'. After a final single, 'EVERLASTING LOVE', however, The WILD HORSES finally trotted into the rock graveyard later that year, ROBERTSON joining MOTORHEAD while BAIN went on to play with DIO.

Album rating: WILD HORSES (*4) / STAND YOUR GROUND (*5)

JIMMY BAIN (b. Edinburgh, Scotland) – vocals, bass, guitar, keyboards (ex-RAINBOW, ex-HARLOT, ex-THREE'S A CROWD) / **BRIAN ROBERTSON** (b.12 Sep'56, Glasgow, Scotland) – guitar, bass, vocals (ex-THIN LIZZY) / **NEIL CARTER** – guitar, keyboards (ex-GILBERT O'SULLIVAN) / **CLIVE EDWARDS** – drums (ex-PAT TRAVERS)

EMI Int. not iss.

Nov 79. (7") *(INT 599)* **CRIMINAL TENDENCIES. / THE RAPIST** [ ] [-]

E.M.I. not iss.

Mar 80. (7") *(EMI 5047)* **FACE DOWN. / DEALER** [ ] [-]

Apr 80. (lp/c) *(EMC/TC-EMC 3324)* **WILD HORSES** [38] [-]
– Reservation / Face down / Blackmail / Fly away / Dealer / Street girl / No strings attached / Criminal tendencies / Nights on the town / Woman.

May 80. (7"white/12"white) *(EMI/12EMI 5078)* **FLY AWAY. / BLACKMAIL** [ ] [-]

— **JOHN LOCKTON** – guitar; repl. CARTER who joined GARY MOORE

Apr 81. (7") *(EMI 5149)* **I'LL GIVE YOU LOVE. / ROCKY MOUNTAIN WAY** [ ] [-]
(free 7"w.a.) *(PSR 45)* – THE KID. / ON A SATURDAY NIGHT

May 81. (lp/c) *(EMC/TC-EMC 3368)* **STAND YOUR GROUND** [ ] [-]
– I'll give you love / In the city / Another lover / Back in the U.S.A. / Stand your ground / The axe / Miami justice / Precious / New York City / Stake out.

— **DIXIE LEE** – drums (ex-LONE STAR) repl. EDWARDS

Jun 81. (7") *(EMI 5199)* **EVERLASTING LOVE. / THE AXE** [ ] [-]

— folded in 1981, ROBERTSON joining MOTORHEAD, while BAIN sessioned for PHIL LYNOTT, KATE BUSH and went on to DIO; the latter also played bass for GARY MOORE and JOHN CALE

WILDLIFE (see under ⇒ FM)

WILLARD

Formed: Seattle, Washington, USA . . . 1991 by JOHNNY CLINT, MARK SPIDERS, OTIS P. OTIS, DARREN PETERS and STEVE WIED. Taking the name WILLARD from a character out of James Herbert's book 'The Rats', they secured a deal with 'Roadracer' who issued their debut, 'STEEL MILL – THE SOUND OF FUCK!' (1992). However, this hardcore, early NIRVANA or BLACK SABBATH influenced album was their only output.

Album rating: STEEL MILL (*6)

JOHNNY CLINT – vocals / **MARK SPIDERS** – guitar / **OTIS P. OTIS** – guitar / **DARREN PETERS** – bass / **STEVE WIED** – drums

Roadracer Roadracer

Jul 92. (cd/lp) *<(RO 9162-2/-1)>* **STEEL MILL** [ ] [ ]
– The sound of fuck! / Fifteen / Seasick / Sweet Kali / No confession / Steel mill / Monotony / Stain / High moon / Hod / Double dragon / Folsom / Water sports / Turn it all the way up!

— nothing has been heard of them since the above album

WILL HAVEN

Formed: Sacramento, California, USA . . . 1995 by high school chums, JEFF IRWIN, GRADY AVENELL, MIKE MARTIN and WAYNE MORSE; all mates of fellow heavies, The DEFTONES. Having opened for the likes of The BEASTIE BOYS and EARTH CRISIS, WILL HAVEN were ready to explode on the scene via an eponymous mail-order-only mini-CD in '96. They certainly come across as a more cheesed-off NEUROSIS, guttural vox backed with primitive, rumbling basslines and huge slab-like riffs on their wild full debut set, 'EL DIABLO' (1997). Heralded by noneother than MAX CAVALERA (of SOULFLY) who subsequently invited the sonic heavy-metal quartet to support his band on a European and Stateside tour the following summer. Now signed to 'Music For Nations' ('Revelation' in the USA), WILL HAVEN delivered their sophomore long-player, 'WHVN' (1999), another remarkable record produced by Eric Stenman.

Album rating: WILL HAVEN (*6) / EL DIABLO (*8) / WHVN (*7)

GRADY AVENELL – vocals / **JEFF IRWIN** – guitar / **MIKE MARTIN** – bass / **WAYNE MORSE** – drums

Landscaped / not iss.

Oct 96. (m-cd) *(LS-001)* **WILL HAVEN** [ ] [-]
– Choke / Rut / Labcoats / Fisk / Veg / Both ways / Asking. *(re-iss. Mar98; same)*

Crisis / Crisis

Jul 97. (lp/cd) *<(CRISIS 15/+CD)>* **EL DIABLO** [ ] [ ]
– Stick up kid / I've seen my fate / Ego's game / Mason / Climbing out this bottle / Extinguish / Baseball theory / June / Foreign film / Escuha! *(re-iss. Mar98; same)*

Music For Nations / Revelation

Sep 99. (cd) *(CDMFN 255) <79>* **WHVN** [ ] [ ]
– Fresno / If she could speak / Jaworski / Slopez / End summary / Genesis 11 / Dallass drake / Death us do part / Muse / Miguel abburido / I've see my fate (mix) / Sign off.

Rozz WILLIAMS (see under ⇒ CHRISTIAN DEATH)

WILT (see under ⇒ KERBDOG)

WINGER

Formed: New York City, New York, USA . . . 1986 by Colorado-born pin-up boy (and ex-ballet dancer!), KIP WINGER and PAUL TAYLOR, the pair first working together as part of ALICE COOPER's backing band. Recruiting experienced sidemen REB BEACH and ROD MORGANSTEIN, WINGER were initially conceived as a studio outfit, although after the surprise success of the eponymous debut album (released on 'Atlantic' in 1988), they subsequently took their airbrushed hard rock out on tour. With his designer-windswept good looks, KIP was a focal point for the band and MTV coverage ensured Top 30 US hits for singles such as 'SEVENTEEN' and 'HEADED FOR A HEARTBREAK'. The album itself almost made the Top 20, ensuring WINGER's profile was high for a follow-up set, 'IN THE HEART OF THE YOUNG' (1990). Due in no small part to the massive success of the 'MILES AWAY' single (adopted as a mascot tune by relatives of servicemen involved in the Gulf conflict), the album went on to sell in bucketloads. While a lighter third set, 'PULL' (1993), featured TAYLOR in a songwriting role, he'd already tired of touring and KIP recruited extra guitarist, JOHN ROTH for subsequent live work. Unable to compete with the grunge takeover, the band inevitably split soon after. KIP went on to record solo material, although the tragic death of his wife Beatrice in a car accident (late '96) dealt the singer a serious blow. The material was nevertheless released in 1997 as 'THIS CONVERSATION SEEMS LIKE A DREAM', WINGER managing a solo acoustic tour to promote the album. The following year saw the release of stop-gap set, 'MADE BY HAND' (released in the US as 'DOWN INCOGNITO' in 1999), featuring acoustic renditions of WINGER nuggets. A second album of new material entitled 'SONGS FROM THE OCEAN FLOOR' (2000) found KIP attempting to come to terms with his wife's death. • **Songwriters:** KIP & REB, except PURPLE HAZE (Jimi Hendrix). • **Trivia:** KIP was once the boyfriend of RACHEL HUNTER who later married ROD STEWART.

Album rating: WINGER (*5) / IN THE HEART OF THE YOUNG (*7) / PULL (*4) / Kip Winger: THIS CONVERSATIONS SEEMS LIKE A DREAM (*3) / MADE BY HAND /or/ DOWN INCOGNITO (*3) / SONGS FROM THE OCEAN FLOOR (*4)

KIP WINGER (b.21 Jun'61, Golden, Colorado) – vocals, bass (ex-ALICE COOPER) / **REB BEACH** (b.31 Aug'63, Baltimore, Maryland) – guitar (ex-ALICE COOPER) / **PAUL TAYLOR** (b.1960, San Francisco) – keyboards / **ROD MORGANSTEIN** (b.19 Apr'57) – drums

Atlantic / Atlantic

Aug 88. (7") *<89041>* **MADELAINE. / HIGHER AND HIGHER** [-] [ ]

Aug 88. (lp/c/cd) *(781 867-1/-4/-2) <81867>* **WINGER** [ ] [21]
– Madelaine / Hungry / Seventeen / Without the night / Purple haze / State of emergency / Time to surrender / Poison angel / Hangin' on / Headed for a heartbreak. *(cd+=)* – Higher and higher.

Feb 89. (7") *<88958>* **SEVENTEEN. / POISON ANGEL** [-] [26]

May 89. (7") *<88922>* **HEADED FOR A HEARTBREAK. / STATE OF EMERGENCY** [-] [19]

Sep 89. (7") *<88859>* **HUNGRY. / TIME TO SURRENDER** [-] [85]

— later in '89, KIP WINGER was credited on FIONA's single, 'Everything You Do (You're Sexing Me)'.

Jul 90. (cd/c/lp) *<(7567 82103-2/-4/-1)>* **IN THE HEART OF THE YOUNG** [ ] [15]
– Can't get enuff / Loosen up / Miles away / Easy come, easy go / Rainbow in the rose / In the day we'll never see / Under one condition / Little dirty blonde / Baptized by fire / You are the saint, I am the sinner / In the heart of the young.

Jul 90. (7") *<87773>* **EASY COME, EASY GO (remix). / YOU ARE THE SAINT, I AM THE SINNER** [ ] [41] Feb91
(12"+=/cd-s+=) – Madelaine (live).

Nov 90. (7") *(A 6112) <87884>* **CAN'T GET ENUFF. / LOOSEN UP** [ ] [42] Jul90
(12"+=/cd-s+=) *(A 6112 T/CD)* – Time to surrender.

Jan 91. (7"/c-s) *(A 7802/+C) <87824>* **MILES AWAY. / IN THE DAY WE'LL NEVER SEE** [56] [12] Oct90
(12"+=/cd-s+=) *(A 7802 T/CD)* – All I ever wanted / Seventeen.

Jun 91. (7") **HEADED FOR A HEARTBREAK ('91 version). / LITTLE DIRTY BLONDE** [ ] [ ]
(12"+=/cd-s+=) – Never.

— (Dec'91) PAUL TAYLOR departed repl. **JOHN ROTH** (b. 5 May'67, Springfield, Illinois) – guitar

May 93. (cd/c) *<(7567 82485-2/-4)>* **PULL** [ ] [83]
– Blind revolution mad / Down incognito / Spell I'm under / In my veins / Junkyard dog / The lucky one / In for the kill / No man's land / Like a ritual / Who's the one. *(re-iss. Feb95; same)*

— WINGER split after above

KIP WINGER

— with various musicians incl. MORGANSTEIN, BEACH + RICH KERN

Domo / Domo

Mar 97. (cd/c) *<(DOMO 71015-2/-4)>* **THIS CONVERSATION SEEMS LIKE A DREAM** [ ] [ ]
– Kiss of life / Monster / Endless circles / Angel of the underground / Steam / It'll be down / Naked son / Daniel / How far will we go? / Don't let go / Here. *(cd re-iss. Jan01 on 'Frontiers'; FRCD 076)*

Feb 98. (cd) *(DOMO 71019-2)* **MADE BY HAND** (acoustic) [ ] [-]
– Another way / Down incognito / Under one condition / Miles away / Steam / Headed for a heartbreak / How far will you go? / Naked son / The spell I'm under / Easy come easy go / Daniel. *<US + re-iss. Oct99 as 'DOWN INCOGNITO' on 'Cleopatra'; CLP 704>* – Rainbow in the rose / Blind revolution mad. *(UK re-iss. Jan01 as 'DOWN INCOGNITO' on 'Frontiers'; FRCD 077)*

Frontiers / Meadowlark

Jan 01. (cd) *(FRCD 075) <101>* **SONGS FROM THE OCEAN FLOOR** [ ] [ ] Nov00
– Cross / Crash the wall / Sure was a wildflower / Two lovers stand / Landslide / Faster / Song of midnight / Free / Only one world / Broken open / Resurrection / Everything you need.

WIPERS

Formed: Portland, Oregon, USA . . . 1977 by GREG SAGE, DAVE KOUPAL and SAM HENRY. The former two had begun their musical career in late 60's rock outfit, BEAUREGARDE, named after a professional wrestler (who actually featured on the sleeve of their one and only eponymous album!). The WIPERS debuted in '78 with the EP, 'BETTER OFF DEAD', a full album, 'IS THIS REAL?', emerging at the turn of the decade, the blitzkrieg 'D-7' later covered by NIRVANA (KURT COBAIN was only one of a number of alt-rock icons to cite The WIPERS as a seminal influence). After another EP, 'ALIEN BOY', some personnal changes took place, drummer HENRY making way for BRAD DAVIDSON and BRAD NAISH before the subsequent release of their second set, 'YOUTH OF AMERICA' (1982). Following the release of a Canadian-only LP, 'OVER THE EDGE' (1984), GREG signed to rising label 'Enigma' issuing a solo album, 'STRAIGHT AHEAD' (1986) in the process. The WIPERS returned to the fold (STEVE PLOUF replacing NAISH) with a fifth set, 'LAND OF THE LOST' (1986), a dirtier, metallic grunge sound which deserved a lot more success than it achieved. They continued ploughing a singular furrow to the end of the decade, remaining largely unsung until the advent of the Seattle grunge scene. SAGE subsequently went solo in the early '90's with the album 'SACRIFICE (FOR LOVE)', although the resulting surge in interest for all things WIPERS, led to a reformation in 1993. The 'SILVER SAIL' single (their first ever!) and an album of the same name appeared the following year, while 'Tim/Kerr' (the label) also issued another, 'THE HERD', in '96. • **Trivia:** May '94 saw the release of a tribute album, 'SONGS FOR GREG SAGE & THE WIPERS', boasting contributions from the likes of NIRVANA, HOLE, POISON IDEA, etc.

Album rating: IS THIS REAL? (*7) / YOUTH OF AMERICA mini (*6) / OVER THE EDGE (*8) / LAND OF THE LOST (*6) / FOLLOW BLIND (*6) / THE CIRCLE (*6) / SILVER SAIL (*6) / THE HERD (*6) / Greg Sage: STRAIGHT AHEAD (*6)

GREG SAGE – vocals, guitar / **DAVE KOUPAL** – bass / **SAM HENRY** – drums

not iss. / Trap

1978. (7"ep) *<810X44>* **BETTER OFF DEAD. / UP IN FLAMES / DOES IT HURT?** [-] [ ]

not iss. / Park Avenue

Feb 80. (lp) **IS THIS REAL?** [-] [ ]
– Return of the rat / Mystery / Up front / Let's go let's go away / Is this real? / Tragedy / Alien boy / D-7 / Potential suicide / Don't know what I am / Window shop for love / Wait a minute. *<re-iss. Apr84 on 'Psycho'; PSYCHO 22> (UK-iss.Mar87 on 'Weird Systems'; WS 024) (cd-iss. Mar93 on 'Sub Pop'+=; SPCD 82-253)* – ALIEN BOY EP

Aug 80. (7"ep) *<PA 10EP>* **ALIEN BOY** [-] [ ]
– Image of man / Telepathic love / Voices in the rain.

— **BRAD DAVIDSON** – bass + **BRAD NAISH** – drums repl. DAVE (on some) + SAM also departed

Feb 82. (m-lp) <82802> **YOUTH OF AMERICA** [-] [ ]
– Taking too long / Can this be / Pushing the extreme / When it's over / No fair / Youth of America. *<re-iss. Apr84 on 'Psycho'; PSYCHO 23> (cd-iss. Dec94 on 'Gift Of Life' lp/cd; GIFT 025/+CD)*

not iss. / Brain Eater

Nov 84. (lp) <EATER 2> **OVER THE EDGE** [-] [-] Canada
– Over the edge / Doom town / So young / Messenger / Romeo / Now is the time / What is / No one wants an alien / The lonely one / No generation gap / This time. *(re-iss. Mar87 on 'Enigma'; 2187-1) (UK-iss.Aug94 on 'Gift Of Life' lp/cd; GIFT 020/+CD)*

Enigma / Enigma

Jan 86. (lp; by GREG SAGE) <2007-1> **STRAIGHT AHEAD** [-] [ ]
– Straight ahead / Soul's tongue / Blue cowboy / Your empathy / The illusion fades / Seems so clear / On the run / Astro clouds / Lost in space / Let it go / World without fear / Keep on keepin' on. *(UK-iss.Aug94 on 'Gift Of Life' lp/cd; GIFT 022/+CD))*

Mar 86. (lp) <(2026-1)> **LIVE: WIPERS (live)** [ ] [ ]
(re-iss. Aug94 & Feb98 on 'Gift Of Life' lp/cd; GIFT 021/+CD)

— **STEVE PLOUF** – drums repl. NAISH

Nov 86. (lp/cd) <(2094-1/-2)> **LAND OF THE LOST** [ ] [ ]
– Just a dream away / Way of love / Let me know / Fair weather friends / Land of the lost / Nothing left to lose / The search / Different ways / Just say. *(cd re-iss. Aug94 & Feb98 on 'Gift Of Life'; GIFT 023CD)*

Dec 87. (lp) <971194> **FOLLOW BLIND** [-] [ ]
– Follow blind / Some place else / Any time you find / The chill remains / Let it slide / Against the wall / No doubt about it / Don't belong to you / Losers town / Coming down / Next time. *(UK-iss.Aug94 & Feb98 on 'Gift Of Life' lp/cd; GIFT 024/+CD)*

Enigma / Restless

Dec 88. (lp/c/cd) *(ENVLP/TCENV/CDENV 516)* <72339> **THE CIRCLE** [ ] [ ]
– I want a way / Time marches on / All the same / True believer / Good thing / Make or break / The circle / Goodbye again / Be there / Blue & red.

Feb 90. (cd/c) <72378-2/-4> **BEST OF WIPERS & GREG SAGE** (compilation) [-] [ ]
– Nothing left to lose / The way of love / Some place else / The chill remains / Soul's tongue / Blue cowboy / Taking too long / The circle / Romeo / Messenger / Better off dead / No solution / My vengeance / Just a dream away / Different ways / Losers town.

Roadrunner / Restless

Oct 91. (cd; by GREG SAGE) *(LS 9237-2)* <772539-2> **SACRIFICE (FOR LOVE)** [ ] [ ]
– Stay by me / Sacrifice (for love) / Know by now / Forever (with BOBBY WOMACK) / The same guitar / No turning back / Ready or not / For your love / This planet Earth / Dreams. *(cd re-iss. Jul95 on 'Restess'; same as US)*

— the WIPERS line-up still:- **SAGE / DAVIDSON / KOUPAL**

Tim/Kerr / Gift Of Life

Jun 94. (7"/cd-s) **SILVER SAIL. /** [ ] [ ]

Jun 94. (cd/lp) <(TK 92 CD/12 031)> **SILVER SAIL** [ ] [ ]
– Y I came / Back to the basics / Warning / Mars / Prisoner / Standing there / Sign of the times / Line / On a roll / Never win / Silver sail. *(re-iss. Nov94 on 'Gift Of Life' lp/cd; GIFT 036/+CD)*

Apr 96. (cd) <(TK 95CD 114)> **THE HERD** [ ] [ ] Feb96
– Psychic vampire / No place safe / Last chance / Wind the clock slowly / The herd / Stormy / Green light region / Sinking as a stone / Sunrise / Defiant / Resist / Insane. *(re-iss. Jul97; same)*

Apr 96. (cd-s) <TK 116> **INSANE /** [-] [ ]

WISEBLOOD (see under ⇒ FOETUS)

WISHBONE ASH

Formed: Torquay, Devon, England ... summer 1969 out of the EMPTY VESSELS, by MARTIN TURNER and STEVE UPTON. They quickly moved to London with two new members; ANDY POWELL and TED TURNER (no relation). In 1970, they signed to 'M.C.A.' and delivered their eponymous debut into the UK Top 40. They were described at the time as Britain's answer to The ALLMAN BROTHERS, albeit with a mystical lyrical element. Fusing heavy-rock with fine harmonies and self-indulgent solos, the second album, the Top 20 'PILGRIMAGE' was more of the same. Their third album, 'ARGUS' (1972) broke them through big time, a compelling hybrid of arcane medieval themes and water-tight prog-rock. This classic Top 3 album featured, 'WARRIOR', 'THE KING WILL COME' and 'THROW DOWN THE SWORD' alongside the more freely flowing, 'BLOWIN' FREE' (a record that should have given them a hit). 'WISHBONE FOUR' was completed the following year, a mellower set with a rootsier country-rock feel, especially on the track, 'BALLAD OF THE BEACON'. After a double live set in '73, they took an even more down-home approach on 'THERE'S THE RUB', although it did contain one highlight, 'F*U*B*B*' (Fucked Up Beyond Belief). Although they managed to retain some (very!) loyal fans, by the end of the decade they had lost all their credibility when most of the original members left. In 1981, they even drafted in folky/new-age vocalist, CLAIRE HAMILL, in an attempt to develop other areas of their sound. They are still treading the boards, churning out new versions of their once classic songs, two live albums of recent material being recorded in Chicago and Geneva respectively. • **Songwriters:** Group compositions / TURNER's.

Album rating: WISHBONE ASH (*5) / PILGRIMAGE (*6) / ARGUS (*8) / WISHBONE FOUR (*6) / LIVE DATES (*8) / THERE'S THE RUB (*5) / LOCKED IN (*4) / NEW ENGLAND (*4) / CLASSIC ASH compilation (*8) / FRONT PAGE NEWS (*5) / NO SMOKE WITHOUT FIRE (*5) / JUST TESTING (*4) / LIVE DATES II (*5) / NUMBER THE BRAVE (*4) / TWIN BARRELS BURNING (*4) / RAW TO THE BONE (*4) / NOUVEAU CALLS (*4) / HERE TO HEAR (*4) / STRANGE AFFAIR (*4) / THE ASH LIVE IN CHICAGO (*4) / BLOWIN' FREE – THE VERY BEST OF... compilation (*7) / LIVE IN GENEVA (*4) / ILLUMINATIONS (*3)

MARTIN TURNER (b. 1 Oct'47) – vocals, bass / **ANDY POWELL** (b. 8 Feb'50) – guitar, vocals repl. GLEN TURNER (no relation) / **TED TURNER** (b.DAVID, 2 Aug'50) – guitar, vocals (ex-KING BISCUIT) / **STEVE UPTON** (b.24 May'46, Wrexham, Wales) – drums

M.C.A. / Decca

Dec 70. (lp) *(MKPS 2014)* <75249> **WISHBONE ASH** [34] [ ]
– Blind eye / Lady Whiskey / Error of my ways / Queen of torture / Handy / Phoenix. *(re-iss. Feb74 lp/c; MCG/TCMCG 3507) (re-iss. 1980; MCA 2343) (cd-iss. Jul91) (cd-iss. Dec94 on 'Beat Goes On'; BGOCD 234)*

Jan 71. (7") *(MK 5061)* <32826> **BLIND EYE. / QUEEN OF TORTURE** [ ] [ ]

Sep 71. (lp) *(MDKS 8004)* <75295> **PILGRIMAGE** [14] [ ]
– Vas dis / The pilgrim / Jail bait / Alone / Lullaby / Valediction / Where were you tomorrow. *(re-iss. Feb74 lp/c; MCG/TCMCG 3504) (re-iss. Dec83 lp/c; MCL/+C 1762) (cd-iss. Jul91; DMCL 1762) (cd re-iss. 1990's; MCLD 19084) (+=)* – Baby what you want me to do / Jail bait (live).

Oct 71. (7") <32902> **JAIL BAIT. / VAS DIS** [-] [ ]

May 72. (lp) *(MDKS 8006)* <75437> **ARGUS** [3] [ ]
– Time was / Sometime world / Blowin' free / The king will come / Leaf and stream / Warrior / Throw down the sword. *(re-iss. Feb74 lp/c; MCG/TCMCG 3510) (re-iss. Feb84 lp/c; MCL/+C 1787) (re-iss. 1987 on 'Castle' lp/c; CLA LP/MC 140) (cd-iss. 1991; DMCL 1787) (cd re-iss. 1990's; MCLD 19085)*

Jun 72. (7") *(MKS 5097)* <33004> **BLOWIN' FREE. / NO EASY ROAD** [ ] [ ]

M.C.A. / M.C.A.

May 73. (lp) *(MDKS 8011)* <327> **WISHBONE FOUR** [12] [44]
– So many things to say / Ballad of the beacon / No easy road / Everybody needs a friend / Doctor / Sorrel / Sing out the song / Rock and roll widow. *(re-iss. Feb74 lp/c; MCG/TCMCG 3505)*

Jul 73. (7") <40041> **ROCK AND ROLL WIDOW. / NO EASY ROAD** [-] [ ]

Jul 73. (7") *(MUS 1210)* **SO MANY THINGS TO SAY. / ROCK'N'ROLL WIDOW** [ ] [-]

Dec 73. (d-lp) *(ULD 1-2)* <2-8006> **LIVE DATES (live)** [ ] [82] Nov73
– The king will come / Warrior / Throw down the sword / Rock'n'roll widow / Ballad of the beacon / Baby what you want me to do / The pilgrim / Blowin' free / Jail bait / Lady Whiskey / Phoenix. *(re-iss. Jun74 d-lp/c; MCSP/+C 254)*

— (Jun74) **LAURIE WISEFIELD** – guitar (ex-HOME) repl. TED who found religion

Nov 74. (7") *(MCA 165)* **HOMETOWN. / PERSEPHONE** [ ] [-]

Nov 74. (lp/c) *(MCF/TCMCF 2585)* <464> **THERE'S THE RUB** [16] [88]
– Silver shoes / Don't come back / Persephone / Hometown / Lady Jay / F*U*B*B.

Feb 75. (7") *(MCA 176)* <40362> **SILVER SHOES. / PERSEPHONE** [ ] [ ]

— added on session **PETER WOODS** – keyboards

M.C.A. / Atlantic

Mar 76. (lp/c) *(MCF/TCMCF 2750)* **LOCKED IN** [36] [ ]
– Rest in peace / No water in the well / Moonshine / She was my best friend / It started in Heaven / Half past lovin' / Trust in you / Say goodbye.

Nov 76. (lp/c) *(MCG/TCMCG 3523)* <18200> **NEW ENGLAND** [22] [ ]
– Mother of pearl / (In all of my dreams) You rescue me / Runaway / Lorelei / Outward bound / Prelude / When you know love / Lonely island / Candle-light. *(re-iss. Jul82 lp/c; MCL/+C 1699)*

Nov 76. (7") *(MCA 261)* <3381> **OUTWARD BOUND. / LORELEI** [ ] [ ]

M.C.A. / M.C.A.

Sep 77. (7") *(MCA 326)* **FRONT PAGE NEWS. / DIAMOND JACK** [ ] [-]

Oct 77. (lp/c) *(MCG/+C 3524)* <2311> **FRONT PAGE NEWS** [31] [ ]
– Front page news / Midnight dancer / Goodbye baby hello friend / Surface to air / 714 / Come in from the rain / Right or wrong / Heart beat / The day I found your love / Diamond Jack. *(re-iss. Feb82 lp/c; MCL/+C 1655)*

Oct 77. (7") <40829> **FRONT PAGE NEWS. / GOODBYE BABY, HELLO FRIEND** [-] [ ]

Nov 77. (7") *(MCA 327)* **GOODBYE BABY, HELLO FRIEND. / COME IN FROM THE RAIN** [ ] [-]

Sep 78. (7"/12") *(MCA/12MCA 392)* **YOU SEE RED. / BAD WEATHER BLUES (live)** [ ] [-]

Oct 78. (lp/c) *(MCG/+C 3528)* <3060> **NO SMOKE WITHOUT FIRE** [43] [ ]
– You see red / Baby the angels are here / Ships in the sky / Stand and deliver / Anger in harmony / Like a child / The way of the world (part 1 & 2) / A stormy weather. *(w/ free live 7")* – COME IN FROM THE RAIN. / LORELEI *(cd-iss. May98; MCLD 19374)*

Aug 79. (7") *(MCA 518)* **COME ON. / FAST JOHNNY** [ ] [ ]

Jan 80. (7") <41214> **HELPLESS. / INSOMNIA** [-] [ ]

Jan 80. (7") *(MCA 549)* **LIVING PROOF. / JAIL BAIT (live)** [ ] [-]

Jan 80. (lp/c) *(MCF/TCMCF 3052)* **JUST TESTING** [41] [ ]
– Living proof / Haunting me / Insomnia / Helpless / Pay the price / New rising star / Master of disguise / Lifeline. *(cd-iss. May98; MCLD 19375)*

Apr 80. (7"/12") *(MCA/+T 577)* **HELPLESS (live). / BLOWIN' FREE (live)** [ ] [-]

Oct 80. (d-lp/c) *(MCG/+C 4012)* **LIVE DATES II (live)** [40] [ ]
– Doctor / Living proof / Runaway / Helpless / F*U*B*B / The way of the world / Lorelei / Persephone / You rescue me / Time was / Goddbye baby hello friend / No easy road. *(ltd. w/ free live lp) (re-iss. Jun84; MCL 1799)*

— **JOHN WETTON** – bass, vocals (ex-URIAH HEEP, ex-FAMILY, ex-KING CRIMSON) repl. MARTIN TURNER to production. / added **CLAIRE HAMILL** – vocals (solo artist)

Mar 81. (7") *(MCA 695)* **UNDERGROUND. / MY MIND IS MADE UP** [ ] [-]

Apr 81. (lp/c) *(MCF/+C 3103)* **NUMBER THE BRAVE** [61] [ ]
– Loaded / Where is the love / Underground / Kicks on the street / Open road / Get ready / Rainstorm / That's that / Rollercoaster / Number the brave.

May 81. (7") *(MCA 726/+/MCL 14)* **GET READY. / KICKS ON THE STREET** [ ] [-]

May 81. (7") <51149> **GET READY. / LOADED** [-] [ ]

— **UPTON, POWELL + WISEFIELD** recruited new member **TREVOR BOLDER** – bass (ex-SPIDERS FROM MARS / Bowie, ex-URIAH HEEP, etc. repl. WETTON to ASIA, etc.

A.V.M. Fantasy

Oct 82. (7") *(WISH 1)* **ENGINE OVERHEAT. / GENEVIEVE** [ ] [-]
Nov 82. (lp/c) *(ASH/+C 1) <F 9629>* **TWIN BARRELS BURNING** [22] [ ] 1983
– Engine overheat / Can't fight love / Genevieve / Me and my guitar / Hold on / Streets of shame / No more lonely nights / Angels have mercy / Wind up. *(cd-iss. Aug93 on 'Castle'; CLACD 389)*
Dec 82. (7") *(1002)* **NO MORE LONELY NIGHTS. / STREETS OF SHAME** [ ] [-]

— **MERVYN 'Spam' SPENCER** – bass (ex-TRAPEZE) repl. BOLDER to URIAH HEEP

Neat not iss.

Jan 85. (lp/pic-lp/c) *(NEAT/+P/C 1027)* **RAW TO THE BONE** [ ] [-]
– Cell of fame / People in motion / Don't cry / Love is blue / Long live the night / Rocket in my pocket / It's only love / Don't you mess / Dreams (searching for an answer) / Perfect timing. *(re-iss. Aug93 on 'Castle'; CLACD 390)*

— **ANDY PYLE** – bass (ex-SAVOY BROWN, ex-BLODWYN PIG) repl. SPENCE

— Originals (**ANDREW, STEVE, MARTIN & TED**) reformed WISHBONE ASH.

I.R.S.-MCA I.R.S.-MCA

Feb 88. (lp/c/cd) *(MIRF/CMIRF/DMIRF 1028)* **NOUVEAU CALLS** (instrumental) [ ] [ ]
– Tangible evidence / Closseau / Flags of convenience / From Soho to Sunset / Arabesque / In the skin / Something's happening in Room 602 / Johnny left home without it / The spirit flies free / A rose is a rose / Real guitars have wings. *(re-iss. 1990 lp/c/cd; ILP/+MC/CD 39) (cd re-iss. Aug99 on 'Power Bright'; PBVP 005CD)*
May 88. (7") *(IRM 164)* **IN THE SKIN. / TANGIBLE EVIDENCE** [ ] [ ]

— In Apr89, TED & ANDY guested on their labels' Various Artists live cd,c,d-lp, video 'NIGHT OF THE GUITAR'.

I.R.S. I.R.S.

Jun 89. (7") *(EIRS 104)* **COSMIC JAZZ. / T-BONE SHUFFLE** [ ] [ ]
(12"+=) *(EIRST 104)* – Bolan's monument.
Aug 89. (lp/c/cd) *(EIRSA/+C/CD 1006) <82006>* **HERE TO HEAR** [ ] [-]
– Cosmic jazz / Keeper of the light / Mental radio / Walk on water / Witness on wonder / Lost cause in Paradise / Why don't we / In the case / Hole in my heart (part 1 & 2).

— **RAY WESTON** – drums repl. MARTIN

May 91. (lp/c/cd) *(EIRSA/+C/CD 1045)* **STRANGE AFFAIR** [ ] [ ]
– Strange affair / Wings of desire / Dream train / You / Hard times / Standing in the rain / Renegade / Say you will / Rollin' / Some conversion.

— **POWELL + TED TURNER + RAY** bring in **ANDY PYLE** – bass / **DAN C. GILLOGLY** – keyboards

Permanent Griffin

Mar 92. (cd/c/lp) *(PERM CD/MC/LP 6)* **THE ASH LIVE IN CHICAGO (live)** [ ] [ ] 1994
– The king will come / Strange affair / Standing in the rain / Lost cause in Paradise / Keeper of the light / Throw down the sword / In the skin / Why don't we? / Hard times / Blowing free / Living proof. *(cd re-iss. Jun99 as 'LIVING PROOF. . .' on 'Right'; RIGHT 005)*

— **POWELL** recruited an entire new line-up:- **ROGER FILGATE** – guitar / **TONY KISHMAN** – bass / **MIKE STURGIS** – drums

Hengest not iss.

Mar 96. (cd) *(HNRCD 03)* **LIVE IN GENEVA (live)** [ ] [-]
– The king will come / Strange affair / Thrown down the sword / In the skin / Hard times / Blowin' free / Keeper of the light / Medley: Blind eye – Lady Whiskey – Jail bait – Phoenix – The pilgrim / Runaway / Sometime world / Vas dis. *(re-iss. Jul99 on 'S.P.V.'; 076-1846-2)*

— **MARK TEMPLETON + MIKE MINDEL** – keyboards (FILGATE now bass); repl. KISHMAN

H.T.D. not iss.

Oct 96. (cd) *(HTDCD 67)* **ILLUMINATIONS** [ ] [-]
– Mountainside / On your own / Top of the world / No joke / Tales of the wise / Another time / A thousand years / The ring / Comfort zone / Mystery man / Wait out the storm / The crack of dawn.

Invisible Hands unknown

Apr 98. (cd) *(IHCD 12)* **TRANCE VISIONARY** [ ] [-]
– Numerology / Wonderful stash / Heritage / Interfaze / Powerbright (black and white screen) / Remnants of a paranormal managerie / Narcissus nervosa / Trance visionary / Flutterby / Banner headlines / The loner / Powerbright volition / Gutterfly / Wronged by righteousness.

Ration-L not iss.

Oct 00. (d-cd) *(RALVP 004CD)* **PSYCHIC TERRORISM** [ ] [-]
– Translitetion / Narcissus stash / Sleeps eternal slave / Monochrome / Breaking out / The son of righteousness / Psychic terrorism / How many times / Bloodline / Back page muse / Powerbright conclusion // Powerbright industrial / Dub visionary / X-ert heritage / Original powerbright / Wonderful nervosa / Powerthrack / Wrong or write / Wonderful stash.

– compilations, others, etc. –

on 'M.C.A.' unless stated otherwise

Apr 77. (7"ep) *(MCA 291)* **PHOENIX. / BLOWIN' FREE / JAIL BAIT** [ ] [-]
May 77. (lp/c) *(MCF/TCMCF 2795)* **CLASSIC ASH** [ ] [ ]
– Blind eye / Phoenix / The pilgrim / Blowin' free / The king will come / Rock'n'roll widow / Persephone / Outward bound / Throw down the sword (live). *(re-iss. Aug81 lp/c; MCL/+C 1621) (re-iss. Jan83 on 'Fame' lp/c; FA/TCFA 3053)*
Jan 82. (lp) *(5283-27126)* **HOT ASH** [-] [ ]
Apr 82. (d-c) *(MCA 2103)* **PILGRIMAGE / ARGUS** [ ] [-]
May 82. (lp) *(MCF 3134)* **THE BEST OF WISHBONE ASH** [ ] [-]
Oct 91. (cd) *Windsong; (WINCD 004)* **LIVE IN CONCERT (live)** [ ] [-]
1993. (d-cd) *<MCAD2 10765>* **TIME WAS** (w/ remixed 'ARGUS') [-] [ ]
Mar 94. (cd/c) *Nectar; (NTR CD/MC 014)* **BLOWIN' FREE – THE VERY BEST OF WISHBONE ASH** [ ] [-]
Sep 94. (cd/c) *(MCLD/MCLC 19249)* **THERE'S THE RUB / LOCKED IN** [ ] [-]
Nov 94. (cd) *Start; (HP 93452)* **IN CONCERT** [ ] [-]
Jan 97. (cd) *Receiver; (RRCD 216)* **LIVE – TIMELINE (live)** [ ] [-]
Nov 97. (cd) *Rialto; (RMCD 224)* **ARCHIVE** [ ] [-]
Apr 98. (cd) *Rhino; <(CP 1002)>* **MOTHER OF PEARL** [ ] [ ]
Jun 98. (4xcd-box) *Repertoire; (REP 4649WX)* **DISTILLATION** [ ] [ ]
Nov 98. (cd) *Power Bright; (PBVP 001CD)* **FROM THE ARCHIVES VOL.1** [ ] [-]
Nov 98. (cd) *Power Bright; (PBVP 002CD)* **FROM THE ARCHIVES VOL.2** [ ] [-]
Jan 99. (cd) *Power Bright; (PBVP 003CD)* **FROM THE ARCHIVES VOL.3** [ ] [-]
Mar 99. (cd) *Beat Goes On; (BGOCD 405)* **NEW ENGLAND / FRONT PAGE NEWS** [ ] [-]
Oct 99. (cd) *Receiver; (<RRCD 276>)* **THE KING WILL COME – LIVE** [ ] [ ]
Nov 99. (cd) *H.T.D.; (HTDCD 104)* **BARE BONES** [ ] [ ]
– Wings of desire / Errors of my way / Master of disguise / You won't take me down / Love abuse / (Won't you give him) One more chance / Baby don't mind / Living proof / Hard times / Strange affair / Everybody needs a friend.

WITCHFINDER GENERAL

Formed: Midlands, England . . . 1979 by ZEEB and PHIL COPE, the line-up completed by ROB HAWKS and GRAHAM DITCHFIELD. Signing to the 'Heavy Metal' label, this motley crew of SABBATH-esque grind merchants rode in on the tail end of the NWOBHM scene rather than the horses of the apocalypse. Preceded by a debut single, 'BURNING A SINNER', their first album, 'DEATH PENALTY', appeared in late '82. It was the cover shot, rather than the music inside, which ensured WITCHFINDER GENERAL a small footnote in metal history; most critics were agreed that the depiction of the group in the process of sacrificing a partially-clad young lady wasn't in the best of taste. Yet despite all the publicity, the album still didn't sell enough to make the charts. Quite literally gluttons for punishment, the group went ahead and did it again with a follow-up set, 'FRIENDS OF HELL' (1983); more scantily-clad ladies, more mock-sacrificial posing, even less taste. Unsurprisingly, the album stiffed and WITCHFINDER GENERAL were court martialled into eternal obscurity – until now!

Album rating: DEATH PENALTY (*4) / FRIENDS OF HELL (*3)

ZEEB PARKES – vocals / **PHIL COPE** – vocals / **WOOLFY TROPE** – bass / **GRAHAM DITCHFIELD** – drums

Heavy Metal not iss.

Sep 81. (7") *(HEAVY 6)* **BURNING A SINNER. / SATAN'S CHILDREN** [ ] [-]
Nov 82. (lp) *(HMRLP 8)* **DEATH PENALTY** [ ] [-]
– Invisible hate / Free country / Death penalty / No stayer / Witchfinder General / Burning a sinner / R.I.P.
Jan 83. (7"m/12"m) *(12HM 17)* **SOVIET INVASION. / RABIES / R.I.P. (live)** [ ] [-]

— **ROB HAWKS** – bass; repl. TROPE

Nov 83. (lp) *(HMRLP 13)* **FRIENDS OF HELL** [ ] [-]
– Love on smack / Last chance / Music / Friends of hell / Requiem for youth / Shadowed images / I lost you / Quietus reprise.
Dec 83. (7"/7"pic-d) *(HEAVY/HMPD 21)* **MUSIC. / LAST CHANCE** [ ] [-]

— disbanded in 1984

WITCHFYNDE

Formed: England . . . 1976 by STEVE BRIDGES, ANDRO COULTON, MONTALO and GRA SCORESBY. Another act who scored a record deal in the slipstream of the NWOBHM, WITCHFYNDE were very much influenced by the heavy rock of the 70's, their occult lyrics marking them out as purveyors of particularly black metal. The label in question, 'Rondelet', released their debut, 'GIVE 'EM HELL' in 1980, which was tracked by 'STAGE FRIGHT' the same year. A three year spell in the ether followed, WITCHFYNDE flying back to vinyl duties with the 'CLOAK & DAGGER' set in 1983. By this point, however, the momentum had all but been lost, and WITCHFYNDE appeared somewhat dated. Inevitably, this spelled the end for the group and following a fourth album, 'LORDS OF SIN' (1984), the group split.

Album rating: GIVE 'EM HELL (*5) / STAGE FRIGHT (*4) / CLOAK & DAGGER (*5) / LORDS OF SIN (*5) / THE BEST OF WITCHFYNDE compilation (*6)

STEVE BRIDGES – vocals / **MONTALO** – guitar / **ANDRO COULTON** – bass / **GRA SCORESBY** – drums

Rondelet not iss.

Feb 80. (7") *(ROUND 1)* **GIVE 'EM HELL. / GETTING HEAVY** [ ] [-]
May 80. (lp/c) *(ABOUT/CARB 1)* **GIVE 'EM HELL** [ ] [-]
– Ready to roll / The divine victim / Leading Nadir / Gettin' heavy / Give 'me hell / Unto the ages of the ages / Pay now – love later.
Sep 80. (7") *(ROUND 4)* **IN THE STARS. / WAKE UP SCREAMING** [ ] [-]
Oct 80. (lp/c) *(ABOUT/CARB 2)* **STAGE FRIGHT** [ ] [-]
– Stage fright / Doing the right thing / Would not be seen dead in Heaven / Wake up screaming / Big deal / Moon magic / In the stars / Trick or treat / Madelaine.

— **LUTHER BELTZ** – vocals; repl. BRIDGES

— **PETE SURGEY** – bass; repl. COULTON

Expulsion not iss.

Jul 83. (7") *(OUT 3)* **I'D RATHER GO WILD. / CRY WOLF** [ ] [-]
Nov 83. (lp) *(EXIT 5)* **CLOAK AND DAGGER** [ ] [-]
– The Devil's playground / Crystal gazing / I'd rather go wild / Somewhere to hide / Cloak and dagger / Cry wolf / Start counting / Living for memories / Rock'n'roll / Stay away / Fra Diabolo.

— **EDD WOLFE** – bass; repl. SURGEY

Mausoleum | not iss.

Dec 84. (lp/c) *(LORD/TAPE7 8352)* **LORDS OF SIN** [ ] [-]
– The lord of sin / Stab in the back / Heartbeat / Scarlet lady / Blue devils / Hall of mirrors / Wall of death / Conspiracy / Red garters / Cloak and dagger / I'd rather go wild / Moon magic / Give 'em hell.

Mar 85. (7") *(GUTS 8404)* **CONSPIRACY. / SCARLET LADY** [ ] [-]

—— disbanded in 1985

– compilations, etc. –

Feb 97. (cd) *British Steel; (CDMETAL 1)* **THE BEST OF WITCHFYNDE** [ ] [-]
– Give 'em hell / Unto the ages of the ages / Ready to roll / Leaving Nadir / Gettin' heavy / Pay now – love later / Stage fright / Wake up screaming / Moon magic / In the stars / The Devil's playground / I'd rather go wild / Cloak and dagger / Cry wolf / Stay away / Fra diabolo.

WOLFSBANE

Formed: Tamworth, Essex, England . . . 1986 by BLAZE BAYLEY, JASE 'The Ace' EDWARDS, JEFF HATELEY D'BRINI and STEVE 'Dangerous' ELLETT. In 1988, they signed to Rick Rubin's new metal incorporated label 'Def American', their debut album, 'LIVE FAST, DIE FAST', making it into the UK Top 50 in 1989. Greasy rockers combining the bombast of Brit-metallers such as IRON MAIDEN, with the good-time party feel of L.A. acts, WOLFSBANE became something of a cause celebre for the UK rock scene at the turn of the decade. They were even into skateboarding, further boosting their street-cred in the metal stakes. Although subsequent teen-adranaline rush singles, 'SHAKIN' and 'I LIKE IT HOT', failed to chart, BLAZE and the boys scored another UK Top 50 with a much-improved second set, 'ALL HELL'S BREAKING LOOSE DOWN AT KATHY WILSON'S PLACE' (1990), the Kathy in question being a movie star of the 50's. A UK tour with IRON MAIDEN gave WOLFSBANE further exposure, and while a third set, 'DOWN FALL THE GOOD GUYS', again brought favourable press, the group couldn't seem to turn critical acclaim into record sales. Dropped by Rubin, the band subsequently signed to the 'Essential' imprint and proceeeded to issue a double album, 'MASSIVE NOISE INJECTION' (1993). The record showcased WOLFSBANE growling at the proverbial moon, finally doing justice to a band whose on stage charisma has often been lost in translation to vinyl. After a final set, 'THERE CAN ONLY BE YOU – WOLFSBANE' (1994), the band splintered as the hyperactive BAYLEY took BRUCE DICKINSON's place in IRON MAIDEN. • **Songwriters:** Group compositions except WILD THING (Troggs).

Album rating: LIVE FAST, DIE FAST (*6) / ALL HELL'S BREAKING LOOSE DOWN AT KATHY'S PLACE mini (*5) / DOWN FALL THE GOOD GUYS (*5) / MASSIVE NOISE INJECTION (*6) / WOLFSBANE (*4)

BLAZE BAYLEY – vocals / **JASE 'The Ace' EDWARDS** – guitar / **JEFF HATELEY D'BRINI** – bass / **STEVE 'Dangerous' ELLETT** – drums

Cops | not iss.

Oct 86. (12"ep) *(WSB 1)* **CLUTCHING AT STRAWS EP** [ ] [-]

Def Jam | Def Jam

Oct 88. (12"ep) *(WSB 2)* **LOCO / DANCE DIRTY. / LIMOUSINE / KILLER** [ ] [-]
(re-iss. Jul89 with 4 diff.mixes)

Def American | Warners

Jul 89. (lp/c/cd) *(838486-1/-4/-2) <24215>* **LIVE FAST, DIE FAST** [48] [ ]
– Manhunt / Shakin' / Killing machine / Fell out of Heaven / Money to burn / Greasy / I like it hot / All or nothing / Tears from a fool / Pretty baby.

Oct 89. (7"/c-s) *(DEFA/+M 2)* **SHAKIN'. / BRANDO** [ ] [-]
(12"+=) *(DEFA 2-12)* – Angel.
(12"pic-d++=/cd-s++=) *(DEFA S/C 2)* – Money to burn.

Mar 90. (7"/7"red) *(DEFA/+T 3)* **I LIKE IT HOT. / LIMOSINE (live)** [ ] [-]
(12"+=) *(DEFAP 3-12)* – Loco (live).
(10"++=)(cd-s++=) *(DEFA 3-10)(DEFAC 3)* – Manhunt (live).

Oct 90. (m-cd/m-c/m-lp) *(846967-2/-4/-1)* **ALL HELL'S BREAKING LOOSE DOWN AT KATHY WILSON'S PLACE** [48] [-]
– Steel / Paint the town red / Loco / Hey babe / Totally nude / Kathy Wilson.

Sep 91. (7") *(DEFA 11)* **EZY. / BLACK LAGOON** [68] [-]
(12") *(DEFA 11-12)* – ('A'side) / You load me down / Dead at last.
(cd-s+=) *(DEFAC 11)* – Fucked off.

Oct 91. (cd/c/lp) *(510413-2/-4/-1)* **DOWN FALL THE GOOD GUYS** [53] [-]
– Smashed and blind / You load me down / Ezy / Black lagoon / Broken doll / Twice as mean / Cathode ray clinic / The loveless / After midnight / Temple of rock / Moonlight / Dead at last.

Feb 92. (7"/c-s) *(DEFA/+M 14)* **AFTER MIDNIGHT. / IDOL** [ ] [-]
(12"+=)(cd-s+=) *(DEFA 14-12)(DEFAC 14)* – Win or lose / Hey babe (acoustic).

Essential | not iss.

Jun 93. (cd/c/d-lp) *(ESS CD/MC/LP 193)* **MASSIVE NOISE INJECTION** (live 20th Feb'93) [ ] [-]
– Protect & survive / Load me down / Black lagoon / Rope & ride / Kathy Wilson / Loco / End of the century / Steel / Temple of rock / Manhunt / Money to burn / Paint the town red / Wild thing / Want me all the time / Hollow man. *(cd re-iss. Aug96; same)*

Feb 94. (cd/c; ltd) **THERE CAN ONLY BE YOU – WOLFSBANE** [ ] [-]

—— split after BLAZE joined IRON MAIDEN to repl. BRUCE DICKINSON

Jan 97. (cd) *(ESMCD 396)* **WOLFSBANE** [ ] [-]
– Wings / Lifestyles of the broke and obscure / My face / Money talks / See how it's done / Beautiful lies / Protect & survive / Black machine / Violence / Die again.

WOOL (see under ⇒ SCREAM)

WORKHORSE MOVEMENT

Formed: Mount Pleasant, Michigan, USA . . . 1994 by MYRON (MATT KOZUCH-REA), JAY, JOE MACKIE and FREEDOM (JEFF PIPER). The original line-up met while attending the Central Michigan University, where they developed their musical abilities at various gigs and student bashes. Their music was a well-cooked blend of rap metal which combined hardcore with heavy stoner rock. Always a self-reliant band, the boys released their debut outing 'DOPAMINE' (1995) under their own steam. Two years on, WORKHOUSE . . . moved to Detroit to try and capitalise more seriously on their ambitions. Here the band were signed up by the label 'Overcore', who released their EP, 'RHYTHM AND SOUL CARTEL', early in 1998. The move to the city of Motown also saw the departure of JAY, who was eventually replaced by PETE BEVER, an old school friend of FREEDOM's, although GRADY was brought into WM in the meantime as a stop-gap bassist for touring purposes. The famous city of soul certainly had an effect on the band's sound, as did the insertion of a second vocalist/rapper in the shape of CORNBREAD (CHRIS SPARKS). This was exemplified on the band's next outing, the full-length album, 'SONS OF THE PIONEERS' (2000), released on the long-standing metal label 'Roadrunner'. On this piece the group skillfully welded their heavy riffing and rapping style with the funkier side of soul; unfortunately the band have now called it a day.

Album rating: DOPAMINE (*5) / RHYTHM & SOUL CARTEL (*6) / SONS OF THE PIONEERS (*6)

MYRON (b.MATT KOZUCH-REA) – vocals / **FREEDOM** (b.JEFF PIPER) – guitar / **JAY** – bass / **JOE MACKIE** – drums

not iss. | own label

1996. (cd) **DOPAMINE** [-] [ ]

not iss. | Overcore

Mar 98. (cd-ep) *<30044>* **RHYTHM AND SOUL CARTEL** [-] [ ]

—— added **CORNBREAD** (b.CHRIS SPARKS) – vocals

—— **PETE BEVER** – bass; repl. GRADY (JEFF WRIGHT who repl. JAY

Roadrunner | Roadrunner

Jun 00. (cd) *<(RR 8583CD)>* **SONS OF THE PIONEERS** [ ] [ ]
– Workhorse and intercourse (intro) / Keep the sabbath dream alive / Livin' evil / Gimme some skin / Zero / Traffic / Heavy / Beotch / Motown / Joe mama / Charlie don't surf / Cosmic highway / Mother Earth / Feel like Bob Marley.

Oct 00. (cd-s) *(RR 2091-3)* **KEEP THE SABBATH DREAM ALIVE / JOE MAMA (big balls mix) / IS** [ ] [-]

WORLD SERVICE (see under ⇒ ZOUNDS)

WORLD TRADE

Formed: USA . . . late 80's as a studio outfit numbering BILLY SHERWOOD, BRUCE COWDY, GUY ALLISON and MARK T. WILLIAMS. A surprisingly brief affair, WORLD TRADE were represented by a sole eponymous album released on 'Polydor', in late '89. Drawing widespread comparisons with classic YES, the band's synth-pomp was characterised by SHERWOOD's Jon Anderson-esque vocal flights of fancy (he had even been invited to join YES at one point!). Despite the interest in the band, they collapsed following SHERWOOD's bid for the solo market.

Album rating: WORLD TRADE (*5)

BILLY SHERWOOD – vocals, bass / **BRUCE COWDY** – guitar / **GUY ALLISON** – keyboards / **MARK T. WILLIAMS** – drums

Polydor | Polygram

Mar 90. (cd/c/lp) *<(839 626-2/-4/-1)>* **WORLD TRADE** [ ] [ ] Dec89
– The painted corner / The moment is here / Can't let you go / Lifetime / Fight to win / Sense of freedom / The revolution song / One last chance / Wasting time / Emotional wasteland / Open the door.

—— split late in '89, and SHERWOOD went solo

WRABIT

Formed: Canada . . . early 80's by LOU NADEAU, DAVID APLIN, JOHN ALBANI, LES PAULHUS, CHRIS BROCKWAY and SCOTT JEFFERSON STECK. Securing a major label deal with 'M.C.A.', this airbrushed ensemble released their eponymous debut at the tail end of '81 (Sping '82 in Britain). Touting hard but harmonious pomp-rock in the mould of JOURNEY or FOREIGNER, the group were much admired by a loyal following in their native Canada. A follow-up set, 'TRACKS' (1983), took a heavier approach with impressive results, although their commercial impact remained relatively minimal. WRABIT eventually retreated into their collective burrow in the mid 80's after a final set, 'WEST SIDE KID', most of the group subsequently joining LEE AARON. • **Songwriters:** Mostly by NADEAU, except some by APLIN or ALBANI.

Album rating: WRABIT (*5) / TRACKS (*5) / WEST SIDE KID (*4)

LOU NADEAU – vocals / **DAVID APLIN** – guitar / **JOHN ALBANI** – guitar / **LES PAULHUS** – keyboards / **CHRIS BROCKWAY** – bass / **SCOTT JEFFERSON STECK** – drums

M.C.A. | M.C.A.

Nov 81. (7") *<52010>* **ANYWAY, ANYTIME. / DON'T SAY GOODNIGHT TO ROCK AND ROLL** [-] [ ]

Feb 82. (7") *(MCA 767)* **TOO MANY YEARS. / JUST GO AWAY**

Apr 82. (lp) *(MCF 3126)* <5268> **WRABIT** Dec81
– Anyway, anytime / Pushin' on / Can't be wrong / Back home / Too many years / Just go away / Tell me what to do / How does she do it / Here I'll stay / Don't say goodnite to rock and roll.

Jun 82. (7") *(MCA 781)* <52048> **BACK HOME. / DON'T SAY GOODNITE TO ROCK AND ROLL**

— **GERALD O'BRIEN** – keyboards; repl. PAULHUS + ALPIN

— **GARY McCRACKEN** – drums; repl. STECK

1983. (7") <52117> **DON'T LOSE THAT FEELING. / BARE KNUCKLES**

1983. (lp) <*MCA 5359*> **TRACKS**
– Run for cover / Soldier of fortune / I'll never run away / See no evil / Bare knuckler / Don't lose that feeling / Unsung hero / Don't stop me now / There was a time / Castles in the sky.

— **GARY CRAIG** – drums; repl. McCRACKEN

— **LOU POMANTI** – keyboards; repl. O'BRIEN

1984. (lp) <*39005*> **WEST SIDE KID**
– Waiting / Hold on to me / Say lady say / Piece of the action / Sing boy / Young girl / Cry cry / Lin / Best of love / West side kid.

— when they folded, most of the band joined LEE AARON

WRATHCHILD

Formed: Evesham, Worcestershire, England . . . 1981 by ROCKY SHADES and MARC ANGEL, initially as a black-metal outfit. Subsequently realising tacky glam posturing was their true calling, the band adopted a KISS / NEW YORK DOLLS style image, LANCE ROCKET and EDDIE STARR completing the line-up. Debuting in 1983 with a 12" EP (released on lurid red vinyl), 'ROCK THE CITY DOWN', the group were subsequently signed to Midlands-based 'Heavy Metal' records. Later that summer, they issued their debut album proper, 'STAKK ATTAKK' (1984), a tottering high heel of an album featuring such low-rent anthems as 'TRASH QUEEN' and the title track. WRATHCHILD were best experienced live, however, and fans had to content themselves with gigs as the studio output ground to a halt. Embroiled in a lengthy dispute with their label, it would be a further four years before the band released 'THE BIZZ SUXX (BUT WE DON'T CARE)'. Many felt that WRATHCHILD had lost their early impetus and, like contemporaries TIGERTAILZ, their attempt at Anglicising an inherently American music style didn't quite catch on. After a final album, 'DELIRIUM' (1989) and a second legal battle (they succeeded in forcing a similarly titled US outfit to suffix their moniker with AMERICA; see below!), WRATHCHILD were sent to bed without any supper. • **Covers:** ALRITE WITH THE BOYZ (Gary Glitter) / PRETTY VACANT (Sex Pistols).

Album rating: STAKK ATTAKK (*5) / TRASH QUEENS collection (*5) / THE BIZZ SUXX (BUT WE DON'T CARE) (*5) / DELIRIUM (*4)

ROCKY SHADES – vocals / **LANCE ROCKET** – guitar / **MARC ANGEL** – bass / **EDDIE STARR** – drums

Bullet / not iss.

Mar 83. (12"red-ep) *(BOLT 2)* **STACKHEEL STRUTT**
– Rock the city down / Lipstik killers / Teenage revolution / Trash queen.

Sep 83. (7"/12"/7"pic-d) *(BOL/BOLT/PBOL 5)* **DO YOU WANT MY LOVE. / TWIST OF THE KNIFE**

Heavy Metal / not iss.

Jun 84. (lp/c/pic-lp) *(HMR LP/MC/PD 18)* **STAKK ATTAKK**
– Stakk attakk / Too wild to tame / Trash queen / Sweet surrender / Kick down the walls / Tonight / Law abuzer / Shokker / Alrite with the boyz / Wreckless. *(cd-iss. Apr89; HMRXD 18)*

Sep 84. (7") *(VHF 3)* **ALRITE WITH THE BOYZ. / SWEET SURRENDER**

— Were left in wilderness for a few years, while they had legal fight with record company.

FM-Revolver / not iss.

Nov 88. (lp/c/cd/pic-lp) *(HMR LP/MC/XD/PD 116)* **THE BIZZ SUXX (BUT WE DON'T CARE)**
– The big suxx / Millionaire / Hooked / (Na na) Nukklear rokket / Wild wild honey / Ring my bell / Hooligunz / She'z no angel / O.K.U.K. / Noo sensation / Stikky fingerz.

Mar 89. (7") *(VHF 50)* **(NA NA) NUKKLEAR ROKKET. / TRASH QUEEN (live)**
(12"+=) *(12VHF 50)* – Pretty vacant (live).

Dec 89. (lp/c/cd) *(WKFM XD/MC/LP 137)* **DELIRIUM**
– Delirium / Watch me shake it / That's what U get / My girlz / Long way 2 go / Good girlz / Do what you want boy / Kid pusher / She's high on luv / Rock me over / Only 4 the fun / Drive me krazee.

– compilations, etc. –

Apr 86. (lp) *Dojo; (DOJOLP 6)* **TRASH QUEENS**
– Do you want my love? / Rock the city down / Lipstik killers / Trash queen / Teenage revolution / Twist of the knife / Cock rock shock / It's a party.

WRATHCHILD AMERICA

Formed: Baltimore, Maryland, USA . . . 1988 by BRAD DIVENS, JAY ABBENE, TERRY CARTER and SHANNON LARKIN. Despite being signed to 'Atlantic', this power-metal/thrash quartet lost some of their early momentum after becoming the subject of legal action by the British glam-metal outfit of the same name. Their debut, 'CLIMBING THE WALLS', eventually emerged in early '89 to minimal interest. A second set, '3-D' (1991) was released to a similarly underwhelming response and the group were ultimately dropped by their major label paymasters. With a change of moniker to SOULS AT ZERO, the band signed to 'Edel' and released an album in '95, 'A TASTE FOR THE PERVERSE'. By this point, however, LARKIN had left for UGLY KID JOE.

Album rating: CLIMBIN' THE WALLS (*6) / 3-D (*5) / Souls At Zero: A TASTE FOR THE PERVERSE (*6)

BRAD DIVENS – vocals, bass / **JAY ABBENE** – guitar / **TERRY CARTER** – guitar, vocals / **SHANNON LARKIN** – drums, vocals

Atlantic / Atlantic

Feb 89. (lp/cd) *(PR 2572-2)* <*781 889-1/-2*> **CLIMBIN' THE WALLS**
– Climbin' the walls / Hell's gate / No deposit, no return / Hernia / London after midnight / Candy from a madman / Silent darkness (smothered life) / Time / Day of thunder.

1991. (cd/lp) <*82186-2/-1*> **3-D**
– 3-D man / Spy / Gentleman death / Forever alone / Draintime / Surrounded by idiots / Desert grins / What's your pleasure? / Prego / Another nameless face / II. *(cd+=)* – I ain't drunk, I'm just drinkin'.

— due to problems with British group of the same name, they changed to . . .

SOULS AT ZERO

— same line-up but now without LARKIN who joined UGLY KID JOE

Edel / Edel

Oct 95. (cd) *(086272CTR)* **A TASTE FOR THE PERVERSE**
– Undecided / Strip / Cold / Taken apart / My fault? / Thrown down / Inside a scream / Needles / Me myself I / Know more.

— SOULS AT ZERO released two others, 'SOULS AT ZERO' and the mini 'SIX-T-SIX'

WRITING ON THE WALL

Formed: Edinburgh, Scotland . . . 1966 as The JURY, by JAKE SCOTT, BILL SCOTT, JIMMY HUSH and WILLY FINLAYSON. They found vocalist LINNIE PATTERSON, formerly part of mod/soul outfit The EMBERS (who released one single in 1963). LINNIE then joined THREE'S A CROWD, who issued the 45, 'LOOK AROUND THE CORNER', in '66. The JURY were initially managed by TAM PATON (later boss of The BAY CITY ROLLERS, until London-born BRIAN WALDMAN took over). The name change came about in late '67 to match their influence by West Coast psychedelia. WALDMAN then opened a club in London, calling it MIDDLE EARTH. Using the same name, he also set up a label and issued a debut 45, 'CHILD ON A CROSSING', in late '69. An album, 'THE POWER OF THE PICTS', soon followed, but an offer from an American promoter was refused unwisely by WALDMAN, who wanted his complete roster taken on. The record was a heavy doom-laden, progressive rock effort, fusing CREAM / YARDBIRDS, ARTHUR BROWN, IRON BUTTERFLY and BLACK SABBATH. Late in 1970, they entered the studio with BOWIE, although the only fruits of these sessions were some rough demos. Early the following year, after a John Peel session, LINNIE and SMIGGY left, although they did persuade FINLAYSON to return. In the summer of '72, they played in front of over 60,000 people at Brazil's Rio Song Festival, which was also televised for South American TV. Although the Brazilians hailed them as heroes, the band returned to London and obscurity. They released one more single, containing the excellent B-side, 'BUFFALO', but the "writing was on the wall" as they say, after their equipment and transport was stolen. • **Songwriters:** Group with DONALD CAMERON (my former music teacher at Woodlands High, who died in the early 80's).

Album rating: THE POWER OF THE PICTS (*7)

ROBERT 'Smiggy' SMITH – guitar (ex-EMBERS) repl. WILLY FINLAYSON (mid-69) / **BILL SCOTT** – keyboards / **JAKE SCOTT** – bass, vocals / **JIMMY HUSH** – drums / **LINNIE PATTERSON** – vocals

Middle Earth / not iss.

Oct 69. (7") *(MDS 101)* **CHILD ON A CROSSING. / LUCIFER'S CORPUS**

Nov 69. (lp) *(MDLS 303)* **THE POWER OF THE PICTS**
– It came on a Sunday / Mrs. Coopers pie / Ladybird / Aries / Bogeyman / Shadow of man / Taskers successor / Hill of dreams / Virginia Water. *(cd-iss. 1991 'Repertoire'; REP 8002SP) (German cd on 'Green Tree'; GTR 001)(+=)* – Child on a crossing / Lucifer's corpus. *(UK re-iss. Aug00 on 'Repertoire'; REP 4854)*

— now without SMIGGY and LINNIE. They both teamed up with JIMMY BAIN to form STREETNOISE. LINNIE joined BEGGAR'S OPERA, while SMIGGY joined BLUE. They were both replaced by returning **WILLIE FINLAYSON**. In the mid-90's, LINNIE died of asbestosis.

Pye / not iss.

Jun 73. (7") *(7N 45251)* **MAN OF RENOWN. / BUFFALO**

— split when only JAKE SCOTT and JIMMY HUSH remained. FINLAYSON joined BEES MAKE HONEY, taking his song 'BURGHLEY ROAD'. He went on to form MEAL TICKET.

– compilations, etc. –

Oct 95. (lp) *Tenth Planet; (TP 017)* **CRACKS IN THE ILLUSION OF LIFE: A HISTORY OF WRITING ON THE WALL**

Jul 96. (lp) *Tenth Planet; (TP 018)* **BURGHLEY ROAD: THE BASEMENT SESSIONS**

Jun 97. (lp) *Pie & Mash; (PAM 003)* **RARITIES FROM THE MIDDLE EARTH**

Zakk WYLDE

Born: New Jersey, USA. Having cut his teeth performing as guitarist with mid-80's act STONEHENGE, the man was signed up to join OZZY OSBOURNE (he made his debut on 1988's 'No Rest For The Wicked'). With Stateside Southern rock trio PRIDE & GLORY (who had a brief Top 200 entry with their eponymous 1994 album), the heavily-maned ZAKK duly took up a brief position with GUNS N' ROSES and SLASH'S SNAKEPIT early in '95. Notorious Becks drinker WYLDE subsequently joined up with OZZY OSBOURNE and he maintained that connection by playing the Ozzfest in 2001 – he's also about to make a cameo in the movie, 'Steel Dragon'. In 1996, ZAKK delivered a one-off solo set, 'BOOK OF SHADOWS', and went on to release three other sets under the BLACK LABEL SOCIETY billing, 'SONIC BREW' (1999), the mini 'STRONGER THAN DEATH' (2000) and the live 'ALCOHOL FUELED BREWTALITY' (2001).

Album rating: Pride & Glory: PRIDE & GLORY (*6) / Zakk Wylde: BOOK OF SHADOWS (*6) / Black Label Society: SONIC BREW (*6) / STRONGER THAN DEATH (*6) / ALCOHOL FUELED BREWTALITY – LIVE + 5 mini (*4)

PRIDE & GLORY

ZAKK WYLDE – vocals, guitar / **JAMES LoMENZO** – bass / **BRIAN TICHY** – drums

Geffen Geffen

May 94. (cd/c) <*(GED/GEC 24703)*> **PRIDE & GLORY** ☐ ☐
– Losin' your mind / A horse called war / Shine on / Lovin' woman / Harvester of pain / Choose one / Sweet Jesus / Troubled wine / Machine gun man / Cry me a river / Toe'n the line / Found a friend / Fadin' away / Hate your guts.

ZAKK WYLDE

Jun 96. (cd) <*SPITCD 014*> **BOOK OF SHADOWS** [-] ☐
– Between Heaven and Hell / Sold my soul / Road back home / Way beyond empty / Throwin' it all away / What you're look'n for / Dead as yesterday / Too numb to cry / The things you do / 1,000,000 miles away / I thank you child. *(UK-iss.Jul99; same)*

BLACK LABEL SOCIETY

ZAKK with **PHIL ONDICH** – drums

Spitfire Spitfire

May 99. (cd) <*(SPITCD 004)*> **SONIC BREW** ☐ ☐
– Bored to tears / The rose petalled garden / Hey you (batch of lies) / Born to lose / Peddlars of death / Mother Mary / Beneath the tree / Low down / T.A.Z / Lost my better half / Black pearl / Black pearl / World of trouble / Spoke in the wheel / The beginning . . . at last.

Apr 00. (cd) *(SPITCD 046)* <*15046*> **STRONGER THAN DEATH** ☐ ☐
– All for you / Phoney smiles and fake hellos / 13 years of grief / Rust / Superterrorizer / Counterfeit god / Ain't life grand / Just killing time / Stronger than death / Love reign down.

May 01. (m-cd) *(SPITCD 112)* <*15112*> **ALCOHOL FUELED BREWTALITY – LIVE + 5** ☐ ☐ Jan01
– Intro – Low down / Lowdown / 13 years of grief / Stronger than death / Super terrorizer / Phoney smiles and fake hellos / Lost my better half / Bored to tears / A.N.D.R.O.T.A.Z. / Born to booze / World of trouble / No more tears / The beginning . . . at last / Heart of gold / Snowblind / Like a bird / Blood in the wall / The beginning . . . at last.

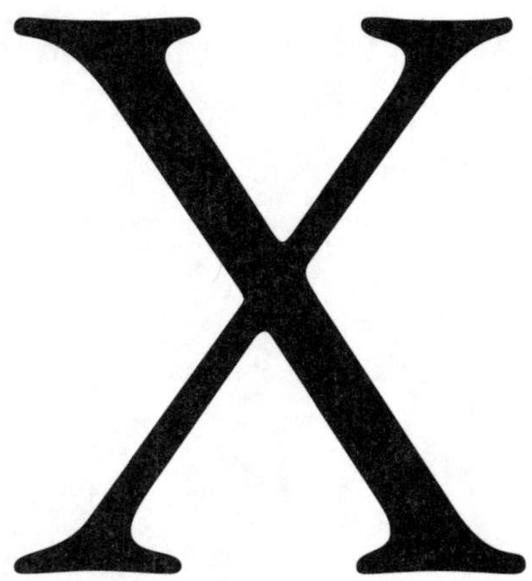

XENTRIX

Formed: Preston, England ... 1986 initially (until 1987) as SWEET VENGEANCE by CHRIS ASTLEY alongside KRISTIAN HOVARD, DENNIS GASSER and PAUL McKENZIE. Signed to 'Roadrunner' in 1988, the group released their debut album, 'SHATTERED EXISTENCE', the following year. Basic Brit thrash leaning heavily on traditional Bay Area stylings, the band became a regular fixture on the UK's toilet circuit along with fellow speedsters such as ACID REIGN, ONSLAUGHT and LAWNMOWER DETH. They shared something of the latter band's off-the-wall sense of humour, issuing an irreverent cover of Ray Parker Jr.'s 'GHOSTBUSTERS' as their debut single in 1990, the track already established among the band's growing grassroots fanbase as a celebratory set closer. A second album, 'SHATTERED EXISTENCE', followed later that year, the record receiving encouraging reviews in the metal press. With the thrash movement dying out somewhat as the 90's wore on, the group moved to a more conventional metal aproach on successive releases, 'DILUTE TO TASTE' (1991) and 'KIN' (1992). • **Songwriters:** ASTLEY, except REWARD (Teardrop Explodes).

Album rating: SHATTERED EXISTENCE (*6) / FOR WHOSE ADVANTAGE (*6) / DILUTE TO TASTE (*5) / KIN (*6) / SCOURGE (*4)

CHRIS ASTLEY – vocals, guitar / **KRISTIAN HOVARD** – guitar / **DENNIS GASSER** – drums / **PAUL McKENZIE** – bass; repl. STEVE HODGSON

Roadracer Roadracer

Sep 89. (lp/c/cd) *(<RO 9444-1/-4/-2>)* **SHATTERED EXISTENCE** ☐ ☐
– No compromise / Balance of power / Crimes / Back in the real world / Dark enemy / Bad blood / Reasons for destruction / Position of security / Heaven cent.

Jun 90. (cd-s) *(RO 2435-2)* **GHOSTBUSTERS. /** ☐ ☐

Sep 90. (cd/c/lp) *(<RO 9366-2/-4/-1>)* **FOR WHOSE ADVANTAGE?** ☐ ☐
– Questions / For whose advantage? / The human condition / False ideals / The bitter end / New beginnings / Desperate remedies / Kept in the dark / Black embrace. *(cd+=)* – Running white faced city boy.

May 91. (cd/c/lp) *(<RO 9320-2/-4/-1>)* **DILUTE TO TASTE** ☐ ☐
– Pure thought / Shadows of doubt / Balance of power / Kept in the dark / Crimes / Ghostbusters.

Apr 92. (12"ep/cd-ep) **THE ORDER OF CHAOS. / ALL BLEED RED / REWARD** ☐ -

May 92. (cd/c/lp) *(RO 9196-2/-4/-1)* **KIN** ☐ ☐
– The order of chaos / A friend to you / All bleed red / No more time / Waiting / Come tomorrow / Release / See through you / Another day.

Heavy Metal not iss.

Nov 95. (cd) *(HMRXD 198)* **SCOURGE** ☐ -
– 13 years / Scourge / Incite / Caught you living / Strength of persuasion / Never be / The hand that feeds itself / Blood nation / Creed / Breathe.

— split after above

XYTRAS (see under ⇒ SAMAEL)

XYZ

Formed: Los Angeles, California . . .1988 by French/Italian descendants, TERRY ILOUS and MARC RICHARD DIGLIO. Eventually signed by 'Enigma', XYZ were graced with DON DOKKEN in a production capacity on their eponymous 1990 album. Unsurprisingly, the record came out sounding fairly similar to DOKKEN's patented brand of melodic heavy rock, although vocalist ILOUS put in a powerful performance. With the album scraping into the US Top 100, the group secured support slots with the likes of ALICE COOPER. Subsequently picked up by 'Capitol', the band cut a harder-edged follow-up set, 'HUNGRY' (1991), which featured a cover of Free's 'FIRE AND WATER'. The record stiffed and XYZ finally came to the end of their particular Alphabet Street.

Album rating: XYZ (*4) / HUNGRY (*5) / TAKE WHAT YOU CAN compilation (*5)

TERRY ILOUS – vocals / **MARC RICHARD DIGLIO** – guitar / **PATT FONTAINE** – bass / **PAUL MONROE** – drums

Enigma Enigma

Feb 90. (cd/c/lp) *(CDENV/TCENV/ENVLP 1002) <73525>* **XYZ** ☐ 99 Nov89
– Maggy / Inside out / What keeps me loving you / Take what you can / Follow the night / Come on n' love me / Souvenirs / Tied up / Nice day to die / After the rain.

Mar 90. (7") *(ENV 16)* **INSIDE OUT. / TAKE WHAT YOU CAN** ☐ ☐
(12"+=/cd-s+=) *(12ENV/ENVCD 16)* – On the blue side of the night.

Capitl Capitol

Sep 91. (cd/c/lp) *<(CD/TC+/EST 2150)>* **HUNGRY** ☐ ☐
– Face down in the gutter / Don't say no / Fire and water / When the night comes down / Off to the sun / Feels good / Shake down the walls / When I find love / H H Boogie / The sun also rises in Hell / Roll of the dice / Whiskey on a heartache. *(cd re-iss. Jun99 on 'Axe Killer'; AXE 305139CD)*

— split after above

- compilations, etc. -

Oct 97. (cd) *Axe Killer; (AXE 302550CD)* **TAKE WHAT YOU CAN . . .. LIVE (live)** ☐ -
– Maggie / Take what you can / Come on 'n love me / What keeps me lovin' you / After the rain / Inside out / Off too the sun / Nice day 2 die / Straight in the night / Only get you on the phone / Connected to you / Slow me down.

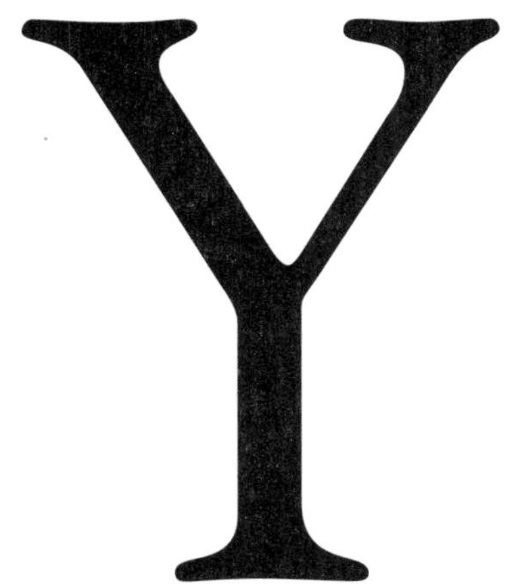

Y & T

Formed: Bay Area, San Francisco, California, USA . . . 1975 as YESTERDAY & TODAY by DAVE MENIKETTI, JOEY ALVES, PHIL KENNEMORE and LEONARD HAZE. This quartet of talented hard/heavy-rock musicians, issued two 'London' albums under this moniker, the eponymous 'YESTERDAY & TODAY' (1976) and 'STRUCK DOWN', before they changed the group name to Y&T. Signing to 'A&M' in the early 80's, they delivered a masterful set in the shape of 'EARTHSHAKER' (1981), although this surprisingly failed to move mountains commercially. The follow-up, 'BLACK TIGER' (1982), picked up where the last album left off, although the fruits of their labour were still not appreciated back home in the States. Y&T finally got tough with the commercial market via 'MEAN STREAK' (1983), hitting the UK Top 40, while it was caught short just outside the US Top 100. 'IN ROCK WE TRUST', unleashed the following year, became a Top 50 seller on both sides of the Atlantic, although it was clear the band were taking a more radio-friendly approach. Two more albums, the live 'OPEN FIRE' and 'DOWN FOR THE COUNT', sold moderately well in 1985, 'Geffen' supplying Y&T with a new home in '87 for 'CONTAGIOUS', an album that featured new members JIMMY DeGRASSO and STEF BURNS who replaced HAZE and ALVES respectively. This line-up finally delivered a long-awaited set, 'TEN' (1990), although this was their last recording (for some time) as the group splintered in many directions (i.e. MENIKETTI to PETER FRAMPTON, DeGRASSO to WHITE LION and BURNS to ALICE COOPER). Y&T reformed in the mid 90's (who didn't?!), signing to 'Music For Nations' (who didn't?!), then littered the bargain bins with the appropriately-titled 'MUSICALLY INCORRECT' (1995) and 'ENDANGERED SPECIES' (1997). • **Covers:** YOUR MAMA DON'T DANCE (Loggins & Messina) / ALL AMERICAN BOY (Val Stephenson / Dave Robbins) LET IT OUT (Moon Over Paris).

Album rating: YESTERDAY & TODAY (*4) / STRUCK DOWN (*4) / EARTHSHAKER (*7) / BLACK TIGER (*6) / MEAN STREAK (*4) / IN ROCK WE TRUST (*4) / OPEN FIRE (*5) / DOWN FOR THE COUNT (*5) / CONTAGIOUS (*5) / ANTHOLOGY compilation (*6) / TEN (*5) / MUSICALLY INCORRECT (*4) / ENDANGERED SPECIES (*4)

DAVE MENIKETTI – vocals, lead guitar / **JOEY ALVES** – guitar / **PHIL KENNEMORE** – bass / **LEONARD HAZE** – drums

not iss. | London

Nov 76. (lp; as YESTERDAY & TODAY) *<PS 677>* **YESTERDAY & TODAY** [-] [ ]
– Animal woman / 23 hours a day / Game playing woman / Come on over / My heart plays too / Earthshaker / Fast ladies (very slow gin) / Alcohol / Beautiful dreamer.

Apr 77. (7"; as YESTERDAY & TODAY) **ALCOHOL. /** [-] [ ]

Jun 78. (lp; as YESTERDAY & TODAY) *<PS 711>* **STRUCK DOWN** [-] [ ]
– Struck down / Pleasure in my heart / Road / Nasty Sadie / Dreams of Egypt / Tired to show you / I'm lost / Stargazer.

A&M | A&M

Jul 81. (lp/c) *(AMLH/CAM 64867) <4867>* **EARTHSHAKER** [ ] [ ]
– Hungry for rock / Dirty girl / Shake it loose / Squeeze / Rescue me / Young and tough / Hurricane / Let me go / Knock you out / I believe in you.

Oct 81. (7") *(AMS 8172)* **DIRTY GIRL. / KNOCK YOU OUT** [ ] [-]
(12"+=) *(AMSX 8172)* – Hungry for you.

May 82. (7"/12") *(AMS/+P 8229)* **I BELIEVE IN YOU. / RESCUE ME** [ ] [-]

Aug 82. (lp/c) *(AMLH/CAM 64910) <4910>* **BLACK TIGER** [53] [ ]
– From the moon / Open fire / Don't wanna lose / Hell or high water / Forever / Black tiger / Barroom boogie / My way or the highway / Winds of change.

Sep 82. (7"/12") *(AMS/+X 8251)* **DON'T WANNA LOSE. / SQUEEZE** [ ] [-]

Nov 82. (7") *<2516>* **BLACK TIGER. / FOREVER** [-] [ ]

Aug 83. (7"/7"pic-d) *(AM/+P 135)* **MEAN STREAK. / STRAIGHT THRU THE HEART** [41] [ ]
(12"+=) *(AMX 135)* – Dirty girl.

Sep 83. (lp/c) *(AMLX/CXM 64960) <4960>* **MEAN STREAK** [35] [ ]
– Mean streak / Straight thru the heart / Lonely side of town / Midnight in Tokyo / Breaking away / Hang 'em high / Take you to the limit / Sentimental fool / Down and dirty.

Nov 83. (7") *(AM 161)* **MIDNIGHT IN TOKYO. / BARROOM BOOGIE** [ ] [-]
(12"+=) *(AMX 161)* – Squeeze.

Aug 84. (lp/c) *(AMLX/CXM 65007) <5007>* **IN ROCK WE TRUST** [33] [46]
– Rock & roll's gonna save the world / Life, life, life / Masters and slaves / I'll keep on believin' (do you know) / Break out tonight! / Lipstick and leather / Don't stop runnin' / (Your love is) Drivin' me crazy / She's a liar / This time. *(cd-iss. 1988; 395007-2)*

Aug 84. (7") *<2669>* **DON'T STOP RUNNIN'. / FOREVER** [-] [ ]

Aug 84. (7") *(AM 208)* **DON'T STOP RUNNIN'. / ROCK & ROLL'S GONNA SAVE THE WORLD** [ ] [-]
(12"+=) *(AMX 208)* – Mean streak / I believe in you.

Jul 85. (7") *<2745>* **SUMMERTIME GIRLS. / ('A'extended)** [-] [55]

Jul 85. (lp/c) *<(AMA/AMC 5076)>* **OPEN FIRE (live)** [ ] [70]
– Open fire / Go for the throat / 25 hours a day / Rescue me / Summertime girls (studio version) / Forever / Barroom boogie / I believe in you. *(cd-iss. 1988; 395076-2)*

Aug 85. (7"/12") *(AM/+Y 264)* **SUMMERTIME GIRLS. / LIPSTICK AND LEATHER** [ ] [-]

Nov 85. (lp/c/cd) *<(AMA/AMC/CDA 5101)>* **DOWN FOR THE COUNT** [ ] [91]
– In the name of rock / All American boy / Anytime at all / Anything for money / Face like an angel / Summertime girls / Looks like trouble / Your mamma don't dance / Don't tell me what to wear / Hands of time.

Jan 86. (7") *<2789>* **ALL AMERICAN BOY. / GO FOR THE THROAT** [-] [ ]

—— **STEF BURNS** – guitar repl. JOEY / **JIMMY DEGRASSO** – drums repl. LEONARD

Geffen | Geffen

Jul 87. (lp/c/cd) *(924142-1/-4/-2) <24142>* **CONTAGIOUS** [ ] [78]
– Contagious / L.A. rocks / Temptation / The kid goes crazy / Fight for your life / Armed and dangerous / Rhythm or not / Bodily harm / Eyes of a stranger / I'll cry for you.

Jun 90. (cd/c/lp) *<(7599 24283-2/-4/-1)>* **TEN** [ ] [ ] May90
– Hard times / Lucy / Don't be afraid of the dark / Girl crazy / City / Come in from the rain / Red, hot & ready / She's gone / Let it out / Ten lovers / Goin' off the deep end / Surrender. *(re-iss. Aug91 cd/c; GEFD/GEFC 24283)*

—— Disbanded in Nov'90 and DEGRASSO joined hard rockin' solo songstress FIONA, before joining WHITE LION and then SUICIDAL TENDENCIES. Y&T reformed in the mid-90's

Music For Nations | Beacon

Sep 95. (cd/c) *(CD/T MFN 191) <51563>* **MUSICALLY INCORRECT** [ ] [ ]
– Long way down / Fly away / Quicksand / Cold day in Hell / Ive got my own / Nowhere land / Pretty prison / Don't know what to do / 21st century / I'm lost / Confusion / No regrets.

Music For Nations | D-Rock

Oct 97. (cd) *(CDMFN 229) <9011>* **ENDANGERED SPECIES** [ ] [ ]
– Hello hello / Black gold / God only knows / Sumthin 4 nuthin / Can't stop the rain / Sail on by / Still fallin' / I wanna cry / Gimme the beat / Voices / Try to believe / Rocco. *(re-iss. Jul00 on 'DeRock'; DERCD 9011)*

– compilations, others, etc. –

Sep 89. (lp/c/cd) *Raw Fruit; (RAW LP/MC/CD 040)* **ANTHOLOGY** [ ] [-]
– Rescue me / I believe in you / Squeeze / Hungry for rock / Don't wanna lose / Hell or highwater / Winds of change / Barroom boogie / Black tiger / In the name of rock / Summertime girls / All American boy / Hands of time / Mean streak / Take you to the limit / Down and dirty / Hang 'em high / Open fire (live) / Go for the throat (live) / Forever (live).

Sep 90. (cd/c) *A&M;* **THE BEST OF Y & T** [-] [ ]

May 91. (cd) *Castle; (CCSCD 286)* **THE COLLECTION** [ ] [-]

Mar 91. (cd/c/d-lp) *Metal Blade; (CD/T+/ZORRO 21) <3984 17017CD>* **YESTERDAY & TODAY LIVE (live)** [ ] [ ] Dec90
– Mean streak / Hurricane / Don't stop runnin' / Struck down / Winds of change / Black tiger / Midnight in Tokyo / Beautiful dreamer / Hard times / I'll cry / I believe in you / Squeeze / Forever. *(cd re-iss. May96; same as US)*

Sep 98. (cd) *Strange Fruit; (SFRSCD 071)* **LIVE ON THE FRIDAY ROCK SHOW – BBC IN CONCERT** [ ] [-]
(re-iss. Jul00 on 'Varese Sarabande' 302061069-2)

Neil YOUNG

Born: 12 Nov'45, Toronto, Canada. He was raised in Winnipeg until 1966, when he drove to America in his Pontiac hearse. NEIL had cut his teeth in local instrumental outfit, The SQUIRES, who released one '45 'THE SULTAN'. / 'AURORA' for 'V' records in September '63. The following year, NEIL formed The MYNHA BIRDS and joined forces with RICKY JAMES MATTHEWS (later to become RICK JAMES). Although many songs were recorded, only one saw the light of day; 'MYNHA BIRD HOP' for 'Columbia' Canada. They signed to 'Motown' (first white people to do so) but were soon dropped when they found out that RICKY had dodged the draft. He subsequently met up with past acquaintance, STEPHEN STILLS, and formed BUFFALO SPRINGFIELD. Constant rivalry led to YOUNG departing for a solo venture after signing for new label, 'Reprise', in Spring '68. His eponymous debut with arranger/producer JACK NITZSCHE, then DAVID BRIGGS, was finally issued in early 1969. A fragile, acoustic affair, the album was a tentative start to YOUNG's mercurial solo career, songs like 'THE OLD LAUGHING LADY' and 'THE LONER' hinting at the genius to come. The album was also a guinea pig for 'Warners' (then) new 'CSG' recording process, YOUNG later complaining bitterly about the resulting sound quality. 'EVERYBODY KNOWS THIS IS NOWHERE' (1969), however, was the sound of YOUNG in full control. Hooking up with a bunch of hard-bitten rockers going by the name of CRAZY HORSE, the record marked the beginning of a long and fruitful partnership that's still going strong almost thirty years on. With 'CINNAMON GIRL', DOWN BY THE RIVER' and 'COWGIRL IN THE SAND', this bruising musical synergy saw YOUNG scaling cathartic new heights and the guitar interplay would become a template for the primal improvisation of YOUNG's live work. Although 'AFTER THE GOLDRUSH' (1970) was partly recorded with CRAZY HORSE and featured the blistering 'SOUTHERN MAN', most of the album was by turns melancholy, bittersweet and charming in the style of the gorgeous ballad, 'HELPLESS', he'd contributed some months earlier to the CSN&Y album, 'DEJA VU'. 'BIRDS' and 'I BELIEVE IN YOU' stand as two of the most poignant love songs of YOUNG's career while the title track was a compelling lament of surreal poetry, based on a script written by actor DEAN STOCKWELL. The album gave YOUNG his breakthrough, going Top 10 in Britain and America but it was the 1972 single, 'HEART OF GOLD' and subsequent album, 'HARVEST', which made YOUNG a household name. Most of the tracks were recorded in Nashville with a band called The STRAY GATORS, piano and production duties falling to JACK NITZSCHE. His biggest selling album to date, the finely crafted country crooning of 'OUT ON THE WEEKEND' and 'HEART OF GOLD' was the closest YOUNG ever came to MOR and true to his contrary style, the next few years saw him trawling the depths of his psyche for some of the most uncompromising and uncommercial material of his career. After the fierce sonic assault of the live 'TIME FADES AWAY' (1973) album, YOUNG went back into the studio with CRAZY HORSE to record a tribute to DANNY WHITTEN, their sad-voiced singer who'd overdosed on heroin the previous year. Just as YOUNG was due to begin recording, another of his friends, BRUCE BERRY (STEPHEN STILLS' guitar roadie), succumbed to smack and the morose, drunken confessionals that resulted from those sessions eventually appeared a couple of years later as the 'TONIGHT'S THE NIGHT' (1975) album. Arguably YOUNG's most essential release, this darkly personal chronicle of drug oblivion veered from the resigned melancholy of 'ALBUQUERQUE' to the detached, twisted country of 'TIRED EYES', while the visceral catharsis of 'COME ON, BABY, LET'S GO DOWNTOWN' (an earlier live recording with a WHITTEN vocal) cranked up the guitars to match the unrelenting intensity level. Following 'Warners' reluctance to release the album, YOUNG set about writing yet another batch of hazy confessionals upon his return from touring the 'TONIGHT'S THE NIGHT' material. Deeply troubled by his increasing estrangement from actress CARRIE SNODGRASS (with whom he'd had a son, ZEKE), he shacked himself up in his new Malibu pad and penned 'ON THE BEACH' (1974). When every other rock star in L.A. was desperately trying to forget they'd ever hung out with CHARLES MANSON, YOUNG wrote 'REVOLUTION BLUES' in response to the Manson Family killings. 'AMBULANCE BLUES' was just as darkly compelling and the album remains an obscure classic. After a brief, ill-starred reunion with CROSBY, STILLS & NASH, YOUNG came up with a set entitled 'HOMEGROWN', which 'Warners' deemed too downbeat to release. Instead, they relented to the belated issue of 'TONIGHT'S THE NIGHT'. Come 1975, YOUNG was back in the studio with CRAZY HORSE, who'd recently recruited FRANK 'PANCHO' SAMPEDRO on guitar as a permanent replacement for WHITTEN. The resulting album, 'ZUMA' (1975), bore the first raw fruits of this new guitar partnership, the lucid imagery and meditative ruminations of 'CORTEZ THE KILLER' bringing the album to a darkly resonant climax while 'DON'T CRY NO TEARS' and 'BARSTOOL BLUES' found YOUNG more animated then he'd sounded for years. Following a disappointing album, 'LONG MAY YOU RUN' (1976), and aborted tour with STEPHEN STILLS, YOUNG cut the 'AMERICAN STARS 'N' BARS' (1977) album. A competent set of country rock, the record featured one of his best loved songs, an aching, soaring testament to the power of romantic obsession entitled 'LIKE A HURRICANE'. With 'COMES A TIME' (1978), he reverted to 'HARVEST'-style mellow country, duetting with then girlfriend, NICOLETTE LARSON. But YOUNG's more abrasive side couldn't be suppressed for long and, rejuvenated by the energy of the punk explosion, YOUNG reunited with CRAZY HORSE once more for the 'RUST NEVER SLEEPS' (1979) album. An electrifying set of passionate rockers and lean acoustic songs, it included such enduring live favourites as 'MY MY, HEY HEY (OUT OF THE BLUE)/(INTO THE BLACK)' (written about SEX PISTOL, JOHNNY ROTTEN) and the wounded 'POWDERFINGER'. The former was YOUNG's own comment on the "live fast, die young" rock'n'roll school of thought (it came back to haunt him when KURT COBAIN quoted the song in his suicide note). 'LIVE RUST' (1979) was the corrosive companion album capturing NEIL YOUNG & CRAZY HORSE live in all their frayed magnificence. Towards the end of 1978, YOUNG's new love, PEGI MORTON, had borne him a second child, BEN. While YOUNG's first son, ZEKE, had been born with cerebral palsy, BEN was a spastic. A stunned YOUNG began to clam up emotionally, with the result that much of his 80's work sounded confused and directionless. After 'REACTOR' (1981) stiffed, YOUNG moved to 'Geffen' where he recorded 'TRANS' (1983), an album that attempted to reflect his son's communication problems. Using a vocoder, YOUNG succeeded in rendering the lyrics almost unintelligible and while the album was almost universally panned, tracks like 'TRANSFORMER MAN' remain oddly affecting. The remainder of his time at 'Geffen' marked an all-time low in his career, both commercially and creatively, during which time he made ill-advised forays into rockabilly and stagnant, MOR country as well as making embarrassing pro-Reagan statments in interviews. Testing his fans to the limit, he was eventually sued by 'Geffen' for making records that didn't sound like NEIL YOUNG! He didn't really get back on track until 1989's 'FREEDOM' album, 'ROCKIN' IN THE FREE WORLD' and 'CRIME IN THE CITY' marking YOUNG's return to searing rock'n'roll. With CRAZY HORSE, he cut 'RAGGED GLORY' (1990) the following year, a frenetic guitar mash-up that was staggering in its intensity for such an elder statesman of rock. 'WELD' (1991), a live document of the subsequent tour, saw YOUNG championed by the new "grunge" vanguard and revered once more by the indie/rock press as the epitome of guitar cool. Influenced by SONIC YOUTH (who supported him for part of the tour), he even recorded a CD collage of feedback, 'ARC', available in a limited quantity as a bonus disc with the 'WELD' double set. His critical rebirth now complete, 'HARVEST MOON' (1992) gave him his biggest commercial success since the 70's. A lilting, careworn set of country-folk, it was billed as a belated follow-up to 1972's 'HARVEST'. Of course, the MTV 'UNPLUGGED' (1993) set was now obligatory, but rather than give the audience a predictable run through of acoustic numbers, he presented radically altered versions of old numbers like 'TRANSFORMER MAN' and 'LIKE A HURRICANE'. 'SLEEPS WITH ANGELS' (1994) was a downbeat elegy for KURT COBAIN while 'MIRRORBALL' (1995) was a misguided collaboration with grunge band, PEARL JAM. The 'DEAD MAN' soundtrack was interesting although 'BROKEN ARROW' (1996) and the live 'YEAR OF THE HORSE' (1997) were given short shrift by the press. In truth, the records were far too inconsistent to warrant parting with hard earned cash. The man's long awaited 'SILVER AND GOLD' (2000) went some way towards redressing the balance although it wasn't quite the dazzling return to form many had hoped for. Much of the album meandered along in a similar fashion to the trio of acoustic songs YOUNG had contributed to the previous year's CSN&Y reunion set, 'Looking Forward'. Bearing in mind that these tracks were by far the most memorable, it follows that 'SILVER AND GOLD' is an enjoyable enough listen without ever hitting those plateaus of inspiration integral to YOUNG's best work. A less obvious comparison than 'HARVEST MOON' might be his transitional 1978 effort, 'COMES A TIME'. New fans could do worse than starting with the 'DECADE' (1977) compilation, a stunning triple set (double CD) gathering the best of YOUNG's earlier work and including such obscure gems as the beautiful 'WINTERLONG'. There are also rumours of a comprehensive boxed set in the offing although there were 'rumours' about a CD reissue of 'ON THE BEACH', and that was four years ago! (take note Warner~s!). While YOUNG seems to be in a bit of a rut at present, and detractors peddle their predictable NEIL 'OLD' jokes, few would doubt the possibility of a blinding return to form or dispute that it's just a matter of when, rather than if. • **Songwriters:** As said, 99% of material is his own with contributions from CRAZY HORSE members, except; FARMER JOHN (Harris-Terry). The album 'EVERYBODY'S ROCKIN'' was full of covers. • **Note:** Entry into the Metal book II is due to his heavy influence on Grunge and in many opinions, NY is one of *thee* hard-rockers of all-time. I make no apologies too, for the inclusion of his non-CRAZY HORSE work – some numbers are even harder than many a hair-rock ballad.

Album rating: NEIL YOUNG (*7) / EVERYBODY KNOWS THIS IS NOWHERE (*8; with Crazy Horse) / AFTER THE GOLD RUSH (*10) / HARVEST (*9) / JOURNEY THROUGH THE PAST soundtrack (*3) / TIME FADES AWAY (*6) / ON THE BEACH (*9) / TONIGHT'S THE NIGHT (*8) / ZUMA (*8; with Crazy Horse) / AMERICAN STARS 'N BARS (*5) / DECADE compilation (*8) / COMES A TIME (*6) / RUST NEVER SLEEPS (*9; with Crazy Horse) / LIVE RUST (*7; with Crazy Horse) / HAWKS & DOVES (*6) / RE-AC-TOR (*5; with Crazy Horse) / TRANS (*5) / EVERYBODY'S ROCKIN' (*4; as Neil & The Shocking Pinks) / OLD WAYS (*5) / LANDING ON WATER (*3) / LIFE (*4; with Crazy Horse) / THIS NOTE'S FOR YOU (*6; as Neil Young & The Bluenotes) / FREEDOM (*7) / RAGGED GLORY (*8; with Crazy Horse) / WELD (*8; with Crazy Horse) / HARVEST MOON (*8) / LUCKY THIRTEEN compilation (*6) / UNPLUGGED (*6) / SLEEPS WITH ANGELS (*8; with Crazy Horse) / MIRRORBALL (*6) / DEAD MAN soundtrack (*4) / BROKEN ARROW (*5; with Crazy Horse) / THE YEAR OF THE HORSE (*5; with Crazy Horse) / SILVER AND GOLD (*6)

NEIL YOUNG – vocals, guitar (ex-BUFFALO SPRINGFIELD) with **JIM MESSINA** – bass / session men, etc.

Reprise Reprise

Jan 69. (lp) *<(RSLP 6317)>* **NEIL YOUNG** [ ] [ ]
– The Emperor of Wyoming / The loner / If I could have her tonight / I've been waiting for you / The old laughing lady / String quartet from Whiskey Boot Hill / Here we are in the years / What did I do to my life / I've loved her so long / The last trip to Tulsa. *(re-iss. 1971 lp/c; K/K4 44059) (cd-iss. 1987; K2 44059)*

Mar 69. (7") *<0785>* **THE LONER. / SUGAR MOUNTAIN** [-] [ ]

Sep 69. (7") *(RS 23405)* **THE LONER. / EVERYBODY KNOWS THIS IS NOWHERE** [ ] [-]

NEIL YOUNG with CRAZY HORSE

— with **DANNY WHITTEN** – guitar / **BILLY TALBOT** – bass / **RALPH MOLINA** – drums / **BOBBY NOTKOFF** – violin

Jul 69. (lp) *<(RSLP 6349)>* **EVERYBODY KNOWS THIS IS NOWHERE** [ ] [24] May69
– Cinnamon girl / Everybody knows this is nowhere / Round and round (it won't be long) / Down by the river / The losing end (when you're on) / Running dry (requiem for the rockets) / Cowgirl in the sand. *(re-iss. 1971 lp/c; K/K4 44073) (cd-iss. 1988; K2 44059)*

Jul 69. (7") *<0836>* **DOWN BY THE RIVER (edit). / THE LOSING END (WHEN YOU'RE ON)** [-] [ ]

— Late 1969, NEIL YOUNG was also added to CROSBY, STILLS, NASH (& YOUNG).

Aug 70. (7") *(RS 23462)* **DOWN BY THE RIVER (edit). / CINNAMON GIRL (alt.take)** [ ] [-]

NEIL YOUNG

— with **NILS LOFGREN** – guitar (of GRIN) repl. NOTKOFF

Aug 70. (7") *<0898>* **OH LONESOME ME (extended). / I'VE BEEN WAITING FOR YOU (alt.mix)** [-] [ ]

Sep 70. (lp) *<(RSLP 6383)>* **AFTER THE GOLD RUSH** 7 8
– Tell me why / After the gold rush / Only love can break your heart / Southern man / Till the morning comes / Oh lonesome me / Don't let it bring you down / Birds / When you dance I can really love / I believe in you / After the goldrush / Cripple Creek ferry. *(re-iss. 1971 lp/c; K/K4 44088) (cd-iss. Jul87; K2 44088)*

Sep 70. (7") *(RS 20861)* **OH LONESOME ME (extended). / SUGAR MOUNTAIN** -

Jun 70. (7") *<0911>* **CINNAMON GIRL (alt.mix). / SUGAR MOUNTAIN** - 55

Oct 70. (7") *(RS 20958) <0958>* **ONLY LOVE CAN BREAK YOUR HEART. / BIRDS** 33

Jan 71. (7") *<0992>* **WHEN YOU DANCE I CAN REALLY LOVE. / SUGAR MOUNTAIN** - 93

Feb 71. (7") *(RS 23488)* **WHEN YOU DANCE I CAN REALLY LOVE. / AFTER THE GOLDRUSH** -

—— solo with The STRAY GATORS. (CRAZY HORSE now recorded on their own). NEIL's musicians: **JACK NITZSCHE** – piano / **BEN KEITH** – steel guitar / **TIM DRUMMOND** – bass / **KENNY BUTTREY** – drums. guests included **CROSBY, STILLS & NASH, LINDA RONSTADT, JAMES TAYLOR** plus The LONDON SYMPHONY ORCHESTRA

Feb 72. (7") *(K 14140) <1065>* **HEART OF GOLD. / SUGAR MOUNTAIN** 10 1

Mar 72. (lp/c) *(K/K4 54005) <MS 2032>* **HARVEST** 1 1
– Out on the weekend / Harvest / A man needs a maid / Heart of gold / Are you ready for the country? / Old man / There's a world / Alabama / The needle and the damage done / Words (between the lines of age). *(cd-iss. May83; K 244131)*

Apr 72. (7") *(K 14167) <1084>* **OLD MAN. / THE NEEDLE AND THE DAMAGE DONE** 31

Jun 72. (7"; by NEIL YOUNG & GRAHAM NASH) *<1099>* **WAR SONG. / THE NEEDLE AND THE DAMAGE DONE** - 61

—— **JOHNNY BARBATA** – drums (ex-CROSBY, STILLS & NASH) repl. BUTTREY

Sep 73. (lp/c) *(K/K4 54010) <MS 2151>* **TIME FADES AWAY (live)** 20 22
– Time fades away / Journey through the past / Yonder stands the sinner / L.A. / Love in mind / Don't be denied / The bridge / Last dance.

Oct 73. (7") *<1184>* **TIME FADES AWAY (live). / LAST TRIP TO TULSA (live)** -

—— now used session people including **CRAZY HORSE** members **BEN KEITH** – steel guitar had now repl. WHITTEN who o.d.'d August 1972.

Jul 74. (7") *(K/K4 54014) <R 2180>* **ON THE BEACH** 42 16
– Walk on / See the sky about to rain / Revolution blues / For the turnstiles / Vampire blues / On the beach / Motion pictures / Ambulance blues.

Jul 74. (7") *(K 14360) <1209>* **WALK ON. / FOR THE TURNSTILES** 69

—— Had just earlier in 1974, re-united with CROSBY, STILLS & NASH

—— recorded solo lp in '73. Musicians: **NILS LOFGREN / BEN KEITH / BILLY TALBOT / RALPH MOLINA**

Jun 75. (lp/c) *(K/K4 54040) <MS 2221>* **TONIGHT'S THE NIGHT** 48 25
– Tonight's the night (part I) / Speakin' out / World on a string / Borrowed tune / Come on baby let's go downtown / Mellow my mind / Roll another number (for the road) / Albuquerque / New mama / Lookout Joe / Tired eyes / Tonight's the night (part II). *(cd-iss. Jul93; 7599 27221-2)*

NEIL YOUNG with CRAZY HORSE

—— (Mar75) **FRANK 'Poncho' SAMPEDRO** – guitar, vocals repl. KEITH + LOFGREN The latter earlier went solo, and later joined BRUCE SPRINGSTEEN band.

Nov 75. (lp/c) *(K/K4 54057) <MS 2242>* **ZUMA** 44 25
– Don't cry no tears / Danger bird / Pardon my heart / Lookin' for a love / Barstool blues / Stupid girl / Drive back / Cortez the killer / Through my sails. *(cd-iss. Jul93; 7599 27222-2)*

Mar 76. (7") *(K 14416) <1344>* **LOOKIN' FOR A LOVE. / SUGAR MOUNTAIN** Dec75

Mar 76. (7") *<1350>* **DRIVE BACK. / STUPID GIRL** -

May 76. (7") *(K 14431)* **DON'T CRY NO TEARS. / STUPID GIRL** -

—— Mid 1976, he teamed up as STILLS-YOUNG BAND with STEPHEN STILLS on album 'LONG MAY YOU RUN'; *K/K4 54081 <MS 2253>*.

Jun 77. (lp/c) *(K/K4 54088) <MSK 2261>* **AMERICAN STARS 'N BARS** 17 21
– The old country waltz / Saddle up the Palomino / Hey babe / Hold back the tears / Bite the bullet / Star of Bethlehem / Will to love / Like a hurricane / Homegrown. *(cd-iss. Dec96; 7599 27234-2)*

Jul 77. (7") *<1390>* **HEY BABE. / HOMEGROWN** -

Sep 77. (7") *(K 14482) <1391>* **LIKE A HURRICANE (edit). / HOLD BACK THE TEARS**

NEIL YOUNG

—— solo with loads on session incl. **NICOLETTE LARSON** – vox

Oct 78. (7") *<1395>* **COMES A TIME. / MOTORCYCLE MAMA** -

Oct 78. (lp/c) *(K/K4 54099) <2266>* **COMES A TIME** 42 7
– Goin' back / Comes a time / Look out for my love / Lotta love / Peace of mind / Human highway / Already one / Field of opportunity / Motorcycle mama / Four strong winds. *(cd-iss. Jul93; 7599 27235-2)*

Nov 78. (7") *(K 14493)* **FOUR STRONG WINDS. / MOTORCYCLE MAMA** 57 -

Dec 78. (7") *<1396>* **FOUR STRONG WINDS. / HUMAN HIGHWAY** - 61

NEIL YOUNG with CRAZY HORSE

—— (YOUNG w / **SAMPEDRO, TALBOT & MOLINA)**

Jun 79. (lp/c) *(K/K4 54105) <2295>* **RUST NEVER SLEEPS** 13 8
– My my, hey hey (out of the blue) / Thrasher / Ride my llama / Pocahontas / Sail away / Powderfinger / Welfare mothers / Sedan delivery / Hey hey, my my (into the black). *(cd-iss. Jul93; 7599 27249-2)*

Aug 79. (7") *(K 14498) <49031>* **HEY HEY, MY MY (INTO THE BLACK). / MY MY, HEY HEY (OUT OF THE BLUE)** 79

Nov 79. (d-lp/d-c) *(K/K4 64041) <2296>* **LIVE RUST (live)** 55 15
– Sugar mountain / I am a child / Comes a time / After the gold rush / My my, hey hey (out of the blue) / When you dance I can really love / The loner / The needle and the damage done / Lotta love / Sedan delivery / Powderfinger / Cortez the killer / Cinnamon girl / Like a hurricane / Hey hey, my my (into the black) / Tonight's the night. *(re-iss. cd Jul93; 7599 27250-2)*

Dec 79. (7") *<49189>* **CINNAMON GIRL (live). / THE LONER (live)** -

NEIL YOUNG

—— solo with **TIM DRUMMOND + DENNIS BELFIELD** – bass / **LEVON HELM + GREG THOMAS** – drums / **BEN KEITH** – steel, dobro / **RUFUS THIBODEAUX** – fiddle

Oct 80. (lp/c) *(K/K4 54109) <2297>* **HAWKS & DOVES** 34 30
– Little wing / The old homestead / Lost in space / Captain Kennedy / Stayin' power / Coastline / Union power / Comin' apart at every nail / Hawks & doves.

Nov 80. (7") *(K 14508) <49555>* **HAWKS & DOVES. / UNION MAN**

Feb 81. (7") *<49641>* **STAYIN' POWER. / CAPTAIN KENNEDY** -

NEIL YOUNG with CRAZY HORSE

—— (see last CRAZY HORSE line-up)

Oct 81. (lp/c) *(K/K4 54116) <2304>* **RE• AC• TOR** 69 27
– Opera star / Surfer Joe and Moe the sleaze / T-bone / Get back on it / Southern Pacific / Motor city / Rapid transit / Shots.

Nov 81. (7"/10"shaped-red) *<498 70/95>* **SOUTHERN PACIFIC. / MOTOR CITY** - 70

Jan 82. (7") *<50014>* **OPERA STAR. / SURFER JOE AND MOE THE SLEAZE** -

NEIL YOUNG

—— solo adding synthesizers, drum machine (sessioners) **BRUCE PALMER** – bass (ex-BUFFALO SPRINGFIELD)

Geffen Geffen

Jan 83. (7") *(GEF 2781) <29887>* **LITTLE THING CALLED LOVE. / WE R IN CONTROL** 71 Dec82

Jan 83. (lp/c) *(GEF/+C 25019) <2018>* **TRANS** 29 19
– Little thing called love / Computer age / We r in control / Transformer man / Computer cowboy (aka Syscrusher) / Hold on to your love / Sample and hold / Mr. Soul / Like an Inca. *(re-iss. Sep86 lp/c; 902018-1/-4) (cd-iss. Apr97; GFLD 19357)*

Jan 83. (12") *<20105>* **SAMPLE AND HOLD (extended). / MR SOUL (extended) / SAMPLE AND HOLD** -

Feb 83. (7") *<29707>* **MR. SOUL. / MR. SOUL (part 2)** -

—— w / **BEN KEITH** – guitar / **TIM DRUMMOND** – bass / **KARL HIMMEL** – drums / **LARRY BYROM** – piano, vocals / **RICK PALOMBI + ANTHONY CRAWFORD** – b.vocals

Sep 83. (lp/c; as NEIL & THE SHOCKING PINKS) *(GEF/+C 25590) <4013>* **EVERYBODY'S ROCKIN'** 50 46 Aug83
– Betty Lou's got a new pair of shoes / Rainin' in my heart / Payola blues / Wonderin' / Kinda fonda Wanda / Jellyroll man / Bright lights, big city / Cry, cry, cry / Mystery train / Everybody's rockin'. *(re-iss. Sep86 lp/c/cd; 904013-1/-4/-2)*

Sep 83. (7") *(GEF 3581) <29574>* **WONDERIN'. / PAYOLA BLUES** -

Oct 83. (7") *<29433>* **CRY, CRY, CRY. / PAYOLA BLUES** -

—— Jul85, with country singer WILLIE NELSON he duets on his ARE THERE ANY MORE REAL COWBOYS single issued on 'Columbia'.

—— solo again with loads of session people.

Aug 85. (lp/c) *(GEF/40 26377) <24068>* **OLD WAYS** 39 75
– The wayward wind / Get back to the country / Are there any more real cowboys? / Once an angel / Misfits / California sunset / Old ways / My boy / Bound for glory / Where is the highway tonight? *(cd-iss. Apr97; GFLD 19356)*

Sep 85. (7") *<28883>* **BACK TO THE COUNTRY. / MISFITS** -

Nov 85. (7") *<28753>* **OLD WAYS. / ONCE AN ANGEL** -

—— w / **STEVE JORDAN** – drums, synths, vox / **DANNY KORTCHMAR** – guitar, synth

Aug 86. (lp/c/cd) *(924109-1/-4/-2) <24109>* **LANDING ON WATER** 52 46
– Weight of the world / Violent side / Hippie dream / Bad news beat / Touch the night / People on the street / Hard luck stories / I got a problem / Pressure / Drifter. *(re-iss. Apr91;) (cd-iss. Nov96; GED 24109)*

Sep 86. (7"/12") *(GEF/+T 7) <28623>* **WEIGHT OF THE WORLD. / PRESSURE** Jul86

NEIL YOUNG & CRAZY HORSE

—— (see last **CRAZY HORSE, + BRYAN BELL** – synth)

May 87. (lp/c)(cd) *(WX 108/+C)(924154-2) <24154>* **LIFE** 71 75
– Mideast vacation / Long walk home / Around the world / Inca queen / Too lonely / Prisoners of rock'n'roll / Cryin' eyes / When your lonely heart breaks / We never danced.

Jun 87. (7") *<28196>* **MIDEAST VACATION. / LONG WALK HOME** -

Jun 87. (7") *(GEF 25)* **LONG WALK HOME. / CRYIN' EYES** -

NEIL YOUNG & THE BLUENOTES

—— with **SAMPEDRO** – keyboards plus others **CHAD CROMWELL** – drums / **RICK ROSAS** – bass / **STEVE LAWRENCE** – tenor sax / **BEN KEITH** – alto sax / **LARRY CRAIG** – baritone sax / **CLAUDE CAILLIET** – trombone / **JOHN FUMO** – trumpet / **TOM BRAY** – trumpet

Reprise Reprise

Apr 88. (7") *<27908>* **TEN MEN WORKIN'. / I'M GOIN'** -

May 88. (lp/c/cd) *(WX 168/+C)(925719-2) <25719>* **THIS NOTE'S FOR YOU** 56 61
– Ten men workin' / This note's for you / Coupe de ville / Life in the city / Twilight / Married man / Sunny inside / Can't believe you're lyin' / Hey hey / One thing. *(re-iss. cd Feb95)*

May 88. (7") *<27848>* **THIS NOTE'S FOR YOU (live). / THIS NOTE'S FOR YOU** -

—— Nov88, NEIL re-joined CROSBY, STILLS, NASH & YOUNG for 'AMERICAN DREAM' lp.

NEIL YOUNG

— solo again with **SAMPEDRO, ROSAS, CROMWELL,** etc.

Oct 89. (lp/c/cd) *(WX 257/+C)(K 925899-2) <25899>* **FREEDOM** [17] [35]
– Rockin' in the free world / Crime in the city (sixty to zero part 1) / Don't cry / Hangin' on a limb / Eldorado / The ways of love / Someday / On Broadway / Wreckin' ball / No more / Too far gone / Rockin' in the free world (live). *(re-iss. cd/c Feb95)*

Apr 90. (7") *(W 2776) <22776>* **ROCKIN' IN THE FREE WORLD. / ('A'live)** [ ] [ ] Aug89
(12"+=/cd-s+=) *(W 2776 T/CD)* – Cocaine eyes.

NEIL YOUNG & CRAZY HORSE

— with **SAMPEDRO, TALBOT + MOLINA**

Sep 90. (cd)(lp/c) *<(7599-26315-2)>(WX 374/+C)* **RAGGED GLORY** [15] [31]
– Country home / White line / Fuckin' up / Over and over / Love to burn / Farmer John / Mansion on the hill / Days that used to be / Love and only love / Mother Earth (natural anthem). *(re-iss. cd/c Feb95)*

Sep 90. (cd-s) *<7599-21759-2>* **MANSION ON THE HILL (edit) / MANSION ON THE HILL / DON'T SPOOK THE HORSE** [-] [ ]

Oct 91. (d-cd/d-c/d-lp) *<(7599 26671-2/-4/-1)>* **WELD (live)** [20] [ ]
– Hey hey, my my (into the black) / Crime in the city / Blowin' in the wind / Live to burn / Welfare mothers / Cinnamon girl / Mansion on the hill / F+!#in' up / Farmer John / Cortez the killer / Powderfinger / Love and only love / Roll another number / Rockin' in the free world / Like a hurricane / Tonight's the night. *(free-cd-ep w.a.+=)* – ARC EP – (feedback).

NEIL YOUNG

solo, with The STRAY GATORS (**KENNY BUTTREY, TIM DRUMMOND, BEN KEITH & SPOONER OLDHAM**) plus **JAMES TAYLOR, LINDA RONSTADT, NICOLETTE LARSON, ASTRID YOUNG & LARRY CRAGG** – backing vocals

Oct 92. (cd/c/lp) *<(9362 45057-2/-4/-1)>* **HARVEST MOON** [9] [16]
– Unknown legend / From Hank to Hendrix / You and me / Harvest moon / War of man / One of these days / Such a woman / Old king / Dreamin' man / Natural beauty.

Feb 93. (7"/c-s) *(W 0139/+C)* **HARVEST MOON. / WINTERLONG** [36] [ ]
(cd-s+=) *(W 0139CD)* – Deep forbidden lake / Campaigner.
(cd-s) *(W 0139CDX)* – ('A'side) / Old king / The needle and the damage done / Goin' back.

Jun 93. (cd/c/lp) *<(9362 45310-2/-4/-1)>* **UNPLUGGED** [4] [23]
– The old laughing lady / Mr. Soul / World on a string / Pocahontas / Strongman / Like a hurricane / The needle and the damage done / Helpless / Harvest Moon / Transformer man / Unknown legend / Look out for my love / Long may you run / From Hank to Hendrix.

Jul 93. (7"/c-s) *(W 0191/+C)* **THE NEEDLE AND THE DAMAGE DONE (live). / YOU AND ME** [75] [ ]
(cd-s+=) *(W 0191CD)* – From Hank to Hendrix.

Oct 93. (7"/c-s) *(W 207/+C)* **LONG MAY YOU RUN (live). / SUGAR MOUNTAIN (live)** [71] [ ]
(cd-s+=) *(W 0207CD)* – Cortez the killer (live) / Cinnamon girl (live).

Feb 94. (7"/c-s) *(W 0231/+C)* **ROCKIN' IN THE FREE WORLD. / ('A'mixes)** [ ] [ ]
(cd-s+=) *(W 0231CD)* – Weld.

Apr 94. (7"/c-s) *(W 0242/+C)* **PHILADELPHIA. / SUCH A WOMAN** [62] [ ]
(12"+=/cd-s+=) *(W 0242 T/CD)* – Stringman (unplugged).

— Above 'A'side was another to be taken from the film 'Philadelphia'.

NEIL YOUNG & CRAZY HORSE

Aug 94. (cd/c/d-lp) *<(9362 45749-2/-4/-1)>* **SLEEPS WITH ANGELS** [2] [9]
– My heart / Prime of life / Drive by / Sleeps with angels / Western hero / Change your mind / Blue Eden / Safeway cart / Train of love / Trans Am / Piece of crap / A dream that can last. *(re-iss. Jan97; same)*

Aug 94. (c-s/cd-s) *(W 0261 C/CD)* **PIECE OF CRAP / TONIGHT'S THE NIGHT** [ ] [ ]

Oct 94. (c-s) *(W 0266C)* **MY HEART / ROLL ANOTHER NUMBER (FOR THE ROAD)** [ ] [ ]
(cd-s+=) *(W 0266CD)* – Tired eyes.

Nov 94. (c-s) **CHANGE YOUR MIND / SPEAKIN' OUT** [ ] [ ]
(cd-s+=) – ('A'full version).

NEIL YOUNG

— with backing from all of PEARL JAM; 8th track written w/ EDDIE VEDDER

Jun 95. (cd/c/lp) *<(9362 45934-2/-4/-1)>* **MIRRORBALL** [4] [5]
– Song X / Act of love / I'm the ocean / Big green country / Truth be known / Downtown / What happened yesterday / Peace and love / Throw your hatred down / Scenery / Fallen angel.

Sep 95. (c-s) *(W 0314C)* **DOWNTOWN / BIG GREEN COUNTRY** [ ] [ ]
(cd-s+=) *(W 0314CD)* – ('A'-lp version).

Feb 96. (cd) *<(9362 46171-2)>* **Music From And Inspired By The Motion Picture DEAD MAN** [ ] [ ]
above was instrumental YOUNG, and based on Jim Jarmusch's film starring Johnny Depp.

NEIL YOUNG WITH CRAZY HORSE

Jun 96. (cd/c) *<(9362 46291-2/-4)>* **BROKEN ARROW** [17] [31]
– Big time / Loose change / Slip away / Changing highways / Scattered (let's think about livin') / This town / Music arcade / Baby what you want me to do.

Jun 97. (cd/c) *<(9362 46652-2/-4)>* **THE YEAR OF THE HORSE (live)** [36] [57]
– When you dance / Barstool blues / When your lonely heart breaks / Mr. Soul / Big time / Pocahontas / Human highway / Slip away / Scattered / Danger bird / Prisoners / Sedan delivery.

NEIL YOUNG

Apr 00. (cd/c) *<(9362 47305-2/-4)>* **SILVER AND GOLD** [10] [22]
– Good to see you / Silver and gold / Daddy went walkin' / Buffalo Springfield again / The great divide / Horseshoe man / Red sun / Distant camera / Razor love / Without rings.

– compilations, others, etc. –

Note; on 'Reprise' until otherwise stated.

1971. (7") *<0746>* **CINNAMON GIRL (alt.mix). / ONLY LOVE CAN BREAK YOUR HEART** [-] [ ]

Nov 72. (d-lp) *(K 64015) <2XS 6480>* **JOURNEY THROUGH THE PAST (Soundtrack featuring live & rare material with past bands)** [ ] [45]
– For what it's worth – Mr. Soul / Rock & roll woman / Find the cost of freedom / Ohio / Southern man / Are you ready for the country / Let me call you sweetheart / Alabama / Words / Relativity invitation / Handel's Messiah / King of kings / Soldier / Let's go away for a while.

Jan 73. (7") *<1152>* **HEART OF GOLD. / OLD MAN** [-] [ ]

Mar 74. (7") *(K 14319)* **ONLY LOVE CAN BREAK YOUR HEART. / AFTER THE GOLDRUSH** [ ] [-]

May 74. (7"ep) *(K 14350)* **SOUTHERN MAN / TILL MORNING COMES. / AFTER THE GOLDRUSH / HEART OF GOLD** [ ] [-]

Nov 77. (t-lp) *(K 54088) <3RS 2257>* **DECADE** [46] [43]
– Down to the wire + Burned + Mr.Soul + Broken arrow + Expecting to fly (BUFFALO SPRINGFIELD) / Sugar mountain / I am a child / The loner / The old laughing lady / Cinnamon girl / Down by the river / Cowgirl in the sand / I believe in you / After the goldrush / Southern man / Helpless + Ohio (CROSBY, STILLS, NASH & YOUNG) / A man needs a maid / Harvest / Heart of gold / Star of Bethlehem / The needle and the damage done / Tonight's the night (part 1) / Turnstiles / Winterlong / Deep forbidden lake / Like a hurricane / Love is a rose / Cortez the killer / Campaigner / Long may you run (w / STEPHEN STILLS). *(re-iss. d-cd Jul93)*

Jan 78. (7") *<1393>* **SUGAR MOUNTAIN. / THE NEEDLE AND THE DAMAGE DONE** [-] [ ]

Oct 82. (d-c) *(K4 64043)* **NEIL YOUNG / EVERYBODY KNOWS THIS IS NOWHERE** [ ] [-]

Oct 82. (d-c) *(K4 64044)* **AFTER THE GOLDRUSH / HARVEST** [ ] [-]

Feb 87. (cd) *(925271-2)* **THE BEST OF NEIL YOUNG** [ ] [-]

Jan 93. (cd) *Movieplay Gold; (MPG 74011)* **THE LOST TAPES** [ ] [-]

Jan 93. (cd/c) *Geffen; (GED/GEC 24452)* **LUCKY THIRTEEN** (80's material) [69] [ ]
– Sample and hold / Transformer man / Depression blues / Get gone / Don't take your love away from me / Once an angel / Where is the highway tonight / Hippie dream / Pressure / Around the world / East vacation / Ain't it the truth / This note's for you. *(cd re-iss. Sep96; GFLD 19328)*

Dec 00. (cd) *Reprise; <48036>* **ROAD ROCK V1 (live)** [-] [ ]

— Note that 1980's 'Where The Buffalo Roam' film contained several YOUNG songs

YOUNG GODS

Formed: Geneva, Switzerland . . . early 1986 . . .by Fribourg-born FRANZ TREICHLER, CESARE PIZZI and FRANK BAGNOUD. Self-financed debut 45 'ENVOYE', which after follow-up 'DID YOU MISS ME', led to a deal with Belgian indie label 'Play It Again Sam'. An eponymous album gained much critical appraisal due to TREICHLER's Euro-gothic stark delivery sung in French and the production techniques of ROLI MOSIMANN (Swans). Second album 'L'EAU ROUGE' continued in the same vein, but it wasn't until 1991's avant-garde 'TV SKY', recorded in English, that they won over the States. Took a break from the studio until 1995, when awesome 'ONLY HEAVEN' was unleashed. Although it didn't chart, it made new friends from the heavy metal brigade, while retaining industrial, indie rock and techno/ambient fans. The latter style was much in evidence on the excellent 15 minute atmospheric soundscape track 'MOON REVOLUTIONS', while 'KISSING THE SUN' was a hard gut-wrenching explosion of sound. • **Songwriters:** Group (TREICHLER – lyrics), except tribute album to KURT WEILL, which included his SEPTEMBER SONG + ALABAMA SONG. Also covered; HELLO HELLO I'M BACK AGAIN (Gary Glitter).

Album rating: YOUNG GODS (*7) / L'EAU ROUGE (*7) / THE YOUNG GODS PLAY KURT WEILL (*5) / T.V. SKY (*6) / LIVE SKY TOUR (*5) / ONLY HEAVEN (*7) / HEAVEN DECONSTRUCTION (*4)

FRANZ TREICHLER – vocals / **CESARE PIZZI** – tapes, synthesizers / **FRANK BAGNOUD** – drums

Organik | not iss.

May 86. (12") *(ORG 89-6)* **ENVOYE. / SOUL IDIOT / CSCLDF** [-] [-] Swiss

Feb 87. (12") *(ORG 87-9)* **DID YOU MISS ME. / THE IRRTUM BOYS** [-] [-] Swiss

Product Inc | Wax Trax!

Apr 87. (12"m) *(12PROD 7)* **DID YOU MISS ME. / HELLO HELLO I'M BACK AGAIN / IRRTUM BOYS** [ ] [-]

Jun 87. (lp/cd) *(LD 8821/+CD) <WAX 7135>* **YOUNG GODS** [ ] [ ]
– Nouse de la lune / Jusqu'au bout / A ciel ouvert / Jimmy / Pais la mouette / Percussione / Feu / Did you miss me / Si tu gardes. *(cd+=)* – The Irrtum boys / Envoye / Soul idiot. *(re-iss. Aug89 lp/cd; 33/CD PROD 10)*

— **USE HEISTAND** – drums; repl. FRANK

Play It Again Sam | Play It Again Sam

Oct 88. (7"/cd-s) *(BIAS 101/+CD)* **L'AMOURIR. / PAS MAL** [ ] [-]
(was to have been issued Aug88; PIAS 99/+CD)

Sep 89. (lp/cd) *(<BIAS/CDBIAS 130>)* **L'EAU ROUGE (THE RED WATER)** [ ] [ ]
– La fille de la morte / Rue des tempetes / L'eau rouge / Charlotte / Longue route / Crier les chiens. *(cd+=)* – Ville notre / Les enfants. *<US re-iss. 1995 on 'Interscope'; 92629>*

Apr 90. (12") *(BIAS 158)* **LONGUE ROUTE (remix). / SEPTEMBER SONG** [ ] [-]
(cd-s+=) *(BIAS 158CD)* – Envoye (live) / Pas mal (live).

—— **AL MONO** – samples; repl. PIZZI

Apr 91. (lp/cd) *(<BIAS 188/+CD>)* **THE YOUNG GODS PLAY KURT WEILL** [ ] [ ]
– Prologue / Salomon song / Mackie messer / Speak low / Alabama song / Seerauber Jenny / Ouverture / September song.

Jan 92. (lp/c/cd) *(<BIAS 201/+C/CD>)* **T.V. SKY** [54] [ ]
– Our house / Gasoline man / T.V. sky / Skinflowers / Dame chance / The night dance / She rains / Summer eyes.

Mar 92. (7") *(7BIAS 206)* **SKINFLOWERS. / SKINFLOWERS (Brain Forest mix)** [ ] [-]
(12"+=/cd-s+=) *(BIAS 206/+CD)* – ('A'-Courtney Speed Love mix) / ('A'edit).

Sep 92. (12"/cd-s) *(BIAS 231/+CD)* **GASOLINE MAN (megadrive mix). / GASOLINE MAN (diesel mix) / ('A'diesel edit)** [ ] [-]

Jul 93. (lp/c/cd) *(<BIAS 241/+C/CD>)* **LIVE SKY TOUR (live Melbourne summer 1992)** [ ] [ ]
– Intro / TV sky / Jimmy / Envoye / Chanson rouge / L'eau rouge / Skinflowers / She rains / Summer eyes / Pas mal / Longue route / September song / Seerauber Jenny.

Jun 95. (lp/c/cd) *(<BIAS 301/+C/CD>)* **ONLY HEAVEN** [ ] [ ]
– Outside / Strangle / Speed of night / Donnez les espirits / Moon revolutions / Kissing the sun / The dreamhouse / Lointaine / Gardez les espirits / Child in the tree. *(lp re-iss. Jun96 on 'Revelation'; REV 2554)*

Nov 95. (cd-ep) *(BIAS 299CD)* **KISSING THE SUN / (remixes)** [ ] [ ]

not iss. Paradigm

Jul 97. (cd) *<15>* **HEAVEN DECONSTRUCTION** [-] [ ]
– December / Aoacu / Acid strange! / Improper / Drun / Riversky / F / Borea / Scores / Landing / Messages / Nano pata / Lova / Light residues / Under / Numiere / Windklang.

Intoxygene Intoxygene

May 00. (cd-s) *(INTOX 005CDS)* **LUCIDOGEN / LUCIDOGEN (Braindance mix) / LUCIDOGEN (Speedfloor mix)** [ ] [ ]

Nov 00. (cd) *(INTOX 008CD)* **SECOND NATURE** [ ] [ ]
– Lucidogen / Supersonic / Laisse couler (le son) / Astronomic / Attends / In the otherland / Stick around / Sound in your eyes / Toi du monde / Love 2.7.

YOUTH BRIGADE

Formed: Washington DC, USA . . . 1980 by NORMAN STREJCEK, TOM CLINTON, BERT QUIEROZ and DANNY INGRAHM. This lot seem to have made only one EP, 1981's '{8 CUTS}', before another group of the same name poached their moniker.

Album rating: er . . . (see below!)

NORMAN STREJCEK – vocals / **TOM CLINTON** – guitar / **BERT QUIEROZ** – bass / **DANNY INGRAHM** – drums

not iss. Dischord

Dec 81. (12"ep) *<DISCHORD 6>* **{8 CUTS}** [-] [ ]

—— must have disbanded

YOUTH BRIGADE

Formed: Hollywood, California, USA . . . 1982, by the STERN brothers, SHAWN, ADAM and MARK. America's answer to SHAM 69, their anthemic barrage of teenage punk rock was first heard on vinyl with their 1984 album, 'SOUND & FURY'. This effort surfaced on their own 'Better Youth Organisation' label, the trio also signing SNFU and The BOUNCING SOULS in the process. From then on, they fought, they split, they reformed, they fought and they didn't conquer.

Album rating: SOUND & FURY / SINK WITH KALIFORNIJA (*5) / HAPPY HOUR (*5) / TO SELL THE TRUTH (*5)

SHAWN STERN – vocals, guitar / **ADAM STERN** – bass, vocals / **MARK STERN** – drums, vocals

Better Youth Org. Better Youth Org.

Jul 84. (lp) *<(BYO 002)>* **SOUND & FURY** [ ] [ ]
– Sink with Kalifornija / Modest proposal / Men in blue (part 1) / Sound & fury / Fight to unite / Jump back / Blown away / Live life / What are you fighting for / Did you wanna die / You don't understand / The circle / Duke of Earl / What will the revolution change. *(cd-iss. Feb91 as 'SINK WITH KALIFORNIJA'; BYO 2CD)*

Nov 84. (12") *<(BYO 6)>* **WHAT PRICE HAPPINESS. /** [ ] [ ]

1985. (lp; as The BRIGADE) *<BYO 012>* **THE DIVIDING LINE** [-] [ ]

1985. (lp; as The BRIGADE) *<BYO 018>* **COME TOGETHER** [-] [ ]

—— split but reformed in the 90's

Lost & Found unknown

Jul 93. (7"; split) *(LF 053)* **GIGANTOR split** [ ] [ ]

EFA EFA

Mar 94. (cd/lp) *(efa 20027-2/-1)* <BYO 27 CD/LP> **HAPPY HOUR** [ ] [ ]
– All style, no substance / Better without you / Punk rock mom / Guns are for / Let me be / It's not enough / Alive by machine / It just doesn't matter / Wanted / Volare / Sad but true / This is a life / Deep inside of me.

May 94. (7") *(efa 40298-7)* **ALL STYLE AND NO SUBSTANCE. /** [ ] [ ]

1996. (cd) *<BYO 038>* **TO SELL THE TRUTH** [-] [ ]
– It's not my fault / Spies for life / Sick / We're in! / Breakdown / Street dominator / Shrinking / Believe in something / Friends / Not gonna take it / My bartender / Tomorrow / Last day of the year / I hate my life.

- compilations, etc. -

all issued on 'Better Youth Org.'

Nov 93. (cd) *<(BYO 025CD)>* **COME AGAIN** [ ] [ ]

Apr 94. (cd/lp) *Beri Beri; <(efa 11655-2/-1)>* **THE GOOD THE BAD . . .** [ ] [ ]

Nov 98. (cd) *<(BYO 050CD)>* **OUT OF PRINT** [ ] [ ]
– Fight to unite / Treachery / Circle / Boys in the brigade / Alienated / You don't understand / Brigade song / Full force / Sound and fury / Confusion / Violence / On the edge / I won't die for you / How can we live like this / Questions / Somebody's gonna get their head kicked in tonight.

Dweezil ZAPPA

Born: 1969, son of the late, great FRANK ZAPPA. Surprisingly not inspired by his father's avant-jazz guitar playing, he cloned himself as another idol, EDDIE VAN HALEN, even to the point of kitting himself out with the same style of clothes and guitar. He guested on two track from his dad's 1984 epic, 'THEM OR US', subsequently signing to 'Chrysalis' records and issuing his debut album, 'HAVIN' A BAD DAY', virtually ignored upon its release 1987. Taking one of his father's tunes, 'MY GUITAR WANTS TO KILL YOUR MAMA' and making it safe for at least MTV to give it an airing, DWEEZIL set out on his own inimitable hard-rock/pop course. The album and video of the same name hit the shops in '88, the latter featuring a 50's style cop pastiche. DWEEZIL released two more albums in the early 90's, 'CONFESSIONS' (1991) and 'SHAMPOO HORN' (1993), both token VAN HALEN mimickry, although the latter featured his brother AHMET (who had also appeared on his father's albums).

Album rating: HAVIN' A BAD DAY (*5) / MY GUITAR WANTS TO KILL YOUR MAMA (*5) / CONFESSIONS (*4) / SHAMPOOHORN (*4)

DWEEZIL ZAPPA – vocals, guitar / with various personnel

Chrysalis Rykodisc

Aug 87. (cd) *(CDL 1581)* <*RCD 10057*> **HAVIN' A BAD DAY**
– Havin' a bad day / Blonde hair, brown nose / You can't imagine / Let's talk about it / Electric hoedown / I want a yacht / I feel like I wanna cry.

—— now with **SCOTT THUNES** – bass / drummers; **STEVE SMITH** (JOURNEY), **BOBBY BLOTZER** (RATT) + **TERRY BOZZIO** (JEFF BECK band) + **FIONA** (FLANNAGAN) – vocals (solo star)

Chrysalis Chrysalis

Apr 88. (lp/c/cd) <*(CHR/ZCHR/CCD 1633)*> **MY GUITAR WANTS TO KILL YOUR MAMA**
– Her eyes don't follow me / The coolest guy in the world / My guitar wants to kill your mama / Comfort of strangers / Bang your groove thang / Your money or your life / Shameless / Before I get old / When you're near me / Nasty bizness.

Jun 88. (7") *(CHS 3247)* **MY GUITAR WANTS TO KILL YOUR MAMA. / NASTY BIZNESS**
(12"+=) *(CHS12 3247)* – Electric hoedown.

—— with different line-up

Food For Thought Barking Pumpkin

Mar 91. (cd/c/d-lp) *(CD/T+/GRUB 19)* <*77334*> **CONFESSIONS**
– Earth / Bad girl / F.W.A.K. / The kiss (Aura resurrects Flash) / Anytime at all / Helpless / Shoogagoogagunga / Stayin' alive / Maybe tonight / Confessions of a deprived youth / Gotta get to you / Pain of love / Obviously influenced by the Devil / Return of the son of Shoogagoogagunga / Vanity.

—— augmented by his brother

May 93. (cd/c/lp) *(CD/T+/GRUB 25)* **SHAMPOOHORN (Z)**

—— took a back seat since the tragic death of his dad, until . . .

Favoured Nations Favoured Nations

Jan 01. (cd) <*(FN 20502)*> **AUTOMATIC**
– Fwakstension / Automatic / Hawaii five-o / You're a mean one Mister Grinch / Therapy / 12 string thing / Secret hedges / Habanera / Les toreadors / Shnook / Dick Cinnamon's office / Purple guitar.

ZEBRA

Formed: New Orleans, USA . . . 1982 by RANDY JACKSON, FELIX HANEMANN and GUY KELSO. Signed to 'Atlantic', ZEBRA's eponymous 1983 debut subsequently became one of the fastest moving releases in the company's distinguished history. Not a bad job from a band whose lead singer could out-helium Rush's GEDDY LEE and Pavlov's Dog's DAVID SURKAMP! Musically, ZEBRA's stripes were characterised by heavy pomp rock of a distinctely 70's hue. Though the record made the US Top 30, a fine follow-up set, 'NO TELLIN' LIES' (1984), barely made the Top 100. By the release of third album, '3.V', the group had matured into one of the most competent exponents of the genre, although ironically, the commercial momentum had dissipated. Finally, after a 1990 live set, ZEBRA set themselves free from the music business zoo.

Album rating: ZEBRA (*5) / NO TELLIN' LIES (*5) / 3.V (*7) / ZEBRA LIVE (*4) / IN BLACK AND WHITE – THE ZEBRA COLLECTION (*6)

RANDY JACKSON – vocals, guitar, keyboards / **FELIX HANEMANN** – bass, keyboards, synthesizer, vocals / **GUY KELSO** – drums, percussion, vocals

Atlantic Atlantic

Jun 83. (7") <*89821*> **WHO'S BEHIND THE DOOR? / AS I SAID BEFORE** - 61

Sep 83. (lp) *(780 054-1)* <*80054*> **ZEBRA** 29 May83
– Tell me what you want / One more chance / Slow down / Blue suede shoes / As I said before / Who's behind the door? / When you get there / Take your fingers from my hair / Don't walk away / La la song.

Dec 84. (lp) *(780 159-1)* <*80159*> **NO TELLIN' LIES** 84 Sep84
– Wait until the summer's gone / I don't like it / Bears / I don't care / Lullaby / No tellin' lies / Takin' a stance / But no more / Little things / Drive me crazy. *(cd-iss. Jan96; 7567 80159-2)*

Sep 84. (7") <*89605*> **BEARS. / ONE MORE CHANCE** -

1986. (7") <*89276*> **YOU'RE ONLY LOSING YOUR HEART. / TAKE YOUR FINGERS FROM MY HAIR** -

1986. (lp) <*7567 81692-1*> **3V** -
– Can't live without you / Your mind's open / You'll never know / Better not call / Isn't that the way / Hard living without you / You're only losing your heart / About to make the time / Time / He's making you the fool. *(UK cd-iss. Jan96; 7567 81692-2)*

1990. (cd/lp) <*82094-2/-1*> **ZEBRA LIVE (live)** -
– Said before / She's waiting for you / The last time / Wait until the summer's gone / One more chance / Take your fingers from my hair / Bears / Better not call / La la song / Time / Who's behind the door? / He's making you the fool / Tell me what you want / The ocean.

—— disbanded around the early 90's

– compilations, etc. –

Nov 98. (cd) *Mayhem;* <*(11133-2)*> **IN BLACK AND WHITE – THE ZEBRA COLLECTION**
– Tell me what you want / One more chance / As I said before / Who's behind the door? / La la song / Wait until the summers gone / Bears / Lullaby / Hard living without you / Better not call / Tim / She's waiting for you (live) / Last time (live) / Take your fingers from my hair (live) / The ocean / But no more / Children at heart.

ZED YAGO

Formed: German-based . . .1987 by female ex-blues singer, JUTTA, along with JIMMY, GUNNAR, TACH and BUBI. Euro metallers who attempted to break the conventional mould with a metaphysical, conceptual approach, ZED YAGO were definitely different if not exactly compelling. After an independently issued domestic release, 'FROM OVER YONDER' (1988), the group were signed up to a major label by 'R.C.A.'. The resulting album, 'PILGRIMAGE' (1989), and accompanying single, 'BLACK BONE SONG' were championed by a few cult enthusiasts although generally, ZED YAGO's rather impenetrable sound didn't catch on.

Album rating: FROM OVER YONDER (*5) / PILGRIMAGE (*4)

JUTTA WEINHOLD – vocals / **JIMMY** – guitar / **GUNNAR** – guitar / **TACH** – bass / **BUBI** – drums

S.P.V. not iss.

1988. (lp) *(08-7517)* **FROM OVER YONDER** - - German
– The spell from over yonder / The flying Dutchman / Zed Yago / Queen and priest / Revenge / United pirate kingdom / Stay the course / Rebel ladies / Rockin' for the nation.

R.C.A. R.C.A.

Jan 89. (lp/c/cd) *(PL/PK/PD 71949)* <*9802*> **PILGRIMAGE**
– Pilgrim's choir / Pilgrimage / The fear of death / Pioneer of the storm / Black bone song / Rose of Martyrdom / The man who stole the holy fire / Achilees heel / The pale man / Omega child. *(cd+=)* – Fallen angel.

May 89. (7") *(PB 49387)* **BLACK BONE SONG. / ZED YAGO** -
(12"+=) *(PT 49388)* – Rocking for the nation.

—— split after above

VELVET VIPER

JUTTA + **BUBI** with **ROY LAST** – guitar / **LARS RATZ** – bass

1992. (lp) *(SPV 008-24791)* **THE 4th QUEST FOR FANTASY** - - German
– The Valkyrie / Savage dream / Highland queen / Modern knights / Mother of all voices / Forefather / Stella / Ancient warriors / Horsewomen / Valkyries.

ZEKE

Formed: Seattle, Washington, USA . . . 1994 by motorbike 'n' girls-fixated songwriter, BLIND MARKY FELCHTONE, along with ABE ZANUEL RIGGS III, DIZZY LEE ROTH and DONNY PAYCHECK. After a handful of rare 45's on numerous labels, these pseudonymous post-grunge sickboys roared into town in 1995 with their turbo-charged debut album, 'SUPER SOUND RACING'. Subsequently moving to their own 'Smooch Pooch' imprint, they delivered their second collection of twisted punk in the shape of 'FLAT TRACKER' (1996), pricking up the ears of 'Epitaph' who issued 1998's 'KICKED IN THE TEETH'.

Album rating: SUPER SOUND RACING (*6) / FLAT TRACKER (*7) / KICKED IN THE TEETH (*5) / DIRTY SANCHEZ (*6)

BLIND MARKY FELCHTONE (b.1966) – vocals, guitar / **ABE ZANUEL RIGGS III** (b.1972) – guitar / **DIZZY LEE ROTH** – bass / **DONNY PAYCHECK** (b.1965) – drums

I.F.A. I.F.A.

Jul 96. (cd) <*(IFACD 001)*> **SUPER SOUND RACING** Oct95
– Slut / Tuned out / Relapse / Chiva / Quicksand / Runnin' shine / Wreckin' machine / Eroded / Holley 750 / Incest / West Seattle acid party / Action / Mainline / 302 cubic inch V-8 powered blues / Hemicuda / Maybe someday / Galaxie 500 / Highway star / Schmidt value pack / Rid. *(re-iss. Oct96 on 'Smooch Pooch' lp/cd; PO 20/+CD)* *(re-iss. Jul97 on 'Epitaph' cd/lp; 20620-2/-1)*

Junk Junk

Jan 96. (2x7") <*(JR 6)*> **SWPR**

— **MARK PIERCE** – bass; repl. ROTH

Scooch Pooch Scooch Pooch

Oct 96. (7") <*(PO 11)*> **CHIVA KNIEVEL. /**
(re-iss. Oct97; same)

Oct 96. (lp) <*(PO 16)*> **FLAT TRACKER**
– T-5000 / Eddie Hill / Chiva Knievel / Overkill / Mystery train / Viva agnostini / Hate / Raped / Wanna fuck / Fight in the storeroom / Flat truck / Bitch / Daytona / Super six / Eliminator. *(cd-iss. Jul97 on 'Epitaph'; 20616-2)*

Jan 97. (7") <*(POOW 001)*> **WEST SEATTLE ACID PARTY. /**

not iss. Man's Ruin

Aug 97. (12"ep) <*MR 064*> **HOLLY 75 – OVERKILL – MYSTERY TRAIN – SLUT (live). / WANNA FUCK – CHIVA KNEVEL – T-5000 – RAPED (live)** -

Collective Fruit Collective Fruit

Oct 97. (7") <*(CF 7009)*> **LOVE GUN. /**

Epitaph Epitaph

Mar 98. (cd/c/lp) <*(6513-2/-4/-1)*> **KICKED IN THE TEETH**
– God of G.S.X.R. / Telepath boy / Rodney / Twisted / Dogfight / Kicked in the teeth / Fuck all night / Revolution / Killer inside / Lawson / Revolution reprise / Goggle boy / Zeke you / Porked / Ages high / Shout it out loud / Mert.

Nov 99. (lp/cd) *(BEHIND 002/+CD)* **TRUE CRIME**
(above issued on 'Drop Kick')

— **JEFFREY PAUL MATZ** – bass; repl. PIERCE

Feb 00. (cd/lp) <*(6562-2/-1)*> **DIRTY SANCHEZ**
– Let's get drugs / Rip and destroy / Now you die / Drunk / Punk rock records / Out of love / Let it rain / Don't give a fuck / Liar / Horror at Red Hook / Fucked up city / Automatic / 1999 / Razor blade / My way / Rhiannon.

ZENO

Formed: Hanover, Germany ...1984 by main songwriter ZENO ROTH (brother of ex-SCORPIONS guitarist ULI ROTH), the line-up completed by MICHAEL FLEXIG, ULE WINSOME RITGEN and ROD MORGENSTEIN. Signed up by EMI subsidiary, 'Parlophone', ZENO's debut album was literally hyped to death with the label pouring in money for the protracted recording sessions as the rumour mill continued to turn. Previewed by the single, 'A LITTLE MORE LOVE', the eponymous debut in question eventually surfaced in Spring '86. Its bombastic BOSTON or QUEEN-like symphonic rock was given a resounding thumbs-down by the press and EMI no doubt looked on in despair as their investment turned to dust before their eyes, album sales hardly a fraction of what they'd anticipated. Following this calamity, ZENO stumbled on for a few years, releasing the 'DELILAH' single in 1990 before quitting.

Album rating: ZENO (*4)

MICHAEL FLEXIG – vocals / **ZENO ROTH** – guitar / **ULE WINSOME RITGEN** – bass / **ROD MORGENSTEIN** – drums

— Also used session men; DON AIREY – keyboards (ex-RAINBOW, ex-OZZY OSBOURNE) / STUART ELLIOT – drums (ex-ALAN PARSONS, etc).

Parlophone Manhattan

Feb 86. (7") *(R 6123)* **A LITTLE MORE LOVE. / SIGNS ON THE SKY**
(12"+=/12"pic-d+=) *(12R/+P 6123)* – Don't tell the wind.

Mar 86. (lp/c) *(PCSD/TCPCSD 102)* <*53025*> **ZENO**
– Eastern sun / A little more love / Love will live / Signs on the sky / Far away / Emergency / Don't tell the wind / Heart on the wing / Circles of dawn / Sent by Heaven / Sunset. *(cd-iss. Jul86; CDP 746270-2)*

Jul 86. (7") *(EMI 5566)* **LOVE WILL LIVE. / FAR AWAY**
(12"+=) *(12EMI 5566)* – ('A'extended).

Stephan not iss.

Aug 90. (7"/12") *(KSR 7/12 07)* **DELILAH. / HANDS OFF (THAT'S MINE)** -

— split after above

ZNOWHITE

Formed: Chicago, Illinois, USA ... 1983 by multi-racial line-up of brothers IAN and SPARKS TAFOYA, plus NICOLE LEE. A unique and popular power-metal trio, ZNOWHITE secured a number of respectable support slots (including METALLICA) in their early career, eventually signing to the American 'Enigma' label. A debut set, 'ALL HAIL TO THEE', displayed their high-octane sound, given a feminine edge by LEE's vocals. A second set, 'KICK 'EM WHILE THEY'RE DOWN' (1986), followed in the same vein, although ZNOWHITE were subsequently enticed by 'Roadrunner' and went for the speed-metal jugular on 'ACT OF GOD' (1988). Despite strong support from the thrashier elements of the metal press, the group failed to crossover from cult status and subsequently evolved into CYCLONE TEMPLE.

Album rating: ALL HAIL TO THEE (*4) / KICK 'EM WHILE THEY'RE DOWN (*5) / LIVE SUICIDE (*4) / ACT OF GOD (*5)

NICOLE LEE – vocals / **IAN TAFOYA** – guitar / **SPARKS TAFOYA** – drums

Thunderbolt Enigma

Aug 85. (lp) *(THBM 002)* <*F 1077*> **ALL HAIL TO THEE** Dec84
– Sledgehammer / Saturday night / Somethin' for nothin' / Bringin' the hammer down / Do or die / Never felt like this / Rock city destination.

1986. (lp) <*72024-1*> **KICK 'EM WHILE THEY'RE DOWN** -
– Live for the weekend / All hail to three / Run like the wind / Too late / Turn up the pain.

not iss. Eriuka

1986. (lp) <*ZER 606*> **LIVE SUICIDE (live)** -
– Hellbent / Bringin' the hammer down / There's no tomorrow / Too late / Rock city destination / Night on parole / Rest in peace.

— added **SCOTT SCHAFFER** – bass

Roadrunner Roadrunner

May 88. (lp/cd) *(RR 9587-1/-2)* **ACT OF GOD**
– To the last breath / Baptised by fire / Pure blood / War machine / Thunderdome / Rest in peace / Disease bigotry / A soldier's creed / Something wicked (this way comes).

— split after above

ZOETROPE

Formed: Chicago, Illinois, USA ... 1981 by KEVIN MICHAEL, KEN BLACK, CALVIN HUMPHREY and BARRY STERN. Signed to US metal indie, 'Combat', ZOETROPE aligned themselves with the burgeoning thrash movement on their debut set, 'BREAK YOUR BACK' (1985). This was quickly followed up the next year with a second set, 'AMNESTY', a marked improvement which added melodic undercurrents. Despite some encouraging press reaction, the band never quite achieved the same success or recognition as their Bay Area contemporaries and split following the impressive 'LIFE OF CRIME' set in late '87. BARRY STERN went on to greater things with retro-rockers, TROUBLE.

Album rating: BREAK YOUR BACK (*5) / AMNESTY (*5) / A LIFE OF CRIME (*6)

KEVIN MICHAEL – vocals, guitar / **KEN BLACK** – guitar / **CALVIN HUMPHREY** – bass / **BARRY STERN** – drums

Music For Nations Combat

1985. (lp) **BREAK YOUR BACK** -

1986. (lp) <*9758*> **AMNESTY** -
– Indecent obsessions / Kill the enemy / Mercenary / Amnesty / Member in a gang / Break your back / Another chance / Creatures / Trip wires. <*(cd-iss. Mar00 on 'Century Media'; 66048-2)*>

Nov 87. (lp) *(MFN 76)* **A LIFE OF CRIME**
– Detention / Seeking asylum / Promiscuity / Nasa / Unbridled energy / Prohibition / Company man / Pickpocket / Hard to survive. <*(cd-iss. Aug99 on 'Century Media'; 66017-2)*>

— split after above, STERN subsequently joined TROUBLE

Rob ZOMBIE (see under ⇒ WHITE ZOMBIE)

ZOUNDS

Formed: Oxford, England ... early 80's by STEVE LAKE and LAURENCE WOOD. Emerging from the same post-punk polemic brigade as CRASS, POISON GIRLS, etc, ZOUNDS actually issued a single, 'CAN'T CHEAT KARMA' on the former band's notorious imprint, hot on the heels of a one-side 7", 'MENAGE'. Subsequently signing to 'Rough Trade', the group released a trio of hard-hitting singles which later turned up on the posthumous 'THE CURSE OF THE ZOUNDS!' (1984). By the time of the latter's release, LAKE had already formed another outfit, WORLD SERVICE and was about to embark upon a low-key solo career.

Album rating: THE CURSE OF THE ZOUNDS! (*4)

STEVE LAKE – vocals / **LAURENCE WOOD** – guitar / **LIBERTY KROPOTKIN** (b. JOSEF PORTER) – drums

Recommended not iss.

1980. (one-sided-7") *(RR 14.15)* **MENAGE** -

Crass not iss.

Jan 81. (7") *(421984-3)* **CAN'T CHEAT KARMA. / WAR / SUBVERT** -

Rough Trade not iss.

Apr 81. (7") *(RT 069)* **DEMYSTIFICATION. / GREAT WHITE HUNTER** -

Mar 82. (7") *(RT 094)* **DANCING. / TRUE LOVE** -

May 82. (7") *(RT 098)* **MORE TROUBLE COMING EVERY DAY. / KNIFE** -

NotSoBrave not iss.

Jun 82. (7"ep) *(NSB 001)* **LA VACHE QUI RIT** -

– compilations, etc. –

1984. (lp) *Rough Trade; (ROUGH 31)* **THE CURSE OF ZOUNDS!** -
– Fear / Did he jump / Little bit more / This land / My mummy's gone / New band / Dirty squatters / Loads of noise / Medley – Target / Mr. Disney / The war goes on. *(cd-iss. Jan94 on 'Rugger Bugger'+=; SEEP 006)* <*US cd-iss. 1997 on 'Broken Rekids'+=; 56*> – Can't cheat karma / War / Subvert / Demystification / Great white hunter / Dancing / True love / More trouble coming everyday / Knife / Not me / Biafra / Wolves.

WORLD SERVICE

STEVE + LAURENCE

		Rough Trade	not iss.
Jun 83.	(12"ep) *(RTT 118)* **CELEBRATION TOWN. / TURN OUT THE LIGHTS / CELEBRATION TOWN (NIGHTMARE)**	[ ]	[-]

STEVE LAKE

		NotSoBrave	not iss.
Mar 84.	(12"ep) *(NSB 5)* **WELCOME TO MONKEY HOUSE EP**	[ ]	[-]
May 85.	(lp) *(NSB 7)* **MURDER VIOLENCE SEX DIVORCE**	[ ]	[-]
Jun 85.	(12"ep) *(NSB 8)* **IN EVERY LIFE**	[ ]	[-]
		Play It Again Sam	not iss.
Apr 87.	(12") *(BIAS 050)* **RUNNING AWAY. /**	[ ]	[-]
May 87.	(lp) *(BIAS 052)* **SO CRUEL**	[ ]	[-]

MOVING SIDEWALKS

BILLY GIBBONS (b.12 Dec'49) – vocals, guitar / **TOM MOORE** – keyboards / **DON SUMMERS** – bass / **DAN MITCHELL** – drums

		not iss.	Tantara
1967.	(7") *<3101>* **99th FLOOR. / WHAT ARE YOU GOING TO DO?** *<re-iss. 1967 on 'Wand'; 1156>*	[-]	[ ]
		not iss.	Wand
1967.	(7") *<1167>* **NEED ME. / EVERY NIGHT A NEW SURPRISE** *<above tracks were re-iss. 1980 as EP on 'Moxie'; 1030>*	[-]	[ ]

—— **LANIER GREIG** – keyboards repl. MOORE

		not iss.	Tantara
1968.	(7") *<3108>* **I WANT TO HOLD YOUR HAND. / JOE BLUES**	[-]	[ ]
1968.	(lp) *<6919>* **FLASH** – Flashback / Crimson witch / Pluto – Sept.31 / Eclipse / Scoun da be / No good to cry / You don't know the life / You make me shake / Reclipse.	[-]	[ ]
1969.	(7") *<3113>* **FLASHBACK. / NO GOOD TO CRY**	[-]	[ ]

ZZ TOP

Formed: Houston, Texas, USA . . . as garage band, THE MOVING SIDEWALKS by BILLY GIBBONS, the now infamous trio/line-up finally emerging in 1970 with the addition of DUSTY HILL and FRANK BEARD. Having initially released a debut single on manager Billy Ham's new 'Scat' label (prior to the arrival of messrs. BEARD and HILL), ZZ TOP subsuquently secured a deal with 'London' records. 'FIRST ALBUM' appeared in 1971, its stark title matching the raw simplicity of the southern blues/boogie contained within the grooves. This straightforward approach also extended to the group's music biz masterplan; ZZ TOP were first and foremost a live band, their punishing touring schedule, largely in the American South initially, would eventually turn grassroots support into record sales as well as honing their musical skills for future glories. A follow-up set, 'RIO GRANDE MUD' (1972) spawned the group's first (US) hit single in 'FRANCENE' although ZZ TOP only really began to make an impact with 1973's 'TRES HOMBRES'. Occasionally reminiscent of 'EXILE . . .'-era 'STONES (see the the smokin' 'LA GRANGE' single), the group had begun to perfect their combination of boot-leather riffing and Texas blues drawl, GIBBONS' nifty axe-work oiling the beast nicely (he'd previously drawn public praise from none other than JIMI HENDRIX). By 1976, the group were popular enough to take their 'Wordwide Texas Tour' on the road, a mammoth operation which certainly equalled The ROLLING STONES in terms of stage set and ticket sales, ZZ TOP now one of America's biggest grossing homegrown acts. The classic 70's grind of 'TUSH' was the group's highest charting single of the decade (Top 20 in '75), although ZZ TOP didn't really garner widespread critical acclaim until the release of 'DEGUELLO' in 1979, their first album for 'Warners'. The record's gristly blues licks and knowing, often surreal sense of humour demonstrating that ZZ TOP were considerably more sussed than the backwoods caricatures which they were often portrayed as (a perception which they often perpetuated), the deadpan 'CHEAP SUNGLASSES' a blistering cover of ELMORE JAMES' 'DUST MY BROOM' and a version of Isaac Hayes' 'I THANK YOU' proving highlights. 'EL LOCO' (1981) was almost as good, the boys insisting that what a woman really wanted was, ahem . . . a 'PEARL NECKLACE'. The tongue-in-cheek smut only really got underway with 'ELIMINATOR' (1983), however, the gleaming videos for the likes of the pounding 'GIMME ALL YOUR LOVIN', 'SHARP DRESSED MAN' and of course, 'LEGS', featuring more leggy lovelies than a ROBERT PALMER video. These MTV staples also introduced ZZ TOP's famous red Ford coupé, the fearsome motor becoming as much of an 80's icon as FRANKIE GOES TO HOLLYWOOD t-shirts. Musically, the album was almost a complete departure, turbo-charging the guitars way up in the mix and boosting the overall sound with a synthesized throb. This trademark electro-boogie would see ZZ TOP through the best part of a decade. Deservedly, the record was a massive worldwide success, a multi-million seller which marked the first instalment in a three-album semi-concept affair, built around the 'Eliminator' car. For 'AFTERBURNER' (1985), the car, don't laugh!, had turned into a space rocket flying high above the earth although it seemed as if they'd also jettisoned the cocksure stomp of old. 'SLEEPING BAG' and 'VELCRO FLY' were competent enough, the videos ensuring another MTV bonanza and healthy sales. 'RECYCLER' (1990) continued in much the same vein, although relatively poor sales subsequently saw the group parting with 'Warners' and starting afresh with 'R.C.A.'. Never the most prolific band, ZZ TOP have only released a further three albums in the 90's, the compilation 'ZZ TOP GREATEST HITS' (1992; and including 'VIVA LAS VEGAS' made famous by Elvis), 'ANTENNA' (1994) and 'RHYTHMEEN' (1996), at last abandoning their outdated 80's sound in favour of a leaner, meaner return to their roots. They mightn't sell as many records these days but they've still got beards (save FRANK BEARD, that is!) as long and grizzly as a DEEP PURPLE guitar solo, and that's what counts! • **Songwriters:** Group penned (plus some early with manager BILL HAM) except; FRANCINE (trad.) / JAILHOUSE ROCK (hit; Elvis Presley)

Album rating: FIRST ALBUM (*6) / RIO GRANDE MUD (*6) / TRES HOMBRES (*8) / FANDANGO (*7) / TEJAS (*6) / THE BEST OF ZZ TOP compilation (*8) / DEGUELLO (*8) / EL LOCO (*6) / ELIMINATOR (*8) / AFTERBURNER (*6) / RECYCLER (*5) / ZZ TOP'S GREATEST HITS compilation (*9) / ANTENNA (*5) / ONE FOOT IN THE BLUES collection (*4) / RHYTHMEEN (*4) / XXX (*3)

ZZ TOP

(GIBBONS, MITCHELL & GREIG)

		not iss.	Scat
1970.	(7") *<45-500>* **SALT LICK. / MILLER'S FARM** *<re-iss. later 1970 on 'London'; 45-131>*	[-]	[ ]

—— **GIBBONS** now sole survivor when LANIER and DAN departed. Newcomers were **DUSTY HILL** (b.JOE, 1949) – bass, vocals (ex-WARLOCKS, ex-AMERICAN BLUES) / **FRANK BEARD** (b.10 Dec'49) – drums (ex-CELLAR DWELLARS)

		London	London
Jan 71.	(lp) *<PS 584>* **FIRST ALBUM** – (Somebody else been) Shaking your tree / Brown sugar / Squank / Goin' down to Mexico / Old man / Neighbor, neighbor / Certified blues / Bedroom thang / Just got back from baby's / Backdoor love affair. *<re-iss. 1980 on 'Warners'; WB 3268> (UK-iss.Sep84 on 'Warners' lp/c; K/K4 56601) (cd-iss. Jan87; K2 56601)*	[-]	[ ]
Feb 71.	(7") *<45-138>* **(SOMEBODY ELSE BEEN) SHAKING YOUR TREE. / NEIGHBOR, NEIGHBOR**	[-]	[ ]
May 72.	(7") *<45-179>* **FRANCENE. / FRANCENE (Spanish)**	[-]	[69]
Jul 72.	(lp) *(SHU 8433) <PS 612>* **RIO GRANDE MUD** – Francene / Just got paid / Mushmouth shoutin' / Ko ko blue / Chevrolet / Apologies to Pearly / Bar-b-q / Sure got cold after the rain fell / Whiskey'n mama / Down Brownie. *<US re-iss. 1980 on 'Warners'; BSK 3269> (re-iss. Sep84 on 'Warners' lp/c; K/K4 56602) (cd-iss. Jan87; K2 56602) (cd re-iss. Mar94 on 'Warners'; 7599 27380-2)*	[ ]	[ ] Apr72
Jul 72.	(7") *(HLU 10376)* **FRANCENE. / DOWN BROWNIE**	[ ]	[-]
Nov 73.	(lp) *(SHU 8459) <PS 631>* **TRES HOMBRES** – Waitin' for the bus / Jesus just left Chicago / Beer drinkers & Hell raisers / Master of sparks / Hot, blue and righteous / Move me on down the line / Precious and Grace / La Grange / Sheik / Have you heard?. *<US re-iss. 1980 on 'Warners'; BSK 3270> (re-iss. Nov83 on 'Warners' lp/c; K/K4 56603)*	[ ]	[8] Aug73
Jun 74.	(7") *(HLU 10458)* **BEER DRINKERS & HELL RAISERS. / LA GRANGE**	[ ]	[-]
Jan 75.	(7") *(HLU 10475) <45-179>* **LA GRANGE. / JUST GOT PAID**	[ ]	[41] Mar74
Jun 75.	(lp) *(SH 8482) <PS 656>* **FANDANGO! (live Warehouse, New Orleans + studio)** – Thunderbird / Jailhouse rock / Back door medley: Backdoor love affair – Mellow down easy – Backdoor love affair No.2 – Long distance boogie / Nasty dogs and funky kings / Blue jean blues / Balinese / Mexican blackbird / Heard it on the X / Tush. *<US re-iss. 1980 on 'Warners'; BSK 3271> (re-iss. Nov83 on 'Warners' lp/c; K/K4 56604) (cd-iss. Jan87; K2 56604)*	[60]	[10] May75
Jul 75.	(7") *(HLU 10495) <5N-220>* **TUSH. / BLUE JEAN BLUES**	[ ]	[20]
Aug 76.	(7") *(HLU 10538) <5N-241>* **IT'S ONLY LOVE. / ASLEEP IN THE DESERT**	[ ]	[44]
Feb 77.	(lp) *(LDU 1) <PS 680>* **TEJAS** – It's only love / Arrested for driving while blind / El Diablo / Snappy kakkie / Enjoy and get it on / Ten dollar man / Pan Am highway blues / Avalon hideaway / She's a heartbreaker / Asleep in the desert. *<US re-iss. 1980 on 'Warners'; BSK 3272> (re-iss. Sep84 on 'Warners' lp/c; K/K4 56605) (cd-iss. Mar87; K2 56605) (cd re-iss. Mar94 on 'Warners'; 7599 27383-2)*	[ ]	[17] Jan77
Mar 77.	(7") *<5N-251>* **ARRESTED FOR DRIVING WHILE BLIND. / IT'S ONLY LOVE**	[-]	[91]
Apr 77.	(7") *(HLU 10547)* **ARRESTED FOR DRIVING WHILE BLIND. / NEIGHBOUR, NEIGHBOUR**	[ ]	[-]
May 77.	(7") *<5N-252>* **EL DIABLO. / ENJOY AND GET IT ON**	[-]	[ ]
Dec 77.	(lp) *<PS 706>* **THE BEST OF ZZ TOP** (compilation) – Tush / Waitin' for the bus / Jesus just left Chicago / Francene / Just got paid / La grange / Blue jean blues / Backdoor love affair / Beer drinkers and Hell raisers / Heard it on the X. *<re-iss. 1980 on 'Warners'; BSK 3273> (UK-iss.Dec83 on 'Warners' lp/c; K/K4 56598) cd-iss. Jan86; K2 56598)*	[-]	[94]
		Warners	Warners
Dec 79.	(lp/c) *(K/K4 56701) <HS 3361>* **DEGUELLO** – I thank you / She loves my automobile / I'm bad, I'm nationwide / A fool for your stockings / Manic mechanic / Dust my broom / Lowdown in the street / Hi fi mama / Cheap sunglasses / Esther be the one. *(re-iss. Jan85 lp/cd; same/K2 56701) (re-iss. Mar94 on 'Warners' cd/c; K2/K4 56701)*	[ ]	[24] Nov79
Mar 80.	(7") *(K 17516) <WB 49163>* **I THANK YOU. / A FOOL FOR YOUR STOCKINGS**	[ ]	[34] Jan80
Jun 80.	(7") *<WB 49220>* **CHEAP SUNGLASSES. / ('A'live)**	[-]	[89]
Jun 80.	(7") *(K 17647)* **CHEAP SUNGLASSES. / ESTHER BE THE ONE**	[ ]	[-]
Jul 81.	(7") *<WB 49782>* **LEILA. / DON'T TEASE ME**	[-]	[77]
Jul 81.	(lp/c) *(K/K4 56929) <BSK 3593>* **EL LOCO** – Tube snake boogie / I wanna drive you home / Ten foot pole / Leila / Don't tease me / It's so hard / Pearl necklace / Groovy little hippy pad / Heaven, Hell or Houston / Party on the patio. *(cd-iss. Mar87; K2 56929) (cd re-iss. Mar94 on 'Warners'; 7599 23593-2)*	[88]	[17]
Jan 82.	(7") *<WB 49865>* **TUBE SNAKE BOOGIE. / HEAVEN, HELL OR HOUSTON**	[-]	[ ]

Jun 83. (7"/7"sha-pic-d) *(W 9693/+P)* <*WB 29693*> **GIMME ALL YOUR LOVIN'. / IF I COULD ONLY FLAG HER DOWN** 61 37 Mar83
(12") *(W 9693T)* – ('A'side) / Jesus just left Chicago / Heard it on the x / Arrested for driving while blind.

Jun 83. (lp/c) *(W 3774/+4)* <*23774-1/-4*> **ELIMINATOR** 3 9 Apr83
– Gimme all your lovin' / Got me under pressure / Sharp dressed man / I need you tonight / I got the six / Legs / Thug / TV dinners / Dirty dog / If I could only flag her down / Bad girl. *(cd-iss. 1984; 9-3774-2) (pic-lp Aug85; W 3774P)*

Nov 83. (7") *(WB 9576)* <*WB 29576*> **SHARP DRESSED MAN. / I GOT THE SIX** 53 56 Jul83
(12"+=) *(WB 9576T)* – La Grange.

Mar 84. (7") *(WB 9334)* **TV DINNERS. / CHEAP SUNGLASSES** 67 -
(c-s+=/d12"+=) *(W 9334 C/T)* – A fool for your stockings.

Sep 84. (single re-issue) *(same)* **GIMME ALL YOUR LOVIN'** 10 -

Dec 84. (single re-issue) *(same)* **SHARP DRESSED MAN** 22 -

Feb 85. (7") *(W 9272)* <*WB 29272*> **LEGS (remix). / BAD GIRL** 16 8 May84
('A'-Metal mix-12") *(W 9272T)* – A fool for your stockings.

Jul 85. (7"ep/c-ep/12"ep) *(W 8946/+C/T)* **THE ZZ TOP SUMMER HOLIDAY EP** 51 -
– Tush / Got me under pressure / Beer drinkers and hell raisers / I'm bad, I'm nationwide.

Oct 85. (7"/7"sha-pic-d/7"interlocking jigsaw pic-d pt.1) *(W 2001/+P/DP)* <*WB 28884*> **SLEEPING BAG. / PARTY ON THE PATIO** 27 8
(12"+=) *(W 2001T)* – Blue jean blues.
(d7+=) *(W 2001D)* – Sharp dressed man / I got the six.

Nov 85. (lp/c)(cd) *(WX 27/+C)(925342-2)* <*25342*> **AFTERBURNER** 2 4
– Sleeping bag / Stages / Woke up with wood / Rough boy / Can't stop rockin' / Planet of women / I got the message / Velcro fly / Dipping low (in the lap of luxury) / Delirious.

Feb 86. (7"/7"jigsaw pic-d pt.2) <US-12"> *(W 2002/+BP)* <*WB 28810T*> **STAGES. / HI-FI MAMA** 43 21 Jan86
(12"+=) *(W 2002T)* – ('A'extended).

Apr 86. (7"/7"pic-d,7"jigsaw pic-d pt.3) *(W 2003/+FP)* <*WB 28733*> **ROUGH BOY. / DELIRIOUS** 23 22 Mar86
(12"shrinkwrapped w/ free jigsaw 'SLEEPING BAG' pic-d+=) – Legs (mix).

Jul 86. (7") <*WB 28650*> **VELCRO FLY. / CAN'T STOP ROCKIN'** - 35

Sep 86. (7") *(W 8515)* **VELCRO FLY. / WOKE UP IN WOOD** 54 -
(12"+=) *(W 8515T)* – Can't stop rockin' ('86 remix).

Jul 90. (7"/c-s/12") *(W 9812/+C/T)* <*19812*> **DOUBLEBACK. / PLANET OF WOMEN** 29 50 May90
(cd-s+=) *(W 9812CD)* – ('A'-AOR mix).

Oct 90. (cd)(lp/c) *(7599 26265-2)(WX 390/+C)* <*26265*> **RECYCLER** 8 6
– Concrete and steel / Lovething / Penthouse eyes / Tell it / My head's in Mississippi / Decision or collision / Give it up / 2000 blues / Burger man / Doubleback. *(re-iss. Mar94 cd/c)*

Nov 90. (7"/c-s) *(W 9509/+C)* **GIVE IT UP. / SHARP DRESSED MAN** -
(12"+=/cd-s+=) *(W 9509 T/CD)* – Cheap sunglasses (live).

Jan 91. (c-s,cd-s) <*19470*> **GIVE IT UP / CONCRETE AND STEEL** - 79

Apr 91. (7"/7"sha-pic-d/c-s) *(W 0009/+P/C)* **MY HEAD'S IN MISSISSIPPI. / A FOOL FOR YOUR STOCKINGS** 37 -
(12"+=/cd-s+=) *(W 0009 T/CD)* – Blue Jean blues.

Mar 92. (7"/c-s) *(W 0098/+C)* <*18979*> **VIVA LAS VEGAS. / 2000 BLUES** 10
(cd-s+=) *(W 0098CD)* – Velcro fly / Stages / Legs.

May 92. (cd/c/lp) <*(7599 26846-2/-4/-1)*> **GREATEST HITS** (compilation) 5 9
– Gimme all your lovin' / Sharp dressed man / Rough boy / Tush / My head's in Mississippi / Pearl necklace / I'm bad, I'm nationwide / Viva Las Vegas / Doubleback / Gun love / Got me under pressure / Give it up / Cheap sunglasses / Sleeping bag / Planet of women / La Grange / Tube snake boogie / Legs.

Jun 92. (7"/c-s) *(W 0111/+C)* **ROUGH BOY. / VIVA LAS VEGAS (remix)** 49 -
(cd-s+=) *(W 0111CD)* – Velcro fly (extended) / Doubleback (AOR mix).
(cd-s) *(W 0111CDX)* – ('A'side) / TV dinners / Jesus has just left Chicago / Beer drinkers and Hell raisers.

R.C.A. R.C.A.

Jan 94. (7"/c-s/cd-s) *(74321 18473-7/-4/-2)* **PINCUSHION. / CHERRY RED** 15
(cd-s+=) *(74321 18261-2)* – ('A'mix).

Jan 94. (cd/c/lp) *(74321 18260-2/-4/-1)* <*66317*> **ANTENNA** 3 14
– Pincushion / Breakaway / World of swirl / Fuzzbox voodoo / Girl in a T-shirt / Antenna head / PCH / Cherry red / Cover your rig / Lizard life / Deal goin' down / Everything.

Apr 94. (c-s/12"/cd-s) *(74321 19228-4/-1/-2)* **BREAKAWAY. / MARY'S / BREAKAWAY (version)** 60

Jun 96. (7"m) *(74321 39482-7)* **WHAT'S UP WITH THAT. / STOP BREAKIN' DOWN BLUES (live) / NASTY DOGS AND FUNKY KINGS (live)** 58
(cd-s+=) *(74321 39482-2)* – ('A'version).

Sep 96. (cd/c) *(74321 39466-2/-4)* <*66958*> **RHYTHMEEN** 32 29
– Rhythmeen / Bang bang / Black fly / What's up with that / Vincent Price blues / Zipper job / Hairdresser / She's just killing me / My mind is gone / Loaded / Prettyhead / Hummbucking, part 2.

— ZZ were back in the UK Top 30 in Oct'99, albeit credited on MARTAY's version of their 'GIMME ALL YOUR LOVIN' 2000'

Sep 99. (cd/c) <*67850*> **XXX** - 100
– Poke chop sandwich / Crucifixx-a-flatt / Fearless boogie / 36-22-36 / Made into a movie / Beatbox / Trippin' / Dreadmonboogaloo / Introduction by Ross Mitchell / Sinpusher / (Let me be your) Teddy bear / Hey Mr. Millionaire / Belt buckle.

– compilations, others, etc. –

on 'Warners' unless mentioned otherwise

Nov 83. (d-c) *(K4 66121)* **TRES HOMBRES / FANDANGO** -

1987. (3xcd-box) *(K 925661-2)* **FIRST ALBUM / RIO GRANDE MUD / / TRES HOMBRES / FANDANGO! / / TEJAS / EL LOCO**

Nov 94. (cd/c) <*(9362 45815-2/-4)*> **ONE FOOT IN THE BLUES**

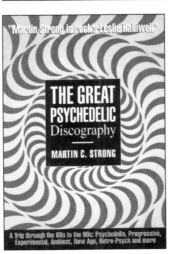